THE EUROPA
WORLD
YEAR BOOK
2013

THE EUROPA WORLD YEAR BOOK 2013

VOLUME 2

KAZAKHSTAN–ZIMBABWE

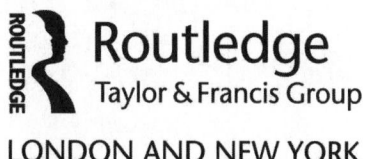

Routledge
Taylor & Francis Group

LONDON AND NEW YORK

54th edition published 2013
by Routledge
2 Park Square, Milton Park, Abingdon, Oxon, OX14 4RN

Simultaneously published in the USA and Canada by Routledge
711 Third Avenue, New York, NY 10017

Routledge is an imprint of the Taylor & Francis Group, an Informa business

© 2013 Routledge

First published 1926

ISBN: 978-1-85743-679-2 (The Set)
       978-1-85743-707-2 (Vol. 2)
ISSN: 0956-2273

Senior Editor: Juliet Love

Senior Editor, Statistics: Philip McIntyre

Senior Editor, Directory: Iain Frame

Regional Editors: Imogen Gladman, Cathy Hartley, Dominic Heaney,
Neil Higgins, Christopher Matthews, Jacqueline West

International Organizations Editor: Helen Canton

Contributing Editors: Catriona Holman, Katharine Murison, Jillian O'Brien

Editorial Assistant: Amy Welmers

Statistics Researchers: Varun Wadhawan *(Team Manager)*,
Mohd Khalid Ansari, Akshay Sharma *(Senior Researchers)*,
Suchi Kedia, Nirbachita Sarkar

Directory Editorial Researchers: Arijit Khasnobis *(Team Manager)*, Rima Kar,
Birendra Pratap Nayak, Thoithoi Pukhrambam, C. Sandhya, K. Nungshithoibi Singha
(Senior Editorial Researchers), Shubha Banerjee *(Editorial Research Associate)*,
Anveshi Gupta, Dinesh Kafle, Sakshi Mathur

Contributors: Christopher Bell, Rebecca Bomford, Katie Dawson, Lucy Dean, Meena Khan,
Joanne Maher, Catriona Marcham, Elizabeth Salzman, Gareth Vaughan

Editorial Director: Paul Kelly

Typeset in New Century Schoolbook
by Data Standards Limited, Frome, Somerset

FSC
www.fsc.org
MIX
Paper from
responsible sources
FSC® C006021

FOREWORD

THE EUROPA WORLD YEAR BOOK was first published in 1926. Since 1960 it has appeared in annual two-volume editions, and has become established as an authoritative reference work, providing a wealth of detailed information on the political, economic and commercial institutions of the world.

Volume 1 contains a comprehensive listing of more than 2,000 international organizations, commissions and specialized bodies, and the first part of the alphabetical survey of countries of the world, from Afghanistan to Jordan. Volume 2 contains countries from Kazakhstan to Zimbabwe. An Index of Territories covered in both volumes is to be found at the end of Volume 2.

The International Organizations section gives extensive coverage to the United Nations and its related agencies and bodies. There are also detailed articles concerning other major international and regional organizations; entries for many affiliated organizations appear within these articles. In addition, the section includes briefer details of some 1,300 other international organizations. A comprehensive Index of International Organizations is included at the end of Volume 1.

Each country is covered by an individual chapter, containing: an introductory survey including contemporary political history, economic affairs, constitution and government, regional and international co-operation, and public holidays; a statistical survey presenting the latest available figures on demographics, labour force, health and welfare, agriculture, forestry, fishing, mining, industry, currency and exchange rates, government finance, international reserves and the monetary sector, cost of living, national accounts, balance of payments, external trade, railways, roads, shipping, civil aviation, tourism, media and telecommunications, and education; and a directory section listing names, addresses and other useful facts about organizations in the fields of government, election commissions, political parties, diplomatic representation, judiciary, religions, the media, telecommunications, banking, insurance, trade and industry, development organizations, chambers of commerce, industrial and trade associations, utilities, trade unions, transport, tourism, defence, and education.

The entire content of the print edition of THE EUROPA WORLD YEAR BOOK is available online at www.europaworld.com. This prestigious resource incorporates sophisticated search and browse functions as well as specially commissioned visual and statistical content. An ongoing programme of updates of key areas of information ensures currency of content, and enhances the richness of the coverage for which THE EUROPA WORLD YEAR BOOK is renowned.

Readers are referred to the nine titles in the Europa Regional Surveys of the World series: AFRICA SOUTH OF THE SAHARA, CENTRAL AND SOUTH-EASTERN EUROPE, EASTERN EUROPE, RUSSIA AND CENTRAL ASIA, THE FAR EAST AND AUSTRALASIA, THE MIDDLE EAST AND NORTH AFRICA, SOUTH AMERICA, CENTRAL AMERICA AND THE CARIBBEAN, SOUTH ASIA, THE USA AND CANADA, and WESTERN EUROPE, available both in print and online, offer comprehensive analysis at regional, sub-regional and country level. More detailed coverage of international organizations is to be found in THE EUROPA DIRECTORY OF INTERNATIONAL ORGANIZATIONS.

The content of THE EUROPA WORLD YEAR BOOK is extensively revised and updated by a variety of methods, including direct mailing. Many other sources are used, such as national statistical offices, government departments and diplomatic missions. The editors thank the innumerable individuals and organizations world-wide whose generous co-operation in providing current information for this edition is invaluable in presenting the most accurate and up-to-date material available.

May 2013

ACKNOWLEDGEMENTS

The editors gratefully acknowledge particular indebtedness for permission to reproduce material from the following sources: the United Nations' statistical databases and *Demographic Yearbook, Statistical Yearbook, Monthly Bulletin of Statistics, Industrial Commodity Statistics Yearbook* and *International Trade Statistics Yearbook*; the United Nations Educational, Scientific and Cultural Organization's *Statistical Yearbook* and Institute for Statistics database; the *Human Development Report* of the United Nations Development Programme; the Food and Agriculture Organization of the United Nations' statistical database; the statistical databases of the World Health Organization; the statistical databases of the UNCTAD/WTO International Trade Centre; the International Labour Office's statistical database and *Yearbook of Labour Statistics*; the World Bank's *World Bank Atlas, Global Development Finance, World Development Report* and *World Development Indicators*; the International Monetary Fund's statistical database, *International Financial Statistics* and *Government Finance Statistics Yearbook*; the World Tourism Organization's *Compendium* and *Yearbook of Tourism Statistics*; the US Geological Survey; the International Telecommunication Union; the International Road Federation's *World Road Statistics*; Lloyd's List; and *The Military Balance 2013*, a publication of the International Institute for Strategic Studies, Arundel House, 13–15 Arundel Street, London WC2R 3DX. Statistics Canada information is used with the permission of Statistics Canada. Users are forbidden to copy this material and/or redisseminate the data, in an original or modified form, for commercial purposes, without the expressed permission of Statistics Canada. Information on the availability of the wide range of data from Statistics Canada can be obtained from Statistics Canada's Regional Offices, its website at www.statcan.ca, and its toll-free access number 1-800-263-1136.

HEALTH AND WELFARE STATISTICS: SOURCES AND DEFINITIONS

Total fertility rate Source: WHO Statistical Information System (part of the Global Health Observatory). The number of children that would be born per woman, assuming no female mortality at child-bearing ages and the age-specific fertility rates of a specified country and reference period.

Under-5 mortality rate Source: WHO Statistical Information System. Defined by WHO as the probability of a child born in a specific year or period dying before reaching the age of five, if subject to the age-specific mortality rates of that year or period.

HIV/AIDS Source: UNAIDS. Estimated percentage of adults aged 15 to 49 years living with HIV/AIDS. < indicates 'fewer than'.

Health expenditure Source: WHO Statistical Information System.
US $ per head (PPP)
International dollar estimates, derived by dividing local currency units by an estimate of their purchasing-power parity (PPP) compared with the US dollar. PPPs are the rates of currency conversion that equalize the purchasing power of different currencies by eliminating the differences in price levels between countries.
% of GDP
GDP levels for OECD countries follow the most recent UN System of National Accounts. For non-OECD countries a value was estimated by utilizing existing UN, IMF and World Bank data.
Public expenditure
Government health-related outlays plus expenditure by social schemes compulsorily affiliated with a sizeable share of the population, and extrabudgetary funds allocated to health services. Figures include grants or loans provided by international agencies, other national authorities, and sometimes commercial banks.

Access to water and sanitation Source: WHO/UNICEF Joint Monitoring Programme on Water Supply and Sanitation (JMP) (Progress on Drinking Water and Sanitation, 2012 Update). Defined in terms of the percentage of the population using improved facilities in terms of the type of technology and levels of service afforded. For water, this includes house connections, public standpipes, boreholes with handpumps, protected dug wells, protected spring and rainwater collection; allowance is also made for other locally defined technologies. Sanitation is defined to include connection to a sewer or septic tank system, pour-flush latrine, simple pit or ventilated improved pit latrine, again with allowance for acceptable local technologies. Access to water and sanitation does not imply that the level of service or quality of water is 'adequate' or 'safe'.

Carbon dioxide emissions Source: World Bank, World Development Indicators database, citing the Carbon Dioxide Information Analysis Center (sponsored by the US Department of Energy). Emissions comprise those resulting from the burning of fossil fuels (including those produced during consumption of solid, liquid and gas fuels and from gas flaring) and from the manufacture of cement.

Human Development Index (HDI) Source: UNDP, *Human Development Report* (2011). A summary of human development measured by three basic dimensions: prospects for a long and healthy life, measured by life expectancy at birth; access to knowledge, measured by a combination of mean years of schooling and expected years of schooling; and standard of living, measured by GNI per head (PPP US $). The index value obtained lies between zero and one. A value above 0.8 indicates very high human development, between 0.7 and 0.8 high human development, between 0.5 and 0.7 medium human development and below 0.5 low human development. A centralized data source for all three dimensions was not available for all countries. In some cases other data sources were used to calculate a substitute value; however, this was excluded from the ranking. Other countries, including non-UNDP members, were excluded from the HDI altogether. In total, 187 countries were ranked for 2011.

CONTENTS

CONTENTS

ABBREVIATIONS

AB   Aktiebolag (Joint-Stock Company); Alberta
Abog.   Abogado (Lawyer)
Acad.   Academician; Academy
ACP   African, Caribbean and Pacific (countries)
ACT   Australian Capital Territory
AD   anno Domini
ADB   African Development Bank; Asian Development Bank
ADC   aide-de-camp
Adm.   Admiral
admin.   administration
AEC   African Economic Community; African Economic Conference
AfDB   African Development Bank
AG   Aktiengesellschaft (Joint-Stock Company)
AGOA   Africa Growth and Opportunity Act
AH   anno Hegirae
a.i.   ad interim
AID   (US) Agency for International Development
AIDS   acquired immunodeficiency syndrome
AK   Alaska
Al.   Aleja (Alley, Avenue)
AL   Alabama
ALADI   Asociación Latinoamericana de Integración
Alt.   Alternate
AM   Amplitude Modulation
a.m.   ante meridiem (before noon)
amalg.   amalgamated
Apdo   Apartado (Post Box)
APEC   Asia-Pacific Economic Cooperation
approx.   approximately
Apt   Apartment
AR   Arkansas
ARV   advanced retroviral
AŞ   Anonim Şirketi (Joint-Stock Company)
A/S   Aktieselskab (Joint-Stock Company)
ASEAN   Association of South East Asian Nations
asscn   association
assoc.   associate
ASSR   Autonomous Soviet Socialist Republic
asst   assistant
AU   African Union
Aug.   August
auth.   authorized
av., Ave   Avenija, Avenue
Av., Avda   Avenida (Avenue)
Avv.   Avvocato (Lawyer)
AZ   Arizona

b.b.   bez broja (without number)
BC   British Columbia
BC   before Christ
Bd   Board
Bd, Bld, Blv., Blvd   Boulevard
b/d   barrels per day
BFPO   British Forces' Post Office
Bhd   Berhad (Public Limited Company)
Bldg   Building
blk   block
Blvr   Bulevar
BP   Boîte postale (Post Box)
br.(s)   branch(es)
Brig.   Brigadier

BSE   bovine spongiform encephalopathy
BSEC   (Organization of the) Black Sea Economic Co-operation
bte   boîte (box)
Bul.   Bulvar (boulevard)
bulv.   bulvarīs (boulevard)

C   Centigrade
c.   circa; cuadra(s) (block(s))
CA   California
CACM   Central American Common Market
Cad.   Caddesi (Street)
CAP   Common Agricultural Policy
cap.   capital
Capt.   Captain
CAR   Central African Republic
CARICOM   Caribbean Community and Common Market
CBSS   Council of Baltic Sea States
CCL   Caribbean Congress of Labour
Cdre   Commodore
CEMAC   Communauté économique et monétaire de l'Afrique centrale
Cen.   Central
CEO   Chief Executive Officer
CET   common external tariff
CFA   Communauté Financière Africaine; Coopération Financière en Afrique centrale
CFE   Treaty on Conventional Armed Forces in Europe
CFP   Common Fisheries Policy; Communauté française du Pacifique; Comptoirs français du Pacifique
Chair.   Chairman/person/woman
Chih.   Chihuahua
CI   Channel Islands
Cia   Companhia
Cía   Compañía
Cie   Compagnie
c.i.f.   cost, insurance and freight
C-in-C   Commander-in-Chief
circ.   circulation
CIS   Commonwealth of Independent States
CJD   Creutzfeldt-Jakob disease
cm   centimetre(s)
cnr   corner
CO   Colorado
Co   Company; County
c/o   care of
Coah.   Coahuila
Col   Colonel
Col.   Colima; Colonia
COMESA   Common Market for Eastern and Southern Africa
Comm.   Commission; Commendatore
Commdr   Commander
Commdt   Commandant
Commr   Commissioner
Cond.   Condiminio
Conf   Confederation
confs   conferences
Cont.   Contador (Accountant)
COO   Chief Operating Officer
COP   Conference of (the) Parties
Corp.   Corporate
Corpn   Corporation
CP   Case Postale, Caixa Postal, Casella Postale (Post Box); Communist Party
C por A   Compañía por Acciones (Joint Stock Company)
CPOB   Central Post Office Box

CPSU   Communist Party of the Soviet Union
Cres.   Crescent
CSCE   Conference on Security and Cooperation in Europe
CSTAL   Confederación Sindical de los Trabajadores de América Latina
CT   Connecticut
CTCA   Confederación de Trabajadores Centro-americanos
Cttee   Committee
cu   cubic
cwt   hundredweight

DC   District of Columbia; Distrito Capital; Distrito Central
d.d.   delniška družba, dioničko društvo (joint stock company)
DE   Delaware; Departamento Estatal
Dec.   December
Del.   Delegación
Dem.   Democrat; Democratic
Dep.   Deputy
dep.   deposits
Dept   Department
devt   development
DF   Distrito Federal
Dgo   Durango
Diag.   Diagonal
Dir   Director
Div.   Division(al)
DM   Deutsche Mark
DMZ   demilitarized zone
DNA   deoxyribonucleic acid
DN   Distrito Nacional
Doc.   Docent
Dott.   Dottore/essa
DPRK   Democratic People's Republic of Korea
Dr   Doctor
Dr.   Drive
Dra   Doctora
Dr Hab.   Doktor Habilitowany (Assistant Professor)
DRC   Democratic Republic of the Congo
DR-CAFTA   Dominican Republic-Central American Free Trade Agreement
Drs   Doctorandus
DU   depleted uranium
dwt   dead weight tons

E   East; Eastern
EAC   East African Community
EBRD   European Bank for Reconstruction and Development
EC   European Community
ECA   (United Nations) Economic Commission for Africa
ECE   (United Nations) Economic Commission for Europe
ECF   Extended Credit Facility
ECLAC   (United Nations) Economic Commission for Latin America and the Caribbean
ECO   Economic Cooperation Organization
Econ.   Economics; Economist
ECOSOC   (United Nations) Economic and Social Council
ECOWAS   Economic Community of West African States
ECU   European Currency Unit

Edif.	Edificio (Building)	HDI	Human Development Index	Jr	Jonkheer (Esquire); Junior
edn	edition	HDTV	high-definition television	Jt	Joint
EEA	European Economic Area	HE	His/Her Eminence; His/Her		
EFTA	European Free Trade		Excellency		
	Association	hf	hlutafelag (Limited Company)	Kav.	Kaveling (Plot)
e.g.	exempli gratia (for example)	HI	Hawaii	kg	kilogram(s)
EIB	European Investment Bank	HIPC	heavily indebted poor country	KG	Kommandit Gesellschaft
EMS	European Monetary System	HIV	human immunodeficiency virus		(Limited Partnership)
EMU	Economic and Monetary Union	hl	hectolitre(s)	kHz	kilohertz
eMv	electron megavolt	HLTF	High Level Task Force	KK	Kaien Kaisha (Limited Company)
Eng.	Engineer; Engineering	HM	His/Her Majesty	km	kilometre(s)
EP	Empresa Pública	Hon.	Honorary, Honourable	kom.	komnata (room)
ERM	Exchange Rate Mechanism	HPAI	highly pathogenic avian	kor.	korpus (block)
ESACA	Emisora de Capital Abierto		influenza	k'och.	k'ochasi (street)
	Sociedad Anónima	HQ	Headquarters	KS	Kansas
Esc.	Escuela; Escudos; Escritorio	HRH	His/Her Royal Highness	küç	küçasi (street)
ESCAP	(United Nations) Economic and	HS	Harmonized System	kv.	kvartal (apartment block);
	Social Commission for Asia and	HSH	His/Her Serene Highness		kvartira (apartment)
	the Pacific	Hwy	Highway	kW	kilowatt(s)
ESCWA	(United Nations) Economic and			kWh	kilowatt hour(s)
	Social Commission for Western	IA	Iowa	KY	Kentucky
	Asia	IBRD	International Bank for		
esq.	esquina (corner)		Reconstruction and		
est.	established; estimate; estimated		Development	LA	Louisiana
etc.	et cetera	ICC	International Chamber of	lauk	laukums (square)
EU	European Union		Commerce; International	lb	pound(s)
eV	eingetragener Verein		Criminal Court	LDCs	Least Developed Countries
excl.	excluding	ICRC	International Committee of the	Lic.	Licenciado
exec.	executive		Red Cross	Licda	Licenciada
Ext.	Extension	ICT	information and communication	LLC	Limited Liability Company
			technology	LNG	liquefied natural gas
F	Fahrenheit	ICTR	International Criminal Tribunal	LPG	liquefied petroleum gas
f.	founded		for Rwanda	Lt, Lieut	Lieutenant
FAO	Food and Agriculture	ICTY	International Criminal Tribunal	Ltd	Limited
	Organization		for the former Yugoslavia		
f.a.s.	free alongside ship	ID	Idaho		
FDI	foreign direct investment	IDA	International Development		
Feb.	February		Association		
Fed.	Federal; Federation	IDB	Inter-American Development	m	metre(s)
feds	federations		Bank	m.	million
FL	Florida	IDPs	internally displaced persons	MA	Massachusetts
FM	frequency modulation	i.e.	id est (that is to say)	Maj.	Major
fmr(ly)	former(ly)	IFC	International Finance	Man.	Manager; managing
f.o.b.	free on board		Corporation	MB	Manitoba
Fr	Father	IGAD	Intergovernmental Authority on	mbH	mit beschränkter Haftung (with
Fr.	Franc		Development		limited liability)
Fri.	Friday	IHL	International Humanitarian Law	MD	Maryland
FRY	Federal Republic of Yugoslavia	IL	Illinois	MDG	Millennium Development Goal
ft	foot (feet)	ILO	International Labour	MDRI	multilateral debt relief initiative
FTA	free trade agreement/area		Organization/Office	ME	Maine
FYRM	former Yugoslav republic of	IMF	International Monetary Fund	Me	Maître
	Macedonia	IML	International Migration Law	mem.(s)	member(s)
		in (ins)	inch (inches)	MEP	Member of the European
		IN	Indiana		Parliament
g	gram(s)	Inc, Incorp.		Mercosul	Mercado Comum do Sul
g.	gatve (street)	Incd	Incorporated		(Southern Common Market)
GA	Georgia	incl.	including	Mercosur	Mercado Común del Sur
GATT	General Agreement on Tariffs	Ind.	Independent		(Southern Common Market)
	and Trade	INF	Intermediate-Range Nuclear	Méx.	México
GCC	Gulf Cooperation Council		Forces	MFN	most favoured nation
Gdns	Gardens	Ing.	Engineer	mfrs	manufacturers
GDP	gross domestic product	Insp.	Inspector	Mgr	Monseigneur; Monsignor
GEF	Gobal Environment Facility	Int.	International	MHz	megahertz
Gen.	General	Inzå.	Engineer	MI	Michigan
GeV	giga electron volts	IP	intellectual property	MIA	missing in action
GM	genetically modified	IPU	Inter-Parliamentary Union	Mich.	Michoacán
GmbH	Gesellschaft mit beschränkter	Ir	Engineer	MIGA	Multilateral Investment
	Haftung (Limited Liability	IRF	International Road Federation		Guarantee Agency
	Company)	irreg.	irregular	Mil.	Military
GMO(s)	genetically modified organism(s)	Is	Islands	Mlle	Mademoiselle
GMT	Greenwich Mean Time	ISIC	International Standard	mm	millimetre(s)
GNI	gross national income		Industrial Classification	Mme	Madame
GNP	gross national product	IT	information technology	MN	Minnesota
Gov.	Governor	ITU	International Telecommunication	mnt.	mante (road)
Govt	Government		Union	MO	Missouri
GPOB	General Post Office Box	ITUC	International Trade Union	Mon.	Monday
Gro	Guerrero		Confederation	Mor.	Morelos
grt	gross registered tons	Iur.	Lawyer	MOU	Memorandum of Understanding
GSM	Global System for Mobile	IUU	illegal, unreported and	movt	movement
	Communications		unregulated	MP	Member of Parliament
Gto	Guanajuato			MS	Mississippi
GWh	gigawatt hour(s)			MSS	Manuscripts
		Jal.	Jalisco	MT	Montana
ha	hectares	Jan.	January	MW	megawatt(s); medium wave
HD	high-definition	Jnr	Junior	MWh	megawatt hour(s)

ABBREVIATIONS

N — North; Northern
n.a. — not available
nab. — naberezhnaya (embankment, quai)
NAFTA — North American Free Trade Agreement
nám. — náměstí (square)
Nat. — National
NATO — North Atlantic Treaty Organization
Nay. — Nayarit
NB — New Brunswick
NC — North Carolina
NCD — National Capital District
NCO — non-commissioned officer
ND — North Dakota
NE — Nebraska; North-East
NEPAD — New Partnership for Africa's Development
NGO — non-governmental organization
NH — New Hampshire
NJ — New Jersey
NL — Newfoundland and Labrador, Nuevo León
NM — New Mexico
NMP — net material product
no — numéro, número (number)
no. — number
Nov. — November
NPT — Non-Proliferation Treaty
nr — near
nrt — net registered tons
NS — Nova Scotia
NSW — New South Wales
NT — Northwest Territories
NU — Nunavut Territory
NV — Naamloze Vennootschap (Limited Company); Nevada
NW — North-West
NY — New York
NZ — New Zealand

OAPEC — Organization of Arab Petroleum Exporting Countries
OAS — Organization of American States
OAU — Organization of African Unity
Oax. — Oaxaca
Oct. — October
OECD — Organisation for Economic Cooperation and Development
OECS — Organisation of Eastern Caribbean States
Of. — Oficina (Office)
OH — Ohio
OIC — Organization of Islamic Cooperation
OK — Oklahoma
ON — Ontario
OPEC — Organization of the Petroleum Exporting Countries
opp. — opposite
OR — Oregon
ORB — OPEC Reference Basket
Org. — Organization
ORIT — Organización Regional Interamericana de Trabajadores
OSCE — Organization for Security and Cooperation in Europe

p. — page
p.a. — per annum
PA — Palestinian Authority; Pennsylvania
Parl. — Parliament(ary)
per. — pereulok (lane, alley)
PE — Prince Edward Island
Perm. Rep. — Permanent Representative
PF — Postfach (Post Box)
PICTs — Pacific Island countries and territories
PK — Posta Kutusu (Post Box)
Pl. — Plac, Plads (square)

pl. — platz; place; ploshchad (square)
PLC — Public Limited Company
PLO — Palestine Liberation Organization
p.m. — post meridiem (after noon)
PMB — Private Mail Bag
PNA — Palestinian National Authority
POB — Post Office Box
pp. — pages
PPP — purchasing-power parity
PQ — Québec
PR — Puerto Rico
pr. — prospekt, prospekti (avenue)
Pres. — President
PRGF — Poverty Reduction and Growth Facility
Prin. — Principal
Prof. — Professor
Propr — Proprietor
Prov. — Province; Provincial; Provinciale (Dutch)
prov. — provulok (lane)
PRSP — Poverty Reduction Strategy Paper
PSI — Policy Support Instrument, Poverty Strategies Initiative
pst. — puistotie (avenue)
PT — Perseroan Terbatas (Limited Company)
Pte — Private; Puente (Bridge)
Pty — Proprietary
p.u. — paid up
publ. — publication; published
Publr — Publisher
Pue. — Puebla
Pvt — Private

QC — Québec
QIP — Quick Impact Project
Qld — Queensland
Qro — Querétaro
Q. Roo — Quintana Roo
q.v. — quod vide (to which refer)

Rag. — Ragioniere (Accountant)
Rd — Road
R(s) — rand; rupee(s)
REC — regional economic communities
reg., regd — register; registered
reorg. — reorganized
Rep. — Republic; Republican; Representative
Repub. — Republic
res — reserve(s)
retd — retired
Rev. — Reverend
RI — Rhode Island
RJ — Rio de Janeiro
Rm — Room
RN — Royal Navy
ro-ro — roll-on roll-off
RP — Recette principale
Rp.(s) — rupiah(s)
Rpto — Reparto (Estate)
RSFSR — Russian Soviet Federative Socialist Republic
Rt — Right

S — South; Southern; San
SA — Société Anonyme, Sociedad Anónima (Limited Company); South Australia
SAARC — South Asian Association for Regional Cooperation
SACN — South American Community of Nations
SADC — Southern African Development Community
SA de CV — Sociedad Anónima de Capital Variable (Variable Capital Company)

SAECA — Sociedad Anónima Emisora de Capital Abierto
SAR — Special Administrative Region
SARL — Sociedade Anônima de Responsabilidade Limitada (Joint-Stock Company of Limited Liability)
SARS — Severe Acute Respiratory Syndrome
Sat. — Saturday
SC — South Carolina
SD — South Dakota
Sdn Bhd — Sendirian Berhad (Private Limited Company)
SDR(s) — Special Drawing Right(s)
SE — South-East
Sec. — Secretary
Secr. — Secretariat
Sen. — Senior; Senator
Sept. — September
SER — Sua Eccellenza Reverendissima (His Eminence)
SFRY — Socialist Federal Republic of Yugoslavia
SGP — Stability and Growth Pact
Sin. — Sinaloa
SIS — Small(er) Island States
SITC — Standard International Trade Classification
SJ — Society of Jesus
SK — Saskatchewan
Skt — Sankt (Saint)
SLP — San Luis Potosí
SMEs — small and medium-sized enterprises
s/n — sin número (without number)
Soc. — Society
Sok. — Sokak (Street)
Son. — Sonora
Şos. — Şosea (Road)
SP — São Paulo
SpA — Società per Azioni (Joint-Stock Company)
Sq. — Square
sq — square (in measurements)
Sr — Senior; Señor
Sra — Señora
Srl — Società a Responsabilità Limitata (Limited Company)
SRSG — Special Representative of the UN Secretary-General
SSR — Soviet Socialist Republic
St — Saint, Sint; Street
Sta — Santa
Ste — Sainte
STI(s) — sexually transmitted infection(s)
Str., str. — Strasse, strada, stradă, strasse (street)
str-la — stradelă (street)
subs. — subscribed; subscriptions
Sun. — Sunday
Supt — Superintendent
SUV — sports utility vehicle
sv. — Saint
SW — South-West

Tab. — Tabasco
Tamps — Tamaulipas
TAŞ — Turkiye Anonim Şirketi (Turkish Joint-Stock Company)
Tas — Tasmania
TD — Teachta Dàla (Member of Parliament)
tech., techn. — technical
tel. — telephone
TEU — 20-ft equivalent unit
Thur. — Thursday
TN — Tennessee
tř — třída (avenue)
Treas. — Treasurer
Tue. — Tuesday
TV — television
TWh — terawatt hour(s)
TX — Texas

ABBREVIATIONS

u.	utca (street)	UNODC	United Nations Office on Drugs and Crime	Vic	Victoria
u/a	unit of account			Vn	Veien (Street)
UAE	United Arab Emirates	UNRWA	United Nations Relief and Works Agency for Palestine Refugees in the Near East	vol.(s)	volume(s)
UEE	Unidade Económica Estatal			VT	Vermont
UEMOA	Union économique et monetaire ouest-africaine			vul.	vulitsa, vulytsa (street)
		UNSMIS	United Nations Supervision Mission in Syria		
UK	United Kingdom				
ul.	ulica, ulitsa (street)	UNWTO	World Tourism Organization	W	West; Western
UM	ouguiya	Urb.	Urbanización (District)	WA	Washington (State); Western Australia
UN	United Nations	US	United States		
UNAIDS	United Nations Joint Programme on HIV/AIDS	USA	United States of America	Wed.	Wednesday
		USAID	United States Agency for International Development	WEU	Western European Union
UNCTAD	United Nations Conference on Trade and Development			WFP	World Food Programme
		USSR	Union of Soviet Socialist Republics	WFTU	World Federation of Trade Unions
UNDP	United Nations Development Programme				
		UT	Utah	WHO	World Health Organization
UNEP	United Nations Environment Programme			WI	Wisconsin
				WSSD	World Summit on Sustainable Development
UNESCO	United Nations Educational, Scientific and Cultural Organization	VA	Virginia		
		VAT	value-added tax	WTO	World Trade Organization
		VEB	Volkseigener Betrieb (Public Company)	WV	West Virginia
UNHCHR	UN High Commissioner for Human Rights			WY	Wyoming
		v-CJD	new variant Creutzfeldt-Jakob disease		
UNHCR	United Nations High Commissioner for Refugees				
		Ven.	Venerable		
UNICEF	United Nations Children's Fund	Ver.	Veracruz	yr	year
Univ.	University	VHF	Very High Frequency	YT	Yukon Territory
		VI	(US) Virgin Islands	Yuc.	Yucatán

INTERNATIONAL TELEPHONE CODES

To make international calls to telephone and fax numbers listed in *The Europa World Year Book*, dial the international access code of the country from which you are calling, followed by the appropriate country code for the organization you wish to call (listed below), followed by the area code (if applicable) and telephone or fax number listed in the entry.

	Country code	+ or − GMT*		Country code	+ or − GMT*
Abkhazia	7	+4	Djibouti	253	+3
Afghanistan	93	+4$\frac{1}{2}$	Dominica	1 767	−4
Åland Islands	358	+2	Dominican Republic	1 809	−4
Albania	355	+1	Ecuador	593	−5
Algeria	213	+1	Egypt	20	+2
American Samoa	1 684	−11	El Salvador	503	−6
Andorra	376	+1	Equatorial Guinea	240	+1
Angola	244	+1	Eritrea	291	+3
Anguilla	1 264	−4	Estonia	372	+2
Antigua and Barbuda	1 268	−4	Ethiopia	251	+3
Argentina	54	−3	Falkland Islands	500	−4
Armenia	374	+4	Faroe Islands	298	0
Aruba	297	−4	Fiji	679	+12
Ascension Island	247	0	Finland	358	+2
Australia	61	+8 to +10	France	33	+1
Austria	43	+1	French Guiana	594	−3
Azerbaijan	994	+5	French Polynesia	689	−9 to −10
Bahamas	1 242	−5	Gabon	241	+1
Bahrain	973	+3	Gambia	220	0
Bangladesh	880	+6	Georgia	995	+4
Barbados	1 246	−4	Germany	49	+1
Belarus	375	+2	Ghana	233	0
Belgium	32	+1	Gibraltar	350	+1
Belize	501	−6	Greece	30	+2
Benin	229	+1	Greenland	299	−1 to −4
Bermuda	1 441	−4	Grenada	1 473	−4
Bhutan	975	+6	Guadeloupe	590	−4
Bolivia	591	−4	Guam	1 671	+10
Bonaire	599	−4	Guatemala	502	−6
Bosnia and Herzegovina	387	+1	Guernsey	44	0
Botswana	267	+2	Guinea	224	0
Brazil	55	−3 to −4	Guinea-Bissau	245	0
British Indian Ocean Territory			Guyana	592	−4
(Diego Garcia)	246	+5	Haiti	509	−5
British Virgin Islands	1 284	−4	Honduras	504	−6
Brunei	673	+8	Hong Kong	852	+8
Bulgaria	359	+2	Hungary	36	+1
Burkina Faso	226	0	Iceland	354	0
Burundi	257	+2	India	91	+5$\frac{1}{2}$
Cambodia	855	+7	Indonesia	62	+7 to +9
Cameroon	237	+1	Iran	98	+3$\frac{1}{2}$
Canada	1	−3 to −8	Iraq	964	+3
Cape Verde	238	−1	Ireland	353	0
Cayman Islands	1 345	−5	Isle of Man	44	0
Central African Republic	236	+1	Israel	972	+2
Ceuta	34	+1	Italy	39	+1
Chad	235	+1	Jamaica	1 876	−5
Chile	56	−4	Japan	81	+9
China, People's Republic	86	+8	Jersey	44	0
Christmas Island	61	+7	Jordan	962	+2
Cocos (Keeling) Islands	61	+6$\frac{1}{2}$	Kazakhstan	7	+6
Colombia	57	−5	Kenya	254	+3
Comoros	269	+3	Kiribati	686	+12 to +13
Congo, Democratic Republic	243	+1	Korea, Democratic People's Republic		
Congo, Republic	242	+1	(North Korea)	850	+9
Cook Islands	682	−10	Korea, Republic (South Korea)	82	+9
Costa Rica	506	−6	Kosovo	381†	+3
Côte d'Ivoire	225	0	Kuwait	965	+3
Croatia	385	+1	Kyrgyzstan	996	+5
Cuba	53	−5	Laos	856	+7
Curaçao	599	−4	Latvia	371	+2
Cyprus	357	+2	Lebanon	961	+2
Czech Republic	420	+1	Lesotho	266	+2
Denmark	45	+1	Liberia	231	0

	Country code	+ or – GMT*		Country code	+ or – GMT*
Libya	218	+1	São Tomé and Príncipe	239	0
Liechtenstein	423	+1	Saudi Arabia	966	+3
Lithuania	370	+2	Senegal	221	0
Luxembourg	352	+1	Serbia	381	+1
Macao	853	+8	Seychelles	248	+4
Macedonia, former Yugoslav republic	389	+1	Sierra Leone	232	0
Madagascar	261	+3	Singapore	65	+8
Malawi	265	+2	Sint Eustatius	1721	–4
Malaysia	60	+8	Sint Maarten	1721	–4
Maldives	960	+5	Slovakia	421	+1
Mali	223	0	Slovenia	386	+1
Malta	356	+1	Solomon Islands	677	+11
Marshall Islands	692	+12	Somalia	252	+3
Martinique	596	–4	South Africa	27	+2
Mauritania	222	0	South Ossetia	7	+4
Mauritius	230	+4	South Sudan	211	+2
Mayotte	262	+3	Spain	34	+1
Melilla	34	+1	Sri Lanka	94	$+5\frac{1}{2}$
Mexico	52	–6 to –7	Sudan	249	+2
Micronesia, Federated States	691	+10 to +11	Suriname	597	–3
Moldova	373	+2	Svalbard	47	+1
Monaco	377	+1	Swaziland	268	+2
Mongolia	976	+7 to +9	Sweden	46	+1
Montenegro	382	+1	Switzerland	41	+1
Montserrat	1 664	–4	Syria	963	+2
Morocco	212	0	Taiwan	886	+8
Mozambique	258	+2	Tajikistan	992	+5
Myanmar	95	$+6\frac{1}{2}$	Tanzania	255	+3
Nagornyi Karabakh	374	+4	Thailand	66	+7
Namibia	264	+2	Timor-Leste	670	+9
Nauru	674	+12	Togo	228	0
Nepal	977	$+5\frac{3}{4}$	Tokelau	690	+15
Netherlands	31	+1	Tonga	676	+13
New Caledonia	687	+11	Transnistria	373	+2
New Zealand	64	+12	Trinidad and Tobago	1 868	–4
Nicaragua	505	–6	Tristan da Cunha	290	0
Niger	227	+1	Tunisia	216	+1
Nigeria	234	+1	Turkey	90	+2
Niue	683	–11	'Turkish Republic of Northern Cyprus'	90 392	+2
Norfolk Island	672	$+11\frac{1}{2}$	Turkmenistan	993	+5
Northern Mariana Islands	1 670	+10	Turks and Caicos Islands	1 649	–5
Norway	47	+1	Tuvalu	688	+12
Oman	968	+4	Uganda	256	+3
Pakistan	92	+5	Ukraine	380	+2
Palau	680	+9	United Arab Emirates	971	+4
Palestinian Territories	970 or 972	+2	United Kingdom	44	0
Panama	507	–5	United States of America	1	–5 to –10
Papua New Guinea	675	+10	United States Virgin Islands	1 340	–4
Paraguay	595	–4	Uruguay	598	–3
Peru	51	–5	Uzbekistan	998	+5
Philippines	63	+8	Vanuatu	678	+11
Pitcairn Islands	872	–8	Vatican City	39	+1
Poland	48	+1	Venezuela	58	$-4\frac{1}{2}$
Portugal	351	0	Viet Nam	84	+7
Puerto Rico	1 787	–4	Wallis and Futuna Islands	681	+12
Qatar	974	+3	Yemen	967	+3
Réunion	262	+4	Zambia	260	+2
Romania	40	+2	Zimbabwe	263	+2
Russian Federation	7	+3 to +12			
Rwanda	250	+2			
Saba	599	–4			
Saint-Barthélemy	590	–4			
Saint Christopher and Nevis	1 869	–4			
Saint Helena	290	0			
Saint Lucia	1 758	–4			
Saint-Martin	590	–4			
Saint Pierre and Miquelon	508	–3			
Saint Vincent and the Grenadines	1 784	–4			
Samoa	685	+13			
San Marino	378	+1			

* The times listed compare the standard (winter) times in the various countries. Some countries adopt Summer (Daylight Saving) Time—i.e. +1 hour—for part of the year.

† Mobile telephone numbers for Kosovo use either the country code for Monaco (377) or the country code for Slovenia (386).

Note: Telephone and fax numbers using the Inmarsat ocean region code 870 are listed in full. No country or area code is required, but it is necessary to precede the number with the international access code of the country from which the call is made.

KAZAKHSTAN

Introductory Survey

LOCATION, CLIMATE, LANGUAGE, RELIGION, FLAG, CAPITAL

The Republic of Kazakhstan extends 1,900 km (1,200 miles) from the Volga river in the west to the Altai mountains in the east, and about 1,300 km (800 miles) from the Siberian plain in the north to the Central Asian deserts in the south. To the south it borders Turkmenistan, Uzbekistan and Kyrgyzstan. To the east the border is with the People's Republic of China. There is a long border in the north with Russia and a coastline of 2,320 km (1,400 miles) on the Caspian Sea in the south-west. The climate is of a strongly continental type, but there are wide variations throughout the territory. Average temperatures in January range from −18°C (0°F) in the north to −3°C (27°F) in the south. In July average temperatures are 19°C (66°F) in the north and 28°C–30°C (82°F–86°F) in the south. Average annual rainfall in mountainous regions reaches 1,600 mm (63 ins), whereas in the central desert areas it is less than 100 mm (4 ins). The state language is Kazakh; however, Russian is employed officially in state and local government bodies. The predominant religion is Islam, most ethnic Kazakhs being Sunni Muslims of the Hanafi school. Other ethnic groups have their own religious communities, notably the (Christian) Russian Orthodox Church, which is attended mainly by Slavs. The national flag (proportions 1 by 2) consists of a light blue field, at the centre of which is a yellow sun (a disc surrounded by 32 rays), framed by the wings of a flying eagle, also in yellow, with a vertical stripe of national ornamentation in yellow near the hoist. In November 1997 the capital was moved from Almatı to Aqmola (formerly Tselinograd); the city was renamed Astana in 1998.

CONTEMPORARY POLITICAL HISTORY

Historical Context

After the February Revolution and the Bolshevik coup in Russia in 1917, there was civil war throughout Kazakhstan, which had come under Russian control in the first half of the 18th century. In 1920, following the victory of Bolshevik forces over those of the White Army and local nationalists, the Kyrgyz Autonomous Soviet Socialist Republic (ASSR) was created within the Russian Soviet Federative Socialist Republic (the Russian Federation): the Kazakhs were known to the Russians as Kyrgyz, to distinguish them from the unrelated Cossacks. In 1925 the Kyrgyz ASSR was renamed the Kazakh ASSR; the Karakalpak region (Qoraqalpog'iston) was detached in 1930, and became an autonomous republic within the Uzbek Soviet Socialist Republic (SSR) in 1936. In December 1936 the Kazakh ASSR became a full Union Republic of the USSR, as the Kazakh SSR.

Under Soviet rule, parts of Kazakhstan were heavily industrialized. More than 1m. people were estimated to have died as a result of the starvation that accompanied the campaign in the early 1930s to collectivize agriculture and settle nomadic peoples. Many of those deported from parts of the USSR during the Second World War (including Germans, Baltic and Caucasian peoples) were sent to the Republic. During Nikita Khrushchev's period in office as Soviet leader (1953–64) large areas of previously uncultivated land in Kazakhstan were transformed into arable land. This, along with intensive industrialization, and the development of nuclear-testing sites and the Baikonur space centre brought large numbers of ethnic Russians to Kazakhstan, the proportion of Russians increased from 19.7% of the population in 1926 to 42.7% in 1959.

In June 1989 Nursultan Nazarbaev, Chairman of the republican Council of Ministers since March 1984, was appointed First Secretary of the Communist Party of Kazakhstan (CPK). As part of political changes instituted in September 1989, a permanent Supreme Kenges (Supreme Council or Supreme Soviet—legislature) was to be established, and multi-candidate elections were to be conducted. The state duties hitherto held by the First Secretary of the CPK were transferred to the Chairman of the Supreme Kenges, to which post Nazarbaev was elected in February 1990. Many candidates stood unopposed at elections to the Supreme Kenges in March, and the system of reserved seats for CPK-affiliated organizations was retained, resulting in a sub-

stantial communist majority. In April the body elected Nazarbaev the first President of Kazakhstan. On 25 October the Supreme Kenges declared its sovereignty. The Kazakhstani Government participated in discussions on the new Union Treaty in early 1991, although Nazarbaev also sought economic sovereignty for Kazakhstan.

In the referendum on the future of the USSR conducted in nine Soviet republics in March 1991, almost 90% of the electorate voted in Kazakhstan, of whom 94% endorsed the proposal to preserve the USSR as a 'union of sovereign states'. In June the Supreme Kenges voted, in principle, to adopt a draft union treaty. Kazakhstan was to sign the treaty in August, but the event was forestalled by an attempted coup, led by conservative communists, in Moscow, the Soviet and Russian capital. As the coup attempt collapsed, Nazarbaev resigned from the Politburo and Central Committee of the Communist Party of the Soviet Union (CPSU). The CPK was ordered to cease activities in state and government organs, and in September the party withdrew from the CPSU; elements from the party went on to form the Socialist Party of Kazakhstan (SPK).

On 1 December 1991 Nazarbaev was elected unopposed as President of Kazakhstan in direct popular elections. On 8 December the leaders of Russia, Ukraine and Belarus signed an agreement establishing the Commonwealth of Independent States (CIS, see p. 251). On 16 December Kazakhstan became the last of the republics to declare independence from the USSR. The country became a co-founder of the CIS on 21 December, when the leaders of 11 former Soviet republics met in Almatı.

Domestic Political Affairs

In June 1992 some 5,000 people demonstrated in Almatı against continued communist predominance in the Government and Supreme Kenges. In October the three most prominent nationalist opposition parties (the Freedom—Azat movement, the Republican Party, and the Jeltoqsan National Democratic Party) united to form the Republican Party—Freedom (RP—F). A new Constitution, which denoted Kazakh as the state language, was adopted in January 1993. The Union of National Unity of Kazakhstan was established in the following month, with the declared aim of countering radical nationalism. Nazarbaev (who held no party affiliation) became Chairman of the Union, which was reorganized as a political party, the People's Unity Party (PUP), later that year.

In December 1993 the Supreme Kenges voted to dissolve itself and to grant Nazarbaev the power to rule by decree pending elections to a new legislature. Kazakhstan's first multi-party elections were duly held on 7 March 1994, with the participation of 74% of the electorate; international observers reported a number of irregularities. The PUP obtained 33 seats, which, when combined with the 42 seats won by candidates from the so-called 'President's List' emerged as the strongest force in the 177-member assembly. The Confederation of Kazakhstani Trade Unions (CKTU) won 11 seats, the People's Congress Party of Kazakhstan (PCPK) nine and the SPK eight. The CPK was granted legal status in March. In that month the CKTU, the SPK and the PCPK formed an opposition bloc in the Supreme Kenges.

In May 1994 some 96 members of the Supreme Kenges endorsed a motion expressing no confidence in the Government's economic, social and legal policies, and in June Nazarbaev announced a major government reorganization. The Government of Sergei Tereshchenko (premier since 1991) resigned in October 1994, admitting its failure to reform the economy. Akejan Kajegeldin, an economist and First Deputy Prime Minister in the outgoing Council of Ministers, was appointed premier.

In February 1995 the Constitutional Court declared the results of the 1994 general election to be invalid, owing to procedural irregularities. In March the Government was forced to tender its resignation, on the grounds that it had been approved by an unconstitutional parliament, although it was subsequently reinstated virtually unchanged. Nazarbaev was thereby effectively empowered to rule by decree pending further legislative elections. At a referendum on 29 April 1995 more than

95% of voters endorsed the extension of Nazarbaev's five-year mandate until December 2000. In May 1995 Nazarbaev ordered the establishment of a special council to prepare a new constitution. The final draft, which was approved by 89.1% of the electorate in a referendum on 30 August, preserved the President's extensive executive powers. The Supreme Kenges was replaced by a bicameral Parliament, comprising a 47-member Senat (Senate), 40 members of which were to be elected by regional administrations and seven appointed by the President, and a directly elected 67-member Majlis (Assembly). The Constitutional Court was replaced by a Constitutional Council, the rulings of which were to be subject to a presidential right of veto. Indirect elections to the Senat took place on 5 December. Some 80.7% of the electorate particiapted in direct elections to the Majlis on 9 December; further rounds of voting took place later in the month and in February 1996. Foreign observers reported procedural violations.

Popular dissatisfaction with the Government's economic and social policies became more pronounced in 1996. In April a new opposition movement, Citizen (Azamat), was established. Prolonged delays in payments of wages in state-owned enterprises were a principal cause of strikes and unauthorized demonstrations throughout 1997 and early 1998, as was the ongoing reform of pensions legislation. Meanwhile, in November 1997 Nazarbaev officially inaugurated the new capital city of Aqmola, in the north of the country. A further ceremony was held in June 1998 to mark the official opening of the capital under the new name of Astana.

In March 1997 Nazarbaev undertook a major reorganization and rationalization of the state apparatus, under which the Ministry of Petroleum and Natural Gas was abolished and replaced by a new state company, KazakhOil, while seven government institutions and ministries were directly subordinated to the President, and the structure of regional government was reorganized. In October Kajegeldin resigned as premier, after a Russian newspaper published an admission by him of his previous involvement with the Soviet state security service (KGB). Nazarbaev appointed Nurlan Balgymbaev, hitherto head of KazakhOil, as his successor.

In September 1998 Nazarbaev outlined proposals for political reforms, including amendments to electoral procedures and enhanced legislative powers. In October, however, a joint session of Parliament rejected Nazarbaev's proposed constitutional reforms, and instead voted to schedule a presidential election before the expiry of Nazarbaev's extended mandate in 2000 and to decrease the quota of the votes required by parties in order to secure representation in the legislature from 10% to 7%.

During November 1998 several opposition figures, including Kajegeldin, were deemed ineligible to contest the presidency by the Central Electoral Commission (CEC), in accordance with a presidential decree, enacted in May, which prevented those convicted of an administrative offence in the 12 months prior to an election from registering as a candidate. Kajegeldin subsequently established a new political party, the Republican People's Party of Kazakhstan (RPPK). Several opposition parties were formed, although some were prevented from registering. Among those to be accorded official status was the pro-presidential Fatherland party (Otan).

Nursultan Nazarbaev re-elected as President

The conduct of the presidential election, contested by four candidates on 10 January 1999, prompted criticism from the Organization for Security and Co-operation in Europe (OSCE, see p. 397) and other international bodies. Nazarbaev was elected to a further term, with 81.0% of the votes cast by 88.3% of the registered electorate. A new Government, headed by Balgymbaev, was appointed later in the month.

In August 1999 the Minister of Defence, Gen. Muxtar Altynbaev, and the Chairman of the National Security Committee (KNB), Nurtai Abykaev, were dismissed, after admitting responsibility for the attempted illegal sale of military aircraft to the Democratic People's Republic of Korea (North Korea). In September Kajegeldin, who had been charged with tax evasion in April, was arrested at an airport in Moscow; he was released following criticism of his detention by the OSCE. Kajegeldin was barred from registering as a candidate for the parliamentary elections in October, and further charges were brought against him in February 2000.

In September 1999 the RPPK announced that it would boycott the forthcoming elections to the Majlis, in protest at the severe restrictions imposed on opposition parties. In early October Balgymbaev resigned as premier and resumed his former pos-

ition as President of KazakhOil. He was succeeded by Kasym-Jomart Tokaev. Elections to the Majlis (and to municipal and local councils) were held in two rounds on 10 and 24 October. Sixty-five candidates from nine political parties contested 10 seats allocated, for the first time, according to a party-list system, while almost 500 candidates contested the remaining 67 single-mandate constituency seats. Of the 10 party-list seats, Fatherland won four, while the CPK, the Agrarian Party of Kazakhstan—APK and the Civic Party of Kazakhstan each won two. Overall, Fatherland was the largest political grouping, with 23 seats; the Civic Party held 13. Three other parties achieved representation, and 34 independent candidates were elected. The rate of participation by voters was reported to be 62.6%.

In June 2000 a law was approved awarding Nazarbaev certain lifetime guarantees and rights. In September 2001 Kajegeldin was sentenced *in absentia* to 10 years' imprisonment, having been found guilty of abuse of power, tax evasion and the illegal possession of weapons. In November Nazarbaev approved the resignation of Rahat Aliev (the husband of his daughter, Darigha Nazarbaeva) as Deputy Chairman of the KNB, amid accusations of abuse of power. Persistent reports that Aliev and Nazarbaeva controlled the majority of Kazakhstan's media outlets and influenced their output prompted the Akim (Governor) of Pavlodar Oblast (region), Galymjan Jakiyanov, and a number of other prominent political and business figures, including the Deputy Prime Minister, Oraz Jandosov, to form a new political movement, the Democratic Choice of Kazakhstan (DCK). Tokaev subsequently announced that two attempts to assassinate the President had been averted, and threatened to resign as Prime Minister unless the President dismissed ministers whom he denounced as disloyal, owing to their involvement in the formation of the DCK. Jandosov and Alixan Baymenov (the Minister of Labour and Social Security) resigned shortly afterwards; Nazarbaev dismissed Jakiyanov on the same day. In December Altynbaev was appointed to his former position of Minister of Defence. In early 2002 the Citizen (Azamat) Democratic Party, the PCPK and the RPPK. merged to form the United Democratic Party

In January 2002 amendments to media legislation came into effect, which required 50% of all radio and television programmes to be broadcast in Kazakh, and imposed restrictions on the rebroadcast of foreign television programmes and on internet media. Later in the month Tokaev resigned, but was appointed State Secretary and Minister of Foreign Affairs in a new Government formed on 31 January and led by a former Deputy Prime Minister, Imangali Tasmagambetov. Meanwhile, divisions emerged within the DCK, and several of its founding members, including Jandosov and Jakiyanov, formed new party, the Bright Road Democratic Party of Kazakhstan (Bright Road—Ak Jol). Jakiyanov, however, was subsequently arrested, and sentenced in August to a seven-year gaol term on charges of abuse of power during his tenure as Akim of Pavlodar Oblast.

In July 2002 Nazarbaev signed into effect new legislation requiring political parties to have a minimum of 50,000 members (rather than the previous 3,000), in order to be permitted to register. In the same month a former Minister of Energy, Industry and Trade and founding member of the DCK, Muxtar Ablyazov, was sentenced to six years' imprisonment, having been found guilty of abuse of office.

In January 2003 it was reported that Jandosov had been appointed as a presidential aide, apparently drawing into question the status of Bright Road as an opposition party. Also in January the Ministry of Justice annulled the DCK's registration. In the same month the establishment of a new opposition bloc, Democracy-Elections-Kazakhstan, was announced, with the aim of uniting those parties prevented from re-registering under the new regulations. By the end of the re-registration period in April, only seven parties had satisfied the requisite criteria. Meanwhile, in January Sergei Duvanov, an independent journalist, was sentenced to three-and-a-half years' imprisonment on charges of rape. In February the European Parliament adopted a resolution condemning the sentences imposed on Duvanov, Ablyazov and Jakiyanov, and demanding that an independent investigation into their trials be carried out. Ablyazov was pardoned in May, and subsequently announced his withdrawal from politics. (Duvanov was released in August 2004, and Jakiyanov was released on parole in January 2006.)

However, on 9 June 2003 Tasmagambetov tendered his resignation, after it emerged that the results of an unsuccessful no confidence vote, conducted in the legislature in May, had been falsified. A new, substantially unchanged Government, led by

Danïal Axmetov, a former Akim of Pavlodar Oblast, was appointed in June. In September Zautbek Turisbekov was appointed as Minister of Internal Affairs, after Nazarbaev decreed that the heads of the law enforcement and security bodies should be civilian appointments.

The 2004 legislative elections

Although newly emerged political parties continued to be refused registration by the Ministry of Justice, in October 2003 a new organization led by Darigha Nazarbaeva, Mutual Help (Asar), was officially registered, as were the Communist People's Party of Kazakhstan (CPPK) and the Democratic Party of Kazakhstan (DPK) in June 2004. On 19 September and 3 October 2003 elections took place to the Majlis. Fatherland obtained 42 seats. An electoral coalition formed by the APK and the Civic Party of Kazakhstan won 11 seats, while Mutual Help obtained four seats. Bright Road and the DPK each obtained one seat, and 18 non-partisan candidates were elected. Monitors from the OSCE criticized the conduct of the polls and media electoral coverage. Baymenov, now a member of Bright Road, and who was effectively the only opposition representative elected to the new legislature, subsequently announced that he would not take up his seat in the Majlis, alleging that the results of the elections had been falsified. The Chairman of the outgoing legislature, Jarmakhan Tuyakbay, resigned from Fatherland in order to protest against the conduct of the elections.

In January 2005, following a declaration by the DCK in the previous month that it regarded the Kazakhstani Government to be illegitimate and urging non-violent civil disobedience, a court ordered that the party be dissolved, on the grounds that it had breached national security laws. Later in the month the DCK, Bright Road and the CPK (which had established an alliance) organized an unsanctioned rally to protest against the court ruling. In February the three parties announced that they were to establish a new movement, to be known as For a Just Kazakhstan. In March former members of the DCK announced the establishment of a new grouping, Forward (Alga), led by Asylbek Kojaxmetov (which was subsequently refused registration). In April another new party, Real Bright Road (Naghyz Ak Jol), held its founding congress, following divisions within Bright Road.

Meanwhile, in December 2004 President Nazarbaev issued a decree allowing the election of village akims (who had hitherto been appointed), as well as the 'experimental' election of several oblast akims. Elections were duly held in villages and in four oblasts during 2005. In the elections to the oblast posts, all the incumbent candidates were returned to office, and all candidates had been nominated by the local authorities.

In April 2005 legislation was introduced to prohibit public demonstrations both during and immediately after elections. In July it was announced that the security agencies were prepared to use force against any unrest that might arise around the time of the forthcoming presidential election (in response to successful popular revolts, following disputed elections, in Georgia, Ukraine and Kyrgyzstan during 2003–05). In early August the For a Just Kazakhstan coalition, led by Tuyakbay, and now comprising the CPK, Forward, the Generation Pensioners' Movement and Real Bright Road, was granted official registration. In September the Majlis confirmed that a presidential election would be held in December, one year earlier than had been anticipated.

In the presidential ballot, conducted on 4 December 2005, Nazarbaev was re-elected as President, with 91.2% of the votes cast, according to official results. Of the four other candidates, Nazarbaev's closest rival was Tuyakbay, who received 6.6% of the votes. The rate of participation was 76.8%. Monitors from the OSCE declared that the conduct of the election had not satisfied international standards of democracy. On 18 January 2006 both legislative chambers unanimously approved Nazarbaev's nomination of Axmetov as Prime Minister. One day later Nazarbaev approved a new, substantially unchanged, Government. New appointments included those of Kärim Mäsımov, a long-standing presidential aide and prominent economist, as Deputy Prime Minister and Natalya Korzhova as Minister of Finance.

In February 2006 Altynbek Sarsenbaev, one of the leaders of Real Bright Road and a prominent supporter of Tuyakbay's presidential campaign, was shot dead in Almatı. Those detained on suspicion of involvement in the case included five KNB officials and the head of the administration of the Senat, Erjan Utembaev. The head of the KNB, Nartai Dutbaev, subsequently resigned as a result of the investigation. In March Real Bright Road was granted official registration. The conviction, in August,

of 10 people (including Utembaev) charged with involvement in the killing of Sarsenbaev attracted international criticism; a former security officer received the death sentence, and Utembaev was sentenced to 20 years' imprisonment. In June the Majlis adopted legislative amendments (strongly criticized by the OSCE) that would enforce greater regulation over media outlets. These were endorsed by the Senat on 29 June and signed into law by the President on 4 July. Also in July, Fatherland merged with Mutual Help, thereby consolidating parliamentary support for Nazarbaev. In December the APK and Civic Party also merged with Fatherland; the new party, known as Light of the Fatherland (Nur Otan) thereby controlled 57 seats in the Majlis.

Constitutional amendments and the 2007 elections

On 8 January 2007 Axmetov resigned as Prime Minister; he had been subject to repeated presidential criticism for poor organization and budget-planning. On 10 January the Majlis voted to approve Nazarbaev's nomination of Mäsımov as premier. Aslan Musin was appointed as Deputy Prime Minister (retaining his existing portfolio as Minister of the Economy and Budgetary Planning), while Axmetov became Minister of Defence. Tokaev became Chairman of the Senat. In May Parliament approved extensive constitutional amendments, proposed by President Nazarbaev, strengthening the powers of an expanded Majlis, which was henceforth to approve prime ministerial appointments. The presidential term of office was to be reduced from seven to five years with effect from 2012, while the restriction on the incumbent President to two terms in office was to be removed.

In June 2007 Rahat Aliev, by then the Kazakhstani ambassador to Austria, was arrested in that country, after Kazakhstan had issued an arrest warrant against him for his alleged involvement in the kidnapping of two banking associates; Kazakhstan officially requested his extradition. (In January 2008 a district court in Almatı imposed *in absentia* a 20-year sentence of imprisonment on Aliev, who had claimed asylum in Austria, for his involvement in the creation of an organized criminal group and the abductions of the banking officials. In March, at a second trial *in absentia*, a military court sentenced Aliev to another 20 years' imprisonment for illegal possession of armaments and ammunition, misappropriation of property and planning a coup.)

In mid-June 2007 President Nazarbaev dissolved the Majlis and announced legislative elections were to be held on 18 August (two years earlier than scheduled). At the elections Light of the Fatherland won 88.4% of the votes cast, securing all 98 contested seats in the enlarged 107-member Majlis. None of the other six parties participating in the poll achieved the 7% minimum of votes required to gain representation in the chamber; the newly established National Social Democratic Party (NSDP) received 4.5% and Bright Road 3.1% of the votes cast. The leaders of the NSDP, Bright Road and the CPPK refused to acknowledge the results and demanded that the poll be repeated. In accordance with the amended Constitution, the Assembly of the Nations of Kazakhstan (representing minority ethnic groups, and which was later renamed the Assembly of the Nation of Kazakhstan) elected the remaining nine deputies to the Majlis on 20 August. A reorganized Government was approved at the first session of the new Parliament on 2 September; Ömirzaq Şökeev, hitherto Akim of Southern Kazakhstan Oblast, became the new Deputy Prime Minister, succeeding Musin, who was elected Chairman of the Majlis. In February 2008, during a party congress, Real Bright Road was renamed Freedom (Azat). Elections were held to one-half of the 32 indirectly elected seats in the Senat on 4 October.

In early 2009 Ablyazov fled to the United Kingdom, where he claimed political asylum, after the Kazakhstani authorities issued an arrest warrant against him for embezzlement in his previous post as Chairman of BTA Bank. (In July 2011 Ablyazov was granted asylum by the United Kingdom, where BTA Bank initiated a court case against him on allegations of fraud. In February 2012 he left the United Kingdom, after he was sentenced to 22 months' imprisonment for failing to disclose his assets.) In February the Constitutional Court revoked legislation restricting freedom of religious worship, which had been adopted the previous November, after a report by the OSCE Office for Democratic Institutions and Human Rights criticized it as being incompatible with Kazakhstan's commitments towards the OSCE (particularly in view of its forthcoming assumption of the body's chairmanship).

In March 2009 a number of significant appointments of government ministers and other public officials were effected. Şökeev received the post of First Deputy Prime Minister, while

Serik Axmetov, hitherto Minister of Transport, became a Deputy Prime Minister. The removal of Daníal Axmetov as Minister of Defence in June was believed to be connected to a contract agreed with an Israeli company in 2007, which had resulted in a substantial loss of government funds and had prompted the arrest of various senior officials on charges of corruption. Adilbek Jaqsıbekov, hitherto ambassador to Russia, was appointed as the new Minister of Defence. In September Qanatbek Sawdabaev was appointed as Minister of Foreign Affairs to succeed Marat Täjïn, who became a presidential aide.

In June 2009 Parliament adopted legislative amendments, designating all online resources as mass media, thereby allowing any websites deemed to be in violation of existing media regulations to be blocked and their owners prosecuted. Although the OSCE urged Nazarbaev to veto the new provisions, they were enacted on 10 July. In September a sentence of four years' imprisonment imposed on human rights activist Yevgeny Jovtis, after he had been convicted of manslaughter resulting from a car accident, prompted protests from domestic and international human rights groups, and from the OSCE. (Jovtis was freed under amnesty in February 2012.) Later that month the deputy leader of Light of the Fatherland urged the adoption of legislation that would permit Nazarbaev to remain as President indefinitely. At a unification congress in October Freedom and the NSDP agreed to form a single party, to be known as the Freedom National Social Democratic Party (FNSDP), which was to be headed jointly by the leaders of the two constituent parties. In November Serik Axmetov resigned from the post of Deputy Prime Minister, following his appointment as Akim of Qarağandi Oblast.

In March 2010 a substantial reorganization of the Government and other state agencies was implemented. The hitherto Minister of Industry and Trade, Aset Isekeşev, was appointed to the posts of Deputy Prime Minister and Minister of Industry and New Technologies, while Sawat Miñbaev, hitherto the Minister of Energy and Mineral Resources became the Minister of Oil and Gas. In May both parliamentary chambers approved legislation awarding Nazarbaev the title 'Leader of the Nation', while also granting him and his relatives immunity from prosecution, and making it a criminal offence to utter or publish insulting remarks about the President. Although Nazarbaev formally refused to sign the legislation into law, it automatically entered into force on 15 June. In September Nazarbaev indicated his intention of contesting the next presidential election in 2012.

The 2011 presidential election

On 29 December 2010 both chambers of the Parliament adopted a motion, which had initially been proposed by a citizen's group, in favour of extending Nazarbaev's term in office until 2020, subject to approval at a national referendum. On 6 January 2011 Nazarbaev issued a decree vetoing the proposal. On 14 January both parliamentary chambers voted unanimously to amend the Constitution to permit the referendum, following the submission of a petition of 5m. signatures in its support. However, Nazarbaev subsequently refused to sign the constitutional amendments into force, instead referring them to the Constitutional Court for consideration. On 31 January the Court ruled against the organization of a referendum on the proposals. Nazarbaev announced his acceptance of the Court's decision and proposed that an early presidential election be conducted (which he subsequently scheduled for 3 April). At a party congress in February, the FNSDP announced that it would boycott the forthcoming presidential election; the three opposition candidates who finally secured registration to contest the poll all declared their support for Nazarbaev.

Nazarbaev was returned to office at the presidential election on 3 April 2011, securing 95.6% of the votes cast, according to official results; voter turn-out of 89.9% was recorded. Nazarbaev was inaugurated for a further five-year term on 8 April, when, in response to the international criticism of the electoral process, he issued pledges to increase anti-corruption efforts and institutional reforms (which included commitments that political parties other than Light of the Fatherland be represented in the Majlis). On the same day Nazarbaev's reappointment of Mäsımov as premier was approved by the Majlis. Nazarbaev subsequently reorganized the Government, notably replacing Sawdabaev as Minister of Foreign Affairs with a former ambassador to the UN, Erjan Qazıxanov, and appointing Qayrat Kelimbetov as Minister of Economic Development and Trade. A new Minister of Internal Affairs, Qalmuxanbet Qasımov was also appointed, while a new ministerial position, of Economic Integration, was created. Meanwhile, on 15 April Kayrat Mami,

hitherto Prosecutor-General, was elected Chairman of the Senat, after he had been appointed to the chamber by Nazarbaev. A new Prosecutor-General was appointed on the same day, and one day later Nazarbaev dismissed six judges of the Supreme Court, who were under investigation for corrupt activity.

Islamist unrest and the 2012 legislative elections

In mid-April 2011 a man blew himself up in the north-western city of Aqtöbe, injuring at least two people, in what was reported to be Kazakhstan's first suicide bombing. (Twelve men were imprisoned in December in connection with the incident.) Violent confrontations in Aqtöbe Oblast between Islamist militants and security forces in June and July reportedly resulted in the deaths of nine fighters and three police officers, while the detonation of a bomb in Aqtöbe in July resulted in three deaths. (In February 2012 five men were sentenced to prison terms for their involvement in this attack.) Meanwhile, in June 2011 two bodies, found in Almatı during the previous month, were identified as being those of the former banking associates of Rahat Aliev who had been kidnapped in 2007. Aliev was charged *in absentia* with involvement in their deaths, but the Austrian Government rejected an extradition request on the grounds that Aliev had taken up residence in Malta. In April 2012 Austrian prosecutors interrogated Aliev about his alleged involvement in the deaths.

In June 2011 the First Secretary of the CPK, Gaziz Aldamjarov, and the leader of Forward, Vladimir Kozlov, together with representatives of several non-governmental organizations, announced the formation of a Popular Front to contest the 2012 legislative elections. Meanwhile, in May 2011 petroleum sector workers in western Kazakhstan commenced strike action in support of wage increases and rights for trade unions. Several activists connected with the strike were arrested and prosecuted, including a lawyer representing the workers, Nataliya Sokolova, who received a six-year prison sentence in August. (She was released on probation in March 2012.) Also in August 2011 Jaqsılıq Dosqalïev, who had been dismissed as Minister of Health in October of the previous year, was sentenced to seven years' imprisonment after he was found guilty of corruption.

On 19 August 2011 Light of the Fatherland secured all 16 contested seats in partial elections in the Senat. In October Valerii Proskuryakov, a prominent member of Light of the Fatherland, was shot dead in the eastern city of Öskemen. Meanwhile, both legislative chambers approved new legislation that required all religious organizations to re-register with the Government, and imposed further restrictions on religious activity. Nazarbaev signed the legislation, which was widely considered to be directed against the influence of fundamentalist Islam, into law in October.

In early October 2011 the CPK's operations were suspended for six months by a court order, on the grounds that the formation of the Popular Front violated the law on public organizations. Aldamjarov claimed that the court's ruling was politically motivated, in light of the Popular Front's support for the strike action by petroleum industry workers, and in April 2012 the suspension was extended by a further six months. In late October 2011 two explosions occurred in the western city of Atiraw, reportedly killing one person. A militant Islamist group based in the territories on the borders of Afghanistan and Pakistan, Jund al-Khilafah (Soldiers of the Caliphate), claimed responsibility for the bombings, and voiced its opposition to the recently introduced religious legislation. (In April 2012 some 47 people were sentenced to between five and 15 years' imprisonment on terrorism charges in connection with the Atiraw bombings.) In November, seven people were shot dead in the southern city of Taraz by an Islamic militant who subsequently blew himself up. (Five men charged with involvement in the incident were sentenced to imprisonment in April 2012.) Jund al-Khilafah also claimed that five men killed in a security operation near Almatı were members of its organization.

In November 2011, in response to a petition from members of the Majlis, President Nazarbaev dissolved the lower house and scheduled pre-term elections for January 2012, seven months before the expiry of the mandate of the chamber. On 16 December, Independence Day, at least 17 people were killed in violent confrontations between striking petroleum workers and security forces in the western town of Jañaözen, in Mañğıstaw Oblast. President Nazarbaev declared a state of emergency and curfew in Jañaözen; this was subsequently extended to the end of January 2012.

At the legislative elections held on 15 January 2012, three parties passed the 7% threshold necessary to achieve representation in the Majlis. Light of the Fatherland won 80.99% of the votes cast, according to the CEC, obtaining 83 of the 98 elective seats, ahead of Bright Road, who won 7.5% of the vote and eight seats, and the CPPK, with 7.2% of the vote and seven seats. Nine further deputies were appointed by the Assembly of the Nation of Kazakhstan. Participation was recorded at 75.4% of registered voters. Observers from the OSCE criticized the poll for failing to meet international democratic standards, citing in particular the denial of registration to the candidates of certain parties—including the entire list of candidates proposed by the Spirituality Party (Ruxniyat)—and the ongoing suspension of the CPK's activities. The new Majlis was formally inaugurated on 20 January. It reconfirmed Mäsımov as Prime Minister, and appointed Nurlan Nigmatulin as its Chairman.

Following the elections, in late January 2012 the authorities began to arrest large numbers of opposition figures and journalists in connection with the unrest in Jañaözen. The offices of Forward were raided by police, and Kozlov was arrested; it was subsequently announced that he was to be charged with inciting the striking workers in Jañaözen to violence. The Government alleged that Ablyazov had been involved in instigating the unrest from his exile, and that earlier in the year a series of terrorist attacks planned by individuals connected to Forward and to Ablyazov had been averted.

In May 2012 five police officers were sentenced to prison terms of between five and seven years for abusing their authority during the suppression of the protests in Jañaözen. Following a separate trial, in June 34 people were convicted on charges of organizing or participating in the violence in the city, of whom 13 received custodial sentences. In August the trial commenced in Aktaw of three opposition activists—Kozlov, Popular Front member Serik Sapargali, and a petroleum worker, Aizhanat Aminov—on charges that included fomenting social unrest during the strike in Jañaözen. In September Orak Sarbopeev, a former Akim of Jañaözen, was found guilty of preparing criminal activity and sentenced to 10 years' imprisonment. (Earlier in the year Sarbopeev had been acquitted of charges of embezzlement.) On 8 October Kozlov was sentenced to seven-and-a-half-years' imprisonment, and Aminova to a suspended term of five years, on charges of inciting social discord, of seeking to overthrow of the constitutional order, and of leading a group intent upon criminal activity; Sapargali received a four-year suspended sentence for inciting the overthrow of the constitutional order. Meanwhile, in September further bomb attacks were staged in Atiraw, including an explosion near a mosque in which one person was killed, and one at interior ministry offices in which two policemen were injured.

Recent developments: government reorganization

On 24 September 2012 President Nazarbaev appointed Serik Axmetov (who had been appointed First Deputy Prime Minister in January) as Prime Minister, replacing Mäsımov, who became presidential Chief of Staff. Qırımbek Köşerbaev, who had resigned as Akim of Mañğıstaw Oblast following the violence there, became First Deputy Prime Minister, Minister of Regional Development, while other government changes included the appointment of Erlan Idırısov, hitherto ambassador to the USA, as Minister of Foreign Affairs. Some observers suggested that the reshuffle was intended to help identify an eventual successor to Nazarbaev, who was reported to have undergone surgery for prostate cancer in Germany in the previous year (although official sources in Kazakhstan neither denied nor confirmed these reports.)

Following the conviction of Kozlov, in November 2012 prosecutors demanded a ban on the activities of Forward and the Popular Front, together with the closure of the main independent media outlets, including the *Respublika* and the *Vzglyad* (Glance) newspapers and two television stations, on the grounds that they had incited the overthrow of the Government prior to the violence in Jañaözen. The authorities claimed that Forward and several opposition organs were financed by Ablyazov, who in the same month was ordered to pay the equivalent of more than US $1,630m., after a British court upheld the charges brought by BTA Bank against him and froze his remaining assets. Also in November a court in the southern town of Qizilorda sentenced former Deputy Akim of Mañğıstaw Amangeldy Aitkulov (who had also been arrested following the violence in Jañaözen), to 12 years' imprisonment for abuse of office and corrupt practices. Following the suspension of their activities, in December an Almatı court upheld the ban on the two opposition movements and the media outlets, which were declared extremist, while other closure orders were pending. In the same month a prominent human rights lawyer, Vadim Kuramshin, was imprisoned

for 12 years for attempting to extort a bribe (after having been cleared of the charges earlier in the year). Opposition supporters staged demonstrations in several towns to mark the anniversary of the police killings of protesters on 16 December.

In mid-December 2012 Nazarbaev announced a programme in accordance with which the Kazakh language would be written solely in the Latin script (rather than predominately in Cyrillic, as had been the case since 1940) by 2025. In January 2013 the President appointed Bakıtjan Sagıntaev, hitherto Deputy Chairman of Light of the Fatherland and a former economy minister, to replace Köşerbaev as First Deputy Prime Minister, Minister of Regional Development (for which portfolio a new ministry was created); Köşerbaev became Akim of Qizilorda Oblast. As part of an extensive reorganization of government administrative structure, which was designed to improve the management of public expenditure, the Ministry of Economic Development and Trade was reconstituted as the Ministry of the Economy and Budgetary Planning.

Foreign Affairs

Regional relations

The question of the legal status of the Caspian Sea—and the division of the substantial mineral resources believed to be located in the seabed—has been a source of tension between the five littoral states: Azerbaijan, Iran, Kazakhstan, Russia and Turkmenistan. In 1998 Nazarbaev and the Russian President, Boris Yeltsin, signed a bilateral agreement on the delineation of their countries' respective boundaries of the Caspian seabed, by which Russia for the first time formally recognized Kazakhstan's claim to its offshore petroleum resources, prompting particular criticism from Iran, which continued to assert that partitioning of the seabed required the consensus of all five littoral states. In 2000 Nazarbaev and the President of Russia, Vladimir Putin, signed an additional agreement, on the definition of the legal status of the Caspian Sea. The 1998 agreement was further augmented in May 2002, when an accord was signed on the equal division of three oilfields in the northern Caspian. Russia and Kazakhstan have also signed a Treaty of Eternal Friendship and Co-operation, which provides for mutual military assistance in the event of aggression by a third party. In November 2001 Kazakhstan concluded a bilateral agreement with Azerbaijan on the two countries' respective mineral rights in the Caspian Sea, prompting further protests from Iran. In May 2003 Azerbaijan, Kazakhstan and Russia signed a trilateral agreement. In November representatives of Azerbaijan, Iran, Kazakhstan, Russia and Turkmenistan, meeting in Tehran, Iran, signed a UN-sponsored framework Convention for the Protection of the Marine Environment of the Caspian Sea, which sought to alleviate environmental damage in the Caspian Sea region. In January 2005 Nazarbaev and Putin signed a treaty in Moscow defining the land border between their two countries. Meeting in the Azerbaijani capital, Baku (Bakı), in November 2010, the Heads of State of Azerbaijan, Iran, Kazakhstan, Russia and Turkmenistan signed an agreement on security co-operation.

In the early 1990s the question of the formerly Soviet, subsequently Russian-controlled, nuclear warheads deployed in Kazakhstan was the focus of international concern. In September 1992 the Kazakhstani legislature ratified the first Strategic Arms Reduction Treaty, signed by the USA and the USSR in July 1991. In December 1993 the Kazakhstani legislature ratified the Treaty on the Non-Proliferation of Nuclear Weapons. By April 1995 all nuclear warheads had been transferred to Russia, and in September 1996 Russia and Kazakhstan signed a final protocol governing the withdrawal of military units linked to the Russian nuclear weapons facilities in Kazakhstan.

In May 2001 the signatories of the CIS Collective Security Treaty (Armenia, Belarus, Kazakhstan, Kyrgyzstan, Russia and Tajikistan) agreed to form a Collective Rapid Response Force, based in Bishkek, Kyrgyzstan, to combat Islamist militancy in Central Asia. An anti-terrorism centre became operational in Bishkek in August 2001. In April 2003 the signatories of the Treaty formally inaugurated the Collective Security Treaty Organization (CSTO, see p. 474), to which Uzbekistan subsequently acceded. Kazakhstan ratified an agreement to join the Collective Rapid Response Force in February 2010.

In 1992 Kazakhstan joined the Economic Cooperation Organization (ECO, see p. 274), founded by Iran, Pakistan and Turkey. In 1994 Kazakhstan, Kyrgyzstan and Uzbekistan formed a trilateral economic area, and in February 1995 an Interstate Council was established to supervise its implementation. In 1997 Tajikistan joined the alliance, which became the Central Asian

Co-operation Organization (CACO) in 2002. Meanwhile, Kazakhstan signed a treaty with Russia, Belarus and Kyrgyzstan in 1996, which envisaged a common market and a customs union between the four countries; Tajikistan signed the agreement in April 1998. In October 2000 a new economic body, the Eurasian Economic Community (EURASEC, see p. 461), was established, and this organization merged with CACO in January 2006. In October 2007 EURASEC leaders approved the legal basis for the establishment of a new customs union that was initially to comprise Belarus, Kazakhstan and Russia. President Nazarbaev and the President of Uzbekistan, Islam Karimov, signed a bilateral agreement in September 2002 on the delimitation of all disputed sectors of their countries' common border. A border agreement with Turkmenistan, which had been signed in July 2001, was ratified by the Senat in June 2003, and in July Nazarbaev signed a number of laws confirming the delimitation of Kazakhstan's borders with Kyrgyzstan, Turkmenistan and Uzbekistan. In June 2009, at a trilateral meeting of Heads of State, it was announced that Russia, Kazakhstan and Belarus were to establish a customs union at the beginning of 2010. Russia, Kazakhstan and Belarus introduced unified customs tariffs on 1 January, and the customs union officially entered into force in July. In December 2011 the Presidents of Russia, Kazakhstan and Belarus signed an agreement to establish an Eurasian Economic Commission (EEC), which was envisioned as the next stage towards the establishment of a Common Economic Space between the three countries, and, ultimately, an Eurasian Economic Union. In September 2012 Russian President Vladimir Putin made an official visit to Kazakhstan, which was followed by a reciprocal visit by Nazarbaev to Moscow in October; it was acknowledged that legislation within the customs union had not yet been fully harmonized. On January 2013 the Kazakhstani and Russian Ministers of Defence, meeting in Astana, signed an agreement providing for the establishment of a joint regional air defence system.

In 1995 Nazarbaev made an official visit to the People's Republic of China. Bilateral relations were further strengthened by two accords concluded in 1997, which granted China permission to exploit two of the largest oilfields in Kazakhstan, and provided for the construction of a petroleum pipeline (completed in 2005) connecting the two countries. In November 1998 Nazarbaev made a state visit to China, which resulted in the signature of a communiqué on the full settlement of outstanding border issues, and of an agreement outlining future bilateral relations. In July 2005 Nazarbaev and Chinese President Hu Jintao signed an agreement on the establishment of a strategic partnership between the two countries. China and Kazakhstan belonged to the so-called Shanghai Five (also comprising Kyrgyzstan, Russia and Tajikistan), which aimed to promote economic co-operation and regional co-ordination on border and security issues. Members of the alliance, which became the Shanghai Co-operation Organization (SCO, see p. 478) upon the accession of Uzbekistan in 2001, signed the Shanghai Convention on Combating Terrorism, Separatism and Extremism in June 2001. In July 2005, at a summit meeting in Astana, members of the SCO approved anti-terrorist measures, and signed a declaration advocating non-interference in the affairs of sovereign states. Several bilateral co-operation agreements were signed during a Chinese official visit to Kazakhstan in November 2007; a second stage in construction of the petroleum pipeline system linking Kazakhstan with China commenced in December. Construction of the pipeline section was completed and entered into operation in July 2009. During an official visit to China in February 2011, Nazarbaev signed a number of major economic and energy agreements with Hu, including a memorandum of understanding to support the construction of a modernized rail link between Astana and Almatı. A further meeting between the two Presidents in Astana in June resulted in the conclusion of a strategic partnership agreement and a commitment to doubling bilateral trade by 2015.

Other external relations

Following the suicide attacks on the USA on 11 September 2001, President Nazarbaev expressed his support for US-led military action against the al-Qa'ida militant Islamist organization and the regime of its hosts, the Taliban, in Afghanistan. Kazakhstan offered the USA the use of airports, airspace and military bases. In February 2006 it was announced that US forces were to participate in Kazakhstani-British military exercises in Kazakhstan in September. Nazarbaev's links with US petroleum companies were subject to legal scrutiny from March 2003, when James H. Giffen, a US businessman and former adviser to

Nazarbaev, was indicted in the USA on charges of offering bribes to prominent Kazakhstani politicians, including Nazarbaev, in return for securing valuable contracts for US petroleum companies. In April 2004 a US federal court indicted Giffen and an executive of the petroleum company, ExxonMobil, on charges of corrupt business practices. In September 2006 Nazarbaev met US President George W. Bush during an official visit to Washington, DC, USA. A Strategic Partnership Dialogue between Kazakhstan and the USA officially began in April 2012, following an agreement in January. The new Minister of Foreign Affairs, Erlan Idırısov (a former ambassador to the USA), met US Secretary of State Hillary Clinton for discussions in the US capital in October.

Despite criticism by the OSCE of the conduct of elections held in August 2007, and continuing international concerns over human rights abuses in the country, on 1 January 2010 Kazakhstan assumed the OSCE rotating chairmanship for the period of one year. Amid considerable publicity, the authorities convened an OSCE summit meeting in Astana in December. In March 2011 Kazakhstan submitted an application for membership of the UN Human Rights Council, which, despite continuing criticism by human rights groups of the country's record, was approved on 12 November 2012. In February 2013 the Iranian Government accepted an offer by Kazakhstan to host further international negotiations on Iran's nuclear programme.

CONSTITUTION AND GOVERNMENT

Under the terms of the 1995 Constitution (as subsequently amended), the President of the Republic is Head of State and commander-in-chief of the armed forces, and holds broad executive powers. The President is directly elected by universal adult suffrage. Under constitutional amendments approved in 2007, the presidential term was reduced from seven to five years, with effect from 2012. The Government, headed by the Prime Minister, is responsible to the President. The supreme legislative organ is the bicameral Parliament, comprising the Senat (Senate, upper chamber) and the Majlis (Assembly, lower chamber). The Senat comprises 47 members, of whom 32 are elected by regional assemblies, while the remaining 15 deputies are appointed by the President. The Majlis comprises 107 deputies, of whom 98 are directly elected; the remaining nine deputies are elected by the Assembly of the Nation of Kazakhstan (a 350-member body representing the country's minority ethnic groups). The Senat's term is six years, and that of the Majlis is five years. One-half of the elected deputies in the Senat are subject to election every three years. Judicial power is exercised by local courts and the Supreme Court. For administrative purposes, Kazakhstan is divided into 16 units (14 regions and the cities of Almatı and Astana). The city of Leninsk (now Turatam) serving the Baikonur space centre, and formerly one of Kazakhstan's administrative units, was transferred to Russian jurisdiction in August 1995. In January 2004 President Nazarbaev and the Russian President, Vladimir Putin, signed an agreement permitting Russia's continued use of the Baikonur space centre until 2050.

REGIONAL AND INTERNATIONAL CO-OPERATION

Kazakhstan is a founder member of the Commonwealth of Independent States (CIS, see p. 251) and participates in the Collective Security Treaty Organization (CSTO, see p. 474), and in the Customs Union of Belarus, Russia and Kazakhstan, which entered into effect in July 2010. It is also a member of the Organization for Security and Co-operation in Europe (OSCE, see p. 397), of which it assumed the rotating chairmanship in 2010. Kazakhstan is a member of the Economic Cooperation Organization (ECO, see p. 274), the Eurasian Economic Community (EURASEC, see p. 461), the Shanghai Co-operation Organization (SCO, see p. 478) and the Organization of Islamic Cooperation (see p. 413). Kazakhstan joined the UN in 1992.

ECONOMIC AFFAIRS

In 2011, according to estimates by the World Bank, Kazakhstan's gross national income (GNI), measured at average 2009–11 prices, was US $136,120m., equivalent to $8,220 per head (or $11,310 per head on an international purchasing-power parity basis). During 2002–11, it was estimated, the population increased at an average annual rate of 1.2%, while gross domestic product (GDP) per head increased, in real terms, by an average annual rate of 6.2%. Overall GDP increased, in real terms, at an average annual rate of 7.5% in 2002–11. Real GDP increased by 7.5% in 2011.

Agriculture (including forestry and fishing) contributed 4.4% of GDP in 2012 and provided 26.5% of total employment in 2011. There are large areas of land suitable for agriculture, and Kazakhstan is a major producer and exporter of agricultural products. The principal crops include fruit, sugar beet, vegetables, potatoes, cotton and, most importantly, cereals. Livestock-breeding is also important, and Kazakhstan is a significant producer of karakul and astrakhan wools. According to the World Bank, the GDP of the agricultural sector increased, in real terms, by an average of 2.5% per year in 2002–11. Agricultural GDP decreased by 11.6% in 2010, largely as result of a drought, but increased by 5.0% in 2011.

Industry (including mining, manufacturing, construction, and power) contributed 39.2% of GDP in 2012 and provided 19.0% of total employment in 2011. The principal branches of industry include the fuel industry and metal-processing. According to World Bank figures, industrial GDP increased, in real terms, at an average annual rate of 7.3% in 2002–11. The GDP of the sector increased by 3.1% in 2011.

Mining and quarrying contributed 18.6% of GDP in 2012 and provided 2.5% of employment in 2011. Kazakhstan possesses immense mineral wealth, and large-scale mining and processing industries have been developed. There are major coalfields, as well as substantial deposits of iron ore, lead, zinc ore, titanium, magnesium, chromium, tungsten, molybdenum, gold, silver, copper and manganese. Petroleum is extracted, and Kazakhstan possesses substantial reserves of natural gas. In January 2004 the state-owned hydrocarbons company KazMunaiGaz awarded the Russian energy company LUKoil a 50% stake in a 40-year production-sharing contract for the development of the Tyub-Karagan field in the Caspian Sea, which has petroleum reserves of an estimated 100m. metric tons. In January 2005 the Kazakhstani and Russian Presidents signed an agreement confirming the equal rights of both countries to the Imashevskoye natural gas field, the second largest natural gas field in Kazakhstan, which was to be developed jointly by KazMunaiGaz and the Russian energy company Gazprom. Also in 2005 a subsidiary of KazMunaiGaz signed a production-sharing agreement with the Russian state-owned petroleum companies Zarubezhneft and Rosneft to develop the offshore Kurmanagazy oilfield, estimated to contain recoverable reserves of petroleum of between 900m. and 1,000m. metric tons. At the end of 2011 Kazakhstan's proven total reserves (on shore and off shore) of petroleum and natural gas were estimated at 30,000m. barrels and 1,881,176m. cu m, respectively.

Manufacturing contributed 11.8% of GDP in 2012 and provided 6.5% of employment in 2011. The GDP of the manufacturing sector increased at an average annual rate of 5.7% in 2002–11, according to the World Bank. This sector's GDP increased by 13.6% in 2010 and by 4.0% in 2011.

The construction sector contributed 6.6% of GDP in 2012 and engaged 7.4% of the employed labour force in 2011. During 2002–11, according to UN estimates, the GDP of the sector increased at an average annual rate of 14.9%. Construction GDP increased by 21.1% in 2010 and by 2.7% in 2011.

In 2009 coal-fired thermal power stations provided around 74.9% of annual domestic electricity production, while natural gas accounted for 13.1% of production, and hydroelectric power stations for a further 8.7%. In 2011 mineral products accounted for 14.6% of total imports.

The services sector contributed some 56.4% of GDP in 2012 and provided 68.2% of employment in 2011. According to the World Bank, the GDP of the services sector increased, in real terms, at an average annual rate of 7.9% during 2002–11. Services GDP increased by 8.3% in 2011.

In 2011 Kazakhstan recorded a visible merchandise trade surplus of US $47,304.0m. and there was a surplus of $14,110.0m. on the current account of the balance of payments. In 2011 the principal source of imports was Russia, which accounted for 41.4% of total imports. Other major suppliers were the People's Republic of China and Germany. The principal

market for exports in that year was the People's Republic of China, which accounted for 18.5% of total exports. Other major purchasers of exports were Italy, Russia, the Netherlands, France and Switzerland. The principal imports in 2011 were machinery and mechanical appliances, mineral products, vehicles, aircraft, and transport equipment, base metals, chemical products, and prepared foodstuffs, beverages, and tobacco. The main exports in that year were mineral products and base metals.

In 2012 Kazakhstan recorded a budgetary deficit of some 833,132.7m. tenge, equivalent to 2.8% of GDP. Kazakhstan's general government gross debt was 2,869,779m. tenge in 2011, equivalent to 10.5% of GDP. At the end of 2010 Kazakhstan's total external debt amounted to US $118,723m. of which only $3,842m. was public and publicly guaranteed. In that year, the cost of servicing long-term public and publicly guaranteed debt and repayments to the IMF was equivalent to 71.4% of the value of exports of goods, services and income (excluding workers' remittances). The annual average rate of inflation was 9.5% during 2002–08, according to ILO. According to the official figure, consumer prices increased by 6.0% in 2012. In 2011 5.4% of the labour force were unemployed.

In late 2008 the international financial crisis prompted the Kazakhstani authorities to initiate an 'anti-crisis' programme, under which savings from the National Oil Fund (established in 2001) were drawn to stabilize the banking system and other affected sectors. In 2010 Russia, Kazakhstan and Belarus established a customs union, and in 2011 it was announced that a Eurasian Economic Commission would be established to co-ordinate the projected integration of the three countries into a Common Economic Space. Trade between Kazakhstan and Russia was reported to have increased by 30% by late 2012. During 2011 workers in the petroleum and other sectors staged strike action to demand higher wages, contributing to social unrest. Although exports of crude petroleum and natural gas rose slightly in 2012, continued delays in the start of operations at the offshore Kashagan oil field, together with production problems at other oil fields, impeded output. The IMF, in a review issued in December, identified reduction of the non-oil deficit as a medium-term priority for the authorities; growth of about 5.0% was projected for that year. The Kazakhstani authorities' success in improving the business and investor environment was reflected by the country's improved rankings (at 47th of 183, and 49th of 185 countries, respectively) in the 2012 and 2013 editions of World Bank's annual *Doing Business* reports. According to official figures, European Union (see p. 281) member states provided nearly one-half of foreign direct investment in 2012 (with the Netherlands accounting for one-third); the USA was also a principal source of investment (in October the Kazakhstani-US Energy Partnership Commission signed a plan for increased co-operation). In January 2013 the head of the World Trade Organization (see p. 444) indicated that Kazakhstan might be admitted to the organization in that year (following its application for membership in 1996). Also in January 2013 Nazarbaev announced the creation of a single pension fund to replace several existing private organizations, and of a new development agency.

PUBLIC HOLIDAYS

2014: 1–2 January (New Year), 7 January (Russian Orthodox Christmas), 8–9 March (International Women's Day), 21–23 March (Nauryz Meyramy, Spring Holiday), 1 May (Day of Unity of the Peoples of Kazakhstan), 9 May (Victory Day, Day of Remembrance), 6 July (Day of the Capital City), 30 August (Constitution Day), 4 October* (Kurban Bayram, Id al-Adha or Feast of the Sacrifice), 1 December (Day of the First President of Kazakhstan), 16–18 December (Independence Day).

* This holiday is dependent on the Islamic lunar calendar and may vary by one or two days from the date given.

Statistical Survey

Source (unless otherwise stated): Statistical Agency of the Republic of Kazakhstan, 050009 Almatı, Abay kosh. 125; tel. (727) 261-13-23; fax (727) 242-08-24; e-mail stat@mail.online.kz; internet www.stat.kz.

Area and Population

AREA, POPULATION AND DENSITY

Area (sq km)	2,724,900*
Population (census results)	
25 February–4 March 1999	14,953,126
25 February–6 March 2009	
Males	7,712,200
Females	8,297,400
Total	16,009,600
Population (official estimates at 1 January)	
2011	16,441,959
2012	16,675,392
2013	16,911,911
Density (per sq km) at 1 January 2013	6.2

* 1,049,150 sq miles.

POPULATION BY AGE AND SEX
(official estimates at 1 January 2012)

	Males	Females	Total
0–14	2,132,271	2,022,985	4,155,256
15–64	5,523,969	5,901,571	11,425,540
65 and over	386,595	708,001	1,094,596
Total	8,042,835	8,632,557	16,675,392

PRINCIPAL ETHNIC GROUPS
(at 2009 census)

	Number ('000)	%
Kazakh	10,096.8	63.1
Russian	3,793.8	23.7
Uzbek	457.0	2.9
Ukrainian	333.0	2.1
Uygur (Uighur)	224.7	1.4
Tatar	204.2	1.3
German	178.4	1.1
Others	721.7	4.5
Total	16,009.6	100.0

ADMINISTRATIVE DIVISIONS
(1 January 2013, official estimates)

	Area (sq km)	Population	Density (per sq km)	Capital city
Oblasts				
Almatı . . .	224,000	1,946,627	8.69	Taldykorgan
Aqmola . . .	146,200	732,947	5.01	Kökşetaw
Aqtöbe . . .	300,600	796,130	2.65	Aqtöbe
Atiraw . . .	118,600	555,198	4.68	Atiraw
Eastern Kazakhstan .	283,200	1,393,964	4.92	Öskemen
Jambıl . . .	144,300	1,070,239	7.42	Taraz
Mañğıstaw . .	165,600	568,086	3.43	Aktaw
Northern Kazakhstan .	98,000	579,636	5.91	Petropavl
Pavlodar . .	124,800	749,154	6.00	Pavlodar
Qarağandi . .	428,000	1,363,264	3.19	Qarağandi
Qizilorda . .	226,000	726,781	3.22	Qizilorda
Qostanay . .	196,000	880,109	4.49	Qostanay
Southern Kazakhstan .	117,300	2,678,335	22.83	Chimkent
Western Kazakhstan .	151,300	617,779	4.08	Oral

—continued	Area (sq km)	Population	Density (per sq km)	Capital city
Cities				
Almatı . . .	700	1,475,579	2,107.97	—
Astana (capital) .	300	778,083	2,593.61	—
Total . . .	2,724,900	16,911,911	6.21	—

PRINCIPAL TOWNS
(population at 1999 census)

Almatı	1,129,400	Petropavl . . .	203,500
Qarağandi . .	436,900	Oral	195,500
Chimkent . .	360,100	Temirtaw . . .	170,500
Taraz	330,100	Qizilorda . . .	157,400
Astana (capital) .	313,000	Aktaw	143,400
Öskemen . .	311,000	Atiraw	142,500
Pavlodar . .	300,500	Ekibastuz . . .	127,200
Semey	269,600	Kökşetaw . . .	123,400
Aqtöbe . . .	253,100	Rudniy . . .	109,500
Qostanay . .	221,400		

IMMIGRATION AND EMIGRATION

	2009	2010	2011
Immigrants	406,251	408,521	402,869
Emigrants	398,749	393,056	397,767

BIRTHS, MARRIAGES AND DEATHS

	Registered live births		Registered marriages		Registered deaths	
	Number	Rate (per 1,000)	Number	Rate (per 1,000)	Number	Rate (per 1,000)
2005 . .	278,977	18.4	123,045	8.1	157,121	10.4
2006 . .	301,756	19.7	137,204	9.0	157,210	10.3
2007 . .	321,963	20.8	146,379	9.5	158,297	10.2
2008 . .	356,555	22.8	135,280	8.6	152,706	9.7
2009 . .	357,552	22.0	140,785	8.0	142,780	8.0
2010 . .	367,752	22.5	146,443	9.0	145,875	8.9
2011 . .	372,208	22.6	160,494	9.8	144,616	8.8
2012 . .	379,121	22.7	164,681	9.9	141,220	8.5

Life expectancy (years at birth): 68.3 (males 63.5; females 73.3) in 2010 (Source: World Bank, World Development Indicators database).

ECONOMICALLY ACTIVE POPULATION
(labour force survey, annual averages, '000 persons)

	2009	2010	2011
Agriculture, forestry and fishing .	2,326.4	2,294.9	2,196.1
Mining and quarrying	197.9	193.7	206.8
Manufacturing	570.6	565.6	542.2
Electricity, gas and water supply .	170.8	189.5	211.3
Construction	551.8	569.8	614.0
Wholesale and retail trade; repair of motor vehicles, motor cycles and personal and household goods	1,170.6	1,224.2	1,233.7
Hotels and restaurants . . .	101.6	105.1	122.5
Transport, storage and communications	586.4	621.1	672.0
Financial intermediation . . .	96.6	104.7	119.2
Real estate, renting and business activities	394.3	455.7	485.4
Public administration and defence; compulsory social security . .	373.1	376.5	391.9
Education	769.5	816.2	851.5
Health and social work . . .	351.4	370.2	392.4
Community, social and personal services	220.9	204.3	238.6
Households with employed persons	21.4	22.6	23.9
Extra-territorial organizations and bodies	0.1	0.1	0.1
Total employed	7,903.4	8,114.2	8,301.6
Unemployed	554.5	496.5	473.0
Total labour force	8,457.9	8,610.7	8,774.6

Health and Welfare

KEY INDICATORS

Total fertility rate (children per woman, 2010) . . .	2.6
Under-5 mortality rate (per 1,000 live births, 2010) . .	33
HIV/AIDS (% of persons aged 15–49, 2009)	0.1
Physicians (per 1,000 head, 2009)	4.1
Hospital beds (per 1,000 head, 2009)	7.6
Health expenditure (2009): US $ per head (PPP) . . .	514
Health expenditure (2009): % of GDP	4.5
Health expenditure (2009): public (% of total) . . .	59.2
Access to water (% of persons, 2010)	95
Access to sanitation (% of persons, 2010) . . .	97
Total carbon dioxide emissions ('000 metric tons, 2008) . .	236,954.2
Carbon dioxide emissions per head (metric tons, 2008) . .	15.1
Human Development Index (2011): ranking . . .	68
Human Development Index (2011): value	0.745

For sources and definitions, see explanatory note on p. vi.

Agriculture

PRINCIPAL CROPS
('000 metric tons)

	2009	2010	2011
Wheat	17,052.0	9,638.4	22,732.0
Rice, paddy	307.0	373.2	346.8
Barley	2,519.0	1,312.8	2,593.1
Maize	471.2	462.0	482.0
Rye	75.1	42.2	28.4
Oats	204.0	133.8	258.3
Millet	31.3	16.5	43.4
Buckwheat	61.6	27.0	37.4
Potatoes	2,755.6	2,554.6	3,076.1
Sugar beet	181.3	152.0	200.4
Beans, dry	0.6	0.7	0.2*
Peas, dry	58.0	55.4	107.8*
Soybeans	94.3	113.9	77.0*
Sunflower seed	367.9	328.9	409.1
Safflower seed	84.1	122.2	82.0*
Seed cotton	270.0	239.9	336.1
Cabbages and other brassicas .	376.3	412.0	460.0*
Tomatoes	580.9	593.4	662.0

—continued	2009	2010	2011
Cucumbers and gherkins . . .	273.0	298.8	334.0
Aubergines (Eggplants) . . .	51.4	63.6	71.0*
Chillies and peppers, green . .	139.2	136.7	153.0
Onions, dry	388.2	440.5	492.3
Carrots and turnips	321.5	331.3	370.0
Watermelons	579.2	783.6	874.6*
Apples	118.0	107.2	114.0
Pears	11.3	11.1	11.4*
Cherries	10.8	9.1	10.0*
Plums and sloes	4.9	4.9	5.2*
Grapes	55.7	56.4	57.1
Tobacco, unmanufactured . .	8.4	3.2	2.8

* Unofficial figure.

Aggregate production ('000 metric tons, may include official, semi-official or estimated data): Total cereals 20,764.0 in 2009, 12,115.9 in 2010, 26,641.5 in 2011; Total roots and tubers 2,755.6 in 2009, 2,554.6 in 2010, 3,076.1 in 2011; Total vegetables (incl. melons) 3,310.2 in 2009, 3,695.7 in 2010, 4,126.3 in 2011; Total fruits (excl. melons) 234.3 in 2009, 222.1 in 2010, 233.3 in 2011.

Source: FAO.

LIVESTOCK
('000 head, year ending September)

	2009	2010	2011
Horses	1,370.5	1,438.7	1,528.3
Asses*	30	30	30
Cattle	5,991.6	6,095.2	6,175.3
Buffaloes*	10.0	10.0	10.0
Camels	148.3	155.5	169.6
Pigs	1,347.3	1,326.3	1,344.0
Sheep	14,126.1	14,660.8	15,110.0†
Goats	2,644.3	2,708.9	2,878.1†
Chickens†	30,000	32,500	3,2600
Turkeys†	150	200	200

* FAO estimates.
† Unofficial figure(s).

Source: FAO.

LIVESTOCK PRODUCTS
('000 metric tons)

	2009	2010	2011
Cattle meat	396.1	406.8	392.8
Sheep meat	116.2	122.6	128.2*
Goat meat	18.8	20.3	21.3*
Horse meat	71.4	73.1	75.6
Pig meat	208.9	206.0	213.6
Chicken meat	79.5	103.0	102.0
Cows' milk	5,269.0	5,347.5	5,200.0
Sheeps' milk*	24.9	23.7	23.0
Goats' milk*	10.0	10.0	9.5
Hen eggs*	184.0	207.3	207.2
Wool, greasy	36.4	37.6	38.5

* Unofficial figure(s).

Source: FAO.

Forestry

ROUNDWOOD REMOVALS
(cubic metres, excl. bark)

	2008*	2009	2010
Sawlogs, veneer logs and logs for sleepers	158,300	—	—
Pulpwood	19,800	—	—
Other industrial roundwood . .	19,800	74,000	73,000
Fuel wood	49,600	243,000†	272,000†
Total	247,500	317,000	345,000

* FAO estimates.
† Unofficial figure.

2011: Production assumed to be unchanged from 2010 (FAO estimates).

Source: FAO.

SAWNWOOD PRODUCTION
(cubic metres, incl. railway sleepers)

	2008	2009	2010*
Coniferous (softwood) . . .	91,500	80,400	97,823
Broadleaved (hardwood) . . .	7,100	6,700	9,977
Total	98,600	87,100	107,800

* Unofficial figures.

2011: Production assumed to be unchanged from 2010 (FAO estimates).

Source: FAO.

Fishing

('000 metric tons, live weight)

	2008	2009	2010
Capture	55.7	35.0	43.0
Freshwater bream	21.3	17.1	22.1
Common carp	0.2	0.2	0.1
Crucian carp	3.8	2.3	2.7
Roaches	4.8	4.2	5.0
Asp	5.2	1.4	1.6
Northern pike	1.9	1.3	1.4
Wels (Som) catfish . . .	3.4	2.5	2.4
Pike-perch	9.8	4.1	5.5
Aquaculture	0.2	0.3	0.2
Total catch	55.9	35.3	43.2

Source: FAO.

Mining

('000 metric tons unless otherwise indicated)

	2010	2011	2012
Hard coal	} 110,929	116,449	120,511
Brown coal (incl. lignite) . .			
Crude petroleum* . . .	79,685	80,061	79,211
Natural gas (million cu m) .	37,406	35,531	40,090
Iron ore (gross weight) . .	24,016	24,736	52,577
Bauxite	5,310	5,495	n.a.
Lead ore (metal content) . .	35	39	88
Zinc ore (metal content) . .	405	377	371
Manganese ore	3,045	2,963	n.a.
Chromite	5,092	5,059	n.a.
Uranium (metric tons)† . . .	17,803	19,451	n.a.
Silver ore (metal content, metric tons) . .	n.a.	n.a.	963,137
Gold (metal content, kg) . .	n.a.	n.a.	61,160
Asbestos	214	223	n.a.

* Including gas condensate.

† Uranium content of ores; Source: World Nuclear Association.

Industry

SELECTED PRODUCTS
('000 metric tons unless otherwise indicated)

	2010	2011	2012
Wheat flour	3,754	3,846	4,020
Raw sugar	364	272	169
Wine ('000 hl)	172	158	n.a.
Beer ('000 hl)	4,952	4,258	4,801
Cigarettes (million) . . .	24,228	25,222	27,053
Motor spirit (petrol) . . .	2,926	2,775	2,874
Kerosene	491	387	421
Gas-diesel (distillate fuel) oils .	4,436	4,665	4,720
Residual fuel oils (Mazout) .	3,806	4,277	3,896
Cement	6,683	7,645	6,392
Copper (unrefined, metric tons) .	323,368	338,524	367,177
Electric energy (million kWh) .	82,647	86,586	90,534

Crude steel ('000 metric tons): 4,243 in 2008.

Woven cotton fabrics (metric tons): 35,491 in 2009.

Finance

CURRENCY AND EXCHANGE RATES

Monetary Units
  100 tein = 1 tenge.

Sterling, Dollar and Euro Equivalents (31 December 2012)
  £1 sterling = 237.868 tenge;
  US $1 = 150.740 tenge;
  €1 = 198.886 tenge;
  1,000 tenge = £4.20 = $6.63 = €5.03.

Average Exchange Rate (tenge per US $)
  2010   147.355
  2011   146.621
  2012   149.113

Note: The tenge was introduced on 15 November 1993, replacing the old Russian (formerly Soviet) rouble at an exchange rate of 1 tenge = 500 roubles. On 18 November the rate was adjusted to 250 roubles per tenge. In April 1999 the tenge was allowed to 'float' on foreign exchange markets.

STATE BUDGET
(million tenge)

Revenue*	2010	2011	2012
Tax revenue	2,934,080.7	3,982,338.0	4,095,366.3
Other current revenue . . .	104,398.2	138,596.6	285,144.1
Capital revenue	60,653.3	49,891.5	52,493.1
Official transfers	1,200,000.0	1,200,000.0	1,380,000.0
Total	4,299,132.2	5,370,826.0	5,813,003.5

Expenditure†	2010	2011	2012
General public services . .	224,944.3	296,481.2	326,128.6
Defence	221,345.1	264,503.3	341,103.7
Public order and security . .	368,776.3	448,495.3	558,217.6
Education	755,294.8	986,773.4	1,210,115.4
Health care	551,325.7	626,309.9	730,819.9
Social security and social assistance	905,272.7	1,133,573.0	1,239,018.4
Housing and communal services .	334,154.8	389,238.2	438,585.7
Recreation and cultural activities .	227,564.3	201,639.6	223,065.3
Agriculture, forestry, water management, fishing and environmental protection . .	207,073.8	270,763.4	292,572.9
Transport and communications .	390,669.5	449,210.7	482,059.8
Other expenditure	270,743.2	356,246.5	427,284.7
Total	4,457,164.6	5,423,234.6	6,268,972.0

* Excluding grants received (million tenge): 22,189.2 in 2010; 69,072.2 in 2011; 28,588.0 in 2012.

† Excluding net expenditure minus repayments (million tenge): 347,042.7 in 2010; 447,117.2 in 2011; 405,752.2 in 2012.

Source: Ministry of Finance, Astana.

INTERNATIONAL RESERVES
(US $ million at 31 December)

	2009	2010	2011
Gold	2,500.7	3,052.2	4,150.8
IMF special drawing rights .	540.2	530.6	529.0
Reserve position in IMF . .	0.0	0.0	0.0
Foreign exchange	20,179.6	24,692.1	24,650.1
Total	23,220.5	28,274.9	29,329.9

Source: IMF, *International Financial Statistics*.

MONEY SUPPLY
(million tenge at 31 December)

	2009	2010	2011
Currency outside depository corporations	913,443	1,148,489	1,365,698
Transferable deposits . . .	2,266,473	2,612,523	3,324,220
Other deposits	4,307,390	4,721,817	5,062,317
Broad money	7,487,306	8,482,828	9,752,236

Source: IMF, *International Financial Statistics*.

COST OF LIVING

(Consumer Price Index at December; base: December of previous year = 100)

	2010	2011	2012
Food and beverages	110.1	109.1	105.3
Other consumer goods	105.5	105.3	103.5
Services	106.8	107.3	109.3
All items	107.8	107.4	106.0

NATIONAL ACCOUNTS

Expenditure on the Gross Domestic Product

(million tenge at current prices)

	2009	2010	2011
Final consumption expenditure.	10,037,360	12,258,756	14,733,828
Households	7,912,607	9,721,100	11,568,531
Non-profit institutions serving households	141,164	178,887	223,332
General government . .	1,983,589	2,358,769	2,941,965
Gross capital formation . . .	5,002,725	5,535,371	6,204,641
Gross fixed capital formation . Acquisitions, less disposals of valuables .	4,726,718	5,307,137	5,771,550
Changes in inventories . .	276,007	228,234	433,091
Total domestic expenditure .	15,040,085	17,794,127	20,938,469
Exports of goods and services .	7,136,356	9,589,504	13,641,182
Less Imports of goods and services	5,770,296	6,373,248	7,603,450
Statistical discrepancy . . .	601,502	805,134	595,688
GDP in market prices . .	17,007,647	21,815,517	27,571,889

Gross Domestic Product by Economic Activity

	2010	2011	2012
Agriculture, hunting, forestry and fishing	983,995	1,409,003	1,233,549
Mining and quarrying	4,249,268	5,003,253	5,234,539
Manufacturing	2,469,804	3,131,187	3,322,918
Electricity, gas and water supply .	458,054	574,003	605,146
Construction	1,680,503	1,816,612	1,864,252
Wholesale and retail trade; repair of motor vehicles, motorcycles and personal and household goods	2,834,219	3,819,299	4,426,764
Hotels and restaurants . . .	188,935	239,580	276,033
Transport, storage and communications	2,426,070	2,635,934	2,815,189
Financial intermediation . . .	792,400	550,693	606,139
Real estate, renting and business activities	3,146,122	4,151,804	4,867,427
Public administration and defence; compulsory social security . .	456,417	551,535	664,236
Education	704,181	886,296	1,046,391
Health and social work . . .	377,937	482,062	573,176
Other community, social and personal services	347,988	495,374	599,483
Sub-total	21,115,891	25,746,635	28,135,243
Less Financial intermediation services indirectly measured .	466,859	—	—
Gross value added in basic prices	20,649,032	25,746,635	28,135,243
Taxes, less subsidies, on products .	1,166,485	1,825,254	1,937,286
GDP in market prices . . .	21,815,517	27,571,889	30,072,529

BALANCE OF PAYMENTS

(US $ million)

	2009	2010	2011
Exports of goods	43,923.4	61,578.6	88,467.0
Imports of goods	−28,919.5	−32,880.4	−41,163.0
Balance on goods	15,003.9	28,698.2	47,304.0
Exports of services	4,243.5	4,258.8	4,511.8
Imports of services	−10,081.7	−11,365.8	−10,965.3
Balance on goods and services	9,165.7	21,591.1	40,850.3
Primary income received . .	2,492.7	1,822.0	1,942.2
Primary income paid	−15,050.0	−20,524.0	−28,426.6
Balance on goods, services and primary income	−3,391.6	2,889.1	14,365.9
Secondary income received . .	952.8	1,466.8	2,755.4
Secondary income paid . . .	−1,675.2	−1,947.4	−3,011.2
Current balance	−4,114.0	2,408.5	14,110.0
Capital account (net)	−29.5	7,890.2	9.3
Direct investment assets . . .	−4,192.6	−3,700.5	−4,847.1
Direct investment liabilities . .	14,275.9	6,631.7	13,227.2
Portfolio investment assets . .	1,868.8	−7,193.7	−13,539.6
Portfolio investment liabilities .	1,179.0	15,716.8	70.0
Financial derivatives and employee stock options (net)	59.4	8.7	126.1
Other investment assets . . .	−1,080.5	−6,470.3	−3,776.0
Other investment liabilities . .	−4,726.4	−13,576.2	737.6
Net errors and omissions . . .	−783.1	3,003.6	−5,822.7
Reserves and related items .	2,457.1	4,718.9	294.8

Source: IMF, *International Financial Statistics*.

External Trade

PRINCIPAL COMMODITIES

(distribution by SITC, US $ million)

Imports c.i.f.	2008	2009	2010
Food and live animals . . .	2,266.2	1,918.8	1,914.8
Mineral fuels, lubricants and related materials	5,431.0	2,834.8	2,379.6
Petroleum and related products .	4,518.0	2,341.1	1,881.9
Chemicals and related products	3,207.3	2,838.6	2,857.7
Manufactured goods classified chiefly by material . . .	8,619.3	7,525.1	4,345.9
Iron and steel	4,158.7	3,893.1	1,432.0
Machinery and transport equipment	14,172.8	10,523.5	9,726.6
Machinery specialized for particular industries . . .	2,608.7	1,704.2	1,639.1
General industrial machinery, equipment and parts . . .	3,799.5	2,987.7	1,883.3
Electrical machinery, apparatus, appliances and parts . . .	1,881.1	1,588.3	1,794.2
Road vehicles	2,438.1	1,444.1	984.8
Passenger cars and other passenger vehicles . . .	1,228.3	771.3	403.6
Miscellaneous manufactured articles	2,121.1	1,926.4	2,084.3
Total (incl. others)	37,815.4	28,408.7	24,023.6

KAZAKHSTAN — Statistical Survey

Exports f.o.b.

Exports f.o.b.	2008	2009	2010
Food and live animals	2,871.7	1,520.1	1,797.6
Crude materials (inedible) except fuels	4,414.7	2,580.6	3,084.7
Metalliferous ore and metal scrap	3,537.3	2,262.8	2,661.2
Mineral fuels, lubricants and related materials	48,910.9	30,027.2	41,032.9
Petroleum and related products	45,965.7	27,632.6	38,836.9
Manufactured goods classified chiefly by material	11,058.6	5,938.8	7,430.2
Iron and steel	5,881.2	2,866.3	3,557.7
Non-ferrous metals	4,507.2	2,598.7	3,671.4
Copper	2,866.1	1,494.0	2,089.6
Total (incl. others)	71,172.0	43,195.8	57,244.1

Exports f.o.b.—continued	2008	2009	2010
Turkey	1,903.8	791.8	1,234.8
Ukraine	2,003.3	1,289.2	665.7
United Kingdom	1,811.2	1,235.1	1,379.5
USA	569.6	612.6	868.1
Uzbekistan	1,272.0	891.8	1,101.2
Total (incl. others)	71,172.0	43,195.8	57,244.1

Source: UN, *International Trade Statistics Yearbook*.

2011 (US $ million): *Imports:* Prepared foodstuffs, beverages, spirits and vinegar and tobacco 2,075.2; Mineral products 5,404.0; Chemicals and related products 3,129.7; Plastics, rubber and articles thereof 1,844.3; Base metals and articles thereof 3,717.0; Machinery and mechanical appliances 9,299.3; Vehicles, aircraft, vessels and associated transport equipment 4,254.3; Total (incl. others) 37,055.7. *Exports:* Mineral products 68,269.0; Chemicals and related products 3,360.3; Base metals and articles thereof 11,609.6; Total (incl. others) 87,964.0.

2011 (US $ million): *Imports:* Belarus 593.8; China, People's Republic 5,021.1; France 687.4; Germany 2,082.3; Italy 1,144.8; Japan 645.0; Korea, Republic 622.0; Russia 15,331.2; Turkey 729.3; Ukraine 1,734.4; United Kingdom 526.0; USA 1,714.0; Uzbekistan 770.5; Total (incl. others) 37,055.7. *Exports:* Austria 3,876.5; Canada 2,629.3; China, People's Republic 16,291.5; France 5,414.7; Germany 1,610.3; Iran 1,077.0; Israel 1,418.5; Italy 15,045.3; Japan 1,043.9; Netherlands 6,637.1; Poland 1,305.5; Romania 2,265.8; Russia 7,359.5; Spain 1,135.4; Switzerland (incl. Liechtenstein) 4,961.3; Turkey 2,574.4; Ukraine 2,670.5; United Kingdom 1,619.2; USA 1,028.9; Uzbekistan 1,179.5; Total (incl. others) 87,964.0.

PRINCIPAL TRADING PARTNERS
(distribution by SITC, US $ million)

Imports c.i.f.	2008	2009	2010
Belarus	396.2	367.1	251.1
China, People's Republic	4,565.1	3,569.5	3,964.5
Finland	506.0	309.7	207.6
France (incl. Monaco)	813.0	460.4	501.7
Germany	2,572.0	2,041.9	1,828.2
Italy	1,239.8	1,915.3	1,580.6
Japan	979.3	635.1	554.8
Korea, Republic	423.2	373.9	527.3
Netherlands	275.8	319.1	301.8
Norway	695.0	274.9	85.6
Poland	426.4	421.6	376.6
Russia	13,753.8	8,896.6	5,475.7
Sweden	301.6	262.2	207.9
Switzerland-Liechtenstein	164.6	156.2	180.2
Turkey	970.8	570.9	616.3
Ukraine	2,104.8	2,131.6	1,358.5
United Kingdom	688.9	702.3	724.7
USA	1,930.8	1,393.6	1,315.8
Uzbekistan	516.1	304.4	473.3
Total (incl. others)	37,815.4	28,408.7	24,023.6

Exports f.o.b.	2008	2009	2010
Canada	398.2	1,385.4	2,439.1
China, People's Republic	7,676.6	5,888.6	10,122.1
France (incl. Monaco)	5,388.7	3,381.5	4,433.1
Germany	614.2	898.1	1,749.7
Iran	2,039.5	1,279.0	1,093.9
Israel	2,226.5	1,121.5	1,279.7
Italy	11,920.3	6,686.8	9,576.8
Japan	803.9	247.5	539.3
Netherlands	4,638.7	2,222.5	4,161.0
Poland	461.5	835.8	1,215.5
Portugal	561.5	274.4	733.5
Romania	1,010.8	840.3	1,281.9
Russia	6,227.0	3,547.0	3,006.5
Spain	896.6	580.3	921.4
Switzerland-Liechtenstein	11,281.3	2,668.2	1,235.0

Transport

RAILWAYS
(estimated traffic)

	2010	2011	2012
Paying passengers (million journeys)	19.1	19.9	24.1
Passenger-km (million)	15,800	16,483	19,081
Freight carried ('000 metric tons)	265,663	277,150	290,874
Freight net ton-km (million)	210,713	219,740	232,940

ROAD TRAFFIC
('000 motor vehicles in use at 31 December)

	2009	2010	2011
Passenger cars	2,656.8	3,087.6	3,553.8
Lorries and vans	410.8	397.6	414.0
Buses and coaches	94.8	94.0	98.4

SHIPPING
Flag Registered Fleet
(at 31 December)

	2010	2011	2012
Number of vessels	146	167	167
Total displacement (grt)	140,472	181,454	183,229

Source: Lloyd's List Intelligence (www.lloydslistintelligence.com).

CIVIL AVIATION
(traffic on scheduled services)

	2010	2011	2012
Passengers carried (million)	3.4	4.1	4.6
Passenger-km (million)	6,517.2	7,859.1	8,795.8
Total ton-km (million)	94.0	89.1	54.9

Tourism

FOREIGN TOURIST ARRIVALS

Country of residence	2008	2009	2010
China, People's Republic . . .	172,083	169,866	133,861
Kyrgyzstan	1,045,781	1,043,015	1,115,711
Russia	1,105,981	1,122,709	1,269,697
Tajikistan	394,125	203,579	173,592
Uzbekistan	1,495,249	1,197,743	1,393,881
Total (incl. others)	4,721,456	4,329,848	4,712,657

Total tourist arrivals ('000): 4,093 in 2011 (provisional).

Tourism receipts (US $ million, excl. passenger transport): 963 in 2009; 1,005 in 2010; 1,209 in 2011 (provisional).

Source: World Tourism Organization.

Communications Media

	2009	2010	2011
Telephones ('000 main lines in use)	3,856.5	4,057.6	4,265.8
Mobile cellular telephones ('000 subscribers)	17,063.2	19,402.6	25,240.8
Internet subscribers ('000) . .	756.5	1,543.4	1,261.5
Broadband subscribers ('000) . .	577.2	1,426.8	1,193.4

Source: International Telecommunication Union.

Education

(state educational institutions 2011/12)

	Institutions	Teachers	Students ('000)
Pre-primary	6,133	52,777	489.4
Primary *and* Secondary: general* .	7,706	304,775	2,522.8
Secondary: vocational	494	28,360	491.7
Professional-technical schools . .	310	7,362	110.1
Higher	146	40,531	629.5

* Excluding secondary-general evening schools.

Note: There were, additionally: 155 independent primary and secondary-general schools, with 20,000 students; 179 independent secondary-vocational schools, with 88,700 students; and 134 non-governmental higher education institutes, with 297,900 students, in 2003/04.

Pupil-teacher ratio (primary education, UNESCO estimate): 16.4 in 2010/11 (Source: UNESCO Institute for Statistics).

Adult literacy rate (UNESCO estimates): 99.7% (males 99.8%; females 99.6%) in 2010 (Source: UNESCO Institute for Statistics).

Directory

The Government

HEAD OF STATE

President: NURSULTAN A. NAZARBAEV (elected indirectly 24 April 1990; elected unopposed 1 December 1991; term extended by referendum 29 April 1995; re-elected 10 January 1999; re-elected 4 December 2005; re-elected 3 April 2011; inaugurated 8 April 2011).

GOVERNMENT
(May 2013)

Prime Minister: SERIK N. AXMETOV.

First Deputy Prime Minister, Minister of Regional Development: BAKITJAN A. SAGINTAEV.

Deputy Prime Minister: ERBOL T. ORINBAEV.

Deputy Prime Minister: QAYRAT N. KELIMBETOV.

Deputy Prime Minister, Minister of Industry and New Technologies: ASET Ö. İSEKEŞEV.

Minister of Internal Affairs: QALMUXANBET N. QASIMOV.

Minister of Health: SALİDAT Z. QAYIRBEKOVA.

Minister of Foreign Affairs: ERLAN Ä. IDIRISOV.

Minister of Culture and Information: MUXTAR A. QUL-MUXAMMED.

Minister of Defence: ÄDILBEK R. JAQSIBEKOV.

Minister of Education and Science: BAQITJAN T. JUMAĞULOV.

Minister of Environmental Protection: NURLAN J. QAPPAROV.

Minister of Agriculture: ASILJAN S. MAMITBEKOV.

Minister of Transport and Communications: ASQAR Q. JUMAĞALİEV.

Minister of Labour and Social Security: SERIK S. ÄBDENOV.

Minister of Finance: BOLAT B. JÄMIŞEV.

Minister of Emergency Situations: VLADİMİR K. BOJKO.

Minister of the Economy and Budgetary Planning: ERBOLAT A. DOSAEV.

Minister of Justice: BERIK M. İMAŞEV.

Minister of Oil and Gas: SAWAT M. MIÑBAEV.

Minister of Economic Integration: JANAR S. AYTJANOVA.

MINISTRIES

Office of the President: 010000 Astana, Beibitshilik kosh. 11; tel. (7172) 32-13-99; fax (7172) 32-61-72; e-mail egov@nitec.kz; internet www.akorda.kz.

Office of the Prime Minister: 010000 Astana, Beibitshilik kosh. 11; tel. (7172) 74-54-00; fax (7172) 32-40-89; internet www.government.kz.

Ministry of Agriculture: 010000 Astana, Kenesary kosh. 36; tel. and fax (7172) 55-57-65; e-mail info@minagri.kz; internet www.minagri.kz.

Ministry of Culture and Information: 010000 Astana, Soljagaw, Ministrilkter uyi, 15 kireberis, 3rd Floor, office 305; tel. (7172) 74-01-07; fax (7172) 50-30-51; e-mail mkis@mki.kz.

Ministry of Defence: 010000 Astana, Soljagaw, AEA, 2-ui Barlyk kukyktar korgalgan; tel. (7172) 72-14-10; fax (7172) 50-41-97; e-mail pressa@mod.gov.kz; internet www.mod.gov.kz.

Ministry of the Economy and Budgetary Planning: 010000 Astana, Orynbor kosh. 8; tel. (7172) 74-28-09; fax (7172) 74-30-49; e-mail info@minplan.kz; internet www.minplan.kz.

Ministry of Education and Science: 010000 Astana, Orynbor kosh. 8; tel. (7172) 91-27-90; fax (7172) 93-86-08; e-mail pressa@edu.gov.kz; internet www.edu.gov.kz.

Ministry of Emergency Situations: 010000 Astana, Beibitshilik kosh. 22; tel. (7172) 60-21-28; fax (7172) 94-48-32; e-mail mchs@emer.kz; internet www.emer.kz.

Ministry of Environmental Protection: 010000 Astana, Soljagaw, ui. Ministrigi 35-8/14; tel. (7172) 74-00-75; fax (7172) 59-19-73; e-mail kulzhanov@eco.gov.kz; internet www.eco.gov.kz.

Ministry of Finance: 010000 Astana, Zhenis d-ly 11; tel. (7172) 71-77-64; fax (7172) 71-77-85; e-mail administrator@minfin.kz; internet www.minfin.kz.

Ministry of Foreign Affairs: 010000 Astana, Soljagaw, Tauelsizdik kosh. 31; tel. (7172) 72-05-18; fax (7172) 72-05-16; e-mail midrk@mid.kz; internet www.mfa.kz.

Ministry of Health: 010000 Astana, Soljagaw, Ministrilkter uyi, 5 kireberis; tel. (7172) 74-32-43; e-mail zdrav@mz.gov.kz; internet www.mz.gov.kz.

Ministry of Industry and New Technologies: 010000 Astana, Kabanbai batyr d-ly 32/1, 'Transport Tauer'; tel. (3172) 24-04-75; fax (3172) 24-12-13; internet www.mint.gov.kz.

Ministry of Internal Affairs: 010000 Astana, Tauelsizdik d-ly 1; tel. (7172) 71-40-10; fax (7172) 34-17-38; e-mail kense@mvd.kz; internet www.mvd.kz.

Ministry of Justice: 010000 Astana, Soljagaw, Orynbor kosh. 8, Ministrilkter uyi, 13 kireberis; tel. (7172) 74-06-37; fax (7172) 74-09-54; e-mail press@minjust.kz; internet www.minjust.kz.

Ministry of Labour and Social Security: 010000 Astana, Orynbor kosh. 8, Ministrilkter uyi, 6 kireberis; tel. (7172) 74-28-51; fax (7172) 74-36-08; e-mail mintrud@enbek.kz; internet www.enbek.gov .kz.

Ministry of Oil and Gas: 010000 Astana, Kabanbai batyr kosh. 19; tel. (7172) 97-68-90; e-mail bogdanova@mgm.gov.kz; internet mgm .gov.kz.

Ministry of Regional Development: 010000 Astana.

Ministry of Transport and Communications: 010000 Astana, Kabanbai batyr d-ly 32/1; tel. (7172) 24-13-12; fax (7172) 24-14-19; e-mail mtc@mtc.gov.kz; internet www.mtk.gov.kz.

President

Presidential Election, 3 April 2011

Candidates	Votes	%
Nursultan A. Nazarbaev	7,850,958	95.55
Gani E. Kasymov	159,036	1.94
Jambyl A. Ahmetbekov	111,924	1.36
Mels H. Yeleussizov	94,452	1.15
Total	**8,216,370**	**100.00**

Legislature

Parliament is a bicameral legislative body, comprising the Senat (Senate) and the Majlis (Assembly).

Majlis

010000 Astana, Parliament House; tel. (7172) 74-71-42; fax (7172) 24-26-19; e-mail smimazh@parlam.kz; internet www.parlam.kz.

Chairman: NURLAN NIGMATULIN.

General Election, 15 January 2012

Parties	Votes	%	Seats
Light of the Fatherland (Nur Otan)	5,621,436	80.99	83
Bright Road Democratic Party of Kazakhstan (Ak Jol)	518,405	7.47	8
Communist People's Party of Kazakhstan (CPPK)	498,788	7.19	7
Freedom National Social Democratic Party (Azat JSDP)	116,534	1.68	—
Village Kazakhstani Social Democratic Party (Auyl)	82,623	1.19	—
Party of Patriots of Kazakhstan	57,732	0.83	—
Justice Democratic Party (Adilet)	45,702	0.66	—
Total	**6,941,220**	**100.00**	**107***

* Including nine deputies elected by the Assembly of the Nation of Kazakhstan (a body representing the country's minority ethnic groups) on 16 January 2012.

Senat

010000 Astana, Abay d-ly 33, Parliament House; tel. (7172) 15-33-76; fax (7172) 33-31-18; e-mail smimazh@parlam.kz; internet www .parlam.kz.

Chairman: KAYRAT A. MAMI.

The 47-member Senat is the upper chamber of Parliament. Elections are held every three years for one-half of the 32 seats elected by special colleges (comprising members of local councils) in Kazakhstan's 14 regions and two cities; the term of office for members of the Senat is six years. Under constitutional amendments adopted on 18 May 2007, the number of deputies appointed by the President increased from seven to 15; the additional eight members were officially appointed to the Senat by presidential decree in August. The most recent partial elections to the Senat were conducted on 4 October 2008 and 19 August 2011.

Election Commission

Ortalyk Sailau Komissiyasy (Central Election Commission): 010000 Astana, Beibitshilik kosh. 4; tel. (7172) 75-21-21; fax (7172) 33-33-88; e-mail info@election.kz; internet www.election.kz; Chair. KUANDYK T. TURGANKULOV.

Political Organizations

A new law was introduced in July 2002, which required all parties to have a minimum of 50,000 members from among all the country's regions in order to qualify for official registration. In 2012 the following nine parties were registered:

Bright Road Democratic Party of Kazakhstan (Ak Jol) (Kazakstannyn 'Ak Jol' Demokratiyalyk Partiyasy): 010000 Astana, Saraishyk kosh. 11; tel. (7172) 50-70-01; fax (7172) 50-70-20; e-mail akzholpress@mail.ru; internet www.akzhol.kz; f. 2002 by former mems of the Democratic Choice of Kazakhstan; merged with Justice Democratic Party (Adilet) in 2007; Chair. AZAT PERUASHEV; 220,000 mems (2008).

Communist Party of Kazakhstan (CPK) (Kazakstan Kommunistik Partiyasy): 010000 Astana, Beibitshilik kosh. 27/49; tel. and fax (7172) 21-32-97; e-mail pravdakz@list.ru; f. 1937; suspended Aug. 1991, re-registered Aug. 1998 and March 2003; mem. of For a Just Kazakhstan opposition bloc formed in 2005; suspended from participation in political activities for a period of six months from Oct. 2011 by court ruling (this period was extended by a further six months in April 2012); Chair. SERIKBOLSYN A. ABDILDIN; First Sec. GALIZ ALDAMJAROV; 54,246 mems (2007).

Communist People's Party of Kazakhstan (Kazakstan Kommunistik Khalyk Partiyasy): 010000 Astana, Karasai batyr 14/7; tel. and fax (7172) 24-06-09; e-mail zenterknpk@mail.ru; internet www.knpk .kz; f. 2004 by fmr mems of the Communist Party of Kazakhstan; Sec. of the Central Cttee VLADISLAV B. KOSAREV; 90,000 mems (2007).

Freedom National Social Democratic Party (Azat JSDP) ('Azat' Jalpyulttyk Sotsial Demokratiyalyk Partiyasy): 050000 Almatı, Kajymukan kosh. 70; tel. (727) 296-52-22; e-mail ocdp@ mail.ru; f. 2009 by merger of Freedom and National Social Democratic Party; supports construction of a democratic, secular, social government and the rule of law, and an open society; Chair. JARMAKHAN A. TUYAKBAY; 400,000 mems (2009).

Justice Democratic Party (Adilet): 050000 Almatı, Abay kosh. 52B; tel. (727) 392-25-27; fax (727) 392-25-36; e-mail dpadilet.kz@ gmail.com; internet dp-adilet.kz; f. 2004; as Democratic Party of Kazakhstan; present name adopted 2006; Chair. MAKSUT NARIKBAEV.

Light of the Fatherland People's Democratic Party (Nur Otan) ('Nur Otan' Khalyktyk Demokratiyalyk Partiyasy): 010000 Astana, Kunaev kosh. 12/1; tel. (7172) 55-55-62; fax (727) 279-40-66; e-mail partyotan@nursat.kz; internet www.ndp-nurotan.kz; f. 2006 by merger of Fatherland, Civic Party of Kazakhstan and Agrarian Party of Kazakhstan; supports administration of President Nazarbaev; Chair. NURSULTAN A. NAZARBAEV; Sec. ERLAN T. KARIN; 607,557 mems (2007).

Party of Patriots of Kazakhstan (PPK) (Kazakstan Patriottary Partiyasy): 050000 Almatı, Jibek-joly kosh. 76/318; tel. and fax (7172) 22-98-34; f. 2000; Chair. GANI E. KASYMOV; 172,000 mems (2007).

Spirituality Party (Ruxaniyat) ('Ruxaniyat' Partiyasy): 010000 Astana, Saryarka kosh. 5; tel. and fax (7172) 97-73-80; e-mail kazayelder@nursat.kz; f. 1995 as Renaissance Party of Kazakhstan; re-registered under new name 2003; supports Govt of President Nazarbaev; party refused permission to participate in 2012 legislative elections; Chair. SERIK SULTANGALIEV; 72,000 mems (2007).

Village Kazakhstani Social Democratic Party (Auyl) ('Auyl' Kazakstandyk Sotsial-Demokratiyalyk Partiyasy): 010000 Astana, Beibitshilik kosh. 46/109; tel. and fax (7172) 31-71-57; e-mail kaliev@ parlam.kz; registered in 2002; seeks to strengthen government support for the agricultural sector; Chair. GANI A. KALIEV; 61,043 mems (2007).

Diplomatic Representation

EMBASSIES IN KAZAKHSTAN

Afghanistan: 010000 Astana, Karaotel kosh. 3; tel. (7172) 57-14-42; fax (7172) 24-04-54; e-mail embassy@afghanembassy.kz; internet www.afghanembassy.kz; Ambassador SOHRAB ALI SAFARI.

Armenia: 010000 Astana, Komsomolskii kosh. 73; tel. (7172) 40-20-15; fax (7172) 40-19-70; e-mail armeniaemb.kz@gmail.com; Ambassador VASILY KAZARIAN.

Austria: 010000 Astana, Kosmonavtov kosh. 62; tel. (7172) 97-78-69; fax (7172) 97-78-50; e-mail astana-ob@bmeia.gv.at; Ambassador (vacant).

Azerbaijan: 010000 Astana, Diplomatiyalyk kalashyk B-6; tel. (7172) 24-15-81; fax (7172) 24-15-32; e-mail astana@azembassy.kz; internet www.azembassy.kz; Ambassador ZAKIR HASHIMOV.

Belarus: 010000 Astana, Kenesary kosh. 35; tel. and fax (7172) 32-48-29; e-mail kazakhstan@mfa.gov.by; internet www.kazakhstan .mfa.gov.by; Ambassador (vacant).

Belgium: 010000 Astana, Kosmonavtov kosh. 62; tel. (7172) 97-44-85; fax (7172) 97-78-49; e-mail embassy.astana@diplobel.fed.be; internet www.diplomatie.be/astana; Ambassador DANIEL BERTRAND.

Brazil: 010000 Astana, Kabanbai batyr kosh. 6/1, Kaskad Business Centre; tel. (7172) 24-46-84; fax (7172) 24-47-43; e-mail brasemb .astana@itamaraty.gov.br; internet www.brasembastana.kz; Ambassador OSWALDO BIATA, Jr.

Bulgaria: 010000 Astana, Saryarka kosh. 15; tel. (7172) 90-15-15; fax (7172) 90-18-19; e-mail embassy.astana@mfa.bg; internet www .mfa.bg/bg/112/; Ambassador STOYAN RIZOV.

Canada: 010000 Almatı, Karasai batyr kosh. 13/1; tel. (727) 47-55-77; fax (727) 47-55-87; e-mail astnag@international.gc.ca; internet www.canadainternational.gc.ca/kazakhstan; Ambassador STEPHEN MILLAR.

China, People's Republic: 010000 Astana, Kabanbai batyr d-ly 28/5; tel. (7172) 79-35-64; fax (7172) 79-35-65; e-mail chinaemb_kz@mfa .gov.cn; internet kz.china-embassy.org; Ambassador ZHOU LI.

Cuba: 010000 Astana, Kabanbai batyr d-ly 18/2; tel. (7172) 24-24-67; fax (7172) 24-26-38; e-mail natembacu@mail.online.kz; internet www.cubadiplomatica.cu/kazajstan; Ambassador ABELARDO HERNÁNDEZ FERRER.

Czech Republic: 010000 Astana, Saryarka kosh. 6, Biznes-Tsentr Arman, 13th Floor; tel. (7172) 66-04-72; fax (7172) 66-01-42; e-mail astana@embassy.mzv.cz; internet www.mzv.cz/astana; Ambassador BEDŘICH KOPECKÝ.

Egypt: 010000 Astana, Sarayshyk kosh. 30; tel. (7172) 28-60-67; fax (7172) 28-60-50; e-mail embassy.astana@mfa.gov.eg; Ambassador NABILA IBRAHIM SALAMA FARHANA.

Estonia: 010000 Astana, Kabanbai batyr kosh. 28; tel. (7172) 24-02-80; fax (7172) 24-02-81; e-mail embassy.astana@mfa.ee; internet www.astana.vm.ee; Ambassador JAAN HEIN.

France: 010000 Astana, Kosmonavtov kosh. 62, 4th Floor; tel. (7172) 79-51-00; fax (7172) 79-51-01; e-mail admin-francais.astana-amba@ diplomatie.gouv.fr; internet ambafrance-kz.org; Ambassador JEAN-CHARLES BERTHONNET.

Georgia: 010000 Astana, Diplomatiyalyk kalashyk C-4; tel. (7172) 24-32-58; fax (7172) 24-34-26; e-mail astana.emb@mfa.gov.ge; internet www.kazakhstan.mfa.gov.ge; Ambassador (vacant).

Germany: 010000 Astana, Kosmonavtov kosh. 62; tel. (7172) 79-12-00; fax (7172) 79-12-13; e-mail info@astana.diplo.de; internet www .astana.diplo.de; Ambassador Dr GUIDO HERZ.

Greece: 010000 Astana, Karaotkel sh-a 2, 109; tel. (7172) 56-37-14; fax (7172) 56-38-26; e-mail gremb.ast@mfa.gr; Ambassador EFTHYMIOS PANTZOPOULOS.

Holy See: 010000 Astana, Zelenaya Alleya kosh. 20; tel. (7172) 24-12-69; fax (7172) 24-16-04; e-mail nuntius_kazakhstan@lycos.com; Apostolic Nuncio Most Rev. MIGUEL MAURY BUENDÍA (Titular Archbishop of Italica).

Hungary: 010000 Astana, Kosmonavtov kosh. 62; tel. (7172) 55-03-23; fax (7172) 55-03-24; e-mail mission.ast@ku.hu; internet www .mfa.gov.hu/emb/astana; Ambassador IMRE LASZLÓCZKI.

India: 010000 Astana, Kabanbai batyr kosh. 6/1, Kaskad Business Centre, 5th Floor; tel. (7172) 92-57-00; fax (7172) 92-57-15; e-mail hoc .astana@mea.gov.in; internet indembastana.in; Ambassador ASHOK KUMAR SHARMA.

Indonesia: 010000 Astana, Saraishyk kosh. 26/1; tel. (7172) 79-06-70; fax (7172) 79-06-73; e-mail embassy@kbri-astana.kz; internet www.kbri-astana.kz; Ambassador FOSTER GULTOM.

Iran: 010000 Astana, Diplomatiyalyk kalashyk B-7; tel. (7272) 79-23-20; fax (7272) 79-23-23; e-mail iranembassy@itte.kz; Ambassador GORBAN SEIFI.

Iraq: 010000 Astana, Konaev kosh. 19; tel. (7127) 28-60-92; fax (7172)-28-60-96; e-mail astemb@iraqmfamail.com; Ambassador RAGEH SABER AL-MOUSSAWI ABBOUD.

Israel: 010000 Astana, Auezov kosh. 8; tel. (7172) 68-87-39; fax (7172) 68-87-35; e-mail info@astana.mfa.gov.il; internet astana.mfa .gov.il; Ambassador ELI TASMAN.

Italy: 010000 Astana, Shuba sh-a, Kosmonavtov kosh. 62; tel. (7172) 24-38-68; fax (7172) 24-36-86; e-mail ambasciata.astana@esteri.it; internet www.ambastana.esteri.it; Ambassador ALBERTO PIERI.

Japan: 010000 Astana, Chubar sh-a, Kosmonavtov kosh. 62, 5th Floor; tel. (7172) 97-78-43; fax (7172) 97-78-42; e-mail info@aq.mofa .go.jp; internet www.kz.emb-japan.go.jp; Ambassador YUZO HARADA.

Jordan: 010000 Astana, Novostroitel kosh. 8/2; tel. (7172) 24-52-54; fax (7172) 24-52-53; e-mail astana@fm.gov.jo; Ambassador SLAIMAN ARABIAT.

Korea, Republic: 010000 Astana, Kabanbai batyr d-ly 6/1/91–93, Kaskad Business Centre; tel. (7172) 92-55-91; fax (7172) 92-55-96; e-mail koreaemb-kz@mofat.go.kr; internet kaz.mofat.go.kr; Ambassador BAIK JOO-HWEON.

Kyrgyzstan: 010000 Astana, Diplomatiyalyk kalashyk B-5; tel. (7172) 24-20-24; fax (7172) 24-24-14; e-mail kz@mail.online.kz; Ambassador ESENGUL OMURALIYEV.

Latvia: 010000 Astana, Kabanbai batyr d-ly 6/1/122, Kaskad Business Centre; tel. (7172) 92-53-16; fax (7172) 92-53-19; e-mail embassy .kazakhstan@mfa.gov.lv; Ambassador JURIS MAKLAKOVS.

Lebanon: 010000 Astana, Kunayev 2, 13th Floor; tel. (7172) 79-35-15; fax (7172) 79-35-16; e-mail embassylebanon-kz@hotmail.com; Ambassador VAZKEN KAVLAKIAN.

Libya: 010000 Astana, Karaokel sh-a, 36-8 kosh. 6; tel. (7172) 56-37-65; fax (7172) 24-27-57; e-mail lpb_ast@yahoo.com; Ambassador AHMED EDDEB.

Lithuania: 010000 Astana, Kabanbai batyr kosh. 6/1, Kaskad Business Centre 10A; tel. (7172) 92-58-50; fax (7172) 92-58-53; e-mail amb.kz@urm.lt; internet kz.mfa.lt; Ambassador Dr ROKAS BERNOTAS.

Malaysia: 010000 Astana, Diplomatiyalyk kalashyk 26; tel. (7272) 79-06-90; fax (7272) 79-06-92; e-mail malastana@kln.gov.my; internet www.kln.gov.my/web/kaz_astana/home; Ambassador DATO AHMAD RASIDI HAZIZI.

Mongolia: 050000 Almatı, Musabaev kosh. 1; tel. (727) 269-35-70; fax (727) 229-37-90; e-mail info@mongemb.kz; Ambassador JAGIRYN SÜKHEE.

Netherlands: 010000 Astana, Kosmonavtov kosh. 62; tel. (7172) 55-54-50; fax (7172) 55-54-74; e-mail ast@minbuza.nl; internet www .netherlands-embassy.kz; Ambassador PETER VAN LEEUWEN.

Oman: 010000 Astana, Chubar sh-a, Novostroitel kosh. 1; tel. (7172) 52-85-70; fax (7172) 52-86-75; e-mail astana@mofa.gov.om; Ambassador ABDULLAH KHALID SULAIMAN AL-SULEIMANI.

Pakistan: 050004 Almatı, Tulebaev kosh. 25; tel. (727) 79-93-75; e-mail parepalmaty@yahoo.com; Ambassador MOHAMMAD AKHTAR TUFAIL.

Poland: 010000 Astana, Saryarka kosh. 15; tel. (7172) 94-44-00; fax (7172) 94-44-01; e-mail astana.sekretariat@msz.gov.pl; internet astana.msz.gov.pl; Ambassador JACEK KLUCZKOWSKI.

Qatar: 010000 Astana, Saraishyk kosh. 20A; tel. (7172) 28-61-23; fax (7172) 28-61-33; Ambassador NASSER BIN RASHID AL-NUAIMI.

Romania: 010000 Astana, Saraishyk kosh. 28; tel. (7172) 28-62-01; fax (7172) 28-62-03; e-mail amb@romania.kz; internet astana.mae .ro; Ambassador NICOLAE URECHE.

Russia: 010000 Astana, Baraev kosh. 4; tel. (7172) 44-07-83; fax (7172) 44-08-07; e-mail rfekz@yandex.ru; internet www.rfembassy .kz; Ambassador MIKHAIL N. BOCHARNIKOV.

Saudi Arabia: 010000 Astana, Akyn Sary kosh. 19; tel. (7172) 92-57-52; fax (7172) 92-57-62; e-mail kzemb@mofa.gov.sa; Ambassador ABDUL MAZHID KHAKIM.

Serbia: 010000 Astana, Saraishyk kosh. 6; tel. (7172) 99-00-27; fax (7172) 99-00-26; e-mail ambasada_rs_astana@yahoo.com; internet www.astana.mfa.gov.rs; Ambassador VLADIMIR MIRKOVIĆ.

Slovakia: 010000 Astana, Karaotkel sh-a 2, Tanbalytas St 13; tel. (7172) 56-37-90; fax (7172) 24-20-48; e-mail emb.astana@mzv.sk; internet www.mzv.sk/astana; Chargé d'affaires a.i. JANA SVECOVÁ.

South Africa: 010000 Astana, Kabanbai batyr d-ly 6/1, Kaskad Business Centre; tel. (7172) 92-53-26; fax (7172) 92-53-29; e-mail administration@saembassy.kz; Ambassador SHIRISH M. SONI.

Spain: 010000 Astana, Kenesary kosh. 47/25; tel. (7172) 20-15-35; fax (7172) 20-03-17; e-mail emb.astana@maec.es; Ambassador MANUEL LARROTCHA PARADA.

Switzerland: 010000 Astana, Kosmonavtov kosh. 62; tel. (7172) 97-98-92; fax (7172) 97-98-94; e-mail ast.vertretung@eda.admin.ch; internet www.eda.admin.ch/astana; Ambassador MAURO REINA.

Tajikistan: 010000 Astana, Chubar sh-a, Marsovaya kosh. 15; tel. and fax (7172) 24-09-29; e-mail embassy_tajic@mbox.kz; Ambassador BAHROM M. HOLNAZAROV.

Turkey: 010000 Astana, Tashenov kosh. 3; tel. (7172) 70-47-04; fax (7172) 20-45-31; e-mail embassy.astana@mfa.gov.tr; internet astana .be.mfa.gov.tr; Ambassador ÖMER BURHAN TÜZEL.

Turkmenistan: 010000 Astana, Otyrar kosh. 8/1; tel. and fax (7172) 21-08-82; e-mail tm_emb@astanatelecom.kz; Ambassador MAGTYMGULY AKMYRADOV.

Ukraine: 010000 Astana, Kenesary kosh. 41; tel. (7172) 32-60-42; fax (7172) 32-68-11; e-mail embassy_ua1@mail.kz; internet www .mfa.gov.ua/kazakhstan; Ambassador OLEH DYOMIN.

United Arab Emirates: 010000 Astana, Diplomatiyalyk kalashyk C-15; tel. (7172) 24-36-75; fax (7172) 24-36-76; e-mail emaratembassy_kz@yahoo.com; Ambassador (vacant).

United Kingdom: 010000 Astana, Shubar sh-a, Kosmonavtov kosh. 62; tel. (7172) 55-62-00; fax (7172) 55-62-11; e-mail ukinkz@fco.gov .uk; internet www.ukinkz.fco.gov.uk; Ambassador Dr CAROLYN BROWNE.

USA: 010010 Astana, Ak Bulak 4/23-22/3; tel. (7172) 70-21-00; fax (7172) 54-09-14; e-mail astanainfo@state.gov; internet kazakhstan .usembassy.gov; Ambassador KENNETH J. FAIRFAX.

Uzbekistan: 050010 Almatı, Beribaev kosh. 36; tel. (727) 291-78-86; fax (727) 291-10-55; e-mail emb-uzbekistan@mail.ru; Ambassador ALISHER A. SALAXITDINOV.

Viet Nam: 010000 Astana, Saryarka kosh. 6; tel. (7172) 99-03-75; fax (7172) 66-03-79; Ambassador NGUYEN VAN HOA.

Judicial System

Supreme Court of the Republic of Kazakhstan (Kazakstan Respublikasynyn Zhogargy Soty): 010000 Astana, D. Kunaev kosh. 39; tel. (7172) 74-75-85; fax (7172) 74-78-13; e-mail ms@ supcourt.kz; internet www.supcourt.kz; Chair. BEKTAS BEKNAZAROV.

Constitutional Council of the Republic of Kazakhstan (Kazakstan Respublikasy Konstitutsiyalyk Keneci): 010000 Astana, Soljagaw, Tauelsizdik kosh. 39; tel. (7172) 74-79-58; fax (7172) 74-76-51; e-mail liaison@constcouncil.kz; internet www.constcouncil.kz; f. 1995; seven mems; Chair. IGOR I. ROGOV.

Prosecutor-General: ASKAT K. DAUYLBAEV, 010000 Astana, Orynbor kosh. 8; tel. (7172) 71-24-07; e-mail gp-rk@mail.online.kz; internet www.procuror.kz.

Religion

The major religion of the Kazakhs is Islam. They are almost exclusively Sunni Muslims of the Hanafi school. The Russian Orthodox Church is the dominant Christian denomination; it is attended mainly by Slavs. There are also Protestant Churches (mainly Baptists), as well as a Roman Catholic presence and a Jewish community. In mid-2005 legislation was introduced, which required all religious organizations and communities to register with the state authorities.

ISLAM

The Kazakhs were converted to Islam only in the early 19th century, and for many years elements of animist practices remained. Over the period 1985–90 the number of mosques in Kazakhstan increased from 25 to 60. By 1991 there were an estimated 230 Muslim religious communities functioning in Kazakhstan and an Islamic institute had been opened in Almatı. The Islamic revival intensified following Kazakhstan's independence from the USSR, and during 1991–94 some 4,000 mosques were reported to have been opened.

Religious Administration of Muslims of Kazakhstan (Kazakstan musylmandary dini baskarmasy): 050000 Almatı; tel. (727) 230-63-65; fax (727) 297-94-23; e-mail susaev@bk.ru; internet www .muftyat.kz; Chair. Chief Mufti Haji ERJAN MAYAMEROV.

CHRISTIANITY

The Roman Catholic Church

The organization of the Roman Catholic Church in Kazakhstan comprises one archdiocese, two dioceses and one apostolic administration. Most Catholics in Kazakhstan are enrolled in the Latin Rite, and there are also a number of Byzantine Rite communities. There were an estimated 250,000 adherents at April 2008. A newly constructed cathedral at Qarağandi was consecrated in September 2012.

Catholic Bishops' Conference of Kazakhstan: 010010 Astana, Tashenov kosh. 3, POB 622; tel. (7172) 37-25-53; e-mail bishops-conf .kz@mail.ru; internet www.catholic-kazakhstan.org; f. 2003; Pres. Rt Rev. TOMASZ PETA (Archbishop of the Archdiocese of the Most Holy Virgin Mary at Astana).

Archbishop of the Archdiocese of the Most Holy Virgin Mary at Astana: Rt Rev. TOMASZ PETA, 010010 Astana, Tashenov kosh. 3, POB 622; tel. (7172) 37-29-35; fax (7172) 37-29-27; e-mail catholic_astana@mail.ru; internet www.catholic-kazakhstan.org.

Apostolic Administrator of Atiraw: Most Rev. JANUSZ KALETA (Titular Bishop of Phelbes), 060009 Atiraw, Avangard 3/34A; tel. (7122) 28-16-86; fax (7122) 28-16-84; e-mail catholic.atyrau@gmail .com.

The Russian Orthodox Church

The Russian Orthodox Church of the Moscow Patriarchate in Kazakhstan is represented by a Metropolitan District, established in 2003, comprising three dioceses. In 2009 there were 112 parishes.

Metropolitan District of Kazakhstan: 010000 Astana, pl. Respubliki 12; tel. (7172) 28-60-49; fax (7172) 28-69-84; e-mail cross@ orthodox.kz; internet www.mitropolia.kz; f. 2003; three dioceses (of Astana and Almatı, Chimkent and Aqmola, and Oral and Guriyev—Atiraw) Metropolitan of Astana and Almatı ALEKSANDR (MOGILEV).

JUDAISM

Mitsva Association of Kazakhstan: Almatı; tel. (727) 273-54-49; fax (727) 258-34-59; e-mail contact@mitsva.kz; internet www.mitsva .kz; f. 1992; unites Jewish communities across Kazakhstan; Pres. ALEKSANDR BARON.

Rabbi of Almatı: Rabbi MENACHEM GERSHOVICH.

The Press

PRINCIPAL DAILY NEWSPAPERS

Aikyn/Liter (Travel Warrant): 050029 Almatı, Mukanova kosh. 223B; tel. (727) 295-24-52; fax (727) 315-24-57; e-mail info@liter.kz; internet www.aikyn.kz; internet www.liter.kz; f. 2004; five a week; Kazakh and Russian edns; weekly arts and information supplement, *Aikyn apta/Liter nedelya* (Thurs); Editor-in-Chief LEV TARAKOV; circ. 39,300 (Kazakh edn, *Aikyn*), 33,600 (Russian edn, *Liter*).

Almaty Herald: 050000 Almatı, Rozybakiev kosh. 37; tel. (727) 241-45-69; fax (727) 241-40-78; e-mail herald@nursat.kz; Editor-in-Chief OLESSYA IVANOVA.

Egemen Kazakhstan (Sovereign Kazakhstan): Astana, Egemen Kazakhstan kosh. 5/13; tel. (7172) 37-65-27; e-mail egemenkz@mail .online.kz; internet www.egemen.kz; f. 1919; 6 a week; organ of the Govt; in Kazakh; Pres. SAUYTBEK ABDRAXMANOV; Editor-in-Chief JANBOLAT AUPBAEV.

Ekspress–K: 010000 Almatı, Kabanbai batyr kosh. 30A; tel. (727) 259-24-27; fax (727) 259-24-02; e-mail daily@express-k.kz; internet www.express-k.kz; f. 1920; 5 a week; in Russian; Editor-in-Chief TLEPBERGEN BEKMAGANBETOV; circ. 19,500.

Kazakhstanskaya Pravda (Kazakhstani Truth): 010000 Astana, Jenis kosh. 18A; tel. (727) 232-17-29; fax (727) 250-18-73; e-mail kpam@kaznet.kz; internet www.kazpravda.kz; f. 1920; 5 a week; publ. by the Govt; in Russian; Editor-in-Chief TATIANA V. KOSTINA; circ. 100,000 (2010).

Vechernii Almaty (Evening Almatı): 050016 Almatı, Abylai-xan d-ly 2; tel. and fax (727) 279-28-90; e-mail info@vecher.kz; internet www.vecher.kz; f. 1968; in Russian; Editor-in-Chief NIKOLAI N. ZHOROV.

Vremya (Time): 050000 Almatı, Raiymbek d-ly 115; tel. (727) 259-71-96; e-mail info@time.kz; internet www.time.kz; f. 1999; in Russian; general; Editor-in-Chief VADIM N. BOREIKO; circ. 250,000 (2004).

OTHER PUBLICATIONS

Akikat (Justice): 050044 Almatı, Gogol kosh. 39; tel. (727) 273-84-03; f. 1921; monthly; social and political.

Ana Tili (Native Language): 050044 Almatı, Dostyk d-ly 7; tel. (727) 233-22-21; fax (727) 233-34-73; f. 1990; weekly; in Kazakh; Editor-in-Chief J. BEISENBAY-ULI; circ. 11,073.

Dala Men Qala: 050029 Almatı, Abilaijan kosh. 79; tel. (727) 315-06-86; fax (727) 315-06-89; e-mail dalamenkala@mail.ru; internet dmk .kz; f. 2003; weekly; politics, society; Editor-in-Chief SAPARBAY PARMANKULOV.

Delovaya Nedelya (Business Week): 050044 Almatı, Jibek-joly d-ly 64; tel. (727) 250-62-72; fax (727) 273-91-48; e-mail info@dn.kz; internet www.dn.kz; f. 1992; weekly; business, politics, finance of Kazakhstan and Central Asia; in Russian; Editor-in-Chief S. A. KORJUMBAEV; circ. 15,000.

Delovoi Kazakhstan (Business Kazakhstan): 050013 Almatı, pl. Respubliki 15/553, POB 388; tel. (727) 250-72-68; fax (727) 295-23-02; e-mail dk@intelsoft.kz; internet www.dknews.kz; in Russian; weekly; f. 2006; Chief Editor SERIK KORJUMBAEV; circ. 15,000 (2009).

Druzhnye Rebyata (Friendly Chaps): 050009 Almatı, Abay d-ly 143/508; tel. (727) 242-77-89; e-mail jorken@mail.ru; f. 1933 as *Pioner Kazakhstana* (Kazakhstani Pioneer); present name adopted 1956; weekly; in Russian; for children.

Ekologicheskii Kuryer int (Ecological Courier International): 050000 Almatı, Panfilov kosh. 106A; tel. (727) 261-12-23; fax (727) 261-12-10; e-mail ecocourier@nursat.kz; every two weeks; in Russian; environmental concerns; Editor EDUARD MATSKEVICH; circ. 3,000.

Ekspert Kazakhstan: 050000 Almatı, Furmanov kosh. 122; tel. (727) 272-73-69; fax (727) 295-28-33; e-mail skir@expert.ru; internet www.expert.ru/printissues/kazakhstan; f. 2003; weekly; business and economics; in Russian; Chief Editor YURII DOROKHOV; circ. 10,000 (2011).

Jas Alash (Young Generation): 050002 Almatı, Jibek-joly kosh. 50; tel. (727) 273-75-59; fax (727) 273-87-55; e-mail zhasalash2010@mail.ru; internet www.zhasalash.kz; f. 1921; publ. by the Kazakhstan Youth Union; two a week; in Kazakh; Editor-in-Chief RYSBEK SARSENBAY.

Karavan (Caravan): 050000 Almatı, pl. Respubliki 13; tel. (727) 258-36-24; fax (727) 258-36-25; e-mail kaztag@caravan.kz; internet www.caravan.kz; f. 1991; weekly; in Russian; Editor-in-Chief ADIL IBRAEV; circ. 250,000.

Kazak Adebiety (Kazakh Literature): 050000 Almatı, Ablai-xan kosh. 105; tel. and fax (727) 269-54-62; f. 1934; weekly; organ of the Union of Writers of Kazakhstan; in Kazakh; Editor-in-Chief A. JAKSYBAEV; circ. 7,874.

Kazakhstan: 050044 Almatı, Jibek-joly d-ly 50; tel. (727) 233-13-56; f. 1992; weekly; analytical publication on the extractive industry intended for an audience of international investors; in Russian and English; Editor-in-Chief N. ORAZBEKOV.

Kazakstan Aielderi (Women of Kazakhstan): 050044 Almatı, Jibek-joly d-ly 50; tel. (727) 233-06-23; fax (727) 246-15-53; f. 1925; monthly; culture and housekeeping; in Kazakh; Editor-in-Chief ALTYNSHASH K. JAGANOVA; circ. 15,200.

Kazakstan Mektebi (Kazakhstani School): 050004 Almatı, Ablai-xan d-ly 34; tel. (727) 239-76-65; f. 1925; monthly; publ. by the Ministry of Education and Science; in Kazakh; Editor-in-Chief S. ABISHEVA; circ. 10,000.

Kazakstan Zaman (Kazakh Time): 050002 Almatı, Dostyk d-ly 106G; tel. (727) 265-07-39; e-mail info@kazakzaman.kz; internet www.kazakzaman.kz; f. 1992; in Kazakh and Turkish; weekly; Gen. Dir ERTAY AIGALYEVICH; circ. 15,000.

Kazakstannyn zher resurstary/Zemelnye Resursy Kazakhstana (Land Resources of Kazakhstan): 010000 Astana, 8 Orynbor kosh., 12 kireberis, 5th Floor; tel. and fax (7172) 74-16-52; e-mail info@auzr.kz; internet www.auzr.kz; every two months; in Kazakh and Russian edns; publication of Republican Agency for the Management of Land Resources; Chair. of Editorial Bd ALJANBAY SHAYAHMETOV.

Kontinent (Continent): 050000 Almatı, POB 271; tel. (727) 250-10-39; fax (727) 250-10-41; e-mail bzchyt@kaznet.kz; f. 1999; every two weeks; policy and society journal; Editor-in-Chief ANDREI KUKUSHKIN; circ. 10,000.

Korye Ilbo (Korean News): 050044 Almatı, Jibek-joly d-ly 50; tel. (727) 233-90-10; fax (727) 263-25-46; f. 1923; weekly; in Korean and Russian; Editor-in-Chief YAN WON SIK.

Kredo (Credo): 100029 Qarağandi, Oktyabrskaya 25; tel. (721) 222-38-40; e-mail credogazeta@gmail.com; internet www.catholic-kazakhstan.org/credo; f. 1995; monthly; Catholic; in Russian; Chief Editor N. MAMAEV.

Megapolis (Megalopolis): 050060 Almatı, P. Tajibaevoy kosh. 155; tel. and fax (727) 315-09-87; e-mail info@megapolis.kz; internet www.megapolis.kz; f. 2000; general; weekly; CEO RINAT ASKAROV; Editor-in-Chief IGOR SHAXNOVICH.

Novoye Pokoleniye (New Generation): 050091 Almatı, Bogenbai batyr kosh. 156A/505; tel. (727) 334-09-11; fax (727) 250-95-46; e-mail np@np.kz; internet www.np.kz; f. 1998; weekly; economic and political affairs of Kazakhstan and the CIS, with supplement on the arts; in Russian; Editor-in-Chief SERGEI APARIN; circ. 40,000.

Panorama: 050013 Almatı, pl. Respubliki 15/647; tel. (727) 291-50-46; fax (727) 291-50-36; e-mail panorama@intelsoft.kz; internet www.panorama.kz; f. 1992; weekly; analytical coverage of politics, economics, business and international relations; in Russian; Dir ALEKSANDR NESUKANNYI; Editor-in-Chief LERA TSOY; circ. 20,000.

Petroleum of Kazakhstan: 050000 Almatı, Nauryzbai batyr kosh. 58; tel. (727) 258-28-38; fax (727) 250-50-82; e-mail office@petroleumjournal.kz; internet www.petroleumjournal.kz; every two months; in Russian and English; Editor-in-Chief OLEG C. CHERVINSKY; circ. 1,000.

Pro Sport Kazakhstan: 050008 Almatı, Bogenbai batyr kosh. 34A/87A; tel. and fax (727) 250-90-30; two a week; in Russian; sport.

Rukh-Miras (Heritage Movement): 050013 Almatı, Abay d-ly 14; tel. (727) 267-28-83; e-mail ieshua@front.ru; internet www.nlrk.kz; f. 2004; quarterly; literature, fine arts; in Kazakh and Russian; Chair. of Editorial Bd MURAT AUEZOV; Chief Editor TALASBEK ASEMKULOV.

Russkii Yazyk i Literatura v Kazakhskoye Shkole (Russian Language and Literature in the Kazakh School): 050091 Almatı, Abylai-xan kosh. 34; tel. (727) 239-76-68; f. 1962; every two months; in Russian; Editor-in-Chief B. S. MUKANOV.

Strana i Mir (The Country and The World): 050029 Almatı, Abylai-xan kosh. 79; tel. (727) 315-06-85; fax (727) 315-06-89; e-mail reklamanyr@liter.kz; internet sim.kz; politics; weekly; in Russian; f. 2003; Editor-in-Chief RASHID GARIPOV.

Turkistan: 050009 Almatı, Abay kosh. 143; tel. (727) 394-42-51; fax (727) 394-41-80; e-mail turkestan_gazeta@mail.ru; internet www.turkystan.kz; f. 1994; weekly; political analysis; in Kazakh; Editor-in-chief SHAMSHIDIN A. PATTEEV; circ. 10,000.

Uigur Avazi (Uigur Voice): 050044 Almatı, Jibek-joly d-ly 50; tel. (727) 233-84-59; f. 1957; two a week; publ. by the Govt; socio-political; in Uighur; Editor-in-Chief I. AZAMATOV; circ. 9,000.

Ulan (Man Alive): 050044 Almatı, Jibek-joly d-ly 50; tel. (727) 233-80-03; f. 1930; weekly; in Kazakh; for children and teenagers; Editor-in-Chief S. KALIEV; circ. 183,014.

Zerde (Intellect): 050044 Almatı, Jibek-joly d-ly 50; tel. (727) 233-83-81; f. 1960; monthly; popular, scientific, technical; in Kazakh; Editor-in-Chief E. RAUSHAN-ULY; circ. 68,600.

NEWS AGENCY

National Information Agency 'Kazinform': 010000 Astana, Beibitshilik kosh. 10; tel. and fax (7172) 32-75-67; e-mail product@inform.kz; internet www.inform.kz; f. 1997; 100% state-owned open jt-stock co; provides information on govt activities in Kazakhstan and abroad; Chair. of Bd DAUREN DIYAROV.

Publishers

Almatykitap: 050012 Almatı, Jambıl 111; tel. (727) 250-29-58; fax (727) 292-81-10; art, educational and children's books; Pres. A. LOMEYKO.

Civil Engineering & Architecture Publishing House: 050043 Almatı, Ryskulbekov kosh. 28; tel. (727) 309-63-49; fax (727) 309-61-53; e-mail esengalieva_b@email.ru; f. 2002; publr of KazGASA Kazakh Chief Architectural-Construction Academy; Dir BATIMA ESENGALIEVA.

Gylym (Science): 050010 Almatı, Pushkin kosh. 111–113; tel. (727) 291-18-77; fax (727) 261-88-45; f. 1946; books on natural sciences, humanities and scientific research journals; Dir S. G. BAIMENOV.

Kainar (Spring): 050009 Almatı, Abay d-ly 143; tel. (727) 242-27-96; e-mail kainar_baspasy@mail.ru; f. 1962; agriculture, history, culture, religion; Dir ORAZBEK S. SARSENBAEV.

Kazakhskaya Entsiklopediya (Kazakh Encyclopedia): 050000 Almatı; tel. (727) 262-55-66; f. 1968; Editor-in-Chief BAURZHAN JAKYP.

Kazakhstan Publishing House: 050000 Almatı, Abay d-ly 143; tel. and fax (727) 242-29-29; f. 1920; political science, economics, medicine, general and social sciences; Dir E.X. SYZDYKOV; Editors-in-Chief M. D. SITKO, M. A. RASHEV.

Mektep: 050009 Almatı, Abay d-ly 143; tel. (727) 394-42-34; fax (727) 394-37-58; e-mail mektep@mail.ru; internet www.mektep.kz; f. 1947; mainly literature for educational institutions; dictionaries, phrase books, children's textbooks, teaching materials, reference books; publishes books in Kazakh, Russian, Uighur and Uzbek; Gen. Dir ERLAN SATYBALDIEV.

Oner (Art): 050000 Almatı, Abay d-ly 143; tel. (727) 242-08-88; f. 1980; Dir S. S. ORAZALINOV; Editor-in-Chief A. A. ASKAROV.

Zhazushy (Writer): 050000 Almatı, Abay d-ly 143; tel. (727) 242-28-49; e-mail zhazushi@mail.ru; internet www.adai@mail.ru; f. 1934; literature, literary criticism, essays, poetry, textbooks; Dir YESSEN-GALI RAUSHANOV.

Broadcasting and Communications

GOVERNMENT AGENCY

Republican Agency for Information and Communications: 010000 Astana, Ministry Bldg, Soljagaw, Ishim; tel. (7172) 74-01-35; fax (7172) 74-10-03; e-mail press@aic.gov.kz; internet www.aic.gov.kz; Chair. KUANYSHBEK B. YESEKEEV.

TELECOMMUNICATIONS

The telecommunications sector in Kazakhstan experienced rapid growth in the 2000s. The fixed-line telecommunications market is dominated by the state-owned company, Kazakhtelekom, while the mobile telecommunications sector has three main operators. In 2010 the market shares of fixed-line and mobile telecommunications services were 74.7% and 25.3%, respectively; 22.2% of households had a fixed-line telephone and the rate of subscription to mobile services was equivalent to 100.2% of the population.

Altel: 050000 Almatı, Jarokov kosh. 189; tel. (727) 259-81-20; fax (727) 259-81-21; e-mail info@altel.kz; internet www.altel.kz; f. 1994; provides mobile cellular communications and wireless internet services in Kazakhstan (under the brand names City, Dalacom, Jet and PAThWORD).

GSM Kazakhstan (Kcell): 050013 Almatı, Timiriyazev kosh. 2G; tel. (727) 258-11-48; fax (727) 258-89-10; e-mail info@kcell.kz; internet www.kcell.kz; f. 1998; 51% owned by TeliaSonera (Sweden), 49% by Kazakhtelekom; provides mobile cellular telecommunications services (as Kcell and Activ) in 1,449 settlements across Kazakhstan; provides internet services; 7.5m. subscribers (May 2009); Chief Exec. VEYSEL ARAL.

KaR-tel (K-Mobile): 050000 Almatı, Tole bi 55; tel. (727) 266-23-33; fax (727) 250-16-11; e-mail info@beeline.kz; internet www.beeline.kz; f. 1999; wholly—owned subsidiary of VympelKom-Bilain (Russia); provides mobile cellular telecommunications services (as K-Mobile, Excess and Beeline) in more than 100 settlements and along principal roads across Kazakhstan; Gen. Dir ANATOLII POPOV; 1.6m. subscribers (mid-2005).

Kazakhtelekom: 010000 Astana, Abai kosh. 31; tel. (717) 258-06-59; fax (717) 258-77-24; e-mail webmaster@telecom.kz; internet www.telecom.kz; f. 1994; internet and telecommunications services; public limited co; Dir AIDAN KARIBJANOV.

KazTransCom: 050009 Almatı, Radostovets kosh. 69/204A; tel. (727) 237-73-10; fax (727) 237-73-18; e-mail ktc@kaztranscom.kz; internet www.kaztranscom.kz; f. 2001 as a result of merger of CaspiMunayBailanys, Aktjubneftesviaz and Bailanys; jt-stock co; provides telecommunications services to the petroleum and natural gas sectors; won licence in 2004 to provide long-distance and international telephone calls country-wide, becoming Kazakhstan's second long-distance provider

BROADCASTING

Private radio and television stations began operating in Kazakhstan in the 1990s.

Kazakh State Television and Radio Broadcasting Corpn: 050013 Almatı, Jeltoksan kosh. 175A; tel. (727) 263-37-16; f. 1920; Pres. YERMEK TURSUNOV.

Radio

Kazakh Radio: 050013 Almatı, Jeltoksan kosh. 177; tel. (727) 393-22-33; fax (727) 265-03-87; internet www.kazradio.kaztrk.kz; f. 1921; broadcasts in Kazakh, Russian, Uighur, German and other minority languages; Gen. Dir TOREXAN DANIYAR.

Radio 31: 050060 Almatı, Tajibaevoi kosh. 155; tel. and fax (727) 315-31-31; e-mail tv_31@31.kz; internet www.31.kz; f. 1994; news and music; Dir NURJAN MUHAMEJANOVA.

Television

Khabar News Agency: 050013 Almatı, Jeltosan kosh. 185; tel. (727) 270-10-01; fax (727) 270-10-40; e-mail astananews@khabar.kz; internet www.khabar.kz; f. 1959; international broadcasts in Kazakh, Uighur, Russian and German; two television channels; Chair. of the Bd of Dirs MAULEN ASHIMBAEV; Dir ASEL E. BALGAEVA.

KTK (Kazakh Commercial Television): 050013 Almatı, pl. Respubliki 13; tel. and fax (727) 258-36-55; e-mail ktk@ktk-tv.kz; internet www.ktk-tv.kz; f. 1990; independent; Gen. Dir ARMAN SHURAEV.

NTK (Association of TV and Radio Broadcasters of Kazakhstan): 050013 Almatı, pl. Respubliki 13, 6th Floor; tel. (727) 270-01-83; fax (727) 270-01-85; e-mail kaztvradio@nursat.kz; f. 2000; privately owned; Pres. AIDAR JUMABAEV.

STV: 050010 Almatı, Karasai batyr kosh. 88; tel. (727) 292-74-74; internet www.rakhattv.kz; f. 1994; privately owned; fmrly Rakhat-TV, present name adopted 2009; information and entertainment broadcasts to Aktaw, Almatı, Astana, Atiraw, Pavlodar, Petropavl and Toldykorgan, also available on cable networks and satellite.

Finance

(cap. = capital; res = reserves; dep. = deposits; m. = million; brs = branches; amounts in tenge, unless otherwise indicated)

BANKING

Central Bank

National Bank of Kazakhstan (NBK): 050040 Almatı, Koktem-3 21; tel. (727) 270-45-91; fax (727) 250-60-90; e-mail hq@nationalbank.kz; internet www.nationalbank.kz; f. 1990; cap. 20,000.0m., res 668,713.7m., dep. 2,555,829.3m. (Dec. 2009); Gov. GRIGORII A. MARCHENKO; 19 brs.

Major Commercial Banks

Alliance Bank: 050000 Almatı, Furmanov kosh. 50; tel. (727) 258-40-40; fax (727) 259-80-71; e-mail ir@alb.kz; internet www.alb.kz; f. 1993; cap. 273,090m., res −21,483m., dep. 302,477m. (Dec. 2011); Chair. MAXAT KABASHEV.

ATFBank: 050000 Almatı, Furmanov kosh. 100; tel. (727) 250-30-40; fax (727) 250-19-95; e-mail info@atfbank.kz; internet www.atfbank.kz; f. 1995; present name adopted 2002; cap. 152,878.4m., res 16,574.9m., dep. 608,351.9m. (Dec. 2011); Chair. TIMUR ISSATAEV; 10 brs.

Bank Centercredit: 050000 Almatı, Panfilov kosh. 98; tel. (727) 259-85-98; fax (727) 258-45-10; e-mail info@centercredit.kz; internet www.centercredit.kz; f. 1988; present name adopted 1996; 30.5% owned by Kookmin Bank (Rep. of Korea); cap. 69,797m., res 1,680m., dep. 733,978m. (Dec. 2011); Chair. of Bd BAXYTBEK R. BAYSEITOV; 19 brs.

BTA Bank: 050051 Almatı, Samal 2, Joldasbekov kosh. 97; tel. (727) 250-40-70; fax (727) 250-02-24; e-mail post@bta.kz; internet www.bta.kz; f. 1997 as Bank TuranAlem; name changed as above 2008; 75.1% state-owned; cap. 1,187,023m., res −143,516m., dep. 835,162m. (Dec. 2011); Chair. of Bd YELENA BAKHMUTOVA; Chair. of Managing Bd ANVAR G. SAIDENOV; 23 brs.

Development Bank of Kazakhstan: 010000 Astana, pl. Respublika 32; tel. (7172) 58-02-60; fax (7172) 58-02-76; e-mail info@kdb.kz; internet www.kdb.kz; f. 2001; wholly state-owned; cap. 255,976.0m., res 20,742.6m., dep. 428.6m. (Dec. 2011); Chair. of Bd NURLAN KUSSAINOV.

Eurasian Bank (Yevraziiskii Bank): 050002 Almatı, Kunaev kosh. 56; tel. (727) 250-77-05; fax (727) 250-86-50; e-mail info@eurasian-bank.kz; internet www.eurasian-bank.kz; f. 1994; cap. 24,210.2m., res 5,114.6m., dep. 248,832.8m. (Dec. 2011); Chair. MICHAEL EGGLETON; 18 brs.

Eurasian Development Bank: 050000 Almatı, Panfilov kosh. 98; tel. (727) 244-40-44; fax (727) 244-65-70; e-mail info@eabr.org; internet www.eabr.org; f. 2006; cap. US $1,515.7m., res $96.5m., dep. $49.9m. (Dec. 2012); Chair. IGOR FINOGENOV.

Halyk Bank: 050046 Almatı, Rozybakiev kosh. 97; tel. (727) 259-00-00; fax (727) 259-02-71; e-mail halykbank@halykbank.kz; internet www.halykbank.kz; f. 1936 as br. of Savings Bank of USSR; fully privatized in Nov. 2001; cap. 143,695m., res −54,730m., dep. 1,701,711m. (Dec. 2012); Chair. and Chief Exec. UMUT SHAYAKHMETOVA.

HSBC Bank Kazakhstan: 050010 Almatı, Dostyk d-ly 43; tel. (727) 259-69-00; fax (727) 259-69-02; e-mail info@hsbc.kz; internet www.hsbc.kz; f. 1998; 100% owned by HSBC Bank PLC (United Kingdom); cap. 7,050.0m., res 1,966.4m., dep. 138,679m. (Dec. 2011); Chair. of Bd DEREK P. LUNT.

Kaspi Bank: 050012 Almatı, Adi Sharipov kosh. 90; tel. (727) 250-18-00; fax (727) 250-95-96; e-mail office@bankcaspian.kz; internet www.bc.kz; 96% owned by Caspian Group (Netherlands); fmrly Caspian Bank; present name adopted 2008; cap. 17,001.2m., res 2,120.7m., dep. 336,545.7m. (Dec. 2011); Chair. MIXEIL LOMTADZE; 17 brs.

KazInvestBank: 050051 Almatı, Dostyk d-ly 176; tel. (727) 261-90-60; fax (727) 259-86-58; e-mail info@kib.kz; internet www.kib.kz; f. 1993; open jt-stock co; cap. 7,432.8m., res 2,778.3m., dep. 64,352.2m. (Dec. 2011); Chair. ADNAN ALLY AGHA; 3 brs.

Kazkommertsbank (KKB): 050060 Almatı, Gagarin kosh. 135; tel. (727) 258-53-01; fax (727) 258-51-61; e-mail mailbox@kkb.kz; internet www.kkb.kz; f. 1991; cap. 9,023m., res 370,929m., dep. 1,512,575m. (Dec. 2011); Chair. NURJAN S. SUBXANBERDIN; Man. Dir ANDREI I. TIMCHENKO; 23 brs.

Nurbank: 050010 Almatı, Dostyk d-ly 38; tel. (727) 259-97-10; fax (727) 250-16-09; e-mail bank@nurbank.kz; internet www.nurbank.kz; f. 1992; cap. 127,611.2m., res 1,323.8m., dep. 162,445.9m. (Dec. 2011); Chair. NURMUXAMED BEKTEMISSOV; 56 brs.

Temirbank: 050008 Almatı, Abay d-ly 68/74; tel. (727) 257-88-88; fax (727) 250-62-41; e-mail board@temirbank.kz; internet www.temirbank.kz; f. 1992; 80% owned by Samruk-Kazyna National Welfare Fund; cap. 59,725.9m., res −25.2m., dep. 163,365.3m. (Dec. 2012); CEO YERZHAN SHAIKENOV; 15 brs.

Tsesnabank: 010000 Astana, Jengis d-ly 29; tel. (7172) 77-07-70; fax (7172) 77-01-95; e-mail info@tsb.kz; internet www.tsb.kz; f. 1992; cap. 27,480.8m., res 2,992.8m., dep. 345,975m. (Dec. 2011); Chair. YERKEGALI YEDENBAEV; 21 brs.

Islamic Bank

Al Hilal Bank Kazakhstan: 050059 Almatı, Al Farabi kosh. 36, Bldg B, 6th Floor; tel. (727) 233-00-00; internet www.alhilalbank.kz; f. 2010; owned by Al Hilal Bank Abu Dhabi (United Arab Emirates); Chair. AHMED ATEEQ AL-MAZROUEI; Gen. Man. PRASAD JOSE ABRAHAM.

Bankers' Organization

Bank Association of Kazakhstan: 010000 Almatı, Panfilov kosh. 98; tel. (727) 273-16-89; fax (727) 273-90-85; Pres. BAXYTBEK BAISEI-TOV.

STOCK EXCHANGES

Kazakhstan Stock Exchange (KASE): 050040 Almatı, Baizakov kosh. 280; tel. (727) 237-53-00; fax (727) 296-64-02; e-mail info@kase.kz; internet www.kase.kz; f. 1993; Pres. KADYRZHAN DAMITOV.

Regional Financial Centre of Almatı City: 050059 Almatı, Al-Farabi kosh. 17/1, Biznes-Tsentr 'Nurly-Taw' 4B, 9th Floor; tel. (727) 311-09-31; fax (727) 311-09-42; e-mail info@rfca.kz; internet www.rfca.gov.kz; f. 2007; Chair. of Bd DAUREN B. UTKELBAEV.

INSURANCE

Almatı International Insurance Group: 050000 Almatı, Kabanbai batyr kosh. 112; tel. and fax (727) 250-12-31; f. 1994; Chair. SUREN AMBARTSUMIAN.

Centras Insurance: 050008 Almatı, Manas kosh. 32A; tel. (727) 259-77-55; fax (727) 259-77-66; e-mail insurance@centras.kz; internet www.cic.kz; f. 1997; non-life insurance and reinsurance; Chair. TALGAT USENOV.

Dynasty Life Insurance Co: 050000 Almatı, Seifullin kosh. 410; tel. (727) 250-73-95; e-mail dynasty@bta.nursat.kz; Chair. SERIK TEMIRGALEEV.

Industrial Insurance Group (IIG): 050046 Almatı, Nauryzbai batyr kosh. 65–69; tel. (727) 250-96-95; fax (727) 250-96-98; e-mail iig@kaznet.kz; f. 1998; Pres. IVAN MIXAILOV.

Interteach Kazakhstani Health and Medical Insurance Corpn: 050059 Almatı, Furmanov kosh. 275D; tel. and fax (727) 320-02-00; e-mail interteach@interteach.kz; internet www.interteach.kz; f. 1989; medical and travel insurance, health care, accident and employee liability insurance; 290 employees; 48 brs; Gen. Dir ERNST M. KURLEUTOV.

KazAgroPolits Insurance Co: 050000 Almatı, Nauryzbai batyr kosh. 49–61; tel. (727) 232-13-24; fax (727) 232-13-26; e-mail kazagropolise@mail.banknet.kz; Chair. YERMEK USPANOV.

Kazakhinstrakh (Kazakh International Insurance Co): 050044 Almatı, Jibek-joly d-ly 69; tel. (727) 233-73-49; fax (727) 250-74-37; e-mail kiscentr@nursat.kz; Chair. NURLAN MOLDAXMETOV.

Kazkommerts-Polits Insurance Co: 050013 Almatı, Satpaev kosh. 24; tel. (727) 258-48-08; fax (727) 292-73-97; e-mail info@kkp.kz; internet www.kkp.kz; f. 1996; non-life; Chair. MEIRAM B. SERGAZIN; Dir TALGAT K. USSENOV.

Trade and Industry

GOVERNMENT AGENCY

Republican Agency for the Regulation of Natural Monopolies: 010000 Astana, Bukei-xan kosh. 14; tel. (7172) 59-16-77; fax (7172) 21-54-73; e-mail info@arem.kz; internet www.regulator.kz; Chair. NURLAN SH. ALDABERGENOV.

CHAMBERS OF COMMERCE

Union of Chambers of Commerce and Industry of Kazakhstan: 050000 Almatı, Masanchi kosh. 26; tel. (727) 292-00-52; fax (727) 250-70-29; e-mail tpprkaz@online.ru; internet www.ccikaz.kz; f. 1959; Chair. ABLAI MYRZAXMETOV.

Almatı City Chamber of Commerce and Industry: 050000 Almatı, Tole bi 45; tel. (727) 262-03-01; e-mail alcci@nursat.kz; internet www.atpp.marketcenter.ru; Chair. ABLAI MYRZAXMETOV.

Astana City Chamber of Commerce and Industry: 010000 Astana, Auezov kosh. 66, POB 1966; tel. (7172) 32-38-33; e-mail akmcci@dan.kz; internet www.chamber.kz; Chair. TATYANA I. KONONOVA.

Jambıl Oblast Chamber of Commerce and Industry: 080012 Jambıl obl., Taraz, Karaxan kosh. 2; tel. (7262) 43-05-98; Chair. ADILXAN JAPARBEKOV.

Qarağandi Oblast Chamber of Commerce and Industry: 100008 Qarağandi, bulv. Mira 31; tel. (7212) 30-06-84; fax (7212) 30-05-05; e-mail karcci@karcci.kz; internet www.karcci.kz; f. 1959; Chair. of Presidium NESSIP SEITOVA.

Southern Kazakhstan Oblast Chamber of Commerce and Industry: 160000 Southern Kazakhstan obl., Chimkent, Tauke-xan kosh. 31; tel. (7252) 21-14-05; Chair. SYRLYBAJ ORDABEKOV.

EMPLOYERS' ORGANIZATIONS

Confederation of Employers of the Republic of Kazakhstan (KRRK): 050060 Almatı, Radostovets kosh. 212; tel. (727) 390-17-14;

fax (727) 395-66-58; e-mail krrk@krrk.kz; internet www.krrk.kz; Pres. KADYR BAYIKENOV.

Kazakhstan Petroleum Association: 050010 Almatı, Zenkov 59; tel. (727) 311-67-05; fax (727) 311-67-04; e-mail kpa@arna.kz; internet www.kpakz.kz; f. 1998; Chair. RZABEK ARTYGALIEV; 40 mem. cos.

UTILITIES

Electricity

KEGOS—Kazakhstan Electricity Grid Operating Co (Elektr zhelilerin baskaru zhanindegi Kazakstan kompaniyasy): 050000 Almatı, Kozybaev kosh. 23; tel. (727) 271-93-59; internet www.kegoc.kz; f. 1997; technical electricity network operator; Pres. BAKYTJAN KAJIEV.

Water

Almatı Vodokanal: 050057 Almatı, Jarokov kosh. 196; tel. (727) 274-84-02; fax (727) 274-98-41; e-mail vk.prm@itte.kz; f. 1936; state-owned; responsible for water supply and sewerage in Almatı and surrounding villages; Gen. Dir VLADISLAV GALIEV.

STATE HYDROCARBONS COMPANIES

KazMunaiGaz: 010000 Astana, Kabanbai batyr kosh. 22; tel. (7172) 97-60-00; fax (7172) 97-60-01; e-mail info@kmg.kz; internet www.kmg.kz; f. 2002 by merger of KazakhOil and Transneftegas; national jt-stock co; subsidiaries include petroleum transportation co KazTransOil, and gas transportation co KazTransGas; CEO ASKAR BALJANOV.

Munaigaz: 010000 Astana, Jeltoksan kosh. 7/1; tel. and fax (7172) 39-03-11; e-mail info@munaygas.com; internet www.munaygas.com; f. 2004; prospecting for, and production of, petroleum and gas; Pres. JENISHBEK JUMASHEV (acting).

TRADE UNIONS

Confederation of Free Trade Unions of Coal and Mining Industries: 050000 Almatı; Chair. V. GAIPOV.

Confederation of Free Trade Unions of Kazakhstan: f. 1991; fmrly Independent Trade Union Centre of Kazakhstan; 9 regional brs with 2,200 mems; Chair. SERGEI BELKIN.

Federation of Trade Unions of Kazakhstan: 010000 Astana, pr. Abay 38; tel. (7172) 216-68-14; fax (7172) 21-68-35; e-mail fprkastana@fprk.kz; internet www.fprk.kz; 26 affiliated unions with 2,047,185 mems (2009); Chair. SIYAZBEK MUKASHEV.

Transport

RAILWAYS

In 2010 the total length of rail track in use was 14,184 km (4,054 km of which were electrified). Much of the rail network is in the north of the country, where it joins the rail lines of Russia. There are also connections with Kyrgyzstan, Uzbekistan and the People's Republic of China.

An underground railway in Almatı opened to passengers in December 2011. In Astana the construction of a rapid transit system was planned.

Kazakstan Temir Joly (Kazakhstan Railways): 010000 Astana, Konaev kosh. 6; tel. (7172) 93-01-13; fax (7172) 32-82-30; e-mail temirzhol@railways.kz; internet www.railways.kz; f. 1991; Pres. ASKAR U. MAMIN.

ROADS

In 2010 Kazakhstan's total road network was 96,018 km, including 23,494 km of main roads. Some 89.5% of the total network was hard-surfaced.

INLAND WATERWAYS

Kazakhstan has an inland waterway network extending over some 4,000 km. The main navigable river is the Ertis (Irtysh).

Committee of Transport and Railways (Ministry of Transport and Communications): 010000 Astana, Kabanbai batyr kosh. 32/1; tel. (7172) 24-10-79; fax (7172) 24-12-98; e-mail ktps_info@mtc.gov.kz; internet www.ktps.gov.kz; f. 2008; Chair. NURDAULET I. KILYBAY.

SHIPPING

A ferry port was inaugurated on the Caspian Sea at Aktaw in 2001, with services operating to Azerbaijan, Iran and Russia. At 31 December 2012 Kazakhstan's flag registered fleet comprised 167 vessels, with a combined displacement of 183,229 grt.

Aktau (Aktaw) International Commercial Sea Port: 130000 Mañğıstaw obl., Aktaw akimat, Ömırzaq; tel. (7292) 51-45-49; fax

(7292) 44-51-01; e-mail aktauport@aktauport.kz; f. 1963; Dir Talgat B. Abylgazin; 609 employees.

CIVIL AVIATION

There are 18 domestic airports, and four airports with international services, located at Aktaw, Almatı, Astana and Atiraw.

Department of Aviation (Ministry of Transport and Communications): 010000 Astana, Kabanbai batyr kosh. 32/1; tel. (7172) 24-26-05; fax (7172) 24-31-65; e-mail kga_info@mtc.gov.kz; internet www.caa.gov.kz; Chair. Radilbek Adimolda.

Air Astana: 050039 Almatı, Zakarpatska kosh. 4a; tel. (7172) 58-41-35; fax (7172) 59-87-01; internet www.airastana.com; f. 2001 jointly by the Samruk-Kazyna National Welfare Fund (51%) and BAE Systems (United Kingdom—49%); domestic and international flights; Pres. Peter Foster.

Tourism

Tourism is not widely developed in Kazakhstan. In 2011 there were 4.1m. tourist arrivals in Kazakhstan, while receipts from tourism (excluding passenger transport) amounted to US $1,209m., according to provisional figures.

Kazakhstan Tourist Association (KTA): 050022 Almatı, Abay d-ly 42/44/302; tel. (727) 292-53-31; fax (727) 292-48-53; e-mail kta@mail.kz; f. 1999.

Defence

Kazakhstan was one of the four former Union Republics to become a nuclear power in succession to the USSR, but dismantled its final nuclear-testing capabilities at Semey (Semipalatinsk) in July 2000. In mid-1992 Kazakhstan signed a Collective Security Treaty with five other members of the Commonwealth of Independent States (CIS); in May 2001 it was announced that the signatory countries were to form a Collective Rapid Reaction Force to combat Islamist militancy in Central Asia. In April 2003 the Collective Security Treaty Organization (CSTO) was inaugurated as the successor to the CIS collective security system, comprising Armenia, Belarus, Kazakhstan, Kyrgyzstan, Russia and Tajikistan. Kazakhstan participates, with Russia and Azerbaijan, in the operation of the Caspian Sea Flotilla, based at Astrakhan, Russia, and established its own navy in 2003. In May 1994 Kazakhstan joined the North Atlantic Treaty Organization's (NATO) 'Partnership for Peace' programme of military co-operation. As assessed at November 2012, the country's total armed forces numbered some 39,000, with an army of 20,000, an air force of 12,000, a navy of 3,000 and 4,000 joint troops answerable to the Ministry of Defence. There were also 31,500 paramilitary troops, including 20,000 internal security troops under the command of the Ministry of Internal Affairs, a 2,000-strong Presidential Guard, a 500-member Government Guard, and 9,000 state border protection forces answerable to the Ministry of Internal Affairs. Conscripts serve for a period of 12 months.

Chairman of Joint Chiefs of Staff: Gen.-Col Saken A. Jasuzakov.

Defence Expenditure: Budgeted at 340,000m. tenge in 2012.

Education

General education (pre-primary, primary and secondary) is compulsory, and is fully funded by the state. Since 2010 primary education, which begins at seven years of age and lasts for four years, has been preceded by one year of pre-primary education, while secondary education continues for a further seven years. In 2009/10 total enrolment at primary schools included 90% of children in the relevant age-group, while the comparable ratio for secondary enrolment was 88%. In 2011/12 there were 7,706 state general schools. After completing general education, pupils may continue their studies at vocational secondary schools; there were 494 such schools in the state sector in 2011/12. In addition, there were 310 professional-technical schools.

In 2011/12 there was a total of 146 state higher schools (including universities), attended by 629,500 students, and in 2003/04 there were 134 non-governmental higher education institutes, attended by 297,900 students. Government expenditure on education in 2012 was 1,210,115.4m. tenge (19.3% of total spending).

KENYA

Introductory Survey

LOCATION, CLIMATE, LANGUAGE, RELIGION, FLAG, CAPITAL

The Republic of Kenya lies astride the equator on the east coast of Africa, with Somalia to the north-east, Ethiopia and South Sudan to the north, Uganda to the west and Tanzania to the south. The climate varies with altitude: the coastal region is hot and humid, with temperatures averaging between 20°C and 32°C (69°F–90°F), while inland, at more than 1,500 m (5,000 ft) above sea-level, temperatures average 7°C–27°C (45°F–80°F). The highlands and western areas receive ample rainfall (an annual average of 1,000 mm–1,250 mm) but most of northern Kenya is very dry (about 250 mm). Kiswahili is the official language, while English is widely spoken and 22% and 13% of the population, respectively, speak Kikuyu and Luo as their mother tongue. Most of the country's inhabitants follow traditional beliefs. There is a sizeable Christian community, while Muslims form a smaller proportion of the population. The national flag (proportions 2 by 3) has three broad horizontal stripes, of black, red and green, separated by two narrow white stripes. Superimposed in the centre is a red shield, with black and white markings, upon crossed white spears. The capital is Nairobi.

CONTEMPORARY POLITICAL HISTORY

Historical Context

Formerly a British colony (inland) and protectorate (along the coast), Kenya became independent, within the Commonwealth, on 12 December 1963, and a republic exactly one year later. Jomo Kenyatta, a Kikuyu, and leader of the Kenya African National Union (KANU), was appointed Prime Minister in June 1963 and became the country's first President in December 1964. (He was subsequently re-elected to the presidency, unopposed, in 1969 and 1974.)

Kenyatta died in August 1978; the Vice-President, Daniel arap Moi, was proclaimed President in October, and was the sole candidate at a presidential election held (concurrently with a KANU-only general election) in November 1979. In June 1982 the National Assembly officially declared Kenya a one-party state. Moi was returned unopposed in presidential elections in 1983 and 1988.

Domestic Political Affairs

By the early 1990s pressure for political reform had grown and in November 1991 several members of the Forum for the Restoration of Democracy (FORD), an outlawed political movement, were arrested prior to a planned pro-democracy rally in Nairobi, which was suppressed by the security forces. The Kenyan authorities were condemned internationally and bilateral and multilateral creditors suspended aid to Kenya indefinitely, pending the acceleration of both economic and political reforms. In December a special conference of KANU delegates acceded to the demands for reform, resolving to introduce a multi-party political system. The National Assembly subsequently endorsed appropriate amendments to the Constitution. Former Vice-President Mwai Kibaki resigned as Minister of Health later in the month, in protest against alleged electoral malpractice by KANU, and founded the Democratic Party (DP).

During the first half of 1992 some 2,000 people were reportedly killed in tribal clashes in western Kenya. In March the Government banned all political rallies, and restrictions were placed on the activities of the press. Following a general strike in April, organized by FORD, the Government ended the ban on political rallies. In August FORD split into two opposing factions, which were registered in October as separate political parties, FORD—Asili and FORD—Kenya, respectively led by Kenneth Matiba and Oginga Odinga.

At multi-party presidential and legislative elections held in December 1992 Moi was elected for a fourth term of office as President, winning 36.3% of the votes cast, ahead of Matiba (26.0%), Kibaki (19.5%) and Odinga (17.5%). Of the 188 elective seats in the National Assembly, KANU won 100 (including 16 uncontested); FORD—Asili and FORD—Kenya secured 31 seats

each, and the DP took 23. Votes were cast predominantly in accordance with ethnic affiliations, with the two largest tribes, the Kikuyu and Luo, overwhelmingly rejecting KANU. An extensive reorganization of cabinet posts was subsequently effected. In 1993 the international donor community agreed to resume the provision of aid to Kenya, in response to the Government's progress in implementing political and economic reforms.

During the mid-1990s Kenya's human rights record came under intense domestic and international scrutiny. In response to its critics, the Moi administration provisionally withdrew controversial draft legislation in January 1996 that would have severely restricted the freedom of the press and, in July, inaugurated a human rights committee to investigate alleged humanitarian abuses (including the torture of criminal suspects and opposition activists by security forces).

Divisions within opposition parties continued to undermine efforts to present a cohesive challenge to Moi and KANU prior to the 1997 elections. A renewed attempt to establish a coalition of opposition organizations, initiated in November 1995, was short-lived. Meanwhile, following an unsuccessful attempt to assume the leadership of FORD—Kenya, Raila Odinga (the son of Oginga Odinga, who died in January 1994, and a prominent opposition activist) left that party and subsequently became leader of the National Development Party (NDP). In October 1997 Matiba's faction of FORD—Asili registered as an independent party, the Forum for the Restoration of Democracy for the People (FORD—People). During the mid-1990s several opposition deputies, disaffected by these internal rivalries, defected to KANU.

In August 1997 the IMF suspended assistance to Kenya, pending the implementation of decisive action to eliminate official corruption and to improve the system of revenue collection; the Government consequently announced the inauguration of an anti-corruption body. In the following month the National Assembly approved legislation that amended the Constitution with the stated aim of ensuring free and fair democratic elections. All political parties were granted equal access to the media, and detention without trial was prohibited. In addition, the new legislation enabled the opposition to participate in selecting the 12 nominated members of the National Assembly and 10 of the 12 members of the supervisory Electoral Commission.

The presidential and legislative elections, which took place concurrently on 29 December 1997, were undermined by allegations of widespread fraud, as well as by logistical difficulties. Moi was re-elected President, winning 40.6% of the valid votes cast, while Kibaki came second, with 31.5% of the votes. KANU secured 107 of the 210 elected seats in the enlarged National Assembly, and the remainder were divided between nine opposition parties, with the DP taking 39 seats, the NDP 21, FORD—Kenya 17 and the Social Democratic Party 15. Moi was inaugurated for a fifth (and final) term as President in January 1998. Shortly afterwards Moi appointed a new Cabinet. However, he postponed the designation of a new Vice-President, evidently in order not to give an indication of his preferred successor to the presidency.

In early August 1998 a carbomb exploded at the US embassy in central Nairobi, concurrently with a similar attack on the US mission in Dar es Salaam, Tanzania. Some 254 people were killed in Nairobi, and more than 5,000 suffered injuries. The attacks were believed to have been co-ordinated by international Islamist terrorists, and, in mid-August, the USA retaliated by launching air-strikes against targets in Afghanistan and Sudan. Four men were convicted of involvement in the bombings by a court in New York, USA, in May 2001 and were later sentenced to life imprisonment. (Osama bin Laden, the fugitive Saudi-born Islamist activist whom the US authorities held ultimately responsible for the bombings, was killed by US forces in Pakistan in May 2011.)

Meanwhile, during late 2000 a parliamentary anti-graft committee sought the adoption by the National Assembly of a report in which the alleged perpetrators of corruption were named, and also proposed legislation that would allow the anti-corruption authority significant powers of prosecution. In January 2001, however, the IMF and the World Bank expressed concern over delays in the implementation of the reforms, particularly the failure to approve legislation on public service ethics and economic crimes. In August the National Assembly again refused to approve anti-corruption legislation, and the IMF suspended aid to Kenya indefinitely. Moi subsequently created a new police body to combat corruption.

In January 2001 Odinga, on behalf of the Luo-dominated NDP, signed a memorandum of understanding with KANU, which allowed Moi to appoint ministers from the NDP. In June Moi reorganized the Cabinet and appointed Odinga as Minister of Energy, thereby creating the first coalition Government in Kenya's history. Moi reshuffled the Cabinet again in November, introducing younger KANU ministers in an apparent attempt to provide suitable candidates for his succession; most notably Uhuru Kenyatta (son of the late President Jomo Kenyatta) was appointed as Minister for Local Government.

The NDP was dissolved and absorbed into KANU in mid-March 2002, despite opposition from elements within both parties; Moi was elected as party Chairman, while Odinga became Secretary-General. In July some 12 opposition parties, including the DP, FORD—Kenya and the National Party of Kenya, formed an electoral alliance, the National Alliance Party of Kenya (NAK).

The 2002 elections

In August 2002 Moi publicly announced that he favoured Uhuru Kenyatta as KANU's presidential candidate. However, several senior KANU members, including the Vice-President, Prof. George Saitoti, and Odinga, subsequently announced their intention to seek the party's presidential nomination and formed the Rainbow Alliance (RA) to campaign within KANU for a democratic vote to select its candidate. Moi responded by dismissing Saitoti. In mid-October, in protest against Moi's attempts to impose his preferred successor, members of the RA resigned from their posts in the Government and from KANU, together with some 30 KANU deputies. The RA subsequently boycotted the KANU conference, at which Kenyatta's presidential candidacy was endorsed. Later in October the RA established a new party, the Liberal Democratic Party (LDP), and joined with the NAK to form the National Rainbow Coalition (NARC), with Kibaki as its presidential candidate.

At the presidential and legislative elections, held concurrently on 27 December 2002, the opposition secured an emphatic victory, with Kibaki winning 62.3% of the votes cast in the presidential election, and the NARC securing 125 of the 210 elected seats in the National Assembly, while Kenyatta received 31.2% of the votes cast for the presidency, and KANU won 64 seats in the legislature. The NARC was allocated a further seven appointed seats, increasing their representation to 132, and KANU a further four seats, bringing their total to 68. The electoral turnout was 56.1%.

Following his inauguration as President on 30 December 2002, Kibaki promised reforms, including the adoption of a new constitution, under which certain powers would be transferred from the President to the legislature, and the adoption of anti-corruption legislation. In January 2003 Kibaki appointed a new Cabinet; however, divisions within the ruling coalition soon became apparent, as a group of 25 LDP deputies accused Kibaki of breaching a power-sharing agreement signed by the constituent parties of the NARC prior to the elections. In May the Anti-Corruption and Economic Crimes Act, which provided for the establishment of the Kenya AntiCorruption Commission (KACC), and the Public Service (Code of Conduct and Ethics) Act, requiring elected officials and senior civil servants to declare their wealth, came into effect.

In February 2003 Kibaki appointed a commission of inquiry into a financial scandal, in which public funds had been paid to the company Goldenberg International in 1990–93 as subsidies for non-existent exports of gold and diamonds. The illicit payments to Goldenberg were estimated at Ks. 25,000m. (US $600m.), equivalent to more than 10% of Kenya's annual GDP, although it was indicated that the total amount misappropriated could reach $4,000m. Public hearings ended in November 2004, and the commission's findings were reported to Kibaki in February 2005. It had initially been expected that prosecutions would follow from the report; however, the Minister of Justice and Constitutional Affairs, Martha Karua, stated that further investigations were necessary before any charges could be brought.

Meanwhile, a constitutional review conference opened in April 2003, but divisions persisted over the proposed post of Prime Minister. The LDP advocated an executive Prime Minister with powers to appoint the Cabinet, while Kibaki and his supporters sought to maintain a strong presidency. In August the death of Vice-President Michael Wamalwa, who had been regarded as a moderating influence within the Government, led to an intensification of the power struggle. In September Kibaki named the Minister of Home Affairs, Arthur Moody Awori (a Luhya), as Vice-President and effected a minor government reshuffle. In March 2004 the constitutional review conference voted to reduce the powers vested in the presidency and to create the new post of Prime Minister following the next elections, which were scheduled to be held in December 2007. Under the recommendations adopted by the conference, greater power was to be accorded to the National Assembly. The Government withdrew from the conference in protest; however, the draft constitution was successfully presented to the Attorney-General, after which it was to be considered by the National Assembly. The High Court subsequently ruled that the document required the endorsement of a simple majority at a referendum. The draft constitution, which retained the executive functions of the President, was approved by the National Assembly in July 2005.

Several months of campaigning, punctuated by often violent demonstrations, ensued. Seven ministers announced their opposition to the proposed new constitution, including, most notably, Raila Odinga, whose LDP split from the NARC coalition and joined with KANU to form the Orange Democratic Movement (ODM). At the referendum, held on 21 November 2005, the draft constitution was rejected by 58.1% of voters. Some 53% of the electorate participated in the poll. Kibaki conceded defeat, but dismissed the entire Cabinet, and in early December announced a new administration, from which those ministers who had opposed the draft constitution were removed. Those NARC members who maintained their support for Kibaki subsequently formed a new coalition party, the National Rainbow Coalition—Kenya (NARC—Kenya), to contest the 2007 elections.

Corruption

During 2004 evidence emerged of continuing endemic corruption in Kenya, despite the NARC Government's pledge to take measures to combat it. Four senior civil servants were suspended in May following their involvement in awarding contracts to supply passport-printing equipment to a fictitious British company, Anglo Leasing Ltd. In July the British High Commissioner, Sir Edward Clay, claimed that corruption had cost Kenya some Ks. 15,000m. since Kibaki took office and warned that it could lead to a reduction in donor assistance; later that month the European Union (see p. 281) withheld substantial aid. Clay subsequently produced a dossier of some 20 allegedly dubious contracts involving corruption in four ministries.

Against a background of increasing public resentment, in February 2005 the Permanent Secretary for Governance and Ethics in the Office of the President, John Githongo, resigned. Kibaki did not appoint a replacement for Githongo, and in November disbanded the Office of Governance and Ethics. Following Githongo's resignation, the USA and Germany announced that they would withhold anti-corruption aid, and the United Kingdom imposed travel restrictions on government ministers and others implicated in corruption. Following demands from within the Government for the resignations of corrupt ministers, Kibaki reorganized the Cabinet, dismissing several high-ranking civil servants and effectively demoting a key presidential aide, the Minister of State for Provincial Administration and National Security in the Office of the President, Christopher Murungaru, to the Ministry of Transport.

Meanwhile, in February 2005 the Kenya Law Society announced that it was to prosecute senior figures on corruption charges, including Awori, the Attorney-General, Amos Wako, and the Minister of Finance, David Mwiraria. It was also revealed that the four senior civil servants suspended in May 2004 had agreed to act as prosecution witnesses and to testify that they had received instructions from government ministers to pursue the transactions for which they were being prosecuted. However, Wako invoked a provision in the Constitution granting him the power to take over private prosecutions initiated by individuals or institutions, and terminated the case.

In November 2005 Githongo presented Kibaki with a dossier detailing his investigations into corruption in Kenya and death threats made against him. Awori, Mwiraria, Murungaru and Kiraitu Murungi (the Minister of Energy) were implicated by

Githongo in the Anglo Leasing scandal, and it was claimed that they had intended to embezzle a total of US $700m. through false military and security contracts. The four accused were subsequently summoned to appear before the KACC; they all denied the allegations. In January 2006 Githongo, who considered that Kibaki had failed to act upon the information supplied, released a copy of his dossier to the British media. (Githongo remained in exile in the United Kingdom.) Following Githongo's disclosure, a delegation of deputies representing the parliamentary Public Accounts Committee (PAC) travelled to the United Kingdom and interviewed him at the Kenyan High Commission in London. In early February Mwiraria resigned from the Cabinet. Pressure increased on the Government and later that month Kibaki announced the resignations of Murungi and Saitoti, the Minister of Education. All three denied any wrongdoing. Kibaki reshuffled the Cabinet following the resignations, with Amos Kimunya assuming the finance portfolio, although Awori retained his position as Vice-President despite growing demands for his resignation. The PAC questioned Awori, Mwiraria, Murungi and Saitoti in late February. In March Saitoti was also questioned by the police about his role in the Goldenberg affair, but the High Court of Kenya later rejected recommendations that he be charged. In a further cabinet reorganization in November, he was readmitted to the Government as Minister of Education, alongside Murungi, who resumed responsibility for the energy portfolio.

Division among the main parties intending to contest the forthcoming presidential and legislative elections emerged during 2007. In June NARC—Kenya indicated that Kibaki was to be named as its presidential candidate. In November, however, when primary elections were held, Kibaki defected from the ruling NARC—Kenya and chose to contest the elections under his newly established Party of National Unity (PNU). Odinga was named the presidential candidate for the ODM.

Post-election violence

At the legislative elections, held on 27 December 2007, the ODM secured 99 of the 210 seats in the National Assembly, the PNU won 43, the ODM—Kenya, which had broken away from the main party in August, 16 and KANU 14. Results in three constituencies were not released. The presidential election was held concurrently and the Electoral Commission of Kenya (ECK) announced that, despite indications prior to the vote that Odinga had garnered greater popular support, Kibaki had narrowly been re-elected to the presidency with 4,584,721 votes; Odinga was reported to have secured 4,352,993 votes. Odinga and other opposition candidates vehemently denounced the results, while independent international observers expressed scepticism regarding the credibility of the election, which had taken place amid allegations of widespread procedural violations. The results led to an upsurge in tribal conflict between Kibaki's Kikuyu supporters and Odinga's Luo followers. Nevertheless, on 30 December Kibaki was sworn in for a second term.

On 8 January 2008 Kibaki announced the partial composition of his new Cabinet; despite the ODM having secured the largest number of seats in the legislature, no representatives from that party were included in the new Government. Proposed African Union (AU, see p. 191) mediation was rejected by the Kenyan Government, and on 16 January the ODM, defying a ban on public demonstrations, commenced nation-wide protests scheduled to last for three days. These were violently dispersed by the security forces, resulting in additional fatalities.

On 29 January 2008 the former UN Secretary-General, Kofi Annan, formally launched a round of negotiations. However, ethnic fighting intensified and two senior ODM officials were killed. As a result Annan suspended discussions temporarily and the ODM appealed for calm. Following the resumption of talks in early February, the establishment of a power-sharing transitional government was proposed; on 28 February Kibaki and Odinga signed an agreement on the division of power and the creation of the posts of Prime Minister and two Deputy Prime Ministers, pending a full constitutional review to be carried out within 12 months. Odinga conceded the presidency to Kibaki and accepted the role of Prime Minister. Despite the agreement, attacks were carried out in early March ahead of the opening of a new parliamentary session during which members were to debate the legislation required to endorse the power-sharing agreement. The National Accord and Reconciliation Act, which provided, *inter alia*, for the creation of the position of Prime Minister and allowed a new coalition government to begin to implement a recovery programme and to assist internally displaced persons across the country in returning to their homes,

was ratified by the National Assembly later that month. (By that time over 1,000 people had been killed and some 600,000 displaced as a result of the violence.)

Meanwhile, following prolonged negotiations, in mid-April 2008 Kibaki named a new coalition Government, comprising members of the PNU, the ODM and ODM—Kenya, including Kenyatta as Deputy Prime Minister and Minister of Trade and Wycliffe Musalia Mudavadi as Deputy Prime Minister and Minister of Local Government; Stephen Kalonzo Musyoka, who had been appointed as Vice-President and Minister of Home Affairs in January, and Moses Wetangula, who assumed responsibility for the foreign affairs portfolio at the same time, retained their positions in the new Cabinet. It was agreed that a commission of inquiry to investigate the causes and perpetrators of the post-election violence should be established with immediate effect, which would be chaired by Appellate Judge Philip Waki. However, divisions soon emerged within the Cabinet as Odinga and ministers allied to the ODM sought an amnesty for all those arrested in the violence, which was ultimately rejected. Waki's report, published in mid-October, recommended the establishment of a tribunal, to be known as the Special Tribunal for Kenya, to 'seek accountability against persons bearing the greatest responsibility for crimes, particularly crimes against humanity' relating to the 2007 elections. It also recommended that a comprehensive reform of the Kenya Police Service be undertaken. Kibaki and Odinga agreed to the establishment of the Special Tribunal in December 2008 and the following month legislation providing for its creation was introduced before the National Assembly.

Election inquiry

On 10 June 2008 the Minister of Roads, Kipkalya Kones, and the Assistant Minister of Home Affairs, Lorna Laboso, died when the aircraft they were travelling in crashed in the Enoosupkia Forest (near the Maasai Mara game reserve). The following day by-elections were held for five seats in the National Assembly: the killings of two ODM deputies and the failure to announce the results in two Rift Valley constituencies during the unrest that followed the 2007 elections had left four seats vacant (while the other seat was had previously been occupied by the newly elected speaker of the National Assembly). The by-elections were conducted peacefully, despite fears of further unrest, with the ODM winning three of the seats and the PNU securing two, taking their total representations in the legislature to 102 and 45 seats, respectively.

The issue of corruption remained significant for the Government during 2008. In July Kimunya resigned from his position as Minister of Finance, owing to the commencement of an investigation into claims that he had given false information regarding the sale of a hotel to Libyan investors, although a government inquiry later cleared him of any wrongdoing. In January 2009 Kimunya was named as Minister of Trade in a minor government reorganization. At the same time Kenyatta was appointed as the new Minister of Finance (retaining the deputy premiership).

In September 2008 a report was published by the independent commission of inquiry, chaired by Johann Kriegler, a South African judge and the former Chairperson of that country's Independent Electoral Commission, set up to investigate the disputed elections in December 2007. It concluded that the conduct of the elections made it impossible to verify results reliably, and recommended that the ECK should undergo major reforms or be replaced by a new body. In December 2008 the ECK was disbanded and provision was made for its replacement by a new nine-member body, the Interim Independent Electoral Commission.

In February 2009 the UN Special Rapporteur on Extrajudicial, Summary or Arbitrary Executions, Philip Alston, issued a report in which he accused Kenya's security forces of widespread extrajudicial killings, and demanded the removal of Kenya's Police Commissioner, Hussein Ali, and Attorney-General Wako. The report concluded that death squads had been formed on the orders of senior police officials to exterminate members of the Mungiki (an illegal religious sect allegedly responsible for a number of murders and involved in extortion), although the Kenyan Government rejected the findings. In early March two leading members of the Oscar Foundation, a civil rights advocacy group which had been accused by the Government of having links with the Mungiki, were killed by unidentified gunmen. Prior to the murders, the Oscar Foundation had led demonstrations in the capital, expressing anger at government corruption and accusing the Kenyan police of brutality and widespread extrajudicial killings and arrests, especially of suspected

Mungiki members. The deaths of the two activists precipitated further demonstrations in which one student was shot dead, and on 10 March violent protests were staged in Nairobi. The Government suffered a further reverse later in March when Minister of Justice, National Cohesion and Constitutional Affairs Martha Karua announced her resignation, citing Kibaki's appointment of judges without her knowledge as the main reason for her departure. In May Mutula Kilonzo was appointed to replace her in a government reorganization.

In July 2009 the Kenya National Commission on Human Rights (KNCHR) named 219 people suspected of involvement in the violence that took place after the 2007 elections; these included Deputy Prime Minister and Minister of Finance Uhuru Kenyatta and a number of other government ministers. In the same month former UN Secretary-General Kofi Annan submitted a list of 10 suspects to be investigated by the International Criminal Court (ICC) with regard to their involvement in the post-election violence. The Kenyan authorities were divided on whether suspects would be tried at a local tribunal or at the ICC, in The Hague, Netherlands. Also in July President Kibaki announced the formation of a nine-member Kenya Truth, Justice, and Reconciliation Commission to investigate a number of 'injustices' including land allocation and regional imbalances.

It was reported that five people had been killed during violent demonstrations in the mainly Somali Nairobi suburb of Eastleigh against the detention of a radical, Jamaican-born Muslim cleric, Sheikh Abdullah al-Faisal, in mid-January 2010. Al-Faisal had entered Kenya from Tanzania in late 2009 with the intention of carrying out a preaching tour, but was arrested in early January 2010 after the Kenyan Government stated that he was a threat to national security. Some 328 people were believed to have been arrested in the days following the protests, including a number of citizens with alleged links to a Somali militant Islamist group, al-Shabaab ('The Youth'), and Al-Amin Kimathi, the Chairman of Kenya's Muslim Human Rights Forum. Kimathi was among eight of those charged with incitement to violence later in January. Al-Faisal was deported to Jamaica on 22 January.

In February 2010 President Kibaki suspended a number of senior officials from the National Cereals and Produce Board, and from the agriculture, education and special programmes ministries, after inquiries into the work of a subsidized maize scheme and Kenya's free primary education programme revealed corrupt practices. Shortly afterwards Prime Minister Odinga announced the suspension of Minister of Agriculture William Ruto (who had also featured on the KNCHR list of those suspected of major involvement in the post-election violence) and Minister of Education Samson Ongeri to allow independent investigations into the corruption allegations to proceed. However, Kibaki overturned Odinga's decision, maintaining that he had not been consulted on the matter and that Odinga did not have the constitutional powers to suspend the two ministers. (In April Ruto was removed as Minister of Agriculture and appointed Minister of Higher Education.)

In early March 2010 the Chief Prosecutor of the ICC, Luis Moreno-Ocampo, presented evidence relating to the potential prosecution of 20 people (whose identities remained confidential) for their role in the post-election violence in which an estimated 1,100 people had been killed, stating that senior political and business leaders from both the ODM and the PNU had organized and financed post-election attacks against civilians in 2008. At the end of March the ICC's pre-trial chamber, at Moreno-Ocampo's recommendation, announced that it was to initiate an investigation into the alleged crimes against humanity.

New Constitution

Following its submission in mid-March 2010, on 1 April 2010 the National Assembly unanimously approved the text of a draft constitution, which was presented to the Attorney-General later that month. In May the draft was officially published and a referendum on its adoption was scheduled to take place in August. On 4 August the new Constitution was endorsed by 66.9% of votes cast, according to official results released by the Interim Independent Electoral Commission, with a participation rate of 72.2%. However, ethnic differences over the issue were prominent, reflecting the continued divisions in the country. In Central and Nyanza provinces, dominated by the Kikuyu and Luo, respectively, an overwhelming majority voted in favour of the new Constitution, which had been supported by Odinga and Kenyatta; however, in Rift Valley, dominated by the Kalenjin, a significant majority had voted against it, following a campaign led by former President Moi and William Ruto. The new Constitution notably provided for the abolition of the post of Prime Minister and creation of a deputy presidency, and the devolution of some powers to 47 new counties, which were to be represented by a second legislative chamber, the Senate. On 16 August a ministerial reorganization was announced. On the following day the Government established a committee, to be chaired by Kibaki and Odinga, which was to supervise the implementation of the constitutional reforms (the full enactment of which was expected to be slow). The new Constitution was officially signed into law by President Kibaki on 27 August.

In October 2010 Ruto was suspended as Minister of Higher Education, following a court ruling that he be tried on charges of illegally selling forest land during his tenure of the agriculture portfolio. (He was cleared of the charges in April 2011.) Later that month the Minister of Foreign Affairs, Moses Wetangula, submitted his resignation, after being implicated in allegedly irregular property agreements conducted by Kenyan embassies overseas. In November Kiplagat was obliged to resign as Chairman of the Kenya Truth, Justice, and Reconciliation Commission, after he was accused of being implicated in a 1984 massacre by security forces. In December Moreno-Ocampo issued indictment requests formally naming six principal suspects accused of organizing the post-election violence, the most notable being Deputy Prime Minister and Minister of Finance Kenyatta. The other accused were: the Cabinet Secretary and close associate of Kibaki, Francis Muthaura; Ruto, who had travelled to the ICC in The Hague shortly beforehand in an effort to reach a compromise agreement; Henry Kosgey, the Chairman of the ODM and Minister of Industrialization; a former police commissioner, Mohammed Hussein Ali; and a radio broadcaster, Joshua Arap Sang. The announcement of the high-level suspects (all of whom denied the charges) prompted public controversy and later in December, following a motion submitted by Ruto, the National Assembly voted overwhelmingly for Kenya to withdraw from the jurisdiction of the ICC. The Minister of Justice and 13 foreign envoys subsequently urged Kibaki and Odinga to ignore the parliamentary resolution. In early 2011 Kosgey resigned from the post of Minister of Industrialization, following allegations of corruption against him. On 8 March the ICC issued summonses for the six accused to appear before the Court on 7 April; hearings to confirm the charges against them were conducted in September.

In May 2011 the Government of the British Crown Dependency island of Jersey issued arrest warrants for a former head of Kenya Power and Lighting, Samuel Gichuru, and a former Minister of Energy, Chris Okemo, for corruption, alleging they had both received bribes from European engineering companies and a US communications company. However, the Kenyan Government refused to extradite either suspect. In the following month the KACC announced that it was to investigate 1,600 police officers to establish whether any were implicated in corrupt practices. In July the British High Court ruled that four former members of the Mau Mau movement, which had fought against the British colonial authority in Kenya during 1952–60, were entitled to take legal action against the Government of the United Kingdom to seek compensation for their alleged torture at detention camps (the United Kingdom having contested that liabilities had been assumed by Kenya when it gained independence in 1963). (In October 2012 the British High Court further ruled that three claimants—the fourth having died—were able to proceed with their legal appeals.) In August 2011 Ruto was dismissed in a government reorganization, in which Wetangula was reinstated as Minister of Foreign Affairs. In October one person was killed and a further 23 injured in two grenade attacks in Nairobi; later that month a Kenyan national, who confessed to being a member of al-Shabaab (see below), was sentenced to life imprisonment, after pleading guilty to involvement in one of the incidents.

ICC announcement and terrorist attacks

On 23 January 2012 the ICC officially announced that Ruto was to stand trial, together with Arap Sang, for crimes against humanity perpetrated against supporters of Kibaki, while Kenyatta was to be tried with Muthaura for crimes against humanity directed at Odinga supporters; the charges against Kosgey and Ali were not confirmed. On 26 January Kenyatta and Muthaura both resigned their government posts; President Kibaki accepted Kenyatta's resignation as Minister of Finance, but announced that he was to retain the post of Deputy Prime Minister in accordance with the Constitution. Minister of Nairobi Metropolitan Development Benjamin Githae subsequently assumed additional responsibilities as acting Minister of Finance. In March allegations made by an ODM deputy during a session of

Parliament that European states, notably the United Kingdom, had also sought the indictment of Kibaki at the ICC prompted outrage, and demands that Kenya suspend diplomatic relations with the United Kingdom. (On 24 May the ICC rejected an appeal by the accused challenging its jurisdiction.)

In March 2012 six people were killed and 69 injured in a grenade attack in central Nairobi, which was widely attributed to al-Shabaab (following several attacks in border regions in late 2011 that were regarded as retaliation for Kenyan involvement in Somalia—see Foreign Affairs). An increasing number of similar attacks took place in the capital and other principal towns in following months, including one in a church in Nairobi in April, in which one person was killed and 16 injured, one in a nightclub in the eastern coastal town of Mombasa in May, in which one person was killed and five injured, and two simultaneous attacks on churches in the north-eastern city of Garissa in July, in which 17 people were killed and 40 injured.

Meanwhile, in early May 2012 Mudavadi tendered his resignation as Deputy Prime Minister and Minister of Local Government, announcing that he was to leave the ODM to join the United Democratic Forum Party (UDFP), which had been formed in the previous month by supporters of Kibaki. Kenyatta also established a new political organization, The National Alliance (TNA), later that month, in preparation for forthcoming elections. In June the Minister of Provincial Administration and Internal Security, Saitoti, and five others were killed when a police helicopter crashed in the outskirts of Nairobi. (Katoo Ole Metito was appointed to replace Saitoti as part of a government reorganization in September.) After the withdrawal of the corruption charges against Kosgey in July, in early August Kibaki reappointed him as Minister of Industrialization. Following controversy over the scheduling of the legislative and presidential elections, in September the High Court ruled that they would take place in March 2013, following the expiry of the National Assembly's term in January.

In August 2012 a radical Muslim cleric, who had been arrested in January for possession of armaments and subsequently also charged with membership of al-Shabaab, was shot dead by unknown assailants in Mombasa, prompting violent rioting and attacks against police in the town, in which five people were killed. (In early September Muslim cleric Abubaker Sharif was charged with inciting the violence.) It was reported in September that two suspects, who were arrested with a cache of armaments in Nairobi, had confessed that they were part of a terrorist group affiliated to al-Shabaab that had planned to attack the parliamentary building and assassinate senior politicians. In early October a meeting addressed by the Minister of Fisheries Development, Amason Jeffah Kingi, in the coastal town of Kilifi was attacked by suspected members of Muslim separatist Mombasa Republican Council (MRC), who killed three people and injured Kingi. Later that month the MRC leader, Omar Mwamnuadzi, and a number of his supporters were arrested in the nearby town of Kwale, following an exchange of fire in which two people were killed; a local government official was subsequently murdered in an apparent retaliatory attack. Mwamnuadzi was later charged with possession of armaments and incitement to violence. In early December at least six people were killed in a grenade attack outside a mosque in Nairobi, which was followed by violent protests by youths. Meanwhile, more than 150 people had been killed since August in increasing ethnic clashes between the Pokomo and Orma tribes over land in the Tana River area of south-eastern Kenya; human rights groups expressed concerns that the tensions had been exacerbated by rivalries between potential candidates in the forthcoming legislative elections. In January 2013 five people were shot dead in a further terrorist attack against a hotel in Garissa.

Recent developments: the 2013 elections

Kenya's first pre-election presidential debate was broadcast on 11 February 2013 (with a second later that month), by which time Odinga and Kenyatta had emerged as the two leading presidential candidates. Following a challenge by opposition activists, on 15 February the Kenyan High Court ruled that Kenyatta, together with his running mate, Ruto, were entitled to contest the presidential election, despite the ICC indictments against them. Later that month Annan and other international representatives expressed concerns of renewed large-scale violence ensuing from the elections.

The presidential, legislative and gubernatorial elections, held on on 4 March 2013, were generally conducted peacefully, although some 18 people, including six police officers, were killed

in attacks in Mombasa, Kilifi and Kwale shortly beforehand. The MRC (which had opposed the organization of the elections) denied accusations by the authorities that its members were responsible for the violence. According to official results, which were announced on 9 March, the ODM won 78 of the 290 directly elected constituency seats in the expanded National Assembly, while the TNA received 72 seats, and the United Republican Party (URP), newly established by Ruto, 62. (Of 47 additional women members elected in each of the counties, 15 represented the ODM, 14 the TNA and 10 the URP.) Under the terms of the 2010 Constitution, elections were also held for a new Senate, at which the ODM and the TNA both obtained 11 of the 47 directly elected seats, and the URP nine. Overall, following the additional nomination of deputies, the Jubilee Coalition, an alliance including both the TNA and the URP, had secured 167 of the total 349 seats in the National Assembly, and 30 of the 67 seats in the Senate, while the ODM-led Coalition for Reforms and Democracy (CORD) had taken 141 seats in the lower and 28 in the upper chamber. CORD elected 23 and the Jubilee Coalition 18 of the 47 governors. The results of the presidential election, which was contested by eight candidates, indicated a victory for Kenyatta, with about 50.5% of the valid votes cast, followed by Odinga, with 43.7%, and Mudavadi, with 4.0%. A voter turn-out of about 86% was recorded.

In response to an appeal by Odinga, who alleged malpractice following delays and technical malfunctions in the vote-counting, on 25 March 2013 the Supreme Court ordered a partial recount of the votes. However, on 30 March the Supreme Court issued a ruling upholding Kenyatta's victory; two people were killed and 11 injured when police violently suppressed ensuing protests. Meanwhile, on 11 March the ICC announced that the charges against Muthaura had been withdrawn, owing to lack of witness evidence; the trial of Ruto and Arap Sang had been postponed until 28 May, and that of Kenyatta to 9 July, following defence applications. Seven people were killed in a further attack on a casino in the coastal town of Malindi in late March.

Kenyatta was sworn in as President on 9 April 2013, and on 18 April he announced major revisions to the structure of the Kenyan Government, reducing the number of ministries from 44 to 18. Later that month Kenyatta released the names of 16 ministerial nominees, all of whom underwent an intensive vetting procedure by the National Assembly's Committee on Appointments in mid-May. The new Government was sworn in on 15 May, although the posts of Minister of the Interior and Co-ordination of National Government and Minister of Labour, Social Security and Services were yet to be designated.

Foreign Affairs

Following an improvement in relations between Kenya and Uganda from the late 1980s, in November 1994 President Moi, Ugandan President Yoweri Museveni and Tanzanian President Ali Hassan Mwinyi met in Arusha, Tanzania, and established a commission for co-operation. In March 1996 the Secretariat of the Permanent Tripartite Commission for East African Co-operation was formally inaugurated, with a view to reviving the East African Community (EAC), which had been dissolved in 1977. A treaty for the re-establishment of the EAC, providing for the promotion of free trade between the member states, the development of the region's infrastructure and economy and the creation of a regional legislative assembly and court, was ratified by the Kenyan, Tanzanian and Ugandan Heads of State in November 1999. The new EAC (see p. 460) was officially inaugurated in Arusha in January 2001. Talks on integrating the economies of the three EAC members followed, and in March 2004 President Mwai Kibaki, Museveni and President Benjamin Mkapa of Tanzania signed a protocol on the creation of a customs union, eliminating most duties on goods traded within the Community, which took effect from January 2005. In November 2009 the Heads of State of Tanzania, Kenya, Uganda, Rwanda and Burundi signed a common market protocol in Arusha (Rwanda and Burundi having joined the EAC in 2007), allowing the free movement of goods, services, people and capital within the EAC. The common market protocol entered into force in July 2010. In May 2011 the Kenyan Government demanded the immediate removal of Ugandan security personnel from the disputed Ugingo Island in Lake Victoria, which had been occupied by Ugandan soldiers. In the same month about 30 Ugandan police officers were deployed on neighbouring Migingo Island; Kenyan security forces arrived on the island in August, following appeals from Kenyan fishermen and traders for protection. Meanwhile, a survey team was dispatched in an effort to resolve the sovereignty issue.

In early 1989 Sudan renewed a long-standing dispute with Kenya over the sovereignty of territory on the Kenyan side of the two countries' common border, known as the 'Elemi triangle'. During the late 1990s Kenya hosted a series of peace talks between the Sudanese Government and opposition leaders, under the auspices of the Intergovernmental Authority on Development (IGAD, see p. 344), in an attempt to resolve the conflict in southern Sudan. Further negotiations were held in Nairobi in September 2000 and June 2001, and in July 2002 the Sudanese Government and the opposition Sudan People's Liberation Movement (SPLM) signed an accord in Machakos, Kenya, which provided for the holding of a referendum on self-determination for southern Sudan after a transitional period of six years. In September 2003 Kenya and Sudan agreed to form a joint border committee. Talks aimed at achieving a final peace settlement between the Sudanese Government and the SPLM continued in Kenya throughout 2003 and 2004, and in January 2005 the Sudanese Government and southern rebels signed a peace accord in Nairobi, which officially ended the 21-year civil war. Following South Sudan's secession in July 2011, its links with Kenya strengthened (although its claim to the 'Elemi triangle' remained unresolved), while Kenya's relations with Sudan consequently became strained; amidst a protracted oil transit dispute between the authorities of South Sudan and Sudan, in January 2012 an agreement was reached for the construction of a pipeline linking oil fields in South Sudan to Kenya's Lamu port. In January 2013 it was announced that a 960-km road connecting Eldoret, in north-western Kenya, to South Sudan's capital, Juba, would be constructed with World Bank funding.

Following an increased incidence of cross-border attacks in 1997, a number of communiqués were signed by the Kenyan and Ethiopian Governments, agreeing to reinforce border security, and to take measures to prevent the smuggling of arms and drugs. In January 1999 the Kenyan Government protested to the Ethiopian authorities, following an incursion into Kenya by Ethiopian security forces, who were alleged to be in pursuit of Ethiopian rebels. Bilateral relations again became strained during late 2000, after it was reported that some 50 Kenyans had been killed, allegedly by Ethiopian militia forces, in cross-border clashes. In January 2001 representatives from both countries met in Nairobi and agreed to initiate measures aimed at ending border disputes. In April 2006 Kenya closed part of its border with Ethiopia when militia forces allegedly entered Kenyan territory and fighting ensued. In May 2011 more than 50 people were reported to have been killed in the border area, following a cross-border raid by militia from the Ethiopia-based Merille tribe. In May 2012 it was reported that Kenya and Ethiopia had agreed to renegotiate the demarcation of their international boundary, in response to further incidents.

Somalia has traditionally laid claim to part of north-eastern Kenya. After Moi agreed to mediate between an interim Government and opposing rebel factions in Somalia, an IGAD-sponsored Somali reconciliation conference opened in the Kenyan town of Eldoret in October 2002 and was moved to Nairobi in February 2003. In January 2004 the conference reached agreement on the establishment of a new Somali parliament, which was based in Nairobi until mid-2005.

In October 2011 Kenya dispatched troops into southern Somalia in pursuit of insurgents of the al-Shabaab militant Islamist group, who were held responsible for a number of abductions of Western tourists and aid workers from Kenyan territory following a marked increase in Somali banditry and piracy. Al-Shabaab subsequently staged a large number of violent reprisal attacks, including one against a bus carrying soldiers and civilians in the north-eastern border town of Mandera in late October, in which eight people were killed. (Terrorist attacks in Nairobi and other principal towns continued during 2012—see Domestic Political Affairs.) In early 2012 Kenyan ground troops and fighter aircraft staged attacks against al-Shabaab bases in southern Somalia, in which large numbers of insurgents were reportedly killed. In February a UN Security Council resolution endorsed an AU request that Kenyan troops reinforce an expanded African Union Mission in Somalia (AMISOM), which had been established to counter the al-Shabaab insurgency in the country. A total of 4,664 Kenyan personnel deployed in Somalia were officially integrated into AMISOM in July. In December the new Somali President, Abdi Farah Shirdon Saaid, made an official visit to Kenya, where he and Kibaki pledged continued co-operation in operations against al-Shabaab, and finalized a border security agreement.

Continuing conflict in Somalia has resulted in large influxes of refugees to Kenya. In late 2010 the office of the UN High Commissioner for Refugees (UNHCR) urged the Kenyan authorities, which claimed that the Somali refugees placed an intolerable burden on the country's resources, to halt their forced repatriation. In 2011 further refugee arrivals from Somalia to north-eastern Kenya resulted in severe overcrowding at three refugee camps in Dadaab which also affected the surrounding area, obliging the Kenyan Government to allocate additional land to settle refugees. According to UNHCR, at February 2013 the number of Somalian refugees in Kenya totalled 510,191. In January UNHCR expressed concern at a government directive for all refugees to be relocated from Nairobi and other urban centres to refugees camps, which, following an application by refugee rights groups, was temporarily suspended by the High Court.

CONSTITUTION AND GOVERNMENT

Under the terms of the Constitution that was approved at a national referendum on 4 August 2010 and entered into force on 27 August, legislative power is vested in and exercised by Parliament, which consists of the National Assembly and the Senate. Members of Parliament serve concurrent five-year terms. The National Assembly consists of 290 members, each elected by the registered voters of single member constituencies; 47 women (one elected in each county); 12 members nominated by parliamentary political parties according to their proportion of members of the National Assembly to represent special interests including the youth, persons with disabilities and workers; and the Speaker, who is an ex officio member. The Senate consists of 47 members each elected by the registered voters of the counties, each county constituting a single member constituency; 16 women members who shall be nominated by political parties according to their proportion of members of the Senate; two members representing the youth; two members representing persons with disabilities; and the Speaker, who is an ex officio member. The President is the Head of State and Government and exercises the executive authority of the Republic, with the assistance of the Deputy President and Cabinet Secretaries. The Cabinet consists of the President, the Deputy President, the Attorney-General and not fewer than 14 and not more than 22 Cabinet Secretaries.

REGIONAL AND INTERNATIONAL CO-OPERATION

Kenya is a member of the Common Market for Eastern and Southern Africa (see p. 241) and, with Burundi, Rwanda, Tanzania and Uganda, of the East African Community (see p. 460).

Kenya became a member of the UN in 1963. As a contracting party to the General Agreement on Tariffs and Trade, Kenya joined the World Trade Organization (WTO, see p. 444) on its establishment in 1995. Kenya participates in the Group of 15 (G15, see p. 461) and the Group of 77 (G77, see p. 461) developing countries.

ECONOMIC AFFAIRS

In 2011, according to estimates by the World Bank, Kenya's gross national income (GNI), measured at average 2009–11 prices, was US $34,211m., equivalent to $820 per head (or $1,720 per head on an international purchasing-power parity basis). During 2002–11, it was estimated, the population increased at an average annual rate of 2.6%, while gross domestic product (GDP) per head grew, in real terms, by an average of 1.9% per year. Overall GDP increased, in real terms, at an average annual rate of 4.6% in 2002–11. Real GDP rose by 4.5% in 2011.

Agriculture (including forestry and fishing) contributed 27.4% of GDP in 2011, according to provisional official figures, and accounted for 16.5% of workers engaged in paid employment in the formal sector in that year. (According to FAO, some 69.0% of the labour force were employed in the agriculture sector in mid-2013.) The principal cash crops are coffee (which contributed 24.9% of total export earnings in 2010) and tea. Horticultural produce (Kenya is the world's fourth largest exporter of cut flowers), pyrethrum, sisal, sugar cane and cotton are also important. Maize is the principal subsistence crop. There is a significant dairy industry for domestic consumption and export. During 2002–11, according to the World Bank, agricultural GDP increased at an average annual rate of 2.1%. According to provisional official figures, agricultural GDP increased by 1.6% in 2011.

Industry (including mining, manufacturing, construction and power) contributed 16.9% of GDP in 2011, according to provisional official figures, and employed an estimated 19.7% of workers engaged in paid employment in the formal sector in the same year. During 2002–11, according to the World Bank, industrial GDP increased at an average annual rate of 5.2%. Industrial GDP grew by 5.4% in 2010 and by a provisional 2.8% in 2011, according to official figures.

Mining contributed 0.8% of GDP, according to provisional figures, and employed an estimated 0.4% of those in paid formal-sector employment in 2011. Soda ash is the principal mineral export. Fluorspar, iron ore, salt, limestone, gold, gemstones (including rubies and sapphires), vermiculite and lead are also mined. Kenya has substantial reserves of titanium. According to official figures, the GDP of the mining sector increased at an average annual rate of 3.7% during 2007–11; sectoral GDP increased by a provisional 7.1% in 2011.

Manufacturing contributed 10.6% of GDP, according to provisional official figures, and employed an estimated 13.1% of workers engaged in paid employment in the formal sector in 2011. During 2002–11, according to the World Bank, manufacturing GDP increased at an average annual rate of 4.6%. According to provisional official figures, manufacturing GDP grew by 3.3% in 2011.

Construction contributed 4.6% of GDP in 2011, according to provisional official figures, and employed an estimated 5.2% of workers engaged in paid employment in the formal sector in that year. The GDP of the construction sector grew at an average annual rate of 7.4% during 2007–11; it increased by an estimated 4.3% in 2011.

Hydroelectric power accounted for 31.6% of total electricity generated in 2009. It had accounted for an average of 81.9% of annual electricity generated during 1990–98, whereafter recurrent droughts began to affect hydroelectric production. This shortfall was taken up by petroleum, which accounted for 44.1% in 2009 (as opposed to an average of 9.2% per year during 1990–98). Kenya does not produce electricity from coal, natural gas or nuclear power. Energy for domestic use is derived principally from fuel wood and charcoal. The prolonged drought led to severe power shortages in 2000 and threatened to affect hydroelectric production in 2005–06. In February 2004 it was announced that the Kenyan and Tanzanian national grids were to be connected to that of Zambia under a cross-border energy project; the first phase of the project, which was to cost some US $300m., was commissioned in 2007, followed by a second phase in 2012. In 2010 imports of mineral fuels and lubricants (including crude petroleum intended for refining) comprised 22.1% of the value of total imports.

The services sector contributed 55.7% of GDP in 2011, according to provisional official figures, and employed an estimated 63.8% of workers engaged in paid employment in the formal sector in that year. Tourism makes an important contribution to Kenya's economy and has been the country's principal source of foreign exchange since 1987. Following terrorist attacks in 2001, however, and subsequent warnings against travel to Kenya by the United Kingdom and the USA, the tourism industry experienced difficulties for several years. The industry was also adversely affected by the violence that followed the 2007 elections. By 2010, however, tourist arrivals had recovered to reach a total of an estimated 1,609,000 (in 2011 receipts from tourism—excluding passenger transport—amounted to an estimated US $884m.). The GDP of the services sector increased at an average annual rate of 4.7% in 2002–11, according to the World Bank. Services GDP increased by an estimated 5.1% in 2011, according to provisional official figures.

In 2011 Kenya recorded a visible merchandise trade deficit of US $8,370.3m. and there was a deficit of $3,333.2m. on the current account of the balance of payments. In 2010 the principal source of imports was the People's Republic of China (which supplied 12.6% of total imports in that year); other major suppliers were the United Arab Emirates, India, South Africa, Japan and the United Kingdom. Uganda was the principal market for Kenya's exports (purchasing 12.7%) in 2010; other important purchasers were the United Kingdom, Tanzania, the Netherlands and the USA. The principal exports in 2010 were coffee, tea, vegetables and fruit, cut flowers and foliage, basic manufactures, and chemicals and related products. The principal imports in that year were machinery and transport equipment, petroleum and petroleum products, chemicals and related products, and food and live animals.

In the financial year ending 30 June 2012 there was a preliminary budgetary deficit of Ks. 184,400m. Kenya's general government gross debt was Ks. 1,271,120m. in 2010, equivalent to 49.9% of GDP. The country's external debt was US $8,400m. at the end of 2010, of which $6,978m. was public and publicly guaranteed debt. In that year the cost of servicing long-term public and publicly guaranteed debt and repayments to the IMF was equivalent to 4.4% of the value of exports of goods, services and income (excluding workers' remittances). According to the IMF, the annual rate of inflation averaged 12.7% in 2005–11; consumer prices increased by 4.0% in 2010 and by 14.0% in 2011. Some 23% of the labour force were estimated to be unemployed in late 2000.

Kenya's economy is reasonably diversified, although most employment is dependent on agriculture, and the country is highly vulnerable to fluctuations in international prices for its cash crops, most notably tea and coffee. Poverty is widespread, and the revelation in the mid-2000s of large-scale state corruption adversely affected investment and led international donors to withhold aid. Large-scale post-election violence in early 2008 had a further negative impact on growth. In mid-2009 an agreement was signed with the Canadian firm Africa Oil Corpn and Dubai-based East Exploration Ltd on the joint exploration of oilfields in Kenya. Kenya also benefited following the ratification of East African Community (see p. 460) common market protocol in July 2010. In January 2011 the IMF approved a three-year Extended Credit Facility (ECF) arrangement, totalling US $508.7m., to support the Government's implementation of economic reforms. In October 2012 the IMF completed a favourable fourth review of economic progress under the ECF-supported programme, and approved a credit of about $110.5m. bringing total disbursements under the arrangement to about $529.6m. Following a slowdown resulting from the 2008–09 global economic crisis, GDP growth continued to strengthen, principally generated by foreign investment in oil and natural gas exploitation, and large infrastructure projects (although exports had been adversely affected by a continuing debt crisis within the European Union, see p. 281). Public debt had declined, despite the budgetary strains of maintaining security operations in Somalia, implementing a new Constitution, and organizing forthcoming elections. However, an increase in abductions of tourists from Kenyan territory by Somali bandits and pirates from 2011, and numerous terrorist attacks in principal towns attributed to the al-Shabaab militant Islamist group (see Foreign Affairs) presented a significant obstacle to the country's tourism industry. The presidential and legislative polls in March 2013 took place relatively peacefully, and the election to the presidency of Uhuru Kenyatta (a former Chairman of the Kenya Tourism Board) was welcomed by some businesses. The new authorities were urged by the IMF to continue fiscal reforms, including the adoption of value-added tax legislation.

PUBLIC HOLIDAYS

2014: 1 January (New Year's Day), 18–21 April (Easter), 1 May (Labour Day), 1 June (Madaraka Day, anniversary of self-government), 28 July* (Id al Fitr, end of Ramadan), 20 October (Mashujaa Day), 12 December (Jamhuri Day), 25–26 December (Christmas).

* This holiday is determined by the Islamic lunar calendar and may vary by one or two days from the date given.

Statistical Survey

Source (unless otherwise stated): Kenya National Bureau of Statistics, POB 30266, Nairobi; tel. (20) 317583; fax (20) 315977; e-mail director@knbs.go.ke; internet www.knbs.or.ke.

Area and Population

AREA, POPULATION AND DENSITY

Area (sq km)	
Land area	571,416
Inland water	11,230
Total	582,646*
Population (census results)†	
24 August 1999	28,686,607
24 August 2009	
Males	19,192,378
Females	19,417,719
Total	38,610,097
Population (UN estimates at mid-year)‡	
2011	41,609,729
2012	42,749,417
2013	43,923,725
Density (per sq km) at mid-2013§	76.9

* 224,961 sq miles.
† Excluding adjustment for underenumeration.
‡ Source: UN, *World Population Prospects: The 2010 Revision*.
§ Land area only.

POPULATION BY AGE AND SEX
(UN estimates at mid-2013)

	Males	Females	Total
0–14	9,362,866	9,253,807	18,616,673
15–64	12,042,506	12,080,258	24,122,764
65 and over	537,823	646,465	1,184,288
Total	21,943,195	21,980,530	43,923,725

Source: UN, *World Population Prospects: The 2010 Revision*.

PRINCIPAL ETHNIC GROUPS
(population at 2009 census)

African	38,445,941		European	32,338
Arab	40,760		Other	9,267
Asian	81,791		**Total**	38,610,097

POPULATION BY PROVINCE
(2010, projected estimates)

Nairobi	3,240,155		Nyanza	5,201,996
Central	3,908,907		Rift Valley	9,101,524
Coast	3,205,175		Western	4,552,522
Eastern	5,587,781		**Total**	36,287,423
North-Eastern	1,489,363			

Note: Projections not adjusted to take account of 2009 census results.

PRINCIPAL TOWNS
(estimated population at census of August 1999)

Nairobi (capital)	2,143,020		Meru	78,100
Mombasa	660,800		Kitale	63,245
Nakuru	219,366		Malindi*	53,805
Kisumu*	194,390		Nyeri*	46,969
Eldoret*	167,016		Kericho	30,023
Thika	82,665		Kisii	29,634

* Boundaries extended between 1979 and 1989.

Mid-2011 (incl. suburbs, UN estimate): Nairobi (capital) 3,363,130 (Source: UN, *World Urbanization Prospects: The 2011 Revision*).

BIRTHS AND DEATHS
(annual averages, UN estimates)

	1995–2000	2000–05	2005–10
Birth rate (per 1,000)	38.0	38.7	38.0
Death rate (per 1,000)	11.8	12.8	11.3

Source: UN, *World Population Prospects: The 2010 Revision*.

Life expectancy (years at birth): 57.1 (males 56.0; females 58.3) in 2011 (Source: World Bank, World Development Indicators database).

EMPLOYMENT
(labour force survey, selected urban and rural settlements, '000s)*

	2009	2010	2011
Agriculture and forestry	340.3	343.8	345.9
Mining and quarrying	6.5	6.6	8.8
Manufacturing	266.4	268.1	275.7
Electricity and water	19.6	19.6	20.7
Construction	93.4	101.3	109.0
Wholesale and retail trade	215.4	226.9	238.6
Transport and communications	143.5	151.3	157.4
Finance, insurance, real estate and business services	97.2	99.3	107.3
Community, social and personal services	817.7	843.7	835.7
Total	2,000.0	2,060.6	2,099.1

* Data are for salaried employees in the formal sector only, and therefore exclude self-employed and unpaid family workers and a vast number of workers in the informal sector (8,388.9 in 2009; 8,826.2 in 2010; 9,272.1 in 2011, according to official estimates). According to ILO, the 1999 census recorded an employed population of 14,474,200.

Health and Welfare

KEY INDICATORS

Total fertility rate (children per woman, 2010)	4.7
Under-5 mortality rate (per 1,000 live births, 2010)	85
HIV/AIDS (% of persons aged 15–49, 2009)	6.3
Physicians (per 1,000 head, 2002)	0.1
Hospital beds (per 1,000 head, 2010)	1.4
Health expenditure (2009): US $ per head (PPP)	75
Health expenditure (2009): % of GDP	4.8
Health expenditure (2009): public (% of total)	43.3
Access to water (% of persons, 2010)	59
Access to sanitation (% of persons, 2010)	32
Total carbon dioxide emissions ('000 metric tons, 2008)	10,392.3
Carbon dioxide emissions per head (metric tons, 2008)	0.3
Human Development Index (2011): ranking	143
Human Development Index (2011): value	0.509

For sources and definitions, see explanatory note on p. vi.

Agriculture

PRINCIPAL CROPS
('000 metric tons)

	2009	2010	2011
Wheat	219.3	512.0	268.5
Barley	42.1	64.2	65.2
Maize	2,439.0	3,464.5	3,376.9
Millet	54.0	53.9	73.4
Sorghum	99.0	164.1	159.9
Potatoes	2,299.1	2,725.9	2,365.3
Sweet potatoes	930.8	821.0	759.5
Cassava (Manioc)	820.0	323.4	679.2
Sugar cane	5,610.7	5,709.6	5,338.6
Beans, dry	465.4	390.6	577.7
Cow peas, dry	60.2	72.3	81.5

—*continued*	2009	2010	2011
Pigeon peas	46.5	103.3	84.3
Cashew nuts	17.7	17.6	20.9
Coconuts	61.2	74.6	87.5
Seed cotton	14.9	11.8	22.1
Cottonseed*	9.7	7.7	14.4
Cabbages and other brassicas	511.7	784.9	599.6
Tomatoes	526.9	539.2	407.4
Onions, dry	88.7	96.4	112.0
Carrots and turnips	82.3	76.9	61.3
Bananas	1,686.9	1,583.1	1,198.0
Plantains*	32.0	35.0	31.0
Guavas, mangoes and mangosteens	528.8	593.5	636.6
Avocados	145.2	202.3	201.5
Pineapples	296.1	328.2	371.3
Papayas	71.2	98.1	18.4
Coffee, green	54.0	42.0	36.3
Tea (made)	314.2	399.0	377.9
Tobacco, unmanufactured	10.3	14.2	14.0
Sisal	19.0	23.9	27.6

* FAO estimates.

Aggregate production ('000 metric tons, may include official, semi-official or estimated data): Total cereals 2,898.9 in 2009, 4,346.7 in 2010, 4,057.8 in 2011; Total roots and tubers 4,072.9 in 2009, 3,896.6 in 2010, 3,831.5 in 2011; Total vegetables (incl. melons) 1,971.5 in 2009, 2,527.3 in 2010, 2,030.6 in 2011; Total fruits (excl. melons) 3,168.5 in 2009, 3,258.3 in 2010, 2,862.4 in 2011.

Source: FAO.

LIVESTOCK
('000 head, year ending September)

	2009	2010	2011*
Cattle	17,468	17,863	18,000
Sheep	9,903	9,899*	10,000
Goats	13,872	13,300*	13,400
Pigs	344	347	350
Camels	947	1,347	1,350
Chickens	31,827	30,398	30,000

* FAO estimate(s).

Source: FAO.

LIVESTOCK PRODUCTS
('000 metric tons)

	2009	2010	2011
Cattle meat	483.0	462.0	458.0
Sheep meat	40.8	41.5	43.0
Goats' meat	46.3	46.9	47.2
Pig meat	18.1	15.3	12.8
Chicken meat	25.2	27.1	21.5
Game meat*	21.4	25.1	25.1
Camel meat	16.6	23.6	25.0*
Cows' milk	3,893.0	3,967.8	4,058.8
Sheep's milk*	29.7	30.8	30.8
Goats' milk	192.4	196.1	197.2
Camels' milk*	29.2	30.1	30.1
Hen eggs	81.0	80.6	85.8
Honey*	25.1	24.0	24.0

* FAO estimate(s).

Source: FAO.

Forestry

ROUNDWOOD REMOVALS
('000 cubic metres, excluding bark, FAO estimates)

	2007	2008	2009
Sawlogs, veneer logs and logs for sleepers	607.0	607.0	607.0
Pulpwood	450.0	450.0	450.0
Other industrial wood	189.0	189.0	189.0
Fuel wood	26,400.0	26,400.0	26,400.0
Total	27,646.0	27,646.0	27,646.0

2010–11: Production assumed to be unchanged from 2009 (FAO estimates).

Source: FAO.

SAWNWOOD PRODUCTION
('000 cubic metres, including railway sleepers)

	2004	2005	2006
Coniferous (softwood)	70	116	121
Broadleaved (hardwood)	8	20	21
Total	78	136	142

2007–11: Production assumed to be unchanged from 2006 (FAO estimates).

Source: FAO.

Fishing

('000 metric tons, live weight)

	2008	2009	2010
Capture	135.4	133.6	143.1
Silver cyprinid	47.0	49.3	47.7
Nile tilapia	12.7	17.3	26.1
Nile perch	45.0	43.7	39.4
Aquaculture	4.5	4.9	12.2
Total catch	139.9	138.5	155.3

Note: Figures exclude crocodiles, recorded by number rather than by weight. The number of Nile crocodiles caught was: 4,504 in 2008; 6,906 in 2009; 5,259 in 2010.

Source: FAO.

Mining

('000 metric tons)

	2008	2009	2010
Soda ash	513.4	404.9	473.7
Fluorspar	98.2	15.7	44.5
Salt	24.3	24.1	25.0*
Limestone flux*	42.0	38.0	40.0

* Estimated production.

Source: US Geological Survey.

Industry

SELECTED PRODUCTS
('000 metric tons unless otherwise indicated)

	2007	2008	2009
Wheat flour	370.3	310.7	359.3
Raw sugar	520.4	511.9	548.2
Beer ('000 hectolitres)	3,934.2	4,248.6	3,968.2
Cigarettes (million)	12,203.7	12,169.0	11,012.8
Cement	2,615.0	2,829.6	3,320.3
Jet fuel	236	221	217
Motor gasoline (petrol)	207	182	157
Gas-diesel oils	397	374	372
Residual fuel oils	534	515	498
Electric energy (million kWh)	6,772	7,055	6,450

Source: UN Industrial Commodity Statistics Database.

Finance

CURRENCY AND EXCHANGE RATES

Monetary Units
100 cents = 1 Kenya shilling (Ks.).
Ks. 20 = 1 Kenya pound (K£).

Sterling, Dollar and Euro Equivalents (31 December 2012)
£1 sterling = Ks. 135.71;
US $1 = Ks. 86.00;
€1 = Ks. 113.47;
Ks. 1,000 = £7.37 sterling = $11.63 = €8.81.

Average Exchange Rate (Ks. per US $)
2010   79.233
2011   88.811
2012   84.530

Note: The foregoing information refers to the Central Bank's mid-point exchange rate. However, with the introduction of a foreign exchange bearer certificate (FEBC) scheme in October 1991, a dual exchange rate system is in effect. In May 1994 foreign exchange transactions were liberalized and the Kenya shilling became fully convertible against other currencies.

BUDGET
(Ks. '000 million, year ending 30 June)

Revenue*	2010/11	2011/12†	2012/13‡
Tax revenue	557.2	626.5	748.6
Taxes on income and profits .	258.7	312.5	366.5
Taxes on goods and services .	252.5	262.3	323.0
Value-added tax . . .	171.9	183.4	231.9
Excise duties	80.6	78.9	91.1
Taxes on international trade .	46.1	51.7	59.1
Import duties	46.1	51.7	59.1
Non-tax revenue	110.4	121.7	158.2
Total (incl. others)	667.5	748.2	906.8

Expenditure§	2010/11	2011/12†	2012/13‡
Recurrent expenditure . . .	578.5	642.3	818.2
Wages and benefits . . .	198.5	224.6	278.0
Defence	60.6	78.7	83.5
Interest payments . . .	76.2	91.2	105.8
Internal	69.2	82.3	94.5
External	7.0	8.9	11.3
Development expenditure . .	216.9	297.9	329.3
Domestically financed . .	149.9	211.8	205.6
Foreign financed	67.0	86.1	123.7
Drought expenditure . . .	8.3	4.9	—
Constitutional reform . . .	5.6	—	5.0
Contingencies	—	—	5.0
Total	809.3	945.1	1,157.5

* Excluding grants received (Ks. '000 million): 18.8 in 2010/11; 15.3 in 2011/12 (preliminary estimate); 56.2 in 2012/13 (projected figure).
† Preliminary estimates.
‡ Projected figures.
§ Excluding net lending (Ks. '000 million): 2.5 in 2010/11; 2.8 in 2011/12 (preliminary estimate); 2.5 in 2012/13 (projected figure).

Source: IMF, *Kenya: Fourth Review Under the Three-Year Arrangement Under the Extended Credit Facility, Request for a Waiver and Modification of Performance Criteria—Staff Report; Press Release on the Executive Board Discussion; and Statement by the Executive Director for Kenya* (November 2012).

INTERNATIONAL RESERVES
(excl. gold, US $ million at 31 December)

	2009	2010	2011
IMF special drawing rights . .	350.6	318.5	16.9
Reserve position in IMF . . .	20.2	20.0	20.0
Foreign exchange	3,478.1	3,981.7	4,227.5
Total	3,849.0	4,320.2	4,264.4

Source: IMF, *International Financial Statistics*.

MONEY SUPPLY
(Ks. million at 31 December)

	2009	2010	2011
Currency depository corporations .	100,850	122,925	136,983
Transferable deposits	427,532	557,124	621,196
Other deposits	515,682	597,485	764,029
Broad money	1,044,064	1,277,534	1,522,208

Source: IMF, *International Financial Statistics*.

COST OF LIVING
(Consumer Price Index at December; base: October 1997 = 100)

	2001	2002	2003
Food and non-alcoholic beverages .	135	142	162
Alcohol and tobacco	138	139	147
Clothing and footwear . . .	110	111	112
Housing	128	132	134
Fuel and power	156	169	170
Household goods and services .	119	120	123
Medical goods and services . .	153	160	169
Transport and communications .	128	131	139
Recreation and education . .	130	133	137
Personal goods and services . .	121	123	124
All items (incl. others)	131	137	148

Source: IMF, *Kenya: Statistical Appendix* (June 2009).

All items (Consumer Price Index, annual averages; base 2005 = 100): 173.2 in 2009; 180.1 in 2010; 205.3 in 2011 (Source: IMF, *International Financial Statistics*).

NATIONAL ACCOUNTS
(Ks. million at current prices)

Expenditure on the Gross Domestic Product

	2009	2010	2011*
Government final consumption expenditure	383,847	449,339	538,541
Private final consumption expenditure	1,849,582	1,983,496	2,350,129
Changes in inventories . .	6,365	−14,015	23,537
Gross fixed capital formation .	465,111	518,504	608,982
Total domestic expenditure .	2,704,905	2,937,324	3,521,189
Exports of goods and services .	571,305	709,209	869,222
Less Imports of goods and services	886,480	1,021,873	1,374,101
Statistical discrepancy . . .	−22,745	−74,834	8,471
GDP at market prices . . .	2,366,984	2,549,825	3,024,782
GDP at constant 2001 prices .	1,394,387	1,474,763	1,539,306

Gross Domestic Product by Economic Activity

	2009	2010	2011*
Agriculture, forestry and fishing .	565,191	560,564	741,251
Mining and quarrying	12,083	17,650	20,621
Manufacturing	234,556	252,122	285,698
Electricity, gas and water . .	44,185	35,592	26,071
Construction	97,445	109,146	125,046
Wholesale and retail trade, restaurants and hotels . .	272,422	303,415	371,507
Transport, storage and communications	234,752	253,958	292,601
Finance, insurance, real estate and business services	245,389	266,644	327,790
Public administration and defence	118,662	141,648	151,321
Other services	292,025	319,540	361,166
Sub-total	2,116,710	2,260,280	2,703,072
Less Financial intermediation services indirectly measured .	25,762	21,652	31,787
Indirect taxes, less subsidies . .	276,036	311,196	353,497
GDP in market prices . . .	2,366,984	2,549,825	3,024,782

* Provisional figures.

BALANCE OF PAYMENTS
(US $ million)

	2009	2010	2011
Exports of goods	4,492.1	5,210.9	5,791.8
Imports of goods	−9,461.2	−11,442.2	−14,162.1
Balance on goods	**−4,969.1**	**−6,231.3**	**−8,370.3**
Exports of services	2,893.0	3,772.2	4,114.5
Imports of services	−1,840.4	−2,089.1	−2,186.5
Balance on goods and services	**−3,916.5**	**−4,548.3**	**−6,442.2**
Primary income received . . .	181.9	144.2	289.5
Secondary income paid . . .	−212.4	−291.9	−282.5
Balance on goods, services and primary income	**−3,947.0**	**−4,695.9**	**−6,435.3**
Secondary income received . .	2,341.3	2,370.4	3,148.5
Secondary income paid . . .	−82.8	−43.2	−46.4
Current balance	**−1,688.5**	**−2,368.7**	**−3,333.2**
Capital account	260.9	240.2	234.9
Direct investment assets . . .	−46.0	−1.6	−9.4
Direct investment liabilities . .	116.3	178.1	335.2
Portfolio investment assets . .	−23.7	−51.2	−81.2
Portfolio investment liabilities .	2.8	22.2	23.8
Other investment assets . .	544.6	94.7	−668.5
Other investment liabilities . .	1,871.9	1,886.0	2,269.4
Net errors and omissions . .	79.8	142.1	17.3
Reserves and related items .	**1,118.0**	**141.9**	**−1,211.7**

Source: IMF, *International Financial Statistics*.

External Trade

PRINCIPAL COMMODITIES
(distribution by SITC, US $ million)

Imports c.i.f.	2008	2009	2010
Food and live animals . . .	**688.9**	**1,117.0**	**846.2**
Cereals and cereal preparations .	421.7	811.4	437.3
Crude materials (inedible) except fuels	**225.3**	**224.2**	**262.9**
Mineral fuels, lubricants, etc. .	**3,029.4**	**2,187.1**	**2,670.2**
Petroleum, petroleum products, etc.	2,976.7	2,138.7	2,596.1
Crude petroleum oils . . .	1,176.5	705.8	915.2
Refined petroleum products .	1,769.6	1,399.2	1,646.3
Animal and vegetable oils, fats and waxes	**496.8**	**356.9**	**490.8**
Chemicals and related products	**1,454.0**	**1,325.7**	**1,602.7**
Medicinal and pharmaceutical products	301.6	297.8	351.4
Plastics in primary forms . . .	341.0	288.4	378.6
Basic manufactures	**1,602.3**	**1,408.8**	**1,774.6**
Iron and steel	512.9	437.3	548.7
Machinery and transport equipment	**3,110.1**	**3,097.3**	**3,841.1**
Power-generating machinery and equipment	350.8	317.2	306.5
Machinery specialized for particular industries . . .	365.5	339.3	369.5
General industrial machinery, equipment and parts . . .	329.6	272.0	356.4
Electrical machinery, apparatus, etc.	185.1	196.5	233.8
Road vehicles and parts . . .	817.7	785.2	869.6
Passenger motor cars (excl. buses)	311.9	296.0	345.5
Motor vehicles for goods transport and special purposes	190.8	165.3	212.8
Aircraft, associated equipment and parts	235.5	349.5	517.6
Miscellaneous manufactured articles	**431.5**	**417.2**	**504.0**
Total (incl. others)	**11,127.8**	**10,202.0**	**12,092.9**

Exports f.o.b.	2008	2009	2010
Food and live animals . . .	**1,827.7**	**1,681.1**	**2,095.9**
Vegetables and fruit	451.6	358.9	451.6
Fresh or simply preserved vegetables	274.1	224.7	270.4
Coffee, tea, cocoa and spices . .	1,098.8	1,110.4	1,388.9
Tea	931.8	894.1	1,163.8
Crude materials (inedible) except fuels	**763.1**	**638.3**	**612.8**
Cut flowers and foliage . . .	527.4	422.5	397.4
Mineral fuels, lubricants, etc. .	**197.7**	**187.5**	**216.9**
Petroleum, petroleum products, etc.	192.3	183.9	211.4
Refined petroleum products .	173.3	177.9	205.2
Chemicals and related products	**574.0**	**457.2**	**466.5**
Basic manufactures	**654.1**	**547.8**	**625.6**
Iron and steel	158.4	118.1	153.5
Miscellaneous manufactured articles	**510.6**	**429.5**	**449.2**
Total (incl. others)	**5,000.9**	**4,463.4**	**5,169.1**

Source: UN, *International Trade Statistics Yearbook*.

PRINCIPAL TRADING PARTNERS
(US $ million)

Imports c.i.f.	2008	2009	2010
Bahrain	198.8	97.9	57.9
Belgium	119.7	91.2	96.3
China, People's Repub. . . .	932.2	965.2	1,522.5
Egypt	157.4	124.3	232.1
Finland	77.2	55.7	178.6
France (incl. Monaco) . . .	237.6	206.8	235.8
Germany	389.7	294.4	332.6
India	1,309.5	1,078.1	1,301.6
Indonesia	335.7	243.1	339.8
Italy	181.7	179.9	151.1
Japan	649.3	632.7	734.6
Korea, Repub.	119.3	138.6	248.7
Netherlands	192.1	225.9	232.7
Russia	166.2	63.3	122.1
Saudi Arabia	373.1	356.4	406.8
Singapore	360.7	342.2	400.1
South Africa	678.2	913.8	754.2
Switzerland-Liechtenstein . .	80.4	69.8	143.0
Tanzania	105.5	101.1	133.0
Thailand	131.4	91.6	107.3
Ukraine	82.7	131.9	110.4
United Arab Emirates . . .	1,655.7	1,161.8	1,462.9
United Kingdom	402.6	473.2	626.3
USA	402.3	649.1	496.0
Total (incl. others)	**11,127.8**	**10,202.0**	**12,092.9**

Exports f.o.b.	2008	2009	2010
Afghanistan	62.6	98.9	150.5
Belgium	40.9	43.9	52.5
Burundi	50.5	59.5	68.8
Congo, Democratic Repub. . .	143.6	146.5	161.4
Egypt	224.7	153.8	228.5
Ethiopia	63.9	55.9	55.3
France (incl. Monaco) . . .	72.1	56.1	65.5
Germany	89.3	95.1	97.3
India	98.2	66.5	106.9
Malawi	58.2	40.7	53.8
Netherlands	380.1	340.7	338.9
Pakistan	202.3	196.3	227.9
Russia	49.5	46.8	57.0
Rwanda	130.4	123.4	132.9
Somalia	186.7	145.1	164.7

Exports f.o.b.—*continued*	2008	2009	2010
South Africa	52.9	46.3	30.8
Sudan	204.6	165.1	237.5
Tanzania	424.9	389.3	420.2
Uganda	614.7	598.3	657.3
United Arab Emirates	109.8	138.7	237.8
United Kingdom	550.6	498.1	507.2
USA	299.6	226.1	284.9
Yemen	40.7	42.9	57.0
Zambia	79.9	62.5	59.1
Total (incl. others)	5,000.9	4,463.4	5,169.1

Source: UN, *International Trade Statistics Yearbook*.

2011 (Ks. million): Total imports 1,315.7; Total exports 511.0.

Transport

RAILWAYS
(traffic)

	2000	2001	2002*
Passenger-km (million)	302	216	288
Freight ton-km (million)	1,557	1,603	1,538

* Provisional figures.

Freight carried ('000 metric tons): 1,532 in 2009; 1,572 in 2010; 1,596 in 2011 (provisional).

ROAD TRAFFIC
(motor vehicles in use)

	2009	2010	2011*
Motor cars	499,679	553,397	598,622
Light vans	219,901	226,876	234,318
Lorries, trucks and heavy vans	91,431	96,355	101,602
Buses and mini-buses	84,844	89,708	91,821
Motorcycles and autocycles	252,960	371,747	514,102
Other motor vehicles	45,229	50,038	53,941

* Provisional figures.

SHIPPING

Flag Registered Fleet
(at 31 December)

	2010	2011	2012
Number of vessels	34	34	32
Total displacement (grt)	20,068	20,068	15,949

Source: Lloyd's List Intelligence (www.lloydslistintelligence.com).

International Sea-borne Freight Traffic
('000 metric tons)

	1999	2000	2001*
Goods loaded	1,845	1,722	1,998
Goods unloaded	6,200	7,209	8,299

* Provisional figures.

Freight handled ('000 metric tons at Kenyan ports): 19,062 in 2009; 18,977 in 2010; 19,953 in 2011 (provisional).

CIVIL AVIATION
(traffic on scheduled services)

	2007	2008	2009
Kilometres flown (million)	57	61	64
Passengers carried ('000)	2,858	2,881	2,949
Passenger-km (million)	7,952	8,047	7,925
Total ton-km (million)	1,023	1,022	987

Source: UN, *Statistical Yearbook*.

Passengers carried ('000, all services): 7,516 in 2010; 8,722 in 2011 (provisional).

Tourism

FOREIGN TOURIST ARRIVALS
('000 overnight stays at accommodation establishments)

	2008	2009	2010
France	63.8	231.8	222.7
Germany	339.5	685.6	563.2
India	51.2	83.3	91.1
Italy	158.2	383.2	651.0
Switzerland	66.8	127.5	83.1
Tanzania	43.1	71.1	61.5
Uganda	43.2	103.0	67.9
United Kingdom	486.6	909.7	964.7
USA	148.1	233.8	254.2
Total (incl. others)	2,080.1	4,062.4	4,260.1

Tourism receipts (US $ million, excl. passenger transport): 800 in 2010; 884 in 2011 (provisional).

Source: World Tourism Organization.

Total tourist arrivals ('000): 1,490 in 2009; 1,609 in 2010; 1,823 in 2011 (provisional).

Communications Media

	2009	2010	2011
Telephones ('000 main lines in use)	664	381	284
Mobile cellular telephones ('000 subscribers)	19,365	24,969	28,081
Internet subscribers ('000)	8.3	12.2	n.a.
Broadband subscribers ('000)	8.3	4.2	42.4

Personal computers: 492,000 (13.7 per 1,000 persons) in 2005.

Source: International Telecommunication Union.

Education

(2008/09 unless otherwise indicated)

	Institutions	Teachers	Pupils
Pre-primary	23,977[1]	92,555	1,914,222
Primary	17,611[1]	152,848	7,150,259
Secondary:			
general secondary	3,057[1]	106,033	3,188,707
technical	36[2]	1,937	15,672
teacher training	26[3]	808[4]	18,992[5]
Higher	n.a.[6]	n.a.[6]	167,983

[1] 1998/99 figures.
[2] 1988 figure.
[3] 1995 figure.
[4] 1985 figure.
[5] 1992 figure.
[6] In 1990 there were four universities, with 4,392 teachers.

2009/10 (provisional figures) *Institutions:* Primary 27,489; Secondary 7,308; Higher 32. *Pupils:* Primary 9,381,211; Secondary 1,701,501; Higher 21,106.

2010/11 (provisional figures) *Pupils:* Primary 9,857,890; Secondary 1,767,720; Higher 25,533.

Sources: Ministry of Education, Nairobi; UNESCO Institute for Statistics.

Pupil-teacher ratio (primary education, UNESCO estimate): 46.8 in 2008/09 (Source: UNESCO Institute for Statistics).

Adult literacy rate (UNESCO estimates): 87.4% (males 90.6%; females 84.2%) in 2010 (Source: UNESCO Institute for Statistics).

Directory

The Government

HEAD OF STATE

President: UHURU KENYATTA (inaugurated 9 April 2013).

Deputy President: WILLIAM SAMOEI RUTO.

CABINET
(May 2013)

Secretary for Information, Communication and Technology: Dr FRED OKENGO MATIANG'I.

Secretary for the National Treasury: HENRY K. ROTICH.

Secretary for Health: JAMES WAINAINA MACHARIA.

Secretary for Foreign Affairs: AMINA MOHAMED.

Secretary for Industrialization and Enterprise Development: ADAN ABDULLA MOHAMED.

Secretary for Devolution and Planning: ANNE WAIGURU.

Secretary for Defence: RAYCHELLE OMAMO.

Secretary for Sports, Culture and the Arts: Dr HASSAN WARIO ARERO.

Secretary for Education, Science and Technology: Prof. JACOB KAIMENYI.

Secretary for Agriculture, Livestock and Fisheries: FELIX KIPTARUS KOSKEI.

Secretary for Transport and Infrastructure: MICHAEL S. KAMAU.

Secretary for East African Affairs, Commerce and Tourism: PHYLLIS JEPKOSGEI KIPKINGOR-KANDIE.

Secretary for Energy and Petroleum: DAVIS CHIRCHIR.

Secretary for the Environment, Water and Natural Resources: JUDI WANGALWA WAKHUNGU.

Secretary for Mining: NAJIB BALALA.

Secretary for Land, Housing and Urban Development: CHARITY NGILU.

MINISTRIES

Office of the President: Harambee House, Harambee Ave, POB 62345, 00200 Nairobi; tel. (20) 2227411; e-mail president@statehousekenya.go.ke; internet www.cabinetoffice.go.ke.

Office of the Vice-President: Jogoo House 'A', Taifa Rd, POB 30478, 00100 Nairobi; tel. (20) 228411; fax (20) 243620; internet www.homeaffairs.go.ke.

Ministry of Agriculture, Livestock and Fisheries: Kilimo House, Cathedral Rd, POB 30028, Nairobi; tel. (20) 2718870; internet www.kilimo.go.ke.

Ministry of Defence: Nairobi.

Ministry of Devolution and Planning: Nairobi.

Ministry of East African Affairs, Commerce and Tourism: Co-operative House, 16th Floor, Haile Selassie Ave, POB 8846, 00200 Nairobi; tel. (20) 2245741; fax (20) 2229650; e-mail ps@meac.go.ke; internet www.meac.go.ke.

Ministry of Education, Science and Technology: Jogoo House 'B', Harambee Ave, POB 30040, 00100 Nairobi; tel. (20) 318581; fax (20) 214287; e-mail info@education.go.ke; internet www.education.go.ke.

Ministry of Energy and Petroleum: Nyayo House, 23rd Floor, Kenyatta Ave, POB 30582, 00100 Nairobi; tel. (20) 310112; fax (20) 228314; e-mail info@energy.go.ke; internet www.energy.go.ke.

Ministry of the Environment, Water and Natural Resources: NHIF Bldg, Ragati Rd, POB 30126, 00100 Nairobi; tel. (20) 2730808; fax (20) 2725707; internet www.environment.go.ke.

Ministry of Foreign Affairs: Old Treasury Bldg, Harambee Ave, POB 30551, 00100 Nairobi; tel. (20) 318888; fax (20) 240066; e-mail press@mfa.go.ke; internet www.mfa.go.ke.

Ministry of Health: Medical HQ, Afya House, Cathedral Rd, POB 30016, 00100 Nairobi; tel. (20) 2717077; fax (20) 2713234; e-mail psph@health.go.ke; internet www.publichealth.go.ke.

Ministry of Industrialization and Enterprise Development: Teleposta Towers, GPO 11th Floor, POB 30418, 00100 Nairobi; tel. (20) 315001; e-mail info@industrialization.go.ke; internet www.tradeandindustry.go.ke.

Ministry of Information, Communication and Technology: Teleposta Towers, Kenyatta Ave, POB 30025, 00100 Nairobi; tel. (20) 2251152; fax (20) 315147; internet www.information.go.ke.

Ministry of Land, Housing and Urban Development: Ardhi House, Ngong Rd, POB 30450, 00100 Nairobi; tel. (20) 2718050; fax (20) 2721248; internet www.ardhi.go.ke.

Ministry of Mining: Nairobi.

National Treasury: Treasury Bldg, Harambee Ave, POB 30007, Nairobi; tel. (20) 228411; internet www.treasury.go.ke.

Ministry of Transport and Infrastructure: Transcom House, Ngong Rd, POB 52692, 00200 Nairobi; tel. (20) 2729200; fax (20) 2730330; e-mail ps@transport.go.ke; internet www.transport.go.ke.

Ministry of Sports, Culture and the Arts: Kencom House, 3rd Floor, Moi Ave, POB 34303, 00100 Nairobi; tel. (20) 240068; fax (20) 312351; e-mail infor@youthaffairs.go.ke; internet www.youthaffairs.go.ke.

President and Legislature

PRESIDENT

Election, 4 March 2013

Candidate	Votes	% of valid votes
Uhuru Kenyetta (TNA)	6,173,433	50.51
Raila Amollo Odinga (ODM) . .	5,340,546	43.70
Wycliffe Musalia Mudavadi (UDF)	483,981	3.96
Peter Kenneth (KNC) . .	72,786	0.60
Mohamed Abduba Dida (ARK) . .	52,848	0.40
Martha Wangari Karua (NARC—Kenya)	43,881	0.36
James Legilisho Kiyiapi (RBK) . .	40,998	0.34
Paul Kibugi Muite (Safina) . . .	12,580	0.10
Total	**12,221,053***	**100.00**

* In addition, there were 108,975 invalid votes.

NATIONAL ASSEMBLY

Speaker: JUSTIN MUTURI.

General Election, 4 March 2013

Party	Constituency seats	Women members	Total seats
ODM	78	15	93
TNA	72	14	86
URP	62	10	72
WDM—Kenya . .	19	6	25
UDFP	11	—	11
FRD—Kenya . .	9	—	9
KANU	6	—	6
New FORD—Kenya .	4	2	6
APK	5	—	5
FORD—People . .	3	—	3
FPK	3	—	3
NRC	3	—	3
CCU	2	—	2
KNC	2	—	2
FORD—Kenya . .	1	—	1
KADU—Asili . .	1	—	1
IP	1	—	1
MDP	1	—	1
MP	1	—	1
NARC—Kenya . .	1	—	1
PDP	1	—	1
Independents . .	4	—	4
Total	**290**	**47**	**337***

* In addition to the 290 directly elected constituency seats and 47 women members elected in each of the counties, 12 members (three from the ODM the TNA and the URP, and one each from Ford—Kenya, the UDFP and the WDM—Kenya) were nominated by parliamentary political parties according to their proportion of members of the National Assembly to represent special interests including the youth, persons with disabilities and workers. The Speaker is also, ex officio, a member of the National Assembly.

SENATE

Speaker: EKWEE DAVID ETHURO.
General Election, 4 March 2013

Party	Seats
ODM	11
TNA	11
URP	9
FORD—Kenya	4
WDM—Kenya	4
APK	2
KANU	2
UDF	2
FPK	1
NARC	1
Total	**47***

* In addition, 16 women members were nominated by political parties according to their proportion of members of the Senate (four from the ODM and the TNA, three from the URP and one each from the APK, FORD—Kenya, KANU, the UDFP and the WDM—Kenya). A further two members, represent the youth (one ODM, one TNA) and two members (also one from the ODM and one from the TNA) represent persons with disabilities. The Speaker is also an ex officio member.

Election Commission

Independent Electoral and Boundaries Commission (IEBC): Loita St, Anniversary Towers, 6th Floor, POB 45371, 00100 Nairobi; tel. (20) 2769000; e-mail info@iebc.or.ke; internet www.iebc.or.ke; f. 2011 to replace Electoral Commission of Kenya, which was disbanded following disputed elections in 2007; Chair. AHMED ISSACK HASSAN.

Political Organizations

In early 2013 there were 59 political parties registered with the Office of the Registrar of Political Parties. At the March 2013 elections the TNA, the NARC and the URP were members of the Jubilee Alliance, while the ODM, the WDM—Kenya and the FORD—Kenya were part of the Coalition for Reforms and Democracy.

Alliance Party of Kenya (APK): El-Molo Dr., Lavington, POB 21398, 00100 Nairobi; tel. (20) 2094424; e-mail info@alliancepartyofkenya.net; Sec.-Gen. BEATRICE ELACHI.

Alliance for Real Change (ARK): Gilfillan House, 2nd Floor, Kenyatta Ave, Suite No. 203, POB 1462, 00100 Nairobi; tel. (20) 2496334; e-mail info@allianceforrealchange.com; internet www.allianceforrealchange.com; f. 2010; Leader MOHAMED ABDUBA DIDA; Sec.-Gen. AMINA GUYO.

Chama Cha Uzalendo (CCU): Danpark Apartment, off Airport, Embakasi, Nairobi; tel. 738836701 (mobile); e-mail chamachauzalendokenya@gmail.com; Chair. MAUR ABDALLAH BWANAMAKA.

Democratic Party of Kenya (DP): Gitanga Rd, POB 53695, 00200 Nairobi; tel. (20) 2625977; f. 1991; Leader JOSEPH MUNYAO; rival faction led by NGENGI MUIGAI.

Federal Party of Kenya (FPK): POB 25091, Nairobi; tel. 722302368 (mobile); e-mail info@federalpartykenya.org; Chair. CALEB BURUDI; Sec.-Gen. KENNEDY OKELLO OLUOCH.

Forum for the Restoration of Democracy—Asili (FORD—Asili): 58 Duplex Apt, Upper Hill, Matumbato Rd, POB 69564, 00400 Nairobi; e-mail fordasili@gmail.com; tel. 722779005 (mobile); f. 1992; Chair. ISSAC ONEKA MUNANAIRI.

Forum for the Restoration of Democracy—Kenya (FORD—Kenya): Simba House, Gatundu Cres., Kileleshwa, off Gatundu Rd, POB 43591, 00100 Nairobi; tel. (20) 3869338; e-mail fordkenya@yahoo.com; internet www.fordkenya.or.ke; f. 1992; predominantly Luo support; Leader MOSES WETANGULA; Sec.-Gen. Dr DAVID ESELI SIMIYU.

Forum for the Restoration of Democracy for the People (FORD—People): Muchai Dr., off Ngong Rd, POB 5938, 00200 Nairobi; tel. (20) 2737015; f. 1997 by fmr mems of FORD—Asili; Nat. Chair. REUBEN OYONDI.

The Independent Party (TIP): Karesh Complex Inn, Mlolongo, POB 6854, 00200 Nairobi; tel. 722352009 (mobile); e-mail tiptipamanikenya@yahoo.com; Leader KALEMBE NDILE; Sec.-Gen. JANE WILLY.

Kenya African Democratic Union—Asili (KADU—Asili): Door 1, Dockworkers Union Bldg, Makuli Fagia, Kenyatta Ave, 2nd Floor, POB 83229, Mombasa; Sec.-Gen. PATIENCE M. CHOME.

Kenya African National Union (KANU): Yaya Center, Chania Rd, POB 72394, 00200 Nairobi; tel. (20) 245791; e-mail info@kanuparty.com; internet www.kanuparty.com; f. 1960; sole legal party 1982–91; absorbed the National Development Party (f. 1994) in 2002; Chair. UHURU KENYATTA; Sec.-Gen. NICK SALAT.

Kenya National Congress (KNC): Mbabane Rd, POB 1498, 00100 Nairobi; tel. (20) 2604013; e-mail info@kenyanationalcongress.com; internet www.kenyanationalcongress.com; f. 1992; Chair. HERBERT MWACHIRO.

Maendeleo Democratic Party (MDP): Mwalimu Centre, 2nd Floor, Room No. 207, Muril Rd, POB 1980, 50100 Kakamega; tel. 722635506 (mobile); e-mail mdpparty@yahoo.com; Sec.-Gen. ALEX AMASAKHA.

Mazingira Greens Party of Kenya (MPK): POB 14832, Nairobi; tel. 737444901 (mobile); e-mail info@greenspartyofkenya.com; internet www.greenspartyofkenya.com; f. 2007; campaigns for the equitable sharing of wealth, sustainable use of natural resources, women's rights and the defence of Kenyan cultural values; Leader WANGARI MAATHAI.

Muungano Party (MP): Nyahururu House, Kilome Rd, POB 19080, 00100 Nairobi; tel. and fax (20) 8059439; e-mail muunganodevelopmentparty@yahoo.com; internet muunganoparty.or.ke.

The National Alliance (TNA): Promiso Plaza, Jogoo Rd, POB 13913, 00800 Nairobi; e-mail info@tna.co.ke; internet tna.co.ke; Chair. JOHNSON SAKAJA; Sec.-Gen. ONYANGO OLOO.

National Party of Kenya (NPK): Ole Shapara Rd, POB 2013–00200, Nairobi; internet nationalpartyofkenya.org; f. 1992; Chair. CHARITY KALUKI NGILU; Sec.-Gen. FIDELIS MWEKE.

National Rainbow Coalition (NRC): Othaya Road, House No. 18, POB 51498–00200, Nairobi; tel. (20) 2022617; f. 2002; Chair. CHARITY KALUKI NGILU; Sec.-Gen. FIDELLIS NGULLI.

National Rainbow Coalition—Kenya (NARC—Kenya): Woodlands Rd, off Lenana Rd, Kilimani, POB 34200, 00100 Nairobi; tel. (20) 2726783; fax (20) 2726784; e-mail narckenya06@yahoo.com; internet www.narckenya.org; f. 2006 by former mems of NARC; Chair. MARTHA W. KARUA.

New FORD—Kenya: Magumo Rd, House No. 33, POB 49416–00100 Nairobi; tel. 721399626 (mobile); e-mail newfordkenya@gmail.com; f. 2007; Chair. SOITA SHITANDA.

Orange Democratic Movement (ODM): Orange House, Menelik Rd, Kilimani Area, POB 2478, 00202 Nairobi; tel. (20) 2053481; f. 2005; Leader RAILA AMOLO ODINGA.

Peoples Democratic Party (PDP): Cannon Annex, Parliament Lane, POB 10734, 00400 Nairobi; tel. 7212019203 (mobile); e-mail info@peoples-democratic-party.com; internet peoples-democratic-party.com; Leader JAMES OMINGO MAGARA; Sec.-Gen. ERIC MBIU.

Restore and Build Kenya (RBK): Juma House, Makasembo St, POB 2670, 30100 Eldoret; tel. 720661812 (mobile); Leader JAMES LEGILISHO KIYIAPI.

Safina ('Noah's Ark'): Amboseli Rd, off Gitanga Rd, Lavington, POB 14746-00100 Nairobi; tel. (20) 5202211; fax (20) 3864242; e-mail info@safinaparty.org; internet www.safinaparty.org; f. 1995; aims to combat corruption and human rights abuses and to introduce proportional representation; Chair. PAUL KIBUGI MUITE.

Social Democratic Party of Kenya (SDP): Tena Estate House No. 574, Manyanja Rd, POB 4403, 00100 Nairobi; tel. 729497009 (mobile); e-mail info@sdpkenya.org; internet www.sdpkenya.org; f. 1992; Chair. MWANDAWIRO MGHANGA; Sec. Gen. BENEDICT WACHIRA.

United Democratic Forum Party (UDFP): POB 50905, 00100 Nairobi; tel. (20) 8020819; e-mail info@udfparty.org; internet udfparty.org; Chair. HASSAN A. OSMAN; Sec.-Gen. ABRAHAM K. LIMO.

United Democratic Movement (UDM): Matambato Rd, Upperhill, POB 44820, Nairobi; tel. 722752156 (mobile); e-mail uniteddemocraticmovement@yahoo.com; internet www.uniteddemocraticmovement.com; Chair. Rev. PAUL CHEBOI; Sec.-Gen. STANLEY K. ROTICH.

United Republican Party (URP): POB 2169, 00200 Nairobi; tel. (20) 2166885; e-mail info@urp.co.ke; Leader WILLIAM KIPCHIRCHIR SAMOEI RUTO; Sec.-Gen. DAVID KIMUTAI CHIRCHIR.

Wiper Democratic Movement—Kenya (WDM—Kenya): Wiper House, 408 Othaya Rd, POB 403-00100, Nairobi; tel. (20) 2663336; fax (20) 3864498; e-mail wiper@wipermovement.com; internet www.wipermovement.com; f. 2007 following split in the ODM; Leader STEPHEN KALONZO MUSYOKA.

Diplomatic Representation

EMBASSIES AND HIGH COMMISSIONS IN KENYA

Algeria: Mobil Plaza, POB 64140, 00620 Nairobi; tel. (20) 3755559; fax (20) 3755560; e-mail algerianembassy@wananchi.com; Ambassador ALI BENZERGA.

Argentina: Kitisuru Rd, POB 30283, 00100 Nairobi; tel. (20) 4183119; fax (20) 4183054; e-mail ekeny@bidii.com; internet www.ekeny.mrecic.gob.ar; Chargé d'affaires a.i. FERNANDO ROLANDELLI.

Australia: ICIPE House, Riverside Dr., off Chiromo Rd, POB 39341, 00623 Nairobi; tel. (20) 4277100; fax (20) 4277139; e-mail australian.hc.kenya@dfat.gov.au; internet www.kenya.embassy.gov.au; High Commissioner GEOFFREY PETER TOOTH.

Austria: 536 Limuru Rd, Muthaiga, POB 30560, 00100 Nairobi; tel. (20) 4060022; fax (20) 4060025; e-mail nairobi-ob@bmeia.gv.at; internet www.bmeia.gv.at/botschaft/nairobi; Ambassador CHRISTIAN HASENBICHLER.

Bangladesh: Lenana Rd, POB 41645, Nairobi; tel. (20) 8562816; fax (20) 8562817; e-mail bdhc@bdootnairobi.com; High Commissioner A. K. M. SHAMSUDDIN.

Belgium: Muthaiga, Limuru Rd, POB 30461, 00100 Nairobi; tel. (20) 7122011; fax (20) 7123050; e-mail nairobi@diplobel.fed.be; internet www.diplomatie.be/nairobi; Ambassador BART OUVRY.

Botswana: LR Block 91/238, Gigiri Dr., off United Nations Ave, Nairobi; tel. (20) 7123412; fax (20) 7123418; e-mail botkena@gov.bw; internet botswanamission.or.ke; High Commissioner JOHN MORETI.

Brazil: Tanar Center, UN Crescent Rd, UN Close, Gigiri, POB 30754, 00100 Nairobi; tel. (20) 7125765; fax (20) 7125767; e-mail geral@kenbrem.co.ke; Ambassador (vacant).

Burundi: Coop Trust Plaza, Upper Hill, off Bunyala Rd, POB 61165, 00200 Nairobi; tel. (20) 2719200; fax (20) 2719211; e-mail embunai@yahoo.fr; Ambassador EZECHIEL NIBIGIRA.

Canada: Limuru Rd, Gigiri, POB 1013, 00621 Nairobi; tel. (20) 3663000; fax (20) 3663900; e-mail nrobi@international.gc.ca; internet www.canadainternational.gc.ca/kenya; High Commissioner DAVID ANGELL.

Chile: Riverside Dr. 66, Riverside, POB 45554, 00100 Nairobi; tel. (20) 4452950; fax (20) 4443209; e-mail echile@echile.co.ke; Ambassador KONRAD PAULSEN.

China, People's Republic: Woodlands Rd, Kilimani District, POB 30508, Nairobi; tel. (20) 2722559; fax (20) 2726402; e-mail chinaemb_ke@mfa.gov.cn; internet ke.china-embassy.org; Ambassador LIU GUANGYUAN.

Colombia: UN Cresent House No 91/244, POB 48494, 00100 Nairobi; tel. (20) 7120850; fax (20) 7120304; e-mail enairobi@cancilleria.gov.co; Chargé d'affaires a.i. JOSÉ MIGUEL CASTIBLANCO MUÑOZ.

Congo, Democratic Republic: Electricity House, 12th Floor, Harambee Ave, POB 48106, 00100 Nairobi; tel. (20) 2229772; fax (20) 3754253; e-mail ambardckenyal@yahoo.com; Ambassador TADUMI ON'OKOKO.

Cuba: International House, Mama Ngina St, 13th Floor, POB 41931, 00606 Nairobi; tel. (20) 2241003; fax (20) 2241023; e-mail embacuba@swiftkenya.com; internet emba.cubaminrex.cu/kenyaing; Ambassador PAUL RODRIGUEZ RAMOS.

Cyprus: Eagle House, 5th Floor, Kimathi St, POB 30739, 00100 Nairobi; tel. (20) 2220881; fax (20) 312202; e-mail cyphc@nbnet.co.ke; High Commissioner AGIS LOIZOU.

Denmark: 13 Runda Dr., Runda, POB 40412, 00100 Nairobi; tel. (20) 7122848; fax (20) 7120638; e-mail nboamb@um.dk; internet www.ambnairobi.um.dk; Ambassador GEERT AAGAARD ANDERSEN.

Djibouti: Comcraft House, 2nd Floor, Haile Selassie Ave, POB 59528, Nairobi; tel. (20) 339640; Ambassador ADEN MARIAM AHMED GOUMEH.

Egypt: Othaya Rd, Kileleshwa, POB 30285, 00100 Nairobi; tel. (20) 3870360; fax (20) 3870383; Ambassador KADRI FATHI ABDEL-MOTTALEB.

Eritrea: New Rehema House, 2nd Floor, Westlands, POB 38651, Nairobi; tel. (20) 4443164; fax (20) 4443165; Ambassador BEYENE RUSSOM.

Ethiopia: State House Ave, POB 45198, 00100 Nairobi; tel. (20) 2732052; fax (20) 2732054; e-mail ethiopian22embassy@yahoo.com; Ambassador SHEMSUDIN ROBELE.

Finland: Eden Sq., Blk 3, 6th Floor, Greenway Rd, off Westlands Rd, POB 30379, 00100 Nairobi; tel. (20) 3750721; fax (20) 3750714; e-mail sanomat.nai@formin.fi; internet www.finland.or.ke; Ambassador ANNA BRITA SOFIE FROM-EMMESBERGER.

France: Barclays Plaza, 9th Floor, Loita St, POB 41784, 00100 Nairobi; tel. (20) 2778000; fax (20) 2778180; e-mail ambafrance.nairobi@diplomatie.gouv.fr; internet www.ambafrance-ke.org; Ambassador ETIENNE DE PONCINS.

Germany: Ludwig Krapf House, Riverside Dr. 113, POB 30180, Nairobi; tel. (20) 4262100; fax (20) 4262129; e-mail info@nairobi.diplo.de; internet www.nairobi.diplo.de; Ambassador MARGIT HELLWIG-BÖTTE.

Greece: Nation Centre, 13th Floor, Kimathi St, POB 30543, 00100 Nairobi; tel. (20) 340722; fax (20) 2216044; e-mail gremb.nai@mfa.gr; Ambassador ELEFTHERIOS KOVARITAKIS.

Holy See: 151 Manyani Rd West, Waiyaki Way, POB 14326, 00800 Nairobi; tel. (20) 2148971; fax (20) 2631120; e-mail nunciokenya@nunciokenya.org; Apostolic Nuncio Most Rev. CHARLES DANIEL BALVO (Titular Archbishop of Castello).

Hungary: Kabarsiran Ave, off James Gichuru Rd, Lavington, POB 61146, Nairobi; tel. (20) 4442612; fax (20) 4442101; e-mail mission.nai@kum.hu; internet www.mfa.gov.hu/kulkepviselet/ke; Ambassador SÁNDOR JUHÁSZ.

India: Jeevan Bharati Bldg, 2nd Floor, Harambee Ave, POB 30074, Nairobi; tel. (20) 2225104; fax (20) 316242; e-mail hcindia@kenyaweb.com; internet www.hcinairobi.co.ke; High Commissioner SIBABRATA TRIPATHI.

Indonesia: Menengai Rd, Upper Hill, POB 48868, Nairobi; tel. (20) 2714196; fax (20) 2713475; e-mail indonbi@indonesia.or.ke; internet www.indonesia.or.ke; Ambassador BUDI BOWOLEKSONO.

Iran: Dennis Pritt Rd, POB 49170, Nairobi; tel. (20) 711257; fax (20) 339936; Ambassador MALEK HOSSEIN GIVZAD.

Israel: Bishop's Rd, POB 30354, 00100 Nairobi; tel. (20) 4927500; fax (20) 2715966; e-mail info@nairobi.mfa.gov.il; internet nairobi.mfa.gov.il; Ambassador GIL HASKELL.

Italy: Int. House, 9th Floor, Mama Ngina St, POB 30107, 00100 Nairobi; tel. (20) 2247750; fax (20) 2247086; e-mail ambasciata.nairobi@esteri.it; internet www.ambnairobi.esteri.it; Ambassador PAOLA IMPERIALE.

Japan: Mara Rd, Upper Hill, POB 60202, 00200 Nairobi; tel. (20) 2898000; fax (20) 2898531; e-mail jinfocul@eojkenya.org; internet www.ke.emb-japan.go.jp; Ambassador TOSHIHISA TOKATA.

Korea, Republic: Misha Tower, 1st and 2nd Floors, Westlands Rd, POB 30455, 00100 Nairobi; tel. (20) 3749931; fax (20) 3741337; e-mail emb-ke@mofat.go.kr; internet ken.mofat.go.kr; Ambassador KIM CHAN-WOO.

Kuwait: Muthaiga Rd, POB 42353, Nairobi; tel. (20) 761614; fax (20) 762837; Ambassador YAQOUB YOUSEF EID AL-SANAD.

Libya: Jamahiriya House, Loita St, POB 47190, Nairobi; tel. (20) 250380; fax (20) 243730; e-mail jamahiriyanbi@wananchi.com; Chargé d'affaires HESHAM ALI SHARIF.

Malawi: Nairobi; Deputy High Commissioner Brig.-Gen. MARCEL CHIRWA.

Malaysia: Block 91/404, Gigiri Grove, Gigiri, POB 42286, 00200 Nairobi; tel. (20) 7123373; fax (20) 7123371; e-mail malnairobi@kln.gov.my; High Commissioner ISMAIL SALAM.

Mexico: Kibagare Way, off Loresho Ridge, POB 14145, 00800 Nairobi; tel. (20) 4182593; fax (20) 4181500; e-mail mexico@embamex.co.ke; internet www.sre.gob.mx/kenia; Ambassador LUIS JAVIER CAMPUZANO PINA.

Morocco: UN Ave, POB 617, 00621 Nairobi; tel. (20) 7120765; fax (20) 7120817; e-mail sifmanbi@clubinternetk.com; Ambassador ABDELILAH BENRYANE.

Mozambique: Bruce House, 3rd Floor, Standard St, POB 66923, Nairobi; tel. (20) 221979; fax (20) 222446; e-mail embamoc.quenia@minec.gov.mz; High Commissioner MANUEL JOSÉ GONCALVES.

Netherlands: Riverside Lane, off Riverside Dr., POB 41537, 00100 Nairobi; tel. (20) 4288000; fax (20) 4288264; e-mail nlgovnai@africaonline.co.ke; internet kenia.nlembassy.org; Ambassador JOOST REINTJES.

Nigeria: Lenana Rd, Hurlingham, POB 30516, Nairobi; tel. (20) 3864116; fax (20) 3875871; e-mail info@nhc.org; internet www.nigeriahckenya.org; High Commissioner SOLOMON OYATERU.

Norway: 58 Red Hill Rd, Gigiri, POB POB 2472-00621, 00100 Nairobi; tel. (20) 4251000; fax (20) 4451517; e-mail emb.nairobi@mfa.no; internet www.norway.or.ke; Ambassador PER LUDVIG MAGNUS.

Pakistan: St Michel Rd, Westlands Ave, POB 30045, 00100 Nairobi; tel. (20) 4443911; fax (20) 4446507; e-mail parepnairobi@iwayafrica.com; internet www.pakhc.or.ke; High Commissioner RAFUZZAMAN SIDDIQUI.

Poland: 58 Red Hill Rd, POB 30086, 00100 Nairobi; tel. (20) 7120019; fax (20) 7120106; e-mail ambnairo@kenyaweb.com; internet www.nairobi.msz.gov.pl/en; Ambassador MAREK ZIÓŁKOWSKI.

Romania: Eliud Mathu St, Runda, POB 63240, 00619 Nairobi; tel. (20) 721214073; e-mail secretariat@romanianembassy.co.ke; Ambassador JULIA PATAKI.

Russia: Lenana Rd, POB 30049, Nairobi; tel. (20) 2728700; fax (20) 2721888; e-mail russembkenya@mail.ru; Ambassador ALEXANDER MAKARENKO.

Rwanda: International House, 12th Floor, Mama Ngina St, POB 48579, Nairobi; tel. (20) 560178; fax (20) 561932; internet kenya .embassy.gov.rw; High Commissioner YAMINA KARITANYI.

Saudi Arabia: Muthaiga Rd, POB 58297, Nairobi; tel. (20) 762781; fax (20) 760939; Ambassador GHORM SAID MALHAN.

Senegal: Nairobi; Ambassador MOMAR GUEYE.

Serbia: State House Ave, POB 30504, 00100 Nairobi; tel. (20) 2710076; fax (20) 2714126; e-mail nairobi@embassyofserbia.or.ke; internet www.embassyofserbia.or.ke; Ambassador IVAN ZIVKOVIĆ.

Slovakia: Milimani Rd, POB 30204, Nairobi; tel. (20) 2721896; fax (20) 2717291; e-mail slovakembassy@jambo.co.ke; Ambassador MICHAEL MLYNÁR.

Somalia: POB 30769, Nairobi; tel. (20) 580165; fax (20) 581683; internet www.kenya.somaligov.net; Ambassador MOHAMMED ALI NUR.

South Africa: Roshanmaer Place, Lenana Rd, POB 42441, 00100 Nairobi; tel. (20) 2827100; fax (20) 2827236; e-mail nairobi@foreign .gov.za; High Commissioner RATUBATSI SUPER MOLOI.

South Sudan: Bishops Gate, 6th Floor, 5 Ngong Ave, cnr Bishop Rd, POB 73699, 00200 Nairobi; tel. (20) 4349107; fax (20) 4349109; Ambassador MICHAEL MAJOK AYOM DOR.

Spain: CBA Bldg, Mara and Ragati Rds, Upper Hill, POB 45503, 00100 Nairobi; tel. (20) 2720222; fax (20) 2720226; e-mail emb .nairobi@maec.es; Ambassador JAVIER HERRERA GARCÍA-CANTURRI.

Sri Lanka: Lenana Rd, POB 48145, Nairobi; tel. (20) 3872627; fax (20) 3872141; e-mail slhckeny@africaonline.co.ke; High Commissioner THAMBIRAJAH RAVEENTHIRAN.

Sudan: Kabarnet Rd, off Ngong Rd, POB 48784, 00100 Nairobi; tel. (20) 3875159; fax (20) 3878187; e-mail embassy@sudanebassyke.org; internet www.sudanembassyke.org; Ambassador KAMAL ISMAIL SAEED (recalled Nov. 2011).

Sweden: United Nations Cres., Gigiri, POB 30600, 00100 Nairobi; tel. (20) 4234000; fax (20) 4234339; e-mail embassy.nairobi@gov.se; internet www.swedenabroad.com/nairobi; Ambassador JOHAN BORG-STAM.

Switzerland: General Mathenge Dr. 89, POB 2600, 00100 Nairobi; tel. (20) 2673282; fax (20) 2673535; e-mail nai.vertretung@eda .admin.ch; internet www.eda.admin.ch/nairobi; Ambassador JAC-QUES PITTELOUD.

Tanzania: Re-Insurance Plaza, 9th Floor, Taifa Rd, POB 47790, 0100 Nairobi; tel. (20) 312027; fax (20) 2218269; e-mail highcom@ tanzaniahc.or.ke; High Commissioner Dr BATILDA BURIAN.

Thailand: Rose Ave, off Denis Pritt Rd, POB 58349, 00200 Nairobi; tel. (20) 2715243; fax (20) 2715801; e-mail thainbi@thainbi.or.ke; internet www.thaiembassy.org/nairobi; Ambassador ITTIPORN BOON-PRACONG.

Turkey: 30 Gigiri Rd, off Limuru Rd, POB 64748, 00620 Nairobi; tel. and fax (20) 7126929; fax (20) 7126931; e-mail embassy.nairobi@mfa .gov.tr; internet www.nairobi.emb.mfa.gov.tr; Ambassador HUSEYIN AVNI AKSOY.

Uganda: Uganda House, 1st Floor, Kenyatta Ave, POB 60853, 00200 Nairobi; tel. (20) 4449096; fax (20) 4443772; e-mail info@ugahicom.co .ke; internet www.ugahicom.co.ke; High Commissioner ANGELINA WAPAKHABULO.

Ukraine: Limuru Rd 674, Muthaiga, POB 63566, 00619 Nairobi; tel. (20) 5224545; fax (20) 5224545; e-mail emb_ke@mfa.gov.ua; internet kenya.mfa.gov.ua/ua; Ambassador VOLODYMYR BUTYAGA.

United Kingdom: Upper Hill Rd, POB 30465, 00100 Nairobi; tel. (20) 2844000; fax (20) 2844088; e-mail nairobi.enquiries@fco.gov.uk; internet ukinkenya.fco.gov.uk; High Commissioner Dr CHRISTIAN TURNER.

USA: UN Ave, Village Market, POB 606, 00621 Nairobi; tel. (20) 3636000; fax (20) 3633410; internet nairobi.usembassy.gov; Ambassador ROBERT F. GODEC.

Venezuela: Int. House, 3rd Floor, Mama Ngina St, POB 34477, 00100 Nairobi; tel. (20) 340134; fax (20) 248105; e-mail embavene@ swiftkenya.com; Ambassador (vacant).

Yemen: cnr Ngong and Kabarnet Rds, POB 44642, Nairobi; tel. (20) 564379; fax (20) 564394; Ambassador AHMAD MAYSARI.

Zambia: Nyerere Rd, POB 48741, Nairobi; tel. (20) 7224850; fax (20) 2718494; e-mail zambiacom@swiftkenya.com; High Commissioner MARY MIDRED ZAMBEZI.

Zimbabwe: 2 Westlands Close, Westlands, POB 30806, 00100 Nairobi; tel. (20) 3744052; fax (20) 3748079; e-mail zimna@ africaonline.co.ke; Ambassador KELEBERT NKOMANI.

Judicial System

The superior courts are the Supreme Court, the Court of Appeal and the High Court.

Chief Justice: Dr WILLY MUNYWOKI MUTUNGA.

Supreme Court: Nairobi; comprises the Chief Justice, who shall be the president of the court, the Deputy Chief Justice and five other judges; has jurisdiction to hear and determine disputes relating to the elections to the office of President and appellate jurisdiction to hear and determine appeals from the Court of Appeal and any other court or tribunal as prescribed by national legislation.

Court of Appeal: POB 30187, Nairobi; comprises not fewer than 12 judges; the final court of appeal for Kenya in civil and criminal process; sits at Nairobi, Mombasa, Kisumu, Nakuru and Nyeri; Pres. PAUL KIHARA KARIUKI.

High Court: Between Taifa Rd and City Hall Way, POB 30041, Nairobi; tel. (20) 221221; e-mail hck-lib@nbnet.co.ke; has unlimited criminal and civil jurisdiction at first instance; jurisdiction to determine the question whether a right or fundamental freedom in the Bill of Rights has been denied, violated, infringed or threatened; jurisdiction to hear an appeal from a decision of a tribunal appointed under the Constitution to consider the removal of a person from office; and jurisdiction to hear any question respecting the interpretation of this Constitution; Principal Judge MSAGHA MBOGHOLI.

The subordinate courts are the Magistrates' courts, the Kadhis' courts, the Courts Martial and any other court or local tribunal as may be established by an Act of Parliament.

Resident Magistrates' Courts: have country-wide jurisdiction, with powers of punishment by imprisonment for up to five years or by fines of up to K£500. If presided over by a chief magistrate or senior resident magistrate, the court is empowered to pass any sentence authorized by law. For certain offences, a resident magistrate may pass minimum sentences authorized by law.

District Magistrates' Courts: of first, second and third class; have jurisdiction within districts and powers of punishment by imprisonment for up to five years, or by fines of up to K£500.

Kadhis' Courts: have jurisdiction within districts, to determine questions of Islamic law; comprise a Chief Kadhi and no fewer than three other Kadhis.

Religion

According to the 2009 census, Protestants, the largest religious group, represent approximately 48% of the population. Approximately 24% of the population is Roman Catholic, 11% of the population practises Islam, 0.1% practises Hinduism and the remainder follow various traditional indigenous religions or offshoots of Christian religions. There are very few atheists. Muslim groups dispute government estimates; most often they claim to represent 15% to 20% of the population, sometimes higher. Members of most religious groups are active throughout the country, although certain religions dominate particular regions. Muslims dominate North-Eastern Province, where the population is chiefly Somali. Muslims also dominate Coast Province, except for the western areas of the Province, which are predominantly Christian. Eastern Province is approximately 50% Muslim (mostly in the north) and 50% Christian (mostly in the south). The rest of the country is largely Christian. Many foreign missionary groups operate in the country, the largest of which are the African Inland Mission (Evangelical Protestant), the Southern Baptist Church, the Pentecostal Assembly of Kenya, and the Church Missionary Society of Britain (Anglican). The Government generally has permitted these missionary groups to assist the poor and to operate schools and hospitals. The missionaries openly promote their religious beliefs and have encountered little resistance.

CHRISTIANITY

National Council of Churches of Kenya: Jumuia Pl., POB 45009, 00100 Nairobi; tel. (20) 2711862; fax (20) 2724183; e-mail gsoffice@ ncck.org; internet www.ncck.org; f. 1943 as Christian Council of Kenya; 24 mem. churches and 18 Christian orgs; Chair. Rev. JOSEPH WAITHONGA; Sec.-Gen. Rev. Canon PETER KARANJA MWANGI.

The Anglican Communion

Anglicans are adherents of the Church of the Province of Kenya, which was established in 1970. It comprises 28 dioceses, and has about 2.5m. members.

Archbishop of Kenya and Bishop of Nairobi: Most Rev. Dr DAVID M. GITARI, POB 40502, Nairobi; tel. (20) 2714755; fax (20) 2718442; e-mail davidgitari@insightkenya.com.

Greek Orthodox Church

Archbishop of East Africa: NICADEMUS OF IRINOUPOULIS, Nairobi; jurisdiction covers Kenya, Tanzania and Uganda.

The Roman Catholic Church

Kenya comprises four archdioceses, 20 dioceses and one Apostolic Vicariate. Some 24% of the total population are adherents of the Roman Catholic Church.

Kenya Episcopal Conference

Kenya Catholic Secretariat, Waumini House, 4th Floor Westlands, POB 13475, Nairobi; tel. (20) 443133; fax (20) 442910; e-mail csk@users.africaonline.co.ke; internet www.catholicchurch.or.ke.

f. 1976; Pres. Cardinal JOHN NJUE (Archbishop of Nairobi); Sec.-Gen. Rev. Fr VINCENT WAMBUGU.

Archbishop of Kisumu: Most Rev. ZACCHAEUS OKOTH, POB 1728, 40100 Kisumu; tel. (57) 2020725; fax (57) 2022203; e-mail archdiocese-kisumu@africaonline.co.ke.

Archbishop of Mombasa: Most Rev. BONIFACE LELE, Catholic Secretariat, Nyerere Ave, POB 84425, Mombasa; tel. (41) 2311801; fax (41) 2228217; e-mail catholicsecretariat@msarchdiocese.org.

Archbishop of Nairobi: Cardinal JOHN NJUE, Archbishop's House, POB 14231, 00800 Nairobi; tel. (20) 241391; fax (20) 4447027; e-mail arch-nbo@wananchi.com.

Archbishop of Nyeri: Most Rev. PETER J. CAIRO, POB 288, 10100 Nyeri; tel. (61) 2030446; fax (61) 2030435; e-mail adn@wananchi.com.

Other Christian Churches

Africa Gospel Church: POB 458, Kericho 20200; tel. (52) 20123; e-mail agc@agckenya.org; internet www.agckenya.org; Admin. Sec. JOSEPH TONUI.

African Christian Church and Schools: POB 1365, Thika; e-mail accsheadoffice@yahoo.com; f. 1948; Moderator Rt Rev. JOHN NJUN-GUNA; Gen. Sec. Rev. SAMUEL MWANGI; 50,000 mems.

African Israel Nineveh Church: Nineveh HQ, POB 701, Kisumu; f. 1942; High Priest Rt Rev. JOHN KIVULI, II; Gen. Sec. Rev. JOHN ARAP TONUI; 350,000 mems.

Baptist Convention of Kenya: POB 14907, Nairobi; internet bcok.org; f. 1972; Pres. Rev. Bishop Dr JULIUS A. MBAGAYA; Gen. Sec. GIDEON MAKUTHI.

Church of God in East Africa: Pres. Rev. Dr BYRUM MAKOKHA.

Evangelical Alliance of Kenya (EAK): Valley Rd, POB 20571, 00100 Nairobi; tel. (20) 2721269; e-mail secretariat@eakenya.org; internet eakenya.org; Co-ordinator Rt Rev. Bishop Dr BONIFES ADOYO; Sec.-Gen. Rev. Dr WELLINGTON MUTISO.

Evangelical Lutheran Church in Kenya (ELCK): POB 44685, 00100 Nairobi; tel. and fax 38131231; e-mail bishopobarewa@yahoo.com; internet elckenya.com; f. 1948; Presiding Bishop Most Rev. WALTER OBARE OMWANZA; Gen. Sec. Rev. JOHN HALAKHE; 100,000 mems (2010).

Kenya African Church of the Holy Spirit: POB 183, Kakamega; internet kenyaafricanchurchoftheholyspirit.org; f. 1927; 20,000 mems.

Kenya Evangelical Lutheran Church: POB 54128, 00200 City Sq., Jogoo Rd, off Nile Rd, Nairobi; tel. and fax (20) 78-04-54; e-mail info@kelc.or.ke; internet www.kelc.or.ke; Bishop ZACHARIAH W. KAHUTHU; 44,000 mems (2010).

Methodist Church in Kenya: POB 47633, 00100 Nairobi; tel. (20) 2724828; fax (20) 2729790; e-mail mckconf@insightkenya.com; internet www.methodistchurchkenya.org; f. 1862; autonomous since 1967; Presiding Bishop Rev. Dr STEPHEN KANYARU M'IMPWII; 900,000 mems (2005).

Presbyterian Church of East Africa: Jitegemea House, Muhoho Ave, South C, POB 27573, 00506 Nairobi; tel. (20) 6008848; fax (20) 6009102; e-mail info@pcea.or.ke; internet www.pceaheadoffice.or.ke; f. 1891; Moderator Rt Rev. Dr DAVID RIITHO GATHANJU; Sec.-Gen. Rev. FESTUS KABURU GITONGA.

Other denominations active in Kenya include the African Brotherhood Church, the African Independent Pentecostal Church, Africa Inland Church in Kenya, the African Interior Church, the Episcopal Church of Kenya, the Free Pentecostal Fellowship of Kenya, the Full Gospel Churches of Kenya, the National Independent Church of Africa, the Pentecostal Assemblies of God, the Pentecostal Evangelistic Fellowship of God and the Reformed Church of East Africa.

BAHÁ'Í FAITH

National Spiritual Assembly: POB 47562, Nairobi; tel. (20) 725447; e-mail nsakenya@yahoo.com; mems resident in 9,654 localities.

ISLAM

Supreme Council of Kenyan Muslims (SUPKEM)

Islamia House, 2nd and 3rd Floors, Njugu Lane, POB 415163, Nairobi 00100; tel. and fax (20) 243109; e-mail admin@supkem.com; internet supkem.com; Nat. Chair. Prof. ABD AL-GHAFUR AL-BUSAIDY; Sec.-Gen. ADAN WACHU.

Chief Kadhi: SHEIKH AHMED MUHDHAR.

The Press

PRINCIPAL DAILIES

Business Daily: Nation Center, 2nd Floor, Kimathi St, POB 49010, 00100 Nairobi; tel. (20) 3288104; fax (20) 211130; e-mail bdfeedback@ke.nationmedia.com; internet www.businessdailyafrica.com; Editorial Dir JOSEPH ODINDO; Man. Editor OCHIENG RAPURO.

Daily Nation: Nation Centre, Kimathi St, POB 49010, 00100 Nairobi; tel. (20) 3288000; fax (20) 2337710; e-mail newsdesk@nation.co.ke; internet www.nation.co.ke; f. 1960; English; owned by Nation Media Group; Man. Editor MUTUMA MATHIU; Editorial Dir JOSEPH ODINDO; circ. 195,000.

The People: POB 10296, 00100 Nairobi; tel. (20) 2249686; fax (20) 2228503; e-mail info@people.co.ke; internet www.people.co.ke; f. 1993; Man. Editor MUGO THEURI; circ. 40,000.

The Standard: Mombasa Rd, POB 30080, 00100 Nairobi; tel. (20) 3222111; fax (20) 214467; e-mail ads@standardmedia.co.ke; internet www.standardmedia.co.ke; f. 1902 as African Standard; renamed East African Standard before adopting present name in 2004; Editor OKETCH KENDO; circ. 59,000.

The Star: Lion Place, Waiyaki Way, POB 74497-0200, Nairobi; tel. (20) 4244000; fax (20) 4447410; e-mail webmaster@the-star.co.ke; internet www.the-star.co.ke; Editor CATHERINE GICHERU.

Taifa Leo: POB 49010, Nairobi 00100; tel. (20) 3288419; e-mail taifa@ke.nationmedia.com; Kiswahili; f. 1960; daily and weekly edns; Kiswahili; owned by Nation Media Group; Man. Editor NICHOLAS MUEMA; circ. 15,000.

Kenya also has a thriving vernacular press, but titles are often short-lived.

SELECTED PERIODICALS

Weeklies and Fortnightlies

The Business Chronicle: POB 53328, Nairobi; tel. (20) 544283; fax (20) 532736; f. 1994; weekly; Man. Editor MUSYOKA KYENDO.

Coastweek: Oriental Bldg, 2nd Floor, Nkrumah Rd, POB 87270, Mombasa; tel. (41) 2230125; fax (41) 2225003; e-mail coastwk@africaonline.co.ke; internet www.coastweek.com; f. 1978; English, with German section; Friday; Editor ADRIAN GRIMWOOD; Man. Dir SHIRAZ D. ALIBHAI; circ. 54,000.

Diplomat East Africa: Vision Plaza, Ground Floor, Suite 37, Mombasa Rd, POB 23399, Nairobi; tel. (20) 2525253; e-mail editor@diplomateastafrica.com; internet www.diplomateastafrica.com.

The East African: POB 49010, 00506 Nairobi; tel. (20) 3288000; fax (20) 2213946; e-mail newsdesk@nation.co.ke; internet www.theeastafrican.co.ke; f. 1994; weekly; English; owned by Nation Media Group; Editor-in-Chief JOE ODINDO; Man. Editor MBATAU WA NGAI.

Kenya Gazette: POB 30746, Nairobi; tel. (20) 334075; internet www.kenyalaw.org/KenyaGazette; f. 1898; official notices; weekly; circ. 8,000.

Kenya Today: c/o Office of Public Communications, KICC Bldg, 3rd Floor, POB 45617, 00100 Nairobi; e-mail comms@comms.go.ke; f. 2009; govt-owned; weekly; Dir JERRY OKUNGU.

Sunday Nation: POB 49010, Nairobi; f. 1960; English; owned by Nation Media Group; Man. Editor BERNARD NDERITU; circ. 170,000.

Sunday Standard: POB 30080, Nairobi; tel. (20) 552510; fax (20) 553939; English; Man. Editor DAVID MAKALI; circ. 90,000.

Taifa Jumapili: POB 49010, Nairobi; tel. (20) 3288419; e-mail taifa@ke.nationmedia.com; f. 1987; Kiswahili; owned by Nation Media Group; Man. Editor NICHOLAS MUEMA; circ. 15,000.

Other Periodicals

African Ecclesiastical Review: POB 4002, 30100 Eldoret; tel. (53) 2061218; fax (53) 2062570; e-mail gabapubs@africaonline.co.ke;

internet www.gabapublications.org; f. 1969; scripture, religion and devt; 4 a year; Editor and Dir Sister JUSTIN C. NABUSHAWO; circ. 2,500.

Afya: POB 30125, Nairobi; tel. (20) 501301; fax (20) 506112; e-mail amrefkco@africaonline.co.ke; journal for medical and health workers; quarterly.

Azania: POB 30710, 00100 Nairobi; tel. (20) 4343190; fax (20) 4343365; f. 1966; annual (Dec.); English and French; history, archaeology, ethnography and linguistics of East African region; circ. 650.

Defender: AMREF, POB 30125, Nairobi; tel. (20) 201301; f. 1968; quarterly; English; health and fitness; Editor WILLIAM OKEDI; circ. 100,000.

Inside Kenya Today: POB 8053, Nairobi; tel. (20) 340010; fax (20) 340659; English; publ. by Ministry of Tourism; quarterly; Editor M. NDAVI; circ. 10,000.

Kenya Statistical Digest: POB 30007, Nairobi; tel. (20) 338111; fax (20) 330426; publ. by Ministry of Finance; quarterly.

Safari: Norwich Bldg, 4th Floor, Mama Ngina St, POB 30339, Nairobi; tel. (20) 2246612; fax (20) 2215127; 6 a year; English.

NEWS AGENCY

Kenya News Agency (KNA): Information House, POB 8053, Nairobi; tel. (20) 223201; internet www.kenyanewsagency.go.ke; f. 1963; Dir S. MUSANDU.

Publishers

Academy Science Publishers: POB 24916, Nairobi; tel. (20) 884401; fax (20) 884406; e-mail asp@africaonline.co.ke; f. 1989; part of the African Academy of Sciences; Editor-in-Chief Prof. KETO E. MSHIGENI.

AMECEA Gaba Publications: Amecea Pastoral Institute, POB 4002, 30100 Eldoret; tel. (53) 2061218; fax (53) 2062570; e-mail gabapubs@africaonline.co.ke; internet www.gabapublications.org; f. 1958; anthropology, religious; owned by AMECEA Bishops; Editor and Dir Sister JUSTINE C. NABUSHAWO.

Camerapix Publishers International: POB 45048, GPO 00100, Nairobi; tel. (20) 4448923; fax (20) 4448818; e-mail rukhsana@camerapix.co.ke; internet www.camerapix.com; f. 1960; travel, topography, natural history; Man. Dir RUKHSANA HAQ.

East African Educational Publishers: cnr Mpaka Rd and Woodvale Grove, Westlands, POB 45314, 00100 Nairobi; tel. (20) 4444700; fax (20) 2324761; e-mail eaep@eastafricanpublishers.com; internet www.eastafricanpublishers.com; f. 1965 as Heinemann Kenya Ltd; present name adopted 1992; academic, educational, creative writing; some books in Kenyan languages; Chair. Dr HENRY CHAKAVA; Gen. Man. KIARIE KAMAU.

Evangel Publishing House: Lumumba Drive, off Kamiti Rd, Thika Rd, Private Bag 28963, 00200 Nairobi; tel. (20) 8560839; fax (20) 8562050; e-mail info@evangelpublishing.org; internet www.evangelpublishing.org; f. 1952; Christian literature; current backlist of over 300 titles; marriage and family, leadership, Theological Education by Extension (TEE); Gen. Man. LUCY NDUTA (acting).

Jomo Kenyatta Foundation: Industrial Area, Enterprise Rd, POB 30533, 00100 Nairobi; tel. (20) 557222; fax (20) 531966; e-mail publish@jomokenyattaf.com; internet www.jkf.co.ke; f. 1966; primary, secondary, university textbooks; Man. Dir NANCY W. KARIMI.

East African Publishers Ltd: POB 45314, Nairobi; tel. (20) 2324761; fax (20) 4451532; e-mail info@eastafricanpublishers.com; internet www.eastafricanpublishers.com; f. 1964; school, university and general; Man. Dir SIMON NGIGI.

Kenya Literature Bureau: Bellevue Area, Popo Rd, off Mombasa Rd, POB 30022, 00100 Nairobi; tel. (20) 600839; fax (20) 601474; e-mail info@klb.com; f. 1947 as East African Literature Bureau; name changed as above in 1980; educational and general books; CEO E. A. OBARA.

Longman Kenya Ltd: Banda School, Magadi Rd, POB 24722, Nairobi; tel. (20) 8891220; fax (20) 8890004; e-mail bandaschool@swiftkenya.com; internet www.bandaschool.com; f. 1966.

Moran (EA) Publishers Ltd: Judda Complex, Forest Rd, POB 30797, 00100 Nairobi; tel. (20) 2013580; fax (20) 2013583; e-mail info@moranpublishers.co.ke; internet www.moranpublishers.co.ke; f. 1970; as Macmillan Kenya Publishers Ltd; renamed as above in 2010; atlases, children's educational, guide books, literature; Man. Dir DAVID MUITA.

Newspread International: POB 46854, Nairobi; tel. (20) 331402; fax (20) 607252; f. 1971; reference, economic devt; Exec. Editor KUL BHUSHAN.

Oxford University Press (Eastern Africa): Elgon Rd, Upper Hill, The Oxford Place, POB 72532, Nairobi; tel. (20) 2732047; fax (20) 2732011; e-mail enq@oxford.co.ke; internet www.oxford.co.ke;

f. 1954; children's, educational and general; Regional Man. MURIUKI NJERU.

Paulines Publications Africa: POB 49026, 00100 Nairobi; tel. (20) 447202; fax (20) 442097; e-mail publications@paulinesafrica.org; internet www.paulinesafrica.org; f. 1985; African bible, theology, children's, educational, religious, psychology, audio CDs, tapes, videos; Pres. Sister MARIA KIMANI; Dir Sister TERESA MARCAZZAN.

Storymoja Publishers: Njamba House, Shanzu Rd, off Lower Kabete Rd, Westlands, POB 264, 00606 Nairobi; tel. (20) 208959; e-mail info@storymojaafrica.co.ke; internet www.storymojaafrica.co.ke; Gen. Man. MARTIN NJAGA.

GOVERNMENT PUBLISHING HOUSE

Government Printing Press: POB 30128, Nairobi; tel. (20) 317840.

PUBLISHERS' ORGANIZATION

Kenya Publishers' Association: POB 42767, 00100 Nairobi; tel. (20) 3752344; fax (20) 3754076; internet www.kenyapublishers.org; f. 1971; organizes Nairobi International Book Fair each Sept; Chair. DAVID MUITA.

Broadcasting and Communications

TELECOMMUNICATIONS

In 2011 there were four providers of mobile telephone services in Kenya, one of which, Telkom Kenya Ltd, was also the sole provider of fixed-line services. At September 2011 there were 355,493 subscribers to fixed-line telephone services and 26,493,940 subscribers to mobile telephone services.

Airtel Kenya: Parkside Towers, Mombasa Rd, Nairobi; tel. (20) 6910000; e-mail info.africa@airtel.com; internet africa.airtel.com/kenya; f. 2004; mobile cellular telephone network provider; fmrly Celtel; name changed as above in 2010; Man. Dir SHIVAN BHARGAVA.

Essar Telecom Kenya Ltd: Brookside Grove, Muguga Green Lane, Westlands, POB 45742, 00100 Nairobi; tel. (20) 750049003; e-mail communications@yu.co.ke; internet www.yu.co.ke; f. 2008; owner of yuMobile brand; Country Man. MADHUR TANEJA.

Telkom Kenya Ltd: Telkom Plaza, Ralph Bunche Rd, POB 30301, Nairobi; tel. (20) 2221000; e-mail customercare@orange-tkl.co.ke; internet www.telkom.co.ke; f. 1999; 51% owned by France Telecom; provides both fixed-line and mobile telephone services; Chair. EDDY NJOROGE; Man. Dir MICKAËL GHOSSEIN.

Safaricom Ltd: Safaricom House, Waiyaki Way, Westlands, POB 66827, 00800 Nairobi; tel. (20) 4273272; e-mail info@safaricom.co.ke; internet www.safaricom.co.ke; f. 1999; owned by Telkom Kenya Ltd and Vodafone Airtouch (UK); operates a national mobile cellular telephone network; Chair. NICHOLAS NG'ANG'A; CEO ROBERT WILLIAM COLLYMORE.

Regulatory Authority

Communications Commission of Kenya (CCK): Waiyaki Way, POB 14448, 00800 Westlands, Nairobi; tel. (20) 4242000; fax (20) 4451866; e-mail info@cck.go.ke; internet www.cck.go.ke; f. 1999; Chair. Eng. PHILIP O. OKUNDI; Dir-Gen. CHARLES J. K. NJOROGE.

BROADCASTING

Radio

Kenya Broadcasting Corpn (KBC): Broadcasting House, Harry Thuku Rd, POB 30456, Nairobi; tel. (20) 223757; fax (20) 220675; e-mail md@kbc.co.ke; internet www.kbc.co.ke; f. 1989; state corpn responsible for radio and television services; Chair. CHARLES MUSYOKI MUOKI; Man. Dir WAITHAKA WAIHENYA.

    Radio: National service (Kiswahili); General service (English); Vernacular services (Borana, Burji, Hindustani, Kalenjin, Kikamba, Kikuyu, Kimasai, Kimeru, Kisii, Kuria, Luo, Luhya, Rendile, Somali, Suba, Teso and Turkana).

Capital FM: Lonrho House, 19th Floor, City Sq., POB 74933, Nairobi; tel. (20) 2210020; fax (20) 340621; e-mail info@capitalfm.co.ke; internet www.capitalfm.co.ke; f. 1999; commercial station broadcasting to Nairobi and environs.

Easy FM: Nation Centre, Kimathi St, POB 49010, Nairobi; tel. (20) 32088801; fax (20) 241892; e-mail info@nation.co.ke; internet www.nationmedia.com; f. 1999; commercial radio station broadcasting in English and Kiwahili; fmrly Nation FM; owned by Nation Media Group; Man. Dir IAN FERNANDES.

IQRA Broadcasting Network: Kilimani Rd, off Elgeyo Marakwet Rd, POB 21186, 00505 Nairobi; tel. (20) 3861542; fax (20) 4443978; e-mail iqrafm@swiftkenya.com; Islamic radio station broadcasting religious programmes in Nairobi; Man. Dir SHARIF HUSSEIN OMAR.

Kameme FM: Longonot Pl., Kijabe St, POB 49640, 00100 Nairobi; tel. (20) 2217963; fax (20) 2249781; e-mail info@kamemefm.com; internet www.kameme.co.ke; commercial radio station broadcasting in Kikuyu in Nairobi and its environs; Man. Dir Rose Kimotho.

Kitambo Communications Ltd: Bishop's Tower, 4th Floor, Bishop's Rd, POB 56155, Nairobi; tel. (20) 4244000; commercial radio and television station broadcasting Christian programmes in Mombasa and Nairobi; Man. Dir Dr R. Ayah.

Radio Africa Ltd (KISS FM): 2nd Floor, Lion Pl., Waiyaki Way, POB 74497, 00200 Nairobi; tel. (20) 4244000; Man. Dir Kiprono Kittony.

Radio Citizen: Communication Centre, Maalim Juma Rd, off Dennis Pritt Rd, POB 7468, Nairobi; tel. (20) 2721415; fax (20) 2724220; e-mail citizen@royalmedia.co.ke; internet radiocitizen.co.ke; commercial radio station broadcasting in Nairobi and its environs; owned by Royal Media Services Ltd; Chair. Samuel Kamau Macharia.

Sauti ya Rehema RTV Network: Gulab Lochab Bldg, Oginga Oginga St, POB 4139, Eldoret; tel. (20) 2045239; e-mail elirop2003@gmail.com; f. 1999; Christian, broadcasts in Eldoret and its environs; Man. Dir Rev. Eli Rop.

Television

Kenya Broadcasting Corpn (KBC): see Radio

Television: KBC–TV; services in Kiswahili and English; operates three channels—KBC1, KBC2 and Metro TV.

Citizen TV: Communication Centre, Maalim Juma Rd, off Dennis Pritt Rd, POB 7468, Nairobi; tel. (20) 2721415; fax (20) 2724220; e-mail citizen@royalmedia.co.ke; internet www.citizentv.co.ke; f. 1999, relaunced 2006; commercial station broadcasting in Nairobi and its environs; Chair. Samuel Kamau Macharia.

Family Media: Dik Dik Gardens, off Gatundu Rd, Kileleshwa, POB 2330, Nairobi; tel. (20) 4200000; fax (20) 4200100; e-mail info@familykenya.com; internet www.familykenya.com; f. 1999; Gen. Man. Paul Coogan.

Kenya Television Network (KTN–TV): Nyayo House, 22nd Floor, POB 56985, Nairobi; tel. (20) 3222111; fax (20) 215400; e-mail news@ktnkenya.com; internet www.ktnkenya.tv; f. 1990; commercial station operating in Nairobi and Mombasa; Man. Dir D. J. Davies.

NTV: POB 49010, Nairobi; e-mail ntv@nation.co.ke; internet www.nationmedia.com/ntv; f. 1999 as Nation TV; commercial station; owned by Nation Media Group; Man. Dir Ian Fernandes.

Stellagraphics TV (STV): NSSF Bldg, 22nd Floor, POB 42271, Nairobi; tel. (20) 218043; fax (20) 222555; f. 1998; commercial station broadcasting in Nairobi; Gen. Man. Kanja Waruru.

Finance

(cap. = capital; res = reserves; dep. = deposits; m. = million; brs = branches; amounts in Kenya shillings)

BANKING

At the end of 2010 there were 43 licensed commercial banks and one mortgage finance company operating in Kenya, of which 31 were locally owned and 13 were foreign owned.

Central Bank

Central Bank of Kenya (Banki Kuu Ya Kenya): City Sq., Haile Selassie Ave, POB 60000, 00200 Nairobi; tel. (20) 22863000; fax (20) 2250783; e-mail info@centralbank.go.ke; internet www.centralbank.go.ke; f. 1966; bank of issue; cap. 5,000m., res 34,005m., dep. 125,637m. (June 2009); Gov. Prof. Njuguna Ndung'u.

Commercial Banks

African Banking Corpn Ltd: ABC-Bank House, Mezzanine Floor, Koinange St, POB 46452, Nairobi; tel. (20) 2223922; fax (20) 2222437; e-mail headoffice@abcthebank.com; internet www.abcthebank.com; f. 1984 as Consolidated Finance Co; converted to commercial bank and adopted present name 1995; cap. 525.0m., res 5.5m., dep. 7,505.3m. (Dec. 2009); Chair. Ashraf Savani; CEO Shamaz Savani; 7 brs.

Bank of Africa—Kenya: Re-Insurance Plaza, Taifa Rd, POB 69562, 00400 Nairobi; tel. (20) 3275000; fax (20) 2214166; e-mail bkofkenya@boakenya.com; internet www.boakenya.com; f. 2004; cap. 2,000.0m., res 364.3m., dep. 20,829.1m. (Dec. 2009); Chair. Paul Derreumaux; Man. Dir Kwame Ahadzi.

Barclays Bank of Kenya Ltd: West End Bldg, Level 6, POB 30120, 00100 Nairobi; tel. (20) 4254000; fax (20) 2213915; e-mail barclays.kenya@barclays.com; internet www.barclays.com/africa/kenya; f. 1916; cap. 2,716m., res 4,612m., dep. 131,654m. (Dec. 2009); Chair. Francis Okomo-Okello; Man. Dir Jeremy Awori; 119 brs.

CFC Stanbic Bank Ltd: CFC Centre, Chiromo Rd, Westlands, POB 30550, 00100 Nairobi; tel. (20) 3268000; fax (20) 3752905; e-mail customercare@stanbic.com; internet www.cfcstanbicbank.co.ke; formed by merger of CFC Bank Ltd and Stanbic Bank Kenya Ltd in June 2008; 100% owned by CFC Stanbic Holdings Ltd; cap. 2,441.3m., res 1,177.8m., dep. 82,799.7m. (Dec. 2009); Man. Dir Greg Brackenridge.

Chase Bank (Kenya) Ltd: Riverside Mews, Ring Rd Riverside and Riverside Westlane, POB 66015, 00800 Nairobi; tel. (20) 2774000; fax (20) 4454816; e-mail info@chasebank.co.ke; internet www.chasebankkenya.co.ke; cap. 1,000.0m., res 85.4m., dep. 10,863.7m. (Dec. 2009); Chair. Osman Murgian; Man. Dir and Pres. Mohamed Zafrullah Khan.

Commercial Bank of Africa Ltd: Commercial Bank Bldg, Upper Hill, cnr Mara and Ragati Rds, POB 30437, Nairobi; tel. (20) 2884000; fax (20) 335827; e-mail cba@cba.co.ke; internet www.cba.co.ke; f. 1962; owned by Kenyan shareholders; cap. 4,515.4m., res 2,334.9m., dep. 57,492.7m. (Dec. 2009); Chair. Mirabeau H. da Gama-Rose; Pres. and Man. Dir Isaac O. Awuondo; 12 brs.

Consolidated Bank of Kenya Ltd: Consolidated Bank House, Koinange St, POB 51133, 00200 Nairobi; tel. (20) 340551; fax (20) 340213; e-mail headoffice@consolidated-bank.com; internet www.consolidated-bank.com; f. 1989; state-owned; cap. 1,119.5m., res 186.8m., dep. 5,678.3m. (Dec. 2009); Chair. Eunice W. Kagane; Man. Dir David Ndegwa Wachira.

Dubai Bank Kenya Ltd: ICEA Bldg, Kenyatta Ave, POB 11129-00400, Nairobi; tel. (20) 311109; fax (20) 2245242; e-mail info@dubaibank.co.ke; internet www.dubaibank.co.ke; 20% owned by World of Marble and Granite, Dubai (United Arab Emirates), 22.4% owned by Abdul Hassan Ahmed, 16% owned by Hassan Bin Hassan Trading Co LLC, Dubai (United Arab Emirates), 17.6% owned by Ahmed Mohamed; cap. 411.4m., res 12.0m., dep. 986.2m. (Dec. 2009); Chair. Hassan Ahmed Zubeidi; Man. Dir Mayank Sharma.

Ecobank Kenya Ltd: Ecobank Towers, 5th Floor, Muindi Mbingu St, POB 49584, 00100 Nairobi; tel. (20) 22883000; fax (20) 22883304; e-mail eke-fedhamgr@ecobank.com; internet www.ecobank.com; f. 1972 as Akiba Bank Ltd, present name adopted 2008; cap. 2,519.3m., res 161.7m., dep. 11,308.5m. (Dec. 2009); Chair. N. P. G. Warren; Man. Dir Tony Okpanachi; 3 brs.

Equatorial Commercial Bank Ltd: Waiyaki Way, POB 52467, Nairobi; tel. (20) 4981000; fax (20) 2719625; e-mail ecbcustomerservice@ecb.co.ke; internet www.equatorialbank.co.ke; f. 1983; cap. 600m., res 41.1m., dep. 3,702.0m. (Dec. 2009); Chair. Dan Ameyo; Man. Dir Peter Harris.

Equity Bank: 14th Floor, NHIF Bldg, Ragati Rd, POB 75104, 00200 Nairobi; tel. (20) 2262000; fax (20) 2737276; e-mail info@equitybank.co.ke; internet www.equitybank.co.ke; f. 1984; Chair. Peter Munga; CEO James Mwangi.

Family Bank: Fourways Tower, Muindi Mbingu St, POB 74145, 00200 Nairobi; tel. (20) 318173; fax (20) 318174; e-mail info@familybank.co.ke; internet www.familybank.co.ke; f. 1984; Chair. Titus K. Muya; CEO Peter Munyiri.

Fidelity Commercial Bank Ltd: IPS Bldg, 7th Floor, Kimathi St, POB 34886, Nairobi; tel. (20) 2242348; fax (20) 2243389; e-mail customerservice@fidelitybankkenya.com; internet www.fidelitybank.co.ke; f. 1993 as Fidelity Finance; present name adopted 1996; cap. 323.5m., res 101.9m., dep. 3,820.1m. (Dec. 2008); Exec. Dir Sultan Khimji; Man. Dir Rana Sengupta.

Fina Bank Ltd: Fina House, Kimathi St, POB 20613, 00200 Nairobi; tel. (20) 2246943; fax (20) 2247164; e-mail banking@finabank.com; internet www.finabank.com; f. 1986 as The Finance Institute of Africa Ltd; converted to commercial bank as above in 1996; cap. 528.3m., res 239.8m., dep. 15,932.4m. (Dec. 2009); Chair. Dhanji Hansraj Chandaria; Man. Dir Tim Marshall.

Giro Commercial Bank Ltd: POB 46739, Giro House, Kimathi St, 00100 Nairobi; tel. (20) 22217776; fax (20) 22230600; e-mail info@girobankltd.com; f. 1992 as Giro Bank Ltd; name changed as above in 1999 after merging with Commerce Bank Ltd; 21.76% owned by Blandford Investments Ltd, Nairobi; cap. 309.5m., res 218.0m., dep. 4,959.3m. (Dec. 2007); Chair. Chandan Jethanand Gidoomal; Man. Dir T. K. Krishnan.

Gulf African Bank (GAB): Geminia Insurance Plaza, Kilimanjaro Ave, Upper Hill, POB 43683, Nairobi; tel. (20) 2740000; fax (20) 2729031; e-mail info@gulfafricanbank.com; internet www.gulfafricanbank.com; f. 2007; 20% owned by Bank Muscat International (BMI), 10% owned by the International Finance Corpn (IFC); cap. 250m., res 1,547m., dep. 6,425m. (Dec. 2009); Chair. Suleiman Said Shahbal; CEO Najmul Hassan.

Imperial Bank Ltd: Bunyala Rd, Upper Hill, POB 44905, 00100 Nairobi; tel. (20) 22719612; fax (20) 22719498; e-mail info@imperialbank.co.ke; internet www.imperialbank.co.ke; f. 1992 as Imperial Finance and Securities Company; converted to a bank and name changed as above in 1995; 100% owned by Kenyan shareholders; cap. 1,085.0m., res 205.2m., dep. 12,862.2m. (Dec. 2009); Chair. ALNASHIR POPAT; Man. Dir ABDULMALEK JANMOHAMED.

Kenya Commercial Bank Ltd: Kencom House, Moi Ave, POB 48400, 00100 Nairobi; tel. (20) 3270000; fax (20) 2216405; e-mail kcbhq@kcb.co.ke; internet www.kcb.co.ke; f. 1970; 23.1% state-owned; cap. 2,217.8m., res 18,368.3m., dep. 169,212.9m. (Dec. 2009); Chair. PETER W. MUTHOKA; Man. Dir JOSHUA NYAMWEYA OIGARA; 123 brs and sub-brs.

Middle East Bank Kenya Ltd: Mebank Tower, Milimani Rd, POB 47387, 00100 Nairobi; tel. (20) 2723120; fax (20) 343776; e-mail ho@mebkenya.com; internet www.mebkenya.com; f. 1981; 25% owned by Banque Belgolaise SA (Belgium), 75% owned by Kenyan shareholders; cap. 506.8m., res 31.0m., dep. 2,199.4m. (Dec. 2009); Chair. A. A. K. ESMAIL; Man. Dir PHILIP B. ILAKO; 2 brs.

National Bank of Kenya Ltd (Banki ya Taifa La Kenya Ltd): National Bank Bldg, Harambee Ave, POB 72866, Nairobi; tel. (20) 2226471; fax (20) 311444; e-mail info@nationalbank.co.ke; internet www.nationalbank.co.ke; f. 1968; 42% owned by National Social Security Fund, 22.5% state-owned; cap. 6,675.0m., res 906.9m., dep. 34,347.0m. (Dec. 2008); Chair. M. E. G. MUHINDI; Man. Dir REUBEN M. MARAMBII; 23 brs.

Oriental Commercial Bank Ltd: POB 14357, Apollo Centre, Ring Rd, 00800 Nairobi; tel. (20) 3743289; fax (20) 3743270; e-mail info@orientalbank.co.ke; internet www.orientalbank.co.ke; f. 1991; name changed as above in 2003; cap. 1,643.8m., res 10.4m., dep. 822.9m. (Dec. 2007); Chair. SHANTI SHAH; Man. Dir and CEO R. B. SINGH; 4 brs.

Paramount Universal Bank Ltd: Sound Plaza, 4th Floor, Woodvale Grove, Westlands, POB 14001, 00800 Nairobi; tel. (20) 44492668; fax (20) 4449265; e-mail info@paramountbank.co.ke; internet www.paramountbank.co.ke; f. 1993 as Combined Finance Ltd; name changed as above in 2000; 25% owned by Tormount Holdings Ltd, St Helier, 25% owned by Anwarali Merali, 25% owned by Tasneem Padamshi; Chair. ANWARALI MERALI; Man. Dir AYAZ MERALI.

Standard Chartered Bank Kenya Ltd: Stanbank House, Moi Ave, POB 30003, Nairobi; tel. (20) 32093000; fax (20) 2214086; e-mail mds.office@ke.standardchartered.com; internet www.standardchartered.com/ke; f. 1987; 74.5% owned by Standard Chartered Holdings (Africa) BV (Netherlands); cap. 1,639.8m., res 4,191.7m., dep. 67,750.5m. (Dec. 2006); Chair. HARRINGTON AWORI; CEO RICHARD M. ETEMESI; 29 brs.

Trans-National Bank Ltd: Transnational Plaza, 2nd Floor, Mama Ngina St, POB 34353, 00100 Nairobi; tel. (20) 2224235; fax (20) 339227; e-mail info@tnbl.co.ke; internet www.tnbl.co.ke; f. 1985; cap. 583.7m., res 19.5m., dep. 1,907.1m. (Dec. 2008); Chair. MICHAEL CHERWON; CEO DHIRENDRA RANA; 9 brs.

Merchant Banks

Diamond Trust Bank Ltd: Nation Centre, 8th Floor, Kimathi St, POB 61711, 00200 Nairobi; tel. (20) 2849000; fax (20) 2245495; e-mail info@dtbkenya.co.ke; internet www.dtbafrica.com; f. 1945; cap. 652.1m., res 2,670.8m., dep. 45,853.3m. (Dec. 2008); Chair. MAHMOOD MANJI; Man. Dir NASIM MOHAMED DEVJI.

National Industrial Credit Bank Ltd (NIC): NIC House, Masaba Rd, POB 44599, 00100 Nairobi; tel. (20) 718200; fax (20) 718232; e-mail info@nic-bank.com; internet www.nic-bank.com; Chair. J. P. M. NDEGWA; Man. Dir JAMES MACHARIA.

Co-operative Bank

Co-operative Bank of Kenya Ltd: Co-operative Bank House, Haile Selassie Ave, POB 48231, Nairobi; tel. (20) 3276100; fax (20) 2219831; e-mail md@co-opbank.co.ke; internet www.co-opbank.co.ke; f. 1968; cap. 2,856.5m., res 1,596.9m., dep. 56,198.0m., total assets 65,708.9m. (Dec. 2007); Chair. STANLEY C. MUCHIRI; Man. Dir GIDEON MURIUKI; 29 brs.

Development Banks

Development Bank of Kenya Ltd: Finance House, 16th Floor, Loita St, POB 30483, 00100 Nairobi; tel. (20) 340426; fax (20) 2250399; e-mail dbk@devbank.com; internet www.devbank.com; f. 1963 as Development Finance Co of Kenya; current name adopted 1996; owned by Industrial and Commercial Devt Corpn (89.3%), the Commonwealth Development Corpn (10.7%); cap. 347.5m., res 884.7m., dep. 3,774.0m. (Dec. 2008); Chair. Prof. HAROUN NGENY KIPKEMBOI MENGECH; CEO VICTOR J. O. KIDIWA.

East African Development Bank: Rahimtulla Tower, 2nd Floor, Upper Hill Rd, POB 47685, Nairobi; tel. (20) 340642; fax (20) 2731590; e-mail cok@eadb.org; internet www.eadb.org; Dirs J. KINYUA, F. KARUIRU.

IDB Capital Ltd: National Bank Bldg, 18th Floor, Harambee Ave, POB 44036, Nairobi; tel. (20) 247142; fax (20) 334594; e-mail idbkenya@swiftkenya.com; internet www.idbkenya.com; f. 1973 as

Industrial Development Bank Ltd; adopted present name in 2005; 49% state-owned; cap. 272m., res 83m., dep. 190m. (Dec. 2002); Chair. DAVID LANGAT; Man. Dir JAMES B. OCHAMI.

STOCK EXCHANGE

Nairobi Securities Exchange (NSE): Nation Centre, 1st Floor, Kimathi St, POB 43633, 00100 Nairobi; tel. (20) 2831000; fax (20) 2224200; e-mail info@nse.co.ke; internet www.nse.co.ke; f. 1954; Chair. EDWARD NJOROGE; CEO PETER MWANGI.

INSURANCE

In 2009 there were 52 insurance companies operating in Kenya

Insurance Regulatory Authority: Zep-Re Place, off Mara Road, Upper Hill, POB 43505, 00100 Nairobi; tel. 20-4996000; fax (20) 2710126; internet www.ira.go.ke; f. 2006; Chair. STEVE O. MAINDA; CEO SAMMY MUTUA MAKOVE.

Africa Merchant Assurance Co Ltd: Transnational Plaza, 2nd Floor, Mama Ngina St, POB 61599, 00200 Nairobi; tel. (20) 312121; fax (20) 340022; e-mail marketing@amaco.co.ke; internet www.amaco.co.ke; f. 2000; Gen. Man. KENNEDY ABINCHA.

APA Insurance Ltd: Ring Rd Parklands, Westlands, POB 30065, 00100 Nairobi; tel. (20) 2862000; e-mail info@apainsurance.org; internet www.apainsurance.org; f. 2003; Chair. JOHN P. N. SIMBA; Man. Dir ASHOK K. M. SHAH.

Apollo Life Assurance Ltd: Apollo Centre, 3rd Floor, Vale Close, off Ring Rd, Westlands, POB 30389, 00100 Nairobi; tel. (20) 223562; fax (20) 339260; e-mail insurance@apollo.co.ke; internet www.apollo.co.ke; f. 1977; life and general; Chair. BUDHICHAND M. SHAH; CEO PIYUSH SHAH.

Blue Shield Insurance Co Ltd: Blue Shield Towers, Upper Hill, Hospital Rd, off Mara Rd, POB 49610, 00100 Nairobi; tel. (20) 2712600; fax (20) 2712625; e-mail info@blueshield.co.ke; internet www.blueshield.co.ke; f. 1983; life and general; Chair. BETH MUIGAI; Man. Dir KULOVA WANJALA.

British-American Insurance Co: Mara and Ragati Rds Junction, Upper Hill, POB 30375, 00100 Nairobi; tel. (20) 2710927; e-mail insurance@british-american.co.ke; internet www.british-american.co.ke; f. 1965; Man. Dir STEPHEN WANDERA.

Cannon Assurance (Kenya) Ltd: Gateway Business Park, Mombasa Rd, Block D, POB 30216, Nairobi; tel. (20) 3966000; fax (20) 829075; e-mail info@cannonassurance.com; internet www.cannonassurance.com; f. 1964; life and general; Man. Dir MAINA MUKOMA.

CfC Life Assurance Co Ltd: CfC House, Mamlaka Rd, POB 30364, 00100 Nairobi; tel. (20) 2866000; fax (20) 2718365; e-mail cfclife@cfclife.co.ke; internet www.cfclife-kenya.com; f. 1964; life and general; Man. Dir ABEL MUNDA.

Chartis Kenya Insurance Co Ltd: Eden Sq. Complex, Chiromo Rd, POB 49460, 00100 Nairobi; tel. (20) 3676000; fax (20) 3676001; e-mail chartiskenya@chartisinsurance.com; internet www.chartisinsurance.com; Man. Dir JAPH OLENDE.

The Co-operative Insurance Co of Kenya Ltd: Mara Rd, Upper Hill, POB 59485, 00200 Nairobi; tel. (20) 2823000; fax (20) 2823333; e-mail cic@cic.co.ke; internet www.cic.co.ke; Chair. JAPHETH ANAVILA MAGOMERE; Man. Dir NELSON C. KURIA.

East Africa Reinsurance Co Ltd: EARe House, 98 Riverside Dr., POB 20196, 00200 Nairobi; tel. (20) 4443588; fax (20) 4455391; e-mail info@eastafricare.com; internet www.eastafricare.com; Chair. J. P. M. NDEGWA; Man. Dir HAROON MOTARA.

Fidelity Shield Insurance Ltd: 4th Floor, Rank Xerox House, Parklands Rd, Westlands, POB 47435, 00100 Nairobi; tel. (20) 4443063; fax (20) 4445699; e-mail info@fidelityshield.com; internet www.fidelityshield.com; Man. Dir SHEHNAZ SUMAR.

First Assurance Co Ltd: Gitanga Rd, Lavington, POB 30064, 00100, Nairobi; tel. (20) 3867374; fax (20) 3872204; f. 1979 as Prudential Assurance Co. of Kenya Ltd; present name adopted 1991; life and general; Chair. M. H. DA GAMA ROSE; Man. Dir STEPHEN GITHIGA.

GA Insurance Ltd: GA Insurance House, 4th Floor, Ralph Bunche Rd, POB 42166, 00100 Nairobi; tel. (20) 2711633; fax (20) 2714542; e-mail insure@gakenya.com; internet www.gakenya.com; general; Chair. SURESH B. R. SHAH; CEO VIJAY SRIVASTAVA.

Heritage Insurance Co Ltd: CFC House, Mamlaka Rd, POB 30390, 00100 Nairobi; tel. (20) 2783000; fax (20) 2727800; e-mail info@heriaii.com; internet www.heritageinsurance.co.ke; f. 1976; general; Chair. J. G. KIEREINI; Man. Dir JOHN H. D. MILNE.

Jubilee Insurance Co Ltd: Jubilee Insurance House, 5th Floor, Wabera St, POB 30376, 00100 Nairobi; tel. (20) 3281000; fax (20) 3281150; e-mail jic@jubileekenya.com; internet www.jubileeafrica.com; f. 1937; long term (life and pensions) and short term (general and medical) insurance; Chair. NIZAR JUMA; Gen. Man. PATRICK TUMBO NYAMEMBA.

Kenindia Assurance Co Ltd: Kenindia House, 11th Floor, Loita St, POB 40512, Nairobi; tel. (20) 316099; fax (20) 218380; e-mail kenindia@kenindia.com; internet www.kenindia.com; f. 1978; life and general; Chair. M. N. MEHTA; Man. Dir M. N. SARMA.

Kenya Reinsurance Corpn Ltd (KenyaRe): Reinsurance Plaza, Taifa Rd, POB 30271, Nairobi; tel. (20) 2240188; fax (20) 2252106; e-mail kenyare@kenyare.co.ke; internet www.kenyare.co.ke; f. 1970; Chair. NELIUS KARIUKI; Man. Dir JADIAH MWARANIA.

Madison Insurance Co Kenya Ltd: Upper Hill Rd, POB 47382, 00100 Nairobi; tel. (20) 2721970; e-mail madison@madison.co.ke; internet www.madison.co.ke; life and general; Chair. SAMUEL G. NGARUIYA; Man. Dir F. MUCHIRI; 14 brs.

Mercantile Insurance Co Ltd: Fedha Towers, 16th Floor, Muindi Mbingu St, Nairobi; tel. (20) 2219486; fax (20) 215528; e-mail mercantile@mercantile.co.ke; internet www.mercantile.co.ke; Chair. N. P. G. WARREN; Man. Dir SUPRIYO SEN.

Monarch Insurance Co Ltd: Prudential Assurance Bldg, 4th Floor, Wabera St, POB 44003, Nairobi; tel. (20) 310032; fax (20) 340691; e-mail info@themonarchinsco.com; internet www .themonarchinsco.com; f. 1975; life and general; Man. Dir CHARLES MAKONE.

Pan Africa Life Assurance Ltd: Pan Africa House, Kenyatta Ave, POB 44041, 00100 Nairobi; tel. (20) 247600; fax (20) 217675; e-mail insure@pan-africa.com; internet www.panafrica.co.ke; f. 1946; life and general; Chair. JOHN SIMBA; CEO TOM GITOGO.

Phoenix of East Africa Assurance Co Ltd: Ambank House, 17th and 18th Floors, University Way, POB 30129, 00100 Nairobi; tel. (20) 2251350; fax (20) 2211848; e-mail general@phoenix.co.ke; general; Gen. Man. KAUSHAL KUMAR.

PTA Reinsurance Co (ZEP-RE): Zep-Re Pl., Longonot Rd, Upper Hill, POB 42769, Nairobi; tel. (20) 212792; fax (20) 224102; e-mail mail@zep-re.com; internet www.zep-re.com; f. 1992; Chair. MICHAEL GONDWE; Man. Dir RAJNI VARIA.

REAL Insurance Co: Royal Ngao House, Hospital Rd, POB 40001, 00100 Nairobi; e-mail general@realinsurance.co.ke; tel. (20) 717888; fax (20) 712620; internet www.realinsurance.co.ke; f. 1979; general; Chair. S. K. KAMAU; CEO JOSEPH W. KIUNA.

Standard Assurance (Kenya) Ltd: POB 42996, Nairobi; tel. (20) 224721; fax (20) 224862; Man. Dir WILSON K. KAPKOTI.

UAP Provincial Insurance Co of East Africa Ltd: Bishop Garden Towers, Bishops Rd, POB 43013, 00100 Nairobi; tel. (20) 850000; fax (20) 719030; e-mail uapinsurance@uapkenya.com; f. 1980; general; Chair. FRANCIS OGUTU; CEO JAMES WAMBUGU.

Insurance Association

Association of Kenya Insurers (AKI): Victoria Towers, 3rd Floor, Kilimanjaro Ave, Upper Hill, POB 45338, 00100 Nairobi; tel. (20) 2731330; fax (20) 2731339; e-mail info@akinsure.com; internet www .akinsure.or.ke; Chair. STEPHEN WANDERA.

Trade and Industry

GOVERNMENT AGENCIES

Export Processing Zones Authority: Administration Bldg, Viwanda Rd, Athi River Export Processing Zone, off Nairobi-Namanga Highway, Athi River, POB 50563, Nairobi; tel. (45) 26421; fax (45) 26427; e-mail info@epzakenya.com; internet www .epzakenya.com; established by the Govt to promote investment in Export Processing Zones; Chief Exec. J. O. B. AKARA.

Export Promotion Council: Anniversary Towers, 1st and 16th Floors, University Way, POB 40247, Nairobi; tel. (20) 228534; fax (20) 218013; e-mail chiefexe@epc.or.ke; internet www.epckenya.org; f. 1992; Chair. Prof. PETER NJERU NDWIGA; CEO RUTH MWANIKI.

Kenya Investment Authority: Railways HQ, Block D, 3rd Floor, Workshops Rd, POB 55704, 00200 Nairobi; tel. (20) 2221401; fax (20) 2243862; e-mail info@investmentkenya.com; internet www .investmentkenya.com; f. 1986; promotes and facilitates local and foreign investment; Man. Dir SUSAN KIKWAI.

Kenya National Trading Corpn Ltd: Yarrow Rd, off Nanyuki Rd, POB 30587, Nairobi; tel. (20) 2430861; fax (20) 556331; e-mail customercare@kntcl.com; internet www.kntcl.com; f. 1965; promotes wholesale and retail trade; Chair. MOHAMMED HASSAN; Man. Dir GLADYS MAINA.

DEVELOPMENT ORGANIZATIONS

Agricultural Development Corpn: Development House, 10th Floor, POB 47101, Nairobi; tel. (20) 250695; fax (20) 243571; e-mail info@adc.co.ke; internet www.adc.co.ke; f. 1965 to promote agricultural devt and reconstruction; Chair. L. W. WARUINGI; CEO WILLIAM K. KIRWA.

Agricultural Finance Corpn: POB 30367, Nairobi; tel. (20) 317199; fax (20) 219390; e-mail info@agrifinance.org; internet www.agrifinance.org; a statutory organization providing agricultural loans; Man. Dir OMUREMBE IYADI.

Horticultural Crops Development Authority: POB 42601, Nairobi; tel. (20) 8272601; fax (20) 827264; e-mail md@hcda.or.ke; internet www.hcda.or.ke; f. 1968; invests in production, dehydration, processing and freezing of fruit and vegetables; exports of fresh fruit and vegetables; Chair. JOSEPH G. KIBE; Man. Dir ALFRED SEREM.

Housing Finance Co of Kenya Ltd: Rehani House, cnr Kenyatta Ave and Koinange St, POB 30088, 00100 Nairobi; tel. (20) 317474; fax (20) 340299; e-mail housing@housing.co.ke; internet www.housing .co.ke; f. 1965; Chair. STEVE MAINDA; Man. Dir FRANK M. IRERI.

Industrial and Commercial Development Corpn: Uchumi House, 17th Floor, Aga Khan Walk, POB 45519, Nairobi; tel. (20) 2229213; fax (20) 317456; e-mail info@icdc.co.ke; internet www.icdc .co.ke; f. 1954; govt-financed; assists industrial and commercial devt; Chair. MARTIN KARIUKI MURAGU; Exec. Dir PETER KIMURWA.

Kenya Industrial Estates Ltd: Nairobi Industrial Estate, Likoni Rd, POB 78029, Nairobi; tel. (20) 651348; fax (20) 651355; e-mail admin@kie.co.ke; internet www.kie.co.ke; f. 1967 to finance and develop small-scale industries; Chair. AHMED MOHAMMED; Man. Dir JULIUS OBARE MOKOGI.

Kenya Industrial Research and Development Institute: POB 30650, Nairobi; tel. (20) 6003842; fax (20) 6007023; e-mail kirdi .go.ke; internet www.kirdi.go.ke; f. 1942; reorg. 1979; restructured 1995; research and devt in industrial and allied technologies including engineering, agro-industrial, mining and environmental technologies; Chair. Eng. Dr SIPHILA MUMENYA; Dir Dr CHARLES M. Z. MOTURI.

Kenya Tea Development Agency: Moi Ave, POB 30213, Nairobi; tel. and fax (20) 3227000; e-mail info@ktdateas.com; internet www .ktdateas.com; f. 1964 as Kenya Tea Development Authority to develop tea growing, manufacturing and marketing among African smallholders; operates 65 tea factories and six subsidiaries; privatized in 2000; Chair. PETER KANYAGO; CEO LERIONKA TIAMPATI.

CHAMBER OF COMMERCE

Kenya National Chamber of Commerce and Industry: Ufanisi House, Haile Selassie Ave, POB 47024, Nairobi; tel. (20) 220867; fax (20) 334293; internet www.kncci.org; f. 1965; 69 brs; Nat. Chair. DAVID M. GITHERE; Chief Exec. TITUS G. RUHIU.

INDUSTRIAL AND TRADE ASSOCIATIONS

Coffee Board of Kenya: Coffee Plaza, 10th Floor, Exchange Lane, off Haile Selassie Ave, POB 30566, Nairobi; tel. and fax (20) 315754; fax (20) 311079; e-mail info@coffeeboard.co.ke; internet www .coffeeboard.co.ke; f. 1947; Chair. RICHARD MORRIS GITONGA; Man. Dir LOISE W. NJERU.

East African Tea Trade Association (EATTA): Tea Trade Centre, Nyerere Ave, POB 85174, 80100 Mombasa; tel. (41) 2220093; fax (41) 2225823; e-mail info@eatta.co.ke; internet www .eatta.com; f. 1957; organizes Mombasa weekly tea auctions; Chair. PETER KIMANGA; Man. Dir EDWARD MUDIBO; 178 mems in 9 countries.

Fresh Produce Exporters' Association of Kenya (FPEAK): New Rehema House, 4th Floor, Rhapta Rd, Westlands, POB 40312, 00100 Nairobi; tel. (20) 4451488; fax (20) 445189; e-mail info@fpeak.org; internet www.fpeak.org; Chair. RICHARD COLLINS; CEO Dr STEPHEN MBITHI MWIKYA.

Kenya Association of Manufacturers (KAM): Mwanzi Rd, off Peponi Rd, Westlands, POB 30225, Nairobi; tel. (20) 3746005; fax (20) 3746028; e-mail kam@users.africaonline.co.ke; internet www.kam .co.ke; Chair. JASWINDER BEDI; Exec. Sec. LUCY MICHENI; 200 mems.

Kenya Dairy Board: NSSF Bldg, 10th and 11th Floors, Bishops Rd, POB 30406, Nairobi; tel. (20) 310559; fax (20) 244064; e-mail info@ kdb.co.ke; internet www.kdb.co.ke; f. 1958; Chair. MARTHA MULWA; Man. Dir MACHIRA GICHOHI.

Kenya Fish Processors' and Exporters' Association: 5th Floor, New Rehema House, Raphta Rd, Westlands, POB 345, 00606 Nairobi; tel. and fax (20) 4440858; e-mail info@afipek.org; internet www.afipek.org; f. 2000; Chair. NADIR JESSA; CEO BETH WAGUDE.

Kenya Flower Council: Muthangari Gardens, off Gitanga Rd, POB 56325, 00200 Nairobi; tel. and fax (20) 3876597; e-mail info@ kenyaflowercouncil.org; internet www.kenyaflowercouncil.org; regulates production of cut flowers; CEO JANE NGIGE.

Kenya Meat Commission: POB 30414, Nairobi; tel. (45) 6626041; fax (45) 6626520; e-mail info@kenyameat.co.ke; internet www .kenyameat.co.ke; state-owned; f. 1953; purchasing, processing and marketing of beef livestock; Man. Commr ALI HASSAN MOHAMMED.

Kenya Planters' Co-operative Union Ltd: Nairobi; e-mail gm@ kpcu.co.ke; coffee processing and marketing; Chair. J. M. MACHARIA; Gen. Man. RUTH MWANIKI.

Kenya Sisal Board: Mutual Bldg, Kimathi St, POB 41179, Nairobi; tel. (20) 248919; fax (20) 240091; e-mail kensisal@sisalboardkenya .go.ke; internet www.sisalboardkenya.go.ke; f. 1946; Man. Dir CHARLES K. KAGWIMI.

Kenya Sugar Board: Sukari Plaza, off Waiyaki Way, POB 51500, Nairobi; tel. (20) 2023316; fax (20) 593273; e-mail info@kenyasugar .co.ke; internet www.kenyasugar.co.ke; f. 2002 to succeed the Kenya Sugar Authority; Chair. OKOTH OBADO; CEO ROSEMARY MKOK.

Mild Coffee Trade Association of Eastern Africa (MCTA): Nairobi; Chair. F. J. MWANGI.

National Cereals and Produce Board (NCPB): POB 30586, Nairobi; tel. (20) 536028; fax (20) 557622; e-mail info@ncpb.co.ke; internet www.ncpb.co.ke; f. 1985; grain marketing and handling, provides drying, weighing, storage and fumigation services to farmers and traders, stores and manages strategic national food reserves, distributes famine relief; Chair. Prof. WILFRED MWANGI; Man. Dir Prof. GIDEON MISOI.

Pyrethrum Board of Kenya (PBK): POB 420, Nakuru; tel. (51) 2211567; fax (51) 2210466; e-mail pbk@pyrethrum.co.ke; internet www.kenya-pyrethrum.com; f. 1935; 14 mems; Chair. SOLOMON BOIT; Man. Dir ISAAC MULAGOLI.

Tea Board of Kenya: Naivasha Rd, off Ngong Rd, POB 20064, 00200 Nairobi; tel. (20) 3874446; fax (20) 3862120; e-mail info@ teaboard.or.ke; internet www.teaboard.or.ke; f. 1950; regulates tea industry on all matters of policy, licenses tea processing, carries out research on tea through **Tea Research Foundation of Kenya**, monitors tea planting and trade through registration, promotes Kenyan tea internationally; Chair. TITUS G. KIPYAB; Man. Dir SICILY K. KARIUKI.

EMPLOYERS' ORGANIZATIONS

Federation of Kenya Employers (FKE): Waajiri House, Argwings Kodhek Rd, POB 48311, Nairobi; tel. (20) 2721929; fax (20) 2721990; e-mail fkehq@fke-kenya.org; internet fke-kenya.org; Chair. PATRICK OBATH; Exec. Dir JACQUELINE MUGO.

Association of Local Government Employers (ALGAE): POB 52, Muranga; Chair. SAMUEL NYANGESO.

Kenya Association of Hotelkeepers and Caterers: Heidelberg House, 2nd Floor, Mombasa Rd, POB 9977, 00100 Nairobi; tel. (20) 6004419; fax (20) 6002539; e-mail info@kahc.co.ke; internet www.kahc.co.ke; f. 1944; CEO MIKE MACHARIA.

Kenya Bankers' Association: POB 73100, 00200 Nairobi; tel. (20) 2221704; fax (20) 2221792; e-mail info@kba.co.ke; internet www.kba.co.ke; f. 1962; Chair. RICHARD ETEMESI; CEO HABIL O. OLAKA; 43 mem orgs.

Kenya Coffee Producers' Association (KCPA): Wakulima House, 4th Floor, Room 408, Haile Selassie Ave, Ronald Ngala, POB 8100, 00300 Nairobi; tel. (20) 311235; e-mail info@kcpa.or.ke; internet www.kcpa.or.ke; f. 2009; Chair. JAMES K. GITAO.

Kenya Vehicle Manufacturers' Association: POB 1436, Thika; tel. (20) 350309; fax (67) 31434; e-mail kvm@kvm.co.ke; internet www.kvm.co.ke; f. 1974; name changed as above in 1989; Chair. KENNETH KEBAARA.

UTILITIES
Electricity

Energy Regulatory Commission (ERC): Integrity Centre, 1st Floor, cnr Valley and Milimani Rds, POB 42681, 00100 Nairobi; tel. (20) 2717627; fax (20) 2717603; e-mail info@erc.go.ke; internet www .erc.go.ke; f. 1997 as Energy Regulatory Board; present name assumed in 2007; govt-owned; regulates the generation, distribution, supply and use of electric power; Chair. HINDPAL SINGH JABBAL; Dir-Gen. Eng. KABURU MWIRICHIA.

Kenya Electricity Generating Co Ltd (KenGen): Stima Plaza, Phase 3, Kolobot Rd, Parklands, POB 47936, Nairobi; tel. (20) 3666000; fax (20) 248848; e-mail comms@kengen.co.ke; internet www.kengen.co.ke; f. 1997 as Kenya Power Co; present name adopted 1998; generates 82% of Kenya's electricity requirements; partially privatized in 2006; Chair. TITUS KITILI MBATHI; Man. Dir and CEO EDWARD NJOROGE.

Kenya Power and Lighting Co (KPLC): Electricity House, Harambee Ave, POB 301779, Nairobi; tel. (20) 221251; fax (20) 337351; e-mail custcare@kplc.co.ke; internet www.kplc.co.ke; partially privatized in 2006; 4% owned by Transcentury Group; co-ordinates electricity transmission and distribution; Man. Dir JOSEPH K. NJOROGE.

WATER

Nairobi City Water and Sewerage Co (NWSC): Kampala Rd, off Enterprise Rd, POB 30656, 00100 Nairobi; tel. (20) 3988000; internet www.nairobiwater.co.ke; f. 2002; Chair. PETER KUGURU; Man. Dir PATRICK OMUTIA.

TRADE UNIONS

Central Organization of Trade Unions (Kenya) (COTU): Solidarity Bldg, Digo Rd, POB 13000, Nairobi; tel. (20) 6761375; fax (20) 6762695; e-mail info@cotu-kenya.org; internet www.cotu-kenya.org; f. 1965 as the sole trade union fed.; Chair. RAJABU W. MWONDI; Sec.-Gen. FRANCIS ATWOLI.

Independent Union

Kenya National Union of Teachers: POB 30407, 00100 Nairobi; tel. (20) 2220387; fax (20) 2222701; e-mail knut@nbnet.co.ke; internet www.knut.or.ke; f. 1957; Sec.-Gen. DAVID OKUTAH OSIANY.

Transport
RAILWAYS

In 2004 there were some 1,920 km of track open for traffic. In 2006 the Rift Valley Railways consortium assumed management of the Kenya Railways Corpn. In 2009 plans were announced to construct a railway line connecting Mombasa with Malaba, with a possible extension to Kampala, Uganda. The project was expected to start in late 2011 and be completed in 2016. In 2010 a new railway project was under way to connect Jomo Kenyatta International Airport (JKIA) with Embakasi and the Nairobi city centre to relieve congestion on the road system. In 2011 plans were announced to construct a railway line linking the proposed port of Lamu with oil fields in South Sudan and eventually with Ethiopia. Construction work on the project began in 2012.

Kenya Railways Corpn: POB 30121, Nairobi; tel. (20) 221211; fax (20) 224156; internet www.krc.co.ke; f. 1977; management of operations assumed by Rift Valley Railways consortium in Nov. 2006; Chair. Gen. (retd) JEREMIAH KIANGA; Man. Dir NDUVA MULI.

ROADS

At the end of 2010 there were an estimated 61,947 km of classified roads, of which 14,098 km were main roads and 10,722 km were secondary roads. Only an estimated 14.3% of road surfaces were paved. An all-weather road links Nairobi to Addis Ababa, in Ethiopia, and there is a 590-km road link between Kitale (Kenya) and Juba (South Sudan). The rehabilitation of the important internal road link between Nairobi and Mombasa (funded by a US $165m. loan from the World Bank) was undertaken during the late 1990s.

Akamba Public Road Services: Industrial Area, POB 40322, Nairobi; tel. (20) 556062; fax (20) 559885; e-mail info@akambabus .com; internet www.akambabus.com; operates bus services from Nairobi to all major towns in Kenya and to some major towns in Uganda and Tanzania.

East African Road Services Ltd: Nairobi; tel. (20) 764622; f. 1947; operates bus services from Nairobi to all major towns in Kenya; Chair. S. H. NATHOO.

Kenya Bus Service Management Ltd: Utali Lane, View Park Towers, 10th Floor, Rm 1010, POB 41001, 00100 Nairobi; tel. (20) 2223235; fax (20) 2223110; e-mail info@kenyabus.net; internet kenyabus.net; promotes and develops transport enterprises; Man. Dir EDWINS MUKABANAH.

Kenya Roads Board: Kenya Re Towers, 3rd Floor, Ragati Rd, Upper Hill, POB 73718, Nairobi; tel. (20) 722865; internet www.krb .go.ke; f. 2000 to co-ordinate maintenance, rehabilitation and devt of the road network; Chair. ALFRED JUMA.

Kenya National Highways Authority (KeNHA): Blue Shield Towers, Hospital Rd, Upper Hill, POB 49712, 00100 Nairobi; tel. (20) 8013842; e-mail info@kenha.co.ke; internet www.kenha.co.ke; Chair. HANNAH W. MURIITHI; Dir-Gen. Eng. M.O. KIDENDA.

Kenya Rural Roads Authority: Blue Shield Towers, 6th Floor, Hospital Rd, Upperhill, POB 48151, 00100 Nairobi; tel. (20) 2710464; e-mail kerra@roadsnet.go.ke; internet www.kerra.go.ke; Dir-Gen. Eng. MWANGI MAINGI.

Kenya Urban Roads Authority: 2nd Floor, IKM Place, 5th Ngong Ave, POB 41727, 00100 Nairobi; tel. (20) 8013844; e-mail info@kura .go.ke; internet www.kura.go.ke; Chair. Prof. Eng. SIXTUS K. MWEA; Dir-Gen. Eng. JOSEPH NKADAYO.

SHIPPING

The major international seaport of Mombasa has 16 deep-water berths, with a total length of 3,044 m, and facilities for the off-loading of bulk carriers, tankers and container vessels. Kenyan ports handled some 16.4m. metric tons of cargo in 2008. In December 2012 the Kenyan flag registered fleet comprised 32 vessels with a total displacement of 15,949 grt. In 2011 plans were announced for the construction of a second international port at Lamu.

Kenya Maritime Authority: White House, Moi Ave, Mombasa; tel. (41) 2318398; fax (41) 2318397; e-mail info@maritimeauthority.co

.ke; internet www.maritimeauthority.co.ke; f. 2004; regulates, co-ordinates and oversees maritime affairs; Chair. Col. JOSEPH NGURU; Dir-Gen. NANCY W. KARIGITH.

Kenya Ports Authority: POB 95009, Mombasa; tel. (41) 2112999; fax (41) 311867; internet www.kpa.co.ke; f. 1978; sole operator of coastal port facilities; also operates two inland container depots at Nairobi and Kisumu; Chair. SHUKRI BARAMADI; Man. Dir JAMES MLEWA.

Inchcape Shipping Services Kenya Ltd: Inchcape House, Archbishop Makarios Cl., off Moi Ave, POB 90194, 80100 Mombasa; tel. (41) 2221885; fax (41) 2314662; e-mail mail@iss-shipping.com; internet www.iss-shipping.com; covers all ports in Kenya, Tanzania, Uganda, South Africa, Namibia, Nigeria, Ghana and Mauritius; Vice-Pres. (Africa Operations) DAVID MACKAY.

Mackenzie Maritime Ltd: Maritime Centre, Archbishop Makarios Close, POB 90120, Mombasa; tel. (11) 221273; fax (11) 316260; e-mail mml@africaonline.co.ke; shipping agents; Man. Dir M. M. BROWN.

Marship Ltd: Mombasa; tel. (11) 314705; fax (11) 316654; f. 1986; shipbrokers, ship management and chartering agents; Man. Dir MICHELE ESPOSITO.

Mitchell Cotts Kenya Ltd: Voi St, Shimanzi, POB 42485, 80100 Mombasa; tel. (20) 2315780; fax (20) 2226181; e-mail sales@mitchellcotts.co.ke; internet www.mitchellcottskenya.com; f. 1926; transport and shipping agents; freight handling and distribution; warehousing; Man. Dir DANIEL TANUI.

Motaku Shipping Agencies Ltd: Motaku House, Tangana Rd, POB 80419, 80100 Mombasa; tel. (41) 2229065; fax (41) 2220777; e-mail motaku@motakushipping.com; internet motakushipping.googlepages.com/home; f. 1977; ship managers and shipping agents, freight broker and charter; Man. Dir KARIM KUDRATI.

PIL (Kenya) Ltd: Liberty Plaza, Mombasa Rd, POB 40109, Nairobi; tel. (20) 825082; fax (20) 821086; e-mail admin@nbo.pilship.com; internet www.pilship.com.

Shipmarc Ltd: POB 99553, Mombasa; tel. (41) 229241; fax (41) 221390; e-mail info@shipmarckenya.com.

Southern Line Ltd: POB 90102, 80107 Mombasa; tel. (11) 229241; fax (11) 221390; e-mail shipmarc@africaonline.co.ke; operating dry cargo and tanker vessels between East African ports, Red Sea ports, the Persian (Arabian) Gulf and Indian Ocean islands.

Spanfreight Shipping Ltd: Cannon Towers, Moi Ave, POB 99760, Mombasa; tel. (11) 315623; fax (11) 312092; e-mail a23ke464@gncomtext.com; Exec. Dir DILIPKUMAR AMRITLAL SHAH.

CIVIL AVIATION

Kenya has four major international airports: Jomo Kenyatta International Airport (JKIA), in south-eastern Nairobi, Moi International Airport, at Mombasa, Eldoret International Airport, in Eldoret, and Kisumu International Airport, at Kisumu. Wilson Airport, in south-western Nairobi, and the airport at Malindi handle internal flights. Kenya also has about 250 smaller airfields.

Kenya Airports Authority: Jomo Kenyatta International Airport, POB 19001, Nairobi; tel. (20) 825400; fax (20) 822300; e-mail info@kenyaairports.co.ke; internet www.kenyaairports.co.ke; f. 1991; state-owned; responsible for the provision, management and operation of all airports and private airstrips; Man. Dir GEORGE MUHOHO.

Aero Kenya: Shelter Afrique House, Mamlaka Rd, Nairobi; tel. (20) 2719091; fax (20) 2719264; e-mail info@aerokenya.com; f. 1997; operates domestic charter and schedule services; Man. Dir Capt. CHARLES K. MUTHAMA.

African Express Airways: Airport North Rd, Jomo Kenyatta International Airport, POB 19202, 00501 Nairobi; tel. (20) 2014746; fax (20) 2049888; e-mail afex@africanexpress.co.ke; internet www.africanexpress.co.ke.

Airkenya Express Ltd: Wilson Airport, POB 30357, 00100 Nairobi; tel. (20) 605745; fax (20) 602951; e-mail info@airkenya.com; internet www.airkenya.com; f. 1985; operates internal scheduled and charter passenger services; Gen. Man. DINO BISLETI.

Astral Aviation: 1st Floor, Mechanised Freight Terminal, Specialised Freight Rd, 1st Ave, Jomo Kenyatta International Airport, POB 594, 00606 Nairobi; tel. (20) 827222; fax (20) 827243; e-mail info@astral-aviation.com; internet www.astral-aviation.com; f. 2001; cargo services; CEO SANJEEV S. GADHIA.

Blue Bird Aviation Ltd: Wilson Airport, Langata Rd, POB 52382, Nairobi; tel. (20) 602338; fax (20) 602337.

Eagle Aviation (African Eagle): POB 93926, Mombasa; tel. (11) 434502; fax (11) 434249; e-mail eaglemsa@africaonline.co.ke; f. 1986; scheduled regional and domestic passenger and cargo services; Chair. RAJA TANUJ; CEO Capt. KIRAN PATEL.

Five Forty Aviation Ltd (fly540.corp): ABC Pl. Westlands, POB 10293, Nairobi; tel. (20) 4453252; fax (20) 4453257; e-mail info@fly540.com; internet www.fly540.com; f. 2006; low-cost airline operating domestic and regional flights; COO NEIL STEFFEN.

Jetlink Express: Unit 3, Jomo Kenyatta International Airport, Nairobi; tel. (20) 827915; e-mail customercare@jetlink.co.ke; internet www.jetlink.co.ke; f. 2006; provides internal services and also operates flights to Juba (South Sudan), Goma (DRC) and Kigali (Rwanda); Man. Dir and CEO Capt. ELLY ALUVALE.

Kenya Airways Ltd (KQ): Airport North Road, Jomo Kenyatta International Airport, POB 19142, Nairobi; tel. (20) 6422000; fax (20) 823488; e-mail contact@kenya-airways.com; internet www.kenya-airways.com; f. 1977; in private sector ownership since 1996; passenger services to Africa, Asia, Europe and Middle East; freight services to Europe; internal services from Nairobi to Kisumu, Mombasa and Malindi; also operates a freight subsidiary; Chair. EVANSON MWANIKI; Man. Dir and CEO TITUS NAIKUNI.

CIVIL AVIATION AUTHORITY

Kenya Civil Aviation Authority: Jomo Kenyatta International Airport, POB 30163, 00100 Nairobi; tel. (20) 827470; fax (20) 822300; e-mail info@kcaa.or.ke; internet www.kcaa.or.ke; f. 2002; regulatory and advisory services for air navigation; Chair. KEVIN KARIUKI; Dir-Gen. HILARY KIOKO.

Tourism

Kenya's main attractions for visitors are its wildlife, with 25 National Parks and 23 game reserves, the Indian Ocean coast and an equable year-round climate. In 2011 there were an estimated 1.8m. foreign visitors. Earnings from the sector totalled an estimated US $844m. (excluding passenger transport) in that year.

Kenya Tourism Board: Kenya-Re Towers, Ragati Rd, POB 30630, 00100 Nairobi; tel. (20) 2711262; fax (20) 2719925; e-mail info@kenyatourism.org; internet www.magicalkenya.com; f. 1997; promotes Kenya as a tourist destination, monitors the standard of tourist facilities; Man. Dir JACINTA NZIOKA-MBITHI (acting).

Kenya Tourist Development Corpn: Utalii House, 11th Floor, Uhuru Highway, POB 42013, Nairobi; tel. (20) 2229751; fax (20) 2227817; e-mail info@ktdc.co.ke; internet www.ktdc.co.ke; f. 1965; Chair. MOHAMMED SHAIYA; Man. Dir MARIANNE NDEGWA-JORDAN.

Defence

As assessed at November 2012, Kenya's armed forces numbered 24,120, comprising an army of 20,000, an air force of 2,500 and a navy of 1,620. Military service is voluntary. The paramilitary police general service unit was 5,000 strong. In 2012 a total of 3,962 troops were stationed abroad, of which 30 were observers.

Defence Expenditure: Budgeted at Ks. 64,300m. for 2013.

Commander-in-Chief of the Armed Forces: Pres. MWAI KIBAKI.

Chief of General Staff: Gen. JULIUS WAWERU KARANGI.

Army Commander: Lt-Gen. JOHN KASAON.

Air Force Commander: Maj.-Gen. JOFF OTIENO.

Navy Commander: Brig.-Gen. NGEWA MUKALA.

Education

The Government provides, or assists in the provision of, schools. In 2007/08 enrolment at pre-primary level was 26% (26% of boys; 26% of girls). Primary education, which is compulsory, is provided free of charge. The education system involves eight years of primary education (beginning at six years of age), four years at secondary school and four years of university education. According to UNESCO estimates, in 2008/09 enrolment at primary schools included 83% of pupils in the relevant age-group (males 82%; females 83%), while enrolment at secondary schools included 50% of children in the relevant age-group (males 52%; females 49%). Tertiary enrolment in 2009/10 was equivalent to 7% of those in the relevant age-group (8% males; 5% females), according to UNESCO estimates. There are six state universities and seven private universities. In 2008/09 a total of 167,983 students were enrolled in higher education. In 2010 spending on education represented 17.2% of total budgetary expenditure.

KIRIBATI

Introductory Survey

LOCATION, CLIMATE, LANGUAGE, RELIGION, FLAG, CAPITAL

The Republic of Kiribati (pronounced 'Kir-i-bas') comprises 32 atolls, in three principal groups, scattered within an area of about 5m. sq km (2m. sq miles) in the mid-Pacific Ocean, and the island of Banaba (formerly Ocean Island). The country extends about 3,870 km (2,400 miles) from east to west and about 2,050 km (1,275 miles) from north to south. Its nearest neighbours are Nauru, to the west, and Tuvalu and Tokelau, to the south. The climate varies between maritime equatorial in the central islands and tropical in the north and south, with daytime temperatures varying between 26°C (79°F) and 32°C (90°F). There is a season of north-westerly trade winds from March to October and a season of rains and gales from October to March. However, average annual rainfall varies greatly, from 3,000 mm (118 ins) in the northern islands to 1,500 mm (59 ins) in Tarawa and 700 mm (28 ins) in the Line Islands. Droughts often occur in the central and southern islands. The principal languages are I-Kiribati (Gilbertese) and English, and the islands' inhabitants are mostly Christians. The national flag (proportions 1 by 2) depicts a golden frigate bird in flight, on a red background, above a rising sun and six alternating wavy horizontal lines of blue and white, representing the sea. The capital is the island of Bairiki, in Tarawa Atoll.

CONTEMPORARY POLITICAL HISTORY

Historical Context

In 1892 the United Kingdom established a protectorate over the 16 atolls of the Gilbert Islands and the nine Ellice Islands (now Tuvalu). The two groups were administered together by the Western Pacific High Commission (WPHC), which was based in Fiji until its removal to the British Solomon Islands (now Solomon Islands) in 1953. The phosphate-rich Ocean Island (now Banaba), west of the Gilberts, was annexed by the United Kingdom in 1900. The Gilbert and Ellice Islands were annexed in 1915, effective from January 1916, when the protectorate became a colony. The local representative of the WPHC was the Resident Commissioner, based on Tarawa Atoll in the Gilbert group. Later in 1916 the new Gilbert and Ellice Islands Colony (GEIC) was extended to include Ocean Island and two of the Line Islands, far to the east. Christmas Island (now Kiritimati), another of the Line Islands, was added in 1919, and the eight Phoenix Islands (then uninhabited) in 1937. The Line and Phoenix Islands, south of Hawaii, were also claimed by the USA. A joint British-US administration for two of the Phoenix group, Canton (now Kanton) and Enderbury, was agreed in April 1939. During the Second World War the GEIC was invaded by Japanese forces, who occupied the Gilbert Islands in 1942–43. Tarawa Atoll was the scene of some of the fiercest fighting in the Pacific between Japan and the USA.

In 1963, to prepare the GEIC for self-government, the first of a series of legislative and executive bodies was established. In 1972 a Governor of the GEIC was appointed to assume almost all the functions previously exercised in the colony by the High Commissioner. The five uninhabited Central and Southern Line Islands, previously administered directly by the High Commissioner, became part of the GEIC at this time. In 1974 the Legislative Council was replaced by a House of Assembly, with 28 elected members and three official members. The House elected Naboua Ratieta as Chief Minister.

In October 1975 the Ellice Islands were allowed to secede from the GEIC to form a separate territory, Tuvalu (q.v.). The remainder of the GEIC was renamed the Gilbert Islands, and the House of Assembly's membership was reduced. The Gilbert Islands obtained internal self-government on 1 January 1977. Later in that year the number of elected members in the House of Assembly was increased to 36, and provision was subsequently made for a member appointed by the Rabi Council of Leaders. Following a general election in 1978, Ieremia Tabai, Leader of the Opposition in the previous House, was elected Chief Minister. On 12 July 1979 the Gilbert Islands became an independent republic within the Commonwealth, under the name of Kiribati.

The House of Assembly was renamed the Maneaba ni Maungatabu, and Ieremia Tabai became the country's first President (Beretitenti). In September Kiribati signed a treaty of friendship with the USA, which relinquished its claim to the Line and Phoenix Islands, including Kanton and Enderbury. Kiribati did not become a member of the UN until September 1999, although it had previously joined some of the organization's agencies.

In 1975, meanwhile, the United Kingdom refused to recognize as legitimate a demand for independence by the people of Ocean Island (Banaba), who had been in litigation with the British Government since 1971 over revenues derived from exports of phosphate. Open-cast mining had adversely affected the island's environment to such an extent that most Banabans had been resettled on Rabi Island, 2,600 km (1,600 miles) away in Fiji. The Banabans rejected the British Government's argument that phosphate revenues should be distributed over the whole territory of the Gilbert Islands. In 1976 the High Court in London dismissed the Banabans' claim for unpaid royalties but upheld that for damages. An offer made by the British Government in 1977 of an *ex gratia* payment of $A10m., without admission of liability and on condition that no further judicial appeal would be made, was rejected. In 1981, however, the Banaban community on Rabi decided to accept the British Government's *ex gratia* offer of compensation, although it continued to seek self-government. The 1979 Constitution provided for the establishment of an independent commission of inquiry to review the political status of the Banabans three years after Kiribati had achieved independence; however, the inquiry was not commissioned until 1985. (In 2009 it was reported that rehabilitation work was being undertaken on Banaba. The work was expected to cost $A50m. and to take 20 years to complete, whereupon the Banaban community hoped to return to the island. In 2010 Banabans appealed to Australia, New Zealand, Japan and the United Kingdom for additional funding for the project.)

As part of the United Kingdom's programme to develop its own nuclear weapons, the first test of a British hydrogen bomb was conducted near Christmas Island in May 1957. Two further thermonuclear tests in the same vicinity followed later in the year. Serious concerns with regard to the monitoring of radioactivity levels in the area were subsequently raised. In addition to the potential effects on the health of both islanders and service personnel, millions of birds were reported to have died as a direct result of the high-altitude tests. The USA also operated a test programme, conducting 26 nuclear experiments in the vicinity of Christmas Island in 1962. The United Kingdom announced its withdrawal from the Christmas Island base in 1964. Despite various 'clean-up' operations, including one financed by the British Government in 2005–06, concerns arising from the environmental impact of the testing programmes remained.

Domestic Political Affairs

The first general election since independence took place in March–April 1982. The members of the new Maneaba all sat as independents. In accordance with the 1979 Constitution, the legislature nominated from among its members candidates for the country's first presidential election, to be held on the basis of direct popular vote. President Ieremia Tabai was confirmed in office at the election in May 1982. The Government resigned in December, after the Maneaba had twice rejected proposals to increase the salaries of civil servants. The legislature was dissolved, and a fresh general election took place in January 1983. The formation of the new Maneaba necessitated a further presidential election in February, at which Tabai was re-elected for a third term of office. He was returned to office in May 1987 (following a general election in March). The May 1991 legislative election was followed by a presidential election in July, at which the former Vice-President, Teatao Teannaki, narrowly defeated Roniti Teiwaki to replace Tabai, who had served the maximum number of presidential terms permitted by the Constitution.

In May 1994 the Government was defeated on a motion of confidence, following opposition allegations that cabinet ministers had misused travel allowances. The Maneaba was dissolved, and at a legislative election in July five ministers lost their seats.

Of the newly elected members, 13 were supporters of the Maneaban Te Mauri (Protect the Maneaba), while only eight were known to support the previously dominant National Progressive Party grouping. At the presidential election in September, Teburoro Tito, of the Maneaban Te Mauri, was elected, receiving 51.1% of the votes cast. The new President declared that reducing Kiribati's dependence on foreign aid would be a major objective for his Government. He also announced his intention to pursue civil and criminal action against members of the previous administration for alleged misuse of public funds while in office.

In 1995 a committee was created with the aim of assessing public opinion regarding possible amendments to the Constitution. In March 1998 more than 200 delegates attended a Constitutional Review Convention in Bairiki to consider the recommendations of a report presented to the Government in 1996, which included equalizing the status of men and women with regard to the citizenship rights of foreigners marrying I-Kiribati and changes to the structure of the Council of State.

At a general election, held in September 1998 and contested by a record 191 candidates, the Government and opposition each lost seven seats. Tito was re-elected as President in November, with 52.3% of the votes cast, defeating Dr Harry Tong, who obtained 45.8% of the votes, and Ambreroti Nikora (1.8%).

Controversy continued in 1999 regarding the renamed Millennium Island (previously known as Caroline Island). Following an adjustment to the International Date Line, the island had been renamed in 1997 in an attempt to promote it as a tourist destination for the year 2000. However, despite expenditure of more than $A1m., the Government failed to attract the predicted numbers to the island's millennium celebrations.

The Government was accused of attempting to stifle freedom of expression in late 1999, when a New Zealand journalist working for Agence France-Presse was banned from entering Kiribati. It had claimed that articles by the correspondent, published in a regional magazine and unfavourable to Kiribati, were biased and sensationalist. Moreover, in December former President Ieremia Tabai and a former member of the Maneaba, Atiera Tetoa, were fined for importing telecommunications equipment without a permit. They had launched Newair FM, an independent commercial radio station, 12 months previously; it had been immediately suspended. Tabai subsequently established Kiribati's first private newspaper, the *Kiribati Newstar*, in an attempt to reduce the Government's control over the media in the islands. The radio station was finally granted a licence to broadcast in December 2002.

In November 2000 the Vice-President and Minister for Home Affairs and Rural Development, Tewarika Tentoa, collapsed while addressing the Maneaba and died. The post of Vice-President was subsequently combined with the cabinet portfolio of finance and economic planning.

Campaigning for the general election during late 2002 was characterized by numerous allegations of improper conduct. Observers noted that officials from the Chinese embassy in Tarawa, accompanied by government candidates, had been donating gifts to the local community in the weeks preceding the election. (The Government had recently amended the Elections Act to allow gifts to be distributed to the public by candidates during their electoral campaigns, a practice that had been banned hitherto.) Moreover, under a newly amended Newspaper Registration Act, President Tito ordered police to seize opposition election pamphlets in November.

A total of 176 candidates contested the general election held in November 2002. The Government suffered significant losses, with 14 of its supporters (including seven ministers) failing to retain their seats. At a presidential election in February 2003, Tito narrowly secured a third term, receiving 14,160 votes, while opposition candidate Taberannang Timeon secured 13,613. However, in the following month Tito was narrowly defeated in a motion of no confidence and his Government was replaced by an interim administration, the Council of State (comprising the Speaker, the Chief Justice and the Public Service Commissioner). In accordance with the Constitution, another general election was held in May, when supporters of Tito secured a majority of seats. At a presidential election in July, the opposition candidate, Anote Tong, narrowly defeated his brother, Harry Tong. Anote Tong's electoral campaign, which had focused on his pledge to review the lease of the Chinese satellite-tracking station on South Tarawa (opened in 1997), had been characterized by a series of personal criticisms of his brother.

In November 2003 several hundred people staged a protest in Tarawa against the Government's decision to establish diplomatic relations with Taiwan, in place of the People's Republic of China, claiming that it had been made in return for Taiwanese funding of Anote Tong's election campaign. The President strongly denied this allegation, but did confirm that Taiwan had offered extensive development funds to Kiribati for adopting its position (see Regional Affairs).

The 2007 general election

A legislative election, contested by a total of 146 candidates, was held on 22 and 30 August 2007. The ministers of the incumbent Government, with one exception, were re-elected to the Maneaba. The Boutokan Te Koaua (Pillars of Truth) grouping of Anote Tong secured 18 seats, defeating the Maneaban Te Mauri grouping, which won seven. Anote Tong was re-elected as President on 17 October, having received almost twice as many votes as his nearest rival, Nabuti Mwemwenikarawa.

In May 2008 the Minister for Communications, Transport and Tourism Development, Patrick Tatireta, was forced to resign after a motion of no confidence was raised against him in the Maneaba. Controversy surrounded his dismissal of the chairman and members of the board of directors of the country's shipping corporation, Kiribati Shipping Services Ltd (KSSL), owing to their refusal to authorize payment for the purchase of a new ship. The vessel was to have been purchased from the WKK Shipping Line, a company owned by a close associate of Tatireta, but was deemed unseaworthy by maritime inspectors. However, in April 2009 the High Court of Kiribati ruled that KSSL was to honour the agreement to purchase the ship from the WKK Shipping Line, and ordered that a payment of US $390,000 be made.

A four-member parliamentary select committee was established in June 2009 to investigate the operations of foreign investors in the country, amid allegations of the involvement of government officials in corrupt practices. The committee was to focus on the activities of the Chinese business community, which in recent years had expanded considerably in Kiribati.

In August 2009 there was an outbreak of violence on the island of Maiana between the two ruling bodies, Te Bau Ni Maiana (the traditional elders' association) and the democratically elected council. The mayor and the council refused to comply with an order from Te Bau Ni Maiana to vacate their seats so that a fresh election could take place. Following a High Court ruling in favour of the council, the mayor's house was destroyed in an arson attack. The council subsequently acceded to Te Bau Ni Maiana's demands. The Minister for Environment, Lands and Agricultural Development, Tetabo Nakara, resigned in response to criticism of the Government's handling of the issue.

An report on domestic abuse by the Social Welfare Division of the Ministry for Internal and Social Affairs was published in December 2009. According to its findings, nearly 70% of women in Kiribati had experienced abuse by their husbands, close relatives or others; of those, 19% were under 15 years of age. In response to the report, human rights organizations urged the Government to take action to address the problem.

Recent developments: the 2011 general election

A general election held on 21 and 28 October 2011 was contested by 138 candidates, of whom only 12 were women. A total of 30 members, including seven government ministers, retained their seats in the Maneaba, with Anote Tong's Boutokan Te Koaua grouping securing 15 of the 42 elective seats and Tetaua Taitai's Karikirakean Tei-Kiribati (United Coalition Party, which had been formed in August 2010 by the merger of the Maneaban Te Mauri grouping and the Kiribati Tabomoa party) taking 10 seats. The Maurin Kiribati Party secured three seats and the remainder were won by independents. Among the elected members, supporters and opponents of Tong's outgoing Government were thought to be fairly evenly divided. During the campaign period Tong had alleged that Chinese interests had provided funding for opposition candidates, in the hope that a new government would switch recognition from Taiwan back to China. The claims were denied by the opposition.

At a presidential election held on 13 January 2012, Anote Tong was re-elected, albeit with a smaller proportion of the vote than in 2007, receiving 42.2%, compared with 35.0% for Tetaua Taitai and 22.8% for Rimeta Beniamina (of the Maurin Kiribati Party). A relatively high rate of voter participation, estimated at 68%, was recorded, following a campaign by the electoral office to increase turn-out. Tong was inaugurated as President for a third term on 19 January 2012, naming Teima Onorio, once again, as Vice-President.

The issue of press freedom re-emerged in June 2012, when a fortnightly newspaper, the *Kiribati Independent*, which had begun publication in December 2011, was ordered to cease operating on the grounds that it had not been registered. The editor, Taberannang Korauaba, stated that the newspaper's application to register, lodged in late 2011, had been ignored by the authorities. In defiance of the ban, the newspaper resumed publication in January 2013. Kiribati's sole television station, state-owned Kiribati Television, was suspended by the Government in March on the grounds of financial difficulties and a lack of expertise in programming and production; a review into whether the closure should be permanent was subsequently initiated.

In August 2012 the Government proposed a constitutional revision providing for the creation of a new Ministry of Women and Youth. However, the draft amendment did not receive the requisite approval of a two-thirds' majority in the Maneaba. The decision of the opposition not to support the proposal, leading to its defeat in the legislature, was condemned by human rights and women's groups. In April 2013 President Tong again proposed a constitutional amendment to allow the establishment of a Ministry of Women.

Environmental Concerns and Other Issues

In addition to the legacies of phosphate-mining operations and of the testing of hydrogen bombs, by the end of the 20th century the impact of climate change on the islands had begun to assume major significance. In 1989 a UN report on the greenhouse effect (the heating of the earth's atmosphere, and a resultant rise in sea level, as a consequence of pollution) listed Kiribati as one of the countries that would completely disappear beneath the sea in the 21st century, unless drastic action were taken. None of the land on the islands was more than 3m above sea level, making the country extremely vulnerable to the potential effects of climate change. It was feared that a rise in sea level would not only cause flooding but would also upset the balance between sea and fresh water (below the coral sands), rendering water supplies undrinkable. A report by the World Bank in 2000 listed the flooding and loss of low-lying areas, more intense cyclones and droughts, the failure of subsistence crops and coastal fisheries, the death of coral reefs and the spread of mosquito-borne diseases such as malaria and dengue fever as consequences of climate change on Pacific island nations. Meanwhile, a state of emergency was declared in Kiribati in early 1999, owing to one of the worst droughts ever recorded in the islands, and later that year it was announced that two of the country's uninhabited coral reefs had been submerged as a result of rising sea levels. During the early 2000s the causeways linking villages on Tarawa atoll were flooded by high tides, and shortages of drinking water, which had become common, were reported to be approaching critical levels by 2009. The UN Development Programme (UNDP, see p. 56) signed an agreement with the Government of Kiribati in September 2009 to assist in the implementation of environmental projects. In July 2010 boreholes were drilled on Tarawa atoll to measure the extent of the underground fresh water supply and assist in preventing contamination by salt water. The work was undertaken as part of the Kiribati Adaptation Program, financed by the World Bank, Australia and New Zealand. The planting of more than 37,000 mangroves to alleviate the problem of coastal erosion was undertaken with international support in early 2011.

In late 1997 President Tito strongly criticized the Australian Government's refusal, at the Conference of the Parties to the Framework Convention on Climate Change (under the auspices of the UN Environment Programme, see p. 61) in Kyoto, Japan, to reduce its emission of gases known to contribute to the greenhouse effect. In April 2001 the USA's decision to reject the Kyoto Protocol to the UN's Framework Convention on Climate Change was widely criticized. Kiribati continued to urge the UN to work towards a co-ordinated response to the challenge of global warming. In December 2007 the new Australian Government of Kevin Rudd reversed the country's previous position, immediately signing the Kyoto Protocol, and in early 2009 the incoming US Administration of Barack Obama also confirmed its commitment to addressing climate change. President Anote Tong addressed the UN Climate Change Conference in the Danish capital of Copenhagen in December, criticizing the lack of agreement among nations on the issue. Tong expressed profound disappointment when the conference failed to reach consensus on a legally binding agreement to reduce carbon emissions. In November 2010 Kiribati hosted a conference on climate change, at which the 19 countries and numerous organizations represented drew up a declaration urging the adoption of definite measures to prevent disastrous levels of global warming and emphasizing the need for funding to combat the effects of climate change in vulnerable developing countries. The declaration was submitted at the UN conference on climate change held in Cancún, Mexico, in the following month. In September 2011 the UN Secretary-General Ban Ki-moon appealed for urgent action by developed countries to reduce their carbon emissions, naming Kiribati as one of the island nations most vulnerable to the effects of climate change. Furthermore, following an official visit to Kiribati in November 2012, the Commonwealth Secretary-General, Kamalesh Sharma, spoke of the devastating impact of rising sea levels on the islands and similarly urged governments of developed countries to do more to mitigate the effects of climate change on small island states.

In March 2012 it was reported that the Government of Kiribati was seeking to purchase a 23 sq km plot of land in Fiji, at a cost of US $9.6m. President Anote Tong announced that the land was intended primarily for economic development but, following intense speculation in the media, admitted that it could be used for the relocation of I-Kiribati residents when their islands are rendered uninhabitable by climate change.

In 2003 the UN Children's Fund (UNICEF) established a field office in Kiribati as part of a wider strategy to increase the UN's presence in the region. In 2007 the efforts of a team of Cuban doctors were reported to have resulted in an 80% decrease in infant mortality rates. In September 2008, furthermore, President Anote Tong became the first leader of a Pacific nation to undertake a state visit to Cuba. Discussions with Cuban President Raúl Castro led to an agreement for the training of I-Kiribati medical students by Cuban doctors in Kiribati. In 2012, however, child mortality rates in Kiribati remained the highest in the region, and an official UN mission to the islands in July of that year urged the Government to make improved sanitation and the provision of clean water a national priority.

Owing to Kiribati's high rate of population growth and, in particular, the overpopulation of South Tarawa with associated social and economic problems, in 1988 it was announced that nearly 5,000 inhabitants were to be resettled on outlying atolls, mainly in the Line Islands. In 2004 the Government announced a major new initiative, supported by UNDP and the Asian Development Bank, to establish up to four new urban areas in the outer islands as part of ongoing efforts to ease the overcrowding on South Tarawa. However, persistent water shortages hindered efforts to resettle people on the island of Kiritimati.

In 1976 a Japanese company established a satellite-tracking station on Kiritimati, the management of which was subsequently transferred to the Japan Aerospace Exploration Agency. A Chinese satellite-tracking station was opened on South Tarawa in 1997 but was dismantled in 2003, following the suspension of diplomatic relations between Kiribati and the People's Republic of China. Sea Launch, an international consortium led by the US Boeing Commercial Space Company, began a rocket-launching operation from a converted oil-rig near the islands in 1999. Kiribati, which did not benefit financially from the project, as the consortium had sought to carry out its activities in international waters near the outer limits of the islands' exclusive economic zone (EEZ), had, together with the South Pacific Regional Environment Programme (see p. 472), expressed concerns regarding the adverse environmental impact of the site (particularly the dumping of large quantities of waste fuel in the islands' waters). These fears were compounded in March 2000 when a rocket launched from the site crashed and Sea Launch refused to disclose where it had landed.

In March 2006 President Anote Tong announced that a large marine reserve was to be established in Kiribati. Commercial fishing was to be banned in the Phoenix Islands Protected Area (PIPA), which would afford protection to more than 500 species of fish, along with other marine life such as coral and birds. In August 2010 PIPA, which at 408,250 sq km constituted the largest marine protected area in the world, was designated by UNESCO as a World Heritage site. In 2012 the Pacific Oceanscape initiative, modelled on Kiribati's PIPA, outlined plans to establish a protected area of 38m. sq km, covering all the Pacific islands' EEZs and the areas between these boundaries. The initiative, which had been endorsed by all the leaders of the Pacific Islands Forum (see p. 426) member nations at a meeting of the group in 2010, proposed the establishment of a framework to manage the EEZs in an integrated way and to respond more effectively to the impact of climate change on the marine environment.

Regional Affairs

Following its accession to independence in 1979, Kiribati maintained good relations with other island nations of the Pacific region, as well as with Australia and New Zealand, both of which continued to provide significant development assistance. Through the Pacific Patrol Boat Program, for example, Australia supported Kiribati in the area of maritime surveillance. During 2009 Australia announced a programme to provide training for I-Kiribati nursing students and signed a partnership development agreement with Kiribati and Solomon Islands to assist in improving education, work-force skills and economic management.

In June 2008 President Anote Tong embarked upon a state visit to New Zealand. Tong and Prime Minister Helen Clark signed a declaration aimed at increasing political and economic links. New Zealand confirmed its support for the Marine Training Centre, and offered financial assistance of \$NZ15m. over a five-year period for the Kiribati Sustainable Towns Programme, established in order to address the issue of rapid urbanization, particularly on South Tarawa. In 2010 the New Zealand Minister of Foreign Affairs, Murray McCully, undertook to double New Zealand's annual aid for Kiribati, emphasizing the need to improve water supplies and sanitation.

In November 2003 President Anote Tong announced the establishment of diplomatic relations with Taiwan. The Government's decision to transfer its recognition from the People's Republic of China to Taiwan caused considerable controversy, prompting a demonstration in Tarawa in protest against the decision. During that month it was reported that Chinese technicians were dismantling the satellite-tracking station, which had played an important role in China's recent first manned space flight. Despite Chinese efforts to persuade Kiribati to reconsider its decision, which many observers believed were motivated by the islands' strategic importance, in late November China suspended its diplomatic relations with Kiribati. Following Kiribati's transfer of diplomatic allegiance, a Taiwanese embassy was opened in Tarawa in January 2004, and in May 2005 President Chen Shui-bian of Taiwan reportedly became the first foreign head of state to visit Kiribati in an official capacity. During a reciprocal visit by President Tong to Taiwan in May of the following year, President Chen described Kiribati as a 'staunch ally'. Further official visits to both countries took place during 2010, when the issues of climate change and bilateral co-operation in fisheries and aquaculture were discussed.

Relations with Japan have been tested by various issues. In 1992 the legislature approved an opposition motion urging the Government to seek compensation from Japan for damage caused to the islands during the Second World War. The intention to seek compensation was reiterated by President Teburoro Tito in 1994. As a result of discussions held at the Pacific Islands Forum summit meeting in Kiribati in October 2000, Japan announced that it was willing to negotiate compensation claims. Furthermore, a visit by Tito to Japan in February 2001 resulted in a number of informal agreements aimed at enhancing relations between the two countries, particularly regarding the contentious issues of tuna fishing, whaling and nuclear fuel shipments. In June 2010 the Kiribati Government denied allegations that Kiribati had accepted financial assistance from Japan in return for voting, at that month's annual meeting of the International Whaling Commission, in favour of an end to the moratorium on commercial whaling.

In June 2010 President Tong affirmed his Government's intention to maintain cordial bilateral relations with Fiji, despite the latter's exclusion from the Pacific Islands Forum (from May 2009) because of its failure to restore democratic rule. In January 2011 a delegation from Fiji visited Kiribati with the aim of developing the two countries' co-operation in economic and environmental matters.

CONSTITUTION AND GOVERNMENT

Under the Constitution of 1979, legislative power is vested in the unicameral Maneaba ni Maungatabu. It has 42 members elected by universal adult suffrage for four years (subject to dissolution), one nominated representative of the Banaban community and, if he is not an elected member, the Attorney-General as an ex-officio member. The head of state is the Beretitenti (President), who is also Head of Government. The President is elected by direct popular vote. The President governs with the assistance of the Vice-President and Cabinet, whom he appoints from among members of the Maneaba. Executive authority is vested in the Cabinet, which is responsible to the Maneaba.

REGIONAL AND INTERNATIONAL CO-OPERATION

Kiribati is a member of the Pacific Community (see p. 422), the Pacific Islands Forum (see p. 426) and the Asian Development Bank (ADB, see p. 214). The country is an associate member of the UN's Economic and Social Commission for Asia and the Pacific (ESCAP, see p. 31) and is a signatory to the South Pacific Regional Trade and Economic Co-operation Agreement (SPARTECA, see p. 427).

Kiribati became a member of the UN in 1999. It is a signatory to the Lomé Conventions and successor Cotonou Agreement (see p. 334) with the European Union.

ECONOMIC AFFAIRS

In 2011, according to estimates by the World Bank, Kiribati's gross national income (GNI), measured at average 2009–11 prices, was US \$213m., equivalent to \$2,110 per head (or \$3,480 on an international purchasing-power parity basis). During 2002–11, it was estimated, the population increased at an average annual rate of 1.7%, while gross domestic product (GDP) per head declined, in real terms, by an estimated average of 0.6% per year. Overall GDP increased, in real terms, at an average annual rate of 1.6% in 2002–11, according to official figures. According to the Asian Development Bank (ADB), GDP rose by 3.3% in 2011 and by 3.0% in 2012.

Agriculture and fishing contributed 26.3% of GDP in 2011. In 2005, according to official estimates, agriculture engaged 7.4% of the economically active population (excluding subsistence workers). FAO projected that 21.2% of the population would be engaged in agriculture in mid-2013. The principal cash crop is coconut, yielding copra as well as coconut oil. In 2010 exports of crude coconut oil accounted for 43.5% of the country's total receipts from exports and re-exports. Export revenue from copra and copra cake declined from \$A1.8m. in 2008, accounting for 21.0% of the total, to \$A681,000 in 2009 (8.5%). Bananas, taro, screw-pine (*Pandanus*), breadfruit and papaya are cultivated as food crops. The cultivation of seaweed began in the mid-1980s. In 2010 seaweed provided 1.1% of total export earnings. Sea cucumbers (*bêches-de-mer*) have become an increasingly important source of export revenue, accounting for 10.6% of the total in 2010. Pigs and chickens are kept. The sale of fishing licences to foreign fleets (notably from South Korea, Japan, the People's Republic of China, Taiwan and the USA) has provided an important source of income. In September 2006 a new six-year agreement with the European Union (EU) entered into force: 16 Spanish vessels were permitted to fish for tuna in Kiribati waters, while the EU's annual financial contribution was to remain at US \$0.6m. Revenue from the sale of fishing licences reached a record \$A52m. in 2001, but declined in subsequent years. Receipts from fishing licences rose from \$A25.4m. in 2007 to \$A32.2m. in 2008, before decreasing to \$A29.5m. in 2009, when they accounted for 42.4% of total government revenue. However, income from licence fees increased by 41.4% in 2010, to \$A41.7m. (51.5% of total revenue), mainly owing to the introduction in September of that year of an auction scheme for fishing rights, which was intended to replace bilateral access agreements. According to official figures, the GDP of the agricultural sector increased at an average annual rate of 2.9% in 2002–11. Agricultural GDP decreased by 2.5% in 2010, but rose by 5.7% in 2011.

Industry (including manufacturing, construction and utilities) contributed 8.2% of GDP in 2011. The sector engaged 8.7% of the economically active population in 2005. Industrial GDP expanded by an average of 4.8% per year in 2002–11. Industrial GDP contracted by 9.9% in 2010, but grew by 11.8% in 2011.

Mining of phosphate rock on the island of Banaba, which ceased in 1979, formerly provided some 80% of export earnings. Interest from a phosphate reserve fund, the Revenue Equalization Reserve Fund (RERF, which was established in 1956), became an important source of income (see below). The production of solar-evaporated salt for export to other islands of the Pacific (for use on fishing vessels with brine refrigeration systems) began on Kiritimati in 1985.

Manufacturing, which contributed 5.8% of GDP in 2011, is confined to the small-scale production of coconut-based products, soap, foods, handicrafts, furniture, leather goods and garments. Manufacturing GDP increased by an average of 1.4% per year in 2002–11. The GDP of the manufacturing sector increased by 0.8% in 2011.

The construction sector contributed 1.4% of GDP in 2011. The sector engaged 3.9% of the economically active population in 2005. Construction GDP decreased at an average annual rate of

13.6% in 2002–11. The GDP of the construction sector decreased by 24.8% in 2010, but increased by 33.0% in 2011.

Production of electrical energy increased from 13.3m. kWh in 2000 to 21.6m. kWh in 2010. Mineral fuels accounted for 24.7% of total import costs in 2010. The use of solar energy is of increasing significance.

The services sector provided 65.5% of GDP in 2011. Services engaged 83.9% of the economically active population in 2005. Although impeded by factors such as the high costs of transport to Kiribati, the tourism sector makes a significant contribution to the economy. Receipts from tourism totalled US $3.0m. in 2009. Details of a five-year plan to revitalize the country's tourism sector, which aimed to increase the number of visitors to 10,000 annually by 2015, were announced in December 2009, and a new promotional campaign was launched in April 2010. International visitor arrivals increased by 19.2% in 2010, to 4,701, rising further, to a provisional 5,000, in 2011. The GDP of the services sector increased at an average annual rate of 2.0% in 2002–11. The services sector's GDP expanded by 1.4% in 2010, but contracted by 1.2% in 2011.

In 2011, according to the ADB, Kiribati recorded a visible merchandise trade deficit of $A80.9m., and there was a deficit of $A45.7m. on the current account of the balance of payments. Kiribati depends on imports for almost all essential commodities, and import duties are a major source of government revenue. In 2011 the principal source of imports was Fiji (36.1% of the total); other major suppliers were Japan, Australia, the USA, the People's Republic of China and New Zealand. The principal recipient of exports in that year was Thailand (57.4%); other major purchasers were Ecuador and Japan. The major imports in 2010 were food and live animals, mineral fuels, machinery and transport equipment, basic manufactures, beverages and tobacco, and chemicals. The major exports in 2010 included coconut oil and bêche-de-mer.

A central government budgetary deficit of $A13.2m., equivalent to 8.0% of GDP, was recorded in 2010, according to the IMF. The fiscal deficit widened to 14.2% of GDP in 2011 and to 20.0% of GDP in 2012, according to the ADB. Budgetary deficits continued to be financed by drawdowns from the RERF. However, it was feared that the Government's repeated recourse to such drawdowns, estimated at $A37.5m. in 2012 (above the Government's target limit of $A15m.), would be unsustainable in the longer term (see below). The country is reliant on foreign assistance for its development budget. Australia is a major provider of development assistance, with emphasis on the management of human resources, training, governance, health, education and improved customs procedures, within the framework of a new co-operation strategy. In 2012/13 aid from Australia was budgeted at $A26.9m. Aid from New Zealand was expected to total $NZ12.0m. in 2011/12. Through the ADB, Taiwan has provided aid to finance various development projects, as has Japan. Kiribati's total external debt was estimated by the ADB to total US $34m. in 2012. The cost of debt-servicing was estimated to be the equivalent of 2.8% of the value of exports of goods and services in that year. The annual rate of inflation averaged 2.2% in 2002–11, according to ADB figures. Consumer prices rose by 1.2% in 2011, but declined by 1.8% in 2012. About 6.1% of the labour force were unemployed in 2005. Opportunities for formal employment are limited, the majority of jobs available being in the public sector.

With its isolated location and extremely limited export base, Kiribati is one of the world's least developed nations. Remittances from Kiribati's emigrant workers, the majority of whom have traditionally been seafarers employed on foreign ships, are a vital source of income for many families, reaching an estimated A$11.6m. in 2009. However, global economic conditions subsequently resulted in fewer opportunities for I-Kiribati seafarers. In a report published in 2011, the IMF predicted that the real per-head balance of the RERF would be depleted to one-third of its 2000 value by 2030, in view of the substantial drawdowns of recent years, as well as losses on investments. Having exceeded $A637m. in 2007, the value of the RERF was reported to have declined to $A571m. in 2009. The Government aimed to limit the annual drawdown to a maximum of $A15m. in 2011–15. The Government also holds substantial offshore assets through the Kiribati Provident Fund. In March 2011 the World Bank announced a Country Assistance Strategy for Kiribati, which aimed primarily to address the threats associated with climate change and problems relating to the islands' geographical isolation, with grants totalling some US $50m. during 2011–14. According to the ADB, GDP grew by 3.0% in 2012, driven by infrastructure projects financed by development partners, and was forecast to increase by 3.5% in 2013. Following his re-election in January 2012, President Tong stated that his Government intended to strengthen the country's economy by deriving greater revenue from its fishing industry, primarily by increasing the capacity for processing fish domestically. He also reiterated his intention to develop the skills of the islands' young people, many of whom would need to seek employment overseas, through the Marine Training Centre and the Technical Institute.

PUBLIC HOLIDAYS

2014: 1 January (New Year), 3 March (for International Women's Day), 28 March (National Health Day), 18 April (Good Friday), 21 April (Easter Monday), 9 July (National Church Day), 12–16 July (National Day Celebrations), 6 August (for Youth Day), 7 December (for Human Rights and Peace Day), 25–26 December (Christmas).

Statistical Survey

Source (unless otherwise stated): Statistics Office, Ministry of Finance and Economic Development, POB 67, Bairiki, Tarawa; tel. 21082; fax 21307; e-mail statistics@mfep.gov.ki; internet www.spc.int/prism/country/KI/Stats.

AREA AND POPULATION

Area: 810.5 sq km (312.9 sq miles). *Principal Atolls* (sq km): Banaba (island) 6.3, Tarawa 31.0 (North 15.3, South 15.8), Abemama 27.4, Tabiteuea 37.6 (North 25.8, South 11.9), Total Gilbert group (incl. others) 285.5; Kanton (Phoenix Is) 9.2, Tabuaeran (Fanning—Line Is) 33.7, Kiritimati (Christmas—Line Is) 388.4, Total Line and Phoenix group (incl. others) 525.0 (Line Is 496.6, Phoenix Is 28.5).

Population: 92,533 at census of 7 November 2005; 103,058 (males 50,796, females 52,262) at census of 7 November 2010. *Principal Atolls* (2010): Banaba (island) 295; Abaiang 5,502; Tarawa 40,529 (North 6,102, South 34,427); Tabiteuea 4,979 (North 3,689, South 1,290); Total Gilbert group (incl. others) 93,791; Kanton (Phoenix Is) 31; Kiritimati 5,586; Total Line and Phoenix Group (incl. others) 9,267. *Mid-2013* (Secretariat of the Pacific Community estimate): 106,461 (Source: Pacific Regional Information System).

Density (mid-2013): 131.4 per sq km.

Population by Age and Sex (Secretariat of the Pacific Community estimates at mid-2013): *0–14:* 36,215 (males 18,686, females 17,529); *15–64:* 66,443 (males 32,740, females 33,703); *65 and over:* 3,804 (males 1,511, females 2,293); *Total* 106,461 (males 52,937, females 53,524) (Source: Pacific Regional Information System).

Ethnic Groups (census of 2000): Micronesians 83,452; Polynesians 641; Europeans 154; Others 247; Total 84,494.

Principal Villages: (population at 2010 census): Betio 15,755; Bikenibeu 6,568; Teaoraereke 4,171; Bairiki (capital) 3,524; Eita 3,061; Temwaiku 3,135; Bonriki 2,355. Note: All of the listed villages are in South Tarawa atoll.

Births, Marriages and Deaths (Secretariat of the Pacific Community estimates, 2010, unless otherwise indicated): Registered live births 2,774 (birth rate 27.8 per 1,000); Marriages (registrations, 1988) 352 (marriage rate 5.2 per 1,000); Registered deaths 827 (death rate 8.3 per 1,000) (Source: mainly Pacific Regional Information System).

Life Expectancy (years at birth, WHO estimates): 68 (males 65; females 70) in 2009. Source: WHO, *World Health Statistics*.

Economically Active Population (paid employees aged 15 years and over, 2005 census): Agriculture, hunting, forestry and fishing 936; Manufacturing 305; Electricity, gas and water 293; Construction 511; Trade, restaurants and hotels 1,873; Transport, storage and communications 1,473; Financing, insurance, real estate and business services 356; Public administration 6,953; *Sub-total* 12,700; Activities not adequately defined 433; *Total employed* 13,133 (males 8,095, females 5,038); Unemployed 2,254 (males 1,130, females

1,124); *Total cash labour force* 15,387 (males 9,225, females 6,162). Note: Subsistence workers (not included) numbered 21,582 (males 10,788, females 10,794). *Mid-2013:* Agriculture, etc. 11,000; Total labour force 52,000 (Source: FAO).

HEALTH AND WELFARE

Key Indicators

Total Fertility Rate (children per woman, 2010): 2.9.

Under-5 Mortality Rate (per 1,000 live births, 2010): 49.

Physicians (per 1,000 head, 2010): 0.4.

Hospital Beds (per 1,000 head, 2010): 1.4.

Health Expenditure (2009): US $ per head (PPP): 294.

Health Expenditure (2009): % of GDP: 13.0.

Health Expenditure (2009): public (% of total): 84.7.

Access to Water (% of persons, 2006): 65.

Access to Sanitation (% of persons, 2006): 33.

Total Carbon Dioxide Emissions ('000 metric tons, 2008): 29.3.

Total Carbon Dioxide Emissions Per Head (metric tons, 2008): 0.3.

Human Development Index (2011): ranking: 122.

Human Development Index (2011): value: 0.624.

For sources and definitions, see explanatory note on p. vi.

AGRICULTURE, ETC.

Principal Crops ('000 metric tons, 2011, FAO estimates): Taro (Cocoyam) 1.7; Other roots and tubers 8.9; Coconuts 169.5; Vegetables 5.5; Bananas 4.5.

Livestock ('000 head, year ending September 2011, FAO estimates): Pigs 12.6; Chickens 570.

Livestock Products (metric tons, 2011, unless otherwise indicated, FAO estimates): Pig meat 888; Poultry meat 740; Hen eggs 320.

Fishing (metric tons, live weight, 2010): Capture 44,599* (Emperors 118*; Mullets 350*; Snappers and jobfishes 162*; Jacks and crevalles 102*; Skipjack tuna 8,438; Yellowfin tuna 4,533; Other marine fishes 40; Marine molluscs 3,004*); Aquaculture 11; *Total catch* 44,610*. Figures exclude aquatic plants (metric tons, FAO estimate): 4,745 (all aquaculture).

* FAO estimate.

Source: FAO.

INDUSTRY

Copra Production (processed, metric tons): 9,686 in 2006; 8,808 in 2007; 9,135 in 2008.

Electric Energy (million kWh): 22.45 in 2008; 22.19 in 2009; 21.60 in 2010.

Sources: Asian Development Bank; UN Industrial Commodity Statistics Database.

FINANCE

Currency and Exchange Rates: Australian currency: 100 cents = 1 Australian dollar ($A). *Sterling, US Dollar and Euro Equivalents* (31 December 2012): £1 sterling = $A1.517; US $1 = $A0.961; €1 = $A1.268; $A100 = £65.94 = US $104.05 = €78.86. *Average Exchange Rate* (Australian dollars per US $): 1.0902 in 2010; 0.9695 in 2011; 0.9658 in 2012.

Budget (central government operations, $A '000, year ending 31 December 2010): *Revenue:* Current 122,078 (Tax 31,880, Non-tax 90,198); Capital receipts 50; Total 122,128. *Current Expenditure:* General public services 10,580; Public order and safety 7,977; Education 16,259; Health 14,259; Welfare and environment 2,688; Community and culture 2,579; Agriculture, etc. 1,803; Construction affairs 2,483; Communications 3,272; Commerce and labour affairs 4,132; Other 21,488; Total 87,520.

Cost of Living (Consumer Price Index; base: 2000 = 100): All items 108.3 in 2006; 112.9 in 2007; 125.3 in 2008. Source: ILO.

Gross Domestic Product ($A '000 at constant 2006 prices): 152,479 in 2009; 151,719 in 2010; 156,681 in 2011.

Expenditure on the Gross Domestic Product ($A million at current prices, 2011): Government final consumption expenditure 66.5; Private final consumption expenditure 172.8; Gross fixed capital formation 74.6; Change in stocks 0.4; *Total domestic expenditure* 314.3; Exports of goods and services 22.9; *Less* Imports of goods and services 160.5; *GDP in purchasers' values* 176.7. Source: UN Statistics Division, National Accounts Main Aggregates Database.

Gross Domestic Product by Economic Activity ($A '000 at current prices, 2011): Agriculture and fishing 43,009; Mining 45; Manufacturing 9,461; Electricity, gas and water 1,700; Construction 2,250; Wholesale and retail trade, hotels and restaurants 13,608; Transport and communications 14,435; Financial intermediation 28,536; Government administration 47,494; Other community, social and personal service activities 2,914; *Sub-total* 163,452; *Less* Imputed bank service charge 7,000; Indirect taxes, less subsidies 11,499; *GDP in purchasers' values* 167,952.

Balance of Payments ($A '000, 2011): Exports of goods 11,439.6; Imports of goods –92,292.6; *Trade balance* –80,853.0.; Exports of services and income 74,260.6; Imports of services and income –60,300.4; *Balance on goods, services and income* –66,892.8; Current transfers received 27,241.8; Current transfers paid –6,010.7; *Current balance* –45,661.6; Capital account (net) 33,155.5; Direct investment (net) 1,163.4; Portfolio investment (net) –18,032.0; *Overall balance* 6,689.3. Source: Asian Development Bank.

EXTERNAL TRADE

Principal Commodities ($A '000, 2010): *Imports:* Food and live animals 27,471; Beverages and tobacco 4,591; Crude materials (excl. fuels) 954; Mineral fuels, lubricants, etc. 19,719; Chemicals 4,092; Basic manufactures 6,979; Machinery and transport equipment 11,489; Total (incl. others) 79,686. *Exports (incl. re-exports):* Copra cake (meal) 122; Coconut oil (crude) 1,845; Bêche-de-mer 448; Seaweed 47; Total (incl. others) 4,245 (Re-exports 1,347).

Principal Trading Partners (US $, 2011): *Imports:* Australia 12,284; China, People's Republic 6,452; Fiji 33,089; Japan 16,265; New Zealand 5,009; USA 6,456; Total (incl. others) 91,703. *Exports:* Ecuador 1,136; Japan 580; Thailand 4,934; Total (incl. others) 8,594. Source: Asian Development Bank.

TRANSPORT

Road Traffic (vehicles in use, 2008): Passenger cars 9,600; Buses 160; Trucks 4,320; Motorcycles 2,080. Source: IRF, *World Road Statistics.*

Shipping: *Flag Registered Fleet* (at 31 December 2012): 139 vessels; total displacement 385,170 grt. (Source: Lloyd's List Intelligence— www.lloydslistintelligence.com). *International Sea-borne Freight Traffic* ('000 metric tons, 1990): Goods loaded 15; Goods unloaded 26 (Source: UN, *Monthly Bulletin of Statistics*).

Civil Aviation (traffic on scheduled services, 1998): Passengers carried 28,000; Passenger-km 11 million; Total ton-km 2 million. Source: UN, *Statistical Yearbook.*

TOURISM

Foreign Tourist Arrivals: 3,944 in 2009; 4,701 in 2010; 5,000 in 2011 (provisional).

Tourist Arrivals by Country of Residence (2010): Australia 913; France 72; Japan 244; New Zealand 470; United Kingdom 153; USA 776; Total (incl. others) 4,701.

Tourism Receipts (US $ million): 3.0 in 2009.

Source: World Tourism Organization.

COMMUNICATIONS MEDIA

Telephones (main lines in use, 2011): 8,500.

Mobile Cellular Telephones (subscribers, 2011): 13,800.

Personal Computers (2005): 1,000.

Internet Users (2009): 7,800.

Broadband Subscribers (2011): 900.

Source: International Telecommunication Union.

EDUCATION

Primary (2008): 91 schools; 16,123 students (males 8,044, females 8,079); 645 teachers (males 119, females 526).

Secondary (2005 unless otherwise indicated): 40 schools (2008); 7,487 students (males 3,716, females 3,771); 665 teachers (males 350, females 315).

Teacher-training (2001): 198 students; 22 teachers.

Vocational (2001): 1,303 students; 17 teachers.

Pupil-teacher Ratio (primary education, UNESCO estimate): 25.0 in 2007/08. Source: UNESCO Institute for Statistics.

Adult Literacy Rate (UNESCO estimates): 92.5% (males 93%; females 92%) in 2001. Source: UNESCO, *Assessment of Resources, Best Practices and Gaps in Gender, Science and Technology in Kiribati.*

Directory

The Government

HEAD OF STATE

President (Beretitenti): ANOTE TONG (elected 4 July 2003; re-elected 17 October 2007; re-elected 13 January 2012).

Vice-President (Kauoman-ni-Beretitenti): TEIMA ONORIO.

CABINET
(May 2013)

President and Minister for Foreign Affairs and Immigration: ANOTE TONG.

Vice-President and Minister for Internal and Social Affairs: TEIMA ONORIO.

Minister for Public Works and Utilities: KIRABUKE TEIAUA.

Minister for Education, Youth and Sports Development: MAERE TEKANENE.

Minister for Communications, Transport and Tourism Development: TABERANNANG TIMEON.

Minister for Health and Medical Services: Dr KAUTU TENAUA.

Minister for Environment, Lands and Agricultural Development: TIARITE KWONG.

Minister for Commerce, Industry and Co-operatives: PINTO KATIA.

Minister for Finance and Economic Development: TOM MURDOCH.

Minister for Fisheries and Marine Resource Development: TINIAN REIHER.

Minister for the Line and Phoenix Islands: TAWITA TEMOKU.

Minister for Labour and Human Resource Development: BOUTU BATERIKI.

Attorney-General: TITABU TABANE.

MINISTRIES

Office of the President (Beretitenti): POB 68, Bairiki, Tarawa; tel. 21183; fax 21145.

Ministry of Commerce, Industry and Co-operatives: POB 510, Betio, Tarawa; tel. 26158; fax 26233; e-mail enquiry@mcic.gov.ki; internet www.mcic.gov.ki.

Ministry of Communications, Transport and Tourism Development: POB 487, Betio, Tarawa; tel. 26003; fax 26193.

Ministry of Education, Youth and Sports Development: POB 263, Bikenibeu, Tarawa; tel. 28091; fax 28222.

Ministry of Environment, Lands and Agricultural Development: POB 234, Bikenibeu, Tarawa; tel. 28211; fax 28334.

Ministry of Finance and Economic Development: POB 67, Bairiki, Tarawa; tel. 21801; fax 21307; e-mail account@mfep.gov.ki; internet www.mfep.gov.ki.

Ministry of Fisheries and Marine Resource Development: POB 64, Bairiki, Tarawa; tel. 21099; fax 21120.

Ministry of Foreign Affairs and Immigration: POB 68, Bairiki, Tarawa; tel. 21342; fax 21466; e-mail mfa@tskl.net.ki.

Ministry of Health and Medical Services: POB 268, Bikenibeu, Tarawa; tel. 28100; fax 28152; e-mail mhfp@tskl.net.ki.

Ministry of Internal and Social Affairs: POB 75, Bairiki, Tarawa; tel. 21092; fax 21133; e-mail homeaffairs@tskl.net.ki.

Ministry of Labour and Human Resource Development: POB 69, Bairiki, Tarawa; tel. 21097; fax 21452; internet www.labour.gov.ki.

Ministry of the Line and Phoenix Islands: Kiritimati Island; tel. 81211; fax 81278.

Ministry of Public Works and Utilities: POB 498, Betio, Tarawa; tel. 26192; fax 26172.

President and Legislature

PRESIDENT

Election, 13 January 2012

Candidate	Votes	% of votes
Anote Tong	14,315	42.20
Tetaua Taitai	11,866	34.98
Rimeta Beniamina	7,738	22.81
Total	33,919	100.00

MANEABA NI MAUNGATABU
(House of Assembly)

This is a unicameral body comprising 42 elected members (most of whom formally present themselves for election as independent candidates), and one nominated representative of the Banaban community, along with the Attorney-General in an ex officio capacity (if the latter is not elected). An election was held on 21 October 2011, with a second round of voting being conducted on 28 October. A total of 30 members of the outgoing Maneaba were re-elected in 2011. Boutokan Te Koaua (Pillars of Truth) secured 15 of the 42 elective seats, while Karikirakean Tei-Kiribati (United Coalition Party) won 10 and the Maurin Kiribati Party three, with the remainder obtained by independents.

Speaker: TAOMATI IUTA.

Election Commission

Election Commission: Tarawa; Electoral Commr RINE UEARA.

Political Organizations

Political organizations in Kiribati are not conventional organized bodies but loose groupings of individuals supporting similar policies. In addition to the groupings listed below, also in existence are the National Progressive Party, led by Teatao Teannaki, and the Liberal Party, led by Tewareka Tentoa.

Boutokan Te Koaua (Pillars of Truth): c/o Maneaba Ni Maungatabu, Tarawa; tel. 21880; fax 21278; mems affiliated to Anote Tong.

Karikirakean Tei-Kiribati (United Coalition Party): c/o Maneaba Ni Maungatabu, Tawara; tel. 21880; fax 21278; f. 2010; est. by merger of Maneaban Te Mauri and Kiribati Tabomoa groupings; mems affiliated to Tetaua Taitai.

Maurin Kiribati Party: c/o Maneaba Ni Maungatabu, Tawara; Sec. NABUTI MWEMWENIKARAWA.

Diplomatic Representation

EMBASSY AND HIGH COMMISSIONS IN KIRIBATI

Australia: POB 77, Bairiki, Tarawa; tel. 21184; fax 21904; e-mail ahc.tarawa@dfat.gov.au; internet www.kiribati.embassy.gov.au; High Commissioner GEORGE FRASER.

New Zealand: POB 53, Bairiki, Tarawa; tel. 21400; fax 21402; e-mail nzhc@tskl.net.ki; High Commissioner MIKE WALSH.

Taiwan (Republic of China): Bairiki, Tarawa; tel. 22557; fax 22535; e-mail Kir@mofa.gov.tw; Ambassador ABRAHAM CHU.

Judicial System

There are 24 Magistrates' Courts (each consisting of one presiding magistrate and up to eight other magistrates) hearing civil, criminal and land cases. When hearing civil or criminal cases, the presiding magistrate sits with two other magistrates, and when hearing land cases with four other magistrates. A single magistrate has national jurisdiction in civil and criminal matters. Appeal from the Magistrates' Courts lies, in civil and criminal matters, to a single judge of the High Court, and, in matters concerning land, divorce and inheritance, to the High Court's Land Division, which consists of a judge and two Land Appeal Magistrates.

The High Court of Kiribati is a superior court of record and has unlimited jurisdiction. It consists of the Chief Justice and a Puisne Judge. Appeal from a single judge of the High Court, both as a Court of the First Instance and in its appellate capacity, lies to the Kiribati Court of Appeal, which is also a court of record and consists of a panel of three judges.

All judicial appointments are made by the Beretitenti (President).

High Court: POB 501, Betio, Tarawa; tel. 26007; fax 26149; Chief Justice Sir JOHN BAPTIST MURIA.

Religion

CHRISTIANITY

Most of the population are Christians: 53.4% Roman Catholic and 39.2% members of the Kiribati Protestant Church, according to the 1990 census.

The Roman Catholic Church

Kiribati forms part of the diocese of Tarawa and Nauru, suffragan to the archdiocese of Suva (Fiji). At 31 December 2007 the diocese contained an estimated 60,686 adherents. The Bishop participates in the Catholic Bishops' Conference of the Pacific, based in Suva (Fiji).

Bishop of Tarawa and Nauru: Most Rev. PAUL EUSEBIUS MEA KAIUEA, Bishop's House, POB 79, Bairiki, Tarawa; tel. 21279; fax 21401; e-mail diocesetarawa@tskl.net.ki.

The Anglican Communion

Kiribati is within the diocese of Polynesia, part of the Anglican Church in Aotearoa, New Zealand and Polynesia. The Bishop in Polynesia is resident in Fiji.

Protestant Church

Kiribati Protestant Church: POB 80, Bairiki, Tarawa; tel. 21195; fax 21453; e-mail kpc@tskl.net.ki; f. 1988; Moderator Rev. BAITEKE NABETARI; Gen. Sec. Rev. MAREWEIA RITETI; over 30,000 mems.

Other Churches

Seventh-day Adventist, Church of God and Assembly of God communities are also represented, as is the Church of Jesus Christ of Latter-day Saints (Mormon).

BAHÁ'Í FAITH

National Spiritual Assembly: POB 269, Bikenibeu, Tarawa; tel. and fax 28074; e-mail natbahaikiribati@gmail.com; 2,400 mems resident in 100 localities in 1995.

The Press

Butim'aea Manin te Euangkerio: POB 80, Bairiki, Tarawa; tel. 21195; e-mail kpc@tskl.net.ki; f. 1913; Protestant Church newspaper; weekly; a monthly publication *Te Kaotan te Ota* is also produced; Editor Rev. TOOM TOAKAI.

Kiribati Business Link: Bairiki, Tarawa; English.

Kiribati Independent: Tarawa; f. 2011; fortnightly; Editor TABERANNANG KORAUABA.

Kiribati Newstar: POB 10, Bairiki, Tarawa; tel. 21652; fax 21671; f. 2000; independent; weekly; English and I-Kiribati; Editor-in-Chief NGAUEA UATIOA.

Te Itoi ni Kiribati: POB 231, Bikenibeu, Tarawa; tel. 28138; fax 21341; f. 1914; Roman Catholic Church newsletter; monthly; circ. 2,300.

Te Mauri: Protestant Church newspaper; Editor BATIRI BATAUA.

Te Uekera: Broadcasting and Publications Authority, POB 78, Bairiki, Tarawa; tel. 21162; fax 21096; e-mail bpa_admin@tskl.net.ki; f. 1945; bi-weekly; English and I-Kiribati; Editor ROOTI TERUBEA; circ. 2,000.

Broadcasting and Communications

TELECOMMUNICATIONS

Telecom Kiribati Ltd: Bairiki, Tarawa; govt-owned; Gen. Man. ENOTA INGINTAU.

Telecom Services Kiribati Ltd: POB 72, Bairiki, Tarawa; tel. 20700; fax 21424; e-mail admin@tskl.net.ki; internet www.tskl.net.ki; f. 1990; Chair. ELLIOT ALI; CEO BARANIKO TONGANIBEIA.

BROADCASTING

Regulatory Authority

Broadcasting and Publications Authority: POB 78, Bairiki, Tarawa; tel. 21187; fax 21096; Gen. Man. BETARIM RIMON.

Radio

Radio Kiribati: Broadcasting and Publications Authority, POB 78, Bairiki, Tarawa; tel. 21187; fax 21096; f. 1954; statutory body; station Radio Kiribati broadcasting on SW and MW transmitters; programmes in I-Kiribati (90%) and English (10%); some advertising; Gen. Man. TANIERI TEIBUAKO.

Television

Television Kiribati Ltd: Betio, Tarawa; tel. 26036; fax 26045; f. 1987; suspended by the Govt in March 2013 owing to financial difficulties; a review to decide whether the closure should be permanent was subsequently initiated; CEO TAOM KAITARA.

Finance

(cap. = capital; dep. = deposits; res = reserves)

BANKING

ANZ Bank (Kiribati) Ltd: POB 66, Bairiki, Tarawa; tel. 21095; fax 21200; e-mail anzkiribati@anz.com; internet www.anz.com/kiribati; f. 1984; 75% owned by ANZ Bank, 25% by Govt of Kiribati; fmrly The Bank of Kiribati Ltd, name changed as above 2009; CEO ISIKELI TUITUKU; 3 brs.

Development Bank of Kiribati: POB 33, Bairiki, Tarawa; tel. 21345; fax 21297; e-mail dbk@tskl.net.ki; f. 1986; took over the assets of the National Loans Board; identifies, promotes and finances small-scale projects; auth. cap. \$A5m.; Gen. Man. KIETAU TABWEBWEITI; 5 brs.

A network of lending entities known as 'village banks' operates throughout the islands, as do a number of credit unions under the management of the Credit Union League.

INSURANCE

Kiribati Insurance Corpn: POB 509, Betio, Tarawa; tel. 253367; fax 25338; e-mail enquire@kic.org.ki; internet www.kic.org.ki; f. 1981; govt-owned; sole insurance co; reinsures overseas; Gen. Man. TEIBABA ABERA.

Trade and Industry

GOVERNMENT AGENCIES

Kiribati Copra Mill Co Ltd: POB 607, Betio, Tarawa; tel. 26831; fax 26635; e-mail kcmc@tskl.net.ki; internet www.kcmcl.ki; f. 2001.

Kiribati Housing Corporation: Bairiki, Tarawa; tel. 21092; operates the Housing Loan and Advice Centre; Chair. TOKOREAUA KAIRORO.

Kiribati Provident Fund: POB 76, Bairiki, Tarawa; tel. 21153; fax 21300; internet www.kpf.com.ki; f. 1977; Chair. TEKIERA ABERA.

CHAMBER OF COMMERCE

Kiribati Chamber of Commerce: POB 550, Betio, Tarawa; tel. 26351; fax 26332; Pres. MARTIN TOFINGA.

UTILITIES

Public Utilities Board: POB 443, Betio, Tarawa; tel. 26292; fax 26106; e-mail ceo.pub@tskl.net.ki; f. 1977; govt-owned; provides electricity, water and sewerage services in Tarawa; CEO TABOIA METUTERA.

Solar Energy Company (SEC): POB 493 Betio, Tarawa; tel. 26058; fax 26210; e-mail sec@tskl.net.ki; a co-operative administering and implementing solar-generated electricity projects in North Tarawa and the outer islands.

CO-OPERATIVE SOCIETIES

Co-operative societies dominate trading in Tarawa and enjoy a virtual monopoly outside the capital, except for Banaba and Kiritimati.

Bobotin Kiribati Ltd (BKL): POB 485, Betio, Tarawa; tel. 26092; fax 26224; replaced Kiribati Co-operative Wholesale Society; govt-owned; Gen. Man. AKAU TIARE.

The Kiribati Copra Co-operative Society Ltd: POB 489, Betio, Tarawa; tel. 26534; fax 26391; e-mail kccs@tskl.net.ki; f. 1976; the sole exporter of copra; 7 cttee mems; 29 mem. socs; Chair. RAIMON TAAKE; CEO RUTIANO BENETITO.

TRADE UNIONS

Kiribati Trades Union Congress (KTUC): POB 166, Bairiki, Tarawa; tel. 28157; fax 28712; e-mail ktc@tskl.net.ki; f. 1982; unions and asscns affiliated to the KTUC include: Fishermen's Union, Co-operative Workers' Union, Seamen's Union, Teachers' Union, Nurses' Asscn, Public Employees' Asscn, Bankers' Union, Butaritari Rural Workers' Union, Christmas Island Union of Federated Workers, Pre-School Teachers' Asscn, Makim Island Rural Workers' Org., Nanolelei Retailers' Union, Plantation Workers' Union of Fanning Island and Overseas Fishermen's Union; 2,500 mems; Pres. TATOA KAITEIE; Gen. Sec. TAMARETI TAAU.

Transport

ROADS

Wherever practicable, roads are built on all atolls, and connecting causeways between islets are also being constructed as funds and labour permit. Kiribati has about 670 km of roads that are suitable for motor vehicles; all-weather roads exist in Tarawa and Kiritimati. In March 2011 it was announced that, with a loan of US $12m. from the Asian Development Bank, the road network in South Tarawa was to be upgraded.

SHIPPING

A major project to rehabilitate the port terminal and facilities at Betio, with finance totalling some US $22m. from Japan, was completed in 2000. There are other port facilities at Banaba, Kanton and English Harbour.

Kiribati Shipping Services Ltd (KSSL): POB 495, Betio, Tarawa; tel. 26195; fax 26204; e-mail kssl@tskl.net.ki; govt-owned; operates 3 passenger/freight vessels on inter-island services connecting Kiribati, Nauru, Tuvalu, the Wallis and Futuna Islands, and Suva (Fiji), and 1 landing craft and multi-purpose cargo vessels between Fiji, Tuvalu, Nauru and Marshall Islands; Gen. Man. Capt. ITIBWINNANG AIAIMOA.

Nikoraoi Shipping: Betio, Tarawa; tel. 26536; fax 26367.

CIVIL AVIATION

There are five international airports (Bonriki on South Tarawa, Cassidy on Kiritimati, Antekana on Butaritari, as well as two others on Kanton and Tabuaeran) and several other airfields in Kiribati. Air Pacific, the Fijian carrier, operates services to Tarawa and Kiritimati, with links to Nadi (Fiji) and Honolulu (Hawaii, USA).

Air Kiribati Ltd: POB 274, Bonriki, Tarawa; tel. 28533; fax 29716; e-mail admin@airkiribati.net; internet www.airkiribati.net; f. 1977; fmrly Air Tungaru; national airline; operates scheduled services to outer islands; CEO Capt. IOSABATA NAMAKIN.

Tourism

Kiribati's attractions include fishing and bird-watching opportunities, as well as the sites of Second World War battles. In 1997 Caroline Island, situated close to the recently realigned International Date Line, was renamed Millennium Island, in an attempt to maximize its potential for attracting visitors. The Phoenix Islands Protected Area (PIPA), a 408,250-sq km expanse of marine and terrestrial habitats, was inscribed by UNESCO on its World Heritage List in 2010. PIPA contains about 800 species of fauna, including 200 coral species, 500 fish species, 18 marine mammals and 44 bird species. The objectives of the 2010–15 plan for the development of the tourism sector included an increase in the annual number of visitors to 10,000 by the end of the plan period. A campaign to attract more visitors was launched in April 2010. International visitor arrivals increased significantly after the campaign, reaching 4,701 in 2010 and a provisional 5,000 in 2011, largely supported by the Australian, US and New Zealand markets. Tourism receipts totalled US $3m. in 2009.

Kiribati National Tourism Office: Ministry of Communications, Transport and Tourism Development, POB 487, Betio, Tarawa; tel. 25573; fax 26193; e-mail info@kiribatitourism.gov.ki; internet www.visit-kiribati.com; Senior Tourist Officer IATAAKE KING.

Defence

Kiribati has no professional defence forces. Assistance is provided by Australia and New Zealand. In 2010 expenditure by Kiribati on the islands' defence totalled nearly $A8.0m. (equivalent to 9.1% of total government spending).

Education

Education is compulsory for children between six and 15 years of age. This generally involves six years at a primary school and at least three years at a secondary school. Every atoll is provided with at least one primary school. In 2008 there were 91 primary schools and 40 secondary schools. There were 16,123 pupils enrolled at primary schools in 2008; 7,487 pupils attended secondary schools in 2005. Teaching staff at primary level numbered 645 in 2008; in 2005 there were 665 secondary school teachers. In 2001/02 enrolment at primary schools reached 97% of pupils in the relevant age-group, according to UNESCO estimates. In 2004/05 enrolment at secondary schools included 69% of students in the relevant age-group, according to UNESCO estimates. The tertiary sector is based on Tarawa, except for one of the two private colleges, which is based on Abemama. The Government administers a technical college and training colleges for teachers, nurses and seafarers (the last, the Marine Training Centre, trains about 200 students each year for employment by overseas shipping companies). There were 198 students enrolled in teacher-training and 1,303 in other vocational training in 2001. An extra-mural centre of the University of the South Pacific (based in Fiji) is also located on South Tarawa. In 2010 government expenditure on education totalled $A16.3m. (equivalent to 18.6% of total expenditure).

THE DEMOCRATIC PEOPLE'S REPUBLIC OF KOREA

Introductory Survey

LOCATION, CLIMATE, LANGUAGE, RELIGION, FLAG, CAPITAL

The Democratic People's Republic of Korea (North Korea) occupies the northern part of the Korean peninsula, bordered to the north by the People's Republic of China and, for a very short section to the north-east, by the Russian Federation, and to the south by the Republic of Korea (South Korea). The climate is continental, with cold, dry winters and hot, humid summers; temperatures range from −6°C to 25°C (21°F to 77°F). The language is Korean. Buddhism, Christianity and Chundo Kyo are officially cited as the principal religions. The national flag (proportions 33 by 65) is red, with blue stripes on the upper and lower edges, each separated from the red by a narrow white stripe. Left of centre is a white disc containing a five-pointed red star. The capital is Pyongyang.

CONTEMPORARY POLITICAL HISTORY

Historical Context

Korea was formerly an independent monarchy. It was occupied by Japanese forces in 1905 and annexed by Japan in 1910, when the Emperor was deposed. Following Japan's surrender in August 1945, ending the Second World War, Korea was divided at latitude 38°N into military occupation zones, with Soviet forces in the North and US forces in the South. A Provisional People's Committee, led by Kim Il Sung of the Korean Communist Party (KCP), was established in the North in February 1946 and accorded government status by the Soviet occupation forces. In July the KCP merged with another group to form the North Korean Workers' Party. In 1947 a legislative body, the Choe Ko In Min Hoe Ui (Supreme People's Assembly—SPA), was established, and Kim Il Sung became Premier. A new Assembly was elected in August 1948, and the Democratic People's Republic of Korea (North Korea) was proclaimed on 9 September. In the same year the Republic of Korea (South Korea) was proclaimed in the South. Initially, North Korea was recognized only by the USSR and other communist countries. Soviet forces withdrew from North Korea in December 1948. In the following year, as a result of a merger between communists in the North and South, the Korean Workers' Party (KWP) was formed, under the leadership of Kim Il Sung. The KWP continued to hold power in the 21st century.

The two republics each claimed to have legitimate jurisdiction over the whole Korean peninsula. North Korean forces crossed the 38th parallel in June 1950, precipitating a three-year war between North and South. The UN mounted a collective defence action in support of South Korea, and the invasion was repelled. North Korean forces were supported by the People's Republic of China from October 1950. The heavy bombardment of the North resulted in a high number of civilian casualties. Peace talks began in July 1951 and an armistice agreement was concluded in July 1953. The cease-fire line, which approximately followed the 38th parallel, became the frontier between North and South Korea, with a demilitarized zone (DMZ), supervised by UN forces, separating the two countries. No final peace agreement was concluded, and North and South Korea remained technically at war.

Domestic Political Affairs

Through the 'personality cult' of Kim Il Sung (the 'Great Leader') and of his son Kim Jong Il (the 'Dear Leader'), and a policy of strict surveillance of the entire population, overt opposition to the KWP was effectively eliminated. The only organized opposition to the regime (albeit in exile) appeared to be the Salvation Front for the Democratic Unification of Chosun, established by former military and other officials of North Korea in the early 1990s, with branches in Russia, Japan and China. International human rights organizations indicated that they believed there to be a number of concentration camps in North Korea, in which many thousands of political prisoners were being held (see Humanitarian Issues).

A new Constitution, adopted in December 1972, created the office of President, and Kim Il Sung was duly elected to the post. Kim Jong Il was appointed to several key positions within the KWP in 1980. In July 1984 Radio Pyongyang referred to Kim Jong Il, for the first time, as the 'sole successor' to his father, but there were reports of opposition to the President's heir, particularly among older members of the KWP.

Following elections to the eighth SPA, in November 1986 (when the 655 members were returned unopposed), Kim Il Sung was re-elected President, and a new Administration Council (cabinet) was formed. In March 1990 Kim Il Sung was returned to the post of President, and Kim Jong Il was appointed to his first state (as distinct from party) post, as First Vice-Chairman of the National Defence Commission. In February 1991 it was rumoured that there had been an unsuccessful military coup against Kim Jong Il. In December he was appointed Supreme Commander of the Korean People's Army (KPA), in place of his father, and in January 1992 he was reported to have been given control of foreign policy. In April Kim Jong Il was appointed to the rank of Marshal, while his father assumed the title of Grand Marshal.

In what was interpreted as a partial attempt to adapt to the change in international conditions following the collapse of communist regimes world-wide, the SPA (according to South Korean reports) made several amendments to North Korea's Constitution in April 1992. Principal among these were the deletion of all references to Marxism-Leninism, and the promotion of 'economic openness' to allow limited foreign investment in North Korea (although the KWP's guiding principle of *Juche*, or self-reliance, was strongly emphasized). In September measures to address the deteriorating economic situation included a drastic devaluation of the national currency. At the fifth session of the ninth SPA in April 1993 Kim Jong Il was elected Chairman of the National Defence Commission. In July Kim Il Sung's younger brother, Kim Yong Ju, unexpectedly returned to political life after a 17-year absence, and was subsequently elevated to the position of Vice-President and to membership of the Central Committee of the KWP's Political Bureau (Politburo).

The death of Kim Il Sung and rise of Kim Jong Il

Kim Il Sung died of heart failure on 8 July 1994. One hundred days of national mourning were observed, but, contrary to expectations, Kim Jong Il was not appointed to the leading post of President of North Korea. Kim Jong Il did not appear in public during this period, reviving earlier speculation that he was either in poor health or that a struggle for power was taking place. It was thought that Kim Song Ae, the widow of Kim Il Sung and stepmother of Kim Jong Il, favoured her eldest son, Kim Pyong Il, for the presidency. In February 1995 the Minister of the People's Armed Forces, Marshal O Jin U, died; O had been a significant supporter within the military of Kim Jong Il's succession. Scheduled elections to the SPA did not take place in April 1995, and no session of the Assembly was convened in 1996.

Meanwhile, from the mid-1990s, the influence of the KPA expanded significantly, as Kim Jong Il increasingly relied upon the military to maintain his power, and the policy of *Songun* ('military first') was emphasized as the regime's central doctrine. The 50th anniversary of the establishment of the KWP in October 1995 was dominated by the military rather than the party, and several generals were promoted. However, Kim Jong Il did not assume any new posts. In February 1996 Sung Hye Rim, a former consort of Kim Jong Il and mother of his eldest son, defected to a Western European country. In February 1997 Premier Kang Song San, who had made no public appearance since early 1996, was dismissed, and replaced on an acting basis by Hong Song Nam. Deepening social unrest was indicated by an increase in the rate of defections. In February 1997 Hwang Jang Yop, a close adviser to Kim Jong Il, sought political asylum in the

South Korean embassy in the People's Republic of China while returning from an official visit to Japan, and warned that North Korea was preparing to launch a military assault on South Korea. Hwang's defection appeared to precipitate significant changes in the KWP and military high command, as did the deaths of the Minister of the People's Armed Forces, Marshal Choe Kwang, and of his deputy, Kim Kwang Jin. Many senior officials were replaced, and some 123 generals, including many allies of Kim Jong Il, were promoted in rank in April. In August two senior North Korean diplomats, including the ambassador to Egypt, defected to the USA. There were also rumours of unrest and coup attempts, and several senior officials disappeared from public view without explanation. The official mourning period for Kim Il Sung was formally declared to be at an end in July 1997, on the third anniversary of his death. It was announced that, henceforth, the country was to use the *Juche* calendar, with 1912, the year of Kim Il Sung's birth, designated the first year of the new calendar. On 8 October 1997 Kim Jong Il was elected General Secretary of the KWP.

Elections to the SPA finally took place in July 1998, at which the single list of candidates received 100% of the votes cast. Some two-thirds of the 687 deputies were newcomers to the Assembly, while the military reportedly doubled its representation. The first session of the 10th SPA was convened in September. However, the anticipated appointment of Kim Jong Il as President of North Korea did not occur, as the post was effectively abolished under major amendments to the Constitution that extensively revised the structure of government. The deceased Kim Il Sung was designated 'Eternal President', thus remaining *de jure* head of state, while Kim Jong Il, who had been re-elected Chairman of the National Defence Commission (now apparently the highest office in the state hierarchy), was reported to have assumed the role of de facto head of state. Vice-Marshal Jo Myong Rok, the Director of the General Political Bureau of the KPA, was appointed First Vice-Chairman of the Commission, becoming the de facto second-ranking official in North Korea. The Cabinet, as the Administration Council was redesignated, assumed many of the functions of the Central People's Committee, which was abolished. A new Presidium of the SPA was established, the President of which was to represent the State in diplomatic affairs; Kim Yong Nam, hitherto Minister of Foreign Affairs, was appointed to this position. Hong Song Nam was formally appointed Premier of the new Cabinet. Jo Chang Dok and Kwak Pom Gi, were appointed as Vice-Premiers.

In October 2000 the Minister of Finance, Rim Kyong Suk, and the President of the Central Bank of North Korea, Jong Song Thaek, were dismissed. They were replaced, respectively, by Mun Il Bong and Kim Wan Su. The replacement of the Minister of Foreign Trade in December was similarly unexplained. The Minister of Agriculture was replaced in March 2001.

In January 2001 the Government urged a 'new way of thinking' to address the country's economic problems and to complement the *Kangsong Taeguk* ('prosperous and powerful nation') philosophy. Meanwhile, the number of people defecting from the North to the South continued to increase, bringing the total to 650 since 1996. At the fifth session of the 10th SPA held in March 2002, a new land planning law was adopted. Premier Hong Song Nam also urged improved trade and economic co-operation, including joint ventures with other countries. In April Kim Jong Il promoted some 55 military leaders, including Jang Song U, the elder brother of Kim's brother-in-law, Jang Song Thaek.

The question of the succession of the next generation of leadership became increasingly important following Kim Jong Il's 60th birthday in February 2002. Kim was initially believed to have been preparing his eldest son, Kim Jong Nam, who had served in the Ministry of Public Security and as head of the country's information technology industry since the late 1990s; however, in May 2001 he was detained in Tokyo, Japan, on charges of entering that country with a false passport, and subsequently deported to China. Thenceforth it was reported that Kim Jong Il was preparing for leadership Kim Jong Chol, the elder son of Ko Yong Hui, described as Kim Jong Il's unofficial wife.

In September 2002 the Government designated the city of Sinuiju a 'Special Administrative Region' designed to attract foreign investment, and appointed Yang Bin, a Chinese-born Dutch citizen, as its first governor. However, within days of his appointment, Yang was arrested by the Chinese authorities on corruption charges, and he was unable to assume his post. In late 2004 there were indications that the Sinuiju project had been abandoned, although in July 2006 it was reported that loyalists and foreign-currency management groups were being moved into the area. In mid-2007 it was reported that 3,000 families were being relocated from Pyongyang to Sinuiju, which had apparently been declared a special economic zone. In late 2002 the Government also established a special industrial zone in Kaesong, with South Korean investment, and a special tourist zone in the region of Mount Kumgang, although these did not have the same special status as Sinuiju. A meeting of senior law enforcement officials was held in Pyongyang in December during which Premier Hong urged the elimination of 'non-socialist elements'. In early 2003 it was reported that travel restrictions within the country had been reintroduced.

Kim Jong Il did not attend the sixth session of the 10th SPA, held in March 2003. Having reportedly disappeared from public view for 50 days, Kim reappeared in April, in which month celebrations were organized in Pyongyang to mark the 10th anniversary of Kim's election as Chairman of the National Defence Commission. Further celebrations took place in July to commemorate the 50th anniversary of the Korean War truce (celebrated as a triumph for North Korea by the country's media). In August elections were held to form the 11th SPA. Voter turn-out was reported to be have been 99.9%, and all 687 candidates were elected unopposed. At the first session of the 11th SPA in September, Kim Jong Il was re-elected as Chairman of the National Defence Commission. The appointment of Pak Pong Ju, hitherto Minister of Chemical Industry, as Premier was endorsed.

In July 2004 Ju Sang Song was appointed as Minister of People's Security, replacing Choe Ryong Su. Choe had been removed from his post only one year after being appointed, and the reason for his removal was unclear. In November there was speculation that Kim's power might be weakening, following reports that portraits of him had been removed from public locations. It was also noted that official news reports no longer referred to Kim by the honorific title of 'Dear Leader'. Some sources claimed that Kim himself was attempting to diminish the personality cult surrounding him. However, there were tentative suggestions throughout 2004 that a power struggle was taking place in Pyongyang. It was believed that in April Kim had removed his brother-in-law, Jang Song Thaek, from his position as vice-director of the KWP Central Committee and placed him under house arrest. Later in the year Jang's wife, Kim Jong Il's sister Kim Kyong Hui, was injured in a traffic incident, which was believed to have been a deliberate attack. Meanwhile, in April Kim's eldest son, Kim Jong Nam, reportedly survived an assassination attempt in Austria.

In May 2005 South Korean media reported that the North Korean Minister of Post and Telecommunications, Ri Kum Bom, had been dismissed, apparently as a result of his failure to control the revelation of information earlier in the year disclosing that North Korea was in the process of combating outbreaks of avian influenza ('bird flu'). In August an unspecified number of prisoners were granted an amnesty to mark the 60th anniversary of the liberation of the Korean peninsula from Japanese rule. In October the 60th anniversary of the KWP was celebrated with a national meeting in Pyongyang, at which the primacy of the *Songun* policy was reaffirmed, as was the need for economic development in order to achieve the objective of *Kangsong Taeguk*. In January 2006 Jang Song Thaek made his first public appearance since 2003, prompting speculation that he had been rehabilitated following his apparent removal from favour in 2004.

While thousands took to the streets in October 2006 for mass rallies to celebrate the country's first nuclear test, in November a rare protest against the authorities occurred in a town in North Hamgyong Province. Although the number of protesters was said to be little more than 100, the demonstration was highly significant, since private mass activities were forbidden by North Korean law. According to a report on *Daily NK*, a website maintained by a group campaigning for democracy in North Korea, residents of Hoiryeong were demonstrating against 'refurbishment fees' for a local market imposed on them by the town's officials. North Korean refugees arriving in China also reported growing discontent under the regime, with 90% of the 1,300 refugees questioned by the bipartisan US Committee on Human Rights in North Korea agreeing that North Koreans were expressing their concerns about persistent food shortages.

At the fifth session of the 11th SPA in April 2007, Premier Pak Pong Ju was replaced by Kim Yong Il, hitherto Minister of Land and Marine Transport. Although no official explanation was given, observers later suggested that Pak had unsuccessfully attempted to introduce economic reforms, including allowing greater autonomy for state enterprises. At the same time Vice-Marshal Kim Yong Chun, hitherto Chief of General Staff of the KPA, was appointed as a Vice-Chairman of the National Defence Commission, filling the vacancy left by the death of Yon Hyong Muk in October 2005. Gen. Kim Kyok Sik became the new KPA Chief of General Staff. The permanent staff of the National Defence Commission was expanded as part of a further reorganization of senior military officials in May 2007, with the appointment of Gen. Ri Myong Su, the former operations director of the KPA, as a standing member. The changes at the National Defence Commission were generally interpreted as an attempt to enhance its role and powers. Rumours suggesting that Kim Jong Il's health was deteriorating prompted renewed speculation regarding his successor, which intensified in August following reports that Kim's eldest son, Kim Jong Nam, had returned from exile to work in the organization and guidance bureau of the KWP. In November it was reported that Jang Song Thaek had been promoted from the position of vice-director within the KWP to the directorship of the party's department responsible for state internal security, while Kim's second eldest son, Kim Jong Chol, had been appointed as a vice-director of another department of the KWP.

The future leadership question

Several government changes were reported to have been implemented at senior level in 2008–09. Meanwhile, elections to the new SPA, originally due to be held in August 2008, were postponed, thereby further increasing speculation about the health of Kim Jong Il, who failed to attend a parade commemorating the country's 60th anniversary in early September and was not seen in public for three months subsequently. Although he had resumed his public duties by the beginning of 2009, Kim Jong Il did not appear to be in robust health, and it was widely concluded that he had suffered a stroke.

In January 2009 it was announced that the elections for the 12th SPA would take place on 8 March. A total of 687 candidates were duly elected unopposed; 316 deputies were reported to be entering the SPA for the first time, fewer than the number of new members elected in 2003. The level of voter participation was declared to have been 99.98%. Observers noted that the list of incoming deputies included none of Kim Jong Il's three sons, the youngest of whom, Kim Jong Un (the younger son of Ko Yong Hui), had become the subject of much speculation with regard to the succession issue. In February 2009 Gen. Ri Yong Ho replaced Kim Kyok Sik as KPA Chief of General Staff. Various changes to the leadership were effected at the first session of the SPA, which opened on 9 April. Notable appointments were those of Kim Wan Su as Minister of Finance and Ri Kwang Gon as President of the Central Bank, who exchanged responsibilities. Ro Tu Chol remained as a Vice-Premier, in addition being appointed as Chairman of the State Planning Commission. O Su Yong relinquished the electronics industry portfolio upon his appointment as a Vice-Premier, in place of Jon Sung Hun. Kim Jong Il's influential brother-in-law, Jang Song Thaek, became a member of the National Defence Commission, of which Vice-Marshal O Kuk Ryol (a former Chief of General Staff of the KPA) was appointed a Vice-Chairman, as was the Minister of the People's Armed Forces, Vice-Marshal Kim Yong Chun. Also joining the National Defence Commission were Gen. U Tong Chuk Chuk (the deputy director of the State Security Agency) and Ju Kyu Chang, a senior party official and aide of Kim Jong Il.

Also in April 2009 the SPA adopted the text of a revised Constitution (although this was not published until the end of September): for the first time, this gave official recognition to the Chairman of the National Defence Commission (the post held by Kim Jong Il) as the 'supreme leader' of the nation, and added a reference to *Songun* alongside *Juche* as guiding principles. In June South Korean media quoted intelligence reports that Kim Jong Un had formally been declared his father's successor; however, this was not confirmed in the North Korean state media, and it appeared possible that Kim Jong Un's youth (he was believed to be only 27 or 28 years of age) would be an obstacle to his acceptance by the political establishment.

In early December 2009 the Government announced a revaluation of the currency, obliging North Koreans to exchange existing bank-notes for new notes worth 1% of the old currency. A limit on the amount per family that could be exchanged meant that savings above a modest level became worthless. The aim of the revaluation was apparently to reduce inflation and to eliminate profiteering by unofficial traders; however, it resulted in price rises, disruption to the distribution of goods, and food shortages. Furthermore, there were reports of considerable public resentment. In February 2010 it was reported that the official responsible for the revaluation, Pak Nam Gi (the director of the KWP's department for planning and finance), had been dismissed, and in March he was reported to have been executed.

In January 2010 An Tong Chun (hitherto chairman of the central committee of the Korean Writers' Union) was appointed Minister of Culture. Between April and June the deaths of three senior members of the KWP were reported, namely: Ri Yong Chol, deputy director of the party's organization and guidance department, with responsibility for the supervision of military organization; Ri Je Gang, a senior deputy director of the same department, who died in a car crash in June; and Kim Jung Rin, responsible for workers' organizations. In addition, the retirement was reported in May of Kim Il Chol, a member of the National Defence Commission and hitherto the Vice-Minister of the People's Armed Forces. Also in May, the Government condemned as a 'fabrication' a report by international experts that concluded that the sinking of a South Korean naval vessel in March had been caused by a North Korean torpedo (see Inter-Korean Relations), leading to speculation by observers that the attack might have been perpetrated by officers who had not been duly authorized, or alternatively that the attack had been deliberately ordered by the Government in an attempt to associate the possible future leader, Kim Jong Un, with a successful military action.

In an unusual development, after its regular meeting in April 2010 the SPA convened for a second session in June, when the appointment of Choe Yong Rim (hitherto chief secretary of the KWP's Pyongyang city committee) as Premier was announced, replacing Kim Yong Il, possibly because the latter had presided over the unsuccessful currency revaluation at the end of the previous year. Six new Vice-Premiers were appointed and three recalled; several cabinet portfolios were reallocated. The appointments as Vice-Premier included that of Jo Pyong Ju, retaining his previous post as Minister of Machine-Building Industries, and Han Kwang Bok, retaining her previous post as Minister of the Electronics Industry; the four other new Vice-Premiers were Kang Nung Su (hitherto chairman of the State Film Commission), Kim Rak Hui, Ri Tae Nam and Jon Ha Chol (senior KWP officials reportedly specializing in agricultural management, steel production and financial planning, respectively). Other appointments were to the ministries responsible for light industry (An Song Ju), foodstuff and daily necessities industry (Jo Yong Chol), and physical culture and sports (Pak Myong Chol). The promotion of Jang Song Thaek, Kim Jong Il's brother-in-law, to the powerful position of a Vice-Chairman of the National Defence Commission was also announced. Both Jang and Choe Yong Rim were reported to be supporters of Kim Jong Un as a successor to his father.

In August 2010 the former Premier, Pak Pong Ju, was described as a First Deputy Director of the KWP Central Committee, having apparently been reinstated after his demotion in 2007; Pak was believed to be a close ally of Jang Song Thaek. In September 2010 Kang Sok Ju, a cousin of Kim Jong Il and hitherto the Vice-Minister of Foreign Affairs, was promoted to Vice-Premier, while two senior negotiators in the six-nation talks on North Korea's nuclear policy, Kim Kye Gwan and Ri Yong Ho (as distinct from Gen. Ri, the Chief of General Staff of the armed forces), became Vice-Ministers of Foreign Affairs. Later in September a delegates' conference of the KWP was convened, the first such meeting since 1980. Widespread speculation that the conference would be the setting for the official appearance of Kim Jong Un as Kim Jong Il's heir appeared to be confirmed when, shortly beforehand, Kim Jong Un (who had no record of military service) was awarded the rank of general. The same rank was conferred on Kim Kyong Hui (the sister of Kim Jong Il and wife of Jang Song Thaek), and on two other civilians: Choe Ryong Hae (whose father, Choe Hyon, had been a close colleague of Kim Il Sung), and Kim Kyong Ok (deputy director of the KWP's organization and guidance department).

At the conference itself, Kim Jong Il was re-elected General Secretary of the KWP. Kim Jong Un was appointed a Vice-Chairman of the KWP's Central Military Commission (a newly created post), and a member of the party's Central Committee; however, he was not given membership of the Politburo or the National Defence Commission. The KPA Chief of General Staff, Gen. Ri Yong Ho, was promoted to the rank of Vice-Marshal and became a member of the Presidium of the Politburo, and was also, alongside Kim Jong Un, appointed a Vice-Chairman of the

KWP's Central Military Commission. Jang Song Thaek was elected an alternate member of the Politburo and a member of the KWP's Central Military Commission, while his wife, Kim Kyong Hui, was also elected to the KWP's Politburo. Reports and photographs of Kim Jong Un published after the conference were believed to represent the first time that he had been mentioned by name in the North Korean media.

The 'Young General', as Kim Jong Un was now often called, appeared with Kim Jong Il at a large military parade held in Pyongyang in October 2010 to celebrate the 65th anniversary of the KWP, and was subsequently reported to be accompanying his father on various official visits. In November Kim Jong Un was reported to be in charge of an investigation into corrupt officials. In the same month Vice-Marshal Jo Myong Rok, the Director of the KPA General Political Department and First Vice-Chairman of the National Defence Commission, died, and there was speculation that Kim Jong Un might shortly be appointed to the latter post. Observing the year's events, analysts generally concluded that, in the event of Kim Jong Il's death or incapacity, while Kim Jong Un might be his nominal successor, the latter's youth and inexperience would mean that real power would be exercised collectively by older party members, in particular Jang Song Thaek, Kim Kyong Hui, and Vice-Marshal Ri Yong Ho.

In January 2011 Yi Kyong Sik replaced Kim Chang Sik as Minister of Agriculture, a post Yi was reported to have held previously between 2003 and 2008. Following a meeting of the SPA in April 2011 there were, contrary to expectations, no announcements of any new appointment for Kim Jong Un. A Vice-Premier, Ri Tae Nam, left his post for reasons of health. Ri Myong Su was appointed as Minister of People's Security, a position vacated in March by Ju Sang Song, also reportedly owing to ill health. Pak To Chun, an alternate member of the KWP Politburo, joined the membership of the National Defence Commission, replacing Jon Pyong Ho who was transferred to another post. In September Kim Sok Jun was reported to have replaced Pae Tae Jun as Minister of Land Development and Construction Affairs.

Recent developments: the succession of Kim Jong Un

Kim Jong Il died suddenly of heart failure on 17 December 2011. His death was followed by widespread public demonstrations of grief. Kim Jong Un was immediately described as the 'great successor' by the official media, and at his father's funeral ceremonies he was described as 'supreme leader of the party, the armed forces and the people' by the titular head of state, Kim Yong Nam. Kim Jong Un's uncle by marriage, Jang Song Thaek, was observed to be in close attendance during the ceremonies (unprecedentedly wearing military uniform, with insignia indicating that he had been awarded the rank of general). A meeting of the Politburo in late December was reported to have confirmed Kim Jong Un as Supreme Commander of the KPA. Official pronouncements during the early weeks of Kim Jong Un's leadership emphasized continuity and the maintenance of the *Songun* policy. In March 2012, however, South Korean media reported that, in an apparent purge, some senior North Korean military officers had been executed.

A KWP conference was convened in April 2012, at which Kim Jong Un was appointed to the newly created post of First Secretary of the party, while his deceased father, Kim Jong Il, was designated Eternal General Secretary. Kim Jong Un was also appointed Chairman of the party's Central Military Commission and elected to the Presidium of the Politburo. Choe Ryong Hae, recently promoted to the rank of Vice-Marshal, and reported as having recently been appointed (although he was a civilian) to the influential position of Director of the KPA General Political Department in succession to the late Jo Myong Rok, now became a Vice-Chairman of the party's Central Military Commission, and was also elected to the Presidium of the Politburo. (Besides Kim Jong Un and Choe Ryong Hae, the Presidium's other three members were Kim Yong Nam, Choe Yong Rim, the Premier, and Vice-Marshal Ri Yong Ho.) Two days later the transfer of power to Kim Jong Un was consolidated when a session of the SPA appointed him First Chairman of the National Defence Commission, in practice regarded as the highest office in the state hierarchy (with the late Kim Jong Il being designated Eternal Chairman); Choe Ryong Hae became a member of the National Defence Commission, as did Ri Myong Su, the Minister of People's Security. Also in April, as part of the celebrations to mark the 100th anniversary of the birth of Kim Il Sung, North Korea defied international protests and launched a long-range rocket, ostensibly with the intention of putting a satellite into orbit. It was widely suspected (as on previous occasions) that the operation was in fact intended to test long-range missile technology. The launch was promoted in North Korea as a symbol of the country's technological advances, but in the event the rocket was reported by US and South Korean agencies to have broken up shortly after take-off and fallen into the sea. In an unusual admission of failure, the North Korean authorities confirmed that the satellite had failed to go into orbit. The Government reacted indignantly to international condemnation of the launch, and throughout 2012 it maintained its traditionally belligerent attitude towards South Korea and the USA (see Inter-Korean Relations and Foreign Affairs).

During 2012 the official North Korean media encouraged public adulation of Kim Jong Un similar to that directed at his father and grandfather, although he appeared to be cultivating a more informal and affable image, sometimes appearing in the company of his wife, Ri Sol Ju. In July the sudden removal of Vice-Marshal Ri Yong Ho from all his political and military posts, officially due to illness, gave rise to speculation that Ri Yong Ho had objected to the increasing prominence of Choe Ryong Hae, and that Kim Jong Un (who assumed the rank of Marshal shortly afterwards) was attempting to exert his own authority over the armed forces. A little-known army general, Hyon Yong Chol, replaced Ri as Chief of General Staff. In November there were reports that Ri Yong Ho was under house arrest. Also in November Vice-Marshal Kim Jong Gak, who had replaced Vice-Marshal Kim Yong Chun as Minister of People's Armed Forces in April, was reported to have been replaced in his turn by Gen. Kim Kyok Sik, hitherto First Vice-Minister in the same department and reputed to favour a confrontational attitude to South Korea. It was observed that the state media gave greater prominence to economic affairs during 2012, and in August it was reported that reforms had been announced, including permitting farmers to keep and sell 30% of their output and allowing manufacturers to set their own prices; however, it was not clear whether these changes were already being implemented. In October it was announced that Hwang Min had replaced Yi Kyong Sik as Minister of Agriculture, while Kim Jae Song had replaced Han Kwang Bok (a Vice-Premier) as Minister of the Electronics Industry.

The North Korean Government again defied international opinion by launching another long-range rocket, ostensibly bearing a satellite (this time with apparent success) in December 2012 and by conducting a third test of a nuclear device in February 2013, encouraging public celebrations of both events. The Government's extremely bellicose reaction to joint exercises by South Korean and US forces in March and April also appeared to have the aim of increasing domestic support in the face of supposed external threats: mass rallies were held in Pyongyang and other cities, denouncing the military exercises and the UN Security Council's recent intensification of sanctions against North Korea (see Increasing tensions on the Korean peninsula). In May the reputedly hardline Minister of the People's Armed Forces, Gen. Kim Kyok Sik, was replaced by the younger Gen. Jang Jong Nam.

Humanitarian Issues

During the 1990s intermittent severe flooding interspersed with drought exacerbated food shortages in North Korea. Humanitarian assistance was provided by China, the USA, South Korea and Japan. (Subsequent provision of aid fluctuated in accordance with political developments: see Inter-Korean Relations and Foreign Affairs). In 1997 and 1998 the UN's World Food Programme (WFP, see p. 110) issued appeals for food and medical supplies. UN representatives sent to North Korea to assess the extent of the crisis confirmed that chronic malnutrition was widespread, particularly among infants, and that the medical system was no longer able to provide even basic health care. In 1998 agreement was reached with North Korea whereby additional UN staff were to be permitted to enter the country in order to monitor the distribution of aid, following allegations that previous supplies had been diverted to the army.

From 2000 intermittent severe weather conditions, including both drought and flooding, exacerbated the situation. A survey conducted by WFP in 2004 concluded that 37% of North Korean children aged six years and under were chronically malnourished. In September 2005, however, the North Korean Government announced that it had asked humanitarian aid agencies operating in North Korea to terminate food aid programmes and withdraw the majority of their foreign staff by the end of the year. The Government asserted that, following a harvest that year reported to be the best in a decade, it was able to feed its people without assistance, and expressed a desire to progress from humanitarian to developmental aid. (Analysts speculated that the Government of North Korea preferred to rely on food aid from China and South Korea, as the distribution of aid from these countries was monitored less closely and the political implications of allowing Westerners access to the country were thereby avoided.)

Severe flooding in July 2006 prompted the North Korean Government to seek further humanitarian aid, and by October WFP was warning of renewed famine conditions. The shortage of food was exacerbated by the reluctance of donor nations (including South Korea) to give aid to North Korea following its missile tests in July and October. After further flooding in August 2007 the UN and the Red Cross launched international appeals for funding. South Korea resumed deliveries of fertilizer to the North in March and of food aid in June. In April 2008 WFP warned of a humanitarian crisis, the food deficit for the coming year having been revised upwards to 1.66m. metric tons, more than double that of the previous year. In September, following an appeal from North Korea, WFP initiated an emergency operation, envisaging expenditure of US \$504m. In March 2009, however, it was revealed that WFP operations in the country had been substantially scaled down, owing to serious funding difficulties, and that aid had reached only 15% of the extent originally planned. The revaluation of the currency in December led to further hardship, with widespread food shortages being reported.

In August and September 2010 heavy flooding, followed by typhoon damage, was reported. South Korea suspended aid to the North following the attacks by North Korea on South Korean targets in 2010 (see Inter-Korean Relations). In March 2011 the UN reported that more than 6m. North Koreans were in urgent need of food aid. Following further flooding in North Korea in June and July 2011, South Korea resumed humanitarian assistance through the Red Cross and UN agencies. In March 2012, after North Korea had agreed to suspend its nuclear activities (see The Inception of North Korea's Nuclear Programme) the USA agreed to provide 240,000 tons of food aid, intended primarily for children and expectant mothers; however, the agreement was suspended when North Korea announced the forthcoming launch of a long-range rocket, which took place (unsuccessfully) in April. Continuing drought combined with flooding in mid-2012 led to a fresh appeal by the North Korean authorities for emergency aid from WFP.

In May 2011 Amnesty International reported that, according to satellite photographs, labour camps for political prisoners in remote areas of North Korea had expanded in size over the previous decade: the number of detainees was estimated to be as many as 200,000. Former inmates reported extremely harsh and inhumane conditions, forced labour and summary executions. The existence of the camps was denied by the North Korean Government. In early 2012 protests took place in South Korea concerning the fate of about 30 North Koreans who had fled to China and were facing forcible repatriation. It was reported by South Korean human rights groups that harsher penalties had recently been announced in the North for defectors and their families. The South Korean authorities reported a decline in the number of refugees from North Korea arriving in 2012, to just over 1,500, compared with some 2,700 in 2011. (See Inter-Korean Relations and Relations with China concerning policy with regard to defectors in previous years.) In January 2013 the UN High Commissioner for Human Rights, Navi Pillay, described North Korea's human rights situation as 'one of the worst, but least understood and reported, in the world'. In March the UN Human Rights Council resolved to establish an inquiry into abuses of human rights in North Korea, particularly in prison camps; the North Korean Government denounced the resolution as displaying 'serious distortions' and was thought to be unlikely to allow access by investigators.

Inter-Korean Relations

After the consolidation of power in the North by Kim Il Sung, North Korea's relations with South Korea remained tense. In 1971 discussions took place for the first time between the Red Cross Societies of North and South Korea. However, negotiations were suspended in 1973, and hopes for better relations were undermined by a series of clashes between North and South Korean vessels in disputed waters during 1974. Propaganda campaigns, suspended by agreement in 1972, were resumed by both sides. In October 1978 the UN Command (UNC—under which troops were stationed in South Korea) accused North Korea of threatening the 1953 truce, after the discovery of an underground tunnel (the third since 1974) beneath the DMZ.

During the 1980s the increasing prominence of Kim Jong Il, who advocated an uncompromising policy towards the South, appeared to aggravate the situation. In 1983 some 17 South Koreans, including four government ministers, were killed in a bomb explosion in Burma (now Myanmar), in what appeared to be an assassination attempt on the South Korean President, Chun Doo-Hwan. North Korea was held responsible for the attack, and Burma severed relations with the country. In January 1984, none the less, North Korea suggested tripartite discussions on reunification, involving North and South Korea and the USA, but the proposal was rejected by South Korea, which favoured bilateral talks. North Korea's propaganda campaign was moderated, and in September North Korea provided emergency relief to flood-stricken areas of the South. In November the first discussions, on possible economic co-operation, were held, and negotiations continued in 1985. However, in February 1986, during the annual South Korean-US 'Team Spirit' military manoeuvres, North Korea suspended all negotiations with the South. North Korea denied accusations of involvement in the explosion of a South Korean airliner over Burma in November 1987, despite the subsequent confession of an alleged North Korean agent. In August 1988 three sessions of talks were held at the 'peace village' of Panmunjom (in the DMZ) between delegates of the legislatures of North and South Korea, although the discussions (the first formal contact between the two countries since 1986) produced no conclusive results. Further negotiations in 1989 were suspended by North Korea.

Inter-Korean discussions resumed in mid-1990, and in September the North Korean Premier visited the South Korean capital, Seoul, for discussions with his counterpart: this was the most senior-level bilateral contact since the end of the Korean War. Subsequent discussions culminated in the signing of an 'Agreement on Reconciliation, Non-aggression and Exchanges and Co-operation between the South and the North', in Seoul in December 1991. Both states pledged, *inter alia*, to desist from mutual slander, vilification and sabotage; to promote economic and other co-operation; to facilitate the reunion of families separated by the war; and to work towards a full peace treaty to replace the 1953 armistice agreement. In November 1992, however, North Korea threatened a complete suspension of contacts with the South, in protest against the latter's decision to resume the 'Team Spirit' military exercises in March 1993. (The 1992 exercises had been cancelled, owing to the improvement in relations between the two states.) Relations had also been seriously impaired by the South's announcement, in October 1992, that an extensive North Korean espionage network had been discovered in South Korea, and by the North's repeated refusals to agree to simultaneous nuclear inspections in both countries.

While the controversy surrounding North Korea's suspected nuclear programme continued, inter-Korean relations were strained by North Korea's withdrawal in May 1994 of its mission to the Military Armistice Commission (the Panmunjom-based body overseeing the maintenance of the 1953 truce). Following discussions between Kim Il Sung and former US President Jimmy Carter, who visited North Korea in June 1994, it was announced that the first summit meeting at presidential level between the two Korean states would be held in Pyongyang in July. However, the death of Kim Il Sung led to the indefinite postponement of the meeting. The signature of the US-North Korean nuclear accord in October caused South Korea to make renewed efforts to resume the inter-Korean negotiations, and in February 1995 the South announced the cancellation of the annual 'Team Spirit' manoeuvres (for the second consecutive year).

Tension increased markedly in April 1996, when North Korea announced its decision to abandon the 1953 armistice. North Korean troops subsequently made a number of incursions into the DMZ, thereby violating the provisions of the agreement. Later in the month, in an attempt to revitalize the peace process and replace the armistice agreement with a formal peace treaty, President Bill Clinton of the USA and President Kim Young-Sam of South Korea proposed four-way talks, involving the two Koreas, the USA and China. China responded positively, but North Korea declared its willingness to hold discussions only with the USA. In September 1996 a submarine from North Korea was discovered abandoned in South Korean waters. One of the two surviving crew members claimed that this was the fourth such mission by armed North Koreans. South Korea suspended all contact with North Korea; the UN Security Council expressed 'serious concern' at the incident. Following mediation by the

USA, an unprecedented apology was broadcast in South Korea by the official North Korean news agency.

After exploratory talks in March 1997 involving delegates from North Korea, South Korea and the USA, North Korea announced that its participation in full quadripartite negoti- ations was conditional upon the receipt of substantial food aid. In May representatives of the Red Cross organizations of North and South Korea reached agreement on the provision of grain to North Korea. Negotiations were concluded in October to allow foreign airlines, including those from South Korea, to use North Korean airspace.Full quadripartite negotiations, aimed at con- cluding a peace treaty between North and South Korea, finally opened in Geneva, Switzerland, in December. A second round, in March 1998, proved unsuccessful, since North Korea continued to insist on the inclusion on the agenda of the withdrawal of US troops from the Korean peninsula. In December 1997, mean- while, negotiations in the Chinese capital of Beijing between the South and North Korean Red Cross organizations foundered, owing to North Korea's reluctance to allow South Korean officials access to North Korea to monitor the distribution of food aid. At a subsequent meeting, in March 1998, the provision of additional food aid was agreed.

Following the inauguration of the new South Korean President, Kim Dae-Jung, in February 1998, North Korea urged 'dialogue and negotiation' with the South Korean administra- tion. In April, as part of Kim Dae-Jung's 'sunshine' policy of co- operation with North Korea, the South Korean Government announced measures to encourage inter-Korean economic con- tacts However, during a permitted visit by the founder of the South Korean conglomerate Hyundai to deliver a gift of cattle to his home town, a North Korean submarine was caught in the nets of a South Korean fishing boat; all nine crew members were found dead inside the vessel. The UNC condemned the incursion during a meeting with North Korean army officers in Panmun- jom, the first such discussions to be held in seven years. A further delivery of cattle was made by Chung Ju-Yung in October, when he also met with Kim Jong Il, and in November some 800 tourists from South Korea participated in the first tour to Mount Kumgang. In December, during Chung's third visit to North Korea, a proposal for the construction of an industrial complex at Haeju was approved. Following further visits in early 1999, it was announced that these would continue on a monthly basis. In December 1998, meanwhile, South Korean naval forces sank a suspected North Korean spy boat, after pursuing it into inter- national waters.

In June 1999 a week-long confrontation between North and South Korean naval forces in the Yellow Sea resulted in a brief gun battle, during which one North Korean torpedo boat was sunk. Two rounds of bilateral discussions in Beijing in June and July ended in failure. In September North Korea declared invalid the Northern Limit Line (the maritime border that had separ- ated the territorial waters of the two Koreas since 1953), in protest against the UNC's refusal to renegotiate its demarcation. In August 2000 Hyundai agreed to establish a technologically advanced industrial compound in Kaesong, and agreements with two other major South Korean companies on joint industrial projects (comprising electronics manufacture and motor vehicle assembly) followed.

The summit meeting of 2000 and subsequent events

In June 2000 an historic summit meeting took place between Kim Jong Il and Kim Dae-Jung in Pyongyang, following which detailed agreements were signed pledging the promotion of economic co-operation, the building of mutual trust and the resolution of reunification issues. In July ministerial-level dele- gations from both countries met in Seoul. This was the first visit to the South by North Korean officials since 1991. A joint communiqué was issued allowing for, *inter alia*, the reopening of liaison offices at Panmunjom, which had been closed in 1996, and the reconnection of the inter-Korean Kyongui railway line. In September 2000 Kim Dae-Jung formally inaugurated the project to remove thousands of land-mines and rebuild the railway line and an adjacent highway. Meanwhile, in August 100 North Korean families travelled to Seoul and 100 South Korean families visited Pyongyang simultaneously to meet with relatives from whom they had been separated by the Korean War.

In a symbolic display of unity, in September 2000 the two countries marched under the same flag in the opening ceremony of the Olympic Games in Sydney, Australia. In late September North Korea's Minister of the People's Armed Forces, Vice- Marshal Kim Il Chol, visited the South and met his counterpart,

Cho Seong-Tae, the first such ministerial meeting ever held. In October Kim Dae-Jung was awarded the Nobel Peace Prize in recognition of his reunification efforts. Further sessions of inter- ministerial, military and economic talks took place during 2000 and early 2001, and further family reunions were arranged by the North and South Korean Red Cross organizations. However, in its annual defence policy document published in December 2000, South Korea described the North as its main enemy and alleged that North Korea had expanded its military capacity along the DMZ. The North Korean Government was also dis- pleased by the approval of a resolution in the South Korean legislature to demand the repatriation of prisoners of war who, it alleged, remained in detention in the North.

The uncompromising attitude towards North Korea displayed by the new US Administration of President George W. Bush, inaugurated in 2001, threatened to undermine the reconciliation process. However, in April 2002 Kim Jong Il received Kim Dae- Jung's special envoy, Lim Dong-Won, and the two sides agreed to further reunions for separated families and to continuing dis- cussions on economic co-operation. North Korea also agreed to Lim's request that it renew dialogue with the USA and Japan. In May the increasing number of defectors from the North received international attention as several groups sought asylum at Canadian, Japanese and South Korean diplomatic buildings in China. They were eventually allowed to travel to the South, via the Philippines. At the end of June a gun battle between North and South Korean vessels in the Yellow Sea resulted in the sinking of a Southern patrol boat and the deaths of six crew members. South Korean military sources estimated that 30 North Korean crewmen were also killed in the confrontation, which had started when two North Korean vessels accompany- ing a fishing boat reportedly crossed the Northern Limit Line. Following the incident, in July South Korea suspended rice shipments to the North and economic co-operation projects, reflecting widespread public anger. None the less, Kim Dae- Jung maintained his 'sunshine' policy towards the North. In August North and South Korea held a seventh round of minis- terial discussions in Seoul, aimed at improving relations in the aftermath of the latest naval confrontation, and focusing on the issue of future family reunions, railway links and cultural exchanges. In September the first inter-Korean military 'hotline' was inaugurated to allow for improved communications in cir- cumstances of potential tension.

The eighth round of ministerial talks was held in Pyongyang in October 2002 and mainly focused on economic co-operation issues, despite the fact that the USA had earlier revealed the existence of a secret nuclear weapons programme in the North. At the end of that month a North Korean economic delegation began a nine-day tour of the South, including several major industrial facilities in the itinerary. At the end of December the South Korean Ministry of National Defence published a 'white paper', which, for the first time, excluded any reference to the North as its main enemy.

The election in December 2002 of Roh Moo-Hyun, the candi- date of Kim Dae-Jung's party, as President of South Korea heralded a continuation of Kim's 'sunshine' policy. In February 2003 the first road reconnecting the North with the South was completed, on the eastern coast of the Korean peninsula. How- ever, in May 2003 North Korea announced that it no longer recognized a Joint Declaration of the Denuclearization of the Korean Peninsula, signed with the South in 1992. North Korea warned that the South would risk 'unspeakable disaster' if it became too confrontational in co-operating with the USA on the nuclear issue (the threat followed a summit meeting between Roh and US President George W. Bush). Attempts to develop inter-Korean relations were also complicated by confirmation in June 2003 by South Korean investigators that former President Kim Dae-Jung had arranged for the Korea Development Bank to give a Hyundai affiliate substantial funds to transfer to the North in order to finance the historic inter-Korean summit meeting of 2000.

In May 2004 senior-level military discussions took place between the two sides, at which the establishment of a radio communication line between the North and South Korean navies was agreed. It was believed that the new communication line would reduce naval conflicts between the two sides, although later in the year there were, none the less, incidents of warning shots being fired by the South Korean navy at North Korean vessels considered to have intruded across the maritime border. In July more than 450 North Korean defectors arrived in Seoul. North Korea subsequently accused South Korean officials of kidnapping its citizens and suspended bilateral dialogue. By the end of 2004 the number of North Koreans who had defected to South Korea had reportedly exceeded 6,000.

In May 2005 South Korea undertook to provide 200,000 metric tons of fertilizer to ease North Korea's food supply problems. Three North Korean freighters reportedly docked at Ulsan in South Korea to load the fertilizer later in the month, this being the first time since 1984 that North Korean ships had docked in a South Korean port. In July 2005 the 15th ministerial discussions between North and South Korea, held in Seoul, concluded with a 12-point joint statement in which the two sides pledged, *inter alia*, to reopen military talks, continue reunions for separated families and hold North-South Red Cross discussions on the question of South Korean soldiers and civilians allegedly abducted to North Korea during and after the 1950–53 war, more than 1,000 of whom, according to the South Korean Government, remained in detention in the North. In November it was announced that North and South Korea would present joint teams at the 2006 Asian Games in Doha, Qatar, and at the 2008 Olympic Games in Beijing, China. In March 2006 military negotiations were held between the two Koreas in the DMZ, following a break of some two years; these were reportedly the most senior-level military talks between the two sides since the 1953 armistice. However, the North Korean Government postponed the scheduled 18th round of ministerial discussions between the two sides in protest against the South's conduct of joint military exercises with the USA.

Relations between the two Koreas were strained further throughout 2006, mainly as a result of North Korea's missile tests. The testing of the intercontinental *Taepodong-2* missile on 5 July prompted South Korea to announce an indefinite suspension of food aid; however, it insisted that business co-operation, notably at Kaesong and Mount Kumgang, would not be affected. In response, North Korea suspended family reunions. Aid was resumed after North Korea suffered severe flooding later in that month, with the South Korean Government granting US $10.5m. to the North via non-governmental organizations (NGOs) in August, followed by supplies of rice and equipment. However, the testing of a nuclear device by the North on 9 October placed this emergency aid programme in jeopardy. While again pledging to continue its economic co-operation in Kaesong and Mount Kumgang (despite express US pleas for these links to be severed), the South Korean Government announced an indefinite suspension of humanitarian aid. (However, NGOs continued to provide relief shipments.) Although the South Korean Minister of Foreign Affairs, Ban Ki-Moon, reportedly stated that North Korea deserved sanctions under the UN Security Council Resolution, he also urged a resumption of dialogue. The South Korean Government refused to join the US-led Proliferation Security Initiative, which provided for the stopping and searching of North Korean ships that were suspected of carrying materials for use in nuclear, chemical or biological weapons, and in early November President Roh undertook to continue his policy of engagement with the North Korean Government. None the less, in a reversal of previous policy, in mid-November South Korea supported a UN resolution condemning North Korea's human rights record (in previous votes it had been absent or abstained). Furthermore, a South Korean defence policy document published at the end of December described North Korea as a 'serious threat' to the South—the most strongly worded assessment since the inception of the latter's policy of engagement in 2000. It was reported in February 2007 that the number of defectors from North to South Korea since 1953 had reached 10,000.

Following the progress made in mid-February 2007 at six-party talks on North Korea's nuclear programme, North and South Korea held ministerial discussions later in that month, South Korea shipped 12,500 metric tons of fertilizer to the North in March and family reunions were resumed in May. Inter-Korean talks on economic co-operation were held in Pyongyang in April, shortly after North Korea had failed to meet a deadline agreed in February for the closure of its nuclear reactor at Yongbyon. South Korea agreed to revive its food aid programme to the North, with the provision of 400,000 metric tons of rice, but only on condition that North Korea demonstrate some progress in complying with its commitments under the February six-party accord. Following senior-level military talks at Panmunjom, in May 2007 cross-border rail links were finally completed when, for the first time in more than 50 years, passengers were conveyed on trains travelling in each direction. Agreement was also reached in principle, on the creation of a joint fishing zone in the disputed Yellow Sea, where naval clashes had previously occurred. However, ministerial discussions in Seoul in late May and early June ended without progress, as South Korea continued to refuse to dispatch any rice to the North while the latter's pledge to shut down the Yongbyon reactor remained unfulfilled. In late June, as inspectors of the International Atomic Energy Agency (IAEA, see p. 122) were permitted to enter North Korea for the first time since December 2002, South Korea announced the resumption of food aid to the North with a first shipment of rice, and the first instalment of heavy fuel oil followed in July. None the less, senior-level military talks ended in late July 2007 without agreement on the disputed maritime boundary, the Northern Limit Line, which North Korea refused to recognize, and in early August North and South Korean soldiers exchanged gunfire across the DMZ.

In early October 2007, in only the second meeting between the two countries' leaders since the Korean War, Kim Jong Il welcomed President Roh to Pyongyang for a three-day summit. Kim and Roh, who was approaching the end of his term of office, issued a declaration, in which they committed North and South Korea, *inter alia*, to working towards the replacement of the 1953 armistice agreement with a peace treaty; to making joint efforts for the smooth implementation of the six-party nuclear agreements; to creating a special 'peace zone' around Haeju; to establishing the planned joint fishing zone in the Yellow Sea; to expanding co-operation on economic and humanitarian projects; and to developing co-operation in a wide range of other areas (including education and technology). It was also decided to resume a cross-border freight rail service. (A daily freight service, connecting the South with Kaesong, was duly launched in December, although North Korea continued to oppose the introduction of regular passenger services.) Several bilateral ministerial exchanges followed. In November 2007, during the first bilateral prime ministerial discussions since 1992, Premier Kim Yong Il and the South Korean Prime Minister, Han Duck-Soo, agreed on a timetable for resuming cross-border freight rail services and on the establishment of a joint committee to advance the creation of the 'peace zone' at Haeju.

Increasing tensions on the Korean peninsula

The conservative Lee Myung-Bak, who was elected President of South Korea in December 2007, advocated the adoption of a more uncompromising approach towards North Korea than that pursued over the preceding 10 years by Presidents Kim Dae-Jung and Roh Moo-Hyun: he demanded increased progress on denuclearization in return for the continuation of economic co-operation. In January 2008 President Lee announced plans to review the agreements reached at the inter-Korean summit in the previous October, and the Ministry of Unification was reduced in importance. None the less, Lee proposed the creation of a 37,500m. won investment fund for North Korea if it abandoned its nuclear weapons programme, with the aim of raising the North's per caput income to US $3,000 within 10 years. In March North Korea expelled South Korean officials from Kaesong and test-fired missiles in the Yellow Sea. The North Korean Government was reportedly dissatisfied with Lee's association of humanitarian assistance with preconditions on nuclear disarmament and human rights. Tensions rose further in July, when a South Korean tourist was shot dead by a North Korean soldier at Mount Kumgang, having allegedly crossed into a restricted area. In response, the South Korean Government halted tours to the area, while the North refused to participate in a joint investigation into the death, warning that it would expel all 'unnecessary' South Korean nationals from the resort. (In August 2011 the North Korean Government announced that it was seizing South Korean assets at the site, considering them to have been abandoned, and expelling the remaining South Korean staff: tourist visits were to resume once an alternative investment partner had been found.) In November 2007 South Korea acted as the co-sponsor of a UN resolution criticizing human rights violations in North Korea. Later in that month the North announced the suspension of non-military telephone connections with the South, as well as the closure of the border. The rail service between the two sides was discontinued by the North in November 2008. In early March 2009, in their first, albeit brief, meeting since 2002, North Korean officials and UNC representatives had discussions at Panmunjom, in an attempt to reduce tensions.

In early March 2009 the North Korean Government again temporarily closed the border, in response to the holding of joint US-South Korean military exercises. In the same month a South Korean worker at Kaesong was arrested by the North Korean authorities for allegedly criticizing North Korea. In April the South Korean Government condemned the launch by North Korea of a rocket-mounted satellite, which was believed to be, in reality, a pretext for testing a long-range missile. In May, following North Korea's testing of a nuclear device, South Korea undertook to join the Proliferation Security Initiative, whereupon North Korea declared that it no longer considered itself bound by the armistice agreement with the South, and would respond with military action if any of its vessels were seized and searched. In August, however, following a meeting between Kim Jong Il and the chairwoman of the Hyundai group, the North Korean Government announced that it would reopen the border and permit tourism and family reunions to resume, as well as release the Kaesong worker who had been detained since March. The first family reunions since 2007 duly took place in September 2009. It was reported that in October, during further discussions on family reunions, North Korea requested 100,000 metric tons of food aid, but South Korea agreed to provide only about 20,000 tons.

In November 2009 North and South Korean naval vessels exchanged fire across the disputed maritime boundary (the first such incident for seven years), and in January 2010 there was a further exchange of land-based artillery fire across the maritime boundary. In March a South Korean naval vessel, the *Cheonan*, exploded and sank near the boundary, with the loss of 46 lives. The South Korean Government did not immediately accuse North Korea of deliberately causing the disaster, but in May a multinational team of experts concluded that the only plausible explanation for the explosion was that it had been caused by a torpedo from a North Korean submarine. This was vehemently denied by the North Korean Government, which threatened to respond aggressively to any retaliation. Joint naval exercises undertaken by South Korea and the USA in July were described as an 'intolerable provocation' by North Korea. In September, following severe flooding in the North, South Korea offered food aid, although the amount was criticized as inadequate by the Government of North Korea. In the same month North Korea suggested the organizing of further family reunions (which took place in late October). Also in September, discussions took place at Panmunjom between senior military officers, for the first time in two years, but they ended without agreement, reportedly after the South Korean representatives urged the North to apologize for the sinking of the *Cheonan* and to punish those responsible.

In November 2010 North Korea fired artillery shells at the South Korean island of Yeonpyeong, where South Korean forces had been conducting a military exercise. The bombardment killed four people, including two civilians, injured several more and caused widespread damage. In the same month South Korea and the USA conducted further (previously planned) naval exercises in the Yellow Sea. South Korea announced the suspension of the aid that it had promised to North Korea in September, after the floods. In February 2011 further discussions between military officers at Panmunjom again failed to lead to agreement on a possible meeting at a more senior level. After further flooding in North Korea in June and July, South Korea offered to resume humanitarian aid. In August the South Korean Minister for Unification, Hyun In-Taek, was replaced by Yu Woo-Ik; although the South Korean Government denied that the replacement indicated a change in policy, Yu was believed to favour a less confrontational attitude to the North than that of his predecessor. Following the death of Kim Jong Il in December, the bellicose language used by his successor, Kim Jong Un, in February 2012, when denouncing forthcoming joint South Korean and US military exercises, and in March, when visiting Panmunjom, suggested that no immediate change in policy was likely. The South Korean Government described as a 'grave provocation' North Korea's announcement in March that it was to launch a rocket-mounted satellite in the following month, suspecting that the event would actually be a long-range missile test (as had been generally assumed in similar circumstances in April 2009). South Korea condemned the launch in April, which proved unsuccessful, as a breach of the UN resolution prohibiting the use of ballistic missile technology, and later in April announced that it had deployed new cruise missiles with a range of 1,000 km, which could reach any North Korean nuclear or missile site.

During the South Korean presidential election campaign in the second half of 2012 both the principal candidates undertook to improve inter-Korean relations; the North Korean state media, which had routinely denounced the incumbent President Lee and his Saenuri Party as 'traitors', urged South Koreans to support the opposition. Tensions were increased by North Korea's successful launch of another long-range rocket in December, a few days before the election. Following the electoral victory of the Saenuri Party candidate, Park Geun-Hye, however, it was observed that the North Korean media desisted from vilifying her. President-elect Park promised to conduct 'trust-based diplomacy' with the North and offered economic co-operation if progress were made in denuclearization. Kim Jong Un's new year message for 2013 urged an end to confrontation between north and south, but later in January, after the UN Security Council voted to extend sanctions against North Korea as a result of the recent rocket launch, the North Korean Government reacted defiantly, declaring its intention to proceed with a third nuclear test, which it duly conducted in February. President-elect Park described the test as undermining efforts for peace, but following her inauguration in late February she undertook to continue the 'trust-building process', urging the North to stop wasting its resources on the development of nuclear missiles. However, the North Korean authorities described as a 'war of aggression' the forthcoming annual joint military exercises to be held by US and South Korean forces in March and April, and after a new UN Security Council resolution in March, which further extended sanctions, the North's belligerent rhetoric intensified: it announced an end to the 1953 armistice and all non-aggression agreements with the South, the closure of the 'hot-line' military telephone link and the closure of the border crossing-point at Panmunjom in the DMZ. During March the North Korean authorities alleged that state internet servers had been subject to a cyber attack by 'hostile forces', and shortly afterwards the computer systems of several South Korean broadcasters and financial institutions were temporarily shut down by the implantation of malicious codes from an unknown source. At the end of March, following the inclusion of US B-52 bomber aircraft and 'stealth' bomber and fighter aircraft in the joint military exercises with South Korea, a North Korean Government statement declared that North–South relations were now in a 'state of war'. Operations at the joint Kaesong industrial complex (currently employing more than 50,000 North Koreans working for 123 South Korean companies) were suspended by North Korea in April 2013 for the first time since its establishment, with the last South Korean workers departing at the beginning of May.

The Inception of North Korea's Nuclear Programme

In the early 1990s there was growing international concern that North Korea had intensified its clandestine nuclear programme at Yongbyon, north of Pyongyang, and would soon be capable of manufacturing a nuclear weapon. During 1991 pressure was applied, by the USA and Japan in particular, for North Korea to sign the Nuclear Safeguards Agreement (NSA) with the IAEA. This was required by North Korea's signature, in 1985, of the Treaty on the Non-Proliferation of Nuclear Weapons (the Non-Proliferation Treaty—NPT), in order that IAEA representatives might be permitted to inspect the country's nuclear facilities. However, North Korea consistently refused to allow such inspections to take place unless there was to be a simultaneous inspection (or withdrawal) of US nuclear weapons sited in South Korea. Tension was eased considerably by the USA's decision, in October 1991, to remove all its tactical nuclear weapons from South Korea, and by South Korea's subsequent declaration that it would not manufacture, deploy or use nuclear, chemical or biological weapons. In December the South Korean Government stated that all US nuclear weapons had been withdrawn, and proposed that simultaneous inspections of military bases in the South and nuclear facilities in the North be conducted. Later in the month the two Korean states concluded an agreement 'to create a non-nuclear Korean peninsula', and in January 1992 North Korea signed the NSA. In March delegates of North and South, meeting at Panmunjom, agreed to form a Joint Nuclear Control Commission (JNCC) to permit inter-Korean nuclear inspections.

In 1992 IAEA inspectors were permitted to make several visits to North Korean nuclear facilities. Despite the findings of the inspectors (who concluded that the Yongbyon plant was 'primitive' and far from completion, although potentially capable of producing plutonium), suspicions persisted regarding North Korean nuclear ambitions. Moreover, North Korea repeatedly failed to agree to separate nuclear inspections by the JNCC, finally announcing in January 1993 its intention to boycott all future inter-Korean nuclear talks (in protest against the imminent resumption of the joint US-South Korean 'Team Spirit' military manoeuvres). In February North Korea refused to allow

IAEA inspections of two 'undeclared' sites near Yongbyon, claiming that these were military installations unrelated to nuclear activities. North Korea announced in March that it was to withdraw from the NPT. In May the UN Security Council adopted a resolution urging North Korea to reconsider its decision to withdraw from the NPT and to allow an inspection by the IAEA of the country's nuclear facilities. Following negotiations with the USA, North Korea agreed to suspend its withdrawal from the NPT; in return, the USA agreed to assist North Korea in the development of its non-military nuclear programme. International concern regarding the North Korean weapons programme was further heightened by the successful testing of a medium-range missile in May.

In February 1994, following further discussions between North Korea and the USA, an agreement was reached whereby the IAEA would be allowed to visit all the country's declared nuclear facilities. In March, however, the inspectors were impeded in their efforts to remove samples from nuclear installations, and it was discovered that seals placed on nuclear materials by IAEA representatives during previous visits had been broken, leading the IAEA to conclude that North Korea had probably produced more plutonium than had been admitted. In August the USA and North Korea reached an agreement on the replacement of the latter's existing nuclear reactors by two light-water reactors, which were considered to be less easily adapted to the production of nuclear weaponry. Under an agreement concluded in October the USA undertook to establish an international consortium to finance and supply the light-water reactors, while North Korea agreed to suspend operation of its existing reactors and halt construction at two further sites. To compensate for North Korea's consequent shortfall in energy production until the new reactors were fully operational, the USA agreed to donate to North Korea 500,000 metric tons annually of heavy fuel oil. IAEA inspectors travelled to Pyongyang to oversee the suspension of the country's nuclear programme.

In March 1995 several countries, led by the USA, South Korea and Japan, created the Korean Peninsula Energy Development Organization (KEDO). In December North Korea and KEDO reached agreement on the details of implementing the October 1994 accord. In January 1996 North Korea announced its willingness to permit routine inspections of its nuclear installations by the IAEA. In March the Korea Electric Power Corporation (KEPCO) was commissioned by KEDO as the principal contractor for the construction of the light-water reactors. Discussions between KEDO and North Korea to negotiate the terms of repayment by the latter of the construction costs of the light-water reactors were successfully concluded in April 1997.

Meanwhile, US energy experts began the sealing of spent fuel rods at North Korea's nuclear facilities. However, North Korea's continued refusal to grant IAEA inspectors access to several contentious laboratories again provoked concern that North Korea was developing its nuclear programme. Preparation of the nuclear-reactor site at Sinpo formally began in August 1997. Negotiations held in early 1998 between the participants in KEDO (which the European Union—EU—had joined in mid-1997) concerning the financing of the light-water reactors (estimated at US $5,170m.) proved difficult, and were further complicated by South Korea's financial problems, raising fears that progress on the project would be hindered. In June 1998 the North Korean Government admitted to having sold nuclear missiles abroad, claiming that such exports were necessary, given ongoing US economic sanctions against North Korea. In September North Korea agreed to resume sealing of spent fuel rods (which had been suspended earlier that year), while the USA promised to deliver the delayed shipment of heavy fuel oil. However, the US Congress was increasingly reluctant to approve financing for the purchase of fuel oil, obliging President Bill Clinton personally to authorize the disbursement of funds in October, in order to safeguard the 1994 nuclear accord.

Talks held during mid-1999 between the USA and North Korea culminated in September in a decision by the USA to ease several long-standing economic sanctions (principally on non-military trade, travel and banking) against North Korea. In return, the country agreed to suspend missile test-firing for the duration of negotiations with the USA. Discussions aimed at improving US-North Korean relations were held in Beijing in November 1999 and January 2000. Meanwhile, in November 1999 it was reported that the IAEA was supervising the final stage of the sealing of spent fuel rods at Yongbyon. After several months of delays caused by disputes over the division of the costs

of the project, in December KEDO and KEPCO finally signed the contract for the construction of the two light-water reactors; in February 2000 it was reported that construction of the reactors was unlikely to be completed before 2007, some four years later than scheduled. In November 2000 North Korea, frustrated by the delay, threatened to restart missile testing unless construction of the reactors was accelerated. North Korea denied the IAEA's claim that delays were due to the former's refusal to allow nuclear inspections.

In June 2000 the North Korean Government confirmed its moratorium on test flights of ballistic missiles. In July the USA rejected North Korea's demand for annual payments from the USA of US $1,000m. in return for the curtailment of weapons exports. The fundamental issues of missile development and export remained unresolved. A planned visit to Pyongyang by the outgoing US President, Bill Clinton, was cancelled in December when North Korea rejected a US proposal that the two sides prepare a draft missile accord to form a basis for talks. In early 2001 the new Administration of George W. Bush adopted a less conciliatory stance towards North Korea, refusing to grant economic aid unless transparency in North Korea's missile production and export was assured and verified. Since the late 1990s elements in Bush's Republican Party had been strongly arguing in favour of a planned 'national missile defence' (NMD) system to protect the USA from long-range missile attack, and had frequently cited North Korea as a developer and exporter of such missiles; it was feared that North Korea had developed an intercontinental ballistic missile, the *Taepodong-2*, capable of striking the west coast of the USA. Bush's commitment to develop NMD was denounced by North Korea, which responded by threatening to abandon the 1994 framework, and to resume ballistic missile testing. In June 2001 President Bush sought to broaden discussions with North Korea about its missile programme to include nuclear technology and a reduction of the country's conventional forces. The North responded that discussions on the latter would take place only following the withdrawal of the 37,000 US troops from the South, and that it was also seeking financial compensation for the delay in building KEDO's two light-water reactors, which were now not expected to be completed until 2008 at the earliest. In October 2001 the North rejected suggestions by the head of the IAEA and later by US officials that inspections of its nuclear facilities were necessary; however, in December it agreed to limited international access to certain laboratories. (See Foreign Affairs for subsequent developments.)

Foreign Affairs

North Korea's international relations have been dominated by its hostility to the USA and to perceived US influence in South Korea, resulting in belligerent official rhetoric and actions, despite the country's chronic need for economic assistance. China, North Korea's principal ally, has played an important role in persuading North Korea to take part in international negotiations. North Korea's unilateral application for UN membership, first announced in May 1991, represented a radical departure from its earlier insistence that the two Koreas should occupy a single UN seat. This development was welcomed by South Korea, and both countries were admitted separately to the UN in September of that year.

Relations with China

North Korea's relations with the People's Republic of China remained a crucial focus of North Korean foreign policy. During the years of the so-called Sino-Soviet dispute North Korea fluctuated in its allegiance to each of its powerful northern neighbours, China and the USSR. Kim Il Sung made several official visits to China in the late 1980s, which were interpreted by some Western observers as an attempt to establish closer relations in view of the erosion of communist power in many Eastern European countries. However, North Korea was aggrieved at China's establishment of full diplomatic relations with South Korea in August 1992. China appeared largely conciliatory with regard to North Korea's nuclear programme, and during 1993 and the first months of 1994 indicated that it would veto any attempt by the UN Security Council to impose economic sanctions on North Korea. In 1997 China agreed to provide substantial food aid to North Korea to alleviate the effects of flooding. Later in that year China accepted US and South Korean proposals for quadripartite negotiations with North Korea to conclude a new peace agreement with the South, and between December 1997 and August 1999 it participated in all six rounds of these negotiations. In June 1999 China announced that it would provide North Korea with 150,000 metric tons of food aid and 400,000 tons of coke over the following months.

In late 1999 international attention was focused on the uncertain situation of the large number of North Koreans (estimated at some 30,000 by South Korean sources and at 200,000 by the voluntary organization Médecins Sans Frontières) who had crossed the border into China in recent years. In early 2000 it was reported that China had returned some 10,000 escapees to North Korea during 1999. The number of migrants was thought to fluctuate, according to the season.

In February 2000 China permitted North Korea to open a consulate-general in Hong Kong. In May Kim Jong Il visited China, his first official trip abroad for 17 years. In January 2001 the North Korean leader paid a second visit to the People's Republic. During this visit Kim had extensive discussions with Chinese leaders in Beijing, and also toured the new business zones of Shanghai and Shenzhen. In September the Chinese President, Jiang Zemin, undertook an official visit to North Korea, the first such visit since 1990. Jiang promised an additional 200,000 metric tons of food aid and 30,000 tons of diesel oil to alleviate North Korea's economic crisis.

During 2002 North Korea and China continued to seek the reconnection of the inter-Korean railway lines and their subsequent linking to China's own railway system. In May, however, China's forcible removal of North Korean refugees from South Korean embassy premises in the People's Republic again brought the issue of the refugees to international attention. Several groups of North Korean refugees had, in 2002, fled to Western, Japanese and South Korean diplomatic offices in China, embarrassing the latter, since the Chinese Government had signed a treaty with North Korea providing for the repatriation of refugees. In June China allowed 24 North Korean refugees who had been concealed in the embassy of South Korea to leave for that country. After that incident, China began an operation against South Korean activists and missionaries who had been helping North Koreans to flee via China. It was estimated that as many as 300,000 North Korean refugees were already residing in China, with US sources stating that as many as 50,000 had fled to China in 2001 alone.

In February 2003 the President of North Korea's SPA Presidium, Kim Yong Nam, visited Beijing and undertook to maintain strong bilateral relations. In March China suspended its oil supply to North Korea via a pipeline from Liaoning Province for three days, following North Korean missile tests. In April China hosted and participated in senior-level meetings between North Korea and the USA over the North Korean nuclear weapons programme. Immediately prior to the discussions, Vice-Marshal Jo Myong Rok, North Korea's second highest ranking official, led a military delegation to China, and held meetings with President Hu Jintao and senior military leaders. Chinese diplomatic efforts played a major role in ensuring North Korean participation in the first round of six-party talks on the nuclear issue that were held in Beijing in August (as well as in subsequent rounds—see above). In April 2004 Kim Jong Il made a secretive visit to China, where he held talks with President Hu and other officials. Topics under discussion included the nuclear issue, with China reportedly urging North Korea to modify its stance, and economic matters. During 2004 repeated instances of defectors from North Korea seeking refuge in foreign embassies in Beijing posed a dilemma for China, which as an official ally of North Korea continued to refuse to grant refugee status to such persons. Many defectors were none the less able to travel to Seoul via a third country. In November, however, China forcibly repatriated a group of 70 North Korean nationals. It was believed that they would be imprisoned and possibly executed upon their return to North Korea. In March 2005 the North Korean Premier, Pak Pong Ju, visited Beijing and Shanghai. Chinese diplomacy received considerable credit for the achievement of the joint draft agreement at the end of the fourth round of six-party talks in September. In October President Hu made his first official visit to Pyongyang, in advance of the fifth round of discussions in November. In January 2006 reports emerged that Kim Jong Il had travelled incognito to the People's Republic and was again visiting the special economic zone of Shenzhen, to observe China's economic modernization. The visit was confirmed by North Korean media only after Kim's return.

North Korea's relations with China deteriorated in October 2006, however, following the North Korean nuclear weapon test. The test embarrassed the Chinese Government, which had repeatedly urged North Korea to forgo its plans. Somewhat unexpectedly, China agreed to UN sanctions against the coun-

try, while ensuring that they did not contain a threat of military action. Moreover, the Chinese Government indicated that North Korean refugees being sheltered in a US consulate in northeastern China would be allowed to travel to South Korea or the USA (a transfer that China had originally opposed), and stated that it would no longer object to Japan raising the issue of the abduction of Japanese citizens by North Korea at the six-party talks. China helped to broker another diplomatic advance at the end of October, when North Korea indicated that it was willing to rejoin the six-way nuclear talks. In September 2007 China provided North Korea with 50,000 metric tons of fuel oil, in accordance with the agreement reached in February at the six-party talks, which China continued to host. Following North Korea's failure to meet the deadline for the disablement of its nuclear facilities and disclosure of its nuclear activities, in late January 2008 the head of the Chinese Communist Party's international liaison department visited Pyongyang to urge Kim Jong Il to comply with his commitments under the six-party agreement. During a visit to Beijing in late February US Secretary of State Condoleezza Rice urged the Chinese Government to use its influence to persuade North Korea to implement the agreement fully. The newly appointed Chinese Vice-President, Xi Jinping, who was frequently described as a potential successor to President Hu Jintao, chose North Korea as the destination for his first official visit, meeting with Kim Jong Il and other senior officials in June 2008.

Following North Korea's launch of a long-range ballistic missile, purporting to be a satellite, in April 2009, China joined the UN Security Council's unanimous condemnation of the launch, but expressed opposition to any new sanctions that might exacerbate the situation. After North Korea tested its second nuclear device in late May, China stated that it was resolutely opposed to the test, urged North Korea to return to negotiations, and concurred with the UN Security Council's resolution on stricter sanctions, agreed in June. In October Chinese Premier Wen Jiabao visited North Korea, and it was reportedly his influence that led Kim Jong Il to announce, during the visit, that North Korea was ready to return to the six-party negotiations on its nuclear programme. In May 2010 Kim Jong Il embarked upon a visit to China, holding discussions with both the Chinese President and Prime Minister: it was reported that the North Korean leader had declared his commitment to ending the country's nuclear programme and expressed his intention to create conditions favourable to the resumption of the six-party talks. Kim Jong Il paid another visit to China in August 2010, reportedly accompanied by his son, Kim Jong Un, and in November the Premier of North Korea, Choe Yong Rim, spent eight days touring various industrial sites in China, particularly in Jilin Province, adjoining North Korea. Meanwhile, despite the conclusion by international investigators in May that the sinking of a South Korean naval vessel in March had been caused by a North Korean torpedo (see Inter-Korean Relations), China had refused to support a UN Security Council resolution condemning the action: China merely referred to the incident as unfortunate, and described subsequent joint South Korean and US naval exercises as unnecessarily confrontational. Following the bombardment of the South Korean island of Yeonpyeong by North Korea in November, China expressed concern and urged both countries to display restraint.

Kim Jong Il paid further official visits to China in May and August 2011, visiting industrial sites. Following his death in December, the Chinese Government quickly endorsed Kim Jong Un as his successor. In March 2012 China expressed concern when North Korea announced plans to launch a rocket-mounted satellite in the following month: it was widely suspected that in reality the operation would be the testing of a long-range missile. After the failed launch of the rocket in April, China urged South Korea, the USA and Japan not to aggravate regional tensions by overreacting, and later in the month President Hu pledged to strengthen China's relations with North Korea. In August a large North Korean delegation, led by Jang Song Thaek, toured the neighbouring Chinese provinces of Jilin and Liaoning, and an agreement was signed on the joint development of two special economic zones. The Chinese Government expressed 'regret' after North Korea's successful launch of another long-range rocket in December, and agreed to approve a UN Security Council resolution condemning the launch and extending the scope of sanctions against North Korean institutions and individuals. In early 2013 the Chinese authorities urged North Korea not to proceed with its threat to conduct a third nuclear test, and expressed 'firm opposition' once the test had taken place in February, again supporting a UN Security Council resolution that condemned the test and further expanded sanctions. In what was widely perceived to be a rebuke to North Korea, in April the Chinese President stated that 'no one should be allowed to throw the region, or the whole world, into chaos for selfish gains'. Unprecedented financial pressure from China was applied from May as leading Chinese banks suspended transactions with North Korea.

Relations with Japan

North Korea's relations with Japan have been characterized by continuing hostility towards the latter as a result of the atrocities committed in Korea during the Japanese occupation of 1910–45. The North Korean Government had demanded thousands of millions of dollars in compensation from Japan, before normal relations could be restored. In the 1980s, following the testimony of defectors, Japan began to suspect that North Korean agents had kidnapped a number of Japanese citizens during the late 1970s and early 1980s. Japan imposed sanctions on North Korea after North Korean agents were accused of attempting to assassinate the South Korean President in Burma in 1983. Following the destruction of a South Korean aircraft in 1987, allegedly by North Korean agents posing as Japanese citizens, Japan reimposed sanctions during 1988; North Korea then severed diplomatic contacts with Japan, although mutual trade continued. From late 1990 there was a significant rapprochement between North Korea and Japan, and in January 1991 a Japanese government delegation visited Pyongyang for discussions concerning the possible normalization of diplomatic relations. The Japanese delegation offered apologies, on behalf of its Government, for Japanese colonial aggression on the Korean peninsula between 1910 and 1945. Moreover, the Japanese Government expressed its willingness to make reparations for Japanese abuses of human rights in Korea during this period. However, subsequent negotiations in 1991 foundered, owing to North Korea's demand for reparations for damage inflicted after 1945 (which the Japanese Government denied) and to Japan's insistence that North Korea's nuclear installations be opened to outside inspection; normalization talks collapsed in November 1992, as the North Korean delegation abandoned the proceedings. Relations with Japan were further strained after North Korea's testing of the *Rodong-1* missile in the Sea of Japan (also known as the East Sea) in May 1993. The missile, according to US intelligence reports, would be capable of reaching most of Japan's major cities (and possibly of carrying either a conventional or a nuclear warhead). None the less, Japan, like South Korea, opposed the possible imposition of international economic sanctions on North Korea in response to North Korea's refusal to allow inspections of its nuclear facilities. In March 1995 a Japanese parliamentary group visited North Korea and reached an agreement for the resumption of normalization talks later in that year. In May Japan agreed to North Korea's request for emergency rice aid, and later in the year Japan provided aid to help North Korea overcome the effects of serious flooding. In early 1996 Japan provided a shipment of fuel oil to alleviate North Korea's energy shortfall.

Relations were complicated in 1997 by Japanese allegations that North Korea had abducted several Japanese citizens during the 1970s. However, in August 1997, for the first time since 1992, negotiations opened on the restoration of normal bilateral relations. An agreement was signed whereby some 1,800 Japanese women married to North Koreans, who had never been permitted to leave North Korea, were to be allowed to visit their relatives in Japan for short periods; the first such visits took place in November 1997 and January 1998. Moreover, in October 1997 the Japanese Government resumed the provision of aid to North Korea, suspended since mid-1996, donating food and medical supplies in response to the renewed appeals issued by the UN. In mid-1998, however, the North Korean Government cancelled a third visit of the Japanese women to their homeland, following Japan's rejection of a North Korean investigation into the alleged abduction of Japanese nationals. The testing by North Korea of a suspected *Taepodong* missile over Japanese territory in August prompted Japan to break off normalization talks, suspend food aid and postpone its contribution to the KEDO project. North Korea subsequently claimed that the object launched was in fact a satellite.

In March 1999 Japanese naval forces pursued and opened fire on suspected North Korean spy ships that had infiltrated Japanese waters. However, relations improved following North Korea's agreement with the USA, in September, to suspend its reported plans to test a new long-range missile. In December,

following a successful visit to North Korea by a group of Japanese parliamentarians, Japan announced an end to its ban on food aid. Later in that month intergovernmental preparatory discussions on re-establishing diplomatic relations were held in Beijing. Progress was achieved by the Japanese and North Korean Red Cross Societies at a meeting in March 2000. It was reported that North Korea had agreed to co-operate in a further investigation into the fate of some 10 missing Japanese nationals, while Japan had agreed to a search for Korean citizens who had disappeared prior to 1945. In addition, visits to their homeland by Japanese women married to North Koreans were to resume, and Japan was to provide some 100,000 metric tons of rice to North Korea through WFP. In late April 2000 Japanese charter flights to North Korea resumed. Following informal contacts between the North Korean and Japanese Governments, full normalization talks commenced in April; further rounds of discussions took place during the year.

In September 2000 the long-delayed third visits home by the Japanese wives of North Korean men took place. In October Japan decided, on humanitarian grounds, to provide 500,000 metric tons of rice to North Korea. In December North Korea reiterated that normal relations with Japan could be restored only after the latter delivered an apology and compensation for its earlier colonial rule. In May 2001 Japan deported Kim Jong Nam, son of Kim Jong Il, for entering the country on a false passport. In December a suspected North Korean spy vessel was sunk by Japanese coastguard forces after it had been expelled from Japan's exclusive economic zone. North Korea condemned the incident, accusing Japan of seeking to mislead world opinion. In February 2002 North Korea released a Japanese journalist who had been detained on spying charges since December 1999.

Junichiro Koizumi visited Pyongyang in September 2002, becoming the first incumbent Japanese Prime Minister to do so. His one-day visit, during which he held discussions with Kim Jong Il, elicited the latter's admission that North Korean agents had abducted 12 Japanese citizens in the 1970s and 1980s, of whom five were still alive. Kim apologized for the incidents, attributing them to rogue elements within the security services. The surviving captives were temporarily allowed to return to Japan in October 2002, although they had to leave behind any spouses or children. The Japanese authorities then refused to allow the abductees to return to North Korea.

In October 2002 the alleged admission by North Korean officials to their visiting US counterparts that North Korea was pursuing a secret nuclear weapons programme greatly alarmed Japan. In separate incidents in February and March 2003, North Korea test-launched two short-range ground-to-ship missiles in the Sea of Japan, and in April tested a third missile in the Yellow Sea. However, it refrained from testing longer-range ballistic missiles, which Japan considered a threat to its security. In March the North Korean Government condemned Japan's launching of two spy satellites, believed to be part of a programme of intelligence-gathering on North Korea initiated following the suspected testing of the North Korean *Taepodong* missile over Japan in 1998. In October 2003 North Korea announced that it did not wish Japan to participate in future negotiations on its nuclear weapons programme.

In January 2004 the Japanese House of Representatives approved legislation to permit the imposition of economic sanctions on North Korea; in April legislation was approved requiring all ships entering Japanese ports from March 2005 to be insured against oil damage. This in practice amounted to a ban on entry of all but 16 of an estimated 100 North Korean ships that were involved in trade with Japan. Following a second visit by Japanese Prime Minister Koizumi to Pyongyang in May 2004, five children of the abductees who had returned to Japan in 2002 (see above) were permitted to fly to Tokyo. Their release had been secured in return for pledges of food aid and medical supplies. However, suspicions remained over the fate of other missing Japanese nationals.

Japan remained reluctant to impose direct economic sanctions on North Korea, not wishing to jeopardize negotiations on the nuclear weapons programme. The six-party agreement of September 2005 contained a clause whereby the two countries undertook to 'take steps to normalize their relations'. In February 2006 inconclusive bilateral discussions incorporated the issues of the alleged abductions of Japanese citizens, the development of ballistic missiles by North Korea and the resumption of the nuclear negotiations.

In June 2006 the Japanese legislature enacted the North Korean Human Rights Act, which expressly linked the imposition of sanctions to issues of human rights in North Korea. The Act stated that economic sanctions would be imposed unless North Korea worked to resolve human rights issues, including the abduction of Japanese nationals. When North Korea conducted missile tests in July, Japan was one of its most vehement critics, announcing unilateral sanctions against North Korea in September: these included the suspension of transfers of funds to North Korea by groups suspected of having links to the country's nuclear weapons or missiles programmes.

When Shinzo Abe became Japanese Prime Minister in September 2006, he adopted a firmer stance on North Korea. Abe appointed a prime ministerial adviser on the issue of Japanese abductees, and also established a special government panel on the subject. Following the North Korean nuclear test on 9 October, Japan not only supported sanctions under the UN Security Council, but also imposed firm measures of its own, banning all North Korean imports and prohibiting North Korean ships from entering Japanese waters, and banning the export of luxury goods to North Korea. However, the restoration of normal relations between North Korea and Japan was one of the tenets of the agreement reached during six-party talks in February 2007, and a working group was established to conduct negotiations. Bilateral discussions were held in Viet Nam in March, but they broke down over the issue of the Japanese abductees. In July the North Korean Government accused Japan of attempting to obstruct the talks on the normalization of bilateral relations and to disrupt the six-party process with its refusal to provide energy aid and its insistence on the resolution of the abduction issue, which North Korea claimed had already been settled. In October Japan announced that it would not resume aid to North Korea and extended its sanctions for a further six months, again renewing them in April 2008. In June North Korea and Japan attended bilateral talks in Beijing, with the former agreeing to carry out another investigation into the abduction issue in exchange for the withdrawal of certain Japanese sanctions, including restrictions on port visits by North Korean vessels carrying humanitarian cargo. In October, with little progress having been made on the abduction issue, Japan sought to withhold aid for North Korea under the six-party agreement.

In March 2009, following the revelation that North Korea was shortly to launch a satellite (widely believed to represent, in reality, a test of long-range missile technology), Japan mobilized its missile interceptors, in the country's first deployment of this technology. The Japanese Government reiterated its warning that it would attempt to destroy any North Korean missile or debris that threatened Japanese territory. In June, following North Korea's testing of a nuclear device in the previous month, Japan banned all exports to North Korea. In May 2010, following the conclusion by multinational investigators that North Korea had been responsible for the sinking of a South Korean naval vessel in March (see Inter-Korean Relations), the Japanese Government expressed its support for South Korea and stated that it would consider imposing additional sanctions on North Korea. In March 2012 the Japanese Government urged North Korea not to proceed with its announced intention to launch another rocket-mounted 'satellite' in the following month, and stated that the country's missile defence systems would be deployed if the rocket passed over Japanese territory. Although the launch in April failed as the rocket broke up over the sea, Japan condemned it as a threat to its security and a violation of UN resolutions. In August discussions between diplomatic representatives of Japan and North Korea—the first for four years—took place in China, followed by discussions at a more senior level in Mongolia in November, covering the habitual topics of reparations and abduction as obstacles to establishing normal diplomatic relations. In September it was announced that the US and Japanese Governments had agreed to establish a second missile defence system in Japan, in order to counter the threat of North Korean ballistic missiles. Japan strongly protested at North Korea's successful launch of a long-range rocket in December and condemned, as a 'grave threat' to Japan and the region, the testing of a nuclear device that ensued in February 2013. In April Japan deployed missile defence systems to protect against a potential missile launch from North Korea.

Other regional relations

In April 2000 North Korea formally applied to join the Association of Southeast Asian Nations (ASEAN, see p. 218). Following North Korea's admittance to the ASEAN Regional Forum (ARF), a meeting in Thailand in July was attended for the first time by the North Korean Minister of Foreign Affairs, Paek Nam Sun, who held unprecedented meetings with his South Korean,

Japanese and US counterparts; North Korea was regularly represented at the ARF thereafter, and the meetings provided an important opportunity for informal contacts. In November the Asia-Pacific Economic Co-operation (APEC, see p. 208) forum supported North Korea's guest status in that organization.

In May 2000 Australia restored diplomatic links with North Korea. Diplomatic relations were established with the Philippines in 2000 and with New Zealand in 2001. Relations with Timor-Leste were established in late 2002. In 2003 there were reports that military relations with Myanmar were being developed; diplomatic relations were re-established (after a hiatus of 25 years) in April 2007. A UN report released in November 2010 stated that North Korea was supplying nuclear-related technology to Myanmar, but this was denied by the Myanma Government: in September 2012, following progress towards democratic reform in Myanmar, the US Government urged the Myanma Government to reduce its links with North Korea. In June 2009, meanwhile, ASEAN leaders, attending a summit meeting in Seoul, condemned North Korea's recent testing of a nuclear device, urging the elimination of nuclear weapons on the Korean peninsula and North Korea's return to the six-party negotiations; ASEAN member governments again expressed serious concern at North Korea's long-range rocket launches in April and December 2012 and at its testing of a third nuclear device in February 2013.

Relations with the USA and multilateral talks

From the time of the Korean War, North Korea continued to depict the USA as its main enemy and repeatedly accused South Korea of being a US 'puppet' state. Relations deteriorated after North Korea seized a US naval vessel, the *USS Pueblo*, in 1968 and detained its crew for several months. In 1969 North Korea shot down a US reconnaissance aircraft, which had apparently violated North Korean airspace, resulting in the deaths of 31 US servicemen. In 1987, in response to alleged North Korean involvement in the bombing of a South Korean airliner, the USA placed North Korea on its list of countries supporting terrorism, and restricted contacts between US and North Korean diplomats. From the 1990s relations with the USA were largely dominated by North Korea's nuclear ambitions. In December 1994 it was announced that agreement had been reached to establish liaison offices in Washington, DC, and Pyongyang in 1995, in preparation for an eventual resumption of full diplomatic relations. However, the USA insisted that normal relations would be restored only when North Korea ceased to export ballistic missiles and withdrew its troops from the border with South Korea; North Korea, in turn, stated that liaison offices could only be opened when light-water nuclear reactors, in accordance with the October 1994 agreement between North Korea and the USA, had been supplied. In January 1995 North Korea opened its ports to US commercial shipping and removed restrictions on the import of goods from the USA. Following severe flooding in North Korea in 1995 and 1996, the USA provided relief aid.

The issue of four-way talks dominated relations between the USA and North Korea in 1996, but parallel negotiations were conducted concerning the estimated 8,100 US soldiers who were listed as 'missing in action' following the Korean War. The USA agreed to provide funds to assist in locating the remains. In early 1997 the USA responded to a renewed appeal issued by the UN for food aid and humanitarian assistance for North Korea, as a result of which North Korea announced its intention to take part in exploratory discussions about the proposed quadripartite talks. Bilateral discussions with the USA focused on the establishment of liaison offices, missile non-proliferation and procedures for the exhumation of the US servicemen listed as 'missing in action'. In August, however, the defection to the USA of two North Korean diplomats (the most senior officials yet to seek asylum in North America) resulted in the suspension of the third round of missile non-proliferation talks. North Korea was unsuccessful in attempting to make its participation in full quadripartite talks conditional upon the withdrawal of US forces from the Korean peninsula and upon the provision of food aid. None the less, the USA responded positively, on humanitarian grounds, to two further UN appeals for food aid during the year.

Relations with the USA were dominated by nuclear issues and other concerns regarding North Korea's missile development programme in 1998 and 1999. The exhumation of US soldiers listed as 'missing in action' proceeded, with the remains of more than 40 soldiers being returned in 1998–2000.

In October 2000 Kim Jong Il's special envoy, Vice-Marshal Jo Myong Rok, paid a state visit to the USA, the most senior North

Korean official ever to do so. The US Secretary of State, Madeleine Albright, reciprocated the visit and met Kim Jong Il, who agreed in principle to halt his country's long-range missile-testing programme. However, relations between North Korea and the USA deteriorated during 2001 following the inauguration of George W. Bush as US President. Bush adopted a more hostile position towards North Korea than that of his predecessor, and this also adversely affected inter-Korean relations. North Korea condemned the joint US-South Korean military exercises held in April. In May a non-governmental delegation from the USA visited North Korea to examine evidence of atrocities committed by US troops during the Korean War. In June Bush stated that he was willing to resume negotiations with North Korea, albeit linking these to a reduction in North Korea's missile programme and military deployments—terms rejected by the North. Following the terrorist attacks on the USA in September, the US Administration paid increasing attention to the possibility of North Korea having developed biological, chemical and nuclear weapons. Despite signing two UN treaties against terrorism in November, North Korea remained on the USA's list of states sponsoring terrorism.

In January 2002 President Bush referred to North Korea as forming an 'axis of evil' with Iran and Iraq. Bush's comments were believed to reflect concern that North Korea was exporting weapons technology to countries the USA considered to be 'rogue states'. (During the 1990s North Korea had exported missiles and related technology to Egypt, Iran, Libya, Pakistan and Syria, allegedly earning up to US $1,000m. a year.) In April the North accepted a South Korean request to reopen dialogue with the USA. At the same time the USA announced that it would release $95m. to North Korea in order to accelerate the building of replacement nuclear reactors—construction of which finally began in August 2002.

In October 2002 the USA revealed that senior North Korean officials had confirmed US intelligence reports that North Korea was pursuing a secret nuclear weapons programme; the USA declared the agreement concluded in October 1994 to be null and void and placed renewed pressure on North Korea to halt its nuclear activities. North Korea responded by stating that it would consider halting its nuclear programme if the USA would sign a non-aggression treaty guaranteeing it sovereignty, a demand rejected by the USA. In November 2002 the USA finally halted petroleum shipments to North Korea, citing the latter's violation of the 1994 framework. It was widely reported that Pakistan had provided the technical expertise for North Korea's nuclear programme in exchange for ballistic missiles.

In December 2002 North Korea announced that it would restart its nuclear reactor at Yongbyon and removed the IAEA's monitoring and surveillance equipment from the facility. Security analysts, meanwhile, concluded that North Korea already possessed between two and five nuclear devices. The IAEA reported that North Korean technicians had transferred 1,000 fuel rods (of the 8,000 necessary to reactivate it) to the Yongbyon reactor, ostensibly for the production of electricity, but probably for the production of plutonium required to manufacture nuclear devices. North Korea expelled the two remaining IAEA inspectors at the end of the year.

In January 2003 North Korea announced its withdrawal from the NPT. In February North Korea stated that the Yongbyon reactor was operating normally, and that any US military build-up in the region could lead the North to launch a pre-emptive strike on US forces anywhere in the world. In March the USA and South Korea began their annual joint military exercises, as usual incurring condemnation by the North, which announced at the end of the month that it was severing military contacts with the USA at the liaison office in the DMZ. Between late February and the beginning of April North Korea test-fired three short-range missiles, although it refrained from testing its longer-range ballistic missiles. By early April the USA had imposed new sanctions on North Korea's Government and its Changgwang Sinyong Corporation, for exporting ballistic missiles to Pakistan. However, the sanctions were largely symbolic, since the USA had minimal economic links with North Korea. The seizure by Australian authorities of a North Korean ship carrying 50 kg of heroin confirmed US claims that North Korea was involved in drugs-trafficking. Also in April, the UN Security Council held its first discussions on the North Korean crisis. North Korea had stated that the imposition of economic sanctions through the Security Council would be tantamount to a declaration of war.

In June 2003 North Korea for the first time publicly defended its nuclear weapons strategy, declaring that the development of nuclear weapons was a 'deterrent'. In July there were new indications from US and Asian intelligence sources that North Korea was operating a second secret nuclear facility, in addition to the plant at Yongbyon. At the end of July it was announced that North Korea had agreed to take part in multilateral talks on its nuclear weapons programme with the USA, South Korea, Japan, China and Russia. The six-party talks duly took place in Beijing in August, but little progress was achieved, the USA insisting that North Korea unconditionally abandon its nuclear weapons programme, while North Korea reiterated that it would continue to develop its nuclear capacity unless the USA provided a guarantee of non-aggression. In September the US Government indicated that verifiable progress on dismantling might be sufficient to elicit concessions, but that a bilateral non-aggression treaty, as desired by North Korea, was not a possibility, and that any guarantee would involve China, Russia, South Korea and Japan, as well as the USA. In October the North Korean state news agency claimed that North Korea had successfully generated sufficient plutonium to build a nuclear bomb. In November the Central Intelligence Agency (CIA) reported to the US Congress that it believed North Korea had the technology to turn its nuclear fuel into functioning weapons. In early December KEDO (the international consortium established in 1995, following the 1994 agreement with the USA on assistance for energy development in North Korea in return for nuclear non-proliferation) announced that it would be suspending for one year its construction in North Korea of two non-military nuclear reactors. Also in December 2003, the USA rejected an offer from North Korea to freeze its nuclear programme in return for concessions on security and energy aid.

In January 2004 there was speculation about the existence of a second nuclear programme for enriching uranium (in addition to the plutonium-reprocessing activities at Yongbyon). In February and June further six-party talks took place, but no significant resolutions were reached, with North Korea continuing to deny the existence of a uranium enrichment programme. In August it was reported that North Korea was developing a new sea-based long-range missile system, which would possibly be capable of targeting the USA. A fourth round of six-party talks scheduled for September 2004 was suspended when North Korea refused to attend, citing US hostility. Tensions in relations with the USA increased further following the re-election of George W. Bush as US President in November. Later in that month KEDO announced its intention to suspend plans for the construction in North Korea of two non-military nuclear reactors.

In a state radio broadcast in February 2005 North Korea for the first time explicitly stated that it possessed nuclear weapons, and that it intended to postpone its participation in six-party negotiations for an indefinite period. Subsequent suggestions by North Korea for bilateral discussions with the USA were rejected by the latter. In May North Korea test-fired a ballistic missile into the Sea of Japan. An apparent improvement in relations in June included a US pledge of 50,000 metric tons of food aid, and the fourth round of six-party talks began in Beijing in late July. Meanwhile, in bilateral discussions the USA continued to insist that the restoration of normal relations, removal of sanctions and guarantees of security could only follow the 'complete, verifiable and irreversible dismantling' of North Korea's nuclear weapons programme, while the latter reiterated that only after the normalization of relations, including the signing of a peace treaty ending the Korean War, and the removal of US nuclear weapons from South Korea (the presence of which the US side denied) would the North agree to abandon its military nuclear aspirations.

In mid-September 2005 a draft joint agreement was signed by all sides in the six-party negotiations, in which North Korea committed itself to dismantling its nuclear weapons programme, returning to the NPT and permitting IAEA inspectors to visit its nuclear facilities. In return, the USA declared that it maintained no nuclear weapons on the Korean peninsula and had no intention of attacking North Korea. North Korea's right to peaceful nuclear energy was acknowledged, and it was envisaged that the provision of a civilian light-water nuclear reactor to North Korea would be discussed 'at an appropriate time'. The other five parties also undertook to provide North Korea with energy assistance. Although significant, the agreement was compromised almost immediately when the North Korean Government insisted that it would take no steps towards dismantling its nuclear weapons programme until provided with a light-water reactor as specified in the agreement. The USA insisted that concessions such as the provision of the reactor could be expected to come into force only after North Korea had fulfilled its dismantlement obligations. The fifth round of talks, which began in Beijing in November, ended without agreement. Later in November KEDO announced that it was considering the termination of its light-water reactor construction project in North Korea, which had been suspended since 2003. (All workers were withdrawn from KEDO's construction site in Kumho, North Korea, in January 2006, and in December KEDO's executive board signed an agreement to terminate the project.)

Meanwhile, the resumption of the six-party nuclear negotiations appeared to be jeopardized by US allegations of financial crimes on the part of North Korea. In September 2005 the US Government had ordered that all transactions with Banco Delta Asia in the Chinese Special Administrative Region of Macao be terminated, in relation to suspected money-laundering activities conducted with the bank by the North Korean Government, and had also frozen the assets of eight North Korean companies, which it accused of proliferating weapons of mass destruction. In October the US Department of Justice accused North Korea of having forged millions of US dollars' worth of counterfeit $100 bills since 1989, and in December 2005 the US ambassador to South Korea publicly described North Korea as a 'criminal regime'. Although the US Administration insisted that the sanctions were purely a legal matter and had no political connection to the nuclear issue, the North Korean Government declared that no further six-party negotiations could be held until sanctions against it were removed. In April 2006 the US Administration rejected North Korean overtures for bilateral discussions in Tokyo, to coincide with a regional security forum at which all six participants in the nuclear discussions were present, insisting that communication between the two sides was only possible within the context of the six-party talks.

By mid-2006 speculation was rife that North Korea was soon to test-launch an intercontinental ballistic missile, thus breaking the moratorium on tests imposed in 1999. The US Government warned that a test would be regarded as a provocative act. Japan threatened stern action should a test missile be launched. However, North Korea continued to insist that it might be prepared to halt the planned test should the USA agree to direct bilateral talks, a request that the US Government once again rejected. Instead, the USA announced that it would deploy advanced *Patriot* missiles (capable of intercepting North Korean ballistic missiles, as well as cruise missiles and aircraft) on Japanese soil for the first time. North Korea's decision to test seven missiles on 5 July 2006 was regarded as a deliberate attempt to provoke the USA. Of the missiles tested, at least one was a *Taepodong-2* missile, thought to be capable of reaching Alaska; although the US Department of State claimed that the *Taepodong-2* failed in mid-air after about 42 seconds of flight, the North Korean Government hailed the tests as a success, announcing that more test launches were planned.

While the international community broadly condemned the tests, harsh criticism from the USA and Japan was tempered by the more cautious stance adopted by China, Russia and South Korea. The USA and Japan urged the UN Security Council to adopt sanctions against North Korea, while Russia and China, which as permanent members of the Council held the power of veto, emphasized the importance of the resumption of dialogue. The UN Security Council adopted Resolution 1695 on 15 July 2006, requiring member states to ban the import and export of missile-related material to and from North Korea. The USA attempted once more to revive the six-party talks in September, but reiterated that its position had not changed.

In defiance of international opinion North Korea conducted a nuclear test in October 2006, reportedly from a test site near Kimchaek city in North Hamgyong Province. The South Korean Minister for Unification, Lee Jong-Seok, denounced the test as a clear challenge to world peace and stability. Although the size of the device tested was thought to be very small, the detection of airborne radiation by US analysts confirmed that the device was nuclear in nature. The test prompted an emergency meeting of the UN Security Council in New York, USA, amid strong condemnation from many governments. The Security Council approved a unanimous resolution imposing sanctions on North Korea, with Russia and China unexpectedly agreeing to a range of sanctions, albeit measures that were purely economic and commercial, rather than military, in nature. Resolution 1718 urged North Korea to suspend immediately its ballistic weapons programme and further nuclear tests and to return to the six-party talks without precondition. Sanctions included provision for the inspection of cargo entering and leaving North Korean

ports, a ban on weapons-related imports, a travel ban on North Korean officials thought to be involved in the weapons programme and a freezing of their assets, and also a ban on the import of luxury goods. At the end of October North Korea indicated that it would return to the six-party talks, following discussions among Chinese, US and North Korean officials. While North Korea set no conditions for its return to the discussions, it expressed the hope that one of the topics would be the removal of financial sanctions and the release of North Korean assets.

Intense diplomatic activity resulted in the resumption of the six-party talks in December 2006. However, North Korea stated that it would consider halting its nuclear programme only if the US and UN sanctions were removed. The country also reiterated demands for a nuclear reactor to generate electricity. The US negotiators, meanwhile, were reported by South Korean sources to have offered a fresh programme of incentives, which would give North Korea aid and security guarantees if it agreed to declare all its nuclear-related programmes and place them under permanent external inspection. In February 2007 North Korea agreed to permit IAEA inspections and to shut down its nuclear reactor at Yongbyon within 60 days in exchange for the equivalent of 50,000 metric tons of heavy fuel oil and the assurance of negotiations on the restoration of normal relations with Japan and the USA, with the latter notably agreeing to begin the process of ending the designation of North Korea as a state sponsoring terrorism. Five working groups were to be established to address North Korean relations with both Japan and the USA, economic and energy co-operation, denuclearization of the Korean peninsula, and the establishment of a North-East Asia peace and security mechanism. North Korea was given an incentive of a further 950,000 tons of heavy fuel oil for immobilizing its nuclear facilities and providing a complete declaration of all its nuclear programmes as part of the next phase of the agreement. Although the formal accord did not directly mention the North Korean funds in the Banco Delta Asia in Macao that had been frozen by the USA in 2005, this issue was covered by a reference to 'resolving pending bilateral issues', and the USA subsequently agreed to return the funds. In March a further round of six-party talks faltered over delays to the release of the North Korean funds in Macao, and North Korea missed the 14 April closure deadline for the Yongbyon reactor. As progress on the implementation of the February 2007 agreement remained stalled, with commercial banks reportedly unwilling to transfer the Banco Delta Asia funds, North Korea test-fired three short-range missiles in late May and early June.

US Assistant Secretary of State Christopher Hill visited Pyongyang for the first time in late June 2007. Shortly afterwards North Korea confirmed that it had received the Banco Delta Asia funds, which amounted to US $25m. and had been transferred via a Russian bank, and on the following day IAEA inspectors arrived on their first visit to North Korea since their expulsion in December 2002. In mid-July 2007 North Korea announced that it had shut down Yongbyon, and this was subsequently verified by the IAEA. Participants in the six-party talks met in Beijing a few days later, but failed to agree upon a timetable for the second phase of the February accord, i.e. the disclosure and disablement of all North Korea's nuclear facilities. Following the discussions, North Korea renewed its demands for a light-water reactor in exchange for immobilizing its Yongbyon nuclear reactor. Working groups established by the six nations involved in the talks on ending North Korea's nuclear weapons programme held meetings in Panmunjom in August to discuss the technical details of the next stage of the process. Following talks between North Korea and the USA on improving their bilateral relations, which were held in Geneva in early September, Hill announced that North Korea had agreed to declare and disable all its nuclear facilities by the end of the year.

A new round of six-party talks, which was held in Beijing in late September 2007, resulted in formal agreement on a deadline of 31 December for the completion of the second phase of the February accord, under which North Korea would receive a further 900,000 metric tons of heavy fuel oil (100,000 tons having already been supplied by South Korea and China). In mid-October a US team of government officials and nuclear experts spent a week in North Korea discussing detailed plans for disablement. Work on immobilizing the Yongbyon reactor, which was to entail the removal of 8,000 fuel rods, commenced in early November under US supervision. However, North Korea failed to meet the deadline to disclose details of its nuclear activities. The disablement of the country's nuclear facilities had also not been completed by the end of 2007, although this was attributed to technical difficulties.

At discussions between US and North Korean negotiators, held in February 2008, disagreement remained over North Korea's continued denial of US claims of the existence of a covert North Korean nuclear programme for enriching uranium; this was followed in April by the USA's contention that North Korea had passed sensitive nuclear information to Syria. In May North Korea accepted the USA's offer of substantial amounts of food aid, the bulk of which was to be delivered by WFP. The provision of documentation on the nuclear programme in May and June prompted President Bush to announce that North Korea would be removed from the USA's list of state sponsors of terrorism and that US trade sanctions would be withdrawn. Soon afterwards, the cooling tower of the Yongbyon reactor was destroyed by the North Korean authorities. However, further movement on the terms of the agreement was slow, owing to disputes over the method of authentication of the North Korean progress reports and delays to North Korea's official redesignation as a non-terrorist nation. In August these disagreements resulted in an announcement from North Korea that it would stop dismantling its Yongbyon reactor, and, in early September, that the reactor was to be restarted. The impasse appeared to have been resolved in October, when the USA implemented the redesignation of North Korea in return for the latter's assurance of compliance with nuclear inspections, albeit with conditions. However, the issue of the verification procedure continued to impede progress when the six-party talks resumed in Beijing in December.

After Barack Obama had taken office as President of the USA in January 2009, his Secretary of State, Hillary Clinton, declared that if North Korea were to eliminate its nuclear weapons programme 'genuinely and verifiably' the new Administration would be prepared to establish normal diplomatic relations and provide economic assistance. In March, however, following the closure of the border in response to South Korea's participation in its customary joint military exercises with the USA, and as speculation mounted with regard to the precise nature of an imminent satellite launch announced by North Korea, the North Korean Government refused to accept any further supplies of US food aid and instructed five US aid groups to leave the country by the end of the month.

North Korea's announcement of its forthcoming launch of a communications satellite aroused much concern. The US, South Korean and Japanese Governments suspected that the operation might prove to be a long-range ballistic missile test. In April 2009 North Korea proceeded to launch its rocket, in defiance of international warnings. The rocket dropped a booster stage to the west of Japan before flying over the country towards the Pacific Ocean, where a second booster stage was released. North Korea announced that the launch had permitted the placement of a communications satellite into orbit; however, this was contested by the US military, which asserted that the rocket's payload had landed in the Pacific Ocean. The Japanese Government requested an emergency session of the UN Security Council. The session ended without agreement after divisions emerged with regard to the response to the launch. Chinese and Russian envoys urged restraint, while the USA and Japan advocated a reinforcement of sanctions against North Korea. However, later in April the Security Council released a statement condemning the rocket launch and the violation of the ban on missile tests by North Korea. The country then expelled all UN nuclear inspectors and announced its withdrawal from the six-party talks and the resumption of its nuclear programme.

On 25 May 2009 North Korea exploded an underground nuclear device, believed to be larger than the one tested in October 2006. On the same day three short-range ballistic missiles were also fired, followed by several more in the ensuing days. The nuclear test was condemned by the USA, China, Russia and numerous other countries, and in June 2009 the UN Security Council unanimously approved a resolution condemning the test 'in the strongest terms', demanding that North Korea not conduct any further nuclear test or any launch using ballistic missile technology, urging the country to reverse its withdrawal from the NPT and strengthening the sanctions that had been imposed on North Korea in 2006: the resolution prohibited the export of all weapons from North Korea and the import of all except minor weapons, and urged member states to inspect North Korean cargo ships and aircraft for materials related to the production of nuclear weapons. North Korea responded by firing several short-range and medium-range ballistic missiles in early July 2009. Later in July the Security

Council's committee on sanctions nominated five companies and five individuals to be subject to a freeze of financial assets and a ban on foreign travel, including North Korea's General Bureau of Atomic Energy and its director, and three trading companies.

In June 2009 two US journalists who had been detained in North Korea in March were tried, convicted of illegal entry into the country and 'hostile acts', and sentenced to 12 years' labour. In August, however, the former US President, Bill Clinton, travelled to Pyongyang (reportedly at the indirect invitation of the North Korean Government) and secured the release of the two women: his visit, although unofficial, included a meeting with Kim Jong Il. In October, during a visit to Pyongyang by the Chinese Premier, Wen Jiabao, Kim Jong Il expressed readiness to resume multilateral talks on the nuclear programme, depending on the outcome of bilateral discussions with the USA. The Obama Administration, for its part, stated that bilateral dialogue was acceptable, provided that it led to a resumption of the six-party talks, and in November it was announced that a special US envoy to North Korea, Stephen Bosworth, had been appointed. During a visit to South Korea in that month, President Obama offered economic assistance to North Korea if it demonstrated an irreversible halt to its development of nuclear weapons. Bosworth paid a visit to Pyongyang in December, but no date for a subsequent meeting was announced.

In April 2010 North Korea's principal negotiator on nuclear affairs, Kim Kye Gwan, was reported to have been refused entry to the USA for bilateral discussions, since no North Korean undertaking to resume the six-party talks had been made. In May, following the conclusion by expert investigators that North Korea had been responsible for the sinking of the South Korean naval vessel *Cheonan* in March (see Inter-Korean Relations), the US Government condemned the incident as an unacceptable provocation. In the same month a preliminary report by a group of experts, commissioned by the UN, reported that North Korea had been exporting nuclear technology to Iran, Myanmar and Syria, in defiance of sanctions imposed by the UN Security Council. In June President Obama announced an extension of US sanctions against North Korea. In July North Korea reacted with outrage to four days of large-scale joint naval exercises by South Korea and the USA, in international waters off North Korea. In August Jimmy Carter, the former US President, visited North Korea in a successful attempt to secure the freedom of a US citizen who had been imprisoned after entering the country illegally in January; although the visit was private, Carter met Kim Kye Gwan and Kim Yong Nam (a senior member of the KWP and the country's titular head of state), and the latter was reported by the North Korean media to have expressed willingness to resume the six-party negotiations. Later in August the US Government imposed new sanctions and travel bans on North Korean organizations and individuals, including a clandestine branch of the KWP, known as Office 39, which was alleged to have been dealing in illicit drugs, and the Green Pine Corporation, which was believed to export weapons. In November a senior US nuclear scientist visited North Korea and reported that he had been shown an advanced uranium enrichment facility, which was much more extensive and up-to-date than expected; the facility was intended to supply a new light-water reactor that was under construction at Yongbyon, ostensibly for the peaceful production of electricity. Later in November, after North Korea's bombardment of the South Korean island of Yeonpyeong, President Obama reaffirmed the USA's commitment to South Korea's defence, and the two countries again undertook joint naval exercises in the Yellow Sea.

In July 2011 discussions took place in New York between the representatives of North Korea and the USA, Kim Kye Gwan and Bosworth, after which the North Korean Government announced that it was willing to resume the six-party talks from which it had withdrawn in April 2009. In August 2011 North Korea also agreed to resume negotiations on repatriating the remains of US soldiers: repatriations had been halted in 2005. Also in August 2011 the USA agreed to provide emergency aid for flood victims in North Korea. In October a new US special envoy, Glyn Davies, was appointed to replace Bosworth. In late February 2012, after a third session of bilateral talks, held in Beijing, the North Korean Government announced that it would suspend its uranium enrichment activities, long-range missile tests and the testing of nuclear weapons, and allow IAEA inspectors to return to the country. In response, the US Government announced the provision of 240,000 metric tons of food aid. In March, however, the agreement was cancelled after North Korea's announcement that in the following month it was to launch another rocket-mounted satellite (an operation again generally suspected to be, in reality, the testing of a long-range missile). Visiting South Korea in March, President Obama reaffirmed his wish to improve relations with North Korea, but declared that there would be no 'rewards for provocation', and urged the North Korean leadership to 'have the courage to pursue peace'. Despite international protests, the launch took place in April, although the rocket failed soon after take-off. The US Government condemned the launch and reaffirmed its commitment to the security of its allies in the area. The North Korean Government subsequently announced that it was no longer bound by the moratorium on missile and nuclear tests agreed with the US Government in February, accusing the latter of violating the accord. In early May the UN Security Council imposed sanctions on three North Korean state-owned companies (reportedly involved in weapons trading) in response to the failed rocket launch.

In early December 2012 the North Korean authorities announced that another satellite was to be launched for peaceful purposes, using a long-range rocket, and this time the attempt was apparently successful. As on previous occasions, it was widely suspected that the launch represented a test of long-range missile technology, and it was described by the US Government as a 'highly provocative act'. In January 2013 the UN Security Council unanimously condemned the launch and extended sanctions against North Korea to include more individuals and state-owned trading companies, a bank and the national space agency. The North Korean Government promptly announced that it was proceeding with plans to test a third nuclear device, which it duly did in February. The test, which as on previous occasions took place underground, involved a 'miniaturized' device which could possibly be mounted on a long-range rocket and was believed to be twice as powerful as that used in the 2009 test. In March 2013 a new UN Security Council resolution (the fifth since 2006) further expanded sanctions on financial transactions and strengthened states' authority to inspect North Korean ships and aircraft suspected of carrying weapons-related cargoes. Meanwhile, in anticipation of the annual joint military exercises to be undertaken by South Korean and US forces in March and April, there was a marked increase in anti-US rhetoric on the part of the North Korean authorities, which threatened 'pre-emptive nuclear strikes' and declared that artillery units were ready to target US bases in South Korea and the Pacific region. The US deployment of B-52 bomber aircraft and 'stealth' bombers and fighter jets (for the first time) over South Korea, as part of the exercises, was viewed as particularly provocative. In early April North Korea announced that it was recommencing activities at the Yongbyon nuclear plant, the source for plutonium for the country's nuclear programme; the Yongbyon facility has been officially suspended since 2007. Also in early April the US Government announced that it was to move an advanced missile defence system to the US Pacific territory of Guam in response to North Korean threats, but also postponed planned tests of its own long-range ballistic missile, for fear of exacerbating the crisis. However, in early May two North Korean medium-range missiles that had been moved to a coastal launch site in April were reportedly removed in an apparent lowering of tension.

Other external relations

In the mid-1980s North Korea placed increased emphasis on its relations with the USSR. North Korea's diplomatic isolation became more pronounced in the early 1990s, as former communist bloc countries attempted to foster relations with South Korea. Furthermore, the USSR announced that, from January 1991, its barter trading system with North Korea would be abolished in favour of trade in convertible currencies at world market prices. However, an agreement was reported to have been signed in May 1993 by North Korea and the Russian Federation (which, following the dissolution of the USSR, had assumed responsibility for many of the USSR's international undertakings) on technological and scientific co-operation. In February 2000 the two countries concluded a new bilateral treaty of friendship, good neighbourliness and co-operation (to replace a 1961 bilateral treaty). In July President Vladimir Putin became the first Russian (or Soviet) leader to visit North Korea. Following Putin's visit, co-operation between Russia and North Korea placed a strong emphasis on connecting the latter's rail system to the Trans-Siberian railway, and in March 2001 the two countries signed a railway co-operation agreement. In August Kim Jong Il undertook a 24-day visit across Russia to Moscow, where he and President Putin signed a new declaration of co-operation in

politics, the economy, military matters, science and technology, and culture. However, Russia also urged North Korea to settle the latter's outstanding bilateral debt.

As the diplomatic crisis over North Korea's nuclear weapons programme intensified in January 2003, Russia sought to defuse the situation by urging a three-stage formula whereby the international community would accept a nuclear-free Korean peninsula, guarantees for the regime's security, and a resumption of aid. North Korea reiterated that the crisis could be resolved only through discussions with the USA.

In July 2006, following the North's missile tests, Russia and China ensured that attempts by the UN Security Council to impose sanctions on North Korea were obstructed. However, Russia modified its strong anti-sanctions policy following the nuclear test of 9 October, like China using its power of veto and ensuring that UN Security Council Resolution 1718 did not include the threat of military action. The Russian authorities assisted in the process of transferring previously frozen North Korean funds from the Banco Delta Asia in Macao to North Korea via a Russian bank in June 2007, thus removing the main obstacle to the implementation of the February agreement on North Korea's nuclear programme (see Relations with the USA and multilateral talks). In January 2008 Russia provided North Korea with 50,000 metric tons of fuel oil as part of its commitment under the six-party agreement on the dismantling of North Korea's nuclear facilities. In April Russia and North Korea signed an agreement to restore an existing railway line between Khasan on the Russian border and Rajin in North Korea. Russia condemned North Korea's launch of a long-range missile in April 2009, but opposed the imposition of stricter sanctions; however, after North Korea had conducted a nuclear test in the following month, Russia agreed to accept the new sanctions imposed by the UN Security Council. Following the conclusion by an expert inquiry in May 2010 that the sinking of a South Korean naval vessel in March had been caused by a torpedo fired by a North Korean submarine, the Russian Government undertook to 'closely consult' South Korea, and urged restraint on both sides.

In August 2011 Kim Jong Il paid a visit to Russia (his first since 2002) and held discussions with President Dmitrii Medvedev concerning North Korea's outstanding debt, the resumption of the six-party talks on North Korean nuclear facilities, and the possible construction of a pipeline supplying Russian gas to South Korea via North Korea. In September 2012 the Russian Government agreed to cancel 90% of the total of some US $11,000m. owed to it by North Korea, and to reinvest the remaining 10% as 'debt-for-aid' in the fields of energy, health and education. In April, meanwhile, Russia condemned the failed launch by North Korea of a long-range rocket, accusing North Korea of defying the UN Security Council. Russia likewise expressed 'regret' when North Korea launched another rocket, this time successfully, in December; following the testing of a North Korean nuclear device in February 2013 the Russian Government urged North Korea to 'cease its unlawful acts'. Russia gave its support to the respective UN Security Council resolutions that followed both events. During the marked increase in tension in March and April between North Korea on the one side and South Korea and the USA on the other, Russia urged all sides to prevent the situation from escalating.

North Korea has maintained close relations with a number of Middle Eastern countries, including Egypt, Libya, Syria and Iran, and with many African nations. In May 2004 it was reported that an IAEA investigation of uranium delivered to the USA by Libya in late 2003 had revealed that the material had been supplied to Libya by North Korea through an illicit nuclear technology procurement network operated by a Pakistani nuclear scientist. Further evidence concerning the transfer of nuclear material from North Korea to Libya emerged in early 2005. In January 2007 North Korea was reported to have agreed to share its data from the October 2006 nuclear test with scientists from Iran, but denied the allegations. In September 2007 North Korea similarly rejected claims that it was assisting Syria to develop a nuclear weapons programme. In March 2008 a visit by Kim Yong Nam and senior ministers to Namibia prompted speculation regarding North Korea's interest in the country's uranium resources. In September 2012 an agreement on scientific co-operation was concluded between North Korea and Iran, arousing suspicions that the co-operation was likely to include nuclear technology.

In January 2000 Italy became the first member of the Group of Seven (G7) Western industrialized nations (and the sixth member of the EU) to establish diplomatic relations with North

Korea. Diplomatic relations were established with the United Kingdom in December 2000. During 2001 North Korea further expanded its range of diplomatic partners, opening relations with the EU and several European countries, including Germany and Spain, and also with Canada, Brazil and Turkey. The EU and individual member states strongly condemned North Korea's tests of nuclear devices in 2006, 2009 and 2012, urging the North Korean Government to resume negotiations on nuclear non-proliferation.

CONSTITUTION AND GOVERNMENT

Under the Constitution of 1972, the highest organ of state power is the unicameral Supreme People's Assembly (SPA), with 687 members, elected (unopposed) for five years by universal adult suffrage. The SPA elects, for its duration, the Chairman of the National Defence Commission, who, since the effective abolition of the presidency in September 1998, holds the most senior accessible office of state. This position was designated as that of 'supreme leader' in 2009. The SPA elects the Premier and, on the latter's recommendation, appoints other Ministers to form the Cabinet. The President of the SPA Presidium, the members of which are elected by the SPA, represents the state in its relations with foreign countries.

Political power is held by the communist Korean Workers' Party (KWP), which is the most influential party in the Democratic Front for the Reunification of the Fatherland (comprising the KWP and two minor parties). The Front presents an approved list of candidates for elections to representative bodies. The KWP's highest authority is the Party Congress, which elects a Central Committee to supervise party work. The Committee elects a Political Bureau (Politburo) to direct policy. The Presidium of the Politburo is the KWP's most powerful policy-making body.

North Korea comprises nine provinces and two cities, each with an elected Local People's Assembly.

REGIONAL AND INTERNATIONAL CO-OPERATION

North Korea formally applied to join the Association of Southeast Asian Nations (ASEAN, see p. 218) in 2000, and the country was subsequently admitted to the ASEAN Regional Forum (ARF). The country has guest status in the Asia-Pacific Economic Co-operation (APEC, see p. 208) forum. North Korea is a member of the UN's Economic and Social Commission for Asia and the Pacific (ESCAP, see p. 31), having been admitted to the UN in 1991.

ECONOMIC AFFAIRS

In 2011, according to the Bank of Korea (the South Korean central bank), the gross national income (GNI) of North Korea was estimated to total US $28,100m., equivalent to about $1,154 per head. According to UN estimates (based on a different method of calculation), North Korea's GNI per head increased from $499 in 2010 to $506 in 2011. During 2002–11, according to estimates by the World Bank, the population increased by an annual average of 0.6%. In 2002–11, according to UN estimates, GDP grew at an average rate of 0.8%. According to estimates published by the South Korean central bank, North Korea's GDP contracted by 0.5% in 2010, but increased by 0.8% in 2011.

Agriculture (including hunting, forestry and fishing) contributed 21.1% of GDP in 2011, according to UN estimates. According to FAO, some 17.1% of the active labour force were estimated to be employed in the agricultural sector in mid-2013. The principal crops are rice, maize and potatoes. North Korea is not self-sufficient in food, and imports substantial amounts of wheat, rice and maize annually. Intermittent food shortages became a serious problem from the mid-1990s, and considerable support has been provided by the World Food Programme (WFP—see Contemporary Political History). According to FAO estimates, cereal production increased from 4.0m. metric tons in 2007 to 4.7m. tons in 2011. Potato production was 1.8m. tons in 2011, compared with 2.0m. metric tons in 2006, according to estimates. The raising of livestock (principally cattle and pigs), forestry and fishing are important. An outbreak of foot-and-mouth disease was confirmed in February 2011. During 2002–11, according to UN estimates, agricultural GDP increased by an average of 0.5% per year; the sector's GDP was estimated to have decreased by 2.1% in 2010, before increasing by 1.1% in 2011.

In 2011, according to UN estimates, industry (including mining, manufacturing, construction and utilities) contributed 47.1% of GDP, and 34.3% of the employed population were engaged in the sector at the time of the 2008 census, according to official figures. During 2002–11, according to estimates from the UN, industrial GDP was estimated to have increased by an annual average of 1.0%. Industrial GDP decreased by 0.1% in 2011.

Mining contributed 14.6% of GDP in 2011, according to South Korean estimates. At the time of the 2008 census 5.9% of the employed population were engaged in the sector, according to official estimates. North Korea possesses considerable mineral wealth, with large deposits of coal, iron, lead, copper, zinc, tin, silver and gold. Output of hard coal totalled an estimated 41.0m. metric tons in 2011. There are unexploited offshore deposits of petroleum and natural gas. South Korean sources estimated that the output of the mining sector decreased by 0.2% in 2010, before increasing by 0.9% in 2011.

In 2011, according to UN estimates, the manufacturing sector contributed 22.2% of GDP, and 23.7% of the employed population were engaged in the sector at the time of the 2008 census, according to official figures. In the 1990s industrial development concentrated on heavy industry (metallurgy—notably steel production, machine-building, cement and chemicals). The textiles industry has provided significant exports. According to UN estimates, the GDP of the manufacturing sector increased at an average annual rate of 1.0% in 2002–11. Manufacturing GDP declined by 0.3% in 2010, but expanded by 0.5% in 2011.

Construction, according to UN estimates, contributed 8.1% of GDP in 2011. The sector engaged 3.0% of the employed population at the time of the 2008 census, according to official figures. The GDP of the construction sector was estimated to have decreased at an average annual rate of 0.5% in 2002–11. The sector's GDP increased by 0.3% in 2010, before decreasing by 1.2% in 2011.

In 2009 it was estimated that 59.1% of North Korea's energy supply was derived from hydroelectricity, followed in importance by coal (38.1%) and petroleum (2.8%). A 30-MW nuclear reactor was believed to have been inaugurated in 1987. From the 1990s North Korea experienced increasing power shortages, as generation declined and transmission infrastructure deteriorated. Furthermore, the production of hydroelectric power was adversely affected by intermittent drought. In 2009 North Korea's electricity production totalled 21,096m. kWh, compared with 23,206m. kWh in 2008. Fuel oil shipments to North Korea have been intermittently suspended owing to international concerns with regard to the country's nuclear programme.

According to UN estimates, the services sector contributed 31.7% of GDP in 2011, and the sector engaged 29.6% of the employed population at the time of the 2008 census, according to official figures. The GDP of the services sector was estimated to have increased at an average annual rate of 0.7% in 2002–11; services GDP increased by 0.2% in 2010, before decreasing by 0.9% in 2011.

According to South Korean sources, in 2008 total exports, excluding trade with South Korea, reached US $113m. and imports totalled $269m. North Korea's principal source of imports in 2009 (again excluding South Korea) was the People's Republic of China, which accounted for 80.4% of total imports. China was North Korea's principal market for exports in 2009, purchasing 74.5% of goods. Other major trading partners in that year were Germany, Russia, India and Singapore. China was a source of crude petroleum (imports of this commodity were sourced exclusively from China in 2009, when the cost of petroleum imports greatly decreased, by 44.2% to reach $330.0m.), electrical equipment and coal, while Japan was a destination for industrial and agricultural goods. The principal exports in 2008 were mineral products (an increase of 33.5% in the value of exports compared with the previous year, and, at $465.4m., accounting for 41.3% of the total value of exports), non-ferrous minerals (16.8%), textiles (10.6%), chemical plastics (7.6%), and machinery and electrical equipment. The principal imports in 2008 were mineral products (25.9% of the value of total imports), textile fibres (11.9%), machinery and electrical equipment (11.5%), and processed food items (8.8%). In 2009, according to data from the Bank of Korea, in comparison with the previous year inter-Korean trade decreased by 7.8%, to total $1,680m.

The Government planned an increase in overall budgetary spending in 2010 of 8.3%, while revenue was projected to rise by 6.3%. The 2011 budget, endorsed in April of that year, provided for expenditure of 567,000m. won. By 2008, according to one source, North Korea's total external debt was estimated to have reached US $18,000m. Following the introduction of market-orientated reforms in 2002, the inflation rate was believed to have reached 4,000% in that year. Between mid-2007 and mid-2008 the prices of staple foods reportedly increased by 100% in Pyongyang. The revaluation of the currency in December 2009 had major repercussions, and prices of basic commodities were reported to have risen substantially in 2010.

North Korea is one of the poorest countries in Asia, in contrast with South Korea, where income per head was estimated to be about 19 times that of the North in 2011. North Korea's centrally planned economy has not overcome the difficulties caused by high external debt, lack of domestic and foreign investment, international economic sanctions and disproportionate military spending, while agricultural production has been affected by recurrent adverse weather conditions, causing both drought and flooding. Since the 1990s the country has intermittently depended on foreign aid (especially from China) to avert famine. In 2002 limited reforms allowed private agricultural production and marketing, and many citizens are believed to be dependent on 'unofficial' economic activities. The establishment of a special industrial zone at Kaesong from 2002 allowed South Korean companies based there to employ North Korean workers, providing an important source of revenue for North Korea. In a report released in February 2009, the US Department of State reiterated its belief that activities such as the forging of US currency and the counterfeiting of brand cigarettes remained significant sources of revenue for the North Korean Government, along with trade in illicit drugs and the sale of weapons. A revaluation of the currency in December 2009 apparently aimed to reduce inflation and the hoarding of currency by unofficial traders, but eliminated many citizens' savings and resulted in food shortages: the price of rice was subsequently reported to have increased 40-fold within a year. North Korea's GDP reportedly contracted in 2009 and 2010, with adverse weather affecting agricultural production, while manufacturing was constrained by energy shortages, outdated equipment and a lack of raw materials. In January 2011 the State Strategy Plan for Economic Development, a new 10-year plan encompassing the period to 2020, was revealed: it included projects in 12 areas, including agricultural development; petroleum and energy development; and the improvement of the transport network. The budget for 2011, approved by the legislature in April, envisaged total expenditure of 567,000m. won; as was customary, few details were released, but according to the South Korean Ministry of Unification 15.8% was allocated to defence (the same percentage as in the previous year, although this was regarded by many observers as a substantial understatement), while expenditure on construction (of housing in Pyongyang and a major power plant) was to increase by some 15% compared with the previous year. In June 2011 North Korea and Chinese Governments announced the expansion of a (previously unsuccessful) special economic zone at Rason (on the east coast of North Korea near the border with China) and the creation of a similar zone on the island of Hwanggumpyong, near the North Korean border city of Sinuiju, the principal centre for trade between the two countries (the city had been the site of another previously unsuccessful venture in 2002). In October 2012 a joint conference identified specific projects in the special economic zones for investment by Chinese enterprises. The South Korean Bank of Korea (BOK) estimated that the North Korean economy had grown by 0.8% (year-on-year) in 2011 after two years of contraction: relatively favourable weather was reported to have allowed an increase of more than 5% in agricultural production, but manufacturing was believed to have declined by some 3%, according to the BOK. During the second half of 2012 there were reports (not officially confirmed) of significant policy changes, namely that the North Korean authorities were to allow manufacturers to set their own prices, and that farmers were to be allowed to keep 30% of their output to consume or sell, thus having an incentive to produce more food. In April 2013, amid rising tensions between North and South Korea, operations were suspended at the Kaesong industrial complex, one of North Korea's principal sources of foreign exchange.

PUBLIC HOLIDAYS

The *Juche* calendar was introduced in North Korea in 1997; 1912, the year of the late Kim Il Sung's birth, was designated the first year of the new calendar.

2014: 1 January (New Year), 31 January–2 February (Seollal), 16–17 February (Day of the Shining Star, Kim Jong Il's Birthday), 5 April (Chungmyung Day), 15–16 April (Day of the Sun, Kim Il Sung's Birthday), 1 May (May Day), 27 July (Fatherland Liberation War Day), 15 August (Anniversary of Liberation), 8 September (Chuseok), 9 September (Independence Day), 10 October (Anniversary of the foundation of the Korean Workers' Party), 27 December (Anniversary of the Constitution).

Statistical Survey

Area and Population

AREA, POPULATION AND DENSITY*

Area (sq km)	122,762†
Population (census results)	
31 December 1993	21,213,378
1 October 2008	
Males	11,721,838
Females	12,330,393
Total	24,052,231
Population (UN estimates at mid-year)‡	
2011	24,451,282
2012	24,553,670
2013	24,654,355
Density (per sq km) at mid-2013	200.8

* Excluding the demilitarized zone between North and South Korea, with an area of 1,262 sq km (487 sq miles).
† 47,399 sq miles.
‡ Source: UN, *World Population Prospects: The 2010 Revision*.

POPULATION BY AGE AND SEX
(UN estimates at mid-2013)

	Males	Females	Total
0–14	2,725,138	2,602,122	5,327,260
15–64	8,502,399	8,356,476	16,858,875
65 and over	878,201	1,590,019	2,468,220
Total	**12,105,738**	**12,548,617**	**24,654,355**

Source: UN, *World Population Prospects: The 2010 Revision*.

ADMINISTRATIVE DIVISIONS
(population at 2008 census)

	Area (sq km)	Population ('000)	Density (per sq km)
Chagang Province	16,968	1,299,830	76.6
Hamgyong North Province* . .	17,570	2,327,362	132.5
Hamgyong South Province . .	18,970	3,066,013	161.6
Hwanghae North Province . .	9,262	2,113,672	228.2
Hwanghae South Province . .	8,002	2,310,485	288.7
Kangwon Province	11,152	1,477,582	132.5
Pyongan North Province . .	12,191	2,728,662	223.8
Pyongan South Province . .	12,330	4,051,696	328.6
Yanggang (Ryanggang) Province .	14,317	719,269	50.2
Pyongyang City	2,000	3,255,288	1,627.6
Total	122,762	24,052,231†	195.9

* Includes Najin-Sonbong, which enjoys the administrative status of Special City.

† Total includes population living in military camps.

Source: partly Thomas Brinkhoff, *City Population* (www.citypopulation.de).

PRINCIPAL TOWNS
(population at 2008 census)*

Pyongyang (capital).	2,581,076	Sariwon . . .	271,434
Hamhung . . .	703,610	Kaechon . . .	262,389
Chongjin . . .	614,892	Kanggye . . .	251,971
Sinuiju . . .	334,031	Sunchon . . .	250,738
Wonsan . . .	328,467	Haeju . . .	241,599
Nampo . . .	310,531	Tanchon . . .	240,873

* Population for urban areas of cities, as enumerated at census.

Mid-2011 (incl. suburbs, UN estimate): Pyongyang 2,842,570 (Source: UN, *World Urbanization Prospects: The 2011 Revision*).

BIRTHS AND DEATHS
(annual averages, UN estimates)

	1995–2000	2000–05	2005–10
Birth rate (per 1,000)	19.8	16.3	14.6
Death rate (per 1,000)	9.8	9.0	9.6

Source: UN, *World Population Prospects: The 2010 Revision*.

2008 census (12 months ending 1 October 2008): Live births 345,630; deaths 216,616.

Life expectancy (years at birth): 68.7 (males 65.5; females 72.0) in 2011 (Source: World Bank, World development Indicators database).

EMPLOYMENT
(persons aged 16 years and over at 2008 census)

	Males	Females	Total
Agriculture, forestry and fishing .	2,082,297	2,304,598	4,386,895
Mining and quarrying	458,484	259,711	718,195
Manufacturing	1,507,014	1,375,968	2,882,982
Electricity, gas and water . .	161,098	55,184	216,282
Construction	285,941	81,709	367,650
Wholesale and retail trade; repair of motor vehicles	173,962	383,393	557,355
Transport, storage and communications	337,983	144,175	482,158
Hotels and restaurants . . .	26,591	114,614	141,205
Finance and insurance activities .	12,374	13,854	26,228
Professional, scientific and technical activities	80,574	37,558	118,132
Administrative and support service activities	287,951	163,385	451,336
Public administration and defence; compulsory social security . .	439,586	284,592	724,178
Education	263,635	284,497	548,132
Health and social welfare . . .	134,306	196,396	330,702
Arts, entertainment and recreation	72,290	58,292	130,582
Other services	35,852	66,856	102,708
Total employed	6,359,938	5,824,782	12,184,720

Note: Of the remaining total population aged 16 years and over, 940,886 were studying, 155,093 were disabled, 3,147,553 were retired, 921,191 were engaged in housework and 17,326 were described as 'other'.

Mid-2013 (estimates in '000): Agriculture, etc. 2,949; Total labour force 13,741 (Source: FAO).

Health and Welfare

KEY INDICATORS

Total fertility rate (children per woman, 2010)	2.0
Under-5 mortality rate (per 1,000 live births, 2010) . . .	33
HIV/AIDS (% of persons aged 15–49, 1994)	<0.01
Physicians (per 1,000 head, 2003)	3.3
Health expenditure (2006): US $ per head (PPP)	1
Health expenditure (2006): % of GDP	3.5
Health expenditure (2006): public (% of total)	85.6
Access to water (% of persons, 2010)	98
Access to sanitation (% of persons, 2010)	80
Total carbon dioxide emissions ('000 metric tons, 2008) . .	78,371.1
Carbon dioxide emissions per head (metric tons, 2008) . .	3.2

For sources and definitions, see explanatory note on p. vi.

Agriculture

PRINCIPAL CROPS
('000 metric tons)

	2009	2010	2011
Wheat*	169	160	127
Rice, paddy	2,336	2,426	2,479
Barley*	63	80	55
Maize	1,705	1,683	1,857
Rye†	69	70	73
Oats†	17	18	18
Millet†	62	63	66
Sorghum†	28	29	30
Potatoes	1,560	1,708	1,756
Sweet potatoes	390	427	439
Beans, dry†	335	304	355
Soybeans (Soya beans)* . .	350	350	350
Cabbages and other brassicas†	722	725	772
Tomatoes†	69	71	74
Pumpkins, squash and gourds† .	79	76	76
Cucumbers and gherkins† . .	72	74	76
Aubergines (Eggplants)† . .	49	51	53
Chillies and peppers, green† . .	53	48	43
Onions and shallots, green† . .	103	106	110
Onions, dry†	85	83	89
Garlic†	101	104	108
Apples†	720	752	807
Pears†	137	143	150
Peaches and nectarines† . .	147	118	139
Watermelons†	115	118	123
Cantaloupes and other melons† .	92	95	98
Tobacco, unmanufactured† . .	73	71	74

* Unofficial figures.
† FAO estimates.

Aggregate production ('000 metric tons, may include official, semi-official or estimated data): Total cereals 4,449 in 2009, 4,528 in 2010, 4,704 in 2011; Total roots and tubers 1,950 in 2009, 2,135 in 2010, 2,195 in 2011; Total vegetables (incl. melons) 3,999 in 2009, 3,847 in 2010, 4,006 in 2011; Total fruits (excl. melons) 1,530 in 2009, 1,562 in 2010, 1,705 in 2011.

Source: FAO.

LIVESTOCK
('000 head)

	2009	2010	2011*
Horses*	48	48	48
Cattle	576	577	580
Pigs	2,150	2,248	2,325
Sheep	165	166	167
Goats	3,570	3,556	3,600
Chickens	13,859	14,943	15,500
Ducks	5,900	5,936	6,000

* FAO estimates.

Source: FAO.

LIVESTOCK PRODUCTS
('000 metric tons, FAO estimates)

	2009	2010	2011
Cattle meat	21.8	21.9	22.0
Goat meat	14.6	14.9	15.0
Pig meat	110.0	110.0	115.0
Chicken meat	31.9	31.9	33.0
Cows' milk	95.2	95.4	95.4
Hen eggs	150.8	155.0	155.0

Source: FAO.

Forestry

ROUNDWOOD REMOVALS
('000 cubic metres, excl. bark, FAO estimates)

	2008	2009	2010
Sawlogs, veneer logs and logs for sleepers	1,000	1,000	1,000
Other industrial wood	500	500	500
Fuel wood	5,911	5,949	5,987
Total	7,411	7,449	7,487

2011: Production assumed to be unchanged from 2010 (FAO estimates).

Sawnwood production ('000 cubic metres, incl. railway sleepers): 280 (coniferous 185, broadleaved 95) per year in 1970–2011 (FAO estimates).

Source: FAO.

Fishing

('000 metric tons, live weight, FAO estimates)

	2007	2008	2009
Capture	205.0	205.0	205.0
Freshwater fishes	5.0	5.0	5.0
Alaska pollock	60.0	60.0	60.0
Other marine fishes	107.6	107.6	107.6
Marine crustaceans	16.0	16.0	16.0
Squids	9.5	9.5	9.5
Aquaculture	63.9	64.0	64.1
Molluscs	63.0	60.0	60.0
Total catch	268.9	269.0	269.1

2010: Figures assumed to be unchanged from 2009 (FAO estimates).

Note: Figures exclude aquatic plants (FAO estimates, '000 metric tons, aquaculture only): 444.3 in 2007–10.

Source: FAO.

Mining

('000 metric tons, unless otherwise indicated, estimates)

	2008	2009	2010
Hard coal	25,060	36,000	41,000
Iron ore: gross weight	5,316	5,300	5,300
Iron ore: metal content	1,488	1,500	1,500
Copper ore*	12	12	12
Lead ore*	13	13	13
Zinc ore*	70	70	70
Tungsten concentrates (metric tons)*	270	100	100
Silver (metric tons)*	20	20	20
Gold (kg)*	2,000	2,000	2,000

—continued	2008	2009	2010
Magnesite (crude)	150,000	150,000	150,000
Phosphate rock†	300	300	300
Fluorspar‡	13	13	13
Salt (unrefined)	500	500	500
Graphite (natural)	30	30	30
Talc, soapstone and pyrophyllite	50	50	50

* Figures refer to the metal content of ores and concentrates.
† Figures refer to gross weight.
‡ Metallurgical grade.

Note: No recent data were available for the production of molybdenum ore and asbestos.

2011: Production assumed to be unchanged from 2010.

Source: US Geological Survey.

Industry

SELECTED PRODUCTS
('000 metric tons unless otherwise indicated)

	2007	2008	2009
Motor spirit (petrol)	146	151	116
Kerosene	29	30	23
Gas-diesel (distillate fuel) oils	157	161	n.a.
Residual fuel oils	90	92	n.a.
Cement*	6,415	6,415	6,400
Pig-iron*	900	900	900
Crude steel*	1,230	1,279	1,300
Refined copper (primary and secondary metal)*	15	15	15
Refined lead (primary and secondary metal)*	9	9	9
Zinc (primary and secondary metal)	75	75	75
Electric energy (million kWh)	21,523	23,206	21,093

* US Geological Survey estimates.

Source: mostly UN Industrial Commodity Statistics Database.

2011 ('000 metric tons, estimates): Cement 6,400; Pig-iron 900; Crude steel 1,300; Refined copper (primary and secondary metal) 15; Refined lead (primary and secondary metal) 9; Refined zinc (primary and secondary metal) 75 (Source: US Geological Survey).

Finance

CURRENCY AND EXCHANGE RATES

Monetary Units
100 chon (jun) = 1 won.

Sterling, Dollar and Euro Equivalents (30 November 2012)
£1 sterling = 161.196 won;
US $1 = 100.390 won;
€1 = 130.366 won;
1,000 won = £6.20 = $9.96 = €7.67.

Note: In August 2002 it was reported that a currency reform had been introduced, whereby the exchange rate was adjusted from US $1 = 2.15 won to $1 = 150 won: a devaluation of 98.6%. In November 2009 reports of further currency reform emerged; a 'currency exchange' was believed to have been implemented in December, whereby denominations of the former currency were exchanged for new currency at a rate of 100 old won for 1 new won. In January 2010 it was reported that an exchange rate of US $1 = 96.9 won had been established by some financial institutions.

BUDGET
(million won, reported)

	2004	2005	2006
Revenue	337,546	n.a.	n.a.
Expenditure	348,807	419,700	388,950

2007 (million won, reported, estimate): Total expenditure 440,200 (Defence 69,200).

2008 (million won, reported): Total expenditure 451,500 (Defence 71,300).

2009 (million won, reported): Total expenditure 482,600 (Defence 76,300).

NATIONAL ACCOUNTS
(million won, UN estimates)

Expenditure on the Gross Domestic Product

	2009	2010	2011
Total domestic expenditure . .	1,761,724.5	2,004,429.3	2,035,362.8
Exports of goods and services . .	97,858.0	112,168.5	113,522.5
Less Imports of goods and services	186,696.3	212,008.9	215,459.0
GDP in purchasers' values	1,672,886.2	1,904,588.8	1,933,426.2
GDP in constant 2005 prices	1,799,957.3	1,791,457.7	1,789,684.9

Gross Domestic Product by Economic Activity

	2009	2010	2011
Agriculture, hunting, forestry and fishing	350,141.2	396,803.4	408,110.4
Mining, manufacturing and utilities	651,834.5	765,516.0	754,870.4
Manufacturing	370,004.2	417,366.4	429,098.9
Construction	134,037.6	152,679.9	156,679.0
Services	536,878.8	589,595.9	613,768.5
Sub-total	1,672,892.1	1,904,595.2	1,933,428.3
Indirect taxes (net)*	−5.9	−6.4	−2.1
GDP in purchasers' values .	1,672,886.2	1,904,588.8	1,933,426.2

* Figures obtained as a residual.

Source: UN National Accounts Main Aggregates Database.

External Trade

PRINCIPAL COMMODITIES
(US $ million)*

Imports	2000	2001	2002
Live animals and animal products	20.3	73.9	103.4
Vegetable products	159.0	221.0	118.4
Animal or vegetable fats and oils; prepared edible fats; animal or vegetable waxes . . . . Prepared foodstuffs; beverages, spirits and vinegar; tobacco and manufactured substitutes . .	89.1	89.9	72.3
Mineral products	171.2	231.1	235.9
Products of chemical or allied industries	108.4	123.4	122.1
Plastics, rubber and articles thereof	67.5	66.0	66.0
Textiles and textile articles .	171.9	203.9	158.5
Base metals and articles thereof	85.2	100.4	88.2
Machinery and mechanical appliances; electrical equipment; sound and television apparatus . .	205.1	243.8	234.7
Vehicles, aircraft, vessels and associated transport equipment	146.2	88.4	76.1
Total (incl. others) . . .	1,406.5	1,620.3	1,525.4

Exports	2000	2001	2002
Live animals and animal products	97.9	158.4	261.1
Vegetable products	30.3	42.0	27.5
Mineral products	43.2	50.5	69.8
Products of chemical or allied industries . . . . . . Plastics, rubber and articles thereof	44.9	44.6	42.4
Wood, cork and articles thereof; wood charcoal; manufactures of straw, esparto, etc. . .	10.9	5.6	10.2
Textiles and textile articles .	140.0	140.5	123.1

Exports—*continued*	2000	2001	2002
Natural or cultured pearls, precious or semi-precious stones, precious metals and articles thereof; imitation jewellery; coin	9.8	14.1	14.6
Base metals and articles thereof	43.9	60.2	57.4
Machinery and mechanical appliances; electrical equipment, sound and television apparatus . . .	105.2	97.9	85.6
Total (incl. others)	565.8	650.2	735.0

* Excluding trade with the Republic of Korea (US $ million): *Imports:* 272.8 in 2000; 226.8 in 2001; 370.2 in 2002. *Exports:* 152.4 in 2000; 176.2 in 2001; 271.6 in 2002.

Source: Korea Trade-Investment Promotion Agency (KOTRA), Republic of Korea.

2006 (US $ million, unofficial estimates): *Excluding Republic of Korea:* Total imports 205; Total exports 95. *Republic of Korea only:* Total imports 830.2; Total exports 519.5 (Source: Bank of Korea, Republic of Korea).

2007 (US $ million, unofficial estimates): *Excluding Republic of Korea:* Total imports 202; Total exports 92. *Republic of Korea only:* Total imports 1,032.6; Total exports 765.3 (Source: Bank of Korea, Republic of Korea).

2008 (US $ million, unofficial estimates): *Excluding Republic of Korea:* Total imports 269; Total exports 113. *Republic of Korea only:* Total imports 888.1; Total exports 932.3 (Source: Bank of Korea, Republic of Korea).

PRINCIPAL TRADING PARTNERS
(US $ million)*

Imports	2001	2002	2003
China, People's Republic . . .	570.7	467.3	627.6
Germany	82.1	140.4	n.a.
Hong Kong	42.6	29.2	n.a.
India	154.8	186.6	157.9
Japan	249.1	135.1	91.5
Netherlands	9.1	27.6	n.a.
Russia	63.8	77.0	115.6
Singapore	112.3	83.0	n.a.
Spain	31.6	n.a.	n.a.
Thailand	106.0	172.0	203.6
United Kingdom	40.7	n.a.	n.a.
Total (incl. others)	1,620.3	1,525.4	1,614.4

Exports	2001	2002	2003
Bangladesh	38.0	32.3	n.a.
China, People's Republic . . .	166.8	270.9	395.3
Germany	22.8	27.8	n.a.
Hong Kong	38.0	21.9	n.a.
India	3.1	4.8	1.6
Japan	225.6	234.4	173.8
Netherlands	10.4	6.4	n.a.
Russia	4.5	3.6	2.8
Spain	12.6	n.a.	n.a.
Thailand	24.9	44.6	50.7
Total (incl. others)	650.2	735.0	777.0

* Excluding trade with the Republic of Korea (US $ million): *Imports:* 226.8 in 2001; 370.2 in 2002; 435.0 in 2003. *Exports:* 176.2 in 2001; 271.6 in 2002; 289.3 in 2003.

Source: Korea Trade-Investment Promotion Agency (KOTRA).

2004 (US $ million): *Imports:* China, People's Republic 800; Japan 89; Korea, Republic 439; Total (incl. others) 2,280. *Exports:* China, People's Republic 586; Japan 163; Korea, Republic 258; Total (incl. others) 1,280 (Source: Ministry of Unification, Republic of Korea).

Trade with Republic of Korea (US $ million, unofficial estimates): *Total imports:* 830.2 in 2006; 1,032.6 in 2007; 888.1 in 2008. *Total exports:* 519.5 in 2006; 765.3 in 2007; 932.3 in 2008 (Source: Bank of Korea, Republic of Korea).

Transport

SHIPPING

Flag Registered Fleet
(at 31 December)

	2010	2011	2012
Number of vessels	315	310	316
Total displacement ('000 grt) . .	991.1	908.7	879.7

Source: Lloyd's List Intelligence (www.lloydslistintelligence.com).

International Sea-borne Freight Traffic
(estimates, '000 metric tons)

	1988	1989	1990
Goods loaded	630	640	635
Goods unloaded	5,386	5,500	5,520

Source: UN, *Monthly Bulletin of Statistics*.

CIVIL AVIATION
(traffic on scheduled services)

	2007	2008	2009
Kilometres flown (million) . .	1	1	1
Passengers carried ('000) . .	111	109	101
Passenger-km (million) . . .	45	44	41
Total ton-km (million)	7	7	6

Source: UN, *Statistical Yearbook*.

Passengers carried ('000): 83.8 in 2010 (Source: World Bank, World Development Indicators database).

Tourism

	1996	1997	1998
Tourist arrivals ('000)	127	128	130

Source: World Tourism Organization.

Communications Media

	2009	2010	2011
Telephones ('000 main lines in use)	1,180	1,180	1,180
Mobile cellular telephones ('000 subscribers)	69.3	431.9	1,000.0

Source: International Telecommunication Union.

Education

(2000)

	Institutions	Students
Kindergartens	14,167	748,416
Primary	4,886	1,609,865
Senior middle schools	4,772	2,181,524

Source: mainly Government of the Democratic People's Republic of Korea, *UNESCO Education for All Assessment Report 2000*.

Universities and Colleges: The *UNESCO Education for All Assessment Report 2000* identified more than 300 universities and colleges with 1.89m. students and academics.

Teachers (1987/88, UNESCO estimates): Pre-primary 35,000, Primary 59,000, Secondary 111,000, Universities and colleges 23,000, Other tertiary 4,000 (Source: UNESCO, *Statistical Yearbook*).

Directory

The Government

HEAD OF STATE

Following the death of the General Secretary of the Korean Workers' Party and the Chairman of the National Defence Commission, Kim Jong Il, who had ruled the country since the death of his father Kim Il Sung in 1994, his third son, Kim Jong Un, was declared the Supreme Leader at the memorial service on 29 December 2011 that followed a period of official mourning, by the Titular Head of State, Kim Yong Nam. The following day Kim Jong Un was formally confirmed as Supreme Commander of the Korean People's Army and was referred to by the state media as the Great Leader. He was appointed First Chairman of the National Defence Commission on 14 April 2012, while Kim Jong Il was named Eternal Chairman.

President: President KIM IL SUNG died on 8 July 1994 and was declared Eternal President in September 1998.

First Chairman of the National Defence Commission: MARSHAL KIM JONG UN.

Titular Head of State: KIM YONG NAM.

CABINET
(May 2013)

The Government is formed by the Korean Workers' Party (KWP).

Premier: PAK PONG JU.

Vice-Premiers: KANG NUNG SU, KIM RAK HUI, JON HA CHOL, KANG SOK JU.

Vice-Premier and Chairman of the State Planning Commission: RO TU CHOL.

Vice-Premier and Minister of Capital City Construction: KIM IN SIK.

Vice-Premier and Minister of Machine-Building Industries: JO PYONG JU.

Vice-Premier and Minister of Chemical Industry: RI MU YONG.

Vice-Premier and Minister of Agriculture: RI CHOL MAN.

Minister of Foreign Affairs: PAK UI CHUN.

Minister of the People's Armed Forces: Gen. JANG JONG NAM.

Minister of State Security: Gen. KIM WON HONG.

Minister of People's Security: Col Gen. CHOE PU IL.

Minister of Electric Power Industry: HO TAEK.

Minister of the Electronics Industry: KIM JAE SONG.

Minister of the Coal Industry: KIM HYONG SIK.

Minister of the Mining Industry: KANG MIN CHOL.

Minister of the Oil Industry: PAE HAK YI.

Minister of the Metal Industry: KIM THAE BONG.

Minister of National Resource Development: RI CHUN SAM.

Minister of Construction and Building Materials Industries: TONG JONG HO.

Minister of Railways: JON KIL SU.

Minister of Land and Marine Transport: RA TONG HUI.

Minister of Light Industry: AN JONG SU.

Minister of Foreign Trade: RI RYONG NAM.

Minister of Forestry: KIM KWANG YONG.

Minister of Fisheries: RI HYUK.

Minister of Urban Management: KANG YONG SU.

Minister of Land and Environmental Protection: KIM KYUNG JUN.

Minister of Land Development and Construction Affairs: KIM SOK JUN.

Minister of Commerce: KIM PONG CHOL.

Minister of Food Procurement and Administration: MUN UNG JO.

Minister of Education: (vacant).

Minister of Higher Education: SONG JA RIP.

Minister of Post and Telecommunications: RYU YONG SOP.

Minister of Culture: HONG KWANG-SUN.

Minister of Labour: JONG YONG SU.

Minister of Public Health: (vacant).

Minister of State Inspection: KIM UI SUN.

Minister of Finance: CHOE KWANG JIN.

Minister of the Foodstuff and Daily Necessities Industry: JO YONG CHOL.

Minister of Physical Culture and Sports: RI JONG MU.

President of the National Academy of Sciences: PYON YONG RIP.

President of the Central Bank: PAEK RYONG CHON.

Director of the Central Statistical Board: KIM CHANG SU.

Director of the Secretariat of the Cabinet: KIM YONG HO.

MINISTRIES
All Ministries and Commissions are in Pyongyang.

Legislature

CHOE KO IN MIN HOE UI
(Supreme People's Assembly)

The 687 members of the 12th Supreme People's Assembly (SPA) were elected unopposed for a five-year term on 8 March 2009. The SPA's permanent body is the Presidium.

Chairman: CHOE TAE BOK.

President of the Presidium: KIM YONG NAM.

Vice-Presidents of the Presidium: YANG HYONG SOP, KIM YONG DAE.

Political Organizations

Democratic Front for the Reunification of the Fatherland: Pyongyang; f. 1946; vanguard org. comprising political parties and mass working people's orgs seeking the unification of North and South Korea; Dir KIM YANG GON.

The component parties are:

Chondoist Chongu Party: Pyongyang; tel. (2) 334241; f. 1946; follows the guiding principle of *Innaechon* (the realization of 'heaven on earth'); satellite party of the KWP; Chair. RYU MI YONG.

Korean Social Democratic Party (KSDP) (Joson Sahoeminju-dang): Pyongyang; tel. (2) 5591323; fax (2) 3814410; f. 1945; advocates national independence and a democratic socialist society; satellite party of the KWP; Chair. KIM YONG DAE.

Korean Workers' Party (KWP): Pyongyang; internet www.rodong .rep.kp; f. 1945; merged with South Korean Workers' Party in 1949; follows the guiding principle of *Juche*, based on the concept that man is the master and arbiter of all things; most significant political entity in the DPRK; Central Cttee of 124 full mems and 105 alternate mems; 3m. mems; First Sec. Marshal KIM JONG UN.

SEVENTH CENTRAL COMMITTEE OF THE KWP

Eternal General Secretary: Generalissimo KIM JONG IL.

POLITICAL BUREAU (POLITBURO) OF THE KWP

Presidium: Marshal KIM JONG UN, KIM YONG NAM, JANG SONG TAEK, PAK PONG JU, Gen. CHOE RYONG HAE.

Full Members: Vice-Marshal KIM YONG CHUN, KIM KUK THAE, KIM KI NAM, CHOE THAE BOK, YANG HYONG SOP, KANG SOK JU, Vice-Marshal RI YONG MU, KIM KYONG HUI, Vice-Marshal KIM JONG GAK, PAK TO CHUN, Vice-Marshal HYON CHOL HAE, Gen. RI MYONG SU, Gen. KIM WON HONG.

Alternate Members: KIM YANG GON, KIM YONG IL, JU KYU CHANG, Gen. HYON YONG CHOL, KIM KYOK SIK, CHOE PU IL, THAE JONG SU, KIM PYONG HAE, Col Gen. KIM CHANG SOP, MUN KYONG DOK, KWAK POM GI, Gen. O KUK RYOL, RO TU CHOL, Col Gen. RI PYONG SAM, JO YON JUN.

Secretariat: Marshal KIM JONG UN, KIM KI NAM, CHOE THAE BOK, CHOE RYONG HAE, MUN KYONG DOK, PAK TO CHUN, KIM YONG IL, KIM YANG GOK, TAE JONG SU, KIM PYONG HAE, KIM KYONG HUI, KWAK POM GI.

The component mass working people's organizations (see under Trade Unions) are:

General Federation of Trade Unions of Korea (GFTUK).

Kim Il Sung Socialist Youth League.

Korean Democratic Women's Union (KDWU).

Union of Agricultural Working People of Korea.

Diplomatic Representation

EMBASSIES IN THE DEMOCRATIC PEOPLE'S REPUBLIC OF KOREA

Brazil: 3 Munsudong, Taedongkang District, Pyongyang; tel. (2) 3817955; fax (2) 3817699; Ambassador ARNALDO CARRILHO.

Bulgaria: Munsudong, Taedongkang District, Pyongyang; tel. (2) 3827343; fax (2) 3817342; e-mail embassy.pyongyang@mfa.bg; internet www.mfa.bg/embassies/nordkorea; Chargé d'affaires a.i. SERGEY MICHEV.

Cambodia: Munsudong, Taedongkang District, Pyongyang; tel. (2) 3817283; fax (2) 3817625; e-mail recpyongyang@gmail.com; Ambassador CHHORN HAY.

China, People's Republic: Kinmauldong, Moranbong District, Pyongyang; tel. (2) 3813116; fax (2) 3813425; e-mail chinaemb_kp@mfa.gov.cn; internet kp.china-embassy.org; Ambassador LIU HONGCAI.

Cuba: Munsudong, Taedongkang District, POB 5, Pyongyang; tel. (2) 3817370; fax (2) 3817703; e-mail embajada@rpdc.cubaminrex.cu; Ambassador GERMÁN HERMÍN FERRAS ALVAREZ.

Czech Republic: Taedongkang Guyok 38, Taehakgori, Puksudong, Pyongyang; tel. (2) 3817021; fax (2) 3817022; e-mail pyongyang@ embassy.mzv.cz; internet www.mzv.cz/pyongyang; Ambassador DUŠAN STRAUCH.

Egypt: 39 Munsudong, Taedongkang District, Pyongyang; tel. (2) 3817414; fax (2) 3817410; e-mail embassy.pyongyang@mfa.gov.eg; internet www.mfa.gov.eg/english/embassies/ egyptian_embassy_north_korea; Ambassador ISMAIL ABDEL RAHMAN GHONEIM HUSSEIN.

Ethiopia: Munsudong, Taedongkang District, POB 55, Pyongyang; tel. (2) 3827554; fax (2) 3827550; Chargé d'affaires a.i. FEKADE S. G. MESKEL.

Germany: Munsudong, Pyongyang; tel. (2) 3817385; fax (2) 3817397; e-mail info@pjoengjang.diplo.de; Ambassador GERHARD THIEDEMANN.

India: 6 Taehak St, Munsudong, Taedongkang District, Pyongyang; tel. (2) 3817274; fax (2) 3817619; e-mail amb.pyongyang@mea.gov.in; Ambassador AJAY K. SHARMA.

Indonesia: 5 Foreigners' Bldg, Munsudong, Taedongkang District, Pyongyang; tel. (2) 3827439; fax (2) 3817620; e-mail kompyg2@ public2.bta.net.cn; Ambassador NASRI GUSTAMAN.

Iran: Munhungdong, Monsu St, Taedongkang District, Pyongyang; tel. (2) 3817214; fax (2) 3817612; e-mail embpyong@mfa.gov.ir; Ambassador MANSOUR CHAVOSHI.

Laos: Munhungdong, Taedongkang District, Pyongyang; tel. (2) 3827363; fax (2) 3817722; Ambassador KIETTISAK KEOBANHDITH.

Malaysia: Munhungdong, Taedongkang District, Pyongyang; tel. (2) 3817125; fax (2) 3817845; e-mail malpygyang@kln.gov.my; internet www.kln.gov.my/web/prk_pyongyang/home; Ambassador RAHIMI BIN HARUN.

Mongolia: 17 Taehak St, Munsudong, Taedongkang District, Pyongyang; tel. (2) 3827322; fax (2) 3817616; e-mail mon-emb@kcckp.net; Ambassador MANIBADRAKHYN GANBOLD.

Nigeria: Munsudong, Taedongkang District, POB 535, Pyongyang; tel. (2) 3827558; fax (2) 3817293; e-mail empngrdprk@yahoo.com; Ambassador ALEXANDER NWOFE.

Pakistan: 23, Blk 66, Munsudong, Taedongkang District, Pyongyang; tel. (2) 3827479; fax 3817622; e-mail parep.pyongyang@gmail .com; internet www.mofa.gov.pk/northkorea; Ambassador ARIF MAHMOOD (outgoing).

Poland: Munsudong, Taedongkang District, Pyongyang; tel. (2) 3817325; fax (2) 3817634; e-mail pjongjang.amb.sekretariat@msz .gov.pl; internet www.pjongjang.polemb.net; Ambassador EDWARD PIETRZYK.

Romania: Munhungdong, Taedongkang District, Pyongyang; tel. (2) 3827336; fax (2) 3817336; e-mail ambrophe@gmail.com; Chargé d'affaires a.i. ADRIAN BIANU.

Russia: Sinyangdong, Central District, Pyongyang; tel. (2) 3813101; fax (2) 3813427; e-mail embassy@rusembdprk.ru; internet www .dprk.mid.ru; Ambassador ALEKSANDR ANDREEVICH TIMONIN.

Sweden: Munsudong, Taedongkang District, Pyongyang; tel. (2) 3817485; fax (2) 3817663; e-mail ambassaden.pyongyang@foreign .ministry.se; Ambassador KARL-OLOF ANDERSSON.

Syria: Munsudong, Taedongkang District, Pyongyang; tel. (2) 3827473; fax (2) 3817635; Chargé d'affaires a.i. HAISSAM SAAD.

United Kingdom: Munsudong, Taedongkang District, Pyongyang; tel. (2) 3817980; fax (2) 3817985; e-mail postmaster.PYONX@fco.gov .uk; internet ukindprk.fco.gov.uk/en; Ambassador MICHAEL JOHN GIFFORD.

Viet Nam: 7 Munsudong, Taedongkang District, Pyongyang; tel. (2) 3817358; fax (2) 3817649; e-mail vnembassydprk@mofa.gov.vn; internet www.vietnamembassy-pyongyang.org; Ambassador LE QUANG BA.

Judicial System

Central Court (Supreme Court): Pyongyang; the highest judicial organ, which supervises the work of all courts (the Court of the Province—or city under central authority—and the People's Court, each constituted by judges and people's assessors; Pres. KIM PYONG RYUL.

Central Procurator's Office: Pyongyang; supervises the work of procurator's offices in provinces, counties and cities; procurators examine the ordinances and regulations of all ministries and the decisions and directives of local organs of state power to ensure that they conform to the Constitution, laws and decrees, as well as to the decisions and other measures of the Cabinet; procurators can bring suits against criminals in the name of the state, and participate in civil cases to protect the interests of the state and citizens; Procurator-General RI KIL SONG.

Religion

The religions that are officially reported to be practised in North Korea are Buddhism, Christianity and Chundo Kyo, a religion peculiar to Korea combining elements of Buddhism and Christianity. Religious co-ordinating bodies are believed to be under strict state control. The exact number of religious believers is unknown.

Korean Religious Believers Council: Pyongyang; f. 1989; brings together members of religious organizations in North Korea; Chair. JANG JAE ON.

BUDDHISM

In 2002 it was reported that there were an estimated 300 Buddhist temples in the DPRK; the number of believers was estimated at about 10,000 in 2003.

Korean Buddhists Federation: POB 77, Pyongyang; tel. (2) 43698; fax (2) 3812100; f. 1945; Chair. Cen. Cttee SHIM SANG JIN; Sec. JONG SO JONG.

CHRISTIANITY

In 2003 it was reported that there were approximately 13,000 Protestants and 3,000 Roman Catholics in the country, many of whom worshipped in house churches (of which there were said to be about 500 in 2002). The construction of North Korea's first Russian Orthodox church was completed in August 2006.

Korean Christians Federation: Pyongyang; f. 1946; Chair. Cen. Cttee KANG YONG SOP; Sec. O KYONG U.

The Roman Catholic Church

For ecclesiastical purposes, North and South Korea are nominally under a unified jurisdiction. North Korea contains two dioceses (Hamhung and Pyongyang), both suffragan to the archdiocese of Seoul (in South Korea), and the territorial abbacy of Tokwon (Tokugen), directly responsible to the Holy See.

Diocese of Hamhung: Catholic Mission, Hamhung; 134-1 Waekwan-dong Kwan Eub, Chil kok kun, Gyeongbuk 718-800, Republic of Korea; tel. (545) 970-2000; Bishop (vacant); Apostolic Administrator of Hamhung and of the Abbacy of Tokwon Fr PLACIDUS DONG-HO RI.

Diocese of Pyongyang: Catholic Mission, Pyongyang; Bishop Rt Rev. FRANCIS HONG YONG HO (absent); Apostolic Administrator Most Rev. NICHOLAS CHEONG JIN-SUK (Archbishop of Seoul, South Korea).

Korean Catholics Association: Changchung 1-dong, Songyo District, Pyongyang; tel. (2) 23492; f. 1988; Chair. Cen. Cttee JANG JAE ON; Vice-Chair. MUN CHANG HAK.

CHUNDO KYO

According to officials quoted in 2002, there were approximately 40,000 practitioners of Chundo Kyo in North Korea.

Korean Chundoists Association: Pyongyang; tel. (2) 334241; f. 1946; Chair. of Central Guidance Cttee RYU MI YONG.

The Press

PRINCIPAL NEWSPAPERS

Choldo Sinmun: Pyongyang; f. 1947; every two days.

Joson Inmingun (Korean People's Army Daily): Pyongyang; f. 1948; daily; Editor-in-Chief RI TAE BONG.

Kyowon Sinmun: Pyongyang; f. 1948; publ. by the Education Commission; weekly.

Minju Choson (Democratic Korea): Pyongyang; f. 1946; govt organ; 6 a week; Editor-in-Chief KIM JONG SUK; circ. 200,000.

Nongup Kunroja: Pyongyang; publ. of Cen. Cttee of the Union of Agricultural Working People of Korea.

Pyongyang Sinmun: Pyongyang; f. 1957; general news; 6 a week; Editor-in-Chief SONG RAK GYUN.

Rodong Chongnyon (Working Youth): Pyongyang; f. 1946; organ of the Cen. Cttee of the Kim Il Sung Socialist Youth League; 6 a week; Editor-in-Chief RI JONG GI.

Rodong Sinmun (Labour Daily): Pyongyang; internet www.kcna .co.jp/today-rodong/rodong.htm; f. 1946; organ of the Cen. Cttee of the Korean Workers' Party; daily; Editor-in-Chief YUN U CHOL; circ. 1.5m.

Rodongja Sinmun (Workers' Newspaper): Pyongyang; f. 1945; organ of the Gen. Fed. of Trade Unions of Korea; Editor-in-Chief RI SONG JU.

Saenal (New Day): Pyongyang; f. 1971; publ. by the Kim Il Sung Socialist Youth League; 2 a week; Deputy Editor CHOE SANG IN.

Sonyon Sinmun: Pyongyang; f. 1946; publ. by the Kim Il Sung Socialist Youth League; 2 a week; circ. 120,000.

Tongil Sinbo: Kangan 1-dong, Youth Ave, Songyo District, Pyongyang; f. 1972; non-affiliated; weekly; Chief Editor PAK JIN SIK; circ. 300,000.

PRINCIPAL PERIODICALS

Chollima: Pyongyang; popular magazine; monthly.

Choson (Korea): Pyongyang; social, economic, political and cultural; bi-monthly.

Choson Minju Juuiinmin Gonghwaguk Palmyonggongbo (Official Report of Inventions in the DPRK): Pyongyang; 6 a year.

Choson Munhak (Korean Literature): Pyongyang; organ of the Cen. Cttee of the Korean Writers' Union; monthly.

Choson Yesul (Korean Arts): Pyongyang; organ of the Cen. Cttee of the Gen. Fed. of Unions of Literature and Arts of Korea; monthly.

Economics: POB 73, Pyongyang; fax (2) 3814410; quarterly.

History: POB 73, Pyongyang; fax (2) 3814410; quarterly.

Hwahakgwa Hwahakgoneop: Pyongyang; organ of the Hamhung br. of the Korean Acad. of Sciences; chemistry and chemical engineering; 6 a year.

Jokook Tongil: Kangan 1-dong, Youth Ave, Songyo District, Pyongyang; organ of the Cttee for the Peaceful Unification of Korea; f. 1961; monthly; Chief Editor LI MYONG GYU; circ. 70,000.

Korean Medicine: POB 73, Pyongyang; fax (2) 3814410; quarterly.

Kunroja (Workers): 1 Munshindong, Tongdaewon, Pyongyang; f. 1946; organ of the Cen. Cttee of the Korean Workers' Party; monthly; Editor-in-Chief RYANG KYONG BOK; circ. 300,000.

Kwahakwon Tongbo (Bulletins of the Academy of Science): POB 73, Pyongyang; fax (2) 3814410; organ of the Standing Cttee of the Korean Acad. of Sciences; 6 a year.

Mulri (Physics): POB 73, Pyongyang; fax (2) 3814410; quarterly.

Munhwao Haksup (Study of Korean Language): POB 73, Pyongyang; fax (2) 3814410; publ. by the Publishing House of the Acad. of Social Sciences; quarterly.

Philosophy: POB 73, Pyongyang; fax (2) 3814410; quarterly.

Punsok Hwahak (Analysis): POB 73, Pyongyang; fax (2) 3814410; organ of the Cen. Analytical Inst. of the Korean Acad. of Sciences; quarterly.

Ryoksagwahak (Historical Science): Pyongyang; publ. by the Acad. of Social Sciences; quarterly.

Saengmulhak (Biology): Pyongyang; fax (2) 3814410; publ. by the Korea Science and Encyclopedia Publishing House; quarterly.

Sahoekwahak (Social Science): Pyongyang; publ. by the Acad. of Social Sciences; 6 a year.

Suhakkwa Mulli: Pyongyang; organ of the Physics and Mathematics Cttee of the Korean Acad. of Sciences; quarterly.

FOREIGN LANGUAGE PUBLICATIONS

The Democratic People's Republic of Korea: Korea Pictorial, Pyongyang; f. 1956; illustrated news; Korean, Russian, Chinese, English, French, Arabic and Spanish edns; monthly; Editor-in-Chief HAN POM CHIK.

Foreign Trade of the DPRK: Foreign Trade Publishing House, Potonggang District, Pyongyang; economic developments and export promotion; English, French, Japanese, Russian and Spanish edns; monthly.

Korea: Pyongyang; f. 1956; illustrated; Korean, Arabic, Chinese, English, French, Spanish and Russian edns; monthly.

Korea Today: Foreign Languages Publishing House, Pyongyang; current affairs; Chinese, English, French, Russian and Spanish edns; monthly; Vice-Dir and Editor-in-Chief HAN PONG CHAN.

Korean Women: Pyongyang; English and French edns; quarterly.

Korean Youth and Students: Pyongyang; English and French edns; monthly.

The Pyongyang Times: Sochondong, Sosong District, Pyongyang; tel. (2) 51951; English, Spanish and French edns; weekly.

NEWS AGENCY

Korean Central News Agency (KCNA): Potonggangdong 1, Potonggang District, Pyongyang; e-mail eng-info@kcna.co.jp; internet www.kcna.co.jp; f. 1946; sole distributing agency for news in the DPRK; publs daily bulletins in English, Russian, French and Spanish; Dir-Gen. KIM PYONG HO.

PRESS ASSOCIATION

Korean Journalists Union: Pyongyang; tel. (2) 36897; f. 1946; assists in the ideological work of the Korean Workers' Party; Chair. Cen. Cttee KIM SONG GUK.

Publishers

Academy of Sciences Publishing House: Nammundong, Central District, Pyongyang; tel. (2) 51956; f. 1953.

Academy of Social Sciences Publishing House: Pyongyang; Dir CHOE KWAN SHIK.

Agricultural Press: Pyongyang; labour, industrial relations; Pres. HO KYONG PIL.

Central Science and Technology Information Agency: Pyongyang; f. 1963; Dir JU SONG RYONG.

Education Publishing House: Pyongyang; f. 1945; Pres. KIM CHANG SON.

Foreign Language Press Group: Sochondong, Sosong District, Pyongyang; tel. (2) 841342; fax (2) 812100; f. 1949; Dir CHOE KYONG GUK.

Foreign Language Publishing House: Oesong District, Pyongyang; Dir KIM YONG MU.

Higher Educational Books Publishing House: Pyongyang; f. 1960; Pres. PAK KUN SONG.

Kim Il Sung University Publishing House: Pyongyang; f. 1965.

Korea Science and Encyclopedia Publishing House: POB 73, Pyongyang; tel. (2) 18111; fax (2) 3814410; publishes numerous periodicals and monographs; f. 1952; Dir-Gen. KIM JUNG HYOP; Dir of International Co-operation JEAN BAHNG.

Korean People's Army Publishing House: Pyongyang; Pres. YUN MYONG DO.

Korean Social Democratic Party Publishing House: Pyongyang; tel. (2) 5591709; fax (2) 3814410; f. 1946; publishes quarterly journal *Joson Sahoemingjudang* (in Korean) and *KSDP Says* (in English); Dir RI KANG SIK.

Korean Workers' Party Publishing House: Pyongyang; f. 1945; fiction, politics; Dir RYANG KYONG BOK.

Kumsong Youth Publishing House: Pyongyang; f. 1946; Dir HAN JONG SOP.

Literature and Art Publishing House: Pyongyang; f. by merger of Mass Culture Publishing House and Publishing House of the Gen. Fed. of Literary and Art Unions; Dir-Gen. RI PHYO U.

Transportation Publishing House: Namgyodong, Hyongjaesan District, Pyongyang; f. 1952; travel; Editor PAEK JONG HAN.

Working People's Organizations Publishing House: Pyongyang; f. 1946; fiction, government, political science; Dir MIN SANG HYON.

WRITERS' UNION

Korean Writers' Union: Pyongyang; Chair. Cen. Cttee KIM PYONG HUN.

Broadcasting and Communications

Information flow within North Korea is still mainly conducted via a closed intranet system (Kwangmyong), which was opened in 2000, with access to the global internet severely limited. In October 2001 North Korea launched its first e-mail service provider in co-operation with the China-based company Silibank, which can be used by registered users for business and trade purposes. Although a mobile telephone network was established in 2002, the use of mobile telephones was banned in 2004. However, the ban was subsequently removed, and Orascom Telecom Holding, a provider based in Egypt, was permitted to establish a 3G mobile service, Koryolink, as a joint venture with the state-owned Korea Post and Telecommunications Corporation in 2008. There were reported to be over 1m. subscribers to Koryolink by February 2013. In January 2013 a previous policy was reversed and foreign visitors were permitted to bring mobile telephones into North Korea and purchase a SIM card for the local network; in March Koryolink launched a mobile internet service for foreign visitors. As at April 2013 North Korean citizens were not permitted to call overseas and were also unable to call numbers owned by foreign residents. Foreign residents were usually allowed to call overseas, but were unable to call the numbers of ordinary North Koreans.

TELECOMMUNICATIONS

Korea Post and Telecommunications Co: Pyongyang; Dir KIM HYON JONG.

BROADCASTING

Regulatory Authorities

Central Broadcasting Committee of the DPRK: Jonsungdong, Moranbong District, Pyongyang; tel. (2) 3816035; fax (2) 3812100.

Radio

There are 17 AM radio stations, 14 FM stations and 11 shortwave stations.

Korean Central Broadcasting Station: Pyongyang; programmes relayed nationally with local programmes supplied by local radio cttees; loudspeakers are installed in factories and in open spaces in all towns; home broadcasting 22 hours daily; foreign broadcasts in Russian, Chinese, English, French, German, Japanese, Spanish and Arabic.

Television

There are four television stations in operation.

General Bureau of Television: Gen. Dir CHA SUNG SU.

DPRK Radio and Television Broadcasting Committee: see Radio.

Kaesong Television: Kaesong; broadcasts five hours on weekdays, 11 hours at weekends.

Korean Central Television Station: Ministry of Post and Telecommunications, Pyongyang; broadcasts five hours daily; satellite broadcasts commenced Oct. 1999.

Mansudae Television Station: Mansudae, Pyongyang; f. 1983; broadcasts nine hours of cultural programmes, music and dance, foreign films and news reports at weekends.

Finance

(cap. = capital; res = reserves; dep. = deposits; m. = million; br(s) = branch(es); amounts in won)

BANKING

A total of 18 banks were reported to be in operation in mid-2011.

Central Bank

Central Bank of the DPRK: Munsudong, Seungri St 58-1, Central District, Pyongyang; tel. (2) 3338196; fax (2) 3814624; e-mail kcb_idkb@co.chesin.com; f. 1946; bank of issue; supervisory and control bank; Pres. PAEK RYONG CHON; 13 brs.

State Banks

Credit Bank of Korea: Chongryu 1-dong, Munsu St, Otandong, Central District, Pyongyang; tel. (2) 3818285; fax (2) 3817806;

f. 1986; est. as International Credit Bank, name changed 1989; Pres. Li Sun Bok; Vice-Pres. Son Yong Sun.

Foreign Trade Bank of the DPRK: FTB Bldg, Jungsongdong, Seungri St, Central District, Pyongyang; tel. (2) 3815270; fax (2) 3814467; e-mail ftb@co.chesin.com; f. 1959; deals in international settlements and all banking business; Pres. and Chair. O Kwang Chol; 12 brs.

International Industrial Development Bank: Jongpyong-dong, Pyongchon District, Pyongyang; tel. (2) 3818610; fax (2) 3814427; f. 2001; Pres. Shin Dok Song.

Korea Daesong Bank: Segoridong, Gyongheung St, Potonggang District, Pyongyang; tel. (2) 3818221; fax (2) 3814576; f. 1978; cap. 158,205.8m., res 25,917.6m., dep. 1,990,582.5m. (Dec. 2006); Pres. Ri Gyong Ha.

Koryo Bank: Ponghwadong, Potonggang District, Pyongyang; tel. (2) 18333; fax (2) 3814410; e-mail krbankpy@co.chesin.com; f. 1989; est. as Koryo Finance Joint Venture Co, name changed 1994; co-operative, devt, regional, savings and universal bank; Pres. Pak Yong Chil.

Kumgang Bank: Jungsongdong, Central District, Pyongyang; tel. (2) 3818532; fax (2) 3814467; f. 1979; Chair. Kim Jang Ho.

State Development Bank: Pyongyang; f. 2010; Dir-Gen. Jeon Il Chun.

Private Banks

Bank of East Land: BEL Bldg, Jonseung-dong, Moranbong District, POB 32, Pyongyang; tel. (2) 3818923; fax (2) 3814410; f. 2001; commercial, investment, merchant, private and retail banking; Pres. Pak Hyong Gil.

Tanchon Commercial Bank: Saemaeul 1-dong, Pyongchon District, Pyongyang; tel. (2) 18111999; fax (2) 3814793; e-mail cbktm828@co.chesin.com; f. 1983; fmrly Changgwang Credit Bank, merged with Samchon-ri Bank and named as above Nov. 2003; cap. 50,043.9m., res 93,817.9m., dep. 875,021.9m. (Dec. 2003); Chair. Kim Chol Hwan; Pres. Kye Chang Ho.

Joint-Venture Banks

Korea Joint Bank (KJB): Ryugyongdong, Potonggang District, Pyongyang; tel. (2) 3818151; fax (2) 3814410; f. 1989; est. with co-operation of Fed. of Korean Traders and Industrialists in Japan; 50% owned by Korea Int. General Jt Venture Co, 50% owned by Gen. Assen of Koreans in Japan; Gen. Man. O Ho Ryol; 6 domestic brs, 1 br. in Tokyo.

Korea Joint Financial Co: f. 1988; jt venture with Koreans resident in the USA.

Korea Nagwon Joint Financial Co: f. 1987; est. by Nagwon Trade Co and a Japanese co.

Korea Rakwon Joint Banking Co: Pyongyang; Man. Dir Ho Pok Dok.

Korea United Development Bank: Central District, Pyongyang; tel. (2) 3814165; fax (2) 3814483; e-mail kudb888@yahoo.com; f. 1991; 51% owned by Zhongce Investment Corpn (Hong Kong), 49% owned by Osandok Gen. Bureau; Pres. Kim Se Ho.

Koryo Commercial Bank: tel. (2) 3812060; fax (2) 3814441; f. 1988; jt venture with Koreans resident in the USA.

Foreign Investment Banks

Daedong Credit Bank: Potonggang Hotel, 401 Ansan-dong, Pyongchon District, Pyongyang; tel. (2) 3814866; fax (2) 3814723; internet www.daedongcreditbank.com; f. 1996; est. as Peregrine-Daesong Devt Bank; jt venture between Oriental Commercial Holdings Ltd (Hong Kong) and Korea Daesong Bank; Gen. Man. and CEO Nigel Cowie.

Golden Triangle Bank: Rajin-Sonbong Free Economic and Trade Zone; f. 1995.

INSURANCE

State Insurance Bureau: Central District, Pyongyang; tel. (2) 38196; handles all life, fire, accident, marine, hull insurance and reinsurance.

Korea Foreign Insurance Co (Chosunbohom): Central District, Pyongyang; tel. (2) 3818024; fax (2) 3814464; f. 1974; conducts marine, motor, aviation and fire insurance, reinsurance of all classes, and all foreign insurance; brs in Chongjin, Hungnam and Nampo, and agencies in foreign ports; overseas representative offices in Chile, France, Germany, Pakistan, Singapore; Pres. Ri Jang Su.

Korea International Insurance Co: Pyongyang; Dir Paek Myong Ron.

Korea Mannyon Insurance Co: Pyongyang; Pres. Pak Il Hyong.

Trade and Industry

GOVERNMENT AGENCIES

DPRK Committee for the Promotion of External Economic Co-operation: Jungsongdong, Central District, Pyongyang; tel. (2) 333974; fax (2) 3814498; Chair. Paek Hong Bong.

DPRK Committee for the Promotion of International Trade: Central District, Pyongyang; Pres. Ri Song Rok; Chair. Kim Yong Jae.

Economic Co-operation Management Bureau: Ministry of Foreign Trade, Pyongyang; f. 1998; Dir Kim Yong Sul.

Korea International Joint Venture Promotion Committee: Pyongyang; Chair. Chae Hui Jong.

Korean Association for the Promotion of Asian Trade: Pyongyang; Pres. Ri Song Rok.

Korean International General Joint Venture Co: Pyongyang; f. 1986; promotes jt economic ventures with foreign countries; Man. Dir Ro Tu Chol.

CHAMBER OF COMMERCE

DPRK Chamber of Commerce: Jungsongdong, Central District, POB 89, Pyongyang; tel. (2) 3815926; fax (2) 3815827; e-mail micom@co.chesin.com.

INDUSTRIAL AND TRADE ASSOCIATIONS

Korea Building Materials Trading Co: Tongdaewon District, Pyongyang; tel. (2) 18111-3818085; fax (2) 3814555; chemical building materials, woods, timbers, cement, sheet glass, etc.; Dir Shin Tong Bom.

Korea Cereals Export and Import Corpn: Jungsongdong, Central District, Pyongyang; tel. (2) 18111-3818278; fax (2) 3813451; high-quality vegetable starches, etc.

Korea Chemicals Export and Import Corpn: Central District, Pyongyang; petroleum and petroleum products, raw materials for the chemical industry, rubber and rubber products, fertilizers, etc.

Korea Daesong General Trading Corpn: Pulgungori 1-dong, Potonggang District, Pyongyang; tel. (2) 18111; fax (2) 3814432; e-mail Daesong@silibank.com; Gen. Dir Choe Jong Son.

Korea Daesong Jei Trading Corpn: Pulgungori 1-dong, Potonggang District, Pyongyang; tel. (2) 18111-3818213; fax (2) 3814431; machinery and equipment, chemical products, textiles, agricultural products, etc.

Korea Daesong Jesam Trading Corpn: Pulgungori 1-dong, Potonggang District, Pyongyang; tel. (2) 18111-3818562; fax (2) 3814431; remedies for diabetes, tonics, etc.

Korea Ferrous Metals Export and Import Corpn: Potonggang 2-dong, Potonggang District, Pyongyang; tel. (2) 18111-3818078; fax (2) 3814581; steel products.

Korea Film Export and Import Corpn: Taedongmundong, Central District, POB 113, Pyongyang; tel. (2) 180008034; fax (2) 3814410; f. 1956; feature films, cartoons, scientific and documentary films; Dir-Gen. Choe Hyok U.

Korea First Equipment Export and Import Co: Central District, Pyongyang; tel. (2) 334825; f. 1960; export and import of ferrous and non-ferrous metallurgical plant, geological exploration and mining equipment, communication equipment, machine-building plant, etc.; construction of public facilities such as airports, hotels, tourist facilities, etc.; jt-venture business in similar projects; Pres. Chae Won Chol.

Korea Foodstuffs Export and Import Corpn: Kangan 2-dong, Songyo District, Pyongyang; tel. (2) 18111-3818289; fax (2) 3814417; cereals, wines, meat, canned foods, fruits, cigarettes, etc.

Korea Fruit and Vegetables Export Corpn: Central District, Pyongyang; tel. (2) 35117; vegetables, fruit and their products.

Korea General Corpn for External Construction (GENCO): Sungri St 25, Jungsongdong, Central District, Pyongyang; tel. (2) 18111-3818090; fax (2) 3814611; e-mail gen122@co.chesin.com; f. 1961; construction of dwelling houses, public establishments, factories, hydroelectric and thermal power stations, irrigation systems, ports, bridges, transport services, technical services; Gen. Dir Choe Bong Su.

Korea General Machine Co: Tongsin 3-dong, Tongdaewon, Pyongyang; tel. (2) 18555-3818102; fax (2) 3814495; Dir Ra In Gyun.

Korea Hyopdong Trading Corpn: Othan-dong, Kangan St, Central District, Pyongyang; tel. (2) 18111-3818011; fax (2) 3814454; fabrics, glass products, ceramics, chemical goods, building materials, foodstuffs, machinery, etc.

Korea Industrial Technology Co: Jungsongdong, Central District, Pyongyang; tel. (2) 18111-3818025; fax (2) 3814537; Pres. Kwon Yong Son.

Korea International Chemical Joint Venture Co: Pyongyang; Chair. RYO SONG GUN.

Korea Jangsu Trading Co: Kyogudong, Central District, Pyongyang; tel. (2) 18111-3818834; fax (2) 3814410; medicinal products and clinical equipment.

Korea Jeil Equipment Export and Import Corpn: Jungsongdong, Central District, Pyongyang; tel. (2) 334825; f. 1960; ferrous and non-ferrous metallurgical plant, geological exploration and mining equipment, power plant, communications and broadcasting equipment, machine-building equipment, railway equipment, construction of public facilities; Pres. CHO JANG DOK.

Korea Koryo Trading Corpn: Jongpyongdong, Pyongchon District, Pyongyang; tel. (2) 18111-3818104; fax (2) 3814646; Dir KIM HUI DUK.

Korea Kwangmyong Trading Corpn: Jungsongdong, Central District, Pyongyang; tel. (2) 18111-3818111; fax (2) 3814410; dried herbs, dried and pickled vegetables; Dir CHOE JONG HUN.

Korea Light Industry Import-Export Co: Juchetab St, Tongdaewon District, Pyongyang; tel. (2) 37661; exports silk, cigarettes, canned goods, drinking glasses, ceramics, handbags, pens, plastic flowers, musical instruments, etc.; imports chemicals, dyestuffs, machinery, etc.; Dir CHOE PYONG HYON.

Korea Machine Tool Trading Corpn: Tongdaewon District, Pyongyang; tel. (2) 18555-381810; fax (2) 3814495; Dir KIM KWANG RYOP.

Korea Machinery and Equipment Export and Import Corpn: Potonggang District, Pyongyang; tel. (2) 333449; f. 1948; metallurgical machinery and equipment, electric machines, building machinery, farm machinery, diesel engines, etc.

Korea Mansu Trading Corpn: Chollima St, Central District, POB 250, Pyongyang; tel. (2) 43075; fax (2) 812100; f. 1974; antibiotics, pharmaceuticals, vitamin compounds, drugs, medicinal herbs; Dir KIM JANG HUN.

Korea Marine Products Export and Import Corpn: Central District, Pyongyang; canned, frozen, dried, salted and smoked fish, fishing equipment and supplies.

Korea Minerals Export and Import Corpn: Central District, Pyongyang; minerals, solid fuel, graphite, precious stones, etc.

Korea Namheung Trading Co: Sinri-dong, Tongdaewon District, Pyongyang; tel. (2) 18111-3818974; fax (2) 3814623; high-purity reagents, synthetic resins, vinyl films, essential oils, menthol and peppermint oil.

Korea Non-ferrous Metals Export and Import Corpn: Potonggang 2-dong, Potonggang District, Pyongyang; tel. (2) 18111-3818247; fax (2) 3814569.

Korea Okyru Trading Corpn: Kansongdong, Pyongchon District, Pyongyang; tel. (2) 18111-3818110; fax (2) 3814618; agricultural and marine products, household goods, clothing, chemical and light industrial products.

Korea Ponghwa Contractual Joint Venture Co: Pyongyang; Dir MUN YONG OK.

Korea Ponghwa General Trading Corpn: Jungsongdong, Central District, Pyongyang; tel. (2) 18111-3818023; fax (2) 3814444; machinery, metal products, minerals and chemicals.

Korea Publications Export and Import Corpn: Yokjondong, Yonggwang St, Central District, Pyongyang; tel. (2) 3818536; fax (2) 3814404; f. 1948; export of books, periodicals, postcards, paintings, cassettes, videos, CDs, CD-ROMs, postage stamps and records; import of books; Pres. RI YONG.

Korea Rungra Co: Sinwondong, Potonggang District, Pyongyang; tel. (2) 18111-3818112; fax (2) 3814608; Dir CHOE HENG UNG.

Korea Rungrado Trading Corpn: Segori-dong, Potonggang District, Pyongyang; tel. (2) 18111-3818022; fax (2) 3814507; food and animal products; Gen. Dir PAK KYU HONG.

Korea Ryongaksan General Trading Corpn: Pyongyang; Gen. Dir HAN YU RO.

Korea Samcholli General Corpn: Pyongyang; Dir JONG UN OP.

Korea Technology Corpn: Jungsongdong, Central District, Pyongyang; tel. (2) 18111-3818090; fax (2) 3814410; scientific and technical co-operation.

Korea Unha Trading Corpn: Rungra 1-dong, Taedongkang District, Pyongyang; tel. (2) 18111-3818236; fax (2) 3814506; clothing and fibres.

Korea Yonghung Trading Co: Tongan-dong, Central District, Pyongyang; tel. (2) 18111-3818223; fax (2) 3814527; e-mail greenlam@co.chesin.com; f. 1979; export of freight cars, vehicle parts, marine products, electronic goods; import of steel, chemical products; Pres. CHOE YONG DOK.

Pyongsu JV Co Ltd: Pyongyang; f. 2004; pharmaceutical mfr, medical products incl. analgesics; jt venture with Interpacific/Zuellig Pharma (Switzerland).

TRADE UNIONS

General Federation of Trade Unions of Korea (GFTUK): Dongmun-dong, Taedongkang District, POB 333, Pyongyang; fax (2) 3814427; f. 1945; 1.6m. mems (2003); seven affiliated unions (2003); Pres. RYOM SUN GIL.

Transport

RAILWAYS

In 2009 the total length of track was estimated at 5,242 km, of which at least 70% was electrified. There are international train services to Moscow (Russia) and Beijing (People's Republic of China). Construction work on the reconnection of the Kyongui (West Coast, Sinuiju to Seoul, in South Korea) and East Coast Line (Wonsan–Seoul) began in September 2002. The two lines were officially opened in June 2003, but were not yet open to traffic, as construction work on the Northern side remained to be completed. The lines were reportedly completed in 2005, and in May 2007 the first cross-border trial runs were conducted. In the long term, the two were to be linked to the Trans-China and Trans-Siberian railways, respectively, greatly enhancing the region's transport links.

There is an underground railway system in Pyongyang, with two public lines serving 17 stations.

ROADS

In 2010 the road network was estimated at 25,554 km, of which most were unpaved. As part of the Government's 10-year plan, an additional 3,000 km of expressways were to be constructed by 2020.

INLAND WATERWAYS

In 2005 the total length of inland waterways was estimated at 2,253 km, most of which was navigable only by small craft. The Yalu (Amnok-gang), Taedong, Tumen and Ryesong are the most important commercial rivers. Regular passenger and freight services: Nampo–Chosan–Supung; Chungsu–Sinuiju–Dasado; Nampo–Jeudo; Pyongyang–Nampo.

SHIPPING

The principal ports are Nampo, Wonsan, Chongjin, Rajin, Hungnam, Songnim and Haeju. At 31 December 2012 North Korea's flag registered fleet comprised 316 vessels, with a combined displacement of 879,672 grt.

Bochon Shipping Co: Pyongchon District, Pyongyang.

Chon Song Shipping Co Ltd: Sochang-dong, Potonggang District, Pyongyang.

Korea Ansan Shipping Co: Nampo.

Korea Chartering Corpn: Central District, Pyongyang; arranges cargo transport and chartering.

Korea Daehung Shipping Co: Ansan 1-dong, Pyongchon District, Pyongyang; tel. (2) 18111, ext. 8695; fax (2) 3814508; f. 1994; owns 6 reefers, 3 oil tankers, 1 cargo ship.

Korea East Sea Shipping Co: Pyongyang; Dir RI TUK HYON.

Korea Foreign Transportation Corpn: Central District, Pyongyang; arranges transport of cargoes for export and import (transit goods and charters).

Korea Myohyang Shipping Co: Ryonhwadong Changgoan St, Chung District, Pyongyang; tel. (3) 8160590; fax (3) 8146420.

Korea Myongsang Shipping Co: Chongpyong-dong, Pyongchon District, Pyongyang; tel. (2) 3815842; fax (2) 3815942.

Korea Tonghae Shipping Co: Changgwang St, Central District, POB 120, Pyongyang; tel. (2) 345805; fax (2) 3814583; arranges transport by Korean vessels.

Korea Undok Shipping Co Ltd: Nampo.

Korean-Polish Shipping Co Ltd: Moranbong District, Pyongyang; tel. (2) 3814384; fax (2) 3814607; f. 1967; maritime trade mainly with Polish and Far East ports.

Ocean Maritime Management Co Ltd: Tonghungdong, Central District, Pyongyang.

Ocean Shipping Agency of the DPRK: Moranbong District, POB 21, Pyongyang; tel. (2) 3818100; fax (2) 3814531; Pres. O JONG HO.

CIVIL AVIATION

In 2012 there were 81 airports, 39 of which possessed paved runways. The international airport is at Sunan, 22 km north-west of the centre of Pyongyang. The airport has two runways, and a new terminal building opened in mid-2011.

Chosonminhang/General Civil Aviation Bureau of the DPRK: Sunan Airport, Sunan District, Pyongyang; tel. (2) 37917; fax (2) 3814625; f. 1954; internal services and external flights by Air Koryo to Beijing and Shenyang (People's Republic of China), Bangkok (Thailand), Macao, Nagoya (Japan), Kuala Lumpur (Malaysia), Moscow, Khabarovsk and Vladivostok (Russia), Sofia (Bulgaria) and Berlin (Germany); charter services are operated to Asia, Africa and Europe; Pres. KIM YO UNG.

Tourism

Tourism is permitted only in officially accompanied parties. In 1999 there were more than 60 international hotels (including nine in Pyongyang) with 7,500 beds. Mount Kumgang has been developed as a tourist attraction, as part of a joint venture between North Korea and Hyundai, the South Korean conglomerate. Mount Paekdu, Korea's highest mountain, is another tourist attraction. In 2012 it was estimated that around 4,000 Western tourists visited North Korea. It was estimated that more than 101,700 South Koreans visited the North in 2006 (of whom about 88,000 were business travellers to Kaesong), excluding visitors to Mount Kumgang.

Korea International Tourist Bureau: Central District, Pyongyang; tel. (2) 3817201; fax (2) 3817607; Pres. HAN PYONG UN.

Korean International Youth Tourist Co: Mankyongdae District, Pyongyang; tel. (2) 73406; f. 1985; Dir HWANG CHUN YONG.

Kumgangsan International Tourist Co: Central District, Pyongyang; tel. (2) 31562; fax (2) 3812100; f. 1988.

Ryohaengsa (Korea International Travel Company): Central District, Pyongyang; tel. (2) 3817201; fax (2) 3817607; f. 1953; has relations with more than 200 tourist companies throughout the world; Pres. CHO SONG HUN.

State General Bureau of Tourism: Mangyongdae District, Pyongyang; e-mail kitc_1@silibank.com; Pres. KIM DO JUN.

Defence

The estimated total strength of the armed forces as assessed at November 2012 was 1,190,000: army 1,020,000, air force 110,000 and navy 60,000. Security and border troops numbered 189,000, and there was a workers' and peasants' militia ('Red Guards') numbering about 5.7m. Military service is selective: army for five to 12 years; navy for five to 10 years; and air force for three to four years. Reserve forces were estimated to total 600,000 in 2012.

Defence Expenditure: total expenditure was estimated at 76,300m. won in 2009.

Supreme Commander of the Korean People's Army and First Chairman of the National Defence Commission: Marshal KIM JONG UN.

Vice-Chairmen of the National Defence Commission: Vice-Marshal RI YONG MU, Vice-Marshal KIM YONG CHUN, Vice-Marshal O KUK RYOL, Gen. JANG SONG THAEK.

Chief of General Staff of the Korean People's Army: Vice-Marshal HYON YONG CHOL.

Commander of the Air Force: Col-Gen. RI PYONG CHOL.

Commander of the Navy: Gen. KIM YUN SHIM.

Education

Universal, compulsory primary and secondary education were introduced in 1956 and 1958, respectively, and are provided at state expense. Free and compulsory 11-year education in state schools was introduced in 1975, and was planned to be extended by one more year in 2012. Children enter kindergarten at five years of age, and primary school at the age of six. After four years, they advance to senior middle school for six years which was proposed in 2012 to be divided into two three-year curricula. English is compulsory as a second language from the age of 14. A report submitted to UNESCO by the North Korean Government in 2000 stated that there were 27,017 nurseries for 1,575,000 pupils, 14,167 kindergartens for 748,416 pupils, 4,886 primary schools for 1,609,865 pupils, 4,772 senior middle schools for 2,181,524 pupils, and more than 300 universities and colleges with 1.89m. students and academics. The adult literacy rate was reported to be 100% in 2008. In June 2010 it was reported that the Ministry of Education was to be reorganized as the Education Commission, comprising the Ministry of Higher Education and the Ministry of Common Education. The Pyongyang University of Science and Technology (PUST), established in October 2010 in co-operation with a South Korean education foundation, was the first private university in the country. The university had initially offered courses in information science and technology and had planned to include management courses. In 2013 it was reported that the University would open schools in public health care and construction engineering.

THE REPUBLIC OF KOREA

Introductory Survey

LOCATION, CLIMATE, LANGUAGE, RELIGION, FLAG, CAPITAL

The Republic of Korea (South Korea) forms the southern part of the Korean peninsula, in eastern Asia. To the north, separated by a frontier that roughly follows the 38th parallel, is the country's only neighbour, the Democratic People's Republic of Korea (North Korea). To the west is the Yellow Sea, to the south is the East China Sea, and to the east is the Sea of Japan. The climate is marked by cold, dry winters, with an average temperature of −6°C (21°F), and hot, humid summers, with an average temperature of 25°C (77°F). The language is Korean. Confucianism, Mahayana Buddhism, and Chundo Kyo are the principal traditional religions. Chundo Kyo is peculiar to Korea, and combines elements of Shaman, Buddhist and Christian doctrines. There are some 17.5m. Christians, of whom about 83% are Protestants. The national flag (proportions 2 by 3) comprises, in the centre of a white field, a disc divided horizontally by an S-shaped line, red above and blue below, surrounded by four configurations of parallel, broken and unbroken black bars. The capital is Seoul.

CONTEMPORARY POLITICAL HISTORY

Historical Context

(For more details of the history of Korea up to 1953, including the Korean War, and subsequent bilateral relations see the Democratic People's Republic of Korea—North Korea.)

UN-supervised elections to a new legislature, the National Assembly (Kuk Hoe), took place in May 1948. The Assembly adopted a democratic Constitution, and South Korea became the independent Republic of Korea on 15 August 1948, with Dr Syngman Rhee, leader of the Liberal Party, as the country's first President. He remained in the post until his resignation in April 1960. Elections in July were won by the Democratic Party, led by Chang Myon, but his Government was deposed in May 1961 by a military coup, led by Gen. Park Chung-Hee. Power was assumed by the Supreme Council for National Reconstruction, which dissolved the National Assembly, suspended the Constitution and disbanded all existing political parties. In January 1963 the military leadership formed the Democratic Republican Party (DRP). Under a new Constitution, Gen. Park became President of the Third Republic in December.

Domestic Political Affairs

Opposition to Park's regime led to the imposition of martial law in October 1972. A Constitution for the Fourth Republic, giving the President greatly increased powers, was approved by national referendum in November. A new body, the National Conference for Unification (NCU), was elected in December. The NCU re-elected President Park for a six-year term, and the DRP obtained a decisive majority in elections to the new National Assembly. In May 1975 opposition to the Government was effectively banned, and political trials followed. Elections to the NCU were held in May 1978, and the President was re-elected for a further six-year term in July. In October 1979 serious rioting erupted when Kim Young-Sam, the leader of the opposition New Democratic Party (NDP), was accused of subversive activities and expelled from the National Assembly. On 26 October Park was assassinated in an alleged coup attempt, led by the head of the Korean Central Intelligence Agency. Martial law was reintroduced, and in December the Prime Minister, Choi Kyu-Hah, was elected President by the NCU. A military coup in December was led by the head of the Defence Security Command, Lt-Gen. Chun Doo-Hwan, who arrested the Army Chief of Staff and effectively took power. Nevertheless, President Choi was inaugurated on 21 December to complete his predecessor's term of office (to 1984).

Choi promised liberalizing reforms, but in May 1980 demonstrations by students and confrontation with the army led to the arrest of about 30 political leaders, including Kim Dae-Jung, former head of the NDP. Martial law was extended throughout the country, the National Assembly was suspended, and all political activity was banned. Almost 200 people were killed

when troops stormed the southern city of Gwangju, which had been occupied by students and dissidents. In August Choi resigned, and Gen. Chun was elected President. Acting Prime Minister Nam Duck-Woo formed a new State Council (cabinet) in September. In the same month the sentencing to death of Kim Dae-Jung for plotting rebellion was condemned internationally. (This sentence was subsequently suspended.) In October a new Constitution was overwhelmingly approved by referendum.

Martial law was ended in January 1981, and new political parties were formed. In the following month President Chun was re-elected: the start of his new term, in March, inaugurated the Fifth Republic. Chun's Democratic Justice Party (DJP) became the majority party in the new National Assembly, which was elected shortly afterwards. Amid opposition demands for liberalization, Chun pledged that he would retire at the end of his term in 1988, thus becoming the country's first head of state to transfer power constitutionally.

During 1984, following an escalation of student unrest, the Government adopted a more flexible attitude towards dissidents. Several thousand prisoners were released, and the political 'blacklist' was finally abolished in March 1985. In January 1985 the New Korea Democratic Party (NKDP) was established by supporters of Kim Young-Sam and Kim Dae-Jung. At the general election to the National Assembly held in February, the DJP retained its majority, but the NKDP emerged as the major opposition force, boosted by the return from exile of Kim Dae-Jung. The new party secured 67 of the Assembly's 276 seats, while the DJP won 148 seats. Chun appointed a new State Council, with Lho Shin-Yong as Prime Minister. Before the opening session of the new National Assembly many deputies defected to the NKDP.

In April 1987 internal divisions within the NKDP led to the formation of a new opposition party, the Reunification Democratic Party (RDP); Kim Young-Sam was elected to its presidency in May. In April Chun unexpectedly announced the suspension of the process of reform until after the Olympic Games (due to be held in Seoul in September 1988). While confirming that he would leave office in February 1988, Chun indicated that his successor would be elected by the existing electoral college system, precipitating violent clashes between anti-Government demonstrators and riot police.

In June 1987 Roh Tae-Woo was nominated as the DJP's presidential candidate. However, Roh subsequently informed Chun that he would relinquish both the DJP chairmanship and his presidential candidature if the principal demands of the opposition for constitutional and electoral reform were not satisfied. Under international pressure, Chun acceded, and negotiations on constitutional amendments were announced. In August the DJP and the RDP announced that a bipartisan committee had agreed a draft constitution. Among its provisions were the reintroduction of direct presidential elections by universal suffrage, and the restriction of the presidential mandate to a single five-year term; the President's emergency powers were also to be reduced, and serving military officers were to be prohibited from taking government office. Having been approved by the National Assembly, the amendments were endorsed in a national referendum in October, and the amended Constitution was promulgated shortly thereafter.

Kim Dae-Jung joined the RDP in August 1987; however, in November he became President of a new Peace and Democracy Party (PDP), and declared himself a rival presidential candidate. At the election, in December, Roh Tae-Woo won some 36% of the votes, while Kim Dae-Jung and Kim Young-Sam each achieved about 27%. Roh Tae-Woo was inaugurated as President on 25 February 1988, whereupon the Sixth Republic was established. At the general election to the National Assembly, in April, the DJP failed to achieve an overall majority, securing 125 of the 299 seats. The PDP achieved 70 seats, thus becoming the main opposition party; the remainder went to the RDP and the New Democratic Republican Party (NDRP—the revived and renamed DRP), led by Kim Jong-Pil.

In February 1990 the DJP merged with the RDP and the NDRP to form the Democratic Liberal Party (DLP). Roh was subsequently elected President of the DLP, while Kim Young-Sam and Kim Jong-Pil were elected as two of the party's three Chairmen. The DLP thus controlled more than two-thirds of the seats in the National Assembly. The PDP, effectively isolated as the sole opposition party, condemned the merger and demanded new elections. In March a new opposition group, the Democratic Party (DP), was formed, largely comprising members of the RDP who had opposed the merger.

In July 1990 a large rally was held in Seoul to denounce the adoption by the National Assembly of several items of controversial legislation, including proposals to restructure the military leadership and to reorganize the broadcasting media. In protest, all the opposition members of the National Assembly tendered their resignations. Although the Assembly's Speaker refused to accept the resignations, the PDP deputies returned to the National Assembly only in November, following an agreement with the DLP that local council elections would take place in the first half of 1991, to be followed by gubernatorial and mayoral elections in 1992. The DLP also agreed to abandon plans for the transfer, by constitutional amendment, of executive powers to the State Council. The first local elections to be held in the Republic of Korea (South Korea) for 30 years took place in March and June 1991, and resulted in a decisive victory for the DLP.

Meanwhile, in April 1991 the PDP merged with the smaller opposition Party for New Democratic Alliance to form the New Democratic Party (NDP). In September the NDP and the DP agreed to merge (under the latter's name) to form a stronger opposition front. A further opposition group, the Unification National Party (UNP), was established in January 1992 by Chung Ju-Yung, the founder and Honorary Chairman of the powerful Hyundai industrial conglomerate.

At elections to the National Assembly in March 1992, the DLP unexpectedly failed to secure an absolute majority, obtaining a total of 149 of the 299 seats. The remainder of the seats were won by the DP (97), the UNP (31), the New Political Reform Party (NPRP—one) and independent candidates (21). In May Kim Young-Sam was chosen as the DLP's candidate for the presidential election, scheduled for December, and in August he replaced Roh as the party's President; divisions within the DLP led to defections from the party by opponents of Kim Young-Sam.

The presidency of Kim Young-Sam

The presidential election, on 18 December 1992, was won by Kim Young-Sam, with some 42% of the votes cast. Kim (who was inaugurated on 25 February 1993) was the first South Korean President since 1960 without military connections. In February 1993 Chung Ju-Yung resigned as President of the United People's Party (UPP—as the UNP had been renamed), following allegations that he had embezzled Hyundai finances to fund his election campaign; he was given a three-year suspended sentence in November. Kim Young-Sam appointed Hwang In-Sung as Prime Minister, and a new State Council was formed.

Kim Young-Sam acted swiftly to honour his campaign pledge to eliminate corruption in business and politics; in all, during 1993, Kim's anti-corruption measures were reported to have resulted in the dismissal of, or disciplinary action against, some 3,000 business, government and military officials, and new regulations to restrict the activities of the country's industrial conglomerates (*chaebol*) were announced.

Hwang In-Sung resigned as Prime Minister in December 1993 and was succeeded by Lee Hoi-Chang, hitherto Chairman of the Board of Audit and Inspection (BAI). However, he resigned in April 1994 and was replaced by Lee Yung-Duk, latterly Deputy Prime Minister responsible for national unification.

In July 1994 the UPP and the NPRP merged to form the New People's Party (NPP). In October the Government announced that its inquiry into the role played by former Presidents Chun and Roh in the 1979 coup had found that both had participated in a 'premeditated military rebellion'. In December 1994 Lee Hong-Koo (hitherto the Deputy Prime Minister responsible for national unification) was appointed Prime Minister, as part of a major restructuring of the State Council.

The DLP fared badly at elections for gubernatorial, mayoral and other municipal and provincial posts in May 1995, in contrast to the success of a new party, the United Liberal Democrats (ULD), established in March by defectors from the DLP and led by Kim Jong-Pil (who had resigned as DLP Chairman earlier in the year). In September Kim Dae-Jung returned to politics, establishing his own party, the National Congress for New

Politics (NCNP). The DP was severely undermined when many of its members left to join the NCNP.

A major scandal erupted in October 1995, when Roh Tae-Woo admitted in a televised address that he had amassed a large sum of money during his term of office. He was arrested in the following month; at his trial, which opened in December, Roh confessed to having received donations from South Korean businesses, but denied that these constituted bribes. Many senior politicians and business leaders were also detained and interrogated in connection with the affair. Kim Dae-Jung, meanwhile, unexpectedly admitted that his campaign for the 1992 presidential election had been supported by a donation of money from Roh's 'slush fund'. Kim Young-Sam denied opposition allegations that he too had benefited from a similar donation. In December 1995, in an effort to distance his party from the deepening scandal, Kim Young-Sam changed the DLP's name to the New Korea Party (NKP). A major reorganization of the State Council was effected, in which Lee Hong-Koo was replaced as Prime Minister by Lee Soo-Sung, the President of Seoul National University.

In late 1995 it was announced that Roh Tae-Woo and Chun Doo-Hwan were to be prosecuted for their involvement in the 1979 coup and the 1980 Gwangju massacre. Chun was arrested in December 1995, and in the following month he was additionally accused of accumulating political funds through bribe-taking. Legal proceedings in connection with the events of 1979 and 1980 opened in March 1996: Chun was charged with mutiny for his organization of the 1979 coup, and with sedition in connection with the Gwangju massacre, while Roh was charged with aiding Chun. Roh and Chun were convicted as charged in August 1996, receiving lengthy prison sentences; each was heavily fined in the corruption cases.

Elections to the National Assembly took place in April 1996. Contrary to widespread predictions, the NKP only narrowly failed to retain its parliamentary majority, winning a total of 139 of the 299 seats. Recent incursions into the demilitarized zone (DMZ, separating North and South Korea) by North Korean troops had apparently caused many voters to favour the ruling party out of concern for national security. The NCNP took 79 seats, and the party's leader, Kim Dae-Jung, failed to win a seat. By the time the National Assembly convened in June, the NKP had secured a working majority with the support of several opposition and independent members.

The revision of the country's labour laws, to introduce greater flexibility into the employment market (a condition of South Korea's impending membership of the Organisation for Economic Co-operation and Development—OECD, see p. 388), was initiated in May 1996. Reforms proposed by the Government in early December were severely criticized by trade unions and opposition parties. Many thousands of factory workers, as well as public sector employees, participated in a strike called by the country's principal workers' confederation, the Federation of Korean Trade Unions (FKTU), after the Government convened a dawn session of the National Assembly, which approved the labour reform bill in the absence of opposition deputies. Anti-Government demonstrators in Seoul and other major cities repeatedly clashed with riot police, and warrants were issued for the arrest of several leaders of the Korean Confederation of Trade Unions (KCTU). By mid-January 1997 support for the strikes was abating; the KCTU suggested that it might accept a modification of the labour law, having previously insisted on its complete annulment. OECD issued a severe rebuke to the Government for failing to honour its pledges on labour reform, and, in a significant concession, Kim agreed to meet the leaders of the opposition parties to discuss amendments to the law; warrants for the arrest of union leaders were also suspended. In March the National Assembly approved a revised version of the legislation, whereby the implementation of certain proposals was delayed for two years, while the KCTU was granted immediate official recognition.

Meanwhile, bribery scandals persisted, prompting several government resignations during 1996. The infiltration of a North Korean submarine into South Korean waters in September resulted in the dismissal of the Minister of Defence, Lee Yang-Ho. He was subsequently charged with divulging classified information and with receiving bribes in connection with the procurement of helicopters for the army, and in December was sentenced to four years' imprisonment.

In January 1997 a further major scandal erupted when Hanbo, one of the country's largest steel and construction conglomerates, was declared bankrupt. Allegations were made that Hanbo had bribed the Government to exert pressure on banks to provide substantial loans to the conglomerate. The chief executives of several large Korean banks were arrested on charges of receiving bribes, and in February the Minister of Home Affairs, Kim Woo-Suk, resigned following allegations that he too had accepted payments from the company. President Kim issued an official apology for the loan scandal, and in March Lee Soo-Sung resigned as Prime Minister in a gesture of contrition. He was replaced by Goh Kun, hitherto President of Myongju University. The repercussions of the Hanbo affair widened further, implicating, among others, Kim Soo-Han, the Speaker of the National Assembly, and President Kim himself, whose 1992 election campaign was alleged to have been funded partially by the conglomerate. In June 1997 the former Chairman of Hanbo and several senior banking officials and politicians, including Kim Woo-Suk, were convicted on charges relating to the scandal.

In July 1997 Lee Hoi-Chang, former Prime Minister and Chairman of the NKP, was nominated as the ruling party's candidate for the presidential election, scheduled for December. Lee's candidacy was severely affected by various scandals surrounding the NKP and his family. In September Lee was elected President of the NKP, replacing Kim Young-Sam, who subsequently resigned from the party in order to ensure his neutrality in the forthcoming election. In October the NCNP and the ULD established an alliance, uniting behind the NCNP presidential nominee, Kim Dae-Jung. In November the NKP announced its merger with the DP, to form the Grand National Party (GNP).

However, internal party politics were overshadowed by the crisis experienced by the Korean economy in the latter half of 1997 and the revelation that many of the *chaebol* had amassed huge debts. Following the rejection by the legislature of the Government's financial liberalization measures, President Kim dismissed Kang Kyung-Shik, the Deputy Prime Minister and Minister of Finance and the Economy, in November, replacing him with Lim Chang-Yul, latterly Minister of Trade, Industry and Energy. An economic stabilization programme failed to curb the depreciation of the national currency, and the Government was forced to request the assistance of the IMF, a decision that was condemned by opposition politicians and the media as a 'national shame'. In December the IMF agreed to allocate substantial funds to prevent South Korea from defaulting on its repayments of external debt, subject to the implementation of a programme of extensive reforms.

The presidency of Kim Dae-Jung

The presidential election, held on 18 December 1997, was narrowly won by Kim Dae-Jung, representing the first peaceful transfer of power to an opposition politician in South Korea's history. Six other candidates contested the election. In a gesture to promote a sense of national unity, former Presidents Chun Doo-Hwan and Roh Tae-Woo were granted a presidential pardon and released from prison.

Legislation for financial reforms, to comply with the terms of the IMF agreement, was approved by the National Assembly in late December 1997. Discussions with South Korea's overseas creditors to renegotiate the terms of the country's debt repayments were successfully concluded at the end of January 1998. Compulsory reform of the *chaebol*, which had been widely criticized for contributing to the debt-repayment crisis through their extensive borrowing, and legislation to allow foreign investors to acquire majority shareholdings in South Korean companies, were among reform measures promulgated in early 1998.

Kim Dae-Jung was formally inaugurated as President in late February 1998. Despite resistance from the opposition, Kim Dae-Jung designated Kim Jong-Pil, the leader of the ULD, as acting Prime Minister, and a cabinet was formed in early March, with the ministries divided equally between the NCNP and the ULD. Various administrative reforms were implemented, including the abolition of the two posts of Deputy Prime Minister and a reduction in the powers of the Ministry of Finance and the Economy.

In May 1998 a two-day strike was called to demand that the Government fully honour its pledge to improve unemployment benefits and to reform the *chaebol*. As the economic recession deepened, labour unrest increased. Tens of thousands participated in strikes in July to protest against rising unemployment, the Government's privatization proposals and plans from Hyundai Motor and Daewoo Motor for mass redundancies.

In August 1998 the National Assembly formally confirmed Kim Jong-Pil as Prime Minister, following months of legislative inactivity, during which the GNP had refused to support his

nomination. However, the GNP boycotted parliamentary sessions throughout September and into October, further delaying the consideration of urgent economic reforms, in protest against a government anti-corruption campaign, which it claimed was partisan and aimed at dividing the opposition. In December the GNP claimed that the intelligence agency had been carrying out surveillance of opposition deputies and subsequently boycotted legislative proceedings. In early January 1999, as the boycott continued, the ruling parties unilaterally endorsed 130 bills without debate, including legislation on banking reform and a controversial fishing agreement with Japan. In mid-January, however, the ruling and opposition parties agreed that all issues relating to the anti-corruption investigations be referred to the National Assembly's steering committee. In May a major reorganization of the State Council was effected. However, in June corruption scandals led to the replacement of the newly appointed Ministers of Justice and of the Environment.

As the next legislative elections approached, in January 2000 Kim Jong-Pil resigned as Prime Minister to chair the ULD, nominating Park Tae-Joon, the founder of Pohang Iron and Steel Company, as his successor. Kim Dae-Jung reorganized the State Council, as a number of ministers resigned to concentrate on campaigning for parliamentary seats. Lee Hun-Jai, hitherto Chairman of the Financial Supervisory Commission, was appointed as Minister of Finance and the Economy. Kim Dae-Jung established a new party, the Millennium Democratic Party (MDP), to succeed the ruling NCNP, having reportedly failed in attempts to effect a merger with the ULD. In February the National Assembly approved revisions to the election law, which reduced the number of legislative seats from 299 to 273 (227 directly elected and 46 allocated by proportional representation), and reversed a ban on campaigning by civic groups against candidates. Lee Han-Dong, recently elected as President of the ULD, subsequently announced the party's withdrawal from the ruling coalition, claiming that the MDP had failed to fulfil its electoral pledges, although Prime Minister Park was to remain in the Government.

The elections to the National Assembly were held on 13 April 2000. The GNP, which won 133 of the 273 seats, retained its position as the largest party in the Assembly, but remained four seats short of a majority. The ruling MDP secured 115 seats, while the ULD suffered a serious reverse, taking only 17 seats (compared with 50 in the 1996 elections). Only two seats were won by the Democratic People's Party (DPP), which had been formed in February by defectors from the GNP who had failed to be nominated as parliamentary candidates by their former party. In mid-May Park resigned as Prime Minister, amid increasing controversy over allegations of tax evasion. The designation of Lee Han-Dong as Park's successor indicated a restoration of MDP-ULD co-operation. Amid criticism that reform of the *chaebol* was proceeding too slowly, President Kim Dae-Jung effected a major government reorganization in August, which primarily concerned the economic portfolios.

President Kim enjoyed increasing respect within the international community, in October 2000 being awarded the Nobel Peace Prize for his contribution to democracy and human rights (and particularly for his successful attempts at reconciliation with North Korea). However, his pursuit of reunification was criticized domestically by those who felt that, with its own economic problems, South Korea could ill afford assistance to North Korea.

During 2000 and early 2001 dissatisfaction with the Government manifested itself on numerous occasions in the form of industrial and agricultural unrest. In November 2000 farmers held a strike to demand that their debts be cancelled and that the Government intervene on their behalf at the World Trade Organization (WTO, see p. 444). Meanwhile, as the Daewoo Motor Company had been declared bankrupt, some 15,000 workers protested in November in Seoul against government-led corporate restructuring, which it was feared would result in large-scale retrenchment.

In January 2001 a minor reorganization of the State Council was effected, when changes included Jin Nyum's elevation to the post of Deputy Prime Minister for Finance and the Economy. In March there was a major reorganization of the State Council, following the resignation of the Minister of Foreign Affairs and Trade, Lee Joung-Binn, who had caused controversy by signing a joint statement with Russia criticizing the USA's planned 'national missile defence' system. Han Seung-Soo, a member of the DPP, replaced him. The former Minister of Culture, Park Jie-Won, who had resigned in September 2000 following allegations of corruption, was appointed chief presidential policy adviser. Park had organized the historic inter-Korean summit in June 2000.

In early April 2001 the minor opposition DPP joined the ruling MDP-led coalition, despite protests from within the MDP. Later in that month the MDP suffered a defeat in local by-elections, and by May Kim Dae-Jung's popularity had declined sharply, as voters grew disillusioned by his failure to implement political reforms. In August the Minister of Unification, Lim Dong-Won, came under heavy criticism from the opposition after delegates from several South Korean non-governmental organizations (NGOs) travelled to the North to mark the anniversary of Korean liberation from Japanese rule, on 15 August. In September Lim was forced to resign after the National Assembly approved a motion of no confidence in him, organized by the GNP and supported by the MDP's coalition partner, the ULD. The latter's actions effectively dissolved the ruling coalition, and President Kim appointed four new ministers. Lim was immediately appointed presidential adviser on reunification, national security and foreign affairs, reaffirming Kim's confidence in him.

In October 2001 the GNP won three by-elections, increasing its seats in the National Assembly to 136—just one short of a majority. The opposition victory created new rifts within the ruling MDP between younger reformers and party veterans, and President Kim resigned from the party presidency in November, ostensibly in order to administer state affairs without being involved in party disputes. He was succeeded, on an interim basis, by Han Kwang-Ok.

In late January 2002 President Kim again reorganized the State Council, dismissing the Minister of Unification, Hong Soon-Young (who had been appointed only in September 2001), and reallocating seven other posts, as well as the positions of six of the eight senior presidential secretaries and his chief of staff. Park Jie-Won returned as Kim's special aide for policy, emphasizing his close relationship with the President. Within days, the Minister of Foreign Affairs and Trade, Han Seung-Soo, was also dismissed, owing to the country's strained relations with the USA.

A power struggle within the opposition GNP resulted in the departure of the party's Vice-President, Park Geun-Hye (daughter of former President Park Chung-Hee). In May 2002 Park established a new party, the Korean Coalition for the Future (KCF), but the KCF merged with the GNP in November.

The GNP's eight vice-presidents all resigned on 24 March 2002 in order to 'renew the face of the party', and were succeeded by a collective leadership. In mid-April President Kim replaced the Deputy Prime Minister for Finance and the Economy, Jin Nyum, with Jeon Yun-Churl, hitherto the chief of staff to the President.

President Kim and six of his ministers resigned from the MDP in May 2002, in order to focus on state affairs during the final months of Kim's presidency. Kim had become increasingly embarrassed by corruption scandals involving his second and third sons, Kim Hong-Up and Kim Hong-Gul, respectively, and he publicly apologized for their behaviour. The scandals adversely affected the MDP's performance in local elections held in mid-June.

In July 2002 President Kim announced a cabinet reorganization, nominating Chang Sang, hitherto President of Ewha Woman's University, as the country's first female Prime Minister. At the same time, six ministers were replaced. However, at the end of the month the National Assembly rejected Chang's appointment on the grounds of dubious property dealings and the fact that her son had adopted US citizenship. In her place, President Kim nominated Chang Dae-Whan, a former newspaper proprietor, but he too was rejected by the National Assembly in late August on the grounds of questionable financial practices. A third nominee, Kim Suk-Soo, a former Supreme Court judge and previously Head of the National Election Commission, was finally accepted by the National Assembly in October, thus ending months of political paralysis.

The MDP suffered further setbacks in by-elections held in August 2002 when the GNP won 11 out of 13 seats contested, giving it an overall majority in the National Assembly. In September Chung Mong-Joon (the sixth son of Hyundai founder Chung Ju-Yung), who was President of the Korean Football Association, announced that he was standing for the country's presidency. Chung's popularity had risen sharply following South Korea's successful co-hosting of the 2002 football World Cup. In November Chung formally established his 'National Unity 21' party, receiving support from a broad political spectrum. However, later in that month Chung and Roh, who had

secured the presidential nomination of the MDP earlier in the year, agreed to present a joint candidate for the presidency, namely the latter, in order to prevent Lee Hoi-Chang's election as President in December. Under the terms of the Roh-Chung partnership, there was to be a constitutional amendment whereby the powers of the presidency would be reduced in favour of those of the Prime Minister. In October it emerged that President Kim and Chung Mong-Joon had arranged for a Hyundai subsidiary to transfer a substantial sum of money to North Korea via the (South Korean) state-owned Korea Development Bank prior to the historic inter-Korean summit of June 2000, effectively 'buying' the meeting.

The presidency of Roh Moo-Hyun

The presidential election, held on 19 December 2002, was narrowly won by Roh Moo-Hyun, who received 48.9% of the votes cast, against 46.6% for Lee Hoi-Chang, representing the GNP. The level of participation was estimated at 70.8%. Roh's victory, despite the late withdrawal of Chung Mong-Joon's support, was generally attributed to his uncompromising stance in favour of a foreign policy more independent from the USA, whereas Lee was widely seen as having very close relations with the US Government. The MDP accused the USA of supporting Lee in the election, citing a meeting between him and the US ambassador.

In January 2003 President-elect Roh began making various appointments. Goh Kun, hitherto the president of Transparency International Korea, an anti-corruption agency, and himself a former Prime Minister, was reappointed to that post, while Moon Hee-Sang, an MDP legislator, was appointed chief of staff, and concurrently Chairman of the Civil Service Commission. Roh was inaugurated on 25 February and promptly appointed a new cabinet. President Roh also reorganized the military and intelligence services, appointing Gen. Kim Jong-Hwan as Chairman of the Joint Chiefs of Staff and Ko Young-Koo, a human rights lawyer, as director of the National Intelligence Service (NIS). The latter appointment reflected Roh's determination to depoliticize the agency, which had been responsible for surveillance of political figures even after the transition to democracy. In March Roh appointed a special counsel to investigate the alleged transfer of funds by Hyundai to North Korea in connection with the 2000 presidential summit meeting (see below). In the longer term Roh aimed to address regional imbalances and the disparity between rich and poor, to reduce corruption in business and the economy, and to improve living standards and labour management.

In April 2003 the GNP won two out of three seats in by-elections to the National Assembly, raising its total representation to 153. However, the victory of a reformist ally of the MDP, Rhyu Si-Min, was welcomed by the Government as an indication of support for the reform process. Also in April, the National Assembly voted in favour of the dispatch of South Korean troops to support US military action in Iraq in a non-combat capacity. Despite his independent stance on relations with the USA, President Roh justified the decision in terms of strengthening Korean-US relations. Several hundred South Korean military medical and engineering personnel were sent to Iraq in May, despite widespread public opposition to the deployment.

In June 2003 two aides of former President Kim Dae-Jung, former Minister of Unification Lim Dong-Won and former Minister of Culture and Tourism Park Jie-Won, were charged in connection with illegal payments made through the Hyundai group to North Korea to arrange the 2000 presidential summit meeting (Lim received an 18-month prison sentence in September, and Park was sentenced to 12 years' imprisonment in December). Also implicated in the scandal was Hyundai heir Chung Mong-Hun, who committed suicide in August.

In September 2003 a faction of the MDP announced its intention to form a new party, owing to internal divisions over corruption and other issues. President Roh subsequently relinquished his membership of the MDP, although he did not commit himself to joining the new organization, which was named the Uri (meaning 'our') Party in October. A large number of MDP legislators, including MDP Chairman Chyung Dai-Chul, joined the Uri Party, thus leaving the MDP with only 62 seats in the National Assembly. The Uri Party was officially inaugurated in November under a temporary leadership (Chung Dong-Young was elected Uri Party Chairman in early 2004). Another development in September 2003, meanwhile, was the resignation of the Minister of Home Affairs, Kim Doo-Kwan, following an incident in which protesters had infiltrated a US base in Pocheon.

President Roh's declining popularity was further undermined in October 2003 by the investigation and subsequent arrest of his former aide Choi Do-Sul, who was accused of having received illegal funds from the SK Group, a major *chaebol*, following the 2002 presidential election. In an attempt to restore his popularity, Roh announced proposals for a referendum to be held on the issue of his presidency later in the year. However, the proposed referendum prompted further political instability, with Prime Minister Goh Kun and other government ministers offering their resignations (which were rejected by President Roh). Both the GNP and the MDP dismissed the referendum proposal as unconstitutional.

Official investigations into illegal campaign funding from leading *chaebol* during the 2002 presidential election, involving both the MDP and the GNP, were instigated in October 2003. Initially focusing on donations from the SK Group, the investigation widened in November, with forcible searches taking place at the offices of other *chaebol*, including Hyundai, LG Group and Samsung. At the end of November President Roh vetoed a bill, already approved by the National Assembly, which urged an independent investigation into the funding allegations. In December the National Assembly voted to rescind the veto, in the first reversal of a presidential decision since 1954. An independent investigator was subsequently appointed. In the same month President Roh announced that he would step down if the MDP were found by the investigation to have received one-10th of the illegal funding taken by the GNP. Also in December 2003, the GNP's Lee Hoi-Chang, Roh's rival in the 2002 election, publicly admitted that his party had accepted US $42m. in illegal donations.

In January 2004 the Minister of Foreign Affairs and Trade, Yoon Young-Kwan, relinquished his post, reportedly following a dispute related to President Roh's policy on independence from the USA over issues such as the North Korean nuclear weapons programme, but there was also a suggestion that Yoon Young-Kwan's departure was due to unrelated internal divisions. Yoon Young-Kwan was replaced by Ban Ki-Moon. There were further government changes in February, following the resignation of Kim Jin-Pyo, the Deputy Prime Minister for Finance and the Economy, in order to stand as a Uri Party candidate in the legislative elections scheduled for April. Kim was replaced as Deputy Prime Minister by Lee Hun-Jai. Also in February, the National Assembly approved the deployment of an additional 3,000 non-combat troops to Iraq (the deployment was later delayed owing to security concerns—see below).

Meanwhile, investigations into political corruption continued in early 2004, and both the former MDP Chairman, Chyung Dai-Chul (now of the Uri Party), and the former Secretary-General of the GNP, Kim Young-Iel, were arrested. In February there was also speculation that Park Geun-Hye had received undeclared funds from the GNP for the purposes of a merger with her KCF. In March it was reported that President Roh's MDP election campaign had received 12,500m. won in illicit funds, amounting to one-seventh of the 84,000m. allegedly received by the GNP and thus to more than the proportion of one-10th that Roh had previously stated would prompt his resignation. At the end of March it was confirmed that Roh's former aide Choi Do-Sul (see above) had received US $530,000 in illegal funding.

As the legislative elections of April 2004 approached, there were dramatic developments in mid-March when President Roh was impeached over the issue of his support for the pro-Government Uri Party, whereby he had allegedly violated electoral law. A total of 193 legislators, mostly from the GNP and Roh's former party, the MDP, voted in favour of the impeachment. There were vehement protests from supporters of President Roh in the National Assembly and members of the public following the vote, with opinion polls indicating that around 70% of the population did not support the impeachment. President Roh's position was to be reviewed by the Constitutional Court within six months, with Prime Minister Goh Kun becoming acting head of state for this period.

At the elections to the National Assembly on 15 April 2004, the Uri Party won a narrow majority in the legislature, securing 152 seats of the total of 299 in the newly expanded chamber (243 of which were determined by direct election and the remainder by proportional representation). The GNP, now under the leadership of Park Geun-Hye, secured 121 seats. Roh's former party, the MDP, won only nine seats. The success of the Uri Party was regarded as a victory for Roh and an expression of public disapproval of his impeachment. In May Roh was reinstated following the decision of the Constitutional Court to dismiss the case for

impeachment. He became a formal member of the Uri Party in the same month.

Following the reinstatement of President Roh, Prime Minister Goh Kun resigned from his post; Lee Hae-Chan, a former education minister, was approved by the National Assembly as Prime Minister in June 2004. Three new ministerial appointments were then made, including that of Chung Dong-Young as Minister of Unification. Also in June, the Government announced that the deployment of 3,000 South Korean troops to Iraq, originally approved in February (see above), would take place in August. Public opposition to this decision increased dramatically a few days later when a South Korean translator, Kim Sun-Il, who had been taken hostage in Iraq, was beheaded by his captors. In July the Minister of National Defence, Cho Young-Kil, resigned, taking responsibility for an incident in which a South Korean ship had fired warning shots at a North Korean vessel believed to be intruding in South Korean waters, with naval staff reportedly having failed to report radio communication with the North Korean ship. Cho was replaced by Yoon Kwang-Woong. Meanwhile, during mid-2004 there were various instances of labour unrest, including strikes by subway workers and by employees of a major oil company. In August President Roh announced that investigations were to be held into the past conduct of politicians during the period of Japanese rule and of dictatorial governments extending into the 1980s. The first senior politician to be adversely affected by these investigations was Shin Ki-Nam, who had replaced Chung Dong-Young as leader of the Uri Party in May 2004; he was forced to resign after it was found that his father had committed human rights abuses as a police officer during the period of Japanese colonization. Shin was replaced by Lee Bu-Young. In September controversy arose over the anti-communist national security law, which dated back to the country's pre-democratic era. Human rights groups, supported by President Roh, claimed that the law was outdated and subject to abuse. However, proposals to abolish the law were rejected by the Supreme Court. In November there were further instances of labour unrest in protest against government plans to reform labour legislation to prohibit strikes by public sector workers and to allow employers to hire staff on a temporary basis. In December the National Assembly approved a proposal for South Korean troops in Iraq to remain there until the end of 2005, despite continuing strong public opposition to the deployment.

A number of government changes took place in January 2005. In March the Deputy Prime Minister for Finance and the Economy, Lee Hun-Jai, resigned as a result of controversy over his wife's real estate investments. He was replaced by Han Duck-Soo, hitherto the Minister of Government Policy Co-ordination. Further government changes took place in June, when Roh appointed Chun Jung-Bae as Minister of Justice and Lee Jae-Yong as Minister of the Environment.

In January 2005 Lee Bu-Young resigned from the leadership of the Uri Party, citing his party's failure to realize its reform aims such as the abolition of the anti-communist national security law. Moon Hee-Sang was elected party leader in April. The Uri Party had lost its majority in the National Assembly in the previous month when the Supreme Court upheld the convictions of two party legislators for malpractice in the elections of April 2004, thereby depriving them of their seats and reducing the party's representation to 146. In all, six of the legislators elected in April 2004 had subsequently lost their seats as a result of malpractice convictions, temporarily reducing the National Assembly to 293 seats. At by-elections held in late April 2005 to fill these vacancies, the opposition GNP took five of the six contested seats, with the sixth being won by an independent candidate. In May it was announced that the MDP was changing its name to the Democratic Party (DP). Another round of by-elections was held in October to replace two legislators from the Uri Party and two from the GNP who had lost their seats, again owing to convictions for electoral malpractice. The GNP won all four contested seats, thereby further reducing the Uri Party's parliamentary representation to 144 and prompting the resignation of the party's senior leadership, including Chairman Moon. Chung Sye-Kyun was appointed acting Chairman pending a leadership election in February 2006. Former party Chairman Chung Dong-Young resigned as Minister of Unification in December 2005 in order to stand in the leadership election, as did Kim Geun-Tae, the Minister of Health and Welfare.

Consequently, in January 2006 President Roh effected a government reorganization. Notably, Rhyu Si-Min was appointed Minister of Health and Welfare, while Lee Jong-Seok became

Minister of Unification and acting Uri Party Chairman Chung Sye-Kyun was appointed Minister of Commerce, Industry and Energy. At the Uri Party's national convention in February, Chung Dong-Young was elected to the post of Chairman for a second time. A scandal developed in March with regard to the conduct of the Prime Minister, Lee Hae-Chan, after he chose to play golf rather than oversee the Government's reaction to the first day of a national strike. Furthermore, objections were raised to his choice of golfing partners, who reportedly included a businessman with a criminal record for the manipulation of share prices. Lee resigned in mid-March. Roh's nomination of Han Myeong-Sook as Lee's successor was approved by a vote in the National Assembly in mid-April, and she was thus appointed as the country's first female Prime Minister.

None the less, the appointment of a new Prime Minister failed to improve the fortunes of the Uri Party. (Conversely, the resignation of the Secretary-General of the GNP, Choi Yeon-Hee, following charges of sexual harassment, did little to boost the Uri Party's popularity.) Local elections held at the end of May 2006 resulted in victory for the GNP, which garnered 54.5% of the votes cast nation-wide, compared with just 21.2% received by the Uri Party. Significantly, of the 16 provincial governor and city mayoral positions, the Uri Party took only one, while the GNP secured 12, the DP two and an independent candidate the remaining one. In June, taking responsibility for the party's disastrous election performance, Chairman Chung Dong-Young resigned and was replaced by Kim Kun-Tae. By-elections held in July further emphasized the Uri Party's declining popularity: the GNP won three of the four seats contested, while the DP took the fourth.

Also in July 2006, President Roh effected a minor cabinet reorganization, appointing three new Deputy Prime Ministers: Kwon O-Kyu with responsibility for Finance and the Economy, Chang Byoung-Wan with responsibility for Planning and Budget, and Kim Shin-Il for Education and Human Resources Development. In the following month Kim Sung-Ho, hitherto deputy head of the Commission Against Corruption, was named as Minister of Justice, replacing Chun Jung-Bae.

The North Korean nuclear test on 9 October 2006 (see below) resulted in a further ministerial reorganization. Both the Minister of Unification, Lee Jong-Seok, and the Minister of National Defence, Yoon Kwang-Woong, resigned amid both domestic and international criticism of the South Korean Government's continuing policy of engagement with the North. The new Minister of Unification was Lee Jae-Joung, a former Uri Party legislator, while the Army Chief of Staff, Kim Jang-Soo, took the defence portfolio. Another new appointment was that of Song Min-Soon, who was nominated to the post of Minister of Foreign Affairs and Trade (a position vacated by Ban Ki-Moon, following his appointment as UN Secretary-General). Parliamentary by-elections and local elections held that month resulted in defeat for the Uri Party's candidates.

In addition to the issue of engagement with North Korea, public dissatisfaction with President Roh's handling of the economy also increased; house prices had risen rapidly and the education system had undergone a controversial restructuring. Many South Koreans were also deeply suspicious of the Government's plans to sign a free trade agreement (FTA) with the USA, and in November 2006 thousands took to the streets to protest against the proposed deal, leading to violent clashes with the police (see Relations with the USA).

In January 2007 the Uri Party formally announced that it would disband and establish a new party. Initial reports suggested that the party would seek an alliance with the DP (defectors from which had originally formed the Uri Party in 2003), and that a number of Uri Party legislators had already switched their party allegiance to the DP. However, in February 2007, before these plans could be implemented, 23 legislators announced their defection from the Uri Party, joining six others who had resigned in the previous fortnight. Following this mass defection, the GNP held 127 seats and the Uri Party 110 in the National Assembly. President Roh finally announced his departure from the Uri Party, in the hope of reversing its decline in popularity. This decision forced the President to engage more deeply with the GNP and other parties; without their support, the Roh administration would be unable to secure the approval of important legislation.

In March 2007, after only 10 months in office, Prime Minister Han Myeong-Sook resigned and was succeeded by Han Duck-Soo, who had been special adviser to the President on free trade affairs since being replaced as Deputy Prime Minister for Finance and the Economy in July 2006. Further government changes followed in April 2007.

The GNP suffered a reverse in by-elections held in late April 2007, securing only one of the three seats contested. It was defeated by the recently formed People First Party and the DP in the other two constituencies, where the Uri Party had opted not to field candidates, instead supporting the minor opposition parties, with which it hoped to form a 'grand alliance' in advance of the forthcoming presidential and legislative elections. Voter participation in the by-elections was only 27.7%. Moreover, the GNP lost five of six mayoral and gubernatorial posts being contested concurrently. The poor performance of the GNP, which some observers attributed to bribery allegations connected with the nomination of candidates, prompted the resignation of several senior officials from the party's leadership, although its Chairman, Kang Jae-Seop, remained in his post. The party was also damaged by the extreme antagonism between its two rival presidential contenders for the election due to be held in December: Park Geun-Hye, the former GNP Chairwoman, thought to be popular among conservative voters, and Lee Myung-Bak, the former mayor of Seoul and Chief Executive of Hyundai Engineering and Construction Company. The GNP elected Lee as its presidential candidate by a narrow margin in August, despite his reputation haveing been undermined by allegations that he had been involved in fraudulent business transactions.

Meanwhile, the disintegration of the Uri Party continued, with a series of further defections in June and July 2007, including that of former Chairman Chung Dong-Young, which left the party with only 58 seats in the National Assembly. In early August Chung and 79 other former legislators of the Uri Party joined with five defectors from the DP to form the United New Democratic Party (UNDP). Later that month the Uri Party finally disbanded and was absorbed into the UNDP, thus making the new party the largest in the National Assembly, with 143 seats.

In early August 2007 Roh announced a minor government reorganization, in which Chung Soung-Jin, hitherto Chairman of the Commission Against Corruption, was allocated the justice portfolio, replacing Kim Sung-Ho, who had resigned following disagreements with the President. Also appointed to the State Council were Im Sang-Gyu as Minister of Agriculture and Forestry and Yoo Young-Hwan as Minister of Information and Communication.

Chung Dong-Young was elected as the UNDP's presidential candidate in October 2007. In early November, in a development that threatened to split the conservative vote, former Prime Minister Lee Hoi-Chang unexpectedly announced that he was leaving the GNP to stand as an independent candidate, in a third attempt to secure the country's presidency.

A major corruption scandal at Samsung arose in late October 2007, when the former head of its legal department, Kim Yong-Chul, claimed that senior executives at the *chaebol* had regularly bribed politicians, government officials and prosecutors using a 'slush fund' totalling 200,000m. won. In late November the National Assembly approved legislation authorizing an independent investigation into Kim's allegations, which Samsung vigorously denied. Also to be examined were claims that the conglomerate had made improper payments to candidates in the 2002 presidential election. (The investigation commenced in January 2008. In April, having been charged with tax evasion and breach of trust, the Chairman of Samsung, Lee Kun-Hee, resigned, and in July he was convicted on the former charge and given a three-year suspended prison sentence. He was pardoned by President Lee Myung-Bak in December 2009.) Meanwhile, the head of the National Tax Service and two of Roh's former presidential aides were also arrested on various corruption charges. These developments proved embarrassing for Roh, who had pledged to reduce corruption.

Corruption allegations against Lee Myung-Bak gained renewed momentum in mid-November 2007, when one of his former business partners was extradited from the USA to answer charges of embezzlement and money-laundering. In early December prosecutors concluded that there was no evidence to link Lee to the financial crimes with which his former associate had been charged, but later in that month, only two days before the presidential election, the National Assembly voted to appoint an independent counsel to reinvestigate fraud claims against Lee, following the emergence of a video that purported to show the presidential candidate stating that he had established the investment company at the centre of the allegations. Lee denied any involvement in the scandal.

The presidency of Lee Myung-Bak

At the presidential election, which was held on 19 December 2007, the GNP's Lee Myung-Bak achieved a decisive victory, securing 48.7% of the votes cast, despite the allegations that had overshadowed the electoral campaign. Of the nine other candidates, his nearest rivals were Chung Dong-Young, with 26.1% of the votes, and Lee Hoi-Chang, with 15.1%. However, the level of voter participation, at 62.9%, was relatively low. Lee's win (by the largest margin since the reintroduction of direct elections in 1987) was attributed to a combination of the electorate's dissatisfaction with the achievements of the incumbent centre-left administration and its attraction to the President-elect's focus on the economy. During the election campaign he had pledged to improve the country's economic prospects with his so-called '7.4.7' vision: achieving annual growth of 7%, raising average annual income per caput to US $40,000 and making South Korea one of the world's seven largest economies by 2017. More controversially, Lee also proposed the construction of a 540-km inland canal, traversing the country from Seoul in the northwest to the port city of Busan in the south-east, at a cost of 14,000,000m. won, with the aim of easing road and rail congestion, creating employment and improving growth.

Lee Myung-Bak was inaugurated as President on 25 February 2008. Four days previously he had been exonerated by the independent counsel re-examining the accusations of financial impropriety against him. The National Assembly subsequently approved Lee's nomination of Han Seung-Soo for the post of Prime Minister. An experienced politician and diplomat, Han had previously held various cabinet positions and was currently serving as a UN special envoy on climate change. The other members of the State Council were also designated in February, although several nominees, including Lee's choice to head the Ministry of Unification, Nam Joo-Hong, withdrew following criticism of misconduct in property dealings, of tax evasion and of malpractice in other areas. Among the nominees subsequently confirmed were Kang Man-Soo as Minister of Strategy and Finance; Kim Ha-Joong as Minister of Unification; and Yu Myung-Hwan as Minister of Foreign Affairs and Trade. The position of Deputy Prime Minister was terminated. Meanwhile, there was some realignment of political parties in early 2008 in advance of the forthcoming legislative elections. Lee Hoi-Chang created the Liberty Forward Party, which later absorbed the People First Party, and the UNDP and the DP merged to form the United Democratic Party (UDP).

At the legislative elections conducted on 9 April 2008, the GNP secured a narrow majority, winning 153 of the 299 seats in the National Assembly. The UDP won 81 seats and the Liberty Forward Party 18 seats, while the pro-Park coalition (comprising former GNP members allied to the party's defeated presidential nominee, Park Geun-Hye) took 14 seats. A total of 245 candidates were directly elected, with the remaining seats being determined by proportional representation. The rate of participation by voters, at some 46%, was the lowest ever recorded at a general election. The GNP's lack of a strong majority was expected to curtail the new President's programme of economic reform, while the presence of more than 50 supporters of Park Geun-Hye within the GNP contingent, as well as the pro-Park coalition and independents, was another possible constraint on Lee's ambitions.

One of President Lee's first challenges emerged in April 2008, when he agreed to rescind the country's ban on beef imports from the USA, reportedly to improve bilateral relations and expedite the FTA process. Amid widespread public fear of bovine spongiform encephalopathy (BSE) contamination, daily demonstrations were attended by thousands of South Koreans; although initially peaceful, the protests subsequently escalated into violence, prompting the Government to offer concessions, such as a restriction on imports of cattle older than 30 months. As the protests continued, the issue became symbolic of wider public dissatisfaction with major government initiatives, including Lee's plans for the transnational canal system (which was subsequently reported to have been abandoned) and the privatization of several state-owned businesses. The GNP's defeat at local elections in early June, when it secured only 10 of 52 positions (in comparison with the 22 won by the UDP, now known as the Democratic Party—DP), was a further sign of this decline in popularity. With the BSE affair rapidly becoming a national crisis, the members of the State Council offered to resign. In July President Lee responded by effecting a cabinet reorganization, replacing the Minister of Food, Agriculture, Forestry and Fisheries, Chung Woon-Chun, with Jang Tae-Pyoung.

President Lee implemented another cabinet reorganization in January 2009, appointing Hyun In-Taek to succeed Kim Ha-Joong as Minister of Unification and dismissing Kang Man-Soo as Minister of Strategy and Finance, to be replaced by Yoon Jeung-Hyun. In the same month Won Sei-Hoon, the Minister of Public Administration and Security, was transferred to a senior intelligence position; Lee Dal-Gon was nominated to replace him. By-elections for five seats in the National Assembly were held in April. In a rebuke to the ruling GNP, voters elected three independents (including former UNDP presidential candidate Chung Dong-Young) and one DP member to the Assembly, while the New Progressive Party, which had been founded in the previous year by a breakaway faction of the Democratic Labour Party, secured its first seat in the legislature.

Former President Roh Moo-Hyun became embroiled in a corruption scandal in April 2009, when he was questioned by prosecutors in connection with allegations that he and members of his family had accepted US $6m. in bribes from a businessman, Park Yeon-Cha. Roh denied any knowledge of the payments, and his supporters claimed that the investigation was motivated by political factors. With the former President's indictment believed to be imminent and his reputation severely damaged (combating corruption had been a central tenet of his presidency), Roh committed suicide on 23 May. Meanwhile, in August two former senior aides to Roh were sentenced to prison terms after being convicted on bribery charges. In December former Prime Minister Han Myeong-Sook, appointed by Roh in 2006, was arrested on charges of accepting bribes. She was acquitted in April 2010, describing her trial as having been politically motivated. She was indicted in July on further charges of accepting bribes, but was acquitted of the separate offences in October 2011 and January 2012.

In July 2009, despite a DP-led opposition boycott and amid scuffles in the National Assembly, the GNP deputies in the legislature approved controversial reforms permitting newspaper companies to own stakes in broadcasting concerns. The Government argued that this was vital to the sector's competitiveness, but the opposition asserted that the reforms would lead to a conservative monopoly of the broadcasting industry. (The Constitutional Court upheld the approval of the reforms in October, despite acknowledging that procedural violations, highlighted by the DP, had occurred during the parliamentary vote.)

President Lee announced a major reorganization of the State Council in September 2009, which included the appointment of a new Prime Minister, Chung Un-Chan, hitherto president of Seoul National University and a vocal critic of Lee's economic policies. Gen. Kim Tae-Young, the former Chairman of the Joint Chiefs of Staff, was appointed as Minister of National Defence, Lee Kwi-Nam was allocated the justice portfolio, and Joo Ho-Young became the Minister for Special Affairs, a new position created to enhance cross-party co-operation. In October by-elections were held for five seats in the National Assembly: the DP won three seats and the GNP secured the remaining two. In the same month Chung Mong-Joon assumed the chairmanship of the GNP, replacing Park Hee-Tae, who had resigned in order to contest a seat at the by-elections.

The 2010 budget was approved unilaterally in December 2009, following another boycott of the National Assembly by the DP. Controversially, the budget incorporated significant funding for the President's plan to rehabilitate South Korea's four main rivers. Critics had expressed concern about the cost of the scheme and potential environmental damage, while many believed that Lee's ultimate objective was to revive his ambitious scheme for a national canal network.

Resignation of Chun Un-Chan as Prime Minister and appointment of Kim Hwang-Sik

The GNP performed poorly in local elections held on 2 June 2010, securing only six of the 16 contested mayoral and gubernatorial posts, compared with seven for the DP, despite predictions that the GNP would benefit from President Lee's firm attitude to North Korea following the sinking of the *Cheonan* warship in March (see North Korea). Chung Mong-Joon resigned as GNP Chairman along with the party's entire Supreme Council in response to the electoral defeats; Ahn Sang-Soo was elected to replace Chung in July. Meanwhile, Lee announced a review of his policy priorities and a reorganization of his administrative office, including the appointment of Yim Tae-Hee, hitherto Minister of Labour, as presidential chief of staff.

At eight by-elections to the National Assembly held in July 2010, the GNP won five seats in comparison with the DP's three.

None the less, on the following day Chun Un-Chan announced his resignation as Prime Minister, claiming responsibility for a series of reverses suffered by the Government during his 10 months in office: in particular, he cited his failure to secure legislative approval for the Government's revised development plan for Sejong City, a new town under construction in the Chungcheong region. President Roh Moo-Hyun had originally proposed establishing the city as a new capital, before modifying the plan to entail transferring a limited number of ministries and government agencies from Seoul; the Lee administration had proposed abandoning Roh's plan and instead turning Sejong City into an industrial and scientific centre. Following the National Assembly's defeat of Lee's proposal in June, in mid-July the Government announced that 35 state agencies would relocate to Sejong by the end of 2014.

In early August 2010 President Lee nominated Kim Tae-Ho for the premiership, also naming seven other ministers (although the principal portfolios remained unchanged) and other senior officials. However, during August Kim and several of the other nominees were subjected to fierce criticism from opposition legislators at their confirmation hearings before the National Assembly, amid allegations of impropriety. At the end of the month Kim resigned as Prime Minister-designate, having failed to refute claims that he had accepted bribes from Park Yeon-Cha while Governor of South Gyeongsang province in 2004–09; Kim was one of several leading politicians, in addition to former President Roh, who had been implicated in the corruption scandal surrounding Park. The Ministers-designate of Culture, Sports and Tourism and of Knowledge Economy also resigned after admitting unethical conduct. In mid-September Lee nominated Kim Hwang-Sik, the Chairman of the Board of Audit and Inspection, for the post of Prime Minister, and his nomination was finally confirmed by the National Assembly in early October. Shortly afterwards Kim Sung-Hwan was appointed Minister of Foreign Affairs and Trade, filling a vacancy left in early September by Yu Myung-Hwan: Yu had tendered his resignation after being accused of nepotism following the revelation that his daughter had secured a mid-level job at his ministry, having previously been rejected for the post.

Sohn Hak-Kyu was elected Chairman of the DP at the party's convention in October 2010, defeating Chung Dong-Young, the former UNDP presidential candidate, and Chung Sye-Kyun, the outgoing Chairman. Chung Sye-Kyun had submitted his resignation following the DP's poor performance at the by-elections in July.

The Government was severely criticized by both opposition and GNP politicians for its hesitant response to the fatal shelling of Yeonpyeong island by North Korean artillery in November 2010 (see North Korea), and for the armed forces' apparent lack of preparedness for the attack. The incident prompted the resignation as Minister of National Defence of Kim Tae-Young, whose earlier offer to resign in March over the sinking of the *Cheonan* had been refused by the President; he was replaced by Kim Kwan-Jin, a former Chairman of the Joint Chiefs of Staff. At the end of December President Lee finally nominated Choung Byoung-Gug as Minister of Culture, Sports and Tourism, and Choi Joong-Kyung as Minister of Knowledge Economy.

At by-elections in April 2011 the GNP secured only one of the three contested National Assembly seats. In May Lee replaced five ministers. Bahk Jae-Wan, hitherto Minister of Employment and Labour, became Minister of Strategy and Finance, while his previous position was assumed by Lee Chae-Pil. Other appointments were those of Kwon Do-Yup as Minister of Land, Transport and Maritime Affairs, Suh Kyu-Yong as Minister of Food, Agriculture, Forestry and Fisheries, and Yoo Young-Sook as Minister of Environment. In August further ministerial changes included the replacement of Hyun In-Taek as Minister of Unification by Yu Woo-Ik, formerly (until May) the ambassador to China and regarded as likely to favour a less confrontational attitude to North Korea than his predecessor. New appointments were also made to the Ministries of Justice (Kwon Jae-Jin), Culture, Sports and Tourism (Choe Kwang-Sik), Health and Welfare (Rim Che-Min) and Gender Equality and Family (Kim Kum-Lae), and in October a new Minister of Knowledge Economy, Hong Suk-Woo, was appointed. Public concern over stagnating property prices and high levels of household indebtedness was exacerbated during 2011 by reports that officials of the financial supervisory service had accepted bribes in return for not reporting financial problems (particularly loss-making property developments) and corruption in a number of savings banks, and by September the Government had suspended the oper-

ations of 16 of the country's savings banks, including the largest, the Busan Savings Bank. In November the Government encountered vociferous opposition within the legislature, as well as public protests outside, when it finally succeeded in gaining ratification of the long-delayed FTA with the USA (see Relations with the USA).

Party reorganizations and the 2012 elections

Both the principal political parties undertook major changes during 2011, in anticipation of the general election to be held in April 2012 and the presidential election due to take place in December 2012. The GNP Chairman, Ahn Sang-Soo, and other members of the ruling party's leadership resigned after the by-election defeats in April 2011, and a new Chairman, Hong Joon-Pyo, and Supreme Council were elected in July. In October an independent candidate, Park Won-Soon, was successful at the election to the important post of mayor of Seoul, unexpectedly defeating the GNP candidate. The GNP's popularity was further eroded by allegations that its supporters had been responsible for a 'cyber-attack' on the website of the National Election Commission on the day of the Seoul mayoral election. In December Hong Joon-Pyo responded to critics within the GNP by resigning as Chairman, and Park Geun-Hye assumed the chair in an 'emergency' capacity, undertaking to introduce reforms. In February 2012 the Speaker of the National Assembly, Park Hee-Tae, resigned after being accused of offering bribes while contesting the GNP leadership election in 2008; he was later convicted of the offence. Also in February 2012 the GNP absorbed the small Future Hope Alliance, and later in the month the party's 'emergency committee' announced that the party was to be 'reborn' as the Saenuri Party (variously translated as the New Frontier or New World Party). The party then embarked on a review of nominations for the forthcoming general election, eliminating those incumbent candidates who were perceived, according to opinion polls, to be the least likely to succeed: most of those rejected were adherents of President Lee Myung-Bak. Some party members whose candidacy had been rejected were reported to have formed a new conservative party, the Korea Vision Party, led by Park Se-Il.

In December 2011, meanwhile, the main opposition party, the DP, merged with the small Civil Unity Party, with the support of the FKTU, to form the Democratic United Party (DUP); Sohn Hak-Kyu, who had supported the merger, then retired from the party chair. In January 2012 (following her acquittal earlier in that month, and in the previous October, on separate charges of accepting bribes) the former Prime Minister, Han Myeong-Sook, was elected as Chairwoman of the DUP. In the same month she reached an agreement with Park Geun-Hye on adopting a revision of electoral rules to allow an 'open primary system', whereby members of the public would be allowed to nominate candidates for election. In February Park Won-Soon, the mayor of Seoul (elected in the previous October as an independent candidate) announced that he was joining the DUP. In March the Unified Progressive Party (UPP, which had been formed in the previous December by a merger of three smaller groupings, the People's Participation Party, the Democratic Labour Party and a faction of the New Progressive Party) agreed to form an electoral alliance with the DUP and the remainder of the New Progressive Party: joint candidates for the general election were nominated by 'primary' voting in over 70 constituencies. However, the co-Chairwoman of the UPP, Lee Jung-Hee, was obliged to withdraw her nomination as a constituency candidate after allegations that her supporters had falsified replies in a telephone survey.

A general election to the National Assembly (enlarged to 300 seats, of which 246 were for directly elected candidates and 54 for candidates chosen by proportional representation) was held on 11 April 2012. Despite losing control of 13 seats, the Saenuri Party retained a narrow majority, winning 152 seats, while the DUP won 127, the UPP 13, the Liberty Forward Party (which subsequently changed its name to the Advancement and Unification Party) five and independents the remaining three; 54.3% of the electorate participated. The ruling party's victory was regarded as advancing the prospects of the Saenuri Party's presumed candidate, Park Geun-Hye, in the presidential election due to be held in December. Han Myeong-Sook subsequently announced her resignation from the chair of the DUP, taking responsibility for the party's defeat. She was replaced in an acting capacity by Moon Sung-Keun, who had been the runner-up in the leadership election in January. In June Lee Hae-Chan, Prime Minister during 2004–06, was elected DUP Chairman.

During 2012 the problem of corruption in public life remained conspicuous. In July President Lee made an apology to the nation when his brother, Lee Sang-Deuk, a former member of the National Assembly, was implicated in the savings banks scandal (see above): Lee Sang-Deuk had been arrested for having allegedly received bribes from officials of two savings banks (and was convicted of the offence in January 2013). In August 2012 the Chairman of Hanwha, one of South Korea's largest *chaebol*, was convicted of embezzlement. In November the Chief Prosecutor, Han Sang-Dae, resigned after the revelation of corruption scandals within the prosecution service, although not implicated himself. In January 2013, shortly before the end of his term of office, President Lee controversially issued a pardon for more than 50 associates who had been convicted of corruption or malpractice, including the former Speaker of the National Assembly, Park Tee-Hae; Park Geun-Hye strongly criticized the pardon. In February the Chairman of another major *chaebol*, SK Group, was sentenced to a prison term for misuse of funds.

In August 2012, meanwhile, Park Geun-Hye was officially nominated as the Saenuri Party's presidential candidate, while in September the DUP selected as its candidate Moon Jae-In, who had been chief of staff of former President Roh Moo-Hyun. Moon had been imprisoned during the 1970s for protesting against the actions of Park Geun-Hye's father, President Park Chung-Hee. Later in September 2012 Park Geun-Hye apologized for human rights violations that had taken place under her father's rule. Prominent among several independent presidential candidates was Ahn Cheol-Soo, a wealthy businessman and academic who had urged the reform of the political system. In November the Chairman of the DUP, Lee Hae-Chan, and other senior party members resigned, apparently in response to Ahn's criticisms. Later in November Ahn relinquished his candidacy so as not to split the liberal vote, encouraging his supporters to vote for Moon. The UPP candidate, Lee Jung-Hee, also stood down in favour of Moon. The two remaining principal candidates both undertook, if elected, to increase spending on social welfare, to make an effort to reduce the gap between rich and poor, and to curtail the influence of the *chaebol*. They also both declared that they would seek more cordial relations with North Korea, although Park stated that this would depend on progress towards North Korea's renunciation of its nuclear weapons programme, while Moon favoured an unconditional improvement in relations. At the election on 19 December, Park Geun-Hye won 51.6% of the votes, while Moon Jae-In won 48.0%; voter participation was 75.8%. In January 2013 the DUP chose Moon Hee-Sang, a long-standing member of the National Assembly, as its 'emergency' Chairman.

Recent developments: presidency of Park Geun-Hye

Park Geun-Hye, South Korea's first female head of state, took office as President on 25 February 2013. She promised to undertake a 'trust-building process' with North Korea, but almost immediately had to confront an extreme intensification in hostile utterances from the North, denouncing the routine military exercises conducted by South Korea jointly with the USA in March and April (see North Korea). Park also encountered difficulties in her attempts to form a new administration and reorganize some government departments. She was accused of failing to observe adequate vetting procedures when her original nominees as Prime Minister, Kim Yong-Joon, and as Minister of National Defence, Kim Byung-Kwan, were obliged to decline their nominations following various allegations of past misconduct (as were several other nominees for less senior posts). Park then appointed Chung Hong-Won, a prominent lawyer, as Prime Minister and retained the incumbent Minister of National Defence, Kim Kwan-Jin, in his post. The new Minister of Foreign Affairs was Yun Byung-Se, a former diplomat; responsibility for trade, formerly assigned to this ministry, was transferred to a new Ministry of Trade, Industry and Energy (replacing the Ministry of Knowledge Economy), headed by Yoon Sang-Jick, hitherto Vice-Minister for Industry and Technology. The new Minister of Strategy and Finance, Hyun Oh-Seok, the erstwhile President of the Korea Development Institute, was given the additional post of Deputy Prime Minister. A new Ministry of Science, ICT (information and communications technology) and Future Planning was created, for which Choi Mun-Kee was allocated ministerial responsibility. A ministry in charge of maritime affairs, the Ministry of Oceans and Fisheries, was re-established, headed by Yoon Jin-Sook, who was appointed in mid-April, despite strong objections from the DUP, which expressed concern that the new minister's earlier performance at her parliamentary confirmation hearing had been poor. A new Office of National Security, headed by Kim Jang-Soo (a former Minister of National Defence), was established within the presi-

dential office. In April Park's Government proposed a supplementary budget, which included additional defence expenditure, amid continued heightened tensions with North Korea, and announced other measures to stimulate the economy, to encourage exports and to create some 2.3m. jobs over the next five years. In May the DUP elected Kim Han-Gil as its new Chairman and voted to revert to its previous name, the Democratic Party.

Relations with North Korea

For details of relations between North and South Korea, see the Democratic People's Republic of Korea (North Korea), Inter-Korean Relations.

Foreign Affairs

The foreign policy of the Republic of Korea (South Korea) has been dominated by its relations with the major powers of Japan, China, the USA and Russia, owing to its geographical position, and by the quest for stability on the Korean peninsula.

Relations with Japan

Relations between South Korea and Japan, which had long been strained, were eased by President Chun's official visit to Japan in September 1984 (the first such visit undertaken by a South Korean head of state), during which Emperor Hirohito and Prime Minister Yasuhiro Nakasone formally expressed their regret for Japanese aggression in Korea in the past. In May 1990, during President Roh's visit to Japan, Emperor Akihito offered official apologies for the cruelties of Japanese colonial rule in Korea. In January 1992 the Japanese Prime Minister, Kiichi Miyazawa, visited South Korea, where he publicly expressed regret at the enslavement during the Second World War of an estimated 100,000 Korean women, who were used by the Japanese military for sexual purposes ('comfort women'). In late 1994 the Japanese Government announced that it would not make compensation payments directly to individuals, but would finance a programme to construct vocational training centres for the women concerned. In August 1995, on the 50th anniversary of the end of the Second World War, the Japanese Prime Minister, Tomiichi Murayama, issued a statement expressing 'deep reflection and sincere apologies' for Japanese colonial aggression. At the end of a summit meeting with President Kim Young-Sam in June 1996, the Japanese Prime Minister, Ryutaro Hashimoto, issued a public apology to the 'comfort women'. However, the South Korean Government regarded Japanese proposals to provide compensation through private sources of funding, rather than government money, as tantamount to a denial of moral responsibility. The conclusion of new defence co-operation guidelines between Japan and the USA in September 1997 was of concern for South Korea, which feared an expansion in Japanese military capability. Negotiations for a new fisheries agreement, under way since mid-1996, were unilaterally terminated by Japan in January 1998, following the continuing disagreement regarding sovereignty of the Dokdo islands (or Takeshima in Japanese, located between South Korea and Japan in the East Sea—also known as the Sea of Japan), to which both countries laid claim. In April 1998 the South Korean Government announced its intention to make payments itself to surviving 'comfort women'.

In October 1998, during a visit to Tokyo, Japan, by President Kim Dae-Jung, a joint declaration was signed, in which Japan apologized for the suffering inflicted on the Korean people during Japanese colonial rule. In addition, South Korea agreed to revoke a ban on the import of various Japanese goods, while Japan promised financial aid to South Korea in support of its efforts to stimulate economic recovery. In November the two countries concluded negotiations on the renewal of their bilateral fisheries agreement, which came into effect in January 1999, despite the objections of the main South Korean opposition party, which protested that it failed positively to affirm South Korea's claim to sovereignty over the disputed Dokdo/Takeshima islands. In early 1999 protests by South Korean fishermen, who were apparently suffering heavy losses because of the revised agreement, forced the resignation of the Minister of Maritime Affairs and Fisheries. In March, during a visit to South Korea by the Japanese Prime Minister, Keizo Obuchi, both countries agreed to strengthen bilateral economic relations, and Japan pledged a further US $1,000m. in aid to South Korea.

During 2001 relations with Japan deteriorated owing to the publication in February of new Japanese history textbooks, which sought to justify Japan's aggression towards its Asian neighbours during the Second World War, and neglected to mention the forced prostitution of Asian (mainly Korean) 'comfort women' by the Japanese army and the forcible transfer and use of Koreans as slave labour in Japan. Large-scale protests were held in Seoul, and bilateral military co-operation was suspended. In August South Korean opinion was further outraged by the visit of the Japanese Prime Minister, Junichiro Koizumi, to the controversial Yasukuni Shrine in Tokyo honouring Japan's war dead. Amid popular protests, Koizumi visited Seoul in October and delivered an apology for the suffering of Koreans under Japanese rule. He was forced to cancel a visit to the National Assembly owing to the hostile sentiment of some legislators.

Along with China and North Korea, South Korea condemned Koizumi's visits to the Yasukuni Shrine in April 2002 and January 2003. However, in March 2002 Koizumi and Kim Dae-Jung agreed to begin discussions on a possible bilateral FTA, and mutual hostility between the two countries was superseded by the need for co-operation in engaging with the North. In June 2003 Roh made his first state visit to Japan and had discussions with Koizumi on the issue of North Korea's nuclear weapons programme. Although both leaders opposed any development of nuclear weapons in North Korea, Roh urged dialogue with that country, whereas Koizumi favoured stricter measures. Japan and South Korea continued efforts towards reaching an FTA from 2003, but negotiations faltered in November 2004, reportedly over disagreement regarding the liberalization of trade in agricultural and fisheries products.

In March 2005 the local legislature of Japan's Shimane Prefecture, which claimed the Dokdo/Takeshima islands as part of its territory, voted to establish a 'Takeshima Day'. In response, the South Korean Minister of Foreign Affairs and Trade, Ban Ki-Moon, cancelled a scheduled visit to Japan, while protests were held outside the Japanese embassy in Seoul. Further public demonstrations took place in April in reaction to the approval for use in Japanese schools of history textbooks, including one first published in 2001 (see above), which were regarded by Koreans (and Chinese) as failing to address the true nature of Japanese wartime conduct. Another visit to the Yasukuni Shrine by Prime Minister Koizumi in October 2005 provoked condemnation from South Korea, and prompted President Roh to cancel a scheduled visit to Japan in December. Throughout 2006 South Korea's continued requests for the shrine visits to end were disregarded by the Japanese Government. South Korea antagonized the Japanese authorities in July when it conducted a survey of the waters around the Dokdo/Takeshima islands, against the express wishes of Japan (which, in turn, had announced plans to conduct a similar survey in April, prompting the South Korean Government to declare a five-year plan to develop facilities on the islands and to explore the area's marine and mineral resources).

Relations deteriorated further in early 2007 after the new Japanese Prime Minister, Shinzo Abe, made comments inferring that there was no direct evidence to prove that South Korean 'comfort women' had been coerced into sexual servitude; however, Abe did not emulate his predecessor with regard to visits to the Yasukuni Shrine. Yasuo Fukuda, who succeeded Abe as Japanese Prime Minister in September, identified strengthening relations with South Korea as a priority, notably pledging not to visit the controversial Yasukuni Shrine. Fukuda attended Lee Myung-Bak's inauguration as South Korean President in February 2008, following which the two leaders agreed to undertake regular reciprocal visits and to promote the resumption of negotiations on the establishment of an FTA (which had not progressed since late 2004). In July 2008, however, the dispute over the Dokdo/Takeshima islands re-emerged when the Japanese Government announced that the islands would be described as Japanese in teachers' materials, and a defence document reiterating Japan's stance placed further strain on bilateral relations in September.

During a visit to South Korea in February 2010 the Japanese Minister for Foreign Affairs, Katsuya Okada, apologized for the colonial occupation of Korea by Japan during the first half of the 20th century. In August, in a statement made in advance of the centenary of Japan's annexation of the peninsula, the new Japanese Prime Minister, Naoto Kan, expressed 'deep remorse' for the period of colonial rule and announced the repatriation to South Korea of a number of cultural artefacts seized during the occupation. However, new textbooks and an official foreign affairs report published earlier in the year, and the Japanese Government's annual defence review published in September, once again reiterated Japan's claim to the Dokdo/Takeshima islands, prompting protests by South Korea.

In March 2012 South Korea, Japan and China completed negotiations on the terms of a trilateral agreement on investment, which was signed in May in Beijing, China. At this meeting, the three countries announced that they had reached agreement to begin negotiations on a trilateral FTA. In June, following protests in South Korea, the Government postponed the signing of an agreement with Japan on the sharing of military intelligence. In August Japan strongly criticized a visit by President Lee to the Dokdo/Takeshima islands (the first such visit by a South Korean head of state). In the same month the South Korean Government declined a Japanese offer to submit the dispute over the islands to the International Court of Justice in The Hague, Netherlands. Renewed visits to the Yasukuni Shrine during October by Japanese politicians, including the leader of the main opposition party, Shinzo Abe, again offended South Korean opinion, and there was apprehension that tension would be increased further after Abe became Prime Minister (for the second time) in December. None the less, the first session of negotiations on the trilateral FTA took place in March 2013. In the following month, however, South Korea's Minister of Foreign Affairs cancelled a visit to Tokyo, after senior Japanese government ministers, including Deputy Prime Minister Taro Aso, visited the Yasukuni Shrine and Prime Minister Abe made a ritual offering.

Other regional relations

Full diplomatic relations with the People's Republic of China were established in 1992 (a development that was denounced by North Korea, of which China had been the principal ally hitherto). Relations with China were strengthened by numerous subsequent reciprocal ministerial visits. In October 2000 agreement was reached on the resumption of the quadripartite conference, incorporating the two Koreas, China and the USA, with the aim of establishing a peace mechanism for the Korean Peninsula (see North Korea). Later in the month, following strong opposition from China, South Korea refused to grant a visa to the Dalai Lama, Tibet's spiritual leader, on the grounds that it would be 'inappropriate'.

A diplomatic dispute arose between South Korea and China in October 2001, following the execution in China of a South Korean national and the alleged torture of another Korean prisoner, both convicted of drugs-trafficking. In November the ministers of economics, finance and foreign affairs from China, South Korea and Japan agreed to hold regular meetings to foster closer co-operation. In mid-2002 the Chinese authorities sought to prevent North Korean refugees from seeking asylum in various diplomatic buildings in China, including the South Korean embassy in Beijing.

The growing diplomatic crisis over North Korea's nuclear programme from late 2002 led South Korea to seek China's assistance in persuading the North to work towards a peaceful solution. Chinese diplomatic efforts subsequently played a major role (see North Korea). In August 2004, however, relations between South Korea and China were damaged by controversy over the issue of the historical kingdom of Koguryo, which had covered the area of modern North Korea and part of South Korea, as well as areas of northern China. Following the deletion of references to Koguryo from the Chinese Ministry of Foreign Affairs website, the South Korean Government feared that China was planning to claim Koguryo as part of Chinese, rather than Korean, history, and to use this historical 'distortion' as a basis for present-day expansionism. In September, however, the Chinese Ministry of Foreign Affairs issued a statement declaring that its reference to Koguryo as an ancient Chinese province had been a mistake. The issue of Koguryo dominated discussions between President Roh and Chinese Prime Minister Wen Jiabao held in September 2006, not least because China was in the process of applying to the UN to register Mount Paekdu (half of which belonged to North Korea, half to China, and regarded by Korean nationalists as a sacred symbol) as an historic site.

China's continuing policy of forcibly repatriating North Korean defectors who had been apprehended in China (regarding them as illegal migrants) attracted criticism in South Korea and was condemned by human rights organizations, including Amnesty International and the office of the UN High Commissioner for Refugees, particularly in early 2012 after the new North Korean leadership was reported to have increased the severity of punishments for captured defectors. In February and March there were protests in South Korea concerning the fate of some 30 North Korean defectors who were facing repatriation from China, and the South Korean Government urged China to fulfil its obligations as a signatory to international treaties on the status of refugees.

A further cause of tension was illegal fishing by Chinese vessels in South Korean territorial waters, particularly after the killing of a South Korean coastguard by the captain of a Chinese fishing boat in December 2011: more than 400 Chinese fishing boats had been seized by the Korean authorities in that year. The matter was raised by President Lee on a state visit to China in January 2012. Nevertheless, the strengthening of economic ties with China (South Korea's principal export market) remained a priority, and during the visit the two Governments agreed to prepare for formal negotiations on a bilateral FTA, for which feasibility studies had been initiated in 2007. A trilateral agreement with China and Japan on investment was signed in May 2012, and agreement was reached to begin negotiations on a trilateral FTA: the first session duly took place in March 2013.

In November 2000, after eight years' suspension, the 25th Joint Conference of Korea-Taiwan Business Councils took place in Seoul. It was agreed that henceforth annual conferences would be held alternately in the respective capitals of Seoul and Taipei. In the same month a Korean passenger aircraft flew from Seoul to Taipei for the first time since 1992, when diplomatic relations had been severed. South Korea also maintained close relations with South-East Asian countries, and an agreement on free trade in merchandise goods was reached between South Korea and nine of the 10 members of the Association of Southeast Asian Nations (ASEAN, see p. 218) in August 2006. Under the agreement, which was ratified by the South Korean National Assembly in May 2007 and took effect on 1 June, 97% of South Korean products exported to the nine ASEAN countries were exempt from tariffs or would carry tariffs of less than 5% by 2010. The South Korean Government thus envisaged a substantial increase in its trade surplus with the nine South-East Asian signatories. Although more commonly known as the South Korea-ASEAN FTA, the arrangement did not include Thailand, which refused to participate in protest against South Korea's insistence on the exclusion of rice from the agreement. However, several rounds of free trade negotiations were held between the two countries during 2007, and in January 2008 it was reported that an agreement had been reached whereby Thailand would be allowed more flexibility in reducing or waiving its tariffs compared with the other ASEAN nations. Meanwhile, in November 2007 South Korea and all 10 members of ASEAN signed an agreement on free trade in services; a further accord, covering investment, was concluded in 2009. In October 2011 the first official meeting of the ministers of foreign affairs of South Korea and the Mekong River nations (Cambodia, Laos, Myanmar, Thailand and Viet Nam) discussed South Korean development co-operation and investment in the region, and in November the South Korean and Vietnamese Governments agreed to conduct a joint study on the building of nuclear power plants by South Korea in Viet Nam. Negotiations on a bilateral FTA with Viet Nam began in September 2012.

In 2006 trade negotiations commenced between South Korea and India, and in August 2009 a Comprehensive Economic Partnership Agreement was signed by both countries, entering into effect in January 2010. In July 2011 an agreement was concluded on the export of South Korean nuclear technology to India.

Relations with the USA

Relations between South Korea and the USA were frequently strained from the late 1970s, in particular by the proposal to withdraw US ground troops from South Korea (which was abandoned in 1979) and by the trial of Kim Dae-Jung (see above). Disputes between South Korea and the USA in the late 1980s over trade issues had subsided by mid-1991. President George Bush of the USA visited the country in January 1992, and it was agreed to cancel that year's 'Team Spirit' joint military exercises. In December 1991 it had been announced that all US nuclear weapons had been withdrawn from South Korean territory. The 'Team Spirit' exercises were resumed in 1993. In July, during a visit to Seoul, US President Bill Clinton affirmed his country's continuing commitment to the defence of South Korea. In January 1994 it was announced that the USA was to deploy air-defence missiles on South Korean territory. In April 1996, during a visit to Seoul, President Clinton issued a joint US-South Korean proposal for quadripartite negotiations with North Korea and the People's Republic of China (see above). In October 1997 the US Government asked the South Korean administration to reconsider its decision to order an air-defence missile

system from France. However, South Korea was seeking to reduce its dependence on the USA for military technology. Later in that year the USA pledged financial support for South Korea, following the conclusion of an agreement with the IMF.

President Kim Dae-Jung was warmly received on a state visit to the USA in June 1998, during which he outlined his 'sunshine' policy of engagement with North Korea. In March 1999 the South Korean Government welcomed a major advance in negotiations between North Korea and the USA on US access to a suspected nuclear site in North Korea. In October the US and South Korean Governments began investigations into the alleged massacre of as many as 300 Korean refugees by US troops near Nogun-ri, in the South Korean province of North Chungcheong, shortly after the beginning of the Korean War. Revelations of the use of defoliants in the DMZ in the late 1960s created further controversy in November 1999. The herbicides, which had apparently been provided by the USA but applied by South Korean troops, included Agent Orange, which had later been found to be highly toxic. The South Korean Government announced that it was prepared to compensate both soldiers and civilians adversely affected by the defoliants, but the USA reportedly refused to accept any liability. In December a lawsuit was filed against seven US chemical companies by a group of Koreans demanding compensation for damage they claimed to have suffered as a consequence of the herbicides. (In January 2006, in the first such ruling, a South Korean court ordered the US manufacturers to pay 68,000m. won in compensation to 6,800 individuals.)

In May 2000 violent protests took place after a US aircraft accidentally released several bombs close to a village south-west of Seoul, causing minor injuries and damage to property. Following the incident, opposition politicians demanded a review of the Status of Forces Agreement (SOFA), which governed the 37,000 US troops stationed in South Korea. Negotiations held in August and December successfully revised the agreement, which was signed in January 2001. However, South Korean civic groups protested that the partnership between the two countries remained biased in favour of the USA. A missile accord was signed between South Korea and the USA, permitting the former to develop missiles with greatly increased ranges and payloads. Also in January outgoing US President Bill Clinton made an unprecedented statement of regret for the massacre near Nogun-ri, but many South Koreans were angry that no apology was forthcoming.

South Korea immediately pledged support to the USA following terrorist attacks on the latter in September 2001, and in December the National Assembly endorsed the deployment of non-combat troops to assist the US-led campaign in Afghanistan, mainly in a logistical capacity. Meanwhile, in November the USA and South Korea agreed to a major 'land-swap' whereby existing US bases would relocate to other areas within the country, allowing a consolidation of bases and training facilities over the next 10 years.

In November 2002 two US soldiers, whose vehicle had accidentally killed two South Korean girls in June, were acquitted of negligent homicide by a US military court, leading to a significant increase in anti-US sentiment among the public. Although President George W. Bush apologized for the incident, in December hundreds of thousands of people attended anti-US rallies in Seoul and across the country. The rallies became a forum of protest against the country's perceived dependency on the USA and that country's policy towards North Korea. Meanwhile, in October a new joint base pact came into force whereby the US military would reduce the number of its bases from 41 to 23 and return 50% of the land it used to South Korea. However, there had yet to be changes to the SOFA that governed the conduct of US troops in Korea—amendments to which had long been demanded by South Koreans.

Before his election as President, Roh Moo-Hyun had campaigned for a foreign policy more independent from the USA. However, in January 2003 he indicated a more conciliatory stance, but nevertheless warned the USA against attacking North Korea, instead urging the USA to resume dialogue with North Korea. The USA announced that it planned to remove its 15,000 troops stationed between Seoul and the DMZ and deploy them in the south of the country. In February the commander of the United States Forces Korea, Gen. Leon LaPorte, stated that the USA and South Korea would review their 1953 Mutual Defense Treaty, with the possibility of ending provisions under the 'Combined Forces Command' for the transfer of control over South Korea's military to the USA in wartime. However, it was noted that South Korea still remained dependent on the USA for military intelligence. Despite domestic protests, meanwhile, Roh arranged to send 700 non-combatant troops to Iraq in support of the US-led military operation. In June plans were confirmed to withdraw US troops to locations 120 km south of the DMZ, as part of a wider reorganization of US forces in South Korea. In January 2004 the two countries agreed to relocate US troops out of Seoul. In September it was announced that US troops would withdraw from the DMZ by the end of October (South Korean forces duly assumed responsibility for patrolling the border zone from the beginning of November). In October an agreement for the planned withdrawal of one-third of all US troops in South Korea was reached, to take place in three phases extending to 2008.

Meanwhile, the deployment of 3,000 South Korean troops to Iraq at the request of the USA, which had been approved by the National Assembly in February 2004, went ahead in August, despite public outrage at the beheading of a South Korean hostage in that country in June. In December 2004, following a vote in the National Assembly, it was announced that South Korean troops in Iraq (now numbering around 3,600) would remain there throughout 2005. In December 2005 the National Assembly voted to reduce the number of South Korean troops in Iraq to 2,300 and to extend their deployment until the end of 2006.

In February 2007 the two Governments agreed to transfer operational control of South Korean military forces from the USA to South Korea in the event of war and to disband the Combined Forces Command in April 2012 (three years later than the USA had proposed). A new 'supporting-supported command relationship' was to be established, under which the United States Forces Korea would continue to support the South Korean military. The two Governments also reaffirmed earlier agreements on the relocation of US forces from Seoul to the Osan-Pyeongtaek and Daegu-Busan regions and on a reduction in the number of US troops stationed in South Korea from around 30,000 to 25,000 by 2008. The election of Lee Myung-Bak as South Korean President in December 2007 prompted speculation that the new administration might attempt to renegotiate the arrangement on the transfer of wartime military control. The GNP remained staunchly opposed to the agreement concluded under Roh earlier in the year. Lee pledged to forge closer relations with the USA, asserting that South Korea continued to require US protection. The National Assembly voted to extend the deployment of South Korean troops in Iraq until the end of 2008, but to reduce their number from around 1,250 to 650. The South Korean Government had come under pressure from the Bush Administration to maintain its military presence in Iraq, despite continued domestic public opposition to the deployment. In December 2008 South Korea withdrew its remaining soldiers from Iraq.

Meanwhile, in February 2006 it was announced that discussions had commenced with regard to an important FTA between South Korea and the USA. However, as negotiations proceeded in July an estimated 30,000 demonstrators took to the streets of Seoul to protest against what they described as 'economic subjugation'. South Korean farmers, in particular, were concerned that the proposed FTA might prove detrimental to their livelihoods. Major corporations expressed reservations with regard to US demands that trade-related legislation, including fair trade laws, be applied to the South Korean *chaebol*. A further obstacle was the pharmaceutical sector, owing to the USA's strong objections to a new South Korean drugs-pricing system intended to ensure that medicines were available at reasonable cost to those on low incomes. The USA, moreover, insisted that goods produced in the North Korean industrial complex of Kaesong should be exempt from the trade pact, while the South Korean Government regarded Kaesong as a symbol of reconciliation, serving to promote peace and stability on the Korean Peninsula. In November at least 65,000 people joined protests across South Korea, as part of a general strike organized by the KCTU, to demonstrate their disapproval of the proposed FTA.

In April 2007 South Korea and the USA finally reached a compromise on the terms of the FTA. The principal elements of the agreement included wider access to the US market for South Korean car manufacturers, a reduction of taxes payable by television and mobile phone manufacturers and the cessation of duties levied on beef imports. Critics claimed that these measures would have a drastic impact on South Korean farmers, although the agreement did not encompass rice imports, as South Korea objected to the liberalization of that particular market. The conclusion of the FTA led to renewed protests by

various sections of South Korean society. Many argued that increased US imports would render local businesses uncompetitive, thus threatening numerous livelihoods. Several amendments to the FTA, incorporating stricter labour and environmental provisions (mainly to facilitate ratification in the US Congress), were agreed before it was formally signed at the end of June 2007. In April 2008, prior to a visit to the USA by the newly elected President Lee Myung-Bak, the South Korean Government agreed to relax restrictions on imports of US beef (imposed in 2003). The decision prompted large-scale public protests in mid-2008 and, along with other factors, was responsible for a sharp decline in support for Lee (see above). In April 2009 a parliamentary committee approved a bill to allow the ratification of the FTA; however, ratification was subsequently delayed in both the South Korean National Assembly and the US Congress (which had expressed concern that the FTA would negatively affect the troubled US car industry). In December 2010, following talks between Lee and US President Barack Obama in the previous month, the two countries signed a revised version of the FTA that sought to address some of the concerns raised by both legislatures, in particular by delaying the elimination of tariffs on vehicle imports. The agreement was finally ratified by the US legislature in October 2011, and by the South Korean National Assembly (accompanied by violent protests both within and outside the legislature) in November. It entered into effect in March 2012: tariffs on 80% of goods traded between the two countries were immediately abolished, and the proportion was to rise to 95% within five years.

In November 2009, meanwhile, President Obama travelled to South Korea and held discussions with Lee on the resumption of the six-party talks to address the issue of North Korea's nuclear programme; Obama reiterated that the USA's commitment to the defence of South Korea had 'never been stronger'. The US Secretary of State, Hillary Clinton, visited the DMZ in July 2010, when she reaffirmed the USA's commitment to South Korea's defence in the aftermath of the sinking of the *Cheonan* in March; the visit coincided with the annual joint US-South Korean naval exercises. In early 2012 the US Government urged South Korea to reduce its imports of petroleum from Iran (which provided about 10% of South Korea's petroleum imports) in compliance with international sanctions intended to deter Iran from developing nuclear weapons. In June South Korea announced that it was suspending imports of petroleum from Iran, having arranged other sources of supply. In September an agreement with the USA was announced whereby South Korea was to increase the range of its ballistic missile system to 800 km, to counteract threats of military action by North Korea (the previous agreement, concluded in 2001, had limited the range to 300 km). After North Korea reacted with an unusual degree of belligerence to the beginning of annual joint military exercises conducted by South Korea and the USA in March 2013, the USA and South Korea concluded an agreement allowing a joint response to possible limited-scale attacks by the North. In early April it was announced that South Korea and the USA were to begin negotiations on revising a bilateral agreement (dating from 1974) that limited South Korea's civilian nuclear activities (in particular, by banning the reprocessing of spent fuel, a potential source of plutonium for military use). Co-operation on resisting 'cyber-warfare' against South Korea's computer networks was also to be increased. Clinton's successor as US Secretary of State, John Kerry, visited Seoul in mid-April, holding talks with President Park Geun-Hye on tensions with North Korea and reaffirming the USA's commitment to protecting South Korea.

Other external relations

South Korea established full diplomatic relations with the USSR in 1990. In 1991 South Korea extended a substantial loan to the USSR; this debt was subsequently transferred to the Russian Federation (Russia) following the disintegration of the USSR later in that year. In September 1993 it was announced that South Korea and Russia were to participate in joint naval exercises, and in 1994 it was reported that Russia was to supply 'defensive missiles' in order to repay a part of its debt to South Korea. Further arrangements were made concerning the settlement of Russia's debt, through the provision of commodities, in July 1997. President Vladimir Putin of Russia paid a three-day state visit to South Korea in February 2001, when he agreed to proceed with a tripartite framework of co-operation between Russia and both Koreas. Arrangements were made for Russia to supply weapons to South Korea, which were to be partially paid for by the cancellation of some Soviet-era debt. South Korea and

Russia also issued a joint statement supporting the 1972 Anti-Ballistic Missile treaty; however, US displeasure with this led to the resignation of the Minister of Foreign Affairs and Trade, Lee Joung-Binn. In December 2002 the South Korean Government agreed to accept military equipment worth US $534m. from Russia as further debt repayment.

There were indications that Roh Moo-Hyun would seek to improve relations with Russia during his presidency, as part of a broader policy of reducing dependency on the USA. In March 2003 Roh revived the idea of building a 4,000-km pipeline that would provide North Korea with Russian natural gas from Sakhalin in exchange for the abandonment of its nuclear weapons programme. At a summit meeting in Bangkok, Thailand, in October 2003 Roh and Putin agreed to co-operate on the North Korean nuclear issue. In September 2004 President Roh visited Russia. A significant agreement between state-owned oil companies of the two countries (Korean National Oil Corporation—KNOC—and Russia's Rosneft) was signed. In April 2005 the Minister of Defence, Yoon Kwang-Woong, visited Russia, where he met his Russian counterpart, Sergei Ivanov, to discuss the provision of Russian 'advanced weapons technology' by way of further repaying the Russian debt to South Korea. In November 2011, during a visit to Russia by President Lee Myung-Bak, the two Governments agreed to undertake studies on the construction of a pipeline to bring Russian natural gas to South Korea (via North Korea), instead of transporting it by sea as was currently the case; they also agreed to encourage the resumption of the six-party talks on North Korea's nuclear programme (see above).

Taliban militants seized a group of 23 South Korean Christians in Afghanistan in mid-July 2007. Following the killing of two of the hostages later in that month, direct talks between South Korean officials and the Taliban were held in August. By the end of August the Taliban had released the remaining 21 hostages, who claimed to have been undertaking aid work rather than missionary activities. The South Korean authorities refused to confirm or deny speculation that a ransom had been paid to the Taliban, but stated that it had agreed to withdraw its troops from Afghanistan by the end of the year, as scheduled, and to prevent missionary groups from travelling to the country. The withdrawal of South Korea's 210-strong contingent (comprising military medical and engineering personnel) in the International Security Assistance Force in Afghanistan was completed by mid-December. None the less, in February 2010 the GNP-dominated National Assembly approved the deployment of some 350 troops to Afghanistan to protect the South Korean Provincial Reconstruction Team, in spite of an opposition boycott of the parliamentary vote, demonstrations outside the National Assembly Building and a warning by Taliban insurgents of 'bad consequences' if the deployment were carried out. The troops began operating in Afghanistan in July and all but 70 were withdrawn by the end of 2012.

As the country continued to sign various bilateral accords providing for free trade, in May 2007 South Korea and the European Union (EU) commenced negotiations on the establishment of an FTA; the final agreement was signed in October 2009. Despite the opposition of the EU's vehicle-manufacturing industry and South Korean farmers, the FTA was ratified by the European Parliament in February 2011 and by the South Korean National Assembly in May; it entered into force in July. Meanwhile, an FTA between South Korea and Peru was signed in March 2011. Negotiations aimed at concluding an FTA between South Korea and Canada, which commenced in July 2005, continued in early 2013. An FTA with Turkey was to enter into effect in May 2013.

In March 2009 President Lee Myung-Bak embarked upon a state visit to Australia, where he and Prime Minister Kevin Rudd signed a pact relating to closer co-operation in the area of security, including counter-terrorism strategies and the combating of transnational crime. The commencement of formal negotiations on an FTA between the two countries was also announced, and discussions were ongoing in early 2013.

CONSTITUTION AND GOVERNMENT

Under the Constitution of the Sixth Republic (adopted in October 1987), executive power is held by the President, who is directly elected for one term of five years by universal suffrage. The President appoints and governs with the assistance of the State Council (cabinet), led by the Prime Minister. Legislative power is vested in the unicameral National Assembly (Kuk Hoe), popularly elected for a four-year term. The Assembly has 300 members; 246 are directly elected and 54 are chosen by proportional representation.

REGIONAL AND INTERNATIONAL CO-OPERATION

The Republic of Korea (South Korea) is a member of the Asian Development Bank (ADB, see p. 214), Asia-Pacific Economic Cooperation (APEC, see p. 208), the Colombo Plan (see p. 460) and the UN's Economic and Social Commission for Asia and the Pacific (ESCAP, see p. 31). In 1991 South Korea was accepted as a dialogue partner of the Association of Southeast Asian Nations (ASEAN, see p. 218), subsequently becoming one of the three additional partners of ASEAN + 3.

South Korea joined the UN in 1991, and commenced a two-year mandate as a non-permanent member of the UN Security Council on 1 January 2013. As a contracting party to the General Agreement on Tariffs and Trade (GATT), the country joined the World Trade Organization (WTO, see p. 444) upon its establishment in 1995. South Korea is also a member of the Organisation for Economic Co-operation and Development (OECD, see p. 388).

ECONOMIC AFFAIRS

In 2011, according to estimates by the World Bank, the gross national income (GNI) of the Republic of Korea (South Korea), measured at average 2009–11 prices, was US $1,038,981m., equivalent to $20,870 per head (or $30,340 per head on an international purchasing-power parity basis). During 2002–11, it was estimated, the population increased at an average annual rate of 0.5%, while gross domestic product (GDP) per head increased, in real terms, by an average of 3.3% per year. Overall GDP increased, in real terms, at an average annual rate of 3.8% in 2002–11. According to the Asian Development Bank (ADB), GDP rose by 3.7% in 2011, but growth slowed to 2.0% in 2012.

Agriculture (including forestry and fishing) contributed 2.7% of GDP and engaged 6.4% of the employed labour force in 2011. The principal crop is rice, but barley, potatoes, sweet potatoes and fruit are also important, as is the raising of livestock (principally poultry, pigs and cattle). Fishing provides food for domestic consumption, as well as a substantial surplus for export. South Korea is one of the world's leading ocean-fishing nations. During 2002–10, according to figures from the World Bank, the GDP of the agricultural sector increased by an average of 1.8% per year. Agricultural GDP declined by 2.1% in 2011 and by 0.6% in 2012, according to the ADB.

In 2011 industry (including mining and quarrying, manufacturing, utilities and construction) contributed 39.2% of GDP and (excluding utilities) engaged 24.2% of the employed labour force. Industry is dominated by large conglomerate companies (*chaebol*), with greatly diversified interests, especially in construction and manufacturing. According to figures from the World Bank, during 2002–10 industrial GDP increased at an average annual rate of 5.5%. The sector's GDP expanded by 5.1% in 2011 and by 1.7% in 2012, according to the ADB.

South Korea is not richly endowed with natural resources. Mining and quarrying contributed 0.2% of GDP in 2011, employing a negligible percentage of the labour force. There are deposits of coal (mainly anthracite). Other minerals include iron ore, lead, zinc, silver, gold and limestone. Substantial offshore reserves of natural gas have been discovered. According to the ADB, the sector's GDP declined by 4.6% in 2011.

Manufacturing contributed 31.2% of GDP and engaged 16.9% of the employed labour force in 2011. The most important branches of manufacturing include electrical machinery, transport equipment (mainly road motor vehicles and shipbuilding), non-electrical machinery, chemicals, food products, iron and steel, and textiles. During 2002–10 manufacturing GDP increased by an average of 6.5% per year, according to figures from the World Bank. The sector's GDP expanded by by 7.2% in 2011, according to the ADB.

Construction contributed 5.9% of GDP and engaged 7.2% of the employed labour force in 2011. Construction GDP contracted by 4.6% in 2011.

Energy is derived principally from nuclear power and coal. In 2010 31.1% of total electricity output was generated by nuclear power and 44.1% from coal. In April 2013 there were 23 nuclear units in operation in the country. South Korea also produces liquefied natural gas for domestic and industrial consumption. Imports of petroleum and its products comprised 23.8% of the value of merchandise imports in 2011.

The services sector contributed 58.1% of GDP and (including utilities) engaged 69.5% of the employed labour force in 2011.

Receipts from tourism are significant, totalling an estimated US $14,176m. in 2012. The number of visitor arrivals rose by 13.7% in that year, to reach 11.1m. During 2002–10, according to figures from the World Bank, the GDP of the services sector increased at an average annual rate of 3.1%. The GDP of the services sector increased by 2.6% in 2011 and by 2.5% in 2012, according to the ADB.

In 2011 South Korea recorded a visible merchandise trade surplus of US $30,950m., and there was a surplus of $26,505m. on the current account of the balance of payments. The People's Republic of China (accounting for 16.5%) was the principal source of imports in 2011; other important suppliers were Japan, the USA, Saudi Arabia and Australia. China was the principal market for exports in that year (purchasing 24.2%). Other important markets included the USA, Japan and Hong Kong. The main exports in 2011 were machinery and transport equipment, basic manufactures, chemical products, petroleum and petroleum products, and miscellaneous manufactured articles. The principal imports in that year were mineral fuels and lubricants (notably petroleum and petroleum products), machinery and transport equipment, basic manufactures, chemical products, crude materials and miscellaneous manufactured articles.

South Korea recorded a budget deficit equivalent to 2.9% of GDP in 2012. The general government gross debt was 392,237,500m. won in 2010, equivalent to 33.4% of GDP. At the end of 2012, according to the ADB, the total external debt reached US $413,437m. In that year the cost of debt-servicing was equivalent to 7.4% of the value of exports of goods and services. According to the International Labour Organization, the average annual rate of inflation was 1.4% in 2002–11. According to the ADB, consumer prices increased by 2.2% in 2012. The seasonally adjusted rate of unemployment was 3.4% at March 2013.

Strong growth in both domestic consumption and private investment prevailed until the deterioration in global economic conditions in mid-2008. From November the Government introduced a series of fiscal stimulus measures, including reductions in taxation. A substantial decline in the value of exports in 2009 was alleviated by demand from China (South Korea's leading market). The greater diversification of the South Korean manufacturing sector in recent years also afforded some resilience to changing global conditions, although the domination of the economy by a small number of major conglomerates (*chaebol*), hindering the development of small and medium-sized enterprises, was identified as a cause for concern. Following minimal GDP growth in 2009, a robust recovery ensued in 2010, with expansion of 6.3% in GDP, propelled by increased investment and revitalized domestic consumption. GDP growth of 3.7% in 2011 was slower than anticipated, as high levels of personal and household debt, together with stagnating property prices, placed a limit on domestic demand, while exports to the European Union (EU), South Korea's second largest export market, were adversely affected by the debt crisis in the eurozone. The implementation of a free trade agreement (FTA) with the EU, with effect from July, was expected to yield major benefits to the South Korean economy. A controversial FTA with the USA (see Relations with the USA) was also ratified by both legislatures in 2011 and entered into effect in March 2012. However, GDP growth slowed to 2.0% in 2012, as exports continued to be adversely affected by global problems, while the weakness of the Japanese currency made that country's exports more competitive, at the expense of rival South Korean enterprises. The Bank of Korea, the central bank, reduced interest rates twice during 2012 (to 2.75% at the end of the year), and inflation remained low. The new Government of President Park Geun-Hye, inaugurated in February 2013, identified job creation and the reduction of household debt as economic priorities, and undertook to support the development of small and medium-sized enterprises. A trilateral trade agreement with China and Japan, which together accounted for nearly one-third of South Korean trade, was under negotiation in 2013. In April 2013 the Government proposed a supplementary budget worth 17,300,000m. won in an effort to stimulate the economy, amid weak domestic and external demand, having recently reduced its forecast for GDP growth that year to 2.3% (from 3.0%).

PUBLIC HOLIDAYS

2014: 1 January (New Year's Day), 30 January–1 February (Seollal, Lunar New Year), 1 March (Sam Il Jol, Independence Movement Day), 5 May (Children's Day), 6 May (Buddha's Birthday), 6 June (Memorial Day), 15 August (Liberation Day), 7–9 September (Juseok, Korean Thanksgiving Day), 3 October (National Foundation Day), 9 October (Hangeul, Korean Alphabet Day), 25 December (Christmas).

Statistical Survey

Source (unless otherwise stated): Statistics Korea, Bldg III, Government Complex-Daejeon 920, Dunsan-dong, Seo-gu, Daejeon 302-701; tel. (42) 481-2120; fax (42) 481-2460; internet kostat.go.kr.

Area and Population

AREA, POPULATION AND DENSITY*

Area (sq km)	99,646†
Population (census results)	
1 November 2005	47,041,434
1 November 2010	
Males	24,167,098
Females	24,413,195
Total	48,580,293
Population (official estimates at mid-year)	
2011	49,779,440
2012	50,004,441
2013	50,219,669
Density (per sq km) at mid-2013	503.4

* Excluding the demilitarized zone between North and South Korea, with an area of 1,262 sq km (487 sq miles).
† 38,474 sq miles. The figure indicates territory under the jurisdiction of the Republic of Korea, surveyed on the basis of land register in 2005.

POPULATION BY AGE AND SEX
(official estimates at mid-2013)

	Males	Females	Total
0–14	3,820,046	3,550,072	7,370,118
15–64	18,769,462	17,942,387	36,711,849
65 and over	2,543,104	3,594,598	6,137,702
Total	25,132,612	25,087,057	50,219,669

ADMINISTRATIVE DIVISIONS
(official estimates at mid-2013)

Province	Area (sq km)	Population	Density (per sq km)
Seoul	605.4	9,991,064	16,503.2
Busan	764.4	3,430,473	4,487.8
Daegu	884.5	2,471,357	2,794.1
Incheon	994.1	2,816,025	2,832.7
Gwangju	501.4	1,518,006	3,027.5
Daejeon	539.8	1,546,251	2,864.5
Ulsan	1,057.1	1,120,444	1,059.9
Gyeonggi-do . . .	10,130.9	12,080,585	1,192.4
Gangwon-do . . .	16,613.5	1,504,986	90.6
Chungcheongbuk-do . .	7,431.4	1,561,471	210.1
Chungcheongnam-do . .	8,600.5	2,147,980	249.8
Jeollabuk-do	8,054.6	1,803,230	223.9
Jeollanam-do	12,073.5	1,762,178	146.0
Gyeongsangbuk-do . .	19,026.0	2,642,329	138.9
Gyeongsangnam-do . .	10,520.8	3,263,050	310.2
Jeju-do	1,848.3	560,240	303.1
Total	99,646.2	50,219,669	504.0

PRINCIPAL TOWNS
(population at 1995 census)

Seoul (capital) .	10,231,217	Jeonju (Chonju) .	563,153
Busan (Pusan) .	3,814,325	Jeongju (Chongju) .	531,376
Daegu (Taegu) .	2,449,420	Masan	441,242
Incheon (Inchon) .	2,308,188	Jinju (Chinju) . .	329,886
Daejeon (Taejon) .	1,272,121	Kunsan . . .	266,559
Gwangju (Kwangju)	1,257,636	Jeju (Cheju) . .	258,511
Ulsan . . .	967,429	Mokpo	247,452
Seongnam		Chuncheon	
(Songnam) . .	869,094	(Chunchon) . .	234,528
Suwon	755,550		

2000 census: Seoul 9,853,972; Busan 3,655,437; Daegu 2,473,990; Incheon 2,466,338; Daejeon 1,365,961; Gwangju 1,350,948; Ulsan 1,012,110.

Mid-2011 (incl. suburbs, UN estimate): Seoul 9,735,860 (Source: UN, *World Urbanization Prospects: The 2011 Revision*).

BIRTHS, MARRIAGES AND DEATHS*

	Registered live births		Registered marriages		Registered deaths	
	Number	Rate (per 1,000)	Number	Rate (per 1,000)	Number	Rate (per 1,000)
2005	435,031	8.9	314,304	6.5	243,883	5.0
2006	448,153	9.2	330,634	6.8	242,266	5.0
2007	493,189	10.0	343,559	7.0	244,874	5.0
2008	465,892	9.4	327,715	6.6	246,113	5.0
2009	444,849	9.0	309,759	6.2	246,942	5.0
2010	470,171	9.4	326,104	6.5	255,405	5.1
2011	471,265	9.4	329,087	6.6	257,396	5.1

* Owing to late registration, figures are subject to continuous revision.

Life expectancy (years at birth): 80.8 (males 77.4; females 84.3) in 2010 (Source: World Bank, World Development Indicators database).

ECONOMICALLY ACTIVE POPULATION*
(labour force survey, '000 persons aged 15 years and over)

	2006	2007	2008
Agriculture, forestry and fishing .	1,785	1,779	1,686
Mining and quarrying	18	18	23
Manufacturing	4,167	4,014	3,963
Electricity, gas and water . . .	76	86	90
Construction	1,835	1,849	1,812
Wholesale and retail trade, repair of motor vehicles and personal and household goods . .	3,713	3,673	3,631
Restaurants and hotels . . .	2,049	2,049	2,044
Transport, storage and communications	1,470	1,498	1,875
Financial intermediation . . .	786	806	821
Real estate, renting and business activities	2,168	2,350	2,219

—continued	2006	2007	2008
Public administration and defence; compulsory social security . .	801	797	840
Education	1,658	1,740	1,784
Health and social work . .	686	740	842
Other community, social and personal service activities . .	1,781	1,845	1,782
Households with employed persons	138	161	150
Extra-territorial organizations and bodies	20	15	16
Statistical discrepancy	—	13	—
Total employed	23,151	23,433	23,578
Unemployed	827	783	769
Total labour force	23,978	24,216	24,347
Males	13,978	14,124	14,208
Females	10,000	10,092	10,139

* Excluding armed forces.

Source: ILO.

2011 ('000 persons aged 15 years and over): Agriculture, forestry and fishing 1,542; Mining 17; Manufacturing 4,091; Construction 1,751; Services (incl. power) 16,844; *Total employed* 24,244; Unemployed 855; *Total labour force* 25,099.

Health and Welfare

KEY INDICATORS

Total fertility rate (children per woman, 2010)	1.3
Under-5 mortality rate (per 1,000 live births, 2010) . . .	5
HIV/AIDS (% of persons aged 15–49, 2009)	<0.1
Physicians (per 1,000 head, 2010)	2.0
Hospital beds (per 1,000 head, 2009)	10.3
Health expenditure (2009): US $ per head (PPP) . . .	1,879
Health expenditure (2009): % of GDP	6.9
Health expenditure (2009): public (% of total)	58.2
Access to water (% of persons, 2010)	98
Total carbon dioxide emissions ('000 metric tons, 2008) .	509,170.3
Carbon dioxide emissions per head (metric tons, 2008) . .	10.5
Human Development Index (2011): ranking	15
Human Development Index (2011): value	0.897

For sources and definitions, see explanatory note on p. vi.

Agriculture

PRINCIPAL CROPS
('000 metric tons)

	2009	2010	2011
Rice, paddy	7,023.0	6,136.3	6,304.0*
Barley	148.6	81.2	75.5
Maize	77.0	74.3	73.6
Potatoes	591.1	616.7	622.2
Sweet potatoes	350.7	298.9	255.3
Beans, dry	7.4	6.1	5.5
Chestnuts	75.9	68.6	55.8†
Soybeans (Soya beans) . . .	139.3	105.3	129.4
Sesame seed	12.8	12.7	9.5
Cabbages and other brassicas .	2,848.1	2,035.7	3,049.3
Lettuce and chicory	146.1	141.3	116.8
Spinach	104.6	87.9	104.5
Tomatoes	383.8	324.8	368.2
Pumpkins, squash and gourds .	341.2	302.9	300.4
Cucumbers and gherkins . . .	352.0	306.1	303.8
Chillies and peppers, green . .	350.4	310.5	262.3
Onions and shallots, green . .	447.0	417.2	482.1
Onions, dry	1,372.3	1,411.7	1,520.0
Garlic	357.3	271.6	295.0
Carrots and turnips	98.8	102.1	93.7
Mushrooms	27.0	26.3	30.6†
Watermelons	846.9	678.8	609.0

—*continued*	2009	2010	2011
Cantaloupes and other melons .	227.8	207.7	180.0
Tangerines, mandarins,			
clementines and satsumas . .	752.8	614.9	680.5
Apples	494.5	460.3	379.5
Pears	418.4	307.8	290.5
Peaches and nectarines . .	198.3	138.6	185.1
Plums and sloes . . .	63.6	62.9	57.4
Strawberries	203.8	231.8	171.5
Grapes	333.0	305.5	269.2
Persimmons	416.7	390.6	390.8
Tobacco, unmanufactured† . .	34.0	33.2	34.6

* Unofficial figure.
† FAO estimate(s).

Aggregate production ('000 metric tons, may include official, semi-official or estimated data): Total cereals 7,278 in 2009, 6,345 in 2010, 6,513 in 2011; Total vegetables (incl. melons) 11,269 in 2009, 9,757 in 2010, 11,364 in 2011; Total fruits (excl. melons) 3,099 in 2009, 2,734 in 2010, 2,642 in 2011.

Source: FAO.

LIVESTOCK
('000 head)

	2009	2010	2011
Cattle	3,079	3,351	3,353
Pigs	9,585	9,881	8,171
Goats	250	244	245*
Chickens	138,768	149,200	154,000*

* FAO estimate.

Source: FAO.

LIVESTOCK PRODUCTS
('000 metric tons)

	2009	2010	2011
Cattle meat	283.0	247.0	280.0
Pig meat*	1,062.0	1,110.0	837.0
Chicken meat*	551.0	588.0	617.0
Duck meat*	62.0	65.0	69.0
Cows' milk	2,222.0	2,073.0	1,869.0
Goats' milk†	4.1	3.8	3.8
Hen eggs†	602.0	590.0	595.0
Other poultry eggs† . . .	31.5	31.5	31.5
Honey†	28.0	24.0	24.0

* Unofficial figures.
† FAO estimates.

Source: FAO.

Forestry

ROUNDWOOD REMOVALS
('000 cubic metres, excl. bark, FAO estimates)

	2009	2010	2011
Sawlogs, veneer logs and logs for			
sleepers	451	451	451
Pulpwood	1,919	1,919	1,919
Other industrial wood . . .	806	806	806
Fuel wood	2,477	2,477	2,479
Total	5,653	5,653	5,655

Source: FAO.

SAWNWOOD PRODUCTION
('000 cubic metres, incl. sleepers)

	2005*	2006*	2007
Coniferous (softwood)	4,200	4,200	3,654†
Broadleaved (hardwood) . . .	166	166	144†
Total	4,366	4,366	3,798*

* FAO estimate(s).
† Unofficial figure.

2008–11: Production assumed to be unchanged from 2007 (FAO estimates).

Source: FAO.

Fishing

('000 metric tons, live weight)

	2008	2009	2010
Capture	1,956.6	1,858.6	1,732.9
Croakers and drums	39.6	35.6	33.0
Japanese anchovy . . .	261.5	203.7	249.6
Skipjack tuna	187.3	257.5	216.7
Chub mackerel	188.2	119.0	94.4
Largehead hairtail . . .	72.9	85.5	59.2
Argentine shortfin squid . .	157.8	57.0	25.0
Japanese flying squid . . .	186.2	189.2	159.1
Aquaculture	473.8	473.1	475.6
Pacific cupped oyster . . .	250.0	240.9	267.8
Total catch	2,430.4	2,331.6	2,208.5

Note: Figures exclude aquatic plants ('000 metric tons): 934.9 (capture 13.9, aquaculture 921.0) in 2008; 869.5 (capture 10.8, aquaculture 858.7) in 2009; 914.7 (capture 13.0, aquaculture 901.7) in 2010. Also excluded are aquatic mammals, recorded by number rather than by weight; the number of dolphins and whales caught was: 728 in 2008; 556 in 2009; 577 in 2010.

Source: FAO.

Mining

('000 metric tons unless otherwise indicated)

	2008	2009	2010
Hard coal (Anthracite) . . .	2,773	2,519	2,500*
Iron ore: gross weight . . .	366	455	513
Iron ore: metal content . . .	205	274	308
Lead ore (metric tons)† . . .	449	2,064	1,168
Zinc ore (metric tons)† . . .	3,672	3,672	710
Kaolin	955	659	764
Feldspar	344.3	622.7	496.5
Salt (unrefined)	384.3	382.3	222.5
Mica (metric tons)	49,474	27,078	36,486
Talc (metric tons)	6,438	5,996	5,729
Pyrophyllite	892.6	617.4	673.9

* Estimate.
† Figures refer to the metal content of ores.

Source: US Geological Survey.

Industry

SELECTED PRODUCTS
('000 metric tons unless otherwise indicated)

	2006	2007	2008
Wheat flour	1,850	1,760	1,681
Refined sugar	1,317	n.a.	n.a.
Beer (million litres)	17,400	18,200	19,073
Cigarettes (million)	119,966	124,570	129,543
Cotton yarn—pure and mixed	217	216	206
Plywood ('000 cu m)	736	716	682
Newsprint	1,654	1,666	1,600
Rubber tyres ('000)*	65,231	68,771	n.a.
Caustic soda	1,477	1,578	1,590
Liquefied petroleum gas	3,098	2,927	2,977
Naphtha	21,537	23,147	20,441
Kerosene	5,410	3,827	4,116
Gas-diesel (distillate fuel oil)	32,392	34,314	35,860
Residual fuel oil	30,793	27,363	22,370
Cement	55,021	58,188	56,010
Pig-iron	27,559	29,437	31,043
Crude steel	48,259	51,003	52,129
Passenger cars—produced ('000 units)	3,489	n.a.	n.a.
Electric energy (million kWh)	404,021	427,316	446,428
Carbon black†	484.3	497.2	484.0‡
Products of petroleum refineries ('000 barrels)†	717,493	770,523	747,827‡

* Tyres for passenger cars and commercial vehicles.
† Source: US Geological Survey.
‡ Estimate.

Source: mostly UN, *Industrial Commodity Statistics Yearbook*.

2009 ('000 metric tons unless otherwise indicated): Liquefied petroleum gas 3,026; Naphtha 19,034; Kerosene 4,642; Residual fuel oil 18,470; Cement 50,127; Pig-iron 27,475; Crude steel 48,572; Electric energy (million kWh) 454,504; Carbon black 500.0 (estimate); Products of petroleum refineries ('000 barrels) 750,000 (estimate) (Sources: US Geological Survey; UN Industrial Commodity Statistics Database).

2010 ('000 metric tons unless otherwise indicated): Cement 47,236; Pig-iron 31,228; Crude steel 58,912; Carbon black 500.0 (estimate); Products of petroleum refineries ('000 barrels) 750,000 (estimate) (Source: US Geological Survey).

Finance

CURRENCY AND EXCHANGE RATES

Monetary Units
100 chun (jeon) = 10 hwan = 1 won.

Sterling, Dollar and Euro Equivalents (31 December 2012)
£1 sterling = 1,692.41 won;
US $1 = 1,072.50 won;
€1 = 1,415.06 won;
10,000 won = £5.91 = $9.32 = €7.07.

Average Exchange Rate (won per US $)
2010   1,156.06
2011   1,108.29
2012   1,126.53

BUDGET
('000 million won)

Revenue	2009	2010	2011
Current revenue	252,720	268,540	289,785
Tax revenue	164,542	177,718	192,381
Non-tax revenue	88,178	90,822	97,404
Capital revenue	2,532	2,383	2,528
Total	255,252	270,923	292,312

Expenditure	2009	2010	2011
General public services	27,409	25,885	27,844
Defence	27,719	27,772	30,134
Education	38,894	37,676	40,988
Health	2,821	2,972	2,641
Social security and welfare	53,998	56,350	60,107
Housing and community amenities	16,965	12,330	12,758
Economic services	54,432	47,607	48,546
Transport and communications	19,954	16,451	15,497
Others	47,088	40,564	47,638
Total	269,326	251,156	270,655

Source: Asian Development Bank.

INTERNATIONAL RESERVES
(US $ million at 31 December)

	2009	2010	2011
Gold (national valuation)	79.0	79.6	2,166.6
IMF special drawing rights	3,745.5	3,540.0	3,457.7
Reserve position in IMF	985.2	1,024.8	2,564.3
Foreign exchange	265,202.3	286,926.4	298,232.9
Total	270,012.0	291,570.7	306,421.5

Source: IMF, *International Financial Statistics*.

MONEY SUPPLY
('000 million won at 31 December)

	2009	2010	2011
Currency outside banks	31,209	36,983	41,687
Demand deposits at deposit money banks	72,953	77,028	81,982
Total money (incl. others)	105,398	114,214	123,955

Source: IMF, *International Financial Statistics*.

COST OF LIVING
(Consumer Price Index; base: 2005 = 100)

	2008	2009	2010
Food and non-alcoholic beverages	108.2	116.3	123.8
Alcoholic beverages and cigarettes	100.8	101.9	102.3
Housing, water and fuels	109.7	110.9	113.6
Furnishings and household goods	111.2	116.3	117.3
Clothing and footwear	108.1	113.6	116.9
Health	105.8	108.1	110.2
Education	117.2	120.1	122.8
Communication	95.3	95.2	94.3
Transport	117.9	113.7	119.3
All items (incl. others)	109.7	112.8	116.1

2011 (base 2010 = 100): Food and non-alcoholic beverages 108.1; Alcoholic beverages and cigarettes 100.8; Housing, water and fuels 104.5; Furnishings and household goods 103.7; Clothing and footwear 103.3; Health 101.8; Education 101.7; Communication 98.4; Transport 107.0; All items (incl. others) 104.0.

2012 (base 2010 = 100): Food and non-alcoholic beverages 112.4; Alcoholic beverages and cigarettes 102.3; Housing, water and fuels 109.3; Furnishings and household goods 106.7; Clothing and footwear 108.3; Health 102.7; Education 103.2; Communication 95.9; Transport 110.5; All items (incl. others) 106.3.

NATIONAL ACCOUNTS
('000 million won at current prices)

National Income and Product

	2009	2010	2011
Compensation of employees	493,685.7	525,072.1	556,857.4
Operating surplus	310,604.0	365,108.0	383,119.5
Domestic factor incomes	804,289.7	890,180.1	939,976.9
Consumption of fixed capital	142,094.1	150,910.9	161,105.4
Gross domestic product (GDP) at factor cost	946,383.8	1,041,091.0	1,101,082.3
Indirect taxes, *less* subsidies	118,653.1	132,183.9	136,045.9
GDP in purchasers' values	1,065,036.8	1,173,274.9	1,237,128.2
Net factor income from abroad	4,746.2	1,478.1	3,375.7
Gross national income	1,069,783.1	1,174,753.0	1,240,503.9
Less Consumption of fixed capital	142,094.1	150,910.9	161,105.4
National income in market prices	927,689	1,023,842.1	1,079,398.5

Expenditure on the Gross Domestic Product

	2009	2010	2011
Final consumption expenditure	746,294.9	795,378.8	845,343.3
Households (incl. non-profit institutions serving households)	575,970.2	616,982.6	654,857.7
General government	170,324.7	178,396.1	190,485.6
Gross capital formation	279,858.0	346,430.2	364,339.8
Gross fixed capital formation	309,714.0	331,734.1	339,416.8
Changes in inventories	−29,856.0	14,696.1	24,923.0
Total domestic expenditure	1,026,152.9	1,141,809.0	1,209,683.1
Exports of goods and services	529,645.1	613,368.3	694,765.8
Less Imports of goods and services	490,188.3	583,157.3	669,746.4
Statistical discrepancy	−573.0	1,254.8	2,425.5
GDP in market prices	1,065,036.8	1,173,274.9	1,237,128.2

Gross Domestic Product by Economic Activity

	2009	2010	2011
Agriculture, forestry and fishing	26,615.0	27,832.1	30,095.6
Mining and quarrying	2,220.5	2,223.2	2,241.1
Manufacturing	266,578.2	319,275.2	347,371.1
Electricity, gas and water	17,258.2	21,473.6	21,835.1
Construction	66,576.6	66,156.6	65,444.6
Wholesale and retail trade, restaurants and hotels	103,994.8	114,858.5	123,625.5
Transport, storage and communications	81,387.5	86,634.6	83,714.7
Financial intermediation	65,035.5	71,846.9	78,115.2
Real estate, renting and business activities	125,363.0	131,540.4	137,315.3
Public administration and defence, compulsory social security	63,706.6	65,079.2	69,595.8
Education	63,448.7	64,887.0	67,746.6
Health and social work	43,092.1	47,228.9	50,788.6
Other service activities	33,559.3	34,896.5	36,837.0
Gross value added at basic prices	958,836.0	1,053,932.6	1,114,726.3
Taxes, less subsidies, on products	106,200.8	119,342.2	122,401.9
Total	1,065,036.8	1,173,274.9	1,237,128.2

Source: Bank of Korea.

BALANCE OF PAYMENTS
(US $ million)

	2009	2010	2011
Exports of goods	358,190	461,445	552,564
Imports of goods	−320,324	−421,362	−521,614
Balance on goods	37,866	40,083	30,950
Exports of services	73,580	87,282	95,000
Imports of services	−80,221	−95,908	−99,378
Balance on goods and services	31,226	31,457	26,573
Primary income received	14,514	16,354	17,422
Primary income paid	−12,238	−15,338	−14,967
Balance on goods, services and primary income	33,502	32,472	29,029
Secondary income received	12,700	13,424	15,345
Secondary income paid	−13,412	−16,503	−17,869
Current balance	32,791	29,394	26,505
Capital account (net)	290	−218	150
Direct investment assets	−17,197	−23,278	−20,355
Direct investment liabilities	2,249	1,094	4,661
Portfolio investment assets	1,436	−1,190	−5,231
Portfolio investment liabilities	48,292	43,669	15,543
Financial derivatives and employee stock options (net)	−3,093	829	−1,735
Other investment assets	1,688	−15,981	−23,615
Other investment liabilities	394	−5,434	12,530
Net errors and omissions	1,804	−1,838	5,530
Reserves and related items	68,652	27,048	13,983

Source: IMF, *International Financial Statistics*.

External Trade

PRINCIPAL COMMODITIES
(distribution by SITC, US $ million)*

Imports c.i.f.	2009	2010	2011
Food and live animals	13,438.4	16,335.1	21,900.2
Crude materials (inedible) except fuels	20,310.1	30,632.2	42,262.7
Mineral fuels, lubricants, etc.	91,669.2	122,596.2	173,673.7
Petroleum, petroleum products, etc.	64,527.6	87,676.7	125,013.9
Gas (natural and manufactured)	17,146.7	21,788.7	30,182.7
Chemicals and related products	31,504.9	41,147.7	48,251.0
Organic chemicals	8,907.4	12,136.9	15,060.0
Basic manufactures	43,250.4	56,142.6	64,231.1
Iron and steel	17,430.2	22,726.5	25,760.7
Machinery and transport equipment	96,881.6	123,316.7	133,256.9
Machinery specialized for particular industries	9,634.3	18,148.8	17,885.0
General industrial machinery, equipment and parts	12,367.7	13,779.1	14,572.0
Office machines and automatic data-processing machines	6,443.6	8,855.1	8,682.1
Telecommunications and sound equipment	8,631.0	10,486.6	12,917.5
Other electrical machinery, apparatus, etc.	41,913.0	48,856.3	53,180.3
Thermionic valves and tubes, microprocessors, transistors, etc.	25,261.4	28,637.0	30,163.3
Miscellaneous manufactured articles	23,292.6	31,597.6	36,845.8
Total (incl. others)	323,084.5	425,212.2	524,413.1

Exports f.o.b.	2009	2010	2011
Mineral fuels, lubricants, etc. .	23,786.0	32,579.7	53,086.9
Petroleum, petroleum products, etc.	23,663.4	32,375.2	52,801.6
Chemicals and related products	37,414.7	48,951.5	60,709.2
Organic chemicals	12,847.5	16,531.1	22,178.4
Plastics in primary forms . .	13,874.9	17,817.3	20,460.3
Basic manufactures	48,114.5	60,430.1	76,748.8
Textile yarn, fabrics, etc. . .	9,155.4	10,967.7	12,368.8
Iron and steel	17,468.0	24,432.9	31,792.8
Machinery and transport equipment	206,334.1	263,902.6	300,067.4
Office machines and automatic data-processing machines . .	8,991.8	12,889.8	10,388.3
Automatic data-processing machines and units, etc. . .	2,377.2	2,987.5	3,312.0
Parts and accessories for office machines and automatic data-processing equipment . . .	5,074.9	8,266.8	5,090.1
Telecommunications and sound equipment	41,226.4	40,403.0	40,351.2
Other electrical machinery, apparatus, etc.	47,500.1	70,194.3	77,570.1
Thermionic valves and tubes, microprocessors, transistors, etc.	26,957.9	43,291.1	45,211.4
Road vehicles	36,294.6	53,209.0	66,781.4
Motor cars and other motor vehicles	22,399.1	31,781.7	40,909.9
Other transport equipment . .	43,592.6	48,617.7	55,783.2
Ships, boats and floating structures	42,483.4	46,735.3	54,133.1
Miscellaneous manufactured articles	36,906.7	46,860.0	47,009.1
Total (incl. others)	363,533.6	466,383.8	555,213.7

* Excluding trade with the Democratic People's Republic of Korea.

Source: Korea International Trade Association.

PRINCIPAL TRADING PARTNERS
(US $ million)*

Imports c.i.f.	2009	2010	2011
Australia	14,756.1	20,456.2	26,316.3
Brazil	3,743.5	4,712.1	6,342.9
Canada	3,535.3	4,350.9	6,611.9
China, People's Republic . .	54,246.1	71,573.6	86,432.2
France	4,006.1	4,283.5	6,314.9
Germany	12,298.5	14,304.9	16,962.6
Hong Kong	1,487.2	1,945.9	2,315.1
India	4,141.6	5,674.4	7,893.6
Indonesia	9,264.1	13,985.8	17,216.4
Iran	5,745.7	6,940.2	11,358.4
Iraq	3,812.2	4,427.7	9,137.8
Italy	3,512.9	3,723.3	4,373.9
Japan	49,427.5	64,296.1	68,320.2
Kuwait	7,991.5	10,850.1	16,959.6
Malaysia	7,574.1	9,531.0	10,467.8
Oman	4,124.5	4,095.9	5,362.8
Philippines	2,651.6	3,488.1	3,571.5
Qatar	8,386.5	11,915.5	20,749.4
Russia	5,788.7	9,899.5	10,852.2
Saudi Arabia	19,736.8	26,820.0	36,972.6
Singapore	7,871.8	7,849.5	8,966.7
Taiwan	9,851.4	13,647.1	14,693.6
Thailand	3,238.6	4,168.8	5,413.4
United Arab Emirates . . .	9,310.0	12,170.1	14,759.4
United Kingdom	2,895.8	3,265.5	3,818.1
USA	29,039.5	40,402.7	44,569.0
Total (incl. others)	323,084.5	425,212.2	524,413.1

Exports f.o.b.	2009	2010	2011
Australia	5,243.1	6,641.6	8,163.8
Brazil	5,311.2	7,752.6	11,821.4
Canada	3,439.6	4,101.9	4,927.7
China, People's Republic . .	86,703.2	116,837.8	134,185.0
France	2,910.6	3,004.3	5,707.4
Germany	8,820.9	10,702.2	9,500.9
Hong Kong	19,661.1	25,294.3	30,968.4
India	8,013.3	11,434.6	12,654.1
Indonesia	5,999.9	8,897.3	13,564.5
Iran	3,991.9	4,596.7	6,068.3
Italy	2,797.3	3,569.1	4,107.5
Japan	21,770.8	28,176.3	39,679.7
Liberia	4,884.6	5,401.7	7,389.3
Malaysia	4,324.8	6,114.8	6,275.1
Mexico	7,132.8	8,845.5	9,729.1
Netherlands	4,527.5	5,306.2	4,627.0
Philippines	4,567.3	5,838.0	7,338.9
Russia	4,194.1	7,759.8	10,304.9
Singapore	13,617.0	15,244.2	20,839.0
Spain	1,737.1	1,858.0	1,856.6
Taiwan	9,501.1	14,830.5	18,206.0
Thailand	4,528.2	6,459.8	8,459.0
Turkey	2,660.7	3,752.9	5,071.0
United Arab Emirates . .	4,977.8	5,487.0	7,267.8
United Kingdom	3,796.6	5,555.1	4,969.1
USA	37,649.9	49,816.1	56,207.7
Viet Nam	7,149.5	9,652.1	13,464.9
Total (incl. others)	363,533.6	466,383.8	555,213.7

* Excluding trade with the Democratic People's Republic of Korea.

Source: Korea International Trade Association.

Trade with the Democratic People's Republic of Korea (US $ million, unofficial estimates): *Total imports:* 519.5 in 2006; 765.3 in 2007; 932.3 in 2008. *Total exports:* 830.2 in 2006; 1,032.6 in 2007; 888.1 in 2008 (Source: Bank of Korea, Republic of Korea).

Transport

RAILWAYS
(traffic)

	2003	2004	2005
Passengers carried ('000) . . .	894,620	921,223	950,995
Passenger-km (million) . . .	27,228	28,459	31,004
Freight ('000 metric tons) . . .	47,110	44,512	41,669
Freight ton-km (million) . . .	11,057	10,641	10,108

ROAD TRAFFIC
(motor vehicles in use at 31 December)

	2008	2009	2010
Passenger cars	12,483,809	13,023,819	13,631,769
Goods vehicles	3,213,712	3,220,704	3,259,862
Buses and coaches	1,096,698	1,080,687	1,049,725
Motorcycles and mopeds . . .	1,814,399	1,820,729	1,825,474

Source: IRF, *World Road Statistics.*

SHIPPING

Flag Registered Fleet
(at 31 December)

	2010	2011	2012
Number of vessels	2,022	2,036	2,029
Total displacement ('000 grt) . .	13,021.9	12,620.1	11,913.0

Source: Lloyd's List Intelligence (www.lloydslistintelligence.com).

Sea-borne Freight Traffic
('000 metric tons)*

	2002	2003	2004
Goods loaded	319,570	340,527	317,799
Goods unloaded	615,555	616,326	593,361

* Including coastwise traffic loaded and unloaded.

CIVIL AVIATION
(scheduled services)

	2007	2008	2009
Kilometres flown (million) . .	488	516	513
Passengers carried ('000) . . .	36,655	36,078	34,169
Passenger-km (million) . . .	81,387	83,192	82,264
Total ton-km (million)	16,404	16,283	16,059

Source: UN, *Statistical Yearbook*.

2010: Passengers carried ('000) 42,763 (Source: World Bank, World Development Indicators database).

Tourism

FOREIGN VISITOR ARRIVALS*

Country of residence	2007	2008	2009
China, People's Republic . . .	1,068,925	1,167,891	1,342,317
Hong Kong	140,138	160,325	215,769
Japan	2,235,963	2,378,102	3,053,311
Philippines	263,799	276,710	271,962
Russia	140,426	136,342	137,054
Taiwan	335,224	320,244	380,628
Thailand	146,792	160,687	190,972
USA	587,324	610,083	611,327
Total (incl. others)	6,448,240	6,890,841	7,817,533

* Including same-day visitors (excursionists) and crew members from ships; also including Korean nationals resident abroad.

Total foreign visitor arrivals ('000): 8,798 in 2010; 9,795 in 2011 (provisional).

Receipts from tourism (US $ million, excl. passenger transport): 9,819 in 2009; 10,359 in 2010; 12,304 in 2011 (provisional).

Source: World Tourism Organization.

Communications Media

	2009	2010	2011
Telephones ('000 main lines in use)	26,893.8	28,543.2	29,468.5
Mobile cellular telephones ('000 subscribers)	47,944.2	50,767.2	52,506.8
Internet subscribers ('000)* . .	16,347.7	17,193.6	17,859.0
Broadband subscribers ('000) . .	16,347.7	17,193.6	17,859.0

* Estimates based on percentage.

Source: International Telecommunication Union.

Education

(2007)

	Institutions	Teachers	Pupils
Kindergarten	8,294	33,504	541,550
Primary schools	5,756	167,182	3,829,998
Middle schools	3,032	107,986	2,063,159
General high schools . .	1,457	83,662	1,347,363
Vocational high schools . .	702	36,549	494,011
Junior colleges	148	11,685	795,519
Teachers' colleges . . .	11	855	25,834
Universities and colleges . .	175	52,763	1,919,504
Graduate schools	1,042	2,895	296,576

2009/10 (UNESCO estimates): *Pupils:* Pre-primary 1,538,067; Primary 3,306,192; Secondary 3,950,500 (General 3,484,371, Vocational 466,129); Tertiary 3,269,509; *Teachers:* Primary 158,056; Secondary 224,503 (General 190,765, Vocational 33,738); Tertiary 222,525 (Source: UNESCO Institute for Statistics).

Pupil-teacher ratio (primary education, UNESCO estimate): 20.9 in 2009/10 (Source: UNESCO Institute for Statistics).

Adult literacy rate (UNESCO estimates): 97.9% (males 99.2%; females 96.6%) in 2001 (Source: UN Development Programme, *Human Development Report*).

Directory

The Government

HEAD OF STATE

President: PARK GEUN-HYE (took office 25 February 2013).

STATE COUNCIL
(May 2013)

The Government is formed by the Saenuri Party (New Frontier Party).

Prime Minister: CHUNG HONG-WON.

Deputy Prime Minister and Minister of Strategy and Finance: HYUN OH-SEOK.

Minister of Unification: YOO KIL-JAE.

Minister of Foreign Affairs: YUN BYUNG-SE.

Minister of Security and Public Administration: YOO JEONG-BOK.

Minister of Justice: HWANG KYO-AHN.

Minister of National Defence: KIM KWAN-JIN.

Minister of Education: SEO NAM-SOO.

Minister of Culture, Sports and Tourism: YOO JIN-RYONG.

Minister of Agriculture, Food and Rural Affairs: LEE DONG-PIL.

Minister of Science, ICT and Future Planning: CHOI MUN-KEE.

Minister of Trade, Industry and Energy: YOON SANG-JICK.

Minister of Health and Welfare: CHIN YOUNG.

Minister of Environment: YOON SEONG-KYU.

Minister of Employment and Labour: PHANG HA-NAM.

Minister of Gender Equality and Family: CHO YOON-SUN.

Minister of Land, Infrastructure and Transport: SUH SEUNG-HWAN.

Minister of Oceans and Fisheries: YOON JIN-SOOK.

MINISTRIES

Office of the President: Chong Wa Dae (The Blue House), 1, Sejong-no, Jongno-gu, Seoul; tel. (2) 730-5800; e-mail foreign@president.go.kr; internet www.president.go.kr.

Prime Minister's Office: 55, Sejong-no, Jongno-gu, Seoul 110-760; tel. (2) 2100-2114; fax (2) 739-5830; e-mail webmaster@pmo.go.kr; internet www.pmo.go.kr.

Ministry of Agriculture, Food and Rural Affairs: Govt Complex, 94 Euhjin-dong, Sejong City 339-012; tel. (2) 1577-1020; fax (44) 868-0846; e-mail webmaster@mafra.go.kr; internet www.mafra.go.kr.

Ministry of Culture, Sports and Tourism: 215, Changgyeong-gung-ro, Jongno-gu, Seoul 110-630; tel. (2) 3704-9114; fax (2) 3704-9154; e-mail webadmin@www.mct.go.kr; internet www.mcst.go.kr.

Ministry of Education: 77-6, Sejong-no, Jongno-gu, Seoul 110-760; tel. (2) 6222-6060; fax (2) 2100-6133; e-mail webmaster@moe.go.kr; internet www.moe.go.kr.

Ministry of Employment and Labour: Govt Complex, 2, 47 Gwanmun-ro, Gwacheon City, Gyeonggi-do 427-718; tel. (2) 2110-7497; fax (2) 503-6623; internet www.moel.go.kr.

Ministry of Environment: Govt Complex, 11, Doum 6-ro, Sejong City 339-012; tel. (44) 201-6568; e-mail webmaster@me.go.kr; internet www.me.go.kr.

Ministry of Foreign Affairs: 37, Sejong-no, Seoul 110-787; tel. (2) 2100-2114; fax (2) 2100-7999; e-mail web@mofa.go.kr; internet www.mofa.go.kr.

Ministry of Gender Equality and Family: Premiere Place Bldg, 96, Mugyo-dong, Jung-gu, Seoul 100-777; tel. (2) 2075-4500; fax (2) 2075-4780; e-mail webadmin@mogef.go.kr; internet www.mogef.go.kr.

Ministry for Health and Welfare: 75, Yulgong-ro, Jongno-gu, Seoul 110-793; internet www.mohw.go.kr.

Ministry of Justice: Bldg 5, 1, Jungang-dong, Gwacheon City, Gyeonggi Prov. 427-720; tel. (2) 2110-3009; fax (2) 503-7113; e-mail webmaster@moj.go.kr; internet www.moj.go.kr.

Ministry of Land, Infrastructure and Transport: Govt Complex, 11, Doum 6-ro, Sejong City 339-012; tel. (44) 201-4672; fax (44) 860-9500; e-mail webmaster@molit.go.kr; internet www.molit.go.kr.

Ministry of National Defence: 1, 3-ga, Yeongsan-dong, Yeongsan-gu, Seoul 140-701; tel. (2) 795-0071; fax (2) 703-3109; e-mail cyber@mnd.go.kr; internet www.mnd.go.kr.

Ministry of Oceans and Fisheries: 94 Govt Complex, 5-dong, Sejong City 339-012; tel. (44) 200-5555; internet www.mof.go.kr.

Ministry of Science, ICT and Future Planning: Govt Complex, Gwacheon City, Gyeonggi Prov. 427-700; internet www.msip.go.kr.

Ministry of Security and Public Administration: Govt Complex, 77-6, Sejong-no, 1-ga, Jongno-gu, Seoul 110-760; tel. (2) 2100-3399; internet www.mospa.go.kr.

Ministry of Strategy and Finance: Govt Complex, 477, Galmae-ro, Sejong City 339-012; tel. (44) 215-2114; fax (44) 215-4000; e-mail forumnet@mosf.go.kr; internet www.mosf.go.kr.

Ministry of Trade, Industry and Energy: 47, Gwanmunro, Gwacheon City, Gyeonggi Prov. 427-723; tel. (2) 1577-0900; e-mail webmke@mke.go.kr; internet www.motie.go.kr.

Ministry of Unification: Govt Complex, 77-6, Sejong-no, Jongno-gu, Seoul 110-760; tel. (2) 2100-5722; fax (2) 2100-5799; e-mail hanabyun@unikorea.go.kr; internet www.unikorea.go.kr.

President and Legislature

PRESIDENT

Election, 19 December 2012

Candidate	Votes	% of total
Park Geun-Hye (Saenuri Party) . .	15,773,128	51.55
Moon Jae-In (Democratic United Party*)	14,692,632	48.02
Kang Ji-Won (Independent) . . .	53,303	0.17
Kim Soon-Ja (Independent) . . .	46,017	0.15
Kim So-Yeon (Independent) . . .	16,687	0.05
Park Jong-Sun (Independent) . . .	12,854	0.04
Total (incl. others)	30,721,459	100.00

* In May 2013 the Democratic United Party changed its name to the Democratic Party.

LEGISLATURE

Kuk Hoe
(National Assembly)

1 Yeouido-dong, Yeongdeungpo-gu, Seoul 150-701; tel. (2) 788-2001; fax (2) 788-3375; e-mail webmaster@assembly.go.kr; internet www.assembly.go.kr.

Speaker: KANG CHANG-HEE.

General Election, 11 April 2012

Party	Representatives		
	Elected	Proportional	Total
Saenuri Party . . .	127	25	152
Democratic United Party* . .	106	21	127
Unified Progressive Party . .	7	6	13
Liberty Forward Party† . .	3	2	5
Independents	3	—	3
Total	246	54	300

* In May 2013 the Democratic United Party changed its name to the Democratic Party.

† In May 2012 the Liberty Forward Party changed its name to the Advancement and Unification Party.

Election Commission

National Election Commission: 2-3 Junggang-dong, Gwacheon-si, Gyeonggi-do 427-727; tel. (2) 503-1114; e-mail nec@nec.go.kr; internet www.nec.go.kr; Chair. KIM NUNG-HWAN.

Political Organizations

Advancement and Unification Party (AUP): Yeongsan Bldg, 3rd Floor, 14-14, Yeouido-dong, Yeoungdeungpo-gu, Seoul; tel. (2) 780-3988; fax (2) 780-3983; e-mail webmaster@jayou.or.kr; internet www.aup.or.kr; conservative; merged with People First Union Sept. 2011; fmrly Liberty Forward Party; renamed as above May 2012; Leader RHEE IN-JE.

Democratic Party (DP): 133-6, Youngdeungpo-dong, Youngdeungpo-gu, Seoul 150-036; fax (2) 2630-0145; internet www.minjoo.kr; f. 2011; est. as the Democratic United Party, following the merger of the Democratic Party with the Civil Unity Party; renamed as above May 2013; formed electoral alliance with Unified Progressive Party and New Progressive Party to contest April 2012 elections; supported by Federation of Korean Trade Unions; Chair. KIM HAN-GIL; Sec.-Gen. LIM JONG-SEOK.

New Progressive Party (NPP): 371-12, Seogyo-dong, Mapo-gu, Seoul 121-893; tel. (2) 6004-2000; fax (2) 6004-2001; e-mail newjinbo@gmail.com; internet www.newjinbo.org; f. 2008; left-wing; est. by splinter group of DLP; absorbed the Korea Socialist Party in 2012; Pres. ROH HOE-CHAN .

Saenuri Party (New Frontier Party): 14-31, Yeouido-dong, Yeongdeungpo-gu, Seoul 156-768; tel. (2) 3786-3000; fax (2) 3786-3610; internet www.saenuriparty.kr; f. 1997; est. as Grand National Party by merger of the original Democratic Party (f. 1990) and New Korea Party; renamed as above in 2012; Chair. HWANG WOO-YEA; Sec.-Gen. SUH BYUNG-SOO.

Unified Progressive Party: f. 2011; est. by amalgamation of Democratic Labour Party, People's Participation Party and a faction of the New Progressive Party; in electoral alliance with the Democratic United Party for April 2012 election; Chair. KANG KI-KAB.

Civic groups play an increasingly significant role in South Korean politics. These include: the People's Solidarity for Participatory Democracy (Dir JANG HASUNG); the Citizens' Coalition for Economic Justice (Sec.-Gen. PARK BYEONG-OK); and the Citizens' Alliance for Political Reform (Leader KIM SOK-SU).

Diplomatic Representation

EMBASSIES IN THE REPUBLIC OF KOREA

Afghanistan: 27-2, Hannam-dong, Yeongsan-gu, Seoul 140-210; tel. (2) 793-3535; fax (2) 795-2662; e-mail info@afghanistanembassy.or.kr; internet www.afghanistanembassy.or.kr; Ambassador MOHAMMAD YOUNOS FARMAN.

Algeria: 2-6, Itaewon 2-dong, Yeongsan-gu, Seoul 140-857; tel. (2) 794-5034; fax (2) 794-5040; e-mail sifdja01@kornet.net; internet www.algerianemb.or.kr; Ambassador HOCINE SAHRAOUI.

Angola: 737-11, Hannam 2-dong, Yeongsan-gu, Seoul 140-212; tel. (2) 792-8463; fax (2) 792-8467; e-mail embassy@angolaembassy.or.kr; internet www.angolaembassy.or.kr; Ambassador ALBINO MALUNGO.

Argentina: Chun Woo Bldg, 5th Floor, 534, Itaewon-dong, Yeongsan-gu, Seoul 140-861; tel. (2) 793-4062; fax (2) 792-5820; e-mail info@argentina.or.kr; internet www.argentina.or.kr; Chargé d'affaires a.i. AUGUSTO CESAR GRANADA.

Australia: Kyobo Bldg, 19th Floor, 1, Jongno 1-ga, Jongno-gu, Seoul 110-714; tel. (2) 2003-0100; fax (2) 2003-0196; e-mail seoul-inform@dfat.gov.au; internet www.southkorea.embassy.gov.au; Ambassador WILLIAM PATERSON.

Austria: Kyobo Bldg, 21st Floor, 1-1, Jongno 1-ga, Jongno-gu, Seoul 110-714; tel. (2) 732-9071; fax (2) 732-9486; e-mail seoul-ob@bmeia.gv.at; internet www.bmeia.gv.at/seoul; Ambassador Dr JOSEF MÜLLNER.

Azerbaijan: Hannam Tower, Annex Bldg, 3rd Floor, 730, Hannam-dong, Yeongsan-gu, Seoul 140-893; tel. (2) 797-1765; fax (2) 797-1767; e-mail info@azembassy.co.kr; internet www.azembassy.co.kr; Ambassador ROVSHAN JAMSHIDOV.

Bangladesh: 310-22, Dongbinggo-dong, Yeongsan-gu, Seoul; tel. (2) 796-4056; fax (2) 790-5313; e-mail bdootseoul@kornet.net; internet www.bdembseoul.org; Ambassador M. ENAMUL KABIR.

Belarus: 432-1636, Sindang 2-dong, Jung-gu, Seoul 100-835; tel. (2) 2237-8171; fax (2) 2237-8174; e-mail korea@mfa.gov.by; internet korea.mfa.gov.by; Ambassador NATALLIA ZHYLEVICH.

Belgium: 737-10, Hannam-dong, Yeongsan-gu, Seoul 140-893; tel. (2) 749-0381; fax (2) 797-1688; e-mail seoul@diplobel.fed.be; internet www.diplomatie.be/seoul; Ambassador FRANÇOIS BONTEMPS.

Brazil: Ihn Gallery Bldg, 4th and 5th Floors, 141, Palpan-dong, Jongno-gu, Seoul; tel. (2) 738-4970; fax (2) 738-4974; e-mail braseul@kornet.net; internet seul.itamaraty.gov.br; Ambassador EDMUNDO SUSSUMU FUJITA.

Brunei: 39-1, Cheongun-dong, Jongno-gu, Seoul 110-030; tel. (2) 790-1078; fax (2) 790-1084; e-mail kbnbd_seoul@yahoo.com; Ambassador Dato' Paduka Haji HARUN BIN Haji ISMAIL.

Bulgaria: 723-42, Hannam 2-dong, Yeongsan-gu, Seoul 140-894; tel. (2) 794-8626; fax (2) 794-8627; e-mail embassy.seoul@mfa.bg; internet www.mfa.bg/embassies/korea; Ambassador PETAR ANDONOV.

Cambodia: 653-110, Hannam-dong, Yeongsan-gu, Seoul 140-887; tel. (2) 3785-1041; fax (2) 3785-1040; e-mail camboemb@korea.com; Ambassador KY SIM CHAN.

Canada: 16-1, Jeong-dong, Jung-gu, CPOB 6299, Seoul 100-662; tel. (2) 3783-6000; fax (2) 3783-6239; e-mail seoul@international.gc.ca; internet www.canadainternational.gc.ca/korea-coree; Ambassador DAVID CHATTERSON.

Chile: Coryo Daeyungak Tower, Unit 1801, 25-5, Chungmoro 1-ga, Jung-gu, Seoul 100-706; tel. (2) 779-2610; fax (2) 779-2615; e-mail echilekr@yahoo.co.kr; internet www.coreachile.org; Ambassador HERNÁN BRANTES.

China, People's Republic: 54, Hyoja-dong, Jongno-gu, Seoul 110-033; tel. (2) 738-1038; fax (2) 738-1046; e-mail chinaemb_kr@mfa.gov.cn; internet www.chinaemb.or.kr; Ambassador ZHANG XINSEN.

Colombia: Kyobo Bldg, 11th Floor, Jongno 1-ga, Jongno-gu, Seoul 110-714; tel. (2) 720-1369; fax (2) 725-6959; e-mail cseul@cancilleria.gov.co; Ambassador MANUEL HERNANDO SOLANO SOSSA.

Congo, Democratic Republic: Daewoo Complex Bldg, Unit 702, 167, Naesu-dong, Jongno-gu, Seoul 110-070; tel. (2) 722-7958; fax (2) 722-7998; e-mail congokoreaembassy@yahoo.com; Ambassador NDAMBO CHRISTOPHE NGWEY.

Costa Rica: Iljin Bldg, Unit 8, 50-1, Dohwa-dong, Mapo-gu, Seoul 121-040; tel. (2) 707-9249; fax (2) 707-9255; e-mail embajadacr@ecostarica.or.kr; internet www.ecostarica.or.kr; Ambassador FERNANDO BORBÓN ARIAS.

Côte d'Ivoire: Chungam Bldg, 2nd Floor, 794-4, Hannam-dong, Yeongsan-gu, Seoul 140-894; tel. (2) 3785-0561; fax (2) 3785-0564; e-mail ambaciseoul@gmail.com; internet cotedivoireembassy.or.kr; Ambassador KOUASSI FLORENT EKRA.

Czech Republic: 1-121, Sinmun-no 2-ga, Jongno-gu, Seoul 110-062; tel. (2) 725-6765; fax (2) 734-6452; e-mail seoul@embassy.mzv.cz; internet www.mzv.cz/seoul; Ambassador JAROSLAV OLŠA, Jr.

Denmark: Namsong Bldg, 5th Floor, 260-199, Itaewon-dong, Yeongsan-gu, Seoul 140-200; tel. (2) 795-4187; fax (2) 796-0986; e-mail selamb@um.dk; internet sydkorea.um.dk; Ambassador PETER LYSHOLT HANSEN.

Dominican Republic: Taepyeong-no Bldg, 19th Floor, 310, Taepyeong-no 2-ga, Jung-gu, Seoul; tel. (2) 756-3513; fax (2) 756-3514; e-mail embadom@kornet.net; internet embadom.or.kr; Ambassador GRECIA FIORDALICIA PICHARDO POLANCO.

Ecuador: SC First Bank Bldg, 19th Floor, 100, Gongpyeong-dong, Jongno-gu, Seoul 110-702; tel. (2) 739-2401; fax (2) 739-2355; e-mail ecuadorkoreaembassy@gmail.com; internet ecuadorkorea.org; Ambassador NICOLÁS TRUJILLO NEWLIN.

Egypt: 46-1, Hannam-dong, Yeongsan-gu, Seoul 140-210; tel. (2) 749-0787; fax (2) 795-2588; e-mail embassyegyptkorea@yahoo.com; internet www.mfa.gov.eg/Seoul_Emb; Ambassador MOHAMED ABDEL RAHIM EL-ZORKANY.

El Salvador: Samsung Life Insurance Bldg, 20th Floor, 150, Taepyeong-no 2-ga, Jung-gu, Seoul 100-716; tel. (2) 753-3432; fax (2) 753-3456; e-mail koresal@kornet.net; Ambassador HÉCTOR ROBERTO GONZÁLEZ URRUTIA.

Fiji: 210-69, Itaewon-dong, Yeongsan-gu, Seoul; Ambassador FILIMONE KAU.

Finland: Kyobo Bldg, 18th Floor, Jongno 1, Jongno-gu, Seoul 110-714; tel. (2) 732-6737; fax (2) 723-4969; e-mail sanomat.seo@formin.fi; internet www.finland.or.kr; Ambassador MATTI HEIMONEN.

France: 30, Hap-dong, Seodaemun-gu, Seoul 120-030; tel. (2) 3149-4300; fax (2) 3149-4310; e-mail ambafrance@hanafos.com; internet www.ambafrance-kr.org; Ambassador JÉRÔME PASQUIER.

Gabon: Yoosung Bldg, 4th Floor, 738-20, Hannam-dong, Yeongsan-gu, Seoul; tel. (2) 793-9575; fax (2) 793-9574; e-mail amgabsel@unitel.co.kr; Ambassador CARLOS VICTOR BOUNGOU.

Germany: 32, Jangmun-ro, Yeongsan-gu, Seoul 140-816; tel. (2) 748-4114; fax (2) 748-4161; e-mail info@seoul.diplo.de; internet www.seoul.diplo.de; Ambassador ROLF MAFAEL.

Ghana: 5-4, Hannam-dong, Yeongsan-gu, CPOB 3887, Seoul 140-884; tel. (2) 3785-1427; fax (2) 3785-1428; e-mail ghana3@kornet.net; internet www.ghanaembassy.or.kr; Ambassador MARGARET CLARKE-KWESIE.

Greece: Hanwha Bldg, 27th Floor, 1, Janggyo-dong, Jung-gu, Seoul 100-797; tel. (2) 729-1401; fax (2) 729-1402; e-mail greekemb@kornet.net; Ambassador DIONISIOS SOURVANOS.

Guatemala: 614, Lotte Hotel, 1, Sogong-dong, Jung-gu, Seoul 100-635; tel. (2) 771-7582; fax (2) 771-7584; e-mail embcorea@minex.gob.gt; Chargé d'affaires a.i. ALEJANDRO JOSÉ MONTUFAR CHÁVEZ.

Holy See: 2, Gungjeong-dong, Jongno-gu, Seoul 110-031 (Apostolic Nunciature); tel. (2) 736-5725; fax (2) 739-5738; e-mail apnunkr@yahoo.com; Apostolic Nuncio Most Rev. OSVALDO PADILLA (Titular Archbishop of Voli).

Honduras: Jongno Tower Bldg, 22nd Floor, 6, Jongno 2-ga, Jongno-gu, Seoul 110-160; tel. (2) 738-8402; fax (2) 738-8403; e-mail hondurasembassy@hotmail.com; Ambassador MICHEL IDIAQUEZ BARADAT.

Hungary: 58, Jangmun-ro, Dongbinggo-dong, Yeongsan-gu, Seoul 140-809; tel. (2) 792-2105; fax (2) 792-2109; e-mail mission.sel@mfa.gov.hu; internet www.mfa.gov.hu/emb/seoul; Ambassador MIKLÓS LENGYEL.

India: 37-3, Hannam-dong, Yeongsan-gu, CPOB 3466, Seoul 140-210; tel. (2) 798-4257; fax (2) 796-9534; e-mail eoiseoul@sinbiro.com; internet www.indembassy.or.kr; Ambassador VISHNU PRAKASH.

Indonesia: 55, Yeouido-dong, Yeongdeungpo-gu, Seoul 150-010; tel. (2) 783-5675; fax (2) 780-4280; e-mail kbriseoul@kornet.net; internet www.kemlu.go.id/seoul; Ambassador JOHN A. PRASETIO.

Iran: 1-93, Dongbinggo-dong, Yeongsan-gu, Seoul 140-809; tel. (2) 793-7751; fax (2) 792-7052; e-mail iranssy@chol.com; Ambassador AHMAD MASOUMIFAR.

Iraq: 1-94, Dongbinggo-dong, Yeongsan-gu, Seoul 140-811; tel. (2) 790-4202; fax (2) 790-4206; e-mail sulemb@iraqmfamail.com; internet www.mofamission.gov.iq/kor; Ambassador KHALIL AL-MOSAWI.

Ireland: Leema Bldg, 13th Floor, 146-1, Susong-dong, Jongno-gu, Seoul 110-755; tel. (2) 774-6455; fax (2) 774-6458; e-mail seoulembassy@dfa.ie; internet www.embassyofireland.or.kr; Ambassador EAMONN MCKEE.

Israel: Cheonggye 11 Bldg, 18th Floor, 149, Seorin-dong, Jongno-gu, Seoul 110-726; tel. (2) 3210-8500; fax (2) 3210-8555; e-mail info@seoul.mfa.gov.il; internet seoul.mfa.gov.il; Ambassador TUVIA ISRAELI.

Italy: Ilshin Bldg, 3rd Floor, 714, Hannam-dong, Yongsan-gu, Seoul 140-894; tel. (2) 796-0491; fax (2) 797-5560; e-mail embassy.seoul@esteri.it; internet www.ambseoul.esteri.it; Ambassador SERGIO MERCURI.

Japan: 18-11, Junghak-dong, Jongno-gu, Seoul 110-150; tel. (2) 2170-5200; fax (2) 734-4528; e-mail info@so.mofa.go.jp; internet www.kr.emb-japan.go.jp; Ambassador KORO BESSHO.

Jordan: Twin-Tree Tower, Bldg B, 6th Floor, 14 Joonghak-dong, Jongno-gu, Seoul 110-792; tel. (2) 318-2897; fax (2) 318-3644; e-mail jdembassy@gmail.com; Ambassador OMAR AL-NAHAR.

Kazakhstan: 53, Jangmun-ro, Yeongsan-gu, Seoul 140-809; tel. (2) 379-9714; fax (2) 395-9766; e-mail seoul@mfa.kz; internet www.kazembassy.org; Ambassador DULAT BAKISHEV.

Kenya: 243-36, Itaewon-dong, Yeongsan-gu, Seoul 140-200; tel. (2) 3785-2903; fax (2) 3785-2905; e-mail info@kenya-embassy.or.kr; internet www.kenya-embassy.or.kr; Ambassador NGOVI KITAU.

Kuwait: 309-15, Dongbinggo-dong, Yeongsan-gu, Seoul; tel. (2) 749-3688; fax (2) 749-3687; e-mail kuwaitembassy@kornet.net; Ambassador MUTEB AL-MUTOTEH.

Kyrgyzstan: Namsong Bldg, Unit 403, 260-199, Itaewon-dong, Yeongsan-gu, Seoul 140-200; tel. (2) 379-0951; fax (2) 379-0953; e-mail seoulembassykg@gmail.com; Ambassador DUISHONKUL CHOTONOV.

Laos: 657-9, Hannam-dong, Yeongsan-gu, Seoul 140-887; tel. (2) 796-1713; fax (2) 796-1771; Ambassador KHAMLA SAYACHAK.

Lebanon: 310-49, Dongbinggo-dong, Yeongsan-gu, Seoul 140-230; tel. (2) 794-6482; fax (2) 794-6485; e-mail emleb@lebanonembassy.net; internet www.lebanonembassy.net; Chargé d'affaires a.i. JAD AL-HASSAN.

Malaysia: 4-1, Hannam-dong, Yeongsan-gu, Seoul 140-884; tel. (2) 2077-8600; fax (2) 794-5480; e-mail malseoul@kln.gov.my; internet www.malaysia.or.kr; Ambassador Dato' RAMLAN BIN IBRAHIM.

Mexico: 33-6, Hannam 1-dong, Yeongsan-gu, Seoul 140-885; tel. (2) 798-1694; fax (2) 790-0939; e-mail embajada@embamexcor.org; internet portal.sre.gob.mx/corea; Ambassador MARTHA ORTIZ DE ROSAS GÓMEZ.

Mongolia: 33-5, Hannam-dong, Yeongsan-gu, Seoul 140-885; tel. (2) 794-1350; fax (2) 794-7605; e-mail mongol6@kornet.net; internet www.mongolembassy.com; Ambassador BAASANJAVYN GANBOLD.

Morocco: Hannam Tower, Annex Bldg, 4th Floor, 730, Hannam-dong, Yeongsan-gu, Seoul; tel. (2) 793-6249; fax (2) 792-8178; e-mail sifamase@kornet.net; Ambassador MOHAMED CHRAÏBI.

Myanmar: 724-1, Hannam-dong, Yeongsan-gu, Seoul 140-210; tel. (2) 790-3814; fax (2) 790-3817; e-mail myanmar@kotis.net; Ambassador NYUNT HLAING.

Nepal: 445-7, Huam-dong, Yeongsan-gu, Seoul; tel. (2) 3789-9770; fax (2) 736-8848; e-mail info@nepembseoul.gov.np; internet www.nepembseoul.gov.np; Ambassador KAMAN SINGH LAMA.

Netherlands: Jeongdong Bldg, 10/F, 15-5 Jeong-dong, Jung-gu, Seoul; tel. (2) 311-8600; fax (2) 311-8650; e-mail seo@minbuza.nl; internet southkorea.nlembassy.org; Ambassador PAUL ALEX MENK-VELD.

New Zealand: Jeong-dong Bldg, 8th Floor, Jeong-dong, Jung-gu, Seoul 100-784; tel. (2) 3701-7700; fax (2) 3701-7701; e-mail nzembsel@kornet.net; internet www.nzembassy.com/korea; Ambassador PATRICK RATA.

Nigeria: 310-19, Dongbinggo-dong, Yeongsan-gu, CPOB 3754, Seoul 140-230; tel. (2) 797-2370; fax (2) 796-1848; e-mail chancery@nigerianembassy.or.kr; internet www.nigerianembassy.or.kr; Ambassador DESMOND AKAWOR.

Norway: Jeong-dong Bldg, 13th Floor, 15-5 Jeong-dong, Jung-gu, Seoul 100-784; tel. (2) 727-7100; fax (2) 727-7199; e-mail emb.seoul@mfa.no; internet www.norway.or.kr; Ambassador TORBJØRN HOLTHE.

Oman: 58-1, Shinmoon-ro 1-ga, Jongno-gu, Seoul 110-700; tel. (2) 790-2431; fax (2) 790-2430; e-mail omanembs@kornet.net; Ambassador MOHAMED SALIM AL-HARTHY.

Pakistan: 124-13, Itaewon-dong, Yeongsan-gu, Seoul 140-200; tel. (2) 796-8252; fax (2) 796-0313; e-mail consular@pkembassy.or.kr; internet www.pkembassy.or.kr; Ambassador SHAUKAT ALI MUKA-DAM.

Panama: 407, Somerset Palace, Soosong-dong, Jongno-gu, Seoul 110-885; tel. (2) 734-8610; fax (2) 734-8613; e-mail panaemba@kornet.net; Ambassador ARAM B. CISNEROS NAYLOR.

Papua New Guinea: Doosan We've Pavilion Bldg, Unit 210, 58, Soosong-dong, Jongno-gu, Seoul 110-858; tel. (2) 2198-5771; fax (2) 2198-5779; e-mail ambassador@kunduseoul.kr; Ambassador BILL VERI.

Paraguay: 302, Hannam Tower, Annex Bldg, 3rd Floor, 730, Hannam-dong, Yeongsan-gu, Seoul; tel. (2) 792-8335; fax (2) 792-8334; e-mail pyemc2@kornet.net; internet www.embaparcorea.org; Ambassador JOSE FÉLIZ FERNÁNDEZ ESTIGARRIBIA.

Peru: Daeyungak Bldg, Unit 2002, 25-5, Jungmu-no 1-ga, Jung-gu, Seoul 100-706; tel. (2) 757-1735; fax (2) 757-1738; e-mail embaperuencorea@gmail.com; internet www.embassyperu.or.kr; Ambassador JAIME POMAREDA MONTENEGRO.

Philippines: 5-1, Itaewon 2-dong, Yeongsan-gu, Seoul; tel. (2) 796-7387; fax (2) 796-0827; e-mail seoulpe@philembassy-seoul.com; internet www.philembassy-seoul.com; Ambassador LUIS TEODORO CRUZ.

Poland: 70, Sagan-dong, Jongno-gu, Seoul; tel. (2) 723-9681; fax (2) 723-9680; e-mail seul.amb.sekretariat@msz.gov.pl; internet www.seul.polemb.net; Ambassador KRZYSZTOF MAJKA.

Portugal: Wonseo Bldg, 2nd Floor, 171, Wonseo-dong, Jongno-gu, Seoul 110-280; tel. (2) 3675-2251; fax (2) 3675-2250; e-mail embport@chol.com; internet www.portugalseoul.com; Ambassador ANTÓNIO QUINTEIRO NOBRE.

Qatar: 309-5, Dongbinggo-dong, Yeongsan-gu, Seoul 140-817; tel. (2) 798-2444; fax (2) 790-1027; e-mail qatarembassy@koreamail.com; Ambassador ALI HAMAD MUBARAK AL-MARRI.

Romania: 1-104, Dongbinggo-dong, Yongsan-gu, Seoul 140-809; tel. (2) 797-4924; fax (2) 794-3114; e-mail romemb@uriel.net; Ambassador CALIN FABIAN.

Russia: 34-16, Jeong-dong, Jung-gu, Seoul 100-120; tel. (2) 318-2116; fax (2) 754-0417; e-mail russemb@gmail.com; internet www.russian-embassy.org; Ambassador KONSTANTIN VNUKOV.

Rwanda: Sooyong Bldg, Unit 503, 64-1, Hannam-dong, Yeongsan-gu, Seoul 140-889; tel. (2) 798-1052; fax (2) 798-1054; e-mail info@rwanda-embassy.or.kr; internet rwanda-embassy.or.kr; Ambassador EUGENE S. KAYIHURA.

Saudi Arabia: 36-37, Itaewon 1-dong, Yeongsan-gu, Seoul 140-201; tel. (2) 739-0631; fax (2) 739-0041; e-mail embassysaudi@yahoo.co.kr; Ambassador AHMED BIN YUNUS AL-BARRAK.

Senegal: Coryo Daeyungak Tower, 13th Floor, Unit 1302, 25-5, Chungmuro 1-ga, Jung-gu, Seoul 100-706; tel. (2) 745-5554; fax (2) 745-5524; Ambassador AMADOU DABO.

Serbia: 730, Hannam-dong, Yeongsan-gu, Seoul; tel. (2) 797-5109; fax (2) 790-6109; e-mail emserbseul@yahoo.com; internet www.embserb.or.kr; Ambassador SLOBODAN MARINKOVIĆ.

Singapore: Seoul Finance Bldg, 28th Floor, 84, Taepyeong-no 1-ga, Jung-gu, Seoul 100-101; tel. (2) 774-2464; fax (2) 773-2463; e-mail singemb_seo@sgmfa.gov.sg; internet www.mfa.gov.sg/seoul; Ambassador PETER TAN HAI CHUAN.

Slovakia: 389-1, Hannam-dong, Yeongsan-gu, Seoul 140-210; tel. (2) 794-3981; fax (2) 794-3982; e-mail emb.seoul@mzv.sk; internet www.mzv.sk/seoul; Ambassador DUŠAN BELLA.

South Africa: 1-37, Hannam-dong, Yeongsan-gu, Seoul 140-885; tel. (2) 792-4855; fax (2) 792-4856; e-mail general@southafrica-embassy.or.kr; internet www.southafrica-embassy.or.kr; Ambassador HILTON ANTHONY DENNIS.

Spain: 726-52, Hannam-dong, Yeongsan-gu, Seoul 140-894; tel. (2) 794-3581; fax (2) 796-8207; e-mail emb.seul@maec.es; internet www.maec.es/subwebs/Embajadas/Seul; Ambassador LUIS ARIAS ROMERO.

Sri Lanka: 347-359, Shindang-dong, Jung-gu, Seoul 100-450; tel. (2) 735-2966; fax (2) 737-9577; e-mail lankaemb@kornet.net; Ambassador W. W. T. WIJERATNE.

Sudan: Vivien Bldg, 3rd Floor, 4-52, Seobinggo-dong, Yeongsan-gu, Seoul 140-240; tel. (2) 793-8692; fax (2) 793-8693; e-mail sudanembassykorea@gmail.com; internet www.sudanembassy.co.kr; Ambassador TAGELDIN EL-HADI.

Sweden: Danam Bldg, 8th Floor, 120, Namdaemunro 5-ga, Jung-gu, CPOB 3577, Seoul 100-635; tel. (2) 3703-3700; fax (2) 3703-3701; e-mail embassy@swedemb.or.kr; internet www.swedenabroad.com/seoul; Ambassador LARS DANIELSSON.

Switzerland: 32-10, Songwol-dong, Jongno-gu, CPOB 2900, Seoul 110-101; tel. (2) 739-9511; fax (2) 737-9392; e-mail seo.vertretung@eda.admin.ch; internet www.eda.admin.ch/seoul; Ambassador JÖRG ALOIS REDING.

Thailand: 653-7, Hannam-dong, Yeongsan-gu, Seoul 140-210; tel. (2) 795-3098; fax (2) 798-3448; e-mail rteseoul@kornet.net; internet www.thaiembassy.or.kr; Ambassador Dr KITTIPHONG NA-RANONG.

Timor-Leste: Hannam Tower Bldg II, Unit 405, 725-23, Hannam-dong, Yeongsan-gu, Seoul 140-894; tel. (2) 797-6151; fax (2) 797-6152; e-mail tlembseoul@gmail.com; Chargé d'affaires a.i. CAETANO GUTERRES.

Tunisia: 1-17, Dongbinggo-dong, Yeongsan-gu, Seoul 140-809; tel. (2) 790-4334; fax (2) 790-4333; e-mail ambtnkor@kornet.net; Ambassador MOHAMED ALI NAFTI.

Turkey: Vivien Corpn Bldg, 4th Floor, 4-52, Seobinggo-dong, Yeongsan-gu, Seoul 140-240; tel. (2) 794-0255; fax (2) 797-8546; e-mail turkemb.seoul@hotmail.com; internet www.seul.be.mfa.gov.tr; Ambassador NACI SARIBAŞ.

Ukraine: 1-97, Dongbinggo-dong, Yeongsan-gu, Seoul; tel. (2) 790-5696; fax (2) 790-5697; e-mail emb_kr@mfa.gov.ua; internet www.mfa.gov.ua/korea; Ambassador VASYL MARMAZOV.

United Arab Emirates: 5-5, Hannam-dong, Yeongsan-gu, Seoul 140-884; tel. (2) 790-3235; fax (2) 790-3238; e-mail uaeemb@kornet.net; Ambassador ABDULLA AL-ROMAITHI.

United Kingdom: 19-gil 24, Sejong-no, Jung-gu, Seoul 100-120; tel. (2) 3210-5500; fax (2) 725-1738; e-mail enquiry.seoul@fco.gov.uk; internet www.ukinkorea.fco.gov.uk; Ambassador SCOTT WIGHTMAN.

USA: 188, Sejong-no, Jongno-gu, Seoul 110-710; tel. (2) 397-4114; fax (2) 397-4080; e-mail embassyseoulpa@state.gov; internet seoul.usembassy.gov; Ambassador SUNG KIM.

Uruguay: 653-30, Hannam 1-dong, Yeongsan-gu, Seoul 140-887; tel. (2) 6245-3179; fax (2) 6245-3181; e-mail uruseul@embrou.or.kr; internet www.embrou.or.kr; Ambassador ALBA ROSA FLORIO LEGNANI.

Uzbekistan: Diplomatic Center, Unit 701, 1376-1, Seocho 2-dong, Seocho-gu, Seoul; tel. (2) 574-6554; fax (2) 578-0576; internet www.uzbekistan.or.kr; Ambassador VITALI V. FEN.

Venezuela: SC First Bank Bldg, 16th Floor, 100, Gongpyeong-dong, Jongno-gu, CPOB 10043, Seoul 110-702; tel. (2) 732-1546; fax (2) 732-1548; e-mail emvesel@soback.kornet.net; internet www.venezuelaemb.or.kr; Chargé d'affaires a.i. YADIRA HIDALGO DE ORTIZ.

Viet Nam: 28-58, Samcheong-dong, Jongno-gu, Seoul 140-210; tel. (2) 738-2318; fax (2) 739-2064; e-mail vndsq@yahoo.com; internet www.vietnamembassy-seoul.org; Ambassador TRAN TRONG TOAN.

Judicial System

Supreme Court: 219 Seocho-dong, Seocho-gu, Seoul; tel. (2) 533-2824; fax (2) 533-1911; e-mail webmaster@scourt.go.kr; internet www.scourt.go.kr; the Supreme Court is empowered to receive and decide on appeals against decisions of the High Courts, the Patent

Court, and the appellate panels of the District Courts or the Family Court in civil, criminal, administrative, patent and domestic relations cases; the Court is also authorized to act as the final tribunal to review decisions of courts-martial and to consider cases arising from presidential and parliamentary elections; consists of 13 Justices, including the Chief Justice, who are appointed for six years by the President, subject to the consent of the National Assembly; other sitting judges are appointed on the recommendation of the Chief Justice; Chief Justice YANG SUNG-TAE.

Constitutional Court: 15 Gahoero, Jongno-gu, Seoul 110-250; tel. (2) 708-3629; fax (2) 708-3566; e-mail interdiv@ccourt.go.kr; internet www.ccourt.go.kr; adjudicates the following matters: constitutionality of a law (when requested by the other courts); impeachment; dissolution of a political party; disputes between state agencies, or between state agencies and local governments; and petitions relating to the Constitution; composed of nine adjudicators appointed by the President, of whom three are chosen from among persons selected by the National Assembly and three from persons nominated by the Chief Justice; Pres. PARK HAN-CHUL.

High Courts: there are five High Courts, situated in Seoul, Daegu, Busan, Gwangju and Daejeon, with five chief, 78 presiding and 145 other judges; the courts have appellate jurisdiction in civil and criminal cases and can also pass judgment on administrative litigation against government decisions.

Patent Court: 45 Cheongsodong-ro, Seo-gu, Daejeon 302-784; tel. (42) 480-1400; established in March 1998 to deal with cases in which the decisions of the Intellectual Property Tribunal are challenged; cases are conducted by a judge, with the assistance of technical examiners.

District Courts: there are 13 District Courts, with 13 chief, 241 presiding and 966 other judges; they exercise jurisdiction over all civil and criminal cases in the first instance.

Municipal Courts: there are 103 Municipal Courts within the District Court system, dealing with small claims, minor criminal offences, and settlement cases.

Family Court: there is one Family Court, in Seoul, with a chief judge, four presiding judges and 16 other judges; the court has jurisdiction in domestic matters and cases of juvenile delinquency.

Administrative Court: established in Seoul in March 1998 to deal with cases that are specified in the Administrative Litigation Act; the Court has jurisdiction over cities and counties adjacent to Seoul, and deals with administrative matters, including taxes, expropriations of land, labour and other general administrative matters.

Courts-Martial: exercise jurisdiction over all offences committed by armed forces personnel and civilian employees and are also authorized to try civilians accused of military espionage or interference with the execution of military duties.

Religion

BUDDHISM

Korean Mahayana Buddhism has about 80 denominations. The Chogye-jong is the largest Buddhist order in Korea, having been introduced from China in AD 372. The Chogye Order accounts for almost two-thirds of all Korean Buddhists. Won Buddhism combines elements of Buddhism and Confucianism.

Korean United Buddhist Association (KUBA): 46-19, Soosong-dong, Jongno-gu, Seoul 110-140; tel. (2) 732-4885; 28 mem. Buddhist orders; Pres. SONG WOL-JOO.

CHRISTIANITY

National Council of Churches in Korea: Christian Bldg, Rm 706, 136-46, Yeonchi-dong, Jongno-gu, Seoul 110-736; tel. (2) 744-8981; fax (2) 744-6189; e-mail kncc@kncc.or.kr; internet www.kncc.or.kr; f. 1924; est. as National Christian Council; present name adopted 1946; eight mem. churches; Pres. Rev. LEE YOUNG-HOON; Gen. Sec. Rev. KIM YOUNG-JU.

The Anglican Communion

South Korea has three Anglican dioceses, collectively forming the Anglican Church of Korea (founded as a separate province in April 1993), under its own Primate, the Bishop of Seoul.

Archbishop of Korea and Bishop of Seoul: Most Rev. PAUL KIM KEUN-SANG, 3, Jeong-dong, Jung-gu, Seoul 100-120; tel. (2) 738-6597; fax (2) 738-3982; e-mail skhseoul@skhseoul.or.kr; internet www.skhseoul.or.kr.

Bishop of Pusan (Busan): Rt Rev. SOLOMON JONG-MO YOON, 18, 2-ga, Daechung-dong, Jung-gu, Busan 600-600; tel. (51) 463-5742; fax (51) 463-5957; e-mail adpusan@hanmail.net; internet skhpusan.onmam.com.

Bishop of Taejon (Daejeon): Rt Rev. MICHAEL KWON HI-YEON, POB 22, Daejeon 300-600; tel. (42) 256-9988; fax (42) 255-8918; e-mail djdio@djdio.or.kr; internet www.djdio.or.kr.

The Roman Catholic Church

For ecclesiastical purposes, North and South Korea are nominally under a unified jurisdiction. South Korea comprises three archdioceses, 12 dioceses and one military ordinate. At 31 December 2007 some 4,821,020 people were adherents of the Roman Catholic Church.

Bishops' Conference

Catholic Bishops' Conference of Korea, 643-1, Junggok-dong, Gwangjin-gu, Seoul 143-912; tel. (2) 460-7500; fax (2) 460-7505; e-mail cbck@cbck.or.kr; internet www.cbck.or.kr.

f. 1857; Pres. Most Rev. PETER KANG (Bishop of Cheju—Jeju).

Archbishop of Kwangju (Gwangju): Most Rev. HYGINUS KIM HEE-JONG, Archdiocesan Office, 997-1, Sangmu 2-dong, Gwangju 502-855; tel. (62) 380-2801; fax (62) 380-2806; e-mail biseo1@kjcatholic.or.kr; internet www.kjcatholic.or.kr.

Archbishop of Seoul: Cardinal ANDREW YEOM SOO-JUNG, Archdiocesan Office, 1, 2-ga, Myeong-dong, Jung-gu, Seoul 100-022; tel. (2) 727-2114; fax (2) 773-1947; e-mail ao@seoul.catholic.or.kr; internet www.catholic.or.kr.

Archbishop of Daegu (Taegu): THADDEUS CHO HWAN-KIL, Archdiocesan Office, 225-1, Namsan 3-dong, Jung-gu, Daegu 700-804; tel. (53) 253-7011; fax (53) 253-9441; e-mail taegu@tgcatholic.or.kr; internet www.tgcatholic.or.kr.

Protestant Churches

Korean Methodist Church: 64-8, 1-ga, Taepyeong-no, Jung-gu, Seoul 100-101; KPO Box 285, Seoul 110-602; tel. (2) 399-4300; fax (2) 399-4307; e-mail bishop@kmcweb.or.kr; internet www.kmcweb.or.kr; f. 1885; 1,534,504 mems (2007); Bishop KANG HEUNG-BOK.

Presbyterian Church in the Republic of Korea (PROK): Academy House, San 76, Suyu 6-dong, Kangbuk-ku, Seoul 142-714; tel. (2) 3499-7600; fax (2) 3499-7630; e-mail prok3000@chol.com; internet www.prok.org; f. 1953; 337,570 mems (2007); Gen. Sec. Rev. BAE TAE-JIN.

Presbyterian Church of Korea (PCK): The Korean Church Centennial Memorial Bldg, 135, Yunji-dong, Jongno-gu, Seoul 110-470; tel. (2) 741-4350; fax (2) 766-2427; e-mail thepck@pck.or.kr; internet www.pck.or.kr; 2,395,323 mems (Dec. 2003); Moderator Rev. JUNG SUH-KIM; Gen. Sec. Rev. SEONGI CHO.

There are some 160 other Protestant denominations in the country, including the Korea Baptist Convention and the Korea Evangelical Church.

OTHER RELIGIONS

Chundo Kyo, a religion indigenous and unique to Korea, combines elements of Shamanistic, Buddhist, and Christian doctrines. Confucianism also has a significant number of followers. Taejong Gyo is Korea's oldest religion, dating back 4,000 years, and comprising beliefs in the national foundation myth, and the triune god, Hanul. By the 15th century the religion had largely disappeared, but a revival began in the late 19th century.

The Press

NATIONAL DAILIES
(In Korean, unless otherwise indicated)

Chosun Ilbo: 61, 1-ga, Taepyeong-no, Jung-gu, Seoul 100-756; tel. (2) 724-5114; fax (2) 724-5059; e-mail englishnews@chosun.com; internet www.chosun.com; f. 1920; morning, weekly and children's edns; independent; Korean, English, Chinese and Japanese; Exec. Editor BYUN YONG-SHIK; circ. 2,470,000.

Daily Sports Seoul: 25, 1-ga, Taepyeong-no, Jung-gu, Seoul; tel. (2) 721-5114; fax (2) 721-5396; internet www.seoul.co.kr; f. 1985; morning; sports and leisure; Pres. LEE HAN-SOO; Man. Editor SON CHU-WHAN.

Dong-A Ilbo: 139-1, 3-ga, Sejong-no, Jongno-gu, Seoul 100-715; tel. (2) 2020-0114; fax (2) 2020-1239; e-mail newsroom@donga.com; internet www.donga.com; f. 1920; morning; independent; Publr and CEO KIM JAE-HO; Editor-in-Chief LEE HYUN-NAK; circ. 2,150,000.

Han-Joong Daily News: 91-1, 2-ga, Myeong-dong, Jung-gu, Seoul; tel. (2) 776-2801; fax (2) 778-2803; Chinese.

Hankook Ilbo: 14, Junghak-dong, Jongno-gu, Seoul; tel. (2) 724-2114; fax (2) 724-2244; internet www.hankooki.com; f. 1954; morning; independent; Pres. PARK JIN-YEOL; Editor-in-Chief YOON KOOK-BYUNG; circ. 2,000,000.

Hankuk Kyungje Shinmun (Korea Economic Daily): 441, Junglim-dong, Jung-gu, Seoul 100-791; tel. (2) 360-4114; fax (2) 779-4447; e-mail hkinfo@hankyung.com; internet www.hankyung.com; f. 1964; morning; Pres. and CEO KIM KI-WOONG; Man. Dir and Editor-in-Chief CHOI KYU-YOUNG.

Hankyoreh (One Nation): 116-25, Gongdeok-dong, Mapo-gu, Seoul 121-750; tel. (2) 1566-9595; internet www.hani.co.kr; f. 1988; centre-left; Korean, English; CEO and Publr YANG SANG-WOO; Editor-in-Chief PARK CHAN-SU; circ. 500,000.

Ilgan Sports (The Daily Sports): 14, Junghak-dong, Jongno-gu, Seoul 110-792; tel. (2) 724-2114; fax (2) 724-2299; internet www.dailysports.co.kr; morning; f. 1969; Pres. CHANG CHAE-KEUN; Editor KIM JIN-DONG; circ. 600,000.

Jeil Economic Daily: 146, Ssangrin-dong, Jung-gu, Seoul; tel. (2) 6325-3114; e-mail ysk@jed.co.kr; internet www.jed.co.kr; f. 1988; morning; Pres. PARK JUNG-GU; Editor-in-Chief JANG CHANG-YONG.

JoongAng Ilbo (JoongAng Daily News): 7, Soonhwa-dong, Jung-gu, 100-759 Seoul; tel. (2) 751-9215; fax (2) 751-9219; e-mail iht@joongang.co.kr; internet joongangdaily.joins.com; f. 1965; morning; Korean and English; Publr LHO CHOL-SOO; Exec. Dir KIM DONG-KYUN; circ. 2,300,000.

Kookmin Ilbo: Kookmin Ilbo Bldg, 5/F, 12, Yeouido-dong, Yeongdeungpo-gu, Seoul; tel. (2) 781-9114; fax (2) 781-9781; e-mail kimyh@kmib.co.kr; internet www.kukminilbo.co.kr; Pres. RO SEUNG-SOOK; Editorial Dir KIM Y. H.

Korea Daily News: 25, 1-ga, Taepyeong-no, Jung-gu, Seoul; tel. (2) 2000-9000; fax (2) 2000-9659; e-mail webmaster@seoul.co.kr; internet www.kdaily.com; f. 1945; morning; independent; Publr and Pres. SON CHU-HWAN; Man. Editor LEE DONG-HWA; circ. 700,000.

The Korea Herald: 1-17, Jeong-dong, Jung-gu, Seoul; tel. (2) 727-0205; fax (2) 727-0670; e-mail editor@heraldm.com; internet www.koreaherald.co.kr; f. 1953; morning; English; independent; Pres. WOOK HONG-JUNG; Man. Editor CHON SHI-YONG; circ. 150,000.

The Korea Times: 43, Chungmuro 3-ga, Chung-gu, Seoul 100-013; tel. (2) 724-2859; fax (2) 723-1623; e-mail webmaster@koreatimes.co.kr; internet www.koreatimes.co.kr; f. 1950; morning; English; independent; Pres. PARK MOO-JONG; Man. Editor OH YOUNG-JIN; circ. 100,000.

Kyung-hyang Shinmun: 22, Jeong-dong, Jung-gu, Seoul; tel. (2) 3701-1114; fax (2) 737-6362; internet www.khan.co.kr; f. 1946; evening; independent; Pres. HONG SUNG-MAN; Exec. Editor KIM JI-YOUNG; circ. 350,000.

Maeil Business Newspaper: 30-1, 1-ga, Bil-dong, Jung-gu, Seoul 100-728; tel. (2) 2000-2114; fax (2) 2269-6200; internet www.mk.co.kr; f. 1966; evening; economics and business; Korean, English; Pres. CHANG DAE-WHAN; Chief Editor JANG YONG-SUNG; circ. 235,000.

Munhwa Ilbo: 68, 1-ga, Chungjeong-no, Jung-gu, Seoul 110-170; tel. (2) 3701-5114; fax (2) 3701-5566; internet www.munhwa.co.kr; f. 1991; evening; Pres. and Publr LEE BYUN-KYU; Editor-in-Chief KANG SIN-KU.

Naeway Economic Daily: 1-12, 3-ga, Hoehyon-dong, Jung-gu, Seoul 100; tel. (2) 727-0114; fax (2) 727-0661; f. 1973; morning; Pres. KIM CHIN-OUK; Man. Editor HAN DONG-HEE; circ. 300,000.

Segye Times: 550-15, Gasan-dong, Seoul; tel. (2) 2000-1160; fax (2) 2000-1349; e-mail webmaster@segye.com; internet www.segyetimes.co.kr; f. 1989; morning; Pres. SA KWANG-KEE; Editor MOK JUNG-GYUM.

Seoul Kyungje Shinmun (Seoul Economic Daily): 14, Junghak-dong, Jongno-gu, Seoul; tel. (2) 724-2114; fax (2) 732-2140; e-mail webmaster@hanooki.com; internet economy.hankooki.com; f. 1960; morning; Pres. LIM KONG-JON; Man. Editor LEE JONG-WHAN; circ. 500,000.

Sports Chosun: 61, 1-ga, Taepyeong-no, Jung-gu, Seoul; tel. (2) 3219-8114; fax (2) 724-6979; e-mail readers@sportschosun.com; internet www.sportschosun.com; f. 1964; Publr BANG SANG-HOON; circ. 400,000.

LOCAL DAILIES

Chungcheong Daily News: 304, Sachang-dong, Hungduk-gu, Cheongju, N. Chungcheong Prov.; tel. (43) 279-5000; fax (43) 279-5050; e-mail webmaster@ccilbo.com; internet www.ccilbo.com; f. 1946; morning; Pres. SEO JEONG-OK; Editor IM BAIK-SOO.

Daegu Ilbo: 177-10, Sincheon 2-dong, Dong-gu, Daegu; tel. (53) 757-5700; fax (53) 757-5757; internet www.idaegu.com; f. 1953; morning; Pres. LEE TAE-YEUL; Editor KIM KYUNG-PAL.

Daejon Ilbo: 1-135, Munhwa 1-dong, Jung-gu, Daejeon; tel. (42) 251-3311; fax (42) 253-3320; f. 1950; evening; Pres. CHO JOON-HO; Editor KWAK DAE-YEON.

Halla Ilbo: 568-1, Samdo 1-dong, Jeju; tel. (64) 750-2114; fax (64) 750-2520; e-mail webmaster@ihalla.com; internet www.ihalla.com; f. 1989; evening; Chair. KANG YONG-SOK; Man. Editor HONG SONG-MOK.

Incheon Ilbo: 18-1, 4-ga, Hang-dong, Jung-gu, Incheon; tel. (32) 763-8811; fax (32) 763-7711; e-mail webmaster@itimes.co.kr; internet www.itimes.co.kr; f. 1988; evening; Chair. MUN PYONG-HA; Man. Editor LEE JAE-HO.

Jeju Daily News: 2324-6, Yeon-dong, Jeju; tel. (64) 740-6114; fax (64) 740-6500; e-mail webmaster@jejunews.com; internet www.jejunews.com; f. 1945; evening; Pres. KIM DAE-SUNG; Man. Editor KANG BYUNG-HEE.

Jeonbuk Domin Ilbo: 417-62, 2-ga, Deokjin-dong, Deokjin-gu, Jeonju, N. Jeolla Prov.; tel. (63) 251-7113; fax (63) 251-7127; internet www.domin.co.kr; f. 1988; morning; Pres. LIM BYOUNG-CHAN; Man. Editor YANG CHAE-SUK.

Jeonbuk Ilbo: 710-5, Kumam-dong, Deokjin-gu, Jeonju, N. Jeolla Prov.; tel. (63) 250-5500; fax (63) 250-5550; f. 1950; evening; Chair. SUH CHANG-HOON; Man. Editor LEE KON-WOONG.

Jeonju Ilbo: 568-132, Sonosong-dong, Deokjin-gu, Jeonju, N. Jeolla Prov.; tel. (63) 285-0114; fax (63) 285-2060; f. 1991; morning; Chair. KANG DAE-SOON; Man. Editor SO CHAE-CHOL.

Jeonnam Ilbo: 700-5, Jungheung-dong, Buk-gu, Gwangju 500-758; tel. (62) 527-0015; fax (62) 510-0436; f. 1989; morning; Pres. PARK KEE-JUNG; Editor-in-Chief KIM YONG-OK.

Joongdo Ilbo: 274-7, Galma-dong, Seo-gu, Daejeon; tel. (42) 530-4114; fax (42) 535-5334; f. 1951; morning; CEO KIM WOK-SIK; Man. Editor SONG HYOUNG-SOP.

Kangwon Ilbo: 23, Jungang-no, Chuncheon, Gangwon Prov.; tel. (33) 258-1000; fax (33) 258-1114; internet www.kwnews.co.kr; f. 1945; evening; Pres. CHOI SEUNG-IK; Editor-in-Chief KIM SUNG-KEE.

Kookje Daily News: 76-2, Goje-dong, Yeonje-gu, Busan 611-702; tel. (51) 500-5114; fax (51) 500-4274; e-mail jahwang@ms.kookje.co.kr; internet www.kookje.co.kr; f. 1947; morning; Pres. ROH KI-TAE; Editor-in-Chief JEONG WON-YOUNG.

Kwangju Ilbo: 20-2, Geumnam-no, Dong-gu, Gwangju; tel. (62) 222-8111; fax (62) 227-9500; e-mail kwangju@kwangju.co.kr; internet www.kwangju.co.kr; f. 1952; evening; Chair. KIM CHONG-TAE; Man. Editor CHO DONG-SU.

Kyeonggi Ilbo: 452-1, Songjuk-dong, Changan-gu, Suwon, Gyeonggi Prov.; tel. (31) 250-3333; fax (31) 250-3306; e-mail webmaster@ekgib.co.kr; internet www.kgib.co.kr; f. 1988; evening; Pres. SHIN CHANG-GI; Man. Editor LEE CHIN-YONG.

Kyeongin Ilbo: 1276, Maetan-dong, Yeongtong-gu, Suwon, Gyeonggi-do; tel. (31) 231-5114; fax (31) 232-1231; e-mail webmaster@kyeongin.com; internet www.kyeongin.com; f. 1960; evening; Pres. WOO JE-CHAN; Man. Editor KIM HWA-YANG.

Kyungnam Shinmun: 100-5, Sinwol-dong, Changwon, S. Gyeongsang Prov.; tel. (55) 283-2211; fax (55) 210-6048; internet www.knnews.co.kr; f. 1946; evening; Pres. KIM DONG-KYU; Editor PARK SUNG-KWAN.

Maeil Shinmun: 71, 2-ga, Gyesan-dong, Jung-gu, Daegu; tel. (53) 255-5001; fax (53) 255-8902; e-mail imaeil@msnet.co.kr; internet www.imaeil.com; f. 1946; evening; Pres. CHO HWAN-KIL; Editor LEE YONG-KEUN; circ. 300,000.

Pusan Daily News: 1-10, Sujeong-dong, Dong-gu, Busan 601-738; tel. (51) 461-4114; fax (51) 463-8880; internet www.pusanilbo.co.kr; f. 1946; Pres. JEONG HAN-SANG; Man. Editor AHN KI-HO; circ. 427,000.

Yeongnam Ilbo: 111, Sincheon-dong, Dong-gu, Daegu; tel. (53) 756-8001; fax (53) 756-9011; internet www.yeongnam.co.kr; f. 1945; morning; Chair. PARK CHANG-HO; Man. Editor KIM SANG-TAE.

SELECTED PERIODICALS

Academy News: 50, Unjung-dong, Bundang-gu, Seongnam, Gyeonggi Prov. 463-791; tel. (31) 709-8111; fax (31) 709-9945; organ of the Acad. of Korean Studies; Pres. HAN SANG-JIN.

Eumak Dong-A: 139, Sejong-no, Jongno-gu, Seoul 110-715; tel. (2) 781-0640; fax (2) 705-4547; f. 1984; monthly; music; Publr KIM BYUNG-KWAN; Editor KWON O-KIE; circ. 85,000.

Han Kuk No Chong (FKTU News): 35, Yeouido-dong, Yeongdeungpo-gu, Seoul 150-885; tel. (2) 6277-0026; fax (2) 6277-0068; internet www.fktu.or.kr; f. 1961; labour news; circ. 20,000.

Hyundae Munhak: Seoul; tel. (2) 516-3770; fax (2) 516-5433; e-mail webmaster@hdmh.co.kr; internet www.hdmh.co.kr; f. 1955; literature; Publr KIM SUNG-SIK; circ. 200,000.

Korea Business World: Yeouido, POB 720, Seoul 150-607; tel. (2) 532-1364; fax (2) 594-7663; f. 1985; monthly; English; Publr and Pres. LEE KIE-HONG; circ. 40,200.

Korea Buyers Guide: Rm 2301, Korea World Trade Center, 159, Samseong-dong, Gangnam-gu, Seoul; tel. (2) 551-2376; fax (2) 551-2377; e-mail info@buyersguide.co.kr; internet www.buykorea21.com; f. 1973; monthly, consumer goods; quarterly, hardware; Pres. YOU YOUNG-PYO; circ. 30,000.

Korea Journal: Korean National Commission for UNESCO, CPOB 64, Seoul 100-600; tel. (2) 6958-4110; e-mail kj@unesco.or.kr; internet www.ekoreajournal.net; f. 1961; quarterly; organ of the Korean National Commission for UNESCO; focus on Korean Studies; Editor HAHM SEONG-DEUK; Publr MIN DONG-SEOK.

Korea Newsreview: 1-12, 3-ga, Hoehyeon-dong, Jung-gu, Seoul 100-771; tel. (2) 756-7711; weekly; English; Publr and Editor PARK CHUNG-WOONG.

Korea and World Affairs: Rm 1723, Daewoo Center Bldg, 5-541, Namdaemun-no, Jung-gu, Seoul 100-714; tel. (2) 777-2628; fax (2) 319-9591; organ of the Research Center for Peace and Unification of Korea; Pres. CHANG DONG-HOON.

Korean Business Review: FKI Bldg, 28-1, Yeouido-dong, Yeong-deungpo-gu, Seoul 150-756; tel. (2) 3771-0114; fax (2) 3771-0138; monthly; publ. by Fed. of Korean Industries; Publr KIM KAK-CHOONG; Editor SOHN BYUNG-DOO.

Literature and Thought: Seoul; tel. (2) 738-0542; fax (2) 738-2997; f. 1972; monthly; Pres. LIM HONG-BIN; circ. 10,000.

Monthly Travel: Cross Bldg, 2nd Floor, 46-6, 2-ga, Namsan-dong, Jung-gu, Seoul 100-042; tel. (2) 757-6161; fax (2) 757-6089; e-mail kotfa@unitel.co.kr; Pres. SHIN JOONG-MOK; circ. 50,000.

News Maker: 22, Jung-dong, Jung-gu, Seoul 110-702; tel. (2) 3701-1114; fax (2) 739-6190; e-mail hudy@kyunghyang.com; internet www .kyunghyang.com/newsmaker; f. 1992; Pres. JANG JUN-BONG; Editor PARK MYUNG-HUN.

Reader's Digest: 295-15, Deoksan 1-dong, Geumcheon-gu, Seoul 153-011; tel. (2) 3670-5497; fax (2) 3670-5001; internet www .readersdigest.co.kr; f. 1978; monthly; general; Pres. YANG SUNG-MO; Editor PARK SOON-HWANG; circ. 115,000.

Shin Dong-A (New East Asia): 139, Chungjeong-no, Seodaemun-gu, Seoul 120-715; tel. (2) 361-0974; fax (2) 361-0988; e-mail hans@donga .com; internet shindonga.donga.com; f. 1931; monthly; general; Publr KIM JAE-HO; Editor LEE HYUNG-SAM; circ. 150,000.

Taekwondo: Joyang Bldg 113, 4/F, Samseong-dong, Gangnam-gu, Seoul; tel. (2) 566-2505; fax (2) 553-4728; e-mail wtf@wtf.org; internet www.wtf.org; f. 1973; annual; organ of the World Taekwondo Federation; Pres. Dr CHOUE CHUNG-WON.

Vantage Point: 85-1, Susong-dong, Jongno-gu, Seoul, 110-140; tel. (2) 398-3114; fax (2) 398-3539; e-mail master@yna.co.kr; internet www.yonhapnews.co.kr; f. 1978; monthly; developments in North Korea; Editor KWAK SEUNG-JI.

Weekly Chosun: 61, Taepyong-no 1, Jung-gu, Seoul; tel. (2) 724-5114; fax (2) 724-6899; e-mail weekly@chosun.com; internet weekly .chosun.com; Publr KIM CHANG-KI; Editor CHOI JOON-SUK; circ. 350,000.

The Weekly Hankook: 14, Junghak-dong, Jongno-gu, Seoul; tel. (2) 732-4151; fax (2) 724-2444; f. 1964; Publr CHANG CHAE-KUK; circ. 400,000.

Wolgan Mot: 139, Sejong-no, Jongno-gu, Seoul 110-715; tel. (2) 733-5221; f. 1984; monthly; fashion; Publr KIM SEUNG-YUL; Editor KWON O-KIE; circ. 120,000.

Women's Weekly: 14, Junghak-dong, Jongno-gu, Seoul; tel. (2) 735-9216; fax (2) 732-4125.

Yosong Dong-A (Women's Far East): 139, Sejong-no, Jongno-gu, Seoul 110-715; tel. (2) 721-7621; fax (2) 721-7676; f. 1933; monthly; women's magazine; Publr KIM BYUNG-KWAN; Editor KWON O-KIE; circ. 237,000.

NEWS AGENCY

Yonhap News Agency: 85-1, Susong-dong, Jongno-gu, Seoul; tel. (2) 398-3114; fax (2) 398-3567; e-mail ldm@yna.co.kr; internet www .yonhapnews.co.kr; f. 1980; Pres. KIM KUN.

PRESS ASSOCIATIONS

Journalists Association of Korea (JAK): Korea Press Center Bldg, 25 1-ga, Taepyeong-no, Jung-gu, Seoul; tel. (2) 737-2483; fax (2) 738-1003; e-mail jakmaster@journalist.or.kr; internet www .journalist.or.kr; Pres. JANG KYUNG-WOO.

Korean Association of Newspapers: Korea Press Center, 13th Floor, 25, 1-ga, Taepyeong-no, Jung-gu, Seoul 100-745; tel. (2) 733-2251; fax (2) 720-3291; e-mail iwelcome@presskorea.or.kr; internet www.presskorea.or.kr; f. 1962; 48 mems; Pres. JAE-HO; Sec.-Gen. MOON HAN-KWON.

Korean Newspaper Editors' Association: Korea Press Center, 13th Floor, 25, 1-ga, Taepyeong-no, Jung-gu, Seoul; tel. (2) 732-1726; fax (2) 739-1985; f. 1957; 416 mems; Pres. SEONG BYONG-WUK.

Seoul Foreign Correspondents' Club: Korea Press Center, 18/F, 1-ga, Taepyeong-no, Jung-gu, Seoul; tel. (2) 734-3272; fax (2) 734-7712; e-mail master@sfcc.or.kr; internet www.sfcc.or.kr; f. 1956; Pres. RYOJI ITO.

Publishers

Ahn Graphics Ltd: 260-288, Seongbuk-dong, Seongbuk-gu, Seoul 136-823; tel. (2) 743-8065; fax (2) 744-3251; e-mail ask@ag.co.kr; internet www.ag.co.kr; f. 1985; art, literature, computer graphics; Pres. KIM OK-CHUL.

BIR Publishing Co Ltd: 4/F, Gangnam Publishing Culture Center, 506 Sinsa-dong, Gangnam-Gu, Seoul 135-887; tel. (2) 515-2000; fax (2) 3442-4661; e-mail bir@bir.co.kr; internet www.bir.co.kr; children's books; Pres. PARK SANG-HEE.

Bobmun Sa Publishing Co: 526-3, Munbal-ri, Gyoha-eup, Paju-si, Gyeonggi-do 413-756; tel. (31) 955-6500; fax (31) 955-6525; internet www.bobmunsa.co.kr; f. 1954; law, politics, philosophy, history; Pres. BAE HYO-SEON.

Bookhouse Publishing Co Ltd: 6/F, Dongsomun Bldg, Seoul 136-034; tel. (2) 3144-3123; e-mail editor@bookhouse.co.kr; internet www .bookhouse.co.kr; business, foreign novels, health; CEO KIM JEONG-SUN.

Bumwoo Publishing Co: 525-2, Paju Book City, Munbal-ri, Gyoha-eup, Paju-si, Gyeonggi-do; tel. (31) 955-6900; fax (31) 955-6905; e-mail bumwoosa@chol.com; internet www.bumwoosa.co.kr; f. 1966; philosophy, religion, social science, technology, art, literature, history; Pres. YOON HYUNG-DOO.

Chaeksesang Publishing Co (Book World): 68-7, Sinsu-dong, Mapu-gu, Seoul 121-854; tel. (2) 704-1251; fax (2) 719-1258; e-mail webmaster@bkworld.co.kr; internet www.bkworld.co.kr; f. 1975; art, literature, religion, science and technology; Pres. KIM JIK-SEUNG.

Changhae Publishing: 336-10, Ahyun 2-dong, Seoul 121-012; tel. (2) 313-3200; fax (2) 313-3204.

Cheong Moon Gak Publishing Co Ltd: 486-9, Kirum 3-dong, Seongbuk-gu, Seoul 136-800; tel. (2) 985-1451; fax (2) 988-1456; e-mail cmgbook@cmgbook.co.kr; internet www.cmgbook.co.kr; f. 1974; science, technology, business; subsidiaries HanSeung Publishers, Lux Media; Pres. KIM HONG-SEOK; Man. Dir HANS KIM.

Crayon House Co Ltd: 5/F, Crayon House Bldg, Seoul; tel. (2) 3436-1711; fax (2) 3436-1410; e-mail crayong@korea.com; internet www .crayonhouse.co.kr; f. 1996; children's books.

Dai Won Publishing Co: 40-456, Hangangno 3-ga, Yeongsan-gu, Seoul 140-880; tel. (2) 2071-2000; fax (2) 793-8994; e-mail webmaster@dwci.co.kr; internet www.dwci.co.kr; f. 1990; comics.

Design House Publishing Co: Taekwang Bldg, 162-1, Jangchung-dong, 2-ga, Jung-gu, Seoul 100-855; tel. (2) 2275-6151; fax (2) 2267-6158; e-mail yhlee@design.co.kr; internet www.design.co.kr; f. 1987; social science, art, literature, languages, children's periodicals; Pres. LEE YOUNG-HEE.

Dong-Hwa Publishing Co Ltd: 509-3, Munbal-ri, Gyoha-eup, Paju-si, Gyeonggi-do 413-756; tel. (31) 955-4961; fax (31) 955-4960; f. 1968; art, children's books, literature; Pres. LIM IN-KYU.

Dongmoonsun Publishing Co: 21 Insa-dong-gil, Jongno-gu, Seoul 110-300; tel. (2) 737-2795; fax (2) 723-4518; e-mail dmspub@hanmail .net; humanities; Pres. SIN SUNG-DAE.

Doosan Corporation Publishing BG: 14-34, Yeouido-dong, Yeongdeungpo-gu, Seoul; tel. (2) 2167-0601; fax (2) 2167-0668; e-mail dudvkf@doosan.com; internet www.bookdonga.com; f. 1951; general works, school reference, social science, periodicals; Pres. CHOI TAE-KYUNG.

E*Public Co: 923-11, Mok 1-dong, Yangcheon-gu, Seoul 158-051; tel. (2) 2653-5131; fax (2) 2653-2454; e-mail webmaster@epublic.co .kr; internet www.epublic.co.kr; f. 1955; social science, pure science, technology, medicine, linguistics; Pres. and CEO LIU SUNG-KWON.

Eulyoo Publishing Co Ltd: 46-1, Susong-dong, Jongno-gu, Seoul 110-603; tel. (2) 733-8151; fax (2) 732-9154; e-mail eulyoo1945@gmail .com; internet www.eulyoo.co.kr; f. 1945; linguistics, literature, social science, history, philosophy; Pres. CHUNG JEE-YOUNG.

Gilbut Publishing Co Ltd: 467-9, Seogyo-dong, Mapo-gu, Seoul 121-842; tel. (2) 332-0931; fax (2) 323-0586; e-mail gilbut@gilbut.co .kr; internet www.gilbut.co.kr; f. 1991.

Gimm-Young Publishers Inc: 515-1, Munbal-ri, Gyoha-eup, Paju-si, Gyeonggi-do 413-756; tel. (31) 955-3100; fax (31) 955-3111; e-mail marketing@gimmyoung.com; internet www.gimmyoung.com; f. 1979; current affairs, humanities, history, religion, children's books; Pres. PARK EUN-JU.

Hainaim Publishing Co Ltd: 5/F, Hainaim Bldg, 368-4, Seogyo-dong, Mapo-gu, Seoul; tel. (2) 326-1600; fax (2) 326-1624; e-mail jwlee@hainaim.com; internet www.hainaim.com; f. 1983; philosophy, literature, children's; Pres. SONG YOUNG-SUK.

Haksan Publishing Co: Haksan Bldg, 777-1, Sangdo-dong, Dong-jak-gu, Seoul 156-830; tel. (2) 828-8988; fax (2) 828-8890; internet www.haksanpub.co.kr; f. 1995; children's books, comics, magazines.

Hakwon Publishing Co Ltd: Seocho Plaza, 4th Floor, 1573-1, Seocho-dong, Seocho-gu, Seoul; tel. (2) 587-2396; fax (2) 584-9306;

f. 1945; general, languages, literature, periodicals; Pres. KIM YOUNG-SU.

Hangilsa Corpn: 520-11, Paju Book City, Munbal-ri, Gyoha-eup, Paju-si, Gyeonggi-do; tel. (31) 955-2000; fax (31) 955-2005; e-mail hangilsaone@hangilsa.co.kr; internet www.hangilsa.co.kr; f. 1976; social science, history, literature; Pres. KIM EOUN-HO.

Hanul Publishing Company: 3/F Seoul Bldg, 105-90 Gongdeok-dong, Mapo-gu, Seoul 121-801; tel. (2) 336-6183; fax (2) 333-7543; e-mail hanul@hanulbooks.co.kr; internet www.hanulbooks.co.kr; f. 1980; general, philosophy, university books, periodicals; Pres. KIM CHONG-SU.

Hollym Corporation: 13-13, Gwancheol-dong, Jongno-gu, Seoul 110-111; tel. (2) 735-7551; fax (2) 730-5149; e-mail info@hollym.co.kr; internet www.hollym.co.kr; f. 1963; academic and general books on Korea in English; Pres. SANGBEK RHIMM.

Hyang Mun Sa Publishing Co: 3/F, Burim Bldg, 1668-14, Seocho 1-dong, Seocho-gu, Seoul 137-881; tel. (2) 584-5671; fax (2) 584-5673; f. 1950; science, agriculture, history, engineering, home economics; Pres. NAH JOONG-RYOL.

Hyeonam Publishing Co Ltd: 481-12, Seogyo-dong, Mapo-gu, Seoul 121-841; tel. (2) 365-5051; fax (2) 365-2729; e-mail ks@hyeonamsa.com; internet www.hyeonamsa.com; f. 1951; general, children's, literature, periodicals; Pres. CHO KEUN-TAE.

Hyungseul Publishing Co: 7-33, Tongeui-dong, Jongno-gu, Seoul; tel. (2) 738-6052; fax (2) 736-7134; e-mail hs@hyungseul.co.kr; internet www.hyungseul.co.kr; social science, university books.

Il Jin Sa Publishing Co: Iljin Bldg, 3rd Floor, 5-104, Hyochang-dong, Yeongsan-gu, Seoul; tel. (2) 704-1616; fax (2) 715-3536; e-mail webmaster@iljinsa.com; internet www.iljinsa.com; f. 1979; vocation, science and technology, social sciences, fine arts; CEO LEE JUNG-IL.

Ilchokak Publishing Co Ltd: 1-335, Sinmunno 2-ga, Jongno-gu, Seoul 110-062; tel. (2) 733-5430; fax (2) 738-5857; e-mail ilchokak@hanmail.net; internet www.ilchokak.co.kr; f. 1953; history, literature, sociology, linguistics, medicine, law, engineering; Pres. KIM SI-YEON.

Jigyungsa Publishers Ltd: 790-14, Yeoksam-dong, Gangnam-gu, Seoul 135-080; tel. (2) 557-6351; fax (2) 557-6352; e-mail jigyung@uriel.net; internet www.jigyung.co.kr; f. 1979; children's, periodicals; Pres. KIM BYUNG-JOON.

Jihak Publishing Co Ltd: 180-20, Dongkyo-dong, Mapo-gu, Seoul 121-200; tel. (2) 330-5200; fax (2) 325-4488; e-mail webmaster@jihak.co.kr; internet www.jihak.co.kr; f. 1965; philosophy, language, literature; Pres. KWON BYONG-IL.

Jimoondang: 95, Waryon-dong, Jongno-gu, Seoul 110-360; tel. (2) 743-0227; fax (2) 742-4657; e-mail plan@jipmoon.co.kr; internet www.jimoon.co.kr; f. 1970; scholarly books on Korean history, society, language, literature, religion, art, folklore, politics and economy; Pres. LIM SAM-KYU.

Jisik Sanup Publications Co Ltd: 35-18, Dongui-dong, Jongno-gu, Seoul 110-040; tel. (2) 734-1978; fax (2) 720-7900; e-mail jsp@jisik.co.kr; internet www.jisik.co.kr; f. 1969; religion, social science, art, literature, history, children's; Pres. KIM KYUNG-HEE.

Kemongsa Publishing Co Ltd: 772, Yeoksam-dong, Gangnam-gu, Seoul 135-080; tel. (2) 531-5335; fax (2) 531-5520; internet www.kemongsa.co.kr; f. 1946; picture books, juvenile, encyclopaedias, history, fiction; Pres. RHU SEUNG-HEE.

Kookminbooks Co Ltd: 514-4, Paju Book City, Munbal-ri, Gyoha-eup, Paju-si, Gyeonggi-do; tel. (31) 955-7851; fax (31) 955-7855; internet www.kmbooks.com; f. 1961; children's books.

Korea Britannica Corpn: 117, 1-ga, Jungchung-dong, Seoul 100-391; tel. (2) 272-2151; fax (2) 278-9983; e-mail webmaster@britannica.co.kr; internet www.britannica.co.kr; f. 1968; encyclopaedias, dictionaries; Pres JANG HO-SANG, SUJAN ELEN TAPANI.

Korea University Press: 1-2, Anam-dong, 5-ga, Seongbuk-gu, Seoul 136-701; tel. (2) 3290-4232; fax (2) 923-6311; e-mail kupress@korea.ac.kr; internet www.kupress.com; f. 1956; philosophy, history, language, literature, Korean studies, education, psychology, social science, natural science, engineering, agriculture, medicine; Pres. LEE KI-SU.

Kum Sung Publishing Co: 242-63, Gongdeok-dong, Mapo-gu, Seoul 121-022; tel. (2) 713-9651; fax (2) 701-9345; e-mail webmaster@kumsungpub.co.kr; internet www.kumsung.co.kr; f. 1965; literature, juvenile, social sciences, history, fine arts; Pres. KIM NAK-JOON.

Kyohak-sa Publishing Co Ltd: 105-67, Gongdeok-dong, Mapo-gu, Seoul 121-020; tel. (2) 707-5110; fax (2) 707-5160; internet www.kyohak.co.kr; f. 1952; dictionaries, educational, children's; Pres. YANG CHEOL-WOO.

Kyung Hee University Press: 1, Hoeki-dong, Dongdaemun-gu, Seoul 130-701; tel. (2) 961-0106; fax (2) 962-8840; f. 1960; general, social science, technology, language, literature; Pres. CHOE YOUNG-SEEK.

Kyungnam University Press: 28-7, Samchung-dong, Jongno-gu, Seoul 110-230; tel. and fax (2) 3700-0700; e-mail ifes@kyungnam.ac.kr; internet ifes.kyungnam.ac.kr; Pres. PARK JAE-KYU.

Minumsa Publishing Co Ltd: 5/F Kangnam Publishing Culture Centre, 506, Sinsa-dong, Gangnam-gu, Seoul 135-120; tel. (2) 515-2000; fax (2) 514-3249; e-mail webmaster@minumsa.com; internet www.minumsa.com; f. 1966; literature, philosophy, linguistics, pure science; Pres. PARK MAENG-HO.

Munhakdongne Publishing Co Ltd: 513-8, Paju Book City, Munbal-ri, Gyoha-eup, Paju-si, Gyeonggi-do 413-756; tel. (31) 955-8888; fax (31) 955-8855; e-mail editor@munhak.com; internet www.munhak.com; f. 1993; art, literature, science, philosophy, non-fiction, children's, periodicals; Pres. KANG BYUNG-SUN.

Sakyejul Publishing Ltd: 513-3, Paju Book City, Munbal-ri, Gyoha-eup, Paju-si, Gyeonggi-do; tel. (31) 955-8558; fax (31) 955-8596; e-mail skj@sakyejul.co.kr; internet www.sakyejul.co.kr; f. 1982; social sciences, art, literature, history, children's; Pres. KANG MAR-XILL.

Sam Joong Dang Publishing Co: 261-23, Soke-dong, Yeongsan-gu, Seoul 140-140; tel. (2) 704-6816; fax (2) 704-6819; f. 1931; literature, history, philosophy, social sciences, dictionaries; Pres. LEE MIN-CHUL.

Sam Seong Dang Publishing Co: 101-14, Non Hyun-dong, Gangnam-gu, Seoul 135-010; tel. (2) 3442-6767; fax (2) 3442-6768; e-mail kyk@ssdp.co.kr; f. 1968; literature, fine arts, history, philosophy; Pres. KANG MYUNG-CHAE.

Samseongdang Publishing Co Ltd: 9/F, Samsungdang Bldg, 101-14, Nonhyeon-dong, Gangnam-gu, Seoul 135-820; tel. (2) 3443-2681; fax (2) 3443-2683; internet www.ssdp.co.kr; children's; Pres. KANG JEAN-KYUN.

Samsung Publishing Co Ltd: Samsung Publishing Bldg, 1516-2, Seocho 3-dong, Seocho-gu 137-871; tel. (2) 3470-6800; fax (2) 525-5057; e-mail jykim@samsungbooks.com; internet www.samsungbooks.com; children's books, comics, cooking, parenting, health, travel; f. 1951; Pres. KIM JIN-YONG.

Segyesa Publishing Co Ltd: 529-2, Munbal-ri, Gyoha-eup, Paju-si, Gyeonggi-do 413-756; tel. (31) 955-8080; fax (31) 955-8070; e-mail info@segyesa.co.kr; internet www.segyesa.co.kr; f. 1988; general, philosophy, literature, periodicals; Pres. CHOI SUN-HO.

Se-Kwang Music Publishing Co: 232-32, Seogye-dong, Yeongsan-gu, Seoul 140-140; tel. (2) 719-2652; fax (2) 719-2191; e-mail sekwang@sekwang.co.kr; internet www.sekwang.co.kr; f. 1953; music, art; Pres. PARK SEI-WON; Chair. PARK SHIN-JOON.

Seong An Dang Publishing Co: 4579, Singil-6-dong, Yeongdeungpo-gu, Seoul 150-056; tel. (2) 3142-4151; fax (2) 323-5324; f. 1972; technology, text books, university books, periodicals; Pres. LEE JONG-CHOON.

Seoul National University Press: 599, Gwanak-ro, Gwanak-gu, Seoul 151-742; tel. (2) 889-0785; fax (2) 888-4148; e-mail snubook@snu.ac.kr; internet www.snupress.com; f. 1961; philosophy, engineering, social science, art, literature; Pres. LEE KI-JUN.

Si-sa-young-o-sa, Inc: 55-1, 2-ga, Jongno, Jongno-gu, Seoul 110-122; tel. (2) 274-0509; fax (2) 271-3980; internet www.ybmsisa.co.kr; f. 1959; language, literature; Pres. CHUNG YOUNG-SAM.

Sogang University Press: Rm 332, Kim Daegon Hall, 35 Baekbeom-ro, Mapo-gu, Seoul 121-742; tel. (2) 705-8212; fax (2) 705-8612; e-mail kje@sogang.ac.kr; internet sgpress.sogang.ac.kr; f. 1978; philosophy, religion, science, art, history; Pres. LEE JONG-WOOK.

Sookmyung Women's University Press: 53-12, 2-ga, Jongpa-dong, Yeongsan-gu, Seoul 140-742; tel. (2) 710-9162; fax (2) 710-9090; f. 1968; general; Pres. LEE KYUNG-SOOK.

Sungkyunkwan University Press: 53, Myeongnyun-dong 3-ga, Jongno-gu, Seoul; tel. (2) 760-1252; fax (2) 762-7452; internet www.skku.edu.

Sungshin Women's University Press: 249-1, Dongsun-dong 3-ga, Seongbuk-gu, Seoul; tel. (2) 920-7327; fax (2) 920-7326; internet www.sungshin.ac.kr/press.

Tam Gu Dang Publishing Co: 158, 1-ga, Hanggangno, Yeongsan-gu, Seoul 140-011; tel. (2) 3785-2211; fax (2) 3785-2272; e-mail tamgudang@tamgudang.co.kr; internet www.tamgudang.co.kr; f. 1950; linguistics, literature, social sciences, history, fine arts; Pres. HONG YOUNG-SOO.

Woongjin Think Big Co Ltd: Kukdong Bldg, 24th Floor, Chungmuro 3-ga, Jung-gu, Seoul; tel. (2) 3670-1832; fax (2) 766-2722; e-mail webmaster@wjholdings.co.kr; internet www.woongjin.com; children's; Pres. YOON SEOK-KEUM.

Yearimdang Publishing Co Ltd: Yearim Bldg, 153-3, Samseong-dong, Gangnam-gu, Seoul 135-090; tel. (2) 566-1004; fax (2) 567-9660; e-mail yearim@yearim.co.kr; internet www.yearim.kr; f. 1973; children's; Pres. NA CHOON-HO.

Yonsei University Press: 134, Sincheon-dong, Seodaemun-gu, Seoul 120-749; tel. (2) 2123-3380; fax (2) 2123-6673; e-mail dykim@yonsei.ac.kr; internet www.yonsei.ac.kr/press; f. 1955; philosophy, religion, literature, history, art, social science, pure science; Pres. KIM BYUNG-SOO.

Youl Hwa Dang: Paju Book City, 520-10, Munbal-ri, Gyoha-eup, Paju-si, Gyeonggi-do 413-832; tel. (31) 955-7000; fax (31) 955-7010; e-mail yhdp@youlhwadang.co.kr; internet www.youlhwadang.co.kr; f. 1971; art; Pres. YI KI-UNG.

Younglim Cardinal Inc: Hyecheon Bldg, 831, Yeoksam-dong, Gangnam-gu, Seoul 135-792; tel. (2) 553-8516; fax (2) 552-0436; e-mail edit@ylc21.co.kr; internet www.ylc21.co.kr; f. 1987.

PUBLISHERS' ASSOCIATION

Korean Publishers' Association: 105-2, Sagan-dong, Jongno-gu, Seoul 110-190; tel. (2) 735-2702; fax (2) 738-5414; e-mail kpa@kpa21.or.kr; internet www.kpa21.or.kr; f. 1947; Pres. BAEK SOK-GHEE; Sec.-Gen. KO HUNG-SIK.

Broadcasting and Communications

TELECOMMUNICATIONS

Korea Telecom: 206, Jungja-dong, Bundang-gu, Seongnam-si, Gyeonggi Prov. 463-711; tel. (2) 727-0114; fax (2) 750-3994; internet www.kt.co.kr; domestic and international telecommunications services and broadband internet services; privatized in June 2002; CEO LEE SUK-CHAE.

Korea Telecom (KT) Freetel: Seoul; internet www.ktf.co.kr; subsidiary of Korea Telecom; 10m. subscribers (2002); CEO JOONG SOO-NAM.

LG UPlus: 827, Namdaemunno 5-ga, Jung-gu, Seoul 100-095; tel. (70) 4080-1114; e-mail ir@lguplus.co.kr; internet www.uplus.co.kr; subsidiary of LG Corpn; mobile telecommunications and wireless internet services; CEO SANG CHUL-LEE.

Onse Telecom: 192-2, Gumi-dong, Bundang-gu, Seongnam-si, Gyeonggi Prov. 463-500; tel. and fax (31) 738-6000; internet www.onse.net; domestic and international telecommunications services; Jt CEO SONG YIN-GWON; KIM HYEONG JIN.

SK Telecom Co Ltd: 11, Euljiro, 2-ga, Jung-gu, Seoul 100-999; tel. (2) 6100-2114; fax (2) 2121-3999; e-mail webmaster@sktelecom.com; internet www.sktelecom.com; cellular mobile telecommunications and wireless internet services; merged with Shinsegi Telecom in Jan. 2002; 16m. subscribers (2002); Pres. and CEO HA SUNG-MIN.

BROADCASTING

Regulatory Authority

Broadcasting and Communications Commission: KBS Bldg, 923-5, Mok-dong, Yangcheon-gu, Seoul 158-715; tel. (2) 3219-5117; fax (2) 3219-5371; e-mail admin@kbc.go.kr; internet www.kbc.go.kr; Chair. LEE KYE-CHEOL.

Radio

Korean Broadcasting System (KBS): 18, Yeouido-dong, Yeongdeungpo-gu, Seoul 150-790; tel. (2) 781-1000; fax (2) 781-4179; internet www.kbs.co.kr; f. 1926; publicly owned corpn with 26 local broadcasting and 855 relay stations; overseas service in Korean, English, German, Indonesian, Chinese, Japanese, French, Spanish, Russian and Arabic; Pres. KIM IN-KYU.

Buddhist Broadcasting System (BBS): 140, Mapo-dong, Mapo-gu, Seoul 121-050; tel. (2) 705-5114; fax (2) 705-5229; e-mail webmaster@bbsfm.co.kr; internet www.bbsfm.co.kr; f. 1990; Pres. CHO HAE-HYONG.

Christian Broadcasting System (CBS): 917-1, Mok-dong, Yangcheon-gu, Seoul 158-701; tel. (2) 650-0500; fax (2) 654-0505; e-mail help@cbs.co.kr; internet www.cbs.co.kr; f. 1954; independent religious network with 14 network stations, incl. Seoul, Daegu, Busan and Gwangju; also satellite, cable and digital media broadcasting; programmes in Korean; Pres. LEE JEONG-SIK.

Educational Broadcasting System (EBS): 463-2, Dogok-dong, Gangnam-gu, Seoul 135-854; tel. (2) 526-2000; fax (2) 526-2179; e-mail hotline@ebs.co.kr; internet www.ebs.co.kr; f. 1990; Pres. Dr PARK HEUNG-SOO.

Far East Broadcasting Co (FEBC): 89, Sangsu-dong, Mapo-gu, Seoul 121-707; tel. (2) 320-0114; fax (2) 320-0229; e-mail febcadm@febc.net; internet www.febc.net; Christian programmes; 11 local stations; Chair. Dr BILLY KIM.

  Radio Station HLAZ: MPO Box 88, Seoul 121-707; tel. (2) 320-0114; fax (2) 320-0129; e-mail febcadm@febc.net; internet www.febc.net; f. 1973; religious, educational service operated by Far East Broadcasting Co; programmes in Korean, Chinese, Russian and Japanese; Chair. Dr BILLY KIM.

  Radio Station HLKX: MPO Box 88, Seoul 121-707; tel. (2) 320-0114; fax (2) 320-0129; e-mail febcadm@febc.net; internet www.febc.net; f. 1956; religious, educational service operated by Far East Broadcasting Co; programmes in Korean, Chinese and English; Chair. Dr BILLY KIM.

Munhwa Broadcasting Corpn (MBC): 31, Yeouido-dong, Yeongdeungpo-gu, Seoul 150-728; tel. (2) 784-2000; fax (2) 784-0880; e-mail mbcir@imbc.com; internet www.imbc.com; f. 1961; public; Pres. and CEO KIM JAE-CHEOL.

Pyong Hwa Broadcasting Corpn (PBC): 2-3, 1-ga, Jeo-dong, Jung-gu, Seoul 100-031; tel. (2) 270-2114; fax (2) 270-2210; internet www.pbc.co.kr; f. 1990; religious and educational programmes; Pres. OH JI-YEONG.

Seoul Broadcasting System (SBS): SBS Broadcasting Center, 920-1, Mok-dong, Yangcheon-gu, Seoul 158-051; tel. (2) 786-0792; fax (2) 780-2530; e-mail webmaster@sbs.co.kr; internet www.sbs.co.kr; f. 1991; Pres. WOO WONGIL.

US Forces Network Korea (AFN Korea): Seoul; tel. (2) 7914-6495; fax (2) 7914-5870; e-mail info@afnkorea.net; internet www.afnkorea.net; f. 1950; six originating stations and 19 relay stations; 24 hours a day.

Television

There are numerous large national and regional television broadcasting companies. The switch to digital services was completed by the end of 2012.

Educational Broadcasting System (EBS): see Radio.

Jeonju Television Corpn (JTV): 656-3, Sonosong-dong, Deokjin-gu, Jeonju, Jeollabuk-do; tel. (63) 250-5200; fax (63) 250-5249; e-mail jtv@jtv.co.kr; internet www.jtv.co.kr; f. 1997; Pres. KIM TAEK-GON.

Korean Broadcasting System (KBS): 18, Yeouido-dong, Yeongdeungpo-gu, Seoul 150-790; tel. (2) 781-1000; fax (2) 781-4179; e-mail webmaster@kbs.co.kr; internet www.kbs.co.kr; f. 1961; publicly owned corpn with 25 local broadcasting and 770 relay stations; Pres. KIM IN-KYU.

Munhwa Broadcasting Corpn (MBC-R/TV): 31, Yeouido-dong, Yeongdeungpo-gu, Seoul 150-728; tel. (2) 789-2851; fax (2) 782-3094; e-mail song@mbc.co.kr; internet www.imbc.com; f. 1961; public; owned by the Foundation for Broadcast Culture (70%) and the Chung-Soo Scholarship Foundation (30%); includes terrestrial, cable and satellite TV stations, regional stations and radio stations; Pres. and CEO KIM JAE-CHEOL.

Seoul Broadcasting System (SBS): see Radio.

US Forces Network Korea (AFN Korea): Seoul; tel. (2) 7914-2711; fax (2) 7914-5870; internet www.afnkorea.net; f. 1950; main transmitting station in Seoul; 19 rebroadcast transmitters and translators; 168 hours weekly.

Finance

(cap. = capital; res = reserves; dep. = deposits; m. = million; brs = branches; amounts in won, unless otherwise indicated)

REGULATORY AUTHORITIES

Financial Services Commission: 38, Yeoui-daero, Yeongdeungpo-gu, Seoul 150-743; tel. (2) 2156-8000; fax (2) 2156-9538; internet www.fsc.go.kr; f. 1998; deliberates on and resolves financial supervision issues; oversees Financial Supervisory Service; Chair. KIM SEOK-DONG.

Financial Supervisory Service: 38, Yeoui-daero, Yeongdeungpo-gu, Seoul 150-743; tel. (2) 3145-5114; fax (2) 785-3475; e-mail fssintl@fss.or.kr; internet www.fss.or.kr; f. 1999; examines and supervises financial institutions; Gov. KWON HYOUK-SE.

BANKING

At August 2012 there were 58 commercial banks in South Korea, comprising six specialized banks and 39 branches of foreign banks. The Financial Supervisory Service oversees the operations of commercial banks and the financial services sector.

Central Bank

Bank of Korea: 110, 3-ga, Namdaemun-no, Jung-gu, Seoul 100-794; tel. (2) 759-4114; fax (2) 759-4060; e-mail bokdplp@bok.or.kr; internet www.bok.or.kr; f. 1950; bank of issue; res 3,342m., dep. 283,785m. (Dec. 2009); Gov. KIM CHOONG-SOO; Sr Dep. Gov. PARK WON-SHIK; 16 domestic brs, 6 overseas offices.

Commercial Banks

Citibank Korea Inc: 39, Da-dong, Jung-gu, Seoul 100-180; tel. (2) 3455-2114; fax (2) 3455-2969; internet www.citibank.co.kr; f. 1983; fmrly KorAm Bank, name changed as above 2004; acquired by Citigroup in 2004; cap. 1,518,322m., res 1,963,247m., dep. 34,458,803m. (Dec. 2010); CEO and Chair. HA YUNG-KU; 215 brs.

Hana Bank: 101-1, 1-ga, Ulchi-no, Jung-gu, Seoul 100-191; tel. (2) 2002-1111; fax (2) 775-7472; e-mail webmaster@hanabank.co.kr; internet www.hanabank.co.kr; f. 1991; merged with Boram Bank in Jan. 1999; merged with Seoulbank in Dec. 2002; cap. 1,147,404m., res 2,958,344m., dep. 106,424,262m. (Dec. 2011); Chair. and CEO KIM JONG-JUN; 604 brs.

Kookmin Bank: 9-1, 2-ga, Namdaemun-no, Jung-gu, Seoul 100-703; tel. (2) 2073-7114; fax (2) 2073-3296; e-mail corres@kookminbank.com; internet www.kookminbank.com; f. 1963; est. as Citizen's National Bank, renamed 1995; re-est. Jan. 1999, following merger with Korea Long Term Credit Bank; merged with H & CB in Nov. 2001; cap. 2,481,896m., res 7,912,460m., dep. 185,504,184m. (Dec. 2010); Chair. EUH YOON-DAE; Pres. and CEO MIN BYUNG-DUK; 1,122 domestic brs, 6 overseas brs.

Korea Exchange Bank: 181, 2-ga, Ulchi-no, Jung-gu, Seoul 100-793; tel. (2) 729-0114; fax (2) 775-2565; internet www.keb.co.kr; f. 1967; merged with Korea International Merchant Bank in Jan. 1999; acquired by Hana Financial Group in 2012; cap. 3,224,534m., res 1,112,486m., dep. 68,781,556m. (Dec. 2010); CEO RO YUN-YONG; 345 domestic brs, 19 overseas brs.

Shinhan Bank: 120, 2-ga, Taepyeong-no, Jung-gu, Seoul 100-102; tel. (2) 6360-3000; fax (2) 6360-3082; e-mail irshy@shinhan.com; internet www.shinhan.com; f. 1982; merged with Chohung Bank in April 2006; cap. 7,928,078m., res 8,653,091m., dep. 162,996,416m. (Dec. 2011); Pres. and CEO SUH JIN-WON; 957 domestic brs, 12 overseas brs.

Standard Chartered Bank Korea Limited: 100, Gongpyeong-dong, Jongno-gu, Seoul 110702; tel. (2) 3702-3114; fax (2) 3702-4934; e-mail scbk.webmaster@sc.com; internet www.scfirstbank.com; f. 1929; acquired by Standard Chartered Bank in Jan. 2005; name changed from Standard Chartered First Bank Korea Limited to above in Jan. 2012; cap. 1,313,043m., res 1,032,407m., dep. 46,535,388m. (Dec. 2011); Chair. ROBERT T. BARNUM; Pres. and CEO RICHARD HILL; 414 brs.

Woori Bank: 203, 1-ga, Hoehyeon-dong, Jung-gu, Seoul; tel. (2) 2002-3000; fax (2) 2002-5687; internet www.wooribank.com; f. 2002; est. by merger of Hanvit Bank and Peace Bank of Korea; 78% govt-owned; privatization plans deferred in 2008; cap. 3,829,783m., res 3,032,208., dep. 164,092,476m. (Dec. 2011); CEO LEE SOON-WOO; 712 domestic brs.

Development Banks

Export-Import Bank of Korea: 16-1, Yeouido-dong, Yeong-deungpo-gu, Seoul 150-996; tel. (2) 3779-6114; fax (2) 784-1030; e-mail iro@koreaexim.go.kr; internet www.koreaexim.go.kr; f. 1976; cap. 6,258,755m., res −50,307m., dep. 2,103,275m. (Dec. 2011); Chair. and Pres. KIM YONG-HWAN; 10 brs.

Korea Development Bank: 16-3, Yeouido-dong, Yeongdeungpo-gu, Seoul 150-973; tel. (2) 787-6934; fax (2) 787-6991; e-mail KDBir@kdb.co.kr; internet www.kdb.co.kr; f. 1954; cap. 9,251,861m., res 617,033m., dep. 33,116,805m. (June 2012); Chair. and CEO HONG KY-TTACK; 69 domestic brs, 16 overseas brs.

Specialized Banks

Industrial Bank of Korea: 50, 2-ga, Ulchi-no, Jung-gu, Seoul 100-758; tel. (2) 729-6114; fax (2) 729-6402; e-mail ifd@ibk.co.kr; internet www.ibk.co.kr; f. 1961; est. as the Small and Medium Industry Bank; 85.5% govt-owned; cap. 3,219,869m., res 7,048,604m., dep. 66,919,658m. (Dec. 2011); Chair. and CEO YOON YONG-RO; 417 domestic brs, 5 overseas brs.

Meritz Investment Bank: Seoul Financial Center, 5th Floor, 84, Taepyeong-no 1-ga, Jung-gu, Seoul 100-768; tel. (2) 777-7711; fax (2) 318-7060; internet home.imeritz.com; f. 1977; fmrly Korean-French Banking Corpn (SogeKo).

Provincial Banks

Daegu Bank Ltd: 118, 2-ga, Susong-dong, Susong-gu, Daegu 706-712; tel. (53) 756-2001; fax (53) 756-2095; internet www.daegubank.co.kr; f. 1967; cap. 660,625m., res 53,303m., dep. 19,094,668m. (Dec. 2010); Chair. and CEO HA CHUN-SOO; 209 brs.

Jeju Bank: 1349, Ido-1-dong, Jeju 690-021, Jeju Prov.; tel. (64) 720-0200; fax (64) 753-4132; internet www.e-jejubank.com; f. 1969; cap. 110,644m., dep. 2,442,222m. (Dec. 2011); merged with Central Banking Co in 2000, joined the Shinhan Financial Group in 2002; CEO HEO CHANG-GI; 34 brs.

Jeonbuk Bank Ltd: 669-2, Geumam-dong, Deokjin-gu, Jeonju 561-711, N. Jeolla Prov.; tel. (63) 250-7114; fax (63) 250-7078; internet www.jbbank.co.kr; f. 1969; cap. 277,539m., res 17,998m., dep. 6,797,837m. (2010); Chair. and Pres. HONG SUNG-JOO; 74 brs.

Kwangju Bank Ltd: 7-12, Daein-dong, Dong-gu, Gwangju 501-719; tel. (62) 239-5000; fax (62) 239-5199; e-mail kbjint1@nuri.net; internet www.kjbank.com; f. 1968; cap. 247,069m., res 98,899m., dep. 11,424,534m. (Dec. 2010); Chair. JEONG TAE-SEOK; 124 brs.

Kyongnam Bank: 315 Main St, Masan, Hoiwon-gu, Changwon-si, Gyeongsangnam-do 630-807; tel. (551) 290-8000; fax (551) 294-9426; internet www.knbank.co.kr; f. 1970; est. as Gyeongnam Bank Ltd, name changed 1987; cap. 290,250m., res 120,770m., dep. 16,486,459m. (Dec. 2010); Chair. and CEO PARK YOUNG-BEEN; 155 brs.

Banking Association

Korea Federation of Banks: 19, 1-ga, Myeong-dong, Jung-gu, Seoul 100-021; tel. (2) 3705-5000; fax (2) 3705-5337; e-mail webmaster@kfb.or.kr; internet www.kfb.or.kr; f. 1928; 61 mems; Chair. BAHK BYONG-WON; Vice-Chair. KIM KONG-JIN.

STOCK EXCHANGE

Korea Exchange (KRX): Nulwon Bldg, 825-3, Beomil-dong, Dong-gu, Busan 601-720; tel. (51) 662-2000; fax (51) 662-2478; internet www.krx.co.kr; f. 2005; formed by merger of Korea Stock Exchange, Korea Futures Exchange, Kosdaq Stock Market, Korea Securities Dealers Association; Chair. and CEO KIM BONG-SOO.

INSURANCE

Principal Life Companies

Allianz Life Insurance Co Ltd: Allianz Tower, 45-21, Yeouido-dong, Yeongdeungpo-gu, Seoul 150-978; tel. (2) 3787-7000; e-mail webadmin@allianzlife.co.kr; internet www.allianzlife.co.kr; fmrly Allianz Jeil Life Insurance; formed in 2000 following acquisition of Jeil (First Life) by Allianz Group; renamed as above in 2002; Pres. and CEO MANUEL BAUER.

American International Assurance Korea: Shinil Bldg, 5/F, 64-5, 2-ga, Chungmu-ro, Jung-gu, Seoul; tel. (2) 3707-4800; fax (67) 725-0783; e-mail kr.webmaster@aia.com; internet www.aia.co.kr; f. 1977; CEO SANG LEE.

Dongbu Life Insurance Co Ltd: Dongbu Bldg, 7th Floor, 891-10, Daechi-dong, Gangnam-gu, Seoul 135-820; tel. (2) 1588-3131; fax (2) 3011-4100; internet www.dongbulife.co.kr; f. 1989; cap. 85,200m. (2003); CEO CHO JAE-HONG.

Green Cross Life Insurance Co Ltd: 395-68, Shindaebang-dong, Dongjak-gu, Seoul; tel. (2) 3284-7000; fax (2) 3284-7455; internet www.healthcare.co.kr; CEO LEE JUNG-SANG.

Hana HSBC Life Insurance Ltd: Hana Bank HQ Bldg, 17/F, 101-1 Ulchiro-1ga, Jung-gu, Seoul 100-191; tel. (2) 3709-7300; fax (2) 755-0668; internet www.hanahsbclife.co.kr; jt venture between HSBC Insurance (Asia-Pacific) Holdings Ltd and Hana Financial Group; CEO DAVID YOON.

Hungkuk Life Insurance Co Ltd: 226, Sinmun-no 1-ga, Jongno-gu, Seoul 100-061; tel. (2) 2002-7000; fax (2) 2002-7804; e-mail webmaster@hungkuk.co.kr; internet www.hungkuk.co.kr; f. 1958; CEO JIN HUN-JIN.

ING Life Insurance Co Korea Ltd: ING Center, 53 Sunhwa-dong, Jung-gu, Seoul 100-130; tel. (2) 3703-9500; fax (2) 734-3309; e-mail webmaster@inglife.co.kr; internet www.inglife.co.kr; f. 1991; cap. 64,820m. (2002); Pres. and CEO JOHN WYLIE.

KB Life Insurance Co Ltd: 2–5/F, 16-49, Hangangro-3 ga, Yong-san-gu, Seoul; tel. (2) 398-6800; fax (2) 398-6843; e-mail webmaster@kbli.co.kr; internet www.kbli.co.kr.

Korea Life Insurance Co Ltd: 60, Yeouido-dong, Yeongdeungpo-gu, Seoul 150-603; tel. (2) 789-5114; fax (2) 789-8173; internet www.korealife.com; f. 1946; cap. 3,550,000m. (2002); CEO SHIN EUN-CHUL.

Korean Reinsurance Company: 80, Susong-dong, Jongno-gu, Seoul 110-733; tel. (2) 3702-6000; fax (2) 739-3754; internet www.koreanre.co.kr; f. 1963; cap. 57,000m. (2010); Pres. PARK JONG-WON.

Kumho Life Insurance Co Ltd: 57, 1-ga, Sinmun-no, Jongno-gu, Seoul 110-061; tel. (2) 1588-4040; fax (2) 771-7561; internet www.kumholife.co.kr; f. 1988; acquired Dong-Ah Life Insurance in 2000; cap. 211,249m. (2002); Pres. CHOI BYEONG-GIL.

Kyobo Life Insurance Co Ltd: 1, 1-ga, Jongno, Jongno-gu, Seoul 110-714; tel. (2) 721-2121; fax (2) 737-9970; internet www.kyobo.co.kr; f. 1958; cap. 92,500m.; Chair. and CEO SHIN CHANG-JAE; 84 main brs.

Life Insurance Association of North America: Seoul City Tower, 14/F, 581, Namdaemunro-5-ga, Jung-gu, Seoul; tel. (2)

3781-1000; fax (2) 792-6063; internet www.lina.co.kr; f. 1987; CEO BENJAMIN HONG.

MetLife Insurance Co of Korea Ltd: Sungwon Bldg, 8/F, 141, Samseong-dong, Gangnam-gu, Seoul 135-716; tel. (2) 3469-9600; fax (2) 3469-9700; internet www.metlifekorea.co.kr; f. 1989; cap. 97,700m. (2002); Pres. STUART B. SOLOMON.

Mirae Asset Life Insurance: Times Sq. Bldg A, 442, 4-ga, Yeong-deungpo-dong, Seoul 150-034; tel. (2) 3271-4114; fax (2) 3271-4400; e-mail msp@miraeasset.com; internet www.miraeassetlife.com; f. 2005; CEO PARK HYEON-JOO.

New York Life Insurance Ltd: 10/F, Shinyoung Bldg, 68-5, Chung Dam-dong, Gangnam-gu, Seoul; tel. (2) 2107-4600; fax (2) 2107-4700; f. 1990.

PCA Life Insurance Co Ltd: PCA Life Tower, 706, Yeoksam-dong, Gangnam-gu, Seoul; tel. (2) 6960-1700; fax (2) 6960-1606; internet www.pcakorea.co.kr; f. 1990; cap. 52,100m. (2002); Pres. MIKE BISHOP.

Prudential Life Insurance Co of Korea Ltd: Prudential Bldg, Yeoksam-dong, Gangnam-gu, Seoul; tel. (2) 2144-2000; fax (2) 2144-2100; internet www.prudential.co.kr; f. 1989; cap. 26,400m.; Pres. HWANG OU-JIN.

Samsung Life Insurance Co Ltd: 150, 2-ga, Taepyeong-no, Jung-gu, Seoul 100-716; tel. (2) 751-8000; fax (2) 751-8100; e-mail samsunglife.ir@samsung.com; internet www.samsunglife.com; f. 1957; cap. 100,000m. (2002); Pres. LEE SOO-CHANG; 1,300 brs.

Shinhan Life Insurance Co Ltd: 120, 2-ga, Taepyeong-no, Jung-gu, Seoul 100-102; tel. (2) 3455-4000; fax (2) 775-3286; internet www.shinhanlife.co.kr; f. 1990; CEO GWEON JEUM-JOO.

Tong Yang Life Insurance Co Ltd: 185, Ulchi-no 2-ga, Jung-gu, Seoul 100-192; tel. (2) 728-9114; fax (2) 728-9563; internet www.myangel.co.kr; f. 1989; cap. 340,325m. (2002); Pres. KU JA-HONG.

Woori Aviva Life Insurance Co Ltd: Woori Aviva Life Insurance Bldg, Sujung 3-dong, Dong-gu, Busan 601-716; tel. (2) 2087-9337; fax (2) 2087-93258; internet www.wooriaviva.com; f. 1988; fmrly LIG Life Insurance Co Ltd; name changed as above after joint acquisition by Woori Finance Holdings Co Ltd and Aviva Life Insurance Co; Pres. SEON HWAN-KYU.

Non-Life Companies

American Home Insurance Co: Seoul Central Bldg, 15–18/F, 136 Seorin-dong, Jongno-gu, Seoul; tel. (2) 2260-6800; fax (2) 2260-6707; e-mail ask.chartis@chartisinsurance.com; internet www.chartisinsurance.com; f. 1947; operates under the brand name Chartis; Pres. BRAD BENNETT.

Dongbu Insurance Co Ltd: Dongbu Financial Center, 12/F, 891-10, Daechi-dong, Gangnam-gu, Seoul 135-840; tel. (2) 2262-3450; fax (2) 3001-3159; e-mail dongbu@dongbuinsurance.co.kr; internet www.idongbu.com; f. 1962; cap. 30,000m.; Pres. KIM JING-NAM.

First Fire and Marine Insurance Co Ltd: 12-1, Seosomun-dong, Jung-gu, CPOB 530, Seoul 100-110; tel. (2) 316-8114; fax (2) 771-7319; f. 1949; cap. 17,200m.; Pres. KIM WOO-HOANG.

Green Non-Life Insurance Co Ltd: Green Non-Life Insurance Co Bldg, 705-19, Yeoksam-dong, Gangnam-gu, Seoul; tel. (2) 3788-2000; fax (2) 774-8368; internet www.greenfire.co.kr; Pres. LEE YOUNG-DOO.

Heungkuk Fire and Marine Insurance Co Ltd: 226, Sinmun-no, 1-ga, Jongno-gu, Seoul; tel. (2) 724-9000; fax (2) 774-8368; e-mail sfmi@ssy.insurance.co.kr; internet www.insurance.co.kr; f. 1948; fmrly Ssangyong Fire and Marine Insurance Co; cap. 27,400m.; Pres. KIM YOUNG-GWON.

Hyundai Marine and Fire Insurance Co Ltd: 178, Sejongno, Jongno-gu, Seoul 110-731; tel. (2) 732-1212; fax (2) 732-5687; e-mail webpd@hdinsurance.co.kr; internet www.hi.co.kr; f. 1955; cap. 30,000m.; Pres. and CEO SEO TAI-CHANG.

Korean Reinsurance Co: 80, Susong-dong, Jongno-gu, Seoul 100-733; tel. (2) 3702-6000; fax (2) 739-3754; e-mail service@koreanre.co.kr; internet www.koreanre.co.kr; f. 1963; cap. 57,000m.; Pres. PARK JONG-WON.

Kyobo AXA General Insurance Co Ltd: 395-70, Sindaebang-dong, Dongjak-gu, Seoul; tel. (2) 3479-4900; fax (2) 3479-4800; internet www.kyobodirect.com; fmrly Kyobo Auto Insurance Co Ltd, name changed as above in 2007; Pres. GUY MARCILLAT.

LIG Insurance Co Ltd: 649-11, Yeoksam-dong, Gangnam-gu, Seoul; tel. (2) 310-2391; fax (2) 753-1002; e-mail webmaster@lginsure.com; internet www.lig.co.kr; f. 1959; fmrly LG Insurance Co; Pres. JANG NAM-SIK.

Lotte Insurance Co Ltd: 51-1, Namchang-dong, Jung-gu, Seoul 100-778; tel. (2) 1588-3344; fax (2) 754-5220; internet www.lotteins.co.kr; f. 1946; cap. 19,500m.; fmrly Daehan Fire and Marine Insurance Co Ltd, name changed as above in 2008; Pres. and CEO KIM CHANG-JAE.

Meritz Fire and Marine Insurance Co Ltd: 825-2, Yeoksam-dong, Gangnam-gu, Seoul 135-080; tel. (2) 3786-1910; fax (2) 3786-1940; e-mail ir@meritzfire.com; internet www.meritzfire.com; f. 1922; Vice-Chair. and CEO WOHN MYUNG-SOO.

Samsung Fire and Marine Insurance Co Ltd: Samsung Insurance Bldg, 87, 1-ga, Ulchi-no, Jung-gu, Seoul 100-191; tel. (2) 758-7948; fax (2) 758-7831; internet www.samsungfire.com; f. 1952; cap. 6,566m.; Pres. LEE SOO-CHANG.

Seoul Guarantee Insurance Co: 136-74, Yeonchi-dong, Jongno-gu, Seoul 110-470; tel. (2) 3671-7459; fax (2) 3671-7480; internet www.sgic.co.kr; f. 1969; CEO BAANG YOUNG-MIN.

Shindongah Fire and Marine Insurance Co Ltd: 43, 2-ga, Taepyeong-no, Jung-gu, Seoul; tel. (2) 6366-7000; fax (2) 755-8006; internet www.sdafire.com; f. 1946; cap. 60,220m.; CEO KWON CHU-SIN.

Insurance Associations

General Insurance Association of Korea: KRIC Bldg, 6th Floor, 80, Susong-dong, Jongno-gu, Seoul; tel. (2) 3702-8539; fax (2) 3702-8549; e-mail jhero@knia.or.kr; internet www.knia.or.kr; f. 1946; 16 corporate mems; fmrly Korea Non-Life Insurance Asscn; Chair. MOON JAE-WOO.

Korea Life Insurance Association: Kukdong Bldg, 16th Floor, 60-1, 3-ga, Jungmu-no, Jung-gu, Seoul 100-705; tel. (2) 2262-6685; fax (2) 2262-6580; e-mail info@klia.or.kr; internet www.klia.or.kr; f. 1950; Chair. KIM GYU-BOK.

Trade and Industry

GOVERNMENT AGENCIES

Fair Trade Commission: 217, Banpo-dong, Seocho-gu, Seoul; tel. (2) 2023-4248; fax (2) 2023-4241; e-mail kftc@korea.kr; internet www.ftc.go.kr; Chair. KIM DONG-SOO; Sec.-Gen. LEE DONG-KYU.

Federation of Korean Industries: FKI Bldg, 14/F, 28-2, Yeouido-dong, Yeongdeungpo-gu, Seoul 150-756; tel. (2) 3771-0354; fax (2) 3771-0110; e-mail webmaster@fki.or.kr; internet www.fki.or.kr; f. 1961; conducts research and survey work on domestic and overseas economic conditions and trends; advises the Govt and other interested parties on economic matters; exchanges economic and trade missions with other countries; sponsors business conferences; 366 corporate mems and 63 business asscns; Chair. HUH CHANG-SOO.

Korea Appraisal Board: 171-2, Samseong-dong, Gangnam-gu, Seoul; tel. (2) 2189-8000; fax (2) 561-6133; internet www.kab.co.kr; Chair. KWAN JIN-BONG.

Korea Asset Management Corpn (KAMCO): 450, Gangnam-daero, Gangnam-gu, Seoul; tel. (2) 3420-5000; fax (2) 3420-5030; e-mail irkamco@kamco.or.kr; internet www.kamco.or.kr; f. 1963; collection and foreclosure agency; appointed following Asian financial crisis as sole institution to manage and dispose of non-performing loans for financial institutions; Chair. and CEO CHANG YONG-CHUL.

Korea Export Industrial Corpn: 33, Seorin-dong, Jongno-gu, Seoul; tel. (2) 853-5573; f. 1964; encourages industrial exports, provides assistance and operating capital, conducts market surveys; Pres. KIM KI-BAE.

Korea Industrial Research Institutes: FKI Bldg, 28-1, Yeouido-dong, Yeongdeungpo-gu, Seoul; tel. (2) 780-7601; fax (2) 785-5771; f. 1979; analyses industrial and technological information from abroad; Pres. KIM CHAE-KYUM.

Korea Institute for Industrial Economics and Trade (KIET): 66 Hoegi-ro, Dongdaemun-gu, Seoul; tel. (2) 3299-3114; fax (2) 963-8540; e-mail webmaster@kiet.re.kr; internet www.kiet.re.kr; f. 1976; economic and industrial research; Pres. SONG BYOUNG-JUN.

Korea Land and Housing Corpn: 217, Jeongja-dong, Seongnam-shi, Gyeonggi-do; tel. (31) 738-7114; fax (31) 717-5431; internet www.lh.or.kr; f. 1975; land development; est. by merging Korea Land Corpn and Korea National Housing Corpn; CEO LEE JI-SONG.

Korea Resources Corpn (KORES): 606, Siheung-daero, Dongjak-gu, Seoul; tel. (2) 840-5600; e-mail csmaster@kores.or.kr; internet www.kores.or.kr; f. 1967; provides technical and financial support for the national mining industry; Pres. KIM SHIN-JONG.

Korea Trade Insurance Corpn: Seoul Central Bldg, 2/F, 136, Seorin-dong, Jongno-gu, Seoul 110-729; tel. (2) 399-6800; fax (2) 399-7439; internet www.ksure.or.kr; f. 1992; financial support services for traders; fmrly Korea Export Insurance Corpn; Chair. and Pres. RYU CHANG-MOO.

Korea Trade-Investment Promotion Agency (KOTRA): 300-9, Yeomgok-dong, Seocho-gu, Seoul; tel. (2) 3460-7114; fax (2) 3460-7777; e-mail digitalkotra@kotra.or.kr; internet www.kotra.or.kr; f. 1962; various trade promotion activities, market research, cross-border investment promotion, etc.; 102 overseas brs; Pres. CHO HWAN-EIK.

Korean Intellectual Property Office: Government Complex-Daejeon Bldg 4, 189, Cheongsa-ro, Seo-gu, Daejeon; tel. (42) 481-5071; fax (42) 472-9314; e-mail kipoicd@kipo.go.kr; internet www.kipo.go.kr; Commissioner LEE SOO-WON.

CHAMBER OF COMMERCE

Korea Chamber of Commerce and Industry: 45, 4-ga, Namdaemun-no, Jung-gu, Seoul 100-743; tel. (2) 6050-3114; fax (2) 6050-3400; e-mail webmaster@korcham.net; internet www.korcham.net; f. 1884; over 47,000 mems; 70 local chambers; promotes development of the economy and of international economic co-operation; Chair. SOHN KYUNG-SHIK.

INDUSTRIAL AND TRADE ASSOCIATIONS

Construction Association of Korea: Construction Bldg, 8th Floor, 71-2, Nonhyon-dong, Gangnam-gu, Seoul 135-701; tel. (2) 3485-0200; fax (2) 542-6264; internet www.cak.or.kr; f. 1947; national licensed contractors' asscn; 6,823 mem. firms (2006); Pres. KWON HONG-SA.

Korea Agro-Fisheries Trade Corpn (aT): aT Center, 232 Yang-jae-dong, Seocho-gu, Seoul; tel. (2) 6300-1114; fax (2) 6300-1600; internet www.at.or.kr; f. 1967; fmrly Agricultural and Fishery Marketing Corpn; integrated devt for secondary processing and marketing distribution for agricultural products and fisheries products; Pres. JANG BAE-YOO; Exec. Vice-Pres. KIM JIN-KYU.

Korea Automobile Manufacturers Association (KAMA): 1461-15, Seocho 3-dong, Seocho-gu, Seoul 137-720; tel. (2) 3660-1854; fax (2) 3660-1900; e-mail webmaster@kama.or.kr; internet www.kama.or.kr/index.jsp; f. 1988; Chair. YOUN YEO-CHUL.

Korea Electronics Association: Digital Innovation Center, 11–12/F, 1599, Sangnam-dong, Mapo-gu, Seoul; tel. (2) 6388-6000; fax (2) 6388-6009; e-mail webmaster@gokea.org; internet www.gokea.org; f. 1976; 328 mems; Chair. YUN JONG-YONG.

Korea Federation of Textile Industries: Textile Center, 16/F, 944-31, Daechi 3-dong, Gangnam-gu, Seoul 135-713; tel. (2) 528-4052; fax (2) 528-4069; e-mail kofoti@kofoti.or.kr; internet www.kofoti.or.kr; f. 1980; 50 corporate mems; Chair. CHAN RO-HEE.

Korea Foods Industry Association: 1002-6, Bangbae-dong, Seo-cho-gu, Seoul; tel. (2) 3470-8100; fax (2) 3471-3492; internet www.kfia.or.kr; f. 1969; 104 corporate mems; Pres. CHUN MYUNG-KE.

Korea Importers Association (KOIMA): 218, Hangang-no, 2-ga, Yeongsan-gu, Seoul 140-875; tel. (2) 792-1581; fax (2) 785-4373; e-mail koima@koima.or.kr; internet www.koima.or.kr; f. 1970; 6,804 mems; Chair. Dr LEE JU-TAE.

Korea International Trade Association: 159-1, Samseong-dong, Gangnam-gu, Seoul; tel. (2) 6000-5114; fax (2) 6000-5115; e-mail kitainfo@kita.net; internet www.kita.org; f. 1946; private, non-profitmaking business org. representing all licensed traders in South Korea; provides foreign businesses with information, contacts and advice; 80,000 corporate mems; Chair. and CEO HAN DUCK-SOO.

Korea Iron and Steel Association: Posteel Tower, 19th Floor, 735-3, Yeoksam-dong, Gangnam-gu, Seoul; tel. (2) 559-3500; fax (2) 559-3508; internet www.kosa.or.kr; f. 1975; 39 corporate mems; Chair. YOO SANG-BOO.

Korea Oil Association: 28-1, Yeouido-dong, Yeongdeungpo-gu, Seoul; tel. (2) 555-8322; fax (2) 555-7825; e-mail oilassn@yahoo.co.kr; internet www.koreaoil.or.kr; f. 1980; Pres. CHOI DOO-HWAN.

Korea Productivity Center: 122-1, Jeokseon-dong, Jongno-gu, Seoul 110-751; tel. (2) 724-1114; fax (2) 736-0322; internet www.kpc.or.kr; f. 1957; services to increase productivity of industries, consulting services, education and training of specialized personnel; Chair. and CEO CHOI DONG-KYU.

Korea Sericultural Association: 17-9, Yeouido-dong, Yeongdeungpo-gu, Seoul; tel. (2) 783-6072; fax (2) 780-0706; e-mail jamsa@silktopia.or.kr; internet ksa.silktopia.or.kr; f. 1946; improvement and promotion of silk production; 50,227 corporate mems; Pres. PARK DONGCHUI.

Korea Shipbuilders' Association: Landmark Tower, 18/F, 837-36, Yeoksam-dong, Gangnam-gu, Seoul 135-937; tel. (2) 2112-8181; fax (2) 2112-8182; internet www.koshipa.or.kr; f. 1977; 9 mems; Chair. NAM SANG-TAE.

Korea Textiles Trade Association: Textile Center, 16/F, 944-31, Daechi 3-dong, Gangnam-gu, Seoul 135-713; tel. (2) 528-5158; fax (2) 528-5188; e-mail keat@kotis.net; internet www.textra.or.kr; f. 1981; 947 corporate mems; Pres. KANG TAE-SEUNG.

Korean Apparel Industry Association: Textile Center, 16/F, 944-31, Daechi 3-dong, Gangnam-gu, Seoul 135-713; tel. (2) 528-0114; fax (2) 528-0120; internet www.kaia.or.kr; f. 1993; 741 corporate mems; Chair. LEE IN-SUNG.

Mining Association of Korea: 35-24, Dongui-dong, Jongno-gu, Seoul 110; tel. (2) 737-7748; fax (2) 720-5592; f. 1918; 128 corporate mems; Pres. KIM SANG-BONG.

Spinners and Weavers Association of Korea: 43-8, Gwancheol-dong, Jongno-gu, Seoul 110; tel. (2) 735-5741; fax (2) 735-5749; internet www.swak.org; f. 1947; 20 corporate mems; Chair. KIM HYONG-SANG.

EMPLOYERS' ORGANIZATION

Korea Employers' Federation: KEF Bldg, 276-1, Daeheung-dong, Mapo-gu, Seoul 121-726; tel. (2) 3270-7310; fax (2) 3270-7431; e-mail admin@kef.or.kr; internet www.kef.or.kr; f. 1970; advocates employers' interests with regard to labour and social affairs; 13 regional employers' asscns, 20 economic and trade asscns, and 4,000 major enterprises; Chair. LEE HEE-BEOM.

UTILITIES

Electricity

Korea Electric Power Corpn (KEPCO): 167, Samseong-dong, Gangnam-gu, Seoul; tel. (2) 3456-3114; fax (2) 3456-3699; internet www.kepco.co.kr; f. 1961; transmission and distribution of electric power, and development of electric power sources; six power generation subsidiaries formed in 2001; Pres. and CEO (vacant).

Oil and Gas

Daegu City Gas Co Ltd: 2268-1, Namsan 4-dong, Jung-gu, Daegu; tel. (53) 606-1000; fax (53) 606-1004; e-mail kej@taegugas.co.kr; internet www.taegugas.co.kr; f. 1983; Pres. and CEO LEE CHONG-MOO.

Daehan City Gas: 27-1, Daechi-dong, Kangnam-gu, Seoul; tel. (2) 3410-8000; internet www.daehancitygas.com; f. 1978; supplies liquefied natural gas (LNG) to customers in Seoul and Gyeonggi Province; Co-CEOs NAH SEONG-HWA, KIM BOK-HWAN.

GS Caltex: GS Tower, 679 Yeoksam-dong, Gangnam-gu, Seoul; tel. (2) 2005-1114; internet www.gscaltex.com; subsidiary of GS Holdings Corpn; fmrly LG Caltex Oil, renamed as above March 2005; Chair. and CEO HUR DONG-SOO.

Hanjin City Gas: 711, Sanggye 6-dong, Nowon-gu, Seoul; tel. (2) 950-5000; fax (2) 950-5001; e-mail webmaster@daeryunens.com; internet www.daeryunens.com; f. 1985; supplies natural gas to Seoul and Gyeonggi; CEO LEE SEUNG-CHIL.

Incheon City Gas Corpn: 178-24, Gajoa-dong, Seo-gu, Incheon; tel. (32) 1600-0002; fax (32) 576-2710; internet www.icgas.co.kr; f. 1983; CEO PARK DAE-YONG.

Jungbu City Gas Co Ltd: Asan, Chungcheongnam-do; fax (41) 530-1800; f. 1992; Pres. YOO TAE-PEO.

Korea Gas Corpn: 215, Jeongja-dong, Bundang-gu, Seongnam, Gyeonggi-do; tel. (31) 710-0114; fax (31) 710-0117; e-mail kogasmaster@kogas.or.kr; internet www.kogas.or.kr; f. 1983; state-owned; privatization pending; Pres. and CEO CHOO KANG-SOO.

Korea National Oil Corpn (KNOC): 57, Gwanpyeong-ro, 212 Beon-gil, Anyang-S Dongan-gu, Gyeonggi-do; tel. 380-2114; fax 387-9321; e-mail webmaster@knoc.co.kr; internet www.knoc.co.kr; CEO SUH MOON-KYU.

KyungDong City Gas Co: 939, Jinjang-dong, Book-gu, Ulsan; tel. (52) 219-5300; internet www.kdgas.co.kr; distributes liquefied natural gas (LNG) to residential, commercial and industrial customers in Ulsan and Yangsan; CEO SONG JAE-HO.

Kyungnam Energy Co Ltd: 55-5, Ungnam-dong, Changwon, Gyeongsangnam-do 641-290; tel. (55) 260-4432; fax (55) 285-9861; e-mail admin@knenergy.co.kr; internet www.knenergy.co.kr; f. 1972; supplies natural gas to Changwon and the surrounding area; Pres. and CEO CHUNG YEUN-WOOK.

Samchully Co Ltd: 35-6, Yeouido-dong, Yeongdeungpo-gu, Seoul; tel. (2) 368-3300; fax (2) 783-1206; e-mail webmaster@samchully.co.kr; internet www.samchully.co.kr; f. 1966; gas supply co for Seoul metropolitan area and Gyeonggi Prov; Pres. and CEO SHIN MAN-JOONG.

Seoul City Gas Co: 281, Yeomchang-dong, Gangseo-gu, Seoul 157-864; tel. (2) 810-8000; fax (2) 828-6740; internet www.seoulgas.co.kr; f. 1983; distributes gas in Seoul and Gyeonggi Province; Chair. and CEO KIM YOUNG-MIN.

SK E & S: 99, Seorin-dong, Jongno-gu, Seoul; tel. (2) 2121-3114; fax (2) 2121-3198; internet www.skens.net; f. 1999; jt venture between SK Corpn and Enron Corpn (USA); supplies natural gas through various cos, incl.: Chongju City Gas, Chonnam City Gas, Chungnam City Gas, Iksan City Gas, Iksan Energy, Kangwon City Gas, Kumi City Gas and Pusan City Gas; Pres. and CEO MOON DUK-KYU.

Yesco Co Ltd: 249-8, Yongdap-dong, Sungdong-gu, Seoul; tel. (2) 1644-0303; fax (2) 3390-3117; e-mail webmaster@lsyesco.com; internet www.gaspia.com; f. 1981; fmrly Kukdong City Gas Co;

part of the LS Group; supplies liquefied natural gas (LNG) to the Seoul metropolitan area; Pres. and CEO CHOI KYUNG-HOON.

Water

Korea Water Resources Corpn: 6-2, Yeonchuk-dong, Daedeok-gu, Daejeon; tel. (42) 629-3114; fax (42) 623-0963; e-mail limetree@kwater.or.kr; internet www.kowaco.or.kr; CEO KIM JUNG-YUN.

Office of Waterworks, Seoul Metropolitan Govt: 27-1 Hap-dong, Seodaemun-gu, Seoul; tel. (2) 390-7332; fax (2) 362-3653; internet arisu.seoul.go.kr; f. 1908; responsible for water supply in Seoul; Head CHOI DONG-YON.

Ulsan City Water and Sewerage Board: 646-4, Sin-Jung 1-dong, Nam-gu, Ulsan; tel. (52) 743-020; fax (52) 746-928; f. 1979; responsible for water supply and sewerage in Ulsan; Dir HO KUN-SONG.

CO-OPERATIVES

Korea Auto Industries Co-operative Association: 1638-3, Seocho-dong, Seocho-gu, Seoul 137-070; tel. (2) 587-0014; fax (2) 583-7340; e-mail kaica@kaica.or.kr; internet www.kaica.or.kr; f. 1962; Chair. SHIN DAL-CHUK.

Korea Computers Co-operative: 14-8, Yeouido-dong, Yeongdeungpo-gu, Seoul; tel. (2) 780-0511; fax (2) 780-7509; f. 1981; Pres. MIN KYUNG-HYUN.

Korea Federation of Knitting Industry Co-operatives: 586-1, Sinsa-dong, Gangnam-gu, Seoul; tel. (2) 548-2131; fax (2) 3444-9929; e-mail kts01@korea.com; internet www.knit.or.kr; f. 1962; Chair. JOUNG MAN-SUB.

Korea Federation of Non-ferrous Metal Industry Co-operatives: Backsang Bldg, Rm 715, 35-2, Yeouido-dong, Yeongdeungpo-gu, Seoul; tel. (2) 780-8551; fax (2) 784-9473; f. 1962; Chair. PARK WON-SIK.

Korea Federation of Plastic Industry Co-operatives: 146-2, Ssangrim-dong, Jung-gu, Seoul; tel. (2) 2280-8200; fax (2) 2277-3915; internet www.koreaplastic.or.kr; f. 1973.

Korea Federation of Small and Medium Business (Kbiz): 16-2, Yeouido-dong, Yeongdeungpo-gu, Seoul 150-740; tel. (2) 2124-3114; fax (2) 3775-1981; e-mail webmaster@kbiz.or.kr; internet www.kbiz.or.kr; f. 1962; Chair. KIM KI-MUN.

Korea Federation of Weaving Industry Co-operatives: tel. (2) 752-8097; fax (2) 755-6994; e-mail weaving3@hanmail.net; internet www.weaving.or.kr; f. 1964.

Korea Information and Communication Industry Co-operative: tel. (2) 711-2266; fax (2) 7111-2272; e-mail webmaster@kicic.or.kr; internet www.kicic.or.kr; f. 1962; CEO JOO DAE-CHULL.

Korea Metal Industry Co-operative: tel. (2) 780-4411; fax (2) 785-5067; e-mail master@koreametal.or.kr; internet www.koreametal.or.kr; f. 1962.

Korea Mining Industry Co-operative: 35-24, Dongui-dong, Jongno-gu, Seoul; tel. (2) 735-3490; fax (2) 735-4658; f. 1966; Chair. JEON HYANG-SIK.

Korea Steel Industry Co-operative: 915-14, Bangbae-dong, Seocho-gu, Seoul; tel. (2) 587-3121; fax (2) 588-3671; internet www.kosic.or.kr; f. 1962; Pres. KIM DUK-NAM.

National Agricultural Co-operative Federation (NACF): Saemunangil 91, Jung-gu, Seoul; tel. (2) 2080-5114; fax (2) 1544-2100; internet www.nonghyup.com; f. 1961; international banking, marketing, co-operative trade, utilization and processing, supply, co-operative insurance, banking and credit services, education and research; Chair. CHOI WUN-BYUNG.

National Federation of Fisheries Co-operatives: 11-6, Sincheon-dong, Songpa-gu, Seoul; tel. (2) 2240-2114; fax (2) 2240-3024; e-mail webmaster@suhyup.co.kr; internet www.suhyup.co.kr; f. 1962; CEO LEE JONG-KOO.

TRADE UNIONS

Federation of Korean Trade Unions (FKTU): 35, Yeouido-dong, Yeongdeungpo-gu, Seoul 150-885; tel. (2) 6277-0026; fax (2) 6277-0068; e-mail fktu@fktu.or.kr; internet www.fktu.or.kr; f. 1941; Pres. LEE YONG-DEUK; affiliated to ITUC; 26 affiliated union federations.

Korean Confederation of Trade Unions: 5th Daeyoung Bldg, 139, 2-ga, Yeouido-dong, Yeongdeungpo-gu, Seoul 150-032; tel. (2) 2670-9234; fax (2) 2635-1134; internet www.kctu.org; f. 1995; legalized 1999; Chair. KIM YOUNG-HOON; 600,000 mems.

Transport

RAILWAYS

In 2010 there were 3,379 km of railways in operation. The first phase of construction of a new high-speed rail system connecting Seoul to Busan (412 km) via Cheonan, Daejeon, Daegu, and Gyungju, was completed in early 2004. The second phase, Daejeon–Busan, became operational in November 2010.

Korean National Railroad (Korail): 293-74 Soje-dong, Dong-gu, Daejeon 300-720; tel. (42) 472-3014; fax (42) 259-2197; e-mail admin@korail.com; internet www.korail.com; f. 1963; operates all railways under the supervision of the Ministry of Land, Transport and Maritime Affairs; Pres. and CEO CHING CHANG-YOUNG.

City Underground Railways

Busan Subway: Gyotonggongsa 1-ro, Busanjin-gu, Busan 614-722; tel. (51) 640-7186; fax (51) 640-7010; e-mail ipsubway@buta.or.kr; internet www.subway.busan.kr; f. 1988; length of 71.6 km (2 lines, with a further line under construction); Pres. BAE TAE-SOO.

Daegu Metropolitan Transit Corpn: 1500, Sangin 1-dong, Dalseo-gu, Daegu 704-808; tel. (53) 643-2114; fax (53) 640-2189; e-mail webmaster@daegusubway.co.kr; internet www.dtro.co.kr; length of 57.3 km (two lines, with further routes totalling 125.4 km planned or under construction); CEO BAE SANG-MIN.

Daejeon Metropolitan Express Transit Corpn: tel. (42) 539-3114; fax (42) 539-3119; e-mail qnsdlqkr@hanmail.net; internet www.djet.co.kr; f. 2006; operates one line, with a further four lines planned.

Gwangju Metropolitan Rapid Transit Corpn: 165-27 Mareuk-dong, Seo-gu, Gwangju 502-750; tel. (62) 604-8000; fax (62) 604-8069; internet www.gwangjusubway.co.kr; f. 2004; one line, with a further line planned; Pres. LEE HO-JOON.

Incheon Rapid Transit Corpn: 67-2, Gansok-dong, Namdong-gu, Incheon 405-233; tel. (32) 451-2114; fax (32) 451-2200; e-mail webmaster@ictr.or.kr; internet www.ictr.or.kr; length of 31.1 km (29 stations, 1 line), with two further lines planned; Pres. LEE KWANG-YUONG.

Seoul Metropolitan Rapid Transit Corporation: 133-783, Seongdong-gu, Yongdap-dong 223-3, Seoul; tel. (2) 6311-2200; internet www.smrt.co.kr; operates lines 5–8; Pres. KIM KI-CHUN.

Seoul Metropolitan Subway Corpn: 447-7, Bangbae-dong, Seocho-gu, Seoul; tel. (2) 520-5020; fax (2) 520-5039; internet www.seoulsubway.co.kr; f. 1981; length of 134.9 km (115 stations, lines 1–4); Pres. KIM IK-HWAN.

ROADS

In 2009 there were 104,983 km of roads. A network of motorways (approximately 3,779 km) links all the principal towns, the most important being the 428-km Gyeongbu (Seoul–Busan) motorway. Improvements in relations with North Korea resulted in the commencement of work on a highway to link Seoul and the North Korean capital, Pyongyang, in September 2000. In February 2003 a road link between the two countries was completed.

Korea Expressway Corpn: 293-1, Kumto-dong, Sujong-gu, Seongnam, Gyeonggi-do 461-703; tel. (822) 2230-4114; fax (822) 2230-4308; internet www.ex.co.kr; f. 1969; responsible for construction, maintenance and management of toll roads; CEO CHANG SEOK-HYO.

SHIPPING

In December 2012 South Korea's flag registered fleet (2,029 vessels) had a total displacement of 11.9m. grt, and included 388 general cargo ships, 287 tankers, 171 bulk carriers, 65 gas tankers and 429 fishing vessels. Major ports include Busan, Incheon, Donghae, Masan, Yeosu, Gunsan, Mokpo, Pohang, Ulsan, Jeju and Gwangyang.

Busan Port Authority: 79-9, Jungangdong 4-ga, Junggu, Busan 600-817; tel. (2) 999-3000; fax (2) 988-8878; e-mail bpmaster@busanpa.com; internet www.busanpa.com; f. 2004; Pres. LIM KI-TACK.

Korea Shipowners' Association: Sejong Bldg, 10th Floor, 100, Dangju-dong, Jongro-gu, Seoul 110-071; tel. (2) 739-1551; fax (2) 739-1558; e-mail korea@shipowners.or.kr; internet www.shipowners.or.kr; f. 1960; 181 shipping co mems (March 2011); Chair. LEE JONG-CHUL.

Korea Shipping Association: 660-10, Dungchon 3-dong, Gangseo-gu, Seoul 157-033; tel. (2) 6096-2000; fax (2) 6096-2029; e-mail kimny@haewoon.co.kr; internet www.haewoon.co.kr; f. 1962; management consulting and investigation, mutual insurance; 1,189 mems; CEO LEE IN-SOO.

Principal Companies

DooYang Line Co Ltd: 170-8, Samseong-dong, Gangnam-gu, Seoul 135-091; tel. (2) 569-7722; fax (2) 550-1777; f. 1984; world-wide tramping and conventional liner trade; Pres. CHO DONG-HYUN.

Hanjin Shipping Ltd: 25-11, Yeouido-dong, Yeongdeungpo-gu, Seoul; tel. (2) 3770-6114; fax (2) 3770-6748; e-mail micaela@hanjin.com; internet www.hanjin.com; f. 1977; marine transport, harbour service, warehousing, shipping and repair, vessel sales, harbour department and cargo service; Chair. and CEO CHOI EUN-YOUNG.

Hyundai Merchant Marine Co Ltd: 1-7, Yeonje-dong, Jongno-gu, Seoul 110-052; tel. (2) 3706-5114; fax (2) 778-4341; internet www.hmm.co.kr; f. 1976; Pres. and CEO LEE SUK-HUI.

Korea Line Corpn: 135-878 KLC Bldg, 145-9, Samseong-dong, Gangnam-gu, Seoul; tel. (2) 3701-0114; fax (2) 733-1610; internet www.korealines.co.kr; f. 1968; world-wide transport service and shipping agency service; Pres. KIM CHANG-SHIK.

STX Pan Ocean Co Ltd: STX Namsan Tower, 631 Namdaemunno 5-ga, Jung-nu, Seoul; tel. (2) 316-5114; fax (2) 316-5209; internet www.stxpanocean.co.kr; f. 1966; transport of passenger cars and trucks, chemical and petroleum products, dry bulk cargo; STX Shipbuilding Co Ltd became the majority shareholder in 2004; CEO PAE SEON-RYUNG.

CIVIL AVIATION

There are international airports at Incheon (Seoul), Gimpo (Seoul), Busan, Jeongju, Daegu, Gwangju, Jeju and Yangyang. The main gateway into Seoul is Incheon International Airport, located 52 km from Seoul, which opened for service in 2001. The second phase of construction was completed in mid-2008.

Asiana Airlines Inc: 47, Osae-dong, Gangseo-gu, Seoul; tel. (2) 2669-8000; fax (2) 2669-8180; internet flyasiana.com; f. 1988; serves 12 domestic cities and 67 destinations in 20 countries; fmrly Seoul Air International; CEO YOON YOUNG-DOO.

Jeju Air: Jeju; tel. (64) 746-7003; fax (64) 746-7011; internet www.jejuair.net; f. 2005; 25% owned by Jeju provincial govt, 75% by the Aekyung Group; operates low-cost domestic and international services; CEO CHOI KYU-NAM.

Jin Air Co Ltd: 653-25 Deungchon-dong, Gangseo-gu, Seoul; internet www.jinair.com; f. 2008; low-cost subsidiary of Korean Air; CEO KIM JAE-KUN.

Korean Air: 1370, Gonghang-dong, Gangseo-gu, Seoul 157-712; tel. (2) 2656-7857; fax (2) 656-7289; internet www.koreanair.com; f. 1962; est. by the Govt, privately owned since 1969; fmrly Korean Air Lines (KAL); operates domestic and regional services and routes in Asia and to the Americas, Europe, the Far East and the Middle East; Chair. and CEO CHO YANG-HO.

T'way Airlines: 18/F, Tomato Tower, Yeoksam-dong, Gangnam-gu, Seoul; tel. (43) 1599-1090; fax (43) 210-0520; internet www.twayair.com; f. 2004 as Hansung Airlines, relaunched in 2010 under above name; operates low-cost flights between Jeongju and Jeju City; CEO SHIN DONG-CHUN.

Tourism

South Korea's mountain scenery and historic sites are the principal attractions for tourists. Jeju Island, located some 100 km off the southern coast, is a popular resort. In 2011 the city of Pyeongchang was selected to host the 2018 Winter Olympics. The number of visitor arrivals increased by 13.7% in 2012, to exceed 11.1m. Japan and the People's Republic of China are the leading sources of visitors. Receipts from tourism totalled an estimated US $14,176m. in 2012.

Korea Tourism Organization: KTO Bldg, 40, Cheonggyecheon-ro, Jung-gu, Seoul 100-180; tel. (2) 729-9600; fax (2) 757-5997; e-mail webmaster@mail.knto.or.kr; internet kto.visitkorea.or.kr; f. 1962; est. as International Tourism Corpn; name changed to Korea National Tourism Corpn in 1982 and to Korea National Tourism Organization in 1996, before present name was adopted; Chair. and CEO LEE CHARM.

Korea Tourism Association: KTO Bldg, 8th Floor, 40, Cheonggyecheon-ro, Jung-gu, Seoul 100-180; tel. (2) 757-7485; fax (2) 757-7489; internet www.koreatravel.or.kr; f. 1963; Chair. SHIN JOONG-MOK.

Defence

As assessed at November 2012, the strength of the active armed forces was 655,000 (including an estimated 140,000 conscripts): army 522,000, navy 68,000, air force 65,000. Paramilitary forces included a 3m.-strong civilian defence corps. Military service is compulsory and lasts for 26 months. In November 2012 US forces stationed in South Korea comprised 28,500 army personnel, 250 navy, 8,800 air force and 250 marines.

Defence Expenditure: Budgeted at 34,600,000m. won for 2013.

Chairman of the Joint Chiefs of Staff: Gen. JUNG SEUNG-JO.

Chief of Staff (Army): Gen. CHO JUNG-HWAN.

Chief of Staff (Air Force): Gen. SUNG IL-HWAN.

Chief of Naval Operations: Adm. CHOI YOON-HEE.

Education

Education, available free of charge, is compulsory for nine years between the ages of six and 15 years. Primary education begins at six years of age and lasts for six years. In 2009/10 enrolment at primary schools included 99% of children in the appropriate age-group. Secondary education begins at 12 years of age and lasts for up to six years, comprising two cycles of three years each. UNESCO estimated that enrolment at secondary schools in 2009/10 included 96% of children in the relevant age-group. A five-day school week was introduced in 2012. (From 2006 school pupils had been granted two Saturdays off school every month; previously, they had attended school six days every week.) In 2007 there were 175 colleges and universities and 1,042 graduate schools. In 2011 approximately 3.8m. students were enrolled in undergraduate and graduate courses. In 2001, according to UNESCO estimates, the rate of adult literacy averaged 97.9% (males 99.2%, females 96.6%). Expenditure on education by the central Government in 2011 was 40,988,000m. won, representing 15.1% of total spending.

KOSOVO

Introductory Survey

LOCATION, CLIMATE, LANGUAGE, RELIGION, FLAG, CAPITAL

The Republic of Kosovo (Kosova), formerly the province officially named Kosovo and Metohija within the Republic of Serbia, is situated in the central Balkan peninsula in south-eastern Europe. There are borders with Serbia in the north-west and north-east, the former Yugoslav republic of Macedonia in the south, Albania in the south-west, and Montenegro to the west. The climate is continental. Under a new Constitution, approved in April 2008, the official languages of Kosovo are Albanian and Serbian, while the Turkish, Bosnian and Roma languages are also accorded official status at municipal level. The principal religion in Kosovo is Islam. Serbs are principally adherents of Orthodox Christianity, as represented by the Serbian Orthodox Church. The state flag (proportions 2 by 3) is blue, with an arc of six white stars above a golden map of Kosovo. The capital is Prishtina (Prishtinë—Priština).

CONTEMPORARY POLITICAL HISTORY

Historical Context

Kosovo was part of the Serbian state established by the Nemanja dynasty in 1166. The Serbian Orthodox Patriarchate was established in Kosovo in the 13th century, and the territory was the location of the defeat of the Serbs by the Turkish Ottoman Empire at Fushë Kosovë (Kosovo Polje—'the Field of Blackbirds') in 1389. After continued Albanian resistance to Ottoman rule, the League of Prizren political organization was established in 1878. Kosovo remained under Ottoman rule until its annexation by Serbia during the First Balkan War in 1912. During the Second World War (1939–45) Kosovo was annexed by Albania (in personal union with the Italian Crown). Following the establishment of the Federative People's Republic of Yugoslavia, the 1946 Constitution provided for the establishment of Kosovo and Metohija (as the region was renamed) and the northern territory of Vojvodina as autonomous units within Serbia. In 1963 the autonomous region of Kosovo and Metohija was formally upgraded in status to that of an autonomous province, a status that was confirmed by the 1974 Constitution, which also renamed the territory as Kosovo and increased the powers of the two autonomous provinces at the federal level of the state.

From the mid-1980s increasing Serb nationalism, and the rise to power of Slobodan Milošević (President of Serbia in 1989–97), exacerbated tensions in the province. A new Serbian Constitution, adopted in 1990, revoked the autonomy of Kosovo and Vojvodina; this was confirmed by the April 1992 Constitution that created the Federal Republic of Yugoslavia (FRY). A republic-wide referendum, largely boycotted by the ethnic Albanians, was conducted on 2 July 1990, when a majority of Serbs approved the new Constitution. It was formally promulgated on 28 September, whereupon the designation of Kosovo reverted to that of Kosovo and Metohija. Following the constitutional referendum, 114 of 180 deputies in the Kosovo Assembly (Kuvendi i Kosovës/Skupština Kosova) met and declared Kosovo independent of Serbia. On 5 July the Serbian authorities dissolved the provincial Assembly and Government. The Kosovo presidency resigned in protest, and Serbia introduced a special administration. On 7 September members of the former representative body declared the Kosovo Assembly to have been reconvened and subsequently proclaimed a basic law of a 'Republic of Kosovo'. Meanwhile, elections, declared illegal by the Serbian authorities, were held in the province on 24 May. The Democratic Alliance of Kosovo (DAK) secured the most seats in the 130-member Assembly, and the DAK leader, Ibrahim Rugova, was elected President of the self-proclaimed 'Republic of Kosovo'.

Domestic Political Affairs

Throughout the mid-1990s there were reports of harassment of Kosovo Albanians by Serbian police. In early 1996 an ethnic Albanian militant organization, the Kosovo Liberation Army (KLA), announced its intention to achieve independence for Kosovo through armed resistance against the Serbian au-

thorities, and began attacks against security forces. Special Serbian security units undertook reprisals.

Negotiations regarding the implementation of a cease-fire in Kosovo and the withdrawal of Serbian forces were conducted throughout 1998. In October, following a North Atlantic Treaty Organization (NATO, see p. 380) ultimatum, Milošević, President of the FRY (Serbia and Montenegro) since the previous year, agreed to the presence in Kosovo of an Organization for Security and Co-operation in Europe (OSCE, see p. 397) mission, which began deployment in early November. Nevertheless, armed clashes between Serbian forces and the KLA increased. In January 1999 the bodies of 45 Albanians were discovered in the village of Reçak (Račak), increasing international concerns of a humanitarian crisis. In February a peace conference in Rambouillet, France, attended by Serbian and ethnic Albanian delegations, including KLA representatives, commenced. Although the Albanian delegation signed a peace agreement on 18 March, the Serbian delegation continued to present objections to the plan. On 23 March the Serbian legislature adopted a resolution condemning aggression against its country and opposing the deployment of NATO forces in Kosovo.

On 24 March 1999 a NATO-led aerial bombardment of military and civilian installations in the FRY commenced. Serbian security forces in Kosovo subsequently conducted mass expulsions and large-scale massacres of the Albanian civilian population. According to the Office of the UN High Commissioner for Refugees (UNHCR), a total of 848,100 Albanians fled or were expelled from Kosovo. On 3 June a peace agreement providing for the withdrawal of Serbian forces from Kosovo and the deployment of a joint NATO-Russian peace-keeping force was approved by the Serbian legislature. On 10 June, following a Military Technical Agreement between NATO and the Federal Government, the withdrawal of Serbian forces from Kosovo commenced, and NATO officially suspended its air operations. On the same day a UN Security Council resolution was approved, authorizing the deployment of international civil and security presences in Kosovo, and providing for the establishment of the UN Interim Administration Mission in Kosovo (UNMIK) as the supreme legal and executive authority in the region. On 12 June both Russian and NATO troops entered Kosovo. By 20 June the Serb withdrawal had been completed and the multinational NATO-led Kosovo Force (KFOR), which had an authorized strength of up to 50,000 personnel, was established. Some three weeks after the end of the conflict, an estimated 600,000 Albanians had returned to Kosovo. Over the same period some 180,000 Serbs and Roma fled the province.

Kosovo under UN administration

In February 2000 Rugova announced the dissolution of the 'Republic of Kosovo' and of the DAK. In local government elections, held in Kosovo on 28 October, Rugova's Democratic League of Kosovo (DLK—a successor organization to the DAK) secured 58% of the votes cast to 30 municipal councils, while the Democratic Party of Kosovo (DPK), led by a former KLA commander, Hashim Thaçi, won 27% of the votes. Elections to 100 seats of the 120-member Kosovo Assembly were conducted on 17 November 2001, under an UNMIK programme for establishing partial and provisional self-government in the province. (The remaining 20 seats were reserved for representatives of Serbs and other minority ethnic groups.) The DLK secured 47 seats, while the DPK won 26 seats and a coalition of Serb parties 22 seats. On 4 March 2002, following protracted inter-party discussions, Rugova was elected President of Kosovo. Under a coalition agreement, a member of the DPK, Bajram Rexhepi, became Prime Minister, and a 10-member Government was subsequently established. In April the Serb coalition agreed to join the administration.

In March 2004 the deaths of three Albanian boys, who had allegedly been pursued by a group of Serbs into the Ibar River, precipitated rioting in Mitrovicë (Kosovska Mitrovica), escalating into several days of clashes between the Serbian and Albanian communities throughout Kosovo. Some 2,000 KFOR reinforcements were dispatched to quell the violence, in which 19 civilians (11 Albanians and eight Serbs) were killed. At elections to the Kosovo Assembly on 23 October, the DLK secured 45.4% of the votes cast, retaining 47 seats in the 120-member legislature. The DPK won 28.9% of the votes, increasing its representation to 30 seats, while the Alliance for the Future of Kosovo (AFK) obtained 8.4% of the votes and nine seats. The DLK negotiated a coalition agreement, whereby the leader of the AFK, Ramush Haradinaj, became the new Prime Minister on 3 December. The election of Haradinaj, a former senior KLA leader who had been under investigation by the International Criminal Tribunal for the former Yugoslavia (ICTY, see p. 23) for alleged war crimes in Kosovo, was strongly criticized by Serbian parties. Although the overall rate of participation was recorded at some 53.6% of the registered electorate, only about 0.3% of the Serb community voted. (Serbs retained an allocation of 10 seats in the Assembly, but continued to boycott the provisional institutions.) On 8 March 2005 Haradinaj, indicted by the ICTY on a total of 37 charges, resigned as Prime Minister and surrendered to the Tribunal, amid widespread protests. On 23 March a new Government, led by Bajram Kosumi, also of the AFK, was established. (In April 2008 the ICTY acquitted Haradinaj.)

The resolution of Kosovo's future status became an increasingly pressing issue. On 4 October 2005 a UN Special Envoy submitted a review to the Secretary-General of the organization, stating that the Kosovo Government had made significant progress towards establishing executive, legislative and judicial institutions. On 24 October the UN Security Council endorsed the initiation of final status negotiations on Kosovo. In November the Serbian Government adopted a resolution rejecting the independence of Kosovo, while the Kosovo Assembly approved a motion stating that it would accept only independence as the final status of the territory. Later that month former Finnish President Martti Ahtisaari, who had been appointed UN Special Envoy for the Future Status Process for Kosovo, commenced separate discussions with Serbian and Kosovo leaders. Following Rugova's death on 21 January 2006, on 10 February Fatmir Sejdiu of the DLK was elected unopposed as the new President by the Kosovo Assembly. On 1 March Kosumi resigned as Prime Minister. Nine days later, the Kosovo Assembly approved Agim Çeku, a former KLA chief of staff, as his successor. Meanwhile, final status negotiations between Kosovo and Serbian government delegations commenced in Vienna, Austria, on 20–21 February. The Presidents and Prime Ministers of Serbia and Kosovo attended the discussions in Vienna for the first time in July; however, the Kosovo delegation reiterated demands for full independence for the province, while the Serbian leaders maintained that Serbia would not accept a loss of territory.

On 2 February 2007 Ahtisaari presented his recommendations for the future status of Kosovo and invited the Serbian and Kosovo delegations to engage in consultations on the draft in Vienna. After the discussions ended without success in March, Ahtisaari concluded that there was no further prospect of achieving a negotiated agreement. On 26 March Ahtisaari submitted to the UN Security Council the finalized Comprehensive Proposal for the Kosovo Status Settlement, which recommended independence for the province, initially under international military and civilian supervision. Kosovo was to adopt a constitution, flag and anthem, and be granted rights to membership of international organizations; the rights of all minority groups living in the province were to be protected. Under the Proposal, an International Civilian Representative, operating under a UN and European Union (EU, see p. 281) mandate, would be appointed to supervise the implementation of the Settlement, and would be empowered to veto legislation and dismiss local officials. KFOR would continue to provide security in the province, while the EU would deploy a police mission to assist in the development of institutions of law enforcement. On 3 April Koštunica announced to the UN Security Council that Serbia rejected the Proposal, following a vote in the Serbian legislature in February. On 5 April Ahtisaari's Proposal was approved by 100 of the 101 votes cast in the Kosovo Assembly. Prime Minister Çeku stated that Kosovo was prepared to declare unilateral independence in the event of a protracted delay. During April–July intensive, but unsuccessful, discussions on the Comprehensive Proposal continued in the UN Security Council. A further series of negotiations between the Serbian and Kosovo delegations from August failed to resolve the impasse. On 10 December the UN Secretary-General was informed that no agreement could be reached.

Meanwhile, legislative elections were conducted in Kosovo on 17 November 2007. According to official results, the DPK secured the highest number of votes cast, with 34.3% of the total, taking 37 seats in the Assembly, while the DLK received some 22.6% of the votes and 25 seats. With a boycott of the elections by Serb parties, a rate of participation of about 43% of the electorate was recorded. Following a coalition agreement between the DPK and the DLK, on 9 January 2008 a Government headed by Thaçi, and comprising eight members of the DPK, six members of the DLK, two representatives of Serb groups and one representative of the ethnic Turkish community, was approved by the Assembly. With both main ruling parties in favour of independence, Thaçi confirmed to the Assembly that a declaration of independence was imminent. On the same day Sejdiu was re-elected President in a third round of voting in the Assembly for a term that was extended to five years. Jakup Krasniqi of the DPK was elected President of the Assembly.

Declaration of independence

On 17 February 2008 the Assembly of Kosovo endorsed a declaration establishing the province as the Republic of Kosovo (Kosova), a sovereign state independent from Serbia, the resolution adopted being based on Ahtisaari's Comprehensive Proposal for the Kosovo Status Settlement and in accordance with UN Security Council Resolution 1244 (of 1999). Serbia immediately protested that the declaration of independence contravened international law and demanded that it be annulled. An emergency meeting of the UN Security Council failed to agree on a new resolution, with Russia, in continued strong support of Serbia, and the People's Republic of China opposing Kosovo's sovereignty among the permanent members of the Council. Several countries, including Albania, France, the USA and the United Kingdom, extended recognition to Kosovo on 18 February, and were rapidly followed by a number of other states. On 28 February the International Steering Group for Kosovo appointed a Dutch diplomat, Pieter Feith, already the EU Special Representative, as an International Civilian Representative, to supervise the implementation of the Settlement. An EU Rule of Law Mission in Kosovo (EULEX), comprising some 1,900 foreign personnel, was to be deployed in Kosovo to support the authorities in maintaining public order. In March a member of UNMIK was killed in fierce clashes between Serb protesters and UNMIK and KFOR troops in Mitrovica. Also in March Serbia announced that it intended to submit a legal challenge against Kosovo's declaration of independence at the International Court of Justice (ICJ, see p. 26) in The Hague, Netherlands, and would seek international support at the UN General Assembly. A new Constitution, which had been drafted by a Constitutional Commission in accordance with the principles of the Settlement, was adopted by the Assembly on 9 April, after being approved by Feith. The Constitution, which declared Kosovo to be an independent and sovereign state, was to enter into effect on 15 June, when UNMIK was officially to transfer its functions to the Kosovo authorities. However, it became increasingly evident that the deployment of EULEX would not proceed as envisaged, owing to the refusal of Kosovo Serbs and the Serbian Government to accept an EU mission. A report by the UN Secretary-General on developments in Kosovo, published in April, stated that UNMIK's mandate would remain in force under Resolution 1244, pending a further decision by the UN Security Council.

The new Constitution entered into effect on 15 June 2008, as scheduled. The NATO Secretary-General announced that the remaining KFOR contingent was to organize the dissolution of the Kosovo Protection Corps (KPC—formed in 1999 largely on the basis of the KLA) and the establishment of a 2,500-member multi-ethnic Kosovo Security Force. Following polls conducted among Kosovo Serbs on 11 May 2008, without the recognition of the Kosovo Government, but supported by Serbia, on 28 June a parallel legislature comprising representatives of the Serb community from 26 municipalities, the 'Assembly of the Community of Municipalities of the Autonomous Province of Kosovo and Metohija', was convened in Mitrovica.

In September 2008 it was announced that Kosovo had appointed its first 10 envoys to countries that had recognized its statehood, while a number of diplomatic missions in Prishtina had become embassies. In October the decision of Montenegro and the former Yugoslav republic of Macedonia to extend recognition to Kosovo prompted strong protests from the Serbian Government. In the same month the UN General Assembly, in support of Serbia, voted in favour of referring to the ICJ the question of whether Kosovo's unilateral declaration of independence from Serbia was in accordance with international law.

Following the continued refusal of Kosovo Serbs to accept the deployment of EULEX, in early November 2008 the UN

Secretary-General presented an amended six-point plan on the reconfiguration of the international presence in Kosovo, under which officials in the Serb-majority areas would receive directives from a reduced UNMIK contingent, while those in Albanian-majority areas would be the responsibility of EULEX. On 26 November the UN Security Council unanimously endorsed the six-point plan under the stipulated terms. On 9 December EULEX began deployment throughout the country, including in Mitrovica; it was later confirmed that a reduced UNMIK presence was to remain in the country indefinitely under Resolution 1244. In January 2009 the KPC was dissolved and replaced by the Kosovo Security Force. Celebrations for the first anniversary of Kosovo's declaration of independence took place peacefully; however, 80 opposition deputies of the Serbian legislature joined the Kosovo Serb 'Assembly' in approving a declaration affirming the constitutional status of Kosovo within Serbia and rejecting the activities of the Kosovo institutions.

Municipal elections

In June 2009 former Prime Minister Agim Çeku was arrested in Bulgaria, under an international warrant issued by Serbia for alleged war crimes committed while he was a KLA military commander; however, a Bulgarian court rejected the request for Çeku's extradition and he returned to Kosovo. In August seven people were injured in clashes between Serbs and Albanians in Mitrovica, following Serb protests against the reconstruction of Albanian houses in the ethnically divided Brđani district of the town.

The first elections since independence to elect councils and mayors in Kosovo's 36 municipalities (including six new municipalities) took place on 15 November 2009. The rate of voter participation was recorded at about 45.4%, after a Serb boycott urged by the Serbian Government was only partially observed. A mission from the European Network of Election Monitoring Organizations released a report concluding that the elections had generally met international standards. A second round of voting was conducted on 13 December. According to the Central Election Commission (CEC), the DPK secured the largest number of municipalities, with 16. Voting was repeated in two municipalities on 31 January 2010, and in a further constituency on 14 March, after allegations of irregularities were upheld.

In February 2010 Fejzullah Hasani was appointed President of the Supreme Court, and 21 other judges and prosecutors were nominated, as part of efforts to create an independent, multi-ethnic judiciary. At the end of March the DPK and the DLK agreed to the replacement of three ministers from each party in a government reorganization (which also included the creation of a new Ministry of Integration); notably, former Prime Minister Bajram Rexhepi was appointed as the new Minister of Internal Affairs. On 30 May unauthorized elections were organized to the Serb 'Assembly' in Mitrovica. In July one protester was killed when two bombs were thrown into a crowd of Kosovo Serbs who were demonstrating against the Government's plan to open an office in Mitrovica. Later that month the appeals chamber of the ICTY overturned the acquittal of Haradinaj and an associate in April 2008, on the grounds that witnesses had been intimidated, and ordered their retrial.

Early legislative elections

On 22 July 2010 the ICJ issued a non-binding, advisory opinion that Kosovo's declaration of independence had not breached international law, UN Security Council Resolution 1244, or the constitutional framework. The ruling prompted public celebrations in Prishtina, while Serbia reaffirmed its intention to continue to withhold recognition of the independence of Kosovo. In early September the UN General Assembly adopted a resolution, supported by Serbia and the 27 EU member states, urging a direct dialogue between Serbia and Kosovo on ensuing issues. On 27 September Sejdiu tendered his resignation as President of Kosovo, following a ruling by the Constitutional Council that holding the office was incompatible with his chairmanship of the DLK. (He was subsequently replaced on an acting basis by parliamentary President Krasniqi.) In October Sejdiu withdrew the DLK from the coalition Government, which consequently lost its majority in the Assembly. In November the Assembly adopted a motion of no confidence in the Government, after Thaçi urged DPK deputies to support it and thereby bring an end to the institutional crisis; early legislative elections were subsequently scheduled for 12 December. On 7 November the mayor of Prishtina, Isa Mustafa, was elected Chairman of the DLK, replacing Sejdiu.

In December 2010 Swiss senator and Council of Europe rapporteur Dick Marty presented a report (which was subsequently adopted by the Parliamentary Assembly of the Council of Europe—PACE) claiming that the trafficking of human organs had taken place during and after the 1999 conflict in Kosovo, and implicating Thaçi. EULEX was charged with investigating the allegations, which the Governments of Kosovo and Albania denied.

The legislative elections on 7 December 2010 were monitored by officials from embassies in Kosovo, together with local observers; Serb voters again boycotted the elections. Following allegations by all parties of voter intimidation and major electoral irregularities, complaints were upheld in five municipalities, where polls were repeated on 9 January and (in the case of Mitrovica) on 23 January 2011. The final election results were released by the CEC on 7 February: the DPK, with 32.1% of the votes cast, secured 34 seats, while the DLK won 24.7% of the votes and 27 seats; an ethnic Albanian nationalist party that opposed international involvement in Kosovo, Self-Determination!, was placed third, with 12.7% of the votes and 14 seats, followed by the AFK, with 11.0% and 12 seats, and a coalition led by the New Kosovo Alliance (NKA), with 7.3% and eight seats. The rate of participation by the registered electorate was recorded at about 45%. On 22 February, under a coalition agreement reached between the DPK and the NKA, a construction industry magnate and President of the NKA, Behgjet Pacolli, was elected unopposed as the President of Kosovo in a third round of voting in the new Assembly (with opposition parties boycotting the session). On the same day Thaçi was re-elected as Prime Minister and the appointment of a new coalition Government was approved. The five Deputy Prime Ministers in the new administration included for the first time a Kosovo Serb, the Chairman of the ILP, Slobodan Petrović. In March Kosovo and Serbian delegations began an EU-supported dialogue in Brussels, Belgium, which was subsequently endorsed by a resolution in the Kosovo Assembly. Following a challenge by the DLK, on 28 March the Constitutional Court ruled the election of Pacolli to be illegitimate, owing to the absence of the requisite parliamentary quorum; Pacolli resigned from the presidency on 30 March. Following an unprecedented agreement between the DPK, the DLK and the NKA on a consensus candidate, on 7 April the deputy director of the Kosovo police, Maj.-Gen. Atifete Jahjaga, was elected President with 80 of 100 votes cast in the Assembly, becoming the country's first female head of state. The Government announced that Jahjaga would serve in an interim capacity (pending constitutional reforms that would allow the direct election of a President), with her mandate to expire no later than 2013. Also in April 2011 Pacolli was appointed as First Deputy Prime Minister.

In July 2011 it was announced that the EU-mediated discussions in Brussels had resulted in agreement on free movement between Kosovo and Serbia, the mutual recognition of university diplomas, and the establishment of a civil registry for Kosovo. In August the trial began of DPK Deputy Chairman and parliamentary deputy Fatmir Limaj and a further nine former members of the KLA, on charges of committing war crimes against prisoners and civilians during 1997–99. Six of the defendants were acquitted in March 2012, and Limaj and the remaining three in May. (In November, however, the Supreme Court ordered their retrial, prompting public protests.)

Clashes at the border with Serbia

In July 2011 a Kosovo special police officer was killed and four others were injured by Kosovo Serbs, who resisted an attempt by the police to assume control of two crossing-points at the border with Serbia, which were supervised by KFOR and EULEX. Kosovo Serbs continued to obstruct government efforts to establish authority throughout the state; in September EULEX units were deployed to take control of two border posts that the Kosovo police had been unable to reach owing to road blocks erected by local Serbs, and a number of people were injured in further attacks by Serbs against KFOR and EULEX forces in the border region. In October two Serbs were killed in separate incidents in predominantly ethnic Albanian areas of Kosovo, increasing ethnic tensions. In November some 30 members of KFOR were injured in clashes with Serbs, following an attempt by the troops to dismantle a road block preventing Kosovo police and customs officers from gaining access to border crossing-points. Serbian President Boris Tadić (who aspired to secure EU candidate status for Serbia) subsequently urged Serb protesters to remove the barricades. On 2 December the ongoing discussions in Brussels resulted in an agreement that would allow Kosovo officials to establish control of the border crossing-points, although most of the road blocks subsequently remained in place. In January 2012 the Serbian Government urged Kosovo Serbs in four northern municipalities to abandon a planned referendum; nevertheless, the non-binding plebiscite took place on 14–15 February, with 99.7% of those participating in the municipalities rejecting the authority of Kosovo state institutions. On 15 February the Kosovo Assembly adopted a resolution declaring the referendum to be illegal.

On 18 February 2012 the Kosovo Government signed a Status of Forces Agreement with the USA, providing for military co-operation between the two states. The barricades at the border with Serbia were removed on 23 February, following an agreement between the Serb authorities in northern Kosovo and EULEX, which allowed the mission free movement in the region. Also in February it was announced that the negotiations in Brussels had resulted in a significant compromise, welcomed by EU officials, that Kosovo be represented in regional meetings under the name 'Kosovo', rather than 'Kosovo-UNMIK' (with an explanatory addendum). At the beginning of May the Kosovo and Serbian Governments reached an agreement, permitting voting to take place in northern Kosovo for Serbia's legislative and presidential elections on 6 May, under OSCE supervision. Following his election to the Serbian presidency, the nationalist victor, Tomislav Nikolić, indicated that he would make no concessions regarding Serbia's perceived claim to Kosovo. In early June the Kosovo Government announced that the discussions in Brussels had effectively been suspended, owing to the failure to implement the measures already agreed.

In June 2012 dissension increased within the DPK over controversial articles in the new penal code, approved by the Assembly in April, which required journalists to reveal their sources in cases involving national security, and made defamation a criminal offence. Although President Jahjaga had refused to endorse the new code, parliamentary deputies, including some DPK members, continued to demand that the articles be retained, prompting the resignation of the Deputy Prime Minister and Minister of Justice, Hajredin Kuçi of the DPK, in late June. However, Kuçi returned to his post on 10 July, after the Assembly voted in favour of a penal code that did not include the contentious articles, at the instigation of Prime Minister Thaçi.

Recent developments: unsupervised independence

Following an official visit to Kosovo by UN Secretary-General Ban Ki-Moon on 24 June 2012, the International Steering Group announced on 2 July that Kosovo's period of supervised independence would end in September, three months earlier than anticipated. On 11 July Thaçi submitted an application for membership of NATO's 'Partnership for Peace' (see p. 383) programme. Also in July the Constitutional Court ruled that the parliamentary resolution of April 2011, which had elected Jahjaga as President on an interim basis, had been illegitimate (thereby entitling her to remain in office until 2016).

On 7 September 2012 the Assembly adopted a number of constitutional amendments required in order to permit the end of supervised independence. Kosovo officially attained full independence on 10 September, with the closure of the International Civilian Office; however, under an agreement reached between the Kosovo Government and the EU on 1 August, the mandate of EULEX had been renewed until June 2014, while KFOR troops (numbering some 5,000) and a small UNMIK contingent also remained in the country. Following EU and US pressure, in October 2012 dialogue on the normalization of relations between Kosovo and Serbia formally resumed in Brussels, with a meeting between Thaçi and the new Serbian Prime Minister, Ivica Dačić. Self-Determination! organized a further protest against the negotiations in Prishtina. A border management agreement between Kosovo and Serbia that would allow the opening of crossing-points was reached in November, and its implementation began in December. Meanwhile, on 29 November Haradinaj was acquitted following his retrial at the ICTY; the verdict prompted outrage in Serbia.

In January 2013 the EU-mediated discussions resulted in Kosovo's appointment of a liaison officer to Serbia, the hitherto ambassador to Sweden, Lulzim Peci; the Serbian Government subsequently appointed a counterpart, Dejan Pavićević. In the same month, however, Kosovo Serbs in the north erected further road blocks to obstruct Kosovo border police from gaining access to crossing-points, while continued attacks were staged on Kosovo government targets in Prishtina, in protest at the negotiations in Brussels. In early February Jahjaga and Nikolić met

for the first time, with EU mediation, in Brussels; both Presidents pledged commitment to continued dialogue, which subsequently gained momentum, as the Serbian Government sought to secure the opening of EU accession negotiations. The EU High Representative for Foreign Affairs and Security Policy, Catherine Ashton, visited Prishtina in March, and subsequently declared that the two sides were close to agreement on the dismantling of the Serb 'Assembly', financed by Serbia, in northern Kosovo, and the operation of a legitimate 'Association of Serbian Municipalities'. On 19 April it was announced that Thaçi and Dačić had initialled a provisional accord in Brussels, which confirmed that ethnic Serb-dominated northern Kosovo was to be administered by Kosovo, while retaining autonomy in the areas of education, health care and culture, and with provision made for the appointment of a police commander for the region, and the establishment of a separate court of appeal; the deal also allowed both Kosovo and Serbia to seek EU accession without obstruction. The agreement, which was immediately rejected by Kosovo Serbs, was approved by the Kosovo Assembly on 21 April.

CONSTITUTION AND GOVERNMENT

A new Constitution entered into effect in Kosovo on 15 June 2008, after the Kosovo Assembly (Kuvendi i Kosovës/Skupština Kosova) adopted a declaration of independence on 17 February. This declaration was based on the Comprehensive Proposal for the Kosovo Status Settlement drawn up by the UN Special Envoy of the Secretary-General for the Future Status Process for Kosovo, Martti Ahtisaari, and in accordance with UN Security Council Resolution 1244 (of 1999). An International Civilian Representative, who was also the Special Representative of the European Union (EU, see p. 281), was appointed by an International Steering Group on 28 February 2008 to supervise the implementation of the Settlement. An EU Rule of Law Mission in Kosovo (EULEX), which became operational under the overall authority of the UN in December, was deployed in Kosovo to maintain public order and security, and to assist in the development of judicial institutions. A reduced UN Interim Administration Mission in Kosovo (UNMIK) was to remain in the country under Resolution 1244. Kosovo's period of supervised independence officially ended on 10 September 2012, with the closure of the International Civilian Office.

Under the Constitution, the Kosovo Assembly comprises 120 deputies, of whom 100 are directly elected (the remaining 20 seats are reserved for the elected representatives of specified minority ethnic communities, including eight allocated to Serbs). The Assembly has a nine-member Presidency. The President of Kosovo is elected by the Assembly for a five-year term (renewable only once). The President nominates a Prime Minister, who proposes a Government, for approval by the Assembly. Kosovo comprises seven regions, which are divided into 36 municipalities.

REGIONAL AND INTERNATIONAL CO-OPERATION

Following Kosovo's unilateral declaration of independence on 17 February 2008, a total of 98 UN member states, including 22 of the 27 member states of the European Union (EU, see p. 281), recognized Kosovo as an independent sovereign state at April 2013. Kosovo joined the Central European Free Trade Agreement (CEFTA, see p. 459) in July 2007, and the European Bank for Reconstruction and Development (EBRD, see p. 276) in December 2012.

ECONOMIC AFFAIRS

In 2011, according to estimates by the World Bank, the gross national income (GNI) of Kosovo, measured at average 2009–11 prices, was US $6,310m., equivalent to $3,520 per head. During 2002–11, it was estimated, the population increased at an average annual rate of 0.6%. During 2002–11 gross domestic product (GDP) per head increased, in real terms, at an average annual rate of 4.1%. Overall GDP grew, in real terms, at an average annual rate of 4.8% in 2002–11; growth was 5.0% in 2011.

Agriculture contributed some 17.4% of GDP in 2011. In 2009 about 6.2% of the total employed labour force were engaged in agriculture (including hunting, forestry and fishing). Kosovo's principal crops are wheat, potatoes, maize and peppers. According to UN figures, agricultural production increased at an average annual rate of 8.3% in 2002–11; the sector's GDP increased by 4.7% in 2011.

Industry contributed some 26.4% of GDP in 2011. The sector (including mining, manufacturing, construction and power) engaged around 23.4% of the employed labour force in 2009.

Industrial production increased at an average annual rate of 2.7% in 2002–11, according to UN figures. Output increased by 5.6% in 2011.

The mining sector contributed some 2.0% of GDP in 2011, and mining and quarrying engaged around 1.1% of the employed labour force in 2009. One of the principal minerals extracted is halloysite, a clay mineral used in the production of porcelain and bone china. More significantly, Kosovo has some 14.7m. metric tons of proven lignite reserves. Lead, zinc, chromium and bauxite are also mined. According to UN figures, the GDP of mining and utilities together increased at an average annual rate of 2.6% in 2002–11; growth was 3.2% in 2011.

Manufacturing contributed 9.9% of GDP in 2011. The manufacturing sector employed about 9.9% of the population in 2009. Manufacturing increased at an average annual rate of 1.6% in 2002–11, according to UN figures; sectoral GDP increased by 7.4% in 2011.

The construction sector contributed some 9.8% of GDP in 2011, and engaged around 7.9% of the employed labour force in 2009. According to UN figures, the GDP of the sector grew at an average annual rate of 4.3% in 2002–11. Sectoral GDP increased by 3.4% in 2011.

Energy in Kosovo is derived principally from coal (which contributes, on average, 97% of total electricity generated). Imports of mineral fuels accounted for some 18.1% of the value of total imports to Kosovo in 2011.

Services contributed some 56.1% of GDP in 2011, and engaged around 70.6% of the employed labour force in 2009. Important areas of the services sector include wholesale and retail trade, education and administration. According to UN estimates, GDP in the services sector increased at an average annual rate of 1.8% in 2002–11; sectoral GDP rose by 6.2% in 2011.

In 2011 Kosovo recorded a visible merchandise trade deficit of €2,848m. and there was a deficit of €1,028m. on the current account of the balance of payments. In 2011 the principal source of imports to Kosovo was the former Yugoslav republic of Macedonia (FYRM), accounting for 14.7% of the total; other major sources were Germany, Serbia, Turkey, the People's Republic of China and Italy. The principal market for exports in that year was Italy (taking 26.3% of total exports); other important purchasers were Albania, the FYRM, the People's Republic of China, Germany and Switzerland. The main exports in 2011 were base metals (accounting for 60.5% of export trade), in particular iron and steel. Exports of mineral products were also significant. The principal imports in that year were mineral products (which accounted for 21.6% of imports); prepared foodstuffs, beverages, alcohol and tobacco; machinery and mechanical products; base metals; chemical products; vehicles and transport equipment; vegetable products; and plastics and rubber.

In 2011 the overall budgetary deficit for Kosovo was estimated to be €101.0m., equivalent to 2.1% of GDP. In 2002–12 the rate of inflation in Kosovo increased at an average annual rate of 2.2%.

Consumer prices increased by 2.5% in 2012. The rate of unemployment in Kosovo was 45.4% in 2009, according to official estimates.

Following its declaration of independence in 2008, Kosovo remained one of the poorest territories in Europe and was highly reliant upon remittances from abroad. Kosovo was officially admitted to the IMF and the World Bank in June 2009. However, the continuing inability of the Kosovo institutions to exert authority in northern Serb-dominated areas obstructed economic development. In June 2011 the IMF suspended a credit arrangement agreed in the previous year, owing to dissatisfaction with the Government's budgetary expenditure, which notably incorporated wage increases; consequently, the European Commission also failed to extend €50m. in pledged assistance. The resumption of disbursements was dependent on the reduction of state expenditure and the satisfactory implementation of structural adjustment reforms. In February 2012 the Kosovo authorities adopted a number of tax reforms intended to stimulate growth, and established an Anti-organized Crime Council. In April the IMF approved a 20-month stand-by credit arrangement totalling €106.6m. for Kosovo, after noting a significant improvement in policy implementation, and disbursed €5m. Further loan tranches, of €48.0m. and €40.7m., respectively, were released after favourable economic performance reviews in July and December. GDP growth was projected by the IMF at 2.7% in 2012 and 3.2% in 2013. In October 2012 the Government signed an agreement on the sale of the Kosovo Energy Corporation for €26.3m. to a private Turkish consortium, which pledged to invest €300m. in the business. Meanwhile, in a progress report released in October, the European Commission emphasized that the continued failure of five European Union (EU, see p. 281) member states to extend recognition to Kosovo presented a major impediment to the signature of a Stabilization and Association Agreement (SAA) with Kosovo. An EU feasibility study had also identified four areas in which further progress was required, including the rule of law, and the reform of public administration. Nevertheless, after an accord was signed between the Governments of Kosovo and Serbia in April 2013, the European Commission recommended the opening of SAA negotiations with Kosovo, as well as the state's participation in 22 EU programmes (although this was subject to approval by EU member states).

PUBLIC HOLIDAYS

2014: 1–2 January (New Year's Day), 7 January (Orthodox Christmas), 17 February (Independence Day), 9 April (Constitution Day), 21 April (Catholic Easter Monday), 1 May (Labour Day), 9 May (Europe Day), 28 July* (Small Bayram, end of Ramadan), 4 October* (Great Bayram, Feast of the Sacrifice), 25 December (Catholic Christmas).

*These holidays are dependent on the Islamic lunar calendar and may vary by one or two days from the dates given.

Statistical Survey

Source (unless otherwise indicated): Statistical Office of Kosovo, 10000 Prishtina, Rruga Zenel Salihu 4; e-mail eskinfo@ks-gov.net; internet esk.rks-gov.net.

Area and Population

AREA, POPULATION AND DENSITY

Area (sq km)	10,908*
Population (census results)	
31 March 1991†	1,956,196
1–15 April 2011	
Males	875,900
Females	863,925
Total	1,739,825
Density (per sq km) at 2011 census	159.5

* 4,212 sq miles.

† Assessment of the Office of Statistics of the Socialist Federal Republic of Yugoslavia.

POPULATION BY AGE AND SEX
(at 2011 census)

	Males	Females	Total
0–14	252,405	235,172	487,577
15–64	568,903	566,560	1,135,463
65 and over	54,592	62,193	116,785
Total	**875,900**	**863,925**	**1,739,825**

POPULATION BY ETHNIC GROUP
(at 2011 census)

Ethnic group	Population	%
Albanian	1,616,869	92.9
Bosniak	27,533	1.6
Serb	25,532	1.5
Turk	18,738	1.1
Ashkali	15,436	0.9
Egyptian	11,524	0.7
Goran	10,265	0.5
Roma	8,824	0.5
Others*	5,104	0.3
Total	**1,739,825**	**100.0**

* Including other groups, non-declared persons and those of unknown ethnicity.

MUNICIPALITIES
(population at 2011 census)

Municipality*	Area (sq km)	Population	Density (per sq km)
Deçan/Dečani	294	40,019	136.1
Dragash/Dragaš	434	33,997	78.3
Ferizaj/Uroševac	345	108,610	314.8
Fushë Kosovë/Kosovo Polje	84	34,827	414.6
Gjakovë/Đakovica	587	94,556	161.1
Gjilan/Gnjilane	392	90,178	230.0
Gllogovc/Glogovac	276	58,531	212.1
Graçanicë/Gračanica	131	10,675	81.5
Hani i Elezit/Đeneral Jankovič	83	9,403	113.3
Istog/Istok	454	39,289	86.5
Junik	78	6,084	78.0
Kaçanik/Kačanik	211	36,085	171.0
Kamenicë/Kamenica	405	33,409	82.5
Klinë/Klina	309	38,496	124.6
Kllokot/Klokot	29	2,556	88.1
Leposaviq/Leposavić†	n.a.	n.a.	n.a.
Lipjan/Lipljan	338	57,605	170.4
Malishevë/Mališevo	306	54,613	178.5
Mamushë/Mamuša	11	5,507	500.6
Mitrovicë/Mitrovica	336	71,909	214.0
Novobërdë/Novo Brdo	204	6,729	33.0
Obiliq/Obilić	105	21,549	205.2
Partesh/Parteš	23	1,787	77.7
Pejë/Peć	603	96,450	160.0
Podujevë/Podujevo	633	88,499	139.8
Prishtina (Prishtinë)/Priština	514	198,897	387.0
Prizren	627	177,781	283.5
Rahovec/Orahovac	276	56,208	203.7
Ranillug/Ranilug	89	3,866	43.4
Shtërpcë/Štrpce	248	6,949	28.0
Shtime/Štimlje	134	27,324	203.9
Skënderaj/Srbica	374	50,858	136.0
Suharekë/Suva Reka	361	59,722	165.4
Viti/Vitina	270	46,987	174.0
Vushtrri/Vučitrn	345	69,870	202.5
Zubin Potok†	n.a.	n.a.	n.a.
Zveçan/Zvečan†	n.a.	n.a.	n.a.
Total	**10,908**	**1,739,825**	**159.5**

* The Serbian names are given after the Albanian names, where they differ.
† No census conducted; estimates for these municipalities will be published at a later date.

BIRTHS, MARRIAGES AND DEATHS

	Registered live births		Registered marriages		Registered deaths	
	Number	Rate (per 1,000)	Number	Rate (per 1,000)	Number	Rate (per 1,000)
2004	35,063	17.2	16,989	8.3	6,399	3.1
2005	37,218	18.0	15,732	7.6	7,207	3.5
2006	34,187	16.3	15,825	7.5	7,479	3.6
2007	33,112	15.6	16,824	7.9	6,681	3.1
2008	34,399	16.0	17,950	8.3	6,852	3.2
2009	34,240	15.7	20,209	9.3	7,030	3.2
2010	33,751	15.3	18,289	8.3	7,234	3.3
2011	34,262	19.7	17,343	10.0	7,556	4.3

Life expectancy (years at birth): 69.9 (males 67.9; females 72.0) in 2010 (Source: World Bank, World Development Indicators database).

EMPLOYMENT
(labour force survey, percentage distribution)

	2007	2008	2009
Agriculture, hunting, forestry and fishing	14.6	8.0	6.2
Mining and quarrying	1.0	1.5	1.1
Manufacturing	10.4	8.7	9.9
Electricity, gas and water supply	2.7	5.2	4.5
Construction	6.6	8.6	7.9
Wholesale and retail trade; repair of motor vehicles, motorcycles and personal and household goods	16.9	17.1	17.4
Hotels and restaurants	3.9	4.5	4.6
Transport, storage and communications	4.5	5.6	5.8
Financial intermediation	1.1	1.8	2.2
Real estate, renting and business activities	1.4	2.6	2.9
Public administration and defence; compulsory social security	9.6	9.7	9.8
Education	12.1	13.6	13.4
Health and social work	7.0	6.5	7.0
Other community, social and personal service activities	8.3	6.7	7.5

Note: Reliable estimates of the number of employed people were not available. According to the results of an official agricultural household survey conducted at the end of 2005, some 500,000 farm residents of working age were engaged in some level of farming activity (of which 135,000 were employed in this activity on a full-time basis). An official statistical overview of some 54,000 registered private sector businesses at the end of 2002 recorded 186,000 employees, while the number of people engaged in public administration at the end of 2005 totalled 74,081.

Registered unemployed (at 31 December): 338,895 in 2009; 335,260 in 2010; 325,261 in 2011. Note: According to official estimates, some 45.4% of the total labour force were unemployed in 2009.

Agriculture

PRINCIPAL CROPS
('000 metric tons)

	2005	2007	2008
Wheat	273.4	207.2	293.1
Barley	11.3	3.7	6.4
Oats	9.8	7.8	8.9
Maize (incl. mixed crops)	79.9	37.5	58.5
Potatoes	87.4	95.1	104.0
Tomatoes	15.0	14.7	20.6
Peppers	55.0	36.0	51.3
Pumpkins (incl. mixed crops)	8.3	5.0	11.6
Cabbages	18.9	15.4	19.0
Onions	11.0	10.9	16.0
Beans (incl. mixed crops)	7.5	2.5	6.2

—continued	2005	2007	2008
Cucumbers	6.1	7.1	9.0
Watermelons	13.5	15.0	24.7
Apples	7.1	6.3	12.6
Pears	2.8	1.8	2.9
Plums	12.0	8.0	10.9
Vine grapes	2.2	2.8	1.9
Other grapes	3.5	3.5	8.6

Note: Data exclude second crops and autumn crops; production from state-owned enterprises is also excluded. Data for 2006 are not available.

LIVESTOCK
('000 head, October–December, unless otherwise indicated)

	2006	2007	2008
Horses	6.7	6.1	5.0
Cattle	382.0	321.6	341.6
Pigs	68.2	39.6	26.8
Sheep	100.8	139.2	124.1
Goats	12.1	12.6	8.9
Chickens	2,337.1	2,058.8	2,046.9
Other poultry	187.4	219.4	166.5

Note: Data exclude livestock belonging to state-owned enterprises.

LIVESTOCK PRODUCTS
(total value of products sold, € '000)

	2007	2008
Meat	2,955.5	2,331.4
Milk	15,266.4	20,995.6
Fat	85.8	343.9
Other dairy products	463.6	1,480.3
Eggs	616.6	1,389.7
Honey	871.6	958.7
Total (incl. others)	24,135.2	33,139.7

Note: Data exclude production by state-owned enterprises.

Forestry

FORESTRY REMOVALS
('000 cubic metres)

	2005	2007	2008
Fuel wood	393.1	468.9	451.7
Total (incl. others)	400.5	482.9	456.0

Note: Data exclude removals by state-owned enterprises. Data for 2006 are not available.

Mining
('000 metric tons)

	2009	2010	2011
Coal	7,870.7	7,991.0	8,212.1

Industry
(million kWh)

	2009	2010	2011
Electric energy	5,349	5,596	5,712

Finance

CURRENCY AND EXCHANGE RATES
Monetary Units
100 cent = 1 euro (€).

Sterling, Dollar and Euro Equivalents (31 December 2012)
£1 sterling = 1.196 euros;
US $1 = 0.758 euros;
€10 = £8.36 = $13.19.

Average Exchange Rate (euros per US $)
2010   0.7550
2011   0.7194
2012   0.7779

BUDGET
(consolidated accounts, € million)

Revenue	2010	2011*	2012†
Tax revenue	894	1,059	1,120
Non-tax revenue	148	159	171
Dividends	85	60	35
Total (incl. others)	1,169	1,312	1,361

Expenditure	2010	2011*	2012†
Current expenditure	746	845	887
Wages and salaries	311	386	407
Goods and services	182	187	198
Subsidies and transfers	253	272	282
Capital expenditure and net lending	455	535	617
Total (incl. others)	1,262	1,413	1,520

* Estimates.
† Budgeted figures.

Source: Ministry of Finance, Prishtina.

COST OF LIVING
(Consumer Price Index; base: May 2002 = 100)

	2010	2011	2012
All items	113.5	121.8	124.8

NATIONAL ACCOUNTS
(€ million at current prices)
Expenditure on the Gross Domestic Product

	2009	2010	2011
Government final consumption expenditure	670.5	709.3	772.3
Private final consumption expenditure	3,630.4	3,847.9	4,250.9
Gross fixed capital formation	1,026.5	1,192.6	1,374.3
Changes in inventories	137.6	149.4	156.5
Total domestic expenditure	5,465.0	5,899.2	6,554.0
Exports of goods and services	657.0	835.1	958.9
Less Imports of goods and services	2,114.2	2,443.1	2,736.7
GDP at market prices	4,007.8	4,291.1	4,776.1

Note: Data include contributions from UN Interim Mission in Kosovo operations.

Gross Domestic Product by Economic Activity

	2009	2010	2011
Agriculture, hunting, forestry and fishing	532.7	630.3	705.5
Mining	29.9	48.8	81.1
Manufacturing	465.9	411.9	399.4
Construction	336.2	371.9	398.2
Electricity and water supply . .	171.0	179.9	190.3
Wholesale and retail trade; repair of motor vehicles, motorcycles and personal and household goods	574.5	615.1	723.3
Hotels and restaurants . . .	30.8	61.1	37.1
Transport, storage and communications	149.1	157.9	207.8
Financial intermediation . . .	190.6	194.6	231.2
Real estate, renting and business activities	382.1	356.9	267.1
Public administration and defence; compulsory social security . .	542.4	563.7	636.5
Other community, social and personal service activities . .	127.8	104.6	165.6
Sub-total	3,532.9	3,696.8	4,043.2
Less Financial intermediation services indirectly measured .	111.1	120.5	136.7
GDP at basic prices	3,421.8	3,576.3	3,906.5
Taxes, *less* subsidies, on products .	585.9	714.8	869.7
GDP in purchasers' values .	4,007.8	4,291.1	4,776.1

BALANCE OF PAYMENTS
(€ million)

	2009	2010	2011
Exports of goods	243.0	394.9	441.2
Imports of goods	−2,549.2	−2,695.6	−3,289.1
Balance on goods	−2,306.2	−2,300.7	−2,847.9
Exports of services	673.0	703.9	893.1
Imports of services	−412.4	−527.9	−535.6
Balance on goods and services	−2,045.6	−2,124.7	−2,490.4
Primary income received . . .	253.8	234.3	336.1
Primary income paid	−139.2	−153.9	−193.7
Balance on goods, services and primary income	−1,931.0	−2,044.2	−2,348.0
Secondary income received . .	1,556.4	1,415.7	1,476.2
Secondary income paid . . .	−172.3	−139.3	−156.5
Current balance	−547.0	−767.9	−1,028.2
Capital account (net)	15.9	28.3	29.4
Direct investment assets . . .	−14.6	−32.4	−6.9
Direct investment liabilities . .	408.1	486.6	546.2
Portfolio investment assets . .	−85.6	−37.9	−83.2
Other investment assets . . .	−344.9	−365.9	−132.8
Other investment liabilities . .	67.3	391.6	243.2
Net errors and omissions . . .	223.2	343.4	350.2
Reserves and related items .	−277.7	45.7	−82.2

Source: IMF, *International Financial Statistics*.

External Trade

PRINCIPAL COMMODITIES
(€ '000, distribution by Harmonized System)

Imports c.i.f.	2009	2010	2011
Live animals and animal products	84,598	87,898	98,433
Vegetable products	90,035	108,622	136,877
Prepared foodstuffs, beverages, alcohol and tobacco	241,566	267,005	304,095
Beverages, spirits and vinegar .	49,102	55,409	57,900
Tobacco and manufactured tobacco substitutes	38,532	47,071	57,067
Mineral products	331,303	413,074	539,579
Mineral fuels, mineral oils and products of their distillation .	283,846	339,261	452,779
Chemical products	142,902	144,625	181,179
Pharmaceutical products . . .	37,997	34,541	50,757
Plastics, rubber and articles thereof	95,748	108,147	137,563
Plastics and articles thereof . .	78,640	92,148	114,430
Wood and articles of wood .	44,922	49,077	53,885
Paper and paper articles . .	45,412	41,787	46,669
Textiles and textile articles .	69,089	71,691	88,598
Articles of stone, plaster, ceramics and glass . . .	73,465	84,765	91,174
Ceramic products	47,344	52,253	57,083
Base metals and articles thereof	159,368	190,140	228,156
Iron and steel	76,434	101,255	119,302
Machinery and mechanical appliances; electrical equipment; sound and television apparatus . . .	278,689	298,714	273,047
Vehicles, aircraft, vessels and associated transport equipment	162,215	143,066	155,650
Total (incl. others)	1,935,541	2,157,725	2,492,348

Exports f.o.b.	2009	2010	2011
Vegetable products	9,484	12,217	12,766
Edible vegetables (incl. some roots and tubers)	4,175	3,686	2,642
Prepared foodstuffs, beverages, alcohol and tobacco	9,356	11,505	12,937
Beverages, spirits and vinegars .	4,578	5,313	8,106
Mineral products	24,952	38,944	40,575
Ores, slag and ash	12,065	27,545	20,104
Mineral fuels, mineral oils and products of their distillation .	7,213	10,869	17,758
Plastics, rubber and articles thereof	6,357	8,153	12,429
Leather and leather articles .	4,454	9,683	9,406
Raw hides and skins (other than fur)	4,452	9,644	9,399
Base metals and articles thereof	88,363	186,131	193,143
Iron and steel	73,229	158,776	162,038
Articles of iron and steel . . .	5,390	6,823	7,766
Copper and articles thereof . .	4,764	12,213	14,461
Aluminium and articles thereof .	3,393	6,370	7,561
Machinery and mechanical appliances; electrical equipment; sound and television apparatus . . .	7,206	10,872	15,276
Total (incl. others)	165,328	295,957	319,165

PRINCIPAL TRADING PARTNERS
(€ '000)

Imports c.i.f.	2009	2010	2011
Albania	58,385	69,714	96,400
Austria	38,886	33,126	38,669
Bosnia and Herzegovina	59,739	82,986	79,835
Brazil	37,888	27,188	40,925
Bulgaria	44,493	35,211	50,541
China, People's Republic	128,318	135,406	170,285
Croatia	58,544	58,542	64,063
France	27,166	33,635	34,755
Germany	246,120	280,617	293,441
Greece	79,107	96,267	103,179
Hungary	26,892	28,950	35,020
Italy	87,646	100,603	159,444
Macedonia, former Yugoslav republic	291,837	319,313	365,961
Netherlands	30,926	14,876	18,195
Poland	24,146	39,876	32,963
Serbia	210,901	260,471	254,917
Slovenia	66,249	65,738	71,614
Switzerland	21,949	20,981	22,194
Turkey	141,545	150,360	184,452
United Kingdom	14,133	13,457	17,084
USA	26,703	35,311	42,847
Total (incl. others)	1,935,541	2,157,725	2,492,348

Exports f.o.b.	2009	2010	2011
Albania	26,182	30,841	34,566
Austria	1,978	5,670	5,711
Belgium	5,176	11,455	5,085
Bosnia and Herzegovina	1,206	1,847	612
Bulgaria	2,709	6,765	936
China, People's Republic	1,596	14,779	28,268
Croatia	2,151	2,744	2,794
Germany	7,563	15,587	24,144
Italy	46,218	80,193	83,924
Macedonia, former Yugoslav republic	17,355	26,308	30,949
Montenegro	3,084	3,920	6,988
Serbia	3,504	3,941	7,198
Slovenia	2,882	6,203	6,001
Switzerland	10,510	17,786	17,611
Turkey	6,512	9,357	7,831
Total (incl. others)	165,328	295,957	319,165

Transport

RAILWAYS

	2005	2006
Passenger train journeys	3,427	5,662
Passenger train-kilometres	214,731	317,320
Freight train journeys	1,440	1,494
Freight train-kilometres	69,245	82,459
Total freight transported (metric tons)	297,555	354,835

Source: Kosovo Railways, *Annual Report 2006*.

2011: Passengers carried ('000) 358; Freight carried ('000 metric tons) 1,001; Freight ton-km (million) 56.

ROAD TRAFFIC
(vehicles registered at 31 December)

	2004	2005	2006
Passenger cars	137,981	145,546	146,744
Buses and coaches	1,142	13,757	239
Lorries and vans	21,565	13,887	20,611
Heavy goods vehicles	7,213	4,769	6,457
Total (incl. others)	169,072	200,000	178,185

CIVIL AVIATION
(traffic at Prishtina International Airport)

	2009	2010	2011
Aircraft movements	5,709	5,541	6,738
Passengers arrivals	578,451	641,406	696,033
Passenger departures	613,527	664,126	716,269

Education

(2010/11)

	Institutions	Pupils	Teachers
Kindergarten	52	24,655	1,303
Primary	1,030	302,253	17,856
Secondary	137	108,503	5,957
Special	50	905	191
Primary	46	807	155
Secondary	4	98	36
University level	n.a.	35,910	1,023

Directory

The Government

HEAD OF STATE

President: ATIFETE JAHJAGA (inaugurated 7 April 2011).

GOVERNMENT
(May 2013)

A coalition of the Democratic Party of Kosovo (DPK), the New Kosovo Alliance (NKA), the Independent Liberal Party (ILP), the Democratic League of Kosovo (DLK), the Justice Party (JP), the Social Democratic Party (SDP) and the Turkish Democratic Party of Kosovo (TDPK).

Prime Minister: HASHIM THAÇI (DPK).

First Deputy Prime Minister: BEHGJET PACOLLI (NKA).

Deputy Prime Minister and Minister of Justice: HAJREDIN KUÇI (DPK).

Deputy Prime Minister and Minister of Trade and Industry: MIMOZA KUSARI-LILA (NKA).

Deputy Prime Minister and Minister of Local Government: SLOBODAN PETROVIĆ (ILP).

Deputy Prime Minister: EDITA TAHIRI (DPK).

Deputy Prime Minister: BUJAR BUKOSHI (DLK).

Minister of Foreign Affairs: ENVER HOXHAJ (DPK).

Minister of European Integration: VLORA ÇITAKU (DPK).

Minister of the Kosovo Security Force: AGIM ÇEKU (SDP).

Minister of Internal Affairs: BAJRAM REXHEPI (DPK).

Minister of Finance: (vacant).

Minister of Culture, Youth and Sports: MEMLI KRASNIQI (DPK).

Minister of Economic Development: BESIM BEQAJ (DPK).

Minister of Education, Science and Technology: RAMË BUJA (DPK).

Minister of Public Administration: MAHIR YAĞCILAR (TDPK).

Minister of Infrastructure: FEHMI MUJOTA (DPK).

Minister of Agriculture, Forestry and Rural Development: BLERAND STAVILECI (DPK).

Minister of Health: FERID AGANI (JP).

Minister of Labour and Social Welfare: NENAD RAŠIĆ (ILP).

Minister of the Environment and Spatial Planning: DARDAN GASHI (DLK).

Minister of Communities and Resettlement: RADOJICA TOMIĆ (ILP).

Minister of the Diaspora: IBRAHIM MAKOLLI (NKA).

MINISTRIES

Office of the President: 10000 Prishtina, Rruga Nënë Terezë; tel. (38) 211972; fax (38) 211651; e-mail fehmi@president-ksgov.net; internet www.president-ksgov.net.

Office of the Prime Minister: 10000 Prishtina, Rruga Nënë Terezë; tel. (38) 20114635; fax (38) 20014671; e-mail info_pmo@ks-gov.net; internet www.kryeministri-ks.net.

Ministry of Agriculture, Forestry and Rural Development: 10000 Prishtina, Rruga Nënë Terezë; tel. (38) 211821; e-mail jusuf.salihu@ks-gov.net; internet www.mbpzhr-ks.net.

Ministry of Communities and Resettlement: 12000 Fushë Kosova, Sheshi Nënë Terezë; tel. (38) 552045; e-mail snezana.palocevic@ks-gov.net; internet www.mkk-ks.org.

Ministry of Culture, Youth and Sports: 10000 Prishtina, Sheshi Nënë Terezë; tel. (38) 211637; fax (38) 211440; e-mail info@mkrs-ks.org; internet www.mkrs-ks.org.

Ministry of the Diaspora: 10000 Prishtina, Nëna Terezë; tel. (38) 20017001; e-mail ministriaediaspores@ks-gov.net; internet med.rks-gov.net.

Ministry of Economic Development: 10000 Prishtina, Sheshi Nënë Terezë; tel. (38) 200215; e-mail mzhe.informimi@gmail.com; internet www.mzhe.rks-gov.net.

Ministry of Education, Science and Technology: 10000 Prishtina, Rruga Agim Ramadani; tel. (38) 213327; e-mail masht@ks-gov.net; internet www.masht-gov.net.

Ministry of the Environment and Spatial Planning: 10000 Prishtina, Ish Pallati i Mediave, Kati 14-17; tel. (38) 20032517; fax (38) 20032041; e-mail webmaster.mmph@ks-gov.net; internet www.mmph.rks-gov.net.

Ministry of European Integration: 10000 Prishtina, Rruga Nënë Terezë, Ndërtesa e Qeverisë, Kati 9; tel. (38) 20027001; e-mail bardha.ajvazi@rks-gov.net; internet www.mei-ks.net.

Ministry of Finance: 10000 Prishtina, Sheshi Nënë Terezë; tel. (38) 20034101; fax (38) 213113; e-mail abeiqi@mfe-ks.org; internet www.mf.rks-gov.net.

Ministry of Foreign Affairs: 10000 Prishtina, Ndërtesa e Qeverisë, Rruga Nënë Terezë; tel. (38) 213963; fax (38) 213985; e-mail mfa@rks-gov.net; internet www.mfa-ks.net.

Ministry of Health: 10000 Prishtina, Rruga Zagrebi; tel. (38) 213886; e-mail faik.hoti@ks-gov.net; internet www.msh-ks.org.

Ministry of Infrastructure: 10000 Prishtina, Ndërtesa e Kuvendit të Kosovës, Aneksi i Ri, Rruga Nënë Terezë; tel. (38) 211022; e-mail ministria.infrastruktures@gmail.com; internet mi-ks.net.

Ministry of Internal Affairs: 10000 Prishtina, Rruga Luan Haradinaj; tel. (38) 213007; fax (38) 20019640; e-mail merita.vidishiq@ks-gov.net; internet www.mpb-ks.org.

Ministry of Justice: 10000 Prishtina, Ndërtesa e ish Rilindjes, Kati VIII, Zyra 817/A; tel. (38) 20018009; e-mail astrit.kolaj@ks-gov.net; internet www.md-ks.org.

Ministry of the Kosovo Security Force: 10000 Prishtina, Lagjja Emshiri-1; tel. (38) 551437; e-mail violeta.reka@ks-gov.net; internet mksf-ks.org.

Ministry of Labour and Social Welfare: 10000 Prishtina, Rruga UÇK-së 1; tel. and fax (38) 20026049; e-mail behxhet.gaxhiqi@ks-gov.net; internet mpms.rks-gov.net.

Ministry of Local Government: 10000 Prishtina, Ndërtesa e ish Rilindjes, Katet 10–13; tel. (38) 20035630; e-mail blerta.miftari@rks-gov.net; internet mapl.rks-gov.net.

Ministry of Public Administration: 10000 Prishtina, Kati V, Zyra 534, Ndërtesa e ish Rilindjes; tel. (38) 20060005; fax (38) 20030008; e-mail mahir.yagcilar@rks-gov.net; internet map.rks-gov.net.

Ministry of Trade and Industry: 10000 Prishtina, Lagjja e Spitalit, Rruga Muharrem Fejza; tel. (38) 512059; fax (38) 512798; e-mail zkp.mti@rks-gov.net; internet mti-ks.org.

INTERNATIONAL REPRESENTATIVES

Special Representative of the Secretary-General of the UN, Head of the UN Interim Administration Mission in Kosovo (UNMIK): FARID ZARIF.

Special Representative of the European Union and International Civilian Representative in Kosovo: PIETER FEITH.

International Civilian Office (ICO): 10000 Prishtina, Rruga Ahmet Krasniqi, Blue Bldg; tel. (38) 2044100; fax (38) 2044210; e-mail office@ico-kos.org; internet www.ico-kos.org.

President

In voting by the members of the Kosovo Assembly (Kuvendi i Kosovës/Skupština Kosova), held on 7 April 2011, the sole candidate for the presidency, Maj.-Gen. ATIFETE JAHJAGA, was elected President. (A previous presidential election, conducted on 22 February, of which BEHGJET PACOLLI had been declared the winner, was subsequently ruled to have been unconstitutional.) It was announced that JAHJAGA was to serve in an interim capacity until no later than 2013, pending the drafting, approval and implementation of proposed constitutional reforms providing for the election of the President by direct popular vote.

Legislature

Kosovo Assembly
(Kuvendi i Kosovës/Skupština Kosova)

10000 Prishtina, Rruga Nënë Terezë; tel. (38) 211186; fax (38) 211188; e-mail info@assembly-kosova.org; internet www.assembly-kosova.org.

President: JAKUP KRASNIQI.

Election, 12 December 2010*

Parties and Coalitions	Votes	% of votes	Seats
Democratic Party of Kosovo .	224,339	32.11	34
Democratic League of Kosovo .	172,552	24.69	27
Self-Determination!	88,652	12.69	14
Alliance for the Future of Kosovo .	77,130	11.04	12
New Kosovo Alliance-led coalition†	50,951	7.29	8
Independent Liberal Party .	14,352	2.05	8
United Serbian List	6,004	0.86	4
Turkish Democratic Party of Kosovo	8,548	1.22	3
Vakat Coalition	5,296	0.76	2
New Spirit	15,156	2.17	—
Democratic League of Dardania .	14,924	2.14	—
Others	20,847	2.98	8‡
Total	**698,751**	**100.00**	**120**

* Including the results of re-run elections, held in the municipalities of Skënderaj/Srbica, Gllogovc/Glogovac and Deçan/Dečani and in certain polling stations in the municipalities of Malishevë/Mališevo and Lipjan/Lipljan on 9 January 2011, and in the municipality of Mitrovicë/Mitrovica on 23 January. The figures shown in this table incorporate the results of voting to the 20 seats reserved for representatives of designated minority ethnic groups (10 seats are elected by Serbs, four by a constituency comprising Roma, Ashkali and 'Egyptian' Roma, three by Bosniaks, two by Turks and one by Gorani).

† An alliance of seven parties, comprising: the New Kosovo Alliance; the Justice Party; the Social Democratic Party; the Pensioners' and Disabled People's Party; the Pensioners' Party of Kosovo; the Albanian National Democratic Party; and the Green Party of Kosovo.

‡ The other parties to obtain representation (one seat apiece) were: the Civic Initiative of Gora; the Democratic Ashkali Party of Kosovo; New Democratic Party; the New Democratic Initiative of Kosovo; the Serb Democratic Party of Kosovo and Metohija; the United Roma Party of Kosovo; the Bosniak Party of Democratic Action of Kosovo; and the Ashkali Party for Integration.

Election Commission

Central Election Commission (Komisioni Qendror i Zgjedhjeve): 10000 Prishtina, Rruga Migjeni p.n.; tel. (38) 246599; fax (38) 246602; e-mail kqz.sekretariati@kqz-ks.org; internet www.kqz-ks.org; f. 2004; Chair. VALDETE DAKA.

Political Organizations

Albanian Christian Democratic Party of Kosovo (Partia Shqiptare Demokristane e Kosovës): 10000 Prishtina, Mustafa Kruja, Dorona; tel. (38) 221536; e-mail info@pshdk-ks.org; f. 2000; Chair. NIKË GJELOSHI.

Alliance for the Future of Kosovo (AFK) (Aleanca për Ardhmër-inë e Kosovës): 10000 Prishtina, Bulevardi i Dëshmorëve 49; tel. and fax (38) 544188; e-mail info@aak-ks.com; f. 2001; Chair. RAMUSH HARADINAJ.

Democratic League of Dardania (Lidhja Demokratike e Darda-nisë): 10000 Prishtina, Rruga Edmond Hoxha 86; tel. (45) 277755; e-mail info@ldd-kosova.org; internet www.ldd-kosova.org; f. Jan. 2007 by fmr mems of Democratic League of Kosovo; Leader NEXHAT DAÇI.

Democratic League of Kosovo (DLK) (Lidhja Demokratike e Kosovës): 10000 Prishtina, Kompleksi Qafa; tel. (38) 242242; fax (38) 245305; e-mail info@ldk-ks.eu; internet www.ldk-ks.eu; f. 2000 as successor to the Democratic Alliance of Kosovo; Chair. ISA MUSTAFA.

Democratic Party of Kosovo (DPK) (Partia Demokratike e Kosovës): 10000 Prishtina, Rruga Nënë Terezë 20; tel. (44) 183445; e-mail separikosova@pdk49.com; internet www.pdk49 .com; f. 1999; est. as Party for the Democratic Progress of Kosovo; renamed as above 2000; Chair. HASHIM THAÇI.

Independent Liberal Party (ILP) (Samostalna liberalna stranka—SLS): Gračanica, Poslovni centar 'Lazic'; tel. (38) 566680; e-mail office@sls-ks.org; internet www.sls-ks.org; f. 2006; represents Serb interests; Chair. SLOBODAN PETROVIĆ.

Justice Party (JP) (Partia e Drejtësisë—PD): 10000 Prishtina, Vellusha, Rruga Bajram Kelmendi 22; tel. and fax (44) 248920; internet www.drejtesia.org; f. 2000; Chair. FERID AGANI.

Liberal Party of Kosovo (Partia Liberale e Kosovës—PLK): 10000 Prishtina, Goleshi St 10/2; tel. and fax (38) 244780; e-mail info@ plk-kosova.org; Chair. Prof. GJERGJ DEDAJ.

New Democracy (Nova Demokratija): 10000 Prishtina; f. 2007; represents Serb interests; Leader BRANISLAV GRBIĆ.

New Kosovo Alliance (NKA) (Aleanca Kosova e Re—AKR): 10000 Prishtina, Rruga UÇK 55; tel. (38) 224021; fax (38) 247988; e-mail akr.kosova@gmail.com; internet www.akr-ks.eu; f. 2006; Pres. BEHGJET PACOLLI.

Self-Determination! (Vetëvendosje!): 10000 Prishtina, Qyteza Pejton, Rruga Bajram Kelmendi 10; tel. (44) 411174; e-mail info@ vetevendosje.org; internet www.vetevendosje.org; f. 2005; ethnic Albanian nationalist party; Pres. ALBIN KURTI.

Serb List for Kosovo and Metohija (Srpska Lista za Kosovo i Metohiju): Mitrovica; coalition of representatives of the Serbian Renewal Movement, the Democratic Party of Kosovo and the Social Democratic Party; Leader OLIVER IVANOVIĆ.

Social Democratic Party (SDP) (Partia Social Demokrate—PSD): 10000 Prishtina, Rruga Rexhep Mala 5; tel. (38) 225645; e-mail info@ psd-ks.org; internet www.psd-ks.org; Pres. AGIM ÇEKU.

Socialist Party of Kosovo (Partia Socialiste e Kosovës): 10000 Prishtina, Rruga Thimi Mitko 6; tel. (44) 131832; e-mail info@ps-ks .org; internet www.ps-ks.org; f. 1982; Chair. ILAZ KADOLLI.

Turkish Democratic Party of Kosovo (TDPK) (Kosova Demo-kratik Türk Partisi): 10000 Prizren, Sheshi e Lidhjes Cad. 47; tel. (29) 242534; fax (38) 20030008; e-mail info@kdtp.org; internet www.kdtp .org; f. 1990; Chair. MAHIR YAĞCILAR.

Vakat Coalition (Koalicija Vakat): Dragaš; f. 2004; coalition of representatives of the Bosniak Democratic Party, the Fatherland (Vatan) Democratic Party and the Bosniak Party of Kosovo; Leader SADIK IDRIZI.

Other political parties include: the **Democratic Ashkali Party of Kosovo** (Partia Demokratike e Ashkanlive të Kosovës); the **Serb Democratic Party of Kosovo and Metohija** (Srpska Demo-kratska Stranka Kosova i Metohije), led by SLAVIŠA PETKOVIĆ; the **Party of Democratic Action** (Stranka Demokratske Akcije); the **Serb People's Party** (Srpska Narodna Stranka), led by MIHAJL SĆEPANOVIĆ; the **Civic Initiative of Gora** (Građanska Inicijativa Gore); the **Serb Kosovo and Metohija Party** (Srpska Kosovsko-Metohijka Stranka), led by DRAGIŠA MIRIĆ; the **New Democratic Initiative of Kosovo** (Iniciativa e re Demokrarike e Kosovës), representing the 'Egyptian' Roma; the **Union of Independent Social Democrats of Kosovo and Metohija** (Savez Nezavisnih Socijaldemokrata Kosova i Metohije), led by NEBOJŠA ŽIVIĆ; and the **United Roma Party of Kosovo** (Partia Rome e Bashkuar e Kosovës).

Diplomatic Representation

EMBASSIES IN KOSOVO

At May 2013 98 countries had officially recognized Kosovo.

Albania: 10000 Prishtina, Qyteza Pejton, Rruga Mujo Ulqinaku 18; tel. (38) 248208; fax (38) 248209; e-mail embassy.pristina@mfa.gov .al; Ambassador ISLAM LAUKA.

Austria: 10000 Prishtina, Fan Noli 22, Arbëria 1; tel. (38) 249284; fax (38) 249285; e-mail pristina-as@bmeia.gv.at; Ambassador JOHANN BRIEGER.

Bulgaria: 10000 Prishtina, Arbëria 1, Rruga Ismail Qemali 12; tel. (38) 245540; fax (38) 245543; e-mail embassy.pristina@mfa.bg; internet www.mfa.bg/embassies/kosovo; Ambassador BOBI BOBEV.

Croatia: 10000 Prishtina, Rruga Mujo Ulqinaku 20; tel. (38) 223320; fax (38) 223979; e-mail croemb.pristina@mvpei.hr; Ambassador ZORAN VODOPIJA.

Czech Republic: 10000 Prishtina, Dragodan, Rruga Ismail Qemali 31; tel. (38) 246676; fax (38) 248782; e-mail pristina@embassy.mzv .cz; Ambassador JIŘÍ DOLEŽEL.

Finland: 10000 Prishtina, Lagja Payton, Perandori Justinian 19; tel. (43) 737000; fax (43) 732863; e-mail sanomat.pri@formin.fi; internet www.finlandkosovo.org; Chargé d'affaires a.i. ANNE MES-KANEN.

France: 10000 Prishtina, Dragodan, Rruga Ismail Qemali 67; tel. (38) 22458800; fax (38) 22458801; e-mail admin-etrangers .pristina-amba@diplomatie.gouv.fr; internet www.ambafrance -kosovo.org; Ambassador MARYSE DAVIET.

Germany: 10000 Prishtina, Arbëri, Rruga Azem Jashanica 17; tel. (38) 254500; fax (38) 254536; e-mail info@pristina.diplo.de; internet www.pristina.diplo.de; Ambassador Dr PETER BLOMEYER.

Hungary: 10000 Prishtina, Arbëri, 24 Maj 23; tel. (38) 247763; fax (38) 248004; e-mail mission.prs@mfa.gov.hu; internet www.mfa.gov .hu/pristina; Ambassador LÓRÁNT BALLA.

Italy: 10000 Prishtina, Dragodan, Rruga Azem Jashanica 5; tel. (38) 244925; fax (38) 244929; e-mail pubblico.pristina@esteri.it; Ambas-sador MICHAEL LOUIS GIFFONI.

Macedonia, former Yugoslav republic: 10000 Prishtina, Rruga 24 Maji 121; tel. (38) 247462; fax (38) 247463; Ambassador STOJAN KARAJANOV.

Netherlands: 10000 Prishtina, Velania, Xhemajl Berisha 12; tel. (38) 516101; fax (38) 516103; e-mail pri@minbuza.nl; internet www .kosovo.nlambassade.org; Ambassador ROBERT BOSCH.

Norway: 10000 Prishtina, Pejton, Sejdi Kryeziu 6; tel. (38) 23211100; fax (38) 23211122; e-mail embpri@mfa.no; internet www.norway-kosovo.no; Ambassador JAN BRAATHU.

Slovenia: 10000 Prishtina, Anton Ceta 6; tel. (38) 246255; fax (38) 246256; e-mail mpi@gov.si; Ambassador JOŽEF HLEB.

Switzerland: 10060 Prishtina, Adrian Krasniqi 11; tel. (38) 248088; fax (38) 248078; e-mail pri.vertretung@eda.admin.ch; internet www .eda.admin.ch/pristina; Ambassador KRYSTYNA MARTY LANG.

Turkey: 10000 Prishtina, Arbëri, Rruga Ismail Qemali 59; tel. (38) 226044; fax (38) 226031; e-mail embassy.prishtina@mfa.gov.tr; internet www.prishtina.emb.mfa.gov.tr; Ambassador SONGÜL OZAN BÜYÜKELÇI.

United Kingdom: 10000 Prishtina, Arbëri, Rruga Ismail Qemali 6; tel. (38) 254700; fax (38) 243062; e-mail britishoffice.pristina@fco.gov .uk; internet ukinkosovo.fco.gov.uk; Ambassador IAN CAMERON CLIFF.

USA: 10000 Prishtina, Arbëri, Nazim Hikmet 30; tel. (38) 593000; fax (38) 549890; e-mail papristina@state.gov; internet pristina .usembassy.gov; Ambassador TRACEY ANN JACOBSON.

Judicial System

The court system comprises a Supreme Court, Constitutional Court, district courts, municipal courts and minor offences courts.

Supreme Court: 10000 Prishtina; tel. (38) 243345; fax (38) 245219; internet www.gjykatasupreme-ks.org; Pres. FEJZULLAH HASANI.

Constitutional Court: 10000 Prishtina, Rruga Perandori Justi-nian; tel. (38) 220103; fax (38) 220112; e-mail info@gjk-ks.org; internet www.gjk-ks.org; f. 2009; Chair. Prof. ENVER HASANI; Dep. Chair. Prof. Dr IVAN ČUKALOVIĆ.

Religion

Most of the inhabitants of Kosovo are adherents of Islam, although most Serbs are Orthodox Christians, and several sites of historic importance to Serbian Orthodoxy are located within Kosovo. A significant minority of the Kosovo Albanian population are Roman Catholics.

ISLAM

Islamic Community: 10000 Prishtina; tel. and fax (38) 245700; internet www.bislame.net; f. 1951; Pres. of the Islamic Community NAIM TERNAVA.

CHRISTIANITY

The Eastern Orthodox Church
The Patriarchate of the Serbian Orthodox Church is located at Pej (Peć), in central Kosovo.

The Roman Catholic Church
There are an estimated 65,000 Roman Catholics within the Apostolic Administration of Prizren. In the early 2010s a Catholic co-cathedral was under construction in Prishtina.

Apostolic Administrator of Prizren: GJERGJU DODË, 20000 Prizren, Rruga I. L. Ribar 7; tel. (29) 41933; fax (29) 41232; e-mail ipeshkvia_pz@yahoo.com.

The Press

PRINCIPAL DAILIES

Bota Sot (The World Today): 10000 Prishtina, Rruga Jakove Xoxa 18; tel. and fax (38) 226881; e-mail bota-sot@ipko.org; in Albanian; Editor IDRIZ MORINA.

Epoka e Re (The New Age): 10000 Prishtina, opp. UNMIK HQ; tel. (44) 127434; e-mail info@epokaere.com; internet www.epokaere.com; f. 1999; Man. MUHAMET MAVRAJ.

Express: 10000 Prishtina, Dardania 1/1; tel. (38) 767676; fax (38) 767678; e-mail info@gazetaexpress.com; internet www.gazetaexpress.com; f. 2005; in Albanian; Chief Editor LEONARD KERQUKI.

Infopress: 10000 Prishtina, Shtypshkronja Rilindja; tel. (38) 222464; fax (38) 222510; e-mail info@infopress-rh.com; popular; supports Democratic Party of Kosovo; Editor AVNI AZEMI.

Koha Ditore: 10000 Prishtina, Rruga Nënë Terezë, POB 202; tel. (38) 249104; fax (38) 249106; e-mail redaksia@kohaditore.com; internet www.kohaditore.com; in Albanian; Editor-in-Chief AGRON BAJRAMI.

Kosova Sot (Kosovo Today): 10000 Prishtina, Zona Industriale; tel. (38) 601007; fax (38) 601010; e-mail redaksia@kosova-sot.info; internet www.kosova-sot.info; f. 1998; in Albanian; Editor-in-Chief MARGARITA KADRIU.

Lajm (The News): 10000 Prishtina, UÇK 58; tel. (38) 243021; fax (38) 243009; e-mail redaksia@gazetalajm.info; internet www.gazetalajm.info; f. 2004; in Albanian; supports the New Kosovo Alliance; Chief Exec. BEHGJET PACOLLI.

Prishtina Post: 10000 Prishtina, Bulevardi Bil Klinton; tel. and fax (38) 555566; e-mail redaksia@prishtinapost.info; in Albanian; Editor FATON ABDULLAHU.

PERIODICALS

Alem: 1000 Prishtina, Rruga Hajdar Dushi 1A; tel. (44) 185099; fax (38) 243800; e-mail info@alemnet.info; f. 2001; weekly; in Bosnian; Editor-in-Chief NADIRA A. VLASSI.

Drita: 20000 Prizren, Rruga I. L. Ribar 7; e-mail ipeshkvia_pz@yahoo.com; review publ. by Catholic Church in Kosovo; Editor Mgr LUSH GJERGJI.

Fokus Kosova/Fokus Kosovo/Focus Kosovo: 10000 Prishtina, UNMIK Administrative HQ; e-mail focuskosovo@un.org; f. 2001; publ. by UNMIK; Albanian, Serbian and English edns; seven a year; Publr ALEXANDER IVANKO; Editors MYRIAM DESSABLES (Albanian and Serbian edns), RICARDO Z. DUNN.

Gradanski Glasnik (The Civil Herald): 10000 Prishtina, Tringe Ismaili 34A; tel. (44) 431106; e-mail gg@gradjanskiglasnik.com; every two weeks; in Serbian; Editor-in-Chief JELENA BJELICA.

Official Gazette of the Republic of Kosovo (Gazeta Zyrtare e Republikës së Kosovës/Sluzbeni list Republike Kosova/Kosova Cumhuriyeti Resmi Gazetesi/Sluzbeni Novine Republike Kosova): 10000 Prishtina, Ndërtesa e re e Qeverisë; tel. (38) 20114039; fax (38) 20114180; e-mail info-gzk@ks-gov.net; internet www.ks-gov.net/GazetaZyrtare; f. 2005; monthly; publishes official text of laws adopted by the Kosovo Assembly as promulgated by the Special Representative of the Secretary-General, resolutions adopted by the Kosovo Assembly, secondary and other legislation issued by the Government and ministries of Kosovo, international agreements, etc.; edns in Albanian, Serbian, English, Turkish and Bosnian; administered by the Office of the Prime Minister; Editorial Dir NASER CANOLLI.

Yeni Dönem (New Era): Prizren, Rruga Ceraviqa 13A; tel. (29) 630230; fax (29) 44788; e-mail yenidonem@hotmail.com; in Turkish; weekly.

Zëri (The Voice): 10000 Prishtina, Media House Annex II; tel. (38) 249071; fax (38) 222451; e-mail redaksia@zeri.info; f. 1945; in Albanian; weekly; Editor-in-Chief ASTRIT GASHI.

NEWS AGENCIES

Infosot: Prishtina; tel. (44) 383333; e-mail info@infosot.com; internet www.infosot.com; f. 2007; Exec. Dir FATLUM RRAHMANI.

KosovaLive: 1000 Prishtina, Aneksi te Pallati i Shtypit, Kati II; tel. (38) 248276; fax (38) 248277; e-mail editor@kosovalive.com; internet www.kosovalive.com; f. 2000; Editor-in-Chief KELMEND HAPÇIU.

Kosovapress: 10000 Prishtina, Rruga Hamez Jashari 28/22A; tel. and fax (38) 248721; e-mail kryeredaktori@kosovapress.com; internet www.kosovapress.com; f. 1999; Dir and Editor SKENDER KRASNIQI.

Press Association

Press Council of Kosovo: 10000 Prishtina, Rruga Hajdar Dushi 17; tel. (44) 291810; e-mail presscouncil.kosovo@gmail.com; internet www.presscouncil-ks.org; self-regulatory body of the print media; Chair. of Bd WILLEM HOUWEN; Dir NEHAT ISLAMI.

Publishers

Dukagjini Publishing House: 10000 Pejë, Rruga Fehmi Agani 16; tel. (39) 432025; fax (39) 434281; internet books.dukagjinigroup.com; literature and contemporary philosophy; titles publ. in three series: Rozafa, Ballkan and Fryma; owned by Dukagjini Group; Pres. RAMADAN MEHMETI.

Gjon Buzuku Publishing House: 10000 Prishtina, Rruga Brigadat e Kosovës; tel. and fax (38) 530873; e-mail buzuku@prishtina.com; f. 1990; Pres. HANA ZENELI.

Panorama: 10000 Prishtina; f. 1994; publishes newspapers and journals in Serbian, Albanian and Turkish; Dir JORDAN RISTIĆ.

Rilindja Publishing House: 10000 Prishtina, Pallati i mediave, Dom štampe pa nr; tel. (38) 549675; popular science, literature, children's fiction, travel books, textbooks in Albanian; Dir DAUT DEMAKU.

Broadcasting and Communications

TELECOMMUNICATIONS
Kosovo's telecommunications industry has been liberalized, with one licensed fixed-line telecommunication service provider and two licensed mobile operators in 2010. As Kosovo's independence is not recognized by the International Telecommunication Union, it has been unable to obtain an international dialling code of its own, and network operators in Kosovo at present use one of the country codes of Monaco, Slovenia or Serbia.

iPKO: 10000 Prishtina, Rruga Zija Shemsiu, Lagjja Ulpiana; tel. (38) 643700700; e-mail info@ipko.com; internet www.ipko.com; f. 1999; subsidiary of Telekom Slovenije (Slovenia); mobile cellular telecommunications services, and provider of internet and digital cable television.

PTK (Post and Telecommunications of Kosovo): 10100 Prishtina, Dardania pa nr, Kati VIII, Zyra 808; tel. (38) 500555; e-mail postaekosoves@ptkonline.com; internet www.ptkonline.com; f. 1959; became jt-stock co in 2005; provides postal and telecommunications services; CEO EJUP QERIMI.

Regulatory Authority

Telecommunications Regulatory Authority (Kosovo) (ART) (Autoriteti Rregullator i Telekomunikacionit): 10000 Prishtina, Qyteza Pejton, Rruga Pashko Vasa; tel. (38) 212345; e-mail info@art-ks.org; internet www.art-ks.org; f. 2004; Chair. EKREM HOXHA.

BROADCASTING
In 2010 there were 118 broadcasters of television and radio in Kosovo, including three national television channels and four national radio stations.

Radio Televizioni i Kosovës (RTK) (Radio-Television Kosovo): 10000 Prishtina, Rruga Xhemail 12; tel. (38) 230102; fax (38) 235336; e-mail post@rtklive.com; internet www.rtklive.com; subsidiaries include Radio Kosova and Radio Blue Sky; Chair. Dr VJOSA DOBRUNA; Dir-Gen. SYLEJMAN SHAQIRI; Editor-in-Chief MUFAIL LIMANI.

RadioTelevizioni21 (RTV21): 10000 Prishtina, Pallati i Mediave, Aneks II; tel. and fax (38) 241522; e-mail lajmet@rtv21.tv; internet www.rtv21.tv; radio and television broadcaster.

Finance

(cap. = capital; res = reserves; dep. = deposits; m. = million; amounts in euros; brs = branches)

BANKING

Regulatory Authority

Central Bank of the Republic of Kosovo (Banka Qendrore Republikës së Kosoves): 10000 Prishtina, Rruga Garibaldi 33; tel. (38) 222055; fax (38) 243763; e-mail publicrelations@cbak-kos.org; internet www.bqk-kos.org; f. 1999 as the Banking and Payments Authority of Kosovo; became Central Banking Authority of Kosovo 2006; total assets 1,113.2m. (Dec. 2008); Gov. BEDRI HAMZA; Chair. GAZMEND LUBOTENI.

Registered Banks

There are 10 registered commercial banks operating in Kosovo, of which seven are foreign owned.

Banka Kombëtare Tregtare: 10000 Prishtina, Qyteza Pejton, Rruga Kosta Novakoviç 9; tel. (38) 222910; fax (38) 222907; e-mail infobktkosova@bkt.com; internet www.bkt.com.al; f. 1993; total assets 18.3m. (Dec. 2008).

Bank for Business (Banka për Biznes—BpB): Prishtina, Rruga UÇK 41; tel. (38) 244666; fax (38) 243656; e-mail info@bpbbank.com; internet www.bpbbank.com; f. 2001; total assets 41.2m. (Dec. 2007); Dir-Gen. SELVINAZE SHEHOLLI.

Economic Bank: 10000 Prishtina, Rruga Migjeni 1; tel. (38) 225353; fax (38) 225454; e-mail bek@bekonomike.com; internet www.bekonomike.com; f. 2001; total assets 86.1m. (Dec. 2008); Pres. HAJRULLAH ZAITI.

Komercijalna Banka a.d. Beograd: 40000 Mitrovica, Rruga Kralja Petra Prvog 33; tel. (28) 423822; fax (28) 425295; e-mail posta@kombank.com; internet www.kombank.com; f. 1970; Chair. VLADISLAV CVETKOVIĆ.

NLB Prishtina: 10000 Prishtina, Rruga Rexhep Luci 5; tel. (38) 234111; fax (38) 246189; e-mail info@nlbprishtina-kos.com; internet www.nlbprishtina-kos.com; f. Jan. 2008 by merger of NLB Kasabank and NLB New Bank of Kosova; 80.4% owned by NLB d.d.; cap. 20.5m., dep. 256.0m., total assets 298.4m. (Dec. 2009); Gen. Man. ALBERT LUMEZI.

ProCredit Bank Kosova: 10000 Prishtina, Nënë Terezë 16; tel. (38) 555777; fax (38) 555776; e-mail info@procreditbank-kos.com; internet www.procreditbank-kos.com; f. 2000 as Micro Enterprise Bank; present name adopted 2003; cap. 36.3m., res 3.5m., dep. 665.1m. (Dec. 2011); CEO ILIR I. ALIU.

Raiffeisen Bank Kosovo: Rruga UÇK 51; tel. (38) 222222; e-mail info@raiffeisen-kosovo.com; internet www.raiffeisen-kosovo.com; fmrly American Bank of Kosovo; acquired by Raiffeisen International (Austria) and name changed in 2003; cap. 58.0m., res 0.3m., dep. 548.6m. (Dec. 2009); Chair. and CEO BOGDAN MERFEA; 43 brs.

TEB sh. a.: 10000 Prishtina, Rruga Agim Ramadani 15; tel. (38) 230000; fax (38) 224699; e-mail info@teb-kos.com; internet www.teb-kos.com; f. Jan. 2008; joint venture of TEB (Turkey) and BNP Paribas (France); cap. 21.5m., dep. 184.0m., total assets 212.6m. (Dec. 2011).

INSURANCE

In early 2009 there were 14 registered insurance companies operating in Kosovo.

Croatia Sigurimi-Kosovo: 10000 Prishtina, Rruga Luan Haradinaj 5D; tel. (38) 246956; fax (38) 426957; e-mail ivopcro@yahoo.com; owned by Croatia Sigurimi (Croatia); Dir IVICA PEZO.

Dardania Kompania e Sigurimeve (Dardania Insurance Co): 10000 Prishtina, Rruga Sylejman Vokshi 4; tel. (38) 244080; fax (38) 244081; e-mail info@dardaniainsurance.com; internet www.dardaniainsurance.com; Dir RYZA LLUKA.

Elsig: 10000 Prishtina, Rruga e Trepçës 15; tel. (38) 221112; fax (38) 221115; e-mail office@kselsig.com; internet www.kselsig.com; f. 2008; non-life; Dir REXHEP IDRIZAJ.

Illyria Insurance Co: 10000 Prishtina, Nënë Terezë 33; tel. (38) 225385; fax (38) 225384; e-mail fatgashi@hotmail.com; Dir FATMIR GASHI.

Insig Kosovo: 10000 Prishtina, Mujo Ulqinaku, Pejton 6; tel. (38) 249900; fax (38) 249901; e-mail shberisha@insig-ks.com; Dir ILDA KEKEZI.

Kompania e Sigurimeve Illyria (Illyria Insurance Co): 10000 Prishtina, Sheshi Nënë Terezë 33; tel. (38) 225385; fax (38) 225384; e-mail info@illyriainsurance.com; internet www.illyriainsurance.com; f. 2002; 100% owned by Sava Re (Slovenia); Dir UROŠ LORENČIČ.

Kosova e Re Insurance Co (New Kosova Insurance Co): 10000 Prishtina, Lagja Kalabria 5/1B; tel. (38) 770777; fax (38) 770888;

e-mail info@kosovaere.com; internet www.kosovaere.com; f. 2002; owned by Kürüm Holding; Dir VISAR RRUSTEMI.

Sigal Kosove: 10000 Prishtina, Rruga Vaso Pasha; tel. and fax (38) 240241; e-mail info@sigal-ks.com; internet www.sigal-ks.com; f. 2003; owned by Uniqa Group Austria; five main brs in Prishtina, Prizren, Peja, Ferizaj and Gjilan; two sub-brs in Gjakova and Mitrovica; more than 50 agencies throughout Kosovo; Dir SOFO LIMAJ.

Sigkos: 10000 Prishtina, Rruga Sylejman Vokshi, Pallati i Kuq; tel. (38) 240022; fax (38) 240222; e-mail info@sigkos.com; internet www.sigkos.com; f. 2006; Dir IBRAHIM KASTRATI.

Sigma Kosovo: 10000 Prishtina, Qyteza Pejton, Rruga Pashko Vasa; tel. (38) 246301; fax (38) 246302; e-mail info@sigma-ks.net; internet www.sigma-ks.net; f. 2004; part of Vienna Insurance Gp; Dir ROLAND KACANI.

Siguria: 10000 Prishtina, Rruga Luan Haradinaj; tel. (38) 248848; fax (38) 248850; e-mail info@ks-siguria.com; internet www.ks-siguria.com; f. 2000; Dir RRAHIM PACOLLI.

Trade and Industry

GOVERNMENT AGENCIES

Investment Promotion Agency of Kosovo (IPAK): 10000 Prishtina, Rruga Muharrem Fejza; tel. (38) 20036527; fax (38) 212807; e-mail info@invest-ks.org; internet www.invest-ks.org; CEO VALDRIN LLUKA.

Privatization Agency of Kosovo: 10000 Prishtina, Rruga Ilir Konushevci 8; tel. (38) 500400; e-mail info@pak-ks.org; internet www.pak-ks.org; fmrly Kosovo Trust Agency, supervised by UNMIK; restructured as above in June 2008; Vice-Chair. and Dir HAXHI ARIFI.

CHAMBERS OF COMMERCE

American Chamber of Commerce: 10000 Prishtina, Fehmi Agani 36/3; tel. (38) 246012; fax (38) 248012; e-mail info@amchamksv.org; internet www.amchamksv.org; f. 2004; Exec. Dir VISAR BAJRA; 90 mem. cos.

Kosovo Chamber of Commerce (Oda Ekonomike e Kosovës): 10000 Prishtina, Rruga Nënë Terezë 20; tel. and fax (38) 224299; e-mail info@oek-kcc.org; internet www.oek-kcc.org; Pres. SAFET GËRXHALIU; Sec.-Gen. BERAT RUKIQI.

UTILITIES

Kosovo Energy Corpn (Korporata Energetike e Kosovës/Energetska Korporacija Kosova—KEK): 10000 Prishtina; e-mail komunikime@kek-energy.com; internet www.kek-energy.com; generation and distribution of electricity; Chair. FADIL ÇITAKU.

Prishtina Regional Water Company (Kompania Ujësjellësi Rajonal 'Prishtina'): 10000 Prishtina, Rruga Tahir Zajmi; tel. (38) 551010; e-mail info@kur-prishtina.com; internet www.kur-prishtina.com; f. 2007; offers services in central Kosovo, 550,000 customers (est.); Dir SKENDER BUBLAKU.

TRADE UNIONS

Union of Independent Trade Unions of Kosovo (BSPK) (Bashkimi i Sindikatave të Pavarura të Kosovës): 10000 Prishtina, Rruga Nënë Terezë 35; tel. and fax (38) 222859; e-mail info@bspk.org; internet www.bspk.org; 120,000 mems in 18 federations (2006); Chair. HAXHI ARIFI.

Transport

RAILWAYS

In 2005 there were 436 km of railways and 33 railway stations in operation in Kosovo.

Hekurudhat e Kosovës/Kosovske Železnice (Kosovo Railways): Fushë Kosovë, Sheshi i lirisë pn; tel. (38) 536355; fax (38) 536307; e-mail info@kosovorailway.com; internet www.kosovorailway.com; f. 2005 to replace UNMIK Railway; jt-stock co; operates railway services within Kosovo and international services to Skopje, former Yugoslav republic of Macedonia; Man. Dir XHEVAT RAMOSAJ.

ROADS

Kosovo's road network totalled 6,955 km in 2010 including 36 km of motorways; 26.02% of roads were paved.

CIVIL AVIATION

There is an international airport at Prishtina.

Defence

Under an agreement between the North Atlantic Treaty Organization (NATO) and the Federal Government, reached in June 1999, and a subsequent UN resolution, the NATO-led Kosovo Force (KFOR—with a maximum authorized strength of 50,000 personnel) was deployed in the province of Kosovo, and the UN Interim Administration Mission in Kosovo (UNMIK) was installed. In September, following the disarmament of the Kosovo Liberation Army paramilitary organization, the movement was reconstituted as a 5,000-member civil emergency security force, the Kosovo Protection Corps. After Kosovo's declaration of independence in February 2008, an EU Rule of Law Mission (EULEX Kosovo), comprising some 1,900 foreign personnel and 1,100 local staff, became operational under the overall authority of the UN in December. In August 2012 the mandate of EULEX was extended until mid-2014. In January 2009 the Kosovo Protection Corps was dissolved and a new, multi-ethnic, Kosovo Security Force was launched, with 2,500 active members, plus 800 reserves. A reduced UNMIK presence was to continue in the country indefinitely under UN Resolution 1244. At the end of December 2010 UNMIK comprised 418 personnel. At January 2013 5,134 multi-national KFOR troops, led by NATO, were maintaining security, in support of Kosovo's institutions.

Commander of KFOR: Maj.-Gen. VOLKER HALBAUER.

Education

Responsibility for education was transferred to the Ministry of Education, Science and Technology in 2002. The system of compulsory education was extended from eight to nine years in 2003/04. The education system comprises a five-year period of primary education, beginning at seven years, and two cycles of secondary education, lasting four years and three years, respectively. The higher education system operates through two state universities, the University of Prishtina, and the University of Mitrovica; a total of 35,910 students were enrolled in higher education in 2010/11.

KUWAIT

Introductory Survey

LOCATION, CLIMATE, LANGUAGE, RELIGION, FLAG, CAPITAL

The State of Kuwait lies at the north-west extreme of the Persian (Arabian) Gulf, bordered to the north-west by Iraq and to the south by Saudi Arabia. The state comprises a mainland region and nine small islands, of which the largest is Bubiyan and the most populous is Failaka. Immediately to the south of Kuwait, along the Gulf, lies a Neutral (Partitioned) Zone of 5,700 sq km, which is shared between Kuwait and Saudi Arabia. Much of Kuwait is arid desert, and the climate is generally hot and humid. Temperatures in July and August often exceed 45°C (113°F), and in the winter months are frequently above 20°C (68°F)—although there is often frost at night. Average annual rainfall is only 111 mm. The official language is Arabic, which is spoken by the majority of Kuwaiti nationals (estimated to have comprised 32.1% of Kuwait's population in 2011) and by many of the country's non-Kuwaiti residents. Apart from other Arabs, the non-Kuwaitis are mainly Iranians, Indians and Pakistanis. The majority of Kuwaitis are Muslims, around 70% of whom are thought to belong to the Sunni sect. The national flag (proportions 1 by 2) has three equal horizontal stripes, of green, white and red, with a superimposed black trapezoid at the hoist. The capital is Kuwait City.

CONTEMPORARY POLITICAL HISTORY

Historical Context

Kuwait became part of Turkey's Ottoman Empire in the 16th century. During the later years of Ottoman rule Kuwait became a semi-autonomous Arab monarchy, with local administration controlled by a Sheikh of the al-Sabah family, which is still the ruling dynasty. In 1899, fearing an extension of Turkish control, the ruler of Kuwait made a treaty with the United Kingdom, accepting British protection while surrendering control over external relations. Nominal Turkish suzerainty over Kuwait ended in 1918, with the dissolution of the Ottoman Empire.

Petroleum was first discovered in Kuwait in 1938, but exploration was interrupted by the Second World War (1939–45). After 1945 drilling resumed on a large scale, and extensive deposits of petroleum were found. Sheikh Ahmad (ruler since 1921) was succeeded in 1950 by his cousin, Sheikh Abdullah al-Salim al-Sabah, who inaugurated a programme of public works and educational development, funded by petroleum revenues, which transformed Kuwait's infrastructure and introduced a comprehensive system of welfare services.

Domestic Political Affairs

Kuwait became fully independent on 19 June 1961, when the United Kingdom and Kuwait agreed to terminate the 1899 treaty. The ruler took the title of Amir and assumed full executive power. Kuwait was admitted to the League of Arab States (the Arab League, see p. 372) despite opposition from Iraq, which claimed that Kuwait was historically part of Iraqi territory. Kuwait's first election took place in December 1961, when voters chose 20 members of a Constituent Assembly (the other members being government ministers appointed by the Amir). The Assembly drafted a new Constitution, which was adopted in December 1962. A 50-member Majlis al-Umma (National Assembly) was elected, under a limited franchise, in January 1963. In the absence of formal political parties (which remain illegal), candidates contested the poll as independents, although some known opponents of the Government were elected. In the same month the Amir appointed his brother, Sheikh Sabah al-Salim al-Sabah (the heir apparent), to be Prime Minister. Iraq renounced its claim to Kuwait in October, and diplomatic relations between the two countries were established.

In January 1965, following conflict between the paternalistic ruling family and the democratically inclined Majlis, the powers of the Council of Ministers were strengthened. The Amir died in November 1965, and Sheikh Sabah succeeded to the throne. He was replaced as Prime Minister by his cousin, Sheikh Jaber al-Ahmad al-Sabah, who was named heir apparent in May 1966.

The Neutral (Partitioned) Zone between Kuwait and Saudi Arabia was formally divided between the two countries in 1969: revenues from oil production in the area are shared equally.

As Kuwait's petroleum sector expanded during the 1960s, the country became increasingly wealthy. The Government effected an extensive redistribution of income, through public expenditure and a land compensation scheme, but there was some popular discontent concerning corruption, and official manipulation of the media and the Majlis. A more representative legislature was elected in January 1971 (again under a limited franchise). A further general election took place in January 1975, but in August 1976 the Amir dissolved the Majlis, on the grounds that it was acting against the best interests of the state. Sheikh Sabah died in December 1977 and was succeeded by Crown Prince Jaber. In January 1978 the new Amir appointed Sheikh Saad al-Abdullah al-Salim al-Sabah to be his heir apparent. The new Crown Prince, hitherto Minister of Defence and the Interior, became Prime Minister in the following month. In accordance with an Amiri decree of August 1980, a new Majlis was elected in February 1981, although only one-half of the eligible 6% of the population registered to vote.

The collapse of Kuwait's unofficial stock exchange, the Souk al-Manakh, in September 1982 caused a prolonged financial crisis, and eventually led to the resignations of the Ministers of Finance (in 1983) and of Justice (in 1985). The Majlis subsequently opposed several government measures, including proposed price increases for public services, educational reforms and legislation to restrict the press, and questioned the competence of certain ministers. In July 1986 the Council of Ministers submitted its resignation to the Amir, who then dissolved the Majlis and suspended some articles of the Constitution, declaring his intention to rule by decree. The Crown Prince was immediately reappointed Prime Minister. An Amiri decree accorded the Council of Ministers greater powers of censorship, including the right to suspend publication of newspapers for up to two years.

In late 1989 the Amir refused to accept a petition, signed by more than 20,000 Kuwaiti citizens, seeking the restoration of the Majlis. In January 1990 police dispersed two pro-democracy demonstrations, although later in the month the Government agreed to relax press censorship. In June 62% of eligible voters participated in a general election for 50 members of a 'provisional' National Council; a further 25 members were appointed by the Amir. The election was boycotted by pro-democracy activists, who continued to demand the full restoration of the Majlis.

Relations between Kuwait and Iraq were stable until 1973, when Iraqi troops occupied a Kuwaiti outpost on their joint border. Kuwait none the less supplied aid to Iraq from the outbreak of the Iran–Iraq War in 1980. As a result, Kuwaiti petroleum installations and shipping in the Persian (Arabian) Gulf were targeted intermittently by Iranian forces, and by pro-Iranian groups within Kuwait, for much of the 1980s. A large number of Iranians were among 27,000 expatriates deported in 1985–86, and in 1987 the Government initiated a five-year plan to reduce the number of expatriates in the Kuwaiti work-force. Kuwait resumed diplomatic relations with Iran following the 1988 cease-fire between Iran and Iraq.

Iraqi invasion of Kuwait

In July 1990 the Iraqi Government implicitly criticized Kuwait (among other states) for disregarding the petroleum production quotas stipulated by the Organization of the Petroleum Exporting Countries (OPEC, see p. 418). It also declared that Kuwait should cancel Iraq's war debt and compensate it for losses of revenue incurred during the war with Iran, and as a result of Kuwait's overproduction of petroleum—to which Iraq attributed a decline in international oil prices. In addition, Iraq alleged that Kuwait had established military posts and drilled oil wells on Iraqi territory. Despite regional mediation efforts, Iraq subsequently began to deploy armed forces on the Kuwait–Iraq border. Direct negotiations in Jeddah, Saudi Arabia, at the end of the month between Kuwaiti and Iraqi officials collapsed, and on 2 August some 100,000 Iraqi troops invaded Kuwait (the total military strength of which was about 20,000): Iraq stated that it had entered at the invitation of insurgents who had overthrown the Kuwaiti Government. The Amir and other government members fled to Saudi Arabia, where they established a 'Government-in-exile', while Iraq declared that a provisional Government had been formed in Kuwait comprising Iraqi-sponsored Kuwaiti dissidents. The UN Security Council immediately adopted a series of resolutions, of which the first (Resolution 660) condemned the invasion, demanded the immediate and unconditional withdrawal of Iraqi forces from Kuwait, and appealed for a negotiated settlement of the conflict. A trade embargo was then imposed on Iraq and Kuwait. Meanwhile, the USA and member states of the European Community (now European Union—EU, see p. 281) froze all Kuwait's overseas assets to prevent their repatriation. Five days after the invasion US troops and aircraft were deployed in Saudi Arabia, with the stated aim of securing that country's borders with Kuwait in the event of further Iraqi territorial expansion. A number of European governments, together with some Arab League states, agreed to provide military support for the US forces. The Iraqi Government subsequently announced the formal annexation of Kuwait, and ordered the closure of foreign diplomatic missions there. At the end of August most of Kuwait was officially declared to be the 19th Governorate of Iraq, while a northern strip was incorporated into the Basra Governorate.

In the months following the invasion apparent attempts at demographic manipulation—by settling Iraqis and Palestinians in Kuwait and by forcing Kuwaitis to assume Iraqi citizenship—were documented. The population was estimated to have decreased from approximately 2m. prior to the invasion to some 700,000, of whom Kuwaitis constituted about 300,000, Palestinians 200,000, and the remainder comprised other Arab and Asian expatriates. Many Kuwaitis, and Arab and Asian expatriates, had fled Iraq and Kuwait into Jordan, while most European and US expatriates were temporarily detained as hostages.

UN Security Council Resolution 678, adopted in November 1990, authorized the multinational force by now stationed in Saudi Arabia and the Gulf region to use 'all necessary means' to liberate Kuwait. It was implied that should Iraq not begin, by 15 January 1991, to implement the terms of 10 resolutions hitherto adopted regarding the invasion, military action would ensue. Renewed international diplomatic attempts failed to avert a military confrontation. On the night of 16–17 January the US-led multinational force launched an intensive aerial bombardment of Iraq. Ground forces entered Kuwait during the night of 23–24 February, encountering relatively little effective Iraqi opposition. Within three days the Iraqi Government had agreed to comply with the terms of all Security Council resolutions concerning Kuwait, and on 28 February the USA announced a suspension of military operations. Resolutions 686 and 687, adopted by the UN Security Council in March and April, respectively, dictated the terms to Iraq for a permanent ceasefire: Iraq was required to release all allied prisoners of war and Kuwaitis detained as hostages, repeal all laws and decrees concerning the annexation of Kuwait, and recognize the inviolability of the Iraq–Kuwait border. Iraq promptly announced its compliance with both resolutions. Resolution 689, adopted in April, provided for the establishment of a demilitarized zone, to be supervised by a UN Iraq-Kuwait Observation Mission (UNIKOM).

Meanwhile, in October 1990, at a conference in Jeddah of some 1,000 prominent Kuwaitis, the exiled Crown Prince Saad agreed to establish government advisory committees on political, social and financial matters, and pledged to restore the country's Constitution and legislature and to organize free elections after Kuwait's eventual liberation. In February 1991, however, the Government-in-exile excluded the possibility of early elections, maintaining that the need to rebuild and repopulate the country took precedence over that for political reform. Immediately following liberation an Amiri decree imposed martial law in Kuwait, and in March the formation of a state security committee was announced: its objectives included the investigation of individuals suspected of collaboration with the Iraqi authorities in Kuwait, the prevention of unofficial acts of reprisal and the identification of those civilians relocated to Kuwait by Iraq. Palestinians in Kuwait were a particular target of reprisals, and it was alleged by several human rights organizations that they were subject to torture by Kuwaiti security forces. Kuwait's Palestinian population, which had totalled around 400,000 prior

to the Iraqi invasion, was estimated to have declined to less than 50,000 by early 1992.

The Amir, the Prime Minister and other members of the exiled regime returned to Kuwait in March 1991. The Council of Ministers resigned later that month, apparently in response to public discontent at the Government's failure to restore essential services. Although several specialists were appointed to strategic posts within the new Government named by Sheikh Saad in April (most notably to the finance, planning and oil portfolios), other important positions (including the foreign affairs, interior and defence ministries) were allocated to members of the al-Sabah family.

In May 1991 it was revealed that some 900 people were under investigation in Kuwait in connection with crimes committed during the Iraqi occupation; about 200 of these were accused of collaboration. The Government undertook to investigate alleged abuses documented by the human rights organization Amnesty International, which claimed that trials were being conducted without the provision of adequate defence counsel and that in some cases torture had been used to extract confessions. Martial law was ended in June, and 29 death sentences hitherto imposed on convicted collaborators were commuted to custodial terms. Outstanding trials relating to the occupation were to be referred to civilian courts, and in August a tribunal, said to guarantee defendants the right to greater legal protection as well as a right of appeal, was established to replace the martial law courts.

It was announced in August 1991 that the USA would maintain 1,500 troops in Kuwait for several more months, after little progress had been achieved in negotiations for the establishment of a regional defence force. In September the US and Kuwaiti Governments signed a 10-year military co-operation agreement, permitting the storage of US supplies and equipment in Kuwait, and providing for joint military training and exercises. (The agreement was renewed for a further 10 years in February 2001 and was presumed to have been renewed again in 2011, although no specific announcement was made by the US Department of Defense.) Defence accords were signed with both the United Kingdom and France in 1992.

In June 1993 the State Security Court was reported to have issued death sentences against 17 people who had been found guilty of collaborating with Iraq in 1990–91; Alaa Hussein Ali, the leader of the provisional Government installed by Iraq in August 1990, was convicted *in absentia*. In February 1994 Amnesty International asserted that at least 120 alleged collaborators had been convicted by trials that failed to satisfy international minimum standards. Human rights organizations therefore welcomed the endorsement by the Majlis, in August 1995, of government proposals to abolish the State Security Court. In January 1997 the Government announced the creation of a new human rights committee within the Ministry of the Interior.

Political developments following the Gulf War

Elections to the new Majlis, on 5 October 1992, were contested by some 280 candidates, many of whom (although nominally independent) were affiliated to one of several quasi-political organizations. The franchise was again restricted, with only about 81,400 men eligible to vote. Anti-Government candidates, notably those representing Islamist groups, were unexpectedly successful, securing 31 of the chamber's 50 seats. The Prime Minister subsequently formed a new Government, including six members of the Majlis, who were allocated, *inter alia*, the oil and justice portfolios; members of the ruling family retained control of foreign affairs, the interior and defence.

The Majlis voted in December 1992 to establish a commission of inquiry into the circumstances surrounding the 1990 invasion. The commission's report, published in May 1995, revealed profound negligence on the part of government and military officials, who had apparently ignored warnings of an imminent invasion. The report also claimed that the immediate flight of members of the royal family and the Council of Ministers had deprived the country of political leadership and military organization.

In June 1994 the Majlis approved legislation extending the franchise to sons of naturalized Kuwaitis, and in July 1995 it approved a bill reducing from 30 years to 20 the minimum period after which naturalized Kuwaitis would become eligible to vote. In July 1996 the Ministry of the Interior announced that an electorate of just over 107,000 men was entitled to vote in the forthcoming elections to the Majlis, scheduled for 7 October. Pro-Government candidates were the most successful, securing the majority of the 50 seats, and Sheikh Saad was reappointed Prime Minister.

Sheikh Saad submitted his Government's resignation in March 1998, after members of the Majlis proposed a motion of no confidence in the Minister of Information, Sheikh Sa'ud Nasir al-Sa'ud al-Sabah, who had allowed what were deemed 'un-Islamic' publications to be exhibited at a book fair in Kuwait. The Amir immediately reappointed the Crown Prince as Prime Minister, and a new Government was named at the end of the month. Despite the recent action against him, Sheikh Sa'ud was promoted to the post of Minister of Oil.

In May 1999 the Amir dissolved the Majlis and ordered fresh elections, after deputies had in the previous month questioned the Minister of Justice and of Awqaf (Religious Endowments) and Islamic Affairs over errors that had appeared in copies of the Koran printed and distributed by his ministry. At the election, which took place on 3 July, pro-Government candidates recorded the greatest losses, taking only 12 seats; Islamist candidates won 20 seats and liberals 14, with the remaining four seats going to independents. Sheikh Saad was again reappointed Prime Minister, and the ruling family retained control of the strategic foreign affairs, oil, interior and defence portfolios, although a number of liberal deputies joined the Government.

Alaa Hussein Ali, who had been in self-imposed exile since Kuwait's liberation, returned to Kuwait in January 2000 in order to appeal against the death sentence pronounced in June 1993 (see above). In May 2000 it was announced that Hussein had lost his appeal at the Court of First Instance, and that he planned a further challenge to his sentence. The Court of Appeal upheld the previous ruling in July, but in March 2001 commuted Hussein's death sentence to one of life imprisonment.

In July 2000 unrest was reported in the Al-Jahra region, where a community of *bidoun* ('stateless' Arabs) form the majority of the population. (About 100,000 *bidoun* reside in Kuwait, but the authorities refuse to recognize their claims to Kuwaiti nationality.) The unrest followed the approval, in May, of a draft amendment to the Citizenship Law that would grant only a small number of *bidoun* the right to Kuwaiti citizenship. Some 1,000 *bidoun* obtained citizenship in early 2001, leading to protests by those whose applications had been refused.

Sheikh Saad tendered his Government's resignation in January 2001. The Crown Prince denied that this constituted an attempt to prevent parliamentary scrutiny of the Minister of Justice and of Awqaf and Islamic Affairs, Saad Jasem Yousuf al-Hashil, relating to allegations of inefficiency and corruption in his ministry. The Amir immediately reappointed Sheikh Saad as Prime Minister, and a new Government was named in February.

In January 2002 four people died following a major explosion at Raudhatain, Kuwait's second largest oilfield, to the north of Kuwait City. Dr Adil Khalid al-Sabih immediately submitted his resignation as Minister of Oil, and was replaced in an acting capacity by the Minister of Information, Sheikh Ahmad al-Fahd al-Ahmad al-Sabah. Meanwhile, several members of the increasingly assertive Majlis demanded the resignation of the entire Government, alleging that the explosion at Raudhatain was the result of state corruption and mismanagement.

After a campaign that was overshadowed by the US-led military intervention in Iraq (which was largely conducted from Kuwaiti territory), parliamentary elections were held, as scheduled, on 5 July 2003. Islamist candidates secured 21 of the 50 seats in the Majlis, while pro-Government candidates won 14 seats, independents (regarded as being aligned with the Government) 12 and liberals three.

Sheikh Sabah appointed Prime Minister

Following the elections, in July 2003 the ailing Crown Prince relinquished the position of Prime Minister. The appointment of Sheikh Sabah al-Ahmad al-Sabah as his replacement represented an unprecedented separation between the post of Prime Minister and the position of Crown Prince, and provided some encouragement to reformists after their heavy electoral losses. A new Council of Ministers was also announced in mid-July.

In October 2003 and May 2004 the Council of Ministers approved legislation that would permit women to vote in and contest municipal and parliamentary elections, respectively. The Majlis gave provisional approval for the former piece of legislation in April 2005, but subsequently failed to ratify the legislation at a second vote in May. Both new laws were approved later in the month. In April 2005 the Minister of Health, Muhammad Ahmad al-Jarallah, became the third member of the Council of Ministers to resign in connection with hostile parliamentary questioning since the elections to the Majlis in

July 2003 (the Ministers of Finance and of Information having stood down in March 2004 and January 2005, respectively). In June the Prime Minister appointed Dr Massouma Saleh al-Mubarak as Minister of Planning and Minister of State for Administrative Development Affairs, making her Kuwait's first female member of the Council of Ministers.

The accession of Sheikh Sabah

On 15 January 2006 the death of the Amir, Sheikh Jaber, was announced. He was automatically succeeded by the Crown Prince, Sheikh Saad. However, in an unprecedented development, on 24 January Sheikh Saad, who had yet to take the oath of office, was removed from the position of Amir on health grounds, following a formal request from the Council of Ministers that the Majlis debate the issue. The parliamentary vote in favour of replacing Sheikh Saad was unanimous. In the absence of a nominated Crown Prince, the Prime Minister, Sheikh Sabah, who was in any case regarded as the de facto ruler of the emirate, temporarily assumed the powers of the Amir. After his nomination as a permanent head of state by the Council of Ministers had been unanimously approved by the Majlis, Sheikh Sabah was duly sworn in as Amir on 29 January. The sole controversy attached to Sheikh Sabah's accession was that, like the late Sheikh Jaber, he belonged to the al-Jaber branch of the ruling al-Sabah family, which, by tradition, alternated the position of Amir with the al-Salim branch of the family, of which Sheikh Saad was a member.

The new Amir accepted the resignation of the Council of Ministers in January 2006. In February Sheikh Sabah appointed his nephew, former diplomat Sheikh Nasser al-Muhammad al-Ahmad al-Sabah, as the new Prime Minister, and his brother, Sheikh Nawwaf al-Ahmad al-Jaber al-Sabah, as Crown Prince. The appointments, which maintained the post-2003 separation between the roles of premier and Crown Prince, emphasized the channelling of power towards the al-Jaber branch of the ruling family, although both men possessed extensive political experience. Later that month the Amir approved Sheikh Nasser's first Council of Ministers; a notable change was the addition of the interior portfolio to the responsibilities of the Minister of Defence, Sheikh Jaber Mubarak al-Hamad al-Sabah, who also became First Deputy Prime Minister.

A long-running campaign for electoral reform, which sought to reduce the number of electoral constituencies in Kuwait in order to diminish the opportunities for vote-buying, began to attract extensive popular support from May 2006. A proposal by the Government to reduce the number of constituencies from 25 to 10 was rejected by the opposition, which advocated a more comprehensive reduction, to just five constituencies. Following efforts by the Majlis to cross-examine the Prime Minister on the matter, the Amir dissolved parliament and called for elections to be held at the end of June. A loose alliance of 29 pro-reform members of the outgoing legislature was formed to contest the elections, comprising candidates from across the political spectrum. Reformists made significant gains at the polls, winning 34 of the 50 seats contested. The remaining 16 seats were won by independents and pro-Government candidates. A reform bill drafted by the new Majlis proposing the introduction of a five-constituency electoral system was passed into law in July. Also that month a new Council of Ministers was named under Prime Minister Sheikh Nasser.

In December 2006 the Minister of Information, Muhammad Nasser al-Sanousi, resigned following a request by the increasingly confrontational Majlis to question him over allegations that he had curbed media freedom during the recent election campaign. In February 2007 deputies cross-examined the Minister of Health, Sheikh Ahmad Abdullah al-Ahmad al-Sabah, on charges related to the deteriorating state of the health service. However, in early March, one day before the Majlis was due to debate a motion of no confidence in the minister, the entire Council of Ministers resigned. Sheikh Ahmad was excluded from the new, largely unchanged Government that was approved by the Amir in late March. The reorganization also included the division of the recently created Ministry of Energy into the Ministry of Oil and the Ministry of Electricity and Water. In June Sheikh Ali al-Jarrah al-Sabah resigned as Minister of Oil; the Majlis had been scheduled to debate a motion of no confidence in the minister after having questioned him over allegations of corruption. In October Prime Minister Sheikh Nasser instigated an extensive reorganization of the Council of Ministers. New appointments included Sheikh Jaber Khalid al-Jaber al-Sabah as Minister of the Interior, Bader Mishari al-Humaidhi as Minister of Oil and Mustafa Jassem al-Shamali as Minister of Finance. However, in

November al-Humaidhi resigned amid continuing controversy relating to his previous role as Minister of Finance.

In January 2008 the liberal Minister of Education, Nouriya al-Subeeh, survived a no-confidence vote in the Majlis, following an interrogation by Islamist and tribal deputies. The fact that political infighting was increasingly damaging Kuwait's prospects for economic and social development was said to be causing growing frustration among the population. In mid-March the entire Council of Ministers resigned, stating that relations with the Majlis had become untenable, and that the legislature was continuing to obstruct ministers' attempts to carry out their duties effectively. The immediate cause of the crisis involved a dispute concerning salary increases for state employees, with deputies asserting that the pay rise was too low. Having cut short a visit to Morocco, Sheikh Sabah ordered the dissolution of the Majlis in order for fresh elections to take place in May. The elections would be the first to use the five-constituency system adopted into law in July 2006.

Meanwhile, in February 2008 tensions increased between Sunni and Shi'a Muslims in the emirate after several hundred people from the minority Shi'a community had held a rally to commemorate the death of a senior commander of the militant Shi'a organization Hezbollah in Lebanon. Imad Mughniyeh, who had been killed earlier that month in a bomb attack in the Syrian capital, Damascus, was described by the Kuwaiti Government as a 'terrorist'. It was claimed that Mughniyeh had been responsible for the hijacking of a Kuwait Airways plane in 1988, in which two Kuwaiti passengers were murdered. A number of prominent Shi'a politicians and clerics were questioned by the authorities over their involvement in the rally, and many arrests were reported; In October 2008 it was reported that two prominent Shi'a members of the Majlis were among seven people acquitted by a court in Kuwait for their alleged membership of an illegal opposition group, Hezbollah Kuwait.

Escalating tension between the Majlis and the Government following the election of May 2008

At the legislative election held on 17 May 2008, Islamist candidates performed strongly, with Sunni Islamists winning 21 of the 50 seats in the Majlis and Shi'ite Islamists (including the Popular Action Bloc) nine; liberals and their allies garnered seven and the remaining 13 seats were won by independents. In spite of opposition from several parliamentarians, the Amir subsequently reappointed Sheikh Nasser to the post of Prime Minister. In late May Sheikh Nasser appointed a new Council of Ministers, which included two women. At the first session of the new Majlis, held in June, a number of members withdrew in protest against the composition of the new Government, in which many previous incumbents retained their posts.

In July 2008 hundreds of Bangladeshi workers protested about low and irregular wages and poor working conditions. The demonstration, which followed several similar ones in recent months, turned violent, and the police reportedly arrested and subsequently deported some 1,000 of the protesters. The incident reignited international discussion of Kuwait's human rights record. The Council of Ministers subsequently announced that it would introduce a minimum monthly wage of KD 40 (US $150) for workers employed by companies contracted by the Government. In October the Government announced its intention to draft legislation abolishing its much-criticized employee sponsorship system (which stipulates that foreign workers must be sponsored by a Kuwaiti employer); however, a package of labour market reforms aimed at improving the conditions of expatriate workers approved by the Majlis in December did not address this system. Although the Government pledged in December 2010 to terminate the system during 2011, it remained in place in early 2013. In early March the Government was reported to have proposed a new system whereby foreigners employed in Kuwait's private sector would henceforth be employed directly by the Ministry of Social Affairs and Labour; it was unclear precisely when such a reform would be implemented.

Meanwhile, parliamentarians continued to express disquiet over the Prime Minister's handling of the Government and his alleged mismanagement of public funds. In early November 2008 three Sunni Islamist members of the Majlis submitted a request to question Sheikh Nasser over the decision to allow the controversial Iranian Shi'a cleric, Muhammad Baqer al-Fali, to visit Kuwait (al-Fali had been banned from entering Kuwait after being convicted of religious slurs that had offended Sunni Muslims and of 'threatening national unity'). To avert parliamentary questioning of the Prime Minister, on 25 November the entire Council of Ministers resigned. The Amir accepted its resignation on 1 December, and on 12 January 2009 approved the formation of a new, largely unchanged Government under Sheikh Nasser. Several deputies walked out of the opening parliamentary session in protest at the lack of new appointments. Moreover, in February some asserted that the nomination of Sheikh Ahmad Abdullah al-Ahmad al-Sabah as Minister of Oil was unconstitutional, given that he had been subject to a motion of no confidence in his capacity as Minister of Health two years previously.

In March 2009 several Islamist members of the legislature sought to question the Prime Minister about allegations of mismanagement, misuse of public funds and the failure to adapt economic policy to the worsening global financial climate. The continued refusal by Sheikh Nasser to submit to scrutiny precipitated the resignation of the entire Council of Ministers in mid-March, as a result of which the Amir ordered the dissolution of parliament; fresh elections were subsequently called for May. Meanwhile, in late March the outgoing Government finally approved a programme of economic stimulus, envisaging expenditure of up to US $5,200m. to support Kuwait's beleaguered financial markets. The initiative was ratified by the Amir and entered into effect in April.

An estimated 59% of eligible voters participated in parliamentary elections on 16 May 2009: Sunni Islamists retained only 11 seats in the 50-member Majlis, losing out to Shi'ite Islamists (who won nine seats) and liberals (eight seats), with the balance gained by the tribal-based independents. For the first time since women were allowed to participate in electoral politics in 2005, four female candidates were successful. Sheikh Nasser was reappointed Prime Minister and a new Council of Ministers was named in late May 2009.

Political events after the 2009 elections

In his speech at the inaugural session of the new legislature in late May 2009, the Amir stressed the urgent need for renewed co-operation at all levels of government in order to safeguard national unity and promote economic development. However, the session was boycotted by 14 Islamist and tribal deputies in protest at the composition of the new Council of Ministers. Several Islamist deputies also lodged objections against the presence of Dr Moudhi Abd al-Aziz al-Homoud, the Minister of Education and Higher Education, and two female members of parliament, who declined to wear the *hijab* (Islamic headscarf) during the opening session, accusing them of violating legislation requiring women to adhere to *Shari'a* (Islamic) law. Tensions between the Majlis and the Council of Ministers thus resumed immediately, with the conduct and performance of the ministers responsible for defence, finance and the interior being severely criticized by deputies in June.

In an unprecedented move, on 8 December 2009 Prime Minister Sheikh Nasser agreed to submit himself to formal scrutiny by members of parliament, concerning allegations of misuse of public funds; similar motions were lodged against three other senior government ministers. Following the interrogation of the Prime Minister and the Ministers of Defence, the Interior, and Public Works and Municipal Affairs in a closed parliamentary session on 9 December, 10 deputies proposed a motion of non-co-operation against Sheikh Nasser; a motion of no confidence was lodged against Sheikh Jaber, the Minister of the Interior. The Prime Minister comfortably survived the vote against him, which was conducted in the Majlis on 16 December. The no-confidence motion against Sheikh Jaber was also defeated on the same day.

Despite the ongoing tensions between the executive and the legislature, a four-year economic development plan proposed by the Government received parliamentary support in February 2010, and was duly implemented in April. In May the Majlis approved legislation allowing the privatization of certain state assets—excluding the production of petroleum and natural gas, oil refineries and the health and education sectors—but stipulating that all privatized companies should be *Shari'a*-compliant.

Human rights issues continued to be a source of considerable anti-Government sentiment throughout 2010. In April Muhammad Abd al-Qader al-Jassem, a prominent Kuwaiti journalist, author and former editor of *Al-Watan* newspaper, was convicted of criticizing government policy and defaming Prime Minister Sheikh Nasser; he was sentenced to six months' imprisonment and ordered to pay a fine of US $17,500. In May al-Jassem, who had remained free pending an appeal, was ordered to be detained for further investigation into new charges, including inciting the overthrow of the Government, undermining the status of the Amir and damaging national interests. The charges were all reported to have been brought in response to criticism of Sheikh Nasser and the Government made by al-Jassem in three books on Kuwaiti politics, as well as articles posted on his internet site. Opposition and human rights groups urged the authorities to release al-Jassem, the charges against whom, they argued, were politically motivated. Al-Jassem, who had begun a hunger strike in protest against his detention, was released on bail in June, amid concerns about his health.

Al-Jassem's conviction for defaming the Prime Minister was overturned on appeal in July 2010, and later that month he was acquitted of further charges of defamation, as well as the charges of inciting the overthrow of the Government and undermining the status of the Amir. However, in the same month the Prime Minister and Minister of Information declared that public criticism of the Amir, Prime Minister, government ministers and countries with which Kuwait enjoyed close relations constituted a threat to national unity, and announced that the Government intended to amend the press and publications law accordingly. In November al-Jassem was convicted on a further charge of defaming the Prime Minister and was sentenced to one year's imprisonment; in the following month this was reduced to three months. Although al-Jassem was released in January 2011, after the Supreme Court overturned his original conviction, a new series of similar charges was levelled against the writer at the end of that month. In October 2012 the Ministry of Foreign Affairs threatened to take legal action against al-Jassem (who was acting as the lawyer of former Majlis deputy Musallam al-Barrak—see Recent Developments), after he was accused of damaging the close diplomatic relations between Kuwait and both Saudi Arabia and the United Arab Emirates (UAE) by comments he had made in a recent blog concerning their 'unacceptable interference' in Kuwait's domestic affairs.

Further claims that the Government was intent on suppressing freedom of expression were provoked by its decision to shut down the local offices of the Qatar-based broadcaster *Al Jazeera* in mid-December 2010, accusing it of interference in Kuwait's internal affairs. A few days previously *Al Jazeera* had broadcast video footage that purported to show Kuwaiti security forces using excessive force to disperse people attending an opposition rally earlier that month. At least 14 people, including four parliamentary deputies, were reported to have been injured in the resulting clashes. In late December a motion of non co-operation was filed against Sheikh Nasser by members of a broad-based opposition grouping within the Majlis, which blamed the Prime Minister for the violence, claiming that the authorities' heavy-handed response had represented an attempt to intimidate dissenters. Sheikh Nasser again survived the motion, voting on which was conducted in early January 2011; however, unlike in December 2009, the motion against the Prime Minister was only narrowly defeated.

Opposition members thus pledged to continue to fight for the removal from office of the Prime Minister and Government, and tensions continued to escalate. On 6 February 2011 the resignation of Deputy Prime Minister and Minister of the Interior, Sheikh Jaber, was accepted; he had resigned from office on 13 January in advance of parliamentary questioning over allegations that a man arrested by police in that month had been tortured to death while in custody. Sheikh Jaber was immediately replaced by Sheikh Ahmad Homoud al-Jaber al-Sabah. In early March a number of youth opposition groups began protests in the capital demanding the resignation of Sheikh Nasser and reform of the political system; the pro-democracy rallies mirrored similar ones taking place across much of the Arab world, having initially begun in Tunisia at the end of 2010. Later in March 2011 parliamentarians filed requests to interrogate (in addition to the Prime Minister) the Minister of Oil and Information, the Deputy Prime Minister for Economic Affairs and Minister of State for Development Affairs and for Housing Affairs, and the Deputy Prime Minister and Minister of Foreign Affairs, all of whom were members of the ruling family. The first two ministers were required to submit to questioning related to allegations of corruption and financial mismanagement, while the third was to be questioned over his perceived weak response to a broadcast by Bahraini state television which was deemed to be critical of Kuwait and its ruling family. On 1 April the Amir accepted the resignation of the Council of Ministers, which had been announced the previous day by the Prime Minister.

However, on 5 April 2011 Sheikh Nasser was reappointed as Prime Minister and instructed to form his seventh government since assuming the premiership in 2006. The new Council of Ministers was appointed on 8 May 2011 and sworn in two days later. Members of the ruling family again retained the key foreign affairs, interior and defence portfolios.

Meanwhile, in late February 2011 Kuwaiti security forces had acted forcefully to bring to an end anti-Government protests being held by groups of *bidoun* in Al-Jahra and elsewhere against their continued failure to secure certain basic rights, principally the right to gain Kuwaiti citizenship; a number of the demonstrators were detained by the authorities. Further unrest occurred in Al-Jahra in March, after it was revealed that the passage through the Majlis of draft legislation that would grant basic entitlements to the *bidoun*, such as free provision of medical and educational services, had been blocked by the Government. In early December legal proceedings began against 52 of those who had participated in the protests, the charges against whom included holding illegal public gatherings and attacking security forces. Renewed protests were held by stateless Arabs in Al-Jahra in that month, leading to further arrests. Nevertheless, in late December the head of the government agency concerned with *bidoun* affairs pledged to consider granting citizenship to around 34,000 of the stateless provided that they fulfilled certain eligibility criteria. A bill allowing up to 4,000 foreigners to gain Kuwaiti citizenship during 2013, adopted by the Majlis in March of that year, was widely expected to be used to naturalize a further group of stateless Arabs; the bill was awaiting the endorsement of Sheikh Sabah.

On 10 May 2011, when his new Council of Ministers was inaugurated, Prime Minister Sheikh Nasser was again asked by opposition members of the Majlis to answer questions relating to several issues, among them his management of Kuwait's four-year economic development plan and his alleged involvement in corrupt practices. A week later, however, parliament agreed to allow a postponement of Sheikh Nasser's interrogation until May 2012, while the Constitutional Court examined the Prime Minister's case. A further demonstration by opposition activists calling for the resignation of the Prime Minister and his administration was held in front of the parliament building on 27 May 2011. On 13 June the Deputy Prime Minister and Minister for Housing Affairs, Sheikh Ahmad Fahad al-Sabah, resigned from the Government, reportedly as the result of a disagreement with the premier. Sheikh Ahmad, who had been responsible for leading the Government's 'mega projects' strategy, had stated that a request for a group of Majlis deputies to question him over claims of corruption and mismanagement was unconstitutional.

As the opposition continued to increase their pressure on the Council of Ministers, in a private session held on 14 June 2011 Prime Minister Sheikh Nasser was questioned by two Sunni Islamist deputies and one independent legislator with regard to his Government's close relationship with Iran. This was, they claimed, to the detriment of Kuwait's relations with other Cooperation Council for the Arab States of the Gulf (Gulf Cooperation Council—GCC) member states and thus to the emirate's security. The request to interrogate Sheikh Nasser was made after Kuwait had been slow to respond to calls from the Bahraini Government for military support to quell the Shi'a-led pro-democracy protests that were taking place there, and after a controversial visit by the Iranian Minister of Foreign Affairs, Ali Akbar Salehi, to Kuwait in May. (Kuwait did eventually send a small naval force to Bahrain in May 2011 to assist the GCC 'Peninsula Shield' forces that had arrived in March.) There was evidence of an increase in tensions between Kuwait's Sunni and Shi'a communities as a result of the 'Arab spring' protests erupting across the Middle East and North Africa, and particularly the situation in Bahrain: Shi'a and moderate Kuwaitis strongly opposed the Bahraini authorities' harsh crackdown on the anti-Government protests. On 23 June Sheikh Nasser survived the third no-confidence motion he had faced since becoming Prime Minister, although the opposition pledged to continue their attempts to force him from office.

Recent developments: early election in 2012 and annulment of result leading to fresh polls

The Deputy Prime Minister and Minister of Foreign Affairs, Sheikh Muhammad al-Sabah, resigned on 17 October 2011; he had held the foreign affairs portfolio since 2003. Sheikh Muhammad had been implicated in a judicial investigation—initiated in the previous month—into allegations of official corruption, which reportedly involved the transfer of US $350m. of public funds as bribes to foreign bank accounts owned by some 16 pro-Government Majlis deputies through Kuwaiti embassies. It was alleged by the opposition that the Government had paid the money in return for securing the deputies' support in important parliamentary votes. On 23 October 2011 Sheikh Sabah al-Khaled al-Hamad al-Sabah was appointed to succeed Sheikh Muhammad in both his former roles. Following a recurrence of pro-democracy demonstrations and strikes in November, to which the security forces responded forcefully, on 16 November pro-reform campaigners, opposition deputies, intellectuals and doctors forced entry into the Majlis building, and demanded the resignation of the Prime Minister. Their action came after a further demand to interrogate Sheikh Nasser by opposition parliamentarians, relating to the same corruption scandal, was defeated by pro-Government deputies. Many of the protesters were arrested, and trial proceedings were subsequently launched against 24 young opposition activists. The Amir responded by warning on 17 November that henceforth the Ministry of the Interior would take 'all necessary steps' to guarantee Kuwait's national security.

On 28 November 2011 the Prime Minister and his entire Council of Ministers resigned, and on 30 November Sheikh Sabah asked Sheikh Jaber Mubarak al-Hamad al-Sabah, the outgoing First Deputy Prime Minister and Minister of Defence, to serve as premier at the head of a transitional government. Sheikh Jaber was sworn in on 4 December, and, in an attempt to resolve the dispute between the Government and parliament over allegations of corruption and amid increasing public protests against the Government, on 6 December the Amir dissolved the Majlis and ordered new parliamentary elections to be held more than one year ahead of schedule. A new Council of Ministers to take charge in the lead-up to the polls was inaugurated on 14 December. Sheikh Ahmad Homoud al-Sabah became Minister of Defence, in addition to retaining his role as Deputy Prime Minister and Minister of the Interior; however, no other changes were made to key portfolios.

Elections to the Majlis were held on 2 February 2012, in which voter turn-out was estimated at 60%. For the first time, foreign and local election monitors were officially permitted to observe the conduct of the polls. Sunni Islamists opposed to the Government won 23 seats; liberals and their allies secured nine; Shi'ite Islamists took seven; and the remaining seats were won by independent candidates. The result therefore represented significant electoral progress for Kuwait's Islamist opposition groups, many of which had pledged to take action against official corruption if they achieved success at the ballot. Unlike in 2009 (when four female candidates were successful), no women were elected to the Assembly. The Prime Minister tendered his resignation on 5 February, but on the following day was asked by the Amir to lead a new government. A new Council of Ministers was sworn in on 14 February; besides the notable absence of any female or Islamist cabinet members, the most high-profile appointment was that of ex-military chief of staff Sheikh Ahmad Khaled al-Hamad al-Sabah as Deputy Prime Minister and Minister of Defence. There was also only one elected Majlis deputy in the new Government (the minimum number required according to the Constitution). The interior, finance and foreign affairs portfolios remained in the same hands, while 10 new appointments were made. On 15 February, in an apparent concession to the opposition, Ahmad al-Saadoun, the leader of the Shi'ite Popular Action Bloc, which had won five parliamentary seats, was elected as Speaker of the Majlis. On 24 April the Majlis voted to remove the immunity from prosecution of nine opposition deputies (including Musallam al-Barrak—see below), who had been charged with forced entry, damage to property and disruption of the assembly's proceedings in connection with the brief takeover of parliament in November 2011.

On 17 May 2012 Sheikh Sabah rejected a proposal by a parliamentary faction called the Islamic Justice Bloc to amend the Constitution in order to change the reference to Islam as a 'major source' of legislation to the 'only source' of legislation. The campaign to render all Kuwaiti laws subject to *Shari'a* law had reportedly been endorsed by 31 of the 50 newly elected deputies. The Amir also, on 6 June, refused to endorse a bill recently adopted by the Majlis which proposed introducing the death penalty for those convicted of blasphemy. Meanwhile, on 24 May 2012 the Deputy Prime Minister and Minister of Finance, Mustafa al-Shamali, resigned after he was interrogated by opposition members of the Majlis about a range of alleged financial irregularities, which included squandering public funds and having links with Iran and its Lebanese ally Hezbollah through his chairmanship of a pension fund. Al-Shamali's resignation was accepted four days later. On 10 June former Prime

Minister Sheikh Nasser refused for a second time to appear before a parliamentary committee which was undertaking investigations into the massive corruption scandal revealed in late 2011. (In mid-May 2012 Sheikh Nasser had declined to attend a session of the committee to answer questions on the scandal, having recently been cleared of wrongdoing by a special judicial tribunal set up to look into the matter, owing to a lack of evidence.) On 11 June the Minister of Social Affairs and Labour, Ahmad Abd al-Latif al-Rujeib, also tendered his resignation, after the Majlis had sought to question him regarding the issuing of work permits. Later that month the Deputy Prime Minister and Minister of the Interior, Sheikh Ahmad Homoud, was also asked by opposition deputies to appear before parliament to answer questions relating to the country's Citizenship Law and *bidoun* affairs.

In a dramatic development, on 20 June 2012 the Constitutional Court annulled the results of the Majlis elections held in February, having ruled that the approval by the Council of Ministers of the Amiri decrees dissolving the previous legislature and scheduling elections for that month had been unconstitutional. The ruling prompted the effective restoration of the more pro-Government Majlis elected in 2009; however, more than one-half of its members immediately resigned their seats in protest against the decision, citing the fact that the previous assembly had been implicated in several cases of corruption. The Government under Sheikh Jaber resigned on 25 June 2012; its resignation was accepted by the Amir on 1 July. Meanwhile, a reported 30,000 Islamist and other demonstrators took part in a protest rally held in Kuwait City on 29 June 2012, at which they demanded the restoration of parliament and introduction of a constitutional monarchy with full democratic rights for Kuwaiti citizens. On 5 July Sheikh Sabah asked Sheikh Jaber to lead a new, interim administration. The new Council of Ministers was approved by the Amir on 19 July. The scheduled inauguration of the Council of Ministers before a session of the recently reinstated Majlis on 31 July was delayed by the fact that so many deputies had chosen not to take up their seats; only five deputies and five members of the cabinet were reported to have attended the session.

The restored Majlis was itself dissolved by Amiri decree on 7 October 2012, and early elections were subsequently scheduled for December. Leading opposition groups declared that they would boycott the poll in protest against amendments to the electoral law, announced in another decree signed by Sheikh Sabah on 19 October, which reintroduced a system of one vote (rather than four) for each constituency. On 25 September the Constitutional Court had rejected draft legislation put forward by the Council of Ministers which involved a redrawing of the country's electoral boundaries (from the five-constituency system created in 2006). Large-scale protests were held during October 2012, as opposition activists sought urgently to persuade the Council of Ministers not to approve amendments that would favour pro-Government candidates at the forthcoming polls by making it harder for opposition groups, including Islamists, to form coalitions. Around 20,000 demonstrators reportedly engaged in violent clashes with security forces in front of the Majlis building on 21 October; more than 100 protesters and several police officers were injured. The authorities responded to the upsurge in demonstrations by introducing measures such as using tear gas against protesters, banning groups of more than 20 people from holding public gatherings and launching trial proceedings against those deemed to be involved in anti-Government dissent—including opposition deputies, journalists and bloggers. The former Majlis deputy Musallam al-Barrak was arrested on 29 October, having been accused of 'undermining the status of the Amir' by criticizing Sheikh Sabah's 'autocratic' rule during a rally outside the parliament building on 15 October; however, he was freed on bail on 1 November. A number of opposition activists were charged with offences such as insulting Kuwait's ruler in comments either made during political speeches or on news or social media websites. In early 2013 several more online commentators had been given substantial prison sentences, including a five-year term imposed upon Bader al-Rashidi in March; al-Rashidi had initially been sentenced to two years in gaol in November 2011, having been found guilty of threatening national security and of insulting the Amir in comments published online.

Meanwhile, at the elections held on 1 December 2012, Shi'ite Islamist candidates secured 17 seats (compared with just seven in February), while Sunni Islamists won four seats (compared with 23). It was reported that 30 new deputies had been elected to parliament, including three women. As a result of the electoral boycott by Islamist, liberal and nationalist opposition movements, the new Majlis was reported to be strongly pro-Government. According to the Ministry of Information, voter turn-out was recorded at 38.8%, although opponents of the Government claimed that the figure was in fact only 27%. On 3 December Sheikh Sabah accepted the resignation of Sheikh Jaber and his interim Council of Ministers, before asking the incumbent Prime Minister to begin discussions concerning the formation of a new administration. A new Government led by Sheikh Jaber was sworn into office by the Amir on 12 December. The most notable change was the reappointment of Mustafa al-Shamali as Deputy Prime Minister and Minister of Finance. At the inaugural session of the Majlis on 16 December, Ali Fahad al-Rashed was elected Speaker. Meanwhile, significant anti-Government rallies continued throughout Kuwait during the latter part of December and into early 2013, with many protesters urging the authorities to annul the results of the recent poll.

On 8 January 2013 the newly elected Majlis voted to adopt the amendment to the electoral law decreed by the Amir in October 2012, which had prompted the opposition's electoral boycott. On 5 February 2013 three former parliamentarians were given three-year prison terms, having been convicted of the charges of insulting Sheikh Sabah during an anti-Government rally against the proposed electoral law changes on 10 October 2012. However, on 10 February 2013 an appeals court overturned the verdict and the three politicians were subsequently released on bail pending further court hearings. Meanwhile, as tensions persisted between the Government and Majlis, during February several deputies sought to interrogate government ministers alleged to have committed a range of legal violations—with al-Shamali and the Minister of Oil, Hani Abd al-Aziz Hussein, being the latest proposed targets of questioning. Some opposition politicians alleged that the deputies' actions represented an attempt to force the dissolution of parliament in advance of a scheduled ruling by the Constitutional Court on the recent amendment to Kuwait's election legislation. On 3 March al-Barrak announced the formation of the Opposition Coalition, which included a wide range of Islamist, nationalist, leftist, trade union and youth groups, in the hope that a stronger anti-Government alliance would be able to persuade the authorities to dissolve the current parliament, reverse the recent electoral amendment and ultimately transform Kuwait into a genuine parliamentary democracy. In mid-March parliament approved a proposal to award Kuwaiti citizenship to up to 4,000 people, most of whom, it was intended, would be *bidoun*; the legislation required ratification by the Amir.

Regional Relations

Friction between Kuwait and Iraq in the aftermath of the Gulf War was exacerbated by the issue of the demarcation of their joint border. The UN commission with responsibility for delineating the frontier formalized the land border as it had been defined by British administrators in 1932 (and officially agreed by Kuwait and Iraq in 1963). The boundary, the validity of which was now rejected by Iraq, was established some 570 m north of its pre-war position, dividing the Iraqi port of Umm Qasr, with the effect that Iraq retained the town and much of the harbour, while Kuwait was awarded hinterland that included an abandoned Iraqi naval base; the border also situated several Iraqi oil wells on Kuwaiti territory. In January 1993 the USA led air attacks on Iraq, and more than 1,000 US troops were dispatched to Kuwait, in response to a series of incursions by Iraqi forces into Kuwaiti territory in the days immediately preceding the designated entry into force of the new border; its formal delineation was completed in March, when the UN commission defined the maritime border along the median line of the Khawr Abd Allah waterway. Allegations made by Kuwait of Iraqi violations of the border, and of attempts to impede construction of a trench along the land border, intensified during the second half of 1993, and there were sporadic reports of exchanges of fire in the border region. In November a 775-strong armed UNIKOM reinforcement was deployed in northern Kuwait, with authorization (under specific circumstances) to use its weapons to assist the unarmed force already in the demilitarized zone.

In October 1994 Iraq deployed some 70,000 troops and 700 tanks near the border with Kuwait, in an apparent attempt to force an easing of UN economic sanctions. Kuwait immediately mobilized its army reserves, and dispatched some 20,000 troops to the border region. The USA committed almost 40,000 land, naval and air forces to the region; France and the United Kingdom deployed naval vessels, and the United Kingdom

dispatched about 1,200 troops. Following Russian mediation, Iraq announced its willingness to recognize Kuwait's sovereignty and borders, on condition that the UN ease sanctions against Iraq after six months. However, the UN Security Council adopted a resolution (No. 949) requiring Iraq's unconditional recognition of Kuwait's sovereignty and borders and restricting the movement of Iraqi troops in the border area. In November Iraq officially recognized Kuwait's sovereignty, territorial integrity and political independence, as well as its UN-defined borders. Most of the US and British reinforcements deployed in the region in October had been withdrawn by the end of the year.

Kuwait's relations with Iraq deteriorated sharply in September 1996, after the Kuwaiti Government agreed to the deployment in Kuwait of US military aircraft and troops in support of a US operation to force the withdrawal of Iraqi armed forces from the Kurdish 'safe haven' in northern Iraq. In December the USA announced that some 4,200 US troops deployed in Kuwait during 1996 would be withdrawn by the end of the year, although the deployment of US F-117 *Stealth* fighter aircraft was to be extended.

As the crisis involving weapons inspections in Iraq by the UN Special Commission deepened in February 1998, fears were expressed for Kuwait's security—in particular that an attack on Iraq might result in the use of chemical or other weapons of mass destruction against Kuwait. By the end of the month, when the UN Secretary-General and the Iraqi Government reached a compromise agreement regarding weapons inspections, some 6,000 US ground troops—supported by the British military—had been dispatched to Kuwait. Iraq accused Kuwait of collaborating in a series of air-strikes against targets in Iraq by US and British forces from December, and frequently reiterated claims to Kuwaiti territory. In December 1999 the Kuwaiti Government welcomed UN Security Council Resolution 1284 (establishing a new weapons inspectorate for Iraq), which incorporated demands for: the repatriation of Kuwaiti and other prisoners from Iraq, Iraq's co-operation with the International Committee of the Red Cross, and the return of Kuwaiti property seized during the occupation.

In September 2000 Iraq renewed its long-standing accusation that Kuwait was drilling oil wells on Iraqi territory, and accused Kuwait and Saudi Arabia of inflicting suffering on the Iraqi population through the maintenance of UN sanctions. In November 2001 Kuwait issued a formal complaint to the UN, following an alleged violation of its territory by Iraq. In January 2002 the Kuwaiti leadership was reported to have rejected attempts by the Arab League to persuade it to accept Iraqi proposals apparently aimed at improving bilateral relations: the proposals were part of Iraq's diplomatic offensive to secure the support of the Arab world in view of the threat of US-led military action against Saddam Hussain's regime. However, at the Arab League summit held in Beirut, Lebanon, in March, it was announced that Kuwait and Iraq had reached agreement on the resolution of outstanding differences.

Relations with Iraq were profoundly affected by the political repercussions of the suicide attacks against New York and Washington, DC, USA, in September 2001. Kuwait, which strongly condemned the attacks, thereafter assumed an important role in persuading other Gulf states to join the US-led 'coalition against terror'. US bases in Kuwait were subsequently used to provide logistical support to the US-led campaign against al-Qa'ida (held by the USA to be principally responsible for the suicide attacks) and its Taliban hosts in Afghanistan during late 2001. Meanwhile, in October the Kuwaiti authorities revoked the citizenship of the official spokesperson of al-Qa'ida, Sulayman Abu Ghaith, after remarks that he had made via *Al Jazeera*.

During the course of 2002 increased speculation that the US Administration of George W. Bush intended to extend the 'war on terror' to target the regime of Saddam Hussain in Iraq threatened to fuel opposition to a continued US presence in the region and exacerbate an increasingly tense political situation in Kuwait. In December some 12,000 US troops were stationed in Kuwait, and the entire northern half of Kuwait was designated a closed military zone from February 2003. At the outset of military action, which commenced in late March, US-led troops in Kuwait, the base for the main ground assault on Iraq, numbered some 140,000. Iraqi armed forces launched several missiles at Kuwaiti territory, although little damage was caused in the emirate during the course of the conflict. In the aftermath of the most intense period of fighting, which President Bush declared to have ended by early May, Kuwait renewed its financial demands against Iraq, while a number of Kuwaiti firms entered into agreements with the US-led occupying powers. In October the demilitarized zone between Iraq and Kuwait was ended and, having fulfilled its mandate, UNIKOM's operations were terminated.

The resumption of diplomatic relations between Iraq and Kuwait was announced in mid-2004. In 2005 Kuwait began the construction of a 200-km steel barrier along the border with Iraq, parts of which were destroyed by Iraqi militants who claimed that it was encroaching upon their land; however, in November 2006 Iraq agreed to allow the fence to be completed. In October 2008 the first Kuwaiti ambassador since the Iraqi invasion of 1990, Ali Muhammad al-Momen, took up his post in the Iraqi capital, Baghdad. Iraq had earlier reopened its embassy in Kuwait, which was initially headed by a chargé d'affaires; Muhammad Hussain Bahr al-Ulum was subsequently appointed, in April 2010, as Iraq's first ambassador to Kuwait since the Iraqi invasion.

In June 2009 Iraq's Permanent Representative to the UN, Hamid al-Bayati, lodged an official request with the Security Council requesting a reduction in the reparation payments owed to Kuwait (see below). In July the issue of reparations was the primary topic in talks between Iraqi Prime Minister Nuri al-Maliki and UN Secretary-General Ban Ki-Moon in New York. However, later that month Kuwait's Deputy Prime Minister and Minister of Foreign Affairs, Sheikh Dr Muhammad Sabah al-Salim al-Sabah, stated in a newspaper interview that Iraqi 'violations' of their common border continued to represent a serious threat to regional security and bilateral relations, and urged Iraq to respect all existing UN resolutions relating to the Gulf War. Bilateral negotiations aimed at resolving all outstanding differences between Kuwait and Iraq, under the auspices of the UN, continued throughout 2009–10. In January 2011 Prime Minister Sheikh Nasser paid an official visit to Baghdad, the first visit to Iraq by a Kuwaiti premier since the Gulf War. At the inauguration of a new building for the Kuwaiti embassy in Baghdad later that month, the Kuwaiti ambassador and Iraqi Minister of Foreign Affairs Hoshyar al-Zibari pledged to work toward resolving remaining issues of bilateral contention, notably issues pertaining to Iraqi reparation payments. In February the Kuwaiti authorities approved the construction of a large seaport, the Mubarak al-Kabir Port, on Bubiyan Island, which the Iraqi Government claimed violated international legislation governing maritime borders and would severely restrict its vessels' access to international shipping lanes in the Gulf. Iraq initially demanded an end to construction of the port, which began in April (with a completion date of 2016); concerns were also expressed about security at the port, after Iraqi militants threatened to target it.

The improvement in relations between Kuwait and Iraq was assisted by the completion of the US military withdrawal from Iraq in December 2011. Sheikh Sabah attended the historic meeting of the Arab League which took place in Baghdad in March 2012. In April, following a high-profile visit by the Amir to Iraq, the Kuwaiti and Iraqi Governments reached a settlement concerning their land and maritime border dispute; this included the formation of a joint commission to ensure that both sides abided by the terms of the deal. Nevertheless, the bilateral dispute over construction of the Mubarak al-Kabir Port remained a source of tension during 2012. In July it was reported that the Kuwaiti authorities had agreed to build the port in three, rather than four, phases, in order to reduce the number of shipping berths under construction. However, many Iraqi officials continued to insist that the project would be detrimental to the country's access to international shipping lanes. In February 2013 an Iraqi Airways plane became the first Iraqi aircraft to land in Kuwait since the 1990–91 Gulf crisis, after the two countries had agreed to the resumption of direct flights in April 2012. (For further details on bilateral relations, see the chapter on Iraq.)

Meanwhile, in May 1994 the governing body of the UN Compensation Commission (UNCC), responsible for considering claims for compensation arising from the 1990–91 Gulf crisis, approved the first disbursements (to 670 families or individuals in 16 countries), totalling US $2.7m. By late 1996 payments amounting to $3,000m. (to be financed partly by Iraqi petroleum revenues) had been endorsed by the UN, which had yet to consider claims for a further $190,000m. In December international arbitrators recommended that a payment of $610m. should be made to the Kuwait Oil Company (KOC), in compensation for the cost of extinguishing oil wells set alight by retreating Iraqi troops in early 1991. In March 1997 the Kuwaiti general

committee responsible for evaluating war damages stated that it was to begin compensation payments, initially to some 4,500 citizens who had incurred losses valued at less than $100,000. The disbursement of a further $84m. to some 33,800 individuals was authorized by the UN in February 1999. In September 2000 the UN Security Council approved the payment to the Kuwait Petroleum Corporation (which controls the KOC) of $15,900m. in compensation for lost petroleum revenues arising from the Iraqi occupation. However, the Security Council decided at the same time to reduce the share of Iraqi petroleum revenues to be paid into the compensation fund from 30% to 25%.

By mid-2003 the majority of individual claimants (Kuwaitis and expatriates in Kuwait and Iraq during the Gulf War) had received compensation, with total disbursements being valued at some US $17,600m. In May UN Security Council Resolution 1483 reduced the share of Iraqi petroleum revenue to be used for compensation payments from 25% to 5%, which was expected to result in outstanding compensation payments believed to total more than $30,000m. remaining unpaid for several decades. In June the UNCC authorized the payment of only $1,500m. of a claim of $86,000m. by the Kuwait Investment Agency, principally in recompense for lost earnings during the conflict. Following similar announcements by the Governments of the UAE and Qatar in January 2004, Sheikh Sabah stated that Kuwait was prepared to waive a 'significant proportion' of the estimated $16,000m. owed by Iraq. This did not, however, include any war reparations still claimed by the Government. In March 2005 the UN panel overseeing payments to victims of the Gulf crisis approved a further disbursement of $265m. to families of those who had died in Iraqi detention. At a final session of the UNCC governing body, held in June, a further $367m. in compensation was awarded to successful claimants. The claims assessment process was concluded thereafter, and payments to individuals ceased in 2007. In 2009 payments worth a total of $1,040m. were made by the UNCC, principally to Kuwaiti state-owned and private companies and government agencies for losses incurred as a result of the Iraqi invasion and occupation. A further $1,240m. was disbursed in 2010, while some $3,657m. was paid out during 2011 and $4,430m. during 2012. Following a further compensation payment of $1,300m. in January 2013, the total value of payments issued by the UNCC since 1994 reached around $40,100m.; according to the UNCC, some $12,300m. remained owing to Kuwait.

In July 2000 Kuwait and Saudi Arabia signed an agreement finalizing the delineation of their maritime borders. Kuwait subsequently began negotiations with Iran on the demarcation of respective rights to the continental shelf, following complaints by the Kuwaiti and Saudi authorities over Iran's decision to begin drilling for gas in the disputed Arash/Dorra offshore field. Iraq asserted that, as a concerned party, it should be included in the Kuwaiti-Iranian discussions. Iran suspended drilling pending the conclusion of the dispute. Despite issuing remarks in early 2012 threatening to recommence drilling without Kuwaiti permission, by mid-2012 the managing director of the National Iranian Offshore Oil Co indicated that the Islamic Republic was keen to reach an agreement with the Kuwaiti authorities for the joint development of the gas field; the dispute remained unresolved in early 2013. Meanwhile, in December 2000 a defence agreement was signed by the six member states of the GCC. In July 2007 the US Administration unveiled a US $20,000m. package of military assistance and weapons sales to Kuwait and the other GCC member states, in an attempt to bolster security in the Gulf region and to encourage the GCC to side with the USA in its dispute with the Iranian regime regarding the latter's nuclear programme. However, Kuwait opposes any military action being taken by the USA against Iran, and supports the Iranian Government's right to develop a peaceful nuclear energy programme.

Prime Minister Sheikh Nasser made an official visit to Tehran, Iran, in November 2009, the first such visit by a Kuwaiti premier since the foundation of the Islamic Republic of Iran in 1979. Sheikh Nasser, accompanied by a senior-level ministerial delegation, held talks encompassing economic co-operation and bilateral relations with Iranian First Vice-President Muhammad Reza Rahimi. The premier also met with Ayatollah Sayed Ali Khamenei, Iran's Supreme Religious Leader. Discussions on the possible construction of a sub-marine gas pipeline connecting Kuwait with Iran's gas network were also conducted between Kuwait's Minister of Oil and Information, Sheikh Ahmad Abdullah al-Ahmad al-Sabah, and his Iranian counterpart. In April 2010 a delegation of senior Kuwaiti officials concluded several bilateral co-operation agreements in Tehran, including understandings concerning the import of Iranian water and gas. However, relations were threatened by the discovery in the following month of an allegedly Iranian-led network of spies in Kuwait; seven people (three Iranians, one Syrian, one Kuwaiti soldier and two *bidoun*), were arrested on suspicion of belonging to the network. Several legislators demanded the expulsion of the Iranian ambassador in Kuwait, while Iranian officials denied any involvement in espionage in Kuwait. The seven were charged in early August with, *inter alia*, passing confidential military information relating to both Kuwaiti and US forces to Iran's Islamic Revolutionary Guards Corps, and their trial, *in camera*, commenced later that month. The defendants initially confessed to the charges against them, but their lawyer subsequently claimed that these confessions had been extracted under duress.

In March 2011, having been found guilty of involvement in the espionage network, two of the Iranian defendants and the Kuwaiti were given death sentences, while the Syrian and one *bidoun* received terms of life imprisonment; the third Iranian and second *bidoun* were both acquitted. Iran reacted strongly to the announcement of the verdicts, and the case was subsequently referred to Kuwait's Court of Appeal. In its ruling issued in late May 2012, the Court commuted the three death sentences to those of life imprisonment, confirmed the life sentence given to the convicted *bidoun* but acquitted the Syrian defendant. A further appeal against the verdicts was expected to be brought before the Court of Cassation. Meanwhile, at the end of March 2011 Kuwait withdrew its ambassador from Tehran and ordered three Iranian diplomats to leave the country. The Iranian authorities responded in early April by expelling a similar number of Kuwaiti diplomats from Tehran. After high-level bilateral discussions aimed at resolving the dispute, by late May both ambassadors had been returned to their respective capitals. However, at the same time the Kuwaiti Government alleged that another spy network, linked both to Iran and the Lebanese Hezbollah, was operating within Kuwait and plotting terrorist acts against civilians.

CONSTITUTION AND GOVERNMENT

Under the 1962 Constitution, executive power is vested in the Amir, the head of state (who is chosen by and from members of the ruling family), and is exercised through the Council of Ministers. The Amir appoints the Prime Minister and, on the latter's recommendation, other ministers. Legislative power is vested in the unicameral Majlis al-Umma (National Assembly), with 50 elected members who serve for four years (subject to dissolution), along with some 15 government ministers who sit as *ex officio* members. In May 2005 legislation was approved allowing women to vote in legislative and municipal elections for the first time. The country is divided administratively into six governorates.

REGIONAL AND INTERNATIONAL CO-OPERATION

Kuwait is a member of the Cooperation Council for the Arab States of the Gulf (Gulf Cooperation Council—GCC, see p. 255); the six GCC states established a unified regional customs tariff in January 2003, and agreed to create a single market and currency. The economic convergence criteria for the monetary union were agreed at a GCC summit in Abu Dhabi, the UAE, in December 2005, and in January 2008 the GCC launched its common market. Kuwait also participates in the League of Arab States (the Arab League, see p. 372) and the Organization of Arab Petroleum Exporting Countries (OAPEC, see p. 410).

Kuwait became a member of the UN in May 1963 and, as a contracting party to the General Agreement on Tariffs and Trade, joined the World Trade Organization (WTO, see p. 444) upon its establishment in 1995. The country is also a participant in the Organization of the Petroleum Exporting Countries (OPEC, see p. 418), the Organization of Islamic Cooperation (OIC, see p. 413) and the Group of 77 developing countries (G77, see p. 461).

ECONOMIC AFFAIRS

In 2010, according to estimates by the World Bank, Kuwait's gross national income (GNI), measured at average 2008–10 prices, was US $133,823m., equivalent to $48,900 per head (or $53,820 on an international purchasing-power parity basis). During 2002–11, it was estimated, the population increased at an average annual rate of 3.5%, while gross domestic product (GDP) per head grew, in real terms, by an average of 2.8% per

year. According to the World Bank, overall GDP was estimated to have increased, in real terms, at an average annual rate of 6.4% in 2002–11. Real GDP rose by 8.2% in 2011.

Agriculture (including hunting, forestry and fishing) contributed 0.2% of GDP in 2011. The sector engaged 2.2% of the classified labour force in mid-2011. The principal crops are potatoes, tomatoes, cucumbers, aubergines and dates. Owing to scarcity of water, little grain is produced, and the bulk of food requirements is imported. (Imports of food and live animals accounted for 14.5% of merchandise imports in 2009.) Livestock, poultry and fishing are also important. According to the Central Bank of Kuwait (CBK), agricultural GDP decreased, in real terms, by an average annual rate of 2.7% in 2002–10. The agricultural sector expanded by 25.6% in 2009, before contracting by 15.5% in 2010.

Industry (including mining, manufacturing, construction and power) provided 67.4% of GDP in 2011, and employed 17.1% of the classified labour force in mid-2011. During 2002–10 industrial GDP increased, in real terms, at an average annual rate of 4.3%, according to the CBK. The GDP of the sector decreased by 13.9% in 2009, but increased by 3.0% in 2010.

Mining and quarrying contributed 60.0% of GDP in 2011, although the sector engaged only 0.4% of the classified labour force in mid-2011. The production of petroleum and its derivatives is the most important industry in Kuwait, providing an estimated 92.1% of export revenue in 2010. At the end of 2011 the country's proven recoverable reserves of petroleum were 101,500m. barrels, representing about 6.1% of world reserves. Kuwait's petroleum production averaged 2.87m. barrels per day (b/d) in 2011; the Government aimed to increase its production capacity to 4.0m. b/d by 2020. As a member of the Organization of the Petroleum Exporting Countries (OPEC, see p. 418), Kuwait is subject to production quotas agreed by the Organization's Conference. There are significant reserves of natural gas (1,784,000m. cu m at the end of 2011) associated with the petroleum deposits. Output was 12,950m. cu m in that year. However, although in March 2006 a major discovery of non-associated gas in the north of the country was announced, Kuwait remains a net importer of natural gas. According to the CBK, during 2002–10 the GDP of the mining sector increased, in real terms, at an average rate of 3.4% per year. The sector's GDP decreased by 16.9% in 2009, but increased by 1.6% in 2010.

Manufacturing provided 4.5% of GDP in 2011, and employed 6.3% of the classified labour force in mid-2011. Petroleum refineries accounted for 52.3% of manufacturing activity, measured by gross value of output, in 2010. Of the other branches of manufacturing, the most important are the production of building materials (and related activities such as aluminium extrusion), fertilizer production, food-processing and the extraction of salt and chlorine. During 2002–10 manufacturing GDP increased, in real terms, at an average annual rate of 2.4%, according to the CBK; the sector's GDP declined by 3.4% in 2010.

Construction contributed 1.7% of GDP in 2011, and engaged 9.6% of the classified labour force in mid-2011. According to the CBK, during 2002–10 construction GDP increased, in real terms, at an average annual rate of 2.9%. The GDP of the sector declined by 0.9% in 2010.

Electrical energy is derived from Kuwait's own resources of petroleum (providing 71.2% of total electricity production in 2009) and both local and imported natural gas (28.8%).

Services contributed 32.4% of GDP in 2011, and employed 80.8% of the classified labour force in mid-2011. Kuwait's second most important source of revenue is investment abroad, both in petroleum-related ventures and in other industries, chiefly in the USA, Western Europe and Japan; many such investments are held by the Reserve Fund for Future Generations (to which 10% of petroleum revenues must by law be contributed each year, and which is intended to provide an income after hydrocarbon resources have been exhausted) and managed by the Kuwait Investment Authority. As part of its efforts to diversify the economy, the Government plans to develop the islands of Bubiyan and Failaka into major tourist resorts. The combined GDP of the service sectors increased, in real terms, at an average rate of 10.5% per year during 2002–10, according to the CBK. The services sector contracted by 2.6% in 2009, before expanding by 16.5% in 2010.

In 2010 Kuwait recorded a visible merchandise trade surplus of US $47,908m., and there was a surplus of $36,822m. on the current account of the balance of payments. In 2010 the principal source of imports was the People's Republic of China (12.5%);

other important suppliers in that year were the USA, Japan, Germany, India and Saudi Arabia. Details concerning the destination of Kuwait's petroleum exports are not available for recent years; however, the major markets for non-petroleum exports in 2010 included the People's Republic of China (14.2%), the UAE, Saudi Arabia and India. The principal imports are machinery and transport equipment (which accounted for 40.2% of total imports in 2009), basic manufactures and other manufactured goods, food and live animals, and chemicals and related products.

A budget surplus of KD 13,229m. was recorded for the financial year ending 30 June 2012. Kuwait's general government gross debt was KD 3,751m. in 2010, equivalent to 10.9% of GDP. The average annual rate of inflation in 2005–11 was 5.3%; consumer prices increased by an estimated average of 4.7% in 2011. The rate of unemployment among Kuwaiti nationals was estimated at 3.4% in 2011; however, underemployment was unofficially reported to be up to 50% in June 2009.

Despite its significant, oil-based wealth, Kuwait has a number of fundamental weaknesses in its economic structure: instability in its relations with Iraq have necessitated a high level of defence expenditure; reliance on petroleum revenues has impeded diversification into other industries; and its constitutional commitment to provide employment for all Kuwaitis has resulted in a heavy burden on government spending. Plans to allow foreign participation in a development project for the northern oilfields (known as 'Project Kuwait'), which aimed to increase national production from 2.5m. b/d to 4m. b/d by 2020, were first proposed by the Kuwait Petroleum Corpn (KPC) in 1997. However, the project was hampered by consistent opposition from the Majlis, and the petroleum sector was exempted from legislation approved by parliament in April 2010 permitting the privatization of certain state assets. In November 2012 it was announced that the Government planned to spend US $100,000m. on oil projects over a five-year period to reach its production target from the current level of 3m. b/d. In February 2010 the Majlis approved a four-year economic development plan that envisaged expenditure of up to $125,000m. on energy, transport, social and utilities projects, with special provisions for private sector participation. Nevertheless, progress has been slow, and foreign investors have been deterred by the ongoing disputes between the Council of Ministers and the Majlis, which have led to frequent changes of government. The budget for 2011/12 envisaged a significant increase in government expenditure, much of which was to be allocated to social spending, in response to a series of anti-Government protests taking place from early 2011. However, following lower-than-anticipated spending levels and significantly higher revenues, a record budget surplus of around $47,000m. was achieved. The escalating tensions between the Government and Majlis during 2012 meant that the adoption of important financial legislation and the progress of several major capital projects was postponed. Following protracted delays in its announcement, in October 2012 the Government approved the 2012/13 budget, which forecast a deficit of $26,000m. In that month the value of shares on the Kuwait Stock Exchange declined by their largest daily rate since July 2009, amid an intensification of opposition protests over planned amendments to electoral legislation. Following GDP growth of 8.2% in 2011, in October 2012 the IMF projected growth of 6.3% for that year. For 2013, the Fund projected growth of only 1.9%, partly due to an anticipated decline in oil GDP.

PUBLIC HOLIDAYS

2014: 1 January (New Year's Day), 13 January* (Mouloud, Birth of the Prophet), 25 February (Kuwaiti National Day), 26 February (Liberation Day), 26 May* (Leilat al-Meiraj, Ascension of the Prophet), 28 July* (Id al-Fitr, end of Ramadan), 4 October* (Id al-Adha, Feast of the Sacrifice), 24 October (Muharram, Islamic New Year).

* These holidays are dependent on the Islamic lunar calendar and may vary by one or two days from the dates given.

Statistical Survey

Sources (unless otherwise stated): Economic Research Department, Central Bank of Kuwait, POB 526, 13006 Safat, Kuwait City; tel. 22403257; fax 22440887; e-mail cbk@cbk.gov.kw; internet www.cbk.gov.kw; Central Statistical Bureau, Arabian Gulf St, Sharq, Kuwait City; tel. 22428200; fax 2430470; e-mail ppd@cso .gov.kw; internet www.csb.gov.kw.

Note: Unless otherwise indicated, data refer to the State of Kuwait as constituted at 1 August 1990, prior to the Iraqi invasion and annexation of the territory and its subsequent liberation. Furthermore, no account has been taken of the increase in the area of Kuwait as a result of the adjustment to the border with Iraq that came into force on 15 January 1993.

Area and Population

AREA, POPULATION AND DENSITY

Area (sq km)	17,818*
Population (census results)†	
20 April 2005‡	
Males	1,300,347
Females	893,304
Total	2,193,651
21 April 2011 (preliminary)§	3,065,850
Population (official estimates at mid-year)‖	
2009	3,442,945
2010	3,566,437
2011	3,632,009
Density (per sq km) at mid-2011	203.8

* 6,880 sq miles.
† Figures include Kuwaiti nationals abroad.
‡ Excluding adjustment for underenumeration; the total population at the 2005 census comprised 860,324 Kuwaiti nationals (425,279 males, 435,045 females) and 1,333,327 non-Kuwaitis (875,068 males, 458,259 females).
§ Comprising 1,089,969 Kuwaitis and 1,975,881 non-Kuwaitis.
‖ Estimates based on new methodology used by the Public Authority for Civil Information, not revised to take account of results of 2011 census.

POPULATION BY AGE AND SEX
(UN estimates at mid-2013)

	Males	Females	Total
0–14	400,507	378,880	779,387
15–64	1,313,923	787,925	2,101,848
65 and over	48,410	29,371	77,781
Total	**1,762,840**	**1,196,176**	**2,959,016**

Source: UN, *World Population Prospects: The 2010 Revision.*

GOVERNORATES
(population at 2005 census)

Governorate	Area (sq km)*	Population	Density (per sq km)
Capital	199.8	254,503	1,273.8
Hawalli		482,127	
Mubarak al-Kabir .	368.4	175,244	3,469.9
Farwaniya . . .		620,935	
Al-Jahra	11,230.2	269,915	24.0
Al-Ahmadi . . .	5,119.6	390,927	76.4
Total	**16,918.0**	**2,193,651**	**129.7**

* Excluding the islands of Bubiyan and Warba (combined area 900 sq km).

PRINCIPAL TOWNS
(population at 2005 census)

Kuwait City (capital)	31,574	Farwaniya . . .	83,478
Jaleeb al-Shuyukh .	179,425	Salwa . . .	62,822
Salmiya . . .	145,314	Subbah al-Salem .	55,927
Hawalli . . .	104,901	Sulaibiah . . .	54,693
South Kheetan . .	92,475	Subahiya . . .	50,607

Mid-2011 (incl. suburbs, UN estimate): Kuwait City 2,406,410 (Source: UN, *World Urbanization Prospects: The 2011 Revision*).

BIRTHS, MARRIAGES AND DEATHS

	Registered live births		Registered marriages		Registered deaths	
	Number	Rate (per 1,000)	Number	Rate (per 1,000)	Number	Rate (per 1,000)
1993 . .	37,379	25.6	10,077	6.9	3,441	2.4
1994 . .	38,868	24.0	9,550	5.9	3,464	2.1
1995 . .	41,169	22.8	9,515	5.3	3,781	2.1
1996 . .	44,620	23.6	9,022	4.8	3,812	2.0
1997 . .	42,817	21.6	9,610	4.9	4,017	2.0
1998 . .	41,424	20.4	10,335	5.1	4,216	2.1
1999 . .	41,135	19.5	10,847	5.1	4,187	2.0
2000 . .	41,843	19.1	10,785	4.9	4,227	1.9

2008: Total births 54,571; Total deaths 5,701; Total marriages 14,709.

2009: Total births 56,503; Total deaths 5,935; Total marriages 14,526.

2010: Total births 57,533; Total deaths 5,448; Total marriages 13,993.

Life expectancy (years at birth): 65.2 (males 63.5; females 66.9) in 2011 (Source: World Bank, World Development Indicators database).

ECONOMICALLY ACTIVE POPULATION
('000 persons aged 15 years and over, mid-2011)

	Kuwaitis	Non-Kuwaitis	Total
Agriculture, hunting and fishing .	0.4	41.4	41.8
Mining and quarrying . . .	4.9	2.1	7.1
Manufacturing	9.0	112.7	121.6
Electricity, gas and water . .	13.1	2.0	15.1
Construction	10.9	175.8	186.8
Wholesale and retail trade . .	14.5	331.2	345.7
Transport, storage and communications . . .	9.3	59.9	69.1
Finance, insurance, real estate and business services . .	19.3	95.7	114.9
Public administration	270.6	764.0	1,034.6
Sub-total	352.0	1,584.9	1,936.7
Activities not adequately defined	37.9	252.8	290.7
Total labour force	389.7	1,837.7	2,227.4

Note: Totals may not be equal to the sum of components, owing to rounding.

Source: IMF, *Kuwait: Selected Issues and Statistical Appendix* (June 2012).

Health and Welfare

KEY INDICATORS

Total fertility rate (children per woman, 2010)	2.3
Under-5 mortality rate (per 1,000 live births, 2010) . . .	11
HIV/AIDS (% of persons aged 15–49, 1994)	<0.2
Physicians (per 1,000 head, 2009)	1.8
Hospital beds (per 1,000 head, 2009)	2.0
Health expenditure (2009): US $ per head (PPP)	1,671
Health expenditure (2009): % of GDP	3.8
Health expenditure (2009): public (% of total)	85.4
Access to water (% of persons, 2010)	99
Total carbon dioxide emissions ('000 metric tons, 2008) . .	76,743.0
Carbon dioxide emissions per head (metric tons, 2008) . .	30.1
Human Development Index (2011): ranking	63
Human Development Index (2011): value	0.760

For sources and definitions, see explanatory note on p. vi.

Agriculture

PRINCIPAL CROPS
('000 metric tons)

	2009	2010	2011*
Potatoes	34.0	36.8	44.6
Cabbages and other brassicas .	16.6	15.1	13.7
Lettuce	11.3	12.8	12.3
Tomatoes	74.4	73.7	71.3
Cauliflowers and broccoli . . .	17.9	16.8	22.1
Pumpkins, squash and gourds .	10.3	12.2	12.5
Cucumbers and gherkins . .	44.5	48.7	53.1
Aubergines (Eggplants) . .	26.7	25.0	25.0
Chillies and peppers, green . .	16.4	16.3	16.3
Onions, dry	15.6	18.6	19.7
Dates	29.8	32.6	33.6

*FAO estimates.

Aggregate production ('000 metric tons, may include official, semi-official or estimated data): Total cereals 14.2 in 2009, 21.4 in 2010–11; Total roots and tubers 34.0 in 2009, 36.8 in 2010, 44.6 in 2011; Total vegetables (incl. melons) 290.6 in 2009, 298.5 in 2010, 321.4 in 2011; Total fruits (excl. melons) 32.2 in 2009, 35.2 in 2010, 36.5 in 2011.

Source: FAO.

LIVESTOCK
('000 head, year ending September)

	2009	2010	2011
Cattle	35.8	35.7	35.0*
Camels	10.4	10.3	11.0*
Sheep	455	462	470*
Goats	145.0†	181.6	178.7
Chickens	40,902	30,559	32,000*

*FAO estimate.
† Unofficial figure.

Source: FAO.

LIVESTOCK PRODUCTS
('000 metric tons)

	2009	2010	2011*
Cattle meat*	2.5	2.6	2.6
Sheep meat*	37.5	35.7	35.7
Chicken meat*	41.3	39.9	39.0
Cows' milk*	40.1	55.2	55.2
Goats' milk*	3.5	4.2	4.2
Hen eggs	35.0	40.0	40.0

*FAO estimates.

Source: FAO.

Fishing

(metric tons, live weight)

	2007	2008	2009*
Capture	4,373	3,979	4,000
Hilsa shad	78	84	80
Mullets	259	22	100
Groupers	169	129	140
Grunts and sweetlips	140	119	130
Croakers and drums	45	649	300
Yellowfin seabream	305	299	300
Indo-Pacific king mackerel	58	57	55
Carangids	92	39	60
Natantian decapods	1,540	1,807	1,700
Silver pomfret	101	115	110
Aquaculture	348	360*	360
Nile tilapia	293	300*	300
Total catch	4,721	4,339*	4,360

* FAO estimate(s).

2010: Figures assumed to be unchanged from 2009 (FAO estimates).

Source: FAO.

Mining

	2009	2010	2011
Crude petroleum ('000 metric tons)	120,951	122,689	140,041
Natural gas (million cu m)	11,190	11,730	12,950

Source: BP, *Statistical Review of World Energy*.

Industry

SELECTED PRODUCTS

('000 metric tons unless otherwise stated)

	2009	2010	2011
Bran and flour*	340.2	336.2	n.a.
Sulphur (by-product)†	800	820	830
Chlorine*	24.5	21.8	n.a.
Caustic soda (Sodium hydroxide)*.	36.9	35.5	n.a.
Salt†	13.0	14.0	15.0
Nitrogenous fertilizers†‡	450	340	460
Motor spirit (petrol) (million barrels)†§	20	22	23
Kerosene (million barrels)†§	60	68	66
Gas-diesel (distillate fuel) oils (million barrels)†§	80	85	94
Residual fuel oils (mazout—million barrels)†§	69	68	70
Quicklime†	45	50	50
Cement†	2,000	2,000	2,250
Electric energy (million kWh)*§	53,200	57,000	n.a.

* Source: IMF, *Kuwait: Selected Issues and Statistical Appendix* (June 2012).
† Source: US Geological Survey; estimates.
‡ Production in terms of nitrogen.
§ Including an equal share of production with Saudi Arabia from the Neutral (Partitioned) Zone.

Finance

CURRENCY AND EXCHANGE RATES

Monetary Units
1,000 fils = 10 dirhams = 1 Kuwaiti dinar (KD).

Sterling, Dollar and Euro Equivalents (31 December 2012)
£1 sterling = 443.66 fils;
US $1 = 281.15 fils;
€1 = 370.95 fils;
10 Kuwaiti dinars = £22.54 = $35.57 = €26.96.

Average Exchange Rate (fils per US $)
2010   286.6
2011   276.0
2012   279.9

From 1 January 2003 the official exchange rate was fixed within the range of US $1 = 289 fils to $1 = 310 fils (KD 1 = $3.4602 to KD 1 = $3.2258), but this 'peg' to the US dollar was abandoned in May 2007 in favour of a basket of currencies including the pound sterling, the euro and the yen.

GENERAL BUDGET

(KD million, year ending 30 June)

Revenue	2009/10	2010/11	2011/12
Tax revenue	296.4	320.1	326.1
International trade and transactions	190.8	218.4	222.9
Non-tax revenue	17,391.6	21,181.9	29,910.0
Oil revenue	16,584.9	19,947.4	28,569.6
Total operating revenue of government enterprises	566.3	566.6	576.7
Total	17,687.9	21,502.0	30,236.1

Expenditure	2009/10	2010/11	2011/12
Current expenditure	8,095.0	11,329.2	11,097.4
Land acquisitions	10.1	3.6	21.0
Capital expenditure	226.5	152.9	147.0
Construction expenditure	1,071.2	1,684.5	1,631.0
Other expenditure	1,847.8	3,050.8	4,111.1
Total	11,250.7	16,221.0	17,007.4

INTERNATIONAL RESERVES

(US $ million at 31 December)

	2009	2010	2011
Gold (national valuation)	110.7	n.a.	113.9
IMF special drawing rights	2,261.3	2,222.9	2,219.0
Reserve position in IMF	397.8	390.8	654.7
Foreign exchange	17,608.4	18,623.0	22,921.4
Total	20,378.2	21,236.7*	25,909.0

* Excluding data for gold, which was not available.

Source: IMF, *International Financial Statistics*.

MONEY SUPPLY

(KD million at 31 December)

	2009	2010	2011
Currency outside depository corporations	775.7	842.9	1,024.6
Transferable deposits	4,383.5	5,285.1	6,304.2
Other deposits	19,736.5	19,506.2	20,495.3
Broad money	24,895.8	25,634.2	27,824.2

Source: IMF, *International Financial Statistics*.

COST OF LIVING
(Consumer Price Index; base: 2000 = 100)

	2009	2010	2011
Food	149.6	162.1	177.7
Beverages and tobacco	159.1	167.9	163.6
Clothing and footwear	144.7	151.7	157.0
Housing	137.7	143.8	149.2
Transport and communication	114.9	113.4	115.8
Education and medical care	151.3	155.0	161.1
All items (incl. others)	136.0	141.5	148.2

NATIONAL ACCOUNTS
(KD million at current prices)

Expenditure on the Gross Domestic Product

	2009	2010	2011
Government final consumption expenditure	5,635.5	5,946.6	6,719.8
Private final consumption expenditure	10,215.9	9,444.5	10,125.4
Increase in stocks ⎫			
Gross fixed capital formation ⎬	5,478.9	6,964.1	6,921.1
Total domestic expenditure	21,330.3	22,355.2	23,766.3
Exports of goods and services	18,125.0	22,055.0	31,578.0
Less Imports of goods and services	8,959.0	10,041.0	10,935.0
GDP in purchasers' values	30,496.2	34,369.2	44,409.3
GDP at constant 2000 prices	18,882.3	21,040.1	n.a.

Gross Domestic Product by Economic Activity

	2009	2010	2011
Agriculture, hunting, forestry and fishing	80.0	80.0	85.5
Mining and quarrying	15,059.9	18,483.9	27,575.4
Manufacturing	1,562.0	1,933.0	2,058.7
Electricity, gas and water	432.1	510.1	587.3
Construction	583.0	730.2	774.5
Trade	1,154.0	1,273.5	1,335.1
Restaurants and hotels	259.4	272.4	288.0
Transport, storage and communications	2,741.3	2,405.6	2,539.3
Finance, insurance, real estate and business services	5,058.7	4,649.8	4,444.3
Community, social and personal services	5,091.8	5,583.9	6,287.3
Sub-total	32,022.1	35,922.4	45,975.4
Import duties	196.8	211.5	206.4
Less Imputed bank service charges	−1,722.7	−1,764.7	−1,772.5
GDP in purchasers' values	30,496.2	34,369.2	44,409.3

BALANCE OF PAYMENTS
(US $ million)

	2008	2009	2010
Exports of goods f.o.b.	86,944	51,675	66,973
Imports of goods f.o.b.	−22,939	−17,285	−19,065
Trade balance	64,004	34,390	47,908
Exports of services	11,959	11,309	7,716
Imports of services	−15,777	−13,850	−13,617
Balance on goods and services	60,186	31,849	42,007
Other income received	13,962	8,599	9,619
Other income paid	−3,219	−1,671	−1,801
Balance on goods, services and income	70,929	38,776	49,825
Current transfers (net)	−10,689	−13,002	−13,003

—continued	2008	2009	2010
Current balance	60,239	25,774	36,822
Capital account (net)	1,729	1,065	2,158
Direct investment abroad	−9,091	−8,635	−2,068
Direct investment from abroad	−6	1,114	81
Portfolio investment assets	−32,085	−8,674	−6,921
Portfolio investment liabilities	3,955	−480	−815
Other investment assets	−18,281	3,148	−14,498
Other investment liabilities	4,227	−13,842	−10,461
Net errors and omissions	−10,040	3,376	−3,683
Overall balance	647	3,759	611

Source: IMF, *International Financial Statistics*.

External Trade

PRINCIPAL COMMODITIES
(KD million)

Imports c.i.f.	2007	2008	2009
Food and live animals	698	880	849
Chemicals and related products	484	558	571
Basic manufactures	1,394	1,478	973
Machinery and transport equipment	2,527	2,721	2,351
Miscellaneous manufactured articles	715	758	823
Total (incl. others)	6,062	6,679	5,852

Total imports: 6,428 in 2010; 6,972 in 2011 (preliminary).

Exports f.o.b.*	2008	2009	2010
Petroleum, petroleum products, etc.	22,092	13,415	17,681
Crude petroleum	15,492	8,882	11,409
Refinery products	5,976	4,736	5,554
Non-petroleum products	1,281	1,456	1,514
Plastics in primary forms	174	673	n.a.
Road vehicles	228	194	n.a.
Total	23,373	14,871	19,195

* Including re-exports (KD million): 460 in 2008; 466 in 2009; 512 in 2010.

Source: IMF, *Kuwait: Statistical Appendix* (June 2012).

PRINCIPAL TRADING PARTNERS
(KD million)*

Imports c.i.f.	2008	2009	2010
Australia	141.0	127.9	152.7
Brazil	162.5	78.2	74.1
Canada	93.1	50.0	78.4
China, People's Repub.	780.7	707.0	812.2
France (incl. Monaco)	136.8	160.4	153.1
Germany	489.1	445.7	475.0
India	302.7	315.5	369.2
Iran	58.8	35.3	31.2
Italy	322.8	261.2	307.1
Japan	641.1	419.4	517.0
Korea, Repub.	223.5	247.7	293.2
Malaysia	77.8	60.5	70.5
Netherlands	91.3	92.9	85.2
Saudi Arabia	374.6	346.8	344.3
Spain	64.7	59.7	66.5
Switzerland-Liechtenstein	102.1	91.8	143.6
Syria	25.3	32.3	28.4
Taiwan	52.3	106.7	55.3
Thailand	100.9	142.4	101.8
Turkey	152.1	76.3	137.0
United Arab Emirates	264.1	249.7	289.4
United Kingdom	190.2	188.4	200.0
USA	719.1	635.3	743.6
Total (incl. others)	6,678.7	5,852.2	6,498.6

Exports f.o.b.†	2008	2009	2010
Bahrain	45.2	41.2	29.7
Belgium-Luxembourg	2.3	5.1	3.6
China, People's Repub.	25.9	326.4	194.4
Egypt	20.4	23.3	19.3
India	143.9	94.4	118.5
Indonesia	56.4	41.8	58.1
Iran	34.5	26.8	32.2
Japan	8.7	2.1	1.6
Jordan	58.1	64.8	50.3
Korea, Repub.	4.1	3.4	25.5
Lebanon	13.9	13.4	13.7
Malaysia	9.3	10.1	38.1
Oman	16.0	18.9	24.1
Pakistan	69.1	37.0	44.6
Philippines	3.3	3.9	2.9
Qatar	55.9	42.3	36.0
Saudi Arabia	114.2	127.0	140.4
Spain	4.8	8.0	7.7
Syria	25.0	26.2	22.5
Taiwan	2.7	1.1	9.8
Turkey	34.3	65.9	37.4
United Arab Emirates	185.4	168.5	173.9
USA	125.8	51.8	49.4
Total (incl. others)	1,281.4	1,456.0	1,370.9

* Imports by country of production; exports by country of last consignment.
† Excluding petroleum exports.

Transport

ROAD TRAFFIC
(motor vehicles in use at 31 December)

	2009	2010
Passenger cars	1,150,840	1,202,704
Buses and coaches	24,759	25,668
Motorcycles and mopeds	7,664	8,765

Source: IRF, *World Road Statistics*.

SHIPPING

Flag Registered Fleet
(at 31 December)

	2010	2011	2012
Number of vessels	148	155	155
Displacement ('000 grt)	1,957.8	2,392.9	2,479.5

Source: Lloyd's List Intelligence (www.lloydslistintelligence.com).

International Sea-borne Freight Traffic
('000 metric tons)*

	1988	1989	1990
Goods loaded	61,778	69,097	51,400
Goods unloaded	7,123	7,015	4,522

* Including Kuwait's share of traffic in the Neutral (Partitioned) Zone.
Source: UN, *Monthly Bulletin of Statistics*.
Goods loaded ('000 metric tons): 89,945 in 1997.
Goods unloaded ('000 metric tons): 6,049 in 1997.

CIVIL AVIATION
(traffic on scheduled services)

	2007	2008	2009
Kilometres flown (million)	42	43	44
Passengers carried ('000)	2,660	2,524	2,597
Passenger-km (million)	7,721	7,368	7,670
Total ton-km (million)	967	945	976

Source: UN, *Statistical Yearbook*.
2010 ('000): Total passengers carried 2,741.

Tourism

VISITOR ARRIVALS BY COUNTRY OF ORIGIN
(incl. excursionists)

	2008	2009	2010
Bahrain	112,910	125,962	122,192
Bangladesh	93,585	104,757	102,390
Egypt	532,753	540,708	569,452
India	673,671	733,117	751,059
Iran	90,839	89,219	81,136
Lebanon	117,055	119,998	117,686
Pakistan	214,427	219,502	228,028
Philippines	117,812	130,417	135,182
Saudi Arabia	1,425,049	1,613,460	1,708,661
Sri Lanka	90,896	95,250	99,330
Syria	304,605	306,561	307,949
Total (incl. others)	4,735,910	5,087,781	5,207,785

Tourism receipts (US $ million, excl. passenger transport): 354 in 2009; 241 in 2010; 199 in 2011 (provisional).

Source: World Tourism Organization.

Communications Media

	2009	2010	2011
Telephones ('000 main lines in use)	528.5	519.4	514.7
Mobile cellular telephones ('000 subscribers)	2,618.4	3,979.1	4,934.2
Internet users ('000)	1,100	n.a.	n.a.
Broadband subscribers ('000)	45	46	n.a.

Source: International Telecommunication Union.

Education

(state-controlled schools, 2011/12)

	Schools	Teachers	Students Males	Females	Total
Kindergarten	201	5,755	22,876	21,867	44,743
Primary	253	21,520	70,707	65,171	135,878
Intermediate	204	17,404	55,180	52,436	107,616
Secondary	136	12,363	39,233	29,803	69,036
Religious institutes	9	699	1,059	1,649	2,708
Special training institutes	29	1,285	663	1,031	1,694

Private education (2011/12): 105 kindergarten schools (1,888 teachers, 37,433 students); 132 primary schools (5,204 teachers, 94,260 students); 133 intermediate schools (3,065 teachers, 57,743 students); 105 secondary schools (2,872 teachers, 34,832 students).

Pupil-teacher ratio (primary education, UNESCO estimate): 8.4 in 2009/10 (Source: UNESCO Institute for Statistics).

Adult literacy rate (UNESCO estimates): 93.9% (males 95.0%; females 91.8%) in 2008 (Source: UNESCO Institute for Statistics).

Directory

The Government

HEAD OF STATE

Amir of Kuwait: His Highness Sheikh SABAH AL-AHMAD AL-JABER AL-SABAH (acceded 29 January 2006).

COUNCIL OF MINISTERS
(May 2013)

Prime Minister: Sheikh JABER MUBARAK AL-HAMAD AL-SABAH.

First Deputy Prime Minister and Minister of the Interior: Sheikh AHMAD HOMOUD AL-JABER AL-SABAH.

Deputy Prime Minister and Minister of Foreign Affairs: Sheikh SABAH AL-KHALED AL-HAMAD AL-SABAH.

Deputy Prime Minister and Minister of Defence: Sheikh AHMAD KHALED AL-HAMAD AL-SABAH.

Deputy Prime Minister and Minister of Finance: MUSTAFA AL-SHAMALI.

Minister of Oil: HANI ABD AL-AZIZ HUSSEIN.

Minister of Education and Higher Education: Dr NAYEF FALAH AL-HAJRAF.

Minister of Commerce and Industry: ANAS KHALED AL-SALEH.

Minister of Justice and Minister of Awqaf (Religious Endowments) and Islamic Affairs: SHARIDA ABDULLAH AL-MUOSHERJI.

Minister of Communications and Minister of State for Housing Affairs: SALEM MUTHEYEB AHMED AL-UTHAINA.

Minister of State for Cabinet Affairs and Minister of State for Municipal Affairs: Sheikh MUHAMMAD ABDULLAH AL-MUBARAK AL-SABAH.

Minister of Health: Dr MUHAMMAD BARRAK AL-HAIFI.

Minister of Electricity and Water and Minister of Public Works: ABD AL-AZIZ ABD AL-LATIF AL-IBRAHIM.

Minister of State for Planning and Development and Minister of State for National Assembly Affairs: Dr ROLA ABDULLAH DASHTI.

Minister of Social Affairs and Labour: THEKRA AYED AL-RASHIDI.

Minister of Information and Minister of State for Youth Affairs: Sheikh SALMAN SABAH SALEM AL-HUMOUD AL-SABAH.

MINISTRIES

Diwan of the Prime Minister: POB 1397, 13014 Kuwait City; tel. 22000000; fax 22223150; e-mail contact@pm.gov.kw; internet www.pm.gov.kw.

Ministry of Awqaf (Religious Endowments) and Islamic Affairs: POB 13, 13001 Safat, Kuwait City; tel. 22487225; internet www.islam.gov.kw.

Ministry of Commerce and Industry: POB 2944, 13030 Safat, Kuwait City; tel. 2248000; fax 22424411; e-mail admin@moci.gov.kw; internet www.moci.gov.kw.

Ministry of Communications: POB 15, 13001 Safat, Kuwait City; tel. 24840606; fax 24814448; internet www.moc.kw.

Ministry of Defence: POB 1170, 13012 Safat, Kuwait City; tel. 24848300; fax 24846059; e-mail mod_info@mod.gov.kw; internet www.mod.gov.kw.

Ministry of Education: POB 7, 13001 Safat, Hilali St, Kuwait City; tel. 24839452; fax 22423676; e-mail webmaster@moe.edu.kw; internet www.moe.edu.kw.

Ministry of Electricity and Water: POB 12, South al-Sourra St, Ministries Area, Al Assimah, 13001 Safat, Kuwait City; tel. 25371000; fax 25371420; internet www.mew.gov.kw.

Ministry of Finance: POB 9, 13001 Safat, al-Morkab St, Ministries Complex, Kuwait City; tel. 22480000; fax 22404025; e-mail webmaster@mof.gov.kw; internet www.mof.gov.kw.

Ministry of Foreign Affairs: POB 3, 13001 Safat, Gulf St, Kuwait City; tel. 22425141; fax 22420429; e-mail mofa.site@mofa.gov.kw; internet www.mofa.gov.kw.

Ministry of Health: POB 5, 13001 Safat, Arabian Gulf St, Kuwait City; tel. 24863840; fax 24863485; e-mail health@moh.gov.kw; internet www.moh.gov.kw.

Ministry of Higher Education: tel. 24925177; fax 24925260; e-mail info_minister@mohe.edu.kw; internet www.mohe.edu.kw.

Ministry of Information: POB 193, 13002 Safat, al-Sour St, Kuwait City; tel. 22415301; fax 22418605; e-mail info@moinfo.gov.kw; internet www.moinfo.gov.kw.

Ministry of the Interior: POB 11, 13001 Safat, Kuwait City; tel. 22430500; fax 24348821; e-mail contact@moi.gov.kw; internet www.moi.gov.kw.

Ministry of Justice: POB 6, 13001 Safat, al-Morkab St, Ministries Complex, Kuwait City; tel. 22486218; fax 22442257; e-mail info@moj.gov.kw; internet www.moj.gov.kw.

Ministry of Oil: POB 5077, 13051 Safat, Kuwait City; tel. 22406990; e-mail alnaft@moo.gov.kw; internet www.moo.gov.kw.

Ministry of Planning and Development: POB 15, 13001 Safat, Kuwait City; tel. 22428200; fax 22430403; e-mail info@mop.gov.kw; internet www.mop.gov.kw.

Ministry of Public Works: POB 8, 13001 Safat, Kuwait City; tel. 25385520; fax 25380829; e-mail undersecretary@mpw.gov.kw; internet www.mpw.gov.kw.

Ministry of Social Affairs and Labour: POB 563, 13006 Safat, Kuwait City; tel. 22480000; fax 22419877; internet www.mosal.gov.kw.

Legislature

Majlis al-Umma
(National Assembly)

POB 716, Safat 13008; tel. 22436336; fax 22436331; e-mail kwt-ipu-grp@majlesalommah.net; internet www.kna.kw.

Speaker: ALI FAHAD AL-RASHED.

Elections to the 50-seat National Assembly took place more than one year early on 2 February 2012, following the dissolution of the legislature by Sheikh Sabah in December 2011 (precipitated by a dispute between the Government and parliament over allegations of corruption and public protests against the Government). Sunni Islamists opposed to the Government won 23 seats; liberals and their allies secured nine; Shi'ite Islamists took seven; and the remaining seats were won by independent candidates. No female candidates won election to the Assembly, in contrast to 2009, when four women were elected. On 20 June 2012 the National Assembly was dissolved and the Assembly members elected in 2009 reinstated, following a ruling by the Constitutional Court that declared the results of the 2 February 2012 elections to be null and void. However, more than one-half of those reinstated members immediately resigned their seats in protest against the decision. The restored Assembly was itself dissolved by Amiri decree on 7 October, and early elections were subsequently scheduled for 1 December. Despite a boycott organized by leading opponents of the Government and ongoing anti-Government protests, the election took place as scheduled. Shi'ite Islamist candidates secured 17 seats (compared with just seven at the February 2012 election), while Sunni Islamists won four seats (compared with 23 in February). Some 30 new deputies were reported to have been elected to the Assembly, including three women. According to the Ministry of Information, the rate of voter participation was recorded at 38.8%, although opponents of the Government claimed that the true figure was as low as 27%.

Political Organizations

Political parties are not permitted in Kuwait. However, several quasi-political organizations are in existence. Among those that have been represented in the Majlis since 1992 are:

Islamic Constitutional Movement (Hadas): internet www.icmkw.org; f. 1991; Sunni Muslim; political arm of the Muslim Brotherhood; Sec.-Gen. NASSER AL-SANE.

Islamic Salafi Alliance: Sunni Muslim; Sec.-Gen. ALI AL-OMAIR (acting).

Justice and Peace Alliance: Shi'a Muslim; Leader HASSAN NASIR.

Kuwait Democratic Forum: f. 1991; loose asscn of secular, liberal and Arab nationalist groups; campaigned for the extension of voting rights to women.

National Action Bloc: liberal, nationalist.

National Democratic Alliance (NDA): f. 1997; secular, liberal; Sec.-Gen. KHALED AL-KHALED.

National Islamic Alliance: Shi'a Muslim; Leader HUSSAIN AL-MA'TOUQ.

Popular Action Bloc: loose asscn of nationalists and Shi'a Muslims; Leader AHMAD AL-SAADOUN.

Diplomatic Representation

EMBASSIES IN KUWAIT

Afghanistan: POB 33186, 73452 Rawdah, Block 6, Surra St, Across Surra Co-op Society House 16, Kuwait City; tel. 25329461; fax 25326274; e-mail afg_emb_kuw@hotmail.com; Ambassador Dr ASADULLAH HANIF BALKHI.

Algeria: POB 578, 13006 Safat, Istiqlal St, Kuwait City; tel. 24820791; fax 24820853; e-mail ambalgkt@qualitynet.net; Ambassador KHAMISI ARIF.

Argentina: POB 3788, 40188 Mishref, Kuwait City; tel. 25379211; fax 25379212; e-mail ekuwa@mrecic.gov.ar; Ambassador JORGE OMAR ANTONIO BIGA.

Armenia: Jabriya District, Blk 8, St 3, Villa 8, Kuwait City; tel. 25322175; fax 25314656; e-mail embassy.kuwait@mfa.am; internet kuwait.mfa.am; Ambassador FADEY CHARCHOGHLYAN.

Australia: Dar al-Awadi Bldg (Level 12), Ahmad al-Jaber St, Sharq, Kuwait City; tel. 22322422; fax 22322430; e-mail austemb.kuwait@dfat.gov.au; internet www.kuwait.embassy.gov.au; Ambassador ROBERT TYSON.

Austria: POB 15013, Daiyah, Ahmed Shawki St, House 10, 35451 Kuwait City; tel. 22552532; fax 22563052; e-mail kuwait-ob@bmaa .gv.at; internet www.bmeia.gv.at/botschaft/kuwait; Ambassador ULRICH FRANK.

Azerbaijan: al-Yarmouk, Block 2, Villa 15, Kuwait City; tel. 25355247; fax 25355246; e-mail embazerbaijan@yahoo.com; internet www.azerembassy-kuwait.org; Ambassador TURAL RZAYEV.

Bahrain: POB 196, al-Surrah, Plot 5, al-Surrah Rd, Villa 27, Kuwait City; tel. 25318530; fax 25330882; e-mail Kuwait.mission@mofa.gov .bh; internet www.mofa.gov.bh/kuwait; Ambassador Sheikh KHALIFA BIN HAMAD AL KHALIFA.

Bangladesh: House 11, St 29, Blk 2, Khaldiya, Kuwait City; tel. 24913219; fax 24913205; e-mail ambassador.kuwait@mofa.gov.bd; internet kuwait.mofa.gov.bd; Ambassador SYED SHAHED REZA.

Belgium: POB 3280, Bayan, Blk 13, St 4, Villa 8, Safat, 13033 Kuwait City; tel. 25384582; fax 25384583; e-mail kuwait@diplobel .fed.be; internet www.diplomatie.be/kuwait; Ambassador DAMIEN ANGELET.

Bhutan: POB 1510, 13016 Safat, Adailiya-Block 3, Issa Abd al-Rahman al-Assoussi St, Jadda 32, Villa 7, Kuwait City; tel. 22516640; fax 22516550; e-mail bhutankuwait@hotmail.com; Ambassador Dasho TASHI PHUNTSOG.

Bosnia and Herzegovina: Bayan, Blk 5, Rd 2, St 5, Villa 18, Kuwait City; tel. 25392637; fax 25392106; Ambassador SENAHID BRISTRIĆ.

Brazil: POB 39761, 73058 Nuzha, Blk 1, St 116, House 47, Kuwait City; tel. 25378561; fax 25378560; e-mail embassy@brazil.org.kw; internet www.brazil.org.kw; Ambassador ROBERTO ABDALLA.

Bulgaria: POB 12090, 71651 Shamiya, Jabriya, Area 11, St 107 and St 1, Kuwait City; tel. 25314458; fax 25321453; e-mail Embassy .Kuwait@mfa.bg; internet www.mfa.bg/embassies/kuwait; Ambassador ALEXANDAR OLSHEVSKI.

Canada: POB 25281, 13113 Safat, Daiyah, Blk 4, al-Mutawakkel St, Villa 24, Kuwait City; tel. 22563025; fax 22560173; e-mail kwait@international.gc.ca; internet www.canadainternational.gc.ca/kuwait-koweit; Ambassador DOUGLAS GEORGE.

China, People's Republic: POB 2346, 13024 Safat, Yarmouk, Sheikh Ahmad al-Jaber Bldgs 4 & 5, St 1, Villa 82, Kuwait City; tel. 25333340; fax 25333341; e-mail chinakwt@hotmail.com; internet kw.chineseembassy.org; Ambassador CUI JIANCHUN.

Czech Republic: Nuzha, Blk 3, St 34, House 13, Kuwait City; tel. 22529018; fax 22529021; e-mail kuwait@embassy.mzv.cz; internet www.mzv.cz/kuwait; Ambassador MARTIN VÁVRA.

Egypt: POB 11252, 35153 Dasmah, Istiqlal St, Kuwait City; tel. 22519955; fax 22563877; e-mail embassy.kuwait@mfa.gov.eg; Ambassador ABD AL-KARIM SULEIMAN.

Eritrea: POB 53016, 73015 Nuzha, Jabriya, Block 9, St 21, House 9, Kuwait City; tel. 25317427; fax 26631304; Ambassador MAHMOUD OMAR CHURUM.

Ethiopia: POB 939, 45710 Safat, Jabriya, Block 10, St 107, Villa 30, Kuwait City; tel. 25330128; fax 25331179; e-mail ethiokwt@qualitynet.net; Ambassador MUHAMMAD GUDETA CHEBSA.

France: POB 1037, 13011 Safat, Mansouriah, Blk 1, St 13, Villa 24, Kuwait City; tel. 22582020; fax 22571058; e-mail cad.koweit-amba@diplomatie.gouv.fr; Ambassador NADA YAFI.

Georgia: Qurtoba, Blk 2, Area 1, Ave 3, Villa 6, Kuwait City; tel. 25352909; fax 25354707; e-mail kuwait.emb@mfa.gov.ge; internet www.kuwait.mfa.gov.ge; Chargé d'affaires a.i. BEZHAN SHONIA.

Germany: POB 805, 13009 Safat, Dahiya Abdullah al-Salem, Area 1, Ave 14, Branch of al-Yousef St, Villa 13, Kuwait City; tel. 22520827; fax 22520763; e-mail info@kuwait.diplo.de; internet www.kuwait.diplo.de; Ambassador FRANK M. MANN.

Greece: POB 23812, 13099 Safat, Khaldiya, Block 4, St 44, House 4, Kuwait City; tel. 24817100; fax 24817103; e-mail gremb.kuw@mfa .gr; Ambassador KONSTANTINOS DRAKAKIS.

Holy See: POB 29724, 13158 Safat, Kuwait City; tel. 22562248; fax 22562213; e-mail nuntiuskuwait@gmail.com; Apostolic Nuncio Most Rev. Archbishop PETAR RAJIC (Titular Archbishop of Sarsenterum).

Hungary: POB 23955, 13100 Safat, Bayan, Blk 13, St 30, Villa 381, Kuwait City; tel. 25379351; fax 25379350; e-mail mission.kwi@mfa .gov.hu; internet www.mfa.gov.hu/emb/kuwait; Ambassador FERENC CSILLAG.

India: POB 1450, 13015 Safat, Diplomatic Enclave, Arabian Gulf St, Kuwait City; tel. 22530600; fax 22546958; e-mail contact@indembkwt.org; internet www.indembkwt.org; Ambassador SATISH C. MEHTA.

Indonesia: POB 21560, 13076 Safat, Kaifan, Blk 6, al-Andalus St, House 29, Kuwait City; tel. 24839927; fax 24819250; e-mail unitkom@kbrikuwait.org; internet kuwaitcity.kemlu.go.id; Ambassador FERRY ADAMHAR.

Iran: POB 4686, 13047 Safat, Daiyah, Embassies Area, Block B, Kuwait City; tel. 22560694; fax 22529868; e-mail iranembassy@hotmail.com; Ambassador RUHOLLAH QAHREMANI CHABOK.

Iraq: Kuwait City; e-mail kuwemb@iraqmfamail.com; Ambassador MUHAMMAD HUSSAIN BAHR AL-ULUM.

Italy: POB 4453, 13045 Safat, Jabriya, Blk 9, St 1, Villa 84, Kuwait City; tel. 25356010; fax 25356030; e-mail ambasciata.alkuwait@esteri.it; internet www.ambalkuwait.esteri.it; Ambassador FABRIZIO NICOLETTI.

Japan: POB 2304, 13024 Safat, Plot 57, Blk 7A, Diplomatic Zone, Mishref, Kuwait City; tel. 25309400; fax 25309401; e-mail info@embjp-kw.org; internet www.kw.emb-japan.go.jp; Ambassador YASUYOSHI KOMIZO.

Jordan: POB 39891, 73059 Kuwait City; tel. 22533261; fax 22533270; e-mail kujor@qualitynet.net; Ambassador MUHAMMAD AL-KAYED.

Korea, Republic: POB 4272, 13043 Safat, Plot 6, Blk 7A, Diplomatic Zone 2, Mishref, Kuwait City; tel. 25378621; fax 25378628; e-mail kuwait@mofat.go.kr; internet kwt.mofat.go.kr; Ambassador KIM KYUNG-SIK.

Lebanon: POB 253, 13003 Safat, Da'Yiah Diplomatic Area, Plot 6, Kuwait City; tel. 22562103; fax 22571682; e-mail lebembassy@lebanonembassy.org.kw; internet www.lebanonembassy.org.kw; Ambassador Dr BASSEM ABD AL-QADIR AL-NO'MANI.

Libya: POB 21460, 13075 Safat, 27 Istiqlal St, Kuwait City; tel. 22575183; fax 22575182; Ambassador Dr MUHAMMAD SALEM EMAISH.

Malaysia: POB 4105, 13042 Safat, Daiya, Diplomatic Enclave, Area 5, Yemen St, Plot 5, Kuwait City; tel. 22550394; fax 22550384; e-mail malkuwait@kln.gov.my; internet www.kln.gov.my/perwakilan/kuwait; Ambassador Dato' ADNAN Haji OTHMAN.

Mongolia: Block 8, St 806, Villa 161, al-Zahra Area, Kuwait City; tel. 25216551; fax 25216557; e-mail kuwait@mfat.gov.mn; Ambassador SODNOMYN ENKHBAT.

Morocco: Yarmouk, Blk 2, St 2, Villa 14, Kuwait City; tel. 25312980; fax 25317423; e-mail ambkow@yahoo.fr; Ambassador YAHYA BANANI.

Netherlands: Blk 6, St 11, House 7, Jabriya, Kuwait City; tel. 25312650; fax 25326334; e-mail kwe@minbuza.nl; internet www .netherlandsembassy.gov.kw; Ambassador NICOLAAS BEETS.

Niger: POB 44451, 32059 Hawalli, Salwa Block 12, St 6, Villa 183, Kuwait City; tel. 25652943; fax 25640478; Ambassador ABDOUL-KARIMOU SEINI.

Nigeria: POB 6432, 32039 Hawalli, Surra, Area 1, St 14, House 24, Kuwait City; tel. 18278813; fax 18278896; Ambassador HARUNA GARBA.

Oman: POB 21975, 13080 Safat, al-Odeilia Block 3, St 3, Villa 25, Kuwait City; tel. 22561956; fax 22561963; e-mail kuwait@mofa.gov .om; Ambassador Sheikh SALIM BIN SUHAIL AL-MA'ASHANI.

Pakistan: POB 988, 13010 Safat, Jabriya, Police Station Rd, St 101, Plot 5, Blk 11, Villa 46, Kuwait City; tel. 25327649; fax 25327648; e-mail parepkwt@yahoo.com; internet www.mofa.gov.pk/kuwait; Ambassador (vacant).

Philippines: POB 26288, 13123 Safat, Blk 6, Villa 153, Nouman Bin Basher St, corner Damascus St, Faiha, Kuwait City; tel. 22528422; fax 22511805; e-mail kuwaitpe@philembassykuwait.gov.kw; internet www.philembassykuwait.gov.kw; Ambassador SHULAN O. PRIMAVERA.

Poland: POB 5066, 13051 Safat, Jabriya, Blk 7, St 3, Villa 20, Kuwait City; tel. 25311571; fax 25311576; e-mail kuwejt.amb .sekretariat@msz.gov.pl; internet www.kuwejt.polemb.net; Ambassador JANUSZ SZWEDO.

Qatar: POB 1825, 13019 Safat, Diiyah, Istiqlal St, Kuwait City; tel. 22523107; fax 22513604; e-mail kuwait@mofa.gov.qa; Ambassador ABD AL-AZIZ BIN SAAD AL-FEHAID.

Romania: POB 13574, 35152 Dasmah, Keifan, Area 4, Moona St, House 34, Kuwait City; tel. 24845079; fax 24848929; e-mail ambsa@kems.net; Ambassador VASILE SOFINETI.

Russia: POB 1765, Safat, Daya Diplomatic Area, Plot 17, Blk 5, Kuwait City; tel. 22560427; fax 22524969; e-mail rusposkuw@mail.ru; internet www.kuwait.mid.ru; Ambassador ALEKSANDR KINSHCHAK.

Saudi Arabia: POB 20498, 13065 Safat, Istiqlal St, Kuwait City; tel. 22550021; fax 22551858; Ambassador ABD AL-AZIZ AL-FAYEZ.

Senegal: POB 23892, 13099 Safat, Rawdah, Block 3, St 35, Villa 9, Kuwait City; tel. 22573477; fax 22542044; e-mail senegal_embassy@yahoo.com; Ambassador ABDOU LAHAD MBACKE.

Serbia: POB 20511, 13066 Safat, Surra, Blk 5, St 1, Villa 71, Kuwait City; tel. 25327548; fax 25327568; e-mail embrskw@qualitynet.net; internet kuwait.mfa.gov.rs; Ambassador MIHAILO BRKIĆ.

Somalia: POB 22766, 13088 Safat, Bayan, St 1, Block 7, Villa 25, Kuwait City; tel. 25394795; fax 25394829; e-mail webmaster@somaligov.net; internet www.kuwait.somaligov.net; Ambassador Dr ABDUL KHADIR AMIN SHEIKH ABUBAKER.

South Africa: POB 2262, 40173 Mishref, Salwa Block 10, St 1, Villa 91, Unit 3, Kuwait City; tel. 25617988; fax 25617917; e-mail kuwait.political@dirco.gov.za; Ambassador DELAREY VAN TONDER.

Spain: POB 22207, 13083 Safat, Surra, Block 3, St 14, Bldg 19, Kuwait City; tel. 25325827; fax 25325826; e-mail emb.kuwait@mae.es; Ambassador ÁNGEL LOSADA FERNÁNDEZ.

Sri Lanka: POB 44650, Jabriya, Blk 10, St 107, Bldg 1, Kuwait City; tel. 25339140; fax 25339154; e-mail lankaemb@qualitynet.net; internet www.slembkwt.org; Ambassador C. A. H. M. WIJERATNE.

Switzerland: POB 23954, 13100 Safat, Qortuba, Blk 2, St 1, House 122, Kuwait City; tel. 25340172; fax 25340176; e-mail kow.vertretung@eda.admin.ch; internet www.eda.admin.ch/kuwait; Ambassador ETIENNE THÉVOZ.

Syria: POB 25600, 13116 Safat, Kuwait City; tel. 25396560; fax 25396509; Ambassador (vacant).

Thailand: POB 66647, 43757 Bayan, Blk 6, St 8, Villa 1, Jabriya, Kuwait City; tel. 25317530; fax 25317532; e-mail thaiemkw@kems.net; internet www.thaiembassy.org/kuwait; Ambassador SURASAK CHUASUKONTHIP.

Tunisia: POB 5976, 13060 Safat, Nuzha, Plot 2, Nuzha St, Villa 45, Kuwait City; tel. 2542144; fax 2528995; e-mail tunemrku@ncc.moc.kw; Ambassador MUSTAPHA BAHIA.

Turkey: POB 20627, 13067 Safat, Blk 5, Plot 16, Istiqlal St, Kuwait City; tel. 22277400; fax 22560653; e-mail embassy.kuwait@mfa.gov.tr; internet kuwait.emb.mfa.gov.tr; Ambassador MURAT TAMER.

Ukraine: POB 7588, 32096 Hawalli, Jabriya, Blk 10, St 6, House 5, Kuwait City; tel. 25318507; fax 25318508; e-mail emb_kw@mfa.gov.ua; internet www.mfa.gov.ua/kuwait; Ambassador VOLODYMYR TOLKACH.

United Arab Emirates: POB 1828, 13019 Safat, Blk 5, Yemen St, Bldg 7, Kuwait City; tel. 22528544; fax 22526382; e-mail kuwait@mofa.gov.ae; internet uae-embassy.ae/Embassies/kw; Ambassador ALI AHMAD BIN SHUKR AL-ZA'ABI.

United Kingdom: POB 2, 13001 Safat, Arabian Gulf St, Kuwait City; tel. 22594320; fax 22594339; e-mail kuwait.generalenquiries@fco.gov.uk; internet ukinkuwait.fco.gov.uk; Ambassador FRANCIS RAYMOND (FRANK) BAKER.

USA: POB 77, 13001 Safat, Bayan, al-Masjed al-Aqsa St, Plot 14, Block 14, Kuwait City; tel. 22591001; fax 25380282; e-mail paskuwaitm@state.gov; internet kuwait.usembassy.gov; Ambassador MATTHEW H. TUELLER.

Uzbekistan: Mishref, Blk 2, St 5, Villa 18A, Kuwait City; Ambassador ABDURAFIK A. HOSHIMOV.

Venezuela: POB 24440, 13105 Safat, Block 5, St 7, Area 356, Surra, Kuwait City; tel. 25324367; fax 25324368; e-mail embavene@qualitynet.net; Ambassador ELOY FERNÁNDEZ AZUAJE.

Yemen: POB 7182, al-Jabriya St, Kuwait City; tel. 25349416; fax 25349415; Ambassador KHALED SHEIKH.

Zimbabwe: POB 36484, 24755 Salmiya, Kuwait City; tel. 25620845; fax 25621491; e-mail zimkuwait@hotmail.com; Ambassador MARK GREY MARONGWE.

Judicial System

Constitutional Court: Comprises five judges. Interprets the provisions of the Constitution; considers disputes regarding the constitutionality of legislation, decrees and rules; has jurisdiction in challenges relating to the election of members, or eligibility for election, to the Majlis al-Umma.

Court of Cassation: Comprises five judges. Is competent to consider the legality of verdicts of the Court of Appeal and State Security Court; Chief Justice MUHAMMAD YOUSUF AL-RIFA'I.

Court of Appeal: Comprises three judges. Considers verdicts of the Court of First Instance; Chief Justice RASHED AL-HAMMAD.

Court of First Instance: Comprises the following divisions: Civil and Commercial (one judge), Personal Status Affairs (one judge), Lease (three judges), Labour (one judge), Crime (three judges), Administrative Disputes (three judges), Appeal (three judges), Challenged Misdemeanours (three judges); Chief Justice MUHAMMAD AL-SAKHOBY.

Summary Courts: Each governorate has a Summary Court, comprising one or more divisions. The courts have jurisdiction in the following areas: Civil and Commercial, Urgent Cases, Lease, Misdemeanours. The verdict in each case is delivered by one judge.

There is also a **Traffic Court**, with one presiding judge.

Prosecutor-General: HAMAD AL-OTHMAN.

Religion

ISLAM

The majority of Kuwaitis are Muslims of the Sunni or Shi'a sects. The Shi'ite community comprises about 30% of the total.

CHRISTIANITY

The Roman Catholic Church

Latin Rite

For ecclesiastical purposes, Kuwait forms part of the Apostolic Vicariate of Northern Arabia.

Vicar Apostolic: CAMILLO BALLIN (Titular Bishop of Arna), Bishop's House, POB 25362, Rd 4603, House 137/125, Blk 946, Awali, Bahrain; tel. (+973) 39504488; fax 22420297; e-mail mail@camilloballin.com; internet www.avona.org.

Melkite Rite

Exarch Patriarchal: Rev. BOUTROS GHARIB, Vicariat Patriarchal Greek-Melkite, POB 1205, Salwa Block 12, St 6, House 58, 22013 Salmiya, Kuwait City; tel. and fax 25652802; e-mail greekcatholickuwait@yahoo.com.

Syrian Rite

The Syrian Catholic Patriarch of Antioch is resident in Beirut, Lebanon. The Patriarchal Exarchate of Basra and the Gulf, is based in Basra, Iraq.

The Anglican Communion

Within the Episcopal Church in Jerusalem and the Middle East, Kuwait forms part of the diocese of Cyprus and the Gulf. The Anglican congregation in Kuwait is entirely expatriate. The Bishop in Cyprus and the Gulf is resident in Cyprus, while the Archdeacon in the Gulf is resident in Bahrain.

Other Christian Churches

National Evangelical Church in Kuwait: POB 80, 13001 Safat, Kuwait City; tel. 22407195; fax 22431087; e-mail elc@ncc.moc.kw; Rev. NABIL ATTALLAH (pastor of the Arabic-language congregation), Rev. JERRY A. ZANDSTRA (senior pastor of the English-speaking congregation); an independent Protestant Church founded by the Reformed Church in America; services in Arabic, English, Korean, Malayalam and other Indian languages; combined weekly congregation of some 20,000.

The Armenian, Greek, Coptic and Syrian Orthodox Churches are also represented in Kuwait.

The Press

Freedom of the press and publishing is guaranteed in the Constitution, although press censorship was in force between mid-1986 and early 1992 (when journalists adopted a voluntary code of practice). In February 1995 a ruling by the Constitutional Court effectively endorsed the Government's right to suspend publication of newspapers; however, legislation passed in 2006 rendered this illegal without a court order. The Government provides financial support to newspapers and magazines.

DAILIES

Al-Anbaa (The News): POB 23915, 13100 Safat, Kuwait City; tel. 24830322; fax 24832647; e-mail editorial@alanba.com.kw; internet www.alanba.com.kw; f. 1976; Arabic; general; Editor-in-Chief BIBI KHALID AL-MARZOOQ; circ. 85,000.

Arab Times: POB 2270, Airport Road, Shuwaikh, 13023 Safat, Kuwait City; tel. 24849144; fax 24818267; e-mail arabtimes@arabtimesonline.com; internet www.arabtimesonline.com; f. 1977; English; political and financial; no Fri. edn; Editor-in-Chief AHMAD ABD AL-AZIZ AL-JARALLAH; Man. Editor MISHAL AL-JARALLAH; circ. 41,922.

Al-Jarida (The Newspaper): POB 29846, 13159 Safat, Kuwait City; tel. 22257036; fax 22257035; e-mail info@aljarida.com; internet www.aljarida.com; f. 2007; Arabic; affiliated with the Nat. Democratic Alliance; Editor-in-Chief KHALID HILAL AL-MUTAIRI.

Kuwait Times: POB 1301, 13014 Safat, Kuwait City; tel. 24833199; fax 24835621; e-mail info@kuwaittimes.net; internet www.kuwaittimes.net; f. 1961; English, Malayalam and Urdu; political; Editor-in-Chief ABD AL-RAHMAN ALYAN; circ. 32,000.

Al-Qabas (Firebrand): POB 21800, 13078 Safat, Kuwait City; tel. 24812822; fax 24834355; e-mail info@alqabas.com.kw; internet www.alqabas.com.kw; f. 1972; Arabic; independent; Gen. Man. FOUZAN AL-FARES; Editor-in-Chief WALEED ABD AL-LATIF AL-NISF; circ. 60,000.

Al-Ra'i al-'Aam (Public Opinion): POB 761, 13008 Safat, Kuwait City; tel. 24817777; fax 24838352; e-mail editor@alraialaam.com; internet www.alraialaam.com; f. 1961; Arabic; political, social and cultural; Editor-in-Chief YOUSUF AL-JALAHMA; circ. 101,500.

Al-Seyassah (Policy): POB 2270, Shuwaikh, Kuwait City; tel. 24813566; fax 24846905; internet www.al-seyassah.com; f. 1965; Arabic; political and financial; Editor-in-Chief AHMAD ABD AL-AZIZ AL-JARALLAH; circ. 70,000.

Al-Watan (The Homeland): POB 1142, 13012 Safat, Kuwait City; tel. 24840950; fax 24818481; e-mail alwatan@alwatan.com.kw; internet www.alwatan.com.kw; f. 1962; Arabic; political; Editor-in-Chief Sheikh KHALIFA ALI AL-KHALIFA AL-SABAH; Gen. Man. DINA AL-MALLAK; circ. 91,726.

WEEKLIES AND PERIODICALS

Al-Balagh (Communiqué): POB 4558, 13046 Safat, Kuwait City; tel. 24818820; fax 24812735; e-mail albalagh5@yahoo.com; internet www.al-balagh.com; f. 1969; weekly; Arabic; general, political and Islamic affairs; Editor-in-Chief ABD AL-RAHMAN RASHID AL-WALAYATI; circ. 29,000.

Byzance: Kuwait City; f. 2007; bi-monthly; Arabic and French; lifestyle magazine, incl. features on fashion, jewellery, furniture and art; Man. Editor JEAN-PIERRE GUEIRARD; Exec. Editor-in-Chief ANTOINE DAHER.

Al-Dakhiliya (The Interior): POB 71655, 12500 Shamiah, Kuwait City; tel. 22410091; fax 22410609; e-mail moipr@qualitynet.net; monthly; Arabic; official reports, transactions and proceedings; publ. by Public Relations Dept, Ministry of the Interior; Editor-in-Chief Lt-Col AHMAD A. AL-SHARQAWI.

Dalal Magazine: POB 6000, 13060 Safat, Kuwait City; tel. 24832098; fax 24832039; internet www.dalal-kw.com; f. 1997; monthly; Arabic; family affairs, beauty, fashion; Editor-in-Chief AHMAD YOUSUF BEHBEHANI.

Friday Times: POB 1301, 13014 Safat, Kuwait City; tel. 24833199; fax 24835627; e-mail info@kuwaittimes.net; internet www.kuwaittimes.net; f. 2005; weekend edn of *Kuwait Times*.

Al-Hadaf (The Objective): POB 2270, 13023 Safat, Kuwait City; tel. 24813566; fax 24816042; internet www.al-seyassah.com/alhadaf; f. 1964; weekly; Arabic; social and cultural; Editor-in-Chief AHMAD ABD AL-AZIZ AL-JARALLAH; circ. 268,904.

Al-Iqtisadi al-Kuwaiti (Kuwaiti Economist): POB 775, 13008 Safat, Kuwait City; tel. 1805580; fax 22404110; e-mail kcci@kcci.org.kw; internet www.kcci.org.kw; f. 1960; monthly; Arabic; commerce, trade and economics; publ. by Kuwait Chamber of Commerce and Industry; Editor MAJED B. JAMALUDDIN; circ. 6,000.

Journal of the Gulf and Arabian Peninsula Studies: POB 17073, 72451 Khaldiya, Kuwait University, Kuwait City; tel. 24833215; fax 24833705; e-mail jotgaaps@kuc01.kuniv.edu.kw; internet pubcouncil.kuniv.edu.kw/jgaps; f. 1975; quarterly; Arabic and English; publ. by Academic Publication Council of Kuwait Univ; Editor-in-Chief Dr FATIMA HUSSAIN ABD AL-RAZZAQ.

Al-Khaleej Business Magazine: POB 25725, 13118 Safat, Kuwait City; tel. 22433765; e-mail aljabriya@gulfweb.com; Editor-in-Chief AHMAD ISMAIL BEHBEHANI.

Kuwait Medical Journal (KMJ): POB 1202, 13013 Safat, Kuwait City; tel. 25316023; fax 25317972; e-mail kmj@kma.org.kw; internet www.kma.org.kw/KMJ; f. 1967; quarterly; English; publ. by the Kuwait Medical Asscn; original articles, review articles, case reports,

short communications, letters to the editor and book reviews; Editor-in-Chief Prof. FOUAD ABDULLAH M. HASSAN; circ. 5,000.

Kuwait al-Youm (Kuwait Today): POB 193, 13002 Safat, Kuwait City; tel. 24842167; fax 24831044; e-mail info@ipd.gov.kw; internet www.ipd.gov.kw; f. 1954; weekly; Arabic; statistics, Amiri decrees, laws, govt announcements, decisions, invitations for tenders, etc.; publ. by the Ministry of Information; circ. 5,000.

Al-Kuwaiti (The Kuwaiti): Information Dept, POB 9758, 61008 Ahmadi, Kuwait City; tel. 23981076; fax 23983661; e-mail kocinfo@kockw.com; f. 1961; monthly journal of the Kuwait Oil Co; Arabic; Editor-in-Chief KHALED AL-KHAMEES; circ. 6,500.

The Kuwaiti Digest: Information Dept, POB 9758, 61008 Ahmadi, Kuwait City; tel. 23981076; fax 23983661; e-mail kocinfo@kockw.com; f. 1972; quarterly journal of Kuwait Oil Co; English; Editor-in-Chief KHALED AL-KHAMEES; circ. 7,000.

Al-Majaless (Meetings): POB 5605, 13057 Safat, Kuwait City; tel. 24841178; fax 24847126; e-mail qasem@almajaless.com; weekly; Arabic; current affairs; Editor-in-Chief QASIM ABD AL-QADIR; circ. 60,206.

Mejallat al-Kuwait (Kuwait Magazine): POB 193, 13002 Safat, Kuwait City; tel. 22415300; fax 22419642; f. 1961; monthly; Arabic; illustrated magazine; science, arts and literature; publ. by the Ministry of Information.

Mirat al-Umma (Mirror of the Nation): POB 1142, 13012 Safat, Kuwait City; tel. 24837212; fax 24838671; weekly; Arabic; Editor-in-Chief MUHAMMAD AL-JASSEM; circ. 79,500.

Al-Nahdha (The Renaissance): POB 695, 13007 Safat, Kuwait City; tel. 24813133; fax 24849298; f. 1967; weekly; Arabic; social and political; Editor-in-Chief THAMER AL-SALAH; circ. 170,000.

Osrati (My Family): POB 2995, 13030 Safat, Kuwait City; tel. 24813233; fax 24838933; e-mail info@osratimag.com; internet www.osratimag.com; f. 1964; weekly; Arabic; women's magazine; publ. by Fahad al-Marzouk Establishment; Editor GHANIMA F. AL-MARZOUK; circ. 10,500.

Al-Talia (The Ascendant): POB 1082, 13011 Safat, Kuwait City; tel. 24831200; fax 24840471; f. 1962; weekly; Arabic; politics and literature; Editor AHMAD YOUSUF AL-NAFISI; circ. 10,000.

Al-Yaqza (The Awakening): POB 6000, 13060 Safat, Kuwait City; tel. 24831318; fax 24832039; internet www.alyaqza.com; f. 1966; weekly; Arabic; political, economic, social and general; Editor-in-Chief AHMAD YOUSUF BEHBEHANI; circ. 91,340.

NEWS AGENCY

Kuwait News Agency (KUNA): POB 24063, 13101 Safat, Kuwait City; tel. 24834546; fax 24813424; e-mail kuna@kuna.net.kw; internet www.kuna.net.kw; f. 1979; public corporate body; independent; also publishes research digests on topics of common and special interest; Chair. and Dir-Gen. Sheikh MUBARAK AL-DUAIJ AL-SABAH.

PRESS ASSOCIATION

Kuwait Journalists Association: POB 5454, 13055 Safat, Kuwait City; tel. 24843351; fax 24842874; e-mail kja@kja-kw.com; internet www.kja-kw.com; Chair. AHMAD YOUSUF BEHBEHANI.

Publishers

Al-Abraj Translation and Publishing Co WLL: POB 26177, 13122 Safat, Kuwait City; tel. 22442310; fax 22407024; Man. Dir Dr TARIQ ABDULLAH.

Dar al-Seyassah Publishing, Printing and Distribution Co: POB 2270, 13023 Safat, Kuwait City; tel. 24813566; fax 24833628; internet www.dar-al-seyassah.com; publ. *Arab Times, Al-Seyassah* and *Al-Hadaf.*

Gulf Centre Publishing and Publicity: POB 2722, 13028 Safat, Kuwait City; tel. 22402760; fax 22458833; Propr HAMZA ISMAIL ESSLAH.

Kuwait National Advertising and Publishing Co (KNAPCO): POB 2268, Safat 13023, Kuwait City; tel. 25745770; fax 25745779; e-mail support@knapco.com; internet www.knapco.com; f. 1995; publ. annual commercial business directory, *Teledymag*; Founder NAWAF ABD AL-RAZAK.

Kuwait Publishing House Co: POB 1446, 13015 Safat, Kuwait City; tel. 22449686; fax 22436956; e-mail info@kuwaitpocketguide.com; f. 1970; Dir ESAM AS'AD ABU AL-FARAJ.

Kuwait United Co for Advertising, Publishing and Distribution WLL: POB 29359, 13153 Safat, Kuwait City; tel. 24817111; fax 24817797.

Al-Talia Printing and Publishing Co: POB 1082, Airport Rd, Shuwaikh, 13011 Safat, Kuwait City; tel. 24840470; fax 24815611; Man. AHMAD YOUSUF AL-NAFISI.

GOVERNMENT PUBLISHING HOUSE

Ministry of Information: see Ministries.

Broadcasting and Communications

TELECOMMUNICATIONS

National Mobile Telecommunications Co KSC (Wataniya Telecom): POB 613, 13007 Safat, Kuwait City; tel. 65805555; fax 22423369; e-mail info@wataniya.com; internet www.wataniya.com; f. 1999; Qatar Telecommunications Corpn (Q-Tel) acquired 51% stake 2007; Chair. and Man. Dir Sheikh ABDULLAH BIN MUHAMMAD BIN SAUD AL THANI; CEO and Gen. Man. Dr BASSAM HANNOUN.

VIVA: POB 181, Salmiya 22002, Kuwait City; tel. 55670000; fax 55676666; e-mail info@viva.com.kw; internet www.viva.com.kw; f. 2008; mobile cellular communications; commercial brand of Kuwait Telecom Co; Chair. ADEL MUHAMMAD AL-ROUMI; CEO NAJEEB AL-AWADI.

Zain Kuwait: POB 22244, 13083 Safat, Kuwait City; tel. 24644444; fax 24641111; e-mail info.kw@zain.com; internet www.kw.zain.com; f. 1983 as Mobile Telecommunications Co; in Sept. 2007 began operating under new global brand, Zain; group operates in 24 countries in the Middle East and Africa; 1.8m. subscribers in Kuwait, 69.5m. total group subscribers (30 June 2009); Chair. ASAAD AL-BANWAN; CEO SCOTT GEGENHEIMER.

BROADCASTING

Radio

Radio of the State of Kuwait: POB 397, 13004 Safat, Kuwait City; tel. 22423774; fax 22456660; e-mail info@moinfo.gov.kw; internet www.moinfo.gov.kw; f. 1951; broadcasts daily in Arabic, Farsi, English and Urdu, some in stereo; Dir of Radio Dr ABD AL-AZIZ ALI MANSOUR; Dir of Radio Programmes ABD AL-RAHMAN HADI.

Television

Kuwait Television: POB 193, 13002 Safat, Kuwait City; tel. 22415301; fax 22438403; e-mail info@moinfo.gov.kw; internet www.moinfo.gov.kw; f. 1961; transmission began privately in Kuwait in 1957; transmits in Arabic; colour television service began in 1973; has a total of five channels; Head of News Broadcasting MUHAMMAD AL-KAHTANI.

Al-Rai: Kuwait City; tel. 24817777; fax 24953002; e-mail alraitv@alrai.tv; internet www.alrai.tv; f. 2004; first private satellite television station in Kuwait; admin. offices in Kuwait and transmission facilities in Dubai (United Arab Emirates); owned by Al-Rai Media Group.

Finance

(cap. = capital; res = reserves; dep. = deposits; m. = million; br(s) = branch(es); amounts in Kuwaiti dinars, unless otherwise stated)

BANKING

Central Bank

Central Bank of Kuwait: POB 526, 13006 Safat, Abdullah al-Salem St, Kuwait City; tel. 22449200; fax 22464887; e-mail cbk@cbk.gov.kw; internet www.cbk.gov.kw; f. 1969; cap. 5m., res 562m., dep. 3,369m. (March 2010); Governor Dr MUHAMMAD AL-HASHEL.

National Banks

Al-Ahli Bank of Kuwait KSC (ABK): POB 1387, 13014 Safat, Ahmad al-Jaber St, Kuwait City; tel. 22400900; fax 22424557; e-mail marketing@abkuwait.com; internet www.eahli.com/abk; f. 1967; wholly owned by private Kuwaiti interests; cap. 144m., res 266m., dep. 2,525m. (Dec. 2011); Chair. AHMAD YOUSUF BEHBEHANI; Dep. Chair. and Man. Dir ALI HILAL AL-MUTAIRI; 25 domestic brs and 2 foreign brs.

Ahli United Bank KSC (BKME): POB 71, 13001 Safat, Joint Banking Centre, East Tower, Darwazat Abd al-Razzak, Kuwait City; tel. 22459771; fax 22461430; e-mail hayakom@bkme.com.kw; internet www.bkme.com; f. 1971; fmrly Bank of Kuwait and the Middle East KSC; current name adopted in April 2010 after acquiring Kuwaiti brs of British Bank of the Middle East; 75% owned by Ahli United Bank (Bahrain); cap. 112m., res 69m., dep.

2,312m. (Dec. 2011); Chair. and Man. Dir HAMAD ABD AL-MOHSEN AL-MARZOUQ; 26 brs.

BBK: POB 24396, 13104 Safat, Ahmad al-Jaber St, Kuwait City; tel. 22417140; fax 22440937; e-mail bbkp@batelco.com.bh; internet www.bbkonline.com; f. 1971 as Bank of Bahrain and Kuwait BSC; name changed as above in 2005; dep. BD 1,756.4m. (Dec. 2009); Chair. MURAD ALI MURAD; Chief Exec. ABD AL-KARIM AHMAD BUCHEERI.

Boubyan Bank KSC: POB 25507, 13116 Safat, Kuwait City; tel. 22325000; fax 22454263; e-mail info@bankboubyan.com; internet www.bankboubyan.com; f. 2004; cap. 174m., res 63m., dep. 1,282m. (Dec. 2011); Chair. and Man. Dir ADEL ABD AL-WAHAB AL-MAJID.

Burgan Bank SAK: POB 5389, 12170 Safat, Abd al-Haih al-Ahmad St, Kuwait City; tel. 22439000; fax 22461148; e-mail info@burgan.com; internet www.burgan.com; f. 1975; 33.9% owned by Kuwait Projects Co (Holding), Safat; cap. 147m., res 229m., dep. 3,737m. (Dec. 2011); Chair. MAJID EISA AL-AJEEL; CEO EDUARDO EGUREN LINSEN; 20 brs.

Commercial Bank of Kuwait SAK: POB 2861, 13029 Safat, Mubarak al-Kabir St, Kuwait City; tel. 22411001; fax 22464870; e-mail cbking@cbk.com; internet www.cbk.com; f. 1960 by Amiri decree; cap. 127m., res 289m., dep. 3,140m. (Dec. 2011); Chair. and Man. Dir ALI MOUSA M. AL-MOUSA; CEO NUHAD KALIM SALIBA; 51 brs.

Gulf Bank KSC: POB 3200, 13032 Safat, Mubarak al-Kabir St, Kuwait City; tel. 22449501; fax 22445212; e-mail customerservice@gulfbank.com.kw; internet www.e-gulfbank.com; f. 1960; cap. 250m., res 171m., dep. 4,183m. (Dec. 2011); Chair. MAHMOUD ABD AL-KHALEQ AL-NOURI; CEO and Chief Gen. Man. MICHEL ACCAD; 52 brs.

Industrial Bank of Kuwait KSC (IBK): POB 3146, 13032 Safat, Joint Banking Centre, Darwazzat Abd al-Razaq, Commercial Area 9, Kuwait City; tel. 22457661; fax 22406595; e-mail ibk@ibkuwt.com; internet www.ibkuwt.com; 31.4% state-owned; f. 1973; cap. 20m., res 172m., dep. 133m. (Dec. 2011); Chair. and Man. Dir ABD AL-MOHSEN YOUSUF AL-HANIF; Gen. Man. ALI ABD AL-NABI KHAJA.

Kuwait Finance House KSC (KFH): POB 24989, 13110 Safat, Abdullah al-Mubarak St, Kuwait City; tel. 22445050; fax 22455135; e-mail kfh@kfh.com; internet www.kfh.com; f. 1977; 45% state-owned; Islamic banking and investment co; cap. 268m., res 943m., dep. 8,927m. (Dec. 2011); Chair. SAMIR YACOUB AL-NAFISI; Chief Exec. MUHAMMAD SULAYMAN AL-OMAR; 44 brs.

Kuwait International Bank (KIB): POB 22822, 13089 Safat, West Tower, Joint Banking Centre, Mubarak al-Kabir St, Kuwait City; tel. 22458177; fax 22462516; e-mail contact@kib.com.kw; internet www.kib.com.kw; f. 1973 as Kuwait Real Estate Bank KSC; name changed as above upon conversion into an Islamic bank in 2007; wholly owned by private Kuwaiti interests; cap. 103m., res 85m., dep. 699m. (Dec. 2011); Chair. MUHAMMAD JARRAH AL-SABAH; CEO LOAI MAQAMIS (acting); 11 brs.

National Bank of Kuwait SAK (NBK): POB 95, 13001 Safat, Abdullah al-Ahmad St, Kuwait City; tel. 22422011; fax 22462469; e-mail webmaster@nbk.com; internet www.nbk.com; f. 1952; cap. 395m., res 1,199m., dep. 11,109m. (Dec. 2011); Chair. MUHAMMAD ABD AL-RAHMAN AL-BAHAR; CEO IBRAHIM S. DABDOUB; 66 brs in Kuwait, 44 brs abroad.

INSURANCE

Al-Ahleia Insurance Co SAK: POB 1602, Ahmad al-Jaber St, 13017 Safat, Kuwait City; tel. 1888444; fax 22416495; e-mail aic@alahleia.com; internet www.alahleia.com; f. 1962; all forms of insurance; cap. 15.6m. (July 2007); Chair. and Man. Dir SULAYMAN HAMAD MUHAMMAD AL-DALALI.

Arab Commercial Enterprises WLL (Kuwait): POB 2474, 13025 Safat, Kuwait City; tel. 22413854; fax 22409450; e-mail acekwt@ace-ins.com; f. 1952; Man. SALIM ABOU HAIDAR.

First Takaful Insurance Co (FTIC): Abdullah al-Mubarak St, Alenma'a Tower, POB 5713, 13058 Safat, Kuwait City; tel. 21880055; fax 22444599; e-mail info@firsttakaful.com; internet www.firsttakaful.com; f. 2000; Islamic insurance; Chair. and Man. Dir KHALIL IBRAHIM MUHAMMAD AL-SHAMI; 5 brs.

Gulf Insurance Co KSC: POB 1040, 13011 Safat, Ahmad al-Jaber St, Kuwait City; tel. 1802080; fax 22961998; e-mail contacts@gulfins.com.kw; internet www.gulfins.com.kw; f. 1962; cap. 11.3m. (2002); all forms of insurance; Chair. FARKAD ABDULLAH AL-SANEA; CEO and Man. Dir KHALED SAOUD AL-HASSAN.

Al-Ittihad al-Watani Insurance Co for the Near East SAL: 4th Floor, Bahman Bldg, Ahmad al-Jaber St, POB 781, 13008 Safat, Kuwait City; tel. 22420390; fax 22420366; e-mail webmaster@alittihadalwatani.com.lb; Man. JOSEPH ZACCOUR.

Kuwait Insurance Co SAK (KIC): POB 769, 13008 Safat, Abdullah al-Salem St, Kuwait City; tel. 1884433; fax 22428530; e-mail info@kic-kw.com; internet www.kic-kw.com; f. 1960; cap. US $64.6m.; all life and non-life insurance; Chair. MUHAMMAD SALEH BEHBEHANI; Gen. Man. Dr ALI HAMAD AL-BAHAR.

Kuwait Reinsurance Co KSCC: POB 21929, 13080 Safat, Kuwait City; tel. 22432011; fax 22427823; e-mail kuwaitre@kuwaitre.com; internet www.kuwaitre.com; f. 1972; cap. 10.0m., total assets 59.3m. (2006); Chair. FAHED AL-IBRAHIM; Gen. Man. AMIR AL-MUHANNA.

Mohd Saleh Behbehani & Co: POB 341, 13004 Safat, Kuwait City; tel. 24721670; fax 24760070; e-mail msrybco@qualitynet.net; f. 1963; Pres. MUHAMMAD SALEH YOUSUF BEHBEHANI.

New India Assurance Co: 19th Floor, Behbehani Bldg, Jaber al-Mubarak St, Sharq, POB 370, 13004 Safat, Kuwait City; tel. 22404258; fax 22412089; e-mail newindia@qualitynet.net; f. 1919; Man. Dr G. VENKATAIAH.

The Oriental Insurance Co Ltd: Burj Jassim, 9th floor, Al Soor St, Kuwait City; tel. 22960500; fax 22960499; e-mail insurance@almullagroup.com; internet www.orientalinsurance.org.in; f. 1947; Man. ANIL KUMAR PARASHER.

Sumitomo Marine & Fire Insurance Co (Kuwait Agency): POB 3458, 13035 Safat, Kuwait City; tel. 22433087; fax 22430853; Contact ABDULLAH BOUDROS.

Warba Insurance Co SAK: POB 24282, 13103 Safat, Kuwait City; tel. 22445140; fax 22466131; e-mail warba@warbaonline.com; internet www.warbaonline.com; f. 1976; cap. 7.7m. (2002), total assets 80.1m. (Dec. 2005); all forms of insurance; Chair. ANWAR JAWAD KHAMSEEN; Man. Dir TAWFIK SHAMLAN AL-BAHAR; 3 brs.

Wethaq Takaful Insurance Co: Khaled bin al-Waleed St, City Tower, Kuwait City; tel. 21866662; fax 22491280; f. 2000; Islamic insurance; Chair. ABDULLAH YOUSUF AL-SAIF; Gen. Man. MAJID Y. AL-ALI.

STOCK EXCHANGE

Kuwait Stock Exchange (KSE): POB 22235, 13083 Safat, Mubarak al-Kabir St, Kuwait City; tel. 22992000; fax 22420779; e-mail webmaster@kuwaitse.com; internet www.kuwaitse.com; f. 1983; 226 cos and one mutual fund listed (Aug. 2009); Dir-Gen. SALEH MUBARAK AL-FALAH.

Markets Association

Kuwait Financial Markets Association (KFMA): 6th Floor, Deema Bldg, POB 25228, 13113 Safat, Block 3, St 64, Kuwait City; tel. 22498560; fax 22498561; e-mail kfma@kfma.org.kw; internet www.kfma.org.kw; f. 1977; represents treasury, financial and capital markets and their mems; Pres. AQEEL NASSER HABIB; Sec.-Gen. FERAS FAISAL AL-KANDARY.

Trade and Industry

GOVERNMENT AGENCY

Kuwait Investment Authority (KIA): POB 64, 13001 Safat, Kuwait City; tel. 22485600; fax 22454059; e-mail information@kia.gov.kw; internet www.kia.gov.kw; oversees the Kuwait Investment Office (London, United Kingdom); sovereign wealth fund; responsible for the Kuwaiti General Reserve; Chair. MUSTAFA AL-SHAMALI (Deputy Prime Minister and Minister of Finance); Man. Dir BADER MUHAMMAD AL-SAAD.

DEVELOPMENT ORGANIZATIONS

Arab Planning Institute (API): POB 5834, 13059 Safat, Kuwait City; tel. 24843130; fax 24842935; e-mail api@api.org.kw; internet www.arab-api.org; f. 1966; 15 Arab mem. states; publishes *Journal of Development and Economic Policies* (twice-yearly) and proceedings of seminars and discussion group meetings, offers research, training programmes and advisory services; Dir-Gen. BADER MALALLAH.

Industrial and Financial Investments Co (IFIC): POB 26019, 13121 Safat, Joint Banking Complex, 8th Floor, Industrial Bank Bldg, Derwaza Abd al-Razak, Kuwait City; tel. 22429073; fax 22448850; e-mail ific@ific.net; internet www.ific.net; f. 1983; privatized in 1996; invests directly in industry; Chair. and Man. Dir Dr TALEB AHMAD ALI.

Kuwait Fund for Arab Economic Development (KFAED): POB 2921, 13030 Safat, cnr Mubarak al-Kabir St and al-Hilali St, Kuwait City; tel. 22999000; fax 22999090; e-mail info@kuwait-fund.org; internet www.kuwait-fund.org; f. 1961; cap. KD 2,000m.; state-owned; provides and administers financial and technical assistance to developing countries; Chair. Sheikh SABAH AL-KHALED AL-HAMAD AL-SABAH (Deputy Prime Minister and Minister of Foreign Affairs); Dir-Gen. ABD AL-WAHAB A. AL-BADER.

Kuwait International Investment Co SAK (KIIC): POB 22792, 13088 Safat, al-Salhiya Commercial Complex, Kuwait City; tel. 22438273; fax 22454931; 30% state-owned; domestic real estate and share markets; Chair. and Man. Dir JASEM MUHAMMAD AL-BAHAR.

Kuwait Investment Co SAK (KIC): POB 1005, 13011 Safat, 5th Floor, al-Manakh Bldg, Mubarak al-Kabir St, Kuwait City; tel. 65888852; fax 22444896; e-mail info@kic.com.kw; internet www.kic.com.kw; f. 1981; 88% state-owned, 12% owned by private Kuwaiti interests; cap. KD 50.0m. (2002); international banking and investment; Chair. and Man. Dir BADER NASSER AL-SUBAIEE.

Kuwait Planning Board: POB 15, 13001 Safat, Kuwait City; tel. 22428200; fax 22414734; f. 1962; supervises long-term devt plans; through its Central Statistical Office publishes information on Kuwait's economic activity; Dir-Gen. AHMAD ALI AL-DUAIJ.

Mega Projects Agency (MPA): c/o Ministry of Public Works, POB 8, 13001 Safat, Kuwait City; tel. 25385520; fax 25385234; e-mail hmansour@mpa.gov.kw; f. 2005; supervises the progress of Failaka and Bubiyan island devts; Chair. BADER AL-HUMAIDI.

Public Authority for Industry (PAI): POB 4690, 13047 Safat, Kuwait City; POB 10033, Shuaiba; tel. 25302222; fax 25302190; e-mail indust@pai.gov.kw; internet www.pai.gov.kw; f. 1997; successor to Shuaiba Area Authority (f. 1964); develops, promotes and supervises industry in Kuwait; CEO ANAS KHALED AL-SALEH (Minister of Commerce and Industry); Gen. Man. ALI FAHAD AL-MUDHAF.

CHAMBER OF COMMERCE

Kuwait Chamber of Commerce and Industry: POB 775, 13008 Safat, Commercial Area 9, al-Shuhadaa St, Kuwait City; tel. 1805580; fax 22404110; e-mail kcci@kcci.org.kw; internet www.kuwaitchamber.org.kw; f. 1959; 36,000 mems; Chair. ALI MUHAMMAD THUNAYAN AL-GHANIM; Dir-Gen. RABAH AL-RABAH.

STATE HYDROCARBONS COMPANIES

Supreme Petroleum Council (SPC): Kuwait City; f. 1974; highest energy decision-making body, responsible for national oil policy; Chair. Sheikh JABER MUBARAK AL-HAMAD AL-SABAH (Prime Minister).

Kuwait Petroleum Corpn (KPC): POB 26565, 13126 Safat, al-Salhiya Commercial Complex, Fahed al-Salem St, Kuwait City; tel. 22455455; fax 22467159; e-mail info@kpc.com.kw; internet www.kpc.com.kw; f. 1980; co-ordinating org. to manage the petroleum industry; Chair. HANI ABD AL-AZIZ HUSSEIN (Minister of Oil); CEO FARUK HUSSAIN AL-ZANKI; subsidiaries include:

Kuwait Aviation Fuelling Co KSC (KAFCO): POB 1654, 13017 Safat, Kuwait City; tel. 24378500; fax 24378505; e-mail airfuel@kafco.com; internet www.kafco.com; f. 1963; Chair. and Man. Dir ASAAD AHMED AL-SAAD; 200 employees.

Kuwait Foreign Petroleum Exploration Co KSC (KUFPEC): POB 5291, 13053 Safat, Kuwait City; tel. 1836000; fax 24921818; internet www.kufpec.com; f. 1981; state-owned; overseas oil and gas exploration and devt; Chair. and Man. Dir FAHED AL-AJMI; 169 employees.

Kuwait Gulf Oil Co KSC (KGOC): POB 9919, Ahmadi 61010; tel. 25454254; e-mail info@kgoc.com; internet www.kgoc.com; f. 2002 to take over Kuwait's interest in the Neutral (Partitioned) Zone's offshore operator, Khafji Joint Operations, and all of Kuwait's other offshore exploration and production activities; Chair. and Man. Dir HASHIM MUSTAFA AL-RIFAAI.

Kuwait National Petroleum Co KSC (KNPC): POB 70, 13001 Safat, Ali al-Salem St, Kuwait City; tel. 23989900; fax 23986188; internet www.knpc.com.kw; f. 1960; oil refining, production of liquefied petroleum gas, and domestic marketing and distribution of petroleum by-products; Chair. and Man. Dir FAROUK HUSSAIN AL-ZANKI; 5,611 employees.

Kuwait Oil Co KSC (KOC): POB 9758, 61008 Ahmadi; tel. 23983661; fax 23984971; e-mail kocinfo@kockw.com; internet www.kockw.com; f. 1934; state-owned; Chair. and Man. Dir SAMI FAHED AL-RUSHAID; 4,815 employees.

Kuwait Petroleum International (Q8): POB 1819, 13019 Safat, Kuwait City; tel. 22332800; fax 22332776; e-mail info-kuwait@q8.com; internet www.q8.com; marketing division of KPC; controls 4,000 petrol retail stations in Europe, and European refineries with capacity of 235,000 b/d; Man. Dir HUSSEIN AL-ISMAIL.

UTILITIES

The Government planned to create regulatory bodies for each of Kuwait's utilities, with a view to facilitating their privatization.

Ministry of Electricity and Water: see Ministries; provides subsidized services throughout Kuwait.

TRADE UNIONS

Kuwait Trade Union Federation (KTUF): POB 5185, 13052 Safat, Kuwait City; tel. 25636389; fax 25627159; e-mail ktuf@hotmail.com; internet www.ktuf.org; f. 1967; central authority to which all trade unions are affiliated; Pres. FAIEZ ALI AL-MUTAIRI; Gen. Sec. FARES AL-SAWAGH AL-AZEMI.

Transport

RAILWAYS

There are currently no railways in Kuwait. However, plans for a 518-km national rail network, which would be linked to a regional rail network, connecting Kuwait with member countries of the Cooperation Council for the Arab States of the Gulf (or Gulf Cooperation Council—GCC), were announced in 2008. Construction work on the first phase of a four-line, 171-km metro system in Kuwait City were expected to begin in 2013. The project, the total cost of which was estimated at US $7,000m., was scheduled to commence operations in 2016.

ROADS

In 2010 the total road network was estimated at 6,608 km. Roads in the towns are metalled, and the most important are motorways or dual carriageways. There are metalled roads linking Kuwait City to Ahmadi, Mina al-Ahmadi and other centres of population in Kuwait, and to the Iraqi and Saudi Arabian borders. A 72-km Subiya–Jahra highway and a ring-road at Sabah al-Ahmad City are currently under construction; work on a 42-km, six-lane Nawaseeb Highway was expected to be completed in 2013. In late 2012 a US $3,700m. design-and-build contract for a causeway linking Kuwait City with Madinat al-Hareer (Silk City—a new development under construction in Subiya) was awarded to Hyundai Engineering and Construction Co of the Republic of Korea (South Korea).

Kuwait Public Transport Co SAK (KPTC): POB 375, 13004 Safat, Murghab, Safat Sq., Kuwait City; tel. 22328501; fax 22328870; e-mail info@kptc.com.kw; internet www.kptc.com.kw; f. 1962; state-owned; provides internal bus service; regular service to Mecca, Saudi Arabia; Chair. and Man. Dir MAHMOUD A. AL-NOURI.

SHIPPING

Kuwait has three commercial seaports. The largest, Shuwaikh, situated about 3 km from Kuwait City, comprises 21 deep-water berths, with a total length of 4 km, three shallow-water berths and three basins for small craft, each with a depth of 3.35 m. Shuaiba Commercial Port, 56 km south of Kuwait City, comprises 20 berths with a total length of 4 km. Since 2003 the port has been used by the US Army as a base for supplying its troops in Iraq. Expansion plans were announced in 2009. Doha, the smallest port, has 20 small berths, each 100 m long. An oil port at Mina al-Ahmadi, 40 km south of Kuwait City, comprises 12 tanker berths, one bitumen-carrier berth, two LPG export berths and bunkering facilities, and is able to load more than 2m. barrels of oil per day.

Plans for the privatization of Kuwait's ports were under development in the late 2000s. In 2010 a contract for the construction of a new US $1,200m. international port at Bubiyan island was awarded to Hyundai Engineering and Construction Co. The Mubarak al-Kabir port was expected to commence operations in 2016.

At 31 December 2012 Kuwait's flag registered fleet numbered 155 vessels, with a total displacement of 2,479,501 grt, of which two were bulk carriers, one was a fish carrier, four were gas tankers and two were general cargo ships.

Port Authority

Kuwait Ports Authority: POB 3874, 13039 Safat, Kuwait City; tel. 24812622; fax 24819714; e-mail info@kpa.gov.kw; internet www.kpa.gov.kw; f. 1977; Dir-Gen. Dr SABER JABER AL-ALI AL-SABAH.

Principal Shipping Companies

Arab Maritime Petroleum Transport Co (AMPTC): POB 22525, 13086 Safat, Kuwait City; tel. 24959400; fax 24842996; e-mail amptc.kuwait@amptc.net; internet www.amptc.net; f. 1973; six crude petroleum tankers, four LPG carriers and one product carrier; owned by Algeria, Bahrain, Egypt, Iraq, Kuwait, Libya, Qatar, Saudi Arabia and the UAE; Gen. Man. SULAYMAN I. AL-BASSAM.

Heavy Engineering Industries and Shipbuilding Co (Heisco): POB 21998, 13080 Safat, Kuwait City; tel. 24835488; fax 24830291; e-mail heisco@heisco.com; internet www.heisco.com; f. 1974 as Kuwait Shipbuilding and Repairyard Co; name changed as above in 2003; ship repairs and engineering services, underwater services, maintenance of refineries, power stations and storage tanks; maintains floating dock for vessels up to 35,000 dwt; synchrolift for vessels up to 5,000 dwt with transfer yard; seven repair jetties up to 550 m in length and floating workshop for vessels lying at anchor; Chair. JUHAIL MUHAMMAD AL-JUHAIL.

KGL Ports Int. Co (KGL PI): POB 42438, Shuwaikh 70655; tel. 22245155; fax 22245166; e-mail info@kglpi.com; internet www.kglpi.com; f. 2004; subsidiary of Kuwait and Gulf Link Transport Co; port management and stevedoring; operates Shuaiba Commercial Port Container Terminal; also operations and management contracts with ports in United Arab Emirates and Saudi Arabia; Chair. and Man. Dir FADHEL AL-BAGHLI; CEO ALLAN ROSENBERG.

Kuwait Maritime Transport Co KSC (KMTC): POB 22595, 13086 Safat, Nafisi and Khatrash Bldg, Jaber al-Mubarak St, Kuwait City; tel. 22449974; fax 22420513; f. 1981; Chair. YOUSUF AL-MAJID.

Kuwait Oil Tanker Co SAK (KOTC): POB 810, 13009 Safat, Shuwaikh Administrative Sector (P), Gamal Abdel Nasser St, Kuwait City; tel. 24625050; fax 24913597; e-mail nakilat@kotc.com.kw; internet www.kotc.com.kw; f. 1957; state-owned; operates eight crude oil tankers, 11 product tankers and five LPG vessels; sole tanker agents for Mina al-Ahmadi, Shuaiba and Mina al-Abdullah and agents for other ports; LPG filling and distribution; Chair. and Man. Dir NABIL M. BOURISLI.

United Arab Shipping Co SAG (UASC): POB 20722, 13068 Safat, UASC Bldg, Old Airport Rd, Beside Zain Bldg, Kuwait City; tel. 24848190; fax 24831263; e-mail gencom.uasackwt@uasc.net; internet www.uasc.net; f. 1976; nat shipping co of six Arabian Gulf countries; services between Europe, Far East, Mediterranean ports, Japan and east coast of USA and South America, and ports of participant states on Persian (Arabian) Gulf and Red Sea; operates 42 vessels; subsidiary cos include: United Arab Shipping Agencies Co (Kuwait), Arab Transport Co (Aratrans), United Arab Chartering Ltd (United Kingdom), Middle East Container Repair Co (UAE), Arabian Chemicals Carriers (Saudi Arabia), United Arab Agencies Inc (USA) and United Arab Shipping Agencies Co (Saudi Arabia); Chair. OTHMAN IBRAHIM AL-ISSA; Pres. and CEO JØRN HINGE.

CIVIL AVIATION

Kuwait International Airport opened in 1980, and by 2011 handled 8.5m. passengers, compared with 3.8m. in 2001. The airport is undergoing a major programme of expansion: the first phase of the project was to expand the airport's annual capacity to 20m. passengers and to modernize facilities, with a further final phase of development intended to achieve passenger capacity of 55m.

Directorate-General of Civil Aviation (DGCA): POB 17, 13001 Safat, Kuwait City; tel. 24744256; fax 24744396; e-mail president@dgca.gov.kw; internet www.dgca.gov.kw; Pres. FAWAZ AL-FARAH; Dir-Gen. Eng. BADER BOUTAIBAN.

Jazeera Airways: POB 29288, 13153 Safat, Kuwait City; e-mail helpdesk@jazeeraairways.com; internet www.jazeeraairways.com; f. 2005; low-cost airline owned by Boodai Group; serves 26 destinations in the Middle East, North Africa, Europe and Asia; Chair. MARWAN BOODAI; CEO STEFAN PICHLER.

Kuwait Airways Corpn (KAC): POB 394, Kuwait International Airport, 13004 Safat, Kuwait City; tel. 22248560; fax 22441304; e-mail kwi@kuwaitairways.com; internet www.kuwait-airways.com; f. 1954; scheduled and charter passenger and cargo services to the Arabian peninsula, Asia, Africa, the USA and Europe; scheduled for privatization; Chair. and Man. Dir HAMAD A. LATIF AL-FALAH.

Tourism

Attractions for visitors include the Kuwait Towers leisure and reservoir complex, the Entertainment City theme park, the Kuwait Zoological Garden in Omariya and the Khiran Resort tourist village near the border with Saudi Arabia, as well as extensive facilities for sailing and other water sports. In 2010 foreign tourist arrivals totalled some 5.2m. According to provisional data, tourism receipts (excluding passenger transport) of US $199m. were recorded in 2011.

Department of Tourism: Ministry of Information, Tourism Affairs, POB 193, 13002 Safat, al-Sour St, Kuwait City; tel. 22457591; fax 22401540; e-mail tourism_kw@media.gov.kw.

Kuwait Tourism Services Co: POB 21774, 13078 Safat, Kuwait City; tel. 2451734; fax 2451731; e-mail ktsc@qualitynet.net; internet www.ktsc-q8.com; f. 1997; Chair. KHALID AL-DUWAISAN.

Touristic Enterprises Co (TEC): POB 23310, 13094 Safat, Kuwait City; tel. 24965555; fax 24965055; e-mail info@tec.com.kw; internet www.kuwaittourism.com; f. 1976; 92% state-owned; manages 23 tourist facilities; Chair. BADER AL-BAHAR; Vice-Chair. SHAKER AL-OTHMAN.

Defence

Chief of Staff of Armed Forces: Lt-Gen. KHALID AL-JARRAH AL-SABAH.

Defence Budget (2012): KD 1,280m.

Military Service: voluntary.

Total Armed Forces (as assessed at November 2012): 15,500: army 11,000; navy est. 2,000 (including 500 coast guards); air force 2,500. Reserves 23,700.

Paramilitary Forces (as assessed at November 2012): est. 7,100 (national guard est. 6,600; coast guard 500).

Education

Compulsory education for children between six and 14 years of age was introduced in 1966–67. However, many children spend two years prior to this in a kindergarten, and go on to complete their general education at the age of 18 years. It is government policy to provide free education to all Kuwaiti children from kindergarten stage to the University. In 2011/12 a total of 357,273 pupils attended 794 government schools (201 kindergarten, 253 primary, 204 intermediate and 136 secondary). In 2011/12 a total of 224,268 pupils attended 475 private schools (105 kindergarten, 132 primary, 133 intermediate and 105 secondary).

Primary education lasts for five years between the ages of six and 10, after which the pupils move on to an intermediate school for another four years. Secondary education, which is optional and lasts between the ages of 14 and 18, is given mainly in general schools. There are also commercial institutes, a Faculty of Technological Studies, a health institute, religious institutes (with intermediate and secondary stages) and 11 institutes for handicapped children. In 2008/09 enrolment at primary schools was equivalent to 95% of

children in the relevant age-group, while at secondary schools the rate was equivalent to 90% of children in the relevant age-group.

Scholarships are granted to students to pursue courses not offered by Kuwait University. Such scholarships are mainly used to study in Egypt, Lebanon, the United Kingdom and the USA. There are also pupils from Arab, African and Asian states studying in Kuwait schools on scholarships provided by the Kuwaiti Government. Kuwait University had about 20,000 students in 2006, and also provides scholarships for a number of Arab, Asian and African students. In May 1996 the Majlis approved a draft law to regulate students' behaviour, dress and activities, with regard to observance of the teachings of *Shari'a* (Islamic) law, and to eradicate co-educational classes at Kuwait University over a five-year period. A KD 1,000m. project to build a new university campus and to gather the institution's dispersed facilities onto one site was expected to be completed by 2025. In 2008/09 an estimated 61,920 students were enrolled in tertiary education. Expenditure on education by the central Government in 2010/11 totalled KD 1,441m. (12.0% of total expenditure).

KYRGYZSTAN

Introductory Survey

LOCATION, CLIMATE, LANGUAGE, RELIGION, FLAG, CAPITAL

The Kyrgyz Republic is a small, landlocked state situated in eastern Central Asia. It borders Kazakhstan to the north, Uzbekistan to the west, Tajikistan to the south and west, and the People's Republic of China to the east. There are distinct variations in climate between low-lying and high-altitude areas. In the valleys the mean July temperature is 28°C (82°F), falling to an average of −18°C (−0.5°F) in January. Annual rainfall ranges from 180 mm (7 ins) in the eastern Tien Shan mountains to 750 mm–1,000 mm (30 ins–39 ins) in the Farg'ona (Fergana) mountain range. In the settled valleys the annual average varies between 100 mm and 500 mm (4 ins–20 ins). The state language is Kyrgyz; in addition, Russian has the status of an official language. The main religion is Islam, with the majority of ethnic Kyrgyz being Sunni Muslims of the Hanafi school. The national flag (proportions 3 by 5) consists of a red field, at the centre of which is a yellow sun, with 40 counter-clockwise rays surrounding a red-bordered yellow disc, on which are superimposed two intersecting sets of three red, curved, narrow bands. The capital is Bishkek.

CONTEMPORARY POLITICAL HISTORY

Historical Context

Following the October Revolution of 1917 in Russia, Kyrgyzstan (which had been formally incorporated into the Russian Empire in 1876) experienced civil war, with anti-Bolshevik forces, including the Russian White Army and local armed groups (*basmachi*), fighting against the Bolshevik Red Army. In 1918 the Turkestan Autonomous Soviet Socialist Republic (ASSR) was established within the Russian Soviet Federative Socialist Republic (the Russian Federation), and Soviet power was established in the region by 1919. In 1924 the Kara-Kyrgyz Autonomous Oblast (Region) was created. In 1925 the region was renamed the Kyrgyz Autonomous Oblast, and became the Kyrgyz ASSR in February 1926. In December 1936 the Kyrgyz Soviet Socialist Republic (SSR) was established as a full union republic of the USSR.

During the 1920s considerable economic and social developments were made in Kyrgyzstan, when land reforms resulted in the settlement of many of the nomadic Kyrgyz. The agricultural collectivization programme implemented under Stalin (Iosif V. Dzhugashvili—Soviet leader in 1924–53) in the early 1930s was strongly opposed in the republic, and many so-called 'national communists' were expelled from the Kyrgyz Communist Party (KCP) and imprisoned or exiled, particularly during the late 1930s.

The election of Mikhail Gorbachev as Soviet leader in 1985, and his introduction of the policies of perestroika (restructuring) and glasnost (openness), led to the resignation of Turdakan Usubaliyev as First Secretary of the KCP and the dismissal from office of his allies by Absamat Masaliyev, his successor. The republic's Supreme Soviet (Jogorku Kenesh or Supreme Council—legislature) adopted Kyrgyz as the official language, although Russian was retained as a 'language of inter-ethnic communication'. The republican leadership opposed the development of unofficial quasi-political groups, although one such group, Ashar, which was tolerated by the authorities, developed a wider political role. A notable group at this time was Osh Aymaghi, based in Osh Oblast, in the south of the Republic and located in the Farg'ona (Fergana) valley (which is shared between Kyrgyzstan, Tajikistan and Uzbekistan). Osh Aymaghi attempted to obtain land and housing provision for Kyrgyz in the Uzbek-dominated region, where demands for the establishment of an Uzbek autonomous region were voiced. In 1990 disputes over land developed into violent inter-ethnic confrontations. According to official reports, more than 300 people died, and a state of emergency and a curfew were introduced, the former remaining in force until 1995; the Uzbekistani–Kyrgyzstani border was also closed.

At elections to the 350-member Kyrgyzstani Supreme Soviet held in February 1990 KCP candidates won most seats unopposed, and in April Masaliyev was elected to the new office of Chairman of the Supreme Soviet. In October an extraordinary session of the Supreme Soviet was convened to elect the President. The growth in support for the opposition Democratic Movement of Kyrgyzstan (DMK), combined with the discrediting of Masaliyev as a consequence of the conflict in Osh meant that Masaliyev failed to be elected in the first round of voting. In a further round of voting a compromise candidate, Askar Akayev, the President of the Kyrgyz Academy of Sciences, was elected to the executive presidency. Akayev rapidly allied himself with reformist factions. In December Masaliyev resigned as Chairman of the Supreme Soviet, and was replaced by Medetkan Sherimkulov. (In April 1991 he also resigned as First Secretary of the KCP.) Also in December 1990, the Supreme Soviet voted to change the name of the republic from the Kyrgyz SSR to the Republic of Kyrgyzstan. In January 1991 Akayev replaced the Council of Ministers with a smaller, largely reformist, cabinet. In February the capital, Frunze, reverted to its pre-1926 name of Bishkek. In a referendum held in nine Soviet Union Republics in March, 87.7% of eligible voters in Kyrgyzstan approved the proposal to retain the USSR as a 'renewed federation'.

Domestic Political Affairs

In August 1991, when the conservative communist State Committee for the State of Emergency (SCSE) announced that it had assumed power in the Russian and Soviet capital, Moscow, there was an attempt to depose Akayev in Kyrgyzstan. Akayev dismissed the Chairman of the republican Committee of State Security (KGB) and ordered interior ministry troops to guard strategic buildings in Bishkek. Akayev publicly denounced the coup (which the KCP had supported) and issued a decree prohibiting activity by any political party in government or state bodies. After the coup had collapsed in Moscow, Akayev renounced his membership of the Communist Party of the Soviet Union, and the entire politburo and secretariat of the KCP resigned. On 31 August the Kyrgyzstani Supreme Soviet voted to declare independence from the USSR. Akayev (the sole candidate) was re-elected President of Kyrgyzstan by direct popular vote on 12 October, receiving 95% of the votes cast.

In October 1991 Akayev signed, with representatives of seven other republics, a treaty to establish a new economic community. On 21 December Kyrgyzstan was among the 11 signatories to the Almatı (Alma-Ata) Declaration, which formally established the Commonwealth of Independent States (CIS, see p. 251).

Discussions were held throughout 1992 to draft a new constitution. The Constitution, which was finally promulgated on 5 May 1993, provided for a parliamentary system of government. Legislative power was to be vested in a 105-member Jogorku Kenesh. The country's official name was changed from the Republic of Kyrgyzstan to the less ethnically neutral Kyrgyz Republic. In July Akayev's attempts to encourage non-Kyrgyz to remain in the republic suffered a serious reverse when German Kuznetsov, the First Deputy Prime Minister, announced his decision to return to Russia. By mid-1993 some 145,000 Russians were estimated to have left the republic since 1989.

Akayev's presidency was destabilized during 1993 by a series of corruption scandals. Two commissions of inquiry were established to investigate the business dealings of Vice-President Feliks Kulov and to examine allegations that senior politicians—including the Prime Minister since February 1992, Tursunbek Chyngyshev—had been involved in unauthorized gold exports. In December 1993 Kulov resigned and the legislature subsequently held a vote of confidence in Chyngyshev's Government: the motion failed to secure the required two-thirds' majority and Akayev dismissed the entire cabinet. A new Government, headed by Apas Jumagulov (Chairman of the Council of Ministers in 1986–91), was approved later in the month. A referendum of confidence in the presidency was held in January 1994, at which 96.2% of voters endorsed Akayev's leadership. In June, in an attempt to curb the rate of emigration, Akayev issued a decree promoting the use of Russian, simplifying the procedure of application for dual citizenship, and guaranteeing the equitable representation of ethnic Russians in the state administration.

In September 1994 more than 180 deputies demanded the dissolution of the Kenesh and the holding of fresh elections, in protest at the continuing obstruction of economic reforms. The Government tendered its resignation, and Akayev announced that fresh parliamentary elections would be held. The Government was promptly reinstated by Akayev, who announced the holding of a referendum in October on constitutional amendments, at which the majority of the electorate endorsed proposals for a bicameral Jogorku Kenesh, to comprise a 70-member El Okuldor Palatasy (People's Assembly, the upper chamber) to represent regional interests at twice-yearly sessions and a permanent 35-member Myizam Chygaru Palatasy (Legislative Assembly—lower chamber). Elections to the two legislative chambers were held in February 1995. The two chambers of the Jogorku Kenesh held their inaugural sessions on 28 March. A new Government, again led by Jumagulov, was appointed in April.

In September 1995 the Myizam Chygaru Palatasy vetoed a proposal to hold a referendum on extending the President's term of office until 2000. On 24 December 1995 Akayev received 71.6% of the votes cast in a direct presidential election; Masaliyev (who had recently been reinstated as the leader of the revived KCP) won 24.4% of the votes. The rate of participation by the electorate was some 82%. Akayev was inaugurated on 30 December. Following a decree issued by Akayev, a referendum was held on 10 February 1996, at which the majority of the electorate endorsed amendments to the Constitution increasing presidential powers and decreasing those of the legislature. The Government resigned later that month; Jumagulov was reinstated as Prime Minister in March and Akayev approved a new Government shortly afterwards.

In March 1998, after Jumagulov announced his retirement, the Jogorku Kenesh endorsed the appointment of Kuvachbek Jumaliyev as Prime Minister. In July the Constitutional Court ruled that Akayev was permitted to seek a third residential term in the election due in 2000. A referendum held on 17 October overwhelmingly approved numerous constitutional amendments, including an increase in the number of deputies in the Myizam Chygaru Palatasy to 60, alongside a reduction in the membership of the El Okuldor Palatasy to 45, the introduction of restrictions on parliamentary immunity, the legalization of private land ownership, and the prohibition of the adoption of any legislation restricting freedom of speech or of the press. The Jogorku Kenesh and the majority of political parties declared their opposition to the constitutional changes and, in particular, to the introduction of private land ownership. By mid-December some 383 government officials had been dismissed on grounds of corruption, and later in the month the President dissolved the Government for its failure to address the country's economic problems. Jumabek Ibraimov was appointed Prime Minister and a new Government was formed, in which 10 ministers from the previous administration retained their portfolios. Akayev strengthened the Prime Minister's mandate, empowering him to appoint and dismiss ministers and heads of departments (hitherto the prerogative of the President). Ibraimov died in April 1999, and Amangeldy Muraliyev was appointed as his successor.

The 2000 legislative and presidential elections

A new electoral law was introduced in May 1999. Henceforth, 15 seats in the Myizam Chygaru Palatasy were to be allocated on a proportional basis for those parties that secured a minimum of 5% of the votes; the legislation also banned the use of foreign funding in electoral campaigns. In June legislation came into effect banning political organizations considered a threat to Kyrgyzstan's stability and ethnic harmony. In July two new opposition parties were established: the Dignity Party (Ar-Namys), led by Kulov—by this time Mayor of Bishkek—and the Justice (Adilettuuluk) Party.

Two rounds of elections were held to both chambers of the Jogorku Kenesh on 20 February and 12 March 2000. In the first round, six parties surpassed the 5% threshold required to secure party-list seats in the Myizam Chygaru Palatasy. The Organization for Security and Co-operation in Europe (OSCE, see p. 397) recorded a number of electoral violations. Overall, nominally independent candidates took 73 of the 105 seats in the two chambers, while the Union of Democratic Forces achieved the greatest representation of any party or bloc overall, securing a total of 12 seats, compared with the KCP's six. Kulov (who contested the poll as an independent after the Dignity Party was prohibited from participating) failed to win a seat.

Meanwhile, at the presidential election, held on 29 October 2000, Akayev was re-elected, securing 74.5% of the votes cast. His closest rival was Omurbek Tekebayev, the leader of the Fatherland Socialist Political Party (Ata-Meken), with 13.9%, while Almazbek Atambayev, the leader of the Social Democratic Party of Kyrgyzstan (SDPK), obtained 6.0% of the ballot. According to official figures, 74% of the electorate participated. On the day of the election a criminal case opened in Bishkek following the discovery, by international observers, of several hundred ballot papers, marked in favour of Akayev, before polling had begun officially. The Chairman of the Central Commission for Elections and Referendums was forced to concede that electoral violations had taken place, but in spite of this, on 10 November the Constitutional Court formally endorsed the results.

Akayev was inaugurated for a third term on 9 December 2000 and on 21 December Kurmanbek Bakiyev, hitherto the Governor of Chui Oblast, was appointed Prime Minister; a new Government was announced in January 2001. In the same month Kulov was sentenced to seven years' imprisonment, having been found guilty of abuse of office during his tenure as Minister of National Security. An appeal was rejected in March, and in May 2002 Kulov was also found guilty of embezzlement. In April 2001 the leaders of nine opposition parties formally announced the establishment of an alliance, the People's Patriotic Movement. The movement organized demonstrations against the erosion of the independent media and against the imprisonment of Kulov. In November opposition parties including the Dignity Party, the Fatherland Socialist Political Party and the Liberty Party announced the formation of a new People's Congress, and elected the imprisoned Kulov its Chairman. In the following month the President signed into law a constitutional amendment granting Russian the status of official language, alongside Kyrgyz.

In January 2002 the arrest of Azimbek Beknazarov, an opposition deputy, was denounced as politically motivated. In March six demonstrators were shot dead by security forces in the village of Aksy, in the southern Jalal-Abad region, where Beknazarov's trial was being held; the trial was subsequently suspended. In May the Myizam Chygaru Palatasy ratified a controversial Sino-Kyrgyzstani border treaty signed in 1999, prompting two weeks of anti-Government demonstrations, hunger strikes and civil disobedience. Protesters demanded that the Government accept responsibility for the violence of March 2002, rescind the ratification of the border treaty (which they claimed had been signed illegally by President Akayev, as the transfer of territory had not been authorized by the legislature), and close the criminal case against Beknazarov. Nevertheless, the El Okuldor Palatasy ratified the treaty later in May, and it was duly signed into law by the President.

As controversy continued about his alleged responsibility for ordering the killings by the security forces, in May 2002 Prime Minister Bakiyev tendered his resignation. The First Deputy Prime Minister, Nikolai Tanayev, was appointed Prime Minister, and a new Government was formed. Meanwhile, in May Beknazarov received a one-year suspended prison sentence. Following an appeal and further large-scale demonstrations, Beknazorov's sentence was annulled (although the initial guilty verdict was upheld), enabling him to retain his parliamentary seat. In June the Myizam Chygaru Palatasy approved an amnesty, proposed by Tanayev for both protesters and law enforcement officials involved in the disturbances of March.

In January 2003 President Akayev announced that a referendum on several constitutional amendments was to be held on 2 February. The amendments, which provided for the introduction of a unicameral legislature with effect from 2005, in which all deputies were to be elected in single-member constituencies, were duly approved by 76.6% of the electorate, while 78.7% of voters supported Akayev's remaining in office until 2005; the reported rate of participation was 86.7%.

A major government reorganization took place in February 2004. In April the President introduced a new law designating Kyrgyz the state language, and stipulating measures for its promotion, apparently in order to encourage bilingualism in Kyrgyz and Russian, which was to remain an official language. In May, in advance of legislative elections, opposition parties, including the Dignity Party, the Fatherland Socialist Political Party and the SDPK, announced the formation of an electoral bloc, the Civic Union For Fair Elections. The formation of a larger electoral bloc, the People's Movement of Kyrgyzstan, was announced in September, under Bakiyev's leadership.

'The Tulip Revolution'

In January 2005 Roza Otunbayeva the leader of the recently formed opposition Homeland Idealistic Democratic Party (Ata-Jurt), was refused permission to register as a candidate in the parliamentary elections, on the grounds that, as the former ambassador to the United Kingdom, she had not been resident in Kyrgyzstan for the previous five years. Protests against the exclusion of candidates and opposition rallies demanding free and fair parliamentary elections, or the impeachment of Akayev, continued throughout February. In the first round of legislative voting on 27 February the rate of participation by the electorate was reported as 60%. Some 31 candidates (each of whom had received an absolute majority of votes cast in their respective electoral districts) were elected to the restructured, unicameral, 75-member Jogorku Kenesh. Most of those elected were nominally independent candidates. Forward, Kyrgyzstan, regarded as generally sympathetic to Akayev's administration, became the largest party faction to achieve representation, with 10 deputies. OSCE monitors concluded that the elections had not fully complied with democratic standards, while opposition and independent observers asserted that large-scale electoral fraud had taken place. Protests to dispute polling results took place in various regions in advance of the second round of elections, held on 13 March, and media outlets supportive of the opposition or critical of the authorities were suppressed. Following the second round of voting, a further 37 candidates were elected (with a participation rate of 55%); only six opposition candidates obtained representation in the new legislature.

Dissatisfaction at the conduct and outcome of the elections resulted in large-scale protests in a number of cities, particularly in the south. None the less, on 22 March 2005 the Central Commission for Elections and Referendums declared that the results of voting for 69 of the 75 seats were valid; investigations into the conduct of voting in the remaining six districts were to continue. The Supreme Court, however revoked the mandate of the newly elected Jogorku Kenesh, asserting that the previous bicameral legislature continued to hold authority. On 23 March Akayev dismissed the Minister of Internal Affairs, Bakirdin Subanbekov, who had declared that he would not use force to end the protests; the Prosecutor-General was also removed from office.

By 24 March 2005 demonstrations had spread to Bishkek, and protesters stormed the presidential palace and government buildings. Akayev fled the country, while maintaining that he remained Kyrgyzstan's Head of State, and Tanayev resigned as Prime Minister. Meanwhile, protesters freed Kulov from gaol. On the same day, at an emergency session, the lower chamber of the legislature elected in 2000 named Bakiyev acting Prime Minister (he automatically became acting President in Akayev's absence) and Kulov was given responsibility for overseeing the country's law enforcement agencies and armed forces. After the Central Commission for Elections and Referendums announced that the powers of the bicameral legislature elected in 2000 were terminated, the lower and upper chambers dissolved themselves on 28 and 29 March, respectively, thereby effectively confirming the legitimacy of the recently elected legislature. Meanwhile, on 28 March the new Jogorku Kenesh voted to confirm Bakiyev as interim Prime Minister, and to elect Tekebayev as legislative Chairman. (In late April Tekebayev was also appointed as Chairman of the Constitutional Court.) On 30 March Kulov resigned, reportedly owing to disagreement with Bakiyev.

On 4 April 2005 Akayev, speaking at the Kyrgyzstani embassy in Moscow, announced his resignation as President (the Jogorku Kenesh approved this decision on 11 April). On 8 April the Jogorku Kenesh voted to remove immunity from prosecution from members of Akayev's family, and it subsequently scheduled a presidential election for 10 July. From mid-April protests were staged outside the Supreme Court against the conduct of the legislative elections, demanding the resignation of the Court's Chairman, Kurmanbek Osmonov. In mid-April the Court overturned Kulov's convictions. Although Osmonov submitted his resignation later in the month, Bakiyev rejected it. In mid-May Bakiyev reached an agreement with Kulov, according to which the latter agreed to withdraw his candidacy in the presidential election (in which he had been regarded as Bakiyev's principal rival) in return for a guarantee that he would be appointed Prime Minister in the event that Bakiyev was elected President.

On 10 July 2005 Bakiyev won 88.7% of the votes cast in the presidential election, defeating five other candidates. The OSCE reported some irregularities in the counting of votes. Bakiyev was inaugurated as President on 14 August, and on 1 September the Jogorku Kenesh confirmed Kulov's appointment as Prime Minister. In late September the Jogorku Kenesh approved 10 of the 16 ministers proposed by Bakiyev. Many ministers in the outgoing interim administration retained their portfolios. In October the Office of the Prosecutor-General charged former Prime Minister Tanayev, who was under house arrest in Bishkek, with abuse of power and corruption. (In May 2006 it was reported that the criminal case against Tanayev had been closed.) The Jogorku Kenesh rejected Bakiyev's nomination of Daniyar Usenov, an opponent of Kulov, as First Deputy Prime Minister, instead approving the appointment, in November 2005, of Medetbek Kerimkulov. The Government was sworn in on 20 December.

Meanwhile, in September 2005 Bayaman Erkinbayev, a parliamentary deputy and businessman who had actively participated in Akayev's removal from power, was murdered in Bishkek; another parliamentary deputy had been assassinated in July. In October a further deputy, Tynychbek Akmatbayev, was killed by inmates during an official visit to a gaol. Large rallies, led by Akmatbayev's brother, Ryspek, a prominent and controversial figure alleged to be involved in organized crime, subsequently took place to demand the dismissal of Kulov, whom the protesters accused of having collaborated with prisoners to organize the killing of Akmatbayev.

In January 2006 Bakiyev (who had pledged to increase the powers of the legislature) decreed that measures be taken to organize a referendum on the division of powers between the President and parliament. Later in the month Kulov demanded reform of the judicial and law enforcement systems, and accused the Chairman of the National Security Service (SNB), Tashtemir Aitbayev, of having allowed criminal elements to infiltrate the organization. In early February Bakiyev removed the deputy head of the SNB, and accepted the resignation of the Deputy Secretary of the Security Council. In the same month Bakiyev accused the legislature of fomenting political instability and exceeding its mandate, in response to which Tekebayev resigned as parliamentary chairman; he was succeeded by Marat Sultanov in the following month. In early March Bakiyev signed a decree designating 24 March, the anniversary of Akayev's effective removal from power as a result of the so-called 'tulip revolution', a national holiday, to be known as the Day of the People's Revolution.

Parliamentary by-elections, scheduled to take place in three districts in April 2006, generated considerable controversy owing to the candidacy of Rysbek Akmatbayev. Akmatbayev, convicted twice during the 1990s for assault and robbery, had been tried, but acquitted, in early 2006 for the murder of a police officer; however, his acquittal was in the process of being appealed at the time of the polls, thus rendering his candidacy constitutionally illegitimate. In protest at Akmatbayev's participation, thousands of demonstrators amassed in the streets of Bishkek, urging the Government to adopt a tougher stance against organized crime. The by-elections proceeded as planned on 9 April, and Akmatbayev secured a comfortable victory in the constituency that he contested. Another large-scale demonstration took place in the capital in late April when several thousand people gathered to protest against widespread corruption among state officials. In May Akmatbayev was shot dead by unknown assailants in Bishkek. Meanwhile, in late April the Jogorku Kenesh voted to evaluate the performance of individual members of the Government: only Prime Minister Kulov, two ministers and the head of a state committee were given positive appraisals, and in early May 14 ministers resigned. Although President Bakiyev rejected their resignations and the ministers subsequently agreed to remain in their posts, Bakiyev effected a cabinet reorganization in mid-May, which included the appointment of Usenov as First Deputy Prime Minister.

Constitutional disputes

In November 2006 thousands of opposition supporters attended a rally in Bishkek demanding constitutional reform and the resignation of Bakiyev. Following a week of mass protests, the Jogorku Kenesh approved a new Constitution on 8 November, which was to diminish the power afforded to the President and to augment that of the legislature, the capacity of which was to be enlarged to 90 members; the membership of governments was henceforth to be determined by the Jogorku Kenesh, rather than the President. Bakiyev signed the new Constitution into effect on 9 November. In mid-December Prime Minister Kulov tendered his resignation (together with that of his Government), with the stated aim of forcing early parliamentary elections and thereby addressing the ongoing political crisis.

In late December 2006 the legislature voted to adopt a number of amendments to the new Constitution, including the retraction of the legislature's power to appoint the Government, which was henceforth to be appointed by the President at the suggestion of the Prime Minister, without the need for legislative approval. These amendments were signed into law on 17 January 2007. In late January the Jogorku Kenesh formally approved Bakiyev's nomination of Azim Isabekov as Prime Minister, having twice rejected his nomination of Kulov. In February Isabekov formed a new Government, in which the majority of key posts were allocated to close associates of President Bakiyev, including Usenov, who was re-appointed First Deputy Prime Minister. In the same month Kulov added his voice to opposition demands for the President's resignation. On 29 March Isabekov resigned as premier, after Bakiyev reversed his decision, taken in response to continuing mass protests, to dismiss five government ministers. One day later the Jogorku Kenesh approved the appointment of Atambayev as Prime Minister; Usenov was dismissed in an ensuing governmental reorganization. Later in April security forces dispersed large-scale protests in Bishkek organized by Kulov's recently established opposition grouping, the United Front For A Worthy Future For Kyrgyzstan; some 100 demonstrators were arrested and two prominent opposition leaders were detained on charges of inciting unrest.

In September 2007 the Constitutional Court ruled that the adoption of the two Constitutions of November 2006 and January 2007 had been illegal, since the drafts had not been submitted to a national referendum; consequently the Constitution in place prior to November 2006 again entered into force. Bakiyev subsequently announced that a further new constitutional text was to be proposed. In October Bakiyev established a political party, Bright Road (Ak Jol). The Constitution proposed at the national referendum on 21 October was endorsed by 76.1% of the electorate (with a voter turnout of 81.6%); henceforth, the number of parliamentary deputies was to increase from 75 to 90, all of whom were to be elected from party lists. One day later Bakiyev dissolved the Jorgorku Kenesh; early legislative elections were subsequently scheduled for 16 December. The Government submitted its resignation on 24 October, remaining in office in an interim capacity.

On 29 November 2007 Bakiyev dismissed Atambayev as premier; on the same day he appointed Iskenderbek Aidaraliyev First Deputy Prime Minister and also assigned him the role of acting Prime Minister. At the elections, held on 16 December, Bright Road won 47.0% of votes cast, securing 71 legislative seats, ahead of the SDPK, with 5.1% of the votes cast and 11 seats, and the Communist Party of Kyrgyzstan, with 5.1% of the votes cast and eight seats. The Fatherland Socialist Political Party, despite gaining 8.3% of votes overall, narrowly failed to qualify for representation, owing to a new electoral requirement that each party obtain at least 0.5% of the votes cast in each of the country's seven oblasts and two largest cities. Although this stipulation was particularly criticized by OSCE observers, who stated that the conduct of the elections failed to meet democratic standards, the electoral commission upheld the results. On 24 December Igor Chudinov was appointed Prime Minister, while Adahan Madumarov (of Bright Road) was elected legislative Chairman. A new Government, which retained the principal ministers of the former administration, was approved in the Jorgorku Kenesh on 27 December.

On 26 May 2008 Bakytbek Kalyev, hitherto the head of the State Border Guard Service, was appointed Minister of Defence, succeeding Gen. Ismail Isakov, who became Secretary of the National Security Council. On 29 May Madumarov resigned as legislative Chairman, after he was found to have contravened regulations concerning expenditure; he was replaced by a close ally of President Bakiyev, Aitibai Tagayev. In September Bakiyev dismissed the Minister of Justice, Marat Kaiyypov, and the head of the penal service, following an investigation into a prison riot, in which two officers had been killed. Later that month, the Chairman of the electoral commission, Klara Kabilova, fled the country, subsequently accusing Maksim Bakiyev, the son of the President and a prominent businessman, of issuing threats against her. In local elections, held on 5 October, observers from local non-governmental organizations (NGOs) alleged that numerous irregularities had enabled pro-Government candidates to win most seats in municipal councils. In November the Minister of Industry, Energy and Fuel Resources was replaced, following criticism over energy shortages. In the same month the Government imposed restrictions on the operation of religious organizations, stating that the legislation had been introduced in response to a growth in support for extremist Islamist groups, particularly in the south of the country. In late December an alliance of the major opposition parties, the United People's Movement (UPM), was established to demand the resignation of Bakiyev and to oppose the proposed privatization of various important facilities. In January 2009 Bakiyev removed numerous ministers, senior government officials, regional officials and ambassadors. Aidaraliyev was replaced as First Deputy Prime Minister by Omurbek Babanov.

The 2009 presidential election

Following the announcement of his decision (rescinded in June) to close the Manas airbase (see Foreign Affairs) in February 2009, Bakiyev indicated that he intended to seek a second term in office; several opposition leaders had appealed to the Constitutional Court to bring forward the next poll (due to take place in October 2010). Opposition parties threatened to begin a campaign of protests to demand that the Government end repressive measures against opposition leaders and activists. In March 2009, shortly after Bakiyev had agreed to negotiate with opposition leaders, a prominent supporter of Tekebayev and member of the opposition For Justice Movement, Alikbek Jekshenkulov, was arrested on suspicion of involvement in the killing of a Turkish businessman in 2007. Jekshenkulov was also charged with abuse of office while serving as Minister of Foreign Affairs in 2005–07; his trial commenced in June, and in August he was released from custody on remand, instead being placed under house arrest. He was given a five years' suspended sentence, including three years under probation (during which period he was additionally prohibited from seeking public office) in March 2010. Also in March 2009 Medet Sadyrkulov, who had been replaced as the head of the presidential administration in January, was killed in an allegedly suspicious automobile collision. On 19 March the Constitutional Court ruled that the next presidential election must take place no later than 25 October. In late March the UPM, led by Beknazarov, staged large anti-Government demonstrations in Bishkek and other major towns. In April the UPM announced that it had selected Atambayev as its presidential candidate. In April a Bright Road deputy, Sanjarbek Kadyraliyev, was assassinated outside his home in Bishkek; he was the fifth parliamentarian to have been killed since Bakiyev became President. In early May Bright Road confirmed its endorsement of Bakiyev as its presidential candidate. In early July a journalist who had often criticized the Government for its social policies, Almaz Tashiyev, was severely beaten by several police officers; he died a few days later.

In the presidential election, held on 23 July 2009, Bakiyev was re-elected, obtaining 76.4% of the votes cast, according to official results. Shortly after polling began Atambayev, announced his withdrawal from the election on the grounds that officials had perpetrated extensive fraud. He, none the less, was the second-placed candidate, with 8.4%. Some 79.1% of the electorate were recorded to have participated. Observers from the OSCE described the election as falling short of full democratic standards, while it was reported that around 20 opposition supporters had been detained by the police on polling day. On 29 July clashes broke out between demonstrators protesting at the conduct of the election and police in Bishkek, precipitating the imposition of a ban of mass gatherings.

On 1 September 2009, in an address to the Jogorku Kenesh, Bakiyev proposed a series of administrative reforms. These proposed reforms were opposed by Prime Minister Chudinov, who consequently resigned on 21 October. He was succeeded as premier by Usenov, who had served as the Chairman of the Presidential Administration since January. Many members of the outgoing administration were reappointed to the new Government formed one day later. Responsibility for foreign affairs was transferred to the Office of the President, and consequently the post of Minister of Foreign Affairs was abolished. On 22 December 2009 a prominent Kyrgyzstani journalist critical of Bakiyev, Gennadii Pavlyuk (also known as Ibragim Rustamek), was killed after he was thrown to the ground from a high-rise building in Almatı, Kazakhstan. The Kazakhstani police stated that they regarded Pavlyuk's death as murder, prompting speculation that his killing was politically motivated, particularly as Pavlyuk had recently been involved in negotiations with Atambayev on the establishment of an online news site. (Two other journalists operating in Kyrgyzstan were physically attacked during that month.) The European Union (EU, see p. 281) subsequently demanded that a full investigation into Pavlyuk's killing be conducted; two people were arrested in Almatı in October 2010 in connection with the killing, while a third, the prime suspect, was apprehended two months later. In March 2010 the Government imposed a number of measures that inhibited the freedom of the media; two opposition newspapers, *Achyk Sayasat* and *Nazar*, were ordered to close, and the rebroadcasting on local FM radio stations of the Kyrgyz programming of the Czech Republic-based (and US-funded) Radio Free Europe/Radio Liberty was halted, while access to two prominent independent online news websites was blocked. In April a further newspaper, *Forum*, was ordered by a court in Bishkek to cease publication, after it had allegedly called for the overthrow by force of the Government.

The April 2010 uprising

On 3 April 2010 a visit by UN Secretary-General Ban Ki-Moon to Kyrgyzstan was a focus for protests in Bishkek, led by members of civil rights organizations. On 6 April, following the arrest of opposition leader Bolotbek Sherniyazov, several thousand protesters demanding the resignation of President Bakiyev stormed the regional government offices in the north-western town of Talas, holding the regional governor hostage, while rioting ensued throughout the town. (Smaller demonstrations against the Government took place in other cities.) A further cause of discontent was the recent appointment of relatives of the President to senior positions in the security services, and of Maksim Bakiyev as Chairman of a state committee responsible for the control of all financial inflows into the country and several major companies. The police succeeded in freeing the regional governor later in the day, but demonstrators regained control of the administrative building. On the same day Atambayev was arrested and accused of inciting the unrest in Talas, while other prominent opposition leaders, including Tekebayev, were detained in Bishkek.

On 7 April 2010 demonstrations in Bishkek attended by an estimated 5,000 people demanding the resignation of Bakiyev, expressing opposition to increases in fuel tariffs and the arrest of opposition leaders, rapidly degenerated into widespread violent disorder, as unruly crowds undertook extensive looting of commercial and government premises in the city. The demonstrations appeared to have no clear leader. Opposition supporters gained control of the state TV channel and broadcast speeches in support of the uprising. The First Deputy Prime Minister, Akylbek Japarov, was taken hostage, and the Minister of the Interior, Moldomusa Kongantiyev, was severely beaten. Anti-Bakiyev protesters also seized control of government and police buildings in the provincial cities of Naryn and Tokmak. In Bishkek, police officers opened fire on demonstrators when the protesters attempted to storm the principal government building. In the ensuing violence around 80 people were killed and more than 1,000 injured. Kazakhstan closed its border with Kyrgyzstan until 20 May. By the end of 7 April the Government had effectively lost control, and President Bakiyev, having been forced to flee Bishkek, flew to Osh, from where he announced his refusal to resign from office. Meanwhile, Otunbayeva, now the leader of the parliamentary faction of the SDPK, declared herself to be the leader of a transitional administration, the Interim Government of National Trust (later designated simply the Interim Government), which would hold office for a period of six months prior to the organization of a presidential election. Other senior members of the transitional administration included Temir Sarayev, the leader of the White Falcon Political Party (Ak Shumkar), Atambayev, Tekebayev and Beknazarov. On 11 April the transitional administration dissolved the Jogorku Kenesh and temporarily assumed all legislative functions.

On 12 April 2010 Bakiyev led a rally in Jalal-Abad, attended by around 4,000 people. On 15 April officials of the Interim Government announced that Bakiyev had resigned as President. Following negotiations (mediated by the OSCE) between the transitional administration and the leaders of Kazakhstan, Russia and the USA, Bakiyev was granted safe passage to Kazakhstan, from where he denied that he had resigned. Meanwhile, the Minister of Defence in the Bakiyev administration, Bakytbek Kalyyev, was arrested on charges related to the use of force against unarmed civilians in Bishkek during the uprising. On 22 April Tekebayev announced that a referendum on a new Constitution, which would reduce presidential powers, would be held on 27 June, and that a presidential election would be scheduled for 10 October. Meanwhile, as sporadic unrest continued in various regions of the country, Otunbayeva declared that the state would take firm action to restore order. Meanwhile, the President of Belarus, Alyaksandr Lukashenka, announced that he had granted asylum to Bakiyev, who continued to state that he was the legitimate Head of State of Kyrgyzstan, and that his letter of resignation had been written under pressure and against his will, following a telephone conversation with the Russian Chairman of the Government, Vladimir Putin. On 4 May Otunbayeva signed an agreement seeking the extradition of Bakiyev and ordered the opening of a criminal investigation against him in connection with his involvement in the violent suppression of protests on 7 April. However, Lukashenka stated that he would not permit Bakiyev's extradition from Belarus. On the same day an investigation began into apparent corruption by companies allegedly controlled by Maksim Bakiyev that were responsible for the supply of fuel to the US airbase at Manas. On 17 May KCP leader Iskhak Masaliyev (the son of the party's former leader) was charged with organizing mass protests in Osh, Batken and Jalal-Abad. Violent clashes erupted on 19 May between Kyrgyz and Uzbek groups in Jalal-Abad and Osh, in which two people died and more than 70 were injured; a state of emergency was declared in Jalal-Abad. Also on 19 May the Interim Government announced that Otunbayeva was to serve additionally as interim President until the end of 2011, and that she would be prohibited from contesting the next presidential election (to be held in October 2011 and not, as previously announced, in 2010) and, in the mean time, from membership of any political party. On 21 May the Interim Government published a new draft Constitution, which defined the country as a secular state with a parliamentary system of government. Voters in the constitutional referendum would also be required to approve Otunbayeva as interim President until December 2011, while the scheduling of parliamentary elections for 10 October 2010 was confirmed.

Ethnic unrest and the 2010 Constitution

On 9–10 June 2010 there was renewed ethnic violence in Osh, after a fight broke out between Kyrgyz and Uzbek groups at a casino. A series of subsequent attacks against Kyrgyz resulted in reprisals against the city's Uzbek population, prompting the Interim Government to send troops to the region and to declare a state of emergency. In the ensuing days the ethnic unrest spread to other cities, including Jalal-Abad, while tens of thousands of Uzbeks attempted to flee across the border into Uzbekistan. The Interim Government declared a partial mobilization of the armed forces and appealed to Russia for help in restoring peace. On 14 June Uzbekistan closed its border to prevent any further influx of refugees. The UN stated that there was evidence that the violence was 'orchestrated, targeted and well-planned'. While the Interim Government accused supporters of Bakiyev of inciting the unrest, a subsequent report by the international organization Human Rights Watch stated that the Kyrgyzstani military had played a role in facilitating the attacks against the Uzbek population. At least 400 people were officially reported to have died in the conflict, which lasted just four days, and 400,000 people were displaced, of whom at least 100,000 had crossed into Uzbekistan. On 17 June the Russian-led Collective Security Treaty Organization (CSTO) announced that it would not deploy a peace-keeping mission to Kyrgyzstan. On 25 June it was reported that Sanjarbek Bakiyev, a nephew of the ousted president, had been detained on charges of organizing the ethnic unrest in Jalal-Abad in May. (He was found guilty and sentenced to 10 years in prison in November)

Despite the unrest, the Kyrgyzstani authorities proceeded with the scheduled constitutional referendum on 27 June 2010, the conduct of which the OSCE described as 'largely transparent'. Some 90.6% of votes cast supported the Constitution, and voter participation was estimated at 72%. The Constitution came into force on 2 July; one day later Otunbayeva was sworn in as interim President, while remaining Prime Minister. Subsequently, several prominent members of the Interim Government, including deputy premiers Atambayev, Tekebayev and Sarayev resigned in order to participate in the forthcoming legislative elections. On 14 July several new senior ministers were appointed to the Interim Government, including former Prime Minister Muraliyev as First Deputy Prime Minister and Kubatbek Baibolov as Minister of the Interior (replacing Sherniyazov). The Interim Government announced that it would establish a national commission to investigate the events of the previous month. The following week the OSCE approved the deployment of a 52-strong police force to Osh and Jalal-Abad. The move was met with protests, led by the Mayor of Osh, Melisbek Myrzakmatov, a supporter of Bakiyev who was accused of inciting the violence. (Having postponed the deployment of the police force owing to security threats, in November the OSCE announced that the mission would be reduced to around 30 personnel.)

On 2 August 2010 the official investigation began into the ethnic violence that had occurred in June. On 5 August Urmat Baryktabasov, the leader of the nationalist Flag of the Fatherland (Meken Tuu) party, and more than 20 associates were arrested, on charges of plotting a coup. Police dispersed around 2,000 of Baryktabasov's supporters in Bishkek, after officials banned a demonstration against his prosecution for economic crimes. On 15 September a prominent Uzbek activist, Azimjan Askarov, and seven other Uzbeks were found guilty of the murder of a Kyrgyz policemen during the conflict in June. Askarov and four of his co-defendants were sentenced to life imprisonment. The verdict, which was criticized by several human rights groups, came amid growing concern that a disproportionately high number of Uzbeks were standing trial for atrocities committed during that time.

The 2010 legislative elections

On 10 September 2010 political campaigning for the legislative elections began. In early October around 100 people attacked the Bishkek offices of the Homeland Idealistic Democratic Party, which enjoyed strong support among Kyrgyz in the south of the country, following reports (subsequently denied) that its leader, Kamchybek Tashiyev, had called for the return to power of Bakiyev. Some 29 political parties contested the elections to the new 120-seat legislature, held on 10 October and which were widely reported to be free and fair. The announcement of the final results of the legislative elections was delayed until 1 November 2010, owing to allegations of procedural irregularities and confusion over the number of voters. Five parties won the requisite number of votes (5% of the total registered electorate) for representation in the Jogorku Kenesh: the Homeland Idealistic Democratic Party won 15.3% of the votes cast (equivalent to 8.5% of the registered electorate), and obtained 28 seats; the SDPK, won 14.2% (26 seats); the Dignity Party 13.7% (25 seats); the Republic Political Party (Respublika), a new party led by Babanov, 12.5% (23 seats); and Tekebayev's Fatherland Socialist Political Party won 9.9% (18 seats). The White Falcon Political Party won 4.7% of the votes cast, and consequently failed to secure representation. Some 55.3% of the registered electorate participated in the ballot. Supporters of the United Kyrgyzstan Political Party (Butun Kyrgyzstan), which won 8.3% of the votes cast, and which also failed to obtain legislative representation, subsequently staged protests outside the parliamentary building in Bishkek and in Osh, and presented a legal challenge to the results. Meanwhile, on 24 October, following claims by Tashiyev that he had been the target of an assassination attempt by state security forces, hundreds of his supporters held a rally in Bishkek.

The first session of the new Jogorku Kenesh was held on 10 November 2010, when some 150 activists from the Martyrs of the Fatherland (Meken Sheyitteri) movement, comprising relatives of those killed during the clashes between protesters and security forces on 7 April, attempted to prevent the delegates from entering the parliament building. The following day, with no coalition agreement having been reached among the five parties represented in the Jogorku Kenesh, Otunbayeva issued a mandate to SDPK leader Atambayev to form a parliamentary coalition within 15 days.

On 7 November 2010 some 500 Kyrgyz activists illegally occupied land in Osh Oblast, in the Uzbek-populated villages of Ishkevan and Kyzyl-Kyshtak, with the intention of dividing it into plots. The following day at least 20 Kyrgyz were arrested after several hundred activists joined the protesters. At a meeting on 9 November the regional governor promised representatives of the group, whose homes had been destroyed during the ethnic violence in June, that they would be allocated land near Osh. On 17 November the trial of ousted President Bakiyev opened in Bishkek. Bakiyev, along with 27 of his aides, was being tried *in absentia* for ordering special forces to open fire on civilians during the protests on 7 April. However, the hearing was immediately adjourned after relatives of those killed in the violence disrupted proceedings. On 30 November a bomb exploded outside the stadium in which the trial was being held, injuring at least three people. One day earlier four people alleged to have connections with the Islamic Movement of Uzbekistan (IMU) had been killed by security forces in Osh, while interior ministry officials announced that nine people suspected of planning to carry out terrorist attacks had been arrested.

On 30 November 2010 the SDPK formed a coalition with the Republic Political Party and the Fatherland Socialist Political Party. Atambayev was nominated Prime Minister with Babanov his deputy; Tekebayev was to become parliamentary speaker. On 2 December, however, Tekebayev's nomination failed by three votes to obtain a majority in the Jogorku Kenesh, and the coalition subsequently collapsed. Consequently, on 4 December Otunbayeva instructed Babanov to form a government. On 15 December it was announced that the Republic Political Party was to join a new coalition with the SDPK and the Homeland Idealistic Democratic Party. On the same day the trial began of Akmat Bakiyev, brother of the ousted President, who had been arrested in June on charges relating to the ethnic violence in the south of the country in 2010. Also in December Amnesty International announced that ethnic Uzbeks were being disproportionately targeted in the investigations relating to the June unrest; the organization claimed that by early November 271 people had been detained and the 'overwhelming majority' of those brought to trial had been Uzbeks, the fact that Uzbek casualties during the violence far exceeded those of ethnic Kyrgyz notwithstanding.

On 20 December 2010 the Jogorku Kenesh endorsed the nominations of Atambayev as Prime Minister and of Akhmatbek Keldibekov as legislative Chairman. A new Government was formed, including Babanov as First Deputy Prime Minister, Ruslan Kazakbayev of the SDPK as Minister of Foreign Affairs and Zarylbek Rysaliyev of the SDPK as Minister of Internal Affairs. A ministerial position for the reconstruction and development of Osh and Jalal-Abad was created. Later in December a vehicle packed with explosives was discovered outside Bishkek's main police headquarters, in connection with which nine people were later arrested. In early January 2011 three policemen were killed while carrying out identity checks in Bishkek; two suspects were killed and a third was detained by security forces the following day. Rysaliyev later announced that the men had been responsible for the recent bombing in Bishkek and the attempted car bomb, and had been planning further terrorist attacks.

On 11 January 2011 the national commission appointed to investigate the violence of June 2010 published its findings, concluding that a combination of Uzbek leaders in Southern Kyrgyzstan, relatives of ousted President Bakiyev, drugs dealers, Islamist extremists and 'outside forces' were responsible for the violence. The commission's report criticized several high-ranking officials serving in the Interim Government at the time of the crisis, including Sherniyazov, as well as the head of the National Security Committee and the Prosecutor-General, for having failed to act with sufficient rapidity to curb the violence. Isakov and Former Deputy Prime Minister Azimbek Beknazarov were also criticized. Maksim Bakiyev and a prominent Uzbek businessman, Kadyrjon Batyrov, both of whom had left the country, were among those found to be implicated in initiating the violence, while the elder brother of the former President, Janysh Bakiyev, a former head of the State Security Service, was accused of having financed the unrest. Also on 11 January the National Security Committee announced the arrest of a local leader of the transnational, Islamist Hizb-ut-Tahrir al-Islami (Party of Islamic Liberation) in Jalal-Abad Oblast. At least four other members of the organization were apprehended in southern Kyrgyzstan in that month. In March Iskhak Masaliyev was acquitted by a Bishkek court of the charges of organizing the ethnic violence. In April Baryktabasov was sentenced to four years' imprisonment, after he and 14 associates were convicted of possession of armaments and attempting to seize power. (In August, however, Baryktabasov was released under an amnesty.) In August Akmat Bakiyev was sentenced to seven and a half years' imprisonment. (In March 2012 it was reported that he had escaped from detention, after being hospitalized.)

Meanwhile, in February 2011 Otunbayeva appointed two non-partisan ministers to the Government, including Melis Mambetjanov as Minister of Finance. In early March two visiting deputies from the Russian State Duma accused First Deputy Prime Minister Babanov of corruption in relation to Megacom, a mobile telecommunications service provider and one of Kyrgyzstan's leading companies, which was 51% owned by the Russian enterprise, Eventis Telecom. On 13 April Atambayev agreed to Babanov's request that he temporarily resign from office, for the period of one month; Babanov also requested that the Zhogorku Kenesh form a special commission to investigate the accusations against him (which he denied) during that period. In September 15 of the 25 parliamentary deputies representing the Dignity Party voted to remove Kulov as the leader of their parliamentary faction and party, electing Kamila Taliyeva as their leader, and announcing that, henceforth, the party leadership would serve on an annual rotational basis. However, Kulov refused to accept these decisions, stating that such appointments could only be made by the entire party membership, and he retained effective control of the party.

The 2011 presidential election

On 25 September 2011 Atambayev resigned as Prime Minister in order to contest the forthcoming presidential election. Consequently, Babanov became acting premier. A total of 16 candidates (of a reported 86 who had applied for registration) contested the presidential election on 30 October. Atambayev was decisively elected as President, securing 62.5% of the votes cast; Madumarov, representing United Kyrgyzstan, was placed second, with 14.8%; and Tashiyev, the leader of the Homeland Idealistic Democratic Party, was third, with 14.3%. A rate of participation of 61.3% was recorded. OSCE observers reported that the voting process had been peaceful, but subject to significant violations, while noting that the pre-election campaign had largely met democratic standards. Atambayev was officially inaugurated on 1 December. On 16 December the SDPK formed a new parliamentary coalition with the Republic Political Party, the Fatherland Socialist Political Party and the Dignity Party, which together held 92 parliamentary seats. The Jogorku Kenesh confirmed Babanov's appointment as Prime Minister on 23 December; the opposition criticized the inclusion of several members of previous administrations, notably First Deputy Prime Minister Aaly Karashev and Minister of Finance Akylbek Japarov, who had both served under Bakiyev, in the new Government.

In January 2012 an ongoing protest in prisons throughout Kyrgyzstan at poor living conditions escalated when some 1,300 of 7,000 prisoners on hunger strike sewed their lips together; a few days later, however, the authorities announced that nearly all prisoners had ended their hunger strike, following a government pledge to address living standards in the penal system.

Recent developments: collapse of the coalition Government

On 22 August 2012, following ongoing allegations of corruption against Babanov, the Fatherland Socialist Political Party and the Dignity Party both withdrew from the Government. The Fatherland Socialist Political Party had accused the premier earlier in the month of having accepted a race horse as a bribe from a Turkish businessman in exchange for a construction contract relating to facilities at the US airbase at Manas. Following the collapse of the Government, a new coalition was rapidly formed. On 12 September a new Government was sworn in, comprising members of the SDPK, the Fatherland Socialist Political Party and the Dignity Party; the coalition parties between them held a slim parliamentary majority, with 67 of the 120 seats. The Republic Political Party and the Homeland Idealistic Democratic Party, which had recently formed a new alliance, Law and Justice, were excluded from the coalition. President Atambayev nominated independent Jantoro Satybaldiyev, the hitherto presidential Chief of Staff and a former Governor of Osh Oblast, as Prime Minister. On 5 September the Jogorku Kenesh overwhelmingly endorsed his nomination. Other ministerial appointments included Djoomart Otorbayev as First Deputy Prime Minister, and Taiyrbek Sarpashev and Taliyeva as Deputy Prime Ministers; Erlan Abdyldayev and Olga Lavrova were appointed Minister of Foreign Affairs and Minister of Finance, respectively. On 29 October Shamil Atahanov, erstwhile chairman of the State National Security Committee of Kyrgyzstan, was appointed Minister of Internal Affairs, replacing Rysaliyev.

On 3 October 2012 Tashiyev and two other senior members of the Homeland Idealistic Democratic Party were detained and charged with inciting unrest during a protest rally in Bishkek. The rally, attended by around 1,000 people, had been called to demand the renationalization of the Kumtor gold mine, partly as a result of concerns about the social and environmental costs of the project. On 5 October, when the pre-trial detention of the opposition leaders had been due to end, some 700 protesters gathered in Jalal-Abad to demand their release, but a court in Bishkek extended their pre-trial detention to two months, precipitating further demonstrations across the country in their support. Also in October Maksim Bakiyev (who was also subject to charges of money-laundering and corruption in Kyrgyzstan) was arrested in London, United Kingdom at the request of the US Department of Justice, on charges of fraud and conspiracy to pervert the course of justice in the USA in 2010–12, in connection with the supply of fuel to the US airbase at Manas. The trial of Tashiyev and his associates began on 10 January 2013, and in March 2013 around 1,000 protesters gathered in Jalal-Abad to demand their immediate release.

Meanwhile, in February 2013 former President Bakiyev was sentenced *in absentia* to 24 years imprisonment for abuse of power. Meanwhile, his brother Janysh Bakiyev (who was also in exile in Belarus) was sentenced *in absentia* to life in prison, having been found guilty of the murder of Sadyrkulov in March 2009. In late February 2013 the Government was reorganized. The hitherto Minister of Internal Affairs, Shamil Atakhanov, was appointed as a Deputy Prime Minister; he was succeeded in his former role, in an acting capacity, by Abdulda Suranchiyev.

Foreign Affairs

Regional relations

Kyrgyzstan is a member of the Eurasian Economic Community (EURASEC, see p. 461), an organization formed in 2000 as the successor to a 'community of integrated states' comprising Kyrgyzstan, Belarus, Kazakhstan and Russia, and which had absorbed the Central Asian Co-operation Organization (CACO) in 2002, which also included Kyrgyzstan among its members. Kyrgyzstan sought to accede to a customs union between Belarus, Kazakhstan and Russia that entered into effect in 2010, and by early 2013 it was anticipated that the country would join the union in 2014. Kyrgyzstan is also a member of the Collective Security Treaty Organization (CSTO, see p. 474) that was inaugurated in 2003 as the successor of the CIS Collective Security Treaty, which had agreed to form a Collective Rapid Reaction Force in Bishkek to combat Islamist militancy in Central Asia.

Kyrgyzstan's campaign against Islamist extremism—particularly against the clandestine, transnational, Islamist Hizb-ut-Tahrir al-Islami (Party of Islamic Liberation)—intensified in 1999, after a number of kidnappings and hostage-taking incidents perpetrated by Islamist groups believed to be based in Uzbekistan and Tajikistan, including the Islamic Movement of Uzbekistan (IMU). From August 2000 Islamist militants made a further series of incursions from Tajikistan, leading to armed conflict with government forces. In April 2001 a local government official accused Uzbekistan of laying landmines along the border with Kyrgyzstan, and demanded the removal of Uzbekistani troops, deployed in an effort to combat the incursions of Islamist militants and drugs-traffickers, from Kyrgyzstani border territories. Meanwhile, reports in May indicated that Islamist rebels were increasingly recruiting from southern Kyrgyzstan. In July 2003 it was reported that Kyrgyzstan was to commence the unilateral removal of landmines along the border with Uzbekistan.

Relations with Uzbekistan were further strained in mid-2005, when the Kyrgyzstani Government refused to return a large number of refugees who had fled Uzbekistan after violence broke out in Andijon in May (see Uzbekistan). In August Uzbekistan annulled a bilateral agreement to supply natural gas to Kyrgyzstan, and in September issued a report accusing Kyrgyzstan of having permitted religious extremists to use bases in the south of the country to prepare to foment unrest in Andijon. In August 2006 the Kyrgyzstani authorities attracted international censure for the decision to repatriate to Uzbekistan a number of refugees from Andijon. In the same month Rafiq Qori Kamoluddin, a prominent imam in Kyrgyzstan and an ethnic Uzbek, was shot dead in an operation targeting alleged Islamist extremists conducted by the Kyrgyzstani and Uzbekistani national security services. Despite the large-scale ethnic unrest that occurred near the border with Uzbekistan in June 2010 and the subsequent influx into Uzbekistan of many thousands of refugees, the Uzbekistani Government refrained from actively intervening in the conflict, although it did briefly close the border. In January 2013 hundreds of residents of Uzbekistan's Sokh district (which forms one of four exclaves of the country, surrounded by Kyrgyzstani territory) clashed with Kyrgyzstani border guards who were installing power lines on disputed territory. According to reports at least three Uzbekistani citizens were shot, while one Kyrgyzstani policeman was severely beaten. On the following day, Sokh residents took hostage 30 Kyrgyzstani from a nearby village. Following negotiations between Uzbekistani and Kyrgyzstani border officials, the hostages were released, but Kyrgyzstani villagers subsequently blocked roads between Sokh and metropolitan Uzbekistan.

In 1992 the Presidents of Kyrgyzstan and Russia signed a treaty of friendship, co-operation and mutual assistance; a further declaration of partnership was signed in 2000. In accordance with an agreement reached in 1997, Russia was to lease four military installations in Kyrgyzstan in return for training Kyrgyzstani army recruits. In October 2003 a Russian airbase became operational at Kant; this was the first Russian military installation to be established outside Russia since the collapse of the USSR, and was located around 30 km from an airbase at Manas, used by the US-led coalition fighting in Afghanistan. In September the Russian Minister of Defence, Sergei Ivanov, declared that Russia was to provide Kyrgyzstan with several million US dollars in military aid. In February 2009 Russian President Dmitrii Medvedev agreed to extend funds equivalent to more than US $2,000m. to Kyrgyzstan (of which some $1,700m. were designated for the development of a major hydro-electric project). Russia harshly criticized the decision of President Bakiyev, announced in June, to reverse the proposed closure of the US airbase at Manas. In August 2009 a summit meeting of the CSTO took place in Cholpon-Ata, in northern Kyrgyzstan, when Presidents Bakiyev and Medvedev signed a preliminary memorandum of understanding on the opening of a second Russian military base in Kyrgyzstan. This base, which was to operate under the auspices of the CSTO, was to be leased to Russia for a period of up to 49 years, extendable for subsequent 25-year periods, and all Russian personnel at the base were to be granted diplomatic immunity. Although final agreement on the base was to have been reached by 1 November, negotiations subsequently stalled, apparently owing to opposition from Uzbekistan.

Shortly after the Interim Government of National Trust came to power in April 2010, Russia announced that it would provide financial aid amounting to US $50m. Following the ethnic unrest in southern Kyrgyzstan in June, however, the Russian Government was reluctant to accept that the proposed new parliamentary system of government in Kyrgyzstan would be the most effective at achieving stability. During the campaign for the October legislative elections several party leaders visited Moscow; of these Feliks Kulov, leader of the Dignity Party, was seen to be most closely allied with the Russian administration, particularly after he signed a co-operation agreement with United Russia on behalf of his party. In January 2011, in what was widely perceived to be an act of support for the new coalition Government, Russia agreed to abolish an export tax on fuel imposed during the final days of Bakiyev's administration. The new President, Almazbek Atambayev, made an official visit to Moscow in February 2012, during which he reportedly pledged commitment to Russian premier (and former and subsequent President) Vladimir Putin's stated aim of greater economic integration between post-Soviet states; however, he failed to secure a requested EURASEC loan and confirmation of continued duty-free exports of Russian fuel. Tensions subsequently emerged, after Atambayev criticized Russia, particularly with regard to its alleged interference in Kyrgyzstan's domestic politics at the time of the October 2011 presidential election, and demanded that it pay US $15m. in rent arrears for the use of the airbase at Kant.

An agreement signed in April 1997 with China, Russia, Kazakhstan and Tajikistan (which, together with Kyrgyzstan, constituted the so-called Shanghai Five) aimed to improve joint border security. The alliance, renamed the Shanghai Co-operation Organization (SCO, see p. 478) upon the accession of Uzbekistan, signed the Shanghai Convention on Combating Terrorism, Separatism and Extremism in mid-2001. In August an SCO anti-terrorism centre became operational in Bishkek. In August 2003 Kyrgyzstani forces participated in major anti-terrorist manoeuvres, hosted by China and Kazakhstan. In September 2004 Tanayev and the Chinese Prime Minister, Wen Jiabao, signed a 10-year co-operation agreement on combating terrorism, separatism and religious extremism, and a protocol on the demarcation of the border between the two countries.

Other external relations

Following the suicide attacks on the US cities of New York and Washington, DC, on 11 September 2001, Kyrgyzstan announced that it would permit US military aircraft access to Kyrgyzstani airspace for the aerial bombardment of militants of the Islamist al-Qa'ida organization (which co-ordinated the attacks) and its Taliban hosts in Afghanistan. In November the US-led coalition was also granted access to the country's military bases and, later, the airbase at Manas airport. Kyrgyzstani and US troops under-

took joint exercises in February 2002. In September Akayev met the US President, George W. Bush, and the US Secretary of State, Colin Powell, in Washington, DC. In early 2006 Kyrgyzstan presented the USA with new conditions for the use of the Manas airbase, apparently proposing to increase the rent payable by the USA from US $2m. to $200m.; President Bakiyev maintained that the proposed charge was in accordance with international norms. In July an agreement was signed allowing the continued US use of the airbase in exchange for an 'assistance and co-operation' payment of $150m. In February 2009 Bakiyev announced that the airbase would be closed; this followed a visit to Moscow during which Russia had offered Kyrgyzstan assistance and loans equivalent to more than US $2,000m. On 19 February the Jogorku Kenesh approved the closure of the airbase; US forces were to be required to withdraw from Kyrgyzstan within a period of 180 days after the US embassy received notice of the termination of the lease. However, in June Kyrgyzstan and the USA concluded an agreement to reverse the decision on the closure of the airbase, although the new agreement stipulated that the USA would use the site as a transit centre, rather than as a full military facility, while the rent charged was to be increased more than three-fold, to an annual rate of US $60m. The five-year agreement was signed into law in July, after it had been approved by the Jogorku Kenesh.

Following the overthrow of President Bakiyev in April 2010, the new interim leader, Otunbayeva, a former Ambassador to the USA, stated that Kyrgyzstan wished to maintain co-operative relations with the USA. The award by the US Administration in November of a $315m. fuel supply contract for the Manas transit centre, as the airbase had been renamed, to the Gibraltar-based Mina Corporation was unpopular with the Interim Government, as the company was implicated in corrupt schemes during Akayev's and Bakiyev's terms in office. In February 2011 the Jogorku Kenesh approved the draft of a new leasing agreement under which a Kyrgyzstani state-owned enterprise, the Manas Refuelling Complex, would share up to 50% of the fuel contract with Mina Corporation. After his election in October, President Atambayev announced that the lease on the US transit centre at Manas airbase would not be renewed after the expiry of the existing agreement in July 2014.

CONSTITUTION AND GOVERNMENT

Under the Constitution adopted on 2 July 2010, following a national referendum, presidential powers in Kyrgyzstan were substantially reduced. Legislative power is vested in the 120-seat Jogorku Kenesh, elected by universal adult suffrage for a term of five years. Executive power is vested in the President, who is directly elected for just one term of six years. The President appoints the members of the Government, including the Prime Minister. Judicial power is exercised by the Supreme Court and regional courts. For administrative purposes, Kyrgyzstan is divided into seven oblasts (regions) and the municipality of Bishkek (the capital).

REGIONAL AND INTERNATIONAL CO-OPERATION

Kyrgyzstan is a member of the Commonwealth of Independent States (CIS, see p. 251), and has also joined the Eurasian Economic Community (EURASEC, see p. 461), the Collective Security Treaty Organization (CSTO, see p. 474), the Shanghai Co-operation Organization (SCO, see p. 478) and the Organization of Islamic Cooperation (see p. 413).

Kyrgyzstan joined the UN in 1992 and became a member of the World Trade Organization (WTO, see p. 444) in 1998.

ECONOMIC AFFAIRS

In 2011, according to estimates by the World Bank, Kyrgyzstan's gross national income (GNI), measured at average 2009–11 prices, was US $5,084m., equivalent to $920 per head (or $2,290 per head on an international purchasing-power parity basis). During 2002–11, it was estimated, the population increased by an annual average of 1.1%, while gross domestic product (GDP) per head increased, in real terms, at an average annual rate of 3.5%. According to the World Bank, overall GDP increased, in real terms, at an estimated average annual rate of 4.7% in 2002–11. Real GDP decreased by 1.4% in 2010 but increased by 7.0% in 2011.

Agriculture (including forestry and fishing) contributed an estimated 19.7% of GDP and engaged 30.7% of the employed labour force in 2011, according to official figures. By tradition, the Kyrgyz are a pastoral nomadic people, and the majority of the population (some 63.3% in 2010, according to UN estimates) reside in rural areas. Livestock-rearing, once the mainstay of agricultural activity, is declining in importance. Only about 7% of the country's land area is arable; of this, some 70% depends on irrigation. The principal crops are grain, potatoes, vegetables and barley. By 2002, according to government figures, collective farms accounted for only around 6% of agricultural production, while state farms accounted for just under 2%. According to the World Bank, the GDP of the agricultural sector increased, in real terms, by an average annual rate of 0.2% per year in 2002–11; agricultural GDP declined by 2.7% in 2010 but grew by 3.5% in 2011.

Industry (comprising manufacturing, mining, utilities and construction) contributed 27.9% of GDP and provided 21.0% of employment in 2011, according to official figures. According to the World Bank, real industrial GDP increased at an average annual rate of 3.2% in 2002–11; the GDP of the sector increased by 11.0% in 2011.

The mining and quarrying sector provided 0.9% of GDP and engaged 0.7% of the employed workforce in 2011, according to official figures. Kyrgyzstan has considerable mineral deposits, including coal, gold, tin, mercury, antimony, zinc, tungsten and uranium. In May 2001 the Government announced the discovery of new deposits of petroleum, estimated to total 70m. barrels, in an oilfield in the west of the country. Production of gold from the Kumtor mine, which is believed to contain the eighth largest deposit of gold in the world (over 200 metric tons), began in January 1997. As a result, by 2001 Kyrgyzstan had become the 10th largest extractor and seller of gold world-wide. The Kumtor mine reportedly produced almost 4.4m. ounces of gold between 1997 and the end of 2003. Production of gold from the Jeruy deposit commenced in 2002. In April 2006 an agreement was signed with a Kazakhstani company on the development of the Taldy Bulak Levoberezhny gold deposit. Gold production totalled 19.7 tons in 2011.

Manufacturing contributed 18.3% of GDP in 2011 and engaged 7.6% of the employed labour force in 2011, according to official figures. Real manufacturing GDP increased by an average of 2.0% per year in 2002–11, according to the World Bank; the GDP of the sector increased by 8.0% in 2011.

Kyrgyzstan's principal source of domestic energy production (and a major export) is hydroelectricity (generated by the country's mountain rivers), which provided 89.3% of the country's total energy requirements in 2009. Kyrgyzstan has insufficient petroleum and natural gas to meet its needs, and substantial imports of hydrocarbons are thus required; Kyrgyzstan exports electricity to Kazakhstan and Uzbekistan in return for coal and natural gas, respectively. Imports of mineral products comprised 23.5% of the value of total recorded imports in 2011.

The construction sector contributed 5.3% of GDP in 2011 and engaged 10.9% of the employed labour force in 2011. During 2002–11, according to UN figures, the GDP of the sector increased at an average annual rate of 8.2%. However, construction GDP decreased by 18.5% in 2010 and further by 3.9% in 2011.

In 2011 the services sector contributed 52.4% of GDP and engaged 48.3% of the employed labour force in 2011. In 2002–11, according to the World Bank, the GDP of the sector increased, in real terms, by an average of 10.0% per year; services GDP decreased by 0.9% in 2010, but increased by 5.5% in 2011.

In 2011 Kyrgyzstan recorded a visible merchandise trade deficit of US $1,664.7m., and there was a deficit of $377.3m. on the current account of the balance of payments. In 2011 the principal source of imports (accounting for 33.5% of the total) was Russia; other major suppliers were the People's Republic of China and Kazakhstan. The main market for exports in that year was Switzerland (which accounted for 44.1% of all exports); other principal markets were Kazakhstan, Russia, the United Arab Emirates and Uzbekistan. The main exports in 2011 were precious and semi-precious stones, mineral products, textiles and fabrics, and vegetable products. The principal imports in that year were mineral products, machinery, vehicle and transport equipment, chemicals, prepared foodstuffs, textiles and fabrics, and metals.

In 2011 Kyrgyzstan recorded an overall budgetary deficit of 29,498.5m. soms, equivalent to 10.8% of GDP. Kyrgyzstan's general government gross debt was 143,210m. soms in 2011, equivalent to 52.4% of GDP. Kyrgyzstan's total external debt was US $3,984m. at the end of 2010, of which $2,442m. was public and publicly guaranteed debt. In that year, the cost of servicing long-term public and publicly guaranteed debt and repayments to the IMF was equivalent to 21.9% of the value of exports of goods, services and income (excluding workers' remittances). The annual rate of inflation averaged 7.3% in 2000–09. According to official figures, consumer prices increased by 19.2% in 2010, by 5.7% in 2011, and by 7.5% in 2012. The average rate of unemployment was 8.5% in 2011.

Political instability following the removal of President Askar Akayev in 2005 led to a contraction in GDP in that year. A steep increase in consumer tariffs for electricity, fuel and water, which exacerbated economic hardship was a principal factor in precipitating protests in that led to the overthrow of President Kurmanbek Bakiyev in April 2010. Shortly after it assumed power, the Interim Government reversed the increase in energy tariffs and introduced key reforms to the energy sector aimed at improving transparency, also recovering US $60.6m. of a $300m. loan from Russia that had allegedly been diverted by the Bakiyev regime. In October 2011 Kyrgyzstan and seven other member states of the Commonwealth of Independent States (CIS, see p. 251) signed a free trade agreement. It was hoped the agreement would enter into effect in 2013. President Almazbek Atambayev, who was elected in October 2011, pledged commitment to Kyrgyzstan's membership of a customs union between Belarus, Kazakhstan and Russia; in March 2013 it was announced that the country expected to join the union by the end of that year. Atambayev's administration also pursued joint projects in the energy sector with the Russian state-controlled natural gas company Gazprom. In late 2012, moreover, Gazprom announced that it was to purchase a 75% stake in the state-controlled and heavily indebted gas distribution company Kyrgyzgaz for the nominal sum of $1 in 2013, and that it sought to purchase the remainder of the company. In late 2012 the IMF released its third review under a three-year Extended Credit Facility (ECF), totalling $106m., to support the authorities' fiscal stimulus measures. At the conclusion of the review, the IMF's Executive Board approved the release of some $14.6m., bringing total disbursements to $58.5m. Authorities noted the continued macroeconomic stability in the country in spite of political uncertainty following the break-up of the coalition Government in August; and significantly lower gold output. (One-third of Kumtor's gold production was deferred to 2013–14 as a result of geological factors.) The downturn in gold output was a major factor behind the substantially lower rate of GDP increase projected for 2012, of 1%.

PUBLIC HOLIDAYS

2014: 1 January (New Year's Day), 7 January (Christmas), 8 March (International Women's Day), 21 March (Nooruz, Spring Holiday), 24 March (Day of the People's Revolution), 1 May (International Labour Day), 5 May (Constitution Day), 9 May (Victory Day), 28 July* (Orozo Ait, Id al-Fitr, end of Ramadan), 31 August (Independence Day), 4 October* (Kurban Ait, Id al-Adha, Feast of the Sacrifice).

* These holidays are dependent on the Islamic lunar calendar and may vary by one or two days from the dates given.

Statistical Survey

Source (unless otherwise stated): National Statistical Committee, 720033 Bishkek, Frunze 374; tel. (312) 22-63-63; fax (312) 22-07-59; e-mail zkudabaev@nsc .bishkek.su; internet www.stat.kg.

Area and Population

AREA, POPULATION AND DENSITY

Area (sq km)	199,900*
Population (census results)†	
24 March 1999	4,822,938
24 March 2009	
Males	2,645,921
Females	2,716,872
Total	5,362,793
Population (official estimates at 1 January)	
2010	5,418,299
2011	5,477,620
2012	5,551,888
Density (per sq km) at 1 January 2012	27.8

* 77,182 sq miles.
† The figures refer to *de jure* population. The total was 4,850,700 at the 1999 census and 5,107,640 in 2009.

POPULATION BY AGE AND SEX
(official estimates at 1 January 2011)

	Males	Females	Total
0–14	844,833	812,074	1,656,907
15–64	1,764,222	1,817,186	3,581,408
65 and over	94,633	144,672	239,305
Total	**2,703,688**	**2,773,932**	**5,477,620**

PRINCIPAL ETHNIC GROUPS
(official estimates at 1 January 2012)

	Number	%
Kyrgyz	4,006,009	72.2
Uzbek	796,291	14.3
Russian	381,562	6.9
Dungan	61,372	1.1
Uigur	50,346	0.9
Tajik	48,033	0.9
Turk	39,913	0.7
Kazakh	32,981	0.6
Tatar	28,656	0.5
Ukrainian	16,657	0.3
Others	90,068	1.6
Total	**5,551,888**	**100.0**

ADMINISTRATIVE DIVISIONS
(official estimates at 1 January 2011)

	Area (sq km)	Population	Density (per sq km)	Principal city
Oblasts (regions) .				
Batken	17,000	441,101	25.9	Batken
Chui	20,200	814,870	40.3	Tokmok
Jalal-Abad . .	33,700	1,036,644	30.8	Jalal-Abad
Naryn	45,200	262,137	5.8	Naryn
Osh	29,200	1,386,734	47.5	Osh*
Talas	11,400	231,819	20.3	Talas
Yssyk-Kul . .	43,100	444,520	10.3	Karakol
City				
Bishkek . .	100	859,795	8,598.0	—
Kyrgyzstan . .	**199,900**	**5,477,620**	**27.4**	

* The city of Osh also constitutes a separate administrative area, with a population numbering 255,847 at 1 January 2011.

PRINCIPAL TOWNS
(official estimates at 1 January 2011)

Bishkek (capital) .	859,800	Karakol	68,000
Osh	255,800	Tokmok	53,800
Jalal-Abad . . .	98,400		

BIRTHS, MARRIAGES AND DEATHS

	Registered live births		Registered marriages		Registered deaths	
	Number	Rate (per 1,000)	Number	Rate (per 1,000)	Number	Rate (per 1,000)
2004 . .	109,939	21.6	34,542	6.8	35,061	6.9
2005 . .	109,839	21.4	37,321	7.3	36,992	7.2
2006 . .	120,737	23.3	43,760	8.4	38,566	7.4
2007 . .	123,251	23.5	44,392	8.5	38,180	7.3
2008 . .	127,332	23.9	44,258	8.3	37,710	7.1
2009 . .	135,494	25.2	47,567	8.8	35,898	6.7
2010 . .	146,123	26.8	50,362	9.2	36,174	6.6
2011 . .	149,612	27.1	56,509	10.2	36,700*	6.7

* Data rounded to nearest hundred deaths.

Life expectancy (years at birth, official estimates): 69.6 (males 65.7; females 73.7) in 2011.

IMMIGRATION AND EMIGRATION

	2009	2010	2011
Immigrants	3,829	3,903	6,337
Emigrants	33,380	54,531	45,740

ECONOMICALLY ACTIVE POPULATION
(annual averages, '000 persons)

	2009	2010	2011
Agriculture, hunting forestry and fishing	718.6	699.1	700.3
Mining and quarrying	14.7	17.5	16.7
Manufacturing	172.6	174.6	173.1
Electricity, gas and water supply .	38.8	41.4	38.7
Construction	244.0	240.1	249.1
Wholesale and retail trade; repair of motor vehicles, motor cycles and personal and household goods	316.0	337.5	345.9
Hotels and restaurants . . .	82.2	82.8	86.5
Transport, storage and communications	144.9	147.5	147.2
Financial intermediation . . .	15.8	18.2	17.7
Real estate, renting and business activities	55.3	58.4	56.0
Public administration and defence; compulsory social security . .	103.6	99.9	102.6
Education	164.3	171.9	177.1
Health and social work . . .	79.4	74.4	78.5
Other services	66.2	80.4	88.3
Total employed	**2,216.4**	**2,243.7**	**2,277.7**
Unemployed	203.7	212.3	212.4
Total labour force	**2,420.1**	**2,456.0**	**2,490.1**
Males	1,395.7	1,427.8	1,448.6
Females	1,024.4	1,028.2	1,041.5

Health and Welfare

KEY INDICATORS

Total fertility rate (children per woman, 2010)	2.7
Under-5 mortality rate (per 1,000 live births, 2010) . . .	38
HIV/AIDS (% of persons aged 15–49, 2009)	0.3
Physicians (per 1,000 head, 2007)	2.3
Hospital beds (per 1,000 head, 2007)	5.1
Health expenditure (2009): US $ per head (PPP)	148
Health expenditure (2009): % of GDP	6.4
Health expenditure (2009): public (% of total)	53.0
Access to water (% of persons, 2010)	90
Access to sanitation (% of persons, 2010)	93
Total carbon dioxide emissions ('000 metric tons, 2008) . .	6,208.2
Carbon dioxide emissions per head (metric tons, 2008) . .	1.2
Human Development Index (2011): ranking	126
Human Development Index (2011): value	0.615

For sources and definitions, see explanatory note on p. vi.

Agriculture

PRINCIPAL CROPS
('000 metric tons)

	2009	2010	2011
Wheat	1,056.7	813.3	799.8
Rice, paddy	20.7	20.9	19.4
Barley	289.7	231.5	233.8
Maize	486.6	440.9	446.4
Potatoes	1,393.1	1,339.4	1,379.2
Sugar beet	54.0	139.2	158.8
Sunflower seed	57.5	48.8	45.6
Cabbages and other brassicas .	123.8	112.1	127.8
Tomatoes	194.0	182.2	176.7
Cucumbers and gherkins . .	68.3	74.0	79.9
Onions, dry	136.4	131.9	138.0
Garlic	32.0	31.0	30.6
Carrots and turnips . . .	168.9	158.9	152.2
Apples*	113.5	142.0	158.3
Apricots*	22.0	16.4	18.2
Peaches and nectarines* . .	15.0	3.8	4.2
Grapes	12.3	4.5	6.7
Watermelons	137.2	157.3	151.6
Seed cotton	49.2	74.0	101.3
Tobacco, unmanufactured . .	12.0	9.9	9.9

* Unofficial figures.

Aggregate production ('000 metric tons, may include official, semi-official or estimated data): Total cereals 1,858.1 in 2009, 1,510.3 in 2010, 1,504.7 in 2011; Total roots and tubers 1,393.1 in 2009, 1,339.4 in 2010, 1,379.2 in 2011; Total vegetables (incl. melons) 967.5 in 2009, 963.1 in 2010, 965.9 in 2011; Total fruits (excl. melons) 212.7 in 2009, 197.6 in 2010, 221.8 in 2011.

Source: FAO.

LIVESTOCK
('000 head at 1 January)

	2009	2010	2011
Horses	373.0	378.4	389.0
Asses	69	73	71
Cattle	1,278.1	1,298.8	1,338.6
Pigs	61.3	59.8	59.2
Sheep	3,881.8	4,095.2	4,314.7
Goats	933.7	942.5	973.4
Chickens	4,238	4,422	4,490
Turkeys	141	156	166

Source: FAO.

LIVESTOCK PRODUCTS
('000 metric tons)

	2009	2010	2011
Cattle meat	94.5	97.7	98.7
Sheep meat	41.2	42.6	50.1
Goat meat	7.6	7.8	9.0
Pig meat	17.3	16.3	16.3
Horse meat	18.7	19.0	18.8
Chicken meat	4.0	4.1	6.1
Cows' milk	1,273.5	1,321.8	1,321.7
Hen eggs*	20.6	20.8	21.9
Honey	1.4	1.5†	1.5†
Wool, greasy	11.0	10.9	11.1

* Unofficial figures.
† FAO estimate.

Source: FAO.

Forestry

ROUNDWOOD REMOVALS
('000 cubic metres, excl. bark, FAO estimates)

	2008	2009	2010
Sawlogs, veneer logs and logs for sleepers	4.7	4.7	4.7
Other industrial wood	4.7	4.7	4.7
Fuel wood	18.0	28.5	36.6
Total	27.4	37.9	46.0

2011: Figures assumed to be unchanged from 2010 (FAO estimates).

Source: FAO.

SAWNWOOD PRODUCTION
('000 cubic metres, incl. railway sleepers, unofficial figures)

	2008	2009	2010
Coniferous (softwood) . . .	30.0	44.5	39.8
Broadleaved (hardwood) . . .	30.0	44.5	39.8
Total	60.0	89.0	79.6

2011: Production assumed to be unchanged from 2010 (FAO estimates).

Source: FAO.

Fishing

(metric tons, live weight)

	2008	2009	2010
Capture	8	10*	27
Common carp	6	6*	15
Silver carp	1	1*	3
Goldfish	1	1*	3
Aquaculture	92	133	319*
Common carp	35	51	120*
Grass carp	6	9	20*
Silver carp	28	40	99*
Rainbow trout	23	33	80*
Total catch	100	143*	346*

* FAO estimate.

Source: FAO.

Mining

('000 metric tons, unless otherwise indicated)

	2009	2010	2011
Coal	606.9	575.0	839.0
Crude petroleum	77.3	82.8	90.3
Natural gas (million cu m) . .	15.4	22.8	26.5

Gold (metric tons): 17.0 in 2009; 18.5 in 2010; 19.7 in 2011 (Source: Gold Fields Mineral Services, *Gold Survey 2012*).

Industry

SELECTED PRODUCTS
('000 metric tons unless otherwise indicated)

	2009	2010	2011
Vegetable oil	20.6	18.1	15.6
Refined sugar	5.8	14.1	17.0
Vodka ('000 hl)	13.6	12.0	15.6
Beer ('000 hl)	15.2	18.0	20.2
Cigarettes (million)	3,586.0	3,649.3	2,443.5
Textile fabrics ('000 sq m) . . .	1,413.6	985.7	727.8
Footwear	5,089.1	3,095.6	4,581.4
Motor spirit (petrol)	9.9	15.3	13.5
Gas-diesel (distillate fuel) oil . .	48.0	38.2	27.4
Residual fuel oils (mazout) . . .	39.0	43.8	41.9
Cement	579.4	759.7	1,014.8
Electric energy (million kWh) .	11,083.2	12,062.7	15,222.7

Finance

CURRENCY AND EXCHANGE RATES

Monetary Units
100 tyiyns = 1 som.

Sterling, Dollar and Euro Equivalents (31 December 2012)
£1 sterling = 74.799 soms;
US $1 = 47.401 soms;
€1 = 62.541 soms;
1,000 soms = £13.37 = $21.10 = €15.99.

Average Exchange Rate (soms per US $)
2010   45.964
2011   46.144
2012   47.004

Note: In May 1993 Kyrgyzstan introduced its own currency, the som, replacing the Russian (former Soviet) rouble at an exchange rate of 1 som = 200 roubles.

BUDGET
(million soms)*

Revenue†	2009	2010	2011
Taxation	36,097.8	36,365.1	53,017.4
Corporate income taxes . . .	2,661.6	2,407.9	2,652.8
Personal income taxes . . .	5,657.1	6,338.6	8,402.6
Value-added tax	13,467.4	14,602.0	20,352.9
Excise taxes	1,668.6	1,689.3	2,187.0
Taxes on international trade and transactions	4,138.9	4,350.1	7,146.8
Other current revenue	9,061.4	10,997.3	15,654.8
Capital revenue	312.3	628.6	456.1
Total	45,471.5	47,991.1	69,128.3

Expenditure‡	2009	2010	2011
Current expenditure	50,034.3	61,583.2	82,393.8
General public services . .	8,333.4	8,191.5	10,121.0
Defence and public security .	6,391.0	8,475.8	9,719.0
Economic affairs	8,008.1	10,801.8	15,370.3
Environmental protection . .	581.8	567.7	562.0
Education	11,498.4	11,993.6	18,231.3
Health care	5,809.8	6,413.3	9,079.9
Social insurance and security .	5,587.5	11,075.2	14,182.5
Housing and public utilities .	2,441.8	2,504.3	2,893.3
Cultural and religious activity .	1,382.5	1,560.1	2,234.5
Capital expenditure	8,523.4	7,197.8	8,944.5
Total	58,557.7	68,781.1	91,338.3

* Figures represent a consolidation of the budgetary transactions of the central Government and local governments. The operations of extra-budgetary accounts, including the Social Fund (formed in 1994 by an amalgamation of the Pension Fund, the Unemployment Fund and the Social Insurance Fund), are excluded.
† Excluding grants received (million soms): 10,162.9 in 2009; 7,022.1 in 2010; 8,672.3 in 2011.
‡ Excluding lending minus repayments (million soms): 2,601.1 in 2009; 11,652.3 in 2010; 15,960.8 in 2011.

Source: National Bank of the Kyrgyz Republic.

INTERNATIONAL RESERVES
(US $ million at 31 December)

	2009	2010	2011
Gold	90.8	116.8	132.1
IMF special drawing rights . .	162.1	171.7	177.0
Foreign exchange	1,331.9	1,431.9	1,525.9
Total	1,584.8	1,720.4	1,835.0

Source: IMF, *International Financial Statistics*.

MONEY SUPPLY
(million soms at 31 December)

	2005	2006	2007
Currency outside banks . . .	13,065	19,410	26,675
Demand deposits at banking institutions	2,123	3,655	5,669
Total money	15,188	23,065	32,343

Source: IMF, *International Financial Statistics*.

COST OF LIVING
(Consumer Price Index; base: previous year = 100)

	2010	2011	2012
Food and non-alcoholic drinks .	127.0	103.5	104.5
Alcoholic drinks and tobacco products	112.9	109.8	110.2
Non-food products	114.2	109.2	109.8
Services	111.9	111.1	109.8
All items (incl. others) . . .	119.2	105.7	107.5

NATIONAL ACCOUNTS
(million soms at current prices)

Expenditure on the Gross Domestic Product

	2009	2010	2011
Government final consumption expenditure	37,088.5	39,946.5	50,422.7
Private final consumption expenditure	157,518.4	186,422.6	229,600.9
Changes in inventories . . .	−2,671.9	−1,565.3	2,480.3
Gross fixed capital formation . .	57,546.1	61,950.0	66,725.2
Total domestic expenditure .	249,481.1	286,753.8	349,229.1
Exports of goods and services . .	110,065.6	113,609.9	156,237.3
Less Imports of goods and services	158,323.8	179,994.4	233,420.2
Statistical discrepancy	—	—	1,061.6
GDP in market prices . . .	201,222.9	220,369.3	273,107.8

Gross Domestic Product by Economic Activity

	2009	2010	2011
Agriculture, forestry and fishing .	37,743.9	38,444.1	49,228.8
Mining	1,072.3	1,384.8	2,227.7
Manufacturing	28,630.5	37,356.5	45,823.1
Electricity, gas and water supply .	4,369.1	6,848.5	8,445.7
Construction	13,488.6	12,169.1	13,317.8
Wholesale and retail trade; repair of motor vehicles, motorcycles and personal and household goods	33,865.4	35,179.7	43,856.9
Transport and communication .	17,670.8	18,894.0	22,464.6
Financial intermediation . .	8,023.4	8,573.9	9,759.7
Public administration and defence; compulsory social security . .	10,757.7	12,448.2	14,814.5
Others*	30,095.4	33,759.3	40,104.8
Sub-total	185,717.1	205,058.1	250,043.6
Less Financial intermediation services indirectly measured .	6,647.0	7,271.2	8,286.7
Gross value added in basic prices	179,070.1	197,786.9	241,756.9
Taxes, less subsidies, on products .	22,152.8	22,582.4	31,350.9
GDP in market prices . . .	201,222.9	220,369.3	273,107.8

* Including hotels and restaurants; real estate, renting and business activities; education; health and social work; and other community, social and personal services.

Source: Asian Development Bank.

BALANCE OF PAYMENTS
(US $ million)

	2009	2010	2011
Exports of goods	1,693.8	1,778.7	2,271.2
Imports of goods	−2,813.6	−2,980.9	−3,935.9
Balance on goods . . .	−1,119.8	−1,202.2	−1,664.7
Exports of services . . .	859.8	693.1	1,117.1
Imports of services	−868.9	−924.2	−1,138.0
Balance on goods and services	−1,128.8	−1,433.3	−1,685.6
Primary income received . .	21.7	29.7	31.6
Primary income paid . . .	−203.2	−334.9	−562.0
Balance on goods, services and primary income	−1,310.4	−1,738.6	−2,215.9
Secondary income received . .	1,094.1	1,450.9	2,044.1
Secondary income paid . .	−85.1	−141.4	−205.4
Current balance	−301.3	−429.1	−377.3
Capital account (net) . . .	−14.0	−62.1	−37.5
Direct investment assets . .	0.3	—	0.1
Direct investment liabilities .	189.4	437.6	693.5
Portfolio investment assets . .	161.2	182.5	−166.8
Portfolio investment liabilities .	0.7	−18.2	5.5
Other investment assets . .	−217.2	127.3	−227.4
Other investment liabilities .	489.0	−145.2	346.5
Net errors and omissions . .	−241.2	−71.4	−129.4
Reserves and related items .	66.8	21.4	107.3

Source: IMF, *International Financial Statistics.*

External Trade

PRINCIPAL COMMODITIES
(distribution by Harmonized System Classification, US $ million)

Imports c.i.f.	2009	2010	2011
Vegetable products	142.7	121.6	166.3
Prepared foodstuffs, beverages and tobacco	245.9	267.3	376.3
Mineral products	839.0	876.0	1,002.2
Products of chemical or allied industries	305.9	300.8	405.1
Plastics, rubber and articles thereof	99.1	121.3	172.2
Textiles and fabrics	189.1	209.0	296.0
Metals and articles thereof . .	185.4	183.1	284.9
Machinery, electrical equipment and parts	330.0	408.5	485.8
Vehicles and transport equipment	276.5	280.0	482.0
Total (incl. others)	3,040.2	3,223.1	4,261.2

Exports f.o.b.	2009	2010	2011
Vegetable products	86.2	104.1	138.5
Prepared foodstuffs, beverages and tobacco	36.4	45.2	46.3
Mineral products	236.3	125.9	216.5
Products of chemical or allied industries	258.5	166.9	49.1
Raw hides and skins, leather, fur, travel articles and bags . . .	6.6	6.7	12.0
Textiles and fabrics	103.1	161.8	189.0
Natural and cultured pearls, precious and semi-precious stones, precious metals and products, and coins . . .	533.7	671.7	1,017.1
Metals and articles thereof . .	19.0	36.9	70.6
Machinery, electrical equipment and parts	49.5	49.8	55.7
Vehicles and transport equipment	34.1	36.7	69.4
Total (incl. others)	1,443.5	1,488.4	1,978.9

PRINCIPAL TRADING PARTNERS
(US $ million)

Imports c.i.f.	2009	2010	2011
Belarus	74.0	53.4	109.5
Canada	19.3	19.0	22.4
China, People's Republic (incl. Hong Kong)	623.6	666.3	923.5
Germany	100.7	88.6	144.6
Japan	66.0	86.7	164.5
Kazakhstan	339.9	385.6	411.4
Korea, Republic	51.2	49.5	63.2
Netherlands	49.5	25.7	40.9
Russia	1,090.4	1,083.9	1,429.6
Turkey	72.8	84.7	117.1
Ukraine	89.3	81.5	124.9
USA	101.6	191.3	210.3
Uzbekistan	111.7	93.8	84.3
Total (incl. others)	3,040.2	3,223.1	4,261.2

Exports f.o.b.	2009	2010	2011
Afghanistan	18.8	9.0	23.5
China, People's Republic (incl. Hong Kong)	19.4	28.3	42.0
Kazakhstan	140.7	181.7	289.7
Russia	185.8	257.8	284.4
Switzerland	444.8	387.9	873.6
Tajikistan	15.8	15.4	7.6
Turkey	36.7	37.2	54.5
United Arab Emirates . . .	101.7	302.2	150.0
USA	38.1	90.3	0.6
Uzbekistan	167.6	40.2	124.4
Total (incl. others)	1,443.5	1,488.4	1,978.9

Transport

RAILWAYS
(traffic)

	2009	2010	2011
Paying passengers ('000 journeys).	751.5	711.3	596.9
Passenger-km (million) . . .	106.1	98.7	82.8
Freight carried ('000 metric tons) .	1,044.4	1,032.1	1,033.7
Freight net ton-km (million) . .	744.5	737.7	798.3

ROAD TRAFFIC
(vehicles in use at 31 December)

	2005	2006	2007
Passenger cars	201,430	218,718	229,735
Motorcycles and mopeds . . .	10,059	9,948	9,099

2010: Passenger cars 342,439; Motorcycles and mopeds 6,443.

Source: IRF, *World Road Statistics*.

CIVIL AVIATION
(traffic on scheduled services)

	2009	2010	2011
Passengers carried ('000) . . .	357.8	464.6	707.9
Passenger-km (million) . . .	571.9	814.2	1,400.4
Total ton-km (million) . . .	45.4	64.4	111.0

Tourism

FOREIGN VISITOR ARRIVALS
(selected countries)

Country of residence	2009	2010	2011
China, People's Republic . . .	21,879	18,167	25,059
Germany	9,374	6,980	8,432
Kazakhstan	1,036,322	837,609	1,437,739
Korea, Republic	4,790	4,207	3,681
Russia	157,008	132,493	1,020,102
Turkey	12,265	11,098	15,237
Uzbekistan	474,751	140,644	433,363
Total (incl. others)	2,146,740	1,316,207	3,114,372

Tourism receipts (US $ million, excl. passenger transport): 459 in 2009; 284 in 2010 (Source: World Tourism Organization).

Communications Media

	2009	2010	2011
Telephones ('000 main lines in use)	498.3	489.1	502.0
Mobile cellular telephones ('000 subscribers)	4,487.1	5,275.5	6,277.1
Internet subscribers ('000) . .	47.5	68.9	115.1
Broadband subscribers ('000) . .	15.3	20.9	37.0
Book production (incl. brochures):			
titles	820	800	1,070
copies ('000)	699.5	730.4	1,705.1
Newspapers (incl. periodicals):			
titles	199	212	195
copies ('000)	31,500	38,700	37,900
Magazines:			
titles	66	57	48
copies ('000)	495.7	1,608.5	310.9

Source: partly International Telecommunication Union.

Education

(2011)

	Institutions	Teachers	Students
Pre-primary	741	3,647	98,706
Primary and Secondary: general .	2,204	75,502	1,015,172
Secondary: vocational . . .	235	9,573	103,355
Higher (all institutions) . . .	54	12,830	239,208

Pupil-teacher ratio (primary education, UNESCO estimate): 24.3 in 2009/10 (Source: UNESCO Institute for Statistics).

Adult literacy rate (UNESCO estimates): 99.2% (males 99.5%; females 99.0%) in 2009 (Source: UNESCO Institute for Statistics).

Directory

The Government

HEAD OF STATE

President: ALMAZBEK ATAMBAYEV (elected 30 October 2011, inaugurated 1 December).

THE GOVERNMENT
(May 2013)

A coalition, principally comprising members of the Dignity Political Party (Ar-Namys), the Fatherland Socialist Political Party (Ata Meken) and the Social Democratic Party of Kyrgyzstan (SDPK). The Republic Political Party (Respublika) additionally contributed one minister to the Government.

Prime Minister: JANTORO SATYBALDIYEV (Independent).

First Deputy Prime Minister: DJOOMART OTORBAYEV (Ata Meken).

Deputy Prime Minister: SHAMIL ATAKHANOV (SDPK).

Deputy Prime Minister: TAIYRBEK SARPASHEV (Independent).

Deputy Prime Minister: KAMILA TALIYEVA (Ar-Namys).

Minister, Head of the Government Staff: NURHANBEK MOMUNA-LIYEV (Independent).

Minister of Foreign Affairs: ERLAN ABDYLDAYEV (Independent).

Minister of Defence: TAALAIBEK OMURALIYEV (Independent).

Minister of Internal Affairs: ABDULDA SURANCHIYEV (acting) (SDPK).

Minister of Justice: ALMAMBET SHYKMAMATOV (Ata Meken).

Minister of Finance: OLGA LAVROVA (Ar-Namys).

Minister of Economics and Anti-monopoly Policy: TEMIR SARIYEV (Independent).

Minister of Agriculture and Land Reclamation: CHYNGYSBEK UZAKBAYEV (Ar-Namys).

Minister of Transport and Communications: KALYKBEK SULTANOV (Ata Meken).

Minister of Emergency Situations: KUBATBEK BORONOV (Respublika).

Minister of Energy and Industry: (vacant).

Minister of Education and Science: KANAT SADYKOV (SDPK).

Minister of Health: DINARA SAGIMBAYEVA (SDPK).

Minister of Culture, Information and Tourism: SULTAN RAYEV (Independent).

Minister of Social Development: (vacant).

Minister of Labour, Migration and Youth: ALIYASBEK ALYMKU-LOV (SDPK).

Chairman of the State Committee for National Security: BEYSHENBAY ZHUNUSOV (Independent).

MINISTRIES

Office of the President: 720003 Bishkek, pr. Chui 205; tel. (312) 63-89-20; e-mail psp@adm.gov.kg; internet www.president.kg.

Office of the Government: 720003 Bishkek, Dom Pravitelstva; tel. (312) 66-49-23; e-mail okmotkg@mail.gov.kg; internet www.gov.kg.

Ministry of Agriculture and Land Reclamation: 720040 Bishkek, Kiyevskaya 96A; tel. (312) 62-36-16; fax (312) 62-36-22; e-mail agroprod@agroprod.kg; internet www.agroprod.kg.

Ministry of Culture, Information and Tourism: 720026 Bishkek, Pushkina 78; tel. (312) 62-04-82; fax 62-35-89; e-mail info@mincultinfo.kg; internet www.minculture.gov.kg.

Ministry of Defence: 720001 Bishkek, Logvinenko 26; tel. (312) 66-18-04; fax (312) 66-19-04; e-mail ud@bishkek.gov.kg; internet www.mil.kg.

Ministry of Economics and Anti-monopoly Policy: 720002 Bishkek, pr. Chui 106; tel. (312) 62-52-41; fax (312) 66-18-37; e-mail mert@mert.kg.

Ministry of Education and Science: 720040 Bishkek, Tynysta-nova 257; tel. (312) 62-24-42; e-mail minedukg@gmail.com; internet edu.gov.kg.

Ministry of Emergency Situations: 720055 Bishkek, Toktona-liyeva 2/1; tel. (312) 54-79-86; fax (312) 25-60-77; e-mail mchs@elcat.kg; internet mes.kg.

Ministry of Energy and Industry: 720055 Bishkek, Akhunbayeva 119; tel. (312) 56-18-22; fax (312) 56-20-28; internet energo.gov.kg.

Ministry of Finance: 720040 Bishkek, bul. Erkindik 58; tel. (312) 66-12-27; fax (312) 66-16-45; e-mail minfin@mf.gov.kg; internet www.minfin.kg.

Ministry of Foreign Affairs: 720040 Bishkek, bul. Erkindik 57; tel. (312) 62-05-45; fax (312) 66-05-01; e-mail gendep@mfa.gov.kg; internet www.mfa.kg.

Ministry of Health: 720040 Bishkek, Moskovskaya 148; tel. (312) 62-26-80; fax (312) 66-07-17; e-mail mz@med.kg; internet www.med.kg.

Ministry of Internal Affairs: 720000 Bishkek, Frunze 469; tel. (312) 66-24-50; fax (312) 26-62-80; e-mail pressa@mvd.kg; internet www.mvd.kg.

Ministry of Justice: 720010 Bishkek, M. Gandi 32; tel. (312) 65-64-90; fax (312) 65-65-02; e-mail minjust.ep@mail.ru; internet www.minjust.gov.kg.

Ministry of Labour, Migration and Youth: 720000 Bishkek, Razzakova 8/1; tel. (312) 30-02-32; internet www.mz.kg.

Ministry of Social Development: 720000 Bishkek, ul. Tynysta-nova 215; tel. (312) 66-34-00; fax (312) 66-57-24; e-mail mlsp@mlsp.kg; internet www.mlsp.kg.

Ministry of Transport and Communications: 720017 Bishkek, Isanova 42; tel. (312) 31-43-85; fax (312) 31-28-11; e-mail mtk@mtk.gov.kg; internet mtc.gov.kg.

President

Presidential Election, 30 October 2011

Candidates							Votes	%
Almazbek Atambayev	.	.	.	.	.	.	1,161,929	62.52
Adahan Madumarov	.	.	.	.	.	.	274,639	14.78
Kamchibek Tashiyev	.	.	.	.	.	.	266,189	14.32
Temirbek Asanbekov	.	.	.	.	.	.	17,232	0.93
Omurbek Suvanaliyev	.	.	.	.	.	.	16,143	0.87
Kubatbek Baibolov	.	.	.	.	.	.	15,427	0.83
Tursunbai Bakir uulu	.	.	.	.	.	.	15,195	0.82
Anarbek Kalmatov	.	.	.	.	.	.	13,609	0.73
Others	.	.	.	.	.	.	26,075	1.42
Against all candidates	.	.	.	.	.	.	13,419	0.72
Total*	.	.	.	.	.	.	**1,858,632**	**100.00**

* Including 38,145 invalid votes (2.05% of the total).

Legislature

Jogorku Kenesh
(Supreme Council)

720053 Bishkek, Abdymomunov 207; tel. (312) 61-16-04; fax (312) 62-50-12; e-mail zs@kenesh.gov.kg; internet www.kenesh.kg.

Chairman: ASILBEK JEENBEKOV.

General Election, 10 October 2010

Parties	Votes	%*	Seats
Homeland Idealistic Democratic Political Party (Ata-Jurt) . . .	257,100	15.31	28
Social Democratic Party of Kyrgyzstan	237,634	14.15	26
Dignity Political Party (Ar-Namys).	229,916	13.69	25
Republic Political Party (Respublika)	210,594	12.54	23
Fatherland Socialist Political Party (Ata-Meken)	166,714	9.93	18
United Kyrgyzstan Political Party .	139,548	8.31	—
White Falcon Political Party (Ak Shumkar)	78,673	4.68	—
Zamandash Political Party . . .	55,907	3.33	—
Harmonious Fatherland Party (Meken Yntymagy)	46,070	2.74	—
Others	246,715	14.69	—
Against all	10,839	0.65	—
Total valid votes	**1,679,710**	**100.00**	**120**

* Parties were required to obtain the support of at least 5% of the total registered electorate (3,036,703 persons) in order to be eligible for legislative representation. (44.69% of the registered electorate either did not participate or cast invalid votes.) The results announced by the Central Commission for Elections and Referendums presented the share of the vote received by each party as a proportion of the total electorate, rather than of the valid votes cast. The five parties that obtained legislative representation received the support of the following share of the total electorate: Homeland Idealistic Democratic Political Party (Ata-Jurt) 8.47%; Social Democratic Party of Kyrgyzstan 7.83%; Dignity Political Party (Ar-Namys) 7.57%; Republic Political Party (Respublika) 6.93%; Fatherland Socialist Political Party (Ata-Meken) 5.49%.

Election Commission

Central Commission for Elections and Referendums (Shailoo Jana Referendum Otkoruu Boyuncha Borborduk Komissiyasy): 720040 Bishkek, ul. Razzakova 59; tel. (312) 62-68-25; fax (312) 66-58-60; e-mail cec@shailoo.gov.kg; internet www.shailoo.gov.kg; independent govt organ; one-third of mems nominated by President; Chair. TUIGUNAALY ABDRAIMOV.

Political Organizations

At December 2007 some 50 political organizations were registered with the Central Election Commission. A total of 29 parties contested the legislative elections held in October 2010. The following were among the most important operating in 2013.

Bright Road People's Party (Ak Jol) (Ak Jol Eldik Partiyasy): 720000 Bishkek, Panfilov 152; tel. (312) 62-62-06; fax (312) 66-34-03; internet www.akjolnarod.kg; f. Oct. 2007; Chair. KURMANBEK S. BAKIYEV (in exile).

Dignity Political Party (Ar-Namys): 720033 Bishkek, Togolok Moldo 60A; tel. (312) 32-46-01; e-mail ar-namys@mail.kg; internet www.ar-namys.org; f. 1999; pro-democracy; mem. of political bloc For a Worthy Future of Kyrgyzstan United Front, formed Feb. 2007; Chair. FELIKS KULOV; c. 11,000 mems.

Fatherland Socialist Political Party (Ata Meken) (Ata Meken Sotsialisttik Partiyasy): 720040 Bishkek, Ibraimova 108; tel. (312) 89-55-12; fax (312) 66-46-38; e-mail pr@atameken.kg; internet www.atameken.kg; f. 1992; nationalist; supports state control of the economy; supports parliamentary system of govt; mem. of the opposition United People's Movement formed in late 2008; supported Interim Govt that assumed power in April 2010; Chair. OMURBEK CH. TEKEBAYEV; more than 2,000 mems.

Great Unification National Democratic Party (Uluu Birim-dik): Bishkek; f. 2005; moderate nationalist party; supported Interim Govt that assumed power in April 2010; Leader EMILBEK KAPTAGAYEV.

Harmonious Fatherland Party (Meken Yntymagy): Bishkek; f. 2010; represents interests of Kyrgyz diaspora; Leader TEMIRBEK ASANBEKOV.

Homeland Idealistic Democratic Political Party (Ata-Jurt): Bishkek, pr. Chui 34/11; tel. (312) 43-78-14; fax (312) 90-02-68; e-mail iyikatajurt@gmail.com; internet www.atajurt.kg; f. 2004; opposed fmr regime of President Akayev, and supported fmr regime of President Bakiyev; Chair. KAMCHYBEK TASHIYEV.

Party of Communists of Kyrgyzstan (KCP): 720001 Bishkek, pr. Chui 114/206; tel. (312) 62-49-99; fax (312) 67-02-55; disbanded 1991, re-established 1992, re-registered 2007; successor to the Communist Party of Kyrgyz SSR; Chair. BUMAYRAM MAMASEYITOVA; 20,000 mems.

Republic Political Party (Respublika): 720000 Bishkek, Toktogula 126; tel. (312) 66-31-21; e-mail pr@republic.kg; internet www.republic.kg; f. 2010; supportive of fmr Pres. Bakiyev; Leader OMURBEK BABANOV.

Social Democratic Party of Kyrgyzstan (SDPK) (Kyrgyzstandyn Sotsial-Demokratiyalyk Partiyasy): 720000 Bishkek, Shabdan Batyr 46D; tel. (312) 53-16-84; fax (312) 53-16-87; e-mail sdpkkenesh@gmail.com; internet www.sdpk.kg; f. 1993; supports parliamentary system of govt; mem. of the opposition United People's Movement formed in late 2008; supported Interim Govt that assumed power in April 2010; Chair. ALMAZBEK ATAMBAYEV.

United Kyrgyzstan Political Party (Butun Kyrgyzstan): 720000 Bishkek, Turusbekov 109/1; tel. (312) 39-40-48; fax (312) 39-40-70; e-mail pressa@bytyn.kg; internet bytyn.kg; f. 2010; supportive of former President Bakiyev; Chair. ADAHAN MADUMAROV.

White Falcon Political Party (Ak Shumkar): 720000 Bishkek, pr. Manasa 40; tel. (312) 31-17-54; e-mail p.akshumkar@gmail.com; internet www.akshumkar.kg; f. 2008; supported Interim Govt that assumed power in April 2010; Chair. TEMIR SARIYEV.

Zamandash Political Party (Zamadash Sayasiy Partiyasy): 720001 Bishkek, Turusbekov 118; tel. (312) 34-02-08; fax (312) 34-01-88; e-mail partiya.zamandash@gmail.com; internet zamandash.kg; f. 2010; represents interests of Kyrgyz diaspora; Leader MUKTARBEK OMURAKUNOV.

Diplomatic Representation

EMBASSIES IN KYRGYZSTAN

Azerbaijan: 720040 Bishkek, Shurukova 41; tel. (312) 51-07-70; fax (312) 51-31-72; e-mail bishkek@mission.mfa.az; Ambassador HIDAYAT HUDUSH ORUJOV.

Belarus: 720040 Bishkek, Moskovskaya 210; tel. (312) 35-28-35; fax (312) 35-34-33; e-mail kyrgyzstan@mfa.gov.by; internet www.kyrgyzstan.mfa.gov.by; Ambassador VIKTOR DENISENKO.

China, People's Republic: 720016 Bishkek, pr. Mira 299/7; tel. (312) 31-74-86; fax (312) 59-74-84; e-mail chinaemb_kg@mfa.gov.cn; internet kg.chineseembassy.org; Ambassador WANG KAIWEN.

Germany: 720040 Bishkek, Razzakova 28; tel. (312) 90-50-00; fax (312) 30-07-43; internet www.bischkek.diplo.de; Ambassador GUDRUN SRÄGA.

India: 720044 Bishkek, Aeroportinskaya 15A; tel. (312) 54-92-14; fax (312) 54-32-45; e-mail indembas@infotel.kg; internet www.embassyofindia.kg; Ambassador PHUNCHOK STOBDAN.

Iran: 720026 Bishkek, Razzakova 36; tel. (312) 62-49-17; fax (312) 66-02-09; e-mail embiran@mail.kg; Ambassador MANOUCHEHR MORADI.

Japan: 720040 Bishkek, Razzakova 16; tel. (312) 30-00-50; fax (312) 30-00-5232-54-08; internet www.kg.emb-japan.go.jp; Ambassador TAKAYUKI KOIKE.

Kazakhstan: 720044 Bishkek, pr. Mira 95 A; tel. (312) 69-20-98; fax (312) 69-20-94; e-mail kaz_emb@kazemb.elcat.kg; internet www.kaz-emb.kg; Ambassador BEYBIT O. ISABAEV.

Korea, Republic: 720005 Bishkek, Matrosova 67/8; tel. (312) 56-02-71; fax (312) 57-60-04; e-mail korea.kg@gmail.com; internet kgz.mofat.go.kr; Ambassador KIM CHANG GYU.

Pakistan: 720040 Bishkek, Serova 37; tel. (312) 37-39-01; fax (312) 37-39-05; e-mail parepbishkek@elcat.kg; internet www.mofa.gov.pk/kyrgyzstan; Ambassador (vacant).

Russia: 720001 Bishkek, Manas 55; tel. (312) 61-09-05; fax (312) 90-33-84; e-mail rusemb@infotel.kg; internet www.kyrgyz.mid.ru; Ambassador ANDREI A. KRUTKO.

Switzerland: 720040 Bishkek, Panfilov 144; tel. (312) 30-10-36; fax (312) 30-10-31; e-mail bik.vertretung@eda.admin.ch; Ambassador LAURENT GUYE.

Tajikistan: 720031 Bishkek, Karadarynskaya 36; tel. (312) 51-23-43; e-mail tjemb@ktnet.kg; internet www.tajikemb.kg; Ambassador OLIM RAHIMOV.

Turkey: 720040 Bishkek, Moskovskaya 89; tel. (312) 90-59-00; fax (312) 90-99-12; e-mail embassy.bishkek@mfa.gov.tr; internet bishkek.emb.mfa.gov.tr; Ambassador NEJAT AKÇAL.

Ukraine: 720040 Bishkek, bulv. Akhunbayeva 201; tel. (312) 25-17-67; fax (312) 25-17-80; e-mail emb_kg@mfa.gov.ua; internet www.mfa.gov.ua/kirgizia; Ambassador VOLODYMYR V. SOLOVEY.

United Kingdom: 720010 Bishkek, bul. Erkindik 21/404; tel. (312) 69-02-32; e-mail ukin.kyrgyzrepublic@fco.gov.uk; Ambassador JUDITH MARGARET FARNWORTH.

USA: 720016 Bishkek, pr. Mira 171; tel. (312) 55-12-41; fax (312) 55-12-64; internet bishkek.usembassy.gov; Ambassador PAMELA SPRATLEN.

Uzbekistan: 720040 Bishkek, Tynystanova 213; tel. (312) 66-20-65; fax (312) 66-44-03; e-mail uzbembish@infotel.kg; internet www.uzbekistan.kg; Ambassador K. RASHIDOV.

Judicial System

Supreme Court: 720000 Bishkek, Orozbekova 37; tel. (312) 66-33-18; fax (312) 66-29-46; e-mail scourt@bishkek.gov.kg; to be reformed to include a Constitutional Chamber, in accordance with the 2010 Constitution, to replace the former Constitutional Court; Chair. FERUZA DJAMASHEVA (acting).

Office of the Prosecutor-General: 720040 Bishkek; Prosecutor-General AIDA J. SALYANOVA.

Religion

ISLAM

The majority of Kyrgyz are Sunni Muslims (Hanafi school), as are the Uzbeks and Tajiks living in Kazakhstan.

Chief Mufti of the Muslims of Kyrgyzstan: RAHMATILLA EGEMBERDIEV (acting), 720000 Bishkek.

International Islamic Centre of Kyrgyzstan: 714018 Osh; Pres. Haji SADYKJAN KAMALUDDIN.

CHRISTIANITY

Roman Catholic Church

The Church is represented in Kyrgyzstan by an Apostolic Administration, established in March 2006. There were an estimated 500 adherents in the country at 31 December 2007.

Apostolic Administrator of Kyrgyzstan: Most Rev. NIKOLAUS MESSMER (Titular Bishop of Carmeiano), 720040 Bishkek, Mayakovskogo 25; tel. (312) 28-50-03; fax (312) 67-03-92; e-mail nikmessmer@hotmail.com; internet www.catholic-kyrgyzstan.org.

Russian Orthodox Church (Moscow Patriarchate)

The Russian Orthodox Church (Moscow Patriarchate) in Kyrgyzstan comes under the jurisdiction of the Eparchy of Tashkent and Central Asia, based in Uzbekistan.

JUDAISM

At the 1989 census, around 6,000 Jews were enumerated as living within the Kyrgyz SSR, although around one-half of this number had emigrated, mostly to Israel, by 1993, and emigration continued subsequently.

Chief Rabbi: Rabbi ARIYE RAICHMAN, 720000 Bishkek, Sutombayev 193, Khabad Lyubavich Synagogue; tel. and fax (312) 68-19-66; e-mail arier@mail.ru.

The Press

In 2004 there were 83 non-daily newspapers, with an average circulation of 427,800 copies. Two daily newspapers were published in that year, with an average circulation of 21,000 copies.

PRINCIPAL NEWSPAPERS

Bishkek Observer: 720001 Bishkek, Ibraimova 105; tel. (312) 28-95-96; fax (312) 29-28-21; e-mail dssuri@elcat.kg; f. 2000; weekly; independent; in English; Editor AVTAR SINGH.

Bishkek Taims (Bishkek Times): 720040 Bishkek, Pushkina 70; tel. (312) 62-15-70; fax (312) 62-15-68; e-mail b-times@yandex.ru; internet www.presskg.com/bt; Editor-in-Chief NURALY KAPAROV.

Chuy Baayni/Chuyskiye Izvestiya (Chui News): 720300 Bishkek, Ibraimova 24; tel. (312) 42-83-31; weekly; organ of Chui Oblast administration; Kyrgyz and Russian edns; Editor (Kyrgyz edn) KURMANBEK RAMATOV; Editor (Russian edn) A. BLINDINA.

Delo N°... (Case Number. . .): 720000 Bishkek, Sovetskaya 190; tel. (312) 22-84-62; fax (312) 66-36-03; e-mail cactus@elcat.kg; f. 1991; weekly; in Russian; independent; politics, crime; Editor VIKTOR ZAPOLSKII; circ. 40,000.

Erkin Too (Free Mountain): 720040 Bishkek, Ibraimova 24; tel. (312) 59-15-30; fax (312) 59-16-31; f. 1991; 2 a week; organ of the Govt; publishes laws, presidential, parliamentary and govt decrees, and other legal documents; in Kyrgyz; Chief Editor ABDUVAKHAB MONIYEV; circ. 10,000.

Gazeta.kg: 720000 Bishkek; e-mail info@gazeta.kg; internet gazeta .kg; online only, in Russian and English; independent; politics and analysis of current affairs; culture; regional news; f. 2003; Chief Editor ANTON NOSIK.

Kyrgyz Madaniyaty (Kyrgyz Culture): 720301 Bishkek, Bokonbayeva 99; tel. (312) 26-14-58; f. 1967; weekly; organ of the Union of Writers; Editor NURALY KAPAROV; circ. 15,940.

Kyrgyz Rukhu: 720040 Bishkek, Abdymomunova 193; tel. (312) 62-76-60; fax (312) 66-11-60; f. 1991; weekly; in Kyrgyz; Editor-in-Chief BAKBYRBEK ALENOV; circ. 7,000.

Kyrgyz Tuusu (Flag of Kyrgyzstan): 720040 Bishkek, Abdymomunova 193; tel. (312) 62-20-29; fax (312) 62-20-25; e-mail tuusu@infotel .kg; f. 1924; fmrly *Sovettik Kyrgyzstan*; daily; organ of the Govt; in Kyrgyz; Chief Editor KYAZ MOLDOKASYMOV; circ. 20,000.

Limon (Lemon): 720040 Bishkek, Moskovskaya 189; tel. (312) 45-66-72; fax (312) 65-02-04; e-mail limon@akipress.org; internet www .limon.kg; f. 1994; in Russian; youth newspaper; independent; Editor-in-Chief VENERA JAMONA KULOVA.

MSN—Moya Stolitsa—Novosti (My Capital City—News): 720001 Bishkek, Turusbekova 47; tel. (312) 48-62-15; fax (312) 48-61-24; e-mail city@infotel.kg; internet www.msn.kg; f. 2001; independent; 3 a week; in Russian; Editor-in-Chief ALEXANDER KIM; circ. 5,000 (Tues. and Thurs.), 50,000 (Fri.).

Slovo Kyrgyzstana (Word of Kyrgyzstan): 720004 Bishkek, Abdymomunova 193; tel. (312) 66-60-88; fax (312) 66-59-28; e-mail slovo@ infotel.kg; f. 1925; daily; organ of the Govt; in Russian; Chief Editor TAMARA SLASHCHEVA.

The Times of Central Asia: 720000 Bishkek, Abdrahmanova 175A; tel. (312) 66-17-37; fax (312) 66-01-67; e-mail edittimes@timesca .com; internet www.timesca.com; f. 1999; weekly; in English; also distributed in Kazakhstan, Turkmenistan, Tajikistan and Uzbekistan, and internationally; Publr GIORGIO FIACCONI.

Vechernii Bishkek (Bishkek Evening News): 720021 Bishkek, Usenbayeva 2; tel. (312) 48-65-65; fax (312) 68-02-68; e-mail webmaster@vb.kg; internet www.vb.kg; f. 1974; daily; independent; in Russian; Editor-in-Chief GENNADII A. KUZMIN; circ. 700,000.

Zaman Kyrgyzstan (Herald of Kyrgyzstan): 720040 Bishkek, Ibraimova 24; tel. (312) 61-46-42; fax (312) 61-46-20; e-mail zamantur@hotmail.com; f. 1992; weekly; independent; in Kyrgyz, Turkish and English; Editor-in-Chief MUSTAFA BASHKURT; circ. 7,500.

PRINCIPAL PERIODICALS

AKIpress: 720010 Bishkek, Moskovskaya 189; tel. and fax (312) 45-54-38; e-mail admin@akipress.org; internet www.akipress.org; f. 1993; monthly; in Russian; independent; analysis of political and economic affairs; Editor-in-Chief SAMAGAN AITYMBETOV; circ. 1,000.

Kut Bilim (Good Knowledge): 720001 Bishkek, Tynystanova 257; tel. (312) 62-04-86; e-mail kutbilim@elcat.kg; internet kb.host.net .kg; f. 1953 as *Mugalimder Gazetasy*; current name adopted 1993; organ of the Ministry of Education and Science; weekly; in Kyrgyz; Editor-in-Chief KUBATBEK CHEKIROV; circ. 6,000.

Literaturnyi Kyrgyzstan (Literary Kyrgyzstan): 720301 Bishkek, Pushkina 70; tel. (312) 626-16-01; e-mail literary_kyrgyzstan@ rambler.ru; f. 1955; journal of the Union of Writers; fiction, literary criticism, journalism; monthly; in Russian; Editor-in-Chief A. I. IVANOV; circ. 3,000.

Zhany Agym (Current): 720021 Bishkek, Usenbayeva 2; tel. (312) 38-67-73; fax (312) 48-61-24; e-mail agym@vb.kg; internet presskg .com/agym; f. 1992 as Agym; renamed as above in 2010; 2 a week; in Kyrgyz; political; Editor-in-Chief ASKER SAKYBAEVA.

NEWS AGENCY

Kabar Kyrgyz News Agency: 720011 Bishkek, Abdrahmanova 175; tel. (312) 62-05-74; fax (312) 66-11-68; e-mail kabar@kabar.kg; internet www.kabar.kg; f. 1937; Dir KUBANYCHBEK A. TAABALDIEV.

Publishers

Ilim (Science): 720071 Bishkek, pr. Chui 265A; tel. (312) 39-20-70; e-mail ilimph@mail.ru; f. 1954; state-owned; scientific and science fiction; Dir L. V. TARASOVA.

Kyrgyz-Russian Slavic University Publishing House (Izdatelstvo Kyrgyzsko-Rossiiskogo slavyanskogo universiteta): 720000 Bishkek, Kiyevskaya 44; tel. (312) 25-53-60; internet www .krsu.edu.kg/Rus/EduIzd.htm; f. 1995; academic works of university staff; textbooks; Dir LARISA V. TARASOVA.

Kyrgyzstan: Bishkek, bul. Bokonbayev 5/43; tel. (312) 68-26-85; fax (312) 65-42-79; politics, science, economics, literature; Dir BERIK N. CHALAGYZOV.

Tsentr Gosudarstvennogo Yazyka i Kyrgyzskoi Entsiklopedii (Centre for the State Language and the Kyrgyz Encyclopedia): 720040 Bishkek, bul. Erkindik 56; tel. (312) 62-50-72; fax (312) 62-50-03; e-mail gocst.ensk@mail.ru; dictionaries and encyclopedias; Dir BAKTYGUL KALDYBAYEVA; Editor-in-Chief USEN A. ASANOV.

Broadcasting and Communications

National Communications Agency of the Kyrgyz Republic: 720005 Bishkek, Baytik Baatyra 7B; tel. (312) 54-30-55; fax (312) 54-41-05; internet www.nas.kg; f. 1997; Dir KUBAT S. KYDYRALIYEV.

TELECOMMUNICATIONS

Kyrgyzstan's telecommunications sector was liberalized in 1998, and competition across all segments of the market has been permitted since 2007. There are four providers of mobile cellular telecommunications services in Kyrgyzstan. In 2010 9% of households had a fixed-line telephone, while the rate of mobile network subscription was equivalent to 85% of the population.

BiMoKom: 720040 Bishkek, Razzakova 33/2; tel. (312) 90-52-21; fax (312) 90-52-40; e-mail pr@megacom.kg; internet www.megacom.kg; f. 2006; provides mobile cellular telecommunications services in Bishkek, Manas Airport, the shores of Lake Yssyk-Kul and in Chui, Yssyk-Kul, Osh, Jalal-Abad, Naryn, Talas and Batken Oblasts under the Megacom brand name; provides internet services; Dir ANDREI G. SILICH; c. 1.65m. subscribers (Oct. 2009).

Kyrgyztelekom AO: 720000 Bishkek, pr. Chui 96; tel. (312) 68-16-16; fax (312) 66-24-24; e-mail info@kt.kg; internet www.kt.kg; f. 1993, transformed into joint stock co in 1997; 77.8% state-owned; provides mobile and fixed telephone and internet services; Chair. of the Bd of Dirs TALAIBEK S. OROZOV; Pres. of the Bd of Management ASKAR S. BARATBAYEV.

Sky Mobile: 720011 Bishkek, pr. Chui 121; tel. (312) 58-79-15; fax (312) 90-09-16; f. 1997; provides mobile cellular telecommunications services under the Bitel and Mobi brand names; 50.1% owned by VympelKom-BiLain (Russia); Dir-Gen. D. V. SHERSHNEV; over 1m. subscribers (Jan. 2008).

BROADCASTING

Radio and Television

Public Broadcasting Corporation of the Kyrgyz Republic: 720010 Bishkek, Molodoi Gvardii 59; tel. (312) 65-56-77; fax (312) 65-10-64; f. 1958; fmrly National TV and Radio Broadcasting Corporation of the Kyrgyz Republic; name changed as above in 2010; Dir-Gen. KUBAT OTORBAEV.

Channel Five: 720031 Bishkek, Ibraimova 24; tel. (312) 54-77-27; fax (312) 54-77-15; e-mail office@koort.kg; f. 1997; fmrly Kyrgyz Public Educational Radio and Television; renamed as above in 2007; broadcasts in Kyrgyz and Russian; educational programmes and entertainment; Gen. Dir AZIMA ABDIMAMINOVA; 103 employees.

Radio

Public Broadcasting Corporation of the Kyrgyz Republic: 720010 Bishkek, Molodoi Gvardii 59; tel. (312) 65-98-18; fax (312) 65-10-64; f. 1931; broadcasts in Kyrgyz, Russian, English, German, Ukrainian, Uzbek, Dungan and Uigur; Chair. KUBAT OTORBAEV.

Radio Azattyk: 720000 Bishkek; tel. (312) 31-61-53; fax (312) 31-60-80; e-mail djumataevav@rferl.org; internet www.azattyk.org; Kyrgyz language news broadcasts by Radio Free Europe/Radio Liberty (USA—based in the Czech Republic); Dir VENERA JUMATAEVA; Bureau Chief SULTAN JUMAGULOV.

Radio Television Pyramid: 720300 Bishkek, Jantosheva 70; tel. and fax (312) 51-15-50; e-mail pyramid@tom.kg; f. 1992; privately owned; broadcasts to Bishkek and neighbouring regions; Pres. MIRBEK OROZOV.

There are several other private radio stations operating in Kyrgyzstan.

Television

In addition to two state-owned television stations, there are four major private national and six major private regional television stations in Kyrgyzstan.

Kyrgyz Television: 720300 Bishkek, Molodoi Gvardii 63; tel. (312) 25-79-36; fax (312) 25-79-30; subsidiary of Public Broadcasting Corporation of the Kyrgyz Republic (q.v.); Pres. KYYAS MOLDOKASYMOV.

TV Pyramid: 720005 Bishkek, Jantosheva 70; tel. (312) 51-15-50; fax (312) 51-00-12; e-mail pyramid@ss5-22.kyrnet.kg; f. 1991; privately owned; broadcasts to Bishkek and neighbouring regions; Pres. ADYLBEK T. BIINAZAROV.

Finance

(cap. = capital; res = reserves; dep. = deposits; m. = million; brs = branches; amounts in soms, unless otherwise indicated)

BANKING

Central Bank

National Bank of the Kyrgyz Republic (Kyrgyz Respublikasy-nyn Uluttuk Banky): 720040 Bishkek, Umetaliyeva 101; tel. (312) 66-90-08; fax (312) 61-07-30; e-mail mail@nbkr.kg; internet www.nbkr.kg; f. 1991, name changed in 1992, and as above in 1993; cap. 300.0m., res 10,331.5m., dep. 27,047.0m. (Dec. 2009); Gov. ZINA ASANKOJOEVA.

Other Banks

Bank Bakai: 720001 Bishkek, Isanov 77; tel. (312) 61-02-42; fax (312) 61-02-43; e-mail bank@bakai.kg; internet www.bakai.kg; f. 1998; cap. 265.2m., dep. 905.9m., total assets 1,323.1m. (Dec. 2011); Chair. BAKYT MURZALIEV (acting); Pres. SERGEI IBRAGIMOV; 5 brs.

BTA Bank: 720040 Bishkek, Moskovskaya 118; tel. (312) 90-50-50; fax (312) 62-45-65; e-mail info@ineximbank.com; internet www.bta.kg; f. 1996; name changed as above 2008; cap. 1,000.0m., res 120.8m., dep. 1,894.5m. (Dec. 2011); Chair. of Bd MURAT KUNAKUNOV; 4 brs.

Commercial Bank Kyrgyzstan: 720001 Bishkek, Togolok Moldo 54A; tel. (312) 21-95-98; fax (312) 61-02-20; e-mail akb@bankkg.kg; internet www.bankkg.kg; f. 1991; name changed as above in 2006; cap. 420.2m., res 0.04m., dep. 2,810.9m. (Dec. 2011); Chair. ABIROV NURBEK; 29 brs.

Demir Kyrgyz International Bank (DKIB): 720001 Bishkek, pr. Chui 245; tel. (312) 61-04-44; fax (312) 66-64-44; e-mail demir@demirbank.kg; internet www.demirbank.kg; f. 1997; cap. 132.5m., res 1.3m., 5,642.6m. (Dec. 2011); Gen. Man. L. SEVKI SARILAR; 5 brs.

Kyrgyz Investment and Credit Bank: 720001 Bishkek, Ibraimova 115A, Dordoi Plaza Business Centre; tel. (312) 69-05-55; fax (312) 69-05-60; e-mail kicb@kicb.net; internet www.kicb.net; f. 2001; 21% owned by Aga Khan Fund for Economic Development, 18% by Habib Bank (Pakistan), 17% by Deutsche Investitions und Entwicklungsgesellschaft GmbH (Germany), 17% by European Bank for Reconstruction and Development (United Kingdom), 17% by International Finance Corpn; cap. US $17.5m., res $0.5m., dep. $100.1m. (Dec. 2011); Chief Exec. KUANG YOUNG CHOI; 8 brs.

Tolubay Bank: 720040 Bishkek, Umetaliyeva 105; tel. (312) 65-88-88; fax (312) 25-63-14; e-mail tolubay@infotel.kg; internet www.tolubaybank.kg; f. 1996; cap. 63.0m., res 12.5m., dep. 293.1m. (Dec. 2006); Chair. JENISHBEK S. BAIGUTTIYEV; 1 br.

UniCredit Bank: 720070 Bishkek, Jibek Jolu 493; tel. and fax (312) 67-04-71; e-mail bank@atfbank.kg; internet www.unicreditbank.kg; f. 1992; fmrly ATFBank-Kyrgyzstan, present name adopted 2010; cap. 700.0m., res 2.7m., dep. 5,632.3m. (Dec. 2011); Chair. of Bd of Dirs MUHABBAT SEITOVA; 14 brs.

Zalkar Bank: 720001 Bishkek, Moskovskaya 80/1; tel. (312) 55-44-44; fax (312) 31-31-00; e-mail call-center@zalkar.kg; internet zalkar.kg; f. 2010 in succession to AsiaUniversal Bank; cap. 40.9m., res 533.3m., dep. 2,776.2m. (Dec. 2011); 59 brs and sub-brs; state-owned; transfer to private ownership pending in 2013; Chair. of Board of Dirs SAIDBEK ZULLUYEV; Chair. of Management ERKEBAI MURZABEKOV; 2 brs.

COMMODITY EXCHANGE

Kyrgyzstan Commodity and Raw Materials Exchange: 720001 Bishkek, Belinskaya 40; tel. (312) 22-13-75; fax (312) 22-27-44; f. 1990; Gen. Dir TEMIR SARIYEV.

STOCK EXCHANGE

Kyrgyz Stock Exchange (Kyrgyz Fonduluk Birjasy/ Kyrgyzskaya Fondovaya Birzha): 720010 Bishkek, Moskovskaya 172; tel. (312) 31-14-84; fax (312) 31-14-83; e-mail kse@kse.kg; internet www.kse.kg; f. 1994; privately owned; Pres. AIBEK TOLUBAEV.

INSURANCE

At July 2011 there were 19 registered insurance companies in Kyrgyzstan.

Anglo-Kyrgyz Insurance Co: 720000 Bishkek, ul. Akhunbaeva 100; tel. (312) 54-90-23; fax (312) 54-90-49; e-mail anglokgz@elcat.kg.

ATN Polis: 720000 Bishkek, ul. Isanova 42/1; tel. (312) 93-79-37; fax (312) 90-32-52; e-mail info@atnpolis.kg; internet www.atnpolis.kg; f. 2001; life and non-life.

Insurance Group of Central Asia: 720000 Bishkek, Baitik Baatyra 191, Hyatt Hotel, room 103; tel. (312) 68-12-21.

Kyrgyzinstrakh: 720001 Bishkek, pr. Chui 219; tel. (312) 61-45-88; fax (312) 61-46-45; e-mail kinstrakh@ingo.kg; internet www.ingo.kg; f. 1996 by the Russian joint stock insurance company Investstrakh and the Kyrgyz Government to insure foreign investors; brs in Karakol and Osh; insurance and reinsurance; Chair. of Bd E. M. SEIDAKHMETOVA.

Kyrgyzstan Insurance Co: 720000 Bishkek, ul. Moskovskaya 76B; tel. (312) 28-28-15; e-mail office@insurance.kg; internet www.insurance.kg; f. 1991; Dir MARIYA ADENOVA.

Trade and Industry

GOVERNMENT AGENCIES

Centre for Standardization and Metrology: 720040 Bishkek, Panfilova 197; tel. (312) 62-68-70; fax (312) 66-13-67; e-mail nism@nism.gov.kg; internet www.nism.gov.kg; f. 1927 as the Division of the Chamber of Measures and Weights; present name adopted 2010; certification, control and testing of products and services; Dir ALIMBEK KURMANBAEV.

State Agency for Geology and Mineral Resources: 720739 Bishkek, pr. Erkindik 2; tel. (312) 66-49-01; fax (312) 66-03-91; e-mail mail@geoagency.bishkek.gov.kg; f. 1938; Chair. SHEISHENALY MURZAGAZIYEV.

State Committee for Management of State Property: 720017 Bishkek, Moskovskaya 151; tel. (312) 61-51-87; fax (312) 66-02-36; e-mail goskomitet@ktnet.kg; internet www.spf.gov.kg; f. 1991; responsible for the privatization of state-owned enterprises and dealing with bankruptcies; Dir MARAT AMANKULOV.

CHAMBER OF COMMERCE

Chamber of Commerce and Industry of the Kyrgyz Republic: 720001 Bishkek, Kiyevskaya 107; tel. (312) 61-38-72; fax (312) 61-38-75; e-mail info@cci.kg; internet www.cci.kg; f. 1959; supports foreign economic relations and the development of small and medium-sized enterprises; regional brs in Balykchy, Batken, Jalal-Abad, Karakol, Naryn, Osh, Talas and Tokmok; Pres. MARAT D. SHARSHEKEEV.

UTILITIES

Electricity

NES Kyrgyzstana (National Electric Grid of Kyrgyzstan) (NESK): 720070 Bishkek, pr. Jibek Jolu 326; tel. (312) 66-10-01; fax (312) 66-16-09; e-mail nesk@elcat.kg; internet www.energo.kg; f. 2001; comprises five companies, including three regional distribution companies, Oshelektro, Jalabadelektro, Vostokelektro and one heating company, Bishkekteploset; 80.49% owned by State Cttee for State Property, 13.16% owned by Social Fund of the Kyrgyz Republic; cap. 1,597.4m. soms (June 2006); Gen. Dir MEDETBEK AITKULOV.

Severelektro: 722160 Chui obl., Lebedinovka, ul. Chkalov 3; tel. (312) 33-33-93; fax (312) 33-85-68; e-mail severpiu@mail.ru; internet www.severelectro.kg; f. 2001; state-owned; distribution of electricity in northern regions of Kyrgyzstan, including Bishkek, Chui and Talas Oblasts; Gen. Dir ISKENDER KADYRKULOV.

Gas

Kyrgyzgaz: 720661 Bishkek, Gorkogo 22; tel. (312) 53-45-10; fax (312) 53-00-33; e-mail admin@kg.elcat.kg; gas distribution co; 87% state-owned; sale of 75% stake to Gazprom (Russia) pending in early 2013; Dir-Gen. TURGUNBEK N. KULMURZAYEV.

TRADE UNIONS

TRADE UNIONS

Trade Unions Federation of Kyrgyzstan: 720032 Bishkek, Chui 207; tel. (312) 21-77-08; fax (312) 62-57-53; e-mail fpk.kg@mail.ru; f. 1925; affiliated with the General Confed. of Trade Unions; Chair. IMANKADYR RYSALIEV.

Transport

RAILWAYS

Kyrgyzstan's railway network consists of one main line (417 km) in northern Kyrgyzstan, which connects the country to Kazakhstan and Russia, and some local lines that connect Osh and Jalal-Abad with Uzbekistan.

Kyrgyz Railway Administration (Kyrgyz Temir Jolu): 720009 Bishkek, L. Tolstogo 83; tel. (312) 65-69-32; fax (312) 65-06-90; e-mail asoup@imfiko.bishkek.su; internet railway.aknet.kg; f. 1992; Pres. I. S. OMURKULOV.

ROADS

In 2007 Kyrgyzstan's road network totalled an estimated 34,000 km; in 1996 there were 3,200 km of main roads and 6,380 km of secondary roads.

CIVIL AVIATION

There are three international airports at Bishkek (Manas), Osh and Tamchy (in the Yssyk-Kul region).

Aviakompaniya Kyrgyzstan—Kyrgyzstan Aircompany: 720017 Bishkek, pr. Manasa 12 A; tel. (312) 31-30-03; fax (312) 31-27-42; e-mail company@air.kg; internet kyrgyzaero.com; f. 2006 by merger of Altyn Air and Kyrgyzstan Airlines; state-owned; charter passenger services; Pres. EGEMBERDI B. MYRZABEKOV.

Tourism

In 2011 there were 3,114,372 foreign tourist arrivals, compared with 398,078 in 2004. Tourism receipts (including passenger transport) amounted to US $284m. in 2010.

State Committee for Tourism, Sport and Youth Policy: 720033 Bishkek, Togolok Moldo 17; tel. (312) 62-24-99; fax (312) 21-28-45; e-mail gktsm@gks.gov.kg; Chair. TURUSBEK CH. MAMASHEV.

Defence

Military service is compulsory, and lasts for 18 months. As assessed at November 2012, Kyrgyzstan's total armed forces numbered 10,900, comprising an army of 8,500 and an air force of 2,400. There were 9,500 paramilitary forces (comprising 5,000 border guards—including both Kyrgyzstani conscripts and Russian officers, 3,500 troops attached to the Ministry of Internal Affairs and a national guard of 1,000). About 500 Russian troops were deployed at the Kant airbase (established by Russia in October 2003). In August 2009 a preliminary memorandum of understanding was signed on the establishment of a second Russian military base in Kyrgyzstan for a period of up to 49 years. Meanwhile, in February 2009 the Kyrgyzstani legislature approved a government decision for the closure of the US military base at Manas airport (where some 1,000 US forces had been stationed); however, in June the legislature endorsed a bilateral agreement to maintain the US presence at Manas, although the facility's official legal status was to be amended to that of a logistics centre rather than an airbase. In late 2011 the Kyrgyzstani authorities announced that the lease on the US transit centre at Manas would not be renewed after the expiry of the existing agreement in July 2014.

Defence Expenditure: Budgeted at 4,910m. soms in 2013.

Chief of the General Staff: Col ILYYAZBEK SUBANKULOV.

Education

Compulsory education comprises four years of primary education (between the ages of seven and 10), followed by five years of lower secondary school (ages 11 to 15). Pupils may then attend upper secondary schools, specialized secondary schools or technical and vocational schools. In 2009/10 total enrolment at primary schools included 87% of children in the relevant age-group; enrolment at secondary schools included 79% of the school-age population. In 1993/94 some 63.6% of primary and secondary schools used Kyrgyz as the sole language of instruction, 23.4% Russian, 12.7% Uzbek and 0.3% Tajik. Russian, however, was the principal language of instruction in higher educational establishments. In 2011 there were 54 institutes of higher education in Kyrgyzstan, attended by 239,208 students. Government budgetary expenditure on education in 2011 was 18,231.3m. soms (representing 20.0% of total spending).

LAOS

Introductory Survey

LOCATION, CLIMATE, LANGUAGE, RELIGION, FLAG, CAPITAL

The Lao People's Democratic Republic is a land-locked country in South-East Asia, bordered by the People's Republic of China to the north, by Viet Nam to the east, by Cambodia to the south, by Thailand to the west and by Myanmar (formerly Burma) to the north-west. The climate is tropical, with a rainy monsoon season lasting from May to September. The temperature in the capital ranges between 23°C and 38°C in the hottest month, April, and between 14°C and 28°C in the coolest month, January. Laos comprises 47 ethnic groups. The official language, Lao or Laotian, is spoken by about two-thirds of the population. French is also spoken, and there are numerous tribal languages, including Meo. The principal religion is Buddhism. There are also some Christians and followers of animist beliefs. The national flag (proportions 2 by 3) has three horizontal stripes, of red, blue (half the total depth) and red, with a white disc in the centre. The capital is Vientiane (Viangchan).

CONTEMPORARY POLITICAL HISTORY

Historical Context

Laos was formerly a part of French Indo-China and comprised the three principalities of Luang Prabang, Vientiane and Champasak. These were merged in 1946, when France recognized Sisavang Vong, ruler of Luang Prabang since 1904, as King of Laos. In May 1947 the King promulgated a democratic constitution (although women were not allowed to vote until 1957). The Kingdom of Laos became independent, within the French Union, in July 1949, and full sovereignty was recognized by France in October 1953. The leading royalist politician was Prince Souvanna Phouma, who was Prime Minister in 1951–54, 1956–58, 1960 and in 1962–75. King Sisavang Vong died in October 1959, and was succeeded by his son, Savang Vatthana.

Domestic Political Affairs

From 1950 the Royal Government was opposed by the Neo Lao Haksat (Lao Patriotic Front—LPF), an insurgent movement established by a group of former anti-French activists. The LPF's Chairman was Prince Souphanouvong, a half-brother of Prince Souvanna Phouma, but its dominant element was the communist People's Party of Laos (PPL), led by Kaysone Phomvihane. During the 1950s the LPF's armed forces, the Pathet Lao, gradually secured control of the north-east of the country with the assistance of the Vietnamese communists, the Viet Minh, who were engaged in war with the French (until 1954). Several agreements between the Royal Government and the LPF, attempting to end the guerrilla war and reunite the country, failed during the 1950s and early 1960s. By 1965 the de facto partition of Laos was established, with the LPF refusing to participate in national elections and consolidating its power over the north-eastern provinces.

During the 1960s, as the 'Ho Chi Minh Trail' (the communist supply route to South Viet Nam) ran through Pathet Lao-controlled areas, Laos remained closely involved with the war between communist forces and anti-communist troops (supported by the USA) in Viet Nam. In 1973 the Viet Nam peace negotiations included provisions for a cease-fire in Laos. A new Government was formed in April 1974 under Prince Souvanna Phouma, with royalist, neutralist and LPF participation; Prince Souphanouvong was appointed Chairman of the Joint National Political Council. However, the LPF increased its power and eventually gained effective control of the country. This was confirmed by election victories in October and November 1975. In November King Savang Vatthana abdicated, and Prince Souvanna Phouma resigned as head of government.

In December 1975 the National Congress of People's Representatives (264 delegates elected by local authorities) abolished the monarchy and elected a 45-member legislative body, the Supreme People's Council. Souphanouvong was appointed President of the renamed Lao People's Democratic Republic and President of the Supreme People's Council. Kaysone Phomvihane, who had become Secretary-General of the Phak Pasaon Pativat Lao (Lao People's Revolutionary Party—LPRP, a successor to the PPL), was appointed Chairman of the Council of Ministers. The former King, Savang Vatthana, was designated Supreme Counsellor to the President, but he refused to co-operate with the new regime and was arrested in March 1977. (He was subsequently stated to have died in a 're-education camp'.) The LPF was replaced in February 1979 by the Lao Front for National Construction (LFNC), under the leadership of the LPRP.

In October 1986 the ailing Souphanouvong announced his resignation from his duties as President of the Republic (while retaining the title) and of the Supreme People's Assembly (as the Supreme People's Council had been renamed). Phoumi Vongvichit, formerly a Vice-Chairman in the Council of Ministers, became acting President of the Republic, while Sisomphon Lovansai, a Vice-President of the Supreme People's Assembly and a member of the LPRP Political Bureau (Politburo), became acting President of the Assembly. In November Kaysone Phomvihane was re-elected Secretary-General of the LPRP. In September 1987 it was announced that Phoumi Vongvichit had also replaced Souphanouvong as Chairman of the LFNC.

In June 1988 elections (the first since the formation of the Lao People's Democratic Republic) took place to the district-level People's Councils, and provincial prefectural elections were held in November; all of the electoral candidates had been approved by the LFNC prior to polling. At the legislative elections of March 1989, 121 candidates contested 79 seats in the enlarged Supreme People's Assembly. At its inaugural session in May, Nouhak Phoumsavanh (a Vice-Chairman of the Council of Ministers) was elected President of the Assembly.

In June 1990 a draft Constitution, enshrining free-market principles, was published, and the Supreme People's Assembly approved legislation providing for the ownership of property, for inheritance rights and contractual obligations. In October three former government officials were arrested in connection with what were termed 'activities aimed at overthrowing the regime'. It was reported in Thailand that they had formed part of a 'Social Democrat Group', which was actively seeking the introduction of multi-party democracy. In November 1992 all three were sentenced to 14 years' imprisonment.

In March 1991, at the Fifth Congress of the LPRP, Souphanouvong stood down from all his party posts. Phoumi Vongvichit and Sisomphon Lovansai also retired, and the three were appointed to a newly created advisory board to the LPRP Central Committee. Kaysone Phomvihane's title was altered to President of the LPRP, and his power was slightly enhanced following the abolition of the party Secretariat. A new Politburo and (younger) Party Central Committee were elected. Gen. Sisavat Keobounphan, the military Chief of the General Staff, was not re-elected to the Politburo. The leadership pledged a continuance of free-market economic reforms, but denied the need for political pluralism.

On 14 August 1991 the Supreme People's Assembly adopted a new Constitution, which provided for a National Assembly, confirmed the leading role of the LPRP, enshrined the right to private ownership and endowed the presidency with executive powers. Kaysone Phomvihane was appointed President of Laos. Gen. Khamtay Siphandone, a Vice-Chairman of the Council of Ministers, Minister of National Defence and Supreme Commander of the Lao People's Army, replaced Kaysone Phomvihane as Chairman of the Council of Ministers, the position being restyled Prime Minister.

Kaysone Phomvihane died in November 1992. He was replaced as President of the LPRP by Gen. Khamtay Siphandone, and a specially convened meeting of the Supreme People's Assembly elected Nouhak Phoumsavanh as the country's President. At elections to the new National Assembly in December, 99.3% of eligible voters participated in the polls, in which 154 LFNC-approved candidates contested 85 seats. In February 1993 the new National Assembly re-elected Nouhak Phoumsavanh as President, confirmed Khamtay Siphandone as Prime Minister, and implemented the most extensive reorganization of the Council of Ministers since the LPRP's accession to power in

1975. Phoumi Vongvichit died in January 1994, and Souphanouvong in January 1995.

Although the 20th anniversary of the beginning of communist rule was celebrated in 1995, the Laotian Government was attempting gradually to replace communist ideology with Lao nationalism, as Laos developed a market economy with increasing foreign participation. In July senior Buddhist monks were assembled in Vientiane (as Buddhism was deemed central to Laotian cultural identity) and were encouraged by the Government to lead a 'cultural renaissance'. Meanwhile, the Government urged the security forces to suppress social problems, particularly corruption and prostitution, perceived as arising from increasing external influences.

The outcome of the Sixth LPRP Congress at the end of March 1996 consolidated the country's apparent progress towards a form of military-dominated authoritarian government. The armed forces gained a majority of seats on the new Politburo; Khamtay Siphandone was elected as its President (replacing Nouhak Phoumsavanh, who retired from this post), and the Minister of National Defence and Commander-in-Chief of the armed forces, Lt-Gen. Choummaly Sayasone, was promoted to third position, after the President of the National Assembly, Lt-Gen. Saman Vignaket. The most significant development was the failure of Khamphoui Keoboualapha, a Deputy Prime Minister responsible for many of Laos's reforms, to be re-elected either to the Politburo or to the Central Committee. Lts-Gen. Choummaly Sayasone and Saman Vignaket were widely reported to be opposed to rapid economic and political reform.

At the opening session of the National Assembly in April 1996 Nouhak Phoumsavanh was, despite his retirement from the Politburo, confirmed as head of state until the end of his term of office in February 1998. Sisavat Keobounphan (who had been restored to the Politburo at the previous month's elections) was elected to the new office of Vice-President, in order to relieve Nouhak Phoumsavanh of a number of presidential duties. Contrary to expectation, the reformist Khamphoui Keoboualapha was retained as Deputy Prime Minister and Chairman of the State Committee for Planning and Co-operation. However, his influence was diminished both by his exclusion from the Politburo and by the establishment of a new State Planning Committee, which assumed some of the responsibilities hitherto exercised by Khamphoui's Committee.

Elections to the National Assembly took place in December 1997, when 159 LFNC-approved candidates contested 99 seats. The three members of the LPRP Politburo and 10 Central Committee members who stood for election were all successful; one of the four 'independent' candidates without affiliation to the LPRP was elected. Electoral turn-out was officially recorded as 99.4%. The first session of the new National Assembly was held in February 1998, when Gen. Khamtay Siphandone was elected to succeed Phoumsavanh as President of Laos. The Assembly also endorsed the appointment of Sisavat Keobounphan as Prime Minister and of Oudom Khattigna in his place as Vice-President, re-elected Saman Vignaket as President of the National Assembly, and approved a redistribution of ministerial posts.

In March 2001 the Seventh Congress of the LPRP confirmed the military's control of the Politburo. In a further reorganization of the Council of Ministers, Oudom was replaced as the country's Vice-President by Lt-Gen. Choummaly Sayasone, who had withdrawn his candidacy for the premiership owing to ill health. Prime Minister Sisavat Keobounphan was forced to resign, in order to take responsibility for the mismanagement of the economy following the Asian financial crisis of 1997/98. His successor, the former Deputy Prime Minister and Minister of Finance, Boungnang Volachit, provided a civilian balance to the entirely military executive branch. The appointment of Thongloun Sisolit to the post of Deputy Prime Minister further increased the civilian representation on the Council of Ministers.

In February 2002 elections took place from among 166 LFNC-approved candidates for the 109 contested seats in the National Assembly. Only one of the elected members was not affiliated to the LPRP, ensuring that the ruling party secured a comprehensive victory. In April, at the opening session of the National Assembly, the existing Council of Ministers was almost wholly re-elected. The former Minister of the Interior, Maj.-Gen. Asang Laoli, became Deputy Prime Minister and Maj.-Gen. Soudchai Thammasith subsequently assumed the interior portfolio. In January 2003 a cabinet reorganization was announced in an apparent attempt to strengthen the national economy. The former Governor of the central bank, Chansy Phosikham, was

appointed Minister of Finance, Onneua Phommachanh became Minister of Industry and Handicrafts and Soulivong Daravong was placed in charge of the Ministry of Commerce and Tourism. In October Politburo member Bouasone Bouphavanh was appointed fourth Deputy Prime Minister, with responsibility for home affairs.

The 2006 legislative elections

In February 2006 it was announced that legislative elections would be held at the end of April, almost a year ahead of schedule. President Khamtay Siphandone stated that the decision to hold early elections had been made in order to enable the new Council of Ministers and the incoming legislature to commence their respective terms of office within close proximity of one another, in order to facilitate the forging of a strong working relationship. In March the LPRP held its Eighth Party Congress, during which Gen. Khamtay tendered his resignation from the Politburo; he was replaced as party leader by Vice-President Lt-Gen. Choummaly Sayasone. Two new members were elected to the Politburo, including Pany Yathotou (a Vice-President of the National Assembly), the only female member. Elections for a new Central Committee were also held, at which 55 members were selected. The party Secretariat, comprising seven members, was revived.

In the legislative elections held on 30 April 2006, two nominally independent candidates (of the three independents who had contested the elections) were elected, alongside 113 members of the LPRP. However, some 71 of the incoming deputies had not previously been members of the National Assembly, and therefore were described by some commentators as constituting a new generation of legislators. The new National Assembly was convened in June, electing Thongsing Thammavong, Politburo member and Governor of Vientiane, as the chamber's President. Lt-Gen. Choummaly Sayasone was chosen to succeed Gen. Khamtay as President of Laos. Boungnang Volachit became Vice-President, and was replaced as Prime Minister by Bouasone Bouphavanh. Two women were among the new cabinet appointments; other notable changes included the transfer of the foreign affairs portfolio from Somsavat Lengsavat to Thongloun Sisolit, both of whom remained as Deputy Prime Ministers, as did Maj.-Gen. Asong Laoli. Lt-Gen. Douangchai Phichit retained the defence portfolio and was promoted to the position of Deputy Prime Minister. The National Assembly approved several ministerial changes proposed by Prime Minister Bouasone in July 2007, including Chansy Phosikham's replacement as Minister of Finance by his deputy, Somdy Douangdy. Addressing the legislature in the previous month, Bouasone had emphasized the need to combat rising corruption among government officials.

Recent developments: Thongsing's appointment as Prime Minister, the Ninth LPRP Congress and legislative elections

In mid-December 2010 Bouasone Bouphavanh unexpectedly announced his resignation as Prime Minister three months prior to the expiry of his term of office, citing family issues. However, some observers speculated that the decision was more likely to have been due to a shift in the balance of power within the Politburo. Bouasone had been widely expected to be reappointed Prime Minister at the forthcoming LPRP Congress. Thongsing Thammavong was elected unanimously by the National Assembly as the new premier. Thongsing was replaced as President of the National Assembly by Pany Yathotou, hitherto one of his deputies, who thus became the first woman to assume the role.

The Ninth Congress of the LPRP, which was convened in mid-March 2011, was attended by 576 delegates. Following the appointment of a new, 61-member Central Committee, Choummaly Sayasone was re-elected as Secretary-General of the party for a further five-year term. Former Prime Minister Bouasone Bouphavanh was removed from both the Politburo and from the Central Committee. Another former Prime Minister, Sisavat Keobounphan, and Saman Vignaket retired from the Politburo. The incoming 11-member body thus incorporated three new members. A nine-member Secretariat was also appointed.

A total of 190 candidates contested the legislative elections held on 30 April 2011. Although, as in previous polls, the LPRP was the sole party permitted to present candidates, four of the 132 seats in the expanded National Assembly were won by candidates described as independent; 33 seats were taken by female candidates. The level of participation was reported to have been 99.6% of the electorate. On 15 June the National Assembly re-elected Choummaly Sayasone as the country's President for a further five-year term. Thongsing Thammavong was similarly confirmed in the position of Prime Minister, and a new cabinet was formally approved by the National Assembly. The incoming Council of Ministers incorporated several new members. Phouphet Khamphounvong, hitherto Governor of the central bank, replaced Somdy Douangdy as Minister of Finance. Somdy was appointed Minister of Planning and Investment, while Sompao Phaysith became Governor of the central bank. Thongloun Sisolit was retained as Deputy Prime Minister and Minister of Foreign Affairs, while four new ministries—with responsibility for the interior, for science and technology, for natural resources and environment, and for post, telecommunication and communication—were established.

Dissidence and Civil Unrest

Armed opposition to the Government persisted during the 1980s, particularly among hill tribes. In December 1989 the right-wing United Lao National Liberation Front (ULNLF) proclaimed the 'Revolutionary Provisional Government' of Laos. The self-styled Government, which was headed by Outhong Souvannavong (the former President of the Royal Council of King Savang Vatthana), claimed to have used military force to 'liberate' one-third of Laotian territory. Although there were reports of attacks by insurgent guerrillas in northern Laos at this time, it was widely assumed that the ULNLF's claims were exaggerated and that its proclamation was an attempt to elicit popular support. Responsibility for defence in the 'Revolutionary Provisional Government' was reportedly allocated to Gen. Vang Pao, a leader of the Hmong tribe who in the 1970s had been a commander of the Royalist army (and who had lived in exile in the USA since 1975). In October 1992 Gen. Vang Pao's brother, Vang Fung, and another Hmong rebel, Moua Yee Julan (who were allegedly preparing an incursion into Laos under Gen. Vang Pao's command), were arrested in Thailand. In September 1993 Thai troops launched an offensive against Gen. Vang Pao's forces, expelling 320 rebels from Thai territory.

From the mid-1990s uprisings against the Government became more frequent. In July 1995 an army unit based near Luang Prabang mutinied after its commander, a Hmong general, was passed over for promotion. Five members of the armed forces died in the rebellion, which was believed to be symptomatic of the resentment felt by hill tribes over the political and military dominance by the lowland Lao. About 2,000 troops were dispatched to Luang Prabang to restore order. In October a shipment of explosives, allegedly destined for Hmong insurgents, was intercepted on the Mekong River. Several incidents in the Luang Prabang region during late 1995 and 1996 were ascribed to Hmong rebels.

In October 1999 an anti-Government demonstration by students and teachers was held in Vientiane—an extremely rare overt demonstration of public dissatisfaction, which was reportedly swiftly dispersed by police. The Government subsequently denied that the demonstration had taken place; however, it was claimed that about 50 people suspected to have been involved in the protest had been arrested, and in March 2000 it was reported that the whereabouts of six of these alleged detainees—one professor and five students—remained unknown.

Civil unrest intensified throughout 2000, with a spate of bomb explosions, including two separate attacks in Vientiane in May, coinciding with the respective visits of the Thai Prime Minister and his Minister of Foreign Affairs. By June at least two people had been killed in the bombing campaign and more than 20 others had been injured. The Government attributed the attacks to Hmong insurgents, claiming to have arrested two men (one Lao and one Hmong) carrying explosive devices in June. However, the bombings continued unabated. A bomb was defused near the Vietnamese embassy in Vientiane in July, appearing to lend credence to the suspicion that the campaign was part of an internal power struggle between pro-Chinese and pro-Vietnamese governmental factions. In total, at least nine bombs exploded between March 2000 and January 2001, including an attack prior to a summit meeting of the European Union (EU) and the Association of Southeast Asian Nations (ASEAN, see p. 218) in December 2000.

In October 2001 five European activists, including Olivier Dupuis, a Belgian member of the European Parliament, were arrested for distributing pro-democracy leaflets at a peaceful protest in Vientiane. The protest was held to commemorate the second anniversary of the disappearance of the five students who had participated in the demonstration of October 1999. In November 2001, following expressions of concern at the conditions under which the detainees were being held, the President of the European Commission warned the Laotian authorities that the continued detention of the activists would threaten diplomatic relations with the EU. In the same month, following a swift trial, the prisoners were convicted of attempting to spread unrest and ordered to be deported.

In September 2002 a bomb exploded at the Si Muang temple in Vientiane, injuring two children. Fears that tourists might be deterred from visiting Laos were intensified by three separate attacks on buses, thought to have been perpetrated by Hmong rebels, in February, April and August 2003; the ambushes claimed the lives of at least 30 people, including several foreign nationals. In October three bombs exploded in Vientiane. A previously unknown group, the Free Democratic People's Government of Laos (FDPGL), claimed responsibility for the bombings, as well as for the spate of bomb attacks in the capital since 2000. It was believed that the group consisted of disaffected former members of the armed forces. However, a German-based organization, the Committee for Independence and Democracy in Laos, later claimed responsibility for the bombings, including two further attacks in February 2004—one in Vientiane, which killed two people, and one in the southern town of Savannakhet, where tourism ministers from ASEAN countries had convened.

In March 2004 an official from the Ministry of National Defence claimed that some 700 Hmong, including five senior commanders, had recently surrendered to the authorities, having been offered amnesty. Five bomb attacks occurred in April and May. In September the human rights organization Amnesty International alleged that up to 40 government troops had murdered five Hmong children in the Xaysomboun special zone in northern Laos in May; the Government denied the accusations. Two minor bomb explosions occurred in a village near Vientiane in November, prompting a heightening of security in advance of the ASEAN summit meeting, which was held in the capital at the end of the month.

In June 2007 10 Hmong resident in the USA and a former officer of the California National Guard were arrested and charged in connection with an alleged plot to overthrow the Laos Government, which had been uncovered by US federal agents. Most of the 11 defendants, including Gen. Vang Pao, the purported leader of the group, were released on bail in July. The charges against all 11 defendants were withdrawn in 2009; Vang Pao died in the USA in January 2011.

Foreign Affairs

Regional relations

Laos was formally admitted as a full member of ASEAN in 1997. Laos hosted the 10th summit meeting of the Association in November 2004 and the 38th Ministerial Meeting in July 2005. Despite bomb threats made to staff at the US embassy in Vientiane, apparently by groups opposed to the Laotian Government, in the period prior to the summit meeting in November 2004, both the meeting itself and the subsequent ministerial conference proceeded without incident and did much to raise the international profile of Laos. In February 2008 Laos ratified the new ASEAN Charter, which codified the principles and purposes of the Association.

Laos hosted the ninth summit of the Asia-Europe Meeting (ASEM), in Vientiane, in November 2012. The summit meeting constituted the largest international event ever to be held in Laos. It was hoped that Laos's successful hosting of the event would result in an increase in foreign investment inflows and a spate of new infrastructure projects.

Laos's closest regional partner for many years was Viet Nam. However, in recent years Vietnamese influence in Laos has begun to be eclipsed by that exerted by the People's Republic of China. From 1975 Laos was dependent on Vietnamese economic and military assistance, permitting the stationing of Vietnamese troops (estimated in 1987 to number between 30,000 and 50,000) on its territory. In 1977 a 25-year treaty of friendship between the two countries was signed, and Laos supported the Vietnamese-led overthrow of the Khmer Rouge regime in Kampuchea (Cambodia) in January 1979. Following the outbreak of hostilities between Viet Nam and China in that year, Laos allied itself with the former. Viet Nam withdrew its military presence from Laos during 1988. The two countries signed a protocol governing military co-operation in March 1994. In July 2001 Prime Minister Boungnang Volachit visited Viet Nam on his first foreign trip since assuming office in March. In May 2002 President Khamtay Siphandone paid an official friendship visit to Viet Nam, which was reciprocated in October by the Chairman of the Vietnamese National Assembly, Nguyen Van An. The visits affirmed the strength of relations between the two countries. In February 2006 a major border crossing was opened between Sekong province in Laos and Quang Nam province in Viet Nam. It was hoped that this would facilitate economic exchanges and help to control smuggling along the common border. Discussions held during an official visit to Laos by the Vietnamese President, Nguyen Minh Triet, in February 2007 also focused on the expansion of economic co-operation. In February 2008 it was reported that Viet Nam had become the second largest foreign investor in Laos after Thailand. An official visit to Laos in April 2010 by Nong Duc Manh, General Secretary of the Communist Party of Viet Nam (CPV), was reciprocated by a state visit to Viet Nam in September by Prime Minister Bouasone, accompanied by a senior-level ministerial delegation. Nguyen Phu Trong, the General Secretary of the CPV Central Committee, made an official visit to Vientiane in June 2011, during which both countries stressed the importance of bilateral relations and proclaimed 2012 as the 'Year of Viet Nam-Laos Friendship and Solidarity'. In November 2012 Laos and Viet Nam signed an agreement to construct a 220-km high-speed rail link between the two countries (from Savannakhet province in southern Laos to the Vietnamese border town of Lao Bao) at an estimated cost of US $5,000m.; the project was to be undertaken by a Malaysian company and was expected to take five years to complete.

Relations with China improved from the mid-1980s. In December 1986 a Chinese delegation, led by the Deputy Minister of Foreign Affairs, made the first official Chinese visit to Laos since 1978. After an assurance that Chinese support would be withdrawn from Laotian resistance groups operating from within China, full diplomatic relations between the LPRP and the Chinese Communist Party were restored in August 1989. In October 1991 the Laotian and Chinese Prime Ministers signed a border treaty, which established a framework for meetings of a Laotian-Chinese joint border committee. In January 1992 the committee adopted a resolution providing for the demarcation of the common border, and in June an agreement on the delineation of boundaries was signed. In November 1994 Laos and China signed a reciprocal agreement on the transport of passengers and goods on each other's sections of the Mekong River. In February 1996 the two countries opened a section of their border to highway traffic. The first ever visit by a Chinese head of state to Laos was undertaken by President Jiang Zemin in November 2000.

As the volume of bilateral trade continued to increase, Laotian-Chinese relations were further strengthened by a state visit by Chinese President Hu Jintao to Vientiane in November 2006 and by a seven-day official visit to China by Laotian Prime Minister Bouasone in August 2007, during which six agreements on co-operation in a range of areas were signed. In March 2008 Chinese Premier Wen Jiabao undertook a three-day visit to Laos for discussions with Bouasone. The two leaders broadly agreed to increase exchanges, to collaborate closely on important projects and to promote strategic industries. However, China's increasing involvement in the economy of Laos, mainly in infrastructural development projects, had begun to concern the Laotian people. Many were perturbed by the influx of Chinese workers and business entrepreneurs, who, according to some estimates, totalled as many as 300,000 by 2008. In particular, in return for the granting of a concession to develop a large residential and economic zone in Vientiane, thousands of Chinese labourers were engaged to work on the construction of a new sports stadium. Financed by the China Development Bank, the national stadium was completed in time for the South-East Asian Games, hosted by Laos in December 2009. In April 2010 Laos and China signed a memorandum of understanding agreeing to co-operate as joint stakeholders in the development of a 420-km high-speed railway from their joint border to Vientiane, from where it would connect to the rail network in Viet Nam. The planned railway, which was forecast to cost some US $7,000m. and was to be funded by a long-term loan from the Chinese Government, prompted further consternation in Laos on account of the high number of Chinese workers expected to be involved (some 64,000, according to Laotian officials). Although the project appeared unlikely to proceed when the participating Chinese construction company withdrew from the venture in October 2012, reportedly owing to concerns about profitability, the Laotian authorities, having been offered another loan by the China Exim Bank in November, decided to assume sole ownership of the project. At January 2013, however, construction work on the railway had not yet started.

In June 2010 Laos received a senior-level Chinese delegation; during its stay, the two countries signed 18 co-operation agreements on bilateral trade and development, among other fields. In the following month Laotian Deputy Prime Minister and Minister of National Defence Lt-Gen. Douangchai Phichit visited the Chinese capital, Beijing, where he signed a military co-operation agreement with his Chinese counterpart. A series of high-level bilateral visits was conducted in 2011, and in April of that year Laotian and Chinese companies signed an agreement providing for the construction of a 25-ha urban development project (at a cost of some US $180m.) in Vientiane. Furthermore, in December 2012 another Chinese company reached an agreement with the Laotian Government to develop an area of 365 ha around That Luang Lake into a commercial, residential and tourism complex; the project was forecast to cost around $1,600m. China's total investment in Laos during 2012 totalled some $3,300m., making it the third largest foreign investor after Thailand and Viet Nam. Meanwhile, in December 2011, following the murder of 13 Chinese nationals on the Mekong, China deployed armed patrols in Laos (as well as in Thailand and Viet Nam) to provide security along the river.

Following a visit to Japan in 1989 by LPRP Secretary-General Kaysone Phomvihane (his first official visit to a non-communist country), the Japanese Government agreed to increase grant aid to Laos. Japan resumed the provision of official loans to Laos in 1996. In January 2000 the Japanese Prime Minister, Keizo Obuchi, undertook an official visit to Laos, and in August a bridge over the Mekong, built with a 5,460m.-yen grant from the Japanese Government, was officially opened in Paksé. In September 2001 Japan agreed a further loan to fund the construction of the second Mekong Friendship Bridge. During a visit to Japan by Bouasone Bouphavanh in May 2007, the Laotian Prime Minister held a meeting with his Japanese counterpart, Shinzo Abe, who pledged to provide continued economic assistance to Laos; the financial aid was to include approximately US $1m. for the clearance of unexploded ordnance remaining from the Viet Nam War. Furthermore, it was hoped that a bilateral agreement on investment, which was signed in January 2008, would encourage the participation of Japanese businesses in the Laotian economy. Relations were further strengthened by a five-day official visit to Japan by President Choummaly Sayasone in March 2010, when he met with the Emperor of Japan, Akihito, and the Japanese Prime Minister, Yukio Hatoyama. Prime Minister Bouasone made an official visit to Japan in May, during which Japan pledged further aid for Laos, to be divested primarily towards poverty reduction measures. In March 2012 Prime Minister Thongsing Thammavong visited Japan and held discussions with Prime Minister Yoshihiko Noda on Japanese aid and investment in Laos, with particular emphasis on strengthening regional connectivity; during his visit the Laotian Prime Minister expressed his especial gratitude for Japan's recommencement of yen loans to Laos. The two premiers conducted further talks with each other in November during the ASEM summit in Vientiane.

In February 1993 Laos, Thailand, Viet Nam and Cambodia signed a joint communiqué providing for the resumption of co-operation in the development of the Mekong River. In April 1995 in Chiang Rai, Thailand, representatives of the four countries signed an agreement on the joint exploitation and development of the lower Mekong. The accord provided for the establishment of the Mekong River Commission (MRC, see p. 462) as a successor to the Committee for Co-ordination of Investigations of the Lower Mekong Basin. The first summit meeting of the Commission, the primary focus of which was to examine means of enhancing the sustainable use and development of the Mekong River, was held in the Thai resort of Hua Hin in April 2010, and was attended by Laotian Prime Minister Bouasone Bouphavanh and his Cambodian, Thai and Vietnamese counterparts. Meanwhile, in August 2008 Laos, Cambodia and Viet Nam signed a border-crossing agreement that defined the intersection point of their borders and affirmed their resolve to complete works related to the demarcation of their land borders. A joint Laotian-Cambodian border demarcation survey in an area between the Laotian province of Attapeu and the Cambodian province of Ratanakiri was conducted in 2010; at May 2012 the Laotian authorities claimed to have reached agreement with Cambodia on some 86% of their 535-km mutual border. In November 2010 Laos and Viet Nam commenced a joint border demarcation survey along the Mo River, and in December the two countries signed an agreement pledging to enhance border security co-operation. The Laotian-Vietnamese border demarcation process was scheduled to be completed in 2014. In June 2011 the Laotian, Cambodian and Vietnamese Governments signed an agreement providing for the establishment of a trilateral economic development zone, which called for an acceleration of the border demarcation process. A controversial plan to build a hydropower dam on the Mekong River at Xayaburi in northern Laos was further delayed in December, pending more environmental studies, by a decision of the MRC, which had also failed to approve the project in April. Environmental groups claimed that the hydropower project, which would be the first to be built in the Lower Mekong Basin (although other dams were planned by both Laos and Cambodia), would adversely affect agriculture and fish stocks downstream.

Relations with Thailand from 1975 were characterized by mutual suspicion. Thailand intermittently closed its border to Laotian imports and exports, causing considerable hardship. Disputed sovereignty claims in border areas were a cause of friction, and led to clashes between Laotian and Thai troops in 1984. Further hostilities began in December 1987, resulting in hundreds of casualties. In February 1988 the two sides agreed to declare a cease-fire, to withdraw their troops from the combat area and to attempt to negotiate a peaceful solution. In March 1991 (following a military coup in Thailand) representatives of the two countries signed an agreement providing for the immediate withdrawal of troops from disputed areas. The Thai Government also undertook to suppress the activities of Laotian insurgents operating from Thai territory. In December Thailand and Laos signed a border co-operation agreement.

The first bridge linking Laos and Thailand, the so-called 'Friendship Bridge', was opened in April 1994; the bridge (over the Mekong River) connected Vientiane and Nong Khai province in north-eastern Thailand. In September 1996 the countries' Joint Co-operation Commission agreed to establish a boundary commission, in an effort to resolve demarcation problems. Despite various diplomatic efforts to stimulate further co-operation between the two countries, the relationship was strained by an assault launched in July 2000 from Thai territory on a customs outpost in the border town of Vang Tao, carried out by suspected royalist rebels. (In July 2004, following a lengthy legal dispute, Thailand handed over to the Laotian authorities 16 Lao nationals who were allegedly involved in the incursion; in October all were convicted of robbery in connection with the raid and sentenced to prison terms of between two and 12 years.) Meanwhile, the situation deteriorated further in August 2000 after Laotian troops occupied two islands in the Mekong River, evicting 65 Thai farming families. Laos claimed that, under a treaty of 1926, it had sovereignty over all the islands in the Mekong, while Thailand merely requested the withdrawal of the troops.

In March 2004, for the first time, the Thai and Laotian Governments held a joint cabinet meeting to discuss bilateral co-operation. The meeting ended with Prime Ministers Thaksin Shinawatra and Boungnang Volachit presiding over a ceremony to lay the foundation stone for a second Mekong Friendship Bridge (the third bridge over the river in total), connecting Savannakhet in Laos to the Thai province of Mukdahan; the bridge was officially opened in December 2006. In February 2008 Laos and Thailand agreed to complete the demarcation of their 735-km land border in that year, as the area remaining under dispute covered only 12 km, followed by that of the 1,100-km water border in 2010; however, with a number of difficult points of contention remaining unresolved, neither of these deadlines were met, and in March 2012 the two countries drew up two new deadlines: 2014 for the land border and 2016 for the water border. Meanwhile, in March 2009 the first rail link between Laos and Thailand was inaugurated, with the route between Vientiane and Nong Khai province in north-eastern Thailand. Construction of a fourth Mekong bridge, between the Laotian province of Khammouane and the Thai province of Nakhon Pathom, commenced in May, and the bridge was inaugurated in November 2011, at a ceremony co-chaired by the Lao Vice-President, Boungnang Volachit, and the Thai Prime Minister, Yingluck Shinawatra. A fifth bridge over the Mekong, which would link the Laotian province of Bokeo and the northernmost Thai province, Chiang Rai, was originally scheduled for completion by the end of 2012. However, following numerous delays, largely owing to funding problems as a result of the global financial downturn, construction did not commence until May 2010; as a result, completion was not expected until September 2013. When completed, the new bridge (the fourth 'Friendship Bridge') would, for the first time, provide a direct road link from the Chinese province of Yunnan, through Laos, to the Thai capital of Bangkok. The project was to be financed jointly by the Laotian and Thai Governments, although the Chinese Govern-

ment contributed US \$20m. to the Laotian share of the cost. Also in May 2010 it was announced that Laos had secured financing of some \$50m. from the Chinese Government for a sixth bridge over the Mekong, which would connect the Laotian province of Oudomxay with Thailand's Nan province. Work on the project was scheduled to begin in the second half of 2011 and to be completed by 2015; however, owing to a subsequent dispute between the Laotian and Chinese Governments over the terms of the deal, construction of the bridge did not commence until December 2012. The construction of another bridge over the Mekong (the fifth 'Friendship Bridge'), which would connect the Laotian province of Bolikhamsai with Thailand's Bueng Karn province, was due to start in December 2013; the project, which was to be financed by the Thai Government, was expected to be completed by the end of 2015.

Meanwhile, at a meeting in October 2010 of the Joint Co-operation Commission, co-chaired by the Laotian Deputy Prime Minister and Minister of Foreign Affairs, Thongloun Sisolit, and by Thai Minister of Foreign Affairs Kasit Piromya, the two countries reiterated their commitment to expand bilateral co-operation; Thailand confirmed a prior agreement to purchase 7,000 MW of electricity from Laos by 2015. In April 2012 a Thai company, CH. Karnchang, signed a contract with the Laotian authorities to proceed with the construction of the planned hydropower dam at Xayaburi, across the lower reaches of the Mekong River. It was alleged that funding for the controversial project had been secured on the understanding that, once the dam was completed (at a projected cost of US 3,500m.), Thailand would purchase some 95% of the electricity produced. Despite continuing opposition from Viet Nam and Cambodia and from environmentalists (who were concerned about the potential impact of the dam on fish migration and sediment flow), in November the Laotian Government gave official approval to the commencement of full construction work at the site, claiming that the requisite environmental studies had been completed.

During the 1970s and 1980s thousands of Laotian refugees fled to Thailand to escape from civil war and food shortages. The office of the UN High Commissioner for Refugees (UNHCR) began a programme of voluntary repatriation in 1980. In June 1991 UNHCR, Laos and Thailand signed an agreement guaranteeing the repatriation or resettlement in a third country of the remaining 60,000 Laotian refugees in Thailand by the end of 1994; however, this deadline was subsequently revised on several occasions. In December 1997 UNHCR announced that a final review of the status of the last remaining refugees at Ban Napho camp in Thailand would be completed by January 1998, whereupon they would be repatriated or resettled in a third country. Among the camp's 1,344 refugees were reportedly 964 Hmong, most of whom were unwilling to return to Laos. In December 2003 the USA agreed to accept around 15,000 Laotian Hmong refugees living in refugee camps in Thailand.

In September 2006 UNHCR urged the Thai Government to abandon its plan for the forcible repatriation of 158 Hmong migrants (including 92 children, and all recognized by UNHCR as political refugees), arguing that they would be at risk if they returned to Laos. In response, the Thai Ministry of Foreign Affairs stated that Thai and Laotian immigration officials were determining the nationality of the migrants, who, it was stated, would not be repatriated against their will. Meanwhile, Laotian officials insisted that the Government had not persecuted the Hmong. In January 2007 the Thai Government agreed to halt the deportation process for the group of 158 Hmong after the several third countries agreed to provide asylum to the migrants.

Meanwhile, an agreement between the Thai and Laotian Governments in December 2006 to repatriate the 8,000 or so Hmong living in refugee camps in Thailand's Phetchabun province, who were alleged to be economic migrants (and to whom UNHCR did not have access), prompted widespread international criticism. In January 2007 UNHCR urged the suspension of all deportations pending the introduction of procedures to allow a proper assessment of the needs and claims of the Hmong. None the less, the Thai authorities proceeded with the repatriation process, claiming to have received assurances from the Laotian authorities that the Hmong would be treated well upon their return to Laos. Following a mass protest at the Ban Huay Nam Khao camp in Phetchabun in June 2008, the Thai authorities promptly deported 837 Hmong refugees to Laos. However, some 1,300 refugees remained unaccounted for after the incident. Although the 837 repatriations were described by the Thai army as voluntary, concerns were raised by human rights organizations, including Amnesty International and Human

Rights Watch. In December 2009 the Thai Government forcibly deported to Laos the final 4,000 or so Hmong remaining at the Ban Huay Nam Khao camp, as well as the 158 UNHCR-recognized political refugees being held in an immigration detention centre, despite protests by UNHCR, the USA and other members of the international community. In July 2010 the USA urged the Laotian Government to allow the group of 158 UNHCR-recognized political refugees to leave Laos for a third country. However, the Laotian authorities claimed that the group wished to remain in Laos. Although foreign diplomats who had been allowed access to the refugees earlier in the year had stated that there was no evidence to suggest that the group had been mistreated, media reports indicated that the refugees' living conditions were extremely poor and that they were being kept under the constant supervision of armed guards. At early 2013 little was known of their whereabouts.

Other external relations

During the Viet Nam War US aircraft completed almost 600,000 bombing missions over Laos, leaving large amounts of undetonated explosives, which were estimated to have caused 50–100 fatalities per year in the 1990s and which continued to claim the lives of Laotians in the 21st century. The National Unexploded Ordnance Awareness and Clearance Programme was established in Laos in 1995, with support from the UN. Following the adoption by 107 countries in May 2008 of the Convention on Cluster Munitions, banning the use, production, stockpiling and transfer of cluster bombs, the treaty was opened for signature in December. The First Meeting of States Parties to the Convention on Cluster Munitions was held in Vientiane in November 2010. About 1,200 foreign delegates attended the meeting, during which the Convention adopted the Vientiane Declaration, which included a pledge by the signatories to foster greater international co-operation in order better to assist victims of cluster bombs and to accelerate efforts to destroy cluster munition stockpiles and clear buried remnants.

Relations with the USA have traditionally been dominated by the issue of US soldiers listed as 'missing in action' in Laos during the Viet Nam War. In 1985 Laos agreed to co-operate with the USA in tracing missing soldiers. The first remains of US soldiers were passed to the US Government in February 1988; further operations to locate the remains of US soldiers took place in the 1990s and 2000s. In November 1991, in response to continued Laotian co-operation and the implementation of limited political and economic reforms, the US Government announced that diplomatic relations with Laos were to be upgraded to ambassadorial level. In May 1995 the USA announced the ending of a 20-year embargo on aid to Laos. In November 1997 the US Deputy Secretary of State, Strobe Talbott, led the most senior-level US delegation to Laos since the mid-1970s; during the visit further US support was pledged for a programme to clear unexploded ordnance left behind from the Viet Nam War. In December 2004, following its adoption by Congress, President George W. Bush of the USA signed legislation according normal trade relations (NTR) status to Laos: this status had been suspended in 1975. The US Senate had separately adopted a resolution condemning Laos's human rights record, concerns over which had delayed the approval of NTR status. A bilateral trade agreement signed by the USA and Laos in September 2003 consequently entered into force in February 2005; according to the US Department of State, trade between the two countries almost tripled between 2007 and 2010. A meeting in Washington, DC, USA, between Deputy Prime Minister and Minister of Foreign Affairs Thongloun Sisolit and US Secretary of State Hillary Clinton in July 2010 represented the first official visit to the USA by a Laotian minister responsible for foreign affairs since the establishment of the Lao People's Democratic Republic in 1975. An air travel co-operation agreement was signed, which it was hoped would bolster bilateral tourism; other areas of discussion included US aid, and trade and military co-operation. Two years later, in July 2012, in the course of a major tour of Asia, Hillary Clinton made the first visit to Laos by a US Secretary of State since 1955. During her visit, Clinton held discussions with Prime Minister Thongsing Thammavong and other senior officials on a variety of topics, including economic ties, the legacies of the Viet Nam War (unexploded ordnance and missing personnel), the Mekong dam and Laos's pending entry into the World Trade Organization (see p. 444).

Meanwhile, in November 2002 Indian Prime Minister Atal Bihari Vajpayee paid the first visit to Laos by an Indian head of government in more than 45 years. During his stay, bilateral agreements on defence co-operation and the control of drugs-

trafficking were signed. The Indian Government also agreed to provide US $10m. of credit to Laos at low interest rates. Regular meetings of the Laos-India Joint Commission for Bilateral Co-operation subsequently took place. During a visit to Laos by Indian President Pratibha Patil in September 2010, the two countries signed an agreement whereby India would provide funding of $72.5m. for two Laotian power projects, as part of a wider programme of monetary and technical assistance for Laos across several fields. A free trade agreement signed between India and ASEAN in August 2009 was implemented between India and Laos in January 2011; as a result of the pact, the import duties of 80% of goods currently traded between the two countries were to be eliminated by 2019, with tariffs on chemicals, electronics, garments and machinery significantly reduced with immediate effect.

In April 2009 Ban Ki-Moon visited Vientiane, the first official visit to Laos by a UN Secretary-General for almost 25 years. During his visit, Ban Ki-Moon met with senior officials, including President Choummaly Sayasone. He praised the Laotian Government for its poverty reduction efforts and pledged a continuance of UN support for Laos's goal of eliminating poverty by 2020. In December 2012 the office of the UN High Commissioner for Human Rights urged the Laotian Government to ensure the safe return of a prominent human rights activist, Sombath Somphone, who had gone missing in Vientiane (in an apparent abduction) earlier that month; the Laotian authorities denied having played any part in his disappearance.

CONSTITUTION AND GOVERNMENT

Under the terms of the 1991 Constitution, executive power is vested in the President of State, while legislative power resides with the National Assembly. The President is elected for five years by the National Assembly. Members of the National Assembly are elected for a period of five years by universal adult suffrage. The Lao People's Revolutionary Party remains the sole legal political party. With the approval of the National Assembly, the President appoints the Prime Minister and members of the Council of Ministers, who conduct the government of the country. The President also appoints provincial governors and mayors of municipalities, who are responsible for local administration.

REGIONAL AND INTERNATIONAL CO-OPERATION

Laos is a member of the Association of Southeast Asian Nations (ASEAN, see p. 218), the Asian Development Bank (ADB, see p. 214), the UN's Economic and Social Commission for Asia and the Pacific (ESCAP, see p. 31), the Colombo Plan (see p. 460), which promotes economic and social development in Asia and the Pacific, and the Mekong River Commission (see p. 462).

Laos became a member of the UN in 1955. In February 2013, following a 15-year-long bid for admission, the country was finally admitted as a full member of the World Trade Organization (WTO, see p. 444). Laos is a member of the International Labour Organization (ILO, see p. 142) and the Non-aligned Movement (see p. 477).

ECONOMIC AFFAIRS

In 2011, according to estimates by the World Bank, Laos's gross national income (GNI), measured at average 2009–11 prices, was US $7,105m., equivalent to $1,130 per head (or $2,600 per head on an international purchasing-power parity basis). During 2002–11, it was estimated, the population increased at an average annual rate of 1.5%, while gross domestic product (GDP) per head increased, in real terms, by an average of 5.9% per year. Overall GDP increased, in real terms, at an average annual rate of 7.5% in 2002–11. According to the Asian Development Bank (ADB), GDP expanded by 7.9% in 2012.

Agriculture (including forestry and fishing) contributed 30.3% of GDP in 2010. According to the ADB, an estimated 78.5% of the working population were employed in the sector in 2005; FAO projected that 74.4% of the labour force would be employed in the sector in mid-2013. Rice is the staple crop. Other crops include sweet potatoes, maize, cassava, sugar cane and fruit. Coffee is grown for export. In 2012 natural forest covered about 42% of the country's total land area (compared with 70% in 1940). Although declining, timber remained a significant export commodity in 2008, accounting for an estimated 8.0% of total export revenue in that year (compared with 27.2% in 2003, prior to the growth of copper exports). The illicit cultivation of narcotic drugs has been widespread. Although the UN Office on Drugs and Crime (UNODC) estimated that the area under opium poppy cultivation in Laos had declined from 26,800 ha in 1998 to 1,500 ha in 2007, thereafter there were five successive years of increases, reaching 6,800 ha in 2012. During 2002–11 agricultural GDP increased at an average annual rate of 3.1%, according to the World Bank. Growth in the sector was estimated by the ADB at 2.5% in 2012.

Industry (including mining, manufacturing, construction and utilities) contributed 27.7% of GDP in 2010. According to the ADB, the sector employed 9.3% of the working population in 2003. During 2002–11 industrial GDP increased at an average annual rate of 14.1%, according to the World Bank. Growth in the industrial sector was estimated by the ADB at 13.7% in 2012.

Mining contributed 8.1% of GDP in 2010 (in comparison with just 1.5% in 2004). Laos has considerable mineral resources: copper, gold, tin, coal, iron ore, gemstones and gypsum are among the minerals exploited. Other mineral deposits include zinc, nickel, potash, lead, limestone and silver. Copper production totalled 64,241 metric tons in 2010. Exports of copper increased from US $446.0m. in 2007 to an estimated $620.3m. in 2008. The value of gold exports (including re-exports) rose from $93.2m. in 2007 to an estimated $118.9m. in 2008. According to ADB figures, during 2001–10 the GDP of the mining sector increased by an average of 58.9% per year. The start of gold production in 2003 greatly enhanced the sector's output. Mining GDP expanded by 49.3% in 2009 and by 12.6% in 2010.

Manufacturing contributed 9.9% of GDP in 2010. The sector is mainly confined to the processing of raw materials (chiefly sawmilling) and agricultural produce, the production of garments (a significant export, accounting for an estimated 11.6% of total exports in 2008), and the manufacture of handicrafts and basic consumer goods for the domestic market. According to the World Bank, manufacturing GDP increased at an average annual rate of 9.6% in 2002–11; manufacturing GDP grew by 10.4% in 2011.

Construction contributed 5.5% of GDP in 2010. In 2001–10 the GDP of the sector increased at an average annual rate of 10.6%, according to ADB figures; growth in the construction sector reached 20.0% in 2010.

Electrical energy is principally derived from hydroelectric power. Electricity is exported to Thailand and Viet Nam, and is an important source of foreign exchange. Laos's total hydroelectric power potential is estimated at around 23,000 MW. Hydroelectricity production reached 13,800m. kWh in 2012. The 1,070-MW Nam Theun 2 hydroelectric project began commercial operations in March 2010. Initial operations at the 615-MW Nam Ngum 2 hydropower plant commenced in late 2010. In November 2011 the ADB approved funding of some US $465m. to support the construction of the 440-MW Nam Ngum 3 hydropower plant, which was expected to provide 2,072 GWh of clean energy annually for export to Thailand upon completion (scheduled by 2017), generating around $770m. for the Laotian Government. Several other power projects have been commissioned. Laos is dependent on imports, mainly from Thailand, for supplies of mineral fuels. Petroleum accounted for 15.0% of total import costs in 2008.

The services sector contributed 42.0% of GDP in 2010, and engaged 8.6% of the total labour force in 2003. Visitor arrivals were reported to have increased by 22.3% in 2012, to 3.3m. In 2011 receipts from tourism were estimated to have reached US $406m. The country's first stock exchange commenced trading in early 2011. According to the World Bank, the GDP of the services sector increased at an average annual rate of 7.4% in 2002–11. The GDP of the sector grew by 8.0% in 2012, according to the ADB.

In 2011 Laos recorded a visible merchandise trade deficit of US $568.9m. and there was a deficit of $150.6m. on the current account of the balance of payments. Remittances from relatives residing overseas are a significant source of income for many Lao. In 2011 Thailand was the principal source of imports, supplying 65.9% (including any goods in transit) of the total. The People's Republic of China was also an important source of imports in that year, along with Viet Nam. The principal destination of exports from Laos in 2011 was Thailand, which purchased 34.8% (including any goods in transit) of the total. Other significant purchasers in that year were China and Viet Nam. The main export in 2008 was copper, followed by garments, timber, gold and electricity. The principal imports were capital goods, petroleum and material for the garment industry.

An overall budget deficit of 1,121,000m. new kips was recorded in 2010/11. Laos's general government gross debt was 35,766.1m. new kips in 2011, equivalent to 55.9% of GDP. According to the ADB, at the end of 2012 the country's public external debt totalled US $3,100m. In 2011 the cost of servicing external public debt was equivalent to 4.6% of the value of exports of goods and services. According to ILO, consumer prices increased by an average of 7.2% per year in 2002–11. Consumer prices rose by 4.3% in 2012. The unemployment rate was estimated by the ADB at 1.4% of the labour force in 2005.

Despite being a communist country, Laos implemented gradual economic reforms to liberalize its economy moderately in the 2000s. Although historically one of the world's poorer nations and still very much dependent on foreign aid, Laos's economy grew at an average annual rate of 7.9% over the period of its Sixth National Socio-economic Development Plan (2006–10), largely due to the development of mining and hydropower projects. The country intends to expand its hydropower production significantly, exploiting its abundant natural resources, and more than 70 new projects were planned or under construction in early 2013 (including the controversial Mekong dam project). In order to comply with the requirements of the World Trade Organization (WTO, see p. 444), which Laos joined in February 2013, the Government implemented numerous measures to improve trade and investment conditions. Revenue generated by the introduction in January 2010 of value-added tax, levied at a rate of 10%, was largely to finance wider development. Furthermore, it was hoped that equity and bond sales on the Lao Securities Exchange, which was established in 2010 with financial support from the Republic of Korea and which began operations in January 2011, would fund investment in the country, as well as attracting foreign investors; at early 2013, however, the exchange had only two listed companies (both of which were large, state-operated firms). According to the World Bank, foreign direct investment was projected to increase from US $1,100m. in 2011 to $1,500m. in 2012. The Seventh National Socio-economic Development Plan (2011–15) forecast an annual economic growth rate of at least 8%, supporting the Government's objective to graduate from least developed country status by 2020. Considerable progress had already been made towards alleviating poverty, which remained a priority for the Government, as well as a focus on the greater integration of Laos into the regional economy. To this end, in 2010 the Laotian Government signed an agreement with China to build a high-speed rail link between the two countries, and drew up plans in 2012 for a similar project with Viet Nam. In 2010–11 Laos benefited from strong prices for its principal commodity exports of copper and gold, and increasing revenue from sales of electricity. Inflation reached 7.6% in 2011, mainly owing to rising food and fuel prices, but moderated to 4.3% in 2012, partly as a result of a good rice harvest and a decrease in fuel prices. Following the robust GDP growth of 2010–12 (despite severe flooding in 2011), the ADB envisaged similarly strong expansion, of 7.7%, in 2013, bolstered by continued development in the mining, hydropower and construction sectors. In addition, membership of the WTO was expected to encourage greater, longer-term and more diverse foreign investment and thereby help to sustain healthy growth rates.

PUBLIC HOLIDAYS

2014: 1 January (New Year's Day), 6 January (Pathet Lao Day), 20 January (Army Day), 31 January (Chinese New Year), 7 March (for International Women's Day), 21 March (for People's Party Day), 14–16 April (Lao New Year), 1 May (Labour Day), 2 June (for Children's Day), 13 August (Free Laos Day), 22 August (for Liberation Day), 13 October (for Liberation from the French Day, Vientiane only), 2 December (Independence Day).

Statistical Survey

Source (unless otherwise stated): National Statistics Centre, rue Luang Prabang, Vientiane; tel. (21) 214740; fax (21) 219129; e-mail nscp@laotel.com; internet www.nsc.gov.la.

Area and Population

AREA, POPULATION AND DENSITY

Area (sq km)	236,800*
Population (census results)	
1 March 1995	4,581,258
1 March 2005	
Males	2,800,551
Females	2,821,431
Total	5,621,982
Population (UN estimates at mid-year)†	
2011	6,288,039
2012	6,373,930
2013	6,458,910
Density (per sq km) at mid-2013	27.3

* 91,400 sq miles.
† Source: UN, _World Population Prospects: The 2010 Revision._

POPULATION BY AGE AND SEX
(UN estimates at mid-2013)

	Males	Females	Total
0–14	1,058,916	1,016,158	2,075,074
15–64	2,054,595	2,071,771	4,126,366
65 and over	112,882	144,588	257,470
Total	**3,226,393**	**3,232,517**	**6,458,910**

Source: UN, _World Population Prospects: The 2010 Revision._

PROVINCES
(population at mid-2011, official estimates)

	Area (sq km)	Population	Density (per sq km)
Vientiane (municipality) . . .	3,920	783,032	199.8
Phongsali	16,270	178,006	10.9
Luang Namtha	9,325	168,140	18.0
Oudomxay	15,370	307,065	20.0
Bokeo	6,196	169,807	27.4
Luang Prabang	16,875	455,532	27.0
Houaphanh	16,500	325,757	19.7
Sayabouri	16,389	381,908	23.3
Xiangkhouang	16,358	276,242	16.9
Vientiane	22,554	493,593	21.9
Bolikhamsai	14,863	272,794	18.4
Khammouane	16,315	383,099	23.5
Savannakhet	21,774	922,210	42.4
Saravan	10,691	375,517	35.1
Sekong	7,665	100,595	13.1
Champasak	15,415	661,358	42.9
Attopu	10,320	130,402	12.6
Total	**236,800**	**6,385,057**	**27.0**

PRINCIPAL TOWNS
(population at 1995 census)

Viangchan			
(Vientiane—		Xam Nua (Sam	
capital) . .	160,000	Neua) . . .	33,500
Savannakhet			
(Khanthaboury) .	58,500	Luang Prabang .	25,500
		Thakhek	
Pakxe (Paksé) . .	47,000	(Khammouane) .	22,500

Source: Stefan Helders, _World Gazetteer_ (internet www.world-gazetteer.com).

Mid-2011 (incl. suburbs, UN estimate): Vientiane 810,054 (Source: UN, _World Urbanization Prospects: The 2011 Revision_).

BIRTHS AND DEATHS
(annual averages, UN estimates)

	1995–2000	2000–05	2005–10
Birth rate (per 1,000)	33.6	27.8	24.1
Death rate (per 1,000)	9.4	7.9	6.6

Source: UN, _World Population Prospects: The 2010 Revision._

Life expectancy (years at birth): 67.4 (males 66.0; females 68.9) in 2011 (Source: World Bank, World Development Indicators database).

ECONOMICALLY ACTIVE POPULATION
('000 persons in 2003)

	Total
Agriculture, etc.	2,085
Industry	235
Services	217
Total employed	**2,537**
Unemployed	136
Total labour force	**2,673**

2005 ('000 persons): Agriculture 2,091; Total employed 2,664; Unemployed 38; Total labour force 2,701.

Source: Asian Development Bank.

Mid-2013 (estimates in '000): Agriculture, etc. 2,534; Total labour force 3,407 (Source: FAO).

Health and Welfare

KEY INDICATORS

Total fertility rate (children per woman, 2010)	2.7
Under-5 mortality rate (per 1,000 live births, 2010) . . .	54
HIV/AIDS (% of persons aged 15–49, 2009)	0.2
Physicians (per 1,000 head, 2005)	0.3
Hospital beds (per 1,000 head, 2010)	0.7
Health expenditure (2009): US $ per head (PPP)	92
Health expenditure (2009): % of GDP	4.3
Health expenditure (2009): public (% of total)	28.3
Access to adequate water (% of persons, 2010)	67
Access to adequate sanitation (% of persons, 2010)	63
Total carbon dioxide emissions ('000 metric tons, 2008) . .	1,532.8
Carbon dioxide emissions per head (metric tons, 2008) . .	0.3
Human Development Index (2011): ranking	138
Human Development Index (2011): value	0.524

For sources and definitions, see explanatory note on p. vi.

Agriculture

PRINCIPAL CROPS
('000 metric tons)

	2009	2010	2011
Rice, paddy	3,145	3,071	3,066
Maize	1,134	1,021	1,098
Potatoes*	40	39	33
Sweet potatoes	171	226	237
Cassava (Manioc)	153	500	743
Sugar cane	434	819	1,222
Watermelons	115	106	137
Cantaloupes and other melons*	40	42	54
Bananas*	56	52	53
Oranges*	49	45	40
Tangerines, mandarins, clementines and satsumas*	44	41	38
Pineapples	46	42	49*
Coffee, green	46	47*	47*
Tobacco, unmanufactured	26†	24*	25*

* FAO estimate(s).
† Unofficial figure.

Aggregate production ('000 metric tons, may include official, semi-official or estimated data): Total cereals 4,279 in 2009, 4,092 in 2010, 4,164 in 2011; Total vegetables (incl. melons) 1,203 in 2009, 1,108 in 2010, 1,431 in 2011; Total fruits (excl. melons) 286 in 2009, 266 in 2010, 250 in 2011.

Source: FAO.

LIVESTOCK
('000 head, year ending September)

	2009	2010	2011
Horses*	31	31	31
Cattle	1,430	1,474	1,520*
Buffaloes	1,178	1,186	1,186*
Pigs	2,554	2,752	2,965*
Goats	339	367	431
Chickens	22,529	25,105	27,000*
Ducks*	3,300	3,200	3,350

* FAO estimate(s).
Source: FAO.

LIVESTOCK PRODUCTS
('000 metric tons, FAO estimates)

	2009	2010	2011
Cattle meat	25.7	25.8	26.5
Buffalo meat	19.3	19.5	19.5
Pig meat	62.0	59.4	64.0
Chicken meat	17.6	19.6	20.4
Cows' milk	7.2	7.0	7.0
Hen eggs	14.8	15.0	15.0

Source: FAO.

Forestry

ROUNDWOOD REMOVALS
('000 cubic metres, excl. bark, FAO estimates)

	2009	2010	2011
Sawlogs, veneer logs and logs for sleepers	86	86	86
Other industrial wood	132	132	132
Fuel wood	5,946	5,948	5,935
Total	6,164	6,166	6,153

Source: FAO.

SAWNWOOD PRODUCTION
('000 cubic metres, incl. railway sleepers)

	2003	2004	2005
Total (all broadleaved)	125	125	130

2006–11: Production assumed to be unchanged from 2005 (FAO estimate).
Source: FAO.

Fishing
('000 metric tons, live weight)

	2008*	2009*	2010
Capture	29.2	30.0	30.9
Cyprinids	4.4	4.5	4.9
Other freshwater fishes	24.8	25.5	26.0
Aquaculture	64.3	75.0	82.1*
Common carp	4.8	5.6	6.1*
Roho labeo	4.4	5.1	5.6*
Mrigal carp	3.9	4.5	4.9*
Bighead carp	5.4	6.3	6.9*
Silver carp	6.6	7.6	8.4*
Nile tilapia	16.1	18.8	20.6*
Total catch	93.5	105.0	113.0*

Source: FAO.
* FAO estimate(s).

Mining
('000 metric tons unless otherwise indicated)

	2008	2009	2010
Coal (all grades)*	600.0	600.0	600.0
Gemstones, sapphire ('000 carats)*	1,200.0	1,200.0	1,200.0
Gold (kg)	4,333	5,033	5,061
Gypsum*	775.0	775.0	775.0
Salt*	35.0	35.0	35.0
Copper (metric tons)†	64,075	67,561	64,241
Tin (metric tons)*†	450	240	350

* Estimates.
† Figures refer to metal content.
Source: US Geological Survey.

Industry

SELECTED PRODUCTS

	2008	2009	2010
Beer ('000 hectolitres)	1,363	1,391	2,391
Soft drinks ('000 hectolitres)	270	273	430
Cigarettes (million packs)	136	137	212
Garments (million pieces)	53	51	61
Plastic products (metric tons)	7,625	7,750	11,271
Detergent (metric tons)	1,613	1,713	2,112
Agricultural tools ('000 metric tons)	46,500	52,750	61,579
Nails (metric tons)	2,225	2,313	2,590
Bricks (million)	266	269	771
Hydroelectric energy (million kWh)	3,705	3,428	8,623
Tobacco (metric tons)	4,738	5,063	5,908
Plywood (million sheets)	996	1,009	3,645

Source: Ministry of Industry and Commerce, Vientiane.

Finance

CURRENCY AND EXCHANGE RATES

Monetary Units
100 at (cents) = 1 new kip.

Sterling, Dollar and Euro Equivalents (29 June 2012)
£1 sterling = 12,518.7 new kips;
US $1 = 8,023.3 new kips;
€1 = 10,101.3 new kips;
100,000 new kips = £7.99 = $12.46 = €9.90.

Average Exchange Rate (new kips per US $)
2009	8,516.1
2010	8,258.8
2011	8,030.1

Note: In September 1995 a policy of 'floating' exchange rates was adopted, with commercial banks permitted to set their rates.

GENERAL BUDGET
('000 million new kips, year ending 30 September)*

Revenue†	2009/10	2010/11‡	2011/12‡
Tax revenue	7,503	8,287	10,058
Profits tax	1,125	1,474	2,003
Income tax	462	486	500
Turnover tax	1,869	2,028	2,240
Excise tax	1,687	1,832	2,166
Import duties	832	1,010	1,208
Timber royalties	560	607	894
Other taxes	968	849	1,047
Non-tax revenue	1,035	1,042	1,282
Total	**8,538**	**9,329**	**11,340**

Expenditure	2009/10	2010/11‡	2011/12‡
Current expenditure	6,656	7,786	9,112
Wages and salaries	2,525	2,947	3,450
Transfers	1,698	1,917	2,131
Interest	398	498	553
Other recurrent expenditure	2,034	2,424	2,979
Net acquisition of non-financial assets	5,646	4,553	5,385
Domestically financed	3,271	1,703	2,640
Foreign-financed and net onlending	2,376	2,850	2,744
Total	**12,302**	**12,339**	**14,497**

* Since 1992 there has been a unified budget covering the operations of the central Government, provincial administrations and state enterprises.
† Excluding grants received ('000 million new kips): 1,242 in 2009/10; 1,188 in 2010/11 (budget forecasts); 1,169 in 2011/12 (budget forecasts).
‡ Budget forecasts.

Source: IMF, *Lao People's Democratic Republic—Staff Report for the 2012 Article IV Consultation.* (October 2012).

INTERNATIONAL RESERVES
(US $ million at 31 December)

	2009	2010	2011
Gold (national valuation)	9.99	9.99	16.00
IMF special drawing rights	80.06	78.65	78.41
Foreign exchange	528.54	624.70	662.80
Total	**618.59**	**713.34**	**757.21**

Source: IMF, *International Financial Statistics.*

MONEY SUPPLY
(million new kips at 31 December*)

	2008	2009	2010
Currency outside banks	2,223,230	3,085,780	3,790,530
Demand deposits at commercial banks	1,491,680	1,704,000	2,555,300
Total (incl. others)	**3,715,330**	**4,790,490**	**6,349,830**

* Figures rounded to the nearest ten million.

Source: IMF, *International Financial Statistics.*

2011 ('000 million new kips at 31 December): Currency outside banks 4,899.7; Demand deposits at commercial banks 2,347.0; *Total* 7,246.7 (Source: Asian Development Bank).

COST OF LIVING
(Consumer Price Index; base: December 1999 = 100)

	2008	2009	2010
Food	231.9	237.3	258.6
Others	196.2	191.9	200.4
All items	**212.1**	**212.4**	**225.1**

2011 (base December 2010 = 100): Food 108.8; All items (incl. others) 106.0.
Source: Asian Development Bank.

NATIONAL ACCOUNTS

Gross Domestic Product by Economic Activity
('000 million new kips at current prices)

	2008	2009	2010
Agriculture, hunting, forestry and fishing	13,889.3	14,510.8	16,056.0
Mining and quarrying	4,595.0	3,289.4	4,273.4
Manufacturing	3,998.8	4,833.2	5,231.7
Electricity, gas and water	1,172.9	1,280.9	2,238.9
Construction	2,187.3	2,265.4	2,913.2
Wholesale and retail trade	8,741.8	9,333.2	11,485.2
Transport, storage and communications	2,120.0	2,309.6	2,847.4
Finance	1,483.5	1,619.9	2,040.1
Government services	2,123.7	2,171.9	2,527.0
Other services	2,812.7	2,985.3	3,327.2
Sub-total	**43,125.0**	**44,599.5**	**52,940.3**
Taxes on imports	3,089.7	2,962.8	3,582.3
GDP in purchasers' values	**46,214.7**	**47,562.2**	**56,522.6**

Source: Asian Development Bank.

BALANCE OF PAYMENTS
(US $ million)

	2009	2010	2011
Exports of goods	1,052.7	1,746.4	1,854.0
Imports of goods	−1,461.1	−2,060.4	−2,422.9
Balance on goods	**−408.4**	**−314.0**	**−568.9**
Services and primary income (net)	214.6	164.7	195.5
Balance on goods, services and primary income	**−193.8**	**−149.3**	**−373.4**
Secondary income (net)	132.9	178.6	222.8
Current balance	**−60.9**	**29.3**	**−150.6**
Direct investment (net)	318.6	278.8	300.7
Portfolio investment (net)	—	53.8	11.0
Other investments (net)	325.8	69.3	154.1
Net errors and omissions	−559.8	−327.7	−372.4
Reserves and related items	**23.7**	**103.5**	**−57.2**

Source: Asian Development Bank.

External Trade

PRINCIPAL COMMODITIES
(US $ million)

Imports c.i.f.	2006	2007	2008*
Petroleum	208.7	311.0	421.8
Capital goods	728.1	1,084.8	1,171.8
Materials for garments industry .	98.7	80.3	143.7
Electricity	28.0	37.4	43.3
Total (incl. others)	1,589.3	2,156.1	2,816.1

Exports f.o.b.	2006	2007	2008*
Timber	195.6	179.0	131.4
Coffee	9.8	28.9	18.5
Garments	151.2	152.8	189.7
Electricity	122.6	114.1	118.3
Copper	409.3	446.0	620.3
Gold (incl. re-exports) . . .	117.9	93.2	118.9
Total (incl. others)	1,132.6	1,320.7	1,638.6

* Estimates.

Source: IMF, *Lao People's Democratic Republic: Statistical Appendix* (September 2009).

PRINCIPAL TRADING PARTNERS
(US $ million)

Imports	2009	2010	2011
Belgium	30.5	20.4	34.2
China, People's Republic . . .	413.9	524.1	519.3
France	62.7	15.7	146.7
Germany	18.1	21.4	37.9
Hong Kong	18.5	30.0	32.4
Japan	83.5	68.3	85.9
Korea, Republic	61.3	123.5	169.9
Singapore	40.4	25.3	38.2
Thailand*	1,800.5	2,348.4	3,035.0
Viet Nam	186.2	218.3	244.5
Total (incl. others)	2,892.5	3,575.3	4,603.0

Exports	2009	2010	2011
Belgium	14.7	17.1	16.4
China, People's Republic . . .	306.0	510.9	729.0
France	12.8	15.7	16.8
Germany	48.0	53.1	71.3
Japan	24.4	34.2	88.3
Korea, Republic	15.9	18.2	3.9
Thailand*	423.7	689.7	1,028.5
United Kingdom	62.3	69.9	95.1
USA	41.7	56.3	54.8
Viet Nam	225.9	265.2	297.1
Total (incl. others)	1,521.0	2,195.9	2,959.4

* Trade with Thailand may be overestimated, as it may include goods in transit to and from other countries.

Note: Data reflect the IMF's direction of trade methodology and, as a result, the totals may not be equal to those presented for trade in commodities.

Source: Asian Development Bank.

Transport

ROAD TRAFFIC
(motor vehicles in use at 31 December, estimates)

	1994	1995	1996
Passenger cars	18,240	17,280	16,320
Motorcycles and mopeds . . .	169,000	200,000	231,000

2007: Passenger cars 12,822; Buses and coaches 6,411; Lorries and vans 108,984; Motorcycles and mopeds 506,454.

Source: IRF, *World Road Statistics.*

SHIPPING
Inland Waterways
(traffic)

	2007	2008	2009
Freight ('000 metric tons) . . .	767.0	883.0	961.0
Freight ton-kilometres (million) .	60.9	67.6	69.5
Passengers ('000)	1,953.0	1,811.0	1,810.0
Passenger-kilometres (million) .	50.5	48.9	48.7

Source: Ministry of Communications, Transport, Post and Construction, Vientiane.

Merchant Fleet
(registered at 31 December)

	2007	2008	2009
Number of vessels	2	1	1
Displacement ('000 grt) . . .	2.9	0.5	0.5

Source: IHS Fairplay, *World Fleet Statistics.*

Flag Registered Fleet (at 31 December): Number of vessels 1 in 2010–12; Displacement (grt) 1,091 in 2010–12 (Source: Lloyd's List Intelligence (www.lloydslistintelligence.com)).

CIVIL AVIATION
(traffic on scheduled services)

	2007	2008	2009
Kilometres flown (million) . .	4	4	4
Passengers carried ('000) . . .	328	323	303
Passenger-kilometres (million) .	144	142	133
Total ton-kilometres (million) .	15	14	13

Source: UN, *Statistical Yearbook.*

2010: Passengers carried ('000) 645 (Source: World Bank, World Development Indicators database).

Tourism

FOREIGN VISITOR ARRIVALS
(incl. excursionists)

Country of nationality	2008	2009	2010
Australia	28,180	24,209	30,538
China, People's Republic . . .	105,852	128,226	161,854
France	39,077	31,775	44,844
Japan	31,569	28,081	34,076
Thailand	891,448	1,274,064	1,517,064
United Kingdom	36,038	27,044	37,272
USA	54,717	39,339	49,782
Viet Nam	351,384	296,763	431,011
Total (incl. others)	1,736,787	2,008,363	2,513,028

Tourism receipts (US $ million, excl. passenger transport): 268 in 2009; 382 in 2010; 406 in 2011 (provisional) (Source: World Tourism Organization).

Communications Media

	2009	2010	2011
Telephones ('000 main lines in use)	100.2	103.1	107.6
Mobile cellular telephones ('000 subscribers)	3,234.6	4,003.4	5,480.9
Internet subscribers ('000) . .	15.6	n.a.	n.a.
Broadband subscribers ('000) . .	8.4	12.0	41.7

Sources: International Telecommunication Union.

Education

(2011/12 unless otherwise indicated)

	Institutions	Teachers	Students
Pre-primary	1,358	5,623	103,200
Primary	8,902	34,000	900,000
Secondary:			
lower	844	24,000	345,000
upper	34	6,000†	143,000
vocational	39	884	18,859
University level	5	3,236	70,231
Other higher	108	1,655	40,134

* 2008/09 figure.

Source: Ministry of Education, Vientiane.

Pupil-teacher ratio (primary education, UNESCO estimate): 28.8 in 2009/10 (Source: UNESCO Institute for Statistics).

Adult literacy rate (UNESCO estimates): 73.2% (males 80.0%; females 66.6%) in 2007 (Source: UNESCO Institute for Statistics).

Directory

The Government

HEAD OF STATE

President of State: Lt-Gen. CHOUMMALY SAYASONE (elected 8 June 2006; re-elected 15 June 2011).

Vice-President: BOUNGNANG VOLACHIT.

COUNCIL OF MINISTERS
(May 2013)

The Council of Ministers comprises members of the Phak Pasason Pativat Lao (Lao People's Revolutionary Party—LPRP).

Prime Minister: THONGSING THAMMAVONG.

Deputy Prime Minister and Minister of Foreign Affairs: THONGLOUN SISOLIT.

Deputy Prime Minister and Minister of National Defence: Lt-Gen. DOUANGCHAI PHICHIT.

Deputy Prime Ministers: Maj.-Gen. ASANG LAOLI, SOMSAVAT LENGSAVAT.

Minister of Finance: PHOUPHET KHAMPHOUNVONG.

Minister of Public Security: Dr THONGBANH SENGAPHONE.

Minister of Justice: CHALEUN YIAPAOHEU.

Minister of Agriculture and Forestry: VILAYVANH PHOMKHE.

Minister of Post, Telecommunication and Communication: HIEM PHOMMACHANH.

Minister of Industry and Commerce: Dr NAM VIYAKET.

Minister of Information, Culture and Tourism: Dr BOSENGKHAM VONGDARA.

Minister of Labour and Social Welfare: ONECHANH THAMMAVONG.

Minister of Education and Sports: Dr PHANKHAM VIPHAVANH.

Minister of Public Health: Dr EKSAVANG VONGVICHIT.

Minister of Energy and Mining: SOULIVONG DALAVONG.

Minister of Planning and Investment: SOMDY DOUANGDY.

Minister of Interior: KHAMPANE PHILAVONG.

Minister of Natural Resources and Environment: NOULIN SINBANDITH.

Minister of Public Works and Transport: SOMMAD PHOLSENA.

Minister of Science and Technology: Dr BOVIENGKHAM VONGDARA.

Minister to the Office of the President: PHONGSAVATH BOUPHA.

Ministers to the Office of the Prime Minister: SINLAVONG KHOUPHAYTHOUNE, Dr BOUNTIEM PHITSAMAY, BOUNPHENG MOUNPHOSAY, KHEMPHENG PHOLSENA, Dr DOUANGSAVAT SOUPHANAOUVONG, BOUNHEUANG DUANGPHACHANH.

Governor of the Central Bank: SOMPAO PHAYSITH.

MINISTRIES

Office of the President: rue Lane Xang, Vientiane; tel. (21) 214200; fax (21) 214208.

Office of the Prime Minister: Ban Sisavat, Vientiane; tel. (21) 213653; fax (21) 213560.

Ministry of Agriculture and Forestry: Ban Phonxay, Vientiane; tel. (21) 412359; fax (21) 412344; internet www.maf.gov.la.

Ministry of Education and Sports: 1 rue Lane Xang, BP 67, Vientiane; tel. (21) 216013; fax (21) 216006; e-mail esitc@moe.gov.la; internet www.moe.gov.la.

Ministry of Energy and Mining: rue Nongbone, Ban Hatsady, BP 4708, Vientiane; tel. (21) 414319; fax (21) 413013.

Ministry of Finance: 23 rue Singha, Ban Phonxay, BP 24, Vientiane; tel. and fax (21) 900798; e-mail ict@mof.gov.la; internet www.mof.gov.la.

Ministry of Foreign Affairs: 23 rue Singha, Ban Phonxay, Vientiane; tel. (21) 413148; fax (21) 414009; e-mail ict@mofa.gov.la; internet www.mofa.gov.la.

Ministry of Industry and Commerce: rue Phonxay, BP 4107, Vientiane; tel. (21) 412009; fax (21) 412434; internet www.moic.gov.la.

Ministry of Information, Culture and Tourism: rue Setthathirath, Ban Xiengnyeun, Chanthaboury, BP 122, Vientiane; tel. (21) 212406; fax (21) 212408; e-mail email@mic.gov.la.

Ministry of Interior: rue Samsenthai, Vientiane; tel. (21) 212529.

Ministry of Justice: ave Lane Xang, Vientiane; tel. (21) 414105; fax (21) 414102.

Ministry of Labour and Social Welfare: rue Pangkham, Ban Sisaket, BP 347, Vientiane; tel. (21) 213000; fax (21) 213287.

Ministry of National Defence: ave Kaysone Phomvihane, Ban Phone Kheng, Vientiane; tel. (21) 911017; fax (21) 911118; e-mail kongthap@yahoo.com; internet www.kongthap.gov.la.

Ministry of Natural Resources and Environment: That Dam, Vientiane; tel. (21) 263799; fax (21) 260984; e-mail monre@monre.gov.la; internet www.monre.gov.la.

Ministry of Planning and Investment: rue Luang Prabang, Vientiane 01001; tel. (21) 218377; fax (21) 215491; internet www.investlaos.gov.la.

Ministry of Post, Telecommunication and Communication: ave Lane Xang, Ban Hatsadi, Chanthaboury, Vientiane; tel. (21) 218897; fax (21) 285257; e-mail info@mpt.gov.la; internet www.mpt.gov.la.

Ministry of Public Health: rue Samsenthai, Ban That Khao, Sisattanak, Vientiane; tel. (21) 214000; fax (21) 214003; e-mail contact@moh.gov.la.

Ministry of Public Security: rue Nongbone, Xaysettha, Vientiane; tel. (21) 951084.

Ministry of Public Works and Transport: rue Dongpalane, Ponesavanh, Sisattanak, Vientiane; tel. (21) 412285; fax (21) 451826.

Ministry of Science and Technology: Vientiane.

Legislature

The National Assembly was expanded from 115 to 132 members in 2011. At the election held on 30 April 128 candidates of the Lao People's Revolutionary Party (LPRP) and four independents were elected to the legislature.

President of the National Assembly: PANY YATHOTOU.

Vice-Presidents: Dr XAYSOMPHONE PHOMVIHANE, SOMPHANH PHENG-KHAMMY.

Political Organizations

COMMUNIST PARTY

Phak Pasason Pativat Lao (Lao People's Revolutionary Party—LPRP): Vientiane; f. 1955; est. as People's Party of Laos; reorg. under present name in 1972; 191,700 mems (2011); Cen. Cttee of 61 full mems elected at Ninth Party Congress in March 2011; Sec.-Gen. Lt-Gen. CHOUMMALY SAYASONE.

Political Bureau (Politburo)

Full members: Lt-Gen. CHOUMMALY SAYASONE, THONGSING THAM-MAVONG, BOUNGNANG VOLACHIT, Maj.-Gen. ASANG LAOLI, THONGLOUN SISOLIT, Lt-Gen. DOUANGCHAI PHICHIT, SOMSAVAT LENGSAVAT, PANY YATHOTOU, Dr BOUNTHONG CHITMANY, Dr BOUNPONE BOUTTANAVONG, Dr PHANKHAM VIPHAVANH.

OTHER POLITICAL ORGANIZATIONS

Lao Front for National Construction (LFNC): Thanon Khou-vieng, Ban Sisakhet, Chanthaboury, Vientiane; tel. and fax (21) 213752; f. 1979; est. to replace Lao Liberal Front and Lao Patriotic Front; comprises representatives of various political and social groups, of which the LPRP is the dominant force; fosters national solidarity; 165-mem. cttee elected in July 2011; Chair. PHANDOUANG-CHIT VONGSA; Vice-Chair. TONG YERTHOR.

Numerous factions are in armed opposition to the Government. The principal groups are:

Democratic Chao Fa Party of Laos: led by PA KAO HER until his death in Oct. 2002; Pres. SOUA HER; Vice-Pres. TENG TANG.

Free Democratic Lao National Salvation Force: based in Thailand.

United Front for the Liberation of Laos: Leader PHOUNGPHET PHANARETH.

United Front for the National Liberation of the Lao People: f. 1980; led by Gen. PHOUMI NOSAVAN until his death in 1985.

United Lao National Liberation Front: Sayabouri Province; comprises an est. 8,000 mems, mostly Hmong (Meo) tribesmen; Sec.-Gen. VANG SHUR.

Diplomatic Representation

EMBASSIES IN LAOS

Australia: rue Thadeua, Ban Wat Nak, Km 4, Sisattanak, Vientiane; tel. (21) 353800; fax (21) 353801; e-mail austemb.laos@dfat.gov.au; internet www.laos.embassy.gov.au; Ambassador LYNDA WORTHAISONG.

Brunei: Unit 12, 30 Lao-Thai Friendship Rd, Ban Thoungkang, Sisattanak, Vientiane; tel. (21) 352294; fax (21) 352290; e-mail vientiane.laos@mfa.gov.bn; Chargé d'affaires a.i. ANI SURAINI Dato' Haji ABDUL AZIZ.

Cambodia: rue Thadeua, Km 2, BP 34, Vientiane; tel. (21) 314952; fax (21) 314951; e-mail recamlao@laotel.com; Ambassador DAN YI.

China, People's Republic: rue Wat Nak, Sisattanak, BP 898, Vientiane; tel. (21) 315100; fax (21) 315104; e-mail chinaemb_la@mfa.gov.cn; internet la.china-embassy.org/chn; Ambassador BU JIANGUO.

Cuba: rue Bourichanne 422, Xaysettha, Vientiane; tel. (21) 453813; fax (21) 453814; e-mail embajada@laotel.com; internet www.cubadiplomatica.cu/laos; Ambassador WALDO REYES SARDIÑAS.

France: rue Setthathirath, BP 06, Vientiane; tel. (21) 267400; fax (21) 267439; e-mail contact@ambafrance-laos.org; internet www.ambafrance-laos.org; Ambassador YVES CARMONA.

Germany: rue Sok Paluang 26, Sisattanak, BP 314, Vientiane; tel. (21) 312110; fax (21) 351152; e-mail info@vientiane.diplo.de; internet www.vientiane.diplo.de; Ambassador ROBERT VON RIMSCHA.

India: 2 Ban Wat Nak, rue Thadeua, Km 3, Sisattanak, BP 225, Vientiane; tel. (21) 352301; fax (21) 352300; e-mail indiaemb@laotel.com; internet indemblao.nic.in; Ambassador C. GURURAJ RAO.

Indonesia: ave Kaysone Phomvihane, BP 277, Vientiane; tel. (21) 413909; fax (21) 214828; e-mail kbrivte@laotel.com; internet www.kbrivientiane.org; Ambassador KRIA FAHMI PASARIBU.

Japan: rue Sisangvone, Vientiane; tel. (21) 414401; fax (21) 414406; internet www.la.emb-japan.go.jp; Ambassador JUNKO YOKOTA.

Korea, Democratic People's Republic: Ban Wat Nak, Vientiane; tel. (21) 315261; fax (21) 315260; Ambassador HAN PONG HO.

Korea, Republic: Lao-Thai Friendship Rd, Ban Wat Nak, Sisatta-nak, BP 7567, Vientiane; tel. (21) 352031; fax (21) 352035; e-mail laos@mofat.go.kr; internet lao.mofat.go.kr; Ambassador LEE GUN-TAE.

Malaysia: 23 rue Singha, Ban Phonxay, BP 789, Vientiane; tel. (21) 414205; fax (21) 414201; e-mail malvntian@kln.gov.my; internet www.kln.gov.my/web/lao_vientiane; Ambassador Dato' THAN TAI HING.

Mongolia: Ban Wat Nak, Km 3, BP 370, Vientiane; tel. (21) 315220; fax (21) 315221; e-mail embmong@laotel.com; Ambassador TÜVA-DENDORJIIN JANABAZAR.

Myanmar: Lao-Thai Friendship Rd, Ban Wat Nak, Sisattanak, BP 11, Vientiane; tel. (21) 314910; fax (21) 314913; e-mail mevlao@laotel.com; Ambassador KYAW SOE WIN.

Philippines: Ban Saphanthong Kang, Sisattanak, BP 2415, Vientiane; tel. (21) 452490; fax (21) 452493; e-mail vientiane.pe@dfa.gov.ph; Ambassador MARIA LUMEN ISLETA.

Russia: rue Thadeua, Ban Thaphalanxay, Km 4, BP 490, Vientiane; tel. (21) 312222; fax (21) 312210; e-mail embrus_lao@mail.ru; internet www.laos.mid.ru; Ambassador OLEG V. K. KABANOV.

Singapore: Unit 4, rue Thadeua, Ban Wat Nak, Km 3, Sisattanak, Vientiane; tel. (21) 353939; fax (21) 353938; e-mail singemb_vte@sgmfa.gov.sg; internet www.mfa.gov.sg/vientiane; Ambassador KANG SIEW KHENG.

Thailand: ave Kaysone Phomvihane, Xaysettha, Vientiane; tel. (21) 214581; fax (21) 214580; e-mail thaivte@mfa.go.th; internet www.thaiembassy.org/vientiane; Ambassador PISANU CHANVITAN.

United Kingdom: rue Nehru, Phonexay, Xaysettha, Vientiane; e-mail bevientiane@gmail.com; internet www.gov.uk/government/world/laos; Ambassador PHILIP MALONE.

USA: 19 rue Bartholonie, That Dam, BP 114, Vientiane; tel. (21) 267000; fax (21) 267190; e-mail webmastervientiane@state.gov; internet laos.usembassy.gov; Ambassador KAREN BREVARD STEWART.

Viet Nam: Unit 85, 23 rue Singha, Ban Phonxay, Xaysettha, Vientiane; tel. (21) 990986; fax (21) 416720; e-mail vnemba.la@mofa.gov.vn; internet www.mofa.gov.vn/vnemb.la; Ambassador NGUYEN MANH HUNG.

Judicial System

People's Supreme Court: the highest judiciary body in Laos; supervises decisions made by the People's Provincial and Municipal Courts and military courts; judges are elected by the National Assembly Standing Committee; with the President being elected by the National Assembly on the recommendation of the Standing Committee; Pres. KHAMPANH SITTHIDAMPHA.

Office of the Public Prosecutor: monitors the observance of laws by ministries, government organizations, local administrative bodies, state employees and citizens; supervises public prosecutors at the lower (province, prefecture, district) level and military prosecutors; the Public Prosecutor-General is appointed by the National Assembly on the recommendation of the Standing Committee; Public Prosecutor-General KHAMSAN SOUVONG.

Religion

The 1991 Constitution guarantees freedom of religious belief. The principal religion of Laos is Buddhism.

BUDDHISM

Lao Unified Buddhists' Association: Maha Kudy, Wat That Luang, Vientiane; f. 1964; Pres. (vacant); Sec.-Gen. Rev. SIHO SIHAVONG.

CHRISTIANITY

The Roman Catholic Church

For ecclesiastical purposes, Laos comprises four Apostolic Vicariates. At 31 December 2007 an estimated 0.6% of the population were adherents.

Episcopal Conference of Laos and Cambodia
c/o 787 Preah Monivong Blvd, Boeung Trabek, Chamkarmon, Phnom-Penh.
f. 1971; Pres. Mgr LOUIS-MARIE LING MANGKHANEKHOUN (Vicar of Paksé).

Vicar Apostolic of Luang Prabang: (vacant), Evêché, BP 74, Luang Prabang.

Vicar Apostolic of Paksé: Mgr LOUIS-MARIE LING MANGKHANE-KHOUN (Titular Bishop of Proconsulari), Centre Catholique, BP 77, Paksé, Champasak; tel. (31) 212879; fax (31) 251439.

Vicar Apostolic of Savannakhet: Fr JEAN MARIE PRIDA INTHIRATH (Titular Bishop of Lemfocta), Centre Catholique, BP 12, Thakhek, Khammouane; tel. (51) 212184; fax (51) 213070.

Vicar Apostolic of Vientiane: Mgr JEAN KHAMSÉ VITHAVONG (Titular Bishop of Moglaena), Centre Catholique, BP 113, Vientiane; tel. (21) 216593; fax (21) 215085.

The Anglican Communion

Laos is within the jurisdiction of the Anglican Bishop of Singapore.

The Protestant Church

Lao Evangelical Church: BP 4200, Vientiane; tel. (21) 169136; Exec. Pres. Rev. KHAMPHONE KOUTHAPANYA.

BAHÁ'Í FAITH

National Spiritual Assembly: BP 189, Vientiane; tel. and fax (21) 216996; e-mail usme@laotel.com; f. 1956; Sec. SUSADA SENCHANTHISAY.

The Press

Aloun Mai (New Dawn): rue That Luang, Ban Nongbone, Xaysettha, Vientiane; tel. (21) 413029; fax (21) 413037; f. 1985; quarterly; theoretical and political organ of the LPRP; Editor-in-Chief SISOUK PHILAVONG.

Finance: rue That Luang, Ban Phonxay, Vientiane; tel. (21) 412401; fax (21) 412415; organ of Ministry of Finance.

Heng Ngan: 87 ave Lane Xang, BP 780, Vientiane; tel. (21) 212756; fax (21) 219750; fortnightly; organ of the Federation of Lao Trade Unions; Editor CHANSING KOKKEOBOUNMA.

Khao Tourakit (Business News): rue Sihom, Ban Sihom, Chanthaboury, Vientiane; tel. (21) 219244; fax (21) 219223; e-mail bsnews@laotel.com; f. 1999; fortnightly; organ of the Lao National Chamber of Commerce and Industry; Editor-in-Chief SOMCHIT THIPTHIENGTHAM.

Khaokila (Sports Daily News): Ban Mixay, Chanthaboury, Vientiane; tel. (21) 252908; fax (21) 252909; e-mail khaokila@hotmail.com; f. 1999; Editor-in-Chief SUKSAKHONE SIPRASEUTH.

Lao Dong (Labour): 87 ave Lane Xang, Vientiane; f. 1986; fortnightly; organ of the Federation of Lao Trade Unions; circ. 46,000.

Laos: 80 rue Setthathirath, BP 3770, Vientiane; tel. (21) 21447; fax (21) 21445; quarterly; published in Lao and English; illustrated; Editor V. PHOMCHANHEUANG; English Editor O. PHRAKHAMSAY.

Meying Lao: rue Manthatoarath, BP 59, Vientiane; e-mail chansoda@hotmail.com; f. 1980; monthly; women's magazine; organ of the Lao Women's Union; Editor-in-Chief VATSADY KHUTNGOTHA; Editor CHANSODA PHONETHIP; circ. 7,000.

Noum Lao (Lao Youth): rue Phonthan, Ban Phonthan Neua, Xaysettha, Vientiane; tel. (21) 951067; fax (21) 416727; f. 1979; fortnightly; organ of the Lao People's Revolutionary Youth Union; Editor KHANKAB BUDARAT; circ. 1,500.

Pasason Van Athit: rue Pangkham, Ban Xiengyeun Thong, Chanthaboury, Vientiane; tel. (21) 212471; fax (21) 212470; weekly; Editor THONGLITH LIEMXAYYACHAK; circ. 2,000.

Pasason (The People): 80 rue Setthathirath, BP 110, Vientiane; tel. (21) 212466; fax (21) 212470; e-mail infonews@pasaxon.org.la; internet www.pasaxon.org.la; f. 1940; daily; Lao; organ of the Cen. Cttee of the LPRP; Editor-in-Chief BOUALAPHANH THANPHILOM; circ. 28,000.

Pathet Lao: 80 rue Setthathirath, Vientiane; tel. (21) 212447; f. 2001; daily; Lao and English; organ of the Lao News Agency, Khao San Pathet Lao (KPL); Editor KHEMTHONG SANOUBAN.

Sciences and Technics: Science, Technology and the Environment Agency (STEA), BP 2279, Vientiane; f. 1991; est. as Technical Science Magazine; quarterly; organ of the Ministry of Science and Technology; scientific research and development.

Siang Khong Gnaovason Song Thanva (Voice of the 2 December Youths): Vientiane; monthly; youth journal.

Sieng Khene Lao: Vientiane; monthly; organ of the Lao Writers' Association.

Suksa Mai: Vientiane; e-mail sm.touk1@gmail.com; monthly; organ of the Ministry of Education.

Valasan Khosana (Propaganda Journal): Vientiane; f. 1987; organ of the Cen. Cttee of the LPRP.

Vannasinh: Vientiane; monthly; literature magazine.

Vientiane Mai (New Vientiane): 36 rue Setthathirath, BP 989, Vientiane; tel. (21) 212623; fax (21) 215989; e-mail admin@vientianemai.net; internet www.vientianemai.net; f. 1975; morning daily; organ of the LPRP Cttee of Vientiane province and city; Editor SOMPHET INTHISARATH; circ. 2,500.

Vientiane Times: rue Pangkham, BP 5723, Vientiane; tel. (21) 216364; fax (21) 216365; e-mail info@vientianetimes.gov.la; internet www.vientianetimes.org.la; f. 1994; daily; English; Editor-in-Chief SAVANKHONE RAZMOUNTRY; circ. 3,000.

Vientiane Tourakit Sangkhom (Vientiane Business-Social): 36 rue Setthathirath, Vientiane; tel. (21) 2623; fax (21) 6365; weekly; publ. in conjunction with Vientiane Mai; Editor SOMPHET INTHISARATH; circ. 2,000.

There is also a newspaper published by the Lao People's Army, and several provinces have their own newsletters.

NEWS AGENCY

Khao San Pathet Lao (Lao News Agency—KPL): 80 rue Setthathirath, BP 3770, Vientiane; tel. (21) 215402; fax (21) 212446; e-mail kplnews@yahoo.com; internet www.kplnet.net; f. 1968; dept of the Ministry of Information, Culture and Tourism; news service for press, radio and television broadcasting; daily bulletins in Lao, English and French; Gen. Dir KHAMSENE PHONGSA; English Editor BOUNLERT LOUANEDOUANGCHANH.

PRESS ASSOCIATION

Lao Journalists' Association (LJA): BP 122, Vientiane; tel. (21) 212420; fax (21) 212408; Pres. Dr BOSENGKHAM VONGDARA; Sec.-Gen. KHAM KHONG KONGVONGSA.

Publishers

Khoualuang Kanphim: 2–6 Khoualuang Market, Vientiane.

Lao-phanit: Ministry of Education, Bureau des Manuels Scolaires, rue Lane Xang, Ban Sisavat, Vientiane; educational, cookery, art, music, fiction.

Pakpassak Kanphin: 9–11 quai Fa-Hguun, Vientiane.

Department of Publishing, Printing, Distribution and Libraries: Ministry of Information, Culture and Tourism, BP 122, Vientiane; tel. (21) 212421; fax (21) 212408; oversees the State Publishing and Book Distribution House and the State Printing Enterprise; Dir NOUPHAY KOUNLAVONG.

Broadcasting and Communications

TELECOMMUNICATIONS

Entreprise de Télécommunications de Laos (ETL): rue Saylom, Ban Saylom, Chanthaboury, Vientiane; tel. (21) 260015; fax (21) 260051; e-mail csd@etllao.com; internet www.etllao.com; state enterprise, telephone, mobile and Voice over Internet Protocol (VoIP) services; Dir-Gen. KHAMMOUANE XOMSIHAPANYA.

Lao Télécommunications Co Ltd: ave Lane Xang, BP 5607, 01000 Vientiane; tel. (21) 244212; fax (21) 241638; e-mail ltc-webmaster@laotel.com; internet laotel.com; f. 1996; jt venture between a subsidiary of Shinawatra Group of Thailand and Entreprises des Postes et Télécommunications de Laos; awarded 25-year contract by Govt in 1996 to undertake all telecommunications projects in Laos; Dir-Gen. THANSAMAY KOMMASITH.

Star Telecom Co Ltd (Unitel): rue Nongbone, Ban Phonxay, Xaysettha, Vientiane; tel. (21) 998888; fax (21) 988988; e-mail startelecom@unitel.com.la; internet www.unitel.com.la; f. 2009; jt venture between Viettel Global Joint Stock Co and Lao Asia Telecom (LAT); operates mobile, fixed-line and internet services; Chair. OULAHA THONGVANHTHA.

VimpelCom Lao Co. Ltd (Beeline): Lane Xang Business Center, 14 ave Lane Xang, Unit 4, Ban Hatsadi, Chanthaboury, BP 4693, Vientiane; tel. 77800700 (mobile); fax 77800701; e-mail customer.care@beeline.la; internet www.beeline.la; f. 2011; CEO ALEXANDER IZOSIMOV.

Regulatory Authority

National Authority of Posts and Telecommunications (NAPT): ave Lane Xang, Vientiane 01000; tel. (21) 219857; fax (21) 219858; e-mail depostel@laotel.com; Dir-Gen. SNITH XAPHAKDY.

BROADCASTING

Radio

In 2010 there were 44 radio stations broadcasting throughout Laos.

Lao National Radio: rue Phangkham, Km 6, BP 310, Vientiane; tel. (21) 212468; fax (21) 212430; e-mail laonradio@lnr.org.la; internet www.lnr.org.la; f. 1960; state-owned; programmes in Lao, French, English, Thai, Khmer and Vietnamese; domestic and international services; Dir-Gen. SIPHA NONGLATH.

Television

A domestic television service began in December 1983.

Lao National Television (TVNL): rue Sivilay, BP 5635, Vientiane; tel. (21) 710067; fax (21) 710182; e-mail tnlinfo@tnl.gov.la; internet www.tnl.gov.la; f. 1983; colour television service; Dir-Gen. BOUNCHOM VONGPHET.

Laos Television 3: BP 860, Vientiane; tel. (21) 315449; fax (21) 215628; f. 1994; est. as IBC Channel 3; 30% govt-owned, 70% owned by Int. Broadcasting Corpn Co Ltd (Thailand); operated by latter; programmes in Lao.

Finance

(cap. = capital; res = reserves; dep. = deposits; br.(s) = branch(es); m. = million)

BANKING

The banking system was reorganized in 1988–89, ending the state monopoly of banking. Some commercial banking functions were transferred from the central bank and the state commercial bank to a new network of autonomous banks. The establishment of joint ventures with foreign financial institutions was permitted.

Central Bank

Banque de la RDP Lao: rue Yonnet, BP 19, Vientiane; tel. (21) 213109; fax (21) 213108; e-mail bol@bol.gov.la; internet www.bol.gov.la; f. 1959; est. as the bank of issue; became Banque Pathetlao 1968; took over the operations of Banque Nationale du Laos 1975; known as Banque d'Etat de la RDP Lao from 1982 until adoption of present name; dep. 23,532,240m. kips (Dec. 2011); Gov. SOMPAO PHAYSITH.

Commercial Banks

Acleda Bank Lao: 372 cnr rues Dongpalane and Dongpaina, Unit 21, Ponesavanh, Sisattanak, Vientiane; tel. (21) 264994; fax (21) 264995; e-mail acledabank@acledabank.com.la; internet www.acledabank.com.la; f. 2008; cap. 220,000m. kips, res 3,809m. kips, dep. 243,297m. kips (Dec. 2011); Chair. CHEA SOK; Pres. and CEO PHON NARIN.

Agriculture Promotion Bank: 58 rue Hengboun, Ban Haysok, BP 5456, Vientiane; tel. (21) 241394; fax (21) 223714; e-mail apblao@laotel.com; internet www.apblao.com.la; Dir BOUANGEUN PHONGSAVATH.

ANZ Vientiane Commercial Bank Ltd: 33 ave Lane Xang, Ban Hatsady, Chanthaboury, Vientiane; tel. (21) 222700; fax (21) 213513; e-mail vccbank@laotel.com; internet www.anz.com/laos; f. 1993; renamed as above in 2007; private jt venture owned by Laotian, Thai, Taiwanese and Australian investors; Man. Dir KERROD THOMAS.

Banque pour le Commerce Extérieur Lao (BCEL): 1 rue Pangkham, Ban Xiengnheun, Chanthaboury, Vientiane; tel. (21) 213200; fax (21) 213202; e-mail bcelhqv@bcel.com.la; internet www.bcel.com.la; f. 1975; 100% state-owned; cap. 682,888m. kips, res 90,096m. kips, dep. 11,666,795m. kips (Dec. 2011); Chair. SALSAMONE SAYSOULIEN; Man. Dir VANKHAM VORAVONG.

Banque Franco-Lao: ave Lane Xang, Ban Hatsady, Chanthaboury, Vientiane; tel. (21) 285111; fax (21) 285222; e-mail contact@bfl.la; internet www.banquefrancolao.com; f. 2010; Laotian-French jt venture; Man. Dir GUILLAUME PERDON.

Indochina Bank: 116 Capital Tower, 23 rue Singha, BP 6029, Vientiane; tel. (21) 455000; fax (21) 455111; e-mail info@indochinabank.com; internet www.indochinabank.com; f. 2009; Laotian-South Korean jt venture; Man. Dir TAY HONG HENG.

International Commercial Bank: 127/07, rue Hatsady, Ban Hatsady Tai, Chanthaboury, Vientiane; tel. (21) 250388; fax (21) 250479; e-mail enquiry@icb-lao.com; internet www.icb-lao.com; f. 2008; Man. Dir ZHUKIBLI KUAN.

Joint Development Bank: 82 rue Lane Xang, Vientiane; tel. (21) 213531; fax (21) 213530; e-mail jdb@jdbbank.com; internet www.jdbbank.com; f. 1989; 100% owned by Phrom Suwan Silo and Drying Co Ltd; cap. US $5m.; Gen. Man. SAROGE SINGSOMBOON.

Lao Development Bank (LDB): 13 ave Souphanouvong, Ban Sihome, Chanthaboury, BP 2700, Vientiane; tel. (21) 213300; fax (21) 213304; e-mail ldbhovte@ldblao.com; internet www.ldblao.com; f. 1999; est. as Lao May Bank upon consolidation by the Govt of ParkTai Bank, Lao May Bank and Nakornluang Bank; merged with Lane Xang Bank Ltd in 2001; name changed as above in 2003; 100% govt-owned; lends mainly to SMEs; Man. Dir BOUALIANE PHOMMAVONGSA; 18 brs.

Lao-Viet Bank (LVB): 44 ave Lane Xang, Ban Hatsady, Chanthaboury, Vientiane; tel. (21) 216316; fax (21) 212197; e-mail lvbho@laotel.com; f. 1999; jt venture between BCEL and Bank for Investment and Devt of Vietnam; cap. US $15m.; Chair. PHANSANA KHOUNNOUVONG; Man. Dir NGUYEN VANHEING; 3 brs.

Nayobay Bank: ave Kaysone Phomvihane, Ban Phonphanao, Xaysettha, Vientiane; tel. (21) 264407; fax (21) 264408; e-mail nbb_ho@nayobybank.org; internet www.nayobybank.org; f. 2007; 100% state-owned; Man. Dir BOUALONG XAYAVONG.

Phongsavanh Bank Ltd: Unit 1, ave Kaysone Phomvihane, Ban Phakhao, Xaythany, Vientiane; tel. (21) 711566; fax (21) 711556; e-mail info@phongsavanhbank.com; internet www.phongsavanhbank.com; f. 2007; Man. Dir SENGDAO BOUPHAKONEKHAM; cap. US $10m. (2007).

STOCK EXCHANGE

Lao Securities Exchange (LSX): Ban Phonethan Neue, rue T4, Xaysettha, Vientiane; internet www.lsx.com.la; f. 2010; establishment funded by the Banque de la RDP Lao (51% of capital) and Republic of Korea (49%); trading began in 2011; Chair. and CEO DETHPHOUVANG MOULARAT.

INSURANCE

Assurances Générales du Laos (AGL): Vientiane Commercial Bank Bldg, 33 ave Lane Xang, BP 4223, Vientiane; tel. (21) 215903; fax (21) 215904; e-mail agl@agl-allianz.com; internet www.agl-allianz.com; f. 1990; jt venture between Laotian Govt (49%) and Assurances Générales de France (51%); Group Chair. Dr MICHAEL DIEKMANN; Man. Dir GUY APOVY.

Lane Xang Assurance Co (LAP): Vientiane; f. 2010; equal jt venture between Lao Development Bank and Post and Telecommunication Joint Venture Insurance Corpn; life and general.

Trade and Industry

GOVERNMENT AGENCY

National Economic Research Institute (NERI): ave Kaysone Phomvihane, Ban Sivilay, Xaythany, Vientiane; tel. and fax (21) 711181; e-mail nerilaos@yahoo.com; govt policy development unit; Dir SOUPHAN KEOMISAY.

DEVELOPMENT ORGANIZATIONS

Department of Domestic and Foreign Investment (DDFI): rue Luang Prabang, 01001 Vientiane; tel. (21) 222690; fax (21) 215491; e-mail fimc@laotel.com; internet invest.laopdr.org; fmrly Foreign Investment Management Committee (FIMC); provides information and assistance to existing and potential investors.

Department of Livestock and Fisheries: Ministry of Agriculture and Forestry, Ban Phonxay, BP 811, Vientiane; tel. (21) 416932; fax (21) 415674; e-mail eulaodlf@laotel.com; public enterprise; imports and markets agricultural commodities; produces and distributes feed and animals; Dir-Gen. BOUAPHAN KONEDAVONG.

National Agriculture and Forestry Research Institute (NAFRI): Nongviengkham, BP 7170, Vientiane; tel. (21) 770084; fax (21) 770047; e-mail bounthong@nafri.org.la; internet www.nafri.org.la; f. 1999; supports sectoral devt and formulation of strategies and programmes in accordance with govt policy; Dir-Gen. Dr BOUNTHONG BOUAHOM.

State Committee for State Planning: Office of the Prime Minister, Ban Sisavat, Vientiane; tel. (21) 213653; fax (21) 213560.

CHAMBER OF COMMERCE

Lao National Chamber of Commerce and Industry (LNCCI): ave Kaysone Phomvihane, Ban Phonphanao, Xaysettha, BP 4596, Vientiane; tel. (21) 452579; fax (21) 452580; e-mail lncci@laopdr.com; internet www.lncci.laotel.com; f. 1989; 800 mems; Pres. KISSANA VONGSAY; Sec.-Gen. KHAMPANH SENGTHONGKHAM.

TRADE ASSOCIATION

Société Lao Import-Export (SOLIMPEX): 43–47 ave Lane Xang, BP 2789, Vientiane; tel. (21) 213818; fax (21) 217054; Dir KANHKEO SAYCOCIE; Dep. Dir PHONGSAMOUTH VONGKOT.

UTILITIES
Electricity

Electricité du Laos (EDL): Lao-Thai Friendship Rd, BP 2392, Sisattanak, Vientiane; tel. (21) 312791; fax (21) 314236; e-mail eedlmdo@edl.com.la; internet www.edl.com.la; f. 1959; state-owned corpn; responsible for production and distribution of electricity; shares in subsidiary EDL-Generation Co offered in 2011; Chair. and Man. Dir SISAVATH THIRAVONG.

Lao National Grid Co: Vientiane; responsible for Mekong hydro-electricity exports.

Water

Nam Papa Nakhoneluang (Laos Water Supply State Enterprise): ave Kaysone Phomvihane, Ban Thatluang, Xaysettha, Vientiane; tel. (21) 412880; fax (21) 414378; e-mail nampapalao@laotel.com; internet www.nampapa.com.la; f. 1962; Gen. Man. DAOPHET BOUAPHA.

Water Supply Authority (WASA): Dept of Housing and Urban Planning, Ministry of Public Works and Transport, ave Lane Xang, Vientiane; tel. and fax (21) 415764; fax (21) 451826; e-mail mctpcwwa@laotel.com; f. 1998; regulates the urban water industry; Dir NOUPHEUAK VIRABOUTH.

STATE ENTERPRISES

Agricultural Forestry Development Import-Export and General Service Co: trading co of the armed forces.

Bolisat Phatthana Khet Phoudoi Import-Export Co: rue Khoun Boulom, Vientiane; tel. (21) 216234; fax (21) 215046; f. 1984; trading co of the armed forces.

Dao-Heuang Import-Export Co: 242-7 Route 13 South, Ban Thaluang, Paksé, Champasak Province; tel. (31) 212250; fax (31) 212438; e-mail daoheuangcafe@laopdr.com; internet www .daoheuangcoffee.com; f. 1990; imports and distributes whisky, beer, mineral water, coffee and foodstuffs; Pres. LEUANG LITDANG.

Lao Commodities Export Co Ltd (Lacomex): Ban Wattuang, Paksé, Champasak Province; tel. (31) 212552; fax (31) 212553; e-mail sisanouk@laotel.com; f. 1994; exports coffee under the Paksong Cafe Lao brand; Man. Dir SISANOUK SISOMBAT.

Lao Houng Heuang Export-Import Co: rue Nongbone, Vientiane; tel. (21) 217344; fax (21) 212107.

Lao State Material Import-Export Co (Lasmac): 59 Ban Hatsady Tai, Chanthaboury, Vientiane; tel. (21) 216578; fax (21) 217149; e-mail lasmac@laotel.com; internet www.lasmac.laopdr.com; f. 1983; mfr of wood products and woven plastic; exports agricultural and wood products; imports construction materials.

Luen Fat Hong Lao Plywood Industry Co: BP 83, Vientiane; tel. (21) 314990; fax (21) 314992; e-mail lfhsdsj@laotel.com; internet www.luenfathongyada.laopdr.com; devt and management of forests, logging and timber production.

CO-OPERATIVES

Central Leading Committee to Guide Agricultural Co-operatives: Vientiane; f. 1978; helps to organize and plan regulations and policies for co-operatives; by the end of 1986 there were some 4,000 co-operatives, employing about 74% of the agricultural labour force; Chair. (vacant).

TRADE UNION ORGANIZATION

Federation of Lao Trade Unions: 87 ave Lane Xang, BP 780, Vientiane; tel. (21) 212754; e-mail kammabanlao@pan-laos.net.la; f. 1956; 21-mem. Cen. Cttee and five-mem. Control Cttee; Pres. KHAMLA LORLONESY; 70,000 mems.

Transport
RAILWAYS

In 2003 the Thai Government agreed to finance a 3.5-km rail link from Tha Naleng (near Vientiane) to Nong Khai, in north-eastern Thailand; construction was completed in April 2008, and the first passenger train service commenced in March 2009. Proposals to extend the track, to link Tha Naleng with Vientiane and to extend southwards and eastwards to Vinh in Viet Nam via Thakhek in central Laos, were also announced. In November 2012 plans were announced for the construction of a 220-km high-speed rail link from

Savannakhet province to the Vietnamese border town of Lao Bao; the project was expected to take five years to complete. The construction of a 420-km high-speed railway from the Chinese–Laotian border to Vientiane was also planned.

ROADS

The Asian Development Bank has supported an extensive development programme for the road network in Laos. In 2010 there were an estimated 39,586 km of roads. The main routes link Vientiane and Luang Prabang with Ho Chi Minh City in southern Viet Nam and with northern Viet Nam and the Cambodian border, Vientiane with Savannakhet, Phongsali to the Chinese border, Vientiane with Luang Prabang and the port of Ha Tinh (northern Viet Nam), and Savannakhet with the port of Da Nang (Viet Nam). Laos, Thailand and China are linked by the Kunming–Bangkok Highway, 250 km of which traverse Laos. In February 2004 construction of a 245-km national road (Route 9) was completed, linking Laos with Thailand and Viet Nam.

A number of bridges across the Mekong River link Laos to Thailand. The fourth bridge, linking Khammouane in Laos with the Thai province of Nakhon Pathom, was completed in November 2011. Construction of a fifth bridge, between the Laotian province of Bokeo and the northernmost Thai province of Chiang Rai, was expected to be completed by September 2013, with a further two bridges scheduled for completion in 2015.

INLAND WATERWAYS

The Mekong River, which forms the western frontier of Laos for much of its length, is the country's greatest transport artery. However, the size of river vessels is limited by rapids, and traffic is seasonal. There are about 4,600 km of navigable waterways.

CIVIL AVIATION

Wattay airport, Vientiane, is the principal international airport. In 1998 Luang Prabang airport also gained formal approval to receive international flights. Construction of a new airport in Oudomxay Province was completed in the late 1990s. Savannakhet Airport was to be developed into an international facility, as part of plans for the east–west economic corridor project, a proposed transport network linking Laos with Myanmar, Thailand and Viet Nam.

Lao Civil Aviation Department: BP 119, Vientiane; tel. (21) 512163; fax (21) 520236; e-mail laodca@laotel.com; internet www .dca.mpwt.gov.la; Dir-Gen. YAKUA LOPANGKAO.

Lao Air: rue Asiane, Ban Akat, Wattay Airport, BP 6618, Vientiane; tel. (21) 513022; fax (21) 512027; e-mail info@lao-air.com; internet www.lao-air.com; f. 2002; domestic flight services; Man. Dir BOUNMA CHANTHAVONGSA.

Lao Airlines: National Air Transport Co, 2 rue Pangkham, BP 6441, Vientiane; tel. (21) 212057; fax (21) 212065; e-mail laoairlines@ laoairlines.com; internet www.laoairlines.com; f. 1975; state airline, fmrly Lao Aviation; operates internal and international passenger and cargo transport services within South-East Asia; CEO SOMPHONE DOUANGDARA.

Lao Central Airlines: Vientiane; internet www.flylaocentral.com; f. 2012; 3 flights a week from Vientiane to Bangkok and Luang Prabang; CEO SAVANHPHONE PHONGSAVANH.

Tourism

Laos has spectacular scenery and ancient pagodas. Luang Prabang was approved by UNESCO as a World Heritage site in 1995, as was the Wat Phu temple complex in southern Laos in 2001. Foreign visitor arrivals were reported to have increased by 22.3% in 2012 to reach 3.3m., with the largest number of visitors coming from Thailand and Viet Nam. Receipts were estimated at US $406m. in 2011.

National Tourism Administration of Lao PDR: ave Lane Xang, BP 3556, Hatsady, Chanthaboury, Vientiane; tel. (21) 212251; fax (21) 212769; e-mail tmpd_lnta@yahoo.com; internet www .tourismlaos.org; parastatal org.; promotes Laos as a tourist destination and regulates the tourism industry; 17 provincial offices; Chair. SOMPHONG MONGKHONVILAY.

Defence

As assessed at November 2012, the total strength of the armed forces was an estimated 29,100: army 25,600 (including an army marine section of an estimated 600); air force 3,500. Conscription lasts a minimum of 18 months. Paramilitary forces comprise militia self-defence forces numbering about 100,000 men.

Defence Expenditure: Budgeted for 2012: 179,000m. kips.

Supreme Commander of the Lao People's Army (Commander-in-Chief): Lt-Gen. CHOUMMALY SAYASONE.

Chief of the General Staff: Brig.-Gen. SOUVENE LEUALG BOUNMY.

Education

A comprehensive educational system is in force, and Lao is the language of instruction.

In 2010/11 enrolment in pre-primary education included 24% of pupils in the relevant age-group (males 23%; females 24%). In the same year enrolment in primary education, which begins at six years of age and lasts for five years, included 97% of children in the relevant age-group (males 98%; females 96%). Secondary education, begin-ning at the age of 11, lasts for six years, comprising two three-year cycles. In 2010/11 enrolment in secondary education included 41% of pupils in the relevant age-group (males 43%; females 39%).

In the 2011/12 academic year there were 1,358 pre-primary institutions, which were attended by 103,200 children, and 8,902 primary schools, attended by 900,000 pupils. The 917 secondary schools provided education for a total of 506,859 students (including 39 vocational schools at which 18,859 students were enrolled). There were 113 tertiary institutions, including five universities at which 70,231 students were enrolled, while 40,134 were studying at other institutions of higher education. There are several regional technical colleges. The National University of Laos was founded in 1995. Government spending on education in 2010 was an estimated 13.2% of total budgetary expenditure.

LATVIA

Introductory Survey

LOCATION, CLIMATE, LANGUAGE, RELIGION, FLAG, CAPITAL

The Republic of Latvia is situated in north-eastern Europe, on the east coast of the Baltic Sea. The country is bounded by Estonia to the north and by Lithuania to the south and south-west. To the east it borders Russia, and to the south-east Belarus. Owing to the influence of maritime factors, the climate is relatively temperate, but changeable. Average temperatures in January range from −2.8°C (26.6°F) in the western coastal town of Liepāja to −6.6°C (20.1°F) in the inland town of Daugavpils. Mean temperatures for July range from 16.7°C (62.1°F) in Liepāja to 17.6°C (63.7°F) in Daugavpils. Average annual rainfall in Rīga is 617 mm (24 ins). The official language is Latvian. The major religion is Christianity: most ethnic Latvians are traditionally Lutherans or Latin-rite Catholics, whereas ethnic Russians are mainly adherents of the Russian Orthodox Church. The national flag (proportions 1 by 2) has a maroon background, with a narrow white horizontal stripe superimposed across the central part. The capital is Rīga (Riga).

CONTEMPORARY POLITICAL HISTORY

Historical Context

In November 1917 representatives of Latvian nationalist groups elected a provisional national council, which informed the Russian Government of its intention to establish an independent Latvian state. On 18 November 1918 the newly constituted Latvian National Council proclaimed the independent Republic of Latvia, with Jānis Čakste as President. Independence, under the Government of Kārlis Ulmanis, was fully achieved after the expulsion of the Bolsheviks from Rīga in May 1919, with the aid of German troops, and from the eastern province of Latgale, with Polish and Estonian assistance, in January 1920. A Latvian-Soviet peace treaty was signed in August. Latvia's first Constitution was adopted in 1922. An electoral system based on proportional representation permitted many small parties to be represented in the Saeima (Parliament), resulting in administrative instability, and 18 changes of government in 1922–34. None the less, under the dominant party, the Latvian Farmers' Union (LZS, led by Ulmanis), agrarian reforms were successfully introduced. The world-wide economic decline of the early 1930s prompted a (bloodless) coup in May 1934, led by Ulmanis. Martial law was introduced, the Saeima was dissolved and all political parties, including the LZS, were banned. A Government of National Unity assumed the legislative functions of the Saeima, and Ulmanis (hitherto the Prime Minister) became President in 1936.

Under the Treaty of Non-Aggression signed by Germany and the USSR in August 1939, the incorporation of Latvia into the Soviet 'sphere of interests' was agreed by the two powers. A 'treaty of mutual aid' with the USSR allowed the establishment of Soviet military bases in Latvia, and in June 1940 Soviet forces occupied the country. A 'puppet' administration, under Augusts Kirhenšteins, was installed, and the election to the Saeima of Soviet-approved candidates took place in July. The new legislature proclaimed the Latvian Soviet Socialist Republic, which was formally incorporated into the USSR as a constituent union republic in August.

In the first year of Soviet rule almost 33,000 Latvians were deported to Russia and Kazakhstan, and a further 1,350 were killed. Latvian language, traditions and culture were suppressed. In July 1941 Soviet rule in Latvia was interrupted by German occupation. Most German troops had withdrawn by 1944, although the Kurzeme region, in south-western Latvia, was retained by Germany until the end of the Second World War. Soviet Latvia was re-established in 1944–45 and the process of 'sovietization' was resumed. There were further mass deportations of Latvians to Russia and Central Asia. Independent political activities were prohibited and the Communist Party of Latvia (LKP) exercised exclusive political power. Industrialization encouraged significant and sustained Russian and other Soviet immigration into the republic.

There was a revival in Latvian national culture from the late 1970s. In 1986 anti-Soviet demonstrations were suppressed by the police. In 1987 there were further demonstrations on the anniversaries of significant events in Latvian history, which were strongly opposed by the LKP. In October 1988 representatives of the leading opposition movements established the Latvian Popular Front (LTF), which resolved to seek Latvian sovereignty within a renewed Soviet federation. Meanwhile, in September Jānis Vagris was appointed First Secretary of the LKP, and the new leadership of the party came increasingly under the influence of the LTF. Later that month Latvian was designated the state language. In March 1989 LTF-supported candidates won 26 of the 34 contested seats representing Latvia in elections to the USSR's Congress of People's Deputies. On 28 July, following similar measures in Lithuania and Estonia, the Latvian Supreme Soviet (Supreme Council—legislature) adopted a declaration of sovereignty and economic independence. Meanwhile, there was growing support within the republic for full independence, as advocated by the Latvian National Independence Movement (LNNK), formed in 1988, particularly among ethnic Latvians—who, however, were outnumbered by Slavs (mostly Russians and Ukrainians) in Rīga and the other large cities in the republic. In December 1989 candidates supported by the LTF won some 75% of seats contested in local elections.

In January 1990 the Latvian Supreme Soviet voted to abolish the constitutional guarantees of the LKP's political predominance. In February the Supreme Soviet formally condemned the Latvian legislature's decision to request admission to the USSR in 1940, and restored to official use the flag, state emblems and anthem of pre-1940 Latvia. At elections to the Supreme Soviet in March–April 1990, LTF-endorsed candidates won 131 of the 201 seats; the LKP and the anti-independence Interfront (dominated by members of the Russian-speaking population) together won 59 seats. The LKP subsequently split into two parties: the majority of delegates at an extraordinary congress rejected a motion to leave the Communist Party of the Soviet Union (CPSU), and elected Alfrēds Rubiks, an opponent of independence, as First Secretary.

The new Supreme Council, convened in May 1990, elected Anatolijs Gorbunovs of the LKP as its Chairman (de facto president of the Republic). On 4 May the Supreme Council announced the beginning of a transition towards full political and economic independence. Four articles of the 1922 Constitution, defining the Republic of Latvia as an independent democratic state and asserting the sovereignty of the Latvian people, were restored. Ivars Godmanis, the Deputy Chairman of the LTF, was elected Prime Minister in a new Government. Meanwhile, a rival body to the Supreme Soviet had been convened at the end of April 1990. This Congress of Latvia had been elected in an unofficial poll, in which only citizens of the pre-1940 republic and their descendants had been entitled to vote. The Congress, in which members of the LNNK predominated, declared Latvia to be an occupied country and adopted resolutions on independence and the withdrawal of Soviet troops.

The Supreme Council's resolutions, although more cautious than the independence declarations adopted in Lithuania and Estonia, severely strained relations with the Soviet authorities. On 14 May 1990 the Soviet President, Mikhail Gorbachev, issued a decree annulling the Latvian declaration of independence. The declaration was also opposed within the republic by some Slavs, who organized protest strikes and demonstrations. In December the Latvian Government claimed that special OMON units of the Soviet Ministry of Internal Affairs had caused a series of explosions in Rīga, and in January 1991 OMON troops seized the Rīga Press House. Later in January a 'Committee of Public Salvation', headed by Rubiks, declared itself as a rival Government to the Godmanis administration; on the same day five people died when OMON troops attacked the Ministry of the Interior in Rīga.

Latvia refused to conduct the all-Union referendum on the future of the USSR, which was scheduled for 17 March 1991 (although some 680,000 people, mostly Slavs, did participate, unofficially). Instead, a referendum on Latvian independence took place on 3 March. Of those eligible to vote, 87.6% participated, of whom, according to official results, 73.7% supported independence.

During the attempted overthrow by conservative communists of the Gorbachev administration in the Russian and Soviet capital, Moscow, in August 1991, an emergency session of the Latvian Supreme Council was convened and the full independence of the country proclaimed. As the coup collapsed, the Godmanis Government banned the LKP and detained Rubiks. (In July 1995 Rubiks was found guilty of involvement in the coup attempt. He was released in November 1997.) On 6 September 1991 the USSR State Council formally acknowledged Latvian independence; Latvia was admitted to the UN later that month. In late 1991 the Supreme Council adopted legislation guaranteeing the right of citizenship to all citizens of the pre-1940 republic and their descendants. Other residents of Latvia were to be required to apply for naturalization after final legislation governing citizenship had been determined.

Domestic Political Affairs

Around 90% of the electorate participated in legislative elections held in June 1993. (Around 27% of the adult population, mostly Slavs, were ineligible to participate). Eight groups secured representation in the 100-seat Saeima. Latvian Way (LC), a broadly based movement, emerged as the largest party, with 32% of the votes cast and 36 seats. The more moderate nationalist parties obtained strong popular support, while socialist-orientated parties (including the successor of the LKP, the Latvian Socialist Party—LSP) failed to win representation. Only 11 of the elected deputies were not ethnically Latvian.

Restoration of the 1922 Constitution

The new Saeima voted to restore the 1922 Constitution, and undertook to elect the President of the Republic from among three prominent deputies. At a third round of voting on 7 July 1993 Guntis Ulmanis (great-nephew of Kārlis Ulmanis) of the revived LZS succeeded in winning a majority, with 53 votes. He was inaugurated as President the following day, when he appointed Valdis Birkavs of LC as Prime Minister. The Cabinet of Ministers represented a coalition agreement between LC (the majority partner) and the LZS.

The requirements for naturalization proposed by the Government's draft citizenship law included a minimum of 10 years' permanent residence in Latvia, a knowledge of Latvian to conversational level and an oath of loyalty to the republic. In July 1994 the Saeima amended the legislation on citizenship, thereby placating some international criticism of Latvia. In the same month the LZS announced its withdrawal from the governing coalition, following disagreements with LC over economic and agricultural policy. A new Cabinet of Ministers, appointed in September, was dominated by LC members, including the Prime Minister, Māris Gailis; Birkavs became Deputy Prime Minister and Minister of Foreign Affairs. Latvia was admitted to the Council of Europe (see p. 260) in February 1995.

A general election was held on 30 September–1 October 1995. Nine parties and coalitions succeeded in obtaining the 5% of the votes required for legislative representation. LC's share of the 100 seats was reduced significantly, to 17, while the largest number of seats (18) was won by the newly established, leftist Saimnieks Democratic Party (DPS). The People's Movement for Latvia (Zigerists' Party), an extreme nationalist party led by a German-Latvian, Joahims Zigerists, won 16 seats. In December the Saeima finally endorsed a Cabinet of Ministers led by an entrepreneur with no party affiliation, Andris Šķēle. The new Government was a coalition of the DPS, LC, the For Fatherland and Freedom Union (TB), the LNNK (now renamed the Latvian National Conservative Party), the LZS and the Latvian Unity Party (LVP).

On 18 June 1996 the Saeima re-elected Ulmanis for a second three-year term as President. In July it was announced that the LVP was to merge into the DPS. In January 1997 Šķēle resigned as Prime Minister, but was swiftly reappointed by Ulmanis. Local elections conducted in March demonstrated a marked increase in support for the LZS.

By July 1997 the governing coalition had begun to disintegrate, following a series of corruption scandals, and at the end of the month Šķēle's Government resigned. Ulmanis invited Guntars Krasts, the outgoing Minister of the Economy, to form a new administration. In August the Saeima approved Krasts's proposals for a five-party coalition, comprising his own party, the TB/LNNK (formed in the previous month by the merger of the TB and the LNNK—which had reverted to its original designation),

the DPS, LC, the LZS and the Christian Democratic Union of Latvia. In March 1998 Šķēle announced the formation of a new political party, later named the People's Party (TP).

In April 1998 the Minister of the Economy, Ātis Sausnītis, was dismissed. Shortly afterwards the DPS withdrew from the governing coalition. Later in the month Krasts survived a parliamentary vote of no confidence proposed by the LZS and LC. At the same session the Saeima approved appointments to a new coalition Government, with members of the Cabinet of Ministers drawn from the LZS, LC, and an alliance of the Latvian National Reform Party and the Latvian Green Party.

In April 1998 draft amendments to the strict legislation regulating rights to citizenship were adopted, in response to recommendations made by the Organization for Security and Co-operation in Europe (OSCE, see p. 397). In June the Saeima approved the amendments, which removed the age-related system of naturalization that allocated dates for application by age-group, granted citizenship to stateless children permanently resident in Latvia born after the 1991 declaration of independence and relaxed the citizenship requirements for Russian-speakers. However, nationalist groups within the Saeima secured sufficient support to force a delay to the enactment of the new legislation and the organization of a referendum on the subject. The referendum was conducted concurrently with legislative elections on 3 October; 52.5% of the votes were cast in favour of the amendments, which were promulgated later in the month.

The Presidency of Vaira Vīķe-Freiberga

At the legislative elections of 3 October 1998, the TP was the most successful party, taking 21.2% of the votes (and 24 of the 100 legislative seats), ahead of LC with 18.1% (21 seats) and the TB/LNNK with 14.7% (17 seats). Six parties secured the minimum 5% of the votes necessary for representation in the Saeima. In November 1998 the Saeima approved a minority coalition Government, headed by Vilis Krištopans of LC. The Government, comprising LC, the TB/LNNK and the New Party (which held eight legislative seats), also drew support from the Latvian Social Democratic Alliance, with 14 deputies, which subsequently formally joined the coalition.

On 17 June 1999 Vaira Vīķe-Freiberga was elected President at a seventh round of voting in the Saeima, with the support of 53 deputies. Vīķe-Freiberga, a non-partisan figure who had been resident in Canada in 1954–98, became the first female President in central or eastern Europe. At her inauguration on 8 July 1999 Vīķe-Freiberga identified as priorities for her presidency Latvia's entry into the European Union (EU, see p. 281) and the North Atlantic Treaty Organization (NATO, see p. 380). Three days before her inauguration, Krištopans announced his Government's resignation, apparently in response to the recent signing by the TB/LNNK of a co-operation accord with the opposition TP. After Vīķe-Freiberga asked Šķēle to form a new government, he led a coalition administration comprising TP, the TB/LNNK and LC.

In July 1999 the Saeima adopted legislation requiring all business and state- and municipally-organized gatherings to be conducted in Latvian. Russia denounced the legislation, which was also condemned by the OSCE, the Council of Europe, the European Commission and, within Latvia, by groups representing Russophones. Revised legislation, which incorporated amendments urged by the OSCE, was approved in December and took effect in September 2000.

Šķēle resigned from the premiership in April 2000, after LC withdrew from the governing coalition. President Vīķe-Freiberga asked Andris Bērziņš, hitherto the Mayor of Rīga, to form a new government; a coalition administration, principally comprising the TP, LC and the TB/LNNK, was approved by the Saeima in early May. In November 2001 Einars Repše resigned as Governor of the Bank of Latvia, in order to found a new rightist political party, New Era (JL). In May a new Christian democratic party, the Latvian First Party (LPP), was formed.

In legislative elections, held on 5 October 2002, JL won 23.9% of the votes cast, obtaining 26 seats; the leftist, pro-Russian electoral bloc For Human Rights in a United Latvia (PCTVL), including the People's Harmony Party (TSP) and the LSP, obtained 18.9% of the votes (25 seats); and the TP received 16.7% (20 seats). Other groups to achieve representation in the Saeima were the Greens' and Farmers' Union (ZZS—an alliance of the Centre Party, the LZS and the Latvian Green Party—LZP), with 12 seats, the LPP (10 seats) and the TB/LNNK (seven); LC failed to obtain a seat in the Saeima. The rate of participation by the electorate was some 72.5%. Repše formed a coalition government comprising members of JL, the LPP, the ZZS and the TB/LNNK, which was approved by the Saeima on 7 November. A new post of Deputy Prime Minister was established, to which Ainārs Slesers of the LPP was appointed. In late November Atis Slakteris replaced Šķēle as Chairman of the TP.

In February 2003 the TSP withdrew from the PCTVL alliance, apparently in order to pursue more moderate policies. In June the LSP also announced its withdrawal; the remainder of PCTVL was officially reconstituted as a united organization later that year. On 20 June Vīķe-Freiberga was re-elected unopposed to serve a second term of office as President; she was inaugurated on 8 July. In September tensions emerged within the Government, when its constituent parties (other than JL) issued a statement expressing a lack of confidence in Repše as premier. Following inter-party discussions, a compromise agreement was reached, and Repše remained in office. In January 2004 Repše dismissed Slesers as Deputy Prime Minister; Slesers alleged that his removal had been prompted by a proposal to establish a special investigative committee to examine the premier's property dealings. The LPP subsequently withdrew from the Government and on 5 February Repše's administration resigned. On 20 February President Vīķe-Freiberga nominated the Co-Chairman of the LZP, Indulis Emsis, as premier. Emsis secured the support of the ZZS, the LPP and the TP, and on 9 March the Saeima approved a new coalition Government.

After accession to the European Union

Following Latvia's accession to the EU on 1 May 2004 (see Regional relations), elections to the European Parliament were conducted on 13 June; the opposition TB/LNNK won four of Latvia's nine seats, while its ally JL won two, and PCTVL, the LPP and LC each won one seat. Neither of the two main parties in the ruling coalition obtained representation. Rihards Piks resigned as Minister of Foreign Affairs in order to take his seat in the European Parliament; he was replaced by Artis Pabriks. On 28 October the Saeima voted to reject the draft budget, precipitating the collapse of the ruling coalition. President Vīķe-Freiberga nominated Aigars Kalvītis of the TP (which had led opposition to the proposed budget) to form a new government, and on 2 December, following prolonged negotiations, the Saeima approved the formation of a Government comprising members of the TP, JL, the ZZS and the LPP. Several members of the outgoing administration were retained in the same posts, including Pabriks and Oskars Spurdziņš (both of the TP), as Minister of Foreign Affairs and Minister of Finance, respectively. A revised draft budget was approved in the Saeima on 20 December.

In July 2005 Jānis Jurkāns resigned as leader of the TSP, in protest at the party's decision, following electoral defeats at both European and local level, to form an alliance with the New Centre, a breakaway party headed by Sergejs Dolgopolovs, who had been expelled from the TSP in 2003. The new union, the Harmony Centre (SC) alliance, was joined by the LSP in December 2005. Meanwhile, in October LC and the LPP also formed a political alliance. In November Jānis Urbanovičs was elected as leader of the TSP.

In October 2005 the Minister of the Interior, Ēriks Jēkabsons, tendered his resignation, after attracting criticism for his performance; Dzintars Jaundzeikars of the LPP was appointed as his successor in the following month. In December Repše resigned as Minister of Defence, following the announcement of a criminal investigation into his property investments; he also resigned his parliamentary seat and withdrew from the leadership of JL. Linda Mūrniece succeeded Repše as Minister of Defence. In March 2006 Kalvītis dismissed Slesers as Minister of Transport, after evidence emerged implicating him in electoral malpractice in the 2005 municipal elections. In April 2006 the Ministry of the Interior launched an inquiry into allegations of financial misconduct by the JL Minister of the Economy, Krišjānis Kariņš. JL accused the LPP of misusing its control of the interior ministry and subsequently withdrew its seven representatives from the Government, after Kalvītis (of the TP) rejected its demand that the LPP be removed from the governing coalition. On 8 April the Saeima approved a three-party minority Government, in which JL was not represented.

At elections to the Saeima on 7 October 2006 the TP won 19.6% of the votes cast and 23 seats, the ZZS alliance 16.7% (18 seats), JL 16.4% (18 seats), the SC alliance 14.4% (17 seats), the LPP, allied with LC, 8.6% (10 seats), the TB/LNNK 6.9% (eight seats) and PCTVL 6.0% (six seats). The outgoing governing coalition of

the TP, the ZZS and the LPP thus secured a narrow parliamentary majority. Around 62.3% of the electorate participated in the elections. Kalvītis invited the TB/LNNK to join the governing coalition in order to strengthen its parliamentary majority and subsequently formed a new, four-party administration, which was approved by the Saeima on 7 November. In December a congress of the TSP approved the consolidation of the SC alliance as a merged association (although the LSP retained its separate status as an affiliated party).

On 31 May 2007 the Saeima elected Valdis Zatlers, the candidate proposed by the ruling coalition, as President, to succeed Vīķe-Freiberga. Žatlers (a medical doctor without political experience) was inaugurated on 8 July. In August the LPP officially merged with LC; the reconstituted LPP/LC was jointly chaired by Slesers and Godmanis.

In mid-September 2007 Jurijs Strods of the TB/LNNK resigned as Minister of the Economy. On 22 September the Chairman of the Saeima, Emsis, resigned, after the opening of a criminal investigation into allegations that he had given false testimony in a case related to corruption in the city of Ventspils. He was succeeded by Gundars Daudze, a close ally of the controversial Mayor of Ventspils, Aivars Lembergs, who had been arrested for corruption and abuse of public office in March. In October Kalvītis dismissed the Minister of Regional Development and Local Government, who had voted against a government motion to remove the director of the anti-corruption bureau, Aleksejs Loskutovs, who had been suspended from his post in connection with accounting irregularities. Later in the month Artis Pabriks resigned as Minister of Foreign Affairs in protest at the suspension of Loskutovs, which opponents of Kalvītis claimed was motivated by the bureau's investigations into official corruption. Although the crisis precipitated a mass anti-Government demonstration in Rīga, a Saeima motion of no confidence was defeated. At the end of October the Minister of Welfare resigned, following opposition to her proposed pensions reforms. In early December Kalvītis finally tendered the resignation of his Government. Zatlers, after rejecting an attempt by the TP to propose a further candidate as Prime Minister, nominated Godmanis (who had hitherto held the interior portfolio) to the premiership. On 20 December the Saeima approved a new coalition Government, comprising representatives of the TP, the LPP/LC, the ZZS and the TB/LNNK.

In April 2008 a new, centre-right political party, the Civic Union (PS), was founded by two prominent politicians, Sandra Kalniete (formerly a member of JL) and Valdis Kristovskis (formerly of the TB/LNNK). Also in April it was announced that at least 10% of the electorate had signed a petition in support of a constitutional amendment that would enable voters to dissolve the legislature by referendum, thereby requiring a national referendum to be held on the matter. In June Loskutovs (who remained under investigation) was removed from his post by a vote in the Saeima. On 2 August the proposed constitutional amendment failed to secure sufficient support (a minimum of 50% of the registered electorate) at the referendum. However, Zatlers described the referendum result, which was equivalent to about 40.2% of the electorate voting in favour, as significant, and submitted a legal initiative to the Saeima for consideration of the amendment.

In January 2009, following the severe impact of the international financial crisis upon Latvia, around 10,000 people attended a demonstration in Rīga to protest against perceived economic mismanagement by the Government and in support of the holding of early legislative elections; after ensuing riots, some 100 protesters were arrested. On the following day Zatlers issued an ultimatum threatening to dissolve the Saeima in the event that it (and the Government) had not, by the end of March, implemented certain political reforms (including the adoption of the constitutional amendment on the dissolution of the legislature by a national referendum initiated by voters). In early February the Government survived a parliamentary motion of no confidence, initiated by JL. However, following protests by farmers about increasing hardship in the sector, the Minister of Agriculture resigned. After the Cabinet of Ministers failed to adopt proposed measures to reduce the number of existing government ministries, Zatlers declared that he had lost confidence in Godmanis as Prime Minister. On 20 February, after the TP and the ZZS threatened to withdraw from the governing coalition, Godmanis tendered his resignation.

The Government of Valdis Dombrovskis

President Zatlers nominated Valdis Dombrovskis, a member of JL and a former Minister of Finance, as Prime Minister. Subsequently, JL invited all parties represented in the Saeima, except PCTVL, to enter into consultations on the formation of a new administration. On 12 March 2009 a new coalition Government, comprising representatives of JL, the TP, the ZZS alliance, the TB/LNNK and the PS and headed by Dombrovskis (who also held the portfolio of children, the family and social integration), was approved by the Saeima; new appointments included those of Repše as Minister of Finance and Artis Kampars of JL as Minister of the Economy. On the same day the Saeima appointed a new director of the anti-corruption bureau (thereby fulfilling one of the political reforms stipulated by Zatlers). Later in March Zatlers announced that he would not act upon his threat to dissolve the Saeima, owing to the installation of a new Government and progress towards the adoption of political and economic reforms. On 8 April the Saeima approved amendments to two articles of the Constitution, enabling voters to initiate a referendum on the dissolution of the legislature during the second and third years of its term; the changes were to enter into effect following the next parliamentary elections.

On 6 June 2009 elections to the European Parliament took place. Of the eight seats allocated to Latvia, the PS and the SC both won two, while PCTVL, the LPP/LC, the TB/LNNK and JL each won one. On the same day local elections were held, prior to the introduction of a new, single-tier structure of local government across the country from the beginning of July. The SC performed strongly in the local elections, and secured just over one-third of the vote in Rīga. In mid-June the Minister of Health, Ivars Eglītis, resigned, in protest at spending reductions in the health sector, approved as part of efforts to satisfy conditions for the disbursement of EU funds. In March 2010 the founding congress was held of a new right-wing alliance, Unity, comprising JL, the PS and the Society for a Different Politics. (The admission of the TB/LNNK to the alliance, sought by the leadership of that party, was rejected.) In mid-March the TP withdrew its five ministers (including the Minister of Foreign Affairs) from the governing coalition, after Dombrovskis refused to sign an economic agreement with the party. Dombrovskis henceforth led a minority Government. At the end of April Aivis Ronis, a former ambassador to the USA and to NATO, was appointed as Minister of Foreign Affairs. Meanwhile, another right-wing electoral coalition, the Alliance for A Good Latvia, headed by Ulmanis and comprising the TP and the LPP/LC, was established.

At the legislative elections, held as scheduled on 2 October 2010, the Unity coalition was the most successful group, securing 31.9% of the votes cast and a total of 33 seats. The SC (which was strongly opposed to recently introduced economic austerity measures) demonstrated an increase in support, receiving 26.6% of the vote and 29 seats. The ZZS alliance obtained 20.1% of the vote and 22 seats; a coalition of the nationalist All For Latvia (VL) party and the TB/LNNK, and the Alliance for A Good Latvia each obtained 7.8% of the votes cast; each won seats. Dombrovskis formed a coalition Government comprising the parties of the Unity coalition and the ZZS alliance, although attempts to negotiate the inclusion of the TB/LNNK proved unsuccessful. None the less, the ruling coalition held 55 of the 100 seats in the Saeima. Among the principal appointments in the new Government were Ģirts Kristovskis of the PS as Minister of Foreign Affairs, Artis Kampars of JL as Minister of the Economy and Aigars Stokenbergs as Minister of Justice. Mūrniece was one of three ministers from the outgoing Government to be reappointed, retaining her position as Minister of the Interior.

In mid-February 2011 Mūrniece tendered her resignation as Minister of the Interior, after persistent concerns about corruption within the police and security forces were exacerbated by an incident, in late January, in which a group of police officers were discovered robbing a casino in Jekabpils; one of the officers dispatched to the casino to apprehend the criminals was shot dead, and two others were injured. At the request of Dombrovskis, Mūrniece remained in office until early June, when Stokenbergs assumed the interior portfolio in an acting capacity.

The 2011 presidential and legislative elections

An investigation was launched in May 2011 into charges of corruption brought against Lembergs, Šķēle and Slesers. However, the Anti-Corruption Bureau was refused permission to search their residences, and there were allegations that the Saeima was obstructing the course of justice. Later that month President Zatlers announced that a referendum on the dissolution of the Saeima would be held. The referendum proceeded as planned on 23 July, when 94.3% of voters supported the motion to dissolve the Saeima.

On 2 June 2011, in the first round of the presidential election in the Saeima, Zatlers obtained the support of only 43 deputies, while 50 voted for Andris Bērziņš (no relation to the former Prime Minister of the same name), a former banking and business executive, and the candidate of the ZZS. In a second ballot, which took place on the same day, Bērziņš secured the requisite majority of votes, with 53, to be elected President; he was inaugurated on 8 July. Zatlers's defeat was ascribed to his earlier decision to call the referendum on the dissolution of the Saeima. Zatlers later announced he would establish a new party, the Zatlers Reform Party (ZRP), which would not co-operate with the ZZS, the LPP/LC and the TP. Meanwhile, a campaign led by the National Alliance (recently formed by the TB and VL) to gather support for the organization of a referendum on the compulsory use of Latvian as the sole language of instruction in state-funded schools failed to obtain the requisite quantity of signatures (equivalent to 10% of those who voted in the most recent elections to the Saeima). However, Russophones, led by the Mother Tongue organization, subsequently began a petition for a referendum on the amendment of the Constitution to grant Russian the status of second official language.

Following the dissolution of the Saeima, legislative elections were conducted on 17 September 2011. The SC alliance secured 28.4% of the votes cast, winning 31 seats in the Saeima; the ZRP (founded in July, and which later renamed itself as the Reform Party, while remaining under Zatlers's leadership) won 20.8% of the votes and 22 seats, while the Unity coalition took 18.8% and 20 seats. The National Alliance and the ZZS took 14 and 13 seats, respectively. On 25 October Prime Minister Dombrovskis formed a new coalition Government, which obtained approval of 57 votes to 38 in the Saeima. Gaidis Bērziņš of the National Alliance was appointed Minister of Justice; ZRP member Rihards Kozlovskis assumed the interior portfolio; and Edgars Rinkēvičs became Minister of Foreign Affairs. Unity member Pabriks retained his position as Minister of Defence, while Andris Vilks, also of Unity, continued as Minister of Finance.

By mid-November 2011 it had been confirmed that sufficient signatures had been collected for a referendum on the constitutional status of the Russian language to be held, and in December the plebiscite was scheduled to take place on 18 February 2012. (In order to be approved, the proposals would require the approval of at least one-half of the registered electorate.) In the referendum, the proposals were overwhelmingly defeated, with some 74.8% of the votes cast being against the proposed amendments (71.1% of the electorate participated), although a majority of those who voted in some eastern regions were in support. However, some 290,000 Russophones, who continued to lack Latvian citizenship, were not entitled to vote. Questions of entitlement to Latvian citizenship remained an important topic of political debate during 2012; in March Saeima Chairman Solvita Āboltiņa spoke in favour of the eventual introduction of legislation permitting Latvian citizens dual citizenship, in order to simplify the situation of children born to Latvian families resident abroad. In August PCTVL succeeded in securing sufficient signatures to demand that a referendum be conducted on the granting of automatic citizenship to the Russophone population. In November, however, the members of the Central Election Commission voted to ban the referendum, claiming that the proposed measure would contravene the Constitution and international law.

Recent developments: euro area application

Following the intensification of the sovereign debt crisis within the euro area in 2011–12, questions had been raised regarding a suitable exit strategy for Latvia from the euro adoption programme should this become necessary. Although opinion polls indicated that some 63% of Latvians continued to oppose introduction of the euro, legislation providing for its adoption on 1 January 2014 was nevertheless endorsed by the Saeima on 31 January 2013, and signed into effect by President Bērziņš on 15 February. On 4 March Latvia submitted a formal application to join the euro area; a decision by the European Commission and European Central Bank was expected in mid-2013. Meanwhile, in mid-January 2013 Ronis, the non-partisan Minister of Transport announced his resignation, to take effect from 1 March; he was succeeded by Anrijs Matīss.

Foreign Affairs

Regional relations

A priority of Latvian foreign policy was attaining full membership of the EU. Latvia applied for membership in October 1995, and formal negotiations on accession commenced in February 2000. In December 2002 Latvia, together with nine other countries, was formally invited to become a full member of the EU in 2004. A referendum on EU membership was held on 20 September 2003. Of the 72.5% of the electorate who participated in the plebiscite, 66.8% voted in support of Latvia's accession to the EU, although in certain areas of the country, particularly in the predominantly Russian-speaking, south-eastern regions around the second city of Daugavpils, a majority of votes were cast against EU membership. The country became a full member on 1 May 2004. In December 2007 Latvia, together with eight other countries, implemented the EU's Schengen Agreement, enabling its citizens to travel to and from other member states, without border controls. On 8 May 2008 the Saeima voted to ratify the EU's Lisbon Treaty.

Latvia enjoys close relations with Estonia and Lithuania, and the three countries have established institutions to promote co-operation, including the interparliamentary Baltic Assembly and the Baltic Council of Ministers (which meets twice yearly). In 1992 Latvia became a founder member, with Estonia, Lithuania and other countries of the region, of the Council of the Baltic Sea States, a principal aim of which was to assist the political and economic development of its former communist member states (including Russia). Agreement on the delimitation of the maritime border with Estonia was reached in May 1996, and the document was ratified by both countries' legislatures in August. A further agreement on fishing rights was concluded in 1997, in which year the demarcation of the land border between the two countries was completed. Negotiations between Latvia and Lithuania on their maritime border were complicated in 1996 by the Saeima's ratification of an agreement with two foreign petroleum companies to explore and develop offshore oilfields in disputed maritime areas. Although the two countries signed an agreement on the delimitation of their territorial waters in 1999, the Saeima refused to ratify the agreement. In 2000 a protocol was signed on the re-demarcation of the land border with Lithuania. In 2006 the leaders of all three Baltic countries reached agreement on the construction of a new nuclear power plant to replace that at Ignalina, Lithuania, and on various other measures aimed at reducing Russian dominance in the supply of energy.

Latvia's post-independence relations with Russia were troubled by two questions. The first concerned the citizenship and linguistic rights of Latvia's large Russian-speaking community. The second was the question of the 100,000 former Soviet troops still stationed in Latvia (jurisdiction over whom had been transferred, following the dissolution of the USSR, to Russia). Following negotiations, withdrawal of the troops began in 1992. The process was hampered by a series of disagreements, in particular concerning a Russian military radar station at Skrunda, in western Latvia. In April 1994 agreements were concluded on the complete withdrawal of the remaining 10,000 Russian troops by the end of August, as well as on social guarantees for the estimated 22,000 Russian military pensioners residing in Latvia. Installations at the Skrunda base were subsequently dismantled.

Negotiations regarding the demarcation of the Latvian–Russian border, and Latvia's claim to 1,640 sq km of land transferred to Russia during the Soviet era, commenced in 1996. Latvia initially insisted that any future border agreement should include a reference to the 1920 treaty in which Russia recognized Latvia's independence. However, Latvia abandoned this demand in 1997, and agreed that claims to property in the disputed territory should be discussed separately from the main border agreement. Full agreement on a border treaty was reached in October, although it remained unratified. In January 2007 Latvia agreed to remove a declaration from the draft treaty, which Russia had interpreted as making a territorial claim over the land that had formerly constituted part of Latvia. On 27 March Kalvītis and the Russian premier, Mikhail Fradkov, signed the treaty in Moscow. The treaty was endorsed by Vīķe-Freiberga in May and by Russian President Vladimir Putin in October. In August 2008 Zatlers, together with the Presidents of Estonia, Lithuania and Poland, condemned a Russian military offensive in Georgia (see Georgia).

Meanwhile, relations with Russia became strained in March 1998, following the organization, in Rīga, of a rally of Latvian veterans of Nazi German *Waffen SS* units, who had fought Soviet forces during the Second World War; the participation of senior Latvian politicians and military personnel attracted particular criticism from the Russian authorities. Government officials and serving military officers were not permitted to participate in a further veterans' rally held in March 2000. Meanwhile, tensions arising from repeated Russian threats to impose economic sanctions against Latvia, if the Government did not promptly address perceived infringements of minority rights, were exacerbated by Latvia's 1999 state language law. The revised language law, approved by the Saeima in December, was denounced by Russia. Economic issues threatened to raise further tensions between the two countries in early 2003, following Russia's decision to cease using the port of Ventspils for its petroleum exports, primarily owing to the opening of a new Russian petroleum terminal on the Baltic coast. Russia also condemned amendments to legislation on education, which took effect from September 2004, in accordance with which 60% of lessons in minority schools were to be taught in the Latvian language.

On 9 May 2005 President Vīķe-Freiberga travelled to Moscow to attend celebrations to commemorate the 60th anniversary of the end of the Second World War in Europe (her Estonian and Lithuanian counterparts declined to attend.) Three days later the Saeima adopted a declaration denouncing the Soviet occupation of Latvia and urging Russia to accept moral, legal and financial responsibility for the losses incurred by the Latvian people under Soviet rule. In late May the Saeima ratified the Council of Europe's Framework Convention for the Protection of National Minorities; however, a declaration was appended, stipulating that only Latvian citizens would be regarded as members of a national minority. Latvia (together with Estonia and Lithuania) expressed concerns at the signature in September of an agreement between Russia and Germany on the construction of a North European Gas Pipeline, which was to carry natural gas from Russia to Germany under the Baltic Sea, bypassing the Baltic countries. In August 2006 the Latvian authorities introduced a new citizenship law provision, stipulating that applicants who failed a Latvian language test three times would be disqualified permanently from obtaining citizenship. Proposals on granting Russian the status of a second official language in Latvia, were overwhelmingly rejected at a national referendum in February 2012, while later that year the Central Election Commission ruled against the organization of a further poll on the granting of automatic citizenship to the Russophone population (see Domestic Political Affairs), prompting Russian Minister of Foreign Affairs Sergei Lavrov to reiterate criticism of Latvia's citizenship laws.

CONSTITUTION AND GOVERNMENT

Under the terms of the 1922 Constitution, which was restored in July 1993 and subsequently amended, Latvia is an independent democratic parliamentary republic. The supreme legislative body is the Saeima (Parliament), the 100 members of which are elected by universal adult suffrage for a four-year term. The President of the Republic, who is Head of State, is elected by a secret ballot of the Saeima, also for a period of four years. The President, who is also Head of the Armed Forces, may not serve for more than two consecutive terms. Executive power is held by the Cabinet of Ministers, which is headed by the Prime Minister. The Prime Minister is appointed by the President; the remaining members of the Cabinet are nominated by the Prime Minister. Judges are independent, and their appointment is confirmed by the Saeima. For administrative purposes, Latvia is divided into nine cities (including the capital, Rīga) and 109 municipalities.

REGIONAL AND INTERNATIONAL CO-OPERATION

Latvia is a member of the European Bank for Reconstruction and Development (EBRD, see p. 276), the Council of the Baltic Sea States (see p. 258), the Baltic Council (see p. 474), the Council of Europe (see p. 260) and the Organization for Security and Co-operation in Europe (see p. 397). In 2004 it acceded to the European Union (see p. 281).

Latvia joined the UN in 1991, and was admitted to the World Trade Organization (see p. 444) in 1999. The country joined the North Atlantic Treaty Organization (see p. 380) in 2004.

ECONOMIC AFFAIRS

In 2011, according to estimates by the World Bank, Latvia's gross national income (GNI), measured at average 2009–11 prices, was US $27,418m., equivalent to $12,350 per head (or $17,820 per head on an international purchasing-power parity basis). During

2002–11, it was estimated, the population decreased by an annual average of 0.6%, while gross domestic product (GDP) per head increased at an average annual rate of 3.7%, in real terms. Overall GDP increased, in real terms, at an average annual rate of 3.1% in 2002–11, according to World Bank estimates. According to chain-linked methodologies, real GDP declined by 0.9% in 2010, but increased by 5.5% in 2011.

Agriculture (including hunting, forestry and fishing) contributed 5.1% of GDP and provided 8.9% of employment in 2011. The principal sectors are dairy farming and pig-breeding. Cereals, potatoes and fodder crops are the main crops grown. As part of the process of land reform and privatization, the dissolution of collective and state farms was undertaken in the early 1990s. Fishing makes an important contribution to the economy (an estimated 70% of the total annual catch is exported). Output of the forestry industry increased from 1996. According to World Bank estimates, agricultural GDP increased, in real terms, by an average of 2.4% per year in 2002–10. According to chain-linked methodologies, the real GDP of the sector decreased by 8.9% in 2010 and by 0.5% in 2011.

Industry (comprising mining and quarrying, manufacturing, construction and utilities) contributed 24.7% of GDP and provided 22.9% of employment in 2011. According to World Bank estimates, industrial GDP increased, in real terms, at an average annual rate of 1.5% in 2002–10. In 2011, the GDP of the industrial sector decreased, in real terms, by 8.7%, according to chain-linked methodologies.

Mining and quarrying contributed just 0.6% of GDP and employed 0.3% of workers in 2010. Latvia has limited mineral resources, the most important being peat, dolomite, limestone, gypsum, amber, gravel and sand. Offshore and onshore petroleum reserves have been located. According to chain-linked methodologies, the sector's GDP increased, in real terms, by 2.4% in 2010.

The manufacturing sector contributed 14.1% of GDP and (along with utilities) provided 15.8% of employment in 2011. According to World Bank estimates, real manufacturing GDP increased by an average of 1.4% per year in 2002–10. According to chain-linked methodologies, the GDP of the sector increased, in real terms, by 11.7% in 2011.

The construction sector contributed 5.5% of GDP and provided 7.1% of employment in 2011. During 2001–10, according to UN estimates, the GDP of the sector increased at an average annual rate of 2.3%. According to chain-linked methodologies, construction GDP declined by 31.1% in 2010, but increased by 11.9% in 2011.

Latvia is highly dependent on imported fuels to provide energy. In 2011 mineral products represented 17.3% of the total value of Latvia's imports. Electric energy is supplied primarily by Estonia and Lithuania, and petroleum products are supplied by Russia and Lithuania. In 2009 hydroelectric plants provided some 62.1% of annual domestic electricity production in Latvia; a further 36.0% was derived from natural gas.

The services sector contributed 70.2% of GDP and accounted for 68.2% of employment in 2011. According to World Bank estimates, the GDP of the sector increased, in real terms, by an annual average of 3.7% in 2002–10. According to chain-linked methodologies, real services GDP declined by 4.8% in 2011. The tourism sector expanded markedly in the mid-2000s, following a significant expansion in air services between Rīga and cities in central and western Europe. Total visitor arrivals numbered 1,063,294 in 2011, compared with 545,366 in 2004.

In 2011 Latvia recorded a visible merchandise trade deficit of US $3,241m., and there was a deficit of $628m. on the current account of the balance of payments. The principal source of imports in 2011 was Lithuania, which accounted for 18.8% of total imports; other major sources were Germany, Russia, Poland and Estonia. The main market for exports in that year was Lithuania, which accounted for 18.1% of the total; other significant purchasers were Estonia, Russia, Germany, Sweden and Poland. The principal exports in 2011 were wood and wood articles, followed by base metals and manufactures, machinery and electrical equipment, mineral products, chemicals, and prepared foodstuffs, beverages and tobacco. The principal imports in that year were mineral products, machinery and electrical equipment, base metals, chemicals, vehicles and transport equipment, prepared foodstuffs, beverages and tobacco, and plastics and rubber.

In 2011 there was a budgetary deficit of 490m. lats (equivalent to 3.4% of GDP). Latvia's general government gross debt was 5,349m. lats in 2011, equivalent to 37.8% of GDP. At the end of 2010 Latvia's external debt totalled US $39,555m., of which $6,891m. was public and publicly guaranteed debt. In that year the cost of debt-servicing was equivalent to 76.4% of the value of exports of goods and services. Annual consumer-price inflation averaged 5.9% in 2003–12. Consumer prices increased by 2.3% in 2012. According to official statistics, some 16.2% of the population were unemployed in 2011.

Latvian GDP declined by an estimated 18% in 2009, as a consequence of the international financial crisis. In early 2010 the IMF stated that the economic situation in Latvia had stabilized, following the introduction of an IMF- and European Union (EU, see p. 281)-funded programme of austerity measures. In May of that year, however, the Constitutional Court ruled that a government decision to reduce pensions by 70% for retired people in employment, and by 10% for other pensioners, was unconstitutional, forcing the Government to seek further financial assistance. Despite early legislative elections in September 2011, the authorities continued to meet IMF-recommended performance criteria and objectives in that year. The Government made an early repayment of €211.4m. to the IMF in September 2012, and in December, following the successful issuance of an international bond, announced its intention to repay all its outstanding obligations to the Fund earlier than scheduled. In a January 2013 report, the IMF continued to commend Latvia's significant economic recovery, and concluded that the country was well placed to meet all criteria for its planned adoption of the euro in 2014. Continued economic growth of 5.2% was estimated for 2012, while the budget deficit was reduced to 1.5% of GDP. Despite lack of public support for Latvia's accession to the euro area, particularly in view of the continuing sovereign debt crisis in Europe during 2012, legislation providing for the adoption of the euro as the national currency on 1 January 2014 was enacted in February 2013. On 4 March Latvia submitted a formal application to enter the euro area (having been admitted to the EU's exchange rate mechanism—ERM II—in 2005). The Government confirmed that it had fulfilled all the necessary fiscal criteria; however, the country's banking system, deemed vulnerable owing to its large proportion of non-resident deposits, was a potential source of concern for EU officials. Legislation had been adopted in January to enforce the stipulations of the EU's 'fiscal compact' treaty that government debt remain below 60% and the general budget deficit below 3% of GDP. A decision on Latvia's euro area application was expected in mid-2013.

PUBLIC HOLIDAYS

2014: 1 January (New Year's Day), 18–21 April (Easter), 1 May (Labour Day), 4 May (Declaration of Independence Day), 23–24 June (Midsummer Festival), 18 November (National Day, proclamation of the Republic), 25–26 December (Christmas—Gregorian), 31 December (New Year's Eve).

Statistical Survey

Source (unless otherwise stated): Central Statistical Bureau of Latvia, Lāčplēša iela 1, Rīga 1301; tel. 6736-6850; fax 6783-0137; e-mail csb@csb.lv; internet www.csb.lv.

Area and Population

AREA, POPULATION AND DENSITY

Area (sq km)	64,559*
Population (census results)†	
31 March 2000	2,377,383
1 March 2011	
Males	946,102
Females	1,124,269
Total	2,070,371
Density (per sq km) at 2011 census	32.1

* 24,926 sq miles.
† Figures refer to the resident population.

POPULATION BY AGE AND SEX
(population at 2011 census)

	Males	Females	Total
0–14	150,506	143,644	294,150
15–64	672,616	723,149	1,395,765
65 and over	122,980	257,476	380,456
Total	946,102	1,124,269	2,070,371

POPULATION BY ETHNIC GROUP
(population at 2011 census)

	Number	%
Latvian	1,285,136	62.1
Russian	557,119	26.9
Belarusian	68,202	3.3
Ukrainian	45,798	2.2
Polish	44,772	2.2
Lithuanian	24,479	1.2
Others	44,865	2.1
Total	2,070,371	100.0

PRINCIPAL TOWNS
(population at 2011 census)

Rīga (Riga, capital) .	658,640	Jūrmala . . .	50,840
Daugavpils . . .	93,312	Ventspils . . .	38,750
Liepāja . . .	76,731	Rēzekne . . .	32,328
Jelgava	59,511		

BIRTHS, MARRIAGES AND DEATHS

	Registered live births		Registered marriages		Registered deaths	
	Number	Rate (per 1,000)	Number	Rate (per 1,000)	Number	Rate (per 1,000)
2004 . .	20,334	8.8	10,370	4.5	32,024	13.8
2005 . .	21,497	9.3	12,554	5.5	32,777	14.2
2006 . .	22,264	9.7	14,616	6.4	33,098	14.5
2007 . .	23,273	10.2	15,486	6.8	33,042	14.5
2008 . .	23,948	10.6	12,946	5.7	31,006	13.7
2009 . .	21,677	9.6	9,925	4.4	29,897	13.3
2010 . .	19,219	8.6	9,290	4.1	30,040	13.4
2011 . .	18,586	9.0	10,760	5.2	28,519	13.8

Life expectancy (years at birth): 73.5 (males 68.8; females 78.4) in 2010 (Source: World Bank, World Development Indicators database).

IMMIGRATION AND EMIGRATION

	2009	2010	2011
Immigrants	2,688	2,790	5,589
Emigrants	7,388	10,702	17,709

ECONOMICALLY ACTIVE POPULATION
(annual averages, '000 persons aged 15–74 years)

	2009	2010	2011
Agriculture, forestry and fishing	86.9	82.5	76.6
Manufacturing; electricity, gas and water supply	159.8	159.2	136.5
Construction	76.8	66.4	60.9
Wholesale and retail trade; repair of motor vehicles, motorcycles and personal and household goods; hotels and restaurants .	188.0	179.0	161.4
Transport, storage and communications	112.6	111.0	98.5
Financial intermediation; real estate, renting and other business activities	90.5	92.8	91.1
Public administration and defence, compulsory social security . .	78.2	62.5	59.4
Education	89.5	95.5	88.8
Health and social work . . .	52.3	47.5	51.6
Other community, social and personal service activities . .	51.7	44.1	36.6
Sub-total	986.4	940.5	861.4
Activities not adequately defined .	0.3	0.4	0.2
Total employed	986.7	940.9	861.6
Males	480.3	454.8	416.2
Females	506.4	486.1	445.4
Unemployed	200.7	216.1	166.6
Total labour force	1,187.4	1,157.0	1,028.2

Health and Welfare

KEY INDICATORS

Total fertility rate (children per woman, 2010) . . .	1.5
Under-5 mortality rate (per 1,000 live births, 2009) .	8
HIV/AIDS (% of persons aged 15–49, 2009)	0.7
Physicians (per 1,000 head, 2006)	3.1
Hospital beds (per 1,000 head, 2006)	7.6
Health expenditure (2009): US $ per head (PPP) . . .	1,066
Health expenditure (2009): % of GDP	6.6
Health expenditure (2009): public (% of total) . . .	61.6
Access to water (% of persons, 2010)	99
Access to sanitation (% of persons, 2008)	78
Total carbon dioxide emissions ('000 metric tons, 2008) . .	7,590.7
Carbon dioxide emissions per head (metric tons, 2008) . .	3.3
Human Development Index (2011): ranking	43
Human Development Index (2011): value	0.805

For sources and definitions, see explanatory note on p. vi.

Agriculture

PRINCIPAL CROPS
('000 metric tons)

	2009	2010	2011
Wheat	1,036.4	1,035.4	937.0
Barley	265.5	228.4	236.7
Rye	162.2	70.2	76.4
Oats	141.4	100.6	120.9
Triticale (wheat-rye hybrid)	33.3	26.4	21.4
Potatoes	525.4	484.0	499.0
Peas, dry	2.6	2.6	2.9
Rapeseed	204.7	226.3	219.1
Cabbages and other brassicas	61.9	60.0	61.2
Cucumbers and gherkins	7.8	8.0	10.0
Onions, dry	29.8	16.3	20.2
Carrots and turnips	43.3	34.3	38.6
Apples	12.8	10.3	7.5
Currants	0.4	0.4	0.4

Aggregate production ('000 metric tons, may include official, semi-official or estimated data): Total cereals 1,663.2 in 2009, 1,481.5 in 2010, 1,421.9 in 2011; Total roots and tubers 525.4 in 2009, 484.0 in 2010, 499.0 in 2011; Total vegetables (incl. melons) 182.9 in 2009, 151.1 in 2010, 168.6 in 2011; Total fruits (excl. melons) 16.9 in 2009, 13.8 in 2010, 11.4 in 2011.

Source: FAO.

LIVESTOCK
('000 head at 1 January)

	2009	2010	2011
Cattle	380	378	380
Pigs	384	377	390
Sheep	67	71	77
Goats	13	13	14
Horses	13	13	12
Chickens*	3,920	4,105	4,208
Turkeys*	701	724	741

* Unofficial figures.
Source: FAO.

LIVESTOCK PRODUCTS
('000 metric tons unless otherwise indicated)

	2009	2010	2011
Cattle meat	20.5	18.4	18.0
Pig meat	38.8	37.2	37.6
Chicken meat	23.2	23.5	23.0
Cows' milk	828.1	830.9	841.7
Hen eggs	42.9	45.0	41.9

Source: FAO.

Forestry

ROUNDWOOD REMOVALS
('000 cubic metres, excl. bark)

	2009	2010	2011
Sawlogs, veneer logs and logs for sleepers	6,247	6,667	7,652
Pulpwood	1,701	2,704	3,254
Other industrial wood	759	851	743
Fuel wood	1,736	2,312	1,184
Total	10,442	12,534	12,833

Source: FAO.

SAWNWOOD PRODUCTION
('000 cubic metres, incl. railway sleepers)

	2009	2010	2011
Coniferous (softwood)	2,260	2,600	2,870
Broadleaved (hardwood)	260	550	562
Total	2,520	3,150	3,432

Source: FAO.

Fishing

('000 metric tons, live weight)

	2008	2009	2010
Capture	157.9	163.2	164.8
Atlantic cod	4.0	4.6	5.2
Jack and horse mackerels	31.3	35.1	40.2
Atlantic herring	22.5	21.6	21.4
Sardinellas	11.5	11.7	14.2
European sprat	57.3	49.6	45.9
Chub mackerel	8.1	10.5	8.1
Northern prawn	1.6	1.5	1.0
Aquaculture	0.6	0.5*	0.5
Total catch	158.5	163.7*	165.4

* FAO estimate.
Source: FAO.

Mining

('000 metric tons)

	2006	2007	2008
Peat	1,000.0	541.2	865.5
Gypsum	235.7	346.1	349.1
Limestone	468.1	388.1	515.9

Industry

SELECTED PRODUCTS
('000 metric tons, unless otherwise indicated)

	2007	2008	2009
Sausages	42	43	37
Preserved fish	65	64	40
Yoghurt	73	69	66
Ice-cream (million litres)	12.4	10.1	8.3
Beer ('000 hectolitres)	1,402	1,339	1,283
Plywood ('000 cu metres)	258	266	199
Electric energy (million kWh)	4,771	5,274	5,569

Source: UN Industrial Commodity Statistics Database.

Finance

CURRENCY AND EXCHANGE RATES

Monetary Units
100 santimi = 1 lats.

Sterling, Dollar and Euro Equivalents (31 December 2012)
£1 sterling = 83.79 santimi;
US $1 = 53.10 santimi;
€1 = 70.06 santimi;
10 lats = £11.93 = $18.83 = €14.27.

Average Exchange Rate (lats per US $)
2010	0.5305
2011	0.5012
2012	0.5469

GOVERNMENT FINANCE
(general government operations, million lats)

Summary of Balances

	2008	2009	2010
Revenue	5,719.0	4,723.8	4,592.1
Less Expense	5,534.0	5,202.2	5,012.6
Net operating balance	185.0	−478.4	−420.5
Less Net acquisition of non-financial assets	724.0	420.0	377.0
Net lending/borrowing	−539.0	−898.0	−797.5

Revenue

	2008	2009	2010
Tax revenue	3,335.0	2,434.4	2,346.5
Social contributions	1,402.0	1,166.7	1,093.2
Grants	431.0	528.1	600.0
Other revenue	551.0	594.7	552.3
Total	5,719.0	4,723.8	4,592.1

Expense/Outlays

Expense by economic type	2008	2009	2010
Compensation of employees	1,679.0	1,338.2	1,087.1
Use of goods and services	933.0	671.1	688.3
Interest	64.0	150.5	177.1
Subsidies	1,293.0	1,209.5	1,171.0
Social benefits	1,385.0	1,647.6	1,744.3
Other expense	180.0	185.4	144.7
Total	5,534.0	5,202.2	5,012.6

Outlays by function of government	2008	2009	2010
General public services	678.0	606.7	554.7
Defence	244.0	152.2	131.3
Public order and safety	357.0	280.7	253.8
Education	1,052.0	874.8	759.8
Health care	579.0	482.9	475.0
Social security and social welfare	1,515.0	1,742.1	1,800.3
Housing and community amenities	201.0	129.8	148.2
Recreation, sport, cultural and religious affairs	282.0	207.8	181.8
Economic affairs	1,183.0	979.2	973.5
Environmental protection	167.0	165.5	111.7
Total	6,258.0	5,621.8	5,390.1

Source: IMF, *Government Finance Statistics Yearbook*.

2011 (general government operations, million lats): Total revenue 4,993.4; Total expenditure 5,483.4.

INTERNATIONAL RESERVES
(US $ million at 31 December)

	2009	2010	2011
Gold (national valuation)	274.78	349.87	386.15
IMF special drawing rights	186.72	186.60	144.69
Reserve position in IMF	0.09	0.09	0.09
Foreign exchange	6,444.99	7,069.48	5,852.50
Total	6,906.58	7,606.04	6,383.43

Source: IMF, *International Financial Statistics*.

MONEY SUPPLY
(million lats at 31 December)

	2009	2010	2011
Currency outside depository corporations	667	807	1,040
Transferable deposits	2,313	2,964	3,317
Other deposits	2,816	2,674	2,105
Securities other than shares	77	103	199
Broad money	5,873	6,548	6,661

Source: IMF, *International Financial Statistics*.

COST OF LIVING
(Consumer Price Index; base: 2000 = 100)

	2010	2011	2012
Food and non-alcoholic beverages	188.7	204.7	209.4
Fuel and light	235.6	261.8	286.8
Clothing (incl. footwear)	96.9	98.7	96.9
Rent	154.3	163.0	178.5
Transport	162.3	175.0	180.4
Education	249.2	249.7	245.9
All items (incl. others)	169.0	176.4	180.4

NATIONAL ACCOUNTS
(million lats at current prices)*

Expenditure on the Gross Domestic Product

	2009	2010	2011
Government final consumption expenditure	2,557.2	2,349.1	2,470.3
Private final consumption expenditure	8,025.7	8,070.8	8,874.7
Gross fixed capital formation	2,820.3	2,329.7	3,044.5
Changes in inventories	−139.1	207.9	574.0
Total domestic expenditure	13,264.1	12,957.5	14,963.5
Exports of goods and services	5,741.7	6,847.0	8,392.4
Less Imports of goods and services	5,935.3	7,020.3	9,080.7
GDP in market prices	13,070.4	12,784.1	14,275.2

Gross Domestic Product by Economic Activity

	2009	2010	2011
Agriculture, forestry and fishing .	444.5	575.9	653.0
Mining and quarrying; electricity, gas and water supply . . .	581.9	602.3	657.4
Manufacturing	1,280.0	1,526.7	1,806.2
Construction	942.7	606.5	697.2
Wholesale and retail trade; repair of motor vehicles, motorcycles and personal and household goods	1,805.7	1,811.5	2,034.0
Hotels and restaurants . . .	184.1	170.3	220.3
Transport, storage and communications	1,818.1	1,817.5	2,107.5
Financial intermediation . . .	472.7	367.6	453.9
Real estate, renting and business activities	1,957.9	1,958.7	2,149.9
Public administration and defence; compulsory social security . .	992.1	865.7	893.4
Education	633.6	521.9	536.6
Health and social work . . .	377.2	352.0	360.6
Other community, social and personal service activities . .	304.2	286.5	221.0
GDP at basic prices	11,794.7	11,463.1	12,791.1
Taxes *less* subsidies on products .	1,275.7	1,321.0	1,484.2
GDP in purchasers' values .	13,070.4	12,784.1	14,275.2

* Figures revised in accordance with standard EU classification.

BALANCE OF PAYMENTS
(US $ million)

	2009	2010	2011
Exports of goods	6,987	8,777	11,499
Imports of goods	−8,979	−10,623	−14,740
Balance on goods	−1,992	−1,847	−3,241
Exports of services	4,013	3,819	4,617
Imports of services	−2,276	−2,182	−2,607
Balance on goods and services	−255	−210	−1,231
Primary income received . . .	1,324	992	1,251
Primary income paid . . .	331	−930	−1,517
Balance on goods, services and primary income	1,400	−148	−1,497
Secondary income received . .	1,984	1,643	1,816
Secondary income paid . . .	−1,100	−772	−947
Current balance	2,284	724	−628
Capital account (net)	622	470	607
Direct investment assets . . .	194	−82	−107
Direct investment liabilities . .	−44	433	1,502
Portfolio investment assets . .	161	−370	−857
Portfolio investment liabilities .	11	−34	237
Financial derivatives and employee stock options assets	639	349	581
Financial derivatives and employee stock options liabilities . .	−236	−616	−458
Other investment assets . . .	−1,046	−792	−404
Other investment liabilities . .	−1,481	214	−1,557
Net errors and omissions . . .	180	274	−103
Reserves and related items .	1,285	570	−1,186

Source: IMF, *International Financial Statistics*.

External Trade

PRINCIPAL COMMODITIES
(million lats)

Imports c.i.f.	2009	2010	2011
Live animals and animal products	181.7	211.9	265.9
Vegetable products	222.9	266.0	315.3
Prepared foodstuffs; beverages, spirits and vinegar; tobacco and manufactured substitutes .	416.9	435.3	510.5
Mineral products	808.6	907.6	1,337.9
Diesel oil	223.4	288.2	438.7
Natural gas	249.6	246.4	261.6
Products of chemical or allied industries	557.3	663.0	736.8
Pharmaceutical products . .	284.0	324.0	327.1
Plastics, rubber and articles thereof	237.8	333.2	416.2
Textiles and textile articles .	230.4	269.0	328.1
Base metals and articles thereof	379.7	605.9	843.7
Iron and steel	123.9	197.9	317.1
Machinery and mechanical appliances; electrical equipment; sound and television apparatus . . .	740.3	972.3	1,337.1
Electrical machinery and equipment	377.4	518.1	595.8
Vehicles, aircraft, vessels and associated transport equipment	304.6	423.9	694.4
Total (incl. others)	4,709.8	5,911.9	7,719.1

Exports f.o.b.	2009	2010	2011
Live animals and animal products	157.3	200.7	263.8
Vegetable products	214.9	267.7	257.5
Prepared foodstuffs; beverages, spirits and vinegar; tobacco and manufactured substitutes .	290.3	353.8	441.7
Mineral products	199.6	283.1	548.6
Products of chemical or allied industries	307.0	348.5	443.6
Pharmaceutical products . . .	158.7	197.1	217.0
Plastics, rubber and articles thereof	102.9	154.3	186.5
Wood, cork and articles thereof; wood charcoal; manufactures of straw, esparto, etc.	595.4	890.3	1,010.1
Textiles and textile articles .	178.8	206.7	242.8
Base metals and articles thereof	447.8	650.0	868.0
Iron and steel	212.4	278.2	310.6
Machinery and mechanical appliances; electrical equipment; sound and television apparatus . . .	509.4	609.1	763.1
Machinery and mechanical appliances	262.6	277.2	332.2
Electrical machinery and equipment	246.8	331.9	430.9
Miscellaneous manufactured articles	121.0	134.1	153.4
Total (incl. others)	3,602.2	4,694.9	5,998.5

2012: Total Imports 8,697.0; Total Exports 6,897.8.

PRINCIPAL TRADING PARTNERS
(million lats)*

Imports c.i.f.	2009	2010	2011
Austria	51.7	68.3	83.1
Belarus	163.3	202.4	341.3
Belgium	72.3	102.2	144.8
China, People's Republic	99.5	151.9	206.9
Czech Republic	69.1	86.5	113.8
Denmark	126.6	135.4	172.4
Estonia	375.7	422.9	574.9
Finland	168.6	290.0	355.6
France	120.7	143.1	182.8
Germany	543.1	680.1	935.5
Hungary	64.1	78.4	81.2
Italy	160.7	196.7	248.5
Lithuania	800.9	1,008.1	1,449.6
Netherlands	190.5	234.0	277.7
Poland	397.2	465.6	624.9
Russia	505.7	591.8	659.1
Spain	63.8	70.0	84.4
Sweden	168.3	209.9	295.6
Switzerland	85.0	86.0	97.6
Ukraine	57.1	65.4	97.1
United Kingdom	64.5	93.7	135.6
Total (incl. others)	4,709.8	5,911.9	7,719.1

Exports f.o.b.	2009	2010	2011
Belarus	92.2	99.8	107.4
Belgium	43.0	57.8	64.4
Denmark	148.6	181.7	201.4
Estonia	518.4	633.0	818.3
Finland	102.5	148.4	184.3
France	66.8	75.8	86.8
Germany	314.0	409.6	496.4
Italy	58.2	91.7	91.8
Lithuania	590.4	762.2	1,086.7
Netherlands	92.6	105.8	136.9
Norway	94.7	131.1	142.9
Poland	138.3	232.4	351.9
Russia	316.4	497.1	633.6
Spain	38.4	53.3	45.5
Sweden	219.5	295.6	380.5
Ukraine	37.7	52.8	52.9
United Kingdom	115.3	164.7	183.1
USA	58.6	65.7	71.5
Total (incl. others)	3,602.2	4,694.9	5,998.5

* Imports by country of origin; exports by country of destination.

2012: Total Imports 8,697.0; Total Exports 6,897.8.

Transport

RAILWAYS
(traffic)*

	2009	2010	2011
Passenger journeys (million)	21.6	20.9	20.5
Passenger-kilometres (million)	756	749	741
Freight transported (million metric tons)	53.7	49.2	59.4
Freight ton-kilometres (million)	18,725	17,179	21,410

* Data relating to passengers include railway personnel, and data on freight include passengers' baggage, parcel post and mail.

ROAD TRAFFIC
(motor vehicles in use at 31 December)

	2009	2010	2011
Passenger cars	904,308	636,664	612,321
Buses and coaches	9,687	5,377	5,186
Lorries and vans (incl. road tractors)	120,571	71,575	72,622

SHIPPING
Flag Registered Fleet
(at 31 December)

	2010	2011	2012
Number of vessels	151	148	153
Total displacement ('000 grt)	312.3	234.8	181.4

Source: Lloyd's List Intelligence (www.lloydslistintelligence.com).

International Sea-borne Freight Traffic
('000 metric tons)

	2010	2011	2012
Goods loaded	55,724	61,028	66,130
Goods unloaded	5,436	7,793	9,063

CIVIL AVIATION
(traffic)

	2009	2010	2011
Passengers carried (million)	2.9	3.4	3.5
Passenger-kilometres (million)	3,474	4,136	4,113
Cargo carried ('000 metric tons)	14	15	13
Cargo ton-kilometres (million)	19	18	13

Tourism

FOREIGN TOURIST ARRIVALS*

Country of residence	2009	2010	2011
Denmark	12,686	12,859	15,075
Estonia	58,762	62,906	81,979
Finland	72,024	79,655	90,991
Germany	93,739	98,305	113,064
Italy	27,303	27,510	37,963
Lithuania	71,811	84,509	100,561
Norway	49,190	64,273	72,309
Poland	24,038	27,447	35,309
Russia	72,227	119,007	174,343
Sweden	55,609	61,155	63,135
United Kingdom	35,596	39,524	43,959
USA	14,829	17,863	18,115
Total (incl. others)	753,875	877,774	1,063,294

* Figures refer to the number of visitors arriving at accommodation establishments.

Tourism receipts (US $ million, excl. passenger transport): 723 in 2009; 640 in 2010; 771 in 2011 (provisional) (Source: World Tourism Organization).

Communications Media

	2009	2010	2011
Telephones ('000 main lines in use)*	562	532	516
Mobile cellular telephones ('000 subscribers)	2,304	2,306	2,309
Broadband subscribers ('000)	437.0	434.9	457.4
Book production: titles	2,244	2,035	2,128
Book production: copies ('000)	3,500	3,300	3,500
Newspapers: number	244	197	208
Newspapers: average annual circulation (million copies)	153	117	111
Other periodicals: number	370	368	339
Other periodicals: average annual circulation (million copies)	35.4	36.2	36.1

* At 31 December.

Personal computers: 748,000 (326.9 per 1,000 persons) in 2006.

Source: partly International Telecommunication Union.

Education

(2011/12)

	Institutions	Students
Pre-primary (children ages 3–6)	605	90,859
General schools*	814	206,440
Primary (Grades 1–4)	37	5,428
Basic (Grades 5–9)	354	45,772
Secondary (Grades 10–12)	362	147,269
Special	61	7,971
Vocational schools	65	34,638
Higher education institutions	59	97,041

* Full-time education.

Teachers (2002, unless otherwise indicated): Pre-primary 7,996 (2004); Primary (including basic schools) 9,252; Secondary 16,495; Special schools 1,837; Vocational 5,639; Higher 4,864 (2011/12).

Pupil-teacher ratio (primary education, UNESCO estimate): 11.9 in 2009/10 (Source: UNESCO Institute for Statistics).

Adult literacy rate (UNESCO estimates): 99.8% (males 99.8%; females 99.8%) in 2010 (Source: UNESCO Institute for Statistics)

Directory

The Government

HEAD OF STATE

President: Andris Bērziņš (inaugurated 8 July 2011).

CABINET OF MINISTERS
(May 2013)

A coalition of the Reform Party (RP), Unity and the National Alliance.

Prime Minister: Valdis Dombrovskis (Unity).

Minister of Defence: Artis Pabriks (Unity).

Minister of Foreign Affairs: Edgars Rinkēvičs (RP).

Minister of the Economy: Daniels Pavļuts (RP).

Minister of Finance: Andris Vilks (Unity).

Minister of Education and Science: Vjačeslavs Dombrovskis (RP).

Minister of Culture: Žaneta Jaunzeme-Grende (National Alliance).

Minister of Welfare: Ilze Viņķele (Unity).

Minister of Transport: Anrijs Matīss (Independent).

Minister of Justice: Jānis Bordāns (National Alliance).

Minister of the Interior: Rihards Kozlovskis (RP).

Minister of Environmental Protection and Regional Development: Edmunds Sprūdžs (RP).

Minister of Health: Ingrīda Circene (Unity).

Minister of Agriculture: Laimdota Straujama (Unity).

MINISTRIES

Chancery of the President: Pils lauk. 3, Rīga 1900; tel. 6709-2106; fax 6709-2157; e-mail prese@president.lv; internet www.president.lv.

Office of the Cabinet of Ministers: Brīvības bulv. 36, Rīga 1520; tel. 6708-2800; fax 6728-0469; e-mail vk@mk.gov.lv; internet www.mk.gov.lv.

Ministry of Agriculture: Republikas lauk. 2, Rīga 1981; tel. 6702-7010; fax 6702-7512; e-mail zm@zm.gov.lv; internet www.zm.gov.lv.

Ministry of Culture: K. Valdemāra iela 11A, Rīga 1364; tel. 6733-0200; fax 6733-0293; e-mail mail@km.gov.lv; internet www.km.gov.lv.

Ministry of Defence: K. Valdemāra iela 10–12, Rīga 1473; tel. 6733-5114; fax 6721-2307; e-mail kanceleja@mod.gov.lv; internet www.mod.gov.lv.

Ministry of the Economy: Brīvības iela 55, Rīga 1519; tel. 6701-3101; fax 6728-0882; e-mail pasts@em.gov.lv; internet www.em.gov.lv.

Ministry of Education and Science: Vaļņu iela 2, Rīga 1050; tel. 6722-6209; fax 6722-3905; e-mail info@izm.gov.lv; internet www.izm.gov.lv.

Ministry of Environmental Protection and Regional Development: Peldu iela 25, Rīga 1494; tel. 6702-6533; fax 6782-0442; e-mail pasts@varam.gov.lv; internet www.varam.gov.lv.

Ministry of Finance: Smilšu iela 1, Rīga 1919; tel. 6709-5405; fax 6709-5503; e-mail info@fm.gov.lv; internet www.fm.gov.lv.

Ministry of Foreign Affairs: K. Valdemāra iela 3, Rīga 1395; tel. 6701-6201; fax 6782-8121; e-mail mfa.cha@mfa.gov.lv; internet www.mfa.gov.lv.

Ministry of Health: Brīvības iela 72, Rīga 1011; tel. 6787-6000; fax 6787-6002; e-mail vm@vm.gov.lv; internet www.vm.gov.lv.

Ministry of the Interior: Čiekurkalna 1, līnija 1, korp. 2, Rīga 1026; tel. 6721-9263; fax 6782-9686; e-mail kanceleja@iem.gov.lv; internet www.iem.gov.lv.

Ministry of Justice: Brīvības bulv. 36, Rīga 1536; tel. 6703-6801; fax 6721-0823; e-mail tm.kanceleja@tm.gov.lv; internet www.tm.gov.lv.

Ministry of Transport: Gogoļa iela 3, Rīga 1743; tel. 6702-8205; fax 6782-0630; e-mail una.vitola@sam.gov.lv; internet www.sam.gov.lv.

Ministry of Welfare: Skolas iela 28, Rīga 1331; tel. 6702-1600; fax 6727-6445; e-mail lm@lm.gov.lv; internet www.lm.gov.lv.

President

In voting by members of the Saeima (Parliament), conducted on 2 June 2011, Andris Bērziņš was elected President. In a first round of voting (in which a successful candidate was required to obtain 51 votes) he obtained the support of 50 deputies, compared with the 43 who voted in favour of the incumbent, Valdis Zatlers. In a second round of voting, held on the same day, Bērziņš was duly elected, receiving 53 votes, while Zatlers obtained 41. Bērziņš was inaugurated on 8 July.

Legislature

Saeima
(Parliament)

Jēkaba iela 11, Rīga 1811; tel. 6708-7321; fax 6708-7100; e-mail saeima@saeima.lv; internet www.saeima.lv.

Chairman: SOLVITA ĀBOLTIŅA.

General Election, 17 September 2011

Coalitions		Votes	%	Seats
Harmony Centre*	. . . .	259,930	28.36	31
Zatlers Reform Party	. . . .	190,853	20.82	22
Unity†	. . . . .	172,567	18.83	20
National Alliance	. . . .	127,208	13.88	14
Greens' and Farmer's Union‡	. . .	111,955	12.22	13
Others	. . . . . .	53,956	5.89	—
Total‖	. . . .	916,469	100.00	100

* Coalition comprising the Harmony Social Democratic Party and the Latvian Socialist Party.

† Coalition comprising the Civic Union, New Era and Society for a Different Politics.

‡ Comprising the Latvian Green Party and the Centre Party Latvian Farmers' Union.

‖ Excluding 1,211 invalid votes (0.13% of the total votes cast).

Election Commission

Central Election Commission (Centrālā vēlēšanu komisija—CVK): Smilšu iela 4, Rīga 1050; tel. 6732-2688; fax 6732-5251; e-mail cvk@cvk.lv; internet www.cvk.lv; Chair. ARNIS CIMDARS.

Political Organizations

The following are among the most influential political parties in Latvia:

Centre Party Latvian Farmers' Union (CP LZS) (Centriskā partija Latvijas Zemnieku savienība): Republikas lauk. 2, Rīga 1010; tel. 6732-3628; fax 6702-7467; e-mail info@lzs.lv; internet www.lzs.lv; f. 1990; rural, centrist; forms part of the Greens' and Farmers' Union; Chair. AUGUSTS BRIGMANIS.

For Human Rights in a United Latvia (PCTVL/ZaPChEL) (Par cilvēka tiesībām vienotā Latvijā/Za prava cheloveka v yedinoi Latvii): Rūpniecības iela 9, Rīga 1010; tel. and fax 6732-0290; e-mail pctvl.info@gmail.com; internet www.pctvl.lv; f. 1998 as electoral alliance; became united party Nov. 2003; represents interests of Russian-speaking communities in Latvia; opposed to Latvian membership of NATO; Leaders TATJANA ŽDANOKA, JAKOVS PLINERS, MIROSLAV MITROFANOV.

Harmony Centre (SC) (Saskaņas Centrs/ Tsentr soglasiya): Jūra Alunana 8/3, Rīga 1010; tel. 6733-3515; e-mail office@saskanascentrs.lv; internet www.saskanascentrs.lv; formed in 2005 by merger of the National Harmony Party and the New Centre, subsequently joined by the Latvian Socialist Party (q.v.), the Social Democratic Union and by the Harmony Social Democratic Party (q.v.); Chair. NILS UŠAKOVS.

Harmony Social Democratic Party (SDPS) (Sociāldemokrātiskā Partija 'Saskaņa'): Jēkaba iela 16, Rīga 1811; tel. 67087239; fax 67087227; e-mail saskanas.centrs@saeima.lv; internet www.saskanascentrs.lv; f. 2010; absorbed Daugavpils City Party in 2011; Chair. JĀNIS URBANOVIČS.

Latvian Green Party (LZP) (Latvijas Zaļā partija): Kalnciema iela 30, Rīga 1046; tel. and fax 6761-4272; e-mail birojs@zp.lv; internet www.zp.lv; f. 1990; forms part of the Greens' and Farmers' Union; Co-Chair. VIESTURS SILENIEKS, RAIMONDS VĒJONIS.

Latvian Social Democratic Workers' Party (LSDSP) (Latvijas Sociāl-demokrātiskā strādnieku partija): Aldaru iela 8, Rīga 1050; tel. 6735-6585; fax 6735-6588; e-mail lsdsp@lis.lv; internet www.lsdsp.lv; f. 1904; Chair. AIVARS TIMOFEJEVS.

Latvian Socialist Party (LSP) (Latvijas Sociālistiskā partija/Sotsialisticheskaya partiya Latvii): Citadeles iela 2, Rīga 1010; tel. and fax 6755-5535; e-mail latsocpartija@inbox.lv; internet www.latsocpartija.lv; f. 1994; joined the Harmony Centre alliance in Dec. 2005, remained affiliated to Harmony Centre at 2006 and 2010 legislative elections; Chair. ALFRĒDS RUBIKS.

National Alliance (Nacionālā apvienība): Rīga; e-mail tb@tb.lv; internet www.visulatvijaidodu.lv; f. 2011 by merger of For Fatherland and Freedom Union/Latvian National Independence Movement and All for Latvia; Leaders GAIDIS BĒRZIŅŠ, RAIVIS DZINTARS.

Reform Party (RP) (Reformu partija): Vīlandes iela 14-1/6, Rīga 1050; tel. 6728-3908; e-mail birojs@reformupartija.lv; internet www.reformupartija.lv; f. 2011 by fmr President Valdis Zatlers; centre-right; Chair. VALDIS ZATLERS.

Unity (Vienotība): K. Barona iela 3, Rīga 1050; tel. 6720-5472; e-mail birojs@vienotiba.lv; internet vienotiba.lv; f. 2010 as coalition of the Civic Union (f. 2008), New Era (f. 2002) and Society for a Different Politics (f. 2008); constituted as a party 2011; Pres. SOLVITA ĀBOLTIŅA.

Diplomatic Representation

EMBASSIES IN LATVIA

Austria: Elizabetes iela 15, Rīga 1010; tel. 6721-6125; fax 6721-6126; e-mail riga-ob@bmeia.gv.at; internet www.bmeia.gv.at/riga; Ambassador STEFAN PEHRINGER.

Azerbaijan: Raiņa bulv. 2–5, Rīga 1050; tel. 6714-2889; fax 6714-2896; e-mail office@azembassy.lv; internet www.azembassy.lv; f. 2005; Ambassador ELMAN ZEYNALOV.

Belarus: Jēzusbaznīcas iela 12, Rīga 1050; tel. 6722-2560; fax 6732-2891; e-mail latvia@mfa.gov.by; internet www.latvia.mfa.gov.by; Ambassador ALYAKSANDR GERASIMENKA.

Belgium: Alberta iela 13, Rīga 1010; tel. 6711-4852; fax 6711-4855; e-mail riga@diplobel.fed.be; internet www.diplomatie.be/riga; Ambassador FRANK ARNAUTS.

Canada: Baznicas iela 20–22, Rīga 1010; tel. 6781-3945; fax 6781-3960; e-mail riga@international.gc.ca; internet latvia.gc.ca; Ambassador JOHN MORRISON.

China, People's Republic: Ganību dambis 5, Rīga 1045; tel. 6735-7023; fax 6735-7025; e-mail chinaemb_lv@mfa.gov.cn; internet lv.chineseembassy.org; Ambassador HU YESHUN.

Czech Republic: Elizabetes iela 29A, Rīga 1010; tel. 6721-7814; fax 6721-7821; e-mail riga@embassy.mzv.cz; internet www.mfa.cz/riga; Ambassador PAVOL SEPEĻÁK.

Denmark: Pils iela 11, Rīga 1863; tel. 6722-6210; fax 6782-0234; e-mail rixamb@um.dk; internet letland.um.dk; Ambassador PER CARLSEN.

Estonia: Skolas iela 13, Rīga 1010; tel. 6781-2020; fax 6781-2029; e-mail embassy.riga@mfa.ee; internet www.estemb.lv; Ambassador MATI VAARMANN.

Finland: Kalpaka bulv. 1, Rīga 1605; tel. 6707-8800; fax 6707-8814; e-mail sanomat.rii@formin.fi; internet www.finland.lv; Ambassador PIRKKO HÄMÄLÄINEN.

France: Raiņa bulv. 9, Rīga 1050; tel. 6703-6600; fax 6703-6616; e-mail webmastre.ambafrance-lv@diplomatie.gouv.fr; internet www.ambafrance-lv.org; Ambassador STÉPHANE VISCONTI.

Georgia: Raiņa bulv. 3/2, Rīga 1050; tel. and fax 6721-3136; e-mail riga.emb@mfa.gov.ge; internet www.latvia.mfa.gov.ge; Ambassador TEIMURAZ JANJALIA.

Germany: Raiņa bulv. 13, Rīga 1050; tel. 6708-5100; fax 6708-5149; e-mail info@riga.diplo.de; internet www.riga.diplo.de; Ambassador ANDREA WIKTORIN.

Greece: Elizabetes iela 11/5, Rīga 1010; tel. 6735-6345; fax 6735-6351; e-mail gremb.rig@mfa.gr; Ambassador GEORGIOS CHATZIMI-CHELAKIS.

Hungary: Baznicas iela 20/22, Rīga 1010; tel. 6721-7500; fax 6721-7878; e-mail mission.rix@mfa.gov.hu; internet www.mfa.gov.hu/emb/riga; Ambassador GÁBOR DOBOKAY.

Ireland: Alberta iela 13, Rīga 1010; tel. 6703-9370; fax 6703-9371; e-mail irijas.vestnieciba@gmail.com; internet www.embassyofireland.lv; Ambassador AIDAN KIRWAN.

Israel: Elizabetes iela 2, Rīga 1010; tel. 6763-5574; fax 6763-5555; e-mail press@riga.mfa.gov.il; internet embassies.gov.il/riga; Ambassador HAGIT BEN-YAAKOV.

Italy: Teātra iela 9, Rīga 1050; tel. 6721-6069; fax 6721-6084; e-mail ambitalia.riga@esteri.it; internet www.ambriga.esteri.it; Ambassador GIOVANNI POLIZZI.

Japan: Vesetas iela 7, Rīga 1013; tel. 6781-2001; fax 6781-2004; internet www.lv.emb-japan.go.jp; Ambassador TOSHIYUKI TAGA.

Lithuania: Rūpniecibas iela 24, Rīga 1010; tel. 6732-1519; fax 6732-1589; e-mail info@lv.mfa.lt; internet lv.mfa.lt; Ambassador RIČARDAS DEGUTIS.

Moldova: Zigfrīda Annas Meierovica bulv. 14, Rīga 1050; tel. 6735-9160; fax 6735-9165; e-mail riga@moldovaembassy.lv; internet www.letonia.mfa.md; Ambassador ALEKSEI CRACAN.

Netherlands: Torņa iela 4, Jēkaba Kazarmas 1A, Rīga 1050; tel. 6732-6147; fax 6732-6151; e-mail rig@minbuza.nl; internet latvia.nlembassy.org; Ambassador HENDRIK G. C. VAN DEN DOOL.

Norway: Zirgu iela 14, POB 181, Rīga 1050; tel. 6781-4100; fax 6781-4108; e-mail emb.riga@mfa.no; internet www.norvegija.lv; Ambassador Jāns Grēvstads.

Poland: Mednieku iela 6B, Rīga 1010; tel. 6703-1500; fax 6703-1549; e-mail ryga.ambasada@msz.gov.pl; internet ryga.msz.gov.pl; Ambassador Jerzy Marek Nowakowski.

Portugal: Balasta Dambis 60, Oglu iela, Ķīpsala, Rīga 1048; tel. 6782-1926; fax 6767-1626; e-mail embporturiga@gmail.com; Ambassador Manuel Marcel Monteiro Curto.

Russia: Antonijas iela 2, Rīga 1010; tel. 6733-2151; fax 6783-0209; e-mail rusembas@delfi.lv; internet www.latvia.mid.ru; Ambassador Aleksandr A. Veshnyakov.

Slovakia: Smilšu iela 8, Rīga 1050; tel. 6781-4280; fax 6781-4290; e-mail emb.riga@mzv.sk; internet www.mzv.sk/riga; Ambassador Dušan Krištofik.

Spain: Elizabetes iela 11, 3rd Floor, Rīga 1010; tel. 6732-0281; fax 6732-5005; e-mail emb.riga@maec.es; internet www.maec.es/embajadas/riga; Ambassador María Consuelo Femenía Guardiola.

Sweden: A. Pumpura iela 8, Rīga 1010; tel. 6768-6600; fax 6768-6601; e-mail ambassaden.riga@gov.se; internet www.swedenemb.lv; Ambassador Mats Staffansson.

Switzerland: World Trade Centre, Elizabetes iela 2, Rīga 1340; tel. 6733-8351; fax 6733-8354; e-mail rig.vertretung@eda.admin.ch; internet www.eda.admin.ch/riga; Ambassador Markus Dutly.

Turkey: A. Pumpura iela 2, Rīga 1010; tel. 6782-1600; fax 6732-0334; e-mail embassy.riga@mfa.gov.tr; internet riga.emb.mfa.gov .tr; Ambassador Şerife Serap Özcoşkun.

Ukraine: Kalpaka bulv. 3, Rīga 1010; tel. 6724-3082; fax 6732-5583; e-mail emb_lv@mfa.gov.ua; internet www.mfa.gov.ua/latvia; Ambassador Anatoliy T. Oliynyk.

United Kingdom: J. Alunāna iela 5, Rīga 1010; tel. 6777-4700; fax 6777-4707; e-mail britishembassy.riga@fco.gov.uk; internet ukinlatvia.fco.gov.uk; CAmbassador Sarah Cowley (designate).

USA: Samnera Velsa iela 1, Rīga 1510; tel. 6710-7000; fax 6710-7050; e-mail ambassador-riga@state.gov; internet riga.usembassy.gov; Ambassador Mark Pekala.

Uzbekistan: Elizabetes iela 11/11, Rīga 1010; tel. 6732-2424; fax 6732-2306; e-mail posoluz@apollo.lv; Ambassador Afzal Artykov.

Judicial System

Constitutional Court (Latvijas Republikas Satversmes tiesa): J. Alunāna iela 1, Rīga 1010; tel. 6721-0274; fax 6783-0770; e-mail tiesa@satv.tiesa.gov.lv; internet www.satv.tiesa.gov.lv; f. 1996; comprises seven judges, appointed by the Saeima for a term of 10 years; Chair. Gunārs Kūtris.

Supreme Court (Latvijas Republikas Augstākā tiesa): Brīvības bulv. 36, Rīga 1511; tel. 6702-0350; fax 6702-0351; e-mail at@at.gov .lv; internet www.at.gov.lv; Chair. Ivars Bičkovičs.

Office of the Prosecutor-General: Kalpaka bulv. 6, Rīga 1801; tel. 6704-4400; fax 6704-4449; e-mail gen@lrp.gov.lv; internet www.lrp .gov.lv; Prosecutor-General Ēriks Kalnmeiers.

Religion

From the 16th century the traditional religion of the Latvians was Lutheran Christianity, although there remained a substantial Roman Catholic population. Russian Orthodoxy is the religion of much of the Slavic population. During the period of Soviet rule many places of religious worship were closed. Following the restoration of independence in 1991, religious organizations regained their legal rights and property.

Board of Religious Affairs: Pils lauk. 4, Rīga 1050; tel. 6722-0585; e-mail zlp@zlp.gov.lv; f. 2000; govt agency, attached to the Ministry of Justice; Principal Ireta Romanovska.

CHRISTIANITY

Protestant Churches

Evangelical Lutheran Church of Latvia: Pils iela 4, Rīga 1050; tel. 6782-0041; fax 6722-5436; e-mail lelb@lelb.lv; internet www.lelb .lv; f. 1922; 708,000 mems; Archbishop Jānis Vanags.

Latvian Conference of Seventh-day Adventists in Latvia: Baznīcas iela 12A, Rīga 1010; tel. and fax 6724-0013; e-mail viesturs@baznica.lv; internet www.adventistu.baznica.lv; f. 1920; Pres. of Council Viesturs Reķis.

Latvian Pentecostal Union: J. Asara iela 8, Jelgava 3001; tel. 6308-1401; fax 6308-1407; e-mail lvdaddf@hotmail.com; f. 1989; Bishop Jānis Ozolinkevičs.

Union of Baptist Churches in Latvia: Lāčplēša iela 37, Rīga 1011; tel. and fax 6722-3379; internet www.lbds.lv; e-mail kanceleja@lbds .lv; f. 1860; Bishop Dr Pēteris Sproģis.

United Methodist Church in Latvia: Klaipēdas iela 56, Liepāja 3401; tel. 6343-2161; fax 6346-9848; re-est. 1991; Supt Ārijs Vīksna.

The Roman Catholic Church

Latvia comprises one archdiocese and three dioceses.

Bishops' Conference

M. Pils iela 2A, Rīga 1050; tel. 6722-7266; fax 6722-0775; Pres. Cardinal Jānis Pujats (Archbishop of Rīga).

Archbishop of Rīga: Cardinal Jānis Pujats, Pils iela 2A, Rīga 1050; tel. 6722-7266; fax 6722-0775; e-mail curia@e-apollo.lv; internet www.catholic.lv.

The Orthodox Church

Although the Latvian Orthodox Church has close ties with the Moscow Patriarchate, it has administrative independence.

Latvian Orthodox Church: Pils iela 14, Rīga 1050; tel. 6722-5855; fax 6722-4345; e-mail sinode@orthodoxy.lv; internet www .pareizticiba.lv; f. 1850; Metropolitan of Rīga and all Latvia Aleksandr (Kudrjashov).

Latvian Old Believer (Old Ritualist) Pomor Church: Krasta iela 73, Rīga 1003; tel. 6711-3083; fax 6714-4513; e-mail oldbel@junik .lv; f. 1760 in split from Moscow Patriarchate; Head of Central Council Ivans Mizoļubovs.

JUDAISM

Jewish Religious Community of Rīga: Peitavas iela 6/8, Rīga 1050; tel. 6722-4549; f. 1764; Rabbi Natan Barkan.

The Press

The joint-stock company Preses nams (Press House—q.v.) is the leading publisher of newspapers and magazines in Latvia. In 2002 there were eight daily newspapers, with an average circulation of 183,000. In 2010 a total of 197 daily and non-daily newspapers and 368 other periodicals were published. The publications listed below are in Latvian, unless otherwise indicated.

DAILIES

Bizness & Baltiya (Business and the Baltics): K. Valdemāra iela 149, Rīga 1013; tel. 6703-3011; fax 6703-3010; e-mail media@bb.lv; internet www.bb.lv; f. 1991; 5 a week; in Russian; Editor-in-Chief Aleksei Sherbakov; circ. 12,000 (2007).

Chas (Hour): Peldu iela 15, Rīga 1050; tel. 6708-8733; fax 6721-1067; internet www.chas-daily.com; f. 1997; 5 a week; in Russian; Editor-in-Chief Pavel Kirillov; circ. 13,100 (2010).

Diena (Day): Mūkusalas iela 15, Rīga 1004; tel. 6706-3300; fax 6706-3190; e-mail info@dienasmediji.lv; internet www.diena.lv; f. 1990; social and political issues; associated with free newspaper *5min*, launched in Sept. 2005; Editor-in-Chief Guntis Bojārs; circ. 85,000 (2009).

Neatkarīgā Rīta Avīze (Independent Morning Paper): Balasta dambis 3, Rīga 1081; tel. 6706-2462; fax 6706-2465; e-mail redakcija@nra.lv; internet www.nra.lv; f. 1990; Editor-in-Chief Aldis Bērziņš; circ. 40,000.

Rīgas Balss (RB) (Voice of Rīga): Rīga; tel. 6706-2420; fax 6706-2400; e-mail balss@rb.lv; internet www.rigasbalss.lv; f. 1957; city evening newspaper; Editor-in-Chief Iveta Mediņa; circ. 18,100 (Mon.–Thur.), 42,700 (Fri.).

Vakara Ziņas (The Evening News): Bezdelīgas iela 12, Rīga 1007; tel. 6761-7595; fax 6761-2383; e-mail vakara.zinas@vz.lv; internet www.vz.lv; f. 1993; popular; Editor-in-Chief Ainārs Vladimirovs; circ. 53,000.

Vesti Segodnya (News Today): Martiņa 9, Rīga 1048; tel. 6706-6130; fax 6706-8131; e-mail sm@fenster.lv; internet www.ves.lv; f. 1945; in Russian; 6 a week; Editor-in-Chief Aleksandrs Bļinovs; circ. 25,500.

OTHER NEWSPAPERS

The Baltic Times: Katrinas iela 2–3, Rīga 1010; tel. 6722-9978; fax 6722-6041; e-mail editor@baltictimes.com; internet www .baltictimes.com; f. 1996; news from Estonia, Latvia and Lithuania; in English; Man. Dir Sergei Alekseyev; Editor-in-Chief Dorian Ziedonis; circ. 12,000 (2007).

Dienas Bizness (Daily Business): Mūkusalas iela 15, Rīga 1004; tel. 6706-3100; fax 6706-3190; e-mail redakcija@db.lv; internet www.db .lv; f. 1992; Man. Editor Indra Lazdiņa; circ. 17,000.

Ieva (Eve): Stabu iela 34, Rīga 1880; tel. 6700-6102; fax 6700-6111; e-mail ieva@santa.lv; internet www.ieva.lv; f. 1997; weekly; illustrated journal for women; Editor-in-Chief INITA SILA; circ. 73,650.

Izglitība un Kultūra (Education and Culture): Marijas iela 2/5, Rīga 1050; tel. 6735-7585; fax 6735-7584; e-mail redakcija@ izglitiba-kultura.lv; internet www.izglitiba-kultura.lv; f. 1948; Man. Editor VIOLETA BRENČEVA.

Latvijas Avīze (Latvian Newspaper): Dzirnavu iela 21, Rīga 1010; tel. 6709-6600; fax 6709-6645; e-mail redakcija@la.lv; internet www2 .la.lv; f. 1987; fmrly *Lauku Avīze* (Country Newspaper); present name adopted 2004; 6 issues a week; popular; agriculture, politics and sport; Editor-in-Chief LINDA RASA; circ. 59,500.

Latvijas Vēstnesis (Latvian Herald): Bruņinieku iela 41, Rīga 1011; tel. 6729-8833; fax 6731-2190; e-mail info@lv.lv; internet www.lv.lv; f. 1993; official newspaper; 4 a week; Editor-in-Chief OSKARS GERTS; circ. 3,500.

Privātā Dzīve (Private Life): Stabu iela 34, Rīga 1011; tel. 6700-6104; fax 6700-6111; e-mail pdz@santa.lv; weekly; Man. Editor ZITA RAMMA; circ. 56,000 (2010).

Rīgas Viļņi (Riga Waves): Lāčplēša iela 20A, Rīga 1011; tel. 6784-2577; fax 6784-2578; e-mail info@rigasvilni.lv; internet www.abone .rigasvilni.lv; weekly.

PRINCIPAL PERIODICALS

Baltiskii Kurs/The Baltic Course: Lāčplēša iela 53, Rīga 1011; tel. 2926-9645; fax 2926-9645; e-mail olga.pavuk@baltic-course.com; internet www.baltic-course.com; f. 1996; quarterly; business; in Russian and English; Int. Editor EUGENE ETERIS; Editor-in-Chief OLGA PAVUK.

Karogs (Banner): Kuršu iela 24, Rīga 1006; tel. 6755-4128; fax 6755-4146; e-mail karogs@apollo.lv; internet www.ekarogs.lv; f. 1940; literary monthly; Editor-in-Chief IEVA KOLMANE; circ. 1,500.

Klubs (Club): Stabu iela 34, Rīga 1011; tel. 6700-6103; fax 6700-6111; e-mail klubs@santa.lv; internet www.klubs.lv; f. 1994; monthly; politics, business, fashion; Editor-in-Chief JURIS ŠLEIERS; circ. 17,000 (Jan. 2010).

Latvijas Ekonomists: Alūksnes iela 5, Rīga 1045; tel. 6779-0631; fax 6779-0619; e-mail birojs@ekonomists.lv; internet www .ekonomists.lv; f. 1992; monthly; in Latvian and Russian; Dir INESE LAPIŅA.

Māksla Plus (M+): Akadēmijas lauk. 1, a.k. 41, Rīga 1027; tel. 6722-0722; fax 6782-0608; e-mail makslap@latnet.lv; internet www .makslaplus.lv; cultural magazine (cinema, music, theatre, photography); Editor-in-Chief SANITA BUČINIECE.

Mans Mazais (My Little One): Stabu iela 34, Rīga 1880; tel. 6700-6105; fax 6700-6111; e-mail mansmazais@santa.lv; internet www .mansmazais.lv; f. 1994; monthly; illustrated journal for parents; Editor-in-Chief SINDIJA MELUŠKĀNE; circ. 20,000.

Mūsmājas (Our Home): Mūkusalas iela 15, Rīga 1004; tel. 6729-9105; fax 6729-2701; e-mail musmajas@musmajas.lv; internet www .musmajas.lv; f. 1993; monthly; home and family magazine; Editor-in-Chief AIVA KALVE; circ. 50,000.

Mūzikas Saule (Musical Sun): K. Barona iela 37/5, Rīga 1011; tel. 2935-9688; fax 2678-9826; e-mail saule@muzikassaule.lv; internet www.muzikassaule.lv; music; Editor-in-Chief ORESTS SILABRIEDIS.

Rīgas Laiks (Rīga Times): Zaļā iela 5-1, Rīga 1010; tel. 6728-7922; e-mail pasts@rigaslaiks.lv; internet www.rigaslaiks.lv; f. 1993; monthly; Editor-in-Chief ULDIS TĪRONS; circ. 6,000.

Santa: Stabu iela 34, Rīga 1011; tel. 6700-6103; fax 6700-6111; e-mail santa@santa.lv; internet www.zurnalssanta.lv; f. 1991; monthly; illustrated journal for women; Editor-in-Chief SANTA DANSBERGA-ANČA; circ. 42,000.

Zinātnes Vēstnesis (Scientific Herald): Akadēmijas lauk. 1, Rīga 1050; tel. 6721-2706; fax 6782-1109; e-mail lza@lza.lv; internet www .lza.lv/zv00.htm; f. 1989; published by the Latvian Scientific Council, the Latvian Academy of Science and the Latvian Society of Scientists; two a month; Man. Editor JURIS EKMANIS.

NEWS AGENCIES

Baltic News Service: Berga Bazārs, Marijas iela 13/1, Rīga 1050; tel. 6708-8600; fax 6708-8601; e-mail bns@bns.lv; internet www.bns .lv; f. 1990; news from Latvia, Lithuania, Estonia and the CIS; in English, Russian and the Baltic languages; Dir SIGITA KIRILKA.

LETA Latvian News Agency: Marijas iela 2, Rīga 1050; tel. 6722-2509; fax 6722-3850; e-mail redaktori@leta.lv; internet www.leta.lv; independent; Chair. MĀRTIŅŠ BARKĀNS.

PRESS ASSOCIATION

Latvian Union of Journalists (Latvijas Žurnālistu savienība): K. Valdemāra iela 118–211, Rīga 1013; tel. 6721-1433; e-mail zurnalistu

.savieniba@e-apollo.lv; internet www.zurnalistusavieniba.lv; f. 1992; 600 mems; Pres. JURIS PAIDERS.

Publishers

AGB: K. Barona iela 31, Rīga 1011; tel. 6728-0464; fax 6728-0356; e-mail info@izdevnieciba.com; internet www.izdevnieciba.com.

Avots (Spring): Puškina iela 1A, Rīga 1050; tel. 6721-1394; fax 6722-5824; e-mail avots@apollo.lv; f. 1980; non-fiction, dictionaries, crafts, hobbies, etc.; Pres. JĀNIS LEJA.

Elpa (Breath): Doma lauk. 1, Rīga 1050; tel. 6721-1776; fax 6722-6497; e-mail elpa@apollo.lv; f. 1990; books and newspapers; Pres. MAIRITA SOLIMA.

Jāņa sēta: Elizabetes iela 83–85, Rīga 1050; tel. 6709-2290; fax 6709-2292; e-mail janaseta@janaseta.lv; internet www.janaseta.lv; f. 1991; travel and culinary books; Dir AIVARS ZVIRBULIS.

Jumava: Dzirnavu iela 73, Rīga 1011; tel. and fax 6728-0314; e-mail jumava@parks.lv; internet www.jumava.lv; f. 1994; translations, dictionaries, fiction, etc.; Pres. JURIS VISOCKIS.

Kontinents: Elijas iela 17, Rīga 1050; tel. 6720-4130; fax 6720-4129; e-mail kontinent@ml.lv; internet www.kontinents.lv; f. 1991; translated fiction, non-fiction and colour children's books; Chair. of Bd OLEG MIHALEVICH.

Nordik: Daugavgrīvas 36–9, Rīga 1048; tel. 6760-2672; fax 6760-2818; e-mail nordik@nordik.lv; internet www.nordik.lv; f. 1992; sister co, Tapals, at same address; Dir JĀNIS JUŠKA; Editor-in-Chief IEVA JANAITE.

Preses nams (Press House): Balasta dambis 3, Rīga 1081; tel. 6246-5732; internet www.presesnams.lv; f. 1990; newspapers, magazines, encyclopedias and scientific literature; controlling interest owned by Ventspils Nafta; Dir EGONS LAPIŅŠ.

Smaile (Peak): Rīga; tel. 6731-5137; f. 1999; fiction, poetry, fine arts; Dir ANDREJS BRIMERBERGS.

Zinātne Publishers Ltd (Science): Akadēmijas lauk. 1, Rīga 1050; tel. 6721-2797; fax 6722-7825; e-mail zinatne@navigator.lv; f. 1951; non-fiction, text books, dictionaries, reference books; Dir INGRĪDA SEGLINA.

Zvaigzne ABC: K. Valdemāra iela 6, Rīga 1010; tel. 6750-8799; fax 6750-8798; e-mail info@zvaigzne.lv; internet www.zvaigzne.lv; f. 1966; privately owned; educational literature, textbooks, dictionaries, non-fiction for children and adults, fiction; Head of Bd VIJA KILBLOKA.

PUBLISHERS' ASSOCIATION

Latvian Publishers' Asscn (Latvijas Grāmatizdevēju asociācija): Rīga; tel. 6728-2392; fax 6728-0549; e-mail lga@gramatizdeveji.lv; internet www.gramatizdeveji.lv; f. 1993; 40 mems; Pres. JĀNIS LEJA.

Broadcasting and Communications

TELECOMMUNICATIONS

In 2011 there were 516,000 main telephone lines in use and 2.3m. mobile phone subscribers.

Lattelecom SIA: Dzirnavu iela 105, Rīga 1011; tel. 6700-0177; fax 8000-8041; e-mail lattelecom@lattelecom.lv; internet www .lattelecom.lv; f. 1992; 51% state-owned, 49% by TeliaSonera AB (Sweden); telecommunications and internet service provider; CEO JURIS GULBIS; 3,000 employees.

Latvian Mobile Telephone Co (Latvijas Mobilais Telefons SIA—LMT): Ropažu iela 6, Rīga 1039; tel. 8000-0076; fax 6777-3517; e-mail info@lmt.lv; internet www.lmt.lv; f. 1992; 24.5% owned by Sonera Holding BV (Finland), 24.5% owned by TeliaSonera AB (Sweden), 23.0% owned by SIA Lattelekom, 23.0% owned by Digitālais Latvijas radio un televīzijas centrs; telecommunications and internet service provider; Gen. Man. JURIS BINDE.

SIA Bite Latvija: Uriekstes iela 2A, Rīga 1005; tel. 2585-0600; fax 2585-0610; e-mail info@bite.lv; internet www.bite.lv; f. 2005; mobile cellular telecommunications; CEO FRED HRENCHUK.

SIA Radiokoms: Elizabetes iela 45–47, Rīga 1010; tel. 6733-3355; fax 6782-0013; e-mail radiokoms@radiokoms.lv; internet www .radiokoms.lv; Dir PETERIS GRAZULS.

Tele2: Rīga; tel. 6706-0069; fax 6706-0176; internet www.tele2.lv; f. 1991; owned by Tele2 AB (Sweden); fmrly Baltkom GSM; telecommunications and internet service provider; Pres. BILL BUTLER; 110 employees.

Regulatory Organizations

Dept of Communications (Ministry of Transport): Gogoļa iela 3, Rīga 1190; tel. 6724-2321; fax 6782-0636; e-mail diana.ainep@sam .gov.lv; f. 1991; Dir INĀRA RUDAKA.

Public Utilities Commission (Sabiedrisko Pakalpojumu Regulē-šanas Komisija): see Trade and Industry (Utilities) section.

BROADCASTING

Regulatory Organization

National Broadcasting Council of Latvia (Nacionālā Radio un Televizijas Padome): Smilšu iela 1/3, Rīga 1939; tel. 6722-1848; fax 6722-0448; e-mail neplpadome@neplpadome.lv; internet www.nrtp .lv; f. 1995; independent regulatory authority; Chair. ABRAMS KLECKINS.

Radio

Latvijas Radio (Radio Latvia): Doma lauk. 8, Rīga 1505; tel. 6720-6722; fax 6720-6709; e-mail radio@radio.org.lv; internet www .latvijasradio.lv; f. 1925; state-operated service; broadcasts in Latvian and Russian; Member of the Bd JĀNIS SIKSNIS.

Alise Plus: Raiņa iela 28, Daugavpils 5403; e-mail radio@aliseplus .eu; internet www.aliseplus.eu; 24-hour transmissions in Russian and Latvian.

European Hit Radio: Elijas iela 17, Rīga 1050; tel. 2957-5757; e-mail radio@superfm.lv; internet www.europeanhitradio.com; f. 1994; 24-hour transmissions in Latvian and English; Pres. UGIS POLIS; Dir RICHARD ZAKSS.

Latvijas Kristīgais Radio (Latvian Christian Radio): Lāčplēša iela 37, Rīga 1011; tel. 6721-3704; fax 6782-0633; e-mail lkr@lkr.lv; internet www.lkr.lv; f. 1993; 24-hour transmissions in Latvian and Russian.

Radio Ef-Ei: Atbrvōsanas aleja 98, Rēzekne 4600; e-mail efei@ mailbox.riga.lv; 24-hour transmissions in Russian and Latvian.

Radio Imanta: Tērbatas iela 1, Valmiera 4201; tel. 6420-7349; fax 6420-7350; e-mail radio.imanta@tl.lv; internet www.radioimanta.lv; 24-hour transmissions in Russian and Latvian; Chief Editor NILS INTERBERGS.

Radio Mix FM: L. Nometņu iela 62, Rīga 1002; 24-hour transmissions in Russian.

Radio Sigulda: L. Paegles iela 3, Sigulda 2150; tel. 6797-2678; fax 6797-3786; e-mail mail@radiosigulda.lv; internet www.radiosigulda .lv; f. 1991; 24-hour transmissions in Latvian; music radio; Dir AIVARS PLUCIS.

Radio SWH: Skanstes iela 13, Rīga 1013; tel. 6737-0067; fax 6782-8283; e-mail radio@radioswh.lv; internet www.radioswh.lv; Pres. ZITMARS LIEPINSCH.

Radio Trīs: Vaļņu iela 5, Cēsis 4101; tel. 6412-4566; fax 6412-7041; e-mail radio@radio3.lv; internet www.radio3.lv; f. 1994; Di EGILS VISKRINTS.

Radio Zemgale: Grāfa lauk. 6, Lecava 3913; e-mail rz@apollo.lv; f. 2000; 24-hour transmissions in Latvian; Dir DACE DUBKEVIČA.

Television

Latvia has one publicly owned television network and nine private stations. In 2010 satellite television reached approximately 10% of the population.

Latvijas Televīzija (Latvian Television): Zaķusalas krastmala 3, Rīga 1509; tel. 6720-0315; fax 6720-0025; e-mail ltv@ltv.lv; internet www.ltv.lv; f. 1954; state-operated service; two channels in Latvian, LTV1 and LTV7 (LTV7 also includes programmes in Russian, English and French); Dir-Gen. EDGARS KOTS.

Latvijas Neatkariga Televizija (Latvian Independent Television—LNT): Elijas iela 17, Rīga 1050; tel. 6707-0200; fax 6782-1128; e-mail lnt@lnt.lv; internet www.lnt.lv; f. 1996; entertainment, news reports; Dir-Gen. ANDREJS ĒĶIS.

TV3 Latvia: Dzelzavas iela 120G, Rīga 1021; tel. 6747-9100; fax 7479-2996; e-mail tv3@tv3.lv; internet www.tv3.lv; f. 1998; owned by Modern Times Group–MTG (Sweden); affiliated with channel 3+; targeted at a Russian-speaking audience; Dir KASPARS OZOLINS.

Finance

(cap. = capital; res = reserves; dep. = deposits; m. = million; brs = branches; amounts in lats)

BANKING

Central Bank

Bank of Latvia (Latvijas Banka): K. Valdemāra iela 2A, Rīga 1050; tel. 6702-2300; fax 6702-2420; e-mail info@bank.lv; internet www

.bank.lv; f. 1990; cap. 25.0m., res 163.5m., dep. 2,135.9m. (Dec. 2008); Gov. and Chair. of Council ILMĀRS RIMŠĒVIČS.

Commercial Banks

ABLV Bank AS: Elizabetes iela 23, Rīga 1010; tel. 6777-5222; fax 6777-5200; e-mail bank@ab.lv; internet www.ab.lv; f. 1993; present name adopted 2011; cap. 19.7m., res 22.5m., dep. 1,865.6m. (Dec. 2012); Chair. of Bd ALEKSANDRS BERGMANIS.

Citadele banka: Republikas lauk. 2A, Rīga 1522; tel. 6701-0000; fax 6701-0001; e-mail info@citadele.lv; internet www.citadele.lv; f. 2010; founded on the basis of Parex banka; 75% state-owned; 25% owned by the European Bank for Reconstruction and Development; cap. 103.0m., res 3.6m., dep. 1,398.4m. (Dec. 2012); Pres. and Chair. of Bd NILS MELNGAILIS; 72 brs.

DNB Banka: Skanstes iela 12, Rīga 1013; tel. 6717-1880; fax 6732-3449; e-mail info@dnb.lv; internet www.dnb.lv; f. 1989; present name adopted 2011; 100% owned by Bank DnB A/S (Denmark); cap. 134.4m., res 206.5m., dep. 1,467.8m. (Dec. 2012); Pres. and Chair. of Bd ANDRIS OZOLINS; 10 brs.

Expobank AS: Grēcinieku iela 22, Rīga 1050; tel. 6704-3510; fax 6704-3511; e-mail ltb@ltblv.com; internet www.expobank.eu; f. 1991; fmrly LTB Bank; present name adopted 2012; owned by MDM Bank (Russian Federation); cap. 8.2m., res 4.5m., dep. 196.1m. (Dec. 2011); Chair. ARMANDS STEINBERGS.

GE Money Bank: 13 Janvāra iela 3, Rīga 1050; tel. 6702-4747; fax 6782-0319; e-mail info@gemoneybank.lv; internet www .gemoneybank.lv; f. 2008 by merger of Baltic Trust Bank (BTB) and GE Money; 99.48% owned by Finstar Baltic Investments; cap. 26.4m., res 42.7m., dep. 65.1m. (Dec. 2012); Chair. RICHARD GASKIN; 31 brs.

Latvijas Biznesa Banka (Latvian Business Bank): 3 Antonijas iela, Rīga 1010; tel. 6777-5888; fax 6777-5849; e-mail info@lbb.lv; internet www.lbb.lv; f. 1992; present name adopted 2004; 99.87% owned by Bank of Moscow (Russia); cap. 10.8m., res 5.4m., dep. 113.9m. (Dec. 2008); Chair. and Pres. ANDREY BORODIN.

Latvijas Hipotēku un Zemes Banka (Hipotēku Banka) (Mortgage and Land Bank of Latvia): Doma lauk. 4, Rīga 1977; tel. 6800-0100; fax 6777-4152; e-mail banka@hipo.lv; internet www.hipo.lv; f. 1993; present name adopted in 2000; state-owned; cap. 216.6m., res 3.3m., dep. 192.7m. (Dec. 2012); Chair. of Bd ROLAND PAŅKO; 32 brs.

Norvik Banka: E. Birznieka-Upiša iela 21, Rīga 1011; tel. 6704-1100; fax 6704-1111; e-mail welcome@norvik.lv; internet www .norvik.lv; f. 1992; fmrly Lateko Bank; present name adopted 2006; cap. 57.4m., res 1.2m., dep. 520.7m. (Dec. 2011); Chair. of Bd ANDREJS SVIRČENKOVS; 15 brs.

PrivatBank: Terbatas iela 4, Rīga 1134; tel. 6704-1300; fax 6728-2981; e-mail info@privatbank.lv; internet www.privatbank.lv; f. 1992; fmrly Paritate Banka; present name adopted 2007; cap. 56.5m., res 3.8m., dep. 489.1m. (Dec. 2012); Chair. of Bd OLEKSANDR TRUBAKOV; 21 brs.

Rietumu Banka: Vesetas iela 7, Rīga 1013; tel. 6702-5555; fax 6702-5588; e-mail info@rietumu.lv; internet www.rietumu.lv; f. 1992; cap. 100.0m., res 16.9m., dep. 1,461.4m. (Dec. 2012); Pres. and Chair. of Exec. Bd ALEXANDER KALINOVSKI.

SEB Banka: SEB finanšu centrs, Meistaru iela 1, Valdlauci 1076; tel. 2777-8777; fax 6721-5335; e-mail info@seb.lv; internet www.seb .lv; f. 1993; fmrly SEB Latvijas Unibanka; present name adopted 2008; owned by SEB (Skandinaviska Enskilda Banken AB, Sweden); cap. 102.1m., res 7.2m., dep. 2,323.5m. (Dec. 2012); CEO AINĀRS OZOLS; 68 brs.

Swedbank Latvia: Balasta dambis 1A, Rīga 1048; tel. 6744-4444; fax 6744-4344; e-mail info@swedbank.lv; internet www.swedbank .lv; f. 1992; present name adopted 2008, following merger between Hansabank and Swedbank; cap. 662.6m., res 0.3m., dep. 2,703.7m. (Dec. 2012); Pres. and CEO MARIS MANCINSKIS; 59 brs.

Trasta komercbanka—TKB (Trust Commercial Bank): Miesnieku iela 9, Rīga 1050; tel. 6702-7777; fax 6702-7700; e-mail info@tkb.lv; internet www.tkb.lv; f. 1989; present name adopted 1996; cap. 14.5m., res 5.4m., dep. 251.6m. (Dec. 2012); Pres. and Chair. GUNDARS GRIEZE.

UniCredit Bank: Elizabetes iela 63, Rīga 1050; tel. 6708-5500; fax 6708-5507; e-mail info@unicreditbank.lv; internet www .unicreditbank.lv; f. 1997; fmrly Vereinsbank Rīga; present name adopted 2005; 100% owned by Bank Austria Creditanstalt AG (Austria); cap. 86.1m., res 0.2m., dep. 490.2m. (Dec. 2012); Chair. of Bd RALF CYMANEK.

Savings Bank

Latvijas Krājbanka (Latvian Savings Bank): Dalina iela 15, Rīga 1013; tel. 6709-2020; fax 6709-2070; e-mail info@lkb.lv; internet www.krajbanka.lv; f. 1924; present name adopted 1998; 76.65% owned by Snoras Bankas (Lithuania); operations suspended in Nov.

2011; cap. 12.1m., res 18.2m., dep. 624.1m. (Dec. 2008); Chair. JANIS BRAZOVSKIS; 10 brs.

Regulatory Authority

Financial and Capital Market Commission (Finanšu un kapitāla tirgus komisija—FKTK): Kungu iela 1, Rīga 1050; tel. 6777-4800; fax 6722-5755; e-mail fktk@fktk.lv; internet www.fktk.lv; f. 2001; Chair. KRISTAPS ZAKULIS.

Banking Association

Association of Latvian Commercial Banks (Latvijas Komercbanku asociācija): Pērses iela 9–11, Rīga 1011; tel. 6728-4528; fax 6782-8170; e-mail asoc@bankasoc.lv; internet www.bankasoc.lv; f. 1992; 23 mems; Pres. ANDRIS TVERIJONS.

INSURANCE

At September 2004 there were 18 insurance companies in Latvia, of which six were involved in life insurance and 12 in non-life insurance operations.

Balta Insurance Co: Raunas iela 10/12, Rīga 1039; tel. 6708-2333; fax 6708-2345; e-mail balta@balta.lv; internet www.balta.lv; f. 1992; automobile, property, freight, travel, agricultural insurance; Chair. ANDREW KIRKLAND.

Balva: Vīlandes iela 14, Rīga 1010; tel. 6750-6955; fax 6750-6956; e-mail balva@balva.lv; internet www.balva.lv; f. 1992; partly owned by Ingosstrakh (Russia); non-life insurance; Chair. of Bd RUŽENA OZERNOVA; 31 brs.

BTA Apdrošināšana: K. Valdemāra iela 63, Rīga 1142; tel. 6702-5100; fax 6702-5190; e-mail bta@bta.lv; internet www.bta.lv; f. 1993; Chair. of Bd GINTS DANDZBERGS.

Colemont FKB Latvia: Dārzauglu iela 1–50, Rīga 1012; tel. 6724-0066; fax 6720-1737; e-mail info@colemont.lv; internet www.colemont.lv; f. 2000; 60% owned by Colemont Insurance Brokers (USA); fmrly Finansu Konsultanti Un Brokeri (FKB); name changed in 2006; Chair. of Bd ARVILS PŪPOLS.

ERGO Latvija: Ūnijas iela 45, Rīga 1039; tel. 6708-1700; fax 6708-1715; e-mail info@ergo.lv; internet www.ergo.lv; owned by Alte Leipziger (Germany); life and non-life; Chair. of Bd THOMAS HANS SCHIRMER.

Estora Reinsurance Co: Elizabetes iela 14, Rīga 1010; tel. 6733-3335; fax 6733-3898; e-mail estora@estora.com; internet www.estora.com; f. 1992; reinsurance; Dir-Gen. JERGENIJS TOLOČKOVS.

SEB Dzīvības Apdrošināšana (SEB Life Insurance): Antonijas iela 9, Rīga 1010; tel. 6707-9800; fax 6707-9808; e-mail dziviba@seb.lv; internet www.seb.lv; f. 1940; present name adopted 2005; Chair. of Bd UĢIS VORONS.

Seesam Latvia: Vienības gatve 87H, Rīga 1004; tel. 6706-1000; fax 6706-1022; e-mail seesam@seesam.lv; internet www.seesam.lv; f. 1993; owned by Pohjola Group Plc (Finland); Chair. of Bd IVO KULDMÄE.

COMMODITY AND STOCK EXCHANGE

NASDAQ OMX Riga (NASDAQ OMX Riga AS): Valnu iela 1, Rīga 1050; tel. 6721-2431; fax 6722-9411; e-mail riga@nasdaqomx.com; internet www.nasdaqomxbaltic.com; f. 1993; owned by the NASDAQ OMX Group (USA); Chair. of Managing Bd DAIGA AUZIŅA-MELALKSNE.

Trade and Industry

GOVERNMENT AGENCY

Corruption Prevention and Combating Bureau (Korupcuas Novēršanas un Apkarošanas Birojs—KNAB): Brīvības iela 104, blk 2, Rīga 1001; tel. 6735-6161; fax 6733-1150; e-mail knab@knab.gov.lv; internet www.knab.gov.lv; f. 2002; ind. authority under government supervision; Dir JAROSLAVS STRELČENOKS.

Latvian Privatization Agency (Latvijas Privatizācijas agentūra): K. Valdemāra iela 31, Rīga 1887; tel. 6702-1358; fax 6783-0363; e-mail lpa@mail.bkc.lv; internet www.lpa.bkc.lv; f. 1994; became state joint-stock co in 2004; Dir-Gen. ARTIS KAMPARS.

DEVELOPMENT ORGANIZATIONS

Investment and Development Agency of Latvia (Latvijas Investīciju un Attīstības Agentūra—LIAA): Pērses iela 2, Rīga 1442; tel. 6703-9400; fax 6703-9401; e-mail liaa@liaa.gov.lv; internet www.liaa.gov.lv; f. 1993; promotion of business development in Latvia and foreign markets; Dir ANDRIS OZOLS.

CHAMBER OF COMMERCE

Latvian Chamber of Commerce and Industry (Latvijas Tirdzniecības un rūpniecības kamera): K. Valdemāra iela 35, Rīga 1010; tel. 6722-5595; fax 6782-0092; e-mail info@chamber.lv; internet www.chamber.lv; f. 1934; re-est. 1990; Pres. ANDRIS BĒRZIŅŠ; Chair. of Bd ŽANETA JAUNZEME-GRENDE.

INDUSTRIAL AND TRADE ASSOCIATIONS

Employers' Confederation of Latvia: Baznicas iela 25-3, Rīga 1010; tel. 6722-5162; fax 6722-4469; e-mail lddk@lddk.lv; internet www.lddk.lv; f. 1993; Pres. VITĀLIJS GAVRILOVS.

Latvian Construction Contractors' Association (LCCA) (Latvijas būvnieku asociācija—LBA): Grēcinieku iela 22/24, kab. 201, Rīga 1050; tel. 6722-8584; fax 6721-0023; e-mail lba@latnet.lv; internet www.building.lv/lba; f. 1996; Pres. VIKTORS PURIŅŠ; 6 brs.

Latvian Electrical Engineering and Electronics Industry Association (LETERA): Dzirnavu iela 93, Rīga 1011; tel. 6728-8360; fax 6728-8390; e-mail letera@latnet.lv; internet www.letera.lv; f. 1995; 50 mems (enterprises and education institutions); Pres. NORMUNDS BERGS.

Latvian Fuel Traders' Association (Latvijas Degvielas Tirgotāju Asociācija): Citadeles iela 1A, Rīga 1010; tel. 6732-0229; fax 6732-0228; e-mail birojs@ldta.lv; internet www.ldta.lv; f. 1998; Chair. of Bd MĀRTIŅŠ STIRĀNS; Pres. OJĀRS KARČVSKIS.

Latvian Information Technology and Telecommunications Association (Latvijas Informācijas un Komunikācijas Tehnologijas Asociācija—LIKTA): Stabu iela 47–1, Rīga 1011; tel. 6731-1821; fax 6731-5567; e-mail office@likta.lv; internet www.likta.lv; f. 1998; Pres. SIGNE BĀLIŅA.

Latvian Timber Exporters' Association (LTEA) (Latvijas Kokmateriālu Eksportētāju Asociācija): Skaistkalnes iela 1, Rīga 1004; tel. 6706-7369; fax 6786-0268; e-mail office@latvianwood.lv; internet www.latvianwood.lv; f. 1998; Pres. JANIS APSITIS.

UTILITIES

Regulatory Authority

Public Utilities Commission (PUC) (Sabiedrisko Pakalpojumu Regulēšanas Komisija): Brīvības iela 55, Rīga 1010; tel. 6709-7220; fax 6709-7277; e-mail sprk@sprk.gov.lv; internet www.sprk.gov.lv; f. 2001; multi-sector regulator overseeing electricity, gas, electronic communications, post, water, district heating and railway sectors; Chair. VALDIS LOKENBAHS.

Electricity

Latvenergo: Pulkveža Brieža iela 12, Rīga 1230; tel. 6772-8222; fax 6772-8778; e-mail info@latvenergo.lv; internet www.latvenergo.lv; state-owned joint-stock co; transmits and distributes electricity and thermal energy; five regional subsidiary cos and two associated cos; Chair. of Bd KĀRLIS MIĶELSONS.

Gas

Latvian Gas (Latvijas gāze): Vagonu iela 20, Rīga 1009; tel. 6704-1818; fax 6782-1604; e-mail latvijas_gaze@lg.lv; internet www.lg.lv; partially privatized in 2000–01; jt-stock co; 8% state-owned; Chair. ADRIAN DAVIS; 2,817 employees.

Water

Major suppliers include:

Aizkraukle Water Co (Aizkraukles ūdens): Torņu iela 1, Aizkraukle 5101; fax 6512-2150; e-mail udensall@inbox.lv.

Daugavpils Water Co (Daugavpils ūdens): Ūdensvada iela 3, Daugavpils 5401; tel. 6544-4608; fax 6542-5547; e-mail kontakti@daugavpils.udens.lv; internet www.daugavpils.udens.lv; f. 1889.

Liepāja Water Co (Liepājas ūdens): K. Valdemāra iela 12, Liepāja 3401; tel. 6541-1416; fax 6541-0769; e-mail dmeu@dpu.lv.

Rīga Water Co (Rīgas ūdens): Zigfrīda Annas Meierovica bulv. 1, Rīga 1495; tel. 6708-8555; fax 6722-2660; e-mail office@rw.lv; internet www.rw.lv; water supply and sewage treatment.

TRADE UNIONS

Free Trade Union Confederation of Latvia (Latvijas Brīvo Arodbiedrību Savienība—LBAS): Bruņinieku iela 29–31, Rīga 1001; tel. 6727-0351; fax 6727-6649; e-mail lbas@lbas.lv; internet www.lbas.lv; f. 1990; 21 branch or professional affiliated unions; Pres. PETERIS KRIGERS; 110,602 mems (2009).

Transport

RAILWAYS

In 2010 there were 1,897 km of railways on the territory of Latvia. In 2011 Latvian railways carried 20.5m. passengers and 59.4m. metric tons of freight.

Latvian Railways (Latvijas Dzelzceļš): Gogoļa iela 3, Rīga 1547; tel. 6723-4940; fax 6782-0231; e-mail biruta.sakse@ldz.lv; internet www .ldz.lv; f. 1993; state joint-stock co; Chair. of Bd UGIS MAGONIS.

ROADS

In 2010 Latvia's total road network was 68,941 km, of which 6,966 km were main roads.

Latvian State Roads (Latvijas Valsts Ceļi): Gogoļa iela 3, Rīga 1050; tel. 6702-8169; fax 6702-8171; e-mail lad@lvceli.lv; internet www.lvceli.lv; f. 2004 to replace Latvian Road Administration; state jt-stock co; manages state road network, administers State Road Fund; Chair. TĀLIS STRAUME.

SHIPPING

At 31 December 2012 the Latvian flag registered fleet numbered 153 vessels, with a combined total displacement of 181,360 grt. In 2012 some 75.2m. metric tons of sea-borne freight were transported through the country's three main ports (Ventspils, Rīga and Liepāja) and seven smaller ports.

Maritime Department (Ministry of Transport): Gogoļa iela 3, Rīga 1743; tel. 6702-8198; fax 6733-1406; e-mail aigars.krastins@ sam.gov.lv; internet www.sam.gov.lv; Dir AIGARS KRASTIŅŠ.

Port Authorities and Ports

Freeport of Rīga Authority (Rīgas Brīvostas Pārvalde): Kalpaka bulv. 12, Rīga 1010; tel. 6703-0800; fax 6703-0835; e-mail info@ freeportofriga.lv; internet www.rop.lv; f. 1994; CEO LEONIDS LOGINOVS; Chair. of Bd ANDRIS AMERIKS.

Liepāja Port Authority: Liepāja Special Economic Zone, Feniksa iela 4, Liepāja 3401; tel. 6342-7605; fax 6348-0252; e-mail authority@ lsez.lv; internet www.lsez.lv; Man. Dir AIVARS BOJA.

Rīga Commercial Port (Rīgas Tirdzniecības osta): Katrinas iela 5A, Rīga 1227; tel. 6732-9224; fax 6783-0215; e-mail rto@mail.bkc.lv; internet www.rto.lv; f. 1996.

Ventspils Commercial Port (Ventspils Tirdzniecības Ostā): Dzintaru iela 22, Ventspils 3602; tel. 6366-8706; fax 6366-8860; e-mail vcp@vto.lv; internet www.vcp.lv; Chair. of Bd VALERIJ PASHUTA.

Ventspils Free Port Authority (Ventspils brīvostas pārvalde): Jāņa iela 19, Ventspils 3601; tel. 6362-2586; fax 6362-1297; e-mail info@vbp.lv; internet portofventspils.lv; f. 1991; Chief Exec. IMANTS SARMULIS.

Shipping Company

Latvijas kuģniecība (LASCO) (Latvian Shipping Co): Elizabetes iela 1, Rīga 1807; tel. 6702-0111; fax 6782-8106; e-mail lsc@lscgroup .lv; internet www.lk.lv; f. 1991; tanker, reefer, liquid petroleum gas and dry-cargo transportation; 49.94% owned by Ventspils Nafta (q.v.); Chair. of Bd POLS TOMASS.

CIVIL AVIATION

There is an international airport at Rīga.

airBaltic Corpn: Rīga Airport, Rīga 1053; tel. 6720-7069; fax 6720-7369; e-mail info@airbaltic.lv; internet www.airbaltic.com; f. 1995; 52.6% govt-owned; Pres. and Chief Exec. BERTOLT FLICK; Chair. of Bd VIGO LEGZDINS.

Civil Aviation Agency of Latvia (Latvijas Civilās Aviācijas Administrācija): Rīga Airport 1011, Rīga 1053; tel. 6783-0936; fax 6783-0967; internet www.caa.lv; Dir MĀRIS GORODCOVS.

Tourism

Among Latvia's principal tourist attractions are the historic centre of Rīga, with its medieval and art nouveau buildings, the extensive beaches of the Baltic coastline, and Gauja National Park, which stretches east of the historic town of Sigulda for nearly 100 km. Revenue from tourism was some US $771m. in 2011, according to provisional figures. Foreign tourist arrivals at accommodation establishments numbered 1.1m. in 2011.

Latvian Tourism Development Agency: Brīvības iela 55, Rīga 1519; tel. and fax 6722-9945; fax 6735-8128; e-mail info@latvia .travel; internet www.latvia.travel; f. 1993; Dir ARMANDS SLOKENBERGS.

Defence

A Latvian Ministry of Defence was established in November 1991. In August 1994 the withdrawal from Latvia of all former Soviet forces was completed. As assessed at November 2012, Latvia's total armed forces numbered 5,350, comprising an army of 1,400, a navy of 550, an air force of 300, joint staff of 2,500, and a national guard of 600. Army volunteer reservists numbered 7,800. Conscription ended in 2006. Latvia joined the North Atlantic Treaty Organization's (NATO) 'Partnership for Peace' programme in February 1994, and became a full member of the Alliance on 29 March 2004.

Defence Expenditure: Budgeted at 147m. lats for 2012.

Commander of the National Armed Forces: Brig.-Gen. RAIMONDS GRAUBE.

Commander of the Air Force: Col AIVARS MEZRS.

Commander in Chief of the Navy: Capt. RIMANTAS STRIMAITIS.

Education

Primary education begins at seven years of age and lasts for four years. Secondary education, beginning at the age of 11, comprises a first cycle of five years and a second of three years. Only the first nine years of education are officially compulsory. In 2009/10 enrolment at primary schools included 95% of pupils in the relevant age-group; in that year enrolment at secondary schools included 84% of pupils in the relevant age-group. In the 2004/05 academic year some 65% of school-age pupils were taught in Latvian-language schools and some 25% were taught in Russian-language schools; 10% were taught in schools offering instruction in both Latvian and Russian. In 2011/12 higher education was offered at 59 institutions and enrolment totalled 97,041 students. According to official figures, in 2009 consolidated central government expenditure on education amounted to 759.8m. lats (representing 14.1% of expenditure).

LEBANON

Introductory Survey

LOCATION, CLIMATE, LANGUAGE, RELIGION, FLAG, CAPITAL

The Republic of Lebanon lies in western Asia, bordered by Syria to the north and east, and by Israel and the Palestinian Territories to the south. The country has a coastline of about 220 km (135 miles) on the eastern shore of the Mediterranean Sea. The climate varies widely with altitude. The coastal lowlands are hot and humid in summer, becoming mild (cool and damp) in winter. In the mountains, which occupy much of Lebanon, the weather is cool in summer, with heavy snowfalls in winter. Rainfall is generally abundant. The official language is Arabic, which is spoken by almost all of the inhabitants. French is widely used as a second language, while Kurdish and Armenian are spoken by small ethnic minorities. According to the UN Relief and Works Agency for Palestine Refugees in the Near East (UNRWA), at 1 January 2012 there were 436,154 Palestinian refugees registered in Lebanon. The major religions are Islam and Christianity, and there is a very small Jewish community. In the early 1980s it was estimated that 57% of Lebanon's inhabitants were Muslims, with about 43% Christians; these figures were believed to have changed to 60% and 39%, respectively, by 2008. The principal Muslim sects are Shi'a and Sunni, while there is also a significant Druze community. Most Christians adhere to the Roman Catholic Church, principally the Maronite rite. There are also Armenian, Greek and Syrian sects (both Catholic and Eastern Orthodox) and small groups of Protestants. The national flag (proportions 2 by 3) has three horizontal stripes, of red, white (half the depth) and red, with a representation of a cedar tree (in green and brown) in the centre of the white stripe. The capital is Beirut.

CONTEMPORARY POLITICAL HISTORY

Historical Context

Lebanon, the homeland of the ancient Phoenicians, became part of the Turkish Ottoman Empire in the 16th century, and following the dissolution of the Ottoman Empire after the First World War (1914–18), a Greater Lebanese state was created by the Allied powers. The new state was formed in order to meet the nationalist aspirations of the area's predominantly Christian population, but it also included largely Muslim-populated territories traditionally considered to be part of Syria. Lebanon was administered by France, under a League of Nations mandate, from 1920 until independence was declared on 26 November 1941. A republic was established in 1943, and full autonomy was granted in January 1944.

Religious and cultural diversity is Lebanon's defining feature. At the time of independence Christians formed a slight majority of the population, the largest single community (nearly 30% of the total) being the Maronite Christians, who mostly inhabited the north of the country and the capital, Beirut. Other Christian groups included Greek Orthodox communities, Greek Catholics and Armenians. The Muslim groups were the Sunnis, living mainly in the coastal towns of Sur (Tyre), Saida (Sidon) and Beirut, the Shi'ites, a predominantly rural community in southern Lebanon and the northern Beqa'a valley, and, in much smaller numbers, the Druzes, an ancient community in central Lebanon. The relative size of the various communities provided the basis for the unwritten 'national pact' of 1943, whereby executive and legislative posts were to be shared in the ratio of six Christians to five Muslims, and seats in the Chamber of Deputies (renamed the National Assembly in March 1979) were distributed on a religious, rather than a politico-ideological, basis. The convention according to this 'confessional' arrangement was that the President was a Maronite Christian, the Prime Minister a Sunni Muslim, and the President of the National Assembly a Shi'a Muslim.

Lebanon's first President, during 1943–52, was Sheikh Bishara el-Khoury. His successor was Camille Chamoun, whose reforms included the enfranchisement of women. Following elections to the Chamber of Deputies in 1957 there was considerable unrest, mainly among Muslims who mistrusted Chamoun's pro-Western foreign policy and advocated Lebanon's closer alignment with Syria and Egypt. In July 1958 Chamoun appealed to the USA for military assistance; US forces remained in Beirut until October, by which time peace had been restored. Meanwhile, Chamoun was persuaded not to seek a further presidential term, and the Chamber elected Gen. Fouad Chehab as his successor. Chehab, who took office in September 1958, adopted a foreign policy of non-alignment, and introduced state provision of health, education and other services. In 1964 he was succeeded by Charles Hélou, who was faced by increasing controversy over the status of Palestinians in Lebanon.

After the establishment of Israel in 1948, and during the subsequent Arab–Israeli wars, thousands of Palestinians fled to Lebanon, where most were housed in refugee camps in the south of the country. Following the creation of the Palestine Liberation Organization (PLO) in 1964, military training centres for Palestinian guerrilla fighters were established in the camps. From 1968 these self-styled *fedayeen* ('martyrs') began making raids into Israel, provoking retaliatory attacks by Israeli forces. In 1969 there were clashes between Lebanese security forces and the *fedayeen*. Many Christians, particularly the Maronites, advocated strict government control over the Palestinians' activities, but the majority of Muslims strongly supported Palestinian operations against Israel.

Domestic Political Affairs

Charles Hélou's successor as President, Sulayman Franjiya, took office in 1970. In July 1971 a further influx of Palestinian fighters expelled from Jordan led to fierce fighting between Israeli forces and Palestinians based in Lebanon, while Christian groups began their own armed campaign against the *fedayeen*. In July 1974 Palestinian forces clashed with militia of the Phalangist Party (the Phalanges libanaises or al-Kataeb, a militant right-wing Maronite Christian group now also known as the Lebanese Social Democratic Party). From April 1975 the conflict between the Palestinians and Phalangists quickly descended into full-scale civil war between the Lebanese National Movement (LNM) of left-wing Muslims (including Palestinians), led by Kamal Joumblatt of the Parti socialiste progressiste (PSP, a mainly Druze-supported group), and conservative Christian groups, mainly the Phalangist militia. Constitutional matters overtook the status of Palestinians as the main divisive issue, with the LNM advocating an end to the 'confessional' system, claiming that this unduly favoured Christians (who by now formed a minority of the population). Despite diplomatic efforts by Arab and Western countries, no durable cease-fire was achieved until October 1976, largely as a result of intervention in the conflict (in order to prevent an outright LNM victory) by Syrian forces in mid-1976. Under the terms of the cease-fire, a 30,000-strong Arab Deterrent Force (ADF), composed mainly of Syrian troops, entered Lebanon.

President Franjiya was succeeded by Elias Sarkis in September 1976, and Prime Minister Rashid Karami by Selim al-Hoss in December. Legislative elections, due in April 1976, were postponed for an initial period of 26 months—the term of the Chamber of Deputies was subsequently extended further. Although the constitutional status quo remained intact, more than 30,000 people had already died in the civil war and the militias of the various warring factions controlled most of the country. East Beirut and much of northern Lebanon was controlled by the Lebanese Forces (LF), a coalition of Maronite militias formed in September 1976; west Beirut was controlled by Muslim groups; and Palestinians dominated much of southwest Lebanon.

In March 1978 Israeli forces advanced into southern Lebanon in a counter-attack against forces of Fatah (the Palestine National Liberation Movement), the main guerrilla group within the PLO. UN Security Council Resolution 425, adopted on 17 March, demanded an Israeli withdrawal from Lebanon (thereby respecting its territorial integrity, sovereignty and independence) and also established a UN Interim Force in Lebanon (UNIFIL, see p. 87), initially of 4,000 troops. Israeli forces withdrew in June, but transferred control of a border strip to the pro-Israeli Christian militia which in May 1980 became known as the South Lebanon Army (SLA). Meanwhile, in October 1978, following several months of renewed fighting in Beirut between Syrian troops of the ADF and right-wing Christian militias, the ADF states agreed on a peace plan (the Beiteddin Declaration), which aimed to restore the authority of the Lebanese Government and army. Attempts to implement the plan were unsuccessful, however, and Lebanon's fragmentation deepened.

Al-Hoss resigned as premier in June 1980 and was replaced in October by Chafic al-Wazzan. In August 1982, in an election boycotted by most Muslim deputies, the renamed National Assembly designated Bashir Gemayel (the younger son of the founder of the Phalangist Party and commander of the LF) to succeed President Sarkis. The President-elect was assassinated in September, and his brother, Amin, was elected in his place. Following the assassination, Phalangist forces (with the apparent complicity of occupying Israeli forces) entered the Palestinian refugee camps of Sabra and Chatila, in west Beirut, killing some 2,000 refugees. Israeli forces had re-entered Lebanon in June 1982, with the declared aim of finally eliminating the PLO's military threat to Israel's northern border; they quickly defeated Palestinian forces in south-west Lebanon and surrounded the western sector of Beirut, trapping more than 6,000 Palestinian fighters. A US-led diplomatic initiative resulted in an agreement enabling the PLO fighters to disperse among several Arab states, and a multinational peace-keeping force was deployed in Beirut. (In September 1983 intense fighting between rival factions of Fatah resulted in a truce agreement, brokered by Saudi Arabia and Syria, which led to a second evacuation of some 4,000 Palestinian fighters, most notably of the PLO Chairman, Yasser Arafat, who was exiled to Tunisia.) Meanwhile, in May 1983 Lebanon and Israel agreed to end all hostilities (including the theoretical state of war that had existed between them since 1948) and to withdraw all foreign troops from Lebanon. However, Syria did not recognize the accord, leaving 40,000 of its own troops and 7,000 PLO fighters in the Beqa'a valley and northern Lebanon. Israel, meanwhile, redeployed a reduced force of 10,000 troops along the Awali river, south of Beirut. The SLA was to police southern areas as Israel's role lessened. Meanwhile, the multinational force in Beirut (comprising some 5,800 mainly French, Italian and US personnel) came under frequent attack from Muslim militias who opposed its tantamount support for the Christian-led Government. In October 1983 241 US and 58 French marines were killed in suicide bombings by Muslim groups.

The resumption of heavy fighting in February 1984 (which the reconstituted, US-trained Lebanese army was unable to suppress) led to the resignation of Prime Minister al-Wazzan, followed shortly afterwards by the withdrawal of the USA, Italy, France and the United Kingdom from the peace-keeping force. By March successive defeats had left Gemayel's forces with effective control only in the mainly Christian-populated east Beirut. In that month President Gemayel abrogated the May 1983 agreement with Israel, and in April 1984, with Syrian support, he formed a Government of national unity under former premier Rashid Karami. The Israeli Government formed by Shimon Peres in September pledged to withdraw Israeli forces from Lebanon. However, while the Lebanese authorities demanded that UNIFIL police the Israeli–Lebanese border, by the time the Israeli withdrawal was completed, in June 1985, Israel had ensured that a narrow security zone, policed by the SLA, was in place along the border. With the Israeli presence in Lebanon reduced to a token force, Syria withdrew about one-third of its troops from the Beqa'a valley in July, leaving some 25,000 in position.

In December 1985 the leaders of the three main Lebanese militias (the Druze forces, Amal and the LF) signed an accord in the Syrian capital, Damascus, providing for an immediate cease-fire and for the cessation of the civil war within one year. The militias were to be disarmed and disbanded, and a new constitutional regime was to be introduced within three years. However, the militias of the Sunni Murabitoun and the Iranian-backed Shi'ite Hezbollah were not parties to the agreement, which was also opposed by influential Christian elements. Furthermore, there were clashes later in December between supporters of the agreement within the LF and those who resented the concessions made by their leader, Elie Hobeika. In January 1986 Hobeika was forced into exile and replaced as leader of the LF by Samir Geagea, who urged renegotiation of the Damascus accord.

During 1986 Palestinian guerrillas resumed rocket attacks on settlements in northern Israel, provoking retaliatory air attacks by Israel on targets in the Beqa'a valley and southern Lebanon. Meanwhile, Hezbollah escalated its attacks on SLA positions within the Israeli security zone, and also clashed with UNIFIL. Fighting between Palestinian guerrillas and Shi'ite Amal militiamen for control of the refugee camps in south Beirut escalated in May, before a cease-fire was imposed around the camps in June, as part of a Syrian-sponsored peace plan for Muslim west Beirut. The activities of the Amal, Druze and Sunni militias in west Beirut were temporarily curtailed by the deployment of Lebanese and Syrian troops, but fighting across the so-called 'Green Line', which had effectively divided the area from Christian east Beirut since early 1984, continued. By the time Amal and the PLO agreed in September 1987 to end hostilities, more than 2,500 people had died in the 'war of the camps'. Despite renewed fighting near Sidon in October, the Amal leader, Nabih Berri, in January 1988 announced an end to the siege of the Palestinian refugee camps in Beirut and southern Lebanon, avowedly as a gesture of support for the *intifada* (uprising) by Palestinians in the Israeli-occupied territories.

After Prime Minister Karami was killed in a bomb explosion in June 1987, Selim al-Hoss was appointed acting premier. In 1988 a political crisis developed as it proved impossible to find a successor to President Gemayel who was acceptable to all the warring factions. Sulayman Franjiya was Syria's preferred candidate but was notably opposed by Geagea, who apparently ensured that the National Assembly was inquorate when it convened for the presidential election in August 1988. Gemayel's term of office expired later in the month, at which time the outgoing President appointed an interim military administration, comprising three Christians and three Muslims, with Gen. Michel Aoun (Commander-in-Chief of the Lebanese army) as Prime Minister. However, the three nominated Muslim officers immediately refused to serve in the new administration. The constitutional crisis, with two governments claiming legitimacy, was further complicated in November, when the Minister of Defence in the al-Hoss administration dismissed Aoun as army commander; however, Aoun retained the loyalty of large sections of the military and thus remained its de facto leader.

The Ta'if agreement

In September 1989, following six months of fighting in Beirut between Aoun's Lebanese army and Syrian forces, a Tripartite Arab Committee—formed in May by an emergency session of Arab leaders, and comprising King Hassan of Morocco, King Fahd of Saudi Arabia and President Ben Djedid Chadli of Algeria—announced a peace plan whereby, most notably, the Lebanese National Assembly would meet to discuss a draft charter of national reconciliation. The Committee's charter was approved by the Syrian Government and the leaders of Lebanon's Muslim militias. Aoun initially rejected its terms, on the grounds that it did not provide for the withdrawal of Syrian forces, but he was forced to relent, in view of support for the charter by almost every Arab country, as well as the USA, the USSR, the United Kingdom and France; a cease-fire accordingly took effect. The National Assembly subsequently met in Ta'if, Saudi Arabia, to discuss the charter, which was finally approved (with some amendments) in October by 58 of the 62 attending deputies (of the 99 deputies elected in May 1972, only 73 survived); it became known as the 'Ta'if agreement'. The charter provided for the transfer of executive power from the presidency to a cabinet, with portfolios divided equally between Christian and Muslim ministers. The number of seats in the National Assembly was to be increased to 108, comprising equal numbers of Christian and Muslim deputies. Following the election of a President and the formation of a new government, all militias involved in the Lebanese conflict were to be disbanded within six months, while the internal security forces would be strengthened; the Syrian armed forces would assist the new Government in implementing the security plan for a maximum of two years.

In early November 1989 the National Assembly unanimously endorsed the Ta'if agreement, and elected René Mouawad as President. However, Aoun, who denounced the agreement as a betrayal of Lebanese sovereignty, declared the presidential election unconstitutional and its result null and void, proclaiming himself President. Mouawad was assassinated only 17 days after his election. The National Assembly again convened and elected Elias Hrawi as the new President; the legislature also voted to extend its own term until 1994. A new Cabinet was formed by al-Hoss in late November 1989.

The Christian communities were divided over the Ta'if agreement, and Geagea's refusal to reject it precipitated violent clashes between his LF and Aoun's forces in January 1990: by March more than 800 people had been killed in inter-Christian fighting. In August the National Assembly duly approved amendments to the Constitution, increasing the number of seats in the legislature to 108, to be divided equally between Muslims and Christians. On 21 September the Second Lebanese Republic was officially inaugurated when President Hrawi formally endorsed the amendments. In October Aoun and his forces were expelled from east Beirut by Syrian forces and units of the Lebanese army loyal to Hrawi; Aoun sought refuge in the French embassy. The Lebanese army began to deploy in Beirut in December, by which time all militia forces had withdrawn from the city. In the same month al-Hoss submitted his Government's resignation, and Hrawi invited Omar Karami to form a government of national unity, as stipulated by the Ta'if agreement. By early 1991 the Lebanese army was established in most major southern Lebanese towns; by September the militias had been largely disbanded (although Hezbollah maintained armaments in southern Lebanon and the Beqa'a valley). In May the National Assembly approved amendments to the electoral law, and in June the Cabinet appointed 40 deputies to fill the seats that had become vacant since the 1972 election, as well as the nine new seats created under the Ta'if agreement. In August 1991 the National Assembly approved a general amnesty for crimes perpetrated during the civil war, although its terms excluded several specified crimes committed during 1975–90. Under a presidential pardon, Aoun was permitted to depart for exile in France.

In May 1991 Lebanon and Syria signed a bilateral treaty establishing formal relations in political, military and economic affairs, and confirming the role of the Syrian army as guarantor of the security plans enshrined in the Ta'if agreement. Israel immediately condemned the treaty as a further step towards the formal transformation of Lebanon into a Syrian protectorate, while its opponents within Lebanon denounced it as a threat to the country's independence. In September Lebanon and Syria concluded a mutual security agreement. Syrian forces began to withdraw from Beirut in March 1992, in preparation for their scheduled withdrawal to eastern Lebanon by September. Israel, meanwhile, reasserted its intention of maintaining a military presence in the security zone, and its support for the SLA, by launching fierce attacks on Palestinian bases in southern Lebanon in June 1991. Lebanese forces began to take up positions in Sidon in July. Initial resistance from Palestinians loyal to Arafat was swiftly overcome, and an agreement was concluded with the PLO to allow the Lebanese army to assume control of the area. The conflict escalated further in February 1992, following the assassination by the Israeli air force of the Secretary-General of Hezbollah, Sheikh Abbas Moussawi.

The deteriorating economic situation in early 1992, combined with allegations of government corruption and incompetence, and a series of general strikes, provoked the resignation of Karami and his Cabinet in May. Subsequent talks in Damascus between President Hrawi and the Syrian leadership led to the reappointment of Rashid Solh (Prime Minister in 1974–75) as premier. In July 1992 the National Assembly approved a new electoral law whereby the number of seats in the Assembly was raised from 108 to 128, to be divided equally between Christian and Muslim deputies.

The 1992 and 1996 elections to the National Assembly

Lebanon's first legislative elections for 20 years were held in three rounds, on 23 August 1992 (in the governorates of the North and the Beqa'a valley), 30 August (Beirut and Mount Lebanon) and 6 September 1992 (South and Nabatiyah). Electoral turn-out was low (averaging 32%), especially in Maronite districts where leaders had urged a boycott. Hezbollah, contesting the elections for the first time as a political party, enjoyed considerable success in southern constituencies. The Amal leader, Nabih Berri, was appointed President of the new National Assembly in October, and Hrawi invited Rafiq Hariri, a Lebanese-born Saudi Arabian business executive, to form a new government. Hariri's Cabinet was dominated by technocrats, and the system of distributing portfolios on an entirely 'confessional' basis was somewhat diluted.

In December 1992 the Lebanese army took up positions in southern suburbs of Beirut for the first time in eight years, apparently meeting no resistance from Hezbollah, which had hitherto effectively controlled the areas. From mid-1993 the Lebanese Government was said to be attempting to curtail the activities of the Damascus-based Popular Front for the Liberation of Palestine—General Command (PFLP—GC), which had begun to mount guerrilla attacks on Israeli military positions from bases in southern Lebanon. In July Israeli armed forces launched their heaviest artillery and air attacks on targets in southern Lebanon since 1982. The declared aim of 'Operation Accountability' was to eradicate the threat posed by Hezbollah and Palestinian guerrillas, and to create a flow of refugees so as to compel the Lebanese and Syrian authorities to take action against these groups. According to Lebanese sources, the week-long offensive displaced some 300,000 civilians towards the north and resulted in 128 (mainly civilian) deaths. Although a US-brokered cease-fire understanding took effect in July 1993, hostilities continued. In October 1994 an Israeli attack on the town of Nabatiyah, in which seven civilians died, was apparently provoked by the deaths of 22 people in a bomb attack, attributed to Palestinian militants of the Islamic Resistance Movement (Hamas), in the Israeli city of Tel-Aviv.

Meanwhile, in March 1994 the National Assembly approved legislation instituting the death penalty for 'politically motivated' murders. Shortly afterwards the Maronite LF was proscribed (on the grounds that it had sought the country's partition) and its leader, Samir Geagea, was arrested and charged, along with several of his associates, in connection with the murder, in October 1990, of Dany Chamoun, son of former President Camille Chamoun and the leader of the right-wing Maronite Parti national libéral (PNL), and with the bombing of a Maronite church outside Beirut in January 1994. In September Geagea was reportedly relieved of the organization's leadership and his recognition of the Ta'if agreement revoked; the LF command had also reportedly countermanded the formal dissolution of the organization's militia status. (A successor political organization, the Lebanese Forces Party, had been created in September 1990.) In June 1995 Geagea and a co-defendant were convicted of instigating the murder of Chamoun, and were (together with seven others convicted *in absentia*) sentenced to death; the sentences were immediately commuted to life imprisonment with hard labour. In July 1996 Geagea was acquitted of involvement in the Maronite church bombing. However, by mid-1997 Geagea had received another two death sentences (one for ordering the assassination of another Maronite rival in 1990, and the other for attempting to assassinate the Minister of Defence, Michel Murr, in 1991—both of which were later commuted to life imprisonment); another life sentence for orchestrating the death of Prime Minister Rashid Karami in 1987; and a 10-year prison term for attempting illegally to recruit and arm militiamen after 1991.

In October 1995 the National Assembly voted to amend the Constitution to extend President Hrawi's mandate for a further three years. Prime Minister Hariri had sought an extension of the presidential term in the stated interest of promoting stability in the economic reconstruction process, and the amendment had been facilitated following intervention by Syria to resolve a procedural dispute between Hariri and National Assembly President Berri.

Elections to the National Assembly took place in five rounds during August–September 1996. Pro-Hariri candidates enjoyed considerable success in the first three rounds of voting (in Mount Lebanon, North Lebanon and Beirut governorates), with the Prime Minister himself winning the largest number of votes at the third round; there were, however, allegations of vote-buying involving Hariri's supporters in Beirut. In the fourth and fifth rounds (in the South and Nabatiyah, and in the Beqa'a valley) an electoral alliance led by Amal and Hezbollah was reported to have won all but one of the 46 seats. Prior to the fifth round Syria had effected the redeployment (delayed since 1992) of some 12,000 of its estimated 30,000 troops in Lebanon to the eastern Beqa'a valley. The overall rate of voter participation averaged about 45%. Berri was re-elected President of the legislature in October 1996, and in the following month a new Government was formed under Hariri.

In April 1996 Israel commenced a sustained military offensive (code-named 'Operation Grapes of Wrath') in southern Lebanon and suburbs to the south of Beirut, aimed at preventing rocket attacks by Hezbollah on settlements in northern Israel. After more than two weeks of hostilities a cease-fire understanding took effect in late April. According to the Israeli authorities, the operation had resulted in no Israeli deaths, while 170–200 Lebanese civilians, in addition to some 50 fighters, were killed. Hezbollah claimed to have sustained minimal casualties, and its military capacity appeared largely undiminished. In July Israel and Hezbollah reportedly exchanged prisoners and the bodies of members of their armed forces for the first time since 1991.

Voting in Lebanon's first municipal elections since 1963 took place in four rounds during May–June 1998. At the first round (in Mount Lebanon governorate), Hezbollah won convincing victories in Beirut's southern suburbs, while right-wing organizations opposed to the Government also took control of several councils. At the second round (in North Lebanon), efforts failed to achieve an inter-community balance in Tripoli, where a council comprising 23 Muslims and only one Christian was elected; elsewhere in the governorate there was notable success for candidates loyal to Samir Geagea. However, a joint list of candidates supported by Hariri and Berri won control of the Beirut council at the third round, while Berri's Amal gained overall control in Tyre. At the final round of voting (in the Beqa'a valley), Hezbollah candidates were largely defeated by their pro-Syrian secular rivals and by members of the governorate's leading families. Other than in Beirut, the rate of voter participation was high (about 70%). (Municipal elections did not take place in southern Lebanon until September 2001, following the withdrawal of Israeli troops in 2000.)

Emile Lahoud's accession to the presidency and the Israeli withdrawal from the south

As President Hrawi's mandate neared completion in 1998, the Commander-in-Chief of the Army, Gen. Emile Lahoud, emerged as a suitable successor: his firm stance on corruption and his success in having reconstructed the army following the civil war were expected to assist the process of political reform and economic regeneration. Moreover, despite his strong nationalist tendency, Lahoud's candidacy was endorsed by Syria. To enable his appointment, the National Assembly overwhelmingly adopted an exceptional amendment to Article 49 of the Constitution—which requires that senior civil servants resign from their posts two years prior to seeking political office—and Lahoud was duly elected President on 15 October, with the approval of all 118 National Assembly deputies present (the vote was boycotted by the Druze leader, Walid Joumblatt, and his supporters). Lahoud took office on 24 November. Hariri unexpectedly declined an invitation from him to form a new government, and at the beginning of December Selim al-Hoss was again designated Prime Minister. Several reformists were appointed to the Cabinet, which excluded representatives of the various 'confessional' blocs and former militia leaders whose rivalries had frequently undermined previous governments. At the Cabinet's first session later that month, Gen. Michel Suleiman was appointed to succeed Lahoud as head of the armed forces.

Clashes persisted in southern Lebanon following Israel's 'adoption' of Resolution 425, amid continuing protests of violations of the April 1996 cease-fire understanding. In January 1999 Israel's Security Cabinet voted to respond to future Hezbollah offensives by targeting infrastructure in central and northern Lebanon, as well as suspected guerrilla bases in the south. In July the Lebanese Government was angered by an announcement made by the new Israeli Prime Minister, Ehud Barak, that Palestinian refugees residing in Lebanon would under no circumstances be permitted to return to Israel. President Lahoud demanded that any permanent peace agreement should guarantee the right of Palestinians to return home; he subsequently initiated legislation to prevent Palestinian refugees in Lebanon from being granted Lebanese citizenship.

During his election campaign Barak had pledged to withdraw Israeli forces from southern Lebanon by July 2000. In June 1999 the SLA completed a unilateral withdrawal from the enclave of Jezzine, in the north-east of the occupied zone. Following further Hezbollah attacks on northern Israel, in late June the outgoing administration of Binyamin Netanyahu ordered a series of airstrikes against infrastructure targets in central and southern Lebanon—the heaviest aerial bombardment since Operation Grapes of Wrath in 1996. In December 1999 an 'understanding in principle' was reportedly reached between Israel and Syria in order to curb the fighting in southern Lebanon, although the informal cease-fire ended in January 2000 when a senior SLA commander was killed; moreover, the deaths of three Israeli soldiers led Israel to declare that peace talks with Syria (again postponed indefinitely) could resume only if Syria took action to restrain Hezbollah. In February, after suffering further military casualties in the security zone, Israel announced that its Prime Minister would henceforth be empowered to order immediate retaliatory raids against Hezbollah without discussion with the Security Cabinet. In March the Israeli Cabinet voted

unanimously to withdraw its forces from southern Lebanon by July, even if no agreement had been reached on the Israeli-Syrian track of the Middle East peace process. In April, having released 13 Lebanese prisoners held without trial for more than a decade as 'bargaining counters' for Israeli soldiers missing in Lebanon, Israel gave the UN official notification that it intended to withdraw its forces from southern Lebanon 'in one phase' by 7 July. The Lebanese Government made the unprecedented admission that it would accept a UN peace-keeping force in southern Lebanon after the Israeli withdrawal.

On 23 May 2000 Israel's Security Cabinet voted to accelerate the withdrawal of its remaining troops from Lebanon, after Hezbollah had taken control of about one-third of southern Lebanon following the evacuation by the SLA of outposts transferred to its control by the Israeli army. Both the Israeli Government and the UN had expected the withdrawal to take place on 1 June; however, the rapid and chaotic withdrawal of Israeli forces from southern Lebanon was completed on 24 May, almost six weeks ahead of Barak's original deadline. In June the UN Security Council officially declared that the Israeli withdrawal had been completed. However, both the Lebanese Government and Hezbollah maintained that Israel was still required to depart from territory known as Shebaa Farms and to release all Lebanese prisoners. (The UN maintains that Shebaa Farms is part of territory captured by Israel from Syria, and as such must be considered under the Israeli-Syrian track of the peace process.) In July a limited contingent of UNIFIL troops assumed responsibility for the Lebanese border with Israel; they numbered some 5,600 by August. In that month a Joint Security Force of some 1,000 Lebanese troops and Internal Security Forces was reportedly deployed in southern Lebanon (other than in the border area), charged with the provision of general security in the territory. By January 2001 an estimated 2,041 SLA militiamen were reported to have been convicted of having collaborated with Israel during its occupation of southern Lebanon.

Redefinition of Syria's role after the 2000 legislative elections

Elections to the National Assembly took place on 27 August (Mount Lebanon and North Lebanon) and 3 September 2000 (Beirut, the Beqa'a valley, Nabatiyah and the South). For the first time since 1972 Lebanese citizens in the former Israeli-occupied zone of southern Lebanon participated in the elections. Voting patterns in the first round swiftly indicated a rejection of al-Hoss's premiership, as the Druze leader, Walid Joumblatt (one of former premier Rafiq Hariri's staunchest allies), secured an overwhelming victory in Mount Lebanon governorate. Moreover, the election of Pierre Gemayel, son of Amin Gemayel, in the Maronite Northern Metn district (north-east of Beirut) was regarded as a considerable reverse for President Lahoud. At the second round of voting, Hariri's Al-Karamah (Dignity) list secured 18 of the 19 assembly seats in Beirut; al-Hoss lost his own seat in the legislature. In the south an alliance of Hezbollah and Amal candidates took all the governorate's 23 seats, while Hezbollah enjoyed similar successes in the Beqa'a valley. Independent monitors reported numerous instances of electoral malpractice. Overall, Hariri was reported to have the support of between 92 and 106 of the 128 seats in the new legislature. In October President Lahoud formally appointed Rafiq Hariri to the premiership.

Divisions between pro- and anti-Syrian elements within Lebanon had become increasingly vocal in the aftermath of the Israeli withdrawal from southern Lebanon in May 2000 and the death of Syria's President Hafiz al-Assad in the following month. An unofficial visit to Beirut by his successor, Bashar al-Assad, for meetings with key Lebanese politicians shortly before the legislative elections, appeared to indicate that he intended to continue his late father's role as power-broker in Lebanon. In December Syria—which had never previously confirmed that it was holding Lebanese prisoners—freed 46 Lebanese political prisoners (including many Christians who had been detained by Syrian troops during 1975–90), apparently as a goodwill gesture. In April 2001, following student protests demanding the withdrawal of Syrian troops, the Government banned all unlicensed demonstrations against Syria.

The outbreak of the so-called 'al-Aqsa *intifada*' in the Palestinian Territories in September 2000 prompted uncertainty in Lebanon about the permanence of the Israeli withdrawal, particularly as Hezbollah had renewed its campaign against the Israeli military. In October Hezbollah fighters captured three Israeli soldiers in Shebaa Farms, with the demand that Israel release 19 Lebanese and tens of Palestinians from Israeli detention. In the following week a senior Israeli army reservist and businessman, Elhanan Tannenbaum, was kidnapped in Switzerland, apparently by Hezbollah (which claimed that the officer was working for Israeli intelligence). The killing of an Israeli soldier in Shebaa Farms at the end of November prompted Israel to launch air-strikes against suspected Hezbollah targets in southern Lebanon. In mid-November the UN Security Council had urged the Lebanese Government to comply with international law by deploying its armed forces on the Israeli border with southern Lebanon (where Hezbollah still controlled the line of withdrawal, or 'Blue Line'), but Lebanon rejected such a deployment until Israel had signed a comprehensive peace treaty with both Lebanon and Syria. In January 2001 the UN Security Council voted to extend UNIFIL's mandate in Lebanon until July, when its operational strength was to be reduced to about 4,500—the number of troops deployed prior to the Israeli withdrawal. In April 2001 at least one Syrian soldier died when Israel responded to the killing by Hezbollah of one of its soldiers in Shebaa Farms by attacking a radar base to the east of Beirut which was operated by Syria (alleged by Israel to be sponsoring Hezbollah).

In June 2001 Syria withdrew an estimated 6,000–10,000 troops from the largely Christian eastern and southern suburbs of Beirut and from Mount Lebanon, and redeployed the majority to the Beqa'a valley. However, Syria retained 15 military bases in strategic parts of Beirut. In early August the Maronite patriarch, Cardinal Sfeir, and the Druze leader, Walid Joumblatt, held discussions, apparently to indicate a new era of reconciliation between the two communities. Within days, however, the mainly pro-Syrian army intelligence service began mass arrests of Maronite Christians (mostly members of the banned LF or supporters of the exiled Michel Aoun) who were again demanding a complete Syrian withdrawal from Lebanon. Many Christian and Muslim deputies condemned the detentions as 'unconstitutional'. Indeed, Hariri's political standing appeared to have been weakened by the security forces' actions, which had been undertaken when he was out of the country, as in mid-August the National Assembly approved legislation granting increased powers to President Lahoud.

Israel launched a further air attack on a Syrian radar station in eastern Lebanon at the beginning of July 2001, again apparently in response to an assault by Hezbollah against the Israeli military in Shebaa Farms. At the end of July the UN Security Council voted for an extension of UNIFIL's mandate for a further six months; prior to the expiry of this mandate, the status of the peace-keeping force—now numbering 3,600 troops—was downgraded to that of an observer mission. In October Israel alleged that Hezbollah was directly involved in the Palestinian *intifada*, and was supplying weapons to Palestinians in the West Bank and Gaza. (In April 2006 Hezbollah Secretary-General Sheikh Hasan Nasrallah acknowledged for the first time that Hezbollah funded Palestinian militant groups.) In January 2002 the UN Security Council expressed concern regarding recent Israeli violations of Lebanese airspace, and criticized Hezbollah for its frequent interference with the freedom of movement of UNIFIL. The UN again urged the Lebanese Government to deploy its army along the Blue Line. The observer mission's mandate was extended for further six-month periods in January and July; by the end of 2002 the strength of the force had been reduced to some 2,000 troops.

In January 2002 Elie Hobeika, the former leader of the Christian LF militia, was killed (along with three aides and two bystanders) in a car bombing in Beirut. A previously unknown anti-Syrian group claimed responsibility for the attack, alleging that Hobeika was a 'Syrian agent'. Israel strongly denied assertions made by some Lebanese sources that Israeli interests had instigated the killing, since Hobeika had declared his willingness to give evidence to an investigation being carried out by a Belgian court into alleged 'crimes against humanity' by Israeli premier Ariel Sharon related to the massacre of Palestinians in the Sabra and Chatila refugee camps in 1982 (at which time Sharon had been Israel's Minister of Defence). Hobeika was the first prominent Lebanese politician to be assassinated since the civil war ended in 1990. (A Belgian appeals court judged the case against Sharon to be inadmissible in June 2002.)

Amid rising tensions between Israel and Lebanon, in February 2002 Iran denied allegations made by Israeli officials that it was supplying Hezbollah with vast consignments of *Katyusha* rockets and had sent a number of its Revolutionary Guards to Lebanon. In March and August Hezbollah initiated cross-border mortar, missile and machine-gun attacks against Israeli military targets in Shebaa Farms, asserting that these were in retaliation for Israeli violations of Lebanese airspace. Israel responded by shelling suspected militant bases in southern Lebanon. In April the UN had condemned Hezbollah for increasing the instability along the Blue Line, and also for an incident in which five UNIFIL personnel allegedly came under attack by Hezbollah guerrillas near Shebaa Farms.

President Assad of Syria undertook an historic visit to Beirut in March 2002 for discussions with President Lahoud. This first official visit by a Syrian leader to Beirut since 1947 was welcomed by many Lebanese as a formal recognition by Syria of Lebanese sovereignty. The talks resulted in several agreements regarding closer economic co-operation. It was reported in April 2002 that Syrian troops were soon to redeploy from central Lebanon to the Beqa'a valley, thus fulfilling one of the requirements of the 1989 Ta'if agreement. However, hundreds of Syrian intelligence officers were expected to remain in central Lebanon.

In March 2002 Beirut hosted the annual summit meeting of the Council of the Arab League, at which the principal issue under discussion was a peace initiative for the Middle East proposed by Crown Prince Abdullah of Saudi Arabia. However, only 10 out of 22 Arab heads of state attended the summit, while President Hosni Mubarak of Egypt and King Abdullah ibn al-Hussein of Jordan reportedly declined to participate in the discussions as a demonstration of solidarity with the President of the Palestinian (National) Authority (PA), Yasser Arafat, who was effectively blockaded by Israeli forces in the West Bank. At the conclusion of the summit Arab leaders unanimously endorsed the Saudi peace initiative. Incorporated in the Beirut Declaration, this required from Israel a complete withdrawal from all Arab territories occupied in June 1967, and what were termed 'territories still occupied in southern Lebanon', a 'just solution' to the issue of Palestinian refugees, and acceptance of the establishment of a sovereign Palestinian state in the West Bank and Gaza Strip, with East Jerusalem as its capital. In return, the Arab states undertook to consider the Arab–Israeli conflict at an end, to sign a peace agreement with Israel, and to establish normal relations with Israel within this comprehensive peace framework. The initiative was rejected by the Israeli Government, however, which maintained that it would lead to the destruction of the State of Israel.

In April 2003, following weeks of reported disagreements between members of the Cabinet over economic and other domestic policies, the Prime Minister, Rafiq Hariri, tendered his resignation and that of his Government. However, after his premiership was endorsed by the Lebanese parliament, Hariri was asked by President Lahoud to form a new cabinet. The new Government was widely considered to be the most pro-Syrian for more than a decade; it contained no members of the Christian opposition, nor of Hezbollah. Nevertheless, in February Syria had commenced the gradual redeployment of more than 4,000 troops stationed in northern Lebanon, under the terms of the Ta'if agreement.

It was reported in May 2003 that Lebanese security forces had arrested at least nine suspected members of the militant Islamist al-Qa'ida organization in Sidon. The suspects were accused of plotting to attack the US embassy in Beirut and to kidnap members of the Lebanese Cabinet. Moreover, they were believed to be linked to alleged al-Qa'ida militants thought to be in hiding in the Ain al-Hilweh refugee camp. In December 27 Lebanese were found guilty, and given varying prison sentences, on charges of carrying out bomb attacks against mostly US and British businesses in Lebanon between the end of 2002 and April 2003. However, a military court in Beirut acquitted three defendants of plotting to assassinate the US ambassador to Lebanon.

The Israeli Cabinet agreed in November 2003 to release more than 400 Palestinian, Lebanese (mostly Hezbollah) and other Arab prisoners in exchange for the remains of three soldiers kidnapped by Hezbollah in Shebaa Farms in 2000, as well as the return of the abducted Israeli businessman, Elhanan Tannenbaum. Germany, which had mediated the negotiations between Israel and Hezbollah, oversaw the exchange, and in January 2004 the first 30 Lebanese and other Arab prisoners to be released by Israel were flown to the airport at Cologne, Germany, where they were exchanged for Tannenbaum and the remains of the Israeli soldiers. The other Palestinian prisoners, and the remains of 59 Lebanese militants held by Israel, were later released at Israeli border posts.

In January 2005 at least one Israeli officer and two UN observers were killed when Israeli soldiers retaliated against Hezbollah guerrilla attacks on an Israeli military vehicle patrolling Shebaa Farms. The UN Secretary-General, Kofi Annan, criticized Israel's persistent violations of Lebanese airspace and also Hezbollah's recent launching of a remote-controlled drone aircraft over Israel, both of which he considered to be provocative acts; moreover, he urged Lebanon to respect the Blue Line. In November Hezbollah launched what was apparently its heaviest attack on Israeli troops in the Shebaa Farms area since October 2000. Four Hezbollah militants were killed and 11 Israeli soldiers injured in the ensuing violence, in which the two sides exchanged heavy artillery fire across the border.

In August 2004, in advance of the expiry of President Lahoud's six-year term of office in November, the Cabinet voted to amend the Constitution, which prevented Lahoud from seeking a second term, to extend Lahoud's mandate by three years. Both Muslim and Christian politicians and Hariri protested against the decision, but Hariri eventually offered his support for the amendment after a meeting with Syrian politicians, including President Assad. The USA and France expressed their opposition to the move, and presented a resolution to the UN in early September in an attempt to forestall it. The UN subsequently adopted Resolution 1559, demanding that: Lebanon's sovereignty be respected; a 'free and fair' presidential election be held; the Government assert its power throughout the whole country; all foreign forces leave Lebanon; and all militias in the country, both Lebanese and non-Lebanese, disband and disarm. However, the resolution did not explicitly refer to Syria or its forces and agents. The Security Council gave Lebanon 30 days to comply with the resolution's demands, threatening to take measures against the country if it failed to meet them. Nevertheless, the National Assembly approved the constitutional amendment by 96 votes to 29, prompting the resignation of four cabinet ministers in protest.

The Syrian army responded to Resolution 1559 by redeploying about 3,000 special forces from positions to the south of Beirut, although some 14,000 Syrian troops remained in Lebanon. (Further redeployments of Syrian troops took place in December 2004, from the northern town of Batrun and from Beirut's southern suburbs and the airport to the Beqa'a valley.) In October 2004, after UN Secretary-General Kofi Annan had reported Lebanon's non-compliance with the resolution, the Security Council ordered Annan to provide a report every six months detailing steps towards its fulfilment. Hariri dissolved his Cabinet a day after the release of the statement, declaring that he would not attempt to head the next government. The following day he was replaced by Omar Karami, who revealed the composition of his Cabinet five days later (which for the first time included two women). The new Government was considered to be still more favourable than its predecessor to continued Syrian influence in Lebanese affairs. Prime Minister Karami criticized the recent UN Security Council resolution, asserting that the fulfilment of its demands would destabilize Lebanon.

On 22 November 2004 (Independence Day) some 3,000 university students and right-wing Christian activists demonstrated in Beirut against Syria's influence in Lebanon, in defiance of a government ban. At the end of the month the Government supported a march by over 100,000 demonstrators in Beirut in praise of Syria's role and rejecting the terms of UN Resolution 1559. In December parties including the main Christian opposition group, the Qornet Shehwan Gathering, Kamal Joumblatt's mainly Druze-supported PSP and the proscribed Lebanese Forces Party issued a joint statement demanding a cessation of foreign interference in Lebanon and calling for the release of Lebanese Forces Party leader Samir Geagea, who had been imprisoned on murder charges in 1994. They also demanded an electoral law that would allow people of all political sensibilities to participate in governing the country.

The assassination of Rafiq Hariri

On 14 February 2005 a car bomb in Beirut killed former Prime Minister Rafiq Hariri and 22 other people; at least 100 were injured in the blast. The attack provoked condemnation from Syrian President Assad. However, the USA, emphasizing the problems caused by the Syrian military presence in Lebanon and the inability of the Syrian-dominated intelligence services to forestall the attack, removed its ambassador to Syria for consultations, and subsequently demanded that all Syrian troops and security forces withdraw from Lebanon. Later in the month Syria announced that it would redeploy its troops in Lebanon to the Beqa'a valley. On 28 February, following a general strike and

mass protests in Beirut advocated by opposition parties, at which demonstrators demanded the complete withdrawal of Syrian troops from Lebanon and an end to Syrian influence in Lebanese politics, Karami dissolved his Cabinet and resigned as premier.

Lebanese opposition groups demanded in March 2005 that the public prosecutor and senior security officials in Lebanon resign from their posts in order to ensure that the investigation into Hariri's death be conducted legitimately and with integrity. They also announced their refusal to participate in any discussions on the formation of a new government until their demands were met. Assad and Lahoud agreed at a summit meeting to the withdrawal of Syrian troops to the Beqa'a valley by the end of the month; Syria later pledged to withdraw all troops prior to Lebanon's general election, scheduled to begin in May. Meanwhile, protests took place in Beirut in support of Syria's influence and military presence. Syria reportedly withdrew 4,000–6,000 of its soldiers and intelligence agents from Lebanon to Syria in mid-March; 8,000–10,000 troops remained in the Beqa'a valley. A UN report released later that month accused Syria of allowing political tension in Lebanon to be heightened before the murder of Hariri, and criticized Lebanon's initial attempts to investigate the incident. In April the UN Security Council approved Resolution 1595, establishing an International Independent Investigation Commission (UNIIIC) to investigate Hariri's murder. After Syria declared that it had fulfilled its promise to withdraw all troops, military assets and intelligence apparatus, in May a UN team dispatched to Lebanon verified the absence of Syrian military personnel in areas that it had inspected.

President Lahoud reappointed Karami to the post of Prime Minister on 10 March 2005. Yet in the following month Karami, having failed to form a new administration, tendered his resignation for a second time, and Najib Miqati was appointed to the post of caretaker Prime Minister. Miqati named a new Cabinet (approved by the National Assembly on 27 April), which was to be responsible for the implementation of legislation facilitating a general election. In late April three senior Lebanese security officials with close ties to Syria announced their resignations, and by mid-May a number of other pro-Syrian security officials had been dismissed from their posts.

Elections to the National Assembly were held in four rounds between 29 May and 19 June 2005. The first round of voting took place in the Beirut region, where turn-out was a reported 28%. The anti-Syrian Rafiq Hariri Martyr List, headed by the Future Movement of Rafiq Hariri's son, Saad Hariri, and including the PSP, the Lebanese Forces Party—which now functioned legally—and the Qornet Shehwan Gathering, won all 19 seats. Four days later the prominent anti-Syrian journalist Dr Samir Kassir was killed in a car bombing in a Christian district of Beirut. The anti-Syrian opposition accused remaining Syrian intelligence agents of involvement in the murder, and called on President Lahoud to resign. Syria, however, insisted that it had removed all its security personnel. An estimated 45% of registered voters participated in the second round of elections conducted on 5 June in southern Lebanon; as in the first round, turn-out was reportedly lower in Christian than in Muslim districts. The Resistance and Development Bloc, consisting of the pro-Syrian Shi'a organizations Amal and Hezbollah and their allies, secured all 23 seats. The third round was held on 12 June in Mount Lebanon, where candidates contested 35 seats and turn-out was unofficially estimated at 54%, and the Beqa'a valley, where an estimated 49% of registered voters elected deputies to 23 seats. Immediately prior to the poll, Michel Aoun allied himself with pro-Syrian factions as the Free Patriotic Movement (FPM), declaring that he was no longer hostile to Syria since it had withdrawn its troops from Lebanon. Aoun's alliance took 21 seats, while Hariri's list secured 25. However, in the final round in north Lebanon on 19 June, at which turn-out was officially estimated at 49%, Hariri's list won all 28 seats. Consequently, according to final results, the Rafiq Hariri Martyr List secured 72 of the National Assembly's 128 seats, allowing the Lebanese Forces Party to achieve parliamentary representation for the first time; the Resistance and Development Bloc won 35 seats; and the FPM took 21.

In June 2005 George Hawi, the former Secretary-General of the Parti communiste libanais (PCL) and an outspoken critic of Syrian interference in Lebanese politics, was killed by a car bomb in Beirut. The anti-Syrian opposition attributed the attack to Syrian agents and their allies in the Lebanese security services. Further bomb explosions took place in the capital throughout 2005, causing a number of fatalities. In July two people were killed in an explosion that injured pro-Syrian Deputy Prime

Minister and Minister of National Defence Elias Murr, and in December the anti-Syrian publisher of the daily newspaper *An-Nahar* and three others were killed in a car bombing.

Meanwhile, pro-Syrian Nabih Berri was re-elected President of the National Assembly in June 2005. Two days later President Lahoud appointed Fouad Siniora of the Future Movement, a close ally of Rafiq Hariri, as Prime Minister, and asked him to form a new government. In July Siniora announced the composition of a new Cabinet: Fawzi Salloukh was appointed Minister of Foreign Affairs and Emigrants, while Muhammad Fneish became the first representative of Hezbollah to hold cabinet office, assuming responsibility for energy and water. In the same month the National Assembly passed a law pardoning Lebanese Forces Party leader Samir Geagea, as demanded by some of the opposition. (Geagea survived an assassination attempt outside his home in Beirut in early April 2012, amid rising sectarian tensions as a result of the unrest in Syria from early 2011 and subsequent civil conflict—see below.) Almost 40 Islamist militants, some of whom were allegedly linked to al-Qa'ida, were also released by parliamentary approval.

UNIIIC began its inquiry into Rafiq Hariri's assassination in June 2005, with a three-month mandate. In August UNIIIC arrested the three former security officials who had tendered their resignations in April for questioning regarding the assassination. A fourth security chief, who had retained his post after Hariri's murder, was also sought, and subsequently handed himself in to the organization; a former pro-Syrian parliamentary deputy was also detained. In October, shortly before UNIIIC issued its first report on the investigation, the Syrian Minister of the Interior, Maj.-Gen. Ghazi Kanaan, was found shot dead in his office. The official Syrian Arab News Agency announced that he had committed suicide. A former head of Syrian military intelligence in Lebanon, Kanaan had become Chief of Political Intelligence in Syria in 2002, and had been appointed Minister of the Interior in October 2004. Shortly before his apparent suicide, Kanaan had told a Lebanese radio station that he had been questioned by UNIIIC, but had not given any evidence against Syria. According to its report, issued in October 2005, UNIIIC had found evidence that senior Lebanese and Syrian intelligence and security officials were directly involved in Hariri's assassination. Moreover, the report reasoned, the act was too complex and too well-planned to have taken place without their approval. Both Lebanon and Syria denounced the investigation's findings as being politically motivated, and Syria announced that it had established a special judicial commission to deal with all matters relating to UNIIIC's mission. The commission was granted an extension to its mandate until December.

The UN Security Council responded to the first UNIIIC report by adopting in October 2005 a resolution, sponsored by the USA, France and the United Kingdom, establishing measures against suspects in the assassination, including prohibitions on travel and the freezing of assets. The Security Council urged Syria to co-operate fully with the investigation commission and detain suspects identified by the inquiry, threatening unspecified 'further action' should Syria fail to comply with the resolution's demands by 15 December. Syria reported in November that it had arrested six government officials for questioning. Meanwhile, in October the UN Special Envoy, Terje Rød-Larsen, issued his report on the implementation of UN Security Council Resolution 1559, in which he praised the withdrawal of Syrian troops from Lebanon, but noted that Lebanon had still not complied with the demands that all militias disarm and disband, and that government authority be extended throughout the country. Lebanon rejected the report, asserting that the Government would deal with armed groups through national dialogue.

In December 2005 UNIIIC began questioning five Syrian officials suspected of involvement in Hariri's assassination in Vienna, Austria. Prosecutor Detlev Mehlis presented his second report on the investigating body's work to the UN Security Council later in the month. While noting that Syria had presented the five officials to the commission for interrogation, the report repeated accusations that Syria was hindering the investigation. It stated that UNIIIC had found further evidence that the Lebanese and Syrian intelligence and security services had been involved in the assassination, and revealed that Mehlis had identified 19 suspects, six of whom were Syrian (including the five being questioned in Vienna). Mehlis resigned as the head of UNIIIC shortly afterwards, citing personal and professional reasons; he was replaced by Serge Brammertz.

In January 2006 UNIIIC investigators declared that they wished to question Syrian President Assad and Minister of Foreign Affairs Farouk al-Shara' in relation to Hariri's murder. (A few days earlier the Vice-President of Syria, Abd al-Halim Khaddam, who had been living in exile in Paris, having resigned from his post in June 2005, had accused Assad of personally threatening Hariri. He subsequently declared that, in his view, Assad had ordered Hariri's assassination, although he awaited the final decision of the investigating commission.) However, the following day the Syrian Minister of Information announced that Syria would not permit UNIIIC to interview Assad. Al-Shara' announced in March 2006 that he had reached an agreement with UNIIIC that provided for full Syrian co-operation with the investigation, while preserving the country's 'sovereignty and dignity'.

Ministers from Hezbollah and Amal announced in February 2006 that they were ending a boycott of cabinet meetings begun in December 2005 in protest against the Government's decision to allow an international investigation into Hariri's assassination. The announcement came shortly after Prime Minister Fouad Siniora declared to the National Assembly that the Government had always considered Hezbollah to be a movement of national resistance rather than a militia (a further demand of the ministers).

The 2006 conflict with Israel

On 12 July 2006 Hezbollah soldiers conducted a cross-border raid in which three Israeli troops were killed and two were captured; five more Israeli soldiers were killed during an attempt to rescue the kidnapped men. Prime Minister Siniora denied Israeli claims that his Government had organized the soldiers' abduction. Later that same day Israel launched a series of air raids on a number of suspected Hezbollah positions across southern Lebanon. Further strikes during the night caused extensive damage to civilian infrastructure in the area. Hezbollah declared 'open war' on 14 July, firing barrages of rockets into northern Israel in response to Israeli air-strikes. On the same day the UN Security Council held an emergency meeting, at which Lebanon accused Israel of instigating the violence.

Numerous strikes were exchanged between the two warring factions on a daily basis and, despite claims to the contrary from both sides, who insisted that they were targeting political and military targets exclusively, many civilians were killed or injured in the conflict and thousands of homes were destroyed. Israel systematically targeted Lebanese infrastructure—roads and bridges were destroyed, seaports were blockaded and Beirut International Airport was bombed, forcing all international flights to be diverted to Cyprus. An estimated 70% of civilians living in southern Lebanon fled to the north of the country to escape the worst of the violence. In late July 2006 at least 28 civilians, including 19 children, were reported to have been killed when a residential building in the Lebanese village of Qana was struck by missiles during an Israeli air raid. At a further emergency session of the UN Security Council, convened on the following day, members issued a statement expressing 'extreme shock and distress' at the attack; UN Secretary-General Kofi Annan, while apportioning blame for the initial outbreak of the conflict to Hezbollah, denounced the scale of the Israeli response as excessive and unacceptable. Nevertheless, in early August the Israeli Cabinet approved a plan to send a large number of ground troops further into Lebanon, as far as the Litani river (approximately 30 km north of the Israeli–Lebanese border).

On 11 August 2006 the UN Security Council adopted Resolution 1701, which had been unanimously approved and which called for: an immediate and full cessation of hostilities; the extension of the Lebanese Government's authority over the whole country; and the delineation of Lebanese international boundaries, with particular regard to disputed sectors such as Shebaa Farms. (The USA had come under criticism for apparently blocking earlier attempts to impose a cease-fire, which had led to allegations that the Administration of President George W. Bush was implicitly encouraging Israel to wreak damage upon Hezbollah.) The resolution was endorsed by the Lebanese Government on 12 August, and Nasrallah announced that Hezbollah would honour the call for a cease-fire; however, 24 Israeli soldiers were killed on that same day—the greatest loss of life on any single day since the conflict began. Similarly, despite Israel's Cabinet approving the resolution on 13 August, on the following day Israeli troops launched an attack on a refugee camp in Sidon, killing an UNRWA staff member approximately one hour before the cease-fire was scheduled to take effect.

Nasrallah acknowledged in late August 2006 that Hezbollah's kidnapping of the two Israeli soldiers that had triggered the conflict had, with hindsight, been deeply regrettable and that talks concerning their possible return, in exchange for Lebanese nationals detained by Israel, were ongoing. However, he remained defiant, claiming during a rally staged in Beirut in September that Hezbollah was stronger than it had been prior to the conflict and that the organization possessed in excess of 20,000 rockets in its arsenal. Earlier that month Israel had lifted its naval blockade of Lebanon and rescinded its restrictions on air travel to and from Lebanon, thereby formalizing the end of the conflict. However, much of southern Lebanon remained uninhabitable owing to the presence of unexploded cluster bombs. According to figures released by Lebanon's Higher Relief Council, an estimated 1,191 Lebanese civilians were killed during the conflict, and a further 4,410 were thought to have been injured. According to the Israeli Ministry of Foreign Affairs, 119 Israeli troops and 44 Israeli civilians had died in the fighting, and more than 530 Hezbollah members had also been killed. In November the findings of an official UN investigation into the conflict determined that Israel had fired artillery shells containing white phosphorus, an incendiary substance the use of which against civilians, or against legitimate military targets within residential areas, is banned under the terms of the Geneva Convention. However, the Israeli Government insisted that the shells had been aimed solely at military targets in open ground. Meanwhile, in September 2006 the human rights group Amnesty International accused Hezbollah of having committed war crimes by deliberately targeting Israeli civilians in its recent missile launches.

Increasing political and sectarian division

In October 2006 Nasrallah demanded that Hezbollah be allocated one-third of the seats in an expanded national unity government, prompting accusations that he was attempting to attain the right of veto in order to protect the Syrian Government from prosecution in the ongoing investigation into the assassination of Rafiq Hariri. Nasrallah's demands were ignored, however, and in the following month five ministers—two members of Hezbollah and three from its ally, Amal—resigned from the Cabinet, thereby removing any Shi'a presence from the Government. A sixth resignation, that of a Christian pro-Syrian minister, followed soon afterwards. The assassination later in November of Pierre Gemayel, the Minister of Industry since 2005, rendered the political situation even more unstable. Gemayel was shot dead in his car in a suburb of Beirut, and many Lebanese leaders were quick to blame Syria for his murder. Since the Lebanese Constitution decrees that any government in which one-third of the ministers have vacated their posts must automatically be dissolved and a new administration formed, Gemayel's assassination meant that the departure of just one further minister would force the collapse of the Government.

In December 2006 thousands of demonstrators gathered in Beirut and erected tents in the capital's main square, besieging government buildings and proclaiming that the Cabinet was now constitutionally invalid and should therefore resign. When the protests had failed to achieve this result by late January 2007, the opposition intensified its efforts and called for a general strike, which brought commercial districts of the capital to a virtual standstill; at least three people were killed during clashes between protesters and the authorities. Yet, despite the Government's refusal to submit to the wishes of the opposition, the presence of two separate Lebanese delegations at the annual summit meeting of the Arab League, held in Saudi Arabia in March 2007, aptly symbolized the endemic divisions threatening the country's future stability.

Meanwhile, a disagreement between pro-Government Sunni and anti-Government Shi'a students at Beirut Arab University in January 2007 escalated into violent clashes; up to four people were killed and more than 150 injured. The incident fuelled concerns that Lebanon was about to spiral into full-scale sectarian conflict again; in an effort to prevent further violence, the Government imposed an overnight curfew in Beirut for the first time in a decade. In February two bombs were detonated on commuter buses travelling through Ein Alaq, a village to the north-east of Beirut, killing three people. The attacks, which took place on the eve of the second anniversary of Hariri's assassination, were thought to have been intended to deter people from travelling to Beirut to attend a large rally to mark the occasion. In March the Lebanese authorities announced that four Syrian members of Fatah al-Islam—a militant Islamist

Palestinian group inspired by al-Qa'ida and which they alleged to be supported by Syria—had been arrested on suspicion of involvement in the bus explosions.

In March 2007 UNIIIC released its latest report into the assassination of Rafiq Hariri, in which Brammertz stated that the Commission had identified 250 individuals whom it wanted to question. In the same month recently appointed UN Secretary-General Ban Ki-Moon issued his report on the implementation of UN Security Council Resolution 1701, in which he rebuked both Israel and Lebanon for failing to adhere to all of its terms. However, the Secretary-General praised both sides' overall commitment to maintaining the cease-fire, and proposed the establishment of an independent assessment mission to assist with the monitoring of the Israeli–Lebanese border and thereby to facilitate the full implementation of the resolution.

In May 2007 the UN Security Council adopted Resolution 1757, authorizing the formation of an international tribunal to try suspects in Hariri's assassination. The Special Tribunal for Lebanon (STL) was to comprise 11 independent judges (or 14, should a second trial chamber be created), of whom seven were to be international judges and four Lebanese; should a second trial chamber be created, there were to be nine international and five Lebanese judges. While the creation of the STL was welcomed by the Siniora Government, the Hezbollah-led opposition was quick to challenge its validity. Nasrallah insisted that any such tribunal not approved by the Lebanese legislature was illegitimate.

Walid Eido, an anti-Syrian legislator and member of the Future Movement, was killed in a car bombing in Beirut in June 2007; nine others, including Eido's son, also died. Once again, Syrian officials vehemently denied allegations of the country's involvement. A few days later, following a request by Prime Minister Siniora, the UN Security Council announced that UNIIIC was to assist with the investigation into Eido's assassination. By-elections to select replacements for Eido, in Beirut's second district, and for Pierre Gemayel, in the Metn district, were held in August. The former seat was won comfortably by the pro-Government Muhammad Amin Itani, of the Future Movement, while the latter was secured by pro-Syrian Camille Khoury, of the FPM, in a very tight contest against his closest rival, former President Amin Gemayel.

The sixth UNIIIC report compiled during the tenure of Serge Brammertz was released in July 2007. It asserted that a 'number of persons' had now been identified who might have been involved in Hariri's assassination, and stated that Syria and other states had continued to provide a 'mostly positive response' to UNIIIC's requests for co-operation and information. In the same month Lebanese investigators concluded that Fatah al-Islam had been responsible for the killing of Pierre Gemayel. Meanwhile, the 10th UNIIIC report, and the first to be published since the appointment in early 2008 of Daniel Bellemare in place of Brammertz, was issued in March of that year. In the report, the UN body revealed that the evidence it had examined thus far indicated that a network of people was behind Hariri's murder, without mentioning specific individuals.

In September 2007 a 105-day siege of the Nahr al-Bared refugee camp in Tripoli was finally concluded when the Lebanese army seized control from Islamist militants. More than 300 people were believed to have been killed in fierce clashes between the army and militants within the camp, which forced an estimated 40,000 Palestinian refugees to flee the violence. The Syrian Government commended the efforts of the Lebanese army in ending the siege, and continued to deny claims that it supported the activities of Fatah al-Islam. In March 2008 Fatah al-Islam's leader, Shaker al-Abassi (who was reported to have gone missing), was charged with incitement to murder, in connection with the bus explosions at Ein Alaq in February 2007.

The 2007 constitutional crisis

With the scheduled expiry, in November 2007, of Lahoud's presidential term, the attention of the Government and the opposition in the preceding months came increasingly to focus on the election of his successor. The first session of the National Assembly to elect a new president was duly arranged for 25 September 2007—the first time that the legislature was to have met since October 2006. In a conciliatory overture, the President of the Assembly, Nabih Berri, proposed an initiative whereby the opposition would relinquish its long-standing demand for a national unity government if the rival factions could agree on a presidential candidate, although the response from Siniora and his supporters to the proposal was muted. The ambiguity of the Lebanese Constitution meant that, in the event of political divisions between the two camps preventing agreement on a common candidate, the likely eventuality remained deeply uncertain. According to the Constitution, if a new president was not elected by 23 November 2007, then Siniora and his Cabinet would automatically assume executive control. However, the Constitution also authorized the President to decree the resignation of the Cabinet, allowing Lahoud, should he have chosen, to appoint a new, opposition cabinet, which would almost certainly have elected a pro-Syrian, anti-Government president. In late September, just six days before the scheduled presidential election, Antoine Ghanem, a Christian Phalangist legislator, was killed in a car bombing in a predominantly Christian district of Beirut; five others died in the explosion. Since the Government and opposition were unwilling to co-operate in order to elect a new president, leading to an opposition boycott, the National Assembly failed to achieve the requisite two-thirds' quorum of members on 25 September; a second vote was thus scheduled for 23 October.

Following mediation by German diplomats and representatives of the International Committee of the Red Cross, Hezbollah and Israel carried out a limited exchange of prisoners and bodies in October 2007. However, the two Israeli soldiers whose abduction by Hezbollah militants in July 2006 had apparently provoked the month-long conflict were not included in the arrangement. At the start of June 2008 Hezbollah handed over to Israel the remains of several Israeli soldiers killed during the conflict, while the Israeli authorities returned a Lebanese civilian who had served a six-year prison term for espionage. At the end of June the Israeli Cabinet controversially voted to exchange the bodies of the two soldiers abducted by Hezbollah in 2006 (who it now transpired were certainly dead) for five Lebanese detainees; the exchange occurred in July 2008.

The second postponement of the scheduled ballot to elect a successor to President Lahoud was announced by Berri on 22 October 2007, the day before the vote was to take place; a new date of 12 November was declared. In early October US President Bush had warned the Syrian Government not to interfere in Lebanon's internal affairs, since it was a boycott of the National Assembly by pro-Syrian opposition members that had rendered the parliament inquorate. Thus began a seven-month period during which no fewer than 17 further postponements of the presidential election were ordered, owing to a failure by the opposing factions to agree first on a mutually acceptable candidate, and then on the exact nature of administration to be formed after a new president had been elected. When the parliamentary session scheduled for 23 November—at the end of which Lahoud's term of office expired—was postponed until 30 November, the Constitution dictated that presidential duties would be assumed by the Siniora Government in an acting capacity. However, shortly before the expiry of his mandate, Lahoud had issued a statement asserting that, owing to conditions being present for a 'state of emergency', he would hand over responsibility for the country's security to the armed forces. (He and other representatives of the pro-Syrian opposition refused to recognize the legitimacy of the Government following the ministerial resignations of November 2006.) Lahoud's stance was firmly rejected by the Prime Minister, who insisted that no head of state could call a state of emergency without the approval of the Cabinet. This represented the first time that Lebanon had been without a president since the civil war ended in 1990.

Although the Commander-in-Chief of the Army, Gen. Michel Suleiman (a Maronite Christian), was chosen as a 'compromise candidate' acceptable to both pro-Government and pro-opposition politicians towards the end of November 2007, disagreements remained as to how to amend the Constitution in order to permit Suleiman, as a serving senior state official, to assume the office of head of state. Finally, in early January 2008, the ministers responsible for the foreign affairs of Arab League member states, meeting in Cairo, Egypt, approved details of a plan intended to bring to an end Lebanon's presidential vacuum. The three-phase proposals included the election of Suleiman as president, establishment of a Lebanese government of national unity (where Suleiman would have the deciding vote in any dispute) and approval of new electoral legislation. It was reported that the Arab League plan had received the support of both the Lebanese and Syrian administrations, but that Hezbollah and its principal allies continued to demand that they receive at least one-third of government portfolios in any new cabinet, thus granting them the right to veto important decisions. A National Assembly session to elect a president was postponed (for the 19th time) on 13 May. In April, meanwhile,

Suleiman had announced his intention to retire from his military post in August, three months in advance of the scheduled date.

In December 2007 Brig.-Gen. François al-Hajj, the army's head of operations, was killed, along with three other people, in a car bomb attack in east Beirut. Al-Hajj had been widely expected to be promoted to Commander-in-Chief should Suleiman be elected as Lahoud's successor. It was, however, unclear as to which group had carried out the assassination, with Syria, Israel and Fatah al-Islam all being accused by various parties of responsibility for the blast. Towards the end of January 2008 Capt. Wissam Eid, a senior member of the police team charged with investigating the recent bombings and assassinations, was killed in another car bomb attack in a suburb of the capital; Eid's driver and up to 10 others also died in the explosion. In February Imad Mughniyeh, one of Hezbollah's most senior militants, was killed in a car bombing in the Syrian capital. Hezbollah representatives immediately blamed Israel for Mughniyeh's death; however, Israeli officials rejected such claims. Mughniyeh had been implicated in a number of high-profile kidnappings of Western journalists, military personnel and religious envoys in Lebanon during the 1980s, as well as in several bomb attacks against principally US interests in the 1980s and 1990s.

Lebanon's political situation deteriorated rapidly in early May 2008, when a decision taken by the Government to close both a private telecommunications network controlled by Hezbollah and Beirut International Airport (where Hezbollah was accused of using surveillance equipment to spy on pro-Government politicians) prompted fierce clashes between members of the Shi'a opposition group and government loyalists. Moreover, a general strike called by the opposition in protest against price increases and to demand higher salaries descended into violence. As Nasrallah called the Government's actions against his organization a 'declaration of war', gunmen from Hezbollah and its allies besieged the Beirut offices of the media controlled by the Future Movement's Saad Hariri, while major roads were blocked. Observers noted that west Beirut was now effectively controlled by militants of the Hezbollah-led opposition. After several days of violent clashes, which spread to other cities such as Tripoli, at least 81 people had been killed, and up to 250 wounded, in Lebanon's worst period of unrest since the civil war. However, by mid-May the Government and army claimed to have regained control, and, following mediation by the Arab League, the Cabinet voted to revoke the measures that had provoked the recent violence—an outcome widely viewed as a demonstration of Hezbollah's growing military strength and influence. This development meant that the lengthy sit-in by demonstrators in the centre of Beirut came to an end and businesses began to resume trading.

The Doha Agreement

On 21 May 2008 18 months of conflict between the Lebanese Government and Hezbollah and its allies was apparently ended through the signing of the Doha Agreement, following mediation by the Qatari leadership under the auspices of the Arab League. The Agreement encompassed: the election of a new president; formation of a national unity government, which would involve power-sharing with Hezbollah; and introduction of a new electoral law. A few days after the signing of the unity accord, Fouad Siniora was chosen by the National Assembly to remain as Prime Minister. Yet, notwithstanding the election of a new President and formation of a 30-member national unity Cabinet on 11 July (the administration consisted of 16 ministers of the Western-supported majority coalition, 11 linked to Hezbollah and its allies, and three appointed by President Suleiman), the security situation remained uneasy. Heavy fighting between supporters of the Government and pro-opposition activists was reported in the eastern Beqa'a valley and Tripoli, resulting in tens of fatalities. Michel Suleiman had been sworn in as President on 25 May. Prior to Suleiman's election by the National Assembly, the chamber's President, Nabih Berri, rejected the demands of some deputies that the Constitution needed to be amended to permit a serving official to become head of state; this occasion was deemed exceptional since the presidency was actually vacant. The new Siniora Government, which was to administer the country until fresh legislative elections were held in 2009, secured a parliamentary vote of confidence on 12 August 2008. At the end of August Brig.-Gen. Jean Kahwaji was chosen to succeed Suleiman as Commander-in-Chief of the Army.

A landmark agreement was reached between Lebanon and Syria in mid-July 2008, when the two countries announced that they were to enter into diplomatic relations and open embassies in one another's capitals for the first time since they had achieved independence in 1943 and 1945, respectively. The announcement was made by the French President, Nicolas Sarkozy, who welcomed Syria's President Assad and President Suleiman to Paris in advance of the summit convened to launch his Union for the Mediterranean initiative. It was also revealed that the work of a committee to demarcate the Lebanese–Syrian border and to investigate the issue of missing persons since Lebanon's civil war would be resumed. Suleiman undertook an official visit to Damascus on 13–14 August 2008 for discussions with Assad, and the Lebanese Cabinet formally adopted a resolution to establish diplomatic relations with Syria on 22 August. On 16 March 2009 Michel al-Khoury duly arrived in Damascus to assume the post of Lebanese ambassador to Syria and on 24 March Syria opened its embassy in Beirut, with Ali Abd al-Karim Ali as ambassador. However, the deployment of some 10,000 Syrian special forces along the border with northern Lebanon in late September 2008 (which the Syrian Government insisted was to prevent cross-border smuggling) made many Lebanese question Syria's long-term intentions towards their country.

In September 2008 the National Assembly adopted new electoral legislation as required under the terms of the Doha Agreement, in preparation for the general election subsequently scheduled for 7 June 2009. The new law involved the redrawing of electoral boundaries and the staging of elections on one day, rather than over several days. In late October Nasrallah and Saad Hariri held their first meeting since 2006, in advance of a second round of discussions between Lebanon's rival political factions as part of the national dialogue that had begun on 16 September 2008. The talks were held in early November and hosted by President Suleiman; however, the 14 participants (representing each of Lebanon's parliamentary blocs) failed to agree on a national defence strategy, largely owing to their lack of consensus on the issue of how to deal with Hezbollah's military arsenal. Further national reconciliation discussions were held during December 2008, and in January and March 2009.

Meanwhile, the UN Secretary-General, Ban Ki-Moon, announced in November 2008 that the STL established to try those charged with the assassination of former premier Rafiq Hariri in February 2005 would commence proceedings in the Netherlands on 1 March 2009. The 11 judges would be led by Daniel Bellemare, with a Lebanese deputy. In the 11th UNIIIC report, issued at the start of December 2008, the Commission asserted that it had discovered evidence of links between Hariri's assassination and other political attacks that had taken place in Lebanon. On 16 December the UN Security Council approved a resolution extending UNIIIC's mandate until 28 February 2009, although Bellemare pledged that the investigation would continue after the STL began operating in March. On 29 February three of the seven suspects being detained on suspicion of withholding information and misleading the investigation of Hariri's murder were released on bail. Four pro-Syrian army generals, including Maj.-Gen. Jamil Sayyed, former head of the General Security Directorate, suspected of involvement in that crime and other terrorist attacks in Lebanon remained in custody, although they had not been formally charged.

The UN-sponsored STL formally opened on 1 March 2009, with a renewable three-year mandate and a 60-day period during which the general prosecutor could request that the Lebanese Government hand over to the tribunal the four generals in Lebanese custody. However, it was unclear when exactly the tribunal proceedings would begin. In late March an Italian judge, Antonio Cassese, was named as President of the STL. In April the four generals were unexpectedly released from custody, after the STL ruled that there was insufficient evidence to charge them. (In December Maj.-Gen. Sayyed launched legal proceedings in Syria against several defendants in the case whom he accused of giving false evidence in order to implicate Syria and pro-Syrian Lebanese individuals in the crime.)

In March 2009 the National Assembly approved a bill which reduced the voter eligibility age in Lebanese parliamentary elections from 21 to 18; the new legislation would not, however, take effect until after the general election due to be held on 7 June as, under the terms of the Constitution, the Cabinet had four months during which to endorse it. The change in electoral law satisfied a long-standing demand of Hezbollah and its ally, Amal, since it would affect the eligibility to vote of a substantial number of young Shi'a voters. Meanwhile, in May the German periodical *Der Spiegel* reported that UNIIIC had discovered evidence indicating Hezbollah's involvement in Hariri's murder. The allegation was denounced by Hezbollah as part of a campaign to persuade Lebanese voters not to support the Shi'a group at the forthcoming elections; Hezbollah also denounced a landmark visit to Beirut in May by the US Vice-President, Joseph Biden.

The 2009 legislative elections

Despite the failure of parliamentarians to approve electoral reforms proposed by the Cabinet, legislative elections were held as scheduled on 7 June 2009. The March 14 Alliance of Saad Hariri—notably including among its constituent parties Hariri's Future Movement, the PSP and the Lebanese Forces Party—retained its status as the largest group in the legislature, winning 71 of the 128 seats in the National Assembly. The March 8 Alliance, which included Amal, the FPM and Hezbollah, secured 57 seats; voter turn-out was recorded at 54%. The following day Hariri, as Prime Minister-designate, proposed a cabinet for the approval of President Suleiman; however, the proposal was denounced by Hezbollah leader Nasrallah, who claimed that his party had not been consulted. Protracted negotiations between the constituent parties of the two main electoral alliances failed to secure an agreement, partly owing to a dispute between the Future Movement and the FPM over the portfolios allocated to the latter. The process was further complicated in August when the leader of the PSP, Walid Joumblatt, announced his party's withdrawal from the March 14 Alliance, although he reiterated his support for the bloc. In early September Hariri resigned as Prime Minister-designate; however, the following week President Suleiman again instructed him to lead talks over the formation of a national unity coalition, and on 9 November a new, 30-member administration was sworn in by the President. In total, 12 cabinet portfolios were assigned to members of the March 14 Alliance, 10 to the March 8 Alliance and three to March 14-affiliated independents. In addition, five ministers were nominated by Suleiman. In December Prime Minister Hariri visited Damascus to meet with President Assad, and, in what appeared to be a further indication of waning anti-Syrian sentiment among the March 14 parties and its allies, in March 2010 Joumblatt also travelled to Damascus for talks with the Syrian President.

Meanwhile, in August 2009 the mandate of UNIFIL was extended until August 2010, following a vote by the UN Security Council. The issue of integrating Hezbollah's weapons and fighters into the Lebanese armed forces, under the terms of the 2008 Doha Agreement, remained a cause for concern among the international community, amid increasing tensions along the Israeli–Lebanese border. Following reports that Hezbollah had acquired Scud missiles capable of reaching targets across Israel, in early April 2010 Israeli President Shimon Peres publicly accused Syria of supplying the weapons; however, both the Lebanese and Syrian Governments denied the allegations. In late April the US Secretary of Defense, Robert Gates, expressed his Administration's concerns that Syria and Iran were supplying Hezbollah with increasingly sophisticated weaponry. In May UNIFIL declared southern Lebanon to be free of Scud missiles. During discussions with Hariri in Washington, DC, in late May—the Lebanese premier's first official visit to the USA—the US President, Barack Obama, also raised the issue of arms-smuggling to Hezbollah militants.

The collapse of the national unity Government

President Assad and King Abdullah of Saudi Arabia held a tripartite summit meeting with President Suleiman in Beirut on 30 July 2010, in an effort to dissuade Lebanon's competing Sunni and Shi'ite political factions from once again resorting to violence. This was the first visit to Lebanon by the Syrian leader since the Arab League summit of 2002, and the first by a Saudi monarch since 1957. The summit meeting was convened amid growing tensions in Lebanon over reports that an indictment by the STL was imminent, and that members of Hezbollah were likely to be named as culprits in the 2005 assassination of Rafiq Hariri.

An exchange of gunfire between Lebanese and Israeli forces across their joint border on 3 August 2010 reportedly led to the deaths of at least two Lebanese soldiers and a journalist, and one Israeli commander. This constituted the most serious violence between the two sides since the conflict between Israel and Hezbollah in mid-2006. Both Israeli and Lebanese officials blamed the other's military for having been first to violate the terms of UN Security Council Resolution 1701; however, the UN urged both sides to exercise restraint. The foreign affairs committee of the US House of Representatives declared on 10 August 2010 that the US Administration had decided to suspend US $100m. of military assistance to Lebanon, and that this recent incident highlighted concerns among many in the USA that its weaponry might be employed by Lebanese troops, with the possible influence of Hezbollah, to attack Israeli targets.

In mid-August 2010 the National Assembly approved legislation granting limited rights to Palestinian refugees resident in Lebanon, including the right to work legally in some areas of the private sector and to contribute to, and claim payments from, the state social security fund. The law was highly controversial and had required a number of amendments, since many of Lebanon's political factions (particularly Christian groups) were fearful of the consequences for the country's fragile sectarian balance of fully integrating Palestinian refugees into Lebanese society.

The following month Prime Minister Saad Hariri stated in an interview with *Asharq al-Awsat*, a United Kingdom-based Arabic newspaper, that he had been mistaken in initially having accused the Syrian Government of involvement in his father's assassination. In mid-October 2010 the Iranian President, Mahmoud Ahmadinejad, undertook his first state visit to Lebanon; he was welcomed by thousands of Hezbollah supporters in southern Beirut and in the south of the country, where a mass rally was held in Bint Jbeil, near the Israeli border. At the end of that month Nasrallah urged all Lebanese people to boycott the STL, stating that the UN-led tribunal was an 'Israeli project' created in order to defeat Hezbollah. In November Israel announced that, in line with the terms of UN Security Council Resolution 1701, its military was preparing to withdraw from the northern part of the disputed village of Ghajar, just north of the Blue Line and thus inside Lebanese territory.

As the country awaited the issuing of the first indictment by the STL, on 12 January 2011 the parties comprising the March 8 Alliance announced the withdrawal from the Cabinet of their 10 ministers, after Prime Minister Hariri refused to accede to Hezbollah demands that the Government end its co-operation with the STL; one of President Suleiman's five appointed ministers also resigned. The resignations of more than one-third of cabinet ministers (including the Minister of Foreign Affairs and Emigrants, Ali Shamy) thus prompted the collapse of the national unity Government after only 14 months in office. The previous day the Saudi and Syrian Governments were reported to have failed in their efforts to secure a compromise agreement for Lebanon. Some sources alleged that the USA had intervened to prevent a political deal being reached which allowed Hezbollah to avoid censure by the STL. Having instructed ministers to remain in office pending the approval of a new cabinet, on 25 January Suleiman invited Najib Miqati—who was briefly Prime Minister in 2005—to begin negotiations to form a new administration. The Prime Minister-designate had received support from the March 8 Alliance, but was widely viewed as a moderate politician, who claimed to be independent and who was acceptable to both the Saudi and Syrian leaderships. However, supporters of Hariri held large-scale protests in Beirut, Tripoli (Miqati's mainly Sunni home town), Sidon and other cities, amid widespread anger about Hezbollah's role in the collapse of the Government and Miqati's subsequent appointment. Meanwhile, on 17 January 2011 the STL prosecutor, Daniel Bellemare, submitted the first sealed indictment for Rafiq Hariri's assassination to pre-trial judge Daniel Fransen; the latter was required to confirm the indictment before any arrest warrants could be issued. In mid-February Saad Hariri announced formally that his March 14 Alliance would decline to join a cabinet led by Miqati.

Sectarian divisions heightened by conflict in Syria and other regional unrest

A growing movement of mainly young Lebanese, who sought to change the country's political system to reduce the level of sectarianism that had been witnessed during 2010, began to hold large-scale rallies from late February 2011. On 20 March a demonstration was attended by thousands of protesters in Beirut, who demanded the abolition of Lebanon's 'sectarian regime' and the introduction of widespread political reforms, including the drafting of new electoral legislation. The President of the National Assembly, Nabih Berri, had angered some in the country's political establishment by urging members of his Amal movement to participate in the protests. A rally had also been held in mid-March by around 2,000 Shi'a protesters who were demonstrating their support for the Shi'a-led demonstrations which were taking place against Bahrain's Sunni Government; the protest in Beirut was believed to have been instigated by members of Hezbollah.

As negotiations concerning the formation of a new government continued in mid-May 2011, there were reports that the Syrian Government was exerting considerable pressure on Lebanese politicians to agree on a cabinet list without delay, particularly in light of the popular uprisings taking place in many countries of the Middle East and North Africa since January, which had already led to the overthrow of the Tunisian and Egyptian Presidents and had spread to Syria itself by April. Tensions between the March 8 Alliance parties and the Future Movement had increased in mid-April, following the broadcast on Syrian state television of a purported confession by members of a 'terrorist cell' which, it was claimed, had attempted to foment unrest in Syria; one of those interviewed stated that Future Movement parliamentarian Jamal al-Jarrah had financed and supplied arms to the group, a claim which al-Jarrah vehemently denied. On 26 May the Minister of the Interior and Municipalities, Ziad Baroud, resigned in connection with a dispute between the rival political factions over what Hezbollah and the FPM claimed was a secret telecommunications network being operated by members of the Internal Security Forces (ISF), with the backing of Saad Hariri's movement. Baroud declared that he was leaving his post in protest against 'the breakdown of the Lebanese state', after the head of the ISF, Gen. Ashraf Rifi, had failed to meet the minister's demand that his forces withdraw from the Ministry of Telecommunications building, where the state-controlled firm OGERO was supposed to be testing equipment prior to launching a third private mobile telephone network. Hezbollah and Aoun's party alleged that the network, to be financed by the Government of the People's Republic of China, was already in operation. On 30 May President Suleiman ordered legal proceedings to be brought against Gen. Rifi in relation to the recent events.

On 4 August 2011, a year after a bill was adopted permitting offshore exploration and drilling of potential oil and gas reserves (see Economic Affairs), legislation outlining Lebanon's maritime boundaries with Israel and Cyprus was endorsed by the National Assembly. In the previous month Lebanese officials had rejected a border map drawn up by the Israeli Government for UN inspection, claiming that it included some of Lebanon's sovereign territory. On 30 August UNIFIL's mandate was extended to 31 August 2012, following a vote in the UN Security Council. The peace-keeping mission was the target of bomb attacks in May, July and December 2011, with a number of French and Italian peace-keepers, as well as Lebanese civilians, being injured in the blasts. No group claimed responsibility for the attacks, although some members of Lebanon's opposition were swift to blame Syria, alleging that they had been perpetrated with Hezbollah's assistance. The Shi'a organization strongly denied such claims. Meanwhile, on 29 November 2011 Islamist militants with alleged links to al-Qa'ida launched a series of rocket attacks across Lebanon's border into northern Israel; however, no casualties were reported. On 30 August 2012 the UN Security Council voted to extend the mandate of UNIFIL to 31 August 2013.

After almost five months of complex discussions had finally resulted in a coalition agreement, on 13 June 2011 a new Cabinet was sworn in by President Suleiman. Miqati was confirmed as Prime Minister, while Marwan Charbel became Minister of the Interior and Municipalities, Fayiz Ghosn Minister of National Defence, and Adnan Mansour Minister of Foreign Affairs and Emigrants. Although Miqati's administration won a parliamentary vote of confidence on 7 July, deputies from the March 14 Alliance refused to participate in the vote, with Saad Hariri claiming that Miqati had formed a 'Hezbollah Government'. (Hezbollah and its allies held a combined total of 17 of the 30 cabinet portfolios, with Hezbollah itself receiving two, while those allied with Aoun's FPM held 10.)

On 17 June 2011 clashes occurred between rival pro- and anti-Syrian gunmen in Tripoli, leading to the deaths of at least six people. The city has a predominantly Sunni population, which was generally supportive of the popular uprising to force President Assad, an Alawite (a follower of a branch of Shi'a Islam), from power. The fighting started after a rally was held in support of the anti-Government protests in Syria. Further violence was reported in Tripoli in subsequent months, with several deaths being reported. In October 2011 the Lebanese security forces held the Syrian regime responsible for the abduction of a number of Syrian dissidents who had travelled to Beirut to flee the worsening conflict in Syria, even alleging the direct involvement of the Syrian embassy. Some Syrian opposition activists were reported to have been arrested and handed over to the Syrian authorities as soon as they arrived in Lebanon, prompting politicians from the March 14 Alliance to accuse the Miqati Government of acting on behalf of the Assad regime.

After the formation of the new Cabinet in June 2011, Miqati had promised to support the work of the STL, as long as it did not place Lebanon's stability under threat. The opposition, however, insisted that the Government must pledge its full commitment to the UN tribunal. On 28 June pre-trial judge Fransen confirmed the STL indictment that had been submitted in January (and subsequently amended). On 30 June the STL formally issued the arrest warrants relating to Rafiq Hariri's murder in 2005 to the General Prosecutor, Said Mirza, in Beirut. The authorities were supposed to arrest the suspects within 30 days, after which time they would be summoned by the court. Saad Hariri called the formal issuing of the indictments a 'historic moment' for the country. Although the indictment was supposed to be confidential, it was leaked to the Lebanese media, which named the four suspects as all belonging to Hezbollah. On 29 July Fransen ordered that the requirement for confidentiality could be removed in order to facilitate the arrest of the men. Thus, on 17 August the STL published details of the indictment, and the four suspects were summoned to appear before the STL. It was alleged that Hezbollah's head of operations, Mustafa Amine Badreddine (the brother-in-law of Imad Mughniyeh), had been the most senior militant responsible for carrying out Hariri's assassination. Another leading member of Hezbollah, Salim Jamil Ayyash, and two lower-ranking operatives, Assad Hassan Sabra and Hussein Hassan Oneissi, were also formally named. Following the death of STL President Cassese in October, David Baragwanath—a judge from New Zealand—was appointed to lead the tribunal. On 30 November Miqati unexpectedly announced that he had transferred the share of the STL finances required to be paid by the Lebanese Government, thereby avoiding the certain need for a new administration to be formed, should the authorities have failed to honour their international commitments. It was not known, however, which government ministers had supported the Prime Minister's action, since the finance had come from a funding source within Miqati's office that did not require cabinet authorization. In mid-December it was revealed that the entire STL payment would in fact be made by private Lebanese banks, a decision that had presumably allowed Hezbollah to support the move. In early February 2012, by which time the four suspects had neither been handed over by the Hezbollah leadership nor arrested by Lebanese security forces, the STL declared that the men would be tried *in absentia*; no date for the start of trial proceedings was given.

Meanwhile, in late October 2011, in a further report on the implementation of UN Security Council Resolution 1559, UN Secretary-General Ban Ki-Moon urged the Syrian Government to order an immediate halt to military incursions being carried out in parts of northern Lebanon close to the Syrian border (as a result of which at least three Syrians had been killed) and in disputed territory. The Secretary-General warned that a continuation of such actions risked escalating the conflict, and emphasized the need for both sides to reach agreement on the delineation of their border. On 2 November the Syrian leadership had agreed to consider a plan submitted by the Arab League for a political resolution of the conflict. Meeting on 12 November, Arab League ministers responsible for foreign affairs threatened to expel Syria from the organization and impose punitive sanctions if it did not comply with the terms of the peace initiative by 19 November. However, Lebanon joined Yemen in voting against the decision, prompting Saad Hariri to call the situation 'shameful'. As the crisis unfolded, Hezbollah was forced to deny that it was providing military support to the Assad regime, its traditional ally. Following an upsurge in the fighting, amid an intensification of government efforts to eradicate the opposition threat, particularly in the city of Homs, by early March 2012 it was estimated that more than 7,000 Syrians had been displaced to Lebanon since April 2011. Moreover, human rights groups estimated that the death toll in Syria had increased to 7,000 by February 2012. In February 2012 Lebanon joined 14 other member states in abstaining from a UN General Assembly motion on a resolution condemning the actions of the Syrian leadership and demanding that President Assad step down.

In May 2012 fighting again broke out between members of the Sunni and Alawite communities in Tripoli over their opposing positions on the conflict in Syria. On 20 May a leading Sunni cleric, Sheikh Ahmad Abd al-Wahid, was shot dead by Lebanese armed forces at a military checkpoint close to the northern city, along with another religious official with whom he was travelling. It was alleged that their car had failed to stop at the checkpoint, although both men were known to be opponents of the Syrian regime. Sunni demonstrators reacted to the deaths by staging a series of protests, which further aggravated the sectarian tensions across Lebanon. On 22 May some 11 Lebanese Shi'a pilgrims were abducted by Syrian militants in the city of Aleppo while travelling home from Iran. The kidnappings again provoked a vociferous response within Lebanon, with a number of Syrian workers being targeted in retaliatory attacks. The Syrian opposition's Free Syrian Army denied reports in both the Lebanese and Syrian state media that it had carried out the abductions. Meanwhile, Hezbollah denied that the group of pilgrims were members of the organization, although it appeared that the abductors had acted partly in protest against Hezbollah's alleged military support for the Assad regime; they also demanded the release of detainees from Syrian prisons. Mediation by the Turkish Government had reportedly resulted in the release of two of the hostages by early January 2013. During June 2012 there was a serious escalation of the clashes taking place between rival pro- and anti-Syrian gunmen in Tripoli, with many warning that the country risked returning once again to the levels of violence seen during the 1975–90 civil war. At least 12 people were reportedly killed in the latest clashes between the two groups, which had been provoked by a speech made by President Assad on 3 June 2012 in which he had denied that his armed forces had been responsible for the murders of more than 100 civilians in the Syrian town of Houla on 25 May.

Amid continuing disagreements at cabinet level as far as the funding of the STL was concerned, Fransen announced on 19 July 2012 that he had scheduled 25 March 2013 as a possible date for the start of trial proceedings at the UN tribunal in the Netherlands. On 21 February 2013 it was announced that the STL proceedings would now be postponed from 25 March 2013, with no new date having been agreed by the start of April.

In August 2012, amid a spate of retaliatory sectarian kidnappings, a number of Gulf states (Bahrain, Kuwait, Qatar, Saudi Arabia and the United Arab Emirates—UAE) recommended that their citizens leave Lebanon in order to avoid the risk of abduction. Renewed fighting in Tripoli between Sunni and Alawite gunmen from 20 August resulted in at least 11 further deaths in subsequent days. The Prime Minister urged all of Lebanon's rival factions to exercise restraint for the sake of national unity, and secured a tentative cease-fire on 22 August.

On 19 October 2012 Brig.-Gen. Wissam al-Hassan, the anti-Syrian head of intelligence at the ISF, was killed, together with seven others, in a car bomb attack in east Beirut. Large numbers of protesters subsequently took to the streets of the Lebanese capital to blame the Syrian regime for the assassination, and, when the demonstrations turned violent, the Lebanese authorities were forced to deploy armed forces and use tear gas to bring the situation under control. Meanwhile, Hariri's Future Movement publicly criticized the Miqati Government for its failure to prevent al-Hassan's assassination and for its decision not to refer the case to the STL; there were widespread demands by the opposition for the Prime Minister to resign. However, although Miqati had reportedly offered to resign in the wake of the assassination, President Suleiman had asked him to retain his post 'in the national interest'.

The upsurge in sectarian violence between more radical elements of the Sunni and Alawite communities of Tripoli and Beirut from mid-2012 continued into early 2013, with a number of additional fatalities being reported. Meanwhile, from mid-2012 clashes took place between Syrian armed forces and rebel fighters who had crossed the border and reportedly established bases in Lebanon from which they were attempting to oust President Assad's regime. Further civilian deaths were also reported as rocket fire from Syrian forces landed in Lebanese territory. In mid-March 2013 Syrian military aircraft fired four rockets over the border into northern Lebanon, near the town of Arsal in the Beqa'a valley, as Lebanon appeared to be increasingly drawn into the Syrian conflict. The air-strike followed warnings by the Assad leadership that it would target anti-Government fighters (whom it described as 'armed terrorist gangs') who had sought refuge across the border; Arsal was also home to many civilian refugees from the Syrian conflict. Both the US and French Governments condemned the rocket attack as representing a violation of Lebanese sovereignty and a dangerous escalation of the conflict—which was believed by the UN to have claimed more than 70,000 lives by mid-February 2013. At the same time, the numbers of Syrian refugees entering Lebanon increased at a rapid rate, further aggravating the country's widening sectarian divisions. A report issued by the UN High Commissioner for

Refugees (UNHCR) at the end of March estimated that there were now 402,000 Syrian refugees living in Lebanon: of these, 262,000 had registered with UNHCR, while 140,000 were awaiting registration. More than 30% of the refugees were reported to have sought refuge among the Lebanese population rather than in designated refugee camps. A further Syrian rocket attack was reported close to Arsal in early April.

Recent developments: The Miqati Government resigns in advance of the 2013 legislative elections

In mid-March 2013 three Sunni clerics were injured as the result of attacks by Shi'a militants in two predominantly Shi'a districts of Beirut. The attacks provoked angry demonstrations in the capital, leading the Commander-in-Chief of the Army, Brig.-Gen. Jean Kahwaji, to warn that Lebanon was in the midst of its most dangerous period since the events following Rafiq Hariri's assassination in 2005. Prime Minister Miqati issued a plea for calm to be restored, while both Hezbollah and Amal publicly condemned the incidents.

Miqati submitted his resignation and that of his entire Government on 22 March 2013, amid considerable differences within the Cabinet over the way in which the legislative elections scheduled for June should be organized. The Prime Minister's decision also came as the result of opposition by the ministers representing the March 8 Alliance (particularly those from Hezbollah) to the reappointment as head of the ISF of the anti-Syrian Gen. Rifi, whose term was due to expire on 1 April. The March 8 Alliance parties had rejected the appointment of members to the commission which was to be established to monitor the forthcoming polls, amid their continuing opposition to Lebanon's current electoral law. The March 14 Alliance was also predominantly in favour of agreeing a new electoral law prior to the convening of the elections, while Miqati and the PSP leader, Walid Joumblatt, supported the retention of the existing legislation. Miqati, who—along with his ministers—was to remain in office pending the approval of a new administration, urged the leaders of all Lebanese political parties to work together in forming a national unity government to prevent the already precarious situation in the country from deteriorating further. On 6 April a former Minister of Culture, Tammam Salam, was asked by President Suleiman to begin discussions on the formation of a new cabinet, after his nomination had received almost unanimous support from the National Assembly.

CONSTITUTION AND GOVERNMENT

The Constitution was promulgated on 23 May 1926 and amended by the Constitutional Laws of 1927, 1929, 1943, 1947 and 1990. Legislative power is held by the National Assembly, with 128 members elected by universal adult suffrage for four years (subject to dissolution), on the basis of proportional representation. Seats are allocated on a religious or 'confessional' basis (divided equally between Christians and Muslims); according to convention, the President of the Assembly is usually a Shi'a Muslim. The President of the Republic (who must be a Maronite Christian) is elected for six years by the National Assembly. The President, in consultation with deputies and the President of the National Assembly, appoints the Prime Minister (a Sunni Muslim) and other ministers to form the Cabinet, in which executive power is vested. The Ta'if agreement of October 1989 (see Contemporary Political History) stated that cabinet portfolios must be distributed equally between Christian and Muslim ministers.

REGIONAL AND INTERNATIONAL CO-OPERATION

Lebanon is a member of the League of Arab States (the Arab League, see p. 372). A Euro-Mediterranean Association Agreement was signed with the European Union (EU, see p. 281) in 2002. Lebanon joined the UN on 10 October 1966. The country also participates in the Organization of Islamic Cooperation (OIC, see p. 413). Lebanon has observer status at the World Trade Organization (WTO, see p. 444), membership of which organization was applied for in 1999.

ECONOMIC AFFAIRS

In 2011, according to estimates by the World Bank, Lebanon's gross national income (GNI), measured at average 2009–11 prices, was US $38,792m., equivalent to $9,110 per head (or $14,000 per head on an international purchasing-power parity basis). During 2002–11, it was estimated, the population increased at an average annual rate of 1.1%, while gross domestic product (GDP) per head grew, in real terms, by an average of 4.1% per year. Overall GDP increased, in real terms, at an average annual rate of 5.2% in 2002–11; GDP growth of 3.0% was recorded in 2011.

Agriculture (including hunting, forestry and fishing) contributed an estimated 6.2% of GDP in 2011, according to the World Bank. Some 5.1% of the employed labour force were engaged in the sector in 2007. According to FAO estimates, the sector employed 1.5% of the labour force in mid-2013. The principal crops are potatoes, tomatoes, cucumbers, citrus fruits and grapes. Viticulture is also significant. The cultivation of hashish is a notable, albeit illegal, activity in the Beqa'a valley, despite official efforts to eradicate crops and switch land to other production. According to World Bank estimates, the GDP of the agricultural sector increased at an average annual rate of 1.2% in 2002–11; agricultural GDP grew by 4.0% in 2011.

The industrial sector (including manufacturing, construction and power) contributed an estimated 21.4% of GDP in 2011, according to the World Bank. Some 25.9% of the labour force were employed in industry in 1997. Lebanon's only mineral resources consist of small reserves of lignite and iron ore, and their contribution to GDP is insignificant. According to World Bank estimates, the GDP of the industrial sector increased by an average of 4.4% per year in 2002–11; industrial GDP expanded by 4.0% in 2011.

Manufacturing (including mining and quarrying) contributed an estimated 8.2% of GDP in 2011, according to the World Bank. The sector employed about 10% of the labour force in 1985. The most important branches have traditionally been food-processing, petroleum-refining, textiles, and furniture and woodworking. According to World Bank estimates, manufacturing GDP increased at an average annual rate of 0.9% in 2002–11; the GDP of the sector grew by 4.0% in 2011.

Construction contributed an estimated 15.2% of GDP in 2010. The sector employed about 5.5% of the labour force in 1985. According to the UN, the GDP of the construction sector increased at an average annual rate of 8.2% in 2002–11; real GDP grew by 18.5% in 2010, but declined by 5.3% in 2011.

Energy is derived principally from thermal power stations, mainly using imported petroleum (which accounted for 94.1% of total electricity production in 2009). Generating capacity is inadequate to meet Lebanon's peak requirements, and interruptions to supply are frequent. Since 2009 Lebanon has been supplied with electricity from the regional power grid, and has imported natural gas from Egypt. In January 2010 Turkey also agreed to supply electricity and natural gas via Syria. In September 2011 parliament ratified a new government strategy for the power sector, which aimed to improve infrastructure and to encourage the use of liquefied petroleum gas and renewable energy sources over a four-year period. Meanwhile, in August 2010 legislation was approved permitting the exploration and drilling of potential oil and gas reserves off Lebanon's Mediterranean coast. The new law increased tensions with Israel since no formal maritime border exists between the two states (see Contemporary Political History). In November 2012 a Petroleum Administration Board was established to oversee future licensing rounds for the exploration of these reserves. Imports of mineral products accounted for 28.4% of the value of total imports in 2012.

According to the World Bank, the services sector contributed an estimated 72.4% of GDP in 2011. In 1997 some 65.1% of the working population were employed in the sector. Financial services, particularly banking, withstood many of the disruptions inflicted on the economy by the civil conflict during 1975–90 (although trading on the Beirut Stock Exchange was suspended in 1983–96). The revival of tourism, which was of considerable importance prior to the civil conflict, remains vulnerable to the political and security situation. Nevertheless, the sector contributed around 22% of GDP in 2011. Although tourism experienced strong growth in 2008–10, arrivals of foreign tourists decreased from 2.2m. in 2010 to 1.7m. in 2011. This decline was attributed both to domestic and regional instability. In February 2012 the Ministry of Tourism revealed a plan for the sector that aimed to increase the annual number of visitors to 4.0m. by 2015; however, the number of arrivals declined further, to 1.4m., in 2012. According to World Bank estimates, the GDP of the services sector increased at an average annual rate of 6.4% in 2002–11; the sector's GDP expanded by 9.1% in 2011.

In 2011 Lebanon recorded a merchandise trade deficit of US $13,918.9m. and there was a deficit of $4,163.3m. on the current account of the balance of payments. The principal market for exports in 2012 was Switzerland (which took 12.2% of

Lebanese exports); other significant purchasers included Saudi Arabia, the United Arab Emirates and Syria. In 2012 the principal supplier of imports was the USA (11.2%); Italy, the People's Republic of China, France and Germany were also important suppliers. The principal exports in 2012 were pearls and precious or semi-precious stones, machinery and electrical equipment, base metal and base metal products, food, beverages and tobacco, and chemical products. The principal imports in that year were mineral products, machinery and electrical equipment, chemical products, pearls and precious or semi-precious stones, base metals and base metal products, vehicles and transport equipment, and food, beverages and tobacco.

In 2011, according to official estimates, Lebanon recorded an overall budget deficit of £L3,530,000m. Lebanon's general government gross debt was £L80,887,000m. in 2011, equivalent to 137.4% of GDP. At the end of 2010 Lebanon's total external debt was US $24,293m., of which $20,213m. was public and publicly guaranteed debt. In that year, the cost of servicing long-term public and publicly guaranteed debt and repayments to the IMF was equivalent to 19.1% of the value of exports of goods, services and income (excluding workers' remittances). According to ILO, the annual rate of inflation averaged 3.4% in 2008–11. According to official figures, the annual rate of inflation reached 10.1% in 2012. Some 6.4% of the adult labour force were unemployed in 2009.

Lebanon's economy performed strongly following the Doha Agreement of May 2008, particularly enjoying strong growth in its vital tourism industry during 2008–10. In 2009 there was a record increase of 26% in capital inflow, from tourists, foreign direct investment and remittances from Lebanese abroad. After an initial disbursement by the IMF in 2007 under the Emergency Post-Conflict Assistance and a further US $37.6m. in November 2008, the organization in its 2009 report praised the Government's prudent macroeconomic policies that had led to the doubling of international reserves since 2007. While efforts to reduce the debt-to-GDP ratio had proceeded at a faster rate than envisaged under the Paris III programme, the ratio—137% of GDP at the end of 2011—remained one of the highest in the world. By 2012 progress on structural reforms also remained slow. Meanwhile, the increase in sectarian tensions, which led to the collapse of the Hariri Government in January 2011 (see Contemporary Political History), had a negative impact on Lebanon's hitherto impressive rates of economic growth. Amid considerable domestic and regional instability, GDP growth declined to an estimated 3.0% in 2011 from 7.0% in 2010. The five-month political stalemate prior to the formation of a new Government under Prime Minister Najib Miqati in June 2011, as well as regional unrest—particularly that in neighbouring Syria—led to a slowdown in the tourism, trade, real estate and banking sectors, with many foreign companies being deterred from investing in Lebanon. In May 2012 the IMF urged the Lebanese authorities to restore confidence in the economy and to guarantee fiscal discipline in order to reduce further the debt-to-GDP ratio. The Fund also emphasized the need to improve Lebanon's infrastructural framework to attract new investment and create jobs. The rate of youth unemployment— estimated by some economists to be as high as 19% in early 2012—remains a major concern. In January 2012 the National Assembly rejected the Government's draft budget for that year, amid disagreements over proposed tax increases; although a revised budget received cabinet approval in July, it was not ratified by parliament. The Ministry of Finance reported a 67% increase in the budget deficit recorded in 2012 compared with that of 2011. In early 2013, as worsening sectarian divisions hindered the implementation of vital political and economic reforms, and the rapid influx of Syrian refugees placed an additional strain on the economy, the IMF forecast GDP growth of 2.0% for 2012 and of 2.5% for 2013.

PUBLIC HOLIDAYS

2014: 1 January (New Year's Day), 6 January (Christmas Day— Armenian Orthodox Church only), 13 January* (Mouloud/Yum al-Nabi, birth of Muhammad), 9 February (Feast of St Maron), 20 March (Easter, Western and Greek Orthodox Churches), 25 March (Feast of the Annunciation), 1 May (Labour Day), 2 May (Martyrs' Day), 9 May (Ascension Day, Western and Greek Orthodox Churches), 26 May* (Leilat al-Meiraj, ascension of Muhammad), 28 July* (Id al-Fitr, end of Ramadan), 15 August (Assumption), 4 October* (Id al-Adha, Feast of the Sacrifice), 24 October* (Muharram, Islamic New Year), 1 November (All Saints' Day), 2 November* (Ashoura), 22 November (Independence Day), 25 December (Christmas Day).

* These holidays are determined by the Islamic lunar calendar and may vary by one or two days from the dates given.

Statistical Survey

Sources (unless otherwise stated): Central Administration for Statistics, Beirut; tel. (1) 373169; internet www.cas.gov.lb; Direction Générale des Douanes, Beirut.

Area and Population

AREA, POPULATION AND DENSITY

Area (sq km)	10,452*
Population (official estimate)	
15 November 1970†	
Males	1,080,015
Females	1,046,310
Total	2,126,325
Population (UN estimates at mid-year)‡	
2011	4,259,403
2012	4,291,717
2013	4,324,062
Density (per sq km) at mid-2013	413.7

* 4,036 sq miles.

† Figures are based on the results of a sample survey, excluding Palestinian refugees in camps. According to UNRWA, the total number of registered Palestinian refugees in Lebanon was around 436,000 at January 2012, although the actual resident number in refugee camps was estimated to be 230,000–240,000.

‡ Source: UN, *World Population Prospects: The 2010 Revision*.

2007 (official estimate): Total resident population 3,759,134 (males 1,857,659, females 1,901,475).

POPULATION BY AGE AND SEX
(UN estimates at mid-2013)

	Males	Females	Total
0–14	507,640	487,997	995,637
15–64	1,458,050	1,549,014	3,007,064
65 and over	144,883	176,478	321,361
Total	**2,110,573**	**2,213,489**	**4,324,062**

Source: UN, *World Population Prospects: The 2010 Revision*.

PRINCIPAL TOWNS
(population in 2003)*

Beirut (capital) . .	1,171,000	Jounieh	79,800
Tarabulus (Tripoli) .	212,900	Zahle	76,600
Saida (Sidon) . .	149,000	Baabda	58,500
Sur (Tyre) . . .	117,100	Ba'albak (Ba'albek) .	29,800
Al-Nabatiyah al-Tahta (Nabatiyah)	89,400	Alayh	26,700

* Figures are rounded.

Source: Stefan Helders, *World Gazetteer* (internet www.world-gazetteer.com).

Mid-2011 (incl. suburbs, UN estimate): Beirut 2,022,350 (Source: UN, *World Urbanization Prospects: The 2011 Revision*).

BIRTHS, MARRIAGES AND DEATHS
(annual averages, UN estimates)

	1995–2000	2000–05	2005–10
Birth rate (per 1,000)	22.6	17.7	15.9
Death rate (per 1,000)	7.1	6.9	6.9

Source: UN, *World Population Prospects: The 2010 Revision*.

Live births (numbers registered, official estimates): 90,388 in 2009; 95,218 in 2010; 98,569 in 2011.

Marriages (numbers registered, official estimates): 40,565 in 2009; 41,758 in 2010; 42,500 in 2011.

Deaths (numbers registered, official estimates): 22,260 in 2009; 25,500 in 2010; 26,070 in 2011.

Life expectancy (years at birth): 72.6 (males 70.5; females 74.8) in 2011 (Source: World Bank, World Development Indicators database).

EMPLOYMENT
(ISIC major divisions)

	1975	1985*
Agriculture, hunting, forestry and fishing . .	147,724	103,400
Manufacturing	139,471	45,000
Electricity, gas and water	6,381	10,000
Construction	47,356	25,000
Trade, restaurants and hotels	129,716	78,000
Transport, storage and communications . .	45,529	20,500
Other services	227,921	171,000
Total	**744,098**	**452,900**

* Estimates.

1997 (provisional estimates at mid-year): Total employed 1,246,000; Unemployed 116,000; Total labour force 1,362,000.

2007 (household survey, persons aged 15 years and over): Total employed 1,033,572 (Agriculture and fishing 52,528, Unskilled 126,684, Skilled 188,168, Intermediate professions 108,051, Specialists 115,420, Office employees 84,269, Service sector workers and salespersons 131,950, General and corporate managers 132,761, Drivers 93,741). Note: Figures exclude members of the armed forces (84,224) and non-respondents (585).

Source: partly National Employment Office.

Mid-2013 ('000, estimates): Agriculture, etc. 24; Total labour force 1,611 (Source: FAO).

Health and Welfare

KEY INDICATORS

Total fertility rate (children per woman, 2010)	1.8
Under-5 mortality rate (per 1,000 live births, 2010) . . .	22
HIV/AIDS (% of persons aged 15–49, 2009)	0.1
Physicians (per 1,000 head, 2009)	3.5
Hospital beds (per 1,000 head, 2009)	3.5
Health expenditure (2009): US $ per head (PPP) . . .	965
Health expenditure (2009): % of GDP	7.4
Health expenditure (2009): public (% of total) . . .	41.9
Access to sanitation (% of persons, 2006)	97
Total carbon dioxide emissions ('000 metric tons, 2008) . .	17,099.2
Carbon dioxide emissions per head (metric tons, 2008) . .	4.1
Human Development Index (2011): ranking	71
Human Development Index (2011): value	0.739

For sources and definitions, see explanatory note on p. vi.

Agriculture

PRINCIPAL CROPS
('000 metric tons)

	2009	2010*	2011*
Wheat	111	83†	90
Barley	30	24	24
Potatoes	425	260	275
Almonds, with shell*	34	28	40
Olives	87	90	91
Cabbages and other brassicas . .	49	50	46
Lettuce and chicory*	37	50	55
Tomatoes	195	310	315
Cauliflowers and broccoli . . .	13	17	20
Pumpkins, squash and gourds* . .	31	26	25
Cucumbers and gherkins . . .	87	163	170
Aubergines (Eggplants) . . .	22	45	43
Onions, dry	87	90	91
Garlic	3	3	4
Beans, green	16	27	25
Carrots and turnips	6	4	4
Watermelons	53	74	70
Cantaloupes and other melons . .	14	21	22
Bananas	96	115	120
Oranges	177	130	110
Tangerines, mandarins, clementines and satsumas . .	31	28	23
Lemons and limes	121	85	80
Grapefruit and pomelos . . .	17	8	7
Apples	138	140	150
Pears	36	22	20
Apricots	29	24	22
Sweet cherries	31	25	21
Peaches and nectarines . . .	31	34	36
Plums and sloes*	24	23	23
Strawberries	3	2	2
Grapes	108	90	89
Figs*	6	9	9

* FAO estimates.
† Unofficial figure.

Aggregate production ('000 metric tons, may include official, semi-official or estimated data): Total cereals 147 in 2009, 113 in 2010, 121 in 2011; Total roots and tubers 426 in 2009, 261 in 2010, 276 in 2011; Total vegetables (incl. melons) 656 in 2009, 942 in 2010, 957 in 2011; Total fruits (excl. melons) 902 in 2009, 793 in 2010, 777 in 2011.

Source: FAO.

LIVESTOCK
('000 head, year ending September)

	2009	2010	2011*
Horses	4†	4†	4
Asses*	15	15	15
Mules*	5	5	5
Cattle	75	69	65
Pigs	8*	8	8
Sheep	372	265	255
Goats	430	404	400
Chickens*	37,500	37,000	38,000

* FAO estimate(s).
† Unofficial figure.

Source: FAO.

LIVESTOCK PRODUCTS
('000 metric tons)

	2009	2010	2011
Cattle meat*	67.7	69.3	68.6
Sheep meat*	13.4	9.5	10.5
Goat meat*	3.0	2.7	2.6
Pig meat*	0.8	0.8	0.8
Chicken meat*	129.9	129.2	131.0
Cows' milk	168.2	165.0*	165.0*
Sheep's milk	14.8	13.0*	13.0*
Goats' milk	21.7	32.0*	32.0*
Hen eggs	47.0†	47.0*	47.0*
Wool, greasy*	2.1	2.2	2.2

* FAO estimate(s).
† Unofficial figure.

Source: FAO.

Forestry

ROUNDWOOD REMOVALS
('000 cubic metres, excluding bark, FAO estimates)

	2009	2010	2011
Sawlogs, veneer logs and logs for sleepers*	7.2	7.2	7.2
Fuel wood	18.9	18.8	18.8
Total	26.1	26.0	26.0

* Assumed to be unchanged since 1992.

Source: FAO.

SAWNWOOD PRODUCTION
('000 cubic metres, including railway sleepers)

	1991	1992	1993
Total (all broadleaved)	10.9	9.1	9.1*

* FAO estimate.

1994–2011: Figures assumed to be unchanged from 1993 (FAO estimates).

Source: FAO.

Fishing

(metric tons, live weight)

	2004	2005	2006
Capture	3,866	3,798	3,811
Groupers and seabasses	245	250	252
Porgies and seabreams	365	370	371
Surmullets (Red mullets)	200	190	190
Barracudas	250	240	240
Mullets	360	365	360
Scorpionfishes	125	110	115
Carangids	400	380	383
Clupeoids	600	580	580
Tuna-like fishes	400	385	389
Mackerel-like fishes	300	320	322
Marine crustaceans	60	55	57
Aquaculture	790	803	803
Rainbow trout	700	708	708
Total catch	4,656	4,601	4,614

2007–10: Catch assumed to be unchanged from 2006 (FAO estimates).

Source: FAO.

Mining

('000 metric tons, estimates)

	2008	2009	2010
Gypsum	85	100	105
Salt (unrefined)	20	20	20
Phosphoric acid	51	51	51

Source: US Geological Survey.

Industry

SELECTED PRODUCTS
('000 metric tons unless otherwise indicated)

	2007	2008	2009
Flour and derivatives thereof	379	n.a.	n.a.
Cigarettes (metric tons)	431.9	433.1	647.5
Cement	3,945	4,219	4,897
Bottled water and soda (million litres)	497	532	n.a.
Wine*	11	15	13
Electric energy (million kWh)	9,072	11,188	11,909

* FAO estimates (Source: FAO).

2010: Cement 5,226,621 metric tons; Electric energy 12,459m. kWh; Wine 14,200 metric tons (FAO estimate).

2011: Cement 5,549,769 metric tons; Electric energy 12,469m. kWh; Wine 14,200 metric tons (FAO estimate).

Finance

CURRENCY AND EXCHANGE RATES

Monetary Units:
100 piastres = 1 Lebanese pound (£L).

Sterling, Dollar and Euro Equivalents (31 December 2012):
£1 sterling = £L2,378.8;
US $1 = £L1,507.5;
€1 = £L1,989.0;
£L10,000 = £4.20 sterling = $6.63 = €5.03.

Exchange Rate: The official exchange rate has been maintained at US $1 = £L1,507.5 since September 1999.

BUDGET
(£L '000 million):

Revenue	2009	2010	2011
Tax revenue	8,967	9,976	9,885
Taxes on income, profits and capital gains	1,839	2,050	2,423
Taxes on property	809	1,088	1,144
Domestic taxes on goods and services	3,260	3,583	3,685
Taxes on international trade	2,664	2,802	2,179
Other taxes	396	453	454
Non-tax revenue	3,069	2,043	3,468
Income from public enterprises	2,456	1,382	2,679
Administrative fees and charges	505	535	570
Fines and confiscations	7	8	10
Other	100	118	208
Treasury revenue	669	666	718
Total	12,705	12,684	14,070

Expenditure	2009	2010	2011
Personnel costs	4,936	5,066	5,533
Salaries and wages	3,325	3,354	3,818
Interest payments and financial charges	5,784	5,893	5,655
Foreign debt principal repayment .	303	324	379
Materials and supplies . . .	238	277	329
External services	114	103	135
Various transfers	717	2,503	3,278
Acquisitions of land, buildings, for the construction of roads, ports, airports and water networks .	4	1	1
Equipment	35	40	52
Construction in progress . . .	356	467	402
Maintenance	103	129	186
Other expenditures (including current capital and treasury expenditures)	4,524	2,239	1,650
Unclassified expenditure . . .	3	4	1
Customs cashiers	50	—	—
Total	**17,167**	**17,047**	**17,600**

Source: Ministry of Finance, Beirut.

INTERNATIONAL RESERVES
(US $ million at 31 December)

	2009	2010	2011
Gold (national valuation) . . .	10,062.0	13,010.0	14,400.7
IMF special drawing rights . .	328.9	321.8	295.7
Reserve position in IMF . . .	29.5	29.0	53.2
Foreign exchange	28,744.5	31,163.3	33,391.6
Total	**39,164.9**	**44,524.1**	**48,141.2**

Source: IMF, *International Financial Statistics*.

MONEY SUPPLY
(£L '000 million at 31 December)

	2009	2010	2011
Currency outside banks . . .	2,383.0	2,712.9	2,891.0
Demand deposits at commercial banks	2,410.3	2,950.8	3,200.6
Total money (incl. others) . .	**4,839.7**	**5,728.3**	**6,138.4**

Source: IMF, *International Financial Statistics*.

COST OF LIVING
(Consumer Price Index for Beirut; December of each year; base: December 2007 = 100)

	2010	2011	2012
Food and non-alcoholic beverages .	125.1	132.4	138.0
Alcoholic beverages and tobacco .	108.6	121.0	131.1
Clothing and footwear	113.4	118.2	123.3
Water, electricity and gas . . .	106.4	112.7	120.1
Housing	111.2	111.2	160.2
Health	103.9	107.2	106.9
Transport	124.6	121.3	124.1
All items (incl. others) . . .	**114.1**	**117.6**	**129.5**

NATIONAL ACCOUNTS
(£L '000 million)
Expenditure on the Gross Domestic Product

	2008	2009	2010
Government final consumption expenditure	6,686	7,399	7,999
Private final consumption expenditure	38,018	41,215	44,672
Gross fixed capital formation . }	13,810	18,114	18,986
Changes in stocks . . . . }			
Total domestic expenditure .	**58,514**	**66,728**	**71,657**
Exports of goods and services .	11,077	10,772	12,410
Less Imports of goods and services	24,244	25,265	28,102
GDP in purchasers' values .	**45,346**	**52,235**	**55,965**

Gross Domestic Product by Economic Activity

	2007	2008	2009*
Agriculture, hunting, forestry and fishing	2,279	2,646	2,574
Manufacturing (including mining and quarrying)	3,325	3,545	3,947
Electricity, gas and water . .	−608	−1,341	−756
Construction	4,286	6,090	7,012
Wholesale and retail trade; repair of motor vehicles, motorcycles and personal and household goods	8,532	11,778	14,531
Hotels and restaurants . . .	1,223	1,602	1,993
Transport, storage and communications	3,089	3,376	4,026
Financial intermediation . . .	3,439	4,166	4,322
Real estate, renting and business activities	4,269	4,733	5,084
Government services . . .	3,662	4,270	4,766
Education	3,509	3,837	4,105
Health	2,376	2,614	2,983
Other services	971	1,112	1,123
Sub-total	**40,352**	**48,428**	**55,710**
Less Financial intermediation services indirectly measured .	2,579	3,084	3,061
GDP in purchasers' values .	**37,774**	**45,346**	**52,650**

* Preliminary.

Note: Indirect taxes assumed to be distributed at origin.

2009 (revised figures): Agriculture, hunting, forestry and fishing 2,660; Manufacturing (including mining and quarrying) 3,982; Electricity, gas and water −867; Construction 7,018; Services 39,442 (Transport, storage and communications 3,426, Wholesale and retail trade and repair of motor vehicles, motorcycles and personal and household goods 14,658, Other market services 16,578, Government services 4,780); *GDP in purchasers' values* 52,235.

2010: Agriculture, hunting, forestry and fishing 2,650; Manufacturing (including mining and quarrying) 4,002; Electricity, gas and water −1,473; Construction 8,515; Services 42,271 (Transport, storage and communications 3,084, Wholesale and retail trade and repair of motor vehicles, motorcycles and personal and household goods 15,395, Other market services 18,721, Government services 5,071); *GDP in purchasers' values* 55,965.

Source: Presidency of the Council of Ministers, *Economic Accounts of Lebanon*.

BALANCE OF PAYMENTS
(US $ million)

	2009	2010	2011
Exports of goods	4,187.1	4,688.7	5,385.5
Imports of goods	−15,394.3	−17,187.8	−19,304.4
Balance on goods	**−11,207.2**	**−12,499.0**	**−13,918.9**
Exports of services	16,909.9	16,113.9	19,758.5
Imports of services	−14,042.7	−13,324.3	−12,989.4
Balance on goods and services	**−8,340.0**	**−9,709.5**	**−7,149.7**
Primary income received . .	2,040.2	1,448.1	1,615.9
Primary income paid . . .	−2,268.3	−1,957.0	−1,200.6
Balance on goods, services and primary income	**−8,568.1**	**−10,218.4**	**−6,734.4**
Secondary income received . .	6,642.0	8,393.5	8,360.8
Secondary income paid . . .	−4,814.9	−5,637.2	−5,789.7
Current balance	**−6,740.9**	**−7,462.1**	**−4,163.3**
Capital account (net) . . .	18.0	267.9	165.0
Direct investment assets . .	−1,125.8	−486.7	−744.6
Direct investment liabilities .	4,803.6	4,279.9	3,476.0
Portfolio investment assets . .	−825.9	−1,016.2	−687.9
Portfolio investment liabilities .	2,690.5	−693.5	−1,141.4
Other investment assets . .	5,083.0	2,081.7	6,110.9
Other investment liabilities .	8,075.0	388.6	3,924.2
Net errors and omissions . .	−3,042.1	5,699.8	−4,644.8
Reserves and related items .	**8,935.4**	**3,059.4**	**2,294.2**

Source: IMF, *International Financial Statistics*.

External Trade

PRINCIPAL COMMODITIES
(£L '000 million)

Imports c.i.f.	2010	2011	2012
Live animals and animal products	1,306.0	1,307.6	1,243.0
Vegetable products	1,079.2	1,281.2	1,308.4
Prepared foodstuffs; beverages, spirits and vinegar; tobacco and manufactured substitutes . .	1,721.8	1,947.0	2,115.3
Mineral products	5,716.2	6,972.3	9,100.2
Products of chemical or allied industries	2,336.9	2,602.0	2,622.8
Plastics, rubber and articles thereof	966.2	1,062.1	1,148.7
Textiles and textile articles . .	1,059.8	1,060.0	1,133.5
Natural or cultured pearls, precious or semi-precious stones, precious metals and articles thereof; imitation jewellery; coin	1,747.8	3,229.2	2,390.4
Base metals and articles thereof .	1,916.8	2,297.0	2,304.9
Machinery and mechanical appliances; electrical equipment; sound and television apparatus .	3,271.3	3,212.1	3,126.1
Vehicles, aircraft, vessels and associated transport equipment .	2,920.1	2,231.2	2,282.1
Total (incl. others)	27,089.5	30,398.7	32,090.0

Exports f.o.b.	2010	2011	2012
Vegetable products	232.4	242.2	258.2
Prepared foodstuffs; beverages, spirits and vinegar; tobacco and manufactured substitutes . .	488.9	572.8	591.4
Mineral products	84.1	52.3	198.7
Products of chemical or allied industries	467.5	578.6	516.5
Plastics, rubber and articles thereof	179.2	202.5	220.7
Paper and paperboard and articles thereof	356.7	326.6	274.8
Textiles and textile articles . .	162.5	194.7	175.6
Natural or cultured pearls, precious or semi-precious stones, precious metals and articles thereof; imitation jewellery; coin	1,671.9	2,250.3	2,600.5
Base metals and articles thereof .	694.4	792.2	709.8
Machinery and mechanical appliances; electrical equipment; sound and television apparatus .	1,118.6	782.9	721.3
Total (incl. others)	6,413.3	6,432.3	6,760.6

Source: Ministry of Finance, Lebanese Customs Administration, Beirut.

PRINCIPAL TRADING PARTNERS
(£L '000 million)

Imports c.i.f.	2010	2011	2012
Belgium	371.5	377.2	421.3
Brazil	402.7	459.3	455.5
China, People's Republic . . .	2,470.0	2,449.1	2,672.6
Egypt	648.4	1,421.1	1,267.7
France	1,802.9	2,277.1	2,323.6
Germany	1,899.2	1,719.1	1,812.2
Italy	2,101.9	2,816.6	2,759.1
Japan	938.1	609.1	548.4
Korea, Republic	446.0	396.2	463.3
Kuwait	536.9	456.3	950.6
Netherlands	363.1	519.8	613.3
Romania	350.6	314.9	293.9
Russia	764.5	775.5	637.9
Saudi Arabia	613.2	801.7	638.8
Spain	462.9	510.2	642.4
Switzerland	843.0	1,499.1	765.7
Syria	511.8	467.7	401.4
Turkey	1,031.1	1,267.2	1,456.0
Ukraine	510.1	580.3	638.7
United Arab Emirates . . .	557.4	896.0	627.8
United Kingdom	794.3	786.0	782.0
USA	2,878.8	3,001.2	3,582.3
Total (incl. others)	27,089.5	30,398.7	32,090.0

Exports f.o.b.	2010	2011	2012
Belgium	153.5	196.7	168.2
Egypt	303.1	102.0	132.9
France	524.3	86.5	90.0
Germany	73.7	68.2	52.0
Greece	49.9	41.8	44.2
Iran	60.3	19.9	7.5
Italy	46.2	55.4	55.3
Jordan	156.3	191.7	214.5
Korea, Republic	37.3	40.3	85.5
Kuwait	108.6	115.7	102.7
Netherlands	55.2	39.9	28.9
Nigeria	72.5	74.2	65.2
Qatar	124.7	120.4	128.9
Saudi Arabia	370.9	464.3	541.3
Spain	95.2	73.8	66.3
Switzerland	757.7	776.2	825.4
Syria	332.9	324.0	443.8
Turkey	347.7	416.2	237.0
United Arab Emirates . . .	631.0	486.0	530.9
United Kingdom	73.4	92.2	67.3
USA	92.7	96.9	97.4
Total (incl. others)	6,413.3	6,432.3	6,760.6

Source: Ministry of Finance, Lebanese Customs Administration, Beirut.

Transport

ROAD TRAFFIC
(motor vehicles in use)

	1995	1996*	1997*
Passenger cars (incl. taxis) . .	1,197,521	1,217,000	1,299,398
Buses and coaches	5,514	5,640	6,833
Lorries and vans	79,222	81,000	85,242
Motorcycles and mopeds . .	53,317	54,450	61,471

* Estimates.

Source: IRF, *World Road Statistics*.

Passenger cars ('000, incl. taxis): 1,370.6 in 1999; 1,370.8 in 2000; 1,370.9 in 2001 (Source: UN, *Statistical Yearbook*).

SHIPPING

Flag Registered Fleet
(at 31 December)

	2010	2011	2012
Number of vessels	53	53	52
Total displacement ('000 grt) . .	136.4	146.4	151.8

Source: Lloyd's List Intelligence (www.lloydslistintelligence.com).

International Sea-borne Freight Traffic
('000 metric tons)

	2007	2008	2009
Goods loaded	891	841	669
Goods unloaded	4,426	4,906	5,641

CIVIL AVIATION
(traffic on scheduled services)

	2007	2008	2009
Kilometres flown (million) . .	27	29	30
Passengers carried ('000) . . .	1,074	1,330	1,308
Passenger-km (million) . . .	2,225	2,727	2,711
Total ton-km (million)	294	330	313

Source: UN, *Statistical Yearbook*.

2010: Passengers carried ('000) 1,600 (Source: World Bank, World Development Indicators database).

Tourism

FOREIGN TOURIST ARRIVALS
('000)*

Country of nationality	2008	2009	2010
Australia	40.9	62.1	58.2
Canada	66.8	87.1	88.0
Egypt	41.7	57.4	67.8
France	91.1	120.4	139.5
Germany	53.9	69.8	76.9
Iran	92.5	145.7	241.5
Iraq	72.8	101.6	129.8
Jordan	180.9	223.8	274.6
Kuwait	68.9	102.5	95.8
Philippines	28.0	39.4	41.2
Saudi Arabia	101.7	173.3	191.1
United Kingdom	38.1	50.0	60.2
USA	83.8	111.9	123.3
Total (incl. others)	1,332.5	1,844.1	2,168.0

* Figures exclude arrivals of Syrian nationals, Palestinians and students.

Total tourist arrivals ('000): 1,655 in 2011 (provisional).

Tourism receipts (US $ million, incl. passenger transport, unless otherwise indicated): 6,317 in 2008; 7,157 in 2009; 8,012 in 2010 (excl. passenger transport).

Source: World Tourism Organization.

Communications Media

	2009	2010	2011
Telephones ('000 main lines in use)	803.7	887.8	900.0
Mobile cellular telephones ('000 subscribers)	2,390.3	2,874.8	3,350.0
Broadband subscribers ('000)	197	200	220

Internet subscribers ('000): 315.0 in 2008; 468.5 in 2011.

Source: International Telecommunication Union.

Education

(2009/10, unless otherwise indicated)

	Institutions	Teachers	Students
Pre-primary	1,938*	9,735	154,159
Primary	2,160*	32,649	461,719
Secondary:			
general	n.a.	31,802	326,513
vocational	275†	11,056	56,713
Higher	n.a.	25,251	202,345

* 1996/97 figure.
† 1994 figure.

Sources: UNESCO Institute for Statistics; Banque du Liban, *Annual Report*.

Pupil-teacher ratio (primary education, UNESCO estimates): 14.1 in 2009/10 (Source: UNESCO Institute for Statistics).

Adult literacy rate (UNESCO estimates): 89.6% (males 93.4%; females 86.0%) in 2007 (Source: UNESCO Institute for Statistics).

Directory

The Government

HEAD OF STATE

President: Gen. MICHEL SULEIMAN (inaugurated 25 May 2008).

CABINET
(May 2013)

On 23 March 2013 the Prime Minister, Najib Miqati, tendered the resignation of his administration, citing disagreement among the constituent parties. The resignation followed the failure of the Government to agree the composition of a committee to supervise the conduct of legislative elections scheduled for June. President Michel Suleiman requested that Miqati remain in office until a new Cabinet could be formed. On 6 April Tammam Salam was appointed as Prime Minister-designate, having won a vote of confidence at the National Assembly the previous day.

Prime Minister: NAJIB MIQATI.

Deputy Prime Minister: SAMIR MOQBEL.

Minister of the Interior and Municipalities: MARWAN CHARBEL.

Minister of Foreign Affairs and Emigrants: ADNAN MANSOUR.

Minister of Justice: SHAKIB QORTBAWI.

Minister of Industry: VREJ SABOUNJIAN.

Minister of Energy and Water: GEBRAN BASSIL.

Minister of Public Works and Transportation: GHAZI ARIDI.

Minister of Finance: MUHAMMAD SAFADI.

Minister of Economy and Trade: NICOLAS NAHHAS.

Minister of Education and Higher Education: HASSAN DIAB.

Minister of Culture: GABY LAYOUN.

Minister of Information: WALID AL-DAOUK.

Minister of Tourism: FADI ABBOUD.

Minister of Telecommunications: NICOLAS SEHNAWI.

Minister of Labour: SALIM JREISSATI.

Minister of Agriculture: HUSSEIN HAJJ HASSAN.

Minister of the Environment: NAZIM AL-KHOURY.

Minister of National Defence: FAYIZ GHOSN.

Minister of Public Health: ALI HASSAN KHALIL.

Minister of Social Affairs: WAEL ABU FAOUR.

Minister of the Displaced: ALAA EL-DIN TERRO.

Minister of Youth and Sports: FAISAL KARAMI.

Minister of State for Administrative Reform: MUHAMMAD FNEISH.

Minister of State for Parliamentary Affairs: NICOLAS FATTOUSH.

Ministers of State: ALI QANSO, SALIM KARAM, AHMAD KARAMI, PANOS MANJIAN, MARWAN KHEIREDDINE.

MINISTRIES

Presidency of the Republic of Lebanon: Presidential Palace, Baabda, Beirut; tel. (5) 900900; fax (5) 900919; e-mail president_office@presidency.gov.lb; internet www.presidency.gov.lb.

Office of the President of the Council of Ministers: Grand Sérail, place Riad el-Solh, Beirut; tel. (1) 746800; fax (1) 983065; e-mail Conseilm@pcm.gov.lb; internet www.pcm.gov.lb.

Ministry of Agriculture: Embassies St, Bir Hassan, Beirut; tel. (1) 849600; fax (1) 849620; e-mail ministry@agriculture.gov.lb; internet www.agriculture.gov.lb.

Ministry of Culture: Immeuble Hatab, rue Madame Curie, Verdun, Beirut; tel. (1) 744250; fax (1) 756322; e-mail amalm@culture.gov.lb; internet www.culture.gov.lb.

Ministry of the Displaced: POB 9150, Minet el-Hosn, Starco Centre, Beirut; tel. (1) 366373; fax (1) 366087; e-mail modbeirut@hotmail.com; internet www.ministryofdisplaced.gov.lb.

Ministry of Economy and Trade: 5th Floor, Azarieh Bldg, rue Riad el-Solh, Hamra, Beirut; tel. (1) 982360; fax (1) 982293; e-mail Info@economy.gov.lb; internet www.economy.gov.lb.

Ministry of Education and Higher Education: Unesco Quarter, Habib Abi Chahla, Beirut; tel. (1) 789611; fax (1) 789606; e-mail info@higher-edu.gov.lb; internet www.higher-edu.gov.lb.

Ministry of Energy and Water: Beirut River Highway, Beirut; tel. (1) 565100; e-mail mew@terra.net.lb; internet www.energyandwater.gov.lb.

Ministry of the Environment: POB 11-2727, 7th and 8th Floors, Lazarieh Centre, Beirut; tel. (1) 976555; fax (1) 976530; e-mail webmaster@moe.gov.lb; internet www.moe.gov.lb.

Ministry of Finance: MOF Bldg, place Riad el-Solh, Beirut; tel. (1) 981001; fax (1) 981059; e-mail infocenter@finance.gov.lb; internet www.finance.gov.lb.

Ministry of Foreign Affairs and Emigrants: al-Sultana Bldg, al-Jnah, Sultan Ibrahim, Beirut; tel. (1) 8470767; fax (1) 840924; e-mail director@emigrants.gov.lb; internet www.emigrants.gov.lb.

Ministry of Industry: Ministry of Industry and Petroleum Bldg, ave Sami Solh, Beirut; tel. (1) 423338; fax (1) 427112; e-mail ministry@industry.gov.lb; internet www.industry.gov.lb.

Ministry of Information: rue Hamra, Beirut; tel. (1) 754400; fax (1) 754776; internet www.ministryinfo.gov.lb.

Ministry of the Interior and Municipalities: Grand Sérail, place Riad el-Solh, Beirut; tel. (1) 751601; fax (1) 084750; e-mail info@moim.gov.lb; internet www.moim.gov.lb.

Ministry of Justice: rue Sami Solh, Beirut; tel. (1) 422112; fax (1) 427957; e-mail info@justice.gov.lb; internet www.justice.gov.lb.

Ministry of Labour: Shiah, Beirut; tel. (1) 556804; fax (1) 556806; e-mail mol@labor.gov.lb; internet www.labor.gov.lb.

Ministry of National Defence: Yarze, Beirut; tel. (5) 420000; fax (5) 951014; e-mail cmdarm@lebarmy.gov.lb; internet www.lebarmy.gov.lb.

Ministry of Public Health: Hussein Mansour Bldg, Museum St, Beirut; tel. (1) 615774; fax (1) 615771; e-mail ministry@public-health.gov.lb; internet www.moph.gov.lb.

Ministry of Public Works and Transportation: Shiah, Beirut; tel. (5) 456482; fax (5) 455840.

Ministry of Social Affairs: rue Badro, Beirut; tel. (1) 260611; fax (1) 242611; e-mail info@socialaffairs.gov.lb; internet www.socialaffairs.gov.lb.

Ministry of State for Administrative Reform: 5th Floor, Immeuble Starco, rue Omar Daouk, place Minet el-Hosn 2020 3313, Beirut; tel. (1) 371510; fax (1) 371599; e-mail www.omsar.gov.lb; internet www.omsar.gov.lb.

Ministry of State for Parliamentary Affairs: Beirut.

Ministry of Telecommunications: Ministry of Telecom Bldg, 1st Floor, place Riad el-Solh, Beirut; tel. (1) 979161; fax (1) 979164; e-mail webmaster@mpt.gov.lb; internet www.mpt.gov.lb.

Ministry of Tourism: POB 11-5344, rue Banque du Liban 550, Beirut; tel. (1) 340940; fax (1) 340945; e-mail mot@inco.com.lb; internet www.destinationlebanon.gov.lb.

Ministry of Youth and Sports: rue Sami Solh, Beirut; tel. (1) 425770; fax (1) 424387; e-mail minijes@cyberia.net.lb.

Legislature

Majlis al-Nuab
(National Assembly)

Place de l'Etoile, Beirut; tel. (1) 982047; fax (1) 982059; e-mail lp@lp.gov.lb; internet www.lp.gov.lb.

The equal distribution of seats among Christians and Muslims is determined by law, and the Cabinet must reflect the level of representation achieved by the various religious denominations within that principal division. Deputies of the same religious denomination do not necessarily share the same political or party allegiances. The distribution of seats is as follows: Maronite Catholics 34; Sunni Muslims 27; Shi'a Muslims 27; Greek Orthodox 14; Druzes 8; Greek-Melkite Catholics 8; Armenian Orthodox 5; Alawites 2; Armenian Catholics 1; Protestants 1; Others 1.

President: NABIH BERRI.

General Election, 7 June 2009

Party list	Seats
March 14 Alliance*	71
March 8 Alliance†	57
Total	**128**

* Electoral list comprising the Future Movement, Parti socialiste progressiste, Lebanese Forces Party, Al-Kataeb, Democratic Left, Parti national libéral, Ramgavar Party, Al-Jama'a al-Islamiya and independents.

† Electoral list comprising Amal, Hezbollah, the Free Patriotic Movement, Armenian Revolutionary Federation, Syrian Social Nationalist Party, Al-Baath, Islamic Action Front, El-Marada Movement, Lebanese Democratic Party and independents.

Political Organizations

Amal (Hope—Afwaj al-Muqawamah al-Lubnaniyyah—Lebanese Resistance Detachments): e-mail info@amal-movement.com; internet www.amal-movement.com; f. 1975 as a politico-military organization; Shi'ite political party; contested 2009 legislative elections as part of March 8 Alliance; Leader NABIH BERRI.

Armenian Revolutionary Federation (ARF) (Tashnag): rue Spears, Beirut; internet www.arfd.am; f. 1890; principal Armenian party; historically the dominant nationalist party in the independent Armenian Republic of Yerevan of 1917–21, prior to its becoming part of the USSR; socialist ideology; contested 2009 legislative elections as part of March 8 Alliance; Leader HRANT MARKARIAN.

Al-Baath (Baath Arab Socialist Party): Beirut; f. 1948; local branch of secular pro-Syrian party with policy of Arab union; contested 2009 legislative elections as part of March 8 Alliance; Leader FAYEZ SHUKER.

Bloc national libanais (Lebanese National Bloc): rue Pasteur, Gemmayze, Beirut; tel. (1) 584585; fax (1) 584591; e-mail ketleh@ketleh.org; internet www.ketleh.org; f. 1943; right-wing Lebanese party with policy of power-sharing between Christians and Muslims and the exclusion of the military from politics; Pres. CARLOS EDDÉ.

Free Patriotic Movement (FPM) (Tayar al-Watani al-Horr): Beirut; tel. (3) 122858; e-mail info@tayyar.org; internet www.tayyar.org; aims to recover sovereignty and complete independence for Lebanon; majority of leaders and supporters are from the Christian community, although is officially secular; largest party in the Change and Reform parliamentary bloc; contested 2009 legislative elections as part of March 8 Alliance; Leader Gen. MICHEL AOUN.

Future Movement (Tayar al-Mustaqbal): POB 123, Koraytem, Hamra, Beirut; tel. (3) 375442; fax (1) 375442; e-mail info@almustaqbal.org; internet www.almustaqbal.org; opposed to Syrian influence in Lebanese affairs; contested 2009 legislative elections as largest party of the March 14 Alliance; Leader SAAD EL-DIN HARIRI.

Hezbollah (Party of God): Beirut; e-mail moqawama@moqawama.org; internet www.moqawama.org; f. 1982 by Iranian Revolutionary Guards who were sent to Lebanon; militant Shi'ite faction, which has become the leading organization of Lebanon's Shi'a community and a recognized political party; demands the withdrawal of Israeli forces from the occupied Shebaa Farms area of what it considers to be southern Lebanon (but which is designated by the UN as being part of Syria) and the release of all Lebanese prisoners from Israeli detention; contested 2009 legislative elections as part of March 8 Alliance; Chair. MUHAMMAD RA'D; Leader and Sec.-Gen. Sheikh HASAN NASRALLAH; Spiritual Leader Ayatollah MUHAMMAD HUSSAIN FADLALLAH.

Hizb-ut-Tahrir al-Islami (Party of Islamic Liberation): e-mail info@hizb-ut-tahrir.org; internet www.hizb-ut-tahrir.org; f. 1953; transnational org. granted a political parties licence in Lebanon in 2006; aims to establish Islamic caliphate throughout the world; denies claims that it is a militant group; Global Leader Sheikh ABU YASIN ATA IBN KHALIL ABU RASHTA (Sheikh Ata Abu Rashta).

Al-Kataeb (Lebanese Social Democratic Party): POB 992, place Charles Hélou, Beirut; tel. (1) 584107; internet www.kataeb.org; f. 1936 as the Phalangist Party (Phalanges libanaises); nationalist, reformist, democratic social party; largest Maronite party, although is officially secular; contested 2009 legislative elections as part of March 14 Alliance; 100,000 mems; Pres. AMIN GEMAYEL.

Lebanese Democratic Party (LDP): Beirut; e-mail webmaster@ldparty.org; internet www.ldparty.org; f. 2001; contested 2009 legislative elections as part of March 8 Alliance; Leader TALAL ARSLAN; Sec.-Gen. WALID BARAKAT.

Lebanese Forces Party: Beirut; internet www.lebanese-forces.com; political successor to the **Lebanese Forces** (f. 1976); coalition of Maronite Christian militias; launched as political party in 1989; proscribed by the Government in 1994; resumed activities as a legal party in 2005; contested 2009 legislative elections as part of March 14 Alliance, securing five seats; Leader SAMIR GEAGEA.

Lebanese Option Gathering: POB 45-489, Hazmieh, Mar Takla, La Diva Bldg, Beirut; tel. (5) 957257; fax (5) 957357; e-mail lebaneseoption@lebaneseoption.org; internet lebaneseoption.org; f. 2007; aims to contest Hezbollah's monopoly over Shi'ite political representation in Lebanon, and to reform and develop the south of the country; Leader AHMAD AL-ASSAD.

El-Marada Movement: Zgharta; internet elmarada.org; f. as the Marada Brigade, relaunched in 1996 as a political party; advocates Lebanese unity, sovereignty and independence; contested 2009 legislative elections as part of March 8 Alliance; Leader SULAYMAN FRANJIYA.

March 8 Alliance: contested 2009 legislative elections as an electoral bloc comprising Hezbollah, Amal, the Free Patriotic Movement, the Armenian Revolutionary Federation, the Syrian Social

Nationalist Party, Al-Baath, the Islamic Action Front, the El-Marada Movement, the Lebanese Democratic Party and independents.

March 14 Alliance: contested 2009 legislative elections as an electoral bloc comprising Future Movement, Parti socialiste progressiste (PSP), the Lebanese Forces Party, Al-Kataeb and other smaller parties and independents; following disagreements over the formation of a new government, the PSP withdrew from the alliance in August 2009.

National Dialogue Party: POB 15-5060, Immeuble Marj el-Zouhour, 1st Floor, rue Donna Maria, Ras el-Nabeh, Beirut; tel. (1) 637000; fax (1) 631234; e-mail info@alhiwar.com; internet www.alhiwar.com; f. 2004; advocates a comprehensive national dialogue to bring about political, social and judicial reforms; also seeks to target corruption and to ensure that the State has authority over the whole of Lebanon; Founder and Chair. FOUAD MUSTAFA MAKHZOUMI.

Parti communiste libanais (PCL) (Lebanese Communist Party): rue al-Bahatri, al-Watuat, Beirut; tel. and fax (1) 739615; e-mail lcparty@lcparty.org; internet www.lcparty.org; f. 1924; officially dissolved 1948–71; Marxist, with much support among intellectuals; Sec.-Gen. KHALID HADDADEH.

Parti national libéral (PNL) (Al-Wataniyin al-Ahrar): POB 165576, rue du Liban, Beirut; tel. (1) 338000; fax (1) 200335; e-mail ahrar@ahrar.org.lb; internet www.ahrar.org.lb; f. 1958; liberal reformist secular party, although has traditionally had a predominantly Maronite Christian membership; contested 2009 legislative elections as part of March 14 Alliance; Pres. DORY CHAMOUN.

Parti socialiste progressiste (PSP) (Al-Takadumi al-Ishteraki): POB 11-2893, Beirut 1107 2120; tel. (1) 303455; fax (1) 301231; e-mail internationalrelation@psp.org.lb; internet www.psp.org.lb; f. 1949; progressive party, advocates constitutional road to socialism and democracy; over 25,000 mems; mainly Druze support; contested 2009 legislative elections as part of March 14 Alliance; Pres. WALID JOUMBLATT; Sec.-Gen. SHARIF FAYAD.

Syrian Social Nationalist Party (al-Hizb al-Suri al-Qawmi al-Ijtima'i): internet www.ssnp.net; f. 1932 in Beirut; banned 1962–69; seeks creation of a 'Greater Syrian' state, incl. Lebanon, Syria, Iraq, Jordan, the Palestinian territories, Kuwait, Cyprus and parts of Egypt, Iran and Turkey; advocates separation of church and State, the redistribution of wealth and a strong military; supports Syrian involvement in Lebanese affairs; contested 2009 legislative elections as part of March 8 Alliance; Leader ASSAD HARDANE.

Al-Wa'ad (National Secular Democratic Party—Pledge): Beirut; f. 1986 by the late Elie Hobeika; pro-Syrian splinter group of Lebanese Forces; officially secular, although most supporters are Maronite Christians; aligned with March 8 Alliance; did not achieve parliamentary representation in June 2009 legislative elections; Leader JOSEPH HOBEIKA.

Other parties include the **Independent Nasserite Movement** (Murabitoun; Sunni Muslim Militia; Leader IBRAHIM QULAYAT) and the **Lebanese Popular Congress** (Pres. KAMAL SHATILA). The **Nasserite Popular Organization** and the **Arab Socialist Union** merged in January 1987, retaining the name of the former. The **Islamic Amal** is a breakaway group from Amal, based in Ba'albek (Leader HUSSEIN MOUSSAVI). **Islamic Jihad** is a pro-Iranian fundamentalist guerrilla group. The **Popular Liberation Army** (f. 1985 by the late MUSTAFA SAAD) is a Sunni Muslim faction, active in the south of Lebanon. **Tawhid Islami** (the Islamic Unification Movement; f. 1982; Sunni Muslim) and the **Arab Democratic Party** (or the Red Knights; Alawites; pro-Syrian; Leader ALI EID) are based in Tripoli.

Diplomatic Representation

EMBASSIES IN LEBANON

Algeria: POB 4794, face Hôtel Summerland, 1 rue Jnah, Sector 8, Beirut; tel. (1) 826712; fax (1) 826711; e-mail ambalbey@dm.nt.lb; Ambassador IBRAHIM BENAOUDA HASSI.

Argentina: Residence des Jardins, Immeuble Moutran, 2e étage, 161 rue Sursock, Achrafieh, Beirut; tel. (1) 210800; fax (1) 210802; e-mail elbno@mrecic.gov.ar; internet www.elbno.mrecic.gov.ar; Ambassador JOSÉ MAXWELL.

Armenia: rue Jasmin 28, Mtaileb, Beirut; tel. (4) 418860; fax (4) 402952; e-mail armlebanonembassy@mfa.am; Ambassador ASHOT KOCHARIAN.

Australia: Embassy Complex, Sérail Hill, Beirut; tel. (1) 960600; fax (1) 960601; e-mail austemle@dfat.gov.au; internet www.lebanon.embassy.gov.au; Ambassador LEX BARTLEM.

Austria: POB 11-3924, Immeuble Tabaris, 8e étage, 812 ave Charles Malek, Achrafieh, Beirut 2071 1606; tel. (1) 213017; fax (1) 217772; e-mail beirut-ob@bmeia.gv.at; internet www.bmeia.gv.at/en/embassy/beirut; Ambassador URSULA FAHRINGER.

Belgium: Bloc A, Immeuble Lazarie, 10e étage, rue Emir Béchir, Beirut; tel. (1) 976001; fax (1) 976007; e-mail beirut@diplobel.fed.be; internet www.diplomatie.be/beirut; Ambassador COLETTE TAQUET.

Brazil: POB 11-562, rue de l'Armée, Colline du Sérail, Beirut; tel. (1) 982161; fax (1) 982159; e-mail brasemb.beirute@itamaraty.gov.br; internet www.brazillebanon.org.lb; Ambassador PAULO ROBERTO CAMPOS TARRISSE DA FONTOURA.

Bulgaria: POB 11-6544, Sector 6, Mar-Takla, Hazmieh, Beirut; tel. (5) 452883; fax (5) 452892; e-mail embassy.beirut@mfa.bg; internet www.mfa.bg/embassies/lebanon; Chargé d'affaires PLAMEN TSOLOV.

Canada: POB 60163, Immeuble Coolrite, 1er et 2e étage, Autoroute Jal el-Dib 43, Beirut; tel. (4) 726700; fax (4) 726701; e-mail berut@international.gc.ca; internet www.lebanon.gc.ca; Ambassador HILARY CHILDS-ADAMS.

Chile: Nouvelle Naccache, Sector 2, rue 64, Immeuble Antoine Boukather, 1er étage, Beirut; tel. (4) 418670; fax (4) 418672; e-mail echilelb@dm.net.lb; internet chileabroad.gov.cl/libano; Ambassador JOSÉ MIGUEL MENCHACA.

China, People's Republic: POB 11-8227, 72 rue Nicolas Ibrahim Sursock, Ramlet el-Baida, Beirut 1107 2260; tel. (1) 856133; fax (1) 822492; e-mail chinaemb_lb@mfa.gov.cn; internet lb.china-embassy.org; Ambassador WU ZEXIAN.

Colombia: Immeuble Mazda, 5e étage, Jal el-Dib, Beirut; tel. (4) 712646; fax (4) 712656; e-mail colombia@cyberia.net.lb; Ambassador RIDA MARIETTE ALJURE-SALAME.

Cuba: Center Farrania, 2e étage, rue Saïd Freiha, Mar-Takla, Hazmieh, Beirut 2901 6727; tel. (1) 459925; fax (1) 950070; e-mail libancub@cyberia.net.lb; Ambassador MANUEL MARÍA SERRANO ACOSTA.

Cyprus: Immeuble M.N.C., 1er étage, rue Debbas, Achrafieh, Beirut; tel. (1) 326461; fax (1) 326471; e-mail info@cyprusembbeirut.org; internet www.cyprusembbeirut.org; Ambassador HOMER MAVROMMATIS.

Czech Republic: POB 40195, Baabda, Beirut; tel. (5) 929010; fax (5) 922120; e-mail beirut@embassy.mzv.cz; internet www.mzv.cz/beirut; Ambassador SVATOPLUK CUMBA.

Denmark: POB 11-5190, rue de l'Armée, Colline du Sérail, Beirut; tel. (1) 991001; fax (1) 991006; e-mail beyamb@um.dk; internet www.libanon.um.dk; Ambassador JAN TOP CHRISTENSEN.

Egypt: POB 5037, rue Dr Mohamad el-Bezri, Bir Hassan, Beirut; tel. (1) 825566; fax (1) 859988; Ambassador ASHRAF HAMDI.

France: rue de Damas, Beirut; tel. (1) 420000; fax (1) 420013; e-mail cad.beyrouth-amb@diplomatie.gouv.fr; internet www.ambafrance-lb.org; Ambassador PATRICE PAOLI.

Gabon: POB 11-1252, Riad el-Solh, Hadath, Beirut 1107 2080; tel. (5) 924649; fax (5) 924643; Ambassador SIMON NTOUTOUME EMANE.

Germany: POB 11-2820, Riad el-Solh, Beirut 1102 2110; tel. (4) 935000; fax (4) 935001; e-mail info@beirut.diplo.de; internet www.beirut.diplo.de; Ambassador BIRGITTA SIEFKER-EBERLE.

Greece: POB 11-0309, Immeuble Boukhater, rue des Ambassades, Nouvelle Naccache, Beirut; tel. (4) 418772; fax (4) 418774; e-mail gremb.bei@mfa.gr; internet www.mfa.gr/beirut; Ambassador AIKATERINI BOURA.

Holy See: POB 1061, Jounieh (Apostolic Nunciature); tel. (9) 263102; fax (9) 264488; e-mail naliban@terra.net.lb; Apostolic Nuncio Most Rev. GABRIELE GIORDANO CACCIA (Titular Archbishop of Sepino).

Hungary: POB 113-5259, Immeuble BAC, 9e étage, rue Justinien, Sanayeh, Beirut; tel. (1) 730083; fax (1) 741261; e-mail mission.bej@mfa.gov.hu; internet www.mfa.gov.hu/emb/beirut; Ambassador LÁSZLÓ VÁRADI.

India: POB 113-5240, 239 rue Ibrahim Abed el-Aal, Beirut; tel. (1) 741270; fax (1) 741283; e-mail amb.beirut@mea.gov.in; Ambassador RAVI THAPAR.

Indonesia: POB 40007, ave Palais Presidential, rue 68, Secteur 3, Baabda, Beirut; tel. (5) 924682; fax (5) 924678; e-mail kbri@kbri-beirut.org; internet kbri-beirut.org; Ambassador DIMAS SAMODRA RUM.

Iran: POB 5030, Bir Hassan, Beirut; tel. (1) 821224; fax (1) 821229; Ambassador GHANDAFAR RUKUN ABADI.

Iraq: Beirut; tel. (1) 453209; fax (1) 459850; e-mail brtemb@iraqmofamail.net; Ambassador OMAR AL-BARZENJI.

Italy: POB 57, rue du Palais Présidentiel, Baabda, Beirut 2902 2633; tel. (5) 954955; fax (5) 959616; e-mail amba.beirut@esteri.it; internet www.ambbeirut.esteri.it; Ambassador GIUSEPPE MORABITO.

Japan: POB 11-3360, rue de l'Armée, Zkak al-Blat, Colline du Sérail, Beirut; tel. (1) 989751; fax (1) 989754; e-mail japanemb@japanemb.org.lb; internet www.lb.emb-japan.go.jp; Ambassador SEIICHI OTSUKA.

Jordan: POB 109, Beirut 5113; tel. (5) 922500; fax (5) 922502; e-mail joremb@dm.net.lb; Ambassador ZEID ZREIQAT.

Korea, Republic: POB 40-290, Baabda, Beirut; tel. (5) 953167; fax (5) 953170; e-mail lbkor@mofa.go.kr; internet lbn.mofa.go.kr; Ambassador KIM BYOUNG-GI.

Kuwait: POB 4580, Rond-point du Stade, Bir Hassan, Beirut; tel. (1) 756100; fax (1) 842220; e-mail info@kuwaitinfo.net; Ambassador ABD AL-AAL AL-QINAI.

Mexico: POB 70-1150, 1er étage, Immeuble Mansour 90, rue 53, Sector 2, New Naccache, Antélias, Beirut; tel. and fax (4) 418871; e-mail mail@embassyofmexicoinlebanon.org; internet www .embassyofmexicoinlebanon.org; Ambassador JORGE ÁLVAREZ FUENTES.

Morocco: Bir Hassan, Beirut; tel. (1) 859851; fax (1) 859839; e-mail sifmar@cyberia.net.lb; Ambassador ALI OUMLIL.

Netherlands: POB 167190, Netherlands Tower, ave Charles Malek, Achrafieh, Beirut 2073 0802; tel. (1) 211150; fax (1) 211173; e-mail bei@minbuza.nl; internet lebanon.nlembassy.org; Ambassador HEERE E. G. DE BOER.

Norway: POB 113-7001, Immeuble Dimashki, rue Bliss, Ras Beirut, Hamra, Beirut 1103 2150; tel. (1) 960000; fax (1) 960099; e-mail emb .bey@mfa.no; internet www.norway-lebanon.org; Ambassador SVEIN AASS.

Pakistan: POB 135506, UNESCO Centre Crossroad, 8e étage, rue Saeb Salam, Immeuble 1, Verdun, Beirut; tel. (1) 790327; fax (1) 790471; e-mail pakemblb@gmail.com; internet www.mofa.gov.pk/ lebanon; Ambassador RAANA RAHIM.

Paraguay: Immeuble La Rosa, Rez-de-chaussée, rue Farid Zeidan, Hazmieh, Mar Takla, Beirut; tel. and fax (1) 5458502; e-mail embaparlibano@hotmail.com; Ambassador HASSAN KHALIL DAY.

Philippines: POB 136631, rue Mar Geries, Immeuble W, Hadath, Baabda, Beirut; tel. (5) 953522; fax (5) 953521; e-mail beirut.pe@dfa .gov.ph; Ambassador LEAH M. BASINANG-RUIZ.

Poland: POB 40-215, Immeuble Khalifa, ave Président Sulayman Franjiya 52, Baabda, Beirut; tel. (5) 924591; fax (5) 924882; e-mail bejrut.amb.sekretariat@msz.gov.pl; internet www.bejrut.polemb .net; Ambassador TOMASZ NIEGODZISZ.

Qatar: POB 11-6717, Immeuble Deebs, 1er étage, Shouran, Beirut; tel. (1) 865271; fax (1) 810460; e-mail beirut@mofa.gov.qa; Ambassador SAAD BIN ALI AL-MUHANNADI.

Romania: route du Palais Présidentiel, Baabda, Beirut; tel. (5) 924848; fax (5) 924747; e-mail romembey@inco.com.lb; internet beirut.mae.ro; Ambassador DANIEL TANASE.

Russia: POB 5220, rue Mar Elias el-Tineh, Wata Mseitbeh, Beirut; tel. (1) 300041; fax (1) 303837; e-mail rusembei@cyberia.net.lb; internet www.lebanon.mid.ru; Ambassador ALEKSANDR ZASYPKIN.

Saudi Arabia: POB 136144, Kuraitem, Beirut; tel. (1) 860242; fax (1) 861524; e-mail lbemb@mofa.gov.sa; Ambassador ALI BIN AWADH ASSERI.

Spain: POB 11-3039, Palais Chehab, Hadath Antounie, Beirut; tel. (5) 464120; fax (5) 464030; e-mail emb.beirut@maec.es; Ambassador MILAGROS HERNANDO ECHEVARRÍA.

Sri Lanka: Immeuble Muhammad K. Awad 549, Beirut; tel. (5) 956031; fax (5) 956033; e-mail slemblbn@cyberia.net.lb; Ambassador RANJITH GUNARATHNA.

Sudan: POB 2504, Hamra, Beirut; tel. (1) 350057; fax (1) 353271; Ambassador AHMED HASSAN.

Switzerland: POB 11-172, Immeuble Bourj al-Ghazal, ave Fouad Chehab, Achrafieh, Beirut 1107 2020; tel. (1) 324129; fax (1) 324167; e-mail bey.vertretung@eda.admin.ch; internet www.eda.admin.ch/ beirut; Ambassador RUTH FLINT.

Syria: rue Makdessi, Hamra, Beirut; Ambassador ALI ABD AL-KARIM ALI.

Tunisia: Mar-Takla, Hazmieh, Beirut; tel. (5) 457431; fax (5) 950434; Ambassador MUHAMMAD FAWZI BALLOUT.

Turkey: POB 70-666, zone II, rue 1, Rabieh, Beirut; tel. (4) 520929; fax (4) 407557; e-mail ambassade.beyrouth@mfa.gov.tr; internet beirut.emb.mfa.gov.tr; Ambassador SÜLEYMAN INAN OZYILDIZ.

Ukraine: POB 40268, rue Antoine El Rayes, Mount Lebanon, Casa Baabda, Beirut; tel. (5) 921975; fax (5) 921972; e-mail emb_lb@mfa .gov.ua; internet www.mfa.gov.ua/lebanon; Ambassador VOLODYMYR KOVAL.

United Arab Emirates: Ramla al-Bayda, Jnah, Beirut; tel. (1) 857000; fax (1) 857009; e-mail beirut@mofa.gov.ae; internet uae-embassy.ae/embassies/lb; Ambassador YOUSSEF ALI AL-ASSIMI.

United Kingdom: POB 11-471, Embassies Complex, rue de l'Armée, Colline du Sérail, Zkak al-Blat, Beirut; tel. (1) 960800; fax (1) 990420; e-mail chancery@cyberia.net.lb; internet ukinlebanon.fco.gov.uk; Ambassador TOM FLETCHER.

USA: POB 70-840, Antélias, Beirut; tel. (4) 542600; fax (4) 544861; e-mail beirutpd@state.gov; internet lebanon.usembassy.gov; Ambassador MAURA CONNELLY.

Uruguay: POB 2051, Centre Stella Marris, 7e étage, rue Banque du Liban, Jounieh; tel. (9) 636529; fax (9) 636531; e-mail uruliban@dm .net.lb; internet www.embauruguaybeirut.org; Ambassador Dr MARTA INÉS PIZZANELLI.

Venezuela: POB 11-603, rue Amaret Chalhoub, Immeuble Baeze-vale House, 5e étage, Zalka, Beirut; tel. (1) 888701; fax (1) 900757; e-mail embajadora@embavenelibano.com; internet www .embavenelibano.com; Ambassador ZOED KARAM.

Yemen: Bir Hassan, Beirut; tel. (1) 852688; fax (1) 821610; Ambassador (vacant).

Judicial System

Law and justice in Lebanon are administered in accordance with the following codes, which are based upon modern theories of civil and criminal legislation:

Code de la Propriété (1930).

Code des Obligations et des Contrats (1932).

Code de Procédure Civile (1933).

Code Maritime (1947).

Code de Procédure Pénale (Code Ottoman Modifié).

Code Pénal (1943).

Code Pénal Militaire (1946).

Code d'Instruction Criminelle.

Courts of First Instance: Fifty-six courts, each consisting of a single judge, and dealing in the first instance with both civil and criminal cases; there are 17 such courts in Beirut and seven in Tripoli; Pres. Dr FADI ELIAS.

Courts of Appeal: Eleven courts, each consisting of three judges, including a President and a Public Prosecutor, and dealing with civil and criminal cases; there are five such courts in Beirut; First Pres. JEAN FAHD.

Courts of Cassation: Four courts, three dealing with civil and commercial cases and the fourth with criminal cases. A Court of Cassation, to be properly constituted, must have at least three judges, one being the President and the other two Councillors. If the Court of Cassation reverses the judgment of a lower court, it does not refer the case back but retries it itself; General Prosecutor of Cassation SAMIR HAMMOUD (acting).

State Consultative Council: deals with administrative cases; Pres. SHUKRI SADER.

Court of Justice: a special court consisting of a President and four judges, deals with matters affecting the security of the State; there is no appeal against its verdicts.

Constitutional Council: considers matters pertaining to the constitutionality of legislation; Pres. ISSAM SULEIMAN.

Higher Judicial Council: considers matters involving members of the executive branch; Pres. JEAN FAHED.

Military Court: competent to try crimes and misdemeanours involving the armed and security forces; Chief of the Military Court Brig.-Gen. MAHER SAFI EL-DIN.

In addition, Islamic (*Shari'a*), Christian and Jewish religious courts deal with affairs of personal status (marriage, death, inheritance, etc.).

Religion

Of all the countries of the Middle East, Lebanon probably presents the closest juxtaposition of sects and peoples within a small territory. In 1994 it was estimated that 29%–32% of the population of Lebanon were Shi'a Muslims, 25%–28% Maronites, 16%–20% Sunni Muslims and 3.5% Druzes. The Maronites, a uniate sect of the Roman Catholic Church, inhabited the old territory of Mount Lebanon, i.e. immediately east of Beirut. In the south, towards the Israeli frontier, Shi'a villages are most common, while between the Shi'a and the Maronites live the Druzes (divided between the Yazbakis and the Joumblatis). The Beqa'a valley has many Greek Christians (both Roman Catholic and Orthodox), while the Tripoli area is mainly Sunni Muslim.

CHRISTIANITY
The Roman Catholic Church
Armenian Rite

Patriarchate of Cilicia: Patriarcat Arménien Catholique, rue de l'Hôpital orthodoxe, Jeitawi, Beirut 2078 5605; tel. (1) 570555; fax (1) 570563; e-mail nerbed19@magnarama.com; f. 1742; est. in Beirut since 1929; includes patriarchal diocese of Beirut, with an estimated 12,000 adherents (31 December 2007); Patriarch Most Rev. NERSES BEDROS XIX TARMOUNI; Protosyncellus Rt Rev. VARTAN ACHKARIAN (Titular Bishop of Tokat—Armenian Rite).

Chaldean Rite

Diocese of Beirut: Evêché Chaldéen de Beyrouth, POB 373, Hazmieh, Beirut; tel. (5) 457732; fax (5) 457731; e-mail chaldepiscopus@hotmail.com; an estimated 10,000 adherents (31 December 2007); Bishop of Beirut MICHEL KASSARJI.

Latin Rite

Apostolic Vicariate of Beirut: Vicariat Apostolique, POB 11-4224, Riad el-Solh, Beirut 1107 2160; tel. (9) 236101; fax (9) 236102; e-mail vicariatlat@hotmail.com; an estimated 15,000 adherents (31 December 2007); Vicar Apostolic PAUL DAHDAH (Titular Archbishop of Arae in Numidia).

Maronite Rite

Patriarchate of Antioch and all the East: Patriarcat Maronite, Bkerké; tel. (9) 915441; fax (9) 938844; e-mail jtawk@bkerke.org.lb; includes patriarchal dioceses of Jounieh, Sarba and Jobbé; the Maronite Church in Lebanon comprises four archdioceses and six dioceses; Patriarch Cardinal BÉCHARA BOUTROS RAÏ.

Archbishop of Antélias: Most Rev. JOSEPH MOHSEN BÉCHARA, Archevêché Maronite, POB 70400, Antélias; tel. (4) 410020; fax (4) 415872.

Archbishop of Beirut: Most Rev. PAUL YOUSUF MATAR, Archevêché Maronite, 10 rue Collège de la Sagesse, Achrafieh, Beirut; tel. (1) 561980; fax (1) 561930; e-mail maronitebeyrouth@yahoo.fr; also representative of the Holy See for Roman Catholics of the Coptic Rite in Lebanon.

Archbishop of Tripoli: Most Rev. GEORGES BOU-JAOUDÉ, Archevêché Maronite, POB 104, rue al-Moutran, Karm Sada, Tripoli; tel. (6) 624324; fax (6) 629393; e-mail rahmat@inco.com.lb.

Archbishop of Tyre: Most Rev. CHUCRALLAH-NABIL HAGE, Archevêché Maronite, Tyre; tel. (7) 740059; fax (7) 344891; e-mail abounacharbel@cyberia.net.lb.

Melkite Rite

Patriarch of Antioch: Patriarcat Grec-Melkite Catholique, POB 22249, 12 ave al-Zeitoon, Bab Charki, Damascus, Syria; tel. (11) 5441030; fax (11) 5417900; e-mail pat.melk@scs-net.org; internet www.pgc-lb.org; f. 1724; the Melkite Church in Lebanon comprises seven archdioceses, with an estimated 393,000 adherents (31 December 2009); Patriarch of Antioch and all the East, of Alexandria and of Jerusalem His Beatitude GREGORIOS III LAHAM.

Archbishop of Ba'albek: Most Rev. ELIAS RAHAL, Archevêché Grec-Catholique, Ba'albek; tel. (8) 370200; fax (8) 373986.

Archbishop of Baniyas: Most Rev. GEORGES NICOLAS HADDAD, Archevêché de Panéas, Jdeidet Marjeyoun; tel. and fax (3) 830007.

Archbishop of Beirut and Jbeil: CYRILLE SALIM BUSTROS, Archevêché Grec-Melkite-Catholique, POB 11-901, 655 rue de Damas, Beirut; tel. (1) 616104; fax (1) 616109; e-mail agmcb@terra.net.lb.

Archbishop of Saida (Sidon): Most Rev. ELIE BÉCHARA HADDAD, Archevêché Grec-Melkite-Catholique, POB 247, rue el-Moutran, Sidon; tel. (7) 720100; fax (7) 722055; e-mail mhaddad.saida@hotmail.com.

Archbishop of Tripoli: Most Rev. GEORGE RIASHI, Archevêché Grec-Catholique, POB 72, rue al-Kanaess, Tripoli; tel. (6) 431602; fax (6) 441716.

Archbishop of Tyre: Most Rev. GEORGES BAKOUNY, Archevêché Grec-Melkite-Catholique, POB 257, Tyre; tel. (7) 740015; fax (7) 349180; e-mail pbacouni@yahoo.com.

Archbishop of Zahleh and Furzol: Most Rev. ISSAM JOHN DARWISH, Archevêché Grec-Melkite-Catholique, Saidat el-Najat, Zahleh; tel. (8) 800333; fax (8) 822406; e-mail info@catholiczahle.org; internet www.catholiczahle.org.

Syrian Rite

Patriarchate of Antioch: Patriarcat Syrien Catholique d'Antioche, rue de Damas, POB 116/5087, Beirut 1106 2010; tel. (1) 615892; fax (1) 616573; e-mail psc_lb@yahoo.com; jurisdiction over about 150,000 Syrian Catholics in the Middle East; Patriarch Most Rev. IGNACE JOSEPH III YOUNAN; Protosyncellus Mgr GEORGES MASRI.

The Anglican Communion

Within the Episcopal Church in Jerusalem and the Middle East, Lebanon forms part of the diocese of Jerusalem (see the chapter on Israel).

Other Christian Groups

Armenian Apostolic Orthodox Church: Armenian Catholicosate of Cilicia, POB 70317, Antélias; tel. (4) 410001; fax (4) 419724; e-mail info@armenianorthodoxchurch.org; internet www.armenianorthodoxchurch.org; f. 301 AD in Armenia, re-established in 1293 in Cilicia (now in Turkey), transferred to Antélias, Lebanon, 1930; Leader His Holiness ARAM KESHISHIAN I (Catholicos of Cilicia); jurisdiction over an estimated 3.5m. adherents in Lebanon, Syria, Cyprus, Kuwait, Greece, Iran, Qatar, the United Arab Emirates, South America, the USA and Canada.

National Evangelical Synod of Syria and Lebanon: POB 70890, Antélias; tel. (4) 525030; fax (4) 411184; e-mail nessl@synod-sl.org; internet www.synod-sl.org; f. 1959; 20,000 adherents (2010); Gen. Sec. Rev. FADI DAGHER.

Patriarchate of Antioch and all the East (Greek Orthodox): Patriarcat Grec-Orthodoxe, POB 9, Damascus, Syria; tel. (11) 5424400; fax (11) 5424404; e-mail info@antiochpat.org; internet www.antiochpat.org; Patriarch His Beatitude IGNATIUS (HAZIM) IV.

Patriarchate of Antioch and all the East (Syrian Orthodox): Patriarcat Syrien Orthodoxe, Bab Toma, POB 22260, Damascus, Syria; tel. (11) 5951870; fax (11) 5951880; internet www.syrian-orthodox.com; Patriarch IGNATIUS ZAKKA I IWAS.

Supreme Council of the Evangelical Community in Syria and Lebanon: POB 70/1065, rue Rabieh 34, Antélias; tel. (4) 525036; fax (4) 405490; e-mail suprcoun@minero.net; Pres. Rev. Dr SALIM SAHIOUNY.

Union of the Armenian Evangelical Churches in the Near East: POB 11-377, Beirut; tel. (1) 565628; fax (1) 565629; e-mail uaecne@cyberia.net.lb; f. 1846 in Turkey; comprises about 30 Armenian Evangelical Churches in Syria, Lebanon, Egypt, Cyprus, Greece, Iran, Turkey and Australia; Pres. Rev. MEGRDICH KARAGOEZIAN; Gen. Sec. SEBOUH TERZIAN.

ISLAM

Shi'a Muslims: Leader Imam Sheikh SAYED MOUSSA AL-SADR (went missing during visit to Libya in August 1978); Vice-Pres. of the Supreme Islamic Council of the Shi'a Community of Lebanon ABD AL-AMIR QABALAN; Beirut.

Sunni Muslims: Grand Mufti of Lebanon, Dar el-Fatwa, rue Ilewi Rushed, Beirut; tel. (1) 422340; Leader Sheikh Dr MUHAMMAD RASHID QABBANI.

Druzes: Supreme Spiritual Leader of the Druze Community, Beirut; tel. (1) 341116; Supreme Spiritual Leader Sheikh AL-AQL BAHJAT GHAITH; Political Leader WALID JOUMBLATT.

Alawites: a schism of Shi'ite Islam; there are an estimated 50,000 Alawites in northern Lebanon, in and around Tripoli.

JUDAISM

A small Jewish community, thought to number less than 100 people, remains in Lebanon.

Jewish Community: Pres. ISAAC ARAZI (Beirut).

The Press
DAILIES

Al-Akhbar (The News): POB 5963-113, Concorde Centre, 6th Floor, rue Verdun, Beirut; tel. (1) 759500; fax (1) 759597; internet www.al-akhbar.com; f. 2006; Arabic; independent; Editor-in-Chief IBRAHIM AL-AMIN.

Al-Anwar (Lights): c/o Dar Assayad, POB 11-1038, Hazmieh, Beirut; tel. (5) 456374; fax (5) 452700; e-mail info@alanwar.com; internet www.alanwar-leb.com; f. 1959; Arabic; independent; supplement, Sunday; cultural and social; publ. by Dar Assayad SAL; Editors-in-Chief MICHEL RAAD, RAFIK KHOURY; circ. 14,419.

Aztag: POB 80-860, Shaghzoyan Cultural Centre, Bourj Hammoud; tel. (1) 258526; fax (1) 258529; e-mail info@aztagdaily.com; internet www.aztagdaily.com; f. 1927; Armenian; Editor-in-Chief SHAHAN KANDAHARIAN; circ. 6,500.

Al-Balad: Beirut; tel. (1) 494694; fax (1) 494894; e-mail crm@albaladonline.com; internet albaladonline.com; Arabic; Chair. AHMAD BADRANI; Man. Editor GEORGE JABARA.

Al-Bayrak (The Standard): Immeuble Dimitri Trad, rue Issa Maalouf, Achrafieh, Beirut; tel. (1) 216393; fax (1) 338928; e-mail dalwl@dm.net.lb; internet www.albayrakonline.com; f. 1913; Arabic; publ. by Dar Alf Leila wa Leila Publishing House; politics and society; Editor-in-Chief MELHEM KARAM; circ. 10,000.

Daily Star: Markaziah Centre, 3rd Floor, Umm Gelias St, Beirut Central District, Beirut; tel. (1) 587277; fax (1) 561333; e-mail editorial@dailystar.com.lb; internet www.dailystar.com.lb; f. 1952; English; Publr SALMA EL-BISSAR; Editor-in-Chief NADIM LADKI; circ. 10,550.

Al-Diyar (The Homeland): al-Nahda Bldg, Yarze, Beirut; tel. (5) 923830; fax (5) 923773; e-mail info@addiyaronline.com; internet www.aldiyaronline.com; f. 1987; Arabic; Propr and Editor-in-Chief CHARLES AYYUB.

Al-Hayat (Life): POB 11-1242, rue Maarad, place Riad el-Solh, Beirut; tel. (1) 987990; fax (1) 983921; e-mail information@alhayat .com; internet www.daralhayat.com; f. 1946; Arabic; independent; Editor-in-Chief GHASSAN CHARBEL; circ. 196,800.

Al-Liwa' (The Standard): POB 11-2402, Beirut; tel. (1) 735745; fax (1) 735749; e-mail events@aliwaa.com.lb; internet www.aliwaa.com; f. 1963; Arabic; Propr ABD AL-GHANI SALAM; Editor SALAH SALAM; circ. 26,000.

Al-Mustaqbal: POB 14-5426, Beirut; tel. (1) 797770; fax (1) 869264; e-mail rnakib@almustaqbal.com.lb; internet www.almustaqbal.com .lb; f. 1999; Dir RAFIQ NAKIB; Editor-in-Chief HANI HAMMOUD; circ. 20,000.

An-Nahar (The Day): Immeuble An-Nahar, place des Martyrs, Marfa', Beirut 2014 5401; tel. (1) 994888; fax (1) 996777; e-mail webmaster@annahar.com.lb; internet www.annahar.com; f. 1933; Arabic; independent; publ. by Editions Dar an-Nahar SAL; Editor-in-Chief NAYLA TUENI; circ. 50,000.

L'Orient-Le Jour: POB 11-2488, Route de Damas, montée Fiyaddiyé, 200m aprés station Total, Beirut; tel. (5) 956444; fax (5) 957444; e-mail administration@lorientlejour.com; internet www .lorientlejour.com; f. 1970; by merger of two newspapers, *L'Orient* and *Le Jour*; French; independent; Pres. and CEO MICHEL EDDÉ; Editor-in-Chief NAGIB AOUN; circ. 23,000.

As-Safir: POB 113/5015, Immeuble as-Safir, rue Monimina, Hamra, Beirut 1103-2010; tel. and fax (1) 350001; fax (1) 743602; e-mail mail@assafir.com; internet www.assafir.com; f. 1974; Arabic; political; Publr and Editor-in-Chief TALAL SALMAN; circ. 45,000.

Zartonk: POB 11-617, rue Nahr Ibrahim, Beirut; tel. and fax (1) 566709; e-mail info@zartonkdaily.com; internet www.zartonkdaily .com; f. 1937; Armenian, Arabic and English; official organ of Armenian Liberal Democratic Party; Man. Editor BAROUYR H. AGHBASHIAN.

WEEKLIES

Achabaka (The Net): c/o Dar Assayad SAL, POB 11-1038, Said Freiha St, Hazmieh, Beirut; tel. (5) 453673; fax (5) 452700; e-mail info@dar-assayad.com; internet www.achabaka.com; f. 1956; Arabic; society and features; Founder SAID FREIHA; Editor ELHAM FREIHA; circ. 139,775.

Al-Anwar Supplement: c/o Dar Assayad, POB 11-1038, Hazmieh, Beirut; tel. (5) 450406; fax (5) 452700; e-mail info@alanwar.com; internet www.alanwar.com; cultural and social; every Sun.; supplement to daily *Al-Anwar*; Editor ISSAM FREIHA; circ. 90,000.

Assayad (The Hunter): c/o Dar Assayad, POB 11-1038, Hazmieh, Beirut; tel. (5) 450933; fax (5) 452700; e-mail assayad@inco.com.lb; internet www.al-sayad.com; f. 1943; Arabic; political and social; Editor-in-Chief MOUNIR NAJJAR; circ. 76,192.

Attamaddon: POB 90, Aljmizzat St, Tripoli; tel. (6) 441164; fax (6) 435252; e-mail info@attamaddon.com; internet www.attamaddon .com; f. 1972; political.

Al-Bayan: 5th Floor, Karim Centre, Tripoli; tel. and fax (6) 425555; e-mail info@albayanlebanon.com; internet albayanlebanon.com; political.

Ad-Dabbour: place du Musée, Beirut; tel. and fax (1) 616771; e-mail addabbour@yahoo.com; f. 1922; Arabic; CEO JOSEPH RICHARD MOUKARZEL; circ. 12,000.

L'Hebdo Magazine: POB 11-1404, Immeuble Sayegh, rue Sursock, Beirut; tel. (1) 202070; fax (1) 202663; e-mail info@ediori.com.lb; internet www.magazine.com.lb; f. 1956; French; political, economic and social; publ. by Editions Orientales SAL; Pres. CHARLES ABOU ADAL; Editor-in-Chief PAUL KHALIFEH; circ. 18,000.

Al-Hiwar (Dialogue): rue Donna Maria, Beirut; tel. (1) 637000; fax (1) 631282; e-mail info@alhiwar.info; internet www.alhiwar.info; f. 2000; Arabic; publ. by the National Dialogue Party; Chair. FOUAD MAKHZOUMI; Editor-in-Chief SAM MOUNASSA.

Al-Hurriya (Freedom): Beirut; e-mail info@alhourriah.org; internet www.alhourriah.org; f. 1960; Arabic; organ of the Democratic Front for the Liberation of Palestine; Editor DAOUD TALHAME; circ. 30,000.

Al-Intiqad: internet www.alintiqad.com; Arabic; political; organ of Hezbollah; Editor IBRAHIM MOUSSAWI.

Al-Kifah al-Arabi (The Arab Struggle): POB 5158-14, Immeuble Rouche-Shams, Beirut; tel. (1) 809300; fax (1) 808281; e-mail editor@kifaharabi.com; internet www.kifaharabi.com; f. 1974; Arabic; political, socialist, pan-Arab; Publr WALID HUSSEINI.

Massis: Immeuble Eglise Ste Croix des Arméniens Catholiques, rue Zoghbi, Zalka, Beirut; tel. (4) 715263; e-mail hebdomassis@sodetel .net.lb; internet www.armeniancatholic.org; f. 1947; Armenian; Catholic; Editor-in-Chief SARKIS NADJARIAN; circ. 2,500.

Al-Moharrer (The Liberator): POB 136702, rue Hamra, Beirut; tel. (1) 750516; fax (1) 750515; e-mail almoharrer@almoharrer.net; internet www.almoharrer.net; f. 1962; Arabic; circ. 87,000; Gen. Man. WALID ABOU ZAHR.

Monday Morning: POB 165612, Immeuble Dimitri Trad, rue Issa Maalouf, Achrafieh, Beirut; tel. (1) 200961; fax (1) 335079; e-mail info@mmorning.com; internet www.mmorning.com; f. 1971; political and social affairs; publ. by Dar Alf Leila wa Leila; circ. 15,000; Editor-in-Chief MELHEM KARAM.

Al-Nass (The People): POB 145583, ave Fouad Chehab, Beirut; tel. (3) 376185; fax (8) 376610; e-mail an-nass@live.com; f. 1959; Arabic; weekly news magazine; Editor-in-Chief HASSAN YAGHI; circ. 22,000.

Al-Ousbou' al-Arabi (Arab Week): POB 11-1404, Immeuble Sayegh, rue Sursock, Beirut; tel. (1) 202070; fax (1) 202752; e-mail info@arabweek.com.lb; internet www.arabweek.com.lb; f. 1959; Arabic; political and social; publ. by Editions Orientales SAL; Chair. and Editor-in-Chief CHARLES ABOU ADAL; circ. 88,407 (circulates throughout the Arab world).

La Revue du Liban (Lebanon Review): POB 165612, Immeuble Dimitri Trad, rue Issa Maalouf, Achrafieh, Beirut; tel. (1) 200961; fax (1) 338929; e-mail rdl@rdl.com.lb; internet www.rdl.com.lb; f. 1928; French; political, social, cultural; publ. by Dar Alf Leila wa Leila; Publr MELHEM KARAM; Gen. Man. MICHEL MISK; circ. 22,000.

Al-Shiraa (The Sail): POB 13-5250, Beirut; tel. (1) 703000; fax (1) 866050; e-mail alshiraa@alshiraa.com; internet www.alshiraa.com; Arabic; Chief Editor HASSAN SABRA; circ. 40,000.

OTHER SELECTED PERIODICALS

Alam Attijarat (Business World): Immeuble Strand, rue Hamra, Beirut; f. 1965; monthly; commercial; Editor (vacant); international circ. 17,500.

Al Computer, Communications and Electronics (ACCE): c/o Dar Assayad, POB 1038, Hazmieh, Beirut; tel. (5) 450935; fax (5) 452700; e-mail assayad@inco.com.lb; internet www.accemagazine .com; f. 1984; monthly; computer technology; publ. by Dar Assayad Int; Chief Editor ANTOINE BOUTROS; circ. 31,912 (Jan.–June 2006).

Arab Construction World: POB 13-5121, Chouran, Beirut 1102 2802; tel. (1) 352413; fax (1) 352419; e-mail info@acwmag.com; internet www.acwmag.com; f. 1983; monthly; English and Arabic; publ. by CPH World Media; Publr FATHI CHATILA; Pres. and CEO MUHAMMAD RABIH CHATILA; circ. 10,100.

Arab Defence Journal: c/o Dar Assayad, POB 11-1038, Hazmieh, Beirut; tel. (5) 457261; fax (5) 452700; e-mail info@dar-assayad.com; internet www.arabdefencejournal.com; f. 1976; monthly; military; publ. by Dar Assayad Int; Editor-in-Chief FAWZI ABOU FARHAT; circ. 24,831 (July–Dec. 2005).

Arab Water World: POB 13-5121, Chouran, Beirut 1102-2802; tel. (1) 748333; fax (1) 352419; e-mail editorial@awwmag.com; internet www.awwmag.com; f. 1977; monthly; English and Arabic; publ. by CPH World Media; Pres., Publr and Editor-in-Chief FATHI CHATILA; circ. 8,400.

The Arab World: POB 567, Jounieh; tel. and fax (9) 935096; e-mail info@naamanculture.com; internet www.naamanculture.com; f. 1985; 24 a yr; publ. by Dar Naamān lith-Thaqāfa (Maison Naaman pour la Culture); Editor NAJI NAAMAN.

BusinessWeek Al-Arabiya: POB 11-4355, Beirut; tel. (1) 739777; fax (1) 749090; f. 2005; monthly; Arabic edn of US weekly business publ; publ. by InfoPro SA; distributed across 22 countries; Regional Dir SYLVIE GYURAN.

Le Commerce du Levant: POB 45-332 Baabda, Route de Damas, Immeuble l'Orient-Le Jour, 3e étage, Hazmieh, Beirut; tel. (1) 952259; fax (1) 453644; e-mail redaction@lecommercedulevant .com; internet www.lecommercedulevant.com; f. 1929; monthly; French; commercial and financial; publ. by Société de la Presse Economique; Chief Editor SIBYLLE RIZK; circ. 15,000.

Déco: POB 11-1404, Immeuble Sayegh, rue Sursock, Beirut; tel. (1) 202070; fax (1) 202663; e-mail info@decomag.com.lb; internet www .decomag.com.lb; f. 2000; quarterly; French; architecture and interior design; publ. by Editions Orientales SAL; Pres. CHARLES ABOU ADAL; circ. 14,000.

Fairuz International: Dar Assayad, POB 11-1038, Hazmieh, Beirut; tel. (5) 456373; fax (5) 450609; e-mail assayad@inco.com.lb;

internet www.darassayad.net; f. 1982; monthly; Arabic; for women; publ. by Dar Assayad Int; Chief Editor ELHAM FREIHA; circ. 93,892 (July–Dec. 2005).

Al-Fares: c/o Dar Assayad, POB 11-1038, Hazmieh, Beirut; tel. (5) 450406; fax (5) 450609; e-mail assayad@inco.com.lb; internet www .alfaresmagazine.com; f. 1991; monthly; Arabic; men's interest; publ. by Dar Assayad Int; Chief Editor ELHAM FREIHA; circ. 79,237 (July–Dec. 2005).

Al-Idari (The Manager): c/o Dar Assayad, POB 11-1038, Hazmieh, Beirut; tel. (5) 450406; fax (5) 450609; e-mail assayad@inco.com.lb; internet www.alidarimagazine.com; f. 1975; monthly; Arabic; business management, economics, finance and investment; publ. by Dar Assayad Int; Pres. BASSAM FREIHA; Gen. Man. ELHAM FREIHA; circ. 31,867.

Lebanese and Arab Economy: POB 11-1801, Sanayeh, Beirut; tel. (1) 744160; fax (1) 353395; e-mail information@ccib.org.lb; internet www.ccib.org.lb; f. 1951; monthly; Arabic, English and French; publ. by Chamber of Commerce, Industry and Agriculture of Beirut and Mount Lebanon.

Lebanon Opportunities: c/o InfoPro sal, POB 11-4355, 2nd Floor, rue Hamra, Piccadilly Center, Beirut; tel. (1) 739777; fax (1) 749090; e-mail infopro@infopro.com.lb; internet www.opportunities.com.lb; monthly; English; real estate, business and general finance and economy; publ. by InfoPro SA; Publr and Editor-in-Chief RAMZI EL-HAFEZ.

Al-Mar'a: POB 11-1404, Immeuble Sayegh, rue Sursock, Beirut; tel. (1) 202070; fax (1) 202663; e-mail info@almara.com.lb; internet www .almara.com.lb; f. 2000; monthly; Arabic; for women; publ. by Editions Orientales SAL; Dir MOUNA BÉCHARA; Chief Editor PAUL KHALIFEH; circ. 20,000.

MENA Health World: POB 13-5121, Chouran, Beirut 1102 2802; tel. (1) 748333; fax (1) 352419; e-mail editorial@mhwmag.net; internet www.mhwmag.net; f. 1986 as Arab Health World magazine, but publ. suspended in 1993; relaunched as above 2006; bi-monthly; English and Arabic; publ. by CPH World Media; Pres. and Publr FATHI CHATILA; Editor-in-Chief Dr RAJAA CHATILA ALAYLI.

Middle East Food: POB 13-5121, Chouran, Beirut 1102 2802; tel. (1) 352413; fax (1) 352419; e-mail content@mefmag.com; internet www.mefmag.com; f. 1985; monthly; publ. by CPH World Media; Pres. and CEO MUHAMMAD RABIH CHATILA; Editor-in-Chief ROULA HAMDAN; circ. 8,650.

Siyassa was Strategia (Politics and Strategy): POB 567, Jounieh; tel. and fax (9) 935096; e-mail naamanculture@lynx.net.lb; internet www.naamanculture.com; f. 1981; 36 a year; Arabic; publ. by Dar Naaman lith-Thaqāfa (Maison Naaman pour la Culture); Editor NAJI NAAMAN.

Takarir Wa Khalfiyat (Background Reports): c/o Dar Assayad, POB 11-1038, Hazmieh, Beirut; tel. (5) 456374; fax (5) 452700; internet www.darassayad.net; f. 1976; monthly; Arabic; political and economic bulletin; publ. by Dar Assayad SAL; Editor-in-Chief HASSAN EL-KHOURY.

Al-Tarik (The Road): Beirut; monthly; Arabic; cultural and theoretical; publ. by the Parti communiste libanais; circ. 5,000.

Travaux et Jours (Works and Days): Rectorat de l'Université Saint-Joseph, rue de Damas, Beirut; tel. (1) 421157; fax (1) 421005; e-mail travauxetjours@usj.edu.lb; internet www.usj.edu.lb; f. 1961; 2 a year; French; political, social and cultural; Editor MOUNIR CHAMOUN.

NEWS AGENCY

National News Agency (NNA): Hamra, Beirut; tel. (1) 754400; fax (1) 745776; e-mail akassas@nna-leb.gov.lb; internet www.nna-leb .gov.lb; state-owned; Dir LAURE SLEIMAN; Chief Editor ALI LAHHAM.

PRESS ASSOCIATION

Lebanese Press Order: POB 3084, ave Saeb Salam, Beirut; tel. (1) 865519; fax (1) 865516; e-mail mail@pressorder.org; internet www .pressorder.org; f. 1911; 18 mems; Pres. MUHAMMAD AL-BAALBAKI; Sec. ABD AL-KARIM EL-KHALIL.

Publishers

Dar al-Adab: POB 4123, Beirut; tel. (1) 795135; fax (1) 861633; e-mail d_aladab@cyberia.net.lb; internet www.adabmag.com; f. 1953; dictionaries, literary and general; Man. AIDA MATRAJI IDRISS; Editor-in-Chief SAMAH IDRISS.

Arab Institute for Research and Publishing (Al-Mouasasah al-Arabiyah Lildirasat Walnashr): POB 11-5460, Beirut; tel. and fax (1) 751438; e-mail info@airpbooks.com; internet www.airpbooks.com; f. 1969; works in Arabic and English; Dir MAHER KAYYALI.

Arab Scientific Publishers BP: POB 13-5574, Immeuble Ein al-Tenah Reem, rue Sakiet al-Janzir, Beirut; tel. (1) 786233; fax (1)

786230; e-mail asp@asp.com.lb; internet www.asp.com.lb; computer science, biological sciences, cookery, travel, politics, fiction, children's; Pres. BASSAM CHEBARO.

Dar Assayad Group (SAL and International): POB 11-1038, Hazmieh, Beirut; tel. (5) 456376; fax (5) 452700; e-mail info@dar-assayad.com; internet www.dar-assayad.com; Dar Assayad SAL f. 1943; Dar Assayad Int. f. 1983 and provides publishing, advertising and distribution services; publishes in Arabic *Al-Anwar* (daily), *Assayad* (weekly), *Achabaka* (weekly), *Background Reports*, *Arab Defense Journal* (monthly), *Fairuz* (international monthly edition), *Al-Idari* (monthly), *Al Computer, Communications and Electronics* (monthly), *Al-Fares* (monthly); also publishes monthly background reports; has offices and correspondents in Arab countries and most parts of the world; Chair. ISSAM FREIHA; CEO BASSAM FREIHA; Man. Dir ELHAM FREIHA.

CPH World Media SARL: POB 13-5121, Chouran, Beirut 1102 2802; tel. (1) 352413; fax (1) 352419; e-mail marketing@cphworldmedia.com; internet www.cphworldmedia.com; f. 1977 as Chatila Publishing House; adopted present name 2008; magazine publishing, events and research; publishes *Arab Construction World* (monthly), *Arab Water World* (monthly), *MENA Health World* (monthly), *Middle East Food* (monthly); Pres. and Publr FATHI CHATILA; CEO MUHAMMAD RABIH CHATILA.

Edition Française pour le Monde Arabe (EDIFRAMO): POB 113-6140, Immeuble Élissar, rue Bliss, Beirut; tel. (1) 862437; Man. TAHSEEN S. KHAYAT.

Editions Orientales SAL: POB 11-1404, Immeuble Sayegh, rue Sursock, Beirut; tel. (1) 202070; fax (1) 202663; e-mail info@ediori .com.lb; internet www.ediori.com.lb; political and social newspapers and magazines; Pres. and Editor-in-Chief CHARLES ABOU ADAL.

GeoProjects SARL: POB 113-5294, Immeuble Barakat, 13 rue Jeanne d'Arc, Beirut; tel. (1) 344236; fax (1) 342217; e-mail info@geo-publishers.com; internet www.geo-publishers.com; f. 1978; cartographers, researchers, school textbook publrs; Dir-Gen. RIDA ISMAIL.

Dar el-Ilm Lilmalayin: POB 1085, Centre Metco, rue Mar Elias, Beirut 2045 8402; tel. (1) 306666; fax (1) 701657; e-mail info@malayin .com; internet www.malayin.com; f. 1945; dictionaries, encyclopaedias, reference books, textbooks, Islamic cultural books; CEO TAREF OSMAN.

InfoPro SARL: POB 11-4355, Centre Piccadilly, rue Hamra, Beirut; tel. (1) 739777; fax (1) 749090; e-mail infopro@infopro.com.lb; internet www.infopro.com.lb; f. 1997; information-based magazines, incl. *BusinessWeek Al-Arabiya* and *Lebanon Opportunities*, as well as reference books; Pres. RAMZI EL-HAFEZ.

Institute for Palestine Studies, Publishing and Research Organization (IPS): POB 11-7164, rue Anis Nsouli, Verdun, Beirut 1107 2230; tel. (1) 868387; fax (1) 814193; e-mail ipsbrt@palestine-studies.org; internet www.palestine-studies.org; f. 1963; independent non-profit Arab research org., which promotes better understanding of the Palestine problem and the Arab–Israeli conflict; publishes books, reprints, research papers, etc.; Chair. Dr HISHAM NASHABE; Gen. Dir MAHMOUD SOUEID.

The International Documentary Center of Arab Manuscripts: POB 2668, Immeuble Hanna, Ras Beirut, Beirut; e-mail alafaq@cyberia.net.lb; f. 1965; publishes and reproduces ancient and rare Arabic texts; Propr ZOUHAIR BAALBAKI.

Dar al-Kashaf: POB 11-2091, rue Assad Malhamee, Beirut; tel. (1) 249952; e-mail dakashaf4@yahoo.com; f. 1930; publrs of *Al-Kashaf* (Arab Youth Magazine), maps, atlases and business books; printers and distributors; Propr M. A. FATHALLAH.

Dar al-Kitab al-Lubnani: POB 11-8330, Beirut; tel. (1) 735731; fax (1) 351433; e-mail info@daralkitabalmasri.com; internet www .daralkitabalmasri.com; f. 1929; publr of books on Islamic studies, history, sciences and literature; Pres. and Gen. Dir Dr HASSAN EL-ZEIN.

Dar Alf Leila wa Leila: BP 165612, rue Issa Maalouf, Immeuble Dimitri Trad, Achrafieh, Beirut; tel. (1) 200961; fax (1) 338929; e-mail rdl@rdl.com.lb; internet www.rdl.com.lb; publishes *Al-Bayraq* (Arabic, daily), *Al-Hawadeth* (Arabic, weekly), *La Revue du Liban* (French, weekly), *Monday Morning* (English, weekly); Editor-in-Chief MELHEM KARAM.

Librairie du Liban Publishers: POB 11-9232, Beirut; tel. (9) 217944; fax (9) 217734; e-mail info@ldlp.com; internet www.ldlp .com; f. 1944; publr of children's books, dictionaries and reference books; distributor of books in English and French; Man. Dirs HABIB SAYEGH, PIERRE SAYEGH.

Dar al-Maaref Liban SARL: POB 2320, Riad el-Solh, Beirut; tel. (1) 931243; f. 1959; children's books and textbooks in Arabic; Man. Dir Dr FOUAD IBRAHIM; Gen. Man. JOSEPH NACHOU.

Dar al-Machreq SARL: POB 166778, Beirut 1100 2150; tel. (1) 202423; fax (1) 202424; e-mail info@darelmachreq.com; internet www.darelmachreq.com; f. 1848; religion, art, Arabic and Islamic literature, history, languages, science, philosophy, school books, dictionaries and periodicals; Man. Dir SALAH ABOUJAOUDE.

Dar Naamān lith-Thaqāfa (Maison Naaman pour la Culture): POB 567, Jounieh; tel. and fax (9) 935096; e-mail info@najinaaman .org; internet www.naamanculture.com; f. 1979; publishes *Mawsou'atul 'Alamil 'Arabiyyil Mu'asser* (Encyclopaedia of the Contemporary Arab World), *Mawsou'atul Waqa'e'il 'Arabiyya* (Encyclopaedia of Arab Events), and *Qitāboul A'lamil A'rabi* ; Propr NAJI NAAMAN; Exec. Man. MARCELLE AL-ASHKAR.

Editions Dar an-Nahar SAL: BP 11-226, Immeuble an-Nahar, rue Banque du Liban, Hamra, Beirut; tel. (1) 747620; fax (1) 747623; e-mail darannahar@darannahar.com; internet www.darannahar .com; f. 1967; pan-Arab publishing house; Pres. GHASSAN TUÉNI; Dir JANA TAMER.

Naufal Group SARL: POB 11-2161, Immeuble Naufal, rue Sourati, Beirut; tel. (1) 354898; fax (1) 354394; e-mail naufalgroup@terra.net .lb; f. 1970; encyclopaedias, fiction, children's books, history, law and literature; subsidiary cos: Macdonald Middle East Sarl, Les Editions Arabes; Man. Dir TONY NAUFAL.

Publitec Publications: POB 16-6142, Beirut; tel. (1) 495401; fax (1) 493330; e-mail info@whoswhointhearabworld.info; f. 1965; publishes *Who's Who in Lebanon* and *Who's Who in the Arab World* (both bi-annual); Pres. CHARLES GEDEON; Man. KRIKOR AYVAZIAN.

Rihani Printing and Publishing House: 13-5378, Beirut; tel. (1) 838281; fax (1) 868384; f. 1963; Propr ALBERT RIHANI; Man. DAOUD STEPHAN.

Sader Publishers: POB 55530, Immeuble Sader, Dekwaneh, Beirut; tel. (1) 488776; e-mail sader@saderpublishers.com; internet www.saderpublishers.com; f. 1863; legal publr; Chair. JOSEPH SADER.

Samir Éditeur: POB 175132, rue Gouraud Gemmayzé, Sin el-Fil, Beirut; tel. (1) 448181; fax (1) 482541; e-mail samir@samirediteur .com; internet www.samirediteur.com; children's books in Arabic, English and French.

World Book Publishing: POB 11-3176, 282 rue Emile Eddé, Sanayeh, Beirut; tel. (1) 349370; fax (1) 351226; e-mail info@ wbpbooks.com; internet www.wbpbooks.com; f. 1926; literature, education, philosophy, current affairs, self-help, children's books; Chair. M. SAID EL-ZEIN; Man. Dir RAFIK EL-ZEIN.

Broadcasting and Communications

TELECOMMUNICATIONS

OGERO (Organisme de Gestion et d'Exploitation de l'ex Radio Orient): POB 11-1226, Bir Hassan, Beirut 1107 2070; tel. (1) 840000; fax (1) 826823; internet www.ogero.gov.lb; f. 1972; 100% state-owned; plans for the incorporation of OGERO and two depts of the Ministry of Telecommunications into a single operator, Liban Télécom, were announced in 2005; however, no progress has since been made; fixed-line operator.

In late 2008 it was announced that the planned privatization of Lebanon's two state-owned mobile telephone networks would be deferred until after the 2009 legislative elections. New management contracts to operate the Mobile Interim Company (MIC) networks until April 2010 were awarded with effect from February 2009 to Orascom Telecom Holding of Egypt (which was to operate the MIC1 network) and Zain Group of Kuwait (MIC2); those contracts have subsequently been extended on an annual basis.

Alfa: Palm Center, rond-point Chevrolet, Beirut; tel. (3) 391111; fax (3) 391109; e-mail customercare@alfamobile.com.lb; internet www .alfa.com.lb; managed by Orascom Telecom Holding (Egypt); operates the state-owned MIC1 mobile telephone network under licence; Chair. and CEO MARWAN HAYEK.

touch: POB 17-5051, Immeuble MTC Touch, ave Charles Helou, Beirut; tel. (3) 792000; e-mail info@mtc.com.lb; internet www.touch .com.lb; f. 2004 as MTC Touch; present name adopted 2012; managed by Zain Group (fmrly Mobile Telecommunications Co—Kuwait); operates the state-owned MIC2 mobile telephone network under licence; Gen. Man. CLAUDE BASSIL.

Regulatory Authority

Telecommunications Regulatory Authority (TRA): Marfaa Bldg 200, 2nd Floor, Beirut Central District, Beirut; tel. (1) 964300; fax (1) 964341; e-mail info@tra.gov.lb; internet www.tra .gov.lb; f. 2007; Chair. and CEO Dr IMAD HOBALLAH.

BROADCASTING

Radio

Radio Liban: rue Emile Edée, Sanayeh, Hamra, Beirut; tel. (1) 756185; fax (1) 347489; internet www.96-2.com; run by the Ministry of Information in conjunction with Radio France International;

f. 1937; Arabic programmes broadcast on 98.1 FM and 98.5 FM; scheduled for privatization; Dir-Gen. FOUAD KABALAN HAMDAN; Dir of Programmes MICHÈLE DE FREIGE.

The Home Service broadcasts in Arabic on short wave, and the Foreign Service broadcasts in Portuguese, Armenian, Arabic, Spanish, French and English.

Television

Lebanese Broadcasting Corpn (LBC) Sat Ltd: POB 111, Zouk, Beirut 165853; tel. (9) 850850; fax (9) 850916; e-mail lbcsat@lbcsat .com.lb; internet www.lbcgroup.tv; f. 1985 as Lebanese Broadcasting Corpn Int. SAL; name changed 1996; operates satellite channel on Arabsat 2C, Arabsat 3A and Nilesat 102; programmes in Arabic, French and English; broadcasts to Lebanon, the Middle East, Europe, the USA and Australia; Chair. Sheikh PIERRE EL-DAHER.

Future Television (Al-Mustaqbal): POB 13-6052, White House, rue Spears, Sanayeh, Beirut; tel. (1) 355355; fax (1) 753434; e-mail future@future.com.lb; internet www.future.com.lb; f. 1993; privately owned; commercial; Gen. Man. NADIM AL-MONLA.

Al-Manar (Lighthouse): Bir Hassan, Beirut; tel. (1) 540440; fax (1) 553138; e-mail info@manartv.com.lb; internet www.almanar.com .lb; f. 1991; television station owned by Lebanese Communication Group; broadcasts to Arab and Muslim audiences world-wide; operates satellite channel since May 2000; partially controlled by Hezbollah; Chair. of Bd ABDALLAH KASSIR.

Murr Television: Naccache, Beirut; internet www.mtv.com.lb; f. 1991; closed down in 2002 for contravening electoral laws; relaunched April 2009; privately owned; CEO MICHEL EL-MURR.

Finance

(cap. = capital; dep. = deposits; res = reserves; m. = million;
br(s) = branch(es); amounts in Lebanese pounds)

BANKING

Beirut was, for many years, the leading financial and commercial centre in the Middle East, but this role was destroyed by the civil conflict during 1975–90. To restore the city as a regional focus for investment banking has been a key element of the reconstruction plans of successive governments.

Central Bank

Banque du Liban: POB 11-5544, rue Masraf Loubnane, Beirut; tel. (1) 750000; fax (1) 747600; e-mail bdlfx@bdl.gov.lb; internet www.bdl .gov.lb; f. 1964 as successor in Lebanon to the Banque de Syrie et du Liban; cap. and res 3,342,331m., dep. 63,932,268m. (Dec. 2009); Gov. RIAD T. SALAMEH; 9 brs.

Principal Commercial Banks

Bank Audi SAL—Audi Saradar Group: POB 11-2560, Riad el-Solh, Beirut 1107 2808; tel. (1) 994000; fax (1) 990555; e-mail contactus@banqueaudi.com; internet www.banqueaudi.com; f. 1962 as Bank Audi; acquired Orient Credit Bank 1997 and Banque Nasr 1998; absorbed into Audi Saradar Group in 2004; cap. 455,440m., res 2,083,782m., dep. 38,066,066m. (Dec. 2011); Chair. and Gen. Man. RAYMOND W. AUDI; CEO SAMIR HANNA; 80 brs in Lebanon, 12 brs in Jordan.

Bank of Beirut SAL: POB 11-7354, Bank of Beirut SAL Bldg, Foch St, Beirut Central District, Beirut; tel. (1) 983999; fax (1) 972972; e-mail contactus@bankofbeirut.com; internet www.bankofbeirut .com.lb; f. 1973; acquired Transorient Bank 1999, Beirut Riyad Bank 2002; cap. 603,500m., res 491,519m., dep. 9,443,966m. (Dec. 2010); Chair. and Gen. Man. SALIM G. SFEIR; 46 brs.

BankMed SAL: POB 11-0348, Centre Groupe Méditerranée, 482 rue Clémenceau, Beirut 2022 9302; tel. (1) 373937; fax (1) 362706; internet www.bankmed.com.lb; f. 1944 as Banque Naaman et Soussou; name changed to Eastern Commercial Bank 1955, Banque de la Méditerranée SAL 1970 and as above 2006; acquired Allied Bank SAL in 2006; cap. 680,750m., res 478,488m., dep. 14,280,785m. (Dec. 2010); Chair. and Gen. Man. MUHAMMAD HARIRI; 51 brs.

Banque Bemo SAL: POB 16-6353, Immeuble Bemo, place Sassine, ave Elias Sarkis, Achrafieh, Beirut 1100 2120; tel. (1) 200505; fax (1) 217860; e-mail bemosal@dm.net.lb; internet www.bemobank.com; f. 1964 as Future Bank SAL; name changed to BEMO (Banque Européenne pour le Moyen-Orient) SAL 1994 and as above 2006; cap. 46,150m., res 59,815m., dep. 1,578,742m. (Dec. 2010); Chair. and Gen. Man. RIAD BECHARA OBEGI; Man. Dir and Gen. Man. SAMIH H. SAADEH; 9 brs in Lebanon, 1 br. in Cyprus.

Banque Libano-Française SAL: POB 11-0808, Tour Liberty, 5 rue de Rome, Beirut 1107 2804; tel. and fax (1) 791332; e-mail info@eblf .com; internet www.eblf.com; f. 1967; cap. 586,828m., res 392,458m., dep. 13,616,363m. (Dec. 2011); Chair. FARID RAPHAËL; 47 brs.

LEBANON

Banque Misr-Liban SAL: rue Riad el-Solh, Beirut 2011 9301; tel. (1) 986666; fax (1) 964296; e-mail mail@bml.com.lb; internet www.bml.com.lb; f. 1929 as Banque Misr Syrie Liban; name changed as above 1958; cap. 100,000m., res 29,425m., dep. 1,279,432m. (Dec. 2011); Chair. MUHAMMAD KAMAL EL-DIN BARAKAT; Exec. Gen. Man. HADI NAFFI; 14 brs.

BBAC (Bank of Beirut and the Arab Countries) SAL: POB 11-1536, Immeuble de la Banque, 250 rue Clémenceau, Riad el-Solh, Beirut 1107 2080; tel. (1) 360460; fax (1) 365200; e-mail contactus@bbac.com.lb; internet www.bbacbank.com; f. 1956; cap. 147,375m., res 192,566m., dep. 5,625,310m. (Dec. 2010); Chair. and Gen. Man. GHASSAN T. ASSAF; 37 domestic brs and 1 foreign rep. office.

BLC Bank SAL: POB 11-1126, BLC Bldg, Adlieh Intersection, Beirut 2064 5809; tel. and fax (1) 429000; e-mail info@blcbank.com; internet www.blcbank.com; f. 1950; 74.8% owned by Fransabank SAL; cap. 152,700m., res 149,087m., dep. 3,971,891m. (Dec. 2010); Chair. and Gen. Man. MAURICE SEHNAOUI; 35 brs.

BLOM Bank SAL: POB 11-1912, Immeuble BLOM Bank, rue Rachid Karameh, Verdun, Beirut 1107 2807; tel. (1) 743300; fax (1) 738946; e-mail blommail@blom.com.lb; internet www.blom.com.lb; f. 1951 as Banque du Liban et d'Outre-Mer; name changed as above 2000; cap. 282,000m., res 1,545,471m., dep. 30,933,706m. (Dec. 2011); Chair. and Gen. Man. SAAD AZHARI; 62 domestic brs and 11 foreign brs.

Byblos Bank SAL: POB 11-5605, ave Elias Sarkis, Achrafieh, Beirut 1107 2811; tel. (1) 335200; fax (1) 339436; e-mail byblosbk@byblosbank.com.lb; internet www.byblosbank.com; f. 1959; merged with Banque Beyrouth pour le Commerce SAL 1997; acquired Byblos Bank Europe SA 1998, Wedge Bank Middle East SAL 2001 and ABN AMRO Bank Lebanon 2002; cap. 689,113m., res 1,304,378m., dep. 20,713,778m. (Dec. 2011); Chair. and Gen. Man. Dr FRANÇOIS S. BASSIL; 78 brs in Lebanon, 23 brs abroad.

Creditbank SAL: POB 16-5795, Immeuble Crédit Bancaire SAL, 680 blvd Bachir Gemayel, Achrafieh, Beirut 1100 2822; tel. (1) 501600; fax (1) 485245; e-mail info@creditbank.com.lb; internet www.creditbank.com.lb; f. 1981 as Crédit Bancaire SAL; name changed as above following merger with Crédit Lyonnais Liban SAL 2002; cap. 55,526m., res 99,477m., dep. 1,834,873m. (Dec. 2010); Chair. and Gen. Man. TAREK JOSEPH KHALIFÉ; 15 brs.

Crédit Libanais SAL: POB 16-6729, Centre Sofil, 5e étage, ave Charles Malek, Beirut 1100 2811; tel. (1) 200028; fax (1) 325713; e-mail info@creditlibanais.com.lb; internet www.creditlibanais.com.lb; f. 1961; cap. 250,000m., res 352,920m., dep. 8,564,329m. (Dec. 2010); Chair. and Gen. Man. Dr JOSEPH M. TORBEY; 57 brs in Lebanon, 2 brs abroad.

Fenicia Bank SAL: POB 113-6248, Immeuble Fenicia Bank, rue Foch, Beirut Central District, Beirut 1103 2110; tel. (1) 957800; e-mail info@feniciabank.com; internet www.bkawbank.com; f. 1959; as Bank of Kuwait and the Arab World SAL; name changed as above 2010; 74% owned by Achour Group, 15% by Maacaron Group, 10% by Merhi Group and 1% by Dr Cheaib; cap. 100,000m., res 17,258m., dep. 1,554,368m. (Dec. 2010); Chair. and Gen. Man. ABD AL-RAZZAK ACHOUR; 14 brs in Lebanon.

First National Bank SAL: POB 11-0435, Immeuble 147, rue Allenby, Riad el-Solh, Beirut 2012 6004; tel. (1) 963000; fax (1) 973090; e-mail info@fnb.com.lb; internet www.fnb.com.lb; f. 1996; acquired Société Bancaire du Liban SAL 2002; cap. 137,605m., res 91,951m., dep. 2,922,936m. (Dec. 2009); Chair. RAMI REFAAT EL-NIMER; Gen. Man. ELIAS SALIM BAZ; 21 brs.

Fransabank SAL: POB 11-0393, rue Hamra, Riad el-Solh, Beirut 1107 2803; tel. (1) 745761; fax (1) 354572; e-mail fsb@fransabank.com; internet www.fransabank.com; f. 1921; acquired Banque Tohmé SAL 1993, Universal Bank SAL 1999, United Bank of Saudi and Lebanon SAL 2001 and Banque de la Beka'a SAL 2003; Banque de la Beka'a was subsequently sold to Bank of Sharjah Ltd (United Arab Emirates) in July 2007; cap. 438,500m., res 778,709m., dep. 15,612,755m. (Dec. 2010); Chair. ADNAN KASSAR; 63 brs.

IBL Bank SAL: POB 11-5292, Immeuble Ittihadiah, ave Charles Malek, Beirut 1107 2190; tel. (1) 200350; fax (1) 204505; e-mail info@ibl.com.lb; internet www.ibl.com.lb; f. 1961 as Intercontinental Bank of Lebanon SAL; cap. 151,657m., res 54,933m., dep. 4,456,678m. (Dec. 2010); Chair. and Gen. Man. SALIM Y. HABIB; 17 brs.

Jammal Trust Bank SAL: POB 11-5640, Immeuble Jammal, rue Verdun, Beirut; tel. (1) 781999; fax (1) 800361; e-mail services@jammalbank.com.lb; internet www.jammalbank.com.lb/home.html; f. 1963 as Investment Bank SAL; cap. 58,000m., res 22,869m., dep. 743,164m. (Dec. 2010); Chair. and Gen. Man. ANWAR A. AL-JAMMAL; 22 brs in Lebanon, 3 rep. offices abroad.

Lebanese Swiss Bank SAL: POB 11-9552, Immeuble Hoss, 6e étage, rue Emile Eddé, place Hamra, Ras Beirut, Beirut; tel. (1) 354501; fax (1) 346242; e-mail lbs@t-net.net.lb; internet www.lebaneseswissbank.com; f. 1962; cap. 70,000m., res 48,382m., dep. 1,265,653m. (Dec. 2010); Chair. and Gen. Man. Dr TANAL SABBAH; 14 brs.

Lebanon and Gulf Bank SAL: POB 11-3360, 124 Allenby St, Beirut Central District, Beirut; tel. (1) 965000; fax (1) 965199; e-mail info@lgb.com.lb; internet www.lgb.com.lb; f. 1963 as Banque de Crédit Agricole; name changed as above 1980; cap. 106,000m., res 86,350m., dep. 2,526,227m. (Dec. 2010); Chair. and Gen. Man. ABD AL-HAFIZ MAHMOUD ITANI; 13 domestic brs, 1 foreign br.

MEAB SAL: POB 14-5958, Immeuble Hejeij, ave Adnan al-Hakim, Beirut 1105 2080; tel. (1) 826740; fax (1) 841190; e-mail meab@meabank.com; internet www.meabank.com; f. 1991 as Middle East and Africa Bank SAL; name changed as above 2003; cap. 41,000m., res 26,617m., dep. 1,144,214m. (Dec. 2010); Chair. and Gen. Man. KASSEM HEJEIJ; 6 brs.

Société Nouvelle de la Banque de Syrie et du Liban SAL (SNBSL): POB 11-957, rue Riad el-Solh, Beirut; tel. (1) 980080; fax (1) 980991; e-mail info@bsl.com.lb; internet www.bsl.com.lb; f. 1963; cap. 46,920m., res 64,676m., dep. 1,084,953m. (Dec. 2010); Chair. and Man. Dir RAMSAY A. EL-KHOURI; Gen. Man. SÉLIM STÉPHAN; 17 brs.

Syrian Lebanese Commercial Bank SAL: SLCB Bldg, Makdessi St, Beirut; tel. (1) 741666; fax (1) 736629; e-mail hamra@slcbk.com; internet www.slcb.com.lb; f. 1974; cap. 132,000m., res 29,497m., dep. 137,097m. (Dec. 2010); Chair. ANTOINE FRANJIEH; 3 brs in Lebanon.

Development Bank

Audi Saradar Investment Bank SAL: POB 16-5110, Bank Audi Plaza, Omar al-Daouk St, Beirut; tel. (1) 994000; fax (1) 999406; e-mail contactus@asib.com; internet www.asib.com; f. 1974 as Investment and Finance Bank; name changed to Audi Investment Bank SAL 1996 and as above 2004; medium- and long-term loans, 100% from Lebanese sources; owned by Bank Audi SAL—Audi Saradar Group; cap. 25,075m., res 164,154m., dep. 763,983m. (Dec. 2010); Chair. and Gen. Man. Dr MARWAN M. GHANDOUR; Gen. Man. RAMZI N. SALIBA.

Supervisory Body

Banking Control Commission of Lebanon: POB 11-5544, rue Masraf Loubnane, Beirut; tel. (1) 350167; fax (1) 750040; internet www.bccl.gov.lb; f. 1967; Chair. OSAMA MEKDASHI.

Banking Association

Association of Banks in Lebanon: POB 976, Gouraud St, Saifi, Beirut; tel. (1) 970500; e-mail abl@abl.org.lb; internet www.abl.org.lb; f. 1959; serves and promotes the interests of the banking community in Lebanon; mems: 64 banks and 7 foreign rep. offices; Chair. JOSEPH TORBEY.

STOCK EXCHANGE

Beirut Stock Exchange (BSE): POB 11-3552, Immeuble Azareih, 4e étage, Bloc O1, Beirut; tel. (1) 993555; fax (1) 993444; e-mail bse@bse.com.lb; internet www.bse.com.lb; f. 1920; recommended trading in Jan. 1996; 10 cttee mems; Vice-Chair. GHALEB MAHMASSANI.

INSURANCE

About 80 insurance companies were registered in Lebanon in the late 1990s, although fewer than one-half of these were operational. An insurance law enacted in 1999 increased the required capital base for insurance firms and provided tax incentives for mergers within the sector.

Allianz SNA SAL: POB 16-6528, Immeuble Allianz SNA, Hazmieh, Beirut 1100 2130; tel. (1) 956600; fax (1) 956624; e-mail info@allianzsna.com; internet www.allianzsna.com; f. 1963 as Société Nationale d'Assurances SAL; renamed as above 2008; part of Allianz Group; cap. 13,264m. (2007); Chair. ANTOINE WAKIM; CEO XAVIER DENYS.

Arabia Insurance Co SAL: POB 11-2172, Arabia House, rue de Phénicie, Beirut; tel. (1) 363610; fax (1) 365139; e-mail arabia@arabia-ins.com.lb; internet www.arabiainsurance.com; f. 1944; cap. 51,000m.; Chair. WAHBÉ A. TAMARI; CEO FADY SHAMMAS.

Bankers Assurance SAL: POB 11-4293, 4th Floor, Immeuble Asseily, rue El Mir Bechir, Riad el-Solh Sq., Beirut; tel. (1) 962700; fax (1) 984004; e-mail mail@bankers-assurance.com; internet www.bankers-assurance.com; f. 1972; Chair. SABA NADER; Gen. Man. EUGÈNE S. NADER.

Commercial Insurance Co (Lebanon) SAL: POB 11-4351, Centre Starco, North Block, 9th Floor, Beirut; tel. (1) 373070; fax (1) 373071; e-mail comins@commercialinsurance.com.lb; internet www.commercialinsurance.com.lb; f. 1962; cap. 6,000m. (March 2006); Chair. MAX R. ZACCAR; 2 brs.

Compagnie Libanaise d'Assurances SAL: POB 3685, rue Riad el-Solh, Beirut; tel. (1) 868988; e-mail lebanese@sodetel.net.lb; internet www.lebaneseinsurance.com; f. 1951; cap. 22,500m.; Chair. PEDRO ABOUJAOUDÉ; Gen. Man. JIHAD SAKR.

Al-Ittihad al-Watani: POB 11-1270, Jisr al-Wati, Immeuble Al-Ittihad al-Watani, Beirut; tel. (1) 426480; fax (1) 426486; e-mail webmaster@alittihadalwatani.com.lb; internet www.alittihadalwatani.com.lb; f. 1947; cap. 20.6m. (2005); Chair. and Gen. Man. TANNOUS FEGHALI.

Libano-Suisse Insurance Co SAL: POB 11-3821, Immeuble Commerce and Finance, Beirut 1107 2150; tel. (1) 374900; fax (1) 368724; e-mail libano-suisse@libano-suisse.com; internet www.libano-suisse.com; f. 1959; Chair. MICHEL PIERRE PHARAON; Gen. Man. LUCIEN LETAYEF, Jr.

Al-Mashrek Insurance and Reinsurance SAL: POB 16-6154, Immeuble Al-Mashrek, Antélias Main Rd, Rabieh, Beirut 1100 2100; tel. (4) 408666; fax (4) 417688; e-mail almashrek@almashrek.com.lb; internet www.almashrek.com.lb; f. 1962; Chair. and CEO ABRAHAM MATOSSIAN.

'La Phénicienne' SAL: POB 11-5652, Immeuble Hanna Haddad, rue Amine Gemayel, Sioufi, Beirut; tel. (1) 425484; fax (1) 424532; e-mail phenicienne@sodetel.net.lb; f. 1964; cap. 3,167m.; Chair. and Gen. Man. CAROLE FÉGHALI CHAMOUN.

Trade and Industry

DEVELOPMENT ORGANIZATIONS

Council for Development and Reconstruction (CDR): POB 116-5351, Tallet el-Serail, Beirut; tel. (1) 980096; fax (1) 981252; e-mail general@cdr.gov.lb; internet www.cdr.gov.lb; f. 1977; an autonomous public institution reporting to the Cabinet, the CDR is charged with the co-ordination, planning and execution of Lebanon's public reconstruction programme; it plays a major role in attracting foreign funds; Pres. NABIL ADNAN EL-JISR.

Investment Development Authority of Lebanon (IDAL): POB 113-7251, Azarieh Tower, 4th Floor, Emir Bechir St, Riad el-Solh, Beirut; tel. (1) 983306; fax (1) 983302; e-mail invest@idal.com.lb; internet www.idal.com.lb; f. 1994; state-owned; Chair. and Gen. Man. NABIL ITANI.

Société Libanaise pour le Développement et la Reconstruction de Beyrouth (Solidere): POB 11-9493, 149 rue Saad Zaghoul, Beirut 2012-7305; tel. (1) 980650; fax (1) 980662; e-mail solidere@solidere.com.lb; internet www.solidere.com.lb; f. 1994; real estate co responsible for reconstruction of Beirut Central District after the civil war; Chair. NASSER CHAMMAA; Gen. Man. MOUNIR DOUAIDY.

CHAMBERS OF COMMERCE AND INDUSTRY

Federation of the Chambers of Commerce, Industry and Agriculture in Lebanon: POB 11-1801, Immeuble CCIAB, rue Justinien, Sanayeh, Beirut; tel. (1) 744702; fax (1) 349614; e-mail fccial@cci-fed.org.lb; internet www.cci-fed.org.lb; f. 1996; Pres. MUHAMMAD CHOUCAIR.

Chamber of Commerce, Industry and Agriculture of Beirut and Mount Lebanon: POB 11-1801, 1 rue Justinian, Sanayeh, Beirut; tel. (1) 353390; fax (1) 353395; e-mail information@ccib.org.lb; internet www.ccib.org.lb; f. 1898; 16,000 mems; Pres. MUHAMMAD CHOUCAIR.

Chamber of Commerce, Industry and Agriculture in Sidon and South Lebanon: POB 41, rue Maarouf Saad, Sidon; tel. (7) 720123; fax (7) 722986; e-mail chamber@ccias.org.lb; internet www.ccias.org.lb; f. 1933; Pres. MUHAMMAD SALEH.

Chamber of Commerce, Industry and Agriculture of Tripoli and North Lebanon: POB 47, rue Bechara Khoury, Tripoli; tel. (6) 627162; fax (6) 442042; e-mail abdallahg@cciat.org.lb; internet www.cciat.org.lb; Chair. ABDALLAH GHANDOUR.

Chamber of Commerce, Industry and Agriculture of Zahleh and Beqa'a: POB 100, Zahleh; tel. (8) 802602; fax (8) 800050; e-mail info@cciaz.org.lb; internet www.cciaz.org.lb; f. 1939; 2,500 mems; Pres. EDMOND JREISSATI.

EMPLOYERS' ASSOCIATION

Association of Lebanese Industrialists: POB 11-1520, Chamber of Commerce and Industry Bldg, 5e étage, rue Justinien, Sanayeh, Beirut; tel. (1) 350280; fax (1) 351167; e-mail ali@ali.org.lb; internet www.ali.org.lb; Pres. FADY ABBOUD; Gen. Man. SAAD S. OUEINI.

UTILITIES

Electricity

Electricité du Liban (EDL): POB 131, Immeuble de l'Electricité du Liban, 22 rue du Fleuve, Beirut; tel. (1) 442720; fax (1) 443828; e-mail info@edl.gov.lb; internet www.edl.gov.lb; f. 1954; state-owned; Chair. and Dir-Gen. KAMAL F. HAYEK.

Water

Legislation introduced in 2000 allowed for the merging of 21 water authorities into four new regional establishments for water exploitation—Beirut and the Mount of Lebanon; North Lebanon; South Lebanon; and the Beqa'a. Under the reorganization the new authorities were to operate under the supervision of the Ministry of Energy and Water.

The Water Establishment of Beirut and the Mount of Lebanon: Beirut; internet www.ebml.gov.lb; f. 2000.

The Water Establishment of North Lebanon: Tripoli; f. 2000; Chair. JAMAL KRAYYEM.

The Water Establishment of the Beqa'a: Zahleh; f. 2000; Gen. Dir JAMAL KRAYEM.

The Water Establishment of South Lebanon: Sidon; f. 2000; Chair. and Dir-Gen. Eng. AHMAD HASSAN NIZAM.

Litani River Authority: rue Bechara el-Khoury, Beirut; tel. (1) 666662; fax (1) 660476; e-mail litani@litani.gov.lb; internet www.litani.gov.lb; f. 1954; responsible for water resources management, irrigation, and the devt of dams and hydroelectric facilities.

TRADE UNION FEDERATION

Confédération Générale des Travailleurs du Liban (CGTL): POB 4381, Beirut; f. 1958; 300,000 mems; only national labour centre in Lebanon and sole rep. of working classes; comprises 18 affiliated feds incl. all 150 unions in Lebanon; Pres. GHASSAN GHOSN.

Transport

RAILWAYS

Office des Chemins de Fer et des Transports en Commun (OCFTC): POB 11-109, Gare St Michel, Nahr, Beirut; tel. (1) 587211; fax (1) 447007; since 1961 all railways in Lebanon have been state-owned; the original network of some 412 km is no longer functioning; however, in 2004 work began on a project to reconstruct a section of the railway network between Tripoli and the Syrian border; Dir-Gen. and Pres. RADWAN BOU NASSER EL-DIN.

ROADS

In 2005 Lebanon had an estimated 6,970 km of roads, of which some 170 km were motorways and 6,800 km were other roads. The two international motorways are the north–south coastal road and the road connecting Beirut with Damascus in Syria. Among the major roads are those crossing the Beqa'a and continuing south to Bent-Jbail and the Shtaura–Ba'albek road. It was reported that up to 80% of Lebanon's major roads, and almost all of its bridges, were destroyed as a result of the Israeli military offensive in mid-2006.

SHIPPING

In the 1990s a two-phase programme to rehabilitate and expand the port of Beirut commenced, involving the construction of an industrial free zone, a fifth basin and a major container terminal, at an estimated cost of US $1,000m.; the container terminal became operational in February 2005. The first phase of a further extension to the container terminal began in 2009 and was expected be completed in 2012. Tripoli, the northern Mediterranean terminus of the oil pipeline from Iraq, is also a busy port, with good equipment and facilities. Jounieh, north of Beirut, is Lebanon's third most important port. A new deep-water sea port was to be constructed south of Sidon. The reconstructed port of al-Naqoura, in what was then the 'security zone' along the border with Israel, was inaugurated in June 1987. Several ports were bombed by Israeli forces during the conflict of mid-2006.

At 31 December 2012 Lebanon's flag registered fleet totalled 52 vessels, with an aggregate displacement of 151,817 grt, of which two were bulk carriers and 17 were general cargo ships.

Port Authorities

Gestion et Exploitation du Port de Beyrouth: POB 1490, Beirut; tel. (1) 580211; fax (1) 585835; e-mail gepb@portdebeyrouth.com; internet www.portdebeyrouth.com; Pres., Dir-Gen. and Man. Dir HASSAN KAMEL KRAYTEM; Harbour Master MAROUN KHOURY.

Service d'Exploitation du Port de Tripoli: rond point Tripoli, rue Mina, Tripoli; tel. (6) 600413; fax (6) 220180; e-mail tport@terra.net.lb; f. 1959; Harbour Master MARWAN BAROUDI.

Principal Shipping Companies

Ademar Shipping Lines: POB 175-231, rue Shafaka, al-Medawar, Beirut; tel. and fax (1) 444100; fax (1) 444101; e-mail ademar@ademarlb.com; internet www.ademarlb.com; f. 1992.

Amin Kawar & Sons (Jordan): POB 11-4230, Beirut; tel. (1) 352525; fax (1) 353802; e-mail amkawar@travelkawar.com; internet www .kawar.com; f. 1963; Chair. TAWFIQ AMIN KAWAR; CEO RUDAIN KAWAR; Pres. KARIM KAWAR.

Beirut Cargo Center: Kurban Bldg, Corniche al-Nahr, Beirut; tel. (1) 585582; fax (1) 585580; e-mail bcc@bcc.com.lb; internet www.bcc .com.lb; f. 1993; air, sea and land freight forwarder; CEO JOSEPH HARB.

Consolidated Bulk Inc (CBI): POB 70-152, Centre St Elie, blk A, 6e étage, Antélias, Beirut; tel. (4) 410724; fax (4) 402842; e-mail info@ bulkgroup.com; internet www.bulkgroup.com; f. 1993; Gen. Man. SAMI P. ZACCA.

Continental Shipping Agencies SARL: POB 17-5039, Immeuble Medawar, 5e étage, rue Saifi-Pasteur, Beirut; tel. (1) 567130; fax (1) 567132; e-mail info@csa-continental.com; internet www .csa-continental.com; f. 1991; member of The Lebanese Shipping Agents Syndicates and The Lebanese Shipping Association.

O. D. Debbas & Sons: POB 3, blvd Corniche du Fleuve, Achrafieh, Beirut; tel. (1) 585253; fax (1) 587135; e-mail oddebbas@oddebbas .com; internet www.oddebbas.com; f. 1892; Man. Dir OIDIH ELIE DEBBAS.

Freight Leader SARL: POB 175530, Immeuble Medawar, 5th Floor, rue Pasteur, Saifi, Beirut; tel. (1) 581870; fax (1) 564387; e-mail info@freightleader.com; internet www.freightleader.com; f. 2001; transportation services and logistics; Exec. Man. MOUSSA SALAMOUN.

Gezairi Ltd (GEZACHART): POB 11-1402, Immeuble Oseili, place Riad Solh, Beirut 2034 0716; tel. (1) 783783; fax (1) 784784; e-mail gezairi@gezairi.com; internet www.gezairi.com; f. 1945; ship management, chartering, brokerage; Pres. and CEO MONA BOUAZZA BAWARSHI.

Gulf Agency Co (Lebanon) Ltd: Immeuble Modern, 7e étage, rue el Arz, Beirut; tel. (1) 446189; fax (1) 446097; e-mail lebanon@gac .com; internet www.gac.com/lebanon; f. 1967; Man. Dir SIMON G. BEJJANI.

Lebanese Navigators Co SARL: POB 175179, Immeuble Pasteur 40, 1e étage, Achrafieh, Beirut; tel. (1) 570571; fax (1) 575730; e-mail navigators@navigators-lb.com; internet www.navigators-lb.com; Man. Dir ANTOINE MOUHAYAR.

Orient Shipping and Trading Co SARL: POB 11-2561, Immeuble Moumneh 72, rue Ain al-Mraisseh 54, Beirut; tel. (1) 364455; fax (1) 365570; e-mail ortship@inco.com.lb; internet orientgroup.net/ lebanon.swf; Dirs ELIE ZAROUBY, EMILE ZAROUBY.

Ets Paul Adem: Centre Moucarri, 6e étage, autostrade Dora, Bourj Hammoud, Beirut; tel. (1) 244610; fax (1) 244612; e-mail padco@inco .com.lb; f. 1971; ship owners, operators, maritime agents, brokers, consultants; Gen. Man. PAUL ADEM.

G. Sahyouni & Co SARL: POB 17-5452, Mar Mikhael, Beirut 1104 2040; tel. (1) 257046; fax (1) 241317; e-mail postmaster@ georgesahyouni.com; internet www.georgesahyouni.com; f. 1989; agents for Baltic Control Lebanon Ltd, SARL, and Lloyds; Man. Dir GEORGE SAHYOUNI.

CIVIL AVIATION

In late 2001 a major expansion project at Beirut International Airport was completed, at an estimated cost of US $600m.; facilities included a new terminal building and two new runways, increasing handling capacity to 6m. passengers a year. In May 2005 the airport was renamed Beirut Rafiq Hariri International Airport in honour of the former Prime Minister who had been killed in February of that year. The airport was targeted by Israeli armed forces in 2006, and was closed to commercial flights during the conflict between Israel and Hezbollah. Following extensive repairs to damaged runways and other infrastructure, the airport reopened to commercial operations in August. In 2008 some 4.1m. passengers used the airport.

MEA (Middle East Airlines, Air Liban SAL): POB 11-206, blvd de l'Aéroport, Beirut 1107 2801; tel. (1) 628888; fax (1) 629260; e-mail mikaouir@mea.com.lb; internet www.mea.com.lb; f. 1945; acquired Lebanese Int. Airways in 1969; regular services throughout Europe, the Middle East, N. and W. Africa, and the Far East; Chair. and Dir-Gen. MUHAMMAD A. EL-HOUT.

Trans-Mediterranean Airways SAL (TMA): POB 30-1001, Beirut Rafiq Hariri International Airport, Beirut; tel. (1) 629210; fax (1) 629219; e-mail cargo@tmacargo.com; internet www.tma.com.lb; f. 1953; cargo services covering Europe, the Middle East, Africa

and the Far East; also provides handling, storage and maintenance services; CEO MAZEN BISSAT.

Tourism

Since the end of the civil conflict in 1990 Lebanon's scenic beauty, sunny climate and historic sites have once again attracted foreign visitors. The Government has chosen to concentrate its efforts on the promotion of cultural as well as conference and exhibition-based tourism, while the country is also being promoted as an 'eco-tourism' destination. Excluding Syrian visitors, the annual total of tourist arrivals increased from 177,503 in 1992 to some 1.28m. in 2004. The Lebanese tourism industry experienced a significant downturn in the aftermath of the conflict between Israel and Hezbollah in 2006. However, there was a marked revival in the sector following the Doha Agreement of May 2008, and by 2010 annual foreign tourist arrivals reached some 2.2m. Receipts from tourism totalled US $8,012m. in that year.

Ministry of Tourism: see section on The Government—Ministries.

Defence

Commander-in-Chief of the Army: Brig.-Gen. JEAN KAHWAJI.

Chief of Staff of Armed Forces: Maj.-Gen. WALID SALMAN.

Commander of the Air Force: Brig.-Gen. GHASSAN CHAHINE.

Commander of the Navy: Col JOSEPH GHADBAN (acting).

Director-General of State Security Forces: Maj.-Gen. GEORGES KARAA.

Defence Budget (2012): £L1,730,000m.

Total armed forces (as assessed at November 2012): 60,000: army 56,600; navy 1,800; air force 1,600.

Paramilitary forces included an est. 20,000 members of the Internal Security Force, attached to the Ministry of the Interior. Compulsory military service was formally abolished in February 2007. Hezbollah's active members numbered some 2,000, as assessed at November 2009.

Following conflict in Lebanon between Hezbollah and Israeli armed forces in July–August 2006, the UN Security Council unanimously adopted Resolution 1701, calling for a full cessation of hostilities, upon which Lebanon was to deploy government forces in southern Lebanon and the presence there of the UN Interim Force in Lebanon (UNIFIL) was to be expanded to a maximum authorized strength of 15,000 troops, while Israel was to commence the parallel withdrawal of all its forces from that region. A formal cease-fire entered into effect on 14 August. At the end of July 2012 there were 11,530 UNIFIL military personnel deployed in Lebanon.

Education

Education is compulsory for a period of nine years between six and 15 years of age. Primary education has been available free of charge in state schools since 1960, but private institutions still provide the main facilities for secondary and university education. Private schools enjoy almost complete autonomy, except for a certain number that receive government financial aid and are supervised by inspectors from the Ministry of Education and Higher Education. In the 2010 budget some £L1,293,000m. was allocated to the Ministry of Education and Higher Education (representing 5.9% of total budgetary expenditure).

Primary education begins at six years of age and lasts for six years, comprising two cycles of three years each. Secondary education, beginning at the age of 13, lasts for up to six years, comprising two cycles of three years each. Technical education is provided mainly at the National School of Arts and Crafts, which offers four-year courses in electronics, mechanics, architectural and industrial drawing, and other subjects. There are also public vocational schools providing courses for lower levels. In 2009/10 enrolment at primary schools included 92% of the relevant age-group, while the comparable rate for secondary schools was 75%. Higher education is provided by at least 14 institutions, including 12 universities, an arts academy and a school of theology. Some 202,345 students were enrolled in higher education institutes in 2009/10.

LESOTHO

Introductory Survey

LOCATION, CLIMATE, LANGUAGE, RELIGION, FLAG, CAPITAL

The Kingdom of Lesotho is a land-locked country, entirely surrounded by South Africa. The climate is generally mild, although cooler in the highlands: lowland temperatures range from a maximum of 32°C (90°F) in summer (October to April) to a minimum of −7°C (20°F) in winter. Rainfall averages about 725 mm (29 ins) per year, mostly falling in summer. The official languages are English and Sesotho; other languages spoken include Zulu and Xhosa. About 90% of the population are Christians. The largest denominations are the Roman Catholic, Lesotho Evangelical and Anglican Churches. The national flag (official proportions 2 by 3) has three horizontal stripes from top to bottom of blue, white and green, with a black traditional Basotho hat in the centre of the white stripe. The capital is Maseru.

CONTEMPORARY POLITICAL HISTORY

Historical Context

Lesotho was formerly Basutoland, which became a separate British colony in 1884 and was administered as one of the High Commission Territories in southern Africa (the others being the protectorates of Bechuanaland, now Botswana, and Swaziland). The British Act of Parliament that established the Union of South Africa in 1910 also provided for the possible inclusion in South Africa of the three High Commission Territories, subject to local consent: the native chiefs opposed requests by successive South African Governments for the transfer of the three territories.

Within Basutoland a revised Constitution, which established the colony's first Legislative Council, was introduced in 1956. A new document, granting limited powers of self-government, was adopted in September 1959. Basutoland's first general election, on the basis of universal adult suffrage, took place on 29 April 1965, and full internal self-government was achieved the following day. Moshoeshoe II, Paramount Chief since 1960, was recognized as King. The Basutoland National Party (BNP), a conservative group supporting limited co-operation with South Africa, narrowly won a majority of the seats in the new Legislative Assembly. The BNP's leader, Chief Leabua Jonathan, was appointed Prime Minister in July 1965. Basutoland became independent, as Lesotho, on 4 October 1966. The new Constitution provided for a bicameral legislature, comprising the 60-seat National Assembly and the 33-member Senate; executive power was vested in the Cabinet, which was presided over by the Prime Minister. The King was designated Head of State.

Domestic Political Affairs

The BNP, restyled the Basotho National Party, remained in power at independence. A general election was held in January 1970, at which the opposition Basotho Congress Party (BCP), a pan-Africanist group led by Dr Ntsu Mokhehle, appeared to have won a majority of seats in the National Assembly. Chief Jonathan declared a state of emergency, suspended the Constitution and arrested several BCP organizers. The election was annulled, and the legislature prorogued. King Moshoeshoe II was placed under house arrest and subsequently exiled, although he returned in December after accepting a government order banning him from participating in politics. The country was thus effectively under the Prime Minister's personal control. An interim National Assembly, comprising the former Senate (mainly chiefs) and 60 members nominated by the Cabinet, was inaugurated in April 1973 and the state of emergency was revoked in July. However, following a failed coup attempt in January 1974 by alleged supporters of the BCP, Chief Jonathan introduced stringent security laws. Mokhehle and other prominent members of the BCP went into exile abroad, and the party split into two factions, internal and external, the latter led by Mokhehle.

Although Lesotho was economically dependent on South Africa, and the Government's official policy during the 1970s was one of 'dialogue' with its neighbour, Chief Jonathan repeatedly criticized the apartheid regime, and supported the then banned African National Congress of South Africa (ANC). In December 1982 South African forces launched a major assault on the homes of ANC members in Maseru, killing more than 40 people. Lesotho's persistent refusal to sign a joint non-aggression pact led South Africa to impound consignments of armaments destined for Lesotho, and the imposition of a blockade on the common border from early 1986.

On 20 January 1986 Chief Jonathan's Government was overthrown in a coup led by Maj.-Gen. Justin Lekhanya, the head of the armed forces. A Military Council, chaired by Lekhanya, was established and executive and legislative powers were to be vested in King Moshoeshoe, assisted by the Military Council and a (mainly civilian) Council of Ministers. In March 1986 the Military Council suspended all formal political activity.

Although the South African Government denied having any part in the coup, the Lekhanya regime proved to be more amenable to South Africa's regional security policy. In March 1986 it was announced that the two countries had reached an informal agreement whereby neither would allow its territory to be used for attacks against the other. Moreover, the Lesotho Government did not join other African states in pressing for international economic sanctions against South Africa. In March 1988 Lesotho and South Africa reached final agreement on the Lesotho Highlands Water Project (LHWP), a major scheme to supply water to South Africa.

In May 1988 Mokhehle was allowed to return to Lesotho after 14 years of exile and by 1990 the two factions of the BCP had apparently reunited under Mokhehle's leadership.

In February 1990 Lekhanya dismissed three members of the Military Council and one member of the Council of Ministers, accusing them of 'insubordination'. When Moshoeshoe refused to approve new appointments to the Military Council, Lekhanya suspended the monarch's executive and legislative powers, which were assumed by the Military Council in March. Moshoeshoe (who remained Head of State) was exiled in the United Kingdom. Lekhanya announced that a general election would take place during 1992; however, party political activity remained outlawed. In June 1990 a National Constituent Assembly (including Lekhanya, members of the Council of Ministers, representatives of banned political parties, traditional chiefs and business leaders) was inaugurated to draft a new constitution. In October Lekhanya invited the King to return from exile. Moshoeshoe responded that his return would be conditional upon the ending of military rule and the establishment of an interim government, pending the readoption of the 1966 Constitution. On 6 November 1990 Lekhanya promulgated an order dethroning the King with immediate effect. Lesotho's 22 principal chiefs elected Moshoeshoe's elder son, Prince David Mohato Bereng Seeiso, as the new King; on 12 November he acceded to the throne, as King Letsie III, having undertaken to remain detached from politics.

On 30 April 1991 Lekhanya was deposed in a coup organized by disaffected army officers. Col (later Maj.-Gen.) Elias Phitsoane Ramaema succeeded Lekhanya as Chairman of the Military Council. Ramaema repealed the ban on party political activity, and by July the National Constituent Assembly had completed the draft Constitution. In May 1992 Lesotho and South Africa agreed to establish diplomatic relations at ambassadorial level. Following talks in the United Kingdom with Ramaema, former King Moshoeshoe returned from exile in July.

The general election was eventually held in March 1993. The BCP secured all 65 seats in the new National Assembly, winning 54% of the votes cast. In April Mokhehle was inaugurated as Prime Minister, and King Letsie swore allegiance to the new Constitution, under the terms of which he remained Head of State with no executive or legislative powers; executive authority was vested in the Cabinet.

Suspension of constitutional government

A mutiny by the Royal Lesotho Defence Force (RLDF) took place in November 1993 following which four senior army officers were reported to have resigned their posts. Skirmishes near Maseru in

January 1994 escalated into more serious fighting between some 600 rebel troops and a 150-strong contingent of forces loyal to the Government, reportedly resulting in the deaths of at least five soldiers and three civilians. Following mediation efforts involving representatives of Botswana, South Africa, Zimbabwe, the Commonwealth (see p. 244), the Organization of African Unity (OAU, now the African Union—AU, see p. 191) and the UN, a truce entered into force, and at the beginning of February the rival factions surrendered their weapons and returned to barracks. In April, however, the Deputy Prime Minister, Selometsi Baholo (who also held the finance portfolio), was killed during an abduction attempt by disaffected troops.

A commission to investigate the armed forces unrest of January and April 1994 began work in July. In that month Mokhehle appointed a commission of inquiry into the dethronement of King Moshoeshoe II. On 17 August Letsie announced that he had dissolved the National Assembly, dismissed the Government and suspended sections of the Constitution, citing 'popular dissatisfaction' with the BCP administration. Although several thousand people gathered outside the royal palace in Maseru in support of the deposed Government, army and police support for Letsie's 'royal coup' was evident, and subsequent clashes between demonstrators and the security forces reportedly resulted in five deaths. A well-known human rights lawyer, Hae Phoofolo, was appointed Chairman of a transitional Council of Ministers, and the Secretary-General of the BNP, Evaristus Retselisitsoe Sekhonyana, was appointed Minister of Foreign Affairs. Phoofolo identified as a priority for his administration the amendment of the Constitution to facilitate the restoration of Moshoeshoe; in the meantime, King Letsie was to act as executive and legislative Head of State.

The suspension of constitutional government was widely condemned outside Lesotho. The Presidents of Botswana, South Africa and Zimbabwe led diplomatic efforts to restore the elected Government, supported by the OAU and the Commonwealth. The USA withdrew financial assistance, and several other countries threatened sanctions. Following negotiations in South Africa, in September 1994 King Letsie and Mokhehle signed an agreement, guaranteed by Botswana, South Africa and Zimbabwe, providing for the restoration of Moshoeshoe II as reigning monarch and for the restitution of the elected organs of government; the commission of inquiry into Moshoeshoe's dethronement was to be abandoned; all those involved in the 'royal coup' were to be immune from prosecution; the political neutrality of the armed forces and public service was to be guaranteed, and consultations were to be undertaken with the aim of broadening the democratic process. Moshoeshoe was restored to the throne on 25 January 1995, undertaking not to interfere in politics. Letsie took the title of Crown Prince.

King Moshoeshoe was killed in a motor accident on 15 January 1996. The College of Chiefs subsequently elected Crown Prince David to succeed his father, and the prince was restored to the throne, resuming the title King Letsie III, on 7 February. Letsie undertook not to involve the monarchy in any aspect of political life.

In June 1997, following a protracted struggle between rival factions for control of the party, Mokhehle resigned from the BCP and formed the Lesotho Congress for Democracy (LCD), to which he transferred executive power. Some 38 members of the National Assembly joined the LCD. In July Molapo Qhobela was elected leader of the BCP. There was further controversy in August, when the Speaker of the National Assembly designated the BCP as the official opposition party. In October members of the Senate (most of whom apparently refused to recognize the legitimacy of Mokhehle's Government) voted to suspend discussion of proposed legislation, pending the King's response to appeals for the dissolution of the National Assembly. At the first annual conference of the LCD, held in January 1998, Mokhehle resigned as leader, and was made Honorary Life President of the party. In February Deputy Prime Minister Bethuel Pakalitha Mosisili was elected to succeed him as party leader. (Mokhehle died in January 1999.)

Elections to an expanded National Assembly took place on 23 May 1998, at which the LCD secured an overwhelming victory, winning 78 of the Assembly's 80 seats; the BNP was the only other party to win representation. The Independent Electoral Commission (IEC) and observers representing the Southern African Development Community (SADC, see p. 434) and the Commonwealth concluded that the polls had been generally free and fair. Mosisili was elected Prime Minister by

the National Assembly in late May, and a new Government was appointed in June.

In August 1998 opposition activists began a mass vigil outside the royal palace to protest against the outcome of the May elections. Tensions escalated as LCD militants blocked access roads to the capital, in a stated attempt to prevent supplies of weapons to the protesters. Following consultations involving the Lesotho Government and the main opposition parties, with mediation by the Government of South Africa, Mosisili announced the establishment of an independent commission, comprising representatives of the SADC 'troika' of Botswana, South Africa and Zimbabwe, to investigate the conduct and results of the May election. The commission was chaired by Pius Langa, the Deputy President of South Africa's Constitutional Court.

SADC intervention

The Langa Commission's report, which was finally released on 17 September 1998, expressed serious concerns at apparent irregularities and discrepancies in the conduct of the May general election, but the Commission was 'unable to state that the invalidity of the elections had been conclusively established'. On 22 September an SADC peace-keeping force, initially comprising 600 South African troops and 200 from Botswana, entered Lesotho. In response to criticism that he had not consulted King Letsie prior to requesting external military assistance, Mosisili stated that the monarch had, by harbouring opposition protesters in the palace grounds, contributed to the instability that had necessitated SADC intervention. (It was subsequently reported that the King had been prevented from making a broadcast to the nation.) Within Lesotho, there was widespread outrage at what was perceived as an effective 'invasion' by South Africa, and the SADC force encountered unexpectedly strong resistance. There was sustained fighting between the intervention force and rebel units of the Lesotho Defence Force (LDF, as the RLDF had been redesignated), while rioting in Maseru and other towns targeted in particular South African interests and caused widespread destruction.

Following meetings with representatives of the SADC 'troika', in early October 1998 it was reported that the LCD and the main opposition parties had agreed in principle that fresh elections should be held within 15–18 months. In the meantime, the IEC was to be restructured, and the electoral system was to be reviewed, with the aim of ensuring wider inclusion in political affairs (many parties felt that the simple majority voting system was incompatible with the nature of Lesotho's political evolution). In mid-October agreement was reached on a transitional structure, designated the Interim Political Authority (IPA), to comprise representatives of 12 political parties, as well as government and parliamentary delegates, to oversee preparations for fresh elections to the National Assembly.

The withdrawal of the SADC intervention force was completed in May 1999. This force was immediately succeeded by a new SADC mission, comprising some 300 military personnel from South Africa, Botswana and (subsequently) Zimbabwe, which remained until May 2000, assisting in the retraining and restructuring of the LDF.

Meanwhile, the 24-member IPA was inaugurated on 9 December 1998. After protracted consultations, it was announced that the number of seats in the National Assembly was to be increased by 50, to 130, effective from the elections scheduled for April 2000, with 80 seats to be allocated on the basis of simple majority in single-member constituencies, and 50 by proportional representation. In the meantime, the Presidents of South Africa, Botswana, Mozambique and Zimbabwe, together with the UN, the OAU and the Commonwealth Secretaries-General, were to act as guarantors to ensure the implementation of the accord. The elections were subsequently postponed due to delays in enacting legislation concerning voter registration and the electoral model.

In April 2000 the establishment of a commission of inquiry to investigate political events during July–November 1998 was announced. The commission, comprising three senior judges and chaired by Nigel Leon, met for the first time in June 2000 and heard evidence from several public figures. However, a number of opposition politicians criticized the commission, expressing doubts as to its impartiality. In August three LDF members were convicted by a court martial of participation in the mutiny of September 1998 and sentenced to a combined 29 years' imprisonment; a further 33 LDF members were convicted in November. The Leon commission of inquiry, which submitted its report to Prime Minister Mosisili in October 2001, rejected demands for a general amnesty to be granted to perpetrators of violence during the period under review, recommending the indictment of a number of opposition politicians and members of the armed forces.

In January 2001 a congress of the LCD re-elected Mosisili as leader of the party, for a five-year term. Deputy Prime Minister Kelebone Maope resigned from the Government in September and broke away from the LCD, together with Shakhane Mokhehle, to form a new opposition party, the Lesotho People's Congress (LPC), to prepare for forthcoming elections. By mid-October a total of 27 deputies had defected from the LCD to join the LPC. Mosisili made new cabinet appointments in October, in an effort to consolidate his position ahead of the elections.

In January 2002 Parliament finally approved amendments to the electoral legislation, providing for the expansion of the National Assembly to 120 members, with 80 to be elected on a constituency basis and 40 selected by proportional representation.

The LCD won a resounding victory at the general election, which took place on 25 May 2002, retaining 77 of the 78 contested constituency seats, with 54.9% of the valid votes cast. The BNP became the second largest legislative party, securing 21 of the 40 seats allocated by proportional representation (known as compensatory seats), with 22.4% of the votes cast; the LPC won one constituency seat and four compensatory seats. Voting in two constituencies was postponed, owing to the deaths of candidates. Of the remaining 15 compensatory seats, the National Independent Party (NIP) secured five, the Basutoland African Congress (BAC) and the BCP both won three, while four smaller parties each took one seat. Mosisili was re-elected Prime Minister by the National Assembly in early June and a new Cabinet was subsequently appointed.

Political realignments and a new ruling party

In late January 2006 Khauhelo Raditapole and Kelebone Maope, the leaders of the BAC and the LPC, respectively, announced that their parties would form an alliance, following appeals by the BCP for reconciliation between political parties. Legislative elections took place on 17 February 2007, at which the LCD retained its parliamentary majority, although the party's total number of seats in the National Assembly was reduced from 77 to 61. The NIP took 21 of the 40 compensatory seats, thus becoming the second largest legislative party, while the All Basotho Convention (ABC) secured 17 constituency seats and the Lesotho Workers' Party (LWP) 10 compensatory seats. The Alliance of Congress Parties and five other parties each secured one compensatory seat. Observers from SADC and the AU declared the elections to have been free and fair. It emerged that an alliance had formed between the LCD and the NIP and that the NIP had fielded candidates from the LCD at the elections, giving the coalition a total of 82 seats in the National Assembly; a similar arrangement was made between the ABC and the LWP, resulting in that alliance securing 27 seats in total. Mosisili was reappointed Prime Minister later that month and in early March a new Cabinet was sworn in.

In April 2009 Mosisili's residence was attacked by 16 gunmen in an apparent assassination attempt. Four of the attackers were reported to have been killed and a number of individuals suspected of involvement in the incident were detained in South Africa; the Prime Minister escaped unharmed. Makotoko Lerotholi, who was suspected of organizing the attack, died of an illness while in custody in South Africa. In the following month it was reported that one of the suspects, Simon Mnguni, had agreed to testify for the prosecution.

In an attempt to resolve the long-standing dispute over the distribution of compensatory seats following the 2007 elections (opposition parties had argued that the allocation of these seats to the LCD-NIP alliance had been unfair), in February 2010 the SADC organ on political, defence and security co-operation requested that a 'road map' be drawn up to address the main points of disagreement among the country's political organizations and to examine the possibility of modifying the Constitution and the legislation governing elections. A further meeting was held by SADC in April 2011 to discuss the issue of allocation of seats. On this occasion an agreement to amend the electoral law was reached between the Government, political parties and the IEC.

Doubts were raised in April 2010 regarding the future viability of Lesotho as an independent nation following, in accordance with the AU's African Peer Review Mechanism, the presentation of a report detailing the dire social and economic conditions within the country. In the following month the People's Charter

Movement (PCM) organized a march through the capital to present to the South African High Commission a document, signed by some 30,000 Basotho, appealing for annexation. The PCM's campaign gained further impetus in June following South Africa's imposition of new border restrictions, denying entry to Basotho without passports.

Opposition threats to boycott the May 2010 local elections—in protest against, *inter alia*, proposed 'affirmative action' laws (which had been criticized for being too heavily weighted in favour of female candidates), constituency boundaries and the unreformed simple majority electoral system still employed in local ballots—led Parliament in April to postpone the vote until 2011. The decision to suspend the elections received cross-party support and was intended to facilitate the parliamentary approval of amendments to the existing legislation regulating local elections. The IEC implemented a restructuring of constituency boundaries in July 2010, although the leader of the ABC, Thomas Thabane, argued that the alterations would benefit the LCD, alleging that the IEC was 'directly working' for the ruling party.

Mosisili effected a cabinet reorganization in October 2010. The ministers responsible for trade, tourism, agriculture and employment—all of whom were believed to be members of an influential faction within the LCD reportedly led by Mothejoa Metsing, the Minister of Communications, Science and Technology—were replaced by close associates of the Prime Minister. Following the reorganization, supporters of the dismissed ministers besieged the LCD's headquarters in protest and accused Monyane Moleleki, the Minister of Natural Resources and alleged leader of a rival wing of the LCD, of pressuring Mosisili to remove Metsing's allies from the Cabinet. The discord within the ruling party was confirmed in November, when Mosisili publicly criticized the 'hatred and divisions' afflicting the LCD. Infighting was also evident within the opposition parties during 2010. The fragile ABC-LWP alliance ended in July due to continued disagreements between the leaders of the respective parties, precipitating a dispute over control of the compensatory seats allocated to the now-defunct coalition after the 2007 elections. Meanwhile, after losing a vote of confidence in December, BNP leader Justin Lekhanya was replaced by his deputy, Thesele Maseribane.

Following continued factional infighting and a series of disagreements with the national executive committee of the LCD, Prime Minister Mosisili left the ruling party in February 2012, but remained Prime Minister. The previous month he had dismissed Metsing, along with two junior members of the Government. Mosisili subsequently announced the formation of a new political party, the Democratic Congress (DC), which swiftly garnered the support of 44 deputies, sufficient to give it a slight majority and move the LCD into opposition. Mosisili, who won a confidence vote in the National Assembly after leaving the LCD, emphasized that the Cabinet would not be reorganized based on new political loyalties, confirming that members of the LCD who refused to defect to the DC would not lose their ministerial portfolios. On 15 March King Letsie dissolved the National Assembly ahead of legislative elections, which were scheduled to take place on 26 May.

Recent developments: the 2012 legislative elections

In legislative elections held on 26 May 2012 the DC secured 39.6% of the votes cast and the largest number of seats in the National Assembly (of which 41 were constituency seats and seven compensatory seats). However, the party's total number of parliamentary seats had declined by 13 since the previous election. The ABC, under the leadership of Thabane, won 25.2% of the votes cast (26 constituency and 4 compensatory seats), while the LCD, under the leadership of Metsing, won 22.0% (12 constituency and 14 compensatory seats). The BNP, the Popular Front for Democracy (PFD) and the NIP secured five, three and two total seats, respectively. Voter turnout was recorded at 50.0%. International observers, including the AU and SADC, declared the election to be free, fair and credible. It was reported that the ABC performed strongly in urban areas, while the DC continued to dominate in rural areas. Despite the DC winning more votes and securing more seats than any other single party, the ABC and LCD formed a coalition government (the first in Lesotho's history) following the DC's failure to win an absolute majority; erstwhile Prime Minister Mosisili accepted defeat after failing to form a coalition of his own. The BNP, PFD and the Marematlou Freedom Party also joined the coalition. On 7 June King Letsie named Thabane as Prime Minister; Thabane also assumed the role of Minister of Defence, Police and National

Security. Later that month Thabane named his new Cabinet, in which Mothetjoa Metsing was appointed Deputy Prime Minister, while Dr Leketekete Victor Ketso (of the LCD) took over the finance portfolio and Tlali Khasu (of the ABC) was named Minister of Mining. Meanwhile, BNP leader Thesele 'Maseribane, who had been at the forefront of anti-government riots following Mosisili's election victory in 1998, was named Minister of Gender, Youth, Sports and Recreation. Soon after forming the coalition Thabane promised to focus attention on poverty, unemployment, education, infrastructure development and health.

In late 2012 the UN World Food Programme announced a feeding programme in Malawi, Zimbabwe and Lesotho after severe droughts had limited food production and increased the price of maize by some 60%. It was reported that the food harvest was the worst for 10 years. The programme was expected to feed around 3.5m. people in the affected countries, and some 200,000 people in rural Lesotho. However, it was estimated that around one-third of Lesotho's population (725,000 people) had been affected by the food crisis.

Foreign Affairs

As exemplified by South Africa's prominent role in the resolution of the 1994 constitutional crisis and by its intervention in the political crisis of September 1998, Lesotho's internal affairs continue to be strongly influenced by South Africa. Long-standing problems of border security and, in particular, the issue of disputed land in South Africa's Free State (formerly Orange Free State) have periodically caused friction between the two countries. Relations between the two countries were strained in August 2000 when Lesotho withdrew its support shortly before the scheduled signing of an agreement with Botswana, Namibia and South Africa on the management of water resources from the Orange river. In September an official at the South African High Commission was killed in Maseru. Representatives of both countries met in Pretoria in November and recommended increased co-operation in areas including education and criminal justice. During a visit to Lesotho by President Thabo Mbeki of South Africa in April 2001, it was agreed to replace an intergovernmental liaison committee that had been established following SADC intervention in 1998 (see above) with a joint binational commission at ministerial level, with the aim of enhancing bilateral relations. Relations between Lesotho and South Africa were further enhanced in May 2002, when their ministers of foreign affairs signed the Joint Bilateral Commission of Co-operation programme, which aimed to raise Lesotho from its current status as a 'least developed country'.

CONSTITUTION AND GOVERNMENT

Lesotho is an hereditary monarchy. Under the terms of the Constitution, which came into effect following the March 1993 election, the King, who is Head of State, has no executive or legislative powers. The College of Chiefs is theoretically empowered, under traditional law, to elect and depose the King by a majority vote. Executive power is vested in the Cabinet, which is headed by the Prime Minister. Legislative power is exercised by the National Assembly, which is elected, at intervals of no more than five years, by universal adult suffrage in the context of a multi-party political system. A system of mixed member proportional representation was introduced at the general election of May 2002, when the National Assembly was expanded to 120 members (80 elected by simple majority in single-member constituencies and 40 selected from party lists). The upper house, the Senate, comprises traditional chiefs and 11 nominated members. Lesotho comprises 10 administrative districts, each with an appointed district co-ordinator.

REGIONAL AND INTERNATIONAL CO-OPERATION

Lesotho is a member of the Common Monetary Area (with Namibia, South Africa and Swaziland), and a member of the Southern African Customs Union (SACU—with Botswana, Namibia, South Africa and Swaziland). Lesotho also belongs to the Southern African Development Community (SADC, see p. 434) and the African Union (see p. 191).

Lesotho became a member of the UN in 1966 and was admitted to the World Trade Organization (WTO, see p. 444) in 1995. Lesotho participates in the Group of 77 (G77, see p. 461) developing countries.

ECONOMIC AFFAIRS

In 2011, according to estimates by the World Bank, Lesotho's gross national income (GNI), measured at average 2009–11 prices, was US $2,679m., equivalent to $1,220 per head (or $2,070 per head on an international purchasing-power parity basis). During 2002–11, it was estimated, the population increased at an average annual rate of 1.0%, while gross domestic product (GDP) per head increased, in real terms, by an average of 3.2% per year. Overall GDP increased, in real terms, at an average annual rate of 4.2% in 2002–11; growth in 2011 was 5.8%.

Agriculture, forestry and fishing contributed 7.8% of GDP in 2011, according to the World Bank. The sector engaged some 38.0% of the labour force in mid-2013, according to FAO estimates. The principal agricultural export is tobacco. The main subsistence crops are maize, potatoes, sorghum and wheat. Lesotho remains a net importer of staple foodstuffs, largely owing to its vulnerability to adverse climatic conditions, especially drought. According to the World Food Programme, less than 10% of land is arable and there is no irrigation. It was reported in late 2011 that the International Fund for Agriculture Development would provide US $10m. to farmers in four of Lesotho's districts in order to help increase agricultural production. Some 15,000 households were expected to benefit from the provision. According to the World Bank, during 2002–11 agricultural GDP declined at an average annual rate of 0.7%; the sector's GDP increased by 10.8% in 2010, but declined by 5.8% in 2011.

Industry (including mining, manufacturing, construction and power) provided 33.7% of GDP in 2011, according to the World Bank. The sector engaged 9.3% of the labour force in 1999. During 2002–11 industrial GDP increased by an average annual rate of 5.1% per year. Industrial GDP increased by 8.3% in 2011.

Mining contributed 6.6% of GDP in 2010, according to the AfDB. Lesotho has reserves of diamonds, which during the late 1970s provided more than 50% of visible export earnings, but large-scale exploitation of these ceased in 1982. The Lets'eng-la-Terae diamond mine reopened in April 2004 and by the time of its official inauguration in November gems with an estimated value of US $28m. had been recovered. Industrial mining at other sites was also envisaged, including a second diamond mine at Liqhobong. Lesotho also possesses deposits of uranium, lead and iron ore, and is believed to have petroleum deposits. According to the AfDB, the GDP of the mining sector declined by an average of 6.7% per year in 2000–08; the GDP of the sector increased by 10.6% in 2010.

Manufacturing contributed 11.7% of GDP in 2011, according to the World Bank. The sector employed 3.5% of the total labour force in 1999. During 2002–11 manufacturing GDP increased by an average of 2.4% per year; it increased by 3.5% in 2011.

According to the AfDB, the construction sector contributed 4.8% of GDP in 2010. The sector engaged 4.8% of the employed labour force in 1999. According to the AfDB, during 2000–08 construction GDP declined by an average of 17.1% per year; the GDP of the sector increased by 5.0% in 2010.

The Lesotho Highlands Water Project (LHWP) provides hydroelectricity sufficient for all Lesotho's needs and for export to South Africa; phases 1A and 1B were inaugurated in 1998 and 2004, respectively. In late September 2005 an agreement was signed for a feasibility study concerning the location of the second phase of the project. The scheme was expected to be completed by about 2030. The R200m. (US $30m.) that Lesotho receives annually in royalties from South Africa for the LHWP represents the country's largest single source of foreign exchange. Prior to the LHWP more than 90% of Lesotho's energy requirements were imported from South Africa. Imports of mineral fuels and lubricants comprised 0.6% of the total value of imports in 2008. In October 2011 it was announced that the country would embark on a large-scale wind and hydroelectric power project—the largest in Africa—in the Maluti mountains, at a cost of some $15,000m. The Lesotho Highlands Power Project (LHPP), 80% of the cost of which was to be financed with loans from China, was expected to generate some 10,000 MW of energy on completion.

The services sector contributed 58.5% of GDP in 2011, according to the World Bank. Only 18.3% of the labour force was employed in the services sector in 1999. During 2002–11 the GDP of the services sector increased at an average annual rate of 1.8%; growth was 4.2% in 2011.

In 2011 Lesotho recorded a visible merchandise trade deficit of US $983.2m., and there was a deficit of $520.1m. on the current account of the balance of payments. In 2008 the principal source of imports 95.2%) was South Africa, which was also the largest market for exports (82.7%). The principal exports in that year were miscellaneous manufactured articles. The principal imports in 2007 were industrial supplies, food and beverages, and machinery and other capital equipment.

In the financial year ending 31 March 2012 there was an estimated budgetary surplus of M944.0m. Lesotho's general government gross debt was M6,238m. in 2009, equivalent to 44.0% of GDP. Lesotho's external debt totalled US $726m. at the end of 2010, of which $698m. was public and publicly guaranteed debt. In that year, the cost of servicing long-term public and publicly guaranteed debt and repayments to the IMF was equivalent to 1.9% of the value of exports of goods, services and income (excluding workers' remittances). According to ILO, the annual rate of inflation averaged 6.3% in 2002–11; consumer prices increased by 5.0% in 2011. In 1999 231,742 people were registered as unemployed, equivalent to 27.3% of the labour force. In 2006 51,595 Basotho were employed as miners in South Africa, compared with 129,000 in 1989. The number was expected to continue to decrease in the coming years. According to the Central Bank of Lesotho, in 2004 Basotho miners' remittances amounted to M1,795.0m. and accounted for more than 70% of total earnings during the period 1997–2004. South African officials estimated that around 300,000 Basotho were employed in South Africa at any given time.

Impediments to economic development in Lesotho include vulnerability to drought and serious land shortages, combined with the country's dependence on South Africa (the Lesotho currency, the loti, is fixed at par with the South African rand, exposing Lesotho to fluctuations within the South African economy). The textile industry benefited considerably from the USA's African Growth and Opportunities Act (AGOA), for which Lesotho was first declared eligible in April 2001. However, faced with increasing competition from producers in Asia and the global financial crisis in late 2008 and early 2009, the industry suffered through job losses, factory closures and reduced production levels. Declining SACU revenues, which provide some 60% of the country's total income, and a proposed restructuring of SACU tariffs presented additional challenges for the Lesotho authorities in meeting the ambitious targets of the 'Vision 2020' long-term economic development programme. Notwithstanding these difficulties, a wind and hydroelectric project, announced in late 2011, was expected to provide a stimulus for the economy. It was hoped that the LHPP would create some 25,000 jobs over a 15-year period; while 1,500 technicians and engineers would be employed on a permanent basis. Upon completion of the project, some of the electricity generated would be sold to neighbouring South Africa, which continued to have difficulty meeting its rapidly growing energy requirements. In December 2012 an IMF mission declared itself broadly satisfied with the country's performance, though it noted weakened economic growth as a result of a recent drought and lower revenues from SACU. It was reported in early 2013 that drought had severely reduced crop production and led to concerns over food security. Lesotho's Government and the UN had appealed for international assistance to respond to the crisis. None the less, real GDP growth has remained relatively strong as a result of increased mining investment (and strong demand internationally for diamonds in particular) and ongoing public infrastructure projects. Growth was estimated at 3.2% for the year ending 31 March 2012, according to the IMF; it was forecast to reach 4% in 2012/13. Meanwhile, IMF observers praised the new Government's commitment to maintaining the policy of fiscal consolidation.

PUBLIC HOLIDAYS

2014: 1 January (New Year's Day), 11 March (Moshoeshoe Day), 18–21 April (Easter), 1 May (Workers' Day), 25 May (Africa Day and Heroes' Day), 29 May (Ascension Day), 17 July (King's Birthday), 4 October (National Independence Day), 25 December (Christmas Day), 26 December (Boxing Day).

Statistical Survey

Sources (unless otherwise stated): Bureau of Statistics, POB 455, Maseru 100; tel. 22323852; fax 22310177; internet www.bos.gov.ls; Central Bank of Lesotho, POB 1184, Maseru 100; tel. 22314281; fax 22310051; e-mail cbl@centralbank.org.ls; internet www.centralbank.org.ls.

Area and Population

AREA, POPULATION AND DENSITY

Area (sq km)	30,355*
Population (*de jure* census results)	
14 April 1996	1,862,275
9 April 2006	
Males	912,798
Females	963,835
Total	1,876,633
Population (UN estimates at mid-year)†	
2011	2,193,842
2012	2,216,850
2013	2,240,129
Density (per sq km) at mid-2012	73.8

* 11,720 sq miles.

† Source: UN, *World Population Prospects: The 2010 Revision*.

POPULATION BY AGE AND SEX
(UN estimates at mid-2013)

	Males	Females	Total
0–14	407,559	402,064	809,623
15–64	661,371	673,176	1,334,547
65 and over	38,523	57,436	95,959
Total	1,107,453	1,132,676	2,240,129

Source: UN, *World Population Prospects: The 2010 Revision*.

DISTRICTS
(population at 2006 census)

District	Population
Berea	250,006
Butha-Buthe	110,320
Leribe	293,369
Mafeteng	192,621
Maseru	431,998
Mohale's Hoek	176,928
Mokhotlong	97,713
Qacha's Nek	69,749
Quthing	124,048
Thaba-Tseka	129,881
Total	1,876,633

PRINCIPAL TOWNS
(population at 1986 census)

Maseru (capital) .	109,400	Hlotse	9,600
Maputsoa . .	20,000	Mohale's Hoek . .	8,500
Teyateyaneng .	14,300	Quthing	6,000
Mafeteng . . .	12,700		

Source: Stefan Helders, *World Gazetteer* (www.world-gazetteer.com).

Mid-2011 (including suburbs, UN estimate): Maseru 238,553 (Source: UN, *World Urbanization Prospects: The 2011 Revision*).

BIRTHS AND DEATHS
(annual averages, UN estimates)

	1995–2000	2000–05	2005–10
Birth rate (per 1,000)	33.7	30.7	28.5
Death rate (per 1,000)	13.5	17.9	16.7

Source: UN, *World Population Prospects: The 2010 Revision*.

Life expectancy (years at birth): 48.0 (males 48.7; females 47.2) in 2011 (Source: World Bank, World Development Indicators database).

ECONOMICALLY ACTIVE POPULATION
(household survey, persons aged 10 years and over, 1999)

	Males	Females	Total
Agriculture	270,919	175,760	446,679
Fishing	125	—	125
Mining and quarrying	2,392	611	3,003
Manufacturing	7,957	13,839	21,795
Electricity, gas and water supply .	1,722	1,541	3,263
Construction	18,947	10,548	29,495
Wholesale and retail trade; repair of motor vehicles, motorcycles and household goods . . .	11,099	17,915	29,014
Hotels and restaurants . . .	918	3,529	4,447
Transport, storage and communications	9,307	1,363	10,670
Financial intermediation . . .	1,041	810	1,851
Real estate, renting and business activities	3,405	2,032	5,437
Public administration and defence; compulsory social security . .	5,181	2,395	7,576
Education	5,125	8,099	13,224
Health and social work	2,070	2,895	4,965
Other community, social and personal service activities . .	1,765	7,686	9,451
Households with employed persons	4,474	21,970	26,444
Extra-territorial organizations and bodies	126	—	126
Total employed	346,573	270,993	617,566
Unemployed	90,964	140,778	231,742
Total labour force	437,537	411,771	849,308

Source: ILO.

2008 (labour force survey, persons aged 15 years and over): Subsistence agriculture 247,258; Government and parastatals 43,762; Private sector 182,868; Private households 135,263; *Total employed* 609,152; Unemployed 179,390; *Total labour force* 788,541.

Mid-2013 (estimates in '000): Agriculture, etc. 371; Total labour force 977 (Source: FAO).

Health and Welfare

KEY INDICATORS

Total fertility rate (children per woman, 2010)	3.2
Under-5 mortality rate (per 1,000 live births, 2010) . . .	85
HIV/AIDS (% of persons aged 15–49, 2009)	23.6
Physicians (per 1,000 head, 2003)	0.05
Hospital beds (per 1,000 head, 2006)	1.30
Health expenditure (2009): US $ per head (PPP)	139
Health expenditure (2009): % of GDP	9.4
Health expenditure (2009): public (% of total)	74.3
Access to water (% of persons, 2010)	78
Access to sanitation (% of persons, 2010)	26
Human Development Index (2011): ranking	160
Human Development Index (2011): value	0.450

For sources and definitions, see explanatory note on p. vi.

Agriculture

PRINCIPAL CROPS
('000 metric tons)

	2009	2010	2011
Wheat	7.4	20.1	20.1
Maize	57.1	128.2	73.4
Sorghum	10.2	23.8	9.6
Potatoes*	88.5	99.1	104.1
Beans, dry	3.5	8.9	7.1
Peas, dry	1.4	1.4	0.7
Vegetables*	28	31	30

* FAO estimates.

Source: FAO.

LIVESTOCK
('000 head, year ending September)

	2009	2010	2011*
Cattle	615	626	650
Sheep	1,242	1,229	1,215
Goats	953	875	845
Pigs	92	84	80
Horses	74	70	69
Asses	160	136	136
Chickens	771	502	485

* FAO estimates.

Source: FAO.

LIVESTOCK PRODUCTS
('000 metric tons, FAO estimates)

	2009	2010	2011
Cattle meat	10.4	10.7	12.5
Cows' milk	33.8	33.7	39.1
Pig meat	4.0	3.8	3.6
Chicken meat	1.9	1.6	1.6
Game meat	4.7	5.1	5.1
Hen eggs	1.7	1.7	1.7
Wool, greasy	3.9	3.7	3.7

Source: FAO.

Forestry

ROUNDWOOD REMOVALS
('000 cubic metres, excluding bark, FAO estimates)

	2009	2010	2011
Total (all fuel wood)	2,084.0	2,091.9	2,099.7

Source: FAO.

Fishing

(metric tons, live weight)

	2008	2009	2010
Capture	50	45	45
Common carp	16	15	15
North African catfish . .	2	5	5
Other freshwater fishes . .	32	25	25
Aquaculture	91	108	300
Common carp	1	1	—
Rainbow trout	90	107	300
Total catch	141	153	345

Source: FAO.

Mining

(cubic metres unless otherwise indicated)

	2008	2009	2010
Fire clay*	15,000	15,000	15,000
Diamond (carats)	253,053	91,815	100,000
Gravel and crushed rock*	300,000	300,000	300,000

* Estimated production.

Source: US Geological Survey.

Finance

CURRENCY AND EXCHANGE RATES

Monetary Units
100 lisente (singular: sente) = 1 loti (plural: maloti).

Sterling, Dollar and Euro Equivalents (31 December 2012)
£1 sterling = 13.415 maloti;
US $1 = 8.501 maloti;
€1 = 11.216 maloti;
100 maloti = £7.45 = $11.76 = €8.92.

Average Exchange Rate (maloti per US $)
2010   7.3212
2011   7.2611
2012   8.2100

Note: The loti is fixed at par with the South African rand.

BUDGET
(million maloti, year ending 31 March)

Revenue*	2010/11	2011/12†	2012/13‡
Tax revenue	3,499	4,258	4,896
Taxes on net income and profits	1,957	2,395	2,686
Taxes on property	106	125	148
Taxes on goods and services	1,414	1,565	1,861
Taxes on international trade	18	151	200
Other taxes	109	22	1
Non-tax revenue	1,232	1,156	926
Property income	652	433	120
Sales of goods and services	530	692	757
Other non-tax revenue	50	31	49
SACU	2,628	2,753	5,966
Total	7,359	8,167	11,788

Expenditure and net lending	2010/11	2011/12†	2012/13‡
Compensation of employees	3,199	3,614	4,084
Wages and salaries	2,881	3,102	3,594
Goods and services	1,918	2,179	2,946
Subsidies	232	237	273
Interest payments	96	137	172
Grants	707	962	896
Social benefits	600	587	739
Other expenditures	707	943	720
Total	7,459	8,660	9,830

* Excluding grants received (million maloti): 1,200 in 2010/11; 1,437 in 2011/12 (estimate); 1,792 in 2012/13 (projection).
† Estimates.
‡ Projections.
Source: IMF, *Fourth Review Under the Three-Year Arrangement Under the Extended Credit Facility, Request for Waiver of Nonobservance of Performance Criterion, and Request for Modification of Performance Criteria* (December 2012).

INTERNATIONAL RESERVES
(excl. gold, US $ million at 31 December)

	2004	2005	2006
IMF special drawing rights	0.62	0.44	0.22
Reserve position in IMF	5.53	5.15	5.45
Foreign exchange	495.35	513.52	652.74
Total	501.50	519.11	658.41

2009: IMF special drawing rights 49.00; Reserve position in IMF 5.66.
2010: IMF special drawing rights 52.61; Reserve position in IMF 5.56.
2011: IMF special drawing rights 54.22; Reserve position in IMF 5.55.
Source: IMF, *International Financial Statistics*.

MONEY SUPPLY
(million maloti at 31 December)

	2009	2010	2011
Currency outside depository corporations	487.18	538.96	688.70
Transferable deposits	3,692.06	4,450.05	2,132.83
Other deposits	1,567.63	1,588.82	3,858.58
Broad money	5,746.87	6,577.83	6,680.10

Source: IMF, *International Financial Statistics*.

COST OF LIVING
(Consumer Price Index; base: March 2010 = 100)

	2009	2010	2011
Food (incl. non-alcoholic beverages)	97.7	101.1	108.1
Alcoholic beverages and tobacco	93.1	101.7	108.3
Housing, water, electricity, and other fuels	99.2	102.5	114.3
Clothing (incl. footwear)	97.2	100.4	101.8
Health	98.5	100.8	102.2
Transport	96.3	100.2	103.2
Communication	99.2	100.6	101.7
Education	94.1	100.0	101.0
All items (incl. others)	97.4	100.9	105.9

NATIONAL ACCOUNTS
(million maloti at current prices)

Expenditure on the Gross Domestic Product

	2008	2009	2010
Government final consumption expenditure	4,959	5,776	5,941
Private final consumption expenditure	13,427	14,779	16,724
Changes in inventories	−46	5	−77
Gross fixed capital formation	3,787	4,057	4,547
Total domestic expenditure	22,127	24,617	27,135
Exports of goods and services	7,560	6,644	6,990
Less Imports of goods and services	16,255	16,760	18,171
GDP in purchasers' values	13,433	14,502	15,956

Gross Domestic Product by Economic Activity

	2008	2009	2010
Agriculture	992	1,025	1,222
Mining and quarrying	1,145	926	1,121
Manufacturing	2,343	2,105	1,816
Electricity, gas and water	510	532	662
Construction	614	790	915
Wholesale and retail trade, restaurants and hotels	1,171	1,157	1,282
Transport and communication	756	848	956
Finance, insurance, real estate and business services	2,417	2,655	2,799
Public administration and defence	1,354	1,753	1,764
Other services	1,345	1,756	1,927
Sub-total	12,647	13,547	14,464
Less Imputed bank service charge	270	304	297
Indirect taxes, less subsidies	1,056	1,258	1,788
GDP in purchasers' prices	13,433	14,502	15,956

Source: African Development Bank.

BALANCE OF PAYMENTS
(US $ million)

	2009	2010	2011
Exports of goods	734.1	877.7	1172.2
Imports of goods	−1,583.3	−1,968.7	−2155.4
Balance on goods	−849.2	−1,091.0	−983.2
Exports of services	43.7	40.9	47.5
Imports of services	−371.9	−475.6	−542.1
Balance on goods and services	−1,177.4	−1,525.7	−1477.8
Primary income received	698.0	743.9	727.1
Primary income paid	−294.8	−325.2	−394.9
Balance on goods, services and primary income	−774.2	−1,107.0	−1145.7
Secondary income received	747.9	687.2	646.6
Secondary income paid	−23.5	−20.5	−21.0
Current balance	−49.8	−440.3	−520.1
Capital account (net)	74.6	136.2	184.0
Direct investment assets	1.9	2.3	3.9
Direct investment from liabilities	99.9	113.7	132.1
Portfolio investment assets	−0.2	−0.2	−0.2
Portfolio investment liabilities	0.1	0.2	0.2
Other investment assets	−125.7	−158.6	24.5
Other investment liabilities	84.0	−9.6	5.2
Net errors and omissions	−112.4	142.7	237.9
Reserves and related items	−27.5	−213.8	67.6

Source: IMF, *International Financial Statistics.*

External Trade

PRINCIPAL COMMODITIES
(million maloti)

Imports	2005	2006	2007
Food and beverages	1,135	1,198	1,549
Industrial supplies	2,015	1,917	2,803
Fuel and lubricants	415	474	684
Machinery and other capital equipment	275	288	553
Parts and accessories	182	298	326
Transport equipment	129	206	418
Parts and accessories for transport equipment	169	191	254
Consumer goods	1,175	1,294	1,488
Goods not specified elsewhere	2	0	2
Unspecified imports	2,932	3,564	2,828
Total	8,429	9,430	10,905

Exports	2006	2007	2008
Food and live animals	126	196	326
Crude materials, inedible except fuels	45	74	74
Mineral fuels and electricity	1	1	—
Chemicals and related products	24	4	6
Manufactured goods	668	1,213	1,663
Machinery and transport equipment	394	545	1,014
Miscellaneous manufactured articles	3,364	3,506	3,738
Other commodities	16	6	49
Total	4,638	5,543	6,870

PRINCIPAL TRADING PARTNERS
(million maloti)

Imports c.i.f.*	2005	2006	2007
Africa	7,709.9	8,574.3	10,473.7
SACU†	7,665.2	8,524.6	10,613.0
Asia	1,315.3	1,462.8	1,786.8
China, People's Repub.	238.9	265.7	324.5
Hong Kong	386.3	429.6	524.5
Taiwan	448.4	498.7	609.2
European Union	61.5	68.4	83.6
North America	38.1	42.3	51.7
USA	31.8	35.4	43.2
Total (incl. others)	9,135.7	10,160.0	12,420.7

Exports f.o.b.	2005	2006	2007
Africa	813.3	930.9	1,113.1
SACU†	714.2	817.5	1,077.5
European Union	711.0	813.8	973.1
North America	2,600.0	2,976.1	3,558.6
Canada	56.1	64.3	76.8
USA	2,543.8	2,911.8	3,381.7
Total (incl. others)	4,138.1	4,736.7	5,663.8

* Valuation exclusive of import duties. Figures also exclude donated food.
† Southern African Customs Union, of which Lesotho is a member; also including Botswana, Namibia, South Africa and Swaziland.

Source: IMF, *Kingdom of Lesotho: Statistical Appendix* (January 2010).

2008 (US $ million): *Imports:* Germany 14.6; Japan 19.4; South Africa 1,015.2; Total (incl. others) 1,066.2. *Exports:* Canada 1.1; South Africa 202.4; USA 35.8; Total (incl. others) 244.7 (Source: UN, *International Trade Statistics Yearbook*).

Transport

ROAD TRAFFIC
(motor vehicles in use at 31 December, estimates)

	1994	1995	1996
Passenger cars	9,900	11,160	12,610
Lorries and vans	20,790	22,310	25,000

Source: International Road Federation, *World Road Statistics.*

CIVIL AVIATION
(traffic on scheduled services)

	1997	1998	1999
Kilometres flown (million)	0	1	0
Passengers carried ('000)	10	28	1
Passenger-km (million)	3	9	0
Total ton-km (million)	0	1	0

Source: UN, *Statistical Yearbook.*

Tourism

FOREIGN TOURIST ARRIVALS BY COUNTRY OF RESIDENCE

	2007	2008	2009
Botswana	1,679	1,796	2,060
Germany	5,778	3,349	5,015
South Africa	261,099	246,014	302,655
Swaziland	1,246	1,233	1,406
United Kingdom	4,168	2,245	4,619
USA	621	1,311	3,212
Zimbabwe	3,457	4,149	4,513
Total (incl. others)	300,350	293,073	343,743

Total tourist arrivals ('000): 414 in 2010.

Tourism receipts (US $ million, excl. passenger transport, unless otherwise indicated): 24 in 2008; 40 in 2009; 34 in 2010.

Source: World Tourism Organization.

Communications Media

	2009	2010	2011
Telephones ('000 main lines in use)	40.0	38.6	38.6
Mobile cellular telephones ('000 subscribers)	661.0	987.4	1,232.4
Internet subscribers	300	980	n.a.
Broadband subscribers	400	400	1,300

Personal computers: 5,000 (2.5 per 1,000 persons) in 2005.

Source: International Telecommunication Union.

Education

(2009/10 unless otherwise indicated)

	Institutions	Teachers	Students		
			Males	Females	Total
Pre-primary	n.a.	2,159	n.a.	n.a.	52,646
Primary	1,455*	11,508	197,909	190,769	388,678
Secondary:					
general	240*	5,837†	51,622	69,169	120,791
technical and					
vocational	8‡	200†	526	1,990	2,516
teacher					
training	1‡	108§	n.a.	n.a.	2,335‖
University	1‡	638*	3,810*	4,690*	8,500*

* 2005/06.
† 2006/07.
‡ 2002/03.
§ 2001/02.
‖ 2004/05.

Source: partly UNESCO Institute for Statistics.

Pupil-teacher ratio (primary education, UNESCO estimate): 33.8 in 2009/10 (Source: UNESCO Institute for Statistics).

Adult literacy rate (UNESCO estimates): 89.6% (males 83.3%; females 95.6%) in 2010 (Source: UNESCO Institute for Statistics).

Directory

The Government

HEAD OF STATE

King: HM King LETSIE III (acceded to the throne 7 February 1996).

CABINET
(May 2013)

The Cabinet is a coalition formed by the All Basotho Convention (ABC), the Basotho National Party (BNP) and the Lesotho Congress for Democracy (LCD).

Prime Minister and Minister of Defence, Police and National Security: THOMAS MOTSOAHAE THABANE (ABC).

Deputy Prime Minister and Minister of Local Government and Chieftainship Affairs: MOTHETJOA METSING (LCD).

Minister of Gender, Youth, Sports and Recreation: THESELE 'MASERIBANE (BNP).

Minister of Public Service: Dr MOTLOHELOA PHOOKO (LCD).

Minister of Energy, Meteorology and Water Affairs: THAHANE TIMOTHY THAHANE (LCD).

Minister of Finance: Dr LEKETEKETE VICTOR KETSO (LCD).

Minister of Tourism, the Environment and Culture: 'MAMAHELE RADEBE (ABC).

Minister of Public Works and Transport: KEKETSO RANTŠO (LCD).

Minister of Law and Human Rights: HAAE EDWARD PHOOFOLO (ABC).

Minister of Communications, Science and Technology: TŠELISO MOKHOSI (LCD).

Minister of Forestry and Land Reclamation: KHOTSO MATLA (LCD).

Minister of Trade, Industry, Co-operatives and Marketing: TEMEKI PHOENIX TŠOLO (ABC).

Minister of Mining: TLALI KHASU (ABC).

Minister of Agriculture and Food Security: LITŠOANE SIMON LITŠOANE (ABC).

Minister of Education and Training: 'MAKABELO PRISCILLA MOSOTHOANE (LCD).

Minister of Social Development: 'MATEBATSO DOTI (ABC).

Minister of Labour and Employment: LEBESA MALOI (LCD).

Minister in the Prime Minister's Office: MOLOBELI SOULU (ABC).

Minister of Justice and Correctional Services: MOPHATO MOSHOETE MONYAKE (ABC).

Minister of Foreign Affairs and International Relations: MOHLABI TSEKOA (LCD).

Minister of Health: Dr PINKIE MANAMOLELA (ABC).

Minister of Home Affairs and Public Safety and Parliamentary Affairs: JOANG MOLAPO (BNP).

Minister of Development Planning: Dr MOEKETSI MAJORO (ABC).

In addition there were seven deputy ministers.

MINISTRIES

Office of the Prime Minister: POB 527, Maseru 100; tel. 22311000; fax 22320662; internet www.gov.ls/pm.

Ministry of Agriculture and Food Security: POB 24, Maseru 100; tel. 22316407; fax 22310186; e-mail minagric@leo.co.ls; internet www.gov.ls/agric.

Ministry of Communications, Science and Technology: Moposo House, 3rd Floor, POB 36, Maseru 100; tel. 22324715; fax 22325682; e-mail m.makhorole@mcst.gov.ls; internet www.gov.ls/comms.

Ministry of Defence, Police and National Security: POB 527, Maseru 100; tel. 22311000; fax 22310518; e-mail nmokatsa@yahoo.co.uk; internet www.gov.ls/defence.

Ministry of Development Planning: Maseru 100.

Ministry of Education and Training: POB 47, Maseru 100; tel. 22317900; fax 22326119; e-mail letsoelam@education.gov.ls; internet www.education.gov.ls.

Ministry of Energy, Meteorology and Water Affairs: Maseru 100.

Ministry of Finance: POB 395, Maseru 100; tel. 22311101; e-mail hmf@finance.gov.ls; internet www.finance.gov.ls.

Ministry of Foreign Affairs and International Relations: POB 1387, Maseru 100; tel. 22311150; fax 22310178; e-mail information@foreign.gov.ls; internet www.gov.ls/foreign.

Ministry of Forestry and Land Reclamation: POB 92, Maseru 100; tel. 22313057; fax 22310515; e-mail lincmox@ilesotho.com.

Ministry of Gender, Youth, Sports and Recreation: POB 729, Maseru 100; tel. and fax 22311006; e-mail honsec@mgysr.gov.ls; internet www.gov.ls/gender.

Ministry of Health: POB 514, Maseru 100; tel. 22317707; fax 22321014; e-mail lesenyehom@health.gov.ls; internet www.health.gov.ls.

Ministry of Home Affairs and Public Safety and Parliamentary Affairs: POB 174, Maseru 100; tel. 22320017; fax 22310013; e-mail mohonoel@homeaffairs.gov.ls; internet www.gov.ls/safety.

Ministry of Justice and Correctional Services: POB 402, Maseru 100; tel. 22322683; fax 22311092; e-mail dps@justice.gov.ls; internet www.justice.gov.ls.

Ministry of Labour and Employment: Private Bag A1164, Maseru 100; tel. 22322602; fax 22325163; e-mail infolabour@leo.co.ls; internet www.labour.gov.ls.

Ministry of Law and Human Rights: Maseru.

Ministry of Local Government and Chieftainship Affairs: POB 686, Maseru 100; tel. 22323415; fax 22327782; e-mail minmolg@leo.co.ls; internet www.localgovt.gov.ls.

Ministry of Mining: POB 772, Maseru 100; tel. 22323163; fax 22310527; internet www.gov.ls/natural.

Ministry of Public Service: POB 228, Maseru 100; tel. 22315946; fax 22310883; e-mail minister@mps.gov.ls; internet www.gov.ls/service.

Ministry of Public Works and Transport: POB 20, Maseru 100; tel. 22324697; fax 22310658; e-mail cio@mopwt.gov.ls; internet www.gov.ls/works.

Ministry of Social Development: Maseru 100.

Ministry of Tourism, the Environment and Culture: POB 52, Maseru 100; tel. 22313034; fax 22310194; e-mail pmasita.mohale@mtec.gov.ls; internet www.mtec.gov.ls.

Ministry of Trade, Industry, Co-operatives and Marketing: POB 747, Maseru 100; tel. 22312938; fax 22310644; e-mail mafura@mticm.gov.ls; internet www.trade.gov.ls.

Legislature

PARLIAMENT

National Assembly

POB 190, Maseru; tel. 22323035; fax 22310023; internet www.parliament.ls/TheNationalAssembly/About.aspx.

Speaker: SEPHIRI MOTANYANE.

General Election, 26 May 2012

Party	Constituency seats	Compensatory seats*	Total seats
Democratic Congress (DC)	41	7	48
All Basotho Convention (ABC)	26	4	30
Lesotho Congress for Democracy (LCD)	12	14	26
Basotho National Party (BNP)	—	5	5
Popular Front for Democracy (PFD)	1	2	3
National Independent Party (NIP)	—	2	2
Basotho Batho Democratic Party (BBDP)	—	1	1
Basutoland Congress Party (BCP)	—	1	1
Basotho Democratic National Party (BDNP)	—	1	1
Lesotho People's Congress (LPC)	—	1	1
Lesotho Workers' Party (LWP)	—	1	1
Marematlou Freedom Party (MFP)	—	1	1
Total	80	40	120

* Allocated by proportional representation.

Senate

POB 553, Maseru 100; tel. 22315338; fax 22310023; internet www.parliament.ls/Senate/AboutSenate.aspx.

President: Chief LETAPATA MAKHAOLA.

The Senate is an advisory chamber, comprising 22 traditional chiefs and 11 members appointed by the monarch.

Election Commission

Independent Electoral Commission (IEC): Moposo House, 7th Floor, Kingsway, POB 12698, Maseru 100; tel. 22314991; fax 22310398; internet www.iec.org.ls; f. 1997 as successor to the Constituency Delimitation Commission; Chair. LIMAKATSO MOKHOTHU.

Political Organizations

In March 2012 a total of 15 parties were registered by the Independent Electoral Commission. At least a further 10 parties had applied to be registered to participate in the May legislative elections.

All Basotho Convention (ABC): Maseru; f. 2006 by fmr mems of the Lesotho Congress for Democracy; Pres. THOMAS MOTSOAHAE THABANE.

Basotho Batho Democratic Party (BBDP): f. 2006; Leader JEREMANE RAMATHEBANE.

Basotho Democratic National Party (BDNP): e-mail joangmolapo@hotmail.com; internet bdnp.blogspot.com; f. 2006; Leader THABANG NYEOE; Sec.-Gen. PELELE LETSOALA.

Basotho National Party (BNP): POB 124, Maseru 100; f. 1958; Leader THESELE MASERIBANE; Sec.-Gen. MOLETSANE JONATHAN; 280,000 mems.

Basutoland Congress Party (BCP): POB 111, Maseru 100; tel. 8737076; f. 1952; Leader THULO MAHLAKENG.

Democratic Congress: Maseru; f. 2012; formed by Prime Minister Mosisili who broke away from the ruling LCD; Leader BETHUEL PAKALITHA MOSISILI.

Lesotho Congress for Democracy (LCD): POB 7, Mohole's Hoek; tel. 785207; f. 1997 as a result of divisions within the BCP; Chair. MOEKETSI MOLETSANE; Sec.-Gen. MOTHETJOA METSING; 200,000 mems.

Lesotho People's Congress (LPC): f. 2001 following split in the LCD; Leader KELEBONE ALBERT MAOPE; Sec.-Gen. SHAKHANE MOKHEHLE.

Lesotho Workers' Party (LWP): Maseru; f. 2001; Leader MACAEFA BILLY.

Marematlou Freedom Party (MFP): POB 0443, Maseru 105; tel. 22315804; f. 1962 following merger between the Marema Tlou Party and Basutoland Freedom Party; Leader MOEKETSE MALEBO; Dep. Leader THABO LEANYA.

National Independent Party (NIP): Maseru; f. 1984; Pres. ANTHONY CLOVIS MANYELI.

Popular Front for Democracy (PFD): Maseru; f. 1991; left-wing; Leader LEKHETHO RAKUOANE.

Diplomatic Representation

EMBASSIES AND HIGH COMMISSIONS IN LESOTHO

China, People's Republic: POB 380, Maseru 100; tel. 22316521; fax 22310489; e-mail chinaemb_ls@mfa.gov.cn; internet ls.china-embassy.org; Ambassador HU DINGXIAN.

Ireland: Tona-Kholo Rd, Private Bag A67, Maseru 100; tel. 22314068; fax 22310028; e-mail maseruembassy@dfa.ie; internet www.embassyofireland.org.ls; Ambassador PADDY FAY.

Libya: 173 Tona-Kholo Rd, Maseru West, POB 432, Maseru 100; tel. 22320148; fax 22327750; Chargé d'affaires a.i. ABDUL-MOEINE GARGOUM.

South Africa: Lesotho Bank Tower, 10th Floor, Kingsway, Private Bag A266, Maseru 100; tel. 22315758; fax 22310128; e-mail dlokovam@dirco.gov.za; High Commissioner HAPPY MAHLANGU.

USA: 254 Kingsway, POB 333, Maseru 100; tel. 22312666; fax 22310116; e-mail infomaseru@state.gov; internet maseru.usembassy.gov; Ambassador MICHELE CARL B. FOX.

Judicial System

The Constitution provides for an independent judicial system, consisting of a Court of Appeal, a High Court, Magistrate's Courts, and traditional courts that exist predominately in rural areas. All but one of the Justices on the Court of Appeal are South African jurists.

Court of Appeal: POB 90, Maseru; tel. 22312188; Pres. MATHEALIRA RAMODIBEDI.

High Court: POB 90, Maseru; tel. 22312188; the High Court is a superior court of record, and in addition to any other jurisdiction conferred by statute it is vested with unlimited original jurisdiction to determine any civil or criminal matter; it also has appellate jurisdiction to hear appeals and reviews from the subordinate courts; appeals may be made to the Court of Appeal; Chief Justice MAHAPELA LEHOHLA.

Subordinate Courts: each of the 10 districts possesses subordinate courts, presided over by magistrates; Chief Magistrate MOLEFI MAKARA.

Judicial Commissioners' Courts: these courts hear civil and criminal appeals from central and local courts; further appeal may be made to the High Court and finally to the Court of Appeal.

Central and Local Courts: there are 71 such courts, of which 58 are local courts and 13 are central courts, which also serve as courts of appeal from the local courts; they have limited civil and criminal jurisdiction.

Religion

About 90% of the population profess Christianity.

CHRISTIANITY

African Federal Church Council (AFCC): POB 70, Peka 340; f. 1927; co-ordinating org. for 48 African independent churches.

Christian Council of Lesotho (CCL): POB 547, Maseru 100; tel. 22313639; fax 22310310; f. 1833; 112 congregations; 261,350 mems (2003); Chair. Rev. PHILLIP MOKUKU; Sec. CATHERINE RAMOKHELE.

The Anglican Communion

Anglicans in Lesotho are adherents of the Anglican Church of Southern Africa (formerly the Church of the Province of Southern Africa). The Metropolitan of the Province is the Archbishop of Cape Town, South Africa. Lesotho forms a single diocese, with an estimated 200,000 members.

Bishop of Lesotho: MALLANE ADAM TAASO, Bishop's House, POB 87, Maseru 100; tel. 22311974; fax 22310161; e-mail diocese@ilesotho.com.

The Roman Catholic Church

Lesotho comprises one archdiocese and three dioceses. Some 52% of the total population are Roman Catholics.

Lesotho Catholic Bishops' Conference

Catholic Secretariat, POB 200, Maseru 100; tel. 22312525; fax 22310294.

f. 1972; Pres. (vacant).

Archbishop of Maseru: Most Rev. GERARD TLALI LEROTHOLI, Archbishop's House, 19 Orpen Rd, POB 267, Maseru 100; tel. 22312565; fax 22310425; e-mail archmase@lesoff.co.za.

Other Christian Churches

At mid-2000 there were an estimated 279,000 Protestants and 257,000 adherents professing other forms of Christianity.

African Methodist Episcopal Church: POB 223, Maseru 100; tel. 22311801; fax 22310548; e-mail bishopsarah@leo.co.ls; f. 1903; Presiding Prelate Rt Rev. SARAH F. DAVIS; 15,000 mems.

Lesotho Evangelical Church: POB 260, Maseru 100; tel. 22323942; f. 1833; independent since 1964; Pres. Rev. TSELISO MASEMENE; Exec. Sec. Rev. GILBERT RAMATLAPENG; 230,000 mems (2003).

Other denominations active in Lesotho include the Apostolic Faith Mission, the Assemblies of God, the Dutch Reformed Church in Africa, the Full Gospel Church of God, Methodist Church of Southern Africa and the Seventh-day Adventists. There are also numerous African independent churches.

BAHÁ'Í FAITH

National Spiritual Assembly of the Bahá'ís of Lesotho: POB 508, Maseru 100; tel. 22312346; e-mail bahailesotho@leo.co.ls.

The Press

Lesotho does not have a daily newspaper.

Leseli ka Sepolesa (The Police Witness): Press Dept, Police Headquarters, Maseru CBD, POB 13, Maseru 100; tel. 22317262; fax 22310045; fortnightly; Sesotho; publ. by the Lesotho Mounted Police Services; Editor-in-Chief CLIFFORD MOLEFE.

Leselinyana la Lesotho (Light of Lesotho): Morija Printing Works, POB 7, Morija 190; tel. 22360244; fax 22360005; e-mail mpw@lesoff.co.ls; f. 1863; fortnightly; Sesotho, with occasional articles in English; publ. by the Lesotho Evangelical Church; Editor MABAT-SOENENG EMELY SIBOLLA; circ. 12,000.

Lesotho Times: Maseru; tel. 22315335; fax 22315352; e-mail editor@lestimes.co.ls; internet www.lestimes.com.

Lesotho Today/Lentsoe la Basotho (Voice of the Lesotho Nation): POB 353, Maseru 100; tel. 22323561; fax 22322764; internet www.lesothotoday.co.ls; f. 1974; weekly; Sesotho; publ. by Ministry of Communications, Science and Technology; Editor KAHLISO LESE-NYANE; circ. 14,000.

Makatolle: POB 111, Maseru 100; tel. 22850990; f. 1963; weekly; Sesotho; Editor M. RAMANGOEI; circ. 2,000.

MoAfrika: MoAfrika Broadcasting and Publishing Services, Carlton Centre Bldg, 1st Floor, POB 7234, Maseru 100; tel. 22321854; fax 22321956; f. 1990 as *The African*; weekly; Sesotho and English; Editor-in-Chief Prof. SEBONONOLA R. K. RAMAINOANE; circ. 5,000.

Moeletsi oa Basotho: Mazenod Institute, POB 18, Mazenod 160; tel. 22350465; fax 22350010; e-mail mzpwrks@lesoff.co.za; f. 1933; weekly; Sesotho; publ. by the Roman Catholic Church; Editor FRANCIS KHOARIPE; circ. 20,000.

Mohahlaula: Allied Bldg, 1st Floor, Manonyane Centre, POB 14430, Maseru 100; tel. 22312777; fax 22320941; weekly; Sesotho; publ. by Makaung Printers and Publrs; Editor WILLY MOLLUNGOA.

Mololi: Cooperatives Bldg, Main North 1 Rd, POB 9933, Maseru 100; tel. 22312287; fax 22327912; f. 1997; Sesotho; organ of the Lesotho Congress for Democracy; Editor (vacant).

Mopheme (The Survivor): Allied Bldg, 1st Floor, Manonyane Centre, POB 14184, Maseru; tel. and fax 22311670; e-mail mopheme@lesoff.co.za; weekly; English and Sesotho; publ. by Newsshare Foundation; Owner and Editor LAWRENCE KEKETSO; circ. 2,500.

Public Eye/Mosotho: House No. 14A3, Princess Margaret Rd, POB 14129, Old Europa, Maseru 100; tel. 22321414; fax 22310614; e-mail editor@publiceye.co.ls; internet www.publiceye.co.ls; f. 1997; weekly; 80% English, 20% Sesotho; publ. by Voice Multimedia; also publ. *Eye on Tourism* and *Family Mirror* magazines; Editor-in-Chief BETHUEL THAI; circ. 20,000 (Lesotho and South Africa).

PERIODICALS

Justice and Peace: Catholic Bishops' Conference, Our Lady of Victories Cathedral Catholic Centre, POB 200, Maseru 100; tel. 22312750; fax 22312751; quarterly; publ. by the Roman Catholic Church.

Moqolotsi (The Journalist): House No. 1B, Happy Villa, POB 14139, Maseru 100; tel. and fax 22320941; e-mail medinles@lesoff.co.za; monthly newsletter; English; publ. by the Media Institute of Lesotho (MILES).

NGO Web: 544 Hoohlo Extension, Florida, Maseru 100; tel. 22325798; fax 22317205; e-mail lecongo@lecongo.org.ls; quarterly; English and Sesotho; publ. of the Lesotho Council of NGOs; circ. 2,000.

Shoeshoe: POB 36, Maseru 100; tel. 22323561; fax 22310003; quarterly; women's interest; publ. by Ministry of Communications, Science and Technology.

Other publications include *Mara LDF Airwing/Airsquadron* and *The Sun/Thebe*.

NEWS AGENCY

Lesotho News Agency (LENA): Lesotho News Agency Complex, Lerotholi St, opp. Royal Palace, POB 36, Maseru 100; tel. 22325317; fax 22324608; e-mail l_lenanews@hotmail.com; internet www.lena.gov.ls; f. 1985; Dir MOTHEPANE KOTELE; Editors MOROA MOPELI, LITEBOHO MAHULA.

Publishers

Longman Lesotho (Pty) Ltd: 104 Christie House, 1st Floor, Orpen Rd, Old Europa, POB 1174, Maseru 100; tel. 22314254; fax 22310118; e-mail connie.burford@pearsoned.com; Man. Dir SEYMOUR R. KIKINE.

Macmillan Boleswa Publishers Lesotho (Pty) Ltd: 523 Sun Cabanas Hotel, POB 7545, Maseru 100; tel. 22317340; fax 22310047; e-mail macmillan@lesoff.co.ls; Man. Dir PAUL MOROLONG.

Mazenod Institute: POB 39, Mazenod 160; tel. 22350224; f. 1933; Roman Catholic; Man. Fr B. MOHLALISI.

Morija Sesuto Book Depot: POB 4, Morija 190; tel. and fax 22360204; f. 1862; owned by the Lesotho Evangelical Church; religious, educational and Sesotho language and literature.

St Michael's Mission: The Social Centre, POB 25, Roma; tel. 22316234; f. 1968; religious and educational; Man. Dir Fr M. FERRANGE.

GOVERNMENT PUBLISHING HOUSE

Government Printer: POB 268, Maseru; tel. 22313023.

Broadcasting and Communications

TELECOMMUNICATIONS

In 2011 there were two providers of mobile cellular telephone services and one provider of fixed-line telephone services.

Lesotho Communications Authority (LCA): Moposo House, 6th Floor, Kingsway Rd, POB 15896, Maseru 100; tel. 22224300; fax 22310984; e-mail lca@lca.org.ls; internet www.lca.org.ls; f. 2000; regulates telecommunications and broadcasting; Chief Exec. MONEHELA POSHOLI.

Econet Telecom Lesotho (ETL): POB 1037, Maseru 100; tel. 22211000; fax 22310600; e-mail enquiries@telecom.co.ls; internet www.telecom.co.ls; 70% holding acquired by the Econet Wireless Group in 2007; 30% state-owned; Chair. PAKO PETLANE; CEO NICO HEYNS.

Vodacom Lesotho (Pty) Ltd: Block B, 7th Floor, Development House, Kingsway Rd, POB 7387, Maseru 100; tel. 52212201; fax 22311079; internet www.vodacom.co.za; f. 1996; jt venture between Telecom Lesotho and Vodacom (Pty) Ltd; fmrly VCL Communications; mobile cellular telecommunications provider; CEO PIETER UYS.

BROADCASTING

RADIO

The first licences for private radio stations were issued in 1998. Licences are issued by the Lesotho Telecommunications Authority. Radio Lesotho is the only station to broadcast nation-wide; all the other stations are restricted to urban areas and their peripheries.

Catholic Radio FM: Our Lady of Victories Cathedral, Catholic Centre POB 200, Maseru 100; tel. 22323247; fax 22310294; f. 1999.

Harvest FM: Carlton Centre, 3rd Floor, Room No. 312, POB 442, Maseru 100; tel. 22313168; fax 22313858; e-mail mlekhoaba@harvestfm.co.ls; internet www.harvestfm.co.ls; operated by Harvest FM Trust; affiliated to United Christian Broadcasters Africa, South Africa; evangelical religious programming; Station Man. MARY MOSHOESHOE.

Joy FM: Lesotho Sun Hotel, Suites 2204–2206, Private Bag A457, Maseru 100; tel. 22310920; fax 22310104; internet www.joyfm.co.ls; f. 2001; Sesotho and English; relays Voice of America broadcasts.

Khotso FM: Institute of Extramural Studies, National University of Lesotho POB 180, Roma; Private Bag A47, Maseru 100; tel. 22322038; fax 22340000; community radio station; sister station of DOPE FM (f. 2004).

MoAfrika FM: Carlton Centre, 2nd Floor, Kingsway, POB 7234, Maseru 100; tel. and fax 22321956; e-mail info@moafrika.co.ls; internet www.moafrika.co.ls; affiliated to the *MoAfrika* newspaper; Sesotho, Xhosa and Mandarin; news and entertainment; Man. and Editor-in-Chief Prof. SEBONONOLA R. K. RAMAINOANE.

People's Choice Radio (PCFM): LNDC Centre, Development House, Level 9, Block D, POB 8800, Maseru 100; tel. 22322122; fax 22310888; internet www.pcfm.co.ls; f. 1998; news and entertainment; Man. Dir MOTLATSI MAJARA.

Radio Lesotho: Lesotho News Agency Complex, Lerotholi St, opp. Royal Palace, POB 36, Maseru 100; tel. and fax 22322714; e-mail enquiries@africanextension.com; internet www.radiolesotho.co.ls; f. 1964; state-owned; part of Lesotho Nat. Broadcasting Services; Sesotho and English; Dir of Broadcasting LEBOHANG DADA MOQASA.

TELEVISION

Lesotho Television (LTV): Lesotho News Agency Complex, Lerotholi St, opp. Royal Palace, POB 36, Maseru 100; tel. 22324735; fax 22310149; e-mail mfalatsa@yahoo.com; f. 1988 in association with M-Net, South Africa; state-owned; part of Lesotho Nat. Broadcasting Services; Sesotho and English.

Finance

(cap. = capital; res = reserves; dep. = deposits; m. = million; brs = branches; amounts in maloti)

BANKING

In 2008 there were four commercial banks in Lesotho.

Central Bank

Central Bank of Lesotho: cnr Airport and Moshoeshoe Rds, POB 1184, Maseru 100; tel. 22314281; fax 22310051; e-mail cbl@centralbank.org.ls; internet www.centralbank.org.ls; f. 1978 as the Lesotho Monetary Authority; present name adopted in 1982; bank of issue; cap. 25.0m., res 1,479.1m., dep. 5,093.2m. (Dec. 2009); Gov. and Chair. Dr M. SENAOANA.

Commercial Banks

First National Bank Lesotho: POB 11902, Maseru 100; tel. 22222200; f. 2004; CEO J. JORDAAN; 1 br.

Lesotho PostBank (LPB): Oblate House, Kingsway Rd, Private Bag A121, Maseru 100; tel. 22317842; fax 22313170; e-mail info@lpb.co.ls; internet www.lpb.co.ls; f. 2004; state-owned; Chair. TŠELISO MOKELA; CEO MPHO VUMBUKANI; 12 brs.

Nedbank (Lesotho) Ltd: 115–117 Griffith Hill, Kingsway St, POB 1001, Maseru 100; tel. 22312696; fax 22310025; e-mail georgego@nedcor.co.za; internet www.nedbank.co.ls; f. 1997; fmrly Standard Chartered Bank Lesotho Ltd; 100% owned by Nedbank Ltd (South Africa); cap. 20m., res 205m., dep. 1,969m. (Dec. 2009); Chair. SOPHIA MOHAPI; Man. Dir LAZARUS MURAHWA; 3 brs and 7 agencies.

Standard Lesotho Bank: Banking Bldg, 1st Floor, Kingsway Rd, Kingsway Town Centre, POB 1053, Maseru 100; tel. 22315737; fax 22317321; internet www.standardbank.co.ls; f. 2006 following merger between Lesotho Bank (1999) Ltd (f. 1972) and Standard Bank Lesotho Ltd (fmrly Stanbic Bank Lesotho Ltd); Chair. THABO MAKEBA; Man. Dir COLIN ADDIS; 11 brs.

INSURANCE

In 2008 there were five insurance companies in Lesotho.

Alliance Insurance Co Ltd: Alliance House, 4 Bowker Rd, POB 01118, Maseru West 105; tel. 22312357; fax 22310313; e-mail alliance@alliance.co.ls; internet www.alliance.co.ls; f. 1993; life and short-term insurance; Man. Dir ROB DUNCAN; Gen. Mans MOK'HAPHEK'HA LAZARO, THABISO MADIBA.

Lesotho National General Insurance Co Ltd (LNIG): Lesotho Insurance House, Kingsway, Private Bag A65, Maseru 100; tel. 22313031; fax 22310007; e-mail manager@lngic.com; f. 1977 as Lesotho National Insurance Group; 60% owned by Regent Insurance Co Ltd (South Africa), 20% state-owned, 20% owned by Molepe Investment Holdings (Pty) Ltd; part-privatized in 1995; incorporating subsidiaries specializing in life and short-term insurance; Chair. Dr TIMOTHY THAHANE; Man. Dir R. J. LETSOELA.

Metropolitan Lesotho Ltd: Metropolitan Bldg, Kingsway St, POB 645, Maseru; tel. 22222300; fax 22317278; internet www.metropolitan.co.ls; f. 2003; subsidiary of Metropolitan Holdings Ltd, South Africa; Man. Dir NKAU MATETE.

Trade and Industry

GOVERNMENT AGENCIES

Privatisation Unit: Privatisation Project, Lesotho Utilities Sector Reform Project, Ministry of Finance and Development Planning, Lesotho Bank Mortgage Division Bldg, 2nd Floor, Kingsway St, Private Bag A249, Maseru 100; tel. 22317902; fax 22317551; e-mail mntsasa@privatisation.gov.ls; internet www.privatisation.gov.ls; CEO MOSITO KHETHISA.

Trade Promotion Unit: c/o Ministry of Trade, Industry, Cooperatives and Marketing, POB 747, Maseru 100; tel. 322138; fax 310121; e-mail tradepu@lesoff.co.za.

DEVELOPMENT ORGANIZATIONS

Basotho Enterprises Development Corpn (BEDCO): Sebaboleng Trade and Industrial Centre, POB 1216, Maseru 100; tel. 22312094; fax 22310455; e-mail info@bedco.org.ls; internet www.bedco.org.ls; f. 1980; promotes and assists in the establishment and devt of Basotho-owned enterprises, with emphasis on small- and medium-scale; Chair. MOHLOMI D. RANTEKOA; CEO TS'ELISO MOKHOSI.

Lesotho Co-operative Handicrafts: Basotho Hat Bldg, Kingsway, PO Box 148, Maseru; tel. 22322523; e-mail lch@ilesotho.com; internet www.basothohat.co.ls; f. 1978; marketing and distribution of handicrafts; Gen. Man. KHOTSO MATLA.

Lesotho Council of Non-Governmental Organizations: House 544, Hoohlo Extension, Private Bag A445, Maseru 100; tel. 22317205; fax 22310412; e-mail lecongo@lecongo.org.ls; internet www.lecongo.org.ls; f. 1990; promotes sustainable management of natural resources, socio-economic devt and social justice; Exec. Dir Mabulara Ts'uene (acting).

Lesotho Highlands Development Authority (LHDA): Lesotho Bank Tower, 3rd Floor, Kingsway, POB 7332, Maseru 100; tel. 22311280; fax 22310665; e-mail lhwp@lhda.org.ls; internet www .lhda.org.ls; f. 1986 to implement the Lesotho Highlands Water Project, being undertaken jtly with South Africa; Chair. J. Eagar; CEO Peter Makuta (acting).

Lesotho National Dairy Board: Maseru; f. 1991; prescribes standards of production, storage, packaging, processing and distribution of dairy products.

Lesotho National Development Corpn (LNDC): Development House, Block A, Kingsway, Private Bag A96, Maseru 100; tel. 22312012; fax 22310038; e-mail info@lndc.org.ls; internet www .lndc.org.ls; f. 1967; state-owned; total assets M477.5m. (March 2006); interests in manufacturing, mining, food-processing and leisure; Chair. Mohlomi Rantekoa; CEO Joshua Setipa.

CHAMBER OF COMMERCE

Lesotho Chamber of Commerce and Industry: Kingsway Ave, POB 79, Maseru 100; tel. 22316937; fax 22322794; Pres. Simon Kuena Phafane.

INDUSTRIAL AND TRADE ASSOCIATIONS

Livestock Marketing Corpn: POB 800, Maseru 100; tel. 22322444; f. 1973; sole org. for marketing livestock and livestock products; liaises with marketing boards in South Africa; projects incl. an abattoir, tannery, poultry and wool and mohair scouring plants; Gen. Man. S. R. Matlanyane.

EMPLOYERS' ORGANIZATION

Association of Lesotho Employers: 18 Bowker Rd, POB 1509, Maseru 100; tel. 22315736; fax 22325384; e-mail makeka@leo.co.ls; f. 1961; represents mems in industrial relations and on govt bodies, and advises the Govt on employers' concerns; Pres. Raditapole Letsoela; Exec. Dir Thabo Makeka.

UTILITIES

Lesotho Electricity Authority (LEA): Moposo House, 6th Floor, Kingsway, Private Bag A315, Maseru; tel. 22312479; fax 22315094; e-mail secretary@lea.org.ls; internet www.lea.org.ls; f. 2004; Chair. Francina Liako Moloi; Chief Exec. Ntoi Paul Rapapa.

Lesotho Electricity Co (LEC): 53 Moshoeshoe Rd, POB 423, Maseru 100; tel. 22312236; fax 22310093; e-mail info@lec.co.ls; internet www.lec.co.ls; f. 1969; 100% state-owned; Chair. Dr K. Lesoetsa; Man. Dir F. M. Hloaele.

Lesotho Water and Sewerage Authority (WASA): POB 426, Maseru 100; tel. 22312449; fax 22312006; internet www.wasa.co.ls; Chair. Refiloe Tlali.

TRADE UNIONS

Congress of Lesotho Trade Unions (COLETU): POB 13282, Maseru 100; tel. 22320958; fax 22310081; f. 1998; Sec.-Gen. Vuyani Tyhali; 15,587 mems.

Lesotho Congress of Democratic Unions (LECODU): POB 15851, Maseru 100; tel. and fax 22323559; f. 2004; Sec.-Gen. Daniel Maraisane; 15,279 mems (2005).

Transport

RAILWAYS

Lesotho is linked with the South African railway system by a short line (2.6 km in length) from Maseru to Marseilles, on the Bloemfontein–Natal main line.

ROADS

In 2007 Lesotho's road network totalled 2,371 km, of which some 58% of roads was paved. In March 2000 a major road network was opened, linking Maseru with the Mohale Dam.

CIVIL AVIATION

King Moshoeshoe I International Airport is at Thota-Moli, some 20 km from Maseru. International services between Maseru and Johannesburg are operated by South African Airlink. The national airline company, Lesotho Airways, was sold to a South African company in 1997 as part of the Government's ongoing privatization programme; however, after two years of losses the company was liquidated in 1999.

Tourism

Spectacular mountain scenery is the principal tourist attraction, and a new ski resort was opened in 2003. Tourist arrivals totalled 414,000 in 2010, and receipts from tourism amounted to an estimated US $34m. in that year.

Lesotho Tourism Development Corpn (LTDC): cnr Linare and Parliament Rds, POB 1378, Maseru 100; tel. 22312238; fax 22310189; e-mail ltdc@ltdc.org.ls; internet www.ltdc.org.ls; f. 2000; successor to the Lesotho Tourist Board; Chair. Mamoruti Malie.

Defence

Military service is voluntary. As assessed at November 2012, the Lesotho Defence Force (LDF, formerly the Royal Lesotho Defence Force) comprised 2,000 men, including an air wing of 110 men. The creation of a new commando force unit, the first professional unit in the LDF, was announced in October 2001, as part of ongoing efforts to restructure the armed forces.

Defence Expenditure: Estimated at M1,020m. for 2013.

Commander of the Lesotho Defence Force: Lt-Gen. Thuso Motanyane.

Education

All primary education is available free of charge, and is provided mainly by the three main Christian missions (Lesotho Evangelical, Roman Catholic and Anglican), under the direction of the Ministry of Education. Education at primary schools is officially compulsory for seven years between six and 13 years of age. Secondary education, beginning at the age of 13, lasts for up to five years, comprising a first cycle of three years and a second of two years. According to UNESCO estimates, in 2009/10 total enrolment at primary schools included 73% of children in the appropriate age-group (72% of boys; 75% of girls); in that year enrolment at secondary schools included 30% of children in the relevant age-group (23% of boys; 37% of girls). Some 8,500 students were enrolled at the National University of Lesotho, at Roma, in 2005/06. Proposed expenditure on education in 2008 represented 23.7% of total government expenditure. In January 2006 17 new schools, constructed with the assistance of the Government of Japan, were opened; they were expected to accommodate some 14,000 pupils.

LIBERIA

Introductory Survey

LOCATION, CLIMATE, LANGUAGE, RELIGION, FLAG, CAPITAL

The Republic of Liberia lies on the west coast of Africa, with Sierra Leone and Guinea to the north, and Côte d'Ivoire to the east. The climate is tropical, with temperatures ranging from 18°C (65°F) to 49°C (120°F). English is the official language but the 16 major ethnic groups speak their own languages and dialects. Liberia is officially a Christian state, although some Liberians hold traditional beliefs. There are about 670,000 Muslims. The national flag (proportions 10 by 19) has 11 horizontal stripes, alternately of red and white, with a dark blue square canton, containing a five-pointed white star, in the upper hoist. The capital is Monrovia.

CONTEMPORARY POLITICAL HISTORY

Historical Context

Founded by liberated black slaves from the southern USA, Liberia became an independent republic in 1847. The leader of the True Whig Party (TWP), William Tubman, who had been President of Liberia since 1944, died in July 1971 and was succeeded by his Vice-President, William R. Tolbert, who was re-elected in October 1975.

In April 1980 Tolbert was assassinated in a military coup, led by Master Sgt (later Commander-in-Chief) Samuel Doe, who assumed power as Chairman of the newly established People's Redemption Council (PRC), suspending the Constitution and proscribing all political parties. The new regime attracted international criticism for its summary execution of 13 former senior government officials who had been accused of corruption and mismanagement. In July 1981 all civilian ministers received commissions, thus installing total military rule.

A draft Constitution was approved by 78.3% of registered voters in a national referendum in July 1984. In the same month Doe dissolved the PRC and appointed a 58-member Interim National Assembly. The ban on political organizations was repealed in the same month, to enable parties to secure registration prior to presidential and legislative elections, which were due to take place in October 1985. In August 1984 Doe established the National Democratic Party of Liberia (NDPL) and formally announced his candidature for the presidency. By early 1985 a total of 11 political associations had been formed; however, two influential parties, the Liberian People's Party (LPP) and the United People's Party (UPP), were proscribed, and apart from the NDPL only three parties—the Liberian Action Party (LAP), the Liberia Unification Party (LUP) and the Unity Party (UP)—were eventually permitted to participate in the elections. Doe won the presidential election, receiving 50.9% of the votes. At the concurrent elections to the bicameral National Assembly the NDPL won 22 of the 26 seats in the Senate and 51 of the 64 seats in the House of Representatives. On 6 January 1986 Doe was inaugurated as President.

Domestic Political Affairs

In December 1989 an armed insurrection by rebel forces began in the north-eastern border region of Nimba County. In early 1990 several hundred deaths ensued in fighting between the Liberian army (the Armed Forces of Liberia—AFL) and the rebels, who claimed to be members of a hitherto unknown opposition group, the National Patriotic Front of Liberia (NPFL), led by a former government official, Charles Taylor. The fighting swiftly degenerated into a war between Doe's ethnic group, the Krahn, and the local Gio and Mano tribes, and many thousands of people took refuge in neighbouring Guinea and Côte d'Ivoire. Taylor's authority as self-proclaimed President of his own interim administration, known as the National Patriotic Reconstruction Assembly, was challenged by a faction of the NPFL, led by Prince Yormie Johnson, which rapidly secured control of parts of Monrovia in July. In the subsequent conflict both government and rebel forces were responsible for numerous atrocities against civilians. The Economic Community of West African States (ECOWAS, see p. 268) repeatedly failed to negotiate a cease-fire, and in late August it dispatched a military force to restore peace in the region. Doe and Johnson accepted this Monitoring Group (ECOMOG), but its initial occupation of the port area of Monrovia encountered armed opposition by Taylor's forces.

On 30 August 1990 exiled representatives of Liberia's principal political parties and other influential groups met at a conference convened by ECOWAS in the Gambian capital, Banjul, where they elected Dr Amos Sawyer, the leader of the LPP, as President of an Interim Government of National Unity (IGNU). Doe was taken prisoner by Johnson's rebel Independent National Patriotic Front of Liberia (INPFL) on 9 September, and was killed on the following day. In early October, following Taylor's rejection of a proposed peace settlement, ECOMOG began an offensive aimed at establishing a neutral zone in Monrovia separating the three warring factions. By mid-October ECOMOG had gained control of central Monrovia. On 22 November Sawyer was inaugurated as Interim President, under the auspices of ECOWAS, in Monrovia. By January 1991 all rebel forces had withdrawn from Monrovia, and in that month Sawyer nominated ministers to the IGNU. Legislative power was vested in a 28-member Interim National Assembly, which represented the principal political factions, including the INPFL; however, the NPFL refused to participate. On 19 April a national conference re-elected Sawyer as Interim President and appointed a member of the INPFL, Peter Naigow (a former minister in Doe's administration), as Vice-President. In June Sawyer nominated a new Council of Ministers, which was subsequently approved by the Interim National Assembly. In August, however, the INPFL representatives, including Naigow, resigned from the IGNU, after Sawyer denounced the execution of four members of the INPFL who had reportedly complied with arrangements to relinquish weapons to ECOMOG.

In April 1991, after several incursions by members of the NPFL into Sierra Leone, Sierra Leonean forces entered Liberian territory and launched retaliatory attacks. It was claimed that NPFL forces were supporting a Sierra Leonean resistance movement, the Revolutionary United Front (RUF), in hostilities against government forces of that country. In September members of a newly emerged rebel movement, comprising former supporters of Doe, the United Liberation Movement of Liberia for Democracy (ULIMO), began attacks from Sierra Leone against NPFL forces in north-western Liberia.

At the end of October 1991 a summit meeting between Sawyer and Taylor, which took place in Yamoussoukro, Côte d'Ivoire, resulted in a peace agreement whereby the troops of all warring factions were to be disarmed and restricted to camps, while the NPFL was to relinquish the territory under its control to ECOMOG. In January 1992 an Interim Election Commission and Supreme Court were established, in accordance with the peace accord.

In August 1992 ULIMO launched a renewed offensive in western Liberia, gaining control of Bomi and Grand Cape Mount Counties. In October the NPFL claimed that Nigerian aircraft under ECOMOG command had bombed its bases at Kakata and Harbel (the site of the Robertsfield International Airport and the country's principal rubber plantation), and at Buchanan. The NPFL subsequently seized a number of strategic areas on the outskirts of Monrovia. ECOMOG forces (who were supported by members of the AFL and militia loyal to the IGNU) began retaliatory attacks against NPFL positions around the capital. In October ECOMOG units succeeded in capturing the INPFL base at Caldwell, near Monrovia, and forcing Johnson to surrender. (The INPFL was subsequently disbanded.) In November the UN Security Council adopted a resolution imposing a mandatory embargo on the supply of armaments to Liberia, and authorized the UN Secretary-General to send a special representative to the country. In March 1993 ULIMO accepted an invitation from Sawyer to join the IGNU; ULIMO forces in Monrovia were subsequently disarmed. Following a major offensive, ECOMOG had by April regained control of the areas seized by the NPFL, including its bases of Harbel and Buchanan.

Installation of transitional institutions

In July 1993 a conference, attended by the factions involved in the hostilities, was convened (under the auspices of the UN and ECOWAS) in Geneva, Switzerland. Following several days of negotiations, the IGNU, the NPFL and ULIMO agreed to a cease-fire (to be monitored by UN observers and a reconstituted peace-keeping force), and to the establishment of a transitional administration. The peace accord was formally signed in Cotonou, Benin, on 25 July. Under its terms, the IGNU was to be replaced by the Liberian National Transitional Government (LNTG), with a five-member transitional Council of State and a 35-member Transitional Legislative Assembly (comprising 13 representatives of the IGNU, 13 of the NPFL and nine of ULIMO), pending elections.

The cease-fire came into effect at the end of July 1993. In August the IGNU, the NPFL and ULIMO each appointed a representative to the Council of State, while nine candidates, nominated by the three factions, elected the two remaining members (who were representatives of the IGNU and ULIMO, respectively) from among their number. Dr Bismark Kuyon, a member of the IGNU, was subsequently elected Chairman of the Council of State. In September the UN Security Council approved the establishment of a 300-member UN Observer Mission in Liberia (UNOMIL), which was to co-operate with ECOMOG and the Organization of African Unity (now the African Union, see p. 191) in monitoring the transitional process. In October the Transitional Legislative Assembly was established, in accordance with the peace agreement. Sawyer dismissed Kuyon (who had reportedly dissociated himself from the IGNU's refusal to relinquish power prior to disarmament) and appointed Philip Banks, hitherto Minister of Justice, in his place.

Meanwhile, it was feared that renewed hostilities in several areas of the country would jeopardize the peace accord. An armed faction styling itself the Liberia Peace Council (LPC), which reportedly comprised members of the Krahn ethnic group from Grand Gedeh County, joined by a number of disaffected AFL troops, emerged in September 1993 and subsequently entered into conflict with the NPFL in south-eastern Liberia. In December fighting between ULIMO and a newly formed movement, the Lofa Defence Force (LDF), was also reported in Lofa County.

In February 1994 the Council of State elected David Kpomakpor, a representative of the IGNU, as its Chairman. In early March units belonging to UNOMIL and the reinforced ECOMOG force were deployed, and the disarmament of all factions commenced. On 7 March the Council of State was inaugurated; it was envisaged that the presidential and legislative elections (originally scheduled for February) would take place in September. However, the disarmament process was subsequently impeded by an increase in rebel activity, which included fighting between members of the Krahn and Mandingo ethnic groups within ULIMO, particularly in the region of Tubmanburg (in Bomi County, where the movement was officially based).

UNOMIL's mandate was renewed in April 1994. In May a 19-member Cabinet was installed, comprising seven representatives of the NPFL, seven of ULIMO and five of the former IGNU. In July, however, a faction known as ULIMO—K (led by Alhaji G. V. Kromah) launched an offensive to recapture Tubmanburg, which was under the control of Maj.-Gen. Roosevelt Johnson's forces (ULIMO—J). On 12 September Taylor, Kromah and the Chief of Staff of the AFL, Lt-Gen. Hezekiah Bowen, meeting in Akosombo, Ghana, signed a peace accord providing for the cessation of hostilities and for the establishment of a reconstituted Council of State, in which four of the five members were to be nominated, respectively, by the three factions and a civilian Liberian National Conference (LNC—which had been convened in Monrovia at the end of August). Meanwhile, following clashes between dissident members of the NPFL and troops loyal to Taylor, the dissidents' Central Revolutionary Council (CRC) announced that Taylor had been deposed and replaced by the Minister of Labour in the LNTG, Thomas Woewiyu, who indicated that he was not prepared to accept the Akosombo agreement. In September the CRC, apparently in alliance with elements of the AFL, ULIMO, the LPC and the LDF, took control of Taylor's base at Gbarnga (in central Bong County); Taylor was reported to have fled to Côte d'Ivoire.

In December 1994 a cease-fire entered into force and reaffirmed the terms of the Akosombo agreement, including provisions for the establishment of demilitarized zones throughout Liberia and for the installation of a reconstituted Council of State, to comprise a single representative of each of the NPFL, ULIMO, the 'Coalition Forces' (a loose alliance comprising the CRC, the LPC, the LDF and elements of the AFL), and the LNC, with a fifth member elected jointly by the NPFL and ULIMO from traditional rulers. At the end of December the UN Security Council extended the mandate of UNOMIL (now comprising some 90 observers) until April 1995, while the Nigerian Government reduced its ECOMOG contingent to 6,000 (from about 10,000).

Regional peace initiatives continue

On 19 August 1995, following protracted negotiations, the armed factions (the NPFL, ULIMO—K, the LPC, the CRC, the LDF, ULIMO—J and the AFL) finally signed a compromise agreement providing for the installation of a reconstituted Council of State, which was to remain in power, pending elections, for one year. An academic with no factional affiliations, Prof. Wilton Sankawulo, was to assume the office of Chairman, while the other seats were to be allocated to Taylor, Kromah, George Boley, the LNC representative, Oscar Quiah, and Chief Tamba Taylor, who had been nominated by ULIMO and the NPFL. Later that month a cease-fire entered into force, in compliance with the terms of the peace accord. The Council of State was formally installed on 1 September, and was to remain in place pending elections, scheduled for August 1996. The Council of State subsequently appointed a transitional Council of Ministers. In September 1995 the UN Security Council extended UNOMIL's mandate until the end of January 1996.

In November 1995 a demilitarized zone was established between NPFL and ULIMO—K forces in the region of the St Paul River (between Bong and Lofa Counties). Deployment of ECOMOG forces commenced, in accordance with the Abuja peace terms, in December. Following continued clashes between the ULIMO factions, however, ULIMO—J attacked ECOMOG troops near Tubmanburg. ECOMOG suspended deployment of its forces, and launched a counter-offensive in an attempt to restore order.

In February 1996 ULIMO—J officials stated that Johnson had been replaced as leader of the movement in the interests of the peace process. In March the Council of State announced his removal from the Council of Ministers. In subsequent clashes between the two factions of ULIMO—J, forces loyal to Johnson allegedly killed a supporter of the new leadership, prompting the Council of State to order that he be arrested on charges of murder. Johnson, however, refused to surrender to the authorities, and became effectively besieged in his private residence in Monrovia. In April government forces, led by Charles Taylor, engaged in hostilities with Johnson's supporters, in an effort to force him to surrender. The principal factions represented in the transitional authorities thus became involved in the conflict: elements of the LPC and AFL (which were predominantly Krahn) supported Johnson's forces, while the NPFL and ULIMO—K opposed them. Fighting rapidly intensified in central Monrovia and ECOMOG deployed its forces in the region. However, some of Johnson's supporters launched attacks in the residential area of Mamba Point (where embassies and offices of humanitarian organizations were situated) and seized a number of civilians as hostages. Later in April a further cease-fire agreement was negotiated under the aegis of the US Government, the UN and ECOWAS, allowing the deployment of ECOMOG troops throughout Monrovia, while most of the remaining hostages were released by Johnson's supporters.

In May 1996, during the absence of Johnson (who had left the country under US protection, to attend a planned ECOWAS summit meeting), the NPFL launched a further attack against the Barclay Training Centre, prompting large numbers of civilians to flee to Monrovia Freeport. At the end of May the UN Security Council renewed the mandate of UNOMIL for a further three months; the mission was henceforth to comprise only the remaining five military and 20 civilian personnel, following the evacuation of the main mission of about 90 observers in April.

In August 1996, at an ECOWAS conference in Abuja, the principal faction leaders (apart from Johnson, who remained abroad) signed a further peace agreement, whereby a reconstituted Council of State was to be installed by the end of that month, with a former senator, Ruth Perry, replacing Sankawulo as Chairman; Taylor and Boley were to remain members of the new administration. Under a revised schedule, elections were to take place at the end of May 1997, and power was to be transferred to an elected government by mid-June, following the dissolution of the armed factions by the end of January of that year. At the end of August 1996 the mandate of UNOMIL was again extended. Perry was inaugurated as Chairman of the Council of State in early September; Johnson was again allocated a ministerial portfolio in a subsequent reorganization of the Cabinet. Following the expiry of the deadline for the completion of the disarmament process, which had been extended to early February 1997, ECOMOG announced that about 91% of the rebel forces (who numbered 30,000–35,000, according to revised estimates) had relinquished their armaments.

In January 1997 Taylor announced that the NPFL had been officially dissolved, in accordance with the peace agreement; the movement was subsequently reconstituted as a political organization, the National Patriotic Party (NPP). In the same month Kromah declared that ULIMO—K had also ceased to exist as a military organization, and was to be reconstituted as the All Liberian Coalition Party (ALCOP). In March Taylor, Kromah and Boley resigned from the Council of State, in compliance with the peace agreement, to allow their candidacy in the forthcoming elections. From March a number of West African countries began to dispatch additional contingents to reinforce ECOMOG (which was to be increased in size to about 16,000 personnel prior to the elections), with the USA providing logistical and financial assistance.

Charles Taylor elected President

By mid-1997 a total of 13 presidential candidates had emerged, amongst them Ellen Johnson-Sirleaf (a former minister in the Tolbert administration and subsequently a World Bank official, who was to contest the election on behalf of the UP). Following a postponement, the elections proceeded on 19 July. The elections commission announced on 23 July that Taylor had been elected President, with 75.3% of votes cast; Johnson-Sirleaf (who had been widely expected to be Taylor's strongest opponent) received only 9.6% of the votes. In the concurrent elections to the bicameral legislature (at which seats were allocated on a proportionate basis), the NPP secured 49 seats in the 64-member House of Representatives and 21 seats in the 26-member Senate, the UP won seven seats in the House of Representatives and three in the Senate, while ALCOP obtained three seats in the House of Representatives and two in the Senate. International observers declared the conduct of the elections to have been 'free and fair'. Taylor's overwhelming victory was generally ascribed to the widely held perception that he was the candidate most likely to achieve long-term stability in the country.

Taylor was inaugurated as President on 2 August 1997, and subsequently nominated a 19-member Cabinet, which was approved by the Senate. The new Government retained several members of the previous transitional administration, including Johnson and Woewiyu. A nine-member National Security Council, comprising several government ministers, the Chief of Staff of the Armed Forces and the Commander of ECOMOG, was also established.

At an ECOWAS summit meeting, convened in Abuja, at the end of August 1997, it was agreed that ECOMOG was to be reconstituted and would henceforth assist in the process of national reconstruction, including the restructuring of the armed and security forces, and the maintenance of security. Following the military coup in Sierra Leone in May 1997, ECOMOG was additionally authorized to enforce international sanctions against the new junta led by Maj. Johnny Paul Koroma. In October, however, Taylor announced that he opposed the use of military force to oust the Koroma regime, and that ECOMOG would no longer be permitted to launch offensives against Sierra Leone from Liberian territory. At the end of October Taylor established a National Human Rights Commission, which was empowered to investigate complaints of human rights violations. In December Taylor appointed Kromah (who had taken up residence in Guinea following his electoral defeat in July) to the post of Chairman of a National Commission on Reconciliation. After the seizure of the Sierra Leonean capital, Freetown, by Nigerian-led ECOMOG troops in February 1998, Taylor protested that the arrest by ECOMOG of about 25 senior members of Sierra Leone's ousted junta at James Spriggs Payne Airport was an infringement of Liberian territory. The Liberian Government recalled its ambassador in Nigeria for consultations, and subsequently submitted a formal complaint to ECOWAS.

In March 1998 violent clashes erupted in Monrovia between the security forces and Johnson's supporters; Johnson subsequently claimed that members of Taylor's special security forces had attacked his private residence. ECOMOG troops were deployed to prevent further violence, and, in an attempt to ease tension in the capital, Johnson was removed from the Cabinet and appointed ambassador to India. In the same month Kromah, who had expressed concern regarding his own safety,

was removed from his position as Chairman of the National Commission on Reconciliation. Later that month the Government and ECOWAS signed an agreement revising ECOMOG's mandate in the country; the contingent was henceforth banned from intervening in civil disputes.

In September 1998 security forces attempted to arrest Johnson (who had not yet assumed his ambassadorial post), pursuing him to the US embassy compound, where he and a number of his supporters had taken refuge. The Government subsequently announced that Johnson, Kromah and 21 of their associates had been charged with treason, following an abortive coup attempt, and demanded that US embassy officials relinquish Johnson to Liberian authority. After discussions with the Liberian authorities, however, US officials transported Johnson to Sierra Leone. In response to an incursion by Liberian security forces into the US embassy compound during the fighting, the US Government temporarily closed the embassy and deployed a naval vessel near the Liberian coast. The Liberian Government subsequently issued a formal apology to the USA and announced that an investigation would be conducted into the incident, in co-operation with the US authorities. In October 32 people (several, including Johnson, *in absentia*) were formally charged with treason; their trial commenced in November.

Regional instability

In December 1998 the Government closed Liberia's border with Sierra Leone, in response to the escalation in civil conflict in the neighbouring country, and pledged support for the administration of President Ahmed Kabbah. In January 1999 it was announced that most of the remaining ECOMOG troops in Liberia were to be redeployed to Sierra Leone, following a major offensive by RUF forces against Freetown. A small number of ECOMOG forces remained in Liberia to provide military assistance to the armed forces. In April 13 of the defendants on trial for treason were convicted and sentenced to 10 years' imprisonment.

In August 1999 members of a rebel movement reported to comprise former members of ULIMO—K, known as the Joint Forces for the Liberation of Liberia (JFLL), attacked principal towns in Lofa County from Guinea. Taylor declared a temporary state of emergency in Lofa County and ordered the closure of the border with Guinea (which was reopened in February 2000). In July 2000 rebel forces again launched an offensive from Guinean territory against Voinjama. Another hitherto unknown movement, Liberians United for Reconciliation and Democracy (LURD), believed to be a grouping of former members of the armed factions (particularly ULIMO–K), claimed responsibility for the attacks. In August Johnson-Sirleaf and a further 14 prominent opposition leaders (many of whom were abroad) were charged with alleged involvement with the LURD dissidents.

In January 2001 the Liberian Government withdrew its ambassador in Guinea, following a further bombardment of towns in the Foya district of northern Liberia from Guinea. In the same month a committee of the UN Security Council reported that the Liberian Government actively supported the RUF and proposed the imposition of UN sanctions against Liberia. In February the authorities announced that the Commander of the RUF, Sam Bockarie, had left the country, and that the rebels' liaison office had been closed. In March the UN Security Council renewed the embargo on the supply of armaments to Liberia and voted in favour of a 12-month ban on diamond exports from Liberia and restrictions on the foreign travel of senior government and military officials; these latter measures were, however, deferred for a period of two months to allow the Government time to comply with demands that it expel RUF members from Liberia and end financial and military aid to the rebels. (In October 2000 the US Government had announced the imposition of diplomatic sanctions against Taylor, his relatives and close associates, prohibiting them from entering the USA until Liberia withdrew support for the RUF.)

In May 2001, in response to Taylor's perceived failure to comply with UN demands, the embargo on exports of diamonds from Liberia, together with the travel restrictions on senior government and military officials, entered into effect. In October a five-member UN commission issued a report recommending the extension of the existing sanctions against Liberia. The UN report also stated that the Liberian Government continued to use revenue generated by the timber industry and maritime activities to finance illicit trade in armaments with the RUF, and proposed the imposition of additional sanctions on timber exports.

By early 2002 LURD forces had gained considerable territory from government troops, and continued to advance southwards towards Monrovia. In response, Taylor declared a national state of emergency on 8 February (which was subsequently ratified by the legislature). Later that month the Government announced that it was to establish a permanent security presence at the country's northern border with Sierra Leone and Guinea. At the beginning of March the leader of LURD, Sekou Damate Conneh, announced that his forces aimed to depose Taylor and install a transitional administration in Monrovia. Later that month representatives of LURD failed to attend negotiations between the Liberian authorities and opposition, which were held in Abuja, under the aegis of ECOWAS. At the conclusion of the meeting delegates representing 29 political and civil society associations, including major opposition leaders, urged the Government and LURD forces to declare a cease-fire. Nevertheless, fighting continued, particularly at Liberia's northern border with Guinea.

On 6 May 2002 the UN Security Council adopted a resolution extending the armaments and diamond embargoes, and the travel ban, for a further 12 months. Also in May the Liberian legislature extended for a further six months the national state of emergency, after LURD forces gained further territory, seizing control of Gbarnga, in Bong County. In September Taylor ended the national state of emergency and the ban on political demonstrations, announcing that government forces had regained control of much of the territory captured by LURD.

During early 2003 hostilities frequently crossed into the territory of Côte d'Ivoire, and reports emerged that Ivorian rebel groups, notably the Mouvement pour la Justice et la Paix (MJP) and the Mouvement Populaire Ivoirien du Grand Ouest (MPIGO), had become allied with LURD. By March LURD had advanced to only 20 km from Monrovia, causing large numbers of civilians to take refuge in the capital. Simultaneous heavy fighting for control of Gbarnga was reported; LURD forces had recaptured the town by April. Meanwhile, a new rebel faction, the Movement for Democracy in Liberia (MODEL), attacked and secured Zwedru in Grand Gedeh County. MODEL was believed to comprise former members of the AFL and Doe loyalists, who were mainly based in Côte d'Ivoire (and reportedly supported by the Ivorian Government). On 6 May the UN Security Council renewed the existing embargoes in force against Liberia for a further year, and imposed an additional ban on timber exports (which entered into effect in early July). Also in early May the Liberian authorities announced that Bockarie (who had been indicted by the Special Court established in Sierra Leone to try suspects of war crimes committed during the 10-year conflict in the country) had been killed in Liberia during an attempt to arrest him. Subsequently, however, officials at the Special Court claimed that Bockarie and his immediate family had been captured and murdered by Liberian security forces to prevent him from testifying against prominent regional leaders.

Removal of Taylor

The international community repeatedly urged unconditional negotiations within the framework of a mediation process led by ECOWAS, and in March 2003 LURD finally agreed, in principle, to enter into dialogue with Taylor. Peace discussions, attended by Taylor and LURD, commenced in Accra, Ghana, on 4 June, but were disrupted by the announcement of Taylor's indictment for war crimes by the Special Court, in connection with his alleged long-standing involvement with the RUF. On the following day Taylor returned to Monrovia, where he immediately announced that the authorities had suppressed an attempted coup. On the same day LURD forces launched a major attack on Monrovia from the movement's base in Tubmanburg, and rapidly reached the capital's western outskirts, causing an exodus from refugee camps towards the city centre. LURD's political leadership issued an ultimatum demanding Taylor's resignation, and French military forces commenced the evacuation of foreign nationals. Following the arrival of a MODEL delegation, the peace discussions in Ghana resumed on 9 June. On 17 June a cease-fire agreement was signed by the LURD and MODEL leaders, and by the Minister of Defence, Daniel Chea. Immediately beforehand, government troops recaptured Greenville, forcing LURD to withdraw to positions some 35 km from Monrovia.

Shortly after the cease-fire agreement was signed in Accra, however, Taylor declared that he would remain in office at least until the end of his presidential term in January 2004, and rejected the Special Court indictment against him. Serious breaches of the cease-fire were reported, and on 26 June 2003, after the resumption of heavy fighting between government and rebel forces in and around Monrovia, in which about 300 civilians

were killed, US President George W. Bush urged Taylor to resign. At the end of June the UN Secretary-General recommended to the Security Council that a multinational peace-keeping force be deployed in Liberia in response to the critical humanitarian situation, and urged US military intervention. On 6 July Taylor announced that he had accepted, in principle, an offer of asylum from the Nigerian Head of State, Olusegun Obasanjo, but stipulated that he would not leave the country until a peace-keeping operation was installed. Following continued appeals from Liberian civilians for foreign intervention to prevent a humanitarian disaster, a US mission of military observers was dispatched to Liberia. Later in July, after the rebel offensive to oust Taylor had reached the centre of the capital, the US embassy compound (in which some 10,000 Liberian civilians had taken refuge) was repeatedly bombarded. Some 100 US marines were flown in to defend the building, while US naval vessels were stationed off the Liberian coast. Meanwhile, following the resumption of discussions between the government, LURD and MODEL delegations in Accra, it was announced that a peace accord, based on the terms of the failed cease-fire agreement, had been drafted.

On 22 July 2003 a summit meeting of ECOWAS Heads of State was convened in the Senegalese capital, Dakar. Following pressure from the UN Secretary-General, the West African delegates agreed to dispatch an initial 1,300 Nigerian peace-keeping troops to Liberia. On 1 August the UN Security Council officially authorized the establishment of a multinational force with a maximum strength of 3,250 troops, to be known as the ECOWAS Mission in Liberia (ECOMIL), which was to restore security to allow the distribution of emergency humanitarian assistance, and prepare for the deployment of a longer-term UN stabilization force. On 11 August, following continued pressure from West African Governments and the international community, Taylor relinquished power to the Vice-President, Moses Zeh Blah, before leaving Liberia for exile in the town of Calabar, in south-eastern Nigeria. Blah was inaugurated as interim Head of State, pending the installation of a government of national unity, which was the subject of continuing negotiations between the government and rebel delegations in Accra. Taylor's departure fulfilled the main demand of the rebel leadership, who ceded control of Monrovia Freeport to ECOMIL, and a further 200 US military personnel arrived in Liberia to support the peace operation. On 18 August delegates of the incumbent Government, rebel factions, political opposition and civil organizations, under the aegis of the UN, reached a comprehensive peace agreement, which provided for the establishment of a transitional power-sharing government and legislature, to comprise representatives of the participating groupings. Under the accord, Blah was to transfer power to the new administration on 14 October, all armed militia were to be disbanded, and democratic elections were to be conducted by October 2005. On 21 August 2003 the delegations elected Gyude Bryant, a prominent church figure and leader of the LAP, as Chairman of the transitional administration. By the end of August a UN Joint Monitoring Committee had been dispatched to Monrovia, and ECOMIL troops (then numbering 1,500) were taking control of rebel-held territory.

The National Transitional Government

On 19 September 2003 the UN Security Council formally established the UN Mission in Liberia (UNMIL, see p. 90), which was mandated to support the transitional authorities and the implementation of the August peace agreement; the first contingent, of about 4,000, commenced deployment in the country (replacing ECOMIL) on 1 October. On 14 October, under the terms of the peace agreement, Bryant was officially inaugurated as Chairman of the two-year power-sharing administration, the National Transitional Government, while the leader of the UPP, Wesley Johnson, became Vice-Chairman. At the same time a 76-member unicameral legislature, the National Transitional Legislative Assembly (NTLA), comprising representatives of the groupings signatory to the August agreement and 15 deputies nominated by the counties, was installed. A prominent member of LURD, George Dweh, was subsequently elected Speaker of the new Assembly. Later in October LURD and MODEL (which were each allocated five ministries in the National Transitional Government) submitted ministerial nominees for approval by the legislature. Of the former Taylor loyalists, Chea retained the post of Minister of Defence, while LURD representatives were awarded the portfolios of justice and finance, and the leader of MODEL, Thomas Nimely Yaya, became Minister of Foreign Affairs. In early December the International Criminal Police Organization (INTERPOL) issued an arrest notice against

Taylor (who remained in Nigeria) for suspected war crimes. Later that month the UN Security Council adopted a resolution maintaining the embargoes on imports of armaments and on exports of timber and diamonds for a minimum of one year

In March 2004, after the remaining ministerial portfolios were finally designated, Bryant inaugurated the National Transitional Government. Following a further struggle for leadership within LURD, its national executive council announced the removal of Sekou Conneh and his replacement by Chayee Doe (a brother of the former President). Conneh refused to acknowledge the statement, and continued to reject demands by his opponents within the movement for the replacement of the LURD Minister of Finance, Lusine Kamara. In September the International Criminal Court (ICC, see p. 349) announced that Liberia had ratified the signatory treaty, thereby allowing the Court jurisdiction to prosecute crimes committed during the civil conflict. On 17 September the UN Security Council adopted a resolution extending the mandate of UNMIL for a further year (while welcoming the progress made in the peace process).

A disarmament process organized by UNMIL, under which a total of some 96,000 former combatants had relinquished armaments, officially ended on 31 October 2004, with a ceremony at which the three former armed factions were also officially dissolved (although operations continued after that date). In December the UN Security Council renewed the sanctions in force on armaments, timber and travel for a further year, while the embargo on the export of diamonds was extended for six months (and again extended in mid-2005).

Meanwhile, disputes over electoral reform legislation between the NTLA and the Government were resolved only by sustained pressure from Bryant and the US Ambassador, thereby delaying the adoption of the legislation until December 2004. Nevertheless, in February 2005 the National Elections Commission (NEC) announced that the presidential and legislative elections would be conducted on 11 October, as scheduled. Some 40 prospective presidential candidates had emerged, notably including George Manneh Weah, a Liberian national and an international association footballer. In mid-March NTLA Speaker Dweh, together with the Deputy Speaker and two parliamentary deputies, were suspended from office on suspicion of corruption, following a report by a parliamentary committee.

The 2005 elections

At the first round of presidential voting on 11 October 2005, which was contested by a total of 22 candidates, Weah secured 28.3% of votes cast, while Johnson-Sirleaf won 19.8% of votes and Charles Brumskine of the Liberty Party (LP) 13.9% of votes. At the elections to the 64-member lower House of Representatives Weah's party, the Congress for Democratic Change (CDC), won 15 seats, the LP nine seats, an alliance known as the Coalition for the Transformation of Liberia (COTOL) eight seats and the UP eight seats. At the elections to the 30-member Senate the COTOL secured seven seats, while the CDC, the UP and the LP each received three seats. Some 74.9% of the registered electorate voted in the presidential ballot and 76.5% in the legislative elections. Since no presidential candidate had secured an absolute majority, a second round was conducted on 8 November: Johnson-Sirleaf defeated Weah by securing 59.4% of votes cast (with 61.0% of the electorate participating). On 23 November, despite claims of electoral malpractice, the NEC officially declared that Johnson-Sirleaf had won the presidential election. Violent demonstrations by Weah's supporters in Monrovia resulted in clashes with security forces and the arrest of some 40 protesters. In mid-December, following international pressure, however, Weah agreed to suspend his legal challenge to Johnson-Sirleaf's election at the Supreme Court, and subsequently announced that he would abandon his claim to the presidency in the interests of national reconciliation. Later that month the UN Security Council again extended the sanctions on armaments and travel for a further year and those on diamonds and timber for six months. (UN sanctions on the export of timber were finally lifted in September 2006, and those on diamond exports in April 2007.)

Johnson-Sirleaf was inaugurated as President on 16 January 2006, thereby becoming the first woman to be elected Head of State in Africa. The two legislative chambers were officially installed on the same day. The election of a close former associate of Taylor, Edwin Snowe, as Speaker of the House of Representatives attracted controversy. In February Johnson-Sirleaf established a seven-member Truth and Reconciliation Commission (TRC), which was to investigate human rights abuses perpetrated during the civil conflict. In March the Nigerian Government announced that it had received an official request from Johnson-Sirleaf for Taylor's extradition. Later in March, shortly after President Obasanjo declared that Nigeria would agree his extradition, Taylor fled from his residence in Calabar; he was apprehended two days later in Borno State, near the border with Cameroon, and dispatched to Liberia, from where he was immediately extradited by UNMIL peace-keepers to the Special Court. In early April Taylor pleaded 'not guilty' to all charges at the Special Court. Tribunal officials subsequently requested that his trial be transferred to the ICC at The Hague, the Netherlands, (while remaining under the jurisdiction of the Special Court), in the interests of regional stability. The Dutch authorities acceded to that request on the condition that any sentence handed down to Taylor was served in another country. The United Kingdom subsequently agreed to host Taylor should he be imprisoned, and, following the unanimous approval of the UN Security Council, on 20 June Taylor was transferred to The Hague, where his trial officially commenced in June 2007.

In November 2006 the Minister of Information, Culture and Tourism, Johnny McClain, resigned from office citing insufficient funding and a lack of support from the Government. He was replaced by Rev. Dr Lawrence Bropleh. In August Johnson-Sirleaf implemented a major reorganization of the Government, in which Olubanke King Akerele replaced George W. Wallace as Minister of Foreign Affairs, and Philip Banks became Minister of Justice, replacing Frances Johnson-Morris, who assumed the commerce and industry portfolio.

In February 2007 Gyude Bryant was charged with misappropriating US $1.3m. during his period as Chairman of the National Transitional Government. In January 2009 Charles 'Chuckie' Taylor, Jr, son of the former President, was sentenced to 97 years' imprisonment, after being found guilty of charges relating to torture and executions committed while he was head of a security unit during the civil conflict. In March the President of the Senate, Isaac Nyenabo (who had been suspended from the post in the previous August on grounds of incompetence), announced his resignation, following a sustained boycott of the Senate by many of its members and the adoption of a vote of no confidence in him. In April Bryant, former parliamentary Speaker and head of the Liberia Petroleum Refining Corporation (LPRC) Edwin Snowe, and three others charged with embezzling funds from the LPRC during Bryant's presidency were acquitted of all charges of corruption while holding public office.

On 1 July 2009 the TRC submitted its final report recommending the establishment of an Extraordinary Criminal Tribunal for Liberia, and the prosecution or investigation of a number of individuals, corporations and institutions for human rights violations. The Commission also recommended that some 50 people who had associated with or financed the warring factions should be barred from public office for a period of 30 years; they included Johnson-Sirleaf, following her admission to the Commission in February that she had supported Taylor's NPFL after its insurrection in 1989, and had donated US $10,000 to the movement. The proposed ban against Johnson-Sirleaf prompted domestic and international consternation, and speculation that it had been instigated in view of the forthcoming 2011 elections. (Nevertheless, Johnson-Sirleaf subsequently declared her intention to seek re-election in 2011.) The National Assembly was required to adopt a resolution on the TRC's report to allow its enactment; in late August 2009 the legislature announced that it would consult with the public for about one year before deciding whether or not to implement the Commission's recommendations. In September the UN Security Council extended the mandate of UNMIL for a further year and authorized a reduction in its total strength to about 8,200 personnel (while maintaining the strength of its police component). In December the UN Security Council relaxed for a trial period of one year the armaments embargo imposed on Liberia to allow the Government and UNMIL to receive military supplies, in view of the progress made in national reconstruction; the freeze on the assets of former associates of Taylor and the travel embargo were extended for a further year. (However, the armaments embargo, together with the sanctions on members of the former regime, was renewed in December 2010 and December 2011.)

In December 2009 the General Auditing Commission concluded that Minister of Information, Culture and Tourism Bropleh, who had been suspended from office pending investigations, had embezzled some US $358,000 and recommended his prosecution. (Cletus Sieh was subsequently appointed to replace Bropleh.) In February 2010 George Boley was arrested in the USA on grounds of lack of proper documentation. Later that month the Minister of Internal Affairs, Ambulai Johnson, resigned from his post, owing to his alleged mismanagement of the Social Development Fund; he was replaced by Harrison Kahnweah.

The 2011 elections

In July 2010 the National Assembly adopted legislation creating nine additional parliamentary seats to be distributed among the six most populated counties, thereby increasing the total number of seats in the House of Representatives to 73 (with effect from the next elections). At the end of August the National Assembly approved four constitutional amendments, including a provision that the two-round system used in legislative elections would be replaced by a single-round, first-past-the-post system. The NEC announced in September that the amendments were to be submitted for endorsement at a pre-election national referendum, which was scheduled for 23 August 2011. At a party convention in October 2010, Johnson-Sirleaf was nominated as the presidential candidate of the UP (which had previously merged with the LUP and LAP, under the chairmanship of former presidential candidate Varney Sherman); the incumbent Vice-President, Joseph Nyumah Boakai, was confirmed as the party's vice-presidential candidate. Former rebel leader Prince Yormie Johnson had also announced that he intended to contest the forthcoming presidential election. In November Johnson-Sirleaf reorganized her Government; new appointments included the replacement of long-standing Minister of Lands, Mines, and Energy, Eugene Shannon, by a former ECOWAS official, Roosevelt Jayjay. In January 2011 the Supreme Court, ruling on a challenge brought by one of those prohibited from holding public office by the TRC report of July 2009, declared that the TRC's recommendation was an unconstitutional violation of the rights of those individuals banned (including Johnson-Sirleaf). Only an estimated 34.2% of the electorate participated in the national referendum on 23 August 2011, when all four constitutional amendments failed to secure the requisite approval of two-thirds of votes cast.

At the legislative elections, which were conducted on 11 October 2011, the UP won the highest number of seats in the expanded, 73-member House of Representatives, taking 24, while the CDC retained only 11 seats. The UP also secured the highest representation in the Senate, holding nine seats in total, after receiving four seats in the partial elections to the chamber. In the first round of the concurrent presidential election, Johnson-Sirleaf won 43.9% of votes cast, and long-standing politician Winston Tubman, representing the CDC, 32.7%; Prince Yormie Johnson, the candidate of the National Union for Democratic Progress, took only 11.6% of votes. The CDC subsequently protested that NEC officials had perpetrated malpractice on behalf of the UP, prompting the head of the Commission to resign. A number of violent incidents were reported during the ensuing unrest, including an arson attack against the UP party headquarters in mid-October and the killing of two supporters of Tubman when security forces opened fire on a gathering in early November. Shortly before the second presidential round took place, Tubman announced the withdrawal of his candidacy and urged an opposition boycott of the poll, in protest at the alleged fraud. In the event, only an estimated 38.6% of the electorate participated in the second round on 8 November: Johnson-Sirleaf was re-elected with some 90.7% of votes cast (Tubman, nevertheless, receiving the remaining 9.3% of the votes). In December Johnson-Sirleaf removed the Minister of Information, Culture and Tourism, Cletus Sieh, reportedly owing to the release of information regarding protests in Monrovia by students. Tubman finally conceded the legitimacy of Johnson-Sirleaf's election to the presidency in January 2012. After her inauguration on 16 January, Johnson-Sirleaf formed a new Government, which notably included Augustine Ngafuan (formerly Minister of Finance) as Minister of Foreign Affairs and Amara Konneh (hitherto Minister of Planning and Economic Affairs) as Minister of Finance. In early March the CDC announced the expulsion of Tubman from the party, accusing him of corruption and unethical behaviour, and the reinstatement of George Weah as party leader; Tubman subsequently declared that he was to retire from politics. Meanwhile, following an assessment mission to Liberia in February, UN officials confirmed that UNMIL (whose mandate had again been extended in September 2010 and September 2011, and which

then numbered some 10,900) was to be reduced in size to about 8,000.

Recent developments: conviction of Taylor

Meanwhile, Taylor's trial at the Special Court had reached completion in March 2011, despite frequent boycotts of proceedings by Taylor and his defence counsel. On 26 April 2012 Taylor was found guilty of aiding and abetting the commission of war crimes, but was acquitted of the charges of directing crimes to be carried out. On 30 May he was sentenced to 50 years' imprisonment (which he was to serve in the United Kingdom). Taylor's lawyers gave formal notice that he would submit an appeal against his conviction (which began at the ICC on 22 January 2013).

In July 2012 the UN Security Council announced that it had ended the travel bans and asset freezes imposed on 17 Liberian citizens. In a report issued in September, however, the UN Secretary-General criticized the failure of the Liberian authorities to control illegal trade in diamonds in accordance with the Kimberley Process Certification Scheme (which had been established under a UN resolution in 2003). Later in September the UN Security Council adopted a resolution that authorized the extension of UNMIL's mandate for a further year, but provided for a staged reduction of 4,200 in its military strength, to about 3,750 personnel by mid-2015, with a concomitant increase of 420 in the number of police officers; concerns were nevertheless expressed at the heightened border instability. Meanwhile, in August Johnson-Sirleaf suspended from office 46 government officials, including one of her sons (who had held the post of Deputy Governor of the Central Bank), for failing to declare their assets to an Anti-Corruption Commission. In October the head of a government Peace and Reconciliation Commission, Leymah Gbowee, resigned, after denouncing perceived corruption and nepotism in Johnson-Sirleaf's administration (Johnson-Sirleaf had attracted repeated criticism for appointing her sons to government posts). In February 2013 it was reported that the director of Roberts International Airport had been dismissed, following allegations of financial malpractice. In the same month the Guinean Chief of Staff, together with four other military personnel and five civilians, who had been travelling to attend Armed Forces Day celebrations in Liberia, were killed in an air crash near Roberts International Airport; a full investigation into the incident was announced.

In March 2013 President Johnson-Sirleaf announced a reorganization of the Cabinet in which new ministers of labour, transport and commerce and industry were appointed. Further changes to the Government were effected in May.

Foreign Affairs

Following the election of Ellen Johnson-Sirleaf as President in November 2005, Liberia's relations with its neighbouring states improved significantly. Johnson-Sirleaf chairs the Mano River Union (initially comprising Liberia, Guinea and Sierra Leone), which was reactivated in 2004 and joined by Côte d'Ivoire in 2008. A non-aggression pact was signed with Sierra Leone when the country's President, Ernest Bai Koroma, visited Liberia in September 2007. During the political crisis that followed the 2010 presidential election in Côte d'Ivoire, reports emerged that President Laurent Gbagbo (prior to his arrest in April 2011) had recruited Liberian mercenaries to abduct opponents and carry out extrajudicial executions. Cross-border raids on western Côte d'Ivoire, which were believed to involve Liberian mercenaries together with Ivorian armed elements loyal to Gbagbo operating from Liberia, became larger in scale during 2012. In June the Liberian Government closed the border with Côte d'Ivoire and dispatched troops to the area, in response to an attack near the Ivorian town of Tai, in which seven members of the UN Operation in Côte d'Ivoire were killed. Four Liberian mercenaries were subsequently arrested on suspicion of perpetrating the attack, while a number of Ivorian nationals were also held in detention in Liberia. In October Johnson-Sirleaf, meeting President Alassane Ouattara in Abidjan, Côte d'Ivoire, announced the organization of a joint security operation along the border.

The election of Johnson-Sirleaf (a former World Bank official) was widely welcomed by the international community, and also resulted in a dramatic improvement in Liberia's relations with the USA and other major aid donors. US President George W. Bush made an official visit to Liberia in February 2008, the first by a US President in 30 years. US Secretary of State Hillary Clinton visited Liberia in August 2009. In October 2003 the National Transitional Government signed an agreement for the resumption of diplomatic relations with the People's Republic of China (thereby ending links with Taiwan); the Chinese Government subsequently provided substantial funding for reconstruction projects in the country. Bilateral relations with Russia were restored in March 2010. Johnson-Sirleaf, together with a Liberian peace activist, Leymah Gbowee, jointly received the Nobel Peace Prize in 2011.

CONSTITUTION AND GOVERNMENT

Under the Constitution of January 1986, legislative power is vested in the bicameral National Assembly, comprising the 73-member House of Representatives and the 30-member Senate. Members of the House of Representatives are elected by legislative constituency for a term of six years, while each county elects two members of the Senate (one for a term of nine years and one for six years). Executive power is vested in the President, who is elected to office for a six-year term (renewable only once), and who appoints the Government (subject to the approval of the Senate). Following a peace agreement in August 2003, a democratically elected administration was installed in January 2006 (replacing the power-sharing National Transitional Government). The country comprises 15 counties, which are divided into 64 districts.

REGIONAL AND INTERNATIONAL CO-OPERATION

Liberia is a member of the Economic Community of West African States (ECOWAS, see p. 268) and the Mano River Union (see p. 462), both of which aim to promote closer economic co-operation in the region. Liberia is also a member of the African Union (see p. 191)

Liberia was a founder member of the UN on its establishment in 1945, and has observer status at the World Trade Organization (WTO, see p. 444). Liberia participates in the Group of 77 (G77, see p. 461) developing countries.

ECONOMIC AFFAIRS

In 2011, according to the World Bank, Liberia's gross national income (GNI), measured at average 2009–11 prices, was US $996m., equivalent to $240 per head (or $520 per head on an international purchasing-power parity basis). During 2002–11, it was estimated, the population increased at an average annual rate of 3.6%, while gross domestic product (GDP) per head declined by 0.4%. Overall GDP increased by 3.2%, in real terms, in 2002–11; real GDP increased by 8.5% in 2011.

Agriculture and forestry contributed an estimated 72.7% of GDP in 2011, according to the African Development Bank (AfDB). An estimated 26.7% of the formal labour force were employed in the sector in 2010. The principal cash crops are rubber (which accounted for an estimated 67.1% of export earnings in 2011), cocoa beans and coffee. The principal food crops are cassava, rice, bananas, plantains, sweet potatoes and yams. Timber production traditionally represented an important source of export revenue, providing an estimated 50.1% of export earnings in 2003 (when, however, sanctions on timber exports were imposed). Agricultural GDP increased at an average annual rate of 0.3% in 2002–11. The GDP of the agricultural sector increased by 4.0% in 2011.

Industry (including mining, manufacturing, construction and power) contributed 11.8% of GDP in 2011, according to the AfDB, and employed an estimated 4.8% of the formal labour force in 2010. Industrial GDP, according to World Bank figures, increased at an average annual rate of 16.2% in 2002–11; the GDP of the industrial sector increased by 9.8% in 2010 and by 36.3% in 2011.

The mining sector contributed an estimated 2.4% of GDP in 2011, according to the AfDB, and engaged an estimated 1.2% of the formal labour force in 2010. Gold and diamonds are mined, and Liberia possesses significant amounts of barytes and kyanite. The production and export of mineral products were severely disrupted from 1990, as a result of the civil conflict. In 1997 total mineral reserves were estimated to include more than 10m. carats of diamonds and 3m. troy oz of gold. In January 2005 the Government prohibited diamond-mining in order to support the enforcement of UN sanctions on the export of diamonds (imposed in 2001). However, mineral exports recommenced in 2007 and, in that year, foreign sales of gold accounted for 2.7% of total export revenue; diamonds contributed 1.3%. In 2011 these commodities contributed 5.5% and 5.0% of total exports, respectively. The GDP of the mining sector increased at an average annual rate of 59.3% in 2002–11; mining GDP increased by 9.1% in 2010 and by 134.4% in 2011.

Manufacturing provided an estimated 6.0% of GDP in 2011, according to the AfDB, and engaged an estimated 0.9% of the formal labour force in 2010. Manufacturing GDP increased at an average annual rate of 13.6% in 2002–11; the GDP of the manufacturing sector increased by 3.2% in 2011.

Construction provided an estimated 2.7% of GDP in 2011, according to the AfDB, and engaged an estimated 2.7% of the formal labour force in 2010.

Energy is derived from the consumption of fossil fuels (62.2%) and from hydroelectric power (37.8%). In 2003 the authorities announced plans to restore power throughout the country by a programme to rehabilitate a major hydroelectric power installation, which had been damaged in the civil conflict. Liberia is dependent on imports of petroleum, which comprised an estimated 21.6% of the value of total imports in 2011.

The services sector contributed 15.6% of GDP in 2011, according to the AfDB, and employed an estimated 68.5% of the formal labour force in 2010. The GDP of the services sector increased at an average annual rate of 11.0% in 2002–11; the GDP of the sector increased by 6.6% in 2011.

Liberia's large open-registry ('flag of convenience') merchant shipping fleet has become an increasingly significant source of foreign exchange. In 2007 revenue from Liberia's maritime programme accounted for an estimated 7.0% of total revenue.

In 2010 Liberia recorded an estimated visible merchandise trade deficit of US $477.9m., and there was a deficit of $736.9m. on the current account of the balance of payments. In 2004 the principal source of imports (37.8%) was the Republic of Korea. The principal market for exports in 2006 was the USA (73.7%); the other major purchaser was Belgium. The principal export in 2011 was rubber, accounting for 67.1% of total exports. The principal imports in that year were food (particularly rice) and live animals, petroleum, machinery and transport equipment, basic manufactures, mineral fuels and lubricants, and miscellaneous manufactured articles.

Liberia's overall budgetary deficit was projected to be US $111.0m. in 2012/13, according to IMF figures. Liberia's general government gross debt was L $421m. in 2011, equivalent to 27.2% of GDP. The country's external debt totalled US $228m. at the end of 2010, of which US $184m. was public and publicly guaranteed debt. In that year the cost of servicing long-term public and publicly guaranteed debt and repayments to the IMF was equivalent to 1.3% of the value of exports of goods, services and income (excluding workers' remittances). The annual rate of inflation averaged 8.9% in 2002–11; consumer prices increased by 8.5% in 2011. In 2006 unemployment was estimated at about 85.0% of the labour force.

The inauguration of Ellen Johnson-Sirleaf, a former World Bank economist, as President in January 2006 marked a turning point in Liberia's economy, which had been ravaged by civil conflict. She appealed for international support for reconstruction, and announced measures to end endemic corruption. UN sanctions on the export of timber were lifted in September and those on diamond exports in April 2007; shortly afterwards Liberia joined the Extractive Industries Transparency Initiative. In December the AfDB cancelled US $255.2m. of Liberia's debt, and in March 2008 the country cleared its long-standing overdue obligations with the IMF; the Fund fully restored Liberia's rights and designated it eligible for debt relief under the initiative for heavily indebted poor countries (HIPC). The Government instigated a three-year poverty reduction strategy, supported by an IMF Extended Credit Facility (ECF) arrangement. In June 2010 the IMF and World Bank, having determined that Liberia had made the required progress to reach completion point under the HIPC initiative, approved $4,600m. of debt relief, thereby reducing the country's external debt by more than 90%. Foreign investment in the country rose significantly in 2011, with the approval of several new concessions in the iron ore and palm oil sectors, and following the acquisition by US corporation Chevron of a 70% interest in three offshore exploration areas. In June iron ore exports were resumed after a suspension of about 20 years, following funding by international steel and mining company ArcelorMittal under a 2005 agreement. However, the Government of Johnson-Sirleaf (which retained power following elections in late 2011) was subject to continued criticism for corruption. In September 2012 Johnson-Sirleaf ordered an investigation into widespread illegal practices in the timber industry, and announced that a large number of logging contracts were to be renegotiated, following a report by an advocacy group that one-quarter of Liberia's land area had been sold to timber companies, frequently under illicit agreements. Also in

September the UN criticized the failure of the Liberian Government to control illegal trade in diamonds, and reported that the US Agency for International Development intended to suspend funding for a programme to support the authorities' compliance with the Kimberley Process Certification Scheme, partly owing to their lack of commitment. Following the successful conclusion of the previous IMF-supported programme (which had been extended until the end of May), in November the IMF approved a new, three-year ECF arrangement for Liberia, totalling about $78.9m., to finance continued poverty reduction efforts. The IMF projected GDP growth of 8.9% for 2012 and 8.3% for 2013,

generated by the resumption of iron ore exports and construction projects.

PUBLIC HOLIDAYS

2014: 1 January (New Year's Day), 11 February (Armed Forces Day), 12 March (Decoration Day), 15 March (J. J. Robert's Birthday), 11 April (Fast and Prayer Day), 14 May (National Unification Day), 26 July (Independence Day), 24 August (Flag Day), 6 November (Thanksgiving Day), 29 November (President Tubman's Birthday), 25 December (Christmas Day).

Statistical Survey

Sources (unless otherwise stated): Liberia Institute of Statistics and Geo-Information Services, POB 629, Tubman Blvd, Sinkor, Monrovia; internet www.tlcafrica.com/lisgis/lisgis.htm; Central Bank of Liberia, POB 2048, cnr of Warren and Carey Sts, Monrovia; tel. 6225685 (mobile); fax 6226114 (mobile); internet www.cbl.org.lr.

Area and Population

AREA, POPULATION AND DENSITY

Area (sq km)	97,754*
Population (census results)	
1 February 1984	2,101,628
21 March 2008	
Males	1,739,945
Females	1,736,663
Total	3,476,608
Population (UN estimates at mid-year)†	
2011	4,128,572
2012	4,244,683
2013	4,348,741
Density (per sq km) at mid-2013	44.5

* 37,743 sq miles.
† Source: UN, *World Population Prospects: The 2010 Revision*.

POPULATION BY AGE AND SEX
(UN estimates at mid-2013)

	Males	Females	Total
0–14	958,975	922,614	1,881,589
15–64	1,175,364	1,170,699	2,346,063
65 and over	53,898	67,191	121,089
Total	**2,188,237**	**2,160,504**	**4,348,741**

Source: UN, *World Population Prospects: The 2010 Revision*.

COUNTIES
(population at 2008 census)

Bomi	84,119	Margibi . . .	209,923
Bong	333,481	Maryland . . .	135,938
Gbarpolu . . .	83,388	Montserrado . .	1,118,241
Grand Bassa . . .	221,693	Nimba	462,026
Grand Cape Mount .	127,076	Rivercess . . .	71,509
Grand Gedeh . . .	125,258	River Gee . . .	66,789
Grand Kru . . .	57,913	Sinoe	102,391
Lofa	276,863	**Total**	3,476,608

PRINCIPAL TOWNS
(2003)

Monrovia (capital) .	550,200	Harbel	17,700
Zwedru	35,300	Tubmanburg . .	16,700
Buchanan . . .	27,300	Gbarnga . . .	14,200
Yekepa	22,900	Greenville . . .	13,500
Harper	20,000	Ganta	11,200
Bensonville . . .	19,600		

Source: Stefan Helders, *World Gazetteer* (internet www.world-gazetteer.com).

Mid-2011 (incl. suburbs, UN estimate): Monrovia 750,376 (Source: UN, *World Urbanization Prospects: The 2011 Revision*).

BIRTHS AND DEATHS
(annual averages, UN estimates)

	1995–2000	2000–05	2005–10
Birth rate (per 1,000)	44.0	42.4	40.5
Death rate (per 1,000)	19.8	15.4	12.0

Source: UN, *World Population Prospects: The 2010 Revision*.

Life expectancy (years at birth): 56.7 (males 55.7; females 57.8) in 2011 (Source: World Bank, World Development Indicators database).

ECONOMICALLY ACTIVE POPULATION
(formal sector only)

	2008	2009	2010*
Agriculture and forestry . . .	22,616	34,882	38,615
Mining	1,421	1,907	1,691
Manufacturing	2,215	2,075	1,367
Construction	390	1,659	3,856
Wholesale and retail trade . .	10,028	10,998	7,536
Transport and communications .	4,984	5,563	9,423
Banking and insurance . . .	2,189	4,044	6,426
Business services	6,231	9,467	10,179
Social and community services .	9,213	20,160	28,020
Government	47,681	34,000	37,532
Total	**106,968**	**124,755**	**144,647**

* Estimates.

Total employed in informal sector: 487,000 in 2008; 569,790 in 2009; 672,352 (estimate) in 2010.

Health and Welfare

KEY INDICATORS

Total fertility rate (children per woman, 2010)	5.2
Under-5 mortality rate (per 1,000 live births, 2010) . .	103
HIV/AIDS (% of persons aged 15–49, 2009)	1.5
Physicians (per 1,000 head, 2004)	0.03
Hospital beds (per 1,000 head, 2009)	0.7
Health expenditure (2009): US $ per head (PPP)	50
Health expenditure (2009): % of GDP	12.2
Health expenditure (2009): public (% of total)	34.5
Access to water (% of persons, 2010)	73
Access to sanitation (% of persons, 2010)	18
Total carbon dioxide emissions ('000 metric tons, 2008) . .	608.7
Carbon dioxide emissions per head (metric tons, 2008) . .	0.2
Human Development Index (2011): ranking	182
Human Development Index (2011): value	0.329

For sources and definitions, see explanatory note on p. vi.

Agriculture

PRINCIPAL CROPS
('000 metric tons)

	2009	2010	2011
Rice, paddy	293*	296*	300†
Cassava (Manioc)	495*	493*	495†
Taro (Cocoyam)†	27	26	26
Yams†	18	19	20
Sweet potatoes†	20	20	22
Sugar cane†	265	265	265
Oil palm fruit	174*	174*	174†
Bananas†	123	125	125
Plantains†	47	46	46
Natural rubber	60*	62*	63†

* Unofficial figure(s).
† FAO estimate(s).

Aggregate production ('000 metric tons, may include official, semi-official or estimated data): Total cereals 293 in 2009, 296 in 2010, 300 in 2011; Total roots and tubers 560 in 2009; 558 in 2010, 563 in 2011; Total vegetables (incl. melons) 83 in 2009, 107 in 2010, 109 in 2011; Total fruits (excl. melons) 190 in 2009, 189 in 2010, 190 in 2011.

Source: FAO.

LIVESTOCK
('000 head, year ending September, FAO estimates)

	2009	2010	2011
Cattle	39	40	40
Pigs	230	265	288
Sheep	252	264	268
Goats	311	338	340
Chickens	6,500	6,800	7,100
Ducks	290	300	320

Source: FAO.

LIVESTOCK PRODUCTS
(metric tons, FAO estimates)

	2009	2010	2011
Pig meat	7,822	9,020	9,720
Chicken meat	10,400	10,880	11,440
Game meat	7,146	7,500	8,000
Cows' milk	799	819	839
Hen eggs	4,950	5,200	5,375

Source: FAO.

Forestry

ROUNDWOOD REMOVALS
('000 cubic metres, excluding bark)

	2009	2010	2011
Sawlogs, veneer logs and logs for sleepers	240	300	358
Other industrial wood* . . .	180	180	180
Fuel wood*	6,751	7,008	7,254
Total	7,171	7,488	7,792

* FAO estimates.
Source: FAO.

SAWNWOOD PRODUCTION
('000 cubic metres, including railway sleepers)

	2006	2007	2008
Total (all broadleaved) . . .	60	60	80

2009–11: Figure assumed to unchanged from 2008 (FAO estimate).
Source: FAO.

Fishing

(metric tons, live weight of capture)

	2007	2008	2009*
Freshwater fishes	1,743	763	750
African sicklefish	150	185	180
Barracudas	356	126	130
Bobo croaker	201	260	260
Cassava croaker	381	229	220
Clupeoids	n.a.	1	1
Hammerhead sharks . . .	332	n.a.	100
Marlins, sailfishes, etc. . . .	459	180	180
Sardinellas	1,599	626	630
Sharks, rays, skates, etc. . . .	504	108	100
Snappers	243	251	250
Total catch (incl. others) . .	14,488	7,890	8,000

* FAO estimates.

2010: Figures assumed to be unchanged from 2009 (FAO estimates).
Source: FAO.

Mining

	2009	2010	2011
Diamonds ('000 carats) . . .	28	27	42*
Gold (kilograms)	524	666	469

* Preliminary.

Note: In addition to the commodities listed, Liberia produced significant quantities of a variety of industrial minerals and construction materials (clays, gypsum, sand and gravel, and stone), but insufficient information is available to make reliable estimates of output levels.

Source: US Geological Survey.

Industry

SELECTED PRODUCTS
(litres, unless otherwise indicated)

	2009	2010	2011*
Beverages	19,979,814	25,457,394	30,986,250
Cement (metric tons) . . .	70,584	71,733	60,764
Paint	211,694	270,217	284,072
Candles (kilograms) . . .	323,200	578,844	473,383
Bleach	529,396	662,285	816,152
Rubbing alcohol	231,060	743,960	309,767
Mattresses (number) . . .	47,278	122,029	142,066
Treated (finished) water (million gallons)	299.7	1,408.4	1,821.1

* Estimates.

Electric energy (million kWh): 353 in 2007; 353 in 2008; 353 in 2009 (Source: UN Industrial Commodity Statistics Database).

Finance

CURRENCY AND EXCHANGE RATES

Monetary Units
100 cents = 1 Liberian dollar (L $).

Sterling, Dollar and Euro Equivalents (31 July 2012)
£1 sterling = L $115.292;
US $1 = L $73.500;
€1 = L $90.287;
L $1,000 = £8.67 = US $13.61 = €11.08.

Average Exchange Rate (L $ per US $)
2009   68.2867
2010   71.4033
2011   72.2267

Note: The aforementioned data are based on market-determined rates of exchange. Prior to January 1998 the exchange rate was a fixed parity with the US dollar (L $1 = US $1).

BUDGET
(US $ million)

Revenue*	2010/11	2011/12†	2012/13†
Tax revenue	269.2	357.0	364.2
Taxes on income, profits and capital gains	111.2	145.4	131.3
Taxes on goods and services .	48.4	53.7	61.0
Taxes on international trade and transactions	105.4	149.0	162.4
Other taxes	4.3	8.9	9.5
Non-tax revenue	65.3	75.8	96.6
Total	334.6	432.7	460.8

Expenditure‡	2010/11	2011/12†	2012/13†
Current expenditure . .	309.4	446.6	473.1
Wages and salaries . . .	138.6	187.3	204.0
Other goods and services . .	86.3	134.0	141.3
Subsidies and transfers .	80.5	120.2	121.3
Interest on debt . . .	4.0	5.1	6.6
Capital expenditure . . .	73.5	67.8	143.5
Total	382.9	514.3	616.6

* Excluding grants received (US $ million): 40.3 in 2010/11; 28.3 in 2011/12 (budget projection); 44.8 in 2012/13 (budget projection).
† Budget projections.
‡ Includes net lending.
Source: IMF, *Liberia: 2012 Article IV Consultation.* (December 2012).

INTERNATIONAL RESERVES
(US $ million at 31 December)

	2009	2010	2011
IMF special drawing rights . .	201.43	210.49	223.56
Reserve position in IMF . .	0.05	0.05	0.05
Foreign exchange	170.97	—	—
Total	372.46	210.54	223.61

Source: IMF, *International Financial Statistics.*

MONEY SUPPLY
(L $ million at 31 December)

	2009	2010	2011
Currency outside banks* . .	4,161.8	5,007.9	6,704.3
Demand deposits at commercial banks	12,686.0	18,204.7	23,364.7
Total money (incl. others) . .	17,610.5	24,170.1	31,295.3

* Figures refer only to amounts of Liberian coin in circulation. US notes and coin also circulate, but the amount of these in private holdings is unknown. The amount of Liberian coin in circulation is small in comparison to US currency.
Source: IMF, *International Financial Statistics.*

COST OF LIVING
(Consumer Price Index; base: May 1998 = 100)

	2003	2004	2005
Food	140.9	153.8	167.0
Fuel and light	154.4	217.6	342.1
Clothing	121.2	128.7	137.3
Rent	131.8	156.1	180.9
All items (incl. others) . . .	157.0	169.3	187.6

Source: IMF, *Liberia: Selected Issues and Statistical Appendix* (May 2006).

All items (Consumer Price Index; base 2000 = 100): 167.6 in 2006; 186.7 in 2007; 219.4 in 2008; 235.7 in 2009; 253.3 in 2010; 274.8 in 2011 (Source: African Development Bank).

NATIONAL ACCOUNTS

Expenditure on the Gross Domestic Product
(US $ million at current prices)

	2009	2010	2011
Government final consumption expenditure	131	142	147
Private final consumption expenditure	1,186	1,218	1,292
Gross capital formation . . .	201	209	221
Total domestic expenditure .	1,518	1,569	1,660
Exports of goods and services . .	325	352	374
Less Imports of goods and services	819	847	887
GDP in purchasers' values .	1,024	1,074	1,147
GDP at constant 2005 prices .	873	936	1,013

Source: UN Statistics Division, National Accounts Main Aggregates Database.

Gross Domestic Product by Economic Activity
(L $ million at current prices)

	2009	2010	2011
Agriculture	663	696	745
Mining and quarrying . . .	22	23	25
Manufacturing	54	57	61
Electricity, gas and water . . .	6	6	7
Construction	25	26	28
Trade, restaurants and hotels .	23	24	25
Transport and communications .	53	54	58
Finance, insurance and real estate, etc.	17	18	19
Public administration and defence	33	35	37
Other services	19	20	21
Sub-total	915	959	1,025
Less Imputed bank service charge.	8	9	9
GDP at factor cost	906	950	1,015
Indirect taxes, less subsidies . .	85	89	95
GDP in market prices . . .	991	1,039	1,110

Source: African Development Bank.

BALANCE OF PAYMENTS
(US $ million)

	2008	2009	2010
Exports of goods	249.0	180.0	241.2
Imports of goods	−728.8	−559.0	−719.1
Balance on goods	−479.8	−379.0	−477.9
Exports of services	509.6	274.1	158.0
Imports of services	−1,411.1	−1,145.2	−1,078.6
Balance on goods and services	−1,381.4	−1,250.1	−1,398.5
Primary income received	22.4	18.1	31.2
Primary income paid	−170.7	−145.9	−7.0
Balance on goods, services and primary income	−1,529.7	−1,377.9	−1,374.2
Secondary income (net)	911.5	836.8	637.3
Current balance	−618.2	−541.1	−736.9
Capital account (net)	1,197.0	1,526.0	1,594.3
Direct investment liabilities	394.5	217.8	452.3
Other investment assets	−33.2	200.4	1.4
Other investment liabilities	−13.4	158.5	−6.8
Net errors and omissions	−465.1	10.8	847.1
Reserves and related items	461.6	1,572.4	2,151.4

Source: IMF, *International Financial Statistics*.

External Trade

PRINCIPAL COMMODITIES
(US $ million)

Imports c.i.f.	2009	2010	2011*
Food and live animals	161.8	185.4	225.2
Rice	65.7	47.3	77.8
Beverages and tobacco	18.6	17.6	18.0
Mineral fuels and lubricants	10.5	64.5	53.4
Petroleum	68.5	150.8	176.0
Chemicals and related products	29.6	31.8	32.9
Basic manufactures	84.0	70.7	83.4
Machinery and transport equipment	125.1	126.7	172.1
Miscellaneous manufactured articles	27.0	44.8	41.0
Total (incl. others)	551.6	709.8	814.3

Exports f.o.b.	2009	2010	2011*
Rubber	93.1	157.0	198.1
Cocoa beans and coffee	3.7	5.3	13.3
Diamonds	6.9	15.3	14.8
Gold	11.9	19.8	16.1
Iron ore	0.9	3.1	6.4
Total (incl. others)	148.8	222.0	295.2

* Preliminary data.

SELECTED TRADING PARTNERS
(US $ million)

Imports c.i.f.	2007	2008	2009
China, People's Republic	13.1	18.0	27.5
Germany	4.4	4.3	1.5
Japan	19.4	19.3	21.8
Korea, Republic	41.0	44.3	71.5
Singapore	28.9	41.6	24.1
Total (incl. others)	1,747.0	2,098.0	1,629.0

Exports f.o.b.	2007	2008	2009
Belgium	0.3	1.0	0.2
Germany	2.1	1.3	5.6
Poland	3.4	2.1	5.1
USA	1.9	2.3	1.2
Total (incl. others)	208.0	254.0	153.0

Source: African Development Bank.

2010 (principal trading partners, US $ million, preliminary): *Imports c.i.f.*: Belgium 11.6; Brazil 13.9; China, People's Republic 107.2; Denmark 7.8; Germany 10.6; France 10.9; India 26.9; Indonesia 7.7; Japan 16.7; Lebanon 13.2; Malaysia 18.9; Spain 8.2; Swaziland 24.5; Switzerland 6.4; Thailand 6.4; Turkey 24.2; Ukraine 14.0; United Arab Emirates 8.0; United Kingdom 10.6; USA 143.6; Total (incl. others) 594.7. *Exports f.o.b.*: Belgium 6.7; Ethiopia 16.7; Sierra Leone 11.6; Senegal 18.1; Spain 3.8; United Arab Emirates 1.9; USA 108.2; Total (incl. others) 168.9.

Total imports (US $ million, official figures): 709.8 in 2010 (revised); 814.3 in 2011 (preliminary).

Total exports (US $ million, official figures): 222.0 in 2010 (revised); 295.2 in 2011 (preliminary).

Transport

RAILWAYS
(estimated traffic)

	1991	1992	1993
Passenger-km (million)	406	417	421
Freight ton-km (million)	200	200	200

Source: UN Economic Commission for Africa, *African Statistical Yearbook*.

ROAD TRAFFIC
(estimates, '000 vehicles in use at 31 December)

	1999	2000	2001
Passenger cars	15.3	17.1	17.1
Commercial vehicles	11.9	12.8	12.8

2002: Figures assumed to be unchanged from 2001.

Source: UN, *Statistical Yearbook*.

2007 (motor vehicles in use at 31 December): Passenger cars 7,428; Buses and coaches 554; Lorries and vans 2,772; Motorcycles and mopeds 333 (Source: IRF, *World Road Statistics*).

SHIPPING

Flag Registered Fleet
(at 31 December)

	2010	2011	2012
Number of vessels	3,389	3,694	3,818
Displacement ('000 grt)	110,137.1	123,665.2	130,379.1

Source: Lloyd's List Intelligence (www.lloydslistintelligence.com).

International Sea-borne Freight Traffic
(estimates, '000 metric tons)

	1991	1992	1993
Goods loaded	16,706	17,338	21,653
Goods unloaded	1,570	1,597	1,608

Source: UN Economic Commission for Africa, *African Statistical Yearbook*.

CIVIL AVIATION
(traffic on scheduled services)

	1990	1991	1992
Passengers carried ('000)	32	32	32
Passenger-km (million)	7	7	7
Total ton-km (million)	1	1	1

Source: UN, *Statistical Yearbook*.

Communications Media

	2009	2010	2011
Telephones ('000 main lines in use)	2.2	5.9*	3.1*
Mobile cellular telephones ('000 subscribers)	1,085.1	1,571.3	2,029.9
Internet users ('000)	20	n.a.	n.a.
Broadband subscribers . . .	200	200	100

* Includes fixed wireless telephones.

Source: International Telecommunication Union.

Education

(2007/08 unless otherwise indicated)

	Teachers	Students		
		Males	Females	Total
Pre-primary	11,778	251,049	240,515	491,564
Primary	22,253	286,584	253,303	539,887
Secondary	11,880	90,383	67,859	158,242
Secondary technical and vocational* . . .	603	26,988	18,079	45,067
Post-secondary technical and vocational* . . .	430	8,842	6,789	15,631
University	772†	25,236*	18,871*	44,107*

* 1999/2000.

† 2000/01.

Source: UNESCO Institute for Statistics.

Pupil-teacher ratio (primary education, UNESCO estimate): 24.3 in 2007/08 (Source: UNESCO Institute for Statistics).

Adult literacy rate (UNESCO estimates): 60.8% (males 64.8%; females 56.8%) in 2010 (Source: UNESCO Institute for Statistics).

Directory

The Government

HEAD OF STATE

President: ELLEN JOHNSON-SIRLEAF (inaugurated 16 January 2006; re-elected 8 November 2011).

Vice-President: JOSEPH NYUMAH BOAKAI.

THE CABINET
(May 2013)

Minister of Agriculture: Dr FLORENCE CHENOWETH.

Minister of Commerce and Industry: AXEL ADDY.

Minister of Defence: BROWNIE SAMUKAI.

Minister of Education: OTHELLO GONGAR.

Minister of Finance: AMARA KONNEH.

Minister of Foreign Affairs: AUGUSTINE NGAFUAN.

Minister of Gender and Development: VARBAH GAYFLOR.

Minister of Health and Social Welfare: Dr WALTER GWENIGALE.

Minister of Information, Culture and Tourism: LEWIS G. BROWN, II.

Minister of Internal Affairs: MORRIS DUKULY.

Minister of Justice: CHRISTIANA TAH.

Minister of Labour: JUAH LAWSON.

Minister of Lands, Mines and Energy: ROOSEVELT JAYJAY.

Minister of National Security: VICTOR HELB.

Minister of Planning and Economic Affairs: (vacant).

Minister of Posts and Telecommunications: FREDERICK NOR-KEH.

Minister of Public Works: SAMUEL KOFI WOODS.

Minister of Transport: TORNOLAH VARPILAH.

Minister of Youth and Sports: LENN EUGENE NAGBE.

MINISTRIES

Office of the President: Executive Mansion, POB 10-9001, Capitol Hill, 1000 Monrovia 10; e-mail gmoore@emansion.gov.lr; internet www.emansion.gov.lr.

Ministry of Agriculture: 19th St, Sinkor, POB 10-9010, 1000 Monrovia 10; tel. 226399; internet www.moa.gov.lr.

Ministry of Commerce and Industry: Ashmun St, POB 10-9014, 1000 Monrovia 10; tel. 226283; internet www.moci.gov.lr.

Ministry of Defence: Benson St, POB 10-9007, 1000 Monrovia 10; tel. 226077; internet www.mod.gov.lr.

Ministry of Education: E. G. N. King Plaza, Broad St, POB 10-1545, 1000 Monrovia 10; tel. and fax 226216; internet www.moe.gov .lr.

Ministry of Finance: Broad St, POB 10-9013, 1000 Monrovia 10; tel. 47510680 (mobile); internet www.mof.gov.lr.

Ministry of Foreign Affairs: Mamba Point, POB 10-9002, 1000 Monrovia 10; tel. 226763; internet www.mofa.gov.lr.

Ministry of Gender and Development: Monrovia; internet www .mogd.gov.lr.

Ministry of Health and Social Welfare: Sinkor, POB 10-9004, 1000 Monrovia 10; tel. 226317; internet www.moh.gov.lr.

Ministry of Information, Culture and Tourism: Capitol Hill, POB 10-9021, 1000 Monrovia 10; tel. and fax 226269; internet www .micat.gov.lr.

Ministry of Internal Affairs: cnr Warren and Benson Sts, POB 10-9008, 1000 Monrovia 10; tel. 226346; internet www.moia.gov.lr.

Ministry of Justice: Ashmun St, POB 10-9006, 1000 Monrovia 10; tel. 227872; internet www.moia.gov.lr.

Ministry of Labour: Mechlin St, POB 10-9040, 1000 Monrovia 10; tel. 226291; internet www.mol.gov.lr.

Ministry of Lands, Mines and Energy: Capitol Hill, POB 10-9024, 1000 Monrovia 10; tel. 226281; internet www.molme.gov.lr.

Ministry of National Security: Monrovia.

Ministry of Planning and Economic Affairs: Broad St, POB 10-9016, 1000 Monrovia 10; tel. 226962; internet www.mopea.gov.lr.

Ministry of Posts and Telecommunications: Carey St, 1000 Monrovia 10; tel. 886552947 (mobile); e-mail internationalbureaurl@ yahoo.com.

Ministry of Public Works: Lynch St, POB 10-9011, 1000 Monrovia 10; tel. 227972; internet www.mopw.gov.lr.

Ministry of Transport: 1000 Monrovia 10; internet www.mopt.gov .lr.

Ministry of Youth and Sports: Monrovia; internet www.lys.gov.lr.

President and Legislature

PRESIDENT

Presidential Election, First Round, 11 October 2011

Candidate	Votes	% of votes
Ellen Johnson-Sirleaf (Unity Party) . .	530,020	43.93
Winston A. Tubman (Congress for Democratic Change)	394,370	32.68
Prince Yormie Johnson (National Union for Democratic Progress)	139,786	11.58
Charles Walker Brumskine (Liberty Party)	65,800	5.45
Others	76,666	6.35
Total	1,206,642	100.00

Presidential Election, Second Round, 8 November 2011

Candidate	Votes	% of votes
Ellen Johnson-Sirleaf (Unity Party) . .	607,618	90.71
Winston A. Tubman (Congress for		
Democratic Change)	62,207	9.29
Total	669,825	100.00

LEGISLATURE

House of Representatives

Speaker: ALEX JANEKAI TYLER.
General Election, 11 October 2011

Party	Seats
Unity Party	24
Congress for Democratic Change	11
Independents	9
Liberty Party	7
National Union for Democratic Progress . .	6
National Democratic Coalition	5
Alliance for Peace and Democracy . . .	3
National Patriotic Party	3
Movement for Progressive Change . . .	2
Liberia Destiny Party	1
Liberia Transformation Party	1
National Reformation Party	1
Total	73

Senate

President: JOSEPH NYUMAH BOAKAI.
General Election, 11 October 2011

Party	Seats
Unity Party	9
Independents	6
National Patriotic Party	4
Congress for Democratic Change . . .	3
Alliance for Peace and Democracy . . .	2
Liberty Party	2
Liberia Destiny Party	1
Liberia Transformation Party . . .	1
National Democratic Coalition	1
National Union for Democratic Progress . .	1
Total	30

Election Commission

National Elections Commission: Tubman Blvd, 16th St, Sinkor, Monrovia; internet www.necliberia.org; independent; Chair. JEROME G. KORKOYA.

Political Organizations

Some 23 political parties were listed by the National Elections Commission in mid-2011 and a further five parties were granted accreditation in June. The most significant of these parties are listed below:

Alliance for Peace and Democracy (APD): Benson St, Monrovia; tel. 6918196 (mobile); e-mail karwease@go.metrostate.edu; internet www.members.tripod.com/tipoteh12/index.html; f. 2005; Chair. MARCUS S. G. DAHN.

All Liberian Coalition Party (ALCOP): Broad St, Monrovia; tel. 6524735; f. 1997 from elements of fmr armed faction the United Liberation Movement of Liberia for Democracy; Leader Alhaji G. V. KROMAH; Chair. ANSU DOLLEY.

Citizens Unification Party (CUP): Monrovia; f. 2011; Chair. MOMOLU FREEMAN.

Congress for Democratic Change (CDC): Tubman Blvd, POB 2799, Monrovia; tel. 6513469 (mobile); internet www.cdcforliberia .org; f. 2004; Leader GEORGE MANNEH WEAH; Chair. GERALDINE DOE-SHERIFF.

Free Democratic Party (FDP): Center St, Monrovia; tel. 6582291 (mobile); Leader DAVID M. FARHAT; Chair. S. CIAPHA GBOLLIE.

Grassroots Democratic Party of Liberia (GDPL): Monrovia; Chair. GLADYS BEYAN.

Liberia Destiny Party (LDP): Congo Town Back Rd, Monrovia; tel. 6511531 (mobile); f. 2005; Chair. BOIMAH TAYLOR; Sec.-Gen. BORBOR B. KROMAH.

Liberia National Union (LINU): 16th St, Sinkor Monrovia; tel. 77059282; Chair. AARON S. M. WESSEH.

Liberia Transformation Party (LTP): Monrovia; f. 1984; Leader KENNEDY GBLEYAH SANDY; Chair. JULIUS SUKU.

Liberty Party (LP): Old Rd, Sinkor Opposite Haywood Mission, POB 1340, Monrovia; tel. 6547921 (mobile); f. 2005; Leader CHARLES WALKER BRUMSKINE; Chair. ISRAEL AKINSANYA.

Movement for Progressive Change (MPC): Monrovia; Leader SIMEON FREEMAN.

Nation Democratic Party of Liberia (NDPL): Capitol By-Pass, Monrovia; f. 1997 from the fmr armed faction the Liberia Peace Council; Chair. D. NYANDEH SIEH, Sr.

National Patriotic Party (NPP): Sinkor, Tubman Bldg, Monrovia; tel. 6515312 (mobile); f. 1997 from the fmr armed faction the National Patriotic Front of Liberia; won the majority of seats in legislative elections in July 1997; Leader ROLAND CHRIS YARKPAH MASSAQUOI; Chair. THEOPHILUS C. GOULD.

National Reformation Party (NRP): Duala Market, Monrovia; tel. 6511531 (mobile); Chair. Rev. MAXIMILLIAN T. W. DIABE.

National Union for Democratic Progress (NUDP): VP Rd, Old Rd, Monrovia; tel. 6645421 (mobile); Chair. GBAWOU KOWOU.

National Democratic Coalition: Monrovia; a coalition of opposition parties formed in 2011; Leader DEW MAYSON.

New Deal Movement (NDM): Randall St, Monrovia; tel. 6567470 (mobile); e-mail info@newdealmovement.com; internet newdealmovement.com; f. 2002; Leader Prof. GEORGE KLAY KIEH, Jr; Chair. HENRY W. YALLAH.

Progressive Democratic Party (PRODEM): McDonald St, Monrovia; tel. 6521091 (mobile); f. early 2005 by mems of fmr rebel movement, Liberians United for Reconciliation and Democracy (emerged 1999); Chair. GARBLA WILLIAMS.

Unity Party (UP): 86 Broad St, Monrovia; tel. 6512528 (mobile); e-mail info@theunityparty.org; f. 1984; Leader ELLEN JOHNSON-SIRLEAF; Chair. HARRY VARNEY GBOTO-NAMBI SHERMAN.

Diplomatic Representation

EMBASSIES IN LIBERIA

Algeria: Capitol By-Pass, POB 2032, Monrovia; tel. 224311; Chargé d'affaires a.i. MUHAMMAD AZZEDINE AZZOUZ.

Cameroon: 18th St and Payne Ave, Sinkor, POB 414, Monrovia; tel. 261374; Ambassador BENG'YELA AUGUSTINE GANG.

China, People's Republic: Tubman Blvd, Congotown, POB 5970, Monrovia; tel. 228024; fax 226740; e-mail Chinaemb_lr@mfa.gov.cn; internet lr.china-embassy.org; Ambassador ZHAO JIANHUA.

Congo, Democratic Republic: Spriggs Payne Airport, Sinkor, POB 1038, Monrovia; tel. 261326; Ambassador (vacant).

Côte d'Ivoire: Tubman Blvd, Sinkor, POB 126, Monrovia; tel. 261123; Ambassador SORO KAPÉLÉTIEN.

Egypt: Coconut Plantation, Randal St, Mamba Point, POB 462, Monrovia; tel. 226226; fax 226122; Ambassador SAMEH LOTFI.

France: German Compound, Congo Town, Monrovia; tel. 6579373 (mobile); e-mail ambafrance.liberia@yahoo.fr; Ambassador GÉRARD LARÔME.

Germany: Tubman Blvd, Monrovia; tel. 886438365 (mobile); e-mail info@monrovia.diplo.de; Ambassador Dr BODO SCHAFF.

Ghana: cnr 11th St and Gardiner Ave, Sinkor, POB 471, Monrovia; tel. 261477; Ambassador KODJO ASIMENG WADEE.

Guinea: Monrovia; Ambassador ABDOULAYE DORÉ.

Holy See: Monrovia; Apostolic Nuncio MIROSŁAW ADAMCZYK.

Lebanon: 12th St, Monrovia; tel. 262537; Ambassador MANSOUR ABDALLAH.

Libya: Monrovia; Ambassador MUHAMMAD UMARAT-TABI.

Morocco: Tubman Blvd, Congotown, Monrovia; tel. 262767; Ambassador MOHAMED LASFAR.

Nigeria: Tubman Blvd, Congotown, POB 366, Monrovia; tel. 6823638 (mobile); fax 226135; e-mail nigerianmonrovia@yahoo .com; Ambassador CHIGOZIE OBI-NNADOZIE.

Russia: Payne Ave, Sinkor, POB 2010, Monrovia; tel. 261304; Ambassador ANDREY V. POKROVSKII.

Sierra Leone: Tubman Blvd, POB 575, Monrovia; tel. 261301; Ambassador Rev. MARIE J. BARNETT.

South Africa: Sophie Rd, House No 5, Congo Town, Monrovia; Ambassador MASILO ESAU MEBETA.

United Kingdom: Monrovia; Ambassador FERGUS COCHRANE-DYET.

USA: POB 98, 502 Benson St, Monrovia; tel. 776777000 (mobile); fax 77010370 (mobile); e-mail ConsularMonrovia@state.gov; internet monrovia.usembassy.gov; Ambassador DEBORAH R. MALAC.

Judicial System

In February 1982 the People's Supreme Tribunal (which had been established following the April 1980 coup) was renamed the People's Supreme Court, and its Chairman and members became the Chief Justice and Associate Justices of the People's Supreme Court. The judicial system also comprised People's Circuit and Magistrate Courts. The five-member Supreme Court was established in January 1992 to adjudicate in electoral disputes.

Supreme Court: Monrovia; consists of a Chief Justice and four Associate Justices; Chief Justice FRANCIS S. KORPKPOR, Sr.

Religion

Liberia is officially a Christian state, although complete religious freedom is guaranteed. Christianity and Islam are the two main religions. There are numerous religious sects, and many Liberians hold traditional beliefs.

CHRISTIANITY

Liberian Council of Churches: 15th St, Sinkor, POB 10-2191, 1000 Monrovia; tel. 886234674 (mobile); e-mail liberiancouncil@yahoo.com; internet www.liberiancouncilofchurches.org; f. 1982; 13 mems, 11 assoc. mems, 4 fraternal mems; Pres. Rev. Dr JONATHAN B. B. HART.

The Anglican Communion

The diocese of Liberia forms part of the Church of the Province of West Africa, incorporating the local Episcopal Church. Anglicanism was established in Liberia in 1836, and the diocese of Liberia was admitted into full membership of the Province in 1982. The Metropolitan of the Province is the Bishop of Koforidua, Ghana.

Bishop of Liberia: Rt Rev. JONATHAN BAU-BAU BONAPARTE HART, POB 10-0277, 1000 Monrovia 10; tel. 224760; fax 227519; e-mail bishop@liberia.net.

The Roman Catholic Church

Liberia comprises the archdiocese of Monrovia and the dioceses of Cape Palmas and Gbarnga. An estimated 9% of the total population were Roman Catholics.

Catholic Bishops' Conference of Liberia

POB 10-2078, 1000 Monrovia 10; tel. 227245; fax 226175.

f. 1998; Pres. Rt Rev. LEWIS ZEIGLER (Archbishop of Monrovia).

Archbishop of Monrovia: Most Rev. LEWIS ZEIGLER, Archbishop's Office, POB 10-2078, 1000 Monrovia 10; tel. 6519766 (mobile); fax 77003719 (mobile); e-mail apostolic_adm@yahoo.com.

Other Christian Churches

Assemblies of God in Liberia: POB 1297, Monrovia; f. 1908; 14,578 adherents, 287 churches; Gen. Supt JIMMY KUOH.

Lutheran Church in Liberia (LCL): POB 10-1046, 13th St, Payne Ave, Sinkor, 1000 Monrovia 10; tel. 886213894 (mobile); e-mail lutheranchurchinliberia@yahoo.com; f. 1947 as Evangelical Lutheran Church, reorg. in 1965 under indigenous leadership as LCL; Pres. Bishop D. JENSEN SEYENKULO; 71,196 mems (2010).

Providence Baptist Church: cnr Broad and Center Sts, Monrovia; tel. 77534172 (mobile); e-mail admin@providencebc.net; internet www.providencebc.net; f. 1821; 2,500 adherents, 300 congregations, 6 ministers, 8 schools; Senior Pastor Rev. Dr SAMUEL BROOMFIELD REEVES, Jr.

Liberia Baptist Missionary and Educational Convention, Inc: POB 390, Monrovia; tel. 222661; f. 1880; 72,000 adherents, 270 churches (2007); Pres. Rev. J. K. LEVEE MOULTON; Nat. Vice-Pres. Rev. J. GBANA HALL; Gen. Sec. CHARLES W. BLAKE.

United Methodist Church in Liberia: cnr 12th St and Tubman Blvd, POB 1010, 1000 Monrovia 10; tel. 223343; e-mail bishop .jinnis@liberiaumc.org; internet www.umcliberia.org; f. 1833; c. 168,300 adherents, 600 congregations, 700 ministers, 394 lay pastors; Resident Bishop Rev. Dr JOHN G. INNIS.

Other active denominations include the National Baptist Mission, the Pentecostal Church, the Presbyterian Church in Liberia, the Prayer Band and the Church of the Lord Aladura.

ISLAM

The total community numbers about 670,000.

National Muslim Council of Liberia: Monrovia; Leader Shaykh KAFUMBA KONNAH.

The Press

NEWSPAPERS

Daily Observer: POB 1858, Monrovia; tel. 6513788 (mobile); e-mail editor@liberianobserver.com; internet www.liberianobserver.com; f. 1981; independent; daily; Dir KENNETH Y. BEST.

Heritage: cnr Broad and Nelson Sts, Monrovia; e-mail info@heritageliberia.net; internet www.news.heritageliberia.net; Man. Editor MOHAMMED M. KANNEH.

Informer: Monrovia; tel. 886519515 (mobile); e-mail editoratinformer@yahoo.com; internet www.informerliberia.net; f. 2003; Man. Dir DARKOLLIE SUMO.

The Inquirer: POB 3600, Monrovia; tel. 6538573 (mobile); fax 227036; e-mail theinquirernews@yahoo.com; internet www .theinquirer.com.lr; daily; Man. Editor PHILIP WESSEH.

National Chronicle: Monrovia; Editor EDWARD MORTEE.

New Dawn: Monrovia; tel. 886484201 (mobile); e-mail mail@thenewdawnliberia.com; internet www.thenewdawnliberia.com; f. 2010; CEO OTHELLO B. GARBLAH.

New Republic: Monrovia; tel. 6568024 (mobile); e-mail etogba2005us@yahoo.com; internet tnrliberia.net; Publr ALPHONSO TOWEH; Editor-in-Chief ELLIS TOGBA.

News: ACDB Bldg, POB 10-3137, Carey Warren St, Monrovia; tel. 227820; independent; weekly; Chair. WILSON TARPEH; Editor-in-Chief JEROME DALIEH.

PERIODICALS

Business Liberia: Monrovia; internet businessliberiamagazine .com; f. 2009; publ. by Baker Pearson Communications, Inc; Editor-in-Chief SEANAN DENIZOT.

The Kpelle Messenger: Kpelle Literacy Center, Lutheran Church, POB 1046, Monrovia; Kpelle-English; monthly; Editor Rev. JOHN J. MANAWU.

Liberia Orbit: Voinjama; e-mail orbit@tekmail.com; internet www .liberiaorbit.org; national current affairs; Editor LLOYD SCOTT.

Liberian Post: e-mail info@liberian.org; internet www.liberian.org; f. 1998; independent internet magazine; tourist information; Publr WILLEM TIJSSEN.

Liberia Travel & Life: Monrovia; e-mail editorial@liberiatravellifemagazine.com; internet www .liberiatravellifemagazine.com; 4 a year; publ. by Baker Pearson Communications, Inc; Editor-in-Chief HESTA BAKER PEARSON.

New Democrat: Clay St, Central Town, Monrovia; tel. 5548626 (mobile); fax 77249415 (mobile); e-mail newdemnews@yahoo.com; internet www.newdemocratnews.com; national news and current affairs; Editor TOM KAMARA.

Patriot: Congo Town 1000, Monrovia; internet www.allaboutliberia .com/patriot.htm.

The People Magazine: Bank of Liberia Bldg, Suite 214, Carey and Warren Sts, POB 3501, Monrovia; tel. 222743; f. 1985; monthly; Editor and Publr CHARLES A. SNETTER.

PRESS ORGANIZATIONS

Liberia Institute of Journalism: Kashour Bldg, 2nd Floor, cnr Broad and Johnson Sts, POB 2314, Monrovia; tel. 227327; Dir VINICIUS HODGES.

Liberia Media Center: LMC Box 1153, 1st St, Sinkor, Jallah Town, Monrovia; tel. 6400206 (mobile); e-mail info@lmcliberia.com; internet www.lmcliberia.com; f. 2005; Pres. PETER QUAQUA.

Press Union of Liberia: Benson St, POB 20-4209, Monrovia; tel. and fax 227105; internet www.pressunionlib.net; f. 1985; Pres. PETER QUAQUA.

NEWS AGENCY

Liberian News Agency (LINA): POB 9021, Capitol Hill, Monrovia; tel. 222229; Dir-Gen. ERNEST KIAZOLY (acting).

Broadcasting and Communications

TELECOMMUNICATIONS

Much of the fixed-line infrastructure in Liberia was destroyed during the civil conflict that ended in 2003. The Liberia Telecommunications Corpn, non-operational since 1990, was restructured as Libtelco in 2007 and began providing fixed wireless services in 2008. In 2011 it was still the sole operator licensed to provide fixed-line services, although its fixed-line network remained non-operational. In that year there were four providers of mobile cellular telephone services in the country.

Cellcom: Haile Selassie Ave, Capitol By-Pass, Monrovia; tel. 77777008 (mobile); fax 77000101 (mobile); e-mail info@cellcomgsm.com; internet www.lr.cellcomgsm.com; mobile cellular telephone provider; CEO AVISHAI MARZIANO; 640,526 subscribers (2010).

Comium: Comium Bldg, Congo Town, Monrovia; tel. 5600600 (mobile); fax 5600611 (mobile); e-mail info@comium.com.lr; internet www.comium.com.lr; mobile cellular telephone provider; CEO MICHAEL CARROLL; 137,848 subscribers (2010).

LiberCell: Monrovia; e-mail info@awli.net; internet www.libercell.info; f. 2004; mobile cellular telephone provider; Chair. AZZAM SBAITY; CEO BACHAR SAGHIR; 29,405 subscribers (2010).

Libtelco: 18th St and Tubman Blvd, Sinkor, Monrovia; tel. 25551000; fax 25551099; e-mail info@libtelco.com.lr; internet www.libtelco.com.lr; f. 1973 as the Liberia Telecommunications Corporation; Chair. MUSA DEAN; Man. Dir BEN WOLO; 4,463 prepaid subscribers (2010).

Lonestar Cell: LBDI Bldg, Congo Town, Monrovia; tel. 6500000 (mobile); fax 6501101 (mobile); internet www.lonestarcell.com; f. 2001; mobile cellular telephone provider; subsidiary of Mobile Telephone Networks (Pty) Ltd, South Africa; CEO MAZEN MROUE; 762,159 subscribers (2010).

Regulatory Authority

Liberia Telecommunications Authority: 12th St, Sinkor, Tubman Blvd, Monrovia; tel. 27302012; e-mail info@lta.gov.lr; internet www.lta.gov.lr; f. 2007; Chair. FRANCIS CHUCHU HORTON.

BROADCASTING

Radio

Liberia Communications Network: Congo Town 1000, Monrovia; govt-operated; broadcasts information, education and entertainment 24 hours daily in English, French and several African languages; short-wave service.

Liberia Rural Communications Network: POB 10-02176, 1000 Monrovia 10; tel. 271368; f. 1981; govt-operated; rural devt and entertainment programmes; Dir J. RUFUS KAINE (acting).

Radio Truth FM: Monrovia.

Radio Veritas: POB 3569, Monrovia; tel. 4712834 (mobile); e-mail radioveritas@hotmail.com; internet radioveritas.org; f. 1981; Catholic; independent; nation-wide shortwave broadcasts; Dirs Fr ANTHONY BOWAH, LEDGERHOOD RENNIE.

Star Radio: 12 Broad St, Snapper Hill, Monrovia; tel. 77104411 (mobile); e-mail star@liberia.net; internet www.starradio.org.lr; independent news and information station; f. July 1997 by Fondation Hirondelle, Switzerland, with funds from the US Agency for International Development; broadcasts in English, French and 14 African languages; Man. JAMES K. MORLU.

Television

Liberia Broadcasting System: POB 594, Monrovia; tel. 224984; internet www.liberiabroadcastingsystem.com; govt-owned; Chair. CLETUS SIEH; Dir-Gen. ALHAJI G. V. KROMAH (acting).

Finance

(cap. = capital; res = reserves; dep. = deposits; m. = million; br. = branch; amounts in Liberian dollars, unless otherwise indicated)

BANKING

In 2010 there were eight commercial banks in Liberia.

Central Bank

Central Bank of Liberia: cnr Warren and Carey Sts, POB 2048, 1000 Monrovia; tel. 6225685 (mobile); fax 6226114 (mobile); e-mail webmaster@cbl.org.lr; internet www.cbl.org.lr; f. 1974 as National Bank of Liberia; name changed March 1999; bank of issue; cap. 7,598.5m., res 3,817.4m., dep. 9,226.7m. (Dec. 2009); Gov. JOSEPH MILLS JONES.

Other Banks

AccessBank Liberia Ltd: Johnson St, Monrovia; tel. 77006688 (mobile); f. 2008; CEO MARY CLARE ODONG.

Ecobank Liberia Ltd: Ashmun and Randall Sts, POB 4825, Monrovia; tel. 880512039 (mobile); fax 227029; e-mail ecobanklr@ecobank.com; internet www.ecobank.com; commenced operations Aug. 1999; cap. and res US $2.1m., total assets US $289m. (Dec. 2001); Chair. CLAVENDA BRIGHT-PARKER; Man. Dir KOLA ADELEKE.

First International Bank (Liberia) Ltd: Luke Bldg, Broad St, Monrovia; tel. 77026241 (mobile); e-mail info@fib-lib.com; internet www.fib-lib.com; f. April 2005; Chair. FRANCIS L. M. HORTON; Exec. Dir ARISA AWA.

Global Bank Liberia Ltd (GBLL): Ashmun and Mechlin Sts, POB 2053, Monrovia; tel. 6425760 (mobile); e-mail mail@globalbankliberia.com; internet www.globalbankliberia.com; f. 2005; Italian-owned; Pres. Dr RICCARDO SEMBIANTE.

Guaranty Trust Bank (Liberia) Ltd (GTBLL): United Nations Dr., Clara Town, Bushrod Island, POB 0382, Monrovia; tel. 77499992 (mobile); fax 77499995 (mobile); internet www.gtbanklr.com; f. 2007; Chair. TAYO ADERINOKUN; CEO DAN OROGUN.

International Bank (Liberia) Ltd: 64 Broad St, POB 10292, 1000 Monrovia; tel. 6557473 (mobile); fax 4074245 (mobile); e-mail jwilliams@ibliberia.com; internet www.ibliberia.com; f. 1948 as International Trust Co of Liberia; name changed April 2000; 75.5% owned by Liberian Financial Holdings; 19.1% Trust Bank Ltd (The Gambia); cap. 2m. (1989), dep. 96.4m. (Dec. 1996); CEO PATRICK ANUMEL (acting); Gen. Man. HENRY SAAMOI; 3 brs.

Liberian Bank for Development and Investment (LBDI): Ashmun and Randall Sts, POB 547, Monrovia; tel. 227140; fax 226359; e-mail lbdi@lbdi.net; internet www.lbdi.net; f. 1961; 18.7% govt-owned; cap. and res US $12.5m., total assets US $26.8m. (Dec. 2001); Chair. AUGUSTINE K. NGAFUAN; Pres. FRANCIS A. DENNIS, Jr.

United Bank for Africa Liberia Ltd: POB 4523, Monrovia; tel. 6569375 (mobile); e-mail ubaliberia@ubagroup.com; internet www.ubagroup.com/ubaliberia; f. 2006; CEO EBELE E. OGBUE.

Banking Association

Liberia Bankers' Association: POB 292, Monrovia; mems include commercial and devt banks; Pres. FRANCIS A. DENNIS, Jr.

INSURANCE

American National Underwriters, Inc: Carter Bldg, 39 Broad St, POB 180, Monrovia; tel. 114921; general; Gen. Man. S. B. MENSAH.

Insurance Co of Africa: 2nd Floor, International Bank Building, 64 Broad St, Monrovia; tel. 6513281 (mobile); internet icaliberia.com; f. 1969; life and general; Pres. SAMUEL OWAREE MINTAH.

National Insurance Corpn of Liberia (NICOL): LBDI Bldg Complex, POB 1528, Sinkor, Monrovia; tel. 262429; f. 1983; state-owned; sole insurer for Govt and parastatal bodies; also provides insurance for the Liberian-registered merchant shipping fleet; Man. Dir MIATTA EDITH SHERMAN.

United Security Insurance Agencies Inc: Randall St, POB 2071, Monrovia; life, personal accident and medical; Dir EPHRAIM O. OKORO.

Trade and Industry

GOVERNMENT AGENCIES

Budget Bureau: Capitol Hill, POB 1518, Monrovia; tel. 226340; Dir-Gen. MATHEW DINGIE.

General Services Agency (GSA): Old USTC Compound, UN Dr., POB 10-9027, Monrovia; tel. 6901333 (mobile); e-mail info@gsa.gov.lr; internet www.gsa.gov.lr; Dir-Gen. ALPHONSO GAYE.

DEVELOPMENT ORGANIZATIONS

Forestry Development Authority: POB 10-3010, Kappa House, Eli Saleby Compound, Monrovia; tel. 224940; fax 226000; e-mail john.woods@fda.gov.lr; internet www.fda.gov.lr; f. 1976; responsible for forest management and conservation; Chair. (vacant); Man. Dir (vacant).

Liberia Industrial Free Zone Authority (LIFZA): One Free Zone, Monrovia; tel. 533671; e-mail mskromah@lifza.com; internet www.lifza.com; f. 1975; 98 mems; Man. Dir MOHAMMED S. KROMAH.

National Investment Commission (NIC): Fmr Executive Mansion Bldg, POB 9043, Monrovia; tel. 7873001 (mobile); internet www.nic.gov.lr; f. 1979; autonomous body negotiating investment incentives agreements on behalf of Govt; promotes agro-based and industrial devt; Chair. O'NATTY B. DAVIS; Exec. Dir CIATA BISHOP.

CHAMBER OF COMMERCE

Liberia Chamber of Commerce: Capitol Hill, POB 92, Monrovia; tel. 77857805 (mobile); e-mail info@lcc.org.lr; internet www.lcc.org .lr; f. 1951; Pres. MONIE RALPH CAPTAN; Sec.-Gen. MASSA R. LANSANAH.

INDUSTRIAL AND TRADE ASSOCIATIONS

Liberian Produce Marketing Corpn: POB 662, Monrovia; tel. 222447; f. 1961; govt-owned; exports Liberian produce, provides industrial facilities for processing of agricultural products and participates in agricultural devt programmes; Man. Dir NYAH MARTEIN.

Liberian Resources Corpn (LIBRESCO): controls Liberia's mineral resources; 60% govt-owned; 40% owned by South African co, Amalia Gold.

EMPLOYERS' ASSOCIATION

National Enterprises Corpn: POB 518, Monrovia; tel. 261370; importer, wholesaler and distributor of foodstuffs, and wire and metal products for local industries; Pres. EMMANUEL SHAW, Sr.

UTILITIES

Electricity

Liberia Electricity Corpn (LEC): Waterside, UN Dr., Monrovia; tel. 6653650 (mobile); e-mail mlackay@libelcorp.com; internet www .libelcorp.com; Chair. DUNSTAN L. D. MACAULEY; Man. Dir JOSEPH MAYAH.

National Oil Co of Liberia (NOCAL): Episcopal Church Plaza, 3rd and 4th Floors, Ashmun and Randall Sts, 1000 Monrovia; tel. 77023859 (mobile); e-mail info@nocal.com.lr; internet www.nocal.lr .com; f. 2000; Chair. ROBERT SIRLEAF; Pres. and CEO CHRISTOPHER NEYOR.

TRADE UNION

Liberian Labor Congress: J. B. McGill Labor Center, Gardnersville Freeway, POB 415, Monrovia; f. 2008 following merger of Liberian Federation of Labor Unions and Congress of National Trade Unions; Pres. ELITHA T. MANNING, Jr; Sec.-Gen. MARCUS S. BLAMAH.

Transport

RAILWAYS

Bong Mine Railway: POB 538, Monrovia; tel. 225222; fax 225770; f. 1958; Gen. Man. HANS-GEORG SCHNEIDER.

ROADS

In 2000 the road network in Liberia totalled an estimated 10,600 km, of which about 657 km were paved. The main trunk road is the Monrovia–Sanniquellie motor road, extending north-east from the capital to the border with Guinea, near Ganta, and eastward through the hinterland to the border with Côte d'Ivoire. Trunk roads run through Tapita, in Nimba County, to Grand Gedeh County and from Monrovia to Buchanan. A bridge over the Mano river connects with the Sierra Leone road network, while a main road links Monrovia and Freetown (Sierra Leone). In 2003 the Liberian authorities announced plans for the extensive rehabilitation of the road network (which had been extensively damaged during the civil conflicts of 1989–1996 and 1999–2003), including a highway linking Monrovia with Harper, which was to be funded by the People's Republic of China.

SHIPPING

At 31 December 2012 Liberia's open-registry fleet comprised 3,818 vessels (of which 105 were gas tankers and 239 were general cargo ships), with a total displacement of 130.4m. grt. The fleet was the second largest in the world (after Panama) in terms of gross tonnage in that year.

Bureau of Maritime Affairs: Tubman Blvd, Sinkor, POB 10-9042, 1000 Monrovia 10; tel. and fax 77206108 (mobile); e-mail info@ bma-liberia.com; internet www.bma-liberia.com; Commissioner BINYAH C. KESSELLY.

Liberia National Shipping Line (LNSL): Monrovia; f. 1987; jt venture by the Liberian Govt and private German interests; routes to Europe, incl. the United Kingdom and Scandinavia.

National Port Authority: Freeport of Monrovia, Bushrod Island, Monrovia; tel. 6402906 (mobile); fax 77861997 (mobile); e-mail natportliberia@yahoo.com; internet www .nationalportauthorityliberia.org; f. 1967; administers Monrovia Freeport and the ports of Buchanan, Greenville and Harper; Chair. Dr C. WILLIAM ALLEN; Man. Dir MATILDA PARKER.

CIVIL AVIATION

Liberia's principal airports are Robertsfield International Airport, at Harbel, 56 km east of Monrovia, and James Spriggs Payne Airport, at Monrovia.

Liberia Civil Aviation Authority: Monrovia; internet www .liberiacaa.com; Dir-Gen. RICHELIEU A. WILLIAMS.

Tourism

Liberia's natural assets, especially its beaches and the Sapo National Park and other areas of primary tropical rainforest, have the potential to support both a beach-based and an eco-tourism industry. However, no such industry has ever been developed in Liberia and tourism has been entirely in abeyance since 1990 because of the almost continuous civil conflict since that time. The development of the country's tourist potential will be limited by high levels of violent crime and a tourism infrastructure that remains meagre or absent.

Defence

As assessed at November 2012, the total strength of the Liberian armed forces was 2,050.

Defence Expenditure: Estimated at US $16m. in 2011.

Chief of Staff of the Armed Forces of Liberia: Maj.-Gen. SURAJ ALAO ABDURRAHMAN.

Education

Education is provided by a mixture of government, private, church and mosque schools. The civil conflicts of 1989–1996 and 1999–2003 devastated the education system as buildings and equipment were damaged and looted, and teachers, parents and children became refugees or internally displaced. By September 2005 3,817 of the country's 4,500 schools were reported to be functioning again. Education in Liberia is officially compulsory for 10 years, between six and 16 years of age. Primary education begins theoretically at six years of age and lasts for six years (grades 1–6). Secondary education, beginning theoretically at 12 years of age, lasts for a further six years, and is divided into two three-year cycles, known in Liberia as 'junior high school' (grades 7–9) and 'senior high school' (grades 10-12). Pre-primary education is undertaken from the age of five or younger and is important for those students whose mother language is not English, since English is the language of instruction throughout the school system. School attendance is not enforced and in 2006 an estimated 61% of primary school age children were out of school (60% of boys and 61% of girls). Although the 1984 Liberian Constitution includes the aspiration to provide universal free education, and fees in public primary schools have been officially abolished, school attendance is discouraged by the poor quality of education offered, by the remaining school fees, by charges and by the cost of uniforms and travel. The higher education sector consists of the University of Liberia in Monrovia, Cuttington University College in Bong County, the Booker Washington Institute in Kakata, Margibi County, and the William V. S. Tubman College in Maryland County. According to UNESCO, a total of 44,107 students were enrolled in tertiary education in 1999/2000.

LIBYA

Introductory Survey

LOCATION, CLIMATE, LANGUAGE, RELIGION, FLAG, CAPITAL

Libya extends along the Mediterranean coast of North Africa. Its neighbours are Tunisia and Algeria to the west, Niger and Chad to the south, Egypt to the east, and Sudan to the south-east. The climate is very hot and dry. Most of the country is part of the Sahara, an arid desert, but the coastal regions are cooler. Average temperatures range from 13°C (55°F) to 38°C (100°F), but a maximum of 57.3°C (135°F) has been recorded in the interior. Arabic is the official language, although English and Italian are also used in trade. Almost all of the population are Sunni Muslims. The national flag (proportions 2 by 3) has three horizontal stripes, of red, black and green; the black stripe is equal in area to the two other stripes together and has, in its centre, a white crescent and a five-pointed white star. During the rule of Col Muammar al-Qaddafi, most government departments and the legislature were relocated from Tarabulus (Tripoli) to Surt (Sirte), although some departments were subsequently moved back. Following Qaddafi's removal from power in August 2011 by forces loyal to the opposition National Transitional Council, an interim Constitutional Declaration designated Tripoli as the capital.

CONTEMPORARY POLITICAL HISTORY

Historical Context

Libya, formerly an Italian colony and occupied by British and French troops in 1942, attained independence as the United Kingdom of Libya in 1951. Muhammad Idris al-Sanusi, Amir of Cyrenaica, became King Idris of Libya. British and US forces maintained bases in Libya in return for economic assistance; however, the discovery of petroleum reserves in 1959 greatly increased the country's potential for financial autonomy.

King Idris was deposed in September 1969, in a bloodless revolution led by a group of nationalist army officers. A Revolutionary Command Council (RCC) was established, with Col Muammar al-Qaddafi as Chairman, and a Libyan Arab Republic was proclaimed. British and US military personnel withdrew from Libya in 1970, and the following year British oil interests in Libya were nationalized.

The Arab Socialist Union (ASU) was established in June 1971 as the country's sole political party. People's Congresses and Popular Committees were formed, and an undertaking was made to administer the country in accordance with Islamic principles. The General National Congress of the ASU (which comprised members of the RCC, and leaders of the People's Congresses and Popular Committees, and of trade unions and professional organizations) held its first session in January 1976; it was subsequently restyled the General People's Congress (GPC).

In March 1977 the GPC endorsed constitutional changes, recommended by Qaddafi, whereby the official name of the country was changed to the Socialist People's Libyan Arab Jamahiriya. Power was vested in the people through the GPC and its constituent parts. The RCC was dissolved, and a General Secretariat of the GPC (with Qaddafi as Secretary) was established. The GPC elected Qaddafi as Revolutionary Leader of the new state. The Council of Ministers was replaced by a General People's Committee, initially with 26 members—each a secretary of a department.

In March 1979 Qaddafi resigned as Secretary of the GPC General Secretariat to devote more time to 'preserving the revolution'. The creation in 1984 of the post of Secretary for External Security and of an office, attached to the Secretariat for Foreign Liaison, to 'combat international terrorism', combined with repressive measures to curb dissident activity, reflected Qaddafi's increasing sensitivity to the growth of opposition groups—principally the National Front for the Salvation of Libya (NFSL), which he accused foreign governments of fostering. In 1986 the country was renamed the Great Socialist People's Libyan Arab Jamahiriya.

Domestic Political Affairs

From 1988, in an apparent attempt to allay domestic dissatisfaction and international criticism, Qaddafi initiated a series of liberalizing economic and political reforms. He encouraged the reopening of private businesses, and declared an amnesty for all prisoners, other than those convicted of violent crimes or of conspiring with foreign powers. Libyan citizens were guaranteed freedom to travel abroad, and the powers of the 'revolutionary committees' were curbed. The GPC created a People's Court and People's Prosecution Bureau to replace the revolutionary courts, and approved a charter of human rights. In August Qaddafi announced that the army was to be replaced by a force of 'Jamahiri Guards', which would be supervised by 'people's defence committees'. In September it was decided to relocate all but two of the GPC secretariats, mostly to the town of Sirte, 400 km east of Tripoli, and in January 1989 Qaddafi announced that all state institutions, including the state intelligence service and the official Libyan news agency, were to be abolished. Extensive changes were effected to the GPC and the General People's Committee during 1990–92.

Western media reported in October 1993 that elements loyal to Qaddafi had suppressed an attempted military coup, and that Libya's second-in-command, Maj. Abd al-Salam Jalloud, was among many placed under house arrest. Qaddafi denied the reports, but the appointment of known loyalists to senior positions in the General People's Committee was announced in January 1994. Additional changes to the composition and structure of the Committee were announced during 1997. The Secretariat for Arab Unity was abolished in December 1998, in accordance with Qaddafi's recently stated intention to forge closer relations with African rather than Arab countries (see Foreign Affairs).

A radical decentralization of the Government was announced in March 2000, whereby almost all of the People's Committees were dissolved and their responsibilities devolved mainly to the local level: only 'sovereign' areas were to remain under the control of the General People's Committee, now led by Secretary Mubarak Abdallah al-Shamikh. Al-Ujayli Abd al-Salam Burayni replaced Muhammad Abdullah Bait al-Mal as Secretary for Finance in October, when a further restructuring of the General People's Committee was announced; it had been reported in July that Bait al-Mal, along with the President of the Central Bank of Libya and a further 22 senior Libyan bankers, had been implicated in allegations of financial impropriety.

Clashes between Libyans and nationals of several other African countries, apparently owing to the local population's resentment at the increasing influx into the country of black African migrants, claimed the lives of more than 100 African migrants in September 2000 and prompted as many as 30,000 others to leave Libya. The GPC announced its intention formally to investigate the incidents, which included the ransacking of the Nigerian embassy in Tripoli and a series of attacks in the town of Zawia, 30 km west of Tripoli. In October the evacuation and deportation of migrant workers from Nigeria, Chad, Niger, Sudan and Ghana commenced. Qaddafi subsequently blamed the incidents on 'foreign hostile hands' opposed to his plans to create an 'African Union'. In May 2001 two Libyans, four Nigerians and one Ghanaian were sentenced to death for their roles in the violence. A further 12 defendants were sentenced to life imprisonment.

In November 2001 it was announced that more than 40 government and bank officials had been sentenced to varying terms of imprisonment for corruption and embezzlement; reportedly among those convicted was Secretary for Finance Burayni, who received a one-year prison sentence for negligence.

In June 2003 Qaddafi dismissed al-Shamikh from the post of Secretary of the General People's Committee, replacing him with Shukri Muhammad Ghanem, hitherto Secretary for the Economy and Trade. It was also announced that the Secretariat for African Unity had been merged with the Secretariat for Foreign Liaison and International Co-operation; Abd al-Rahman Muhammad Shalgam assumed responsibility for both portfolios. Further reorganizations of the General People's Committee in March 2004 and March 2006 resulted in the creation of several new secretariats—including, in the former month, one for national security and the restoration of the Secretariat for Energy (abolished in 2000). In the latter month Dr al-Baghdadi Ali al-Mahmoudi became Secretary of the General People's Committee, in place of Ghanem, who was appointed Chairman of the National Oil Corporation (NOC). The energy secretariat was restructured as the Secretariat for Industry, Electricity and Mines; however, in January 2007 its responsibilities were divided between new Secretariats for Industry and Mineral Resources and for Electricity, Water and Gas.

In June 2006 the US-based organization Human Rights Watch pressed the Libyan Government to allow a full, independent investigation into the deaths of hundreds of inmates at Abu Salim prison in Tripoli in 1996; the alleged massacre was reported to have been caused by security officers opening fire on prisoners protesting against poor living conditions. In September 2006 Human Rights Watch released a report in which it claimed that the Libyan Government routinely subjected refugees and asylum-seekers to violence, arrest without due cause and forcible deportation; the report urged members of the European Union (EU, see p. 281) to apply pressure on Libya to protect the rights of the hundreds of thousands of foreigners residing therein. In October one inmate was killed and 17 other people injured in clashes between prisoners and guards at Abu Salim prison. The disturbance, reported mainly to have involved members of the Libyan Islamic Fighting Group (LIFG), followed the decision by a Tripoli court to uphold the convictions, on charges of having links with the LIFG, of 190 inmates housed at the prison.

An official source in Tripoli announced in November 2006 that Qaddafi's second son, Seif al-Islam was to leave the country to take up employment with an international economic institution. His departure from Libya was widely perceived to have been orchestrated by the Government in reaction to his outspoken criticism of the regime during a speech in Sirte in August. In a televised address in August 2007, Seif al-Islam urged the drafting of a new constitution or 'social contract' that would establish, *inter alia*, an independent central bank and a free media and judiciary. He also criticized the Libyan political system for its lack of a freely elected legislature, its refusal to allow the creation of political parties and its ongoing intolerance of political dissent, and called for political power to be more widely distributed, beyond the GPC and the General People's Committee.

In November 2007 an audio tape purporting to be from Dr Ayman al-Zawahiri, the deputy leader of the militant Islamist organization al-Qa'ida, was released; it included a message from Abu Laith al-Libi, the leader of al-Qa'ida in Afghanistan, who identified himself on the tape as also being a member of the LIFG. Al-Libi declared that the LIFG had pledged allegiance to al-Qa'ida. Al-Zawahiri's own message urged the overthrow of the Libyan, Algerian, Moroccan and Tunisian Governments, and criticized Qaddafi for surrendering Libya's nuclear weapons materials to 'crusader masters'. (Libya had abandoned its programmes to produce weapons of mass destruction in December 2003, having reportedly come close to building a nuclear bomb—see Foreign Affairs.)

Qaddafi effected a reorganization of the General Secretariat of the GPC and of the General People's Committee in March 2008. Muftah Muhammad Kaiba was appointed as Secretary of the GPC. At the same time Qaddafi announced that he intended to abolish the majority of secretariats within the General People's Committee by the end of that year, in an effort to eliminate corruption and maladministration. Through a Wealth Distribution Programme (WDP), oil wealth would be redistributed by transferring the secretariats' powers to the people to enable them to manage their own affairs, requiring privatization of many sectors of Libyan society; only the secretariats for defence, internal security and foreign affairs would be retained, along with those responsible for strategic infrastructural projects, such as the Great Man-made River Project (see Economic Affairs). However, the reforms were subsequently postponed (see below).

In November 2008, meanwhile, there were protests by members of the Tebu tribe in the southern town of Kufra against what they claimed was discrimination practised by the Qaddafi Government against indigenous peoples (including a restriction of access to health and education services). Dozens of people were reported to have been killed in violent confrontations between the Libyan security forces and Tebu tribesmen.

At a meeting of the GPC held in Sirte at the beginning of March 2009, it was announced that the country's Basic People's Congresses had voted in the previous month to defer implementation

of the WDP. At the Sirte meeting Qaddafi implemented a reorganization of the General People's Committee. Notable changes included the appointment of Musa Kusa, hitherto head of Libya's foreign intelligence service, to replace Shalgam as Secretary for Foreign Liaison and International Co-operation; the finance and planning secretariats were among several to be merged. Meanwhile, al-Shamikh was appointed as Secretary of the GPC, replacing Kaiba. The changes fell far short of the large-scale dismantling of secretariats that Qaddafi had previously outlined, but were none the less indicative of the ongoing programme of administrative retrenchment.

Increasing prominence of Seif al-Islam Qaddafi

In March 2009 it was announced that, following two years of talks between the Libyan Human Rights Association—chaired by Seif al-Islam Qaddafi—and the LIFG, 170 imprisoned members of the group were to be released; it was also revealed that 136 LIFG prisoners had already been freed, having completed a rehabilitation programme. In July the LIFG leadership announced that it was renouncing armed violence and reversed the 2007 decision to align the group with al-Qa'ida. In September 2009 six imprisoned members of the LIFG ruling council published a document, described as a new 'code' for *jihad*, which denounced the ideologies of al-Qa'ida. More than 100 LIFG members and other Islamist militants were released from prison in late 2009 and 2010. Human Rights Watch welcomed the development as a positive step, but urged the Libyan authorities to release all those who were 'arbitrarily detained' in Libyan gaols, including many who continued to be imprisoned despite having served the full duration of their sentence or having being acquitted of all charges against them.

Meanwhile, in October 2009 it was announced that, despite having declared in August 2008 his intention to withdraw from the political arena, Seif al-Islam was to be appointed as co-ordinator of social and popular committees, a role that elevated Qaddafi's son to the second most powerful position in the Libyan leadership. The decision was widely interpreted as the formal approval by the Libyan authorities of Seif al-Islam as his father's successor. In January 2010 Qaddafi effected a reorganization of the General Secretariat of the GPC, most notably appointing Muhammad Aboulghasem al-Zwai as Secretary, in place of al-Shamikh. The number of portfolios in the General People's Committee was also reduced from 12 to seven, as part of the ongoing programme of administrative reform.

In December 2009 Seif al-Islam's Human Rights Association published a report detailing wide-ranging examples of the use of torture, wrongful imprisonment and other human rights abuses in Libya, and criticizing the state's dominance of the media. Two days later a report by Human Rights Watch highlighted limited progress in areas such as freedom of expression and freedom of association, and described systemic human rights abuses. Despite significant opposition from human rights groups, Libya was elected to the UN Human Rights Council in May 2010, attracting 155 votes in support of its membership bid from the 192-member body. In early June the human rights organization Amnesty International condemned the execution in Libya of 18 people from Chad, Egypt and Nigeria, following their conviction on charges of murder; it alleged that the defendants had not been granted a fair trial and that foreign nationals were 'disadvantaged' within the Libyan judicial system, often not being allowed access to legal representation. A further report, based on evidence collated during a fact-finding mission's visit to the country in May 2009, was published by Amnesty International in late June. The document detailed a wide array of rights violations that had allegedly been perpetrated by the Libyan Government, including indefinite detentions without trial, the use of torture to extract confessions from prisoners, the disappearance of numerous dissidents, and inhumane treatment of refugees and migrant workers. Meanwhile, in mid-June 2010 the Libyan Government ordered the closure of the office in Tripoli of the UN High Commissioner for Refugees (UNHCR), citing the fact that Libya was not a signatory to the 1951 convention on refugees and had not signed any co-operation agreement with the UNHCR, whose activities in Libya were therefore 'illegal'.

The Libyan authorities were reported to have arrested 20 journalists (15 Libyan citizens, and three Tunisian and two Egyptian nationals) during a four-day period in November 2010, in what some interpreted as evidence of an increasing 'power struggle' between Seif al-Islam and conservatives opposed to what they regarded as his reformist agenda. The detained journalists all worked for media entities controlled by Al-Ghad—a publishing company sponsored by Seif al-Islam. On the day after the journalists were arrested, Col Qaddafi was reported personally to have ordered their release and a full inquiry into the incident.

The Qaddafi International Charity and Development Foundation, a charitable organization headed by Seif al-Islam, announced in December 2010 that it was henceforth to cease advocating political reform and championing human rights causes, and would instead focus on its 'core charitable mission'—namely, the provision of aid and relief to disadvantaged populations, primarily in sub-Saharan Africa. Critics of Seif al-Islam contended that he was merely seeking to protect himself from the ire of conservative forces within Libya, which had strongly objected to the Foundation's pro-reform stance.

Anti-Qaddafi protests and NATO-led intervention

In mid-January 2011 crowds gathered in several Libyan cities, including Benghazi and Bani Walid, to protest against corruption and protracted delays in the transfer of government-subsidized residential buildings to their owners; protesters seized control of hundreds of vacant residential units in the two cities. The Libyan state media made no reference to the protests, but in late January the Government announced the establishment of a US $24,000m. investment fund, the aim of which was to provide affordable housing for lower-income families. Meanwhile, in mid-January the Government announced the elimination of all taxes on food products, in a move believed to be linked to popular unrest in Algeria and Tunisia over, among other things, increased food prices.

At the end of January 2011 a Libyan political writer, Jamal al-Hajji, who had previously been imprisoned for dissidence, posted an article on the internet urging Libyans to stage demonstrations 'in support of greater freedoms in Libya', seemingly inspired by recent events in Tunisia and Egypt that ultimately led to the removal of those countries' ruling regimes in mid-January and mid-February, respectively. Al-Hajji was arrested at the beginning of February and charged with causing injury to another person while driving; however, human rights groups alleged that al-Hajji had been targeted because of his political views and his appeal for the holding of protests. Qaddafi was reported to have met with prominent political activists and journalists shortly thereafter and to have threatened serious repercussions if they should in any way be involved in 'disturbing the peace or creating chaos in Libya'.

Protesters gathered outside the police headquarters in Benghazi on 15 February 2011, following the arrest earlier that day of Fathi Terbil, a prominent critic of the Government and a lawyer who had been campaigning for the release of hundreds of people detained in Abu Salim prison owing to their alleged involvement with militant Islamist groups, including the LIFG. Police officers dispersed the protesters, using violence against those who refused to leave, resulting in more than 40 people being injured. On 16 February Terbil was released, but the protests continued in Benghazi and spread to several other Libyan cities, including al-Bayda and al-Quba, with protesters demanding the resignation of Qaddafi and the Government. Six people were reported to have been killed that day as the authorities attempted to break up the protests. On the same day, in an apparent attempt to appease the protesters, the Government announced the release from prison of 110 LIFG members.

In response to a 'day of revolt' staged by opposition forces on 17 February 2011, when protests took place in Tripoli for the first time, the Government was reported to have hired hundreds of mercenaries from several African countries, notably Chad, to increase the ranks of the Libyan army. The Libyan air force deployed fighter jets and helicopters to launch air-strikes against demonstrators; on 21 February two senior air force pilots flew to Malta, where they requested political asylum from the Qaddafi regime. Violent clashes continued between protesters and the authorities during that month. Some sources, including the Libyan League for Human Rights, estimated that by early March some 6,000 people had been killed as a result of the unrest. Hundreds of thousands of Libyans fled the country in order to escape the violence, and many countries launched rescue missions to help their nationals in Libya to return home. Libyan national flags on buildings were replaced by that of the former Libyan monarchy, while government and police buildings, banks, media premises and construction sites in many towns were looted, set on fire or otherwise damaged, and the protesters seized control of the airport in Benghazi.

By early March 2011 much of eastern Libya was reported to be under opposition control, including Benghazi and Tobruk, and the opposition had also pushed into the central and northern provinces, with a number of cities therein—including the port towns of Mersa Brega and Ras Lanuf—under rebel control, and significant numbers of police and army officers in the region defecting to the opposition. Many of Libya's foreign diplomats, including its ambassador in Washington, DC, USA, had also renounced the Qaddafi regime and urged the international community to take action to stop the violence. Several prominent government officials had also resigned, including Secretary for Justice Mustafa Muhammad Abd al-Jalil, and Secretary for Public Security Gen. Abd al-Fattah Yunis al-Abaidi.

Seif al-Islam Qaddafi gave a televised address on 20 February 2011, in which he blamed the ongoing unrest on 'foreign agents', primarily the Israeli Government, and pledged that the Libyan Government would 'fight to the last man and woman and bullet'. On 22 February Col Qaddafi made his first public statement in response to the protests, appearing briefly on state television to deny external media reports that he had fled to Venezuela. Also that day the UN Security Council issued a statement in which it condemned 'the use of force against civilians' and called for 'an immediate end to the violence and for steps to address the legitimate demands of the population'. Qaddafi appeared on state television again on 23 February, blaming foreign powers and the abuse of hallucinogenic drugs for the unrest, while insisting that, as he had no formal position from which to resign, he would remain the 'head of the revolution'. Qaddafi also condemned the US and British Governments, which he accused of attempting to 'destabilize' Libya. Seif al-Islam's reputation as a reformist within the Qaddafi regime was undermined when video footage materialized on 28 February that purported to show him inciting a crowd of pro-Government supporters to commit violence against the opposition forces, and promising to provide those loyal to his father with weapons.

On 26 February 2011 the opposition forces proclaimed the Transitional National Council of the Libyan Republic (subsequently renamed the National Transitional Council—NTC), which, while not initially serving as a de facto government, was to constitute the 'political face of the revolution', and affirmed its resolve to draft a new national constitution providing for a free and democratically governed Libya. Following its inaugural meeting, convened on 5 March, the Council declared itself to be the sole representative of the country and urged the international community to act to protect Libyan citizens without recourse to direct military action on Libyan soil. A spokesperson for the Council subsequently clarified that UN-mandated air-strikes would not be considered as foreign intervention. Former Secretary for Justice Abd al-Jalil was appointed Chairman of the NTC on 9 March.

Meanwhile, on 21 February 2011 Libya's deputy ambassador to the UN, Ibrahim Dabbashi, urged the Security Council to address the Libyan Government's violent response to the protests, and stated that he could no longer support the Qaddafi regime, which, he argued, was responsible for 'genocide'. Dabbashi's comments prompted the first UN Security Council meeting on the issue of the uprisings in the Middle East and North Africa since the beginning of Tunisia's revolution; the Security Council condemned the Libyan Government's response to the protests and issued a statement demanding an immediate end to the violence. On 26 February the Security Council unanimously adopted Resolution 1970, which imposed sanctions including, *inter alia*, the referral of the situation in Libya to the Chief Prosecutor of the International Criminal Court (ICC), the institution of an embargo upon the sale and transport of arms to Libya, and the imposition of a travel ban and an asset freeze on senior members of Qaddafi's regime and on his family. At the beginning of March the UN General Assembly voted to suspend Libya's membership of the Human Rights Council in response to the Government's 'gross and systematic violations' of human rights.

In late February 2011 US Secretary of State Hillary Clinton pledged her country's assistance, including aid, to those elements within Libya seeking to remove Qaddafi from power, and demanded that Qaddafi step down. On 1 March British Prime Minister David Cameron suggested that the United Kingdom might be prepared to furnish the Libyan rebels with weapons, and that the North Atlantic Treaty Organization (NATO, see p. 380) should impose an air exclusion zone over Libya. Protesters in Benghazi responded by unveiling banners denouncing foreign intervention, and Cameron's stance encountered considerable opposition from France and Russia, while the USA initially distanced itself from Cameron's proposals. However, the US Administration subsequently stated that President Barack

Obama and Prime Minister Cameron had pledged their shared commitment to ensuring an end to the use of violence against Libyan citizens and the departure of Qaddafi from power. Meanwhile, it was reported that Qaddafi had appointed replacements for those members of the General People's Committee who had defected to the opposition in late February: Muhammad Ahmad al-Qamoud became Secretary for Justice, and Masoud Abd al-Hafiz was appointed Secretary for Public Security.

On 17 March 2011 the UN Security Council approved Resolution 1973, which, among other measures, prohibited all flights in Libyan airspace, authorized member states to take 'all necessary measures... to protect civilians and civilian populated areas under threat of attack' by forces loyal to Qaddafi, 'while excluding a foreign occupation force of any form on any part of Libyan territory', and demanded an immediate cease-fire by Libyan government forces. Despite the announcement by Libyan officials the following day of a cease-fire, it was subsequently reported that Qaddafi's forces continued to use violence to counter opposition groups that had taken control of Mersa Brega, Misurata, Ras Lanuf and Zawia. Air-strikes by Allied forces against strategic locations across Libya, including in Tripoli, commenced on 19 March, while on 22 March NATO warships were deployed off the coast of Libya to enforce an arms embargo imposed against Qaddafi's forces. Two days later NATO members determined to enforce the UN-sanctioned air exclusion zone over Libya, alongside a military operation to prevent further attacks on civilians and civilian-populated areas, undertaken by a multinational coalition under British, French and US command, and on 27 March NATO members agreed to assume full command of operations.

Meanwhile, on 23 March 2011 the NTC announced the formation of an Executive Board, which was to serve as the interim executive branch of government for Libya, while the NTC was henceforth to act as the national legislative body, pending the formation of a new permanent government. Mahmoud Jibril was appointed Chairman of the Executive Board.

At the end of March 2011 British officials revealed that Secretary for Foreign Liaison and International Co-operation Musa Kusa had arrived in the United Kingdom, in order to defect. Kusa's former deputy, Abd al-Ati al-Obeidi, was subsequently appointed to replace him. In late 2011 allegations emerged within the British media that, while serving as head of Libya's foreign intelligence service during 1994–2009, Kusa had been involved in the torture of Libyan political detainees, as well as the 1996 massacre at Abu Salim prison; the claims were adamantly denied by Kusa, along with claims of involvement in or knowledge of the 1988 Lockerbie bombing and the killing in 1984 of British police officer Yvonne Fletcher (see Foreign Affairs). Following the rescindment by the EU of sanctions against him, Kusa relocated to Qatar in April 2011, but continued to provide intelligence and other support to assist NATO in locating the Qaddafi regime's secret military sites.

Although the NATO air-strikes against government forces appeared initially to have emboldened opposition forces, in early April 2011 the rebel groups were forced to abandon control of towns in Libya's central coastal area, including Mersa Brega and Ras Lanuf, as Qaddafi's forces continued to bombard opposition-held areas with heavy artillery. On 10 April an African Union (AU, see p. 191) delegation led by South African President Jacob Zuma arrived in Tripoli to present a proposal for a settlement of the conflict, which included, *inter alia*, an immediate cease-fire and negotiations between regime and opposition representatives over a gradual transition to political reform. Qaddafi indicated his approval in principle, but the plan was rejected by opposition figures, who demanded Qaddafi's ouster as a prerequisite for talks. Meanwhile, government forces continued to launch attacks on opposition strongholds, particularly in Misurata, where it was reported that missiles had struck the port area, in an attempt to disrupt the supply by ship of aid to opposition fighters. However, opposition forces took control of Misurata airport on 11 May, as a result of which the supply of weapons and aid was resumed.

Meanwhile, at the end of April 2011 one of Qaddafi's sons, Seif al-Arab, and three of his grandchildren were reportedly killed in a NATO air-strike on the Libyan leader's compound in central Tripoli. Libyan representatives claimed that the strike had been intended to assassinate Qaddafi, although NATO commanders denied this, insisting that the building had been a 'military command and control' facility. Following the attack, large crowds of pro-Qaddafi demonstrators surrounded the residences of diplomats representing NATO member states; the British embassy was reported to have been set alight and others ransacked, prompting the British Secretary of State for Foreign and Commonwealth Affairs, William Hague, to order the expulsion of Libya's head of mission in the United Kingdom. On 17 May foreign media and the NTC reported that the Chairman of the NOC, Shukri Muhammad Ghanem, had defected from the Government and fled to Tunisia; speaking from the Italian capital, Rome, on 1 June, Ghanem confirmed his defection. He died in the Austrian capital, Vienna, at the end of April 2012, having reportedly suffered a heart attack and subsequently drowned in the River Danube; however, the exact circumstances of Ghanem's death were still being investigated by the Austrian authorities later that year.

Assisted by an intensification of NATO air-strikes against government targets from May 2011, including the deployment from late May of ground-attack helicopters by both France and the United Kingdom, opposition forces made significant military gains during May–June. (The use of such helicopters was seen as one step away from the deployment of ground troops, prompting concerns that NATO was overstepping the UN-mandated remit of acting to protect Libyan civilians.) On 7 June, while attending a conference of the International Labour Organization in Geneva, Switzerland, the Secretary for Labour, al-Amin Manfur, confirmed that he had defected. On 19 June a NATO air-strike was reported to have killed nine civilians in a residential area of Tripoli. NATO expressed regret for the incident, which it attributed to a weapons system failure. However, the Libyan Government claimed that the strike was a calculated response to the continued support for Qaddafi among some elements of the Libyan population. By July the vast majority of supply lines to government forces in Tripoli had been severed, with fuel supplies running particularly low, after the rebels had cut the supply of oil to the refinery at Zawia.

Meanwhile, on 27 June 2011 the ICC issued an arrest warrant against Qaddafi in respect of crimes against humanity committed during the early weeks of the popular uprising, on the basis of evidence provided by the Office of the Chief Prosecutor which apparently showed that the Libyan leader had introduced a state policy directly authorizing the use of force against civilians in order to quell the anti-Government protests. Arrest warrants were also issued against Seif al-Islam and Libya's head of intelligence, Abdullah al-Sanoussi, both of whom were also alleged to have been responsible for the killing and persecution of civilians. NATO officials and a spokesperson for the NTC welcomed the development; however, the Libyan Government dismissed the warrants, insisting that it did not recognize the legitimacy of the ICC. Following a meeting in Istanbul, Turkey, in mid-July of the Libya Contact Group—formed in late March and comprising 15 Western and Arab diplomats, including US Secretary of State Clinton, British Secretary of State for Foreign and Commonwealth Affairs Hague, and Qatari Prime Minister and Minister of Foreign Affairs Sheikh Hamad bin Jasim bin Jaber Al Thani—the Group officially recognized the NTC as the sole legitimate authority in Libya. Al-Sanoussi was arrested by the Mauritanian authorities at Nouakchott airport in March 2012; in September he was extradited to Libya, where he was promised a fair trial by the judicial authorities. However, the ICC also sought trial proceedings against al-Sanoussi for alleged 'crimes against humanity' during the uprising in Benghazi in 2011, while France also sought his extradition owing to his alleged involvement in the bombing of a passenger airline over Niger in September 1989 (see Foreign Affairs); al-Sanoussi had been convicted by the French authorities *in absentia* in 1999 and handed a term of life imprisonment.

Opposition forces seize control of Tripoli; the killing of Qaddafi

Concerns about the stability and integrity of the NTC were prompted by the killing on 28 June 2011 in unexplained circumstances of the head of the opposition armed forces, former Secretary for Public Security Gen. Abd al-Fattah Yunis al-Abaidi, together with two aides. Yunis had been summoned to appear before an inquiry by the NTC, following allegations that he had been engaged in secret meetings with the Qaddafi regime, but, according to the NTC, was attacked en route to the meeting by pro-Qaddafi elements seeking to foment division among the opposition. NTC Chairman Abd al-Jalil later announced that the assailant had been captured. However, some observers alleged that the Council had assassinated Yunis amid doubts over his loyalty. In early August the NTC dismissed its Executive Board, citing its inadequate response to Yunis's killing. In December

2012, as part of the ongoing investigation into the assassination, Abd al-Jalil was questioned by military prosecutors, and he was to face a further hearing concerning his possible involvement in the crime in late February 2013.

With the Government's ability to mount operations being increasingly undermined by ongoing NATO air-strikes, opposition forces continued to make military gains and by mid-August 2011 had made further advances on all fronts, having taken, *inter alia*, Zawia, Zlitan (about 160 km east of Tripoli) and Gharyan (one of the largest towns in the Nafusa mountainous area). On the evening of 20 August rebel forces entered Tripoli, clashing with government troops and prompting Qaddafi to appeal for his supporters to help defend the city. Seif al-Islam and Hannibal Qaddafi were apprehended by the opposition forces on 21 August, but subsequently evaded their captors. By 22 August the rebels claimed to have seized control of about 90% of the city, and the following day attacked the Bab al-Aziziya military compound in Tripoli, which had served as Qaddafi's primary base but from which the Libyan leader and his family had already fled; the forces defending the complex surrendered, signalling the effective displacement of the Qaddafi regime.

Following Qaddafi's removal from power, the NTC assumed de facto control of Libya, suspending constitutional decrees issued under his rule and replacing them with an interim Constitutional Declaration, under the terms of which an interim government was to be installed within 30 days and elections for a 210-member legislature were to be held within 240 days; a new constitution was to be formulated and submitted to a national referendum within 60 days of the legislature's inauguration. Islamic law (*Shari'a*) was to be the principal source of legislation, although Abd al-Jalil sought to convince Western governments of the NTC's commitment to moderate Islam. Tripoli was designated as the capital, and the NTC relocated its operations to the city. On 16 September 2011 the UN General Assembly approved a motion to accept the credentials of diplomatic representatives appointed by the NTC, thereby effectively recognizing the Council as the legitimate governing authority in Libya. On the same day the UN Security Council adopted a resolution establishing the UN Support Mission in Libya (UNSMIL), which was to be charged with assisting the transitional authorities in their post-conflict reconstruction efforts. The Security Council also voted to ease sanctions imposed by Resolution 1973, exempting the NOC from the suspension of assets and similarly easing measures against a number of other key state entities, including the central bank and the Libyan Investment Authority. On 3 October the NTC announced the appointment of an interim administration, with Jibril as Prime Minister. On the same day Jibril announced that he would resign from Government following the ultimate defeat of Qaddafi.

A number of mass graves were discovered in and around Tripoli and other towns, including a grave unearthed in Tripoli in mid-September 2011 that was reported to contain the remains of more than 1,270 people, who were widely believed to have been among those killed during the 1996 massacre at Abu Salim prison. In a statement released in October 2011 the International Committee of the Red Cross, which had deployed forensic experts to Libya, at the request of the NTC, to assist in exhuming and identifying the human remains, noted that corpses continued to be discovered on a regular basis at mass graves, hospitals and other sites across Libya.

Fierce fighting occurred between forces loyal to the NTC and pro-Qaddafi forces in Sirte and Bani Walid (the final two remaining strongholds of Qaddafi loyalists) in September–October 2011; both sides incurred heavy casualties and thousands of civilians were displaced by the violence. NTC forces finally asserted control of Bani Walid on 18 October, and two days later the last vestiges of support for Qaddafi in Sirte were defeated. Reports emerged that Qaddafi himself had been captured, having been discovered hiding in a drainage pipe after the convoy in which he was attempting to flee the city was targeted by a NATO air-strike. The NTC confirmed later on 20 October that Qaddafi had died while in the custody of the rebels, initially suggesting that he had been killed in cross-fire following his capture. However, the emergence of video footage depicting Qaddafi injured and being taunted by his captors, and of subsequent footage depicting his corpse, displaying additional bullet wounds to the head and abdomen, being assaulted and dragged through the streets of Sirte by rebel fighters, prompted speculation that the former leader may have been summarily executed by his captors. Qaddafi's fifth son, Mutassim, was killed in Sirte on the same day. It was alleged that he too had been executed by the

rebel fighters who had captured him. Under considerable external pressure from foreign governments and human rights groups, on 24 October, one day after Abd al-Jalil had formally proclaimed the liberation of Libya from Qaddafi's rule, the NTC agreed to conduct a full investigation into the circumstances surrounding Qaddafi's death.

Following the death of Qaddafi, lingering divisions among the NTC's various factions appeared increasingly to come to the fore. On 23 October 2011 Jibril resigned from the interim Government, adhering to the pledge that he had made earlier in the month. Dr Abd al-Rahim al-Keib, a university professor, was elected as the new interim Prime Minister at the end of that month. On 31 October, despite appeals from the NTC to extend the NATO mission to the end of the year, the UN mandate for military action and the air exclusion zone were ended, in accordance with an earlier Security Council vote. On 22 November al-Keib announced the composition of his interim Cabinet, which included Dr Mustafa Abushagur as Deputy Prime Minister, Ashour Ben Khayil as Minister of Foreign Affairs, Col Osama al-Juwaili as Minister of Defence and Fawzi Abdela'ali as Minister of the Interior. Abd al-Jalil was confirmed as interim President on the same day, and the new administration—which was expected to remain in office to oversee the transitional period prior to legislative elections due by mid-2012—was formally inaugurated on 24 November 2011.

On 19 November 2011 Seif al-Islam Qaddafi was captured, together with several aides, near the desert town of Obari in south-western Libya; he had apparently been en route to the Libya–Niger border at the time of his arrest. Seif al-Islam was transported to Zintan, where he remained in detention as of early 2013, amid ongoing wrangling between the NTC and the ICC over the location of his forthcoming trial (see below). The former insisted that he be tried in Libya, and offered assurances that he would be granted a fair trial, while the latter maintained that, in accordance with the arrest warrant issued against Seif al-Islam in June 2011, he should be transferred to face trial in The Hague, Netherlands.

Amid the celebrations over the removal of the Qaddafi regime, a mounting sense of apprehension soon became evident with regard to Libya's future prospects. In mid-December 2011 thousands of protesters gathered in Tripoli and Benghazi to appeal for greater openness and transparency from the interim Government, demanding that the NTC make public the identities of all its members and voting decisions, and appealing for the removal from the Government of former officials of the Qaddafi regime. Interim President Abd al-Jalil in turn appealed for patience on the part of the public and pledged to redistribute central government funds so as to allow greater regional autonomy.

The UN estimated in early 2012 that more than 8,500 prisoners, mostly pro-Qaddafi loyalists, were being held by militia groups, often in unofficial detention centres, and in January Amnesty International alleged that some of the armed militias, as well as officially recognized security forces, were engaged in the use of torture against prisoners. In the same month the international medical humanitarian organization Médecins sans frontières suspended its operations in Misurata after reporting that it had treated 115 patients with injuries that appeared to have been sustained as a result of torture. In early February Human Rights Watch claimed that a former Libyan ambassador to France, Dr Omar Brebesh, who had died in January within 24 hours of being detained by a Tripoli-based militia, had died as a result of injuries sustained during torture. The NTC pledged to investigate the claims.

On 21 January 2012 hundreds of protesters stormed and looted the NTC's headquarters in Benghazi, demanding greater transparency from the Council and voicing anger in particular over its perceived failure properly to consult the public prior to drafting new electoral laws in advance of forthcoming elections for the new legislature. The lack of public consultation on the legislation (which, in the event, was adopted in February) had prompted angry claims that the NTC was eschewing its own stated democratic principles. The following day the NTC Vice-Chairman, Abd al-Hafiz Ghoga, announced his resignation, after he had become a focal point for public anger, and allegations that he was an opportunist who had switched allegiance from the Qaddafi regime to the NTC as the latter gained the ascendancy. Abd al-Jalil, who claimed that 'hidden hands' were driving the protesters, insisted that the NTC would not step down, warning that such action would lead to civil war.

On 23 January 2012 local tribal fighters loyal to Qaddafi, angered by the NTC's perceived unwillingness to co-operate with them, seized control of Bani Walid, with four fighters loyal to the NTC and eight civilians reported to have been killed. On 25 January the interim Government conceded to the restive town's demands, with Minister of Defence al-Juwaili confirming the Government's recognition of a new tribal-based local council, in place of the NTC-appointed local council, as the legitimate authority of Bani Walid. Nevertheless, in mid-October pro-Government militias undertook a large-scale military campaign in the town which they claimed was to prevent a further uprising by pro-Qaddafi tribal fighters and to arrest known fugitives from the ousted regime; by late October more than 22 people had died as a result of the military assault. Meanwhile, in mid-February 2012 more than 100 people were estimated to have died in fighting between ethnic Arab and African tribes in Kufra.

The interim Government adopted new electoral laws in February 2012, providing for a parallel voting system, with 120 constituency seats (to be contested by independent candidates only) and 80 list seats (to be contested by party lists). The age requirement for those seeking to contest the election was lowered to 21 years, while citizens with dual nationality were to be allowed to vote and to present their candidacy. In April the NTC approved further legislation, which prohibited the formation of political organizations formed on the basis of 'religion, ethnicity or tribe', citing the desire to preserve national unity. The legislation was criticized by opposition groups, particularly the Muslim Brotherhood, which had earlier formed the Justice and Construction Party (JCP) to contest the elections to a national assembly (see Recent developments). Also in April the NTC announced that Seif al-Islam Qaddafi would be tried in Libya, contrary to requests by the ICC, which had formally requested that he be transferred to its auspices for trial in The Hague. A spokesman for the NTC stated that the trial would be completed before assembly elections in June. However, later in April 2012 the ICC rejected an appeal by Libya against the request for Seif al-Islam's transfer. In late June Dr al-Baghdadi Ali al-Mahmoudi, the former Secretary of the General People's Committee during Qaddafi's rule, was extradited to Libya from Tunisia, where he had sought refuge in September 2011. Trial proceedings against al-Mahmoudi, who was charged with involvement in the 'unjust killing' of pro-democracy protesters and of using his base in Tunisia to provide some US $25m. in funds to pro-Qaddafi forces during the civil conflict, began in December 2012.

Recent developments: Elections to the General National Congress and formation of a new Government

At elections to the General National Congress (GNC) held on 7 July 2012, the liberal and predominantly secular National Forces Alliance (NFA) of former interim premier Mahmoud Jibril—established in February—won 39 of the 80 seats reserved for political parties. The JCP secured 17 seats and the liberal National Front Party, recently formed as the successor party to the NFSL, won three seats. An additional 120 seats were reserved for independent candidates. Unlike in other countries of the Middle East and North Africa which had held elections as the result of 'Arab Spring' uprisings and subsequent political transitions (including Tunisia and Egypt), Islamists did not, therefore, constitute a majority in the new assembly. International observers commended the conduct of the elections, despite some instances of violence and protests by those in the east of the country who demanded greater political autonomy. On 8 August, almost one year after the end of Qaddafi's rule, the NTC was formally dissolved at a ceremony in Tripoli and its powers transferred to the GNC (being represented by its oldest member, Muhammad Ali Salim). On the following day a moderate Islamist, Muhammad Yousuf Magariaf of the National Front Party, defeated an independent liberal and former diplomat, Ali Zidan, in the vote to elect the President of the GNC; Magariaf thus replaced Abd al-Jalil as Libya's de facto head of state.

Throughout 2012 the Government continued to be involved in the struggle to contain the high levels of inter-tribal and political violence across Libya. After clashes had taken place between supporters of federalism and their pro-NTC opponents in Benghazi in mid-March, in which at least one person died, at the start of July the election commission headquarters in the city was invaded by a group of federalist protesters who set fire to election materials. In mid-June 2012 the mountainous area of western Libya, including Zintan, was officially declared a 'military zone' owing to the fierce fighting that was occurring between pro- and anti-Qaddafi tribes. In late August a series of violent attacks perpetrated by Sunni Islamist militants in a number of locations resulted in the destruction of holy shrines belonging to the Sufi branch of Islam in Misrata, Zlitan and Tripoli, and two car bombings in the capital, in which two people were killed. On 26 August the Minister of the Interior, Fawzi Abdela'ali, tendered his resignation, amid criticism over the failings of the security forces for which he was responsible. However, two days later Abdela'ali decided to remain in office for reasons of national security and continuity. On 20 November, only days after the new Government had been sworn in, Farraj al-Dursi, the chief of police in Benghazi and a former official of the Qaddafi regime, was shot dead outside his home by unknown assailants. At least 10 other security officials were reported to have been assassinated in Benghazi during 2012.

Meanwhile, on 11 September 2012 the US ambassador, J. Christopher Stevens, and three other US staff members were killed when protests targeting the US consulate in Benghazi escalated into attacks by armed assailants. The following day Mustafa Abushagur, the Deputy Prime Minister in the outgoing interim Government, was elected as Prime Minister at a second round of voting by the GNC; Abushagur narrowly defeated former interim premier Jibril, who had won the first round of voting. However, having twice failed to gain the approval of assembly members for his proposed list of ministers during the first week of October (with the NFA and the JCP reportedly seeking a larger number of portfolios), Abushagur was dismissed as premier-designate on 7 October.

Ali Zidan was elected as Prime Minister-designate by the GNC on 14 October 2012, in a fairly close contest against Muhammad al-Hirari, the Minister of Local Government in the outgoing cabinet. On 31 October a Cabinet comprising 27 nominees was approved by the legislature; it was reported to be more representative of Libya's various political factions and regions than the two line-ups proposed by Abushagur, and comprised principally liberal and moderate Islamist ministers. On 14 November 20 ministers, including Zidan, were sworn in to office by the GNC President, Magariaf. The previous day four of the original nominees—including Minister of the Interior Ashour Shuwail—had been deemed unfit to take office by the country's Transparency and Integrity Commission (TIC), owing to alleged links with Qaddafi. A further two nominees remained under investigation by the Commission—including the Minister of Foreign Affairs, Ali Aujali—while another had withdrawn his candidacy earlier that month for separate reasons. Muhammad al-Barghati was appointed as Minister of Defence and Al-Kilani al-Jazi as Minister of Finance. On 25 November 2012 the Minister of International Co-operation, Muhammad Abd al-Aziz, assumed additional responsibility for the foreign affairs portfolio on an interim basis. On the same day the First Deputy Prime Minister, Sadiq Abd al-Karim Abd al-Rahman, was also named as the temporary Minister of the Interior. However, after the TIC, on 4 December, cleared Shuwail of wrongdoing—he had launched an appeal against the initial ruling—the latter was appointed as Minister of the Interior on 11 December. Aujali was also found not guilty by the TIC on 27 November 2012, but he reportedly decided in late December not to take up the post for personal reasons. Abd al-Aziz was thus formally named as the Minister of Foreign Affairs on 7 January 2013. In April it was reported that the GNC had finally agreed that the 60-member committee required to draft a new, permanent constitution would be elected at a national election. The election was expected to take place in time for the committee to begin its work by early 2014.

Foreign Affairs

Relations with the USA and the United Kingdom

Libya's already strained relations with the USA deteriorated significantly under the presidency of Ronald Reagan (1981–89), who accused the Libyan Government of sponsoring international terrorism. In January 1986 Reagan severed all economic and commercial relations with Libya, and in March Libyan forces fired missiles at US fighter aircraft, which were challenging Libya's attempts to enforce recognition of the whole of the Gulf of Sirte as its territorial waters. In retaliatory attacks in April, US military aircraft bombed military installations, airports and official buildings, as well as alleged terrorist training camps and communication centres, in Tripoli and Benghazi; a reported 101 people, including many civilians, died in the raids. The US Administration claimed in justification to have irrefutable proof of Libyan involvement in terrorist attacks and plots against US targets in Europe and the Middle East.

In November 1991 the US and British Governments announced that they would seek to extradite two Libyan citizens, Abd al-Baset Ali Muhammad al-Megrahi (a former head of security at Libyan Arab Airlines) and Al-Amin Khalifa Fhimah (an employee of the airline), alleged to have been responsible for an explosion that destroyed a Pan American World Airways (Pan Am) passenger aircraft over Lockerbie, Scotland, in December 1988, resulting in the deaths of 270 people. The Libyan Government denied any involvement in the bombing, and recommended that the allegations be investigated by a neutral body. In January 1992 the UN Security Council adopted a resolution (No. 731) demanding Libya's compliance with requests for the extradition of its two nationals and its co-operation with a French inquiry into the bombing over Niger, in September 1989, of a Union de Transports Aériens (UTA) passenger airline, in which all 171 passengers and crew had been killed. Libya's offer to try on its own territory the two men accused of the Lockerbie bombing was rejected by the USA, the United Kingdom and France. On 31 March 1992 the UN Security Council adopted a resolution (No. 748) providing for the imposition of economic sanctions against Libya if it refused to comply with Resolution 731, and to commit itself to a renunciation of international terrorism, by 15 April. Sanctions, including the severance of international air links, the prohibition of trade in arms and the reduction of Libya's diplomatic representation abroad, were duly imposed on the specified date.

In June 1992 Libya's GPC announced its decision to allow the two Lockerbie suspects to be tried abroad, provided that the proceedings were 'fair and just'. In October 1993 the UN Secretary-General, Dr Boutros Boutros-Ghali, met the Libyan Secretary for Foreign Liaison and International Co-operation, but failed to secure agreement on a timetable for the surrender of the two suspects to either the USA or the United Kingdom. In November the Security Council adopted a resolution (No. 883) providing for the strengthening of the economic sanctions in force against Libya in the event of the country's failure fully to comply with Resolutions 731 and 748 by 1 December. The sanctions, which were duly applied, included: the closure of all Libyan Arab Airlines' offices abroad; a ban on the sale of equipment and services for the civil aviation sector; the sequestration of all Libyan financial resources overseas; and a ban on the sale to Libya of specified items for use in the petroleum and gas industries. In February 1994 US President Bill Clinton recommended that an embargo be imposed on Libya's sales of petroleum (which accounted for some 98% of its export earnings) if the country continued to defy the international community. In mid-1996, having failed to persuade the UN to agree even tighter sanctions, the US Congress approved unilateral 'secondary' sanctions against Libya (and Iran). The Iran-Libya Sanctions Act (ILSA) sought to penalize companies operating in US markets that were investing more than US $40m. (later amended to $20m.) in Libya's oil and gas industries.

In July 1997 the League of Arab States (the Arab League, see p. 372), which had been criticized by Qaddafi for its lack of support, formally proposed that the two Libyan suspects in the Lockerbie case be tried by Scottish judges under Scottish law in a neutral country. In September the members of the League urged a relaxation of the air embargo on Libya and voted to defy UN sanctions by permitting aircraft carrying Qaddafi, and other flights for religious or humanitarian purposes, to land on their territory. In August 1998 the United Kingdom and the USA proposed that the trial of the two suspects be held in the Netherlands under Scottish law and presided over by Scottish judges. The UN Security Council adopted a resolution (No. 1192) welcoming the initiative and providing for the suspension of sanctions upon the arrival in the Netherlands of the two suspects.

Following a meeting held in December 1998 between the UN Secretary-General, Kofi Annan, and Qaddafi in Libya, the GPC endorsed the principle of a trial of the Lockerbie suspects, but requested that the USA and the United Kingdom remove 'all remaining obstacles'. In a bid to break the impasse arising from Qaddafi's demand that the trial include a panel of international judges, envoys from Saudi Arabia and South Africa were dispatched to Libya in January 1999 to negotiate with the Libyan leader. In February they reportedly reached an understanding whereby UN observers would be allowed to monitor the two Libyan suspects during the trial, to ensure that they were not questioned by US and British agents, and afterwards, if they

were convicted and imprisoned in Scotland. The diplomatic initiative culminated in March with a visit by President Nelson Mandela of South Africa to Libya, during which Qaddafi undertook to surrender the suspects by 6 April. The two Libyans duly arrived for trial in the Netherlands on 5 April and were transferred to Camp Zeist, a former US airbase near Utrecht, designated Scottish territory for the purposes of the trial, where they were formally arrested and charged with murder, conspiracy to murder and contravention of the 1982 Aviation Security Act. The UN Security Council immediately voted to suspend sanctions against Libya indefinitely, although they were not to be permanently revoked until Libya had complied with other conditions stipulated in Resolution 1192 (including the payment of compensation to the families of victims of the Lockerbie bombing). The USA refused to remove the 'secondary' sanctions against Libya, but subsequently announced that it would permit the sale of food and medical items to Libya on a 'case-by-case' basis. In June 1999 the US and Libyan ambassadors to the UN participated in talks; this represented the first official contact between the two countries in 18 years.

The trial of al-Megrahi and Fhimah commenced on 3 May 2000; both pleaded not guilty to all three charges brought against them, and defence lawyers accused a number of organizations, including militant Palestinian resistance groups, of perpetrating the bombing. In January 2001 prosecution lawyers unexpectedly announced that they would no longer pursue charges of conspiracy to murder and contravention of the 1982 Aviation Security Act. Accordingly, the trial proceeded on the sole charge of murder. On 31 January 2001 the judges announced that they had unanimously found al-Megrahi guilty of the murder of 270 people and sentenced him to life imprisonment, with the recommendation that he serve a minimum of 20 years. The judges accepted that al-Megrahi was a member of the Libyan intelligence services, and, while acknowledging 'uncertainties and qualifications' in the case, they concluded that the 'real and convincing pattern' of evidence against him left them with no reasonable doubt as to his guilt. Fhimah, however, was unanimously acquitted, owing to lack of proof, and freed to return to Libya. Despite mounting pressure from Arab League states, the British Government asserted that sanctions against Libya would not be permanently revoked until Libya accepted responsibility for the bombing and paid 'substantial' compensation. The newly inaugurated US President, George W. Bush, indicated his support for this stance, and in July 2001 the ILSA was extended for a further five-year term.

Meanwhile, demands for further investigation into the bombing, and Qaddafi's role in it, were rejected by senior Scottish legal officials, who stated that there was insufficient evidence to justify any further proceedings against those alleged to have abetted al-Megrahi. Lawyers for al-Megrahi subsequently lodged an appeal against his conviction; the hearing, before five Scottish judges, began at Camp Zeist in January 2002. Al-Megrahi's lawyers based their case on what they termed new 'strong circumstantial evidence', which raised the possibility that the bomb had been placed on the aircraft at London, United Kingdom, and not in Malta, as the trial judges had concluded. In February Seif al-Islam Qaddafi indicated that Libya would pay compensation to the families of those killed in the Lockerbie bombing, regardless of the outcome of the appeal. In March the appeal was unanimously rejected, and al-Megrahi was transferred to a prison in Scotland to begin his sentence.

In July 1999 Libya and the United Kingdom reached agreement on the full restoration of diplomatic relations, after Qaddafi issued a statement in which he accepted Libya's 'general responsibility' for the death of Yvonne Fletcher, a British policewoman who was shot outside the Libyan People's Bureau in London in 1984, and agreed to co-operate with the investigation into the killing. The payment by Libya, in November 1999, of compensation to the victim's family facilitated the reopening of the British embassy in Tripoli in the following month, and in March 2001 Libya appointed an ambassador to the United Kingdom for the first time in 17 years.

In April 2003 it was confirmed that, following negotiations in London between senior British, US and Libyan representatives, Libya had agreed to accept civil responsibility for the actions of its officials in the Lockerbie case and would pay US $10m. in compensation to the families of the victims. Payment of the compensation was to be a three-stage process: $4m. would be paid to each family on the permanent lifting of UN sanctions; a further $4m. would follow upon the removal of unilateral US sanctions; and a final payment of $2m. would be made when

Libya was removed from the list of countries that the USA deemed to support international terrorism. However, Libya would pay only an additional $1m. to each family if the USA did not complete the second and third stages.

After further negotiations, on 16 August 2003 Libya delivered a letter to the President of the UN Security Council stating, *inter alia*, that it: accepted 'responsibility for the actions of its officials' in the Lockerbie bombing; agreed to pay compensation to the families of the victims; pledged co-operation in any further Lockerbie inquiry; and agreed to continue its co-operation in the US-led 'war on terror'. Following the transfer of US $2,700m. in compensation to the International Bank of Settlements, on 12 September 13 of the 15 members of the UN Security Council approved a British-drafted resolution lifting the sanctions imposed against Libya; France (which had demanded a similar amount of compensation for families of victims of the UTA bombing in 1989) and the USA abstained from the vote. Later that month Libya announced its intention to commence dialogue with the USA aimed at normalizing bilateral relations. Nevertheless, the US Administration continued to insist that unilateral sanctions would remain in place until the Libyan Government addressed ongoing US concerns such as the infringement of human rights in the country and the pursuit of weapons of mass destruction.

In October 2003 an official of the US Department of State accused Libya of having increased its efforts to purchase components for biological and chemical weapons since the lifting of UN sanctions the previous month, and warned that Libya would be added to the group of countries described by President Bush as forming an 'axis of evil'—comprising Iran, Iraq and the Democratic People's Republic of Korea (North Korea). In mid-December, however, in an unexpected development, the British Prime Minister, Tony Blair, announced that Libya had agreed to disclose and dismantle its programme to develop weapons of mass destruction and long-range ballistic missiles. The statement was the culmination of nine months of clandestine negotiations between Qaddafi and British and US diplomats, during which the Libyan authorities had reportedly shown evidence of a 'well advanced' nuclear weapons programme, as well as the existence of large quantities of chemical weapons and bombs designed to carry poisonous gas. Libya also agreed to adhere to the Chemical Weapons Convention and to sign an additional protocol allowing the International Atomic Energy Agency (IAEA) to carry out random inspections of its facilities. Upon visiting a number of sites in Tripoli in late December, the Director-General of the IAEA, Dr Muhammad el-Baradei, insisted that Libya's weapons development projects had been in the initial stages of development, contradicting the assessment given by the United Kingdom and the USA. In January 2004 the US Department of State confirmed that British and US intelligence agents had, in October 2003, intercepted a shipment of centrifuges capable of developing weapons-grade uranium destined for Tripoli. Also in January 2004 it was announced that Libya had ratified the IAEA's Comprehensive Nuclear Test Ban Treaty. Later in the month it was agreed that US and British officials would be responsible for destroying and removing Libya's nuclear material and that the IAEA would verify that the dismantling process was complete.

In February 2004 it was confirmed that a US diplomat had been stationed in that country's interests section of the Belgian embassy in Tripoli, providing the USA with its first permanent diplomatic presence in Libya for 25 years. Also in February the Libyan Secretary for Foreign Liaison and International Co-operation, Abd al-Rahman Muhammad Shalgam, visited London for talks with his British counterpart and Prime Minister Blair; this represented the first meeting between cabinet-level ministers of the two countries in more than 20 years.

The Secretary of the General People's Committee, Shukri Muhammad Ghanem, caused controversy in late February 2004 when he claimed that compensation was merely being paid to the families of the Lockerbie victims in order to 'buy peace' and avoid sanctions, and denied any Libyan involvement in the murder of Yvonne Fletcher. The following day, however, Shalgam reiterated that Libya stood by its acceptance of responsibility for the Lockerbie bombing. The USA subsequently lifted the restrictions on its citizens travelling to Libya. In March Libya signed an additional IAEA protocol allowing the agency to carry out random inspections of its nuclear facilities; moreover, Libya commenced the destruction of its supplies of chemical weapons and transported all of its remaining nuclear weapons-related equipment to the USA. Later that month the Organisation for

the Prohibition of Chemical Weapons verified that Libya's declaration of its chemical weapons inventory, submitted to the UN in early March, had been accurate. In May it was announced that Libya would no longer conduct military trade with those countries that it believed to be involved in the proliferation of weapons of mass destruction.

Meanwhile, in late March 2004 William Burns, the US Assistant Secretary of the Bureau of Near Eastern Affairs, became the highest-ranking US official to visit Libya in more than 30 years; the principal issues under discussion were further moves towards the lifting of US sanctions on Libya and the restoration of normal bilateral relations. In April the USA announced that it would remove the restrictions that prevented US petroleum companies and banks from conducting commercial activities in Libya. In June it was revealed that Libya had resumed exports of petroleum to the USA. At the end of the month formal diplomatic relations were re-established between the two countries when a US liaison office was opened in Tripoli. In September President Bush lifted all travel restrictions for charter and commercial flights between Libya and the USA. He also announced that the US $1,300m. of Libyan assets held in the USA or in US banks abroad would be unfrozen. In February 2005 the US authorities lifted all restrictions on Libyan diplomats travelling within the USA.

Relations between Libya and the United Kingdom continued to improve in 2004. In March Blair held talks with Qaddafi in Tripoli, after which Qaddafi insisted that he was willing to join the international 'war on terror'. It was also announced that British police officers would travel to Libya in April to continue investigations into the murder of Fletcher. In October 2005 Libya signed a memorandum of understanding with the British Government, which allowed for the deportation from the United Kingdom of Libyans suspected of involvement in terrorist activities. (The United Kingdom is legally prevented from deporting foreign nationals to countries that it suspects of using inhumane or degrading treatment.) In May 2007 the British oil company BP announced that it was to return to Libya, more than three decades after its expulsion from the country when Qaddafi had nationalized its assets in 1971; BP was granted onshore and offshore exploratory rights in a deal worth an estimated US $900m.

Meanwhile, in December 2004, with the unilateral sanctions imposed upon Libya by the USA having been lifted, Libya paid the second instalment of its compensation to the families of those killed in the Lockerbie bombing. In May 2006 the US liaison office in Tripoli was formally upgraded to an embassy in recognition of Libya's 'continued commitment to its renunciation of terrorism'. In June Libya was removed from the US Department of State's list of countries deemed to support international terrorism.

However, tensions arose in that month when Libyan lawyers in the USA insisted that, as a result of the expiration in December 2004 of an agreement concerning the transfer of the final portion of compensation for families of the Lockerbie victims, the Libyan Government was no longer obligated to pay the final US $2m. promised to each family. Nevertheless, in July 2006 the USA lifted all air transport sanctions against Libya. In January 2008 Shalgam held discussions with US Secretary of State Condoleezza Rice in Washington, DC—the first official visit by a Libyan foreign secretary in almost four decades. Following talks between Libyan and US officials in London in May, a statement was issued reiterating the commitment of both parties to resolving all outstanding compensation claims by the families of those killed in the Lockerbie bombing. In August representatives of both countries, meeting in Tripoli, signed a joint agreement on the full and final settlement of mutual claims by victims or their relatives in respect of bombings involving the two countries. Visiting Libya in September, Rice—the first US Secretary of State to visit the country since 1953—stated that their bilateral relationship had entered a new phase, although differences remained. In October 2008 Libya paid $1,500m. into an agreed compensation fund for the relatives of US victims of bombings covered by the agreement.

In December 2008 Gene A. Cretz was sworn in as the first US ambassador to Libya since 1972. In January 2009 Ali Suleiman Aujali assumed the role of Libyan ambassador to the USA, following the upgrading of Libya's liaison office in Washington, DC, to a full embassy in May 2006. From 1 April 2009 the USA began accepting Libyan applications for visas, and in September Qaddafi visited the USA for the first time to address the UN General Assembly in New York.

In August 2009 the Scottish Cabinet Secretary for Justice, Kenny MacAskill, announced that al-Megrahi would be freed on compassionate grounds, after discussions between the British and Libyan authorities over al-Megrahi's declining health (al-Megrahi had been diagnosed with terminal cancer in September 2008). The decision provoked outrage from many of the families of the US victims of the Lockerbie bombing and official condemnation by the US authorities. The British Government attempted to distance itself from the controversy, insisting that al-Megrahi's release had been decided by the Scottish devolved administration. However, one of a series of leaked US diplomatic cables published in late 2010 by the WikiLeaks organization indicated that the decision had enjoyed the full support of the British Government, which had reportedly been warned by Qaddafi of the potential severance of diplomatic ties and the immediate cessation of all British commercial activity in Libya, as well as risks to the personal safety of British diplomatic staff and expatriate workers in Libya. Another leaked communiqué revealed that Cretz had advised the US Administration that public opposition to al-Megrahi's release could result in US interests being subject to similarly punitive measures. In January 2011 Cretz was recalled to Washington, DC, following complaints by the Libyan Government in response to the publication by WikiLeaks of further communiqués, in which the US diplomat commented upon Qaddafi's personal life and eccentricities. Al-Megrahi died in Tripoli in late May 2012.

Meanwhile, a trade and investment agreement signed between the USA and Libya in May 2010 provided for the establishment of a bilateral trade and investment council; the USA also agreed to offer assistance in Libya's bid to accede to the World Trade Organization (WTO, see p. 444). However, the apparent amelioration in bilateral relations was severely undermined by the Qaddafi regime's response to the popular protests in Libya in early 2011, which prompted vociferous condemnation from the Administration of US President Barack Obama. In March US Secretary of State Hillary Clinton announced that the Obama Administration was considering its legal options, following the claims by a number of defecting Libyan government officials, including former Secretary for Justice Mustafa Muhammad Abd al-Jalil, that the 1988 Lockerbie bombing had been carried out on the direct orders of Qaddafi. (For US and British responses to the Libyan Government's handling of the protests and the subsequent installation of the National Transitional Council, see Domestic Political Affairs.)

The USA accepted the NTC as the 'legitimate governing authority' of Libya in July 2011. In September the US embassy in Tripoli, which had been closed, along with many other foreign embassies in Libya, in February, was reopened and Cretz returned to his post in the same month. In late September Scottish prosecutors submitted a formal request to the interim Libyan Government requesting its assistance in uncovering new evidence pertaining to the 1988 Lockerbie bombing. A number of senior government officials who had defected from the Qaddafi regime during mid-2011 had claimed that the bombing had been carried out on the direct orders of the former Libyan leader. Both the US and British Governments praised the new Libyan authorities for having staged the country's first free election for more than four decades in July 2012 (see Domestic Political Affairs). Diplomatic relations between the USA and Libya have continued to grow despite the deaths of Cretz's successor, ambassador J. Christopher Stevens, and three other consular officials following the storming by armed militants of the US consulate in Benghazi in September of that year, with US investigators assisting the Libyan authorities in their efforts to bring the perpetrators of the crime to justice.

In January 2012 the British authorities announced that an investigation was to be launched following claims, which had emerged following the discovery of documents in Tripoli in September 2011, that British intelligence officials had assisted in the rendition of two Libyan nationals, Abd al-Hakim Belhadj and Sami al-Saadi, from Thailand and Hong Kong, respectively, back to their home country in 2004. Both men claimed to have been tortured by the Libyan authorities upon their return, and in late 2011 threatened to begin legal proceedings against the British Government, arguing that it had been complicit in their torture and unlawful detention.

Regional relations

During the late 1990s and 2000s Qaddafi oscillated between identifying Libya as an African nation, and emphasizing Libya's links with the Arab world. In mid-1998 Qaddafi announced his intention to ally Libya more closely with African rather than

Arab countries. In October he changed the name of Libya's mission to the Arab League from 'permanent' to 'resident'. In September 1999, on the 30th anniversary of his seizure of power, Qaddafi hosted an extraordinary summit meeting of the Organization of African Unity (OAU) in Sirte, at which he presented his vision of a United States of Africa and demanded that Africa be given veto power on the UN Security Council. The 'Sirte Declaration', a final document adopted by the 43 attending heads of state and government, called for the strengthening of the OAU, the establishment of a pan-African parliament, African monetary union and an African court of justice. At a further extraordinary summit of the OAU in Sirte in March 2001, it was announced that the organization's member states had overwhelmingly endorsed the proposals to declare the formation of the African Union (AU, see p. 191). In July 2002 Qaddafi travelled to Durban, South Africa, for the 38th and final summit of the OAU, at which the new AU was formally created. During the summit South African President Thabo Mbeki and numerous other African heads of state attempted to persuade Qaddafi to abandon his hostility towards the New Partnership for Africa's Development, a contract between Africa and the international community under which, in exchange for aid and investment, the African states agreed to strive towards democracy and good governance.

Qaddafi's growing influence in Africa was somewhat checked in January 2003, following the removal of some 300 Libyan troops from the Central African Republic, to the Government of which they had been providing protection. In June 2004 allegations were made that in mid-2003 Qaddafi had ordered the assassination of Crown Prince Abdullah of Saudi Arabia, the kingdom's de facto leader, following a dispute at the Arab League summit held in March. (Libya also reportedly accused Saudi Arabia of financing Libyan opposition groups that had attempted to assassinate Qaddafi.) Libyan officials strongly refuted these allegations; however, in December 2004 Saudi Arabia recalled its ambassador from Tripoli and dismissed the Libyan ambassador in the Saudi capital, Riyadh.

In May 2006 Sudanese President Omar Hassan Ahmad al-Bashir expressed gratitude to Qaddafi for the latter's role in finding a resolution to the crisis in Darfur, Sudan, and proposed the establishment of a tripartite committee, comprising representatives of the Libyan and Sudanese Governments and the Sudan Liberation Movement, to oversee the implementation of the peace agreement signed between the two latter parties on 5 May (see the chapter on Sudan). In November Qaddafi, who had emphasized the need for an AU-sponsored resolution of the Darfur crisis rather than external intervention, accused the USA and other Western countries of involving themselves in the crisis to secure oil, and, by means of the deployment of UN troops, to effect the return of colonialism to Africa. In July 2007 Libya hosted an international conference on Darfur, co-chaired by the AU and the UN.

In June 2006 ministers responsible for foreign affairs from Algeria, Libya, Mauritania, Morocco and Tunisia convened in Tripoli to discuss efforts to revive the five-nation Union du Maghreb arabe (UMA—Union of the Arab Maghreb, see p. 464), which had been founded in February 1989 but had remained dormant for more than a decade, predominantly owing to Algerian–Moroccan disagreements concerning Western Sahara. This will to relaunch the UMA was restated in April 2008 during celebrations held in Morocco to mark the 50th anniversary of the summit at which the idea of a union of Arab Maghreb states had initially been proposed. A year later delegates responsible for foreign affairs from the UMA member states again met in Tripoli, where they reiterated their commitment to improving political and economic co-operation among the countries of North Africa.

In March 2007 Qaddafi announced his decision to boycott the Arab League summit meeting in Riyadh, insisting that Libya was an African nation and had 'turned its back to Arabs'. Later that year Qaddafi embarked upon a tour of West Africa, culminating in his attendance in July at an AU summit meeting in the Ghanaian capital, Accra, which focused predominantly on proposals to establish a pan-African government. The majority of those present rejected Qaddafi's appeal for the immediate creation of a 'United States of Africa', and in February 2008 he threatened to sever Libyan ties with Africa, pledging to transfer Libya's African investments to alternative destinations in Arab and European countries if his vision for African unity continued to be ignored. In February 2009 Qaddafi was, none the less, appointed to the chairmanship of the AU and immediately revived his efforts to promote the concept of a 'United States of Africa'. However, at an AU summit meeting in Addis Ababa, Ethiopia, in January 2010, attempts by Qaddafi to be re-elected to the chairmanship were unsuccessful.

In November 2010 Libya and Tunisia agreed to lift all administrative and financial restrictions on the movement of goods and people between the two countries, in a development that was hailed as an important step towards the achievement of greater Maghreb unity. The two countries also agreed to double the value of bilateral investment, to US \$2,000m., and discussed the creation of a free economic zone. In April 2013 the Libyan and Tunisian Governments agreed to establish a joint committee which would supervise the export of Libyan oil to Tunisia, following the conclusion of a bilateral accord in May 2012.

The Arab League suspended Libya's membership of that body in mid-February 2011, citing its disapproval of the Libyan Government's response to the popular protests that commenced earlier that month. During the conflict, both Qatar and the United Arab Emirates contributed aircraft to the NATO coalition, and the former was also reported to have provided the Libyan rebels with significant amounts of financial aid, military training and weapons. Following the ousting of the Qaddafi regime in August, the Arab League formally recognized the NTC as the legitimate representative of the Libyan people and voted to restore the country's membership later that month.

Having at first appeared reluctant to criticize the Qaddafi regime's violent handling of the protesters, the Chairman of the AU Commission issued a statement in late February 2011 condemning the Government's 'disproportionate use of force' against civilians, and demanding 'an immediate end of the repression and violence'. A proposal intended to secure an end to the conflict between the Government and the rebel forces presented by the AU in April secured the approval in principle of Qaddafi but was rejected by the NTC, which insisted on the removal from power of Qaddafi. In July the AU issued a statement in which it declared that its members would not co-operate with the arrest warrants issued by the ICC against Qaddafi, Seif al-Islam and the head of the Libyan intelligence service, contending that the existence of the warrants 'seriously complicates the efforts aimed at finding a negotiated political solution to the crisis'. Following the removal from power of the Qaddafi regime, the AU recognized the NTC as the de facto Libyan Government in mid-September, and stated that it was ready to assist the NTC in its efforts to rebuild the country and form a new, inclusive government.

Other external relations

Relations with the EU, and particularly with France, generally improved following talks in early 1996 between Libyan and EU representatives in Belgium. In July Qaddafi granted the French authorities investigating the 1989 bombing of the UTA passenger aircraft unprecedented access to Libyan evidence. This resulted in February 1998 in a judge's decision to try *in absentia* six Libyans suspected of involvement in the attack, and in March 1999 a French court sentenced the six suspects to life imprisonment. The French authorities issued international arrest warrants for the Libyans, and threatened to intensify sanctions against Libya if it did not impose the verdicts on the accused. In July Libya began payment of some US \$31m. in compensation to the families of those killed in the bomb attack, although attempts by French lawyers on behalf of the victims' families to prosecute Qaddafi for complicity in the bombing of the aircraft were unsuccessful. In September 2003, following an intervention by the French President, Jacques Chirac, the Libyan Government and the families of the UTA bombing reached partial agreement on the payment of additional compensation to the victims' relatives, and in January 2004 Libya agreed to pay them an additional \$170m.; the payment was to be made in four equal instalments, resulting in the families of each victim receiving an additional \$1m. In December 2005 the Libyan Government was ordered by a French court to pay an additional \$4m. in compensation to families of victims of the 1989 bombing not included in the previous agreement.

Relations between the French and Libyan Governments improved in 2005, after France expressed its interest in assisting the development of civil nuclear technology in Libya. In March 2006 a deal on co-operation regarding the development of nuclear energy in Libya was signed by representatives of the two countries during a visit to Tripoli by the Director of France's Commissariat à l'énergie atomique. Meanwhile, in April 2004 Qaddafi, who was visiting Europe for the first time in 15 years, met with several senior EU politicians in Brussels, Belgium, and

addressed the European Commission. The ending of economic sanctions and an arms embargo imposed on Libya by the European Economic Community (now EU) in 1986 was ratified by EU ministers in October 2004.

In December 2007 Qaddafi made an official visit to the French capital at the invitation of President Nicolas Sarkozy—the first such invitation from a Western country since Libya had abandoned its nuclear weapons programme in 2003, and interpreted by some as a reward for the Libyan leader's decision to release the Bulgarian medical workers earlier in 2007 (see below). The visit provoked strong censure from both French and Libyan opposition politicians, as well as international human rights groups, owing to Libya's questionable human rights record. Commercial agreements worth an estimated €10,000m. were signed between the two countries; Libya also expressed a keen interest in the future purchase of military equipment.

Franco-Libyan relations were, however, once more strained in 2008 when Qaddafi criticized President Sarkozy's project to create a Union for the Mediterranean. Qaddafi, who had expressed concerns that French promotion of Mediterranean co-operation represented a reassertion of colonial dominance over former North African colonies, and also that the initiative would undermine the role of the AU, refused to attend the official inauguration of the Union in July. During a state visit to Libya in July 2010, Qaddafi and Sarkozy signed a memorandum of understanding intended to boost nuclear energy co-operation, providing for French access to Libya's uranium resources and the eventual construction of a nuclear desalination plant to provide drinking water to the Libyan population. However, following the onset of conflict in Libya in early 2011, the French Government imposed measures against the Qaddafi regime, and in early March France became the first state officially to recognize the opposition Transitional National Council as the 'legitimate representative of the Libyan people'.

In April 1998, meanwhile, Libya resolved to allow the German authorities to question four Libyans suspected of carrying out a bomb attack on a nightclub in Berlin in 1986. Following a lengthy trial, in November 2001 a court in Berlin sentenced four people, including a Libyan national, to between 12 and 14 years' imprisonment for their involvement in the attack. Although Qaddafi's personal complicity in the incident could not be proven, the presiding judge stated that there was sufficient evidence to ascertain that the bombing had been carried out by members of the Libyan secret service and employees of the Libyan People's Bureau in the former East Germany.

In August 2003 the Qaddafi International Charity and Development Foundation offered to compensate the relatives of the three victims of the Berlin bomb attack. While negotiations between the USA and Libya regarding this compensation continued, a new round of talks between Germany and Libya began in July 2004 to decide upon compensation payments for the non-US citizens injured in the attack. The talks were finalized in the following month, and the Libyan authorities signed a deal in September agreeing to pay US \$35m. to compensate some 160 non-US victims. The agreement signalled the start of improved relations between Germany and Libya.

In July 1998 Italy formally apologized for its colonial rule of Libya, and commitments were made to improve bilateral relations. Following the suspension of international sanctions in April 1999, Italy's Prime Minister, Massimo D'Alema, travelled to Libya in December, thus becoming the first EU premier to visit the country since 1992, and in December 2000 officials from the two countries signed accords regarding political consultation, visas and the removal of landmines during talks in the Italian capital, Rome. In February 2004 the Italian Prime Minister, Silvio Berlusconi, became the first Western leader to meet with Qaddafi following the Libyan renouncement of its nuclear weapons programme. In August Berlusconi exerted pressure on Qaddafi to place stricter border controls on the country's northern coastline, following an influx of illegal immigrants into the Italian island of Lampedusa from Libya. In October, following a sudden increase in the number of illegal immigrants arriving from North Africa (up to 1,700 a week), the Italian Government began a mass expulsion of illegal immigrants to Libya. Having agreed to assist with the immigration problem, Libya returned some 1,000 of these people to Egypt. Also in October Qaddafi agreed to revoke a ban that prohibited some 20,000 Italian settlers who had been expelled from Libya in 1970 (following Qaddafi's rise to power) from visiting the country.

During a meeting with Qaddafi in Benghazi in August 2008, Berlusconi issued an apology for the 'damage inflicted on Libya by Italy during the colonial era'. The two heads of state also signed a treaty of 'friendship, partnership and co-operation' (which was ratified in Sirte in February 2009), committing Italy to annual payments of US $200m. to Libya, over a period of 25 years, via investment and infrastructure projects in the latter country. For its part, Libya agreed to co-operate more fully in efforts to combat illegal immigration, principally through the establishment of joint marine patrols of the Libyan coastline. This issue became particularly salient in early 2009, after a report published by the office of the UN High Commissioner for Refugees stated that the number of migrants arriving in Italy from Libya had risen to 33,000 in 2008 (from 20,000 in 2007). At the end of March 2009 more than 200 migrants were reported to have drowned after their boat, destined for Italy, capsized 30 miles off the Libyan coast. Libya agreed in May to take back more than 200 migrants discovered off the Libyan coastline by Italian marine patrols.

Relations between Libya and Italy, France and Germany, together with most other European countries, were severely compromised in early 2011 as a result of the Libyan Government's response to the widespread popular protests in the country. The Libyan-Italian 'friendship, partnership and co-operation' treaty was suspended by Italy in February, although it was revived in December. At the same time Italian Prime Minister Mario Monti pledged that Italy would continue to release to the control of the Libyan interim administration assets of the former regime held in Italy.

Meanwhile, Libya came under heavy criticism from EU and US officials in May 2004, after five Bulgarian nurses and a Palestinian doctor were sentenced to death for deliberately infecting more than 400 children at a Benghazi hospital in 1999 with blood containing the HIV virus. The trials were denounced by international human rights associations as being unfair, and the nurses stated that their confessions had been extracted through torture. The Bulgarian Government refused Libya's demand for compensation for the families affected by the case, stating that any payment would constitute an admission of the medical workers' guilt. Following an appeal, in December 2005 the sentences of the six medical workers were overturned by the Supreme Court, and a retrial began in May 2006. Notwithstanding data arising from genetic analysis that strongly suggested that the children had been infected with HIV prior to the defendants' arrival in Libya in 1998, the original verdict was upheld in December 2006 and the six death sentences were reinstated. The EU Commissioner for Justice, Franco Frattini, called for the ruling to be reviewed, branding it an 'obstacle' to comfortable EU-Libyan relations, while the office of the UN High Commissioner for Human Rights urged the Libyan Government to intervene, citing 'serious and credible concerns' about the legitimacy of the trial. However, the Government insisted that the Supreme Court had sole jurisdiction as far as the verdict was concerned. A further appeal was rejected in July 2007 and the medical workers' death sentences were upheld. A few days later, however, the High Judicial Court commuted the sentences to terms of life imprisonment, following the successful brokerage of a compensation deal, according to which the victims' families would receive a reported US $1m. for each child infected. After protracted negotiations, Libya finally acquiesced to a request by the Bulgarian Government that the medical workers be allowed to complete their sentences in Bulgaria, and the six were duly released from Libyan custody on 24 July. Upon their return to Bulgaria, they were immediately pardoned by that country's President.

Formal negotiations on an EU-Libya Framework Agreement were inaugurated in November 2008. The agreement, intended to encompass economic, political, social and cultural co-operation, would represent the first such partnership between the EU and Libya. It was also designed to achieve greater consensus regarding the issue of illegal immigration to EU countries via Libya: during a second round of negotiations held in Tripoli in February 2009, Libya was offered some €20m. in assistance to address illegal migration. Negotiations on the Framework Agreement and ongoing co-operation contracts between the EU and Libya were suspended on 22 February 2011, and on 28 February the EU imposed an arms embargo on Libya in line with the UN Security Council resolution adopted two days earlier that implemented similar sanctions against the Qaddafi regime; the EU also prohibited trade with Libya in any equipment that might be used for internal repression and imposed a visa ban and an asset freeze on Qaddafi and other senior officials. After the liberation of Libya from Qaddafi's rule

was formally declared in October, in mid-November the EU High Representative for Foreign Affairs and Security Policy, Catherine Ashton, presided over the opening of a new EU delegation office in the *de jure* capital, Tripoli, and met with NTC Chairman Mustafa Muhammad Abd al-Jalil. Following the conclusion of Ashton's visit, the EU indicated that it was ready to resume negotiations on the Framework Agreement, as well as to allow Libya to rejoin regional initiatives with which the EU was involved. The Union also pledged, in addition to humanitarian aid, up to €30m. towards the NTC's efforts to stabilize the country.

During a visit to Libya in April 2008 by the Russian President, Vladimir Putin, several agreements were signed on co-operation in energy, military and infrastructure projects. Putin agreed to cancel Libyan debts amounting to some US $4,500m. Qaddafi began his first visit to Russia in late October, when Russian assistance for Libya's civilian nuclear programme was among the principal issues discussed. In January 2010 the two countries concluded an agreement worth more than $2,000m. for Libya to purchase more than 20 Russian fighter jets. In February 2011 Russia voted in support of UN Security Council Resolution 1970, implementing an arms embargo and other sanctions against the Qaddafi regime owing to its use of force in response to the popular protests, and referring the actions of the regime to the ICC. However, the Russian Government, which remained opposed to any military action against the regime, abstained from the UN Security Council vote in March on Resolution 1973, which authorized the use of force against Libyan government forces in order to protect civilians.

Increasingly cordial relations with the People's Republic of China have been evident in recent years, fuelled by Chinese interest in Libya's oil resources and Libya's continued adherence to the 'one-China' policy (see the chapter on the People's Republic of China). In September 2009 a special envoy of President Hu Jintao attended celebrations in Tripoli to mark the 40th anniversary of Col Qaddafi's rule. During a visit to China in October 2010 Seif al-Islam Qaddafi pledged to strive for enhanced co-operation between Libya and China on a range of areas including infrastructural development, energy and telecommunications. Like Russia, China voted in support of UN Security Council Resolution 1970 in February 2011 but abstained from the vote on Resolution 1973 in March. In late March both countries appealed for an immediate cease-fire, amid concerns about reports of a growing number of civilian casualties arising from NATO airstrikes against Libyan government forces. Nevertheless, in September the Chinese Government formally recognized the NTC as the sole legitimate governing authority in Libya—the last of the permanent members of the UN Security Council to do so—while expressing its hope that existing bilateral treaties and contracts would continue to be implemented. Controversy had been provoked earlier that month by the discovery in Tripoli of documents that revealed that three Chinese state-owned companies had offered to sell weapons (including rocket launchers and anti-tank missiles) valued at around US $200m. to the Qaddafi regime during its final weeks. A spokesperson for the Chinese Ministry of Foreign Affairs confirmed that Libyan officials had travelled to the Chinese capital, Beijing, in July 2011 with a view to purchasing weaponry, but claimed that the Chinese Government had not been aware of this prior to the discovery of the documents and that no contracts had been signed.

CONSTITUTION AND GOVERNMENT

Following the overthrow of King Idris I in 1969, a Constitutional Proclamation was issued by the Revolutionary Command Council (see Contemporary Political History). In 1977 a further document, the Declaration on the Establishment of the Authority of the People, was approved by the General People's Congress (GPC). Under the system set out in this document, power was vested in the people through People's Congresses, Popular Committees, Trade Unions, and Vocational Syndicates, and with the GPC and its General Secretariat. The head of state was the Revolutionary Leader, elected by the GPC, and executive power was exercised by the General People's Committee. Following the installation of the opposition National Transitional Council (NTC) as the de facto administration in August 2011, all constitutional documents promulgated under Qaddafi's rule were suspended and an interim Constitutional Declaration was issued in its place.

Elections to a 200-member legislature, the General National Congress (GNC), took place in July 2012. Of the total number of seats, 80 were allocated to candidates representing political parties elected on the basis of proportional representation, while the remaining 120 seats were reserved for independents. Following the dissolution of the NTC in August, the President of the legislature assumed the role of head of state. Executive power lies with the Cabinet, led by a Prime Minister. The Cabinet takes office after being approved by a vote of the GNC, to which it is responsible.

REGIONAL AND INTERNATIONAL CO-OPERATION

Libya is a member of the African Union (AU, see p. 191), the League of Arab States (the Arab League, see p. 372), the Organization of Arab Petroleum Exporting Countries (OAPEC, see p. 410) and the Union du Maghreb arabe (UMA—Union of the Arab Maghreb, see p. 464). The Community of Sahel-Saharan States (CEN-SAD, see p. 460) has its headquarters in Tripoli.

Libya joined the UN in September 1990. The country also participates in the Organization of the Petroleum Exporting Countries (OPEC, see p. 418). In 2004 the World Trade Organization (WTO, see p. 444) agreed to commence accession negotiations with Libya, which had applied for membership of the organization in 2001, and a working party was established to examine the application. However, as of early 2013 the working party had yet to convene owing to the Libyan Government's failure to submit a requested memorandum on its foreign trade regime.

ECONOMIC AFFAIRS

In 2009, according to estimates by the World Bank, Libya's gross national income (GNI), measured at average 2007–09 prices, was US $77,140m., equivalent to $12,320 per head (or $16,740 on an international purchasing-power parity basis). During 2002–11, it was estimated, the population increased at an average annual rate of 1.9%, while gross domestic product (GDP) per head increased, in real terms, by an average of 4.3% per year during 2002–09. According to preliminary official figures, overall GDP decreased, in real terms, at an average annual rate of 15.4% in 2006–11. Libya's GDP was estimated to have contracted by around 60% in 2011, owing to a virtual halt in oil production following the outbreak of conflict and political unrest at the beginning of that year

Agriculture (including forestry and fishing) contributed 1.9% of GDP in 2011, according to preliminary official figures, and engaged 2.5% of the employed labour force in mid-2013, according to FAO estimates. The principal subsistence crops are wheat and barley; other crops include potatoes, watermelons, tomatoes, onions, dates, olives and citrus fruits. An aim of the Great Manmade River Project (GMR), in progress since 1984, is to reclaim some 130,000 ha of arable land; more than 70% of water to be delivered by the GMR is intended for agricultural use. The main agricultural activity is animal husbandry, with sheep and goats being the principal livestock. During 2006–11, according to preliminary official data, agricultural GDP decreased at an average annual rate of 19.6%; the sector's GDP decreased by 0.9% in 2010 and by 69.0% in 2011.

Industry (including mining, manufacturing, construction and power) contributed 50.2% of GDP in 2011, according to preliminary official figures, and engaged 16.6% of the employed labour force in 2007. Preliminary official data indicated that the GDP of the industrial sector decreased at an average annual rate of 22.3% in 2006–11; industrial GDP declined by 72.8% in 2011, compared with an increase of 4.0% in 2010.

Mining contributed 43.5% of GDP in 2011, according to preliminary official figures, although the sector engaged just 3.1% of the employed labour force in 2007. Libya's economy is overwhelmingly reliant on its petroleum and natural gas resources. Hydrocarbons contributed 81.6% of total government revenue in 2010. At the end of 2011 proven recoverable reserves of petroleum were estimated at 47,100m. barrels, the largest proven reserves in Africa. The production of oil fell drastically at the end of 2011, averaging 0.48m. barrels per day (b/d) compared to 1.66m. b/d at the end of 2010. As a member of the Organization of the Petroleum Exporting Countries (OPEC, see p. 418), Libya is subject to production quotas agreed by the Organization's Conference. Libya's natural gas reserves are extensive (estimated at 1,495,000m. cu m at the end of 2011). Libya also has reserves of iron ore, salt, limestone, clay, sulphur and gypsum. According to preliminary official figures, the GDP of the mining sector decreased, in real terms, at an average annual rate of 23.0% in 2006–11; mining GDP expanded by 4.0% in 2010, but contracted by 72.1% in 2011.

Manufacturing contributed 2.2% of GDP in 2011, according to preliminary official figures, and engaged 7.9% of the employed labour force in 2007. The principal manufacturing activity is petroleum refining. Other important activities include the production of iron, steel and cement, chemicals-manufacturing, and the processing of agricultural products. Preliminary official figures indicated that the GDP of the manufacturing sector decreased at an average annual rate of 23.9% during 2006–11; the sector's GDP increased by 1.2% in 2010, but declined by 77.0% in 2011.

According to preliminary official figures, construction contributed 3.2% of GDP in 2011. The sector engaged only 2.4% of the employed labour force in 2007. Preliminary official figures indicated that the GDP of the construction sector decreased at an average annual rate of 20.0% during 2006–11; the sector's GDP increased by 5.8% in 2010, but decreased by 79.0% in 2011.

Energy is derived principally from petroleum, which contributed 59.0% of total electricity output in 2009, and natural gas (41.0%). Libya is a net exporter of fuels. Many power stations were damaged during the 2011 conflict, although substantial repairs to the electricity infrastructure had been carried out by the end of 2012. Nevertheless, amid rising annual demand for electricity (estimated at some 7%), infrequent power shortages were still occurring in 2012.

Services contributed 47.9% of GDP in 2011, according to preliminary official figures, and engaged 75.9% of the employed labour force in 2007. Efforts to reform the financial sector, hitherto highly state-controlled, have notably included the sale, in 2007–08, of minority stakes in two banks to foreign interests. A stock exchange was established in 2007. The Government has invested heavily in recent years to expand and rehabilitate Libya's tourism infrastructure. Visitor arrivals neared 1m. in 2004. During 2006–11, according to preliminary official data, the GDP of the services sector decreased at an average annual rate of 5.8%; services GDP increased by 5.4% in 2010, but decreased by 41.9% in 2011.

In 2011 Libya recorded a visible merchandise trade surplus of US $1,786m., and there was a deficit of $2,799m. on the current account of the balance of payments. In 2010 the principal source of imports was Turkey (which provided 10.6% of total imports); the People's Republic of China, Italy, the Republic of Korea (South Korea), Germany, the USA and France (including Monaco) were also important suppliers. The principal market for exports in 2010 was Italy (42.3%); France, China and Spain were also significant purchasers. The petroleum sector is overwhelmingly Libya's principal generator of exports revenue: mineral fuels and related materials accounted for some 97.1% of the value of merchandise exports in 2010. The principal imports in that year were machinery and transport equipment, basic manufactures, food and live animals, miscellaneous products, and chemicals.

According to the IMF, an overall budgetary surplus of LD 8,306m. was recorded in 2009, equivalent to 9.6% of GDP. This was projected to reach LD 15,076m. in 2010, equivalent to 14.7% of GDP. According to the Central Bank of Libya, the annual rate of inflation averaged 5.2% in 2003–11; consumer prices increased at an estimated 15.9% in 2011, compared with an increase of 2.4% in 2010. An estimated 30% of the labour force were unemployed at the end of 2010. The unemployment rate is reported to have increased as a result of the civil conflict in 2011, with a significantly high proportion of young Libyans being out of work in 2012.

As part of efforts to reduce the country's overwhelming reliance on petroleum exports, a new sovereign wealth fund, the Libyan Investment Authority (LIA), began operations in 2007 to manage state-allocated assets, including the Oil Reserve Fund. In 2009 the country's closer diplomatic ties with the West and falling property prices in Western European countries allowed the LIA to make significant foreign investments. With the ending of international sanctions, Libya rapidly became a major centre for hydrocarbons exploration, and output of both oil and natural gas expanded strongly. Furthermore, since large areas of Libyan territory remained hitherto unexplored, it was believed that reserves (already the largest in Africa) could be significantly higher than estimated. However, oil output and exports were severely disrupted by the conflict between the regime of Col Muammar al-Qaddafi and anti-Government forces in 2011; output declined from an average of 1.66m. b/d at the end of 2010 to 48,000 b/d at the end of 2011; by July 2012 it was reported that output had reached 1.4m. b/d. Exports of crude petroleum totalled an average of 1.3m. b/d during that year. Much of Libya's foreign assets (estimated to total some US $168,000m. prior to the conflict) were blocked following the imposition in March 2011 of sanctions by the UN, the USA and the European Union. As a result of the assets freeze, together with the effects of NATO air-strikes in and around Tripoli, fuel shortages increased, and commodity prices rose sharply, owing to severe disruptions to supply lines. Many of the LIA's funds were estimated to have lost up to 40% of their value during the conflict, while in September the interim Government estimated that the Qaddafi regime had sold about one-fifth of the country's gold reserves during its final months. Although the easing of sanctions during late 2011 alleviated economic conditions and improved living standards, many foreign investors were reluctant to return to the country until the political and security climate had become more stable. Trading on the Libyan stock exchange, which was shut down in mid-2011 owing to the civil war, resumed in March 2012. The IMF estimated in April 2013 that GDP contracted by some 62.1% during 2011, as a result of the sharp decline in oil production. However, by mid-2012 a strong recovery in hydrocarbons output was evident, and other sectoral growth was boosted by the

massive reconstruction programme and by efforts being made by Libya's new authorities to improve security. In March 2013 the General National Congress approved a slightly reduced budget for that year, which, none the less, included a significant increase in public sector salaries, partly owing to the absorption of revolutionary fighters into the national security services. The IMF forecast GDP growth of an estimated 104.5% in 2012, followed by a substantially lower growth rate—of around 20.2%—in 2013.

PUBLIC HOLIDAYS

2014: 13 January* (Mouloud, Birth of Muhammad), 17 February (Revolution Day), 1 May (May Day), 26 May* (Leilat al-Meiraj, Ascension of Muhammad), 28 July* (Id al-Fitr, end of Ramadan), 4 October* (Id al-Adha, Feast of the Sacrifice), 23 October (Liberation Day), 24 October* (Muharram, Islamic New Year), 2 November* (Ashoura), 24 December (Independence Day).

* These holidays are dependent on the Islamic lunar calendar and may vary by one or two days from the dates given.

Statistical Survey

Sources (unless otherwise stated): National Corporation for Information and Documentation; Census and Statistical Dept, Sharia Damascus 40, 2nd Floor, Tripoli; tel. (21) 3331731; Central Bank of Libya, POB 1103, Sharia al-Malik Seoud, Tripoli; tel. (21) 3333591; fax (21) 4441488; e-mail info@cbl.gov.ly; internet www.cbl.gov.ly.

Area and Population

AREA, POPULATION AND DENSITY

Area (sq km)	1,676,198*
Population (census results)†	
August 1995	4,404,986
August 2006	
Males	2,610,639
Females	2,687,513
Total	5,298,152
Population (UN estimates at mid-year)	
2011	6,422,770
2012	6,469,496
2013	6,506,097
Density (per sq km) at mid-2013 . . .	3.9

* 647,184 sq miles.
† Excluding non-Libyans: 409,326 in 1995 and 359,540 in 2006.
Sources: National Authority for Information and Authentication; UN, *World Population Prospects: The 2010 Revision.*

POPULATION BY AGE AND SEX
(UN estimates at mid-2013)

	Males	Females	Total
0–14	1,040,854	984,817	2,025,671
15–64	2,026,702	2,146,710	4,173,412
65 and over . . .	147,477	159,537	307,014
Total	3,215,033	3,291,064	6,506,097

Source: UN, *World Population Prospects: The 2010 Revision.*

POPULATION BY REGION
(population at 2006 census)

	Area (sq km)	Population	Density (per sq km)
Al-Butnan	84,996	150,353	1.8
Banghazi (Benghazi) . .	11,372	622,148	54.7
Darnah (Darna) . . .	31,511	155,402	4.9
Ghat	68,482	21,329	0.3
Al-Jabal al-Akhdar . .	11,429	192,689	16.9
Al-Jabal al-Gharbi . .	76,717	288,944	3.8
Al-Jifarah	2,666	422,999	158.7
Al-Jufrah	139,038	46,899	0.3
Al-Kufrah	433,611	42,769	0.1
Al-Marqab	6,796	410,187	60.4
Al-Marj	13,515	175,455	13.0

Marzuq	356,308	72,513	0.2
Misratah (Misurata) . .	29,172	511,628	17.5
Nalut	67,191	87,772	1.3
Al-Nuqat al-Khams . .	6,089	269,553	44.3
Sabha	17,066	119,038	7.0
Surt (Sirte)	86,399	131,786	1.5
Tarabulus (Tripoli) . .	835	997,065	1,194.1
Wadi al-Hayat . . .	31,485	70,711	2.2
Wadi al-Shati . . .	90,244	73,443	0.8
Al-Wahah	108,523	164,718	1.5
Al-Zawiyah (Zawia) . .	2,753	270,751	98.3
Total	1,676,198	5,298,152	3.2

Source: National Authority for Information and Authentication.

PRINCIPAL TOWNS
(population at census of 2006)

Tarabulus (Tripoli, the capital) . .	997,065	Al-Nuquat al-Khams . . .	269,553
Banghazi (Benghazi) . .	622,148	Al-Jabal al-Akhdar .	192,689
Misratah (Misurata) .	511,628	Al-Marj . . .	175,455
Al-Jifarah . . .	422,999	Al-Wahah . . .	164,718
Al-Marqab . . .	410,187	Darnah (Darna) . .	155,402
Al-Jabal al-Gharbi .	288,944	Al-Butnan . . .	150,353
Al-Zawiyah (Zawia) .	270,751	Surt (Sirte) . . .	131,786

Source: National Authority for Information and Authentication.

BIRTHS, MARRIAGES AND DEATHS

	Registered live births		Registered marriages		Registered deaths	
	Number	Rate (per 1,000)	Number	Rate (per 1,000)	Number	Rate (per 1,000)
2004 . .	119,633	23.5	39,105	7.6	15,765	3.1
2005 . .	120,999	23.3	43,979	8.4	16,425	3.2
2006 . .	124,541	23.2	47,219	8.8	17,975	3.4
2007 . .	128,337	23.7	59,583	11.0	20,045	3.7
2008 . .	132,826	24.1	65,326	11.9	21,481	3.9

Source: National Authority for Information and Authentication.

Life expectancy (years at birth): 75.0 (males 72.4; females 77.6) in 2011 (Source: World Bank, World Development Indicators database).

EMPLOYMENT
('000 persons)

	2005	2006	2007
Agriculture, forestry and fishing .	117.0	125.8	135.7
Oil and gas extraction	29.3	31.0	32.8
Mining and quarrying	21.1	22.4	23.7
Manufacturing	131.1	136.3	141.8
Electricity, gas and water . . .	50.4	53.3	56.4
Construction	47.0	44.6	42.4
Trade, restaurants and hotels .	190.1	192.6	195.1
Transport and communications .	121.9	130.5	140.8
Financing, insurance and real estate	35.8	38.4	41.2
Public administration . . .	271.8	280.9	290.4
Education	453.2	468.4	484.2
Health services	196.3	202.9	209.7
Other services	0.1	0.2	0.3
Total	**1,665.2**	**1,727.2**	**1,794.5**
Libyans	1,479.1	1,543.3	1,613.6
Non-Libyans	186.1	183.9	180.9

Source: IMF, *Socialist People's Libyan Arab Jamahiriya: Statistical Appendix* (September 2008).

Mid-2013 ('000, estimates): Agriculture, etc. 60; Total labour force 2,354 (Source: FAO).

Health and Welfare

KEY INDICATORS

Total fertility rate (children per woman, 2010) . . .	2.6
Under-5 mortality rate (per 1,000 live births, 2010) . . .	17
HIV/AIDS (% of persons aged 15–49, 2003)	0.3
Physicians (per 1,000 head, 2009)	1.9
Hospital beds (per 1,000 head, 2009)	3.7
Health expenditure (2009): US $ per head (PPP)	722
Health expenditure (2009): % of GDP	3.9
Health expenditure (2009): public (% of total)	66.1
Access to water (% of persons, 2002)	72
Access to sanitation (% of persons, 2010)	97
Total carbon dioxide emissions ('000 metric tons, 2008) . .	58,331.0
Carbon dioxide emissions per head (metric tons, 2008) . .	9.5
Human Development Index (2011): ranking	64
Human Development Index (2011): value	0.760

For sources and definitions, see explanatory note on p. vi.

Agriculture

PRINCIPAL CROPS
('000 metric tons)

	2009	2010	2011
Wheat*	105	106	111
Barley*	101	102	98
Potatoes*	291	290	352
Broad beans, horse beans, dry* .	2	2	1
Almonds, with shell*	29	30	38
Groundnuts, with shell† . . .	26	22	17
Olives*	203	180	139
Tomatoes*	220	230	223
Pumpkins, squash and gourds* .	32	33	34
Cucumbers and gherkins* . .	12	14	15
Chillies and peppers, green* . .	24	24	24
Onions and shallots, green* . .	59	50	54
Onions, dry*	186	195	206
Peas, green*	6	7	6
Carrots and turnips*	25	26	30
Watermelons*	225	245	243
Cantaloupes and other melons† .	26	26	26

—*continued*	2009	2010	2011
Oranges*	46	46	48
Tangerines, mandarins, etc.* . .	11	11	11
Lemons and limes*	17	18	18
Apples*	20	22	20
Apricots*	21	22	24
Peaches and nectarines* . . .	11	12	13
Plums and sloes*	43	44	51
Grapes*	30	35	35
Figs*	10	11	10
Dates*	155	161	166

* FAO estimates.
† Unofficial figures.

Aggregate production ('000 metric tons, may include official, semi-official or estimated data): Total cereals 216 in 2009, 218 in 2010, 220 in 2011; Total roots and tubers 291 in 2009, 290 in 2010, 352 in 2011; Total vegetables (incl. melons) 912 in 2009, 947 in 2010, 979 in 2011; Total fruits (excl. melons) 370 in 2009, 386 in 2010, 403 in 2011.

Source: FAO.

LIVESTOCK
('000 head, year ending September)

	2009	2010	2011
Horses*	45	45	45
Asses*	29	29	29
Cattle	190†	195†	197*
Camels*	55	56	57
Sheep	6,700†	7,000†	7,100*
Goats	2,600†	2,700†	2,600*
Poultry*	27,000	33,000	34,000

* FAO estimate(s).
† Unofficial figure.

Source: FAO.

LIVESTOCK PRODUCTS
('000 metric tons, FAO estimates)

	2009	2010	2011
Cattle meat	9	9	8
Sheep meat	29	30	31
Goat meat	12	13	13
Chicken meat	125	129	124
Cows' milk	140	141	141
Sheep's milk	67	61	61
Goats' milk	18	19	19
Hen eggs	62	63	63
Wool, greasy	9	9	9

Source: FAO.

Forestry

ROUNDWOOD REMOVALS
('000 cubic metres, excl. bark, FAO estimates)

	2009	2010	2011
Sawlogs, veneer logs and logs for sleepers*	63	63	63
Other industrial wood	53	53	53
Fuel wood	939	952	964
Total	**1,055**	**1,068**	**1,080**

* Annual output assumed to be unchanged since 1978.

Source: FAO.

SAWNWOOD PRODUCTION
('000 cubic metres, incl. railway sleepers, FAO estimates)

	1976	1977	1978
Total (all broadleaved)* . . .	9	21	31

* Annual output to 2011 assumed to be unchanged since 1978 (FAO estimates).

Source: FAO.

Fishing

(metric tons, live weight)

	2008	2009	2010*
Capture	47,645	52,110	50,000
Groupers	1,537	990	950
Common pandora . . .	1,584	7,200	6,950
Bogue	4,009	2,250	2,180
Surmullet	1,519	6,246	6,000
Jack and horse mackerels . .	6,855	2,817	2,720
Sardinellas	19,518	9,450	9,200
'Scomber' mackerels . . .	6,029	n.a.	n.a.
Dogfish sharks	n.a.	7,596	7,300
Aquaculture*	240	240	240
Total catch (incl. others)* . .	47,885	52,350	50,240

* FAO estimates.

Source: FAO.

Mining

('000 metric tons unless otherwise indicated, estimates)

	2008	2009	2010
Salt	40	40	40
Gypsum (crude)	250	250	250

Source: US Geological Survey.

Crude petroleum (million barrels): 592.5 in 2009; 616.0 in 2010; 178.6 in 2011.

Natural gas (incl. flared, '000 million cu ft): 1,051,900 in 2008; 1,035,500 in 2009; 1,078,800 in 2010.

Industry

SELECTED PRODUCTS
('000 metric tons)

	2009	2010	2011
Jet fuels (incl. kerosene) . . .	1,876	1,811	784
Motor spirit (petrol)	751	585	569
Naphthas (raw)	2,474	2,457	649
Gas-diesel (distillate fuel) oil . .	4,178	4,278	1,522
Residual fuel oils	6,719	7,103	2,215

Cement (hydraulic, '000 metric tons, estimates): 6,000 in 2008; 6,500 in 2009; 7,000 in 2010 (Source: US Geological Survey).

Electric energy (million kWh): 25,694 in 2007; 28,667 in 2008; 30,426 in 2009 (Source: UN Industrial Commodity Statistics Database).

Finance

CURRENCY AND EXCHANGE RATES

Monetary Units:
   1,000 dirhams = 1 Libyan dinar (LD).

Sterling, Dollar and Euro Equivalents (29 June 2012):
   £1 sterling = 1.9868 dinars;
   US $1 = 1.2734 dinars;
   €1 = 1.6032 dinars;
   100 Libyan dinars = £50.33 = $78.53 = €62.38.

Average Exchange Rate (Libyan dinar per US $):
   2009   1.2535
   2010   1.2668
   2011   1.2241

BUDGET
(LD million)

Revenue	2008	2009*	2010*
Hydrocarbon budget allocation .	65,365	41,632	50,630
Non-hydrocarbon	7,532	10,353	11,408
Non-hydrocarbon tax revenue .	3,531	4,350	4,817
Taxes on income and profits .	2,790	3,100	3,456
Taxes on international trade .	499	1,000	1,080
Other tax revenue . .	241	250	280
Non-hydrocarbon non-tax revenue	4,002	6,002	6,591
Total	72,898	51,984	62,037

Expenditure	2008	2009*	2010*
Current	17,579	22,039	24,179
Expenditure on goods and services	10,593	12,324	13,494
Wages and salaries . . .	7,764	8,874	9,717
Subsidies and other current transfers†	6,986	9,715	10,684
Capital	27,257	21,639	22,782
Development budget . . .	22,610	18,500	19,333
Total‡	44,835	43,678	46,961

* Projections.
† From 2008 subsidies include food, medicine, fuel, electricity and water.
‡ Including net lending (LD million): 1,350 in 2008; 850 in 2009 (projection); 650 in 2010 (projection).

Source: IMF, *Socialist People's Libyan Arab Jamahiriya: 2009 Article IV Consultation—Staff Report; Public Information Notice on the Executive Board Discussion; and Statement by the Executive Director for the Socialist People's Libyan Arab Jamahiriya* (September 2009).

INTERNATIONAL RESERVES
(US $ million at 31 December)

	2009	2010	2011
Gold (national valuation) . .	194	194	158
IMF special drawing rights . .	2,514	2,473	2,471
Reserve position in IMF . .	595	372	454
Foreign exchange	95,616	96,800	101,872
Total	98,920	99,839	104,955

Source: IMF, *International Financial Statistics*.

MONEY SUPPLY
(LD million at 31 December)

	2009	2010	2011
Currency outside banks . . .	6,962.9	7,609.0	14,840.1
Demand deposits at commercial banks	29,582.9	31,602.2	35,435.3
Total money (incl. others) . .	37,391.7	40,093.9	50,275.4

Source: IMF, *International Financial Statistics*.

COST OF LIVING
(Consumer Price Index; base: 2003 = 100)

	2009	2010	2011
Personal services and others . .	123.5	132.3	162.4
Medical care	134.0	134.0	202.1
Recreation and education . .	100.0	105.3	110.4
Transport and communication .	137.3	136.7	149.2
Clothing and shoes	98.1	106.8	120.8
Furniture	96.7	99.6	122.9
Housing	109.6	109.7	122.6
Food, beverages and tobacco . .	149.3	153.5	178.5
All items	126.7	129.8	150.4

NATIONAL ACCOUNTS
(LD million at current prices)

Expenditure on the Gross Domestic Product

	2009	2010	2011
Government final consumption expenditure	9,310.5	11,365.7	16,323.6
Private final consumption expenditure	26,964.7	32,758.4	13,133.5
Gross fixed capital formation . .	6,861.6	8,380.5	5,241.0
Changes in inventories . .	287.2	351.0	—
Total domestic expenditure .	43,423.9	52,855.6	34,698.1
Exports of goods and services . .	50,139.0	62,314.3	20,189.3
Less Imports of goods and services	19,902.8	24,399.7	16,481.7
GDP in purchasers' values .	73,660.1	90,770.3	38,405.8
GDP at constant 2005 prices .	67,994.1	70,825.1	27,450.9

Source: UN National Accounts Main Aggregates Database.

Gross Domestic Product by Economic Activity

	2009	2010†	2011†
Agriculture, forestry and fishing .	2,382.7	2,543.6	844.3
Mining and quarrying (incl. hydrocarbons)	47,231.2	60,969.8	19,072.8
Manufacturing	5,447.6	5,809.5	978.0
Electricity, gas and water . .	1,334.6	1,420.5	561.2
Construction	7,577.5	8,066.8	1,391.7
Trade, restaurants and hotels .	4,298.1	4,607.5	2,923.1
Transport, storage and communications	4,125.8	4,432.1	3,317.7
Financial intermediation . . .	1,181.8	1,262.0	745.9
Real estate, renting and business activities	6,154.8	6,636.4	1,506.4
Education and health, etc.* . .	298.5	316.5	126.9
Government, defence and mandatory social insurance .	6,870.8	7,128.8	12,319.3
Other services	91.0	98.2	33.7
Sub-total	86,994.4	103,291.6	43,820.9
Less Financial intermediation services indirectly measured .	705.5	753.4	436.0
Total	86,288.9	102,538.2	43,385.1

* Private sector only.
† Preliminary figures.

BALANCE OF PAYMENTS
(US $ million)

	2009	2010	2011
Exports of goods	37,055	48,935	12,986
Imports of goods	−22,002	−24,559	−11,200
Balance on goods	15,053	24,376	1,786
Exports of services	385	410	30
Imports of services	−5,063	−6,127	4,435
Balance on goods and services	10,375	18,659	−2,619
Primary income received . .	2,461	2,318	1,301
Primary income paid	−1,883	−2,348	−800
Balance on goods, services and primary income . . .	10,953	18,629	−2,118
Secondary income (net) . . .	−1,572	−1,828	−681
Current balance	9,381	16,801	−2,799
Direct investment assets . . .	−1,165	−2,722	−257
Direct investment liabilities . .	1,371	1,784	200
Portfolio investment assets . .	−3,352	−4,396	−420
Other investment assets . . .	−3,952	−4,889	1,472
Other investment liabilities . .	1,573	−116	277
Net errors and omissions . . .	1,333	−2,292	687
Reserves and related items .	5,188	4,170	−840

Source: IMF, *International Financial Statistics*.

External Trade

PRINCIPAL COMMODITIES
(LD million)

Imports c.i.f.	2009	2010
Food and live animals	1,663.9	2,320.4
Beverages and tobacco	72.8	101.0
Animal and vegetable oils and fats . . .	72.2	82.1
Crude materials (inedible) except fuels . . .	299.6	604.8
Mineral fuels and related materials . . .	151.5	236.1
Chemical materials	1,056.6	1,287.4
Basic manufactures	3,229.7	4,818.8
Machinery and transport equipment . . .	7,968.9	11,031.6
Miscellaneous products	1,540.8	1,894.1
Total	16,060.6	22,376.3

Exports f.o.b.*	2009	2010
Food and live animals	1.4	0.9
Crude materials (inedible) except fuel . . .	1.2	0.8
Mineral fuels and related products	33,353.3	44,854.1
Chemicals and related products	562.2	989.0
Basic manufactures	151.9	351.4
Total (incl. others)	34,070.9	46,196.3

* Including re-exports.

PRINCIPAL TRADING PARTNERS
(LD million)

Imports c.i.f.	2009	2010
Brazil	96.5	541.5
China, People's Republic	1,949.7	2,183.4
Egypt	383.0	791.3
France (incl. Monaco)	300.8	1,117.2
Germany	779.0	1,523.2
Italy	1,157.9	2,106.6
Japan	598.1	895.3
Korea, Republic	1,467.9	2,060.8
Russia	203.1	290.7
Spain	178.3	296.2
Tunisia	711.9	487.1
Turkey	1,463.8	2,370.1
Ukraine	101.9	311.2
United Kingdom	438.1	711.4
USA	830.2	1,178.6
Total (incl. others)	16,060.6	22,376.3

Exports (incl. re-exports) f.o.b.	2009	2010
Brazil	1,140.5	249.9
Canada	721.1	287.9
China, People's Republic	3,811.6	4,319.4
Egypt	252.2	386.3
France (incl. Monaco)	4,091.0	7,178.7
Germany	2,358.3	1,182.4
Greece	1,216.3	2,059.7
India	584.7	638.8
Ireland	322.1	415.7
Italy	11,670.8	19,527.9
Netherlands	747.3	1,558.6
Portugal	543.6	748.8
Spain	2,637.7	4,264.7
Turkey	405.6	244.6
United Kingdom	1,297.1	494.7
USA	598.4	1,161.2
Total (incl. others)	34,070.9	46,196.3

Transport

ROAD TRAFFIC
(motor vehicles in use at 31 December)

	2000	2001
Passenger cars	549,600	552,700
Commercial vehicles	177,400	195,500

Buses and coaches: 1,424 in 1995; 1,490 in 1996.

Motorcycles and mopeds: 1,078 in 1995; 1,112 in 1996.

2007: Passenger cars 1,388,165; Buses and coaches 91,327; Vans and lorries 310,511; Motorcycles and mopeds 36,531.

Sources: IRF, *World Road Statistics*; UN, *Statistical Yearbook*.

SHIPPING

Flag Registered Fleet
(at 31 December)

	2010	2011	2012
Number of vessels	89	82	81
Total displacement ('000 grt)	1,052.0	1,024.3	1,020.5

Source: Lloyd's List Intelligence (www.lloydslistintelligence.com).

International Sea-borne Freight Traffic
(estimates, '000 metric tons)

	1991	1992	1993
Goods loaded	57,243	59,894	62,491
Goods unloaded	7,630	7,710	7,808

Source: UN Economic Commission for Africa, *African Statistical Yearbook*.

CIVIL AVIATION
(traffic on scheduled services)

	2007	2008	2009
Kilometres flown (million)	18	18	18
Passengers carried ('000)	1,204	1,214	1,147
Passenger-km (million)	1,579	1,597	1,521
Total ton-km (million)	140	148	142

Source: UN, *Statistical Yearbook*.

2010: Passengers carried ('000) 2,345 (Source: World Bank, World Development Indicators database).

Tourism

VISITOR ARRIVALS*

Country of origin	2002	2003	2004
Algeria	70,416	71,657	73,459
Egypt	354,189	429,220	441,230
Morocco	19,076	19,120	20,803
Tunisia	329,145	346,331	366,871
Total (incl. others)	857,952	957,896	999,343

* Including same-day visitors (excursionists).

Tourism receipts (US $ million, excl. passenger transport): 50 in 2009; 60 in 2010.

Source: World Tourism Organization.

Communications Media

	2009	2010	2011
Telephones ('000 main lines in use)	1,063.3	1,228.3	1,000.0
Mobile cellular telephones ('000 subscribers)	9,534.1	10,900.0	10,000.0
Broadband subscribers ('000)	63.0	72.8	70.0
Internet subscribers ('000)	772.5	n.a.	n.a.

Personal computers: 130,000 (21.9 per 1,000 persons) in 2005.

Source: International Telecommunication Union.

Education

(1995/96, unless otherwise indicated)

	Institutions	Teachers	Students
Primary and preparatory: general	2,733*	122,020	1,333,679
Primary and preparatory: vocational	168	n.a.	22,490
Secondary: general	n.a.	17,668	170,573
Secondary: teacher training	n.a.	2,760†	23,919
Secondary: vocational	312	n.a.	109,074
Universities	13	n.a.	126,348

* 1993/94.
† 1992/93.

Source: partly UNESCO, *Statistical Yearbook*.

1998: 1,160,315 primary school students (Source: World Bank).

Students (UNESCO estimates, 2005/06 unless otherwise indicated): Pre-primary 22,246; Primary 755,338; Secondary 732,614; Tertiary 375,028 (2002/03) (Source: UNESCO Institute for Statistics).

Teachers (UNESCO estimates, 2005/06 unless otherwise indicated): Pre-primary 2,486; Primary 148,476; Secondary 152,338; Tertiary 15,711 (2002/03) (Source: UNESCO Institute for Statistics).

Adult literacy rate (UNESCO estimates): 89.2% (males 95.6%; females 82.7%) in 2010 (Source: UNESCO Institute for Statistics).

Directory

The Government

CABINET
(May 2013)

Prime Minister: Dr ALI ZIDAN.

First Deputy Prime Minister: SADIQ ABD AL-KARIM ABD AL-RAHMAN KARIM.

Second Deputy Prime Minister: AWAD AL-BARASI.

Third Deputy Prime Minister: ABDUSSALAM AL-MEHDI AL-QADI.

Minister of Foreign Affairs and of International Co-operation: MUHAMMAD IMHAMID ABD AL-AZIZ.

Minister of Justice: SALAH BASHIR ABAJ MARGANI.

Minister of the Interior: ASHOUR SHUWAIL.

Minister of Defence: MUHAMMAD MAHMOUD MOUSA AL-BARGHATI.

Minister of Oil: ABD AL-BARI ALI AL-HADI AL-ARUSI.

Minister of Health: NURIDEEN ABD AL-HAMID DAGMAN.

Minister of Finance: AL-KILANI ABD AL-KARIM KILANI AL-JAZI.

Minister of Economy: MUSTAFA MUHAMMAD ABUFUNAS.

Minister of Religious Affairs: ABD AL-SALAM MUHAMMAD ABUSAAD.

Minister of Water Resources: AL-HADI SULEIMAN HINSHIR.

Minister of Education: MUHAMMAD HASSAN ABUBAKER.

Minister of Higher Education: ALI MUFTAH OBAID.

Minister of Culture: HABIB MUHAMMAD AL-AMIN.

Minister of Housing: ALI HUSSEIN AL-SHARIF.

Minister of Agriculture: AHMED ALI AL-ORFI.

Minister of Industry: SULAIMAN ALI AL-LATIF AL-FITURI.

Minister of Tourism: IKRAM ABD AL-SALAM BASH IMAM.

Minister of Social Affairs: KAMILA KHAMIS AL-MAZINI.

Minister of Labour and Retraining: MUHAMMAD FITOURI AHMAD SUALIM.

Minister of Transport: ABD AL-QADIR MUHAMMAD AHMAD AL-AYIB.

Minister of the Martyrs and Missing: ALI GADOUR.

Minister of Local Government: ABUBAKER AL-HADI MUHAMMAD.

Minister of Planning: MAHDI ATAHER GENIA.

Minister of Communications: OSAMA ABDURAUF SIALA.

Minister of Sports and Youth: ABD AL-SALAM ABDULLAH GUAILA.

Minister of Information: YOUSEF MUHAMMAD SHERIF.

Minister of Electricity: ALI MUHAMMAD MUHAIRIQ.

Minister of State for the Wounded: RAMADAN ALI MANSOUR ZARMUH.

MINISTRIES

Office of the Prime Minister: Tripoli; internet www.pm.gov.ly.

Ministry of Agriculture: Tripoli; e-mail info@agriculture.gov.ly; internet www.agriculture.gov.ly.

Ministry of Communications: Tripoli; tel. (21) 3619011; fax (21) 3622452; e-mail info@cim.gov.ly; internet www.cim.gov.ly.

Ministry of Culture: Tripoli; internet culture.ly.

Ministry of Defence: Tripoli; tel. (21) 4800734; fax (21) 4800168; e-mail info@defense.gov.ly; internet www.defense.gov.ly.

Ministry of Economy: Tripoli; internet www.ect.gov.ly.

Ministry of Education: Tripoli; internet edu.gov.ly.

Ministry of Electricity: Tripoli.

Ministry of Finance: Tripoli.

Ministry of Foreign Affairs and International Co-operation: Tripoli; tel. (21) 3402121; internet www.foreign.gov.ly.

Ministry of Health: Tripoli; tel. (21) 4630704; fax (21) 4630704; internet www.health.gov.ly.

Ministry of Higher Education: Tripoli; tel. (21) 4630209; e-mail scholarship@edu.gov.ly; internet www.higheredu.gov.ly.

Ministry of Housing: Tripoli.

Ministry of Industry: Tripoli.

Ministry of Information: Tripoli.

Ministry of the Interior: Tripoli.

Ministry of Justice: Tripoli; tel. (21) 4808251; e-mail Secretary@aladel.gov.ly; internet www.aladel.gov.ly.

Ministry of Labour and Retraining: Tripoli.

Ministry of Local Government: Tripoli.

Ministry of the Martyrs and Missing: Tripoli.

Ministry of Oil: Tripoli.

Ministry of Planning: Tripoli; tel. and fax (21) 4447372; internet www.planning.gov.ly.

Ministry of Religious Affairs: Tripoli.

Ministry of Social Affairs: Tripoli.

Ministry of Sports and Youth: Tripoli.

Ministry of State for the Wounded: Tripoli.

Ministry of Tourism: Tripoli.

Ministry of Transport: Tripoli; internet www.ctt.gov.ly.

Ministry of Water Resources: Tripoli.

Legislature

Al-Mu'tamar al-Watani al-Amm
(General National Congress)

Tripoli Congress Centre, Tripoli; tel. (21) 3622897; fax (21) 3622895; e-mail info@gnc.gov.ly; internet www.gnc.gov.ly.

President: MUHAMMAD YOUSUF MAGARIAF.

First Vice-President: JUMAA AHMAD ATIYQA.

Second Vice-President: SALEH MUHAMMAD MAKHZOUM.

Election, 7 July 2012

	Seats
National Forces Alliance (NFA)	39
Justice and Construction Party (JCP)	17
National Front Party	3
Union for Homeland	2
Wadi Al-Hayat Gathering	2
Central National Current	2
Others	15
Independents	120
Total	**200***

* Of the 200 seats, 80 seats were allocated to party lists under a system of proportional representation, while the remaining 120 seats were reserved for individual candidates who were not affiliated to political organizations.

Political Organizations

In June 1971 the Arab Socialist Union (ASU) was established as the country's sole authorized political party. The General National Congress of the ASU held its first session in January 1976 and later became the General People's Congress. Following the ouster of Col Muammar al-Qaddafi, a number of new political organisations were formed, the most prominent among which have been listed below:

Central National Current: f. 2012.

Justice and Construction Party (JCP): internet www.ab.ly; f. 2012; Leader MUHAMMAD SAWAN.

National Forces Alliance (NFA): Tripoli; tel. (21) 4782593; e-mail info@nff.ly; internet www.nff.ly; f. 2012; comprises 58 political parties; Leader MAHMOUD JIBRIL; Sec.-Gen. FAISAL KREKSHI.

National Front Party: Tripoli; e-mail info@jabha.ly; internet www.jabha.ly; f. 2012; offshoot of National Front for the Salvation of Libya; Pres. MUHAMMAD YOUSUF MAGARIAF.

Union for Homeland: Tripoli; tel. (21) 4445315; fax (21) 4443805; e-mail info@ufh.ly; internet www.ufh.ly; f. 2012; Leader ABDURRAHMAN SEWEHLI.

Wadi Al-Hayat Gathering: f. 2012.

Diplomatic Representation

EMBASSIES IN LIBYA

Afghanistan: POB 4245, Sharia Mozhar al-Aftes, Tripoli; tel. (21) 4841441; fax (21) 4841443; e-mail tripoli@afghanistan.mfa.net; Ambassador (vacant).

Algeria: Sharia Kairouan 12, Tripoli; tel. (21) 4440025; fax (21) 3334631; Ambassador ABDELHAMID BOUZAHER.

Argentina: POB 932, Gargaresh, Madina Syahia, Tripoli; tel. (21) 4771107; fax (21) 4782105; e-mail elbia@mrecic.gov.ar; Chargé d'affaires a.i. MAURICIO NINE.

Austria: POB 3207, Sharia Khalid ibn al-Walid, Garden City, Tripoli; tel. (21) 4443379; fax (21) 4440838; e-mail tripolis-ob@bmeia.gv.at; internet www.bmeia.gv.at/tripolis; Ambassador FRANZ HÖRLBERGER.

Bangladesh: POB 5086, Hi Damasq, Tripoli; tel. (21) 4911198; fax (21) 4906616; e-mail bdtripoli@yahoo.com; Ambassador (vacant).

Belarus: POB 1530, Tripoli; tel. (21) 3612555; fax (21) 3614298; e-mail libya@belembassy.org; internet libya.mfa.gov.by; Ambassador ANATOLY STEPUS.

Belgium: POB 91650, Jasmin St, Hay Andalus, Tripoli; tel. (21) 4782044; fax (21) 4782046; e-mail tripoli@diplobel.fed.be; internet www.diplomatie.be/tripoli; Ambassador ANDY DETAILLE.

Benin: POB 6676, Sharia Ghout al-Shaal, Tripoli; tel. (21) 4837663; fax (21) 834569; Ambassador LAFIA CHABI.

Bosnia and Herzegovina: POB 6946, Sharia Abd al-Melik bin Kutn, Tripoli; tel. (21) 4774327; fax (21) 4770652; Ambassador IBRAHIM EFENDIĆ.

Brazil: POB 2270, Sharia Ben Ashour, Tripoli; tel. (21) 3614894; fax (21) 3614895; e-mail brcastripoli@ittnet.net; Ambassador AFONSO CARBONAR.

Bulgaria: POB 2945, Sharia Madinet El Hadeek-Muhammad Farid, Dahra, Tripoli; tel. (21) 3346630; fax (21) 3346633; e-mail embassy.tripoli@mfa.bg; internet www.mfa.bg/embassies/libya; Ambassador VENELIN LAZAROV.

Burkina Faso: POB 81902, Route de Gargaresh, Tripoli; tel. (21) 4771221; fax (21) 4778037; e-mail ambafasolibye@yahoo.fr; Ambassador YOUSSOUF SANGARE.

Burundi: POB 2817, Sharia Ras Hassan, Tripoli; tel. (21) 608848; Ambassador RAPHAËL BITARIHO.

Canada: POB 93392, al-Fateh Tower Post Office, Tripoli; tel. (21) 3351633; fax (21) 3351630; e-mail trpli@international.gc.ca; internet www.canadainternational.gc.ca/libya; Ambassador MICHAEL GRANT.

Chad: POB 1078, Sharia Muhammad Mussadeq 25, Tripoli; tel. (21) 4443955; Ambassador DAOUSSA DEBY.

China, People's Republic: POB 5329, Sharia Menstir, Andalus, Gargaresh, Tripoli; tel. (21) 4832914; fax (21) 4831877; e-mail chinaemb_ly@mfa.gov.cn; internet ly.china-embassy.org; Ambassador WANG WANGSHENG.

Croatia: Great al-Fatah Towers, Tower 2, 12th Floor, Rm 125, Tripoli; tel. (21) 3351097; fax (21) 3351486; e-mail tripoli@mvep.hr; Ambassador PETAR LJUBIČIĆ.

Cyprus: POB 3284, Wassayat Ebderi, Fashloum, Tripoli; tel. (21) 3622610; fax (21) 3622613; e-mail cyprusembassylibya@gmail.com; Ambassador PERICLES D. STIVAROS.

Czech Republic: POB 1097, Sharia Rewaifaa bin Thabet, Ben Ashour, Tripoli; tel. (21) 3615436; fax (21) 3615437; e-mail tripoli@embassy.mzv.cz; internet www.mzv.cz/tripoli; Ambassador JOSEF KOUTSKÝ.

Egypt: Sharia Omar el-Mokhtar, Tripoli; tel. and fax (21) 3339876; e-mail eg.emb_tripoli@mfa.gov.eg; Ambassador HESHAM ABD EL-WAHAB.

Equatorial Guinea: Tripoli.

Eritrea: POB 91279, Tripoli; tel. (21) 4773568; fax (21) 4780152; Ambassador ABDALLA MUSSA.

France: POB 312, Sharia Ben Khafaja, Hay Andalus, Tripoli; tel. (21) 4770452; fax (21) 4770450; e-mail tripoli-amba@diplomatie.gouv.fr; internet www.ambafrance-ly.org; Ambassador ANTOINE SIVAN.

Germany: POB 302, Sharia Hassan al-Mashai, Tripoli; tel. (21) 4448552; fax (21) 4448968; e-mail info@tripolis.diplo.de; internet www.tripolis.diplo.de; Ambassador RAINER EBERLE.

Ghana: POB 4169, Andalus 21A, nr Funduk Shati Gargaresh, Tripoli; tel. (21) 4772534; fax (21) 4773557; e-mail ghaemb@all-computers.com; Ambassador HODARI OKAE.

Greece: POB 5147, Sharia Jalal Bayar 18, Tripoli; tel. (21) 3338563; fax (21) 4441907; e-mail gremb.tri@mfa.gr; internet www.mfa.gr/tripoli; Ambassador KYRIAKOS AMOIRIDIS.

Guinea: POB 10657, Hay Andalus, Tripoli; tel. (21) 4772793; fax (21) 4773441; e-mail magatte@lttnet.net; Ambassador ABDUL AZIZ SOUMAH.

Hungary: POB 4010, Sharia Talha Ben Abdullah, Tripoli; tel. (21) 3618218; fax (21) 3618220; e-mail missions.tpi@kum.hu; Ambassador Dr BÉLA MARTON.

India: POB 3150, Fashloom Area, Nafleen Area, Tripoli; tel. (21) 3409288; fax (21) 3409281; e-mail information@indianembassy.ly; internet indianembassy.ly; Ambassador ANIL TRIGUNAYAT.

Indonesia: POB 5921, Tripoli; tel. (21) 4842067; fax (21) 4842069; e-mail tripoli.kbri@deplu.go.id; internet tripoli.kemlu.go.id; Chargé d'affaires a.i. HERU PRAYITNO.

Iran: POB 6185, Tripoli; tel. (21) 3609552; fax (21) 3611674; e-mail iran_em_tripoli@hotmail.com; Ambassador HOSSEIN AKBARI.

Italy: POB 912, Sharia Vahran 1, Tripoli; tel. (21) 3334131; fax (21) 3331673; e-mail ambasciata.tripoli@esteri.it; internet www.ambtripoli.esteri.it; Ambassador GIUSEPPE BUCCINO GRIMALDI.

Japan: POB 3265, Sharia Jamal al-Din al-Waeli, Hay Andalus, Tripoli; tel. (21) 4781041; fax (21) 4781044; internet www.ly.emb-japan.go.jp; Ambassador WATARU NISHIGAHIRO.

Korea, Democratic People's Republic: Tripoli; Ambassador KIM TONG JE.

Korea, Republic: POB 4781, Abounawas Area, Sharia Gargaresh, Tripoli; tel. (21) 4831322; fax (21) 4831324; e-mail libya@mofat.go.kr; internet lby.mofat.go.kr; Ambassador CHO DAE-SIK.

Kuwait: POB 2225, Beit al-Mal Beach, Tripoli; tel. (21) 4440281; fax (21) 607053; Ambassador MUBARAK ABDULLAH AL-ADWANI.

Lebanon: POB 927, Malek Ben Auss, Al Noflyeen St, Tripoli; tel. (21) 3615744; fax (21) 3611740; e-mail emblebanon_ly@hotmail.com; Ambassador MUHAMMAD SKEINE.

Lesotho: POB 5771, Hay Andalus, Tripoli; tel. (21) 4840900; fax (21) 4840901; e-mail lesotho-tripoli@foreign.gov.ls; Ambassador MALEFETSANE MOHAFA.

Madagascar: POB 652, al-Maidan Zajeir, Tripoli; tel. (21) 3408257; fax (21) 3408256; e-mail ambamtri@yahoo.fr; Ambassador DIEUDONNÉ MARIE MICHEL RAZAFINDRANDRIATSIMANIRY.

Malaysia: POB 6309, Hay Andalus, Sharia Gargaresh, Tripoli; tel. (21) 4830854; fax (21) 4831496; e-mail maltripoli@kln.gov.my; internet kln.gov.my/web/lby_tripoli; Ambassador MUHAMMAD ZULKEPHLI BIN MUHAMMAD NOOR.

Mali: POB 2008, Sharia Jaraba Saniet Zarrouk, Tripoli; tel. (21) 4444924; Ambassador OUSMANE TANDJA.

Malta: POB 2534, Sharia Ubei Ben Ka'ab, Tripoli; tel. (21) 3611181; fax (21) 3611180; e-mail maltaembassy.tripoli@gov.mt; Ambassador VICTOR CAMILLERI.

Mauritania: Sharia Aïssa el-Wakwak, Tripoli; tel. (21) 4443223; Ambassador (vacant).

Morocco: Sharia Ouahchi Ben Harb, Ave Ben Achour, Tripoli; tel. (21) 3617809; fax (21) 3614752; e-mail sifmatripo@hotmail.com; Ambassador MEHDI ALAOUI.

Netherlands: POB 3801, Sharia Jalal Bayar 20, Dahra, Tripoli; tel. (21) 4441549; fax (21) 4440386; e-mail tri@minbuza.nl; internet www.hollandembassy-libya.com; Ambassador A. H. M. LANSINK.

Niger: POB 2251, Fachloun Area, Tripoli; tel. (21) 4443104; Ambassador AMADOU TIDJANI ALI.

Nigeria: POB 4417, Sharia Bashir al-Ibrahim, Tripoli; tel. (21) 4443038; e-mail ambassador@nigeriantripoli.org; internet www.nigeriantripoli.org; Ambassador ISA MUHAMMAD (recalled in March 2010).

Oman: Tripoli; tel. (21) 4772879; fax (21) 4773849; e-mail tripoli@mofa.gov.om; Ambassador Dr QASIM BIN MUHAMMAD BIN SALEM AL-SALEHI.

Pakistan: POB 2169, Sharia al-Jamei, Abu Zaid Dorda Area, Tripoli; tel. (21) 3610937; fax (21) 3600412; e-mail pareptripoli@gmail.com; internet www.mofa.gov.pk/libya; Ambassador SYED AYAZ HUSSAIN.

Philippines: POB 12508, Km 7, Sharia Gargaresh, Abu Nawas, Hay Andalus, Tripoli; tel. (21) 4833966; fax (21) 4836158; e-mail tripoli.pe@dfa.gov.ph; Ambassador OSCAR G. ORCINE.

Poland: POB 519, Sharia Ben Ashour 61, Tripoli; tel. (21) 3608569; fax (21) 3615199; e-mail trypolis.amb.sekretariat@msz.gov.pl; internet www.trypolis.msz.gov.pl; Chargé d'affaires a.i. DARIUSZ NIDERLA.

Portugal: Zaid Bem Thabet, Sharia Ben Ashour, Tripoli; tel. (21) 3621352; fax (21) 3621351; Ambassador RUI NOGUEIRA LOPES ALEIXO.

Qatar: POB 6312, Libay, Tripoli; tel. (21) 4832431; fax (21) 4836660; e-mail tripoli@mofa.gov.qa; Ambassador Sheikh MUHAMMAD BIN NASSER BIN JASSIM AL THANI.

Romania: POB 5085, Sharia Ali bin Talib, Ben Ashour, Tripoli; tel. (21) 3615295; fax (21) 3607597; e-mail tripoli@mae.ro; Chargé d'affaires a.i. LAURENŢIU-MIHAI CRISTEA.

Russia: POB 4792, Sharia Mustapha Kamel, Tripoli; tel. (21) 3330545; fax (21) 4446673; e-mail embr@mail.ru; Ambassador IVAN MOLOTKOV.

Rwanda: POB 6677, Villa Ibrahim Musbah Missalati, Andalus, Tripoli; tel. (21) 72864; fax (21) 70317; Chargé d'affaires CHRISTOPHE HABIMANA.

Saudi Arabia: POB 2551, Sharia Kairouan 2, Tripoli; tel. (21) 3330485; fax (21) 4447180; e-mail lyemb@mofa.gov.sa; Ambassador MUHAMMAD MAHMOUD AL-ALI.

Senegal: POB 6392, el-Arabia Gotchalle 246/5, Gargaresh, Tripoli; tel. (21) 4836090; fax (21) 4838955; e-mail ambassene.tripoli@stcc.presidence.sn; Chargé d'affaires a.i. DIAME SARR.

Serbia: POB 1087, Abdalla Ben Salam St, Ben Ashour Area, Tripoli; tel. (21) 3623205; fax (21) 3623207; e-mail serbianembassy_tripoli@yahoo.com; Ambassador OLIVER POTEZICA.

Sierra Leone: Tripoli; Ambassador Al-Haji ABUBAKARR JALLOH.

Slovakia: POB 5721, Km 3, Gargaresh, Hay Andalus, Tripoli; tel. (21) 4781388; fax (21) 4781387; e-mail slovembtrp@slovembtrp.com; Ambassador (vacant).

Spain: POB 2302, Sharia el-Amir Abd al-Kader al-Jazairi 36, Tripoli; tel. (21) 3620051; fax (21) 3620061; e-mail emb.tripoli@maec.es; internet www.maec.es/embajadas/tripoli; Ambassador JOSÉ RIERA SIQUIER.

Sudan: POB 1076, Sharia Gargaresh, Tripoli; tel. (21) 4775387; fax (21) 4774781; e-mail sudtripoli@hotmail.com; Ambassador MUHAMMAD AMIN AL-KAREB.

Switzerland: POB 439, Sharia el-Moussawer Ben Maghzamah, off Sharia Ben Ashour, Tripoli; tel. (21) 3614118; fax (21) 3614238; e-mail tri.vertretung@eda.admin.ch; internet www.eda.admin.ch/tripoli; Ambassador MICHEL GOTTRET.

Syria: POB 4219, Sharia Muhammad Rashid Reda 4, Tripoli (Relations Office); tel. (21) 3331783; fax (21) 3339030; Ambassador HILAL AL-ATRASH.

Togo: POB 3420, Sharia Khaled ibn al-Walid, Tripoli; tel. (21) 4449565; fax (21) 3332423.

Tunisia: POB 613, Sharia el-Bashir Ibrahimi, Medinat el-Hadaik, Tripoli; tel. (21) 3331051; fax (21) 4447600; Ambassador SALAHEDDINE JEMMALI.

Turkey: POB 947, Sharia Zaviya Dahmani, Tripoli; tel. (21) 3401140; fax (21) 3401146; e-mail embassy.tripoli@mfa.gov.tr; internet tripoli.emb.mfa.gov.tr; Ambassador ALI KEMAL AYDIN.

Uganda: POB 80215, Ben Achour, Sharia Jaraba, Tripoli; tel. (21) 3603083; fax (21) 3634471; e-mail info@ugembassylibya.org; internet www.ugembassylibya.org; Ambassador MOSES KIWA SEBUNYA.

Ukraine: POB 4544, Sharia Dhil, Ben Ashour, Tripoli; tel. (21) 3608665; fax (21) 3608666; e-mail emb_ly@mfa.gov.ua; internet www.mfa.gov.ua/libya; Ambassador MYKOLA NAHORNYI.

United Kingdom: 24th Floor, Tripoli Towers (formerly Bourj al-Fateh), Tripoli; tel. (21) 3351084; fax (21) 3403648; e-mail tripoli.press@fco.gov.uk; internet ukinlibya.fco.gov.uk; Ambassador DOMINIC ASQUITH.

USA: Sidi Slim Area, Sharia Wali al-Ahed, Tripoli; tel. (91) 2203239; e-mail Tripolipao@state.gov; internet libya.usembassy.gov; Chargé d'affaires a.i. WILLIAM ROEBUCK.

Venezuela: POB 2584, Sharia Ben Ashour, Jamaa-Sagaa Bridge, Tripoli; tel. (21) 3600408; fax (21) 3600407; e-mail embavenezlibia@hotmail.com; Ambassador AFIF TAJELDINE.

Viet Nam: POB 587, Sharia Gargaresh, Tripoli; tel. (21) 4901456; fax (21) 4901499; e-mail dsqvnlib@yahoo.com; internet www.vietnamembassy-libya.org; Ambassador DAO DUY TIEN.

Yemen: POB 4839, Sharia Ubei Ben Ka'ab 36, Tripoli; tel. (21) 607472; Ambassador AHMAD ABDULLAH AL-MAJIDI.

Judicial System

The judicial system under the rule of Col Muammar al-Qaddafi was composed, in order of seniority, of the Supreme Court, Courts of Appeal, and Courts of First Instance and Summary Courts.

Supreme Court: The judgments of the Supreme Court are final. It is composed of the President and several Justices. Its judgments are issued by circuits of at least three Justices (the quorum is three). The Court hears appeals from the Courts of Appeal in civil, penal, administrative and civil status matters; Chief Justice KAMAL DHAN.

Courts of Appeal: These courts settle appeals from Courts of First Instance; the quorum is three Justices. Each court of appeal has a court of assize.

Courts of First Instance and Summary Courts: These courts are first-stage courts in the Jamahiriya, and the cases heard in them are heard by one judge. Appeals against summary judgments are heard by the appellate court attached to the court of first instance, the quorum of which is three judges.

Attorney-General: ABD AL-AZIZ AL-HASAIRI.

Religion

ISLAM

The vast majority of Libyan Arabs follow Sunni Muslim rites, although Qaddafi rejected the Sunnah (i.e. the practice, course, way, manner or conduct of the Prophet Muhammad, as followed by Sunnis) as a basis for legislation.

Grand Mufti of Libya: Sheikh SADEQ AL-GHARIANI.

CHRISTIANITY

The Roman Catholic Church

Libya comprises three Apostolic Vicariates and one Apostolic Prefecture.

Apostolic Vicariate of Benghazi: POB 248, Benghazi; tel. and fax (61) 9081599; e-mail apostvicar@yahoo.com; Vicar Apostolic Mgr SYLVESTER CARMEL MAGRO (Titular Bishop of Salde).

Apostolic Vicariate of Tripoli: POB 365, Dahra, Tripoli; tel. (21) 3331863; fax (21) 3334696; e-mail bishoptripolibya@hotmail.com; internet www.catholicinlibya.com; Vicar Apostolic Mgr GIOVANNI INNOCENZO MARTINELLI (Titular Bishop of Tabuda).

The Anglican Communion

Within the Episcopal Church in Jerusalem and the Middle East, Libya forms part of the diocese of Egypt (q.v.).

Other Christian Churches

The Coptic Orthodox Church is represented in Libya.

The Press

Under the rule of Col Muammar al-Qaddafi, most newspapers and periodicals were published either by the Jamahiriya News Agency (JANA), by government secretariats, by the Press Service or by trade unions.

DAILIES

Al-Fajr al-Jadid (The New Dawn): POB 91291, Press Bldg, Sharia al-Jamahiriya, Tripoli; tel. (21) 3606393; fax (21) 3605728; e-mail info@alfajraljadeed.com; f. 1969; publ. by JANA; also publishes bi-monthly English version; Editor AOUN ABDULLAH MADI.

Al-Jamahiriya: POB 4814, Tripoli; tel. (21) 3605731; e-mail info@aljamahiria.com; f. 1980; Arabic; political.

Al-Shams: POB 82331, Al-Sahafa Bldg, Sharia al-Jamhouria, Tripoli; tel. (21) 4442524; fax (21) 609315; e-mail info@alshames.com; Editor MUHAMMAD M. IBRAHIM.

Az-Zahf al-Akhdar (The Green March): POB 14273, Al-Sahafa Bldg, Sharia al-Jamhouria, Tripoli; tel. (21) 4776890; fax (21) 4772502; e-mail info@azzahfalakhder.com; f. 1980; Editor-in-Chief HAMID ABU SALIM.

PERIODICALS

Al-Amal (Hope): POB 4845, Tripoli; e-mail info@alamalmag.com; internet www.alamalmag.com; monthly; social, for children; publ. by the Press Service.

Al-Daawa al-Islamia (Islamic Call): POB 2682, Sharia Sawani, Km 5, Tripoli; tel. (21) 4800294; fax (21) 4800293; f. 1980; weekly (Wed.); Arabic, English, French; cultural; publ. by the World Islamic Call Society; Eds MUHAMMAD IMHEMED AL-BALOUSHI, ABDULAHI MUHAMMAD ABD AL-JALEEL.

Economic Bulletin: POB 2303, Tripoli; tel. (21) 3337106; monthly; publ. by JANA.

Al-Jarida al-Rasmiya (The Official Newspaper): Tripoli; irregular; official state gazette.

Libyan Arab Republic Gazette: Tripoli; weekly; English.

Risalat al-Jihad (Holy War Letter): POB 2682, Tripoli; tel. (21) 3331021; f. 1983; monthly; Arabic, English, French; publ. by the World Islamic Call Society.

Scientific Bulletin: POB 2303, Tripoli; tel. (21) 3337106; monthly; publ. by JANA.

Al-Thaqafa al-Arabiya (Arab Culture): POB 4587, Tripoli; f. 1973; weekly; cultural; circ. 25,000.

The Tripoli Post: 32, 2nd Floor, Tripoli Tower, Tripoli; tel. and fax (21) 3351740; e-mail editor@tripolipost.com; internet www.tripolipost.com; f. 1999; weekly; English; privately owned; Editor-in-Chief Dr SAID LASWAD.

Al-Usbu al-Thaqafi (The Cultural Week): POB 4845, Tripoli; weekly.

Al-Watan al-Arabi al-Kabir (The Greater Arab Homeland): Tripoli; f. 1987.

Publishers

Al-Dar al-Arabia Lilkitab (Maison Arabe du Livre): POB 3185, Tripoli; tel. (21) 4447287; f. 1973 by Libya and Tunisia.

Al-Dar al-Hikma Publishing House: Tripoli; tel. (21) 3606571; fax (21) 3606610; e-mail info@elgabooks.com.

Al-Fatah University, General Administration of Libraries, Printing and Publications: POB 13543, Tripoli; tel. (21) 4628034; fax (21) 4625045; e-mail m.alfituri@hotmail.com; f. 1955; academic books.

General Co for Publishing, Advertising and Distribution: POB 921, Sirte (Surt); tel. (54) 63170; fax (54) 62100; general, educational and academic books in Arabic and other languages; makes and distributes advertisements throughout Libya.

Ghouma Publishing: POB 80092, Tripoli; tel. (21) 3630864; e-mail ghoumapub@hotmail.com; f. 1993; book publishing, distribution and art production; Gen. Man. MUSTAFA FETOURI.

Broadcasting and Communications

TELECOMMUNICATIONS

General Telecommunications Authority (GTA): POB 866, Sharia Zawia, Tripoli; e-mail info@gta.ly; internet www.gta.ly; f. 2006; supervisory body.

General Directorate of Posts and Telecommunications: POB 81686, Tripoli; tel. (21) 3604101; fax (21) 3604102; Dir-Gen. ABU ZAID JUMA AL-MANSURI.

General Post and Telecommunications Co (GPTC): POB 886, Sharia Zawia, Tripoli; tel. (21) 3617945; fax (21) 3619011; internet www.gptc.ly; f. 1984; operates and develops the postal and telecommunications networks; subsidiaries include Libyana Mobile Phone Co and Al-Madar Al-Jadeed (mobile cellular telecommunications operators), and Libya Telecom and Technology (internet service provider); Chair. (vacant).

Libyana Mobile Phone Co: POB 90071, Tripoli; tel. (21) 3406555; internet www.libyana.ly; f. 2004.

Al-Madar Al-Jadeed: Tripoli; internet www.almadar.ly; f. 1997; mobile telecommunications network operator; 1.2m. subscribers; Chief Exec. ABD AL-KHALEK BIN ASHOUR.

BROADCASTING

Radio

Great Socialist People's Libyan Arab Jamahiriya Broadcasting Corporation: POB 80237, Tripoli; tel. (21) 3402107; fax (21) 3403468; e-mail info@en.ljbc.net; internet www.ljbc.net; f. 1968; broadcasts in Arabic; additional satellite channel broadcast for 18 hours a day from 1982; Sec.-Gen. ABDULLAH MANSOUR.

Voice of Africa: POB 4677, Sharia al-Fateh, Tripoli; tel. (21) 4449209; fax (21) 4449875; f. 1973 as Voice of the Greater Arab Homeland; adopted current name in 1998; broadcasts in Arabic, French, English, Swahili and Hausa; Dir-Gen. ABDULLAH AL-MEGRI.

Television

People's Revolution Broadcasting TV: POB 80237, Tripoli; tel. (21) 3402107; fax (21) 3403468; e-mail info@en.ljbc.net; internet www.ljbc.net; f. 1957; broadcasts in Arabic; additional satellite channels broadcast for limited hours in English; Dir ABDULLAH MANSOUR.

Finance

(cap. = capital; res = reserves; dep. = deposits; m. = million; br(s) = branch(es); amounts in Libyan dinars, unless otherwise stated)

BANKING

The Libyan banking sector, hitherto highly state-controlled, was undergoing restructure in the late 2000s. Minority stakes in two state-owned commercial banks were sold to foreign banking interests in 2007–08. It was announced in early 2010 that the Central Bank of Libya (CBL) was to grant two licences to foreign banks for the creation of joint venture banking operations with Libyan investors. However, in August the CBL announced that it had decided to grant just one licence, to UniCredit (Italy); bids from two other European banks and three from the Gulf region were rejected.

Central Bank

Central Bank of Libya (CBL): POB 1103, Sharia al-Malik Seoud, Tripoli; tel. (21) 3333591; fax (21) 4441488; e-mail info@cbl.gov.ly; internet www.cbl.gov.ly; f. 1955 as Nat. Bank of Libya; name changed to Bank of Libya 1963, to Cen. Bank of Libya 1977; state-owned; bank of issue and central bank carrying govt accounts and operating exchange control; commercial operations transferred to Nat. Commercial Bank 1970; cap. 500m., res 909m., dep. 108,079m. (Dec. 2009); Gov. and Chair. SADDEK EL-KABER.

Other Banks

Alwafa Bank: POB 84212, Sharia Alfallah, Tripoli; tel. (21) 4815123; fax (21) 4801247; e-mail info@alwafabank.com; internet www.alwafabank.com; f. 2003; private bank; Chair. and Gen. Man. HADI M. GITELI.

Jumhouria Bank: POB 685, Sharia Omar el-Mokhtar, Tripoli; tel. and fax (21) 4442541; e-mail info@jbank.ly; internet www.jbank.ly; f. 1969 as successor to Barclays Bank Int. in Libya; originally known as Masraf al-Gumhouria; name changed as above 2000; merger with Umma Bank SAL completed mid-2008; cap. 1,000m., res 39m., dep. 19,817m. (Dec. 2009); Chair. MOSBAH MUHAMMAD EL-AKKARI; Gen. Man. AHMED OMAR RAJAB MUHAMMAD; 122 brs.

Libyan Foreign Bank: POB 2542, Tower 2, Dat al-Imad Complex, Tripoli; tel. (21) 3350155; fax (21) 3350164; e-mail it@lafbank.com; internet www.lafbank.com; f. 1972 as Libyan Arab Foreign Bank; present name adopted 2005; 'offshore' bank wholly owned by Cen. Bank of Libya; cap. US $2,000m., res $573m., dep. $10,166m. (Dec. 2009); Chair. Dr AHMED A. HODANA; Gen. Man. MUHAMMAD M. BEN YOUSUF.

National Commercial Bank SAL: POB 543, Aruba Ave, al-Baida; tel. (21) 3610306; fax (21) 3612267; e-mail ncbly@lttnet.net; internet www.ncb.ly; f. 1970 to take over commercial banking division of Cen. Bank (then Bank of Libya) and brs of Aruba Bank and Istiklal Bank; wholly owned by Cen. Bank; cap. 100m., res 4,685m., dep. 6,317m. (Dec. 2008); Chair. ABD AL-WAHAB MUKHTAR; Gen. Man. SULEIMAN AZZABI; 63 brs.

Sahara Bank SPI: POB 70, Sharia 1 September, Tripoli; tel. (21) 3340663; fax (21) 4443836; e-mail sahbankgm1@lttnet.net; internet saharabank.com.ly; f. 1964 to take over br. of Banco di Sicilia; the Govt sold a 19% stake to BNP Paribas (France) in July 2007; cap. and res 208.2m., total assets 1,951.8m. (March 2003); Chair. and Gen. Man. Dr ABD AL-LATIF ABD AL-HAFIZ EL-KIB; CEO CLAUDE RUFIN; 48 brs.

Wahda Bank: POB 452, Sharia Gamal Abd al-Nasser, Benghazi; tel. (61) 2224256; fax (21) 2224122; e-mail wahda@wahdabank.com; internet www.wahdabank.com; f. 1970 to take over Bank of North Africa, Commercial Bank SAL, Nahda Arabia Bank, Société Africaine de Banque SAL, and Kafila al-Ahly Bank; 19% stake acquired by Arab Bank PLC (Jordan) in February 2008; remainder owned by Cen. Bank of Libya; cap. 108m., res 115m., dep. 7,062m. (Dec. 2009); Chair. Dr ANTOINE SREIH; Gen. Man. SELIM K. IHMOUDA; 76 brs.

STOCK EXCHANGE

Libyan Stock Market: Sharia Omar el-Mokhtar, Tripoli; tel. (21) 3365026; fax (61) 9091097; e-mail info@lsm.gov.ly; internet www.lsm.ly; f. 2007; Sec. SULIMAN SALEM AL-SHOHOMIY.

INSURANCE

Libya Insurance Co: POB 80087, Aman Bldg, Sharia al-Taha, Tripoli; tel. (21) 4441499; fax (21) 4444176; e-mail infolt@libtamin.com; internet www.libtamin.com; f. 1964; merged with Al-Mukhtar Insurance Co in 1981; all classes of insurance; Man. ALI AMAR AL-RAGAYEE.

Trade and Industry

There are state trade and industrial organizations responsible for the running of industries at all levels, which supervise production, distribution and sales. There are also central bodies responsible for the power generation industry, agriculture, land reclamation and transport.

GOVERNMENT AGENCIES

Council for Oil and Gas Affairs: Tripoli; f. 2006; holds ultimate responsibility for all matters involving oil, gas and their by-products.

Great Man-made River Water Utilization Authority (GMRA): POB 7217, Benghazi; tel. (61) 2230392; fax (61) 2230393; e-mail info@gmrwua.com; internet www.gmrwua.com; supervises construction of pipeline carrying water to the Libyan coast from beneath the Sahara desert, to provide irrigation for agricultural projects; Sec. for the Great Man-made River Project ABD AL-MAJID AL-AOUD.

Libyan Investment Authority (LIA): Tripoli; e-mail info@lia.ly; internet www.lia.ly; f. 2006, operations commenced 2007; sovereign wealth fund managing state-allocated assets, including Oil Reserve Fund; Chair. Dr ABD AL-HAFID MAHMOUD ZLITNI.

National Economic Development Board (NEDB): Tripoli; internet www.nedb.ly; f. 2007; charged with the drafting and execution of reform campaigns, and the facilitation of decision-making and action on critical economic issues.

DEVELOPMENT ORGANIZATIONS

Arab Organization for Agricultural Development: POB 12898, Zohra, Tripoli; tel. and fax (21) 3619275; e-mail arabagri@lycos.com; internet www.aoad.org; responsible for agricultural devt projects.

General National Organization for Industrialization: Sharia San'a, Tripoli; tel. (21) 3334995; f. 1970; public org. responsible for the devt of industry.

Kufra and Sarir Authority: Council of Agricultural Development, Benghazi; f. 1972 to develop the Kufra oasis and Sarir area in south-eastern Libya.

CHAMBERS OF COMMERCE

Benghazi Chamber of Commerce, Trade, Industry and Agriculture: POB 208 and 1286, Benghazi; tel. (61) 3372319; fax (61) 3380761; f. 1956; Pres. Dr BADIA; Gen. Man. Dr TAREK TARBAGHIA; 150,000 mems.

Tripoli Chamber of Commerce and Industry: POB 2321, Sharia Najed 6–8, Tripoli; tel. (21) 3336855; fax (21) 3332655; f. 1952; Chair. MUHAMMAD KANOON; Dir-Gen. ABD AL-MONEM H. BURAWI; 30,000 mems.

UTILITIES

Electricity

General Electricity Company of Libya (GECOL): POB 668, Tripoli; tel. (21) 4445068; fax (21) 4447023; e-mail gecol@gecol.net; internet www.gecol.ly; Sec. of Management Cttee Eng. ABU AL-GHASSIM ONEAS.

STATE HYDROCARBONS COMPANIES

Until 1986 petroleum affairs in Libya were dealt with primarily by the Secretariat of the General People's Committee for Petroleum. This body was abolished in March 1986, and sole responsibility for the administration of the petroleum industry passed to the national companies that were already in existence. The Secretariat of the General People's Committee for Petroleum was re-established in March 1989 and incorporated into the new Secretariat for the General People's Committee for Energy in October 1992. This was dissolved in March 2000, and responsibility for local oil policy was transferred to the National Oil Corporation, under the supervision of the General People's Committee. From 1973 the Libyan Government entered into participation agreements with some of the foreign oil companies (concession holders), and nationalized others. It concluded 85%:15% production-sharing agreements with various oil companies.

National Oil Corporation (NOC): POB 2655, Sharia Bashier Sadawi, Tripoli; tel. (21) 3337141; fax (21) 3331390; e-mail info@noclibya.com; internet en.noclibya.com.ly; f. 1970 to: undertake jt ventures with foreign cos; build and operate refineries, storage tanks, petrochemical facilities, pipelines and tankers; take part in arranging specifications for local and imported petroleum products; participate in general planning of oil installations in Libya; market crude and refined petroleum and petrochemical products; and establish and operate oil terminals; Chair. and Dir-Gen. NURI BERRUIEN.

Arabian Gulf Oil Co (AGOCO): POB 263, Benghazi; tel. (61) 28931; fax (21) 49031; wholly owned subsidiary of the NOC; Chair. AHMAD MAJBRI.

Oilinvest International NV: Tripoli; f. 1988; wholly owned subsidiary of the NOC; Libya's foreign oil investment arm; Chair. and Gen. Man. AHMAD ABD AL-KARIM AHMAD.

Agip North Africa and Middle East Ltd—Libyan Branch: POB 346, Tripoli; tel. and fax (21) 3335135; Sec. of People's Cttee OMAR AL-SWEIFI.

Azzawiya Oil Refining Co (ARC): POB 6451, Tripoli; tel. (23) 610539; fax (23) 610543; e-mail infoazzawiya@azzawiyaoil.com; internet www.azzawiyaoil.com; f. 1976; Gen. Man. AL-MOAMARE A. SWEDAN.

Brega Oil Marketing Co: POB 402, Sharia Bashir al-Saidawi, Tripoli; tel. (21) 4440830; f. 1971; Chair. Dr DOKALI B. AL-MEGHARIEF.

International Oil Investments Co: Tripoli; f. 1988, with initial capital of US $500m. to acquire 'downstream' facilities abroad; Chair. MUHAMMAD AL-JAWAD.

National Drilling and Workover Co: POB 1454, 208 Sharia Omar Mukhtar, Tripoli; tel. (21) 3332411; f. 1986; Chair. IBRAHIM BAHI.

Ras Lanouf Oil and Gas Processing Co (RASCO): POB 1971, Ras Lanuf, Benghazi; tel. (21) 3605177; fax (21) 607924; f. 1978; Chair. ABULKASIM M. A. ZWARY.

Sirte Oil Co: POB 385, Marsa el-Brega, Tripoli; tel. (21) 607261; fax (21) 601487; internet www.soc.com.ly; f. 1955 as Esso Standard Libya, taken over by Sirte Oil Co 1982; absorbed Nat. Petrochemicals Co in Oct. 1990; exploration, production of crude petroleum, gas and petrochemicals, liquefaction of natural gas; Chair. ABD AL-BASET TAHER AL-REFAE.

Umm al-Jawaby Petroleum Co: POB 693, Tripoli; Chair. and Gen. Man. MUHAMMAD TENTTOUSH.

Waha Oil Co: POB 395, Tripoli; tel. (21) 3331116; fax (21) 3337169; e-mail infowaha@wahaoil.com; internet www.wahaoil.net; Chair. Dr BASHEER MUHAMMAD ELASHAHAB.

Zueitina Oil Co (ZOC): POB 2134, Tripoli; tel. (21) 3338011; fax (21) 3339109; e-mail info@zueitina-ly.com; f. 1986; Chair. of Management Cttee BASHIR BAZAZI.

TRADE UNIONS

General Federation of Producers' Trade Unions: POB 734, Sharia Istanbul 2, Tripoli; tel. (21) 4446011; f. 1952; affiliated to ITUC; Sec.-Gen. BASHIR IHWIJ; 17 trade unions with 700,000 mems.

Transport

Department of Road Transport and Railways: POB 14527, Sharia al-Zawiyah, Tripoli; tel. and fax (21) 3605808; Dir-Gen. (Projects and Research) MUHAMMAD ABU ZIAN.

RAILWAYS

There are, at present, no railways in Libya. In 1998, however, the Government invited bids for the construction of a 3,170-km railway, comprising one branch, 2,178 km in length, running from north to south, and another, 992 km in length, running from east to west along the north coast. The railway may eventually be linked to other North African rail networks. Russian Railways OAO was awarded the contract to build a 554-km section of the network between Sirte and Benghazi in April 2008; construction work commenced in August. In 2008–09 a Chinese company was awarded contracts for a further three sections.

Railway Executive Board: POB 41758, Alkhoms, Tripoli; tel. (21) 3609486; fax (21) 626054; e-mail info@libyanrailways.com; oversees the planning and construction of railways; Sec. SAEED RASHID.

ROADS

The most important road is the 1,822-km national coast road from the Tunisian to the Egyptian border, passing through Tripoli and Benghazi. It has a second link between Barce and Lamluda, 141 km in length. Another national road runs from a point on the coastal road 120 km south of Misurata through Sabha to Ghat near the Algerian border (total length 1,250 km). There is a branch 247 km long running from Vaddan to Sirte. A 690-km road, connecting Tripoli and Sabha, and another 626 km long, from Ajdabiya in the north to Kufra in the south-east, were opened in 1983. The Tripoli–Ghat section (941 km) of the third, 1,352-km national road was opened in September 1984. There is a road crossing the desert from Sabha to the frontiers of Chad and Niger. As part of a wide-ranging agreement signed by Libya and Italy in August 2008, the latter agreed to fund construction of a new coastal motorway between the Tunisian and Egyptian borders. Construction work on the project commenced in mid-2009. In addition to the national highways, the west of Libya has about 1,200 km of paved and macadamized roads and the east about 500 km. All the towns and villages of Libya, including the desert oases, are accessible by motor vehicle. In 2001 Libya had an estimated total road network of 83,200 km, of which 57,200 km was paved.

SHIPPING

The principal ports are Tripoli, Benghazi, Mersa Brega, Misurata and al-Sider. Zueitina, Ras Lanuf, Mersa Hariga, Mersa Brega and al-Sider are mainly oil ports. A pipeline connects the Zelten oilfields with Mersa Brega. Another pipeline joins the Sarir oilfield with Mersa Hariga, and the port of Tobruk, and a pipeline from the Sarir field to Zueitina was opened in 1968. A port is being developed at Darnah, and plans were under way for the expansion of the port of Sirte. Libya also has the use of Tunisian port facilities at Sand Gabès, to alleviate congestion at Tripoli. At 31 December 2012 Libya's flag registered fleet consisted of 81 vessels, with a combined displacement of 1,020,450 grt, of which 12 were fish carriers, two were gas tankers and two were general cargo ships.

Principal Shipping Companies

General National Maritime Transport Co (GNMTC): POB 80173, el-Shaab Terminal, Tripoli; tel. and fax (21) 4843271; e-mail info@gnmtc.com; internet www.gnmtc.com; f. 1975 to handle all projects dealing with maritime trade; state-owned; Chair. Capt. ALI BELHAG AHMED.

Libya Shipping Agency: POB 4288, Abu Seta area, nr Abokmisha Mosque, Tripoli; tel. (21) 3402528; fax (21) 3403496; e-mail info@libyashipping.com; internet www.libyashipping.com; provides chartering, land transportation and customs clearance services; Gen. Man. IMAD FELLAH.

CIVIL AVIATION

There are four international airports: Tripoli International Airport, situated at Ben Gashir, 34 km (21 miles) from Tripoli; Benina Airport 19 km (12 miles) from Benghazi; Sabha Airport; and Misurata Airport. There are a further 10 regional airports. A US $800m. programme to improve the airport infrastructure and air traffic control network was approved in mid-2001. In the mid-2000s plans were announced for the upgrade and expansion of Tripoli International Airport, which were to include the construction of two new terminals, following which the airport's annual passenger capacity was expected to increase to some 20m., compared with 3m. in 2007. Work on the project commenced in September 2007 and was scheduled for completion by 2011. However, progress was halted owing to the outbreak of conflict in February of that year. In April 2012 the National Transitional Council formally regained control of Tripoli International Airport.

Civil Aviation Authority: Tripoli; tel. (21) 3605318; fax (21) 3605322; e-mail info@caa.ly; internet www.lycaa.org; Gen. Dir ABD AL-RAZZAK ZAATUT.

Afriqiyah Airways: 1st Floor, Waha Bldg, Sharia Omar al-Mokhtar, Tripoli; tel. (21) 4449734; fax (21) 4449128; e-mail customerservice@afriqiyah.aero; internet www.afriqiyah.aero; f. 2001; state-owned; flights to 29 destinations in Africa, Asia, Europe and the Middle East; Chair. Capt. SABRI SAAD ABDALLAH SHADI; CEO RAMMAH ETTIR.

Buraq Air: Tripoli International Airport, Tripoli; e-mail lias@buraqair.com; internet www.buraqair.com; f. 2001; first privately owned Libyan airline; scheduled international passenger and cargo flights to Egypt, Morocco, Syria and Turkey; domestic flights from Tripoli, Benghazi and Sabha; Chair. and Man. Dir Capt. MUHAMMAD A. BUBEIDA.

Libyan Airlines: POB 2555, Ben Fernas Bldg, Sharia Haiti, Tripoli; tel. (21) 3614102; fax (21) 3614815; e-mail i.alwani@ln.aero; internet www.libyanairlines.aero; f. 1964 as Kingdom of Libya Airlines; reorg. in 1975 as Libyan Arab Airline; present name adopted 2006; passenger and cargo services from Tripoli, Benghazi and Sabha to destinations in Europe, North Africa, the Middle East and Asia; domestic services throughout Libya; Chair. and CEO Capt. MUHAMMAD M. IBSEM.

Tourism

The principal attractions for visitors to Libya are Tripoli, with its beaches and annual International Fair, the ancient Roman towns of Sabratha, Leptis Magna and Cyrene, and historic oases. There were 999,343 visitor arrivals in 2004; in 2010 receipts from tourism totalled US $60m., excluding passenger transport.

General Board of Fairs: POB 891, Sharia Omar Mukhtar, Tripoli; tel. (21) 3332255; fax (21) 4448385; e-mail info@gbf.com.ly; internet gbf.com.ly; Head of Fairs GAMAL N. A. AL-AMOUSHI.

General Board of Tourism and Traditional Industries: POB 82063, Tripoli; tel. (21) 3334673; fax (21) 4445336; e-mail info@libyan-tourism.net; internet www.libyan-tourism.org; Chair. MUHAMMAD SEALNA.

Defence

The Libyan National Army was founded in 2011 by the National Transitional Council after the overthrow of Col Muammar al-Qaddafi's regime. A restructuring process continued in early 2013.

Chief of Staff of Armed Forces: Gen. YOUSEF AL-MANGOUSH.

Chief of Staff of Air Force: Brig. AHMED HABIB AL-MISMARI (acting).

Chief of Staff of Naval Force: Cdre HASSAN ALI BUSHNAK.

Estimated Defence Expenditure (2012): LD 3,770m.

Military Service: selective conscription; 1–2 years.

Total Armed Forces (as assessed at November 2010): 76,000: army 50,000, incl. (estimated) 25,000 conscripts; navy 8,000; air force 18,000.

People's Militia: (estimated) 40,000.

Education

Education is officially compulsory for nine years between six and 15 years of age. Primary education begins at the age of six and lasts for nine years. Secondary education, beginning at 15 years of age, lasts for a further three or four years. In 2005/06 some 755,338 students were enrolled in primary education. At the secondary level there were 732,614 students in the same year. The teaching of French was abolished in Libyan schools in 1983. Libya also has institutes for agricultural, technical and vocational training, of which there were 84 in 2004.

In 1958 the University of Libya opened in Benghazi with Faculties of Arts and Commerce, followed the next year by the Faculty of Science, near Tripoli. Faculties of Law, Agriculture, Engineering, Teacher Training, and Arabic Language and Islamic Studies have since been added to the University. In 1973 the University was divided into two parts, to form the Universities of Tripoli and Benghazi, later renamed Al-Fatah and Ghar Younis universities. The Faculty of Education at Al-Fatah University became Sabha University in 1983. There is a University of Technology (Bright Star) at Mersa Brega and the Al-Arab Medical University at Benghazi. In 1995 the number of public universities had reached 13. In 2002/03 some 375,028 students were enrolled in tertiary education. The Government's budget for 2012 allocated LD 4,600m. (equivalent to 6.7% of total spending) to the Ministry of Education.

LIECHTENSTEIN

Introductory Survey

LOCATION, CLIMATE, LANGUAGE, RELIGION, FLAG, CAPITAL

The Principality of Liechtenstein is in central Europe. The country lies on the east bank of the Upper Rhine river, bordered by Switzerland to the west and south, and by Austria to the north and east. Liechtenstein has an Alpine climate, with mild winters. The average annual temperature is about 10.5°C, while average annual rainfall is 996 mm. The official language is German, of which a dialect—Alemannish—is spoken. Almost all of the inhabitants profess Christianity, and about 79% are adherents of the Roman Catholic Church. The national flag (proportions 3 by 5) consists of two equal horizontal stripes, of royal blue and red, with a golden princely crown, outlined in black, in the upper hoist. The capital is Vaduz.

CONTEMPORARY POLITICAL HISTORY

Historical Context

Liechtenstein has been an independent state since 1719, except while under French domination briefly in the early 19th century. It joined the German Confederation in 1815, but failed to realign itself with other German states upon the dissolution of the Confederation in 1866. In 1919 Switzerland assumed responsibility for Liechtenstein's diplomatic representation, replacing Austria. In 1920 a postal union with Switzerland was agreed, and in 1924 a treaty was concluded with Switzerland whereby Liechtenstein was incorporated in a joint customs union. Franz Josef II became Reigning Prince in 1938 and was succeeded by his son Prince Hans-Adam II in 1989.

Domestic Political Affairs

After 42 years as the dominant party in government, the Fortschrittliche Bürgerpartei (FBP—Progressive Citizens' Party) was defeated by the centre-right Vaterländische Union (VU—Patriotic Union) at a general election to the Landtag (parliament) in February 1970. Four years later the FBP regained its majority. At the general election in February 1978 the VU, led by Hans Brunhart, won a majority of seats. After protracted negotiations, Brunhart replaced the FBP's Dr Walter Kieber as Prime Minister in April 1978. At the general election in February 1982 the distribution of seats remained unchanged. Following a referendum in July 1984, women were granted the right to vote on a national basis. However, women were still not permitted to vote on communal affairs in three of Liechtenstein's 11 communes until April 1986. (An amendment to the Constitution, declaring equality between women and men, took effect in 1992.) In August 1984 Prince Franz Josef transferred executive power to his son, Prince Hans-Adam, although he remained titular Head of State until his death in November 1989, when he was succeeded by his son (Hans-Adam II).

The composition of the Landtag remained unchanged following a general election in February 1986, when women voted for the first time in a national poll. In January 1989 the Landtag was dissolved by Prince Hans-Adam, following a dispute between the VU and the FBP regarding the construction of a new museum to accommodate the princely art collection. At the subsequent general election, which took place in March, the number of seats in the Landtag was increased from 15 to 25; the VU retained its majority.

In October 1992 almost 2,000 people demonstrated in Vaduz to protest against a threat by Prince Hans-Adam that he would dissolve the Landtag if deputies did not submit to his wish to hold a proposed referendum to endorse Liechtenstein's entry to the nascent European Economic Area (EEA) shortly in advance of a similar vote in Switzerland. The Prince believed that the outcome of the Swiss poll might be prejudicial to that of the Liechtenstein vote, and that, in the event of voters' rejecting EEA membership at an early referendum, Liechtenstein might still be able to join other members of the European Free Trade Association (EFTA, see p. 461) in applying for admission to the European Community (EC, now European Union—EU, see p. 281). A compromise was reached, whereby the referendum was scheduled to take place shortly after the Swiss vote, while the Government agreed actively to promote a vote in favour of the EEA and to explore the possibility of applying to the EC should EEA membership be rejected. (The authorities subsequently decided that admission to the EU would not be beneficial to the Principality.) At the referendum in December, although Switzerland's voters had rejected accession to the EEA, Liechtenstein's membership was approved by 55.8% of those who voted; consequently, the two countries' joint customs union was renegotiated. In April 1995 a further national referendum was held, at which 55.9% of those who voted approved the revised customs arrangements. Liechtenstein joined the EEA in May.

At the general election in February 1993 the VU lost its majority, winning only 11 of the Landtag's 25 seats. The FBP retained 12 seats, and two seats were won by a social democratic, environmentalist party, the Freie Liste (FL—Free List). Lengthy negotiations resulted in the formation of a new coalition between the FBP and the VU, and Markus Büchel of the FBP became Prime Minister. In September, however, following a unanimous vote in the Landtag expressing no confidence in his leadership, Büchel was dismissed from his post, and Prince Hans-Adam dissolved the legislature. At a fresh general election held in October, the VU regained its majority, winning 13 seats, while the FBP took 11 and the FL one. The VU became the dominant party in a new coalition with the FBP, with Mario Frick of the VU as Prime Minister.

In March 1996 the Landtag adopted a unanimous motion of loyalty to the hereditary monarchy, after Prince Hans-Adam offered to resign in response to continued tension between him and the legislature. At the next general election, which took place in February 1997, the VU retained its majority with 13 seats, while the FBP secured 10 and the FL two. Frick remained Prime Minister. In April the FBP withdrew from the ruling coalition, leaving a single party (the VU) to govern alone for the first time since 1938. The constitutional role of the Reigning Prince came under renewed scrutiny in 1997, when, against the wishes of the Landtag, Prince Hans-Adam refused to reappoint Dr Herbert Wille, a senior judge who had advocated that constitutional issues should be decided by the Supreme Court rather than the monarch. Wille subsequently presented a formal complaint to the European Court of Human Rights, which ruled, in November 1999, that Prince Hans-Adam had restricted Wille's right to free speech; the Prince was required to pay 100,000 Swiss francs in costs.

In December 1999 Prince Hans-Adam requested an Austrian prosecutor, Kurt Spitzer, to investigate allegations in the German press based on an unpublished report of April 1999 by the German secret service that international criminals were using financial institutions in Liechtenstein to launder the proceeds of organized crime. As a result, five people were arrested in May 2000; all five were later released without charge. In his final report, which was released in August, Spitzer concluded that Liechtenstein was no more culpable of money-laundering than any other country in Europe. He blamed the current problems on the Principality's inefficient banking system and the poor application of existing legislation designed to combat economic crimes. In June the Financial Action Task Force on Money Laundering (FATF), a commission of the Organisation for Economic Co-operation and Development (OECD, see p. 388), included Liechtenstein on a list of countries considered unco-operative in international attempts to combat money-laundering. In July, in an effort to improve the country's international reputation, the Government approved the establishment of a new financial investigative unit within the police force and measures to accelerate legal assistance to foreign countries in money-laundering investigations. Furthermore, legislation was promulgated in December requiring financial institutions to maintain tighter controls over accounts and transactions, including the abolition of anonymous accounts. Liechtenstein was removed from the FATF's list of unco-operative countries in 2001, and, in October of that year, the Government appointed the former head of the Swiss anti-money-laundering authority, Daniel Thelesklaf, to administer a new financial surveillance unit, which was to enforce new regulations requiring banks and lawyers to be able to verify the identity of their clients. However, in April 2002 Liechtenstein was among seven jurisdictions identified by OECD as 'unco-operative tax havens' lacking financial transparency, under its initiative to abolish 'harmful tax practices'. Liechtenstein remained one of three countries so designated until May 2009.

At the general election held in February 2001 the VU lost its parliamentary majority, securing only 11 of the 25 seats in the Landtag, while the FBP won 13 seats and the FL obtained one. The VU administration's popularity had been adversely affected by an unresolved dispute with Prince Hans-Adam over his demands for constitutional changes, notably with regard to appointments in the judiciary (the Prince advocated that judges be nominated by the monarch rather than by parliamentary deputies). A new Government comprising solely the FBP, under the leadership of Otmar Hasler, took office in April. In December the Prince threatened to abdicate and take up residence in Austria if his proposed constitutional reforms were not enacted.

The issue of constitutional reform was finally resolved by a national referendum, held on 14 and 16 March 2003, in which 64.3% of the votes cast were in favour of granting the Prince new powers; the voter participation rate was 87.7%. As a result of the referendum, the Prince gained the right to dismiss a government even if it retained parliamentary confidence, to appoint an interim administration pending elections, to preside over a panel to select judges, and to veto laws by not signing them within a six-month period. Conversely, the constitutional amendments also divested the Prince of his right to rule by emergency decree for an unlimited period (such a measure was now limited to a maximum of six months) and to nominate government officials. In addition, citizens could now force a referendum on any subject by collecting a minimum of 1,500 signatures. A cross-party group that included former premier Frick presented a compromise proposal, which suggested that a princely veto could be overruled by a referendum and sought to limit the Prince's use of emergency legislation to times of war; this proposal received the support of only 16.5% of the voters. The overwhelming support for the Prince's proposed changes was partially attributed to widespread fear that, if fulfilled, his threat of self-imposed exile as a symbolic monarch would cause economic decline and social upheaval (the royal family owns and operates the LGT Bank, the Principality's largest bank and asset management fund). On 15 August 2004 Prince Hans-Adam transferred his sovereign powers to his son, Prince Alois, in accordance with an announcement that he had made in August 2003. Prince Hans-Adam, however, remained Head of State.

At the general election held in March 2005 the FBP failed to retain an absolute majority, winning 12 of the 25 seats. The VU secured 10 seats, while the FL increased its representation from one seat to three. The FBP and the VU formed a coalition Government, comprising three representatives of the FBP, including Hasler, who remained as Prime Minister, and two of the VU, with Dr Klaus Tschütscher as Deputy Prime Minister.

In August 2005 a conservative group known as the Volksinitiative für das Leben (People's Initiative For Life) submitted 1,889 signatures to the Government in support of its demands for a national referendum to be held on constitutional revisions. The group wished to amend Article 14 of the Constitution so that the highest responsibility of the state would be 'to protect human life from conception until natural death' and also aimed to insert a reference to the state's responsibility to protect human dignity. The initiative was intended to address the potential legalization of abortion and, indirectly, the issues of euthanasia, genetic technology and stem-cell research. Having failed to secure sufficient support in the Landtag, the proposals were to be subject to a national referendum. The FBP and the VU jointly drafted a counterproposal to make the protection of life and human dignity a right for Liechtenstein citizens rather than a duty of the state. A further amendment was added explicitly prohibiting the death penalty (which had already been abolished by a revision of the criminal code in 1985). Following its approval by the Landtag in September, the counterproposal was presented to the referendum concurrently with the People's Initiative For Life. At the referendum, held on 25 and 27 November, the initiative, which opponents claimed would prevent abortion, birth control and assisted suicide, was rejected by 80.9% of the votes cast, while the counterproposal was adopted, with the support of 79.4% of voters.

At the general election held on 8 February 2009 the VU won an absolute majority, securing 13 of the 25 seats and replacing the FBP as the largest party in the Landtag; the rate of participation

by the electorate was 84.6%. The FBP won 11 seats, while the FL's representation declined from three seats to just one. Tschütscher, hitherto Deputy Prime Minister, was sworn in as Prime Minister on 25 March. Despite the VU's absolute majority, the VU and FBP continued to co-operate in a coalition Government; the new administration comprised three members of the VU (including Tschütscher) and two representatives of the FBP. Tschütscher undertook further to improve the reputation of Liechtenstein's financial system by increasing co-operation with other countries in the fight against tax evasion (see Foreign Affairs).

In September 2011 a narrow majority of participants in a referendum rejected the decriminalization of early abortion (a few days prior to the poll Prince Alois had indicated that he would veto any relaxation of the abortion ban). Although the Prince's threat angered a proportion of the population (believing that it rendered the referendum meaningless), in a further referendum held on 1 July 2012 76% of those who participated voted to reject proposals to curb the political power of the Prince by divesting him of his power of veto over decisions reached in national referendums.

The general election of 1 and 3 February 2013 was contested by four groups, rather than the usual three. The new contender was a loose-knit organization entitled Die Unabhängigen (DU, The Independents), which was established by the parliamentary deputy Harry Quaderer, who left the VU in February 2011. In the poll, which attracted a turn-out of 79.8%, the VU lost its majority in the Landtag, securing only eight seats, while the FBP won 10 seats, the DU four seats and the FL three seats. The VU's heavy defeat, in which it lost more than one-third of its parliamentary seats, was largely attributed to the unpopularity of the outgoing administration's proposed economic austerity measures. The FBP's Adrian Hasler, the former chief of the Liechtenstein National Police, formed a new Government on 27 March in coalition with the VU. Two ministerial posts were taken by representatives of the VU, including Thomas Zwiefelhofer, who became Deputy Prime Minister.

Foreign Affairs

In 1950 Liechtenstein became a party to the Statute of the International Court of Justice (ICJ, see p. 26), in 1973 it joined the Organization for Security and Co-operation in Europe (see p. 397) and in 1978 it was admitted to the Council of Europe (see p. 260). Liechtenstein became a full member of the UN in 1990 (hitherto the country had been a member of some UN specialized agencies). In the following year Liechtenstein became a full member of the European Free Trade Association (EFTA, see p. 461). Liechtenstein participates in the European Economic Area (EEA), which since 1994 has incorporated Liechtenstein (together with Iceland and Norway) into the internal market of the European Union (EU, see p. 281).

In February 2008, following a meeting of EU ministers responsible for justice and home affairs in Brussels, Belgium, Liechtenstein became an associate member of the EU's Schengen area (which binds signatories to the abolition of border controls) and the Dublin Convention on Asylum (relating to common formal arrangements on asylum). Although the Landtag ratified the agreement in June, the EU process of ratification was delayed owing to ongoing negotiations between Liechtenstein and the EU on an anti-fraud agreement. Meanwhile, an interim solution to the issue of border control between Liechtenstein and Switzerland was put in place after the latter acceded to the Schengen Agreement in December 2008. Liechtenstein finally became a full member of the Schengen area in December 2011.

Following the Second World War, Liechtenstein's relations with Czechoslovakia (from 1993 the Czech Republic and Slovakia) were strained. This stemmed from the expulsion of ethnic Germans from Czechoslovakia and the confiscation of their land (without compensation) after the war, under the controversial Beneš Decrees. The Liechtenstein princely family lost a large part of its estates during this time. Liechtenstein, which was a sovereign, neutral state throughout both the First and Second World Wars, claimed that it was unfairly grouped together with Germany under the terms of the Decrees. Czechoslovakia, however, considered the Liechtenstein princely family to have been collaborators with the Nazi regime in Germany during the Second World War, and that its action was thus legitimate. As a result of the dispute, Czechoslovakia refused to recognize Liechtenstein as a sovereign state. In October 2003 Prince Hans-Adam blocked the entry of the Czech Republic and Slovakia (along with that of the eight other EU accession states) into the EEA; the 10 countries were due to become members of the EU on 1 May 2004 and would, under normal circumstances, have automatically joined the EEA. Their accession to the EEA was delayed until November 2003, when Liechtenstein agreed to sign the EEA enlargement treaty. Liechtenstein reiterated its demand that the Czech Republic and Slovakia acknowledge that the Principality was a sovereign, neutral state through both World Wars. To do so, however, would expose these two countries to the possibility of legal action being brought against them by Liechtenstein for the illegal seizure of land. None the less, Liechtenstein established diplomatic relations with the Czech Republic in September 2009, although the two countries stressed that any resolution of the dispute over the confiscated property would be subject to separate negotiations. In December diplomatic relations with Slovakia were also established. A joint commission of historians was set up in December 2010 to investigate the background to the dispute between Liechtenstein and the Czech Republic.

Liechtenstein also sought damages from Germany for assets that it claimed Germany had improperly awarded to Czechoslovakia after the Second World War as reparations. The German position was that the assets were seized by Czechoslovakia and that Germany was not responsible. In February 2005, however, the ICJ ruled that it was not competent to make a decision on the claim as it predated the 1980 agreement between Liechtenstein and Germany that disputes between them should be settled by the ICJ.

Following a four-year investigation, in April 2005 an Independent Commission of Historians charged with examining Liechtenstein's role in the Second World War reported that no Jewish assets were confiscated and no forced labour was used during the war, and that while 165 refugees from Nazi-controlled Austria were turned away by Liechtenstein between 1933 and 1945, 400 others were taken in and thousands more allowed safe passage to Switzerland. The Commission was appointed by the Government in 2001 after the World Jewish Congress accused the Principality's financial institutions of having hidden plundered Jewish assets for the Nazis during the war.

Liechtenstein's banking secrecy laws were subject to increased international scrutiny in early 2008, following the revelation that the German Federal Intelligence Service had paid some €4m. to a former employee of Liechtenstein's LGT Bank for access to records detailing accounts held by German nationals. It appeared that members of Germany's business élite had avoided tax by channelling up to €4,000m. into secret foundations established by banks in Liechtenstein. The German Government demanded greater financial transparency in Liechtenstein, as well as greater co-operation regarding tax evasion. In the following months, several more countries (including the USA and the United Kingdom) began investigations into allegations of tax evasion through secret bank accounts held in the country. In response to growing international criticism, Prince Alois announced in August that the country would in future endeavour to co-operate more fully on matters pertaining to tax, but that this should not be at the expense of the country's 'culture of privacy'. A bilateral agreement was reached with the USA in December, whereby Liechtenstein would co-operate with investigations into suspected tax evasion, while Liechtenstein banks would benefit from increased access to US financial markets. The month before the April 2009 meeting of the Group of 20 major industrialized and systemically important emerging market nations (G20, see p. 466), Liechtenstein agreed to amend its secrecy laws to allow for greater transparency and to comply with rules on the sharing of bank data set by OECD to combat tax evasion. Consequently, in May OECD removed Liechtenstein from its list of 'unco-operative tax havens', and in November it recognized Liechtenstein as a jurisdiction that had implemented international co-operation standards in tax matters. A bilateral accord was signed with the United Kingdom in August, under which Liechtenstein agreed to shut down the bank accounts of British investors who refused to disclose details of their Liechtenstein-held assets to the British tax authorities; at the same time, however, Liechtenstein offered favourable terms, including limits on penalties, to customers who voluntarily disclosed details of their unpaid tax, in the hope that tax evaders wishing to regularize their status would move their accounts to the country's banks in order to take advantage of the new arrangements. By mid-2012 some 2,400 United Kingdom taxpayers with accounts in Liechtenstein had taken advantage of the disclosure facility, and the British Government hoped to recover some £3,000m. in unpaid tax by the time the scheme expired in April 2016. Liechtenstein was expected to benefit from

an agreement between the United Kingdom and Switzerland, concluded in August 2011, whereby tax evaders who had accounts in Switzerland incurred harsher penalties than those targeted by the United Kingdom's agreement with Liechtenstein; as a result, the culprits were likely to transfer their funds to Liechtenstein before disclosing them. Co-operation between Liechtenstein and the United Kingdom was further strengthened in June 2012 by the signature, for the first time, of a formal double-taxation agreement between the two countries. By February 2013 Liechtenstein had concluded agreements providing for the exchange of tax information with 32 countries and jurisdictions.

CONSTITUTION AND GOVERNMENT

Under the Constitution of 1921 (as amended in 1969, 1984, 2003 and 2005), the monarchy is hereditary in the male line. The Reigning Prince, who is constitutionally responsible for foreign affairs, exercises legislative power jointly with the Landtag (parliament). The Landtag comprises 25 members, who are elected by universal adult suffrage for a term of four years (subject to dissolution), on the basis of proportional representation. The country is divided into the two election districts of Oberland (Upper Country) and Unterland (Lower Country), which elect 15 and 10 members of the Landtag, respectively. A five-member collegial Government is nominated by the Landtag and appointed by the Reigning Prince for a term of four years. Under constitutional changes approved by referendum in 2003, the Reigning Prince is empowered to dismiss governments (even if they retain parliamentary confidence), appoint an interim administration pending an election, approve judicial nominees, veto laws and invoke emergency legislation. Under the same constitutional changes, citizens can force a referendum on any subject, including the future of the monarchy, by collecting 1,500 signatures. On 15 August 2004 the sovereign rights pertaining to the Reigning Prince were transferred to the Hereditary (Crown) Prince, who was to exercise them as the representative of the Reigning Prince, who remained head of state.

REGIONAL AND INTERNATIONAL CO-OPERATION

Liechtenstein has important links with neighbouring Switzerland: the two countries are joined in a customs union, and Switzerland is responsible for Liechtenstein's diplomatic interests in countries where Liechtenstein is not directly represented. Liechtenstein is a member of the European Free Trade Association (EFTA, see p. 461) and participates in the European Economic Area (EEA), which incorporates Liechtenstein (together with Iceland and Norway) into the internal market of the European Union (EU, see p. 281). Liechtenstein became an associate member of the EU's Schengen Agreement on border controls in 2008, and its accession to full membership was completed in December 2011. It is also a member of the Council of Europe (see p. 260) and the Organization for Security and Co-operation in Europe (OSCE, see p. 397).

Liechtenstein joined the UN in 1990 and the World Trade Organization (WTO, see p. 444) in 1995.

ECONOMIC AFFAIRS

In 2009, according to estimates by the World Bank, Liechtenstein's gross national income (GNI), measured at average 2007–09 prices, was US $4,903m., equivalent to $137,070 per head (although as 50% of the work-force was domiciled abroad in 2009, this figure is not comparable with those for other countries). During 2002–11 the population increased at an average annual rate of 0.9%, while Liechtenstein's gross domestic product (GDP) per head increased, in real terms, by an average of 1.7% per year during 2002–09. Overall GDP increased, in real terms, at an average annual rate of 2.6% in 2002–09; GDP declined by 1.2% in 2009.

According to the UN, in 2011 the agricultural sector (together with forestry and fishing) accounted for just 0.8% of GDP. Within the agricultural sector the emphasis is on cattle-breeding, dairy farming and market gardening. The principal crops are maize and potatoes. In addition, wine is produced, and forestry is a significant activity. In 2011 0.8% of those employed in Liechtenstein worked in agriculture (including forestry).

In 2011, according to the UN, industry (including production of goods) contributed some 26.2% of GDP. Some 39.4% of those employed in Liechtenstein worked in industrial activity (including mining and quarrying, processing industries, energy and water supply, and construction) in that year.

According to the UN, in 2011 the manufacturing sector accounted for 18.4% of GDP. In that year 31.1% of those employed in Liechtenstein worked in the manufacturing sector. The principal branches of manufacturing are mechanical engineering, electrical machinery, vehicle components and dental instruments.

In 2011, according to the UN, the construction sector accounted for 5.6% of GDP. In that year 7.2% of those employed in Liechtenstein worked in the construction sector.

In 2011 more than 90% of energy requirements were imported from other countries. In that year electricity supplied 30.3% of energy requirements, natural gas 22.5%, fuel oil 12.8%, motor fuel (petrol) 12.2%, and diesel 10.5%.

According to the UN, in 2011 73.0% of GDP was generated by the services sector. In that year the sector engaged 59.9% of those employed in Liechtenstein. Financial services are of great importance. Numerous foreign corporations, holding companies and foundations (estimated to number about 75,000) have nominal offices in Liechtenstein, benefiting from the Principality's stable political situation, tradition of bank secrecy (although stricter banking legislation has been introduced in recent years, partly to increase the transparency of the sector) and low fiscal charges. Following the Principality's accession to the European Economic Area (EEA) in 1995, the registration of foreign banks was permitted. New legislation governing insurance companies was approved in 1996, and during the late 1990s the insurance sector expanded rapidly. The building and hotel trades and other service industries (including tourism) are also highly developed.

With a very limited domestic market, Liechtenstein's industry is export-orientated. In 2011 total exports (excluding Switzerland) amounted to 3,328.6m. Swiss francs, while imports (excluding Switzerland) totalled 1,965.2m. Swiss francs. Switzerland is the principal trading partner. In 2005 Switzerland purchased 11.7% of total exports of members of the Liechtenstein Chamber of Commerce and Industry and the EEA accounted for 44.1%. In 2011 other important trading partners were Germany, Austria and the USA. In that year principal imports included specialized machinery and electrical products, dental technology, metals and metal products, chemical products, vehicles and transport equipment and food and related products. Principal exports in 2011 included machinery and electrical products, metals and metal products, vehicles and transport equipment, chemical products, and glass, ceramic and textile products.

In 2011, according to official figures, Liechtenstein recorded a visible merchandise trade surplus of 1,363.4m. Swiss francs (excluding Switzerland), while there was a fiscal deficit of 123.0m. Swiss francs. The average annual rate of inflation was 0.5% during 2006–12; consumer prices increased by 0.2% in 2011, but decreased by 0.7% in 2012. Traditionally the unemployment rate has been negligible (0.1% of the active labour force, or some 20 persons, in 1990); however, it rose during the 1990s and the 2000s, and stood at 1.3% in 2011. More than one-third of Liechtenstein's population are resident foreigners, many of whom provide the labour for industry, while in 2011 18,279 workers crossed the borders (51.9% of workers in Liechtenstein), mainly from Austria and Switzerland each day, to work in the Principality.

During the first decade of the 21st century Liechtenstein's reputation as a financial centre and secretive tax haven was challenged by foreign governments aiming to combat money-laundering and tax evasion (see Domestic Political Affairs and Foreign Affairs). The widespread recession that affected most developed countries in 2008–09 increased governments' determination to recover the revenues that were due to them. During 2008–13 Liechtenstein concluded bilateral agreements on the exchange of tax information with more than 30 countries and jurisdictions, including the USA and the United Kingdom. Liechtenstein's recognition by OECD in November 2009 as a jurisdiction that had implemented international co-operation standards in tax matters was widely viewed as an important development in Liechtenstein's standing as a business location.

In May 2010 Liechtenstein adopted reforms aimed at simplifying the country's own tax system and making it more transparent, while simultaneously increasing its compatibility with EU law: the measures, which came into effect on 1 January 2011, included a uniform corporate tax rate of 12.5% and the abolition of capital gains, inheritance and gift taxes. As a result, the Government expected to receive an additional 66m. Swiss francs in revenue in 2011. It was hoped that the reforms would enhance the attractiveness of Liechtenstein for investors and encourage sustainable growth. In August 2010 the Government introduced revisions to legislation concerning the financial markets, so as to ensure that Liechtenstein's practices would be consistent with international standards. In response to the impact of the ongoing debt crisis in the eurozone and the country's increasing fiscal deficit, the Government implemented a number of austerity measures in 2010–12, including reductions in expenditure on social welfare and health care, and a lowering of state subsidies to the pension system. Following the economic contraction recorded in 2009, there were signs of modest recovery in 2010 and 2011, with GDP returning to positive growth. However, it was estimated that the economy had entered decline once more in 2012, prompting the Government of Dr Tschütscher to propose the expansion of the austerity programme.

PUBLIC HOLIDAYS

2014: 1 January (New Year's Day), 2 January (St Berchtold's Day), 6 January (Epiphany), 2 February (Candlemas), 4 March (Shrove Tuesday), 19 March (St Joseph's Day), 18 April (Good Friday), 21 April (Easter Monday), 1 May (Labour Day), 29 May (Ascension Day), 9 June (Whit Monday), 19 June (Corpus Christi), 15 August (National Holiday and Assumption), 8 September (Nativity of the Virgin Mary), 1 November (All Saints' Day), 8 December (Immaculate Conception), 25 December (Christmas Day), 26 December (St Stephen's Day).

Statistical Survey

Source: Amt für Statistik, Gerberweg 5, 9490 Vaduz; tel. 2366111; fax 2366895; e-mail info.statistik@avw.llv.li; internet www.as.llv.li.

AREA AND POPULATION

Area: 160.5 sq km (62.0 sq miles).

Population: (at 30 June 2012) 36,636 (Liechtensteiners 24,425).

Density (at 30 June 2012): 228.3 per sq km.

Population by Age and Sex (at 30 June 2012): *0–14:* 5,722 (males 2,933, females 2,789); *15–64:* 25,565 (males 12,803, females 12,762); *65 and over:* 5,349 (males 2,387, females 2,962); *Total* 36,636 (males 18,123, females 18,513).

Municipalities (population at 30 June 2012): Schaan 5,914; Vaduz (capital) 5,241; Triesen 4,862; Balzers 4,542; Eschen 4,269; Mauren 4,054; Triesenberg 2,610; Ruggell 2,060; Gamprin 1,620; Schellenberg 1,027; Planken 437; *Total* 36,636.

Births, Marriages and Deaths (2011): Live births 395 (10.9 per 1,000); Marriages 324 (8.9 per 1,000); Deaths 248 (6.8 per 1,000).

Economically Active Population (2011): Agriculture and forestry 277; Industry and skilled trades 13,875 (Mining and quarrying 48, Manufacturing 10,950, Energy and water supply 348, Construction 2,529); Services 21,101 (Retail, repairs, etc. 2,570, Hotels and restaurants 986, Transport and communications 1,800, Banking and insurance 3,223, Real estate, information, business and support services, etc. 3,505, Legal consultancy and trust management 2,579, Public administration 1,788, Education 1,215, Health and social services 2,013, Other services—incl. activities of extraterritorial organizations—1,422); *Total employed* 35,253; Unemployed 463; *Total labour force* 35,716.

HEALTH AND WELFARE

Key Indicators

Under-5 Mortality Rate (per 1,000 live births, 2004): 5.

Physicians (per 1,000 head, 1997): 1.31 (Source: Statistik des Fürstentums Liechtenstein, *Statistisches Jahrbuch—1998*).

For sources (unless specified) and definitions, see explanatory note on p. vi.

AGRICULTURE, ETC.

Note: Figures are for farms with a minimum of either 1 ha of arable land, 30 acres of specialized cultivation, 10 acres of protected cultivation, 8 sows, 80 porkers (or capacity for 80 porkers) or 300 head of poultry, and where livestock owners are covered by the *Tierseuchenfond* (insurance against epidemics).

Principal Crops (metric tons, 1987): Wheat 460; Oats 4; Barley 416; Silo-maize 27,880. *2010:* Potatoes 7,751. *2011* (FAO estimate): Grapes 191 (Source: partly FAO).

Livestock (2011): Cattle 5,993; Pigs 1,690; Horses 489; Sheep 3,656; Goats 434; Hens 12,729.

Dairy Produce (2010, metric tons): Milk delivered to dairies 13,493; Milk for consumption and pasteurization 1,045; Milk for processing 6,159; Cream 1,395; Yoghurt 649.

Forestry ('000 cubic metres, 2011): Roundwood removals (excl. bark) 26.0 (Sawlogs, veneer logs and logs for sleepers 8, Fuel wood 18). Source: FAO.

FINANCE

Currency and Exchange Rates: Swiss currency: 100 Rappen (centimes) = 1 Franken (Swiss franc). *Sterling, Dollar and Euro Equivalents* (31 December 2012): £1 sterling = 1.446 Franken; US $1 = 0.917 Franken; €1 = 1.209 Franken; 10 Franken = £6.91 = $10.90 = €8.27. For average exchange rate, see chapter on Switzerland.

Budget (million Swiss francs, 2010): *Revenue:* Current 1,095 (Taxes and duties 750; Revenues from assets 275); Capital 19; Total 1,114. *Expenditure:* Current 1,053 (Social welfare 231; Finance and taxation 332); Capital 77; Total 1,130. *2011* (million Swiss francs): Total revenue 1,153 (Current 1,108, Capital 45); Total expenditure 1,276 (Current 1,216, Capital 60).

Cost of Living (Consumer Price Index; base: December 2005 = 100, annual averages): All items 103.9 in 2010; 104.1 in 2011; 103.4 in 2012.

Gross Domestic Product (million Swiss francs at current prices, official estimates): 5,504 in 2008; 4,901 in 2009; 5,329 in 2010.

Expenditure on the Gross Domestic Product (million Swiss francs at current prices, 2011): Government final consumption expenditure 610.7; Private final consumption expenditure 3,150.8; Increase in stocks 19.2; Gross fixed capital formation 1,120.7; *Total domestic expenditure* 4,901.4; Exports of goods and services 2,812.4; *Less* Imports of goods and services 2,221.0; *GDP in purchasers' values* 5,492.7 (Source: UN, National Accounts Main Aggregates Database).

Gross Domestic Product by Economic Activity (million Swiss francs at current prices, 2011): Agriculture, forestry and fishing 44.7; Mining and utilities 127.2; Manufacturing 1,058.9; Construction 322.5; Retail trade and hotel and restaurants 1,104.2; Transport, storage and communication 451.8; Other services 2,650.7; *Total gross value added* 5,760.1; Net of taxes on products −267.3 (figure obtained as residual); *GDP in purchasers' values* 5,492.7 (Source: UN, National Accounts Main Aggregates Database).

EXTERNAL TRADE

Note: Imports and exports to and from Liechtenstein presented at Swiss customs, not including trade with Switzerland and goods traffic via Switzerland.

Principal Commodities ('000 Swiss francs, 2011): *Imports:* Food, animals and other products of agriculture 64,849; Raw materials, metals, construction and chemical products 163,787; Vehicles and transport equipment 108,785; Machinery and electrical products 655,627; Metal manufactures and other finished and semi-finished goods 493,173; Glass, ceramic and textile manufactures 161,985; Total (incl. others) 1,965,161. *Exports:* Food, animals and other products of agriculture 228,680; Raw materials, metals, construction and chemical products 288,980; Vehicles and transport equipment 409,108; Machinery and electrical products 1,359,260; Metal manu-

factures and other finished and semi-finished goods 615,965; Glass, ceramic and textile manufactures 231,847; Total (incl. others) 3,328,595.

Principal Trading Partners ('000 Swiss francs, 2011): *Imports:* Austria 737,292; China, People's Republic 43,864; France 36,709; Germany 732,764; Italy 72,681; Netherlands 33,259; Philippines 21,310; Poland 24,472; United Kingdom 28,429; USA 49,095; Total (incl. others) 1,965,161. *Exports:* Australia 34,302; Austria 360,250; China, People's Republic 165,877; France 286,825; Germany 803,966; Hong Kong 52,442; India 42,499; Italy 154,362; Japan 56,250; Mexico 44,257; Russia 56,198; Singapore 63,626; Spain 66,506; Sweden 47,335; Taiwan 52,048; United Arab Emirates 38,898; United Kingdom 88,634; USA 379,463; Total (incl. others) 3,328,595.

TRANSPORT

Road Traffic (registered motor vehicles, 1 July 2011): Passenger cars 27,327; Commercial vehicles 3,788; Motorcycles 3,753; Total (incl. others) 35,867. *2012* (at 1 July): Passenger cars 28,004; Total (incl. others) 36,915.

TOURISM

Arrivals by Country of Residence (arrivals at accommodation establishments, 2011): Austria 2,709; France 1,541; Germany 18,220; Italy 2,119; Switzerland 23,508; United Kingdom 2,613; USA 2,097; Total (incl. others) 72,849. Note: Total includes 5,863 residents of Liechtenstein.

COMMUNICATIONS MEDIA

Telephones (2011): 19,600 main lines in use.

Mobile Cellular Telephones (2011): 37,000 subscribers.

Internet Users (2009): 23,000.

Broadband Subscribers (2011): 26,000.

Source: International Telecommunication Union.

EDUCATION

(2007/08, unless otherwise indicated*)

Kindergarten: 49 classrooms; 79 teachers (males 1, females 78); 711 pupils (males 371, females 340). *2009/10:* 80 teachers; 748 pupils.

Primary†: 138 classrooms; 262 teachers (males 63, females 199); 2,073 pupils (males 1,035, females 1,038). *2009/10:* 262 teachers; 2,067 pupils.

High School: 34 classrooms; 101 teachers (males 45, females 56); 412 pupils (males 221, females 191). *2009/10:* 99 teachers; 396 pupils.

Secondary: 45 classrooms; 127 teachers (males 60, females 67); 732 pupils (males 380, females 352). *2009/10:* 122 teachers; 861 pupils.

Optional 10th School Year: 5 classrooms; 19 teachers (males 10, females 9); 78 pupils (males 32, females 46). *2009/10:* 17 teachers; 72 pupils.

Vocational Training: 8 classrooms; 16 teachers (males 8, females 8); 124 pupils (males 84, females 40).

Grammar Schools (2004/05, unless otherwise indicated): 38 classrooms (2001/02); 103 teachers; 744 pupils.

Music (2004/05): 91 teachers; 2,519 pupils.

Higher Education (2004/05)‡: 527 students.

Pupil-teacher Ratio (primary education, UNESCO estimate): 6.1 in 2009/10 (Source: UNESCO Institute for Statistics).

* Excluding private institutions.
† Including pre-school and reception classes.
‡ Those studying in Liechtenstein only (931 students attended institutions abroad).

Directory

The Government

HEAD OF STATE

Reigning Prince: HSH Prince HANS-ADAM II (succeeded 13 November 1989).

On 15 August 2004 Prince Hans-Adam II transferred the execution of his sovereign powers to his son, Hereditary Prince Alois.

GOVERNMENT
(May 2013)

A coalition of the Fortschrittliche Bürgerpartei (FBP—Progressive Citizens' Party) and the Vaterländische Union (VU—Patriotic Union).

Prime Minister and Minister of General Government Affairs, and of Finance: ADRIAN HASLER (FBP).

Deputy Prime Minister and Minister of Economic Affairs, of Justice and of Home Affairs: Dr THOMAS ZWIEFELHOFER (VU).

Minister of Infrastructure, of the Environment and of Sports: MARLIES AMANN-MARXER (VU).

Minister of Social Affairs: Dr MAURO PEDRAZZINI (FBP).

Minister of Foreign Affairs, of Education and of Cultural Affairs: Dr AURELIA FRICK (FBP).

Alternate Ministers: GEORG WOHLWEND (FBP), ROLAND MOSER (VU), ANDREA KLEIN (VU), CARMEN ZANGHELLINI-PFEIFFER (FBP), ISABEL DONHAUSER-FRICK (FBP).

GOVERNMENT OFFICES

Regierungsgebäude: Regierungsgebäude, Peter-Kaiser-Pl. 1, Postfach 684, 9490 Vaduz; tel. 2366111; fax 2366022; e-mail info@regierung.li; internet www.liechtenstein.li.

Legislature

LANDTAG

Landtagssekretariat des Fürstentums Liechtenstein: Peter-Kaiser-Pl. 3, Postfach 684, 9490 Vaduz; tel. 2366571; fax 2366580; e-mail info@landtag.li; internet www.landtag.li.

President: ALBERT FRICK.

Vice-President: VIOLANDA LANTER-KOLLER.

General Election, 1 and 3 February 2013

Party	Votes*	% of votes	Seats
Fortschrittliche Bürgerpartei (FBP) .	77,644	40.0	10
Vaterländische Union (VU) . . .	65,118	33.5	8
Die Unabhängigen (DU)‡ .	29,739	15.3	4
Freie Liste (FL) . . .	21,604	11.1	3
Total	194,105	100.00	25

* Each elector was permitted to vote for as many candidates as there were seats allocated to the respective electoral district (15 in Oberland and 10 in Unterland). The total number of valid ballots cast was 14,471.

‡ A group of Independent candidates.

Election Commissions

Hauptwahl- oder Hauptabstimmungskommission Oberland: c/o Postfach 684, 9490 Vaduz; independent; Chair. BECK HEINZ.

Hauptwahl- oder Hauptabstimmungskommission Unterland: c/o Postfach 684, 9490 Vaduz; independent; Chair. ELKUCH ROLAND.

Political Organizations

Fortschrittliche Bürgerpartei (FBP) (Progressive Citizens' Party): Aeulestr. 56, Postfach 1213, 9490 Vaduz; tel. 2377940; fax 2377949; e-mail anita.frick@fbp.li; internet www.fbp.li; f. 1918; Pres. ALEXANDER BATLINER.

Freie Liste (FL) (Free List): Landstr. 140, 9494 Schaan; tel. 2311731; fax 2311733; e-mail info@freieliste.li; internet www.freieliste.li; f. 1985; social democratic and ecological party; Pres. WOLFGANG MARXER.

Vaterländische Union (VU) (Patriotic Union): Fürst-Franz-Josef-Str. 13, 9490 Vaduz; tel. 2398282; fax 2398289; e-mail vu@vu-online.li; internet www.vu-online.li; f. 1936 by merger of the People's Party (f. 1918) and the Heimatdienst movement; Pres. JAKOB BÜCHEL; Sec.-Gen. MARTINA BÜCHEL.

Diplomatic Representation

According to an arrangement concluded in 1919, Switzerland has agreed to represent Liechtenstein's interests in countries where it has diplomatic missions and where Liechtenstein is not represented in its own right. In so doing, Switzerland always acts only on the basis of mandates of a general or specific nature, which it may either refuse or accept, while Liechtenstein is free to enter into direct relations with foreign states or to establish its own additional missions. Liechtenstein has nine diplomatic missions abroad, comprising embassies in Berlin (Germany), Bern (Switzerland), Brussels (Belgium, including a permanent mission to the European Union), Washington, DC (USA) and Vienna (Austria, including permanent missions to the Organization for Security and Co-operation in Europe and the UN), as well as a non-resident ambassador to the Holy See, a permanent representative to the Council of Europe in Strasbourg (France), a permanent mission to the UN in New York (USA) and a permanent mission in Geneva (Switzerland).

Judicial System

The Constitution of Liechtenstein provides for an independent judiciary. Jurisdiction in civil and criminal matters is exercised in the first instance by the *Landgericht* (County Court), on appeal by the *Obergericht* (Superior Court) and in the third and last instance by the *Oberster Gerichtshof* (Supreme Court). Cases involving major crime are heard at the *Kriminalgericht* (Criminal Court). Public law cases are heard by the *Staatsgerichtshof* (State Court) and the *Verwaltungsgerichtshof* (Administrative Court of Appeal).

CIVIL AND CRIMINAL COURTS

Landgericht (County Court): Spaniagasse 1, 9490 Vaduz; tel. 2367159; fax 2366539; internet www.gerichte.li; e-mail benedikt.marxer@lg.liv.li; Court of First Instance; 1 presiding judge, and 13 other judges; Presiding Judge Dr PAUL MEIER.

Kriminalgericht (Criminal Court): 9490 Vaduz; bench of 5 judges; Presiding Judge Lic. Iur. DIETMAR BAUR.

Schöffengericht (Court of Assizes): 9490 Vaduz; for minor misdemeanours; bench of 3 judges; Presiding Judge Dr THOMAS SCHMID.

Jugendgericht (Juvenile Court): 9490 Vaduz; bench of 3 judges; Presiding Judge Lic. Iur. NICOLE NETZER.

Obergericht (Superior Court): 9490 Vaduz; internet www.gerichte.li; Court of Second Instance; divided into 3 senates, each with bench of 5 judges; Presiding Judge Lic. Iur. RUDOLF FEHR.

Oberster Gerichtshof (Supreme Court): 9490 Vaduz; internet www.gerichte.li; Court of Third Instance; bench of 5 judges; Presiding Judge Dr GERT DELLE-KARTH.

ADMINISTRATIVE COURTS

Verwaltungsgerichtshof (Administrative Court of Appeal): Peter-Kaiser Pl. 1, 9490 Vaduz; tel. 2366111; appeal against decrees and decisions of the Government may be made to this court; 5 members; Presiding Judge Lic. Iur. ANDREAS BATLINER.

Staatsgerichtshof (State Court): Städtle 36, Postfach 729, 9490 Vaduz; tel. 2391010; fax 2391039; e-mail kontakt@stgh.li; internet www.stgh.li; 5 members; exists for the protection of Public Law; Presiding Judge Lic. Iur. MARZELL BECK.

Religion

CHRISTIANITY

The Principality comprises a single archdiocese of the Roman Catholic Church, Vaduz, created in 1997, which is directly responsible to the Holy See. At 31 December 2006 there were an estimated 26,800 Roman Catholics (some 78.8% of the population). The few Protestants (7.3%) belong to the parish of Vaduz.

Archdiocese of Vaduz: Erzbischöfliche Kanzlei, Fürst-Franz-Josef-Str. 112, Postfach 103, 9490 Vaduz; tel. 2332311; fax 2332324; e-mail erzbistum@powersurf.li; internet www.erzbistum-vaduz.li; f. 1997; Archbishop Most Rev. WOLFGANG HAAS.

The Press

Exclusiv: Aubündt 28, 9490 Vaduz; tel. 2328080; fax 2328081; e-mail info@exclusiv.li; internet www.exclusiv.li; f. 1996; monthly; Publr ALBERT MENNEL.

Liechtensteiner Vaterland: Austr. 81, Postfach 884, 9490 Vaduz; tel. 2361616; fax 2361617; e-mail redaktion@vaterland.li; internet www.vaterland.li; f. 1913; publ. by Vaduzer Medienhaus AG; daily (Mon.–Sat.); organ of the VU; Editor-in-Chief GÜNTHER FRITZ; circ. 10,295.

Liechtensteiner Volksblatt: Im alten Riet 103, 9494 Schaan; tel. 2375151; fax 2375155; e-mail redaktion@volksblatt.li; internet www .volksblatt.li; f. 1878; daily (Mon.–Sat.); organ of the FBP; Editor-in-Chief HEINZ ZÖCHBAUER; circ. 9,000.

Liewo Sonntagszeitung: Austr. 81, 9490 Vaduz; tel. 2361616; fax 2361617; e-mail redaktion@liewo.li; internet www.liewo.li; f. 1993 as *Liechtensteiner Wochenzeitung*; publ. by Vaduzer Medienhaus AG; weekly (Sun.); Editor-in-Chief MICHAEL WINKLER; circ. 32,000.

Wirtschaft Regional: Austr. 81, 9490 Vaduz; tel. 2361616; fax 2361617; e-mail info@wirtschaftregional.li; internet www .wirtschaftregional.li; f. 2001; weekly; publ. by Vaduzer Medienhaus AG; Editor-in-Chief MATTHIAS HASSLER.

PRESS AGENCY

Presse- und Informationsamt (PIA) (Press and Information Office): St Florinsgasse 3, Postfach 684, 9490 Vaduz; tel. 2366721; fax 2366460; internet www.ikr.llv.li; f. 1962; Dir DANIELA CLAVA-DETSCHER.

Publishers

Alpenland Verlag AG: Feldkircher Str. 13, 9494 Schaan; tel. 2395030; fax 2395031; e-mail office@buchzentrum.li; internet www .buchzentrum.li; Man. Dir MARCO NESCHER.

BONAFIDES Verlags-Anstalt: Auring 52, 9490 Vaduz; tel. 2654680; fax 3900594; e-mail bva-fl@adon.li.

BVD Druck+Verlag AG: Landstr. 153, 9494 Schaan; tel. 2361836; fax 2361840; e-mail bvd@bvd.li; internet www.bvd.li; Pres. KURT GÖPPEL.

van Eck Verlag: Haldenweg 8, 9495 Triesen; tel. 3923000; fax 3922277; e-mail info@vaneckverlag.li; internet www.vaneckverlag .li; f. 1982; art, local interest, juvenile, golf, crime fiction; Man. Dirs FRANK P. VAN ECK, PETER GÖPPEL.

Ex Jure Verlagsanstalt: Aeulestr. 74, Postfach 86, 9490 Vaduz; tel. 2360404; fax 2360481; e-mail service@exjure.li; internet www.exjure .net; f. 1968; legal.

A. R. Gantner Verlag KG: Industriestr. 26, Postfach 131, 9491 Ruggell; tel. 3771808; fax 3771802; e-mail bgc@adon.li; internet www .gantner-verlag.com; f. 1966; botany; Dir BRUNI GANTNER-CAPLAN.

GMG Verlag AG: Landstr. 30, 9494 Schaan; tel. 2381166; fax 2381160; e-mail info@gmg.biz; internet www.gmg.biz; f. 1990; Man. Dir ARTHUR GASSNER.

Lehrmittelverlag: Pflugstr. 30, 9490 Vaduz; tel. 2366390; fax 2366391; e-mail lehrmittelverlag@schulen.li; educational materials.

Verlag der Liechtensteinischen Akademischen Gesellschaft (LAG): In der Fina 26, Postfach 829, 9494 Schaan; tel. 2323028; fax 2331449; e-mail info@verlag-lag.li; internet www.verlag-lag.li; f. 1972; Dir NORBERT JANSEN.

Liechtenstein-Verlag AG: Landstr. 30, 9494 Schaan; tel. 2396010; fax 2396019; e-mail books@liechtensteinverlag.com; internet www .liechtensteinverlag.com; f. 1946; belles-lettres, legal and scientific books; agents for international literature; Man. ARTHUR GASSNER.

Litag Anstalt—Literarische, Medien und Künstler Agentur: Industriestr. 26A, Postfach 131, 9491 Ruggell; tel. 3771808; fax 3771802; e-mail bgc@adon.li; f. 1956; Dir BRUNI GANTNER-CAPLAN.

MM-Verlag Buchhandlung Irmgard Meier: Pradafant 20, 9490 Vaduz; tel. 2329448; fax 2329449; e-mail mm.verlag@buchhandlung .li.

Sändig Reprint Verlag Wohlwend: Am Schrägen Weg 12, 9490 Vaduz; tel. 2323627; fax 2323649; e-mail saendig@adon.li; internet www.saendig.com; f. 1981; natural sciences, linguistics, free-masonry, fiction, folklore, music, history; Dir CHRISTIAN WOHLWEND.

Topos Verlag AG: Industriestr. 26, 9491 Ruggell; tel. 3771111; fax 3771119; e-mail topos@supra.net; internet www.topos.li; f. 1977; law, politics, literature, social science, periodicals; Dir GRAHAM A. P. SMITH.

Broadcasting and Communications

REGULATORY AUTHORITY

Amt für Kommunikation: Gerberweg 5, Postfach 684, 9490 Vaduz; tel. 2366488; fax 2366489; e-mail info@ak.llv.li; internet www.ak.llv .li; f. 1999; national regulatory authority; Dir KURT BÜHLER.

TELECOMMUNICATIONS

Mobilkom Liechtenstein AG: Äulestr. 20, 9490 Vaduz; tel. 7970077; fax 7970099; e-mail info@mobilkom.li; internet www.fl1 .li; f. 2000; mobile cellular telephone operator; Man. Dir MICHAEL AMMANN.

Orange Liechtenstein AG: Neugrüt 7, 9496 Balzers; f. 2000; subsidiary of Orange France; mobile cellular telecommunications services.

Telecom Liechtenstein AG: Schaanerstr. 1, 9490 Vaduz; tel. 2377400; fax 2377499; e-mail telecom@telecom.li; internet www .telecom.li; f. 1999; fixed-line and mobile cellular telecommunications, broadband internet access, digital television; Pres. CHRISTIAN WOLF.

BROADCASTING

Radio Liechtenstein: Dorfstr. 24, 9495 Triesen; tel. 3991313; fax 3991366; e-mail admin@radio.li; internet www.radio.li; f. 1995; Pres. CLEMENS LATERNSER; Editor-in-Chief MARTIN FROMMELT.

Finance

(cap. = capital; res = reserves; dep. = deposits; m. = million; brs = branches; amounts in Swiss francs)

REGULATORY AUTHORITY

Finanzmarktaufsicht Liechtenstein (FMA) (Financial Market Authority of Liechtenstein): Landstr. 109, Postfach 279, 9490 Vaduz; tel. 2367373; fax 2367374; e-mail info@fma-li.li; internet www.fma-li .li; f. 2005; independent authority under the auspices of the Landtag; supervises and executes legislation related to financial markets; Pres. URS PHILIPP ROTH-CUONY; CEO MARIO GASSNER.

BANKING

In mid-2010 there were 14 banks in Liechtenstein.

Bank Alpinum AG: Städtle 17, 9490 Vaduz; tel. 2396211; fax 2396221; e-mail info@bankalpinum.com; internet www .bankalpinum.com; fmrly NewCenturyBank, renamed as above April 2006; Chair. WOLFGANG SEEGER; CEO URBAN B. EBERLE.

Bank Frick & Co. AG: Landstr. 14, Postfach 43, 9496 Balzers; tel. 3882121; fax 3882122; e-mail bank@bfc.li; internet www.bfc.li; Chair. MARIO FRICK, Sr; CEO JÜRGEN FRICK.

Bank Vontobel (Liechtenstein) AG: Pflugstr. 20, Postfach 786, 9490 Vaduz; tel. 2364111; fax 2364112; e-mail postmaster@vontobel .li; internet www.vontobel.li; f. 2000; Chair. Dr URS WIDMER; CEO HERBERT J. SCHEIDT.

Banque Pasche (Liechtenstein) SA: Austr. 61, Postfach 832, 9490 Vaduz; tel. 2393333; fax 2393300; e-mail pasche.liechtenstein@ pasche.li; internet www.pasche.li; fmrly Swissfirst Bank (Liechtenstein) AG; 52.5 % owned by Banque Pasche CM-CIC Private Banking (Switzerland); Chair. JEAN-FRANÇOIS KURZ; CEO DANIEL BRÜHWILER.

Centrum Bank AG: Kirchstr. 3, Postfach 1168, 9490 Vaduz; tel. 2383838; fax 2383839; e-mail info@centrumbank.com; internet www .centrumbank.com; f. 1993; cap. 20m., res 10m., dep. 1,598.8m. (Dec. 2011); Chair. Dr PETER MARXER; CEO STEPHAN HÄBERLE.

EFG Bank von Ernst AG: Egertastr. 10, Postfach 112, 9490 Vaduz; tel. 2655353; fax 2655363; e-mail info@bve.li; internet www.bve.li; wholly owned by EFG Bank (Switzerland); name changed as above in 2009; cap. 25m., res 2.5m., dep. 166.1m. (Dec. 2011); Chair. JEAN-PIERRE CUONI; CEO ERNST WEDER.

Kaiser Partner Privatbank AG: Herrengasse 23, 9490 Vaduz; tel. 2378000; fax 2378001; e-mail bank@kaiserpartner.com; internet www.kaiserritterpartner.com; f. 1999; name changed as above in 2011; cap. 10m., res 40.1m., dep. 493.6m. (Dec. 2011); Exec. Chair. FRITZ KAISER; CEO Dr THOMAS TRAUTH.

LGT Bank Ltd (LGT): Herrengasse 12, Postfach 85, 9490 Vaduz; tel. 2351122; fax 2351522; e-mail info@lgt.com; internet www.lgt .com; f. 1920; present name adopted 1996; cap. 291.2m., res 2,145m., dep. 18,502.5m. (Dec. 2011); Group CEO HSH Prince MAXIMILIAN.

Liechtensteinische Landesbank AG (State Bank): Städtle 44, Postfach 384, 9490 Vaduz; tel. 2368811; fax 2368822; e-mail llb@llb .li; internet www.llb.li; f. 1861; present name adopted 1955; cap. 154m., res –208.4m., dep. 16,658.7m. (Dec. 2011); Chair., Bd of Dirs Dr HANS-WERNER GASSNER; Chair., Management Bd Dr JOSEF FEHR; 4 brs.

Neue Bank AG: Marktgass 20, Postfach 1533, 9490 Vaduz; tel. 2360808; fax 2329260; e-mail info@neuebankag.li; internet www .neuebankag.li; f. 1992; cap. 40m., res 75.6m., dep. 1,000.3m. (Dec. 2011); Chair. GEORG VOGT.

Raiffeisen Privatbank Liechtenstein AG: Austr. 51, Postfach 1621, 9490 Vaduz; tel. 2370707; fax 2370777; e-mail info@raiffeisen .li; internet www.raiffeisen.li; f. 1998; name changed as above in

2011; cap. 20m., res 3.4m., dep. 385.9m (Dec. 2011); Chair. GÜNTHER DAPUNT.

Valartis Bank (Liechtenstein) AG: Schaaner Str. 27, 9487 Gamprin-Bendern; tel. 2655656; fax 2655699; e-mail info@valartis.li; internet www.valartis.li; f. 1998 as Hypo Investment Bank (Liechtenstein); cap. 20m., res 11.6m., dep. 710.9m (Dec. 2011); renamed 2009 following takeover by Valartis Group AG; CEO, Management Bd Dr ANDREAS INSAM.

Verwaltungs- und Privat-Bank AG (VP Bank): Aeulestr. 6, 9490 Vaduz; tel. 2356655; fax 2356500; e-mail info@vpbank.com; internet www.vpbank.com; f. 1956; cap. 59.1m., res −59.9m., dep. 1,284.2m. (Dec. 2011); Chair. HANS BRUNHART; CEO ROGER H. HARTMANN; 9 brs.

Volksbank AG: Feldkircher Str. 2, 9494 Schaan; tel. 2390404; fax 2390405; e-mail info@volksbank.li; internet www.volksbank.li; f. 1997; Man. Dir STEFAN WOLF.

Bankers' Association

Liechtensteinischer Bankenverband: Austr. 46, Postfach 254, 9490 Vaduz; tel. 2301323; fax 2301324; e-mail info@bankenverband.li; internet www.bankenverband.li; f. 1969; Pres. ADOLF E. REAL; Dir SIMON TRIBELHORN; 14 mems.

INSURANCE

In 2011 there were 40 insurance companies in Liechtenstein.

Fortuna Lebens-Versicherungs-AG: Städtle 35, 9490 Vaduz; tel. 2361545; fax 2361546; e-mail fl.service@fortuna.li; internet www.fortuna.li; f. 1996; Man. Dir HEINER KEIL.

Liechtensteinische AHV-IV-FAK: Gerberweg 2, Postfach 84, 9490 Vaduz; tel. 2381616; fax 2381600; e-mail ahv@ahv.li; internet www.ahv.li; state-owned; Chair. PETER WOLFF; Dir WALTER KAUFMANN.

Swiss Life (Liechtenstein) AG: In der Specki 3, 9494 Schaan; tel. 3777000; fax 3777099; e-mail slpp@swisslife.com; internet www.swisslife.li; absorbed CapitalLeben Versicherung AG in 2007; life insurance.

Transmarine Insurance Co Ltd: Egertastr. 17, 9490 Vaduz; tel. 2334488; fax 2334489; f. 1996.

Valorlife Lebensversicherungs-AG: Heiligkreuz 43, 9490 Vaduz; tel. 3992950; fax 3992959; e-mail info@valorlife.com; internet www.valorlife.com; f. 1997; subsidiary of Vaudoise Versicherungsgruppe (Switzerland); Pres. ROLF MEHR; Dir SERGE HEDIGER.

Insurance Association

Liechtensteinischer Versicherungsverband eV (LVV): Austr. 46, Postfach 445, 9490 Vaduz; tel. 2374777; fax 2374778; e-mail office@lvv.li; internet www.versicherungsverband.li; f. 1998; Pres. MARKUS BRUGGER; 25 mems.

Trade and Industry

CHAMBER OF COMMERCE

Liechtensteinische Industrie- und Handelskammer (Liechtenstein Chamber of Commerce and Industry): Altenbach 8, 9490 Vaduz; tel. 2375511; fax 2375512; e-mail info@lihk.li; internet www.lihk.li; f. 1947; Pres. KLAUS RISCH; Gen. Man. JOSEF BECK; 40 mems.

INDUSTRIAL ASSOCIATION

Vereinigung Bäuerlicher Organisationen im Fürstentum Liechtenstein (VBO) (Agricultural Union): Duxweg 14, Postfach 351, 9494 Mauren; tel. 3759050; fax 3759051; e-mail vbo@kba.li; Pres. THOMAS BÜCHEL.

UTILITIES

Electricity

Liechtenstein imported some 91% of its electricity in 2009, mainly from Switzerland.

Liechtensteinische Kraftwerke (LKW): Im alten Riet 17, 9494 Schaan; tel. 2360111; fax 2360112; e-mail lkw@lkw.li; internet www.lkw.li; Pres. PATRIK OEHRI; Dir-Gen. GERALD MARXER.

Gas

Liechtensteinische Gasversorgung (LGV): Im Rietacker 4, 9494 Schaan; tel. 2361555; fax 2361566; e-mail lgv@lgv.li; internet www.lgv.li; f. 1985; Dir SILVAN KIEBER.

Water

Gruppenwasserversorgung Liechtensteiner Oberland (GWO): supplies water to Balzers, Planken, Schaan, Triesen, Triesenberg and Vaduz.

Wasserversorgung Liechtensteiner Unterland (WLU): Industriestr. 36, 9487 Gamprin-Bendern; tel. 3732555; fax 3732575; e-mail info@wlu.li; supplies water to Eschen, Gamprin, Mauren, Ruggell, and Schellenberg; Pres. DONATH OEHRI.

TRADE UNIONS

Liechtensteinischer ArbeitnehmerInnenverband (LANV) (Employees' Asscn): Dorfstr. 24, 9495 Triesen; tel. 3993838; fax 3993839; e-mail info@lanv.li; internet www.lanv.li; Pres. SIGI LANGENBAHN; Sec. CHRISTINE SCHÄDLER; 1,200 mems.

Liechtensteinische Ingenieur- und Architektenvereinigung (Engineers' and Architects' Asscn): Postfach 323, 9490 Vaduz; tel. 3751728; fax 3751729; e-mail office@lia.li; internet www.lia.li; Pres. HANSJÖRG VOGT; 153 mems.

Wirtschaftskammer Liechtenstein: Zollstr. 23, 9494 Schaan; tel. 2377788; fax 2377789; e-mail info@wirtschaftskammer.li; internet www.wirtschaftskammer.li; f. 1936; aims to protect the interests of Liechtenstein artisans and tradespeople; Pres. MATT ARNOLD; Gen. Man. JÜRGEN NIGG; 3,000 mems.

Transport

RAILWAYS

Liechtenstein is traversed by some 18.5 km of railway track, which is administered by Austrian Federal Railways. There is a station at Nendeln, as well as two halts at Schaan and Schaanwald. A local 9.5-km service connects Feldkirch in Austria and Buchs in Switzerland via Liechtenstein, and the Arlberg Express (Paris, France, to Vienna, Austria) passes through the Principality.

ROADS

Modern roads connect the capital, Vaduz, with all the towns and villages in the Principality. There are approximately 250 km of roads, all of which are paved. The Rhine and Samina valleys are connected by a tunnel 740 m long. Public transport is provided by a well-developed network of postal buses.

LIEmobil (Verkehrbetrieb LIECHTENSTEINmobil): Postpl. 7, Postfach 459, 9494 Schaan; tel. 2379494; fax 2366311; e-mail info@liemobil.li; internet www.liemobil.li; operates 39 buses on 15 routes over 105 km; Man. Dir ULRICH FEISST.

INLAND WATERWAYS

A canal of 26 km, irrigating the Rhine valley, was opened in 1943.

Tourism

Liechtenstein has an Alpine setting in the Upper Rhine area. The principal tourist attractions include a renowned postal museum, a National Museum and the Liechtenstein State Art Collection at Vaduz, as well as the Prince's castle (although this is closed to the public) and two ruined medieval fortresses at Schellenberg. Annually about two-fifths of foreign tourists visit the winter sports resort at Malbun, in the south-east of the Principality. For summer visitors there are some 400 km of hiking trails and an extensive network of cycling paths. In 2011 the number of foreign guests staying in accommodation establishments was 66,986.

Liechtenstein Tourismus: Postfach 139, Städtle 37, 9490 Vaduz; tel. 2396300; fax 2396301; e-mail info@tourismus.li; internet www.tourismus.li; Dir ROLAND BÜCHEL.

Defence

Although Liechtensteiners under the age of 60 years are liable to military service in an emergency, there has been no standing army since 1868 and there is only a small police force, with some 80 officers.

Education

Pre-primary education starts at the age of four and continues until the age of six. It is not compulsory and is provided free of charge. Compulsory education begins at six years of age. Basic instruction is given for five years at a primary school (*Primarschule*) until the age of 11, after which a pupil may transfer to a lower secondary school (*Oberschule*) or secondary school (*Realschule*) for four years, with the option of an additional year, or to the grammar school (*Liechtensteinisches Gymnasium*) for eight years. In 2010/11 enrolment at pre-primary level included 74% of children in the relevant age-group, while enrolment at primary level included 94% of the children in the relevant age group. There is limited provision for tertiary education in Liechtenstein: a state-run university, the *Universität Liechtenstein*, which offers degrees in architecture and business sciences; the *Private Universität im Fürstentum Liechtenstein* (Private University of the Principality of Liechtenstein), which runs postgraduate-level courses in sciences and jurisprudence; a private institution, the *Liechtenstein-Institut*, a research and academic teaching centre; and the private International Academy of Philosophy. There is also the publicly funded *Liechtensteinische Musikschule* (Liechtenstein Music School) which offers courses at higher education level. Many Liechtensteiners continue their studies at universities in Austria and Switzerland. Liechtenstein also has an art school, an adult education centre and a school for mentally disabled children. Government expenditure on education totalled 163.6m. Swiss francs in 2010 (14.5% of total expenditure).

LITHUANIA

Introductory Survey

LOCATION, CLIMATE, LANGUAGE, RELIGION, FLAG, CAPITAL

The Republic of Lithuania is situated on the eastern coast of the Baltic Sea, in north-eastern Europe. It is bounded by Latvia to the north, by Belarus to the south-east, by Poland to the south-west and by the Russian exclave, Kaliningrad Oblast, to the west. Lithuania's maritime position moderates an otherwise continental-type climate. Temperatures range from an average of −4.9°C (23.2°F) in January to a July mean of 17.0°C (62.6°F). Rainfall levels vary considerably from region to region: in the far west the annual average is 700 mm–850 mm (28 ins–33 ins), but in the central plain it is about 600 mm (24 ins). The official language is Lithuanian. The predominant religion is Christianity. Most ethnic Lithuanians are Latin-rite Catholics, but there are small communities of Lutherans and Calvinists and other Protestants. Adherents of Russian Orthodoxy are almost exclusively ethnic Slavs, while most Tatars have retained an adherence to Islam. The national flag (proportions 3 by 5) consists of three equal horizontal stripes of yellow (top), green and red (bottom). The capital is Vilnius.

CONTEMPORARY POLITICAL HISTORY

Historical Context

Prior to annexation by the Russian Empire in 1795, Lithuania was united in a Commonwealth with Poland. In 1915, after the outbreak of the First World War, it was occupied by German troops. A 'Lithuanian Conference' was convened in September 1917, which elected a 'Lithuanian Council', headed by Antanas Smetona; it proceeded to declare independence on 16 February 1918. The new state survived a Soviet attempt to create a Lithuanian-Belarusian Soviet republic. Soviet Russia recognized Lithuanian independence in the Treaty of Moscow, signed in July 1920. In October Poland annexed the region of Vilnius, but was forced to recognize the rest of Lithuania as an independent state, with its provisional capital at Kaunas. Lithuania's first Constitution, which declared Lithuania a parliamentary democracy, was adopted in August 1922. In December 1926 Smetona seized power in a military coup, establishing an authoritarian regime that endured until 1940.

According to the 'Secret Protocols' to the Treaty of Non-Aggression (the Molotov-Ribbentrop Pact), signed on 23 August 1939 by the USSR and Germany, Lithuania was to be part of the German sphere of influence. However, the Nazi-Soviet Treaty on Friendship and Existing Borders, agreed in September (following the outbreak of the Second World War), permitted the USSR to take control of Lithuania. In October Lithuania was compelled to agree to the stationing of 20,000 Soviet troops on its territory. In return, the USSR granted the city and region of Vilnius (which Soviet troops had seized in September) to Lithuania. In June 1940 the USSR dispatched a further 100,000 troops to Lithuania and forced the Lithuanian Government to resign. A Soviet-approved People's Government was formed. Elections to a People's Seim (parliament), which only pro-Soviet candidates were permitted to contest, took place in July. The Seim proclaimed the Lithuanian Soviet Socialist Republic on 21 July, and on 3 August it formally became a Union Republic of the USSR. The establishment of Soviet rule was followed by the arrest and imprisonment of many Lithuanian politicians and officials.

Some 210,000 people, mainly Jews, were killed during the Nazi occupation of Lithuania (1941–44). The return of the Soviet Army, in 1944, was not welcomed by most Lithuanians, and anti-Soviet partisan warfare continued until 1952. Lithuanian agriculture was forcibly collectivized and rapid industrialization was implemented. Meanwhile, some 150,000 people were deported, many to Kazakhstan or to Russian Siberia and the Far East, and leaders and members of the Catholic Church were persecuted and imprisoned. Political parties were disbanded, and political power became the exclusive preserve of the Communist Party of Lithuania (CPL), the local branch of the Communist Party of the Soviet Union (CPSU).

A significant dissident movement was established from the 1960s. With the introduction of the policy of glasnost (openness) by the Soviet leader, Mikhail Gorbachev, in the mid-1980s, a limited discussion of previously censored aspects of Lithuanian history appeared in the press. Dissident groups organized a demonstration in August 1987 to denounce the Nazi-Soviet Pact. In February 1988 security forces were deployed to prevent the public celebration of the 70th anniversary of Lithuanian independence. This, together with frustration at the slow pace of reform, led to the establishment in June of the Lithuanian Movement for Reconstruction (Sąjūdis). Sąjūdis organized mass demonstrations to protest against environmental pollution, the suppression of national culture and 'russification', and to condemn the signing of the Molotov-Ribbentrop Pact. The movement appealed to the CPL to support a declaration of independence and the recognition of Lithuanian as the state language. The last demand was adopted by the Lithuanian Supreme Soviet (Supreme Council—legislature) in November, and traditional Lithuanian state symbols were restored.

Sąjūdis won 36 of the 42 popularly elected Lithuanian seats at elections to the all-Union Congress of People's Deputies in March 1989. On 18 May the CPL-dominated Supreme Soviet approved a declaration of Lithuanian sovereignty, asserting the supremacy of Lithuania's laws over all-Union legislation. Public debate concerning the legitimacy of Soviet rule in Lithuania intensified: a commission of the Lithuanian Supreme Soviet declared the establishment of Soviet power in 1940 to have been unconstitutional, and, in August 1989, on the 50th anniversary of the signing of the Pact with Nazi Germany, more than 1m. people participated in a 'human chain' extending from Tallinn in Estonia, through Latvia, to Vilnius.

Despite denunciations of Baltic nationalism by the all-Union authorities, the Lithuanian Supreme Soviet continued to adopt reformist legislation, including the establishment of freedom of religion and the legalization of a multi-party system. In December 1989 the CPL declared itself independent of the CPSU, adopting a new programme and declaring support for multi-party democracy and independent statehood. Shortly afterwards a group of former CPL members who were opposed to independence formed a separate movement, the Lithuanian Communist Party on the CPSU Platform (LCP). Meanwhile, Algirdas Brazauskas, First Secretary of the CPL since October 1988, was elected Chairman of the Presidium of the Lithuanian Supreme Soviet, defeating three other candidates, including Romualdas Ozolas of Sąjūdis. None the less, Sąjūdis remained the dominant political force in the republic, and its supporters won an overall majority in the elections to the Lithuanian Supreme Soviet in February–March 1990. This new, pro-independence parliament elected Vytautas Landsbergis, the Chairman of Sąjūdis, to replace Brazauskas as its Chairman (de facto President of Lithuania), and on 11 March declared the restoration of Lithuanian independence: Lithuania thus became the first of the Soviet republics to make such a declaration. The Supreme Council also restored the pre-1940 name of the country (the Republic of Lithuania) and suspended the USSR Constitution on Lithuanian territory. Kazimiera Danutė Prunskienė, a member of the CPL and hitherto a Deputy Chairman of the Council of Ministers, was appointed the first Prime Minister of the restored republic.

Domestic Political Affairs

A special session of the all-Union Congress of People's Deputies condemned the Lithuanian declarations as unconstitutional, and Soviet forces occupied CPL buildings in Vilnius. An economic embargo was imposed on Lithuania in April 1990, and vital fuel supplies were suspended; the embargo remained in force for more than two months, until Lithuania agreed to a six-month moratorium on the independence declaration. However, the Soviet Government soon terminated formal negotiations, which began in August, and in January 1991 Landsbergis revoked the suspension of the declaration of independence. Subsequently, the Soviet authorities dispatched troops (led by the special OMON units of the Soviet Ministry of Internal Affairs) to Vilnius, who occupied former CPSU properties that had been nationalized by the Lithuanian Government. Landsbergis mobilized popular support to help to defend the parliament building.

In mid-January 13 people were killed and about 500 injured when Soviet troops seized the broadcasting centre in Vilnius. (In August 1999 six former officers of the LCP were convicted of complicity in attempts to overthrow the Lithuanian Government in January 1991, and sentenced to between three and 12 years' imprisonment.)

Meanwhile, earlier in January 1991 Prunskienė and her Council of Ministers had resigned after the Supreme Council refused to sanction proposed price increases. Gediminas Vagnorius, a member of the Supreme Council, was appointed Prime Minister. At a referendum on 9 February, 90.5% of voters expressed support for the re-establishment of an independent Lithuania and for the withdrawal of the Soviet army from the republic. In common with five other Soviet republics, Lithuania refused to conduct the all-Union referendum on the future of the USSR, which was held in March.

A series of attacks by OMON forces on members of the nascent Lithuanian defence force and on the customs posts on the border with Belarus, combined with the seizure of power in Moscow, the Russian and Soviet capital, by the conservative communist 'State Committee for the State of Emergency' (SCSE) in August 1991, led to fears that there would be a renewed attempt to reimpose Soviet rule in Lithuania. Soviet military vehicles entered Vilnius, and an emergency session of the Supreme Council condemned the SCSE and issued a statement supporting the Russian President, Boris Yeltsin. As the coup collapsed, the Lithuanian Government ordered the withdrawal of Soviet forces from the republic and banned the LCP. (The successor party to the CPL, the Lithuanian Democratic Labour Party—LDLP, was not banned.) The Government also began to assume effective control of the country's borders. The failed coup prompted the recognition of Lithuanian independence by other states, and on 6 September the USSR State Council recognized the independence of Lithuania along with that of Estonia and Latvia. All three countries were admitted to the UN and the Conference on (now Organization for) Security and Co-operation in Europe (OSCE, see p. 397) later in the month.

During the first half of 1992 there was an increasing polarity within the Supreme Council between Sąjūdis deputies and those of the mainly left-wing opposition parties, most prominently the LDLP, led by Brazauskas. In April 10 members of the Council of Ministers criticized Vagnorius's 'dictatorial' methods, and two ministers subsequently resigned. Vagnorius tendered his resignation as Prime Minister in May, but remained in the post until July, when the legislature approved a motion of no confidence in his leadership. The Seimas (Parliament—as the Supreme Council had been renamed) appointed Aleksandras Abišala, a close associate of Landsbergis, as Prime Minister; a new Council of Ministers was named shortly afterwards.

In July 1992 the Seimas approved a new electoral law, whereby the legislative elections, scheduled for late 1992, would be held under a mixed system of majority voting (for 71 seats) and proportional representation on the basis of party lists (70 seats). The LDLP emerged as the leading party in the elections to the Seimas, held on 25 October and 15 November, winning 73 of the 141 seats, while an alliance of Sąjūdis and the Citizens' Charter of Lithuania secured only 30 seats. The Christian Democratic Party of Lithuania (CDPL), which was closely aligned with Sąjūdis, won 16 seats. A referendum held concurrently with the first round of the elections approved a new Constitution, which was adopted by the Seimas on 6 November. Pending an election to the new post of President of the Republic, Brazauskas was elected by the Seimas to be its Chairman and acting Head of State. In December Brazauskas appointed Bronislovas Lubys Prime Minister. Lubys formed a new coalition Council of Ministers, including only three representatives of the LDLP.

The presidential election on 14 February 1993 was won by Brazauskas, who won some 60% of the votes cast, defeating his only rival, Stasys Lozoraitis, Lithuania's ambassador to the USA. Brazauskas subsequently resigned from the LDLP. Adolfas Šleževičius succeeded Lubys as Prime Minister in March, and was appointed Chairman of the LDLP in April. In May a new political organization, the Conservative Party of Lithuania (CP), also known as the Homeland Union, was formed. Mainly comprising former members of Sąjūdis, and chaired by Landsbergis, the CP rapidly established itself as the principal opposition party.

In December 1995 the operations of Lithuania's two largest commercial banks were suspended on grounds of insolvency. In January 1996 it was revealed that Šleževičius had withdrawn funds from one of these banks, the Lithuanian Joint Stock Innovation Bank (LJIB), only two days before the bank's suspension. Later in the month Romasis Vaitekūnas, who had also withdrawn funds from the LJIB before its closure, resigned as Minister of the Interior. Kazys Ratkevičius, the Chairman of the Bank of Lithuania (the central bank), also resigned. Šleževičius initially disregarded a presidential decree that he should leave office, which was upheld by the Seimas in February. He was replaced as Prime Minister by Laurynas Mindaugas Stankevičius. Šleževičius also resigned as Chairman of the LDLP, and was succeeded by Česlovas Juršėnas, the Chairman of the Seimas.

A general election took place on 20 October and 10 November 1996. The results confirmed the substantial loss of popular support for the LDLP, which obtained only 12 seats in the Seimas. The CP obtained 70 seats, and the CDPL 16. The right-wing Lithuanian Centre Union won 13 seats and the Lithuanian Social Democratic Party (LSDP) 12. Some 53% of eligible voters participated in the first round, and about 40% took part in the second. Following the election, the leaders of the CP and the CDPL signed a coalition agreement. Landsbergis was elected Chairman of the Seimas in late November, and shortly afterwards the Seimas approved the appointment of Vagnorius as Prime Minister. His Government was dominated by members of the CP, with three representatives of the CDPL and two of the Lithuanian Centre Union.

Valdas Adamkus elected as President

The first round of voting in the presidential election held on 21 December 1997 was inconclusive. In a second round on 4 January 1998 the second-placed candidate after the first round, Valdas Adamkus (a former environmental protection executive, who had been naturalized in the USA), narrowly defeated Artūras Paulauskas (a prominent lawyer and deputy Prosecutor-General, supported by the Lithuanian Liberal Union—LLU), with 50.4% of the votes. In April Paulauskas announced the formation of a new, centre-left political party, the New Union (Social Liberals—NU).

A serious conflict of interests between the President and Prime Minister intensified in April 1999, following President Adamkus's criticism of the Government's efforts to combat corruption in the public sector. Vagnorius secured the confidence of the Seimas in a non-binding vote, but at the end of the month announced his intention to resign. In May Adamkus invited the Mayor of Vilnius, Rolandas Paksas (of the CP), to form a new government. His Council of Ministers was again formed from a coalition led by the CP and the CDPL. In October Paksas indicated that he would not endorse an agreement to sell a stake in the state-owned Mažeikiai Nafta petroleum refinery to a US oil company, Williams International. None the less, the Council of Ministers endorsed the sale, prompting the resignations of the Ministers of National Economy and of Finance, and, in late October, of Paksas.

At the end of October 1999 Adamkus nominated Andrius Kubilius, the First Deputy Chairman of the Seimas, as Prime Minister. The new Council of Ministers retained largely the same membership as the previous administration. After the leader of the Lithuanian Centre Union, Ozolas, resigned as a Deputy Chairman of the Seimas, the party went into opposition. Having resigned from the CP in the previous month, Paksas was elected Chairman of the LLU in December. Local elections in March 2000 resulted in considerable successes for parties of the left, most notably the NU. A decline in support for the CP was followed by a split in the party, including within the Seimas, thus depriving the CP-CDPL coalition of an automatic majority in the legislature. In May the LSDP and the LDLP, agreed to contest forthcoming legislative elections in alliance. The New Democracy Party and the Lithuanian Russians' Union subsequently joined the alliance, named the A. Brazauskas Social Democratic Coalition, after the former President, who had been elected Honorary Chairman.

Some 56.2% of eligible voters participated in legislative elections held on 8 October 2000, at which the CP won only nine seats (compared with 70 in 1996). Although the A. Brazauskas Social Democratic Coalition obtained the largest representation, with 51 seats, the LLU and the NU (with 34 and 29 seats, respectively) signed a coalition agreement, forming a parliamentary majority with partners including the Lithuanian Centre Union and the Modern Christian Democratic Union (MCDU). The new Council of Ministers, headed by Paksas, was approved in October; Paulauskas was elected Chairman of the Seimas. The LDLP merged with the LSDP in January 2001; the LSDP thereby became the largest single party in the Seimas, and Brazauskas was elected its Chairman. Further political consolidation took place in May, when the CDPL merged with the Christian Democratic Union to form the Lithuanian Christian Democrats (LCD).

In June 2001 the six NU members of the Council of Ministers resigned their portfolios, following disagreements with the LLU over privatization of the energy sector and economic reform. Paksas, being unable to form a new coalition, resigned on 20 June. After the NU sought a new alliance with the LSDP, President Adamkus offered the post of Prime Minister to Brazauskas, who was confirmed on 3 July. The LSDP agreed to an informal accord, which granted the NU the same six ministerial positions from which it had withdrawn in June. In September Paksas resigned as Chairman of the LLU, in compliance with intra-party demands; he was replaced by Gentvilas. In December Paksas and 10 other deputies left the parliamentary faction of the LLU, owing, in part, to its failure to nominate Paksas as First Deputy Chairman of the Seimas; they were formally expelled from the party in January 2002, and founded the rightist Liberal Democratic Party (LDP) in March, with Paksas as its Chairman.

The results of the first round of voting in the presidential election, held on 22 December 2002, were inconclusive. In a second round, on 5 January 2003, Paksas obtained 54.7% of the votes cast, defeating Adamkus. Paksas was inaugurated as President on 26 February. In March Brazauskas was reappointed as Prime Minister; his Council of Ministers was substantially unchanged. Following the presidential election, Paksas resigned as Chairman of the LDP; Valentinas Mazuronis was elected as his successor. In May Kubilius was elected as Chairman of the CP, in succession to Landsbergis. In the same month the Lithuanian Centre Union, the LLU and the MCDU merged to form the Liberal and Centre Union (LCU), with Artūras Zuokas as Chairman. In February 2004 the CP merged with the Lithuanian Union of Political Prisoners and Deportees to form the Homeland Union—Conservatives, Political Prisoners and Deportees, Christian Democrats (HU).

The impeachment of President Paksas

Meanwhile, in October 2003 a classified report was disclosed, which claimed to provide evidence of links between the presidential adviser on national security, Remigijus Acas, and Yurii Borisov, an ethnic Russian with alleged connections with organized crime groups, who had contributed significant funds to Paksas's presidential election campaign. It was revealed that Paksas had signed a presidential decree permitting Borisov to hold dual citizenship. In November an emergency session of the Seimas established a special parliamentary commission to investigate Paksas's alleged links with Russian organized crime, while the Prosecutor-General launched a criminal investigation into Borisov. In December, after the Seimas approved the commission's conclusion that the President's conduct had jeopardized national security, Brazauskas and Paulauskas appealed for the President's resignation. On 18 December the Seimas approved a draft resolution to initiate impeachment proceedings against Paksas, and an investigative commission was subsequently established to consider the charges.

On 18 February 2004 the investigative commission endorsed six charges, which were to form the basis for the impeachment of the President: that Paksas represented a threat to national security; that he had failed to protect classified information; that he had attempted illegally to influence the operations of private companies; that he was unable to reconcile his public and private interests; that he had hindered the operations of state institutions; and that he had failed to prevent his advisers from abusing their positions. On the following day the Seimas voted to initiate formal impeachment proceedings and, in the mean time, agreed to seek a ruling from the Constitutional Court as to whether the charges constituted a breach of the Constitution. On 31 March the Constitutional Court ruled that the President had severely violated the Constitution by: granting Borisov dual citizenship in exchange for financial support; failing to protect state secrets; and using his presidential office illegally to influence the actions of a company's shareholders. A parliamentary vote on Paksas's impeachment took place on 6 April. Paksas was removed from office, after the necessary three-fifths' majority in the Seimas supported his impeachment. Paulauskas immediately assumed the presidency, in an acting capacity, pending a presidential election, and subsequently suspended his membership of the NU, in compliance with the Constitution. In May the Constitutional Court ruled that legislation recently approved by the Seimas, preventing an impeached head of state from seeking presidential office again, was in accordance with the Constitu-

tion, and Paksas was obliged to withdraw his candidacy from the forthcoming presidential election.

The first round of the presidential election, held on 13 June 2004, proved inconclusive. In the second round, held on 27 June, Adamkus was narrowly elected to the presidency, receiving 52.6% of the votes cast, defeating Prunskienė. Meanwhile, Lithuania's first elections to the European Parliament, following the accession of the country to full membership of the European Union (EU, see p. 281) on 1 May, were held concurrently with the first round of presidential voting, with the participation of 46% of the electorate. The recently founded Labour Party (LP), headed by a controversial, ethnically Russian business executive, Viktor Uspaskich, won five of the 13 mandates allocated to Lithuania; the governing LSDP, the LCU and the HU each obtained two seats, while the LDP and the Peasants' and New Democracy Union (PNDU—led by Prunskienė) each won one seat. Adamkus was inaugurated on 12 July, and on the following day the Seimas approved his nomination of Brazauskas as Prime Minister.

Elections to the Seimas, held in two rounds on 10 and 24 October 2004, demonstrated that the LP had further consolidated its support. It became the largest single party in the Seimas, receiving 28.4% of the votes cast on the basis of party lists, and obtaining 39 of the 141 elective seats. A coalition of the LSDP and the NU received 20.7% of the votes cast on the basis of party lists, and 31 seats. The HU obtained 25 seats, and the LCU 18. The Order and Justice coalition, comprising the LDP and the Lithuanian People's Union for a Free Lithuania, received 11 seats, while the PNDU obtained 10.

The Seimas approved a coalition Government of the LP, the LSDP, the NU and the PNDU in December 2004. Brazauskas remained Prime Minister, while several prominent members of the LSDP and the NU also retained the posts they had held in the outgoing administration. In April 2005 Algirdas Butkevičius resigned as Minister of Finance, after the governing coalition rejected a proposed tax reform programme. He was replaced by Zigmantas Balčytis, hitherto the Minister of Transport, in May. In December the Supreme Court ruled that Paksas was not guilty of divulging confidential state information, while Borisov was granted permission to remain resident in Lithuania.

In April 2006 Paulauskas, the Chairman of the NU, was removed as parliamentary speaker, following a secret ballot in the Seimas, amid accusations that he had been aware of a scandal involving the unauthorized use of official vehicles by government employees. The NU immediately withdrew from the governing coalition. The remaining coalition partners signed a new agreement, and Viktoras Muntianas of the LP was subsequently elected as the new Chairman of the Seimas. At the end of April Paulauskas was re-elected as Chairman of the NU, which in early May declared itself to be in opposition to the Government.

The Government of Gediminas Kirkilas

In May 2006 seven LP deputies renounced their party membership and defected to the newly reconstituted Civil Democracy Party (formerly the Citizens' Union), citing dissatisfaction with the LP leadership, and in particular Uspaskich. The ruling coalition's number of seats in the 141-member Seimas was thereby reduced to just 62. Uspaskich, the subject of ongoing corruption allegations, tendered his resignation as Chairman of the LP later in May. At the end of May the LP withdrew from the ruling coalition, effectively forcing the resignation of the Prime Minister and of the Council of Ministers. Minister of Finance Balčytis was appointed premier in an acting capacity, but in July the Seimas approved the nomination of Gediminas Kirkilas, Vice-Chairman of the LSDP, as Prime Minister. The new Council of Ministers comprised six members of the LSDP, three members of the Lithuanian Peasant Nationalists' Union (LPNU), and two members each of the Civil Democracy Party and of the LCU. Balčytis retained the finance portfolio, while Petras Vaitiekūnas of the LPNU was appointed Minister of Foreign Affairs.

Kęstutis Dauksys was elected Chairman of the LP in August 2006. Uspaskich, meanwhile, fled to Russia, but he was detained there in September, following the issuing of a European warrant for his arrest by the Lithuanian Office of the Prosecutor-General; he was subsequently released without charge.

The rate of participation at the municipal elections held on 25 February 2007 failed to exceed 40% of the electorate. The HU was placed first, with 17.1% of the votes cast, while the LSDP came a close second, with 16.3%; the LP ranked sixth, with 6.4% of the ballot. Uspaskich and Paksas won seats in Kedainiai and Vilnius, respectively. In March Balčytis resigned as Minister of Finance after his son was acquitted of corrupt practices in his position in a state agency responsible for the distribution of EU funds (although the trial had revealed administrative misconduct on his part); Balčytis was replaced by Rimantas Šadžius, also of the LSDP. In May Prime Minister Kirkilas was elected Chairman of the LSDP, following the resignation of Brazauskas. Uspaskich returned to Lithuania from Russia in September, and was subsequently placed under house arrest. Having failed in an attempt to secure a seat in the Seimas at a by-election in October, Uspaskich was re-elected Chairman of the LP in November; he was released on bail in April 2008.

In November 2007 the Minister of the Interior and the head of the police service resigned, after a police official under the influence of alcohol fatally injured three children in an automobile accident. In January 2008 an agreement was signed on the expansion of the ruling coalition to include the NU, thereby giving it a majority in the Seimas, with 73 seats. Later that month NU Chairman Paulauskas joined the Government as Minister of the Environment.

Česlovas Juršėnas of the LSDP was elected Chairman of the Seimas at the beginning of April 2008, following the resignation of Muntianas in response to media allegations of corruption. Also in April the Minister of Education and Science, Roma Žakaitienė, tendered her resignation, following a series of strikes by teachers; she was replaced by Algirdas Monkevičius of the NU, a previous incumbent of the post. The HU merged with the LCD in May, to form the HU—LCD. Also in that month a new political organization, the National Revival Party (NRP), was established by television presenter Arūnas Valinskas.

The HU—LCD became the largest party in the Seimas following legislative elections held in two rounds on 12 and 26 October 2008, winning 19.7% of the votes cast on the basis of party lists and a total of 45 of the 141 seats. In second place, with a total of 25 seats, was Prime Minister Kirkilas's LSDP (which received 11.7% of the votes cast on the basis of party lists), followed by the NRP, with 16 seats, and the Order and Justice Party (OJP), with 15. The Liberal Movement of the Republic of Lithuania (which had been formed by a splinter group of the LCU in 2006) secured 11 seats, while a coalition of the LP and the Youth party took 10, and the LCU itself won eight; three other parties and four independents also obtained representation. In late October President Adamkus invited the Chairman of the HU—LCD, Andrius Kubilius, to form a government. The poor performance of the parties in the outgoing administration was attributed, in part, to a downturn in the economy. The rate of participation by the electorate was 48.6% in the first round, reportedly declining to 32.4% in the second. Uspaskich secured one of the LP's seats in the Seimas, gaining immunity from prosecution, but in December the legislature voted to remove his immunity, as well as that of two other deputies who were standing trial at the time of their election. Arūnas Valinskas, the leader of the NRP, was elected as Chairman of the Seimas in mid-November.

In late November 2008 the Seimas approved the nomination of Kubilius as Prime Minister, to head a four-party coalition Government controlling 80 seats in the Seimas. The new Council of Ministers, which took office in December, comprised six members of the HU—LCD, three members of the Liberal Movement of the Republic of Lithuania, two members each of the LCU and of the NRP, and one independent. The HU—LCD assumed responsibility for the economy, finance and national defence portfolios, while Vygaudas Ušackas, hitherto ambassador to the United Kingdom, was appointed Minister of Foreign Affairs. Addressing the country's economic difficulties was identified as the Government's main priority by Kubilius, who proposed to reform the taxation system, to restructure public finances and to reduce levels of corruption. However, the introduction of austerity measures in January 2009 (see Economic Affairs) aroused public discontent, and a protest organized that month by trade union leaders in Vilnius became violent, with police reportedly forcibly dispersing demonstrators. In February Arvydas Sekmokas was appointed to the newly created post of Minister of Energy.

The presidency of Dalia Grybauskaitė

Dalia Grybauskaitė, hitherto European Commissioner responsible for Financial Programming and the Budget, was elected as President of Lithuania in a first round of voting on 17 May 2009, receiving 69.1% of the valid votes cast. Her nearest rival among the six other candidates was Algirdas Butkevičius, with 11.8%, who had succeeded Kirkilas as Chairman of the LSDP. A rate of electoral participation of 51.7% was recorded. Grybauskaitė's victory was attributed to her political independence and, amid increasing concern regarding the continued deterioration in economic conditions, to her financial experience. She took office

on 12 July. In the same month Ingrida Šimonytė was appointed as Minister of Finance, succeeding Algirdas Gediminas Semeta, who had become Lithuania's representative at the European Commission.

Meanwhile, elections to the European Parliament were conducted on 7 June 2009, with the participation of only 21.0% of the electorate. Of the 12 seats allocated to Lithuania, the HU—LCD won four (increasing its representation two-fold), the LSDP three and the OJP two, while the LP (which had previously held five seats), the Electoral Action of Poles in Lithuania and the Liberal Movement of the Republic of Lithuania each obtained one seat.

The Seimas voted to dismiss Valinskas as its Chairman in September 2009 in response to allegations that he had links to an organized crime group. Irena Degutienė, of the HU—LCD, was elected as his successor. The Minister of Foreign Affairs, Vygaudas Ušackas, resigned in January 2010, shortly after the Seimas approved the findings of a parliamentary investigation that had confirmed the existence in Lithuania of two secret detention centres operated by the US Central Intelligence Agency (CIA) in 2002–06. Audronius Ažubalis was subsequently appointed to replace Ušackas. (In October 2011 a case was brought against Lithuania at the European Court of Human Rights—ECHR by a Saudi Arabian national, who claimed to have been detained and tortured in CIA facilities in Lithuania.) In February 2010 the Minister of Health, Algis Caplikas, of the LCU, announced his resignation, following criticism from members of the HU—LCD of his efforts in health care reform and of the conviction of his former deputy, Artūras Skikas, who had been accused of accepting a bribe. Raimondas Šukys was appointed as the new Minister of Health in mid-March.

Administrative reform

In July 2010, as part of a wider programme of administrative reform, 10 governorships and their corresponding county divisions were abolished. Hitherto the highest level of local governance, county-level powers were redistributed to municipal bodies. On 27 February 2011 municipal elections took place, in which the electorate was able to vote for coalitions of independent candidates, as well as for political parties, for the first time. According to the provisional results of the Central Electoral Committee, the LSDP secured the most votes (21.4%), followed by the CP (16.3%).

Meanwhile, in January 2011 the ECHR returned a verdict stating that the decision by the Constitutional Court to impose a 'permanent and irreversible' ban on the appointment of former President Paksas to a position that required an oath of office was disproportionate, and in contravention of the principals of the Convention for the Protection of Human Rights and Fundamental Freedoms. The ECHR recommended that amendments to Lithuania's Constitution be implemented. Although the ECHR emphasized that it had not assessed the validity of Paksas's 2004 impeachment, Paksas immediately sought to use the ruling as proof that it had been unconstitutional. (Nevertheless, in September 2012 the Constitutional Court prohibited Paksas from contesting the forthcoming elections.) In March 2011 Dainius Kreivys resigned from his position as Minister of the Economy, owing to claims that he had transferred EU funds to a company that was partly owned by his mother; he was replaced by Rimantas Žylius. In April the Government approved a new National Anti-Corruption Programme for 2011–14, which focused on nine areas, including public procurement, legislative bodies and the activities of civil servants. In March 2012 the Minister of the Interior, Raimundus Pailitis, left his post, after his decision to dismiss the directors of the Financial Crime Investigation Service prompted a crisis within the governing coalition. He was replaced by Artūras Melianas in April.

Recent developments: the 2012 legislative elections

Elections to the Seimas were conducted on 14 and 28 October 2012. The parties of the ruling HU—LCD-led coalition received a total of 36 seats, registering a significant loss in support, while the LSDP's representation increased to 34 seats and that of the LP to 30 seats; the Liberal Movement of the Republic of Lithuania took 11 seats, the OJP 10 and the Electoral Action of Poles in Lithuania nine. A party concerned with the combat of corruption, particularly within the judicial system, the Way of Courage, won seven seats. One representative of the Lithuanian Peasant and Greens Union was elected, as were two independent deputies. The election results were widely considered to reflect popular discontent with the austerity measures imposed by the Government. At a referendum held concurrently with the first round of the legislative elections, 64.8% of those participating rejected the Government's proposal that a new nuclear power station be constructed at Ignalina to replace a plant closed at the end of 2009 (see Regional Affairs), thereby reversing the result of a referendum conducted in October 2008. A proposal by LSDP Chairman Butkevičius that his party form a ruling coalition with the LP was initially refused by President Grybauskaitė, on the grounds that Uspaskich and other members of the LP remained under official investigation for tax evasion; three of its new deputies were subsequently also disqualified owing to irregularities in their election. On 19 November, however, Grybauskaitė conceded that only the LSDP was able to form a government coalition with a parliamentary majority. Butkevičius was formally appointed Prime Minister on 7 December, and his new Government, comprising members of the LSDP, the LP (these having been selected by the President as technocrats), the OJP and the Electoral Action of Poles in Lithuania, secured the approval of the Seimas on 12 December.

Minority Ethnic Groups and Citizenship Concerns

Whereas Lithuania's Baltic neighbours, Estonia and Latvia, have large national minorities, ethnic Lithuanians constitute much of the republic's population: in the 2011 census, ethnic Lithuanians represented some 84.1% of the total population, while the two largest minority groups, Poles and Russians, represented 6.6% and 5.8%, respectively (approximately similar figures had been recorded at the 2001 census). Under citizenship laws adopted in late 1989, all residents, regardless of ethnic origin, were eligible to apply for naturalization; by early 1993 more than 90% of the country's non-ethnic Lithuanian residents had been granted citizenship. None the less, the population of Lithuania declined by some 191,000 between 1989 and 2001. In an attempt to counter emigration (in particular to the USA), in September 2002 the Seimas approved legislation permitting Lithuanian citizens to hold dual citizenship, thereby facilitating the eventual return of Lithuanian nationals to the country. However, in November 2006 the Constitutional Court ruled that several provisions of this legislation contravened the Constitution, which only allowed dual citizenship to be held in exceptional cases. In July 2008 the Seimas adopted an amended law on citizenship (which was initially due to expire in January 2010, but which was subsequently extended for a further year), which notably permitted dual citizenship to be held by Lithuanian citizens who had left the country during the occupations of June 1940–March 1990, as well as their children and grandchildren. On 2 December 2010 the Seimas voted on the adoption of new legislation on citizenship, 65 members voting in favour of the proposed law, with amendments and supplements as provided by President Grybauskaitė, 21 voting against, and 40 abstaining.

In May 2012 state-sponsored commemorations of Juozas Brazaitis Ambrazevičius, who served for a brief period in 1941 as acting Prime Minister of a Provisional Government, including the repatriation of his body from the USA and his reburial in an official ceremony in Kaunas were a cause of controversy both domestically and internationally, particularly among Jewish groups. Protesters alleged that Brazaitis Ambrazevičius had failed sufficiently to oppose the Nazi German authorities, despite an investigation by the US immigration authorities having failed to find any evidence of pro-Nazi activity on his part.

Regional Affairs

Lithuania's relations with Russia have generally been less strained than have those of Estonia and Latvia. Agreement was reached in September 1992 on the withdrawal of the estimated 38,000 former Soviet troops remaining in Lithuania, and the final troops left, as scheduled, on 31 August 1993.

In November 1993 Lithuania and Russia signed several agreements, including an accord on most-favoured nation status in bilateral trade, and another concerning the transportation, via Lithuania, of Russian military equipment and troops from the Russian exclave of Kaliningrad Oblast. In October 1997 President Brazauskas undertook the first official visit to Russia by a Baltic head of state since the disintegration of the former USSR: a state border delimitation treaty was signed by both sides, and bilateral co-operation agreements on joint economic zones, and on the Baltic continental shelf, were also concluded. The border treaty was ratified by the Seimas in October 1999, but was not ratified by Russia until May 2003. Lithuania expressed support for an agreement between the EU and Russia in late 2002, which proposed simplified visa arrangements for Russian

citizens traversing Lithuania to reach Kaliningrad. New transit arrangements were implemented in February 2003.

All three Baltic Governments were concerned at an agreement signed between Russia and Germany, in September 2005, on the construction of a North European Gas Pipeline, which was to carry natural gas from Russia to Germany under the Baltic Sea, bypassing the Baltic countries. In June 2006 Russian petroleum supplies to the Mažeikiai Nafta petroleum refinery were indefinitely suspended, on the grounds that its pipeline link had been damaged; Russia subsequently refused assistance to repair the pipeline, prompting speculation that the halt in pipeline exports was in reprisal for the majority acquisition in that year of the refinery by Polish enterprise PKN Orlen, rather than by a Russian company. In May 2008 Lithuania withdrew its earlier objections to the initiation of long-delayed talks between the EU and Russia on a new partnership agreement, after being assured that its concerns regarding the continued closure of the pipeline link to the Mažeikiai Nafta refinery and Russian policy towards Georgia and Moldova would be addressed. Although PKN Orlen bid to purchase the refinery and build a new pipeline to service the facility, the Lithuanian Government refused the offer, amid concerns over national security.

Relations between Lithuania and Russia were further strained in June 2008, when the Seimas adopted legislation prohibiting the public display of Soviet and Nazi symbols. In late June several hundred Lithuanian websites were subject to pro-Russian attacks, their content being replaced by the Soviet flag and anti-Lithuanian propaganda. A dispute over customs inspections arose in August 2009, when the Lithuanian Government accused Russian officials of deliberately delaying Lithuanian lorries attempting to enter Russia from neighbouring Latvia, but was resolved following the intervention of President Grybauskaitė. In February 2010, in the highest level bilateral meeting to take place since 2001, Grybauskaitė and Russian premier Vladimir Putin held talks in Helsinki, Finland to discuss co-operation in a number of areas, including energy.

In June 2010, at the Baltic Development Forum Summit held in Vilnius, Lithuania announced plans to build an offshore liquefied natural gas terminal in an effort to foster greater independence in energy supplies. In December the Lithuanian Government approved the construction of a gas pipeline between the river town of Jurbarkas and the main port of Klaipėda, which was due to be operational before the scheduled completion of the new gas terminal in 2014. Meanwhile, relations between Lithuania and Belarus improved in 2010, and in October the two countries signed a cross-border agreement facilitating travel of residents living within 50 km of the Lithuania–Belarus border.

Lithuania's relations with neighbouring Poland were largely concerned with the status of the Polish minority in Lithuania. In January 1992 Lithuania and Poland signed a 'Declaration on Friendly Relations and Neighbourly Co-operation', which guaranteed the rights of the respective minority ethnic groups and also recognized the existing border between the two countries. A full treaty of friendship and co-operation was signed by the respective Heads of State in April 1994. The treaty, notably, did not include a condemnatory reference to Poland's occupation of the region of Vilnius in 1920–39, as had originally been demanded by Lithuania. In May 2005 the Chairmen of the national legislatures of Lithuania, Poland and Ukraine, meeting in Lutsk, Ukraine, signed a declaration establishing a new Inter-Parliamentary Assembly, which aimed to help fulfil Ukraine's objective of attaining membership of the EU and the North Atlantic Treaty Organization (NATO, see p. 380). In September 2006 President Adamkus made an official visit to the Polish capital, Warsaw, where he signed a joint declaration with President Lech Kaczyński on a plan to connect the electricity grids of Lithuania and Poland; a joint company to manage the project was formed in May 2008. Negotiations to resolve continued tensions over the status of the ethnic Polish population and, in particular, the representation of Polish names on official Lithuanian documentation, including passports, in November 2011 were inconclusive.

Lithuania enjoys close relations with Estonia and Latvia. Relations between the three states are co-ordinated through the consultative inter-parliamentary Baltic Assembly, the Council of the Baltic Sea States (see p. 258) and the Baltic Council (see p. 474). However, in the mid-1990s Lithuania's relations with Latvia came under strain, as a result of disagreement over the demarcation of the countries' maritime border. In October 1995 the Lithuanian Government protested against Latvia's signature of a preliminary agreement with two foreign petroleum companies to explore oilfields in the disputed waters. Tension increased following the ratification of the agreement by the Latvian parliament in October 1996, although in July 1999 the two countries signed an agreement on the Delimitation of the Territorial Sea, Exclusive Economic Zone and Continental Shelf in the Baltic Sea. However, protests from the Latvian fishing industry prevented the agreement from being ratified by the Latvian parliament. In December 2000 a protocol was signed for the re-demarcation of the land border between the two countries. In early 2008 Prime Minister Kirkilas welcomed a decision by the Latvian Government that ratification of the maritime border treaty would proceed separately to the signing of an economic co-operation agreement between the two countries. Meanwhile, in early 2006 the leaders of all three Baltic states reached agreement on the construction of a new nuclear power plant to replace that at Ignalina (see Economic Affairs) and various other co-operative measures aimed at reducing Russian dominance in the supply of regional energy.

Lithuania pursued close co-operation with, and eventual integration into, the political, economic and defence systems of Western Europe, notably NATO and the EU. In December 1999 a summit meeting of EU Heads of State and Government endorsed proposals to begin accession talks with a number of countries, including Lithuania; formal negotiations commenced in February 2000. As a concession to achieve EU membership, the Government approved a draft national energy strategy in September 1999, which provided for the decommissioning of the first unit of the Ignalina nuclear power plant by 2005. In June 2002 Lithuania agreed to decommission the plant's remaining unit in 2009, in return for a significant contribution from the EU towards the cost of the endeavour. The plant eventually closed in December 2010. Proposals for a new nuclear plant to be built on the site were under discussion. In December 2002 Lithuania and nine other countries were formally invited to join the EU on 1 May 2004; at a national referendum, held on 10–11 May 2003, 90.0% of participants voted in favour of membership, and Lithuania duly acceded to the EU as scheduled. In December 2007 Lithuania, together with eight other nations, implemented the EU's Schengen Agreement, enabling its citizens to travel to and from other member states without border controls. In May 2008 the Seimas approved the ratification of the EU's Lisbon Treaty, which was designed to reform the Union's institutions and entered into force in December 2009. Meanwhile, in November 2002 Lithuania was one of seven countries invited to join NATO; Lithuania became a full member of the Alliance on 29 March 2004. From 2010 Lithuania's port of Klaipėda was strategically important in the transport of freight shipments to Afghanistan; in January 2013 Lithuania's part in the impending withdrawal of the NATO-led International Security Assistance Force in Afghanistan was under discussion with the Alliance.

CONSTITUTION AND GOVERNMENT

Under the terms of the Constitution that was approved in a national referendum on 25 October 1992, supreme legislative authority resides with the Seimas (Parliament), which has 141 members, elected by universal adult suffrage for a four-year term (71 deputies are directly elected by majority vote, with 70 being elected from party lists on the basis of proportional representation). The President of the Republic (who is Head of State) is elected by direct popular vote for a period of five years (and a maximum of two consecutive terms). Executive power is vested in the Council of Ministers, headed by the Prime Minister, who is appointed by the President with the approval of the Seimas. Judicial power is exercised by the Constitutional Court, the Supreme Court, the Court of Appeal and district and local courts. Until July 2010 Lithuania was divided into 10 counties. However, in a process of administrative reform, the counties were abolished and their powers were transferred to municipal bodies.

REGIONAL AND INTERNATIONAL CO-OPERATION

Lithuania is a member of the European Bank for Reconstruction and Development (see p. 276), the Council of the Baltic Sea States (see p. 258), of the Baltic Council (see p. 474), of the Council of Europe (see p. 260), and of the Organization for Security and Co-operation in Europe (see p. 397). In 2004 it acceded to the European Union (see p. 281).

Lithuania joined the UN in 1991, and the World Trade Organization (see p. 444) in 2001. The country is also a member of the North Atlantic Treaty Organization (see p. 380).

ECONOMIC AFFAIRS

In 2011, according to estimates by the World Bank, Lithuania's gross national income (GNI), measured at average 2009–11 prices, was US $39,322m., equivalent to $12,280 per head (or $19,690 per head on an international purchasing-power parity basis). During 2002–11 the population decreased at an average annual rate of 0.9%, while gross domestic product (GDP) per head increased, in real terms, by an average of 4.9% per year. Overall GDP increased, in real terms, by an average of 4.0% annually during 2002–11. Real GDP grew by 5.9% according to constant prices, and by 5.9% according to chain linked methodologies, in 2011.

Agriculture (including hunting, forestry and fishing) contributed 3.5% of GDP and engaged an estimated 8.7% of the employed population in 2011. The principal crops are cereals, sugar beet, potatoes and vegetables. According to World Bank estimates, agricultural GDP increased, in real terms, at an average annual rate of 1.6% during 2002–10; the GDP of the sector increased by 7.2% in 2011, according to chain linked methodologies.

Industry (including mining, manufacturing, construction and power) contributed 31.3% of GDP and engaged an estimated 24.5% of the employed population in 2011. According to World Bank estimates, industrial GDP increased by an average of 4.0% per year during 2002–10; the GDP of the sector decreased by 21.1% in 2009, but increased by 3.3% in 2010.

Mining and quarrying contributed 0.4% of GDP and provided an estimated 0.2% of employment in 2011. Lithuania has significant reserves of peat and materials used in construction (limestone, clay, dolomite, chalk, and sand and gravel), as well as small deposits of petroleum and natural gas. In terms of gross value added, the sector registered growth of 3.0% in 2004, according to official data.

The manufacturing sector contributed 20.6% of GDP and engaged 15.4% of the employed labour force in 2011. Based on the value of sales (excluding refined petroleum products), in 2008 the principal branches of manufacturing were food products (particularly dairy products), chemicals (including fertilizers), wood products (particularly furniture), and clothing. According to World Bank estimates, manufacturing GDP increased, in real terms, at an average annual rate of 4.6% during 2002–09; sectoral GDP increased by 10.7% in 2011.

The construction sector contributed 6.5% of GDP, and engaged 6.8% of the employed labour force in 2011.

In 2009 nuclear power accounted for 74.1% of gross electricity production, and natural gas accounted for 14.3%. Lithuania has substantial petroleum-refining and electricity-generating capacities, which enable it to export refined petroleum products and electricity. Lithuania had been a net exporter of electricity, although in June 2002 formal agreement was reached with the European Union (EU, see p. 281) on the closure of the Ignalina nuclear power plant. The plant's two reactors were decommissioned in 2004 and 2009, in return for substantial financial compensation from the EU. In February 2006 the Prime Ministers of Estonia, Latvia and Lithuania reached agreement on the construction of a new nuclear plant in Lithuania by 2015, and Poland became involved in the project in 2007. The connection of the Lithuanian electricity grid to those of Poland and Sweden was also planned. In 2011 imports of mineral fuels accounted for 33.0% of the total value of merchandise imports.

The services sector contributed 65.2% of GDP and provided 66.9% of total employment in 2011. The Baltic port of Klaipėda is a significant entrepôt for regional trade. According to World Bank estimates, the GDP of the services sector increased, in real terms, by an average of 3.8% per year in 2002–10; real services GDP decreased by 12.5% in 2009, but increased by 0.7% in 2010.

According to IMF estimates, in 2011 Lithuania recorded a visible merchandise trade deficit of US $2,494.5m., and there was a deficit of $619.1m. on the current account of the balance of payments. In 2011 the principal source of imports was Russia (accounting for 32.1% of the total); other major sources were Germany, Poland, Latvia and the Netherlands. Russia was also the main market for exports in that year (accounting for 16.6% of the total); other principal markets were Latvia, Germany, Poland, Estonia, the Netherlands and Belarus. In 2011 the principal exports were mineral products, machinery and electrical equipment, chemical products, vehicles and transportation equipment, plastics and rubber, and prepared foodstuffs and beverages. The principal imports were mineral products, machinery and electrical equipment (particularly nuclear reactors and boilers), chemical products, vehicles and transportation equipment, plastics, and prepared foodstuffs and beverages.

According to official sources, in 2011 there was a budgetary deficit of 5,874.8m. litai (equivalent to 5.5% of GDP). Lithuania's general government gross debt was 40,837m. litai in 2011, equivalent to 38.5% of GDP. Lithuania's total external debt was US $29,602m. in 2010, of which $11,664m. was public and publicly guaranteed debt. In that year, the cost of servicing long-term public and publicly guaranteed debt and repayments to the IMF was equivalent to 34.3% of the value of exports of goods, services and income (excluding workers' remittances). According to ILO estimates, annual inflation averaged 3.6% in 2002–11. The rate of inflation was 4.2% in 2011. The average rate of unemployment was 15.3% in 2011.

In February 2002 the national currency's fixed rate of exchange was linked to the common European currency, the euro, instead of the US dollar. Lithuania was admitted to the EU's exchange rate mechanism (ERM II) in June 2004. Meanwhile, legislation approved in January 2003 authorized the sale of agricultural land to foreign owners, although its implementation was to be subject to a seven-year transition period. As a result of the impact of adverse economic conditions associated with the international financial crisis in 2008–09, in January 2009 the Government introduced a number of austerity measures, which included a 15% reduction in public sector salaries, pension reforms and an increase in value-added tax (VAT). Despite signs of recovery, in November 2010 the authorities warned that austerity measures introduced in previous budgets could not be eased and that the budget for 2011 would maintain a tight control on spending, although some state-owned companies were to be reformed with the intent of increasing revenue, while measures to combat illegal trade were to be undertaken. The fiscal deficit, which amounted to 7.1% of GDP in 2010, was a further cause of concern. In addition to the continuing spending freeze on wages and goods and services, as part of its fiscal programme in June 2011 the Government enacted legislation providing for a gradual increase, by 2026, of the pension age to 65 years. Although adherence to the austerity measures had proved successful in stabilizing the economy, with a significant reduction of the budget deficit being recorded in 2011 (as was commended by the IMF), popular discontent contributed to the defeat of the Government in legislative elections in October 2012. Algirdas Butkevičius, the Prime Minister of the new ruling coalition that was established in December, had issued pre-election pledges to increase the minimum wage, impose higher taxes on the rich, and defer the country's entry to the euro area until 2015 (in view of the ongoing economic crisis within the EU). A slower rate of growth, of around 3%, was forecast for 2012.

PUBLIC HOLIDAYS

2014: 1 January (New Year's Day), 16 February (National Day), 11 March (Day of the Re-establishment of Independence), 21 April (Easter Monday), 1 May (Labour Day), 24 June (St John's Day), 6 July (Anniversary of the Coronation of Grand Duke Mindaugas), 15 August (Assumption), 1 November (All Saints' Day), 25–26 December (Christmas).

Statistical Survey

Source (unless otherwise indicated): Department of Statistics to the Government of Lithuania (Statistics Lithuania), Gedimino pr. 29, Vilnius 01500; tel. (5) 236-4800; fax (5) 236-4845; e-mail statistika@stat.gov.lt; internet www.stat.gov.lt.

Area and Population

AREA, POPULATION AND DENSITY

Area (sq km)	65,300*
Population (census results)	
6 April 2001	3,483,972
1 March 2011	
Males	1,402,604
Females	1,640,825
Total	3,043,429
Population (official estimates at 1 January)	
2012	3,007,758
2013	2,979,310
Density (per sq km) at 1 January 2013	45.6

* 25,212 sq miles.

POPULATION BY AGE AND SEX
(official estimates at 1 January 2012)

	Males	Females	Total
0–14	230,173	218,005	448,178
15–64	972,209	1,044,038	2,016,247
65 and over	183,289	360,044	543,333
Total	**1,385,671**	**1,622,087**	**3,007,758**

POPULATION BY ETHNIC GROUP
(at 2011 census)

	Number	%
Lithuanian	2,561,314	84.1
Polish	200,317	6.6
Russian	176,913	5.8
Belarusian	36,227	1.2
Others	68,658	2.3
Total	**3,043,429**	**100.0**

ADMINISTRATIVE DIVISIONS
(official estimates at 1 January 2013)

County	Area (sq km)	Population	Density (per sq km)
Alytus	5,425	152,505	28.1
Kaunas	8,089	594,087	73.4
Klaipėda . . .	5,209	332,488	63.8
Marijampolė . .	4,463	156,795	35.1
Panevėžys . . .	7,881	242,837	30.8
Šiauliai	8,540	291,357	34.1
Tauragė	4,411	106,672	24.2
Telšiai	4,350	148,185	34.1
Utena	7,201	146,080	20.3
Vilnius	9,731	808,304	83.1
Total	**65,300**	**2,979,310**	**45.6**

PRINCIPAL TOWNS
(official estimates at 1 January 2013)

Vilnius (capital) .	527,930		Šiauliai	106,847
Kaunas . . .	307,498		Panevėžys . . .	97,589
Klaipėda . . .	158,891		Alytus	57,452

BIRTHS, MARRIAGES AND DEATHS

	Registered live births		Registered marriages		Registered deaths	
	Number	Rate (per 1,000)	Number	Rate (per 1,000)	Number	Rate (per 1,000)
2005 . .	30,541	8.9	19,938	5.8	43,799	12.8
2006 . .	31,265	9.2	21,246	6.3	44,813	13.2
2007 . .	32,346	9.6	23,065	6.8	45,624	13.5
2008 . .	35,065	10.5	24,063	7.2	43,832	13.1
2009 . .	36,682	11.0	20,542	6.2	42,032	12.5
2010 . .	35,626	10.7	18,688	5.6	42,120	12.7
2011 . .	34,385	10.6	19,221	5.9	41,037	12.6
2012 . .	34,068	11.3	19,329	6.3	40,914	13.5

Life expectancy (years at birth): 73 (males 68; females 79) in 2010 (Source: World Bank, World Development Indicators database).

IMMIGRATION AND EMIGRATION

	2010	2011	2012*
Immigrants	5,213	15,685	21,352
Emigrants	83,157	53,863	42,954

* Provisional.

ECONOMICALLY ACTIVE POPULATION
(annual averages, '000 persons, official estimates)

	2009	2010	2011
Agriculture, hunting, forestry and fishing	130.5	121.4	108.7
Mining and quarrying . . .	3.1	3.3	2.7
Manufacturing	226.0	208.2	193.5
Electricity, gas and water . . .	30.9	26.4	25.6
Construction	122.6	93.3	85.5
Wholesale and retail trade; repair of motor vehicles, motorcycles and personal and household goods	249.7	243.1	223.3
Hotels and restaurants . . .	34.9	33.6	32.5
Transport, storage and communications	115.5	114.7	117.4
Financial intermediation . . .	22.0	22.3	17.7
Real estate, renting and business activities	98.9	105.1	100.2
Public administration and defence; compulsory social security . .	84.9	82.3	75.9
Education	149.0	147.8	136.5
Health and social work . . .	92.6	92.3	86.5
Other community, social and personal service activities . .	53.7	48.3	48.4
Private households with employed persons	1.5	1.6	2.1
Extra-territorial organizations and bodies	0.1	0.2	0.3
Total	1,415.9	1,343.7	1,256.5
Unemployed	225.1	291.1	226.1
Total labour force	1,640.9	1,634.8	1,482.6
Males	819.8	812.6	736.4
Females	821.1	822.3	746.2

2012: Employed 1,278.0; Unemployed 195.6; Total labour force 1,473.6.

Health and Welfare

KEY INDICATORS

Total fertility rate (children per woman, 2010)	1.5
Under-5 mortality rate (per 1,000 live births, 2010) . . .	7
HIV/AIDS (% of persons aged 15–49, 2009)	0.1
Physicians (per 1,000 head, 2009)	3.6
Hospital beds (per 1,000 head, 2009)	6.8
Health expenditure (2009): US $ per head (PPP)	1,292
Health expenditure (2009): % of GDP	7.5
Health expenditure (2009): public (% of total)	73.4
Total carbon dioxide emissions ('000 metric tons, 2008) . .	15,130.0
Carbon dioxide emissions per head (metric tons, 2008) . .	4.5
Human Development Index (2011): ranking	40
Human Development Index (2011): value	0.810

For sources and definitions, see explanatory note on p. vi.

Agriculture

PRINCIPAL CROPS
('000 metric tons)

	2009	2010	2011
Wheat	2,100.2	1,710.4	1,869.0
Barley	858.2	550.0	759.8
Rye	207.9	86.7	85.0
Oats	142.5	93.9	128.5
Triticale (wheat-rye hybrid) . . .	426.0	258.4	237.0
Potatoes	662.5	476.9	587.7
Sugar beet	682.0	706.7	877.8
Peas, dry	50.3	42.5	47.5
Rapeseed	415.8	416.7	484.3
Cabbages and other brassicas .	123.3	53.3	112.9
Onions, dry	20.6	19.0	24.2
Carrots and turnips	63.7	40.9	70.5
Apples	53.3	34.0	49.1

Aggregate production ('000 metric tons, may include official, semi-official or estimated data): Total cereals 3,806.6 in 2009, 2,796.8 in 2010, 3,225.6 in 2011; Total roots and tubers 662.5 in 2009, 476.9 in 2010, 587.7 in 2011; Total vegetables (incl. melons) 335.8 in 2009, 175.6 in 2010, 301.3 in 2011; Total fruits (excl. melons) 70.5 in 2009, 44.5 in 2010, 62.0 in 2011.

Source: FAO.

LIVESTOCK
('000 head at 1 January)

	2009	2010	2011
Horses	54	49	45
Cattle	771	759	748
Pigs	897	928	929
Sheep	48	53	59
Goats	17	15	16
Chickens	8,841	9,034	9,203
Turkeys	194	213	206

Source: FAO.

LIVESTOCK PRODUCTS
('000 metric tons)

	2009	2010	2011
Cattle meat	45.1	43.7	42.0
Pig meat	60.4	73.3	74.9
Chicken meat	66.6	72.9	74.7
Cows' milk	1,786.9	1,732.5	1,782.3
Hen eggs	47.8	46.4	43.8
Honey	1.6	1.8	1.8

Source: FAO.

Forestry

ROUNDWOOD REMOVALS
('000 cubic metres, excl. bark)

	2009	2010	2011
Sawlogs, veneer logs and logs for sleepers	2,742	3,660	3,618
Pulpwood	935	1,494	1,728
Fuel wood	1,783	1,943	1,658
Total	5,460	7,097	7,004

Source: FAO.

SAWNWOOD PRODUCTION
('000 cubic metres, incl. railway sleepers)

	2009	2010	2011
Coniferous (softwood)	635	819	813
Broadleaved (hardwood)	376	453	447
Total	1,011	1,272	1,260

Source: FAO.

Fishing

(metric tons, live weight)

	2008	2009	2010
Capture	182,760	172,692	149,851
Largehead hairtail	28	19	149
Atlantic redfishes	828	5,544	3,833
Jack and horse mackerels	50,321	53,671	50,850
Sardinellas	23,021	16,781	16,611
European sprat	18,296	19,515	10,223
European anchovy	20,610	5,946	n.a.
Chub mackerel	17,768	17,903	14,137
Northern prawn	1,497	—	830
Aquaculture	3,008	3,422	3,191*
Total catch	185,768	176,114	153,042*

* FAO estimate.
Source: FAO.

Mining

('000 metric tons unless otherwise indicated)

	2009	2010	2011
Crude petroleum	115	112	108
Dolomite ('000 cubic metres)	869	1,150	1,147
Limestone	905	917	1,155
Clay ('000 cubic metres)	203	203	250
Peat	476	284	362

Industry

SELECTED PRODUCTS
('000 metric tons unless otherwise indicated)

	2010	2011	2012
Sausages and smoked meat products	62.7	64.4	67.3
Flour	297.9	334.2	341.9
Refined sugar	104.3	134.6	140.8
Beer ('000 hectolitres)	291.8	305.1	284.1
Wine (hectolitres)	7,240	6,123	6,479
Cotton fabrics (million sq m)	0.2	0.2	0.4
Woollen fabrics (million sq m)	2.4	2.3	2.3
Fabrics of man-made fibres	23.2	23.2	15.3
Footwear—excl. rubber and plastic ('000 pairs)*	1,000	900	900
Plywood ('000 cubic metres)	56.2	56.4	44.0
Particle board ('000 cubic metres)	551.1	647.8	664.4
Paper and paperboard	113.1	144.2	123.5
Sulphuric acid	1,153	766	731
Cement*	800	1,000	1,000
Cast iron	0.6	3.0	3.3
Television sets ('000)	416.5	376.9	209.1
Refrigerators and freezers ('000)	173.6	164.5	196.3
Bicycles ('000)	346	327	297
Electric energy (million kWh)	4,770	3,790	n.a.

* Figures are rounded.

Finance

CURRENCY AND EXCHANGE RATES

Monetary Units
100 centas = 1 litas (plural: litai).

Sterling, Dollar and Euro Equivalents (31 December 2012)
£1 sterling = 4.112 litai;
US $1 = 2.606 litai;
€1 = 3.453 litai;
100 litai = £24.32 = $38.37 = €28.96.

Average Exchange Rate (litai per US $)
2010   2.6063
2011   2.4811
2012   2.6863

Note: An official mid-point exchange rate of US $1 = 4.00 litai was in operation from 1 April 1994 until 1 February 2002. From 2 February 2002 the litas was linked to the euro, with the exchange rate set at €1 = 3.4528 litai.

GOVERNMENT FINANCE
(general government transactions, million litai)

Revenue	2009	2010	2011
Taxes	15,992.4	15,673.1	17,007.1
Indirect taxes	10,467.8	11,201.3	12,311.1
Direct taxes	5,518.6	4,468.0	4,692.6
Capital taxes	6.1	3.8	3.5
Social contributions	11,081.0	10,207.1	10,785.8
Sales	1,493.5	1,615.7	1,456.0
Other current revenue	1,463.9	1,965.6	2,237.8
Grants and other capital transfers	1,518.8	2,550.0	2,418.0
Total	31,549.5	32,011.5	33,904.9

Expenditure	2009	2010	2011
Compensation of employees	11,774.2	10,534.9	11,005.9
Intermediate consumption	5,348.0	6,080.8	5,581.0
Interest	1,159.9	1,730.4	1,901.2
Subsidies	588.4	476.4	434.1
Social benefits	15,811.5	14,183.8	14,046.0
Other current expenditure	1,399.7	1,080.8	1,626.1
Capital transfers	545.6	529.9	857.9
Capital investments	3,597.8	4,295.0	4,327.4
Total	40,225.3	38,912.0	39,779.7

INTERNATIONAL RESERVES
(US $ million at 31 December)

	2009	2010	2011
Gold (national valuation) . . .	206.43	263.71	294.45
IMF special drawing rights . .	215.26	211.46	210.81
Reserve position in IMF . . .	0.05	0.05	0.05
Foreign exchange	6,204.51	6,124.01	7,704.51
Total	6,626.25	6,599.23	8,209.82

Source: IMF, *International Financial Statistics.*

MONEY SUPPLY
(million litai at 31 December)

	2009	2010	2011
Currency outside depository corporations	6,972	7,847	9,681
Transferable deposits . . .	15,077	19,550	21,604
Other deposits	21,683	20,347	18,707
Securities other than shares . .	704	415	477
Broad money	44,436	48,159	50,469

Source: IMF, *International Financial Statistics.*

COST OF LIVING
(Consumer Price Index; base: 2000 = 100)

	2008	2009	2010
Food (incl. beverages) . . .	144.1	146.5	145.8
Fuel and light	156.3	181.7	195.5
Clothing	78.0	71.5	67.4
Rent	163.3	218.6	176.3
All items (incl. others) . . .	126.9	132.6	134.3

2011: Food (incl. beverages) 157.8; All items (incl. others) 139.9.

Source: ILO.

NATIONAL ACCOUNTS
(million litai at current prices)

National Income and Profit

	2009	2010	2011
Compensation of employees . .	41,327.5	39,542.6	41,987.5
Operating surplus and mixed income	27,573.3	32,044.9	39,531.6
Domestic primary incomes .	68,900.8	71,587.5	81,519.1
Consumption of fixed capital . .	13,832.8	13,751.8	13,748.3
Gross domestic product (GDP) at factor cost	82,733.6	85,339.3	95,267.4
Taxes on production and imports .	10,831.5	11,512.0	12,641.1
Less Subsidies	1,532.8	1,528.1	1,538.5
GDP in market prices . . .	92,032.4	95,323.2	106,369.9
Primary incomes received from abroad	2,223.4	2,857.0	3,356.8
Less Primary incomes paid abroad	598.9	4,756.8	7,294.8
Gross national income (GNI) .	93,656.9	93,423.5	102,431.9
Less Consumption of fixed capital .	13,832.8	13,751.8	13,748.3
Net national income . . .	79,824.1	79,671.7	88,683.6
Current transfers from abroad .	4,240.8	5,899.7	6,456.5
Less Current transfers paid abroad	2,364.1	2,465.9	3,469.0
Net national disposable income	81,700.8	83,105.5	91,671.2

Expenditure on the Gross Domestic Product

	2009	2010	2011
Final consumption expenditure .	83,126.6	80,279.8	87,554.1
Households	62,807.0	60,586.2	67,149.9
Non-profit institutions serving households	189.4	218.6	249.8
General government	20,130.2	19,474.9	20,154.4
Gross capital formation . . .	10,520.0	16,934.0	21,783.1
Gross fixed capital formation .	15,806.9	15,588.6	18,900.6
Changes in inventories . .	−5,317.2	1,293.4	2,809.0
Acquisitions, less disposals, of valuables	30.3	52.0	73.5
Total domestic expenditure .	93,646.6	97,213.8	109,337.2
Exports of goods and services . .	49,904.9	64,792.4	82,549.0
Less Imports of goods and services	51,519.1	66,682.9	85,516.3
GDP in market prices . . .	92,032.4	95,323.2	106,369.9

Gross Domestic Product by Economic Activity

	2009	2010	2011
Agriculture, hunting, forestry and fishing	2,318.1	2,815.4	3,350.2
Mining and quarrying	263.3	318.0	411.0
Manufacturing	13,940.4	16,215.6	19,720.2
Electricity, gas and water supply .	3,529.5	3,610.9	3,517.1
Construction	5,486.8	5,047.0	6,251.2
Wholesale and retail trade; repair of motor vehicles, motorcycles and personal and household goods	14,566.5	15,287.9	17,763.8
Hotels and restaurants . . .	1,156.0	1,055.8	1,216.2
Transportation and storage . .	8,870.2	10,337.3	11,224.1
Information and communications .	3,253.4	3,133.8	3,010.8
Financial intermediation . . .	1,860.0	2,036.1	2,408.3
Real estate	6,092.9	5,649.3	5,683.5
Professional, scientific and technical activities	3,375.9	3,147.6	3,388.4
Administrative and support service activities	1,943.5	1,843.4	2,018.0
Public administration and defence; compulsory social security . .	6,151.0	5,782.8	5,924.1
Education	5,070.2	4,567.2	4,590.9
Health and social work . . .	3,293.1	3,089.1	3,373.3
Other community, social and personal service activities . .	1,660.8	1,542.1	1,602.8
Private households with employed persons	78.8	82.4	88.9
Gross value added at basic prices	82,910.3	85,561.7	95,543.0
Taxes on products	10,371.0	11,054.9	12,163.1
Less Subsidies on products . .	1,248.9	1,293.3	1,336.1
GDP in market prices . . .	92,032.4	95,323.2	106,369.9

BALANCE OF PAYMENTS
(US $ million)

	2009	2010	2011
Exports of goods	15,420.0	19,652.0	27,029.0
Imports of goods	−17,003.8	−21,799.9	−29,523.5
Balance on goods	−1,583.9	−2,147.9	−2,494.5
Exports of services	4,112.5	4,563.4	5,607.3
Imports of services	−2,983.3	−2,811.9	−3,628.8
Balance on goods and services	−454.7	−396.4	−516.0
Primary income received . . .	821.2	726.5	924.5
Primary income paid	−267.4	−1,554.5	−2,525.8
Balance on goods, services and primary income	99.1	−1,224.3	−2,117.4
Secondary income received . .	2,723.6	2,820.7	3,054.2
Secondary income paid . . .	−1,097.8	−1,062.6	−1,556.0
Current balance	1,724.9	533.8	−619.1

—continued	2009	2010	2011
Capital account (net)	1,261.5	985.8	1,052.5
Direct investment assets . . .	−273.2	−35.7	−389.9
Direct investment liabilities . .	88.5	701.8	1,443.1
Portfolio investment assets .	−1,162.2	−546.7	165.7
Portfolio investment liabilities .	2,293.6	2,456.7	1,376.2
Financial derivatives and employee stock options (net)	38.1	−89.0	5.5
Other investment assets . . .	−709.0	−399.0	−681.5
Other investment liabilities . .	−3,128.3	−2,912.0	−535.2
Net errors and omissions . .	10.3	3.4	60.8
Reserves and related items .	144.4	699.3	1,878.1

Source: IMF, *International Financial Statistics*.

External Trade

PRINCIPAL COMMODITIES
(million litai)

Imports c.i.f.	2009	2010	2011
Prepared foodstuffs; beverages, spirits and vinegar; tobacco and manufactured substitutes . .	2,686.4	2,943.5	3,601.4
Mineral products	13,157.1	20,276.2	27,028.8
Mineral fuels	12,527.8	19,524.4	25,977.4
Products of the chemical or allied industries	5,570.0	6,708.5	8,097.1
Plastics, rubber and articles thereof	2,058.0	2,739.9	3,385.7
Textiles and textile articles .	2,285.3	2,753.9	3,171.8
Base metals and articles thereof .	2,274.4	3,015.9	4,044.3
Machinery and mechanical appliances; electrical equipment; sound and television apparatus .	5,998.2	7,684.5	9,712.9
Nuclear reactors, boilers, etc. .	3,514.3	4,222.2	5,675.1
Electrical machinery, sound and television recorders and parts thereof	2,483.9	3,462.3	4,037.8
Vehicles, aircraft, vessels and associated transport equipment .	2,953.6	4,624.3	7,234.0
Total (incl. others)	45,311.0	60,952.8	78,812.2

Exports f.o.b.	2009	2010	2011
Live animals and animal products	2,289.7	2,723.2	3,353.3
Vegetable products	2,644.8	3,295.1	3,991.8
Prepared foodstuffs; beverages, spirits and vinegar; tobacco and manufactured substitutes . .	2,891.0	3,588.4	4,054.8
Mineral products	8,746.1	12,733.0	17,761.8
Mineral fuels	8,678.2	12,633.6	17,608.3
Products of the chemical or allied industries	3,694.7	4,397.1	6,374.1
Fertilizers	1,814.4	2,082.6	3,356.1
Plastics, rubber and articles thereof	2,750.8	3,677.4	4,314.5
Wood, cork and articles thereof; wood charcoal; manufactures of straw, esparto, etc.	1,337.2	1,875.9	2,324.8
Textiles and textile articles .	2,624.7	3,225.3	3,671.1
Articles of apparel and clothing accessories, not knitted . .	814.5	969.2	1,099.6
Base metals and articles thereof .	1,817.0	2,421.0	3,264.7
Machinery and mechanical appliances; electrical equipment; sound and television apparatus .	4,078.0	5,643.3	7,214.5
Vehicles, aircraft, vessels and associated transport equipment .	2,956.1	4,196.5	5,339.0
Miscellaneous manufactured articles	2,6023.0	3,145.3	3,910.9
Total (incl. others)	40,732.0	54,038.8	69,576.8

PRINCIPAL TRADING PARTNERS
(million litai)

Imports c.i.f.	2009	2010	2011
Belarus	748.7	1,037.0	1,919.7
Belgium	1,345.7	1,991.8	2,496.5
China, People's Republic . . .	1,122.8	1,486.2	1,559.1
Czech Republic	842.8	876.4	1,001.4
Denmark	1,006.6	1,044.9	1,277.2
Estonia	1,188.6	1,743.4	2,216.1
Finland	847.7	1,092.7	1,644.1
France	1,129.9	1,578.8	1,911.5
Germany	5,133.7	6,427.3	7,864.1
Hungary	465.8	493.5	619.0
Italy	1,736.5	2,013.9	2,727.1
Latvia	2,904.9	3,855.3	5,230.5
Netherlands	1,835.4	2,718.6	3,942.8
Poland	4,517.3	5,417.0	7,151.7
Russia	13,537.0	19,880.2	25,259.8
Spain	678.2	755.3	847.6
Sweden	1,226.7	2,000.5	2,598.7
United Kingdom	748.1	971.7	1,285.7
USA	504.8	628.3	917.5
Total (incl. others)	45,311.0	60,952.8	78,812.2

Exports f.o.b.	2009	2010	2011
Belarus	1,923.5	2,840.4	3,602.8
Belgium	702.6	737.1	800.6
Canada	215.0	958.4	783.0
Denmark	1,552.8	1,621.8	1,482.6
Estonia	2,860.7	2,727.3	4,620.0
Finland	673.2	751.7	931.1
France	1,305.3	1,791.2	2,880.5
Germany	3,943.3	5,341.7	6,472.0
Italy	811.8	1,045.4	1,259.3
Kazakhstan	696.6	814.0	1,094.5
Latvia	4,099.1	5,058.0	7,118.8
Netherlands	2,067.9	3,001.9	4,266.0
Norway	1,018.3	1,242.5	1,406.1
Poland	2,927.1	4,178.8	4,832.6
Russia	5,394.4	8,458.7	11,532.7
Spain	674.8	565.7	852.0
Sweden	1,473.4	1,953.5	2,494.0
Ukraine	1,221.5	1,954.4	2,305.6
United Kingdom	1,788.5	2,658.0	2,771.1
USA	1,200.8	1,470.8	1,811.4
Total (incl. others)	40,732.0	54,038.8	69,576.8

Transport

RAILWAYS
(traffic)

	2009	2010	2011
Passenger journeys ('000) . .	4,374.1	4,363.0	4,655.2
Passenger-km (million) . .	356.9	373.1	389.1
Freight transported ('000 metric tons)	42,668.6	48,060.7	52,329.8
Freight ton-km (million) . . .	11,888	13,431	15,088

ROAD TRAFFIC
(motor vehicles in use at 31 December)

	2009	2010	2011
Passenger cars	1,695,286	1,691,855	1,713,277
Buses and coaches	13,360	13,261	13,086
Lorries and vans	126,519	113,113	113,452
Motorcycles and mopeds . . .	51,372	56,217	60,124

INLAND WATERWAYS

	2009	2010	2011
Passenger journeys ('000) . .	2,014.9	1,870.8	1,715.5
Passenger-km (million) . . .	3	4	3
Freight transported ('000 metric tons)	908.5	996.3	1,037.7
Freight ton-km (million) . . .	4	4	4

SHIPPING

Flag Registered Fleet
(at 31 December)

	2010	2011	2012
Number of vessels	148	141	133
Total displacement ('000 grt) . .	447.2	445.8	413.0

Source: Lloyd's List Intelligence (www.lloydslistintelligence.com).

International Sea-borne Freight Traffic
('000 metric tons)

	2009	2010	2011
Goods loaded	21,550	23,613	28,023
Goods unloaded	14,705	16,682	17,504

CIVIL AVIATION
(traffic on scheduled services)

	2009	2010	2011
Passengers carried ('000) . .	715.2	828.2	444.6
Passenger-km (million) . . .	1,528	1,967	797
Freight transported ('000 metric tons)	3.7	2.9	3.5
Freight ton-km (million) . . .	1.9	2.6	2.9

Tourism

FOREIGN VISITORS BY COUNTRY OF ORIGIN
(arrivals at accommodation establishments)

	2009	2010	2011
Belarus	52,193	71,436	92,248
Estonia	30,340	32,527	37,409
Finland	30,211	35,137	36,483
France	21,641	23,248	25,684
Germany	110,163	105,832	128,930
Italy	20,689	22,547	31,490
Latvia	62,815	66,519	66,145
Poland	125,662	135,856	139,632
Russia	78,690	105,869	148,267
Sweden	19,101	19,747	25,303
United Kingdom	25,911	35,398	32,857
USA	16,961	19,666	24,850
Total (incl. others)	752,389	840,368	1,003,843

Receipts from tourism (US $ million, excl. passenger transport): 1,011 in 2009; 1,021 in 2010; 1,353 in 2011 (provisional) (Source: World Tourism Organization).

Communications Media

	2009	2010	2011
Telephones ('000 main lines in use)	747.4	733.7	723.0
Mobile cellular telephones ('000 subscribers)	4,961.5	4,891.0	5,004.2
Internet subscribers ('000) . .	636.0	685.2	n.a.
Broadband subscribers ('000) . .	633.8	684.1	732.0
Book titles (incl. brochures) . .	3,972	3,176	3,278
Newspapers: number . . .	297	276	262
Newspapers: average circulation (million copies)	229.4	188.3	176.2
Magazines and other periodicals .	589	561	558
Magazines and other periodicals: average circulation (million copies)	65.8	59.5	61.7

Personal computers: 812,400 (241.9 per 1,000 persons) in 2008.

Sources: International Telecommunication Union, and Ministry of Education and Science, Vilnius.

Education

(2011/12 unless otherwise indicated)

	Institutions	Teachers	Students
General schools	1,309	37,436	392,922
Vocational schools	75	3,897	46,530
Professional college . . .	1*	120†	16*
Colleges	24	3,729	49,777
Universities	23	9,809	125,046

* 2006/07.
† 2005/06.

Pupil-teacher ratio (primary education, UNESCO estimate): 12.8 in 2009/10 (Source: UNESCO Institute for Statistics).

Adult literacy rate (UNESCO estimates): 99.7% (males 99.7%; females 99.7%) in 2010 (Source: UNESCO Institute for Statistics).

Directory

The Government

HEAD OF STATE

President: DALIA GRYBAUSKAITĖ (inaugurated 12 July 2009).

COUNCIL OF MINISTERS
(May 2013)

A coalition comprising representatives of the Lithuanian Social Democratic Party (LSDP), the Labour Party (LP), the Order and Justice Party (TT) and the Electoral Action of Poles in Lithuania (AWPL).

Prime Minister: ALGIRDAS BUTKEVIČIUS (LSDP).

Minister of Health: VYTENIS ANDRIUKAITIS (LSDP).

Minister of the Interior: DAILIS BARAKAUSKAS (TT).

Minister of Justice: JUOZAS BERNATONIS (LSDP).

Minister of Culture: ŠARŪNAS BIRUTIS (LP).

Minister of Agriculture: VIGILIJUS JUKNA (LP).

Minister of Foreign Affairs: LINAS LINKEVIČIUS (LSDP).

Minister of the Environment: VALENTINAS MAZURONIS (TT).

Minister of Energy: JAROSLAV NEVEROVIČ (Independent).

Minister of National Defence: JUOZAS OLEKAS (LSDP).

Minister of Social Security and Labour: ALGIMANTA PABEDINSKIENĖ (LP).

Minister of Education and Science: DAINIUS PAVALKIS (LP).

Minister of Transport and Communications: RIMANTAS SINKEVIČIUS (LSDP).

Minister of Finance: RIMANTAS ŠADŽIUS (LSDP).

Minister of the Economy: BIRUTĖ VĖSAITĖ (LSDP).

MINISTRIES

Office of the President: S. Daukanto 3, Vilnius 01122; tel. (5) 266-4154; fax (5) 266-4145; e-mail kanceliarija@prezidentas.lt; internet www.president.lt.

Office of the Prime Minister: Gedimino pr. 11, Vilnius 01103; tel. (8) 706-63711; fax (8) 706-63895; e-mail mptarnyba@lrv.lt; internet www.lrv.lt.

Ministry of Agriculture: Gedimino pr. 19, Vilnius 01103; tel. (5) 239-1111; fax (5) 239-1212; e-mail zum@zum.lt; internet www.zum.lt.

Ministry of Culture: J. Basanavičiaus 5, Vilnius 01118; tel. (5) 219-3400; fax (5) 262-3120; e-mail culture@lrkm.lt; internet www.lrkm.lt.

Ministry of the Economy: Gedimino pr. 38, Vasario 16-osios g. 2, Vilnius 01104; tel. (8) 706-64762; fax (8) 706-64845; e-mail kanc@ukmin.lt; internet www.ukmin.lt.

Ministry of Education and Science: A. Volano 2/7, Vilnius 01516; tel. (5) 219-1190; fax (5) 261-2077; e-mail smmin@smm.lt; internet www.smm.lt.

Ministry of Energy: Gedimino pr. 38, Vasario 16-osios g. 2, Vilnius 01104; tel. (8) 706-64715; fax (8) 706-64820; e-mail info@enmin.lt; internet www.enmin.lt.

Ministry of the Environment: A. Jakšto 4/9, Vilnius 01105; tel. (5) 266-3661; fax (5) 266-3663; e-mail info@am.lt; internet www.am.lt.

Ministry of Finance: Lukiškių g. 2, Vilnius 01512; tel. (5) 239-0000; fax (5) 279-1481; e-mail finmin@finmin.lt; internet www.finmin.lt.

Ministry of Foreign Affairs: J. Tumo-Vaižganto g. 2, Vilnius 01511; tel. (5) 236-2444; fax (5) 231-3090; e-mail urm@urm.lt; internet www.urm.lt.

Ministry of Health: Vilniaus g. 33, Vilnius 01506; tel. (5) 268-5110; fax (5) 266-1402; e-mail ministerija@sam.lt; internet www.sam.lt.

Ministry of the Interior: Šventaragio 2, Vilnius 01510; tel. (5) 271-7130; fax (5) 271-8551; e-mail bendrasisd@vrm.lt; internet www.vrm.lt.

Ministry of Justice: Gedimino pr. 30, Vilnius 01104; tel. (5) 266-2981; fax (5) 262-5940; e-mail rastine@tm.lt; internet www.tm.lt.

Ministry of National Defence: Totorių 25/3, Vilnius 01121; tel. (5) 273-5673; fax (5) 264-8517; e-mail pilieciuaptarnavimas@kam.lt; internet www.kam.lt.

Ministry of Social Security and Labour: A. Vivulskio g. 11, Vilnius 03610; tel. (5) 266-4201; fax (5) 266-4209; e-mail post@socmin.lt; internet www.socmin.lt.

Ministry of Transport and Communications: Gedimino pr. 17, Vilnius 01505; tel. (5) 261-2363; fax (5) 212-4335; e-mail sumin@sumin.lt; internet www.transp.lt.

President

Presidential Election, 17 May 2009

Candidates	Valid votes	%
Dalia Grybauskaitė	950,407	69.09
Algirdas Butkevičius	162,665	11.82
Valentinas Mazuronis	84,656	6.15
Valdemar Tomaševski	65,255	4.74
Kazimiera Danutė Prunskienė	53,778	3.91
Loreta Graužinienė	49,686	3.61
Česlovas Jezerskas	9,191	0.67
Total	1,374,319	100.00

Legislature

Seimas
(Parliament)

Gedimino pr. 53, Vilnius 01109; tel. (5) 239-6060; fax (5) 239-6289; e-mail priim@lrs.lt; internet www.lrs.lt.

Chairman: IRENA DEGUTIENĖ.

General Election, 14 and 28 October 2012

	Seats		
Parties and blocs	A*	B*	Total
Homeland Union—Lithuanian Christian Democrats	13	23	36
Lithuanian Social Democratic Party	15	19	34
Labour Party	17	13	30
Liberal Movement of the Republic of Lithuania	7	4	11
Order and Justice Party	6	4	10
Electoral Action of Poles in Lithuania	5	4	9
The Way of Courage	7	—	7
Lithuanian Peasant and Greens Union	—	1	1
Independent candidates	—	2	2
Total†	70	71	141

* Of the 141 seats in the Seimas, 70 (A) are awarded according to proportional representation on the basis of party lists, and 71 (B) are elected in single-mandate constituencies.

†Including one further member who remained to be elected from a single-mandate constituency.

Election Commission

Lietuvos Republikos Vyriausioji rinkimų komisija (Central Electoral Committee of the Republic of Lithuania): Gynėjų g. 8, Vilnius 01109; tel. (5) 239-6969; fax (5) 239-6960; e-mail rinkim@vrk.lt; internet www.vrk.lt; Chair. ZENONAS VAIGAUSKAS.

Political Organizations

In March 2013 some 45 political parties were officially registered. The following were among the most significant:

Christian Party (Krikščionių partija): Odminių g. 5, Vilnius 01122; tel. and fax (5) 212-6874; e-mail info@krikscioniupartija.lt; internet www.krikscioniupartija.lt; f. 2010 by merger of Christian-Conservative Social Union and Lithuanian Christian Democratic Party; Leader GEDIMINAS VAGNORIUS.

Civil Democracy Party (Pilietinės Demokratijos Partija): Kaštonų g. 4, Vilnius 01107; tel. (5) 204-0204; fax (5) 204-0205; e-mail pdpsekretoriatas@gmail.com; internet www.pdp.lt; f. 2006; fmrly Civic Union; joined by fmr members of the Labour Party and the Liberal Democratic Party in 2006; Chair. ALGIMANTAS MATULEVIČIUS.

Electoral Action of Poles in Lithuania (AWPL) (Akcja Wyborcza Polaków na Litwie): Pilies g. 16, Vilnius 01123; tel. (5) 233-3103; fax (5) 233-1266; e-mail info@awpl.lt; internet www.awpl.lt; f. 1994; Chair. WALDEMAR TOMASZEWSKI.

Homeland Union—Lithuanian Christian Democrats (HU—LCD) (Tėvynės Sąjunga—Lietuvos Krikščionys Demokratai—TS—LKD): L. Stuokos-Gucevičiaus g. 11, Vilnius 01122; tel. (5) 212-1657;

fax (5) 278-4722; e-mail sekretoriatas@tsajunga.lt; internet www
.tsajunga.lt; f. 1993 as the Conservative Party of Lithuania (Homeland Union); absorbed the Lithuanian Rightist Union in Nov. 2003;
merged with the Lithuanian Union of Political Prisoners and
Deportees in Feb. 2004; merged with the Lithuanian Christian
Democrats in May 2008, and name changed as above; Chair. ANDRIUS
KUBILIUS; some 18,000 mems.

Labour Party (LP) (Darbo Partija): Ankštoji 3, Vilnius 01109; tel.
(5) 210-7152; fax (5) 210-7153; e-mail info@darbopartija.lt; internet
www.darbopartija.lt; f. 2003; Chair. VIKTORAS USPASKICH; 13,000
mems.

Liberal and Centre Union (Liberalų Centro Sąjunga): Vilniaus g.
22/1, Vilnius 01402; tel. (5) 231-3264; fax (5) 261-9363; e-mail info@
lics.lt; internet www.lics.lt; f. 2003 by a merger of the Lithuanian
Centre Union, the Lithuanian Liberal Union and the Modern
Christian Democratic Union; Chair. ALGIS ČAPLIKAS; over 5,000
mems.

Liberal Movement of the Republic of Lithuania (Lietuvos
Respublikos liberalų sąjūdis): Vašingtono aikštė 1, Vilnius 01108;
tel. (5) 249-6959; fax (5) 212-1083; e-mail info@liberalai.lt; internet
www.liberalai.lt; f. 2006; formed by a splinter group of the Liberal
and Centre Union; Chair. ELIGIJUS MASIULIS.

Lithuanian Peasant and Greens Union (Lietuvos Valstiečių ir
žaliųjų Sąjunga—LVZS): Pamėnkalnio g. 26, Vilnius 01114; tel. (5)
212-0821; fax (5) 212-0822; e-mail info@lvzs.lt; internet www.lvls.lt;
f. 2001 by the merger of the New Democracy Party and the
Lithuanian Peasants' (Farmers') Party; fmrly Peasants' (Farmers')
and New Democratic Party Union (VNDS); name changed to
Lithuanian Peasant Nationalists' Union (LVLS) in Feb. 2006;
present name adopted Jan. 2012; Chair. RAMŪNAS KARBAUSKIS;
3,500 mems (2012).

Lithuanian Polish People's Party (Lietuvos Lenkų Liaudies
Partija/Polska Partia Ludowa): Kauno g. 1A, Vilnius 03212; tel. (5)
216-2874; fax (5) 233-5467; e-mail lllp@zebra.lt; internet www.lllp.lt;
f. 2002; Chair. ANTONINA POŁTAWIEC.

Lithuanian Russians' Union (Lietuvos rusų sąjunga/Soyuz Russkikh Litvy): A. Rotundo g. 5, Vilnius 01400; tel. and fax (5) 262-4248;
e-mail srl@pochta.ru; internet sojuzrus.lt; f. 1995; Chair. SERGEI
DMITRIYEV.

Lithuanian Social Democratic Party (LSDP) (Lietuvos Social-
demokratų Partija): Barboros Radvilaites g. 1, Vilnius 01124; tel. (5)
261-3907; fax (5) 261-5420; e-mail info@lsdp.lt; internet www.lsdp.lt;
absorbed the Lithuanian Democratic Labour Party in 2001; Chair.
ALGIRDAS BUTKEVIČIUS; 11,000 mems.

National Revival Party (NRP) (Tautos prisikėlimo partija):
Pranciškonų g. 4A/10, Vilnius 01133; tel. (8) 698-09686; fax (5)
240-0493; e-mail tppbustine@inbox.lt; internet www
.prisikelimopartija.lt; f. 2008; Leader ARŪNO VALINSKO.

New Union (Social Liberals) (NU) (Naujoji sąjunga—Socialliber-
alai): Gedimino pr. 10/1, Vilnius 01103; tel. (5) 210-7600; fax (5) 210-
7602; e-mail centras@nsajunga.lt; internet www.nsajunga.lt; f. 1998;
centre-left; Chair. ARTŪRAS PAULAUSKAS.

Order and Justice Party (TT) (Partijos Tvarka ir teisingumas):
Gedimino pr. 10/1, Vilnius 01103; tel. and fax (5) 269-1618; e-mail tt@
tvarka.lt; internet www.tvarka.lt; f. 2002; fmrly Liberal Democratic
Party (LDP); present name adopted 2008; right-wing; Chair.
ROLANDAS PAKSAS; 6,500 mems (2007).

The Way of Courage (Drąsos Kelias): Vytauto g. 57-2, Garliava;
e-mail drasoskelias.partija@gmail.com; internet drasiauskelias.lt;
f. 2012; populist, anti-corruption; Leader JONAS VARKALA; 1,019
mems (Sept. 2012).

Diplomatic Representation

EMBASSIES IN LITHUANIA

Armenia: Lenktoji g. 17, Vilnius 08124; tel. (5) 207-5040; fax (5) 207-
5042; e-mail armlithuaniaembassy@mfa.am; Ambassador ARA
AYVAZIAN.

Austria: Gaono g. 6, Vilnius 01131; tel. (5) 266-0580; fax (5) 279-
1363; internet www.bmeia.gv.at/wilna; Ambassador Dr HELMUT
KOLLER.

Azerbaijan: Olimpiečių g. 5–7, Vilnius 02051; tel. (5) 219-0042; fax
(5) 279-1504; e-mail info@azembassy.lt; Ambassador HASAN MAM-
MADZADE.

Belarus: Mindaugo g. 13, Vilnius 03225; tel. (5) 266-2200; fax (5)
266-2212; e-mail lithuania.emb@mfa.gov.by; internet www
.lithuania.belembassy.org; Ambassador ULADZIMIR DRAZHIN.

Belgium: Kalinausko g. 2B, Vilnius 03107; tel. (5) 266-0820; fax (5)
212-6444; e-mail vilnius@diplobel.org; internet www.diplomatie.be/
vilnius; Ambassador PETER LESCOUHIER.

Bulgaria: Pylimo 8, Palangos 2, Vilnius 01118; tel. (5) 249-9274; fax
(5) 261-9174; e-mail vilnius@bgembassy.lt; internet www.mfa.bg/
vilnius; Ambassador MICHAELA TODOROVA.

China, People's Republic: Algirdo g. 36, Vilnius 03218; tel. (5) 216-
2862; fax (5) 216-2682; e-mail chinaemb_lt@mfa.gov.cn; internet
www.chinaembassy.lt; Ambassador LIU ZENGWEN.

Czech Republic: Birutės g. 16, Vilnius 08117; tel. (5) 266-1040; fax
(5) 266-1066; e-mail vilnius@embassy.mzv.cz; internet www.mzv.cz/
vilnius; Ambassador RADEK PECH.

Denmark: T. Kosciuškos g. 36, Vilnius 01100; tel. (5) 264-8760; fax
(5) 231-2300; e-mail vnoamb@um.dk; internet www.litauen.um.dk;
Ambassador JØRGEN MOLDE.

Estonia: A. Mickevičiaus g. 4A, Vilnius 08119; tel. (5) 278-0200; fax
(5) 278-0201; e-mail sekretar@estemb.lt; internet www.estemb.lt;
Ambassador TOOMAS KUKK.

Finland: Klaipėdos g. 24, Vilnius 03107; tel. (5) 266-8010; fax (5)
212-2441; e-mail sanomat.vil@formin.fi; internet www.finland.lt;
Ambassador HARRI MÄKI-REINIKKA.

France: Švarco g. 1, Vilnius 01131; tel. (5) 219-9600; fax (5) 219-
9613; e-mail ambafrance.vilnius@diplomatie.gouv.fr; internet www
.ambafrance-lt.org; Ambassador MARYSE BERNIAU.

Georgia: Poškos g. 13, Vilnius 08123; tel. (5) 273-6959; fax (5) 272-
3623; e-mail embassy@georgia.w3.lt; internet www.lithuania.mfa
.gov.ge; Ambassador GEORGI PANIASHVILI.

Germany: Z. Sierakausko g. 24, Vilnius 03105; tel. (5) 210-6400; fax
(5) 210-6446; e-mail info@wilna.diplo.de; internet www.wilna.diplo
.de; Ambassador MATTHIAS MÜLMENSTÄDT.

Greece: Didžioji 33/Rūdininkų 2, Vilnius 01132; tel. (5) 261-0526;
fax (5) 261-0536; e-mail embassy@grembvil.w3.lt; Ambassador
MICHAEL-EFSTRATIOS C. DARATZIKIS.

Holy See: Kosciuškos g. 28, Vilnius 01100; tel. (5) 212-3696; fax (5)
212-4228; e-mail nuntiusbalt@aiva.lt; Apostolic Nuncio Most Rev.
LUIGI BONAZZI (Titular Archbishop of Glastonia).

Hungary: Jojailos g. 4, Vilnius 01116; tel. (5) 269-0038; fax (5) 269-
0039; e-mail mission.vno@mfa.gov.hu; internet www.mfa.gov.hu/
emb/vilnius; Ambassador ZOLTÁN PECZE.

Ireland: Gedimino pr. 1, Vilnius 01103; tel. (5) 262-9460; fax (5) 262-
9462; e-mail vilniusembassy@dfa.ie; internet www
.embassyofireland.lt; f. 2005; Ambassador PHILOMENA MURNAGHAN.

Italy: Vytauto g. 1, Vilnius 08118; tel. (5) 212-0620; fax (5) 212-0405;
e-mail ambasciata.vilnius@esteri.it; internet www.ambvilnius
.esteri.it; Ambassador RENATO MARIA RICCI.

Japan: M. K. Čiurlionio g. 82B, Vilnius 03100; tel. (5) 231-0462; fax
(5) 231-0461; e-mail info@vn.mofa.go.jp; internet www.lt.emb-japan
.go.jp; Ambassador KAZUKO SHIRAISHI.

Kazakhstan: Birutės g. 20A/35, Vilnius 08117; tel. (5) 212-2123; fax
(5) 231-3580; e-mail vilnius@mfa.kz; internet kazakhstan.embassy
.lt; Ambassador BAURJAN MUHAMEDJANOV.

Latvia: M. K. Čiurlionio g. 76, Vilnius 03100; tel. (5) 213-1260; fax (5)
213-1130; e-mail embassy.lithuania@mfa.gov.lv; internet www
.latvia.lt; Ambassador MARTINŠ VIRSIS.

Moldova: Miglos g. 61A, Vilnius 08102; tel. (5) 260-7914; fax (5) 260-
7915; e-mail vilnius@mfa.md; internet www.lituania.mfa.gov.md;
Ambassador IGOR KLIPII.

Netherlands: Kosciuškos g. 36, Vilnius 01100; tel. (5) 210-4620; fax
(5) 210-4629; internet lithuania.nlembassy.org; Ambassador KOR-
NELIS SPAANS.

Norway: Kalinausko g. 24/3, Vilnius 03107; tel. (5) 261-0000; fax (5)
261-0100; e-mail emb.vilnius@mfa.no; internet www.norvegija.lt;
Ambassador LEIF ARNE ULLAND.

Poland: Smėlio g. 20A, Vilnius 10323; tel. (5) 270-9001; fax (5) 270-
9007; e-mail wilno.amb.sekretariat@msz.gov.pl; internet www
.wilno.polemb.net; Ambassador JANUSZ SKOLIMOWSKI.

Portugal: Gedimino pr. 5, Vilnius 01103; tel. (5) 262-0511; fax (5)
262-0512; e-mail vilnius@embportugal.lt; Ambassador JOÃO MANUEL
DA CRUZ DA SILVA LEITÃO.

Romania: Vivulskio g. 19, Vilnius 03115; tel. (5) 231-0557; fax (5)
231-0652; e-mail ambromania@romania.lt; internet vilnius.mae.ro;
Ambassador DAN ADRIAN BĂLĂNESCU.

Russia: Latvių g. 53/54, Vilnius 08113; tel. (5) 272-1763; fax (5) 272-
3877; e-mail post@rusemb.lt; internet www.lithuania.mid.ru;
Ambassador VLADIMIR V. CHKHIKVADZE.

Spain: Algirdo g. 4, Vilnius 03161; tel. (5) 231-3961; fax (5) 231-3962;
e-mail emb.vilnius@mae.es; Ambassador MIGUEL ARIA ESTÉVEZ.

Sweden: Didžioji g. 16, Vilnius 01128; tel. (5) 268-5010; fax (5) 268-
5030; e-mail ambassaden.vilnius@foreign.ministry.se; internet
www.swedenabroad.com/vilnius; Ambassador CECILIA RUTHSTRÖM-
RUIN.

Turkey: Didžioji g. 37, Vilnius 01128; tel. (5) 264-9570; fax (5) 212-3277; e-mail embassy.vilnius@mfa.gov.tr; internet vilnius.emb.mfa.gov.tr; Ambassador AKIN ALGAN.

Ukraine: Teatro g. 4, Vilnius 03107; tel. (5) 212-1536; fax (5) 212-0475; e-mail emb_lt@mfa.gov.ua; internet www.mfa.gov.ua/lithuania; Ambassador VALERII ZHOVTENKO.

United Kingdom: Antakalnio g. 2, Vilnius 10308; tel. (5) 246-2900; fax (5) 246-2901; e-mail be-vilnius@britain.lt; internet ukinlithuania.fco.gov.uk; Ambassador DAVID HUNT.

USA: Akmenų g. 6, Vilnius 03106; tel. (5) 266-5300; fax (5) 266-5310; e-mail webemailvilnius@state.gov; internet vilnius.usembassy.gov; Ambassador DEBORAH A. MCCARTHY.

Judicial System

The organs of justice are the Supreme Court, the Court of Appeal, district courts, local courts of administrative areas and a special court—the Commercial Court. The Seimas (Parliament) appoints and dismisses from office the judges of the Supreme Court in response to representations made by the President of the Republic (based upon the recommendation of the chairman of the Supreme Court). Judges of the Court of Appeal are appointed by the President with the approval of the Seimas (on the recommendation of the Minister of Justice), while judges of district and local courts are appointed and dismissed by the President. The Council of Judges submits recommendations to the President of the Republic concerning the appointment of judges, as well as their promotion, transfer or dismissal from office.

The Constitutional Court decides on the constitutionality of acts of the Seimas, as well as of the President and the Government. It consists of nine judges, who are appointed by the Seimas for a single term of nine years; one-third of the Court's members are replaced every three years.

The Office of the Prosecutor-General is an autonomous institution of the judiciary, comprising the Prosecutor-General and local and district prosecutors' offices, which are subordinate to him. The Prosecutor-General and his deputies are appointed for terms of seven years by the President, subject to approval by the Seimas, while the prosecutors are appointed by the Prosecutor-General. The Office of the Prosecutor-General incorporates the Department for Crime Investigation. The State Arbitration decides cases of business litigation. A six-volume Civil Code, in accordance with European Union and international law, came into effect in 2001, replacing the Soviet civil legal system, which had, hitherto, remained in operation.

Constitutional Court (Lietuvos Respublikos Konstitucinis Teismas): Gedimino pr. 36, Vilnius 01104; tel. (5) 261-3535; fax (5) 212-7975; e-mail pastas@lrkt.lt; internet www.lrkt.lt; f. 1993; Pres. ROMUALDAS KĘSTUTIS URBAITIS.

Court of Appeal: Gedimino pr. 40/1, Vilnius 01503; tel. (5) 66-3685; fax (5) 66-3060; e-mail apeliacinis@apeliacinis.lt; internet www.apeliacinis.lt; Chair. EGIDIJUS ŽIRONAS.

Supreme Court (Lietuvos Aukščiausiasis Teismas): Gynėjų g. 6, Vilnius 01109; tel. (5) 261-6466; fax (5) 261-6813; e-mail lat@teismas.lt; internet www.lat.lt; Chair. GINTARAS KRYŽEVIČIUS.

Office of the Prosecutor-General: Rinktinės g. 5A, Vilnius 01515; tel. (5) 266-2305; fax (5) 266-2317; e-mail generaline.prokuratura@prokuraturos.lt; internet www.prokuraturos.lt; Prosecutor-General DARIUS VALYS.

Religion

CHRISTIANITY

The Roman Catholic Church

Catholicism has been the principal religious affiliation in Lithuania since its adoption by the Lithuanian State in 1387. The Catholic Church in Lithuania comprises two archdioceses and five dioceses (all of the Latin rite). There were an estimated 2.7m. adherents in Lithuania (equivalent to 84.4% of the population).

Bishops' Conference: Skapo 4, Vilnius 01122; tel. (5) 212-5455; fax (5) 212-0972; e-mail lvk@takas.lt; internet lvk.lcn.lt; f. 1965; Pres. Most Rev. SIGITAS TAMKEVIČIUS (Archbishop of Kaunas).

Archbishop of Kaunas: Most Rev. SIGITAS TAMKEVIČIUS, Rotušės 14A, Kaunas 44279; tel. (37) 409026; fax (37) 320090; e-mail kurija@kn.lcn.lt; internet www.kaunas.lcn.lt.

Archbishop of Vilnius: Cardinal AUDRYS JUOZAS BAČKIS, Šventaragio 4, Vilnius 01122; tel. (5) 262-7098; fax (5) 212-2807; e-mail curia@vilnensis.lt; internet vilnius.lcn.lt.

Orthodox Churches

Russian Orthodox Church (Moscow Patriarchate)

The first Orthodox communities in Lithuania appeared during the 12th century. While Lithuania formed part of the Russian Empire (1795–1915), Orthodoxy was considered the state religion. There were an estimated 180,000 adherents in 2001.

Lithuanian Orthodox Church (Moscow Patriarchate): Aušros Vartų 10/3, Vilnius 01129; tel. (5) 212-7765; internet www.orthodoxy.lt; Metropolitan of Vilnius and Lithuania CHRYZOSTOM (MARTISHKIN).

Lithuanian Old Believers Pomor Church

The first communities settled in Lithuania in 1679 and the Church was established in 1709. In 1996 there were approximately 34,000 adherents.

Supreme Council of the Old Believers Pomor Church in Lithuania: Naujininkų g. 20, Vilnius 02109; tel. (5) 269-5271; f. 1925; Chair. MARK SEMIONOV (acting).

Protestant Churches

Lithuanian Evangelical Lutheran Church

The first parishes were established in 1539–69. The Lithuanian Evangelical Lutheran Church comprises one diocese. In 1998 there were approximately 30,000 adherents.

Consistory of the Lithuanian Evangelical Lutheran Church (Lietuvos Evangeliku-Liuteronu Bažnycia): Tumo-Vaižganto 50, Tauragė 72263; tel. and fax (446) 61145; e-mail redakcija@liuteronai.lt; internet www.liuteronai.lt; Bishop MINDAUGAS SABUTIS.

Lithuanian Evangelical Reformed Church

The first parishes were established after 1563. At 1 January 1996 there were approximately 12,000 adherents.

Lithuanian Evangelical Reformed Church: POB 661, Vilnius 04008; tel. and fax (5) 245-0656; Pres. of Synodie Collegium POVILAS A. JAŠINSKAS.

ISLAM

Sunni Islam is the religion of the ethnic Tatars of Lithuania. The first Tatar communities settled there in the 14th century. The first mosque in Vilnius was erected in 1558. In 2001 there were an estimated 5,000 adherents.

JUDAISM

The first Jewish communities appeared in Lithuania in the 15th century. In the 15th–17th centuries Vilnius was an important centre of Jewish culture and religion. Before the Second World War approximately 200,000 Jews lived in Lithuania; an estimated 90% were murdered during the German occupation (1941–44). At 1 January 1996 there were five religious communities, with two synagogues (in Vilnius and Kaunas). There were an estimated 5,000 adherents in Lithuania in 2001. There is a small number of Karaites (Karaim), who originate from Crimea (now in Ukraine), and who speak a Turkic language and follow a form of Judaism, resident in Lithuania.

The Press

In 2011 there were 262 newspapers and 558 periodicals published in Lithuania.

The publications listed below are in Lithuanian, except where otherwise indicated.

PRINCIPAL NEWSPAPERS

Kauno diena (Kaunas Daily): Kęstučio g. 86, Kaunas 44296; tel. (37) 302250; fax (37) 423404; e-mail redakcija@kaunodiena.lt; internet www.kauno.diena.lt; f. 1945; 6 a week; Editor-in-Chief ŽILVINĖ PETRAUSKAITĖ; circ. 50,000.

Klaipėda: Naujojo Sodo g. 1A, K Centras, Klaipėda 92233; tel. (46) 397750; fax (46) 397700; e-mail redakcija@kl.lt; internet www.klaipeda.daily.lt; Editor-in-Chief SAULIUS POCIUS.

Kurier Wileński (Vilnius Courier): Birbynių g. 4A, Vilnius 02121; tel. and fax (5) 260-8444; e-mail r.mickiewicz@kurierwilenski.lt; internet www.kurierwilenski.lt; f. 1953; 5 a week; in Polish; Editor-in-Chief ROBERT MICKIEWICZ; circ. 8,000.

Lietuvos aidas (Lithuanian Echo): B. Radvilaitės g. 9, Vilnius 01124; tel. (5) 212-4876; e-mail algirdaspilvelis@gmail.com; internet www.aidas.lt; f. 1917; re-est. 1990; 5 a week; Editor-in-Chief ALGIRDAS PILVELIS; circ. 20,000.

Lietuvos rytas (Lithuanian Morning): Gedimino pr. 12A, Vilnius 01103; tel. (5) 274-3600; fax (5) 274-2000; e-mail daily@lrytas.lt;

internet www.lrytas.lt; f. 1990; 6 a week, with 3 supplements per week; Editor-in-Chief RIMVYDAS VALATKA; circ. 65,000 (Mon.–Fri.), 200,000 (Sat.).

Lietuvos žinios (Lithuanian News): Kęstučio g. 4/14, Vilnius 08117; tel. (5) 249-2152; fax (5) 275-3131; e-mail red@lzinios.lt; internet www.lzinios.lt; 6 a week; Gen. Dir and Editor-in-Chief VALDAS VASILIAUSKAS.

Respublika (Republic): A. Smetonos g. 2, Vilnius 01115; tel. (5) 212-3112; fax (5) 212-3538; e-mail press@respublika.net; internet www .respublika.lt; f. 1988; 6 a week in Lithuanian, with 5 Russian editions per week; Editor-in-Chief VITAS TOMKUS; circ. 55,000.

Šiaulių kraštas: P. Višinskio g. 26, Šiauliai 77155; tel. (41) 591555; fax (41) 524581; e-mail redakcija@skrastas.lt; internet www .skrastas.lt; Dir and Editor-in-Chief VLADAS VERTELIS.

Vakaro žinios (Evening News): Jogailos g. 11/2-11, Vilnius 01116; tel. and fax (5) 261-6875; e-mail vakarozinios@takas.lt; daily; circ. 70,000.

Vakarų ekspresas (Western Express): M. Mažvydo 3, Klaipėda 92131; tel. (46) 411308; fax (46) 402408; e-mail sekretore@ve.lt; internet www.ve.lt; f. 1990; 6 a week; Editor-in-Chief GINTARAS TOMKUS; circ. 16,000–22,000.

Verslo žinios (Business News): J. Jasinskio 16A, Vilnius 01112; tel. (5) 252-6300; fax (5) 252-6313; e-mail info@vz.lt; internet www.vz.lt; f. 1994; 5 a week; Editor LINAS KMIELIAUSKAS; circ. 9,000.

PRINCIPAL PERIODICALS

Artuma (Presence): Rotušės a. 23, Kaunas 44279; tel. and fax (37) 209683; e-mail redakcija@artuma.lt; internet www.artuma.lt; f. 1989 as *Caritas*; name changed as above in 1997; monthly; Catholic family magazine; Editor-in-Chief DARIUS CHMIELIAUSKAS; circ. 12,500.

Kultūros barai (Domains of Culture): Latako g. 3, Vilnius 01125; tel. (5) 262-3861; fax (5) 261-0538; e-mail kulturosbarai@takas.lt; internet www.eurozine.com; f. 1965; monthly; independent cultural magazine; Editor-in-Chief LAIMA KANOPKIENE; circ. 2,200.

Laima: J. Jasinskio g. 16, Vilnius 01112; tel. (5) 252-6538; fax (5) 252-6531; e-mail laima@redakcija.lt; internet www.redakcija.lt/ zurnalai/laima; f. 1993; monthly; lifestyle and feature magazine for women; Editor-in-Chief GITANA BUKAUSKIENĖ; circ. 30,000.

Liaudies kultūra (Ethnic Culture): Barboros Radvilaitės 8, Vilnius 01124; tel. (5) 261-3412; fax (5) 261-2607; e-mail llkc@llkc.lt; internet www.llkc.lt; f. 1988; 6 a year; Gen. Editor DALIA ANTANINA RASTENIENĖ; circ. 550.

Literatūra ir menas (Literature and Art): Mesiniu 4, Vilnius 01133; tel. (5) 269-1977; fax (5) 212-6556; e-mail lmenas@takas.lt; internet www.culture.lt/lmenas; f. 1946; weekly; publ. by the Lithuanian Writers' Union; Editor-in-Chief KORNELIJUS PLATELIS; circ. 2,000.

Lithuania in the World: J. Basanavičiaus g. 7, Vilnius 01118; tel. (5) 261-4432; fax (5) 212-5560; e-mail info@liw.lt; internet www.liw .lt; f. 1993; 6 a year; in English and Lithuanian; Exec. Editor JOLANTA LAUMENSKAITĖ; circ. 10,000.

Magazyn Wileński (Vilnius Journal): Laisvės pr. 60, Vilnius 05120; tel. (5) 242-7718; fax (5) 242-9065; e-mail magazyn@magwil.lt; internet www.magwil.lt; f. 1990; monthly; political, cultural; in Polish; Editor HELENA OSTROWSKA; circ. 5,000.

Mano Namai: Ozo g. 10A, Vilnius 08200; tel. (5) 247-7714; e-mail dalia@manomai.lt; internet www.mano-namai.lt; household, interiors and food; Editor DALIA DAUGIRDIENĖ.

Metai (Year): K. Sirvydo g. 6, Vilnius 01101; tel. (5) 261-7344; e-mail metai@takas.lt; f. 1991; monthly; journal of the Lithuanian Writers' Union; Editor-in-Chief DANIELIUS MUŠINSKAS; circ. 2,000.

Mokslas ir gyvenimas (Science and Life): Antakalnio g. 36, Vilnius 10305; tel. and fax (5) 234-1572; e-mail mgredacija@takas.lt; internet ausis.gf.vu.lt/mg; f. 1957; monthly; popular and historical science; Editor-in-Chief JUOZAS BALDAUSKAS; circ. 3,500.

Moteris (Woman): J. Jasinskio 16C, Vilnius 01112; tel. (5) 247-7712; tel. and fax (5) 247-7711; e-mail info@moteris.lt; internet www .moteris.lt; f. 1920; monthly; popular, for women; Editor-in-Chief GRAŽINA MICHNEVIČIŪTĖ; circ. 22,000.

Naujasis Židinys-Aidai (New Hearth–Echoes): Didžioji g. 34, Vilnius 01128; tel. (5) 212-0311; fax (5) 212-2363; e-mail aidai@ aidai.lt; internet www.aidai.lt/zidinys; f. 1991; monthly; religion, culture and social affairs; Editor-in-Chief VIOLETA BOSKAITĖ; circ. 1,000.

Nemunas: Gedimino g. 45, Kaunas 44239; tel. and fax (37) 322244; e-mail nemunasr@gmail.com; internet test.svs.lt/?Nemunas; f. 1967; weekly since 2004; Thursdays; culture and art; journal of the Lithuanian Writers' Union; Editor-in-Chief VIKTORAS RUDŽIANSKAS; circ. 1,500.

Panelė (Young Miss): Ozo g. 10A, Vilnius 08200; tel. (5) 247-7716; fax (5) 210-2557; e-mail magazine@panele.lt; internet www.panele.lt; f. 1994; monthly; popular, for ages 12–25; Editor-in-Chief JURGA BALTRUKONYTĖ; circ. 66,000.

Psihologija Tau: Trakų g. 8, Vilnius 01132; tel. (5) 262-6763; fax (5) 262-7671; e-mail redakcija@psichologijatau.lt; internet www .psichologijatau.lt; popular psychology; Editor RŪTA CHOMENTAUS-KAITĖ.

Septynios meno dienos (7 meno dienos) (Seven Days of Art): Maironio g. 6, Vilnius 01124; tel. (5) 261-3039; fax (5) 261-1926; e-mail 7md@takas.lt; internet www.7md.lt; f. 1992; weekly; media, music, visual arts theatre, dance and cinema; Editor-in-Chief MONIKA KRIKŠTOPAITYTĖ; circ. 1,500.

Tremtinys (Deportee): Laisvės al. 39, Kaunas 44282; tel. (37) 323204; e-mail tremtinys@erdvas.lt; internet www.lpkts.lt/ tremtinys.htm; f. 1988; weekly; publ. of fmr Lithuanian Union of Political Prisoners and Deportees (now part of Homeland Union— Lithuanian Christian Democrats); Editor-in-Chief AUDRONĖ KAMINS-KIENĖ; circ. 4,500.

Valstiečių laikraštis (Farmer's Newspaper): Saltoniškių g. 29/ Sėlių g. 3, Vilnius 08105; tel. (5) 210-0110; fax (5) 242-1281; e-mail redakcija@valstietis.lt; internet www.valstietis.lt; f. 1940; 2 a week; Editor-in-Chief MEILĖ TARAŠKEVIČIENĖ; circ. 68,000.

Vasario 16 (16 February): J. Gruodžio g. 9/404, Kaunas 44293; tel. (37) 225219; f. 1988; fortnightly; journal of Order and Justice Party; Sec. PRIMAS NOREIKA; circ. 1,600.

NEWS AGENCIES

Baltic News Service (BNS): Jogailos g. 9/1, Vilnius 01116; tel. (5) 205-8501; fax (5) 205-8504; e-mail arturas@bns.lt; internet www.bns .lt; f. 1991; Dir and Editor-in-Chief ARTŪRAS RAČAS.

ELTA Lithuanian News Agency (ELTA Lietuvos Naujienų Agentūra): Gedimino pr. 21/2, Vilnius 01103; tel. (5) 262-8864; fax (5) 261-9507; e-mail zinios@elta.lt; internet www.elta.lt; f. 1920; 18.4% owned by Ziniu Partneriai; 39.5% owned by Respublikos Investicija (both cos controlled by Respublika Gp); Dir GRAZINA RAMANAUSKAITĖ-TIUMENEVIENĖ.

Publishers

Alma littera: A. Juozapavičiaus 6/2, Vilnius 09310; tel. (5) 263-8877; fax (5) 272-8026; e-mail post@almali.lt; internet www.almali.lt; f. 1990; fiction, children's books, textbooks; Dir-Gen. ARVYDAS ANDRIJAUSKAS.

Baltos lankos leidykla (White Meadows Publishing House): Aušros Vartų g. 29/1, Vilnius 01129; tel. (5) 240-8673; fax (5) 240-7446; e-mail leidykla@baltoslankos.lt; internet www.baltoslankos.lt; f. 1992; literature, humanities, social sciences, fiction and textbooks; Dir SAULIUS ŽUKAS.

Eugrimas: Kalvariju 98/36, Vilnius 08211; tel. and fax (5) 273-3955; e-mail info@eugrimas.lt; internet www.eugrimas.lt; f. 1995; academic and professional literature, incl. economics, business, law and politics; Dir EUGENIJA PETRULIENĖ.

Katalikų pasaulio leidiniai (Editions of the Catholic World): Pylimo 27/14, Vilnius 01141; tel. (5) 212-2422; fax (5) 212-0375; internet www.katalikuleidiniai.lt; f. 1990; Dir BIRUTĖ BARTASŪNAITE.

Leidykla Vaga: Gedimino pr. 50, Vilnius 01110; tel. (5) 249-8121; fax (5) 249-8122; e-mail info@vaga.lt; internet www.vaga.lt; f. 1945 as Lithuanian State Publishing House of Fiction; privatized and restructured in 1994; fiction, non-fiction, art, children's books; Dir VYTAS V. PETROŠIUS.

Lietuvos rašytojų sąjungos leidykla (Lithuanian Writers' Union Publishers): K. Sirvydo 6, Vilnius 01101; tel. and fax (5) 262-8945; e-mail info@rsleidykla.lt; internet www.rsleidykla.lt; f. 1990; fiction, essays, literary heritage, children's books; Dir GIEDRE SORIENE.

Mintis leidykla (Mintis Publishing House): Z. Sierakausko g. 15, Vilnius 03105; tel. (5) 233-2943; fax (5) 216-3157; e-mail redakcija@ mintis.org; internet www.mintis.org; f. 1949; philosophy, politics, history, law, mythology, textbooks, encyclopedias, biographies, fiction; also book distributor, bookshop; Dir LEONARDAS ARMONAS.

Mokslo ir enciklopedijų leidybos institutas (Science and Encyclopedia Publishing Institute): L. Asanavičiūtės 23, Vilnius 04315; tel. (5) 245-8526; fax (5) 245-8537; e-mail meli@meli.lt; internet www .meli.lt; f. 1992; encyclopedias, science and reference books, dictionaries, higher education textbooks, books for the general reader; Dir RIMANTAS KARECKAS.

Presvika: Kauno g. 28, Vilnius 03202; tel. (5) 262-3182; fax (5) 262-3110; e-mail presvika@presvika.lt; internet www.presvika.lt; f. 1996; psychological and educational literature, textbooks, fiction; Dir VIOLETA BILAIŠYTĖ.

Šviesa (Light): E. Ožeškienės g. 10, Kaunas 44252; tel. (37) 409126; fax (37) 342032; e-mail mail@sviesa.lt; internet www.sviesa.lt; f. 1945; textbooks and pedagogical literature; Dir ASTA VERKIENĖ.

Tyto alba: J. Jasinskio g. 10, Vilnius 01112; tel. (5) 249-7453; fax (5) 298-8602; internet www.tytoalba.lt; f. 1993; contemporary Lithuanian literary fiction and non-fiction, fiction in translation; Dir LOLITA VARANAVIČIENĖ.

Versus Aureus leidykla: Rūdninkų g. 10, Vilnius 01135; tel. and fax (5) 265-2730; e-mail versus@versus.lt; internet www.versus.lt; f. 2003; fiction, non-fiction and educational literature.

PUBLISHERS' ASSOCIATION

Lietuvos Leidėjų Asociacija (Lithuanian Publishers' Association): A. Jakšto 22–13, Vilnius 01105; tel. and fax (5) 261-7740; e-mail lla@centras.lt; internet www.lla.lt; f. 1989; Pres. EUGENIJUS KAZILIŪNAS.

Broadcasting and Communications

TELECOMMUNICATIONS

At the end of 2010 there were 51 fixed-line telecommunications service providers and 13 mobile operators active in Lithuania.

BITĖ Lietuva: Žemaitės 15, Vilnius 03504; tel. (6) 560-0656; fax (6) 990-0111; e-mail info@bite.lt; internet www.bite.lt; f. 1995; mobile telecommunications service provider; 0.2m. subscribers (March 2007); CEO FRED HRENCHUK.

Eurocom: Geležinio Vilko g. 18A, Vilnius 08104; tel. (5) 274-4600; fax (5) 274-4612; e-mail eurocom@eurocom.lt; internet www.eurocom.lt; f. 2003; fixed line and mobile telecommunications, internet service provider; a subsidiary of VP Market; Dir SEDIMINAS JØVAIŠA.

Omnitel: T. Ševčenkos 25, Vilnius 03503; tel. (698) 63333; fax (5) 274-5574; e-mail info@omnitel.net; internet www.omnitel.lt; f. 1991 as Litcom; owned by Telia Sonera (Sweden); telecommunications and internet service provider; Pres. ANTANAS JUOZAS ZABULIS.

Tele2: Sporto 7A, Vilnius 09200; tel. (5) 236-6300; fax (5) 236-6302; e-mail reception.lt@tele2.com; internet www.tele2.lt; f. 1999; owned by Tele2 AB (Sweden); provider of GSM, internet and fixed-line telecommunications services; Chief Exec. PETRAS MASIULIS.

Teo LT AB: Lvovo 25, Vilnius 03501; tel. (5) 262-1511; fax (5) 212-6655; internet www.teo.lt; f. 1992 under the name Lietuvos Telekomas AB; privatized 1998; formerly monopoly provider of telecommunications services; present name adopted 2006; operates public telecommunications network, repairs telecommunications equipment; internet service provider; Chair. ERIK HALLBERG; Gen. Man. ARŪNAS ŠIKŠTA; 3,200 employees.

Regulatory Authority

Communications Regulatory Authority (Ryšių reguliavimo tarnyba): Algirdo 27A, Vilnius 03219; tel. (5) 210-5633; fax (5) 216-1564; e-mail rrt@rrt.lt; internet www.rrt.lt; f. 2001; Dir TOMAS BARAKAUSKAS.

BROADCASTING
Regulatory Authority

Lietuvos radijo ir televizijos komisija (Radio and Television Commission of Lithuania): Vytenio g. 6/23, Vilnius 03113; tel. (5) 233-0660; fax (5) 264-7125; e-mail lrtk@rtk.lt; internet www.rtk.lt; f. 1996; licensing and licence compliance; Chair. PAULIUS SUBAČIUS.

Radio

In 2010, in addition to one publicly owned national radio station, there were 10 private commercial, seven regional and 30 local radio stations.

Lietuvos nacionalinis radijas ir televizija (LRT) (Lithuanian National Radio and Television): S. Konarskio 49, Vilnius 03123; tel. (5) 236-3209; fax (5) 236-3208; e-mail lrt@lrt.lt; internet www.lrt.lt; f. 1926; govt-owned; non-profit public broadcasting co; operates three national radio channels and two national television channels; Chair. of Bd DAINIUS RADZEVIČIUS; Dir-Gen. AUDRIUS SIAURUSEVIČIUS; 650 employees.

A2 Radijo Stotis: Laisvės pr. 3, Vilnius 04215; tel. and fax (5) 245-4922; e-mail a2@a2.lt; internet www.a2.lt; private, commercial; Dir VYDAS IVANAUSKAS.

Aukštaitijos radijas (AR): Laisvės a. 1, Panevėžys 35175; tel. and fax (6) 840-9222; e-mail info@radijas.lt; private, commercial; Dir VYTAUTAS ŽILĖNAS.

FM99: Rotušės a. 2, Alytus 62141; tel. (315) 76120; fax (315) 74646; e-mail fm99@fm99.lt; internet www.fm99.lt; private, commercial; broadcast by Alytaus radijas; Dir LIUDAS RAMANAUSKAS.

Kauno fonas 105.4: Savanorių pr. 192–802, Kaunas 44151; tel. (37) 327427; fax (37) 327447; e-mail info@kf.lt; internet www.kf.lt; f. 2003; private, commercial; Dir ŪDRYS STASELKA.

Laisvoji banga: Gedimino pr. 50, Vilnius 01110; tel. (5) 2333212; fax (5) 2333121; e-mail info@laisvojibanga.lt; internet www.laisvojibanga.lt; private, commercial; broadcasts news and music; Dir MINDAUGAS GAVUTIS.

Laluna: Taikos pr. 81, Klaipėda 94114; tel. (46) 390808; fax (46) 390805; e-mail laluna@laluna.lt; internet www.laluna.lt; private, commercial; Dir TADAS ŽEMAITIS.

M-1: Laisvės pr. 60, Vilnius 05120; tel. (5) 236-0360; fax (5) 236-0366; e-mail m-1@m-1.fm; internet www.m-1.fm; f. 1989; private, commercial; Gen. Man. RŪTA GRUŠNIENĖ.

Mažeikių aidas (MA): POB 17, Mažeikiai 89103; tel. and fax (443) 65055; e-mail info@mazeikiuaidas.lt; internet www.mazeikiuaidas.lt; f. 1996; private, commercial; Dir TOMAS RUGINIS.

Pūkas: Šaldytuvų g. 25, Kaunas 45123; tel. (37) 342424; fax (37) 342434; e-mail pukas@pukas.lt; internet www.pukas.lt; f. 1991; private, commercial; operates two radio stations and a television station; Dir KĘSTUTIS PŪKAS.

Radiocentras: Laisvės pr. 60, Vilnius 05120; tel. (5) 212-8706; fax (5) 242-9073; e-mail biuras@rc.lt; internet www.rc.lt; f. 1991; private, commercial; Gen. Man. MINDAUGAS PLESKEVICIUS.

Saulės radijas: Aušros al. 64, Šiauliai 76235; tel. (41) 525141; fax (41) 424404; e-mail info@saulesradijas.lt; internet www.saulesradijas.lt; private, commercial; Dir RASA AKUČKIENĖ.

Tau: Draugystės g. 19–357, Kaunas 51230; tel. (37) 352790; fax (37) 352128; e-mail info@tau.lt; internet www.tau.lt; private, commercial; Dir GIEDRIUS GIPAS.

Znad Wilii: Laisvės pr. 60, Vilnius 05120; tel. (5) 249-0870; fax (5) 278-4446; e-mail radio@znadwilii.lt; internet www.znadwilii.lt; f. 1992; private, commercial; Dir-Gen. MIROSŁAW JUCHNIEWICZ.

Television

At the end of 2010, in addition to the 28 local and 98 national analogue terrestrial television stations, there were 25 licensed digital terrestrial televisions stations. From October 2012 digital terrestrial television was due to replace analogue terrestrial television throughout the country.

Lietuvos televizija (LTV): S. Konarskio 49, Vilnius 03123; tel. (5) 236-3100; fax (5) 216-3282; e-mail lrt@lrt.lt; internet www.lrt.lt; f. 1957; subsidiary of LRT (see Radio); programmes in Lithuanian, Russian, Polish, Ukrainian and Belarusian; Dir RIMVYDAS PALECKIS.

Aidas (Echo): Birutės g. 42, Trakai 21117; tel. (650) 57171; fax (528) 55656; e-mail tvaidas@gmail.com; mainly relays German programmes; private, commercial; Dir ČESLOVAS RULEVIČIUS.

Baltijos televizija (BTV): Laisvės pr. 60, Vilnius 05120; tel. (5) 278-0805; fax (5) 278-0804; e-mail info@btv.lt; internet www.btv.lt; f. 1993; broadcasts own programmes and relays German, Polish and US broadcasts; private, commercial; Dir-Gen. LIUTAURAS ELKIMAVIČIUS.

KTV plius: Nemuno g. 79, Panevėžys 37355; tel. (45) 514103; fax (45) 443561; e-mail pictura@kateka.lt; internet www.ktvplius.lt; private, commercial; Pres. ROLANDAS MEILIŪNAS.

LNK TV: Šeškinės g. 20, Vilnius 07156; tel. (5) 243-1058; fax (5) 243-1054; e-mail info@lnk.lt; internet www.lnk.lt; f. 1995; private, commercial; broadcasts TV1; Dir-Gen. ZITA SARAKIENĖ.

PAN-TV: Respublikos g. 19, Panevėžys 35185; tel. (8) 606-86686; e-mail info@pantv.lt; private, commercial; Dir SAULIUS BUKELIS.

Raseiniu TV: Vytauto Vilniaus 1A, Raseiniai 60187; tel. (428) 54433; fax (428) 70422; e-mail office@mirkliai.lt; broadcast by Všį Raseinių televizijos ir radijo centras; Dir KĘSTUTIS SKAMARAKAS.

Šiaulių TV: Liejyklos g. 10, Šiauliai 78147; tel. and fax (41) 523808; e-mail info@stv.lt; internet www.stv.lt; private; Dir JUSTINAS SARTAUSKAS.

TV3: Kalvarijų pl. 143, Vilnius 08221; tel. (5) 203-0101; fax (5) 276-4253; e-mail info@tv3.lt; internet www.tv3.lt; f. 1992; broadcasts own programmes (20% of schedule) in Lithuanian and English, and relays international satellite channels; private, commercial; Dir LAURA BLAŽEVIČIŪTĖ.

Finance

(cap. = capital; res = reserves; dep. = deposits; m. = million; brs = branches; amounts in litai)

BANKING
Central Bank

Bank of Lithuania (Lietuvos bankas): Gedimino pr. 6, Vilnius 01103; tel. (5) 268-0029; fax (5) 262-8124; e-mail info@lb.lt; internet www.lb.lt; f. 1922; re-est. 1990; central bank, responsible for bank supervision; cap. 200.0m., res 794.1m., dep. 4,519.6m. (Dec. 2008); Chair. of Bd VITAS VASILIAUSKAS; 2 brs.

Commercial Banks

Citadele Bankas: K. Kalinausko g. 13, Vilnius 03107; tel. (5) 266-4600; fax (5) 266-4601; e-mail info@citadele.lt; internet www.citadele.lt; f. 1996 as Parex Bankas; renamed in 2010; owned by Citadele banka (Latvia); cap. 286.2m., res –2.9m., dep. 750.2m. (June 2011); Chair. and Chief Exec. ALMA VAITKUNSKIENE; 6 brs.

DnB Bankas: J. Basanavičiaus g. 26, Vilnius 03601; tel. (5) 239-3444; fax (5) 213-9056; e-mail info@dnb.lt; internet www.dnb.lt; f. 1924; privatized in March 2002; fmrly DnB NORD Bankas; renamed as above in 2011; 100% owned by Bank DnB A/S (Denmark); cap. 656.7m., res 648.4m., dep. 6,079.5m. (Dec. 2012); Chair. of Management Bd, Pres. and CEO BJØRNAR LUND; 85 brs.

Medicinos Bankas: Pamėnkalnio g. 40, Vilnius 01114; tel. (5) 264-4800; fax (5) 264-4801; e-mail info@medbank.lt; internet www.medbank.lt; f. 1992; cap. 68.9m., res 23.2m., dep. 689.2m. (Dec. 2011); Chair. of Management Bd and CEO GINTARAS TREINYS; 6 brs.

SEB Bankas (SEB Bank): Gedimino pr. 12, Vilnius 01103; tel. (5) 268-2800; fax (5) 268-2333; e-mail info@seb.lt; internet www.seb.lt; f. 1990 as Spaudos Bankas; present name adopted 2008; 100% owned by Skandinaviska Enskilda Banken AB (Sweden); cap. 1,034.6m., res 251.8m., dep. 19,715.4m. (Dec. 2012); Pres. and CEO RAIMONDAS KVEDARAS; 72 brs.

Šiaulių Bankas: Tilžės str. 149, Šiauliai 76348; tel. (41) 595607; fax (41) 430774; e-mail info@sb.lt; internet www.sb.lt; f. 1992; cap. 234.8m., res 57.6m., dep. 2,206.3m. (Dec. 2012); Chair. of Bd ALGIRDAS BUTKUS; CEO AUDRIUS ŽIUGŽDA; 77 brs and agencies (2013).

Swedbank: Konstitucijos pr. 20A, Vilnius 03502; tel. (5) 268-4444; fax (5) 258-2700; e-mail info@swedbank.lt; internet www.swedbank.lt; f. 1919; present name adopted 2009; 99.5% owned by Swedbank AB (Sweden); cap. 1,640.1m., res 185.1m., dep. 15,823.8m. (Dec. 2012); Chair. of Bd ANTANAS DANYS; 84 brs.

Ūkio Bankas: Maironio g. 25, Kaunas 44250; tel. (37) 301301; fax (37) 323188; e-mail ub@ub.lt; internet www.ub.lt; f. 1989; cap. 196.7m., res 189.1m., dep. 3,322.4m. (Dec. 2008); Chair. of Bd EDITA KARPAVIČIENE; Chief Exec. GINTARAS UGIANSKIS; 12 brs.

Banking Association

Association of Lithuanian Banks (Lietuvos Bankų Asociacija): Ankštoji g. 5/3, Vilnius 01109; tel. (5) 249-6669; fax (5) 249-6139; e-mail info@lba.lt; internet www.lba.lt; f. 1991; Pres. STASYS KROPAS; 11 mems.

STOCK EXCHANGE

Vilnius Stock Exchange (VSE) (Vilniaus vertybinių popierių birža): Konstitucijos pr. 7, Vilnius 08501; tel. (5) 272-3871; fax (5) 272-4894; e-mail vilnius@nasdaqomx.com; internet www.nasdaqomxbaltic.com; f. 1993; 93.1% owned by the NASDAQ OMX Group (USA); Chair. of Bd ARMINTA SALADŽIENĖ.

INSURANCE
Principal Insurance Companies

Commercial Union Lietuva Gyvybės draudimas: Lvovo g. 25, Vilnius 09320; tel. (5) 269-0169; fax (5) 269-0269; e-mail info@aviva.lt; internet www.commercialunion.lt; f. 2001; owned by Commercial Union Polska—Towarzystwo Ubezpieczeń na Zycie SA (Poland), part of the Aviva Group (United Kingdom); Dir A. UNGULAITIENĖ.

Ergo Lietuva: Geležinio vilko g. 6A, Vilnius 03507; tel. (5) 268-3000; fax (5) 268-3045; e-mail info@ergo.lt; internet www.ergo.lt; f. 1991; owned by Ergo International AG (Germany); formerly Drauda; name changed as above in 2000; in 2002 merged with Preventa; CEO S. JOKUBAITIS.

Lietuvos draudimas AB (Lithuanian Insurance): J. Basanavičiaus g. 12, Vilnius 03600; tel. (5) 243-1167; fax (5) 231-4138; e-mail info@ldr.lt; internet www.ld.lt; f. 1921; privatized in 1999; part of RSA group (United Kingdom); principal non-life insurance co in Lithuania; CEO KĘSTUTIS SERPYTIS.

PZU Lietuva: Konstitucijos pr. 7, Vilnius 09308; tel. (5) 279-0007; fax (5) 279-0019; e-mail info@pzu.lt; internet www.pzu.lt; f. 1993; owned by Powszechny Zaklad Ubezpieczen (PZU) SA (Poland); Chair. BOGDAN BENCZAK.

SEB VB Gyvybės Draudimas: Gedimino pr. 12, Vilnius 01103; tel. (5) 268-1555; fax (5) 268-1556; e-mail draudimas@seb.lt; internet www.seb.lt; f. 1999; owned by SEB Vilniaus bankas AB; Dir B. KAMUNTAVIČIENĖ.

Swedbank gyvybės draudimas AB (Swedbank Life Insurance): Konstitucijos pr. 20A, Vilnius 03502; tel. (5) 268-4444; fax (5) 258-2700; e-mail info@swedbank.lt; internet www.hansadraudimas.lt;

f. 1995; owned by Swedbank AS (Sweden); formerly Lietuvos Draudimo gyvybės draudimas, then Hansa gyvybės draudimas; present name adopted 2009; life; Dir CARL ERIC STÅLBERG.

Insurance Association

Association of Lithuanian Insurers: Gedimino pr. 45/11, Vilnius 01109; tel. (5) 231-0381; e-mail asociacija@draudikai.lt; internet www.draudikai.lt; f. 1992; Dir ANDRIUS ROMANOVSKIS.

Supervisory Body

Insurance Supervisory Commission: Ukmergės g. 222, Vilnius 07157; tel. (5) 243-1370; fax (5) 272-3689; e-mail dpk@dpk.lt; internet www.dpk.lt; Chair. MINDAUGAS SALČIUS.

Trade and Industry
GOVERNMENT AGENCY

State Property Fund (Valstybės Turto Fondas—VTS): Vilniaus g. 16, Vilnius 01402; tel. (5) 268-4999; fax (5) 268-4997; e-mail info@vtf.lt; internet www.vtf.lt; f. 1995; privatization and management of state-owned and municipal property; Chair. ARNOLDAS BURKOVSKIS; Dir-Gen. JONAS NIAURA.

DEVELOPMENT AGENCY

National Regional Development Agency (Nacionalinė Regionų Plėtros Agentūra): Vilniaus g. 88, Šiauliai 76285; tel. (41) 552061; fax (41) 523903; e-mail info@nrda.lt; internet www.nrda.lt; f. 1999 by the Asscn of Lithuanian Chambers of Commerce, Industry and Crafts; Dir VAIDAS KAZAKEVIČIUS.

CHAMBERS OF COMMERCE

Association of Lithuanian Chambers of Commerce, Industry and Crafts (Lietuvos prekybos, pramonės ir amatų rūmų asociacija): J. Tumo-Vaižganto g. 9/1–63A, Vilnius 01108; tel. (5) 261-2102; fax (5) 261-2112; e-mail info@chambers.lt; internet www.chambers.lt; f. 1992; mem. of International Chamber of Commerce and of Asscn of European Chambers of Commerce and Industry; Pres. RIMANTAS STANKEVIČIUS.

Kaunas Chamber of Commerce, Industry and Crafts: K. Donelaičio g. 8, POB 2111, Kaunas 44213; tel. (37) 229212; fax (37) 208330; e-mail chamber@chamber.lt; internet www.chamber.lt; f. 1925; re-est. 1991; br. at Marijampolė; Pres. Prof. M. RONDOMAN-SKAS.

Klaipėda Chamber of Commerce, Industry and Crafts: Danės g. 17, POB 148, Klaipėda 92117; tel. (46) 390861; fax (46) 410626; e-mail klaipeda@chambers.lt; internet www.kcci.lt; Pres. BENEDIKTAS PETRAUSKA; Gen. Dir VIKTORAS KROLIS; 200 mems.

Panevėžys Chamber of Commerce, Industry and Crafts: Respublikos g. 34, Panevėžys 35173; tel. (45) 463687; fax (45) 500309; e-mail panevezys@chambers.lt; internet www.ccic.lt; f. 1991; Pres. SIGITAS GAILIŪNAS; Gen. Dir VISVALDAS MATKEVIČIUS.

Šiauliai Chamber of Commerce, Industry and Crafts: Vilniaus g. 88, Šiauliai 76285; tel. (41) 523224; fax (41) 523903; e-mail siauliai@chambers.lt; internet www.rumai.lt; f. 1993; Dir-Gen. ALFREDAS JONUŠKA.

Vilnius Chamber of Commerce, Industry and Crafts: Algirdo g. 31, Vilnius 03219; tel. (5) 213-5550; fax (5) 213-5542; e-mail vilnius@cci.lt; internet www.cci.lt; f. 1991; Dir-Gen. BORISAS ZAUBIDOVAS; 480 mems.

INDUSTRIAL ASSOCIATION

Lithuanian Confederation of Industrialists (Lietuvos pramonininkų konfederacija—LPK): A. Vienuolio g. 8, Vilnius 01104; tel. (5) 212-5217; fax (5) 212-5209; e-mail info@lpk.lt; internet www.lpk.lt; f. 1989; Pres. ROBERTAS DARGIS.

EMPLOYERS' ORGANIZATION

Lithuanian Business Employers' Confederation (Lietuvos verslo darbdavių konfederacija—LVDK): Algirdo g. 31, Vilnius 03219; tel. (5) 249-8345; fax (5) 249-6448; e-mail info@lvdk.eu; internet www.lvdk.eu; f. 1999; Gen. Dir DANUKAS ARLAUSKAS.

UTILITIES

Energy Agency (Energetikos agentūra): Gedimino pr. 38/Vasario 16-osios g. 2, Vilnius 01104; tel. (5) 261-9225; fax (5) 262-6845; e-mail eainfo@ena.lt; internet www.ena.lt; f. 1993; state enterprise; attached to the Ministry of Energy; Dir MARIJUS FRANCKEVIČIUS.

Electricity

Lesto: Žvejų g. 14, Vilnius 09310; tel. (5) 277-7524; fax (5) 277-7514; e-mail info@lesto.lt; internet www.lesto.lt; f. 2010 following the reorganization of Rytų Skirstomieji Tinklai and Vakarų Skirstomieji Tinklai; distribution network operator; CEO ARVYDAS TARASEVIČIUS.

Lietuvos Energija AB (Lithuanian Power): Žvejų g. 14, Vilnius 09310; tel. (5) 262-6822; fax (5) 212-6736; e-mail info@lietuvosenergija.lt; internet www.lpc.lt; f. 1995; restructured in 2000; 96.5% owned by LEO LT AB; Chair. of Bd HENRIKAS BERNATAVIČIUS; CEO ALOYZAS KORYZNA.

Gas

Lietuvos Dujos AB (Lithuanian Gas): Aguonų g. 24, Vilnius 03212; tel. (5) 236-0209; fax (5) 236-0200; e-mail ld@lietuvosdujos.lt; internet www.dujos.lt; f. 1995; 17.7% state-owned; 38.9% owned by E.ON Ruhrgas International AG (Germany); 37.1% owned by OAO Gazprom (Russia); natural gas import, sale and transportation; Chair. Dr VALERY GOLUBEV; Gen. Man. VIKTORAS VALENTUKEVIČIUS; 1,900 employees.

TRADE UNIONS

Lithuanian Labour Federation (Lietuvos Darbo Federacija): Vytauto g. 14, Vilnius 03106; tel. and fax (5) 231-2029; e-mail ldforg@ldf.lt; internet www.ldf.lt; f. 1919 as a Christian trade union org.; re-est. 1991; 20,000 mems; Chair. VYDAS PUSKEPALIS; Sec.-Gen. JANINA SVEDIENĖ.

Lithuanian Trade Union Confederation (Lietuvos profesinių sąjungų konfederacija—LPSK): J. Jasinskio g. 9/213, Vilnius 01111; tel. (5) 249-6921; fax (5) 249-8078; e-mail lpsk@lpsk.lt; internet www.lpsk.lt; f. 2002 by merger of Lithuanian Union of Trade Unions (LPSS) and Lithuanian Trade Union Centre (LPSC); 26 branch trade unions with 60,000 mems; Pres. ARTŪRAS ČERNIAUSKAS.

Transport

RAILWAYS

In 2011 there were 1,767 km of railway track in use in Lithuania, of which 122 km were electrified. Main lines link Vilnius with Minsk (Belarus), Kaliningrad (Russia) and Warsaw (Poland), in the latter case by way of the Belarusian town of Grodno (Horadnia).

Lithuanian Railways (Lietuvos geležinkeliai): Mindaugo g. 12–14, Vilnius 03603; tel. (5) 269-2038; fax (5) 269-2028; e-mail lgkanc@litrail.lt; internet www.litrail.lt; f. 1991; Dir-Gen. STASYS DAILYDKA; 10,334 employees.

ROADS

In 2010 the total length of the road network was estimated at 82,131 km; the motorway network totalled 309 km.

Lithuanian Road Administration (Lietuvos automobilių kelių direkcija—LAKD): J. Basanavičiaus g. 36/2, Vilnius 03109; tel. (5) 232-9600; fax (5) 232-9609; e-mail lra@lra.lt; internet www.lra.lt; Dir-Gen. VIRGAUDAS PUODŽIUKAS.

SHIPPING

The main port is at Klaipėda. In 2009 there were 448 km of inland navigable waterways. At 31 December 2012 the flag registered fleet comprised 133 vessels, with a total displacement of 413,019 grt.

Port Authority

Klaipėda State Seaport Authority: J. Janonio g. 24, Klaipėda 92251; tel. (46) 499799; fax (46) 499777; e-mail info@port.lt; internet www.portofklaipeda.lt; multi-purpose, deep-water universal port; connects sea, land and rail routes from east and west; Dir-Gen. EUGENIJUS GENTVILAS.

Shipowning Company

Lithuanian Shipping Company (AB Lietuvos Jūrų Laivininkystė): Malunininku g. 3, Klaipėda 92264; tel. (46) 393105; fax (46) 393119; e-mail gp@ljl.lt; internet www.ljl.lt; f. 1969 as LISCO; partially privatized and renamed as above in June 2001; 73.24%

state-owned; transportation of cargo; owns 18 vessels; Gen. Dir VYTAUTAS VISMANTAS.

CIVIL AVIATION

There are international airports at Vilnius, Kaunas, Palanga and Šiauliai.

Directorate of Civil Aviation (Oro Navigacija): Rodūnios kelias 2, Vilnius 02188; tel. (5) 273-9102; fax (5) 273-9161; e-mail info@ans.lt; internet www.ans.lt; Dir-Gen. ALGIMANTAS RAŠČIUS.

Small Planet Airlines: Smolensko g. 4, Vilnius 03201; tel. (5) 252-5660; fax (5) 252-5661; e-mail info@smallplanet.aero; internet www.smallplanet.aero; f. 2007 as flyLAL Charters; present name adopted 2010; operates passenger and cargo charter flights; CEO VYTAUTAS KAIKARIS.

Tourism

Tourist attractions in Lithuania include the historic cities of Vilnius, Kaunas, Kėdainiai, Trakai and Klaipėda, coastal resorts, such as Palanga and Kuršių Nerija, and picturesque countryside. Some 1.0m. tourists visited the country in 2011, while tourist receipts (excluding passenger transport) totalled US $1,353m., according to provisional figures.

State Dept of Tourism: Švitrigailos 11M, Vilnius 03228; tel. (5) 210-8796; fax (5) 210-8753; e-mail vtd@tourism.lt; internet www.tourism.lt; Dir NIJOLĖ KLIOKIENĖ.

Defence

As assessed at November 2012, Lithuania's armed forces totalled an estimated 11,800, including an army of 7,350 (including 4,150 active reserves), a navy of 650, an air force of 1,100, and 2,700 joint troops. There was also a paramilitary force of 11,550 (including a border guard of 4,000) and a total of 6,700 reserves. Military service is compulsory and lasts for 12 months. Lithuania became a full member of the North Atlantic Treaty Organization (NATO) on 29 March 2004.

Defence Expenditure: Budgeted at 1,120m. litai in 2013.

Commander-in-Chief of the Armed Forces: Lt-Gen. ARVYDAS POCIUS.

Commander of the Land Force: Maj.-Gen. VYTAUTAS JONAS ŽUKAS.

Commander of the Air Force: Maj.-Gen. EDVARDAS MAŽEIKIS.

Commander of the Naval Force: Rear-Adm. KĘSTUTIS MACIJAUSKAS.

Education

Education, beginning at six years of age, is free and compulsory until the age of 16. Pre-school education is available for children aged between one and six years. Children spend four years at primary school (Grades 1–4), followed by six years at lower secondary school (basic education, Grades 5–10) and two years at upper secondary school or gymnasium (Grades 10–12). Vocational training is available. From 2003 a uniform tuition fee was introduced for students in higher education, although there were exemptions for the highest achievers. In 2009/10 enrolment in pre-primary education included 73% of children in the relevant age-group, while the comparable rates of enrolment in primary and secondary education were 93% and 91%, respectively. In the 2011/12 academic year 439,452 students were enrolled in 1,384 general and vocational schools. In that year there were 24 colleges and 23 universities; total enrolment in institutions of higher education was 174,823. In 1991 the first private schools were opened; by 2007/08 there were 26 private schools, 12 private colleges and seven private universities. Lithuanian is the main language of instruction, although in 2007/08 some 4.2% of students at general schools were taught in Russian and 3.4% were taught in Polish. Central government expenditure on education in 2007 amounted to 2,027.1m. litai (9.9% of total expenditure).

LUXEMBOURG

Introductory Survey

LOCATION, CLIMATE, LANGUAGE, RELIGION, FLAG, CAPITAL

The Grand Duchy of Luxembourg is a land-locked country in Western Europe. It is bordered by Belgium to the west and north, by Germany to the east and by France to the south. The climate is temperate, with cool summers and mild winters. The average temperature ranges from 1°C (33°F) in January to 18°C (64°F) in July, while annual rainfall averages 782 mm. Luxembourgish (Lëtzebuergesch), a German-Moselle-Frankish dialect, is the spoken language and became the official language in 1984. French is generally used for administrative purposes, while German is the principal written language of commerce and the press. Almost all of the inhabitants profess Christianity: about 87% are Roman Catholics and a small minority are Protestants. The national flag (proportions 3 by 5) consists of three equal horizontal stripes, of red, white and blue. The capital is the city of Luxembourg.

CONTEMPORARY POLITICAL HISTORY

Historical Context

Luxembourg's independence was affirmed in 1839 under the First Treaty of London, at which time it joined the German Customs Union (Zollverein), to counter French and Belgian influence. However, to prevent war between Prussia and France over the political status of Luxembourg, its independence and neutrality were reaffirmed under the Second Treaty of London in 1867; Luxembourg remained a member of the German Customs Union until 1919. The King of the Netherlands remained as head of state of Luxembourg until 1890, when the Dutch throne passed to his daughter, while he was succeeded as Grand Duke of Luxembourg by Adolphe I, the last Duke of Nassau, in accordance with the Nassau Family Pact, which favoured male heirs.

Luxembourg was invaded and occupied by Germany during the First and Second World Wars. After the Second World War Luxembourg became a founder member of the UN in 1946, the North Atlantic Treaty Organization (NATO, see p. 380) in 1949, and the European Community (later European Union—EU, see p. 281) in 1957. The Belgo-Luxembourg Economic Union (BLEU) has existed since 1922 (following the signing of a treaty in 1921), except during the period of German occupation in 1940–44. In 1948 the Benelux Economic Union (see p. 459) was inaugurated between Belgium, Luxembourg and the Netherlands, becoming effective in 1960, and establishing the three countries as a single customs area in 1970.

Domestic Political Affairs

Pierre Werner, leader of the Chrëschtlech Sozial Vollekspartei (CSV—Christian Social Party), became Prime Minister in February 1959 and, during 1959–74, led successive coalition governments in which the CSV was the dominant partner, along with either the Demokratesch Partei (DP—Democratic Party) or the Lëtzebuerger Sozialistesch Arbechterpartei (LSAP—Socialist Workers' Party of Luxembourg). However, following a general election in May 1974, the CSV entered into opposition for the first time since 1919, and a centre-left coalition between the DP and the LSAP was formed under the premiership of the leader of the DP, Gaston Thorn. At the next general election, which took place in June 1979, the CSV increased its representation in the Chamber of Deputies (Chambre des Députés), and Werner formed a coalition Government comprising the CSV and the DP.

At a general election in June 1984 the CSV again secured the largest number of seats in the legislature. A centre-left coalition was formed between the CSV and the LSAP, which had substantially increased its representation, with Jacques Santer of the CSV as Prime Minister. Following elections in June 1989 and June 1994, Santer renewed the CSV-LSAP coalition.

In January 1995 Santer took office as President of the European Commission. He was succeeded as Prime Minister by Jean-Claude Juncker of the CSV, hitherto Minister of the Budget, of Finance and of Labour. The two coalition partners both recorded losses at the general election in June 1999, the CSV winning 19 of the 60 seats in the Chamber of Deputies and the LSAP 13. The DP increased its representation from 12 to 15 seats, while the conservative Aktiounskomitee fir Demokratie a Rentegerechtegkeet (ADR—Action Committee for Democracy and Pensions Justice) took seven seats (an increase of two). The environmentalist party, Déi Gréng (The Greens), retained its five seats in the legislature. Juncker, who remained as Prime Minister, subsequently formed a new centre-right coalition of the CSV and the DP.

In March 1998 Grand Duke Jean conferred broad constitutional powers upon his eldest son and heir, Prince Henri, permitting him to deputize for the Grand Duke in all official capacities. In October 2000, following a reign of 36 years, Grand Duke Jean abdicated and Prince Henri succeeded his father as head of state.

Luxembourg's banking secrecy laws have for many years been a cause of concern. In April 1993 legislation was introduced that permitted the confiscation of deposits in Luxembourg banks accruing from suspected illegal drugs-related activities, and in 1997 the powers of confiscation were extended to include other illegal activities, including arms-smuggling. During that year the country's financial sector came under renewed scrutiny when the Belgian authorities conducted an investigation into alleged widespread tax evasion by Belgian citizens and companies based in Luxembourg. The German authorities also launched a similar investigation. Luxembourg was further criticized for refusing, as did Switzerland, to endorse the code of conduct with respect to tax havens drafted by the Organisation for Economic Co-operation and Development (OECD, see p. 388) in April 1998. During 1998 Luxembourg also opposed European Commission proposals for European taxation harmonization, which would oblige Luxembourg to impose tax on non-residents' interest and dividend income for the first time, thereby reducing the attraction of Luxembourg as a financial centre. In May 2000, however, Luxembourg endorsed OECD proposals aimed at limiting the use of banking secrecy laws for the purpose of tax evasion. In October the Chamber of Deputies approved a relaxation of such laws to facilitate co-operation with the US Internal Revenue Service in its attempts to halt tax evasion. Luxembourg was exempted for at least six years from a requirement for EU member states to exchange banking information from 2005 under new EU taxation rules concerning overseas investments agreed in 2003 (see Economic Affairs).

At the general election held in June 2004 the CSV increased its representation in the legislature to 24 seats. The LSAP secured 14 seats, while the DP took 10, Déi Gréng seven and the ADR five. A new coalition Government comprising the CSV and the LSAP was sworn in the following month, again under the leadership of Juncker. Jean Asselborn of the LSAP was appointed as Deputy Prime Minister and Minister of Foreign Affairs and Immigration.

In April 2006 the ADR adopted a new name, Alternativ Demokratesch Reformpartei (Alternative Democratic Reform Party), in an attempt to broaden its appeal. However, the concurrent redesign of the party's logo to incorporate the colours of the national flag provoked criticism that it was adopting a more right-wing, nationalist stance. Several members of the ADR subsequently resigned from the party, including one of its five deputies, who remained in the legislature as an independent; the ADR consequently lost its status as an official parliamentary group.

In January 2008 two former members of the state security forces were arrested in connection with a bombing campaign that had targeted a number of public buildings in 1984–86. In September 2008 the General Director and the Secretary-General of the police force, Pierre Reuland and Guy Stebens, were dismissed, after the Attorney-General expressed doubts over the credibility of statements made by the two officials regarding the original investigation into the attacks. In January 2012 it was announced that there was sufficient evidence to try the two detainees in connection with the bombings, although both denied any involvement; the trial commenced in February 2013.

In February 2008 Luxembourg became the third EU member state (along with Belgium and the Netherlands) to approve legislation decriminalizing euthanasia and assisted suicide. However, in December Grand Duke Henri precipitated a constitutional crisis by indicating that he would refuse to ratify the law, citing his religious convictions. Despite his own party's opposition to the bill, Juncker criticized the Grand Duke for disregarding the expressed will of parliament and proposed to amend the Constitution to remove the Grand Duke's powers to veto legislation adopted by the legislature. The amendment received final legislative approval in March 2009, thus, in effect, rendering the monarchy a largely ceremonial role. Meanwhile, the law decriminalizing euthanasia and assisted suicide was approved in December 2008 and was promulgated by Grand Duke Henri in March 2009.

At a general election held on 7 June 2009 the CSV increased its representation in the Chamber of Deputies to 26 seats. The LSAP and the DP each lost one seat, taking 13 and nine, respectively, while Déi Gréng's representation was unchanged at seven seats. The ADR won four seats. On 23 July Junker renewed the outgoing CSV-LSAP coalition; Asselborn remained as Deputy Prime Minister and Minister of Foreign Affairs.

Divisions emerged within the ruling coalition in 2010 over the proposed revision of the wage indexation system, whereby salaries are automatically adjusted according to changes in the cost of living. Fearing that the current system could lead to a loss of economic competitiveness, the CSV Minister of Finance, Luc Frieden, supported by the LSAP Minister of the Economy and External Trade, Jeannot Krecké, advocated the exclusion of energy, alcohol and tobacco prices from the calculation. However, the proposal was strongly opposed by other members of the LSAP and by the trade unions, and appeared to have been abandoned in September, when it was agreed, none the less, to postpone the next index-linked rise in wages until October 2011, the last having occurred in July 2010. Following the continued failure of trade unions and employers to agree on a reform of the wage indexation system, a further compromise was drawn up by the Government in December 2011 and approved by the Chamber of Deputies in the following month: the next indexation of salaries, which would have been due in March 2012 (owing to high inflation), was deferred until October of that year and a minimum delay of 12 months between adjustments to wages was introduced for the period 2012–14.

In February 2012 Krecké resigned as Minister of the Economy and External Trade; although he cited personal reasons as the motivation for his decision, observers noted that he had previously expressed frustration at the slow pace of reform. The LSAP selected Etienne Schneider, hitherto senior adviser at the Ministry of the Economy and External Trade, as Krecké's replacement.

In June 2012 a revision to the laws of succession came into effect, according to which the first-born child of the monarch would henceforth accede to the throne irrespective of gender.

In April 2013 the Minister of Justice, of the Civil Service and Administrative Reform, of Higher Education and Research, of Communications and the Media, and of Religious Affairs, François Biltgen, resigned in order to pursue his candidacy to become a judge at the European Court of Justice. Martine Hansen, new to the Government, succeeded Biltgen as Minister of Higher Education and Research, while his other responsibilities were distributed among the members of the Government; notably, Octavie Modert became Minister of Justice. Marie-Josée Jacobs, Minister of Family Affairs and Integration, of Cooperation and Humanitarian Action and of Relations with Parliament, also resigned in April and was replaced by Marc Spautz.

Foreign Affairs

As a founder member of the European Community (EC, now European Union—EU, see p. 281), of which the city of Luxembourg is one of the main bases, Luxembourg has played a significant role in progress towards European integration since the Second World War. Luxembourg's commitment to such integration was exemplified by its status as one of the original signatories to the Schengen Agreement (named after the town in Luxembourg where the accord was signed by a number of EC member countries in June 1990), which binds signatories to the abolition of internal border controls.

In December 2000 the Luxembourg Government was prominent during negotiations regarding the Treaty of Nice, which aimed to reform the institutions of the EU in light of its forthcoming enlargements. The terms of the treaty substantially safeguarded Luxembourg's privileged position in the EU: Luxembourg was to continue to have a European Commissioner, to maintain its six seats in the European Parliament and to con-

tinue to enjoy a voting weight in the Council of the European Union out of proportion to its size. In July 2001 the Chamber of Deputies ratified the treaty by a large majority. At the same time, Luxembourg continued, much to the frustration of most of its EU partners, to oppose the removal of the Secretariat of the European Parliament from the city of Luxembourg, together with its 1,500 staff, whose continued presence was considered by the Luxembourg Government to be vital to the local economy.

In July 2005 Luxembourg held a national referendum (the first since 1936) on the EU constitutional treaty, which had been approved by the EU in mid-2004. Although there were concerns that the proposed constitution was not wholly advantageous for the smaller member states of the EU, most political parties in Luxembourg supported the treaty, which was approved by some 56.5% of voters in Luxembourg, despite opposition to the document having increased following its rejection by French and Dutch voters at respective referendums in May and June. In December 2007, following a summit meeting in Lisbon, Portugal, EU leaders signed a reform treaty to replace the abandoned constitutional treaty. The so-called Treaty of Lisbon was ratified by the Chamber of Deputies in May 2008 and entered into force in December 2009, following ratification by all 27 EU member states.

As President of the so-called 'Eurogroup' of eurozone finance ministers (a position that he had held since its creation in 2005), Juncker was heavily involved during 2010–12 in negotiations on the provision of assistance to three members of the eurozone in financial difficulties—Greece, Ireland and Portugal—and in wider efforts to safeguard the stability of the eurozone through measures such as the establishment of a temporary European Financial Stability Facility and of a planned permanent European Stability Mechanism (both based in Luxembourg), as well as the introduction of new arrangements designed to increase fiscal discipline. Juncker stood down as Eurogroup President in January 2013.

Meanwhile, popular opposition in Luxembourg to a potential US-led military campaign in Iraq to remove the regime of Saddam Hussain culminated in nation-wide demonstrations in February 2003. The Government's opposition to the military intervention (which was undertaken the following month without the support of a UN resolution) adversely affected relations with the USA. Following the swift removal of the Iraqi regime, however, the Luxembourg Government announced the allocation of €3.5m. towards a humanitarian aid programme for Iraq. In March the Chamber of Deputies approved the secondment of 10 officers and men to the NATO-led International Security Assistance Force in Afghanistan (ISAF). Luxembourg's ISAF contingent numbered 10 troops in March 2013. In early 2013 Luxembourg was also contributing to the NATO-led Kosovo Force (22 troops), to EU missions in Bosnia and Herzegovina and the Democratic Republic of the Congo, and to the UN Interim Force in Lebanon.

In June 2008, at a summit meeting in The Hague, Netherlands, Prime Minister Juncker and his counterparts from Belgium and the Netherlands signed a new Benelux Treaty on political and economic co-operation. The document expanded the scope of the previous treaty, signed in 1958, to provide for greater co-operation between the three Governments on justice and home affairs, as well as customs and cross-border trade. In recognition of this broader scope, the official title was to change from the Benelux Economic Union to the Benelux Union. The treaty was ratified by Luxembourg's Chamber of Deputies in May 2009 and entered into force on 1 January 2012, following its ratification by the national legislatures of the other two countries and by the parliaments of Belgium's five federal units.

CONSTITUTION AND GOVERNMENT

The Constitution dates back to 1868, but in 1919 a constituent assembly introduced some important changes, declaring that the sovereign power resided in the nation, that all secret treaties were denounced and that deputies were to be elected by a list system by means of proportional representation, on the basis of universal adult suffrage. Luxembourg is a hereditary and constitutional monarchy. Legislative power is exercised by the unicameral Chamber of Deputies (Chambre des Députés), with 60 members elected by universal adult suffrage for five years (subject to dissolution). Some legislative functions are also entrusted to the advisory State Council (Conseil d'Etat), with 21 members appointed for life by the Grand Duke, but decisions made by this body can be overruled by the legislature.

Executive power is vested in the Grand Duke, but is normally exercised by the Council of Ministers, led by the President of the Government (Prime Minister). The Grand Duke appoints ministers, but they are responsible to the legislature. Luxembourg is divided into three districts (Luxembourg, Diekirch, Grevenmacher), 12 cantons and 106 municipalities.

REGIONAL AND INTERNATIONAL CO-OPERATION

Luxembourg was a founder member of the European Community, now the European Union (EU, see p. 281), and hosts a number of the EU's institutions. It was also a founder member of the Benelux Economic Union (see p. 459), the Council of Europe (see p. 260) and the Organization for Security and Co-operation in Europe (OSCE, see p. 397).

Luxembourg was a founder member of the UN in 1945. In October 2012 Luxembourg was elected to hold one of the five non-permanent seats on the UN Security Council during 2013–14. As a contracting party to the General Agreement on Tariffs and Trade, Luxembourg joined the World Trade Organization (WTO, see p. 444) on its establishment in 1995. Luxembourg was also a founder member of the North Atlantic Treaty Organization (NATO, see p. 380) and the Organisation for Economic Co-operation and Development (OECD, see p. 388).

ECONOMIC AFFAIRS

In 2011, according to estimates by the World Bank, Luxembourg's gross national income (GNI), measured at average 2009–11 prices, was US $40,393m., equivalent to $78,130 per head (or $64,410 per head on an international purchasing-power parity basis). During 2002–11, it was estimated, the population increased at an average rate of 1.7% per year, while gross domestic product (GDP) per head grew, in real terms, by an average of 0.8% per year during the same period. Overall GDP increased, in real terms, at an average annual rate of 2.5% in 2002–11; in 2011 GDP increased by 1.6%, measured at constant prices, and by 1.7% according to chain-linked methodologies.

In 2011 agriculture (including forestry and fishing) contributed 0.3% of GDP and 1.8% of the employed labour force were engaged in the agricultural sector. The principal crops are cereals, potatoes and wine grapes. Livestock-rearing is also of some importance. According to World Bank estimates, agricultural GDP decreased at an average annual rate of 4.7% in 2002–11. Measured at constant prices, agricultural GDP increased by 0.4% in 2010, but declined by 1.7% in 2011. According to chain-linked methodologies, sectoral GDP declined by 0.1% in 2010 and by 6.1% in 2011.

In 2011 industry (including mining, manufacturing, construction and power) provided 13.5% of GDP and engaged 21.1% of the employed labour force. According to World Bank estimates, industrial GDP decreased, in real terms, at an average annual rate of 0.3% in 2002–11; however, it increased by 5.0% in 2011.

Manufacturing activities constitute the most important industrial sector, contributing 7.2% of GDP and engaging 9.8% of the employed work-force in 2011. Although the country's deposits of iron ore are no longer exploited, the iron and steel industry remains one of the most important sectors of the Luxembourg economy; metal manufactures accounted for 28.8% of total exports in 2011. The Luxembourg steel industry is dominated by ArcelorMittal, which was formed from a merger of Arcelor and Mittal Steel in 2006. Machinery and other equipment provided 15.5% of total exports in 2011. Other important branches of manufacturing are basic manufactures, and chemicals and related products. According to World Bank estimates, real manufacturing GDP decreased by an average of 1.8% per year in 2002–11; in 2011 it increased by 8.7%, measured at constant prices, and by 2.5%, according to chain-linked methodologies.

In 2011 construction contributed 5.4% of GDP and engaged 10.7% of the employed labour force. According to UN figures, during 2002–11 the sector grew at an average annual rate of 2.4%; growth was 3.6% in 2011, measured at constant prices. According to chain-linked methodologies, sectoral GDP increased by 3.2% in 2010, but declined by 1.8% in 2011.

In 2010 90.3% of net electricity production was from natural gas, while 3.3% was from hydroelectric installations. Imports of mineral fuels and lubricants comprised 12.8% of the value of total imports in 2011.

In 2011 the services sector contributed 86.2% of GDP and engaged 77.1% of the employed labour force. Favourable laws governing banking secrecy and taxation encouraged the development of Luxembourg as a major international financial centre. Financial services contributed 23.6% of GDP in 2011. In March 2013 there were 141 banks in Luxembourg, most of which were foreign-owned. In accordance with the demands of the European Commission, however, Luxembourg abolished its preferential tax regime for holding companies from 1 January 2007, although existing companies were permitted to retain their tax benefits until 2010. The replacement regime of 'family private assets management companies', which was aimed at the wealth management sector, was introduced in 2007. Stock exchange activities (notably the Eurobond market and investment portfolio management) are also prominent. Since the mid-1990s Luxembourg has had the largest investment fund sector in Europe: in 2005 investment funds accounted for 8% of GDP. In 2010 there were 95 approved insurance companies in Luxembourg, as well as 244 reinsurance companies. According to World Bank estimates, the GDP of the services sector increased, in real terms, at an average annual rate of 3.1% in 2002–11; it rose by 1.0% in 2011.

In 2011, according to IMF figures, Luxembourg recorded a visible merchandise trade deficit of US $7,462m., while there was a surplus of $4,199m. on the current account of the balance of payments. Other members of the European Union (EU, see p. 281) account for much of Luxembourg's foreign trade. In 2011 the principal source of imports (33.9%) was Belgium; other major providers were Germany, France and the Netherlands. The principal market for exports in that year was Germany (28.0%); other major purchasers were France, Belgium and the Netherlands. The principal exports in 2011 were manufactured goods (particularly metal manufactures), machinery, miscellaneous manufactured articles, transport equipment, chemical products, and food and live animals. The principal imports were transport equipment, mineral fuels and lubricants, machinery, chemical products, crude materials, manufactured articles (notably metal manufactures), and food and live animals.

In 2011 there was a budgetary deficit of €253.2m, equivalent to 0.6% of GDP. Luxembourg's general government gross debt was €7,786m. in 2011, equivalent to 18.2% of GDP. The annual rate of inflation averaged 2.4% in 2002–12; consumer prices rose by 2.7% in 2012. The rate of unemployment averaged 5.7% in 2011. In 2011 net cross-border commuters from neighbouring states totalled 143,400, constituting 38.9% of the total employed in Luxembourg.

Luxembourg's economy expanded at an average annual rate of more than 5% during 1985–2000, its success based on its development as an international financial centre. The rapid economic expansion of the late 1990s slowed significantly in the early 2000s, but high GDP growth resumed in 2005–07, largely led by the banking and insurance sectors. The banking sector suffered as a result of the global financial crisis from mid-2008, but Luxembourg was otherwise well placed to withstand the downturn, owing to its low levels of public debt and strong public finances. Indeed, despite a temporary deterioration in the fiscal situation following the introduction of stimulus measures, the general government deficit in 2009 was the second lowest in the EU (after Sweden), at 0.9% of GDP, and widened only slightly in 2010, to 1.1%, before narrowing to 0.6% in 2011. The Government aimed to return the budget to surplus by 2014. Having contracted by 5.3% in 2009, GDP increased by 2.7% in 2010. More moderate growth of 1.6% was recorded in 2011, mainly owing to the poor performances of exports and the financial sector, which were adversely affected by the sovereign debt crisis in the eurozone; the rate of growth of GDP was estimated to have further decelerated, to 0.2%, in 2012. The unemployment rate remained relatively high, at 5.2% in February 2012 (compared with only 2.7% in 2003), while the rate of inflation declined from 3.4% in 2011 to 2.7% in 2012. Despite the country's relatively strong recovery from the effects of the economic downturn, the Government continued with its policy of fiscal consolidation in 2012, including cuts in public expenditure and proposed changes to the pensions system. In July 2012 the international credit ratings agency Moody's downgraded Luxembourg's economic outlook from 'stable' to 'negative', citing Greece's possible exit from the eurozone and the potential need to provide bail-outs for Spain and Italy. Moreover, the future profitability of Luxembourg's financial sector appeared somewhat uncertain, owing to the effects of EU integration, including the harmonization of taxation and regulatory structures, which threatened the banking secrecy and tax advantages that made the country attractive to investors. Under EU rules, Luxembourg was allowed to retain banking secrecy for a transitional period, levying a withholding tax on non-residents' savings instead, which rose incrementally from 15% in 2005 to 35% from mid-2011. Prime Minister Juncker announced in April 2013 that reforms with regard to the exchange of depositors' banking information in line with EU rules would be implemented in Luxembourg from 2015. However, since any amendments to EU taxation legislation, which require unanimous approval by the EU economy and finance ministers, would almost definitely be opposed by a number of member states, including Luxembourg, it was expected that the latter would retain some comparative economic advantages in the financial services sector at least for the near future.

PUBLIC HOLIDAYS

2014: 1 January (New Year's Day), 21 April (Easter Monday), 1 May (Labour Day), 29 May (Ascension Day), 9 June (Whit Monday), 23 June (National Day), 15 August (Assumption), 1 November (All Saints' Day), 25 December (Christmas Day), 26 December (St Stephen's Day).

Statistical Survey

Source (unless otherwise stated): Service Central de la Statistique et des Etudes Economiques (STATEC), Centre Administratif Pierre Werner, 13 rue Erasme, 1468 Luxembourg; tel. 274-84218; fax 46-42-89; e-mail info@statec.etat.lu; internet www.statec.lu.

AREA AND POPULATION

Area: 2,586 sq km (999 sq miles).

Population: 439,539 at census of 15 February 2001; 512,353 (males 254,967, females 257,386) at census of 1 February 2011. *2012* (official estimate at 1 January): 524,853.

Density (at 1 January 2012): 203.0 per sq km.

Population by Age and Sex (official estimates at 1 January 2012): *0–14:* 89,975 (males 46,210, females 43,765); *15–64:* 361,617 (males 184,003, females 177,614); *65 and over:* 73,261 (males 31,607, females 41,654); *Total* 524,853 (males 261,820, females 263,033).

Principal Towns (official estimates at 1 January 2012): Luxembourg (capital) 99,900; Esch-sur-Alzette 30,900; Differdange 22,300; Dudelange 18,800; Pétange 16,400.

Births, Marriages and Deaths (2011): Live births 5,639 (birth rate 10.9 per 1,000); Marriages 1,714 (marriage rate 3.3 per 1,000); Deaths 3,819 (death rate 7.4 per 1,000).

Life Expectancy (years at birth): 80.1 (males 77.6; females 82.7) in 2010. Source: World Bank, World Development Indicators database.

Immigration and Emigration (2011): Arrivals 20,268; Departures 9,264.

Employment ('000 persons, 2010): Agriculture, hunting, forestry and fishing 6.6; Mining and quarrying 0.3; Manufacturing 35.2; Electricity, gas and water supply 1.8; Construction 38.2; Wholesale and retail trade, repair of motor vehicles, motorcycles and personal and household goods 45.3; Hotels and restaurants 16.6; Transport, storage and communications 28.5; Financial intermediation 41.0; Real estate, renting and business activities 61.3; Public administration and defence and compulsory social security 18.3; Education 16.4; Health and social work 30.3; Other community, social and personal service activities 13.5; Private households with employed persons 5.2; *Total employed* 358.6. *2011* ('000): Total employed 368.4.

HEALTH AND WELFARE
Key Indicators

Total Fertility Rate (children per woman, 2010): 1.6.

Under-5 Mortality Rate (per 1,000 live births, 2010): 3.

HIV/AIDS (% of persons aged 15–49, 2009): 0.3.

Physicians (per 1,000 head, 2009): 2.8.

Hospital Beds (per 1,000 head, 2009): 5.6.

Health Expenditure (2009): US $ per head (PPP): 6,592.

Health Expenditure (2009): % of GDP: 7.9.

Health Expenditure (2009): public (% of total): 84.0.

Total Carbon Dioxide Emissions ('000 metric tons, 2008): 10,502.3.

Carbon Dioxide Emissions Per head (metric tons, 2008): 21.5.

Human Development Index (2011): ranking: 25.

Human Development Index (2011): value: 0.867.

For sources and definitions, see explanatory note on p. vi.

AGRICULTURE, ETC.

Principal Crops ('000 metric tons unless otherwise indicated, 2011): Wheat 76.8; Rye 4.2; Barley 38.5; Oats 4.0; Triticale (wheat-rye hybrid) 22.3; Potatoes 19.7; Rapeseed 15.6; Mushrooms 5.0 (metric tons); Apples 2.1; Grapes 17.6.

Livestock ('000 head, year ending September 2011): Cattle 192.5; Horses 4.6; Pigs 89.2; Sheep 9.0; Chickens 102.0.

Livestock Products (metric tons, 2011): Cattle meat 9,066; Pig meat 10,038; Chicken meat 162 (estimate); Cow milk 292,247.

Forestry ('000 cubic metres, 2011, unofficial figures): *Roundwood Removals:* 261.4 (Sawlogs, veneer logs and logs for sleepers 132.1, Fuel wood 17.5, Pulpwood 92.5, Other 19.3); *Sawnwood Production* (incl. railway sleepers) 78.3 (coniferous 39.2, broadleaved 39.1).

Source: FAO.

INDUSTRY

Selected Products ('000 metric tons, 2011, unless otherwise indicated): Crude steel 2,521; Rolled steel products 2,412; Wine ('000 hl) 132.0; Beer ('000 hl) 373.7 (2005); Electric energy (million kWh) 3,878.0 (2009).

FINANCE

Currency and Exchange Rates: 100 cent = 1 euro (€). *Sterling and Dollar Equivalents* (31 May 2012): £1 sterling = 1.250 euros; US $1 = 0.806 euros; €10 = £8.00 = $12.40. *Average Exchange Rate* (euros per US dollar): 0.7198 in 2009; 0.7550 in 2010; 0.7194 in 2011. Note: The national currency was formerly the Luxembourg franc. From the introduction of the euro, with Luxembourg's participation, on 1 January 1999, a fixed exchange rate of €1 = 40.3399 Luxembourg francs was in operation. Euro notes and coins were introduced on 1 January 2002. The euro and local currency circulated alongside each other until 28 February, after which the euro became the sole legal tender.

Central Budget (€ million): *Revenue:* 15,776.7 in 2009; 16,741.6 in 2010; 17,734.5 in 2011; *Expenditure:* 16,080.4 in 2009; 17,085.2 in 2010; 17,987.7 in 2011.

International Reserves (US $ million at 31 December 2011): Gold 113.36; IMF special drawing rights 374.34; Reserve position in IMF 344.08; Foreign exchange 182.08; Total 1,013.86. Source: IMF, *International Financial Statistics*.

Money Supply (incl. shares, depository corporations, national residency criteria, € million at 31 December 2011): Currency issued 2,260 (Banque centrale du Luxembourg 72,255); Demand deposits 120,261; Other deposits 94,843; Securities other than shares 66,363; Money market fund shares 295,473; Shares and other equity 52,843; Other items (net) –180,333; Total 451,710. Source: IMF, *International Financial Statistics*.

Cost of Living (Consumer Price Index; base: 2005 = 100): All items 111.5 in 2010; 115.3 in 2011; 118.4 in 2012.

Expenditure on the Gross Domestic Product (€ million at current prices, 2011): Final consumption expenditure 20,324.2 (Households 12,608.1, Non-profit institutions serving households 713.6, General government 7,002.5); Gross capital formation 8,992.5; *Total domestic expenditure* 29,316.7; Exports of goods and services 75,228.3; *Less* Imports of goods and services 61,920.4; *GDP in market prices* 42,624.6.

Gross Domestic Product by Economic Activity (€ million at current prices, 2011): Agriculture, hunting, forestry and fishing 129.5; Construction 2,067.8; Other industry 3,138.1; Wholesale and retail trade, repair of motor vehicles, motorcycles and personal and household goods, hotels and restaurants and transport and communications 8,838.6; Financial services, real estate, renting and business activities 17,840.5; Other community, social and personal service activities 6,561.7; *Gross value added in basic prices* 38,576.3; Taxes, less subsidies, on products 4,048.3; *GDP in market prices* 42,624.6.

Balance of Payments (US $ million, 2011): Exports of goods 18,807; Imports of goods –26,269; *Balance on goods* –7,462; Exports of services 71,257; Imports of services –41,581; *Balance on goods and services* 22,214; Primary income received 166,569; Primary income paid –183,090; *Balance on goods, services and primary income* 5,692; Secondary income received 7,306; Secondary income paid –8,799; *Current balance* 4,199; Capital account (net) –206; Direct investment assets –337,740; Direct investment liabilities 379,205; Portfolio investment assets 37,756; Portfolio investment liabilities 53,255; Financial derivatives and employee stock options (net) 14,687; Other investment assets –318,013; Other investment liabilities 167,283; Net errors and omissions –257; *Reserves and related items* 170. Source: IMF, *International Financial Statistics*.

EXTERNAL TRADE

Principal Commodities (€ million, 2011): *Imports:* Food and live animals 1,387.9; Beverages and tobacco 444.9; Crude materials (inedible) except fuels 1,820.3; Mineral fuels, lubricants, etc. 2,382.6; Chemicals and related products 1,822.4; Metal manufactures 1,631.1; Other basic manufactures 1,426.5; Machinery and other equipment 2,369.2; Transport equipment 3,034.4; Miscellaneous manufactured articles 2,279.3; Total 18,598.6. *Exports:* Food and live animals 717.4; Crude materials (inedible) except fuels 507.5; Chemicals and related products 907.8; Metal manufactures 3,461.0; Other basic manufactures 1,962.1; Machinery and other equipment 1,868.2; Transport equipment 1,082.8; Miscellaneous manufactured articles 1,211.8; Total (incl. others) 12,028.8.

Principal Trading Partners (€ million, 2011): *Imports:* Belgium 6,307.4; France 2,227.2; Germany 5,396.6; Italy 439.0; Netherlands 1,178.2; Switzerland 334.4; United Kingdom 369.4; USA 844.8; Total (incl. others) 18,598.6. *Exports:* Austria 198.7; Belgium 1,475.3; China, People's Republic 172.8; France 1,911.4; Germany 3,373.6; Hong Kong 131.9; Italy 517.7; Netherlands 618.5; Poland 250.9; Russia 125.8; Spain 219.3; Sweden 157.1; Switzerland 339.3; Turkey 125.0; United Kingdom 462.1; USA 413.1; Total (incl. others) 12,028.8.

TRANSPORT

Railways (traffic, million, 2011): Passenger-km 349; Freight ton-km (excl. transit traffic) 288.

Road Traffic (motor vehicles in use at 1 January 2012): Cars 344,951; Motorcycles 16,225; Buses and coaches 1,703; Goods vehicles 31,457; Tractors 5,356; Utility vehicles 624; Special vehicles 2,671; Cycles with auxiliary motors 27,110; Total 430,097.

Shipping: *River Traffic* (Port of Mertert, '000 metric tons, 2011): Goods loaded 128, Goods unloaded 484. *Merchant Fleet* (vessels registered at 31 December 2011): Number of vessels 218; Total displacement 1,174,001 grt).

Civil Aviation (traffic on scheduled services, 2011): Passengers carried 1,791,111; Freight (metric tons) 656,651; Mail (metric tons) 279.

TOURISM

Tourist Arrivals (at accommodation establishments): 907,531 in 2009; 841,851 in 2010; 932,629 in 2011.

Arrivals by Country (2011): Belgium 175,805; China, People's Republic 27,009; France 124,687; Germany 118,933; Italy 18,984; Netherlands 167,011; United Kingdom 47,791; USA 22,079; Total (incl. others) 932,629.

Tourism Receipts (US $ million, excl. passenger transport): 4,169 in 2009; 4,116 in 2010; 4,535 in 2011 (provisional). Source: World Tourism Organization.

COMMUNICATIONS MEDIA

Mobile Cellular Telephones: 765,000 in 2011.

Telephones: 279,100 main lines in use in 2011.

Internet Subscribers ('000, estimate): 168.4 in 2010.

Broadband Subscribers ('000): 169.8 in 2011.

Source: International Tele-communication Union.

EDUCATION

(2010/11 unless otherwise indicated)

Nursery: 964 teachers; 10,195 pupils.

Primary: 3,598 teachers; 3,2096 pupils.

Secondary and Technical Secondary: 4,091 teachers; 12,825 pupils (secondary), 25,879 pupils (technical secondary).

University-level: 9,227 students, incl. 6,063 studying abroad (2005/06).

Schools (2004/05): 375 offering a combination of nursery and primary education; 32 secondary (5 private).

Pupil-teacher Ratio (UNESCO estimate): 11.9 in 2007/08. (Source: UNESCO Institute for Statistics).

Directory

The Government

HEAD OF STATE

Grand Duke: HRH Grand Duke HENRI (succeeded to the throne 7 October 2000).

COUNCIL OF MINISTERS
(May 2013)

A coalition of the Chrëschtlech Sozial Volkspartei (CSV) and the Lëtzebuerger Sozialistesch Arbechterpartei (LSAP).

Prime Minister, and Minister of State, of the Treasury and of Religious Affairs: JEAN-CLAUDE JUNCKER (CSV).

Deputy Prime Minister and Minister of Foreign Affairs: JEAN ASSELBORN (LSAP).

Minister of Family Affairs and Integration, of Co-operation and Humanitarian Action and of Relations with Parliament: MARC SPAUTZ (CSV).

Minister of National Education and Vocational Training: MADY DELVAUX-STEHRES (LSAP).

Minister of Finance and of Communications and Media: LUC FRIEDEN (CSV).

Minister of Higher Education and Research: MARTINE HANSEN (CSV).

Minister of Health and of Social Security: MARS DI BARTOLOMEO (LSAP).

Minister of the Interior and the Greater Region and of Defence: JEAN-MARIE HALSDORF (CSV).

Minister of Sustainable Development and Infrastructure: CLAUDE WISELER (CSV).

Minister of Labour, Employment and Immigration: NICOLAS SCHMIT (LSAP).

Minister of Justice, of Culture, of Administrative Simplification in the Prime Minister's Office, and of the Civil Service and Administrative Reform: OCTAVIE MODERT.

Minister of Housing and Minister-delegate of Sustainable Development and Infrastructure: MARCO SCHANK (CSV).

Minister of the Middle Classes and Tourism and of Equal Opportunities: FRANÇOISE HETTO-GAASCH (CSV).

Minister of Agriculture, Viticulture and Rural Development and of Sport, and Minister-delegate of Economic Solidarity: ROMAIN SCHNEIDER (LSAP).

Minister of the Economy and External Trade: ETIENNE SCHNEIDER (LSAP).

MINISTRIES

Office of the Prime Minister: 4 rue de la Congrégation, 1352 Luxembourg; tel. 247-82101; fax 46-17-20; e-mail ministere.etat@me.etat.lu; internet www.gouvernement.lu.

Ministry of Agriculture, Viticulture and Rural Development: 1 rue de la Congrégation, 1352 Luxembourg; tel. 247-82478; fax 46-40-27; e-mail info@ma.public.lu; internet www.ma.public.lu.

Ministry of the Civil Service and Administrative Reform: 63 ave de la Liberté, BP 1807, 1931 Luxembourg; tel. 247-83130; fax 26-48-36-21; e-mail info@fonctionpublique.public.lu; internet www.fonction-publique.public.lu.

Ministry of Culture: 4 blvd Roosevelt, 2450 Luxembourg; tel. 247-86600; fax 26-29-60-38; e-mail info@mc.public.lu; internet www.mc.public.lu.

Ministry of the Economy and External Trade: 19–21 blvd Royal, 2449 Luxembourg; tel. 247-82478; fax 46-04-48; e-mail info@eco.public.lu; internet www.eco.public.lu.

Ministry of Equal Opportunities: 19–21 blvd Royal, 2921 Luxembourg; tel. 247-85814; fax 24-18-86; e-mail info@mega.public.lu; internet www.mega.public.lu.

Ministry of Family Affairs and Integration: 12–14 ave Emile Reuter, 2919 Luxembourg; tel. 247-86500; fax 247-86570; e-mail info@mfi.public.lu; internet www.mfi.public.lu.

Ministry of Finance: 3 rue de la Congrégation, 1352 Luxembourg; tel. 247-82600; fax 47-52-41; internet www.mf.public.lu.

Ministry of Foreign Affairs: Hôtel St Maximin, 5 rue Notre-Dame, 2240 Luxembourg; tel. 247-82300; fax 22-31-44; e-mail boite.officielle@mae.etat.lu; internet www.mae.lu.

Ministry of Health: Villa Louvigny, allée Marconi, 2120 Luxembourg; tel. 247-85505; e-mail info@ms.public.lu; internet www.ms.etat.lu.

Ministry of Higher Education and Research: 20 montée de la Pétrusse, 2327 Luxembourg; tel. 247-85206; fax 40-66-98; e-mail guy.loos@mesr.etat.lu; internet www.mesr.public.lu.

Ministry of Housing: 4 place de l'Europe, 1499 Luxembourg; tel. 247-84819; fax 247-84840; e-mail info@ml.public.lu; internet www.ml.public.lu.

Ministry of the Interior and the Greater Region: 19 rue Beaumont, 1219 Luxembourg; tel. 247-84600; fax 22-11-25; e-mail info@miat.public.lu; internet www.miat.public.lu.

Ministry of Justice: Centre 13 rue Erasme, 2934 Luxembourg; tel. 247-84537; fax 266-84861; e-mail info@mj.public.lu; internet www.mj.public.lu.

Ministry of Labour and Employment: 26 rue Ste Zithe, 2939 Luxembourg; tel. 247-86100; fax 247-86108; e-mail info@mte.public.lu; internet www.mte.public.lu.

Ministry of the Middle Classes and Tourism: 19–21 blvd Royal, 2449 Luxembourg; tel. 247-84715; fax 247-84740; e-mail info@mcm.public.lu; internet www.mcm.public.lu.

Ministry of National Education and Vocational Training: 29 rue Aldringen, 2926 Luxembourg; tel. 247-85100; fax 247-85113; e-mail info@men.public.lu; internet www.men.public.lu.

Ministry of Social Security: 26 rue Ste Zithe, 2763 Luxembourg; tel. 247-86311; fax 247-86328; e-mail mss@mss.etat.lu; internet www.mss.public.lu.

Ministry of State: 4 rue de la Congrégation, 1352 Luxembourg; tel. 247-82101; fax 46-17-20; e-mail ministere.etat@me.etat.lu; internet www.etat.lu; (incorporating Ministry of Religious Affairs).

Ministry of Sustainable Development and Infrastructure: Bâtiment Alcide de Gasperi, 4 place de l'Europe, 1499 Luxembourg; tel. 247-82478; fax 46-27-09; e-mail info@developpement-durable-infrastructures.public.lu; internet www.developpement-durable-infrastructures.public.lu.

Legislature

CHAMBER OF DEPUTIES

Chambre des Députés: Hôtel de la Chambre des Députés, 19 rue du Marché-aux-Herbes, 1728 Luxembourg; tel. 466-966-1; fax 22-02-301; e-mail info@chd.lu; internet www.chd.lu.

President: LAURENT MOSAR.

General Election, 7 June 2009

Party	% of votes	Seats
Chrëschtlech Sozial Vollekspartei	38.04	26
Lëtzebuerger Sozialistesch Arbechterpartei	21.56	13
Demokratesch Partei	14.98	9
Déi Gréng	11.71	7
Alternativ Demokratesch Reformpartei	8.13	4
Déi Lénk	3.29	1
Kommunistesch Partei Lëtzebuerg	1.47	—
BiergerLëscht	0.81	—
Total	**100.00**	**60**

Advisory Councils

Conseil Economique et Social: Centre Administratif Pierre Werner, 13 rue Erasme, BP 1306, 1013 Luxembourg; tel. 43-58-51; fax 42-27-29; e-mail info@ces.public.lu; internet www.ces.public.lu;

f. 1966; consultative body on economics and social affairs; 39 mems; Pres. GARY KNEIP; Sec.-Gen. MARIANNE NATI-STOFFEL.

Conseil d'Etat: 5 rue Sigefroi, 2536 Luxembourg; tel. 47-30-71; fax 46-43-22; e-mail info@conseil-etat.public.lu; internet www.conseil-etat.public.lu; 21 mems nominated by the Sovereign; Pres. VICTOR GILLEN; Sec.-Gen. MARC BESCH.

Political Organizations

Alternativ Demokratesch Reformpartei (ADR) (Alternative Democratic Reform Party): 20 rue de l'Eau, 1449 Luxembourg; tel. 26-203-706; fax 26-20-37-36; e-mail adr@chd.lu; internet www.adr.lu; f. 1987 as Aktiounskomitee 5/6 Pensioun fir jiddfereen (Action Committee 5/6 Pensions for Everyone); name changed to Aktiounskomitee fir Demokratie a Rentegerechtegkeet (Action Committee for Democracy and Pensions Justice) in 1994; present name adopted 2006; conservative; established to campaign for improved pension rights for private sector employees, but subsequently sought to broaden its concerns; Pres. ROBERT (ROBY) MEHLEN.

Chrëschtlech Sozial Vollekspartei (CSV) (Christian Social Party): 4 rue de l'Eau, BP 826, 2018 Luxembourg; tel. 22-57-31-1; fax 47-27-16; e-mail csv@csv.lu; internet www.csv.lu; f. 1914; advocates political stability, sustained economic expansion, ecological and social progress; 9,500 mems; Pres. MICHEL WOLTER; Sec.-Gen. LAURENT ZEIMET.

Déi Gréng (The Greens): 1 rue de Fort Elisabeth, 1463 Luxembourg; tel. 27-48-27-1; fax 27-48-27-22; e-mail greng@greng.lu; internet www.greng.lu; f. 1983; fmrly Déi Gréng Alternativ (Green Alternative Party); merged with the Gréng Lëscht Ekologesch Initiativ (Green List Ecological Initiative) in 1995; advocates grass-roots democracy, environmental protection, social concern and increased aid to developing countries; Spokespersons SAM TANSON, CHRISTIAN GOEBEL.

Déi Lénk (The Left): 5 rue Aldringen, BP 817, 2018 Luxembourg; tel. 26-20-20-72; fax 26-20-20-73; e-mail info@lenk.lu; internet www.dei-lenk.lu; f. 1999; individual membership; Spokespersons FABIENNE LENTZ, DAVID WAGNER.

Demokratesch Partei (DP) (Democratic Party): 5 rue du St Esprit, 1475 Luxembourg; tel. 22-10-21; fax 22-10-13; e-mail secretariat@dp.lu; internet www.dp.lu; liberal; Leader CLAUDE MEISCH; Gen. Sec. FERNAND ETGEN.

Kommunistische Partei Luxemburgs/Parti Communiste Luxembourgeois (KPL) (Communist Party of Luxembourg): 3 rue Zénon Bernard, BP 403, 4005 Esch-sur-Alzette; tel. 44-60-66-21; fax 44-60-66-66; e-mail kpl@zlv.lu; internet www.kp-l.org; f. 1921; Pres. ALI RUCKERT.

Lëtzebuerger Sozialistesch Arbechterpartei (LSAP) (Socialist Workers' Party of Luxembourg): 68 rue de Gasperich, 1617 Luxembourg; tel. 45-65-73-1; fax 45-65-75; e-mail info@lsap.lu; internet www.lsap.lu; f. 1902; social democrat; 6,000 mems; Pres. ALEX BODRY; Sec. YVES CRUCHTEN.

Diplomatic Representation

EMBASSIES IN LUXEMBOURG

Austria: 3 rue des Bains, 1212 Luxembourg; tel. 47-11-88-1; fax 46-39-74; e-mail luxemburg-ob@bmeia.gv.at; internet www.bmeia.gv.at/luxemburg; Ambassador Dr THOMAS OBERREITER.

Belgium: 4 rue des Girondins, 1626 Luxembourg; tel. 44-27-46-1; fax 45-42-82; e-mail luxembourg@diplobel.fed.be; internet www.diplomatie.be/luxemburg; Ambassador LUC TEIRLINCK.

Cape Verde: 117 val de Ste Croix, 1371 Luxembourg; tel. 26-48-09-48; fax 26-48-09-49; e-mail ambcvlux@pt.lu; Chargé d'affaires a.i. CLARA DELGADO.

China, People's Republic: 2 rue Van der Meulen, Dommeldange, 2152 Luxembourg; tel. 43-69-91-1; fax 42-24-23; e-mail chianemb_lu@mfa.gov.cn; internet lu.china-embassy.org; Ambassador ZENG XIANQI.

Czech Republic: 2 rond-point Robert Schuman, 2525 Luxembourg; tel. 26-47-78; fax 26-47-78-20; e-mail luxembourg@embassy.mzv.cz; internet www.mzv.cz/luxembourg; Ambassador VÍT KORSELT.

Denmark: 4 rue des Girondins, 1626 Luxembourg; tel. 22-21-22-1; fax 22-21-24; e-mail luxamb@um.dk; internet www.ambluxembourg.um.dk; Ambassador LOUISE BANG JESPERSEN.

Finland: 2 rue Heine, 1720 Luxembourg; tel. 49-55-51; fax 49-46-40; e-mail sanomat.lux@formin.fi; internet www.finlande.lu; Ambassador MARJA LEHTO.

France: 8B blvd Joseph II, BP 359, 2013 Luxembourg; tel. 45-72-71; fax 45-72-71-227; e-mail ambassade@ambafrance-lu.org; internet www.ambafrance-lu.org; Ambassador GUY YELDA.

Germany: 20–22 ave Emile Reuter, BP 95, 2420 Luxembourg; tel. 45-34-45-1; fax 45-56-04; e-mail info@luxe.diplo.de; internet www .luxemburg.diplo.de; Ambassador CHRISTINE GLÄSER.

Greece: 27 rue Marie-Adélaïde, 2128 Luxembourg; tel. 44-51-93-1; fax 45-01-64; e-mail gremb.lux@mfa.gr; Ambassador IOANNIS RIZO-POULOS.

Ireland: Résidence Christina, 2nd Floor, 28 route d'Arlon, 1140 Luxembourg; tel. 45-06-10-1; fax 45-88-20; e-mail luxembourg@dfa .ie; internet www.embassyofireland.lu; Ambassador DIARMUID O'LEARY.

Italy: 5–7 rue Marie-Adélaïde, 2128 Luxembourg; tel. 44-36-44-1; fax 45-55-23; e-mail ambasciata.lussemburgo@esteri.it; internet www.amblussemburgo.esteri.it; Ambassador STEFANO MARIA CACCIAGUERRA RANGHIERI.

Japan: 62 ave de la Faïencerie, BP 92, 2010 Luxembourg; tel. 46-41-51-1; fax 46-41-76; e-mail embjapan@lx.mofa.go.jp; internet www.lu .emb-japan.go.jp; Ambassador WATARU NISHIGAHIRO.

Netherlands: 6 rue Ste Zithe, 2763 Luxembourg; tel. 22-75-70; fax 40-30-16; e-mail lux@minbuza.nl; internet www.paysbas.lu; Ambassador PETRUS WOUTERUS KOK.

Poland: 2 rue de Pulvermühl, 2356 Luxembourg; tel. 26-00-32; fax 26-68-75-74; e-mail luksemburg.amb.sekretariat@msz.gov.pl; internet www.luksemburg.msz.gov.pl; Ambassador BARTOSZ JAŁOWIECKI.

Portugal: 24 rue Guillaume Schneider, 2522 Luxembourg; tel. 46-61-90-1; fax 46-51-69; e-mail luxemburgo@mne.pt; Ambassador RITA DA FRANCO SOUSA FERRO LEVY GOMES.

Romania: 41 blvd de la Pétrusse, 2320 Luxembourg; tel. 45-51-51; fax 45-51-63; e-mail ambroum@pt.lu; internet luxemburg.mae.ro; Ambassador ROXANA DANIELA IFTIMIE.

Russia: Château de Beggen, 116 rue Cyprien Merjai, 1719 Luxembourg; tel. 42-23-33; fax 42-23-34; e-mail ambruslu@pt.lu; internet www.ruslux.mid.ru; Ambassador MARK LVOVICH ENTIN.

Spain: 4 blvd Emmanuel Servais, BP 290, 2012 Luxembourg; tel. 46-02-55; fax 46-12-88; e-mail emb.luxemburgo@maec.es; internet www .maec.es/embajadas/luxemburgo; Ambassador ARTURO AVELLO DIEZ DEL CORRAL.

Switzerland: Immeuble Forum Royal, 25A blvd Royal, 3rd Floor, 2449 Luxembourg; tel. 22-74-74-1; fax 22-74-74-20; e-mail lux .vertretung@eda.admin.ch; internet www.eda.admin.ch/ luxembourg; Ambassador URS HAMMER.

Turkey: 49 rue Siggy vu Lëtzebuerg, 1933 Luxembourg; tel. 44-32-81; fax 44-32-81-134; e-mail ambassade.luxembourg@mfa.gov.tr; Ambassador CELALETTIN KART.

United Kingdom: 5 blvd Joseph II, 1840 Luxembourg; tel. 22-98-64; fax 22-98-67; e-mail britemb@internet.lu; internet ukinluxembourg .fco.gov.uk; Ambassador ALICE WALPOLE.

USA: 22 blvd Emmanuel Servais, 2535 Luxembourg; tel. 46-01-23; fax 46-14-01; internet luxembourg.usembassy.gov; Ambassador ROBERT A. MANDELL.

Judicial System

The lowest courts in Luxembourg are those of the Justices of the Peace, of which there are three, at Luxembourg city, Esch-sur-Alzette and Diekirch. These are competent to deal with civil, commercial and criminal cases of minor importance. Above these are the two District Courts, Luxembourg being divided into the judicial districts of Luxembourg and Diekirch. These are competent to deal with civil, commercial and criminal cases. The Superior Court of Justice includes both a court of appeal, hearing decisions made by District Courts, and the Cour de Cassation. As the judicial system of the Grand Duchy does not employ the jury system, a defendant is acquitted if a minority of the presiding judges find him or her guilty. The highest administrative court is the Comité du Contentieux du Conseil d'Etat. Special tribunals exist to adjudicate upon various matters of social administration such as social insurance. The department of the Procureur Général (Attorney-General) is responsible for the administration of the judiciary and the supervision of judicial police investigations. In July 1996 an amendment to the Constitution introduced a Constitutional Court.

Judges are appointed for life by the Grand Duke, and are not removable except by judicial sentence.

Superior Court of Justice: Cité Judiciaire, Bâtiment CR, 2080 Luxembourg; tel. 47-59-81-1; fax 47-59-81-396; Pres. GEORGES SANTER.

Attorney-General: ROBERT BIEVER.

Religion

CHRISTIANITY

The Roman Catholic Church

For ecclesiastical purposes, Luxembourg comprises a single archdiocese, directly responsible to the Holy See. At 31 December 2006 adherents numbered 393,800 (around 86.5% of the total population).

Archbishop of Luxembourg: Most Rev. JEAN-CLAUDE HOLLERICH, Archevêché, 4 rue Génistre, BP 419, 2014 Luxembourg; tel. 46-20-23; fax 47-53-81; e-mail archeveche@cathol.lu; internet www.cathol.lu.

The Anglican Communion

Within the Church of England, Luxembourg forms part of the diocese of Gibraltar in Europe.

Chaplain: Rev. CHRISTOPHER LYON, 89 rue de Muhlenbach, 2168 Luxembourg; tel. and fax 43-95-93; e-mail chris.lyon@anglican.lu; internet www.anglican.lu; English-speaking church (Anglican Chaplaincy).

Protestant Churches

Protestant Church of Luxembourg: 5 rue de la Congrégation, 1352 Luxembourg; tel. 22-96-70; fax 22-96-70-70; e-mail mail@ protestant.lu; internet www.protestant.lu; f. 1818 as Protestant Garnison Church, 1868 as multiconfessional community for the Grand Duchy; there are about 1,500 Evangelicals; Pres. Pastor VOLKER STRAUSS.

Protestant Reformed Church of Luxembourg: 11 rue de la Libération, BP 295, 4210 Esch-sur-Alzette; tel. 54-03-45; fax 54-03-46; e-mail eglrefki@pt.lu; internet www.reformiert.lu; f. 1982; 3,500 mems in 4 parishes (2006); Pastor KARL GEORG MARHOFFER.

ISLAM

Centre Culturel Islamique de Luxembourg: 2 route d'Arlon, 8210 Mamer; tel. 31-00-60; fax 26-31-04-26; e-mail info@islam.lu; internet www.islam.lu; f. 1984; Imam HALIL AHMETSPAHIC.

JUDAISM

Chief Rabbi: ALAIN NACACHE, 34 rue Alphouse Munchen, 2172 Luxembourg; tel. 45-23-66; fax 25-04-30.

Consistoire Israélite de Luxembourg (Jewish Community of Luxembourg): 45 ave Monterey, BP 835, 2018 Luxembourg; tel. 45-29-14-20; fax 25-05-30; e-mail info@synagogue.lu; internet www .synagogue.lu; Pres. FRANÇOIS MOYSE.

The Press

DAILIES

L'Essentiel: 53 rue Emile Mark, 4620 Differdange; tel. 26-58-66-1; fax 26-58-66-628; e-mail denis.berche@lessentiel.lu; internet www .lessentiel.lu; f. 2007; Mon.–Fri.; French; distributed free of charge; publ. by Edita SA; Editor-in-Chief DENIS BERCHE; circ. 57,666 (2007).

Lëtzebuerger Journal: Résidence de Beauvoir, 51 rue de Strasbourg, BP 2101, 1021 Luxembourg; tel. 49-30-33-1; fax 49-20-65; e-mail journal@journal.lu; internet www.journal.lu; f. 1948; organ of the Democratic Party; Editor-in-Chief CLAUDE KARGER.

Luxemburger Wort: 2 rue Christophe Plantin, 2988 Luxembourg; tel. 49-93-1; fax 49-93-309; e-mail wort@wort.lu; internet www.wort .lu; f. 1848; German; Catholic; Christian Democrat; Editor-in-Chief PAUL LENERT; circ. 72,745 (2011).

Le Quotidien: 44 rue du Canal, 4050 Esch-sur-Alzette; tel. 44-77-77-1; fax 44-77-33-1; e-mail redaction@lequotidien.lu; internet www .lequotidien.lu; f. 2001; French; owned by Editpress and Le Républicain Lorrain; Dir of Publication JEAN-MARIE MARTINI; circ. 8,445 (2009).

Tageblatt/Zeitung fir Lëtzebuerg: 44 rue du Canal, 4050 Esch-sur-Alzette; tel. 54-71-31-1; fax 54-71-30; e-mail redaktion@tageblatt .lu; internet www.tageblatt.lu; f. 1913; French and German; Editor-in-Chief DANIÈLE FONCK; circ. 20,046 (2007).

Zeitung vum Lëtzebuerger Vollek: 3 rue Zénon Bernard, 4030 Esch-sur-Alzette; tel. 44-60-66-1; fax 44-60-66-66; e-mail info@zlv.lu; internet www.zlv.lu; f. 1946; organ of the Communist Party; Editor-in-Chief ALI RUCKERT.

PERIODICALS

Aktuell: 60 blvd Kennedy, BP 149, 4002 Esch-sur-Alzette; tel. 54-05-45-1; fax 54-16-20; e-mail ogbl@ogbl.lu; internet www.ogbl.lu; f. 1979; articles in both French and German; monthly; journal of the Luxembourg General Confederation of Labour; Editor-in-Chief JEAN-CLAUDE REDING; circ. 62,000.

Auto Moto: Inter Editions SA, 7 rue Robert Stumper, 2557 Luxembourg; tel. 49-50-10-1; fax 49-50-11; monthly; motoring; circ. 72,345 (2007).

Carrière: BP 2535, 1025 Luxembourg; tel. and fax 85-89-19; e-mail carrieremag@logic.lu; internet www.logic.lu/carriere; f. 1988; women's interest; French and German; Editor MONIQUE MATHIEU; circ. 8,000.

Contacto: 2 rue Christophe Plantin, 2988 Luxembourg; tel. 49-93-1; fax 49-93-386; e-mail contacto@saint-paul.lu; internet www .jornal-contacto.lu; Portuguese; weekly; Editor-in-Chief JOSÉ CORREIA; circ. 22,800.

Echo des entreprises: 7 rue Alcide de Gasperi, BP 1304, 1013 Luxembourg; tel. 43-53-66-1; fax 43-23-28; e-mail echo@fedil.lu; internet www.fedil.lu/echo; f. 1920; 6 a year; industry, commerce; publ. by FEDIL—Business Federation Luxembourg; Dir NICOLAS SOISSON.

Femmes Magazine: 74 rue Ermesinde, 1469 Luxembourg; tel. 26-45-85-86; fax 26-45-84-94; e-mail redaction@femmesmagazine.lu; internet www.femmesmagazine.lu; 11 a year; women's interest; Dirs MARIA PIETRANGELI, PATRICIA SCIOTTI; circ. 20,128 (2007).

D'Handwierk: 2 circuit de la Foire Internationale, BP 1604, 1016 Luxembourg; tel. 42-45-11-1; fax 42-45-25; e-mail info@fda.lu; internet www.fda.lu; monthly; organ of the Fédération des Artisans and the Chambre des Métiers; Editor CHRISTIAN REUTER.

Horesca: 7 rue Alcide de Gasperi, BP 2524, 1025 Luxembourg; tel. 42-13-55-1; fax 42-13-55-29-9; e-mail horesca@pt.lu; internet www .horesca.lu; monthly; hotel trade, tourism, gastronomy; Editor DAVE GIANNANDREA; circ. 6,000.

Le Jeudi: 44 rue du Canal, 4050 Esch-sur-Alzette; tel. 22-05-50; fax 22-05-44; e-mail redaction@le-jeudi.lu; internet www.lejeudi.lu; f. 1997; weekly; French; Dir DANIÈLE FONCK; circ. 9,965 (2007).

de Konsument: 55 rue des Bruyères, 1274 Howald; tel. 49-60-22-1; fax 49-49-57; e-mail ulc@pt.lu; internet www.ulc.lu; 11 a year; consumer affairs; Man. GUY GOEDERT.

De Lëtzeburger Bauer: 16 blvd d'Avranches, 2980 Luxembourg; tel. 48-81-61-1; fax 40-03-75; e-mail letzeburger.bauer@netline.lu; f. 1944; weekly; journal of Luxembourg farming; circ. 7,500.

D'Lëtzeburger Land: 59 rue Glesener, BP 2083, 1020 Luxembourg; tel. 48-57-57-1; fax 49-63-09; e-mail land@land.lu; internet www .land.lu; f. 1954; weekly (Fri.); political, economic, cultural affairs; Man. Editor ROMAIN HILGERT; circ. 7,500.

Lux-Post: Editions Saphir, 23 rue des Gênets, 1621 Luxembourg; tel. 49-53-63; fax 48-53-70; local news; 4 regional edns; French and German; circ. 135,283 (2007).

Muselzeidung: 30 rue de Trèves, POB 36, 6701 Grevenmacher; tel. 75-87-47; fax 75-84-32; e-mail burton@pt.lu; internet www .muselzeidung.lu; f. 1981; regional magazine; monthly; German; Editor EUGENE BURTON.

Revue: 2 rue Dicks, BP 2755, 1027 Luxembourg; tel. 49-81-81-1; fax 48-77-22; e-mail revue@revue.lu; internet www.revue.lu; f. 1945; weekly; illustrated; Dir GASTON ZANGERLÉ; circ. approx. 25,000.

Revue Technique Luxembourgeoise: 6 blvd Grande-Duchesse Charlotte, 1330 Luxembourg; tel. 26-73-99; fax 45-09-32; e-mail s.reichert@revue-technique.lu; internet www.revue-technique.lu; f. 1908; organ of the Association Luxembourgeoise des Ingénieurs, Architectes et Industriels; quarterly; technology, architecture, engineering, industry, science; Editor-in-Chief MICHEL PETIT.

Sauerzeidung: 30 rue de Trèves, BP 36, 6701 Grevenmacher; tel. 75-87-47; fax 75-84-32; e-mail burton@pt.lu; internet www .muselzeidung.lu; f. 1988; regional newspaper; monthly; German; Publr EUGENE BURTON; circ. 17,500.

Soziale Fortschrett: 11 rue du Commerce, BP 1208, Luxembourg; tel. 49-94-24-1; fax 49-94-24-49; e-mail infocenter@lcgb.lu; internet lcgb.lu; f. 1921; bimonthly; journal of the Confed. of Christian Trade Unions of Luxembourg; Nat. Pres. PATRICK DURY; circ. 40,000.

Télécran: 2 rue Christophe Plantin, BP 1008, 1010 Luxembourg; tel. 49-93-50-0; fax 49-93-59-0; e-mail telecran@telecran.lu; internet www.telecran.lu; f. 1978; TV and family weekly; illustrated; Editor-in-Chief CLAUDE FRANÇOIS; circ. 36,431 (2007).

Transport: 13 rue du Commerce, BP 2615, 1026 Luxembourg; tel. 22-67-86-1; fax 22-67-09; e-mail syprolux@pt.lu; internet www .fcpt-syprolux.lu; fortnightly; circ. 3,800.

Woxx: 51 ave de la Liberté, 2e étage, BP 684, 2016 Luxembourg; tel. 29-79-99-0; fax 29-79-79; e-mail woxx@woxx.lu; internet www.woxx .lu; f. 1988 as *GréngeSpoun*; weekly; social, ecological, environmental and general issues; circ. 3,000.

NEWS AGENCY

Agence Europe SA: Val Sainte Croix 7, 1371 Luxembourg; e-mail info@agenceurope.eu; internet www.agenceurope.eu; f. 1952.

PRESS ASSOCIATIONS

Association Luxembourgeoise des Editeurs de Journaux: 44 rue du Canal, 4050 Esch-sur-Alzette; tel. 54-71-31; fax 53-05-87; e-mail asold@tageblatt.lu; Pres. ALVIN SOLD.

Association Luxembourgeoise des Journalistes: BP 1732, 1017 Luxembourg; tel. 44-00-44; fax 85-88-40; e-mail rinfalt@tageblatt.lu; Pres. ROGER INFALT.

Publishers

Editions Guy Binsfeld: 14 place du Parc, 2313 Luxembourg; tel. 49-68-68-1; fax 40-76-09; e-mail editions@binsfeld.lu; internet www .editionsguybinsfeld.lu; f. 1979; literature, reference, children's; Dir and Chief Editor ROB KIEFFER.

Editions Mike Koedinger SA: 10 rue des Gaulois, BP 728, 2017 Luxembourg; tel. 29-66-181; fax 29-66-19; e-mail sylvia@ mikekoedinger.com; internet www.mikekoedinger.com; trade and customer magazines, business directories, guidebooks; CEO MIKE KOEDINGER.

Editions Phi: Villa Hadir, 51 rue Emile Mark, 4620 Differdange; tel. 44-44-33-1; fax 44-44-33-55-5; e-mail editions.phi@editpress.lu; internet www.phi.lu; f. 1980; literature, art; owned by Editpress SA; Dir CHRISTINE KREMER.

Editions Schortgen: 108 rue d'Alzette, BP 367, 4004 Esch-sur-Alzette; tel. 54-64-87; fax 53-05-34; e-mail editions@schortgen.lu; internet www.editions-schortgen.lu; art, literature, factual, cuisine, comics; Dir JEAN-PAUL SCHORTGEN.

Editpress Luxembourg SA: 44 rue du Canal, BP 147, 4050 Esch-sur-Alzette; tel. 54-71-31-1; fax 54-71-30; e-mail tageblatt@tageblatt .lu; internet www.tageblatt.lu; Dir ALVIN SOLD.

Edouard Kutter: BP 319, 2013 Luxembourg; tel. 22-35-71; fax 47-18-84; e-mail kuttered@pt.lu; internet www.kutter.lu; art, photography, facsimile edns on Luxembourg.

Imprimerie Beffort SA: 7A rue de Bitbourg, 1273 Luxembourg; tel. 25-44-55-1; fax 25-44-19; e-mail jmkerschen@beffort.lu; f. 1869; scientific, economic reviews; Dir JEAN-MARIE KERSCHEN.

Legitech: 10A rue des Mérovingiens, 8070 Bertrange; tel. 26-31-64-1; fax 26-31-64-99; e-mail contact@legitech.lu; internet www.legitech .lu; f. 2006; law and taxation; Dir NICOLAS HENCKES.

Saint-Paul Luxembourg SA: 2 rue Christophe Plantin, 2988 Luxembourg; tel. 49-93-50-0; fax 49-93-38-6; e-mail direction@ saint-paul.lu; internet www.saint-paul.lu; f. 1887; Man. Dir PAUL LENERT.

PUBLISHERS' ASSOCIATION

Fédération Luxembourgeoise des Editeurs de Livres: 31 blvd Konrad Adenauer, BP 482, 2014 Luxembourg; tel. 43-94-44; fax 43-94-50; e-mail francoise.schlink@clc.lu; internet www.clc.lu; f. 1991; affiliated to Confédération Luxembourgeoise du Commerce (CLC).

Broadcasting and Communications

TELECOMMUNICATIONS

Cegecom SA: 3 rue Jean Piret, 2350 Luxembourg; tel. 26-49-91; fax 26-49-96-99; e-mail info@cegecom.net; internet www.cegecom.lu; f. 1999; Man. Dirs MICHAEL LEIDINGER, GEORGES MULLER, BERTHOLD WEGMANN.

Entreprise des Postes et Télécommunications (P&TLuxembourg): 8A ave Monterey, 2020 Luxembourg; tel. 47-65-1; fax 47-51-10; e-mail contact@pt.lu; internet www.pt.lu; f. 1992; post, telecommunications and internet service provider; Pres. SERGE ALLEGREZZA; CEO CLAUDE STRASSER.

Luxembourg Online SA: 14 ave du X Septembre, 2550 Luxembourg; tel. 27-99-00-00; fax 27-99-35-55; e-mail administration@ internet.lu; internet www.internet.lu; f. 1995; offers fixed-line and mobile telecommunications and broadband internet access.

LUXGSM SA: 90A rue de Strasbourg, 1171 Luxembourg; tel. 24-62-1; fax 24-62-60-00; e-mail communication@luxgsm.lu; internet www .luxgsm.lu; f. 1993; mobile cellular telephone operator; subsidiary of Entreprise des Postes et Télécommunications; Man. Dir MARC ROSENFELD.

Numericable: 283 route d'Arlon, 8011 Strassen; tel. 26-10-23-01; fax 34-93-98; internet www.numericable.lu; fmrly Coditel, name changed 2008; offers digital television, fixed-line telecommunications and broadband internet access; Dir-Gen. PASCAL DORMAL.

Orange SA: 8 rue des Mérovingiens, 8070 Bertrange; fax 27-88-81-00; e-mail clients@orangeluxembourg.lu; internet www.orange.lu; fmrly called VOXmobile; name changed to present in 2009; mobile cellular and fixed-line telecommunications, broadband internet access; owned by Mobistar (Belgium); CEO WERNER DE LAET (acting); 80,678 customers.

Tango: 177 route de Luxembourg, BP 32, 8077 Bertrange; tel. 27-77-71-01; fax 27-77-72-22; e-mail info@tango.lu; internet www.tango.lu; f. 1998; fixed and mobile telephony, as well as broadband internet services; fmrly Tele2Tango; acquired by Belgacom SA (Belgium) in 2008; CEO DIDIER ROUMA.

Regulatory Authority

Institut Luxembourgeois de Régulation (ILR): 45 allée Scheffer, 2520 Luxembourg; tel. 45-88-45-1; fax 45-88-45-88; e-mail info@ilr.lu; internet www.ilr.public.lu; Pres. PAUL LAPLUME; Dir ODETTE WAGENER.

BROADCASTING
Regulatory Authority

Commission Indépendante de la Radiodiffusion: 5 rue Large, 1917 Luxembourg; tel. 24-78-20-75; e-mail monique.fritsch@smc.etat.lu; Pres. GEORGES SANTER.

Radio

Eldoradio: 45 blvd Pierre Frieden, 1543 Luxembourg; tel. 40-95-09-1; fax 40-95-09-509; e-mail eldoradio@eldoradio.lu; internet www.eldoradio.lu; popular music station; Dir CHRISTOPHE GOOSSENS.

Radio 100,7: 45A ave Monterey, BP 1833, 2163 Luxembourg; tel. 44-00-44-1; fax 44-00-44-98-0; e-mail info@100komma7.lu; internet www.100komma7.lu; f. 1993; non-commercial cultural broadcaster; Dir FERNAND WEIDES.

Radio Ara: 2 rue de la Boucherie, BP 266, 1247 Luxembourg; tel. 22-22-89; fax 22-22-66; e-mail radioara@pt.lu; internet www.ara.lu; f. 1992; music broadcaster; Man. Dir LISA MCLEAN.

Radio DNR: 2 rue Christophe Plantin, 2339 Luxembourg; tel. 40-24-01; fax 40-79-98; e-mail dnr@dnr.lu; internet www.dnr.lu; music broadcaster; Dir LUC WAGNER.

Radio Latina: 3 rue du Fort Bourbon, 1249 Luxembourg; tel. 29-95-96-1; fax 40-24-76; e-mail radiolatina@radiolatina.lu; internet www.radiolatina.lu; broadcasts programmes in Portuguese, French, Italian, Spanish and Cape Verdean Créole; Dir LUC WAGNER.

Radio LRB: 4 rue Saint Benoît zu Peppeng, BP 8, 3201 Bettembourg; tel. 52-44-88-22; fax 52-44-88-33; e-mail info@lrb.lu; internet www.lrb.lu; popular music; Man. ANDY CRESTO.

RTL Group: 45 blvd Pierre Frieden, 1543 Luxembourg; tel. 24-86-1; fax 24-86-51-39; e-mail oliver.herrgesell@rtlgroup.com; internet www.rtlgroup.com; f. 2000 by merger of CLT-UFA and Pearson TV; 92.3% owned by Bertelsmann AG (Germany), 7.7% by private shareholders; 29 radio stations and 45 television channels in 9 countries; Co-CEOs GUILLAUME DE POSCH, ANKE SCHÄFERKORDT.

RTL Radio Lëtzebuerg: 45 blvd Pierre Frieden, 1543 Luxembourg; tel. 42-14-28-00; fax 42-14-22-73-7; e-mail news@rtl.lu; internet www.rtl.lu; f. 1959; broadcasts in Lëtzebuergesch; Station Man. FERNAND MATHES; Chief Editor MARC LINSTER.

Television

RTL Télé Lëtzebuerg: 45 blvd Pierre Frieden, 1543 Luxembourg; tel. 42-14-28-10; fax 42-14-27-43-1; e-mail online@rtl.lu; internet www.rtl.lu; f. 1969; 2 channels: RTL Télé Lëtzebuerg and Den 2. RTL; subsidiary of RTL Group; CEO ALAIN BERWICK; Station Man. STEVE SCHMIT.

Finance

(cap. = capital; res = reserves; dep. = deposits; m. = million; brs = branches; amounts in euros, unless otherwise indicated)

REGULATORY BODY

Commission de Surveillance du Secteur Financier (CSSF): 110 route d'Arlon, 2991 Luxembourg; tel. 26-25-11; fax 26-25-1-601; e-mail direction@cssf.lu; internet www.cssf.lu; f. 1998; supervision of financial sector; Dir-Gen. J. GUILL; Dirs ARTHUR PHILIPPE, SIMONE DELCOURT.

BANKING

In March 2013 there were 141 banks in Luxembourg, most of which were subsidiaries or branches of foreign banks; a selection of the principal banks operating internationally is given below.

Central Bank

Banque centrale du Luxembourg: 2 blvd Royal, 2983 Luxembourg; tel. 47-74-1; fax 47-74-49-10; e-mail info@bcl.lu; internet www .bcl.lu; f. 1998; represents Luxembourg within the European System of Central Banks (ESCB); cap. 175m., res 0.2m., dep. 15,080.3m. (Dec. 2009); Pres. YVES MERSCH; Exec. Dirs PIERRE BECK, SERGE KOLB.

Principal Banks

ABN AMRO Bank (Luxembourg) SA: 46 ave J. F. Kennedy, 1855 Luxembourg; tel. 26-07-1; fax 26-07-29-99; internet www .abnamroprivatebanking.com/luxembourg; f. 1991 by merger; cap. 162m., res 342.6m., dep. 1,995.9m. (Dec. 2011); Chair. JAN KOOPMAN; Man. Dir TONIKA HIRDMAN.

Banque et Caisse d'Epargne de l'Etat, Luxembourg: 1–2 pl. de Metz, 1930 Luxembourg; tel. 40-15-1; fax 40-15-20-99; e-mail info@bcee.lu; internet www.bcee.lu; f. 1856 as Caisse de l'Epargne de l'Etat du Grand-Duché de Luxembourg; present name adopted 1989; govt-owned; cap. 173.5m., res 428.6m., dep. 34,042.4m. (Dec. 2011); Chair. VICTOR ROD; Pres. and CEO JEAN-CLAUDE FINCK; 75 brs.

Banque Degroof Luxembourg SA: 12 rue Eugène Ruppert, 2453 Luxembourg; tel. 45-35-45-1; fax 25-07-21; e-mail investors .relation@degroof.lu; internet www.degroof.be; f. 1987; cap. 37m., res 17.4m., dep. 2,211.2m. (Sept. 2011); Chair., Supervisory Cttee ALAIN SIAENS; Chair., Management Cttee REGNIER HAEGELSTEEN.

Banque Internationale à Luxembourg SA: 69 route d'Esch, 2953 Luxembourg; tel. 45-90-1; fax 45-90-20-10; e-mail contact@bil.com; internet www.bil.com; f. 1856 as Banque Internationale à Luxembourg; present name adopted 2000; 99.9% owned by Precision Capital and the state of Luxembourg; cap. 141.2m., res 658.2m., dep. 13,982.3m. (Dec. 2011); Chair. PIERRE MARIANI; 40 brs.

Banque LBLux SA: 3 rue Jean Monnet, BP 602, 2180 Luxembourg; tel. 42-43-41; fax 42-43-45-09-9; e-mail bank@lblux.lu; internet www .lblux.lu; f. 1973; present name adopted 2002; owned by BayernLB (Germany); cap. 300m., res 25.3m., dep. 4,546.9m. (Dec. 2011); Chair., Supervisory Bd NILS NIERMANN; Chair., Management Bd ALAIN WEBER.

Banque de Luxembourg SA: 14 blvd Royal, 2449 Luxembourg; tel. 499-24-1; fax 499-24-55-99; internet www.banquedeluxembourg .com; f. 1937; owned by Banque CIC; cap. 104.8m., res 542.4m., dep. 16,611.9m. (Dec. 2011); Pres. PHILIPPE VIDAL; Man. Dir PIERRE AHLBORN.

Banque Raiffeisen SC: 46 rue Charles Martel, 2134 Luxembourg; tel. 24-50-1; fax 22-75-41; e-mail info@raiffeisen.lu; internet www .raiffeisen.lu; f. 1926 as Caisse Centrale Raiffeisen SC; present name adopted 2001; cap. 213.7m., res 203.3m., dep. 5,350.5m. (Dec. 2011); Chair. PAUL LAUTERBOUR; CEO and Gen. Man. ERNEST CRAVATTE.

Banque Safra-Luxembourg SA: 10A blvd Joseph II, BP 887, 2018 Luxembourg; tel. 45-47-81-1; fax 45-47-86; internet www.safra.lu; f. 1985; cap. 8.8m., res 120.1m., dep. 2,729.9m. (Dec. 2011); Man. Dir JORGE ALBERTO KININSBERG.

BGL BNP Paribas: 50 ave J. F. Kennedy, 2951 Luxembourg; tel. 42-42-20-00; fax 42-42-20-01; internet www.bgl.lu; f. 1919 as Banque Générale du Luxembourg SA; merged with Fortis Bank Luxembourg SA 2001, restyled Fortis Banque Luxembourg SA in 2005; became part of BNP Paribas and adopted present name in 2009; acquired BNP Paribas Luxembourg in 2010; cap. 713.1m., res 4,497.7m., dep. 21,699.9m. (Dec. 2011); Chair. GASTON REINESCH; Chairs, Management Bd CARLO THILL, ERIC MARTIN; 38 brs.

BHF-BANK International: 534 rue de Neudorf, 2220 Luxembourg; tel. 45-76-76-1; fax 45-83-24; e-mail direktion@bhf.lu; f. 1972; present name adopted 2005; subsidiary of BHF-Bank AG (Germany); cap. 26m., res 54m., dep. 774.4m. (Dec. 2011); Mans THILO SCHIERING, ROLAND STEIES.

Clearstream Banking SA: 42 ave J. F. Kennedy, 1855 Luxembourg; tel. 243-38-081; fax 243-63-80-81; e-mail web@clearstream .com; internet www.clearstream.com; f. 1970 as Cedelbank; present name adopted 2000; private bank; acts as the central bank's securities depository; cap. 57.8m., res 301.4m., dep. 14,257.5m. (Dec. 2011); Chair. RETO FRANCIONI; CEO JEFFREY TESSLER.

Commerzbank International SA (CISAL): 25 rue Edward Steichen, 2540 Luxembourg; tel. 47-79-11-1; fax 47-79-11-270; e-mail info@commerzbank.lu; internet www.commerzbank.lu; f. 1969; acquired Dresdner Bank Luxembourg SA 2010; cap. 194.8m., res 286.8m., dep. 3,279.3m. (Dec. 2011); Chair. FALK FISCHER; Man. Dir BERND HOLZENTHAL.

Crédit Agricole Luxembourg: 39 allée Scheffer, BP 1104, 1011 Luxembourg; tel. 24-67-1; fax 24-67-80-00; e-mail marketing@ca-luxembourg.com; internet www.e-private.com; f. 2005; by merger of Crédit Lyonnais Luxembourg and Crédit Agricole Indosuez Luxembourg; merged with Crédit Agricole Luxembourg Bank in 2008; cap. 465m., res 29.1m., dep. 6,518.1m. (Dec. 2011); Chair. ALAIN MASSIERA; Dir-Gen. JEAN-FRANÇOIS ABADIE.

Crédit Suisse (Luxembourg) SA: 56 Grand-Rue, BP 40, 2010 Luxembourg; tel. 46-00-11-1; fax 46-32-70; internet www

.credit-suisse.com; f. 1974; cap. 43m. Swiss francs, res 76.2m. Swiss francs, dep. 4,741.1m. Swiss francs (Dec. 2011); Chair URS ROHNER.

Danske Bank International SA: 13 rue Edward Steichen, BP 173, 2011 Luxembourg; tel. 46-12-75-1; fax 47-30-78; e-mail information@ danskebank.lu; internet www.danskebank.lu; f. 1976 as Den Danske Bank International SA; present name adopted 2000; cap. 90.6m., res 33.9m., dep. 1,331.3m. (Dec. 2011); Man. Dir KLAUS MØNSTED PEDERSEN.

DekaBank Deutsche Girozentrale Luxembourg SA: 38 ave J. F. Kennedy, 1855 Luxembourg; tel. 34-09-35; fax 34-09-34-91; e-mail info@deka.lu; internet www.dekabank.lu; f. 1971 as Deutsche Girozentrale International SA; present name adopted 2002, after merger with DekaBank Luxembourg SA; cap. 50m., res 106.1m., dep. 7,485.7m. (Dec. 2011); Chair. OLIVER BEHRENS; Man. Dir RAINER MACH.

Deutsche Bank Luxembourg SA: 2 blvd Konrad Adenauer, 1115 Luxembourg; tel. 42-12-21; fax 42-12-24-49; internet www.db.com/luxembourg; f. 1970 as Deutsche Bank Compagnie Financière Luxembourg; present name adopted 1987; cap. 2,465m., res 1,000.9m., dep. 84,207.8m. (Dec. 2011); Chair. Dr JOSEF ACKERMANN.

Deutsche Postbank International SA: PB Finance Centre, 18–20 Parc d'Activités Sydrall, 5365 Munsbach; tel. 34-95-31-1; fax 34-62-06; e-mail deutsche.postbank@postbank.lu; internet www.postbank.de; f. 1993; cap. 600m., res 232.4m., dep. 14,874.3m. (Dec. 2011); Chair. STEFAN JÜTTE.

DZ Bank Privatbank SA: 4 rue Thomas Edison, BP 661, 1445 Strassen; tel. 44-90-31; fax 44-90-32-00-1; e-mail info@dzi.lu; internet www.dzi.lu; f. 1978 as DG Bank Luxembourg SA; name changed as above 2010; 89.7% owned by DZ Bank AG Deutsche Zentral-Genossenschaftsbank; cap. 116.6m., res 511.6m., dep. 13,747.5m. (Dec. 2011); Chair. Dr STEFAN SCHWAB.

Eurobank Private Bank Luxembourg SA: 5 rue Jean Monnet, 2180 Luxembourg; tel. 42-07-24-1; fax 42-07-24-650; e-mail info@eurobankefg.lu; internet www.efgnav.lu; f. 1986; fmrly Eurobank EFG Private Bank Luxembourg SA; present name adopted 2012; subsidiary of EFG Eurobank Ergasias (Greece); cap. 70m., res 26.3m., dep. 14,594.9m. (Dec. 2011); Chair. JEAN PIERRE CUONI; CEO LENA LASCARIS.

HSBC Private Bank (Luxembourg) SA: 16 blvd d'Avranches, BP 733, 2017 Luxembourg; tel. 47-93-31-1; fax 47-93-31-22-6; e-mail hrlu@hsbcpb.com; internet www.hsbcpb.com; f. 1985 as Republic National Bank of New York (Luxembourg) SA; present name adopted 2004; cap. 53m., res 7.2m., dep. 4,381.9m. (Dec. 2011); Chair. and CEO STUART GULLIVER.

HSBC Trinkaus & Burkhardt (International) SA: 8 rue Lou Hemmer, 1748 Luxembourg; tel. 47-18-47-1; fax 47-18-47-61-3; e-mail contact@hsbctrinkaus.lu; internet www.hsbctrinkaus.lu; f. 1977 as Trinkaus & Burhardt (International) SA; present name adopted 1999; cap. 15.5m., res 85.5m., dep. 2,219.9m. (Dec. 2011); Pres. Dr OLAF HUTH; Man. Dirs HANS-JOACHIM ROSTECK, JÖRG MEIER.

ING Luxembourg SA: 52 route d'Esch, 2965 Luxembourg; tel. 44-99-11; fax 44-99-20-60; e-mail luc.verbeken@ing.lu; internet www.ing.lu; f. 1960 as Crédit Européen; present name adopted 2003; owned by ING Belgium SA/NV; cap. 83.4m., res 1,302.7m., dep. 9,172m. (Dec. 2011); CEO LUC VERBEKEN; 15 brs.

KBL European Private Bankers SA: 43 blvd Royal, 2955 Luxembourg; tel. 47-97-1; fax 47-97-73-91-2; internet www.kbl.lu; f. 1949; fmrly Kredietbank SA Luxembourgeoise; present name adopted 2008; 99% owned by KBC Bank NV (Belgium); cap. 187.2m., res 265.7m., dep. 10,336m. (Dec. 2011); Chair. JACQUES PETERS; 2 brs.

LBBW Luxemburg SA: 10–12 blvd F.D. Roosevelt, BP 84, 2010 Luxembourg; tel. 47-59-21-1; fax 47-59-21-26-9; e-mail info@lbbw.lu; internet www.lbbw.lu; f. 2008, following acquisition of Landesbank Rheinland-Pfalz International by Landesbank Baden-Württemburg (Germany); cap. 615m., res –717.1m., dep. 3,135.3m. (Dec. 2011); Man. Dirs Dr STEFAN GRABOWSKY, ROBY HAAS.

Norddeutsche Landesbank Luxembourg SA: 26 route d'Arlon, 1140 Luxembourg; tel. 45-22-11-1; fax 45-22-11-30-7; e-mail info@nordlb.lu; internet www.nordlb.lu; f. 1972; cap. 205m., res -126.8m., dep. 15,111.3m. (Dec. 2011); Chair., Management Bd HARRY ROSENBAUM.

Nordea Bank SA: 562 rue de Neudorf, BP 562, 2015 Luxembourg; tel. 43-88-71; fax 43-93-76-11; e-mail nordea@nordea.lu; internet www.nordea.lu; f. 1976 as Privatbanken International (Denmark) SA, Luxembourg; changed name to Unibank SA in 1990, present name adopted 2001; cap. 25m., res 48.1m., dep. 3,494m. (Dec. 2011); Chair. BJÖRN WAHLROOS; CEO CHRISTIAN CLAUSEN.

Skandinaviska Enskilda Banken SA: 6A circuit de la Foire Internationale, BP 487, 2014 Luxembourg; tel. 26-23-1; fax 26-23-20-01; e-mail contact@sebprivatebank.com; internet www.sebgroup.lu; f. 1977; present name adopted 2006; cap. 118m., res 39.5m., dep. 2,321.4m. (Dec. 2011); Man. Dir PETER KUBICKI.

Société Européenne de Banque SA: 19–21 blvd du Prince Henri, BP 21, 2010 Luxembourg; tel. 46-14-11; fax 22-37-55; e-mail contact@seb.lu; internet www.seb.lu; f. 1976; cap. 280m., res 428.7m., dep. 10,996.9m. (Dec. 2011); subsidiary of Intesa Sanpaolo Holding International SA (Luxembourg); Chair. Prof. ANGELO CALOIA; Man. Dir and CEO MARCO BUS.

Société Générale Bank & Trust: 11 ave Emile Reuter, BP 1271, 2420 Luxembourg; tel. 47-93-11-1; fax 22-88-59; internet www.sgbt.lu; f. 1893; present name adopted 1995; cap. 1,389m., res 505.3m., dep. 44,769.4m. (Dec. 2011); Chair. PATRICK SUET; CEO FRÉDÉRIC GENET.

UBS (Luxembourg) SA: 33A ave J. F. Kennedy, 1855 Luxembourg; tel. 45-12-11; fax 45-12-12-70-0; internet www.ubs.lu; f. 1998 by merger of Swiss Bank Corporation (Luxembourg) SA and Union de Banques Suisses (Luxembourg) SA; cap. 150m. Swiss francs, res 754m. Swiss francs, dep. 9,601.3m. Swiss francs (Dec. 2011); Chair. ARTHUR DECURTINS; Group CEO ANDREAS PRZEWLOKA.

UniCredit International Bank (Luxembourg) SA: 8–10 rue Jean Monnet, 2180 Luxembourg; tel. 22-08-42-31-0; fax 46-90-26; e-mail contact@unicreditgroup.lu; internet www.unicreditgroup.eu; fmrly Luxembourg branch of UniCredito Italiano SpA; est. as above 2004; merged with Capitalia Luxembourg SA in 2008; owned by Unicredito Italiano SpA; Group CEO FEDERICO GHIZZONI.

UniCredit Luxembourg SA: 4 rue Alphonse Weicker, 2721 Luxembourg; tel. 42-72-1; fax 42-72-45-00; e-mail contact@hvb.lu; internet www.unicreditbank.lu; f. 1998 by merger of Hypobank International SA and Vereinsbank International SA Luxembourg; fmrly HVB Banque Luxembourg, present name adopted 2009; cap. 238m., res 1,048.2m., dep. 22,517.5m. (Dec. 2011); Pres. and Chair. ANDREAS WÖLFER; CEO ANGELO BRIZI.

Banking Association

Association des Banques et Banquiers Luxembourg (ABBL): 12 rue Erasme, 1468 Luxembourg; tel. 46-36-60-1; fax 46-09-21; e-mail mail@abbl.lu; internet www.abbl.lu; f. 1939; CEO JEAN-JACQUES ROMMES.

STOCK EXCHANGE

Société de la Bourse de Luxembourg SA: 11 ave de la Porte-Neuve, 2227 Luxembourg; tel. 47-79-36-1; fax 47-32-98; e-mail info@bourse.lu; internet www.bourse.lu; f. 1928; Chair. FRANK WAGENER; CEO ROBERT SCHARFE.

INSURANCE

In 2010 there were 95 approved insurance companies and, in addition, 244 reinsurance companies. A selection of insurance companies is given below:

AME Life Lux SA: 7 blvd Joseph II, BP 787, 1840 Luxembourg; tel. 47-46-93; fax 47-46-90; e-mail amelife@ame.lu; internet www.amelife.lu; f. 1989; Man. Dir ROMAIN ROSSETTI.

Aon Luxembourg: 19 rue de Bitbourg, BP 593, 2015 Luxembourg; tel. 31-72-35; fax 31-71-74; e-mail lambert_schroeder@aon.com; internet www.aon.com/luxembourg; f. 1994; insurance and reinsurance broker; subsidiary of Aon Corpn (USA); Pres. and CEO GREGORY C. CASE.

AXA Luxembourg: 7 rue de la Chapelle, 1325 Luxembourg; tel. 44-24-24-1; fax 45-80-23; e-mail info@axa.lu; internet www.axa.lu; f. 1977; all branches and life; Dir-Gen. PAUL DE COOMAN; Chair. HENRI DE CASTRIES.

Cardif Lux Vie: 23–25 ave de la Porte Neuve, 2227 Luxembourg; tel. 26-21-41; fax 26-21-49-37-1; e-mail info@cardifluxvie.lu; internet www.cardifluxvie.lu; f. 2011 by merger of Cardif Lux International and Fortis Luxembourg Vie; owned by BNP Paribas Cardif, BGL BNP Paribas and Ageas; life and non-life insurance; CEO M. FABRICE BAGNE.

Groupe Foyer: 12 rue Léon Laval, 2986 Luxembourg; tel. 43-74-37; fax 43-74-32-49-9; internet www.foyer.lu; f. 1922; all branches and life; CEO FRANÇOIS TESCH.

La Luxembourgeoise Société Anonyme d'Assurances SA (LALUX Assurances): 9 rue Jean Fischbach, 3372 Leudelange; tel. 47-61-1; fax 47-61-30-0; e-mail groupell@lalux.lu; internet www.lalux.lu; f. 1989; all branches of non-life; Pres. and Dir-Gen. PIT HENTGEN.

West of England Shipowners' Mutual Insurance Association (Luxembourg): 33 blvd du Prince Henri, BP 841, 1724 Luxembourg; tel. 47-00-67-1; fax 22-52-53; e-mail carolina.lockwood@westpandi.com; internet www.westpandi.com; f. 1970; marine mutual insurance; Gen. Man. CAROLINA LOCKWOOD.

Insurance Association

Association des Compagnies d'Assurances (ACA): 12 rue de Mamer, 1468 Luxembourg; tel. 44-21-44-1; fax 44-02-89; e-mail aca@ aca.lu; internet www.aca.lu; f. 1956; Pres. PAUL HAMMELMANN; 67 mems.

Trade and Industry

GOVERNMENT AGENCY

Société Nationale de Crédit et d'Investissement (SNCI): 7 rue du Saint Esprit, BP 1207, 1475 Luxembourg; tel. 46-19-71-1; fax 46-19-79; e-mail snci@snci.lu; internet www.snci.lu; f. 1978; cap. €375m., res €185m., dep. €741m., assets €1,036m. (Dec. 2007); SNCI finances participations in certain cos, provides loans for investment and research and devt projects, provides export credit; Pres. GASTON REINESCH; Sec.-Gen. EVA KREMER.

CHAMBER OF COMMERCE

Chambre de Commerce du Grand-Duché de Luxembourg: 7 rue Alcide de Gasperi, 2981 Luxembourg-Kirchberg; tel. 42-39-39-1; fax 43-83-26; e-mail chamcom@cc.lu; internet www.cc.lu; f. 1841; Pres. MICHEL WURTH; 35,000 mems.

INDUSTRIAL AND TRADE ASSOCIATIONS

Centrale Paysanne Luxembourgeoise: BP 48, Agrocenter, 7501 Mersch, Luxembourg; tel. 64-64-48-0; fax 64-64-48-1; e-mail mfiedler@delpa.lu; f. 1945; Pres. MARC FISCH; Sec. LUCIEN HALLER; groups all agricultural organizations.

Chambre d'Agriculture (Landwirtschaftskammer): 261 route d'Arlon, BP 81, 8001 Strassen; tel. 31-38-76; fax 31-38-75; e-mail info@lwk.lu; internet www.lwk.lu; Pres. MARCO GAASCH; Sec.-Gen. POL GANTENBEIN.

Confédération Luxembourgeoise du Commerce (CLC): 7 rue Alcide de Gasperi, BP 482, 2014 Luxembourg; tel. 43-94-44; fax 43-94-50; e-mail info@clc.lu; internet www.clc.lu; f. 1909; Pres. GARY KNEIP; Dir THIERRY NOTHUM; 50,000 individual mems and 11,000 mem. cos.

Fédération des Artisans du Grand-Duché de Luxembourg: 2 circuit de la Foire Internationale, BP 1604, 1016 Luxembourg; tel. 42-45-11-1; fax 42-45-25; e-mail info@fda.lu; internet www.fda.lu; f. 1905; Pres. NORBERT GEISEN; Dir ROMAIN SCHMIT; 51 mem. feds.

FEDIL—Business Federation Luxembourg: 7 rue Alcide de Gasperi, BP 1304, 1013 Luxembourg; tel. 43-53-66-1; fax 43-23-28; e-mail fedil@fedil.lu; internet www.fedil.lu; f. 1918; Pres. ROBERT DENNEWALD; Dir NICOLAS SOISSON; c. 450 mems.

UTILITIES

Regulatory Authority

Institut Luxembourgeois de Régulation (ILR): see Broadcasting and Communications.

Electricity and Gas

Enovos International SA: 19–21 blvd Royal, 2449 Luxembourg; tel. 27-37-1; fax 27-37-91-00; internet www.enovos.eu/lu; f. 2009 from merger of Cegedel SA, Soteg SA and Saar Ferngas AG; produces and distributes electricity and gas; fmrly known as Soteg SA; Mems, Exec. Cttee JEAN LUCIUS, ROMAIN BECKER, NESTOR DIDELOT.

Creos Luxembourg SA: 2 rue Thomas Edison, 1445 Strassen; tel. 26-24-1; fax 26-24-51-00; e-mail info@creos.net; internet www .creos-net.lu; f. 1928 as Cegedel SA; renamed in 2009 following merger of Cegedel SA, Soteg SA and Saar Ferngas AG; owns and manages power grids and natural gas pipelines; Chair. and Man. Dir MARIO GROTZ.

Enovos Luxembourg: 2 rue Thomas Edison, 1445 Strassen; tel. 27-37-1; fax 27-37-61-11; internet www.enovos.eu/lu; f. 1928 as Cegedel SA; name changed in 2009 following merger of Cegedel SA, Soteg SA and Saar Ferngas AG; transportation and supply of natural gas and electricity; Chair. MARCO HOFFMANN; Dir-Gen. JEAN LUCIUS.

Société Electrique de l'Our (SEO): 2 rue Pierre d'Aspelt, BP 37, 2010 Luxembourg; tel. 44-90-21; fax 44-90-28-00; e-mail seo@seo.lu; internet www.seo.lu; f. 1951; electricity production and supply; Pres. TOM EISCHEN.

SOTEL Réseau & Cie: 4 rue de Soleuvre, 4321 Esch-sur-Alzette; tel. 55-19-21; fax 57-22-13; f. 2001; distributor of electricity; Man. Dir NICO WIETOR.

SUDGAZ SA: 150 rue Jean-Pierre Michels, BP 383, 4004 Esch-sur-Alzette; tel. 55-66-55-1; fax 57-20-44; e-mail contact@sudgaz.lu; internet www.sudgaz.lu; f. 1899; gas distribution co; Pres. WILL HOFFMANN.

Water

Responsibility for water supply lies with the municipalities. Many municipalities have formed syndicates to manage water supply, the largest of which is listed below.

Distribution d'Eau des Ardennes (DEA): BP 2, 8701 Useldange; tel. 23-64-24-1; fax 23-63-93-55; e-mail dea@dea.lu; internet www .dea.lu; f. 1929; distribution of drinking water in northern Luxembourg; comprises 36 municipalities; Dir PATRICK KOSTER.

TRADE UNIONS

FNCTTFEL—Landesverband der Eisenbahner, Transportarbeiter, Funktionäre und Beamten, Luxemburg (National Union of Luxembourg Railway and Transport Workers and Employees): 63 rue de Bonnevoie, 1260 Luxembourg; tel. 48-70-44-1; fax 48-85-25; e-mail info@landesverband.lu; internet www.landesverband .lu; f. 1909; affiliated to Confédération Générale du Travail (CGT) and International Transport Workers' Federation; Pres. GUY GREIVELDING; 8,000 mems.

Lëtzebuerger Chrëschtleche Gewerkschaftsbond (LCGB) (Confederation of Luxembourg Christian Trade Unions): 11 rue du Commerce, 1351 Luxembourg; tel. 49-94-24-1; fax 49-94-24-49; e-mail info@lcgb.lu; internet www.lcgb.lu; f. 1921; affiliated to ETUC and World Confederation of Labour; Pres. PATRICK DURY; 40,000 mems.

Onofhängege Gewerkschaftsbond Lëtzebuerg/Confédération Syndicale Indépendente du Luxembourg (OGB-L) (Luxembourg Independent Confederation of Labour): 60 blvd J. F. Kennedy, BP 149, 4002 Esch-sur-Alzette; tel. 54-05-45-1; fax 54-16-20; e-mail ogbl@ogbl.lu; internet www.ogbl.lu; f. 1916; comprises 15 mem. unions; Pres. JEAN-CLAUDE REDING; Sec.-Gen. ANDRÉ ROELTGEN; c. 62,000 mems.

Transport

RAILWAYS

Railways infrastructure is controlled by the state-owned Société Nationale des Chemins de Fer Luxembourgeois (CFL). At 31 December 2009 there were 275 km of railway track, of which 262 km were electrified. A high-speed link from Luxembourg to Paris, France, opened in June 2007.

Société Nationale des Chemins de Fer Luxembourgeois (CFL): 9 place de la Gare, BP 1803, 1018 Luxembourg; tel. 49-90-0; fax 49-90-44-70; e-mail info@cfl.lu; internet www.cfl.lu; f. 1946; Pres. JEANNOT WARINGO; Dir-Gen. and CEO ALEX KREMER.

ROADS

At 1 January 2010 there were 2,899 km of roads, of which motorways comprised 152 km. There are six toll-free motorways linking Luxembourg with cities such as Trier in Germany, Thionville in France and Arlon in Belgium.

INLAND WATERWAYS AND SHIPPING

Rhine shipping has direct access to the Luxembourg inland port of Mertert as a result of the canalization of the Moselle river. An 'offshore' shipping register was established in 1991. In 2012 the merchant fleet numbered 224 vessels with a combined displacement of 1.2m. grt.

Société du Port de Mertert SA: Direction du Port, 6688 Mertert; tel. 74-04-64; fax 74-04-64-30; e-mail info@portmertert.lu; internet www.portmertert.lu; Dir-Gen. JEANNOT POEKER.

CIVIL AVIATION

There is an international airport situated at Findel, north-west of the capital.

Cargolux Airlines International SA: Aéroport de Luxembourg, 2990 Luxembourg; tel. 42-11-1; fax 43-11-37-47; e-mail info@ cargolux.com; internet www.cargolux.com; f. 1970; regular international all-freighter services; technological devt; owned by Luxair, a consortium of Luxembourg banks and SAir Logistics (Switzerland); Pres. and CEO RICHARD FORSON (acting).

Luxair SA (Société Luxembourgeoise de Navigation Aérienne): Aéroport de Luxembourg, 2987 Luxembourg; tel. 24-56-42-42; fax 456-46-05; e-mail callcenter@luxairtours.lu; internet www.luxair.lu; f. 1962; regular services to destinations in Europe and North Africa; Pres. and CEO ADRIEN NEY.

Tourism

Many tourist resorts have developed around the ruins of medieval castles such as Clerf, Esch/Sauer, Vianden and Wiltz. The Benedict-ine Abbey at Echternach is also much visited. There is a thermal centre at Mondorf-les-Bains, supplied by three mineralized springs. In addition, there are numerous footpaths and hiking trails. The city of Luxembourg, with its many cultural events and historical monuments, is an important centre for congresses. In 2011 there were 932,629 tourist arrivals at hotels and other accommodation establishments. Provisional data showed that receipts from tourism totalled US $4,535m. in 2011.

Office National du Tourisme (ONT): 68–70 blvd de la Pétrusse, BP 1001, 1010 Luxembourg; tel. 42-82-82-10; fax 42-82-82-30; e-mail info@ont.lu; internet www.ont.lu; f. 1931; 192 mems; Dir ROBERT L. PHILIPPART.

Defence

Luxembourg was a founder member of the North Atlantic Treaty Organization (NATO) in 1949. Compulsory military service was abolished in 1967, but Luxembourg maintains an army of volunteers, totalling 900, and a gendarmerie numbering 610 (as assessed at November 2012). In March 1987 the country became a signatory of the Benelux military convention, together with Belgium and the Netherlands. This aimed at the standardization of training methods and of military equipment in the three countries. In November 2004 Luxembourg committed to contributing troops to one of the 'battle-groups' of the European Union (EU). The EU battlegroups, two of which were to be ready for deployment at any one time, following a rotational schedule, reached full operational capacity from 1 January 2007. Luxembourg participated in a battlegroup with France, Germany and Belgium.

Defence Expenditure: Budget estimated at €204m. for 2012.

Chief of Staff: Gen. MARIO DAUBENFELD.

Education

Education in Luxembourg is compulsory from the age of four to 16 years. Pre-primary education begins at the age of four years; the Ministry of National Education and Vocational Training has introduced an optional pre-primary level for children at the age of three

years. Luxembourgish is the language of instruction at pre-primary level. Primary education begins at six years of age and lasts for six years. German is the language of instruction in the first year at primary level. French is added to the programme in the second year, and replaces German as the language of instruction at higher secondary level. In 2010/11 the total enrolment in primary education included 92% of children in the relevant age-group, while the total enrolment in secondary education included 87% of children in the relevant age-group. Total enrolment in pre-primary education in 2010/11 included 87% of children in the relevant age-group.

At the age of 12, pupils can choose between secondary school (*lycée*) and technical education (*lycée technique*). The first year of secondary school is a general orientation course on comprehensive lines, which is then followed by a choice between two sections: the Classical Section, with an emphasis on Latin, and the Modern Section, which stresses English and other modern languages. The completed secondary course lasts seven years, and leads to the *Certificat de Fin d'Etudes Secondaires*, which qualifies for university entrance. The technical education course (six to eight years) leads either to a vocational diploma, a technician's diploma (*diplôme de technicien*) or a technical baccalaureate diploma (*bac technique*) and is devised in three parts: an orientation and observation course; an intermediate course; and an upper course.

The *Centre Universitaire* was established in 1969, offering one- or two-year courses in the humanities, sciences and law and economics, as well as training courses for lawyers and teachers, following which the students generally attend other European universities. The *Institut Supérieur de Technologies* (IST) is an institute for higher education at university level in civil engineering, electrical engineering, applied computer sciences and mechanical engineering. In August 2003 the Government founded the University of Luxembourg through the merger of four major institutions: the *Centre Universitaire de Luxembourg*; the Higher Technological Institute, *Institut Supérieur de Technologies*; the Institute for Higher Studies and Research in Teaching, *Institut Supérieur d'Études et de Luxembourg*; and the Institute for Educational and Social Studies, *Institut d'Études Éducatives et Sociales*.

General government expenditure on national education and vocational training in 2010 was €2,068m., equivalent to 5.1% of gross domestic product.

THE FORMER YUGOSLAV REPUBLIC OF MACEDONIA

Introductory Survey

LOCATION, CLIMATE, LANGUAGE, RELIGION, FLAG, CAPITAL

The former Yugoslav republic of Macedonia (FYRM, or, according to its Constitution, the Republic of Macedonia), is situated in south-eastern Europe. The FYRM is a land-locked state and is bounded by Serbia to the north, Kosovo to the north-west, Albania to the west, Greece to the south and Bulgaria to the east. The republic is predominantly mountainous with a continental climate, although the Vardar (Axiós) river valley, which bisects the country from north-west to south-east, across the centre of the republic and into Greece, has a mild Mediterranean climate with an average summertime temperature of 27°C (80°F). The official language of the republic, under the Constitution of November 1991, was originally stipulated as Macedonian, and is most frequently written in the Cyrillic script. It is a South Slavic language most closely related to Bulgarian. Constitutional amendments adopted in November 2001 accorded any minority language, such as Albanian, the status of official language in communities where its speakers constitute 20% of the population. Most of the population is nominally Eastern Orthodox Christian. Most of the ethnic Albanians (officially recorded as 25.2% of the population) are Muslims, as are the majority of the remaining minority groups. The national flag (proportions 1 by 2) comprises, in the centre of a red field, a yellow disc, with eight yellow rays extending to the edges of the flag. The capital is Skopje.

CONTEMPORARY POLITICAL HISTORY

Historical Context

After the First World War, during which Macedonia was occupied by the Bulgarians and the Central Powers of Austria-Hungary and Germany, Vardar Macedonia, the area now known as the former Yugoslav republic of Macedonia (FYRM), became part of the new Kingdom of Serbs, Croats and Slovenes (formally named Yugoslavia in 1929), being widely referred to as 'South Serbia'. In the Second World War, however, the Bulgarian occupation of 1941–44 disillusioned many Yugoslav Macedonians. From 1943 the Partisans of Josip Broz (Tito), the General-Secretary of the Communist Party of Yugoslavia, began to increase their support in the region, and after the war the new Federal People's Republic of Yugoslavia and its communist rulers resolved to include a Macedonian nation as a federal partner. A distinct Macedonian identity was promoted, together with a linguistic policy that encouraged the establishment of a Macedonian literary language distinct from Bulgarian.

The presence of a large ethnic Albanian minority in western Macedonia added to Macedonian insecurities. The proximity of the neighbouring Serbian province of Kosovo, which had a majority ethnic Albanian population, and demands, from the late 1960s, for the creation of an Albanian republic within Yugoslavia, alarmed the Macedonian authorities, which became particularly active against Albanian nationalism from 1981. In 1989 the republican Constitution was amended to allow the introduction of a multi-party system; Macedonia was declared to be a nation state of the ethnic Macedonians, and mention of the Albanian and Turkish minorities was excluded.

Domestic Political Affairs

In November and December 1990 the first multi-party elections to a unicameral Sobranie (Assembly) were held in Macedonia. The Front for Macedonian National Unity, which principally comprised a nationalist party, the Internal Macedonian Revolutionary Organization—Democratic Party for Macedonian National Unity (IMRO—DPMNU), led by Ljubčo Georgievski, and which had previously declared its support for the return of territories within Serbia, alleged irregularities after failing to win any seats at the first round. Following two further rounds of voting, however, the IMRO—DPMNU emerged as the single party with the most seats (37) in the 120-member Sobranie. The League of Communists of Macedonia—Party for Democratic Reform (LCM—PDR, as the League of Communists of Macedonia had renamed itself), led by Petar Gosev, won 31 seats and the two predominantly Albanian parties (the Party for Democratic Prosperity—PDP—and the People's Democratic Party) a total of 25. The republican branch of the federal Alliance of Reform Forces (ARF, subsequently the Liberal Party of Macedonia—LPM) won 19 seats. Following lengthy coalition negotiations, in January 1991 Kiro Gligorov of the LCM—PDR was elected President of the Republic, with Georgievski as Vice-President; Stojan Andov of the ARF was elected President of the Sobranie. The three parties agreed to support a government largely comprising members without political affiliation. In March the Sobranie approved a new administration, headed by Nikola Kljušev. The LCM—PDR was renamed the Social Democratic Alliance of Macedonia (SDAM) in April.

The quest for international recognition

On 25 January 1991 the Sobranie unanimously adopted a motion declaring the republic a sovereign territory. After June declarations of Croatian and Slovenian 'dissociation', Macedonia, wary of the increasing Serbian domination of the remaining federal institutions, declared its neutrality and emphasized its sovereign status. On 8 September a referendum (boycotted by the ethnic Albanian population) approved the sovereignty of Macedonia.

Georgievski resigned the vice-presidency in October 1991, and the IMRO—DPMNU announced that it had joined the opposition, stating that the party had been excluded from the decision-making process. On 17 November the Constitution, which declared the sovereignty of the Republic of Macedonia, was endorsed by 96 of the 120 Assembly members, with opposition from the majority of ethnic Albanian deputies. In January 1992 an unofficial referendum conducted among the ethnic Albanian population reportedly resulted in 99.9% of the vote being cast in favour of territorial and political autonomy for the ethnic Albanian population. The complete withdrawal of federal troops from Macedonia in March, in conjunction with the adoption in April of a new Constitution in Yugoslavia, referring only to Serbia and Montenegro, effectively signalled Yugoslav acceptance of Macedonian secession from the federation.

Macedonian affairs were subsequently dominated by the question of wider international recognition. Bulgaria recognized the state of Macedonia (although not the existence of a distinct Macedonian nationality or language) in January 1992, closely followed by Turkey in February, provoking mass protests in Thessaloníki, the capital of the Greek region of Macedonia. The Greek authorities insisted that 'Macedonia' was a geographical term delineating an area that included a large part of northern Greece, and expressed fears that the republic's independence under the name 'Macedonia' might foster a false claim to future territorial expansion. Greece was instrumental in the formulation of a European Community (EC, now European Union—EU, see p. 281) policy, adopted in early 1992, that the republic should be awarded no formal recognition of independence until stringent constitutional requirements had been fulfilled. In May Gligorov rejected a statement by the EC that it was 'willing to recognize Macedonia as a sovereign and independent state within its existing borders under a name that can be accepted by all concerned'. Negotiations with Greece ended in failure in June. In July, after a motion expressing no confidence in the Government received strong support in the Sobranie (and following large demonstrations against its failure to gain international recognition for an independent Macedonia), the Government resigned. The IMRO—DPMNU failed to form a new alliance, and eventually, in September Branko Crvenkovski, the Chairman of the SDAM, was installed as Prime Minister of a coalition Government.

The adoption of a new flag in August 1992 attracted particular opposition from Greece, which objected to the depiction outside

Greece of the 'Vergina Star' (regarded as an ancient Greek symbol of Philip of Macedon and Alexander the Great). As a result of a blockade of petroleum deliveries imposed on Macedonia by Greece, reserves at the Skopje petroleum refinery were exhausted by September. In February 1993 Greece agreed to international arbitration over the issue of Macedonia's name, undertaking to abide by its final outcome. On 8 April the republic was admitted to the UN under the temporary name of 'the former Yugoslav republic of Macedonia', pending settlement of the issue of a permanent name by international mediators. However, Greece continued to assert that the use of the 'Vergina Star' emblem and the name 'Macedonia' implied territorial claims on Greek territory, and in October Greece withdrew from UN-sponsored negotiations on the issue of a permanent name. In January 1994 Greece requested that the other nations of the EU prevail upon the FYRM (which was, by this time, recognized by all the other EU member states) to make concessions concerning its name, flag and Constitution, and threatened to ban trade with the FYRM. From February (by which time Russia and the USA had formally recognized the FYRM) Greece blocked all non-humanitarian shipments to the FYRM through the port of Thessaloníki, and also road and rail transport links with the FYRM. In April the European Commission initiated legal proceedings against Greece at the Court of Justice of the European Communities. In April 1995 the Court issued a preliminary opinion that the embargo was not in breach of Greece's obligations under the Treaty of Rome. Meanwhile, Greece agreed to resume negotiations in April with the FYRM, under the auspices of the UN; in May the Organization for Security and Co-operation in Europe (OSCE, see p. 397) announced that it was to join the mediation efforts. In September an interim accord was signed at the UN headquarters in New York, USA, by the FYRM Minister of Foreign Affairs and his Greek counterpart. The agreement provided for the mutual recognition of existing frontiers and respect for the sovereignty of each state, and for the free movement of goods and people between the two countries. Greece was to end its trade embargo and veto on the FYRM's entry into international organizations, while the FYRM undertook to abandon its use of the Vergina emblem in any form, and to amend parts of its Constitution that had been regarded by Greece as 'irredentist'. (The question of a permanent name for the FYRM was to be the subject of further UN-mediated negotiations.) In early October the Sobranie approved a new state flag, depicting an eight-rayed sun in place of the Vergina emblem. On 9 October the Sobranie ratified the interim accord, which was formally signed in Skopje by representatives of the FYRM and Greece on 13 October. The border between the two countries was subsequently reopened.

The Albanian Government formally recognized the FYRM in April 1993. However, relations between the FYRM authorities and the minority Albanian population continued to deteriorate. In November several ethnic Albanians were arrested in the western towns of Gostivar and Tetovo, and in Skopje. The Government announced that a conspiracy to form paramilitary groups, with the eventual aim of establishing an Albanian republic in the west of the FYRM, had been discovered. Further arrests followed, and in June 1994 Mithat Emini, the former General Secretary of the PDP, was sentenced to eight years' imprisonment, after being convicted of conspiring to engage in hostile activity; nine others received custodial sentences of between five and eight years. (In February 1995 all the sentences were reduced by two years.)

Ethnic Albanian demands

The PDP split in February 1994, when a faction led by Xheladin Murati (the Deputy President of the Sobranie) and including the party's representatives in the Government and in the legislature, withdrew from the party's congress. The remaining grouping, led by Arben Xhaferi, made more radical demands. The sentencing of Emini and his co-defendants prompted ethnic Albanian deputies to boycott the Sobranie in July. Murati resigned from the leadership of his PDP faction (and from his role in the Sobranie) later that month, reportedly in protest against the sentences; he was succeeded as party leader by Abdurahman Aliti.

Gligorov, representing the Alliance for Macedonia (a coalition of the SDAM, the LPM and the Socialist Party of Macedonia—SPM), was re-elected President on 16 October 1994, winning 78.4% of the valid votes cast, defeating Georgievski. A first round of voting to the new Sobranie took place on the same day. The IMRO—DPMNU, which failed to secure any seats, alleged widespread electoral fraud in both elections, and boycotted the

second round of legislative voting, which took place on 30 October (a third round was necessary in 10 constituencies on 13 November, owing to irregularities in earlier rounds). The final results confirmed that the Alliance for Macedonia had won the majority of seats in the Sobranie (with the SDAM taking 58 seats, the LPM 29 and the SPM eight). Aliti's wing of the PDP, which had been legally recognized as the successor to the original party, secured 10 seats; allies of Xhaferi had been obliged to stand as independent candidates (Xhaferi was among those to be elected). Gligorov subsequently requested that Crvenkovski form a new government, and the SDAM-led administration, which also included members of the LPM, the PDP and the SPM, was approved by the Sobranie in December.

Tensions were exacerbated by efforts by the ethnic Albanian community to establish an Albanian-language university in Tetovo. Despite government objections, the university was formally founded in December 1994. In February 1995 the opening of the university provoked unrest; an ethnic Albanian was killed in clashes with security forces. In July 1996 five of the university's founders, including its rector, received custodial sentences for inciting the riots, prompting further protests. (In May 2000 the Sobranie approved legislation granting the university at Tetovo legal status as a private foundation, and in January 2004 further legislation was adopted, transforming it into a state university.)

In October 1995 Gligorov was injured in a car bomb attack in Skopje; he resumed full presidential duties in January 1996. Meanwhile, divisions had emerged within the governing alliance, which collapsed in February, prompting the LPM to be excluded from the Government. Andov resigned as President of the Sobranie in early March, stating that Crvenkovski had acted unconstitutionally in expelling the LPM from the Government.

In September 1996, prior to local elections scheduled for 17 November, the Sobranie approved legislation reorganizing the territorial division of the FYRM into 123 municipalities. In October three opposition parties, the IMRO—DPMNU, the PDP and the newly established Movement for All-Macedonian Action—Conservative Party, formed a coalition to contest the elections. Xhaferi's faction, which had been reconstituted as the Party of Democratic Prosperity of Albanians in Macedonia (PDPAM), and the (also ethnic Albanian) National Democratic Party (NDP) agreed to present joint candidates in some constituencies. The SDAM received the greatest number of votes, followed by the coalition led by the IMRO—DPMNU, and the PDP. Observers from the Council of Europe (see p. 260) declared that, overall, the elections had been conducted fairly.

In January 1997 legislation was adopted to permit Albanian to become a language of instruction at the teacher-training faculty of the university at Skopje, precipitating outrage among ethnic Macedonian students at the faculty. A financial scandal emerged in the FYRM in March, involving the embezzlement of funds invested in 'pyramid' savings schemes. Crvenkovski pledged an investigation to identify those responsible for the losses sustained by large numbers of investors, and several senior officials were subsequently arrested on suspicion of involvement. In April the Government announced plans to reimburse losses incurred by investors, following the failure of a major savings institution in the south-western town of Bitola, while in May the Governor of the central bank, who was believed to have been involved in the failure of the investment scheme, was replaced. After the IMRO—DPMNU demonstrated in Skopje to demand the resignation of the Government, a reorganized administration was approved by the Sobranie at the end of May.

In May 1997 protests were staged in Gostivar against a Constitutional Court ruling prohibiting the use of the Albanian flag in the FYRM. In the following month the President of the Court demanded that the Government enforce the ruling. In early July the Sobranie adopted legislation stipulating that the use of minority ethnic groups (including Albanians) would only be permitted on national holidays, with the state flag being displayed at the same time. The mayors of Gostivar and Tetovo continued to refuse to comply with the order, and violent clashes, in which three ethnic Albanians were killed, ensued in Gostivar after government officials forcibly removed Albanian flags from municipal buildings; some 500 protesters were arrested. In September the mayor of Gostivar, Rufi Osmani, received a custodial sentence of 13 years (subsequently reduced to seven years), after he was convicted of inciting ethnic tension and rebellion, while the Chairman of the town's municipal council was sentenced to three years' imprisonment for failing to adopt the ruling of the Constitutional Court. In April 1998 the Democratic Party of Albanians (DPA—which had been formed in the previous year by the amalgamation of the PDPAM and the NDP) withdrew its representatives from all government bodies, in protest against Osmani's imprisonment.

Insurgency in northern regions

At legislative elections, conducted in two rounds on 18 October and 1 November 1998, the For Changes coalition, comprising the IMRO—DPMNU and the newly formed Democratic Alternative (DA), secured an absolute majority in the Sobranie, with 58 seats, while the SDAM obtained 29 seats, and an alliance of the PDP and the DPA won 24. Owing to irregularities, a further round of voting took place in two electoral districts, at which one seat was won by the For Changes alliance, and the other by the PDP-DPA alliance. Later in November Georgievski was nominated as Prime Minister. The DPA was subsequently invited to join the governing coalition of the IMRO—DPMNU and the DA. In early December a new Government, comprising 14 representatives of the IMRO—DPMNU, eight of the DA and five of the DPA, was formed. In January 1999 the Sobranie adopted legislation (supported by the new Government) providing for the release of some 8,000 prisoners, among them Osmani.

Six candidates contested the first round of the presidential election on 31 October 1999. Tito Petkovski, representing the SDAM, secured 33.2% of the votes cast, and Boris Trajkovski, the IMRO—DPMNU candidate, won 20.6%; Vasil Tupurkovski, the DA leader, took 16.0%, and Muharem Nexipi, the DPA candidate, 14.8%. Since no candidate had secured an outright majority, Petkovski and Trajkovski progressed to a second round, held on 14 November; Trajkovski was elected to President with 52.8% of the votes cast (after DPA and DA voters transferred support to his candidacy). After the Supreme Court upheld a legal appeal by the SDAM against the results, a further ballot took place in some western regions on 5 December. However, the overall results were almost unchanged, with Trajkovski receiving 52.9% of the votes cast. Trajkovski was formally inaugurated on 15 December. Following negotiations between the two leaders of the For Changes coalition, Georgievski and Tupurkovski, the IMRO—DPMNU, DA and DPA reached agreement on the formation of a new Government. The Sobranie approved the coalition administration, which contained seven new ministers (including Tupurkovski, as a Deputy Prime Minister), on 27 December.

In January 2000 the Government announced that amendments to the Constitution, which would allow higher education to be conducted in the language of ethnic minorities, would be submitted for approval by the Sobranie. In April legislation was adopted obliging the authorities to return property expropriated under the communist regime. In the same month disaffected members of the IMRO—DPMNU established a breakaway faction, which became known as the IMRO—True Macedonian Reform Option (IMRO—TMRO). In July Georgievski reorganized the Government, reducing the number of ministries from 21 to 14. Local elections took place in two rounds on 10 and 24 September, amid reports of numerous violent incidents. After a further round of voting took place, as a result of electoral irregularities, it was announced at the end of the month that the parties of the governing coalition had secured 75 of the 123 municipalities. Following prolonged dissent between Georgievski and Tupurkovski, the DA withdrew from the coalition Government and from the Sobranie at the end of November. Georgievski subsequently formed a new administration, which, for the first time, included members of the Liberal Democratic Party (LDP).

In early 2001 ethnic Albanian militants, members of the self-styled National Liberation Army (NLA), began to infiltrate northern parts of the FYRM from Kosovo, clashing with FYRM security forces. In early March NLA forces seized the border village of Tanusevci, prompting counter-attacks from government troops. The border with Kosovo was closed after senior government officials visiting the border region were attacked and temporarily besieged. Although the authorities succeeded in regaining control of Tanusevci, in mid-March NLA forces attempted to occupy Tetovo, precipitating the imposition of curfew regulations in the city. Following an appeal by the Government to the international community for military assistance, the North Atlantic Treaty Organization (NATO, see p. 380) reinforced its military presence at the Kosovo border to inhibit supplies to the NLA. On 21 March the UN Security Council adopted Resolution 1345, condemning the violence by ethnic Albanian nationalists in the FYRM as constituting a threat to the stability of the region. Despite reports that the rebels aimed to establish a 'greater Albania' (to include some northern and western regions of the FYRM), the NLA insisted that the conflict

had been initiated to put pressure on the FYRM Government to institute constitutional guarantees of equal rights for ethnic Albanians. The prolonged bombardment of rebel positions by government forces resulted in a withdrawal by the NLA from the Tetovo region. At the end of April eight members of the state security forces were killed in an NLA attack near the Kosovo border. Their funeral precipitated rioting and attacks by Macedonians on Albanian-owned property in the southern town of Bitola. Government troops subsequently launched an offensive against rebel positions near Kumanovo, after two further members of the armed forces were killed.

Meanwhile, in early April 2001 inter-party discussions regarding the rebels' demands commenced. After signing a Stabilization and Association Agreement with the EU, the Government pledged to initiate political, social and economic reforms by mid-2001. Rebel proposals included: the postponement of the national census, due to take place in May, until October, to allow the return of refugees who had fled the conflict; state funding for the university at Tetovo; and the conversion of the state television's third service into an Albanian-language channel. However, the Government continued to oppose principal demands that the Constitution be amended to grant the ethnic Albanian population (hitherto officially categorized as a minority) equal group rights with the Macedonian population, and Albanian the status of a second official language.

In early May 2001, following the resumption of intensive hostilities in the north of the country, the Government announced that the declaration of a state of war (which would, subject to the approval of a two-thirds' parliamentary majority, allow the authorities to adopt emergency powers and Trajkovski to rule by decree) was under debate. With EU and NATO mediation, however, it was agreed that the SDAM, the DPA and the PDP would, instead, join a government of national unity. The PDP subsequently demanded that the Government declare a cease-fire in the conflict in the north, as a precondition to its participation in the new administration. After the offensive against the rebels was temporarily suspended, the Sobranie approved the Government of national unity (headed by Georgievski) on 13 May. NLA leaders stated that the rebel movement (which still held several villages) would continue hostilities until the Government agreed to enter into negotiations.

The Ohrid Agreement

On 8 June 2001 Trajkovski announced proposals for a comprehensive peace plan, providing for the proportional representation of ethnic Albanians at all levels of government, the increased official use of the Albanian language, and a partial amnesty for NLA combatants. Despite EU support for the plan, the NLA demanded that the Government end hostilities and enter into negotiations on constitutional reforms, and rebel forces seized the town of Aracinovo, near Skopje. Later in June the Government suspended its offensive against the NLA. In response, violent protests were staged by Macedonian nationalists at the parliament building in Skopje. On 29 June NATO formally approved an operation to deploy a 3,500-member multinational force in the FYRM to assist in the disarmament of the NLA, which was to be conditional on the imposition of a lasting cease-fire. On 5 July the Government announced that both sides had signed an official cease-fire agreement. However, in subsequent negotiations on a permanent settlement Georgievski and his nationalist cabinet supporters strongly opposed proposals, detailed by the EU and US special envoys, for the extension of the use of the Albanian language, and accused them of bias towards the rebels. The cease-fire collapsed after 17 days, when the NLA launched further attacks on government forces deployed near Tetovo. (By that time some 60,000 ethnic Albanians had fled to Kosovo.) International diplomatic efforts subsequently intensified, following renewed fears of widespread civil conflict. On 26 July it was announced that an accord had been reached to restore the cease-fire between government forces and the ethnic Albanian rebels, who had agreed to withdraw from newly captured territory near Tetovo. Further negotiations between government and ethnic Albanian representatives, which commenced at the western town of Ohrid at the end of July, resulted in the resolution of the two main matters of contention (the official use of the Albanian language and the right to proportional representation of ethnic Albanians in the security forces). After the Government announced a unilateral cease-fire, on 13 August the Government and ethnic Albanian leaders at Ohrid signed a framework peace agreement, providing for the amendment of the Constitution to grant greater rights to the ethnic Albanian community. On the following day the NLA leader, Ali Ahmeti, agreed that the organization, numbering an estimated 2,500–3,000, would relinquish its armaments to NATO troops. NATO announced that the cease-fire was generally being observed, and on 22 August the activation order for a NATO mission, Operation Essential Harvest, was released. The force, which comprised 4,500 troops, had a mandate to disarm the ethnic Albanian combatants and destroy their weapons within 30 days of its deployment.

In September 2001 parliamentary debate on constitutional reform was delayed by mass nationalist protests against the peace plan. Meanwhile, investigators from the International Criminal Tribunal for the former Yugoslavia (ICTY, see p. 23) at the Hague, Netherlands, had been dispatched to the FYRM to conduct preliminary inquiries into the killing of six ethnic Albanian civilians in the village of Ljuboten in early August; the Minister of Internal Affairs, Ljube Boškovski, was suspected of responsibility for the operation. On 26 September NATO's 30-day disarmament programme was declared to have been successful, with the collection of some 3,875 armaments. On the same day the establishment of a further, reduced NATO mission, Operation Amber Fox, was authorized. The new mission, comprising 700 troops, together with 300 forces already stationed in the FYRM, was deployed, with a three-month renewable mandate to protect EU and OSCE monitors supervising the implementation of the peace agreement. On 27 September Ahmeti announced that the NLA had been formally dissolved, following the completion of the disarmament process. In October the EU criticized delays in implementing constitutional reforms, after Macedonian parties announced that the legislative process would be suspended pending the release of 14 Macedonian civilians allegedly seized by the NLA earlier that year. Following pressure from Trajkovski, and the international community, discussion on the measures resumed in the Sobranie. Later that month Trajkovski approved plans for the deployment of ethnically mixed security units in regions formerly held by the NLA.

On 16 November 2001, after extensive debate, the Sobranie adopted 15 principal constitutional amendments, including: the revision of the Constitution's preamble to include a reference to members of minority ethnic groups as citizens; the introduction in the Sobranie of a 'double majority' system, whereby certain legislation would require the approval of a minority group; the establishment of Albanian as the second official language in districts in which ethnic Albanians accounted for more than 20% of the population; and the right to proportional representation for ethnic Albanians in the Constitutional Court, all areas of government administration and the security forces. Later in November the SDAM and the LDP withdrew from the coalition Government (which was subsequently reorganized).

Following continued international pressure, in January 2002 new legislation providing for the devolution of greater authority to local government was approved by the Sobranie. In the same month a Deputy Prime Minister, Dosta Dimovska, resigned from the Government, following disagreement with Georgievski over issues relating to the deployment of security units in previously NLA-controlled villages. In February the three principal ethnic Albanian political parties (the DPA, the PDP and the NDP) and the former NLA leadership officially established a co-ordinating council. In March the Sobranie adopted legislation granting immunity from prosecution to several thousand former NLA insurgents (excluding those indictable by the ICTY), in accordance with the peace settlement. The Sobranie was dissolved on 18 July, prior to legislative elections, which were scheduled for 15 September and were to be monitored by the OSCE.

The SDAM administration

In May 2002 Ahmeti established a new political party, the Democratic Union for Integration (DUI), which was believed to comprise mainly former NLA combatants. Later that month two ministers belonging to the IMRO—TMRO resigned from the Government, in protest as what they described as the growing dominance of former NLA members within the principal ethnic Albanian parties. In the same month the Sobranie approved legislation whereby Albanian became an official language. At the end of August ethnic Albanians took hostage five Macedonian civilians at Gostivar; security forces surrounded an ethnic Albanian base and killed two of the kidnappers. None the less, the elections to the legislature took place peacefully on 15 September, and were declared by OSCE observers to have been conducted democratically. Georgievski's Government was removed from power by a 10-party alliance (led by the SDAM and the LDP), Together for Macedonia, which secured 60 of the 120 seats in the Sobranie. The IMRO—DPMNU won 33 seats and

the DUI 16 seats. The Together for Macedonia alliance and the DUI subsequently signed an agreement for the establishment of a coalition Government (which was, however, to exclude former NLA combatants). The Sobranie approved the new administration, comprising members of the SDAM, the LDP and the DUI, and headed by Crvenkovski, on 1 November.

On 14 December 2002 Operation Amber Fox was succeeded by a 450-member mission, Allied Harmony. On 31 March 2003 this contingent was, in turn, replaced by an EU-led mission, Operation Concordia, comprising 350 military personnel from a total of 13 EU member states and 14 non-EU nations. In September, after militants clashed with a security patrol at the border with Kosovo, the authorities dispatched security forces to the region in an operation to suppress dissident activity.

In May 2003 Nikola Gruevski became the new leader of the IMRO—DPMNU. In November Ljupco Jordanovski of the SDAM was elected as the new President of the Sobranie, replacing Nikola Popovski, who had been appointed as Deputy Prime Minister and Minister of Finance. In December Operation Concordia was replaced by a 200-member EU mission, Operation Proxima, which, in addition to maintaining security and combating organized crime in the country, was to advise the FYRM police forces (the mandate of Operation Proxima expired in December 2005).

On 26 February 2004 President Trajkovski, together with eight government officials, was killed, when an aircraft transporting him to a international investment conference in Bosnia and Herzegovina crashed in a southern, mountainous region of that country. Jordanovski, as speaker of the Sobranie, assumed the presidency in an acting capacity. At the ensuing presidential election, held on 14 April, Crvenkovski, representing the SDAM, won 42.5% of the votes cast; he progressed to a second round with Saško Kedev, hitherto a parliamentary deputy and a member of the IMRO—DPMNU (who had won 34.1% of the vote). Two former NLA commanders, the DUI Secretary-General, Gzim Ostreni, and Zudi Xhelili of the DPA, also contested the election, obtaining 14.8% and 8.7% of the votes cast, respectively. On 28 April Crvenkovski was elected to the presidency with 62.7% of the vote; he was inaugurated on 12 May.

On 2 June 2004 the Sobranie approved the formation of a coalition administration, with Hari Kostov of the SDAM as Prime Minister, and comprising members of that party, the DUI and the LDP. The only new ministerial appointment was that of Siljan Avramovski as Minister of Internal Affairs, replacing Kostov. The Government had, meanwhile, announced plans to redemarcate municipal boundaries, as part of a process of administrative decentralization included in the provisions of the Ohrid Agreement, although there was widespread popular opposition to the proposals. In July, under pressure from the international community, the parties of the governing coalition reached an agreement on the planned redemarcation. The total number of administrative districts was to be reduced from 123 to 84, with the ethnic balance of 26 districts becoming predominantly Albanian. On 26 July a large demonstration was staged in Skopje, in protest against the draft agreement on decentralization, which had been submitted for approval to the Sobranie.

On 7 November 2004, following a petition presented by Macedonian nationalist parties, a referendum on the proposed redemarcation of administrative districts was conducted. However, the governing coalition, together with representatives of the international community, urged a boycott and voter participation in the referendum was estimated at only 26%, thereby invalidating the results and allowing the reforms to proceed. In mid-November Kostov resigned as Prime Minister, claiming that the DUI had obstructed the parliamentary approval of reforms essential to attract foreign investment. Later that month Crvenkovski nominated Vlado Buckovski, hitherto Minister of Defence, as Prime Minister. (Buckovski was also elected as Chairman of the SDAM.) On 17 December the Sobranie approved a new Government, again comprising members of the SDAM, the LDP and the DUI. In March 2005 the ICTY issued indictments against Boškovski and a former head of security, Johan Tarculovski, in connection with the August 2001 killings in Ljuboten.

The first round of local government elections, which were to effect the significant devolution of powers to new municipal authorities, took place, with some reported irregularities, on 13 March 2005. A second round of voting in 47 of the 84 municipalities was conducted on 27 March. After upholding claims of irregularities in the first round, the Supreme Court had ordered polls to be repeated in several constituencies, and an OSCE observer mission announced that the second round of the elections in some municipalities again failed to meet OSCE and Council of Europe standards. The DPA and the PDP, which had urged a boycott of the vote, refused to recognize the results. On 10 April further ballots were conducted in those municipalities in which electoral irregularities had occurred. According to official results, 36 of the mayoral contests were won by the Together for Macedonia coalition, and 15 by the DUI, with the IMRO—DPMNU securing 21 mayoralties. In mid-July, in accordance with the Ohrid Agreement, the Sobranie adopted legislation enabling any ethnic minority community to display its flag, together with the state flag, in regions where it constituted at least 50% of the population.

IMRO—DPMNU returns to power

In legislative elections, held on 5 July 2006, the IMRO—DPMNU secured 32.5% of the votes cast, defeating Prime Minister Buckovski's SDAM, which obtained only 23.3% of the vote. A coalition of the DUI and the PDP secured the majority of ethnic Albanian votes, attracting 12.2% of the total ballot, while Xhaferi's DPA received 7.2% of the vote. Reported electoral irregularities caused the Supreme Court to demand that elections be repeated in eight constituencies, following which the IMRO—DPMNU's number of seats in the Sobranie was increased from 44 to 45. In August Gruevski, the Chairman of the IMRO—DPMNU, was formally appointed as Prime Minister and his Government was approved by the Sobranie a few days later. The new coalition administration comprised 10 members of the IMRO—DPMNU, four of the DPA, three of the New Social Democratic Party (formed in the previous year) and one each of the LPM and of the SPM. Ljubiša Georgievski was appointed as President of the Sobranie.

In January 2007 the DUI and the PDP announced a boycott of parliamentary proceedings, in protest against their continued exclusion from Gruevski's Government. In February the Sobranie approved a government reorganization, which included the appointment of Imer Aliu (hitherto Minister of the Environment and Physical Planning) as Deputy Prime Minister, responsible for the implementation of the Ohrid Framework Agreement. In April Boškovski and Tarculovski became the first of those accused of war crimes during the 2001 insurgency to stand trial at the ICTY. In May 2007 the PDP announced that its representatives were to resume participation in the Sobranie, after reaching an agreement with the IMRO—DPMNU permitting it to join the Government. The DUI also officially ended its boycott of the Sobranie (but subsequently withdrew from parliamentary sessions on many occasions). The return of the PDP and the DUI enabled the Sobranie to adopt, on 5 June, legislation providing for full co-operation with the ICTY. In December legislation amending the judicial system was approved, as part of the requirements for NATO accession.

In March 2008 the DPA announced its withdrawal from the Government, in protest against the failure of the IMRO—DPMNU both to recognize the independence of Kosovo, which had been proclaimed in the previous month, and to provide increased rights for the use of the Albanian language and flag. Later that month, however, it was reported that the DPA had retracted its decision (with only Aliu expected to resign from his post), after reaching an agreement with the IMRO—DPMNU on inter-party co-operation to adopt legislation on the use of language. Following the failure of negotiations with Greece on the issue of the country's official name, and Greece's consequent decision to veto NATO membership for the FYRM at a summit meeting of the Alliance held on 2 April, the DUI proposed a motion for the dissolution of the Sobranie. The motion received the support of the IMRO—DPMNU, on the grounds that the existing legislature had obstructed reforms, and was approved on 12 April by the Sobranie, despite a boycott of the vote by the SDAM. Early legislative elections were scheduled for 1 June.

At the elections on 1 June 2008 voting was disrupted in a number of constituencies by outbreaks of violence between rival ethnic Albanian groups, in which at least one person was killed and several injured. The OSCE consequently assessed that the conduct of the elections failed to meet international standards. Elections were repeated on 15 June in those districts in which disorder had prevented voting from taking place, and in a small number of constituencies a further round of voting was necessary on 29 June. According to official results, a 19-party coalition, led by the IMRO—DPMNU, known as For a Better Macedonia, secured 48.8% of the votes cast and 63 of the 120 seats in the legislature, thereby becoming the first grouping to obtain an absolute majority in the Sobranie. The Sun Coalition for Europe, an eight-party coalition led by the SDAM, was placed second,

with 23.7% of the vote, and 27 seats. The DUI received 18 seats (with 12.8%) and the DPA 11 seats (8.5%). It was subsequently announced that the PDP, which failed to obtain legislative representation, was to merge with the DPA. The Sobranie approved the formation of a new Government on 26 July, principally comprising members of the IMRO—DPMNU and the DUI, while the SPM, the Democratic Party of Turks in Macedonia and the (predominantly Roma) United Party for Emancipation were also represented. In the same month Boškovski, having been acquitted of all charges at the ICTY, returned to the FYRM. Meanwhile, Tarculovski was sentenced to 12 years' imprisonment for the Ljuboten killings in 2001.

Gjorge Ivanov is elected President

In January 2009 presidential and municipal elections were scheduled for 22 March; it was also announced that the minimum voter turn-out required for a valid poll would be reduced from 50% to 40%. Later in January the IMRO—DPMNU selected a university professor and non-party member, Gjorge Ivanov, as its presidential candidate, while a former minister, Ljubomir Frčkoski, was nominated by the SDAM. Boškovski also declared his intention to contest the poll as an independent candidate. At the first round of the presidential election, which was contested by seven candidates on 22 March, Ivanov received about 35.1% of the votes cast, while Frčkoski won 20.5%, Imer Selmani of New Democracy 15.0% and Boškovski 14.9%. A second round of voting was scheduled for 5 April, concurrently with run-off ballots for the municipal elections. According to official results, Ivanov was elected to the presidency, with some 63.1% of the votes cast. Voter turn-out at the presidential poll was only 42.6% (owing, in part, to a boycott by ethnic Albanian voters). At the two rounds of municipal elections, held concurrently, the coalition led by the IMRO—DPMNU secured 55 mayoralties; the DUI won 14 and SDAM nine. OSCE and Council of Europe observers declared that the organization of the elections met democratic commitments, but recommended further electoral reforms, including an end to the requirement of the minimum 40% turn-out. Ivanov was inaugurated as President on 12 May.

In late May 2009 Crvenkovski was unanimously elected as Chairman of the SDAM (which position he had held in 1991–2004). At the end of June 2009 the Deputy Prime Minister, responsible for European Integration, Ivica Bocevski, tendered his resignation. In early July, following the dismissal of Trajko Slaveski of the IMRO—DPMNU as Minister of Finance and the resignation of two other ministers, the Sobranie approved a government reorganization. A law professor, Vasko Naumovski, succeeded Bocevski as Deputy Prime Minister, responsible for European Integration. The incumbent Deputy Prime Minister, responsible for Economic Affairs, Zoran Stavreski, became the new Minister of Finance (while remaining a deputy premier), and was replaced in his former position by a business director, Vladimir Peševski. In early August the Chairman of the DPA, Menduh Thaçi, announced a parliamentary boycott by party members, on the grounds that some of the provisions of the Ohrid Framework Agreement were not being observed. In September an encyclopedia published by the Macedonian Academy of Arts and Science (MANU) prompted outrage from Albanian academics and politicians, owing to its portrayal of the Albanian community (which included references to ethnic Albanians resident in the territories of the FYRM as 'settlers'). The publication was denounced by the Governments of Albania and Kosovo, while Greece and Bulgaria also objected to its account of Macedonian history. The MANU subsequently suspended distribution of the encyclopedia, and the Academy's editorial board was subsequently replaced and assurances given that the disputed content would be revised. (In May 2013 it was announced that the FYRM and Albania would establish a joint academic council to produce an encyclopedia with an agreed regional history.)

In December 2010 the SDAM, with the support of the main opposition parties, organized a protest demonstration in Skopje, accusing the Government of economic mismanagement and failing to advance EU integration aspirations. In the same month a parliamentary motion submitted by the SDAM in support of the dissolution of the Sobranie was defeated. Later in December the owner of a major independent television channel, A1 TV, Velija Ramkovski, and 16 executives from associated companies were arrested for suspected tax evasion and other corruption offences. In January 2011 employees of A1 TV broadcast news bulletins from street locations outside government offices in Skopje, rather than from their studios, in protest at the freezing of the station's bank accounts by the authorities, claiming that the corruption investigation was politically motivated. Crvenkovski announced the withdrawal of the SDAM from the Sobranie in support of A1 TV; the LDP and other allied parties, and New Democracy joined the boycott, which was condemned by the IMRO—DPMNU. In February a court in Skopje ruled in favour of reimposing the freezing of the bank accounts of A1 TV and nine associated companies. In the same month clashes, in which eight people were injured, broke out between ethnic Albanian protesters expressing opposition to the planned construction of a museum building, with the appearance of a medieval church, within the historic Skopje Fortress, and supporters of the project. Later in February the Chairman of the State Election Commission, a member of the SDAM, tendered his resignation. In March discussions between government and opposition leaders resulted in some progress towards meeting opposition demands for reforms to electoral regulations. The DPA ended its boycott of the Sobranie later that month in the expectation of early elections (but was only to resume participation in the work of parliamentary commissions relating to electoral legislation). On 30 March Gruevski announced that the IMRO—DPMNU would propose that early legislative elections be scheduled for June, after Crvenkovski agreed that the SDAM would participate in the poll (although the party's boycott of the Sobranie continued). After the Sobranie had approved amendments to the electoral code and the appointment of a new Chairman of the State Election Commission (again of the SDAM), a motion dissolving the legislature was unanimously adopted on 14 April. On the following day it was confirmed that elections to the Sobranie would take place on 5 June.

Early legislative elections

At the pre-term parliamentary elections on 5 June 2011, the coalition of parties led by IMRO—DPMNU won 39.0% of the votes cast, obtaining 56 seats in the Sobranie (thereby losing its absolute majority). The SDAM-led opposition coalition strengthened its position, receiving 32.8% of the votes cast and 42 seats; the DUI obtained 10.2% of the vote and 15 seats, and the DPA 5.9% and eight seats. Under the amendments to electoral legislation approved earlier in the year, the Sobranie had been expanded to 123 deputies, with the additional three seats allocated to representatives of FYRM citizens resident abroad. Prior to the establishment of a new administration, Gruevski reached an agreement with DUI leader Ahmeti on certain concessions; in July the new Sobranie approved legislative amendments, proposed by the DUI, that allowed languages other than Macedonian to be spoken by ministers and other officials (in addition to legislators) during parliamentary sessions and in local self-government bodies if at least 20% were in favour, extended the law on the use of minority flags, and granted amnesty from prosecution on charges of war crimes to four former NLA leaders. On 29 July the Sobranie approved the formation of a new IMRO—DPMNU-led coalition Government, again under the premiership of Gruevski and retaining many members of the previous administration. Several representatives of the DUI again received significant portfolios, including Teuta Arifi, who was appointed as Deputy Prime Minister, responsible for European Integration, and Fatmir Besimi, as Minister of Defence (the first time that the post had been held by an ethnic Albanian). At the end of July it was announced that A1 TV had ceased broadcasting, following bankruptcy proceedings.

An incident, in February 2012, in which a police officer had killed two ethnic Albanians in Gostivar over a reported disagreement about parking, precipitated a series of attacks by ethnic Albanian youths against Macedonians in several towns, particularly Skopje and Tetovo, in early March. Some 30 arrests were made in connection with the violence, in which a number of people were injured, while the main Albanian parties appealed for calm. However, further attacks by ethnic Albanians directed at public transport near Kumanovo were reported. Later in March a 'march for peace' rally, organized by a non-governmental organization in Skopje, was attended by some 2,000 protesters, including President Ivanov. In April five Macedonians were found shot and killed at the village of Smilkovci, near Skopje, precipitating a number of protests directed against the ethnic Albanian community in Skopje and other towns. An operation launched by the special police in May resulted in the arrest of 20 ethnic Albanian suspects, many with alleged connections to a radical Islamist group. Later in the month demonstrations by ethnic Albanians, including Islamist elements, were staged in Skopje to demand the release of the detained suspects. The trial of four ethnic Albanian suspects on charges of terrorism in connection with the killings began in January 2013; the remaining two suspects were detained in

Kosovo in March, after the FYRM authorities issued an international arrest warrant.

Meanwhile, in October 2012 a motion of no confidence in the Government was defeated in the Sobranie. In December the SDAM boycotted the adoption of the 2013 budget by the Sobranie, in protest at what it condemned as excessive government expenditure. SDAM deputies were expelled after disrupting the parliamentary session with violent disturbances, while clashes also occured outside the parliamentary building. Despite EU and US mediation efforts, in early 2013 the SDAM continued its parliamentary boycott and urged followers to stage acts of civil disobedience. In January the SDAM threatened to increase its campaign of protests that blockaded roads in central Skopje, after the ruling coalition rejected opposition demands that early legislative elections be organized concurrently with forthcoming local government polls in March, and that the ministers responsible for internal affairs, justice and finance be replaced. Later that month EU Enlargement Commissioner Stefan Füle mediated a meeting between Gruevski and Crvenkovski, which failed to resolve the crisis.

In February 2013 several DUI members of government were replaced, following the resignation of officials to contest the local elections; these included Arifi, who was succeeded as Deputy Prime Minister, responsible for European Integration by Besimi. However, the appointment of a former commander of the NLA militia, Talat Xhaferi, to replace Besimi as Minister of Defence prompted ethnic Macedonian protests, particularly from a group representing veterans of the police and armed forces; counter-demonstrations by ethnic Albanians degenerated into violent clashes at the beginning of March, in which some 20 people were injured. Meanwhile, Crvenkovski's announcement that the SDAM would boycott the local elections was followed by the resignation of several prominent members from the party in late February. Following further mediation by EU officials, including Füle, on 1 March it was announced that a resolution to the political impasse had been reached: the SDAM had agreed to end its parliamentary boycott and participate in the local elections, while the Government was to enter into dialogue with the opposition on the scheduling of the next legislative elections and on democratic freedoms in the country. Later in March the Constitutional Court began to consider challenges to a new lustration law (intended to remove former secret police informants of the Communist era from certain professions), which had been adopted in June 2012.

Recent developments: local elections

The first round of the local elections took place on 23 March 2013; however, opposition parties immediately complained of alleged violations. A second round of voting was conducted on 7 April. In mid-April the head of the country's Administrative Court resigned, in protest at the Court's annulment of the election of a SDAM candidate in the Skopje municipality of Centar, and of a DPA candidate in Struga. Polls were repeated in those and a further two constituencies on 22 April, in which the victory of the two opposition candidates was confirmed. Overall, an IMRO—DPMNU-led coalition had secured control of 58 mayoralties, while the DUI had obtained 14, a SDAM-led alliance only four and the DUI two. Although the OSCE generally endorsed the conduct of the elections, observers confirmed opposition allegations of voter intimidation and other irregularities, and urged the adoption of further electoral reform legislation. Also in April the Government's announcement of draft media legislation that provided for the establishment of a new regulatory body attracted considerable controversy. Later that month Crvenkovski announced that he would not seek re-election as Chairman of the SDAM upon the expiry of his term in the post in June.

Foreign Affairs

Regional relations

Both the September 1995 interim agreement with Greece and the November Dayton peace accord (for further details, see Bosnia and Herzegovina) were of great significance for the FYRM, despite the unresolved issue of a permanent name for the country. The FYRM was admitted to the Council of Europe in late September, and to the OSCE in October; in the following month the FYRM joined NATO's 'Partnership for Peace' programme (see p. 383). The agreement with Greece facilitated the establishment of full diplomatic relations with the EU from January 1996, and a declaration on co-operation was signed with the European Free Trade Association (see p. 461) in early April. By the end of 1996 more than 75 countries had recognized the

FYRM, with about two-thirds using the country's constitutional name, the Republic of Macedonia.

Under the interim agreement of September 1995 (see above), UN-mediated discussions continued between FYRM and Greek officials regarding the question of a permanent name for the country. By 1999 relations with Greece had improved significantly, and the principal border crossing with Greece was reopened in late 2000. Meanwhile, work on the construction of a 214-km pipeline to transport petroleum from the capital, Skopje, to Thessaloníki, Greece, was officially completed in July 2002. The announcement in December 2006 that the international airport near Skopje was to be renamed after Alexander 'the Great' (considered by Greece to be integral to its cultural heritage) provoked renewed tension. Discussions were resumed in Ohrid in January 2007, but continued to yield little progress. In October Greece announced that it would veto Macedonian NATO and EU applications should no resolution be reached on the matter. In March 2008 the Greek ambassador formally protested to the Government at the public display of posters depicting the Greek flag overprinted with a Nazi swastika during demonstrations in Skopje against changing the country's constitutional name. Following the failure to receive an invitation to join NATO in April, owing to the continued impasse, early legislative elections were scheduled for June. In November the Government submitted a legal challenge against Greece to the International Court of Justice (ICJ, see p. 26), claiming that it had violated the terms of the September 1995 interim accord regulating relations between the two countries, which stipulated that Greece would not veto the country's accession to international institutions under its provisional name; a decision on the issue was expected within four years. On 5 December 2011 the ICJ ruled that Greece had contravened the interim accord by vetoing the country's application to join NATO in 2008 and dismissed Greece's counter-claim that the FYRM had previously breached the accord (while rejecting a court order sought by the FYRM to prevent Greece from violating the accord in the future). The FYRM Government strongly welcomed the verdict of the ICJ. In July 2012 UN Secretary-General Ban Ki-moon visited Skopje in an effort to revive the dialogue with Greece; Prime Minister Gruevski declared commitment to further dialogue, but urged acceptance of the ICJ ruling. Negotiations continued during early 2013; the Government had insisted that any name proposed as a resolution to the dispute would be submitted to a national referendum.

Following the commencement by NATO forces of an intensive aerial bombardment of strategic targets in Yugoslavia in late March 1999 (see Kosovo and Serbia), by early April some 140,000 refugees had fled to the FYRM. Some 14,000 NATO troops were deployed near the border with the Serbian province of Kosovo. Owing to concern over internal destabilization, the FYRM authorities repeatedly closed the border with Kosovo to prevent the continued arrival of large numbers of ethnic Albanians. By late May some 60,000 refugees had been transported from the FYRM for provisional resettlement abroad, while an estimated 250,000 remained in the country. Shortly afterwards the Yugoslav Government accepted a peace plan. On 20 June NATO announced that the air campaign had officially ended, and ethnic Albanian refugees subsequently began to return to Kosovo from the FYRM.

Kosovo's declaration of independence, with the support of many EU member states and the USA, on 17 February 2008 was celebrated by ethnic Albanians in Skopje. In October the FYRM (together with Montenegro) announced the extension of diplomatic recognition to Kosovo, after a motion proposed by the DPA and the DUI was adopted by the Sobranie. The decision prompted an official protest from Serbia, which expelled the FYRM and Montenegrin ambassadors to Serbia in reprisal (but in November invited the appointment of new envoys). Diplomatic relations with Kosovo were formally established in October 2009, following the ratification of an agreement on the demarcation of the common border by the legislatures of both countries. Following economic co-operation accords reached between the FYRM and Kosovo in early 2011, the Ministers of the Interior of the two states in April signed an agreement establishing joint border patrols, in an effort to improve security. In December Serbian President Boris Tadić made an official visit to Skopje, during which he affirmed that relations between Serbia and the FYRM were cordial. Also in December the Governments of the FYRM, Montenegro and Albania signed an agreement providing for the abolition of border controls for citizens of their respective states. Following a visit by the Serbian Prime Minister, Ivica Dačić, to Skopje in January 2013, in March the Governments of the FYRM and Serbia signed an agreement providing for improved bilateral relations and co-operation in the EU integration processes of both states.

Other external relations

The Government signed a Stabilization and Association Agreement with the EU in April 2001, which came into effect in April 2004. A formal application for membership of the EU was submitted in March 2004. Following the recommendation of the European Commission, the country was officially declared to have candidate status at an EU summit meeting in Brussels, Belgium, in mid-December 2005, prompting public celebrations in Skopje. In October 2007 NATO member states adopted a resolution supporting the accession application of the country (together with those of Albania and Croatia). The Government expressed confidence that an official invitation would be extended at a NATO summit meeting in Bucharest, Romania, on 2–4 April 2008; however, the unresolved dispute with Greece over the country's permanent name presented a continued obstacle, and, despite intensified diplomatic efforts by the UN special envoy, Greece vetoed the application. NATO confirmed that the country had fulfilled other membership prerequisites, and that an invitation would be extended upon the settlement of the matter. In July 2009 the European Commission announced that the country had fulfilled all the requirements for the end of visa restrictions, and in November the abolishment of visas for citizens of the FYRM visiting the countries of the Schengen zone was announced, with effect from mid-December. In October the European Commission released a progress report recommending the opening of accession negotiations with the FYRM. However, Greece continued to impose a veto on the beginning of negotiations, and in December EU foreign ministers postponed a decision on establishing a start date for membership negotiations. In March 2011 the European Parliament adopted a draft resolution urging the opening of EU accession talks. Despite the continued impasse, in March 2012 the country began a preliminary dialogue with the EU. In October (as in its annual progress reports of 2010 and 2011) the European Commission reiterated its recommendation that accession negotiations be opened. At a meeting of the European Council in December 2012, however, Bulgaria joined Greece in opposing the initiation of negotiations, on the grounds that the FYRM had failed to foster good bilateral relations (following concerns at perceived discrimination against ethnic Bulgarians in the country). In January 2013, however, in accordance with Bulgarian demands, discussions on the signature of a friendship treaty between the two states began, and the Bulgarian premier subsequently declared that relations had improved.

CONSTITUTION AND GOVERNMENT

According to the 1991 Constitution, which was amended in November 2001, legislative power is vested in the Sobranie (Assembly), with 120 members, elected for a four-year term by universal adult suffrage (85 in single-seat constituencies and 35 members by proportional representation). The President is directly elected for a five-year term, and appoints a Prime Minister to head the Government. The Ministers are elected by the Sobranie. Judicial power is exercised by 27 Courts of First Instance, three Courts of Appeal and the Supreme Court. For the purposes of local government, the FYRM is divided into 84 municipalities.

REGIONAL AND INTERNATIONAL CO-OPERATION

The FYRM is a member of the Council of Europe (see p. 260) the Organization for Security and Co-operation in Europe (OSCE, see p. 397) and the Central European Free Trade Agreement (CEFTA, see p. 459).

The FYRM was admitted to the UN in 1993, provisionally as 'the former Yugoslav Republic of Macedonia', pending settlement of the dispute over its name (see Contemporary Political History). The country became a member of the World Trade Organization (WTO, see p. 444) in 2003.

ECONOMIC AFFAIRS

In 2011, according to World Bank estimates, the FYRM's gross national income (GNI), measured at average 2009–11 prices, was US $9,752m., equivalent to $4,730 per head (or $11,490 per head on an international purchasing-power parity basis). During 2002–11, it was estimated, the population increased by an average of 0.2% per year, while gross domestic product (GDP) per head increased, in real terms, at an average annual rate of 3.3%. Overall GDP increased, in real terms, at an average annual rate of 3.5% in 2002–11; real GDP increased by 2.8% in 2011.

Agriculture (including hunting, forestry and fishing) contributed a preliminary 11.2% of GDP and engaged 18.7% of the employed labour force in 2011. Dairy farming is significant, and the principal agricultural exports are tobacco, vegetables and fruit. The wine industry is of considerable importance, and the FYRM is also a producer of wheat, maize and barley. During 2002–11 the GDP of the agricultural sector increased at an average annual rate of 3.0%, according to the World Bank; real agricultural GDP increased by 1.4% in 2011.

Industry contributed a preliminary 27.6% of GDP and engaged 30.0% of the employed labour force in 2011. During 2002–11, the GDP of the industrial sector increased, in real terms, at an average annual rate of 3.3%, according to the World Bank; real industrial GDP increased by a preliminary 6.0% in 2011.

Mining contributed 1.7% of GDP in 2010 and engaged 0.8% of the employed labour force in 2011. The only major mining activity is the production of lignite (brown coal), although there are also deposits of iron, zinc, lead, copper, chromium, manganese, antimony, silver, gold and nickel.

The manufacturing sector contributed an estimated 14.4% of GDP in 2010 and engaged 19.4% of the employed labour force in 2011. The GDP of the manufacturing sector increased, in real terms, at an average annual rate of 1.1% in 2002–11, according to the World Bank; real manufacturing GDP decreased by 2.9% in 2010, but increased by 2.0% in 2011.

The construction sector contributed a preliminary 6.7% of GDP and engaged 6.2% of the employed labour force in 2011. The GDP of the sector increased, in real terms, at an average annual rate of 2.9% in 2004–11; real construction GDP increased by 12.3% in 2011, according to official estimates.

Energy is derived principally from coal and lignite, which provided 77.7% of the electricity generated in 2009. Hydroelectric sources accounted for another 18.6% of production. The first stage of a pipeline from the Bulgarian border to carry natural gas to the FYRM from Russia became operational in 1995. A 214-km pipeline to transport petroleum from the Greek port of Thessaloníki to Skopje was inaugurated in July 2002. Mineral fuels accounted for 20.5% of the value of total imports in 2011, according to official figures.

Services accounted for a preliminary 61.2% of GDP and engaged 51.3% of the employed labour force in 2011. During 2002–11 the GDP of the services sector increased, in real terms, at an average annual rate of 3.9%, according to the World Bank; services GDP increased by a preliminary 2.2% in 2011.

In 2011 the FYRM recorded a visible merchandise trade deficit of US $2,699.3m., and there was a deficit of $310.6m. on the current account of the balance of payments. In 2011, the principal source of imports was Germany (accounting for 10.4% of total imports); other major sources were Russia, the United Kingdom, Greece, Serbia, Bulgaria, Italy and the People's Republic of China. Germany was also the principal market for exports in that year (accounting for 27.9% of all exports); other important purchasers were Serbia, Bulgaria and Italy. The main imports in 2011 were basic manufactures, mineral fuels and lubricants, machinery and transport equipment, chemical products, food and live animals and miscellaneous manufactured articles. The principal exports in that year were basic manufactures, miscellaneous manufactured articles, chemicals and related products, food and live animals, mineral fuels and lubricants, machinery and transport equipment, inedible crude materials (except fuels), and beverages and tobacco.

The FYRM recorded an overall budgetary deficit of 12,135m. denars in 2012, according to preliminary official figures. General government gross debt was 128,494m. denars in 2011, equivalent to 27.7% of GDP. At the end of 2011 the FYRM's external debt totalled US $5,804m., of which $1,865m. was public and publicly guaranteed debt. In that year the cost of servicing long-term public and publicly guaranteed debt and repayments to the IMF was equivalent to 15.2% of the value of exports of goods, services and income (excluding workers' remittances). The annual rate of inflation averaged 2.0% in 2002–10. Consumer prices increased by 1.3% in 2010. The rate of unemployment was 31.4% in 2011.

Following the entry into force of a Stabilization and Association Agreement with the European Union (EU, see p. 281) in April 2004, the European Commission, in October 2009, released a progress report recommending the opening of accession negotiations with the FYRM; however, the unresolved dispute with Greece over the country's constitutional name subsequently prevented endorsement of the recommendation. In 2010 the Government announced an ambitious 'Skopje 2014' project, involving the construction of public buildings and monuments in the styles of classical antiquity in the capital, with the aim of stimulating tourism and the construction industry. In January 2011 the FYRM was granted a two-year Precautionary Credit Line (PCL) financial arrangement by the IMF. In response to the increasing financial crisis in the euro area, a new Government that was installed in July introduced a number of precautionary measures in the banking sector later that year. The country also continued to benefit from the establishment, in the late 2000s, of four 'technological-industrial development zones', which were designed to attract foreign investment. Despite the continued impasse preventing the agreement of a start date for EU membership negotiations, in March 2012 the FYRM began a preliminary dialogue with the EU, which was to reduce the length of any future official negotiations and maintain the course of reforms. Meanwhile, a sustained reduction in the current account deficit since 2008 (owing to weak growth in both exports and imports) had served to reduce the country's vulnerability to external negative impacts. In September the Government announced an increase in the 2012 budget deficit target from 2.5% of GDP to 3.5%, thereby allowing the payment of public sector arrears; it was envisaged that pensions would be increased by 5% in the following year, although planned rises in public sector wages were to be delayed. In January 2013 the World Bank granted a loan of €155m. to the FYRM. In April the Government estimated that its ongoing 'Skopje 2014' project had cost at least €208m. (far exceeding the €80m. originally projected). The National Bank announced in April that, following growth in the previous two years, the economy had contracted by 0.3% in 2012, reflecting continuing uncertainties in the euro area.

PUBLIC HOLIDAYS

2014: 1 January (New Year), 6–7 January (Orthodox Christmas), 18–21 April (Orthodox Easter), 1 May (Labour Day), 24 May (Day of the Apostles SS Cyril and Methodius), 2 August (National Day), 28 July* (Small Bayram, end of Ramadan), 8 September (Independence Day), 4 October* (Great Bayram, Feast of the Sacrifice), 11 October (Anti-Fascism Day), 23 October (Day of the Macedonian Revolution), 8 December (St Clement of Ohrid Day).

* These holidays are dependent on the Islamic lunar calendar and may vary by one or two days from the dates given.

Statistical Survey

Source (unless otherwise indicated): State Statistical Office of the Republic of Macedonia, 91000 Skopje, Dame Gruev 4, POB 506; tel. (2) 114904; fax (2) 111336; e-mail info@stat.gov.mk; internet www.stat.gov.mk.

Area and Population

AREA, POPULATION AND DENSITY

Area (sq km)	25,713*
Population (census results)†	
20 June 1994	1,945,932
31 October 2002	
Males	1,015,377
Females	1,007,170
Total	2,022,547
Population (UN estimates at mid-year)‡	
2011	2,063,893
2012	2,066,786
2013	2,069,222
Density (per sq km) at mid-2013	80.5

* 9,928 sq miles.

† Comprising persons with an official place of residence in the country (including those temporarily abroad for less than a year), persons from other countries who have been granted a residence permit in the FYRM and have been present there for at least a year, and foreigners with refugee status; excluding foreign diplomatic and military personnel.

‡ Source: UN, *World Population Prospects: The 2010 Revision*.

2011 (official population estimate at 31 December): 2,059,794.

POPULATION BY AGE AND SEX
(UN estimates at mid-2013)

	Males	Females	Total
0–14	179,392	165,980	345,372
15–64	747,378	720,579	1,467,957
65 and over	109,847	146,046	255,893
Total	1,036,617	1,032,605	2,069,222

Source: UN, *World Population Prospects: The 2010 Revision*.

PRINCIPAL ETHNIC GROUPS
(census of 31 October 2002)

	Number	%
Macedonian	1,297,981	64.2
Albanian	509,083	25.2
Turkish	77,959	3.9
Roma (Gypsy)	53,879	2.7
Serb	35,939	1.8
Muslim	17,018	0.8
Vlach	9,695	0.5
Others	20,993	1.0
Total	2,022,547	100.0

PRINCIPAL TOWNS
(2004, official estimates)*

Skopje (capital)	.	515,419	Prilep	76,768
Kumanovo . .	105,484		Struga . . .	63,376
Bitola . . .	95,385		Ohrid	55,749
Tetovo . . .	86,580		Veles	55,108
Gostivar . . .	81,042		Strumica . . .	54,676

* Population by municipality, except for Skopje, which comprises 10 municipalities.

Source: Ministry of Local Self-Government, Skopje.

Mid-2011 (incl. suburbs, UN estimate): Skopje **499,026** (Source: UN, *World Urbanization Prospects: The 2011 Revision*).

BIRTHS, MARRIAGES AND DEATHS

	Registered live births		Registered marriages		Registered deaths	
	Number	Rate (per 1,000)	Number	Rate (per 1,000)	Number	Rate (per 1,000)
2004 . .	26,883	13.2	14,073	6.9	18,265	9.0
2005 . .	22,697	11.1	14,500	7.1	18,406	9.0
2006 . .	22,786	11.2	14,908	7.3	18,630	9.1
2007 . .	22,688	11.1	15,490	7.6	19,594	9.6
2008 . .	22,945	11.2	14,695	7.2	18,982	9.3
2009 . .	23,684	11.5	14,923	7.3	19,060	9.3
2010 . .	24,296	11.8	14,155	6.9	19,113	9.3
2011 . .	22,770	11.1	14,736	7.2	19,465	9.5

Life expectancy (years at birth): 74.8 (males 76.9; females 72.8) in 2011 (Source: World Bank, World Development Indicators database).

ECONOMICALLY ACTIVE POPULATION
(sample surveys, persons aged 15 years and over)

	2009	2010	2011
Agriculture, hunting, forestry and fishing	116,668	121,771	120,894
Mining and quarrying	4,253	4,964	5,316
Manufacturing	126,779	124,282	125,206
Electricity, gas and water . . .	15,296	15,043	23,070
Construction	40,749	40,953	39,961
Wholesale and retail trade, repair of motor vehicles, motorcycles and articles for personal use and for households	96,761	96,206	90,892
Hotels and restaurants	21,193	21,522	23,574
Transport, storage and communications	38,300	35,909	39,986
Financial intermediation . . .	8,654	8,907	10,588
Real estate, renting and business activities	19,560	21,058	22,709
Public administration and defence, compulsory social security . .	44,471	46,415	43,884
Education	37,433	38,862	40,333
Health and social work	35,905	35,959	35,230
Other community, social and personal services	22,133	23,939	21,010
Private households with employed persons	1,103	1,408	1,511
Extra-territorial organizations and bodies	644	656	920
Total employed	629,901	637,855	645,085
Unemployed	298,873	300,439	294,963
Total labour force	928,775	938,294	940,048
Males	570,698	575,349	569,987
Females	358,077	362,945	370,061

Health and Welfare

KEY INDICATORS

Total fertility rate (children per woman, 2010)	1.4
Under-5 mortality rate (per 1,000 live births, 2010) . . .	12
HIV/AIDS (% of persons aged 15–49, 2007)	<0.1
Physicians (per 1,000 head, 2006)	2.6
Hospital beds (per 1,000 head, 2006)	4.6
Health expenditure (2009): US $ per head (PPP) . . .	763
Health expenditure (2009): % of GDP	6.9
Health expenditure (2009): public (% of total)	66.5
Access to sanitation (% of total population, 2010) . . .	88
Total carbon dioxide emissions ('000 metric tons, 2008) . .	11,815.1
Carbon dioxide emissions per head (metric tons, 2008) . .	5.8
Human Development Index (2011): ranking	78
Human Development Index (2011): value	0.728

For sources and definitions, see explanatory note on p. vi.

Agriculture

PRINCIPAL CROPS
('000 metric tons)

	2009	2010	2011
Wheat	271.1	243.1	256.1
Rice, paddy	17.4	25.7	27.0
Barley	146.4	126.3	129.5
Maize	157.5	132.0	129.3
Rye	9.1	8.9	8.3
Potatoes	207.2	202.3	193.9
Sugar beet*	4.8	8.0	8.0
Beans, dry	12.8	12.1	13.0
Olives*	13.8	16.0	15.6
Cabbages and other brassicas .	112.1	149.2	142.7
Tomatoes	145.4	168.0	165.6
Cucumbers and gherkins . .	41.5	46.6	49.9
Chillies and peppers, green . .	154.8	168.2	153.8
Onions, dry	41.9	47.4	44.5
Beans, green	12.8	12.1	13.0
Watermelons	123.9	134.9	127.4
Apples	106.4	121.4	124.6
Peaches and nectarines . . .	10.3	10.2	9.0
Plums and sloes	35.6	38.4	35.4
Grapes	253.5	253.4	235.1
Tobacco, unmanufactured . . .	24.1	30.3	26.5

* FAO estimates.

Aggregate production ('000 metric tons, may include official, semi-official or estimated data): Total cereals 609.0 in 2009, 541.6 in 2010, 554.9 in 2011; Total roots and tubers 207.2 in 2009, 202.3 in 2010, 193.9 in 2011; Total vegetables (incl. melons) 670.4 in 2009, 759.0 in 2010, 728.5 in 2011; Total fruits (excl. melons) 438.9 in 2009, 452.6 in 2010, 436.2 in 2011.

Source: FAO.

LIVESTOCK
('000 head, year ending September)

	2009	2010	2011
Horses	29	27	27*
Cattle	253	260	265
Pigs	194	191	197
Sheep	755	778	767
Chickens	2,118	1,995	1,944

* FAO estimate.

Source: FAO.

LIVESTOCK PRODUCTS
('000 metric tons)

	2009	2010	2011
Cattle meat	7.3	7.1*	5.3
Sheep meat	5.2	5.0*	6.4
Pig meat	8.3	8.0*	8.3
Chicken meat	3.3	3.2*	1.6
Cows' milk	342.6	347.1	376.3
Sheep's milk	34.0	33.2	25.8
Hen eggs*	15.4	18.8	16.6
Honey	0.8	0.8	1.1
Wool, greasy	1.0	1.0	1.0

* Unofficial figure(s).

Source: FAO.

Forestry

ROUNDWOOD REMOVALS
('000 cubic metres, excl. bark)

	2009	2010	2011
Sawlogs, veneer logs and logs for sleepers	84	80	98
Other industrial wood	25	21	23
Fuel wood	530	530	476
Total	639	631	597

Source: FAO.

SAWNWOOD PRODUCTION
('000 cubic metres, incl. railway sleepers)

	2009	2010	2011
Total (all broadleaved) . . .	2	5	3

Source: FAO.

Fishing

(metric tons, live weight)

	2008	2009	2010
Capture	122	141	177
Trouts	36	44	66
Aquaculture	1,331	1,658	1,640
Common carp	247	340	197
Other freshwater fishes . .	130	53	56
Trouts	910	1,147	1,238
Huchen	6	16	11
Total catch	1,453	1,799	1,817

Source: FAO.

Mining

('000 metric tons unless otherwise indicated)

	2009	2010	2011
Lignite	7,454	6,583	7,902
Copper concentrates*†	8	8	8
Lead concentrates†	38	40	40
Gypsum	155	143	163
Crude steel	276	292	386

* Estimated figure.
† Figures refer to the metal content of concentrates.

Gold (estimates): 450 kg in 2006–08.

Silver: 10,000 kg in 2003.

Source: US Geological Survey.

Industry

SELECTED PRODUCTS
('000 metric tons unless otherwise indicated)

	2007	2008	2009
Flour	64	85	77
Refined sugar	36	44	23
Wine ('000 hl)	911	924	1,134
Beer ('000 hl)	695	718	636
Soft drinks ('000 hl)	1,480	1,637	1,717
Cigarettes (million)	5,485	5,919	5,973
Footwear with leather uppers ('000 pairs)	1,563	1,434	1,343
Motor spirit (petrol)	180	177	178
Gas-diesel (distillate fuel) oil	424	451	375
Residual fuel oils	402	360	362
Cement	902	916	909
Ferro-alloys*	171	176	60
Crude steel*	366	253	270
Lead: refined*	29	35	38
Zinc: refined*	24	29	35
Electric energy (million kWh)	6,498	6,311	6,828

* Data from US Geological Survey.

2010: Ferro-alloys 129; Crude steel 292; Lead, refined 40; Zinc, refined 35 (Source: US Geological Survey).

2011: Ferro-alloys 182; Crude steel 386; Lead, refined 40; Zinc, refined 36 (Source: US Geological Survey).

Source (unless otherwise indicated): UN Industrial Commodity Statistics Database.

Finance

CURRENCY AND EXCHANGE RATES

Monetary Units
100 deni = 1 Macedonian denar.

Sterling, Dollar and Euro Equivalents (31 December 2012)
£1 sterling = 73.615 denars;
US $1 = 46.651 denars;
€1 = 61.551 denars;
1,000 denars = £13.58 = $21.44 = €16.25.

Average Exchange Rate (denars per US $)
2010   46.485
2011   44.231
2012   47.890

BUDGET
(million denars)*

Revenue	2010	2011	2012†
Tax revenue	73,619	79,518	81,843
Personal income tax	9,336	10,033	10,223
Profit tax	3,069	3,637	3,900
Value-added tax	37,695	41,247	44,230
Excises	14,810	15,895	15,990
Import duties	5,709	5,706	4,000
Special revenue accounts tax	356	463	452
Social contributions	40,098	42,349	41,471
Pension insurance	26,818	28,637	27,386
Unemployment contributions	1,664	1,765	1,922
Health insurance	11,616	11,947	12,163
Non-tax revenue	15,994	16,071	15,196
Capital revenue	5,314	5,824	5,815
Foreign donations	3,076	3,783	4,155
Repayment of loans	160	400	600
Total	138,617	148,408	149,532

Expenditure	2010	2011	2012†
Current expenditure	131,478	139,000	140,231
Wages, salaries and allowances	23,029	23,309	23,057
Other purchases of goods and services	16,074	17,129	15,918
Transfers	89,194	95,475	70,345
Pensions	37,511	40,485	40,840
Unemployment benefits	2,259	2,224	2,364
Social benefits	4,777	5,175	5,543
Health care	19,902	21,532	21,598
Interest payments	3,181	3,087	3,665
Capital expenditure	17,696	20,992	21,436
Total	149,174	159,992	161,667

* Figures refer to the consolidated accounts of the general Government, comprising the transactions of the central Government and the operations of extra-budgetary funds.
† Preliminary figures.

Source: Ministry of Finance, Skopje.

INTERNATIONAL RESERVES
(US $ million at 31 December)

	2009	2010	2011
Gold (national valuation)	241.0	307.8	345.5
IMF special drawing rights	91.1	1.2	0.8
Foreign exchange	1,959.9	1,968.8	2,330.7
Total	2,292.0	2,277.8	2,677.0

Source: IMF, *International Financial Statistics*.

MONEY SUPPLY
(million denars at 31 December)

	2009	2010	2011
Currency outside depository corporations	16,266	16,958	19,308
Transferable deposits	56,444	62,887	65,859
Other deposits	136,913	155,229	172,212
Broad money	209,623	235,074	257,379

Source: IMF, *International Financial Statistics*.

COST OF LIVING
(Consumer Price Index; base: 2000 = 100)

	2007	2008	2009
Food	109.1	125.8	123.8
Fuel and light	125.0	134.2	142.6
Clothing (incl. footwear)	116.3	118.4	118.4
Housing	127.1	134.8	137.5
All items (incl. others)	114.8	124.4	123.4

2010: Food 125.0; All items (incl. others) 125.3.

Source: ILO.

NATIONAL ACCOUNTS
(million denars at current prices)

Expenditure on the Gross Domestic Product

	2009	2010	2011*
Government final consumption expenditure	78,536	82,957	81,357
Private final consumption expenditure	314,376	321,524	345,219
Changes in inventories†	24,506	27,822	30,861
Gross fixed capital formation	81,872	82,968	94,537
Total domestic expenditure	499,290	515,271	551,974
Exports of goods and services	160,267	202,166	251,866
Less Imports of goods and services	248,822	283,324	342,111
GDP in purchasers' values	410,734	434,112	461,730

* Preliminary figures.
† Including statistical discrepancy.

Gross Domestic Product by Economic Activity

	2008	2009	2010
Agriculture, forestry and fishing .	41,267	39,825	43,739
Mining and quarrying	4,350	4,149	6,662
Manufacturing	70,634	57,628	54,756
Electricity, gas and water supply .	11,159	16,577	20,384
Construction	20,258	21,361	23,902
Wholesale and retail trade . .	50,270	52,889	57,012
Hotels and restaurants . . .	5,952	5,426	4,940
Transport and communications. .	33,143	34,661	33,648
Financial services	11,090	10,541	9,838
Real estate and business services*	45,982	43,377	46,242
Public administration and defence	26,677	29,689	35,922
Education	12,467	14,250	15,315
Health care and social work .	13,577	15,233	15,526
Other community, social and personal services	10,548	13,339	13,262
Sub-total	357,450	358,945	381,148
Value-added tax	50,449	49,706	52,619
Import duties	6,275	5,229	4,712
Less Subsidies on products . .	2,445	3,146	4,367
GDP in purchasers' values .	411,728	410,734	434,112

* Including imputed rents of owner-occupied dwellings.

2011: (preliminary): Agriculture, forestry and fishing 45,185; Mining and quarrying, manufacturing and utilities 84,229; Construction 27,280; Wholesale and retail trade, hotels, restaurants and transport 61,353; Hotels and restaurants 4,386; Transport and communications 36,305; Financial services; real estate and business services 80,508; Public administration and defence, compulsory social security, education, health care and social work 64,978; *Sub-total* 404,224; Taxes on products, less subsidies 57,507; *GDP in purchasers' values* 461,730.

BALANCE OF PAYMENTS
(US $ million)

	2009	2010	2011
Exports of goods f.o.b. . . .	1,891.9	2,618.7	3,299.1
Imports of goods f.o.b. . . .	−4,313.8	−4,649.0	−5,998.4
Balance on goods . . .	−2,421.9	−2,030.4	−2,699.3
Exports of services . . .	1,115.6	1,012.0	1,488.4
Imports of services	−838.4	−853.2	−982.3
Balance on goods and services	−2,144.7	−1,871.5	−2,193.2
Primary income received . .	178.1	194.2	240.5
Primary income paid . . .	−245.0	−325.6	−413.8
Balance on goods, services and primary income . . .	−2,211.6	−2,002.8	−2,366.6
Secondary income received . .	1,668.4	1,867.1	2,120.1
Secondary income paid . .	−66.4	−62.0	−64.0
Current balance	−609.6	−197.8	−310.6
Capital account (net) . . .	28.6	16.5	29.3
Direct investment assets . .	−74.0	−91.7	−31.7
Direct investment from liabilities .	259.5	300.7	495.1
Portfolio investment assets . .	−51.3	−29.0	−10.7
Portfolio investment liabilities .	198.5	−45.5	−47.5
Other investment assets . .	−144.6	−206.0	−575.5
Other investment liabilities .	499.6	330.2	590.2
Net errors and omissions . .	40.2	0.7	−5.8
Reserves and related items .	146.9	78.1	132.8

Source: IMF, *International Financial Statistics*.

External Trade

PRINCIPAL COMMODITIES
(distribution by SITC, US $ million)

Imports c.i.f.	2009	2010	2011
Food and live animals . . .	559.3	558.9	672.0
Meat and meat preparations . .	141.2	125.6	155.2
Mineral fuels, lubricants, etc. .	811.1	966.8	1,436.9
Petroleum, petroleum products, etc.	622.3	744.8	1,055.4
Electric energy	120.9	115.7	228.0
Chemicals and related products	569.4	663.0	827.4
Basic manufactures	1,214.0	1,385.5	1,950.3
Iron and steel	302.4	355.7	437.4
Machinery and transport equipment	1,215.2	1,097.2	1,173.2
General industrial machinery .	171.0	128.6	191.7
Electrical machinery, apparatus, etc. (excl. telecommunications and sound equipment) . .	185.2	188.7	253.6
Road vehicles and transport equipment	361.4	391.6	358.8
Miscellaneous manufactured articles	392.7	399.3	431.7
Total (incl. others)	5,072.8	5,474.5	7,007.3

Exports f.o.b.	2009	2010	2011
Food and live animals . . .	283.6	328.7	373.2
Vegetables and fruit	142.6	181.1	197.0
Beverages and tobacco . . .	197.1	202.5	235.0
Beverages	86.1	79.0	81.5
Tobacco and tobacco manufactures	111.0	123.5	153.5
Crude materials (inedible) except fuels	173.7	260.0	288.4
Mineral fuels, lubricants, etc. .	202.9	257.4	372.4
Petroleum and petroleum products	191.3	218.1	321.3
Chemicals and related products	172.3	381.8	747.1
Basic manufactures	771.5	990.8	1,231.5
Textile yarn, fabrics, etc. . . .	45.7	56.5	59.8
Iron and steel	534.4	778.4	1,010.9
Machinery and transport equipment	153.3	198.8	352.6
Electrical machinery, apparatus, etc. (excl. telecommunications and sound equipment) . . .	76.3	94.3	158.2
Miscellaneous manufactured articles	745.1	717.7	834.5
Clothing and accessories (excl. footwear)	584.6	564.6	658.4
Total (incl. others)	2,708.5	3,351.4	4,455.4

PRINCIPAL TRADING PARTNERS
(US $ million)

Imports c.i.f.	2009	2010	2011
Austria	100.3	94.2	133.1
Bosnia and Herzegovina . . .	46.5	49.1	90.1
Brazil	62.3	60.3	67.4
Bulgaria	244.3	302.0	457.7
China, People's Republic . . .	290.1	288.8	354.7
Croatia	118.4	113.3	133.1
Czech Republic	51.9	51.3	60.5
France	91.8	85.0	125.8
Germany	521.7	613.5	728.9
Greece	441.9	448.9	566.3
Hungary	50.9	47.6	49.7
Italy	368.5	335.2	418.8
Japan	54.6	45.4	52.0
Netherlands	71.0	68.7	68.8
Poland	83.2	69.8	82.1
Romania	108.8	126.8	94.3
Russia	495.1	552.5	683.7
Serbia	398.0	419.4	497.9
Slovenia	190.9	165.1	185.4
Spain	49.0	60.4	62.9
Switzerland-Liechtenstein . .	124.3	99.4	172.0
Turkey	253.4	261.7	343.9
Ukraine	84.5	117.6	157.6
United Kingdom	62.5	285.6	591.0
USA	110.8	102.6	88.7
Total (incl. others)	5,072.8	5,474.5	7,007.3

Exports f.o.b.	2009	2010	2011
Austria	19.1	37.0	38.3
Belgium	36.1	80.8	62.5
Bosnia and Herzegovina . . .	86.7	85.0	93.1
Bulgaria	217.0	294.0	307.7
China, People's Republic . . .	3.2	89.2	127.5
Croatia	152.7	123.7	139.6
Germany	455.9	712.4	1,241.9
Greece	291.6	246.2	215.2
Italy	218.3	235.4	289.7
Netherlands	61.7	70.4	87.5
Romania	20.0	54.3	46.2
Serbia	337.8	271.8	333.4
Slovenia	34.3	69.1	88.2
Spain	38.8	73.7	66.4
Turkey	40.8	50.9	73.3
Ukraine	10.1	21.3	95.8
United Kingdom	42.9	59.3	54.2
Total (incl. others)	2,708.5	3,351.4	4,455.4

Transport

RAILWAYS
(traffic)

	2009	2010	2011
Passenger journeys ('000) . . .	1,523	1,512	1,421
Passenger-km (million) . . .	155	155	145
Freight carried ('000 metric tons)	2,929	3,097	2,770
Freight ton-km (million) . . .	497	525	479

ROAD TRAFFIC
(motor vehicles in use at 31 December)

	2009	2010	2011
Motorcycles	9,097	7,761	8,373
Passenger cars	282,196	310,231	313,080
Buses	2,454	2,695	2,636
Goods vehicles	27,771	28,795	27,917
Tractors, working vehicles and trailers	10,847	11,307	12,013

INLAND WATERS
(lake transport)

	2008	2009	2011*
Passengers carried	55,460	62,530	28,440
Passenger-km ('000)	2,560	2,414	850

* Data for 2010 were not available.

CIVIL AVIATION
(traffic on scheduled services)

	2007	2008	2009
Kilometres flown (million) . .	3	3	1
Passengers carried ('000) . . .	211	196	87
Passenger-km (million) . . .	253	209	87
Total ton-km (million) . . .	23	18	8

Source: UN, *Statistical Yearbook*.

2010: Passengers carried ('000) 137 (Source: World Bank, World Development Indicators database).

Tourism

TOURISTS BY COUNTRY OF ORIGIN*

	2009	2010	2011
Austria	6,437	6,143	5,681
Albania	19,757	17,110	13,614
Bosnia and Herzegovina . . .	4,672	5,619	4,959
Bulgaria	23,619	15,513	18,541
Croatia	12,519	12,791	13,885
Germany	9,795	9,573	9,822
Greece	22,253	26,843	45,509
Israel	6,110	2,885	3,309
Italy	6,050	6,181	7,140
Kosovo	n.a.	9,480	9,829
Netherlands	4,988	6,612	22,219
Poland	5,827	6,182	6,758
Serbia	38,744	35,840	35,692
Slovenia	13,970	12,606	14,063
Turkey	16,962	20,047	39,251
United Kingdom	5,309	5,647	6,139
USA	7,826	7,655	8,082
Total (incl. others)	259,204	261,696	327,471

* Figures refer to arrivals from abroad at all accommodation establishments.

Tourism receipts (US $ million, excl. passenger transport): 218 in 2009; 197 in 2010; 239 in 2011 (provisional) (Source: World Tourism Organization).

Communications Media

	2009	2010	2011
Telephones ('000 main lines in use)	437.3	413.1	422.1
Mobile cellular telephones ('000 subscribers)	1,943.2	2,153.4	2,213.2
Internet subscribers ('000) . .	221.6	239.5	260.3
Broadband subscribers ('000) . .	218.7	237.8	259.2
Newspapers			
Titles	14	15	17
Circulation ('000 copies) . . .	7,131	5,526	4,614
Book production (incl. brochures) .			
Titles	635	498	910
Circulation ('000 copies) . . .	483	528	783
Magazines			
Titles	110	92	100
Circulation ('000 copies) . . .	9,176	1,272	2,334

Personal computers: 749,760 (367.6 per 1,000 persons) in 2007.

Source: partly International Telecommunication Union.

Education

(2011/12 unless otherwise indicated)

	Institutions	Teachers	Students
Primary and lower secondary .	1,041	17,444	200,227
Upper secondary	120	7,379	93,590
University level*	112	2,186	61,148
Other higher*	5	90	2,102

* 2010/11 figures, excluding Tetovo State University.

Pupil-teacher ratio (primary education, UNESCO estimate): 15.9 in 2009/10 (Source: UNESCO Institute for Statistics).

Adult literacy rate (UNESCO estimates): 97.3% (males 98.7%; females 95.9%) in 2010 (Source: UNESCO Institute for Statistics).

Directory

The Government

HEAD OF STATE

President of the Republic: Dr GJORGE IVANOV (elected 5 April 2009; inaugurated 12 May).

COUNCIL OF MINISTERS
(May 2013)

Principally comprising representatives of the Internal Macedonian Revolutionary Organization—Democratic Party for Macedonian National Unity (IMRO—DPMNU), the Democratic Union for Integration (DUI), the Democratic Party of Turks in Macedonia (DPTM) and the United Party for Emancipation (UPE).

Prime Minister: NIKOLA GRUEVSKI (IMRO—DPMNU).

Deputy Prime Minister and Minister of Finance: ZORAN STAVRESKI (IMRO—DPMNU).

Deputy Prime Minister, responsible for the implementation of the Ohrid Framework Agreement: MUSA XHAFERI (DUI).

Deputy Prime Minister, responsible for Economic Affairs: VLADIMIR PEŠEVSKI (IMRO—DPMNU).

Deputy Prime Minister, responsible for European Integration: FATMIR BESIMI (DUI).

Minister of Foreign Affairs: NIKOLA POPOVSKI (IMRO—DPMNU).

Minister of Defence: TALAT XHAFERI (DUI).

Minister of Internal Affairs: GORDANA JANKULOSKA (IMRO—DPMNU).

Minister of Justice: BLERIM BEXHETI (DUI).

Minister of Transport and Communications: MILE JANAKIESKI (IMRO—DPMNU).

Minister of the Economy: VALON SARAČINI (DUI).

Minister of Agriculture, Forestry and Water Resources: LJUPČO DIMOVSKI (SPM).

Minister of Health: NIKOLA TODOROV (IMRO—DPMNU).

Minister of Education and Science: PANČE KRALEV (IMRO—DPMNU).

Minister of the Information Society and Administration: IVO IVANOVSKI (IMRO—DPMNU).

Minister of Local Self-Government: TAHIR HANI (DUI).

Minister of Culture: ELIZABETA KANČESKA MILEVSKA (IMRO—DPMNU).

Minister of Labour and Social Welfare: SPIRO RISTOVSKI (Independent).

Minister of the Environment and Physical Planning: ABDILAQIM ADEMI (DUI).

Minister without Portfolio: HADI NEZIR (DPTM).

Minister without Portfolio: NEŽDET MUSTAFA (UPE).

Minister without Portfolio: VELE SAMAK (IMRO—DPMNU).

Minister without Portfolio: BIL PAVLESKI (Independent).

MINISTRIES

Office of the President: 1000 Skopje, Aco Karamanov 33 A; tel. and fax (2) 3253105; e-mail president@president.gov.mk; internet www .president.gov.mk.

Office of the Prime Minister: 1000 Skopje, Ilindenska bb 2; tel. (2) 3118022; fax (2) 3112561; e-mail primeminister@primeminister.gov .mk; internet www.vlada.mk.

Ministry of Agriculture, Forestry and Water Resources: 1000 Skopje, ul. Leninova 2; tel. (2) 3134477; fax (2) 3230429; e-mail info@ mzsv.gov.mk; internet www.mzsv.gov.mk.

Ministry of Culture: 1000 Skopje, ul. Gjuro Gjakovik 61; tel. (2) 3240500; fax (2) 3240920; e-mail info@kultura.gov.mk; internet www .kultura.gov.mk.

Ministry of Defence: 1000 Skopje, Orce Nikolov 116; tel. (2) 3282042; fax (2) 3283968; e-mail info@morm.gov.mk; internet www.morm.gov.mk.

Ministry of the Economy: 1000 Skopje, Jurij Gagarin 15; tel. (2) 3093408; fax (2) 3084472; e-mail info@economy.gov.mk; internet www.economy.gov.mk.

Ministry of Education and Science: 1000 Skopje, Mito Hadzivasilev Jasmin bb; tel. (2) 3117896; fax (2) 3118414; e-mail contact@ mon.gov.mk; internet www.mon.gov.mk.

Ministry of the Environment and Physical Planning: 1000 Skopje, Goce Delcev, MRTV Bldg; tel. (2) 3251403; fax (2) 3220165; e-mail infoeko@moepp.gov.mk; internet www.moepp.gov.mk.

Ministry of Finance: 1000 Skopje, Dame Gruev 14; tel. (2) 3117288; fax (2) 3106779; e-mail finance@finance.gov.mk; internet www .finance.gov.mk.

Ministry of Foreign Affairs: 1000 Skopje, Dame Gruev 6; tel. and fax (2) 3115790; e-mail cabinet@mfa.gov.mk; internet www.mfa.gov .mk.

Ministry of Health: 1000 Skopje, ul. 50 Divizija 6; tel. (2) 3112500; fax (2) 3113014; internet www.zdravstvo.gov.mk.

Ministry of the Information Society and Administration: 1000 Skopje, Mito Hadzivasilev Jasmin bb; tel. (2) 3200870; fax (2) 3221883; e-mail contact_mis@mis.gov.mk; internet www.mio.gov .mk.

Ministry of Internal Affairs: 1000 Skopje, ul. Dimče Mirčev bb; tel. (2) 3117222; fax (2) 3112468; e-mail kontakt@mvr.gov.mk; internet www.mvr.gov.mk.

Ministry of Justice: 1000 Skopje, Dimitrija Čupovski 9; tel. (2) 3117288; fax (2) 3226975; e-mail contact@mjustice.gov.mk; internet www.pravda.gov.mk.

Ministry of Labour and Social Welfare: 1000 Skopje, Dame Gruev 14; tel. (2) 3106212; fax (2) 3220408; e-mail mtsp@mtsp.gov .mk; internet www.mtsp.gov.mk.

Ministry of Local Self-Government: 1000 Skopje, ul. Mito Hadzivasilev Jasmin bb; tel. 3253921; fax 3253920; e-mail info@mls.gov .mk; internet www.mls.gov.mk.

Ministry of Transport and Communications: 1000 Skopje, ul. Crvena skopska opština 4; tel. (2) 3145497; fax (2) 3126228; e-mail contact@mtc.gov.mk; internet www.mtc.gov.mk.

President

Presidential Election, First Ballot, 22 March 2009

Candidate	Votes	% of votes
Gjorge Ivanov (IMRO—DPMNU)	343,374	35.05
Ljubomir Frčkoski (SDAM)	200,316	20.45
Imer Selmani (ND)	146,795	14.98
Ljube Boškovski (Independent)	145,638	14.87
Agron Buxhaku (DUI)	73,567	7.51
Nano Ružin (LDP)	39,645	4.05
Mirushe Hoxha (DPA)	30,281	3.09
Total	**979,616**	**100.00**

Second Ballot, 5 April 2009

Candidate	Votes	% of votes
Gjorge Ivanov (IMRO—DPMNU)	453,616	63.14
Ljubomir Frčkoski (SDAM)	264,828	36.86
Total	**718,444**	**100.00**

Legislature

Sobranie
(Assembly)

1000 Skopje, 11 Oktomvri bb; tel. (2) 3113268; fax (2) 3237947; e-mail sobranie@sobranie.mk; internet www.sobranie.mk.

President: TRAJKO VELJANOSKI.

General Election, 5 June 2011

Party	Votes	% of votes	Seats
IMRO—DPMNU*	438,138	38.98	56
SDAM†	368,496	32.78	42
DUI	115,092	10.24	15
DPA	66,315	5.90	8
NDR	29,996	2.67	2
IMRO—PP	28,217	2.51	—
ND	19,958	1.78	—
UM	17,081	1.52	—
LDP	16,551	1.47	—
Others	24,220	2.15	—
Total	**1,124,064**	**100.00**	**123**

* In coalition with 21 other parties, including the SPM, the Democratic Union, DRM, the DPTM, the DPSM and the UPE.
† In coalition with 15 other parties, including the NSDP and the LPM.

Election Commission

State Election Commission (Drzhavna izborna komisija): 1000 Skopje, Mito Jasmin bb; tel. (2) 3244744; fax (2) 3244745; e-mail izbori@sec.mk; internet www.sec.mk; Chair. BORIS KONDARKO.

Political Organizations

Democratic Party of Albanians (DPA) (Partia Demokratike Shqiptare) (PDSh): Tetovo, Sheshi i Qytetit 15/1; tel. and fax (44) 333581; e-mail info@gurra-pdsh.org; internet www.pdsh.info; f. 1997; officially registered 2002; absorbed the Party for Democratic Prosperity in 2008; Chair. MENDUH THAÇI.

Democratic Party of Serbs in Macedonia (DPSM): Skopje, 27 Mart 11; tel. (2) 3214556; e-mail dpsm@mt.net.mk; internet www.dpsm.info; f. 1992; contested the 2011 legislative elections as part of a coalition led by the IMRO—DPNMU (q.v.); Pres. IVAN STOILKOVIĆ.

Democratic Party of Turks in Macedonia (DPTM) (Makedonya Türk Demokratik Partisi): 1000 Skopje, Üsküp, ul. Stiv Naumov bb; tel. and fax (2) 3214053; e-mail info@tdp.org.mk; internet www.tdp.org.mk; contested the 2011 legislative elections as part of a coalition led by the IMRO—DPNMU (q.v.); Pres. Dr KENAN HASIPI.

Democratic Renewal of Macedonia (DRM) (Demokratska Obnova na Makedonija): 1000 Skopje, ul. Nikola Vapcarov 18/1; tel. and fax (2) 5112900; e-mail info@dom.org.mk; internet www.dom.org.mk; f. 2006; contested the 2011 legislative elections as part of a coalition led by the IMRO—DPNMU (q.v.); Leader LILJANA POPOVSKA.

Democratic Union for Integration (DUI) (Bashkimi Demokratik për Integrim/Demokratska Unija za Integracija—BDI): 1200 Tetovo, Rruga 170 No 2, Reçicë e Vogël; tel. (4) 4334398; fax (4) 4334397; e-mail bdi@bdi.org.mk; internet www.bdi.org.mk; f. 2002; ethnic Albanian, dominated by fmr mems of rebel National Liberation Army; Chair. ALI AHMETI; Sec.-Gen. ABDILAQIM ADEMI.

Internal Macedonian Revolutionary Organization—Democratic Party for Macedonian National Unity (IMRO—DPMNU) (Vnatrešno-Makedonska Revolucionerna Organizacija—Demokratska Partija za Makedonsko Nacionalno Edinstvo—VMRO—DPMNE): 1000 Skopje, Makedonija 17A; tel. (2) 3215550; fax (2) 3215551; e-mail contact@vmro-dpmne.org.mk; internet www.vmro-dpmne.org.mk; nationalist; Pres. NIKOLA GRUEVSKI; Sec.-Gen. KIRIL BOZHINOVSKI.

Internal Macedonian Revolutionary Organization—People's Party (IMRO—PP) (Vnatrešno Makedonska Revolucionerna Organizacija—Narodna Partija—VMRO—NP): 1000 Skopje, ul. Nikola Vapcarov br. 2; tel. and fax (2) 6145374; e-mail contact@vmro-np.org.mk; internet www.vmro-np.org.mk; f. 2004 by fmr mems of IMRO—DPMNU (q.v.); Chair. LJUBCHO GEORGIEVSKI.

Liberal Democratic Party (LDP) (Liberalno-Demokratska Partija): 1000 Skopje, 11 Oktombri 8; tel. (2) 3298261; fax (2) 3298268; e-mail liberaldemocraticparty@gmail.com; internet www.ldp.org.mk; f. 1996; Chair. ANDREJ ZHERNOVISKI; Sec.-Gen. ROZA TOPUZOVA-KAREVSKA.

Liberal Party of Macedonia (LPM) (Liberalna Partija na Makedonija): 1000 Skopje, ul. Vasko Karangeleski bb; tel. and fax (2) 2464955; e-mail info@lp.org.mk; internet www.lp.org.mk; f. 1990; contested the 2011 legislative election as part of a coalition led by the Social Democratic Alliance of Macedonia (q.v.); centrist, free-market oriented; Pres. IVON VELIČKOVSKI; Sec.-Gen. KIRE BUZLIEV.

National Democratic Revival (NDR) (Rilindja Demokratike Kombëtare—RDK): 1000 Skopje, Bitpazarska 60; tel. (4) 2550551; e-mail info@rdk.org.mk; internet www.rdk.org.mk; f. 2011; Chair. Dr RUFI OSMANI.

New Democracy (ND) (Demokracia e Re): 1000 Skopje, Khristian Todorovski 94A; tel. (2) 2616220; fax (2) 2616217; e-mail info@demokraciaere.org; internet www.demokraciaere.org; f. 2008 by fmr mems of DPA (q.v.); Pres. IMER SELMANI.

New Social Democratic Party (NSDP) (Nova Socijaldemokratska Partija): 1000 Skopje, ul. Veljko Vlahović 4; tel. (2) 3238775; fax (2) 3290465; e-mail contact@nsdp.org.mk; internet www.nsdp.org.mk; f. 2005; contested the 2011 legislative election as part of a coalition led by the Social Democratic Alliance of Macedonia (q.v.); Pres. TAMARA BAARA.

Social Democratic Alliance of Macedonia (SDAM) (Socijaldemokratski Sojuz na Makedonija—SDSM): 1000 Skopje, Bihakjka 8; tel. (2) 3293100; fax (2) 3293109; e-mail web@sdsm.org.mk; internet www.sdsm.org.mk; f. 1943; fmrly League of Communists of Macedonia—Party of Democratic Reform; Chair. BRANKO CRVENKOVSKI; Gen. Sec. ANDREJ PETROV.

Socialist Party of Macedonia (SPM) (Socijalistiska Partija na Makedonija): 1000 Skopje, 11 Oktomvri 17; tel. (2) 3228015; fax (2) 3220025; e-mail contact@spm.org.mk; internet www.spm.org.mk; f. 1990; left-wing; contested the 2011 legislative elections as part of a coalition led by the IMRO—DPNMU (q.v.); Chair. LJUBISAV IVANOV.

United for Macedonia (UM) (Obedineti za Makedonija): 1000 Skopje, Dame Gruev 28; e-mail contact@obedinetizamakedonija.mk; f. 2009; Pres. LJUBE BOŠKOSKI.

United Party for Emancipation (UPE) (Obedinita Partija za Emancipacija): c/o Sobranie, 1000 Oktomvri bb; tel. (2) 3112255 ext. 135; e-mail nezdet.mustafa@gs.gov.mk; f. 2002 by merger of Democratic Progressive Roma Party of Macedonia and First Roma Party of Macedonia; contested the 2011 legislative elections as part of a coalition led by the IMRO—DPNMU (q.v.); Leader NEŽDET MUSTAFA.

Diplomatic Representation

EMBASSIES IN THE FORMER YUGOSLAV REPUBLIC OF MACEDONIA

Albania: 1000 Skopje, Slavej Planina 2; tel. (2) 3246726; fax (2) 3246727; e-mail embassy.skopje@mfa.gov.al; Ambassador ARBEN ÇEJKU.

Austria: 1000 Skopje, Mile Popjordanov 8; tel. (2) 3083400; fax (2) 3083150; e-mail skopje-ob@bmeia.gv.at; internet www .aussenministerium.at/skopje; Ambassador Dr THOMAS MICHAEL BAIER.

Bosnia and Herzegovina: 1000 Skopje, Mile Pop-Jordanov 56; tel. (2) 3086216; fax (2) 3086221; e-mail emb.bih@neotel.net.mk; internet www.ambasadabih.org.mk; Ambassador ZDRAVKO BEGOVIĆ.

Bulgaria: 1000 Skopje, Zlatko Shnajder 3; tel. (2) 3229444; fax (2) 3246493; e-mail embassy.skopje@mfa.bg; internet www.mfa.bg/embassies/macedonia; Ambassador IVAN PETKOV.

China, People's Republic: 1000 Skopje, 474/20; tel. (2) 3213163; fax (2) 3122500; e-mail chinaembmk@mfa.gov.cn; internet mk .china-embassy.org; Ambassador CUI ZHIWEI.

Croatia: 1000 Skopje, Bukureška 91; tel. (2) 3248170; fax (2) 3246004; e-mail croemb.skopje@mvpei.hr; internet mk.mvp.hr; Ambassador ZLATKO KRAMARIĆ.

Czech Republic: 1000 Skopje, Salvador Aljende 35; tel. (2) 3109805; fax (2) 3178380; e-mail embassy.mzv.cz; internet www.mzv .cz/skopje; Ambassador MIROSLAV RAMEŠ.

France: 1000 Skopje, Salvador Aljende 73; tel. (2) 3244300; fax (2) 3244313; e-mail franamba@mt.net.mk; internet www .ambafrance-mk.org; Ambassador JEAN-CLAUDE SCHLUMBERGER.

Germany: 1000 Skopje, Lerinska 59; tel. (2) 3093900; fax (2) 3093899; e-mail info@skop.auswaertiges-amt.de; internet www .skopje.diplo.de; Ambassador GUDRUN ELISABETH STEINACKER.

Hungary: 1000 Skopje, Mirka Ginova 27; tel. (2) 3092041; fax (2) 3063070; e-mail mission.skp@mfa.gov.hu; internet www.mfa.gov .hu/emb/skopje; Ambassador Dr JÓZSEF BENCZE.

Iran: 1000 Skopje, Mile Pop Jordanov 12; tel. and fax (2) 3051759; e-mail iriemb@t-home.mk; Ambassador SAEED SADEQ MOHAMMADI.

Italy: 1000 Skopje, Osma Udarna brig. 22; tel. (2) 3236500; fax (2) 3236505; e-mail segreteria.skopje@esteri.it; internet www .ambskopje.esteri.it; Ambassador FABIO CRISTIANI.

Kosovo: 1000 Skopje, Samoilova 136; tel. (2) 3290320; fax (2) 3290322; Ambassador YLBER HYSA.

Montenegro: 1000 Skopje, Vasil Stefanovski 7; tel. (2) 3227277; fax (2) 3227254; e-mail macedonia@mfa.gov.me; Ambassador DUŠAN MRDOVIĆ.

Netherlands: 1000 Skopje, Leninova bb 69–71; tel. (2) 3109250; fax (2) 3129309; e-mail sko@minbuza.nl; internet www.nlembassy.org .mk; Ambassador MARRIËT SCHUURMAN.

Poland: 1000 Skopje, Djuro Djaković 50; tel. (2) 3112647; fax (2) 3119744; e-mail przemyslaw.czyz@msz.gov.pl; internet www.skopje .polemb.net; Ambassador PRZEMYSŁAW CZYŻ.

Romania: 1000 Skopje, Rajko Zinzifov 42; tel. (2) 3228055; fax (2) 3228036; e-mail romanamb@cabletel.net.mk; internet skopje.mae .ro; Ambassador IUSTINIAN FOCSA.

Russia: 1000 Skopje, Pirinska 44; tel. (2) 3117160; fax (2) 3117808; e-mail embassy@russia.org.mk; internet www.russia.org.mk; Ambassador OLEG N. SHCHERBAK.

Serbia: 1000 Skopje, Pitu Guli 8; tel. (2) 3129298; fax (2) 3129427; e-mail srbamb@unet.com.mk; internet www.scgembassy.org.mk; Ambassador TOMISLAV ĐURIN.

Slovakia: 1000 Skopje, Budimpeštanska 39; tel. (2) 3090360; fax (2) 3090367; e-mail emb.skopje@mzv.sk; Chargé d'affaires RÓBERT KIRNÁG.

Slovenia: 1000 Skopje, Vodnjanska 42; tel. (2) 3103041; fax (2) 3176631; e-mail vsk@gov.si; internet www.skopje.embassy.si; Ambassador BRANKO RAKOVEC.

Spain: 1000 Skopje, 27 Mart 7; tel. (2) 3220717; fax (2) 3215612; e-mail emb.skopje@maec.es; Ambassador FERNANDO DE GALAINENA RODRIGUEZ.

Sweden: 1000 Skopje, Osma Udarna Brigada 2; tel. (2) 3297880; fax (2) 3112065; e-mail ambassaden.skopje@foreign.ministry.se; internet www.swedenabroad.com/skopje; Ambassador LARS WAHLLUND.

Switzerland: 1000 Skopje, Maksim Gorki 19; tel. (2) 3103300; fax (2) 3103301; e-mail sko.vertretung@eda.admin.ch; internet www.eda .admin.ch/skopje; Ambassador STEFANO LAZZAROTTO.

Turkey: 1000 Skopje, Slavej Planina bb; tel. (2) 3104710; fax (2) 3117024; e-mail embassy.skopje@mfa.gov.tr; internet skopje.emb .mfa.gov.tr; Ambassador GÜROL SÖKMENSÜER.

Ukraine: 1000 Skopje, Albert Svjcer 7–9; tel. and fax (2) 3178120; e-mail emb_mk@mfa.gov.ua; internet www.mfa.gov.ua/macedonia; Ambassador YURIY O. HONCHARUK.

United Kingdom: 1000 Skopje, Salvador Aljende 73; tel. (2) 3299299; fax (2) 3179726; e-mail britishembassyskopje@fco.gov.uk; internet ukinmacedonia.fco.gov.uk; Ambassador CHRISTOPHER YVON.

USA: 1000 Skopje, Samoilova 21; tel. (2) 3102000; fax (2) 3102499; e-mail embskowebm@t-home.mk; internet www.macedonia .usembassy.gov; Ambassador PAUL D. WOHLERS.

Judicial System

The former Yugoslav republic of Macedonia has 27 Courts of First Instance and three Courts of Appeal. The Republican Judicial Council, which comprises seven members elected by the Sobranie for a term of six years, proposes the election or dismissal of judges to the Sobranie. The Constitutional Court, comprising nine judges elected by the Sobranie with a mandate of nine years, is responsible for the protection of constitutional and legal rights, and ensures that there is no conflict in the exercise of legislative, executive and judicial powers. The Supreme Court is the highest court in the country, and guarantees the equal administration of legislation by all courts.

Constitutional Court (Ustaven Sud na Republika Makedonija): 1000 Skopje, 12 Udarna brig. 2; tel. and fax (2) 3119355; e-mail mail@ ustavensud.mk; internet www.ustavensud.mk; f. 1964; Pres. BRANKO NAUMOSKI.

Supreme Court: 1000 Skopje, Krste Misirkova bb; tel. (2) 3136044; fax (2) 3237538; internet www.vsrm.mk; Pres. LIDIJA NEDELKOVA.

Republican Judicial Council: 1000 Skopje, Veljko Vlahovikj bb; tel. (2) 3218130; fax (2) 3218131; Pres. ALEKSANDRA ZAFIROVSKA.

Office of the Public Prosecutor (Javno Obvinitelstvo na RM): 1000 Skopje, Krste Misirkova bb; tel. (2) 3219850; fax (2) 3219866; e-mail jorm@jorm.org.mk; internet www.jorm.org.mk; Public Prosecutor LJUPČO SVRGOVSKI.

Religion

Most ethnic Macedonians are adherents of the Eastern Orthodox Church, and since 1967 there has been an autocephalous Macedonian Orthodox Church. However, the Serbian Orthodox Church (of which the Macedonian Church formed a part) does not recognize the autocephalous church, and nor do other Orthodox Churches. There are some adherents of other Orthodox jurisdictions in the country. Those Macedonian (and Bulgarian) Slavs who converted to Islam during the Ottoman era are known as Pomaks or as ethnic Muslims. The substantial Albanian population is mostly Muslim (mainly Sunni, but there are some adherents of a Dervish sect); there are some Catholic Christians (of both Byzantine and Latin rites) and a small Jewish community.

CHRISTIANITY

Macedonian Orthodox Church: 1000 Skopje, Partizanski Odredi 12, POB 69; tel. (2) 3230697; fax (2) 3230685; internet www.mpc.org .mk; Metropolitan See of Ohrid revived in 1958; autocephaly declared 1967; 1.5m. mems; comprises seven bishoprics in the FYRM and three abroad; Head of Church and Archbishop of Ohrid and Macedonia Metropolitan Archbishop of Skopje STEFAN VELJANOVSKI.

The Roman Catholic Church

The diocese of Skopje, suffragan to the archdiocese of Vrhbosna (based in Sarajevo, Bosnia and Herzegovina), covers most of the FYRM. The Bishop is also Apostolic Exarch for Catholics of the Byzantine Rite in the FYRM.

Latin Rite Bishop of Skopje and Apostolic Exarch for the Byzantine Rite Faithful Resident in the former Yugoslav republic of Macedonia: Rt Rev. KIRO STOJANOV, 1000 Skopje, Risto Šiškov 31; tel. and fax (2) 3164123; e-mail katbiskupija@mt.net.mk.

ISLAM

Islamic Community of Macedonia (Bashkësia Fetare Islame e Republikës së Maqedonisë): Skopje, Çairska 52; tel. (2) 3117410; fax (2) 3117883; e-mail bim@bim.org.mk; internet www.bim.org.mk; Leader Haji SULEJMAN REXHEPI.

The Press

In 2010 a total of 15 newspapers and 92 magazines were published in the former Yugoslav republic of Macedonia.

PRINCIPAL DAILY NEWSPAPERS

Denes (Today): 1000 Skopje, M. H. Jasmin 50; tel. (2) 3110239; fax (2) 3110150; e-mail denes@unet.com.mk; Editor NIK DENES.

Dnevnik (Daily): 1000 Skopje, Teodosij Gologanov 28; tel. (2) 3297555; fax (2) 3297554; e-mail dnevnik@dnevnik.com.mk;

internet www.dnevnik.com.mk; independent; Editor-in-Chief SAŠO KOKALANOV.

Nova Makedonija (New Macedonia): 1000 Skopje, Atinska br. 12; tel. and fax (2) 5511711; e-mail nm@novamakedonija.com.mk; internet www.novamakedonija.com.mk; f. 1944; morning; in Macedonian; Dir RATKO LAZAREVSKI; Editor-in-Chief ZORAN ANDONOVSKII; circ. 25,000.

Utrinski Vesnik (Morning Herald): 1000 Skopje, ul. Dimitrie Čuposki br. 11/5; tel. (2) 3236900; fax (2) 3236901; e-mail contact@ utrinski.com.mk; internet www.utrinski.com.mk; Dir Dr SRGJAN KERIM; Editor-in-Chief NINA NINESKA-FIDANOSKA.

Večer (The Evening): 1000 Skopje, Nikola Vapcarov 2; tel. (2) 3219650; fax (2) 3219651; e-mail latas@vecer.com.mk; internet www.vecer.com.mk; f. 1963; evening; Editor-in-Chief DRAGAN PAVLOVIKJ-LATAS; circ. 29,200.

Vest (News): Skopje; internet www.vest.com.mk; popular; Editor-in-Chief GORAN MIHAILOVSKII.

PERIODICALS

Delo: 1000 Skopje, Mihail Cokov bb; tel. (2) 3133306; fax (2) 3136477; e-mail delo@unet.com.mk; internet www.delo.com.mk; f. 1993; weekly; nationalist; Editor-in-Chief VLADO MOKROV.

Fokus: Skopje, Zheležniča 53; tel. (2) 3111327; fax (2) 3111685; weekly; independent.

Makedonsko Vreme/Macedonian Times: 91000 Skopje, Vasil Gjorgov 39/7; tel. and fax (2) 3121182; e-mail mtimes@unet.com.mk; f. 1994; monthly; politics and current affairs; in Macedonian and English; Editor-in-Chief JOVAN PAVLOVSKI.

Puls (Pulse): 1000 Skopje, Mito Hadživasilev bb; tel. (2) 3117124; fax (2) 3118024; internet www.puls.com.mk; weekly; business and technology; Editor-in-Chief MIRČE TOMOVSKI.

Roma Times: Skopje; e-mail mail@dostae.net.mk; internet www .dostae.net.mk/mk/press_mk_roma.htm; f. 2001; 3 a week; circ. 3,000.

Sport Magazine: 1000 Skopje, Mito Hadživasilev Jasmin bb; tel. and fax (2) 3116254; e-mail lav@unet.com.mk; f. 1991; weekly; circ. 6,000.

Trudbenik (Worker): 1000 Skopje, Udarna brigada 12; f. 1945; weekly; organ of Macedonian Trade Unions; Editor SIMO IVANOVSKI.

NEWS AGENCIES

Macedonian Information Agency (Makedonska Informativna Agencija—MIA): 1000 Skopje, Bojmija 2; tel. (2) 2461600; fax (2) 2464048; e-mail mia@mia.mk; internet www.mia.mk; f. 1992; news service in Macedonian, Albanian and English; Exec. Dir LJUPČO JAKIMOSKI.

Macedonian Information Centre (Makedonski Informativen Centar—MIC): 1000 Skopje, Naum Naumovski Borce 73; tel. (2) 3117876; e-mail contact@micnews.com.mk; internet www.micnews .com.mk; f. 1992; English; independent; Man. DRAGAN ANTONOV.

Makfax: 1000 Skopje, 11 Oktomvri 33A; tel. (2) 3227127; fax (2) 3110125; e-mail makfax@makfax.com.mk; internet www.makfax .com.mk; f. 1992; independent; provides daily regional news service; in Macedonian, Albanian and English; Exec. Dir DAVOR PASHOVSKI.

PRESS ASSOCIATION

Journalists' Association of Macedonia: 1000 Skopje, Gradskizid 13, POB 498; tel. (2) 3298139; fax (2) 3116447; e-mail contact@znm .org.mk; internet www.znm.org.mk; Pres. NASER SELMANI.

Publishers

Detska radost/Nova Makedonija (Children's Happiness/New Macedonia) Publishing House: 1000 Skopje, Mito Hadživasilev Jasmin bb; tel. (2) 3213059; fax (2) 3225830; f. 1944; children's books; Dir KIRIL DONEV.

Kultura: 1000 Skopje, Sv. Kliment Ohridski 68A; tel. (2) 3111332; fax (2) 3228608; e-mail ipkultura@kultura.com.mk; internet www .kultura.com.mk; f. 1945; history, philosophy, art, poetry, children's literature and fiction; in Macedonian; Dir DIMITAR BAŠEVSKI.

Kulturen Život (Cultural Life) Publishing House: 1000 Skopje, Ruzveltova 6; tel. (2) 3239134; f. 1971; Editor LJUBICA ARSOVSKA.

Makedonska kniga (Macedonian Book) Publishing House: 1000 Skopje, 11 Oktomvri; tel. (2) 3224055; fax (2) 3236951; f. 1947; arts, non-fiction, novels, children's books; Dir SANDE STOJČEVSKI.

Matica Makedonska: 1000 Skopje, ul. Kliment Ohridski 23; tel. (2) 3221138; fax (2) 3229244; f. 1991; Dir RADE SILJAN.

Metaforum: 1000 Skopje, Goce Delčev 6; tel. (2) 3114890; fax (2) 3115634; f. 1993; Dir RUŽICA BILKO.

Misla (Thought) Publishing House: 1000 Skopje, Partizanski odredi 1; tel. (2) 3221844; fax (2) 3118439; f. 1966; modern and classic Macedonian and translated literature; Pres. ZLATA BUNTESLEA.

Naša kniga (Our Book) Publishing House: 1000 Skopje, M. Gorki 21, POB 132; tel. (2) 3228066; fax (2) 3116872; f. 1948; Dir STOJAN LEKOVSKI.

Prosvetno delo (Educational) Publishing House: 1000 Skopje, Dimitrija Čupovski 15; tel. (2) 3117255; fax (2) 3225434; f. 1945; works of domestic writers and textbooks in Macedonian for elementary, professional and high schools; fiction and scientific works; Dir Dr KRSTE ANGELOVSKI.

Tabernakul: 1000 Skopje, Mihail Tsokov bb, POB 251; tel. (2) 3127073; fax (2) 3115329; e-mail contact@tabernakul.com.mk; internet www.tabernakul.com.mk; f. 1989; religion, history, literature, philosophy, popular science; Dir TSVETAN VRAŽIVIRSKI.

Broadcasting and Communications

TELECOMMUNICATIONS

In 2010 there were three main providers of mobile cellular telecommunications services in the former Yugoslav republic of Macedonia and two principal providers of fixed-line telephone services.

Makedonski Telekom (MT): 1000 Skopje, Orce Nikolov bb; tel. (2) 3100200; fax (2) 3100300; e-mail 171@telekom.mk; internet www .telekom.mk; fmrly Makedonski telekomunikacii; present name adopted 2008; mem. of Deutsche Telekom group (Germany); 34.8% state-owned; CEO NIKOLAJ J. V. BEKERS.

ONE Telecommunications Services: 1000 Skopje, Kuzman Josifovski-Pitu 15; tel. (2) 5411000; e-mail info@one.mk; internet www .one.mk; f. 2003 as Cosmofon; renamed as above after merger with internet services provider on.net in 2009; member of the Telekom Slovenia Group; fixed-line and mobile cellular telecommunications; internet and digital TV services; CEO KLAVDIJ GODNIČ.

T-Mobile Macedonia: 1000 Skopje, Orce Nikolov bb; tel. (2) 3131131; fax (2) 3201267; e-mail kontakt@t-mobile.com.mk; internet www.t-mobile.com.mk; f. 1996 as Mobimak; present name adopted 2006; mobile cellular telecommunications; CEO ZHARKO LUKOVSKI; 1.3 m. subscribers (Aug. 2006).

VIP operator DOOEL Skopje: 1000 Skopje, Vasil Adzilarski bb, 8th Floor; fax (2) 3110077; e-mail kontakt@vipoperator.mk; internet www.vip.mk; f. 2007; subsidiary of MobilKom (Austria); mobile cellular telecommunications services; Gen. Dir NIKOLA LJUŠEV.

BROADCASTING
Radio

Makedonska Radio-Televizija (MRT): 1000 Skopje, bul. Goce Delčev bb; tel. (2) 3236839; fax (2) 3111821; e-mail deskvesti@mrt .com.mk; internet www.mtv.com.mk; f. 1944; fmrly Radiotelevizija Skopje, name changed 1991; three radio channels; broadcasts in Macedonian, Albanian, Turkish, Serbian, Roma and Vlach; Dirs JANEZ SAJOVIC, BORIS STAVROV; Dir of Radio GRIGORI POPOVSKI.

Antenna 5 Radio: 1000 Skopje, Tetovska 35; tel. and fax (2) 3111911; e-mail mail@antenna5.com.mk; internet www.antenna5 .com.mk; f. 1994; 12 transmitters broadcast to 90% of the country; Gen. Man. ZORAN PETROV.

Television

Makedonska Radio-Televizija (MRT): 1000 Skopje, bul. Goce Delčev bb; tel. (2) 3112200; fax (2) 3111821; e-mail gstosic@unet.com .mk; internet www.mtv.com.mk; f. 1964; fmrly Radiotelevizija Skopje, name changed 1991; state broadcasting co; three television services; broadcasts in Macedonian, Albanian, Turkish, Serbian, Roma and Vlach; Dirs JANEZ SAJOVIC, BORIS STAVROV; Dir of Television LJUBČO TOZIJA.

A1 TV: 1000 Skopje, Pero Nakov 60; tel. (2) 2550301; fax (2) 2550330; e-mail marketing@a1.com.mk; internet www.a1.com.mk; Gen. Man. DARKO PERUSEVSKI.

SITEL Television: 1000 Skopje, Gradski Stadion bb; tel. (2) 3116566; fax (2) 3229799; e-mail informativna@sitel.com.mk; internet www.sitel.com.mk; Gen. Man. GOVAN IVANOVSKI.

Finance

(cap. = capital; res = reserves; dep. = deposits; m. = million; amounts in new Macedonian denars; brs = branches)

BANKS

At September 2008 the banking system comprised 18 commercial banks and 11 savings houses; 14 of the banks were majority foreign-owned.

National Bank

National Bank of the Republic of Macedonia (Narodna Banka na Republika Makedonija): 1000 Skopje, bul. Kuzman Josifovski Pitu 1; tel. (2) 3108108; fax (2) 3108357; e-mail governorsoffice@nbrm .mk; internet www.nbrm.mk; f. 1992; central bank and bank of issue; cap. 1,289.7m., res 10,489.7m., dep. 58,924.1m. (Dec. 2008); Gov. DIMITAR BOGOV.

Selected Banks

Alpha Banka a.d. Skopje: 1000 Skopje, ul. Dimitrie Chupovski 2; tel. (2) 3251900; fax (2) 3251911; e-mail contact@alphabank.com.mk; internet www.alphabank.com.mk; f. 1993; wholly owned by Alpha Bank AE Athens (Greece); cap. 929.2m., res 791.9m., dep. 5,004.2m. (Dec. 2011); Chair. ANDREAS A. GALATOULAS; Gen. Man. MILENA P. PERCHINKOVA; 19 brs.

Halk Banka a.d. Skopje: 1000 Skopje, bul. Mito Hadzivasilev Jasmin bb, POB 421; tel. (2) 3240800; fax (2) 3240801; e-mail halkbank@halkbank.mk; internet www.halkbank.mk; f. 1993; fmrly Izvozna I Kreditna Banka; present name adopted 2012; 98.78% owned by Türkiye Halk Bankası AŞ (Turkey); cap. 1,884.2m., res 406.1m., dep. 5,488.6m. (Dec. 2011); Chief Exec. NECDET PALAKCI; 27 brs.

Komercijalna Banka a.d. Skopje: 1000 Skopje, Kej Dimitar Vlahov 4; tel. (2) 3107107; fax (2) 3119627; e-mail contact@kb.com .mk; internet www.kb.com.mk; f. 1955; present name adopted 1991; cap. 2,279.1m., res 6,161.2m., dep. 67,145.7m. (Dec. 2011); CEO HARI KOSTOV.

Makedonska Banka za Poddrshka na Razvojot a.d. Skopje (Macedonian Bank for Development Promotion): 1000 Skopje, Veljko Vlahovikj 26; tel. (2) 3115844; fax (2) 3239688; e-mail info@mbdp.com .mk; internet www.mbdp.com.mk; f. 1998; cap. 1,193.8m., res 660.2m., total assets 10,181.9m. (Dec. 2011); CEO DRAGAN MARTI-NOVSKI.

NLB Tutunska Banka a.d. Skopje: 1000 Skopje, Vodnjanska 1; tel. (2) 3105600; fax (2) 3105681; e-mail tbanka1@tb.com.mk; internet www.tb.com.mk; f. 1985; cap. 854.1m., res 3,265.3m., dep. 47,774.4m. (Dec. 2011); Pres. GORGI JANCEVSKI; 32 brs.

Ohridska Banka (Ohrid Bank): 6000 Ohrid, Makedonski Prosvetiteli 19; tel. (46) 206600; fax (46) 254130; e-mail obinfo@ob.com.mk; internet www.ob.com.mk; cap. 1,162.3m., res 219.5m., dep. 17,130.2m. (Dec. 2011); Pres. JITKA PANTUCHKOVA; 5 brs.

Sparkasse Bank Makedonija: 1000 Skopje, Makedonija 9/11; tel. (2) 3200501; fax (2) 3200515; e-mail contact@sparkasse.mk; internet www.sparkasse.mk; f. 1992; present name adopted 2010; 99.5% owned by Steiermärkische Bank und Sparkassen AG (Austria); cap. 1,171.0m., res 831.7m., dep. 12,290.2m. (Dec. 2011); Pres. ALEKSANDRA RADIĆ.

Stopanska Banka a.d. Bitola: 7000 Bitola, Dobrivoe Radosavljević 21; tel. (47) 207500; fax (47) 207541; e-mail stbbt@stbbt.com.mk; internet www.stbbt.com.mk; f. 1948; present name adopted 1995; cap. 1,172.9m., res 254.4m., dep. 4,815.2m. (Dec. 2011); Pres. VLADIMIR EFTIMOSKI.

Stopanska Banka a.d. Skopje: 1000 Skopje, 11 Oktomvri 7; tel. (2) 3295295; fax (2) 3114503; e-mail sbank@stb.com.mk; internet www .stb.com.mk; f. 1944; cap. 3,511.2m., res 854.4m., dep. 56,847.8m. (Dec. 2011); 94.64% owned by National Bank of Greece; Chair. KONSTANTINOS BRATOS; 25 brs.

UniBanka—Universalna Investiciona Banka a.d. Skopje (Universal Investment Bank): 1000 Skopje, M. Gorki 6; tel. (2) 3111111; fax (2) 3224162; e-mail info@unibank.com.mk; internet www.unibank.com.mk; f. 1993; present name adopted 2004; cap. 546.0m., res 567.9m., dep. 9,028.2m. (Dec. 2011); Pres. KOSTA MITROVSKI.

STOCK EXCHANGE

Macedonian Stock Exchange (Makedonska Berza a.d. Skopje): 1000 Skopje, Orce Nikolov 75; tel. (2) 3122055; fax (2) 3122069; e-mail mse@mse.org.mk; internet www.mse.com.mk; f. 1995; CEO IVAN STERIEV.

INSURANCE

In 2008 the insurance system in the FYRM comprised 12 insurance companies, seven insurance brokerage companies and three insurance agencies.

QBE Makedonija: 1000 Skopje, 11 Oktomvri 25; tel. (2) 3115188; fax (2) 3114020; internet www.qbeeurope.com/makedonija; subsidiary of QBE Insurance Group (Australia); stock company for insurance and reinsurance; CEO FRANK O'HALLORAN.

Sava Tabak a.d. Skopje: 1000 Skopje, Zagreb 28A; tel. (2) 5101500; fax (2) 5101502; e-mail contact@sava.com.mk; internet www.sava .com.mk; fmrly Tabak Osiguravanje; 66.67% owned by Sava Re (Slovenia).

Trade and Industry

CHAMBER OF COMMERCE

Economic Chamber of Macedonia (Stopanska Komora na Makedonija): 1000 Skopje, Dimitrija Čupovski 13; tel. (2) 3244000; fax (2) 3244088; e-mail ic@ic.mchamber.org.mk; internet www.mchamber .org.mk; f. 1962; Pres. BRANKO AZESKI.

UTILITIES

Electricity

EVN Macedonia: 1000 Skopje, 11 Oktombri 9; tel. (2) 3205000; fax (2) 3227827; e-mail lenche.karpuzovska@evn.mk; internet www.evn .mk; production and distribution of electric power; 90% owned by EVN AG (Austria); fmrly Electric Power Co of Macedonia (Elektrostopanstovo na Makedonija); Chair. WERNER HENGST.

TRADE UNIONS

Federation of Trade Unions of Macedonia: 1000 Skopje; tel. (2) 3231374; fax (2) 3115787; 18 affiliated unions; Pres. VANCO MURATOVSKI.

Transport

RAILWAYS

In 2009 the rail network totalled 699 km, of which 233 km were electrified.

Makedonski Železnici (MZ) (Macedonian Railways): 1000 Skopje, Železnička 50; tel. (2) 3227903; fax (2) 3462330; e-mail muzunova@ mz.com.mk; internet www.mz.com.mk; f. 1992; Chair. KOSANA MAZNEVA; Dir-Gen. NIKOLA DIMITROVSKI.

ROADS

In 2010, the FYRM's road network totalled 13,934 km, of which 660 km were main roads.

CIVIL AVIATION

The FYRM has two international airports, at Ohrid, and the Aleksandar Veliki (Alexander the Great) Airport, near Skopje.

Tourism

Tourist arrivals numbered 327,000 in 2011, when receipts from tourism amounted to US $239m.

Tourist Association of Macedonia: 1000 Skopje, Makedonija 39; tel. (2) 3161348; e-mail tarm@mt.net.mk.

Defence

As assessed at November 2012, the armed forces of the FYRM totalled 8,000 in active service. Paramilitary forces comprised a police force of 7,600, of whom some 5,000 were armed. Conscription was abolished with effect from 2007.

Defence Expenditure: Budgeted at 6,180m. new denars in 2012.

Chief of Staff of the Army: Maj.-Gen. GORANCO KOTESKI.

Education

Elementary education is free and compulsory for all children between the ages of seven and 15. Various types of secondary school, beginning at 15 and lasting for four years, are available to those who qualify. In 2009/10 the primary education enrolment ratio included 88% of children in the relevant age-group, while the enrolment ratio in secondary education was equivalent to 84% of children in the relevant age-group. According to the terms of the Constitution, citizens are granted the right to elementary and secondary education in their mother tongue. In 2011/12 some 293,817 students were enrolled in primary and secondary education. There are universities at Skopje, Bitola and Tetovo (the latter of which operates in Albanian). Expenditure on education by the central Government in 2002 was budgeted at 7,591m. new denars (11.4% of total expenditure).

MADAGASCAR

Introductory Survey

LOCATION, CLIMATE, LANGUAGE, RELIGION, FLAG, CAPITAL

The Republic of Madagascar comprises the island of Madagascar, the fourth largest in the world, and several much smaller offshore islands, in the western Indian Ocean, about 500 km (300 miles) east of Mozambique, in southern Africa. The inland climate is temperate; in Antananarivo temperatures are generally between 8°C (48°F) and 27°C (81°F), with cooler, dryer weather between May and October. The coastal region is tropical, with an average daily maximum temperature of 32°C (90°F). The rainy season extends from November to April in the highlands (average annual rainfall is 1,000 mm–1,500 mm) but is more prolonged on the coast, where average annual rainfall can reach 3,500 mm. The official languages are Malagasy and French. Hova and other dialects are also widely spoken. More than 50% of the population follow animist beliefs, while about 41% are Christians and the remainder are Muslims. The national flag (proportions 2 by 3) has a vertical white stripe (one-third of the length) at the hoist and two equal horizontal stripes, of red and green, in the fly. The capital is Antananarivo.

CONTEMPORARY POLITICAL HISTORY

Historical Context

A French possession since 1896, Madagascar became an autonomous state within the French Community in October 1958, as the Malagasy Republic. In May 1959 Philibert Tsiranana, leader of the Parti Social Démocrate (PSD), was elected President. The country achieved full independence on 26 June 1960. Prior to independence France supported the PSD, which was identified with the majority coastal tribes (*côtiers*), as an alternative to the more nationalistic highland people, the Merina, who were the traditional ruling group in the island.

After 1967 there was growing opposition to the Government's alleged authoritarianism and subservience to French interests. In May 1972, following civil unrest, President Tsiranana transferred full powers to the Army Chief of Staff, Gen. Gabriel Ramanantsoa. In October 1973 pro-Government parties secured a decisive victory in legislative elections. A prolonged crisis followed an attempted military coup in December 1974, and in early February 1975 Ramanantsoa transferred power to Col Richard Ratsimandrava, hitherto Minister of the Interior; however, Ratsimandrava was assassinated shortly afterwards. On 12 February Brig.-Gen. Gilles Andriamahazo assumed power and imposed martial law. All political parties were suspended. In June Andriamahazo was succeeded as Head of State by Lt-Commdr (later Adm.) Didier Ratsiraka, a *côtier* and a former Minister of Foreign Affairs, who became Chairman of the Conseil Supreme de la Révolution (CSR—Supreme Revolutionary Council).

In a referendum in December 1975 more than 94% of voters approved a new Constitution, which provided for radical administrative and agrarian reforms, and the appointment of Ratsiraka as President of the Republic for a term of seven years. The country's name was changed to the Democratic Republic of Madagascar, and a 'Second Republic' was proclaimed. In March 1976 the Avant-garde de la Révolution Malgache (AREMA—Antoky Ny Revolosiona Malagasy) was founded as the nucleus of the Front National pour la Défense de la Révolution Socialiste Malgache (FNDR), the only political organization permitted by the Constitution. Ratsiraka was re-elected to the presidency in 1982 and 1989.

Domestic Political Affairs

In August 1989 Ratsiraka assented to opposition demands for discussions about the future role and structure of the FNDR. In December the Assemblée nationale populaire adopted a constitutional amendment abolishing the requirement for political parties to be members of the FNDR (thereby effectively dissolving the FNDR), despite opposition from the Mouvement pour le Progrès de Madagascar (Mpitolona ho amin'ny Fandrosoan'ny Madagasikara—MFM) deputies.

In March 1990 the Government formally permitted the resumption of multi-party politics. Numerous new organizations emerged, while other parties that had hitherto operated within the FNDR became official opposition movements. Several pro-Government political associations joined AREMA to form a new coalition, the Mouvement Militant pour le Socialisme Malgasy (MMSM). The principal opposition movements included the Union Nationale pour le Développement et la Démocratie (UNDD) and MFM. An informal alliance, the Comité des Forces Vives—subsequently known as Forces Vives (FV, Hery Velona)—was formed by 16 opposition factions and other groups.

In May 1991 legislation providing for extensive constitutional amendments was submitted to the Assemblée nationale populaire. Opposition parties criticized the proposals, on the grounds that the revised Constitution would retain references to socialism. In June opposition leaders applied to the Haute Cour Constitutionnelle (HCC—High Constitutional Court) to effect Ratsiraka's removal from office, while the FV organized demonstrations to demand the resignation of the President and the convening of a constitutional conference. Later in June the FV formed a 'parallel' administration, which it termed the 'Provisional Government'.

In July 1991 the FV began a general strike in support of its demands for constitutional reform. The FV appointed Jean Rakotoharison, a retired army general, as President of the 'Provisional Government', and Albert Zafy, the leader of the UNDD, as its Prime Minister. However, Manandafy Rakotonirina, the leader of the MFM, rejected the formation of the 'Provisional Government', favouring further negotiations, and withdrew his party from the FV. Members of the 'Provisional Government' subsequently occupied the premises of six official government ministries. Later in July Ratsiraka ordered the detention of several members of the 'Provisional Government' and imposed a state of emergency in Antananarivo. The FV withdrew from negotiations with the MMSM, in protest against the arrests. In response to increasing public pressure, Ratsiraka dissolved the Council of Ministers and pledged to organize a constitutional referendum before the end of 1991. Members of the 'Provisional Government' were released from custody, and Ratsiraka repealed legislation that authorized the detention of opponents of the Government.

In August 1991 Ratsiraka appointed Guy Razanamasy, the mayor of Antananarivo, as Prime Minister. Later that month Ratsiraka declared Madagascar to be a federation of six states, with himself as President, and claimed to command the support of five provinces where AREMA continued to hold the majority of seats in regional councils. At the end of August Razanamasy formed an interim Government, which did not include any members of the FV or the MFM.

In October 1991 representatives of the Government, the FV, the MFM, church leaders and the armed forces signed an agreement providing for the suspension of the Constitution and the creation of a transitional Government. The CSR and the Assemblée nationale populaire were to be replaced by interim bodies. Ratsiraka was to remain as President of the Republic and Razanamasy as Prime Minister. Zafy was designated President of the High State Authority, while Rakotonirina and Pastor Richard Andriamanjato were appointed as joint Presidents of a 131-member National Committee for Economic and Social Regeneration. The power to appoint or to dismiss government ministers was granted to Razanamasy. A new constitution was to be submitted to a national referendum. Zafy subsequently rejected the agreement, on the grounds that Ratsiraka was to retain the nominal post of Commander-in-Chief of the Armed Forces. In November Razanamasy formed a new interim Government, which included three representatives of the MFM and one MMSM member. Owing to Zafy's refusal to participate in the Government, 10 portfolios that had been allocated to the FV remained vacant. Later in November, however, Zafy agreed to accept the presidency of the High State Authority.

In December 1991 Razanamasy announced that the formation of the coalition Government had proved unsuccessful, and 11 ministers resigned. Razanamasy appointed a larger Government of national consensus, in which 14 (of 36) portfolios were allocated to the FV. In January 1992 it was announced that all political factions had now accepted the terms of the October 1991 agreement; the constitutional referendum was scheduled for mid-1992, and local, presidential and legislative elections were to take place by the end of the year. In February the High State Authority for Transition to the Third Republic announced the dissolution of the CSR and the Assemblée nationale populaire, in accordance with the agreement.

Establishment of the Third Republic

The draft constitution of the Third Republic, as submitted to the Government in April 1992, envisaged a unitary state and provided for a bicameral legislature, comprising a Sénat and an Assemblée nationale. Two-thirds of the members of the Sénat were to be selected by an electoral college, with the remaining one-third to be appointed by the President, while the 184-member Assemblée nationale was to be directly elected for a four-year term. The authority of the President was to be reduced, and executive power vested in the Prime Minister, who was to be appointed by the Assemblée nationale.

The new Constitution was approved by 72.2% of votes cast in a national referendum in August 1992. At the presidential election, held in November, Zafy secured 45.1% of votes cast, while Ratsiraka took 29.2%. A second round of voting took place in February 1993, when Zafy won 66.7% of the votes. Zafy's inauguration the following month was accompanied by violent clashes between security forces and federalists in the north. In accordance with the Constitution, Zafy resigned as President of the UNDD at a party congress in May; Emmanuel Rakotovahiny, the Minister of State for Agriculture and Rural Development, was elected as his successor.

Several constituent parties of the FV subsequently presented independent lists of candidates for the forthcoming legislative elections, while the remaining parties in the alliance became known as Forces Vives Rasalama (Hery Velona Rasalama—HVR). The elections, to a reduced 138-member Assemblée nationale, took place on 16 June 1993; the HVR secured 46 seats, the MFM 15, and a new alliance of pro-Ratsiraka parties 11 seats. The official results indicated that parties supporting Zafy had won 75 seats in the new Assemblée nationale. In August Francisque Ravony was elected Prime Minister and formed a new Council of Ministers. Richard Andriamanjato was elected President of the Assemblée nationale.

In mid-1995 Zafy announced that he was unable to co-operate with Ravony and decreed that a constitutional amendment empowering the President, rather than the Assemblée nationale, to select the Prime Minister be submitted for approval in a national referendum. Ravony indicated that he would resign after the referendum, regardless of the outcome. The referendum proceeded in September, at which the constitutional amendment was approved by 63.6% of votes cast. Ravony duly resigned in October, and Zafy appointed Rakotovahiny as Prime Minister. However, dissension emerged between the parties that supported Zafy over the composition of the new Council of Ministers. In May 1996 a motion of censure against Rakotovahiny's Government was approved by a large majority in the Assemblée nationale. Rakotovahiny submitted his administration's resignation, and Norbert Ratsirahonana, hitherto President of the HCC, was appointed Prime Minister.

Zafy refused to approve the new Government initially proposed by Ratsirahonana, insisting on the inclusion of five UNDD members who had served in the previous Council of Ministers. Ratsirahonana, however, won a vote of confidence in the legislature in July 1996, by associating the vote with legislation providing for the implementation of economic reforms stipulated by the IMF and the World Bank. On 26 July a motion in the Assemblée nationale to remove Zafy from office for numerous contraventions of the Constitution was supported by 99 of 131 votes cast. The HCC endorsed the President's impeachment in September, upholding the majority of the charges against him; Zafy maintained that his impeachment was illegal, but resigned the same day. Ratsirahonana was appointed interim President by the HCC, pending an election; he formed a new interim Government that represented the majority in the Assemblée nationale and excluded members of the UNDD. Zafy announced his intention to contest the forthcoming election to the presidency, as did Ratsiraka and Ratsirahonana.

Fifteen candidates contested the first round of the presidential election on 3 November 1996; Ratsiraka (with 36.6% of the votes cast) and Zafy (with 23.4%) proceeded to a second round. The head of Libéralisme Économique et Action Démocratique pour la Reconstruction Nationale (LEADER/Fanilo), Herizo Razafimahaleo, obtained 15.1%, and Ratsirahonana 10.1%, of the votes. At the second round, which took place on 29 December, Ratsiraka narrowly won, with 50.7% of the valid votes cast, although more than 50% of the registered electorate abstained from voting. Ratsiraka was inaugurated as President on 9 February 1997. He appointed Pascal Rakotomavo (a former Minister of Finance) as Prime Minister. Rakotomavo's Government included Razafimahaleo as Deputy Prime Minister, responsible for Foreign Affairs.

In March 1998 extensive revisions to the Constitution, which provided for a 'federal-style' state, composed of six autonomous provinces, and for an increase in the powers of the President, were narrowly endorsed by 51.0% of votes cast at a referendum. Elections to an expanded Assemblée nationale took place in May, under a new electoral law. Of the 150 seats, 82 were to be filled from single-member constituencies, with the remaining deputies to be elected by a system of proportional representation. Ratsiraka's party, AREMA, performed well in the elections, winning 63 seats, while the pro-presidential LEADER/Fanilo and the Rassemblement pour le Socialisme et la Démocratie (RPSD) secured 16 and 11 seats, respectively. Ratsirahonana's party, Ny asa vita no ifampitsara (AVI), emerged as the strongest opposition party, with 14 seats, while Zafy's new party—Asa, Faharaminana, Fampandrasoana, Arinda (AFFA)—won six seats; independent candidates took 32 seats. The AVI and 24 independent deputies were subsequently reported to have joined the AREMA majority, leaving the AFFA and the remaining independents as the only significant parliamentary opposition. In July Tantely Andrianarivo, hitherto Deputy Prime Minister, was appointed as Prime Minister, retaining responsibility for finance and the economy. The 31-member Council of Ministers was dominated by AREMA, with the key portfolios largely unchanged; 12 new ministers were appointed.

The first local government elections—communal voting for 20,000 councillors and 1,392 mayors—since the reintroduction of the three-tier system of local government (provinces, regions and communes), under the amended Constitution of 1998, took place on 14 November 1999. The greatest successes were recorded by nominally independent candidates. Most notably, Marc Ravalomanana, the head of the country's largest agro-industrial processor, Tiko, was elected mayor of Antananarivo.

Disputed presidential election

A presidential election took place on 16 December 2001, contested by six candidates, including Ratsiraka, Zafy, Razafimahaleo and Ravalomanana. According to the official results, Ravalomanana secured 46.2% of the votes cast and Didier Ratsiraka 40.9%, thereby necessitating a second round of voting. However, Ravalomanana's own electoral observers disputed this result, claiming that he had won an outright victory, with 52.2% of the votes, and demanded a public comparison of voting records. The opposition was supported in these demands by international electoral observers. A recount was subsequently conducted, and on 25 January 2002 the HCC endorsed the official results and ruled that a second round of voting should take place within 30 days. Ravalomanana rejected this verdict and appealed for a national strike in protest. Some 500,000 people responded by gathering in Antananarivo, and public sector services were suspended. Strike action continued, in varying forms, for eight weeks.

On 22 February 2002 Ravalomanana unilaterally declared himself President at a ceremony in Antananarivo attended by 100,000 supporters. The President of the Sénat immediately declared Ravalomanana's proclamation to be illegal, and it was widely condemned by the international community. In response, President Ratsiraka declared a three-month 'state of national necessity', according himself broad powers, including the right to adopt laws by decree. On 26 February Ravalomanana named Jacques Sylla, a former Minister of Foreign Affairs under Zafy's presidency, as his Prime Minister. Violent clashes erupted between supporters of Ratsiraka and Ravalomanana in Antananarivo, prompting Ratsiraka to decree martial law and appoint a military governor, Gen. Léon-Claude Raveloarison, in the capital. None the less, Ravalomanana proceeded with the formation of his rival Government in early March, while opposition supporters erected barricades against the army and set fire to the military headquarters; 17 of those appointed to Ravalomanana's administration were successfully installed in government offices, accompanied by large crowds of supporters and unopposed by the military. A few days later Gen. Marcel Ranjeva resigned as Minister of the Armed Forces, shortly after

Ravalomanana's rival Government had taken control of his offices in Antananarivo. Gen. Raveloarison resigned as military governor of Antananarivo some three weeks after his appointment, having failed to apply martial law and order troops to end protests, on the grounds that this would have incurred deaths. Later in March 58 of Madagascar's 150 deputies attended a parliamentary session called by Ravalomanana and elected an interim President of the Assemblée nationale.

On 10 April 2002 the Supreme Court ruled that there had been irregularities in the appointment, shortly before the presidential election, of six of the nine judges of the HCC, which had endorsed the official results; one week later the Supreme Court annulled the disputed results and ordered a recount of the votes. On the following day Ratsiraka and Ravalomanana signed a peace accord in Dakar, Senegal, where negotiations had been conducted under the auspices of the Organization of African Unity (OAU) and the UN. Following the completion of the recount, in late April, the HCC ruled that Ravalomanana had secured the presidency, with 51.5% of the votes cast, while Ratsiraka had won 35.9%. Ratsiraka refused to accept the Court's decision. Nevertheless, Ravalomanana was inaugurated as President on 6 May, largely without international recognition, and appointed a new Council of Ministers later that month. Four of the country's six provincial governors, who were loyal to Ratsiraka, subsequently threatened to secede. Heavy fighting ensued, as troops loyal to Ravalomanana conducted a military offensive against areas controlled by Ratsiraka.

Ravalomanana's presidency

In mid-June 2002 Ravalomanana dissolved the Government that he had formed in May, immediately reappointing Sylla as Prime Minister; however, despite nominating six new ministers, he failed to appoint a government of national unity. At the end of June the USA recognized Ravalomanana as the legitimate leader of Madagascar; endorsement soon followed from France and, in contravention of the policy of the OAU, Senegal. Meanwhile, the OAU suspended Madagascar from its meetings, pending the staging of free and fair elections leading to the establishment of a legitimate government; this decision was upheld by the African Union (AU, see p. 191), which replaced the OAU in July. In early July Ravalomanana's government troops took control of Antsiranana and Toamasina, and Ratsiraka sought exile in France. The new authorities had gained full control of the island by mid-July. Ravalomanana replaced the 30 presidentially-appointed members of the Sénat, with the approval of the HCC. In August six of the nine members of the HCC were also replaced.

In mid-October 2002 the Assemblée nationale was dissolved in preparation for legislative elections, brought forward from May 2003, in response to pressure from aid donors, in order to finalize the legitimacy of Ravalomanana's mandate. At the elections, which took place on 15 December 2002, Ravalomanana's party, Tiako i Madagasikara (TIM—I Love Madagascar), won 104 of the 160 seats and the pro-Ravalomanana Firaisankinam-Pirenena, an alliance of the AVI and elements of the RPSD, secured a further 22 seats; notably, 23 independent deputies were elected, and the formerly incumbent AREMA party won only three seats. A new Government, appointed in January 2003, included 10 new ministers and was reduced in overall size from 30 to 20 ministers. Madagascar's suspension from meetings of the AU was formally revoked at the organization's General Assembly in July of that year; the legitimacy of the Ravalomanana administration was thus considered finally to have been established. In August former President Ratsiraka was sentenced, *in absentia*, to 10 years' hard labour for the embezzlement of public funds and declared unfit for public office.

A presidential election was held on 3 December 2006. According to results released by the HCC on 23 December, Ravalomanana secured 54.8% of votes cast in the first-round ballot. His closest rival was Jean Lahiniriko, who took 11.7% of the votes. The poll was generally accepted by independent observers as free and fair. President Ravalomanana was formally sworn in for a second term in office on 19 January 2007 and the following day he appointed Lt-Gen. Charles Rabemananjara, hitherto Minister of the Interior and Administrative Reform, as Prime Minister. A new Government was announced later that month, including, most notably, Harison Edmond Randriarimanana, who was appointed to head the newly created Ministry of the Economy, Planning, the Private Sector and Commerce.

At a national referendum conducted on 4 April 2007 75.3% of participants voted in favour of amendments to the Constitution, which included the abolition of autonomous powers for the six provinces. Voter turn-out was reported at just 44%. The new Constitution also adopted English as the country's third official language alongside Malagasy and French and granted extended powers to the President, including the right to legislate by decree in the event of the declaration of a state of emergency.

President Ravalomanana dissolved the Assemblée nationale on 24 July 2007, claiming that its composition was no longer representative of the recently restructured regional and national administrative order. Elections to the 127-seat legislature (reduced from 160) were held on 23 September, in which the TIM secured 105 seats while independent candidates won 11. However, results in two constituencies were annulled owing to alleged voting irregularities. In October, in a governmental reorganization, Cécile Manorohanta was appointed Minister of National Defence, while Haja Nirina Razafinjatovo became Minister of Finance and the Budget. In January 2009 Desiré Rasolofomanana was appointed Minister of Internal Security and Gervais Rakotonirina Minister of the Interior.

The Haute Autorité de la Transition

Relations between President Ravalomanana and the Mayor of Antananarivo and leader of the Tanora malaGasy Vonona (TGV—Determined Malagasy Youth), Andry Rajoelina, had become strained in December 2008 when Ravalomanana closed Rajoelina's television station after it broadcast a number of anti-Government programmes and an interview with former President Ratsiraka. Against a background of increasing social discontent in the country, this prompted violent protests by several thousand of Rajoelina's supporters who attacked state-owned television and radio stations and began looting businesses. A political impasse developed, with Rajoelina, speaking at an opposition rally in late January 2009, accusing the President of failing in his duties and insisting that he resign. Violence continued to escalate and sizeable areas of the capital were destroyed by fire, resulting in at least 44 deaths. Ravalomanana appealed for Rajoelina's co-operation in order to stabilize the situation; however, in early February Rajoelina, who had been gaining popular support, was dismissed from the mayoralty and replaced by Guy Randrianarisoa, resulting in days of further violent disturbances: some 28 people were killed and more than 200 injured when the security forces fired on demonstrators. Days later the Minister of Defence, Manorohanta, announced her resignation in protest at the actions of the security forces; she was replaced by Vice-Adm. Mamy Ranaivoniarivo. Meanwhile, Rajoelina declared himself President of a Haute Autorité de la Transition (HAT—High Transitional Authority) and named, among others, Monja Roindefo as Prime Minister and Manantsoa Masimana as Minister of the Interior. The parallel administration was not recognized by the international community but received widespread internal popular support. Nevertheless, the security forces removed a number of Rajoelina's supporters who had attempted to seize four government buildings.

Ravalomanana and Rajoelina held a series of discussions with the aim of finding a resolution to the crisis; however, in February 2009 Rajoelina announced that the talks had failed and urged his supporters to hold daily protests until Ravalomanana agreed to step down. Pressure continued to increase on Ravalomanana and, following a military assault on the presidential residence and the central bank on 16 March and demands from Rajoelina that the President be arrested, he dissolved the Government and resigned, relinquishing power to a military executive committee led by the most senior figure in the armed forces, Vice-Adm. Hyppolite Ramaroson. Later that day the military transferred executive powers to Rajoelina, despite the terms of the Constitution stipulating that the President should be aged 40 years or above; Rajoelina, at 34 years of age, was too young to fulfil this requirement. Although international organizations refused to acknowledge Rajoelina's authority, and what was perceived as a coup received widespread international condemnation, on 18 March the HCC endorsed Rajoelina's assumption of interim power (he was officially sworn in as President on 21 March), and on 19 March he dissolved the Assemblée nationale and the Sénat. Rajoelina announced that elections would be held within two years and that a new constitution would be drafted. Both the AU and the Southern African Development Community (SADC) subsequently suspended Madagascar's membership pending a return to constitutional order.

In late March 2009 Rajoelina appointed a 22-member Government, retaining those ministers named in February; other appointments included Col Noël Rakotonandrasana as Minister of the Armed Forces, Benja Joas Razafimahaleo as Minister of Finance and the Budget and Ny Hasina Andriamanjato as

Minister of Foreign Affairs. In mid-April Ravalomanana, who had fled to exile in South Africa, named Rakotonirina as his own 'legal' Prime Minister in an attempt to regain his authority and, despite the issuing of a warrant for his arrest, pledged to return to Madagascar. Later in April Rakotonirina was arrested in Antananarivo and charged with threatening the security of the state, illegitimately declaring himself Prime Minister, instigating the destruction of property and the illegal possession of firearms. In early June Ravalomanana was sentenced *in absentia* to four years in prison and fined US $70m.

A summit meeting, mediated by the UN, the AU, SADC and the Organisation Internationale de la Francophonie, was held in Maputo, Mozambique, on 5–9 August 2009. The discussions resulted in agreement between Ravalomanana, Ratsiraka, Zafy and Rajoelina on a Transitional Charter (Charte de la Transition) which was to remain in place for a maximum duration of 15 months, pending presidential and legislative elections. The Charter provided for the establishment of a bicameral transitional legislature, and a National Union Government of Transition (NUGT). The Prime Minister of the NUGT was to be selected by consensus and officially appointed by Rajoelina, who, in his capacity as President of the Transition, would exercise the functions of Head of State. A new constitution was to be drafted, thus bringing an end to the Third Republic.

However, on 5 September 2009 Rajoelina unilaterally, and in contravention of the Maputo accord, named Roindefo as Prime Minister; he subsequently announced the composition of the NUGT. Both decisions were rejected and condemned by the three former Presidents, who declared their determination to implement a power-sharing deal and that they no longer recognized the authority of Rajoelina. Protests in Antananarivo were violently dispersed by the security forces, and several international organizations, including the AU and SADC, expressed their discontent at the violation of the Maputo power-sharing agreement. Negotiations recommenced and the following month Eugène Régis Mangalaza was chosen by consensus as Prime Minister, although further division ensued as a result of an increase in the powers granted to the premiership under the new accord.

By November 2009, following further negotiations in Addis Ababa, Ethiopia, a tentative power-sharing agreement (which was to supplement the Maputo accord) had been reached, under which executive decisions were to be undertaken jointly by the President and two Vice-Presidents. The agreement also endorsed the formation of a 31-member government headed by a Prime Minister. In early December Ravalomanana, Ratsiraka and Zafy proceeded with further negotiations in Maputo regarding the composition of the proposed transitional administration; however, Rajoelina stated that he would no longer participate in power-sharing negotiations, and refused permission for aircraft carrying the three men and their delegations to land in Madagascar. On 18 December Mangalaza was dismissed by Rajoelina, after which Col (later Gen.) Albert Camille Vital was installed as Prime Minister.

Despite dissatisfaction among international organizations and his domestic political rivals, Rajoelina continued to reject external mediation attempts and any proposals for a power-sharing government, insisting instead on holding legislative elections in March 2010. However, following a request by the AU and subsequent pressure from the UN, which urged continued dialogue on the establishment of a power-sharing government, Rajoelina agreed to postpone the elections, initially until May. In February Andriamanjato, the Deputy Prime Minister, responsible for Foreign Affairs, resigned, citing increasing dissension within the NUGT. Shortly afterwards the AU announced that it would impose sanctions on Madagascar if the resolutions of the Maputo and Addis Ababa power-sharing agreements were not implemented by mid-March. Ramaroson was appointed as Andriamanjato's replacement in late February.

The AU's attempts to persuade Rajoelina to attend further negotiations in Addis Ababa in early March 2010 were unsuccessful, and in mid-March the AU duly imposed sanctions, including the freezing of assets and diplomatic isolation, on 109 individuals, including all members of the NUGT and the HAT. In response, Rajoelina announced that the HAT would seek to charge Ravalomanana with 'corruption, threatening state security and plotting high treason with foreign factions'. Furthermore, Ratsiraka and Zafy would be barred from returning to Madagascar, while members of the three former Presidents'

political parties would be prevented from leaving the country and their assets would be frozen.

Vital dismissed Rakotonandrasana from his position as Minister of the Armed Forces in early April 2010, amid rumours of plans to stage a coup. (Some 19 people, including a number of army officers, were subsequently detained by the authorities.) Later in April senior military officials presented Rajoelina with an ultimatum to find a suitable solution to the country's political crisis by the end of the month. Shortly afterwards Rajoelina pledged to appoint a new unity government and indicated his willingness to engage in further talks with Ravalomanana. Discussions between the two, who were also joined by Zafy and Ratsiraka, commenced in late April in Pretoria, South Africa, but ended inconclusively after two days. On 7 May the army retracted its ultimatum, and on 12 May Rajoelina announced that a presidential election would be held on 30 November, following a referendum on constitutional reform on 26 August and legislative elections on 30 September. On 25 May Rajoelina formed a new, 32-member Government; however, the neutrality of the administration (which included five new members of the military) was immediately questioned by senior opposition figures. Meanwhile, on 20 May several people were killed in a confrontation between dissident elements of the gendarmerie (with the support of several hundred anti-Government protesters) and forces loyal to Rajoelina, who accused Ravalomanana of instigating the unrest.

Constitutional referendum

In June 2010 the head of the Commission Électorale Nationale Indépendante (CENI) announced that the referendum would be postponed, since the draft constitution had not been finalized. On 11 August, following consultations with political parties, the Government signed an agreement rescheduling the constitutional referendum for 17 November 2010 and legislative elections for 16 March 2011, to be followed by the first round of a presidential election on 4 May; under the new accord, Rajoelina would continue to hold office as head of the HAT until the inauguration of the next president, while the HAT was to be reconstituted as a transitional parliament. (However, the agreement failed to address several outstanding issues of contention and the political movements of the three former Presidents, Ravalomanana, Ratsiraka and Zafy, which failed to participate in the discussions, denounced what they considered to be the imposition of another unilateral solution.) At the end of August Ravalomanana was sentenced *in absentia* to life imprisonment for the killing of at least 30 people by his presidential guards in the violence of February 2009. In September 2010 the Government organized a conference of representatives of political parties and civil society, which was to resolve issues related to the implementation of the August agreement; delegates endorsed a proposal that Rajoelina remain as Head of State but appoint a consensus prime minister who was not from his native region, and also supported the replacement of mayors and regional authorities by provisional bodies. On 7 October the HCC approved a decree by Rajoelina establishing a Parlement de la Transition. Accordingly, on 11 October a 256-member lower parliamentary chamber, the Congrès de la Transition, was installed, with representation assigned according to the arrangement established in the accord reached in August: notably, a gathering of all the political parties and associations that participated in the drafting of the agreement, known as l'Espace de Concertation des Partis Politiques (ESCOPOL), was allocated 62 seats, the TIM 52, the TGV 52 and a grouping of parties supporting Rajoelina, the Union des Démocrates et Républicains—Fanovana (UDR—Fanovana) 29. On 12 October a 90-member upper chamber, the Conseil Supérieur de la Transition, took office; the deputies included 25 representatives of the UDR—Fanovana, 21 of the TIM, 18 of ESCOPOL and 10 of the TGV.

A draft constitution, which included requirements that presidential candidates be at least 35 years of age (rather than the previous minimum of 40 years) and have lived in Madagascar for at least six months prior to the elections, was submitted to the delayed national referendum on 17 November 2010. On the same day some 20 disaffected senior army officers, led by Rakotonandrasana, staged a coup attempt, announcing from a military barracks near Antananarivo that the Government had been overthrown. However, prominent members of the Government and military announced their support for Rajoelina, and on 21 November troops loyal to the HAT stormed the barracks, arresting a number of the officers for threatening state security. Later that month it was announced that a former International

Court of Justice judge, Raymond Ranjeva, had also been detained, owing to his alleged connections with the rebels. Two days after the referendum, the CENI released official results, according to which the new Constitution had been endorsed by about 74.2% of votes cast, with a voter turn-out of 52.6% (after the opposition urged a boycott). On 23 November the HCC upheld the results of the referendum, despite opposition complaints of electoral irregularities. The new Constitution of the Fourth Republic of Madagascar entered into effect on 11 December. In January 2011 Ravalomanana submitted a legal complaint to the judicial authorities against the instigators of the effective coup in March 2009.

On 9 March 2011 a new transitional programme proposed by the SADC mediators was signed by eight of the 11 principal political groups, but rejected by the parties of Ravalomanana, Ratsiraka and Zafy, which strenuously opposed the legitimacy conferred on Rajoelina's presidency. Under the new plan, Rajoelina was permitted to remain in office pending elections, and to appoint a consensus Prime Minister proposed by the signatory groups. On the following day the Government of Prime Minister Vital resigned; however, on 16 March Rajoelina reappointed Vital as premier, despite the objections of the three main opposition parties that he failed to meet the consensus criteria of the agreement. On 26 March a new, 32-member administration, termed the Government of National Unity, was established under the transitional programme; nine former government members retained their posts, although members of Ravalomanana's TIM were also included. However, a meeting of the main political parties, held at SADC headquarters in Botswana in June, failed to result in progress towards the organization of elections, while the HAT refused to permit the return of Ravalomanana to the country in the interests of reconciliation.

Following continued SADC mediation, on 17 September 2011 10 political groups (including those representing Ravalomanana and Zafy) signed a further agreement for a timetable to restore democratic rule: a new government of national unity would be installed by the end of November, while a presidential election was to be organized within one year. (Rajoelina was authorized to remain in office until that time.) Ravalomanana was to be allowed to return to the country under an amnesty for exiles in order to participate in the transitional process. Accordingly, Vital submitted the resignation of his Government on 17 October, and Rajoelina announced the appointment of a former ambassador to the European Union (EU), Jean Omer Beriziky of LEADER/Fanilo, as the new Prime Minister on 28 October. A new, 35-member Government was formed on 21 November; seven ministerial posts were allocated to supporters of Zafy and five to those of Ravalomanana. Representatives of Ravalomanana and Zafy initially disputed the legitimacy of the new administration, on the grounds that Beriziky's appointment as premier had not been made by consensus, thereby contravening the terms of the agreement. Following discussions with government officials, however, the supporters of the former Presidents declared that they had agreed to join the new Government of National Unity. Later in November Ratsiraka returned to Madagascar at the invitation of Rajoelina, after spending nine years in exile in France. In December the AU's Peace and Security Council announced that the organization would remove the sanctions in force against Madagascar, conditional on SADC confirmation of satisfactory progress in the implementation of the agreement (which, however, proved unforthcoming).

Recent developments: delays in the election process

In January 2012 an attempt by Ravalomanana to return to Madagascar from South Africa in accordance with the transitional agreement was thwarted, after Rajoelina ordered the closure of all major airports, prompting Ravalomanana's supporters to suspend participation in the transitional institutions. Following a subsequent meeting in Pretoria, SADC mediators urged that the terms of the reconciliation process, including the release of political prisoners and the return of exiles, be fulfilled by the end of February. In March a new CENI was established as part of the process towards the organization of elections. On 21 March 11 people, including Raymond Ranjeva and his daughter, were acquitted of complicity in the November 2010 coup attempt, while a senior officer was sentenced to life imprisonment *in absentia* and a further nine defendants received prison terms of between five and seven years. The amnesty law was finally adopted on 12 April 2012, but excluded those who had been found guilty of human rights abuses including those sentenced for murder, amongst them Ravalomanana. In May police violently suppressed an unauthorized protest in Antananarivo

in support of opposition radio station Radio Free FM, which had been staged after the station's director, Lalatiana Rakotondrazafy, and a journalist were detained for broadcasting material critical of Rajoelina. The Government announced in July that an army mutiny had been suppressed, following an operation to regain control of an airport about 10 km from Antananarivo. Radio Free FM was subsequently closed down voluntarily, owing to alleged intimidation by the armed forces. At the instigation of SADC, discussions between Rajoelina and Ravalomanana, mediated by South African President Jacob Zuma, took place in the Seychelles on 25 July; however, the President continued to reject SADC insistence on Ravalomanana's return to Madagascar. At the beginning of August the head of the CENI finally announced that the first round of a presidential election was to be conducted on 8 May 2013, and was to be followed by legislative elections on 3 July (when a possible second presidential round would also be conducted). Further discussions between Rajoelina and Ravalomanana were held in early August 2012, and later that month the proposed dates for the elections were confirmed at a SADC heads of state summit in Maputo. In September Rakotondrazafy, a journalist and another former employee of Radio Free FM were granted refuge in the South African embassy, after they complained of continued harassment by the authorities. (The three left the embassy in early October, and Rakotondrazafy pledged to reopen the station.)

Following Zuma's replacement as senior mediator by Tanzanian President Jakaya Kikwete, a further SADC summit meeting, held in early December 2012, resulted in a proposal that neither Rajoelina nor Ravalomanana would contest the forthcoming elections. Ravalomanana subsequently announced his agreement not to participate in the elections. On 20 December the Government declared a state of emergency in Antananarivo, due to an increasing number of armed attacks in the capital. Despite initial reluctance to comply with the SADC recommendations, in January 2013 President Rajoelina, ceding to international pressure, announced that he would not seek election later that year, but stated that he would contest the next polls in 2018. Later in January 2013 the UN urged the Malagasy Government to permit the return of Ravalomanana to the country. Following a conference in Addis Ababa, the AU declared that significant aspects of the transitional programme remained unimplemented, and expressed concerns at the lack of press and opposition freedoms. On 5 February the CENI announced that, owing to logistical difficulties, including the organization of voter registration, the first round of the presidential election was to be rescheduled to 24 July, with a possible second round and legislative elections on 25 September. Although the UN endorsed the postponement, Rajoelina criticized the extension of the transitional period.

In early May 2013 the Special Elections Court released the names of 41 candidates who had been approved to contest the presidential poll. Despite Rajoelina's earlier confirmation that he would not present himself as a candidate for the presidency, his name was included on the list. He maintained that the decision of Ravalomanana's wife, Lalao, to stand in the election had rendered the agreement concluded in January void. SADC subsequently urged Rajoelina, Ravalomanana and Ratsiraka (who had also featured on the list of approved candidates) to withdraw from the election.

Foreign Affairs

Madagascar's foreign policy is officially non-aligned: while it formerly maintained close links with communist countries (particularly the People's Republic of China, the Democratic People's Republic of Korea and the former USSR), the Zafy Government established relations with Israel, South Africa and the Republic of Korea. Relations with France have been affected by disputes over compensation for nationalized French assets and over the continuing French claim to the Iles Glorieuses, north of Madagascar, and three other islets in the Mozambique Channel. In 1980 the UN voted in favour of restoring all the disputed islets to Madagascar. In early 1986 the Government announced the extension of Madagascar's exclusive economic zone to include the Iles Glorieuses and the three islets. In 1997 government announcements regarding privatization plans in Madagascar prompted renewed appeals from France for compensation for nationalized French assets. In response, the Government allocated some 50,000m. francs MG as initial compensation in the budget for 1998. In February 2000 it was agreed that the Iles Glorieuses would be co-administered by France, Madagascar and Mauritius, without prejudice to the question of sovereignty. During the prolonged political crisis in Madagascar from 2009 the French Government expressed support for SADC's mediation efforts, and continued to provide emergency assistance to the country, including after the impact of severe cyclones in early 2012.

Relations with China were strengthened in January 1999, during a visit by Vice-President Hu Jintao; agreements were signed on the expansion of bilateral economic relations and China's provision of preferential loans to Madagascar. In September 2000 the representative office for Taiwan in Madagascar was closed down, following an official visit by the Malagasy Minister of Foreign Affairs to China. (It was widely believed that this was carried out by the Government in support of the 'one China' policy.) Following the suspension of US and EU donor assistance programmes in Madagascar in response to Andry Rajoelina's assumption of the presidency in March 2009, the transitional Government announced a number of major infrastructure projects in late 2010 that were to be undertaken in collaboration with Chinese companies.

CONSTITUTION AND GOVERNMENT

Under an August 2010 agreement between the Government and about 100 political parties, a Parlement de la Transition, comprising a 256-member lower chamber, the Congrès de la Transition, and a 90-member upper chamber, the Conseil Supérieur de la Transition, was installed in October and was to remain in place pending legislative elections. On 17 November 2010 the Constitution of the Fourth Republic of Madagascar was approved at a national referendum by some 74% of the participating electorate. The President of the Republic is the Head of State and is elected by direct universal suffrage for a five-year mandate, renewable only once. Candidates for the presidency must be at least 35 years of age and have resided in Madagascar for at least six months prior to the date of the submission of candidacies. The President nominates a Prime Minister from the party or group of parties which secures the largest number of seats in the Assemblée nationale. The President also nominates members of the Government, upon the advice of the Prime Minister. Members of the Assemblée nationale are elected by direct universal suffrage for five-year terms. The Constitution also provides for the election of members to the Sénat, each of whom serves a five-year mandate.

REGIONAL AND INTERNATIONAL CO-OPERATION

Madagascar is a member of the Indian Ocean Commission (see p. 462) and of the Common Market for Eastern and Southern Africa (COMESA, see p. 241). In August 2005 Madagascar joined the Southern African Development Community (SADC, see p. 434), although its membership of that organization and of the African Union (see p. 191) was suspended in 2009.

Madagascar became a member of the UN in 1960 and was admitted to the World Trade Organization (WTO, see p. 444) in 1995. Madagascar participates in the Group of 77 (G77, see p. 461) developing countries.

ECONOMIC AFFAIRS

In 2011, according to estimates by the World Bank, Madagascar's gross national income (GNI), measured at average 2009–11 prices, was US $9,070m., equivalent to about $430 per head (or $950 per head on an international purchasing-power parity basis). During 2002–11, it was estimated, the population increased at an average annual rate of 3.0%, while gross domestic product (GDP) per head increased, in real terms, by an average of 0.9% per year. Overall GDP increased, in real terms, at an average annual rate of 3.9% in 2002–11; GDP grew by 1.0% in 2011.

In 2010 the agricultural sector (including forestry and fishing) accounted for an estimated 27.6% of GDP, according to the African Development Bank (AfDB); the sector employed an estimated 81.0% of the economically active population in 2005 and, according to FAO, engaged 68.6% of the total labour force in mid-2013. Rice, the staple food crop, is produced on some 50% of cultivated land. Since 1972, however, imports of rice have been necessary to supplement domestic production. The most important cash crops are spices (which accounted for an estimated 9.0% of total export revenue in 2009, but declined to 5.2% in 2010). Following a long drought in 2003, vanilla production was estimated to have halved in that year, leading to a dramatic escalation in world prices and the development of the crop in other countries, as well as an increase in synthetic alternatives; however, prices had declined significantly at the beginning of 2005, having a negative impact on producers. Sugar, coconuts, tropical fruits, sweet potatoes and maize are also cultivated. Cattle-farming is important. Sea fishing by coastal fishermen (particularly for crustaceans) is being expanded, while vessels from the European Union (EU) fish for tuna and prawns in Madagascar's exclusive maritime zone, within 200 nautical miles (370 km) of the coast, in return for compensation. According to UN figures, agricultural GDP increased by an average of 2.1% per year in 2002–11; the sector's GDP declined by 3.4% in 2010 and further by 0.1% in 2011.

Industry (including mining, manufacturing, construction and power) contributed an estimated 19.6% of Madagascar's GDP in 2010, according to the AfDB, and employed 3.4% of the employed labour force in 2005. According to UN figures, industrial GDP increased at an average annual rate of 4.7% in 2002–11; the sector's GDP rose by 2.4% in 2011.

The mining sector contributed only 0.2% of GDP in 2010, according to the AfDB, and engaged 0.2% of the employed labour force in 2005. However, Madagascar has sizeable deposits of a wide range of minerals, principally chromite (chromium ore), which, with graphite and mica, is exported, together with small quantities of semi-precious stones. A major project to resume the mining of ilmenite (titanium ore) in south-eastern Madagascar, which would generate some US $550m. over a 30-year period, received approval from the Government in 2001. Construction of the mining facilities and rehabilitation of a deep-sea multipurpose port at Ehoala, near Fort Dauphin (Tolagnaro), was completed in early 2009. The facility began ilmenite production operations in January, and produced 287,000 metric tons in 2010. Other potential mineral projects included the exploitation of an estimated 100m. tons of bauxite in the south-east of the country, and of nickel and cobalt deposits in Ambatovy, central Madagascar. The presence of significant grades of the platinum group of metals was confirmed, as well as copper and nickel, in 2004. A large nickel-mining project at Ambatovy began production in 2012, with annual output expected eventually to reach 60,000 tons of nickel, 5,600 tons of cobalt and 210,000 tons of ammonium sulphate fertilizer. The multinational project was expected to provide employment for some 6,000 workers. In early 2008 a pilot project in the north-west produced the first petroleum in the country for some 60 years, improving Madagascar's prospects for generating export revenue. According to UN figures, real GDP of the mining sector together with utilities increased by an average of 5.4% per year in 2002–11; the sector's GDP rose by 23.6% in 2010, but decreased by 5.2% in 2011.

According to the AfDB, manufacturing contributed 14.3% of GDP in 2010, and engaged some 2.8% of the employed labour force in 2005. The petroleum refinery at Toamasina, using imported petroleum, provides a significant share of export revenue. Other important branches of manufacturing are textiles and clothing, food products, beverages and chemical products. According to UN figures, manufacturing GDP increased at an average annual rate of 3.6% in 2002–11; the GDP of the sector declined by 2.1% in 2010, but grew by 3.2% in 2011.

Construction contributed an estimated 3.8% of Madagascar's GDP in 2010, and employed 0.1% of the employed labour force in 2005. According to UN figures, real GDP of the construction sector increased by an average of 14.8% per year in 2002–11; the sector's GDP rose by 3.7% in 2011.

Energy generation depends on imports of petroleum (which accounted for an estimated 21.2% of the value of total imports in 2011) to fuel thermal installations. However, hydroelectric resources have also been majorly developed, and accounted for an estimated 62.0% of electricity production in 2008.

The services sector accounted for an estimated 52.8% of GDP in 2010, according to the AfDB, and engaged some 14.6% of the employed labour force in 2005. An information communication technologies business park was under development in Antananarivo as part of an effort to diversify Madagascar's economic growth. In March 2010 Madagascar was connected to the Eastern Africa Submarine Cable System, a high bandwidth fibre optic cable that links countries on Africa's eastern coast to the rest of the world, and would enable the transfer of data at speeds 40 times faster than the hitherto available dial-up connection. This was expected to allow the development of service outsourcing activities on the island. According to UN figures, the GDP of the services sector increased by an average of 3.6% per year in 2002–11; services GDP grew by 1.6% in 2010, but decreased by 0.9% in 2011.

In 2005 Madagascar recorded a visible merchandise trade deficit of US $592m. and there was a deficit of $626m. on the current account of the balance of payments; the trade deficit was estimated to have increased to $890m. in 2007. The principal source of imports in 2011 was France (accounting for 12.0% of total imports); other major suppliers were the People's Republic of China, South Africa and Mauritius. France was also the principal market for exports (accounting for 33.7% of exports in that year); China and Germany were other important purchasers. The principal exports in 2010 were clothing, crustaceans and spices; miscellaneous manufactures constituted 33.6% of the value of total exports. The principal imports in that year were machinery and transport equipment, basic manufactures, mineral fuels, food and live animals, chemicals and related products, and miscellaneous manufactures.

According to the AfDB, Madagascar's overall budget deficit for 2011 was estimated at 367,000m. ariary. Madagascar's general government gross debt was 11,758.7m. ariary in 2010, equivalent to 64.4% of GDP. Madagascar's external debt totalled US $2,295m. at the end of 2010, of which $1,981m. was public and publicly guaranteed debt. In that year, the cost of servicing long-term public and publicly guaranteed debt and repayments to the IMF was equivalent to 2.6% of the value of exports of goods, services and income (excluding workers' remittances). The annual rate of inflation averaged 9.7% in 2002–11; consumer prices increased by 9.5% in 2011. About 2.8% of the labour force was unemployed in 2005.

Economic activity in Madagascar was impeded by political instability during the 2000s, although, with the assistance of the IMF and the World Bank, the country made enough progress to facilitate the restructuring of the significant external debt by international creditors. The economy was severely affected by the suspension of Madagascar's participation in the Southern African Development Community (see p. 434) and the African Union (AU, see p. 191), and of economic co-operation with international financial institutions, following the removal of President Marc Ravalomanana in March 2009. In May the USA and the World Bank suspended Madagascar from the Millennium Challenge Corporation, while in December the former also suspended trade benefits granted to Madagascar under the African Growth and Opportunity Act. Following his assumption of the presidency, Andry Rajoelina froze all mining contracts and announced a review of the sector. In March 2010 the AU imposed sanctions against members of the transitional authorities as a result of their failure to implement power-sharing arrangements, and in June the EU suspended budgetary and development aid to Madagascar. Despite the negative impact of the political uncertainty on foreign investment, in late 2010 Rajoelina announced a number of significant infrastructure agreements, principally with China International Fund and China Sonangol. In September 2011 a new transitional agreement for the restoration of democratic government was signed by the main political groupings (see Domestic Political Affairs). During 2012, however, progress towards the organization of elections was subject to continued delays, and in January 2013 the AU criticized the authorities' failure to implement critical aspects of the transitional programme. Nevertheless, the EU announced the resumption of development aid to Madagascar in August 2012, with the adoption of a new programme totalling €54m. The budget for 2012 projected economic growth of only 2.0% (although this represented a slight rise compared with the previous year). In addition to the impact of the political unrest and concomitant sanctions, the continuing financial crisis in Europe adversely affected the country's exports and tourism industry. However, following the completion of the major Ambatovy mining project in the east of the country, it was anticipated that government revenue would benefit in subsequent years from exports of nickel and cobalt. In late 2012 the Government announced a budget plan for economic recovery, with an emphasis on renewable energy projects; however, this was dependent on the resumption of donor funding, which was also necessary to support the scheduled elections. In early 2013 lack of external funding and a deteriorating security situation in the south hampered operations to avert severe locust outbreaks which further threatened food supplies.

PUBLIC HOLIDAYS

2014: 1 January (New Year), 29 March (Martyr's Day, Commemoration of 1947 Rebellion), 21 April (Easter Monday), 1 May (Labour Day), 9 May (Ascension Day), 25 May (Organization of African Unity Day), 8 June (Whitsun), 26 June (Independence Day), 15 August (Assumption), 1 November (All Saints' Day), 25 December (Christmas).

Statistical Survey

Source (unless otherwise stated): Institut National de la Statistique de Madagascar, BP 485, Anosy Tana, 101 Antananarivo; tel. (20) 2227418; email dridnstat@wanadoo.mg; internet www.instat.mg; Ministry of the Economy and Industry, Bâtiment Commerce, Ambohidahy, 101 Antananarivo; internet www.mepspc.gov.mg.

Area and Population

AREA, POPULATION AND DENSITY

Area (sq km)	587,295*
Population (census results)	
1974–75†	7,603,790
1–19 August 1993	
Males	6,088,116
Females	6,150,798
Total	12,238,914
Population (UN estimates at mid-year)‡	
2011	21,315,136
2012	21,928,516
2013	22,555,045
Density (per sq km) at mid-2013	38.4

* 226,756 sq miles.

† The census took place in three stages: in provincial capitals on 1 December 1974; in Antananarivo and remaining urban areas on 17 February 1975; and in rural areas on 1 June 1975.

‡ Source: UN, *World Population Prospects: The 2010 Revision*.

POPULATION BY AGE AND SEX
(UN estimates at mid-2013)

	Males	Females	Total
0–14	4,770,836	4,707,059	9,477,895
15–64	6,145,810	6,223,045	12,368,855
65 and over	329,223	379,072	708,295
Total	**11,245,869**	**11,309,176**	**22,555,045**

Source: UN, *World Population Prospects: The 2010 Revision*.

PRINCIPAL ETHNIC GROUPS
(estimated population, 1974)

Merina (Hova) . .	1,993,000		Sakalava . . .	470,156*
Betsimisaraka . .	1,134,000		Antandroy . .	412,500
Betsileo . . .	920,600		Antaisaka . .	406,468*
Tsimihety . . .	558,100			

* 1972 figure.

PRINCIPAL TOWNS
(population at 1993 census)

Antananarivo (capital)	. .	1,103,304	Mahajanga (Majunga) . . .	106,780
Toamasina (Tamatave)	. .	137,782	Toliary (Tuléar) . .	80,826
Antsirabé	. . .	126,062	Antsiranana (Diégo-Suarez) . . .	59,040
Fianarantsoa	. .	109,248		

2001 (estimated population, incl. Renivohitra and Avaradrano): Antananarivo 1,111,392.

Mid-2011 (incl. suburbs, UN estimate): Antananarivo 1,986,710 (Source: UN, *World Urbanization prospects: The 2011 Revision*).

BIRTHS AND DEATHS

	2009	2010	2011
Birth rate (per 1,000)	35.6	35.3	35.0
Death rate (per 1,000)	6.6	6.5	6.4

Source: African Development Bank.

Life expectancy (years at birth): 66.7 (males 65.1; females 68.4) in 2011 (Source: World Bank, World Development Indicators database).

ECONOMICALLY ACTIVE POPULATION
(labour force survey, '000 persons)

	2005
Agriculture, hunting and forestry	7,745.3
Fishing	99.0
Mining and quarrying	18.8
Manufacturing	267.5
Electricity, gas and water	27.5
Construction	13.0
Wholesale and retail trade; repair of motor vehicles, motor cycles and personal and household goods	470.5
Hotels and restaurants	63.9
Transport, storage and communications	86.3
Financial intermediation	4.1
Public administration and defence; compulsory social security	202.4
Education	44.5
Health and social work	9.9
Other community, social and personal service activities . .	517.7
Total employed	**9,570.4**
Unemployed	274.3
Total labour force	**9,844.7**
Males	4,942.2
Females	4,902.4

Source: ILO.

Mid-2013 (estimates in '000): Agriculture, etc. 7,971; Total labour force 11,626 (Source: FAO).

Health and Welfare

KEY INDICATORS

Total fertility rate (children per woman, 2010)	4.7
Under-5 mortality rate (per 1,000 live births, 2010) . . .	62
HIV/AIDS (% of persons aged 15–49, 2009)	0.2
Physicians (per 1,000 head, 2007)	0.2
Hospital beds (per 1,000 head, 2005)	0.3
Health expenditure (2009): US $ per head (PPP) . . .	41
Health expenditure (2009): % of GDP	4.2
Health expenditure (2009): public (% of total)	64.5
Access to water (% of persons, 2009)	46
Access to sanitation (% of persons, 2009)	15
Total carbon dioxide emissions ('000 metric tons, 2008) . .	1,910.5
Carbon dioxide emissions per head (metric tons, 2008) . .	0.1
Human Development Index (2011): ranking	151
Human Development Index (2011): value	0.480

For sources and definitions, see explanatory note on p. vi.

Agriculture

PRINCIPAL CROPS
('000 metric tons)

	2009	2010	2011*
Rice, paddy	4,540	4,738	5,078
Maize	425	412	459
Potatoes	225	225	208
Sweet potatoes	911	919	860
Cassava (Manioc)	3,020	3,009	3,308
Taro (Cocoyam)*	243	243	225
Sugar cane*	3,000	3,000	3,000
Beans, dry	82	82	99
Groundnuts, in shell† . . .	26	30	31
Coconuts	73†	78†	81
Oil palm fruit*	21	21	21
Tomatoes*	35	41	39
Bananas*	352	361	315
Oranges*	66	70	86
Guavas, mangoes and mangosteens* . . .	250	280	301
Avocados*	26	26	26
Pineapples*	72	70	80
Cashewapple*	75	76	74
Coffee, green*	65	81	53
Vanilla*	3	2	2
Cinnamon (Canella)* . . .	1	1	1
Cloves*	8	8	7
Sisal*	14	16	19
Tobacco, unmanufactured* . .	2	2	2

* FAO estimates.
† Unofficial figure(s).

Aggregate production ('000 metric tons, may include official, semi-official or estimated data): Total cereals 4,978 in 2009, 5,163 in 2010, 5,549 in 2011; Total roots and tubers 4,398 in 2009, 4,395 in 2010, 4,601 in 2011; Total vegetables (incl. melons) 346 in 2009, 393 in 2010, 439 in 2011; Total fruits (excl. melons) 1,136 in 2009, 1,182 in 2010, 1,175 in 2011.

Source: FAO.

LIVESTOCK
('000 head, year ending September, FAO estimates)

	2009	2010	2011
Cattle	9,800	9,900	10,000
Pigs	1,370	1,380	1,381
Sheep	725	730	735
Goats	1,270	1,280	1,300
Chickens	26,000	26,500	27,000
Ducks	4,100	4,200	4,300
Geese and guinea fowls .	3,000	3,000	3,000
Turkeys	2,150	2,200	2,250

Source: FAO.

LIVESTOCK PRODUCTS
('000 metric tons, FAO estimates)

	2009	2010	2011
Cattle meat	153.0	159.4	165.8
Sheep meat	2.8	2.8	2.8
Goat meat	10.0	10.0	10.0
Pig meat	55.0	55.4	55.4
Chicken meat	37.5	37.8	38.1
Duck meat	11.6	11.8	12.0
Goose meat	12.6	12.6	12.6
Turkey meat	9.0	9.0	9.0
Cows' milk	555	555	555
Hen eggs	16.2	16.1	16.1
Other eggs	4.5	4.5	4.5
Honey	4.1	4.4	4.4

Source: FAO.

Forestry

ROUNDWOOD REMOVALS
('000 cubic metres, excl. bark)

	2008	2009	2010
Sawlogs, veneer logs and logs for sleepers	267*	235	271*
Pulpwood*	10	10	10
Fuel wood*	13,100	13,100	13,100
Total*	13,377	13,345	13,381

* FAO estimate(s).

2011: Production assumed to be unchanged from 2010 (FAO estimates).

Source: FAO.

SAWNWOOD PRODUCTION
('000 cubic metres, incl. railway sleepers)

	2008	2009*	2010
Coniferous (softwood)	42	42	42*
Broadleaved (hardwood) . . .	50	50	62
Total	92	92	104*

* FAO estimate(s).

2011: Production assumed to be unchanged from 2010 (FAO estimates).

Source: FAO.

Fishing

('000 metric tons, live weight)

	2008	2009	2010
Capture*	120.5	131.3	128.8
Cichlids*	23.4	23.6	25.5
Other freshwater fishes* . .	4.9	4.9	5.3
Narrow-barred Spanish mackerel	6.6	6.6	6.6
Other marine fishes . . .	44.1	52.8	49.2
Shrimps and prawns . . .	6.7	7.3	6.5
Aquaculture*	10.8	6.1	6.9
Giant tiger prawn . . .	8.0	3.3	4.0
Total catch*	131.3	137.4	135.7

* FAO estimates.

Note: Figures exclude aquatic plants ('000 metric tons, capture only): 0.8 in 2008–10. Also excluded are crocodiles, recorded by number rather than weight, and shells. The number of Nile crocodiles caught was: 2,640 in 2008; 2,450 in 2009; n.a. in 2010.

Source: FAO.

Mining

(metric tons)

	2008	2009	2010
Chromite*	84,000	60,000	90,000†
Salt (marine)†	75,000	75,000	75,000
Graphite (natural)‡	4,967	3,437	3,783
Mica‡	1,233	358	2,069

* Figures refer to gross weight. The estimated chromium content is 27%.
† Estimates.
‡ Figures refer to exports.

Source: US Geological Survey.

Industry

SELECTED PRODUCTS
(metric tons unless otherwise indicated)

	2007	2008	2009
Raw sugar	20,000	16,000	60,000
Cement	270,000	460,000	370,000
Electric energy (million kWh)* .	1,222	1,274	1,274

* Production by the state-owned utility only, excluding electricity generated by industries for their own use.

2010: Cement 410,000 (estimate).

Sources: US Geological Survey; UN Industrial Commodity Statistics Database.

Finance

CURRENCY AND EXCHANGE RATES

Monetary Units
5 iraimbilanja = 1 ariary.

Sterling, Dollar and Euro Equivalents (31 December 2012)
£1 sterling = 3,582.94 ariary;
US $1 = 2,270.56 ariary;
€1 = 2,995.78 ariary;
10,000 ariary = £2.79 = $4.40 = €3.34.

Average Exchange Rate (ariary per US $)
2010   2,090.0
2011   2,025.1
2012   2,195.0

BUDGET
('000 million ariary, central government operations)

Revenue and grants	2009	2010	2011
Tax revenue	1,782	1,981	2,180
Non-tax revenue	80	268	43
Grants	192	174	179
Total	2,054	2,423	2,402

Expenditure	2009	2010	2011
Current expenditure . . .	1,753	1,848	2,160
Wages and salaries . . .	803	945	1,115
Capital expenditure . . .	728	733	609
Total	2,480	2,581	2,769

Source: African Development Bank.

INTERNATIONAL RESERVES
(excl. gold, US $ million at 31 December)

	2009	2010	2011
IMF special drawing rights . .	153.2	148.6	144.5
Foreign exchange	982.3	1,022.9	1,134.5
Total	1,135.5	1,171.6	1,279.1

Source: IMF, *International Financial Statistics*.

MONEY SUPPLY
('000 million ariary at 31 December)

	2009	2010	2011
Currency outside banks . . .	1,010.72	1,174.61	1,477.52
Demand deposits at deposit money banks	1,392.18	1,444.17	1,768.94
Total money	2,402.91	2,618.79	3,246.47

Source: IMF, *International Financial Statistics*.

COST OF LIVING
(Consumer Price Index for Malagasy in Antananarivo; base: 2000 = 100)

	2008	2009	2010
Food	223.2	241.6	257.2
Electricity, gas and other fuels .	234.7	n.a.	n.a.
Clothing*	157.5	178.2	205.3
Rent	315.2	277.0	311.4
All items (incl. others) . . .	221.4	241.2	263.5

* Including household linen.

2011: Food 292.0; All items (incl. others) 288.5.

Source: ILO.

NATIONAL ACCOUNTS
('000 million ariary at current prices)

Expenditure on the Gross Domestic Product

	2008	2009	2010
Government final consumption expenditure	1,492	1,581	1,717
Private final consumption expenditure	12,989	14,288	15,767
Increase in stocks . . . . } Gross fixed capital formation . }	6,483	5,309	3,436
Total domestic expenditure .	20,964	21,178	20,920
Exports of goods and services .	4,268	4,186	4,836
Less Imports of goods and services	9,151	8,635	7,491
GDP in purchasers' values .	16,081	16,729	18,264

Gross Domestic Product by Economic Activity

	2008	2009	2010
Agriculture, hunting, forestry and fishing	3,589	4,490	4,700
Mining and quarrying	17	27	41
Manufacturing	2,131	2,250	2,431
Electricity, gas and water . . .	192	191	215
Construction	709	647	654
Wholesale and retail trade, restaurants and hotels . . .	1,909	2,085	2,250
Transport and communications .	3,100	3,063	3,523
Finance, insurance, real estate and business services	203	208	288
Public administration and defence	650	664	777
Other services	2,136	1,967	2,161
Sub-total	14,636	15,592	17,040
Less Imputed bank service charges	187	182	267
Indirect taxes, less subsidies . .	1,630	1,319	1,491
GDP in purchasers' values .	16,081	16,729	18,264

Source: African Development Bank.

BALANCE OF PAYMENTS
(US $ million)

	2003	2004	2005
Exports of goods f.o.b.	854	990	834
Imports of goods f.o.b.	−1,111	−1,427	−1,427
Trade balance	−258	−437	−592
Exports of services	322	425	498
Imports of services	−619	−637	−615
Balance on goods and services	−555	−649	−710
Other income received	16	15	24
Other income paid	−94	−89	−104
Balance on goods, services and income	−632	−723	−790
Current transfers received . .	357	245	208
Current transfers paid	−183	−62	−45
Current balance	−458	−541	−626
Capital account (net)	143	182	192
Direct investment from abroad .	13	53	85
Other investment assets . . .	−29	295	11
Other investment liabilities . .	−110	−97	−102
Net errors and omissions . . .	67	−35	91
Overall balance	−374	−143	−349

Source: IMF, *International Financial Statistics*.

External Trade

PRINCIPAL COMMODITIES
(US $ million)

Imports c.i.f.	2008	2009	2010
Food and live animals . . .	300.3	243.5	274.9
Cereals and cereal preparations .	148.3	105.7	121.7
Rice	74.0	47.2	53.5
Mineral fuels, lubricants and related materials	510.1	327.4	386.0
Petroleum, petroleum products and related materials	501.3	319.4	374.3
Petroleum and oils obtained from bituminous materials (not crude)	490.8	315.0	368.8
Residual petroleum products .	10.5	4.4	5.5
Chemicals and related products	272.5	192.9	221.0
Medicinal and pharmaceutical products	66.9	61.2	67.2
Basic manufactures	1,197.8	1,139.6	634.2
Textile yarn and related products .	536.2	299.0	255.0
Woven cotton fabrics . . .	145.4	56.3	42.1
Machinery and transport equipment	1,214.8	881.1	751.8
Power generating machinery and equipment	147.8	62.3	40.4
Electric machinery, apparatus and appliances	125.6	96.1	128.8
Road vehicles	232.1	133.4	120.6
Miscellaneous manufactures .	207.0	249.8	171.4
Total (incl. others)	3,850.6	3,159.3	2,545.8

Exports f.o.b.	2008	2009	2010
Food and live animals . . .	323.8	285.1	248.4
Fish, crustaceans and molluscs and			
preparations thereof	159.6	115.5	114.1
Crustaceans and molluscs . .	122.0	87.9	71.2
Vegetables and fruit	36.2	32.9	36.7
Coffee, tea, cocoa, spices . . .	117.3	116.4	80.6
Spices	85.5	98.2	56.7
Vanilla	50.1	44.2	17.6
Cloves	30.1	48.4	31.7
Crude materials, inedible,			
except fuels	94.3	82.0	120.1
Basic manufactures . . .	71.8	96.2	72.8
Miscellaneous manufactures .	948.7	474.4	363.4
Articles of apparel and clothing			
accessories	885.8	431.4	302.7
Men's and boys' outerwear . .	315.2	65.2	47.1
Women's, girls' and infants'			
outerwear	250.2	104.7	42.2
Knitted or crocheted outerwear .	19.8	14.6	5.7
Total (incl. others)	1,667.4	1,095.9	1,082.2

Source: UN, *International Trade Statistics Yearbook*.

2011 ('000 million ariary): *Imports:* Rice 173.1; Petroleum products 1,126.9; Pharmaceutical products 127.7; Plastics 151.7; Reinforced steel bars and laminates 129.0; Total (incl. others) 5,303.8. *Exports:* Shrimps and prawns 123.9; Vanilla 36.6; Chrome ores 51.2; Petroleum products 130.0; Clothing 65.2; Total (incl. others) 2,534.4 (Source: African Development Bank).

PRINCIPAL TRADING PARTNERS
(US $ million)

Imports	2008	2009	2010
Argentina	58.5	11.3	n.a.
Bahrain	306.0	109.9	139.7
Belgium	60.0	198.7	96.6
Canada	17.2	63.0	110.8
China, People's Repub. . . .	810.1	355.4	310.1
France	343.7	331.0	367.5
Germany	161.6	68.7	57.3
Hong Kong	11.7	91.3	62.8
India	182.1	124.7	60.1
Indonesia	72.1	32.9	20.2
Italy	49.6	36.1	26.4
Japan	122.1	22.9	18.0
Korea, Republic	80.3	76.4	56.5
Kuwait	—	85.9	82.0
Malaysia	36.3	43.1	32.5
Mauritius	85.5	146.5	133.3
Pakistan	54.7	42.6	65.1
Saudi Arabia	54.2	15.6	42.8
Singapore	20.6	81.9	96.7
South Africa	234.1	142.0	197.1
Thailand	71.9	578.9	45.8
United Arab Emirates . . .	78.4	55.1	73.0
United Kingdom	39.4	n.a.	n.a.
USA	192.5	108.0	146.9
Total (incl. others)	3,850.6	3,159.3	2,545.8

Exports	2008	2009	2010
Belgium	20.0	18.3	16.4
Canada	13.1	11.9	42.3
China, People's Republic . . .	52.3	52.3	56.7
Côte d'Ivoire	0.2	0.1	49.2
France	751.1	362.6	358.6
Germany	108.3	69.9	78.9
Hong Kong	9.5	16.1	9.5
India	10.6	20.8	46.1
Italy	40.4	27.9	30.9
Mauritius	18.1	19.2	22.6
Netherlands	26.7	17.2	17.5
Singapore	22.8	24.0	18.5
South Africa	24.9	15.7	26.2
Spain	30.5	23.5	31.1
United Arab Emirates	4.7	13.1	34.9
United Kingdom	31.3	35.1	35.3
USA	364.7	196.0	44.5
Total (incl. others)	1,667.4	1,095.9	1,082.2

Source: UN, *International Trade Statistics Yearbook*.

2011 ('000 million ariary): *Imports:* China, People's Republic 598.9; France 634.2; Germany 76.8; Mauritius 267.4; South Africa 346.3; Total (incl. others) 5,303.8. *Exports:* China, People's Republic 174.0; France 852.9; Germany 149.0; Italy 56.2; USA 70.8; Total (incl. others) 2,534.4 (Source: African Development Bank).

Transport

RAILWAYS
(traffic)

	1997	1998	1999
Passengers carried ('000) . . .	359	293	273
Passenger-km (million) . . .	37	35	31
Freight carried ('000 metric tons) .	227	213	141
Ton-km (million)	81	71	46

Source: Réseau National des Chemins de Fer Malagasy.

2000: Passenger-km (million) 19; Ton-km (million) 26 (Source: UN, *Statistical Yearbook*).

ROAD TRAFFIC
(vehicles in use)

	1994	1995	1996*
Passenger cars	54,821	58,097	60,480
Buses and coaches	3,797	4,332	4,850
Lorries and vans	35,931	37,232	37,972
Road tractors	488	560	619

* Estimates.

2008: Passenger cars 146,273; Buses and coaches 280,835; Lorries and vans 83,788.

2009: Passenger cars 141,236; Buses and coaches 280,835; Lorries and vans 88,815.

Source: IRF, *World Road Statistics*.

SHIPPING

Flag Registered Fleet
(at 31 December)

	2010	2011	2012
Number of vessels	42	42	42
Displacement ('000 grt) . . .	20.7	20.3	20.3

Source: Lloyd's List Intelligence (www.lloydslistintelligence.com).

International Sea-borne Freight Traffic
('000 metric tons)

	1987	1988	1989
Goods loaded:			
Mahajanga	17	18	29
Toamasina	252	350	361
other ports	79	100	137
Total	348	468	527
Goods unloaded:			
Mahajanga	37	32	31
Toamasina	748	778	709
other ports	48	53	52
Total	833	863	792

1990 ('000 metric tons): Goods loaded 540; Goods unloaded 984 (Source: UN, *Monthly Bulletin of Statistics*).

CIVIL AVIATION
(traffic on scheduled services)

	2007	2008	2009
Kilometres flown (million) . .	16	10	9
Passengers carried ('000) . .	616	559	500
Passenger-km (million) . . .	1,248	1,041	819
Total ton-km (million)	136	106	88

Source: UN, *Statistical Yearbook*.

2010 ('000): Passengers carried 417.0 (Source: World Bank, World Development Indicators database).

Tourism

TOURIST ARRIVALS BY NATIONALITY

	2008	2009	2010
Canada and USA	11,250	4,881	5,882
France	210,000	95,985	111,750
Germany	11,250	3,253	5,882
Italy	15,000	4,881	17,465
Japan	7,500	1,627	1,960
Mauritius	15,000	6,507	7,845
Réunion	52,501	21,149	21,565
Switzerland	7,500	2,278	3,521
United Kingdom	15,000	3,253	3,920
Total (incl. others)	375,010	162,687	196,052

Note: Most data for 2008 are rounded.

2011: ('000, provisional): Total tourist arrivals 225.

Tourism receipts (US $ million, incl. passenger transport, unless otherwise indicated): 620 in 2008; 518 in 2009; 321 in 2010 (excl. passenger transport).

Source: World Tourism Organization.

Communications Media

	2009	2010	2011
Telephones ('000 main lines in use)	186.2	142.1	138.3
Mobile cellular telephones ('000 subscribers)	6,283.8	7,711.7	8,665.2
Internet subscribers ('000) . .	8.3	8.8	17.7
Broadband subscribers ('000) . .	4.6	5.4	6.9

Source: International Telecommunication Union.

Education

(2009/10, unless otherwise indicated, UNESCO estimates, public and private schools)

		Pupils ('000)		
	Teachers	Males	Females	Total
Pre-primary (all programmes)	7,075	81.3	82.4	163.7
Primary (all programmes) .	105,673	2,145.3	2,096.7	4,242.0
Secondary*	43,539	526.5	496.0	1,022.5
General	39,912	582.8	558.6	1,141.4
Vocational†	2,058	21.2	11.9	33.1
Tertiary	4,494	38.8	35.6	74.4

* 2008/09.
† 2007/08.

Source: UNESCO Institute for Statistics.

2005/06: 6 universities; 14 private institutes of higher education.

Pupil-teacher ratio (primary education, UNESCO estimate): 40.1 in 2009/10 (Source: UNESCO Institute for Statistics).

Adult literacy rate (UNESCO estimates): 64.5% (males 67.4%; females 61.6%) in 2009 (Source: UNESCO Institute for Statistics).

Directory

The Government

HEAD OF STATE

President of the Haute Autorité de la Transition: ANDRY RAJOELINA (inaugurated 21 March 2009).

GOVERNMENT OF NATIONAL UNITY
(May 2013)

Prime Minister and Acting Minister of the Environment and Forests: JEAN OMER BERIZIKY.

Deputy Prime Minister, in charge of Development and Land Settlement: HAJO HERIVELONA RANDRIANIAINARIVELO.

Deputy Prime Minister, in charge of the Economy and Industry: PIERROT BOTOZAZA (suspended in mid-July 2012).

Minister of Foreign Affairs: PIERROT RAJAONARIVELO.

Minister of Agriculture: ROLAND RAVATOMANGA (suspended in mid-July 2012).

Minister of Trade: OLGA RAMALASON (suspended in mid-July 2012).

Minister of Communication: HARRY LAURENT RAHAJASON.

Minister of Culture and Heritage: ELIA RAVELOMANANTSOA.

Minister of Decentralization: RUFFINE TSIRANANA (suspended in mid-July 2012).

Minister of Water: JULIEN REBOZA.

Minister of National Education: RÉGIS MANORO.

Minister of Stockbreeding: IHANTA RANDRIAMANDRATO (suspended in mid-July 2012).

Minister of Energy: NESTOR RAZAFINDROARIAKA.

Minister of Higher Education and Scientific Research: AMETTE ETIENNE HILAIRE RAZAFINDEHIBE.

Minister of Technical Education and Professional Training: JEAN ANDRÉ NDREMANJARY.

Minister of Finance and the Budget: HERY RAJAONARIMAMPIANINA.

Minister of the Civil Service, Labour and Social Legislation: TABERA RANDRIAMANANTSOA.

Minister of the Armed Forces: Gen. ANDRÉ LUCIEN RAKOTOARIMASY.

Minister of Hydrocarbons: BERNARD MARCEL.

Minister of the Interior: FLORENT RAKOTOARISOA.

Minister of Youth and Leisure: JACQUES ULRICH RANDRIANTIANA.

Minister of Justice and Keeper of the Seals: CHRISTINE RAZANAMAHASOA.

Minister of Mining: DANIELLA RANDRIANFENO TOLOTRANDRY RAJO.

Minister of Fisheries and Fishing Resources: SYLVAIN MANORIKY.

Minister of Population and Social Affairs: OLGA VAOMALALA.

Minister of Posts, Telecommunications and New Technologies: NY HASINA ANDRIAMANJATO.

Minister of Handicrafts: ELISA ZAFITOMBO ALIBENA.

Minister of Relations with the Institutions: VICTOR MANANTSOA.

Minister of Public Health: JOHANITA NDAHIMANANJARA.

Minister of Internal Security: ARSÈNE RAKOTONDRAZAKA.

Minister of Sport: GÉRARD BOTRALAHY.

Minister of Tourism: JEAN MAX RAKOTOMAMONJY.

Minister of Transport: BENJAMINA RAMARCEL RAMANANTSOA.

Minister of Public Works and Meteorology: Col. BOTO MANOVATSARA.

Secretary of State responsible for the National Gendarmerie: Gen. RANDRIANAZARY.

MINISTRIES

Office of the President: BP 955, 101 Antananarivo; tel. (20) 2254703; fax (20) 2256252; e-mail communication@presidence.gov .mg; internet www.presidence.gov.mg.

Office of the Prime Minister: BP 248, Palais d'Etat Mahazoarivo, 101 Antananarivo; tel. (20) 2264498; fax (20) 2233116; e-mail stp-ca@ primature.gov.mg; internet www.primature.gov.mg.

Ministry of Agriculture: BP 301, Anosy, 101 Antananarivo; tel. (20) 2261002; fax (20) 2264308; e-mail info@agriculture.gov.mg; internet www.agriculture.gov.mg.

Ministry of the Armed Forces: BP 08, Ampahibe, 101 Antananarivo; tel. (20) 2222211; fax (20) 2235420; e-mail mdn@wanadoo.fr; internet www.defense.gov.mg.

Ministry of the Civil Service, Labour and Social Legislation: BP 207, Cité des 67 Hectares, 101 Antananarivo; tel. (20) 2224209; fax (20) 2233856; e-mail ministre@mfptls.gov.mg; internet www .mfptls.gov.mg.

Ministry of Communication: BP 305, 101 Antananarivo.

Ministry of Culture and Heritage: 101 Antananarivo; e-mail ministre@mcp.gov.mg; internet www.mcp.gov.mg.

Ministry of Decentralization: Antananarivo.

Ministry of Development and Land Settlement: Antananarivo; internet www.matd.gov.mg.

Ministry of the Economy and Industry: Bâtiment Commerce, Ambohidahy, 101 Antananarivo; tel. (20) 2264681; fax (20) 2234530; e-mail sg@mepspc.gov.mg; internet www.mei.gov.mg.

Ministry of Energy: BP 280, rue Farafaty Ampandrianomby, 101 Antananarivo; tel. (20) 2257193; fax (20) 2241776; e-mail bsg_mem@ yahoo.fr; internet www.mem.gov.mg.

Ministry of the Environment and Forests: BP 610, rue Fernand Kasanga, Tsimbazaza, 101 Antananarivo; tel. (20) 2266805; fax (20) 2235410; e-mail sp@meeft.gov.mg; internet www.meeft.gov.mg.

Ministry of Finance and the Budget: BP 61, Antaninarenina, Antananarivo; tel. (20) 2230173; fax (20) 2264680; e-mail mrazanajato@mefb.gov.mg; internet www.mefb.gov.mg.

Ministry of Fisheries and Fishing Resources: 101 Antananarivo.

Ministry of Foreign Affairs: BP 836, Anosy, 101 Antananarivo; tel. (20) 2221198; fax (20) 2234484; e-mail contact@ madagascar-diplomatie.net; internet www.madagascar-diplomatie .net.

Ministry of Handicrafts: 101 Antananarivo.

Ministry of Higher Education and Scientific Research: 101 Antananarivo; internet www.mesupres.gov.mg.

Ministry of Hydrocarbons: BP 280, rue Farafaty Ampandrianomby, 101 Antananarivo; tel. (20) 2257193; fax (20) 2241776; e-mail bsg_mem@yahoo.fr.

Ministry of the Interior: BP 833, Anosy, 101 Antananarivo; tel. (20) 2223084; fax (20) 2235579; internet www.mid.gov.mg.

Ministry of Internal Security: BP 23 bis, 101 Antananarivo; tel. (20) 2221029; fax (20) 2231861; internet www.policenationale.gov .mg.

Ministry of Justice: rue Joel Rakotomalala, BP 231, Faravohitra, 101 Antananarivo; tel. (20) 2237684; fax (20) 2264458; e-mail presse .justice@justice.gov.mg; internet www.justice.gov.mg.

Ministry of Mining: rue Farafaty Ampandrianomby, BP 280,101 Antananarivo; tel. 320311099 (mobile); internet www.mines.gov.mg.

Ministry of National Education: BP 247, Anosy, 101 Antananarivo; tel. (20) 2224308; fax (20) 2223897; e-mail mlraharimalala@ yahoo.fr; internet www.education.gov.mg.

Ministry of Population and Social Affairs: 2 rue Razanakombana, Ambohijatovo, 101 Antananarivo; tel. 330968906 (mobile); e-mail hndev@gmail.com; internet www.population.gov.mg.

Ministry of Posts, Telecommunications and New Technologies: pl. de l'Indépendance, Antaninarenina, 101 Antananarivo; tel. (20) 2222902; fax (20) 2234115; internet www.mtpc.gov.mg.

Ministry of Public Health: BP 88, Ambohidahy, 101 Antananarivo; tel. (20) 2263121; fax (20) 2264228; e-mail ministre@sante.gov .mg; internet www.sante.gov.mg.

Ministry of Public Works and Meteorology: BP 295, 101 Antananarivo; tel. (20) 2228715; fax (20) 2220890; e-mail secreab@mtpm .gov.mg; internet www.mtpm.gov.mg.

Ministry of Relations with the Institutions: 101 Antananarivo.

Ministry of Sport: BP 681, Ambohijatovo, pl. Goulette, 101 Antananarivo; tel. (20) 2227780; fax (20) 2234275; e-mail mjs_101@yahoo .fr; internet www.mscl.gov.mg.

Ministry of Stockbreeding: 101 Antananarivo.

Ministry of Technical Education and Professional Training: BP 793, 101 Antananarivo.

Ministry of Tourism: 101 Antananarivo; e-mail mintour@dts.mg; internet www.mtoura.gov.mg.

Ministry of Trade: 101 Antananarivo; internet www.commerce .gov.mg.

Ministry of Transport: BP 610, rue Fernand Kasanga, Tsimbazaza, 101 Antananarivo; tel. (20) 2262816; fax (20) 2235410; internet www.transport.gov.mg.

Ministry of Water: Antananarivo; e-mail dircab@mineau.gov.mg; internet www.mineau.gov.mg.

Ministry of Youth and Leisure: 101 Antananarivo; internet www .mjl.gov.mg.

President and Legislature

PRESIDENT

Presidential Election, 3 December 2006

Candidate	Votes	% of votes
Marc Ravalomanana	2,435,199	54.79
Jean Lahiniriko	517,994	11.65
Iarovana Roland Ratsiraka	450,717	10.14
Herizo J. Razafimahaleo	401,473	9.03
Norbert Lala Ratsirahonana	187,552	4.22
Ny Hasina Andriamanjato	185,624	4.18
Others	266,191	5.99
Total	4,444,750*	100.00

* Excluding 87,196 invalid votes.

LEGISLATURE

On 7 October 2010 the High Constitutional Court approved a decree by President Rajoelina establishing a Parlement de la Transition. Accordingly, on 11 October a 256-member lower parliamentary chamber, the Congrès de la Transition, was installed, with representation assigned according to the arrangement established in an agreement reached in August: notably, a gathering of all the political parties and associations that participated in the drafting of the agreement, known as l'Espace de Concertation des Partis Politiques (ESCOPOL), was allocated 62 seats, Tiako i Madagasikara (TIM) 52, Tanora malaGasy Vonona (TGV) 52 and a grouping of parties supporting Rajoelina, the Union des Démocrates et Républicains—Fanovana (UDR—Fanovana) 29. On 12 October a 90-member upper chamber, the Conseil Supérieur de la Transition, took office; the deputies included 25 representatives of the UDR—Fanovana, 21 of the TIM, 18 of ESCOPOL and 10 of the TGV. The Parlement de la Transition was restructured on 1 December 2011, with the Congrès de la Transition comprising 365 members and the Conseil Supérieur de la Transition comprising 163 members. In the Congrès de la Transition, the ESCOPOL was allocated 62 seats; the Mouvance Ravalomanana (MR) 57 seats; the TGV and the Union des Démocrates et des Républicains pour le Changement (UDR-C) 52 seats each; the President of the HAT, the Monima-Uamad, Hery Politika Mitambatra (HPM), the Mouvement pour la Démocratie de Madagascar (MDM), AREMA and the Autres Sensibilités (AS) 20 seats each; and 22 seats were allocated to eminent persons. In the Conseil Supérieur de la Transition, the MR was allocated 30 seats; the UDR-C and the TGV 25 seats each; the ESCOPOL 18 seats; the President of the HAT, the Monima-Uamad, the MDM, AREMA, the AS and the HPM 10 seats each; and five seats were allocated to eminent persons.

President of the Congrès de la Transition: MAMY RAKOTOAR-IVELO.

President of the Conseil Supérieur de la Transition: Gen. DOLIN RASOLOSOA.

Election Commission

Commission Electorale Nationale Indépendante pour la Transition (CENIT): Immeuble Microréalisation, 4e étage, 67 ha, 101 Antananarivo; tel. (20) 2225179; fax (20) 2225881; e-mail ceni@ceni-madagascar.mg; internet www.ceni-madagascar.mg; 21 mems; Pres. BÉATRICE JEANINE ATALLAH.

Political Organizations

In August 2011 there were some 285 political organizations registered in Madagascar.

Association pour la Renaissance de Madagascar (Andry sy Riana Enti-manavotra an'i Madagasikara) (AREMA): f. 1975 as Avant-garde de la Révolution Malgache; adopted present name 1997; party of fmr Pres. Adm. (retd) Ratsiraka (now in exile); control disputed between two factions, headed by Gen. Sec. PIERROT RAJAONARIVELO (in exile), and Asst Gen. Sec. PIERRE RAHARIJAONA.

Comité pour la Réconciliation Nationale (CRN): Villa la Franchise, Lot II-I 160 A, Alarobia, Antananarivo; tel. (20) 2242022; f. 2002 by fmr President Zafy; radical opposition; formed part of the 3FN (Trois Forces Nationales) group of opposition parties, established in Sept. 2005; Leader ALBERT ZAFY.

FAFI-V: f. 2009; Pres. NAIVO NAIVO RAHOLDINA.

Hasin'i Madagasikara: Lot K 7-97 bis IIA Mamory Ivato, BP 682, 101 Antananarivo; tel. 340220665 (mobile); e-mail madahasin@gmail.com; internet hasinimadagasikara.mg; f. 2009; Pres. SARAHA GEORGET RABEHARISOA.

Herim-Bahoaka Mitambatra (HBM) (Union of Popular Forces): formed part of the coalition supporting Marc Ravalomanana prior to the 2006 presidential election; Leader TOVONANAHARY RABETSITONTA.

Libéralisme Économique et Action Démocratique pour la Reconstruction Nationale (LEADER/Fanilo) (Torch): f. 1993 by Herizo Razafimahaleo; Sec. Gen. MANASSÉ ESOAVELOMANDROSO.

Malagasy Tonga Saina (MTS): Antananarivo; Pres. ROLAND RATSIRAKA.

Mouvement pour la Démocratie à Madagascar (MDM): Villa Khannet, Maibahoaka, Ambohidratrimo; tel. (34) 3118672; internet www.mdm-iarivo.mg; Pres. PIERROT RAJAONARIVELO.

Mouvement pour le Progrès de Madagascar (Mpitolona ho Amin'ny Fandrosoan'ny Madagasikara) (MFM): 42 & 44 Cité Ampefiloha Bldg, 101 Antananarivo; tel. (20) 2437560; e-mail contact@mfm-madagascar.com; internet www.mfm-madagascar.com; f. 1972 as Mouvement pour le Pouvoir Prolétarien (MFM); adopted present name in 1990; advocates liberal and market-orientated policies; Leader MANANDAFY RAKOTONIRINA; Sec.-Gen. OLIVIER RAKOTOVAZAHA.

Ny Asa Vita no Ifampitsara (AVI) (People are judged by the work they do): f. 1997 to promote human rights, hard work and devt; Leader NORBERT RATSIRAHONANA.

Parti Socialiste et Démocratique pour l'Union de Madagascar (PSDUM): f. 2006; Pres. JEAN LAHINIRIKO.

Rassemblement des Forces Nationales (RFN): f. 2005; a coalition of parties comprising the AKFM, LEADER/Fanilo and Fihavanantsika (led by Pasteur Daniel Rajakoba); formed part of the 3FN (Trois Forces Nationales) group of opposition parties, established in Sept. 2005; Leader Pasteur EDMOND RAZAFIMAHEFA.

Rassemblement pour le Socialisme et la Démocratie (RPSD): f. 1993 by fmr mems of PSD; also known as Renaissance du Parti Social-démocratique; Jean-Eugène Voninahitsy formed a breakaway party known as the RPSD Nouveau in 2003; Leader EVARISTE MARSON.

TAMBATRA: Antananarivo; Pres. PETY RAKOTONIAINA.

Tanora malaGasy Vonona (TGV) (Determined Malagasy Youth): Antananarivo; internet www.tgvonona.org; f. 2007; Leader ANDRY RAJOELINA.

Tiako i Madagasikara (TIM) (I Love Madagascar): internet www.tim-madagascar.org; f. 2002; supports former Pres. Ravalomanana; Pres. YVAN RANDRIASANDRATRINIONY.

Diplomatic Representation

EMBASSIES IN MADAGASCAR

China, People's Republic: Ancien Hôtel Panorama, BP 1658, 101 Antananarivo; tel. (20) 2240129; fax (20) 2240215; e-mail chinaemb_mg@mfa.gov.cn; internet mg.china-embassy.org; Ambassador WO RUIDI.

Comoros: Lot IB 50, rue du Dr Théodore Villette, Isoraka, 101 Antananarivo; tel. and fax (20) 2265819; Ambassador CAABI EL-YACHROUTU.

Egypt: Lot MD 378 Ambalatokana Mandrosoa Ivato, BP 4082, 101 Antananarivo; tel. (20) 2245497; fax (20) 2245379; Ambassador MAGID FOAD SALEH FOAD.

France: 3 rue Jean Jaurès, BP 204, 101 Antananarivo; tel. (20) 2239898; fax (20) 2239927; e-mail ambatana@moov.mg; internet www.ambafrance-mada.org; Ambassador FRANÇOIS GOLDBLATT.

Germany: 101 rue du Pasteur Rabeony Hans, BP 516, Ambodirotra, 101 Antananarivo; tel. (20) 2223802; fax (20) 2226627; e-mail info@antananarivo.diplo.de; internet www.antananarivo.diplo.de; Ambassador HANS-DIETER STELL.

Holy See: Amboniloha Ivandry, BP 650, 101 Antananarivo; tel. (20) 2242376; fax (20) 2242384; e-mail nuntiusantana@wanadoo.mg; Apostolic Nuncio Most Rev. EUGENE MARTIN NUGENT (Titular Archbishop of Domnach Sechnaill).

India: 4 Làlana Emile Rajaonson, Tsaralalana, BP 1787, 101 Antananarivo; tel. (20) 2223334; fax (20) 2233790; e-mail indembmd@blueline.mg; Ambassador AZAD SINGH TOOR.

Indonesia: 26–28 rue Patrice Lumumba, BP 3969, 101 Antananarivo; tel. (20) 2224915; fax (20) 2232857; e-mail kbritana@dts.mg; Chargé d'affaires a.i. SLAMET SUYATA SASTRAMIHARDZA.

Iran: route Circulaire, Lot II L43 ter, Ankadivato, 101 Antananarivo; tel. (20) 2228639; fax (20) 2222298; Ambassador ABDOL RAHIM HOMATASH.

Japan: 8 rue du Dr Villette, BP 3863, Isoraka, 101 Antananarivo; tel. (20) 2226102; fax (20) 2221769; Ambassador RYUHEI HOSOYA.

Korea, Democratic People's Republic: 101 Antananarivo; tel. (20) 2244442; Ambassador RI YONG HAK.

Libya: Lot IIB, 37A route Circulaire Ampandrana-Ouest, 101 Antananarivo; tel. (20) 2221892; Chargé d'affaires a.i. Dr MOHAMED ALI SHARFEDIN AL-FITURI.

Mauritius: Villa David IV, Manakambahiny, 101 Antananarivo; tel. (20) 2221864; fax (20) 2221939; e-mail memad@moov.mg; Ambassador ERNEST GÉRARD LEMAIRE.

Morocco: Bâtiment D1, Rez-de-chaussée, Ankorondrano, BP 12, 104 Antananarivo; tel. (20) 2221347; fax (20) 2221124; e-mail amar_med@hotmail.com; Ambassador MUHAMMAD AMAR.

Norway: Explorer Business Park, Bâtiment 2D, Antananarivo; tel. (20) 2230507; fax (20) 2237799; e-mail emb.antananarivo@mfa.no; internet www.amb-norvege.mg; Ambassador DAG NISSEN.

Russia: BP 4006, Ivandry-Ambohijatovo, 101 Antananarivo; tel. (20) 2242827; fax (20) 2242642; e-mail ambrusmad@blueline.mg; internet www.madagascar.mid.ru; Ambassador VLADIMIR B. GONCHARENKO.

South Africa: Lot IVO 68 bis, rue Ravoninahitriniarivo, Ankorondrano, BP 12101-05, 101 Antananarivo; tel. (20) 2243350; fax (20) 2249514; e-mail antananarivo@foreign.gov.za; Ambassador MOKGETHI SAMUEL MONAISA.

Switzerland: Immeuble ARO, Solombavambahoaka, Frantsay 77, BP 118, 101 Antananarivo; tel. (20) 2262997; fax (20) 2228940; e-mail ant.vertretung@eda.admin.ch; internet www.eda.admin.ch/antananarivo; Ambassador ERIC MAYORAZ.

Turkey: Hotel Carlton, Chambre no. 1410, rue Pierre Stibbe, BP 959 Antananarivo; tel. (20) 2226060; fax (20) 2267609; Ambassador AHMET ENÇ ERCEMUND.

United Kingdom: Tour Zital Ankorondrano, Ravoninahitriniarivo St, BP 167, 101 Antananarivo; tel. 333745689 (mobile); e-mail bismada@moov.mg; internet ukinmadagascar.fco.gov.uk; Ambassador TIMOTHY SPENCER SMART.

USA: Lot 207A, Point Liberty, Andranoro–Antehiroka, BP 5253, 105 Antananarivo; tel. (20) 2348000; fax (20) 2348035; e-mail paoantananarivo@state.gov; internet www.antananarivo.usembassy.gov; Chargé d'affaires a.i. ERIC M. WONG.

Judicial System

According to the Constitution of the Fourth Republic of Madagascar, endorsed by national referendum on 17 November 2010, justice is administered by the Supreme Court, the High Constitutional Court, the High Court of Justice and any courts of appeal that may be established.

Supreme Court (Cour Suprême): Palais de Justice, Anosy, 101 Antananarivo; 9 mems; Pres. CLÉMENTINE CÉCILE RAJAONERA DELMOTTE; Attorney-General COLOMBE RAMANANTSOA (acting); Chamber Pres YOLANDE RAMANGASOAVINA, FRANÇOIS RAMANANDRAIBE.

High Constitutional Court (Haute Cour Constitutionnelle): BP 835, Ambohidahy, 101 Antananarivo; tel. (20) 2266061; e-mail hcc@hcc.gov.mg; internet www.hcc.gov.mg; interprets the Constitution and rules on constitutional issues; nine mems; Pres. JEAN-MICHEL RAJAONARIVONY.

High Court of Justice (Haute Cour de Justice): 101 Antananarivo; 9 mems.

Tribunaux de Première Instance: at Antananarivo, Toamasina, Antsiranana, Mahajanga, Fianarantsoa, Toliary, Antsirabé, Ambatondrazaka, Antalaha, Farafangana and Maintirano; for civil, commercial and social matters, and for registration.

Cours Criminelles Ordinaires: tries crimes of common law; attached to the Cour d'Appel in Antananarivo but may sit in any other large town. There are also 31 Cours Criminelles Spéciales dealing with cases concerning cattle.

Tribunaux Spéciaux Economiques: at Antananarivo, Toamasina, Mahajanga, Fianarantsoa, Antsiranana and Toliary; tries crimes specifically relating to economic matters.

Tribunaux Criminels Spéciaux: judges cases of banditry and looting; 31 courts.

Religion

It is estimated that more than 50% of the population follow traditional animist beliefs, some 41% are Christians (about two-thirds of whom are Roman Catholics) and some 7% are Muslims.

CHRISTIANITY

Fiombonan'ny Fiangonana Kristiana eto Madagasikara (FFKM)/Conseil Chrétien des Eglises de Madagascar (Christian Council of Churches in Madagascar): Vohipiraisana, Ambohijatovo-Atsimo, BP 798, 101 Antananarivo; tel. (20) 2623433; e-mail ffkmfoibe@gmail.com; f. 1980; four mems and two assoc. mems; Pres. Pastor Dr ENDOR MODESTE RAKOTO; Gen. Sec. Rev. GILBERT RANDRIANIRINA.

Fiombonan'ny Fiangonana Protestanta eto Madagasikara (FFPM)/Fédération des Eglises Protestantes à Madagascar (Federation of the Protestant Churches in Madagascar): VK 3 Vohipiraisana, Ambohijatovo-Atsimo, BP 4226, 101 Antananarivo; tel. (20) 2415888; e-mail edmrazafi@fuller.edu; f. 1958; two mem. churches; Pres Rev. Dr LALA RASENDRAHASINA; Gen. Sec. Rev. Dr EDMOND RAZAFIMANANTSOA.

The Anglican Communion

Anglicans are adherents of the Church of the Province of the Indian Ocean, comprising seven dioceses (five in Madagascar, one in Mauritius and one in Seychelles). The Archbishop of the Province is the Bishop of Antananarivo. The Church has about 160,000 adherents in Madagascar, including the membership of the Eklesia Episkopaly Malagasy (Malagasy Episcopal Church), founded in 1874.

Bishop of Antananarivo: Rt Rev. SAMOELA JAONA RANARIVELO, Evêché anglican, Lot VK57 ter, Ambohimanoro, 101 Antananarivo; tel. (20) 2220827; fax (20) 2261331; e-mail eemdanta@yahoo.com.

Bishop of Antsiranana: Rt Rev. ROGER CHUNG PO CHEN, Evêché anglican, 4 rue Grandidier, BP 278, 201 Antsiranana; tel. (20) 8222650; e-mail mgrchungpo@blueline.mg; internet www.antsirananadiocese.org.

Bishop of Fianarantsoa: Rt Rev. GILBERT RATELOSON RAKOTONDRAVELO, Evêché anglican, BP 1418, 531 Fianarantsoa.

Bishop of Mahajanga: Rt Rev. JEAN-CLAUDE ANDRIANJAFIMANANA, Evêché anglican, BP 169, 401 Mahajanga; e-mail eemdmaha@dts.mg.

Bishop of Toamasina: Rt Rev. JEAN PAUL SOLO, Evêché anglican, rue James Seth, BP 531, 501 Toamasina; tel. (20) 5332163; fax (20) 5331689.

The Roman Catholic Church

Madagascar comprises five archdioceses and 16 dioceses. About 26% of the total population are Roman Catholics.

Bishops' Conference

Conférence Episcopale de Madagascar, 102 bis, rue Cardinal Jerôme Rakotomalala, BP 667, 101 Antananarivo; tel. (20) 2220478; fax (20) 2224854; e-mail ecar@vitelcom.mg.

f. 1969; Pres. Most Rev. FULGENCE RABEMAHAFALY (Archbishop of Fianarantsoa).

Archbishop of Antananarivo: ODON MARIE ARSÈNE RAZANAKOLONA, Archevêché, Andohalo, BP 3030, 101 Antananarivo; tel. (20) 2220726; fax (20) 2264181; e-mail didih@simicro.org.

Archbishop of Antsiranana: Most Rev. MICHEL MALO, Archevêché, 5 blvd le Myre de Villers, BP 415, 201 Antsiranana; tel. and fax (82) 21605; e-mail archevediego@blueline.mg.

Archbishop of Fianarantsoa: Most Rev. FULGENCE RABEMAHAFALY, Archevêché, pl. Mgr Givelet, BP 1440, Ecar Ambozontany, 301 Fianarantsoa; tel. (20) 7550027; fax (20) 7551436; e-mail ecardiofianar@mel.moov.mg.

Archbishop of Toamasina: Most Rev. DÉSIRÉ TSARAHAZANA, 11 rue du Commerce, BP 98, 501 Toamasina; tel. (20) 5332128.

Archbishop of Toliary: Most Rev. FULGENCE RABEONY, Archevêché, Maison Saint Jean, BP 30, 601 Toliary; tel. (20) 9442416; e-mail diocese_tulcar@wanadoo.mg.

Other Christian Churches

Fiangonan'i Jesoa Kristy eto Madagasikara/Eglise de Jésus-Christ à Madagascar (FJKM): Lot 11 B18, Tohatohabato Ranavalona 1, Trano 'Ifanomezantsoa', BP 623, 101 Antananarivo; tel. (20) 2228237; fax (20) 2227033; e-mail fjkm@wanadoo.mg; internet foibefjkm.mg; f. 1968; Pres. LALA HAJA RASENDRAHASINA; Gen. Sec. Rev. RÉMY RALIBERA; 2m. mems.

Fiangonana Loterana Malagasy (Malagasy Lutheran Church): BP 1741, 19, rue Jules Pochard, 101 Antananarivo; tel. (20) 2422703; e-mail drmodeste@yahoo.fr; internet www.flm-mada.org; f. 1867; Pres. Rev. Dr ENDOR MODESTE RAKOTO; 3m. mems (2009).

The Press

In December 1990 legislation was adopted guaranteeing the freedom of the press and the right of newspapers to be established without prior authorization.

PRINCIPAL DAILIES

Bulletin de l'Agence Nationale d'Information 'TARATRA' (ANTA): 8/10 Làlana Rainizanabololona, Antanimena, BP 194, 101 Antananarivo; tel. (20) 2234308; e-mail administration@taratramada.com; internet www.taratramada.com; f. 1977; Malagasy; Editor-in-Chief HANITRA RABETOKOTANY.

Le Courier de Madagascar: Antananarivo; Dir of Publication FRANCK RAMAROSON; circ. 12,000.

L'Express de Madagascar: BP 3893, 101 Antananarivo; tel. (20) 2221934; fax (20) 2262894; e-mail lexpress@malagasy.com; internet www.lexpressmada.com; f. 1995; French and Malagasy; Editor-in-Chief SYLVAIN RANJALAHY; circ. 10,000.

Gazetiko: rue Ravoninahitriniarivo, BP 1414 Ankorondrano, 101 Antananarivo; tel. (20) 2269779; fax (20) 2227351; e-mail gazetiko@midi-madagasikara.mg; internet www.gazetiko.mg; Malagasy; circ. 50,000.

La Gazette de la Grande Ile: Lot II, W 23 L Ankorahotra, route de l'Université, BP 8678, Antananarivo; tel. 340561396 (mobile); e-mail administration@lagazette-dgi.com; internet www.lagazette-dgi.com; French; 24 pages; Pres. LOLA RASOAMAHARO; Editor-in-Chief CHRISTIAN ANDRIANARISOA; circ. 15,000–30,000.

Imongo Vaovao: 11K 4 bis Andravoahangy, BP 7014, 101 Antananarivo; tel. (20) 2233110; f. 1955; Malagasy; Dir ANDRÉ RATSIFEHERA; circ. 15,000.

Madagascar Matin: Antananarivo; Editor-in-Chef LAHINIRIKO DENIS ALEXANDRE; circ. 18,000.

Madagascar Tribune: Immeuble SME, rue Ravoninahitriniarivo, BP 659, Ankorondrano, 101 Antananarivo; tel. (20) 2222635; fax (20) 2222254; e-mail contact@madagascar-tribune.com; internet www.madagascar-tribune.com; f. 1988; independent; French and Malagasy; Editor RAHAGA RAMAHOLIMIHASO; circ. 12,000.

Maresaka: Cité Logt. 288, Analamahitsy, 101 Antananarivo; tel. (20) 2431665; f. 1953; independent; Malagasy; Editor R. RABEFANA-NINA; circ. 5,000.

Midi Madagasikara: Làlana Ravoninahitriniarivo, BP 1414, Ankorondrano, 101 Antananarivo; tel. (20) 2269779; fax (20) 2227351; e-mail contact@midi-madagasikara.mg; internet www .midi-madagasikara.mg; f. 1983; French and Malagasy; Dir-Gen. JULIANA ANDRIAMBELO RAKOTOARIVELO; circ. 21,000 (Mon.–Fri.), 35,000 (Sat.).

Les Nouvelles: 8/10, rue Rainizanabololona, BP 194, 101 Antananarivo; tel. (20) 2235433; fax (20) 2229993; e-mail administration@ les-nouvelles.com; internet www.les-nouvelles.com; in French and Taratra; f. 2003; Dir-Gen. NAINA ANDRIANTSITOHAINA.

Ny Vaovaontsika: BP 11137, MBS Anosipatrana; tel. (20) 2227717; e-mail nyvaovaontsika@mbs.mg; f. 2004; re-est. as a daily; Malagasy; owned by the Malagasy Broadcasting System; Editor-in-Chief ROLAND ANDRIAMAHENINA; circ. 10,000.

Le Quotidien: BP 11 097, 101 Antananarivo; tel. (20) 2227717; fax (20) 2265447; e-mail lequotidien@mbs.mg; internet www.lequotidien .mg; f. 2003; owned by the Tiko Group plc; French.

La Vérité: Immeuble SODIAT, Mandrosoa Ivato, BP 5068, Antananarivo 105; tel. (20) 2629521; fax (20) 2244953; e-mail laverite@ blueline.com.

PRINCIPAL PERIODICALS

Basy Vava: Lot III E 96, Mahamasina Atsimo, 101 Antananarivo; tel. (20) 2220448; f. 1959; daily; Malagasy; Dir GABRIEL RAMANAN-JATO; circ. 3,000.

Dans les Médias Demain (DMD): 51 rue Tsiombikibo, BP 1734, Ambatovinaky, 101 Antananarivo; tel. (20) 2241664; fax (20) 2241665; e-mail admin@dmd.mg; f. 1986; independent; economic information and analysis; weekly; Editorial Dir JEAN ERIC RAKO-TOARISOA; circ. 4,000.

Gazetinao: Lot IPA 37, BP 1758, Anosimasina, 101 Antananarivo; tel. (33) 1198161; e-mail mitantanasymitarika@yahoo.fr; f. 1976; French and Malagasy; monthly; religion and culture; Editor-in-Chief DAVID ALDEN EINSTEN RAKOTOMAHANINA; circ. 3,000.

L'Hebdo: BP 3893, 101 Antananarivo; tel. (20) 2221934; e-mail courrier@hebdomada.com; f. 2005; French and Malagasy; weekly; Editor-in-Chief NASOLO VALIAVO ANDRIAMIHAJA.

Isika Mianakavy: Ambatomena, 301 Fianarantsoa; f. 1958; Roman Catholic; Malagasy; monthly; Dir J. RANAIVOMANANA; circ. 21,000.

Journal Officiel de la République de Madagascar/Gazetim-Panjakan' Ny Repoblika Malagasy: BP 248, 101 Antananarivo; tel. (20) 2265010; fax (20) 2225319; f. 1883; official announcements; Malagasy and French; weekly; Dir HONORÉE ELIANNE RALALAHAR-ISON; circ. 1,545.

Jureco: BP 6318, Lot IVD 48 bis, rue Razanamaniraka, Behoririka, 101 Antananarivo; tel. (20) 2255271; e-mail jureco@malagasy.com; law and economics; monthly; French; Dir MBOARA ANDRIANARIMA-NANA.

Lakroan'i Madagasikara/La Croix de Madagascar: BP 7524, CNPC Antanimena, 101 Antananarivo; tel. (20) 2266128; fax (20) 2224854; e-mail lakroa@moov.mg; internet www.lakroa.mg; f. 1927; Roman Catholic; French and Malagasy; weekly; Dir Fr JACQUES MANANTO REHAMA; circ. 15,000.

La Lettre de Madagascar (LLM): Antananarivo; f. 2003; 2 a month; in French and English; economic; Editor-in-Chief DANIEL LAMY.

Mpanolotsaina: BP 623, 101 Antananarivo; tel. (20) 2226845; fax (20) 2226372; e-mail fjkm@wanadoo.mg; religious, educational; Malagasy; quarterly; Dir RAYMOND RAJOELISOL.

New Magazine: BP 7581, Newprint, route des Hydrocarbures, 101 Antananarivo; tel. (20) 2233335; fax (20) 2236471; e-mail newmag@ wanadoo.mg; internet www.newmagazine.mg; monthly; in French; Dir CLARA RAVOAVAHY.

Ny Mpamangy-FLM: 9 rue Général Gabriel Ramanantsoa Isoraka, 101 Antananarivo; tel. (20) 2228943; f. 1882; monthly; Dir LUCIE NOROSOANOMENJANAHARY; circ. 3,000.

Ny Sakaizan'ny Tanora: BP 538, Antsahaminitra, 101 Antananarivo; tel. (20) 2228943; f. 1878; monthly; Editor-in-Chief ELISABETH RAHELINORO; circ. 5,000.

Revue de l'Océan Indien: Communication et Médias Océan Indien, rue H. Rabesahala, BP 46, Antsakaviro, 101 Antananarivo; tel. (20) 2222536; fax (20) 2234534; e-mail roi@dts.mg; internet www .madatours.com/roi; f. 1980; monthly; French; Dir-Gen. HERY M. A. RANAIVOSOA; circ. 5,000.

Sahy: Lot VD 42, Ambanidia, 101 Antananarivo; tel. (20) 2222715; f. 1957; political; Malagasy; weekly; Editor ALINE RAKOTO; circ. 9,000.

Sosialisma Mpiasa: BP 1128, 101 Antananarivo; tel. (20) 2221989; f. 1979; trade union affairs; Malagasy; monthly; Dir PAUL RABEMA-NANJARA; circ. 5,000.

Vaovao: BP 271, 101 Antananarivo; tel. (20) 2221193; f. 1985; French and Malagasy; weekly; Dir MARC RAKOTONOELY; circ. 5,000.

NEWS AGENCIES

Agence Nationale d'Information 'TARATRA' (ANTA): 7 rue Jean Ralaimongo, Ambohiday, BP 386, 101 Antananarivo; tel. and fax (20) 2236047; e-mail taratra.mtpc@mtpc.gov.mg; f. 1977; Man. Dir JOÉ ANACLET RAKOTOARISON.

Mada: Villa Joëlle, Lot II J 161 R, Ivandry, 101 Antananarivo; tel. (20) 2242428; e-mail courrier@mada.mg; internet www.mada.mg; f. 2003; independent information agency; Dir RICHARD CLAUDE RATOVONARIVO.

Publishers

Edisiona Salohy: BP 4226, 101 Antananarivo; Dir MIRANA VOLO-LOARISOA RANDRIANARISON.

Editions Ambozontany Analamalintsy: BP 7553, 101 Antananarivo; tel. and fax (20) 2243111; e-mail editionsj@moov.mg; f. 1952; religious, educational, historical, cultural and technical textbooks; Dir Fr GUILLAUME DE SAINT PIERRE RAKOTONANDRATONIARIVO.

Imprimerie Nouvelle: PK 2, Andranomahery, route de Majunga, BP 4330, 101 Antananarivo; tel. (20) 2221036; fax (20) 2269225; e-mail nouvelle@wanadoo.mg; Dir EUGÈNE RAHARIFIDY.

Imprimerie Takariva: 4 rue Radley, BP 1029, Antanimena, 101 Antananarivo; tel. (20) 2222128; f. 1933; fiction, languages, school textbooks; Man. Dir PAUL RAPATSALAHY.

Madagascar Print and Press Co (MADPRINT): rue Rabesahala, Antsakaviro, BP 953, 101 Antananarivo; tel. (20) 2222536; fax (20) 2234534; f. 1969; literary, technical and historical; Dir GEORGES RANAIVOSOA.

Maison d'Edition Protestante Antso: 19 rue Venance Manifatra, Imarivolanitra, BP 660, 101 Antananarivo; tel. (20) 2220886; fax (20) 2226372; e-mail fjkm@dts.mg; f. 1972; religious, school, social, political and general; Dir HANS ANDRIAMAMPIANINA.

Office du Livre Malgache: Lot 111 H29, Andrefan' Ambohijanahary, BP 617, 101 Antananarivo; tel. (20) 2224449; f. 1970; children's and general; Sec.-Gen. JULIETTE RATSIMANDRAVA.

Société Malgache d'Edition (SME): BP 659, Ankorondrano, 101 Antananarivo; tel. (20) 2222635; fax (20) 2222254; e-mail tribune@ wanadoo.mg; f. 1943; general fiction, university and secondary textbooks; Man. Dir RAHAGA RAMAHOLIMIHASO.

Société Nouvelle de l'Imprimerie Centrale (SNIC): Route des Hydrocarbures, BP 1414, 101 Antananarivo; tel. (20) 2221118; fax (20) 2234421; e-mail contact@snic.mg; internet www.snic.mg; f. 1961; books, newspapers and magazines; CEO JEREMY RABESA-HALA.

Société de Presse et d'Edition de Madagascar: Antananarivo; non-fiction, reference, science, university textbooks; Man. Dir RAJAO-FERA ANDRIAMBELO.

Trano Printy Fiangonana Loterana Malagasy (TPFLM): BP 538, 9 rue Général Gabriel Ramanantsoa, 101 Antananarivo; tel. (20) 2224569; fax (20) 2262643; e-mail impluth@yahoo.fr; f. 1877; religious, educational and fiction; Man. RAYMOND RANDRIANATOANDRO.

GOVERNMENT PUBLISHING HOUSE

Imprimerie Nationale: BP 38, 101 Antananarivo; tel. (20) 2223675; e-mail dinm@wanadoo.mg; all official publs; Dir JEAN DENIS RANDRIANIRINA.

Broadcasting and Communications

REGULATORY AUTHORITY

Office Malagasy d'Etudes et de Régulation des Télécommunications (OMERT): BP 99991, route des Hydrocarbures-Alarobia, 101 Antananarivo; tel. (20) 2242119; fax (20) 2321516; e-mail omert@moov.mg; internet www.omert.org; f. 1997; Gen. Man. AUGUSTIN ANDRIAMANANORO.

TELECOMMUNICATIONS

In 2011 there were four providers of mobile telephone services in the country, one of which, TELMA, also provided fixed-line services.

Airtel Madagascar: Explorer Business Park, Ankorondrano, Antananarivo 101; tel. (33) 1100100; e-mail info.africa@airtel.com; internet africa.airtel.com/madagascar; f. 1997 as Madacom; fmrly

Celtel and subsequently Zain Madagascar; name changed as above in 2010; Dir-Gen. HEIKO SCHLITTKE.

Madamobil SA: Immeuble ARO Ampefiloha, 3ème étage, Porte A32, 101 Antananarivo; tel. (20) 2631886; e-mail contact@life.mg; internet www.life.mg; f. 1997; provides mobile telephone services under the brand name 'Life'; Pres. and Dir PATRICK PERTEGNAZZA.

Orange Madagascar: Antananarivo; internet www.orange.mg; f. 1998; fmrly Antaris, la Société Malgache de Mobiles; name changed as above 2003; mobile telecommunication GSM network provider; market leader; Dir-Gen. MICHEL BARRÉ.

Télécom Malagasy SA (TELMA): BP 763, 101 Antananarivo; tel. (20) 2532705; fax (20) 2253871; e-mail telmacorporate@telma.mg; internet www.telma.mg; 68% owned by Distacom (Hong Kong); owns DTS Wanadoo internet service provider; Chair. DAVID WHITE; Dir-Gen. PATRICK PISAL-HAMIDA.

BROADCASTING

In 2010, in addition to the state-owned Radio Nationale Malgache and Télévision Nationale Malagache, there were some 197 private FM radio stations and 21 private television stations in Madagascar.

Radio

Le Messager Radio Evangélique: BP 1374, 101 Antananarivo; tel. (20) 2234495; internet mreradio.com; broadcasts in French, English and Malagasy; Dir JOCELYN RANJARISON.

Radio MBS (Malagasy Broadcasting System): BP 11137, Anosipa-trana, Antananarivo; tel. (20) 2266702; fax (20) 2268941; e-mail marketing@mbs.mg; internet www.mbs.mg; broadcasts by satellite; Man. SARAH RAVALOMANANA.

Radio Antsiva: BP 632, Enceinte STEDIC, Village des Jeux, Zone Industrielle Nord, route des Hydrocarbures, 101 Antananarivo; tel. (20) 2254849; e-mail antsiva@freenet.mg; internet www.antsiva.mg; f. 1994; broadcasts in French and Malagasy.

Radio Don Bosco: Maison Don Bosco, BP 60, 105 Ivato; tel. (20) 2244387; fax (20) 2244511; e-mail rdb@radiodonbosco.org; internet www.radiodonbosco.org; f. 1996; Catholic, educational and cultural; Dir LUCA TREGLIA.

Radio Lazan'iarivo (RLI): Lot V A49, Andafiavaratra, 101 Anta-nanarivo; tel. (20) 2229016; fax (20) 2267559; e-mail rli@simicro.mg; broadcasts in French, English and Malagasy; privately owned; specializes in jazz music; Dir IHOBY RABARIJOHN.

Radio Nationale Malagasy: BP 442, Anosy, 101 Antananarivo; tel. (20) 2221745; fax (20) 2232715; e-mail rnmdir@dts.mg; internet www.rnm.mg; state-controlled; part of the Office de Radiodiffusion et de Télévision de Madagascar (ORTM); broadcasts in French and Malagasy; Dir JOHARY RAVOAJANAHARY.

Radio Viva: Antananarivo; Owner ANDRY RAJOELINA.

Television

MA TV: BP 1414 Ankorondrano, 101 Antananarivo; tel. (20) 2220897; fax (20) 2234421; f. 1995; Pres. FREDY ANDRIAMBELO; Dir-Gen. WILLY FREDY ANDRIAMBELO.

MBS Television (Malagasy Broadcasting System): BP 11137, Anosipatrana, Antananarivo; tel. (20) 2266702; fax (20) 2268941; e-mail journaltv@mbs.mg; internet www.mbs.mg; broadcasts in French and Malagasy.

Radio Télévision Analamanga (RTA): Immeuble Fiaro, 101 Antananarivo; tel. (20) 2224503; e-mail rta@rta.mg; internet www.rta.mg; incl. four provincial radio stations; Dir-Gen. SELVEN NAIDU.

Télévision Nasionale Malagache: BP 1202, Anosy, 101 Antananarivo; tel. (20) 2222381; state-controlled; part of the Office de Radiodiffusion et de Télévision de Madagascar (ORTM); broadcasts in French and Malagasy; Gen. Man. JPHARY RAVAOJANAHARY.

Télévision Viva: Antananarivo; Owner ANDRY RAJOELINA.

Finance

(cap. = capital; res = reserves; dep. = deposits; m. = million; brs = branches; amounts in ariary)

BANKING

Central Bank

Banque Centrale de Madagascar: rue de la Révolution Socialiste Malgache, BP 550, 101 Antananarivo; tel. (20) 2221751; fax (20) 2234532; e-mail sbu@bfm.mg; internet www.banque-centrale.mg; f. 1973; bank of issue; cap. 111,000m., res 32,420m., dep. 1,305,852m. (Dec. 2008); Gov. GUY RATOVONDRAHONA (acting).

Other Banks

Bank of Africa (BOA)—Madagascar: 2 pl. de l'Indépendance, BP 183, 101 Antananarivo; tel. (20) 2239100; fax (20) 2266125; e-mail boa@boa.mg; internet www.boa.mg; f. 1976 as Bankin'ny Tantsaha Mpamokatra; name changed as above 1999; 38.86% owned by Bank of Africa Group (Luxembourg), 10% state-owned; commercial bank, specializes in micro-finance; cap. 33,000.0m., res 36,511.4m., dep. 1,048,790.9m. (Dec. 2008); Chair. and Pres. PAUL DERREUMAUX; Gen. Man. JACQUES DILET; 55 brs.

Banque Industrielle et Commerciale de Madagascar (BICM): 2 rue du Dr Raseta Andraharo, BP 889, 101 Antananarivo; tel. (20) 2356568; fax (20) 2356656; e-mail bicm@bicm.mg; internet www.bicm.mg; f. 2002; successor of the Banque Internationale Chine Madagascar, fmrly Compagnie Malgache de Banque; cap. 5,779.2m., dep. 3,680.4m. (Dec. 2007) res –1,804.6m.(Dec. 2005); Pres. CHI MING HUI; Dir-Gen. Dr HUANG WEI GUANG.

Banque Malgache de l'Océan Indien (BMOI) (Indian Ocean Malagasy Bank): pl. de l'Indépendance, BP 25 bis, Antaninarenina, 101 Antananarivo; tel. (20) 2238251; fax (20) 2238544; e-mail bmoi.st@bnpparibas.com; internet www.bmoi.mg; f. 1989; 75% owned by BNP Paribas SA (France); cap. and res 40,200.0m., dep. 377,700.0m. (Dec. 2006); Pres. GASTON RAMENASON; Dir ALAIN RIPERT; 8 brs.

Banque SBM Madagascar: rue Andrianary Ratianarivo Antsaha-vola 1, 101 Antananarivo; tel. (20) 2266607; fax (20) 2266608; e-mail bsbmmtana@sbm.intnet.mu; f. 1998; 79.99% owned by SBM Global Investments Ltd (Mauritius), 20.01% owned by Nedbank Africa Investments Ltd (South Africa); cap. 7,404.1m., res 2,363.5m., dep. 92,221.2m. (Dec. 2007); Chair. CHAITLALL GUNNESS; Gen. Man. KRISHNADUTT RAMBOJUN.

BFV—Société Générale: 14 rue Général Rabehevitra, BP 196, Antananarivo 101; tel. (20) 2220691; fax (20) 2237140; e-mail relation.client@socgen.com; internet www.bfvsg.mg; f. 1977 as Banky Fampandrosoana ny Varotra; changed name in 1998; 70% owned by Société Générale (France), 28.5% state-owned; cap. 14,000.0m., res 48,833.0m., dep. 583,398.8m. (Dec. 2008); Pres. PHILIPPE LAMÉ; 40 brs.

BNI Madagascar: 74 rue du 26 Juin 1960, BP 174, 101 Antananarivo; tel. (20) 2222800; fax (20) 2233749; e-mail info@bni.mg; internet www.bni.mg; f. 1976 as Bankin 'ny Indostria; 51% owned by IUB Holding (France), 32.58% state-owned; cap. 10,800.0m., res 43,496.2m., dep. 693,056.1m. (Dec. 2007); Pres. and Chair. EVARISTE MARSON; Man. Dir PASCAL FALL; 25 brs.

Mauritius Commercial Bank (Madagascar) SA (MCB): 77 rue Solombavambahoaka Frantsay, Antsahavola, BP 197, 101 Antananarivo; tel. (20) 2227262; fax (20) 2228740; e-mail mcb.int@mcbmadagascar.com; internet www.mcbmadagascar.com; f. 1992 as Union Commercial Bank; name changed as above in 2007; 70% owned by Mauritius Commercial Bank Ltd; cap. 17,913.9m., res 6,753.6m., dep. 134,956.2m. (Dec. 2008); Chair. JEAN FRANÇOIS DESVAUX DE MARIGNY; Gen. Man. MARC MARIE JOSEPH DE BOLLIVIER; 3 brs.

INSURANCE

ARO (Assurances Réassurances Omnibranches): Antsahavola, BP 42, 101 Antananarivo; tel. (20) 2220154; fax (20) 2234464; e-mail aro1@moov.mg; internet www.aro.mg; state-owned; Dir-Gen. PATRICK ANDRIAMBAHINY.

ASCOMA Madagascar: 13 rue Patrice Lumumba, BP 673, 101 Antananarivo; tel. (20) 2223162; fax (20) 2222785; e-mail madagascar@ascoma.com; internet www.ascoma.com; f. 1952; Dir VIVIANE RAMANITRA.

Compagnie Malgache d'Assurances et de Réassurances 'Ny Havana': Immeuble 'Ny Havana', Zone des 67 Ha, BP 3881, 101 Antananarivo; tel. (20) 2226760; fax (20) 2224303; e-mail nyhavana@nyhavana.mg; internet www.nyhavana.mg; f. 1968; state-owned; cap. 7,704m. (2010); Dir-Gen. ROGER EMILE RANAIVOSON.

Mutuelle d'Assurances Malagasy (MAMA): Lot 1F, 12 bis Amba-lavao-Isotry, BP 185, 101 Antananarivo; tel. (20) 2261882; fax (20) 2261883; e-mail assurancemama@moov.mg; f. 1968; Dir SETH AIMÉ RANDRIANARIJAONA.

Trade and Industry

DEVELOPMENT ORGANIZATIONS

Agence Française de Développement: 23 rue Razanakombana Ambohijatovo, BP 557, Antananarivo; tel. (20) 2220046; fax (20) 2234794; e-mail afdantananarivo@groupe-afd.org; internet www.afd.fr; Dir JEAN-DAVID NAUDET.

Bureau d'Information pour les Entreprises (BIPE): Nouvel Immeuble ARO, Ampefiloha, 101 Antananarivo; tel. (20) 2230512;

internet www.bipe.mg; part of the Ministry of the Economy and Industry.

Economic Development Board of Madagascar (EDBM): ave Gabriel Ramanantsoa, Antaninarenina, Antananarivo 101; tel. (20) 2268121; fax (20) 2266105; e-mail edbm@edbm.mg; internet www .edbm.gov.mg; f. 2006; service for the facilitation and promotion of investment in Madagascar; advisory service for starting a business, obtaining visas and land acquisition; CEO ERIC RAKOTO ANDRIANTSI-LAVO.

La Maison de l'Entreprise: rue Samuel Ramahefy Ambatona-kanga, BP 74, 101 Antananarivo; tel. (20) 2225386; fax (20) 2233669; e-mail cite@cite.mg; internet www.cite.mg; f. 1967; supports and promotes Malagasy businesses; Dir-Gen. ISABELLE GACHIE.

Office des Mines Nationales et des Industries Stratégiques (OMNIS): 21 Làlana Razanakombana, BP 1 bis, 101 Antananarivo; tel. (20) 2224283; fax (20) 2222985; e-mail secdg@omnis.mg; internet www.omnis-madagascar.mg; f. 1976; promotes the exploration and exploitation of mining resources, in particular oil resources; Dir-Gen. BONAVENTURE RASOANAIVO.

Société d'Etude et de Réalisation pour le Développement Industriel (SERDI): BP 3180, 101 Antananarivo; tel. (20) 2225204; fax (20) 2229669; f. 1966; Dir-Gen. RAOILISON RAJAONARY.

CHAMBERS OF COMMERCE

Fédération des Chambres de Commerce et d'Industrie de Madagascar (FCCIM): BP 166, 20 rue Henri Razanatseheno, Antaninarenina, Antananarivo 101; tel. (20) 2221322; fax (20) 2220213; e-mail cciaa@tana-cciaa.org; internet www .cci-madagascar.org; 20 mem. chambers; Pres. CHABANI NOURDINE; Dir-Gen. JOSIELLE RAFIDY.

Chambre de Commerce et d'Industrie d'Antananarivo (CCIA): BP 166, 20 rue Henri Razanatseheno, Antaninarenina, 101 Antananarivo; tel. (20) 2220211; fax (20) 202220211; e-mail communication.tnr@cci.mg; internet www.cci.mg; f. 1993; Pres. JEAN MARTIN RAKOTOZAFY.

TRADE ASSOCIATION

Société d'Intérêt National des Produits Agricoles (SINPA): BP 754, rue Fernand-Kasanga, Tsimbazaza, Antananarivo; tel. (20) 2220558; fax (20) 2220665; f. 1973; monopoly purchaser and distributor of agricultural produce; Chair. GUALBERT RAZANAJATOVO; Gen. Man. JEAN CLOVIS RALIJESY.

EMPLOYERS' ORGANIZATIONS

Groupement des Entreprises de Madagascar (GEM): Kianja MDRM sy Tia Tanindrazana, Ambohijatovo, BP 1338, 101 Antananarivo; tel. (20) 2223841; fax (20) 2221965; e-mail gem@iris.mg; internet www.gem-madagascar.com; f. 1975; 16 nat. syndicates and five regional syndicates comprising 1,000 cos and 59 directly affiliated cos; Pres. JOSÉPHINE NORO ANDRIAMAMONJIARISON; Sec.-Gen. ZINAH RASAMUEL RAVALOSON.

Groupement National des Exportateurs de Vanille de Madagascar (GNEV): BP 21, Antalaha; tel. (13) 20714532; fax (13) 20816017; e-mail rama.anta@sat.blueline.mg; 18 mems; Pres. JEAN GEORGES RANDRIAMIHARISOA.

Malagasy Entrepreneurs' Association (FIV.MPA.MA): Immeuble NY HAVANA, 3e étage, Immeuble Santa, Antananarivo; tel. (20) 2267411; e-mail fivmpama@moov.mg; comprises 10 trade assocs, representing 200 mems, and 250 direct business mems; Chair. RAMANANTSOA RANDRIAMIFIDIMANANA.

Syndicat des Industries de Madagascar (SIM): Immeuble Holcim, Lot 1 bis, Tsaralalàna; BP 1695, 101 Antananarivo; tel. (20) 2224007; fax (20) 2222518; e-mail syndusmad@moov.mg; internet www.sim.mg; f. 1958; Pres. HERY STÉPHANE RAVELOSON; 96 mems (2010).

Syndicat des Planteurs de Café: 37 Làlana Razafimahandry, BP 173, 101 Antananarivo.

Syndicat Professionel des Producteurs d'Extraits Aromatiques, Alimentaires et Medicinaux de Madagascar (SYPEAM): 7 rue Rakotoson Toto Radona, Antsahavola, BP 5038, Antananarivo 101; tel. (20) 2235363; e-mail itd.madagascar@moov .mg; f. 1994; Pres. CHARLES RANDRIAMBOLOLONA.

UTILITIES

Electricity and Water

Office de Regulation de l'Electricité (ORE): rue Tsimanindry, Ambatoroka, Antananarivo; tel. (20) 2264813; fax (20) 2264191; e-mail ore@ore.mg; internet www.ore.mg; f. 2004; Pres. AIMÉE ANDRIANASOLO.

Jiro sy Rano Malagasy (JIRAMA): BP 200, 149 rue Rainandriamampandry, Faravohitra, 101 Antananarivo; tel. (20) 2220031; fax (20) 2233806; e-mail dgjirama@jirama.mg; internet www.jirama.mg; f. 1975; controls production and distribution of electricity and water; managed by local manager; Pres. HAJA RESAMPA; Dir-Gen. RASIDY DÉSIRÉ.

TRADE UNIONS

Cartel National des Organisations Syndicales de Madagascar (CARNOSYMA): BP 1035, 101 Antananarivo.

Confédération des Travailleurs Malagasy Révolutionnaires (FISEMARE): Lot IV N 76-A, Ankadifotsy, BP 1128, Befelatanana-Antananarivo 101; tel. (20) 2221989; fax (20) 2267712; f. 1985; Pres. PAUL RABEMANANJARA.

Confédération des Travailleurs Malgaches (Fivomdronamben'ny Mpiasa Malagasy—FMM): Lot IVM 133 A Antetezanafovoany I, BP 846, 101 Antananarivo; tel. (20) 2224565; e-mail rjeannot2002@yahoo.fr; f. 1957; Sec.-Gen. JEANNOT RAMANARIVO; 30,000 mems.

Fédération des Syndicats des Travailleurs de Madagascar (Firaisan'ny Sendika eran'i Madagaskara—FISEMA): Lot III, rue Pasteur Isotry, BP 172, 101 Antananarivo; tel. (33) 1187414; e-mail fisema@gmail.co; internet fisema.org; f. 1956; Sec.-Gen. JOSÉ RANDRIANASOLO; 8 affiliated unions representing 60,000 mems.

Sendika Kristianina Malagasy (SEKRIMA) (Christian Confederation of Malagasy Trade Unions): Soarano, route de Mahajanga, BP 1035, 101 Antananarivo; tel. (20) 2223174; f. 1937; Pres. MARIE RAKOTOANOSY; Gen. Sec. JEANNE CLAIRETTE RAZANARIMANANA; 158 affiliated unions representing 40,000 mems.

Union des Syndicats Autonomes de Madagascar (USAM): Lot III M 33 BC, Andrefan'Ambohijanahary, BP 1038, 101 Antananarivo; tel. and fax (20) 2227485; e-mail usam@moov.mg; f. 1954; Pres. THÉOPHILE JOËL RUFIN RAZAKARIASY; Sec.-Gen. SAMUEL RABEMANANTSOA; 49 affiliated unions representing 30,000 mems.

Transport

RAILWAYS

In 2009 there were 854 km of railway, including four railway lines, all 1-m gauge track. The northern system, which comprised 673 km of track, links the east coast with Antsirabé, in the interior, via Moramanga and Antananarivo, with a branch line from Moramanga to Lake Alaotra, and was privatized in 2001. The southern system, which comprised 163 km of track, links Manakara, on the east coast, with Fianarantsoa.

Fianarantsoa-Côte Est (FCE): FCE Gare, 301 Fianarantsoa; tel. (20) 7551354; e-mail fce@blueline.mg; internet www .fce-fianarantsoa-madagascar.com; f. 1936; southern network, 163 km.

Madarail: Gare de Soarano, 1 ave de l'Indépendance, BP 1175, 101 Antananarivo; tel. (20) 2234599; fax (20) 2221883; e-mail madarail@wanadoo.mg; internet www.comazar.com/madarail.htm; f. 2001; jt venture, operated by Comazar, South Africa; 45% of Comazar is owned by Sheltam Locomotive and Rail Services, South Africa; 31.6% is owned by Transnet Freight Rail, South Africa; operates the northern network of the Malagasy railway (650 km); Chair. ERIC PEIFFER; Gen. Dir PATRICK CLAES; 878 employees.

ROADS

In 2010 there were an estimated 37,476 km of classified roads; about 16.3% of the road network was paved. In 1987 there were 39,500 km of unclassified roads, used only in favourable weather. A road and motorway redevelopment programme, funded by the World Bank (€300m.) and the European Union (EU) (€61m.), began in 2000. In 2002 the EU undertook to disburse US $10m. for the reconstruction of 11 bridges destroyed during the political crisis in that year. In 2003 Japan pledged $28m. to build several bridges and a 15-km bypass. The Government planned to have restored and upgraded 14,000 km of highways and 8,000 km of rural roads to an operational status by 2015. In 2005, according to the IMF, 8,982 km of roads had been maintained or rehabilitated.

INLAND WATERWAYS

The Pangalanes canal runs for 600 km near the east coast from Toamasina to Farafangana. In 1990 432 km of the canal between Toamasina and Mananjary were navigable.

SHIPPING

There are 18 ports, the largest being at Toamasina, which handles about 70% of total traffic, and Mahajanga; several of the smaller ports are prone to silting problems. A new deep-sea port was constructed at Ehoala, near Fort Dauphin, in order to accommodate the activity of an ilmenite mining development; the first vessel docked at the port in December 2008. At 31 December 2012 the country's flag registered fleet numbered 42 vessels and amounted to 20,260 gross registered tons.

CMA—CGM Madagascar: Village des jeux, Bat. C1 Ankorondrano, BP 12042, 101 Antananarivo; tel. (20) 2235949; fax (20) 2266120; e-mail tnr@cma-cgm.mg; internet www.cma-cgm.com; maritime transport; Gen. Man. JOËL LE JULIEN.

Compagnie Générale Maritime Sud (CGM): BP 1185, Lot II U 31 bis, Ampahibe, 101 Antananarivo; tel. (20) 2220113; fax (20) 2226530.

Compagnie Malgache de Navigation (CMN): rue Rabearivelo, BP 1621, 101 Antananarivo; tel. (20) 2225516; fax (20) 2230358; f. 1960; coasters; 13,784 grt; 97.5% state-owned; privatization pending; Pres. ELINAH BAKOLY RAJAONSON; Dir-Gen. ARISTIDE EMMANUEL.

SCAC-SDV Shipping Madagascar: rue Rabearivelo Antsahavola, BP 514, 102 Antananarivo; tel. (20) 2220631; fax (20) 2247862; operates the harbour in Antananarivo Port.

Société Malgache des Transports Maritimes (SMTM): 6 rue Indira Gandhi, BP 4077, 101 Antananarivo; tel. (20) 2227342; fax (20) 2233327; f. 1963; 59% state-owned; privatization pending; services to Europe; Chair. ALEXIS RAZAFINDRATSIRA; Dir-Gen. JEAN RANJEVA.

Société du Port à Gestion Autonome de Toamasina (SPAT): blvd Ratsimilaho, Ampasimazava Est, Toamasina; e-mail spat@port-toamasina.com; internet www.port-toamasina.com; Dir-Gen. CHRISTIAN AVELLIN.

CIVIL AVIATION

The Ivato international airport is at Antananarivo, while the airports at Mahajanga, Toamasina and Nossi-Bé can also accommodate large jet aircraft. There are 211 airfields, two-thirds of which are privately owned. In 1996 the Government authorized private French airlines to operate scheduled and charter flights between Madagascar and Western Europe.

Aeromarine: Zone Industrielle FORELLO, Tanjombato, BP 3844, 102 Antananarivo; tel. (20) 2248286; fax (20) 2258026; e-mail aeromarine@blueline.mg; internet www.aeromarine.mg; f. 1991; Dir-Gen. RIAZ BARDAY.

Air Madagascar (Société Nationale Malgache des Transports Aériens): 31 ave de l'Indépendance, Analakely, BP 437, 101 Antananarivo; tel. (20) 2222222; fax (20) 2233760; e-mail commercial@airmadagascar.com; internet www.airmadagascar.com; f. 1962; 90.60% state-owned; 3.17% owned by Air France (France); transfer to the private sector pending; restructured and managed by Lufthansa Consulting since 2002; extensive internal routes connecting all the principal towns; external services to France, Italy, the Comoros, Kenya, Mauritius, Réunion, South Africa and Thailand; Chair. HERY RAJAONARIMAMPIANINA; Dir-Gen. HUGHES RATSIFERANA.

Air Transport et Transit Régional (ATTR): tel. (32) 0518811; fax (32) 3205218; e-mail attr.reservation@blueline.mg; internet www.attrmada.com; f. 2006; private; regular local and regional services; services suspended in 2008; Dir-Gen. FRÉDÉRIC RABESAHALA.

Aviation Civile de Madagascar (ACM): 13 rue Fernand Kasanga, BP 4414, 101 Tsimbazaza-Antananarivo; tel. (20) 2222438; fax (20) 2224726; e-mail acm@acm.mg; internet www.acm.mg; f. 2000; Chair. RANTO RABARISOA; Dir-Gen. JEAN RAZAFY ROBERT.

Transports et Travaux Aériens de Madagascar (TAM): 17 ave de l'Indépendance, Analakely, Antananarivo; tel. (20) 2222222; fax (20) 2224340; e-mail tamdg@wanadoo.mg; f. 1951; provides airline services; Administrators LALA RAZAFINDRAKOTO, FRANÇOIS DANE.

Tourism

Madagascar's attractions include unspoiled scenery, many unusual varieties of flora and fauna, and the rich cultural diversity of Malagasy life. In 2008 some 375,010 tourists visited Madagascar, the majority were from France (56.0%). There was a dramatic fall in the number of tourists visiting Madagascar in 2009, to 162,687; however, tourist numbers recovered somewhat in 2010 and 2011 rising to 196,052 and an estimated 225,000, respectively. Revenue from tourism in 2008 was an estimated US $620m., declining to $518m. in 2009 and further to $321m. in 2010.

Direction d'Appui aux Investissements Publiques: BP 610, rue Fernand Kasanga Tsimbazaza, 101 Antananarivo; tel. (20) 2262816; fax (20) 2235410; e-mail mintourdati@wandaoo.mg; internet www.tourisme.gov.mg.

Office National du Tourisme de Madagascar: 3 rue Elysée Ravelontsalama, Ambatomena, 101 Antananarivo; tel. (20) 2266115; fax (20) 2266098; e-mail ontm@moov.mg; internet www.madagascar-tourisme.com; Pres. JOEL RANDRIAMANDRANTO.

Defence

As assessed at November 2012, Madagascar's total armed forces numbered 13,500 men: army 12,500, navy 500 and air force 500. There was also a paramilitary gendarmerie of 8,100.

Defence Expenditure: Budgeted at an estimated 146,000m. ariary in 2011.

Chief of Staff of the Armed Forces: Col ANDRÉ ANDRIARIJAONA.

Education

Education is officially compulsory between six and 13 years of age. Madagascar has both public and private schools, although legislation enacted in 1978 envisaged the progressive elimination of private education. Primary education generally begins at the age of six and lasts for five years. Secondary education, beginning at 11 years of age, lasts for a further seven years, comprising a first cycle of four years and a second of three years. A new educational system, comprising 10 years of basic education and two years of secondary education, was intended for gradual introduction from the academic year 2008/09. However, the process of implementation was suspended in March 2009. According to UNESCO estimates, in 2006/07 primary enrolment included 98% of children in the relevant age-group (male 98%; females 99%), while in 2008/09 secondary enrolment included 26% of children in the relevant age-group (males 26%; females 25%). In 2009/10 74,400 students attended institutions providing tertiary education. In 2005/06 there were six universities and 14 private higher education institutes in Madagascar. In 2011 spending on education represented 20.1% of total budgetary expenditure.

MALAWI

Introductory Survey

LOCATION, CLIMATE, LANGUAGE, RELIGION, FLAG, CAPITAL

The Republic of Malawi is a land-locked country in southern central Africa, with Zambia to the west, Mozambique to the south and east, and Tanzania to the north. Lake Malawi forms most of the eastern boundary. The climate is tropical, but much of the country is sufficiently high above sea-level to modify the heat. Temperatures range from 14°C (57°F) to 18°C (64°F) in mountain areas, but can reach 38°C (100°F) in low-lying regions. There is a rainy season between November and April. The official language is English, although Chichewa is being promoted as the basis for a 'Malawi Language'. Chitumbuka, a national language, and Yao are also widely spoken. More than 82% of the population profess Christianity, while a further 13%, largely Asians, are Muslims. Most of the remaining Malawians follow traditional beliefs, although there is also a Hindu minority. The national flag (proportions 2 by 3) has three equal horizontal stripes, of black, red and green, with a rising sun, in red, in the centre of the black stripe. The capital is Lilongwe.

CONTEMPORARY POLITICAL HISTORY

Historical Context

Malawi was formerly the British protectorate of Nyasaland. In 1953 it was linked with two other British dependencies, Northern and Southern Rhodesia (now Zambia and Zimbabwe), to form the Federation of Rhodesia and Nyasaland. The Federation was dissolved in December 1963 and Nyasaland gained independence, as Malawi, on 6 July 1964. The country became a republic and a one-party state, with Dr Hastings Kamuzu Banda, the leader of the Malawi Congress Party (MCP), as its first President, on 6 July 1966. Malawi created a major controversy among African states in 1967 by officially recognizing the Republic of South Africa. In 1971 Banda, named Life President in that year, became the first African head of state to visit South Africa. In 1976, however, Malawi recognized the communist-backed Government in Angola in preference to the South African-supported forces. Malawi did not recognize the 'independence' granted by South Africa to four of its African 'homelands'.

Domestic Political Affairs

Until 1993 all Malawian citizens were obliged to be members of the MCP; no political opposition was tolerated, and only candidates who had been approved by Banda were allowed to contest elections to the National Assembly. Frequent reorganizations of the Cabinet effectively prevented the emergence of any political rival to Banda. However, it was reported in 1983 that a conflict had developed between Dick Matenje, the Minister without Portfolio in the Cabinet and Secretary-General of the MCP, and John Tembo, the Governor of the Reserve Bank of Malawi, concerning the eventual succession to Banda. In May the authorities reported that Matenje and three other senior politicians had died in a road accident; Malawian exiles claimed that the four men had been shot while attempting to flee the country.

Opposition to the Government intensified during 1992 and in September opposition activists formed the Alliance for Democracy (AFORD)—a pressure group operating within Malawi, under the chairmanship of Chakufwa Chihana, a prominent trade union leader—which aimed to campaign for democratic political reform. Another opposition grouping, the United Democratic Front (UDF), was formed in October. In that month Banda conceded that a referendum on the introduction of a multi-party system would take place. However, in November the Government banned AFORD. In the following month Chihana was found guilty of sedition and sentenced to two years' hard labour (reduced to nine months in March 1993).

At the referendum on the introduction of a multi-party system, held on 14 June 1993, 63.2% of those who participated (some 63.5% of the electorate) voted for an end to single-party rule. Banda rejected opposition demands for the immediate installation of an interim government of national unity. He agreed, however, to the establishment of a National Executive Council to oversee the transition to a multi-party system and the holding of

free elections, and of a National Consultative Council to implement the necessary amendments to the Constitution. Both councils were to include members of the Government and the opposition. Banda announced an amnesty for thousands of political exiles, and stated that a general election would be held, on a multi-party basis, within a year. In late June the Constitution was amended to allow the registration of political parties other than the MCP: by mid-August five organizations, including AFORD and the UDF, had been accorded official status.

In September 1993 Banda carried out an extensive cabinet reshuffle, relinquishing the post of Minister of External Affairs, which he had held since 1964. In October 1993 Banda underwent neurological surgery in South Africa. Interim executive power was assumed by a three-member Presidential Council, chaired by the new Secretary-General of the MCP, Gwandaguluwe Chakuamba. In November a further cabinet reorganization relieved Banda of all ministerial responsibilities. Later in November the National Assembly approved a Constitutional Amendment Bill, which, *inter alia*, abolished the institution of life presidency, ended the requirement that election candidates be members of the MCP and repealed the right of the President to nominate members of the legislature exclusively from the MCP.

Having made a rapid and unexpected recovery, Banda resumed full presidential powers in December 1993. Shortly afterwards, in response to increasing pressure from the opposition, the Government amended the Constitution to provide for the appointment of an acting President in the event of the incumbent being incapacitated. In February 1994 the MCP announced that Banda was to be the party's presidential candidate in the forthcoming general election (scheduled for May). Also in February the National Assembly approved an increase in the number of elective seats in the legislature from 141 to 177.

On 16 May 1994 the National Assembly adopted a provisional Constitution, which provided for the appointment of a Constitutional Committee and of a human rights commission, and abolished the system of 'traditional' courts. Malawi's first multi-party parliamentary and presidential elections took place on 17 May. In the presidential election the Secretary-General of the UDF, (Elson) Bakili Muluzi (a former government minister and MCP Secretary-General), took 47.3% of the votes cast, defeating Banda (who won 33.6% of the votes). Eight parties contested the legislative elections: of these, the UDF won 85 seats in the National Assembly, the MCP 56 and AFORD 36. The Constitution was introduced for a one-year period on 18 May; it was to be subject to further review prior to official ratification one year later.

The Muluzi presidency

President Muluzi and his Vice-President, Justin Malewezi, were inaugurated on 21 May 1994. The new UDF-dominated Government proclaimed an amnesty for the country's remaining political prisoners, and commuted all death sentences to terms of life imprisonment. In August it was announced that Banda, while remaining honorary Life President of the MCP, was to retire from active involvement in politics. Chakuamba, as Vice-President of the party, effectively became the leader of the MCP.

In September 1994 a number of AFORD members were appointed to the Government, including Chihana as Second Vice-President and Minister of Irrigation and Water Development. Meanwhile, the creation of the post of Second Vice-President had necessitated a constitutional amendment, and provoked severe criticism from the MCP. In March the National Assembly (in the absence of MCP deputies, who boycotted the vote) approved the retention of the second vice-presidency; the Assembly also endorsed recommendations for the establishment—although not before May 1999—of a second chamber of parliament. The Constitution took effect on 18 May 1995.

In June 1994 Muluzi established an independent commission of inquiry to investigate the deaths of Matenje and his associates in May 1983. In January 1995, in accordance with the findings of the commission, Banda was placed under house arrest and Tembo and two former police officers were detained; the four were charged with murder and conspiracy to murder. A former inspector-general of police was charged later in the month. In April Cecilia Kadzamira, Tembo's niece and the former President's 'Official Hostess', was also charged with conspiracy to murder. The trial opened later that month, but was immediately adjourned after Banda failed to appear in court (his defence counsel asserted that he was too ill to stand trial). Hearings resumed, in Banda's absence, in July. The case against Kadzamira was abandoned in December, owing to the lack of evidence, and later that month Banda, Tembo and the other defendants were found not guilty of conspiracy to murder and conspiracy to defeat justice. In January 1996 an MCP-owned newspaper printed a statement by Banda in which he admitted that he might unknowingly have been responsible for brutalities perpetrated under his regime and apologized to Malawians for 'pain and suffering' inflicted during his presidency. In November 1997 Banda died in South Africa, where he had been undergoing emergency medical treatment.

Meanwhile, it emerged in mid-1995 that President Muluzi had authorized the payment of some 6.2m. kwacha from the state poverty alleviation account to UDF deputies; there was also evidence of the involvement of government ministers in the smuggling of maize to neighbouring countries. In February 1996 Muluzi announced that an independent Anti-Corruption Bureau (ACB) was to be established to investigate allegations of corruption.

In June 1998 the National Assembly approved legislation providing for the introduction of a single-ballot electoral system to replace the existing multiple-ballot system and for a strengthening of the authority and independence of the Malawi Electoral Commission (MEC). In November legislation was adopted to allow presidential and parliamentary elections to run concurrently (as Muluzi's term was due to end several weeks earlier than that of the National Assembly), and the elections were subsequently scheduled for 18 May 1999. In February the National Assembly adopted a controversial report by the MEC that recommended the creation of a further 72 parliamentary seats, including an additional 42 in the Southern Region, a UDF stronghold. In response to widespread opposition to the proposals, however, the establishment of only 16 of the 72 seats was approved.

Having been postponed twice, the presidential and legislative elections were held on 15 June 1999. Muluzi was re-elected to the presidency, securing 51.4% of the votes cast, while Chakuamba obtained 43.3%. Turn-out was high, at 93.8% of the electorate. At the elections to the expanded National Assembly the ruling UDF won 94 seats, while the MCP secured 66 seats, AFORD 29 and independent candidates four. Muluzi was inaugurated later in June, and a new Cabinet was appointed. In August the UDF regained a parliamentary majority when the four independent deputies decided to ally themselves with the UDF, of which they had previously been members.

Chakuamba, who had maintained a boycott of the new parliament pending the result of his party's challenge to the outcome of the elections, was suspended from the chamber in June 2000. Tembo assumed the leadership of the opposition and appointed his supporters to prominent posts within the MCP. Chakuamba was reinstated in September, and a dispute between the two factions ensued. In October the opposition's petitions against the election results were dismissed by the High Court.

Proposed legislation to change the Constitution to allow Muluzi to seek a third presidential term failed to gain the requisite two-thirds' majority in July 2002. A further attempt to introduce a constitutional amendment also failed in January 2003, when the bill was withdrawn. In March Muluzi declared that he would not seek a third presidential term, and proposed Dr Bingu wa Mutharika, recently appointed Minister of Economic Planning and Development, as his successor, to contest the presidential election scheduled for May 2004. (Mutharika had represented the United Party at the 1999 presidential election, but subsequently defected to the UDF.)

In May 2003 Tembo and Chakuamba were elected, respectively, as President and Vice-President of the MCP. Tembo was subsequently named as the MCP's candidate to contest the 2004 presidential election. Chakuamba resigned from the MCP and formed the Republican Party (RP). On 1 January 2004 Justin Malewezi, Malawi's First Vice-President and Minister responsible for Privatization, resigned from the UDF for 'personal reasons', but did not relinquish his position in the Government, stating that he would remain in office, but on leave, until after the presidential election had taken place. Malewezi subsequently joined the People's Progressive Movement (PPM), an opposition party founded the previous year. Later that month Aleke Banda, who had resigned from the UDF in May 2003, was elected as President of the PPM, while Malewezi was chosen as its Vice-President. Also in January 2004 the PPM, the RP and several other opposition parties announced the formation of the Mgwirizano Coalition to contest the forthcoming presidential election; Chakuamba was elected as the coalition's presidential candidate in February. Muluzi appointed Hetherwick Ntaba, the leader of the New Congress for Democracy (NCD), as Minister of Energy and Mining in March, following the NCD's decision to join the UDF-AFORD electoral alliance.

Mutharika elected President

At the presidential election held on 20 May 2004 Mutharika, representing the ruling UDF, secured 35.9% of the valid votes cast. Tembo and Chakuamba took 27.1% and 25.7% of the vote, respectively. Cassim Chilumpha, of the UDF, was elected as Vice-President. At concurrent elections to the National Assembly, however, the MCP emerged as the largest party, winning 56 of the 193 seats in the legislature, while the UDF secured 49 seats and the Mgwirizano Coalition 25; 39 of the remaining seats were taken by independent candidates, while voting in six constituencies was not conducted owing to irregularities. International observers criticized the conduct of the polls and opposition parties disputed the results. Mutharika was sworn in as President on 24 May, amid rioting by opposition supporters, and a new Cabinet was appointed in June. Mutharika, in defiance of critics who believed that he would merely serve to act as Muluzi's 'puppet', pledged to take measures to combat corruption and to effect wide-ranging economic reforms. In October former Minister of Finance Friday Jumbe was arrested in connection with illegal sales of maize during 2001–02 while General Manager of the Agriculture Development and Marketing Corporation; he was subsequently charged with four counts of corruption. Also in October 2004 it was announced that at least 10 former senior ministers were under investigation by the ACB following the disappearance of more than 10,000m. kwacha during the Muluzi presidency.

In February 2005 Mutharika resigned from the leadership of the UDF—of which Muluzi was Chairman—claiming that the party was opposing his campaign against corruption. Prior to the announcement, Mutharika dismissed three members of the Government loyal to Muluzi, including Chihana, who was replaced as Minister of Agriculture, Irrigation and Food Security by Chakuamba. Later that month Mutharika announced his intention to form a new political party, the Democratic Progressive Party (DPP), which was formally registered in March. In May the Minister of Education and Human Resources, Yusuf Mwawa, was arrested on charges of corruption, fraud and misuse of public funds. (In February 2006 Mwawa was sentenced to five years' imprisonment.) In June 2005 the UDF introduced before the National Assembly a motion of impeachment against Mutharika, alleging statutory violations of the Constitution and misuse of public funds.

In October 2005 Muluzi was summoned to appear before the ACB, which was investigating the misappropriation of 1,400m. kwacha in foreign aid during his presidency. It was alleged that much of this money had been diverted to personal bank accounts and had also been used to finance the 2004 presidential campaign. Muluzi was able to obtain an injunction from the High Court, which allowed him to refuse to answer the ACB's questions. In November Vice-President Chilumpha was arrested in connection with the alleged embezzlement of 187m. kwacha during his tenure as Minister of Education. Chilumpha obtained an injunction against criminal proceedings on the grounds that, as the incumbent Vice-President, he was immune from prosecution.

Meanwhile, following an agreement between the UDF and Tembo, in October 2005 the National Assembly voted in favour of instigating proceedings to impeach Mutharika, and he was summoned to face indictment before the legislature later that month. However, the impeachment process was halted by the High Court after concern was expressed over the constitutionality of the process. In December regional leaders brokered talks between Mutharika, Muluzi and Tembo in an attempt to halt the impeachment proceedings; however, they ended without success. The impeachment motion was eventually withdrawn in January 2006, prompting the resignation of seven UDF members, five of whom subsequently joined the DPP.

In February 2006 it was announced that Mutharika had accepted Chilumpha's 'constructive resignation'. In a letter to Chilumpha, the President asserted that Chilumpha had abandoned his duties as Vice-President, leading the Cabinet to conclude that he had resigned. Chilumpha refuted the allegations made against him—*inter alia*, that he had attended only 16 out of 48 cabinet meetings and had left the country without informing Mutharika—and brought the matter before the High Court on the grounds that his dismissal was unconstitutional: as an elected minister he could only be dismissed by Parliament, not by the President. In March the High Court apparently ordered Chilumpha's full restitution; however, the Supreme Court ruled later that month that, although Chilumpha was confirmed in his position as Vice-President, the Government was permitted to divest him of all benefits and entitlements. In April Chilumpha was arrested and charged with treason and conspiring to murder the President. His trial commenced in early 2007 but was subject to numerous delays. (In mid-2012 the incoming administration of Joyce Banda intimated that the charges against Chilumpha would be withdrawn.)

In April 2008 Muluzi was named as the UDF's candidate for the presidential election due to be held concurrently with legislative elections in May 2009; having previously served two terms in office, opponents objected to his candidacy. However, Muluzi's supporters maintained that the Constitution stipulated only that a President may not serve more than two 'consecutive' terms. In March 2009 the MEC ruled that Muluzi was ineligible to contest the election on the grounds that he had already served as President for the maximum period of two five-year terms. Muluzi appealed against the decision, but in May the Constitutional Court rejected his challenge. He subsequently declared his support for Tembo, who had been selected as the presidential candidate for the newly formed UDF-MCP-New Republican Party (NRP) electoral alliance.

Meanwhile, reports emerged in May 2008 that eight high-ranking security officials, including former Commander-in-Chief of the Armed Forces Lt-Gen. Joseph Chimbayo, had been arrested following accusations by Mutharika that they had been acting under instruction from Muluzi in an attempt to remove him from office. Later that month Muluzi was questioned by police and placed under house arrest. Muluzi denied the allegations and was later released without charge. In February 2009 Muluzi was again detained on charges of corruption relating to the misappropriation of donor funds during his presidency. His trial commenced in March 2011, but proceedings were suspended later that month due to the former President's ill health; the trial was scheduled to resume in May 2013.

Mutharika's second term

By April 2009 several smaller parties had indicated their willingness to join the new UDF-MCP-NRP alliance, which had been established earlier that month to contest the forthcoming presidential and legislative elections. Nevertheless, Mutharika won an overwhelming victory in the presidential election, which was held on 19 May, with 64.4% of the votes cast, while the DPP retained control of the National Assembly in the concurrent legislative poll. The DPP won 112 of the 192 available seats (voting in one constituency was postponed owing to the death of a candidate), the MCP took only 27 seats and the UDF, the influence of which was predominantly limited to the south of the country, 18 seats. A further 32 seats were secured by independent candidates, many of whom had connections to the DPP. Tembo, who had secured 29.9% of the votes in the presidential election, claimed that there was evidence of electoral fraud; however, the MEC declared the ballot to have been free and fair. In June President Mutharika announced the formation of a new Government, which included a number of new appointments to key roles. Arthur Peter Mutharika, the President's brother, became Minister of Justice and Constitutional Affairs, amid widespread reports that he was being prepared to take over the presidency in 2014. In December 2009 Muluzi stepped down as Chairman of the UDF; he was replaced as party leader on an interim basis by Friday Jumbe, who assumed the position of President of the UDF.

Malawi's conservative stance on civil liberties came under international scrutiny in May 2010, when a homosexual couple, who had allegedly been forced to endure beatings and intrusive medical examinations while in custody, were convicted of 'gross indecency and unnatural acts' and sentenced to 14 years' imprisonment. Following criticism from Western donor nations and human rights organizations, Mutharika pardoned the two men, and they were released later that month, although the President denied that international pressure had prompted him to take this action.

In August 2010 Mutharika effected a cabinet reorganization. The ministers responsible for health, transport, local government and gender were all dismissed, while Arthur Peter Mutharika was appointed as Minister of Education, Science and Technology. Furthermore, the President controversially allocated his wife, Callista wa Mutharika, responsibility for maternal, infant and child health, although it was later clarified that she would not be a cabinet member, nor receive a ministerial salary. There was speculation that the Minister of Local Government and Rural Development, Goodall Gondwe, had been replaced because of the repeated postponement of the local elections—last held in 2000 and due since 2005—ostensibly owing to procedural delays and a lack of progress in the implementation of local government reforms. (The local elections were subsequently rescheduled for April 2011.) However, a number of reports in the media claimed that the dismissals had been prompted by a dispute within the DPP over who would become the party's presidential candidate in the 2014 election in place of Mutharika, who was constitutionally prohibited from standing for a third term of office. President Mutharika favoured his brother, Arthur Peter Mutharika, and had been manoeuvring against Vice-President Joyce Banda, who was viewed as a potential rival candidate, in an attempt to secure her expulsion from the DPP. The dismissed ministers had reportedly criticized the President's efforts to remove Banda from the ruling party. Amid rising factionalism within the DPP, in September 2010 the party terminated official ties with its youth wing, the allegedly pro-Banda Progressive Democratic Youth Movement, which subsequently denounced the DPP's 'undemocratic endorsement' of Arthur Peter Mutharika's candidature. Meanwhile, in a further attempt to marginalize Banda, President Mutharika had transferred some of the Vice-President's responsibilities to his wife. In December the DPP finally expelled Banda, accusing her of involvement in 'anti-party activities' and of 'forming parallel structures in the party and Government'; however, it was widely believed that Banda's expulsion had resulted from her failure to support Arthur Peter Mutharika as the DPP's official presidential candidate. Hundreds of DPP members nation-wide resigned from the party in protest and formed a new grouping, the Friends of Joyce Banda. Despite reported death threats against her, in early 2011 Vice-President Banda announced the creation of a new political organization, the People's Party (PP), which was officially registered in July. Banda claimed that she had the support of many DPP deputies.

In January 2011, in a move allegedly orchestrated by Muluzi, the UDF's National Executive Committee elected Dr George Nga Ntafu as party Chairman; however, Jumbe denounced the Committee's action as a 'failed *coup d'état*' and refused to cede control of the leadership of the UDF to Ntafu, effectively splitting the party into two factions. In the following month Jumbe's faction held a separate leadership vote, electing former Vice-President Chilumpha as Chairman and Jumbe as President (the latter being a position not recognized under the UDF's charter). In September, in an attempt to resolve the impasse, both factions agreed to hold another leadership contest. At the election, which was held in October 2012, Atupele Muluzi (the son of the former President) was selected as the new UDF leader. Jumbe established a new party, the Labour Party, in the following month.

In May 2011 the MEC announced that long-delayed local elections would again be postponed, until 2014, ostensibly owing to the disruption caused by an incident within the Commission in late 2010 involving the apparent disappearance of US $3m. (subsequently determined to be merely an auditing error). On 19 July 2011, in an apparent attempt to intimidate potential demonstrators, the High Court ruled that anti-Government protests scheduled to take place on the following day would be considered illegal, despite the fact that armed DPP activists had been able to stage a rally of their own earlier that day. Nevertheless, on 20–21 July, in the most serious challenge to the authority of the Mutharika administration since the President took office, large-scale demonstrations, orchestrated by civil society organizations, were held throughout the country to protest against the Government's economic policies, shortages of fuel, power and foreign exchange, and the President's increasingly dictatorial tendencies. The violent suppression of the protests by the security forces resulted in the deaths of 19 demonstrators, more than 150 people being injured and up to 500 arrests. In addition, protest leaders were reportedly subjected to death threats from anonymous sources. This violent response by the authorities attracted domestic and international censure. Discussions, under UN auspices, were held in August between government representatives and protest organizers, although the talks foundered in the following month after the latter suspended their participation due to further violent attacks against their supporters. In October the President announced the establishment of an official inquiry into the July violence, but there were concerns expressed regarding the credibility and independence of this body.

Shortly after the demonstrations, Mutharika replaced numerous members of the DPP and several senior military officials, including the Commander of the Malawi Defence Force. In September 2011 the President announced the formation of a new Cabinet, after having dissolved the incumbent body the previous month. Most notably, Ken Lipenga was appointed as Minister of Finance and Development Planning, Arthur Peter Mutharika became the new Minister of Foreign Affairs and International Co-operation, and Callista wa Mutharika assumed ministerial rank on being given responsibility for combating HIV, malnutrition, malaria and tuberculosis; the latter two appointments prompted claims of nepotism. In an apparent violation of the Constitution, President Mutharika refused to name Vice-President Banda, an outspoken critic of the violence employed by the security forces, in his new Cabinet and accused her of colluding with the demonstrators. Also in September, Mutharika commenced legal proceedings at the High Court to determine if Banda had 'constructively' resigned the vice-presidency by assuming the leadership of the opposition PP and failing to attend cabinet meetings. Banda's office had been further weakened in mid-2011 by a 60% reduction in its funding and by the removal of more of its responsibilities.

A number of contentious laws were under review in late 2011, including regulations concerning homosexuality, restrictions on legal challenges against the Government and legislation approved in January that granted the authorities the power to close down newspapers publishing content regarded as being 'contrary to the public interest'. Western donor nations and international organizations had cited these laws and other governance concerns as factors that had led to the suspension or reduction of aid inflows to Malawi during 2011.

Recent developments: Banda assumes power

On 7 April 2012 the death of President Mutharika was officially announced. The President was reported to have died on 5 April after suffering a heart attack in South Africa where he had been receiving medical attention. In accordance with the country's Constitution, Vice-President Banda was sworn in as Head of State on 7 April and was to serve the remainder of Mutharika's term, which was scheduled to expire in 2014. On 10 April 2012 Banda dismissed the Minister of Information and Civic Education, Patricia Kaliati, and Chief of Police Peter Mukhito. Banda also removed the Governor of the central bank, appointing Charles Chuka to that position. On 26 April Banda announced the formation of a new Government, taking personal responsibility for, *inter alia*, the public service, disaster management and HIV/AIDS. Lipenga was retained as Minister of Finance, one of several government veterans to keep their posts; however, Ephraim Mganda Chiume replaced Peter Mutharika at the foreign affairs ministry, while a number of those who had been expelled from the DPP following the disturbances in mid-2011 were awarded posts in the new administration. Most notable among these were Khumbo Kachale, who was named Vice-President and Minister of Health, and Ralph Kasambara who was appointed as Minister of Justice and Attorney-General. Callista wa Mutharika was stripped of her official duties in early May 2012. The new Government pledged to respect human rights and acted promptly to introduce economic reforms and to normalize relations with the country's major donors. Banda also announced her intention to sell the presidential jet, which Mutharika had controversially purchased at a cost of US $13m. The change in leadership precipitated mass defections from the DPP and the UDF to the PP, giving Banda's party a majority in the National Assembly.

Banda effected a minor cabinet reorganization in December 2012. Anti-Government demonstrations were staged in January 2013 in protest against economic austerity measures and rising inflation. In a further setback for the President, the PP lost its legislative majority in early 2013 due to ongoing political realignments within the National Assembly.

Meanwhile, a commission was established in May 2012 to investigate rumours that Peter Mutharika and his allies had attempted to orchestrate a coup in the immediate aftermath of President Mutharika's death. The commission published its findings in March 2013, and later that month 11 high-ranking members of the late President's administration, including Peter Mutharika, Kaliati and other former cabinet ministers, were arrested on treason charges, while a 12th was indicted *in absentia*. It was also confirmed in the commission's report that Mutharika had died on 5 April 2012 in an ambulance en route to hospital in Lilongwe, but that his personal physician had attempted to conceal the death by requesting that an air ambulance evacuate Mutharika to South Africa while his body was connected to medical equipment, thus creating the impression that he was still alive. Gondwe, who was also implicated in conspiring to prevent Banda's accession, resigned from his position as Minister of Economic Planning and Development and was replaced by Ralph Pachalo Jooma.

Foreign Affairs

Regional relations

Despite being the only African country to have maintained full diplomatic relations with South Africa during the apartheid era, Malawi joined the Southern African Development Co-ordination Conference (subsequently the Southern African Development Community, see p. 434—SADC), which originally aimed to reduce the dependence of southern African countries on South Africa.

Relations with Mozambique were frequently strained during the early and mid-1980s by the widely held belief that the Hastings Banda regime was supporting the Resistência Nacional Moçambicana (Renamo). Following the death of President Samora Machel of Mozambique in an air crash in South Africa in October 1986, the South African Government claimed that documents discovered in the wreckage revealed a plot by Mozambique and Zimbabwe to overthrow the Banda Government. Angry protests from Malawi were answered by denials of the accusations from the Mozambican and Zimbabwean Governments. In December, however, Malawi and Mozambique signed an agreement on defence and security matters, which was believed to include co-operation in eliminating Renamo operations. In July 1988, during an official visit to Malawi, President Joachim Chissano of Mozambique stated that he did not believe Malawi to be supporting Renamo. In December of that year Malawi, Mozambique and the office of the UN High Commissioner for Refugees (UNHCR) signed an agreement to promote the voluntary repatriation of an estimated 650,000 Mozambican refugees who had fled into Malawi during the previous two years. However, by mid-1992 the number of Mozambican refugees in Malawi had reportedly reached 1m. Large numbers of refugees returned to Mozambique in 1993–94, but in May 1995 Malawi demanded the repatriation of the remainder—estimated to total some 39,000—stating that food aid and other assistance to those who failed to leave would be reduced. The programme of the Malawi-Mozambique-UNHCR commission officially ended in November: it was estimated that a total of 1m. refugees had been repatriated.

Malawi and Tanzania held discussions in August 2012 in an attempt to resolve a long-standing disagreement regarding their mutual border in the Lake Malawi region, which was believed to hold significant hydrocarbon reserves. However, Malawi withdrew from the talks in October due to concerns over the production of an official Tanzanian map displaying a revised border, as well as the purported harassment by Tanzania of Malawian fishing vessels operating in the disputed area. Dialogue recommenced in November, but the negotiations soon foundered, prompting both parties to request SADC mediation.

Other external relations

Until early 2008 Malawi was one of a small number of nations that accorded Taiwan recognition as an independent country. In January of that year, however, it was announced that Malawi had withdrawn its support for Taiwan and established diplomatic relations with the People's Republic of China.

The British High Commissioner, Fergus Cochrane-Dyet, was expelled from Malawi in April 2011 owing to his censure of President Mutharika's authoritarian leadership style in a confidential diplomatic cable that had been released by the WikiLeaks organization. In response, the British Government ejected the Malawian High Commissioner from the United Kingdom later that month and suspended aid to Malawi in July, placing the Malawian Government's finances under severe pressure. The United Kingdom, along with other Western nations, had become increasingly critical of the Mutharika administration, expressing disapproval of government corruption, restrictions on press freedom and discriminatory laws against homosexuals.

The violent suppression of anti-Government protests by the Malawian security forces in July prompted further condemnation from Western powers, and the USA also suspended financial assistance to the country. Although the British High Commissioner was invited to return to Malawi in October, the United Kingdom (Malawi's primary source of aid) refused to resume budgetary support due to ongoing concerns over governance and human rights violations. Citing similar considerations, Germany, the European Union, the World Bank and the IMF also withheld funding to Malawi during 2011. In April 2012, however, following Joyce Banda's accession to the presidency, the British Government announced that relations between the two countries would be normalized, and the new High Commissioner commenced his duties in September. Moreover, in mid-2012 Malawi's major bilateral and multilateral development partners confirmed that financial assistance to the country would be restored.

Meanwhile, relations between Malawi and the West deteriorated in October 2011, when Lt-Gen. Omar Hassan Ahmad al-Bashir, the President of Sudan and an alleged war criminal wanted by the International Criminal Court (ICC), attended a regional trade meeting in Lilongwe. Malawi was accused of violating its international obligations, since, as a signatory to the Rome Statute of the ICC, the country had been legally required to arrest al-Bashir and transfer him to ICC custody. Mutharika claimed that, in his capacity as the incumbent President of a non-signatory state, al-Bashir was immune from prosecution. The ICC rejected this argument and in December requested that the UN Security Council investigate the matter, prompting Malawi to threaten to withdraw from the ICC. Upon Banda's assumption of the presidency, however, the Malawian Government altered its stance on this matter. Malawi was due to host an African Union (AU) summit meeting in July 2012, and, with the Banda administration eager to repair relations with the international community, it was made clear that al-Bashir's presence would be unacceptable. Although the AU insisted that al-Bashir be permitted to attend, Malawi refused to modify its position, and it was subsequently agreed that the meeting would be relocated to Ethiopia.

CONSTITUTION AND GOVERNMENT

Under the provisions of the Constitution promulgated on 18 May 1995, the Head of State is the President, who is elected by universal adult suffrage, in the context of a multi-party political system, for a term of five years. Executive power is vested in the President, and legislative power in the National Assembly, which has 193 elective seats. Members of the Assembly are elected for five years, by universal adult suffrage, in the context of a multi-party system. Cabinet ministers are appointed by the President. The country is divided into three administrative regions (Northern, Central and Southern), subdivided into 24 districts.

REGIONAL AND INTERNATIONAL CO-OPERATION

Malawi is a member of the African Union (see p. 191), the Southern African Development Community (SADC, see p. 434) and the Common Market for Eastern and Southern Africa (COMESA, see p. 241). Nine members of COMESA, including Malawi, became inaugural members of the COMESA Free Trade Area in October 2000.

Malawi became a member of the UN in 1964 and was admitted to the World Trade Organization (WTO, see p. 444) in 1995. Malawi participates in the Group of 77 (G77, see p. 461) developing countries. The country also belongs to the International Tobacco Growers' Association (see p. 457).

ECONOMIC AFFAIRS

In 2011, according to estimates by the World Bank, Malawi's gross national income (GNI), measured at average 2009–11 prices, was US $5,186m., equivalent to $340 per head (or $870 per head on an international purchasing-power parity basis). During 2002–11, it was estimated, the population increased at an average annual rate of 3.0%, while gross domestic product (GDP) per head grew, in real terms, by an average of 3.1% per year. Overall GDP increased, in real terms, at an average annual rate of 6.1% in 2002–11; real GDP rose by 4.5% in 2011.

Agriculture (including forestry and fishing) contributed 35.8% of GDP in 2009, according to the African Development Bank (AfDB), and engaged an estimated 77.6% of the labour force in mid-2013, according to FAO. The principal cash crops are tobacco (which accounted for 54.9% of total export earnings in 2010), tea

and sugar cane. The principal food crops are cassava, maize, potatoes, bananas and plantains. Periods of severe drought and flooding have necessitated imports of basic foods in recent years. During 2002–11, according to the World Bank, agricultural GDP increased at an average annual rate of 4.0%; it grew by 6.8% in 2011.

Industry (including manufacturing, mining, construction and power) contributed 16.9% of GDP in 2009, according to the AfDB, and engaged 4.5% of the employed labour force in 1998. During 2002–11 industrial GDP increased by an average of 9.1% per year. Industrial GDP rose by 9.7% in 2011.

Mining and quarrying contributed 4.5% of GDP in 2009, according to the AfDB, and engaged less than 0.1% of the employed labour force in 1998. Limestone, coal and gemstones are mined, and there are plans to develop deposits of bauxite, high-calcium marble and graphite. There are also reserves of phosphates, uranium, glass sands, asbestos and vermiculite. Environmental and financial concerns have delayed plans to exploit an estimated 30m. metric tons of bauxite deposits at Mount Mulanje. Uranium mining, which commenced at Kayelekera, in northern Malawi, in 2009, was expected to increase the country's export revenue by some 25%. The GDP of the mining sector expanded at an average annual rate of 39.7% in 2004–10, according to preliminary official figures; mining GDP grew by 4.9% in 2009 and by 80.2% in 2010.

Manufacturing contributed 5.5% of GDP in 2009, according to the AfDB, and engaged 2.7% of the employed labour force in 1998. During 2002–11 manufacturing GDP increased by an average of 10.0% per year. The GDP of the sector grew by 5.4% in 2011.

Construction contributed 3.8% of GDP in 2009, according to the AfDB, and engaged 1.6% of the employed labour force in 1998. The GDP of the construction sector increased at an average annual rate of 10.8% in 2004–10, according to preliminary official figures; construction GDP rose by 16.5% in 2010.

Production of electrical energy is by hydroelectric (principally) and thermal installations. Some 95% of energy for domestic use is derived from hydroelectric power. In October 2000 a hydroelectric power plant, with a generation capacity of 64 MW, was opened at Kapichira; in February 2009 the Government pledged funds amounting to some 2,500m. kwacha for the Kapichira Hydroelectric Power Phase II Project, which would double the capacity of the plant. In 2011 the total generation capacity of Malawi's hydroelectric power plants was 282.5 MW. Meanwhile, a World Bank-supported project was planned to connect Malawi's electricity system to Mozambique's Cahora Bassa hydroelectric power plant, which would increase Malawi's power supply by some 200 MW. Investment in alternative sources of energy, such as solar power, the production of gel fuel from ethanol and coal-mining, was also being encouraged, with the construction of a coal-fired plant to generate 300 MW of electricity under consideration. In January 2001 the Government introduced a campaign to widen access to electricity, especially in rural areas. Imports of mineral fuels and lubricants comprised 10.0% of the value of total imports in 2010.

According to the AfDB, the services sector contributed 47.3% of GDP in 2009, and engaged 11.0% of the employed labour force in 1998. The GDP of the services sector increased by an average of 7.9% per year in 2002–09. Services GDP grew by 10.4% in 2008, but decreased by 1.9% in 2009.

According to preliminary figures, Malawi recorded a visible merchandise trade deficit of 171,960.1m. kwacha in 2011, and there was a deficit of 119,687.5m. kwacha on the current account of the balance of payments. In 2010 the principal source of imports was South Africa (providing 30.1% of the total); the People's Republic of China, India, Zambia and the United Arab Emirates were also notable suppliers. Belgium was the principal market for exports (accounting for 12.4% of the total) in that year; other important markets were Egypt, Germany, the USA, South Africa and Zimbabwe. The principal imports in 2010 were chemicals and related products, machinery and transport equipment, basic manufactures, mineral fuels and lubricants, and food and live animals. The principal exports in that year were tobacco, food and live animals (particularly tea and raw cane sugars), and crude materials (inedible) except fuels.

Preliminary figures indicated that in the financial year ending 30 June 2012 Malawi's overall budget deficit was an estimated 67,902m. kwacha. Malawi's general government gross debt was 356,613m. kwacha in 2011, equivalent to 40.5% of GDP. The country's external debt in 2010 totalled US $922m., of which $715m. was public and publicly guaranteed debt. In 2009, the cost of servicing long-term public and publicly guaranteed debt and repayments to the IMF was equivalent to 2.1% of the value of exports of goods, services and income (excluding workers' remittances). The annual rate of inflation averaged 10.0% in 2002–11; consumer prices increased by an average of 7.6% in 2011. Some 1.4m. people were unemployed in 2007.

Malawi's natural impediments to growth (including its landlocked position, the vulnerability of the dominant agricultural sector to drought, and a high rate of population growth) were compounded by the severe mismanagement of economic affairs during the early 2000s. Amid concern regarding the country's vulnerability to the effects of the global financial crisis, in January 2009 Malawi became the first recipient country of the IMF's new Exogenous Shock Facility, under which a one-year loan of US $77.1m. was approved. In February 2010 the IMF authorized a three-year arrangement for Malawi under its Extended Credit Facility (ECF), worth $79.4m. However, Malawi's relations with Western donor nations and the IMF deteriorated in mid-2011. A diplomatic dispute regarding alleged declining standards of governance in Malawi resulted in the suspension of budgetary support by the United Kingdom, the source of the majority of Malawi's aid inflows, while the heavy-handed response by the Malawian authorities to anti-Government demonstrations in July led to the withdrawal of US financial assistance. Moreover, the IMF suspended the ECF in June due to the Government's lack of progress in implementing agreed economic reforms. The administration of President Mutharika introduced an austerity budget in that month, which raised taxes and lowered spending in an attempt to compensate

for the sharp decline in external financing. In accordance with the ECF's stipulations, the Government devalued the kwacha by 10% in August, but the IMF declared that this was insufficient and that the exchange rate remained imbalanced, deterring vital investment. The new administration of President Joyce Banda, which took office in April 2012, prioritized the re-establishment of ties with Malawi's traditional international partners. In July the IMF authorized a new three-year ECF arrangement, valued at $156.2m., and additional financial support was provided by the World Bank and the AfDB. British and US funding was also resumed during mid-2012. In May the kwacha was further devalued by around 50% and foreign exchange controls were removed, although a side effect of these measures was a sharp upturn in inflation during 2012, exacerbated by drought-induced food supply deficiencies and increases in fuel and electricity rates. According to IMF estimates, real GDP rose by just 2.0% in 2012 (down from 4.3% in 2011), but growth of 5.5% was expected in 2013.

PUBLIC HOLIDAYS

2014: 1 January (New Year's Day), 15 January (John Chilembwe Day), 3 March (Martyrs' Day), 29 March–1 April (Easter), 1 May (Labour Day), 14 May (President Kamuzu Banda's Birthday), 14 June (Freedom Day), 6 July (Republic Day), 28 July* (Id al-Fitr, end of Ramadan), 13 October (Mothers' Day), 25–26 December (Christmas).

* This holiday is determined by the Islamic lunar calendar and may vary by one or two days from the date given.

Statistical Survey

Sources (unless otherwise indicated): National Statistical Office of Malawi, POB 333, Zomba; tel. 1524377; fax 1525130; e-mail enquiries@statistics.gov.mw; internet www.nsomalawi.mw; Reserve Bank of Malawi, POB 30063, Capital City, Lilongwe 3; tel. 1770600; fax 1772752; e-mail webmaster@rbm.mw; internet www.rbm.mw.

Area and Population

AREA, POPULATION AND DENSITY

Area (sq km)	
Land	94,276
Inland water	24,208
Total	118,484*
Population (census results)	
1–21 September 1998	9,933,868
8–28 June 2008	
Males	6,358,933
Females	6,718,227
Total	13,077,160
Population (official projections at mid-year)	
2011	14,388,550
2012	14,844,822
2013	15,316,860
Density (per sq km) at mid-2013	162.5†

* 45,747 sq miles.
† Land area only.

POPULATION BY AGE AND SEX
(official projections at mid-2013)

	Males	Females	Total
0–14	3,545,170	3,561,505	7,106,675
15–64	3,733,834	3,977,169	7,711,003
65 and over	222,649	276,533	499,182
Total	7,501,653	7,815,207	15,316,860

REGIONS
(population projections at mid-2013)

Region	Area (sq km)*	Population ('000)	Density (per sq km)	Regional capital
Southern	31,753	6,704.5	211.1	Blantyre
Central	35,592	6,590.5	185.1	Lilongwe
Northern	26,931	2,021.9	75.1	Mzuzu
Total	94,276	15,316.9	162.5	

* Excluding inland waters, totalling 24,208 sq km.

PRINCIPAL TOWNS
(population at census of June 2008)

Lilongwe (capital)	674,448	Karonga	40,334
Blantyre	661,256	Kasungu	39,640
Mzuzu	133,968	Mangochi	39,575
Zomba	88,314	Salima	27,852

Mid-2013 (official population projection): Lilongwe 922,625.

BIRTHS AND DEATHS
(annual averages, UN estimates)

	1995–2000	2000–05	2005–10
Birth rate (per 1,000)	45.4	43.4	44.0
Death rate (per 1,000)	17.9	16.6	13.7

Source: UN, *World Population Prospects: The 2010 Revision*.

2008 (official estimates): Live births 609,487 (birth rate 46.5 per 1,000); deaths 195,014 (death rate 14.9 per 1,000).

Life expectancy (years at birth): 54.1 (males 54.1; females 54.2) in 2011 (Source: World Bank, World Development Indicators database).

ECONOMICALLY ACTIVE POPULATION*
(persons aged 10 years and over, 1998 census)

	Males	Females	Total
Agriculture, hunting, forestry and fishing	1,683,006	2,082,821	3,765,827
Mining and quarrying	2,206	293	2,499
Manufacturing	94,545	23,938	118,483
Electricity, gas and water . . .	6,656	663	7,319
Construction	70,196	3,206	73,402
Trade, restaurants and hotels .	176,466	80,923	257,389
Transport, storage and communications	29,438	3,185	32,623
Financing, insurance, real estate and business services . . .	10,473	3,484	13,957
Public administration	82,973	18,460	101,433
Community, social and personal services	52,980	33,016	85,996
Total employed	2,208,940	2,249,989	4,458,929
Unemployed	34,697	15,664	50,361
Total labour force	2,243,637	2,265,653	4,509,290

* Excluding armed forces.

Mid-2013 (estimates in '000): Agriculture, etc. 5,390; Total labour force 6,943 (Source: FAO).

Health and Welfare

KEY INDICATORS

Total fertility rate (children per woman, 2010)	6.0
Under-5 mortality rate (per 1,000 live births, 2010) . . .	92
HIV/AIDS (% of persons aged 15–49, 2009)	11.0
Physicians (per 1,000 head, 2008)	0.02
Hospital beds (per 1,000 head, 2007)	1.1
Health expenditure (2009): US $ per head (PPP) . . .	65
Health expenditure (2009): % of GDP	6.7
Health expenditure (2009): public (% of total)	65.2
Access to water (% of persons, 2010)	83
Access to sanitation (% of persons, 2010)	51
Total carbon dioxide emissions ('000 metric tons, 2008) . .	1,228.4
Carbon dioxide emissions per head (metric tons, 2008) . .	0.1
Human Development Index (2011): ranking	171
Human Development Index (2011): value	0.400

For sources and definitions, see explanatory note on p. vi.

Agriculture

PRINCIPAL CROPS
('000 metric tons)

	2009	2010	2011
Rice, paddy	136.0	110.1	117.7
Maize	3,582.5	3,419.4	3,699.2
Millet	26.9	24.5	32.9
Sorghum	60.0	53.9	73.3
Potatoes	3,427.8	3,673.5	3,124.0
Cassava (Manioc)	3,823.2	4,001.0	4,259.3
Beans, dry	164.7	153.8	288.4
Chickpeas*	48.5	47.9	66.2
Cow peas, dry*	28.5	26.4	31.9
Pigeon peas	184.2	193.0	195.5
Groundnuts, with shell . .	275.2	297.5	304.9
Cabbages and other brassicas* .	66.2	87.4	77.0
Tomatoes*	35.7	41.7	39.2

—continued	2009	2010	2011
Onions, dry*	45.8	51.1	66.7
Guavas, mangoes and mangosteens*	82.7	96.4	112.0
Bananas*	400.0	410.4	357.7
Plantains*	346.3	318.0	312.4
Sugar cane*	2,500	2,500	2,500
Coffee, green	5.5	4.2	4.0
Tea	52.6	51.6	52.0
Tobacco, unmanufactured . . .	208.2	172.9	174.9

* FAO estimates.

Aggregate production ('000 metric tons, may include official, semi-official or estimated data): Total cereals 3,808.0 in 2009, 3,610.3 in 2010, 3,925.0 in 2011; Total roots and tubers 7,251.3 in 2009, 7,674.9 in 2010, 7,383.6 in 2011; Total vegetables (incl. melons) 311.7 in 2009, 364.5 in 2010, 396.4 in 2011; Total fruits (excl. melons) 1,062.6 in 2009, 1,061.4 in 2010, 1,053.7 in 2011.

Source: FAO.

LIVESTOCK
('000 head, year ending September)

	2009	2010	2011
Cattle	983	1,070	1,111
Pigs	1,444	1,862	2,161
Sheep	200	214	229
Goats	3,480	3,894	4,443
Chickens*	15,700	16,000	16,500

* FAO estimates.

Source: FAO.

LIVESTOCK PRODUCTS
('000 metric tons)

	2009	2010	2011
Cattle meat	30.0	32.2	34.1
Goat meat	21.5	23.6	27.8
Pig meat	41.9	31.7	44.2
Chicken meat	21.3	21.6*	22.4*
Cows' milk	40.4	46.7	50.4
Hen eggs*	20.3	20.2	20.2

* FAO estimate(s).

Source: FAO.

Forestry

ROUNDWOOD REMOVALS
('000 cu m, excluding bark, FAO estimates)

	2009	2010	2011
Sawlogs, veneer logs and logs for sleepers	200	200	200
Other industrial wood . . .	1,200	1,200	1,200
Fuel wood	5,348	5,405	5,466
Total	6,748	6,805	6,866

Source: FAO.

SAWNWOOD PRODUCTION
('000 cu m, including railway sleepers)

	1991*	1992†	1993
Coniferous (softwood)	28	28	30
Broadleaved (hardwood)	15	15	15†
Total	43	43	45

* Unofficial figures.
† FAO estimate(s).

1994–2011: Production assumed to be unchanged from 1993 (FAO estimates).

Source: FAO.

Fishing

('000 metric tons, live weight)

	2008	2009	2010
Capture	70.0	69.3	98.2
Cyprinids	27.2	26.8	44.8
Tilapias	11.1	12.4	11.2
Cichlids	22.0	20.2	33.3
Torpedo-shaped catfishes	5.3	5.0	4.3
Other freshwater fishes	4.4	4.9	4.6
Aquaculture	1.7	1.6	3.2
Total catch	**71.7**	**70.9**	**101.4**

Note: Figures exclude aquatic mammals, recorded by number rather than weight. The number of Nile crocodiles caught was: 3,370 in 2008; 3,105 in 2009; 3,250 in 2010.

Source: FAO.

Mining

('000 metric tons unless otherwise indicated)

	2008	2009	2010
Bituminous coal	57.5	59.2	79.2
Lime	23.5	25.9	31.8
Gemstones (kg)	11,946	306,700	206,900
Stone (crushed for aggregate)	522.1	970.6	989.8
Limestone	46.0	47.2	57.3

Source: US Geological Survey.

Industry

SELECTED PRODUCTS
('000 metric tons unless otherwise indicated)

	2000	2001	2002
Raw sugar	96	107	260*
Beer ('000 hectolitres)	739	1,033	n.a.
Blankets ('000)	574	281	n.a.
Cement	198	111	174

* Natural sodium carbonate (Na_2CO_3).

2003 ('000 metric tons): Raw sugar (Na_2CO_3) 257; Cement 161 (Source: US Geological Survey).

Electric energy (million kWh): 1,637 in 2007; 1,801 in 2008, 1,758 in 2009 (estimate).

Raw sugar ('000 metric tons): 230 in 2006; 280 in 2007; 310 in 2008.

Source (unless otherwise indicated): UN Industrial Commodity Statistics Database.

Cement ('000 metric tons, hydraulic, estimates): 240.0 in 2008–09; 250.0 in 2010 (Source: US Geological Survey).

Finance

CURRENCY AND EXCHANGE RATES

Monetary Units
100 tambala = 1 Malawi kwacha (K).

Sterling, Dollar and Euro Equivalents (31 October 2012)
£1 sterling = 506.577 kwacha;
US $1 = 314.332 kwacha;
€1 = 408.411 kwacha;
1,000 Malawi kwacha = £1.97 = $3.18 = €2.45.

Average Exchange Rate (kwacha per US $)
2009   141.167
2010   150.487
2011   156.515

BUDGET
(K million, year ending 30 June)

Revenue	2007/08	2008/09	2009/10
Tax revenue	95,353	119,398	148,550
Taxes on income and profits	39,860	48,638	64,205
Companies	11,300	14,350	20,171
Individuals	28,560	33,738	43,348
Taxes on goods and services	43,928	57,100	68,483
Surtax	31,238	38,700	45,575
Excise duties	12,600	18,400	22,908
Taxes on international trade	11,565	13,660	15,862
Tax refunds	2,400	3,000	8,520
Non-tax revenue	7,740	16,333	31,105
Departmental receipts	4,686	5,145	15,014
Total	**103,093**	**135,731**	**179,655**

Expenditure	2007/08	2008/09	2009/10
General public services	43,871	83,023	83,863
General administration	34,708	65,683	66,347
Defence	4,413	6,351	8,436
Public order and safety	4,750	8,989	9,080
Social and community services	36,438	68,956	69,653
Education	14,040	26,569	26,838
Health	10,450	19,776	19,976
Social security and welfare	8,892	16,828	16,998
Housing and community amenities	2,151	4,070	4,112
Recreational, cultural and other social services	255	482	487
Broadcasting and publishing	650	1,230	1,242
Economic affairs and services	21,940	41,521	41,941
Energy and mining	155	293	296
Agriculture and natural resources	19,363	36,643	37,014
Physical planning and development	615	1,163	1,175
Transport and communications	971	1,838	1,836
Industry and commerce	324	613	619
Labour relations and employment	365	690	697
Scientific and technological services	149	281	281
Total recurrent expenditure	**102,249**	**193,499**	**195,457**
Debt amortization	13,040	—	—
Total	**115,289**	**193,499**	**195,457**

2010/11 (K million, year ending 30 June): *Revenue:* Tax revenue 175,695; Non-tax revenue 31,877; Total 207,572 (excl. grants 64,329). *Expenditure:* Current expenditure 230,225 (Wages and salaries 58,092, Interest payments 22,819, Other 149,314); Development expenditure 64,971; Total 295,195 (Source: IMF (see below)).

2011/12 (K million, year ending 30 June, projected figures): *Revenue:* Tax revenue 180,906; Non-tax revenue 26,619; Total 207,525 (excl. grants 52,678). *Expenditure:* Current expenditure 250,686 (Wages and salaries 69,916, Interest payments 20,243, Other 160,527); Development expenditure 77,419; Total 328,105 (Source: IMF (see below)).

2012/13 (K million, year ending 30 June, programmed figures): *Revenue:* Tax revenue 236,442; Non-tax revenue 33,933; Total 270,375 (excl. grants 124,079). *Expenditure:* Current expenditure 331,715 (Wages and salaries 86,822, Interest payments 28,753, Other 216,140); Development expenditure 76,226; Total 407,941 (Source (2010/11–2012/13): IMF, *Malawi: 2012 Article IV Consultation and Request for a New Arrangement Under the Extended Credit Facility - Staff Report; Staff Supplements; Public Information Notice and Press Release on the Executive Board Discussion; and Statement by the Executive Director for Malawi*—August 2012).

INTERNATIONAL RESERVES
(US $ million at 31 December)

	2009	2010	2011
Gold (national valuation)	14.03	15.68	15.68
IMF special drawing rights	1.93	1.62	0.43
Reserve position in IMF	3.80	3.73	3.72
Foreign exchange	143.63	302.01	193.29
Total	**163.39**	**323.04**	**213.12**

Source: IMF, *International Financial Statistics*.

MONEY SUPPLY
(K million at 31 December)

	2009	2010	2011
Currency outside banks . . .	27,493.1	31,848.3	42,251.0
Demand deposits at commercial banks	54,407.1	70,263.9	99,683.5
Total money	81,900.3	102,112.2	141,934.5

Source: IMF, *International Financial Statistics*.

COST OF LIVING
(Consumer Price Index; base: 2000 = 100)

	2009	2010	2011
Food (incl. beverages) . . .	258.0	271.2	279.8
Clothing (incl. footwear) . . .	259.1	279.5	307.9
Rent	328.3	350.2	392.4
Transportation	380.1	428.4	501.2
All items (incl. others) . . .	287.7	309.0	332.6

NATIONAL ACCOUNTS
(K million at current prices)

Expenditure on the Gross Domestic Product

	2007	2008	2009
Government final consumption expenditure	163,227	108,524	126,526
Private final consumption expenditure	317,938	458,284	534,304
Gross fixed capital formation . .	70,285	134,027	156,262
Changes in inventories . .	14,735	15,933	18,576
Total domestic expenditure .	566,185	716,768	835,668
Exports of goods and services . .	132,707	133,320	155,435
Less Imports of goods and services	201,800	277,665	323,724
GDP in purchasers' values .	497,092	572,423	667,379

Gross Domestic Product by Economic Activity

	2007	2008	2009
Agriculture, forestry and fishing .	153,063	176,258	202,969
Mining and quarrying	19,384	22,321	25,704
Manufacturing	23,691	27,281	31,415
Electricity, gas and water . . .	12,868	14,818	17,063
Construction	16,229	18,688	21,520
Wholesale and retail trade, restaurants and hotels . . .	44,967	51,782	59,629
Transport and communications .	26,087	30,041	34,593
Finance, insurance and real estate	47,767	55,005	63,341
Public administration and defence	48,843	56,244	64,768
Other services	28,385	32,687	45,849
GDP at factor cost	421,283	485,125	566,852
Taxes on products	75,809	87,298	100,527
GDP at purchasers' values .	497,092	572,423	667,379

Note: Deduction for imputed bank service charge assumed to be distributed at source.

Source: African Development Bank.

BALANCE OF PAYMENTS
(K million)

	2009	2010	2011
Exports of goods f.o.b.	179,052.3	171,441.0	239,610.4
Imports of goods f.o.b.	−283,513.0	−344,286.3	−411,570.6
Trade balance	−104,460.7	−172,845.3	−171,960.1
Net services	−22,569.4	−19,722.1	−22,247.5
Balance on goods and services	−127,030.1	−192,567.4	−194,207.6
Net other income	−17,246.8	−28,610.3	−15,376.2
Balance on goods, services and income	−144,276.9	−221,177.7	−209,583.8
Net transfers	66,150.0	84,962.9	89,896.4
Current balance	−78,127.0	−136,214.8	−119,687.5
Capital account (net)	57,691.6	90,705.0	71,503.9
Direct investment assets . . .	187.8	−6,365.6	−1,502.7
Direct investment liabilities . .	6,935.7	14,598.7	14,463.2
Portfolio investment assets . .	−14.1	−15.0	−15.7
Portfolio investment liabilities .	−38.1	149.0	−156.5
Other investment assets . . .	−5,540.8	−5,030.8	−4,603.0
Other investment liabilities . .	11,554.7	30,689.0	34,031.2
Net errors and omissions . . .	−7,743.5	31,865.0	−11,050.8
Overall balance	15,093.8	−20,380.4	17,017.8

External Trade

PRINCIPAL COMMODITIES
(distribution by SITC, US $ million)

Imports c.i.f.	2008	2009	2010
Food and live animals . . .	136.7	158.7	148.5
Cereals and cereal preparations .	94.1	102.0	99.6
Beverages and tobacco . . .	75.2	62.8	97.8
Tobacco and tobacco products .	74.0	58.4	95.5
Mineral fuels, lubricants, etc. .	214.8	210.6	217.1
Petroleum, petroleum products, etc.	211.7	208.9	214.7
Refined petroleum products .	202.0	198.3	198.6
Chemicals and related products	603.5	464.1	532.4
Medicinal and pharmaceutical products	95.4	114.2	133.9
Manufactured fertilizers . . .	367.1	176.8	206.2
Basic manufactures	271.4	328.9	346.6
Paper, paperboard, etc. . . .	38.4	53.8	49.6
Textile yarn, fabrics, etc. . . .	44.2	46.9	41.6
Iron and steel	66.9	63.2	73.7
Machinery and transport equipment	593.8	529.4	515.2
Machinery specialized for particular industries . . .	238.1	96.6	102.3
General industrial machinery, equipment and parts . . .	41.7	53.1	54.4
Office machinery and automatic data-processing equipment . .	23.3	32.1	33.7
Telecommunications, sound recording and reproducing equipment	45.8	74.7	75.5
Road vehicles	181.7	191.7	159.3
Goods vehicles (lorries and trucks)	59.6	61.3	46.9
Miscellaneous manufactured articles	228.3	191.0	222.0
Total (incl. others)	2,203.7	2,021.7	2,173.0

Exports f.o.b.	2008	2009	2010
Food and live animals . . .	139.2	213.6	209.8
Sugar and honey	53.0	70.3	69.4
Raw cane sugars	50.7	70.2	69.0
Coffee, tea, cocoa and spices . .	42.5	84.4	87.8
Tea	36.9	78.3	80.8
Beverages and tobacco . .	593.2	760.5	587.1
Tobacco and tobacco products .	590.0	759.5	585.2
Unstripped tobacco	428.2	472.4	241.6
Stripped or partly stripped tobacco	161.7	268.6	331.1
Crude materials (inedible) except fuels	57.2	109.3	170.2
Textile fibres	23.4	30.1	17.0
Basic manufactures . . .	30.9	12.1	16.0
Machinery and transport equipment	15.5	28.1	27.1
Miscellaneous manufactured articles	35.1	53.2	38.1
Total (incl. others)	879.0	1,187.9	1,066.2

Source: UN, *International Trade Statistics Yearbook*.

PRINCIPAL TRADING PARTNERS
(US $ million)

Imports	2008	2009	2010
Belgium	8.6	6.0	—
China, People's Repub. . . .	72.4	119.7	198.4
Denmark	40.8	35.0	22.4
France (incl. Monaco) . . .	16.7	52.2	62.8
Germany	22.4	34.2	25.2
Hong Kong	15.1	23.7	23.3
India	106.8	95.8	165.0
Indonesia	15.1	18.5	22.9
Italy	7.6	10.3	8.6
Japan	32.7	18.0	62.5
Kenya	54.9	39.8	49.4
Korea, Repub.	18.0	18.2	19.8
Mozambique	447.1	259.5	31.3
Netherlands	46.3	18.9	37.3
South Africa	585.2	691.5	654.2
Tanzania	128.6	79.4	36.9
United Arab Emirates . . .	111.0	80.3	108.0
United Kingdom	74.8	85.3	83.0
USA	45.0	52.7	62.3
Zambia	68.5	72.7	120.5
Zimbabwe	38.5	38.2	32.9
Total (incl. others)	2,203.7	2,021.7	2,173.0

Exports	2008	2009	2010
Belgium	114.7	208.3	132.5
Denmark	2.1	5.3	7.8
Egypt	25.3	73.2	98.3
France (incl. Monaco) . . .	8.1	5.3	—
Germany	36.7	38.5	65.7
India	2.8	27.4	12.4
Kenya	6.9	13.7	19.3
Korea, Repub.	28.2	10.7	14.2
Mozambique	23.9	64.1	36.2
Netherlands	51.8	52.2	49.8
Philippines	8.4	26.8	14.1
Poland	30.6	15.8	17.2
Portugal	34.0	28.7	18.5
Russia	25.0	36.1	11.2
South Africa	88.7	121.6	61.6
Spain	6.3	7.6	8.6
Switzerland (incl. Liechtenstein) .	36.0	52.6	14.1
Turkey	17.3	17.7	6.1
United Kingdom	78.4	50.4	49.1
USA	50.3	48.6	63.7
Zambia	15.4	23.0	35.5
Zimbabwe	22.6	35.8	57.9
Total (incl. others)	879.0	1,187.9	1,066.2

Source: UN, *International Trade Statistics Yearbook*.

Transport

RAILWAYS
(traffic)

	2009	2010	2011
Passengers carried ('000) . . .	572	561	271
Passenger-km ('000) . . .	38,336	35,950	17,360
Net freight ton-km ('000) . . .	46,673	43,990	39,168

ROAD TRAFFIC
(estimates, motor vehicles in use at 31 December)

	1994	1995	1996
Passenger cars	23,520	25,480	27,000
Lorries and vans	26,000	29,000	29,700

2007: Passenger cars 53,300; Lorries and vans 59,800; Buses 6,500; Motorcycles 10,400.

Source: International Road Federation, *World Road Statistics*.

SHIPPING

Inland Waterways
(lake transport)

	2009	2010	2011
Passengers carried ('000) . . .	39	57	57
Passenger-km ('000)	3,300	4,889	4,047
Net freight-ton km	3,110	2,871	1,367

CIVIL AVIATION
(traffic on scheduled services)

	2007	2008	2009
Kilometres flown (million) . . .	3	5	5
Passengers carried ('000) . . .	116	160	157
Passenger-km (million) . . .	83	209	200
Total ton-km (million)	8	24	23

Source: UN, *Statistical Yearbook*.

Passengers carried ('000): 172 in 2010 (Source: World Bank, World Development Indicators database).

Tourism

FOREIGN TOURIST ARRIVALS BY COUNTRY OF RESIDENCE

	2008	2009	2010
Mozambique	139,296	188,694	159,580
North America	43,085	43,766	44,572
Southern Africa*	106,724	100,958	102,342
United Kingdom and Ireland . .	50,786	54,476	53,897
Zambia	76,408	102,956	80,428
Zimbabwe	143,363	77,281	128,387
Total (incl. others)	742,457	755,031	746,129

* Comprising South Africa, Botswana, Lesotho and Swaziland.

Tourism receipts (US $ million, excl. passenger transport): 43 in 2008; 44 in 2009; 47 in 2010.

Source: World Tourism Organization.

Communications Media

	2009	2010	2011
Telephones ('000 main lines in use)	111.3	160.1	173.5
Mobile cellular telephones ('000 subscribers)	2,374.1	3,037.5	3,855.8
Internet subscribers ('000)	150.0	305.0	450.0
Broadband subscribers ('000)	3.9	5.1	9.8

Personal computers: 25,000 (1.8 per 1,000 persons) in 2005.

Source: International Telecommunication Union.

Education

(2011 unless otherwise indicated)

	Institutions	Teachers	Students
Primary	5,395	53,031	4,034,220
Secondary	n.a.	11,300	256,343
Tertiary	6*	897	10,630

* 2003 figure.

Pupil-teacher ratio (primary education): 76.0 in 2011.

Adult literacy rate (UNESCO estimates): 74.8% (males 81.1%; females 68.5%) in 2010 (Source: UNESCO Institute for Statistics).

Directory

The Government

HEAD OF STATE

President: JOYCE BANDA (took office 7 April 2012).
Vice-President: KHUMBO KACHALI.

CABINET
(May 2013)

President, Commander-in-Chief of the Malawi Defence Force and Police Service, and Minister of Statutory Corporations, Civil Service Administration, Nutrition and HIV/AIDS, National Registration Programme and Green Belt Initiative: JOYCE BANDA.

Vice-President, responsible for National Relief and Disaster Management, National Public Events Office, Central Government Stores and Department of Printing Services: KHUMBO KACHALI.

Minister of Economic Planning and Development: RALPH PACHALO JOOMA.

Minister of Finance: Dr KEN LIPENGA.

Minister of Foreign Affairs and International Co-operation: EPHRAIM MGANDA CHIUME.

Minister of Lands and Housing: HENRY DAMA PHOYA.

Minister of Education, Science and Technology: EUNICE KAZEMBE.

Minister of Gender, Children and Social Welfare: ANITA KALINDE.

Minister of Justice: RALPH KASAMBALA.

Minister of Agriculture and Food Security: Prof. PETER NELSON MWANZA.

Minister of Transport and Public Works: MOHAMMED SIDIK MIA.

Minister of Water Development and Irrigation: RICHIE BIZWICK MUHEYA.

Minister of Information: MOSES KUNKUYU.

Minister of Home Affairs: ULADI MUSSA.

Minister of Local Government and Rural Development: GRACE ZINENANI MASEKO.

Minister of Health: CATHERINE GOTANI HARA.

Minister of Labour: EUNICE MAKANGALA.

Minister of National Defence: KEN EDWARD KANDODO.

Minister of Mining: JOHN BANDE.

Minister of Disability and the Elderly: REEN KACHERE.

Minister of Youth and Sport: ENOCK CHAKUFWA CHIHANA.

Minister of Energy: IBRAHIM MATOLA.

Minister of Industry and Trade: SOSTEN GWENGWE.

Minister of the Environment and Climate Change Management: JENNIFER CHILUNGA.

Minister of Tourism and Culture: RACHEL ZULU MAZOMBWE.
There were also 11 Deputy Ministers.

MINISTRIES

Office of the President and Cabinet: Private Bag 301, Capital City, Lilongwe 3; tel. 1789311; fax 1788456; internet www.malawi .gov.mw/opc/opc.htm.

Office of the Vice President: POB 30399, Capital City, Lilongwe; tel. 1788444; fax 1788218; e-mail vicepres@malawi.gov.mw.

Ministry of Agriculture and Food Security: POB 30134, Capital City, Lilongwe 3; tel. 1789033; fax 1789218; e-mail agriculture@ agriculture.gov.mw; internet www.moafsmw.org.

Ministry of Disability and the Elderly: Lilongwe.

Ministry of Economic Planning and Development: Lilongwe.

Ministry of Education, Science and Technology: Private Bag 328, Lilongwe 3; tel. 1789422; fax 1788064; e-mail education@malawi .gov.mw; internet www.malawi.gov.mw/Education/ Home%20%20Education.htm.

Ministry of Energy: Private Bag 350, Lilongwe 3; tel. 1789488; fax 1773379; internet www.malawi.gov.mw/natres/natres.htm.

Ministry of the Environment and Climate Change Management: Lilongwe.

Ministry of Finance: Capital Hill, POB 30049, Lilongwe 3; tel. 1789355; fax 1789173; internet www.finance.gov.mw.

Ministry of Foreign Affairs and International Co-operation: POB 30315, Lilongwe 3; tel. 1789323; fax 1788482; e-mail foreign@ malawi.net; internet www.foreignaffairs.gov.mw.

Ministry of Gender, Children and Social Welfare: Private Bag 330, Capital City, Lilongwe 3; tel. 1770411; fax 1770826.

Ministry of Health: POB 30377, Capital City, Lilongwe 3; tel. 1789400; fax 1789431; e-mail doccentre@malawi.net; internet www .malawi.gov.mw/Health/Home%20Health.htm.

Ministry of Home Affairs: Lilongwe.

Ministry of Industry and Trade: POB 30366, Capital City, Lilongwe 3; tel. 1770244; fax 1770680; e-mail minci@malawi.net; internet www.trade.gov.mw.

Ministry of Information: Private Bag 326, Capital City, Lilongwe 3; tel. 1775499; fax 1770650; e-mail psinfo@sdnp.org.mw; internet www.malawi.gov.mw/Information/Home%20Information.htm.

Ministry of Justice: Private Bag 333, Capital City, Lilongwe 3; tel. 1788411; fax 1788332; e-mail justice@justice.gov.mw; internet www .justice.gov.mw; also comprises the Attorney-General's Chambers and the Directorate of Public Prosecutions.

Ministry of Labour: Private Bag 344, Capital City, Lilongwe 3; tel. 1773277; fax 1773803; e-mail labour@malawi.net; internet www .malawi.gov.mw/Labour/Home%20%20Labour.htm.

Ministry of Lands and Housing: Lilongwe; internet www.lands .gov.mw.

Ministry of Local Government and Rural Development: POB 30312, Lilongwe 3; tel. 1789388; fax 1788083; e-mail mlgrd@ localgovt.mw; internet www.mlgrd.gov.mw.

Ministry of Mining: Lilongwe.

Ministry of National Defence: Private Bag 339, Lilongwe 3; tel. 1789600; fax 1789176; e-mail defence@defence.gov.mw.

Ministry of Tourism and Culture: Lilongwe 3; tel. 1772702; fax 1770650; e-mail tourism@malawi.net.

Ministry of Transport and Public Works: Private Bag 322, Capital City, Lilongwe 3; tel. 1789315; fax 1789328; e-mail c.k .kumangirana@gmail.com; internet www.malawi.gov.mw/ Transport/Home%20Transport.htm.

Ministry of Water Development and Irrigation: Lilongwe.

Ministry of Youth and Sport: Lingadzi House, Private Bag 384, Lilongwe 3; tel. 1774999; fax 1771018; e-mail sports@malawi.gov .mw.

President and Legislature

PRESIDENT

Presidential Election, 19 May 2009

Candidate		Votes	% of votes
Bingu wa Mutharika (DPP)	.	2,961,099	64.36
John Tembo (MCP)	. . . .	1,373,459	29.85
Walter Chibambo (PETRA)	. .	35,296	0.77
Others	. . . . . .	230,903	5.02
Total	. . . .	4,600,757	100.00

NATIONAL ASSEMBLY

National Assembly: Parliament Bldg, Private Bag B362, Lilongwe 3; tel. 1773566; fax 1774196; internet www.parliament.gov.mw.

Speaker: HENRY CHIMUNTHU BANDA.

General Election, 19 May 2009

Party	Seats
Democratic Progressive Party (DPP)	112
Malawi Congress Party (MCP)	27
United Democratic Front (UDF)	18
Alliance for Democracy (AFORD)	1
Malawi Forum for Unity and Development (MAFUNDE)	1
Maravi People's Party (MPP)	1
Independents	32
Total	192*

* Voting in one constituency did not take place owing to the death of a candidate. A by-election held on 14 August 2009 was won by an independent candidate. In 2010 by-elections were held in four constituencies (two in January and two in October) owing to the deaths of three incumbent members and the ineligibility of one member. The DPP won three seats, while the UDF took one. In September 2011 a by-election was held for a vacant seat, which was won by AFORD.

Election Commission

Malawi Electoral Commission (MEC): Old Controller of Stores Bldg, Private Bag 113, Blantyre; tel. 1822033; fax 1821846; e-mail ceo@mec.org.mw; internet www.mec.org.mw; f. 1998; Chair. MAXON MBENDERA; Chief Elections Officer WILLIE KALONGA.

Political Organizations

Alliance for Democracy (AFORD): Private Bag 28, Lilongwe; f. 1992; in March 1993 absorbed membership of fmr Malawi Freedom Movement; Acting Pres. GODFREY SHAWA; Sec.-Gen. NYASULU KHWAULI MSISKA.

Congress of Democrats (CODE): Mzuzu; Pres. RALPH KASAMBARA.

Congress for National Unity (CONU): Lilongwe; f. 1999; Pres. Bishop DANIEL KAMFOSI NKHUMBWA.

Democratic Progressive Party (DPP): Lilongwe 3; internet dppmw.org; f. 2005 following Bingu wa Mutharika's resignation from the UDF; Pres. Prof. ARTHUR PETER MUTHARIKA.

Malawi Congress Party (MCP): Private Bag 388, Lilongwe 3; tel. 999223228; f. 1959; sole legal party 1966–93; Pres. JOHN TEMBO.

Malawi Democratic Party (MDP): Lilongwe; Pres. (vacant).

Malawi Forum for Unity and Development (MAFUNDE): f. 2002; aims to combat corruption and food shortages; Pres. GEORGE MNESA.

National Rainbow Coalition (NARC): POB 40508, Kanengo, Lilongwe 4; tel. 1774007; f. 2008; Pres. LOVENESS GONDWE.

National Solidarity Movement: Leader NGWAZI KAZUNI KUMWENDA.

National Unity Party (NUP): Blantyre; Pres. HARRY CHIUME; Sec.-Gen. HARRY MUYENZA.

New Dawn for Africa (NDA): Legends Compound, Blantyre, POB 76, Liwonde; f. 2003; associated with the UDF; Pres. THOM CHIUMIA; Sec.-Gen. CHIKUMBUTSO MTUMODZI.

New Republican Party (NRP): f. 2005; Pres. GWANDAGULUWE CHAKUAMBA; Vice-Pres. KEN ZIKHALE NG'OMA.

People's Party (PP): Lilongwe; f. 2011 by Joyce Banda following her expulsion from the DPP; Pres. JOYCE BANDA; Sec.-Gen. HENRY CHIBWANA.

People's Progressive Movement (PPM): f. 2003 by fmr mems of the UDF; Pres. MARK KATSONGA; Sec.-Gen. KNOX VARELA.

People's Transformation Party (PETRA): POB 31964, Chichiri, Blantyre 3; tel. 1871577; fax 1871573; e-mail umunthu@sdnp.org.mw; internet www.petra.mw; f. 2002; Pres. KAMUZU CHIBAMBO; Sec.-Gen. DEREK LAKUDZALA.

Republican Party (RP): Lilongwe; Pres. (vacant).

United Democratic Front (UDF): POB 5446, Limbe; internet www.udf.malawi.net; f. 1992; officially merged with the NDA in June 2004 but maintained independent structure; rival faction led by Cassim Chilumpha and Friday Jumbe; Pres. ATUPELE AUSTIN MULUZI; Sec.-Gen. KANDI PADAMBO.

Diplomatic Representation

EMBASSIES AND HIGH COMMISSIONS IN MALAWI

China, People's Republic: No. 342, Area 43, POB 31799, Lilongwe; tel. 1794751; fax 1794752; e-mail chinaemb_mw@mfa.gov.cn; internet mw.chineseembassy.org/eng; Ambassador PAN HEJUN.

Egypt: 10/247 Tsoka Rd, POB 30451, Lilongwe 3; tel. 1780668; fax 1794660; Ambassador AKRAM MOHSEN HAMDY.

Germany: Convention Dr., POB 30046, Lilongwe 3; tel. 1772555; fax 1770250; e-mail info@lilongwe.diplo.de; internet www.lilongwe.diplo.de; Ambassador Dr PETER WOESTE.

Holy See: Lilongwe; Apostolic Nuncio JULIO MURAT.

Ireland: Arwa House, 3rd Floor, Capital City, Lilongwe; tel. 1776405; fax 1776401; e-mail lilongweemdiplomats@dfa.ie; Ambassador ELIZABETH HIGGINS.

Japan: Plot No. 14/191, Petroda Glass House, POB 30780, Lilongwe 3; tel. 1770284; fax 1773528; e-mail embmalawi@lw.mofa.go.jp; internet www.mw.emb-japan.go.jp; Ambassador FUJIO SAMUKAWA.

Mozambique: Area 40/14A, POB 30579, Lilongwe 3; tel. 1774100; fax 1771342; e-mail embamoc.malawi@minec.gov.mz; High Commissioner MARIA LEOCÁDIA TIVANE MATHE.

Nigeria: Lilongwe; High Commissioner MOHAMMED LAWAN GANA.

South Africa: Kang'ombe House, 3rd Floor, City Centre, POB 30043, Lilongwe 3; tel. 1773722; fax 1772571; e-mail sahc@malawi.net; High Commissioner (vacant).

Tanzania: POB 922, Capital City, Lilongwe 3; tel. 1770150; fax 1770148; e-mail tanzanianhighcomm@tz.lilongwe.mw; High Commissioner PATRICK TSERE.

United Kingdom: British High Commission Bldg, Capital Hill, POB 30042, Lilongwe 3; tel. 1772400; fax 1772657; e-mail bhclilongwe@fco.gov.uk; internet ukinmalawi.fco.gov.uk; High Commissioner MICHAEL NEVIN.

USA: Area 40, Plot No. 18, 16 Jomo Kenyatta Rd, POB 30016, Lilongwe 3; tel. 1773166; fax 1770471; e-mail consularlilong@state.gov; internet lilongwe.usembassy.gov; Ambassador JEANINE E. JACKSON.

Zambia: Area 40/2, City Centre, POB 30138, Lilongwe 3; tel. 1772100; fax 1774349; Deputy High Commissioner HENRY NGILAZI.

Zimbabwe: POB 30187, Lilongwe 3; tel. 1774988; fax 1772382; e-mail zimhighcomllw@malawi.net; Ambassador THANDIWE S. DUMBUTSHENA.

Judicial System

The courts administering justice are the Supreme Court of Appeal, High Court and Magistrates' Courts.

The High Court, which has unlimited jurisdiction in civil and criminal matters, consists of the Chief Justice and five puisne judges. Traditional Courts were abolished under the 1994 Constitution. Appeals from the High Court are heard by the Supreme Court of Appeal in Blantyre.

Supreme Court of Appeal: Blantyre; consists of the Chief Justice and not fewer than three other judges.

High Court of Malawi: POB 30244, Chichiri, Blantyre 3; tel. 1670255; fax 1670213; e-mail highcourt@sdnp.org.mw; internet www.judiciary.mw; Registrar H. S. POTANI.

Chief Justice: ANASTAZIA MSOSA (acting).

Attorney-General: ANTHONY KAMANGA.

Religion

According to the census of 2008, 82.7% of the population profess Christianity. Islam is practised by about 13.0% of the population.

CHRISTIANITY

Malawi Council of Churches (MCC): POB 30068, Capital City, Lilongwe 3; tel. 1783499; fax 1783106; f. 1939; Chair. Rev. JOSEPH P. BVUMBWE; Gen. Sec. Rev. Dr OSBORNE JODA-MBEWE; 24 mem. churches.

The Anglican Communion

Anglicans are adherents of the Church of the Province of Central Africa, covering Botswana, Malawi, Zambia and Zimbabwe. The Church comprises 15 dioceses, including four in Malawi. The current Archbishop of the Province is the Bishop of Northern Zambia. There were about 230,000 adherents in Malawi at mid-2000.

Bishop of Lake Malawi: FRANCIS KAULANDA, POB 30349, Capital City, Lilongwe 3; tel. 1797858; fax 1797548; e-mail anglama@eomw.net.

Bishop of Northern Malawi: Rt Rev. FANUEL EMMANUEL CHIOKO MAGANGANI, POB 120, Mzuzu; tel. 1331486; fax 1333805; e-mail angdioofnm@sdnp.org.mw.

Bishop of Southern Malawi: Rt Rev. JAMES TENGATENGA, POB 30220, Chichiri, Blantyre 3; tel. 1641218; fax 1641235; e-mail angsoma@sdnp.org.mw; internet www.angsoma.org.

Bishop of Upper Shire: BRIGHTON MALASA, Private Bag 1, Chilema, Zomba; tel. and fax 1539203; e-mail dionorth@zamnet.zm.

Protestant Churches

At mid-2001 there were an estimated 2.1m. Protestants in Malawi.

Assemblies of God in Malawi: POB 1220, Lilongwe; tel. 1761057; fax 1762056; Pres. Dr LAZARUS CHAKWERA; 639,088 mems in 3,114 churches (2005).

Baptist Convention of Malawi (BACOMA): Lali Lubani Rd, POB 30212, Chichiri, Blantyre 3; tel. 1671170; e-mail bacoma@sdnp.org.mw; 175,000 adherents, 1,375 churches (2007); Gen. Sec. Rev. FLETCHER KAIYA.

Church of Central Africa Presbyterian (CCAP): Blantyre Synod, POB 413, Blantyre; tel. and fax 1633942; e-mail btsynod@malawi.net; internet www.blantyresynod.org; comprises 3 synods in Malawi (Blantyre, Livingstonia and Nkhoma); Co-ordinator Rev. J.J. MPHATSE; Gen. Sec. DANIEL GUNYA; Exec. Dir ROBSON CHITENGO; more than 1m. adherents in Malawi.

Evangelical Association of Malawi: POB 2120, Blantyre; tel. and fax 999936681 (mobile); Chair. Rev. Dr LAZARUS CHAKWERA; Gen. Sec. FRANCIS MKANDAWIRE.

Evangelical Lutheran Church in Malawi: POB 650, Lutheran Church Centre, Plot 22, Chidzanja Rd, Lilongwe; tel. and fax 1726288; fax 1725910; e-mail elcmwi@elcmw.org; Bishop. Dr JOSEPH P. BVUMBWE; 80,000 mems (2010).

Seventh-day Adventist Church: Robins Rd, Kabula Hill, POB 951, Blantyre; tel. 1820264; fax 1820528; e-mail musda@malawi.net; Pres. FRACKSON KUYAMA; Exec. Sec. BAXTER D. CHILUNGA; 360,000 mems.

The African Methodist Episcopal Church, the Churches of Christ, the Free Methodist Church, the New Apostolic Church and the United Evangelical Church in Malawi are also active. At mid-2000 there were an estimated 2m. adherents professing other forms of Christianity.

The Roman Catholic Church

Malawi comprises two archdioceses and five dioceses. There are some 3.9m. adherents of the Roman Catholic Church (equivalent to approximately 23% of the total population).

Episcopal Conference of Malawi

Catholic Secretariat of Malawi, Chimutu Rd, POB 30384, Capital City, Lilongwe 3; tel. 1782066; fax 1782019; e-mail ecm@malawi.net; internet episcopalconferenceofmalawi.org.

f. 1969; Sec.-Gen. Rev. GEORGE BULEYA.

Archbishop of Blantyre: Most Rev. TARCISIUS GERVAZIO ZIYAYE, Archbishop House, POB 385, Blantyre; tel. and fax 1637905; e-mail archdblantyre@africa-online.net.

Archbishop of Lilongwe: Most Rev. RÉMI JOSEPH GUSTAVE SAINTE-MARIE, POB 33, Lilongwe; tel. 1754667; fax 1752767.

ISLAM

Muslim Association of Malawi (MAM): POB 497, Blantyre; tel. 1622060; fax 1623581; f. 1946 as the Nyasaland Muslim Asscn; umbrella body for Muslim orgs; provides secular and Islamic education; Chair. SHEIKH IDRISA; Sec.-Gen. Dr SALMIN OMAR IDRUS.

BAHÁ'Í FAITH

National Spiritual Assembly: POB 30922, Lilongwe 3; tel. 1771177; fax 1771713; e-mail bahaimalawi@africa-online.net; f. 1970; mems resident in over 1,200 localities.

The Press

The Chronicle: Private Bag 77, Lilongwe; tel. 999913457; e-mail thechronicle@africa-online.net; f. 1993; publ. by Jamieson Promotions Ltd; weekly; English and Chichewa; Owner and Editor-in-Chief ROBERT JAMIESON; circ. c. 5,000 (2006).

The Daily Times: Scott Rd, Private Bag 39, Blantyre; tel. 1871663; fax 1871233; e-mail dailytimes@bnltimes.com; internet www .bnltimes.com/index.php/daily-times; f. 1895; fmrly the *Nyasaland Times*; Mon.–Fri., Sun.; English; publ. by Blantyre Newspapers Ltd (Chayamba Trust); affiliated to the MCP; Editor BRIAN LIGOMEKA; circ. Mon.–Fri. c. 20,000, Sun. c. 40,000 (2006).

The Democratus: Aquarius House, Convention Dr., City Centre, Box 1100, Lilongwe 3; tel. 1770033; internet democratusmalawi .blogspot.com; f. 2004; publ. by Democratus Ltd; Wed. and Sun.; Chair. ZIKHALE NG'OMA.

The Dispatch: The Dispatch Publications Ltd, POB 30353, Capital City, Lilongwe 3; tel. 1751639; fax 9510120; e-mail thedispatchmw@sdnp.org.mw; Thur. and Sun; Publr and Man. Editor MARTINES NAMINGAH; circ. Thur. 5,000, Sun. 7,000.

The Enquirer: POB 1745, Blantyre; tel. 1670022; e-mail pillycolette@yahoo.co.uk; English and Nyanja; affiliated to the UDF; Owner LUCIOUS CHIKUNI.

The Guardian: Capital City, Private Bag B341, Lilongwe; tel. 1761996; fax 1761996; Man. Editor DUWA MUTHARIKA-MUBAIRA; circ. c. 5,000 (2006).

The Lamp: Montfort Media, POB 280, Balaka, Zomba; tel. 1545267; e-mail montfortmedia@malawi.net; f. 1995; fortnightly; Roman Catholic and ecumenical; Editor Fr GAMBA PIERGIORGIO; circ. 5,500.

Malawi Government Gazette: Government Printer, POB 37, Zomba; tel. 1523155; fax 1522301; f. 1894; weekly.

Malawi News: Scott Rd, Private Bag 39, Blantyre; tel. 1871679; fax 1871233; internet www.malawinews.bppmw.com; f. 1959; weekly; English and Chichewa; publ. by Blantyre Newspapers Ltd (Chayamba Trust); Man. Editor EDWARD CHISAMBO; Editor STEVEN NHLANE, Jr; circ. c. 40,000 (2006).

The Malawi Standard: POB 31781, Blantyre 3; tel. 1674013; e-mail bligomeka@yahoo.co.uk; fortnightly; Editor BRIAN LIGOMEKA.

The Mirror: POB 30721, Blantyre; tel. 1675043; f. 1994; weekly; English and Nyanja; affiliated to the UDF; Owner and Publr BROWN MPINGANJIRA; circ. 10,000.

The Nation: POB 30408, Chichiri, Blantyre 3; tel. 1673611; fax 1674343; e-mail nation@nationmalawi.com; internet www .nationmw.net; f. 1993; daily; publ. by Nation Publs Ltd; weekly edn of *The Weekend Nation* (circ. 30,000); English and Nyanja; Owner ALEKE BANDA; Editor EDWARD CHITSULO; circ. 15,000.

UDF News: POB 3052, Blantyre; tel. 1645314; fax 1645725; e-mail echapusa@yahoo.co.uk; organ of the UDF; fortnightly; English and Nyanja.

Weekly Courier: Lilongwe 3; affiliated to the Democratic Progressive Party; Man. Editor DENIS MZEMBE; circ. c. 3,000 (2006).

There is also an online newspaper, the **Nyasa Times** (internet www.nyasatimes.com).

PERIODICALS

Boma Lathu: POB 494, Blantyre; tel. 1620266; fax 1620039; f. 1973; quarterly; Chichewa; publ. by the Ministry of Information; circ. 100,000.

Business Monthly: POB 906646, Blantyre 9; tel. 16301114; fax 1620039; f. 1995; English; economic, financial and business news; Editor ANTHONY LIVUZA; circ. 10,000.

Fairlane Magazine: POB 1745, Blantyre; tel. 1880205; e-mail fairlane@sndp.org.mw; internet www.fairlanemagazine.com; f. 2006; 6 a year; lifestyle magazine; English and Chichewa; Man. Dir MARIE FRANCE CHIKUNI.

Kuunika (The Light): POB 17, Nkhoma, Lilongwe; tel. 1722807; e-mail nkhomasynod@globemw.net; f. 1909; monthly; Chichewa; publ. by the Church of Central Africa (Presbyterian) Nkhoma Synod; Presbyterian; Editor Rev. M. C. NKHALAMBAYAUSI; circ. 6,000.

Malawi Medical Journal: College of Medicine and Medical Asscn of Malawi, Private Bag 360, Blantyre 3; tel. and fax 1878254; e-mail mmj@medcol.mw; internet www.mmj.medcol.mw; f. 1980; replaced *Medical Quarterly*; quarterly; Chair. Prof. ERIC BORGSTEIN; Editor-in-Chief Prof. MALCOLM E. MOLYNEUX.

Moni Magazine: POB 5592, Limbe; tel. 1651833; fax 1651171; f. 1964; monthly; Chichewa and English; circ. 40,000.

Moyo Magazine: Health Education Unit, POB 30377, Lilongwe 3; 6 a year; English; publ. by the Ministry of Health; Editor-in-Chief JONATHAN NKHOMA.

Pride: POB 51668, Limbe; tel. 1640569; f. 1999; quarterly; Publr JOHN SAINI.

This is Malawi: POB 494, Blantyre; tel. 1620266; fax 1620807; f. 1964; monthly; English and Chichewa edns; publ. by the Dept of Information; Editor ANTHONY LIVUZA; circ. 12,000.

Together: Montfort Media, POB 280, Balaka, Zomba; tel. 1545267; e-mail together@sdnp.org.mw; f. 1995; quarterly; Roman Catholic and ecumenical, youth; Editor LUIGI GRITTI; circ. 6,000.

Other publications include *Dzukani*, *Inspiration* and *Msilikali*.

NEWS AGENCY

Malawi News Agency (MANA): POB 28, Blantyre; tel. 1622122; fax 1634867; f. 1966; Exec. Dir GEORGE THINDWA.

Publishers

Christian Literature Association in Malawi (CLAIM): POB 503, Blantyre; tel. 1620839; f. 1968; Chichewa and English; general and religious; Gen. Man. J. T. MATENJE.

Likuni Press and Publishing House: POB 133, Lilongwe; tel. 1721388; fax 1721141; f. 1949; English and Chichewa; general and religious.

Macmillan Malawi Ltd: Private Bag 140, Kenyatta Dr., Chitawira, Blantyre; tel. 1676449; fax 1675751; e-mail mayeso@macmillanmw .net; Gen. Man. HASTINGS MATEWERE.

Montfort Press and Popular Publications: POB 5592, Limbe; tel. 1651833; fax 1641126; f. 1961; general and religious; Gen. Man. VALES MACHILA.

GOVERNMENT PUBLISHING HOUSE

Government Press: Government Printer, POB 37, Zomba; tel. 1525515; fax 1525175.

Broadcasting and Communications

REGULATORY AUTHORITY

Malawi Communications Regulatory Authority (MACRA): Salmon Amour Rd, Private Bag 261, Blantyre; tel. 1883611; fax 1883890; e-mail info@macra.org.mw; internet www.macra.org.mw; f. 1998; Chair. MARTHA KWATAINE; Dir-Gen. CHARLES NSALIWA.

TELECOMMUNICATIONS

In early 2012 there were two mobile cellular telephone operators, one fixed-line telephone operator and one fixed wireless operator in Malawi. In March 2011 a mobile telephone service licence was issued to Celcom Ltd, which was expected to commence operations by October 2012. Later in 2011 dual licences were awarded to all telecommunications operators, permitting them to provide both fixed-line and mobile services.

Access Communications Ltd: Accord Centre, Masauko Chipembere Highway, Limbe, POB 343, Blantyre; tel. 212200200; fax 1871887; e-mail switch@access.mw; internet www.access.mw; f. 2010; fixed wireless.

Airtel Malawi: Mwai House, City Centre, POB 57, Lilongwe; tel. 1774800; fax 1774802; e-mail info.africa@airtel.com; internet africa .airtel.com/malawi; f. 1999; fmrly Zain Malawi, present name adopted in 2010; Man. Dir SAULOS CHILIMA.

Malawi Telecommunications Ltd (MTL): Lamya House, Masauko Chipembere Highway, POB 537, Blantyre; tel. 1870278; fax 1846445; e-mail mtlceo@malawi.net; internet www.mtl.mw; f. 2000 following division of Malawi Posts and Telecommunications Corpn into two separate entities; privatized in 2006; 80% owned by Telecom Holdings Ltd, 20% state-owned; CEO PIUS MULIPA (acting).

Telekom Networks Malawi (TNM): Livingstone Towers, 5th Floor, POB 3039, Blantyre; tel. 888800800 (mobile); fax 1830077; e-mail customercare@tnm.co.mw; internet www.tnm.co.mw; f. 1995; owned by Malawi Telecommunications Ltd; operates mobile cellular telephone network; CEO WILLEM SWART.

BROADCASTING

In early 2011 there were 26 licensed broadcasters in Malawi. In November of that year the Malawi Communications Regulatory Authority awarded licences to four television stations (Galaxy,

CAN, ABC and Getway) and four radio stations (Galaxy, Mulakho, Maziko and Usisya).

Radio

Malawi Broadcasting Corpn: POB 30133, Chichiri, Blantyre 3; tel. 1671222; fax 1671257; e-mail dgmbc@malawi.net; internet www .mbcradios.com; f. 1964; merged with Television Malawi in July 2010; state-run; 2 channels: MBC 1 and Radio 2 (MBC 2); programmes in English, Chichewa, Chitonga, Chitumbuka, Kyangonde, Lomwe, Sena and Yao; Chair. INKOSI YA MAKOSI MBELWA IV; Dir.-Gen. BENSON TEMBO.

Private commercial and religious radio stations include:

African Bible College Radio (Radio ABC): POB 1028, Lilongwe; tel. 1761965; fax 1761602; e-mail radioabc@malawi.net; internet africanbiblecolleges.org; f. 1995; regional Christian religious programming; Station Man. MACLEOD MUNTHALI.

Calvary Family Radio: POB 30239, Blantyre 3; tel. 1671627; fax 1671642; e-mail calvaryministries@hotmail.com; operated by the Calvary Family Church; religious community radio station.

Capital Radio 102.5 FM: Umoyo House, 2nd Floor, Victoria Ave, Blantyre; Private Bag 437, Chichiri, Blantyre 3; tel. 1820858; fax 1823382; e-mail stationmanager@capitalradiomalawi.com; internet www.capitalradiomalawi.com; f. 1999; commercial radio station; music, news and entertainment; Man. Dir and Editor-in-Chief ALAUDIN OSMAN.

Channel for All Nations (CAN): POB 1220, Lilongwe; tel. 1761763; fax 1762056; e-mail kawembale@yahoo.com; f. 2004; operated by the Assemblies of God Church; regional Christian religious programming.

Dzimwe Community Radio (DCR): POB 425, Chichiri, Blantyre; tel. 1672288; fax 1624330; e-mail mamwa@yahoo.com; f. 1997; operated by the Malawi Media Women's Asscn; focus on rural women's issues; Station Man. JANET KARIM.

Joy FM: Private Bag 17, Limbe, Blantyre; tel. 1638330; fax 1638329; e-mail joyradio@globemalawi.net; commercial radio station; Owner BAKILI MULUZI.

MIJ FM: POB 30165, Chichiri, Blantyre 3; tel. 1675087; fax 1675649; e-mail mij@clcom.net; internet www.mij.mw/aboutradio.html; f. 1996; operated by students of the Malawi Institute of Journalism; community radio station; closed by the Govt during May 2004.

Nkhota Kota Community Radio: Nkhota Kota; f. 2003 with assistance from UNESCO; focus on social and devt issues.

Power 101 FM: POB 761, Blantyre; tel. 1844101; fax 1841387; e-mail fm101@malawi.net; f. 1998; commercial radio station; music and entertainment; Dir and Station Man. OSCAR THOMSON.

Radio Alinafe: Maula Cathedral, POB 631, Lilongwe; tel. 1759971; fax 1752767; e-mail radioalinafe@sdnp.org.mw; f. 2002; Chichewa and English; operated by the Archdiocese of Lilongwe; regional Roman Catholic religious programming; Dir GABRIEL JANA; Editor MOSES KAUFA.

Radio Islam: Agason Bldg, Milward Rd, PO Box 5400, Limbe; tel. 1841408; fax 1845728; e-mail info@radioislam.org.mw; internet radioislam.org.mw; f. 2001; operated by the Islamic Zakaat Fund; religious programming; Dir MUHAMMAD MUHAMMAD AHMED.

Radio Maria Malawi: POB 408, Mangochi; tel. 1599626; fax 1599691; e-mail radiomaria@malawi.net; internet www .radiomaria.mw; f. 2003; operated by Asscn of Radio Maria Malawi as part of the World Family of Radio Maria, Italy; Roman Catholic religious programming; Chichewa, Chiyao and English; Gen. Man. JOSEPH KIMU; Dir of Programmes HENRY SAINDI.

Star Radio: Plantation House, 4th Floor, 11 Victoria Ave, Blantyre; tel. and fax 1832787; e-mail info@starradiomw.com; internet www .starradiomw.com; f. 2006; commercial radio station; Station Man. KAJOWOLA PHIRI.

Trans World Radio Malawi (TWR): POB 52, Lilongwe; tel. and fax 1751870; e-mail twr@malawi.net; f. 2000; part of Trans World Radio-Africa, South Africa; Christian religious programming; Chair. ISAAC MTAMBO; Nat. Dir VICTOR KAONGA.

Zodiak Broadcasting Station (ZBS): Private Bag 312, Lilongwe 3; tel. 1762557; fax 1762751; internet www.zodiakmalawi.com; f. 2005; operated by Zodiak Broadcasting Services; programmes in Chichewa and English; Man. Dir GOSPEL KAZAKO.

Television

MBC: (see Radio).

Luntha Television: Andiamo Loop, POB 45, Balaka; tel. 1553009; fax 1553492; e-mail info@lunthatv.com; internet luntha.project4 .webfactional.com; f. 2007; religious broadcaster.

Finance

(cap. = capital; res = reserves; dep. = deposits; m. = million;
br(s). = branch(es); amounts in kwacha)

BANKING

In 2010 there were 11 commercial banks and three other financial institutions in Malawi.

Central Bank

Reserve Bank of Malawi: Convention Dr., POB 30063, Capital City, Lilongwe 3; tel. 1770600; fax 1772752; e-mail webmaster@rbm .mw; internet www.rbm.mw; f. 1965; bank of issue; cap. 19,484m., res 12,191m., dep. 48,715m. (Dec. 2009); Gov. CHARLES CHUKA; br. in Blantyre.

Commercial Banks

INDEBank Ltd: INDEBank House, Kaohsiong Rd, Top Mandala, POB 358, Blantyre; tel. 1820055; fax 1823353; e-mail enquiriesho@ indebank.com; internet www.indebank.com; f. 1972 as Investment and Devt Bank of Malawi Ltd; total assets 2,162.6m. (Dec. 2003); 41.38% owned by Trans-Africa Holdings Ltd, 30% owned by Press Trust, 25.67% owned by ADMARC Investments Holding, 2.95% owned by Employee Ownership Scheme; commercial and devt banking; provides loans to statutory corpns and to private enterprises in the agricultural, industrial, tourism, transport and commercial sectors; Chair. FRANKLIN KENNEDY; Man. Dir and CEO WILLIAM CHATSALA; 6 brs.

Loita Bank Ltd: c/o Fintech (Malawi) Ltd, Peoples Bldg, 1st Floor, Victoria Ave, Private Bag 264, Blantyre; tel. 1822099; fax 1822683; e-mail lib@mw.loita.com; internet www.loita.com; total assets 3,100.3m. (Dec. 2003); 100% owned by Loita Capital Partners Int; Chair. and CEO N. JUSTIN CHIMYANTA; 2 brs.

National Bank of Malawi: 19 Victoria Ave, POB 945, Blantyre; tel. 1820622; fax 1820321; e-mail chiefexec@natbankmw.com; internet www.natbank.co.mw; f. 1971; 52% owned by Press Corpn Ltd, 25% owned by Old Mutual Group; cap. 466m., res 2,592m., dep. 55,338m. (Dec. 2009); Chair. Dr MATHEWS CHIKAONDA; CEO GEORGE B. PARTRIDGE; 25 service centres.

NBS Bank Ltd: Ginnery Cnr, Chipembere Highway, off Masajico, POB 32251, Chichiri, Blantyre; tel. 1876222; fax 1875041; e-mail nbs@nbsmw.com; internet www.nbsmw.com; f. 2003; 60% owned by NICO, 8% owned by the Nat. Investment Trust; fmrly New Building Society; cap. 246.7m., res 733.7m., dep. 24,317m. (Dec. 2009); Chair. FELIX L. MLUSU; CEO JOHN S. BIZIWICK.

Nedbank (Malawi) Ltd: Development House, cnr Henderson St and Victoria Ave, POB 750, Blantyre; tel. 1620477; fax 1620102; e-mail office@mw.nedcor.com; f. 1999; fmrly Fincom Bank of Malawi Ltd; 68.8% owned by Nedbank Africa Investments Ltd, 28.4% owned by SBM Nedcor Holdings Ltd; total assets 1,426.9m. (Dec. 2003); Chair. C. DREW; Man. Dir PAUL TUBB.

Standard Bank Ltd: Kaomba Centre, cnr Glyn Jones Rd and Victoria Ave, POB 1111, Blantyre; tel. 1820144; fax 1820117; e-mail stanbicmw@standardbank.co.mw; internet www .standardbank.co.mw; f. 1970 as Commercial Bank of Malawi; present name adopted June 2003; 60.18% owned by Stanbic Africa Holdings Ltd, 20.00% owned by Nat. Insurance Co; cap. 213m., res 2,392m., dep. 38,147m. (Dec. 2009); Chair. ALEX CHITSIME; Man. Dir CHARLES MUDIWA; 8 brs.

Development Bank

Opportunity International Bank of Malawi Ltd (OIBM): Opportunity Bank Bldg, POB 1794, Lilongwe; tel. 1758403; fax 1758400; e-mail lilongwe@oibm.mw; internet www.oibm.mw; f. 2003; 63.7% owned by Opportunity Transformation Investments, USA, 25.3% owned by Opportunity Micro Investments (UK) Ltd, United Kingdom, 11% owned by Trust for Transformation; total assets 967.4m. (Dec. 2005); Chair. FRANCIS PELEKAMOYO; CEO RODGER VOORHIES.

Discount Houses

CDH Investment Bank: Unit House, 5th Floor, Victoria Ave, POB 1444, Blantyre; tel. 1821300; fax 1822826; e-mail info@cdh-malawi .com; internet www.cdh-malawi.com; f. 1998; 84% owned by Trans-Africa Holdings; total assets 6,728.8m. (Dec. 2005); Chair. ROBERT SEKOH ABBEY; Man. Dir and CEO MISHECK ESAU.

First Discount House Ltd: Umoyo House, 1st Floor, 8 Victoria Ave North, POB 512, Blantyre; tel. 1820219; fax 1523044; e-mail fdh@fdh .co.mw; internet www.fdh.co.mw; f. 2000; 40.16% owned by Kingdom Financial Holdings Ltd, 39.84% owned by Thomson F. Mpinganjira Trust, 20% owned by Old Mutual Life Assurance Co (Malawi) Ltd; total assets 5,960.7m. (Dec. 2004); CEO THOMSON F. MPINGANJIRA; Chair. NIGEL M. K. CHAKANIRA.

Merchant Banks

First Merchant Bank Ltd: Livingstone Towers, Glyn Jones Rd, Private Bag 122, Blantyre; tel. 1821955; fax 1821978; e-mail fmb .headoffice@fmbmalawi.com; internet www.fmbmalawi.com; f. 1994; cap. 111.3m., res 2,281.5m., dep. 11,539.5m. (Dec. 2008); 44.9% owned by Zambezi Investments Ltd, 22.5% owned by Simsbury Holdings Ltd, 11.2% owned each by Prime Capital and Credit Ltd, Kenya, and Prime Bank Ltd, Kenya; Chair. RASIKBHAI C. KANTARIA; Man. Dir KASHINATH N. CHATURVEDI; 7 brs.

Leasing and Finance Co of Malawi Ltd: Livingstone Towers, Glyn Jones Rd, POB 1963, Blantyre; tel. 1820233; fax 1820275; f. 1986; total assets 2,087.4m. (Dec. 2006); Chair. HITESH ANADKAT; Gen. Man. MBACHAZWA LUNGU.

Savings Bank

Malawi Savings Bank: Umoyo House, Victoria Ave, POB 521, Blantyre; tel. 1625111; fax 1621929; internet www.msb.mw; f. 1994; 99.9% state-owned; total assets 1,191.7m. (Dec. 2003); Sec.-Treas. P. E. CHILAMBE; Gen. Man. IAN C. BONONGWE.

STOCK EXCHANGE

Malawi Stock Exchange: Old Reserve Bank Bldg, 14 Victoria Ave, Private Bag 270, Blantyre; tel. 1824233; fax 1824636; e-mail mse@ mse-mw.com; internet www.mse.co.mw; f. 1996; owned by the Reserve Bank of Malawi; 14 cos listed in 2011; Chair. AUGUSTINE CHITHENGA; CEO SYMON MSEFULA.

INSURANCE

In 2010 the insurance sector comprised 12 insurance companies and one reinsurance company. Of these, eight companies dealt in non-life insurance.

NICO Holdings Ltd: CHIBISA House, 19 Glyn Jones Rd, POB 501, Blantyre; tel. 1831902; fax 1822364; e-mail info@nicomw.com; internet www.nicomw.com; f. 1970; fmrly National Insurance Co Ltd; transferred to private sector in 1996; incorporates NICO Gen. Insurance Co Ltd, NICO Life Insurance Co Ltd and NICO Technologies Ltd; offices at Blantyre, Lilongwe, Mzuzu and Zomba; agencies country-wide; Chair. GEORGE A. JAFFU; CEO and Man. Dir FELIX L. MLUSU.

Old Mutual Malawi: 30 Glyn Jones Rd, Old Mutual Building, POB 393, Blantyre; tel. 1820677; fax 1822649; e-mail info@oldmutual.co .mw; internet www.oldmutualmalawi.com; f. 1845; subsidiary of Old Mutual PLC, United Kingdom; Chair. SIMON ITAYE; Man. Dir CHRIS KAPANGA.

REAL Insurance Co of Malawi Ltd: Delamere House, Victoria Ave, POB 442, Blantyre; tel. 1824044; fax 1823862; e-mail blantyre@ realinsurance.co.mw; internet www.realinsurance.co.mw; associate of RSA PLC, United Kingdom; Chair. THOMAS O. B. KANYUKA; CEO GRANT MWENECHANYA.

United General Insurance Co Ltd (UGI): Michiru House, Victoria Ave, POB 383, Blantyre; tel. 1821770; fax 1821980; e-mail ugi@ ugimalawi.com; internet www.ugimalawi.com; f. 1986 as Pearl Assurance Co Ltd; latterly Property and Gen. Insurance Co Ltd; present name adopted following merger with Fide Insurance Co Ltd in July 1998; 74% owned by ZimRE Holdings, Zimbabwe; Chair. ALBERT NDUNA; Man. Dir IAN K. KUMWENDA.

Vanguard Life Assurance Co (Pvt) Ltd: MDC House, 2nd Floor, Glyn Jones Rd, POB 1625, Blantyre; tel. 1823326; fax 1823056; e-mail vanguard@vanguardlifemw.com; internet www .vanguardlifemw.com; f. 1999; 90% owned by Fidelity Life Assurance Ltd, Zimbabwe; Chair. S. TEMBO; Man. Dir GEORGE MAZHUDE.

Trade and Industry

GOVERNMENT AGENCIES

Agricultural Development and Marketing Corpn (ADMARC): POB 5052, Limbe; tel. 1840044; fax 1840486; e-mail admce@admarc .co.mw; internet www.admarc.co.mw; f. 1971; involved in cultivation, processing, marketing and export of grain and other crops; Chair. ERNEST MALENGA; CEO Dr CHARLES J. MATABWA.

Malawi Export Promotion Council (MEPC): Kanabar House, 2nd Floor, Victoria Ave, POB 1299, Blantyre; tel. 1820499; fax 1820995; e-mail mepco@malawi.net; internet www.malawiepc .com; f. 1971; promotes and facilitates export and investment, and provides technical assistance and training to exporters; Gen. Man. LAWRENCE M. CHALULUKA.

Malawi Housing Corpn: POB 414, Blantyre; tel. 1876822.

Malawi Investment Promotion Agency (MIPA): Aquarius House, Private Bag 302, Lilongwe 3; tel. 1770800; fax 1771781; e-mail mipa@mipamw.org; internet www.malawi-invest.net; f. 1993;

promotes and facilitates local and foreign investment; CEO James R. Kaphweleza Banda.

Petroleum Control Commission: POB 2827, Blantyre; e-mail sichioko@pccmalawi.com; state-owned; held monopoly on fuel imports until 2000; also serves regulatory role; Chair. Rev. Dr Lazarus Chakwera; Gen. Man. Ishmael Chioko.

Privatisation Commission of Malawi: Livingstone Towers, 2nd Floor, Glyn Jones Rd, POB 937, Blantyre; tel. 1823655; fax 1821248; e-mail info@pcmalawi.org; internet www.pcmalawi.org; f. 1996; has sole authority to oversee divestiture of govt interests in public enterprises; Chair. Alex Chitsime; CEO Jimmy Lipunga; 75 privatizations completed by January 2008.

Tobacco Control Commission: POB 40045, Kanengo, Lilongwe 4; tel. 1712777; fax 1712632; e-mail tcclib@tccmw.com; internet www .tccmw.com; f. 1939; regulates tobacco production and marketing; advises Govt on sale and export of tobacco; Chair. Gamaliel Bandawe; CEO Dr Bruce Munthali; regional offices in Mzuzu and Limbe.

DEVELOPMENT ORGANIZATIONS

Council for Non-Governmental Organizations in Malawi (CONGOMA): Amina House, Ground Floor, Units 11 12, off Paul Kagame Rd, POB 2264, Lilongwe; tel. 111917800; e-mail congoma@ gmail.com; internet www.congoma.mw; f. 1992; promotes social and economic devt; Chair. Voice Mhone; Exec. Dir Ronald Mtonga; 380 mem. orgs (2013).

Small Enterprise Development Organization of Malawi (SEDOM): POB 525, Blantyre; tel. 1622555; fax 1622781; e-mail sedom@sdnp.org.mw; f. 1982; financial services and accommodation for indigenous small- and medium-scale businesses; Chair. Stella Ndau.

CHAMBER OF COMMERCE

Malawi Confederation of Chambers of Commerce and Industry (MCCCI): Masauko Chipembere Highway, Chichiri Trade Fair Grounds, POB 258, Blantyre; tel. 1871988; fax 1871147; e-mail mccci@mccci.org; internet www.mccci.org; f. 1892; promotes trade and encourages competition in the economy; Chair. Matthews J. Chikankheni; CEO Chancellor L. Kaferapanjira; 400 mems.

INDUSTRIAL AND TRADE ASSOCIATIONS

Dwangwa Cane Growers Trust (DCGT): POB 156, Dwangwa; tel. 1295111; fax 1295164; e-mail dcgt@malawi.net; f. 1999; fmrly Smallholder Sugar Authority; CEO Wilfred Chakanika.

National Hawkers and Informal Business Association (NAHIBA): Chichiri Trade Fair, POB 60544, Ndirande, Blantyre; tel. 1945315; fax 1624558; e-mail nazulug@yahoo.com; f. 1995; Exec. Dir Eva Joachim.

Smallholder Coffee Farmers Trust: POB 20133, Luwinga, Mzuzu 2; tel. 1332899; fax 1333902; e-mail mzuzucoffee@malawi .net; f. 1971; successor to the Smallholder Coffee Authority, disbanded in 1999; producers and exporters of Arabica coffee; Gen. Man. Harrison Kalua; 4,000 mems.

Smallholder Tea Co (STECO): POB 135, Mulanje; f. 2002 by merger of Smallholder Tea Authority and Malawi Tea Factory Co Ltd.

Tea Association of Malawi Ltd (TAML): Kidney Crescent Rd, POB 930, Blantyre; tel. 1671182; fax 1671427; e-mail taml@malawi .net; internet www.taml.co.mw; f. 1934; CEO Clement C. Thindwa; 10 mems.

Tobacco Association of Malawi (TAMA): 13/64 Independence Dr., TAMA House, POB 31360, Lilongwe 3; tel. 1773099; fax 1773493; e-mail tama@tamalawi.com; internet www.tamalawi .com; f. 1929; Pres. Rueben Jefred Maigwa; Chief Exec. Felix Mkumba; brs in Mzuzu, Limbe and Chinkhoma; 75,000 mems.

Tobacco Exporters' Association of Malawi Ltd (TEAM): Private Bag 403, Kanengo, Lilongwe 4; tel. 1775839; fax 1774069; f. 1930; Chair. Charles A. M. Graham; Gen. Man. H. M. Mbale; 9 mems.

EMPLOYERS' ORGANIZATIONS

Employers' Consultative Association of Malawi (ECAM): Ndola Cres., House No 498A, POB 2134, Blantyre; tel. and fax 1830075; fax 1830075; e-mail ecam@ecammw.com; internet www .ecammw.com; f. 1963; Pres. Buxton M. Kayuni; Dep. Exec. Dir Odridge J. Khunga; 250 mem. asscns and 6 affiliates representing 80,000 employees.

Motor Traders' Association: POB 311, Blantyre; tel. and fax 1833312; f. 1954; Chair. Jolly Nkhojera; 13 mems (2008).

UTILITIES

Electricity

Electricity Supply Corpn of Malawi (ESCOM): ESCOM House, 9 Haile Selassie Rd, POB 2047, Blantyre; tel. and fax 1822000; fax 1822008; e-mail info@escommw.com; internet www.escom.mw; f. 1966; controls electricity generation and distribution; Chair. Morgan Tembo; CEO Peter Mtonda (acting).

Malawi Energy Regulatory Authority (MERA): Development House, 2nd Floor, City Centre, Private Bag B496, Lilongwe3; tel. 1775810; fax 1772666; e-mail mera@meramalawi.mw; internet www .meramalawi.mw; f. 2004; regulatory autority; Chair. John D. K. Saka; CEO Dr Allexon A. Chiwaya.

Water

Blantyre Water Board: POB 30369, Chichiri, Blantyre 3; tel. 18720000; e-mail bwb@bwb.mw; internet www.bwb.mw; f. 1995; supplies potable water to Blantyre City and its environs; Chair. W. R. G. Mandowa; Chief Exec. Andrew Thawe.

Lilongwe Water Board: Madzi House, off Likuni Rd, POB 96, Lilongwe; tel. 1750366; fax 1752294; e-mail madzi@lwb.mw; internet www.lwb.mw; f. 1947; Chair. Harry Mkandawire; Gen. Man. Gabriel M. Gonani.

There are also three regional water boards—Central Region Water Board, Northern Region Water Board, Southern Region Water Board—serving the population in small towns and rural areas.

TRADE UNIONS

According to the Malawi Congress of Trade Unions, in 2005 some 18% of the workforce was unionized.

Congress of Malawi Trade Unions (COMATU): POB 1443, Lilongwe; tel. 1757255; fax 1770885; Pres. Thomas L. Banda; Gen. Sec. Phillmon E. Chimbalu.

Malawi Congress of Trade Unions (MCTU): POB 1271, Lilongwe; tel. 1752162; fax 1820716; e-mail mctusecretariat@ mctumw.com; f. 1995 as successor to the Trade Union Congress of Malawi (f. 1964); Pres. Luther Mambala; Sec.-Gen. Robert James D. Mkwezalamba; 113,000 paid-up mems (2008).

Transport

RAILWAYS

The Central East African Railways Co (fmrly Malawi Railways) operates between Nsanje (near the southern border with Mozambique) and Mchinji (near the border with Zambia) via Blantyre, Salima and Lilongwe, and between Nkaya and Nayuchi on the eastern border with Mozambique, covering a total of 797 km. The Central East African Railways Co and Mozambique State Railways connect Malawi with the Mozambican ports of Beira and Nacala. There is a rail/lake interchange station at Chipoka on Lake Malawi, from where vessels operate services to other lake ports in Malawi. The construction of a 27-km railway line linking Mchinji with Chipata, Zambia, was completed in 2010.

Central East African Railways Co Ltd (CEAR): Station Rd, POB 5144, Limbe; tel. 1640844; fax 1643496; f. 1994 as Malawi Railways Ltd; owned by the Sociedade de Desenvolvimento do Corredor de Nacala, a consortium of mining companies of Brazil and Mozambique; freight and passenger service; Dir Hendryl Chimwaza.

ROADS

In 2004 Malawi had a total road network of some 15,500 km, of which 3,600 km was paved. In addition, unclassified community roads total an estimated 10,000 km. All main roads, and most secondary roads, are all-weather roads. Major routes link Lilongwe and Blantyre with Harare (Zimbabwe), Lusaka (Zambia) and Mbeya and Dar es Salaam (Tanzania). A 480-km highway along the western shore of Lake Malawi links the remote Northern Region with the Central and Southern Regions. A project to create a new trade route, or 'Northern Corridor', through Tanzania, involving road construction and improvements in Malawi, was completed in 1992.

Department of Road Traffic: c/o Ministry of Transport and Public Works, Private Bag 257, Capital City, Lilongwe 3; tel. 1756138; fax 1752592; comprises the Nat. Roads Authority.

    National Roads Authority: Functional Bldg, off Chilambula Rd, Private Bag B346, Lilongwe 3; tel. 1753699; fax 1750307; e-mail nra@nramw.com; internet www.ra.org.mw; f. 1997; Chair. Inkosi ya Makosi M'belwa; CEO Paul John Kulemeka.

Road Transport Operators' Association: Chitawira Light Industrial Site, POB 30740, Chichiri, Blantyre 3; tel. 1870422; fax 1871423; e-mail rtoa@sdnp.org.mw; f. 1956; Chair. P. Chakhumbira; Exec. Dir Shadreck Matsimbe; 200 mems (2004).

United Bus Co: POB 176, Blantyre; tel. 888863912; fax 1870038; e-mail ubc@ubcmw.com; internet www.ubcmw.com; f. 2008 by fmr employees of Shire Bus Lines Ltd following its liquidation in 2006; operates local and long-distance bus services between Makata, Blantyre, Malangalanga, Mzimba and Mzuzu and rural areas; services to Harare (Zimbabwe) and Johannesburg (South Africa); Chair. Al-haj Sheik ALIDI LIKONDE.

SHIPPING

There are 23 ports and landing points on Lake Malawi. The four main ports are at Chilumba, Nkhata Bay, Chipoka and Monkey Bay. Ferry services carry around 60,000 passengers annually; the principal cargoes transported are sugar, fertilizer, dried fish and maize. A new landing point at Ngala, near Dwangwa, to carry sugar to Chipoka was inaugurated in 2005. Smaller vessels are registered for other activities, including fishing and tourism. Lake Malawi is at the centre of the Mtwara Development Corridor transport initiative agreed between Zambia, Malawi, Tanzania and Mozambique in December 2004.

Department of Marine Services: c/o Department of Transport and Public Works, Private Bag A-81, Lilongwe; tel. 1751531; fax 1756290; e-mail marinedepartment@malawi.net; responsible for vessel safety and control, ports services, and maritime pollution control; Dir LASTON MAKUZULA.

Malawi Lake Services Ltd (MLS): POB 15, Monkey Bay; tel. and fax 1587221; fax 1587309; e-mail ilala@malawi.net; f. 1994; state-owned; operates passenger and freight services to Mozambique, and freight services to Tanzania; Gen. Man. OWEN SINGINI; 9 vessels, incl. 3 passenger and 4 cargo vessels.

CIVIL AVIATION

Kamuzu (formerly Lilongwe) International Airport was opened in 1982. There is also an international airport at Chileka (Blantyre) and domestic airports at Mzuzu and Karonga in the Northern Region and at the Club Makokola resort near Mangochi.

Department of Civil Aviation: c/o Ministry of Transport and Public Works, Private Bag B311, Lilongwe 3; tel. 1770577; fax 1774986; e-mail aviationhq@malawi.net; Dir L. Z. PHESELE.

Air Malawi Ltd: 4 Robins Rd, POB 84, Blantyre; tel. 1820811; fax 1820042; e-mail enquiries@airmalawi.com; internet www.airmalawi.com; f. 1967; privatization, begun in 1999, was postponed in 2005; scheduled domestic and regional services; owns 5 subsidiary cos, incl. Air Cargo Ltd and Lilongwe Handling Co Ltd; CEO PATRICK CHILAMBE.

Tourism

Fine scenery, beaches on Lake Malawi, big game and an excellent climate form the basis of the country's tourist potential. According to the World Tourism Organization, the number of foreign visitor arrivals was 746,129 in 2010. Receipts from tourism (excluding passenger transport) totalled US $47m. in that year.

Department of Tourism: POB 402, Blantyre; tel. 1620300; fax 1620947; f. 1969; responsible for tourism policy; inspects and licenses tourist facilities, sponsors training of hotel staff and publishes tourist literature; Dir of Tourism Services ISAAC K. MSISKA.

Malawi Tourism Association (MTA): POB 1044, Lilongwe; tel. 1770010; fax 1770131; e-mail mta@malawi.net; internet www.malawi-tourism-association.org.mw; f. 1998; Exec. Dir SAM BOTOMANI.

Defence

As assessed at November 2012, Malawi's defence forces comprised a land army of 5,300, a marine force of 220 and an air force of 200; all form part of the army. There was also a paramilitary police force of 1,500.

Defence Expenditure: Estimated at K8,620m. in 2013.

Commander-in-Chief of the Malawi Defence Force: JOYCE BANDA.

Commander of the Malawi Defence Force: Brig.-Gen. HENRY ODILLO.

Education

Primary education, which is provided free of charge but is not compulsory, begins at six years of age and lasts for eight years. Secondary education, which begins at 14 years of age, lasts for four years, comprising two cycles of two years. According to UNESCO, in 2008/09 primary enrolment included 97% of children in the relevant age-group (males 94%; females 99%), while secondary enrolment in 2009/10 included 28% of children in the relevant age-group (males 28%; females 27%). A programme to expand education at all levels has been undertaken; however, the introduction of free primary education in September 1994 led to the influx of more than 1m. additional pupils, resulting in severe overcrowding in schools. In January 1996 the International Development Association granted US $22.5m. for the training of 20,000 new teachers, appointed in response to the influx. In 2008 there were some 46,333 primary school teachers, of whom 18,026 were female. In 1997 additional funding was provided by the African Development Bank for the construction of primary and secondary schools. The five constituent colleges of the University of Malawi had a total of 6,454 students in 2008, while 1,428 students were enrolled at Mzuzu University, 358 at the Catholic University and 148 at the University of Livingstonia. Some students attend institutions in the United Kingdom and the USA. A small number of students attend the Marine College at Monkey Bay, which was established in 1998. Recurrent expenditure on education in 2008/09 was estimated at 21,413m. kwacha (equivalent to 13.7% of total recurrent expenditure).

MALAYSIA

Introductory Survey

LOCATION, CLIMATE, LANGUAGE, RELIGION, FLAG, CAPITAL

The Federation of Malaysia, situated in South-East Asia, consists of 13 states. Eleven of these are in Peninsular Malaysia, in the southern part of the Kra peninsula (with Thailand to the north and the island of Singapore to the south), and two, Sabah and Sarawak, are on the north coast of the island of Borneo, two-thirds of which comprises the Indonesian territory of Kalimantan. Sarawak also borders Brunei, a coastal enclave in the north-east of the state. The climate is tropical, there is rain in all seasons and temperatures are generally between 22°C (72°F) and 33°C (92°F), with little variation throughout the year. The official language is Bahasa Malaysia, based on Malay, but English is also widely used. Chinese, Tamil and Iban are spoken by minorities. Islam is the established religion, practised by about 60% of the population (including virtually all Malays), while some 19%, including most of the Chinese community, follow Buddhism. The Indians are predominantly Hindus. There is a minority of Christians among all races, and traditional beliefs are practised, particularly in Sabah and Sarawak. Malaysia's national flag (proportions 1 by 2) has 14 horizontal stripes, alternating red and white, with a blue rectangular canton, containing a yellow crescent and a 14-pointed yellow star, in the upper hoist. The capital is Kuala Lumpur. A new administrative capital, Putrajaya, has been developed south of Kuala Lumpur.

CONTEMPORARY POLITICAL HISTORY

Historical Context

The 11 states of Malaya, under British protection, were united as the Malayan Union in April 1946 and became the Federation of Malaya in February 1948. An armed communist offensive began in 1948, and was not effectively suppressed until the mid-1950s. After 1960 the remainder of the banned Communist Party of Malaya (CPM) took refuge in southern Thailand. Meanwhile, Malaya was granted independence, within the Commonwealth, on 31 August 1957. Malaysia was established on 16 September 1963, through the union of the independent Federation of Malaya (renamed the States of Malaya), the internally self-governing state of Singapore, and the former British colonies of Sarawak and Sabah (North Borneo). Singapore left the federation in August 1965, reducing the number of Malaysia's component states from 14 to 13. The States of Malaya were designated West Malaysia in 1966 and later styled Peninsular Malaysia.

Domestic Political Affairs

In 1970 serious inter-communal rioting, engendered by Malay resentment of the Chinese community's economic dominance and of certain pro-Chinese electoral results, precipitated the resignation of Tunku Abdul Rahman, who had been Prime Minister of Malaya (and subsequently of Malaysia) since independence. The new Prime Minister, Tun Abdul Razak, widened the government coalition, dominated by the United Malays National Organization (UMNO), to create a national front, Barisan Nasional (BN). The BN originally comprised 10 parties, absorbing most of the former opposition parties. In January 1976 the Prime Minister died and was succeeded by Deputy Prime Minister Dato' Hussein bin Onn.

Political stability was subsequently threatened by the resurgence of the communist guerrilla movement, which conducted a series of terrorist attacks in Peninsular Malaysia during 1976–78. However, CPM activity subsequently declined, owing to co-operation between Malaysia and Thailand in military operations along their common border, and in December 1989, following a year of negotiations with the Thai Government, the remaining 1,188 rebels—including recruits from Thailand and Singapore—agreed to terminate all armed activities.

Meanwhile, in October 1977 the expulsion of the Chief Minister (Menteri Besar) of the state of Kelantan from the dominant Parti Islam se Malaysia (PAS—Islamic Party of Malaysia) resulted in violent disturbances in Kelantan and the declaration

of a state of emergency by the federal Government. Direct rule was imposed in Kelantan, and the PAS was expelled from the BN coalition in December. In the federal and state elections of July 1978 Hussein consolidated the position of the BN, while the PAS, in opposition, suffered a serious reversal. In 1978, following the federal Government's rejection of proposals for the establishment of a Chinese university, racial and religious tensions re-emerged.

In July 1981 Hussein was succeeded as Prime Minister by Dato' Seri Dr Mahathir Mohamad, Deputy Prime Minister since 1976. Mahathir called a general election in April 1982; the BN coalition won convincingly in all states and increased its overall strength in the House of Representatives.

A new political party, the Parti Bersatu Sabah (PBS—Sabah United Party), won control of the Sabah State Legislative Assembly at an election in April 1985. The legality of the new PBS administration was challenged by Muslim opponents, and in February 1986 the Chief Minister (Ketua Menteri) called a further election. In the May election the PBS won an increased majority of seats in the Assembly, and in June the BN agreed to admit the PBS into its ruling coalition, together with the United Sabah National Organization (USNO), which had been expelled in 1984.

In February 1986 Mahathir's leadership of the federal Government and of UMNO was challenged when Deputy Prime Minister Datuk Musa Hitam resigned from the Government, owing to 'irreconcilable differences' with Mahathir. However, Musa retained his position as Deputy President of UMNO. During the following months Musa's supporters became increasingly critical of Mahathir. At an early general election in August, the BN coalition took 148 of the 177 seats in an enlarged House of Representatives: UMNO secured 83 seats, while the Malaysian Chinese Association (MCA) won 17. Of the opposition parties, the Democratic Action Party (DAP) won 24 seats, having gained support from ethnic Chinese voters who were disillusioned with the MCA. In concurrent state elections, the BN retained control of all the State Legislative Assemblies in Peninsular Malaysia. Several ministers who had supported Musa were subsequently demoted or removed from the Government.

In early 1987 there was a serious challenge for the presidency of UMNO from Tengku Razaleigh Hamzah, the Minister of Trade and Industry. At the UMNO General Assembly in April, none the less, Mahathir was elected UMNO President for the third time (and thus retained the position of Prime Minister at the head of the BN coalition), albeit with a greatly reduced majority. The General Assembly also narrowly elected Abdul Ghafar Baba (who had replaced Musa as Deputy Prime Minister in February 1986) as UMNO Deputy President. Mahathir subsequently announced the resignation of Razaleigh from his cabinet post.

Criticism of Mahathir's leadership persisted during 1987, both from within UMNO and from other political parties. At the same time, racial tensions intensified in various parts of the country over Chinese-language education, religion and other issues. In October–November, allegedly to prevent the outbreak of racially motivated riots between Chinese and Malays over politically sensitive issues, 106 people were detained under the provisions of the Internal Security Act (ISA, which allowed detention without trial for up to two years on grounds of national security). Those detained included politicians from all parties (most notably the leader of the DAP, Lim Kit Siang), lawyers, journalists and leaders of pressure groups. Three newspapers were closed by the Government, and political rallies were prohibited. In November the Government introduced legislation to impose stringent penalties on editors and publishers disseminating what the Government regarded as 'false' news. From December the Minister of Information was empowered to monitor all radio and television broadcasts, and to revoke the licence of any private broadcasting company not conforming with 'Malaysian values'. By April 1989 all the detainees under the ISA had been released (although often under restrictive conditions).

In February 1988 the High Court gave a ruling on a suit filed by dissatisfied members of UMNO, who claimed that, since some of the delegations taking part in the UMNO elections of April 1987 had not been legally registered, the elections should be declared null and void. On account of the irregularities, the Court ruled that UMNO was an 'unlawful society' and that there had been 'no election at all'. Mahathir maintained that the ruling did not affect the legal status of the Government, and the Yang di-Pertuan Agong (head of state), Tunku Mahmood Iskandar, expressed support for the Prime Minister. Later in February 1988 Mahathir announced that UMNO Baru (New UMNO) had been formed and that members of the original party would have to re-register in order to join. Razaleigh and his supporters were excluded from UMNO Baru (hereafter referred to as UMNO).

Tension between the executive and the judiciary was intensified by Parliament's approval in March 1988 of constitutional amendments limiting the power of the judiciary to interpret laws. The Lord President of the Supreme Court, Tun Mohammed Salleh bin Abas, wrote to the Yang di-Pertuan Agong to complain about government attempts to reduce the independence of the judiciary, and was subsequently dismissed from office. In June 1989 the Government introduced a security law removing the right of persons being detained under provisions of the ISA to have recourse to the courts.

In September 1988 Razaleigh and 12 others left the BN to join the opposition in the House of Representatives as independents. Razaleigh's movement established an alliance with the fundamentalist PAS in March 1989, and in May registered as Semangat '46 (Spirit of 1946, a reference to the year of foundation of the original UMNO). The DAP, whose followers were largely urban Chinese, agreed to co-operate with Semangat '46 and the PAS, but refused to join a formal alliance, owing to its opposition to the PAS's proclaimed policy of forming an Islamic state in Malaysia. The opposition parties formed an informal electoral alliance, Gagasan Rakyat (People's Might), to contest the general election held in October 1990. None the less, the BN won 127 of the 180 seats in the enlarged House of Representatives, thus retaining the two-thirds' majority necessary to amend the Constitution. Elections to 11 of the 13 State Legislative Assemblies (excluding Sabah and Sarawak) were held concurrently. The BN obtained a majority of seats in all states except Kelantan, where the Angkatan Perpaduan Ummah (APU—Muslim Unity Movement), another coalition including Semangat '46 and the PAS, won every seat in both the federal and state elections. In November 1990 Mahathir and Abdul Ghafar Baba were unanimously re-elected as President and Deputy President of UMNO. Mahathir appointed Anwar Ibrahim as Minister of Finance and Abdullah Badawi as Minister of Foreign Affairs in February 1991.

In January 1991 Datuk Seri Joseph Pairin Kitingan, the Chief Minister of Sabah and President of the PBS, which had contested the election with the opposition, was arrested and charged with corruption. It was widely conjectured that his arrest, under the ISA, was politically motivated. In May UMNO secured its first seat in Sabah, in a by-election necessitated by the defection to UMNO of USNO's founder and President, Tun Mustapha Harun. Shortly afterwards Jeffrey Kitingan (the brother of the Chief Minister) was detained under the ISA, accused of plotting Sabah's secession from Malaysia. In March 1993 constitutional amendments were adopted reducing the privileges of the country's nine hereditary rulers (seven of whom are entitled 'Sultan', one 'Raja' and the other 'Yamtuan Besar'), including ending their legal immunity, curtailing their power to pardon the offences of relatives, and allowing parliamentary criticism of their misdeeds. The action was widely suspected to have been instigated by Mahathir owing, in part, to the Sultan of Kelantan's open support for Razaleigh (a prince of Kelantan) in the 1990 general election.

In October 1993 Mahathir was returned unopposed as President of UMNO. In the following month Anwar was elected Deputy President of the party (a particularly significant post as the incumbent was traditionally also accorded the position of Deputy Prime Minister). Anwar was duly appointed Deputy Prime Minister in December.

In April 1993 USNO, now led by Tun Mustapha Amirkahar (the son of Tun Mustapha Harun), left the opposition in the Sabah State Legislative Assembly to form a coalition with the ruling PBS. Prior to the announcement six of the 11 elected representatives of USNO joined UMNO. USNO's defection prompted the federal Government successfully to seek the party's deregistration in August, on the grounds that it had breached its own statutes. In the same month Tun Mustapha Harun was appointed to the federal post of Minister of Sabah Affairs.

In January 1994 Pairin Kitingan dissolved the Sabah State Legislative Assembly in preparation for an early election. Shortly afterwards Pairin Kitingan was convicted on charges of corruption by the High Court, but fined less than the minimum required to disqualify him from office. Although Pairin Kitingan gained popular sympathy owing both to his perceived victimization in the corruption case and to his resistance to federal encroachment on Sabahan authority, a faction emerged in the PBS that favoured more harmonious relations with the federal Government. Former members of the deregistered USNO joined the PBS for the election, and the party also gained the support of Tun Mustapha Harun, who had resigned as Minister of Sabah Affairs and as a member of UMNO in January. (Tun Mustapha Harun died in January 1995.) At the election in February 1994 the PBS won a narrow majority, securing 25 of the 48 elective seats. In March, however, several PBS members defected to the opposition, among them Jeffrey Kitingan, who had been released from detention under the ISA in December 1993. As a result, the PBS was stripped of its majority and Pairin Kitingan was replaced as Chief Minister by Tan Sri Sakaran Dandai, a leader of the Sabah wing of UMNO.

In June 1994 the BN coalition agreed to admit two breakaway parties from the PBS, the Parti Demokratik Sabah (Sabah Democratic Party), led by Datuk Bernard Dompok, and the Parti Bersatu Rakyat Sabah (PBRS—United Sabah People's Party), led by Joseph Kurup. In August Dompok was appointed Minister in the Prime Minister's Department, while Jeffrey Kitingan, who had been cleared of corruption in the High Court in June, became Deputy Minister for Housing and Local Government.

Meanwhile, in May 1994 the House of Representatives approved the 1994 Constitution (Amendment) Act, which further restricted the powers of the monarchy and provided for the restructuring of the judiciary. Hitherto, the Yang di-Pertuan Agong had been competent to withhold assent from and return legislation, within 30 days, to Parliament for further consideration. The amendment required the Yang di-Pertuan Agong to give his assent to a bill within 30 days; if he failed to do so, the bill would, none the less, become law. The changes to the judiciary included the creation of a Court of Appeal, the restyling of the Supreme Court as the Federal Court and of the Lord President as the Chief Justice.

In the April 1995 general election the BN won an overwhelming majority, taking 162 of the 192 seats in the enlarged House of Representatives and retaining control of 10 of the 11 State Legislative Assemblies for which voting took place. In Kelantan, which remained the only state under opposition control, a coalition of the PAS and Semangat '46 won a majority of the seats. Despite his election victory, Mahathir's position appeared vulnerable during the divisional elections of UMNO in 1995. The defeat of several Mahathir supporters was widely attributed to the influence of Anwar's associates, and, amid speculation that Anwar might challenge Mahathir for the leadership, in November UMNO's General Assembly adopted an unprecedented resolution to avoid any contest for the two senior party positions in 1996. Mahathir subsequently announced that he would retire in the near future and named Anwar as his successor.

Semangat '46 was formally dissolved in October 1996, and its members were admitted to UMNO. At that month's UMNO General Assembly Mahathir and Anwar were, as anticipated, returned unopposed to their posts. In contrast to the 1993 party elections, in which Anwar's supporters had been particularly successful, a large proportion of Mahathir loyalists were now elected.

Mahathir's response to the regional currency crisis that emerged in 1997, following Thailand's effective devaluation of the baht in July, and his criticism of international investors, was widely perceived to have exacerbated Malaysia's economic position. However, international criticism of Mahathir's outspokenness prompted popular demonstrations of support for the premier within Malaysia and near unanimous support for a vote of confidence in his leadership, which was held in the House of Representatives during November. Meanwhile, political opponents of Anwar attempted to undermine his position through the circulation of a series of letters accusing him of sexual indiscretions.

The first trials of Anwar Ibrahim

Evidence of a growing division between Mahathir and Anwar became apparent at the UMNO annual party congress in June 1998, when Dato' Seri Dr Ahmad Zahid bin Hamidi, the head of the youth wing of UMNO and one of Anwar's supporters, made a speech criticizing what he termed the debilitating impact of corruption in the party. Zahid's speech, echoing recent condemnation by Anwar of corruption and political restrictions, was perceived as an attack on the party's leadership; Mahathir responded by publishing a list of hundreds of people and companies who had received privatization contracts in recent years, including close associates of Anwar and members of his family. During the following weeks Mahathir acted to counter the influence of Anwar, promoting allies and dismissing newspaper editors close to Anwar. The resignation in August of the Governor (a close ally of Anwar) and Deputy Governor of the central bank, reportedly owing to a disagreement over policy with Mahathir, indicated the intensification of the rift within the Government. Supporters loyal to the Prime Minister responded to the perceived threat to Mahathir's leadership by circulating a brochure entitled *Fifty Reasons Why Anwar Cannot Become Prime Minister*, in which Anwar was accused of sexual offences and corruption.

Allegations of Anwar's supposed sexual misconduct increased throughout the months following the UMNO congress, and, following Anwar's refusal to resign, culminated in Mahathir's dismissal of Anwar as Deputy Prime Minister and Minister of Finance on 2 September 1998, on the grounds that he was morally unfit to hold office. On the following day Anwar was expelled from UMNO, and affidavits accusing him of sexual impropriety were filed with the High Court. The allegations were denied by Anwar, who asserted that they constituted part of a senior-level political conspiracy to discredit him. Anwar began a tour of the country, drawing extensive support for his calls for the wide-ranging reform of the political system from the many thousands who attended his public appearances. His supporters adopted the slogan 'reformasi' (reform), which had united the popular forces that ousted President Suharto in Indonesia. In mid-September Anwar's adoptive brother, Sukma Darmawan Samitaat Madja, and a former speech-writer for Anwar, Munawar Ahmad Anees, were each sentenced to six months' imprisonment after they confessed to illegal homosexual activity with Anwar. The following day, at a meeting attended by at least 40,000 people in Kuala Lumpur, Anwar called directly for Mahathir's resignation, but he was arrested shortly afterwards and detained under the ISA. A further 17 people, including a number of close associates of Anwar, were also detained under the same act. Anwar's arrest provoked popular protests, which erupted into violence when demonstrations involving up to 60,000 people were forcibly dispersed by the security forces; 132 people were arrested.

Following Anwar's arrest, his wife, Wan Azizah Wan Ismail, emerged as the de facto leader of the opposition movement. Despite a restriction order issued against Wan Azizah, barring her from holding rallies at her residence, demonstrations in protest against Anwar's detention were held throughout September 1998; these became the forum for demands for widespread political reform and for the removal of the restrictions on freedom of speech and assembly imposed under the ISA. At a court hearing in Petaling Jaya, Anwar pleaded not guilty to charges of corruption and sexual impropriety. Allegations made by Anwar, who appeared in court with visible bruising to his face, that he had been severely beaten while in police custody and had subsequently been denied medical attention for a number of days, provoked expressions of extreme concern from foreign governments. Malaysia's Attorney-General publicly admitted in January 1999 that Anwar had been assaulted by the police while in custody.

Anwar's trial on charges of corruption (relating to efforts allegedly made by him in 1997 to obtain through the police written denials that he was guilty of sexual misconduct and sodomy) began in November 1998, and in April 1999 Anwar was found guilty on all charges and sentenced to six years' imprisonment (under Malaysian law, this would be followed by a five-year period of disqualification from political office). Following the verdict, supporters of the former Deputy Prime Minister clashed with security forces outside the court. Violent protests continued for the next three days, resulting in the arrest of 18 demonstrators. Following the trial, three prosecution witnesses who had withdrawn their testimony against Anwar, including his adoptive brother and speech-writer, who claimed that their confessions had been obtained through police coercion, were charged with perjury.

Anwar's second trial, on the charge of illegal homosexual activity, began in June 1999. On the first day of the trial the prosecution amended the wording of its charge, changing (for the second time) the month and year in which the alleged crimes were supposedly committed. The proceedings were beset by numerous delays during the latter half of 1999, including an adjournment in September to allow for medical examination following claims by the defence that Anwar might have been deliberately poisoned while in police custody. (However, the tests detected no clinical signs of any such action.) In April 2000 the Court of Appeal upheld Anwar's conviction on charges of corruption. Anwar suffered a further set-back in June, when the Court of Appeal rejected his plea for a stay of proceedings, ordering the trial on the charge of sodomy to continue. In August the High Court found Anwar guilty of sodomy, sentencing him to a further nine years' imprisonment, thus bringing his term to a total of 15 years. His adoptive brother, Sukma Darmawan, was sentenced to six years' imprisonment for the same offence.

In May 2001 public prosecutors announced that other outstanding charges of corruption and sodomy against Anwar were to be abandoned. In July 2002 Anwar lost his appeal against his corruption conviction, and in April 2003 the appeal against his sodomy conviction was similarly dismissed. A few days previously he had completed his sentence for corruption, the last two years of his six-year sentence having been remitted for good behaviour. In September 2004 Anwar was released from prison after his appeal against his conviction for sodomy was upheld by the Federal Court, which deemed the evidence against Anwar unreliable. Although he remained disqualified from holding political office until April 2008, owing to his corruption conviction, Anwar announced his intention to resume his campaign for political reform.

Consolidation of power and suppression of dissent

In January 1999, meanwhile, prior to the closure of the first trial of Anwar, Mahathir effected a major cabinet reorganization, in which Abdullah Badawi was appointed as Deputy Prime Minister and Minister for Home Affairs (a post relinquished by Mahathir) and Daim Zainuddin was allocated the finance portfolio. Also in January 1999 the UMNO Supreme Council announced its decision to postpone for 18 months elections for senior posts within the party, previously scheduled to be held in June, effectively preventing any potential challenge to Mahathir's leadership from within the party. The BN won a significant victory in the elections to the State Legislative Assembly in Sabah in March, securing 31 of the 48 seats. In April the Parti Keadilan Nasional (PKN—National Justice Party) was launched by Wan Azizah in anticipation of the forthcoming general election; the new party declared that its first act, should it come to power, would be to seek a royal pardon for Anwar. However, Anwar himself did not join the PKN.

In November 1999 the Government unexpectedly announced that a general election was to be held at the end of that month. The opposition expressed dissatisfaction at the limited period of time allowed for campaigning. At the election, a decisive victory was won by the governing BN coalition, which gained 148 of a total of 193 seats in the enlarged House of Representatives, thereby retaining the two-thirds' majority required to amend the Constitution. The opposition coalition, the Barisan Alternatif (Alternative Front), which had been formed by the PAS, the PKN, the DAP and the Parti Rakyat Malaysia (PRM—Malaysian People's Party) in June 1999 (and which subsequently selected Anwar as its prime ministerial candidate), won a total of 42 seats, while the opposition PBS, which remained outside the Barisan Alternatif, secured three seats. Despite the BN's victory, UMNO experienced a significant decline in support among Malay voters (mainly in favour of the PAS, which secured 27 seats) and lost 23 seats, including those of four cabinet ministers. The party also performed poorly (again largely at the expense of the PAS) in the assembly elections held simultaneously in 11 Malaysian states. This erosion of confidence in UMNO was widely believed to be a result of the Government's treatment of Anwar and the concomitant decline of public trust in the country's institutions, including the police and the judicial system. Mahathir's new Cabinet was announced in December, with many of the important portfolios remaining unchanged. Mahathir announced that he intended this (his fifth) term of office to be his last, and for the first time formally identified Abdullah Badawi as his preferred successor. In the same month the Barisan Alternatif nominated Fadzil Nor, President of the PAS, as the new parliamentary leader of the opposition. He replaced Lim Kit Siang, who had lost his seat in the general election and who in December resigned as Secretary-General of the DAP.

At the UMNO party elections in May 2000 Mahathir and Abdullah Badawi were formally elected President and Deputy

President of the party, respectively. In June 2001 the Minister of Finance, Daim Zainuddin, resigned from his post, following widespread allegations that he had misused public funds to help business associates. Mahathir subsequently assumed responsibility for the finance portfolio.

Meanwhile, government suppression of dissent increased significantly. The deputy leader of the DAP and Anwar's legal representative, Karpal Singh, and the Vice-President of the PKN, Marina Yusoff, were charged under the Sedition Act in January 2000 (although the charges against Karpal were dropped in 2002). In the same month the editor and the printer of the popular PAS newspaper, *Harakah*, were also charged with sedition in connection with an article concerning Anwar's trial; in March 2000 the Government ordered that the newspaper be published just twice a month instead of twice weekly and restricted sales of the publication to members of the PAS only. The group editor-in-chief of the *New Straits Times*, Kadir Jasin, was forced to resign in June over an editorial that questioned UMNO's proposed mode of conduct of forthcoming internal party elections.

The Anwar issue continued to incite public unrest, and in April 2000 a protest to mark the anniversary of Anwar's conviction for corruption was broken up by riot police, with 48 PKN activists being arrested. Public criticism of the Government, and subsequent detentions, became more frequent after Anwar's second conviction, as confidence in Mahathir's leadership continued to decline. Mohamad Ezam Mohamad Noor, Anwar's former political secretary, was arrested in March 2001 for having made allegedly seditious comments, despite already being on trial for releasing a secret report on corruption. A month later he was detained again, along with six other opposition leaders, under the ISA. The aim of these arrests seemed to be to dissuade protesters from gathering for the second anniversary of Anwar's conviction later in April. The approach proved successful, as only 2,000 demonstrators defied the authorities' ban to attend the peaceful rally marking this occasion. However, the seven detainees were not immediately released after the rally, and three more arrests were made under the ISA. In August 2002 Mohamad Ezam Mohamad Noor was sentenced to a two-year prison term, having been convicted of divulging state secrets; however, his conviction was overruled by the High Court in April 2004.

In August 2001 Nik Adli Nik Abdul Aziz, son of PAS spiritual leader Datuk Haji Nik Abdul Aziz Nik Mat, was one of 10 men detained under the ISA on suspicion of membership of the Kumpulan Mujahidin Malaysia (KMM), an Islamist fundamentalist group believed to be engaged in a long-term plot to overthrow the Government. Shortly afterwards 25 supporters of Anwar were freed from prison and promptly rearrested on new charges, before being granted bail. In September the Government announced that Nik Adli was to be detained for two years without trial under the provisions of the ISA. Eight of the nine men arrested with him were also imprisoned. Further arrests continued to be made under the ISA.

Meanwhile, in March 2001 Mahathir confirmed that the National Vision Policy (NVP), which had replaced the National Development Plan (NDP) in 2000, was to remain in force until at least 2010. The Prime Minister thus provided for a continuation of the preferential conditions that had been afforded to the Malay majority by the precursor to the NDP—the New Economic Policy (NEP)—upon its implementation in 1971; this favourable treatment prevailed specifically within the fields of education and commerce. (In the event, the NVP was abandoned, and the NEP reinstated, in 2006.)

In September 2001 the opposition was destabilized by the withdrawal of the DAP from the Barisan Alternatif. The party accused the PAS of alienating Chinese voters through its support for an Islamic state. (The PAS subsequently accused the Government of using devious methods to exploit popular fear of Islamist militancy in the aftermath of the September terrorist attacks in the USA.) In the same month the BN won an overwhelming majority in elections to the state legislature in Sarawak. In January 2002 the PBS was formally readmitted to the BN following more than a decade of absence from power.

On 21 November 2001 the Yang di-Pertuan Agong, Sultan Salahuddin Abdul Aziz Shah Al-Haj ibni al-Marhum Sultan Hisamuddin Alam Shah Al-Haj, died at the age of 75. On 13 December the Raja of Perlis, Tuanku Syed Sirajuddin Syed Putra Jamalullail, was sworn in as the new monarch, following his election by secret ballot from among the eight other Malay rulers. The Sultan of Terengganu continued as his deputy.

In June 2002, during a speech to the annual congress of UMNO, Prime Minister Mahathir unexpectedly announced that he intended to resign from the Government with immediate effect. However, he was persuaded to withdraw his resignation shortly afterwards and, following some discussion, it was decided that he would remain in power until October 2003, when he would be succeeded by Abdullah Badawi. During the transition period Abdullah would assume increased responsibility for government operations. Following the death of Fadzil Nor, the President of the PAS, in June 2002, Abdul Hadi Awang assumed the party leadership on an interim basis. In July Abdul Hadi announced the imposition of Islamic law in Terengganu state, of which he was the Chief Minister; however, the Government continued to oppose efforts to enforce the new legal code.

In August 2003 the PKN merged with the smaller PRM, forming the Parti Keadilan Rakyat (PKR—People's Justice Party), in advance of the next general election. The President of the PKN, Wan Azizah, continued as President of the new party. In September it was announced that nine suspected members of the KMM who had been detained under the ISA in August 2001, including Nik Adli Nik Abdul Aziz, would be imprisoned for a further two years. After more than five years of incarceration without charge, Nik Adli was finally released in October 2006.

The Government of Abdullah Badawi

Prime Minister Mahathir Mohamad formally retired in October 2003, after 22 years in power. Abdullah Badawi was then sworn in as Prime Minister, retaining the home affairs portfolio and, in addition, assuming Mahathir's role as Minister of Finance. In November Abdullah was also endorsed as the new Chairman of the BN. In January 2004 Abdullah effected his first cabinet reorganization, nominating Minister of Defence Mohammad Najib Abdul Razak as Deputy Prime Minister.

At an early general election, which took place in March 2004, around eight months ahead of schedule, the BN secured a commanding victory, winning 198 of the 219 seats in the enlarged House of Representatives and taking control of 11 of the 12 contested State Legislative Assemblies, including that of Terengganu, an erstwhile stronghold of the PAS. The PAS retained control of Kelantan only by a narrow margin. The DAP secured 12 seats in the House of Representatives, followed by the PAS, which won seven (compared with 27 at the election of 1999) and the PKR, which retained only one seat, that held by Wan Azizah. Having been sworn in again as head of government, Abdullah Badawi announced a major cabinet reorganization, although Najib Razak continued as Deputy Prime Minister and Minister of Defence. The Prime Minister launched a National Integrity Plan in April 2004, aimed at reducing corruption and abuse of power. In May the Government allowed journalists to visit a detention centre for those held under the ISA, in an attempt to dispel recent allegations, made by the US-based organization Human Rights Watch, that detainees had been tortured.

Abdullah Badawi's control over UMNO was questioned in September 2004, when three members of his Cabinet failed to secure re-election to the party's Supreme Council at its General Assembly; some observers attributed their defeat to a reaction by party members against the Prime Minister's anti-corruption campaign. None the less, Abdullah and Najib Razak were formally endorsed as the party's President and Deputy President, respectively. UMNO leaders ruled out a return to the party for Anwar, who had been freed from prison earlier in September. In December Anwar launched a nation-wide campaign against the ISA. In August 2005 he was awarded RM 4.5m. in damages by the High Court for the false allegations contained within the pamphlet *Fifty Reasons Why Anwar Ibrahim Cannot Become Prime Minister*, published in 1998. In January 2006 Anwar filed a lawsuit against former Prime Minister Mahathir for falsely having depicted him as a homosexual and causing 'irreparable damage' to his reputation. (In September 2005 Mahathir had controversially told reporters that he had dismissed Anwar in 1998 in order to avoid the potential appointment of a homosexual Prime Minister.) However, in July 2007 the High Court dismissed the lawsuit, which Mahathir had claimed was a ploy by Anwar to 'rehabilitate himself for high office'.

In November 2005 Azahari Husin, a notorious Malaysian bomb-maker thought to be responsible for many of the operations of the regional Islamist organization Jemaah Islamiah (JI), was killed in Indonesia during a police operation. In January 2006 another prominent Malaysian Islamist militant, Noordin Mohammad Top, released a message in which he claimed responsibility for the bombings on the Indonesian island of Bali in 2005 and declared himself to be the head of a new South-East Asian Islamist militant organization—Tanzam Qaedat al Jihad (Organization of the Basis of Jihad). The statement served to remind Malaysia of the threat posed by its own nationals to regional security.

Sultan Tuanku Mizan Zainal Abidin ibni al-Marhum Sultan Mahmud, the Sultan of Terengganu, was sworn in as the country's Yang di-Pertuan Agong on 13 December 2006 and was enthroned on 26 April 2007.

Several scandals involving senior officials emerged in early 2007, including opposition attempts to link Deputy Prime Minister Najib Razak to a murder that his political adviser, Abdul Razak Baginda, was charged with abetting in 2006. Najib denied any connection to the killing or to the victim, Altantuya Shaariibuu, a Mongolian translator who had been involved in a relationship with Abdul Razak, whom she had allegedly been blackmailing prior to her death in 2006. (Abdul Razak was subsequently acquitted of Shaariibuu's murder, of which two police officers were convicted in April 2009.)

In November 2007 police used tear gas and water cannons to disperse up to 30,000 protesters who were marching in Kuala Lumpur to campaign for electoral reform. The demonstration, which had been declared illegal, was organized by the Gabungan Pilihanraya Bersih dan Adil (Bersih—the Coalition for Clean and Fair Elections), comprising a number of opposition parties, including the DAP, the PAS and the PKR, and civil society organizations. Bersih's main demands were equal access to the state-controlled media for all parties, a complete revision of the electoral register, the use of indelible ink to prevent multiple voting, and the abolition of postal voting except for diplomats and overseas voters. A second banned demonstration, involving at least 8,000 ethnic Indians, took place outside the British High Commission in Kuala Lumpur later that month, ending in violence, as police clashed with the protesters. The rally was organized by the Hindu Rights Action Force (Hindraf, a coalition of some 30 Hindu non-governmental organizations—NGOs) to highlight perceived discrimination against Indians in Malaysia (who accounted for some 7% of the population) and, more specifically, in support of a lawsuit, filed in the British courts in August, demanding that the British Government pay reparations to the descendants of Indians transported to Malaysia as indentured labourers during the 19th century. In December five Hindraf members were detained under the ISA. A further banned demonstration organized by Hindraf took place in February 2008.

In February 2008 Abdullah Badawi called a general election for 8 March, more than one year earlier than the constitutional deadline, a decision that observers attributed to a desire to secure a renewed mandate in advance of a widely anticipated deterioration in economic conditions. The timing of the election also ensured the exclusion of Anwar, whose disqualification from seeking public office was not due to expire until a month later. Anwar had returned to active politics at a state assembly by-election in Selangor in April 2007, when he had campaigned vigorously on behalf of the losing PKR candidate. Anwar's renewed prominence had not been welcomed by all members of the PKR and prompted the resignation from the party of a number of senior figures.

On 8 March 2008 the BN sustained heavy losses in elections to an enlarged House of Representatives and to 12 of the 13 State Legislative Assemblies. (Elections to the Sarawak State Legislative Assembly had been conducted in May 2006, when the BN had won 62 of the 71 seats in the expanded state legislature.) The ruling coalition failed to retain its two-thirds' majority in the House of Representatives, taking only 140 of the 222 seats, and lost control of the Legislative Assemblies of Kedah, Penang, Perak and Selangor. Of the opposition parties, which had pledged not to present candidates against each other, the PKR made the most significant gains in the House of Representatives, winning a total of 31 seats (compared with only one in 2004), while the DAP and the PAS both increased their representation by 16 seats, to 28 seats and 23 seats, respectively. The PAS also strengthened its majority in the Kelantan state legislature. The BN's poor performance was attributed to public discontent with renewed ethnic tensions and rising inflation, as well as concern about crime levels and corruption. Having dismissed demands for his resignation, including from within UMNO, Abdullah Badawi reorganized his Cabinet. The Prime Minister retained the finance portfolio, while Najib Razak remained Deputy Prime Minister and Minister of Defence, but most other portfolios were

affected by the reallocations. Rais Yatim assumed responsibility for the foreign affairs portfolio. Other new appointees included Datuk Mohd Zaid bin Ibrahim as a Minister in the Prime Minister's Department. Zaid was charged with reforming the judiciary, which had been damaged during the second half of 2007 by allegations of corruption in the appointment process for judges.

In May 2008 Anwar was accused of sodomy by a party aide, Mohd Saiful Bukhari Azlan. Fearing for his safety, Anwar sought temporary refuge at the Turkish embassy in Kuala Lumpur the following month. He was arrested in July, formally charged with sodomy in August and released on bail pending a further hearing. In July, meanwhile, Wan Azizah vacated the seat that she had occupied in the House of Representatives since her husband's conviction in 1999, thus enabling Anwar to stand as a candidate at the ensuing by-election for the seat that he had previously held. Polling took place in August, when Anwar secured victory by a large majority. As the de facto leader of the opposition, he subsequently gained the support of the PAS.

In October 2008 Abdullah Badawi announced his intention to vacate the presidency of UMNO and to resign as Prime Minister in early 2009, having been placed under increasing pressure to depart, owing to the recent electoral losses suffered by the BN and to his perceived failure effectively to address the issue of corruption. Furthermore, the first parliamentary motion of no confidence against a Malaysian Prime Minister had been drafted in June 2008, only to be withdrawn on a technicality. In September Abdullah had transferred the finance portfolio to Najib Razak, his designated successor, in exchange for that of defence.

Datuk Mohd Zaid bin Ibrahim resigned from his position in the Prime Minister's Department in September 2008, expressing his frustration at the pace of legal reforms and criticizing the use of the ISA to imprison three dissidents earlier that month. (Following his resignation, Zaid cautioned against the appointment of Najib Razak as Prime Minister on account of his alleged links to the killing of the Mongolian translator Altantuya Shaariibuu; Zaid was subsequently suspended from UMNO, before joining the PKR in June 2009.) Other cabinet ministers were also reported to have questioned the authorities' increasing recourse to the ISA.

The editor of online newspaper *Malaysia Today*, Raja Petra Kamaruddin, was arrested under the ISA in September 2008 on the grounds that he had published articles provoking racial tension. Later that month Raja Petra received a two-year detention order on charges of insulting Islam, but this was overruled in November when the High Court found that the Government had acted beyond its legal powers in issuing such an order. Raja Petra also implicated Najib Razak and his wife in the murder of Shaariibuu. In March 2009, after accusing Najib Razak of involvement in the murder of the Mongolian translator, Gobind Singh Deo, a member of the DAP, was banned from Parliament for one year, prompting a walkout by opposition members. Gobind's father, DAP Chairman Karpal Singh, who was also an eminent lawyer and was representing the murdered woman's family, was charged with sedition, allegedly having insulted the Sultan of Perak. Karpal accused the Government of using the Sedition Act as a 'political weapon against its political opponents'. Two opposition newspapers, the PAS's *Harakah* and the PKR's *Suara Keadilan*, were banned from publishing for three months by the Government in March 2009, shortly before the appointment of Najib Razak as Prime Minister and the holding of three by-elections in April. Earlier in March riot police in Kuala Lumpur used tear gas to disperse thousands of demonstrators, who were protesting against the use of English as a medium of instruction in mathematics and science classes. More than 100 protesters were reported to have been detained.

Meanwhile, in February 2009 the BN regained control of Perak state after three PKR members of the State Legislative Assembly defected to the BN. The Sultan of Perak confirmed the BN's majority in the state legislature and deposed the Chief Minister, Mohammad Nizar Jamaluddin, appointing a BN member, Datuk Zambry Abdul Kadir, in his place. The formation of a new state Government was strongly contested by the PKR, which argued that the transition was unconstitutional and demanded the holding of fresh state elections. Following a series of protests and parliamentary manoeuvres to obstruct the new Government, PKR legislators were prevented by the police from entering the assembly building. The case was referred to the High Court; however, prior to the Court's ruling, and amid protests and the arrest of dozens of protesters and opposition members, the BN Government forcibly removed the Assembly's Speaker and took control of the state legislature. The next session of the Assembly was then officially opened by the son of the Sultan of Perak. Four days later, in mid-May, the High Court ruled that the opposition was the lawful Government of Perak and that Nizar Jamaluddin was the rightful Chief Minister; on the following day, however, Zambry was reinstated, pending an appeal. In late May the Court of Appeal overruled the High Court's decision and declared that Zambry was in fact the rightful Chief Minister. The Federal Court, Malaysia's highest judicial body, unanimously ruled in February 2010 that the Court of Appeal had been right to rescind the High Court's verdict and reaffirmed Zambry's validity as Chief Minister.

The Government of Najib Razak

Having officially resigned as UMNO President at the party's annual congress in March 2009, Abdullah Badawi formally submitted his resignation as Prime Minister on 2 April; Najib Razak, who had replaced Abdullah as party leader, was inaugurated as Prime Minister on the following day. In a demonstration of support, Mahathir rejoined UMNO. Mahathir had resigned from the party in May 2008, having been outspokenly critical of Abdullah since 2006, insisting that he would not return until Abdullah had resigned. Najib announced the composition of his Cabinet: eight ministers from the outgoing administration were dismissed, while Muhyiddin Yassin, hitherto the Minister of International Trade and Industry, was promoted to the position of Deputy Prime Minister and concurrently awarded the education portfolio; other notable appointments included those of Ahmad Zahid Hamidi as Minister of Defence and Datuk Anifah bin Haji Aman as Minister of Foreign Affairs.

In his inaugural address, the new Prime Minister, who retained the finance portfolio, pledged to make use of the ISA in a more appropriate way and to release a group of 13 detainees held under its provisions; Najib also rescinded the suspensions of *Harakah* and *Suara Keadilan*, and pledged to address the problems encountered by minority communities, notably the grievances of Malaysia's ethnic Indians. In May the 13 detainees were duly released without having been formally charged; among them were members of Hindraf who had been detained since organizing the anti-Government protests of 2007. Furthermore, in June 2009 Najib announced that the Government was to abandon certain aspects of the NEP, which had guided government policy since 1971; non-Malay business people and investors welcomed Najib's proposals, as a result of which, *inter alia*, the majority of public companies would no longer be required to reserve 30% of their shares for ethnic Malays.

In mid-April 2009, despite the seemingly conciliatory tone struck by Najib Razak upon his assumption of the premiership, a new law enhancing the powers of the police to ban demonstrations deemed a threat to public order was approved by the legislature. The new law was denounced by the opposition as a further erosion of human rights. In July P. Uthayakumar, one of the 13 detainees released in May, registered a new, Indian-based political party: the stated aim of the Human Rights Party (HRP) was politically to empower and liberate Malaysia's ethnic Indians.

The death in July 2009 of Teoh Beng Hock, a journalist and political aide to Ean Yong Hian Wah—a member of the Selangor State Legislative Assembly—caused a public outcry; on the previous day Teoh had been questioned by the Malaysian Anti-Corruption Commission (MACC) in connection with corruption allegations against Ean Yong. The Malaysian authorities claimed that Teoh had committed suicide, but others contended that he had died from injuries sustained during his interrogation, highlighting the harsh methods employed by the MACC. During a mass demonstration in Kuala Lumpur in August, when an estimated 20,000 citizens gathered to protest against the ISA, some protesters took the opportunity to decry the authorities' perceived ill treatment of Teoh, as well as of Anwar. Riot police used tear gas and water cannons to disperse the protesters, and more than 600 people were reported to have been arrested. An inquest into Teoh's death commenced later that month, and in October a Thai pathology expert testified that it was likely that Teoh's death had been a case of homicide; as a result of this testimony, Teoh's body was exhumed and a second autopsy was conducted. In January 2011 the coroner recorded an open verdict, declaring that there was insufficient evidence to determine how Teoh had died; although suicide was ruled out as a possible cause of death, the coroner also noted the absence of 'evidence of third-party involvement'. The verdict was strongly condemned by Teoh's supporters and the political opposition, who contended that evidence had been suppressed during the

17-month inquest in order to protect the reputation of the authorities.

In an apparent attempt to appease critics, Najib announced in mid-January 2011 that a Royal Commission of Inquiry was to be held into the MACC's interrogation procedures. However, the Commission's remit was widely denounced as being too limited in its scope, prompting some to question the sincerity of the Government's pursuit of the carriage of justice. Following much criticism, Najib agreed in late January 2011 to widen the scope of the Commission, which commenced its work in February, to include an investigation into the specific circumstances surrounding Teoh's death. The final report of the Commission, which was made available to the public in July, concluded that Teoh had not been killed by third-party involvement, but had committed suicide following his interrogation by three MACC officers who were found to have breached procedural protocols and employed improper, overly aggressive techniques of questioning. The three officers were subsequently suspended pending a police investigation into the claims made against them. The report prompted an angry response from Teoh's family, who continued to insist that he had been murdered, while a coalition of more than 100 NGOs condemned the document and appealed for the resignations of Najib, the Minister of Home Affairs, the head of the MACC and the Inspector-General of the police force, insisting that the Government and the MACC take responsibility for the safety and human rights of all those in custody. However, the Government defended the Commission's findings and urged all parties to accept its conclusions. An application to the High Court seeking a review of the open verdict recorded by the coroner in January was rejected by the High Court in December. However, an appeal subsequently lodged by Teoh's brother, appealing against the High Court ruling was upheld by the Court of Appeal in February 2012, providing for a judicial review of the coroner's verdict; at April 2013 no such review had yet been carried out.

Meanwhile, a minor cabinet reorganization announced by Najib Razak in June 2010 was widely interpreted as an attempt to regain support for the governing coalition among Malaysia's ethnic Chinese and Indian communities: the representation of both ethnic minority groups within the Cabinet was increased as a result of the changes, although the most senior portfolios were unaffected by the reorganization.

The second trial of Anwar Ibrahim

The second trial of Anwar on sodomy charges, which had finally commenced in February 2010, was beset by numerous delays and adjournments. Anwar continued to dismiss the allegations against him as a government conspiracy to end his career, and his supporters noted that the claims had been announced shortly after the PKS had made significant gains in the 2008 legislative elections. The lead defence counsel for Anwar, DAP Chairman Karpal Singh, alleged numerous apparent discrepancies in the prosecution's case and in the testimony of a number of its witnesses, including that of the claimant, Mohd Saiful Bukhari Azlan. Two attempts by Karpal to force the removal of the presiding High Court judge, Datuk Mohad Zabidin Mohd Diah—the first in February 2010 for the judge's alleged lack of objectivity with regard to the case and the second in December following his reported resort to intimidation of the defence during court proceedings—proved unsuccessful, as did appeals (in August 2010 and May 2011) to have the charges against Anwar withdrawn. Meanwhile, in March 2010 the Federal Court ruled that Mahathir's dismissal of Anwar as Deputy Prime Minister and Minister of Finance in September 1998 had been constitutional and valid.

In December 2010 the House of Representatives voted to suspend Anwar for a period of six months, following a parliamentary disciplinary inquiry in response to claims made by Anwar earlier in the year that a government campaign to promote racial unity under the banner of '1Malaysia' had been inspired by the 'One Israel' electoral campaign of the then Israeli Prime Minister, Ehud Barak, in 1999. Anwar was deemed to have misled legislators on the issue, which was a source of considerable embarrassment to the Government. (Muslim-majority Malaysia had no diplomatic relations with Israel and was a staunch proponent of an independent Palestinian state.) Three of Anwar's parliamentary allies, among them Karpal Singh, were also suspended for a six-month period having been cited for contempt, owing to their criticism of the disciplinary action against Anwar. Opposition legislators responded angrily to the four suspensions, as a result of which the opposition constituted less than one-third of parliamentary members;

many deputies walked out of the parliamentary session in protest at what they perceived as an attempt by the governing coalition to discredit the opposition.

Meanwhile, the authorities imposed further restrictions on the media during 2010, prompting renewed speculation that the Government was attempting to silence its critics and appearing to undermine Najib's pledge upon assuming office to strive for a more tolerant and accountable system of governance. In July Human Rights Watch appealed to the Government to repeal the 1984 Printing Presses and Publications Act, which effectively granted the Ministry of Home Affairs the right of censorship over all publication content within Malaysia, highlighting the pledge made by Najib Razak in 2009 to ensure that the media was empowered responsibly to report events without fear of reprisal.

In February 2011 a PKR state legislator, Shuhaimi Shafiei, was charged with sedition after posting a comment on his website in December 2010 that was deemed to be critical of the Sultan of Selangor. Shuhaimi denied any wrongdoing, claiming that he was a victim of political manipulation, as part of a wider effort by the governing coalition to discredit the opposition prior to elections. At elections to the 71-member Sarawak state legislature held in April 2011, the BN's representation declined from 63 to 55 seats, while the DAP increased its representation from six to 12 seats, the PKR won three seats and the remaining seat was taken by an independent candidate.

The trial of Anwar drew to a close in December 2011, after nearly two years of court proceedings. In early January 2012 presiding judge Zabidin announced the High Court's verdict, unexpectedly acquitting Anwar, on the grounds that Saiful's claims remained unsubstantiated since the Court could not be sure that the DNA evidence against Anwar had not been contaminated. While welcoming the verdict, Anwar's supporters maintained that he should not have been charged in the first place, while some members of the opposition speculated that the whole affair had been orchestrated as a cynical ploy to rebuild public trust in the Najib administration prior to the forthcoming general election.

The return of the Bersih movement and the repeal of the Internal Security Act

A significant development during the course of 2011 was the return to prominence of the Bersih movement (see The Government of Abdullah Badawi), which was now under the chairmanship of Ambiga Sreenevasan, a former President of the Malaysian Bar Council, who declared that Bersih's resumption of activity was a direct consequence of the Government's failure to address the electoral demands made by the movement in November 2007. In advance of a major rally planned for July 2011 by the movement, which had rebranded itself 'Bersih 2.0', the Malaysian authorities were reported to have arrested some 150 Bersih supporters during a police operation designated 'Operation Erase Bersih'. Bersih had initially obtained permission to stage the rally, but this was subsequently withdrawn by the authorities. Nevertheless, the rally went ahead as planned, and was attended by an estimated 10,000–20,000 people. As in 2007, the police resorted to the use of tear gas and water cannons in order to disperse the demonstrators, more than 1,600 of whom were arrested, including Ambiga and the President of the PAS, Abdul Hadi Awang. Although Najib dismissed the rally as representing only a minority of Malaysians, plans for an early election, which many observers had expected to be called in late 2011, were abandoned.

Significant consternation was generated by the Malaysian Government's censorship of an article published in the British periodical *The Economist* in July 2011 regarding the authorities' allegedly over-zealous handling of the Bersih 2.0 rally. Amid mounting criticism, in August Najib conceded that media censorship in Malaysia was no longer effective, with the act of censorship often generating more controversy and ill-feeling than that which was censored, and pledged to review the country's current legislation on media censorship. Najib also announced the creation of a bi-partisan panel tasked with reviewing the country's electoral laws. The panel duly recommended a series of reforms, some of which echoed demands made by Bersih 2.0—including the use of indelible ink at polling stations and the cleaning up of electoral rolls to remove deceased and duplicate voters—and these were approved by the legislature in December. Although failing to address a number of key opposition demands, including the introduction of longer electoral campaign periods and automatic voter registration, the reforms were none the less widely welcomed as a significant

initial step towards ensuring a more fair and free electoral system.

Moreover, in a speech broadcast live on all state-controlled television and radio channels in September 2011, Najib made the crucial announcement that the increasingly vilified ISA, together with three emergency declarations that also provided for detention without charge, were to be repealed, insisting that 'no individual will ever be detained simply due to political ideology'. (New security legislation was to be introduced under Article 149 of the Constitution, which would allow for a continuation of detentions without charge in the case of 'preventing subversive activities, organized terrorism and crime to maintain peace and public order'—see below.) Najib also pledged to replace the existing system of annual publishing licences with a system whereby permits, once granted, would not require regular renewal but would be cancelled if regulations were flouted.

Although these reforms—particularly the revocation of the ISA—were widely welcomed, the opposition and other critics of the Government nevertheless questioned the administration's sincere commitment to a sustained process of meaningful democratic reform, claiming that the recently announced measures merely constituted a calculated ploy intended to bolster popular support ahead of the forthcoming general election (due to be held by the end of June 2013). Furthermore, critics stressed the potentially ominous undertones of Najib's announcement that detentions without charge were still to be allowed in cases pertaining to subversion and terrorism, noting that the terms remained overly broad and undefined, and contending that the Government had previously, under the provisions of the ISA, fabricated claims of involvement in subversion and terrorism against its political opponents in its efforts to silence dissent. In addition, legislation approved under Article 149 of the Constitution would not be required to uphold the fundamental human liberties enshrined elsewhere in the Constitution—including the rights to life, personal liberty and property, and the freedom of speech, assembly and association. The opposition also pointed to the introduction in November 2011 of new legislation banning street protests as evidence of the insincerity of the Government's claims to be instigating genuine democratic reforms. Meanwhile, in October the Sultan of Kedah, Tuanku Haji Abdul Halim Mu'adzam Shah ibni al-Marhum Badlishah, was appointed as the country's Yang di-Pertuan Agong. The new head of state was duly inaugurated on 13 December 2011, following the expiry of the Sultan of Terengganu's five-year term of office.

In January 2012 the MACC announced that it was conducting an investigation into the alleged misappropriation of government funds by the National Feedlot Centre (NFC), a government-subsidized company intended to increase cattle production with a view to decreasing Malaysia's dependence on beef imports, which was chaired by the husband, and directed by the children, of the Minister of Women, Family and Community Development, Dato' Seri Shahrizat Abdul Jalil. It was alleged that the NFC had used RM 9.8m. of public funding to purchase a luxury condominium in Bangsar for the personal benefit of Shahrizat's family. The opposition, claiming that the scandal was evidence of systemic corruption within the Government, demanded Shahrizat's resignation. Some UMNO members, among them former Prime Minister Mahathir, also appealed to the minister to step down, arguing that the controversy surrounding her and her family was compromising the integrity of the Government. Shahrizat finally resigned from the Government in April, although she continued in her position as head of the woman's section of UMNO.

The new security legislation intended to replace the ISA, the Security Offences (Special Measures) Act, was adopted by the House of Representatives in mid-April 2012. The new Act specifically stated that no person could be detained merely for his or her political beliefs and also limited periods of detention without charge to a maximum of 28 days. While welcoming the repeal of the ISA, Anwar asserted that the provisions of the new Act still contravened human rights principles. Later that month Bersih (which now comprised some 84 NGOs) staged a further rally, 'Bersih 3.0', in the capital in support of its demands for further electoral reform; estimates of the number of participants ranged from 25,000 to more than 100,000. The demonstration turned violent when the police fired tear gas and water cannon at the protesters after barriers were reportedly breached; hundreds of demonstrators were arrested, a number of whom subsequently claimed to have been beaten by the security forces while in detention. The following month Anwar, who had addressed the mass rally at the end of April, was charged with violating laws regarding street protests by inciting the demonstrators to break through the barriers.

Recent developments: the 2013 general election

The House of Representatives was dissolved on 3 April 2013, at the request of Prime Minister Najib Razak, and a general election was subsequently scheduled for 5 May. During the election campaign the BN focused on the country's solid economic performance during Najib's premiership, promising to raise living standards further and to attract increased foreign investment, while the opposition alliance Pakatan Rakyat (People's Alliance)—comprising the PKR, the DAP and the PAS and headed by Anwar Ibrahim—pledged to combat corruption, to improve transparency and to provide free education up to university level.

With analysts predicting a close contest, turn-out at the election on 5 May 2013 reached a record high, of 84.8% of the electorate. The BN retained its simple majority in the House of Representatives, but recorded it worst ever electoral result, winning 133 of the 222 seats (compared with 140 seats at the 2008 elections). Pakatan Rakyat increased its representation to 89 seats (from 82), the gain being attributable to the success of the DAP, which secured 38 seats, 10 more than in 2008. The BN performed better at the concurrent elections to 12 of the 13 State Legislative Assemblies (the Sarawak state legislature having been renewed in April 2011—see The second trial of Anwar Ibrahim), recovering control of Kedah's state legislature and retaining its majority in eight others. Prime Minister Najib was sworn in to serve a further term of office on 6 May. Two days later up to 40,000 opposition supporters protested against the official election results at a demonstration organized by Anwar, who accused the ruling coalition of perpetrating widespread electoral fraud.

Religious Tensions

The right to religious freedom, as prescribed by the Malaysian Constitution, and the country's multi-faith status were prominent issues during the early 21st century, with ongoing debates about religious conversion laws, the jurisdiction of Islamic and civil courts, and punishments for apostasy. In January 2005, at a nightclub in Kuala Lumpur, about 100 Muslims, including many women, were detained on charges of public indecency and other 'anti-Islamic' crimes. Amid the ensuing public outcry, the legitimacy of these arrests was questioned, as the application of Islamic law in federal territories was restricted to marriage and related matters. The Government subsequently instructed the Federal Territories Islamic Department to abandon the charges. However, such police operations against night-clubs and hotels continued to be reported, with hundreds of Muslims arrested during 2005–12 for *khalwat*, an offence defined as unmarried men and women meeting 'in close proximity . . . in any secluded place or in a house or room under circumstances which may give rise to suspicion that they were engaged in immoral acts', and which carried a maximum penalty of two years' imprisonment and a fine of RM 3,000.

In February 2006, meanwhile, the Malaysian Government suspended indefinitely the licence of the *Sarawak Tribune*, in response to the newspaper's decision to reprint controversial cartoons depicting the Prophet Muhammad, which had been published in a Danish newspaper in 2005 and had provoked outrage in the international Muslim community. This was the first time in almost two decades that the licence of a Malaysian publication had been revoked, and the episode renewed concerns about the status of religious freedom and freedom of expression.

In May 2007 the Federal Court rejected an appeal by a convert from Islam to Christianity to have the word 'Islam' removed from the religion section of her identity card, ruling that Syariah (Islamic law) courts held jurisdiction in this area. Observers noted that the judgment effectively made it impossible to renounce Islam legally, given that apostasy was a criminal offence under Islamic law, and renewed the debate about the constitutionally enshrined right to religious freedom. This was perhaps the most high profile of a number of similar cases that were provoking religious tension in Malaysia. In August the Government suspended publication of the Tamil-language newspaper *Makkal Osai* for one month, after the newspaper published an image of Jesus Christ apparently smoking a cigarette and drinking alcohol. In December controversy arose over the use of the word 'Allah' by non-Muslims, when a Roman Catholic weekly newspaper, *The Herald*, encountered difficulties in renewing its publishing permit because its Malay-language section employed the word 'Allah' when referring to the Christian God, which the Government argued might confuse Muslims. The newspaper's permit was eventually renewed on the condition that it adhere to a government ban on non-Muslims using the word 'Allah'. *The Herald* filed for a judicial review, insisting that it had used the word 'Allah' to refer to the Christian God for decades and had a constitutional right to do so. In December 2009 the High Court ruled in favour of *The Herald*, reversing the government ban on the use of the word by non-Muslims on the grounds that it was 'unconstitutional'; shortly afterwards the Government announced that it intended to appeal against the decision. The ruling resulted in an intensification of Muslim–Christian tensions in Malaysia, provoking a series of violent attacks on churches, mosques and a Sikh temple in early 2010.

Meanwhile, in April 2009, shortly after the inauguration of Najib Razak as Prime Minister, the Government outlawed the religious conversion of children without the prior consent of both parents. The ban followed several controversial cases in which children had been converted to Islam following a divorce, despite vehement objections from the non-Muslim parent. (Such conversions had been aided by rulings issued by Syariah courts.) The Government's decision, in July 2010, to appoint female judges to Syariah courts for the first time was described by Najib as a serious attempt 'to enhance justice in cases involving families and women's rights'. However, while welcoming the appointment of the two female judges as a positive development, a senior figure within the influential Sisters in Islam group, which sought to promote Muslim women's rights, appealed for more extensive reform.

Following a state visit to the Vatican City by Najib Razak in July 2011, during which he held discussions with Pope Benedict XVI, Malaysia and the Vatican announced the establishment of formal diplomatic relations. The development was widely interpreted as an attempt to reassure Christians in Malaysia, who comprised around 9% of the total population, that the Government was committed to fostering strong ties with the Christian Church. Nevertheless, amid mounting claims by the Muslim community of Christians converting Muslims (a practice that is illegal in many Malaysian states), an intensification of tensions between the two religions in Malaysia was reported in the latter half of 2011 and early 2012, and there were a number of arrests made for alleged incitement of religious hatred.

Foreign Affairs

Malaysia's foreign policy has been dominated by its membership of the Association of Southeast Asian Nations (ASEAN, see p. 218), which was founded in 1967. In February 2008 Malaysia ratified the new ASEAN Charter, codifying the principles and purposes of the Association, which had been signed in November 2007 at the 13th summit meeting in Singapore. Prime Minister Mahathir Mohamad was instrumental in bringing Myanmar into ASEAN in 1997 under the Policy of Constructive Engagement. Malaysia has been involved with Brunei, Viet Nam, the People's Republic of China, the Philippines and Taiwan in disputed sovereignty claims over the Spratly Islands in the South China Sea. In November 2002 the ASEAN member states approved a 'code of conduct' for the islands; the agreement was also sanctioned by China. Proposals to formulate a more legally binding code of conduct were espoused in October 2010, but discussions to this end were not reported to have led to any tangible results by early 2013.

Relations with South-East Asian countries

Relations with Singapore have traditionally been characterized by mistrust since the city-state left the Federation of Malaya in 1965. Resentment grew as Singapore advanced more swiftly than Malaysia in economic terms, creating a certain acrimonious competition between the two countries. Yet, as Malaysia also developed, bilateral relations became more cordial, and co-operation increased. From early 2002, however, tensions arose over the renegotiation of a 1961 agreement (due to expire in 2011) by which Malaysia supplied Singapore with water. Following unsuccessful negotiations in 2002, in February 2003 Prime Minister Mahathir stated that, while Malaysia would cease to supply Singapore with untreated water in 2011, it would continue to supply filtered water, at a reasonable price, for as long as necessary. In January 2005 Malaysia and Singapore appeared to have resolved a dispute over the latter's land reclamation project in the Straits of Johor, which separate the two countries; Malaysia accepted that the reclamation work could proceed, while Singapore agreed to co-operate with Malaysia to ensure navigational safety and environmental protection of the waterway. In 2006, however, relations became strained over

Malaysia's construction of a bridge to replace the Johor Straits causeway to Singapore (Singapore opposed the plan and building on the Malaysian side was suspended in 2006), and deteriorated further in September, when Singapore's Minister Mentor and former Prime Minister, Lee Kuan Yew, remarked that Malaysia's Chinese minority was being systematically marginalized because of its success. Lee later apologized to Prime Minister Abdullah Badawi, and stated that he had no wish to interfere in Malaysian politics. Prime Minister Lee Hsien Loong visited Malaysia in May 2007 for informal talks with Abdullah. The most significant outcome of the discussions was a decision to form a joint ministerial committee to oversee collaboration on Malaysia's plan to establish an economic development zone in southern Johor, to be known as the Iskandar Development Region, with both leaders agreeing that outstanding issues of dispute, such as water sales to Singapore and the suspended construction of the Johor Strait bridge, should not be allowed to impede bilateral co-operation in other areas.

A long-standing dispute between Malaysia and Singapore over their conflicting claims to the island of Batu Puteh (Pedra Branca) was finally concluded in May 2008 when the International Court of Justice (ICJ, see p. 26)—to which the dispute had been referred as per an agreement signed by the two countries in February 2003—ruled in favour of Singapore. During a meeting between Prime Ministers Najib Razak and Lee Hsien Loong in May 2010, the two leaders affirmed their commitment to enhancing bilateral co-operation, and agreed to the joint development of a rapid transit system between Johor Bahru and Singapore. In June 2011 a land swap agreement was finalized, under the terms of which Malaysia was to be awarded six parcels of land in exchange for giving up land in Singapore owned by Malayan Railways. Upon the expiry in August 2011 of the 1961 water-sharing agreement, the Singaporean Government transferred ownership of water assets, including water treatment facilities and pump houses, to the Johor state government, and reaffirmed previous claims that Singapore would achieve water self-sufficiency before the scheduled expiry, in August 2061, of the 1962 water-sharing agreement. Following a further meeting between Najib Razak and Lee Hsien Loong, held in Singapore in February 2013, the two premiers announced plans for the construction of a high-speed rail link between their two countries, with completion anticipated in 2020.

While generally remaining cordial, relations with Indonesia have been periodically adversely affected by the flow of illegal Indonesian immigrants into Malaysia. Following rioting by Indonesian labourers (for which the Indonesian Government issued a formal apology), in January 2001 a temporary ban was imposed on new workers arriving from Indonesia. In November the Malaysian Government announced that it would thenceforth deport 10,000 illegal Indonesian immigrants each month in an attempt to tighten controls on foreign labour in the country. In August 2002 the implementation of new legislation requiring that all illegal immigrants leave Malaysia or risk penalties strained relations with both the Philippines and Indonesia, as the majority of the workers affected were citizens of those countries. In September the Malaysian Government announced a temporary halt to deportations, owing to diplomatic pressure, exacerbated by public protests in Indonesia and the Philippines over the apparently inhumane nature of the expulsions.

At the end of October 2004 a 17-day amnesty began for illegal migrant workers to leave Malaysia voluntarily without penalty. Thousands of Indonesians had fled to Malaysia since the Indonesian authorities had commenced military operations against separatists in the province of Aceh in May 2003. In November 2004 Malaysia agreed to extend the amnesty until the end of the year; the amnesty was subsequently further extended following a request from President Susilo Bambang Yudhoyono of Indonesia. It was reported that around 380,000 of an estimated 1.2m. illegal foreign workers had left Malaysia by the end of January 2005. In February, following talks with President Yudhoyono in Kuala Lumpur, the Malaysian Prime Minister announced that the amnesty would expire at the end of the month, and in March the forced repatriation of illegal immigrants recommenced. Human rights organizations, including Amnesty International, expressed serious misgivings about the standard of training and supervision given to officers of the Malaysian Immigration Department, amid allegations of widespread physical abuse of immigrants. In July 2006, according to government estimates, approximately 500,000 illegal immigrants were still living in Malaysia. In October 2007 a temporary ban was imposed on Malaysian employers recruiting new workers from Bangladesh,

following a series of cases of ill-treatment of migrants, including the abandonment of several thousand at Kuala Lumpur airport. In January 2008 it was reported that the Malaysian Government aimed to reduce the number of foreign workers in the country from some 2.3m. to 1.5m. by 2015, by introducing stricter regulations on their employment. In early 2009 the Government announced the cancellation of work permits for nearly 100,000 Indonesian and 55,000 Bangladeshi migrant workers, amid increasing demands by the Malaysian public that the local work-force be better protected. The Indonesian Government subsequently imposed a moratorium on sending migrant workers to Malaysia. Following the signing in April 2011 of a memorandum of understanding between the two countries intended better to protect Indonesian migrant workers in Malaysia from abuse by their employers, the Indonesian Government rescinded the moratorium imposed in 2009, with effect from May 2011.

In May 2002 Malaysia, Indonesia and the Philippines signed an anti-terrorism pact enabling them to exchange intelligence and to launch joint police operations; Thailand and Cambodia acceded to the pact later in the year. In December the ICJ ruled that Malaysia would be awarded sovereignty of Sipadan and Ligitan, two small islands off the coast of Borneo, thereby bringing to an end a protracted dispute between Malaysia and Indonesia over conflicting claims to the islands. In July 2004 Malaysia and Indonesia, together with Singapore, commenced co-ordinated patrols of the Strait of Melaka between Malaysia and Indonesia, in an attempt to curb piracy.

Relations with Thailand deteriorated in February 1996, owing to Malaysia's construction of a 27-km wall along the border with Thailand, intended to deter illegal immigration from that country. However, in January 1997 the two countries agreed to co-operate in preventing Bangladeshi migrant workers from entering Malaysia and in expediting the return of illegal Thai workers from Malaysia. However, the Thai Minister of Foreign Affairs, Surin Pitsuwan, was among a number of international political figures, including the Presidents of Indonesia and the Philippines, who expressed concern at the arrest and detention of Anwar Ibrahim in September 1998. In January 2004 new Prime Minister Abdullah Badawi visited Thailand for security discussions, following several attacks believed to have been perpetrated by separatists in southern Thailand close to the joint border. The two countries agreed to co-operate in efforts to bring an end to the violence and began joint border patrols. Amid continuing unrest on the Thai side of the border, the Prime Minister of Thailand, Thaksin Shinawatra, visited Malaysia in mid-April for further security talks with Abdullah. In late April Malaysia increased its border security after militants launched a series of attacks on police posts in southern Thailand; the attacks were violently suppressed by the Thai security forces. (Parts of the border were subsequently fenced off, in an attempt to prevent the cross-border transit of those thought to be responsible for the ongoing violence.) Security at the border was heightened again in October following renewed clashes in southern Thailand between government troops and Muslim protesters in which 85 people died, many of whom suffocated after being forced into army trucks. Hundreds of Malaysians demonstrated outside the Thai embassy in Kuala Lumpur in protest against the deaths. Bilateral relations were further strained in December, when the Thai Government claimed to have photographic evidence that militants in southern Thailand had received training in the Malaysian state of Kelantan.

A diplomatic dispute arose between the two countries in October 2005, concerning the fate of 131 Muslim villagers who had fled from the violence-stricken province of Narathiwat, in southern Thailand, to neighbouring Malaysia. The Malaysian authorities insisted that they would not sanction the return of the asylum seekers to Thailand unless they received a guarantee of their safety from the Thai authorities. One of the villagers, suspected of involvement in a raid on a Thai military camp in January 2004, was subsequently handed over to the Thai authorities, while the other 130 refugees remained in a Malaysian detention centre in Terengganu. The dispute was finally resolved in February 2006 when the Thai Government indicated that it was prepared to allow the refugees to remain in Malaysia. There was some improvement in bilateral relations from October, when Gen. Surayud Chulanont was appointed as Thai Prime Minister following a coup in which Thaksin was ousted from power. Surayud visited Malaysia later that month, holding talks with Abdullah on the ongoing insurgency in Thailand's southern provinces. In December Abdullah and Surayud officially opened a new bridge across the Golok River, linking Kelantan to

Narathiwat, as part of efforts to improve the economy of the border region and, as a consequence, reduce violence. During a visit to Thailand in July 2008, the Malaysian Minister of Foreign Affairs, Rais Yatim, pledged a continuation of Malaysian assistance towards the Thai Government's efforts to resolve the ongoing violence in the country's Muslim-dominated southern provinces. In February 2013 Malaysia acted as a mediator in peace talks between the Thai Government and one of the Muslim insurgent groups, the National Revolution Front.

Malaysia played an integral role in bringing together the Myanma military junta and opposition leader Aung San Suu Kyi for negotiations in late 2000, although it was believed that financial considerations might have been significant, with a promise of direct investment in Myanmar by Malaysia's national petroleum corporation, PETRONAS, in return for progress on the part of the junta. In September 2001 the Myanma leader, Gen. Than Shwe, paid an official visit to Malaysia during which a number of bilateral agreements were signed. In March 2006 the Malaysian Minister of Foreign Affairs, Syed Hamid Albar, was denied access to Suu Kyi on a visit to Myanmar in his role as an ASEAN envoy to assess the country's progress towards political reform. Albar, who had held a meeting with Lt-Gen. Soe Win, the Myanma Prime Minister, was initially positive about the visit. However, in July Albar implied that ASEAN's development was being impeded by Myanmar, claiming that the Association could no longer defend Myanmar as the country's regime was 'not making an attempt to co-operate or help itself'. An improvement in bilateral relations was evident following the staging of legislative elections in Myanmar in November 2010. A Malaysian business delegation to Myanmar in the following month identified numerous new opportunities in the country's rapidly developing oil and gas sector. Following a meeting between the Malaysian Minister of Foreign Affairs and the Myanma Deputy Minister of Foreign Affairs in October 2011, the two countries announced that a joint working committee was to be established to address issues pertaining to immigration and trans-national crime, including drugs-, weapon- and people-smuggling. Bilateral relations were further boosted following a visit to Myanmar by Malaysian Prime Minister Najib Razak in March 2012, during which he held cordial talks with Myanma President Thein Sein.

In early February 2013 it was reported that a group of around 200 men from the Philippine island province of Sulu (some of whom were allegedly armed) had landed in Lahad Datu, a remote area of Sabah, and had raised the Philippine flag in the coastal village of Tanduo. The Government of the Philippines denied having sanctioned the actions of the group, which described itself as the 'Royal Security Forces of the Sultanate of Sulu and North Borneo' and which was led by Agbimuddin Kiram, the brother of self-proclaimed Sultan of Sulu Jamalul Kiram III, and urged the men to withdraw at once. The group claimed that Sabah, which had been given to the Sultan of Sulu by the Sultan of Brunei in the 17th century, was still part of Sulu (and, by extension, part of the Philippines). The Malaysian authorities, in turn, maintained that Sabah had, in effect, been sold (rather than simply leased) to the British North Borneo Company by the Sultan of Sulu through a contract drawn up between the two parties in 1878. Following a stand-off between the group and the Malaysian security forces, which had surrounded the village, the situation turned violent at the end of February 2013 when both sides accused the other of opening fire; two police officers and 12 Philippine rebels were reportedly killed in the ensuing shoot-outs. The group demanded that Malaysia recognize it as the rightful owner of Sabah and renegotiate the terms of the 19th-century lease (since Sabah became part of Malaysia in 1963 the latter has paid a token rent to the Sulu Sultanate each year). In early March, as tensions escalated and the death toll rose, the Malaysian authorities dispatched additional troops (including fighter jets) to Sabah, while the Philippine Secretary of Foreign Affairs, Albert del Rosario, was sent to Malaysia to attempt to expedite peace negotiations between the rebels and the Malaysian Government. The Malaysian Government rejected the subsequent offer of a cease-fire made by the rebel group, demanding instead its unconditional surrender. By mid-March more than 70 people had been killed in the conflict between the Philippine clan group and the Malaysian security forces.

Other regional relations

In 1990 a proposal by Mahathir to establish an East Asian Economic Caucus (EAEC), a trade group intended to exclude the USA, met with considerable resistance from the US Government (which continued to promote the US-dominated Asia-Pacific Economic Cooperation forum—APEC, see p. 208) and Australia. In July 1993 ASEAN agreed, despite the continuing reluctance of Japan to participate, that the EAEC should operate as an East Asian interest group within APEC. In November 1999 the third informal summit meeting of the 10 ASEAN countries and the People's Republic of China, Japan and the Republic of Korea (collectively known as 'ASEAN + 3') took place. At the meeting it was agreed to strengthen present economic co-operation with the distant aim of forming an East Asian bloc with a common market and monetary union. This ambition was brought closer in April 2001 when, at a meeting of the ASEAN + 3 group, plans were agreed for a network of currency 'swap' arrangements to prevent a repetition of the regional financial crisis of 1997. At the annual ASEAN summit meeting held in Laos in November 2004 it was agreed to transform the ASEAN + 3 summit meeting, which was first held in 1997, into the East Asia Summit, with the long-term objective of establishing an East Asian Community. In December 2005 Kuala Lumpur hosted the inaugural East Asia Summit, held during the course of the ASEAN summit meeting. It was agreed that the East Asia Summit should convene annually.

Malaysia's relations with the People's Republic of China remained extremely cordial, with Malaysia frequently offering public support to China, particularly in response to US criticism. The importance of bilateral relations was demonstrated in May 2009 when Najib Razak travelled to China in his first official visit to a non-ASEAN country since being inaugurated as Prime Minister the previous month. Relations were further enhanced by a state visit to Kuala Lumpur by Chinese Premier Wen Jiabao in April 2011, during which he met with Najib, with both leaders hailing the increasing significance of bilateral ties. Meanwhile, the implementation in January 2010 of a free trade agreement between ASEAN and China was expected further to deepen Malaysia's growing economic dependence on the People's Republic. In August 2012 Malaysia and China agreed to designate 2014 as 'Malaysia-China Friendship Year' to commemorate the 40th anniversary of the establishment of diplomatic relations.

Malaysia forged closer links with Japan in December 2005 with the signing of a bilateral free trade agreement, which entered into force in July 2006. Under the terms of the accord, the two countries were to eliminate tariffs on all industrial goods and on most agricultural, forestry and fishery products within a 10-year period. In keeping with the spirit of invigorated relations, the Emperor and Empress of Japan paid a state visit to Malaysia in June 2006, their first official trip to the country since 1991, and Japanese Prime Minister Shinzo Abe visited Malaysia in August 2007, marking the 50th anniversary of the establishment of diplomatic relations between the two countries. Malaysian Prime Minister Najib Razak made his first official visit to Japan in April 2010, where he met with his Japanese counterpart, Yukio Hatoyama; the two leaders pledged further to strengthen co-operation, including practical measures towards the realization of the concept of an East Asian Community. Following a meeting between the two countries' foreign affairs ministers in November 2011, the Japanese Government affirmed its desire to support Malaysia in its efforts to achieve developed nation status by 2020.

Malaysia's relations with Australia, which were frequently strained under Mahathir—in particular over Malaysian objections to Australia's leadership of the UN-mandated peacekeeping mission in East Timor (now Timor-Leste), with Mahathir claiming that an ASEAN-led mission would be more appropriate—appeared to improve following the succession of Abdullah Badawi to the Malaysian premiership in October 2003. In June 2004, during a visit to Malaysia by the Australian Minister for Foreign Affairs, Alexander Downer, agreement was reached to hold formal annual talks between the two countries' foreign ministers and separate regular consultations between senior security officials. In April 2005 Abdullah made the first state visit to Australia by a Malaysian premier in more than 20 years. Formal negotiations on a free trade agreement between Malaysia and Australia commenced in the same month. However, relations foundered in February 2010 when more than 50 Australian legislators lodged a protest against the second sodomy trial of Anwar Ibrahim, which had commenced earlier in the month (see Domestic Political Affairs); in a formal statement, the legislators indirectly suggested that the trial was politically motivated and urged that it be abandoned.

During a visit to Canberra, Australia, by Prime Minister Najib Razak in March 2011, and following the successful conclusion of eight rounds of bilateral free trade negotiations, Najib and his Australian counterpart, Julia Gillard, pledged their common commitment to concluding an agreement within 12 months. Following further discussions, a free trade agreement was signed in March 2012 and entered into force on 1 January 2013. The agreement constituted Malaysia's fifth bilateral free trade agreement, following those signed with Japan in December 2005, Pakistan in November 2007, New Zealand in October 2009 and Chile in November 2010. Meanwhile, in November 2011 Malaysia and Australia agreed to bolster co-operation in the fields of people-smuggling and counter-terrorism. In the previous month, owing to staunch opposition from within the Australian legislature and a High Court ruling on its unconstitutionality, the Australian Government was forced to abandon a proposed amendment to its Migration Act that would have provided for the transfer by the Australian authorities of sea-borne asylum seekers to detention centres in Malaysia, where their refugee claims would be processed. The legislative amendment had been proposed as a means of alleviating the strain imposed on the Australian authorities by the increasing number of sea-borne refugees trying to claim asylum in Australia. An agreement on the issue had been signed between the Malaysian and Australian Governments in July. However, members of the Australian opposition had voiced strong concerns over the human rights record of Malaysia, which is not a party to the 1951 UN Convention relating to the Status of Refugees, and noted the country's poor reputation for the treatment of refugees and immigrant workers.

Relations between Malaysia and Australia came under considerable strain in February 2013 following the detention and subsequent deportation from Malaysia of an Australian senator, Nick Xenophon, who had arrived in Kuala Lumpur as part of an unofficial Australian parliamentary fact-finding mission to assess whether the imminent elections would be conducted fairly. The Malaysian authorities claimed that they had refused Xenophon entry on the grounds that he posed a 'security risk'; the senator, who was an outspoken critic of Malaysia's human rights record, had taken part in the Bersih rally held in the Malaysian capital in April 2012 (see Recent developments: the return of the Bersih movement and the repeal of the Internal Security Act).

Following the commencement in 2005 of negotiations on a Malaysian-New Zealand free trade agreement, a deal was formally concluded in October 2009. The agreement, which covered trade in goods, services and investment, entered into force in August 2010.

Other external relations

In June 1997 the inauguration took place of a group that aimed to foster economic co-operation among Muslim developing countries—the Developing-Eight (D-8)—comprising Malaysia, Bangladesh, Egypt, Indonesia, Iran, Nigeria, Pakistan and Turkey. Malaysia continued to express its close relationship with Arab countries through its denouncement of US and British airstrikes against Iraq in February 2001, while demanding the removal of UN sanctions. It was hoped that a D-8 agreement on preferential tariffs signed in May 2006 would further strengthen economic relations between the group's members.

During Mahathir's premiership, Malaysia's desire to foster closer ties with other Muslim countries was, on occasion, the source of friction in its relations with the USA. Malaysian-US ties were strained by the involvement of PETRONAS in a consortium that signed an agreement during September 1997 to invest in Iran, in contravention of US sanctions against that country, and deteriorated further in October following Mahathir's suggestion that the economic crisis in the South-East Asian region was due to hostile Jewish currency speculation aimed at preventing progress among Muslim nations. Bilateral relations were further strained in 1998 following US condemnation of the detention and treatment of former Deputy Prime Minister Anwar Ibrahim and expressions of support by the Administration of US President Bill Clinton for the political reform movement in Malaysia.

However, in September 2001 relations with the USA were considerably strengthened when Mahathir acted quickly to condemn the terrorist attacks on the US mainland for which the al-Qa'ida network claimed responsibility. However, Mahathir refused to lend his Government's support to the US-led retaliatory attacks on Afghanistan that had begun earlier that month, voicing concern at the large numbers of civilian casualties resulting from the raids. In November 2002 Malaysia and the USA co-established the Southeast Asia Regional Centre for Counter-Terrorism; based in Kuala Lumpur, the Centre officially opened in July 2003. While Prime Minister Mahathir made clear his opposition to the US-led campaign to remove the

regime of Saddam Hussain in Iraq in 2003, relations with the USA remained generally stable, owing largely to the Malaysian Government's ongoing operation against suspected domestic terrorists, which was in line with the global anti-terrorism campaign being pursued by the Bush Administration.

In 2006 Malaysia and the USA began negotiations on the establishment of a free trade agreement, which drew opposition from several quarters in Malaysia, including farmers and trade unions fearful of the potential impact of US competition on local livelihoods, as well as from US politicians who disapproved of Malaysia's gas agreement with Iran. Negotiations proved problematic and were suspended on several occasions, and the US focus appeared to shift to the establishment of a regional Asia-Pacific trade pact (the proposed Trans-Pacific Partnership). Bilateral relations were improved by a visit to Washington, DC, in April 2010 by Prime Minister Najib Razak. During separate visits to Malaysia in November, US Secretary of State Hillary Clinton and Secretary of Defence Robert Gates spoke highly of the US-Malaysian relationship, commending the performance of the Malaysian Government and praising the South-East Asian country as a vital regional and global influence. The absence of comment by either US official on the allegations that the criminal charges against Anwar Ibrahim were politically motivated, together with Clinton's refusal to meet with Anwar during her visit, prompted some observers to suggest that the US Administration was compromising its position on human rights in order to preserve cordial relations with the UMNO-led coalition Government; local media reports speculated that this apparent pandering to the Malaysian Government was a reflection of US efforts to counter China's increasing regional prominence. Nevertheless, the US Administration expressed concern over the Malaysian authorities' handling of the 'Bersih 2.0' rally in July 2011 (see Domestic Political Affairs), stressing the importance of democratic freedoms, and stating that the US Administration would continue to monitor closely the human rights situation in Malaysia.

CONSTITUTION AND GOVERNMENT

Malaysia is a federation of 13 states. The capital, Kuala Lumpur, is a separate Federal Territory, as is the island of Labuan and the newly developed administrative capital of Putrajaya. The head of state, or Supreme Head of Malaysia, is a monarch (Yang di-Pertuan Agong), elected for a five-year term (with a deputy head of state) by and from the hereditary rulers of nine of the states. The monarch acts on the advice of Parliament and the Cabinet. Parliament consists of the Dewan Negara (Senate) and the Dewan Rakyat (House of Representatives). The Senate has 70 members, including 44 appointed by the head of state, four of whom are from the Federal Territories, and 26 elected members, two chosen by each of the 13 State Legislative Assemblies. The House of Representatives consists of 222 members, elected for five years by universal adult suffrage: 165 from Peninsular Malaysia (including 11 from Kuala Lumpur and one from Putrajaya), 31 from Sarawak and 26 from Sabah (including one from Labuan). The head of state appoints the Prime Minister and, on the latter's recommendation, other ministers. The Cabinet is responsible to Parliament. The country is divided into 137 administrative districts.

REGIONAL AND INTERNATIONAL CO-OPERATION

Malaysia is a member of the Association of Southeast Asian Nations (ASEAN, see p. 218), the Asia-Pacific Economic Cooperation (APEC, see p. 208) forum, the Asian Development Bank (ADB, see p. 214), the UN's Economic and Social Commission for Asia and the Pacific (ESCAP, see p. 31), and the Colombo Plan (see p. 460), which promotes economic and social development in Asia and the Pacific.

Malaysia became a member of the UN in 1957. As a contracting party to the General Agreement on Tariffs and Trade (GATT), Malaysia joined the World Trade Organization (WTO, see p. 444) upon its establishment in 1995. Malaysia participates in the Organization of Islamic Cooperation (OIC, see p. 413) and the Developing Eight (D-8, see p. 460) group of Muslim states. The country is a member of the Non-aligned Movement (see p. 477) and of the International Labour Organization (ILO, see p. 142). Malaysia also participates in the Five-Power Defence Arrangements with Australia, New Zealand, Singapore and the United Kingdom.

ECONOMIC AFFAIRS

In 2011, according to estimates by the World Bank, Malaysia's gross national income (GNI), measured at average 2009–11 prices, was US \$243,108m., equivalent to \$8,420 per head (or \$15,190 per head on an international purchasing-power parity basis). During 2002–11, it was estimated, the population increased at an average annual rate of 1.8%, while gross domestic product (GDP) per head increased, in real terms, by an average of 3.2% per year. Overall GDP increased, in real terms, at an average annual rate of 5.1% in 2002–11. According to the Central Bank of Malaysia (CBM), GDP expanded by 5.6% in 2012.

In 2011 agriculture (including forestry and fishing) contributed 12.0% of GDP and engaged 12.0% of the employed labour force. Malaysia is one of the world's leading producers of palm oil, exports of which contributed 8.6% of the value of total merchandise exports in 2011. Other important crops include rice, rubber, cocoa, coconuts, bananas, tea and pineapples. During 2002–11, according to the CBM, agricultural GDP increased, in real terms, at an average annual rate of 3.6%; growth in agricultural GDP was 0.8% in 2012.

Industry (including mining, manufacturing, construction and utilities) contributed 40.7% of GDP and engaged 28.5% of the employed labour force in 2011. During 2002–11, according to the CBM, industrial GDP increased, in real terms, at an average annual rate of 3.3%; sectoral GDP expanded by 5.1% in 2012.

In 2011 mining contributed 10.5% of GDP, but engaged only 0.6% of the employed labour force. At the end of 2011 estimated proven gas reserves stood at 2,435,471m. cu m, and petroleum reserves at 5,859m. barrels. Petroleum production in 2011 averaged 572,900 barrels per day, sufficient to maintain production at that year's level for more than 28 years. In 2011 exports of liquefied natural gas accounted for 7.2% of total export revenue, while crude petroleum and condensates provided 4.6% of export earnings. Malaysia is one of the world's leading producers of tin. Bauxite, iron, gold and coal are also mined. The GDP of the mining sector decreased at an average annual rate of 0.5% in 2002–11, according to the CBM. Mining GDP contracted by 5.7% in 2011, but increased by 1.4% in 2012.

Manufacturing (the largest export sector) contributed 24.6% of GDP and engaged 17.1% of the employed labour force in 2011. The most important branches of manufacturing include electrical machinery and appliances, food products, metals and metal products, non-electrical machinery, transport equipment, rubber and plastic products, chemical products, wood products and furniture. According to the CBM, during 2002–11 manufacturing GDP increased, in real terms, at an average annual rate of 4.4%; manufacturing GDP rose by 4.8% in 2012.

In 2011 construction contributed 3.2% of GDP and engaged 9.7% of the employed labour force. According to the CBM, during 2002–11 construction GDP increased, in real terms, at an average annual rate of 2.8%; sectoral GDP growth was 18.5% in 2012.

Energy is derived principally from Malaysia's own reserves of hydrocarbons. The country's dependence on petroleum as a source of electric energy declined from 55.9% in 1990 to 2.0% in 2009. The share contributed by natural gas to electricity output stood at 60.7% in 2009, while coal accounted for 30.9%. Production of electricity reached 119,018m. kWh in 2011. Imports of fuel accounted for 10.1% of total import costs in 2010.

In 2011 services contributed 47.3% of GDP and engaged 59.6% of the employed labour force. Tourism makes a major contribution to the economy. Revenue from this source reached an estimated RM 60,600m. in 2012, in which year tourist arrivals rose to a record 25.0m. In 2011 the financial sub-sector contributed 7.4% of GDP. The GDP of the services sector increased by an average of 6.7% per year in 2002–11, according to CBM data. The sector's GDP grew by 6.5% in 2012.

In 2011 Malaysia recorded a visible merchandise trade surplus of US \$148,071m. and a surplus of \$97,110m. on the current account of the balance of payments. In 2011 the principal sources of imports were the People's Republic of China and Singapore (accounting for 13.2% and 12.8%, respectively, of the total). Other important suppliers included Japan, the USA, Indonesia and Thailand. The principal market for exports (accounting for 13.1%) was China; other significant purchasers were Singapore, Japan, the USA, Thailand and Hong Kong. The principal imports in 2011 were intermediate goods (notably parts and accessories of capital goods, and miscellaneous processed industrial supplies), as well as capital goods and consumption goods. The principal exports were electrical machinery and parts (particularly semiconductors and electronic components), palm oil, liquefied natural gas and chemicals.

In 2011 an overall budget deficit of RM 42,509m. was recorded, equivalent to 4.8% of GDP. Malaysia's general government gross debt was RM 465,781m. in 2011, equivalent to 52.9% of GDP. According to the Asian Development Bank (ADB), at the end of 2012 Malaysia's external debt totalled US \$82,662m. The cost of debt-servicing in that year was equivalent to 10.0% of the value of exports of goods and services. The annual rate of inflation averaged 2.4% in 2002–11. Consumer prices increased by 1.6% in 2012. The rate of unemployment was 3.1% of the total labour force in 2011.

The Malaysian economy recovered strongly from the global recession of 2008–09, following a series of fiscal stimulus measures. The economy expanded more rapidly than anticipated in 2010, driven by rising commodity prices and high private consumption levels, as well as the economic recovery of Malaysia's major trading partners. Net foreign direct investment in Malaysia increased from RM 29,322m. in 2010 to a record RM 36,616m. in 2011, before declining to RM 29,061m. in 2012. GDP growth slowed to 5.1% in 2011, partly as a result of weakening external demand, but recovered to 5.6% in 2012, when strong growth in private investment was recorded, although exports remained sluggish. At early 2013 the ongoing European financial crisis was cause for considerable concern, in the light of the Malaysian banking sector's substantial exposure to eurozone markets. In part owing to the Government's fiscal stimulus measures, the fiscal deficit widened to 6.7% of GDP in 2009 (from 3.1% in 2007), before moderating to 5.4% of GDP in 2010, to 4.8% of GDP in 2011 and to an estimated 4.5% of GDP in 2012. As a result of a deceleration in the rate of growth of food and fuel prices, inflationary pressures decreased in 2012; despite strong domestic demand, the inflation rate fell from 3.2% in 2011 to 1.6% in 2012. While continuing efforts to counter inflation, the Government also implemented a number of measures intended to protect consumer spending, including an increase in fuel subsidies, rises in public sector wages and pensions and the postponement of the planned implementation of a goods-and-services tax. In addition, the 2012 budget included one-off payments for all school pupils and for low- and middle-income households. Legislation introducing, for the first time, a minimum wage entered into force on 1 January 2013. Buoyed by the large number of development projects being carried out under the Government's Economic Transformation Programme (launched in 2010) and by the rising demand for new housing, the construction sector performed particularly strongly in 2012. Among the projects under way was the country's largest ever infrastructure project—the construction of a mass rapid transit rail system in Kuala Lumpur at a cost of an estimated US \$11,500m. With a moderate recovery in the global economy projected for 2013, the high levels of public expenditure and private investment in Malaysia were expected to help to maintain the level of domestic GDP growth in the range of 5%–6%, according to CBM forecasts.

PUBLIC HOLIDAYS

Each state has its own public holidays, and the following federal holidays are also observed:

2014: 13 January* (Mouloud, Prophet Muhammad's Birthday), 31 January† (Chinese New Year), 1 May (Labour Day), 13 May (Vesak Day), 7 June (Official Birthday of HM the Yang di-Pertuan Agong), 28–29 July* (Hari Raya Puasa, end of Ramadan), 31 August (National Independence Day), 16 September (Malaysia Day), 4 October* (Hari Raya Haji, Feast of the Sacrifice), 23 October‡ (Deepavali), 24 October* (Muharram, Islamic New Year), 25 December (Christmas Day).

* These holidays are dependent on the Islamic lunar calendar and may vary by one or two days from the dates given.

† The first two days of the first moon of the lunar calendar.

‡ Except Labuan and Sarawak.

Statistical Survey

Sources (unless otherwise stated): Department of Statistics, Blok C6, Parcel C, Pusat Pentadbiran Kerajaan Persekutuan, 62514 Putrajaya; tel. (3) 88857000; fax (3) 88889248; e-mail jpbpo@stats.gov.my; internet www.statistics.gov.my; Bank Negara Malaysia (Central Bank of Malaysia), Jalan Dato' Onn, POB 10922, 50929 Kuala Lumpur; tel. (3) 26988044; fax (3) 26912990; e-mail info@bnm.gov.my; internet www.bnm.gov.my; Departments of Statistics, Kuching and Kota Kinabalu.
Note: Unless otherwise indicated, statistics refer to all states of Malaysia.

Area and Population

AREA, POPULATION AND DENSITY

Area (sq km)	
Peninsular Malaysia	131,554
Sabah (incl. Labuan)	74,286
Sarawak	124,450
Total	330,290*
Population (census results)†	
5–20 July 2000	23,274,690
6 July 2010	
Males	14,562,638
Females	13,771,497
Total	28,334,135
Population (official estimates at mid-year)	
2011	28,964,300
2012	29,336,800
Density (per sq km) at mid-2012	88.8

* 127,526 sq miles.
† Including adjustment for underenumeration; enumerated totals were 22,198,276 in 2000 and 27,565,821 in 2010.

POPULATION BY AGE AND SEX
(population at 2010 census)

	Males	Females	Total
0–14	4,018,281	3,809,626	7,827,907
15–64	9,855,411	9,223,477	19,078,888
65 and over	688,946	738,394	1,427,340
Total	14,562,638	13,771,497	28,334,135

PRINCIPAL ETHNIC GROUPS
(at 2010 census)

	Peninsular Malaysia	Sabah*	Sarawak	Total
Malays and other indigenous groups	13,735,752	2,027,903	1,759,853	17,523,508
Chinese	5,509,302	305,688	577,646	6,392,636
Indians	1,892,322	8,094	7,411	1,907,827
Others	130,205	50,042	9,138	189,385
Non-Malaysians	1,301,764	901,923	117,092	2,320,779
Total	22,569,345	3,293,650	2,471,140	28,334,135

* Including the Federal Territory of Labuan.

ADMINISTRATIVE DIVISIONS
(population at 2010 census)

States	Area (sq km)	Population ('000)	Density (per sq km)	Capital
Johor (Johore)	19,016	3,348.3	176	Johor Bahru
Kedah	9,425	1,947.7	207	Alor Star
Kelantan	15,105	1,539.6	102	Kota Bharu
Melaka (Malacca)	1,652	821.1	497	Melaka
Negeri Sembilan (Negri Sembilan)	6,657	1,021.1	153	Seremban
Pahang	35,965	1,500.8	42	Kuantan
Perak	21,022	2,352.7	112	Ipoh
Perlis	795	231.5	291	Kangar
Pulau Pinang (Penang)	1,031	1,561.4	1,514	George Town
Sabah	73,902	3,206.7	43	Kota Kinabalu

—continued	Area (sq km)	Population ('000)	Density (per sq km)	Capital
Sarawak	124,450	2,471.1	20	Kuching
Selangor	7,930	5,462.1	689	Shah Alam
Terengganu (Trengganu)	12,956	1,036.0	80	Kuala Terengganu
Federal Territories				
Kuala Lumpur	243	1,674.6	6,891	—
Labuan	92	86.9	945	—
Putrajaya	49	72.4	1,478	—
Total	330,290	28,334.1	86	

PRINCIPAL TOWNS
(population at 2000 census)

Kuala Lumpur (capital)	1,305,792	Sabang Jaya	447,183
Johor Bahru	642,944	Shah Alam	314,440
Kelang (Klang)	626,699	Kota Kinabalu	306,920
Ipoh	536,832	Seremban	290,709
Petaling Jaya	432,619	Kuantan	288,727
Kuching	422,240	Sandakan	276,791

2010 census: Kuala Lumpur 1,674,621.

BIRTHS AND DEATHS*

	Registered live births		Registered deaths	
	Number	Rate (per 1,000)	Number	Rate (per 1,000)
2004	477,800	19.1	112,700	4.5
2005	469,200	18.5	113,700	4.5
2006	465,100	18.1	115,100	4.5
2007	472,000	18.1	118,200	4.5
2008	487,300	18.4	124,900	4.7
2009	496,300	18.5	130,100	4.8
2010†	475,800	17.5	129,300	4.8

* Numbers are rounded to nearest 100.
† Preliminary.

Life expectancy (years at birth, official estimates, 2011): Males 72.0; females 77.1.

ECONOMICALLY ACTIVE POPULATION*
(sample surveys, ISIC major divisions, '000 persons aged 15 to 64 years)

	2009	2010	2011
Agriculture, hunting, forestry and fishing	1,471.1	1,674.2	1,450.5
Mining and quarrying	62.7	56.8	73.5
Manufacturing	1,807.1	1,972.3	2,074.8
Electricity, gas and water	58.1	116.1	121.3
Construction	1,015.9	1,121.0	1,180.2
Wholesale and retail trade; repair of motor vehicles, motorcycles and personal and household goods	1,831.8	1,865.1	1,969.1
Hotels and restaurants	800.5	857.4	940.5
Transport, storage and communications	592.0	705.8	770.1
Financial intermediation	271.5	305.2	299.0
Real estate, renting and business activities	601.9	677.1	818.4

—*continued*	2009	2010	2011
Public administration and defence; compulsory social security . .	813.9	778.9	743.8
Education	731.4	773.2	782.9
Health and social work . . .	271.7	278.0	379.9
Other community, social and personal service activities . .	303.3	270.6	267.8
Private households with employed persons	262.5	321.1	248.8
Extra-territorial organizations and bodies	1.7	4.0	2.5
Total employed	10,897.3	11,776.8	12,123.0
Unemployed	418.0	395.8	382.8
Total labour force	11,315.3	12,172.6	12,505.8

* Excluding members of the armed forces.

Health and Welfare

KEY INDICATORS

Total fertility rate (children per woman, 2010)	2.6
Under-5 mortality rate (per 1,000 live births, 2010) . . .	6
HIV/AIDS (% of persons aged 15–49, 2009) . . .	0.5
Physicians (per 1,000 head, 2008)	0.9
Hospital beds (per 1,000 head, 2010)	1.8
Health expenditure (2009): US $ per head (PPP) . . .	629
Health expenditure (2009): % of GDP . . .	4.6
Health expenditure (2009): public (% of total)	55.7
Access to sanitation (% of persons, 2010)	96
Total carbon dioxide emissions ('000 metric tons, 2008) . .	208,267.3
Carbon dioxide emissions per head (metric tons, 2008) . .	7.6
Human Development Index (2011): ranking	61
Human Development Index (2011): value	0.761

For sources and definitions, see explanatory note on p. vi.

Agriculture

PRINCIPAL CROPS
('000 metric tons)

	2009	2010	2011
Rice, paddy	2,511	2,465	2,665
Maize	33	48	50
Sweet potatoes	13	23	24
Cassava (Manioc)	69	37	39
Sugar cane*	850	800	800
Coconuts	450	550	578
Oil palm fruit*	87,825	87,825	87,825
Cabbages	61	144	144
Tomatoes	30	134	134
Cucumbers and gherkins . . .	76	61	61
Watermelons	239	236	237
Bananas	280	333	334
Pineapples	358	331	333
Papayas	46	45	45
Coffee, green	16	16	16
Cocoa beans	18	19*	16*
Pepper	23	19*	19*
Natural rubber	857	899*	997*

* FAO estimate(s).

Aggregate production ('000 metric tons, may include official, semi-official or estimated data): Total cereals 2,547 in 2009, 2,512 in 2010, 2,715 in 2011; Total oilcrops 19,737 in 2009, 19,090 in 2010, 21,015 in 2011; Total vegetables (incl. melons) 873 in 2009, 1,207 in 2010, 1,213 in 2011; Total fruits (excl. melons) 1,030 in 2009, 1,074 in 2010, 1,079 in 2011.

Source: FAO.

LIVESTOCK
('000 head, year ending September)

	2009	2010	2011*
Cattle	890	910	925
Buffaloes	131	130	130
Goats	506	538	545
Sheep	130	128	125
Pigs	1,726	1,711	1,695
Chickens	208,333	225,790	230,000
Ducks*	48,000	48,200	48,900

* FAO estimates.

Source: FAO.

LIVESTOCK PRODUCTS
('000 metric tons)

	2009	2010	2011
Cattle meat*	23.2	24.9	25.9
Buffalo meat*	4.0	4.0	4.0
Pig meat	206.0	234.0	231.3*
Chicken meat	1,202.0	1,295.6	1,315.0*
Duck meat*	107.9	109.0	112.6
Cows' milk*	62.3	63.0	63.0
Buffaloes' milk*	10.7	11.2	11.2
Hen eggs	510.0	540.4	540.4*
Other poultry eggs*	13.9	14.0	14.0

* FAO estimate(s).

Source: FAO.

Forestry

ROUNDWOOD REMOVALS
('000 cubic metres, excl. bark)

	2008	2009	2010
Sawlogs, veneer logs and logs for sleepers	21,244	18,714	18,202
Pulpwood*	703	703	703
Other industrial roundwood . .	798	710	797
Fuel wood*	2,908	2,858	2,810
Total*	25,653	22,985	22,512

* FAO estimates.

2011: Production assumed to be unchanged from 2010 (FAO estimates).

Source: FAO.

SAWNWOOD PRODUCTION
('000 cubic metres, incl. railway sleepers)

	2009	2010	2011
Total (all broadleaved)* . . .	3,875	4,321	3,875

* Unofficial figures.

Source: FAO.

Fishing

('000 metric tons, live weight)

	2008	2009	2010
Capture	1,398.9	1,397.7	1,433.4
Indian scad	96.9	92.0	82.8
Indian mackerels	170.3	185.5	186.2
Other marine fishes	939.8	903.3	947.5
Natantian decapods	54.6	61.1	63.2
Squids	56.4	56.2	50.1
Aquaculture*	243.1	333.4	373.2
Torpedo-shaped catfishes	41.5	83.7	63.2
Whiteleg shrimp*	36.5	51.9	68.1
Blood cockle	61.1	64.9	78.0
Total catch*	1,642.0	1,731.1	1,806.6

* FAO estimates.

Note: Figures exclude crocodiles, recorded by number rather than by weight. The number of estuarine crocodiles caught was: 1,043 in 2008; 587 in 2009; 861 in 2010. Also excluded are shells and corals. Catches of turban shells (metric tons, FAO estimates) were: 80 in 2008–10. Catches of hard corals (metric tons, FAO estimates) were: 4,000 in 2008–10.

Source: FAO.

Mining

PRODUCTION
(metric tons, unless otherwise indicated)

	2009	2010	2011
Tin-in-concentrates	2,412	2,642	3,343
Bauxite	263,432	124,474	188,141
Iron ore*	1,470,186	3,465,895	7,695,577
Kaolin	463,736	473,273	404,237
Gold (kg)	2,794	3,766	4,242
Hard coal	2,122,651	2,399,699	2,843,532
Ilmenite*†	15,983	16,947	28,782
Crude petroleum ('000 barrels)	240,479	232,965	207,969
Natural gas (net production, million cu ft)	2,119,356	2,159,533	2,164,983
Zirconium*‡	1,145	1,261	n.a.

* Figures refer to the gross weight of ores and concentrates.
† Concentrate from amang retreatment plants.
‡ Source: US Geological Survey.

Industry

SELECTED PRODUCTS
('000 metric tons, unless otherwise indicated)

	2009	2010	2011
Canned fish, frozen shrimps/ prawns	47.7	41.8	38.9
Palm oil (crude)	17,565	16,994	18,300
Refined sugar	1,488.8	1,661.7	1,688.6
Soft drinks ('000 litres)	1,667.0	2,980.7	3,357.3
Cigarettes (metric tons)	20,892	20,935	23,604
Woven cotton fabrics (million metres)	166.3	172.7	276.7
Veneer sheets ('000 cu metres)	753.5	1,016.6	912.4
Plywood ('000 cu metres)	3,655.2	4,094.6	3,797.0
Kerosene and jet fuel	3,402.8	3,350.4	3,559.7
Liquefied petroleum gas	3,265.3	3,054.6	3,036.3
Inner tubes and tyres ('000)	27,647	30,105	30,263
Rubber gloves (million pairs)	23,132.7	26,257.3	30,897.8
Earthen brick and cement roofing tiles (million)	311.6	528.4	739.7
Cement	19,457	19,762	21,198

—continued	2009	2010	2011
Iron and steel bars and rods	1,890.7	2,217.0	2,562.3
Television receivers ('000)	6,361.8	13,163.3	13,966.5
Radio receivers ('000)	58,410	57,350	47,889
Semiconductors (million)	14,885	17,997	16,281
Electronic transistors (million)	29,271	34,184	34,189
Integrated circuits (million)	23,279	38,007	33,380
Passenger motor cars ('000)*	409.4	474.7	441.7
Commercial vehicles ('000)*	67.6	72.6	65.7
Motorcycles and scooters ('000)	306.0	421.7	486.9
Electric energy (million kWh)†	107,116	115,144	119,018

* Vehicles assembled from imported parts.
† Source: Asian Development Bank.

Tin (smelter production of primary metal, metric tons): 31,691 in 2008; 36,407 in 2009; 38,737 in 2010 (Source: US Geological Survey).

Finance

CURRENCY AND EXCHANGE RATES

Monetary Units
100 sen = 1 ringgit Malaysia (RM—also formerly Malaysian dollar).

Sterling, US Dollar and Euro Equivalents (31 December 2012)
£1 sterling = RM 4.8260;
US $1 = RM 3.0583;
€1 = RM 4.0351;
RM 100 = £20.72 = US $32.70 = €24.78.

Average Exchange Rate (ringgit Malaysia per US $)
2010   3.221
2011   3.060
2012   3.089

FEDERAL BUDGET
(RM million)

Revenue	2010	2011*	2012†
Tax revenue	109,515	129,182	135,618
Taxes on income and profits	79,009	96,457	102,099
Companies (excl. petroleum)	36,266	43,970	47,470
Individuals	17,805	19,696	21,347
Petroleum	18,713	25,993	26,182
Export duties	1,810	2,038	2,114
Import duties	1,966	1,976	1,985
Excises on goods	11,770	11,783	11,881
Sales tax	8,171	8,605	8,965
Service tax	3,926	4,968	5,385
Others	2,863	3,355	3,189
Other revenue	50,138	54,193	51,288
Total	159,653	183,375	186,906

Expenditure	2010	2011*	2012†
Emoluments	46,663	49,913	52,017
Pensions and gratuities	11,515	12,957	12,088
Debt service charges	15,621	18,517	20,453
Supplies and services	23,841	29,532	30,480
Subsidies	23,106	32,798	33,197
Grants and transfers to state governments	4,689	5,511	5,846
Other expenditure	26,198	31,055	27,503
Total	151,633	180,283	181,584

* Estimates.
† Budget allocations.

FEDERAL DEVELOPMENT EXPENDITURE
(RM million)

	2009	2010	2011
Defence and security	3,956	3,970	4,569
Social services	17,388	20,784	12,607
Education	10,827	12,046	7,735
Health	2,575	3,780	2,207
Housing	1,395	1,333	762
Economic services	26,440	26,121	28,156
Agriculture and rural			
development	5,508	2,920	1,128
Public utilities	2,899	5,286	6,013
Trade and industry . . .	4,916	6,987	8,364
Transport	9,450	8,665	10,140
General administration . . .	1,731	1,917	1,085
Sub-total	49,515	52,792	46,416
Less Loan recoveries	519	1,496	1,082
Total	48,997	51,296	45,334

INTERNATIONAL RESERVES
(US $ million at 31 December)

	2009	2010	2011
Gold (national valuation) . .	1,281	1,641	1,838
IMF special drawing rights . .	2,124	2,088	1,973
Reserve position in IMF . . .	442	471	843
Foreign exchange	92,865	102,325	128,964
Total	96,712	106,525	133,618

Source: IMF, *International Financial Statistics*.

MONEY SUPPLY
(RM million at 31 December)

	2009	2010	2011
Currency outside depository			
corporations	43,438	47,685	53,488
Transferable deposits . . .	170,431	192,100	219,439
Other deposits	749,555	798,978	919,560
Securities other than shares . .	28,628	26,183	28,058
Broad money	992,052	1,064,945	1,220,545

Source: IMF, *International Financial Statistics*.

COST OF LIVING
(Consumer Price Index; base 2005 = 100)

	2008	2009	2010
Food and non-alcoholic beverages .	115.9	120.7	123.6
Alcoholic beverages and tobacco .	123.6	131.2	136.3
Clothing and footwear . . .	96.8	95.9	94.6
Rent and other housing costs,			
heating and lighting . . .	104.4	105.9	107.1
Furniture, domestic appliances,			
tools and maintenance . . .	105.3	108.4	109.2
Medical care	106.0	108.4	110.1
Transport	123.6	112.0	113.8
Communications	96.8	96.3	96.1
Education	105.8	108.3	110.1
All items (incl. others) . . .	111.4	112.1	114.0

2011 (base 2010 = 100): Food and non-alcoholic beverages 104.8; Alcoholic beverages and tobacco 104.6; Clothing and footwear 99.8; Rent and other housing costs, heating and lighting 101.8; Furniture, domestic appliances, tools and maintenance 101.8; Medical care 102.7; Transport 104.4; Communications 99.7; Education 102.2; All items (incl. others) 103.2.

NATIONAL ACCOUNTS
(RM million at current prices)

Expenditure on the Gross Domestic Product

	2009	2010	2011
Government final consumption			
expenditure	93,017	96,947	114,750
Private final consumption			
expenditure	348,168	377,631	418,473
Changes in inventories . . .	−29,517	7,132	12,795
Gross fixed capital formation . .	156,660	176,903	195,002
Total domestic expenditure .	568,328	658,613	741,020
Exports of goods and services . .	651,671	745,311	806,705
Less Imports of goods and services	507,142	608,887	666,645
GDP in purchasers' values .	712,857	795,037	881,080
GDP at constant 2005 prices .	629,885	674,946	709,261

Gross Domestic Product by Economic Activity

	2009	2010	2011
Agriculture, forestry and fishing .	65,719	82,612	104,581
Mining and quarrying	81,342	86,545	91,786
Manufacturing	169,661	195,280	214,626
Electricity, gas and water . . .	17,852	18,994	20,144
Construction	23,187	25,893	28,306
Trade	96,032	106,634	120,180
Restaurants and hotels . . .	19,231	21,370	23,414
Transport and storage	24,569	26,468	28,273
Communications	22,332	24,664	26,812
Finance and insurance . . .	57,460	61,725	64,166
Real estate and business services .	36,797	39,987	42,876
Government services	56,588	59,984	67,808
Other services	35,123	37,207	39,398
Sub-total	705,893	787,363	872,370
Import duties	6,964	7,672	8,711
GDP in purchasers' values .	712,857	795,037	881,080

BALANCE OF PAYMENTS
(RM million)

	2009	2010	2011
Exports of goods f.o.b.	553,290	640,043	696,614
Imports of goods f.o.b.	−412,565	−505,317	−548,543
Trade balance	140,725	134,726	148,071
Exports of services	98,381	105,268	110,090
Imports of services	−94,578	−103,570	−118,101
Balance on goods and services	144,529	136,424	140,060
Other income received	39,630	38,297	52,449
Other income paid	−53,844	−64,811	−74,421
Balance on goods, services and			
income	130,314	109,910	118,088
Current transfers received . .	3,738	1,855	4,655
Current transfers paid	−23,326	−23,686	−25,634
Current balance	110,727	88,079	97,110
Capital account (net)	−126	−165	−193
Direct investment (net)	−22,315	−13,611	−10,072
Portfolio investment (net) . . .	588	47,756	25,722
Other investment (net) . . .	−58,447	−53,973	6,604
Net errors and omissions . . .	−16,596	−70,713	−24,487
Overall balance	13,831	−2,628	94,682

External Trade

PRINCIPAL COMMODITIES
(RM million)

Imports c.i.f.	2009	2010	2011
Capital goods*	65,769	73,769	80,171
Intermediate goods	297,340	365,681	385,739
Miscellaneous industrial supplies, processed . . .	94,001	115,854	132,883
Parts and accessories of capital goods (excl. transportation equipment)	132,962	161,945	143,482
Consumption goods	31,427	34,477	41,024
Total (incl. others)†	434,670	528,828	573,626

Exports f.o.b.	2009	2010	2011
Palm oil	36,329	44,730	60,310
Crude petroleum and condensates	25,360	30,765	31,982
Liquefied natural gas . . .	29,018	38,742	49,963
Semiconductors	93,057	97,975	107,090
Electronic components	87,686	96,438	75,068
Consumer electrical products . .	18,793	25,804	22,866
Industrial and commercial electrical products . . .	24,606	22,731	24,508
Electrical industrial machinery and equipment	21,641	24,655	27,656
Chemicals and chemical products .	34,079	41,557	47,760
Metal manufactures	22,645	26,201	31,011
Total (incl. others)	552,518	638,822	697,862

* Figures net of re-exports.
† Including re-exports.

PRINCIPAL TRADING PARTNERS
(RM million)

Imports c.i.f.	2009	2010	2011
Australia	9,480	10,188	12,810
China, People's Republic . . .	61,026	66,430	75,706
France	7,058	6,255	9,513
Germany	18,411	21,332	21,976
Hong Kong	10,811	12,681	13,601
India	7,872	7,978	10,191
Indonesia	23,019	29,390	35,113
Japan	54,316	66,535	65,362
Korea, Republic	20,132	28,687	23,271
Philippines	4,006	11,308	4,781
Singapore	49,359	60,278	73,699
Taiwan	18,469	23,829	27,133
Thailand	26,299	32,972	34,480
United Kingdom	5,997	5,826	6,141
USA	48,834	56,259	55,405
Total (incl. others)	434,670	528,828	573,626

Exports f.o.b.	2009	2010	2011
Australia	20,190	24,016	25,683
China, People's Republic . . .	67,359	80,105	91,551
France	5,448	7,109	8,066
Germany	14,854	17,346	18,456
Hong Kong	29,113	32,408	31,253
India	17,306	20,934	28,154
Indonesia	17,235	18,090	20,841
Japan	53,345	66,763	81,368
Korea, Republic	20,318	24,330	26,252
Netherlands	18,525	20,216	19,281
Philippines	6,956	9,968	10,945
Singapore	77,009	85,253	88,191
Taiwan	14,520	20,209	23,228
Thailand	29,808	34,136	35,742
United Kingdom	7,082	7,195	7,157
USA	60,811	60,951	57,653
Total (incl. others)	552,518	638,822	697,862

Transport

RAILWAYS
(traffic)

	2009	2010	2011
Passengers carried ('000) . . .	4,451	4,386	4,279
Passenger-km (million) . . .	1,526	1,532	1,428
Freight ('000 metric tons) . . .	5,388	5,531	6,096
Freight ton-km (million) . . .	1,384	1,483	1,536

ROAD TRAFFIC
(registered motor vehicles at 31 December)

	2008	2009	2010
Passenger cars	8,056,999	8,601,808	9,217,881
Buses and coaches	64,050	66,581	69,149
Lorries and vans	909,243	936,222	966,177
Motorcycles and mopeds . . .	8,487,451	8,940,230	9,441,907

Source: IRF, *World Road Statistics*.

SHIPPING
Flag Registered Fleet
(at 31 December)

	2010	2011	2012
Number of vessels	2,037	2,073	2,168
Total displacement ('000 grt) . .	9,703.3	9,770.0	9,481.7

Source: Lloyd's List Intelligence (www.lloydslistintelligence.com).

Sea-borne Freight Traffic*
(Peninsular Malaysia, international and coastwise, '000 metric tons)

	2009	2010	2011
Goods loaded	101,664	112,404	125,472
Goods unloaded	110,892	136,824	153,048

* Including transshipments.

Source: UN, *Monthly Bulletin of Statistics*.

CIVIL AVIATION
(traffic on scheduled services)

	2007	2008	2009
Kilometres flown (million) . .	311	302	297
Passengers carried ('000) . . .	22,762	22,421	23,766
Passenger-km (million) . . .	49,942	47,323	45,532
Total ton-km (million)	7,161	6,758	6,207

Source: UN, *Statistical Yearbook*.

2010: Passengers carried ('000) 26,255 (Source: World Bank, World Development Indicators database).

Tourism

TOURIST ARRIVALS BY COUNTRY OF RESIDENCE*

	2009	2010	2011
Australia	533,382	580,695	558,411
Brunei	1,061,357	1,124,406	1,239,404
China, People's Republic (incl. Hong Kong and Macao)	1,019,756	1,130,261	1,250,536
India	589,838	690,849	693,056
Indonesia	2,405,360	2,506,509	2,134,381
Singapore	12,733,082	13,042,004	13,372,647
Thailand	1,449,262	1,458,678	1,442,048
Total (incl. others)	23,646,191	24,577,196	24,714,324

* Including Singapore residents crossing the frontier by road through the Johore Causeway.

Source: Malaysia Tourism Promotion Board.

Tourism receipts (US $ million, excl. passenger transport): 15,772 in 2009; 18,276 in 2010; 18,259 in 2011 (provisional) (Source: World Tourism Organization).

Communications Media

	2009	2010	2011
Telephones ('000 main lines in use)	4,524	4,573	4,243
Mobile cellular telephones ('000 subscribers)	30,144	33,859	36,661
Internet subscribers ('000)	5,591.8	n.a.	n.a.
Broadband subscribers ('000)	1,671.8	2,078.5	2,147.8

Personal computers: 6,040,000 (231.5 per 1,000 persons) in 2006.

Source: International Telecommunication Union.

Education

(at 30 June 2008 unless otherwise indicated)

	Institutions	Teachers	Students
Primary	7,644	210,912	3,154,090
Secondary	2,181	159,019	2,310,660
Regular	1,845	139,740	2,126,146
Fully residential	54	3,368	33,289
Technical	90	7,713	69,006
Religious	55	3,306	38,865
Special	4	190	773
Special Model	11	879	10,437*
Sports	2	174	912†
Tertiary‡	48	14,960	210,724
Universities	9	7,823	97,103
Teacher training	31	3,220	46,019
MARA Institute of Technology	1	2,574	42,174

* 2004 figure.
† 2003 figure.
‡ 1995 figures.

2009: *Tertiary:* Institutions 75; Teachers 37,534; Students 589,407.

2011 (provisional): *Primary:* Institutions 7,709; Teachers 232,095; Students 2,859,921; *Secondary:* Institutions 2,271; Teachers 176,669; Students 2,296,034.

Source: Ministry of Education, Putrajaya.

Pupil-teacher ratio (primary education, UNESCO estimate): 13.2 in 2008/09 (Source: UNESCO Institute for Statistics).

Adult literacy rate (UNESCO estimates): 93.1% (males 95.4%; females 90.7%) in 2010 (Source: UNESCO Institute for Statistics).

Directory

The Government

SUPREME HEAD OF STATE

HM Yang di-Pertuan Agong: HRH Sultan Tuanku Haji ABDUL HALIM MU'ADZAM SHAH IBNI AL-MARHUM Sultan BADLISHAH (Sultan of Kedah) (took office 13 December 2011).

Deputy Supreme Head of State

Timbalan Yang di-Pertuan Agong: HRH Sultan MUHAMMAD V (Sultan of Kelantan).

CABINET
(May 2013)

The Government is formed by the Barisan Nasional (National Front), led by the United Malays National Organization (UMNO).

Prime Minister and Minister of Finance I: Dato' Sri MOHD NAJIB BIN Tun Haji ABDUL RAZAK.

Deputy Prime Minister: Tan Sri Dato' Haji MUHYIDDIN BIN MOHD YASSIN.

Ministers in the Prime Minister's Department: Dato' Seri JAMIL KHIR BIN BAHAROM, Dato' Sri ABDUL WAHID BIN OMAR, Dato' Sri IDRIS JALA, Tan Sri Datuk Seri PANGLIMA JOSEPH KURUP, Dato' Seri SHAHIDAN BIN KASSIM, Puan Hajah NANCY BINTI SHUKRI, Datuk JOSEPH ENTULU ANAK BELAUN, Datuk PAUL LOW SENG KUAN.

Minister of Finance II: Dato' Seri Haji AHMAD HUSNI BIN MOHAMAD HANADZLAH.

Minister of Education and Higher Education I: Tan Sri Dato' Haji MUHYIDDIN BIN MOHD YASSIN.

Minister of Education and Higher Education II: Dato' Seri IDRIS BIN JUSOH.

Minister of Defence and Acting Minister of Transport: Dato' Seri HISHAMMUDDIN BIN Tun HUSSEIN.

Minister of Home Affairs: Dato' Seri Dr AHMAD ZAHID BIN HAMID.

Minister of Works: Datuk FADILLAH YUSOF.

Minister of Trade and Industry: Dato' Sri MUSTAPA BIN MOHAMED.

Minister of Foreign Affairs: Dato' Sri ANIFAH BIN Haji AMAN.

Minister of Domestic Trade, Co-operatives and Consumerism: Dato' Haji HASAN BIN MALEK.

Minister of Education and Higher Education I: Tan Sri Dato' Haji MUHYIDDIN BIN MOHD YASSIN.

Minister of Communications and Multimedia: Y. B. Dato' Seri AHMAD SHABERY BIN CHEEK.

Minister of Human Resources: Y. B. Datuk RICHARD RIOT ANAK JAEM.

Minister of Rural and Regional Development: Dato' Seri Haji MOHD SHAFIE BIN Haji APDAL.

Minister of Housing, Local Government and Urban Well-being: Dato' Haji ABDUL RAHMAN BIN DAHLAN.

Minister of Youth and Sports: Tuan KHAIRY JAMALUDDIN BIN ABU BAKAR.

Minister of Health: Datuk Seri Dr S. SUBRAMANIAM.

Minister of Federal Territories: Datuk Seri TENGKU ADNAN BIN TENGKU MANSOR.

Minister of Plantation Industries and Commodities: Dato' Sri DOUGLAS UGGAH EMBAS.

Minister of Energy, Green Technology and Water: Datuk Seri Dr MAXIMUS JOHNITY ONGKILI.

Minister of Agriculture and Agro-Based Industry: Dato' Sri ISMAIL SABRI BIN YAAKOB.

Minister of Tourism and Culture: Dato' Seri MOHAMED NAZRI BIN ABDUL AZIZ.

Minister of Science, Technology and Innovation: Dr EWON EBIN.

Minister of Natural Resources and the Environment: Datuk Seri G. PALANIVEL.

Minister of Women, Family and Community: Datuk Hajah ROHANI BINTI Haji ABDUL KARIM.

MINISTRIES

The new Cabinet was sworn in on 16 May 2013; the reorganization of the Ministries was still pending.

Prime Minister's Office (Jabatan Perdana Menteri): Federal Government Administration Center, Bangunan Perdana Putra, 62502 Putrajaya; tel. (3) 88888000; fax (3) 88883444; e-mail fuad@pmo.gov .my; internet www.pmo.gov.my.

Ministry of Agriculture and Agro-Based Industry: Wisma Tani, 28 Persiaran Perdana, Presint 4, Pusat Pentadbiran Kerajaan Persekutuan, 62624 Putrajaya; tel. (3) 88701000; fax (3) 88886020; e-mail pro@moa.gov.my; internet www.moa.gov.my.

Ministry of Defence (Kementerian Pertahanan): Wisma Pertahanan, Jalan Padang Tembak, 50634 Kuala Lumpur; tel. (3) 26921333; fax (3) 26914163; e-mail szy.ppm@mod.gov.my; internet www.mod .gov.my.

Ministry of Domestic Trade, Co-operatives and Consumerism (Kementerian Perdagangan Dalam Negeri, Koperasi Dan Kepenggunaan): 13 Persianan Perdana, Presint 2, Pusat Pentadbiran Kerajaan Persekutuan, 62623 Putrajaya; tel. (3) 88825500; fax (3) 88825762; e-mail aduan@kpdnkk.gov.my; internet www.kpdnkk .gov.my.

Ministry of Education (Kementerian Pendidikan): Blok E8, Parcel E, Pusat Pentadbiran Kerajaan Persekutuan, 62604 Putrajaya; tel. (3) 88846000; fax (3) 88895235; e-mail kpkpm@moe.gov.my; internet www.moe.gov.my.

Ministry of Energy, Green Technology and Water (Kementerian Tenaga, Teknologi Hijau dan Air): Blok E4–5, Parcel E, Pusat Pentadbiran Kerajaan Persekutuan, 62668 Putrajaya; tel. (3) 80008000; fax (3) 88893712; e-mail webmaster@kettha.gov.my; internet www.kettha.gov.my.

Ministry of Federal Territories and Urban Well-being (Kementerian Wilayah Persekutuan Dan Kesejahteraan Bandar): Aras G-4, Blok 2, Menara PJH, Presint 2, 62100 Putrajaya; tel. (3) 88897888; fax (3) 88880375; e-mail zainor@kwp.gov.my; internet www.kwp.gov.my.

Ministry of Finance (Kementerian Kewangan): Kompleks Kementerian Kewangan, 5 Persiaran Perdana, Presint 2, Pusat Pentadbiran Kerajaan Persekutuan, 62592 Putrajaya; tel. (3) 88823000; fax (3) 88823893; e-mail shafei@treasury.gov.my; internet www .treasury.gov.my.

Ministry of Foreign Affairs (Kementerian Luar Negeri): Wisma Putra, 1 Jalan Wisma Putra, Presint 2, 62602 Putrajaya; tel. (3) 88874000; fax (3) 88891717; e-mail webmaster@kln.gov.my; internet www.kln.gov.my.

Ministry of Health (Kementerian Kesihatan): Blok E1, E6–7 & E10, Parcel E, Pusat Pentadbiran Kerajaan Persekutuan, 62590 Putrajaya; tel. (3) 88833888; fax (3) 26985964; e-mail kkm@moh.gov .my; internet www.moh.gov.my.

Ministry of Higher Education (Kementerian Pengajian Tinggi): Blok E3, Parcel E, Pusat Perbadanan Kerajaan Persekutuan, 62505 Putrajaya; tel. (3) 88835000; fax (3) 88893921; e-mail minister@mohe .gov.my; internet www.portal.mohe.gov.my.

Ministry of Home Affairs (Kementerian Hal Ehwal Dalam Negeri): Blok D1–2, Parcel D, Pusat Pentadbiran Kerajaan Persekutuan, 62546 Putrajaya; tel. (3) 88868000; fax (3) 88891613; e-mail menteri@moha.gov.my; internet www.moha.gov.my.

Ministry of Housing and Local Government (Kementerian Perumahan dan Kerajaan Tempatan): Aras 1–7, Blok K, Pusat Bandar Damansara, 50782 Kuala Lumpur; tel. (3) 20947033; fax (3) 20949720; e-mail pro@kpkt.gov.my; internet www.kpkt.gov.my.

Ministry of Human Resources (Kementerian Sumber Manusia): Tingkat 6–9, Blok D3, Parcel D, Pusat Pentadbiran Kerajaan Persekutuan, 62530 Putrajaya; tel. (3) 88865000; fax (3) 88892381; e-mail ksm1@mohr.gov.my; internet www.mohr.gov.my.

Ministry of Information, Communications and Culture (Kementerian Penerangan Komunikasi Dan Kebudayaan): Tingkat 5, Wisma TV, Angkasapuri, Bukit Putra, 50610 Kuala Lumpur; tel.

(3) 22825333; fax (3) 22848115; e-mail azmi@kpkk.gov.my; internet www.kpkk.gov.my.

Ministry of International Trade and Industry (Kementerian Perdagangan Antarabangsa dan Industri): Blok 10, Kompleks Pejabat Kerajaan, Jalan Duta, 50622 Kuala Lumpur; tel. (3) 62033022; fax (3) 62012337; e-mail webmiti@miti.gov.my; internet www.miti .gov.my.

Ministry of Natural Resources and the Environment (Kementerian Sumber Asli dan Alam Sekitar): Wisma Sumber Asli, 25 Persiaran Perdana, Presint 4, Pusat Pentadbiran Kerajaan Persekutuan, 62574 Putrajaya; tel. (3) 88861111; fax (3) 88892672; e-mail james@nre.gov.my; internet www.nre.gov.my.

Ministry of Plantation Industries and Commodities (Kementerian Perusahaan Perladangan dan Komoditi): Aras 6–13, 15 Persiaran Perdana, Presint 2, Pusat Pentadbiran Kerajaan Persekutuan, 62654 Putrajaya; tel. (3) 88803300; fax (3) 88803441; e-mail aduan@kppk.gov.my; internet www.kppk.gov.my.

Ministry of Rural and Regional Development (Kementerian Kemajuan Luar Bandar dan Wilayah): Aras 32, 47 Persiaran Perdana, Presint 4, 62100 Putrajaya; tel. (3) 88912014; fax (3) 88882026; e-mail sitisarah@rurallink.gov.my; internet www .rurallink.gov.my.

Ministry of Science, Technology and Innovation: Aras 1–7, Blok C4–5, Parcel C, Pusat Pentadbiran Kerajaan Persekutuan, 62662 Putrajaya; tel. (3) 88858000; fax (3) 88889070; e-mail info@ mosti.gov.my; internet www.mosti.gov.my.

Ministry of Tourism (Kementerian Pelancongan): No. 2, Tower 1, Jalan P5/6, Precinct 5, 62200 Putrajaya; tel. (3) 88917000; fax (3) 88917100; e-mail info@motour.gov.my; internet www.motour.gov .my.

Ministry of Transport (Kementerian Pengangkutan): Aras 4–7, Blok D5, Parcel D, Pusat Pentadbiran Kerajaan Persekutuan, 62616 Putrajaya; tel. (3) 88866000; fax (3) 88891569; e-mail woon@mot.gov .my; internet www.mot.gov.my.

Ministry of Women, Family and Community Development (Kementerian Pembangunan Wanita, Keluarga dan Masyarakat): Aras 1–6, Blok E, Kompleks Petabat Kerajaan Bukit Perdana, Jalan Dato' Onn, 50515 Kuala Lumpur; tel. (3) 26930095; fax (3) 26934982; e-mail info@kpwkm.gov.my; internet www.kpwkm.gov.my.

Ministry of Works (Kementerian Kerja Raya): Tingkat 6, Blok B, Kompleks Kerja Raya, Jalan Sultan Salahuddin, 50580 Kuala Lumpur; tel. (3) 27111100; fax (3) 27111590; e-mail pro@kkr.gov .my; internet www.kkr.gov.my.

Ministry of Youth and Sports (Kementerian Belia dan Sukan): Aras 17, Menara KBS, 27 Persiaran Perdana, Presint 4, Pusat Pentadbiran Kerajaan Persekutuan, 62570 Putrajaya; tel. (3) 88713333; fax (3) 88888770; e-mail hanizan@kbs.gov.my; internet www.kbs.gov.my.

Legislature

PARLIAMENT

Dewan Negara
(Senate)

The Senate has 70 members, of whom 26 are elected. Each State Legislative Assembly elects two members. The Supreme Head of State appoints the remaining 44 members, including four from the three Federal Territories.

President: Tan Sri ABU ZAHAR Dato' NIKA UJANG.

Dewan Rakyat
(House of Representatives)

The House of Representatives has a total of 222 members: 165 from Peninsular Malaysia (including 11 from Kuala Lumpur and one from the Federal Territory of Putrajaya), 31 from Sarawak and 26 from Sabah (including one from the Federal Territory of Labuan).

A new Speaker and Deputy Speakers were due to be elected at the first parliamentary session to be held following the general election of 5 May 2013.

Speaker: Tan Sri PANDIKAR AMIN MULIA (outgoing).

Deputy Speakers: Datuk RONALD KIANDEE (outgoing), Datuk Dr WAN JUNAIDI TUANKU JAAFAR (outgoing).

General Election, 5 May 2013

Party	Seats
Barisan Nasional	133
United Malays National Organization	88
Parti Pesaka Bumiputera Bersatu	13
Parti Rakyat Sarawak	7
Malaysian Chinese Association	7
Malaysian Indian Congress	4
Parti Bersatu Sabah	4
Sarawak Progressive Democratic Party	4
United Pasokmomogun Kadazandusun Murut Organisation	3
Parti Gerakan Rakyat Malaysia	1
Parti Bersatu Rakyat Sabah	1
Sarawak United People's Party	1
Pakatan Rakyat	89
Democratic Action Party	38
Parti Keadilan Rakyat	30
Parti Islam se Malaysia	21
Total	**222**

The States

JOHOR
(Capital: Johor Bahru)

Sultan: HRH Tuanku IBRAHIM ISMAIL IBNI AL-MARHUM Sultan ISKANDER.

Menteri Besar: Datuk Seri MOHAMMED KHALED NORDIN.

State Legislative Assembly: Tingkat 1, Bangunan Dato' Jaafar Muhammad, Kota Iskandar, 79503 Nusajaya, Johor Darul Ta'zim; tel. (7) 2666070; fax (7) 2908077; e-mail sukpengurusan@johor.gov .my; internet www.johor.gov.my; 56 seats: Barisan Nasional 38; Pakatan Rakyat 18; elected May 2013.

KEDAH
(Capital: Alor Star)

Council of Regency: appointed by the Sultan of Kedah to fulfil his duties during his tenure as the Yang di-Pertuan Agong; four mems; Chair. Datuk Seri Tuanku ANNUAR Sultan BADLISHAH.

Sultan: HRH Tuanku Haji ABDUL HALIM MU'ADZAM SHAH IBNI AL-MARHUM Sultan BADLISHAH.

Menteri Besar: Dato' Paduka MUKHRIZ BIN TUN Dr MAHATHIR.

State Legislative Assembly: Wisma Darul Aman, Alor Setar, 05150 Kedah; e-mail suk@kedah.gov.my; internet www.kedah.gov .my; 36 seats: Barisan Nasional 21; Pakatan Rakyat 15; elected May 2013.

KELANTAN
(Capital: Kota Bharu)

Sultan: HRH Sultan MUHAMMAD V PETRA.

Menteri Besar: Datok AHMAD YAAKOB.

State Legislative Assembly: Kompleks Kota Darulnaim, 15503 Kota Bharu, Kelantan; tel. (9) 7481957; fax (9) 7443203; e-mail portal@kelantan.gov.my; internet www.kelantan.gov.my; 45 seats: Pakatan Rakyat 33; Barisan Nasional 12; elected May 2013.

MELAKA (MALACCA)
(Capital: Melaka)

Yang di-Pertua Negeri: Tan Sri KHALIL YAAKOB.

Ketua Menteri: Datuk Wira Ir IDRIS HARON.

State Legislative Assembly: Kompleks Seri Negeri, Hang Tuah Jaya, 75450 Ayer Keroh, Melaka; tel. (6) 3333333; fax (6) 2328620; internet www.melaka.gov.my; 28 seats: Barisan Nasional 21; Pakatan Rakyat 7; elected May 2013.

NEGERI SEMBILAN
(Capital: Seremban)

Yang di-Pertuan Besar: Tuanku MUKHRIZ IBNI AL-MARHUM Tuanku MUNAWIR.

Menteri Besar: Dato' Seri Haji MOHAMAD BIN Haji HASAN.

State Legislative Assembly: Tingkat 3, Blok B, Wisma Negeri, Jalan Dato' Abdul Malek, 70503 Seremban, Negeri Sembilan; internet www.ns.gov.my; 36 seats: Barisan Nasional 22; Pakatan Rakyat 14; elected May 2013.

PAHANG
(Capital: Kuantan)

Sultan: HRH Haji AHMAD SHAH AL-MUSTA'IN BILLAH IBNI AL-MARHUM Sultan ABU BAKAR RI'AYATUDDIN AL-MU'ADZAM SHAH.

Menteri Besar: Dato' Sri Diraja Haji ADNAN BIN Haji YAAKOB.

State Legislative Assembly: Pejabat Setiausaha Kerajaan, Negeri Pahang, Wisma Sri Pahang, 25503 Kuantan, Pahang Darul Makmur; tel. (9) 5126600; fax (9) 5157448; e-mail webmast@pahang.gov .my; internet www.pahang.gov.my; 42 seats: Barisan Nasional 30; Pakatan Rakyat 12; elected May 2013.

PERAK
(Capital: Ipoh)

Sultan: HRH Sultan Tuanku AZLAN MUHIBUDDIN SHAH IBNI AL-MARHUM Sultan YUSUF IZUDDIN GHAFARULLAH SHAH.

Menteri Besar: Dato' Seri Dr ZAMBRY ABDUL KADIR.

State Legislative Assembly: Pejabat Setiausaha Kerajaan Negeri Perak, Bangunan Perak Darul Ridzuan, Bahagian Majlis, Jalan Panglima Bukit Gantang Wahab, 30000 Ipoh; tel. (5) 2095000; fax (5) 2555026; e-mail webadmin@perak.gov.my; internet www.perak.gov .my; 59 seats: Barisan Nasional 31; Pakatan Rakyat 28; elected May 2013.

PERLIS
(Capital: Kangar)

Raja: HM Tuanku SYED SIRAJUDDIN IBNI AL-MARHUM SYED PUTRA JAMALULLAIL.

Menteri Besar: AZLAN MAN.

State Legislative Assembly: Tingkat 4, Kompleks Dewan Undangan Negeri Perlis, 01990 Kangar, Perlis; tel. (4) 9738800; fax (4) 9775863; e-mail sukpls@perlis.gov.my; internet www.perlis.gov.my; 15 seats: Barisan Nasional 13; Pakatan Rakyat 2; elected May 2013.

PULAU PINANG (PENANG)
(Capital: George Town)

Yang di-Pertua Negeri: HE Tun Dato' Seri Dr ABDUL RAHMAN BIN Haji ABBAS.

Ketua Menteri: LIM GUAN ENG.

State Legislative Assembly: Dewan Undangan Negeri Pulau Pinang, Lebuh Light, 10200 Georgetown, Pulau Pinang; tel. (4) 2611955; fax (4) 2636008; internet dun.penang.gov.my; 40 seats: Pakatan Rakyat 30; Barisan Nasional 10; elected May 2013.

SABAH
(Capital: Kota Kinabalu)

Yang di-Pertua Negeri: HE Tun Datuk Seri Haji JUHAR Haji MAHIRUDDIN.

Ketua Menteri: Datuk Seri MUSA Haji AMAN.

State Legislative Assembly: Dewan Undangan Negeri Sabah, Aras 4, Bangunan Dewan Undangan Negeri Sabah, Peti Surat 11247, 88813 Kota Kinabalu; tel. (88) 427533; fax (88) 427333; e-mail pejduns@sabah.gov.my; internet www.sabah.gov.my; 60 seats: Barisan Nasional 48; Pakatan Rakyat 11; Independent 1; elected May 2013.

SARAWAK
(Capital: Kuching)

Yang di-Pertua Negeri: HE Tun Datuk Patinggi Abang Haji MUHAMMED SALAHUDDIN.

Ketua Menteri: Pehin Sri Haji ABDUL TAIB BIN MAHMUD.

State Legislative Assembly: Bangunan Dewan Undangan Negeri, Petra Jaya, 93502 Kuching, Sarawak; tel. (82) 441955; fax (82) 440628; e-mail supiantt@sarawak.gov.my; internet www.dun .sarawak.gov.my; f. 1867; 71 seats: Barisan Nasional 55; Pakatan Rakyat 15; Independent 1; elected April 2011.

SELANGOR
(Capital: Shah Alam)

Sultan: Tuanku IDRIS SHARAFUDDIN ALHAJ SHAH.

Menteri Besar: Tan Sri Dato' Seri ABDUL KHALID BIN IBRAHIM.

State Legislative Assembly: Tingkat 2, Bangunan Sultan Salahuddin Abdul Aziz Shah, 40503 Shah Alam, Selangor Darul Ehsan; e-mail webadmin@selangor.gov.my; internet www.selangor.gov.my; 56 seats: Pakatan Rakyat 44; Barisan Nasional 12; elected May 2013.

TERENGGANU
(Capital: Kuala Terengganu)

Sultan: HRH Tuanku MUHAMMAD ISMAIL Sultan MIZAN ZAINAL ABIDIN.

Menteri Besar: Dato' Seri Haji AHMAD BIN SAID.

State Legislative Assembly: Wisma Darul Iman, 20503 Kuala Terengganu; tel. (9) 6231957; e-mail webmaster@terengganu.gov .my; internet www.terengganu.gov.my; 32 seats: Barisan Nasional 17; Pakatan Rakyat 15; elected May 2013.

Election Commission

Suruhanjaya Pilihan Raya (SPR): Aras 4–5, Blok C7, Parcel C, Pusat Pentadbiran Kerajaan Persekutuan, 62690 Putrajaya; tel. (3) 88856500; fax (3) 88889117; e-mail spr@spr.gov.my; internet www .spr.gov.my; f. 1957; Chair. Tan Sri Dato' Seri ABD AL-AZIZ BIN MUHAMMAD YUSOF.

Political Organizations

Barisan Nasional (BN) (National Front): Suites 1–2, Tingkat 8, Menara Dato' Onn, Pusat Dagangan Dunia Putra, Jalan Tun Ismail, 50480 Kuala Lumpur; tel. (3) 40451071; fax (3) 40451075; internet www.barisannasional.org.my; f. 1973; the governing multiracial coalition of 13 parties; Chair. Dato' Sri MOHD NAJIB BIN Tun Haji ABDUL RAZAK; Sec.-Gen. Datuk Sri Tengku ADNAN Tengku MANSOR; comprises:

Liberal Democratic Party: Tingkat 2, B10–3 and B11–3, Kepayan Perdana Office Lot, off Jalan Lintas Kepayan, 88200 Kota Kinabalu, Sabah; tel. (88) 413286; fax (88) 413289; internet ldp.org .my; f. 1989; Chinese-dominated; Pres. Datuk LIEW VUI KEONG; Sec.-Gen. TEO CHEE KANG.

Malaysian Chinese Association (MCA): Wisma MCA, Tingkat 8, 163 Jalan Ampang, POB 10626, 50450 Kuala Lumpur; tel. (3) 21618044; fax (3) 21619772; e-mail info@mca.org.my; internet www.mca.org.my; f. 1949; 900,000 mems; Pres. Datuk Seri Dr CHUA SOI LEK; Sec.-Gen. Dato' Seri KONG CHO HA.

Malaysian Indian Congress (MIC): Menara Manickavasagam, Tingkat 6, 1 Jalan Rahmat, 50350 Kuala Lumpur; tel. (3) 40424377; fax (3) 40427236; e-mail michq@mic.org.my; internet www.mic.org.my; f. 1946; 401,000 mems (1992); Pres. Datuk G. PALANIVEL; Sec.-Gen. Dr S. MURUGESAN.

Parti Bersatu Rakyat Sabah (PBRS) (United Sabah People's Party): POB 20148, Luyang, Kota Kinabalu, 88761 Sabah; tel. and fax (88) 269282; f. 1994; breakaway faction of the PBS; mostly Christian Kadazans; Leader Datuk JOSEPH KURUP.

Parti Bersatu Sabah (PBS) (Sabah United Party): Blok M, Lot 4, Tingkat 2–3, Donggongon New Township, 89500 Penampang, Sabah; tel. (88) 702111; fax (88) 718067; internet www .pbs-sabah.org; f. 1985; left the BN in 1990; rejoined in Jan. 2002; multiracial party; Pres. Datuk Seri JOSEPH PAIRIN KITINGAN; Sec.-Gen. HENRYNUS AMIN.

Parti Gerakan Rakyat Malaysia (GERAKAN) (Malaysian People's Movement): Tingkat 5, Menara PGRM, 8 Jalan Pudu Ulu, Cheras, 56100 Kuala Lumpur; tel. (3) 92876868; fax (3) 92878866; e-mail gerakan@gerakan.org.my; internet www .gerakan.org.my; f. 1968; 300,000 mems; Pres. Tan Sri KOH TSU KOON; Sec.-Gen. TENG CHANG YEOW.

Parti Pesaka Bumiputera Bersatu (PBB) (United Traditional Bumiputra Party): Lot 401, Jalan Bako, POB 1053, 93722 Kuching, Sarawak; tel. (82) 448299; fax (82) 448294; internet www .pesakabumiputerabersatu.org; f. 1983; Pres. Tan Sri Datuk Patinggi Amar Haji ABDUL TAIB MAHMUD; Dep. Pres. Datuk ALFRED JABU AK NUMPANG.

Parti Progresif Penduduk Malaysia (PPP) (People's Progressive Party): 74 Jalan Rotan, Kampung Attap, 50460 Kuala Lumpur; tel. (3) 22738199; fax (3) 22736199; e-mail kvs@ppp.org.my; internet www.ppp.org.my; f. 1953; est. as Perak Progressive Party; joined the BN in 1972; Pres. Datuk M. KAYVEAS.

Parti Rakyat Sarawak (PRS) (Sarawak People's Party): Lot 9162, Tingkat 1–3, Jalan Pending KTLD, 93450 Kuching, Sarawak; tel. (82) 488331; fax (82) 481332; internet www.prs30.org; f. 2003; reported to be considering merger with the SPDP; Pres. Datuk Sri Dr JAMES MASING; Sec.-Gen. Datuk WILFRED NISSOM.

Sarawak Progressive Democratic Party (SPDP): Lot 158–160, Seksyen 20, KTLD 9F/9G/9H, Jalan Badruddin, 93400 Kuching, Sarawak; tel. and fax (82) 232805; internet spdp .barisannasional.org.my; f. 2003; est. by breakaway faction of Sarawak Nat. Party; reported to be considering merger with the PRS; Pres. Datuk WILLIAM MAWAN ANAK IKOM; Sec.-Gen. NELSON BALANG RINING.

Sarawak United People's Party (SUPP): 7 Jalan Tan Sri Ong Kee Hui, POB 454, 93710 Kuching, Sarawak; tel. (82) 246999; fax (82) 256510; e-mail supphq@yahoo.com; internet www.supp.org .my; f. 1959; Sarawak Chinese minority party; Pres. Datuk Seri PETER CHIN FAH KUI; Sec.-Gen. Dr SIM KUI HIAN.

United Kadazan People's Organization (UPKO) (United Pasokmomogun Kadazandusun Murut Organization): Penampang Lot 9 & 10, New World Commercial Centre, Tingkat 2–3, Peti Surat 420, 89507 Penampang, Sabah; tel. (88) 718182; fax (88) 718180; e-mail upkohq@gmail.com; internet www.upko.org.my; f. 1994; est. as Parti Demokratik Sabah (PDS—Sabah Democratic Party) after collapse of PBS Govt by fmr PBS leaders; represents mostly Kadazandusun, Rungus and Murut communities; Pres. Tan Sri BERNARD GILUK DOMPOK; Sec.-Gen. Datuk WILFRED M. TANGAU.

United Malays National Organization (Pertubuhan Kebangsaan Melayu Bersatu—UMNO Baru) (New UMNO): Menara Dato' Onn, 38th Floor, Jalan Tun Ismail, 50480 Kuala Lumpur; tel. (3) 40429511; fax (3) 40412358; e-mail email@umno.net.my; internet www.umno-online.com; f. 1988; replaced the original UMNO (f. 1946), which had been declared an illegal org., owing to the participation of unregistered brs in party elections in April 1987; Supreme Council of 45 mems; 2.5m. mems; Pres. Dato' Sri MOHD NAJIB BIN Tun Haji ABDUL RAZAK; Sec.-Gen. Datuk Seri Tengku ADNAN Tengku MANSOR.

Barisan Jama'ah Islamiah Sa-Malaysia (Berjasa) (Pan-Malaysian Islamic Front): Lot 27, Jalan Besar, 17000 Pasir Mas, Kelantan; e-mail info@berjasa.org; internet berjasa.org; f. 1977; pro-Islamic; 50,000 mems; Pres. Ustaz Haji MOHAMMED YUSSOF BIN HARON.

Bersatu Rakyat Jelata Sabah (Berjaya) (Sabah People's Union): Natikar Bldg, 1st Floor, POB 2130, Kota Kinabalu, Sabah; f. 1975; 400,000 mems; Pres. Haji MOHAMMED NOOR MANSOOR.

Human Rights Party (HRP): 6 Jalan Abdullah, off Jalan Bangsar, 59000 Kuala Lumpur; tel. (3) 22825241; fax (3) 22825245; e-mail info@humanrightspartymalaysia.com; internet www .humanrightspartymalaysia.com; f. 2009; Sec.-Gen. P. UTHAYAKUMAR.

Kongres Indian Muslim Malaysia (KIMMA): Kuala Lumpur; tel. (3) 2324759; f. 1977; aims to unite Malaysian Indian Muslims politically; 25,000 mems; Pres. SAMMY VELLU; Sec.-Gen. MOHAMMED ALI BIN Haji NAINA MOHAMMED.

Malaysia Makkal Sakti Party (MMSP): Shah Alam, Selangor; f. 2009; est. by fmr mems of the Hindu Rights Action Force; represents ethnic Indians in Malaysia; Founder R. S. THANENTHIRAN; Pres. KANNAN RAMASAMY.

Pakatan Rakyat (People's Alliance): internet www.pakatanrakyat .my; f. 2008; est. following the legislative election; opposition alliance of the PKR, the DAP and PAS.

Democratic Action Party (DAP): 24 Jalan 20/9, 46300 Petaling Jaya, Selangor; tel. (3) 79578022; fax (3) 79575718; e-mail dap@ dapmalaysia.org; internet www.dapmalaysia.org; f. 1966; main opposition party; advocates multiracial society based on democratic socialism; 12,000 mems; Chair. KARPAL SINGH; Sec.-Gen. LIM GUAN ENG.

Parti Islam se Malaysia (PAS) (Islamic Party of Malaysia): 318A Jalan Raja Laut, 50350 Kuala Lumpur; tel. (3) 26927400; fax (3) 26938399; e-mail editor@parti-pas.org; internet www.pas.org.my; f. 1951; seeks to establish an Islamic state; 700,000 mems; Pres. Dato' Seri ABDUL HADI AWANG; Sec.-Gen. Dato' Haji MUSTAFA ALI.

Parti Keadilan Rakyat (PKR) (People's Justice Party): A1-09, 1 Merchant Sq., 1 Jalan Tropicana Selatan, 47410 Petaling Jaya; tel. (3) 78850530; fax (3) 78850531; e-mail ibupejabat@keadilanrakyat .org; internet www.keadilanrakyat.org; f. 2003; est. following merger of Parti Keadilan Nasional and Parti Rakyat Malaysia; comprises supporters of Anwar Ibrahim; Pres. Datin Seri Dr WAN AZIZAH WAN ISMAIL; Sec.-Gen. SAIFUDDIN NASUTION ISMAIL.

Parti Kesejahteraan Insan Tanah Air (KITA) (Malaysian People's Welfare Party): B-2-19, Merchant Sq., Jalan Tropicana Selatan 1, PJU 3, 47410 Petaling Jaya, Selangor; tel. (3) 78850023; fax (3) 78850027; e-mail info@partikita.com; internet www.partikita.com; f. 1995; fmrly Angkatan Keadilan Insan Malaysia (AKIM); relaunched as above in 2010; Pres. Datuk ZAMIL IBRAHIM.

Persatuan Rakyat Malaysia Sarawak (PERMAS) (Malaysian Sarawak Party): Kuching, Sarawak; f. 1987; est. by fmr mems of PBB; Leader Datuk IBRAHIM ALI.

Sarawak National Party (SNAP): 304–305 Bangunan Mei Jun, 1 Jalan Rubber, POB 2960, 93758 Kuching, Sarawak; tel. (82) 254244; fax (82) 253562; internet sarawak-national-party.blogspot.com; f. 1961; deregistered Nov. 2002, but deregistration deferred indefinitely in April 2003 following appeal; Pres. EDWIN DUNDANG BUGAK; Sec.-Gen. EDMUND STANLEY JUGOL.

Sabah Progressive Party (SAPP) (Parti Maju Sabah): Lot 23, Tingkat 2, Bornion Centre, 88300 Kota Kinabalu, Sabah; tel. (88) 242107; fax (88) 249188; e-mail sappkk@streamyx.com; internet www.sapp.org.my; f. 1994; non-racial; Pres. Datuk YONG TECK LEE; Sec.-Gen. Datuk RICHARD YONG WE KONG.

Setia (Sabah People's United Democratic Party): Sabah; f. 1994.

Diplomatic Representation

EMBASSIES AND HIGH COMMISSIONS IN MALAYSIA

Afghanistan: Wisma Chinese Chamber, 2nd Floor, 258 Jalan Ampang, 50450 Kuala Lumpur; tel. (3) 42569400; fax (3) 42566400; Ambassador Dr JAMRAD JAMSHED.

Albania: UBN Tower 10, 31st Floor, Jalan P. Ramlee, 50250 Kuala Lumpur; tel. (3) 20788690; fax (3) 20702285; e-mail embassy.kualalumpur@mfa.gov.al; Chargé d'affaires a.i. IDRIZ KONJARI.

Algeria: 5 Jalan Mesra, off Jalan Damai, 55000 Kuala Lumpur; tel. (3) 21488159; fax (3) 21488154; e-mail dz@algerianembassy.org.my; internet www.algerianembassy.org.my; Ambassador ABDELMALEK BOUHEDDOU.

Argentina: Suite 16-03, 16th Floor, Menara Keck Seng, 203 Jalan Bukit Bintang, 55100 Kuala Lumpur; tel. (3) 21441451; fax (3) 21441428; e-mail emsia@mrecic.gov.ar; Ambassador MARÍA ISABEL RENDON.

Australia: 6 Jalan Yap Kwan Seng, 50450 Kuala Lumpur; tel. (3) 21465555; fax (3) 21415773; e-mail public-affairs-klpr@dfat.gov.au; internet www.malaysia.embassy.gov.au; High Commissioner MILES KUPA.

Austria: Suite 10.01-02, Tingkat 10, Wisma Goldhill 67, Jalan Raja Chulan, 50200 Kuala Lumpur; tel. (3) 20570020; fax (3) 23817168; e-mail kuala-lumpur-ob@bmeia.gv.at; internet www.bmeia.gv.at/kualalumpur; Ambassador ANDREA WICKE.

Azerbaijan: Lot 589, Jalan 6 Taman Ampang Utama, 68000 Ampang, Selangor Darul Ehsan; tel. (3) 42526800; fax (3) 42571800; e-mail kualalumpur@mission.mfa.gov.az; internet www.azembassy.com.my; Ambassador TAHIR KARIMOV.

Bangladesh: 114 Jalan U Thant, 55000 Kuala Lumpur; tel. (3) 21487940; fax (3) 21413381; e-mail mission.kualalumpur@mofa.gov.bd; internet www.bangladesh-highcomkl.com; High Commissioner ATIQUR RAHMAN.

Belgium: Suite 10-02, 10th Floor, Menara Tan & Tan, 207 Jalan Tun Razak, 50400 Kuala Lumpur; tel. (3) 21620025; fax (3) 21620023; e-mail kualalumpur@diplobel.fed.be; internet www.diplomatie.be/kualalumpur; Ambassador MARC MULLIE.

Bosnia and Herzegovina: JKR 854, Jalan Bellamy, 50460 Kuala Lumpur; tel. (3) 21440353; fax (3) 21426025; e-mail embbhkl@mfa.gov.ba; Ambassador TARIK BUKVIĆ.

Brazil: Suite 20-01, 20th Floor, Menara Tan & Tan, 207 Jalan Tun Razak, 50400 Kuala Lumpur; tel. (3) 21711420; fax (3) 21711427; e-mail embassy@brazilembassy.org.my; internet www.brazilembassy.org.my; Ambassador MARIA AUXILIADORA FIGUEIREDO.

Brunei: Suite 19-01, 19th Floor, Menara Tan & Tan, 207 Jalan Tun Razak, 50400 Kuala Lumpur; tel. (3) 21612800; fax (3) 21631302; e-mail kualalumpur.malaysia@mfa.gov.bn; High Commissioner Dato' Paduka Haji ISHAAQ BIN Haji ABDULLAH.

Cambodia: 46 Jalan U Thant, 55000 Kuala Lumpur; tel. (3) 42571150; fax (3) 42571157; e-mail camemb.mys@mfa.gov.kh; internet embassyofcambodia-malaysia.org; Ambassador HRH Samdech Preah ANOCH NORODOM ARUNRASMY.

Canada: Menara Tan & Tan, 17th Floor, 207 Jalan Tun Razak, 50400 Kuala Lumpur; tel. (3) 27183333; fax (3) 27183399; e-mail klmpr@international.gc.ca; internet www.canadainternational.gc.ca/malaysia-malaisie; High Commissioner RANDOLPH MANK.

Chile: West Block, 8th Floor, Wisma Selangor Dredging, 142C Jalan Ampang, Peti Surat 27, 50450 Kuala Lumpur; tel. (3) 21616203; fax (3) 21622219; e-mail eochile@embassyofchile.org.my; internet chileabroad.gov.cl/malasia; Ambassador CHRISTIAN REHREN.

China, People's Republic: 229 Jalan Ampang, 50450 Kuala Lumpur; tel. (3) 21428495; fax (3) 21414552; e-mail cn@tm.net.my; internet my.china-embassy.org/eng; Ambassador CHAI XI.

Colombia: UOA Centre, Tingkat 28, 19 Jalan Pinang, 50450 Kuala Lumpur; tel. (3) 21645488; fax (3) 21645487; e-mail ekualalumpur@cancilleria.gov.co; internet www.ecolombia.com.my; Ambassador RODRIGO QUERUBÍN LONDOÑO.

Croatia: 3 Jalan Menkuang, off Jalan Ru Ampang, 55000 Kuala Lumpur; tel. (3) 42535340; fax (3) 42535217; e-mail croemb.kuala-lumpur@mvpei.hr; Ambassador ŽELJKO BOŠNJAK.

Cuba: 18 Jalan Kent 2, off Jalan Maktab, 54000 Kuala Lumpur; tel. (3) 26911066; fax (3) 26911141; e-mail admin@cubemb.com.my; internet www.cubaemb.com.my; Ambassador RUBÉN PÉREZ VALDÉS.

Czech Republic: Suite B, 42nd Floor, Vista Tower, The Intermark, 182 Jalan Tun Razak, 50400 Kuala Lumpur; tel. (3) 21427185; fax (3) 21412727; e-mail kualalumpur@embassy.mzv.cz; internet www.mzv.cz/kualalumpur; Ambassador JAN FÜRY.

Denmark: Sunway Tower, 22nd Floor, 86 Jalan Ampang, 50450 Kuala Lumpur; tel. (3) 20322001; fax (3) 20322015; e-mail kulamb@um.dk; internet www.malaysia.um.dk; Ambassador NICOLAI RUGE.

Ecuador: West Block, 10th Floor, Wisma Selangor Dredging, 142C Jalan Ampang, 50450 Kuala Lumpur; tel. (3) 21635078; fax (3) 21635096; e-mail embecua@po.jaring.my; Ambassador LOURDES PUMA PUMA.

Egypt: 12 Jalan Rhu, off Jalan Ampang, 55000 Kuala Lumpur; tel. (3) 42568184; fax (3) 42573515; e-mail embassy.kualalumpur@mfa.gov.eg; Ambassador MOHAMED SAAD IBRAHIM EBEID.

Fiji: Menara Chan, Tingkat 2, 138 Jalan Ampang, 50450 Kuala Lumpur; tel. (3) 27323335; fax (3) 27327555; e-mail fijihckl@gmail.com; High Commissioner Ratu MELI BAINIMARAMA.

Finland: Wisma Chinese Chamber, 5th Floor, 258 Jalan Ampang, 50450 Kuala Lumpur; tel. (3) 42577746; fax (3) 42577793; e-mail sanomat.kul@formin.fi; internet www.finland.org.my; Ambassador MATTI PULLINEN.

France: 192–196 Jalan Ampang, 50450 Kuala Lumpur; tel. (3) 20535500; fax (3) 20535502; e-mail ambassade.kuala-lumpur-amba@diplomatie.gouv.fr; internet www.ambafrance-my.org; Ambassador MARTINE DORANCE.

Germany: Menara Tan & Tan, 26th Floor, 207 Jalan Tun Razak, 50400 Kuala Lumpur; tel. (3) 21709666; fax (3) 21619800; e-mail info@kuala-lumpur.diplo.de; internet www.kuala-lumpur.diplo.de; Ambassador GÜNTER GRUBER.

Ghana: 14 Ampang Hilir, off Jalan Ampang, 55000 Kuala Lumpur; tel. (3) 42526995; fax (3) 42578698; e-mail ghcomkl@tm.net.my; High Commissioner DANIEL K. ABODAKPI.

Guinea: 5 Jalan Kedondong, off Jalan Ampang Hilir, 55000 Kuala Lumpur; tel. (3) 42576500; fax (3) 42511500; e-mail mwcnakry@sotelgui.net.gn; Ambassador MOHAMED SAMPIL.

Holy See: 9 Lingkungan U Thant, off Jalan U Thant, 55000 Kuala Lumpur; tel. (3) 42604262; Apostolic Nuncio JOSEPH SALVADOR MARINO (Titular Archbishop of Natchitoches).

India: Menara 1 Mont Kiara, 28th Floor, 1 Jalan Mont Kiara, 50480 Kuala Lumpur; tel. (3) 62052350; fax (3) 61431173; e-mail dhc@indianhighcommission.com.my; internet www.indianhighcommission.com.my; High Commissioner VIJAY K. GOKHALE.

Indonesia: 233 Jalan Tun Razak, POB 10889, 50400 Kuala Lumpur; tel. (3) 21164000; fax (3) 21423878; e-mail info@kbrikualalumpur.org; internet www.kbrikualalumpur.org; Ambassador Marshal (retd) HERMAN PRAYINTO.

Iran: 1 Lorong U Thant Satu, off Jalan U Thant, 55000 Kuala Lumpur; tel. (3) 42514824; fax (3) 42521563; e-mail ir_emb@tm.net.my; internet www.iranembassy.com.my; Ambassador MOHAMMAD JALAL FIROUZNIA.

Iraq: 2 Jalan Langgak Golf, off Jalan Tun Razak, 55000 Kuala Lumpur; tel. (3) 21480555; fax (3) 21414331; e-mail quaemb@iraqmofamail.net; Ambassador AMAL MUSSA HUSSAIN ALI AL-RUBAYE.

Ireland: Ireland House, The Amp Walk, 218 Jalan Ampang, POB 10372, 50450 Kuala Lumpur; tel. (3) 21612963; fax (3) 21613427; internet www.embassyofireland.my; Ambassador DECLAN KELLY.

Italy: 99 Jalan U Thant, 55000 Kuala Lumpur; tel. (3) 42565122; fax (3) 42573199; e-mail ambasciata.kualalumpur@esteri.it; internet www.ambkualalumpur.esteri.it; Ambassador MARIO SAMMARTINO.

Japan: 11 Pesiaran Stonor, off Jalan Tun Razak, 50450 Kuala Lumpur; tel. (3) 21772600; fax (3) 21672314; e-mail jis@kl.mofa.go.jp; internet www.my.emb-japan.go.jp; Ambassador SHIGERU NAKAMURA.

Jordan: 2 Jalan Kedondong, off Jalan Ampang Hilir, 55000 Kuala Lumpur; tel. (3) 42521268; fax (3) 42528610; e-mail jorembkl@streamyx.com; internet www.jordanembassy.org.my; Ambassador MAHER LUKASHA.

Kazakhstan: 115 Jalan Ampang Hilir, 55000 Kuala Lumpur; tel. (3) 42522999; fax (3) 42523999; e-mail kuala-lumpur@kazembassy.org.my; internet www.kazembassy.org.my; Chargé d'affaires a.i. YERNUR TUYAKBAYEV.

Kenya: 8 Jalan Taman U Thant, 55000 Kuala Lumpur; tel. (3) 21461163; fax (3) 21451087; e-mail admin@kenyahighcom.org.my; internet www.kenyahighcom.org.my; High Commissioner SAMORI AN'GWA OKWIYA.

Korea, Democratic People's Republic: 7 Jalan Batai, Damansara Heights, 59100 Kuala Lumpur; tel. (3) 42569913; fax (3) 42569933; e-mail dprkorea@streamyx.com; Ambassador JANG YONG CHOL.

Korea, Republic: Lot 9 and 11, Jalan Nipah, off Jalan Ampang, 55000 Kuala Lumpur; tel. (3) 42512336; fax (3) 42521425; e-mail korem-my@mofat.go.kr; internet mys.mofat.go.kr/eng/index.jsp; Ambassador LEE YONG-JOON.

Kuwait: 229 Jalan Tun Razak, 50400 Kuala Lumpur; tel. (3) 21410033; fax (3) 21456121; e-mail kuwait@streamyx.com; Ambassador MONTHER BADER SULAIMAN AL-EISSA.

Kyrgyzstan: Wisma Sin Heap Lee, 10th Floor, 346 Jalan Tun Razak, 50400 Kuala Lumpur; tel. (3) 21632010; fax (3) 21632024; e-mail info@kgembassymy.com; internet www.kgembassymy.com; Ambassador (vacant).

Laos: 7 Jalan Mesra, off Jalan Damai, 55000 Kuala Lumpur; tel. (3) 42511118; e-mail embassylao-kualalumpur@hotmail.com; Ambassador Dr BOUNTHEUANG MOUNLASY.

Lebanon: 56 Jalan Ampang Hilir, 55000 Kuala Lumpur; tel. (3) 42516690; fax (3) 42603426; Ambassador ALI HUSSAIN DAHER.

Libya: 6 Jalan Madge, off Jalan U Thant, 55000 Kuala Lumpur; tel. (3) 21411293; fax (3) 21413549; e-mail ipbkl@yahoo.com; Ambassador Dr ABUBAKAR ALMABROUK AL-MANSOURI.

Maldives: Suite 07-01, Menara See Hoy Chan, 374 Jalan Tun Razak, 50400 Kuala Lumpur; tel. (3) 21637244; fax (3) 21647244; e-mail mail@maldives.org.my; internet www.maldives.org.my; High Commissioner MOHAMED ZAKI.

Mauritius: West Block, 17th Floor, Wisma Selangor Dredging, Jalan Ampang, 50450 Kuala Lumpur; tel. (3) 21411870; e-mail maurhckl@streamyx.com; High Commissioner PREMDUT DOONGOOR.

Mexico: Suite 22-05, 22nd Floor, Menara Tan & Tan, 207 Jalan Tun Razak, 50400 Kuala Lumpur; tel. (3) 21646362; fax (3) 21640964; e-mail embamex@po.jaring.my; internet portal.sre.gob.mx/malasia; Ambassador JORGE ALBERTO LOZOYA LEGORRETA.

Morocco: Unit 9, 3rd Floor, East Block, Wisma Selangor Dredging, 142B Jalan Ampang, 50450 Kuala Lumpur; tel. (3) 21610701; fax (3) 21623081; e-mail moremb@streamyx.com; internet www.moroccoembassy.org.my; Ambassador AHMED FAOUZI.

Myanmar: 8C Jalan Ampang Hilir, 55000 Kuala Lumpur; tel. (3) 42516355; fax (3) 42513855; e-mail mekl@tm.net.my; Ambassador TIN LATT.

Namibia: Suite 15-01, Tingkat 15, Menara HLA, 3 Jalan Kia Peng, 50450 Kuala Lumpur; tel. (3) 21433593; e-mail namhckl@streamyx.com; High Commissioner GEBHARD BENJAMIN KANDANGA.

Nepal: Suite 13A-01, 13th Floor, Wisma MCA, 163 Jalan Ampang, 50450 Kuala Lumpur; tel. (3) 21645934; fax (3) 21648659; e-mail info@nepalembassy.com.my; internet www.nepalembassy.com.my; Ambassador RISHI RAJ ADHIKARI.

Netherlands: The Amp Walk, 7th Floor, South Block, 218 Jalan Ampang, POB 10543, 50450 Kuala Lumpur; tel. (3) 21686200; fax (3) 21686240; e-mail kll@minbuza.nl; internet malaysia.nlembassy.org; Ambassador PAUL BEKKERS.

New Zealand: Menara IMC, 21st Floor, 8 Jalan Sultan Ismail, 50250 Kuala Lumpur; tel. (3) 20782533; fax (3) 20780387; e-mail nzhckl@streamyx.com; internet www.nzembassy.com/malaysia; High Commissioner DAVID PINE.

Nigeria: 85 Jalan Ampang Hilir, 55000 Kuala Lumpur; tel. (3) 42517843; fax (3) 42524302; e-mail info@nigeria.org.my; internet www.nigeria.org.my; High Commissioner BELLO SHEHU RINGIM.

Norway: Suite CD, 53rd Floor, Vista Tower, The Intermark, Jalan Tun Razak, 50400 Kuala Lumpur; tel. (3) 21750300; fax (3) 21750308; e-mail emb.kualalumpur@mfa.no; internet www.norway.org.my; Ambassador (vacant).

Oman: 109 Jalan U Thant, 55000 Kuala Lumpur; tel. (3) 42577378; fax (3) 42571400; e-mail omanemb@po.jaring.my; Ambassador AFLAH BIN SULEIMAN AL-TAEI.

Pakistan: 132 Jalan Ampang, 50450 Kuala Lumpur; tel. (3) 21618877; fax (3) 21645958; e-mail pahickl@gmail.com; internet www.pahickl.com; High Commissioner SHAHID KIANI.

Papua New Guinea: 11 Lingkungan U Thant, off Jalan U Thant, 55000 Kuala Lumpur; tel. (3) 42575405; fax (3) 42576203; High Commissioner VEALI VAGI.

Peru: Wisma Selangor Dredging, 6th Floor, South Block, 142A Jalan Ampang, 50450 Kuala Lumpur; tel. (3) 21633034; fax (3) 21633039; e-mail embperu@streamyx.com; Ambassador WILLIAM BELEVAN MCBRIDE.

Philippines: 1 Changkat Kia Peng, 50450 Kuala Lumpur; tel. (3) 21484233; fax (3) 21483576; e-mail consular@philembassykl.org.my; internet www.philembassykl.org.my; Ambassador JOSE EDUARDO E. MALAYA, III.

Poland: POB 10052, 50704 Kuala Lumpur; tel. (3) 21610780; fax (3) 21649924; e-mail kualalumpur.amb.sekretariat@msz.gov.pl; internet www.kualalumpur.msz.gov.pl; Ambassador ADAM JELONEK.

Qatar: 113 Jalan Ampang Hilir, POB 13118, 55000 Kuala Lumpur; tel. (3) 42565552; fax (3) 42565553; e-mail kualalumpur@mofa.gov.qa; Chargé d'affaires a.i. RASHID MAIRZA AL-MULLA.

Romania: 114 Jalan Damai, off Jalan Ampang, 55000 Kuala Lumpur; tel. (3) 21423172; fax (3) 21448713; e-mail roembdhm@streamyx.com; internet kualalumpur.mae.ro; Ambassador CONSTANTIN VOLODEA NISTOR.

Russia: 263 Jalan Ampang, 50450 Kuala Lumpur; tel. (3) 42567252; fax (3) 42576091; e-mail rusembmalaysia@yandex.ru; internet www.malaysia.mid.ru; Ambassador LYUDMILA GEORGIEVNA VOROBYEVA.

Saudi Arabia: Wisma Chinese Chamber, Tingkat 4, 258 Jalan Ampang, 50450 Kuala Lumpur; tel. (3) 42579433; fax (3) 42578751; e-mail saembssy@tm.net.my; Ambassador MOHAMMED REDA HUSSEIN ABU AL-HAMAYEL.

Senegal: 9 Lorong U Thant, off Jalan U Thant, 55000 Kuala Lumpur; tel. (3) 42567343; fax (3) 42563205; e-mail senamb_mal@yahoo.fr; Ambassador MAME BABA CISSÉ.

Singapore: Level 15, West Wing, The Icon, 1 Jalan 1/68F, Jalan Tun Razak, 50400 Kuala Lumpur; tel. (3) 21616277; fax (3) 21616343; e-mail singhc_kul@sgmfa.gov.sg; internet www.mfa.gov.sg/kl; High Commissioner ONG KENG YONG.

Slovakia: 11 Jalan U Thant, 55000 Kuala Lumpur; tel. (3) 21150016; fax (3) 21150018; e-mail emb.kualalumpur@mzv.sk; internet www.mzv.sk/kualalumpur; Ambassador MILAN LAJČIAK.

Solomon Islands: Kuala Lumpur; High Commissioner (vacant).

Somalia: Kuala Lumpur; Ambassador SALAAD ALI IBRAHIM.

South Africa: Menara HLA, Suite 22-01, 3 Jalan Kia Peng, 50450 Kuala Lumpur; tel. (3) 21702400; fax (3) 21688591; e-mail sahcadm@streamyx.com; internet www.sahighcomkl.com.my; High Commissioner THAMSANQA DENNIS MSELEKU.

Spain: 200 Jalan Ampang, 50450 Kuala Lumpur; tel. (3) 21484868; fax (3) 21424582; e-mail emb.kualalumpur@maec.es; internet www.maec.es/embajadas/kualalumpur; Ambassador MARÍA BASSOLS DELGADO.

Sri Lanka: 12 Jalan Keranji Dua, off Jalan Kedondong, Ampang Hilir, 55000 Kuala Lumpur; tel. (3) 42568987; fax (3) 42532497; e-mail slhicom@streamyx.com; internet www.slhc.com.my; High Commissioner IBRAHIM ANSAR (designate).

Sudan: 2A Persiaran Ampang, off Jalan Ru, 55000 Kuala Lumpur; tel. (3) 42569104; fax (3) 42568107; e-mail assalam12@hotmail.com; Ambassador KHALID ABDELGADIR SHUKRI.

Swaziland: Suite 22-03 & 22-03A, Menara Citibank, 165 Jalan Ampang, 50450 Kuala Lumpur; tel. (3) 21632511; fax (3) 21633326; e-mail swdkl_2@streamyx.com; High Commissioner ZANALE MDLULI.

Switzerland: 16 Persiaran Madge, 55000 Kuala Lumpur; tel. (3) 21480622; fax (3) 21480935; e-mail kua.vertretung@eda.admin.ch; internet www.eda.admin.ch/kualalumpur; Ambassador Dr ROLF LENZ.

Syria: 93 Jalan U Thant, 55000 Kuala Lumpur; tel. (3) 42516364; fax (3) 42516363; e-mail enquiry@syrianembassy.com.my; internet www.syrianembassy.com.my; Chargé d'affaires a.i. Dr MOHAMMAD KHAFIF.

Thailand: 206 Jalan Ampang, 50450 Kuala Lumpur; tel. (3) 21488222; fax (3) 21486527; e-mail thaikula@mfa.go.th; internet www.mfa.go.th/web/1830.php?depcode=23000100; Ambassador THANA DUANGRATANA.

Timor-Leste: 62 Jalan Ampang Hilir, 55000 Kuala Lumpur; tel. (3) 42562046; fax (3) 42562016; e-mail embaixada_tl_kl@yahoo.com; Ambassador JOSÉ ANTÓNIO AMORIM DIAS.

Turkey: 118 Jalan U Thant, 55000 Kuala Lumpur; tel. (3) 42572225; fax (3) 42572227; e-mail embassy.kualalumpur@mfa.gov.tr; internet www.kualalumpur.be.mfa.gov.tr; Ambassador SERAP ATAAY.

Ukraine: Suite 22-02, 22nd Floor, Menara Tan & Tan, 207 Jalan Tun Razak, 50400 Kuala Lumpur; tel. (3) 21669552; fax (3) 21664371; e-mail emb_my@mfa.gov.ua; internet www.mfa.gov.ua/malaysia; Ambassador IHOR V. HUMENNYI.

United Arab Emirates: 1 Gerbang Ampang Hilir, off Persiaran Ampang Hilir, 55000 Kuala Lumpur; tel. (3) 42535221; fax (3) 42535220; e-mail uaemal@tm.net.my; Ambassador NASSER SALMAN AL-ABOODI.

United Kingdom: 185 Jalan Ampang, 50450 Kuala Lumpur; tel. (3) 21702200; fax (3) 21702370; e-mail political.kualalumpur@fco.gov.uk; internet ukinmalaysia.fco.gov.uk; High Commissioner SIMON FEATHERSTONE.

USA: 376 Jalan Tun Razak, POB 10035, 50400 Kuala Lumpur; tel. (3) 21685000; fax (3) 21485801; e-mail klconsular@state.gov; internet malaysia.usembassy.gov; Ambassador PAUL W. JONES.

Uruguay: UBN Tower, 6th Floor, 10 Jalan P. Ramlee, 50250 Kuala Lumpur; tel. (3) 20313669; fax (3) 20315669; e-mail urukuala@streamyx.com; Ambassador GERARDO PRATO.

Uzbekistan: Wisma Chinese Chamber, 2nd Floor, 258 Jalan Ampang, 50450 Kuala Lumpur; tel. (3) 42532406; fax (3) 42535406; e-mail uzbekemb@streamyx.com; internet www .malaysia.mfa.uz; Ambassador SHUKUR SABITOV.

Venezuela: Suite 20-05, 20th Floor, Menara Tan & Tan, 207 Jalan Tun Razak, 50400 Kuala Lumpur; tel. (3) 21633444; fax (3) 21636819; e-mail info@venezuela.org.my; internet www.venezuela .org.my; Ambassador MANUEL ANTONIO GUZMÁN HERNÁNDEZ.

Viet Nam: 4 Jalan Persiaran Stonor, 50450 Kuala Lumpur; tel. (3) 21484036; fax (3) 21483270; e-mail daisevn@putra.net.my; internet www.mofa.gov.vn/vnemb.my; Ambassador NGUYEN HONG THAO.

Yemen: 7 Jalan Kedondong, off Jalan Ampang Hilir, 55000 Kuala Lumpur; tel. (3) 42511793; fax (3) 42511794; e-mail secretary@ yemenembassykl.com; internet yemenembassykl.com; Ambassador Dr ABDULLA MOHAMED ALI AL-MONTSER.

Zambia: Suite C, Menara MBF, 5th Floor, Jalan Sultan Ismail, 50250 Kuala Lumpur; tel. (3) 21453512; fax (3) 21453619; e-mail info@zhckl.com.my; internet www.zhckl.com.my; High Commissioner MILES KAWECHE BANDA.

Zimbabwe: 124 Jalan Sembilan, Taman Ampang Utama, 68000 Ampang, Selangor Darul Ehsan; tel. (3) 42516779; fax (3) 42517252; e-mail zhck@tm.net.my; Ambassador CUTHBERT ZHAKATA.

Judicial System

Federal Court: Palace of Justice, Presint 3, 62506 Putrajaya; tel. (3) 88803502; fax (3) 88803507; e-mail cj@kehakiman.gov.my; internet www.kehakiman.gov.my; has jurisdiction in any dispute between states or between the Federation and any state, as well as special jurisdiction as to the interpretation of the Constitution; headed by the Chief Justice; the other members of the Federal Court are the President of the Court of Appeal, the two Chief Judges of the High Courts and the Federal Court Judges; Chief Justice Tan Sri ARIFIN BIN ZAKARIA.

Court of Appeal: tel. (3) 88803566; fax (3) 88803595; e-mail mdraus@kehakiman.gov.my; f. 1994 as an intermediary court between the Federal Court and the High Court; Pres. Tan Sri Dato' Seri MOHD RAUS BIN SHARIF.

High Court (Peninsular Malaysia): tel. (3) 88803552; fax (3) 88803556; e-mail cjm@kehakiman.gov.my; has original, appellate and revisional jurisdiction as the federal law provides; Chief Judge Tan Sri Dato' Seri ZULKEFLI BIN AHMAD MAKINUDIN.

High Court (Sabah and Serawak): High Court, Jalan Gersik, 93050 Sarawak; e-mail cjss@kehakiman.gov.my; has original, appellate and revisional jurisdiction as the federal law provides; Chief Judge Tan Sri Datuk Seri RICHARD MALANJUM.

Attorney-General's Chambers: 45 Persiaran Perdana, Presint 4, 62100 Putrajaya; tel. (3) 88722000; fax (3) 88905670; e-mail pro@agc .gov.my; internet www.agc.gov.my; Attorney-General Tan Sri ABDUL GANI PATAIL.

Below the Federal Court, the Court of Appeal and the High Courts are the Sessions Courts, which are situated in the principal urban and rural centres. The criminal jurisdiction of the Sessions Courts covers the less serious indictable offences, excluding those that carry the death penalty. Civil jurisdiction of a Sessions Court is up to RM 250,000. The Sessions Judges are appointed by the Yang di-Pertuan Agong. The Magistrates' Courts are also found in the main urban and rural centres and have both civil and criminal jurisdiction, although of a more restricted nature than that of the Sessions Courts. The Magistrates consist of officers from the Judicial and Legal Service of the Federation. They are appointed by the State Authority in which they officiate on the recommendation of the Chief Judge.

There are also Syariah (*Shari'a*) courts for rulings under Islamic law. In July 1996 the Cabinet announced that the Syariah courts were to be restructured with the appointment of a Syariah Chief Judge and four Court of Appeal justices, whose rulings would set precedents for the whole country.

Religion

Islam is the established religion. While freedom of religious practice is enshrined in the Constitution, Malaysia's parallel Islamic judicial system holds great sway over the Muslim majority on religious issues. Almost all ethnic Malays are Muslims, representing 60.4% of the total population in 2000. In that year 19.2% of the population followed Buddhism, 9.1% Christianity and 6.3% Hinduism.

Malaysian Consultative Council of Buddhism, Christianity, Hinduism, Sikhism and Taoism (MCCBCHST): Buddhist Maha Vihara, 123 Jalan Berhala, Brickfields, 50470 Kuala Lumpur; tel. (3)

22739304; fax (3) 22739307; e-mail mccbchst@yahoo.com; f. 1981; a non-Muslim group; Pres. Rev. Dr THOMAS PHILIPS.

ISLAM

President of the Majlis Islam: Datuk Haji MOHD FAUZI BIN Haji ABDUL HAMID (Kuching, Sarawak).

Istitut Kefahaman Islam Malaysia (IKIM) (Institute of Islamic Understanding Malaysia): 2 Langgak Tunku, off Jalan Duta, 50480 Kuala Lumpur; tel. (3) 62046200; fax (3) 62014189; e-mail info@ikim .gov.my; internet www.ikim.gov.my; Chair. TUN ABDULLAH BIN AHMAD BADAWI.

Jabatan Kemajuan Islam Malaysia (JAKIM) (Department of Islamic Development Malaysia): Aras 4–9, Blok D7, Pusat Pentadbiran Kerajaan Persekutuan, 62519 Putrajaya; tel. (3) 88864000; fax (3) 88892039; e-mail webmaster@islam.gov.my; internet www.islam .gov.my; Dir-Gen. Haji OTHMAN BIN MUSTAPHA.

BUDDHISM

Malaysian Buddhist Association (MBA): MBA Bldg, 182 Jalan Burmah, 10050 Pinang; tel. (4) 2262690; fax (4) 2263024; e-mail mba .hq@streamyx.com; internet www.malaysianbuddhistassociation .org; f. 1959; the national body for Chinese and English-speaking monks, nuns and temples from the Mahayana, Theravada and Vajrayana tradition; 13 state brs and 33 other brs nation-wide; 30,000 mems; Pres. Ven. SECK JIT HENG.

Buddhist Missionary Society Malaysia (BMSM): 123 Jalan Berhala, off Jalan Tun Sambanthan, 50470 Kuala Lumpur; tel. (3) 22730150; fax (3) 22733835; e-mail bmsm.malaysia@gmail.com; internet www.bmsm.org.my; f. 1962; Pres. Dato' CHEE PECK KIAT.

Buddhist Tzu-Chi Merit Society (Malaysia): 316 Jalan Macalister, 10450 Pulau Pinang; tel. (4) 2281013; fax (2) 2261013; e-mail info@tzuchi.org.my; internet www.tzuchi.org.my.

Malaysian Fo Kuang Buddhist Association: 2 Jalan SS3/33, Taman University, 47300 Petaling Jaya, Selangor; tel. (3) 78776512; fax (3) 78776511; e-mail myfoguang@yahoo.com.

Sasana Abhiwurdhi Wardhana Society: 123 Jalan Berhala, off Jalan Tun Sambanthan, 50490 Kuala Lumpur; f. 1894; the national body for Sri Lankan Buddhists belonging to the Theravada tradition.

Young Buddhist Association of Malaysia (YBAM): 9 Jalan SS25/24, Taman Mayang, 47301 Petaling Jaya, Selangor; tel. (3) 78049154; fax (3) 78049021; e-mail ybam@streamyx.com; internet www.ybam.org.my; f. 1970; 270 mems; Pres. Dr ONG SEE YEW.

CHRISTIANITY

Majlis Gereja-Gereja Malaysia (Council of Churches of Malaysia): 10 Jalan 11/9, 46200 Petaling Jaya, Selangor; tel. (3) 75967092; fax (3) 79560353; e-mail cchurchm@streamyx.org; internet www .ccmalaysia.org; f. 1947; 18 mem. churches; 10 assoc. mems; Pres. Rev. Dr THOMAS PHILIPS (Mar Thoma Syrian Church); Gen. Sec. Rev. Dr HERMEN SHASTRI.

The Anglican Communion

Malaysia comprises three Anglican dioceses, within the Church of the Province of South East Asia.

Primate: Most Rev. Dr JOHN CHEW (Bishop of Singapore).

Bishop of Kuching: Rt Rev. BOLLY ANAK LAPOK, The House of the Epiphany, POB 347, 93704 Kuching, Sarawak; tel. (82) 240187; fax (82) 426488; e-mail bishopk@streamyx.com; has jurisdiction over Sarawak, Brunei and part of Indonesian Kalimantan (Borneo).

Bishop of Sabah: Most Rev. ALBERT VUN CHEONG FUI, Rumah Bishop, Jalan Tangki, POB 10811, 88809 Kota Kinabalu, Sabah; tel. (88) 245846; fax (88) 245942; e-mail dosabah@streamyx.com.

Bishop of West Malaysia: Rt. Rev. NG MOON HING, Bishop's House, 16 Jalan Pudu Lama, 50200 Kuala Lumpur; tel. (3) 20313213; fax (3) 20312728; e-mail anglican@streamyx.com; internet www .anglicanwestmalaysia.org.my.

The Baptist Church

Malaysia Baptist Convention: 2 Jalan Dispensary 2/38, 46000 Petaling Jaya, Selangor; tel. (3) 77823564; fax (3) 77833603; e-mail mbcpj@tm.net.my; internet www.mbc.org.my; Chair. Rev. BERNARD ANG; Gen. Sec. Rev. KOE CHOON HUAN.

The Methodist Church

Methodist Church in Malaysia: 69 Jalan 5/31, 46000 Petaling Jaya, Selangor; tel. (3) 79541811; fax (3) 79541788; e-mail info@ methodistchurch.org.my; internet www.methodistchurch.org.my; f. 1885; 164,400 mems; Head Rev. Dr HWA YUNG.

The Presbyterian Church

Presbyterian Church in Malaysia: 7 Jalan Sungai Buaya, Batu 3 1/2, off Jalan Klang Lama, 58100 Kuala Lumpur; tel. (3) 79847361; fax (3) 79809037; e-mail presbych@gmail.com; internet www.gpm .org.my; Moderator Rev. CHUA HUA PENG.

The Roman Catholic Church

Malaysia comprises three archdioceses and six dioceses. At 31 December 2007 approximately 3.0% of the population were adherents.

Catholic Bishops' Conference of Malaysia, Singapore and Brunei

Majodi Centre, 2101 Jalan Masai, Johor; tel. (7) 3871121; fax (7) 3872498; e-mail mpakiam@pd.jaring.my; Pres. Most Rev. MURPHY NICHOLAS XAVIER PAKIAM (Archbishop of Kuala Lumpur).

Archbishop of Kota Kinabalu: Most Rev. JOHN LEE HIONG FUN-YIT HAW, Archbishop's House, POB 10289, 88803, Kota Kinabalu, Sabah; tel. (88) 712297; fax (88) 711954; internet www.kkdiocese.net.

Archbishop of Kuala Lumpur: Most Rev. MURPHY NICHOLAS XAVIER PAKIAM, Archbishop's House, 528 Jalan Bukit Nanas, 50250 Kuala Lumpur; tel. (3) 20788828; fax (3) 20313815; e-mail mpakiam@pd.jaring.my; internet www.archway.org.my.

Archbishop of Kuching: Most Rev. JOHN HA TIONG HOCK, Archbishop's Office, 118 Jalan Tun Abang Haji Openg, POB 940, 93000 Kuching, Sarawak; tel. (82) 242634; fax (82) 425724; e-mail abcofku@ pd.jaring.my.

BAHÁ'Í FAITH

Spiritual Assembly of the Bahá'ís of Malaysia: 12 Desa Business Centre, 1–2/F, Jalan 2/109E, Taman Desa, Jalan Klang Lama, 58100 Kuala Lumpur; tel. (3) 79819059; fax (3) 79802058; e-mail nsa-sec@ bahai.org.my; internet www.bahai.org.my; f. 1964; mems resident in 800 localities.

The Press

PENINSULAR MALAYSIA DAILIES
English Language

Business Times: Balai Berita 31, Jalan Riong, 59100 Kuala Lumpur; tel. (3) 22822628; fax (3) 22825424; e-mail support@nstp.com .my; internet www.btimes.com.my; f. 1976; morning; Editor SHAHRIMAN JOHARI; circ. 15,000.

The Edge: 1 Menara KLK, Level 3, Jalan PJU 7/6, Mutiara Damansara, 47810 Petaling Jaya, Selangor; tel. (3) 77218000; fax (3) 77218010; e-mail info@bizedge.com; internet www.theedgedaily .com; f. 1996; weekly, with daily internet edition; business and investment news; Editor AU FOONG YEE; circ. 22,821.

Malay Mail: Lot 2A, Jalan 13/2, 46200 Petaling Jaya, Selangor; tel. (3) 74951288; fax (3) 74951229; e-mail mmnews@mmail.com.my; internet www.mmail.com.my; f. 1896; afternoon; Man. Editor TERENCE FERNANDEZ; circ. 75,000.

Malaysiakini: 48 Jalan Kemuja, Bangsar Utama, 59000 Kuala Lumpur; tel. (3) 22835567; fax (3) 22892579; e-mail enquiries@ malaysiakini.com; internet www.malaysiakini.com; f. 1999; Malaysia's first online newspaper; English and Malay; Editor STEVEN GAN.

New Straits Times: Balai Berita 31, Jalan Riong, 59100 Kuala Lumpur; tel. (3) 22823322; fax (3) 22821434; e-mail news@nstp.com .my; internet www.nst.com.my; f. 1845; morning; Group Editor-in-Chief Dato' SYED NADZRI SYED HARUN; circ. 107,513.

The Star: 15 Jalan 16/11, 46350 Petaling Jaya, POB 12474, Selangor Darul Ehsan; tel. (3) 79671388; fax (3) 79550439; e-mail msd@thestar .com.my; internet www.thestar.com.my; f. 1971; morning; Group Chief Editor Datuk WONG CHUN WAI; circ. 302,658.

The Sun: Sun Media Corpn Sdn Bhd, 4th Floor, Lot 6, Jalan 51/217, Section 51, 46050 Petaling Jaya, Selangor Darul Ehsan; tel. (3) 77846688; fax (3) 77835871; e-mail info@thesundaily.com; internet www.thesundaily.com; f. 1993; free tabloid newspaper in print and online formats; Man. Editor CHONG CHENG HAI; circ. 300,587.

Chinese Language

Chung Kuo Pao (China Press): 80 Jalan Riong, off Jalan Bangsar, 59100 Kuala Lumpur; tel. (3) 22896363; fax (3) 22827125; e-mail enews@chinapress.com.my; internet www.chinapress.com.my; f. 1946; Editor POON CHAU HUAY; Gen. Man. NG BENG LYE; circ. 161,794.

Guang Ming Daily: 19 Jalan Semangat, 46200 Petaling Jaya, Selangor; tel. (3) 79658888; fax (3) 79658477; e-mail gmkl@mail .guangming.com.my; internet www.guangming.com.my; Editor-in-Chief YE NING; circ. 94,287.

Kwong Wah Yit Poh: 19 Jalan Presgrave, 11300 Pinang; tel. (4) 2612312; fax (4) 2628540; e-mail editor@kwongwah.com.my; internet www.kwongwah.com.my; f. 1910; morning; Chief Editor HU JINCHANG; circ. 100,000.

Nanyang Siang Pau (Malaysia): 1st Floor, 1 Jalan SS7/2, 47301 Petaling Jaya, Selangor; tel. (3) 78726888; fax (3) 78726800; e-mail editor@nanyang.com.my; internet www.nanyang.com.my; f. 1923; morning and evening; Editor-in-Chief CHONG CHOONG NAM; circ. 180,000 (daily), 220,000 (Sunday).

Sin Chew Jit Poh (Malaysia): 19 Jalan Semangat, POB 367, Jalan Sultan, 46200 Petaling Jaya, Selangor; tel. (3) 79658888; fax (3) 79556881; e-mail editorial@sinchew.com.my; internet www .sinchew-i.com; f. 1929; morning; Group Editor-in-chief SIEW NYOKE CHOW; circ. 440,002 (daily), 230,000 (Sunday).

Malay Language

Berita Harian: Balai Berita, 31 Jalan Riong, 59100 Kuala Lumpur; tel. (3) 22822323; fax (3) 20567081; e-mail bhnews@bharian.com.my; internet www.bharian.com.my; f. 1957; morning; Group Editor Datuk MIOR KAMARUL SHAHID; circ. 166,400.

Mingguan Perdana: 48 Jalan Siput Akek, Taman Billion, Kuala Lumpur; tel. (3) 619133; Group Chief Editor KHALID JAFRI.

Utusan Malaysia: 46M Jalan Lima, off Jalan Chan Sow Lin, 55200 Kuala Lumpur; tel. (3) 92217055; fax (3) 92227876; e-mail corpcomm@utusan.com.my; internet www.utusan.com.my; Editor ABDUL AZIZ ISHAK; circ. 171,582.

Watan: 23-1 Jalan 9A/55A, Taman Setiawangsa, 54200 Kuala Lumpur; tel. (3) 4523040; fax (3) 4523043; circ. 80,000.

Tamil Language

Makkal Osai: 11B Jalan Murai Dua, Batu Kompleks, off Jalan Ipoh, 52000 Kuala Lumpur; tel. (3) 62512251; fax (3) 62535981; f. 1990; est. as a Sunday newspaper after *Tamil Osai* ceased publication; publ. daily since Dec. 2005; Gen. Man. S.M. PERIASAMY; circ. 52,000 (daily), 95,000 (Sunday).

Malaysia Nanban: 544-3 Batu Complex, off Jalan Ipoh, Batu 3 1/4, 51200 Kuala Lumpur; e-mail news@nanban.com.my; internet www .nanban2u.com; tel. (3) 62515981; fax (3) 62591617; circ. 45,000; Editor M. MALAYANDY.

Tamil Nesan: 23, Jalan SBC 5, Taman Sri Batu Caves, 68100 Batu Caves, Selangor Darul Ehsaan; tel. (3) 61841818; fax (3) 61871818; e-mail mytamilnesan@yahoo.com; internet www.tamilnesan.com .my; f. 1924; morning; Editor-in-Chief PADMANATHAN; circ. 35,000 (daily), 60,000 (Sunday).

SUNDAY NEWSPAPERS
English Language

New Sunday Times: Balai Berita 31, Jalan Riong, 59100 Kuala Lumpur; tel. (3) 2822328; fax (3) 2824482; e-mail news@nstp.com .my; f. 1931; morning; Group Editor Datuk HISHAMUDDIN AUN; circ. 191,562.

Sunday Mail: Balai Berita 31, Jalan Riong, 59100 Kuala Lumpur; tel. (3) 2822328; fax (3) 2824482; e-mail smail@nstp.com.my; f. 1896; morning; Editor JOACHIM S.P. NG; circ. 75,641.

Sunday Star: 13 Jalan 13/6, 46200 Petaling Jaya, POB 12474, Selangor Darul Ehsan; tel. (3) 7581188; fax (3) 7551280; f. 1971; Editor DAVID YEOH; circ. 232,790.

Malay Language

Berita Minggu: Balai Berita 31, Jalan Riong, 59100 Kuala Lumpur; tel. (3) 22822323; fax (3) 20567082; e-mail bhnews@bharian.com.my; f. 1957; morning; Group Editor Datuk MIOR KAMARUL SHAHID; circ. 421,127.

Metro Ahad: Balai Berita 31, Jalan Riong, 59100 Kuala Lumpur; tel. (3) 22822328; fax (3) 22821482; e-mail metahad@nstp.com.my; internet www.nstp.com.my/Corporate/nstp/products/ productMetroAhd.htm; f. 1995; morning; circ. 136,974.

Mingguan Malaysia: 11A The Right Angle, Jalan 14/22, 46100 Petaling Jaya; tel. (3) 7563355; fax (3) 7577755; f. 1964; Editor MOHD HASSAN MOHD NOOR; circ. 543,232.

PENINSULAR MALAYSIA PERIODICALS
English Language

Her World: Lot 7, Jalan Bersatu 13/4, Section 13, 46200 Petaling Jaya, Selangor Darul Ehsan; tel. (3) 79527000; fax (3) 79600148; e-mail herworld@bluinc.com.my; internet www.herworld.com.my; monthly; Editor ALICE CHEE LAN NEO; circ. 35,000.

The Herald: Archdiocesan Pastoral Centre, 5 Jalan Robertson, 50150 Kuala Lumpur; tel. (3) 20268290; fax (3) 20268293; e-mail editor@herald.com.my; internet www.heraldmalaysia.com; weekly; Catholic; Publr Rev. Tan Sri MURPHY PAKIAM; Editor Fr ANDREW LAWRENCE; circ. 15,000.

Malaysia Warta Kerajaan Seri Paduka Baginda (HM Government Gazette): Percetakan Nasional Malaysia Berhad, Jalan Chan Sow Lin, 50554 Kuala Lumpur; tel. (3) 92212022; fax (3) 92220690; e-mail pnmb@po.jaring.my; fortnightly.

Malaysian Agricultural Journal: Ministry of Agriculture and Agro-based Industry, Publications Unit, Wisma Tani, Jalan Sultan Salahuddin, 50624 Kuala Lumpur; tel. (3) 2982011; fax (3) 2913758; f. 1901; 2 a year.

Malaysian Forester: Forestry Department Headquarters, Jalan Sultan Salahuddin, 50660 Kuala Lumpur; tel. (3) 26988244; fax (3) 26925657; e-mail skthai@forestry.gov.my; f. 1931; quarterly; Editor THAI SEE KIAM.

The Planter: Wisma ISP, 29 & 31–33 Jalan Taman U Thant, POB 10262, 50708 Kuala Lumpur; tel. (3) 21425561; fax (3) 21426898; e-mail isphq@tm.net.my; internet www.isp.org.my; f. 1919; publ. by Isp Management (M); monthly; Editor AZIZAN ABDULLAH; circ. 4,000.

The Rocket: 24 Jalan 20/9, 46300 Petaling Jaya, Selangor; tel. (3) 79578022; fax (3) 79575718; e-mail rocket@dapmalaysia.org; internet daprocket.com; monthly; official newsletter of Democratic Action Party; also published in Chinese and Malay; Editor TONY PUA.

Young Generation: 11A The Right Angle, Jalan 14/22, 46100 Petaling Jaya, Selangor; tel. (3) 7563355; fax (3) 7577755; monthly; circ. 50,000.

Chinese Language

Mister Weekly: 2A Jalan 19/1, 46300 Petaling Jaya, Selangor; tel. (3) 7562400; fax (3) 7553826; f. 1976; weekly; Editor WONG AH TAI; circ. 25,000.

Mun Sang Poh: 472 Jalan Pasir Puteh, 31650 Ipoh; tel. (5) 3212919; fax (5) 3214006; fortnightly; circ. 77,958.

New Life Post: 80M Jalan SS21/39, Damansara Utama, 47400 Petaling Jaya, Selangor; tel. (3) 7571833; fax (3) 7181809; f. 1972; bi-weekly; Editor LOW BENG CHEE; circ. 231,000.

New Tide Magazine: Nanyang Siang Pau Bldg, 2nd Floor, Jalan 7/2, 47301 Petaling Jaya, Selangor; tel. (3) 76202118; fax (3) 76202131; e-mail newtidemag@hotmail.com; f. 1974; monthly; Editor NELLIE OOI; circ. 39,000.

Malay Language

Dewan Masyarakat: Dewan Bahasa dan Pustaka, Jalan Wisma Putra, POB 10803, 50926 Kuala Lumpur; tel. (3) 2481011; fax (3) 2484211; f. 1963; monthly; current affairs; Editor ZULKIFLI SALLEH; circ. 48,500.

Dewan Pelajar: Dewan Bahasa dan Pustaka, Jalan Wisma Putra, POB 10803, 50926 Kuala Lumpur; tel. (3) 2481011; fax (3) 2484211; f. 1967; monthly; children's; Editor ZALEHA HASHIM; circ. 100,000.

Dewan Siswa: POB 10803, 50926 Kuala Lumpur; tel. (3) 2481011; fax (3) 2484208; monthly; circ. 140,000.

Gila-Gila: 38-1, Jalan Bangsar Utama Satu, Bangsar Utama, 59000 Kuala Lumpur; tel. (3) 22824970; fax (3) 22824967; fortnightly; circ. 70,000.

Harakah: 5 Jalan, 65C, Off Jalan Pahang Barat, Pekeliling Business Center, 53000 Kuala Lumpur; tel. (3) 40212009; fax (3) 40212037; e-mail harakahenglish@yahoo.com; internet harakahdaily.net; two a week; f. 1980; media organ of the PAS; Group Editor-in-Chief AHMAD LUTFI OTHMAN.

Jelita: Berita Publishing Sdn Bhd, 16–20 Jalan 4/109E, Desa Business Park, Taman Desa, off Jalan Klang Lama, 58100 Kuala Lumpur; tel. (3) 76208111; fax (3) 76208026; e-mail jelita@beritapub.com.my; internet www.beritapublishing.com.my; monthly; fashion and beauty magazine; Editor SARIMAH HUSIN; circ. 133,727.

Mangga: 11A The Right Angle, Jalan 14/22, 46100 Petaling Jaya, Selangor; tel. (3) 7563355; fax (3) 7577755; monthly; circ. 56,609.

Mastika: Utusan Karya Sdn Bhd, Lot 6, Jalan P/10, Seksyen 10, 43650 Bandar Baru Bangi, Selangor Darul Ehsan; tel. (3) 89262999; fax (3) 89259277; f. 1941; monthly; illustrated magazine; Editor SAHIDAN JAAFAR; circ. 350,000.

Utusan Radio dan TV: 11A The Right Angle, Jalan 14/22, 46100 Petaling Jaya, Selangor; tel. (3) 7563355; fax (3) 7577755; fortnightly; Editor NORSHAH TAMBY; circ. 115,000.

Wanita: 11A The Right Angle, Jalan 14/22, 46100 Petaling Jaya, Selangor; tel. (3) 7563355; fax (3) 7577755; monthly; women; Editor Nik RAHIMAH HASSAN; circ. 28,651.

Punjabi Language

Navjiwan Punjabi News: 52 Jalan 8/18, Jalan Toman, 46050 Petaling Jaya, Selangor; tel. (3) 7565725; f. 1950; weekly; Assoc. Editor TARA SINGH; circ. 9,000.

SABAH DAILIES

Api Siang Pau (Kota Kinabalu Commercial Press): 24 Lorong Dewan, POB 170, Kota Kinabalu; f. 1954; morning; Chinese; Editor Datuk LO KWOCK CHUEN; circ. 3,000.

Borneo Post (Nountan Press Sdn Bhd): 1 Jalan Bakau, 1st Floor, off Jalan Gaya, 88999 Kota Kinabulu; tel. (88) 238001; fax (88) 238002; internet www.theborneopost.com; English; Chief Editor JIMMY ADIT; circ. 22,533.

Daily Express: News House, 16 Jalan Pasar Baru, POB 10139, 88801 Kota Kinabalu; tel. (88) 256422; fax (88) 238611; e-mail forum@dailyexpress.com.my; internet www.dailyexpress.com.my; f. 1963; morning; English, Bahasa Malaysia and Kadazan; Editor-in-Chief SARDATHISA JAMES; circ. 28,555.

Hwa Chiaw Jit Pao (Overseas Chinese Daily News): News House, 16 Jalan Pasar Baru, POB 10139, 88801 Kota Kinabalu; tel. (88) 256422; fax (88) 238611; e-mail sph@dailyexpress.com.my; internet www.ocdn.com.my; f. 1936; morning; Chinese; Editor HII YUK SENG; circ. 16,489.

Merdeka Daily News: Lot 56, BDC Estate, Mile $1\frac{1}{2}$ North Road, POB 332, 90703 Sandakan; tel. (89) 214517; fax (89) 275537; e-mail merkk@tm.net.my; f. 1968; morning; Chinese; Editor-in-Chief FUNG KON SHING; circ. 8,000.

New Sabah Times: Jalan Pusat Pembangunan Masyarakat, off Jalan Mat Salleh, 88100 Kota Kinabalu; tel. (88) 230055; fax (88) 231155; e-mail chng.boonheng@newsabahtimes.com.my; internet www.newsabahtimes.com.my; English, Malay and Kadazan; Editor-in-Chief CHENG BOON HENG; circ. 22,525.

Syarikat Sabah Times: Kota Kinabalu; tel. (88) 52217; f. 1952; English, Malay and Kadazan; circ. 25,000.

Tawau Jih Pao: POB 464, 1072 Jalan Kuhara, Tawau; tel. (89) 72576; Chinese; Editor-in-Chief STEPHEN LAI KIM YEAN.

SARAWAK DAILIES

Berita Petang Sarawak: Lot 8322, Lorong 7, Jalan Tun Abdul Razak, 93450 Kuching; POB 1315, 93726 Kuching; tel. (82) 480771; fax (82) 489006; f. 1972; evening; Chinese; Chief Editor HWANG YU CHAI; circ. 12,000.

Borneo Post: 40 Jalan Tuanku Osman, POB 20, 96000 Sibu; tel. (84) 332055; fax (84) 321255; internet www.borneopost.com.my; morning; English; Man. Dir LAU HUI SIONG; Editor NGUOI HOW YIENG; circ. 60,000.

International Times: Lot 2215, Jalan Bengkel, Pending Industrial Estate, POB 1158, 93724 Kuching; tel. (82) 482215; fax (82) 480996; e-mail news@intimes.com; internet www.intimes.com.my; f. 1968; morning; Chinese; Editor LEE FOOK ONN; circ. 24,292.

Malaysia Daily News: 7 Island Rd, POB 237, 96009 Sibu; tel. (84) 330211; tel. (84) 320540; f. 1968; morning; Chinese; Editor WONG SENG KWONG; circ. 22,735.

Sarawak Tribune and Sunday Tribune: Lot 231, Jalan Abell Utara, 93100 Kuching; tel. (82) 424411; fax (82) 415024; e-mail st@tru.my; internet tribune.my; f. 1945; English; licence suspended in Feb. 2006; reappeared in May 2010 as New Sarawak Tribune; Editor (vacant); circ. 2,960.

See Hua Daily News: 40 Jalan Tuanku Osman, POB 20, 96000 Sibu; tel. (84) 332055; fax (84) 321255; f. 1952; morning; Chinese; Man. Editor LAU HUI SIONG; circ. 80,000.

United Daily News: Lot 88, Block 3, Piasau Industrial Estate, POB 377, 98007 Miri ; tel. (84) 219251; fax (84) 215037; internet www.eunited.com.my; f. 2004 following merger between Chinese Daily News and Miri Daily News; morning; Chinese; Man. Editor CHRISTINE LIU QING; circ. 35,000.

SARAWAK PERIODICALS

Pedoman Rakyat: Malaysian Information Dept, Mosque Rd, 93612 Kuching; tel. (82) 240141; f. 1956; monthly; Malay; Editor SAIT BIN Haji YAMAN; circ. 30,000.

Pemberita: Malaysian Information Services, Mosque Rd, 93612 Kuching; tel. (82) 247231; internet www.penerangan.gov.my; f. 1950; every 2 months; Iban; Editor PHILIP NYARU BUNDAK; circ. 20,000.

Sarawak Gazette: Sarawak Museum, Jalan Tun Abang Haji Openg, 93566 Kuching; tel. (82) 244232; fax (82) 246680; e-mail museum@po.jaring.my; f. 1870; 2 a year; English; Chief Editor Datu Haji SALLEH SULAIMAN.

Utusan Sarawak: Lot 231, Jalan Nipah, off Jalan Abell Utara, POB 138, 93100 Kuching; tel. (82) 424411; fax (82) 415024; internet www

.utusansarawak.com.my; f. 1949; Malay; Editor Haji ABDUL AZIZ Haji MALIM; circ. 32,292.

NEWS AGENCY

Bernama (Malaysian National News Agency): Wisma Bernama, 28 Jalan 1/65A, off Jalan Tun Razak, POB 10024, 50400 Kuala Lumpur; tel. (3) 26939933; fax (3) 26913972; e-mail helpdesk@bernama.com; internet www.bernama.com; f. 1968; general and foreign news, economic features and photo services, public relations wire, screen information and data services, stock market online equities service, real-time commodity and monetary information services; daily output in Malay and English; in June 1990 Bernama was given the exclusive right to receive and distribute news in Malaysia; Editor-in-Chief Datuk YONG SOO HEONG.

PRESS ASSOCIATION

Magazine Publishers' Association of Malaysia (MPA): 3-3, Jalan 11/48A, Sentul Blvd, 51000 Kuala Lumpur; tel. (3) 40430500; fax (3) 40437648; e-mail jameselva@brandequity.com.my; internet www.mpamalaysia.org; 16 mems; Chair. ADI SATRIA AHMAD.

Persatuan Penerbit-Penerbit Akhbar Malaysia (Malaysian Newspaper Publishers' Asscn): Unit 706, Blok B, Phileo Damansara 1, 9 Jalan 16/11, off Jalan Damansara, 46350 Petaling Jaya; tel. (3) 76608535; fax (3) 76608532; e-mail mnpa@macomm.com.my; Chair. MOHD NASIR ALI.

Publishers

JOHOR

Penerbitan Pelangi Sdn Bhd: 66 Jalan Pingai, Taman Pelangi, 80400 Johor Bahru; tel. (7) 3316288; fax (7) 3329201; e-mail info@pelangibooks.com; internet www.pelangibooks.com; f. 1979; children's books, guidebooks and reference; Man. Dir SAMUEL SUM KOWN CHEEK.

Perniagaan Jahabersa: 15 Jalan Dataran 3/3, Taman Kempas, Johor Bahru, 81200 Johor; tel. (7) 2351602; fax (7) 2351603; internet www.jahabersa.com.my; f. 1989; Islamist teachings; Man. Dir JAHABAR SATHIK.

KUALA LUMPUR

Arus Intelek Sdn Bhd: Plaza Mont Kiara, Suite E-06-06, Mont Kiara, 50480 Kuala Lumpur; tel. (3) 62011558; fax (3) 62018698; e-mail afusint@streamyx.com; academic; Man. Datin AZIZAH MOKHZANI.

Berita Publishing Sdn Bhd: 16–20 Jalan 4/109E, Desa Business Park, Taman Desa, off Jalan Klang Lama, 58100 Kuala Lumpur; tel. (3) 76208111; fax (3) 76208018; e-mail su@beritapub.com; internet www.beritapublishing.com.my; education, business, fiction, cookery; Chair. A. KADIR JASIN.

Dewan Bahasa dan Pustaka (DBP) (Institute of Language and Literature): Menara DBP, Aras 10, Jalan Dewan Bahasa, 50460 Kuala Lumpur; tel. (3) 21482220; fax (3) 21449614; internet www.dbp.gov.my; f. 1956; textbooks, magazines and general; Vice-Chair. Dato' Dr MOHAMED SALEH BIN YAAPAR.

Jabatan Penerbitan Universiti Malaya (University of Malaya Press): University of Malaya, Lembah Pantai, 50603 Kuala Lumpur; tel. (3) 79574361; fax (3) 79574473; e-mail terbit@um.edu.my; internet umpress.um.edu.my; f. 1954; general fiction, literature, economics, history, medicine, politics, science, social science, law, Islam, engineering, dictionaries; Dir ADAM WONG ABDULLAH.

Pustaka Antara Sdn Bhd: Lot UG 07 and 09, Upper Ground Floor, Kompleks Wilayah, 2 Jalan Munshi Abdullah, 50100 Kuala Lumpur; tel. (3) 26980044; fax (3) 26917997; e-mail pantara4@streamyx.com; textbooks, children's, languages, fiction; Man. Dir Datin HAPSAH BINTI MUHAMAD NOR.

Utusan Publications and Distributors Sdn Bhd: 1 and 3 Jalan 3/91A, Taman Shamelin Perkasa, Cheras, 56100 Kuala Lumpur; tel. (3) 92856577; fax (3) 92856341; e-mail rose@utusan.com.my; f. 1976; school textbooks, children's, languages, fiction, general; Exec. Dir WAN MAHMUD WAN TIJAH.

NEGERI SEMBILAN

Bharathi Press: 166 Taman AST, POB 74, 70700 Seremban, Negeri Sembilan Darul Khusus; tel. (6) 7622911; f. 1939; Mans M. SUBRAMANIA BHARATHI, BHARATHI THASAN.

PULAU PINANG

Syarikat United Book Sdn Bhd: 187–189 Lebuh Carnarvon, 10100 Pulau Pinang; tel. (4) 2626891; fax (4) 2626892; textbooks, children's, reference, fiction, guidebooks; Man. Dir CHEW SING GUAN.

SELANGOR

Aras Mega (M) Sdn Bhd: 18, Jalan Damai 2, Taman Desa Damai, Sungai Merab, Kajang, 43000 Selangor; tel. (3) 89258975; fax (3) 89258985; e-mail amsb@arasmega.com; internet www.arasmega.com; f. 1987; Dir ABDUL RAHMAN BIN ABDUL KARIM.

Cemerlang Publications Sdn Bhd: 29 Jalan PBS 14/3, Taman Perindustrian Bukit Serdang, Seri Kembangan, 43300 Selangor; tel. (3) 89417748; fax (3) 89417750; Dir TAN LIN CHAI.

Golden Books Centre Sdn Bhd: Wisma ILBS, 10 Jalan PJU 8/5G, Perdana Business Centre, Petaling Jaya, 47820 Selangor; tel. (3) 77273890; fax (3) 77273884; internet www.goldenbookscenter.com; f. 1982; textbooks; Dir Dr SYED IBRAHIM.

International Law Book Services: 10 Jalan PJU 8/5G, Perdana Business Centre, Bandar Damansara Perdana, 47820 Petaling Jaya, Selangor Darul Ehsan; tel. (3) 77274121; fax (3) 77273884; e-mail gbc@pc.jaring.my; internet www.malaysialawbooks.com; CEO Dato' Dr Haji SYED IBRAHIM.

Karnadya Solution Sdn Bhd: 12A, Jalan BP 6/6, Bukit Puchong Commercial Centre, Puchong, 47100 Selangor; tel. (3) 80684763; fax (3) 80685814; e-mail info@karnadya.com.my; internet www.karnadya.com.my; f. 2005; Dir FAIZ AL-SHAHAB.

Malaya Press Sdn Bhd: 1 Jalan TSB 10, Taman Perindustrian Sungai Buloh, 47000 Selangor; tel. (3) 61573158; fax (3) 61573957; e-mail tmp@tmpsb.com; internet www.malayapress.com.my; f. 1959; education; Man. Dir KOW CHING CHUAN.

Marshall Cavendish (M) Sdn Bhd: Lot 46, Subang Hi-Tech Industrial Park, Batu Tiga, 40000 Shah Alam, Selangor; tel. (3) 56286888; fax (3) 56364620; e-mail eastview@my.marshallcavendish.com; internet www.marshallcavendish.com; f. 1957; fmrly Federal Publications Sdn Bhd; computer, children's magazines, dictionaries, education; Dir DANNY ONG KIM SOO.

Minerva Publications (NS) Sdn Bhd: 51 Jalan SG 3/1, Tan Sri Gombak, Batu Caves, 68100 Selangor; tel. (3) 61882876; fax (3) 61883876; e-mail minerva@streamyx.com; f. 1974; general, children's, reference, medical, law; Dir and Chief Editor SUJAUDEEN; Man. Dir THANJUDEEN.

Oxford Fajar Sdn Bhd: 4 Jalan U1/15, Sekseyen U1, Hicom-Glenmarie Industrial Park, 40150 Shah Alam, Selangor; tel. (3) 56294005; fax (3) 56294006; e-mail dcs@oxfordfajar.com.my; internet www.oxfordfajar.com.my; fmrly Penerbit Fajar Bakti Sdn Bhd; school, college and university textbooks, children's, general; Man. Dir LOKE FOOK YOON.

Pearson Education Malaysia Sdn Bhd: Lot 2, Jalan 215, off Jalan Templer, 46050 Petaling Jaya, Selangor; tel. (3) 78012000; fax (3) 77831906; e-mail inquirymy@pearson.com; internet www.pearsoned.com.my; textbooks, mathematics, physics, science, general, educational materials; Dir WONG WEE WOON; Man. WONG MEI MEI.

Pelanduk Publications (M) Sdn Bhd: 12 Jalan SS 13/3E, Subang Jaya Industrial Estate, 47500 Subang Jaya, Selangor; tel. (3) 56386885; fax (3) 56386575; e-mail pelpub@tm.net.my; internet www.pelanduk.com; f. 1984; politics, history, anthropology, religion, education, language, economics, business and management, culture, self-improvement, women's studies, law; Man. JACKSON TAN.

Penerbit Universiti Kebangsaan Malaysia: Universiti Kebangsaan Malaysia, 43600 UKM, Selangor; tel. (3) 8292840; fax (3) 8254375; e-mail penerbit@ukm.my; internet www.ukm.my/penerbit; Head KAMARUDDIN M. SAID.

Sasbadi Sdn Bhd: Lot 12, Jalan Teknologi 3/4, Taman Sains Selangor 1, Kota Damansara, 47810 Petaling Jaya, Selangor; tel. (3) 61451188; fax (3) 61569080; e-mail enquiry@sasbadi.com; internet www.sasbadi.com; Man. Dir LAW KING HUI.

United Publishing House (M) Sdn Bhd: 5078 Lorong 18/64A, Taman Sri Serdang, Seri Kembangan, 43300 Selangor; tel. (3) 89430631; fax (3) 89436909; e-mail info@uph.com.my; internet www.uph.com.my; f. 1973; children's, dictionaries, textbooks; Dir WONG CHEE KHEONG.

GOVERNMENT PUBLISHING HOUSE

Percetakan Nasional Malaysia Bhd (Malaysia National Printing Ltd): Jalan Chan Sow Lin, 50554 Kuala Lumpur; tel. (3) 92366888; fax (3) 92366999; e-mail inquiries@printnasional.com.my; internet www.printnasional.com.my; fmrly the Nat. Printing Dept; incorporated as a co under govt control in Jan. 1993; Gen. Man. LOTFI AMER BIN ABDUL HAMID.

PUBLISHERS' ASSOCIATION

Malaysian Book Publishers Association: 7-6, Block E2, Jalan PJU, 1/42A, Dataran Prima, 47301 Petaling Jaya, Selangor; tel. (3) 78805840; fax (3) 78805841; e-mail info@mabopa.com.my; internet www.mabopa.com.my; f. 1968; Pres. Dr HUSSAMUDDIN YAACUB; 190 mems.

Broadcasting and Communications

REGULATORY AUTHORITY

Malaysian Communications and Multimedia Commission: 63000 Cyberjaya, Selangor; tel. (3) 86888000; fax (3) 86881000; e-mail ccd@cmc.gov.my; internet www.skmm.gov.my; monitors the regulatory framework for telecommunications and broadcasting industries and on-line activities; Chair. Dato' MOHAMED SHARIL MOHAMED TARMIZI.

TELECOMMUNICATIONS

Celcom (Malaysia) Sdn Bhd: Menara Celcom, 82 Jalan Raja Muda Abdul Aziz, 50300 Kuala Lumpur; tel. (3) 26883939; fax (3) 36308889; internet www.celcom.com.my; f. 1988; private co licensed to operate mobile cellular telephone service; merged with TM Cellular Sdn Bhd in 2003; Chair. Dato' Sri JAMALUDIN IBRAHIM; CEO Dato' Sri MOHAMMED SHAZALLI RAMLY.

DiGi Telecommunications Sdn Bhd: D'House, Lot 10, Jalan Delima 1/1, Subang Hi-Tech Industrial Park, 40000 Shah Alam, Selangor; tel. (3) 57211800; fax (3) 57210238; internet www.digi.com .my; private co licensed to operate mobile telephone service; Chair. SIGVE BREKKE; CEO HENRIK CLAUSEN.

Maxis Communications Bhd: Menara Maxis, Aras 18, Kuala Lumpur City Centre, off Jalan Ampang, 50088 Kuala Lumpur; tel. (3) 23307000; fax (3) 23300008; internet www.maxis.com.my; f. 1995; provides mobile, fixed-line and multimedia services; approx. 11.4m. subscribers in 2009; Chair. Tan Sri Dato' Seri ARSHAD BIN TUN UDA; CEO JOHAN DENNELIND (from 1 July 2013).

Technology Resources Industries Bhd (TRI): Menara TR, 23rd Floor, 161B Jalan Ampang, 50450 Kuala Lumpur; tel. (3) 2619555; fax (3) 2632018; operates mobile cellular telephone service; Chair. and Chief Exec. Tan Sri Dato' TAJUDIN RAMLI.

Telekom Malaysia Bhd: Tingkat 51, North Wing, Menara Telekom, off Jalan Pantai Baru, 50672 Kuala Lumpur; tel. (3) 22401221; fax (3) 22832415; e-mail help@tm.com.my; internet www.tm.com .my; f. 1984; public listed co responsible for operation of basic telecommunications services; 74% govt-owned; 4.22m. fixed lines (95% of total); Chair. Datuk Dr HALIM SHAFIE; Chief Exec. Dato' Sri MOHD ISA ZAMZAMZAIRANT.

Time dotCom Bhd: 14 Jalan Majistret, U1/26 Hicom Glenmarie Industrial Park, 40150 Shah Alam, Selangor; tel. (3) 50326000; fax (3) 50326010; e-mail customerservice@time.com.my; internet www .time.com.my; f. 1996; est. as Time Telecommunications Holdings Bhd; name changed as above in Jan. 2000; state-controlled co licensed to operate trunk network and mobile cellular telephone service; Chair. ABDUL KADIR MOHAMED KASSIM; CEO AFZAL ABDUL RAHIM.

BROADCASTING

Under the Broadcasting Act (approved in December 1987), the Government is empowered to control and monitor all radio and television broadcasting, and to revoke the licence of any private company violating the Act by broadcasting material 'conflicting with Malaysian values'. The switch from analogue to digital services, initially envisaged for 2012–15, was delayed until 2015–20.

Radio

Radio Televisyen Malaysia (RTM): Dept of Broadcasting, Tingkat 2, Wisma TV, Angkasapuri, 50614 Kuala Lumpur; tel. (3) 22825333; fax (3) 22827146; e-mail feedback@rtm.gov.my; internet www.rtm.gov.my; f. 1946; broadcasts in Bahasa Malaysia, English, Chinese (Mandarin and other dialects), Kadazan, Murut, Dusun and Bajau; TV-broadcasting commenced in 1963; operates TV1 and TV2; Dir-Gen. NORHYATI ISMAIL.

Radio Televisyen Malaysia—Sabah: Jalan Tuaran, 88614 Kota Kinabalu; tel. (88) 213444; fax (88) 223493; internet www .rtmsabah.gov.my; f. 1955; television introduced 1971; a dept of RTM; broadcasts programmes over two networks in Bahasa Malaysia, English, Chinese (two dialects), Kadazan, Murut, Dusun and Bajau; Dir of Broadcasting JUMAT ENGSON.

Radio Televisyen Malaysia—Sarawak: Broadcasting House, Jabatan Penyiaran Kawasan Sarawak, Jalan P. Ramlee, 93614 Kuching; tel. (82) 248422; fax (82) 241914; e-mail rtmkuc@rtm.gov .my; internet www.rtmsarawak.gov.my; f. 1954; a dept of RTM;

broadcasts mainly in Bahasa Malaysia, English, Chinese and Iban; Dir of Broadcasting NORHYATI ISMAIL.

Astro Radio Sdn Bhd: All Asia Broadcast Centre, Technology Park, Lebuhraya Puchong, Simpang Besi, Bukit Jalil, 57000 Kuala Lumpur; tel. (3) 95438888; fax (3) 95433888; e-mail kl_radio@astro.com .my; internet ampradio.my; f. 1997; fmrly Airtime Management and Programming Sdn Bhd; operates 10 stations: Era, Hitz, Lite FM, Mix FM, MY FM, Sinar FM, THR Gegar, THR Raaga, Melody FM and X FM; broadcasts in Chinese, English, Malay and Tamil; Exec. Dir Dato' BORHANUDDIN OSMAN.

Media Prima Bhd: 3 Persiaran Bandar Utama, 47800 Petaling Jaya, Selangor; tel. (3) 77266333; fax (3) 77261333; e-mail communications@mediaprima.com.my; internet www.mediaprima .com.my; owns and operates three networks: Fly FM, Hot FM and One FM; Chair. Datuk JOHAN JAAFFAR; CEO AHMAD IZHAM OMAR.

Rediffusion Sdn Bhd: Rediffusion House, 17 Jalan Pahang, 53000 Kuala Lumpur; tel. (3) 4424544; fax (3) 4424614; e-mail mail@ rediffusion.org; internet www.rediffusion.info/Malaya; f. 1949; two programmes; 44,720 subscribers in Kuala Lumpur; 11,405 subscribers in Pinang; 6,006 subscribers in Province Wellesley; 20,471 subscribers in Ipoh; Gen. Man. ROSNI B. RAHMAT.

Suara Islam (Voice of Islam): Islamic Affairs Division, Prime Minister's Department, Blok Utama, Tingkat 1–5, Pusat Pentadbiran Kerajaan Persekutuan, 62502 Putrajaya; f. 1995; Asia-Pacific region; broadcasts in English and Bahasa Malaysia on Islam.

Suara Malaysia (Voice of Malaysia): Wisma Radio, Tingkat 3, South Wing, Angkasapuri, 50740 Kuala Lumpur; tel. (3) 22887826; fax (3) 22847594; e-mail suaramalaysia@rtm.gov.my; internet www.vom.com.my; f. 1963; overseas service in Bahasa Malaysia, Arabic, Myanmar (Burmese), English, Bahasa Indonesia, Chinese (Mandarin/Cantonese), Tagalog and Thai; Controller of Overseas Service STEPHEN SIPAUN.

Television

Radio Televisyen Malaysia; see Radio; regional offices in Sabah and Sarawak.

Measat Broadcast Network Systems Sdn Bhd: All Asia Broadcast Centre, Technology Park Malaysia, Lebuhraya Puchong, Simpang Besi, Bukit Jalil, 57000 Kuala Lumpur; tel. (3) 95434129; fax (3) 95437333; e-mail custcare@astro.com.my; internet www.astro.com .my; nation-wide subscription service; Malaysia's first satellite, Measat 1, was launched in Jan. 1996; a second satellite was launched in Oct. 1996; Chair. Haji BADRI Haji MASRI.

Media Prima Bhd: see Radio; operates four stations: Metropolitan Television Sdn Bhd (8TV); Sistem Televisyen Malaysia Bhd (TV3); ntv7; and TV9.

Finance

(cap. = capital; auth. = authorized; res = reserves; dep. = deposits; m. = million; brs = branches; amounts in ringgit Malaysia)

BANKING

In January 2013 there were 27 commercial banks, 16 Islamic banks and 13 investments banks in Malaysia. In April 2011 some 58 banks held 'offshore' licences in Labuan.

Central Bank

Bank Negara Malaysia (Central Bank of Malaysia): Jalan Dato' Onn, POB 10922, 50929 Kuala Lumpur; tel. (3) 26988044; fax (3) 26912990; e-mail bnmtelelink@bnm.gov.my; internet www.bnm.gov .my; f. 1959; bank of issue; financial regulatory authority; cap. 100.0m., res 19,614.2m., dep. 288,999.2m. (Dec. 2010); Gov. Tan Sri Dato' Sri Dr ZETI AKHTAR AZIZ; 6 brs.

Commercial Banks

Peninsular Malaysia

Affin Bank Bhd: Menara AFFIN, 17th Floor, 80 Jalan Raja Chulan, 50200 Kuala Lumpur; tel. (3) 20559000; fax (3) 20261415; e-mail head.ccd@affinbank.com.my; internet www.affinbank.com.my; f. 1975; est. as Perwira Habib Bank Malaysia Bhd; name changed to Perwira Affin Bank Bhd in 1994; present name adopted upon merger with BSN Commercial Bank (Malaysia) Bhd in 2001; cap. 1,439.2m., res 1,494.3m., dep. 44,074.3m. (Dec. 2011); Chair. Gen. Tan Sri Dato' Seri ISMAIL Haji OMAR; Pres. and CEO Dato' ZULKIFLEE ABBAS BIN ABDUL HAMID; 106 brs.

Alliance Bank Malaysia Bhd: Menara Multi-Purpose, 3rd Floor, Capital Sq., 8 Jalan Munshi Abdullah, 50100 Kuala Lumpur; tel. (3) 26944888; fax (3) 26946200; e-mail info@alliancebg.com.my; internet www.alliancebank.com.my; f. 1982 as Malaysian French Bank Bhd; name changed to Multi-Purpose Bank Bhd 1996; name changed as above Jan. 2001, following acquisition of six merger partners; cap.

600.5m., res 1,477.1m., dep. 30,949.2m. (March 2011); Chair. Dato' Thomas Mun Lung Lee; CEO Seow Wah; 79 brs.

AmBank Bhd: 22nd Floor, Bangunan AmBank Group, 55 Jalan Raja Chulan, 50200 Kuala Lumpur; tel. (3) 20362633; fax (3) 20321914; e-mail ir@ambankgroup.com; internet www .ambankgroup.com; f. 1969; wholly owned subsidiary of AMMB Holdings Bhd; fmrly Arab-Malaysian Bank Bhd; name changed as above 2002; cap. 820.3m., res 2,701.6m., dep. 64,132.5m. (March 2011); Chair. Tan Sri Azman Hashim; Man. Dir Ashok Ramamurthy; 190 brs.

Bangkok Bank Bhd (Thailand): 105 Jalan Tun H. S. Lee, 50000 Kuala Lumpur; tel. (3) 21737200; fax (3) 21737300; e-mail bbb@ bangkokbank.com; internet www.bangkokbank.com; f. 1958; cap. 400m., res 131.2m., dep. 2,050.4m. (Dec. 2011); Chair. Chatri Sophonpanich; CEO Robert Loke Tan Cheng; 5 brs.

Bank of America Merrill Lynch: Wisma Goldhill, Jalan Raja Chulan, 50200 Kuala Lumpur; tel. (3) 20321133; fax (3) 20319087; internet www.bankofamerica.com/my; cap. 135.8m., res 124.6m., dep. 1,122.1m. (Dec. 2010); Chair. Kristjan Drake.

Bank of Nova Scotia Bhd: Menara Boustead, 69 Jalan Raja Chulan, 50200 Kuala Lumpur; tel. (3) 21410766; fax (3) 21412160; e-mail bns.kualalumpur@scotiabank.com; internet www.scotiabank .com.my; f. 1973; cap. 122.3m., res 166.6m., dep. 2,402.7m. (Oct. 2011); Man. Dir Rasool Khan.

Bank of Tokyo-Mitsubishi UFJ (Malaysia) Bhd (Japan): Tingkat 9–11, Menara IMC, 8 Jalan Sultan Ismail, 50250 Kuala Lumpur; tel. (3) 20348000; fax (3) 20788860; e-mail customercare@my.mufg .jp; f. 1996; est. following merger of Bank of Tokyo and Mitsubishi Bank; fmrly known as Bank of Tokyo-Mitsubishi; present name adopted following merger with UFJ; cap. 200m., res 204.6m., dep. 5,618m. (Dec. 2011); Chair. Tetsuo Tanaka; Pres. and CEO Hajime Washizu.

CIMB Bank Bhd: Bangunan CIMB, 10th Floor, Jalan Semantan Damansara Heights, 50490 Kuala Lumpur; tel. (3) 20848888; fax (3) 20848899; internet www.cimbbank.com.my; f. 1999; est. as Bumiputra Commerce Bank Bhd, following merger of Bank Bumiputra Malaysia Bhd with Bank of Commerce Bhd; name changed as above 2006; cap. 3,994.2m., res 10,096.6m., dep. 197,123m. (Dec. 2011); Chair. Tan Sri Dato' Mohamed Nor Yusof; Group CEO Dato' Mohamed Nazir Abdul Razak Ali; 230 brs.

Citibank Bhd (USA): 165 Jalan Ampang, POB 11725, 50450 Kuala Lumpur; tel. (3) 23830000; fax (3) 23836666; e-mail malaysia .customer.service@citi.com; internet www.citibank.com.my; f. 1959; cap. 121.7m., res 495.3m., dep. 31,111m. (Dec. 2010); Country Officer Ajay Banga; 3 brs.

Deutsche Bank (Malaysia) Bhd (Germany): 18–20 Menara IMC, 8 Jalan Sultan Ismail, 50450 Kuala Lumpur; tel. (3) 20536788; fax (3) 20319822; internet www.db.com/malaysia; f. 1994; cap. 173.5m., res 535.3m., dep. 7,912.4m. (Dec. 2011); Man. Dir Raymond Yeoh.

Hong Leong Bank Bhd: Wisma Hong Leong, Tingkat 8, 18 Jalan Perak, 50450 Kuala Lumpur; tel. (3) 21648228; fax (3) 21642503; internet www.hlb.com.my; f. 1905; fmrly MUI Bank Bhd; merged with Wah Tat Bank Bhd in 2001; acquired EON Bank Bhd in 2012; cap. 1,580.1m., res 1,901.7m., dep. 125,554.2m. (June 2011); Chair. Tan Sri Quek Leng Chan; Man. Dir Yvonne Chia; 329 brs.

HSBC Bank Malaysia Bhd (Hong Kong): 2 Leboh Ampang, POB 10244, 50100 Kuala Lumpur; tel. (3) 20753000; fax (3) 20701146; internet www.hsbc.com.my; f. 1860; fmrly Hongkong Bank Malaysia Bhd; adopted present name in 1999; cap. 114.5m., res 1,346m., dep. 68,433m. (Dec. 2011); Chair. Peter Wong Tun Shun; CEO Makhtar Hussain.

Malayan Banking Bhd (Maybank): Menara Maybank, 14th Floor, 100 Jalan Tun Perak, 50050 Kuala Lumpur; tel. (3) 20708833; fax (3) 20702611; e-mail publicaffairs@maybank.com .my; internet www.maybank2u.com.my; f. 1960; acquired Pacific Bank Bhd Jan. 2001; merged with PhileoAllied Bank (Malaysia) Bhd March 2001; cap. 7,478m., res 14,492m., dep. 315,280m. (June 2011); Chair. Tan Sri Dato' Megat Zaharuddin Megat Mohamed Nor; Pres. and CEO Dato' Sri Abdul Wahid Omar; 327 domestic brs, 30 overseas brs.

OCBC Bank (Malaysia) Bhd: Menara OCBC, 18 Jalan Tun Perak, 50050 Kuala Lumpur; tel. (3) 83175000; fax (3) 26984363; internet www.ocbc.com.my; f. 1932; cap. 291.5m., res 1,398m., dep. 56,346.5m. (Dec. 2011); Group Chair. Tan Sri Dato' Nasruddin bin Bahari; CEO Jeffrey Chew Sun Teong; 25 brs.

Public Bank Bhd: Menara Public Bank, 146 Jalan Ampang, 50450 Kuala Lumpur; tel. (3) 21638888; fax (3) 21639917; e-mail pbbcosec@ publicbank.com.my; internet www.publicbank.com.my; f. 1965; merged with Hock Hua Bank Bhd March 2001; cap. 3,531.9m., res 4,913.7m., dep. 216,177.2m. (Dec. 2011); Chair. Tan Sri Dato' Dr Teh Hong Piow; Man. Dir and CEO Tan Sri Dato' Sri Tay Ah Lek; 252 domestic brs, 4 overseas brs.

RHB Bank Bhd: Towers Two and Three, RHB Centre, Jalan Tun Razak, 50400 Kuala Lumpur; tel. (3) 92878888; fax (3) 92879000; e-mail md_ceo@rhbbank.com.my; internet www.rhb.com.my; f. 1997; est. by merger between Development & Commercial Bank Bhd and Kwong Yik Bank Bhd; acquired Sime Bank Bhd 1999; merged with Bank Utama (Malaysia) Bhd 2003; cap. 3,318m., res 3,502m., dep. 121,635m. (Dec. 2011); Chair. (non-exec.) Tan Sri Azlan Zainol; Man. Dir Johari Abdul Muid; 148 brs.

Royal Bank of Scotland Bhd: Menara Maxis, Level 1, Kuala Lumpur City Centre, 50088 Kuala Lumpur; tel. (3) 21609888; fax (3) 21609993; e-mail my.customer.care@rbs.com; internet www.rbs.my; f. 1888; cap. 203m., res 239.5m., dep. 2,350m. (Dec. 2011); Man. Dir Harry Naysmith.

Standard Chartered Bank Malaysia Bhd: Menara Standard Chartered, Level 16, 30 Jalan Sultan Ismail, 50250 Kuala Lumpur; tel. (3) 21177777; fax (3) 27116006; e-mail Malaysia.Feedback@sc .com; internet www.standardchartered.com.my; cap. 125m., res 524.7m., dep. 37,878.5m. (Dec. 2010); Chair. Tan Sri Dato' Mohd Sheriff bin Mohd Kassim; CEO Osman Tarique Morad; 42 brs.

United Overseas Bank (Malaysia) Bhd: Menara UOB, Tingkat 2, Jalan Raja Laut, 50738 Kuala Lumpur; tel. (3) 26924511; fax (3) 26913110; e-mail uobcustomerservice@uob.com.my; internet www .uob.com.my; f. 1920; merged with Chung Khiaw Bank (Malaysia) Bhd in 1997 and with Overseas Union Bank (Malaysia) Bhd in 2002; cap. 470m., res 866m., dep. 59,172m. (Dec. 2011); Chair. Wee Cho Yaw; CEO Chan Kok Seong; 45 brs.

Merchant Banks

Affin Merchant Bank Bhd: Menara Boustead, 27th Floor, 69 Jalan Raja Chulan, 50200 Kuala Lumpur; tel. (3) 21423700; fax (3) 21423799; e-mail enquiry@affinmerchantbank.com.my; internet www.affininvestmentbank.com.my; f. 1970; est. as Permata Chartered Merchant Bank Bhd; present name adopted 2001; cap. 222.2m., res 323.4m., dep. 4,519.5m. (Dec. 2011); Chair. Tan Sri Yaacob bin Mohamed Zain; Man. Dir Datin Maimoonah Hussain.

Alliance Investment Bank Bhd (AIB): Menara Multi-Purpose, 19th Floor, Capital Sq., 8 Jalan Munshi Abdullah, 50100 Kuala Lumpur; tel. (3) 26927788; fax (3) 26928787; e-mail eallianceshare@ alliancefg.com; internet www.allianceinvestmentbank.com.my; f. 1974; est. as Amanah-Chase Merchant Bank Bhd; name changed to Alliance Merchant Bank Bhd in 2001, following merger with Bumiputra Merchant Bankers Bhd; name changed as above in 2006, following merger with Kuala Lumpur City Securities (KLCS); cap. 365m., res 166m., dep. 1,799m. (March 2011); Chair. Dato' Thomas Mun Lung Lee; CEO Rafidz Rasiddi.

AmInvestment Bank Bhd: Bangunan AmBank Group, 22nd Floor, 55 Jalan Raja Chulan, 50200 Kuala Lumpur; tel. (3) 20362633; fax (3) 20782842; e-mail customercare@ambankgroup.com; internet www .ambankgroup.com; f. 1975; fmrly Arab-Malaysian Merchant Bank Bhd; later known as AmMerchant Bank Bhd; name changed as above 2006; cap. 200m., res 240.5m., dep. 13m. (March 2011); Chair. Tan Sri Dato' Azman Hashim; Man. Dir Kok Tuck Cheong; 5 brs.

CIMB Investment Bank Bhd: Bangunan CIMB, 10th Floor, Jalan Semantan, Damansara Heights, 50490 Kuala Lumpur; tel. (3) 20848888; fax (3) 20943566; e-mail info@cimb.com.my; internet www.cimbbank.com.my; f. 1974; fmrly Commerce Int. Merchant Bankers Bhd; present name adopted 2006; cap. 100m., res 210m., dep. 2,042m. (Dec. 2011); CEO Charon Wardini Mokhzani.

Maybank Investment Bank Bhd: Menara Maybank, 32nd Floor, 100 Jalan Tun Perak, 50050 Kuala Lumpur; tel. (3) 20591888; fax (3) 20784194; e-mail enquiries@maybank-ib.com; internet www .maybank-ib.com; f. 1973; cap. 50.1m., res 242m. (June 2011), dep. 4,095.3m. (June 2009); Chair. Tan Sri Dato' Megat Zaharuddin Megat Mohamed Nor; CEO Tengku Dato' Zafrul Tengku Abdul Aziz; 2 brs.

MIDF Amanah Investment Bank Bhd: Menara MIDF, Level 21, 82 Jalan Raja Chulan, 50200 Kuala Lumpur; tel. (3) 21738888; fax (3) 21738877; e-mail inquiry-feedback@midf.com.my; internet www .midf.com.my; f. 1975; est. as Utama Wardley Bhd; name changed to Utama Merchant Bank Bhd in 1996; present name adopted 2006; cap. 156.5m., res 493.7m., dep. 4,472.1m. (Dec. 2011); Chair. Tan Sri Dato' Mahmood bin Taib; Group CEO Datuk Mohamed Najib Haji Abdullah; 1 br.

RHB Investment Bank Bhd: Tower Three, 13th Floor, RHB Centre, Jalan Tun Razak, 50400 Kuala Lumpur; tel. (3) 92873888; fax (3) 92870888; e-mail publicaffairs@rhb.com.my; internet www .rhb.com.my; f. 1974; fmrly RHB Sakura Merchant Bankers Bhd; present name adopted 2006; cap. 263.6m., res 291m., dep. 4,604m. (Dec. 2011); Chair. Dato' Mohamed Khadar Merican.

Co-operative Bank

Bank Kerjasama Rakyat Malaysia Bhd: Bangunan Bank Rakyat, Jalan Tangsi, Peti Surat 11024, 50732 Kuala Lumpur; tel.

(3) 26129600; fax (3) 26129636; internet www.bankrakyat.com.my; f. 1954; 83,095 mems. of which 823 were co-operatives (Dec. 1996); Chair. Tan Sri Dato' Sri SABBARUDDIN CHIK; Man. Dir Dato' YUSOF ABDUL RAHMAN; 136 brs.

Development Banks

Bank Pembangunan Malaysia Bhd: Menara Bank Pembangunan, Bandar Wawasan, 1016 Jalan Sultan Ismail, 50250 Kuala Lumpur; tel. (3) 26113888; fax (3) 26985701; e-mail feedback@bpmb.com.my; internet www.bankpembangunan.com; f. 1973; govt-owned; fmrly Bank Pembangunana & Infrastruktur Malaysia Bhd; present name adopted upon merger with Bank Industri & Teknologi Malaysia Bhd in 2005; specializes in infrastructure, maritime and high-technology sectors; cap. 3,078.7m., res 2,000m., dep. 7,457.6m. (Dec. 2010); Pres. Dato' ZAFER HASHIM; 15 brs.

Bank Perusahaan Kecil & Sederhana Malaysia Bhd (SME Bank): Menara SME Bank, Jalan Sultan Ismail, Peti Surat 12352, 50774 Kuala Lumpur; tel. (3) 26152020; fax (3) 26928520; e-mail customercare@smebank.com.my; internet www.smebank.com.my; f. 2005; wholly owned subsidiary of Bank Pembangunan Malaysia Bhd; provides both financial and non-financial assistance to SMEs; cap. 1,350m., res 13m., dep 1,664m. (Dec. 2010); Chair. Dato' GUMURI HUSSAIN; Man. Dir Datuk MOHD RADZIF MOHD YUNUS.

Sabah Development Bank Bhd: SDB Tower, Wisma Tun Fuad Stephens, km 2.4, Jalan Tuaran, POB 12172, 88824 Kota Kinabalu, Sabah; tel. (88) 232177; fax (88) 261852; e-mail info@sabahdevbank.com; internet www.sabahdevbank.com; f. 1977; wholly owned by Sabah state govt; cap. 430.0m., res 2.2m., dep. 1,507.1m (Dec. 2010); Chair. PETER SIAU WUI KEE; Man. Dir and CEO Datuk PETER LIM SIONG ENG.

Islamic Banks

Affin Islamic Bank Bhd: Menara Affin, 17th Floor, 80 Jalan Raja Chulan, 50200 Kuala Lumpur; tel. (3) 20559000; fax (3) 20261415; e-mail yourvoice@affinbank.com.my; f. 2006; cap. 260m., res 109.1m., dep. 9,676.3m. (Dec. 2011); CEO KAMARUL ARIFFIN MOHD JAMIL.

AmIslamic Bank Bhd: Bangunan AmBank Group, 22nd Floor, 55 Jalan Raja Chulan, 50200 Kuala Lumpur; tel. (3) 20362633; fax (3) 20321914; e-mail ir@ambankgroup.com; internet www.ambankgroup.com; f. 1994; wholly owned subsidiary of AmBank Bhd; cap. 403m., res 832m., dep. 16,588m. (March 2011); CEO Datuk MAHDI MORAD.

Bank Islam Malaysia Bhd: Wisma Bank Islam, 11th Floor, Jalan Dungun, Bukit Damansara, 50490 Kuala Lumpur; tel. (3) 20888000; fax (3) 20888033; e-mail contactcenter@bankislam.com.my; internet www.bankislam.com.my; f. 1983; cap. 2,265.4m., res 1,659m., dep. 28,664.3m. (June 2011); Chair. Dato' ZAMANI ABDUL GHANI; Man. Dir Dato' Sri ZUKRI SAMAT; 125 brs.

Bank Muamalat Malaysia Bhd: Menara Bumiputra, 5th Floor, 21 Jalan Melaka, 50100 Kuala Lumpur; tel. (3) 26988787; fax (3) 20325997; e-mail webmaster@muamalat.com.my; internet www.muamalat.com.my; f. 1999; cap. 1,000m., res 233.3m., dep. 16,186.7m. (March 2011); Chair. Tan Sri Dato' Dr MOHD MUNIR ABDUL MAJID; CEO Dato' Haji MOHD REDZA SHAH ABDUL WAHID; 40 brs.

OCBC Al-Amin Bank Bhd: Wisma Lee Rubber, 25th Floor, 1 Jelan Melaka, 50100 Kuala Lumpur; tel. (3) 20345034; fax (3) 26984363; subsidiary of OCBC Bank Bhd; cap. 85m., res 205m., dep. 5,053.7m. (Dec. 2011); CEO JEFFREY CHEW SUN TEONG.

Public Islamic Bank Bhd: Menara Public Bank, 27th Floor, 146 Jalan Ampang, 50450 Kuala Lumpur; tel. (3) 21766000; fax (3) 21639917; e-mail islamicbkg@publicislamicbank.com.my; internet www.publicislamicbank.com.my; f. 1973; est. as Asian Int. Merchant Bankers Bhd; became Sime Merchant Bankers Bhd 1996; present name adopted 2008; cap. 186.2m., res 1,630m., dep. 27,209.4m. (Dec. 2011); Chair. Tan Sri Dato' Sri Dr TEH HONG PIOW; CEO ABU HASSAN ASSARI BIN IBRAHIM.

Regulatory Authority

Labuan Financial Services Authority (Labuan FSA): Main Office Tower, Tingkat 17, Financial Park Labuan, Jalan Merdeka, 87000 Labuan; tel. (87) 591200; fax (87) 428200; e-mail communication@labuanfsa.gov.my; internet labuanfsa.gov.my; f. 1996; est. as Labuan Offshore Financial Services Authority (LOFSA); regulatory and supervisory body for international business and financial services industry in Labuan; chaired by Gov. of Bank Negara Malaysia; Dir-Gen. AHMAD HIZZAD BAHARUDDIN.

'Offshore' Banks

AmInternational (L) Ltd: Main Office Tower, Blok 4, Tingkat 12B, Financial Park Labuan, Jalan Merdeka, 87000 Labuan; tel. (87) 413133; fax (87) 425211; e-mail felix-leong@ambankgroup.com.my;

internet www.ambankgroup.com; f. 1995; Head of Br. ISKANDAR MOHAMED HAFIDZ.

AmInvestment Bank Bhd, Labuan Branch: Main Office Tower, Blok 4, Tingkat 12B, Financial Park Labuan, Jalan Merdeka, 87000 Labuan; tel. (87) 439399; fax (87) 425211; Man. Dir CHEAH TEK KUANG.

The Bank of East Asia Ltd, Labuan Branch: Main Office Tower, Tingkat 10C, Financial Park Labuan, Jalan Merdeka, 87000 Labuan; tel. (87) 451145; fax (87) 451148; e-mail arraisag@hkbea.com; Gen. Man. ALVIN ARRAIS.

Bank of Nova Scotia, Labuan Branch: Main Office Tower, Tingkat 10-C2, Financial Park Labuan, Jalan Merdeka, 87000 Labuan; tel. (87) 451101; fax (87) 451099; Man. AUDREY YAP.

Bank of Tokyo-Mitsubishi UFJ Ltd, Labuan Branch: Main Office Tower, Tingkat 12A, Financial Park Labuan, Jalan Merdeka, 87000 Labuan; tel. (87) 410487; fax (87) 410476; e-mail jun_minamoto@hd.mufg.jp; Man. JUN MINAMOTO.

Barclays Bank PLC: Main Office Tower, Tingkat 5A, Financial Park Labuan, Jalan Merdeka, 87000 Labuan; tel. (87) 425571; fax (87) 425575; e-mail siawloong.miaw@barcap.com; Man. MIAW SIAW LOONG.

BNP Paribas, Labuan Branch: Main Office Tower, Tingkat 9F, Financial Park Labuan, Jalan Merdeka, 87000 Labuan; tel. (87) 422328; fax (87) 419328; e-mail krishna.chetti@asia.bnpparibas.com; internet www.bnpparibas.com.my; Head KRISHNA CHETTI.

Cathay United Bank, Labuan Branch: Main Office Tower, Tingkat 3C, Financial Park Labuan, Jalan Merdeka, 87000 Labuan; tel. (87) 452168; fax (87) 453678; e-mail pce@cathaybk.com.tw; Gen. Man. PAN CHUNG-EN.

CIMB Bank (L) Ltd: Main Office Tower, Tingkat 14B, Financial Park Labuan, Jalan Merdeka, 87000 Labuan; tel. (87) 410302; fax (87) 410313; e-mail jemima.haziz@cimb.com; Gen. Man. JEMIMA HAZIZ.

Citibank Malaysia (L) Ltd: Main Office Tower, Tingkat 11F, Financial Park Labuan, Jalan Merdeka, 87000 Labuan; tel. (87) 421181; fax (87) 419671; e-mail clara.ac.lim@citi.com; Gen. Man. CLARA LIM AI CHENG.

City Credit Investment Bank Ltd: Main Office Tower, Tingkat 11-D1, Financial Park Labuan, Jalan Merdeka, 87000 Labuan; tel. (87) 582368; fax (87) 582308; e-mail info@ccibl.net; internet www.citycreditinvestmentbank.com; Chair. Tan Sri Dato' HANAFIAH HUSSAIN; CEO Dato' ABDUL RAHMAN ABDULLAH.

Crédit Agricole CIB, Labuan Branch: Main Office Tower, 6E, Tingkat 6, Financial Park Labuan, Jalan Merdeka, 87000 Labuan; tel. (87) 408331; fax (87) 408335; e-mail hoimeng.chew@ca-cib.com; fmrly known as Crédit Agricole Indosuez, Calyon; Gen. Man. HOI MENG CHEW.

Crédit Suisse AG, Labuan Branch: Main Office Tower, Tingkat 10B, Financial Park Labuan, Jalan Merdeka, 87000 Labuan; tel. (87) 425381; fax (87) 425384; e-mail alfred.lee@credit_suisse.com; investment banking; Gen. Man. LEE CHEE MENG.

Deutsche Bank, Labuan Branch: Main Office Tower, Tingkat 9-G2, Financial Park Labuan, Jalan Merdeka, 87000 Labuan; tel. (87) 439811; fax (87) 439866; internet www.db.com/malaysia; Man. Dir RAYMOND YEOH CHENG SEONG.

Development Bank of Singapore (DBS Bank) Ltd, Labuan Branch: Main Office Tower, Tingkat 10A, Financial Park Labuan, Jalan Merdeka, 87000 Labuan; tel. (87) 595500; fax (87) 423376; internet www.dbs.com/my; Gen. Man. JEFFRY LING.

ECM Libra Investment Bank Ltd: Main Office Tower, Tingkat 3-I1, Financial Park Complex, Jalan Merdeka, 87000 Labuan; tel. (87) 408525; fax (87) 408527; e-mail slchan@ecmlibra.com; Man. CHAN SOON LEE.

Hongkong & Shanghai Banking Corporation, Offshore Banking Unit: Main Office Tower, Tingkat 11-B1, Financial Park Labuan, Jalan Merdeka, 87000 Labuan; tel. (87) 419680; fax (87) 417169; e-mail leechoofoo@hsbc.com.my; Man. FOO LEE CHOO.

ING Bank NV: Main Office Tower, Tingkat 8-B2, Financial Park Labuan, Jalan Merdeka, 87000 Labuan; tel. (87) 425733; fax (87) 425734; e-mail milly.tan@asia.ing.com; Gen. Man. MILLY TAN.

J. P. Morgan Chase Bank, Labuan Branch: Main Office Tower, Tingkat 5F, Financial Park Labuan, Jalan Merdeka, 87000 Labuan; tel. (87) 424384; fax (87) 424390; e-mail alex.law@jpmorgan.com; Gen. Man. ALEX LAW WEI HEONG.

Maybank International (L) Ltd: Main Office Tower, Tingkat 16B, Financial Park Labuan, Jalan Merdeka, 87000 Labuan; tel. (87) 414406; fax (87) 414806; e-mail millmit@streamyx.com; Chair. Dato' JOHAN ARIFFIN.

Mizuho Corporate Bank Ltd, Labuan Branch: Main Office Tower, Tingkat 9B-C, Financial Park Labuan, Jalan Merdeka, 87000 Labuan; tel. (87) 417766; fax (87) 419766; Gen. Man. ISAKU TANIMURA.

Natixis: Main Office Tower, Tingkat 9G, Financial Park Labuan, Jalan Merdeka, 87000 Labuan; tel. (87) 582009; fax (87) 583009; e-mail rizal.abdullah@ap.natixis.com; fmrly Natexis Banque Populaires; Gen. Man. RIZAL ABDULLAH.

OSK Investment Bank (Labuan) Ltd: Lot 3B, Tingkat 5, Wisma Lazenda, Jalan Kemajuan, Labuan; tel. (87) 581885; fax (87) 582885; CEO CHEN HOCK.

Oversea-Chinese Banking Corporation Ltd, Labuan Branch: Main Office Tower, Tingkat 8C, Financial Park Labuan, Jalan Merdeka, 87000 Labuan; tel. (87) 423381; fax (87) 423390; Gen. Man. LEONG WAI MUN.

Public Bank (L) Ltd: Bangunan Lucas Kong, 5 Jalan Merdeka, 87007 Labuan; tel. (87) 414201; fax (87) 412388; e-mail pb11@streamyx.com; Man. ALEXANDER WONG.

RHB Bank (L) Ltd: Main Office Tower, Tingkat 15B, Financial Park Labuan, Jalan Merdeka, 87000 Labuan; tel. (87) 417480; fax (87) 417484; e-mail rhbl@streamyx.com; Gen. Man. TOH AY LENG.

RUSD Investment Bank Inc: Lot 17, Jalan Kemajuan, 87000 Labuan; tel. (87) 452100; fax (87) 453100; e-mail info@rusdbank.com; internet www.rusdbank.com; Chair. Dr SALEH J. MALAIKAH; CEO NASEERUDDIN A. KHAN.

Sumitomo Mitsui Banking Corpn, Labuan Branch: Main Office Tower, Tingkat 12B-C, Financial Park Labuan, Jalan Merdeka, 87000 Labuan; tel. (87) 410955; fax (87) 410959; e-mail naoki_nakano@my.smbc.co.jp; Gen. Man. NAOKI NAKANO.

UBS AG, Labuan Branch: Main Office Tower, Tingkat 4-A1, Financial Park Labuan, Jalan Merdeka, 87000 Labuan; tel. (87) 421743; fax (87) 421746; e-mail zelie.ho@ubs.com; Man. ZELIE HO SWEE LUM.

United Overseas Bank Ltd, Labuan Branch: Main Office Tower, Tingkat 6A, Financial Park Labuan, Jalan Merdeka, 87000 Labuan; tel. (87) 424388; fax (87) 424389; e-mail lai.takkong@uob.com.my; Gen. Man. LAI TAK KONG.

Banking Associations

Association of Banks in Malaysia (ABM): UBN Tower, Tingkat 34, 10 Jalan P. Ramlee, 50250 Kuala Lumpur; tel. (3) 20788041; fax (3) 20788004; e-mail banks@abm.org.my; internet www.abm.org.my; f. 1973; 24 mems; Chair. Dato' Sri ABDUL WAHID OMAR; Exec. Dir CHUAH MEI LIN.

Institute of Bankers Malaysia: Wisma IBI, 5 Jalan Semantan, Damansara Heights, 50490 Kuala Lumpur; tel. (3) 20956833; fax (3) 20958922; e-mail ibbm@ibbm.org.my; internet www.ibbm.org.my; f. 1977; professional and educational body for the banking and finance industry; Chair. Tan Sri Dato' AZMAN HASHIM; Chief Exec. TAY KAY LUAN.

Malayan Commercial Banks' Association: Tingkat 22, Akademi Etiqa, 23 Jalan Melaka, 50100 Kuala Lumpur; tel. (3) 26983991; fax (3) 26942679; internet mcba.my; 21 mems; Exec. Dir Y. Y. LAM.

Persatuan Institusi Perbankan Tanpa Faedah Malaysia (Association of Islamic Banking Institutions Malaysia—AIBIM): Menara Bumiputera, Tingkat 4, 21 Jalan Melaka, 50100 Kuala Lumpur; tel. (3) 20268002; fax (3) 20268012; e-mail admin@aibim.com; internet www.aibim.com; f. 1995; 24 mems; Pres. Dato' MOHAMED REDZA SHAH ABDUL WAHID; Exec. Dir ADDELLAN JUSOP (acting).

STOCK EXCHANGE

Bursa Malaysia: Tingkat 10, Exchange Sq., Bukit Kewangan, 50200 Kuala Lumpur; tel. (3) 20347000; fax (3) 20264122; e-mail customerservice@bursamalaysia.com; internet www.bursamalaysia.com; f. 1973; fmrly Kuala Lumpur Stock Exchange (KLSE); present name adopted 2004; merged with Malaysian Exchange of Securities Dealing and Automated Quotation Bhd (MESDAQ) in March 2002; authorized in 1988 the ownership of up to 49% of Malaysian stockbroking cos by foreign interests; 988 listed cos (Jan. 2008); Chair. TUN MOHAMED DZAIDDIN Haji ABDULLAH; CEO Dato' TAJUDDIN ATAN.

Regulatory Authority

Securities Commission (SC): 3 Persiaran Bukit Kiara, Bukit Kiara, 50490 Kuala Lumpur; tel. (3) 62048777; fax (3) 62015078; e-mail cau@seccom.com.my; internet www.sc.com.my; f. 1993; Chair. Datuk RANJIT AJIT SINGH.

INSURANCE

Principal Insurance Companies

Allianz General Insurance Malaysia Bhd: Plaza Sentral, Suite 3A, Level 15, Blok 3A, Jalan Stesen Sentral 5, 50470 Kuala Lumpur; tel. (3) 22641188; fax (3) 22641199; e-mail partner@allianz.com.my; internet www.allianz.com.my/general; f. 2001; Chair. Tan Sri RAZALI ISMAIL; CEO ZAKRI KHIR.

Allianz Life Insurance Malaysia Bhd: Plaza Sentral, Suite 3A, Level 15, Blok 3A, Jalan Stesen Sentral 5, 50470 Kuala Lumpur; tel. (3) 22641188; fax (3) 22641199; e-mail partner@allianz.com.my; internet www.allianz.com.my; fmrly MBA Life Assurance Sdn Bhd; CEO JENS REISCH.

Commerce Life Assurance Bhd: 338 Jalan Tunku Abdul Rahman, 50100 Kuala Lumpur; tel. (3) 26123600; fax (3) 26987035; f. 1992; est. as AMAL Assurance Bhd; present name adopted 1999.

Great Eastern Life Assurance (Malaysia) Bhd: Menara Great Eastern, 303 Jalan Ampang, 50450 Kuala Lumpur; tel. (3) 42598888; fax (3) 42598000; e-mail wecare@lifeisgreat.com.my; internet www.lifeisgreat.com.my; CEO KOH YAW HUI.

Hong Leong Assurance Sdn Bhd: Petaling Jaya City Development 15A, Menara B, Level 3, Jalan 219, 46100 Selangor; tel. (3) 76501818; fax (3) 76501991; e-mail corpcomm@hla.hongleong.com.my; internet www.hla.com.my; Chair. Tan Sri QUEK LENG CHAN; Man. Dir and CEO LOH GUAT LAN.

ING Insurance Bhd: Menara ING, 84 Jalan Raja Chulan, POB 10846, 50927 Kuala Lumpur; tel. (3) 21617255; fax (3) 27110175; internet www.ing.com.my; f. 1987; fmrly Aetna Universal Insurance Bhd; Chair. Tengku ABDULLAH IBNI AL-MARHUM Sultan ABU BAKAR.

Jerneh Insurance Corpn Sdn Bhd: Wisma Jerneh, 12th Floor, 38 Jalan Sultan Ismail, POB 12420, 50788 Kuala Lumpur; tel. (3) 21163300; fax (3) 21426672; e-mail slim@jerneh.com.my; internet www.jerneh.com.my; f. 1970; general; CEO LIM SUN.

Etiqa Insurance Bhd: Level 12B, Academy Etiqa, 23 Jalan Melaka, 50100 Kuala Lumpur; tel. (3) 26125301; fax (3) 26125068; internet www.etiqa.com.my; life and general; fmrly Malaysia National Insurance Sdn Bhd, name changed as above after merger with Etiqa in 2007; Chair. Dato' MOHAMAD SALLEH Haji HARUN.

Manulife Insurance (Malaysia) Bhd: Menara Manulife RB, 12th Floor, 6 Jalan Gelenggang, Damansara Heights, 50490 Kuala Lumpur; tel. (3) 20948055; fax (3) 20935487; internet www.manulife.com.my; f. 1963; life and non-life insurance; fmrly British American Life and General Insurance Bhd; name then changed to John Hancock Life Insurance (Malaysia) Bhd; present name adopted 2005, following 2004 merger between John Hancock Financial Services, Inc and Manulife Financial Corpn; Chair. Tan Sri Dato' MOHAMED SHERIFF BIN MOHAMED KASSIM.

Mayban Assurance Bhd: Mayban Assurance Tower, Level 15, Dataran Maybank, 1 Jalan Maarof, 59000 Kuala Lumpur; tel. (3) 22972888; fax (3) 22972828; e-mail mayassur@tm.net.my; internet www.maybank2u.com.my; Chair. Dato' JOHAN ARIFFIN.

MBf Insurans Sdn Bhd: Plaza MBf, 5th Floor, Jalan Ampang, POB 10345, 50710 Kuala Lumpur; tel. and fax (3) 2613466; Man. MARC HOOI TUCK KOK.

MCIS Zürich Insurance Bhd: Wisma MCIS Zurich, Jalan Barat, 46200 Petaling Jaya, Selangor; tel. (3) 79552577; fax (3) 79571562; e-mail info@mciszurich.com.my; internet www.mciszurich.com.my; f. 1954; Chair. Dato' BALARAM PETHA NAIDU.

Multi-Purpose Insurans Bhd: Menara Multi-Purpose, 8th Floor, Capital Sq., 8 Jalan Munshi Abdullah, 50100 Kuala Lumpur; tel. (3) 20349888; fax (3) 26945758; e-mail generalenquiries@mpib.com.my; internet www.mpib.com.my; fmrly Kompas Insurans Bhd; Chair. YAHYA BIN AWANG.

Oriental Capital Assurance Bhd: 36 Jalan Ampang, 50450 Kuala Lumpur; tel. (3) 20702828; fax (3) 20724150; e-mail oricap@oricap.com.my; internet www.oricap.com.my; f. 2002; est. by merger of Capital Insurance Bhd and United Oriental Assurance Sdn Bhd; Chair. Dato' VIJAYA KUMAR CHORNALINGAM; CEO LAI POONG SHEN.

Overseas Assurance Corpn (Malaysia) Bhd: Menara Great Eastern, Level 18, 303 Jalan Ampang, 50450 Kuala Lumpur; tel. (3) 42597888; fax (3) 48132737; e-mail enquiry@oac.com.my; internet www.oac.com.my; Chair. FANG AI LIAN.

Progressive Insurance Sdn Bhd: Plaza Berjaya, Menara BGI, 7th, 9th and 10th Floors, 12 Jalan Imbi, 55100 Kuala Lumpur; tel. (3) 21188000; fax (3) 21188101; e-mail progressive@progressiveinsurance.com.my; internet www.progressiveinsurance.com.my; Chair. Datuk DATU HARUN BIN DATU MANSOR.

RHB Insurance Bhd: Tower 1, 8th Floor, RHB Centre, Jalan Tun Razak, 50400 Kuala Lumpur; tel. (3) 92812731; fax (3) 92812729; e-mail rhbi_general@rhbinsurance.com.my; Chair. Haji KHAIRUDDIN BIN AHMAD.

Uni.Asia General Insurance Bhd: Menara Uni.Asia, 10th Floor, 1008 Jalan Sultan Ismail, 50250 Kuala Lumpur; tel. (3) 2938111; fax (3) 26932893; e-mail callcentre@uniasiageneral.com.my; internet www.uniasiageneral.com.my; f. 1931; fmrly South-East Asia Insurance Bhd; Chair. DAVID CHAN MUN WAI.

Trade and Industry

GOVERNMENT AGENCIES

Danamodal Nasional Bhd (Danamodal): Bangunan Sime Bank, 10th Floor, Jalan Sultan Sulaiman, 50000 Kuala Lumpur; tel. (3) 20312255; fax (3) 20310786; e-mail info@danamodal.com.my; f. 1998; est. to recapitalize banks and restructure financial institutions, incl. arranging mergers and consolidations; Chair. Raja Datuk ARSHAD Raja Tun UDA; Man. Dir MARIANUS VONG SHIN TZOI.

Federal Agricultural Marketing Authority (FAMA): Bangunan FAMA Point, Lot 17304, Jalan Persiaran 1, Bandar Baru Selayang, 68100 Batu Caves, Selangor; tel. (3) 61262020; fax (3) 61383650; e-mail fama@fama.gov.my; internet www.fama.gov.my; f. 1965; est. to supervise, co-ordinate and improve marketing of agricultural produce, and to seek and promote new markets and outlets for agricultural produce; Chair. Dato' Paduka Haji BADRUDDIN BIN AMIRULDIN; Dir-Gen. Haji AHMAD B. ISHAK.

Federal Land Development Authority (FELDA): Wisma FELDA, Jalan Perumahan Gurney, 54000 Kuala Lumpur; tel. (3) 26172617; fax (3) 26920087; e-mail upd@felda.net.my; internet www.felda.net.my; f. 1956; govt statutory body formed to develop land into agricultural smallholdings to eradicate rural poverty; involved in rubber, oil palm and sugar-cane cultivation; Chair. Tan Sri MOHD ISA ABDUL SAMAD; Dir-Gen. Dato' AHMAD TARMIZI ALIAS.

Khazanah Nasional: Petronas Twin Towers, Tower 2, Tingkat 33, 50088 Kuala Lumpur; tel. (3) 20340000; fax (3) 20340300; e-mail info@khazanah.com.my; internet www.khazanah.com.my; f. 1994; state-controlled investment co; assumed responsibility for certain assets fmrly under control of the Ministry of Finance; holds 40% of Telekom Malaysia Bhd, 40% of Tenaga Nasional Bhd, 6.6% of HICOM Bhd and 17.8% of Proton; Chair. Dato' Sri MOHD NAJIB BIN Haji ABDUL RAZAK; Man. Dir Tan Sri Dato' AZMAN BIN Haji MOKHTAR.

Malaysia External Trade Development Corpn (MATRADE): Menara MATRADE, Jalan Khidmat Usaha, off Jalan Duta, 50480 Kuala Lumpur; tel. (3) 62077077; fax (3) 62037253; e-mail info@matrade.gov.my; internet www.matrade.gov.my; f. 1993; responsible for external trade devt and promotion; Chair. Dato' MAH SIEW KEONG.

Malaysian Institute of Economic Research: Podium City Point, Level 2, Kompleks Dayabumi, Jalan Sultan Hishamuddin, 50050 Kuala Lumpur; tel. (3) 22725897; fax (3) 22730197; e-mail zakariah@mier.po.my; internet www.mier.org.my; f. 1985; Chair. Tan Sri Dr SULAIMAN MAHBOB; Exec. Dir Dr ZAKARIAH ABDUL RASHID.

Malaysian Palm Oil Board (MPOB): 6 Persiaran Institusi, Bandar Baru Bangi, 43000 Kajang, Selangor; tel. (3) 87694400; fax (3) 89259446; e-mail webmaster@mpob.gov.my; internet www.mpob.gov.my; f. 2000; est. by merger of Palm Oil Registration and Licensing Authority and Palm Oil Research Institute of Malaysia; Chair. Dato' Seri SHAHRIR BIN ABDUL SAMAD.

Malaysian Timber Industry Board (Lembaga Perindustrian Kayu Malaysia): 13–17 Menara PGRM, 8 Jalan Pudu Ulu, 56100 Cheras, Kuala Lumpur; tel. (3) 92822235; fax (3) 92851477; e-mail info@mtib.gov.my; internet www.mtib.gov.my; f. 1973; promotes and regulates the export of timber and timber products from Malaysia; Chair. Datuk WILFRED MADIUS TANGAU; Dir-Gen. Dr JALALUDDIN BIN HARUN.

Muda Agricultural Development Authority (MADA): MADA HQ, Ampang Jajar, 05990 Alor Setar, Kedah; tel. (4) 7728255; fax (4) 7722667; e-mail promada@mada.gov.my; internet www.mada.gov.my; Chair. Dato' Seri MAHDZIR BIN KHALID; Gen. Man. Dato' Haji ABDUL RAHIM BIN SALEH.

National Economic Action Council: NEAC-MTEN, Prime Minister's Office, Menara Usahawan, Blok Utama, Tingkat 5, 18 Persiaran Perdana, Pusat Pentadbiran Kerajaan Persekutuan, 62652 Putrajaya; tel. (3) 88886513; fax (3) 88882902; e-mail feedback@neac.gov.my; internet www.neac.gov.my; Chair. Tan Sri AMIRSHAM AZIZ.

National Information Technology Council (NITC): c/o The Ministry of Science, Technology and Innovation, Aras 1-7, Blok C4–5, Kompleks C, Pusat Pentadbiran Kerajaan Persekutuan, 62662 Putrajaya; tel. (3) 88858000; fax (3) 88884328; internet www.nitc.my; Sec. Datuk Tengku Dr MOHD AZZMAN SHARIFFADEEN.

National Timber Certification Council: C-8-5, Megan Ave II, 12 Jalan Yap Kwan Seng, 50450 Kuala Lumpur; tel. (3) 21612298; fax (3) 21612293; e-mail info@mtcc.com.my; internet www.mtcc.com.my; Chair. Dato' Dr FREEZAILAH CHE YEOM.

Perbadanan Nasional Bhd (PERNAS): Menara Dato' Onn, Level 9B, 45 Jalan Tun Ismail, 50480 Kuala Lumpur; tel. (3) 26986670; fax (3) 26986617; e-mail enquiries@pns.com.my; internet www.pns.com.my; f. 1969; govt-sponsored; promotes trade, banking, property and plantation development, construction, mineral exploration, steel manufacturing, inland container transportation, mining, insurance, industrial development, engineering services, telecommunication equipment, hotels and shipping; cap. p.u. RM 116.25m.; 10 wholly owned subsidiaries, over 60 jointly owned subsidiaries and 18 assoc. cos; Chair. Datuk IDRIS BIN HASHIM; Man. Dir Tuan Syed KAMARULZAMAN BIN Syed ZAINOL KHODKI SHAHABUDIN.

DEVELOPMENT ORGANIZATIONS

Fisheries Development Authority of Malaysia: Plaza Utama Alam Mesra, Kota Kinabalu, Sabah; tel. (3) 26177000; fax (3) 26911931; e-mail info@lkim.gov.my; internet lkim.gov.my; Chair. Dato' Haji JIDIN BIN MOHD SHAFEE; Dir-Gen. Dato' Haji KHAZIN BIN MOHD HAMZAH.

Johor Corpn: Level 2, Persada Johor, Jalan Abdullah Ibrahim, 80000 Johor Bahru; tel. (7) 2232692; fax (7) 2233175; e-mail pdnjohor@jcorp.com.my; internet www.jcorp.com.my; devt agency of the Johor state govt; Chair. Dato' Haji ABDUL GHANI BIN OTHMAN; Chief Exec. Haji KAMARUZZAMAN BIN ABU KASSIM.

Kumpulan FIMA Bhd (Food Industries of Malaysia): Plaza Damansara, Blok C, Tingkat 4, Suite 4.1, 45 Jalan Medan Setia 1, Bukit Damansara, 50490 Kuala Lumpur; tel. (3) 20921211; fax (3) 20925923; e-mail enquiry@fima.com.my; internet www.fima.com.my; f. 1972; fmrly govt corpn; transferred to private sector in 1991; promotes food and related industry through investment on its own or by co-ventures with local or foreign entrepreneurs; oil palm, cocoa and fruit plantation developments; manufacturing and packaging, trading, supermarkets and restaurants; Chair. MUHAMMAD RADZI BIN Haji MANSOR; Man. Dir Encik ROSLAN BIN HAMIR; 1,189 employees.

Majlis Amanah Rakyat (MARA) (Trust Council for the People): Bangunan Medan MARA, 25th Floor, Jalan Raja Laut, 50609 Kuala Lumpur; tel. (3) 26915111; fax (3) 26913620; e-mail webmaster@mara.gov.my; internet www.mara.gov.my; f. 1966; est. to promote, stimulate, facilitate and undertake economic and social development, and to participate in industrial and commercial undertakings and jt ventures; Dir-Gen. IBRAHIM BIN AHMAD.

Malaysian Agricultural Research and Development Institute (MARDI): POB 12301, General Post Office, 50774 Kuala Lumpur; tel. (3) 89437111; fax (3) 89483664; e-mail enquiry@mardi.gov.my; internet www.mardi.gov.my; f. 1969; research and development in food and tropical agriculture; Dir-Gen. Datuk Dr ABD. SHUKOR BIN ABD. RAHMAN.

Malaysian Industrial Development Authority (MIDA): Plaza Sentral, Block 4, 5 Jalan Stesen Sentral, 50470 Kuala Lumpur; tel. (3) 22673633; fax (3) 22747970; e-mail investmalaysia@mida.gov.my; internet www.mida.gov.my; f. 1967; Chair. Tan Sri Dr SULAIMAN MAHBOOB; Dir-Gen. Datuk JALILAH BABA.

Malaysian Industrial Development Finance Bhd (MIDF): Level 21, Menara MIDF, 82 Jalan Raja Chulan, 50200 Kuala Lumpur; tel. (3) 21738888; fax (3) 21738877; e-mail inquiry-feedback@midf.com.my; internet www.midf.com.my; f. 1960 by the Govt; banks, insurance cos, industrial financing, advisory services, project development, merchant and commercial banking services; Chair. Tan Sri Dato' MAHMOOD BIN TAIB; Man. Dir Datuk MOHAMED NAJIB Haji ABDULLAH.

Malaysian Pepper Board: Lot 1115, Jalan Utama, 93916 Kuching, Sarawak; tel. (82) 331811; fax (82) 336877; e-mail info@mpb.gov.my; internet www.mpb.gov.my; f. 2007; govt-owned; est. to replace the Pepper Marketing Bd; responsible for the statutory grading of all Sarawak pepper for export, licensing of pepper dealers and exporters, trading and the development and promotion of pepper grading, storage and processing facilities; Chair. Datuk ALEXANDER NANTA LINGGI; Dir-Gen. GRUNSIN AYOM.

Pinang Development Corpn: 1 Pesiaran Mahsuri, Bandar Bayan Baru, 11909 Bayan Lepas, Pinang; tel. (4) 6340111; fax (4) 6432405; e-mail enquiry@pdc.gov.my; internet www.pdc.gov.my; f. 1969; development agency of the Pinang state government; Gen. Man. Dato' ROSLI JAAFAR.

Sarawak Economic Development Corpn: Menara SEDC, 6th–11th Floors, Sarawak Plaza, Jalan Tunku Abdul Rahman, 93100 Kuching; tel. (82) 416777; fax (82) 424330; e-mail ssedc@po.jaring.my; internet www.sedc.com.my; f. 1972; statutory org. responsible for commercial and industrial development in Sarawak either solely or jtly with foreign and local entrepreneurs; responsible for the development of tourism infrastructure; Chair. Datuk Haji TALIB ZULPILIP.

Selangor State Development Corpn (PKNS): Level 2, Menara HPAIC, Laman Seri Business Park, Seksyen 13, 40100 Shah Alam, Selangor; tel. (3) 55201234; fax (3) 55102149; e-mail wazir@pkns.gov.my; internet www.pkns.gov.my; f. 1964; partially govt-owned; Gen. Man. OTHMAN BIN Haji OMAR.

CHAMBERS OF COMMERCE

Associated Chinese Chambers of Commerce and Industry of Malaysia: Wisma Chinese Chamber, 6th Floor, 258 Jalan Ampang, 50450 Kuala Lumpur; tel. (3) 42603090; fax (3) 42603080; e-mail acccim@acccim.org.my; internet www.acccim.org.my; Pres. Datuk LIM KOK CHEONG; Sec.-Gen. Datuk DAVID CHUA.

Malay Chamber of Commerce Malaysia: 29 & 31 Jalan Lawan Pedang, 13/27 Shah Alam, 40100 Selangor; tel. (3) 55199110; fax (3) 55120801; e-mail info@dpmmns.com.my; internet www.dpmms.com .my; f. 1957; fmrly Associated Malay Chambers of Commerce of Malaya; present name adopted 1992; Pres. Tan Sri ROZALI ISMAIL BIN; Sec.-Gen. ZAKI SAID.

Malaysian Associated Indian Chambers of Commerce and Industry: Megan Ave II, Blok B, 9th Floor, Unit 1, 12 Jalan Yap Kwan Seng, 50450 Kuala Lumpur; tel. (3) 21712616; fax (3) 21711195; e-mail info@maicci.org.my; internet www.maicci.org .my; f. 1950; Pres. Datuk K. K ESWARAN; 8 brs.

Malaysian International Chamber of Commerce and Industry (MICCI) (Dewan Perniagaan dan Perindustrian Antarabangsa Malaysia): C-8-8, Plaza Mont' Kiara, 2 Jalan Kiara, 50480 Kuala Lumpur; tel. (3) 62017708; fax (3) 62017705; e-mail micci@micci.com; internet www.micci.com; f. 1837; brs in Pinang, Perak, Johor, Melaka and Sabah; 1,000 corp. mems; Pres. SIMON WHITELAW; Exec. Dir STEWART J. FORBES.

National Chamber of Commerce and Industry of Malaysia: Menara MATRADE, Level 3, West Wing, Jalan Khidmat Usaha, off Jalan Duta, 50480 Kuala Lumpur; tel. (3) 62049811; fax (3) 62049711; e-mail enquiry@nccim.org.my; internet www.nccim.org .my; f. 1962; Pres. Tuan Syed ALI MOHAMED ALATTAS; Hon. Sec.-Gen. Dato' Syed HUSSEIN AL-HABSHEE.

Sabah Bumiputera Chamber of Commerce (SBCC): Lot 119, 4th Floor, SBCC Bldg, Locked Bag 154, Jalan Gaya, 88999 Kota Kinabalu; tel. (88) 222442; fax (88) 223454; f. 1972; Pres. Datuk Haji AHMAD ALIP LOPE ABDUL AZIZ; Sec.-Gen. JURIL Haji SUDIN.

Sabah United Chinese Chambers of Commerce (SUCCC): POB 12176, 88824 Kota Kinabalu; tel. (88) 225460; fax (88) 218185; e-mail succc01@tm.net.my; internet www.succc.org; f. 1955; Pres. Datuk Seri Panglima SAU WAH GAN.

Sarawak Chamber of Commerce and Industry (SCCI): DUBS Commercial Centre, 2nd Floor, Lot 376, Seksyen 54, Jalan Petanak, 93100 Kuching; tel. (82) 237148; fax (82) 237186; e-mail scci@cdc.net .my; internet www.scci.org.my; f. 1950; Chair. Datuk Abang Haji ABDUL KARIM Tun Abang Haji OPENG.

INDUSTRIAL AND TRADE ASSOCIATIONS

Federation of Malaysian Manufacturers: Wisma FMM, 3 Persiaran Dagang, PJU 9 Bandar Sri Damansara, 52200 Kuala Lumpur; tel. (3) 62867200; fax (3) 62741266; e-mail webmaster@fmm.org.my; internet www.fmm.org.my; f. 1968; offers guidance and advice relating to trade and industry; presents problems and concerns to the Govt; 2,500 mems (Jan. 2012); Pres. Tan Sri Datuk POH KON YONG; CEO LEE CHENG SUAN.

Federation of Rubber Trade Associations of Malaysia: 138 Jalan Bandar, 50000 Kuala Lumpur; tel. (3) 2384006.

Malayan Agricultural Producers' Association: Plaza Ampang City, 16G-L, Jalan Ampang, 50734 Kuala Lumpur; tel. (3) 2545253; fax (3) 2413158; e-mail mapa@myjaring.net; internet www.mapa.net .my; f. 1997; 406 mem. estates and 108 factories/mills; Pres. Tan Sri Dato' Dr MOHD NOOR BIN ISMAIL; Dir MOHAMAD BIN AUDONG.

Malaysian Automotive Association: F-1-47, Blok F, Jalan PJU 1A/3, 2 Taipan Damansara, Parcel 1, Ara Damansara, 47301 Petaling Jaya, Selangor Darul Ehsan; tel. (3) 78439947; fax (3) 78430847; e-mail secretariat@maa.org.my; internet www.maa.org.my; f. 1960 as Fed. of Malaya Motor Traders' Assocn; renamed following merger with Malaysian Motor Vehicle Assemblers' Asscn in 2000; Pres. Datuk AISHAH AHMAD; Sec.-Gen. GOH CHENG MENG.

Malaysian Iron and Steel Industry Federation: 28E–30E, Tingkat 5, Blok 2, Worldwide Business Park, Jalan Tinju 13/50, Seksyen 13, Shah Alam, 40675 Selangor; tel. (3) 55133970; fax (3) 55133891; e-mail enquiry@misif.org.my; internet www.misif.org.my; Pres. CHOW CHONG LONG; 150 mems.

Malaysian Palm Oil Association (MPOA): Bangunan Getah Asli, 12th Floor, 148 Jalan Ampang, 50450 Kuala Lumpur; tel. (3) 27105680; fax (3) 27105679; e-mail mpoa@mpoa.org.my; internet www.mpoa.org.my; f. 1999; est. as result of rationalization of plantation industry; secr. for producers of palm oil; CEO MAMAT SALLEH.

Malaysian Pineapple Industry Board: Wisma Nanas, 5 Jalan Padi Mahsuri, Bandar Baru UDA, 81200 Johor Bahru; tel. (7) 2361211; fax (7) 2365694; e-mail umum@mpib.gov.my; internet www.mpib.gov.my; Dir-Gen. Haji SAHDAN BIN SALIM.

Malaysian Rubber Board: POB 10150, 50908 Kuala Lumpur; tel. (3) 92062000; fax (3) 21634492; e-mail general@lgm.gov.my; internet www.lgm.gov.my; f. 1998; implements policies and development programmes to ensure the viability of the Malaysian rubber industry; regulates the industry (in particular, the packing, grading, shipping and export of rubber); Dir-Gen. Dr SALMIAH AHMAD.

Malaysian Rubber Products Manufacturers' Association: 1 Jalan USJ 11/1J, Subang Jaya, 47620 Petaling Jaya, Selangor; tel. (3) 56316150; fax (3) 56316152; e-mail mrpma@po.jaring.my; f. 1952; Pres. Tan Sri Datuk ARSHAD AYUB; 144 mems.

Malaysian Timber Certification Council (MTCC): C-8-5, Megan Ave II, 12 Jalan Yap Kwan Seng, 50450 Kuala Lumpur; tel. (3) 21612298; fax (3) 21612293; e-mail info@mtcc.com.my; internet www.mtcc.com.my; f. 1999; operates a voluntary national timber certification scheme to encourage sustainable forest management; Chair. Dato' Dr FREEZAILAH CHE YEOM; CEO CHEW LYE TENG.

Malaysian Wood Industries Association: Menara PGRM, 18th Floor, 8 Jalan Pudu Ulu, Cheras, 55100 Kuala Lumpur; tel. (3) 92821778; fax (3) 92821789; e-mail mwia@mwia.com.my; internet www.mwia.com.my; f. 1957; Pres. Dato' LOW KIAN CHUAN.

National Tobacco Board Malaysia (Ibu Pejabat Lembaga Tembakau Negara): Kubang Kerian, POB 198, 15720 Kota Bharu, Kelantan; tel. (9) 7652212; fax (9) 7655640; e-mail ltnm@ltn.gov .my; internet www.ltn.gov.my; Dir-Gen. TEO HUI BEK.

Northern Malaya Rubber Millers' and Packers' Association: 22 Pitt St, 3rd Floor, Suites 301–303, 10200 Pinang; tel. (4) 620037; f. 1919; 153 mems; Pres. HWANG SING LUE; Hon. Sec. LEE SENG KEOK.

Palm Oil Refiners' Association of Malaysia (PORAM): 801 C/ 802A Blok B, Executive Suites, Kelana Business Centre, 97 Jalan SS7/2, 47301 Kelana Jaya, Selangor; tel. (3) 74920006; fax (3) 74920128; e-mail info@poram.org.my; internet www.poram.org .my; f. 1975; est. to promote the palm oil refining industry; Chair. MOHD ZAIN ISMAIL; CEO MOHD JAAFAR AHMAD; 90 mems.

Rubber Industry Smallholders Development Authority (RISDA): Bangunan RISDA, km 7, Jalan Ampang, Karung Berkunci 11067, 50990 Kuala Lumpur; tel. (3) 42564022; fax (3) 42576726; e-mail webmaster@risda.gov.my; internet www.risda .gov.my; f. 1973; Chair. Tan Sri RAHIM TAMBY CHIK; Dir-Gen. Dato' WAN MOHAMMAD ZUKI MOHAMMAD.

Tin Industry Research and Development Board: West Block, 8th Floor, Wisma Selangor Dredging, Jalan Ampang, POB 12560, 50782 Kuala Lumpur; tel. (3) 21616171; fax (3) 21616179; e-mail mcom@mcom.com.my; Chair. MOHAMED AJIB ANUAR; Sec. MUHAMAD NOR MUHAMAD.

EMPLOYERS' ORGANIZATIONS

Malaysian Employers' Federation: 3A06–3A07, Blok A, Pusat Dagangan Phileo Damansara II, 15 Jalan 16/11, off Jalan Damansara, 46350 Petaling Jaya, Selangor; tel. (3) 79557778; fax (3) 79556808; e-mail mef-hq@mef.org.my; internet www.mef.org.my; f. 1959; Pres. Dato' AZMAN SHAH Dato' Seri HARUN; Exec. Dir Haji SHAMSUDDIN BARDAN; private sector org. incorporating 13 employer orgs and 4,611 individual enterprises, incl.:

> **Association of Insurance Employers:** c/o Royal Insurance (M) Sdn Bhd, Menara Boustead, 5th Floor, 69 Jalan Raja Chulan, 50200 Kuala Lumpur; tel. (3) 2410233; fax (3) 2442762; Pres. NG KIM HOONG.
>
> **Commercial Employers' Association of Peninsular Malaysia:** c/o The East Asiatic Co (M) Bhd, 1 Jalan 205, 46050 Petaling Jaya, Selangor; tel. (3) 7913322; fax (3) 7913561; Pres. HAMZAH Haji GHULAM.
>
> **Malaysian Chamber of Mines:** West Block, Wisma Selangor Dredging, 8th Floor, 142c Jalan Ampang, 50450 Kuala Lumpur; tel. (3) 21616171; fax (3) 21616179; e-mail mcom@mcom.com.my; internet www.mcom.com.my; f. 1914; promotes and protects interests of Malaysian mining industry; Pres. MOHAMED AJIB ANUAR; Exec. Dir MUHAMAD NOR MUHAMAD; 100 mems.
>
> **Malaysian Textile Manufacturers' Association:** C-9-4, Megan Ave 1, 189 Jalan Tun Razak, 50400 Kuala Lumpur; tel. (3) 21621454; fax (3) 21625148; e-mail info@mtma.org.my; internet www.fashion-asia.com; Pres. J. C. SURESH; CEO ANDREW HONG; 70 mems.
>
> **Pan Malaysian Bus Operators' Association:** 88 Jalan Sultan Idris Shah, 30300 Ipoh, Perak; tel. (5) 2549421; fax (5) 2550858; Sec. TEOH EWE HUN.
>
> **Sabah Employers' Consultative Association:** Dewan SECA, No. 4, Block A, 1st Floor, Bandar Ramai-Ramai, 90000 Sandakan, Sabah; tel. and fax (89) 272846; Chair. LING AH HONG.
>
> **Stevedore Employers' Association:** 5 Pengkalan Weld, POB 288, 10300 Pinang; tel. (4) 2615091; Pres. ABDUL RAHMAN MAIDIN.

UTILITIES

Energy Commission of Malaysia (Suruhanjaya Tenaga): 12 Jalan Tun Hussein, Precinct 2, 62100 Putrajaya; tel. (3) 88708500; fax (3) 88888637; e-mail fauzih@st.gov.my; internet www.st.gov.my; f. 2002; regulatory body supervising electricity and gas supply; CEO Ir AHMAD FAUZI BIN HASAN.

Electricity

Tenaga Nasional Bhd: 129 Jalan Bangsar, POB 11003, 50732 Kuala Lumpur; tel. (3) 2825566; fax (3) 22833686; e-mail webadmin@tnb.com.my; internet www.tnb.com.my; f. 1990; est. through corporatization and privatization of Nat. Electricity Bd; 53% govt-controlled; generation, transmission and distribution of electricity in Peninsular Malaysia; generating capacity of 7,621 MW (63% of total power generation); also purchases power from 12 licensed independent power producers; Chair. Tan Sri Dato' Amar LEO MOGGIE; Pres. and CEO Dato' Ir AZMAN BIN MOHAMED.

Sabah Electricity Supply Board (SESB): Wisma SESB, Jalan Tunku Abdul Rahman, 88673 Kota Kinabalu; tel. (88) 282500; fax (88) 282314; e-mail webmaster@sesb.com.my; internet www.sesb.com.my; generation, transmission and distribution of electricity in Sabah; Man. Dir Ir Haji ABDUL RAZAK SALLIM.

Syarikat Sesco Bhd (SESCO): POB 149, 93700 Kuching, Sarawak; tel. (82) 441188; fax (82) 444433; e-mail public_enquiry@sesoc.com.my; internet www.sesco.com.my; fmrly Sarawak Electricity Supply Corpn; generation, transmission and distribution of electricity in Sarawak; Chair. Datuk ABDUL HAMED SEPAWI; CEO TORSTEIN DALE SJOTVEIT.

Gas

Gas Malaysia Sdn Bhd: 5 Jalan Serendah 26/17, Seksyen 26, Peti Surat 7901, 40732 Shah Alam, Selangor Darul Ehsan; tel. (3) 51923000; e-mail ccu@gasmalaysia.com; internet www.gasmalaysia.com; f. 1992; Chair. Tan Sri Datuk Dr HAMZAH BAKAR; CEO MUHAMAD NOOR HAMID.

Water

Under the federal Constitution, water supply is the responsibility of the state Governments. In 1998, owing to water shortages, the National Water Resources Council was established to co-ordinate management of water resources at national level. Malaysia's sewerage system is operated by Indah Water Konsortium, owned by Prime Utilities.

National Water Resources Council: c/o Ministry of Works, Jalan Sultan Salahuddin, 50580 Kuala Lumpur; tel. (3) 2919011; fax (3) 2986612; f. 1998; co-ordinates management of water resources at national level through co-operation with state water boards; chaired by the Prime Minister.

Regulatory Authorities

Johor State Regulatory Body: c/o Pejabat Setiausaha Kerajaan Negeri Johor, Aras 1, Bangunan Sultan Ibrahim, Jalan Bukit Timbalan, 80000 Johor Bahru; tel. (7) 223850; Dir Haji OMAR BIN AWAB.

Kelantan Water Department: Tingkat Bawah, Blok 6, Kota Darul Naim, 15503 Kota Bharu, Kelantan; tel. (9) 7475240; fax (9) 7475220; e-mail jank@kelantan.gov.my; internet www.jank.kelantan.gov.my; Dir Tengku ADLI BIN Tengku ABDULLAH.

Water Supply Authorities

Kedah Public Works Department: Bangunan Sultan Abdul Halim, Jalan Sultan Badlishah, 05582 Alor Setar, Kedah; tel. (4) 7334041; fax (4) 7341616; internet kedah.jkr.gov.my; Dir Ir ROSLAND BIN GHANI.

Kelantan Water Sdn Bhd: Bangunan Perbadanan Menteri Besar Kelantan, Lot 2 & 257, Jalan Kuala Krai, 15050 Kota Bharu, Kelantan; tel. (9) 7437777; fax (9) 7472030; internet www.airkelantan.com.my; Gen. Man. Ir Haji HANAPI MOHD BIN MAHMUD.

Kuching Water Board: Jalan Batu Lintang, 93200 Kuching, Sarawak; tel. (82) 240371; fax (82) 244546; e-mail juliab@kwb.gov.my; internet www.kwb.gov.my; Chair. Dato' Sri AHMAD TARMIZI BIN Haji SULAIMAN; Gen. Man. MOHD SABARI BIN SHAKERAN.

Labuan Public Works Department: Jalan Kg. Jawa, POB 2, 87008 Labuan; tel. (87) 414040; fax (87) 412370; Dir Ir ZULKIFLY BIN MADON.

LAKU Management Sdn Bhd: Menara Soon Hup, 6th Floor, Lot 907, Jalan Merbau, 98000 Miri; tel. (85) 442000; fax (85) 442005; e-mail laku@lakumy.po.my; internet www.lakumanagement.com.my; f. 1995; serves Miri, Limbang and Bintulu; Chair. HUBERT THIAN CHONG HUI; CEO WONG TIONG KAI.

Melaka Water Corpn: Tingkat Bawah, 1st and 10th–13th Floors, Graha Maju, Jalan Graha Maju, 75300 Melaka; tel. (6) 2821700; fax (6) 2837266; e-mail baharam@pamwtr.gov.my; Dir Ir Haji BAHARAM BIN Haji MOHAMAD.

Negeri Sembilan Water Department: Wisma Negeri, 70990 Seremban; tel. (6) 7610505; fax (6) 7617841; Dir Ir ZULKFLKRI IBRAHIM.

Pahang Water Supply Department (Jabatan Bekalan Air Pahang): Kompleks JBA, Bandar Indera Mahkota, 25200 Kuantan, Pahang; tel. (9) 5712222; fax (9) 5712221; e-mail p-jba@pahang.gov.my; internet jba.pahang.gov.my; corporatized in 2012; Dir Datuk Seri MUHAMMAD SAFIAN ISMAIL.

Perak Water Board (Lembaga Air Perak): Jalan St John, Peti Surat 589, 30760 Ipoh, Perak; tel. (5) 2551155; fax (5) 2556397; internet www.lap.com.my; Dir Dato' Ir Dato' Seri Diraja Dr ZAMBRY BIN Haji ABDUL KADIR.

Pinang Water Supply Corpn (Perbadanan Bekalan Air Pulau Pinang Sdn Bhd): Menara KOMTAR, Level 32, Jalan Pinang, 10000 Pinang; tel. (4) 2634200; fax (4) 2613581; e-mail customer@pba.com.my; internet www.pba.com.my; f. 1973; Gen. Man. Ir JASENI BIN MAIDINSA.

Sabah State Water Department (Jabatan Air Negeri Sabah): Wisma MUIS, Blok A, Tingkat 6, Beg Berkunci 210, 88825 Kota Kinabalu; tel. (88) 232364; fax (88) 232396; e-mail jans.hq@sabah.gov.my; internet www.sabah.gov.my/air; Man. MOHAMAD TAHIR BIN MOHAMAD TALIB.

SAJ Holdings Sdn Bhd: Bangunan Ibu Pejabat SAJ Holdings, Jalan Garuda, Larkin, POB 262, 80350 Johor Bahru; tel. (7) 2244040; fax (7) 2241990; e-mail support@saj.com.my; internet www.saj.com.my; f. 1999; Exec. Chair. Tan Sri HAMDAN MOHAMED.

Sarawak Public Works Department: Wisma Seberkas, Jalan Tun Haji Openg, 93582 Kuching; tel. (82) 203100; fax (82) 429679; internet www.jkr.sarawak.gov.my; Dir Ir ZURAIMI BIN Haji SABKI.

Selangor Water Supply Co (Syarikat Bekalan Air Selangor Sdn Bhd): POB 5001, Jalan Pantai Baru, 59990 Kuala Lumpur; tel. (3) 2826244; fax (3) 22955168; e-mail puspel@syabas.com.my; internet www.syabas.com.my; f. 1972; CEO Dato' RUSLAN BIN HASSAN.

Sibu Water Board: Km 5, Jalan Salim, POB 405, 96007 Sibu, Sarawak; tel. (84) 211001; fax (84) 211543; e-mail swbs@swb.gov.my; internet www.swb.gov.my; Gen. Man. DANIEL WONG PARK ING.

Terengganu Water Department: Wisma Negeri, Tingkat 3, Jalan Pejabat, 20200 Kuala Terengganu; tel. (9) 6222444; fax (9) 6221510; Dir Ir Haji WAN NGAH BIN WAN.

TRADE UNIONS

Malaysian Trades Union Congress (MTUC): Wisma MTUC, 10-5, Jalan USJ 9/5T, 47620 Subang Jaya, Selangor; POB 3073, 46000 Petaling Jaya, Selangor; tel. (3) 80242953; fax (3) 80243225; e-mail mtuc@tm.net.my; internet www.mtuc.org.my; f. 1949; 247 affiliated unions, representing approx. 500,000 workers; Pres. MOHD KHALID ATAN; Sec.-Gen. ABDUL HALIM MANSOR.

Transport

RAILWAYS

Peninsular Malaysia

The state-owned Malayan Railways had a total length of 1,665 km in Peninsular Malaysia in 2010. The main railway line follows the west coast and extends 782 km from Singapore, south of Peninsular Malaysia, to Butterworth (opposite Pinang Island) in the north. From Bukit Mertajam, close to Butterworth, the Kedah line runs north to the Thai border at Padang Besar where connection is made with the State Railway of Thailand. The East Coast Line, 526 km long, runs from Gemas to Tumpat (in Kelantan). A 21-km branch line from Pasir Mas (27 km south of Tumpat) connects with the State Railway of Thailand at the border station of Sungei Golok. Branch lines serve railway-operated ports at Port Dickson and Telok Anson as well as Port Klang and Jurong (Singapore). Malaysia's first Light Rail Transit (LRT) system was opened in the Kuala Lumpur area in 1996. A second line began operating within the same system in 1998; a second LRT system, comprising one line, also commenced operations in that year. An express rail link connecting central Kuala Lumpur and the new Kuala Lumpur International Airport (KLIA) opened in 2001. The construction of a mass rapid transport system commenced in Kuala Lumpur in 2012, with completion scheduled for 2016. In February 2013 plans were announced for the construction of a high-speed rail link between Kuala Lumpur and Singapore, which would be due for completion in 2020.

Keretapi Tanah Melayu Bhd (KTMB) (Malayan Railways): KTMB Corporate Headquarters, Jalan Sultan Hishamuddin, 50621 Kuala Lumpur; tel. (3) 22631111; fax (3) 27105706; e-mail callcenter@ktmb.com.my; internet www.ktmb.com.my; f. 1885; incorporated as a co under govt control in 1992; privatized in 1997; managed by the consortium Marak Unggal (Renong, DRB and Bolton); Chair. Dato' Sri MOHD ZIN BIN MOHAMED.

Sabah

Sabah State Railway: Karung Berkunci 2047, 88999 Kota Kinabalu; tel. (88) 254611; fax (88) 236395; e-mail webmaster.jkns@sabah.gov.my; internet www.sabah.gov.my/railway; 134 track-km of 1-m gauge (2008); goods and passenger services from Tanjong Aru to

Tenom, serving part of the west coast and the interior; diesel trains are used; Gen. Man. Haji MOHD ZAIN Haji MOHD SAID.

ROADS

Peninsular Malaysia

Peninsular Malaysia's road system is extensive, in contrast to those of Sabah and Sarawak. By 2010 the road network in Malaysia totalled an estimated 144,403 km.

Sabah

Jabatan Kerja Raya Sabah (Sabah Public Works Department): Jalan Sembulan, Locked Bag 2032, 88582 Kota Kinabalu, Sabah; tel. (88) 244333; fax (88) 237234; e-mail jkrweb@sabah.gov.my; internet www.jkr.sabah.gov.my; f. 1881; implements and maintains public infrastructures such as roads, bridges, buildings and sewerage systems throughout Sabah; maintains a road network totalling 15,756.6 km, of which 5,686.5 km are sealed roads; Dir JOHN ANTHONY.

Sarawak

Jabatan Kerja Raya Sarawak (Sarawak Public Works Department): Tingkat 11–18, Wisma Saberkas, Jalan Tun Abang Haji Openg, 93582 Kuching, Sarawak; tel. (82) 203100; fax (82) 251908; e-mail corporatejkr@gmail.com; internet www.jkr.sarawak.gov.my; implements and maintains public infrastructures in Sarawak; road network totalling 10,979 km, of which 3,986 km are sealed roads; Dir Ir ZURAIMI BIN SABKI.

SHIPPING

In 2012 Malaysia's flag registered fleet comprised 2,168 vessels, with a total displacement of 9,481,672 grt, including 178 general cargo ships, 32 gas tankers and seven bulk carriers. The ports in Malaysia are classified as federal ports, under the jurisdiction of the federal Ministry of Transport, or state ports, responsible to the state ministries of Sabah and Sarawak.

Peninsular Malaysia

The federal ports in Peninsular Malaysia are Klang (the principal port), Penang, Johor and Kuantan.

Johor Port Authority: 6A1–8A1 Pusat Perdagangan Pasir Gudang, Jalan Bandar, 81700 Pasir Gudang, Johor; tel. (7) 2534000; fax (7) 2517684; e-mail admin@lpj.gov.my; internet www.lpj.gov.my; f. 1976; Gen. Man. MUHAMMAD RAZIF AHMED.

Johor Port Bhd: POB 151, Wisma Kontena, 81707 Pasir Gudang, Johor; tel. (7) 2535888; fax (7) 2510980; e-mail jpb@johorport.com .my; internet www.johorport.com.my; Chair. Datuk MOHD SIDIK BIN SHAIK OSMAN.

Klang Port Authority: POB 202, Jalan Pelabuhan, 42005 Port Klang, Selangor; tel. (3) 31688211; fax (3) 31689177; e-mail onestopagency@pka.gov.my; internet www.pka.gov.my; f. 1963; Gen. Man. Capt. DAVID RAJAN PADMAN.

Kuantan Port Authority: Tanjung Gelang, POB 161, 25720 Kuantan, Pahang; tel. (9) 5858000; fax (9) 5833866; e-mail lpktn@ lpktn.gov.my; internet www.lpktn.gov.my; f. 1974; Gen. Man. Dato' KHAIRUL ANUAR BIN ABDUL RAHMAN.

Penang Port Commission: Level 2, Swettenham Pier Cruise Terminal 1A, 10300 Penang; tel. (4) 2633211; fax (4) 2626211; e-mail sppp@penangport.gov.my; internet www.penangport.gov .my; f. 1956; Gen. Man. NOOR ARIF BIN YUSOFF.

Sabah

The main ports, which are administered by the Sabah Ports Authority, are Kota Kinabalu, Sandakan, Tawau, Lahad Datu, Kudat, Semporna and Kunak. Many international shipping lines serve Sabah. Local services are operated by smaller vessels.

Sabah Ports Authority: Bangunan SPA, Jalan Tun Fuad, Tanjung Lipat, Locked Bag 2005, 88617 Kota Kinabalu, Sabah; tel. (88) 538400; fax (88) 223036; e-mail sabahport@tm.net.my; internet www.lpps.sabah.gov.my; f. 1968; Gen. Man. Eng. MAYONG OMAR.

Sarawak

There are four port authorities in Sarawak: Kuching, Rajang, Miri and Bintulu. Kuching, Rajang and Miri are state ports, while Bintulu is a federal port. Kuching port serves the southern region of Sarawak, Rajang port the central region, and Miri port the northern region.

Kuching Port Authority: Jalan Pelabuhan, Pending, POB 530, 93450 Kuching, Sarawak; tel. (82) 482144; fax (82) 481696; e-mail hq@kuport.com.my; internet www.kpa.gov.my; f. 1961; Gen. Man. LIU MOI FONG.

Rajang Port Authority: Jalan Pulau, 96000 Sibu, Sarawak; tel. (84) 319004; fax (84) 318754; e-mail rpa@rajangport.gov.my; internet www.rajangport.gov.my; f. 1970; Gen. Man. HELEN LIM HUI SHYAN.

Principal Shipping Companies

Malaysia Shipping Corpn Sdn Bhd: Office Tower, Plaza Berjaya, Suite 14C, 14th Floor, 12 Jalan Imbi, 55100 Kuala Lumpur; tel. (3) 21418788; fax (3) 21429214; Chair. Y. C. CHANG.

Malaysian International Shipping Corpn Bhd (National Shipping Line of Malaysia): Menara Dayabumi, Level 25, Jalan Sultan Hishamuddin, 50050 Kuala Lumpur; tel. (3) 22738088; fax (3) 22736602; e-mail miscweb@miscbhd.com; internet www.misc.com .my; f. 1968; regular services between South-East Asia, South Asia, Australia, Japan and Europe; also operates chartering, tanker, haulage and warehousing and agency services; majority stake owned by Petroliam Nasional Bhd (PETRONAS); Chair. Dato' SHAMSUL AZHAR BIN ABBAS; Pres. and CEO Datuk NASARUDIN BIN MOHD IDRIS.

Perbadanan Nasional Shipping Line Bhd (PNSL): Kuala Lumpur; tel. (3) 2932211; fax (3) 2930493; f. 1982; specializes in bulk cargoes; a wholly owned subsidiary of Konsortium Logistik Bhd; Chair. Tunku Dato' SHAHRIMAN BIN Tunku SULAIMAN; Exec. Dep. Chair. Dato' SULAIMAN ABDULLAH.

Persha Shipping Agencies Sdn Bhd: Bangunan Mayban Trust, Penthouse Suite, Jalan Pinang, 10200 Pinang; tel. (4) 2612400; fax (4) 2623122; Man. Dir MOHD NOOR MOHD KAMALUDIN.

Syarikat Perkapalan Kris Sdn Bhd (The Kris Shipping Co Ltd): POB 8428, 46789 Petaling Jaya, Selangor; tel. (3) 7046477; fax (3) 7048007; domestic services; Chair. Dato' Seri Syed NAHAR SHAHABU-DIN; Gen. Man. ROHANY TALIB.

Trans-Asia Shipping Corpn Sdn Bhd: Lot 1A, Persiaran Jubli Perak, Jalan 22/1, Seksyen 22, 40300 Shah Alam, Selangor; tel. (3) 51018888; fax (3) 55488288; e-mail kytan@tasco.com.my; internet www.tasco.com.my; f. 1974; Man. Dir LEE CHECK POH.

CIVIL AVIATION

The new Kuala Lumpur International Airport (KLIA), situated in Sepang, Selangor (50 km south of Kuala Lumpur) began operations in June 1998, with an initial capacity of 25m.–30m. passengers a year, which was projected to rise to 45m. by 2020. An express rail link between central Kuala Lumpur and KLIA opened in early 2001. There are regional airports at Kota Kinabalu, Pinang, Johor Bahru, Kuching and Pulau Langkawi. In addition, there are airports catering for domestic services at Alor Star, Ipoh, Kota Bharu, Kuala Terengganu, Kuantan and Melaka in Peninsular Malaysia, Sibu, Bintulu and Miri in Sarawak, and Sandakan, Tawau, Lahad Datu and Labuan in Sabah. There are also numerous smaller airstrips.

Department of Civil Aviation (Jabatan Penerbangan Awam Malaysia): 27 Persiaran Perdana, Aras 1–4, Blok Podium, 62618 Putrajaya; tel. (3) 88714000; fax (3) 88901640; e-mail webmaster@ dca.gov.my; internet www.dca.gov.my; Dir-Gen. Dato' AZHARUDDIN ABDUL RAHMAN.

AirAsia Sdn Bhd: LCC Terminal Jalan KLIA S3, Southern Support Zone, KLIA, 64000 Sepang, Selangor; tel. (3) 86604333; fax (3) 87751100; e-mail tellus@airasia.com; internet www.airasia.com; f. 1993; 85% owned by HICOM; low-cost national carrier with licence to operate domestic, regional and international flights; Chair. ABDUL AZIZ BIN ABU BAKAR; CEO AIREEN OMAR.

Berjaya Air Sdn Bhd: Sultan Abdul Aziz Shah Airport, Lot No. G4, SkyPark Terminal, 47200 Subang, Selangor; tel. (3) 78427300; fax (3) 78427330; e-mail enquiry@berjaya-air.com; internet www .berjaya-air.com; f. 1989; scheduled and charter domestic services; Pres. Tan Sri Dato' Seri VINCENT TAN CHEE YIOUN.

Firefly: Sultan Abdul Aziz Shah Airport, Admin Bldg 1, 3rd Floor, Kompleks A, 47200 Subang, Selangor; e-mail contactus@fireflyz.com .my; internet www.fireflyz.com.my; f. 2007; wholly owned by Malaysia Airlines; low-cost domestic and regional flights; CEO IGNATIUS ONG.

Malaysia Airlines: Bangunan Pentadbiran 1, Tingkat 3, MAS Kompleks A, Sultan Abdul Aziz Shah Airport, 47200 Subang, Selangor; tel. (3) 78404550; fax (3) 78463932; e-mail tanwf@ malaysiaairlines.com.my; internet www.malaysiaairlines.com.my; f. 1971; est. as the Malaysian successor to Malaysia Singapore Airlines (MSA); known as Malaysian Airline System (MAS) until Oct. 1987; 114 international routes and 118 domestic routes; Chair. Tan Sri MOHAMED NOR YUSOF; Man. Dir and CEO AHMAD JAUHARI YAHYA.

Malindo Airways Sdn Bhd: N1, Tingkat 4, Main Terminal Bldg, Kuala Lumpur International Airport, 64000 Sepang, Selangor; e-mail info@malindoair.com; internet www.malindoair.com; f. 2013; low-cost domestic services; CEO CHANDRAN RAMAMURTHY.

Transmile Air Services Sdn Bhd: Cargo Kompleks, Sultan Abdul Aziz Shah Airport, 47200 Subang, Selangor; tel. (3) 78849898; fax (3) 78849899; e-mail info@transmile.com; internet www.transmile.com; f. 1993; scheduled and charter regional and domestic services for cargo; Chair. and Man. Dir LIU TAI SHIN.

Tourism

Malaysia has a rapidly growing tourist industry, and tourism is an important source of foreign-exchange earnings. In 2012 a record 25.0m. tourists visited Malaysia, while receipts from tourism reached RM 60,600m. Singapore is the main source of visitors, followed by Indonesia and Thailand.

Malaysia Tourism Promotion Board (Tourism Malaysia): Tingkat 9, No. 2, Tower 1, Jalan P5/6, Precint 5, 62200 Putrajaya; tel. (3) 88918000; fax (3) 26935884; e-mail webmaster@tourism.gov.my; internet www.tourismmalaysia.gov.my; f. 1972; est. to co-ordinate and promote activities relating to tourism in Malaysia; Chair. Datuk Dr VICTOR WEE; Dir-Gen. Dato' MIRZA MOHAMMAD TAIYAB.

Sabah Tourist Association: POB 12181, 88824 Kota Kinabalu, Sabah; tel. and fax (88) 239089; e-mail secretariat@sta.my; internet www.sta.my; f. 1963; independent promotional org.; Chair. TONNY CHEW.

Sabah Tourism Board: Mail Bag 112, 88993 Kota Kinabalu, Sabah; tel. (88) 212121; fax (88) 212075; e-mail info@sabahtourism .com; internet www.sabahtourism.com; f. 1976; parastatal promotion org.; Chair. Datuk Seri Tengku ZAINAL ADLIN Tengku MAHAMOOD.

Sarawak Tourism Board: Levels 6 and 7, Bangunan Yayasan Sarawak, Jalan Masjid, 93400 Kuching; tel. (82) 423600; fax (82) 416700; e-mail stb@sarawaktourism.com; internet www .sarawaktourism.com; f. 1995; CEO Datuk RASHID KHAN.

Defence

As assessed at November 2012, the total strength of the armed forces was 109,000; army 80,000 (although this was to be reduced to 60,000–70,000), navy 14,000, air force 15,000; military service is voluntary. Paramilitary forces included the Police-General Operations Force of 18,000 and the People's Volunteer Corps of 240,000. Malaysia is a participant in the Five-Power Defence Arrangements with Singapore, Australia, New Zealand and the United Kingdom.

Defence Expenditure: RM 15,300m. in 2013.

Chief of the Defence Forces: Gen. Tan Sri Dato' Sri MUHAMMAD ZULKIFELI BIN ZIN.

Chief of Army: Gen. Datuk Haji ZULKIFLI BIN Haji ZAINAL ABIDIN.

Chief of Navy Staff: Adm. Tan Sri Dato' Sri ABDUL AZIZ BIN Haji JAAFAR.

Chief of Air Force Staff: Gen. Dato' Seri RODZALI BIN DAUD.

Education

Under the Malaysian education system, free schooling is provided at government-assisted schools for children between the ages of six and 18. There are also private schools, which receive no government financial aid. Education is compulsory for 11 years between the ages of six and 16 years. The federal Government's expenditure on education was RM 49,476m. in 2011 (21.6% of total expenditure). Scholarships are awarded at all levels and there are many scholarship-holders studying at universities and other institutes of higher education at home and abroad.

PRIMARY EDUCATION

The national language, Bahasa Malaysia, is the main medium of instruction, although English, Chinese and Tamil are also used. Two-thirds of the total primary school enrolment is in National Schools where Malay is used and the remainder in National-Type Primary Schools where Tamil or Chinese is used. A place in primary school is now assured to every child from the age of six onwards, and parents are free to choose the language of instruction. In 2013 some 2.74m. students were enrolled in 7,743 primary schools, at which 239,599 teachers were employed. In 2004/05 the total enrolment at primary level included 96% of all children in the relevant age-group. The primary school course lasts for six years.

SECONDARY EDUCATION

Bahasa Malaysia is the main medium of instruction in secondary schools, while English is taught as a second language and Chinese and Tamil are taught as pupils' own languages. Private Chinese secondary schools are also in operation. Secondary education lasts for seven years, comprising a first cycle of three years and a second of four. In 2013 there were 2.29m. students enrolled in 2,340 secondary institutions, at which 177,588 teachers were employed. In 2009/10 the total enrolment at the secondary level included 69% of students (66% of males; 71% of females) in the relevant age-group.

HIGHER EDUCATION

In 2009 there were 589,407 students enrolled in 75 institutes of tertiary education. Malaysia's universities adhere to a quota system (55% of entrants should be Malays and 45% non-Malays), which, in practice, makes it considerably more difficult for non-Malays to gain a place at university. The Government has attempted to encourage foreign universities to establish campuses in Malaysia to improve standards and reduce the cost of sending Malaysian students abroad to study.

THE MALDIVES

Introductory Survey

LOCATION, CLIMATE, LANGUAGE, RELIGION, FLAG, CAPITAL

The Republic of Maldives (commonly referred to as 'the Maldives') is in southern Asia. The country, lying about 675 km (420 miles) south-west of Sri Lanka, consists of 1,192 small coral islands (of which 194 are inhabited), grouped in 26 natural atolls (but divided, for administrative purposes, into 19 atolls and two cities), in the Indian Ocean. The climate is warm and humid. The annual average temperature is 27°C (80°F), with little daily or seasonal variation, while annual rainfall is generally between 2,540 mm and 3,800 mm (100 ins to 150 ins). The national language is Dhivehi (Maldivian), which is related to Sinhala. Islam is the state religion, and most Maldivians are Sunni Muslims. The national flag (proportions 2 by 3) is red, with a green rectangle, containing a white crescent, in the centre. The capital is Malé.

CONTEMPORARY POLITICAL HISTORY

Historical Context

The Maldives, called the Maldive Islands until April 1969, formerly had an elected Sultan as head of state. The islands were placed under British protection, with internal self-government, in 1887. They became a republic in January 1953, but the sultanate was restored in February 1954. In 1956 the Maldivian and British Governments agreed to the establishment of a Royal Air Force staging post on Gan, an island in the southernmost atoll, Addu. The Maldives became fully independent, outside the Commonwealth, on 26 July 1965. Following a referendum, the country became a republic again in November 1968, with Amir Ibrahim Nasir, Prime Minister since 1957, as President. A new Constitution, promulgated in 1968, vested considerable powers in the President, including the right to appoint and dismiss the Prime Minister and the Cabinet of Ministers. In 1975 the British Government decided to close the airbase on Gan and completed the withdrawal of its forces the following year.

Domestic Political Affairs

President Gayoom in power (1978–2009)

In March 1975, following rumours of a coup conspiracy, President Nasir dismissed the Prime Minister, Ahmed Zaki, and the premiership was abolished. Unexpectedly, President Nasir announced that he would not seek re-election at the end of his second term in 1978. To succeed him, the Majlis (legislature) chose Maumoon Abdul Gayoom, Minister of Transport under Nasir, who was approved by referendum in July 1978 and took office in November. President Gayoom announced that his main priority would be the development of the poor rural regions, while in foreign affairs the existing policy of non-alignment would be continued.

Former President Nasir left the country after his resignation, but the authorities subsequently sought his return to the Maldives, where he was required to answer charges of misappropriating government funds. In 1980 President Gayoom confirmed reports of an attempted coup against the Government and implicated Nasir in the alleged plot. Nasir was to stand trial, in his absence, on these and other charges. In April 1981 Ahmed Naseem, former Deputy Minister of Fisheries and brother-in-law of Nasir, was sentenced to life imprisonment for plotting to overthrow President Gayoom. Nasir himself denied any involvement in the coup, and attempts to extradite him from Singapore proved unsuccessful. (In July 1990, however, President Gayoom officially pardoned Nasir in absentia, in recognition of the role that he had played in achieving national independence.) In September 1983 Gayoom was re-elected as President, for a further five years, by a national referendum (with 95.6% of the popular vote). In September 1988 he was again re-elected unopposed, for a third five-year term, obtaining a record 96.4% of the vote.

Another attempt to depose President Gayoom took place in November 1988, when a sea-borne mercenary force, which was composed of around 80 alleged Sri Lankan Tamil separatists (led by a disaffected Maldivian businessman, Abdullah Luthufi), landed in Malé and endeavoured to seize control of key government installations. At the request of President Gayoom, the Indian Government dispatched an emergency contingent of 1,600 troops, which rapidly and successfully suppressed the attempted coup. Nineteen people were reported to have been killed in the fighting. In September 1989 the President commuted to life imprisonment the death sentences imposed on 12 Sri Lankans and four Maldivians who had participated in the aborted coup.

In February 1990 President Gayoom announced that, as part of proposals for a broad new policy of liberalization and democratic reform, he was planning to introduce legislation enabling him to distribute powers currently enjoyed by the President alone among other official bodies. A further sign of growing democratization in the Maldives was the holding of discussions by the President's Consultative Council, in early 1990, concerning freedom of speech (particularly in the local press). In April, however, it became apparent that some Maldivians opposed political change when three pro-reform members of the Majlis received anonymous death threats. A few months later, following the emergence of several politically outspoken magazines, including *Sangu* (The Conchshell), there was an abrupt reversal of the Government's policy regarding the liberalization of the press. All publications not sanctioned by the Government were banned, and a number of leading writers and publishers were arrested.

As part of a major cabinet reorganization in May 1990, President Gayoom dismissed the Minister of State for Defence and National Security, Ilyas Ibrahim (who also held the Trade and Industries portfolio and headed the State Trading Corporation), following the latter's abrupt departure from the country. The Government later disclosed that Ibrahim (Gayoom's brother-in-law) was to have appeared before a presidential special commission investigating alleged embezzlement of government funds. On his return to the Maldives in August, Ibrahim was placed under house arrest. In March 1991, however, the special commission concluded that there was no evidence of Ibrahim having been involved in the alleged financial misdeeds; in the same month the President appointed Ibrahim as Minister of Atolls Administration. In April the President established an anti-corruption board, which was to investigate allegations of corruption, bribery, fraud, misappropriation of government funds and property, and abuse of government office.

In early August 1993, a few weeks before the Majlis vote on the presidential candidate, Gayoom was informed that Ibrahim, whose position as Minister of Atolls Administration had afforded him the opportunity to build a political base outside Malé (where he already enjoyed considerable popularity), was seeking the presidency and attempting to inveigle members of the Majlis (at that time, the Majlis nominated and elected by secret ballot a single candidate, who was presented to the country in a referendum). In the Majlis vote held in late August, the incumbent President, who had previously been unanimously nominated for the presidency by the legislature, obtained 28 votes, against 18 for his brother-in-law. Ibrahim was charged with unconstitutional behaviour for his alleged attempts to 'influence the members of the Majlis' and he promptly left the country once again. Ibrahim was subsequently tried *in absentia* and sentenced to 15 years' imprisonment. (Upon his return to the Maldives in 1996 Ibrahim was placed under house arrest; this restriction was lifted in 1997.) In October 1993 Gayoom's re-election as President for a further five years was endorsed by a national referendum, in which he obtained 92.8% of the popular vote.

In November 1994 President Gayoom outlined various measures intended to strengthen the political system and to advance the process of democratization. These included the granting of greater autonomy and responsibilities to the Cabinet of Ministers, the implementation of regulations governing the conduct of civil servants (in order to increase their accountability), the introduction of democratic elections to island development committees and atoll committees, and the establishment of a Judicial Advisory Council to enact reforms to the judicial system.

In November 1996 President Gayoom effected an extensive cabinet reshuffle and a reorganization of government bodies, including the establishment of a Supreme Council for Islamic Affairs, which was to be under direct presidential control and was to advise the Government on matters relating to Islam. In early November 1997 the Citizens' Special Majlis, a constituent assembly that was established in 1980 to amend the Constitution, finally completed its 17-year-long task. The revised document was ratified by the President on 27 November and came into effect on 1 January 1998. Under the new 156-article Constitution, a formal, multi-candidate contest was permitted for the legislature's nomination for the presidency; no restriction was placed on the number of terms a president might serve; for administrative purposes, the number of atolls was increased from 19 to 20; the Majlis, which was henceforth known as the People's Majlis, was enlarged from 48 to 50 seats; and the Citizens' Special Majlis, when reconvened, was to be renamed the People's Special Majlis.

In September 1998 five individuals declared their candidacy for the presidency; the People's Majlis unanimously voted by secret ballot for the incumbent President Gayoom to go forward to the national referendum. In the referendum, which was held in October, Gayoom was re-elected as President for a fifth term, obtaining 90.9% of the popular vote. In November 1999 elections for 42 members of the 50-seat People's Majlis were conducted (on a non-partisan basis).

In early 2001 an attempt by 42 prominent Maldivians, including members of the People's Majlis, former cabinet ministers and business executives, to register the newly formed Maldivian Democratic Party (MDP) was blocked by the People's Majlis on the grounds that the existence of political parties would encourage divisions among the public and, therefore, be counterproductive.

In July 2002 three journalists were charged with defamation and inciting violence, and were sentenced to life imprisonment for writing articles criticizing the President and the Government. In the same month a Maldivian businessman was sentenced to life imprisonment for publishing an article via the internet advocating the overthrow of the Government. Later that month the human rights group Amnesty International issued a report citing frequent cases of arbitrary detentions, unfair trials and long-term imprisonment and torture of political opponents in the Maldives.

In September 2003 detainees at the prison on Maafushi Island (in Kaafu Atoll) near Malé protested against the suspicious death of a fellow inmate. Reports of the violent suppression of the rioting by the country's National Security Service (NSS), and the death of another prisoner, prompted major anti-Government protests in the capital, the first since President Gayoom came to power in 1978. Large numbers of alleged demonstrators were arrested, and a state of emergency was declared in Malé and neighbouring islands. Gayoom appealed for calm and announced an investigation into the deaths of the prisoners (the subsequent demise of another two inmates brought the total number of deaths to four). Eleven members of the NSS were arrested for their alleged involvement in the over-zealous curbing of the riots, and the Deputy Chief of the NSS and National Police Commissioner, Brig. Adam Zahir, was removed from office (he was reinstated in February 2004, after the inquiry cleared him of any misconduct). In December 2003 a Human Rights Commission was established in Malé.

Meanwhile, in September 2003 Gayoom was re-elected unanimously by secret ballot in the People's Majlis for a sixth presidential term, defeating three other candidates. His re-election was ratified at a referendum in October, when he secured 90.3% of the votes cast. On assuming office President Gayoom effected a cabinet reorganization, in which the Attorney-General, Dr Mohamed Munavvar, and the Minister of Planning and National Development, Ibrahim Hussain Zaki, were dismissed. Gayoom gave no reason for the dismissals, although it was alleged that the two had been removed for supporting reformers attempting to register a political party. In the same month a group of political activists established the MDP in exile in Sri Lanka, in response to rising discontent with the Maldives Government.

In May 2004 the election, by universal suffrage, took place of 42 members (from among 121 independent candidates) to a People's Special Majlis, which was assigned the task of drawing up and implementing constitutional amendments. The President appointed an additional eight people to serve on the council, which also included members of the People's Majlis and the Cabinet of Ministers. Gayoom invited members of the public to put forward suggestions for constitutional reform and in June the President himself proposed a number of radical constitutional reforms. The People's Special Majlis convened in July to discuss the proposals.

In August 2004 President Gayoom declared an indefinite state of emergency following a violent pro-democracy protest in the capital. Four police officers were reportedly stabbed and about 185 people, including former Attorney-General Dr Mohamed Munavvar and members of the People's Special Majlis, were arrested during the protest. The Government claimed that the demonstration had been a coup attempt, a charge denied by the opposition MDP, whose exiled founding leader, Mohamed Latheef, accused Gayoom's administration of 'ruthlessly suppressing dissent'. In October the state of emergency was revoked and in December President Gayoom announced that all charges of treason and public order offences against those taken into custody following the August protest were to be suspended.

On 26 December 2004 a tsunami generated by a massive earthquake in the Indian Ocean, off the coast of Indonesia, devastated many of the low-lying Maldive islands. While the death toll was not as high as might have been initially feared, several of the islands were rendered uninhabitable and an estimated 15,000 people were left homeless. The economic consequences of the catastrophe on the Maldives were extensive, owing in large part to the major contribution made by the tourism industry to the economy.

In January 2005 a total of 149 independent candidates contested elections to the People's Majlis. Candidates backed by the MDP reportedly won 18 of the 42 elective seats. However, the Government stated that only 12 opposition candidates had been successful, claiming that the results indicated widespread popular support for its reform policies. In June the People's Majlis unanimously approved a constitutional amendment permitting the registration of political parties in the Maldives, reversing its 2001 decision against the establishment of multi-party democracy. The MDP was subsequently officially registered in the Maldives as a political party, together with several others, including the Dhivehi Rayyithunge Party (DRP—Maldivian People's Party), established by President Gayoom.

In August 2005 a protest took place in Malé demanding the release of all political prisoners. Shortly afterwards the Chairman of the MDP, Mohamed Nasheed, was arrested, prompting several days of unrest in the capital and on various other atolls. Nasheed was subsequently charged with terrorism and attempting to perpetrate anti-Government actions.

In a significant development towards the further democratization of the Maldives, from June 2006 representatives of the Government and the MDP conducted informal talks at the British High Commission in Colombo, Sri Lanka. The terms of the resulting agreement included the release of a number of opposition detainees and the advancement of constitutional reform, on the part of the Government, in return for MDP assurances that the party would curb public demonstrations and renounce violent protest. Nasheed was released in September, although the charges against him were not withdrawn. In November more than 100 members of the MDP were arrested in the run-up to a planned demonstration to demand the swifter implementation of reforms; the rally was cancelled by the MDP amid fears for the welfare of protesters.

Meanwhile, in early 2006 meetings of the People's Special Majlis were obstructed by President Gayoom's refusal to permit the removal of presidential appointees from the body. The MDP condemned the continued presence of representatives who had not been elected and in February the party boycotted the opening of the People's Majlis in protest against the President's alleged obstruction of the constitutional amendment process. A Police Integrity Commission was established in August, and in November the Human Rights Commission was reconstituted as legally autonomous; however, the introduction of new regulations on press freedom and access to information was delayed indefinitely by the Government in January 2007.

In January 2007 Mohamed Latheef ended three years of voluntary exile in Sri Lanka with his return to the Maldives. In February a demonstration organized by the MDP in protest against police violence against civilians reportedly attracted some 1,000 participants. In April the Minister of Higher Education, Employment and Social Security, Abdullah Yameen, resigned amid rumours of discord within the Cabinet of Ministers. Yameen also stood down as a member of the DRP, and was reported to be planning the creation of a new political party (he founded the People's Alliance—PA—in 2008).

A press freedom bill was approved by the People's Majlis in August 2007, despite criticism that it fell short of international standards. In the same month there was a significant development within the Government, when Minister of Justice Mohamed Jameel Ahmed, Attorney-General Dr Hassan Saeed and Minister of Foreign Affairs Dr Ahmed Shaheed all resigned, reportedly over their concerns regarding impediments and delays to the programme of democratic reforms. The three dissidents subsequently launched a new organization entitled the New Maldives Movement (NMM) and advocated the formation of a united front of pro-democracy groups. In January 2008 the Government declared that the NMM had not sought official registration and was therefore illegal.

The potential threat of terrorism to the Maldives came to the fore when a bomb exploded in Malé in September 2007, injuring 12 foreign tourists. The explosion—the first recorded terrorist attack to take place in the Maldives—was widely believed to have been perpetrated by Islamist extremists. In December three Maldivian men were each sentenced to 15 years imprisonment for their part in the incident, which they confessed to having planned as a deliberate attack on the country's vital tourism industry. In an attempt to combat the perceived threat of growing Islamic fundamentalism, the Government introduced a number of measures, including arresting suspected extremists, banning the wearing of the full veil in public, advocating the promotion of moderate Islamic views in schools and colleges, forbidding the convention of unlicensed Muslim prayer groups, and banning foreign Islamic clerics from visiting the islands unless they had been explicitly invited by the authorities. While visiting an atoll in the far north of the island chain in January 2008, President Gayoom himself escaped unhurt after an attempted knife attack by a young Maldivian man. The Government claimed that the President's political rivals were the most likely instigators of the apparent assassination attempt, rather than Islamist extremists, as some early reports had suggested.

Democratization and a new Constitution

The results of a referendum on the system of government, which took place on 18 August 2007 (having been postponed from September 2006), indicated popular support for retaining the presidential system in preference to adopting a parliamentary one, with a reported 62% of those who participated in favour. In June 2008 the People's Special Majlis approved final amendments to the draft Constitution, which was then passed to the Cabinet of Ministers and the President in turn. The new Constitution was ratified by the President on 7 August; major points included the direct election by popular vote of the President (and his nominated Vice-President) and the restriction of presidential terms of office to two (whether consecutive or not); the removal of the gender bar on the presidency; the election, rather than presidential appointment, of the Speaker and Deputy Speaker of the People's Majlis; the establishment of a Supreme Court as the highest judicial authority; and the granting to citizens of the right to hold peaceful demonstrations. The People's Special Majlis and Judicial Advisory Council were duly dissolved, while the Speaker of the People's Majlis was replaced by an elected incumbent. By September a total of 12 political parties had registered in the Maldives. In that month the Election Commissioner, who had been assigned the post by President Gayoom, was replaced by a new five-member Elections Commission, which was nominated and appointed by the People's Majlis.

Mohamed Nasheed elected President

The first multi-party presidential election in the Maldives was held on 8 October 2008. Despite opposition to Gayoom standing for a seventh presidential term, the DRP argued that the new two-term limit did not exclude him from contesting what would be the first election under the new Constitution. Five other candidates contested the presidency, including former political prisoner and leader of the MDP Mohamed Nasheed. Gayoom secured 40.3% of the vote, Nasheed won 24.9%, Hassan Saeed, who was running as an independent candidate, secured 16.7%, and he was closely followed by Qasim Ibrahim of the Jumhooree Party (JP—Republican Party), with 15.2% of the vote. The reported turn-out was 85.5% of the electorate. As no candidate secured more than 50% in the first round of voting, the two leading candidates contested a second round on 28 October. In an historic victory, Nasheed secured the presidency, with 53.7% of the vote, and was consequently inaugurated on 11 November. On the same day the country's first elected Vice-President, Dr Mohamed Waheed Hassan Manik of the Gaumee Itthihaad Party (GIP—National Unity Party), was also sworn in. The

new President appointed a coalition Cabinet of Ministers, comprising members of the MDP, the GIP, the JP, the Social Liberal Party and the Adhaalath Party (Justice Party). On appointing his new Government, Nasheed carried out a significant reorganization of the ministries, including the establishment of a Ministry of Islamic Affairs, which replaced the Supreme Council for Islamic Affairs. In addition, despite protests by the DRP at the alleged unconstitutional nature of his action, President Nasheed appointed eight new members of the People's Majlis to replace the eight appointees of former President Gayoom, thus ensuring the Government had a working majority. One of Nasheed's first acts as new Head of State was to request the resignation of the National Police Commissioner, Adam Zahir, who had long been held personally accountable for various human rights abuses on the part of the police, including torture and custodial deaths. In December Nasheed's Cabinet of Ministers suffered its first real setback when the Minister of Home Affairs, Qasim Ibrahim, who was also the leader of the JP, resigned. Ibrahim claimed that his resignation had been prompted by the Government's unwillingness to allocate funds to prison reform, but several sources alleged that his departure came as a result of criticism of his heavy-handed response to a strike by employees at a tourist resort. In February 2009 the President's Special Advisor, Dr Hassan Saeed, stood down from his post; earlier that month he had formed a new political party entitled the Dhivehi Qaumee Party (DQP—Maldivian National Party).

In February 2009 the People's Majlis passed two electoral bills, including the Parliamentary Constituencies Bill (determining the number of constituencies to be created), paving the way for the holding of the Maldives' first multi-party legislative elections. A total of 77 seats were contested in the elections, which were held on 9 May; the DRP won the highest number of seats (28), while the MDP secured 25 seats. Although independent candidates took 13 seats, the predominance of the leading parties in the voting appeared to illustrate the population's willing adoption of a party political system.

In May 2009 a presidential commission was established to investigate the alleged embezzlement of state funds and resources and human rights abuses by the former administration. In August a controversial decentralization bill was presented to the People's Majlis (as part of the process of devolution, the Ministry of Atolls Development had already been dissolved by the President and its responsibilities divided between numerous smaller regional offices). The bill, the main proposal of which was the division of the existing 21 administrative districts into seven provinces—each headed by a provincial state minister (appointed by the President) and a council—was opposed by the DRP and the PA on the grounds that it was unconstitutional, would create additional bureaucracy and posed a threat to representative democracy and the unitary state. A revised Decentralization Act was presented to the Majlis in March 2010, which recognized the creation of the seven provinces (but not as administrative units), retained the existing 21 administrative districts and the atoll and island chiefs, and provided for the election of island, atoll and city councils. The act was approved by the legislature in April and ratified by the President in May. In October the Government issued a finalized list of administrative divisions, including 184 islands, 19 atolls and two designated cities—Malé and Addu City (formerly Addu Atoll). Meanwhile, in April Gayoom was replaced as leader of the DRP by Ahmed Thasmeen Ali.

Political deadlock and growing pressure on the MDP Government

A political crisis arose on 29 June 2010 when the Cabinet of Ministers resigned en masse following threats by the opposition to introduce a parliamentary vote of no confidence against each minister; however, Nasheed and his Vice-President remained in their posts. The Government claimed that it had become impossible to work effectively with the opposition-controlled People's Majlis and that the constant use of blocking tactics by the opposition had made the country virtually ungovernable. On the same day two leading opposition figures, Abdullah Yameen of the PA and Qasim Ibrahim of the JP (who had held the post of Minister of Home Affairs in Nasheed's new Government in late 2008 for less than one month before resigning), were placed under house arrest and accused of bribing fellow parliamentarians and conspiring to overthrow the Government. On 7 July, with the political situation in turmoil and the rift between the Government and the opposition appearing deadlocked, President Mahinda Rajapaksa of Sri Lanka arrived in the

Maldives, at the request of Nasheed, to act as a mediator in talks between the two sides. Later that day President Nasheed reappointed the Cabinet of Ministers (with one change of portfolio), but there were doubts whether all the reinstated ministers would subsequently be approved by the People's Majlis (as required by the Constitution).

Despite the reinstatement of the Cabinet of Ministers and the release from house arrest of Yameen and Ibrahim, the political impasse between the Government and the opposition persisted, with the latter refusing to recognize the legitimacy of Nasheed's administration. The rising tension led to violent protests being staged in Malé by both sides. The constitutional crisis escalated in August 2010 when the People's Majlis voted against legitimizing a number of interim state institutions, including the Supreme Court, the Civil Service Commission and the Human Rights Commission (according to the Constitution, the two-year transition period of these bodies expired on 7 August after which date they required official legitimization by the legislature). In protest against the opposition's continuing intransigence, the Attorney-General, Husnu Suood, resigned. However, a few days later the power struggle over the judiciary was resolved when the People's Majlis unanimously voted to appoint a permanent Supreme Court and Chief Justice (as nominated by the President). None the less, the deadlock over the official recognition of the Cabinet continued, with the opposition insisting that the ministers be endorsed on an individual basis and Nasheed claiming that the approval procedure should be carried out on a 'ceremonial' and collective basis. On 22 November the People's Majlis voted not to endorse seven of the cabinet ministers appointed by the President and demanded that they resign immediately. Despite protests by the MDP that the legislature's action was unconstitutional, on 9 December the Supreme Court ruled that the rejected ministers (including Dr Ahmed Ali Sawad, who had been nominated as the new Attorney-General in August) should not remain in office: they all resigned two days later. Nasheed subsequently carried out an extensive cabinet reorganization, including the appointment of two of the rejected ministers as advisors, and, in defiance of the judicial ruling, reappointed Sawad as Attorney-General on 13 December. On 21 March 2011 the People's Majlis endorsed the appointments of a further four ministers, but again refused to approve the nomination of Sawad. In response, the President installed Abdulla Muiz as Attorney-General and Ahmed Naseem as the new Minister of Foreign Affairs; in early April Ahmed Inaz was appointed Minister of Finance and Treasury. In June the post of Minister of Defence and National Security, vacant since the resignation of the Cabinet in June 2010, was accorded to Lt Tholhath Ibrahim Kaleyfaanu.

Meanwhile, in February 2011 multi-party local council elections were held in the Maldives for the first time: the MDP performed strongly in the city councils, while the DRP won the majority of seats in the atoll and island councils.

In February 2011 a report published in an Indian magazine alleged that during his presidency Gayoom and his half-brother Abdullah Yameen had been involved in an international fraud (worth around US $800m.) involving the illegal sale of petroleum to the military junta in Myanmar. In April the People's Majlis was instructed to examine the allegations (the presidential commission that had been set up in 2009 to investigate accusations of corrupt practices perpetrated by the former regime of Gayoom forwarded the case against Yameen to prosecutors in early February 2012). Meanwhile, during the first few months of 2011 serious rifts within the DRP became increasingly apparent as Gayoom continued to criticize the leadership of his successor, Ahmed Thasmeen Ali, accusing him of 'dictatorial' behaviour; by the end of March the DRP had effectively split into two opposing factions—one led by Thasmeen and the other by Gayoom. In April Gayoom's faction announced the establishment of the Zaeem ('Honorary Leader')-DRP (Z-DRP), claiming that it enjoyed the backing of the vast majority of the 40,000 DRP members.

At the end of April 2011 anti-Government protesters staged a series of large demonstrations in Malé provoked by rising commodity prices. Several hundred protesters were arrested and dozens injured in clashes with riot police during the demonstrations, which continued for eight days in the capital. The Government rejected allegations by the opposition that the police had used excessive force and that journalists had been obstructed in their efforts to report on the unrest.

In September 2011 Gayoom officially resigned from the DRP and established a new party, the Progressive Party of Maldives

(PPM), to replace the breakaway Z-DRP. Later that month, in the wake of a number of disagreements regarding government policy (including the MDP's allegedly un-Islamic stance), the religiously conservative Adhaalath Party withdrew from the governing coalition. In December the Minister of Finance and Treasury, Ahmed Inaz, resigned following allegations by the MDP that he had held covert political meetings with Abdullah Yameen (who had recently left the PA to join Gayoom's PPM).

In November 2011 the issue of Islam came to the fore once again following an official visit to the Maldives by the UN High Commissioner for Human Rights, Navi Pillay, during which she expressed her opposition to the practice of flogging women found guilty of extra-marital sex and urged the authorities to remove the 'discriminatory' constitutional clause stipulating that every Maldivian citizen should be a Muslim. However, the Government, which claimed to be an advocate of moderate, liberal Islam, stated that it would continue to adhere to the recommendations of the Ministry of Islamic Affairs on religious issues, including the continuation of the practice of flogging. In December, following a demonstration in the capital organized by a number of religious organizations and political parties in protest against the Government's allegedly 'un-Islamic' policies, the Ministry of Tourism announced plans to close down all luxury spas and massage parlours in the country, following claims by Islamist groups that such premises were being used for prostitution. However, amid concerns that the country's vital tourism industry would be adversely affected by this measure, the Government reversed its decision with immediate effect in early January and requested that the Supreme Court clarify the situation by issuing a ruling on such services (as well as on the sale of alcohol and pork in tourist resorts).

Recent developments: the ousting of President Nasheed

In late 2011 mistrust between the Government and the judiciary fuelled a growing sense of instability within the Maldives. In October the MDP arranged a public demonstration against alleged maladministration within the judiciary; the ruling party claimed that many judges—the majority of whom had been appointed during Gayoom's presidency—were not adequately qualified to carry out their duties and were open to excessive influence from members of the former regime. The MDP demonstration provoked strong criticism and counter-demonstrations by the opposition, which claimed that the ruling party was attempting to stifle the independence of the judiciary. On 16 January 2012 the Government ordered the arrest of the Chief Judge of the Criminal Court, Abdulla Mohamed, for alleged corruption and political bias. On the previous day Justice Abdulla had overturned the arrest of opposition leader Mohamed Jameel Ahmed, the Deputy Leader of the DQP, who had been detained for alleged defamation of the Government. (In November 2011 the Judicial Service Commission, which regulates the Maldivian judiciary, had ruled that Justice Abdulla was guilty of political bias; however, the ruling had been suspended owing to a legal challenge.) The arrest of Justice Abdulla was criticized as unconstitutional by a number of high-ranking officials, including Fathimath Dhiyana Saeed, the Secretary-General of the South Asian Association for Regional Cooperation (SAARC) and a former Attorney-General of the Maldives, who subsequently resigned from her SAARC post in protest against the Government's action.

Buoyed by their majority in the People's Majlis, the protest movement of the opposition parties gained further momentum in the latter half of January 2012. Hostility regarding the detention of Justice Abdulla, as well as the continual undermining of the Government's Islamic credentials by some opposition politicians, served to incite a wave of increasingly unruly anti-Government demonstrations in Malé. Finally, on 7 February, following concerted assaults on MDP facilities in the capital by anti-Government protesters and alleged police mutineers, in rather confused circumstances Nasheed resigned from the presidency, transferred power to Vice-President Mohamed Waheed Hassan Manik and was taken into police custody for several hours (reportedly for his own safety). On the following day, however, Nasheed claimed that he had been forced to stand down 'at gunpoint' by rogue elements of the police and military and by supporters of former President Gayoom, and that what had taken place was, in effect, a coup. He also asserted that the alleged coup had been carried out with the compliance of Waheed—a claim that was vehemently denied by the new President. On the same day several thousand MDP supporters, led by Nasheed, marched through Malé to protest against his ousting. Numerous violent clashes broke out as riot police used tear gas and batons against the demonstrators. Security forces were also dispatched to Addu City, where there were reports of further violent incidents.

Shortly after President Waheed assumed power, Justice Abdulla was released from detention. Waheed pledged to form a government of national unity, to uphold the rule of law and to re-establish stability in advance of the 2013 elections. A warrant was issued for the arrest of Nasheed, although the nature of the charges against him remained unclear and the authorities showed no sign of actually enforcing the warrant. The new Cabinet of Ministers appointed by President Waheed during February and early March 2012 largely comprised members of parties opposed to the MDP (which refused to participate in the new 'illegitimate' administration) and included several staunch supporters of Gayoom (including his daughter). Notably, Mohamed Jameel Ahmed, whose arrest had played a significant part in events leading to the ousting of President Nasheed, was appointed Minister of Home Affairs. In mid-February Waheed nominated prominent businessman Mohamed Waheed Deen as the new Vice-President. In an attempt to resolve the political crisis, UN Assistant Secretary-General Oscar Fernandez-Taranco held talks with both Waheed and Nasheed, the latter of whom demanded the holding of early elections. Nasheed was reportedly disappointed by the official recognition of the new Maldivian Government by the authorities in the USA and India. On 21 February President Waheed established a three-member Commission of National Inquiry (CNI—chaired by former Minister of Defence and National Security Ismail Shafeeu, widely described as a Gayoom loyalist) whose task it was to investigate the events surrounding Nasheed's resignation and to judge whether or not they constituted a coup. The MDP criticized the new body as lacking impartiality and for not including any independent international experts. On 1 March MDP activists attempted to disrupt the official opening of Parliament, but were forcibly suppressed by police using tear gas. Later that month it was reported that the presidential commission established by Nasheed in 2009 to investigate alleged corruption by the former Gayoom regime had been disbanded. Also in March Nasheed was summoned before the Human Rights Commission for questioning regarding his role in the arrest of Justice Abdulla; Nasheed claimed that he had been informed at the time by the Ministry of Home Affairs that the judge allegedly posed a threat to national security.

In mid-April 2012 two pro-Government parties, the PPM and the JP, recorded victories in parliamentary by-elections, further consolidating the position of the new administration. The PPM's electoral victory enabled the new party to gain official recognition in the People's Majlis (hitherto, PPM members had been designated as independent). Following the polls, it was reported that some 44 of the 77 members of the Majlis now supported the Waheed-led coalition Government, with the PPM described as the largest of the pro-Government parties. None the less, the MDP parliamentary group remained the single largest faction in the parliament, with 32 members. However, internal dissension within the MDP became apparent at the end of April when the party's President, Dr Ibrahim Didi, and Vice-President, Alhan Fahmy, were forced to leave the party on a vote of no confidence; the two subsequently joined the JP, of which Didi was elected the new President in June. In that month Nasheed was elected unopposed as the MDP's candidate in the next presidential election.

Meanwhile, in mid-April 2012 the Commonwealth Ministerial Action Group (CMAG) hosted talks in London, United Kingdom, on the political crisis in the Maldives, which were attended by representatives of the Government and the MDP. In a statement issued following the summit CMAG expressed serious concerns regarding the legality of the recent transfer of presidential power in the Maldives and reiterated its earlier demands for the presidential election, scheduled for the latter half of 2013, to be brought forward to 2012. Furthermore, CMAG questioned the legitimacy of the CNI and urged the Government to revise its composition to include an independent, foreign co-chairman and an MDP nominee; failure to act on these recommendations would elicit 'stronger measures' from the Commonwealth (the Maldives had been suspended from membership of CMAG and placed on its formal investigative agenda since late February). In accordance with CMAG's stipulations, the Government finally accepted (after some 10 rejections) a nominee of Nasheed for the CNI, Ahmed 'Gahaa' Saeed, in early June, having earlier appointed a retired Singaporean judge to join the panel as its co-chairman. In addition, two representatives, one from the UN and the other

from the Commonwealth, were appointed to act as advisers to the CNI.

Against the background of fruitless all-party talks instigated by Waheed, the MDP launched a campaign of anti-Government street protests in Malé from early July 2012 demanding early elections. Violent clashes frequently broke out between the demonstrators and the police and hundreds of protesters were arrested. In mid-July Nasheed, his former Minister of Defence and National Security, Lt Tholhath Ibrahim Kaleyfaanu, and three senior officers of the Maldives National Defence Force were formally charged with ordering the illegal detention of Justice Abdulla in January. Although the MDP had suspended its street protests and indicated its willingness to rejoin political dialogue in early August, the situation deteriorated at the end of the month when Ahmed 'Gahaa' Saeed resigned from the CNI, citing the body's alleged lack of integrity and purpose. The following day the CNI published its report which concluded that Nasheed had not been ousted by a coup but had stood down voluntarily and that the transfer of power had been 'legal and constitutional'; however, the report also noted the existence of serious problems with the rule of law and order in the Maldives, including acts of brutality on the part of the police force. Waheed asserted that the findings upheld the legitimacy of his administration and requested that the CMAG remove the Maldives from its human rights watch-list. The imposition of court-ordered travel restrictions on Nasheed in late September (which prevented him from leaving the capital pending his imminent court case on charges of abuse of power) was denounced by his supporters as a government ploy to stop the former President from campaigning ahead of the 2013 elections. Nasheed blatantly flouted the ban, launching an electoral campaign in the southern atolls, and failed to attend his first court hearing at the beginning of October. Several days later, however, Nasheed was arrested and, following a court appearance in Malé, was released on bail. In order to avoid being arrested as a result of another refusal on his part to attend court proceedings, Nasheed sought refuge in the Indian High Commission in February 2013 (where he remained for 10 days). Despite Indian requests that Nasheed be allowed freely to campaign for the presidential election due to be held in September, the MDP leader was detained by police officers in early March. Nasheed's legal representatives subsequently challenged the legitimacy of the panel of judges assembled to hear the case against the former President; by early May the trial was mired in procedural issues.

In January 2013 President Waheed announced his decision to contest the election for the presidency as a candidate of the GIP. In early March the People's Majlis ratified a Political Parties Bill, which stipulated that parties would require a minimum of 10,000 members to qualify for registration with the Elections Commission. It was reported that 11 political parties, including the GIP, were thus threatened with dissolution. However, following a legal challenge, in mid-March the Supreme Court issued an injunction against the dissolution of political parties. At the end of March Abdullah Yameen was selected as the presidential candidate of the PPM, ending speculation that Gayoom might himself contest the forthcoming presidential election. Following the PPM primary election, Yameen's defeated rival, Umar Naseer, issued allegations of vote-rigging in the party poll and launched a legal challenge against the result. The MDP received a boost in mid-April when the Speaker of the People's Majlis, Abdulla Shahid, joined the party, defecting from the Government-aligned DRP.

Environmental Concerns

Environmental issues have become increasingly important in Maldivian politics, particularly given the fact that around 80% of the islands are no more than one metre above sea level and are thus extremely vulnerable to climate change. In November 1989 the Maldives hosted an international conference with delegates from other small island nations, to discuss the threat posed to low-lying island countries by the predicted rise in sea level caused by heating of the earth's atmosphere as a result of pollution (the greenhouse effect). In June 1990 an Environmental Research Unit, which was to operate under the Ministry of Planning and the Environment, was established in the Maldives. The Maldives reiterated its serious concern with regard to problems of world-wide environmental pollution when it hosted the 13th conference of the UN's Intergovernmental Panel on Climate Change (IPCC, see p. 67) in September 1997. In September 1999 a special session of the UN General Assembly was convened in New York, USA, to address the specific problems faced by the 43-member Alliance of Small Island States (see

p. 473) (including the Maldives), notably climate change, rising sea levels and globalization. The Maldives Government expressed its grave disappointment and concern at the USA's decision in April 2001 to reject the Kyoto Protocol to the UN's Framework Convention on Climate Change. A large part of the international community adopted the protocol in July after many of the emissions targets had been lowered. In March 2002 the Maldives, Kiribati and Tuvalu announced their decision to take legal action against the USA for refusing to sign the Kyoto Protocol and thus, so they claimed, threatening the very survival of the low-lying island states. At the World Summit on Sustainable Development held in September in Johannesburg, South Africa, President Gayoom warned the international community that low-lying islands were at greater risk than ever before. He demanded urgent action, including the universal ratification and implementation of the Kyoto Protocol, to prevent a global environmental catastrophe. In July 2008 a meeting of experts and environment ministers from the Maldives and other SAARC member countries finalized a five-year plan of action, with funding expected to be provided by development partners, to combat the adverse effects of climate change in the region. On assuming the presidency in November, Mohamed Nasheed immediately announced government plans to use some of the revenue from the tourism sector to establish a sovereign wealth fund to finance a long-term plan to purchase land abroad should the relocation of the Maldivian population become necessary owing to rising sea levels. In March 2009 President Nasheed announced plans to make the Maldives the world's first 'carbon neutral' state (i.e. a zero net contributor to greenhouse gas emissions) within 10 years by switching to using only renewable energy sources such as wind, wave and solar power, and through carbon offsetting.

In June 2012, in a speech to the UN Conference on Sustainable Development, in Rio de Janeiro, Brazil, President Mohamed Waheed Hassan Manik announced plans for the conversion of the Maldives' territorial waters into the world's largest marine reserve within five years. In October the Maldives Energy Authority announced the imminent launch of a five-year, US $138m. renewable energy project, the aim of which was that 10 islands would be powered solely by renewable energy and 30% of the electricity supply of 30 other islands would be converted to renewable energy; the project, which was to be funded by the World Bank, the Asian Development Bank and a number of foreign banks, was expected to generate around 26 MW of electricity.

Foreign Affairs
Regional relations

Since independence the Maldives have fostered close relations (economic, cultural and military) with India. In 1976 the two countries (together with Sri Lanka) amicably settled their maritime boundary and in 1981 signed a wide-ranging trade agreement. Relations were further strengthened in November 1988 as a result of India's prompt military intervention in the failed coup attempt in the Maldives. India is a major supplier of economic aid to the islands and has helped in the development of the Maldives' infrastructure, including telecommunications, aviation and health facilities. The close military ties between the countries (which regularly conduct joint naval exercises in the Indian Ocean) were reinforced by the establishment of a Defence Attaché's Office at the Maldivian High Commission in New Delhi in 2005. In August 2009 the Maldives signed an important bilateral defence pact with India, according to which the two countries agreed to bolster defence co-operation aimed at fortifying the security of the islands. As part of their plans, India was to establish a network of 26 radars across the Maldives' atolls, which would be linked to the Indian coastal command. In November 2011 Prime Minister Manmohan Singh became the first foreign head of state to address the People's Majlis. Following President Mohamed Nasheed's resignation in February 2012, India afforded official recognition to the new administration of Dr Mohamed Waheed Hassan Manik. At the same time, India attempted to help to quell the political unrest in the Maldives by dispatching Foreign Secretary Ranjan Mathai to hold conciliatory talks with various Maldivian politicians, including Nasheed and Waheed Hassan. In mid-May President Waheed embarked on his first official visit to India, during which he met with Manmohan Singh for talks on bilateral relations and the troubled political situation in the Maldives; Waheed sought to reassure Singh that his Government would adhere to all existing agreements and business arrangements between the

two countries. President Waheed's trip to India was preceded by a similar visit by Nasheed, in late April, during which the former President held talks with Prime Minister Singh on the Maldivian political situation and sought support for his demands for an early presidential election in the Maldives. Relations between the Maldives and India deteriorated in November 2012 when Waheed's Government declared that a US $511m. contract signed in June 2010 between Nasheed's Government and an Indian-Malaysian consortium to modernize and operate Ibrahim Nasir International Airport for 25 years was legally invalid and thenceforth terminated. The Indian authorities warned that the cancellation of the contract could result in the suspension of vital Indian aid to the Maldives.

Relations between the Maldives and Sri Lanka have traditionally been very amicable. The two countries established diplomatic relations in 1965 and have nurtured close co-operation in many fields, including trade, tourism, energy, fisheries and telecommunications. In August 2011 the Sri Lankan Government granted a US $10m. import credit to the Maldives, which, in turn, pledged to take measures to remove more customs duties on goods imported from Sri Lanka.

In recent years the People's Republic of China has cultivated strong relations with the Maldives. The two countries signed a defence agreement in the late 1990s, providing for military co-operation and arms supplies, but China's aim of establishing a military base on the Maldives was not achieved. Economic ties between the two nations have become more important over the last decade or so, with the volume of bilateral trade increasing, large numbers of Chinese tourists visiting the Maldives and substantial Chinese business investment in the islands' infrastructure. In November 2011 China became the first non-SAARC country to open an embassy in Malé (the two countries established diplomatic relations in 1972). Following an official visit to China by Waheed in September 2012, the Maldivian President confirmed that China had pledged US $500m. in loans to the Maldives.

CONSTITUTION AND GOVERNMENT

On 7 August 2008 the President ratified a new 301-article Constitution, which replaced the 1998 Constitution and which introduced a directly elected presidency and a democratic system of multi-party legislative elections. Legislative authority is vested in the People's Majlis. The People's Majlis consists of 77 members elected from Malé, Addu City and the 19 administrative atolls for five years by universal adult suffrage. Executive power is vested in the President, who is elected directly by the people, with more than 50% of the vote, for a period of five years. The President (who is not permitted to serve for more than two terms) governs with the assistance of an appointed Cabinet of Ministers (including a Vice-President, who is nominated by the President), which is responsible to the People's Majlis. The country has 21 administrative districts (19 atolls, the capital, Malé, and Addu City), which are grouped into seven provinces.

REGIONAL AND INTERNATIONAL CO-OPERATION

The Maldives is a member of the Asian Development Bank (ADB, see p. 214) and a founder member of the South Asian Association for Regional Cooperation (SAARC, see p. 430), which was formally constituted in December 1985. The country is also a member of the Colombo Plan (see p. 460), which seeks to improve regional co-operation, and became a full member of the Commonwealth (see p. 244) in June 1985.

Having joined the UN in 1965, the Maldives is a member of the UN Economic and Social Commission for Asia and the Pacific (ESCAP, see p. 31). As a contracting party to the General Agreement on Tariffs and Trade (GATT), the Maldives became a member of the World Trade Organization (WTO, see p. 444) on its establishment in 1995. The country also participates in the Organization of Islamic Cooperation (OIC, see p. 413).

ECONOMIC AFFAIRS

In 2011, according to estimates by the World Bank, the Maldives' gross national income (GNI), measured at average 2009–11 prices, was US $2,090m., equivalent to $6,530 per head (or $8,540 per head on an international purchasing-power parity basis). During 2002–11, it was estimated, the population increased at an average annual rate of 1.4%, while gross domestic product (GDP) per head grew, in real terms, by an average of 6.0% per year over the same period. Overall GDP increased, in real terms, at an average annual rate of 7.1% in 2002–12; GDP grew by 7.1% in 2011 and by an estimated 3.4% in 2012.

Agriculture, mining (mostly for coral and sand) and fishing contributed an estimated 3.8% of GDP in 2012; of this, the primary fishing sector alone accounted for 1.7%. About 12.0% of the total working population were employed in the agricultural and fishing sector at the March 2006 census. According to FAO estimates, about 12.9% of the total labour force were engaged in the sector at mid-2013. In 2011 revenue from exports of marine products totalled 1,717.1m. rufiyaa, thus accounting for 91.0% of total export earnings. Small quantities of various fruits, vegetables and cereals are produced, but virtually all principal staple foods have to be imported. As a result of salt-water intrusion caused by the Indian Ocean tsunami of December 2004, a significant amount of cultivable land was ruined. The dominant agricultural activity (not including fishing) in the Maldives is coconut production. The GDP of the agriculture, mining and fisheries sector increased, in real terms, at an average annual rate of 0.1% in 2002–12; real agricultural GDP increased by 1.0% in 2011 and by an estimated 4.8% in 2012.

Industry (including manufacturing, construction and utilities) contributed an estimated 20.5% of GDP in 2012, and employed 25.4% of the working population at the March 2006 census. Industrial GDP increased, in real terms, at an average annual rate of 9.5% in 2002–12; sectoral growth was an estimated 14.0% in 2012.

The manufacturing sector contributed an estimated 6.4% of GDP in 2012, and employed 18.3% of the working population at the March 2006 census. There are only a small number of 'modern' manufacturing enterprises in the Maldives, including fish-canning, garment-making and soft-drink bottling. Although cottage industries (such as the weaving of coir yarn and boat-building) employ nearly one-quarter of the total labour force, there is little scope for expansion, owing to the limited size of the domestic market. Because of its lack of manufacturing industries, the Maldives has to import most essential consumer and capital goods. From the late 1980s traditional handicrafts, such as lacquer work and shell craft, revived as a result of the expansion of the tourism sector. Manufacturing GDP increased, in real terms, at an average annual rate of 5.0% in 2002–12; sectoral growth was 12.0% in 2011 and an estimated 17.4% in 2012.

Construction contributed an estimated 12.7% of GDP in 2012, and employed 5.6% of the working population at the March 2006 census. Construction GDP increased, in real terms, at an average annual rate of 12.3% in 2002–12; the sector grew by an estimated 16.2% in 2012.

Energy is derived principally from petroleum, and imports of mineral fuels and oils comprised 27.6% of the cost of imports in 2011. Owing to a surge in commercial activities and a significant increase in construction projects in Malé, demand for electricity in the capital grew rapidly in the late 1980s and early 1990s. Accordingly, plans were formulated to augment the generating capacity of the power station in Malé and to improve the distribution network. By 2004 a total of 21 inhabited islands had been provided with electricity. In 2006 the Asian Development Bank (ADB) supplied a loan of US $8m. to enable the electrification of a further 20 or so islands. In recent years considerable focus has been placed on the development of renewable energy sources.

Following the decline of the shipping industry in the 1980s, tourism gained in importance as an economic sector, and by 1989 it had overtaken the fishing industry as the Maldives' largest source of foreign exchange. The tourism sector recovered well and surprisingly swiftly from the devastating effects of the 2004 tsunami; by the end of 2005 all of the resorts affected by the disaster had reopened. Tourist arrivals rose by 2.9% in 2012, compared with the previous year, to reach a record 958,027; revenue amounted to a total of US $1,873m. in that year. The GDP of the tourism sector increased, in real terms, at an average annual rate of 6.4% in 2002–12. The services sector as a whole contributed 75.7% of GDP in 2012, and employed 62.7% of the labour force at the March 2006 census. The GDP of the services sector increased, in real terms, by an average of 6.9% per year in 2002–12; sectoral growth was 6.0% in 2011 and an estimated 1.4% in 2012.

In 2011 the Maldives recorded a visible merchandise trade deficit of US $1,378.9m. and there was a deficit of $490.1m. on the current account of the balance of payments. In 2011 the principal sources of imports were the United Arab Emirates and Singapore (accounting for 21.8% and 21.6% of the total, respectively); other major providers were India, Sri Lanka, Malaysia and the People's Republic of China. In that year the principal market for exports was Thailand (accounting for 26.6% of the total);

other major purchasers were France, Sri Lanka, Italy, the United Kingdom and Taiwan. The principal exports were marine products (tuna being the largest export commodity). The principal imports were mineral products, machinery and mechanical appliances, prepared foodstuffs, beverages, spirits and vinegar, vegetable products, and live animals and animal products.

In the aftermath of the 2004 tsunami, the Maldives received a significant amount of international aid, in the form of grants and concessional loans, principally from the UN, the ADB, the World Bank and Japan (which has traditionally been the Maldives' largest aid donor). According to government figures, foreign financing rose by 68.4% in 2010, compared with the previous year, to reach an estimated 2,021.6m. rufiyaa, but decreased by 9.0% in 2011 to total an estimated 1,840.3m. rufiyaa; foreign grants and loans totalled an estimated 1,877.1m. rufiyaa in 2012. In 2012, in terms of central government finance, there was an estimated fiscal deficit of 4,313.6m. rufiyaa. The Maldives' total external debt was US $1,229m. at the end of 2010, of which $653m. was public and publicly guaranteed debt. In that year, the cost of servicing long-term public and publicly guaranteed debt and repayments to the IMF was equivalent to 21.3% of the value of exports of goods, services and income (excluding workers' remittances). According to the ILO, during 2002–11 the average annual rate of inflation was 5.4%. Owing to a sharp rise in global commodity prices (notably petroleum and food), consumer prices have increased substantially in recent years, with a rise of 10.9% in 2012. According to the March 2006 census, 14.4% of the total labour force was unemployed at that time (compared with around 2% in 2000).

The tsunami disaster of 2004 resulted in a widening budgetary deficit caused by the high cost of reconstruction projects combined with a decrease in revenue, illustrating the vulnerability of the economy to external events, both economic and environmental, and highlighting the fact that the long-term prosperity of the Maldives required sustained growth and diversification of activities. Partly as a result of the ongoing global financial crisis, GDP growth contracted by 4.7% in 2009, compared with positive growth of 12.2% in 2008. In December 2009 the IMF provided the Maldives with a standby loan of $92.5m. to help the islands in their economic recovery. Although GDP grew by 5.7% in 2010 and by 7.1% in 2011, fuelled by strong performances in the tourism sector (with a notable rise in the numbers of visitors from the more affluent countries in Asia such as India and China), the IMF expressed concern over the islands' persistently large public and fiscal deficits. In January 2011 the UN-designated status of the Maldives was upgraded from that of 'least developed country' to 'middle-income country'; although generally welcomed within the Maldives, there was some concern that the country would, as a result, lose special trade preferences and foreign aid. In the same month a tourism goods and services tax was introduced, which was expected to be vital in helping to reduce the fiscal deficit (which was estimated to have narrowed to 16.1% of GDP in 2010 from 21.0% in 2009). In March 2011 the Maldives Inland Revenue Authority was established to oversee the efficient collection of revenue. In May the IMF and the Maldives Government signed a new three-year agreement based on the latter introducing further tax reforms. A business profit tax and a general goods and services tax were introduced in the following months, while the introduction of a personal income tax was under parliamentary consideration from mid-2011. The resulting increases in revenue, combined with a curb on expenditure (including the lowering of public sector wages), helped to narrow the fiscal deficit to 10.2% of GDP in 2011. The political upheaval and unrest in 2012 did not have a major impact on the tourism sector, which remained relatively robust; however, the rate of growth of GDP in that year moderated to an estimated 3.4%. In August further austerity measures were proposed, including an increase in the tourism goods and services tax, a rise in import duties and the termination of electricity subsidies in Malé. In November, the IMF projected that the fiscal deficit would amount to at least 16% of GDP in 2012 (significantly higher than government estimates), and estimated that the public debt-to-GDP ratio was in excess of 80%. In the same month the Government announced plans to establish an offshore financial centre in an attempt to lessen the economy's reliance on the tourism industry. A fiscal responsibility bill approved by the parliament in April 2013 set limits on government borrowing and stipulated that from 2014 the level of public debt must not exceed 60% of GDP.

PUBLIC HOLIDAYS

2014: 2 January* (National Day), 13 January* (Birth of the Prophet Muhammad), 2 February (The Day Maldives Embraced Islam), 1 May (Labour Day), 28 June* (Ramadan begins), 26 July (Independence Day), 28 July* (Id al-Fitr, end of Ramadan), 4 October* (Id al-Adha, feast of the Sacrifice), 24 October* (Islamic New Year), 3 November (Victory Day), 11 November (Republic Day).

* These holidays are dependent on the Islamic lunar calendar and may vary by one or two days from the dates given.

Statistical Survey

Source (unless otherwise stated): Department of National Planning, Ministry of Finance and Treasury, Ameenee Magu, Malé 20-379; tel. 3349200; fax 3327351; e-mail stat@planning.gov.mv; internet planning.gov.mv.

AREA AND POPULATION

Area: 298 sq km (115 sq miles).

Population: 270,101 at census of 31 March–7 April 2000; 298,968 (males 151,459, females 147,509) at census of 21–28 March 2006. *Mid-2013* (official estimate): 336,224 (males 169,800, females 166,424).

Density (official estimate, mid-2013): 1,128.3 per sq km.

Population by Age and Sex (official estimates at mid-2013): *0–14:* 88,456 (males 45,039, females 43,417); *15–64:* 231,597 (males 116,125, females 115,472); *65 and over:* 16,171 (males 8,636, females 7,535); *Total* 336,224 (males 169,800, females 166,424).

Administrative Divisions (population, 2006 census): *Capital City*: Malé 103,693. *Atolls*: North Thiladhunmathi 13,495; South Thiladhunmathi 16,237; North Miladhunmadulu 11,940; South Miladhunmadulu 10,015; North Maalhosmadulu 14,756; South Maalhosmadulu 9,578; Faadhippolhu 9,190; Malé 15,441; North Ari 5,776; South Ari 8,379; Felidhe 1,606; Mulakatholhu 4,710; North Nilandhe 3,765; South Nilandhe 4,967; Kolhumadulu 8,493; Hadhdhunmathi 11,990; North Huvadhu 8,262; South Huvadhu 11,013; Gnaviyani 7,636; Addu 18,026.

Births, Marriages and Deaths (2011): Registered live births 7,182 (birth rate 22.1 per 1,000); Marriages 6,015 (marriage rate 18.5 per 1,000); Registered deaths 1,137 (death rate 3.5 per 1,000).

Life Expectancy (years at birth): 76.9 (males 75.7; females 78.1) in 2011. Source: World Bank, World Development Indicators database.

Economically Active Population (persons aged 12 years and over, census of March 2006): Agriculture, hunting and forestry 4,236; Fishing 8,388; Mining and quarrying 339; Manufacturing 19,259; Electricity, gas and water 1,229; Construction 5,930; Wholesale and retail trade and repairs 11,711; Restaurants and hotels 12,090; Transport, storage and communications 7,098; Financing, insurance, real estate and business services 1,738; Public administration and defence 15,949; Education 9,872; Health and social work 4,182; Other community, social and personal service activities 3,248; Extraterritorial organizations and bodies 216; Activities not adequately defined 4,746; *Total employed* 110,231 (males 69,701, females 40,530); Unemployed 18,605; *Total labour force* 128,836. *Mid-2013* (estimates in '000): Agriculture, etc. 21; Total labour force 163 (Source: FAO).

HEALTH AND WELFARE

Key Indicators

Total Fertility Rate (children per woman, 2010): 1.8.

Under-5 Mortality Rate (per 1,000 live births, 2010): 15.

HIV/AIDS (% of persons aged 15–49, 2009): <0.1.

Physicians (per 1,000 head, 2007): 1.60.

Hospital Beds (per 1,000 head, 2005): 2.6.

Health Expenditure (2009): US $ per head (PPP): 457.

Health Expenditure (2009): % of GDP: 6.4.

Health Expenditure (2009): public (% of total): 60.7.

Access to Water (% of persons, 2010): 98.

Access to Sanitation (% of persons, 2010): 97.

Total Carbon Dioxide Emissions ('000 metric tons, 2008): 920.4.

Carbon Dioxide Emissions Per Head (metric tons, 2008): 3.0.

Human Development Index (2011): ranking: 109.

Human Development Index (2011): value: 0.661.

For sources and definitions, see explanatory note on p. vi.

AGRICULTURE, ETC.

Principal Crops (production in long-term leased islands*, metric tons, 2007 unless otherwise indicated): Coconuts 94.4; Tender coconuts 116.2; Aubergines 31.7; Cucumbers 48.6; Pumpkins 48.4; Bitter gourds 4.4 (2006); Ridged peppers 63.6; Papayas 631.1; Watermelons 395.7; Bananas 499. *2011* (FAO estimates): Bananas 7,000; Coconuts 6,700; Papayas 1,100. (Source: FAO).

* Comprising the atolls of North Thiladhunmathi, South Thiladhunmathi, North Miladhunmadulu, South Ari, Mulakatholhu, North Nilandhe, Kolhumadulu and Hadhdhunmathi.

Sea Fishing ('000 metric tons, 2010): Total catch 95.0 (Skipjack tuna—Oceanic skipjack 58.5; Yellowfin tuna 12.4). Source: FAO.

INDUSTRY

Selected Products (metric tons, 2011): Frozen fish 31,906.24 (Skipjack 18,520.11); Salted or dried fish 4,057.86; Canned fish 1,463.39.

Electric Energy (million kWh): 288.4 in 2009; 246.8 in 2010; 264.7 in 2011.

FINANCE

Currency and Exchange Rates: 100 laari (larees) = 1 rufiyaa (Maldivian rupee). *Sterling, Dollar and Euro Equivalents* (31 December 2012): £1 sterling = 24.246 rufiyaa; US $1 = 15.365 rufiyaa; €1 = 20.273 rufiyaa; 1,000 rufiyaa = £41.24 = $65.08 = €49.33. *Exchange Rate* (rufiyaa per US dollar): since July 2001 the mid-point rate of exchange has been fixed at US $1 = 12.85 rufiyaa.

Budget (central government finance, million rufiyaa, 2010): *Revenue:* Tax revenue 3,695.9 (Import duty 2091.3); Other current revenue 4,302.9 (Resort lease rents 2,567.4); Capital revenue 1,363.3; Grants 304.2; Total 9,666.3. *Expenditure:* General administration of public services 2,031.1; Defence 561.7; Public order and internal security 1,046.5; Environmental protection 181.1; Education 2,006.3; Health 838.5; Social security and welfare 743.0; Community programmes 1,593.6; Economic services 920.8 (Agriculture and fishing 124.6, Trade and industry 116.0, Electricity, gas and water 104.6, Transport and communications 469.4, Tourism 106.2); Interest on public debt 329.7; Net lending –13.0; Total 10,239.3 (Current 8,216.9, Capital and net lending 2,022.4). *2012* (estimates): *Revenue:* Current revenue 9,352.5; Capital revenue 14.0; Grants 465.5; Total 9,832.0. *Expenditure:* Current expenditure 10,522.1; Capital expenditure 3,693.8; Net lending –70.3; Total 14,145.6.

International Reserves (excl. gold, US $ million at 31 December 2011): IMF special drawing rights 10.70; Reserve position in IMF 3.08; Foreign exchange 334.87; Total 348.65. Source: IMF, *International Financial Statistics*.

Money Supply (million rufiyaa at 31 December 2011): Currency outside depository corporations 1,857.55; Transferable deposits 113,165.39; Other deposits 4,033.87; *Broad money* 19,056.81. Source: IMF, *International Financial Statistics*.

Cost of Living (Consumer Price Index; base: 2005 = 100): All items 129.7 in 2009; 135.8 in 2010; 167.2 in 2011. Source: IMF, *International Financial Statistics*.

Gross Value Added in Basic Prices (million rufiyaa at current prices, 2012, provisional): Agriculture (excl. fishing) and mining 769.5; Fishing and fisheries 595.0; Manufacturing 2,300.1; Electricity and water supply 463.5; Construction 4,548.6; Wholesale and retail trade 1,474.6; Transport and communications 4,813.0; Finance, real estate and business services 4,353.0; Tourism 8,564.2; Public administration 4,789.8; Education, health and social service 3,069.0; *Sub-total* 35,740.3; Financial intermediation services indirectly measured –1,592.8; *Gross value added in basic prices* 34,147.6.

Balance of Payments (US $ million, 2011): Exports of goods 346.4; Imports of goods. –1,725.3; *Balance on goods* –1,378.9; Exports of services 1,981.0; Imports of services –540.0; *Balance on goods and services* 62.1; Primary income received 6.6; Primary income paid –340.0; *Balance on goods, services and primary income* –271.3; Secondary income received 25.9; Secondary income paid –244.7; *Current balance* –490.1; Capital account (net) 30.2; Direct investment liabilities 281.6; Portfolio investment liabilities 0.1; Other investment assets −201.3; Other investment liabilities −19.4; Net errors and omissions 383.7; *Reserves and related items* −15.2. Source: IMF, *International Financial Statistics*.

EXTERNAL TRADE

Principal Commodities (million rufiyaa, 2011): *Imports c.i.f.:* Live animals and animal products 1,215.9; Vegetable products 1,360.3; Prepared foodstuffs, beverages, spirits and vinegar 1,633.1; Mineral products 5,654.9; Intermediate and capital goods 10,041.6 (Plastics and rubber and articles thereof 621.3; Wood, articles of wood, wood charcoal, cork and articles and pulp of wood 949.7; Construction materials 463.6; Base metal and articles of base metal 1,044.7; Machinery and mechanical appliances 3,657.9; Textiles 468.5; Chemicals and chemical products 941.5; Transport equipment and parts 1,208.5; Miscellaneous manufactured goods 685.9); Total (incl. others) 20,486.2. *Exports:* Marine products 1,717.1 (Fresh, chilled or frozen tuna 778.6); Other products (mostly clothing and waste and scrap of alloy steel) 53.2; Total 1,770.3.

Principal Trading Partners (million rufiyaa, 2011): *Imports:* Australia 447.0; Bahamas 235.2; Canada 270.9; China, People's Republic 1,063.0; Denmark 336.6; Germany 362.3; India 2,068.7; Indonesia 286.5; Italy 335.0; Japan 477.3; Malaysia 1,105.5; Singapore 4,419.2; Sri Lanka 1,145.3; Thailand 861.4; United Arab Emirates 4,475.2; United Kingdom 222.4; USA 425.3; Total (incl. others) 20,486.2. *Exports:* France 295.6; Germany 45.6; Hong Kong 19.1; India 35.9; Iran 38.4; Italy 177.2; Japan 54.3; Netherlands 48.3; Spain 42.4; Sri Lanka 191.4; Taiwan 99.1; Thailand 471.4; United Kingdom 125.7; Total (incl. others) 1,770.3.

TRANSPORT

Road Traffic (motor vehicles in use at 31 December 2010): Passenger cars 3,348; Buses and coaches 99; Lorries and vans 3,818; Motorcycles and mopeds 39,147. Source: IRF, *World Road Statistics*.

Shipping: *Flag Registered Fleet* (at 31 December 2012): Vessels 65; Total displacement 77,289 grt (Source: Lloyd's List Intelligence—www.lloydslistintelligence.com). *Freight Traffic* ('000 metric tons, 1990): Goods loaded 27; Goods unloaded 78 (Source: UN, *Monthly Bulletin of Statistics*).

Civil Aviation (traffic at Malé International Airport, 2011): *International Flights:* Arrivals 1,128,238; Departures 1,146,175. *Domestic Flights:* Arrivals 565,097; Departures 579,715.

TOURISM

Tourist Arrivals: 791,917 in 2010; 931,333 in 2011; 958,027 in 2012.

Foreign Visitors by Country of Nationality (2012): China, People's Republic 229,551; France 56,775; Germany 98,351; India 31,721; Italy 62,782; Japan 36,438; Russia 66,378; Switzerland 35,457; United Kingdom 91,776; Total (incl. others) 958,027.

Tourism Receipts (US $ million): 1,713 in 2010; 1,868 in 2011; 1,873 in 2012.

COMMUNICATIONS MEDIA

Telephones (main lines in use): 24,084 in 2011.

Mobile Cellular Telephones: 530,449 in 2011.

Personal Computers: 60,000 (202.4 per 1,000 persons) in 2006.

Internet Subscribers (incl. mobile internet customers): 76,918 in 2011.

Broadband Subscribers: 20,400 in 2011.

Sources: Telecommunications Authority of Maldives, Malé; International Telecommunication Union.

EDUCATION

Schools (2011): 382 (government 212, community 69, private 101). Source: Ministry of Education.

Teachers (2011): Pre-primary 715; Primary 3,275; Lower secondary 2,713; Upper secondary 367. Source: Ministry of Education.

Pupils (2011): Pre-primary 17,885 (males 9,024, females 8,861); Primary 40,435 (males 21,061, females 19,374); Lower secondary 22,788 (males 11,693, females 11,095); Upper secondary 5,604 (males 2,445, females 3,159); Special needs 234 (males 135, females 99). Source: Ministry of Education.

Maldives College of Higher Education: Academic staff 138 (2003); Students 4,388 (2007). Source: Maldives College of Higher Education.

Pupil-Teacher Ratio (primary education, UNESCO estimate): 11.7 in 2010/11 (Source: UNESCO Institute for Statistics).

Adult Literacy Rate (UNESCO estimates): 98.4% (males 98.4%; females 98.4%) in 2006 (Source: UNESCO Institute for Statistics).

Directory

The Government

HEAD OF STATE

President: Dr MOHAMED WAHEED HASSAN MANIK (took office 7 February 2012).

THE CABINET OF MINISTERS
(May 2013)

A coalition of the Dhivehi Rayyithunge Party (DRP, Maldivian People's Party), the Dhivehi Qaumee Party (DQP, Maldivian National Party), the People's Alliance (PA), the Adhaalath Party (AP, Justice Party), the Progressive Party of Maldives (PPM) and the Jumhooree Party (JP).

Vice-President: MOHAMED WAHEED DEEN.

Minister of Economic Development: AHMED MOHAMED (DRP).

Minister of Environment and Energy: Dr MARIYAM SHAKEELA.

Minister of Finance and Treasury: ABDULLA JIHAD.

Minister of Foreign Affairs: Dr ABDUL SAMAD ABDULLA (PPM).

Minister of Housing and Infrastructure: Dr MOHAMED MUIZ (AP).

Minister of Health: Dr AHMED JAMSHEED MOHAMED.

Minister of Defence and National Security: Dr MOHAMED NAZIM (PA).

Minister of Education: ASIM AHMED (DRP).

Minister of Transport and Communication: AMEEN IBRAHIM.

Minister of Tourism, Arts and Culture: Dr AHMED ADHEEB ABDUL GHAFOOR.

Minister of Fisheries and Agriculture and Acting Minister of Home Affairs: AHMED SHAFEEU.

Minister of Human Resources, Youth and Sports: MOHAMED HUSSAIN SHAREEF (PPM).

Minister of Islamic Affairs: Dr SHEIKH MOHAMED SHAHEEM ALI SAEED (AP).

Minister of Gender, Family and Human Rights: Uza AISHATH AZIMA SHAKOORU.

Attorney-General: Uza AISHATH BISAM.

MINISTRIES

President's Office: Boduthakurufaanu Magu, Malé 20-113; tel. 3320701; fax 3325500; e-mail info@presidencymaldives.gov.mv; internet www.presidencymaldives.gov.mv.

Attorney-General's Office: Velaanaage, 6th Floor, Ameer Ahmed Magu, Malé 20-096; tel. 3323809; fax 3314109; e-mail info@agoffice.gov.mv; internet agoffice.gov.mv.

Ministry of Defence and National Security: Ameer Ahmed Magu, Malé 20-126; tel. 3314669; fax 3312800; e-mail admin@defence.gov.mv; internet www.defence.gov.mv.

Ministry of Economic Development: Boduthakurufaanu Magu, Malé 20-125; tel. 3323668; fax 3323840; e-mail info@trade.gov.mv; internet www.trade.gov.mv.

Ministry of Education: Velaanaage 8–9 Floors, Ameer Ahmed Magu, Malé 20-096; tel. and fax 3333262; fax 3321201; e-mail admin@moe.gov.mv; internet www.moe.gov.mv.

Ministry of Environment and Energy: Malé; internet www.mhe.gov.mv.

Ministry of Finance and Treasury: Ameenee Magu, Blk 379, Malé 20-379; tel. 3349200; fax 3324432; e-mail admin@finance.gov.mv; internet www.finance.gov.mv.

Ministry of Fisheries and Agriculture: Velaanaage, 11th Floor, Malé 20-096; tel. 3322625; fax 3326558; e-mail admin@fishagri.gov.mv; internet www.fishagri.gov.mv.

Ministry of Foreign Affairs: Henveiru, Blk 77, Boduthakuru-faanu Magu, Malé 20-077; tel. 3323400; fax 3323841; e-mail info@foreign.gov.mv; internet www.foreign.gov.mv.

Ministry of Gender, Family and Human Rights: Fen Bldg, 2nd Floor, Ameenee Magu, Malé; tel. 3317761; fax 3316237; e-mail info@mgf.gov.mv; internet www.mgf.gov.mv.

Ministry of Health: Ameenee Magu, Machangolhi, Malé 20-379; tel. 3328887; fax 3328889; e-mail mohf@health.gov.mv; internet www.health.gov.mv.

Ministry of Home Affairs: Velaanaage Bldg, 10th Floor, Ameer Ahmed Magu, Malé 20-096; tel. 3323820; fax 3324739; e-mail info@homeaffairs.gov.mv; internet www.homeaffairs.gov.mv.

Ministry of Housing and Infrastructure: Ameenee Magu, Malé 20-392; tel. 3004300; fax 3004301; internet www.mhe.gov.mv.

Ministry of Human Resources, Youth and Sports: Haveeree Hingun, Maafanu, Malé 20-210; tel. 3347300; fax 3347490; e-mail info@mhrys.gov.mv; internet www.mhrys.gov.mv.

Ministry of Islamic Affairs: Islamic Centre, Blk 77, Medhuziyaar-aimagu, Malé 20-156; tel. 3323623; fax 3315161; e-mail info@islamicaffairs.gov.mv; internet www.islamicaffairs.gov.mv.

Department of Judicial Administration: Theemuge, Aabruzu, Malé 20-212; tel. 3322303; fax 3325447; e-mail admin@judiciary.gov.mv; internet www.justice.gov.mv.

Ministry of Tourism, Arts and Culture: Velaanaage, 5th Floor, Ameer Ahmed Magu, Malé 20-096; tel. 3323224; fax 3322512; e-mail info@tourism.gov.mv; internet www.tourism.gov.mv.

Ministry of Transport and Communication: Velaanaage, 11th Floor, Ameer Ahmed Magu, Malé 20-096; tel. 3305808; fax 3307674; e-mail admin@motc.gov.mv; internet motc.gov.mv.

President and Legislature

PRESIDENT

Presidential Election, First Ballot, 8 October 2008

Candidates	Votes	% of votes
Maumoon Abdul Gayoom (Dhivehi Rayyithunge Party)	71,731	40.3
Mohamed Nasheed (Maldivian Democratic Party)	44,293	24.9
Hassan Saeed (Independent)	29,633	16.7
Qasim Ibrahim (Jumhooree Party)	27,056	15.2
Umar Naseer (Islamic Democratic Party)	2,472	1.4
Ibrahim Ismail (Social Liberal Party)	1,382	0.8
Invalid or blank votes	1,235	0.7
Total	177,802	100.0

Presidential Election, Second Ballot, 28 October 2008

Candidates	Votes	% of votes
Mohamed Nasheed (Maldivian Democratic Party)	97,222	53.7
Maumoon Abdul Gayoom (Dhivehi Rayyithunge Party)	82,121	45.3
Other (invalid)	1,861	1.0
Total	181,204	100.0

Note: Mohamed Nasheed resigned as President on 7 February 2012; he was replaced on the same day by former Vice-President Dr Mohamed Waheed Hassan Manik of the Gaumee Itthihaad party

LEGISLATURE

People's Majlis

The People's Majlis (People's Council) comprises members elected by the people of Malé and each of the 20 atolls (for a five-year term).

Speaker: ABDULLA SHAHID.

Deputy Speaker: AHMED NAZIM.

Election, 9 May 2009

Party	Seats
Dhivehi Rayyithunge Party	28
Maldivian Democratic Party	25
Independents	13
People's Alliance	7
Dhivehi Qaumee Party	2
Jumhooree Party	1
Vacant	1
Total	77

Election Commission

Elections Commission of Maldives: PA Complex, 3rd Floor, Hilaalee Magu, Malé; tel. 3324426; fax 3323997; e-mail info@elections.gov.mv; internet www.elections.gov.mv; f. 1998; 5-mem. independent body nominated and appointed by People's Majlis; Pres. MOHAMED IBRAHIM; Vice-Pres. AHMED SHAHID; Commrs MOHAMED MAHIR, FUAD THAUFEEQ; Sec.-Gen. ASIM ABDUL SATTAR.

Political Organizations

In early March 2013 a Political Parties Bill was ratified by the People's Majlis, according to which parties would require a minimum of 10,000 members to qualify for registration with the Elections Commission. It was reported that 11 political parties were thus threatened with dissolution. However, the Supreme Court subsequently issued an injunction against the dissolution of political parties.

Adhaalath Party (AP) (Justice Party): Medhuge, 3rd Floor, Medhu Ziyaarai Magu, Malé; tel. and fax 3342671; e-mail admin@adhaalath.org.mv; internet www.adhaalath.org.mv; f. 2005; Islamic; Leader Sheikh IMRAN ABDULLA.

Dhivehi Qaumee Party (DQP) (Maldivian National Party): M. Maahi, 2nd Floor, Malé; tel. 3304548; fax 3343844; e-mail sitee@qaumee.org.mv; internet qaumee.org.mv; f. 2009; Pres. Dr HASSAN SAEED; Vice-Pres. Dr MOHAMED JAMEEL AHMED; Gen. Sec. ABDULLA AMEEN.

Dhivehi Rayyithunge Party (DRP) (Maldivian People's Party): Sinamalé 3 Galolhu, Malé; tel. 3320456; fax 3344774; e-mail info@drp.mv; internet www.drp.mv; f. 2005; Pres. AHMED THASMEEN ALI; Vice-Pres. ALI WAHEED; Sec.-Gen. Dr ABDULLAH MAUSOOM; 38,149 mems (June 2010); in April 2011 supporters of the founder of the DRP, former President of the Maldives Maumoon Abdul Gayoom, split from the party and formed the Zaeem–DRP (Z–DRP) faction; in September Gayoom officially resigned from the DRP and launched a new party, the PPM.

Gaumee Itthihaad (GIP) (National Unity Party): 1st Floor, Jawahiru Vadhee, Orchid Magu, Malé; tel. 3304002; fax 3308036; e-mail info@gip.org.mv; internet www.gip.org.mv; f. 2008; Chair. Dr MOHAMED WAHEED HASSAN MANIK.

Jumhooree Party (JP) (Republican Party): M. Chan'beyleege, 4th Floor, Malé; tel. 3305546; fax 3306699; e-mail jumhooreepartysg@gmail.com; internet www.jumhooreeparty.org.mv; Leader QASIM IBRAHIM; Pres. Dr IBRAHIM DIDI.

Maldivian Democratic Party (MDP): H. Sharasha, 2nd Floor, Sosun Magu, Malé 20-059; tel. 3340044; fax 3322960; e-mail secretariat@mdp.org.mv; internet www.mdp.org.mv; f. 2001; fmrly based in Colombo, Sri Lanka; official registration in Maldives permitted June 2005; Acting Chair. MOOSA 'REEKO' MANIK; Sec.-Gen. HAMID ABDUL GHAFOOR; Pres. (vacant).

People's Alliance (PA): Melaim 2nd Floor, Boduthakurufaanu Magu, Malé; tel. 3346032; fax 3346031; e-mail info@pa.org.mv; internet pa.org.mv; f. 2008; Vice-Pres. MOOSA ZAMEER.

Progressive Party of Maldives (PPM): Henveiru, Thema, Malé; tel. 3303838; fax 3330524; e-mail info@ppm.mv; internet www.ppm.mv; f. 2011; est. by fmr Pres. of the Maldives (1978–2008) and fmr leader of the DRP Maumoon Abdul Gayoom; Pres. MAUMOON ABDUL GAYOOM; Parliamentary Group Leader ABDULLAH YAMEEN.

Diplomatic Representation

EMBASSIES AND HIGH COMMISSIONS IN THE MALDIVES

Bangladesh: M. Kurinbee Lodge, 5th Floor, Izzudheen Magu, Malé; tel. 3315541; fax 3315543; e-mail bdootmal@dhivehinet.net.mv; High Commissioner Rear Adm. A. S. M. A. AWAL.

China, People's Republic: 6B, Canary Lodge, Majeedhe Magu, Malé; tel. 3307825; fax 3307826; Ambassador YU HONGYAO.

India: H. Athireege-Aage, Ameeru Ahmed Magu, Malé; tel. 3323015; fax 3324778; e-mail hoc.male@mea.gov.in; internet www.hcimaldives.in; High Commissioner RAJEEV SHAHARE.

Pakistan: G. Helengely, Lily Magu, Malé; tel. 3323005; fax 3321832; e-mail pahicmale2010@hotmail.com; internet mofa.gov.pk/maldives; High Commissioner MUHAMMAD SAEED KHAN.

Sri Lanka: 1st Floor, H. Haifa Bldg, Bodufungadu Magu, Malé; tel. 3322845; fax 3321652; e-mail highcom@dhivehinet.net.mv; internet www.slhcmaldives.com; High Commissioner DICKSON SARATHCHANDRA DELA BANDARA.

Judicial System

The administration of justice is undertaken in accordance with Islamic (*Shari'a*) law. In 1980 the Maldives High Court was established. There are four courts in Malé, and one island court in every inhabited island. The island court of each atoll capital oversees the administration of justice in that atoll.

The new Constitution, which was enacted in August 2008, provided for the establishment of a Supreme Court to serve as the highest authority for the administration of justice in the nation. In the following month the President appointed five judges to the interim Supreme Court after consultation with the newly established Judicial Service Commission and confirmation of the appointments by a two-thirds' majority of the People's Majlis. With the establishment of the Supreme Court, there was to be no further recourse of appeal from the High Court to the President. In August 2010 a permanent Supreme Court was established; a new Chief Justice and six judges were appointed.

The Maldives' first Prosecutor-General was appointed by the President in September 2008, following approval by the People's Majlis.

Supreme Court: M. Theemuge, Orchid Magu, Malé 20208; tel. 3009990; fax 3008554; e-mail info@supremecourt.gov.mv; internet www.supremecourt.gov.mv; Chief Justice Uz. AHMED FAIZ HUSSAIN.

High Court of the Maldives: M. Theemuge, Orchid Magu, Malé 20208; tel. 3325029; fax 3316471; e-mail info@highcourt.gov.mv; internet www.highcourt.gov.mv; Chief Judge Uz. AHMED SHAREEF.

Office of the Attorney-General: Huravee Building, 3rd Floor, Malé; tel. 3323809; fax 3314109; e-mail info@agoffice.gov.mv; internet agoffice.gov.mv; Attorney-General Uza AISHATH BISHAM.

Office of the Prosecutor-General: Malé 20040; tel. 3000655; fax 3000644; e-mail pgoffice@pgoffice.gov.mv; internet www.pgoffice.gov.mv; Prosecutor-General AHMED MUIZZU.

Religion

Islam is the state religion, and the majority of Maldivians are Sunni Muslims.

In November 2008 a Ministry of Islamic Affairs was established to replace the Supreme Council for Islamic Affairs, which had been founded in 1996 to authorize state policies with regard to Islam and to advise the Government on Islamic affairs.

The Press

DAILIES

Aafathis Daily News: Silver Cloud, Maafannu, Malé 20-02; tel. 3318609; fax 3312425; e-mail aafathis@dhivehinet.net.mv; internet www.aafathisnews.com.mv; f. 1979; Dhivehi and English; Editor ABDULLAH NAEEM IBRAHIM; circ. 3,000.

Dhives: Malé; e-mail editor@dhives.com; f. 2009; organ of the Dhivehi Rayyithunge Party; Editor AHMED NIHAN.

Haama Daily: Ma. Night Rose, Dhilbahaaru Magu, POB 20232, Malé; tel. 3340077; fax 3343726; e-mail haama@haamadaily.com; internet www.haamadaily.com; Dhivehi and English; Chair. QASIM IBRAHIM.

Haveeru Daily: Ameenee Magu, POB 20103, Malé; tel. 3325671; fax 3323103; e-mail haveeru@haveeru.com.mv; internet www.haveeru.com.mv; f. 1979; Dhivehi and English; Chair. MOHAMED ZAHIR HUSSAIN; Editor ALI RAFEEQ; circ. 4,500.

Jazeera Daily: M. Zenthuram, Izzudheen Magu, Malé; tel. 3343738; fax 3343736; e-mail info@jazeera.com.mv; internet www.jazeera.com.mv.

Miadhu News: G. Maple Leaf, Ameenee Magu, Malé; tel. 3320700; fax 3320500; e-mail admin@miadhu.com.mv; internet www.miadhu.com; Chair. MOHAMED NABEEL; Editor ABDUL LATHEEF.

Minivan News: Malé; tel. 3347889; e-mail editorial@minivannews.com; internet www.minivannews.com; f. 2005; English-language online newspaper; Editor J. J. ROBINSON.

Raajje Daily: Malé; e-mail info@raajje.mv; f. 2008; independent; predominantly Dhivehi with English section; Editor HASSAN SAEED.

PERIODICALS

The Evening Weekly: Ameenee Magu, POB 20103, Malé; tel. 3325671; fax 3323103; e-mail info@eveningweekly.com.mv; internet www.haveeru.com.mv; weekly; English; owned by the Haveeru news group; Chair. MOHAMED ZAHIR HUSSAIN.

Faiythoora: National Centre for Linguistic and Historical Research, Soasun Magu, Malé 20-05; tel. 3323206; fax 3326796; e-mail nclhr@dhivehinet.net.mv; internet www.qaumiyyath.gov.mv; f. 1979; monthly magazine; Dhivehi; Maldivian history, culture and language; Editor Uz ABDULLA HAMEED; circ. 800.

Furadhaana: Dept of Information, Ministry of Tourism, Arts and Culture, Ghazee Bldg, 1st Floor, Ameer Ahmed Magu, Malé 20-05; tel. 3334333; fax 3334334; e-mail print@maldivesinfo.gov.mv; internet www.maldivesinfo.gov.mv; f. 1990; monthly; Dhivehi; Editor IBRAHIM MANIK; circ. 1,000.

Hidhaayathuge Magu (The Road to Steadfastness): Malé; f. 2008; weekly; Dhivehi; religious; publ. by the Ministry of Islamic Affairs.

Huvaas Magazine: Ameenee Magu, POB 20103, Malé; tel. 3325671; fax 3323103; e-mail huvaas@haveeru.com.mv; internet www.haveeru.com.mv/huvaas; f. 2001; fortnightly; Chair. Dr MOHAMED ZAHIR HUSSAIN.

Jamaathuge Khabaru (Community News): Centre for Continuing Education, Salahudeen Bldg, Malé 20-04; tel. 3328772; fax 3322223; internet www.cce.edu.mv; monthly; Dhivehi; Editor AHMED ZAHIR; circ. 1,500.

Maldives News Bulletin: Maldives News Bureau, Department of Information, Ministry of Tourism, Arts and Culture, Ghazee Bldg, 1st Floor, Ameer Ahmed Magu, Malé 20-05; tel. 3334333; fax 3334334; e-mail informat@dhivehinet.net.mv; internet www.maldivesinfo.gov.mv; f. 1980; weekly; English; online only since Feb. 2008.

Marine Research Centre Bulletin: Marine Research Centre, Ministry of Fisheries and Agriculture, H. White Waves, Malé 20-025; tel. 3322328; fax 3322509; e-mail info@mrc.gov.mv; internet www.mrc.gov.mv; f. 1984; bi-annual; fisheries and marine research; Exec. Dir Dr MOHAMED SHIHAM ADAM.

NEWS AGENCY

Haveeru News Service (HNS): POB 20103, Malé; tel. 3325671; fax 3323103; e-mail haveeru@haveeru.com.mv; internet www.haveeru.com.mv; f. 1979; Chair. Dr MOHAMED ZAHIR HUSSAIN; Man. Editor AHMED ZAHIR.

PRESS ORGANIZATIONS AND ASSOCIATIONS

Maldives Journalist Association: M.Seeraazee Kanmatheege, Malé 20026; tel. 7785669 (mobile); e-mail admin@mja.org.mv; internet mja.org.mv; f. 2009; Pres. AHMED ZAHIR.

Maldives Media Council: Reghendhi Hingun, Malé 20144; tel. 3003995; fax 3003994; e-mail info@mmc.org.mv; internet www.mmc.org.mv; f. 2010; development and supervision of the media sector; 15 elected mems; Pres. IBRAHIM KHALEEL.

Publishers

Corona Press: Feeroaz Magu, Maafannu, Malé; tel. 3310052; fax 3314741.

Loamaafaanu Print: Alkariyya Bldg, Ground Floor, Ameenee Magu, Malé 20-354; tel. 3317209; fax 3313815; e-mail haveeru@netlink.net.mv.

Novelty Printers and Publishers: M. Vaarey Villa, Izzudhdheen Magu, Malé 20-317; tel. 3318844; fax 3327039; e-mail novelty@dhivehinet.net.mv; internet www.novelty.com.mv; f. 1965; general and reference books; Man. Dir ASAD ALI.

Ummeedhee Press: M. Aasthaanaa Javaahirumagu, Malé 20-02; tel. 3325110; fax 3326412; e-mail ummpress@dhivehinet.net.mv;

f. 1986; printing and publishing; Principal Officers ABDUL SHAKOOR ALI, MOHAMED SHAKOOR.

Broadcasting and Communications

TELECOMMUNICATIONS

According to the Communications Authority of Maldives, in February 2013 there were 578,010 active mobile telephone subscriptions.

Dhivehi Raajjeyge Gulhun Ltd (Dhiraagu): 19 Medhuziyaaraiy Magu, POB 2082, Malé 20-03; tel. 3322802; fax 3322800; e-mail 123@dhiraagu.com.mv; internet www.dhiraagu.com.mv; f. 1988; jtly owned by the Maldivian Govt (48%) and Cable and Wireless PLC (United Kingdom—52%); operates all nat. and int. telecommunications services in the Maldives (incl. internet service—Dhivehinet); Chair. IBRAHIM ATHIF SHAKOOR; CEO ISMAIL WAHEED.

Wataniya Telecom Maldives Pvt Ltd: 5th Floor, H. Sunleet, Boduthakurufaanu Magu, Malé 20005; tel. 9611000; fax 9611001; e-mail info@wataniya-maldives.com; internet www.wataniya.mv; f. 2005; owned by Qatar Telecom (QTel); provides advanced cellular mobile telephone services throughout the Maldives; Chair. SOLAH FAHUD SULTAN; CEO IBRAHIM HALEEL.

Regulatory Authority

Communications Authority of Maldives: Telecom Bldg, Husnuheena Magu, Malé 20-04; tel. 3323344; fax 3320000; e-mail secretariat@cam.gov.mv; internet www.cam.gov.mv; f. 2003; regulatory authority; CEO ILYAS AHMED.

BROADCASTING

Maldives Broadcasting Commission: Ameene Magu, Galolhu, Malé; tel. 3334333; fax 3334334; e-mail info@broadcom.org.mv; internet www.broadcom.org.mv; f. 2010; regulatory authority; Pres. MOHAMED SHAHYB.

Maldives Broadcasting Corpn (MBC): Malé; internet www.mbc.mv; f. 2009; manages Television Maldives, Youth TV, Voice of Maldives and Raajje FM; state broadcaster; Chair. MOHAMED 'MADULU' WAHEED.

Radio

From May 2007 the Maldives Government permitted private broadcasting. The first private radio station commenced broadcasting operations in July.

Capital Radio: H. Gaadhoo, 1st Floor, Boduthakurufaanu Magu, Malé; tel. 3323223; fax 3325707; e-mail studio@capitalradio936.com; internet www.capitalradio936.com; f. 2007; operated by Asna Maldives Pte Ltd; broadcasts BBC news bulletins, music, current affairs and analysis programmes; Man. Dir MOHAMED NASHEED.

DhiFM 95.2: Malé; e-mail admin@dhifm.com; internet dhifm.mv; f. 2007; operated by Maldives Media Co Pvt; broadcasts news, music and general interest programmes in Dhivehi and English; operates 24-hour nation-wide service; CEO MASOOD HILMY; Editorial Dir MASOOD ALI.

HFM 92.6: Ma. Thimarafusheege, 8th Floor, Dhilbahaaru Magu, POB 20231, Malé; tel. 3301171; fax 3301170; e-mail info@hfm.com.mv; internet www.hfm.com.mv; f. 2008; operated by Haveeru Media Group; broadcasts 24 hrs daily.

Radio Atoll: Ma. Eastern Lagoon, POB 20193, Malé 20; tel. 3349696; fax 3319600; e-mail info@radioatoll.com; internet www.radioatoll.com; broadcasts current affairs, entertainment and general interest programmes; Chair. MOHAMED FAZEEL.

Voice of Maldives (VOM) (Dhivehi Raajjeyge Adu): Voice of Maldives Bldg, Maafannu, Malé; tel. 3314515; fax 3317273; e-mail gs@vom.gov.mv; internet www.vom.gov.mv; radio broadcasting began in 1962 under name of Malé Radio; name changed as above in 1980; operates 1 channel for religious broadcasts and another for music and current affairs; home service in Dhivehi and English; from Feb. 2012 under the control of the MBC; Dir-Gen. BADRU NASEER.

Television

Licences for the establishment of national television stations were made available to private bidders from May 2007.

DhiTV: Champa Bldg, Daisy Magu, Galolhu, Malé 20-02; tel. 3304555; fax 3307666; e-mail info@dhitv.com.mv; internet www.dhitv.com.mv; f. 2008; operated by Maldives Media Co Pvt; launched a 24-hour news and entertainment channel, DhiFM Plus, in mid-2012; Chief Exec. YOOSUF NAWAAL FIRAG.

Rajjee TV: H. Regina, 3rd Floor, Malé; tel. 3307773; fax 3307775; e-mail raajjetelevision@gmail.com; f. 2011; news and current affairs; CEO ABDULLA YAMIN RASHEED.

Television Maldives: Buruzu Magu, Malé 20-144; tel. 3342200; fax 3325083; television broadcasting began in 1978; 2 channels: TVM broadcasts for an average of 18 hrs daily and TVM Plus (f. 1994) broadcasts for 10 hrs daily; from Feb. 2012 controlled by the MBC; covers a 40-km radius around Malé; CEO MOHAMED ASIF.

Villa Television (VTV): ADK Bldg, 1st Floor, M. Fathimath Hiya, Malé; tel. 3303642; fax 3303641; e-mail info@vtv.com.mv; internet vtv.com.mv; f. 2008; operated by the Island Broadcasting Co Pvt. Ltd; Chair. QASIM IBRAHIM.

Finance

(cap. = capital; res = reserves; dep. = deposits; m. = million; brs = branches; amounts in rufiyaas unless otherwise stated)

BANKING

Central Bank

Maldives Monetary Authority (MMA): Boduthakurufaanu Magu, Malé 20182; tel. 3312343; fax 3323862; e-mail mail@mma.gov.mv; internet www.mma.gov.mv; f. 1981; bank of issue; supervises and regulates commercial bank and foreign exchange dealings, and advises the Govt on banking and monetary matters; cap. 1m., res 5,151m., dep. 20m. (Dec. 2009); Gov. and Chair. FAZEEL NAJEEB.

Commercial Banks

Bank of Maldives PLC: 11 Boduthakurufaanu Magu, Malé 20094; tel. 3322948; fax 3328233; e-mail info@bml.com.mv; internet www.bankofmaldives.com.mv; f. 1982; 75% state-owned; cap. 269m., res 497m., dep. 7,518m. (Dec. 2011); Chair. (vacant); CEO PETER HORTON; 25 brs.

Maldives Islamic Bank (MIB): H. Coconut Villa, Ameer Ahmed Magu, Malé 20030; tel. 3325555; fax 3007885; e-mail info@mib.com.mv; internet www.mib.com.mv; f. 2011; 85% owned by the Islamic Corporation for Development and 15% by the Govt; offers banking services compliant with Islamic *Shari'a*; cap. 150m., res 2m., dep. 331m. (Dec. 2011); Chair. KHALED M. AL ABOODI.

DEVELOPMENT FINANCE ORGANIZATION

Housing Development Finance Corpn Plc: 4th Floor, H. Milani, Sosun Magu, Malé; tel. 3338810; fax 3315138; e-mail info@hdfc.com.mv; internet www.hdfc.com.mv; f. 2004 to provide public housing loans; partially privatized in 2008; 49% of shares held by the Govt; Chair. SANJAYA GUPTA; Man. Dir Dr A. D. PRIYANKA BADDEVITHANA.

INSURANCE

Allied Insurance Co of the Maldives (Pte) Ltd: 2nd Floor, Fen Bldg, Ameenee Magu, Machchangolhi Malé 20375; tel. 3341001; fax 3325035; e-mail info@alliedmaldives.net; internet www.alliedmaldives.com; f. 1985; all classes of non-life insurance; operated by State Trading Organization (see below); Chair. SANA MANSOOR; Man. Dir ABDUL WAHID THOWFEEQ.

Amana Takaful (Maldives) PLC: 3rd Floor, H. Mialani, Sosun Magu, Malé; tel. 3315262; e-mail info@takaful.mv; internet www.takaful.mv; f. 2003; subsidiary of Amana Takaful PLC, Sri Lanka; Chair. TYEAB AKBARALLY; CEO EHSAN ZAHEED.

Trade and Industry

GOVERNMENT AGENCIES

Department of National Planning: Ministry of Finance and Treasury, Ameenee Magu, Malé 20-125; tel. 3349200; fax 3327351; e-mail info@planning.gov.mv; internet planning.gov.mv; f. 1978 as the Nat. Planning Agency; designated a government ministry, 1982–2008; re-configured as above in 2008; administered by the Ministry of Finance and Treasury; planning and co-ordination of nat. devt; incorporates the Nat. Planning Council.

Invest Maldives: Ministry of Economic Development, 1st Floor, Malé 20-05; tel. 3324767; fax 3322528; e-mail info@investmaldives.org; internet www.investmaldives.org; govt agency est. to promote, regulate and license foreign investment; Dir-Gen. AHMED NASEEM.

Maldives Privatization Committee: Malé; Chair. MAHMOOD RAZEE.

State Trading Organization PLC (STO): STO Bldg, Boduthakurufaanu Magu, Maafannu, Malé 20-345; tel. 3344333; fax 3344334; e-mail info@stomaldives.net; internet www.stomaldives.com; f. 1964 as Athirimaafannuge Trading Account, renamed as above in 1976; became a PLC in 2001; state-controlled commercial org.; imports and distributes staple foods, fuels, pharmaceuticals and general consumer items; acts as purchaser for govt requirements;

undertakes long-term devt projects; Chair. ABDULLA FAIZ; Man. Dir SHAHID ALI.

CHAMBER OF COMMERCE AND INDUSTRY

Maldives National Chamber of Commerce and Industry (MNCCI): G. Viyafaari Hiya, Ameenee Magu, Malé 20-04; tel. 3326634; fax 3310233; e-mail mncci@dhivehinet.net.mv; internet www.mncci.com.mv; f. 1978; merged with Maldivian Traders' Asscn in 2000; Pres. HAMID ISMAIL.

INDUSTRIAL ASSOCIATION

Maldives Association of Construction Industry (MACI): PA Complex, Ground Floor, Hilaalee Magu, Malé; tel. 3318660; fax 3318796; e-mail maci@dhivehinet.net.mv; internet maldivesconstructionassociationofmaldives.tk; f. 2001; Pres. MOHAMED ALI JANAH; Treas. IBRAHIM MUTHTHALIB.

UTILITIES

In June 2012 the Government announced the establishment of a centralized utilities company, Fenaka Corpn Ltd, which was to assume control for the provision of water, sewerage and electricity outside Malé, replacing seven regional utility boards established by the previous administration.

Fenaka Corpn Ltd: Malé; f. 2012; operates and maintains sewerage systems, electricity and water in islands other than Malé; Chair. AHMED NUMAN.

Electricity

Maldives Energy Authority: Ameenee Magu, Maafannu, Malé 20-392; tel. 3004216; fax 3004217; e-mail secretariat@mea.gov.mv; internet www.mea.gov.mv; f. 2006 to replace Maldives Electricity Bureau; regulatory authority; Dir. MUAWIYATH SHAREEF.

State Electric Co (STELCO) Ltd: Ameenee Magu, POB 2184, Malé; tel. 3320982; fax 3327036; e-mail admin@stelco.com.mv; internet www.stelco.com.mv; f. 1997 to replace Maldives Electricity Board; state owned; generation and distribution of electricity; operates 28 power stations; installed capacity 79,200 kW (2012); Chair. AHMED SHAREEF; 550 employees (2012).

Gas

Maldive Gas Pvt Ltd: H. Maizan, 1st Floor, Sosun Magu, Malé; tel. 3335614; fax 3335615; e-mail info@maldivegas.com; internet www.maldivegas.com; f. 1999 as a jt venture between State Trading Organization and Champa Gas and Oil Co; Chair. ABDULLA SHAFEEU.

Water

Malé Water and Sewerage Co Pvt Ltd: Ameenee Magu, Machangolhi, POB 2148, Malé 20375; tel. 3323209; fax 3324306; e-mail mwsc@dhivehinet.net.mv; internet www.mwsc.com.mv; f. 1995; 76% govt-owned; produces c. 8,500 metric tons of fresh, desalinated water daily, using 7 plants; provides water and sewerage services to the islands of Malé, Hulhumalé and Villingili; provides water services to the islands of Maafushi and L. Gan; Chair. AHMED MANSOOR; Man. Dir MOHAMED AHMED DIDI.

TRADE UNIONS AND WORKERS' ASSOCIATIONS

The 2008 Constitution provides for a minimum wage and grants employees the right to form trade unions and to organize strikes. A number of workers' associations have been established, notably in the tourism and education sectors, although by early 2013 there were still no trade unions in operation.

Tourism Employees' Association of Maldives (TEAM): 2B M. Coral Gardens, Izzudhdheen Magu, Malé; tel. 3338996; fax 3338995; e-mail info@teammaldives.com; internet www.teammaldives.com; f. 2008; works towards reforming labour rights of hotel and resort workers; Gen. Sec. MAUROOF ZAKIR; Pres. AHMED SHIHAM.

Transport

Transport Authority of the Maldives: Huravee Bldg, 2nd Floor, Ameer Ahmed Magu, Malé; tel. 3343433; fax 3343434; e-mail admin@transport.gov.mv; internet www.transport.gov.mv; regulatory and licensing authority for maritime and land transport.

SHIPPING

Vessels operate from the Maldives to Sri Lanka and Singapore at frequent intervals, also calling at points in India, Pakistan, Myanmar, Malaysia, Bangladesh, Thailand, Indonesia and the Middle East. Smaller vessels provide services between the islands on an irregular basis. Malé is the only port handling international traffic. Ambitious government-led plans for the construction of 60 new

harbours and a transshipment port in the north of the country were under development from 2006. At 31 December 2012 the flag registered fleet comprised 65 vessels, including 33 general cargoes and 4 fishing tankers, with a total displacement of 77,289 grt.

Maldives Ports Limited: Boduthakurufaanu Magu, Maafannu, Malé 20-250; tel. 3329339; fax 3325293; e-mail info@port.com.mv; internet www.port.com.mv; f. 2008; replaced the former Maldives Port Authority (f. 1986); operates Malé Port and serves as the national ports operator; govt-owned; Chair. ABDUL MATHEEN AHMED; CEO HUSSAIN HILMY.

Island Enterprises Pvt Ltd: H. Green, 3rd Floor, Majeedee Magu, POB 2169, Malé 20-070; tel. 3323531; fax 3325645; e-mail info@ielmaldives.com; internet www.ielmaldives.com; f. 1978; fleet of 8 vessels; exporters of frozen fish, owners of processing plant, shipping agents, chandlers, cruising agents, surveyors and repairs; Exec. Dir IBRAHIM WASEEM.

Maldives National Shipping Ltd: Ship Plaza, 2nd Floor, 1/6 Orchid Magu, POB 2022, Malé 20-02; tel. 3323871; fax 3324323; e-mail male@maldiveshipping.com.mv; internet www.maldiveshipping.com; f. 1948; 100% state-owned; fleet of 3 container vessels; br. in Singapore; Chair. AIMON JAMEEL.

Maldives Transport and Contracting Co Ltd (MTCC): MTCC Bldg, 5th Floor, Boduthakurufaanu Magu, POB 263, Malé 20-181; tel. 3326822; fax 3323221; e-mail info@mtcc.com.mv; internet www.mtcc.com.mv; f. 1980; 60% state-owned, 40% privately owned; marine transport, civil and technical contracting, harbour devt, shipping agents for general cargo, passenger liners and oil tankers; Chair. HUSSAIN HILMY; Man. Dir MOHAMED NASEEM IBRAHIM.

Precision Marine Pvt Ltd: H. Orchidmaage, Ground Floor, Malé; tel. 3315663; fax 3315107; e-mail info@pmlboatyard.com.mv; internet www.pmlboatyard.com.mv; f. 1990; mfrs and repairers of fibreglass boats, launches, yachts, marine sports equipment, etc.; Man. Dir OMAR MANIKU.

Villa Shipping and Trading Co (Pvt) Ltd: Villa Bldg, POB 2073, Malé 20-02; tel. 3325195; fax 3325177; e-mail info@villa.com.mv; internet www.villa.com.mv; operates 5 tourist resorts and owns a trading operation supported by a fleet of 8 cargo vessels and tankers; Man. Dir QASIM IBRAHIM.

CIVIL AVIATION

The existing airport on Hululé Island near Malé, which was first opened in 1966, was expanded and improved to international standards and, as Malé International Airport, was officially opened in 1981. In 2010 Malé International Airport was transferred to private ownership under a 25-year agreement with an Indian-Malaysian consortium; in mid-2011 the airport was renamed Ibrahim Nasir International. However, in December 2012 the Government revoked the operating agreement and took back full control of the airport.

Facilities at Gan Airport on Addu atoll and Hanimaadhoo Airport on South Thiladhunmathi atoll have also been upgraded to accommodate international services. In addition, there are domestic airports located on Kadhdhoo Island (Hadhdhunmathi atoll), Kaadedhdhoo (Kooddoo) Island (South Huvadhu atoll), Fuvahmulah Island and Dharavandhoo Island on Baa atoll (where operations commenced in October 2012). In 2013 construction work was under way on a further domestic airport at Thimarafushi (Thaa atoll).

Maldives Civil Aviation Authority: Velaanaage, 11th Floor, Ameeru Ahmed Magu, Malé 20096; tel. 3324992; fax 3323039; e-mail civav@aviainfo.gov.mv; internet www.aviainfo.gov.mv; f. 2012; regulatory authority; Chair. IBRAHIM FAISAL; CEO HUSSAIN JALEEL.

Maldives Airport Co Ltd (MACL): Malé International Airport, Hululé 22-000; tel. 3338800; fax 3331515; e-mail info@maclnet.net; internet macl.aero; f. 2000; govt-owned; under admin. of Ministry of Transport and Communication; airport management and aviation services; Chair. of Bd MOHAMED SAEED; Man. Dir MOHAMED IBRAHIM.

Island Aviation Services Ltd: 26 Ameer Ahmed Magu, Malé; tel. 3335566; fax 3314806; e-mail info@island.com.mv; internet www.island.com.mv; f. 2000; 100% govt-owned; operates domestic flights; commenced flights to Sri Lanka in Jan. 2008; Chair. BANDHU IBRAHIM SALEEM; Man. Dir ABDUL HAARIS.

Maldivian Air Taxi: Malé International Airport, POB 2023, Malé; tel. 3315201; fax 3315203; e-mail info@maldivianairtaxi.com; internet www.maldivianairtaxi.com; f. 1993; seaplane services between Malé and outer islands; operates 24 aircraft; Chair. LARS ERIK NIELSEN; Gen. Man. FREDRIK GROTH.

MEGA Maldives Airlines: 5th Floor, H. Sakeena Manzil, Medhu Ziyarah Magu, Malé; tel. 3006670; e-mail info@megamaldivesair.com; internet megamaldivesair.com; f. 2010; operates domestic services and int. services to Hong Kong and the People's Republic of China; Chair. and CEO GEORGE WEINMANN; Man. Dir MIFZAL AHMED.

Trans Maldivian Airways (Pvt) Ltd: Malé International Airport, POB 2079, Malé; tel. 3348400; fax 3348409; e-mail mail@tma.com

.mv; internet www.tma.com.mv; f. 1989 as Hummingbird Island Airways Pvt Ltd; name changed as above in 2000; operates 35 aircraft; Man. Dir EDWARD ALSFORD.

Villa Air (FlyMe): 02-25, 2nd Floor, STO Trade Center, Orchid Magu, Malé; tel. 3013000; e-mail info@villa.com.mv; internet www .flyme.mv; f. 1997; owned by Villa Group; developed a private airport on Maamigili island (South Ari atoll); domestic services under the FlyMe brand launched in 2011; Man. Dir RIDWAN SHAREEF.

Tourism

The tourism industry brings considerable foreign exchange to the Maldives. The islands' attractions include white sandy beaches, excellent diving conditions and impressive coral formations. At the end of 2011 there were 101 island resorts in operation, providing some 22,120 guest beds; a further 2,514 beds were available on live-aboard safari vessels, 1,603 in hotels and 659 in guest houses. In 2002 the Maldives attracted 484,680 foreign tourists; by 2012 visitor arrivals had risen to a record total of 958,027 (an increase of 2.9% compared with the previous year). In 2012 receipts from tourism were estimated at US $1,873m.

Lets Go Maldives Pvt Ltd: Lets Go Tower, 1st Floor, Haveeree Hingun, Malé 20-320; tel. 3347755; fax 3307755; e-mail info@ letsgomaldives.com; internet www.letsgomaldives.com; f. 2006; tourism agency incl. port handling and aviation services; Man. Dir MOHAMED RIYAZ.

Maldives Association of Tourism Industry (MATI): Gadhamoo Bldg, 3rd Floor, Boduthakurufaanu Magu, POB 2056, Malé; tel. 3326640; fax 3326641; e-mail mati@dhivehinet.net.mv; internet www.matimaldives.com; f. 1984; promotes and develops tourism; Chair. MOHAMED UMAR MANIKU; Sec.-Gen. SIM I. MOHAMED.

Maldives Marketing and Public Relations Corpn Ltd (MMPRC): H. Aage, 4th Floor, Ameeru Ahmed Magu, Malé 20-05; tel. 3323228; fax 3323229; e-mail mmprc@visitmaldives.com; internet www.visitmaldives.com; f. 1998; as Maldives Tourism Promotion Board; name changed to above in 2011; Chair. AHMED SHAMEEM; Man. Dir MOHAMED ADAM (acting).

Maldives Tourism Development Corpn Plc (MTDC): 1st Floor, G. Fathuruvehi, Buruzu Magu, Malé 20–123; tel. 3347766; fax 3347733; e-mail info@mtdc.com.mv; internet www.mtdc.com.mv; Chair. IBRAHIM SALEEM; CEO MOHAMED MIHAD.

Defence

There is no army, navy or air force. A voluntary National Security Service, which was founded in 1892 and renamed the Maldives National Defence Force in 2006, undertakes paramilitary security duties (including coastguard duties) and comprises some 2,000 members. The first female recruits were sworn into the former National Security Service in 1989.

Defence Budget: Totalled 561.7 rufiyaa (4.0% of total expenditure) in 2010.

Commander-in-Chief of the Maldives National Defence Force: Pres. MOHAMED WAHEED HASSAN MANIK.

Chief of Staff of the Maldives National Defence Force: Maj.-Gen. AHMED SHIYAM.

Education

Until the late 1970s, education was centred largely on the capital, Malé. In 1976 the 16 schools in existence were all in Malé and catered mainly for children of primary school age. In 1977 the Government established a teacher-training institute (which had produced more than 400 qualified teachers by the end of 1986). UNICEF, in particular, has contributed to provincial development, and in 1978 the first primary school outside Malé opened, on Baa atoll. The construction of the first secondary school outside Malé was completed, on Addu atoll, in 1992. By 2011 there were a total of 382 schools throughout the islands.

Education is not compulsory. There are three types of formal education: traditional Koranic schools (*Makthab*), Dhivehi-medium primary schools (*Madhrasa*) and English-medium primary and secondary schools. Primary education begins at six years of age and lasts for five years. Secondary education, beginning at the age of 11, lasts for up to seven years, comprising a first cycle of five years and a second of two years. In 2007/08 enrolment at primary schools included 96% of children in the relevant age-group; the ratio for secondary enrolment of pupils in the relevant age-group was an estimated 69% in the same year.

In 1989 the Government established a National Council on Education, under the chairmanship of the President, to oversee the development of education in the Maldives. There is a full-time vocational training centre, a teacher-training institute, an Institute of Hotel and Catering Services, an Institute of Management and Administration, a Science Education Centre, a Centre for Social Education, an Institute of Health Sciences, an Institute for Islamic Studies and a Centre for Continuing Education. The Maldives Institute of Technical Education, which was completed in 1996, was expected to help to alleviate the problem of the lack of local skilled labour. The Maldives College of Higher Education (MCHE), which was established to provide a uniform framework and policies for post-secondary education institutes, was opened in 1998. Following the passage of a National University Act in December 2010, the MCHE was redesignated as the country's first university: the Maldives National University (www.mnu.edu.mv) was inaugurated in February 2011.

Budgetary expenditure on education by the central Government in 2010 was 2,006.3m. rufiyaa, representing 14.2% of total spending.

MALI

Introductory Survey

LOCATION, CLIMATE, LANGUAGE, RELIGION, FLAG, CAPITAL

The Republic of Mali is a land-locked country in West Africa, with Algeria to the north, Mauritania and Senegal to the west, Guinea and Côte d'Ivoire to the south, and Burkina Faso and Niger to the east. The climate is hot throughout the country. The northern region of Mali is part of the Sahara, an arid desert. It is wetter in the south, where the rainy season is from June to October. Temperatures in Bamako are generally between 16°C (61°F) and 39°C (103°F). The official language is French but a number of other languages, including Bambara, Fulfulde, Sonrai, Tamashek, Soninke and Dogon, are widely spoken. It is estimated that about 80% of the population are Muslims and 18% follow traditional animist beliefs; under 2% are Christians. The national flag (proportions 2 by 3) has three equal vertical stripes, of green, gold and red. The capital is Bamako.

CONTEMPORARY POLITICAL HISTORY

Historical Context

Mali, as the former French West African colony of Soudan, merged with Senegal in April 1959 to form the Federation of Mali, which became independent on 20 June 1960. Senegal seceded two months later, and the remnant of the Federation was proclaimed the Republic of Mali on 22 September. Mali's first President was Modibo Keita, the leader of the Union Soudanaise—Rassemblement Démocratique Africain (US—RDA), who pursued authoritarian socialist policies. Following a series of purges of US—RDA and public officials, Keita was overthrown in November 1968 by a group of junior army officers, who assumed power as the Comité Militaire pour la Libération Nationale (CMLN). The Constitution was abrogated, and all political activity was banned. Lt (later Gen.) Moussa Traoré became Head of State and President of the CMLN.

A draft Constitution, providing for the establishment of a one-party state at the end of a five-year transitional period of military rule, was approved by a national referendum in June 1974. Keita died in custody in 1977, prompting anti-Government demonstrations. The Union Démocratique du Peuple Malien (UDPM), the lone political party, was officially constituted in March 1979, and presidential and legislative elections took place in June. Traoré, the sole candidate for the presidency, was elected for a five-year term; a single list of UDPM candidates for the 82-member Assemblée nationale was elected for a four-year term. Traoré and the UPDM were re-elected at all subsequent polls.

Domestic Political Affairs

Mali's first cohesive opposition movements began to emerge in 1990, among them the Comité National d'Initiative Démocratique (CNID) and the Alliance pour la Démocratie au Mali (ADEMA). The security forces harshly repressed violent pro-democracy demonstrations in Bamako in March 1991: official figures later revealed that 106 people were killed, and 708 injured, in three days of unrest. On 26 March it was announced that Traoré had been arrested. A military Conseil National de Réconciliation (CNR), led by Lt-Col (later Gen.) Amadou Toumani Touré, the commander of the army's parachute regiment, assumed power, and the Constitution and its institutions were abrogated. The CNR was succeeded by a 25-member Comité de Transition pour le Salut du Peuple (CTSP), chaired by Touré. It was announced that a national conference would be convened, and that the armed forces would relinquish power to democratic institutions in January 1992. Soumana Sacko (who had briefly been Minister of Finance and Trade in 1987) returned to Mali from the Central African Republic to head a transitional, civilian-dominated government.

The transitional regime undertook the reform of Malian political life. Among those arrested in subsequent months were Gen. Sékou Ly, Brig.-Gen. Mamadou Coulibaly (respectively, Minister of the Interior and Basic Development and Minister of Defence at the time of the violently repressed demonstrations in early 1991) and the former army Chief of Staff, Ousmane Coulibaly. In July 1991 an amnesty for most political prisoners

detained under Traoré was proclaimed, and provision made for the legalization of political parties. The CNID was registered as the Congrès National d'Initiative Démocratique, and ADEMA adopted the additional title of Parti Pan-africain pour la Liberté, la Solidarité et la Justice. Pre-independence parties, banned for many years, re-emerged, most notably the US—RDA.

The National Conference, which began in July 1991, adopted a draft Constitution, an electoral code and a charter governing the activities of political parties. In November the period of transition to democratic rule was extended until March 1992. The draft Constitution was submitted to a national referendum on 12 January 1992, when it was endorsed by 99.8% of those who voted (about 43% of the registered electorate).

At municipal elections, held on 19 January 1992, ADEMA enjoyed the greatest success, winning 214 of 751 seats. At the elections to the Assemblée nationale, on 23 February and 8 March, ADEMA won 76 of the 129 seats, the CNID nine seats, and the US—RDA eight. The date for the transition to civilian rule was again postponed, and the first round of the presidential election eventually proceeded on 12 April, contested by nine candidates. The leader of ADEMA, Alpha Oumar Konaré, won the largest share of the votes cast (some 45%). He and his nearest rival, Tiéoulé Mamadou Konaté (of the US—RDA), proceeded to a second round, on 26 April, at which Konaré secured 69% of the votes. Overall, only about 20% of the electorate were reported to have voted in the presidential election; a similar turn-out was reported in the legislative polls. Konaré was inaugurated as President on 8 June. He appointed Younoussi Touré (hitherto the national director of the Banque Centrale des États de l'Afrique de l'Ouest) as Prime Minister. Touré's first Council of Ministers was dominated by members of ADEMA, although a small number of portfolios were allocated to representatives of the US—RDA and of the Parti pour la Démocratie et le Progrès (PDP).

The trial of Traoré and his associates began in November 1992. In February 1993 Traoré, Ly, Mamadou Coulibaly and Ousmane Coulibaly were sentenced to death, having been convicted, inter alia, of premeditated murder at the time of the March 1991 unrest. The Supreme Court rejected appeal proceedings in May 1993; however, Konaré subsequently indicated that no death penalty would be exacted under his presidency. Charges remained against Traoré, his wife and several others in connection with the 'economic crimes' of the former administration.

Touré resigned in April 1993, following violent disturbances in Bamako prompted by the adverse effects of economic austerity measures. The new Prime Minister, Abdoulaye Sekou Sow (hitherto Minister of State, responsible for Defence, and who was not a member of any political party), implemented an extensive reorganization of the Government. The Council of Ministers remained dominated by ADEMA, but also included representatives of other parties, among them the CNID.

A programme of further austerity measures, announced in September 1993, provoked considerable political controversy, which was exacerbated by the 50% devaluation of the CFA franc in January 1994. Sow resigned in February, and was replaced by Ibrahim Boubacar Keïta, a member of ADEMA's 'radical' wing, which was opposed to Sow's economic policies. The withdrawal from the coalition of the CNID and the Rassemblement pour la Démocratie et le Progrès (RDP) prompted the appointment of a new Government, again dominated by ADEMA; the PDP in turn withdrew.

Following the election of Keïta as President of ADEMA in September 1994, ADEMA's Vice-President, Mohamed Lamine Traoré, and other prominent figures resigned from the party and subsequently formed the Mouvement pour l'Indépendance, la Renaissance et l'Intégration Africaine (MIRIA). In January 1995 a party established by supporters of the UDPM, the Mouvement Patriotique pour le Renouveau (MPR), was granted official status. In October the Parti pour la Renaissance Nationale (PARENA), comprising several leading members of the CNID, who alleged excessive dominance by the party Chairman, Mountaga Tall, was registered. PARENA and ADEMA established a political alliance in February 1996, and PARENA's leaders, Yoro

Diakité and Tiébilé Dramé, were appointed to the Government in July.

The 1997 elections

The first round of elections to the enlarged (147-seat) Assemblée nationale was held on 13 April 1997. Since early results indicated that ADEMA was the only party to have won seats outright in this round, the main opposition parties denounced the results as fraudulent and announced their intention to withdraw from the second round. The opposition parties also withdrew their candidates from the forthcoming presidential and municipal elections. On 24 April the Constitutional Court invalidated the results of the first round of voting, citing irregularities in the conduct of the poll.

Konaré, not wishing to be the sole candidate in the presidential election scheduled to be held on 11 May 1997, appealed to the opposition to participate. In early May the leader of the Parti pour l'Unité, la Démocratie et le Progrès, Mamadou Maribatou Diaby, announced that he was prepared to contest the presidency. According to the final results, Konaré was re-elected to the presidency, securing 95.9% of the votes cast. Members of the radical opposition, which had campaigned for a boycott by voters, stated that the low rate of participation (28.4% of the registered electorate) effectively invalidated Konaré's victory. At the end of the month the municipal elections were postponed indefinitely. Violent protests occurred in Bamako in June, as Konaré was sworn in for a second term of office and the first round of the fresh legislative elections (due on 6 July) was postponed by two weeks.

A small number of opposition parties announced their intention to present candidates for the Assemblée nationale, but the radical collective, known as the Collectif des Partis Politiques de l'Opposition (COPPO), at this time numbering 18 parties, reiterated its refusal to re-enter the electoral process. Violent disturbances, in which two deaths were reported, preceded the first round of voting on 20 July 1997, which was contested by 17 parties (including five 'moderate' opposition parties) and a number of independent candidates. COPPO asserted that the low rate of participation by voters (at about 12% of the registered electorate in Bamako, and 22% outside the capital) would render the new parliament illegitimate. A second round of voting was necessary for eight seats on 3 August. The final results allocated 130 of the 147 seats to ADEMA, eight to PARENA, four to the Convention Démocratique et Sociale (CDS), three to the Union pour la Démocratie et le Développement (UDD) and two to the PDP.

In September 1997 Konaré held a meeting with some 20 opposition leaders, including representatives of COPPO, at which he presented proposals for a broadly based coalition government. A new Council of Ministers, under Keïta, was appointed in mid-September. The new administration included, in addition to members of ADEMA and its allies, a small number of representatives of the moderate opposition parties (among them the UDD and PDP). Further measures intended to promote national reconciliation were implemented, and in December Konaré commuted some 21 death sentences, including those imposed on ex-President Traoré and his associates, to terms of life imprisonment.

In October 1998 the trial for 'economic crimes' began in Bamako of ex-President Traoré, his wife Mariam, her brother, Abraham Douah Cissoko (the former head of customs), a former Minister of Finance and Trade, Tiénan Coulibaly, and the former representative in France of the Banque de Développement du Mali, Moussa Koné. In January 1999 Traoré, his wife and brother-in-law were sentenced to death, having been convicted of 'economic crimes' to the value of some US $350,000. Coulibaly and Koné were acquitted. In September Konaré commuted the death sentences to terms of life imprisonment.

In February 2000 Keïta submitted his Government's resignation. An extensively reorganized Council of Ministers was subsequently appointed. The new Prime Minister, Mandé Sidibé, was widely regarded as a supporter of economic reform. In June Choguel Kokala Maïga, the leader of the MPR, was among opposition leaders who announced their intention to participate in the presidential and parliamentary elections in 2002.

The 2002 elections

In July 2000 the Assemblée nationale approved legislation providing for state funding of political parties. In addition, the Assemblée adopted an extensive revision of the Constitution proposed by Konaré. (However, a planned referendum to endorse the constitutional amendments was subsequently postponed indefinitely.) Also in July COPPO, which now comprised 15

parties and was led by Almamy Sylla of the RDP, announced that it would henceforth participate in the electoral process.

Keïta resigned from the leadership of ADEMA in October 2000, following the announcement that his opponents within the party had succeeded in calling an extraordinary congress of the party, to be held in late November. At the congress, several new members were appointed to ADEMA's executive committee, and Dioncounda Traoré was elected as the new Chairman of the party. In July 2001 a new party led by Keïta, the Rassemblement pour le Mali (RPM), was officially registered.

In January 2002 Soumaïla Cissé was elected as ADEMA's candidate for the forthcoming presidential election. In March Modibo Keita, hitherto Secretary-General at the presidency, was appointed as Prime Minister, following Sidibé's resignation to contest the presidency as an independent candidate. In early April 16 opposition parties, including the CNID, the RPM and the MPR, formed an electoral alliance, Espoir 2002, agreeing to support a single opposition candidate (generally expected to be Ibrahim Boubacar Keïta, who was to contest the election on behalf of the RPM) in the event of a second round of voting. Meanwhile, an alliance of 23 political parties, including MIRIA, PARENA and the US—RDA, declared their support for the candidacy of Gen. (retd) Amadou Toumani Touré.

At the first round of the presidential election, which was held on 28 April 2002 and was contested by 24 candidates, Touré secured the largest share of the votes cast, with 28.7%, followed by Cissé, with 21.3%, and Keïta, with 21.0%. Touré and Cissé progressed to a second round of voting, held on 12 May. Touré was elected to the presidency, with 65.0% of the votes cast, having obtained the support of more than 40 parties, including those of Espoir 2002. The electoral process was marred by allegations of fraud and incompetence, which led the Constitutional Court to annul 25% of the votes cast in the first ballot. None the less, international observers described the elections as generally free, fair and open. Touré was inaugurated as President on 8 June, and subsequently formed an interim Government, comprising 21 ministers. The new Prime Minister and Minister of African Integration, Ahmed Mohamed Ag Hamani, who had held various ministerial posts under Traoré, was regarded as a technocrat.

The elections to the Assemblée nationale in July 2002 further demonstrated the lack of any one dominant political grouping in Mali, while the rate of participation in the second round, at 25.7% nation-wide, was low. The RPM emerged as the single largest party, with 46 of the 147 seats (although 20 of its seats had been won in local electoral alliances with other parties of the Espoir 2002 grouping), while other parties of Espoir 2002 obtained a further 21 seats, giving a total of 67 to allies of the RPM. ADEMA secured 45 seats, while the pro-ADEMA Alliance pour la République et la Démocratie won an additional six seats, giving a total of 51. The CNID received 13 seats, while parties belonging to an informal alliance supportive of President Touré, the Convergence pour l'Alternance et le Changement (ACC), including PARENA and the US—RDA, won a total of 10 seats. In early September 19 deputies, comprising those of the ACC parties, several independent deputies and other declared supporters of Touré, formed a grouping within the legislature, with the declared intention of forming a stable presidential majority. Later in the month Ibrahim Boubacar Keïta was elected President of the Assemblée nationale.

In October 2002 Touré announced the formation of a Government of National Unity. Although many of the principal posts remained unchanged from the previous interim administration, one notable appointment was that of Bassari Touré, a former official of the World Bank, as Minister of the Economy and Finance. ADEMA increased its representation in the Assemblée nationale to 53 deputies, becoming the largest party grouping, following its victory in eight by-elections on 20 October.

In April 2004 Ag Hamani tendered his resignation as Prime Minister, apparently in response to a request by President Touré. A new administration, headed by Prime Minister Ousmane Issoufi Maïga, hitherto Minister of Equipment and Transport (and not affiliated to any political party), was formed in early May. Moctar Ouane was appointed Minister of Foreign Affairs and International Co-operation, and Aboubacar Traoré became Minister of the Economy and Finance. ADEMA was the most successful party at municipal elections held on 23 May, winning 28% of the seats contested, followed by the Union pour la République et la Démocratie (URD), which secured 14%, and the RPM, with 13%; the rate of participation by the electorate was relatively high, at 43.6%. ADEMA and the RPM subsequently formed an alliance, which, with ADEMA holding 44 seats and the RPM 35, gave the new grouping a majority in the 147-seat Assemblée nationale (although still short of the two-thirds' majority needed to enact a motion of no confidence against the head of the Government).

There was considerable speculation regarding potential re-alignments of political organizations ahead of the presidential and legislative elections due in 2007. In November 2005 the RPM announced that it would henceforth oppose the Government, stating that it had been increasingly marginalized within the ruling coalition. In February 2006 the executive committee of ADEMA declared that the party would support the candidacy of Touré at the forthcoming presidential election.

Touré's second term

The presidential election was duly held on 29 April 2007; 36.2% of the registered electorate participated. Touré received 71.2% of the total votes cast, securing a second, and final, five-year term while avoiding a second round of voting. His closest rival was Keïta, who received 19.2% of the votes cast. Although a number of opposition candidates challenged the results, most independent observers believed the election to have been conducted fairly.

The legislative elections took place on 1 and 22 July 2007. According to official results, ADEMA secured 51 seats, while the URD took 34 seats and the RPM 11. However, an overall voter turn-out of only 12% was recorded. In total, parties supporting President Touré won 113 seats in the Assemblée nationale. In early September ADEMA leader Dioncounda Traoré was elected President of the legislature.

On 27 September 2007 Prime Minister Maïga tendered his resignation and that of his Government. The following day President Touré named Modibo Sidibé, hitherto Secretary-General of the Presidency, as Maïga's successor. Sidibé announced a new Council of Ministers in early October; the most notable appointments were Gen. Sadio Gassama as Minister of Internal Security and Civil Protection, and a Tuareg, Mohammed El Moctar, as Minister of Culture. Ouane retained the foreign affairs portfolio and Gen. Kafougouna Koné was reappointed as head of the Ministry of Territorial Administration and Local Communities. Further ministerial changes were effected in April 2009, including the appointment of Sanoussi Touré as Minister of the Economy and Finance.

In July 2010 the pro-Government Mouvement Citoyen, launched a new political party, the Parti pour le Développement Économique et la Solidarité (PDES), in a move largely regarded as an attempt to consolidate President Touré's influence ahead of the elections due to be held in 2012. Touré, who had already confirmed that he had no intention of seeking to amend the Constitution in order to be able to contest a third term of office, expressed his support for the PDES and its members, several of whom, including its President, Hamed Diane Séméga, were government ministers.

At the end of March 2011 Sidibé resigned the premiership, amid speculation that he intended to contest the presidency in 2012. Cissé Mariam Kaïdama Sidibé, who was not affiliated to any political party, was appointed as Mali's first female Prime Minister on 3 April. Her new Council of Ministers notably included members of the opposition RPM and PARENA, while Soumeylou Boubèye Maïga, a former Minister of Defence during Konaré's presidency, became Minister of Foreign Affairs and International Co-operation, and Daba Diawara was allocated the newly created portfolio of state reform. In preparation for the 2012 elections, in June 2011 the Council of Ministers finally adopted a draft law on the amendments to the Constitution, which was approved in the Assemblée nationale on 2 August. The proposed constitutional reforms, which included the establishment of an upper legislative chamber, were to be submitted to a national referendum on 29 April 2012 (when the first round of the presidential election was also scheduled to take place). By early 2012 four main candidates had emerged to contest the presidential poll: former premiers Keita and Sidibé, Soumaïla Cissé, and President of the Assemblée nationale Traoré.

Military coup and transitional Government

On 21 March 2012 disaffected members of the armed forces staged a rebellion in protest at the Government's failure to contain the intensifying uprising in the north of the country (see Tuareg Insurgencies); after launching attacks in Bamako and seizing the presidential palace, on the following day the rebels announced the deposition of Touré's Government and the installation of a Comité National pour le Redressement de la Démocratie et la Restauration de l'Etat (CNRDR), headed by

Capt. Amadou Sanogo. On 2 April, after the CNRDR failed to comply with demands by the Economic Community of West African States (ECOWAS, see p. 268) that it relinquish power, the organization imposed a number of sanctions against Mali, including the closure of land borders with the country. The USA and the African Union (AU, see p. 191), which had suspended Mali's membership in late March, joined an ECOWAS travel ban on the coup leaders. On 6 April the CNRDR reached an agreement with ECOWAS, under which it was to cede power to a transitional government, while the sanctions in force against the country were to be removed and all participants in the coup were to be granted amnesty. On 8 April both Touré (who had emerged from hiding) and Sanogo formally resigned. In accordance with the agreement, and following a decision by the Constitutional Court, on 12 April Dioncounda Traoré took office as Interim President for a transitional period of 40 days. Later that month a transitional Government, under the premiership of Cheick Modibo Diarra, was formed. Further arrests of supporters of Touré were reported, and Sanogo's forces clashed with troops loyal to Touré in Bamako. Following a summit meeting in Dakar, Senegal, in early May ECOWAS issued a statement urging the transitional authorities to establish rapidly a timetable for the organization of elections and the full restoration of constitutional order, and also confirmed that it would prepare a military force to counter the Tuareg insurgency. It was agreed later in May that Traoré would remain as Interim President for a transitional period of one year, while Sanogo would be accorded the status of a former head of state. However, the extension of Traoré's presidential term angered supporters of the coup, several of whom entered the presidential palace and assaulted him. The attack, which caused Traoré to travel to France for medical treatment (where he remained until July), was widely condemned, although followers of Sanogo continued to demand his installation as Interim President in place of Traoré. In late June the Assemblée nationale voted to extend the mandate of parliamentary deputies until the end of the transitional period. On 12 August Traoré reappointed Diarra as Prime Minister; the formation of a new, interim Council of Ministers, which included five members nominated by officials of the former CNRDR, was subsequently announced on 20 August. The AU ended the suspension of Mali's membership on 24 October, when it also announced that it had approved a transitional programme, including plans for the organization of legislative elections within one year of a return to constitutional order.

Recent developments: removal of Prime Minister Diarra

On 11 December 2012 it was announced that Diarra had resigned as Prime Minister, shortly after being placed under house arrest by troops loyal to Sanogo (a development that was widely condemned by the UN and the USA, which threatened the reimposition of sanctions). Traoré immediately appointed Diango Cissoko, a longstanding government official and hitherto the state ombudsman, to replace him, and a further transitional Government was formed in mid-December. On 11 January 2013, following French military intervention in the north (see Tuareg Insurgencies), the Malian authorities announced a state of emergency (which later in January was extended for three months), prohibiting public gatherings, rallies and any other potential threats to public order. It was reported in early February that three people had been killed in a further clash between supporters of Sanogo and troops loyal to Touré. In March a newspaper editor who had published an article critical of Sanogo was arrested (prompting strike action in the private media), and subsequently charged with incitement to revolt. According to a provisional timetable announced by the Government in late February, a presidential election was to take place on 7 July, with legislative elections to follow on 21 July. The timetable was subsequently amended with the presidential election scheduled to take place on 28 July.

Tuareg Insurgencies

In the first half of the 1990s a rebellion in the north of Mali began with the return to West Africa of large numbers of Tuareg nomads, who had migrated to Algeria and Libya at times of drought. A peace accord, signed in January 1991 in Tamanrasset, Algeria, by representatives of the Traoré Government and delegates from two Tuareg groups, the Mouvement Populaire de l'Azawad (MPA) and the Front Islamique-Arabe de l'Azawad (FIAA), failed to provide a lasting solution to the conflict. Following the overthrow of the Traoré regime, the transitional authorities affirmed commitment to the Tamanrasset accord.

However, unrest continued, while thousands of Tuaregs, Moors and Bella (the descendants of the Tuaregs' black slaves, some of whom remained with the nomads) fled to neighbouring countries.

In February 1992, following negotiations between representatives of the Malian Government and of the Mouvements et Fronts Unifiés de l'Azawad (MFUA), comprising the MPA, the FIAA and the Armée Révolutionnaire de l'Azawad (ARLA), with Algerian mediation, a truce entered into force, although the more militant Front Populaire de Libération de l'Azawad (FPLA) was not reported to have attended the talks. After further discussions, the Malian authorities and the MFUA signed a draft 'National Pact' in April: joint patrols were duly established, and in November President Konaré visited the north to inaugurate new administrative structures.

In May 1994 the Malian authorities and Tuareg leaders reached agreement regarding the integration of 1,500 former rebels into the Malian army and of a further 4,860 Tuaregs into civilian sectors. The success of the agreement was, however, undermined by an intensification of violence in northern Mali. Meanwhile, a Songhaï-dominated black resistance movement, the Mouvement Patriotique Malien Ganda Koy ('Masters of the Land'), emerged, amid rumours of official complicity in its offensives against the Tuaregs. Meeting in Tamanrasset in June, the Malian authorities and the MFUA endorsed a reinforcement of the army presence in areas affected by the violence, and agreed procedures for the more effective integration of Tuareg fighters.

Further discussions involving Tuareg groups, Ganda Koy and representatives of local communities resulted in the signing, in April 1995, of a co-operation agreement. In June the FIAA announced an end to its armed struggle, and expressed its willingness to join national reconciliation efforts. A programme for the encampment of former rebels, in preparation for their eventual integration into the national army or civilian structures, began in November and ended in February 1996, by which time some 3,000 MFUA fighters and Ganda Koy militiamen had registered and surrendered their weapons. The MFUA and Ganda Koy subsequently issued a joint statement affirming their adherence to Mali's territorial integrity, urging the full implementation of the National Pact and associated accords and proclaiming the 'irreversible dissolution' of their respective movements.

In September 1997 the graduation of MFUA and Ganda Koy contingents in the gendarmerie was reported as marking the accomplishment of the integration of all fighters within the national armed and security forces. In October the former FPLA leader, Rhissa Ag Sidi Mohamed, returned to Mali and expressed willingness to join efforts to consolidate peace. None the less, the Government expressed concern that the continued proliferation of weapons, as well as the inadequacy of military and administrative structures in the north, could result in renewed clashes. In November 2000 it was reported that Malian government forces had been dispatched to end widespread banditry by an armed group, led by Ibrahim Bahanga, a former Tuareg rebel, in the Kidal area, near the border with Algeria.

Tensions arose again in May 2006 when Tuareg rebels launched an attack on the town of Kidal and seized three army bases. Military reinforcements were deployed to the region; however, the rebel group withdrew to an area close to the Niger border, from where it demanded the commencement of negotiations with the Government over the conditions in which the Tuaregs had been forced to live since their integration into the armed forces. Following Algerian-mediated discussions between the Malian Government and the Tuareg group, in July a peace deal was signed in Algiers, Algeria, which included agreement on an investment programme for the region and the reintegration of rebels into the armed forces. A further reconciliation agreement was signed in February 2007 between the Government and the Tuareg rebels, stipulating guidelines for the implementation of the agreement signed in July the previous year. The accord also outlined the establishment of special security units in the Kidal region, and measures for facilitating the reintegration of the Tuaregs into Malian society. In August several attacks on military personnel by Tuareg rebels were reported to have occurred near to the border with Niger. The main Tuareg group insisted that it was continuing to uphold the reconciliation agreement; however, a splinter group announced that it had formed an alliance with Tuareg militia in Niger, who had launched an offensive against the Niger Government.

In April 2008 a new agreement, brokered by Libyan authorities, was signed by the Malian Government and a Tuareg rebel group led by Bahanga, styled the Alliance Tuareg Nord-Mali pour le Changement (ATNMC); the accord committed both parties to reducing the number of troops stationed in the Kidal area. However, fighting subsequently intensified and in May it was reported that 27 soldiers and rebels had been killed in an attack on a military base in Abebara, north of Kidal. Meeting in Algiers in July, the Government and the leaders of a group believed to be allied to the ATNMC, the Alliance Démocratique du 23 Mai pour le Changement (ADC), reached an agreement on peace and security, and in September the rebels released 44 government soldiers who had been held hostage. Despite the establishment in November of the first joint special unit comprising rebel fighters and Malian soldiers, further unrest was reported in the following month. In January 2009 it was announced that three Tuareg factions, including the ADC, had united and agreed to rejoin peace negotiations. The Malian military then claimed in February that it had taken the last of the ATNMC positions, and that Bahanga and an unknown number of fighters had crossed the border into Algeria; Bahanga later sought refuge in Libya. (In August 2011 it was reported that Bahanga, who had been involved in the trafficking of armaments from Libya, had been killed in northern Mali.)

Amid an increase in security concerns, it was reported in late 2011 that many Tuareg combatants returning to Mali from Libya (where they had fought in support of forces loyal to the regime of Col Muammar al-Qaddafi) had joined the Mouvement National pour la Libération de l'Azawad (MNLA), a new rebel group that demanded independence for Mali's northern region. In early 2012 government forces attempted to suppress onslaughts by MNLA forces against the northern towns of Menaka, Aguelhoc and Tessalit. In February, however, the MNLA advanced into southern and western Mali, attacking the towns of Lere and Niafounké. Despite a continued land and air counter-offensive by the Government, in early March it was reported that the MNLA rebels had occupied Tessalit, following a lengthy siege of the garrison town. Later that month the MNLA, which was joined by a newly emerged Islamist movement, Ansar Dine, led by Iyad Ag Agaly, benefited from the disorder resulting from a military coup (see Domestic Political Affairs) to advance its insurgency; by the beginning of April the insurgents had gained control of most of northern Mali, including Tombouctou. On 6 April the MNLA declared Azawad (comprising the regions of Gao, Kidal, Tombouctou and part of Mopti district) to be an independent state, prompting statements of condemnation from the AU and ECO-WAS. Meanwhile, in early April members of a jihadist organization affiliated to Al-Qa'ida in the Islamic Maghreb (AQIM), the Mouvement Unité pour le Jihad en Afrique de l'Ouest (MUJAO), abducted seven diplomats from the Algerian consulate in the town of Gao.

In May 2012 it was announced that the MNLA and Ansar Dine had agreed to merge and to establish the 'Islamic Republic of Azawad'. Following increasing divisions between the insurgents, however, it was reported that the MNLA had withdrawn from the accord, and ensuing clashes between the two movements during June resulted in the expulsion of MNLA forces from the captured regions. Ansar Dine, together with MUJAO, established its authority in several northern towns in the following months, including Tombouctou, where it began to impose *Shari'a* law and to destroy Sufi Islamic shrines. Meanwhile, MNLA and Ansar Dine leaders declared their willingness to engage in negotiations with ECOWAS, which demanded, however, that Ansar Dine's links with AQIM be severed prior to talks. In July the International Criminal Court, based in The Hague, Netherlands, announced that, at the request of the Malian Government, it was to initiate a preliminary inquiry into reported atrocities committed by armed groups in northern Mali. Three of the abducted Algerian diplomats were released in July; following the Algerian authorities' rejection of demands for the release of prisoners, however, in September MUJOA released a statement declaring that it had executed one of their hostages, the Algerian Vice-Consul. Meanwhile, Ansar Dine continued a territorial advance, securing control of the central town of Douentza in September.

The first direct discussions between government officials and MNLA and Ansar Dine leaders took place in the capital of Burkina Faso, Ouagadougou, on 4 December 2012, with the mediation of the Burkinabè Minister of Foreign Affairs, Yipènè Djibril Bassolé; both insurgent movements issued commitments to suspend hostilities. After urgent requests from ECOWAS, however, on 20 December the UN Security Council approved a resolution authorizing the deployment of an African-led International Support Mission to Mali (AFISMA) to assist the Malian armed forces in combating the insurgency. In response to an appeal by President Traoré, following Ansar Dine's capture of the central town of Konna and continuing advance towards Bamako, on 9 January 2013 the French Government began a military intervention (codenamed Operation Serval) of some 4,000 French ground troops, together with military fighter jets, in Mali. Deployment of the first contingents of the UN-endorsed AFISMA began on 17 January. At an AU summit meeting in the Ethiopian capital, Addis Ababa, later in January, African leaders welcomed the French military action and approved funds of US $50m. for AFISMA. In the same month a Tuareg faction broke away from Ansar Dine to form the Mouvement Islamique de l'Azawad, which rejected associations with AQIM. The supported French forces had regained control of Gao (where their arrival was met with jubilation from the civilian population), Tombouctou and Kidal by the end of January, and Tessalit by early February. MUJOA staged retaliatory attacks, including suicide bombings at Tessalit, also targeting MNLA members, in response to that movement's co-operation with government and French forces. Following continued bomb attacks by the French air force, it was confirmed in February that a senior AQIM commander, Abdelhamid Abu Zeid, together with 40 other militants, had been killed in the northern Tigargara region. In late March French-supported government forces repelled a further Ansar Dine offensive against Tombouctou. At the end of that month UN Secretary-General Ban Ki-Moon recommended to the UN Security Council that AFISMA (then numbering about 6,300 forces under the command of ECOWAS) be reconstituted as a UN peace-keeping mission comprising 11,200 troops and 1,440 police officers, prior to a staged withdrawal of French forces. The French withdrawal commenced in early April; following concerns expressed by the Malian authorities, however, the French Government proposed that a permanent force of 1,000 French troops remain in the country to support the UN mission. Also in April, after three Chadian soldiers deployed as part of AFISMA were killed in a suicide attack in Kidal, the Chadian Government announced that it would withdraw its 2,000-member contingent from Mali. Later that month the UN Security Council approved the transfer of authority from AFISMA to the United Nations Multidimensional Integrated Stabilization Mission in Mali (MINUSMA). This was scheduled to take place on 1 July.

Foreign Affairs

President Konaré sought to emphasize the role of Mali in ECOWAS, and in November 2000 a 120-member ECOWAS parliament, which was to promote regional co-operation, was inaugurated in Bamako. Mali has forged close relations with Libya, and was a founder member of the Community of Sahel-Saharan States (see p. 460), established in Tripoli, Libya, in 1997.

The presence of large numbers of refugees from the conflict in northern Mali dominated Mali's relations with its neighbours during the 1990s, and even after the completion of the process of repatriation in mid-1998 (and the conclusion of a programme by the office of the UN High Commissioner for Refugees—UNHCR—in June 1999) the north of the country remained vulnerable to cross-border banditry. In February 1999 Mali and Algeria agreed to revive their joint border committee to promote development and stability in the region. At a meeting in Dakar in August, the Malian, Mauritanian and Senegalese ministers responsible for the interior agreed to establish an operational unit drawn from the police forces of the three countries to enforce security in the border area. Bilateral relations between Mali and Mauritania were further strengthened by a military co-operation agreement regarding border security signed by the countries' respective Presidents in January 2005.

Concerns about insecurity in the region re-emerged in mid-2003, following reports, in July, that some 15 German, Swiss and Dutch tourists, believed to have been kidnapped in February by Islamist militants allegedly associated with the Groupe Salafiste pour la Prédication et le Combat (GSPC) in southern Algeria, had been smuggled into Mali. Following negotiations with the kidnappers, conducted by a former rebel Tuareg leader, Iyad Ag Agaly, 14 hostages were released in August (the remaining hostage had reportedly died earlier from heat-stroke). In March 2004 Mali announced that it was to increase anti-terrorism co-operation with the authorities in Algeria, Chad and Niger.

In February 2009 AQIM, as the GSPC had been restyled, an Islamist militant group largely operating in southern Algeria and northern Mali, claimed responsibility for the kidnapping of four European tourists the previous month and of two diplomats in December 2008. The diplomats and two of the tourists were released in April 2009, and in June a 2,000-strong Malian force, supported by Algerian troops and aircraft, launched an attack on an AQIM base in northern Mali. During the offensive it was reported that 26 Islamist militants were killed and several more detained; 10 Malian soldiers were also killed in the fighting. Of the two remaining hostages, one was reported to have been killed in late May while the other was released in July. In response to the kidnapping of the four European citizens and the seizure in Mauritania (and subsequent transfer to Mali) of three Spanish and two Italian tourists later that year, in January 2010 Mali and Mauritania announced plans to strengthen security co-operation. In the following month, however, relations with neighbouring countries became strained after Mali released four Islamist militants, detained in April 2009 on weapons charges, in exchange for the freeing of a French citizen taken hostage in November. Both Algeria and Mauritania subsequently withdrew their ambassadors from Bamako, claiming that Mali's decision to release the terrorists was an infringement of the agreement on security co-operation reached at the September regional summit. One of the Spanish hostages was set free in March 2010, followed by the other two in August; it was reported that the Spanish Government had paid a ransom to secure the release of the prisoners, although the Spanish authorities denied such claims. The two Italian hostages were released in April. Meanwhile, in mid-March ministers responsible for foreign affairs from seven Saharan states, including Mali, Mauritania and Algeria, meeting in Algiers, agreed that they would commence the sharing of operational information and co-ordinate their operations against AQIM. In November 2011 two French nationals were abducted in the central town of Hombori, while a German tourist was killed and a further three foreign nationals were kidnapped in the northern city of Tombouctou. AQIM subsequently issued a statement claiming responsibility for the kidnapping of the five tourists and denouncing the Malian Government's military co-operation with France. In March 2013 AQIM announced that one of the French citizens had been killed in retaliation for the French Government's military intervention in northern Mali.

The large-scale conflict in northern Mali during 2012 precipitated the internal displacement of an estimated 204,000 Malians, while more than 200,000 fled to Mauritania, Niger and Burkina Faso, according to UNHCR estimates. Following French military intervention in January 2013 (see Tuareg Insurgencies), Belgium dispatched a 40-member military contingent, which was to assist in evacuating injured personnel from the region, while the USA provided logistical assistance and the United Kingdom announced that it would deploy 330 military personnel, including some 40 military advisers, to Mali and neighbouring countries. In late January the European Union (EU) declared that it would contribute €50m. to finance a UN-endorsed force, while an international donors conference pledged US $455.5m. The French President, François Hollande, visited Tombouctou in early February, when he issued assurances that French forces would remain in the country as long as necessary. On 18 February France officially resumed the release of development aid, which had been suspended following the March 2012 coup. Also in February 2013 the first members of a 500-member EU mission that was to assist in the training and reorganization of Mali's armed forces began to arrive in the country.

CONSTITUTION AND GOVERNMENT

The Constitution of the Third Republic, which was approved in a national referendum on 12 January 1992, provides for the separation of the powers of the executive, legislative and judicial organs of state. Executive power is vested in the President of the Republic, who is elected for five years by universal suffrage. The President appoints a Prime Minister, who, in turn, appoints a Council of Ministers. Legislative power is vested in the 147-seat unicameral Assemblée nationale, elected for five years by universal suffrage. Elections take place in the context of a multi-party political system.

Mali has eight administrative regions, each presided over by a governor, and a district government in Bamako. Following a significant revision of local government structures in 1999, and a further minor revision in 2001, the number of elected mayors across Mali increased from 19 to 703.

REGIONAL AND INTERNATIONAL CO-OPERATION

Mali is a member of the African Union (AU, see p. 191), the Economic Community of West African States (ECOWAS, see p. 268), the West African organs of the Franc Zone (see p. 339), the African Groundnut Council (see p. 455), the Niger Basin Authority (see p. 463) and the Organisation pour la Mise en Valeur du Fleuve Sénégal (OMVS, see p. 461).

Mali became a member of the UN in 1960 and was admitted to the World Trade Organization (WTO, see p. 444) in 1995. Mali participates in the Group of 77 (G77, see p. 461) developing countries.

ECONOMIC AFFAIRS

In 2011, according to estimates by the World Bank, Mali's gross national income (GNI), measured at average 2009–11 prices, was US $9,633m., equivalent to $610 per head (or $1,050 on an international purchasing-power parity basis). During 2002–11, it was estimated, the population increased at an average annual rate of 3.1%, while gross domestic product (GDP) per head grew, in real terms, by an average of 1.6% per year. Overall GDP increased, in real terms, at an average annual rate of 4.8% in 2002–11. According to the World Bank, real GDP rose by 2.7% in 2011.

Agriculture (including livestock-rearing, forestry and fishing) contributed 39.0% of GDP in 2011, according to provisional African Development Bank (AfDB) figures. According to FAO, some 72.9% of the labour force were estimated to be employed in the sector in mid-2013. Mali is among Africa's foremost producers and exporters of cotton (exports of which contributed an estimated 8.4% of the value of total exports in 2010). According to the IMF, cotton production increased from 202,397 metric tons in 2008 to 236,000 tons in 2009. Sheanuts (karité nuts), groundnuts, vegetables and mangoes are also cultivated for export. A government project introduced in 2006 to support diversification in the agricultural sector has had considerable success, resulting, for example, in a 135% increase in the value of mango exports between 2005 and 2009. The principal subsistence crops are millet, rice, sorghum and maize. Cereal imports remain necessary in most years. The livestock-rearing and fishing sectors make an important contribution to the domestic food supply and (in the case of the former) to export revenue, providing 2.6% of total exports in 2011, according to provisional AfDB figures, although both are highly vulnerable to drought. According to the World Bank, agricultural GDP increased by an average of 5.5% per year in 2002–07. The sector grew by 11.4% in 2010, before provisionally declining by 1.4% in 2011, according to the AfDB.

Industry (including mining, manufacturing, construction and power) contributed 22.1% of GDP in 2011, according to provisional AfDB figures. It engaged 16.5% of the employed labour force in 2004. According to the World Bank, industrial GDP increased at an average annual rate of 1.2% in 2002–07. It grew by 3.7% in 2007.

Mining contributed 7.8% of GDP in 2011, according to provisional AfDB figures. It engaged 0.5% of the employed labour force in 2004. The importance of the sector has increased with the successful exploitation of the country's gold reserves: exports of gold contributed an estimated 79.1% of the value of total exports in 2010. Output of gold rose significantly in the latter half of the 1990s, as new mining facilities commenced operations, and by 2001 Mali had become the third largest gold producer in Africa. Gold production declined by an estimated 16.5% in 2010, according to the IMF, owing to a delay in the opening of a new mine, but was forecast to rise sharply in 2011, before contracting gradually from 2013 as mines neared the end of their reserves. Two new open-pit mines, at Yalea and Loulo, operated by Randgold Resources (of South Africa), commenced operations in late 2005; underground development began at Loulo in 2010 and was expected to produce 1.2m. oz of gold by 2014. Salt, diamonds, marble and phosphate rock are also mined. The future exploitation of deposits of iron ore and uranium is envisaged. According to the IMF, the GDP of the mining sector increased at an average annual rate of 46.8% in 1996–2002; according to the AfDB, mining GDP grew by 1.5% in 2009 but declined by 14.3% in 2010, and no growth was recorded in 2011.

The manufacturing sector contributed 6.3% of GDP in 2011, according to provisional AfDB figures. It engaged 11.5% of the employed labour force in 2004. The main area of activity is agro-industrial (chiefly the processing of cotton, sugar and rice). Brewing and tobacco industries are also represented, and some construction materials are produced for the domestic market. According to the World Bank, manufacturing GDP increased at an average annual rate of 4.0% in 2002–07. According to the AfDB, the GDP of the sector rose provisionally by 20.8% in 2011.

According to provisional AfDB data, construction contributed 5.8% of GDP in 2011, and engaged 4.3% of the employed labour force in 2004. The GDP of the construction sector grew by a provisional 5.0% in 2011.

Mali began to receive power supplies from the Manantali hydroelectric project (constructed and operated under the auspices of the Organisation pour la Mise en Valeur du Fleuve Sénégal—OMVS) from December 2001, and there were also plans to link the Malian network with those of Côte d'Ivoire, Burkina Faso and Ghana. In addition, an agreement on energy supply was reached with Algeria in February 1998. Imports of petroleum, petroleum products and related materials comprised an estimated 25.7% of the value of merchandise imports in 2010.

The services sector contributed 38.9% of GDP in 2011, according to the AfDB. It engaged 41.9% of the employed labour force in 2004. According to the World Bank, the GDP of the services sector increased at an average annual rate of 7.6% in 2002–07. Services GDP grew by 7.6% in 2007.

In 2010 Mali recorded a visible merchandise trade deficit of US $664.6m. and there was a deficit of $1,189.9m. on the current account of the balance of payments. In 2010 the principal sources of imports were Senegal (which supplied 13.6% of total imports), France, Benin and the People's Republic of China. The largest market for exports in that year was South Africa, which accounted for 57.1% of total exports, followed by Switzerland-Liechtenstein (12.1%). The principal exports in 2010 were gold and cotton, while the principal imports were petroleum, petroleum products and related materials, machinery and transport equipment, manufactured goods, chemicals and related products, and food and live animals.

In 2012, according to IMF estimates, Mali recorded an overall budget deficit of 112,600m. francs CFA. Mali's general government gross debt was 1,531,015m. francs CFA in 2011, equivalent to 30.6% of GDP. Mali's total external debt was US $2,326m. at the end of 2010, of which $2,271m. was public and publicly guaranteed debt. In that year, the cost of servicing long-term public and publicly guaranteed debt and repayments to the IMF was equivalent to 2.5% of the value of exports of goods, services and income (excluding workers' remittances). The annual rate of inflation averaged 2.5% in 2002–12. Consumer prices increased by 5.4% in 2012. An estimated 8.8% of the labour force were unemployed in 2004.

Mali's economic development is hindered by its vulnerability to drought, its dependence on imports and its narrow range of exports. In the first half of the 2000s the cotton sector underwent restructuring, with the partial transfer to private ownership of the cotton-ginning company, the Compagnie Malienne pour le Développement des Textiles, while a number of projects were undertaken to broaden the country's exports and increase rural farming income. Following the successful completion of a supported programme in December 2011, the IMF approved a new Extended Credit Facility (ECF) arrangement for Mali totalling US $46.3m. In response to a military coup on 21 March 2012 (see Domestic Political Affairs), however, the USA, the European Union (EU, see p. 281) and donor organizations suspended aid to Mali, and the African Union (AU, see p. 191) suspended the country's membership. On 6 April an agreement was reached with the Economic Community of West African States (ECOWAS, see p. 268), under which power was ceded to a new Government for a transitional period, in exchange for the removal of the sanctions that had been imposed against Mali. (The AU ended Mali's suspension in October.) Meanwhile, an insurrection by Tuareg and Islamist groups (see Tuareg Insurgencies), which had occupied the north of the country by the end of 2012, intensified a humanitarian crisis in the region. Although military intervention by French and ECOWAS-led forces restored government control in early 2013, hostilities and concomitant severe food shortages persisted in the north. In January the EU announced that it would release emergency aid of €20m.; France officially resumed development assistance in February. In March the World Bank's International Development Association approved a further $20m. credit towards the development of Mali's agricultural sector and food production. Following the cancellation of the ECF arrangement, the IMF agreed to extend an $18.4m. emergency loan to Mali in January. After strong growth in 2010–11, which had been generated by the agricultural and gold sectors, GDP had contracted by an estimated 1.5% in 2012, while the IMF noted increased inflation and a balance of payments deficit. Despite the continued instability, in February 2013 a new transitional Government announced a provisional timetable under which democratic elections would take place in July. It was hoped that greater political stability would facilitate improved economic performance.

PUBLIC HOLIDAYS

2014: 1 January (New Year's Day), 20 January (Armed Forces Day), 13 January* (Mouloud, Birth of the Prophet), 20 January*

(Baptism of the Prophet), 26 March (Commemoration of the overthrow of Moussa Traoré), 21 April (Easter Monday), 1 May (Labour Day), 25 May (Africa Day, anniversary of the OAU's foundation), 28 July* (Korité, end of Ramadan), 22 September (Independence Day), 4 October* (Tabaski, Feast of the Sacrifice), 25 December (Christmas Day).

* These holidays are determined by the Islamic lunar calendar and may vary by one or two days from the dates given.

Statistical Survey

Source (unless otherwise stated): Direction Nationale de la Statistique et de l'Informatique, rue Archinard, porte 233, BP 12, Bamako; tel. 2022-2455; fax 2022-7145; e-mail cnpe.mali@afribonemali.net; internet www.dnsi.gov.ml.

Area and Population

AREA, POPULATION AND DENSITY

Area (sq km)	1,240,192*
Population (census results)	
17 April 1998†	9,790,492
1 April 2009 (provisional)	
Males	7,202,744
Females	7,314,432
Total	14,517,176
Population (UN estimates at mid-year)‡	
2011	15,839,536
2012	16,318,894
2013	16,808,245
Density (per sq km) at mid-2013	13.6

* 478,841 sq miles.
† Figures are provisional and refer to the *de jure* population.
‡ Source: UN, *World Population Prospects: The 2010 Revision*.

POPULATION BY AGE AND SEX
(UN estimates at mid-2013)

	Males	Females	Total
0–14	4,025,951	3,861,993	7,887,944
15–64	4,241,062	4,322,763	8,563,825
65 and over	144,220	212,256	356,476
Total	8,411,233	8,397,012	16,808,245

Source: UN, *World Population Prospects: The 2010 Revision*.

Ethnic Groups (percentage of total, 1995): Bambara 36.5; Peul 13.9; Sénoufo 9.0; Soninké 8.8; Dogon 8.0; Songhaï 7.2; Malinké 6.6; Diola 2.9; Bobo and Oulé 2.4; Tuareg 1.7; Moor 1.2; Others 1.8 (Source: La Francophonie).

ADMINISTRATIVE DIVISIONS
(*de jure* population at 1998 census, provisional figures)

District					
Bamako . . .	1,016,167		Mopti		1,475,274
Regions			Kayes		1,372,019
Sikasso . . .	1,780,042		Tombouctou . .		461,956
Ségou . . .	1,679,201		Gao		397,516
Koulikoro . .	1,565,838		Kidal		42,479

PRINCIPAL TOWNS*
(*de jure* population at 1998 census, provisional figures)

Bamako (capital) .	1,016,167		Koutiala		74,153
Sikasso . . .	113,813		Kayes		67,262
Ségou . . .	90,898		Gao		54,903
Mopti . . .	79,840		Kati		49,756

* With the exception of Bamako, figures refer to the population of communes (municipalities).

Mid-2011 ('000, incl. suburbs, UN estimate): Bamako 2,036,520 (Source: UN, *World Urbanization Prospects: The 2011 Revision*).

BIRTHS AND DEATHS
(annual averages, UN estimates)

	1995–2000	2000–05	2005–10
Birth rate (per 1,000) . . .	49.1	49.0	47.6
Death rate (per 1,000)	18.6	17.2	15.5

Source: UN, *World Population Prospects: The 2010 Revision*.

Life expectancy (years at birth): 51.4 (males 50.3; females 52.5) in 2011 (Source: World Bank, World Development Indicators database).

ECONOMICALLY ACTIVE POPULATION
('000 persons, 2004, estimates)

	Males	Females	Total
Agriculture, hunting and forestry .	657.7	291.7	949.4
Fishing	33.3	2.0	35.2
Mining	8.4	3.0	11.4
Manufacturing	136.1	136.4	272.5
Electricity, gas and water . . .	5.1	—	5.1
Construction	97.5	4.7	102.1
Wholesale and retail trade; repair of motor vehicles, motorcycles and personal household goods .	266.1	402.1	668.1
Hotels and restaurants . . .	1.4	6.3	7.6
Transport, storage and communications . . .	51.8	3.5	55.3
Financial intermediation . . .	4.4	—	4.4
Real estate	3.5	0.6	4.0
Public administration	33.3	6.6	39.9
Education	35.6	18.3	53.9
Health and social work . . .	11.4	9.5	20.9
Other social services . . .	42.6	97.5	140.1
Total employed . . .	1,388.3	982.5	2,370.8
Unemployed	107.0	120.5	227.4
Total labour force	1,495.3	1,103.0	2,598.2

Source: ILO.

Mid-2013 (estimates in '000): Agriculture, etc. 3,277; Total labour force 4,494 (Source: FAO).

Health and Welfare

KEY INDICATORS

Total fertility rate (children per woman, 2010)	6.3
Under-5 mortality rate (per 1,000 live births, 2010) . . .	178
HIV/AIDS (% of persons aged 15–49, 2009)	1.0
Physicians (per 1,000 head, 2008)	0.05
Hospital beds (per 1,000 head, 2010)	0.10
Health expenditure (2009): US $ per head (PPP) . . .	57
Health expenditure (2009): % of GDP	5.5
Health expenditure (2009): public (% of total)	47.2
Access to water (% of persons, 2010)	64
Access to sanitation (% of persons, 2010)	22
Total carbon dioxide emissions ('000 metric tons, 2008) . .	594.1
Carbon dioxide emissions per head (metric tons, 2008) . . .	<0.1
Human Development Index (2011): ranking	175
Human Development Index (2011): value	0.359

For sources and definitions, see explanatory note on p. vi.

Agriculture

PRINCIPAL CROPS
('000 metric tons)

	2009	2010	2011
Rice, paddy	1,950.8	2,305.6	1,741.5
Maize	1,477.0	1,403.6	1,298.2
Millet	1,390.4	1,373.3	1,462.1
Sorghum	1,465.6	1,256.8	1,191.0
Fonio	35.5	52.3	51.0
Sweet potatoes	236.8	204.7	207.0*
Cassava (Manioc)	79.6	38.2	45.9*
Yams	65.4	90.1	92.0*
Sugar cane	377.0	359.0	360.0*
Groundnuts, with shell . . .	300.6	314.5	316.0*
Karité nuts (Sheanuts)* . . .	232.1	199.7	208.0
Cottonseed†	144.0	170.0	290.0
Tomatoes	62.2	41.3	41.5*
Onions, dry*	39.0	40.0	42.0
Guavas, mangoes and mangosteens	47.4	47.8*	57.4*
Cotton (lint)*	72.0	78.0	148.0

* FAO estimate(s).
† Unofficial figures.

Aggregate production ('000 metric tons, may include official, semi-official or estimated data): Total cereals 6,334.6 in 2009, 6,415.7 in 2010, 5,777.9 in 2011; Total pulses 158.7 in 2009, 155.3 in 2010, 158.9 in 2011; Total roots and tubers 472.2 in 2009, 415.5 in 2010, 431.4 in 2011; Total vegetables (incl. melons) 973.1 in 2009, 824.1 in 2010, 796.1 in 2011; Total fruits (excl. melons) 385.6 in 2009, 371.4 in 2010, 392.7 in 2011.

Source: FAO.

LIVESTOCK
('000 head, year ending September)

	2009	2010	2011
Cattle	8,896	9,163	9,438
Sheep	11,300	11,865	12,459
Goats	15,736	16,523	17,349
Pigs	74	75	76
Horses	478	488	498
Asses	862	881	900
Camels	904	923	941
Chickens	35,000	36,750	36,711

Source: FAO.

LIVESTOCK PRODUCTS
('000 metric tons, FAO estimates)

	2009	2010	2011
Cattle meat	136.3	143.7	156.0
Sheep meat	44.5	46.4	48.8
Goat meat	65.8	69.1	74.2
Chicken meat	40.6	41.6	41.2
Game meat	22.1	23.7	23.7
Pig meat	2.5	2.6	2.6
Cows' milk	578.9	596.3	596.3
Sheep's milk	153.0	160.0	156.6
Goats' milk	656.4	689.2	702.6
Camels' milk	295.8	301.9	298.8

Source: FAO.

Forestry

ROUNDWOOD REMOVALS
('000 cubic metres, excl. bark, FAO estimates)

	2008	2009	2010
Sawlogs, veneer logs and logs for sleepers	4	4	4
Other industrial wood	409	409	409
Fuel wood	5,203	5,264	5,326
Total	**5,616**	**5,677**	**5,739**

2011: Production assumed to be unchanged from 2010 (FAO estimates).
Source: FAO.

SAWNWOOD PRODUCTION
('000 cubic metres, incl. railway sleepers)

	1987	1988	1989
Total (all broadleaved) . . .	11	13	13*

* FAO estimate.

1990–2011: Production assumed to be unchanged from 1989 (FAO estimates).

Source: FAO.

Fishing

('000 metric tons, live weight)

	2008	2009*	2010
Capture	100.0*	100.0	100.0
Nile tilapia	30.0	30.0	30.0
Elephantsnout fishes . . .	7.0	7.0	7.0
Characins	5.0	5.0	5.0
Black catfishes	4.0	4.0	4.0
North African catfish . . .	25.0	25.0	25.0
Nile perch	6.0*	6.0	6.0
Other freshwater fishes . .	19.0*	19.0	18.9
Aquaculture	0.8	1.4	2.1*
Total catch	**100.8***	**101.4**	**102.1***

* FAO estimate(s).

Source: FAO.

Mining

(metric tons unless otherwise indicated)

	2009	2010	2011
Gold (kg)	42,364	36,360	35,728
Salt*	6,000	6,000	6,000
Semi-precious stones* . . .	10,000	10,000	10,000

* Estimated figures.

Source: US Geological Survey.

Industry

SELECTED PRODUCTS

('000 metric tons unless otherwise indicated)

	2007	2008	2009
Raw sugar	34	35	35
Fish (dried, salted or in brine); smoked fish and edible fish meal	8.8	n.a.	n.a.
Cigarettes (million)	546.8	276.3	975.9
Electric energy (million kWh) .	495	508	516

Source: mainly UN Industrial Commodity Statistics Database.

Finance

CURRENCY AND EXCHANGE RATES

Monetary Units
100 centimes = 1 franc de la Communauté Financière Africaine (CFA).

Sterling, Dollar and Euro Equivalents (31 December 2012)
£1 sterling = 784.523 francs CFA;
US $1 = 497.163 francs CFA;
€1 = 655.957 francs CFA;
10,000 francs CFA = £12.75 = $20.11 = €15.24.

Average Exchange Rate (francs CFA per US $)
2010   495.28
2011   471.87
2012   510.29

Note: An exchange rate of 1 French franc = 50 francs CFA, established in 1948, remained in force until January 1994, when the CFA franc was devalued by 50%, with the exchange rate adjusted to 1 French franc = 100 francs CFA. This relationship to French currency remained in effect with the introduction of the euro on 1 January 1999. From that date, accordingly, a fixed exchange rate of €1 = 655.957 francs CFA has been in operation.

BUDGET

('000 million francs CFA)*

Revenue†	2010	2011‡	2012§
Budgetary revenue	727.6	770.5	816.9
Tax revenue	681.8	734.2	766.2
Non-tax revenue	45.8	32.9	50.7
Special funds and annexed budgets	78.7	96.1	100.2
Total	806.3	866.6	917.1

Expenditure‖	2010	2011‡	2012§
Budgetary expenditure . . .	971.0	1,143.6	968.7
Current expenditure . . .	601.2	709.0	752.3
Wages and salaries . . .	231.8	265.1	306.7
Interest payments (scheduled)	19.1	30.6	32.0
Other current expenditure	350.3	413.4	413.7
Capital expenditure	369.8	437.9	216.3
Externally financed . .	187.6	253.9	79.7
Special funds and annexed budgets	78.7	96.1	100.2
Total	1,049.7	1,249.5	1,068.9

* Figures represent a consolidation of the central government budget, special funds and annexed budgets.
† Excluding grants received ('000 million francs CFA): 133.7 in 2010; 193.9 in 2011 (estimate); 37.2 in 2012 (programmed figure).
‡ Estimates.
§ Programmed figures.
‖ Excluding net lending ('000 million francs CFA): 14.7 in 2010; −3.1 in 2011 (estimate); −2.0 in 2012 (programmed figure).

Source: IMF, *Mali: 2012 Article IV Consultation, Request for Disbursement Under the Rapid Credit Facility and Cancellation of the Extended Credit Facility Arrangement—Staff Report; Staff Supplements; Public Information Notice and Press Release on the Executive Board Discussion; and Statement by the Executive Director for Mali* (February 2013).

INTERNATIONAL RESERVES

(excl. gold, US $ million at 31 December)

	2009	2010	2011
IMF special drawing rights . .	115.0	113.1	112.7
Reserve position in IMF . .	15.5	15.4	15.4
Foreign exchange	1,473.9	1,215.9	1,250.6
Total	1,604.4	1,344.4	1,378.6

2012: IMF special drawing rights 112.8; Reserve position in IMF 15.4.

Source: IMF, *International Financial Statistics*.

MONEY SUPPLY

('000 million francs CFA at 31 December)

	2009	2010	2011
Currency outside banks . . .	304.6	312.3	415.4
Demand deposits	495.5	610.7	677.2
Total money (incl. others) . .	800.5	923.1	1,092.9

Source: IMF, *International Financial Statistics*.

COST OF LIVING

(Consumer Price Index for Bamako: base: 2000 = 100)

	2008	2009	2010
Food, beverages and tobacco . .	132.6	136.7	103.6
Clothing	105.9	108.7	108.6
Housing, water, electricity and gas	118.2	118.4	116.7
All items (incl. others) . . .	126.3	129.1	130.9

2011: Food, beverages and tobacco 112.8; All items (incl. others) 134.6.

2012: Food, beverages and tobacco 121.8; All items (incl. others) 141.9.

Source: ILO.

NATIONAL ACCOUNTS

(million francs CFA at current prices)

Expenditure on the Gross Domestic Product

	2009	2010	2011*
Government final consumption expenditure	734	788	859
Private final consumption expenditure	2,633	2,831	3,097
Changes in inventories . . .	31	155	32
Gross fixed capital formation .	868	986	1,114
Total domestic expenditure .	4,266	4,760	5,102
Exports of goods and services .	914	1,105	1,254
Less Imports of goods and services	947	1,209	1,345
GDP in purchasers' values .	4,233	4,656	5,012

Gross Domestic Product by Economic Activity

	2009	2010	2011*
Agriculture, hunting, forestry and fishing	1,486	1,698	1,761
Mining and quarrying	284	287	351
Manufacturing	219	227	287
Electricity, gas and water . .	83	91	100
Construction	216	238	263
Wholesale and retail trade, restaurants and hotels . . .	611	669	713
Transport and communications .	233	250	268
Finance, insurance, real estate and other business services . . .	315	333	350
Public administration and defence	378	399	427
Sub-total	**3,825**	**4,192**	**4,520**
Less Imputed bank service charges	15	16	23
Indirect taxes, less subsidies . .	423	480	515
GDP in purchasers' values .	**4,233**	**4,656**	**5,012**

* Provisional figures.

Source: African Development Bank.

BALANCE OF PAYMENTS
(US $ million)

	2008	2009	2010
Exports of goods f.o.b.	2,097.2	1,772.2	2,052.6
Imports of goods f.o.b.	−2,732.9	−1,982.3	−2,717.2
Trade balance	**−635.7**	**−210.1**	**−664.6**
Exports of services	454.3	355.8	383.7
Imports of services	−1,024.3	−829.6	−1,027.6
Balance on goods and services	**−1,205.7**	**−683.9**	**−1,308.5**
Other income received	101.6	81.6	71.7
Other income paid	−414.2	−539.0	−490.7
Balance on goods, services and income	**−1,518.3**	**−1,141.2**	**−1,727.5**
Current transfers received . .	554.0	648.3	700.8
Current transfers paid	−99.2	−162.0	−163.3
Current balance	**−1,063.4**	**−654.9**	**−1,189.9**
Capital account (net)	328.8	384.1	229.6
Direct investment abroad . . .	−49.2	646.6	371.6
Direct investment from abroad .	228.9	102.8	26.9
Portfolio investment assets . .	−117.9	−60.3	−462.2
Portfolio investment liabilities .	22.6	21.3	7.2
Financial derivatives assets . .	3.6	−1.6	−3.9
Other investment assets . . .	205.5	−370.7	304.9
Other investment liabilities . .	330.4	554.3	507.9
Net errors and omissions . . .	31.0	−175.3	31.1
Overall balance	**−79.7**	**446.3**	**−177.0**

Source: IMF, *International Financial Statistics*.

External Trade

PRINCIPAL COMMODITIES
(distribution by SITC, US $ million)

Imports c.i.f.*	2007	2008	2010†
Food and live animals . . .	252.2	320.1	437.4
Cereals and cereal preparations .	91.3	117.9	146.0
Mineral fuels, lubricants, etc..	484.9	713.2	1,221.0
Petroleum, petroleum products and related materials . . .	478.4	704.4	1,211.0
Chemicals and related products	338.9	471.6	692.7
Medicinal and pharmaceutical products	140.2	136.2	336.1
Manufactured goods . . .	399.7	683.1	850.7
Iron and steel	89.0	142.5	188.9
Machinery and transport equipment	534.5	860.2	1,121.6
Road vehicles	158.9	220.5	319.1
Miscellaneous manufactured articles	83.1	162.7	228.6
Total (incl. others)	**2,184.8**	**3,338.9**	**4,703.5**

Exports f.o.b.	2007	2008	2010†
Food and live animals . . .	93.7	127.7	95.8
Crude materials, inedible, excluding fuels	207.4	213.1	177.3
Cotton	198.7	203.1	168.0
Machinery and transport equipment	27.3	58.5	30.8
Road vehicles	5.1	21.7	5.8
Gold, non-monetary, unwrought, in powder or semi-manufactured . . .	1,082.5	1,437.1	1,578.7
Total (incl. others)	**1,440.6**	**1,918.3**	**1,996.3**

* Including commodities and transactions not classified according to kind (US $ million): 492.2 in 2007; 734.0 in 2008; 1,258.9 in 2010.
† Data for 2009 were not available.

Source: UN, *International Trade Statistics Yearbook*.

SELECTED TRADING PARTNERS
(US $ million)

Imports c.i.f.	2007	2008	2010*
Belgium	67.2	86.4	69.9
Benin	97.5	74.6	467.7
Brazil	36.4	58.8	67.0
Burkina Faso	35.8	5.3	n.a.
China, People's Repub. . . .	130.0	342.1	467.4
Côte d'Ivoire	277.0	346.9	371.0
France (incl. Monaco) . . .	325.9	464.8	630.3
Germany	52.3	81.3	111.1
Ghana	65.3	55.7	74.2
India	78.3	66.1	67.7
Italy	21.4	36.9	49.2
Japan	41.1	91.9	121.6
Netherlands	15.8	23.2	110.8
Senegal	432.2	575.7	638.8
South Africa	79.5	151.2	298.0
Thailand	11.2	39.5	16.1
Togo	87.3	45.1	105.4
Ukraine	12.1	37.4	72.8
United Arab Emirates . . .	14.6	40.0	43.6
USA	81.6	221.4	421.3
Total (incl. others)	**2,184.8**	**3,338.9**	**4,703.5**

Exports f.o.b.	2007	2008	2010*
Bangladesh	11.8	5.2	16.1
Belgium	30.4	6.4	7.0
Burkina Faso	10.9	18.5	43.1
China, People's Repub. . . .	32.1	35.4	40.8
Côte d'Ivoire	36.0	49.1	39.9
France (incl. Monaco) . . .	12.6	24.2	22.7
Guinea	11.3	11.8	5.6
Indonesia	25.7	11.8	12.0
Pakistan	30.1	16.5	20.5
Senegal	61.1	131.1	87.8
South Africa	966.0	1,390.1	1,139.2
Switzerland-Liechtenstein . .	65.6	49.0	241.6
Thailand	27.0	27.2	9.3
United Kingdom	26.5	1.3	15.6
Viet Nam	23.5	21.7	8.7
Total (incl. others)	1,440.6	1,918.3	1,996.3

* Data for 2009 were not available.

Source: UN, *International Trade Statistics Yearbook*.

Transport

RAILWAYS
(traffic)

	1999	2000	2001
Passengers ('000)	778.7	682.3	649.0
Freight carried ('000 metric tons) .	535	438	358

Passenger-km (million): 210 in 1999.

Freight ton-km (million): 241 in 1999.

ROAD TRAFFIC
(motor vehicles in use, estimates)

	1994	1995	1996
Passenger cars	24,250	24,750	26,190
Lorries and vans	16,000	17,100	18,240

2009 (motor vehicles in use): Passenger cars 107,194; Vans and lorries 49,074; Motorcycles and mopeds 24,700.

Source: IRF, *World Road Statistics*.

CIVIL AVIATION
(traffic on scheduled services)*

	1999	2000	2001
Kilometres flown (million) . .	3	3	1
Passengers carried ('000) . .	84	77	46
Passenger-km (million) . . .	235	216	130
Total ton-km (million) . . .	36	32	19

* Including an apportionment of the traffic of Air Afrique.

Source: UN, *Statistical Yearbook*.

Tourism

FOREIGN VISITORS BY NATIONALITY*

	2008	2009	2010
Austria	2,638	660	1,906
Belgium, Luxembourg and the Netherlands	8,166	6,642	6,306
Canada	6,940	10,091	6,147
France	41,778	38,261	42,883
Germany	9,033	5,380	4,937
Italy	8,269	5,307	6,878
Japan	4,672	1,307	2,668
Middle Eastern states . . .	4,176	2,946	2,948
Scandinavian states	3,883	1,791	1,875
Spain	10,164	4,388	5,514
Switzerland	5,037	2,723	2,520
United Kingdom	5,357	4,173	4,422
USA	12,579	16,901	17,545
West African states . . .	15,276	27,408	29,872
Total (incl. others)	189,511	160,012	169,305

* Arrivals at hotels and similar establishments.

Receipts from tourism (US $ million, excl. passenger transport): 192 in 2009; 205 in 2010.

Source: World Tourism Organization.

Communications Media

	2009	2010	2011
Telephones ('000 main lines in use)	84.8	114.5	104.7
Mobile cellular telephones ('000 subscribers)	4,460.5	7,440.4	10,821.9
Internet subscribers ('000) . .	19.8	24.4	36.5
Broadband subscribers ('000) . .	3.0	2.3	2.4

Source: International Telecommunication Union.

Education

(2010/11 unless otherwise indicated)

	Institutions*	Teachers	Students ('000)		
			Males	Females	Total
Pre-primary . .	212	1,618	35.5	35.7	71.2
Primary . . .	2,871	43,629	1,145.3	969.5	2,114.8
Secondary . .	n.a.	33,220	487.7	332.7	820.4
Tertiary . . .	n.a.	1,112†	60.6	27.1	87.7

* 1998/99 figures.
† 2004/05 figure.

2005/06: *Pre-primary*: 412 institutions; 1,510 teachers; 51,071 students; *Primary and Secondary (lower)*: 8,079 institutions; 39,109 teachers; 1,990,765 students (1,137,787 males, 852,978 females); *Secondary (higher)*: 121 institutions; 1,904 teachers; 47,279 students (31,724 males, 15,555 females—estimates); *Secondary (technical and vocational)*: 119 institutions; 41,137 students; *Secondary (teacher training)*: 10,467 students (Source: Office of the Secretary-General of the Government, Bamako).

Source: mainly UNESCO Institute for Statistics.

Pupil-teacher ratio (primary education, UNESCO estimate): 48.5 in 2010/11 (Source: UNESCO Institute for Statistics).

Adult literacy rate (UNESCO estimates): 31.1% (males 43.4%; females 20.3%) in 2010 (Source: UNESCO Institute for Statistics).

Directory

The Government

HEAD OF STATE

Interim President: DIONCOUNDA TRAORÉ (took office on 12 April 2012 for an interim period of 40 days, which was subsequently extended to a transitional period of 12 months with effect from 22 May).

COUNCIL OF MINISTERS
(May 2013)

Prime Minister: DIANGO CISSOKO.

Minister of the Economy, Finance and the Budget: TIÉNA COULIBALY.

Minister of Defence and War Veterans: Gen. YAMOUSSA CAMARA.

Minister of Foreign Affairs and International Co-operation: TIEMAM HUBERT COULIBALY.

Minister of Territorial Administration, Decentralization and Land Management: Col MOUSSA SINKO COULIBALY.

Minister of Mining: Dr AMADOU BABA SY.

Minister of Education, Literacy, the Promotion of National Languages and Civic Instruction: BOCAR MOUSSA DIARRA.

Minister of Higher Education and Scientific Research: Prof. MESSA OULD MOHAMED LADY.

Minister of Labour, the Civil Service and Relations with the Institutions: MAMADOU NAMORY TRAORÉ.

Minister of Malians Abroad and African Integration: DEMBA TRAORÉ.

Minister of Internal Security and Civil Protection: Gen. TIÉFING KONATÉ.

Minister of Agriculture: BABA BERTHÉ.

Minister of Justice, Keeper of the Seals: MALICK COULIBALY.

Minister of Equipment and Transport: Lt Col ABDOULAYE KOUMARÉ.

Minister of Health: SOUMANA MAKADJI.

Minister of Trade and Industry: ABDEL KARIM KONATÉ.

Minister of Handicrafts and Tourism: YAYA AG MOHAMED ALI.

Minister of Housing, Town Planning and Land Affairs: DAVID SAGARA.

Minister of Employment and Professional Training: Dr DIALLO DÉDIA MAHAMANE KATTRA.

Minister of Post and New Technologies: BREHIMA TOLO.

Minister of the Family, the Promotion of Women and Children: ALWATA ICHATA SAHI.

Minister of Energy and Water: MAKAN TOUNKARA.

Minister of the Environment and Sanitation: OUSMANE AG RHISSA.

Minister of Youth and Sports: HAMEYE FOUNÉ MAHALMADANE.

Minister of Humanitarian Action, Solidarity and the Elderly: Dr MAMADOU SIDIBÉ.

Minister of Stockbreeding and Fisheries: DIANÉ MARIAM KONÉ.

Minister of Religious Affairs and Cults: Dr YACOUBA TRAORÉ.

Minister of Communication, Government Spokesperson: MANGA DEMBELÉ.

Minister of Culture: BRUNO MAIGA.

Minister-delegate at the Ministry of the Economy, Finance and the Budget, responsible for the Budget: MARIMPA SAMOURA.

Minister-delegate at the Ministry of Territorial Administration, Decentralization and Land Management, responsible for Decentralization and Land Management: ABDOURAHMANE OUMAR TOURÉ.

MINISTRIES

Office of the President: BP 1463, Koulouba, Bamako; tel. 2022-2572; fax 2023-0026; internet www.koulouba.pr.ml.

Office of the Prime Minister: Quartier du Fleuve, BP 790, Bamako; tel. 2022-4310; fax 2023-9595; e-mail ecrireaupm@primature.gov.ml; internet www.primature.gov.ml.

Office of the Secretary-General of the Government: BP 14, Koulouba, Bamako; tel. 2022-2552; fax 2022-7050; e-mail sgg@sgg.gov.ml; internet www.sgg.gov.ml.

Ministry of Agriculture: BP 1676, Bamako; tel. 2022-2785; e-mail ministere@ma.gov.ml; internet www.maliagriculture.org.

Ministry of Communication: ave de l'Yser, Quartier du Fleuve, BP 116, Bamako; tel. and fax 2022-2054.

Ministry of Culture: Badalabougou, Semagesco, BP 2211, Bamako; tel. 2029-6450; fax 2029-3917; e-mail malitourisme@afribone.net.ml; internet www.malitourisme.com.

Ministry of Defence and War Veterans: route de Koulouba, BP 2083, Bamako; tel. 2022-5021; fax 2023-2318.

Ministry of the Economy, Finance and the Budget: Bamako; internet www.finances.gov.ml.

Ministry of Education, Literacy, the Promotion of National Languages and Civic Instruction: Bamako.

Ministry of Employment and Professional Training: Bamako.

Ministry of Energy and Water: Bamako.

Ministry of the Environment and Sanitation: Bamako.

Ministry of Equipment and Transport: Bamako; tel. 2022-3937.

Ministry of the Family, the Promotion of Women and Children: porte G9, rue 109, Badalabougou, BP 2688, Bamako; tel. 2022-6659; fax 2023-6660; e-mail mpfef@cefib.com; internet www.mpfef.gov.ml.

Ministry of Foreign Affairs and International Co-operation: Koulouba, Bamako; tel. 2022-8314; fax 2022-5226.

Ministry of Handicrafts and Tourism: Bamako; tel. 2023-0539.

Ministry of Health: BP 232, Koulouba, Bamako; tel. 2022-5302; fax 2023-0203.

Ministry of Higher Education and Scientific Research: BP 71, Bamako; tel. 2022-5780; fax 2022-2126; e-mail info@education.gov.ml; internet www.education.gov.ml.

Ministry of Housing, Town Planning and Land Affairs: Bamako.

Ministry of Humanitarian Action, Solidarity and the Elderly: Bamako; tel. 2023-2301.

Ministry of Internal Security and Civil Protection: BP E 4771, Bamako; tel. 2022-0082.

Ministry of Justice: Quartier du Fleuve, BP 97, Bamako; tel. 2022-2642; fax 2023-0063; e-mail ucprodej@afribone.net.ml; internet www.justicemali.org.

Ministry of Labour, the Civil Service and Relations with the Institutions: Bamako; tel. 2023-0539; internet www.mlafu.gov.ml.

Ministry of Malians Abroad and African Integration: Cité du Niger, route de l'Hotel Mandé, Bamako; tel. 2021-8148; fax 2021-2505; e-mail maliensdelexterieur@yahoo.fr; internet www.maliensdelexterieur.gov.ml.

Ministry of Mining: BP 238, Bamako; tel. 2022-4184; fax 2022-2160.

Ministry of Post and New Technologies: Bamako.

Ministry of Religious Affairs and Cults: Bamako.

Ministry of Stockbreeding and Fisheries: Bamako; tel. 2023-3696.

Ministry of Territorial Administration, Decentralization and Land Management: face Direction de la RCFM, BP 78, Bamako; tel. 2022-4212; fax 2023-0247; internet www.matcl.gov.ml.

Ministry of Trade and Industry: BP 234, Koulouba, Bamako; tel. 2022-5156; fax 2022-0192.

Ministry of Youth and Sports: route de Koulouba, BP 91, Bamako; tel. 2022-3153; fax 2023-9067; internet www.sports.gouv.ml.

President and Legislature

PRESIDENT

Presidential Election, 29 April 2007

Candidate	Votes	% of votes
Gen. (retd) Amadou Toumani Touré (Independent)	1,612,912	71.20
Ibrahim Boubacar Keïta (RPM)	433,897	19.15
Tiébilé Dramé (PARENA)	68,956	3.04
Oumar Mariko (SADI)	61,670	2.72
Others	88,048	3.89
Total	2,265,483	100.00

LEGISLATURE

Assemblée nationale

BP 284, Bamako; tel. 2021-5724; fax 2021-0374; e-mail mamou@blonba.malinet.ml.

President: DIONCOUNDA TRAORÉ.

General Election, 1 and 22 July 2007

Party	Seats
Alliance pour la Démocratie au Mali—Parti Pan-Africain pour la Liberté, la Solidarité et la Justice (ADEMA)	51
Union pour la République et la Démocratie (URD)	34
Rassemblement pour le Mali (RPM)	11
Mouvement Patriotique pour le Renouveau (MPR)	8
Congrès National d'Initiative Démocratique—Faso Yiriwa Ton (CNID)	7
Parti pour la Renaissance Nationale (PARENA)	4
Parti de la Solidarité Africaine pour la Démocratie et l'Indépendance (SADI)	4
Union pour la Démocratie et le Développement (UDD)	3
Bloc des Alternances pour le Renouveau, l'Intégration et la Coopération Africaine (BARICA)	2
Mouvement pour l'Iindépendance, la Renaissance et l'Intégration Africaine (MIRIA)	2
Parti de la Solidarité et du Progrès (PSP)	2
Bloc pour la Démocratie et l'Intégration Africaine—Faso Jigi (BDIA)	1
Parti Citoyen pour le Renouveau (PCR)	1
Rassemblement National pour la Démocratie (RND)	1
Union Soudanaise—Rassemblement Démocratique Africain (US—RDA)	1
Independents	15
Total	**147**

Election Commission

Commission Electorale Nationale Indépendante (CENI): Bamako; Pres. MAMADOU DIAMOUTANI.

Advisory Councils

Economic, Social and Cultural Council: BP E 15, Koulouba, Bamako; tel. 2022-4368; fax 2022-8452; e-mail cesc@cefib.com; f. 1987; Pres. JEAMILLE BITTAR.

High Council of Communities: Bamako; compulsorily advises the Govt on issues relating to local and regional devt; comprises national councillors, elected indirectly for a term of five years; Pres. OUMAROU AG MOHAMED IBRAHIM HAÏDARA.

Political Organizations

At the end of 2012 there were some 138 political parties registered with the Ministry of the Interior.

Alliance pour la Démocratie au Mali—Parti Pan-Africain pour la Liberté, la Solidarité et la Justice (ADEMA): rue Fankélé, porte 145, BP 1791, Bamako-Coura; tel. 2022-0368; internet www.adema-pasj.org; f. 1990 as Alliance pour la Démocratie au Mali; Pres. DIONCOUNDA TRAORÉ; Sec.-Gen. MARIMATIA DIARRA.

Ansar Dine: f. 2012; Islamist; seeks to impose Shari'a law in Mali; Pres. IYAD AG AGALY.

Bloc des Alternances pour le Renouveau, l'Intégration et la Coopération Africaine (BARICA): Faladié Sema, ave de l'OUA, Bamako; Pres. MAMADOU SINAYOKO.

Congrès National d'Initiative Démocratique—Faso Yiriwa Ton (CNID): rue 426, porte 58, Niarela, BP 2572, Bamako; tel. 2021-4275; fax 2023-1861; e-mail mc_tall@hotmail.com; internet www.cnidmali.net; f. 1991; Chair. Me MOUNTAGA TALL; Sec.-Gen. Dr AMADOU SY.

Convention Démocratique et Sociale (CDS): Quinzambougou, rue 535, porte 112, Bamako; tel. 2029-2625; f. 1996; Chair. MAMADOU BAKARY SANGARÉ.

Convention Parti du Peuple (COPP): Hippodrome, rue 234, angle rue 287, porte 1345, BP 9012, Bamako; fax 2021-3591; e-mail lawyergakou@datatech.toolnet.org; f. 1996; Pres. Me MAMADOU GACKOU.

Mouvement pour l'Indépendance, la Renaissance et l'Intégration Africaine (MIRIA): Dravéla, Bolibana, rue 417, porte 66, Bamako; tel. 2029-2981; fax 2029-2979; e-mail miria12002@yahoo.fr; f. 1994 following split in ADEMA; Pres. MAMADOU KASSA TRAORÉ.

Mouvement Islamique de l'Azawad (MIA): f. 2013 following breakaway from Ansar Dine; Tuareg; Sec.-Gen. ALGABAS AG INTALLA.

Mouvement National de Libération de l'Azawad (MNLA): internet www.mnlamov.net; f. 2011; Tuareg movement seeking independence for the Azawad region; Gen. Sec. BILAL AG ACHERIF.

Mouvement Patriotique pour le Renouveau (MPR): Quinzambougou, BP E 1108, Bamako; tel. 2021-5546; fax 2021-5543; f. 1995; Pres. Dr CHOGUEL KOKALA MAÏGA.

Mouvement Unité pour le Jihad en Afrique de l'Ouest (MUJOA): f. 2011; seeks to launch a *jihad* across West Africa; Leader SULTAN OULD BADI.

Parti Citoyen pour le Renouveau (PCR): Niaréla II, rue 428, porte 592, Bamako; tel. 6672-0988; internet pcrmali.net; f. 2005; Pres. OUSMANE BEN FANA TRAORÉ.

Parti de la Solidarité Africaine pour la Démocratie et l'Indépendance (SADI): Djélibougou, rue 246, porte 559, BP 3140, Bamako; tel. 2024-1004; f. 2002; Leader CHEICK OUMAR SISSOKO.

Parti pour la Démocratie et le Progrès/Parti Socialiste (PDP/PS): Korofina sud, rue 96, porte 437, Bamako; tel. 2024-1675; fax 2020-2314; f. 1991; Leader FRANÇOIS KABORÉ.

Parti pour le Développement Économique et la Solidarité (PDES): Hamdallaye, ACI 2000, rue 320, porte 200, Bamako; f. 2010; Pres. HAMED DIANE SÉMÉGA.

Parti pour l'Indépendance, la Démocratie et la Solidarité (PIDS): Hippodrome, rue 250, porte 1183, BP E 1515, Bamako; tel. 2077-4575; f. 2001; Pres. DABA DIAWARA.

Parti pour la Renaissance Nationale (PARENA): rue Soundiata, porte 1397, BP E 2235, Ouolofobougou, Bamako; tel. 2023-4954; fax 2022-2908; e-mail info@parena.org.ml; f. 1995 following split in CNID; Pres. TIÉBILÉ DRAMÉ; Sec.-Gen. DJIGUIBA KEÏTA.

Parti pour la Solidarité et le Progrès (PSP): rue 552, porte 255, Quinzambougou, Bamako; tel. 2021-9960; f. 1945; Pres. OUMAR HAMMADOUN DICKO.

Rassemblement pour la Démocratie et le Progrès (RDP): Niarela, rue 485, porte 11, BP 2110, Bamako; tel. 2021-3092; fax 2024-6795; f. 1991; Pres. BISSI SANGARÉ.

Rassemblement pour le Mali (RPM): Hippodrome, rue 232, porte 130, BP 9057, Bamako; tel. 2021-1433; fax 2021-1336; e-mail siegerpmbko@yahoo.fr; internet www.rpm.org.ml; f. 2001; Pres. IBRAHIM BOUBACAR KEÏTA; Sec.-Gen. Dr BOCARY TRETA.

Union pour la Démocratie et le Développement (UDD): ave OUA, porte 3626, Sogoniko, BP 2969, Bamako; tel. 2020-3971; f. 1991; Leader Me HASSANE BARRY.

Union des Forces Démocratiques pour le Progrès—Sama-ton (UFDP): Quartier Mali, BP E 37, Bamako; tel. 2023-1766; f. 1991; Sec.-Gen. Col YOUSSOUF TRAORÉ.

Union Malienne du Rassemblement Démocratique Africain Faso Jigi (UM-RDA FASO JIGI): Hippodrome, rue RDA, porte 41, BP E 1413, Bamako; tel. and fax 2021-4522; f. 2010; Leader BOCAR MOUSSA DIARRA.

Union pour la République et la Démocratie (URD): Badalabougou, rue 105, porte 483, Bamako; tel. 2021-8642; e-mail contact@urd-mali.net; internet www.urd-mali.net; f. 2003; Pres. YOUNOUSSI TOURÉ.

Diplomatic Representation

EMBASSIES IN MALI

Algeria: Daoudabougou, BP 02, Bamako; tel. 2020-5176; fax 2022-9374; Ambassador NOUREDDINE AYADI.

Brazil: rue 113, porte 62, Badalabougou-ouest, Bamako; tel. 2022-9817; fax 2022-9906; Ambassador JEORGE JOSÉ FRANTZ RAMOS.

Burkina Faso: Hamdallaye ACI 2000, Commune III, BP 9022, Bamako; tel. 2023-3171; fax 2021-9266; e-mail ambafaso@experco.net; Ambassador Prof. SANNÉ MOHAMED TOPAN.

Canada: route de Koulikoro, Immeuble Séméga, Hippodrome, BP 198, Bamako; tel. 2021-2236; fax 2021-4362; e-mail bmako@international.gc.ca; internet www.bamako.gc.ca; Ambassador VIRGINIE SAINT-LOUIS.

China, People's Republic: route de Koulikoro, Hippodrome, BP 112, Bamako; tel. 2021-3597; fax 2022-3443; e-mail chinaemb_ml@mfa.gov.cn; internet ml.china-embassy.org/fra; Ambassador CAO ZHONGMING.

Côte d'Ivoire: square Patrice Lumumba, Immeuble CNAR, 3e étage, BP E 3644, Bamako; tel. 2022-0389; fax 2022-1376; Ambassador SAMUEL OUATTARA.

Cuba: porte 31, rue 328, Niarela, Bamako; tel. 2021-0289; fax 2021-0293; e-mail emcuba.mali@orangemali.net; internet emba .cubaminrex.cu/malifr; Ambassador SIDENIO ACOSTA ADAY.

Denmark: Immeuble UATT, 2e étage, Quartier du Fleuve, BP E 1733, Bamako; tel. 2023-0377; fax 2023-0194; e-mail bkoamb@um .dk; internet mali.um.dk; Chargé d'affaires ANDERS GARLY ANDERSEN.

Egypt: Badalabougou-est, BP 44, Bamako; tel. 2022-3565; fax 2022-0891; e-mail mostafa@datatech.net.ml; Ambassador HAMED AHMED CHOUKRY HAMED.

France: square Patrice Lumumba, BP 17, Bamako; tel. 4497-5757; fax 2022-3136; e-mail ambassade@france-mali.org.ml; internet www .ambafrance-ml.org; Ambassador GILLES HUBERSON.

Germany: Badalabougou-est, rue 14, porte 330, BP 100, Bamako; tel. 2070-0770; fax 2022-9650; e-mail allemagne@orangemali.net; internet www.bamako.diplo.de; Ambassador KARL FLITTNER.

Ghana: BP 3161, Bamako; Ambassador DONALD ADABERE ADABRE.

Guinea: Immeuble Saybou Maïga, Quartier du Fleuve, BP 118, Bamako; tel. 2022-3007; fax 2021-0806; Ambassador OUSMANE KONATÉ.

India: 101 ave de l'OUA, Badalabougou-est, Bamako; tel. 2023-5420; fax 2023-5417; e-mail hoc.bamako@mea.gov.in; f. 2009; Ambassador K. JOSEPH FRANCIS.

Iran: ave al-Quds, Hippodrome, BP 2136, Bamako; tel. 2021-7638; fax 2021-0731; Chargé d'affaires ABOLMOUHSEN SHARIF MOHAMMADI.

Japan: rue 43 porte 407, Cité du Niger, BP E 4227, Bamako; tel. 2070-0150; fax 2021-7785; internet www.ml.emb-japan.go.jp; Ambassador MASAHIRO KAWADA.

Korea, Democratic People's Republic: Bamako; Ambassador KIM PONG HUI.

Libya: Badalabougou-ouest, face Palais de la Culture, BP 1670, Bamako; tel. 2022-3496; fax 2022-6697; Ambassador Dr ALI MUHAMMAD AL-MAGOURI.

Mauritania: route de Koulikoro, Hippodrome, BP 135, Bamako; tel. 2021-4815; fax 2022-4908; e-mail ambarimbko@yahoo.fr; Ambassador SIDI MOHAMED OULD HANANA.

Morocco: Badalabougou-est, rue 25, porte 80, BP 2013, Bamako; tel. 2022-2123; fax 2022-7787; e-mail sifamali@afribone.net.ml; Ambassador HASSAN NACIRI.

Netherlands: rue 437, BP 2220, Hippodrome, Bamako; tel. 2021-9572; fax 2021-3617; e-mail bam@minbuza.nl; internet www.mfa.nl; Ambassador MAARTEN BROUWER.

Nigeria: Badalabougou-est, BP 57, Bamako; tel. 2021-5328; fax 2022-3974; e-mail ngrbko@malinet.ml; Ambassador ILIYA ALI DUNIYA NUHU.

Russia: BP 300, Niarela, Bamako; tel. 2021-5592; fax 2021-9926; e-mail ambrusse_mali@orangemali.net; Ambassador ALEXEY G. DOULIAN.

Saudi Arabia: Villa Bal Harbour, 28 Cité du Niger, BP 81, Bamako; tel. 2021-2528; fax 2021-5064; e-mail mlemb@mofa.gov.sa; Ambassador NAHID BIN ABD AL-RAHMAN AL-HARBI.

Senegal: porte 341, rue 287, angle ave Nelson Mandela, BP 42, Bamako; tel. 2021-0859; fax 2016-9268; Ambassador (vacant).

South Africa: bât. Diarra, Hamdallaye ACI 2000, BP 2015, Bamako; tel. 2029-2925; fax 2029-2926; e-mail bamako@foreign .gov.za; Ambassador R. W. MOKOU.

Spain: porte 81, rue 13, Badalabougou-est, BP 3230, Bamako; tel. 2023-6527; fax 2023-6524; e-mail emb.bamako@maec.es; Ambassador Dr LOURDES MELÉNDEZ GARCÍA.

Tunisia: Quartier du Fleuve, Bamako; tel. 2023-2891; fax 2022-1755; Ambassador TAREK BEN SALEM.

Turkey: Cité du Niger, M-105/112, Niarela, Bamako; tel. 7770-0007; e-mail ambassade.bamako@mfa.gov.tr; internet bamako.be.mfa.gov .tr; Ambassador KEMAL KAYGISIZ.

USA: ACI 2000, rue 243, porte 297, Bamako; tel. 2070-2300; fax 2070-2479; e-mail webmaster@usa.org.ml; internet mali.usembassy.gov; Ambassador MARY BETH LEONARD.

Venezuela: Badalabougou Ouest, Bamako; tel. 2023-2531; fax 2023-2534; Ambassador JOHNY ERREDDY BALZA ARISMENDI.

Judicial System

The 1992 Constitution guarantees the independence of the judiciary.

High Court of Justice: Bamako; competent to try the President of the Republic and ministers of the Government for high treason and for crimes committed in the course of their duties, and their accomplices in any case where state security is threatened; mems designated by the mems of the Assemblée nationale, and renewed annually.

Supreme Court: BP 7, Bamako; tel. 2022-2406; e-mail csupreme@ afribone.net.ml; internet www.cs.insti.ml; f. 1969; comprises judicial, administrative and auditing sections; judicial section comprises five chambers, administrative section comprises two chambers, auditing section comprises three chambers; Pres. NOUHOUM TAPILY; Sec.-Gen. MAMA SININTA.

Constitutional Court: Hamdallaye ACI 2000, Commune IV, BP E 213, Bamako; tel. 2022-5609; fax 2023-4241; e-mail tawatybouba@ yahoo.fr; internet www.cc.insti.ml; f. 1994; Pres. AMADI TAMBA CAMARA; Sec.-Gen. BOUBACAR TAWATY.

There are three Courts of Appeal, seven Tribunaux de Première Instance (Magistrates' Courts) and also courts for labour disputes.

Religion

According to UN figures, around 80% of the population are Muslims, while 18% follow traditional animist beliefs and under 2% are Christians.

ISLAM

Association Malienne pour l'Unité et le Progrès de l'Islam (AMUPI): Bamako; state-endorsed Islamic governing body.

Chief Mosque: pl. de la République, Bagadadji, Bamako; tel. 2021-2190.

Haut Conseil Islamique: Bamako; f. 2002; responsible for management of relations between the Muslim communities and the State; Pres. MAHMOUD DICKO.

CHRISTIANITY

The Roman Catholic Church

Mali comprises one archdiocese and five dioceses. Approximately 2% of the total population practices Roman Catholicism.

Bishops' Conference

Conférence Episcopale du Mali, Archevêché, BP 298, Bamako; tel. 2222-5499; fax 2222-5214; e-mail cemali@afribone.net.ml. f. 1973; Pres. Most Rev. JEAN-BAPTISTE TIAMA (Bishop of Sikasso).

Archbishop of Bamako: JEAN ZERBO, Archevêché, BP 298, Bamako; tel. 2222-5842; fax 2222-7850; e-mail mgrjeanzerbo@ afribonemali.net.

Other Christian Churches

There are several Protestant mission centres, mainly administered by US societies.

BAHÁ'Í FAITH

National Spiritual Assembly: BP 1657, Bamako; e-mail ntirandaz@aol.com.

The Press

The 1992 Constitution guarantees the freedom of the press.

DAILY NEWSPAPERS

Les Echos: Hamdallaye, ave Cheick Zayed, porte 2694, BP 2043, Bamako; tel. 2029-6289; fax 2026-7639; e-mail lesechos@jamana.org; internet www.jamana.org/lesechos; f. 1989; daily; publ. by Jamana cultural co-operative; circ. 30,000; Dir ALEXIS KALAMBRY; Editor-in-Chief ABOUBACAR SALIPH DIARRA.

L'Essor: square Patrice Lumumba, BP 141, Bamako; tel. 2022-3683; fax 2022-4774; e-mail info@essor.gov.ml; internet www.essor.gov .ml; f. 1949; daily; pro-Govt newspaper; Editor SALIM TOGOLA; circ. 3,500.

Info Matin: 56 rue 350, Bamako Coura, BP E 4020, Bamako; tel. 7541-4141; fax 2023-8227; e-mail redaction@info-matin.com; internet www.info-matin.com; independent; Dir of Publication and Editor-in-Chief SAMBI TOURÉ.

Le Républicain: 116 rue 400, Dravéla-Bolibana, BP 1484, Bamako; tel. 2029-0900; fax 2029-0933; internet lerepublicain-mali.com; f. 1992; independent; Dir BOUKARY DAOU.

PERIODICALS

26 Mars: Badalabougou-Sema Gesco, Lot S13, BP MA 174, Bamako; tel. 2029-0459; f. 1998; weekly; independent; Dir BOUBACAR SANGARÉ.

L'Aurore: Niarela 298, rue 438, BP 3150, Bamako; tel. and fax 2021-6922; e-mail aurore@timbagga.com.ml; f. 1990; 2 a week; independent; Dir KARAMOKO N'DIAYE.

Le Canard Déchaîné: Immeuble Koumara, bloc 104, Centre Commercial, Bamako; tel. 7621-2686; fax 2022-8686; e-mail maison.presse@afribone.net.ml; weekly; satirical; Dir OUMAR BABI; circ. 3,000 (2006).

Le Carrefour: ave Cheick Zayed, Hamdallaye, Bamako; tel. 2023-9808; e-mail journalcarrefour@yahoo.fr; f. 1997; Dir MAHAMANE IMRANE COULIBALY.

Le Continent: AA 16, Banankabougou, BP E 4338, Bamako; tel. and fax 2029-5739; e-mail le_continent@yahoo.fr; f. 2000; weekly; Dir IBRAHIMA TRAORÉ.

Le Courrier: 230 ave Cheick Zayed, Lafiabougou Marché, BP 1258, Bamako; tel. and fax 2029-1862; e-mail journalcourrier@webmails.com; f. 1996; weekly; Dir SADOU A. YATTARA; also *Le Courrier Magazine*, monthly.

L'Indépendant: Immeuble ABK, Hamdallaye ACI, BP E 1040, Bamako; tel. and fax 2023-2727; e-mail independant@cefib.com; 2 a week; Dir El Hadj SAOUTI LABASS HAÏDARA.

L'Inspecteur: Immeuble Nimagala, bloc 262, BP E 4534, Bamako; tel. 6672-4711; e-mail inspecteurmali@yahoo.fr; f. 1992; weekly; Dir ALY DIARRA.

Jamana—Revue Culturelle Malienne: BP 2043, Bamako; BP E 1040; e-mail infos@jamana.org; f. 1983; quarterly; organ of Jamana cultural co-operative.

Journal Officiel de la République du Mali: Koulouba, BP 14, Bamako; tel. 2022-5986; fax 2022-7050; official gazette.

Kabaaru: Village Kibaru, Bozola, BP 24, Bamako; f. 1983; state-owned; monthly; Fulbé (Peul) language; rural interest; Editor BARRY BELCO MOUSSA; circ. 3,000.

Kibaru: Village Kibaru, Bozola, BP 1463, Bamako; f. 1972; monthly; state-owned; Bambara and three other languages; rural interest; Editor NIANZÉ SAMAKÉ; circ. 5,000.

Liberté: Immeuble Sanago, Hamdallaye Marché, BP E 24, Bamako; tel. 2028-1898; e-mail ladji.guindo@cefib.com; f. 1999; weekly; Dir ABDOULAYE LADJI GUINDO.

Le Malien: rue 497, porte 277, Badialan III, BP E 1558, Bamako; tel. 2023-5729; fax 2029-1339; e-mail lemalien2000@yahoo.fr; f. 1993; weekly; Dir SIDI KEITA.

Match: 97 rue 498, Lafiabougou, BP E 3776, Bamako; tel. 2029-1882; e-mail bcissouma@yahoo.fr; f. 1997; 2 a month; sports; Dir BABA CISSOUMA.

Musow: BP E 449, Bamako; tel. 2028-0000; fax 2028-0001; e-mail musow@musow.com; internet www.musow.com; women's interest.

Nyéléni Magazine: Niarela 298, rue 348, BP 13150, Bamako; tel. 2029-2401; f. 1991; monthly; women's interest; Dir MAÏMOUNA TRAORÉ.

L'Observateur: Galérie Djigué, rue du 18 juin, BP E 1002, Bamako; tel. and fax 2023-0689; e-mail belcotamboura@hotmail.com; f. 1992; 2 a week; Dir BELCO TAMBOURA.

Le Reflet: Immeuble Kanadjigui, route de Koulikoro, Boulkassoumbougou, BP E 1688, Bamako; tel. 2024-3952; fax 2023-2308; e-mail lereflet@afribone.malinet.ml; weekly; fmrly *Le Carcan*; present name adopted Jan. 2001; Dir ABDOUL KARIM DRAMÉ.

Royal Sports: BP 98, Sikasso; tel. 6672-4988; weekly; also *Tatou Sports*, publ. monthly; Pres. and Dir-Gen. ALY TOURÉ.

Le Scorpion: 230 ave Cheick Zayed, Lafiabougou Marché, BP 1258, Bamako; tel. and fax 2029-1862; f. 1991; weekly; Dir MAHAMANE HAMÈYE CISSÉ.

Le Tambour: rue 497, porte 295, Badialan III, BP E 289, Bamako; tel. and fax 2022-7568; e-mail tambourj@yahoo.fr; f. 1994; 2 a week; Dir YÉRO DIALLO.

NEWS AGENCY

Agence Malienne de Presse et de Publicité (AMAP): square Patrice Lumumba, BP 141, Bamako; tel. 2022-3683; fax 2022-4774; e-mail amap@afribone.net.ml; internet www.amap.ml; f. 1977; Dir SOULEYMANE DRABO.

PRESS ASSOCIATIONS

Association des Editeurs de la Presse Privée (ASSEP): BP E 1002, Bamako; tel. 6671-3133; e-mail belcotamboura@hotmail.com; Pres. DRAMANE ALIOU KONÉ.

Association des Journalistes Professionels des Médias Privés du Mali (AJPM): BP E 2456, Bamako; tel. 2022-1915; fax 2023-5478; Pres. MOMADOU FOFANA.

Association des Professionnelles Africaines de la Communication (APAC MALI): porte 474, rue 428, BP E 731, Bamako; tel. 2021-2912; Pres. MASSIRÉ YATTASSAYE.

Maison de la Presse de Mali: 17 rue 619, Darsalam, BP E 2456, Bamako; tel. 2022-1915; fax 2023-5478; e-mail maison.presse@afribone.net.ml; internet www.mediamali.org; independent media asscn; Pres. SADOU A. YATTARA.

Union Interprofessionnelle des Journalistes et de la Presse de Langue Française (UIJPLF): rue 42, Hamdallaye Marché, BP 1258, Bamako; tel. 2029-9835; Pres. MAHAMANE HAMÉYE CISSÉ.

Union Nationale des Journalistes Maliens (UNAJOM): BP 1300, Bamako; tel. 2022-1915; fax 2023-5478; e-mail ibrafam@yahoo.fr; Pres. IBRAHIM FAMAKAN COULIBALY.

Publishers

EDIM SA: ave Kassé Keïta, BP 21, Bamako; tel. 2022-4041; fax 2029-3001; e-mail edim@afribone.net.ml; f. 1972 as Editions Imprimeries du Mali; general fiction and non-fiction, textbooks; Chair. and Man. Dir ALOU TOMOTA.

Editions Donniya: Cité du Niger, BP 1273, Bamako; tel. 2021-4646; fax 2021-9031; e-mail imprimcolor@cefib.com; internet www.imprimcolor.cefib.com; f. 1996; general fiction, history, reference and children's books in French and Bambara.

Le Figuier: 151 rue 56, Semal, BP 2605, Bamako; tel. and fax 2023-3211; e-mail lefiguier@afribone.net.ml; f. 1997; fiction and non-fiction.

Editions Jamana: BP 2043, Bamako; tel. 2029-6289; fax 2029-7639; e-mail jamana@timbagga.com.ml; internet www.jamana.org; f. 1988; literary fiction, poetry, reference; Dir BA MAÏRA SOW.

Editions Teriya: BP 1677, Bamako; tel. 2024-1142; theatre, literary fiction; Dir GAOUSSOU DIAWARA.

Broadcasting and Communications
TELECOMMUNICATIONS

At the end of 2011 there were two telecommunications companies in Mali, both of which provided mobile and fixed-line telephone services. In January 2012 a third licence to provide mobile telephone services was awarded to a consortium of Planor and Monaco Telecom. In 2010 there were 80,148 subscribers to fixed-line telephone services and 7.4m. subscribers to mobile telephone services.

Orange Mali SA: Immeuble Orange Mali, Hamdallaye, ACI-2000, BP E 3991, Bamako; tel. 4499-9903; fax 4499-9001; e-mail orange@orangemali.com; internet www.orangemali.com; f. 2003 as Ikatel; repackaged under brand name Orange in 2007; fixed-line and mobile cellular telecommunications; jtly owned by France Télécom and Société Nationale des Télécommunications du Sénégal; Dir-Gen. JEAN-LUC BOHÉ; 1,097 fixed lines and 4.7m. subscribers to mobile cellular telecommunications services (2010).

Société des Télécommunications du Mali—Malitel (SOTELMA): Quartier du Fleuve, près de la BCEAO, BP 740, Bamako; tel. 2021-5280; fax 2021-3022; e-mail segal@sotelma.ml; internet www.sotelma.ml; f. 1990; 51% owned by Itissalat al-Maghrib—Maroc Télécom (Morocco), 20% state-owned; operates fixed-line telephone services, also mobile and cellular telecommunications under the brand name Malitel in Bamako, Kayes, Mopti, Ségou and Sikasso; 79,051 fixed lines and 2.69m. subscribers to mobile cellular telecommunications services (2010); Dir-Gen. NOREDDINE BOUMZEBRA.

Regulatory Authority

Comité de Régulation des Télécommunications (CRT): Hamdallaye ACI 2000, rue 390, porte 1849, BP 2206, Bamako; tel. 2023-1490; fax 2023-1494; e-mail crtmali@crt.ml; internet www.crt-mali.org; f. 1999; Dir Dr CHOGUEL K. MAÏGA.

BROADCASTING
Regulatory Authority

Conseil Supérieur de la Communication: BP 1856, Bamako; tel. 2023-2101; fax 2023-2102; f. 1992; Pres. TOGOLA MARIE JACQUELINE NANA.

Radio

In 2010 there were an estimated 400 community, commercial and religious radio stations broadcasting in Mali. Signals from Radio France International, the Voice of America, Radio Chine Internationale, the British Broadcasting Corporation (BBC) and Deutsche Welle are also received.

Office de Radiodiffusion-Télévision Malienne (ORTM): 287 rue de la Marne, BP 171, Bamako; tel. 2021-2019; fax 2021-4205;

e-mail ortm@ortm.ml; internet www.ortm-mali.tv; Dir-Gen. BALLY IDRISSA SISSOKO; Dir of Radio SEYDOU BABA TRAORÉ.

Radio Mali–Chaîne Nationale: BP 171, Bamako; tel. 2021-2019; fax 2021-4205; e-mail ortm@spider.toolnet.org; f. 1957; state-owned; radio programmes in French, Bambara, Peul, Sarakolé, Tamashek, Sonrai, Moorish, Wolof, English.

Chaîne 2: Bamako; f. 1993; radio broadcasts to Bamako.

Fréquence 3: Bamako; f. 1992; commercial.

Radio Balanzan: BP 419, Ségou; tel. 2132-0288; commercial.

Radio Bamakan: Marché de Médine, BP E 100, Bamako; tel. and fax 2021-2760; e-mail radio.bamakan@ifrance.com; internet bamakan.net; f. 1991; community station; 104 hours of FM broadcasts weekly; Man. MODIBO DIALLO.

Radio Espoir—La Voix du Salut: Sogoniko, rue 130, porte 71, BP E 1399, Bamako; tel. 2020-6708; e-mail accm@mali.maf.net; f. 1998; broadcasts 16 hours of radio programming daily on topics including Christianity, devt and culture; Dir DAOUDA COULIBALY.

Radio Foko de Ségou Jamana: BP 2043, Bamako; tel. 2132-0048; fax 2022-7639; e-mail radiofoko@cefib.com.

Radio Guintan: Magnambougou, BP 2546, Bamako; tel. 2020-0938; f. 1994; community radio station; Dir RAMATA DIA.

Radio Jamana: BP 2043, Bamako; tel. 2029-6289; fax 2029-7639; e-mail radio@jamana.org; internet www.jamana.org.

Radio Kayira: Djélibougou Doumanzana, BP 3140, Bamako; tel. 2024-8782; fax 2022-7568; internet www.kayira.org; f. 1992; community station; Dir OUMAR MARIKO.

Radio Klédu: Cité du Niger, BP 2322, Bamako; tel. 2021-0018; e-mail rkledudirect@cefib.com; internet www.kleducommunication.com; f. 1992; commercial; Dir-Gen. JACQUES DEZ.

Radio Liberté: BP 5015, Bamako; tel. 2023-0581; f. 1991; commercial station broadcasting 24 hours daily; Dir ALMANY TOURÉ.

Radio Patriote: Korofina-Sud, BP E 1406, Bamako; tel. 2024-2292; f. 1995; commercial station; Dir MOUSSA KEÏTA.

Radio Rurale de Kayes: Plateau, BP 94, Kayes; tel. 2158-0081; e-mail rrk@afribone.net.ml; internet www.radioruraledekayes.net; f. 1988; community stations established by the Agence de Coopération Culturelle et Technique (ACTT); transmitters in Niono, Kadiolo, Bandiagara and Kidal; Dir FILY KEÏTA.

Radio Sahel: BP 394, Kayes; tel. 2152-2187; f. 1991; commercial; Dir ALMAMY S. TOURÉ.

Radio Tabalé: Bamako-Coura, BP 697, Bamako; tel. and fax 2022-7870; internet www.radiotabale.org; f. 1992; independent public-service station; broadcasting 57 hours weekly; Dir TIÉMOKO KONÉ.

Radio Wassoulou: BP 24, Yanfolila; tel. 2165-1097; internet wassoulou.radio.org.ml; commercial.

La Voix du Coran et du Hadit: Grande Mosquée, BP 2531, Bamako; tel. 2021-6344; f. 1993; Islamic station broadcasting on FM in Bamako; Dir El Hadj MAHMOUD DICKO.

Television

Office de Radiodiffusion-Télévision Malienne (ORTM): see Radio; a second channel, Télévision Malienne 2, was launched on 31 December 2011; Dir of Television BALLY IDRISSA SISSOKO.

Multicanal SA: Quinzambougou, BP E 1506, Bamako; tel. 2020-2929; e-mail sandrine@multi-canal.com; internet www.multi-canal.com; private subscription broadcaster; relays international broadcasts; Pres. ISMAÏLA SIDIBÉ; Dir-Gen. MOHAMED KEITA.

TV Klédu: 600 ave Modibo Keïta, BP E 1172, Bamako; tel. 2023-9000; fax 2023-7050; e-mail info@tvkledu.com; private cable TV operator; relays international broadcasts; Pres. MAMADOU COULIBALY.

Finance

(cap. = capital; res = reserves; dep. = deposits; m. = million; br(s). = branch(es); amounts in francs CFA)

BANKING

In 2009 there were 13 banks and four other financial institutions in Mali.

Central Bank

Banque Centrale des Etats de l'Afrique de l'Ouest (BCEAO): ave Moussa Travele, BP 206, Bamako; tel. 2022-2541; fax 2022-4786; internet www.bceao.int; f. 1962; HQ in Dakar, Senegal; bank of issue for the mem. states of Union Economique et Monétaire Ouest-Africaine (UEMOA, comprising Benin, Burkina Faso, Côte d'Ivoire, Guinea-Bissau, Mali, Niger, Senegal and Togo); cap. 134,120m., res 1,474,195m., dep. 2,124,051m. (Dec. 2009); Gov. KONÉ TIÉMOKO MEYLIET; Dir in Mali KONZO TRAORÉ; brs at Mopti and Sikasso.

Commercial Banks

Bank of Africa—Mali (BOA—MALI): 418 ave de la Marné, Bozola, BP 2249, Bamako; tel. 2070-0500; fax 2070-0560; e-mail information@boamali.net; internet www.boamali.com; f. 1983; cap. 5,500.0m., res 5,818.0m., dep. 139,178.2m. (Dec. 2009); Pres. BOUREIMA SYLLA; Dir-Gen. MAMADOU SENE; 18 brs.

Banque Commerciale du Sahel (BCS–SA): ave Bozola 127, BP 2372, Bamako; tel. 2021-0535; fax 2021-1660; e-mail dg@bcss.mali.com; f. 1980; fmrly Banque Arabe Libyo-Malienne pour le Commerce Extérieur et le Développement; 96.61% owned by Libyan-Arab Foreign Bank; cap. 7,500m., res 1,046m., total assets. 37,953m. (Dec. 2006); Pres. KABA DIAMINATOU DIALLO; Dir-Gen. IBRAHIM ABOUJAFAR SWEAI; 1 br.

Banque de l'Habitat du Mali (BHM): ACI 2000, ave Kwamé N'Krumah, BP 2614, Bamako; tel. 2022-9190; fax 2022-9350; e-mail bhm@bhm-sa.com; internet www.bhm-sa.com; f. 1990; present name adopted 1996; 25.8% owned by Institut National de Prévoyance Social; cap. and res 5,414.7m., total assets 98,237.5m. (Dec. 2003); Pres. and Dir-Gen. MODIBO CISSÉ; 5 brs.

Banque Internationale pour le Commerce et l'Industrie au Mali (BICI–Mali): blvd du 22 octobre 1946, Quartier du Fleuve, BP 72, Bamako; tel. 2070-0700; fax 2023-3373; e-mail bicim-dg@africa.bnpparibas.com; f. 1998; 85% owned by BNP Paribas BDDI Participations (France); cap. and res 3,678m., total assets 40,076m. (Dec. 2003); Pres. and Dir-Gen. PIERRE BEREGOVOY; 1 br.

Banque Internationale pour le Mali (BIM): ave de l'Indépendance, BP 15, Bamako; tel. 2022-5066; fax 2022-4566; e-mail bim@bim.com.ml; internet www.bim.com.ml; f. 1980; present name adopted 1995; 51% owned by Attijariwafa Bank Group (Morocco), 10.5% state-owned; cap. 4,254m., dep. 120,250m., total assets 131,159m. (Dec. 2006); Pres. and Dir-Gen. MOHAMMED KRISNI; 14 brs.

Ecobank Mali: Immeuble Amadou Sow, pl. de la Nation, Quartier du Fleuve, BP E 1272, Bamako; tel. 2070-0600; fax 2023-3305; e-mail ecobankml@ecobank.com; internet www.ecobank.com; f. 1998; 49.5% owned by Ecobank Transnational Inc, 17.8% by Ecobank Bénin, 14.9% by Ecobank Togo, 9.9% by Ecobank Burkina; total assets 596m. (Dec. 2011); Pres. SAMBA DIALLO; Dir-Gen. BINTA N'DOYE TOURÉ; 2 brs.

Development Banks

Banque de Développement du Mali (BDM–SA): ave Modibo Keita, Quartier du Fleuve, BP 94, Bamako; tel. 2022-2050; fax 2022-5085; e-mail info@bdm-sa.com; internet www.bdm-sa.com; f. 1968; absorbed Banque Malienne de Crédit et de Dépôts in 2001; 27.38% owned by Banque Marocaine du Commerce Extérieur (Morocco), 19.58% state-owned, 15.96% by BCEAO, 15.96% by Banque Ouest-Africaine de Développement; cap. and res 15,658m., total assets 276,148m. (Dec. 2002); Pres. and Dir-Gen. ABDOULAYE DAFFÉ; 14 brs.

Banque Malienne de Solidarité (BMS): ave du Fleuve, Immeuble Dette Publique, 2e étage, BP 1280, Bamako; tel. and fax 2023-5034; e-mail bms-sa@bms-sa.com; f. 2002; cap. 2.4m.; Dir BABALI BAH; 1 br.

Banque Nationale de Développement Agricole—Mali (BNDA—Mali): Immeuble BNDA, blvd du Mali, ACI 2000, BP 2424, Bamako; tel. 2029-6464; fax 2029-2575; e-mail bnda@bndamali.com; internet www.bndamali.com; f. 1981; 36.5% state-owned, 22.8% owned by Agence Française de Développement (France), 21.4% owned by Deutsche Entwicklungsgesellschaft (Germany), 19.4% owned by BCEAO; cap. 12,096.2m., res 2,059.0m., dep. 125,447.5m. (Dec. 2008); Chair., Pres. and Gen. Man. MOUSSA ALASSAME DIALLO; 22 brs.

Financial Institutions

Direction Générale de la Dette Publique: Immeuble ex-Caisse Autonome d'Amortissement, Quartier du Fleuve, BP 1617, Bamako; tel. 2022-2935; fax 2022-0793; management of the public debt; Dir NAMALA KONÉ.

Equibail Mali: rue 376, porte 1319, Niarela, BP E 566, Bamako; tel. 2021-3777; fax 2021-3778; e-mail equip.ma@bkofafrica.com; f. 1999; 50.2% owned by African Financial Holding, 17.5% by Bank of Africa—Benin; cap. 300m. (Dec. 2002); Mems of Administrative Council RAMATOULAYE TRAORÉ, PAUL DERREUMAUX, LÉON NAKA.

Société Malienne de Financement (SOMAFI): Immeuble Air Afrique, blvd du 22 octobre 1946, BP E 3643, Bamako; tel. 2022-1866; fax 2022-1869; e-mail somafi@malinet.ml; f. 1997; cap. and res 96.9m., total assets 3,844.9m. (Dec. 2002); Man. Dir ERIC LECLÈRE.

STOCK EXCHANGE

Bourse Régionale des Valeurs Mobilières (BRVM): Chambre de Commerce et de l'Industrie du Mali, pl. de la Liberté, BP E 1398, Bamako; tel. 2023-2354; fax 2023-2359; e-mail abocoum@brvm.org; f. 1998; nat. branch of BRVM (regional stock exchange based in

Abidjan, Côte d'Ivoire, serving the mem. states of UEMOA); Man.
AMADOU DJÉRI BOCOUM.

INSURANCE

Allianz Mali: ave de la Nation, BP E4447, Bamako; tel. 2022-4165;
fax 2023-0034; e-mail allianz.mali@allianz-ml.com; internet www
.allianz-africa.com/mali/index.php; Dir-Gen. OLIVIER PICARD.

Assurances Lafia: Immeuble Assurances Lafia SA, Hamdallaye
ACI 2000, ave du Mali, BP 1542, Bamako; tel. 2029-0940; fax 2029-
5223; e-mail info@assurancelafia.com; internet www.assurancelafia
.com; f. 1983; cap. 1,000m.; Dir-Gen. AMINATA DEMBÉLÉ CISSÉ; 17 brs.

**Caisse Nationale d'Assurance et de Réassurance du Mali
(CNAR):** square Patrice Lumumba, BP 568, Bamako; tel. 2021-
3117; fax 2021-2369; f. 1969; state-owned; cap. 50m.; Dir-Gen. F.
KEITA; 10 brs.

Colina Mali SA: ave Modibo Keita, BP E 154, Bamako; tel. 2022-
5775; fax 2023-2423; e-mail mali@groupecolina.com; internet www
.groupecolina.com/fr/ml; f. 1990; cap. 1,000m.; Dir-Gen. MARCUS K.
LABAN.

Compagnie d'Assurance Privée—La Soutra: BP 52, Bamako;
tel. 2022-3681; fax 2022-5523; f. 1979; cap. 150m.; Chair. AMADOU
NIONO.

Compagnie d'Assurance et de Réassurance de Mali: BP 1822,
Bamako; tel. 2022-6029.

Compagnie d'Assurance et de Réassurance Sabu Nyuman:
rue 350, porte 129, Bamako-Coura, BP 1822, Bamako; tel. 2022-6029;
fax 2022-5750; e-mail assur.sn@malinet.ml; f. 1984; cap. 250m.; Pres.
MOMADOU SANOGO; Dir-Gen. YAYA DIARRA.

Gras Savoye Mali: Immeuble SOGEFIH, 3e etage, Quartier du
Fleuve, ave Moussa Travele, BP E 5691, Bamako; tel. 2022-6469; fax
2022-6470; e-mail grassavoyemali@ml.grassavoye.com; affiliated to
Gras Savoye (France); Man. FAYEZ SAMB.

Nouvelle Alliance d'Assurance (NALLIAS): BP 12671, Bamako;
tel. 2022-2244; fax 2022-9422; e-mail contact@nalliasmali.com;
f. 2007; Dir-Gen. CHEIKNA DIAWARA.

Nouvelle Société Interafricaine d'Assurance (NSIA Mali):
Immeuble du Patronat, derrière le Gouvernorat, ACI 2000, Bamako;
tel. 2023-2440; fax 2023-2441; f. 2009; Dir-Gen. GEORGES ALAIN
N'GORAN; also (NSIA Vie Mali) ; Dir-Gen. KODJO SALAMI WOROU.

Société Nouvelle d'Assurance—Vie (SONA—VIE): Immeuble
Sonavie, ACI 2000, BP E 2217, Bamako; tel. 2029-5400; fax 2029-
5501; internet www.sonavie.com; f. 1996; Dir-Gen. MAMADOU TOURÉ.

Trade and Industry

GOVERNMENT AGENCIES

Agence Nationale pour l'Emploi (ANPE): BP 211, Bamako; tel.
2022-3187; fax 2023-2624; e-mail anpe@anpe-mali.org; internet
www.anpe-mali.org; f. 2001; Dir-Gen. Prof. MAKAN MOUSSA SISSOKO.

**Agence pour la Promotion des Investissements au Mali (API-
Mali):** Quartier du Fleuve, BP 1980, Bamako; tel. 2022-9525; fax
2022-9527; e-mail contact@apimali.gov.ml; internet www.apimali
.gov.ml; f. 2005; CEO MODIBO KEITA.

**Autorité pour la Promotion de la Recherche Petrolière
(AUREP):** Médina Coura, rue 28, porte 189, BP E 4306, Bamako;
tel. 2021-2948; fax 2021-2882; e-mail diawara.baba@aurep.org;
internet www.aurep.org; f. 2003; Dir-Gen. BABA DIAWARA.

Direction Nationale des Affaires Economiques (DNAE): BP
210, Bamako; tel. 2022-2314; fax 2022-2256; involved in economic
and social affairs.

Direction Nationale des Travaux Publics (DNTP): ave de la
Liberté, BP 1758, Bamako; tel. and fax 2022-2902; administers public
works.

Guichet Unique–Direction Nationale des Industries: rue Titi
Niare, Quinzambougou, BP 96, Bamako; tel. and fax 2022-3166.

Office National des Produits Pétroliers (ONAP): Quartier du
Fleuve, rue 315, porte 141, BP 2070, Bamako; tel. 2022-2827; fax
2022-4483; e-mail onapmali@afribone.net.ml; Dir-Gen. TAPA NOUGA
NADIO.

Office du Niger: BP 106, Ségou; tel. 2132-0292; fax 2132-0143;
e-mail on@office-du-niger.org.ml; internet www.office-du-niger.org
.ml; f. 1932; taken over from the French authorities in 1958;
restructured in mid-1990s; cap. 7,139m. francs CFA; principally
involved in cultivation of food crops, particularly rice; the Office du
Niger zone is the western region of the Central Niger Delta; Pres. and
Dir-Gen. AMADOU BOYE COULIBALY.

Office des Produits Agricoles du Mali (OPAM): BP 132,
Bamako; tel. 2022-3755; fax 2021-0406; e-mail opam@cefib.com;
f. 1965; state-owned; manages National (Cereals) Security Stock,
administers food aid, responsible for sales of cereals and distribution
to deficit areas; cap. 5,800m. francs CFA; Pres. and Dir-Gen. BAKARY
DIALLO.

DEVELOPMENT ORGANIZATIONS

Agence pour le Développement du Nord-Mali (ADN): Gao;
f. 2005 to replace l'Autorité pour le Développement Intégré du Nord-
Mali; govt agency with financial autonomy; promotes devt of regions
of Tombouctou, Gao and Kidal; br. in Bamako.

Agence Française de Développement (AFD): Quinzambougou,
route de Sotuba, BP 32, Bamako; tel. 2021-2842; fax 2021-8646;
e-mail afdbamako@groupe-afd.org; internet www.afd.fr; Country
Dir HERVÉ BOUGAULT.

Office de Développement Intégré du Mali-Ouest (ODIMO): pl.
Patrice Lumumba, Bamako; tel. 2022-5759; f. 1991 to succeed Office
de Développement Intégré des Productions Arachidières et Cér-
éalières; devt of diversified forms of agricultural production; Man.
Dir ZANA SANOGO.

Service de Coopération et d'Action Culturelle: square Patrice
Lumumba, BP 84, Bamako; tel. 2021-8338; fax 2021-8339; e-mail
scac.bamako-amba@diplomatie.gouv.fr; administers bilateral aid
from France; Dir YVES GUEYMARD.

CHAMBERS OF COMMERCE

Chambre de Commerce et d'Industrie du Mali (CCIM): pl. de la
Liberté, BP 46, Bamako; tel. 2022-5036; fax 2022-2120; e-mail ccim@
cimali.org; internet www.ccimmali.org; f. 1906; Pres. JEAMILLE
BITTAR; Sec.-Gen. DABA TRAORÉ.

Chambre des Mines du Mali (CMM): Bamako; f. 2004; Pres.
ABDOULAYE PONA; Sec.-Gen. SÉKOU DIORO DICKO.

EMPLOYERS' ASSOCIATIONS

**Association Malienne des Exportateurs de Légumes (AME-
LEF):** Bamako; tel. 7608-9048; fax 2029-2836; f. 1984; Pres. BAKARY
YAFFA; Sec.-Gen. BIRAMA TRAORÉ.

**Association Malienne des Exportateurs de Ressources Ani-
males (AMERA):** Bamako; tel. 2022-5683; f. 1985; Pres. AMBARKÉ
YERMANGORE; Admin. Sec. ALI HACKO.

Conseil National du Patronat du Mali (CNPM): Immeuble du
Patronat, Hamdallaye, ACI 2000, derrière le Gouvernorat du District, route de Sotuba, BP 2445, Bamako; tel. 2021-6311; fax 2021-
9077; e-mail cnpm@cnpmali.org; internet www.cnpmali.org; f. 1980
as Fédération Nationale des Employeurs du Mali; Pres. MAMADOU
SIDIBÉ; 39 professional groups and 5 regional employers' associations.

UTILITIES

Commission de Régulation de l'Électricité et l'Eau: Bamako;
f. 2000; Pres. MOCTAR TOURÉ.

Electricity

**Agence Malienne pour le Développement de l'Energie Domes-
tique et l'Electrification Rurale** (AMADER): colline de Badalabougou, BP E 715, Bamako; tel. 2023-8567; fax 2023–8239; e-mail
itoure@amadermali.net; internet www.amadermali.org; f. 2003;
Pres. and Dir-Gen. ISMAËL O. TOURÉ.

Energie du Mali (EdM): square Patrice Lumumba, BP 69, Bamako;
tel. 2022-3020; fax 2022-8430; e-mail sekou.edm@cefib.com; internet
www.edm-sa.com.ml; f. 1960; 66% state-owned, 34% owned by
Industrial Promotion Services (West-Africa); planning, construction
and operation of power-sector facilities; cap. 7,880m. francs CFA;
Pres. OUSMANE ISSOUFI MAÏGA; Dir-Gen. SÉKOU ALPHA DJITÈYE.

Enertech GSA: marché de Lafiabougou, BP 1949, Bamako; tel.
2022-3763; fax 2022-5136; f. 1994; cap. 20m. francs CFA; solar energy
producer; Dir MOCTAR DIAKITÉ.

Société de Gestion de l'Energie de Manantali (SOGEM):
Parcelle 2501, ACI 2000, BP E 4015, Bamako; tel. 2023-3286; fax
2023-8350; generates and distributes electricity from the Manantali
hydro-electric project, under the auspices of the Organisation pour la
Mise en Valeur du Fleuve Sénégal; Dir-Gen. SALOUM CISSÉ.

Gas

Air Liquide Maligaz: route de Sotuba, BP 5, Bamako; tel. 2022-
2394; internet www.ml.airliquide.com; gas distribution.

There are four other gas distributors in Mali: Sodigaz, Fasogaz, Sigaz
and Total.

Water

Société Malienne de Gestion de l'Eau Potable (SOMAGEP):
Bamako; f. 2010; responsible for the operation of public drinking
water supplies; Pres. BOUBACAR KANÉ.

Société Malienne du Patrimoine de l'Eau Potable (SOMA-PEP): Bamako; f. 2010; responsible for the management and development of infrastructure for supplying drinking water; Pres. ADAMA TIÉMOKO DIARRA.

TRADE UNION FEDERATION

Union Nationale des Travailleurs du Mali (UNTM): Bourse du Travail, blvd de l'Indépendance, BP 169, Bamako; tel. 2022-3699; fax 2023-5945; f. 1963; 13 nat. and 8 regional unions, and 52 local orgs; Sec.-Gen. SIAKA DIAKITÉ.

There are, in addition, several non-affiliated trade unions.

Transport

RAILWAYS

Mali's only railway runs from Koulikoro, via Bamako, to the Senegal border. The line continues to Dakar, Senegal, a total distance of 1,286 km, of which 729 km is in Mali. The track is in very poor condition, and is frequently closed during the rainy season. In 1995 the Governments of Mali and Senegal agreed to establish a joint company to operate the Bamako–Dakar line, and the line passed fully into private ownership in 2003. Plans exist for the construction of a new rail line linking Bamako with Kouroussa and Kankan, in Guinea.

Transrail SA: Immeuble la Roseraie, 310 ave de la liberté, BP 4150, Bamako; tel. 2022-5967; fax 2022-5433; e-mail ericpeiffer@transrailsa.com; f. 2003 on transfer to private management of fmr Régie du Chemin de Fer du Mali; jt venture of Canac (Canada) and Getma (France); Dir-Gen. ERIC PEIFFER.

ROADS

The Malian road network in 2009 comprised 22,474 km, of which about 5,529 km were paved. A bituminized road between Bamako and Abidjan (Côte d'Ivoire) provides Mali's main economic link to the coast; construction of a road linking Bamako and Dakar (Senegal) is to be financed by the European Development Fund. The African Development Bank also awarded a US $31.66m. loan to fund the Kankan–Kouremale–Bamako road between Mali and Guinea. In addition, there are plans to build a road across the Sahara to link Mali with Algeria.

Autorité Routière du Mali: rue 320, porte 153, Hamdallaye ACI 2000, 03 BP 12, Bamako; tel. 2029-1125; fax 2029-1108; e-mail infos@arfer-mali.net; internet www.arfer-mali.net; f. 2001; Dir-Gen. MORY KANTÉ.

INLAND WATERWAYS

The River Niger is navigable in parts of its course through Mali (1,693 km) during the rainy season from July to late December. The River Senegal was, until the early 1990s, navigable from Kayes to Saint-Louis (Senegal) only between August and November, but its navigability improved following the inauguration, in 1992, of the Manantali dam, and the completion of works to deepen the river-bed.

Compagnie Malienne de Navigation (COMANAV): BP 10, Koulikoro; tel. 2026-2094; fax 2026-2009; f. 1968; 100% state-owned; river transport; Pres. and Dir-Gen. DEMBÉLÉ GOUNDO DIALLO.

Conseil Malien des Chargeurs (CMC): Dar-salam, BP E 4031, Bamako; tel. 2023-0486; fax 2023-0489; e-mail contact@cmchargeurs.com; internet www.cmchargeurs.com; f. 1999; Pres. OUSMANE BABALAYE DAOU.

Société Navale Malienne (SONAM): Bamako-Coura, BP 2581, Bamako; tel. 2021-6066; fax 2022-6066; f. 1981; transferred to private ownership in 1986; Chair. ALIOUNE KEÏTA.

Société Ouest-Africaine d'Entreprise Maritime (SOAEM): rue Mohamed V, BP 2428, Bamako; tel. 2022-5832; fax 2022-4024; maritime transport co.

CIVIL AVIATION

The principal airport is at Bamako-Senou. The other major airports are at Bourem, Gao, Goundam, Kayes, Kita, Mopti, Nioro, Ségou, Tessalit and Tombouctou. There are about 40 small airfields. Mali's airports are being modernized with external financial assistance. In early 2005 the Malian Government announced the creation of a new national airline, in partnership with the Aga Khan Fund for Economic Development and Industrial Promotion Services.

Aéroports du Mali: Bamako; internet www.aeroportsdumali.com; f. 1970; responsible for commercial exploitation, maintenance and development of airports; Pres. and Dir-Gen. AYA THIAM DIALLO.

Agence Nationale de l'Aviation Civile (ANAC): route de l'Aéroport de Bamako, Sénou, BP 227, Bamako; tel. 2020-5524; fax 2020-6175; e-mail anacmali@hotmail.com; internet www.anac-mali.org; f. 2005 to replace Direction Nationale de l'Aéronautique Civile (f. 1990); Pres. TOURÉ ALIMATA TRAORÉ; Dir-Gen. ISSA SALEY MAÏGA.

Air Mali: Immeuble Tomota, ave Cheick Zayed, BP E 2286, Bamako; tel. 2022-2424; fax 2022-7111; e-mail dc.cam@cam-mali.org; internet www.air-mali.com; f. 2005; 51% owned by Fonds Aga Khan pour le Développement Economique (AKAFED), 20% state-owned; domestic and international flights; Dir-Gen. ABDERRAHMANE BERTHÉ.

STA Trans African Airlines: Quartier du Fleuve, BP 775, Bamako; tel. 2022-4444; fax 2021-0981; internet www.sta-airlines.com; f. 1984 as Société des Transports Aériens; privately owned; local, regional and international services; Man. Dir MELHEM ELIE SABBAGUE.

Tourism

Mali's rich cultural heritage is promoted as a tourist attraction. In 2010 169,305 tourists visited Mali, while receipts from tourism totalled some US $205m.

Ministry of Handicrafts and Tourism: see section on The Government.

Defence

As assessed at November 2012, the active Malian army numbered some 7,350 men. Paramilitary forces numbered 4,800 and there was an inactive militia of 3,000 men. Military service is by selective conscription and lasts for two years. Following the escalation of an Islamist insurgency during 2012, in January 2013 some 4,000 French ground troops, together with military fighter jet, undertook an intervention mission in northern Mali. The UN Security Council had in December 2012 authorized the deployment of an African-led International Support Mission to Mali (AFISMA) to assist the Malian armed forces in combating the insurgency. In April 2013 the Security Council approved a resolution providing for the reconstitution of AFISMA (then numbering about 6,300 forces under the command of ECOWAS) into the United Nations Multidimensional Integrated Stabilization Mission in Mali (MINUSMA), comprising 11,200 troops and 1,440 police officers, with a 12-month mandate effective from 1 July.

Defence Expenditure: Estimated at 107,000m. francs CFA in 2011.

Chief of Staff of the Armed Forces: Gen. IBRAHIMA DAHIROU DEMBELE.

Chief of Staff of the Air Force: Col MAMADOU TOGOLO.

Chief of Staff of the Land Army: Col MAMADOU ADAMA DIALLO.

Chief of Staff of the National Guard: Col BROULAYE KONÉ.

Education

Education is provided free of charge and is officially compulsory for nine years between seven and 16 years of age. Basic education, which includes six years of primary education, begins at the age of seven and lasts for nine years. Secondary education, from 16 years of age, lasts for a further three years. The rate of school enrolment in Mali is among the lowest in the world. According to UNESCO, in 2010/11 primary enrolment included 63% of children in the appropriate age-group (males 67%; females 59%), while secondary enrolment included only 31% of those in the appropriate age-group (males 36%; females 25%). Tertiary education facilities include the national university, developed in the mid-1990s. In 2010/11 there were some 87,700 students enrolled in tertiary education. Hitherto many students have received higher education abroad, mainly in France and Senegal. In 2010 spending on education represented 16.4% of total budgetary expenditure.

MALTA

Introductory Survey

LOCATION, CLIMATE, LANGUAGE, RELIGION, FLAG, CAPITAL

The Republic of Malta is in southern Europe. The country comprises an archipelago in the central Mediterranean Sea, consisting of the inhabited islands of Malta, Gozo and Comino, and the uninhabited islets of Cominotto, Filfla and St Paul's. The main island, Malta, lies 93 km (58 miles) south of the Italian island of Sicily and 288 km (179 miles) east of the Tunisian coast, the nearest point on the North African mainland. The climate is warm, with average temperatures of 22.6°C (72.7°F) in summer and 13.7°C (56.6°F) in winter. Average annual rainfall is 578 mm (22.8 ins). Maltese and English are the official languages, although Italian is widely spoken. About 95% of the inhabitants are Christians adhering to the Roman Catholic Church, the country's established religion. The national flag (proportions 2 by 3) consists of two equal vertical stripes, white at the hoist and red at the fly, with a representation of the George Cross, edged with red, in the upper hoist. The capital is Valletta, on the island of Malta.

CONTEMPORARY POLITICAL HISTORY

Historical Context

Malta, which had been a Crown Colony of the United Kingdom since 1814, became an independent sovereign state, within the Commonwealth, in September 1964. The Government, led by Dr Giorgio Borg-Olivier of the Nationalist Party (Partit Nazzjonalista—PN), negotiated defence and financial aid agreements, effective over a 10-year period, with the United Kingdom.

In June 1971 the Malta Labour Party (MLP), led by Dom Mintoff, assumed power after winning a general election. Pursuing a policy of non-alignment, the Government concluded agreements for cultural, economic and commercial co-operation with Italy, Libya, Tunisia, the USSR, several East European countries, the USA, the People's Republic of China and others. The MLP Government abrogated the 1964 Mutual Defence and Assistance Agreement with the United Kingdom. This agreement was replaced in 1972 by a new seven-year agreement, under which Malta was to receive substantially increased rental payments for the use of military facilities by the United Kingdom and other members of the North Atlantic Treaty Organization (NATO, see p. 380). British troops were finally withdrawn in March 1979.

Domestic Political Affairs

Malta became a republic in December 1974. The MLP retained power at general elections held in September 1976 and in December 1981, when it secured a majority of three seats in the 65-seat House of Representatives, although obtaining only 49.1% of the votes cast. The PN, which had received 50.9% of the votes cast, contested the result, refused to take its seats in the legislature and organized a campaign of civil disobedience. In March 1983 the PN terminated its legislative boycott, but immediately withdrew again, in protest against a government resolution to loosen ties with the European Community (EC, now the European Union—EU, see p. 281). Although Mintoff promised constitutional amendments and weekly consultations with the opposition, these arrangements collapsed in June, when the MLP blamed the PN for a bomb attack on government offices. In November a police raid on the PN headquarters was alleged to have discovered a cache of arms and ammunition.

In June 1983 the House of Representatives approved controversial legislation, under which about 75% of church property was to be expropriated to provide finance for a programme of universal free education and the abolition of fee-paying church schools. Opponents of the measure denounced it as unconstitutional and a violation of religious liberty, and in September 1984 the courts disallowed the legislation. In April 1984 the House of Representatives approved legislation forbidding any school to accept fees (including voluntary gifts and donations). The Roman Catholic Archbishop of Malta rejected the government conditions and ordered the closure of all church schools, in response to growing tensions and public unrest. An agreement was finally reached in November, when the schools were re-opened.

Mintoff retired in December 1984 and was replaced as Prime Minister by the new leader of the MLP, Dr Carmelo Mifsud Bonnici. In April 1985 the Government reached agreement with the Roman Catholic Church, providing for the phased introduction of free education in church secondary schools, and guaranteeing the autonomy of church schools. However, in July 1988 the enforced introduction of new licensing procedures for church schools led to demands by the Roman Catholic Church that the state should reduce its supervisory powers over church education.

At a general election held in May 1987 the PN obtained 50.9% of the votes cast, but won only 31 of the 65 seats in the House of Representatives, while the MLP, with 48.9% of the votes cast, won the remaining 34 seats. However, in accordance with a constitutional amendment that had been adopted in January (see Constitution and Government), the PN was allocated four additional seats, giving it a majority of one in the legislature, thus ending the MLP's 16-year tenure in office. The leader of the PN, Dr Eddie Fenech Adami, became Prime Minister. The PN secured an increased majority of three seats over the MLP at a general election held in February 1992. This result was widely interpreted as an endorsement of the PN's pro-EC policies.

Application for EU membership

On becoming Prime Minister in May 1987, Fenech Adami declared that the Government, while retaining Malta's policy of non-alignment, would seek closer relations with the USA and other Western countries, and would apply for full membership of the EC. A formal application for full membership of the EC was submitted by the Maltese Government in July 1990. In June 1993 the European Commission recommended that, subject to the Government of Malta's satisfying the Commission's requirements for regulatory reforms in financial services, competition and consumer protection, favourable consideration should be given to the future accession of Malta to the EU (as the EC had become in 1992).

Domestic opposition to Maltese accession to the EU had been led by the MLP, on the grounds that EU agricultural policies would increase the cost of living, and that integration into the EU would conflict with Malta's traditional neutrality in its foreign relations. In September 1996 the PN Government, seeking to confirm its mandate to pursue the goal of full membership of the EU, called a general election for the following month. Although the PN contested the election on its record of economic success, the Government's introduction of value-added tax (VAT), as a precondition of Malta's admission to the EU, had proved unpopular with the electorate, and its proposed abolition by the MLP (which would concurrently disqualify Malta from EU membership) was widely regarded as the decisive factor in the election. With a participation rate of 97.1% of eligible voters, the MLP won 50.7% of the votes cast, compared with 47.8% for the PN. The MLP obtained 31 seats in the House of Representatives, while the PN received 34. In accordance with the Constitution, the subsequent allocation of an additional four seats to the MLP gave the party a one-seat majority in the legislature. Dr Alfred Sant, the leader of the MLP, formed a new Government with the declared intention of replacing the existing association agreement, signed in 1970, with new arrangements providing for an eventual free trade zone between Malta and the EU.

In February 1997 the Government announced the initiation of a 'national discussion' of proposals to legalize divorce. However, the imposition of tax increases and levies on public utilities substantially diminished the Government's popularity. Sant called a general election for September, three years earlier than constitutionally required, at which the PN, led by Fenech Adami, obtained a five-seat majority. Fenech Adami subsequently reactivated Malta's application for full membership of the EU. Accession negotiations recommenced in February 2000. In November of that year the Commission published a report stating that Malta was among the best-equipped economically of applicant countries. However, further action was required in

Malta to reduce state aid (notably the politically sensitive annual subsidy to the island's dry docks), to implement privatization plans and to strengthen tax and customs administrations.

Talks over EU accession were formally concluded on 13 December 2002. Malta had obtained 77 exemptions in the discussions, aimed largely at protecting its industrial and agricultural sectors, but also including cultural issues, such as the right to maintain the ban on divorce. A non-binding referendum was called for 8 March 2003 to determine whether the country would join the EU. Support for membership of the EU was led by the ruling PN and opposition to it by the MLP. Following an acrimonious campaign, 53.6% of valid votes cast were in favour of EU membership.

In accordance with the Constitution, Fenech Adami called a general election for 12 April 2003 to confirm the referendum result, four days before the proposed signing of the EU accession treaty by Malta and nine other applicant countries. At the election the PN won an absolute majority of 35 seats with 51.8% of the votes, while the MLP secured 30 seats (47.5%). Fenech Adami was sworn in as Prime Minister on 14 April and signed the EU accession treaty in Athens, Greece, on 16 April. The House of Representatives ratified the treaty on 14 July by 34 votes to 25 (with six members boycotting the vote). Malta became a full member of the EU on 1 May 2004.

Developments following EU accession

After the MLP's defeat at the 2003 general election, the party leadership decided to accept the majority public opinion in favour of accession to the EU and work within the reality of EU membership. This decision proved divisive, and was resisted by a faction of the MLP led by Mifsud Bonnici. However, delegates at a subsequent party conference agreed that the MLP would not withdraw Malta from the EU if the party came to power.

In February 2004 Fenech Adami announced his intention to retire as leader of the PN and as Prime Minister. At a party conference later that month the Deputy Prime Minister and Minister for Social Policy, Dr Lawrence Gonzi, was elected as the PN's new leader. On his assumption of the premiership in March, Gonzi stated that his main priorities would be full participation in the EU, the creation of jobs and the improvement of the economy. Gonzi assumed responsibility for the finance portfolio and appointed his former rival for the party leadership, John Dalli, as Minister for Foreign Affairs. Later in March Fenech Adami was elected President by the House of Representatives, by 33 votes to 29, following his nomination by Gonzi. His appointment was controversial, as party leaders had not traditionally stood for the post, and it was bitterly opposed by the MLP. Fenech Adami was sworn in as President in April.

In July 2004 Dalli resigned as Minister of Foreign Affairs, claiming he was unable to continue amid attacks from 'different sides', which was thought to be a reference to criticism from within the PN. There were also allegations, which Dalli denied, of irregularities involving a large shipping deal and the handling of ministry travel expenses. He was replaced by his junior minister, Michael Frendo.

On 8 March 2008 Malta held its first general election since joining the EU. The PN, which had emphasized its economic achievements during the electoral campaign, emerged victorious with 49.3% of the votes cast, while the MLP won 48.8% but secured the majority of parliamentary seats (34 seats, compared with 31 for the PN); 93.3% of the electorate voted. Consequently, the PN was assigned four additional seats to ensure that it had a parliamentary majority. Following the announcement of the results, Sant immediately resigned as MLP leader. In Prime Minister Gonzi's new Cabinet the Minister for Gozo, Giovanna Debono, was the only member of the outgoing administration to retain the same portfolio. Dr Tonio Borg remained as Deputy Prime Minister but was allocated the foreign affairs portfolio in place of justice and home affairs, while the former parliamentary secretaries, Dr Tonio Fenech and Mifsud Bonnici, were appointed Minister for Finance, the Economy and Investment and Minister for Justice and Home Affairs, respectively. Dalli was reappointed to the Cabinet as Minister for Social Policy.

In June 2008 Dr Joseph Muscat was elected as the new leader of the MLP. On assuming the post, Muscat indicated his intention to rejuvenate the party's image and to reform its internal structures. At a special party conference held in November, delegates approved a programme of reforms, most notably including changing the party's official title to Partit Laburista (PL).

On 1 April 2009 Dr George Abela of the PL (Muscat's main rival in the party leadership election) was unanimously elected

President by the House of Representatives, having been nominated by Gonzi, in accordance with an agreement reached by the two main parties earlier that year. It was the first time that a Prime Minister had proposed a member of an opposing party for the presidency. Abela was sworn in on 4 April.

In November 2009 Prime Minister Gonzi nominated Dalli to assume Malta's seat on the European Commission. Dalli duly relinquished his ministerial post in February 2010. Erstwhile parliamentary secretary Joe Cassar assumed much of Dalli's portfolio in his new cabinet role as Minister for Health, the Elderly and Community Care, while the Minister for Education and Culture, Dolores Cristina, was given additional responsibility for family affairs.

In July 2010 a private member's bill proposing the legalization of divorce in Malta (a long-standing point of controversy) was introduced in the House of Representatives by a member of the PN, apparently without the prior knowledge of the party leadership. Support for an amended version of the bill, which was presented in December, was expressed by some members of both the main parties, but opposition appeared to be more prevalent among members of the PN. A motion proposing a referendum on the issue received parliamentary approval in March 2011 after Gonzi, although expressing his personal opposition to divorce, allowed representatives of the PN a free vote. The referendum, which was not legally binding, took place on 28 May 2011 and posed the question of whether a divorce should be permitted after four years of marital separation (provided that adequate maintenance was guaranteed and the welfare of any children safeguarded); of the 72% of the electorate who participated, 53.2% voted in favour of the legalization of divorce. The appropriate legislation was accordingly adopted by the House of Representatives in July, and entered into force on 1 October.

In November 2011, after the introduction of widely criticized changes to the national bus system, the opposition proposed a motion of no confidence in the Minister for Infrastructure, Transport and Communications, Austin Gatt. A member of the ruling PN, Franco Debono (who had criticized the Government on various issues, in particular its failure to reform the judicial system), abstained in the vote, and the Government therefore only escaped defeat when the Speaker of the House of Representatives used his casting vote in its favour.

In January 2012 Gonzi made several changes in the Cabinet, including the division of the Ministry of Justice and Home Affairs into two (an action that Debono had repeatedly demanded): Mifsud Bonnici, formerly responsible for the joint portfolio, became Minister for Home Affairs, Local Government and Parliamentary Affairs, while Chris Said, hitherto a parliamentary secretary, became Minister of Justice, Public Dialogue and the Family. Debono declared that the reorganization was not sufficiently thorough, and urged Gonzi to resign, while fellow members of the PN expressed support for Gonzi and deplored Debono's perceived disloyalty to the party leadership. Later in January the opposition proposed a new motion of no confidence in the Government, citing a long list of alleged shortcomings; Debono again abstained, and once more the Government was only saved from defeat by the Speaker's casting vote. The PL leader, Muscat, urged Gonzi to resolve national uncertainty by holding an early general election.

In February 2012 Gonzi addressed the crisis within the PN by instigating an election to the party leadership; no other candidate was presented, and he was re-elected with 96.5% of the party delegates' votes. Gonzi then announced his intention to restore the party's connection with the electorate by consulting various interest groups. At local council elections in March the PL won some 55% of first-preference votes.

At the end of May 2012 Mifsud Bonnici resigned as Minister for Home Affairs, Local Government and Parliamentary Affairs after losing a motion of no confidence presented to the legislature by the opposition by 34 votes to 35 (in this instance Debono unexpectedly voted in favour of the motion); Gonzi assumed responsibility for the vacated portfolio. The following week the Government survived a parliamentary motion of confidence (by 35 votes to 34) tabled by the Prime Minister; Debono voted in support of the Government, while demanding the implementation of a number of political and democratic reforms (including a law to regulate political party financing).

In mid-October 2012 former cabinet minister Dalli was forced to resign from his post as EU Commissioner for Health and Consumer Policy in the wake of allegations made by the EU antifraud agency that a Maltese entrepreneur had attempted to extract payments from a Swedish oral tobacco ('snus') company by pledging to use his contacts with the commissioner to bring about changes to EU tobacco legislation. Later that month the Deputy Prime Minister and Minister for Foreign Affairs, Tonio Borg, was nominated to replace Dalli; he assumed the EU role in late November and the foreign affairs portfolio in the Maltese Cabinet was assigned to Dr Francis Zammit Dimech.

Recent developments: the fall of the PN Government

Gonzi's Government collapsed on 10 December 2012 (thus bringing to an end some 15 years of PN rule) following the loss of its majority, by 34 votes to 35, in a parliamentary vote on the 2013 budget. The Government's fall was precipitated by Debono's decision to vote against the Government for a variety of reasons, including his opposition to a recent government ruling to transfer management of the country's national bus service to a German operator.

At the general election held on 9 March 2013 the PL won a landslide victory, obtaining an absolute majority of 39 seats (with 54.8% of the votes). The PN secured 26 seats (which was increased to 30 when the party was awarded four at-large seats to adjust for its share of the first-preference votes), with 43.3% of the votes, and the environmentalist Alternattiva Demokratika took 1.8% of the vote but won no seats. Electoral turn-out was about 93%. PL leader Muscat assumed the premiership on 11 March and two days later appointed a large, 22-member Cabinet, including Louis Grech as Deputy Prime Minister and Minister for European Affairs and Implementation of the Electoral Manifesto, Dr George Vella as Minister of Foreign Affairs and Dr Emanuel Mallia as Minister for Home Affairs and National Security.

Immigration Issues

Following its accession to the EU in 2004, illegal immigration became an increasing problem for Malta, partly owing to its proximity to North Africa. According to the Office of the UN High Commissioner for Refugees (UNHCR, see p. 69), of all EU states Malta received the second largest number of asylum seekers per 1,000 inhabitants in 2005 (after Cyprus). Given Malta's extremely high population density the European Commission supported the Government's request in July 2005 that a proportion of the migrants arriving there be transferred to other EU states. An investigation was launched in September to determine whether the recent influx of illegal immigrants was the result of human-trafficking. In October the House of Representatives adopted amendments to refugee legislation aimed at facilitating the repatriation of failed asylum seekers. In December a first group of migrants granted refugee status was transferred to the Netherlands. In February 2006 immigrants housed in detention centres across Malta protested, claiming that they were poorly fed and kept in unsanitary conditions. Malta had previously been criticized by UNHCR over its alleged ill-treatment of asylum seekers.

In July 2006 the EU announced its intention to deploy a police force to patrol the borders of member countries experiencing problems with illegal immigration; the force would include a maritime patrol in the Mediterranean Sea between Malta and North Africa. During 2006–07 there were several incidents in which the Maltese authorities refused to take responsibility for migrants arriving by sea from Africa, usually having set off from Libya. In June 2007 the European Commission accused the Maltese Government of failing to meet its internationally recognized obligation to save lives at sea. The Government insisted, however, that Malta could not accept responsibility for all illegal immigrants rescued in the Mediterranean; it proposed the creation of a system of shared responsibility for rescued migrants between EU member states on a quota basis.

In March 2009 Malta and Libya signed a memorandum of understanding on search and rescue, in order to enhance co-operation between the two countries. In the same month the Maltese Government offered to deploy Maltese military personnel to assist in planned joint patrols of Libyan waters by Italian and Libyan forces, which were intended to curtail the illegal transportation of migrants across the Mediterranean; these patrols commenced in May. Meanwhile, in February Malta, together with Cyprus, Greece and Italy, submitted proposals to the European Commission aimed at strengthening co-operation between member states on immigration and asylum policy, including the establishment of a European Asylum Support Office (EASO). The proposals were adopted at an EU summit in June, and the EASO was formally established in Valletta in 2010. In March of that year Malta disputed new EU rules which stipulated that migrants intercepted by naval patrols in the Mediterranean should be landed in the country whose personnel were leading the patrol in question: the Maltese Government argued that such a policy would only encourage illegal migration, and that, since Maltese officers led many such patrols, Malta would be obliged to receive a larger number of migrants than would otherwise have been the case. In February 2011, following the popular protests in Tunisia and Egypt that led to the resignation of their respective heads of state, and escalating civil unrest in Libya, Malta was among six Mediterranean EU states to request the establishment by the EU of a 'burden-sharing mechanism' and an emergency fund, in anticipation of an increased influx of asylum seekers, particularly from Libya in the event of civil war occurring in that country. In September Malta appealed to the new Libyan administration to adhere to international conventions on immigration and the prevention of people-trafficking. In March 2012 the European Commission urged Malta to improve the facilities provided for the reception of migrants and agreed to provide extra funding for this purpose.

Other Foreign Affairs

In November 2005 Malta hosted the Commonwealth Heads of Government Meeting, at which leaders discussed improving co-operation in development, mass migration and combating terrorism. The British Prime Minister, Tony Blair, attended the meeting and later held talks with Gonzi; this was the first visit to Malta by a British Prime Minister in some 60 years.

In July 2005 Malta extended its maritime jurisdiction and established exclusive fisheries zones in response to similar measures adopted by Libya and Tunisia. In early 2006 Malta and Libya discussed reviving their 1984 friendship and co-operation agreement (a proposal discussed again by the two sides in October 2010) and agreed to consider a number of options with regard to petroleum, not limited to exploration; in March 2008 Libya warned a Canadian petroleum company not to begin operations in an area of the seabed that Malta had licensed the company to explore, but which was claimed by Libya. The disputed delineation of areas of the continental shelf apportioned to Malta and Libya respectively was still under discussion in February 2011, when Prime Minister Gonzi paid a visit to Libya. In February 2006, meanwhile, Malta and Tunisia signed an agreement on joint petroleum exploration and exploitation in zones of the continental shelf located between the two countries. In January 2011 Malta made a formal protest to Italy, after the Italian Government offered licences for petroleum exploration in a contested area of the continental shelf.

The widespread anti-Government unrest that broke out in North Africa and the Middle East during early 2011 was a source of grave concern to Malta, not only because of the expected increase in the number of migrants seeking asylum (see Immigration Issues), but also because of the possible impact of regional instability on Malta's economy, with investment and tourism likely to be particularly adversely affected. In February Malta accepted requests from several countries to provide a transit point for many of the thousands of expatriate workers who were being evacuated from Libya by air and sea. NATO aircraft supervising the 'no-fly' zone imposed by the UN over Libya were allowed to land in Malta when necessary. In August Malta recognized the National Transitional Council as Libya's rightful Government, and urged the deposed ruler, Col Muammar al-Qaddafi, to capitulate and end the conflict in that country. Malta agreed to provide a logistical base for humanitarian aid to Libya, and in November Gonzi and other Maltese ministers visited Libya, holding discussions with the new administration on migration, fishing rights and the continental shelf, and undertaking to restore strong links between the two countries through trade and investment. In April 2012 the Maltese Government announced that it had released some €300m. belonging to Libyan companies, funds to which access had been blocked in the previous year under sanctions imposed by the EU and the UN.

CONSTITUTION AND GOVERNMENT

Under the 1974 Constitution, legislative power is held by the unicameral House of Representatives, whose 69 members are elected by universal adult suffrage for five years (subject to dissolution) on the basis of proportional representation. The Constitution was amended in January 1987 to ensure that a party that received more than 50% of the total votes cast in a general election would obtain a majority of seats in the legislature (by the allocation—if necessary—of additional seats to that party). The President is the constitutional Head of State, elected for a five-year term by the House of Representatives, and executive power is exercised by the Cabinet. The President appoints the Prime Minister and, on the latter's recommendation, other Ministers. The Cabinet is responsible to the House of Representatives.

REGIONAL AND INTERNATIONAL CO-OPERATION

Malta is a member of the European Union (EU, see p. 281) and uses the single currency, the euro. It is also a member of the Council of Europe (see p. 260) and the Organization for Security and Co-operation in Europe (OSCE, see p. 397) and of the Commonwealth (see p. 244).

Malta joined the UN following independence in 1964. As a contracting party to the General Agreement on Tariffs and Trade, Malta joined the World Trade Organization (WTO, see p. 444) on its establishment in 1995. Malta participates in the 'Partnership for Peace' programme of the North Atlantic Treaty Organization (NATO, see p. 380).

ECONOMIC AFFAIRS

In 2010, according to estimates by the World Bank, Malta's gross national income (GNI), measured at average 2008–10 prices, was US $7,747m., equivalent to $18,620 per head (or $24,170 per head on an international purchasing-power parity basis). During 2002–11, it was estimated, the population increased at an average annual rate of 0.6%, while gross domestic product (GDP) per head increased, in real terms, at an average annual rate of 1.2%. According to the World Bank, overall GDP increased, in real terms, at an average annual rate of 1.8% in 2002–11; GDP rose by 2.1% in 2011.

Agriculture (including hunting, forestry and fishing) contributed 1.6% of GDP in 2011, and engaged 1.4% of the working population in August 2012. The principal export crop is potatoes. Tomatoes and other vegetables, cereals (principally wheat and barley) and fruit are also cultivated. Livestock and livestock products are also important, and efforts are being made to develop the fishing industry. During 2002–11, according to the UN, agricultural GDP decreased at an average annual rate of 2.0%. Agricultural GDP decreased by 4.0% in 2010, but increased by 3.2% in 2011.

Industry (including mining, manufacturing, construction and power) provided 18.0% of GDP in 2011, and engaged 23.1% of the employed labour force in August 2012. During 2002–11, according to the UN, industrial GDP decreased at an average annual rate of 0.4%; industrial GDP increased by 3.3% in 2011.

Mining and quarrying (together with utilities) contributed 1.1% of GDP in 2011, and engaged 2.2% of the employed labour force in August 2012. The principal activities are stone- and sand-quarrying. There are reserves of petroleum in Maltese offshore waters, and petroleum and gas exploration is proceeding. During 2002–11, according to the UN, real GDP of the mining sector (together with utilities) increased at an average annual rate of 2.9%; GDP rose by 26.6% in 2010, but declined by 20.1% in 2011.

Manufacturing contributed 12.8% of GDP in 2011, and engaged 13.2% of the working population in August 2012. Based on the gross value of output, the principal branches of manufacturing, excluding ship-repairing, in 2007 were electrical and optical equipment (accounting for around 27.3% of the total), chemicals, chemical products and man-made fibres (15.3%), and food products and beverages (13.7%). During 2002–11, according to the UN, manufacturing GDP decreased at an average annual rate of 1.0%. Manufacturing GDP increased by 6.6% in 2011.

Construction contributed 4.0% of GDP in 2011, and engaged 7.8% of the employed labour force in August 2012.

Energy is derived principally from imports of crude petroleum and coal. Imports of mineral fuels comprised 36.7% of the value of total imports in 2011. In November 2011 the Government announced that the European Union (EU, see p. 281) had agreed to allocate funds for a planned gas pipeline linking Malta to the mainland European gas supply network, and work also began in 2012 on an underwater power cable between Malta and Sicily to link Malta to the mainland electricity grid; the projects were expected to reduce Malta's dependence on its ageing principal power station.

Services provided 80.5% of GDP in 2011, and engaged 75.5% of the employed labour force in August 2012. Tourism is a major source of foreign exchange earnings. In 2011 Malta received 1,415,135 foreign visitors and revenue from the tourism sector amounted to US $1,265m. In August 2012 6.4% of the employed labour force were engaged in employment in the hotels and restaurants sub-sector. The GDP of the services sector increased at an average annual rate of 3.0% in 2002–11, according to the UN; services GDP increased by 4.0% in 2010 but by only 0.7% in 2011.

In 2011 Malta recorded a visible merchandise trade deficit of US $1,364.7m. and there was a deficit of $22.0m. on the current account of the balance of payments. In 2011, according to provisional figures, the principal source of imports (accounting for 27.0% of the total value) was Italy (including San Marino); other major suppliers were France, the United Kingdom and Germany. Germany was the principal market for exports (taking 8.4% of the total value); other significant purchasers were France and Singapore. The principal domestic exports in 2011 were mineral fuels, accounting for 42.0% of the total, followed by machinery and transport equipment, manufactured goods and chemicals. The principal imports were mineral fuels, accounting for 36.7% of the total, followed by machinery and transport equipment, chemicals, food and live animals, manufactured goods and semi-manufactures.

In 2011 Malta recorded an estimated central budget deficit of €218.6m., and a general government deficit of €173.9m., equivalent to 2.7% of GDP. Malta's general government gross debt was €4,250.0m. in 2009, equivalent to 69.1% of GDP. According to the International Labour Organization (ILO), the annual rate of inflation averaged 2.4% in 2002–11; consumer prices increased by 2.7% in 2011. In August 2012 the unemployment rate averaged 4.3%.

Following the closure, in 1979, of the British military base and naval docks, on which Malta's economy had been largely dependent, successive governments pursued a policy of restructuring and diversification. The domestic market is limited, owing to the small population. There are few natural resources, and almost all raw materials have to be imported. Malta's development has therefore been based on the promotion of the island as an international financial centre and on manufacturing for export (notably in non-traditional fields, such as electronics, information technology and pharmaceuticals), together with the continuing development of tourism. From 2004 Malta's membership of the EU entailed a commitment on the part of the Government to reduce Malta's budgetary deficit to below 3.0% of GDP in order to comply with the convergence criteria for participation in Economic and Monetary Union (EMU). Through the implementation of strict monetary policies, institutional reform and a privatization programme, Malta reduced its deficit from more than 10% of GDP in 2003 to 2.2% in 2007. Malta adopted the euro as its currency in January 2008.

Although Malta was affected by the global economic downturn of 2008–09, its banking sector remained relatively unharmed by the financial crisis. Export revenue and tourism declined sharply and GDP contracted by 2.7% in 2009 (compared with positive growth of 4.4% in 2008). The budget deficit increased to 4.5% of GDP in 2008, but declined again to 3.8% in 2009 and 3.6% in 2010, primarily as a result of increased revenue from taxation, including that paid by international companies registered in Malta. Manufacturing output and tourism both recovered in 2010, although investment, particularly in the construction industry, remained at a comparatively low level. Malta's GDP grew by 2.7% in 2010 and by 1.6% in 2011, but growth was expected to slow to 1.0% in 2012. In 2011 the budget deficit, at 2.7% of GDP, was below the stipulated EU limit of 3% and was expected to fall further, to around 2.2%, in 2012. In October 2011 the legislature approved an increase in Malta's commitments to the European Financial Stability Facility for emergency assistance to heavily indebted eurozone countries. In March 2012 Malta was among the 25 EU member states that signed the Treaty on Stability, Co-ordination and Governance, or 'fiscal compact', which placed a legal obligation on signatories to balance their budgets. Unemployment in Malta, at around 6% in 2011, was considerably lower than the EU average (of about 9.8%), and employment levels continued to rise during 2012. Although the country's credit rating was downgraded by credit rating agencies in early 2012, the Government stressed that this was primarily due to external factors. The World Bank estimated Malta's public debt to be equivalent to some 72% of GDP at the end of 2012—higher than the 60% stipulated in the EU's Stability and Growth Pact—and urged the Government to reduce this figure (although it compared favourably with the eurozone average of some 90%). In the budgets for both 2012 and 2013 the Government continued to focus on fiscal consolidation, including reductions in expenditure, the provision of adequate incentives to encourage further investment and job creation, and the safeguarding of social welfare. Following recommendations made by the IMF, during 2012 the Government carried out some restructuring of the national airline, Air Malta, and the energy provider

Enemalta, in order to reduce expenditure and address debt levels within the two state companies.

PUBLIC HOLIDAYS

2014: 1 January (New Year's Day), 10 February (St Paul's Shipwreck), 19 March (St Joseph), 31 March (Freedom Day), 18 April (Good Friday), 1 May (St Joseph the Worker), 7 June (Memorial of the 1919 Riot), 29 June (St Peter and St Paul), 15 August (Assumption), 8 September (Our Lady of Victories), 21 September (Independence Day), 8 December (Immaculate Conception), 13 December (Republic Day), 25 December (Christmas Day).

Statistical Survey

Source (unless otherwise stated): National Statistics Office, Lascaris, Valletta VLT 1921; tel. 21223221; fax 21249841; e-mail nso@magnet.mt; internet www.nso.gov.mt.

AREA AND POPULATION

Area: 316 sq km (122 sq miles).

Population (*de jure* population): 404,962 (males 200,819, females 204,143) at census of 27 November 2005; 416,055 (males 207,185, females 208,870) at census of 21 November 2011 (preliminary).

Density (at 2011 census): 1,316.6 per sq km.

Population by Age and Sex (at 2011 census, preliminary): *0–14:* 61,505 (males 31,584, females 29,921); *15–64:* 286,709 (males 145,966, females 140,743); *65 and over:* 67,841 (males 29,635, females 38,206); *Total* 416,055 (males 207,185, females 208,870).

Principal Towns (at 2011 census): Birkirkara 21,533; Mosta 19,650; San Pawl Il-Baħar 16,478; Qormi 16,312; Żabbar 14,823; Sliema 13,511; Naxxar 12,802; San Gwann 12,128; Żebbuġ 11,542; Valletta (capital) 5,784.

Births, Marriages and Deaths (2011): Registered live births 4,283 (birth rate 10.3 per 1,000); Marriages 2,562 (marriage rate 6.1 per 1,000); Registered deaths 3,266 (death rate 7.8 per 1,000).

Life Expectancy (years at birth): 80.9 (males 78.9; females 83.1) in 2010. Source: World Bank, World Development Indicators database.

Migration (2004, unless otherwise indicated): Emigrants 70 (all to United Kingdom); Returning emigrants 459; Non-Maltese nationals settling in the islands 533 (in 2002). *2010:* Total emigrants 1,863; Total immigrants 1,200.

Economically Active Population (persons in full-time employment, labour force survey, August 2012): Agriculture and hunting 1,613; Fishing 510; Mining and quarrying 284; Manufacturing 20,065; Electricity, gas and water supply 2,990; Construction 11,820; Wholesale and retail trade and repair of motor vehicles, motorcycles and personal and household goods 22,955; Hotels and restaurants 9,773; Transport, storage and communications 14,044; Financial intermediation 7,071; Real estate, renting and business activities 17,036; Public administration and defence and compulsory social security 10,552; Education 13,619; Health and social work 12,426; Other community, social and personal service activities 7,120; Private households with employed persons 3; Extra-territorial organizations and bodies 179; *Total employed* 152,060 (males 99,408, females 52,652); Registered unemployed 6,821; *Total labour force* 158,881. Note: Figures exclude apprentices, trainees and students engaged in holiday work (609 in August 2012).

HEALTH AND WELFARE

Key Indicators

Total Fertility Rate (children per woman, 2010): 1.3.

Under-5 Mortality Rate (per 1,000 live births, 2010): 6.

HIV/AIDS (% of persons aged 15–49, 2009): 0.1.

Physicians (per 1,000 head, 2010): 3.1.

Hospital Beds (per 1,000 head, 2010): 4.5.

Health Expenditure (2009): US $ per head (PPP): 2,141.

Health Expenditure (2009): % of GDP: 8.5.

Health Expenditure (2009): public (% of total): 64.8.

Total Carbon Dioxide Emissions ('000 metric tons, 2008): 2,559.6.

Carbon Dioxide Emissions Per Head (metric tons, 2008): 6.2.

Human Development Index (2011): ranking: 36.

Human Development Index (2011): value: 0.832.

For sources and definitions, see explanatory note on p. vi.

AGRICULTURE, ETC.

Principal Crops ('000 metric tons, 2011): Wheat 15.1*; Barley 1.5*; Potatoes 15.2; Cabbages and other brassicas 3.8; Tomatoes 14.0; Cauliflowers and broccoli 6.2; Pumpkins, squash and gourds 1.5; Onions, dry 8.0; Garlic 0.5; Broad beans, dry 0.7*; Melons 2.9; Citrus fruit 2.6*; Grapes 4.6.
* FAO estimate.

Livestock ('000 head, year ending September 2011): Cattle 15.1; Pigs 46.3; Sheep 11.9; Goats 4.9; Chickens 920*; Horses 1.1*.
* FAO estimate.

Livestock Products ('000 metric tons, 2011): Cattle meat 1.1; Pig meat 7.3; Rabbit meat 1.8*; Chicken meat 4.2; Cows' milk 41.6; Sheep's milk 1.7; Hen eggs 4.5.
* FAO estimate.

Fishing (metric tons, live weight, 2010): Capture 1,836 (Atlantic bluefin tuna 153; Common dolphinfish 530; Swordfish 423); Aquaculture 2,916 (European sea bass 102; Gilthead sea bream 1,755); *Total catch* 4,752.

Source: FAO.

INDUSTRY

Production ('000 metric tons, 2001, unless otherwise indicated): Limestone flux and calcareous stones 2,000 (Limestone only); Cigarettes (1992, million) 1,475; Washing powders and detergents 9.7; Quicklime (1992, incl. other types of lime) 5; Tankers, launched (1996, number, completions) 5; Other seagoing merchant vessels launched (number, 2002) 1 (5 grt); Electricity (2009, million kWh, by public utilities) 2,167 (Source: UN, *Industrial Commodity Statistics Yearbook* and Database).

FINANCE

Currency and Exchange Rates: 100 cent = 1 euro (€). *Sterling and Dollar Equivalents* (31 December 2012): £1 sterling = 1.196 euros; US $1 = 0.758 euros; €10 = £8.36 = $13.19. *Average Exchange Rate* (euros per US dollar): 0.7550 in 2010; 0.7194 in 2011; 0.7779 in 2012. Note: The national currency was formerly the Maltese lira (LM; plural liri). Malta adopted the euro on 1 January 2008 at a fixed exchange rate of €1 = LM 0.429300. The euro and local currency circulated alongside each other until 31 January, after which the euro became the sole legal tender.

Budget (€ million, central government transactions, 2011): *Revenue:* Income tax 776.1; Customs and excise 208.2; Value-added tax 525.1; Social security 585.6; Grants 121.1; Other revenue 427.8; Total 2,643.8. *Expenditure:* Recurrent expenditure 2,361.3 (Education 147.8, Social security 728.0, Others 1,485.5); Interest payments 212.5; Capital expenditure 288.7; Total 2,862.4.

International Reserves (US $ million at 31 December 2011): Gold (national valuation) 15.7; IMF special drawing rights 139.2; Reserve position in IMF 70.4; Foreign exchange 290.2; Total 515.5. Source: IMF, *International Financial Statistics*.

Money Supply (incl. shares, depository corporations, national residence criteria, € million at 31 December 2011): Currency issued 783 (Central Bank of Malta 913); Demand deposits 4,590; Other deposits 5,135; Securities other than shares 354; Money market fund shares 206; Shares and other equity 10,645; Other items (net) –471; *Total* 21,239. Source: IMF, *International Financial Statistics*.

Cost of Living (Consumer Price Index; base: 2005 = 100): All items 110.8 in 2009; 112.4 in 2010; 115.5 in 2011. Source: IMF, *International Financial Statistics*.

Gross Domestic Product (€ million at constant 2000 prices): 4,742.5 in 2009; 4,870.7 in 2010; 4,947.3 in 2011.

National Income and Product (€ million at current prices, 2011): Compensation of employees 2,913.0; Gross operating surplus and mixed income 2,768.0; *Gross domestic product at factor cost* 5,681.0; Taxes on production and imports 928.3; *Less* Subsidies 64.9; *GDP in purchasers' values* 6,544.4.

Expenditure on Gross Domestic Product (€ million at current prices, 2011): Final consumption expenditure 5,378.5 (General government 1,346.8, Households 3,930.0, Non-profit institutes serving households 101.7); Gross capital formation 825.6 (Gross fixed capital formation 986.3, Changes in inventories –135.9, Acquisitions, less disposals, of valuables –24.8); *Total domestic expenditure* 6,204.1; Exports of goods and services 6,634.9; *Less* Imports of goods and services 6,294.7; *GDP in purchasers' values* 6,544.4.

Gross Domestic Product by Economic Activity (€ million at current prices, 2011): Agriculture, hunting, forestry and fishing 89.2; Mining and quarrying, manufacturing and utilities 789.9; Construction 228.8; Trade, transport, accommodation and food services 1,214.2; Information and communication 286.3; Financial intermediation 440.5; Real estate, renting and business activities 908.7; Public administration and defence, compulsory social security, education, health and social work 1,089.8; Other community, social and personal services 624.4; *Gross value added at basic prices* 5,671.8; Indirect taxes 894.3; *Less* Subsidies 21.7; *GDP in purchasers' values* 6,544.4. Note: Financial services indirectly measured assumed to be distributed at origin.

Balance of Payments (US $ million, 2011): Exports of goods 4,237.6; Imports of goods –5,602.3; *Balance on goods* –1,364.7; Exports of services 4,972.5; Imports of services –3,097.0; *Balance on goods and services* 510.7; Primary income received 2,271.1; Primary income paid –2,840.1; *Balance on goods, services and primary income* –58.3; Secondary income received 1,255.3; Secondary income paid –1,219.0; *Current balance* –22.0; Capital account (net) 89.6; Direct investment assets –54.2; Direct investment liabilities 474.5; Portfolio investment assets –4,252.5; Portfolio investment liabilities 0.6; Financial derivatives and employee stock options (net) 37.8; Other investment assets 1,987.2; Other investment liabilities 1,662.7; Net errors and omissions –13.4; *Reserves and related items* –89.6. Source: IMF, *International Financial Statistics*.

EXTERNAL TRADE

Principal Commodities (€ million, 2011, provisional): *Imports:* Food and live animals 416.3; Beverages and tobacco 63.9; Animal and vegetable oils and fats 8.5; Crude materials (inedible) except fuels 23.2; Mineral fuels, lubricants, etc. 1,936.0; Chemicals 424.9; Manufactured goods 369.6; Semi-manufactures 323.8; Machinery and transport equipment 1,670.5; Miscellaneous transactions 34.4; Total 5,271.1. *Exports:* Food and live animals 129.3; Beverages and tobacco 21.6; Crude materials (inedible) except fuels 19.5; Mineral fuels, lubricants, etc. 1,571.7; Chemicals 255.2; Manufactured goods 381.3; Semi-manufactures 131.1; Machinery and transport equipment 1,227.5; Miscellaneous transactions 2.5; Total 3,739.6.

Principal Trading Partners (€ million, 2011, provisional): *Imports:* European Union 3,289.4 (France—incl. Monaco 372.2; Germany 305.2; Italy—incl. San Marino 1,422.3; United Kingdom 352.4); Other Europe 869.7; Africa 35.8; Americas 353.3 (USA 225.1); Asia 641.9 (China, People's Republic 149.7; Singapore 100.5); Australasia 20.4; Total 5,271.1 (incl. ships' and aircraft stores and bunkers 60.7). *Exports:* European Union 1,222.4 (France—incl. Monaco 236.4; Germany 315.3; Italy—incl. San Marino 162.0; United Kingdom 146.3); Other Europe 277.2; Africa 234.3; Americas 226.9 (USA 169.1); Asia 1,092.3 (Japan 98.0; Singapore 206.3); Australasia 5.2; Total 3,739.6 (incl. ships' and aircraft stores and bunkers 681.4).

TRANSPORT

Road Traffic (motor vehicles in use, December 2011): Private cars 239,987; Commercial vehicles 48,367; Motorcycles 15,443; Others 8,150; Total 311,947.

Shipping: *Flag Registered Fleet* (31 December 2012): Vessels 1,961; Total displacement 45,461,879 grt (Source: Lloyd's List Intelligence—www.lloydslistintelligence.com). *International Freight Traffic* ('000 metric tons, 2007): Goods loaded 410.2; Goods unloaded 1,669.2.

Civil Aviation (traffic on scheduled services, 2009): Kilometres flown (million) 27; Passengers carried ('000) 1,993; Passenger-km (million) 3,251; Total ton-km (million) 332 (Source: UN, *Statistical Yearbook*). *2010:* Passengers carried ('000) 2,245 (Source: World Bank, World Development Indicators database).

TOURISM

Tourist Arrivals (based on departures by air and sea): 1,182,490 in 2009; 1,338,841 in 2010; 1,415,135 in 2011.

Arrivals by Country of Origin (based on departures by air and sea, 2011): France 103,753; Germany 134,611; Italy 202,021; Libya 6,208; Netherlands 39,073; United Kingdom 439,802; Total (incl. others) 1,415,135.

Tourism Receipts (US $ million, excl. passenger transport): 892 in 2009; 1,079 in 2010; 1,265 in 2011 (provisional).

Source: partly World Tourism Organization.

COMMUNICATIONS MEDIA

Telephones (main lines, 2011): 232,200 in use.

Mobile Cellular Telephones (2011): 521,700 subscribers.

Internet Subscribers (2011): 129,300.

Broadband Subscribers (2011): 129,300.

Source: International Telecommunication Union.

EDUCATION

Pre-primary (2009/10 unless otherwise stated): 131 schools (1999/2000); 601 teachers; 8,515 students. Source: UNESCO.

Primary (2009/10 unless otherwise stated): 126 schools (1999/2000); 1,748 teachers; 24,985 students. Source: UNESCO.

Secondary (2009/10 unless otherwise stated): *General:* 75 schools (1999/2000); 3,821 teachers; 31,578 students. *Vocational:* 23 schools (1999/2000); 217 teachers; 5,584 students. *Junior College* (1995/96): 1 school; 1,800 students. Source: UNESCO, partly *Statistical Yearbook*.

Universities, etc. (2009/10 unless otherwise stated): 968 teachers (2004/05); 10,840 students. Source: UNESCO.

Pupil-teacher Ratio (primary education, UNESCO estimate): 14.3 in 2009/10. Source: UNESCO Institute for Statistics.

Adult Literacy Rate (UNESCO estimates): 92.4% (males 91.2%; females 93.5%) in 2005. Source: UNESCO Institute for Statistics.

Directory

The Government

HEAD OF STATE

President: Dr GEORGE ABELA (took office 4 April 2009).

THE CABINET
(May 2013)

The Government is formed by the Partit Laburista (PL—Labour Party).

Prime Minister: Dr JOSEPH MUSCAT.

Deputy Prime Minister and Minister for European Affairs and Implementation of the Electoral Manifesto: LOUIS GRECH.

Minister for Foreign Affairs: Dr GEORGE VELLA.

Minister for Tourism: KARMENU VELLA.

Minister for Education and Employment: EVARIST BARTOLO.

Minister for Sustainable Development, the Environment and Climate Change: LEO BRINCAT.

Minister for Transport and Infrastructure: JOE MIZZI.

Minister for Gozo: Dr ANTON REFALO.

Minister for Social Dialogue, Consumer Affairs and Civil Liberties: Dr HELENA DALLI.

Minister for the Economy, Investment and Small Business: Dr CHRISTIAN CARDONA.

Minister for the Family and Social Solidarity: MARIE-LOUISE COLEIRO PRECA.

Minister for Home Affairs and National Security: Dr EMANUEL MALLIA.

Minister of Finance: Prof. EDWARD SCICLUNA.

Minister for Energy and the Conservation of Water: Dr KONRAD MIZZI.

Minister for Health: Dr GODFREY FARRUGIA.

PARLIAMENTARY SECRETARIES (ATTACHED TO MINISTRIES)

Parliamentary Secretary for Planning and Simplification of Administrative Processes in the Office of the Prime Minister: Dr MICHAEL FARRUGIA.

Parliamentary Secretary for the EU Presidency 2017 and EU Funds in the Ministry for European Affairs and Implementation of the Electoral Manifesto: Dr IAN BORG.

Parliamentary Secretary for Culture and Local Government in the Ministry for Tourism: Dr JOSÉ A. HERRERA.

Parliamentary Secretary for Research, Innovation, Youth and Sport in the Ministry for Education and Employment: Dr STEFAN BUONTEMPO.

Parliamentary Secretary for Agriculture, Fisheries and Animal Rights in the Ministry for Sustainable Development, the Environment and Climate Change: RODERICK GALDES.

Parliamentary Secretary for Competitiveness and Economic Growth in the Ministry for the Economy, Investment and Small Business: Dr EDWARD ZAMMIT LEWIS.

Parliamentary Secretary for Rights of Persons with Disability and Active Ageing in the Ministry for the Family and Social Solidarity: Dr FRANCO MERCIECA.

Parliamentary Secretary for Justice in the Ministry for Home Affairs and National Security: Dr OWEN BONNICI.

MINISTRIES

Office of the President: The Palace, Valletta VLT 1190; tel. 21221221; fax 21241241; internet www.president.gov.mt.

Office of the Prime Minister: Auberge de Castille, Valletta VLT 2000; e-mail joseph.muscat@gov.mt.

Ministry of Education and Employment: Great Siege Rd, Floriana VLT 2000; tel. 25689000; fax 25903216; e-mail evarist.bartolo@gov.mt; internet www.education.gov.mt.

Ministry for the Economy, Investment and Small Business: e-mail christian.cardona@gov.mt.

Ministry for Energy and the Conservation of Water: Auberge de Castille, Valletta VLT 2000; tel. 22002570; e-mail konrad.mizzi@gov.mt.

Ministry for European Affairs and Implementation of the Electoral Manifesto: Auberge de Aragaon, Valletta; e-mail louis.grech@gov.mt.

Ministry for the Family and Social Solidarity: 310 Republic St, Valletta VLT 1110; tel. 25903123; e-mail marie-louise.coleiro@gov.mt; internet mfss.gov.mt.

Ministry of Finance: Maison Demandols, South St, Valletta VLT 1102; tel. 25998259; fax 25998429; e-mail info.mfin@gov.mt; internet mfin.gov.mt.

Ministry of Foreign Affairs: Palazzo Parisio, Merchants St, Valletta VLT 1171; tel. 21242191; fax 21236604; e-mail george.vella@gov.mt; internet www.mfa.gov.mt.

Ministry for Gozo: St Francis Sq., Victoria VCT 1335, Gozo; tel. 22156400; fax 21559360; e-mail anton.refalo@gov.mt; internet www.gozo.gov.mt.

Ministry of Health: Palazzo Castellania, 15 Merchants St, Valletta VLT 2000; tel. 21224071; internet ehealth.gov.mt.

Ministry for Home Affairs and National Security: Strait St, Valletta; tel. 22957000; fax 22957348; e-mail manuel.mallia@gov.mt.

Ministry for Social Dialogue, Consumer Affairs and Civil Liberties: Cavalier House, Old Mint St, Valletta VLT 2000; tel. 22985100; e-mail helena.dalli@gov.mt.

Ministry for Sustainable Development, the Environment and Climate Change: Casa Leone, St Venera; e-mail leo.brincat@gov.mt.

Ministry for Transport and Infrastructure: Francesco Buonamici St, Floriana FRN 1700; e-mail joe.mizzi@gov.mt.

Ministry for Tourism: Auberge d'Italie, Merchants St, Valletta VLT 2000; tel. 22915021; fax 22915039; e-mail karmenu.vella@gov.mt.

Legislature

House of Representatives

The Palace, Valletta VLT 1115; tel. 25596000; fax 25596400; e-mail parliament@gov.mt; internet www.parliament.gov.mt.

Speaker: ANGELO FARRUGIA.

General Election, 9 March 2013

Party	Votes	% of votes	Seats
Partit Laburista (Malta Labour Party)	167,533	54.83	39
Partit Nazzjonalista (Nationalist Party)	132,426	43.34	30
Alternattiva Demokratika—The Green Party	5,506	1.80	—
Others	91	0.03	—
Total	305,556	100.00	69

Election Commission

Electoral Commission: Electoral Office, Evans Bldg, St Elmo Pl., Valletta VLT 2000; tel. 21221994; fax 21236380; e-mail electoral.office@gov.mt; internet www.electoral.gov.mt; independent; Chair. and Chief Electoral Commr SAVIOUR GAUCI; Sec. JOE CALLEJA.

Political Organizations

Alternattiva Demokratika—The Green Party (AD): POB 38, Marsa MTP 1001; tel. 99894962; e-mail info@alternattiva.org.mt; internet www.alternattiva.org.mt; f. 1989; emphasizes social and environmental issues; Chair. MICHAEL BRIGUGLIO; Sec.-Gen. RALPH CASSAR.

Partit Laburista (PL) (Labour Party): National Labour Centre, Mile End Rd, Hamrun HMR 1717; tel. 21249900; fax 21244204; e-mail info@partitlaburista.org; internet www.partitlaburista.org; f. 1921; fmrly known as the Malta Labour Party; adopted current name in 2008; democratic socialist; Leader Dr JOSEPH MUSCAT; Pres. STEFAN ZRINZO AZZOPARDI.

Partit Nazzjonalista (PN) (Nationalist Party): Herbert Ganado St, Pietà PTA 1541; tel. 21243641; fax 21243640; e-mail admin@pn.org.mt; internet www.pn.org.mt; f. 1880; Christian democratic; Leader SIMON BUSUTTIL; Sec.-Gen. PAUL BORG OLIVIER.

Diplomatic Representation

EMBASSIES AND HIGH COMMISSIONS IN MALTA

Australia: Villa Ferentina, Ta'Xbiex Terrace, Ta'Xbiex XBX 1034; tel. 21338201; fax 21344059; e-mail aushicom@onvol.net; internet www.malta.embassy.gov.au; High Commr JANE LAMBERT.

Austria: Whitehall Mansions, 3rd Floor, Ta'Xbiex Seafront, Ta'Xbiex XBX 1026; tel. 23279000; fax 21317430; e-mail valletta-ob@bmeia.gv.at; internet www.aussenministerium.at/botschaft/valletta.html; Ambassador PETRA MARIA SCHNEEBAUER.

Belgium: Europa Centre, 8–9 John Lopez St, Floriana FLN 1400; tel. 21228214; fax 21243246; e-mail valletta@diplobel.fed.be; internet www.diplomatie.be/valletta; Chargé d'affaires a.i. JEAN-MICHEL COLAS.

China, People's Republic: Karmnu Court, Lapsi St, St Julian's STJ 1264; tel. 23798804; fax 21344730; e-mail chinaemb_mt@mfa.gov.cn; internet mt.chineseembassy.org; Ambassador CAI JINBIAO.

Egypt: Villa Mon Rêve, 10 Sir Temi Zammit St, Ta'Xbiex XBX 1013; tel. 21314158; fax 21319230; e-mail embegmlt@onvol.net; Ambassador ABD AL-MAWGOUD ELHABASHY.

France: 130 Melita St, POB 408, Valletta VLT 1123; tel. 22480600; fax 22480626; e-mail contact@ambafrance-mt.org; internet www.ambafrance-mt.org; Ambassador MICHEL VANDEPOORTER.

Germany: 'Il-Piazzetta', Entrance B, 1st Floor, Tower Rd, Sliema SLM 1605; POB 48, Marsa MRS 1000; tel. 22604000; fax 22604115; e-mail info@valletta.diplo.de; internet www.valletta.diplo.de; Ambassador Dr HUBERT ZIEGLER.

Greece: Villino Fond Galland, 6 Ir-Rampa, Ta'Xbiex XBX 1035; tel. 21320889; fax 21320788; e-mail gremb.val@mfa.gr; Ambassador ALEXANDROS RALLIS.

Holy See: Apostolic Nunciature, 20/22 Pietru Caxaru St, Tal-Virtù, Rabat RBT 2604; tel. 21453422; fax 21453423; e-mail nuntius@onvol.net; Apostolic Nuncio Most Rev. ALDO CAVALLI (Titular Archbishop of Vibo).

Ireland: Whitehall Mansions, Ta'Xbiex Seafront, Ta'Xbiex XBX 1026; tel. 21334744; fax 21334755; e-mail vallettaembassy@dfa.ie; internet www.embassyofireland.org.mt; Ambassador JIM HENNESSY.

Italy: 5 Vilhena St, Floriana FRN 1040; tel. 21233157; fax 21239217; e-mail ambasciata.lavalletta@esteri.it; internet www.amblavalletta .esteri.it; Chargé d'affaires a.i. GAIA LA COGNATA.

Kuwait: Westin Dragonara Resort, Dragonara Rd, St Julian's STJ 3143; tel. 21381000; fax 23747824; e-mail info@ kuwaitembassy-malta.com; Ambassador FAISAL AL-MSAILEEM.

Libya: Triq l-Imdina, POB 20, Balzan BZN 9033; tel. 21486347; fax 21483939; e-mail libyanpeople@waldonet.net.mt; Chargé d'affaires a.i. MUHAMMAD M. A. ELGHIRANI.

Netherlands: Whitehall Mansions, 3rd Floor, Ta'Xbiex Seafront, Ta'Xbiex XBX 1026; tel. 21313980; fax 21313990; e-mail val@ minbuza.nl; internet malta.nlembassy.org; Ambassador ROBERT JAN GABRIËLSE.

Russia: Ariel House, 25 Anthony Schembri St, Kappara, San Ġwann SGN 08; tel. 21371905; fax 21372131; e-mail rusemb@onvol.net; internet www.malta.mid.ru; Ambassador BORIS YU. MARCHUK.

Spain: Whitehall Mansions, Ta'Xbiex Seafront, Ta'Xbiex XBX 1026; tel. 21317365; fax 21317362; e-mail emb.valletta@maec.es; internet www.maec.es/subwebs/embajadas/lavaleta; Ambassador Dr FELIPE DE LA MORENA CASADO.

Tunisia: Valletta Rd, Attard ATD 9052; tel. 21417070; fax 21413414; e-mail at.lavalette@maltanet.net; internet www.atunisie-mt.org; Ambassador SOUAD GUEBLAOUI.

Turkey: 35 Sir Luigi Preziosi Sq., Floriana FRN 1154; tel. 21223424; fax 21224308; e-mail embassy.valletta@mfa.gov.tr; Ambassador REFIKA NIHAL ÇEVIK.

United Kingdom: Whitehall Mansions, Ta'Xbiex Seafront, Ta'-Xbiex XBX 1026; tel. 23230000; fax 23232216; e-mail bhcvalletta@ fco.gov.uk; internet ukinmalta.fco.gov.uk; High Commr ROBERT HAYDON VERNON LUKE.

USA: Ta' Qali National Park, Ta' Qali, ATD 4000; tel. 25614000; fax 21243229; e-mail usembmalta@state.gov; internet malta.usembassy .gov; Ambassador GINA ABERCROMBIE-WINSTANLEY.

Judicial System

The legal system consists of enactments of the Parliament of Malta, and those of the British Parliament not repealed or replaced by enactments of the Maltese legislature. Maltese Civil Law derives largely from Roman Law, while British Law has significantly influenced Maltese public law.

The Constitutional Court, composed of three judges, is appellate in cases involving alleged violations of human rights, the interpretation of the Constitution and the invalidity of laws. It has jurisdiction to decide questions as to membership of the House of Representatives and any reference made to it relating to voting for election of members of the House of Representatives.

The Court of Appeal is composed of three judges, when it hears appeals from the judgments of the Civil Court, and of one judge, when it hears appeals from the Court of Magistrates in its civil jurisdiction. An appeal also lies to the Court of Appeal from the decisions of a number of administrative tribunals, mostly on points of law.

The Court of Criminal Appeal consists of three judges and hears appeals from persons convicted by the Criminal Court. This court, when formed of one judge, hears appeals from judgments delivered by the Court of Magistrates in its criminal jurisdiction.

The Criminal Court is formed by one judge, who sits with a jury of nine persons to try, on indictment, offences exceeding the competence of the Court of Magistrates. This court may, in certain exceptional cases, sit without a jury.

The Civil Court is divided into three sections. The First Hall takes cognisance of all causes of a civil and a commercial nature, exceeding the jurisdiction of the Courts of Magistrates. The Voluntary Jurisdiction Section is assigned all matters of a civil nature, such as authority to proceed the tutorship of minors, adoption, the interdiction and incapacitation of persons, the opening of successions and the confirmation of testamentary executors. The Family Section is assigned matters of a civil nature regulated by titles I, II and IV of the First Book of the Civil Code; the Maintenance Orders (Facilities for Enforcement) Ordinance; the Maintenance Ordinance (Reciprocal Enforcement) Act; the Marriage Act and the Child Abduction and Child Custody Act. One judge presides in all three sections.

The Magistrates' Court, which is composed of one magistrate, exercises both a civil and a criminal jurisdiction. The Court of Magistrates, in civil matters, has an inferior jurisdiction of first instance, limited to claims exceeding €3,494.06 (LM 1,500) but not exceeding €11,646.87 (LM 5,000). In criminal matters, the court has a two-fold jurisdiction: as a court of criminal judicature for the trial of offences which fall within its jurisdiction, and as a court of inquiry in respect of offences which fall within the jurisdiction of a higher tribunal.

The Court of Magistrates for Gozo, in civil matters, has a two-fold jurisdiction—an inferior jurisdiction comparable to that exercised by its counterpart court in Malta, and a superior jurisdiction, both civil and commercial, in respect of causes which in Malta are cognisable by the First Hall of the Civil Court. Within the limits of its territorial jurisdiction, this court has also the powers of a court of voluntary jurisdiction.

The Small Claims Tribunal is presided over by an adjudicator who decides cases on principles of equity, according to law. The Juvenile Court consists of a Magistrate, as Chairman, and two members.

Chief Justice and President of the Court of Appeal and the Constitutional Court: Dr SILVIO CAMILLERI.

Attorney-General: Dr PETER GRECH.

Religion

CHRISTIANITY

The Roman Catholic Church

Malta comprises one archdiocese and one diocese. The Constitution enshrines Roman Catholicism as the state religion. Adherents comprise an estimated 94% of the population.

Bishops' Conference

Conferenza Episcopale Maltese, Archbishop's Curia, St Calcedonius Sq., Floriana FRN 1535; tel. 25906403; fax 21226457; e-mail joe .magro@maltadiocese.org; internet www.maltadiocese.org.

f. 1971; Pres. Most Rev. PAUL CREMONA (Archbishop of Malta); Sec. Rev. JOE MAGRO.

Archbishop of Malta: Most Rev. PAUL CREMONA, Archbishop's Curia, St Calcedonius Sq., Floriana FRN 1535; POB 29, Valletta; tel. 21235350; fax 21223307; e-mail info@maltadiocese.org.mt.

Bishop of Gozo: Rt Rev. MARIO GRECH, Bishop's Chancery, POB 1, Republic St, Victoria VCT 1000, Gozo; tel. 21556661; fax 21551278; e-mail info@gozodiocese.org; internet gozodiocese.org.

The Anglican Communion

Malta forms part of the Diocese in Europe.

Church of England: Pro-Cathedral of St Paul, Independence Sq., Valletta VLT 1535; tel. 21225714; fax 21225867; e-mail anglican@ onvol.net; internet www.anglicanmalta.org; Senior Chaplain and Chancellor of the Pro-Cathedral Rev. Canon SIMON GODFREY.

Other Christian Churches

In 2004 there were approximately 680 Jehovah's Witnesses and 148 members of the Church of Jesus Christ of Latter-day Saints (Mormons). The Bible Baptist Church had 30 members and the Fellowship of Evangelical Churches had about 100 affiliates.

OTHER RELIGIONS

There is one Muslim mosque and a Muslim primary school. There are an estimated 3,000 Muslims in the country. There is one Jewish congregation. Zen Buddhism and the Bahá'í Faith have about 30 members each.

The Press

DAILY NEWSPAPERS

The Malta Independent: Standard House, Birkirkara Hill, St Julian's STJ 1149; tel. 21345888; fax 21344860; e-mail tmid@ independent.com.mt; internet www.independent.com.mt; English; Editor MICHAEL CARABOTT.

In-Nazzjon (The Nation): Herbert Ganado St, POB 37, Pietà PTA 1450; tel. 21243641; fax 21242886; e-mail news@media.link.com.mt; internet www.mument.com.mt; f. 1970; Maltese; affiliated to Partit Nazzjonalista; Editor ALEX ATTARD.

L-orizzont (The Horizon): Union Print Co, A-41 Industrial Estate, Valletta Rd, Marsa MRS 3000; tel. 25900200; fax 21247870; e-mail info@unionprint.com.mt; internet www.orizzont.com.mt; f. 1962; Maltese; organ of the General Workers' Union; Editor JOSEF CARUANA; circ. 20,000 (2008).

The Times: Allied Newspapers Ltd, Strickland House, 341 St Paul St, Valletta VLT 1211; tel. 25594112; fax 25594116; e-mail daily@ timesofmalta.com; internet www.timesofmalta.com; f. 1935; English; Editor RAY BUGEJA.

OTHER NEWSPAPERS

Business Today: Vjal ir-Ríhan, San Ġwann SGN 07; tel. 21382741; fax 21385075; internet www.businesstoday.com.mt; Wed.; Man. Editor SAVIOUR BALZAN.

Il-Ġensillum (The People Today): Media Centre, National Rd, Blata il-Bajda HMR 1640; tel. 25699119; fax 25699123; e-mail gens@ mediacentre.org.mt; internet www.il-gensillum.com; f. 2004 to succeed *Il-Gens* (The People); Maltese; Roman Catholic; Editor Rev. JOHN AVELLINO; circ. 13,000 (2008).

Illum (Today): MediaToday Co Ltd, Vjal ir-Rihan, San Ġwann SGN 9016; tel. 21382741; fax 21385075; e-mail illum@mediatoday.com .mt; internet www.illum.com.mt; weekly; Maltese; Editor SAVIOUR BALZAN.

KullĦadd: Centru Nazzjonali Laburista, Mile End Rd, Ħamrun HMR 1717; tel. 21235312; fax 21238252; e-mail felix@kullhadd.com; internet www.kullhadd.com; f. 1993; organ of Partit Laburista; Maltese; Editor FELIX AGIUS.

Leħen is-Sewwa: Catholic Institute, Floriana FRN 1441; tel. and fax 21225847; e-mail lehenissewwa@vol.net.mt; f. 1928; Roman Catholic; Editor Rev. JOHN CIARLÓ; circ. 10,000 (2008).

The Malta Business Weekly: Standard House, Birkirkara Hill, St Julian's STJ 1149; tel. 21345888; fax 21344860; e-mail csultana@ independent.com.mt; internet www.independent.com.mt; f. 1994; English; Editor CHRISTOPHER SULTANA.

The Malta Independent on Sunday: Standard House, Birkirkara Hill, St Julian's STJ 1149; tel. 21345888; fax 21344884; e-mail tmis@ independent.com.mt; internet www.independent.com.mt; f. 1992; owned by Standard Publications Ltd; English; Editor DAVID LINDSAY.

MaltaToday: MediaToday Co Ltd, Vjal ir-Rihan, San Ġwann SGN 9016; tel. 21382741; fax 21385075; e-mail maltatoday@mediatoday .com.mt; internet www.maltatoday.com.mt; f. 1998; Wed. and Sun.; English; Man. Editor SAVIOUR BALZAN.

Il-Mument (The Moment): Herbert Ganado St, POB 37, Pietà PTA 1450; tel. 25965333; fax 25965525; e-mail mument@media.link.com .mt; f. 1972; Maltese; affiliated to Partit Nazzjonalista; Editor RODERICK AGIUS (acting).

The Sunday Times: Allied Newspapers Ltd, Strickland House, 341 St Paul St, Valletta VLT 1211; tel. 25594500; fax 25594510; e-mail sunday@timesofmalta.com; internet www.timesofmalta.com; f. 1922; English; Editor STEVE MALLIA; circ. 40,000 (2008).

It-Torċa (The Torch): Union Press, A 41, Marsa Industrial Estate, Marsa MRS 3000; tel. 259000200; fax 21247870; e-mail info@ unionprint.com.mt; internet www.torca.com.mt; f. 1944; Maltese; organ of the General Workers' Union; Editor ALEKS FARRUGIA.

SELECTED PERIODICALS

Commercial Courier: Malta Chamber of Commerce, Enterprise and Industry, Exchange Bldgs, Republic St, Valletta VLT 1117; tel. 21233873; fax 21245223; e-mail info@maltachamber.org.mt; internet www.chamber.org.mt; bi-monthly; Editor KEVIN J. BORG.

Malta Government Gazette: Department of Information, 3 Castille Pl., Valletta VLT 2000; tel. 22001700; fax 22001775; e-mail info .doi@gov.mt; internet www.doi.gov.mt; f. 1813; official notices; Maltese and English; 2 a week.

Malta In Figures: National Statistics Office, Lascaris, Valletta VLT 2000; tel. 25997000; fax 25997205; e-mail nso@gov.mt; internet www .nso.gov.mt; official statistics; annual.

Malta This Month: Advantage Advertising Ltd, 118 St John's St, Valletta VLT 1169; tel. 21249924; fax 21249927; e-mail advantage@ onvol.net; publ. by Air Malta; monthly; Editor PETER DARMANIN.

The Retailer: Association of General Retailers and Traders, Exchange Bldgs, Republic St, Valletta VLT 1117; tel. 21230459; fax 21246925; internet www.grtu.eu; monthly; publ. by Malta Chamber of Small and Medium-sized Enterprises; Editor VINCENT FARRUGIA.

The Teacher: Teachers' Institute, 213 Republic St, Valletta VLT 1118; tel. 21237815; fax 21244074; e-mail info@mut.org.mt; internet www.mut.org.mt; f. 1919; journal of the Malta Union of Teachers; 2 a year; Editor FRANKLIN BARBARA.

Xpress: Alternattiva Demokratika, POB 38, Marsa MTP 1001; e-mail info@alternattiva.org.mt; publ. of the Alternattiva Demokratika—The Green Party; Maltese; monthly; Editor (vacant).

Publishers

Malta University Publishing: Robert Mifsud Bonnici St, Lija LIA 1404; tel. 21248218; fax 21230551; e-mail info@ maltauniversitybooks.com; internet www.maltauniversitybooks .com; f. 1992; owned by University of Malta; Maltese folklore, history, law, bibliography and language; also publishes in languages other than Maltese; Administrator REGINALD BARTOLO.

Publishers Enterprises Group (PEG) Ltd: PEG Bldg, UB7 Industrial Estate, San Gwann SGN 3000; tel. 21440083; fax 21488908; e-mail contact@peg.com.mt; internet www.peg.com.mt; f. 1983;

educational, children's, cookery, technical, tourism, leisure; Man. Dir EMANUEL DEBATTISTA.

Broadcasting and Communications

TELECOMMUNICATIONS

GO PLC: Spencer Hill, POB 40, Marsa MRS 1001; tel. 21210210; fax 25945895; e-mail info@go.com.mt; internet www.go.com.mt; f. 1975; fmrly Maltacom PLC; restyled 2007; mobile cellular and fixed-line telecommunications, broadband internet access, digital television services; 60% owned by TECOM Investments and the Dubai Investment Group, both mems of Dubai Holding; Chair. DEEPAK PADMANABHAN; CEO YIANNOS MICHAELIDES.

GO Mobile: Fra Diego St, Marsa MRS 1501; tel. 21246200; fax 21234314; internet www.go.com.mt/gomobile.

Melita PLC: Gasan Centre, Mriehel Bypass, Mriehel BKR 3000; tel. 27788500; fax 22745050; e-mail customercare@melitaplc.com; internet www.melita.com; f. 1992; offers mobile and fixed-line telecommunications services, and broadband internet access; also digital television services; CEO ANDREI MARC TORRIANI.

Vodafone Malta: Skyparks Business Centre, Malta Int. Airport, Luqa LQA 4000; tel. 99999247; fax 92111369; e-mail 247.mt@ vodafone.com; internet www.vodafone.com.mt; mobile telecommunications and broadband internet services; CEO BALESH SHARMA.

Regulatory Authority

Malta Communications Authority (MCA): Pinto Wharf, Valletta Waterfront, Floriana FRN 1913; tel. 21336840; fax 21336846; e-mail info@mca.org.mt; internet www.mca.org.mt; f. 2001; national agency responsible for regulating electronic communications, postal services and electronic commerce; Chair. ANTONIO GHIO; CEO IAN AGIUS (acting).

BROADCASTING
Regulatory Authority

Broadcasting Authority, Malta: 7 Mile End Rd, Ħamrun HMR 1719; tel. 21247908; fax 21240855; e-mail info.ba@ba-malta.org; internet www.ba-malta.org; f. 1961; statutory body responsible for the supervision and regulation of radio and television broadcasting; Chair. ANTHONY J. TABONE; CEO PIERRE CASSAR.

Radio and Television

Digital terrestrial television was introduced on 1 February 2011.

Bay Radio: Eden Pl., St George's Bay, St Julian's STJ 3310; tel. 23710800; fax 23710845; e-mail info@bay.com.mt; internet www.bay .com.mt; Station Man. KEVIN DECESARE, Jr.

Calypso Radio 101.8 FM: Calypso Media Communications, 28, New St in Valletta Rd, Luqa; tel. 21578022; fax 21578026; e-mail info@calypsoradio.com; internet www.calypsoradio.com; Station Man. FRANK CAMILLERI.

Campus FM: Old Humanities Bldg, University of Malta, Tal-Qroqq, Msida; tel. 21333313; fax 21314485; e-mail campusfm@um.edu.mt; internet maltauniversitybroadcasting.com; Station Man. Rev. JOSEPH BORG.

Education 22: Mile End St, Ħamrun HMR 1716; tel. 21239274; fax 21240701; e-mail info@e22.com.mt; internet www.e22.com.mt; f. 1996; educational television channel.

Media.link Communications Co Ltd: Dar Centrali, Herbert Ganado St, Pietà PTA 1450; tel. 21243641; fax 21243640; e-mail antona@vol.net.mt; internet www.ping.com.mt.

Net TV: Dar Centrali, Herbert Ganado St, Pietà PTA 1450; tel. 21243641; fax 21226645; internet www.nettv.com.mt; f. 1998.

Radio 101: Independence Point, Herbert Ganado St, Pietà PTA 1450; tel. 21241164; fax 21564111; e-mail news@media.link.com .mt; internet www.radio101.com.mt.

ONE Productions Ltd: A28B, Industrial Estate, Marsa MRS 3000; tel. 25682568; fax 25682309; e-mail info@one.com.mt; internet www .one.com.mt; f. 1999; owned by Partit Laburista; Exec. Chair. JASON MICALLEF.

One Television: A28B Industrial Estate, Marsa MRS 3000; tel. 25682800; fax 25682409; e-mail ruth.vella@one.com.mt; broadcasts 126 hours weekly; Dir of Television RUTH VELLA MICALLEF.

Super One Radio: A28B, Industrial Estate, Marsa MRS 3000; tel. 25682600; fax 21231472; e-mail ray.azzopardi@one.com.mt; broadcasts 24 hours daily; Senior Man. RAY AZZOPARDI.

Public Broadcasting Services Ltd (PBS): 75 St Luke's Rd, Gwardamangia PTA 1025; tel. 21225051; fax 21244601; e-mail info@pbs.com.mt; internet tvm.com.mt; f. 1991; govt-owned; operates national radio and television services: Radju Malta, Radju

Parlament, Ten Sixty Six, Magic 91.7 and Television Malta; Chair. TONIO PORTUGHESE; CEO ANTON ATTARD.

Radju Marija: Kunvent Patrijiet Dumnikani, Misrah San Duminku, Rabat RBT 2521; tel. 21453105; fax 21453103; e-mail info.mal@radiomaria.org; internet www.radjumarija.org; f. 1995.

RTK Radio: Media Centre, National Rd, Blata il-Bajda HMR 1640; tel. 25699140; fax 25699147; e-mail jcamilleri@rtk.org.mt; internet www.rtk.org.mt; f. 1992; radio station of the Catholic Church of Malta; Chair. FRANCO AZZOPARDI; CEO MICHAEL FRANCALANZA.

Smash TV and Radio: Smash Bldgs, Triq ix-Xewk, Rahal Gdid; tel. 21667777; e-mail info@smashmalta.com; internet www.smash.com .mt; f. 1992; Man. Dir JOSEPH BALDACCHINO.

XFM 100.2 FM: 111 Annunciation St, St Venera SVR 1021; tel. 21230228; e-mail info@xfmmalta.com; internet www.xfmmalta.com; f. 2003; programmes in Maltese and English; music; Station Man. DAVID AZZOPARDI.

Finance

(cap. = capital; res = reserves; dep. = deposits; m. = million; brs = branches; amounts in euros, unless otherwise indicated)

REGULATORY AUTHORITY

Malta Financial Services Authority: Notabile Rd, Attard BKR 3000; tel. 21441155; fax 21441188; e-mail communications@mfsa .com.mt; internet www.mfsa.com.mt; f. 2002; supervises the financial services sector, incl. banking, insurance and investments; regulates activities of Malta Stock Exchange; houses Malta's Companies Registry; Chair. Prof. JOSEPH V. BANNISTER.

BANKING
Central Bank

Central Bank of Malta: Pjazza Kastilja, Valletta VLT 1060; tel. 25500000; fax 25502500; e-mail info@centralbankmalta.org; internet www.centralbankmalta.org; f. 1968; govt-owned; cap. 20m., res 246.5m., dep. 1,105.6m. (Dec. 2010); Gov. JOSEF BONNICI.

Commercial Banks

APS Bank Ltd: APS Centre, Tower St, Birkirkara BKR 4012; tel. 21226644; fax 25603001; e-mail headoffice@apsbank.com.mt; internet www.apsbank.com.mt; f. 1910; cap. 29.2m., res 5.8m., dep. 738.3m. (Dec. 2011); Chair. EMMANUEL P. DELIA; CEO EDWARD CACHIA; 6 brs.

Banif Bank (Malta) PLC: Level 2, 203 Rue D'Argens, Gzira GZR 1368; tel. 22601000; fax 21312000; e-mail customercare@banif.com .mt; internet www.banif.com.mt; f. 2008; owned by Grupo Banif (Portugal); cap. 32.5m., res –4m., dep. 443.3m. (Dec. 2011); Chair. JOSEPH SAMMUT; CEO JOAQUIM SILVA PINTO; 5 brs.

Bank of Valletta PLC: BOV Centre, Cannon Rd, St Venera SVR 9030; tel. 22751537; fax 22753700; e-mail customercare@bov.com; internet www.bov.com; f. 1974; merged with Valletta Investment Bank Ltd in Oct. 2000; cap. 240m., res 19m., dep. 5,685.8m. (Sept. 2011); Chair. (vacant); CEO CHARLES BORG; 46 brs.

HSBC Bank Malta PLC: 233 Republic St, Valletta VLT 1116; tel. 23802380; fax 23804923; e-mail infomalta@hsbc.com; internet www .hsbc.com.mt; f. 1975 as Mid-Med Bank; 70.03% owned by HSBC Europe BV; cap. 87.6m., res 32.9m., dep. 4,792.1m. (Dec. 2011); CEO MARK WATKINSON; 43 brs.

Lombard Bank Malta PLC: Lombard House, 67 Republic St, Valletta VLT 1117; tel. 25581100; fax 25581150; e-mail mail@ lombardmalta.com; internet www.lombardmalta.com; f. 1969; cap. 9m., res 22.3m., dep. 469.3m. (Dec. 2011); Chair. CHRISTIAN LEMMERICH; Dir and CEO JOSEPH SAID; 6 brs.

Volksbank Malta Ltd: 53 Dingli St, Sliema SLM 09; tel. 27777777; fax 21336090; e-mail info@volksbank.com.mt; f. 1995 as an 'offshore' bank; licensed to operate as a commercial bank in 2002; Chair. WINSTON V. ZAHRA; Man. Dir HERBERT SKOK.

Principal 'Offshore' Bank

FIMBank PLC: Mercury Tower, The Exchange Financial & Business Centre, Elia Zammit St, St Julian's STJ 3155; tel. 21322100; fax 21322122; e-mail info@fimbank.com; internet www.fimbank.com; f. 1994 as First International Merchant Bank PLC; cap. US $68m., dep. $777m., total assets $1,018m. (Dec. 2012); Chair. Dr JOHN C. GRECH; Pres. MARGRITH LÜTSCHG-EMMENEGGER.

Bankers' Association

Malta Bankers' Association: 48/2 Birkirkara Rd, Attard ATD 1210; tel. 21412210; fax 21424580; e-mail info@maltabankers.org; internet www.maltabankers.org; f. 1962; Chair. MARK WATKINSON; Sec.-Gen. JAMES BONELLO; 27 mem banks.

STOCK EXCHANGE

Malta Stock Exchange: Garrison Chapel, Castille Pl., Valletta VLT 1063; tel. 21244051; fax 25696316; e-mail borza@borzamalta .com.mt; internet www.borzamalta.com.mt; f. 1992; Chair. Dr ARTHUR GALEA SALOMONE; Chief Exec. EILEEN V. MUSCAT.

INSURANCE

Mediterranean Insurance Brokers (Malta) Ltd: 53 MIB House, Abate Rigord St, Ta'Xbiex XBX 1122; tel. 23433234; fax 21341599; e-mail info@mib.com.mt; internet www.mib.com.mt; f. 1976; Man. Dir JOSEPH CUTAJAR.

Middlesea Insurance PLC: Middle Sea House, Floriana FRN 1442; tel. 21246262; fax 21248195; internet www.middlesea.com; f. 1981; Pres. and CEO ALFREDO MUNOZ.

Numerous foreign insurance companies, principally British, Canadian and Italian, are represented in Malta by local agents.

Insurance Association

Malta Insurance Association: 43A/2, St Paul's Bldgs, West St, Valletta VLT 1532; tel. 21232640; fax 21248388; e-mail mia@ maltainsurance.org; internet www.maltainsurance.org; Dir-Gen. ADRIAN J. GALEA; 22 mem. cos (2012).

Trade and Industry

GOVERNMENT AGENCIES

Malta Enterprise: Gwardamangia Hill, Pieta MEC 0001; tel. 25420000; fax 25423401; e-mail info@maltaenterprise.com; internet www.maltaenterprise.com; f. 2004; CEO SUE VELLA.

Malta Investment Management Co Ltd (MIMCOL): Clock Tower, Level 1, Tigné Point Sliema TP 01; tel. 21497970; fax 21499568; e-mail info@mgis.com.mt; internet mimcol.com.mt; f. 1988; manages govt investments in domestic commercial enterprises and encourages their transfer to private sector ownership; Chair. JOHN IVAN FALZON; CEO VINCENT MIFSUD.

DEVELOPMENT ORGANIZATION

FinanceMalta: Garrison Chapel, Castille Pl., Valletta VLT 1063; tel. 21224525; fax 21449212; e-mail contact@financemalta.org; internet www.financemalta.org; public-private initiative to promote international investment in Malta; Chair. KENNETH FARRUGIA.

EMPLOYERS' ORGANIZATIONS

The Malta Chamber of Commerce, Enterprise and Industry: Exchange Bldgs, Republic St, Valletta VLT 1117; tel. 21233873; fax 21245223; e-mail info@maltachamber.org.mt; internet www .maltachamber.org.mt; f. 2008 by merger of Malta Chamber of Commerce and Enterprise with Malta Federation of Industry; Pres. TANCRED TABONE; 1,200 mems.

Malta Employers' Association: 35/1 South St, Valletta VLT 1100; tel. 21222992; fax 21230227; e-mail admin@maltaemployers.com; internet www.maltaemployers.com; f. 1965; Pres. JOSHUA ZAMMIT; Dir-Gen. JOSEPH FARRUGIA.

UTILITIES

Malta Resources Authority: Millennia, 2nd Floor, Aldo Moro Rd, Marsa MRS 9065; tel. 22955000; fax 22955200; e-mail enquiry@mra .org.mt; internet www.mra.org.mt; set up by the Maltese Parliament through the Malta Resources Authority Act of 2000; regulates water and energy utilities; Chair. MARIO GALEA (acting); CEO ANTHONY RIZZO.

Electricity and Gas

Easygas (Malta) Ltd: Valletta Rd, Luqa Malta; tel. 21821557; e-mail info@easygas.com; licensed supplier of LPG gas.

Enemalta Corporation: Church Wharf, Marsa HMR 01; tel. 21224600; fax 21246637; e-mail info.emc@enemalta.com.mt; internet www.enemalta.com.mt; f. 1977; state-owned energy corpn responsible for generating and distributing electricity and storing liquefied petroleum gas for the distributors; Exec. Chair. LOUIS GIORDIMAINA.

Liquigas Malta Limited: Freeport Centre, Kalafrana, B'Buga BBG 3011; tel. 21651661; fax 22486060; e-mail info@liquigasmalta .com; internet www.liquigasmalta.com; jt venture of Liquigas SpA (Italy) and Multigas Limited (Malta); responsible for providing LPG gas; CEO ROBERTO CAPELLUTO.

Water

Water Services Corporation: Qormi Rd, Luqa LQA 9043; tel. 22445566; fax 22443900; e-mail customercare@wsc.com.mt; internet www.wsc.com.mt; f. 1992; govt corpn responsible for the production and distribution of drinking water and the local sewerage system; Chair. LOUIS GIORDIMAINA; CEO MARC MUSCAT.

TRADE UNIONS

Confederation of Malta Trade Unions (CMTU): 9C Mikiel Anton Vassalli St, Valletta VLT 1310; tel. 21237313; fax 21250146; e-mail info@cmtu.org.mt; internet www.cmtu.org.mt; f. 1958; affiliated to the World Confed. of Labour, to the Commonwealth Trade Union Council and to the ETUC; Pres. WILLIAM PORTELLI; Gen. Sec. CHARLES MAGRO.

Transport

REGULATORY BODIES

Transport Malta: Sa Maison Rd, Floriana FRN 1612; tel. 21222203; fax 21255740; e-mail info.tm@transport.gov.mt; internet www .transport.gov.mt; regulatory body for transport in Malta; Chair. JAMES PISCOPO.

RAILWAYS

There are no railways in Malta.

ROADS

In 2010 there were 3,096 km of roads, of which about 87.5% of roads were paved. Bus services serve all parts of the main island and most parts of Gozo. In July 2011 a new public transport network of bus services, operated by Arriva Malta, was introduced.

Arriva Malta: Triq l-Imdina, Ħal Qormi QRM 9010; tel. 21222000; e-mail enquiries@arriva.com.mt; internet www.arriva.com.mt; f. 2011; 66% owned by Arriva Germany; 33% owned by Maltese Tumas group; sole operator of bus services in Malta; Man. Dir DAVE KAYE (acting).

SHIPPING

Malta's national shipping register is open to ships of all countries. At 31 December 2012 Malta's flag registered fleet comprised 1,961 vessels, with a total displacement of 45.5m. grt, of which 546 were bulk and 334 general cargo ships. The island's dry dock facilities are also an important source of revenue.

Bianchi & Co (1916) Ltd: Palazzo Marina, 143 St Christopher St, Valletta VLT 1465; tel. 21232241; fax 21232991; e-mail info@bianchi .com.mt; Man. Dir R. BIANCHI.

Cassar & Cooper Ltd: Valletta Bldgs, 54 South St, POB 311, Valletta VLT 11; tel. 25584000; fax 21237864; e-mail info@ cassar-cooper.com; internet www.cassar-cooper.com; cargo shipping; also ship agency; Dir MICHAEL COOPER.

Gollcher Group: 19 Zachary St, POB 268, Valletta VLT 1133; tel. 25691100; fax 21234195; e-mail contact@gollcher.com; internet www .gollcher.com; f. 1854; Dir KARL GOLLCHER.

Malta Freeport Terminals Ltd: Freeport Centre, Port of Marsaxlokk, Kalafrana BBG 3011; tel. 21650200; fax 22251900; e-mail marketing@maltafreeport.com.mt; internet www.maltafreeport .com.mt; f. 1988; 2 container terminals; also operates petroleum products terminal and general warehousing facilities; Man. Dir UWE MALEZKI.

Malta Motorways of the Sea Ltd: 21–22 St Barbara Bastion, Valletta VLT 1961; tel. 21251564; fax 21226876; e-mail info@mmos .com.mt; internet www.mmos.com.mt; f. 2005; owned by Grimaldi Group (Italy); operates ro-ro and passenger ferry services between Malta, Italy (including Sicily) and Libya; Man. Dir ERNEST SULLIVAN; Gen. Man. JOSEPH BUGEJA.

Mifsud Brothers Ltd: 14 Lighters Wharf, Grand Harbour Menqa, Marsa MRS 1442; tel. 21232157; fax 21221331; e-mail info@mbl.com .mt; internet www.mbl.com.mt; f. 1860; shipping and travel agents; Man. Dir IVAN MIFSUD.

SMS Shipping: 27 Birkirkara Hill, St Julian's STJ 1143; tel. 25770000; e-mail info@sms.com.mt; internet www.sms.com.mt; ship and forwarding agency; also ship supplies and bunkering; subsidiary of SMS Group Ltd; Chair. NEVILLE MIFSUD.

Sullivan Shipping Agencies Ltd: Exchange Bldgs, Republic St, Valletta VLT 1117; tel. 22296000; fax 21233417; e-mail info@ sullivanshipping.com.mt; internet www.sullivanshipping.com.mt; f. 1888; owned by Sullivan Consolidated Group; Chair. and CEO JOHN E. SULLIVAN.

Thomas Smith & Co Ltd: 12 St Christopher St, Valletta VLT 1468; tel. 22058000; fax 22058399; e-mail info@tcsmith.com; internet www .tcsmith.com; f. 1848; Man. Dir JOE GERADA.

Virtu Ferries Ltd: Ta'Xbiex Terrace, Ta'Xbiex XBX 1034; tel. 23491000; fax 21314533; e-mail admin@virtuferries.com; internet www.virtuferries.com; f. 1988; Malta–Sicily (Italy) express passenger ferry service.

CIVIL AVIATION

Malta International Airport is situated at Gudja (8 km from Valletta).

Air Malta PLC: Skyparks Business Centre, Level 2, Malta Int. Airport, Luqa LQA 9020; tel. 21662211; e-mail customercare .airmalta@airmalta.com; internet www.airmalta.com; f. 1973; national airline with a 96.4% state shareholding; scheduled passenger and cargo services to mainland Europe, the United Kingdom, North Africa and the Middle East; charter services to the United Kingdom and mainland Europe; Chair. LOUIS FARRUGIA; CEO PETER DAVIES.

Tourism

Malta offers climatic, scenic and historical attractions, including fine beaches. Tourism forms a major sector of Malta's economy, generating provisional receipts of US $1,265m. in 2011. Tourist arrivals totalled 1,338,841 in 2010 and 1,415,135 in 2011.

Malta Tourism Authority (MTA): Auberge d'Italie, Merchants St, Valletta VLT 1170; tel. 22915000; fax 22915394; e-mail info@ visitmalta.com; internet www.mta.com.mt; Chair. RAY FENECH; CEO JOSEF FORMOSA GAUCI.

Defence

As assessed at November 2011, the armed forces of Malta comprised a regular army of 1,950. There was also a reserve of 170. Military service is voluntary.

Defence Expenditure: €41m. in 2012.

Commander of the Armed Forces: Brig. MARTIN G. XUEREB.

Education

The Ministry of Education and Employment is responsible for providing all levels of education. From the age of two years and nine months until the age of four years, children study in kindergarten centres, although it is not compulsory. Provision is free in all government schools and church schools. Education is free and compulsory between the ages of five and 16 years. In 2010/11 enrolment at pre-primary level included 99% of children in the relevant age-group. Primary education begins at five years of age and lasts for six years. In 2010/11 enrolment at primary level included 94% of children in the relevant age-group. Secondary education, beginning at 11 years of age, lasts for a maximum of seven years, but this period is extended in the case of technology and vocational courses. Enrolment at secondary level in 2010/11 included 81% of children in the relevant age-group. After completing five years of secondary-level education, students with the necessary qualifications may opt to follow a higher academic, technical or vocational course. The junior college, administrated by the University of Malta, is attended by students aged between 16 and 18 years. It prepares students specifically for a university course by providing them with a Matriculation Certificate after successful completion of a two-year course. About 30% of the student population attend schools administered by the Roman Catholic Church, from kindergarten to higher secondary level. The Government subsidizes the provision of free education for students in church schools. Higher education is available at the University of Malta. There are also a number of technical institutes, specialist schools and an extended skills training scheme for trade school graduates. There were 10,840 students enrolled in higher education in 2009/10. The Government also provides adult education courses. Central government expenditure on education totalled €147.8m. in 2011.

THE MARSHALL ISLANDS

Introductory Survey

LOCATION, CLIMATE, LANGUAGE, RELIGION, FLAG, CAPITAL

The Republic of the Marshall Islands consists of two groups of islands, the Ratak ('sunrise') and Ralik ('sunset') chains, comprising 29 atolls (some 1,225 islets) and five islands, and covering about 180 sq km (70 sq miles) of land. The territory lies within the area of the Pacific Ocean known as Micronesia (which includes Kiribati, Tuvalu and other territories). The islands lie about 3,200 km (2,000 miles) south-west of Hawaii and about 2,100 km (1,300 miles) south-east of Guam. Rainfall decreases from south to north, with January, February and March being the driest months, although seasonal variations in rainfall and temperature are generally small. The native population comprises various ethno-linguistic groups, but English is widely understood. The principal religion is Christianity. The national flag (proportions 100 by 190) is dark blue, with a representation of a white star (with 20 short and four long rays) in the upper hoist; superimposed across the field are two progressively wider stripes (orange above white), running from near the lower hoist corner to near the upper fly corner. The capital is the Delap-Uliga-Darrit Municipality, on Majuro Atoll.

CONTEMPORARY POLITICAL HISTORY

Historical Context

The first European contact with the Marshall and Caroline Islands was by Spanish expeditions in the 16th century, including those led by Alvaro de Saavedra and Fernão de Magalhães (Ferdinand Magellan), the Portuguese navigator. The islands received their name from the British explorer, John Marshall, who visited them at the end of the 18th century. Spanish sovereignty over the Marshall Islands was recognized in 1886 by the Papal Bull of Pope Leo XIII, which also gave Germany trading rights there (German trading companies had been active in the islands from the 1850s). In 1899 Germany bought from Spain the Caroline Islands and the Northern Mariana Islands (except Guam, which had been ceded to the USA after the Spanish–American War of 1898). In 1914, at the beginning of the First World War, Japan occupied the islands, and received a mandate for their administration from the League of Nations in 1920. After the capture of the islands by US military forces in 1944 and 1945, most of the Japanese settlers were repatriated, and in 1947 the UN established the Trust Territory of the Pacific Islands (comprising the Caroline Islands, the Marshall Islands and the Northern Mariana Islands), to allow the USA to administer the region. The territory was governed by the US Navy from 1947 until 1951, when control passed to a civil administration—although the Northern Mariana Islands remained under military control until 1962.

From 1965 onwards there were increasing demands for local autonomy. In that year the Congress of Micronesia was formed; in 1967 a commission was established to examine the future political status of the islands. In 1970 it declared Micronesians' rights to sovereignty over their own lands, to self-determination, to their own constitution and to revoke any form of free association with the USA. In 1977, after eight years of negotiations, US President Jimmy Carter announced that his Administration intended to adopt measures to terminate the trusteeship agreement by 1981.

On 9 January 1978 the Marianas District achieved separate status as the Commonwealth of the Northern Mariana Islands (q.v.), but remained legally a part of the trusteeship until 1986. The Marshall Islands District drafted its own Constitution, which came into effect on 1 May 1979, and the four districts of Yap, Truk (now Chuuk), Ponape (now Pohnpei) and Kosrae ratified a new Constitution, to become the Federated States of Micronesia (q.v.), on 10 May 1979. In the Palau District a referendum in July 1979 approved a proposed local Constitution, which took effect on 1 January 1981, when the district became the Republic of Palau (q.v.).

The USA signed a Compact of Free Association with the Republic of Palau in August 1982, and reached agreement with the Marshall Islands and the Federated States of Micro-

nesia in October. The trusteeship of the Pacific territory was due to end after the principle and terms of Compacts of Free Association had been approved by the respective peoples and legislatures of the new countries, by the US Congress and by the UN Security Council. Under the Compacts, the four countries (including the Northern Mariana Islands) would be independent of each other and would manage both their internal and foreign affairs separately, while the USA would be responsible for defence and security. Moreover, Marshallese citizens were granted the right to live and work in the USA. The final draft of the Compact of Free Association with the USA was signed by the Marshall Islands in June 1983 and approved by plebiscite in September. Under the terms of the Compact, which took effect on 21 October 1986, the USA was to retain its military bases in the Marshall Islands for at least 15 years and, over the same period, was to provide annual aid of US $30m. The UN Security Council finally ratified the termination of the trusteeship agreement in December 1990.

Domestic Political Affairs

The Marshall Islands' atolls of Bikini and Enewetak were used by the USA for experiments with nuclear weapons: Bikini in 1946–58 and Enewetak in 1948–58. The native inhabitants of Enewetak were evacuated before tests began, and were allowed to return to the atoll in 1980, after much of the contaminated area had supposedly been rendered safe. The inhabitants of Bikini Atoll campaigned for similar treatment, and in 1985 the US Administration agreed to decontaminate Bikini Atoll over a period of 10–15 years. In 1985 the entire population of Rongelap Atoll, which had been engulfed by radioactive fall-out from the tests at Bikini in 1954, was forced to resettle on Mejato Atoll, after surveys suggested that levels of radiation at Rongelap remained dangerous. In April 2001, following the adoption by the USA of a new standard of radioactivity considered to be acceptable, some six times lower than the previous level, the Tribunal announced that Ailuk Atoll was to be evacuated and environmental studies conducted.

Under the terms of the Compact, the US Government consented to establish a US $150m. Nuclear Claims Fund to settle claims against the USA resulting from nuclear testing in the Marshall Islands during the 1940s and 1950s. Accordingly, the Marshall Islands Nuclear Claims Tribunal was established in 1988, with jurisdiction to 'render final determination upon all claims past, present and future, of the Government, citizens and nationals of the Marshall Islands' in respect of the nuclear testing programme. A compensation programme was implemented in 1991 for personal injuries deemed to have resulted from the testing programme. The Tribunal initially identified 25 diseases for which credible evidence demonstrated a significant statistical relationship between exposure to radiation and subsequent development of a disease; in response to the findings of later studies, by 2003 the Tribunal's list had been extended to include 11 further conditions. By the end of 2003 compensation awards totalling $83m. had been made to, or on behalf of, 1,865 individuals who had contracted one or more of these conditions. Additionally, an award of some $578m. had been ordered by the Tribunal in May 2000 in respect of a class action brought by the people of Enewetak for loss of and damage to property; and an award of $563m. had been ordered in March 2002 in settlement of a class action brought by the peoples of Bikini Atoll; settlements of similar class actions by the peoples of Rongelap and Utrik Atolls were being finalized, while a new class action had been submitted by the people of Ailuk Atoll. However, only $45.8m. had been made available for actual payment of awards decided by the Tribunal; furthermore, less than $6m. remained of the original value of the Fund. In view of the inadequacy of the Fund to meet the compensation awards made by the Tribunal, in September 2000 the Marshall Islands Government formally petitioned the US Congress for a renegotiation of the settlement agreed under the Compact; the basis of the petition, which sought additional compensation amounting to some $3,000m., was an article of the agreement providing for what were termed 'Changed Circumstances'. In August 2004 the Tribunal declared a deadline for islanders' compensation claims of the end of that month (subsequently extended to 31 December), owing to a severe shortage of funds.

In January 2005, following the publication of a report by the US Department of State's Bureau of East Asian and Pacific Affairs, the Administration of US President George W. Bush recommended that Congress reject the Marshall Islands' request for additional compensation payments, citing a lack of a scientific or legal basis for the request. The Bush Administration's rejection of the appeal was reiterated at a congressional hearing in May, although several senators expressed support for further consideration of the matter. At a Small Islands Summit meeting held in October in the Papua New Guinean capital of Port Moresby, the Marshall Islands' delegation reiterated its demand for a further US $3,000m. in compensation from the US Government. In April 2006 it was announced that the people of Bikini were suing the US Government in the Court of Federal Claims for $561m. as compensation or damages: the original award of $563m. minus the actual payment of $2.3m. The Marshall Islands Government expressed its support for the action. In April 2007 the Marshall Islands Nuclear Claims Tribunal ruled that claimants of Rongelap should receive $1,000m. in compensation; at the same time, however, the funds available to the Tribunal had decreased to just $1m. In August the Court of Federal Claims dismissed the lawsuit submitted by the people of Bikini Atoll against the US Government on the basis that it had been submitted after the expiry of a six-year statute of limitations for the filing of such claims. The dismissal was upheld by the US Court of Appeals in February 2009 and by the US Supreme Court in April 2010. Meanwhile, in March 2009, following confirmation by France that further consideration was to be given to compensation claims by those affected by its nuclear tests, the Marshall Islands renewed its request for additional compensation from the US Government. An amended version of a US Senate bill first proposed in September 2007, which had sought additional compensation for inhabitants of Bikini, Enewetak, Rongelap and Utrik, was introduced to the upper congressional chamber in February 2011. The bill was subsequently referred to the Senate Committee on Energy and Natural Resources; at early 2013 no subsequent developments had been reported.

In January 1994, meanwhile, several senior members of the Marshall Islands' legislature, the Nitijela, demanded that the US authorities release detailed information on the effects of its nuclear-testing programme in the islands. In July documentation released by the US Department of Energy gave conclusive evidence that Marshall Islanders had been deliberately exposed to high levels of radiation in order that its effects on their health could be studied by US medical researchers. Further evidence emerged during 1995 that the USA had withheld the medical records of islanders involved in radiation experiments (which included tritium and chromium-51 injections and genetic and bone-marrow transplant experiments).

Despite the publication of a study conducted by US scientists (in 1992) into contamination levels on Bikini Atoll, which suggested that radiation levels there remained dangerous, in February 1997 a group of Bikini Islanders returned for the first time since 1946 to assist in the rehabilitation of the atoll for resettlement. The operation was to involve the removal of radioactive topsoil (although the matter of its disposal presented a serious problem) and the saturation of the remaining soil with potassium, which was believed to inhibit the absorption of radioactive material by root crops. A report published by the International Atomic Energy Agency in 1998 found that Bikini Atoll remained unsafe for habitation, owing to continuing dangerous levels of radiation. In early 1999 the Nuclear Claims Tribunal demanded the adoption of US Environmental Protection Agency standards in the rehabilitation of contaminated islands, claiming that Marshall Islanders deserved to receive the same treatment as US citizens would in similar circumstances. The US Department of Energy, however, expressed strong resistance to the demand. In February 2001 a report published by an eminent Japanese scientist stated that radiation levels on Rongelap Island, according to research conducted in 1999, had now declined to such a level that human habitation of the island was again possible. Although the USA funded a clean-up and rehabilitation programme on the island, including the construction of new housing and infrastructure, few islanders had returned to Rongelap by 2012 and concerns remained over the actual safety of resettlement. In September 2012, following a fact-finding mission to the Marshall Islands earlier that year, UN Special Rapporteur Călin Georgescu presented a report on the islands' nuclear legacy to the UN Human Rights Council. The document highlighted the health complications and indefinite displacement that the islanders continued to suffer and called upon the international community to provide greater assistance in dealing with the consequences of the testing by drawing up a comprehensive plan of action for the islands' long-term rehabilitation and sustainable development. The report specifically demanded that the USA provide additional compensation to those islanders affected by the testing and declassify secret documentation on the testing programme. President Christopher Loeak reiterated the report's proposals in his address to the UN General Assembly later that month.

Another atoll in the Marshall Islands, Kwajalein, has been used since 1947 as a target for the testing of missiles fired from California, USA. The Compact as ratified in 1986 committed the US Government to provide an estimated US $170m. in rent over a period of 30 years for land used as the site of a missile-tracking station, and a further $80m. for development projects. The inhabitants of Kwajalein Atoll were concentrated on the small island of Ebeye, adjacent to the US base on Kwajalein Island, before a new programme of weapons-testing began in 1961. Consequent overcrowding reportedly led to numerous social problems on Ebeye. In 1989 the Marshall Islands Government agreed that the USA could lease a further four islands in the atoll, for five years, for the purpose of military tests. A further lease agreement was signed in 1995 for the use of Biken Island (in Aur Atoll) and Wake Island in the missile-testing programme. The issue of the Kwajalein lease proved to be one of the most controversial aspects of the renegotiated terms of the Compact, as signed in 2003 (see below). In January 2003 it was announced that the Marshall Islands Government and the USA had reached agreement on new terms extending the lease of the Kwajalein site, previously scheduled to end in 2016, until 2066 (with the USA retaining the right to extend the lease by a further 20 years). The renegotiated terms envisaged that payments for use of the site would be increased from $13.5m. annually to $16.9m. (including continued provision of $1.9m. annually in social funding for the residents of Ebeye), with a further increase, to more than $19.9m. per year, to enter into effect from 2014. However, Kwajalein landowners asserted that the new arrangement was invalid, since they had not consented to its terms, as constitutionally required, and refused to accept the extension beyond 2016. The dispute appeared finally to have been resolved in May 2011, when the landowners agreed to accept the terms negotiated in 2003 and an agreement was signed.

Meanwhile, following the legislative elections of November 1995, the Marshall Islands President, Iroijlaplap (Paramount Chief) Amata Kabua, who had held the post since its creation in 1979, was re-elected for a fifth term. Upon his death in December 1996, he was replaced by Iroijlaplap Imata Kabua, a cousin, in January 1997.

In 1996 the Nitijela approved legislation allowing for the introduction of gambling in the islands, in order to provide an additional source of revenue. However, following a vociferous campaign against the legislation by local church leaders, in April 1998 the Nitijela voted to repeal the law legalizing gambling: several influential politicians known to have major gambling interests (including Imata Kabua) were disqualified from voting. A second bill containing further measures to ensure the prohibition of all gambling activity in the islands was narrowly approved. Three ministers who had supported the anti-gambling legislation were dismissed in a cabinet reorganization in August. In the following month one of the dismissed ministers proposed a motion of no confidence in Kabua. The President and his supporters boycotted subsequent sessions of the Nitijela, thereby rendering the legislature inquorate and effectively precluding the vote; the motion of no confidence in Kabua was eventually defeated by a margin of one vote in October.

The administrations of President Note (1999–2007)

At the legislative elections of November 1999 the opposition United Democratic Party (UDP) secured a convincing victory over the incumbent administration, winning 18 of the 33 seats in the Nitijela. Five senior members of the outgoing Government were defeated, including the Ministers of Finance and of Foreign Affairs and Trade—both of whom had played a prominent role in the establishment of diplomatic relations with Taiwan in 1998 (see Foreign Affairs). The former Speaker of the Nitijela, Kessai Note, was elected President on 3 January 2000 (the islands' first non-traditional leader to assume the post). The UDP Chairman, Litokwa Tomeing, became the new Speaker of the legislature.

Note subsequently appointed a 10-member Cabinet, and in May established an anti-corruption task-force.

In November 2000 it was reported that finance officials had discovered that Imata Kabua had used funds granted to the Marshall Islands under the terms of the Compact of Free Association to pay off a personal loan, although the former President denied any wrongdoing. In January 2001 Kabua and former ministers in his Government presented a no confidence motion against President Note to the Nitijela, citing a number of failings by the Note Government, including its unwillingness to renegotiate land rental payments with the USA for the use of the military base on Kwajalein Atoll (although it was suggested that the vote had been intended to delay the publication of a report into mismanagement and corruption on the part of the former Government). However, the Government defeated the vote by a margin of 19 to 14.

In September 2000 the Nitijela approved legislation to ensure the closer regulation of the banking and financial sector. In May of that year the Group of Seven industrialized nations (G7) had expressed its view that the Marshall Islands had become a significant centre for the laundering of money generated by international criminal activity, and in June the Marshall Islands was one of more than 30 countries and territories criticized by the Organisation for Economic Co-operation and Development (OECD, see p. 388) for the provision of inappropriate 'offshore' financial establishments; the Marshall Islands remained on the OECD list of unco-operative tax havens until 2007. In October 2002, meanwhile, following a commendation from the IMF on a series of new measures to combat fraud, including specific legislation and the establishment of a Domestic Financial Intelligence Unit, the Financial Action Task Force on Money Laundering (see p. 465) removed the Marshall Islands from its list of countries judged to be unhelpful in the combating of international financial crime. Following the signature of a 12th bilateral tax information exchange agreement in October 2010, the Marshall Islands was considered by OECD to have substantially implemented the internationally agreed tax standard.

Negotiations began between the USA and the Marshall Islands in July 2001 to renew the provisions of the Compact of Free Association ratified in 1986, which was due to expire at the end of September 2001. A two-year extension was permitted while negotiations were under way, during which time annual assistance to the Marshall Islands was to increase by some US $5.5m. An agreement was originally scheduled for early 2002 in order to allow adequate time for the US Congress to review it and to approve the requisite legislation (by 1 October 2003), but the procedure was postponed until early May 2002 after the Marshall Islands Government submitted a proposal seeking financing of more than $1,000m. over 15 years. The Government had also objected to being allocated 25%–30% less in US grant assistance per caput than that apportioned to the Federated States of Micronesia since the year 2000. In a further attempt to increase the national income, the Government sought to raise significantly the level of taxes levied on the Kwajalein base. In November 2002 the USA and the Marshall Islands announced a programme of direct funding of $822m., to be disbursed over 20 years, in addition to the expansion of many US government services in the islands. It was envisaged that the Marshall Islands would receive some $30.5m. a year; furthermore, a trust fund would be established, to which the USA would contribute $7m. annually in order to provide a means of income after the termination of direct US assistance in 2023 (by the end of 2012 the assets of this fund totalled an estimated $165.7m.). The amended Compact of Free Association was signed by the Marshall Islands and the USA in May 2003. Under the new Compact, Marshall Islanders would for the first time require passports in order to enter the USA. They would, however, retain the right to enter the USA to live, work and study, and would no longer be required to obtain work authorization documentation before taking up employment in the USA. Other than the issue of the Kwajalein lease, a principal obstacle to the negotiation of Compact amendments had been that of immigration: the USA, increasingly preoccupied by issues of homeland security, had been notably concerned to prevent future sales of Marshallese passports (although this controversial programme had officially been suspended in 1997). Final terms, including the restoration of some rights of access to US health care and education programmes, were approved by the US Congress in November 2003, and ratified by President George W. Bush in December.

At legislative elections held in November 2003 the UDP won 20 seats in the 33-member Nitijela. The opposition grouping Aelon Kein Ad (Our Islands), which had campaigned against the terms of the renewed Compact and which received particularly strong support from Marshall Islanders resident in the USA, secured 10 seats. Note was re-elected for a second presidential term in a vote held in the Nitijela on 4 January 2004, defeating Justin deBrum, the candidate of Aelon Kein Ad, by 20 votes to nine. He and his new Cabinet were sworn in on 12 January.

The administration of President Tomeing (2007–09)

Legislative elections were held on 19 November 2007. There were complaints in Majuro, where several polling stations failed to open at the appointed time; irregularities in the counting procedure were subsequently criticized. The level of participation was relatively low, at approximately 50%. Neither the incumbent UDP nor the opposition Aelon Kein Ad succeeded in securing the requisite majority of 17 or more seats; both parties contested the results. While the UDP claimed that it should remain in power, Aelon Kein Ad—which had gained former Speaker and UDP leader Litokwa Tomeing as a member prior to the elections—maintained that, with the support of independent candidates, its United People's Party coalition would be able to defeat the UDP. Recounts in two constituencies and negotiations between the parties and independent candidates followed. The United People's Party coalition prevailed in January 2008, when the Nitijela elected Tomeing as the country's President by 18 votes (to 15 for the incumbent President Note), and Jurelang Zedkaia as Speaker by the same margin. Tomeing's new Cabinet included Christopher Loeak as Minister in Assistance to the President and Tony deBrum as Minister of Foreign Affairs.

In February 2008 President Tomeing established a commission of inquiry into the organizational failures of the 2007 elections. The commission published its findings in August 2008; the electoral failures were attributed to the former Minister of Internal Affairs, Rien Morris, and to the Public Service Commission. It was concluded that Morris had unconstitutionally interfered in the election process by appointing Carl Alik as the Chief Electoral Officer against the wishes of the Public Service Commission. The commission of inquiry made numerous recommendations, including the establishment of an election commission of five independent members, who would be responsible for the appointment of the Chief Electoral Officer.

In October 2008 the opposition UDP tabled a no-confidence motion against President Tomeing, citing the Government's alleged failures in negotiations with the USA (notably with regard to the financing of health care for islanders affected by the nuclear tests between 1946 and 1958—see above) and its refusal to proceed with an elementary school project in Majuro. However, the motion was withdrawn after the opposition conceded that it had been unable to secure the requisite support of at least 17 of the 33 members of the Nitijela.

Tony deBrum was dismissed as Minister of Foreign Affairs in February 2009, following his public criticism of President Tomeing's administration. DeBrum had been particularly critical of the President's perceived failure to provide sufficient support to landowners in their attempts to secure an increase in the rents payable to them by the USA for the use of the military base at Kwajalein Atoll (see above). John Silk was subsequently appointed as deBrum's replacement.

In April 2009 the United People's Party coalition presented a motion of no confidence against President Tomeing, which was defeated by 18 ballots to 14, after UDP members of the Nitijela voted in Tomeing's favour. Following the defeat of the motion, President Tomeing announced a cabinet reorganization in which several ministers were dismissed, including Loeak, who was replaced as Minister in Assistance to the President by Ruben Zackhras. All of the incoming ministers were members of the opposition UDP.

President Tomeing was finally ousted from power when a third motion of no confidence was submitted against him in October 2009. In the first successful vote of no confidence in the history of the Marshall Islands, the motion was carried by 17 ballots to 15. A few days later an election was conducted by the Nitijela to appoint Tomeing's replacement; Jurelang Zedkaia, hitherto Speaker of the Nitijela, emerged victorious, defeating former President Note by 17 votes to 15.

The Zedkaia administration (2009–11)

Zedkaia was sworn in as the new President in November 2009, pledging to put an end to the factionalism that had characterized the Nitijela since the 2007 elections. With the exception of the Minister of Justice, David Kramer, who resigned and was replaced by Brenson Wase, Zedkaia retained all the members of his predecessor's Cabinet. Alvin Jacklick was elected as the new Speaker of the Nitijela.

In late 2010 allegations emerged of widespread government fraud, with two criminal cases filed against the Ministry of Finance and the Ministry of Health in December. On the opening day of the new parliamentary session in early January 2011, President Zedkaia pledged to ensure that those persons found to have been complicit in any wrongdoing would be prosecuted 'to the fullest extent of the law'. By June 12 people were reported to have been charged with theft of US federal funding intended for the Ministries of Education, of Finance and of Health, and police investigations were reported to have uncovered evidence of fraud and theft within government departments dating back as far as 2006.

The Minister of Transportation and Communications, Kenneth Kedi, became the first serving cabinet minister to be charged with a criminal offence in the Marshall Islands' history when he was charged, in June 2011, with 10 criminal counts, including theft and misconduct in public office, in connection with the ongoing investigations into government fraud. When Kedi presented a plea of no contest on three counts, the Attorney-General's office withdrew the remaining seven charges against the minister. Despite being sentenced in July to a 30-day suspended prison term and being ordered to pay a fine of US $1,000, Kedi retained his post in the Cabinet. The Marshall Islands amended its criminal code in order to strengthen its provisions on bribery and other corruption offences in September, and acceded to the UN Convention against Corruption in November.

Recent developments: legislative elections of 2011

In advance of the legislative elections scheduled to be held in November 2011, a new political party, Kien Eo Am (Your Government), was formed by a number of cabinet ministers and senators associated with the incumbent administration of President Zedkaia. At the elections, held on 21 November, 96 candidates vied for the 33 seats in the Nitijela, many standing as independents. An announcement by the US Government in July that it was reviewing Marshall Islanders' migration privileges, amid congressional concerns regarding the costs of supporting island migrants, reportedly prompted a large turn-out among voters resident in the USA. Following the elections, Aelon Kein Ad, several members of the UDP and a number of independents formed a parliamentary majority controlling some 20 seats. The new Nitijela was sworn in on 3 January 2012, electing former cabinet minister and traditional chief Christopher Loeak (of Aelon Kein Ad) as President and Donald F. Capelle as Speaker. Loeak, who defeated the incumbent Zedkaia by 21 votes to 11, with one senator casting a vote for Kessai Note (although he had not been officially nominated), was formally inaugurated in mid-January, together with his new, 10-member Cabinet. Veteran politicians Tony deBrum and Phillip Muller were appointed Minister in Assistance to the President and Minister of Foreign Affairs, respectively, while Dennis Momotaro was awarded the finance portfolio and Wilbur Heine was named Minister of Internal Affairs; Hilda Heine was allocated the education portfolio, the only woman to be appointed to the Cabinet.

In March 2012 it was reported that a controversial bill to eliminate postal voting from outside the islands had been delayed in response to staunch opposition on the part of overseas Marshall Islanders (who number around 15,000).

Environmental Concerns

The Marshall Islands Government caused regional environmental concerns with regard to the proposed establishment of large-scale facilities for the storage of nuclear waste. Criticism by the US Government of the plans, announced in 1994, was strongly denounced by the Marshall Islands authorities, which claimed that the project constituted the only opportunity for the country to generate sufficient income for the rehabilitation of contaminated islands and the provision of treatment for illnesses caused by the US nuclear-test programme. However, in mid-1997 President Imata Kabua announced the indefinite suspension of the project.

Meanwhile, in 1989 a UN report on the greenhouse effect (heating of the earth's atmosphere) predicted a possible resultant rise in sea level of some 3.7 m by 2030, which would completely submerge the Marshall Islands. In early 2002 the Intergovernmental Panel on Climate Change (IPCC) projected that global sea level rises during the 21st century would sub-

merge over 80% of Majuro Atoll. The islands appeared to be increasingly vulnerable to adverse weather conditions, as exemplified in December 2008, when a state of emergency was declared owing to widespread flooding that followed unusually high tides; hundreds of people were displaced and considerable damage was caused to property. In his opening address to mark the new parliamentary session in January 2011, President Jurelang Zedkaia identified climate change as 'the single most serious threat' to the Marshall Islands. In February 2013, in an address to the UN Security Council, the Minister in Assistance to the President, Tony deBrum, argued that climate change posed a threat to international security and stressed that the very survival of the Marshall Islands was at stake if global warning were allowed to progress unchecked. In his speech, deBrum highlighted the facts that climate change was making drinking water scarce, adversely affecting food production and causing migration to other Pacific islands, as well as to Australia and the USA. A severe drought in the northern Marshall Islands prompted President Christopher Loeak to declare a state of emergency in April and a state of disaster in May.

Regional Affairs

In February 2010 the leaders of eight western Pacific island states—the Marshall Islands, together with Kiribati, Micronesia, Nauru, Palau, Papua New Guinea, Solomon Islands and Tuvalu—convened in Koror, Palau, for the first Presidential Summit of the Parties to the Nauru Agreement (PNA), a multilateral organization established in 1982 with the aim of protecting the western Pacific region's tuna industry and improving the quality of its tuna fisheries through sustainable management and innovation. (About 25%–30% of the global tuna catch is estimated to be caught in the waters of the eight PNA members.) At the Summit, the member states signed the 'Koror Declaration', which provided for the implementation of a ban on tuna-fishing in an area in the Pacific Ocean. In April the PNA Office was officially opened in Majuro, Marshall Islands.In October the PNA voted substantially to expand the area in which tuna-fishing was prohibited, to encompass some 4.5m. sq km, and to implement further restrictions on tuna-fishing in the wider region, including enhanced observer monitoring of licensed fishing vessels, with effect from 1 January 2011; it was hoped that the new measures would facilitate a 30% targeted reduction in the total tuna catch in the region compared with 2010. At a meeting of the PNA held in Alotau, Papua New Guinea, in May 2012, the fisheries ministers of the member states agreed to implement more stringent measures to minimize the impact of fishing on bycatch species (notably whale sharks).

The Marshall Islands was due to host the 44th annual summit meeting of the Pacific Islands Forum in early September 2013; the summit's main theme was to be climate change.

The Marshall Islands established full diplomatic relations with Taiwan in November 1998. The action was immediately condemned by the People's Republic of China, which in December severed diplomatic relations with the islands, closing its embassy in Majuro and suspending all intergovernmental agreements. The Note administration, which took office in January 2000, emphasized its commitment to the maintenance of diplomatic relations with Taiwan. In August 2004 the Chinese Vice-Minister of Foreign Affairs, Zhou Wenzhong, expressed his country's willingness to restore normal relations, on condition that the Marshall Islands withdraw its diplomatic recognition of Taiwan. In April 2005 it was alleged that members of the ruling UDP had accepted bribes from Chinese officials hoping to expedite a return to normal diplomatic relations and the end of Marshallese recognition of Taiwan; the Government denied the allegations. Meanwhile, in September 2004 it was announced that Taiwan was to contribute more than US $40m. over a 20-year period to the Marshall Islands trust fund established in May. In June 2006 a delegation of Marshall Islands parliamentary representatives visited the mainland Chinese capital of Beijing, at the invitation of the National People's Congress, causing consternation among some government officials over the effect on the Marshall Islands' relations with Taiwan. The leader of the delegation insisted that the Marshall Islands was simply responding to an invitation, while the Ministry of Foreign Affairs reaffirmed the country's commitment to Taiwan. In January 2008 the newly elected President, Litokwa Tomeing, who had previously expressed support for alignment with China, nevertheless confirmed that strong links with Taiwan would continue, and reinforced this position during a visit by the Taiwanese Vice-President, Annette Lu, at the end of the month.

The Minister of Foreign Affairs, Tony deBrum, and President Tomeing visited Taiwan in February and March, respectively.

Relations with Taiwan were further strengthened in March 2010, when Taiwanese President Ma Ying-jeou visited the Marshall Islands during a week-long tour of South Pacific allies. In late June–early July of that year Jurelang Zedkaia made his first official visit to Taiwan since assuming the presidency in November 2009. During his six-day visit Zedkaia met with President Ma, whereupon the two leaders pledged further to enhance bilateral co-operation in a number of areas, including the fisheries industry, education, and arts and culture. President Ma also expressed his gratitude to the Marshall Islands for advocating more meaningful Taiwanese participation within the international community. Taiwan had pledged to donate about US $10m. during 2010, to be disbursed in quarterly payments of around $2.5m., to the Marshall Islands, as in previous years. The funding was intended to support the welfare of the local population through various government projects in the fields of, *inter alia*, construction, education, finance and transport. However, in January 2011 it was announced that the disbursement of the proportion of the fourth quarterly payment intended for development projects in the Marshall Islands, which amounted to some $1.5m., was not to be completed until a progress report detailing the results generated by the third-quarter funds had been submitted by the Marshall Islands Government. With Taiwanese funding accounting for almost 8% of total annual budgetary spending in the Marshall Islands, it was feared that Taiwan's imposition of more stringent accountability requirements for funding would hinder bilateral relations. The overdue payment was released by Taiwan in March. In March 2013 President Christopher Loeak made his first official visit to Taiwan since assuming the presidency in January 2012.

The Marshall Islands Government has consistently supported Japan at the International Whaling Commission (IWC), voting in favour of commercial whaling, and also in the country's attempt to secure a permanent seat on the UN Security Council. By 2008 Japan was reported to be the third largest donor of aid to the Marshall Islands (after the USA and Taiwan). In December of that year it was announced that Japan was to provide a grant of US $2.2m. to support the islands' energy sector. Following a covert investigation conducted by a British newspaper, *The Sunday Times*, it was claimed in June 2010 that the Marshall Islands' vote in favour of commercial whaling, together with those of five other countries, had been secured as a result of Japanese bribery that was purported to include offers of additional aid donations, cash incentives and the funding of delegations' visits to whaling meetings. The Japanese authorities insisted that the issue of whaling played no part in Japan's aid programme. (However, in July 2001 the then head of the Japanese Fisheries Agency, Maseyuku Komatsu, had stated publicly that Japan used overseas aid as a tool with which to secure support for its position on whaling; however, this was swiftly denied in a formal statement issued by the Ministry.) During President Christopher Loeak's first official visit to Japan, in May 2012, he confirmed that the Marshall Islands would continue to support Japan's whaling programme at the IWC and the Japanese bid to be granted a permanent seat on the UN Security Council. The following month, in the largest single Japanese aid project to the islands to date, Japan agreed to fund the construction of two new inter-island ships (a landing craft and a passenger/cargo vessel) at a cost of $16m.

CONSTITUTION AND GOVERNMENT

The Constitution of the Republic of the Marshall Islands, which took effect on 1 May 1979, provides for a parliamentary form of government, with legislative authority vested in the 33-member Nitijela. The Nitijela (members of which are elected, by popular vote, for a four-year term) elects the President of the Marshall Islands (also a four-year mandate) from among its own members. Under the terms of the Compact of Free Association, the Republic of the Marshall Islands is a sovereign, self-governing state. The first Compact was finalized by the Governments of the Marshall Islands and the USA on 25 June 1983, and was effectively ratified by the US Congress on 14 January 1986. A revised Compact was signed by the two countries on 1 May 2003; it was ratified by the US Congress in November 2003, and signed by US President George W. Bush in December of that year. Amendments to the Compact were signed in May 2004.

Local governmental units are the municipalities and villages. Elected Magistrates and Councils govern the municipalities. Village government is largely traditional.

REGIONAL AND INTERNATIONAL CO-OPERATION

The Marshall Islands is a member of the Pacific Community (see p. 422), the Pacific Islands Forum (see p. 426), the South Pacific Regional Trade and Economic Co-operation Agreement (SPARTECA, see p. 427), the UN's Economic and Social Commission for Asia and the Pacific (ESCAP, see p. 31) and the Asian Development Bank (ADB, see p. 214). The Marshall Islands hosts the secretariat of the Parties to the Nauru Agreement, a multilateral organization charged with protecting the tuna industry in the western Pacific region.

The Marshall Islands became a member of the UN in 1991.

ECONOMIC AFFAIRS

In 2011, according to estimates by the World Bank, the Marshall Islands' gross national income (GNI), measured at average 2009–11 prices, was US $214m., equivalent to $3,910 per head. During 2002–11, it was estimated, the population increased at an average annual rate of 0.6%, while gross domestic product (GDP) per head rose, in real terms, at an average rate of 1.0% per year. According to UN figures, overall GDP increased, in real terms, at an average annual rate of 2.7% in 2002–11; real GDP increased by 5.0% in 2011. According to the Asian Development Bank (ADB), real GDP rose by 1.9% in the year ended September 2012.

Agriculture is mainly on a subsistence level. The sector (including fishing and livestock-rearing) contributed 12.7% of GDP in 2011, according to UN figures. According to FAO estimates, some 6,000 people were employed in the sector (mainly in subsistence fishing) at mid-2013. Fishing engaged 24.5% of those employed in the private sector in 2009/10. The principal crops are coconuts, cassava and sweet potatoes. Copra production increased from 4,646 short tons in 2006 to an estimated 6,053 tons in 2007. Reports suggested that in 2007/08 the amount of copra processed exceeded 7,000 tons for only the third time since records began in 1951, assisted by improved shipping services and higher global prices for the commodity. In 2009/10 exports of coconut oil and copra accounted for 7.4% of the total value of exports of goods (including re-exports). The fishing sector incorporates a commercial tuna-fishing industry, including a transshipment base on Majuro. A new tuna-processing plant, employing more than 600 local workers and built by a Chinese company, had become fully operational by 2009. In 2009/10 fish exports accounted for 27.2% of the total value of exports of goods (including re-exports), compared with 1.7% in 2004/05. The sale of fishing licences is an important source of revenue, earning the islands an estimated US $1.0m. in 2009/10. According to UN figures, agricultural GDP increased by an average of 1.9% per year during 2002–11; sectoral GDP rose by 5.0% in 2011.

Industrial activities (including mining, manufacturing, construction and utilities) contributed 12.6% of GDP in 2011, according to UN figures, and engaged 18.9% of the employed labour force in 1999. Construction and manufacturing employed 14.8% of private sector wage-earners in 2009/10. The islands have few mineral resources, although there are high-grade phosphate deposits on Ailinglaplap Atoll. According to UN figures, the GDP of the industrial sector increased at an average annual rate of 2.8% during 2002–11; industrial GDP declined by 5.6% in 2010, but expanded by 15.4% in 2011.

Manufacturing activity, which provided 1.8% of GDP in 2011, according to UN figures, consists mainly of the processing of coconuts (to produce copra and coconut oil) and other agricultural products, and of fish (see above). According to the IMF, manufacturing engaged 1.2% of those employed in the private sector in 2009/10. Manufacturing GDP increased by an average of 6.2% per year during 2002–11; the sector's GDP decreased by 11.4% in 2010, but expanded by 22.3% in 2011.

The construction sector contributed 6.8% of GDP in 2011, according to UN figures. According to the IMF, the sector engaged 13.7% of the employed population in the private sector in 2009/10. Construction GDP grew at an average annual rate of 1.7% during 2002–11; sectoral GDP decreased by 4.8% in 2010, but increased by 14.9% in 2011.

The islands are heavily reliant on imported diesel fuel for energy supplies. Severe difficulties in financing purchases of fuel led to the declaration of a state of economic emergency in 2008 (see below). A rapid energy assessment, funded by the ADB, made numerous recommendations for greater energy efficiency in the islands. The wider use of alternative sources of energy, such as solar power, was under consideration.

The services sector (comprising trade, transport, storage, communications and other activities) provided 74.7% of GDP in 2011, according to UN figures, and engaged 59.8% of the employed labour force in 1999. The international shipping registry experienced considerable expansion following political unrest in Panama in 1989, and subsequently continued to expand (largely as a result of the reflagging of US, Japanese and South Korean ships in the islands). The number of vessels registered rose from 853 in December 2005 to 2,608 at the end of 2012. Tourism receipts totalled US $3.0m. in 2010, and tourist arrivals amounted to some 5,000 in 2011. According to UN figures, services GDP increased at an average annual rate of 2.3% during 2002–11; sectoral GDP increased by 5.7% in 2011.

In 2009/10 the Marshall Islands recorded a visible merchandise trade deficit of US $93.3m., and there was a deficit of $40.7m. on the current account of the balance of payments. The only significant domestic exports in 2009/10 were fish and coconut products. Re-exports accounted for 65.3% of total exports in that year. The principal imports in 2000 included mineral fuels and lubricants (which accounted for 37.3% of total expenditure on merchandise imports), food and live animals, and machinery and transport equipment. In 2006 the principal sources of imports were the USA (which provided 45.8% of total imports), Australia and Japan. In 2000 the USA was also the principal export destination (purchasing 57.1% of total exports).

In accordance with the terms stipulated in the Compact of Free Association, financial assistance from the USA contributes a large part of the islands' revenue. Grants and military payments from the USA for use of the missile-testing site on Kwajalein, along with trust fund contributions, constitute the major part of government revenue. In 2011/12 the USA was to provide US $67.1m. in Compact funding to the islands. Considerable support has also been provided by Taiwan since the late 1990s (see Contemporary Political History). According to preliminary estimates, a budget deficit of some $2.0m., equivalent to 1.1% of GDP, was recorded in 2011/12 (following six years of surpluses). The islands' external debt totalled $101m. in 2012. In 2011 the cost of debt-servicing was estimated to be the equivalent of 11.4% of revenue from the export of goods and services. Annual inflation in Majuro averaged 4.5% in 2003–10. According to the ADB, consumer prices in Majuro increased by 9.5% in 2011. The ADB estimated that 30.9% of the work-force were unemployed in 2008. The rate of youth unemployment was estimated at 60% in 2006.

The amended Compact of Free Association, signed by the Marshall Islands and the USA in 2003 (see Contemporary Political History), planned for the gradual decrease in grant assistance over a 20-year period. The Marshallese Government declared a state of economic emergency in July 2008, following sharp increases in the cost of fuel and food imports. Serious concerns with regard to the Marshall Islands' fiscal management re-emerged in late 2010 as a major investigation into allegations of fraud was initiated (see Contemporary Political History). The IMF reported that foreign direct investment increased from US $14.6m. in 2009 to $37.1m. in 2010 (attributing the rise mainly to investment in the fisheries sector), but declined to an estimated $4.0m. in 2011. Infrastructural deficiencies and poorly performing public enterprises have created considerable budgetary pressures in recent years. Meanwhile, rising international prices for copra and coconut oil resulted in an increase in export earnings in 2010. Tax collection in the islands was also reported to have improved, although the implementation of tax reforms is still required to broaden the local tax base, increase government revenue and compensate for the future reduction in grants. The budget for 2011/12 envisaged total expenditure of $131.2m., of which 62% and 8% was to be provided by the US and Taiwanese Governments, respectively, underscoring the extent of the Marshall Islands' reliance on its two principal sources of funding. In the 12 months to September 2011 GDP growth of 0.8%, according to the ADB, was much weaker than expected, owing to a delay in the upgrade of the international airport in Majuro; growth accelerated to 1.9% in 2011/12, fuelled mainly by the resumption of work on the airport and the continuing expansion of the fishing industry. By early 2011 inflationary pressures were again in evidence. According to the IMF, the rate of inflation in Majuro increased to 9.5% in 2011, from 1.6% in 2010, but was projected to decelerate to 2.5% in 2012.

PUBLIC HOLIDAYS

2014: 1 January (New Year's Day), 28 February (for Nuclear Victims' Remembrance Day), 18 March (Good Friday), 1 May (Constitution Day), 4 July (Fishermen's Day), 5 September (Dri-Jerbal—Labour Day), 26 September (Manit—Culture Day), 17 November (Presidents' Day), 20 November (Kamolol—Thanksgiving Day), 5 December (Gospel Day), 25 December (Christmas Day).

Statistical Survey

Source (unless otherwise indicated): Economic Policy, Planning and Statistics Office (EPPSO), Office of the President, POB 2, Majuro, MH 96960; tel. (625) 3802; fax (625) 3805; e-mail planning@ntamar.net; internet www.spc.int/prism/country/mh/stats.

AREA AND POPULATION

Area: 181.4 sq km (70.0 sq miles) (land only); two island groups, the Ratak Chain (88.1 sq km) and the Ralik Chain (93.3 sq km).

Population: 50,840 at census of 1 June 1999; 53,158 (males 27,243, females 25,915) at census of 4 April 2011. *By Island Group* (2011 census): Ratak Chain 33,892 (Majuro Atoll 27,797); Ralik Chain 19,266 (Kwajalein Atoll 11,408). *Mid-2013* (Secretariat of the Pacific Community estimate): 56,086 (Source: Pacific Regional Information System).

Density (mid-2013, land area only): 309.2 per sq km.

Population by Age and Sex (Secretariat of the Pacific Community estimates at mid-2013): *0–14:* 22,931 (males 11,838, females 11,093); *15–64:* 31,701 (males 16,279, females 15,422); *65 and over:* 1,454 (males 674, females 780); *Total* 56,086 (males 28,791, females 27,295) (Source: Pacific Regional Information System).

Principal Towns (population of urban places, 1999 census): Ebeye 9,345; Darrit (Djarrot) 7,103; Delap 6,339; Rairok 3,846; Laura 2,256; Uliga 2,044. Note: The country's capital is the combined municipality of Delap-Uliga-Darrit.

Births and Deaths (2006): Registered live births 1,576; Registered deaths 318. Note: Registered live births exclude US military personnel, their dependants and contract employees (Source: UN, *Population and Vital Statistics Report*). *2010* (Secretariat of the Pacific Community estimates): Birth rate 31.1 per 1,000; death rate 5.8 per 1,000 (Source: Pacific Regional Information System).

Life Expectancy (years at birth, WHO estimates): 59 (males 58; females 60) in 2009. Source: WHO, *World Health Statistics*.

Economically Active Population (persons aged 15 years and over, 1999 census): Agriculture and fishery 2,114; Manufacturing 761; Electricity, gas and water 258; Construction 848; Wholesale and retail trade 788; Transport, storage and communications 763; Finance, insurance, real estate and business services 559; Community, social and personal services 3,803; *Sub-total* 9,894; Activities not reported 247; *Total employed* 10,141 (males 7,008, females 3,133); Unemployed 4,536 (males 2,671, females 1,865); *Total labour force* 14,677 (males 9,679, females 4,998). *2009/10* (private sector only): Fishing 1,062; Manufacturing 50; Construction 593; Wholesale and retail trade 1,738; Hotels and restaurants 150; Transport, storage and communications 324; Financial intermediation 20; Real estate, renting and business activities 221; Health and social work 47; Other services 126; Total employed 4,331 (Source: IMF, *Republic of the Marshall Islands: Statistical Appendix*—December 2011). *Mid-2013* (estimates): Agriculture, etc. 6,000; Total labour force 28,000 (Source: FAO).

HEALTH AND WELFARE
Key Indicators

Total Fertility Rate (children per woman, 2010): 3.5.

Under-5 Mortality Rate (per 1,000 live births, 2010): 26.

Physicians (per 1,000 head, 2010): 0.4.

Hospital Beds (per 1,000 head, 2010): 2.7.

Health Expenditure (2009): US $ per head (PPP): 392.

Health Expenditure (2009): % of GDP: 18.9.

Health Expenditure (2009): public (% of total): 84.0.

Access to Water (% of persons, 2010): 94.

Access to Sanitation (% of persons, 2010): 75.

Total Carbon Dioxide Emissions ('000 metric tons, 2008): 99.0.

Carbon Dioxide Emissions Per Head (metric tons, 2008): 1.9.

For sources and definitions, see explanatory note on p. vi.

AGRICULTURE, ETC.

Principal Crop ('000 metric tons, 2011, FAO estimate): Coconuts 44.0.

Livestock ('000 head, year ending September 2003): Pigs 12.9; Poultry 86.0.

Fishing ('000 metric tons, live weight, 2010, FAO estimates): Bigeye tuna 0.3; Skipjack tuna 50.0; Yellowfin tuna 7.0; Total catch (incl. others) 59.7.

Source: FAO.

INDUSTRY

Electric Energy (million kWh, Majuro only): 81.0 in 2004; 81.3 in 2005; 78.0 in 2006. Source: Asian Development Bank.

FINANCE

Currency and Exchange Rates: United States currency is used: 100 cents = 1 United States dollar (US $). *Sterling and Euro Equivalents* (31 December 2012): £1 sterling = US $1.5780; €1 = US $1.3194; US $100 = £63.37 = €75.79.

Budget (US $ million, year ending 30 September 2011, estimates): *Revenue:* Tax revenue 24.8; Social contributions 7.2; Grants 68.5; Other revenue 9.9; Total 110.4. *Expenditure:* Recurrent 89.7; Capital 18.2; Total 107.9 (excluding net lending 2.5). Source: IMF, *Republic of the Marshall Islands; Staff Report for the 2011 Article IV Consultation* (December 2011).

Cost of Living (Consumer Price Index for Majuro, average of quarterly figures; base: Jan.–March 2003 = 100): All items 136.4 in 2008; 130.1 in 2009; 136.1 in 2010 (Source: IMF, *Republic of the Marshall Islands: Statistical Appendix*—December 2011).

Gross Domestic Product (US $ million at constant 2004 prices): 136.7 in 2009; 143.8 in 2010; 151.0 in 2011. Source: Asian Development Bank.

Expenditure on the Gross Domestic Product (US $ million at current prices, 2011): Government final consumption expenditure 102.3; Private final consumption expenditure 172.2; Gross capital formation 107.3; *Total domestic expenditure* 381.8; Exports of goods and services 23.5; *Less* Imports of goods and services 216.3; *GDP in purchasers' values* 189.0. Source: UN National Accounts Main Aggregates Database.

Gross Domestic Product by Economic Activity (US $ million at current prices, 2011): Agriculture, hunting, forestry and fishing 23.1; Mining, electricity, gas and water 7.2; Manufacturing 3.3; Construction 12.4; Trade, restaurants and hotels 29.4; Transport, storage and communications 14.4; Other activities 92.2; *Sub-total* 182.0; Net of indirect taxes 7.0 (obtained as a residual); *GDP in purchasers' values* 189.0. Source: UN National Accounts Main Aggregates Database.

Balance of Payments (US $ million, year ending 30 September 2010): Merchandise exports f.o.b. 32.3; Merchandise imports c.i.f. −125.5; *Trade balance* −93.3; Services (net) −42.8; *Balance on goods and services* −136.1; Other income 34.5; *Balance on goods and income* −101.6; Private unrequited transfers (net) 60.9; *Current balance* −40.7. Source: IMF, *Republic of the Marshall Islands; Staff Report for the 2011 Article IV Consultation* (December 2011).

EXTERNAL TRADE

Principal Commodities (US $ million): *Imports* (2000): Food and live animals 5.0; Beverages and tobacco 6.0; Crude materials, ined- ible, except fuels 2.6; Mineral fuels, lubricants and related materials 20.4; Animal and vegetable oils and fats 2.4; Chemicals 0.1; Basic manufactures 3.0; Machinery and transport equipment 8.2; Miscellaneous manufactured articles 1.4; Goods not classified by kind 5.8; Total 54.7. *Exports* (year ending September 2006): Coconut oil (crude) 2.0; Copra cake 0.1; Total (incl. others) 20.3. Sources: IMF, *Republic of the Marshall Islands: Selected Issues and Statistical Appendix* (June 2008). *2009* (US $ million): Total imports 158.3; Total exports 34.3 (Source: Asian Development Bank).

Principal Trading Partners (US $ million): *Imports* (2006): Australia 5.7; Hong Kong 1.2; Japan 5.5; New Zealand 2.2; USA 31.0; Total (incl. others) 67.7 (Source: Asian Development Bank). *Exports* (2000, estimates): USA 5.2; Total (incl. others) 9.1.

TRANSPORT

Road Traffic (vehicles registered, 2004): Trucks 97; Pick-ups 423; Sedans 1,531; Jeeps 55; Buses 62; Vans 62; Scooters 20; Other motor vehicles 154; *Total* 2,404.

Shipping: *Flag Registered Fleet* (at 31 December 2012): Vessels 2,608; Displacement ('000 grt) 88,236.0 (Lloyd's List Intelligence— www.lloydslistintelligence.com). *International Sea-borne Freight Traffic** (estimates, '000 metric tons, 1990): Goods loaded 29; Goods unloaded 123 (Source: UN, *Monthly Bulletin of Statistics*).
*Including the Northern Mariana Islands, the Federated States of Micronesia and Palau.

Civil Aviation (traffic on scheduled services, 2008): Kilometres flown 1m.; Passengers carried 30,000; Passenger-km 42m.; Total ton-km 4m. (Source: UN, *Statistical Yearbook*). *2009:* Passengers carried 27,692 (Source: World Bank, World Development Indicators database).

TOURISM

Tourist Arrivals: 6,022 in 2008; 5,372 in 2009; 5,000 in 2010–11 (rounded figure).

Arrivals by Country (2009): Japan 1,431; Other Asia 2,070; USA 1,475; Total (incl. others) 5,372.

Tourism Receipts (US $ million, excl. passenger transport): 4.0 in 2009; 3.0 in 2010.

Source: World Tourism Organization.

COMMUNICATIONS MEDIA

Telephones (main lines in use, estimate): 4,400 in 2010.

Mobile Cellular Telephones (subscriptions, estimate): 3,800 in 2010.

Personal Computers: 5,000 in 2005.

Internet Users: 2,200 in 2009.

Source: International Telecommunication Union.

EDUCATION

Pre-primary (2010/11 unless otherwise indicated): 126 teachers (2002/03); 1,448 pupils enrolled.

Primary (2010/11 unless otherwise indicated): 103 schools (1998); 526 teachers (2002/03, estimate); 8,546 pupils enrolled.

Secondary (2008/09 unless otherwise indicated): 16 schools (1998); 387 teachers (2002/03, estimate); 5,229 pupils enrolled.

Higher (2002/03 unless otherwise indicated): 1 college (1994); 49 teachers (estimate); 919 students enrolled (estimate).

Pupil-teacher Ratio (primary education, UNESCO estimate): 14.5 in 2002/03.

Source: UNESCO Institute for Statistics.

Directory

The Government

HEAD OF STATE

President: CHRISTOPHER LOEAK (took office 3 January 2012; inaugurated 17 January 2012).

CABINET
(May 2013)

The Government is composed mainly of members of Aelon Kein Ad and the United Democratic Party.

Minister in Assistance to the President: TONY deBRUM.

Minister of Foreign Affairs: PHILLIP MULLER.

Minister of Education: HILDA HEINE.

Minister of Finance: DENNIS MOMOTARO.

Minister of Transportation and Communication: RIEN MORRIS.

Minister of Health: DAVID KABUA.

Minister of Public Works: HIROSHI YAMAMURA.

Minister of Internal Affairs: WILBUR HEINE.

Minister of Justice: THOMAS HEINE.

Minister of Resources and Development: MICHAEL KONELIOS.

MINISTRIES

Office of the President: Govt of the Republic of the Marshall Islands, POB 2, Majuro, MH 96960; tel. (625) 3445; fax (625) 3649; e-mail rmiop.press@gmail.com; internet www.rmi-op.net.

Ministry of Education: POB 3, Majuro, MH 96960; tel. (625) 5262; fax (625) 3861; e-mail rmimoe@rmimoe.net; internet www.rmimoe.net.

Ministry of Finance: POB P, Majuro, MH 96960; tel. (625) 3320; fax (625) 3607; e-mail secfin@ntamar.net.

Ministry of Foreign Affairs: POB 1349, Majuro, MH 96960; tel. (625) 3181; fax (625) 4979; e-mail mofasec@ntamar.net.

Ministry of Health: POB 16, Majuro, MH 96960; tel. (625) 3355; fax (625) 3432; e-mail jusmohe@ntamar.net.

Ministry of Internal Affairs: POB 18, Majuro, MH 96960; tel. (625) 3240; fax (625) 5353; e-mail rmihpo@ntamar.net.

Ministry of Justice: c/o Office of the Attorney General, Majuro, MH 96960; tel. (625) 3244; fax (625) 5218; e-mail agoffice@ntamar.net.

Ministry of Public Works: POB 1727, Majuro, MH 96960; tel. (625) 3720; fax (625) 3005; e-mail secpw@ntamar.net.

Ministry of Resources and Development: POB 1727, Majuro, MH 96960; tel. (625) 3206; fax (625) 7471; e-mail rndsec@ntamar.net; internet rmirnd.net.

Ministry of Transportation and Communication: POB 1079, Majuro, MH 96960; tel. (625) 8869; fax (625) 3486; e-mail rmimotc@ntamar.net.

Legislature

THE NITIJELA

The Nitijela (lower house) consists of 33 elected senators. Following the election held on 21 November 2011, Aelon Kein Ad (Our Islands), several members of the United Democratic Party and a number of independents formed a parliamentary majority controlling some 20 seats.

Speaker: DONALD F. CAPELLE.

THE COUNCIL OF IROIJ

The Council of Iroij is the upper house of the bicameral legislature, comprising 12 tribal chiefs who advise the Presidential Cabinet and review legislation affecting customary law, land tenure or any traditional practice.

Chairman: Iroij KOTAK LOEAK.

Election Commission

Electoral Commission: POB 18, Majuro, MH 96900; e-mail rmielectoral@yahoo.com; Chief Electoral Officer JOSEPH JORLANG.

Political Organizations

Aelon Kein Ad (Our Islands): Majuro; f. 2002; formed United People's Party coalition following 2007 elections; Chair. CHRISTOPHER LOEAK; Leader MICHAEL KABUA.

Kien Eo Am (Your Government): Majuro; f. 2011; est. by supporters of then President Jurelang Zedkaia; Pres. JURELANG ZEDKAIA; Chair. DAVID KRAMER.

United Democratic Party: Majuro; Chair. RUBEN ZACKHRAS; Pres. KESSAI NOTE.

Diplomatic Representation

EMBASSIES IN THE MARSHALL ISLANDS

Japan: A1 Lojkar Village, POB 300, Majuro, MH 96960; tel. (247) 7463; fax (247) 7493; e-mail royoji@ntamar.net; Ambassador EIICHI SUZUKI (resident in Federated States of Micronesia).

Taiwan (Republic of China): A5–6 Lojkar Village, Long Island, POB 1229, Majuro, MH 96960; tel. (247) 4141; fax (247) 4143; e-mail eoroc@ntamar.net; internet www.mofa.gov.tw; Ambassador GEORGE T. K. LI.

USA: POB 1379, Majuro, MH 96960; tel. (247) 4011; fax (247) 4012; e-mail publicmajuro@state.gov; internet majuro.usembassy.gov; Ambassador THOMAS H. ARMBRUSTER.

Judicial System

The judicial system consists of the Supreme Court and the High Court, which preside over District and Community Courts, and the Traditional Rights Court.

Supreme Court of the Republic of the Marshall Islands: POB 378, Majuro, MH 96960; tel. (625) 3201; fax (625) 3323; e-mail jutrep@ntamar.com; internet www.rmicourts.org; Chief Justice DANIEL N. CADRA.

High Court of the Republic of the Marshall Islands: Majuro; e-mail judrep@ntamar.net; Chief Justice CARL B. INGRAM.

District Court of the Republic of the Marshall Islands: Majuro, MH 96960; tel. (625) 3201; fax (625) 3323; Presiding Judge MILTON ZACKIOS.

Traditional Rights Court of the Marshall Islands: Majuro, MH 96960; customary law only; Chief Judge BERSON JOSEPH.

Religion

The population is predominantly Christian, mainly belonging to the Protestant United Church of Christ. The Roman Catholic Church, Assembly of God, Bukot Nan Jesus, Seventh-day Adventists, the Church of Jesus Christ of Latter-day Saints (Mormons), the Full Gospel and the Bahá'í Faith are also represented.

CHRISTIANITY

The Roman Catholic Church

The Apostolic Prefecture of the Marshall Islands included 5,020 adherents at 31 December 2007.

Prefect Apostolic of the Marshall Islands: Rev. Fr RAYMUNDO SABIO, POB 8, Majuro, MH 96960; tel. (625) 6675; fax (625) 5520; e-mail diocesemarshalls@yahoo.com.

Protestant Churches

The Marshall Islands come under the auspices of the United Church Board for World Ministries (475 Riverside Drive, New York, NY 10115, USA); Sec. for Latin America, Caribbean and Oceania Dr PATRICIA RUMER.

BAHÁ'Í FAITH

National Spiritual Assembly: POB 1017, Majuro, MH 96960; tel. (247) 3512; fax (247) 7180; e-mail nsamarshallislands@yahoo.com; internet www.mh.bahai.org; mems resident in 50 localities; Sec. Dr IRENE J. TAAFAKI.

The Press

Kwajalein Hourglass: POB 23, Kwajalein, MH 96555; tel. (355) 3539; e-mail jbennett@kls.usaka.smdc.army.mil; f. 1954; 2 a week; Editor JIM BENNETT; circ. 2,300.

Marshall Islands Gazette: monthly; govt publ.

Marshall Islands Journal: POB 14, Majuro, MH 96960; tel. (625) 8143; fax (625) 3136; e-mail journal@ntamar.net; internet www.marshallislandsjournal.com; f. 1970; weekly; Editor GIFF JOHNSON; circ. 3,700.

Broadcasting and Communications

TELECOMMUNICATIONS

National Telecommunications Authority (NTA): POB 1169, Majuro, MH 96960; tel. (625) 3676; fax (625) 3952; e-mail info@ntamar.net; internet www.ntamar.net; privatized in 1991; sole provider of local and long-distance tel. services and internet communications in the Marshall Islands; Chair. ALEX BING; Pres. and CEO ANTHONY M. MULLER.

BROADCASTING

Radio

Marshall Islands Broadcasting Co: POB 19, Majuro, MH 96960; tel. (625) 3250; fax (625) 3505; Chief Information Officer PETER FUCHS.

Radio Marshalls V7AB: POB 3250, Majuro, MH 96960; tel. (625) 8411; fax (625) 5353; govt-owned; commercial; programmes in English and Marshallese; Station Man. ANTARI ELBON.

Other radio stations include Micronesia Heatwave and V7AA.

Television

Marshalls Broadcasting Co Television: POB 19, Majuro, MH 96960; tel. (625) 3413; Chief Information Officer PETER FUCHS.

The US Department of Defense operates the American Forces Radio and Television Service for the Bucholz Army Airfield on Kwajalein Atoll.

Finance

(cap. = capital; res = reserves; dep. = deposits; amounts in US dollars)

BANKING

Bank of Guam (USA): POB C, Majuro, MH 96960; tel. (625) 3322; fax (625) 3444; Man. LISA LEON GUERRERO.

Bank of the Marshall Islands: POB J, Majuro, MH 96960; tel. (625) 3636; fax (625) 3661; e-mail bankmar@ntamar.net; internet www.bomi.biz; f. 1982; 40% govt-owned; cap. 2.1m., dep. 41.5m. (Dec. 2011); Chair. GRANT LABAUN; Pres. and Gen. Man. PATRICK CHEN; brs in Majuro, Kwajalein, Ebeye and Santo.

Marshall Islands Development Bank: POB 1048, Majuro, MH 96960; tel. (625) 3230; fax (625) 3309; e-mail rmimidb@ntamar.net; f. 1989; lending suspended in 2003; Man. Dir AMON TIBON.

INSURANCE

Majuro Insurance Company: POB 60, Majuro, MH 96960; tel. (625) 8885; fax (625) 8188; Man. LUCY RUBEN.

Marshalls Insurance Agency: POB 113, Majuro, MH 96960; tel. (625) 3366; fax (625) 3189; Man. TOM LIKOVICH.

Moylan's Insurance Underwriters (Marshall) Inc: POB 727, Majuro, MH 96960; tel. (625) 3220; fax (625) 3361; e-mail marshalls@moylans.net; internet www.moylansinsurance.com; Founder, Chair. and Pres. KURT S. MOYLAN; Br. Man. STEVE PHILLIP.

Trade and Industry

DEVELOPMENT ORGANIZATIONS AND STATE AUTHORITIES

Marshall Islands Development Authority: POB 1185, Majuro, MH 96960; tel. (625) 3417; fax (625) 3158; Gen. Man. DAVID KABUA.

Marshall Islands Environmental Protection Authority (RMIEPA): POB 1322, Majuro, MH 96960; tel. (625) 3035; fax (625) 5202; e-mail eparmi@ntamar.net; internet www.rmiepa.org; Gen. Man. DEBORAH BARKER-MANASE.

Marshall Islands Marine Resources Authority (MIMRA): POB 860, Majuro, MH 96960; tel. (625) 8262; fax (625) 5447; e-mail kiko@mimra.com; internet www.mimra.com; specializes in farming techniques and research and devt; Exec. Dir GLEN JOSEPH.

Tobolar Copra Processing Authority: POB G, Majuro, MH 96960; tel. (625) 3116; fax (625) 7206; e-mail wpcandilas@ntamar.net; Plant Man. WILFREDO CANDILAS.

CHAMBER OF COMMERCE

Marshall Islands Chamber of Commerce: POB 1226, Majuro, MH 96960; tel. (625) 3177; fax (625) 2500; e-mail commerce@ntamar.net; internet marshallislandschamber.net; fmrly known as Majuro Chamber of Commerce; Pres. BRENDA ALIK-MADDISON; Sec. JIM McLEAN.

UTILITIES

Electricity

Marshalls Energy Company: POB 1439, Majuro, MH 96960; tel. (625) 3827; fax (625) 3397; e-mail meccorp@ntamar.net; internet www.mecrmi.net; Gen. Man. DAVID PAUL.

Kwajalein Atoll Joint Utility Resource (KAJUR): POB 5819, Ebeye Island, Kwajalein, MH 96970; tel. (329) 3799; fax (329) 6722; e-mail meccorp@ntamar.net; internet www.mecrmi.net/KAJUR .htm; Man. ROMEO ALFRED.

Water

Majuro Water and Sewage Services: POB 1751, Majuro, MH 96960; tel. (625) 8934; fax (625) 3837; e-mail mwsco@ntamar.net; internet www.mecrmi.net/MWSC.htm; Man. TERRY MELLAN.

CO-OPERATIVES

These include the Ebeye Co-op, Farmers' Market Co-operative, Kwajalein Employees' Credit Union, Marshall Is Credit Union, Marshall Is Fishermen's Co-operative, and the Marshall Is Handicraft Co-operative.

Transport

ROADS

Tarmac and concrete roads are found in the more important islands. In 2007 there were 2,028 km of roads in the Marshall Islands, including 75 km of expressways. Many islands have stone and coral-surfaced roads and tracks.

SHIPPING

The Marshall Islands operates an 'offshore' shipping register. At the end of 2012 the flag registered fleet comprised 2,608 vessels, with a combined displacement of some 88,235,995 grt, including 89 gas tankers, 753 bulk carriers and 115 general cargo ships.

Vessel Registry:

International Registries Inc: 11495 Commerce Park Drive, Reston, VA 20191-1506, USA; tel. (703) 620-4880; fax (703) 476-8522; e-mail info@register-iri.com; internet www.register-iri.com; Pres. WILLIAM R. GALLAGHER.

   The Trust Company of the Marshall Islands Inc: Trust Company Complex, Ajeltake Island, POB 1405, Majuro, MH 96960; tel. (247) 3018; fax (247) 3017; e-mail tcmi@ntamar.net; Pres. GUY EDISON CLAY MAITLAND.

Marshall Islands Ports Authority (MIPA): POB 109, Majuro; tel. 625-8269; fax 625-4269; internet rmipa-aip.org; responsible for seaports and airports; Dir JACK CHONG GUM.

CIVIL AVIATION

A major project to upgrade the runway at the Marshall Islands' main airport, Amata Kabua International Airport, commenced in May 2011 and was expected to be completed in 2013.

Air Marshall Islands (AMI): POB 1319, Majuro, MH 96960; tel. (625) 3731; fax (625) 3730; e-mail amisales@ntamar.net; internet www.airmarshallislands.com; f. 1980; internal services for the Marshall Islands; also charter, air ambulance and maritime surveillance operations; agency for Aloha airlines; CEO and Gen. Man. JEFFERSON BARTON.

Continental Airlines Micronesia: POB 156, Majuro; tel. (625) 3209; fax (625) 3730; e-mail cmimaj@ntamar.net; international flights between Majuro, the Federated States of Micronesia, Guam and Honolulu; also internal services between Majuro and Kwajalein; based in Hagåtña, Guam; Man. LEO SION.

Tourism

The islands' attractions include excellent opportunities for diving, game-fishing and the exploration of sites and relics of Second World War battles. Bikini Atoll was listed by UNESCO as a World Heritage site in 2010. In 2008 the Marshall Islands Visitor Authority implemented a four-year tourism development programme focusing on special interest tourism markets. In the longer term, the Visitor Authority planned to promote the development of small island resorts throughout the country. A new resort was scheduled to open on Ailinglaplap Atoll in 2012. Tourism receipts totalled US $3m. in 2010, and there were an estimated 5,000 tourist arrivals in 2011. The leading sources of visitors include the USA and Japan.

Marshall Islands Visitor Authority: POB 5, Majuro, MH 96960; tel. (625) 6482; fax (625) 6771; e-mail tourism@ntamar.net; internet www.visitmarshallislands.com; f. 1997; Gen. Man. BRENDA ALIK MADDISON.

Defence

Defence is the responsibility of the USA, which maintains a military presence on Kwajalein Atoll. The US Pacific Command is based in Hawaii, USA.

Education

There is a school system, based on that of the USA, operated by the state. However, the development of secondary facilities has been constrained by the limitations of resources. In 2010/11 8,546 pupils were enrolled in primary schools, and in 2008/09 5,229 pupils were enrolled in secondary schools. In 2010/11 enrolment at primary schools included 99% of children in the relevant age-group, and the comparable ratio for secondary schools in 2006/07 was 62%. The College of the Marshall Islands, which became independent from the College of Micronesia in 1993, is based on Majuro; in 2002/03 there were 919 students enrolled at the College. The Fisheries and Nautical Center offers vocational courses for islanders seeking employment in the fishing industry or on passenger liners, cargo ships and tankers. In the proposed budget for 2011/12, education was allocated the sum of US $22.2m. (16.9% of total government expenditure).

MAURITANIA

Introductory Survey

LOCATION, CLIMATE, LANGUAGE, RELIGION, FLAG, CAPITAL

The Islamic Republic of Mauritania lies in north-west Africa, with the Atlantic Ocean to the west, Algeria and the disputed territory of Western Sahara (occupied by Morocco) to the north, Mali to the east and south, and Senegal to the south. The climate is hot and dry, particularly in the north, which is mainly desert. Average annual rainfall in the capital in the 1990s was 131 mm (5.1 ins). The 1991 Constitution designates Arabic (which is spoken by the Moorish majority) as the official language, and Arabic, Poular, Wolof and Solinke as the national languages. The black population in the south is largely French-speaking, and French is widely used in commercial and business circles. Islam is the state religion, and the inhabitants are almost all Muslims. The national flag (proportions 2 by 3) comprises a green field, bearing, on the vertical median, a yellow five-pointed star between the upward-pointing horns of a yellow crescent. The capital is Nouakchott.

CONTEMPORARY POLITICAL HISTORY

Historical Context

Mauritania, formerly part of French West Africa, achieved full independence on 28 November 1960 (having become a self-governing member of the French Community two years earlier). Moktar Ould Daddah, leader of the Mauritanian Assembly Party (MAP) and Prime Minister since June 1959, became Head of State, and was elected President in August 1961. All parties subsequently merged with the MAP to form the Mauritanian People's Party (MPP), with Ould Daddah as Secretary-General, and Mauritania became a one-party state in 1964. In 1973 Mauritania joined the League of Arab States (see p. 372), and withdrew from the Franc Zone in the following year.

Under a tripartite agreement of November 1975, Spain ceded Spanish (now Western) Sahara to Mauritania and Morocco, to be apportioned between them. The agreement took effect in February 1976, when Mauritania occupied the southern portion of the territory. Fighting ensued between Moroccan and Mauritanian troops and the guerrilla forces of the Frente Popular para la Liberación de Saguia el-Hamra y Río de Oro (the Polisario Front), which sought independence for Western Sahara. Attacks within Mauritania by Polisario forces proved highly damaging to the economy, and, following the removal of Ould Daddah in a bloodless military coup in July 1978, Mauritania renounced its territorial claims in Western Sahara. A peace treaty was signed with Polisario in August 1979 and Morocco announced its annexation of the entire territory.

Domestic Political Affairs

In December 1984, while the Head of State, Lt-Col Mohamed Khouna Ould Haidalla, was temporarily absent from the country, the Prime Minister and Minister of Defence, Lt-Col (later Col) Maaouiya Ould Sid'Ahmed Taya, assumed the presidency.

At a national referendum on 12 July 1991, a draft Constitution, which accorded extensive powers to the presidency and provided for the introduction of a multi-party political system, was supported by 97.9% of those who voted (85.3% of the registered electorate), according to official reports. Meanwhile, legislation permitting the registration of political parties was promulgated: among the first organizations to be accorded official status was the Democratic and Social Republican Party (DSRP), which was closely linked with Taya.

Taya was elected to the presidency on 17 January 1992, with 62.7% of the votes cast, defeating three other candidates; his nearest rival was Ahmed Ould Daddah, with 32.8%. The rate of voter participation was 51.7%. In legislative elections, which were held on 6 and 13 March, Taya's party took 67 of the 79 seats in the National Assembly, and he was inaugurated as President on 18 April.

In January 1996 Taya appointed Cheikh el Avia Ould Mohamed Khouna as Prime Minister, to head a new Council of Ministers. At legislative elections held on 11 and 18 October the DSRP won 71 of the 79 seats in the National Assembly. The Rally for Democracy and Unity (RDU), closely allied with the administration, also secured a seat. Action for Change (AC), which sought to represent the interests of Harratin (mainly dark-skinned Moors who had formerly been slaves), was the only opposition party to obtain representation in the Assembly; six independent candidates also secured election.

In February 1997 five prominent opposition parties, including the AC, which was chaired by Messaoud Ould Boulkheir, and the Union of Democratic Forces—New Era (UDF—NE), formed a coalition, the Forum of Opposition Parties (FOP). At the presidential election, held on 12 December, Taya was returned to office with 90.9% of the valid votes cast; his nearest rival, Mohamed Lemine Ch'Bih Ould Cheikh Melainine, won 7.0% of the vote. Opposition parties alleged that there had been widespread electoral fraud and disputed the official rate of voter participation, of 73.8%. Taya subsequently appointed Mohamed Lemine Ould Guig, a university academic, as Prime Minister, and a new Council of Ministers was installed. In November 1998 Khouna was again appointed Prime Minister.

Meanwhile, in March 1998 internal divisions in the UDF—NE resulted in a split in the party into two rival factions, led by Ahmed Ould Daddah and Moustapha Ould Bedreddine, respectively. In November the Government banned the pro-Iraqi Baathist National Vanguard Party (Taliaa), a constituent member of the FOP, following its criticism of the Mauritanian Government's decision to establish full diplomatic relations with Israel in the previous month.

From October 2000, following the onset of the second *intifada* (uprising) in the Palestinian Territories, the Mauritanian Government experienced increasing pressure from opposition groups, including the UDF—NE, to break off diplomatic relations with Israel. In October several pro-Palestinian demonstrations in Nouakchott and Nouadhibou led to violent anti-Israeli protests. Arrests of members of clandestine Islamist groups and of UDF—NE activists were reported. In late October the Council of Ministers officially dissolved the UDF—NE, on the grounds that the party had incited violence and sought to damage Mauritanian national interests. Ould Daddah refused to recognize the dissolution of the party, and the UDF—NE's partners in the FOP condemned the Government's action as unconstitutional. Meanwhile, the faction of the UDF—NE led by Moustapha Ould Bedreddine, which remained authorized, restyled itself as the Union of Progressive Forces (UPF).

Legislative and municipal elections were held on 19 and 26 October 2001, at which an electoral turn-out of some 55% was reported. The DSRP won 64 of the 81 seats in the enlarged National Assembly, and the RDU and the Union for Democracy and Progress (UDP), which were now both allied with the ruling party, each secured three seats. The AC was the most successful of the opposition parties, winning four seats, while the UPF and the newly formed Rally of Democratic Forces (RDF), which replaced the banned UDF—NE, also each took three seats, and the Popular Front (PF) secured the remaining seat. In November President Taya reappointed Khouna as Prime Minister, and reorganized the Council of Ministers.

In January 2002 Ould Daddah was elected President of the RDF; four former vice-presidents of the UDF—NE were also appointed to the 12-member executive committee of the RDF. In that month the Government officially dissolved the AC, on the grounds that the party promoted racism and extremism. In August the Convention for Change (CC), an organization including many former members of the AC, and led by Ould Boulkheir, was refused registration as a political party.

In October 2002 the UPF announced that it was to organize a series of meetings intended to promote a 'national dialogue' between the authorities and the opposition parties. However, later that month seven other opposition parties, including the CC (which remained banned), the PF and the RDF, formed a new grouping, the United Opposition Framework (UOF), which also stated as its purpose the co-ordination of dialogue between the opposition and the Government pertaining to democratic reform; the UPF was, notably, excluded from the UOF. Consequently, the initial meeting was postponed indefinitely, and, expressing discontent at the situation, in mid-November the UPF announced its withdrawal from the National Assembly. As a result of the departure of the three UPF deputies from the Assembly, the group of opposition deputies was dissolved, as it was now reduced to eight members, fewer than the 10 required for the formation of a parliamentary group.

In March 2003 US-led military action in Iraq, aimed at ousting the Baathist regime of Saddam Hussain, prompted protests in Mauritania, with widespread demonstrations held to demand that the Government sever diplomatic relations with the two principal nations involved in the conflict, the United Kingdom and the USA, and also with Israel. As opposition to the Government's broadly pro-US stance intensified in early May, police raided the headquarters of a tolerated—although not officially authorized—Baathist party, the National Renaissance Party (NRP—Nouhoudh). Three leaders of the NRP were arrested on unspecified charges; 13 other Baathists were also arrested over the following days. (Ten of those arrested were later charged with attempting to re-establish Taliaa.)

Opposition to Taya

In early May 2003 Taya's appointment of Lembrabott Ould Mohamed Lemine as Minister of Culture and Islamic Affairs was regarded as an attempt to reduce tensions between the Government and Islamic communities. However, at the end of May the publication of a pro-Islamist weekly journal, *Al-Rayah*, was suspended, and nine Baathists were convicted by a Nouakchott court of engaging in illegal political activity. According to opposition reports, more than 100 alleged Islamists were detained in June, 36 of whom were charged with plotting against the constitutional order.

The tensions that had been escalating throughout the first half of 2003 culminated in an attempted coup, which commenced on 8 June. Exchanges of fire were reported near the presidential palace and at other strategic locations in Nouakchott. According to official reports, 15 people (including six civilians) died in ensuing clashes between the insurgents and the security forces, including the Chief of Staff of the Armed Forces, Col Mohamed Lamine Ould Ndiayane. Government forces regained control of the city on 9 June. Taya subsequently stated that Islamists had been responsible for the rebellion, although other sources claimed that the attempted coup had been prompted by tribal rivalries. In the days following the restoration of order at least 12 alleged rebel leaders were arrested, while more than 30 detained Islamists, who had been freed during the disorder, were reported to have surrendered to the authorities. In July 2003 another suspected coup leader, Lt Didi Ould M'Hamed, who had fled to Senegal, was extradited to Mauritania.

In early July 2003 Taya appointed a new Prime Minister: Sghaïr Ould M'Barek, a Harratin, was regarded as a close ally of the President. A new Government was subsequently formed. Further arrests of Islamists were reported throughout the month. In early August more than 80 members of the military who had been arrested following the attempted coup were released, although many more remained in detention. Some 41 Islamists had also been released from detention by the end of the month, although others continued to face charges. In September it was announced that some 30 members of the military, including 20 senior officers, were to be tried in connection with the coup attempt.

In October 2003 the Constitutional Council approved the nominations of six candidates, including Taya, Ould Daddah, Ould Boulkheir and former President Ould Haidalla, for the forthcoming presidential election. Ould Haidalla was widely regarded as the most credible challenger to Taya, but only secured 18.7% of the votes cast, and Taya was re-elected with 66.7%. Some 60.8% of the electorate participated in the election. Opposition candidates accused the Government of perpetrating fraud at the election, which international observers had not been permitted to monitor.

The trial of more than 190 soldiers and civilians accused of participation in the attempted coup in June 2003 and in subsequent conspiracies to overthrow the Head of State commenced in November 2004. The defendants included the alleged leaders of the group, Saleh Ould Hnana, Capt. Adberahmane Ould Mini and Mohammed Ould Sheikhna, the latter being one of 19 people tried *in absentia* (also among this number was Sidi Mohamed Mustapha Ould Limam Chavi, an adviser to Burkinabè President Blaise Compaoré); the civilians on trial included opposition leaders Ould Haidalla, Ould Daddah and Cheikh Ould Horma. Ould Hnana and Ould Mini pleaded guilty to the charge of conspiring to overthrow President Taya, while the remaining accused military personnel entered pleas of not guilty. In February 2005 Ould Hnana, Ould Mini, Ould Sheikhna and a fourth officer, Capt. Mohammed Ould Salek, were sentenced to life imprisonment with hard labour, while 79 others received lesser jail sentences; Ould Haidalla, Ould Daddah and Ould Horma were among the 111 acquitted.

Some 15 soldiers were killed in an attack in June 2005 by some 150 assailants on a military post at Lemgheity, in north-eastern Mauritania, for which an Algerian radical Islamist militant group, the Groupe Salafiste pour la Prédication et le Combat (GSPC), subsequently claimed responsibility. Later in June it was reported that the existence of a radical Islamist group based in Mauritania with links to the GSPC, the Mauritanian Group for Preaching and Jihad, had been uncovered, as had details of proposed targets of attack in the country. At the end of the month the Senate adopted legislation aimed at countering terrorism and money-laundering. (In May 2007 the trial of 25 suspected Islamist militants commenced in Nouakchott; several of the accused were being tried *in absentia*. Some of the defendants were charged in connection with the attack in Lemgheity, while others were accused of having received training from the GSPC (which had reportedly restyled itself as the al-Qa'ida Organization in the Islamic Maghreb—AQIM). In June 24 of the defendants were acquitted owing to lack of evidence, and one defendant, who had escaped from prison in April 2006, was sentenced, *in absentia*, to two years' imprisonment for falsifying identity papers.)

The Military Council for Justice and Democracy

On 3 August 2005, while President Taya was absent from Mauritania, a group of army officers seized control of state broadcasting services and the presidential palace in a bloodless coup. A 16-member Military Council for Justice and Democracy (MCJD) under the leadership of Col Ely Ould Mohamed Vall, hitherto the Director of National Security, who had been regarded as a close ally of Taya, announced that it had assumed power. The Council stated that it would preside over the country for a transitional period of up to two years, at the end of which democratic elections, in which members of the MCJD and the Government would be prohibited from participating, would be held; although the National Assembly elected in 2001 was dissolved, the 1991 Constitution and most of its institutions (including the Constitutional Council and judicial bodies) were to be retained, as supplemented and amended by the charter of the MCJD. Taya was prevented from re-entering the country and was flown initially to Niamey, Niger; he subsequently took up residence in The Gambia.

On 7 August 2005 Vall appointed Sidi Mohamed Ould Boubacar, hitherto Ambassador to France, as Prime Minister, a position that he had previously held in 1992–96; a new, civilian, Government was named on 10 August, and Vall announced the intention of holding a constitutional referendum within one year. None of the ministers in the outgoing Government were reappointed, although, notably, Ahmed Ould Sid'Ahmed, who, in his former capacity as Minister of Foreign Affairs and Co-operation, had been largely responsible for Mauritania's rapprochement with Israel in 1999, was reappointed to that position. In the immediate aftermath of the coup, which was initially widely condemned internationally, the African Union (AU, see p. 191) announced the suspension of Mauritania's membership. However, the overthrow of Taya's regime was reported to have widespread domestic support. In mid-August a delegation from the AU met members of the MCJD, subsequently announcing the willingness of the Union to co-operate with the new leadership of Mauritania, although the country was to remain suspended from the organization pending democratic elections.

In early September 2005 the new administration announced that it was to offer a general amnesty for political prisoners; 32 such detainees, principally from among those imprisoned in February 2005 for their role in attempted coups in 2003 and 2004, were among the first to benefit from the amnesty. However, some Islamist detainees were not freed, and, furthermore, in mid-October the authorities refused to recognize a recently formed Islamist political party, the Party for Democratic Convergence, on the grounds that its programme violated Mauritanian law. Indeed, Ould Vall announced that no Islamist party would be legalized.

In November 2005 the MCJD issued a timetable for the transition to democratic rule: a constitutional referendum was to be held in June 2006, followed by elections to municipal councils and to the National Assembly in November, elections to the Senate in January 2007 and, finally, a presidential election in March. A National Independent Electoral Commission was inaugurated at the end of November 2005. Meanwhile, the former ruling DSRP, which had changed its name to the Republican Party for Democracy and Renewal (RPDR), elected Ethmane Ould Cheikh Ebi el Maali, hitherto Ambassador to Kuwait, as its new President.

In March 2006 the MCJD approved proposals presented by the transitional Government on constitutional amendments to be put to a national referendum on 25 June. The principal changes envisaged included: limiting the presidential term of office to five years, renewable only once; stipulating a maximum age of 75 years for presidential candidates; and prohibiting the President from holding any other official post, particularly the leadership of a political party. The proposed reforms were generally supported by most major political parties, including the RPDR. In May the European Union (EU, see p. 281) announced the resumption of co-operation with Mauritania, which had been suspended following the coup in August 2005.

The constitutional referendum was held, as scheduled, on 25 June 2006. Observers from the AU and the Arab League declared their satisfaction with the conduct of the poll. According to official results, 96.9% of the valid votes cast were in favour of the amendments to the Constitution and a turn-out of 76.5% of the registered electorate was recorded. In late June 10 political parties, including the RDF, the PF, the Popular Progressive Alliance (PPA) and the Rally for Mauritania (RPM—Temam), announced the formation of the Coalition of Forces for Democratic Change (CFDC) to contest the forthcoming legislative and local elections.

Democratic elections

At the legislative elections, which were held as scheduled on 19 November and 3 December 2006, the RDF took 15 seats, the UPF eight, the RPDR seven and the PPA five, while the Centrist Reformists and the Mauritanian Party for Union and Change—Hatem both secured four seats; 41 seats were taken by independent candidates. Indirect elections to the Senate took place on 21 January and 4 February 2007 at which independent candidates secured 34 of the 56 seats, while representatives of the CFDC took 15.

The presidential election took place over two rounds on 11 and 25 March 2007. At the first round, which was contested by 20 candidates, Sidi Mohamed Ould Cheikh Abdellahi took 24.8% of votes cast, while Ould Daddah won 20.7%, Zeine Ould Zeidane 15.3% and Ould Boulkheir 9.8%. The rate of voter participation was recorded at 70.1%. Abdellahi and Ould Daddah thus proceeded to the second round, at which Abdellahi (a government minister under both Moktar Ould Daddah and Taya) was elected President, having secured 52.9% of the valid votes cast. Some 67.5% of the electorate participated in the second round. Ould Boubacar submitted the resignation of his Government on 31 March, although the administration was to remain in office in a 'caretaker' capacity pending the inauguration of the new President, scheduled for 19 April. Abdellahi was duly inaugurated on that date, assuming executive powers in place of the MCJD, which was disbanded, and on the following day he appointed Zeidane as Prime Minister. Later in April a new Government was installed. The elections were largely deemed to have been fair and democratic and on 10 April Mauritania was readmitted to the AU.

In late December 2007 four French tourists were shot dead by a group of gunmen near the town of Aleg, in the south-west of Mauritania, in what was initially believed to be a robbery. However, the Government later attributed the killings to Islamist militants, and in January 2008 two Mauritanian men with previous convictions for training with the GSPC and having links to al-Qa'ida, were arrested in Guinea-Bissau in connection with the incident and were handed over to the Mauritanian authorities. In April one of the suspects, Sidi Ould Sidna, escaped from police custody in Nouakchott, although he was later recaptured, and on 10 April the alleged leader of the group, Marouf Ould Haiba, was arrested. In May Ould Sidna and Ould Haiba were charged for their role in the murder of the French tourists, along with 28 other suspected Islamist militants who faced various charges. In September 12 Mauritanian soldiers who were abducted and later found dead, were believed to have been victims of an attack by al-Qa'ida militants. Ould Sidna, Ould Haiba and Mohammed Ould Chabarnou were sentenced to death in May 2010, having been convicted of the murder of the French tourists.

Meanwhile, in May 2008 Zeidane was dismissed as Prime Minister and replaced by Yahya Ould Ahmed el Waghef, leader of the National Party for Democracy and Development (NPDD). A 31-member Council of Ministers was approved by Abdellahi, which included members of the opposition UPF and the National Rally for Reform and Development (NRRD—Tawassou). However, on 1 July a motion of no confidence was submitted by 39 legislators from the NPDD, and the Government resigned on 3 July. Abdellahi initially threatened to dissolve the legislature, but then accepted the Government's resignation and invited el Waghef to form a new Council of Ministers, which was appointed on 10 July and included 14 new members.

Military coup

On 6 August 2008 President Abdellahi announced the dismissal of four senior military officials, including Gen. Mohamed Ould Abdel Aziz, the Presidential Chief of Staff. Later that day Ould Abdel Aziz led a bloodless military coup to overthrow Abdellahi and declared himself President of a new interim executive, the High Council of State (HCS), which included two other generals—Mohamed Ould Cheik Mohamed Ahmed and Felix Negre—and eight colonels. Prime Minister el Waghef was also removed from office and detained along with Abdellahi, although the former Prime Minister was released later in August, while Abdellahi remained under house arrest until December. There was little opposition to the coup, and 107 of the 146 members of the National Assembly declared their support for the new regime. Ould Abdel Aziz claimed that a presidential election would be held 'as soon as possible'. (A timetable was eventually announced which established the election date as 6 June 2009.) The HCS issued a constitutional ordinance, which stated that it would exercise the powers of the President as defined by the Constitution, and granted Ould Abdel Aziz the power to appoint a prime minister, military officials and civil servants. On 14 August 2008 Ould Abdel Aziz named Moulaye Ould Mohamed Laghdaf, hitherto Mauritania's Ambassador to Belgium and the EU, as the new Prime Minister, and in early September a new Government was formed which featured a number of ministers from the previous administration. The coup received widespread international condemnation and on 9 August the AU again announced Mauritania's suspension from the organization.

In April 2009 Ould Abdel Aziz resigned his position as head of the HCS, in order to contest the presidential election. He was also elected as Chairman of a new political party, the Union for the Republic (UR), which had been formed in March. A spokesman for the National Front for the Defence of Democracy (NFDD), a coalition of political parties opposed to the coup, denounced the planned election, claiming it was a means of legitimizing military rule; in May the NFDD and RDF held a joint demonstration in Nouakchott, in which several thousand people protested against the proposed election.

Meanwhile, in early February 2009 the AU's Peace and Security Council imposed further sanctions, including travel restrictions and a freezing of funds, on some 60 Mauritanian nationals, including five members of the HCS, seven government ministers and 10 parliamentary deputies, and called on AU member states to contribute to efforts to restore political order in Mauritania. However, the Chairman of the AU Assembly, Libyan Revolutionary Leader Col Muammar al-Qaddafi, endorsed the electoral timetable set by the HCS for the presidential election (which had been rejected by the opposition and numerous international bodies), while visiting Mauritania in March.

The Senegalese Government hosted negotiations between representatives of the HCS, the NFDD and the RDF in May 2009, and early the following month all parties agreed upon a resolution to the ongoing political crisis. This provided for the formal resignation of Ould Cheikh Abdellahi (which took place on 27 June), the formation of a transitional unity government and the postponement of the presidential election until 18 July. Furthermore, el Waghef was to be released from custody. Thus, on 27 June the HCS was restyled the Superior Council of National Defence (SCND) and it was announced that Ba Mamadou dit M'Baré, the President of the Senate who had replaced Ould Abdel Aziz as President of the HCS in April, would act as interim President of the SCND until the presidential election. The new Government, which was also installed on 27 June, was headed by Ould Mohamed Laghdaf. In early July the AU removed the sanctions imposed in February and restored Mauritania's membership of the organization.

Ould Abdel Aziz elected President

The presidential election, contested by 10 candidates, was duly held on 18 July 2009, and, according to official figures, Ould Abdel Aziz received 52.6% of the valid votes cast. His closest challenger, Messaoud Ould Boulkheir, representing the NFDD, secured 16.3%, while Ould Daddah—the candidate of the RDF—was placed third, with 13.7%. Some 64.6% of the registered electorate participated in the ballot. Several of Ould Abdel Aziz's challengers alleged that electoral fraud had been perpetrated, and the President of the National Independent Electoral Commission resigned from his position, citing doubts regarding the 'reliability' of the poll. None the less, Ould Abdel Aziz's victory was confirmed later in July by the Constitutional Council, which rejected formal challenges from Ould Boulkheir, Ould Daddah and Col Ely Ould Mohamed Vall (who had contested the election as an independent, receiving 3.8% of the votes). Ould Abdel Aziz was sworn in as President on 5 August. He reappointed Ould Mohamed Laghdaf to the premiership on 11 August and a new Government, which notably included the first female Minister of Foreign Affairs and Co-operation, Naha Mint Mouknass, was installed.

At partial elections to the Senate, held on 8 and 15 November 2009, the UR secured 13 of the 17 seats contested. In July 2010 Mohamed Mahmoud Ould Mohamed Lemine was elected Chairman of the UR at its first congress in Nouakchott. In November Ould Abdel Aziz issued a decree ordering the pardon and release from prison of at least 117 convicted criminals, including 17 Islamist militants. In December the NPDD announced its support for the ruling UR. In the same month eight opposition parties, including the PPA, RDF and the UPF, established a new coalition, the Co-ordination of the Democratic Opposition (COD). A government reorganization was effected in March 2011; Mint Mouknass was replaced as Minister of Foreign Affairs and Co-operation by Hamadi Ould Hamadi, hitherto Minister of National Defence, who was, in turn, succeeded by Ahmedou Ould Idey Ould Mohamed Radhi, formerly Minister-delegate to the Minister of State for National Education, in charge of Primary Education.

Recent developments: anti-Government protests

In early 2011 trade unions and a newly formed group of youth activists, Youth of 25 February, organized a series of protests in Nouakchott and other towns over a number of issues, such as rapidly rising food prices, poor working conditions and youth unemployment. In response, the Government announced various measures intended to appease the protesters, including a programme to distribute land to impoverished people in Nouakchott and plans to create jobs and increase food production. However, in April the Youth of 25 February movement organized a major anti-Government rally in Nouakchott; police forcibly prevented demonstrators from entering a square from which they had been barred, arresting some 22 of them. Sporadic protests continued in May and June. In late September the organization of a nation-wide population census, which had begun in May, prompted protests, and ensuing clashes with security forces, in the southern city of Kaedi by members of a black movement known as Don't Touch My Nationality (DTMN); the leaders of the movement expressed concerns (which were dismissed by the authorities) that the census discriminated against their ethnic group and that its implementation would lead to deportations. The violence spread to other major towns, including Nouakchott, resulting in the arrest of some 56 people; one protester was killed in the southern town of Maghama, when security forces violently dispersed the demonstrators. Although 25 members of the DTMN movement were released in October, continued arrests and arbitrary detentions of a number of its activists were reported in subsequent months.

Meanwhile, in August 2011 elections to the National Assembly, which had been due to take place in October, were postponed in response to demands from the COD, which insisted that an agreement between the political parties first be established to ensure the transparency of the polls; the legislative elections, together with delayed municipal elections, were subsequently rescheduled for 31 March 2012. (Partial elections to the Senate, which had also been postponed in April, were to be conducted concurrently.) In accordance with a political agreement that was reached by pro-Government and opposition parties in October 2011, on 6 March 2012 the National Assembly adopted constitutional amendments prohibiting coups and any unconstitutional change of government, criminalizing slavery, and strengthening the powers of the legislature. Later that month, however, the COD staged a protest in Nouakchott, following the further postponement of the parliamentary elections, purportedly until May.

In April 2012 Biram Ould Abeid, the President of an anti-slavery organization, the Initiative for the Resurgence of the Abolitionist Movement in Mauritania (IRA), prompted a number of protests, when he burned Islamic law texts that he claimed condoned slavery. Ould Abeid, together with a further nine IRA activists were arrested after the incident, and in late May he and six others were charged with threatening state security; their trial commenced in June. On 13 June the Government established a new National Independent Electoral Commission, which was tasked with organizing the legislative elections. However, the COD rejected its authority, and with the NRRD—Tawassou organized a further anti-Government demonstration in the capital. In October President Ould Abdel Aziz was slightly injured after a military patrol fired on his unmarked convoy. Despite speculation attributing the shooting to a failed military coup attempt, it was officially announced that the incident had been accidental. Ould Abdel Aziz subsequently received medical treatment in France, while in November the COD organized a demonstration to demand his resignation. At the end of February 2013 the Electoral Commission announced that the long-delayed legislative and municipal elections would take place in September or October. President Ould Abdel Aziz effected a minor reorganization of the Government in May.

Foreign Affairs

Regional relations

A long-standing border dispute with Senegal was exacerbated by the deaths, in April 1989, of two Senegalese farmers, who had been involved in a dispute regarding grazing rights with Mauritanian livestock-breeders. Mauritanian nationals resident in Senegal were attacked, and their businesses (primarily those of the retail trade) looted, while Senegalese nationals in Mauritania and black Mauritanians suffered similar aggression. Operations to repatriate nationals of both countries commenced, with international assistance. Amid allegations that the Mauritanian authorities had begun to instigate expulsions of the indigenous black population into Senegal or to Mali, prominent human rights organization Amnesty International expressed concern at the reported violation of black Mauritanians' rights. Mauritania and Senegal suspended diplomatic relations in August. In early 1991 Mauritanian naval vessels were reported to have opened fire on Senegalese fishing boats, apparently in Senegal's territorial waters; in March several deaths were reported to have resulted from a military engagement on Senegalese territory, following an incursion by Senegalese troops into Mauritania.

Diplomatic relations with Senegal were resumed in April 1992, and the process of reopening the border began in May. However, Mauritanian refugees in Senegal insisted that, as long as the Taya Government refused to recognize their national identity (*mauritanité*) and land and property rights, they would not return to Mauritania. In June 2000 relations between Mauritania and Senegal deteriorated after Mauritania accused the new Senegalese administration of relaunching an irrigation project, which involved the use of joint waters from the Senegal river, in contravention of the Organisation pour la Mise en Valeur du Fleuve Sénégal project (see p. 463). The dispute escalated when the Mauritanian authorities requested that all of its citizens living in Senegal return home and issued the estimated 100,000 Senegalese nationals living in Mauritania with a 15-day deadline by which to leave the country. In mid-June, following mediation by King Muhammad VI of Morocco and the Presidents of The Gambia and Mali, the Mauritanian Government announced that the decision to expel Senegalese citizens had been withdrawn and that Mauritanians living in Senegal could remain there. President Abdoulaye Wade of Senegal visited Mauritania later that month and announced that the irrigation project had been abandoned. By late 2000 the number of Mauritanian refugees in Senegal had declined to 19,800 (compared with 65,500 in mid-1995). In April 2001 President Taya's presence as guest of honour at a ceremony in Dakar to commemorate the 41st anniversary of the independence of Senegal demonstrated an improvement in relations between the countries. According to the office of the UN High Commissioner for Refugees (UNHCR), by March 2012 more than 24,000 Mauritanian refugees had returned from Senegal since January 2008.

In February 1989 Mauritania was a founder member, with Algeria, Libya, Morocco and Tunisia, of the Union of the Arab Maghreb (UMA, see p. 464), although relations with Libya were reported to have deteriorated from the mid-1990s; Libya was a particularly vehement critic of Mauritania's decision to establish and maintain full diplomatic relations with Israel. Diplomatic relations with Libya, severed in 1995, were none the less restored in 1997. In September 2001 King Muhammad VI of Morocco paid a three-day official visit to Mauritania, aimed at improving bilateral relations between the two countries. In March 2004 President Taya led an official delegation to Morocco, and again met with King Muhammad. King Muhammad returned to Mauritania in March 2005 as part of a tour of West Africa.

Relations with both Libya and Burkina Faso were severely strained in the wake of allegations by the Mauritanian Government that those two countries had provided support to rebel elements in the Mauritanian military, accused of participating in the failed coup of June 2003 and of subsequently conspiring to overthrow President Taya (see Opposition to Taya). It was alleged that Ould Hnana and Ould Sheikhna, who were held responsible by the Mauritanian authorities of leading the 2003 coup, had been granted refuge in Burkina Faso, while the Libyan Government was accused of assisting the rebels. Libya and Burkina Faso strenuously denied the accusations. In March 2005 a ministerial commission appointed by the UMA to investigate the Mauritanian allegations against Libya concluded that Qaddafi had 'no connection' to the events in Mauritania.

In September 2009 delegates from Mali, Mauritania, Niger and Algeria met to discuss a new anti-terror plan and agreed to allow military co-operation in the fight against terrorism in their border regions. In response to the kidnapping of four European citizens by al-Qa'ida in the Islamic Maghreb (AQIM, as the GSPC had been restyled) in early 2009, and the seizure in Mauritania (and subsequent transfer to Mali) of three Spanish aid workers and two Italian tourists later that year, in January 2010 Mali and Mauritania announced plans to strengthen security co-operation further. The following month, however, bilateral relations became strained after the Malian Government approved the release of four Islamist militia (including one Mauritanian citizen), detained in April 2009 on weapons charges, in exchange for the freeing of a French citizen taken hostage in November. Both Algeria and Mauritania subsequently withdrew their ambassadors from Bamako, claiming that Mali's decision to release the terrorists was an infringement of the agreement on security co-operation reached at the September regional summit. In March 2010 foreign ministers from seven Saharan states meeting in Algiers, including Mauritania, Mali and Algeria, agreed that they would commence the sharing of operational information and co-operate their actions against AQIM in an attempt to 'collectively confront the threat of terrorism'. Meanwhile, in February an alleged Mauritanian terrorist, Oumar Ould Sid'Ahmed (also known as 'Sahraoui'), who was believed to have been involved in the seizure of the Spanish and Italian citizens in late 2009, was extradited from Mali to Mauritania; in the following month he and six others were charged with kidnapping offences. In July 2010 Ould Sid'Ahmed was sentenced to 12 years' imprisonment for kidnapping the Spanish aid workers (who were released by AQIM in March and August). In September Mauritania's Ambassador to Mali returned to his post. Shortly afterwards Mauritanian military forces, in co-operation with the Malian Government, launched a series of ground and air attacks against suspected AQIM militants in northern Mali. Following the adoption of a law on terrorism in July, which granted AQIM members who surrendered to the authorities special conditions, five young AQIM militants surrendered to the Mauritanian army in November. In October 2011 it was reported that a senior AQIM commander had been killed during an aerial bombardment launched by Mauritanian forces against suspected AQIM bases near the border with Mali. In December AQIM abducted a paramilitary officer from the south-eastern town of Adel Begrou, subsequently offering to release him in exchange for the release of two of its imprisoned members. Following the overthrow of Qaddafi's regime in 2011, his brother-in-law and former head of military intelligence, Abdullah Senussi, was arrested at Nouakchott airport in March 2012; the Libyan Government submitted a formal request for Senussi's extradition, which was also sought by France and the International Criminal Court. Although in August President Ould Abdel Aziz insisted that Senussi be tried in Mauritania on charges of illegal entry before being extradited, following diplomatic pressure the Mauritanian Government approved his extradition to Libya in early September. Meanwhile, the Mauritanian authorities freed two Islamists from prison in July, in exchange for the release by a splinter group of AQIM, the Movement for Oneness and Jihad in West Africa, of three European aid workers who had been kidnapped in Algeria in October 2011 and subsequently held hostage in Mali. After the intensification of conflict in northern Mali from January 2012,

some 100,000 Malians had sought refuge in Mauritania by the end of August, according to UNHCR.

Other external relations

In November 1995 Mauritania signed an agreement to recognize and establish relations with Israel. In October 1998 Mauritania's Minister of Foreign Affairs and Co-operation visited Israel, where he held talks with the Prime Minister, Binyamin Netanyahu. The Arab League strongly criticized the visit, claiming that it contravened the League's resolutions on the suspension of the normalization of relations with Israel, and threatened to impose sanctions on Mauritania. Widespread controversy was provoked both domestically, and in Arab countries, by the establishment of full diplomatic relations between Mauritania and Israel in October 1999. (Of Arab countries, only Egypt and Jordan had taken such a step, under the terms of their respective peace treaties with Israel.) Following the resumption of the Palestinian uprising in September 2000, the Mauritanian Government came under renewed pressure to suspend diplomatic relations with Israel. A visit by the Mauritanian Minister of Foreign Affairs and Co-operation, Dah Ould Abdi, to Israel in May 2001, when he met Israeli Prime Minister Ariel Sharon and President Moshe Katsav, and entered into negotiations with the Minister of Foreign Affairs, Shimon Peres, provoked further controversy, particularly as a result of an appeal by the Arab League, issued earlier that month, for all member countries to cease political contacts with Israel. A further meeting between Peres, Taya and Ould Abdi, in Nouakchott, in October 2002, provoked further controversy. A visit to Mauritania by the Israeli Deputy Prime Minister and Minister of Foreign Affairs, Silvan Shalom, in early May 2005 was preceded, and followed, by the detention of several Islamists, although the Government denied that the arrests were linked to Shalom's presence. His visit prompted a number of anti-Israeli protests in Nouakchott. Although some concern was initially expressed, following the coup of August 2005, that diplomatic relations between the two countries might be terminated, the appointment, later in the month, of Ahmed Ould Sid'Ahmed as Minister of Foreign Affairs and Co-operation (who had held that position when Mauritania re-established full diplomatic relations with Israel in 1999) appeared to indicate that the new regime intended to maintain amicable relations with Israel. In April 2007 newly elected President Abdellahi appealed for a public debate on the future of Mauritania's diplomatic ties with Israel. The Israeli embassy in Nouakchott was attacked in February 2008 by gunmen who opened fire and injured three people. Nevertheless, relations did not seriously deteriorate until after the assumption of power in Mauritania by the HCS. In January 2009 Mauritania recalled its ambassador from Israel and suspended diplomatic relations in response to the Israeli invasion of the Gaza Strip in December 2008; in March 2009 it was reported that the Israeli embassy in Nouakchott had been closed down and the ambassador ordered to leave the country. The Mauritanian Minister of Foreign Affairs and Co-operation announced the 'complete and definitive' abrogation of diplomatic relations with Israel in March 2010.

CONSTITUTION AND GOVERNMENT

Under the provisions of the Constitution adopted in July 1991 and amended in June 2006 and March 2012, the Head of State is the President, who is elected, by universal adult suffrage, for a term of five years, renewable only once. Legislative power is vested in the National Assembly, which is elected by universal suffrage for a period of five years, and in the Senate, which is elected by municipal leaders for a six-year term, one-third of its membership being renewed every two years. All elections are conducted in the context of a multi-party political system. The President of the Republic appoints the Prime Minister and, on the recommendation of the latter, the members of the Council of Ministers.

For the purpose of local administration, Mauritania is divided into 13 wilayat (regions), comprising a total of 53 moughataa (counties), which are subdivided into 216 communes (districts).

REGIONAL AND INTERNATIONAL CO-OPERATION

Mauritania is a member of the African Union (see p. 191), of the Organisation pour la Mise en Valeur du Fleuve Sénégal (see p. 463) and of the Union of the Arab Maghreb (see p. 464). Mauritania withdrew from the Economic Community of West African States (see p. 268), with effect from 31 December 2000, owing to decisions adopted by the organization at its summit in December 1999, including the integration of the armed forces of member states and the removal of internal border controls and tariffs.

Mauritania became a member of the UN in 1961 and was admitted to the World Trade Organization (WTO, see p. 444) in 1995. Mauritania participates in the Group of 77 (G77, see p. 461) developing countries.

ECONOMIC AFFAIRS

In 2011, according to estimates by the World Bank, Mauritania's gross national income (GNI), measured at average 2009–11 prices, was US $3,528m., equivalent to $1,000 per head (or $2,410 on an international purchasing-power parity basis). During 2002–11, it was estimated, the population increased at an average annual rate of 2.6%, while gross domestic product (GDP) per head increased, in real terms, by an average of 3.1% per year. According to the World Bank, overall GDP increased, in real terms, at an average annual rate of 5.8% in 2002–11; GDP increased by 4.7% in 2011.

Agriculture (including forestry and fishing) contributed 16.3% of GDP in 2011, according to the World Bank. In 2013, according to FAO estimates, about 49.7% of the labour force were employed in the sector. Owing to the unsuitability of much of the land for crop cultivation, output of staple foods (millet, sorghum, rice and pulses) is insufficient for the country's needs. Livestock-rearing is the principal occupation of the rural population. Fishing, which in 2011 provided 17.6% of export earnings, supplies 5%–10% of annual GDP and a sizeable proportion of budgetary revenue, and also makes a significant contribution to domestic food requirements. During 2002–11, according to the World Bank, agricultural GDP increased by an average of 3.6% per year; the sector's GDP increased by 7.0% in 2010, before decreasing by 1.4% in 2011.

Industry (including mining, manufacturing, construction and power) provided 46.3% of GDP in 2011, according to the World Bank, and engaged 9.1% of the economically active population in 2000. During 2002–11, according to the World Bank, industrial GDP increased at an average annual rate of 6.4%; it increased by 6.4% in 2011.

Mining contributed 37.1% of GDP in 2011, according to the African Development Bank (AfDB), and engaged 5.1% of the economically active population in 2000. The principal activity in this sector is the extraction of iron ore, exports of which contributed 56.9% of total merchandise export earnings in 2011. Gypsum, salt, gold and copper are also mined. Other exploitable mineral resources include diamonds, phosphates, sulphur, peat, manganese and uranium. Many international companies were involved in offshore petroleum exploration in Mauritania in the early 2000s, with reserves at the offshore Shafr el Khanjar and Chinguetti fields estimated at 450m.–1,000m. barrels; production commenced at Chinguetti in February 2006. According to the IMF, the GDP of the mining sector increased by an average of 8.9% per year in 1996–2005. According to the AfDB, the sector's GDP increased by 4.2% in 2011.

The manufacturing sector contributed 3.7% of GDP in 2011, according to the World Bank, and engaged 1.0% of the economically active population in 2000. Fish-processing (which contributed 3.9% of GDP in 2002) is the most important activity. The processing of minerals (including imported petroleum) is also of some significance. According to the World Bank, manufacturing GDP decreased at an average annual rate of 2.3% in 2002–11; however, it increased by 6.9% in 2010 and by 12.6% in 2011.

Construction contributed 5.5% of GDP in 2011, according to the World Bank, and engaged 2.6% of the economically active population in 2000. The GDP of the sector increased by 8.0% in 2011, according to the AfDB.

Mauritania began to utilize electricity generated at hydro-electric installations constructed under the auspices of the Organisation pour la Mise en Valeur du Fleuve Sénégal (OMVS) in late 2002, thus reducing the country's dependence on power generated at thermal stations. In 2013 a 15-MW photovoltaic solar power station was officially inaugurated. Imports of petroleum products comprised 27.9% of the total value of merchandise imports in 2011.

The services sector contributed 37.5% of GDP in 2011, according to the World Bank, and engaged 38.1% of the economically active population in 2000. According to the World Bank, the combined GDP of the services sector increased at an average rate of 6.9% per year during 2002–11. Services GDP rose by 9.1% in 2011.

In 2011 Mauritania's visible merchandise trade surplus was estimated at US $274.9m.; however, there was a projected deficit of an estimated $313.3m. on the current account of the balance of payments. In 2011 the principal source of imports (25.9%) was the United Arab Emirates; other major suppliers were Belgium, France, the United Kingdom and the People's Republic of China. The principal markets for exports (excluding exports of petroleum, gold and copper) in that year were the People's Republic of China (36.9%), Italy, France, Spain, Germany and Japan. The principal exports in 2011 were iron ore, fish and petroleum. The principal imports in that year were petroleum products, food products, construction materials, and road vehicles and parts.

Mauritania's overall budget surplus for 2011 was UM 1,000m. According to the IMF, Mauritania was projected to have a budget deficit of UM 43,600m. in 2013. The country's general government gross debt was UM 859,063m. in 2010, equivalent to 86.2% of GDP. Total external debt in 2010 was US $2,461m., of which $2,174m. was public and publicly guaranteed debt. In 2009 the cost of servicing long-term public and publicly guaranteed debt and repayments to the IMF was equivalent to 4.8% of the value of exports of goods, services and income (excluding workers' remittances). The annual rate of inflation averaged 6.7% in 2002–11; consumer prices increased by an average of 5.7% in 2011. The overall rate of unemployment in 2000 was 28.9%.

The exploitation, from the mid-2000s, of previously untapped petroleum reserves, principally at offshore locations, was expected to have a significant impact on Mauritania's economy, and in particular on export revenues, which had hitherto been largely dependent on fishing and on the extraction of iron ore. The first major offshore field, at Chinguetti, began production in 2006, and further potential for growth was represented by ongoing onshore petroleum and natural gas drilling operations. In recent years government revenue has also been bolstered by the sale of fishing licences to foreign fleets. Following the election of Gen. Mohamed Ould Abdel Aziz to the presidency in July 2009, in December the European Union (EU, see p. 281) restored diplomatic relations with Mauritania and resumed its aid programmes. Co-operation with the IMF was also reinstated and a three-year Extended Credit Facility (ECF) agreement, aimed at addressing corruption and poverty and at reviving development initiatives, was approved in March 2010. Although a food security agreement was signed with Italy in December 2009, there were continuing concerns regarding the adverse effect of poor harvests. In July 2012 Mauritania signed a new fishing agreement with the European Commission; however, Spain and other EU member states subsequently protested at reduced access to some fish species under the agreement, and delays in its ratification, and consequently in EU payments were expected to affect government revenue significantly. In November the IMF completed its fifth review economic performance under the ECF-supported programme and approved a tranche equivalent to US $16.9m., increasing total disbursements under the Facility to $101.6m.; at the same time the arrangement was extended for a further three months (the final review was scheduled to take place in May 2013). Following the impact of severe drought in 2011, GDP growth had recovered to a projected 6.2% in 2012, with a similar level anticipated for 2013. In accordance with IMF recommendations, the Mauritanian authorities had pursued a policy of gradual elimination of subsidies, under which domestic fuel prices were raised to international levels in 2012. The country's vulnerability to falling demand for exports in Europe was deemed to have been strengthened by an increase in foreign exchange reserves.

PUBLIC HOLIDAYS

2014: 1 January (New Year's Day), 13 January* (Mouloud, Birth of Muhammad), 1 May (Labour Day), 25 May (African Liberation Day, anniversary of the OAU's foundation), 26 May* (Leilat al-Meiraj, Ascension of Muhammad), 28 July* (Korité—Id al-Fitr, end of Ramadan), 4 October* (Tabaski—Id al-Adha, Feast of the Sacrifice), 24 October* (Islamic New Year), 28 November (Independence Day).

*These holidays are determined by the Islamic lunar calendar and may vary by one or two days from the dates given.

Statistical Survey

Source (unless otherwise stated): Office National de la Statistique, BP 240, Nouakchott; tel. 45-25-28-80; fax 45-25-51-70; e-mail webmaster@ons.mr; internet www.ons.mr.

Area and Population

AREA, POPULATION AND DENSITY

Area (sq km)	1,030,700*
Population (census results)	
5–20 April 1988	1,864,236†
1–15 November 2000‡	
Males	1,241,712
Females	1,266,447
Total	2,508,159
Population (official projections at mid-year)	
2011	3,296,958
2012	3,378,254
2013	3,461,041
Density (per sq km) at mid-2013	3.4

* 397,950 sq miles.
† Including an estimate of 224,095 for the nomad population.
‡ Figures include nomads, totalling 128,163 (males 66,007; females 62,156), enumerated during 10 March–20 April 2001.

Ethnic Groups (percentage of total, 1995): Moor 81.5; Wolof 6.8; Toucouleur 5.3; Sarakholé 2.8; Peul 1.1; Others 2.5 (Source: La Francophonie).

POPULATION BY AGE AND SEX
(official projections at mid-2013)

	Males	Females	Total
0–14	699,162	668,278	1,367,440
15–64	973,858	1,007,055	1,980,913
65 and over	55,520	57,168	112,688
Total	1,728,540	1,732,501	3,461,041

REGIONS
(census of November 2000)

Region	Area ('000 sq km)	Population*	Chief town
Hodh Ech Chargui .	183	281,600	Néma
Hodh el Gharbi . .	53	212,156	Aïoun el Atrous
Assaba	37	242,265	Kiffa
Gorgol	14	242,711	Kaédi
Brakna	33	247,006	Aleg
Trarza	68	268,220	Rosso
Adrar	215	69,542	Atâr
Dakhlet-Nouadhibou .	22	79,516	Nouadhibou
Tagant	95	76,620	Tidjikja
Guidimagha . . .	10	177,707	Sélibaby
Tiris Zemmour . .	253	41,121	Zouïrât
Inchiri	47	11,500	Akjoujt
Nouakchott (district) .	1	558,195	Nouakchott
Total	1,030	2,508,159	

* Including nomad population, enumerated during 10 March–20 April 2001.

PRINCIPAL TOWNS
(population at census of 2000*)

Nouakchott (capital)	558,195	Kiffa	32,716
Nouadhibou . .	72,337	Bougadoum . . .	29,045
Rosso . . .	48,922	Atâr	24,021
Boghé . . .	37,531	Boutilimit . . .	22,257
Adel Bagrou . .	36,007	Theiekane . . .	22,041
Kaédi . . .	34,227	Ghabou	21,700
Zouïrât . . .	33,929	Mal	20,488

* With the exception of Nouakchott, figures refer to the population of communes (municipalities), and include nomads.

Mid-2011 (incl. suburbs, UN estimate): Nouakchott 786,226 (Source: UN, *World Urbanization Prospects: The 2011 Revision*).

BIRTHS AND DEATHS
(annual averages, UN estimates)

	1995–2000	2000–05	2005–10
Birth rate (per 1,000) . . .	38.2	36.6	34.8
Death rate (per 1,000)	10.6	10.3	10.1

Source: UN, *World Population Prospects: The 2010 Revision*.

Life expectancy (years at birth): 58.5 (males 56.9; females 60.3) in 2011 (Source: World Bank, World Development Indicators database).

ECONOMICALLY ACTIVE POPULATION
(census of 2000, persons aged 10 years and over, including nomads)

	Males	Females	Total
Agriculture, hunting, forestry and fishing	219,771	94,535	314,306
Mining and quarrying	5,520	249	5,769
Manufacturing	18,301	11,855	30,156
Electricity, gas and water . . .	2,655	182	2,837
Construction	15,251	311	15,562
Trade, restaurants and hotels .	83,733	24,799	108,532
Transport, storage and communications	17,225	691	17,916
Financing, insurance, real estate and business services . . .	1,557	454	2,011
Community, social and personal services	72,137	26,583	98,720
Other and unspecified	33,350	22,608	55,958
Total	469,500	182,267	651,767

Mid-2013 (estimates in '000): Agriculture, etc. 801; Total labour force 1,612 (Source FAO).

Health and Welfare

KEY INDICATORS

Total fertility rate (children per woman, 2010)	4.5
Under-5 mortality rate (per 1,000 live births, 2010) . . .	111
HIV/AIDS (% of persons aged 15–49, 2009)	0.7
Physicians (per 1,000 head, 2009)	0.13
Hospital beds (per 1,000 head, 2006)	0.40
Health expenditure (2009): US $ per head (PPP) . . .	79
Health expenditure (2009): % of GDP	4.2
Health expenditure (2009): public (% of total)	52.8
Access to water (% of persons, 2010)	50
Access to sanitation (% of persons, 2010)	26
Total carbon dioxide emissions ('000 metric tons, 2008) .	1,998.5
Carbon dioxide emissions per head (metric tons, 2008) . .	0.6
Human Development Index (2011): ranking	159
Human Development Index (2011): value	0.453

For sources and definitions, see explanatory note on p. vi.

Agriculture

PRINCIPAL CROPS
('000 metric tons)

	2009	2010	2011
Rice, paddy	53.6	134.4	161.1
Maize	11.8	19.9	11.6
Sorghum	93.6	114.2	24.6
Millet	8.1	3.3	0.5
Peas, dry*	12.5	10.0	6.7
Cow peas, dry*	10.1	12.4	10.4
Beans, dry*	10.0	11.8	11.9
Dates*	20.0	21.0	21.4

* FAO estimates.

Aggregate production ('000 metric tons, may include official, semi-official or estimated data): Total cereals 172 in 2009, 276 in 2010, 202 in 2011; Total pulses 51 in 2009, 57 in 2010, 48 in 2011; Total roots and tubers 6 in 2009, 7 in 2010–11; Total vegetables (incl. melons) 4 in 2009, 5 in 2010, 5 in 2011; Total fruits (excl. melons) 23 in 2009, 24 in 2010–11.

Source: FAO.

LIVESTOCK
('000 head, year ending September)

	2009	2010	2011
Cattle	1,678	1,680*	1,700*
Goats	5,524	5,500	5,550*
Sheep	8,287	8,860†	8,900*
Asses*	170	170	170
Horses*	20	20	20
Camels	1,351	1,355*	1,400*
Chickens*	4,300	4,300	4,400

* FAO estimate(s).
† Unofficial figure.

Source: FAO.

LIVESTOCK PRODUCTS
('000 metric tons, FAO estimates)

	2009	2010	2011
Goat meat	14.6	14.6	15.0
Camel meat	22.0	23.0	23.5
Chicken meat	4.5	4.5	4.5
Camel milk	29.7	26.3	26.3
Cows' milk	142.3	126.0	126.0
Sheep's milk	113.1	115.5	115.5
Goats' milk	120.1	123.8	123.8
Hen eggs	5.6	5.4	5.5

Source: FAO.

Forestry

ROUNDWOOD REMOVALS
('000 cubic metres, excl. bark, FAO estimates)

	2009	2010	2011
Sawlogs, veneer logs and logs for sleepers	1	1	1
Other industrial wood	2	2	2
Fuel wood	1,791	1,836	1,877
Total	1,794	1,839	1,880

Source: FAO.

SAWNWOOD PRODUCTION
('000 cubic metres, incl. railway sleepers)

	2005	2006	2007*
Broadleaved (hardwood)	7	14	14
Total	7	14	14

* FAO estimates.

2008–11: Production assumed to be unchanged from 2007 (FAO estimates).

Source: FAO.

Fishing

('000 metric tons, live weight)

	2008	2009	2010
Freshwater fishes*	15.0	15.0	15.0
Sardinellas	21.8	89.0*	147.7
European pilchard (sardine)	15.3	13.4	16.7
European anchovy	12.6	7.0	5.0
Jack and horse mackerels	34.2	24.4	33.7
Chub mackerel	6.3	5.1	4.6
Octopuses	7.6	12.3	15.8
Total catch (incl. others)*	195.3	216.9	276.2

* FAO estimate(s).

Source: FAO.

Mining

('000 metric tons)

	2008	2009	2010
Gypsum	44.4	36.9	70.7*
Iron ore: gross weight	10,950	10,275	11,500
Iron ore: metal content*	7,120	6,680	7,480

* Estimate(s).

Source: US Geological Survey.

Industry

SELECTED PRODUCTS
('000 metric tons unless otherwise indicated)

	2008	2009	2010
Cement*	322	340	340†
Crude steel*†	5	5	5
Electric energy (million kWh)	486.9	470.0	516.5

* Data from US Geological Survey.
† Estimated production.

Finance

CURRENCY AND EXCHANGE RATES

Monetary Units
5 khoums = 1 ouguiya (UM).

Sterling, Dollar and Euro Equivalents (31 October 2012)
£1 sterling = 482.239 ouguiyas;
US $1 = 299.230 ouguiyas;
€1 = 388.790 ouguiyas;
1,000 ouguiyas = £2.07 = $3.34 = €2.57.

Average Exchange Rate (ouguiyas per US $)
2009   262.366
2010   275.894
2011   281.118

BUDGET
('000 million ouguiyas)

Revenue*	2009	2010	2011
Tax revenue	106.6	155.6	183.7
Taxes on income and profits	34.6	43.4	54.9
Tax on business profits	16.9	21.4	27.4
Tax on wages and salaries	14.4	18.4	19.7
Taxes on goods and services	53.8	79.3	100.5
Value-added tax	38.7	49.4	64.8
Turnover taxes	7.7	21.8	30.0
Tax on petroleum products	4.5	2.2	2.4
Other excises	1.7	4.0	1.4
Taxes on international trade	14.2	17.6	22.3
Non-tax revenue	75.8	83.1	109.8
Fishing royalties and penalties	41.0	42.3	36.9
Revenue from public enterprises	18.4	13.3	32.7
Capital revenue	0.7	0.7	6.0
Other revenue (incl. special accounts)	9.0	10.0	16.8
Oil revenue	13.7	13.5	22.9
Total	196.1	252.2	316.4

Expenditure†	2009	2010	2011
Current expenditure	170.1	200.9	238.9
Wages and salaries	77.0	83.7	89.1
Equipment maintenance and supplies	51.7	47.1	51.3
Transfers and subsidies	20.3	17.9	60.2
Interest on public debt	16.2	15.0	15.0
Capital expenditure	36.9	51.5	75.2
Restructuring expenditure	—	3.3	—
Total	207.0	255.8	314.1

* Excluding grants received ('000 million ouguiyas): 2.4 in 2009; 9.9 in 2010; 7.7 in 2011.
† Excluding restructuring and net lending ('000 million ouguiyas): 21.0 in 2009; 13.2 in 2010; 9.9 in 2011.

2012 ('000 million ouguiyas, projections): Total revenue 325.3; Total expenditure 383.9 (Source: IMF (see below)).

2013 ('000 million ouguiyas, projections): Total revenue 393.2; Total expenditure 436.8 (Source: IMF, *Islamic Republic of Mauritania: Fifth Review Under the Three-Year Extended Credit Facility Arrangement, Requests for Modification of Performance Criteria and Extension of the Arrangement—Staff Report and Press Release*—December 2012).

INTERNATIONAL RESERVES
(US $ million at 31 December)

	2009	2010	2011
Gold*	12.6	16.1	18.0
IMF special drawing rights	0.2	0.1	1.5
Foreign exchange	225.4	271.7	483.2
Total	238.2	287.9	502.7

* Valued at market-related prices.

Source: IMF, *International Financial Statistics*.

MONEY SUPPLY
(million ouguiyas at 31 December)

	2009	2010	2011
Currency outside banks	82,226	91,252	113,723
Demand deposits at deposit money banks	148,967	172,001	222,926
Total money (incl. others)	232,111	264,517	338,012

Source: IMF, *International Financial Statistics*.

COST OF LIVING
(Consumer Price Index; base: 2000 = 100)

	2008	2009	2010
Food (incl. beverages)	190.6	195.5	223.9
Clothing (incl. footwear)	152.5	163.0	174.1
Rent	169.6	164.3	171.9
All items (incl. others)	170.4	174.1	195.6

2011: Food (incl. beverages) 223.9, All items (incl. others) 195.6.

Source: ILO.

NATIONAL ACCOUNTS
(million ouguiyas at current prices)

Expenditure on the Gross Domestic Product

	2009	2010	2011
Government final consumption expenditure	154,933	165,566	173,626
Private final consumption expenditure	576,563	700,322	792,306
Gross capital formation	195,381	243,948	296,593
Total domestic expenditure	926,877	1,109,836	1,262,525
Exports of goods and services	399,012	602,378	849,802
Less Imports of goods and services	531,703	715,161	965,879
GDP in purchasers' values	794,187	997,054	1,146,447

Gross Domestic Product by Economic Activity

	2009	2010	2011
Agriculture, hunting, forestry and fishing	146,638	157,932	172,377
Mining and quarrying	184,990	320,222	393,514
Manufacturing	29,718	33,822	39,194
Construction	40,726	50,410	58,396
Wholesale and retail trade, restaurants and hotels	81,113	95,814	109,803
Finance, insurance and real estate	92,171	99,092	112,291
Transport and communications	35,071	36,905	39,444
Public administration and defence	116,834	126,894	135,727
Sub-total	727,261	921,091	1,060,746
Indirect taxes, less subsidies	66,925	75,962	85,702
GDP in purchasers' values	794,187	997,054	1,146,447

Source: African Development Bank.

BALANCE OF PAYMENTS
(US $ million)

	2009	2010	2011*
Exports of goods f.o.b.	1,364.2	2,073.5	2,769.2
Imports of goods f.o.b.	−1,390.9	−1,935.3	−2,494.3
Trade balance	−26.7	138.2	274.9
Services (net)	−479.2	−550.9	−528.5
Balance on goods and services	−505.9	−412.7	−253.6
Other income (net)	52.1	−68.5	−176.2
Balance on goods, services and income	−453.8	−481.2	−429.8
Current transfers (net) . .	130.8	162.1	116.4
Private unrequited transfers (net)	66.4	59.3	31.5
Official transfers	64.4	102.8	84.9
Current balance	−323.0	−319.1	−313.3
Capital account (net) . . .	0.0	209.0	0.0
Direct investment (net) . . .	−3.1	128.3	776.4
Official medium- and long-term loans	166.3	79.5	280.6
Other capital	42.6	39.0	−475.1
Net errors and omissions . .	108.8	99.2	−22.5
Overall balance	−8.4	235.9	246.1

* Estimates.

Source: IMF, *Islamic Republic of Mauritania: Fifth Review Under the Three-Year Extended Credit Facility Arrangement, Requests for Modification of Performance Criteria and Extension of the Arrangement—Staff Report and Press Release* (December 2012).

External Trade

PRINCIPAL COMMODITIES
('000 million ouguiyas)

Imports	2009	2010	2011
Food products	96.0	86.5	92.8
Cosmetic chemical products . .	9.4	10.2	11.8
Petroleum products	70.9	126.0	192.5
Construction materials . . .	26.5	38.8	64.9
Road vehicles and parts . . .	26.0	37.8	48.7
Various equipment and appliances	78.7	134.8	224.8
Total (incl. others)	350.7	474.1	689.7

Exports	2009	2010	2011
Iron ore	136.2	247.1	393.1
Fish	83.9	91.6	121.9
Petroleum	57.1	72.7	30.2
Total (incl. others)	402.9	552.4	691.0

PRINCIPAL TRADING PARTNERS
(US $ million)

Imports c.i.f.	2009	2010	2011
Belgium	18.9	46.9	96.5
Brazil	18.2	13.1	9.8
China, People's Republic . .	28.3	32.2	36.1
Côte d'Ivoire	1.7	1.1	1.5
France	64.5	66.9	84.5
Germany	14.1	12.9	18.5
Greece	1.5	1.5	1.9
Italy	3.1	5.2	2.4
Japan	11.0	12.6	13.2
Malaysia	6.8	6.8	7.3
Morocco	4.9	11.0	15.1
Netherlands	18.5	50.4	18.8
Singapore	2.4	21.8	2.4
Spain	9.9	22.4	29.0
United Arab Emirates . . .	4.7	57.4	178.4
United Kingdom	10.1	5.2	41.4
USA	14.2	17.6	20.8
Total (incl. others)	350.7	474.1	689.7

Exports c.i.f.*	2010	2010	2011
China, People's Republic . . .	66.0	141.1	255.3
France	20.0	39.4	58.7
Germany	18.0	31.1	42.5
Italy	34.0	31.7	69.2
Japan	27.5	34.2	35.8
Russia	5.2	8.9	7.5
Spain	30.5	36.3	47.3
United Kingdom	5.3	0.5	0.3
Total (incl. others)	305.4	446.0	691.0

* Excluding exports of petroleum, gold and copper.

Transport

RAILWAYS
(traffic)

	2009	2010
Passengers carried	12,736	11,874
Freight carried (metric tons)	4,432	5,948

Freight ton-km (million, estimates): 6,720 in 1991; 6,810 in 1992; 6,890 in 1993 (Source: UN Economic Commission for Africa, *African Statistical Yearbook*).

ROAD TRAFFIC
(motor vehicles registered)

	2004	2005	2006
Passenger cars	6,033	6,040	6,182
Government vehicles . . .	251	317	369
Specialist vehicles	413	542	504

SHIPPING
Flag Registered Fleet
(at 31 December)

	2010	2011	2012
Number of vessels	72	70	70
Total displacement ('000 grt) . .	38.1	25.9	25.8

Source: Lloyd's List Intelligence (www.lloydslistintelligence.com).

International Sea-borne Freight Traffic
(Port of Nouakchott, '000 metric tons)

	2007	2008	2009
Goods loaded	251	267	283
Goods unloaded	2,045	2,051	2,448

Source: Port Autonome de Nouakchott.

CIVIL AVIATION
(traffic on scheduled services)*

	2007	2008	2009
Kilometres flown (million) . .	1	1	1
Passengers carried ('000) . .	155	154	142
Passenger-km (million) . . .	68	68	64
Total ton-km (million)	6	7	6

* Including an apportionment of the traffic of Air Afrique.

Source: UN, *Statistical Yearbook*.

Passengers carried ('000): 114 in 2010; 118 in 2011.

Tourism

Tourist arrivals (estimates, '000): 24 in 1999.

Receipts from tourism (US $ million, excl. passenger transport): 28 in 1999 (Source: World Tourism Organization).

Communications Media

	2009	2010	2011
Telephones ('000 main lines in use)	74.5	71.6	72.3
Mobile cellular telephones ('000 subscribers)	2,182.2	2,776.0	3,314.8
Internet subscribers . . .	7,600	6,800	6,700
Broadband subscribers . . .	6,800	5,600	6,100

Source: International Telecommunication Union.

Education

(2010/11 unless otherwise indicated)

	Institutions	Teachers	Students		
			Males	Females	Total
Pre-primary .	n.a.	251*	n.a.	n.a.	4,856*
Primary . . .	2,676†	13,640	264,787	271,189	535,976
Secondary . .	n.a.	5,869	67,641	55,608	123,249
Tertiary . . .	4‡	379	10,434	4,102	14,536

* 2004/05.
† 1998/99.
‡ 1995/96.

Pupil-teacher ratio (primary education, UNESCO estimate): 37.2 in 2009/10.

Adult literacy rate (UNESCO estimates): 58.0% (males 64.9%; females 51.2%) in 2010.

Sources: mainly UNESCO Institute for Statistics and Ministry of National Education, Nouakchott.

Directory

While no longer an official language, French is still widely used in Mauritania, especially in the commercial sector. Many organizations are therefore listed under their French names, by which they are generally known.

The Government

HEAD OF STATE

President: MOHAMED OULD ABDEL AZIZ (inaugurated 5 August 2009).

COUNCIL OF MINISTERS
(May 2013)

Prime Minister: MOULAYE OULD MOHAMED LAGHDAF.

Minister, Secretary-General to the President of the Republic: ADAMA SY.

Minister of State for National Education, Higher Education and Scientific Research: AHMED OULD BAHYA.

Minister of Justice: ABIDINE OULD EL KHAIRE.

Minister of Foreign Affairs and Co-operation: HAMADI OULD BABA OULD HAMADI.

Minister of National Defence: AHMEDOU OULD IDEY OULD MOHAMED RADHI.

Minister of the Interior and Decentralization: MOHAMED OULD BOILIL.

Minister of Economic Affairs and Development: SIDI OULD TAH.

Minister of Finance: THIAM DIOMBAR.

Minister of Islamic Affairs and Original Education: AHMED OULD NEINI.

Minister of the Civil Service and the Modernization of the Administration: MATY MINT HAMADY.

Minister of Health: AHMEDOU OULD HADEMINE OULD JERVOUNE.

Minister of Petroleum, Energy and Mines: TALEB OULD ABDI VALL.

Minister of Fisheries and the Maritime Economy: GHDAFNA OULD EYIH.

Minister of Trade, Industry, Crafts and Tourism: BAMBA OULD DARAMANE.

Minister of Housing, Urban Development and Land Settlement: BA YAHYA.

Minister of Rural Development: BRAHIM OULD M'BARECK OULD MOHAMED EL MOCTAR.

Minister of Equipment and Transport: YAHYA OULD HADEMINE.

Minister of Water Resources and Sanitation: MOHAMED LEMINE OULD ABOYE.

Minister of Culture, Youth and Sports: CISSÉ MINT CHEIKH OULD BOYDE.

Minister of Communication and Relations with Parliament: MOHAMED YAHYA OULD HORMA.

Minister of Social Affairs, Childhood and Families: AICHA VALL MINT MICHEL VERGÈS.

Minister-delegate to the Prime Minister, in charge of the Environment and Sustainable Development: AMEDI CAMARA.

Minister-delegate to the Minister of State for National Education, in charge of Primary Education: DIA MOKHTAR MALAL.

Minister-delegate to the Minister of State for National Education, in charge of Secondary Education: OUMAR OULD MATALLA.

Minister-delegate to the Minister of State for National Education, in charge of Employment, Vocational Training and New Technologies: MOHAMED OULD KHOUNA.

Minister-delegate to the Minister of Foreign Affairs and Co-operation, in charge of the Arab Maghreb Union: HAMED HAMOUNI.

Secretary-General of the Government: OUSMANE BA.

MINISTRIES

Office of the President: BP 184, Nouakchott; tel. and fax 45-25-26-36.

Office of the Prime Minister: BP 237, Nouakchott; tel. 45-25-33-37.

Office of the Secretary-General of the Government: BP 184, Nouakchott.

Ministry of the Civil Service and the Modernization of the Administration: BP 193, Nouakchott; tel. and fax 45-25-84-10.

Ministry of Communication and Relations with Parliament: Nouakchott.

Ministry of Culture, Youth and Sports: BP 223, Nouakchott; tel. 45-25-11-30.

Ministry of Economic Affairs and Development: 303 Ilot C, BP 5150, Nouakchott; tel. 45-25-16-12; fax 45-25-51-10; e-mail nfomaed@mauritania.mr; internet www.economie.gov.mr.

Ministry of Equipment and Transport: BP 237, Nouakchott; tel. 45-25-33-37.

Ministry of Finance: BP 181, Nouakchott; tel. 45-25-20-20; internet www.finances.gov.mr.

Ministry of Fisheries and the Maritime Economy: BP 137, Nouakchott; tel. 45-25-46-07; fax 45-25-31-46; e-mail ministre@mpem.mr; internet www.mpem.mr.

Ministry of Foreign Affairs and Co-operation: BP 230, Nouakchott; tel. 45-25-26-82; fax 45-25-28-60.

Ministry of Health: BP 177, Nouakchott; tel. 45-25-20-52; fax 45-25-22-68; internet www.sante.gov.mr.

Ministry of Housing, Urban Development and Land Settlement: Nouakchott.

Ministry of the Interior and Decentralization: BP 195, Nouakchott; tel. 45-25-36-61; fax 45-25-36-40; e-mail paddec@mauritania.mr; internet www.interieur.gov.mr.

Ministry of Islamic Affairs and Original Education: Nouakchott; internet www.affairesislamiques.gov.mr.

Ministry of Justice: BP 350, Nouakchott; tel. 45-25-10-83; fax 45-25-70-02.

Ministry of National Defence: Nouakchott.

Ministry of National Education, Higher Education and Scientific Research: BP 387, Nouakchott; tel. 45-25-12-37; fax 45-25-12-22.

Ministry of Petroleum, Energy and Mines: Nouakchott; tel. 45-25-71-40.

Ministry of Rural Development: BP 366, Nouakchott; tel. 45-25-15-00; fax 45-25-74-75; internet www.agriculture.gov.mr.

Ministry of Social Affairs, Childhood and Families: Nouakchott.

Ministry of Trade, Industry, Crafts and Tourism: BP 182, Nouakchott; tel. 45-25-35-72; fax 45-25-76-71.

Ministry of Water Resources and Sanitation: BP 4913, Nouakchott; tel. 45-25-71-44; fax 45-29-42-87; e-mail saadouebih@yahoo.fr.

President and Legislature

PRESIDENT

Presidential Election, 18 July 2009

Candidate	Votes	% of votes
Mohamed Ould Abdel Aziz	409,100	52.64
Messaoud Ould Boulkheir	126,782	16.31
Ahmed Ould Mohameden Ould Daddah	106,263	13.67
Mohamed Jemil Ould Brahim Ould Mansour	37,059	4.77
Ibrahima Moktar Sarr	35,709	4.60
Ely Ould Mohamed Vall Ould Eleya	29,681	3.82
Kane Hamidou Baba	11,568	1.49
Saleh Ould Mohamedou Ould Hanena	10,219	1.32
Hamady Ould Abdallahi Meymou	8,936	1.15
Sghair Ould M'Bareck	1,788	0.23
Total	**777,105**	**100.00**

Al-Jamiya al-Wataniyah
(National Assembly)

ave de l'Indépendance, BP 185, Nouakchott; tel. 45-25-11-30; fax 45-25-70-78; internet www.mauritania.mr/assemblee.

President: MESSOUD OULD BOULKHEIR.

General Election, 19 November and 3 December 2006

Party	Constituency seats	National list seats	Total seats
Rally of Democratic Forces	12	3	15
Union of Progressive Forces	7	1	8
Republican Party for Democracy and Renewal	5	2	7
Popular Progressive Alliance	4	1	5
Centrist Reformists	2	2	4
Mauritanian Party for Union and Change—Hatem	3	1	4
Union for Democracy and Progress	2	1	3
Rally for Democracy and Unity	2	1	3
Democratic Renewal	1	1	2
Alternative	1	—	1
Union of the Democratic Centre	1	—	1
Popular Front	—	1	1
Independents	41	—	41
Total	**81**	**14**	**95**

Majlis ash-Shuyukh
(Senate)

ave de l'Indépendance, BP 5838, Nouakchott; tel. 45-25-68-77; fax 45-25-73-73; internet www.senat.mr.

First Vice-President: MOHAMED EL HACEN OULD EL HAJ.

The total number of seats in the Senate is 56 with three seats reserved for representatives of the Mauritanian diaspora. After elections held on 21 January and 4 February 2007, the strength of the parties was as follows:

Party	Seats
Independents	34
Coalition of Forces for Democratic Change	15
Republican Party for Democracy and Renewal	3
Total*	**52**

* The result from one constituency was annulled by the Constitutional Council and the remaining three reserved seats were yet to be allocated.

Elections to renew 17 seats were held on 8 and 15 November 2009, at which the Union for the Republic secured 13 seats, the Union for Democracy and Progress and the National Rally for Reform and Development (Tawassoul) one seat each and independent candidates won two seats.

Election Commission

National Independent Electoral Commission: 230 ave Moktar Ould Daddah, BP 4550, Nouakchott; tel. 45-24-15-40; fax 45-24-15-44; e-mail ceni@ceni.mr; internet www.ceni.mr; 15 mems; Pres. ABDALLAHI OULD SOUEID AHMED.

Advisory Council

Economic and Social Council: Nouakchott; Pres. MOHAMED OULD HAIMER.

Political Organizations

Alliance for Justice and Democracy/Mouvement pour la Rénovation (AJD/MR): Nouakchott; internet ajd-mr.org; Leader IBRAHIMA MOCTAR SARR.

Alternative (Al-Badil): Nouakchott; f. 2006; mem. of Co-ordination of the Democratic Opposition coalition, formed in 2010; Leader MOHAMED YEHDHIH OULD MOKTAR EL HASSEN.

Centrist Reformists: Nouakchott; f. 2006; mem. of Coalition of Forces for Democratic Change, formed in advance of legislative and local elections in 2006; moderate Islamist grouping.

Democratic Renewal: Nouakchott; f. 2005; mem. of Coalition of Forces for Democratic Change, formed in advance of legislative and local elections in 2006; Pres. MOUSTAPHA OULD ABEIDERRAHMANE.

El Wiam Démocratique et Social: Leader BOIDEIL OULD HOUMEID.

Mauritanian African Liberation Forces—Renovation (MALF—Renovation): Nouakchott; tel. 22-28-77-40 (mobile); internet www.flam-renovation.org; f. 2006 in split from clandestine, exiled, Mauritanian African Liberation Forces; represents interests of Afro- (Black) Mauritanians; mem. of Coalition of Forces for Democratic Change, formed in advance of legislative and local elections in 2006; Leader MAMADOU BOCAR BÂ.

Mauritanian Labour Party: Nouakchott; f. 2001; Leader MOHAMED EL HAFEDH OULD DENNA.

Mauritanian Party for the Defence of the Environment (MPDE—The Greens): Nouakchott; internet pmde.hautetfort.com; ecologist; mem. of Bloc of Parties for Change, formed in advance of legislative and local elections in 2006; Pres. MOHAMED OULD SIDI OULD DELLAHI.

Mauritanian Party for Renewal and Agreement: Nouakchott; f. 2001; Leader MOULAY EL-HASSEN OULD JIYID.

Mauritanian Party for Union and Change—Hatem: Nouakchott; f. 2005 by leadership of the fmr prohibited Knights of Change militia and reformist elements of the fmr ruling Democratic and Social Republican Party; mem. of Coalition of Forces for Democratic Change, formed in advance of legislative and local elections in 2006; Pres. SALEH OULD HNANA; Sec.-Gen. ABDERAHMANE OULD MINI.

Mauritanian People's Rally Party (MPRP): Nouakchott; f. 2009 by parliamentary deputies in support of ruling military junta; Leader Dr LOULEID OULD WEDAD.

National Party for Democracy and Development (NPDD): Nouakchott; Leader YAHYA OULD EL WAGHEF.

National Rally for Reform and Development (NRRD) (Tawassoul): f. 2007; Islamist; mem. of Co-ordination of the Democratic Opposition coalition, formed in 2010; Leader MOHAMED JEMIL OULD MANSOUR.

Party for Liberty, Equality and Justice (PLEJ): Nouakchott; internet www.plej.biz; mem. of Bloc of Parties for Change, formed in advance of legislative and local elections in 2006; mem. of Co-ordination of the Democratic Opposition coalition, formed in 2010; Pres. MAMADOU ALASSANE BÂ.

Popular Front (PF): Nouakchott; f. 1998; social-liberal; mem. of Coalition of Forces for Democratic Change, formed in advance of legislative and local elections in 2006; Leader MOHAMED LEMINE CH'BIH OULD CHEIKH MELAININE.

Popular Progressive Alliance (PPA): Nouakchott; internet www.app.mr; f. 1991; mem. of Coalition of Forces for Democratic Change, formed in advance of legislative and local elections in 2006; mem. of Co-ordination of the Democratic Opposition coalition, formed in 2010; Pres. MESSAOUD OULD BOULKHAR.

Rally for Democracy and Unity (RDU): Nouakchott; f. 1991; supported regime of fmr Pres. Taya; Chair. AHMED OULD SIDI BABA.

Rally of Democratic Forces (RDF): Ilot K, 120, BP 4986, Nouakchott; tel. 45-25-67-46; fax 45-25-65-70; e-mail info@rfd-mauritanie.org; internet www.rfd-mauritanie.org; f. 2001; mem. of Coalition of Forces for Democratic Change, formed in advance of legislative and local elections in 2006; mem. of Co-ordination of the Democratic Opposition coalition, formed in 2010; Pres. AHMED OULD DADDAH.

Republican Party for Democracy and Renewal (RPDR): ZRB, Tevragh Zeina, Nouakchott; tel. 45-29-18-36; fax 45-29-18-00; e-mail info@prdr.mr; internet www.prdr.mr; f. 2006 to replace Democratic and Social Republican Party, the fmr ruling party, prior to coup of August 2005; Leader SIDI MOHAMED OULD MED VALL dit GHRINY.

Reward (Sawab): Nouakchott; f. 2004; social democratic; Chair. of Central Council MOHAMED MAHMOUD OULD GHOULMA; Pres. Dr CHEIKH OULD SIDI OULD HANENA.

Union for Democracy and Progress (UDP): Ilot V, 70, Tevragh Zeina, BP 816, Nouakchott; tel. 45-25-52-89; fax 45-25-29-95; f. 1993; Pres. NAHA HAMDI MINT.

Union of the Democratic Centre (UDC): Nouakchott; f. 2005 by fmr mems of the Democratic and Social Republican Party, the fmr ruling party; Pres. CHEIKH SID'AHMED OULD BABA.

Union of Democratic Youth (UDY): f. 2008; promotes patriotism and moderate Islamic values, opposes extremism; Pres. JEDDOU OULD AHMAD.

Union of Forces of Presidential Majority: Nouakchott; coalition comprising eight political parties supporting Pres. Mohamed Ould Abdel Aziz.

Union of Progressive Forces (UPF) (Ittihad Quwa al-Taqaddum): Nouakchott; e-mail ufpweb2@yahoo.fr; internet www.ufpweb.org; tel. 45-29-32-66; fax 45-24-35-86; e-mail infos@ufpweb.org; f. 2000; mem. of Coalition of Forces for Democratic Change, formed in advance of legislative and local elections in 2006; mem. of Co-ordination of the Democratic Opposition coalition, formed in 2010; Pres. MOHAMED OULD MAOULOUD; Sec.-Gen. MOHAMED EL MOUSTAPHA OULD BEDREDDINE.

Union for the Republic (UR): Nouakchott; f. 2009; Chair. MOHAMED MAHMOUD OULD MOHAMED LEMINE; Sec.-Gen. OUMAR OULD MAATALLAH.

Unauthorized, but influential, is the Islamic **Ummah Party** (the Constitution prohibits the operation of religious political organizations), founded in 1991 and led by Imam SIDI YAHYA, and the Baathist **National Vanguard Party (Taliaa)**, which was officially dissolved by the Government in 1999 and is led by AHMEDOU OULD BABANA. The clandestine **Mauritanian African Liberation Forces (MALF)** was founded in 1983 in Senegal to represent Afro-Mauritanians (Point d'ébullition, BP 5811, Dakar-Fann, Senegal; tel. +221 822-80-77; e-mail ba_demba@yahoo .fr; internet members .lycos .co .uk/flamnet; Pres. SAMBA THIAM); a faction broke away from this organization and returned to Mauritania in early 2006, forming the Mauritanian African Liberation Forces—Renovation. A further group based in exile is the **Arab-African Salvation Front against Slavery, Racism and Tribalism—AASF** (e-mail faas@caramail .com; internet membres .lycos .fr/faas). In August 2007 a further 18 new parties were registered: included were an Islamist party, the **National Rally for Reform and Development**, and two parties led by women, the **National Party for Development**, led by SAHLA BINT AHMAD ZAYID, and the **Mauritanian Hope Party**, led by TAHI BINT LAHBIB.

Diplomatic Representation

EMBASSIES IN MAURITANIA

Algeria: Ilot A, Tevragh Zeina, BP 625, Nouakchott; tel. 45-25-35-69; fax 45-25-47-77; Ambassador ZAHANI ABDEL HAMID.

China, People's Republic: rue 42-133, Tevragh Zeina, BP 257, Nouakchott; tel. 45-25-20-70; fax 45-25-24-62; e-mail chinaemb_mr@ mfa.gov.cn; internet mr.china-embassy.org; Ambassador CHEN GONGLAI.

Congo, Democratic Republic: Tevragh Zeina, BP 5714, Nouakchott; tel. 45-25-46-12; fax 45-25-50-53; e-mail ambardc.rim@ caramail.com; Chargé d'affaires a.i. TSHIBASU MFUAD.

Egypt: Villa 468, Tevragh Zeina, BP 176, Nouakchott; tel. 45-25-21-92; fax 45-25-33-84; Ambassador Dr YOUSSOUF AHMED CHARGHAOUI.

France: rue Ahmed Ould Hamed, Tevragh Zeina, BP 231, Nouakchott; tel. 45-29-96-99; fax 45-29-69-38; e-mail ambafrance .nouakchott-amba@diplomatie.gouv.fr; internet www .ambafrance-mr.org; Ambassador HERVÉ BESANCENOT.

Germany: Tevragh Zeina, BP 372, Nouakchott; tel. 45-25-17-29; fax 45-25-17-22; e-mail info@nouakchott.diplo.de; internet www .nouakchott.diplo.de; Ambassador DIETMAR BLAAS.

Iraq: Tevragh Zeina, Nord Villa 399, Nouakchott; tel. 45-24-32-52; fax 45-24-32-51; e-mail nokemb@iraqmfamail.com; Ambassador AHMED NAEEF RASHID AL-DULAIMI.

Japan: Tevragh Zeina, BP 7810, Nouakchott; tel. 45-25-09-77; fax 45-25-09-76; Ambassador HIROSHI AZUMA.

Korea, Democratic People's Republic: Nouakchott; Ambassador (vacant).

Kuwait: Tevragh Zeina, BP 345, Nouakchott; tel. 45-25-33-05; fax 45-25-41-45; Ambassador ADNAN ABDELLAH AL-AHMED.

Libya: BP 673, Nouakchott; tel. 45-25-52-02; fax 45-25-50-53; Chargé d'affaires ISSA ALI EL-VENAS.

Mali: Tevragh Zeina, BP 5371, Nouakchott; tel. 45-25-40-81; fax 45-25-40-83; e-mail ambmali@hotmail.com; Ambassador ETHMANE KONÉ.

Morocco: 569 ave de Gaulle, Tevragh Zeina, BP 621, Nouakchott; tel. 45-25-14-11; fax 45-29-72-80; e-mail sifmanktt@mauritel.mr; Ambassador ABDERRAHMANE BENOMAR.

Nigeria: Ilot P9, BP 367, Nouakchott; tel. 45-25-23-04; fax 45-25-23-14; Ambassador Alhaji BALA MOHAMED SANI.

Qatar: BP 609, Nouakchott; tel. 45-25-23-99; fax 45-25-68-87; e-mail nouakchoti@mofa.gov.qa; Ambassador MOHAMMED KURDI TALEB AL-MERRI.

Russia: rue Abu Bakr, BP 221, Nouakchott; tel. 45-25-19-73; fax 45-25-52-96; e-mail ambruss@opt.mr; Ambassador VLADIMIR BAYBAKOV.

Saudi Arabia: Las Balmas, Zinat, BP 498, Nouakchott; tel. 45-25-26-33; fax 45-25-29-49; e-mail mremb@mofa.gov.sa; Ambassador SAOUD BEN ABDEL AZIZ EL-JABIRI.

Senegal: Villa 500, Tevragh Zeina, BP 2511, Nouakchott; tel. 45-25-72-90; fax 45-25-72-91; Ambassador MAHMOUDOU CHEIKH KANE.

South Africa: Hotel Tfeila, Mezzanine Floor, Salon el-Waha, ave Charles de Gaulle, BP 2006, Nouakchott; tel. 45-24-55-90; fax 45-24-55-91; e-mail nouakchott@foreign.gov.za; Ambassador JOHANNES JACOBUS SPIES.

Spain: BP 232, Nouakchott; tel. 45-25-20-80; fax 45-25-40-88; e-mail emb.nouakchott@mae.es; Ambassador ALONSO DEZCALLAR Y MAZAR-REDO.

Syria: Tevragh Zeina, BP 288, Nouakchott; tel. 45-25-27-54; fax 45-25-45-00; Ambassador SAID EL-BENI.

Tunisia: BP 631, Nouakchott; tel. 45-25-28-71; fax 45-25-18-27; Ambassador CHAFIK HAJJI.

United Arab Emirates: Tafarugh Zeena Quarter, ZRA 742 bis, Nouakchott; tel. 45-25-10-98; fax 45-25-09-92; e-mail embeau@ mauritel.mr; Ambassador ABDULLAH MOHAMMED AT-TAKAWI.

USA: rue Abdallaye, BP 222, Nouakchott; tel. 45-25-26-60; fax 45-25-15-92; e-mail tayebho@state.gov; internet mauritania.usembassy .gov; Ambassador JO ELLEN POWELL.

Yemen: Tevragh Zeina, BP 4689, Nouakchott; tel. 45-25-55-91; fax 45-25-56-39; Ambassador MOHAMED ALI YAHYA SHIBAN.

Judicial System

The Code of Law was promulgated in 1961 and subsequently modified to incorporate Islamic institutions and practices. The President of the Republic guarantees the independence of judicial power and is assisted in this task by the Higher Council of the Magistracy. The main courts comprise a Supreme Court, three Courts of Appeal, 13 Regional Tribunals, 13 Labour Tribunals and 53 Departmental Civil Courts. An Audit Court has jurisdiction in financial matters. The members of the High Court of Justice are elected by the National Assembly and the Senate.

Shari'a (Islamic) law was introduced in February 1980. A special Islamic court was established in March of that year, presided over by a magistrate of Islamic law, assisted by two counsellors and two *ulemas* (Muslim jurists and interpreters of the Koran). A five-member High Council of Islam, appointed by the President, advises upon the conformity of national legislation to religious precepts, at the request of the President. A High Council of Fatwas and Appeals for Reprieve, comprising nine members, renewable every two years, was established in 2012.

Audit Court (Cour des Comptes): ave Jemal Abd'Enassir, BP 592, Nouakchott; tel. 45-25-34-04; fax 45-25-49-64; e-mail ccomptes@cc .gov.mr; internet www.cdcmr.mr; audits all govt institutions; Pres. SOW ADAMA SAMBA.

Constitutional Council: f. 1992; includes six mems, three nominated by the Head of State and three designated by the Presidents of the Senate and National Assembly; Pres. SGHAIR OULD M'BAREK; Sec.-Gen. SY ADAMA.

Courts of Appeal: at Nouakchott, Nouadhibou and Kiffa.

High Council of Fatwas and Appeals for Reprieve (Haut Conseil de la Fatwa et des Recours Gracieux): Nouakchott; f. 2012; comprises nine members, renewable every two years; issues fatwas with respect to interpretations of Islamic law; also has the authority to resolve disputes which are not under any court of law; Pres. MOHAMED EL MOCTAR OULD M'BALLA.

High Council of Islam (al-Majlis al-Islamiya al-A'la'): Nouakchott; f. 1992; Pres. AHMED HACEN OULD CHEIKH MOHAMED HAMED.

High Court of Justice: Nouakchott; f. 1961; comprises an equal number of appointees elected from their membership by the National Assembly and the Senate, following each partial or general renewal of those legislative bodies; competent to try the President of the Republic in case of high treason, and the Prime Minister and members of the Government in case of conspiracy against the State.

Supreme Court: BP 201, Palais de Justice, Nouakchott; tel. and fax 45-25-67-40; internet www.coursupreme.ma; f. 1961; comprises an administrative chamber, two civil and social chambers, a commercial chamber and a criminal chamber; Pres. YAHFDHOU OULD MOHAMED YOUSSEF.

Religion

ISLAM

Islam is the official religion, and the population are almost entirely Muslims of the Malekite rite. The major religious groups are the Tijaniya and the Qadiriya. Chinguetti, in the region of Adrar, is the seventh Holy Place in Islam. A High Council of Islam (Haut Conseil Islamique) supervises the conformity of legislation to Muslim orthodoxy.

Haut Conseil Islamique: BP 5949, Nouakchott; tel. 45-25-19-91; fax 45-25-19-17.

CHRISTIANITY

Roman Catholic Church

Mauritania comprises the single diocese of Nouakchott, directly responsible to the Holy See. The Bishop participates in the Bishops' Conference of Senegal, Mauritania, Cape Verde and Guinea-Bissau, based in Dakar, Senegal. There are an estimated 4,500 adherents, mainly non-nationals, in the country.

Bishop of Nouakchott: Most Rev. MARTIN ALBERT HAPPE, Evêché, BP 5377, Nouakchott; tel. 45-25-04-27; fax 45-25-37-51; e-mail mgrmartinhappe@yahoo.fr.

The Press

Of some 400 journals officially registered in Mauritania in 2004, some 30 were regular, widely available publications, of which the following were among the most important:

Al-Akhbar: ave Charles de Gaulles, BP 5346, Nouakchott; tel. 25-00-28-28; fax 25-00-22-33; e-mail fr.redaction@alakhbar.info; internet fr.alakhbar.info; f. 2003; weekly; Arabic and French.

Biladi: Immeuble BMCI, 5ème étage, apt 508, BP 1122, Nouakchott; tel. and fax 45-24-02-75; e-mail oneina1@gmail.com; internet www .rmibiladi.com; French; weekly; Dir of Publication MOUSSA OULD HAMED; Editor-in-Chief ABDELVETAH OULD MOHAMED.

Le Calame/Al-Qalam: rue 42–62, Tevragh Zeina, 348 Kennedy ave Ouest, BP 1059, Nouakchott; tel. 45-24-08-29; fax 45-24-08-30; e-mail lecalame@yahoo.fr; internet www.lecalame.mr; f. 1993; weekly; Arabic and French; independent; Editors-in-Chief RIYAD OULD AHMED EL-HADI (Arabic edn), AHMED OULD CHEIKH (French edn).

Châab: BP 371, Nouakchott; tel. 45-25-29-40; fax 45-25-55-20; e-mail chaab@ami.mr; internet www.ami.mr; f. 1975; daily; Arabic; also publ. in French *Horizons*; publ. by Agence Mauritanienne de l'Information; Dir of Publication YARBA OULD SGHAÏR.

Challenge: BP 1346, Nouakchott; tel. and fax 45-29-22-46; e-mail challengehebdo@yahoo.fr; internet www.challenge-mr.com; weekly.

Ech-tary: BP 1059, Nouakchott; tel. 45-25-50-65; e-mail info@ echtary.net; internet www.echtary.net; fortnightly; Arabic; satirical.

Essirage Hebdo: Nouakchott; tel. 22-01-09-82; e-mail wadiaa@ maktoob.com; internet www.essirage.net; weekly.

L'Essor: BP 5310, Nouakchott; tel. 36-30-21-68 (mobile); fax 45-25-95-95; e-mail sidiel2000@yahoo.fr; monthly; the environment and the economy; Dir SIDI EL-MOCTAR CHEÏGUER; circ. 2,500.

L'Eveil-Hebdo: BP 587, Nouakchott; tel. 45-25-67-14; fax 45-25-87-54; e-mail symoudou@yahoo.fr; f. 1991; weekly; independent; Dir of Publication SY MAMADOU.

Journal Officel: BP 188, Nouakchott; tel. 45-25-33-37; fax 45-25-34-74; fortnightly.

Maghreb Hebdo: BP 5266, Nouakchott; tel. 45-25-98-10; fax 45-25-98-11; f. 1994; weekly; Dir KHATTRI OULD DIÈ.

Mauritanies1: Nouakchott; e-mail contact@mauritanies1.com; internet www.mauritanies1.com; monthly.

Al-Mourabit: Nouakchott; tel. 45-24-95-35; e-mail brahimbakar@ almourabit.mr; internet www.almourabit.mr; weekly; French; Editor-in-Chief BRAHIM OULD BAKAR OULD SNEIBA.

Nouakchott-Info: Immeuble Abbas, Tevragh Zeina, BP 1905, Nouakchott; tel. 45-25-02-71; fax 45-25-54-84; e-mail aboulmaaly@ yahoo.com; internet www.ani.mr; f. 1995; daily; independent; Arabic and French; Dir of Publication and Editor-in-Chief MOHAMED MAHMOUD ABOUL MAALY.

Points Chauds Online: Ilot L prés de la garde Nationale (face de Mauritanie couleur), Nouakchott; tel. 46-57-57-02; fax 45-25-06-04; e-mail info@pointschauds.info; internet www.pointschauds.info; f. 2002; Editor-in-Chief MOULAYE NAJIM MOULAYE ZEINE.

Le Quotidien de Nouakchott: BP 1153 Nouakchott; tel. 45-24–53-74; e-mail khalioubi@yahoo.fr; internet www.quotidien-nouakchott .com; French; Editor-in-Chief KHALILOU DIAGANA.

Al-Rayah (The Banner): Nouakchott; e-mail team@rayah.info; internet www.rayah.info; f. 1997; independent; weekly; pro-Islamist; Editor AHMED OULD WEDIAA.

Tahalil Hebdo: BP 5205, Nouakchott; tel. 45-24-18-00; fax 45-25-80-87; e-mail contact@journaltahalil.com; internet www .journaltahalil.com; weekly; French.

La Tribune: BP 6227, Nouakchott; tel. 46-46-18-82 (mobile); e-mail contact@la-tribune.info; internet www.la-tribune.info; weekly; French; Editor-in-Chief KISSIMA TOCKA DIAGANA.

NEWS AGENCY

Agence Mauritanienne de l'Information (AMI): BP 371, Nouakchott; tel. 45-25-29-40; fax 45-25-45-87; e-mail ami@mauritania.mr; internet www.ami.mr; fmrly Agence Mauritanienne de Presse; state-controlled; news and information services in Arabic and French; Man. Dir YARBA OULD SGHAÏR.

Publishers

Imprimerie Commerciale et Administrative de Mauritanie: BP 164, Nouakchott; textbooks, educational.

Imprimerie Nationale: BP 618, Nouakchott; tel. 45-25-44-38; fax 45-25-44-37; f. 1978; state-owned; Pres. RACHID OULD SALEH; Man. Dir ISSIMOU MAHJOUB.

GOVERNMENT PUBLISHING HOUSE

Société Nationale d'Impression: BP 618, Nouakchott; Pres. MOUSTAPHA SALECK OULD AHMED BRIHIM.

Broadcasting and Communications

TELECOMMUNICATIONS

In 2011 there were three mobile cellular telephone operators in Mauritania, one of which, Mauritel, also provided fixed-line telephone services. In 2011 there were 3,283,400 subscribers to mobile telephone services and 72,300 subscribers to fixed-line services.

Chinguitel: Carrefour Cité SMAR, Nouakchott; tel. 22-00-02-91 (mobile); internet www.chinguitel.mr; provides mobile cellular, fixed-line and internet services; Dir-Gen. ABDERAHMAN MOHAMED AHMED OUSMANE.

Mauritel: 563 ave du Roi Fayçal, BP 7000, Nouakchott; tel. 45-25-76-00; fax 45-25-17-00; e-mail webmaster@mauritel.mr; internet www.mauritel.mr; fmrly Société Mauritanienne des Télécommunications; provides fixed-line and mobile cellular telephone services; 46% state-owned, 51% owned by the Compagnie

Mauritanienne de Communication (created by Maroc Télécom), 3% owned by Mauritel employees; Dir-Gen. KAMAL OKBA.

Société Mauritano-Tunisienne de Télécommunications (Mattel): 441 ave Charles de Gaulle, Tevragh-Zeina, BP 3668, Nouakchott; tel. 45-29-53-54; fax 45-29-81-03; e-mail mattel@mattel.mr; internet www.mattel.mr; f. 2000; operates mobile cellular communications network; Dir-Gen. MOHAMED ALI ESSAHILI.

Regulatory Authority

Autorité de Régulation: 428 rue 23023 Ksar, BP 4908, Nouakchott; tel. 45-29-12-70; fax 45-29-12-79; e-mail webmaster@are.mr; internet www.are.mr; f. 1999; Pres. NANI OULD CHROUGHA.

BROADCASTING

In July 2010 the National Assembly passed legislation allowing the establishment of private broadcasters for the first time in Mauritania, thereby ending almost 50 years of state monopoly. In November 2011 the Haute Autorité de la Presse et de l'Audiovisuel awarded licences to five radio and two television channels: Sahara FM, Radio Cobenni, Mauritanides FM, Radio Tenwir and Radio Nouakchott; Mauri–Vision and Télévision Watanya. A further three licences were issued to television channels in March 2013.

Regulatory Authority

Haute Autorité de la Presse et de l'Audiovisuel (HAPA): ave du Roi Fayçal-Ksar, en face de l'UTM, BP 3192, Nouakchott; tel. 45-24-10-88; fax 45-24-10-51; internet www.hapa.mr; f. 2006; Pres. HAMOUD OULD M'HAMED.

Radio

Radio Mauritanie (RM): ave Gamal Abdel Nasser, BP 200, Nouakchott; tel. and fax 45-25-21-64; e-mail rm@radiomauritanie .com; internet www.radiomauritanie.mr; f. 1958; state-controlled; broadcasts two channels; five transmitters; radio broadcasts in Arabic, French, Sarakolé, Toucouleur and Wolof; Dir MOHAMED LEMINE OULD MOULAYE ELY (acting).

Radio Mauritanie also operates 10 local radio stations. Broadcasts from RFI (FM), Africa N°1 and Radio Monte Carlo Doualiya are also received in the country.

Television

Télévision de Mauritanie (TVM): BP 5522, Nouakchott; tel. 45-25-40-67; fax 45-25-40-69; e-mail dgtvm@tvmsat.mr; internet www .tvm.mr; f. 1982; Dir-Gen. MOHAMED DIEH OULD SIDATY.

Finance

(cap. = capital; res = reserves; dep. = deposits; m. = million; br(s).= branch(es); amounts in ouguiyas)

BANKING

In 2010 there were 10 commercial banks, two other financial institutions and some 80 microfinance institutions operating in Mauritania.

Central Bank

Banque Centrale de Mauritanie (BCM): ave de l'Indépendance, BP 623, Nouakchott; tel. 45-25-22-06; fax 45-25-27-59; e-mail info@ bcm.mr; internet www.bcm.mr; f. 1973; bank of issue; cap. 200m., res 2,869.7m., dep. 96,225.3m. (2009); Gov. SID'AHMED OULD RAISS; 4 brs.

Commercial Banks

Attijari Bank Mauritanie: 91/92 rue Mamadou Konaté, Nouakchott; tel. 45-29-63-74; fax 45-29-64-40; cap. 3,398m. (Dec. 2010).

Banque El Amana (BEA): rue Mamadou Konaté BP 5559, Nouakchott; tel. 45-25-59-53; fax 45-25-34-95; e-mail info@bea.mr; internet www.bea.mr; f. 1996; 72% privately owned, 27% owned by Société Nationale Industrielle et Minière; cap. 4,790.3m. (March 2011); CEO AHMED SALEM BOUNA MOKHTAR; Gen. Man. AHMED SALEM ELY EL KORY.

Banque pour le Commerce et l'Industrie (BCI): ave Gemal Abdel Nasser, BP 5050, Nouakchott; tel. 45-29-28-76; fax 45-29-28-77; e-mail info@bci-banque.com; internet www.bci-banque.com; f. 1999; cap. 4,000m. (Dec. 2010); Pres. and Dir-Gen. ISSELMOU OULD DIDI OULD TAJEDINE; 11 brs.

Banque Mauritanienne pour le Commerce International (BMCI): Immeuble Afarco, ave Nasser, BP 622, Nouakchott; tel. 45-25-28-26; fax 45-25-20-45; e-mail info@bmci.mr; internet www .bmci.mr; f. 1974; 95.82% owned by Group Abbas; cap. 4,000m., res 3,402m., dep. 31,005m. (Dec. 2006); Pres. and Dir-Gen. MOULAY SIDI OULD HACEN OULD ABASS; 18 brs.

Banque Nationale de Mauritanie (BNM): ave Gamal Abdel Nasser, BP 614, Nouakchott; tel. 45-25-26-02; fax 45-25-33-97; e-mail bnm10@bnm.mr; internet www.bnm.mr; f. 1989; privately owned; res 977m., dep. 20,659m. (Dec. 2003); cap. 6,000m. (Dec. 2005); Pres. and Dir-Gen. MOHAMED OULD NOUEIGUED; 10 brs.

Chinguitty Bank: ave Gamal Abdel Nasser, BP 626, Nouakchott; tel. 45-25-21-73; fax 45-25-33-82; e-mail chinguittybank@mauritel .mr; f. 1972; 51% owned by Libyan Arab Foreign Bank, 49% state-owned; cap. and res 4,002.9m., total assets 11,428.7m. (Dec. 2007); Pres. MOHAMED OULD DIDI; Gen. Man. YOUNIS TAHER AS-SOUDI; 2 brs.

Générale de Banque de Mauritanie pour l'Investissement et le Commerce SA (GBM): ave de l'Indépendance, BP 5558, Nouakchott; tel. 45-25-36-36; fax 45-25-46-47; e-mail gbm@gbm.mr.com; f. 1995; 70% privately owned; cap. 7,200m., res 14,037.6m., dep. 15,142.5m. (Dec. 2006); Pres. and Dir-Gen. MOHAMED HMAYEN OULD BOUAMATOU; 1 br.

Orabank Mauritanie: P54, ave du Général Charles de Gaulle 20, rue 42-060, BP 1268, Nouakchott; tel. and fax 45-29-13-60; e-mail info-mr@orabank.net; internet www.orabank.net; f. 2002 as Bacim-Bank; present name adopted 2012; privately owned; cap. 6,921m. (Sep. 2012); Dir-Gen. AZHAR KHAN; 6 brs.

Société Générale Mauritanie (SGM): ave Charles de Gaulle, BP 5085, Nouakchott; tel. 45-29-70-00; fax 45-24-53-00; internet www .sgm.mr; f. 2005; present name adopted 2007; cap. 4,000m. (Jan. 2006); Pres. and Dir-Gen. JEAN-PHILLIPE EQUILBECQ; 1 br.

Islamic Bank

Banque al-Wava Mauritanienne Islamique (BAMIS): 758, rue 22–018, ave du Roi Fayçal, BP 650, Nouakchott; tel. 45-25-14-24; fax 45-25-16-21; e-mail bamis@bamis.mr; internet www.bamis.mr; f. 1985; fmrly Banque al-Baraka Mauritanienne Islamique; majority share privately owned; cap. 7,000m., dep. 27,487m. (Dec. 2011); Pres. MOHAMED ABDELLAHI OULD ABDALLAHI; Dir-Gen. MOHAMED ABDELLAHI OULD SIDI; Exec. Dir MOHAMED OULD TAYA; 8 brs.

INSURANCE

In 2008 there were eight insurance companies in Mauritania.

Assurances Générales de Mauritanie: BP 2141, ave de Gaulle, TZA Ilot A 667, Nouakchott; tel. 45-29-29-00; fax 45-29-29-11; Man. MOULAYE ELY BOUAMATOU.

Compagnie Nationale d'Assurance et de Réassurance (NASR): 12 ave Nasser, BP 163, Nouakchott; tel. 45-25-26-50; fax 45-25-18-18; e-mail nasr@nasr.mr; internet www.nasr.mr; f. 1994; state-owned; Pres. MOHAMED ABDALLAHI OULD SIDI; Dir-Gen. AHMED OULD SIDI BABA.

Mauritanienne d'Assurances et de Réassurances (MAR): Nouakchott; tel. 45-24-12-18; e-mail mar@mar-assur.mr; internet www.mar-assur.mr; f. 2002.

Société Anonyme d'Assurance et de Réassurance (SAAR): ave J. F. Kennedy, Immeuble El-Mamy, BP 2841, Nouakchott; tel. 45-25-30-56; fax 45-25-25-36; e-mail saar@infotel.mr; f. 1999; Pres. and Dir-Gen. AHMED BEZEID OULD MED LEMINE.

TAAMIN: BP 5164, Nouakchott; tel. 45-29-40-00; fax 45-29-40-02; e-mail info@assurancestaamin.com; internet www .assurancestaamin.com; Pres. and Dir-Gen. MOULAYE EL HASSEN OULD MOCTAR EL HASSEN.

Trade and Industry

DEVELOPMENT ORGANIZATIONS

Agence Française de Développement (AFD): rue Mamadou Kouaté prolongée, BP 5211, Nouakchott; tel. 45-25-25-25; fax 45-25-49-10; e-mail afdnouakchott@afd.fr; internet www.afd.fr; Country Dir PATRICK ABBES.

Service de Coopération et d'Action Culturelle: BP 203, Nouakchott; tel. 45-29-95-59; fax 45-29-96-15; e-mail scac .nouakchott-amba@diplomatie.fr; administers bilateral aid from France; Dir SYLVAIN FOURCASSIE.

Société Nationale pour le Développement Rural (SONADER): BP 321, Nouakchott; tel. 45-21-18-00; fax 45-25-32-86; f. 1975; Dir-Gen. MOHAMED OULD AHMAHOULLAH.

CHAMBER OF COMMERCE

Chambre de Commerce, d'Industrie et d'Agriculture de Mauritanie (CCIAM): 303 ave de l'Indépendance, BP 215, Nouakchott; tel. 45-25-22-14; fax 45-25-38-95; e-mail cciam_info@yahoo.fr; internet www.chambredecommerce.mr; f. 1954; Pres. MOHAMEDOU OULD MOHAMED MAHMOUD; Sec.-Gen. ABDEL AZIZ WANE.

EMPLOYERS' ORGANIZATION

Union Nationale du Patronat Mauritanien (UNPM): 824 ave de Roi Fayçal, Ksar, BP 383, Nouakchott; tel. 45-25-33-01; fax 45-25-91-08; e-mail germe@opt.mr; f. 1960; professional asscn for all employers active in Mauritania; Pres. AHMED BABA OULD AZIZI OULD EL MAMY; Sec.-Gen. SEYID OULD ABDALLAHI.

UTILITIES

Electricity

Société Mauritanienne d'Electricité (SOMELEC): 47 ave de l'Indépendance, BP 355, Nouakchott; tel. 45-29-66-04; fax 45-25-39-95; internet www.somelec.mr; f. 2001; state-owned; transfer to majority private sector ownership proposed; production and distribution of electricity; Pres. MEMMED OULD AHMED; Dir-Gen. MOHAMED SALEM OULD BÉCHIR.

Gas

Société Mauritanienne de Gaz (SOMAGAZ): POB 5089, Nouakchott; tel. 45-24-28-58; fax 45-24-29-70; e-mail somagazinfo@somagaz.com; internet www.somagaz.com; f. 1987; production and distribution of butane gas; Dir-Gen. ABDALLAHI OULD BENANE.

Water

Société Nationale d'Eau (SNDE): 106 ave 42-096, Tevragh Zeina, BP 796, Nouakchott; tel. 45-25-52-73; fax 45-25-19-52; e-mail mfoudail@infotel.mr; f. 2001; Pres. CHEIKH OULD BAHA; Dir-Gen. AHMED KHALIVA OULD BEYAH.

TRADE UNIONS

Confédération Générale des Travailleurs de Mauritanie: BP 6164, Nouakchott; tel. 45-25-60-24; fax 45-25-80-57; e-mail admin@cgtm.org; internet cgtm.org; f. 1992; obtained official recognition in 1994; Sec.-Gen. ABDALLAHI OULD MOHAMED.

Confédération Libre des Travailleurs de Mauritanie: BP 6902, Nouakchott; fax 45-25-23-16; f. 1995; Sec.-Gen. SAMORY OULD BÉYE.

Confédération Nationale des Travailleurs de Mauritanie (CNTM): Nouakchott; tel. 45-00-17-01; fax 45-24-35-80; internet www.cntm-rim.org; Sec.-Gen. MOHAMED AHMED OULD SALECK.

Union des Travailleurs de Mauritanie (UTM): Bourse du Travail, BP 630, Nouakchott; f. 1961; Sec.-Gen. ABDERAHMANE OULD BOUBOU; 45,000 mems.

Transport

RAILWAYS

A 704-km railway connects the iron-ore deposits at Zouérate with Nouadhibou; a 40-km extension services the reserves at El Rhein, and a 30-km extension those at M'Haoudat. Motive power is diesel-electric. The Société Nationale Industrielle et Minière (SNIM) operates one of the longest (2.4 km) and heaviest (22,000 metric tons) trains in the world.

SNIM—Direction du Chemin de Fer et du Port: BP 42, Nouadhibou; tel. 45-74-51-74; fax 45-74-53-96; e-mail m.khalifa.beyah@zrt.snim.com; internet www.snim.com; f. 1963; Gen. Man. MOHAMED EL-MOCTAR OULD TALEB.

ROADS

In 2010 there were about 10,628 km of roads and tracks, of which only 3,157 km were paved. The 1,100-km Trans-Mauritania highway, completed in 1985, links Nouakchott with Néma in the east of the country. The construction of a 470-km highway between Nouakchott and Nouadhibou was completed in 2004. Plans exist for the construction of a 7,400-km highway, linking Nouakchott with the Libyan port of Tubruq (Tobruk).

Autorité de Régulation des Transports: Nouakchott; Pres. CHEIKH SID'AHMED OULD BABA.

Entreprise Nationale de l'Entretien Routier: Dir-Gen. MADI OULD TALEB.

Société Mauritanienne des Transports (SOMATRA): Nouakchott; tel. 45-25-29-53; f. 1975; Pres. CHEIKH MALAININE ROBERT; Dir-Gen. MAMADOU SOULEYMANE KANE.

INLAND WATERWAYS

The Senegal river is navigable in the wet season by small coastal vessels as far as Kayes (Mali) and by river vessels as far as Kaédi; in the dry season as far as Rosso and Boghé, respectively. The major river ports are at Rosso, Kaédi and Gouraye.

SHIPPING

The principal port, at Point-Central, 10 km south of Nouadhibou, is almost wholly occupied with mineral exports. There is also a commercial and fishing port at Nouadhibou. The deep-water Port de l'Amitié at Nouakchott, built and maintained with assistance from the People's Republic of China, was inaugurated in 1986, and has a total annual capacity of about 1.5m. metric tons. In 2012 Mauritania's flag registered fleet consisted of 70 vessels and had a total displacement of some 25,752 grt.

Mauritanienne de Transport Maritime: Nouakchott; tel. 45-25-44-79; fax 45-25-44-76; e-mail mtm@mtm.mr; internet www.mtm.mr; f. 1996; Pres. and Dir-Gen. A. KADER KAMIL.

Port Autonome de Nouadhibou: BP 236, Nouadhibou; tel. 45-74-51-36; fax 45-74-51-36; e-mail contact@pan.mr; internet www.portndb.com; f. 1973; state-owned; Pres. BAL MOHAMED EL HABIB; Dir-Gen. MOHAMED ABDERRAHMANE OULD BRAHIM.

Port Autonome de Nouakchott (Port de l'Amitié): BP 5103, El Mina, Nouakchott; tel. 45-25-38-59; fax 45-25-16-15; e-mail info@panpa.mr; internet www.panpa.mr; f. 1986; deep-water port; Dir-Gen. AHMEDOU OULD HAMED.

Shipping Companies

Cie Mauritanienne de Navigation Maritime (COMAUNAM): 119 ave Nasser, BP 799, Nouakchott; tel. 45-25-36-34; fax 45-25-25-04; f. 1973; 51% state-owned, 49% owned by Govt of Algeria; nat. shipping co; forwarding agent, stevedoring; Chair. MOHAND TIGHILT; Dir-Gen. KAMIL ABDELKADER.

Société d'Acconage et de Manutention en Mauritanie (SAMMA): BP 258, Nouadhibou; tel. 45-74-52-63; fax 45-74-52-37; e-mail didi.samma@snim.com; internet www.samma.mr; f. 1960; freight and handling, shipping agent, forwarding agent, stevedoring; Man. Dir DIDI OULD BIHA.

Société Générale de Consignation et d'Entreprises Maritimes (SOGECO): 1765 rue 22-002, Commune du Ksar, BP 351, Nouakchott; tel. 45-25-22-02; fax 45-25-39-03; e-mail sogeco@sogeco.sa.mr; internet www.sogecosa.com; f. 1973; shipping agent, forwarding, stevedoring; Man. Dir SID'AHMED OULD ABEIDNA.

Société Mauritanienne pour la Pêche et la Navigation (SMPN): BP 40254, Nouakchott; tel. 45-25-36-38; fax 45-25-37-87; e-mail smpn@toptechnology.mr; Dir-Gen. ABDALLAHI OULD ISMAIL.

VOTRA: route de l'Aéroport, BP 454, Nouakchott; tel. 45-25-24-10; fax 45-25-31-41; e-mail info@votra.net; internet www.votra.net; Dir-Gen. MOHAMED MAHMOUD OULD MAYE.

CIVIL AVIATION

There are international airports at Nouakchott, Nouadhibou and Néma, and 23 smaller airstrips.

Agence Nationale de l'Aviation Civile (ANAC): BP 91, Nouakchott; tel. 45-24-40-06; fax 45-25-35-78; e-mail abseddigh@anac.mr; internet www.anac.mr; f. 2004; Gen. Man. ABOUBEKRINE SEDDIGH OULD MOAMED EL HACEN.

Mauritania Airlines International: Nouakchott; f. 2010.

Tourism

Mauritania's principal tourist attractions are its historical sites, several of which have been listed by UNESCO under its World Heritage Programme, and its game reserves and national parks. Some 24,000 tourists visited Mauritania in 1999. Receipts from tourism in that year totalled an estimated US $28m.

Office National du Tourisme: BP 2884, Nouakchott; tel. 45-29-03-44; fax 45-29-05-28; internet www.tourisme-mauritanie.com; f. 2002; Dir KHADIJÉTOU MINT BOUBOU.

SOMASERT: BP 42, Nouadhibou; tel. 45-74-29-91; fax 45-74-90-43; e-mail somasert@snim.com; internet www.somasert.com; f. 1987; subsidiary of SNIM; responsible for promoting tourism, managing hotels and organizing tours; Dir-Gen. SAAD CHEIK SAAD BOUH.

Defence

As assessed at November 2010, the total armed forces numbered an estimated 15,870 men: army 15,000, navy about 620, air force 250. Full-time membership of paramilitary forces totalled about 5,000. Military service is by authorized conscription, and lasts for two years.

Defence Expenditure: Estimated at UM 30,100m. in 2009.

Chief of Staff of the Armed Forces: Gen. MOHAMED OULD CHEIKH MOHAMED AHMED.

Chief of Staff of the Navy: Col CHEIKH OULD BAYE.

Chief of Staff of the National Gendarmerie: Col N'DIAGA DIENG.

Education

Primary education, which is officially compulsory, begins at six years of age and lasts for six years. In 2009/10 total enrolment at primary schools included 74% of children in the relevant age-group (72% of boys; 76% of girls), according to UNESCO estimates. Secondary education begins at 12 years of age and lasts for seven years, comprising a first cycle of four years and a second of three years.

Total enrolment at public secondary schools in 2006/07 included only 16% of children in the appropriate age-group (17% of boys; 15% of girls), according to UNESCO estimates. In 2010/11 a total of 14,536 students were enrolled at Mauritania's higher education institutions (including the Université de Nouakchott, which was opened in 1983). In 2010 spending on education represented 15.2% of total budgetary expenditure.

MAURITIUS

Introductory Survey

LOCATION, CLIMATE, LANGUAGE, RELIGION, FLAG, CAPITAL

The Republic of Mauritius lies in the Indian Ocean. The principal island, from which the country takes its name, lies about 800 km (500 miles) east of Madagascar. The other main islands are Rodrigues, the Agalega Islands and the Cargados Carajos Shoals (St Brandon Islands). The climate is maritime sub-tropical and generally humid. The average annual temperature is 23°C (73°F) at sea-level, falling to 19°C (66°F) at an altitude of 600 m (about 2,000 ft). Average annual rainfall varies from 890 mm (35 ins) at sea-level to 5,080 mm (200 ins) on the highest parts. Tropical cyclones, which may be severe, occur between September and May. Most of the population are of Indian descent. The most widely spoken languages in 2000 were Creole (38.6%) and Bhojpuri (30.6%). English is the country's official language, and Creole (derived from French) is the lingua franca. The principal religious group are Hindus, who comprise more than 50% of the population. About 30% are Christians and 17% are Muslims. The national flag (proportions 2 by 3) has four equal horizontal stripes, of red, blue, yellow and green. The capital is Port Louis.

CONTEMPORARY POLITICAL HISTORY

Historical Context

The islands of Mauritius and Rodrigues, formerly French possessions, passed into British control in 1810. Subsequent settlement came mainly from East Africa and India, and the European population has remained largely French-speaking.

A ministerial form of government was introduced in 1957. The first elections under universal adult suffrage, held in 1959, were won by the Mauritius Labour Party (MLP), led by Dr (later Sir) Seewoosagur Ramgoolam. Mauritius became independent, within the Commonwealth, on 12 March 1968, with Ramgoolam as Prime Minister.

In November 1965 the United Kingdom transferred the Chagos Archipelago (including the atoll of Diego Garcia), a Mauritian dependency about 2,000 km (1,250 miles) north-east of the main island, to the newly created British Indian Ocean Territory (BIOT, q.v.). Mauritius has subsequently campaigned for the return of the islands, which have been developed as a major US military base. Mauritius also claims sovereignty of the French-held island of Tromelin, about 550 km (340 miles) to the north-west.

Domestic Political Affairs

During the 1970s political opposition to successive coalition governments formed by Ramgoolam was led by a radical left-wing group, the Mouvement Militant Mauricien (MMM), founded by Paul Bérenger. Although the MMM became the largest single party in the Legislative Assembly following a general election in December 1976, Ramgoolam was able to form a new coalition Government with the support of the Parti Mauricien Social Démocrate (PMSD). However, social unrest and rising unemployment undermined popular support for the Government, and at a general election in June 1982 the MMM, in alliance with the Parti Socialiste Mauricien (PSM), won all 60 contested seats on the main island. Aneerood (later Sir Aneerood) Jugnauth, the leader of the MMM, became Prime Minister, and Bérenger Minister of Finance.

The MMM/PSM coalition collapsed in March 1983, when Bérenger and his supporters resigned, following differences concerning economic policy. Jugnauth formed a new Government and a new party, the Mouvement Socialiste Militant (MSM), which subsequently merged with the PSM. A general election took place in August, at which an electoral alliance of the MSM, the MLP and the PMSD, led by Sir Gaëtan Duval, gained a legislative majority. Jugnauth formed a new coalition Government, in which Duval became Deputy Prime Minister. The MLP, however, withdrew from the coalition in February 1984.

Following a general election in August 1987, the MSM again formed an electoral alliance with the PMSD and the MLP; the three parties obtained 39 of the 62 elective seats. Bérenger, who failed to secure a seat, transferred his functions as leader of the

opposition in the Legislative Assembly to Dr Paramhansa Nababsingh (while Bérenger himself replaced Nababsingh as Secretary-General of the MMM). A new coalition, led by Jugnauth, took office in September; however, in August 1988, following a disagreement over employment policies, the PMSD withdrew from the coalition.

In July 1990 the MSM and the MMM agreed to form an alliance to contest the next general election, and to promote constitutional measures allowing Mauritius to become a republic within the Commonwealth. This proposal, however, was jointly opposed by the MLP and the PMSD, prompting Jugnauth to dismiss the MLP leader, Sir Satcam Boolell, from the Government, together with two dissident ministers from the MSM. A further three ministers representing the MLP resigned, leaving only one MLP member in the Government. Boolell subsequently relinquished the leadership of the MLP to Dr Navinchandra Ramgoolam (the son of the late Sir Seewoosagur Ramgoolam). In September Jugnauth formed a new coalition Government.

At a general election, which took place on 15 September, an alliance of the MSM, the MMM and the small Mouvement des Travaillistes Démocrates (MTD) won 57 of the 62 directly elected seats, while the MLP/PMSD alliance obtained three seats. The two remaining seats were secured by the Organisation du Peuple Rodriguais (OPR). Four 'additional' seats were subsequently allocated to members of the MLP/PMSD alliance. Jugnauth formed a new government coalition, to which nine representatives of the MMM (including Bérenger, who became Minister of External Affairs) and one representative of the MTD were appointed.

In December 1991 the Legislative Assembly approved the constitutional framework for the country's transition to a republic within the Commonwealth. Following the proclamation of the Republic of Mauritius on 12 March 1992, the Legislative Assembly was redesignated as the National Assembly, and the incumbent Governor-General, Sir Veerasamy Ringadoo, became interim President. Later in March the Government announced its choice of Cassam Uteem, the Minister of Industry and Industrial Technology and a member of the MMM, to assume the presidency in June. Uteem was duly elected President by the National Assembly; Sir Rabindrah Ghurburrun, a member of the MMM, took office as Vice-President.

The removal of Bérenger from the Council of Ministers in August 1993, on the grounds that he had repeatedly criticized government policy, precipitated a serious crisis within the MMM, the political bureau of which decided that the other nine members of the party who held ministerial portfolios should remain in the coalition Government. Led by Nababsingh, the Deputy Prime Minister, and Jean-Claude de l'Estrac, the Minister of Industry and Industrial Technology, supporters of the pro-coalition faction announced in October 1993 that Bérenger had been suspended as Secretary-General of the MMM. Bérenger and his supporters responded by expelling 11 MMM officials from the party, and seeking a legal ban on Nababsingh and de l'Estrac from using the party name. The split in the MMM led in November to a government reorganization, in which the remaining two MMM ministers supporting Bérenger were replaced by members of the party's pro-coalition faction. Nababsingh and the dissident faction of the MMM, having lost Bérenger's legal challenge for the use of the party name, formed a new party, the Renouveau Militant Mauricien (RMM), which formally commenced political activity in June 1994.

During the course of a parliamentary debate in November 1994 Bérenger and de l'Estrac accepted a mutual challenge to resign their seats in the National Assembly and to contest by-elections. In the following month the MSM indicated that it would not oppose RMM candidates in the two polls. In January 1995, however, Jugnauth unsuccessfully sought to undermine the MLP/MMM alliance by offering electoral support to the MLP. The by-elections, held in February, were both won by MLP/MMM candidates, and Bérenger was returned to the National Assembly. Following these results, Jugnauth opened political negotiations with the PMSD, the leader of which, Charles Gaëtan Xavier-Luc Duval (the son of Sir Gaëtan Duval), entered the coalition as Minister of Industry and Industrial Technology and Minister of Tourism. The post of Attorney-General and Minister of Justice was also allocated to the PMSD, and Sir Gaëtan Duval agreed to act as an economic adviser to the Prime Minister. As a result, however, of widespread opposition within the PMSD to participation in the coalition, Xavier-Luc Duval left the Government in October, and Sir Gaëtan Duval subsequently resumed the leadership of the party. The Minister for Rodrigues, representing the OPR, also left the Government.

The 1995 general election

At the general election held in December 1995 the MLP/MMM alliance won a decisive victory: of the 62 elected seats, the MLP secured 35, the MMM 25 and the OPR two. Under constitutional arrangements providing representation for unsuccessful candidates attracting the largest number of votes, Sir Gaëtan Duval re-entered the National Assembly, together with two members of the Mouvement Rodriguais (MR) and one representative of Hizbullah, an Islamist fundamentalist group. Ramgoolam became Prime Minister of the new MLP/MMM coalition, with Bérenger as Deputy Prime Minister with responsibility for foreign and regional relations. Sir Gaëtan Duval died in May 1996 and was succeeded in the National Assembly and as leader of the PMSD by his brother, Hervé Duval, although Xavier-Luc Duval continued to command a significant following within the party.

Serious divisions began to emerge within the coalition Government in late 1996, when differences were reported between Ramgoolam and Bérenger over the allocation of ministerial responsibilities and the perception by the MMM of delays in the implementation of social and economic reforms. Bérenger's criticism of the coalition's performance intensified in the following months, and culminated in June in his dismissal from the Government and the consequent withdrawal of the MMM from the coalition. Following unsuccessful efforts by Ramgoolam to draw the PMSD into a new administration, an MLP Council of Ministers was formed by Ramgoolam, who additionally assumed Bérenger's former responsibilities for foreign affairs. In June 1997 the National Assembly re-elected Uteem to a second five-year term as President.

Following the dissolution of the MLP/MMM alliance, Bérenger sought to assume the leadership of a consolidated political opposition to the Government. In August 1997 two small parties, the Mouvement Militant Socialiste Mauricien (MMSM) and the Rassemblement pour la Réforme (RPR), agreed to support Bérenger in this aim. The alliance was extended to include a breakaway faction of the PMSD, the 'Vrais Bleus', under the leadership of Hervé Duval, who had been replaced as party leader by Xavier-Luc Duval, an opponent of co-operation with the MMM.

In April 1998 the MMM, the MMSM, the RPR and the 'Vrais Bleus' formed an electoral coalition, the Alliance Nationale, to contest a by-election for a vacant seat in the National Assembly. In the event, however, the seat was retained by the MLP. Meanwhile, Jugnauth, seeking to revitalize the MSM's prospects in preparation for the next general election, entered negotiations with Bérenger for an electoral alliance, and in December both parties agreed terms for a joint list of candidates.

The MLP announced in mid-1999 its endorsement of the candidature of Xavier-Luc Duval for a legislative by-election to be held in September. Xavier-Luc Duval, after obtaining the vacant seat, joined the Government as Minister of Industry, Commerce, Corporate Affairs and Financial Services, following an extensive government reorganization completed at the end of the month. The selection in October of Pravind Jugnauth, the son of Sir Anerood Jugnauth, as Deputy Leader of the MSM gave rise to speculation that Sir Anerood was contemplating retirement from politics and intended his son to be his successor.

In August 2000 the MSM/MMM formed an alliance, in advance of the imminent general election, on the basis that Jugnauth would lead as Prime Minister for three years in the event of victory, before assuming the more honorary role of President, thus allowing Bérenger to become Prime Minister for the remaining two years.

The premiership of Anerood Jugnauth

A general election was held on 11 September 2000, with 81% of the 790,000 registered electors casting their ballots. The MSM/MMM alliance achieved an overwhelming victory, winning 54 of the 62 directly elected seats in the National Assembly, while the MLP/PMSD alliance gained only six seats and the OPR two seats. As agreed, Sir Anerood Jugnauth became Prime Minister

again, while Paul Bérenger was appointed Deputy Prime Minister and Minister of Finance. A new Council of Ministers was appointed one week later.

In November 2000 the British High Court of Justice ruled that the eviction of several thousand inhabitants of the Chagos Archipelago between 1967 and 1973, to allow the construction of a US military base on the atoll of Diego Garcia, had been unlawful, and overturned a 1971 ordinance preventing the islanders from returning to the Archipelago. (The majority of the displaced islanders had been resettled in Mauritius, which had administered the Chagos Archipelago until its transfer to BIOT in 1965.) Following the ruling, the Mauritian Government declared its right to sovereignty over the islands to be indisputable and sought international recognition as such. Jugnauth stated that he would be prepared to negotiate with the USA over the continued presence of the military base. The United Kingdom responded that it would return the islands if, as had been maintained for many years, the USA was prepared to move out of the base on Diego Garcia. India declared its support for the Mauritian Government's claim to sovereignty, as part of the close relationship being encouraged between the two countries.

In November 2001 exiled Chagos islanders demonstrated outside the British High Commission in Port Louis, in support of their demands for compensation from the British Government. In February 2002 legislation allowing the displaced islanders to apply for British citizenship received royal assent in the United Kingdom. At that time the British Government was also examining the feasibility of a return to the Chagos Archipelago for the islanders, who continued to seek compensation.

In January 2002 a commission on constitutional and electoral reform presented its proposals at a series of public forums, before submitting them to the Government for consideration. Recommendations included the introduction of a system of proportional representation in legislative elections and a reinforcement of presidential powers. In mid-February controversial legislation on the prevention of terrorism was finally promulgated by the Chief Justice of the Supreme Court, Arianga Pillay, acting as interim President, following the resignations of both President Uteem and his successor, Vice-President Angidi Chettiar, over the issue. The legislation had been rejected by opposition parties and proved unpopular with many sections of society for arrogating excessive powers to the authorities and infringing on citizens' rights. On 25 February Karl Offman was elected as President by an extraordinary session of the National Assembly, which was boycotted by opposition deputies. Although formally elected for five years, Offman was to relinquish the presidency to Jugnauth in October 2003; in preparation for this, in April 2003 Jugnauth announced his resignation from the leadership of the MSM, to be succeeded by his son, Pravind.

In August 2003, in preparation for the transfer of governing roles, a constitutional amendment was approved by the National Assembly to increase the powers of the President, giving the incumbent the right to refuse a request from the Prime Minister to dissolve the legislature following a vote of no confidence. As agreed, on 1 October Offman resigned as President and was replaced, in an acting capacity, by the Vice-President, Raouf Bundhun, pending the election by the National Assembly of Sir Anerood Jugnauth as his successor one week later. Jugnauth had resigned as Prime Minister on 30 September and was immediately replaced by Paul Bérenger, who appointed a new Council of Ministers. In early 2004 Bérenger renewed the campaign to reclaim sovereignty of the Chagos Archipelago from the United Kingdom (on the basis that there was no provision under international law for the dismemberment of a country before independence) and of Tromelin from France. It was established in 2004 that Mauritius had the right to pursue the case of the Chagos islands at the International Court of Justice, in spite of British objections on the basis of restrictions imposed by membership of the Commonwealth.

In February 2005 the Minister of Public Infrastructure, Land Transport and Shipping, Anil Bachoo, and the Minister of Local Government and Solid Waste Management, Mookhesswur Choonee, resigned from the Government. The two erstwhile ministers formed a new opposition party the following month, the Mouvement Sociale Démocrate (MSD), having also resigned from the MSM alleging poor leadership of that party by Pravind Jugnauth. Bachoo and Choonee reportedly disapproved of an apparent pre-electoral agreement between the parties of the ruling coalition, whereby, should they successfully be re-elected to office, Bérenger would relinquish the premiership in mid-term in favour of Pravind Jugnauth, just as the incumbent President

(Pravind Jugnauth's father) had in September 2003. The MSD announced the formation of an electoral alliance with the MLP, known as the Social Alliance, thus creating a credible rival political force to the governing parties for the forthcoming legislative elections.

Navinchandra Ramgoolam becomes Prime Minister

At the elections, which were held on 3 July 2005, the Social Alliance bloc defeated the incumbent coalition, winning 38 of the 62 directly elected mandates. The MSM/MMM alliance took 22 seats while the OPR secured two. The rate of voter participation was 81.5%. Ramgoolam was appointed as Prime Minister and a new 19-member Council of Ministers was sworn into office later that month. Following the elections, the PMSD withdrew from the opposition alliance in which it had participated with the MSM and MMM.

The Social Alliance Government continued with efforts to regain sovereignty over the Chagos Archipelago. A group of 102 Chagossians was permitted to visit the Archipelago in March 2006 principally in order to visit the graves of relatives. In May the British High Court of Justice overturned the Orders in Council issued by the British Government under the royal prerogative in June 2004, ruling them to be unlawful, and confirmed the right of the islanders to return to the Archipelago without any conditions. In February 2007 the British Government commenced proceedings in the Court of Appeal to overturn the May 2006 ruling. However, in May 2007 that court confirmed that the residents of the Chagos Archipelago had been unlawfully removed and upheld the displaced islanders' immediate right to return. In November the House of Lords granted the British Government the right to appeal against the Court of Appeal's decision, on the condition that the Chagossians' costs were met by the British Government. In November 2008 the House of Lords ruled in favour of the British Government, thus denying the Chagossians the right to return, citing as its main reason the fact that the United Kingdom would have been obliged to meet the costs of economic, social and educational advancement of the residents. Having exhausted the appeals process in the United Kingdom, the Chagossians announced that they would take their case to the European Court of Human Rights (ECHR). However, in December 2012 the ECHR also ruled in favour of the United Kingdom, declaring that a compensation package agreed in 1982 had constituted a final settlement of the matter.

In April 2010 the British Government announced that it had designated the Chagos Archipelago a marine protection area (MPA), within which all fishing and other activities were to be prohibited. The conservation area, covering some 544,000 sq km, was to be patrolled by a ship vested with the powers to arrest fleets caught fishing illegally, to impose fines of up to £100,000 and to confiscate boats and fishing equipment. The ban on fishing undermined the Chagossians' resettlement plans as it removed the legal means by which they could sustain their standard of living. In December the Mauritian Government announced that it had taken a case against the United Kingdom to the UN International Tribunal for the Law of the Sea on the grounds that the MPA was not compatible with the UN Convention on the Law of the Sea. Furthermore, the Chagossians also appealed for a judicial review of the decision to create the MPA. In January 2013 the Permanent Court of Arbitration adjudged that it was competent to hear the case, in spite of objections by the United Kingdom.

Meanwhile, in April 2006 the opposition was further weakened when the MSM/MMM alliance collapsed following weeks of increasing tension between Pravind Jugnauth and Bérenger, and the PMSD announced that it was joining the government coalition. The MSM withdrew its support from Bérenger as official leader of the opposition, and he was succeeded by Nando Bodha, the Secretary-General of the MSM and a close ally of Pravind Jugnauth (who had failed to retain his seat in the legislature in July 2005), since the MSM held 11 seats in the National Assembly to the MMM's 10. Bodha's nomination was rejected by Ashock Jugnauth, a senior member of the MSM (and uncle of Pravind), who resigned from the party and established a new opposition party, the Union Nationale. In August 2007 Chettiar resumed the position of Vice-President, replacing Bundhun. In September Bodha resigned as leader of the opposition and in October Bérenger once again assumed the role.

Ramgoolam reorganized the Government in mid-September 2008. Most notably, Anil Bachoo was reinstated as Minister of Public Infrastructure, Land Transport and Shipping, and Arvin Boolell became Minister of Foreign Affairs, Regional Integration and International Trade. On 19 September the National Assembly unanimously re-elected Aneerood Jugnauth as President for a second five-year term, and on the following day legislation was approved that allowed for two ministers to hold the title of Vice-Prime Minister: these positions were awarded to Xavier-Luc Duval and Dr Rama Sithanen, with the former also retaining the tourism portfolio, while Sithanen retained the finance portfolio. (The position of Deputy Prime Minister remained the second most senior post in the Council of Ministers—Ahmed Rashid Beebeejaun was appointed to this office and also assumed responsibility for the renewable energy and public utilities portfolio.) In January 2010 Louis Hervé Aimé was appointed Minister of Local Government, Rodrigues and Outer Islands, following the sudden death of James Burty David the previous month.

A total of 65 parties and alliances registered to contest the elections on 5 May 2010, most notably the Alliance de l'Avenir, comprising the MLP, the PMSD and the MSM, and the Alliance du Coeur, formed by the MMM, the Union Nationale and the Mouvement Mauricien Social Démocrate. In the event the Alliance de l'Avenir secured 41 of the 62 directly elected seats and was awarded four additional seats. The Alliance du Coeur took 18 directly elected seats and two additional seats, while the remaining directly elected seats were won by the MR (two) and the Front Solidarité Mauricienne (one). A further additional seat was allocated to the OPR, although the eighth seat remained vacant. The rate of voter participation was reported at some 78%. On 11 May Ramgoolam appointed a new Government (featuring 13 new ministers), in which he also assumed responsibility for the defence, home affairs and external communications portfolio. Beebeejaun was reappointed Deputy Prime Minister, while Xavier-Luc Duval became Vice-Prime Minister and Minister of Social Integration and Economic Empowerment, and Pravind Jugnauth became Vice-Prime Minister and Minister of Finance and Economic Development. Following the death of Chettiar in September, Monique Ohsan-Bellepeau of the MLP was elected Vice-President by the National Assembly in November (becoming the first woman to hold the vice-presidential office).

Recent developments: governmental restructure

In early 2011 11 former senior members of the MSM rejoined the party, leaving the Union Nationale weakened. However, later that year divisions within the ruling coalition resulted in a series of governmental changes. In June the MSM's Showkutally Soodhun, hitherto Minister of Industry and Commerce, was relieved of the commerce portfolio; the PMSD's Michaël Yeung assumed responsibility, becoming Minister of Business, Enterprise, Commerce and Consumer Protection. More significantly, in July Minister of Health and Quality of Life Santi Bai (Maya) Hanoomanjee—of the MSM—was arrested amid allegations of corruption in relation to the government purchase of a private medical clinic, MedPoint. Hanoomanjee subsequently resigned from office, along with five other MSM ministers who stood down in protest against her arrest. In August Jugnauth announced that the MSM had effectively been forced from the ruling coalition and that he would be joining the opposition. At that time, a cabinet reorganization was implemented, whereby Xavier-Luc Duval assumed the position of Vice-Prime Minister and Minister of Finance and Economic Development, and Bachoo, retaining the public infrastructure, national development unit, land transport and shipping portfolios, was promoted to Vice-Prime Minister. In September 2011 Pravind Jugnauth was arrested for his alleged involvement in the fraudulent acquisition of the private medical clinic in which Hanoomanjee had earlier also been implicated. Jugnauth denied charges of a conflict of interest, claiming he had disclosed his shareholder interests in MedPoint at the earliest opportunity and had withdrawn from the cabinet meeting relating to the acquisition. Legal proceedings against both Jugnauth and Hanoomanjee were ongoing in early 2013. Meanwhile, in October 2011 the Privy Council in the United Kingdom, after a two-day hearing to review the allocation of seats in the National Assembly, ruled to refer the case back to the Mauritius Supreme Court for consideration.

Elections to the Rodrigues Regional Assembly were held in February 2012 at which the OPR secured 11 of the Assembly's 21 seats, while the MR took eight and the Front Patriotique Rodriguais two seats. On 30 March Aneerood Jugnauth resigned the presidency and announced his intention to return to party politics. The hitherto Speaker of the National Assembly, Kailash Purryag of the MLP, was elected to the presidency on 20 July following a legislative vote; he was inaugurated on the following day. The role of Speaker was subsequently assumed by Peeroo

Razack (also a member of the MLP). Meanwhile, the MSM and the MMM had announced the reformation of their alliance, and in municipal elections held on 9 December the MSM/MMM coalition won 53 of the country's 90 council seats, defeating the MLP and its allies, which obtained 36 seats. In January 2013 Bérenger stepped down as leader of the opposition and of the MMM due to ill health. Alan Ganoo succeeded him, on an interim basis, in both roles.

CONSTITUTION AND GOVERNMENT

Constitutional amendments, which were approved by the Legislative Assembly (henceforth known as the National Assembly) in December 1991 and came into effect on 12 March 1992, provided for the establishment of a republic. The constitutional Head of State is the President of the Republic, who is elected by a simple majority of the National Assembly for a five-year term of office. Legislative power is vested in the unicameral National Assembly, which comprises the Speaker, 62 members elected by universal adult suffrage for a term of five years, up to eight 'additional' members (unsuccessful candidates who receive the largest number of votes at a legislative election, to whom seats are allocated by the Electoral Supervisory Commission to ensure a balance in representation of the different ethnic groups), and the Attorney-General (if not an elected member). Executive power is vested in the Prime Minister, who is appointed by the President and is the member of the National Assembly best able to command a majority in the Assembly. The President appoints other ministers, on the recommendation of the Prime Minister.

REGIONAL AND INTERNATIONAL CO-OPERATION

Mauritius is a member of the Common Market for Eastern and Southern Africa (COMESA, see p. 241), the Southern African Development Community (SADC, see p. 434) and the Indian Ocean Commission (IOC, see p. 462), which aims to promote regional economic co-operation. Mauritius was among the founder members of the Indian Ocean Rim Association for Regional Co-operation (IOR—ARC, see p. 462) in 1997.

Mauritius became a member of the UN in 1968. As a contracting party to the General Agreement on Tariffs and Trade, Mauritius joined the World Trade Organization (WTO, see p. 444) on its establishment in 1995. Mauritius participates in the Group of 77 (G77, see p. 461) developing countries.

ECONOMIC AFFAIRS

In 2011, according to estimates by the World Bank, Mauritius' gross national income (GNI), measured at average 2009–11 prices, was US $10,592m., equivalent to $8,240 per head (or $14,760 per head on an international purchasing-power parity basis). During 2002–11, it was estimated, the population increased at an average annual rate of 0.7%, while gross domestic product (GDP) per head increased, in real terms, by an average of 3.4% per year. Overall GDP increased, in real terms, at an average annual rate of 4.1% in 2002–11; growth in 2011 was 4.1%.

Agriculture (including hunting, forestry and fishing) contributed an estimated 3.7% of GDP in 2011 and engaged 7.9% of the employed labour force in 2011. The principal cash crops are sugar cane (which contributed 1.3% of GDP in 2011), tea and tobacco. Food crops include potatoes, tomatoes and bananas. Chicken farming is also practised. During 2002–11, according to the World Bank, the GDP of the agricultural sector increased by 1.1%; it decreased by 1.3% in 2010, but increased by 0.8% in 2011.

Industry (including mining, manufacturing, construction and utilities) contributed an estimated 26.1% of GDP in 2011 and engaged 30.5% of the employed labour force in that year. During 2002–11, according to the World Bank, industrial GDP increased, in real terms, at an average annual rate of 2.4%; it increased by 3.00% in 2011. Mining is negligible, accounting for less than 0.1% of employment and less than 0.1% of GDP in 2011.

Manufacturing contributed an estimated 17.7% of GDP and engaged 20.1% of the employed labour force in 2011. The principal branches of manufacturing are clothing and food products, mainly sugar. Clothing (excluding footwear) provided 39.6% of export earnings in 2011, according to official provisional figures. Factories in the Export Processing Zone (EPZ) import raw materials to produce goods for the export market. Other important products include fish preparations, textiles, and precious stones. During 2002–11, according to the World Bank, the GDP of the manufacturing sector increased, in real terms, at an average annual rate of 1.3%; manufacturing GDP increased by 3.6% in 2011.

Construction contributed an estimated 6.5% of GDP in 2011 and engaged 9.8% of the employed labour force in 2011.

Electric energy is derived principally from thermal (oil-fired) and hydroelectric power stations. Bagasse (a by-product of sugar cane) is also used as fuel for generating electricity, and in 2011 it accounted for 20.2% of electricity produced. Imports of mineral fuels comprised 21.6% of the value of merchandise imports in 2011.

The services sector contributed an estimated 70.2% of GDP in 2011 and engaged 61.6% of the employed labour force in 2011. Tourism is the third most important source of revenue, after manufacturing and agriculture. The number of foreign tourist arrivals increased to 964,642 in 2011 from 422,000 in 1995. Gross receipts from tourism were estimated to total Rs 42,717m. in 2011. An 'offshore' banking sector and a stock exchange have operated since 1989. According to the World Bank, the real GDP of the services sector increased at an average annual rate of 5.7% in 2002–11; growth in 2011 was 5.0%.

In 2011 Mauritius recorded a visible merchandise trade deficit of US $2,278.9m., and there was a deficit of $1,421.8m. on the current account of the balance of payments. In 2011, the principal source of imports (23.5%) was India; other major suppliers were the People's Republic of China, France and South Africa. The principal market for exports in that year (20.3%) was the United Kingdom; other significant purchasers were France, the USA, Italy, South Africa, Spain and Madagascar. The principal exports (excluding re-exports) in 2011 were miscellaneous manufactured articles, food and live animals, and basic manufactures. The principal imports in that year were mineral fuels and lubricants (especially refined petroleum products), basic manufactures, food and live animals, machinery and transport equipment, and chemicals.

In 2011, there was an estimated budgetary deficit of Rs 10,384.7m. (equivalent to 3.2% of GDP). Mauritius' general government gross debt was Rs 164,507m. in 2011, equivalent to 50.9% of GDP. Mauritius' external debt totalled US $1,076m. at the end of 2010, of which $972m. was public and publicly guaranteed debt. In that year the cost of servicing long-term public and publicly guaranteed debt and repayments to the IMF was equivalent to 2.4% of the value of exports of goods, services and income (excluding workers' remittances). The annual rate of inflation, according to ILO, averaged 5.9% in 2002–11. Consumer prices increased by an average of 6.5% in 2011. About 7.6% of the labour force were unemployed in 2011.

The geographical location of Mauritius, as well as a number of incentive measures implemented by the Government, has contributed to its successful establishment as an international financial centre. The island is a significant provider of 'offshore' banking and investment services for a number of South Asian countries (particularly India), as well as for members of SADC. Mauritius has also been promoted as a future hub of information and communications technology, with the aim of encouraging the next stage of economic development and transferring the emphasis towards services. Mauritius signed an interim Economic Partnership Agreement with the European Union (EU, see p. 281) in September 2009, providing the country with preferential access to European markets. Later that year development began on a Chinese special economic zone, the Jin Fei Trade and Economic Cooperation Zone, near Port Louis; it was envisaged that the project, which was expected to be completed in 2016, would generate export earnings equivalent to US $220m. annually. Although the banking sector in Mauritius remained relatively unaffected by the global financial crisis that developed in 2008 and 2009, weaker external demand for textiles and tourism and a decline in foreign direct investment (FDI) nevertheless had a negative impact on the country's economy, resulting in a fall in real GDP growth, to 3.0%, in 2009. In August 2010 the Government announced a stimulus programme of Rs 12,000m., which was designed to assist businesses affected by the financial crisis in Europe, develop tourism markets in India and the People's Republic of China, and support the sugar sector. In 2011 tourist arrivals increased by 3.2% and, despite poor rainfall, sugar production rose by an estimated 5%, while the textiles and financial services sectors also performed strongly. The IMF reported that real GDP grew by 4.1% in 2011 (compared with 4.2% in the previous year). Growth moderated to an estimated 3.4% in 2012, owing to a drought-induced decline in sugar output and a negligible increase in the number of tourist arrivals, although FDI inflows and export earnings both rose during the year. The Government expected a slight upturn in economic growth in 2013, to 3.7%, supported predominantly by greater activity in the tourism and financial services sectors.

PUBLIC HOLIDAYS

2014: 1–2 January (New Year), 31 January (Chinese New Year), 1 February (Abolition of Slavery Commemoration), 28 February (Maha Shivaratree), 12 March (National Day), 31 March (Ougadi), 1 May (Labour Day), 28 July* (Id al-Fitr, end of Ramadan), 15 August (Assumption), 29 August (Ganesh Chathurti), 23 October (Diwali), 1 November (All Saints' Day), 2 November (Arrival of Indentured Labourers), 25 December (Christmas Day).

Thaipoosam Cavadee is also celebrated in late January or early February. However, the exact date is dependent on the appearance of a full moon.

* This holiday is dependent on the Islamic lunar calendar and may vary by one or two days from the date given.

Statistical Survey

Source (unless otherwise stated): Central Statistics Office, LIC Bldg, President John F. Kennedy St, Port Louis; tel. 212-2316; fax 211-4150; email cso@mail.gov.mu; internet statsmauritius.gov.mu.

Area and Population

AREA, POPULATION AND DENSITY

Area (sq km)	2,040*
Population (census results)	
2 July 2000	1,179,137
3-4 July 2011	
Males	611,022
Females	626,069
Total	1,237,091
Population (official estimate at mid-year)	
2012	1,291,456
Density (per sq km) at mid-2012	633.1

* 788 sq miles.

POPULATION BY AGE AND SEX
(official estimates at mid-2011)

	Males	Females	Total
0–14	137,682	133,438	271,120
15–64	456,871	462,752	919,623
65 and over	39,171	56,137	95,308
Total	633,724	652,327	1,286,051

Note: Estimates exclude data for Agalega and St Brandon, and have not been revised to take account of the 2011 census.

ISLANDS

		Population	
	Area (sq km)	2000 census	2011 census
Mauritius	1,865	1,143,069	1,196,383
Rodrigues	104	35,779	40,434
Other islands . .	71	289	274
Total	2,040	1,179,137	1,237,091

LANGUAGE GROUPS
(census of 2 July 2000)*

Arabic	806	Marathi	16,587
Bhojpuri . . .	361,250	Tamil	44,731
Chinese	16,972	Telegu	18,802
Creole	454,763	Urdu	34,120
English	1,075	Other languages .	169,619
French	21,171	Not stated . . .	3,170
Hindi	35,782	**Total**	1,178,848

* Figures refer to the languages of cultural origin of the population of the islands of Mauritius and Rodrigues only. The data exclude an adjustment for underenumeration.

POPULATION BY DISTRICT
(official estimates at 1 July 2011)

Black River . . .	77,242	Port Louis . . .	128,319
Flacq	140,670	Riv du Rempart .	109,513
Grand Port . . .	115,772	Rodrigues . . .	37,925
Moka	81,431	Savanne	70,526
Pamplemousses . .	138,904		
Plaine Wilhems .	385,749	**Total**	1,286,051

PRINCIPAL TOWNS
(at 2011 census)

Port Louis (capital) .	118,431	Curepipe . . .	77,466
Vacoas/Phoenix .	104,271	Quatre Bornes . .	71,633
Beau Bassin/Rose Hill . . .	103,098		

BIRTHS, MARRIAGES AND DEATHS*

	Registered live births		Registered marriages		Registered deaths	
	Number	Rate (per 1,000)	Number	Rate (per 1,000)	Number	Rate (per 1,000)
2005	18,829	15.1	11,294	n.a.	8,648	7.0
2006	17,605	14.1	11,471	9.1	9,162	7.3
2007	17,034	13.5	11,547	9.1	8,498	6.7
2008	16,372	12.9	11,197	8.8	9,004	7.1
2009	15,344	12.0	10,619	8.3	9,224	7.2
2010	15,005	11.7	10,555	8.2	9,131	7.1
2011	14,701	11.4	10,499	8.1	9,170	7.1
2012† . . .	14,760	11.4	10,240	7.9	9,210	7.1

* Figures refer to the islands of Mauritius and Rodrigues only. The data are tabulated by year of registration, rather than by year of occurrence.
† Preliminary.

Life expectancy (years at birth): 73.0 (males 69.5; females 76.7) in 2010 (Source: World Bank, World Development Indicators database).

ECONOMICALLY ACTIVE POPULATION
('000 persons aged 16 years and over, incl. foreign workers)

	2009	2010	2011*
Agriculture, forestry and fishing .	44.9	44.9	44.4
Sugar cane	14.2	13.9	13.5
Mining and quarrying	0.2	0.2	0.2
Manufacturing	115.8	114.5	112.3
Electricity, gas and water . . .	3.1	3.3	3.3
Construction	52.4	54.0	55.0
Wholesale and retail trade, repair of motor vehicles and household goods	85.4	88.8	89.7
Hotels and restaurants . . .	35.8	37.3	38.0
Transport, storage and communications	40.0	40.4	40.2
Financial intermediation . . .	12.6	13.2	13.5

—continued	2009	2010	2011*
Real estate, renting and business activities	32.4	34.9	35.8
Public administration and defence; compulsory social security . .	39.4	39.1	38.9
Education	30.1	30.8	31.1
Health and social work . . .	16.7	19.0	19.5
Other services	37.0	37.7	37.8
Total employed	**545.8**	**558.1**	**559.7**
Males	355.3	358.8	358.2
Females	190.5	199.3	201.5
Unemployed	41.5	45.2	46.1
Total labour force	**587.3**	**603.3**	**605.8**

* Provisional.

Health and Welfare

KEY INDICATORS

Total fertility rate (children per woman, 2010)	1.6
Under-5 mortality rate (per 1,000 live births, 2010) . . .	15
HIV/AIDS (% of persons aged 15–49, 2009)	1.0
Physicians (per 1,000 head, 2004)	1.1
Hospital beds (per 1,000 head, 2008)	3.3
Health expenditure (2009): US $ per head (PPP) . . .	714
Health expenditure (2009): % of GDP	5.6
Health expenditure (2009): public (% of total)	37.1
Access to water (% of persons, 2010)	99
Access to sanitation (% of persons, 2010)	89
Total carbon dioxide emissions ('000 metric tons, 2008) . .	3,953.0
Carbon dioxide emissions per head (metric tons, 2008) . .	3.1
Human Development Index (2011): ranking	77
Human Development Index (2011): value	0.728

For sources and definitions, see explanatory note on p. vi.

Agriculture

PRINCIPAL CROPS
('000 metric tons)

	2009	2010	2011
Potatoes	19.8	21.7	21.6
Sugar cane	4,667.2	4,365.8	4,230.2
Coconuts	1.6*	1.7*	1.5†
Cabbages and other brassicas .	4.6	4.8	5.1
Lettuce and chicory	0.9	9	0.9
Tomatoes	12.6	12.3	11.4
Cauliflowers and broccoli . .	1.7	1.3	1.6
Pumpkins, squash and gourds .	17.1	18.6	19.2
Cucumbers and gherkins . . .	11.1	11.3	9.6
Aubergines (Eggplants) . . .	2.8	2.7	3.2
Onions, dry	4.9	5.8	5.2
Carrots and turnips	7.4	5.4	5.3
Bananas	10.9	11.9	10.5
Pineapples	8.9	6.5	10.9
Tea	1.5	1.5	1.8
Tobacco, unmanufactured . .	0.3	0.3	0.3

* Unofficial figure.
† FAO estimate.

Aggregate production ('000 metric tons, may include official, semi-official or estimated data): Total cereals 0.1 in 2009, 0.3 in 2010, 0.3 in 2011; Total roots and tubers 21.6 in 2009, 23.4 in 2010, 23.3 in 2011; Total vegetables (incl. melons) 71.4 in 2009, 72.4 in 2010, 71.1 in 2011; Total fruits (excl. melons) 24.4 in 2009, 22.8 in 2010, 26.5 in 2011.

Source: FAO.

LIVESTOCK
('000 head, year ending September)

	2009	2010	2011
Cattle	7.2	7.5	6.6
Pigs	14	22	23
Sheep*	20	20	21
Goats	26	28	28
Chickens*	13,650	13,650	14,300

* FAO estimates.

Source: FAO.

LIVESTOCK PRODUCTS
('000 metric tons)

	2009	2010	2011
Cattle meat	2	2	2
Chicken meat	44	47	47
Cows' milk	4	4	4
Hen eggs	10	10	10

Source: FAO.

Forestry

ROUNDWOOD REMOVALS
('000 cubic metres, excl. bark)

	2009	2010	2011
Sawlogs, veneer logs and logs for sleepers	4	4	3
Other industrial wood	6	2	1
Fuel wood	6	9	7
Total	**15**	**15**	**11**

Source: FAO.

SAWNWOOD PRODUCTION
('000 cubic metres, incl. railway sleepers)

	2009	2010	2011
Coniferous (softwood)	2.0	2.0	1.8
Broadleaved (hardwood) . . .	0.1	0.1	0.0
Total	**2.1**	**2.1**	**1.8**

Source: FAO.

Fishing

(metric tons, live weight)

	2008	2009	2010
Capture	6,642	7,676	7,786
Groupers and seabasses . .	556	1,033	860
Snappers and jobfishes . . .	404	430	739
Emperors (Scavengers) . . .	3,022	3,454	3,032
Goatfishes	100	497	268
Spinefeet (Rabbitfishes) . . .	111	274	372
Swordfish	308	75	27
Tuna-like fishes	200	100	360
Octopuses	92	89	93
Aquaculture	246	437	568
Red drum	175	330	498
Total catch	**6,888**	**8,113**	**8,354**

Note: Figures exclude aquatic animals, recorded by number rather than weight. The number of Nile crocodiles captured was: n.a. in 2008; 100 in 2009; n.a. in 2011.

Source: FAO.

Industry

SELECTED PRODUCTS
('000 metric tons unless otherwise indicated)

	2009	2010	2011
Fish*	66.1	63.0	54.0
Frozen*	3.5	2.4	2.2
Canned*	61.9	59.8	51.1
Raw sugar*	467.2	452.5	435.3
Molasses*	147.6	143.5	138.6
Beer and stout ('000 hectolitres)*	351.7	367.6	373.7
Iron bars and steel tubes*	31.0	32.0	35.0
Fertilizers*	31.0	24.3	27.0
Electric energy (million kWh)	2,577	2,689	2,730*

* Provisional.

Cigarettes (million): 6 in 2008.

Finance

CURRENCY AND EXCHANGE RATES

Monetary Units
100 cents = 1 Mauritian rupee.

Sterling, Dollar and Euro Equivalents (31 December 2012)
£1 sterling = 48.17 rupees;
US $1 = 30.52 rupees;
€1 = 40.27 rupees;
1,000 Mauritian rupees = £20.76 = $32.76 = €24.83.

Average Exchange Rate (Mauritian rupees per US $)
2010   30.784
2011   28.706
2012   30.050

BUDGET
(million rupees)

Revenue

	2010	2011
Tax revenue	55,209.1	59,180.3
Taxes on income, profits and capital gains	13,976.3	13,619.7
Individual income tax	4,497.1	4,913.3
Corporate tax	8,428.0	7,847.0
Taxes on property	3,904.3	3,939.5
Domestic taxes on goods and services	34,633.4	38,817.9
Excise duties	9,331.0	11,487.1
Value-added tax	21,094.4	22,713.6
Taxes on international trade	1,525.2	1,560.3
Other tax revenue	1,169.9	1,242.9
Non-tax revenue	10,270.4	10,042.9
Social contributions	1,008.2	1,020.4
Grants	1,991.0	2,344.5
Property income	3,812.2	3,312.6
Other non-tax revenue	3,459.0	3,365.4
Total	65,479.5	69,223.2

Expense/Outlays

Expense by economic type	2010	2011
Expenditure	66,983.2	70,975.3
Wages and salaries	17,541.0	18,001.3
Other purchases of goods and services	6,149.6	6,194.5
Interest payments	10,261.9	9,667.1
Subsidies and other current transfers	25,091.9	29,665.2
Transfer to general government units	23,838.3	28,233.2
Social benefits	4,855.8	5,125.4
Other expense	3,083.0	2,321.8
Net Acquisition of non-financial assets	8,076.1	8,632.6
Acquisition of fixed capital assets	7,859.5	8,194.1
Non-produced assets	216.6	438.5
Total	75,059.3	79,607.9

Outlays by function of government	2010	2011
General public services	19,753.6	19,219.6
Public order and safety	6,173.2	7,441.6
Community and social services	38,409.1	41,484.2
Education	10,091.9	10,329.3
Health	7,726.3	7,326.6
Social security and welfare	15,738.5	16,824.5
Housing and community amenities	1,587.0	3,718.7
Recreational, cultural and religious services	649.2	721.8
Environmental protection	2,616.2	2,563.3
Economic services	10,723.4	11,462.5
Agriculture, forestry, fishing and hunting	2,910.9	2,019.3
Fuel and energy	37.4	54.9
Mining, manufacturing, and construction	400.7	262.9
Transportation and communications	4,280.1	3,909.3
Tourism	457.5	540.4
General economic, commercial and labour affairs	458.5	407.6
Other economic affairs	2,178.2	4,268.1
Total expenditure	75,059.3	79,607.9

INTERNATIONAL RESERVES
(US $ million at 31 December)

	2009	2010	2011
Gold (market prices)	124.9	159.6	196.0
IMF special drawing rights	156.7	153.7	153.4
Reserve position in IMF	20.6	34.0	48.4
Foreign exchange	2,001.5	2,254.2	2,380.9
Total	2,303.7	2,601.5	2,778.7

Source: IMF, *International Financial Statistics*.

MONEY SUPPLY
(million rupees at 31 December)

	2009	2010	2011
Currency outside depository corporations	17,152.6	18,975.0	20,307.8
Transferable deposits	70,923.4	70,035.5	73,190.5
Other deposits	207,632.2	227,244.8	236,362.4
Securities other than shares	772.2	2,868.9	4,044.5
Broad money	296,480.4	319,124.2	333,905.2

Source: IMF, *International Financial Statistics*.

COST OF LIVING
(Consumer Price Index; base: July 2006–June 2007 = 100)

	2009	2010	2011
Food and non-alcoholic beverages	129.1	133.9	141.7
Alcoholic beverages and tobacco	116.5	119.8	141.8
Clothing and footwear	115.1	123.6	130.5
Housing, fuel and electricity	105.7	105.4	107.8
Household operations	115.1	119.3	122.6
All items (incl. others)	116.8	120.2	128.1

NATIONAL ACCOUNTS
(million rupees in current prices)
National Income and Product

	2009	2010	2011
Compensation of employees .	95,936	101,735	109,949
Operating surplus			
Consumption of fixed capital . }	153,450	160,610	172,534
Gross domestic product (GDP) at factor cost . .	249,386	262,345	282,483
Taxes on production and imports	33,819	37,279	41,768
Less Subsidies	851	840	1,026
GDP in purchasers' values .	282,354	298,784	323,225
Primary incomes received from abroad . . . . . }			
Less Primary incomes paid abroad	−1,333	3,656	2,416
Gross national income . .	281,021	302,440	325,641
Current transfers from abroad . }			
Less Current transfers paid abroad	6,909	5,630	3,795
Gross national disposable income	287,930	308,070	329,436

Expenditure on the Gross Domestic Product

	2009	2010	2011
Private final consumption expenditure	208,879	220,305	237,148
Government final consumption expenditure	39,751	41,625	43,447
Gross fixed capital formation . .	74,430	74,395	76,722
Increase in stocks	−14,294	−3,746	5,511
Total domestic expenditure .	308,766	332,579	362,828
Exports of goods and services .	138,243	156,939	174,962
Less Imports of goods and services	164,655	190,734	214,566
GDP in purchasers' values .	282,354	298,784	323,225

Gross Domestic Product by Economic Activity

	2009	2010	2011
Agriculture, hunting, forestry, and fishing	9,800	9,677	10,444
Sugar cane	3,489	3,050	3,594
Mining and quarrying	101	107	106
Manufacturing	47,325	47,764	50,461
Electricity, gas and water . . .	5,398	5,401	5,358
Construction	17,471	18,231	18,608
Wholesale and retail trade, repair of motor vehicles and personal goods	28,770	31,178	33,813
Hotels and restaurants . . .	16,749	18,514	20,268
Transport, storage and communications	24,191	25,257	26,404
Financial intermediation . . .	25,834	26,465	28,806
Real estate, renting and business activities	29,776	32,645	36,995
Public administration and defence; compulsory social security . .	15,322	16,159	16,981
Education	11,085	11,686	12,596
Health and social work . . .	8,936	9,694	10,808
Other services	10,857	12,050	13,846
Gross value added in basic prices	251,615	264,828	285,494
Taxes, less subsidies, on products	30,739	33,956	37,731
GDP in market prices . . .	282,354	298,784	323,225

BALANCE OF PAYMENTS
(US $ million)

	2009	2010	2011
Exports of goods	1,938.5	2,261.5	2,646.5
Imports of goods	−3,503.9	−4,156.7	−4,925.4
Balance on goods	−1,565.4	−1,895.2	−2,278.9
Exports of services	2,239.0	2,695.1	3,295.0
Imports of services	−1,607.3	−1,978.9	−2,500.7
Balance on goods and services	−933.7	−1,179.0	−1,484.7
Primary income received . .	457.6	5,009.0	6,018.8
Primary income paid	−402.6	−5,019.1	−6,087.4
Balance on goods, services and primary income	−878.7	−1,189.1	−1,553.3
Secondary income received . .	413.1	404.4	402.8
Secondary income paid	−189.4	−221.1	−271.4
Current balance	−655.0	−1,005.8	−1,421.8
Capital account (net)	−1.9	−4.8	−1.9
Direct investment assets . . .	−37.8	−20,405.4	−24,342.2
Direct investment liabilities . .	256.7	34,248.7	37,748.9
Portfolio investment assets . .	−261.1	−17,584.3	−20,486.6
Portfolio investment liabilities .	204.8	7,767.2	9,334.5
Financial derivatives and employee stock options (net)	—	544.5	675.6
Other investment assets . . .	−357.7	−4,527.4	−2,931.9
Other investment liabilities . .	948.9	1,026.9	1,412.3
Net errors and omissions . .	287.8	149.5	208.3
Reserves and related items .	384.7	209.0	195.1

Source: IMF, *International Financial Statistics*.

External Trade

PRINCIPAL COMMODITIES
(million rupees)

Imports c.i.f.	2009	2010	2011
Food and live animals . . .	22,051	24,610	26,974
Fish and fish preparations .	7,055	7,869	9,280
Mineral fuels, lubricants, etc. .	18,557	25,630	31,945
Refined petroleum products .	15,293	21,302	26,977
Chemicals	10,711	12,462	12,110
Basic manufactures	21,452	25,087	27,634
Textile yarn, fabrics, etc. .	2,012	2,495	3,027
Cotton fabrics	1,965	2,159	2,395
Machinery and transport equipment	27,689	27,239	26,357
Machinery specialized for particular industries . . .	2,614	2,517	2,745
General industrial machinery, equipment and parts . .	4,704	4,179	3,860
Telecommunications and sound equipment	3,483	4,357	3,925
Other electrical machinery, apparatus, etc. . . .	3,853	4,256	4,066
Road motor vehicles . . .	5,446	6,824	7,149
Miscellaneous manufactured articles	11,028	12,202	12,964
Total (incl. others)	118,444	134,882	147,815

Exports f.o.b.*	2009	2010	2011
Food and live animals . . .	18,593	20,854	20,340
Basic manufactures . . .	5,106	5,843	6,533
Chemicals and related products .	1,957	2,218	2,165
Machinery and transport equipment	1,285	1,687	1,437
Miscellaneous manufactured articles	27,709	29,429	29,516
Total (incl. others)	56,162	61,990	62,358

* Excluding stores and bunkers for ships and aircraft (million rupees): 5,519 in 2009; 7,560 in 2010; 11,228 in 2011.

PRINCIPAL TRADING PARTNERS
(million rupees)*

Imports c.i.f.	2009	2010	2011
Argentina	1,772	1,908	2,557
Australia	3,344	4,250	3,860
Belgium	1,703	1,256	1,820
China, People's Repub.	14,903	18,033	20,780
France	13,812	11,787	13,158
Germany	3,123	3,256	3,551
India	22,336	29,629	34,666
Indonesia	2,987	2,997	2,968
Italy	2,727	2,980	3,144
Japan	3,823	4,520	3,701
Korea, Repub.	1,440	1,650	2,261
Malaysia	3,417	3,474	3,320
Netherlands	n.a.	1,518	1,735
New Zealand	n.a.	1,668	2,198
South Africa	10,236	11,433	10,457
Spain	2,800	3,680	4,462
Switzerland	1,107	1,366	1,563
Thailand	3,120	3,080	3,186
Turkey	n.a.	1,506	1,429
United Arab Emirates	803	1,231	1,991
United Kingdom	2,925	2,992	3,403
USA	2,576	3,142	2,633
Total (incl. others)	118,444	134,882	147,815

Exports f.o.b.	2009	2010	2011
Belgium	1,454	1,317	1,441
France	9,317	10,517	8,797
Germany	1,327	1,199	1,382
Italy	3,090	4,609	5,159
Japan	n.a.	666	400
Madagascar	3,587	3,562	3,973
Netherlands	830	840	987
Portugal	1,400	313	194
Réunion	2,321	1,981	1,997
Seychelles	n.a.	702	860
South Africa	2,553	3,602	4,982
Spain	2,549	3,921	4,315
Switzerland	758	1,024	1,176
United Kingdom	15,280	13,373	12,644
USA	4,624	6,189	6,667
Total (incl. others)	56,162	61,990	62,358

* Imports by country of origin; exports by country of destination (including re-exports, excluding ships' stores and bunkers).

Transport

ROAD TRAFFIC
(motor vehicles registered at 31 December)

	2009	2010	2011
Private vehicles:			
Cars	165,036	175,634	185,357
Motorcycles and mopeds	152,935	159,329	165,706
Commercial vehicles:			
Buses	2,803	2,845	2,912
Taxis	6,941	6,924	6,907
Lorries and trucks	12,950	13,186	13,539

SHIPPING

Flag Registered Fleet
(at 31 December)

	2010	2011	2012
Number of vessels	110	112	116
Total displacement ('000 grt)	145.7	187.4	192.4

Source: Lloyd's List Intelligence (www.lloydslistintelligence.com).

Sea-borne Freight Traffic
('000 metric tons)

	2009	2010	2011
Goods unloaded	4,761	5,100	5,386
Goods loaded*	1,117	1,130	1,091

* Excluding ships' bunkers.

CIVIL AVIATION
(traffic)

	2009	2010	2011*
Aircraft landings	9,824	10,160	10,121
Freight unloaded (metric tons)	20,400	23,992	21,707
Freight loaded (metric tons)	21,924	24,267	23,414

* Provisional.

Tourism

FOREIGN TOURIST ARRIVALS

Country of residence	2009	2010	2011*
France	275,599	302,185	302,004
Germany	51,279	52,886	56,331
India	39,252	49,779	53,955
Italy	56,736	56,540	52,747
Réunion	104,946	114,914	113,000
South Africa	74,176	81,458	86,232
Switzerland	15,349	18,577	24,362
United Kingdom	101,996	97,548	88,182
Total (incl. others)	871,356	934,827	964,642

* Provisional.

Tourism earnings (gross, million rupees): 35,693 in 2009; 39,456 in 2010; 42,717 in 2011.

Communications Media

	2009	2010	2011
Telephones ('000 main lines in use)	375.2	387.7	374.6
Mobile cellular telephones ('000 subscribers)	1,086.7	1,190.9	1,294.1
Internet subscribers ('000)	101.0	98.5	126.8
Broadband subscribers ('000)	68.8	79.2	116.8
Television sets licensed ('000)	315.0	314.8	316.4
Daily newspapers	8	12	11*
Non-daily newspapers	54	56	57*

* Provisional.

Personal computers: 220,000 (45.4 per 1,000 persons) in 2006.

Source: partly International Telecommunication Union.

Education

(March 2012)

	Institutions	Teachers	Students*
Pre-primary	1,031	2,508	33,579
Primary	312	5,427	113,634
Secondary	183	8,014	115,677
Technical and vocational	121	629	7,221

* By enrolment.

Pupil-teacher ratio (primary education, UNESCO estimate): 21.5 in 2009/10 (Source: UNESCO Institute for Statistics).

Adult literacy rate (UNESCO estimates): 88.5% (males 90.9%; females 86.2%) in 2010 (Source: UNESCO Institute for Statistics).

Directory

The Government

HEAD OF STATE

President: KAILASH PURRYAG.
Vice-President: MONIQUE OHSAN-BELLEPEAU.

COUNCIL OF MINISTERS
(May 2013)

Prime Minister, Minister of Defence, Home Affairs and External Communications, Minister of Rodrigues: Dr NAVINCHANDRA RAMGOOLAM.

Deputy Prime Minister and Minister of Energy and Public Utilities: Dr AHMED RASHID BEEBEEJAUN.

Vice-Prime Minister and Minister of Finance and Economic Development: CHARLES GAËTAN XAVIER-LUC DUVAL.

Vice-Prime Minister and Minister of Public Infrastructure, the National Development Unit, Land Transport and Shipping: ANIL KUMAR BACHOO.

Minister of Foreign Affairs, Regional Integration and International Trade: Dr ARVIN BOOLELL.

Minister of Housing and Lands: Dr ABU TWALIB KASENALLY.

Minister of Social Security, National Solidarity and Reform Institutions: SHEILABAI BAPPOO.

Minister of Education and Human Resources: Dr VASANT KUMAR BUNWAREE.

Minister of Agro-industry and Food Security: SATYA VEYASH FAUGOO.

Minister of the Environment and Sustainable Development: DEVANAND VIRAHSAWMY.

Minister of Tertiary Education, Science, Research and Technology: Dr RAJESHWAR JEETAH.

Minister of Youth and Sports: SATYAPRAKASH RITOO.

Minister of Local Government and Outer Islands: LOUIS HERVÉ AIMÉE.

Minister of Arts and Culture: MOOKHESSWUR CHOONEE.

Minister of Information and Communication Technology: TASSARAJEN PILLAY CHEDUMBRUM.

Minister of Fisheries: LOUIS JOSEPH VON-MALLY.

Minister of Labour, Industrial Relations and Employment: SHAKEEL AHMED YOUSUF ABDUL RAZACK MOHAMED.

Attorney-General: YATINDRA NATH VARMA.

Minister of Tourism and Leisure: JOHN MICHAEL TZOUN SAO YEUNG SIK YUEN.

Minister of Health and Quality of Life: LORMUS BUNDHOO.

Minister of Industry, Commerce and Consumer Protection: SAYYAD ABD-AL-CADER SAYED-HOSSEN.

Minister of Social Integration and Economic Empowerment: SURENDRA DAYAL.

Minister of Business, Enterprise and Co-operatives: JANGBAHADOORSING ISWURDEO MOLA ROOPCHAND SEETARAM.

Minister of Gender Equality, Child Development and Family Welfare: MARIA FRANCESCA MIREILLE MARTIN.

Minister of the Civil Service and Administrative Reforms: SUTYADEO MOUTIA.

MINISTRIES

Office of the President: State House, Le Réduit, Port Louis; tel. 454-3021; fax 464-5370; e-mail president@mail.gov.mu; internet president.gov.mu.

Office of the Vice-President: 30 Farquhar Ave, Quatre Bornes, Port Louis; tel. 427-1024; fax 427-1487; e-mail ovp@mail.gov.mu; internet vice-president.gov.mu.

Office of the Prime Minister: New Treasury Bldg, Intendance St, Port Louis; tel. 207-9595; fax 208-8619; e-mail primeminister@mail.gov.mu; internet primeminister.gov.mu.

Ministry of Agro-industry and Food Security: Renganaden Seeneevassen Bldg, 8th and 9th Floor, cnr Jules Koenig and Maillard Sts, Port Louis; tel. 212-0854; fax 212-4427; e-mail moa-headoffice@mail.gov.mu; internet agriculture.gov.mu.

Ministry of Arts and Culture: Renganaden Seeneevassen Bldg, 7th Floor, cnr Pope Hennessy and Maillard Sts, Port Louis; tel. 212-2112; fax 210-0681; e-mail moac@mail.gov.mu; internet culture.gov.mu.

Ministry of Business, Enterprise and Co-operatives: Newton Tower, 6th Floor, Sir William Newton St, Port Louis; tel. 405-3100; fax 213-9176; e-mail Mincom@intnet.mu; internet enterbusiness.gov.mu.

Ministry of the Civil Service and Administrative Reforms: New Government Centre, 7th Floor, Port Louis; tel. 201-2886; fax 212-9528; e-mail civser@mail.gov.mu; internet civilservice.gov.mu.

Ministry of Defence, Home Affairs and External Communications: New Government Centre, 4th Floor, Port Louis; tel. 201-2409; fax 212-9393; e-mail pmo@mail.gov.mu; internet dha.pmo.gov.mu.

Ministry of Education and Human Resources: MITD House, Pont Fer, Phoenix; tel. 601-5200; fax 698-9627; e-mail moeps@mail.gov.mu; internet ministry-education.gov.mu.

Ministry of Energy and Public Utilities: Air Mauritius Centre, 10th Floor, John F. Kennedy St, Port Louis; tel. 405-6700; fax 208-6497; e-mail mpu@mail.gov.mu; internet publicutilities.gov.mu.

Ministry of the Environment and Sustainable Development: Ken Lee Tower, cnr Barracks and St Georges Sts, Port Louis; tel. 203-6200; fax 212-8324; e-mail menv@mail.gov.mu; internet environment.gov.mu.

Ministry of Finance and Economic Development: Government House, Ground Floor, Port Louis; tel. 201-1146; fax 211-0096; e-mail mof@mail.gov.mu; internet mof.gov.mu.

Ministry of Fisheries: LIC Centre, 4th Floor, President John Kennedy St, Port Louis; tel. 211-2453; fax 210-3694; e-mail fisheries@mail.gov.mu; internet fisheries.gov.mu.

Ministry of Foreign Affairs, Regional Integration and International Trade: Newton Tower, 9th–11th Floors, Sir William Newton St, Port Louis; tel. 201-1648; fax 208-8087; e-mail mfa@mail.gov.mu; internet foreign.gov.mu.

Ministry of Gender Equality, Child Development and Family Welfare: CSK Bldg, cnr Remy Ollier and Emmanuel Anquetil Sts, Port Louis; tel. 206-3700; fax 240-7717; e-mail mwfwcd@mail.gov.mu; internet gender.gov.mu.

Ministry of Health and Quality of Life: Emmanuel Anquetil Bldg, 5th Floor, Sir Seewoosagur Ramgoolam St, Port Louis; tel. 201-2175; fax 208-7222; e-mail moh@mail.gov.mu; internet health.gov.mu.

Ministry of Housing and Lands: Moorgate House, Port Louis; tel. 212-6022; fax 212-7482; internet housing.gov.mu.

Ministry of Industry, Commerce and Consumer Protection: Paille en Queue Court, 8th Floor, Port Louis; tel. 210-7100; fax 211-0855; e-mail mind@mail.gov.mu; internet industry.gov.mu.

Ministry of Information and Communication Technology: Air Mauritius Centre, 9th Floor, John F. Kennedy St, Port Louis; tel. 210-0201; fax 212-1673; e-mail mict@mail.gov.mu; internet mict.gov.mu.

Ministry of Labour, Industrial Relations and Employment: Victoria House, cnr St Louis and Barracks Sts, Port Louis; tel. 207-2600; fax 212-3070; e-mail mol@mail.gov.mu; internet labour.gov.mu.

Ministry of Local Government and Outer Islands: Emmanuel Anquetil Bldg, 3rd Floor, cnr Sir Seewoosagur Ramgoolam and Jules Koenig Sts, Port Louis; tel. 201-2155; fax 208-9729; e-mail mlg@mail.gov.mu; internet localgovernment.gov.mu.

Ministry of Public Infrastructure, the National Development Unit, Land Transport and Shipping: Moorgate House, 9th Floor, Sir William Newton St, Port Louis; tel. 208-0281; fax 208-7149; e-mail mpi@mail.gov.mu; internet publicinfrastructure.gov.mu.

Ministry of Social Integration and Economic Empowerment: Air Mauritius Centre, 12th Floor, John F. Kennedy St, Port Louis; tel. 213-0633; fax 213-0537; e-mail msiep@mail.gov.mu; internet socialintegration.gov.mu.

Ministry of Social Security, National Solidarity and Reform Institutions: Renganaden Seeneevassen Bldg, 13th Floor, cnr Jules Koenig and Maillard Sts, Port Louis; tel. 207-0625; fax 212-8190; e-mail mss@mail.gov.mu; internet socialsecurity.gov.mu.

Ministry of Tertiary Education, Science, Research and Technology: Wing A, 4th Floor, Cyber Tower 1, Cyber City, Ebene; tel. 4541450; fax 4681440; e-mail tertiary@mail.gov.mu; internet tertiary.gov.mu.

Ministry of Tourism and Leisure: Air Mauritius Centre, 5th Floor, John F. Kennedy St, Port Louis; tel. 211-7930; fax 208-6776; e-mail mtou@mail.gov.mu; internet tourism.gov.mu.

Ministry of Youth and Sports: Emmanuel Anquetil Bldg, 3rd Floor, Sir Seewoosagur Ramgoolam St, Port Louis; tel. 201-2543; fax 211-2986; e-mail mys@mail.gov.mu; internet youthsport.gov.mu.

Legislature

National Assembly

Port Louis; tel. 201-1414; fax 212-8364; e-mail themace@intnet.mu; internet mauritiusassembly.gov.mu.

Speaker: PEEROO RAZACK.

General Election, 5 May 2010

| | Seats | | |
Party	Directly elected	Additional*	Total
Alliance de l'Avenir†	41	4	45
Alliance du Coeur‡	18	2	20
Mouvement Rodriguais (MR) . .	2	—	2
Front Solidarité Mauricienne (FSM)	1	—	1
Organisation du Peuple Rodriguais (OPR)	—	1	1
Total	**62**	**7**	**69**

* Awarded to those among the unsuccessful candidates who attracted the largest number of votes, in order to ensure that a balance of ethnic groups is represented in the Assembly.

† Alliance comprising the Mauritius Labour Party, the Parti Mauricien Social Démocrate and the Mouvement Socialiste Militant.

‡ Alliance comprising the Mouvement Militant Mauricien, the Union Nationale and the Mouvement Mauricien Social Démocrate.

Election Commission

Electoral Commissioner's Office (ECO): Max City Bldg, 4th Floor, cnr Louis Pasteur and Remy Ollier Sts, Port Louis; tel. 240-9690; fax 241-9409; e-mail electcom@mail.gov.mu; internet electoral.gov.mu; under the aegis of the Prime Minister's Office; Commissioner appointed by the Judicial and Legal Service Commission; Electoral Commissioner MOHAMMAD IRFAN ABDOOL RAHMAN.

Political Organizations

Forum des Citoyens Libres (FCL): Leader GEORGES AH-YAN.

Front Solidarité Mauricienne (FSM): Leader CEHL MEEAH.

Mauritius Labour Party (MLP) (Parti Travailliste): 7 Guy Rozemont Sq., Port Louis; tel. 212-6691; fax 210-0189; e-mail info@labourparty.mu; internet www.labourparty.mu; f. 1936; formed part of the Alliance de l'Avenir for the 2010 elections; Leader Dr NAVINCHANDRA RAMGOOLAM; Pres. PATRICK ASSIRVADEN; Sec.-Gen. KAYLANEE JUGGOO.

Mouvement Mauricien Social Démocrate (MMSD): Morcellement Piat, Forest-Side, POB 1, Port Louis; tel. 670-4000; fax 670-1111; e-mail mmsd@orange.mu; internet www.mmsd.mu; f. 2009; formed part of the Alliance du Coeur for the 2010 elections; Leader ERIC GUIMBEAU.

Mouvement Militant Mauricien (MMM): 21 Poudrière St, Port Louis; tel. 212-6553; fax 208-9939; internet www.mmm.mu; f. 1969; socialist; formed part of the Alliance du Coeur for the 2010 elections; Pres. ARIANNE NAVARRE-MARIE; Leader ALAN GANOO; Secs-Gen. STEVEN OBEEGADOO, RAJESH BHAGWAN.

Mouvement Rodriguais (MR): Port Mathurin, Rodrigues; tel. 831-1876 (Port Mathurin); tel. and fax 686-8859 (Vacoas); fax 831-2648; e-mail nvmally@intnet.mu; f. 1992; represents the interests of Rodrigues; Leader LOUIS JOSEPH (NICHOLAS) VON-MALLY.

Mouvement Sociale Démocrate (MSD) (Social Democratic Movement): Port Louis; f. 2005; Leader ANIL BACHOO.

Mouvement Socialiste Militant (MSM): Sun Trust Bldg, 1st Floor, 31 Edith Cavell St, Port Louis; tel. 212-8787; fax 212-9334; e-mail info@msmparty.org; internet www.msmparty.com; f. 1983 by fmr mems of the MMM; formed part of the Alliance de l'Avenir for the 2010 elections; Leader Dr PRAVIND KUMAR JUGNAUTH; Pres. SHOWKUTALLY SOODHUN; Sec.-Gen. NANDO BODHA.

Organisation du Peuple Rodriguais (OPR): Mont Lubin, Rodrigues; represents the interests of Rodrigues; f. 1976; Leader LOUIS SERGE CLAIR.

Parti Mauricien Social Démocrate (PMSD): Melville, Grand Gaube; internet www.pmsd.mu; centre-right; formed part of the Alliance de l'Avenir for the 2010 elections; Leader CHARLES GAËTAN XAVIER-LUC DUVAL; Sec.-Gen. RAMA VALAYDEN.

Union Nationale (UN) (Mauritian National Union): Port Louis; tel. 208-4254; e-mail ashock.jugnauth@unionnationale.mu; internet unionnationale.mu; f. 2006; formed part of the Alliance du Coeur for the 2010 elections; Chair. ASHOCK JUGNAUTH.

Some of the blocs and parties that participated in the 2010 elections include **Les Verts Fraternels/The Greens** (Leader SYLVIO MICHEL), the **Parti du Peuple Mauricien (PPM)**, the **Rezistans ek Alternativ** (Secretary ASHOK SUBRON), **Lalit** (lalitmauritius.com) and the **Tamil Council**.

Diplomatic Representation

EMBASSIES AND HIGH COMMISSIONS IN MAURITIUS

Australia: Rogers House, 2nd Floor, John F. Kennedy St, POB 541, Port Louis; tel. 202-0160; fax 208-8878; e-mail ahc.portlouis@dfat.gov.au; internet www.mauritius.embassy.gov.au; High Commissioner SANDRA VEGTING.

China, People's Republic: Royal Rd, Belle Rose, Rose Hill; tel. 454-9111; fax 464-6012; e-mail chinaemb_mu@mfa.gov.cn; internet www.ambchine.mu; Ambassador LI LI.

Egypt: Sun Trust Bldg, 2nd floor, Edith Cavell St, Port Louis; tel. 213-1765; fax 213-1768; Ambassador ABD-AL HAMEED AHMAD MARZOUK.

France: 14 St George St, Port Louis; tel. 202-0100; fax 202-0110; e-mail ambafr.port-louis@hotmail.fr; internet www.ambafrance-mu.org; Ambassador JEAN-FRANÇOIS DOBELLE.

India: LIC Centre, 6th Floor, John F. Kennedy St, POB 162, Port Louis; tel. 208-8891; fax 208-6859; e-mail hicom.ss@intnet.mu; internet indiahighcom.intnet.mu; High Commissioner T. P. SEETHARAM.

Madagascar: Guiot Pasceau St, Floreal, POB 3, Port Louis; tel. 686-5015; fax 686-7040; e-mail madmail@intnet.mu; internet www.ambamad.mu; Chargé d'affaires a.i. RICHARD VIA.

Pakistan: 9A Queen Mary Ave, Floreal, Port Louis; tel. 698-8501; fax 698-8405; e-mail pareportlouis@hotmail.com; High Commissioner SALEEM MOHAMMAD KHAN.

Russia: Queen Mary Ave, Floreal, POB 10, Port Louis; tel. 696-1545; fax 696-5027; e-mail rusemb.mu@intnet.mu; Ambassador VYACHESLAV NIKIFOROV.

South Africa: BAI Bldg, 4th Floor, 25 Pope Hennessy St, POB 908, Port Louis; tel. 212-6925; fax 212-6936; e-mail sahc@intnet.mu; High Commissioner MADUMANE M. MATABANE.

United Kingdom: Les Cascades Bldg, 7th Floor, Edith Cavell St, POB 1063, Port Louis; tel. 202-9400; fax 202-9408; e-mail bhc@intnet.mu; High Commissioner NICK LEAKE.

USA: Rogers House, 4th Floor, John F. Kennedy St, POB 544, Port Louis; tel. 202-4400; fax 208-9534; e-mail usembass@intnet.mu; internet mauritius.usembassy.gov; Ambassador SHARI ENGLISH WOODS VILLAROSA.

Judicial System

The laws of Mauritius are derived both from the French Code Napoléon and from English Law. The Judicial Department consists of the Supreme Court, presided over by the Chief Justice and such number of Puisne Judges as may be prescribed by Parliament (currently nine), who are also Judges of the Court of Criminal Appeal and the Court of Civil Appeal. These courts hear appeals from the Intermediate Court, the Industrial Court and 10 District Courts (including that of Rodrigues). The Industrial Court has special jurisdiction to protect the constitutional rights of the citizen. There is a right of appeal in certain cases from the Supreme Court to the Judicial Committee of the Privy Council in the United Kingdom.

Supreme Court: Jules Koenig St, Port Louis; tel. 212-0275; fax 212-9946; internet supremecourt.intnet.mu.

Chief Justice: YEUNG KAM JOHN YEUNG SIK YUEN.

Senior Puisne Judge: KESHOE PARSAD MATADEEN.

Religion

Hindus are estimated to comprise more than 50% of the population, with Christians accounting for some 30% and Muslims 17%. There is also a small Buddhist community.

CHRISTIANITY

The Anglican Communion

Anglicans in Mauritius are within the Church of the Province of the Indian Ocean, comprising seven dioceses (five in Madagascar, one in

Mauritius and one in Seychelles). The Archbishop of the Province is the Bishop of Antananarivo, Madagascar.

Bishop of Mauritius (also Archbishop of the Province of the Indian Ocean): Most Rev. GERALD JAMES (IAN) ERNEST, Bishop's House, Phoenix; tel. 686-5158; fax 697-1096; e-mail dioang@intnet .mu.

The Presbyterian Church of Mauritius

Minister: Pasteur ANDRÉ DE RÉLAND, cnr Farquhar and Royal Rds, Coignet, Rose Hill; tel. 464-5265; fax 395-2068; e-mail embrau@bow .intnet.mu; f. 1814.

The Roman Catholic Church

Mauritius comprises a single diocese, directly responsible to the Holy See, and an apostolic vicariate on Rodrigues. Some 26% of the total population are Roman Catholics.

Bishop of Port Louis: Rt Rev. MAURICE PIAT, Evêché, 13 Mgr Gonin St, Port Louis; tel. 208-3068; fax 208-6607; e-mail eveche@intnet.mu.

BAHÁ'Í FAITH

National Spiritual Assembly: Port Louis; tel. 212-2179; mems resident in 190 localities.

ISLAM

World Islamic Mission (Mauritius): Shah Noorani Centre, Old Moka Rd, Bell Village, Port Louis; tel. 211-1092; fax 210-9445; e-mail wim@wimmauritius.org; internet www.wimmauritius.org; f. 1975; Gen. Sec. HAMADE AUBDOOLLAH.

The Press

DAILIES

China Times: 24 Emmanuel Anquetil St, POB 325, Port Louis; tel. 240-3067; f. 1953; Chinese; Editor-in-Chief LONG SIONG AH KENG; circ. 3,000.

Chinese Daily News: 32 Rémy Ollier St, POB 316, Port Louis; tel. 240-0472; f. 1932; Chinese; Editor-in-Chief WONG YUEN MOY; circ. 5,000.

L'Express: 3 rue des Oursins, Riche-Terre, Baie du Tombeau, POB 247, Port Louis; tel. 206-8200; fax 247-1010; internet www.lexpress .mu; f. 1963; owned by La Sentinelle Ltd; English and French; Dir of Publication ARIANE CAVALOT DE L'ESTRAC; Editor-in-Chief JÉRÔME BOULLE; circ. 35,000.

The Independent Daily: Port Louis; internet theindependent.mu.

Le Matinal: AAPCA House, 6 La Poudrière St, Port Louis; tel. 207-0909; fax 213-4069; e-mail editorial@lematinal.com; internet www .lematinal.com; f. 2003; in French and English; owned by AAPCA (Mauritius) Ltd; Editor-in-Chief KIRAN RAMSAHAYE.

Le Mauricien: 8 St George St, POB 7, Port Louis; tel. 208-3251; fax 208-7059; e-mail redaction@lemauricien.com; internet www .lemauricien.com; f. 1907; English and French; Dir of Publication JACQUES RIVET; Editor-in-Chief GAËTAN SÉNÈQUE; circ. 35,000.

Le Quotidien: Pearl House, 4th Floor, 16 Sir Virgile Naz St, Port Louis; tel. 208-2631; fax 211-7479; e-mail quotidien@bow.intnet.mu; f. 1996; English and French; Dirs JACQUES DAVID, PATRICK MICHEL; circ. 30,000.

Le Socialiste: Manilall Bldg, 3rd Floor, Brabant St, Port Louis; tel. 208-8003; fax 211-3890; English and French; Editor-in-Chief VEDI BALLAH; circ. 7,000.

WEEKLIES AND FORTNIGHTLIES

5-Plus Dimanche: 3 Brown Sequard St, Port Louis; tel. 213-5500; fax 213-5551; e-mail comments@5plusltd.com; internet www .5plusltd.com; f. 1994; English and French; Editor-in-Chief FINLAY SALESSE; circ. 30,000.

5-Plus Magazine: 3 Brown Sequard St, Port Louis; tel. 213-5500; fax 213-5551; e-mail comments@5plusltd.com; f. 1990; English and French; Editor-in-Chief PIERRE BENOÎT; circ. 10,000.

Bollywood Massala: Le Défi Bldg, Royal Rd, Port Louis; tel. 211-8131; fax 213-0959; e-mail ledefi.plus@intnet.mu; internet www .defimedia.info.

Business Magazine: 3 Brown-Sequard St, 3rd Floor, Port Louis; tel. 202-2300; fax 211-1926; e-mail businessmag@intnet.mu; internet www.businessmag.mu; f. 1992; owned by Business Publications Ltd; English and French; Editor-in-Chief PIERRICK PEDEL; circ. 7,500.

Le Défi-Plus: Le Défi Bldg, Royal Rd, Port Louis; tel. 211-8131; fax 213-0959; e-mail ledefi.plus@intnet.mu; internet www.defimedia .info; Saturdays; Dir of Publication ESHAN KHODABUX.

L'Hèbdo: Le Défi Bldg, Royal Rd, Port Louis; tel. 211-8131; fax 213-0959; e-mail ledefi.plus@intnet.mu; internet www.defimedia.info.

Impact News: 10 Dr Yves Cantin St, Port Louis; tel. 211-5284; fax 211-7821; e-mail farhadr@wanadoo.mu; internet www.impactnews .info; English and French; Editor-in-Chief FARHAD RAMJAUN.

Lalit de Klas: 153B Royal Rd, GRNW, Port Louis; tel. 208-2132; e-mail lalitmail@intnet.mu; internet www.lalitmauritius.org; English, French and Mauritian Creole; Editor RADA KISTNASAMY.

Mauritius Times: 23 Bourbon St, Port Louis; tel. and fax 212-1313; e-mail mtimes@intnet.mu; internet www.mauritiustimes.com; f. 1954; English and French; Editor-in-Chief MADHUKAR RAMLALLAH; circ. 15,000.

News on Sunday: Dr Eugen Laurent St, POB 230, Port Louis; tel. 211-5902; fax 211-7302; e-mail newsonsunday@news.intnet.mu; f. 1996; owned by Le Défi Group; weekly; in English; Editor NAGUIB LALLMAHOMED; circ. 10,000.

Le Rodriguais: Saint Gabriel, Rodrigues; tel. 831-1613; fax 831-1484; f. 1989; Creole, English and French; Editor JACQUES EDOUARD; circ. 2,000.

Samedi Plus: Port Louis; Editor-in-Chief DHARMANAND DOOHARIKA.

Star: 38 Labourdonnais St, Port Louis; tel. 212-2736; fax 211-7781; e-mail starpress@intnet.mu; internet www.mauriweb.com/star; English and French; Editor-in-Chief REZA ISSACK.

Sunday: Port Louis; tel. 208-9516; fax 208-7059; f. 1966; English and French; Editor-in-Chief SUBASH GOBIN.

Turf Magazine: 8 George St, POB 7, Port Louis; tel. 207-8200; fax 208-7059; e-mail bdlm@intnet.mu; internet www.lemauricien.com/ turfmag; owned by Le Mauricien Ltd.

La Vie Catholique: 28 Nicolay Rd, Port Louis; tel. 242-0975; fax 242-3114; e-mail viecatho@intnet.mu; internet www.laviecatholique .com; f. 1930; weekly; English, French and Creole; Editor-in-Chief DANIÈLE BABOORAM; circ. 8,000.

Week-End: 8 St George St, POB 7, Port Louis; tel. 207-8200; fax 208-3248; e-mail redaction@lemauricien.com; internet www.lemauricien .com/weekend; f. 1966; owned by Le Mauricien Ltd; French and English; Editor JOSIE LEBRASSE; circ. 80,000.

Week-End Scope: 8 St George St, POB 7, Port Louis; tel. 207-8200; fax 208-7059; e-mail wes@lemauricien.com; internet www .lemauricien.com/wes; f. 1989; owned by Le Mauricien Ltd; English and French; Editor-in-Chief JACQUES ACHILLE.

OTHER SELECTED PERIODICALS

CCI–INFO: 3 Royal St, Port Louis; tel. 208-3301; fax 208-0076; e-mail mcci@intnet.mu; internet www.mcci.org; English and French; f. 1995; quarterly; publ. of the Mauritius Chamber of Commerce and Industry; Man. FAEEZA IBRAHIMSAH.

Education News: Edith Cavell St, Port Louis; tel. 212-1303; English and French; monthly; Editor-in-Chief GIAN AUBEELUCK.

Le Message de L'Ahmadiyyat: c/o Ahmadiyya Muslim Asscn, POB 6, Rose Hill; tel. 464-1747; fax 454-2223; e-mail darussalaam@intnet .mu; French; monthly; Editor-in-Chief MOUSSA TAUJOO; circ. 3,000.

Le Progrès Islamique: 51B Solferino St, Rose Hill; tel. 467-1697; fax 467-1696; f. 1948; English and French; monthly; Editor DEVINA SOOKIA.

Publishers

Business Publications Ltd: TN Tower, 2nd Floor, St George St, Port Louis; tel. 211-3048; fax 211-1926; internet www.businessmag .mu; f. 1993; English and French; Dir LYNDSAY RIVIÈRE.

Editions de l'Océan Indien: Stanley, Rose Hill; tel. 464-6761; fax 464-3445; e-mail eoibooks@intnet.mu; internet www.eoi-info.com; f. 1977; general, textbooks, dictionaries, literature; English, French and Asian languages; Gen. Man. DEVANAND DEWKURUN.

Editions Le Printemps: 4 Club Rd, Vacoas; tel. 696-1017; fax 686-7302; e-mail elp@bow.intnet.mu; Man. Dir A. I. SULLIMAN.

Editions Vizavi: 9 St George St, Port Louis; tel. 211-3047; e-mail vizavi@intnet.mu; Dir PASCALE SIEW.

Broadcasting and Communications

TELECOMMUNICATIONS

In 2011 there were 374,694 subscribers to fixed-line telephone services and 1.2m. subscribers to mobile cellular telephone services.

Mauritius Telecom Ltd: Telecom Tower, Edith Cavell St, Port Louis; tel. 203-7000; fax 208-1070; e-mail ceo@mauritiustelecom.com .mu; internet www.mauritiustelecom.com; f. 1992; 60% owned by Govt of Mauritius, State Bank of Mauritius and National Pensions

Fund, 40% owned by France Télécom through RIMCOM; privatized in 2000; provides all telecommunications services, including internet and digital mobile cellular services; Chair. APPALSAMY (DASS) THOMAS; CEO SARAT DUTT LALLAH.

Cellplus Mobile Communications Ltd: Telecom Tower, 9th Floor, Edith Cavell St, Port Louis; tel. 208-5057; fax 211-6996; e-mail contact@orange.mu; internet www.orange.mu/mobile; f. 1996; introduced the first GSM cellular network in Mauritius and recently in Rodrigues (Cell-Oh); a wholly owned subsidiary of Mauritius Telecom.

Emtel: 10 Ebene Cyber City, Ebene; tel. 454-5400; fax 454-1010; e-mail emtel@emtelnet.com; internet www.emtel.com; f. 1989; CEO SHYAM ROY.

Outremer Télécom Maurice: Hassamal Bldg, Rémono St, POB 113, Rose Hill; tel. 401-9400; fax 401-9422; e-mail info@ outremer-telecom.mu; internet www.outremer-telecom.mu; Man. Dir MICHEL RIGOT.

Regulatory Authority

Information and Communication Technologies Authority (ICTA): The Celicourt, 12th Floor, 6 Sir Celicourt Antelme St, Port Louis; tel. 211-5333; fax 211-9444; e-mail icta@intnet.mu; internet www.icta.mu; f. 1999; regulatory authority; Chair. TRILOK DWARKA; Exec. Dir Dr KRISHNA OOLUN.

BROADCASTING

In 1997 the Supreme Court invalidated the broadcasting monopoly held by the Mauritius Broadcasting Corporation.

Independent Broadcasting Authority: The Celicourt, 2nd Floor, 6 Sir Celicourt Antelme St, Port Louis; tel. 213-3890; fax 213-3894; e-mail iba@intnet.mu; internet iba.gov.mu; Chair. TRILOCK DWARKA; Dir DULLIPARSAD SURAJ BALI.

Radio

Mauritius Broadcasting Corpn: 1 Royal Rd, Moka; tel. 402-8000; fax 433-3330; e-mail customercare@mbc.intnet.mu; internet www .mbcradio.tv; f. 1964; parastatal organization operating eight national radio services and nine television channels; Chair. CLAUDE NARAIN; Dir-Gen. DHANJAY CALLIKAN.

Radio One: 3 Brown Sequard St, Port Louis; tel. 211-4555; fax 211-4142; e-mail sales@r1.mu; internet www.r1.mu; f. 2002; owned by Sentinelle media group; news and entertainment; Dir-Gen. NICOLAS ADELSON.

Radio Plus: 4B Labourdonnais St, Port-Louis; tel. 208-6002; fax 212-0047; e-mail radioplus@intnet.mu; internet www.radioplus.mu; f. 2002.

Top FM: The Peninsula, Caudan Bldg, 7th Floor, 2A Falcon St, Caudan, Port Louis; tel. 213-2121; fax 213-2222; e-mail topfm@intnet .mu; internet www.topfmradio.com; f. 2003; Chair. BALKRISHNA KAUNHYE.

Radio France International and France Inter are also broadcast to Mauritius.

Television

Independent television stations commenced broadcasting from 2002, as part of the liberalization of the sector.

Mauritius Broadcasting Corpn: see Radio.

Broadcasts from France 24 and TV5 are received in Mauritius.

Finance

(cap. = capital; res = reserves; dep. = deposits; m. = million; brs = branches; amounts in Mauritian rupees, unless otherwise stated)

BANKING

Central Bank

In 2010 there were 19 commercial banks and 11 non-bank deposit-taking institutions in Mauritius. The first Islamic bank of Mauritius, Century Banking Corpn Ltd, started its operation in 2011.

Bank of Mauritius: Sir William Newton St, POB 29, Port Louis; tel. 202-3800; fax 208-9204; e-mail governor.office@bom.intnet.mu; internet bom.intnet.mu; f. 1966; bank of issue; cap. 1,000.0m., res 19,158.8m., dep. 27,353.7m. (June 2010); Gov. RUNDHEERSING BHEENICK.

Principal Commercial Banks

ABC Banking Corpn Ltd: 7 Duke of Edinburgh Ave, Place d'Armes, Port Louis; tel. 206-8000; fax 208-0088; internet www

.abcbanking.mu; f. 2010; Chair. Prof. DONALD AH CHUEN; CEO MOHAMED KHALIL ALKHUSHAIRI.

AfrAsia Bank Ltd: Bowen Square, 10 Dr Ferriere St, Port Louis; tel. 208-5500; fax 213-8850; e-mail afrasia@afrasiabank.com; internet www.afrasiabank.com; f. 2007; Chair. ARNAUD LAGESSE; CEO JAMES BENOIT.

Bank of Baroda: 32 Sir William Newton St, POB 553, Port Louis; tel. 208-1504; fax 208-3892; e-mail info@bankofbaroda-mu.com; internet www.bankofbaroda-mu.com; f. 1962; total assets 2,655,000m. (June 2007); Vice-Pres. (Mauritius Operations) S. K. CHAWLA; 7 brs.

Bank One Ltd: 16 Sir William Newton St, POB 485, Port Louis; tel. 202-9200; fax 210-4712; e-mail info@firstcitybank-mauritius.com; internet www.bankone.mu; f. 1991 as the Delphis Bank Ltd; merged with Union International Bank in 1997; private bank; taken over by consortium in 2002; name changed as above in 2008; 50% owned by Investments & Mortgages Bank Ltd (Kenya), 50% by Ciel Investments Ltd; cap. 491.4m., res 142.1m., dep. 9,481.3m. (Dec. 2009); Chair. SARIT SHAH; CEO RAJ DUSSOYE.

BanyanTree Bank Ltd: 13 Nexteracom I, Cybercity, Ebene; e-mail info@banyantreebank.com; internet www.banyantreebank.com; f. 2012; CEO PUTHEN VEETTIL GOPAKUMAR.

Barclays Bank PLC, Mauritius: Harbour Front Bldg, 8th Floor, John F. Kennedy St, POB 284, Port Louis; tel. 402-1000; fax 467-0618; e-mail barclays.mauritius@barclays.com; f. 1919; absorbed Banque Nationale de Paris Intercontinentale in 2002; cap. 100.0m., res 616.1m., dep. 6,886.7m. (Dec. 2001); Man. Dir RAVIN DAJEE; 16 brs.

Bramer Banking Corpn Ltd: 26 Bourbon St, Port Louis; tel. 208-8826; fax 213-4792; internet www.bramerbank.com; f. 1989; present name adopted 2008; owned by British American Investment Group (BAI); cap. 200.0m., res 39.9m., dep. 4,301.8m. (Dec. 2009); Chair. HASSAM A. M. VAYID; CEO ASHRAF ESMAEL (acting); 16 brs.

Deutsche Bank Mauritius Ltd: Barkly Wharf East, 4th Floor, Le Caudan Waterfront, POB 615, Port Louis; tel. 202-7878; fax 202-7898; internet www.db.com/mauritius.

Habib Bank Ltd: 30 Louis Pasteur St, Port Louis; tel. 217-7600; fax 216-3829; e-mail habib@intnet.mu; f. 1964; 2 brs.

Hongkong and Shanghai Banking Corpn Ltd (HSBC): HSBC Centre, 5th Floor, 18 Cyber City, Ebene; tel. 403-0701; fax 403-8300; e-mail hsbcmauritius@hsbc.co.mu; internet www.hsbc.co.mu; f. 1916; CEO SANDEEP UPPAL; Man. Dir JAMES BOUCHER.

Investec Bank (Mauritius) Ltd: Dias Pier Bldg, 7th Floor, Le Caudan Waterfront, Port Louis; tel. 207-4000; fax 207-4003; internet www.investec.com; f. 1997; Chair. HUGH S. HERMAN; CEO CRAIG C. MCKENZIE.

Mauritius Commercial Bank Ltd: MCB Centre, 9–15 Sir William Newton St, POB 52, Port Louis; tel. 202-5000; fax 208-7054; e-mail mcb@mcb.co.mu; internet www.mcb.mu; f. 1838; cap. 2,554.9m., res 3,990.0m., dep. 132,569.1m. (June 2010); Pres. GERARD J. HARDY; CEO PIERRE-GUY NOEL; 42 brs.

Mauritius Post and Co-operative Bank Ltd: 1 Sir William Newton St, Port Louis; tel. 207-9999; fax 208-7270; e-mail mpcb@ mpcb.mu; internet www.mpcb.mu; f. 2003; 44.3% owned by The Mauritius Post Ltd, 35.7% state-owned, 10% owned by the Sugar Investment Trust; cap. 384.0m., res 119.4m., dep. 7,131.9m. (Dec. 2009); CEO RAJIV KUMAR BEEHARRY; Gen. Man. PAVADAY THONDRA-YON.

P. T. Bank Internasional Indonesia (Mauritius): Barkly Wharf, 5th Floor, Caudan Waterfront, Port Louis; tel. 210-6365; fax 210-5458; e-mail biimrt@intnet.mu; internet bii.intnet.mu; f. 1998; CEO SARAH JANE KATE NIRSIMLOO.

SBI Mauritius: SBI Tower Mindspace, 6th and 7th Floors, Bhumi Park, 45 Cyber City, Ebene; tel. 404-4900; fax 454-6890; e-mail info@ sbimauritius.com; internet www.sbimauritius.com; f. 1978 as Indian Ocean International Bank Ltd; merged with SBI International in 2008 and renamed as above; cap. 48.6m., res 62.0m., dep. 438.4m. (March 2009); Chair. PRATIP CHAUDHURI; Man. Dir and CEO J. S. HIREMATH; 15 brs.

Standard Chartered Bank (Mauritius) Ltd: Ebene House, 2nd Floor, 33 Cyber City, Ebene; tel. 466-5000; fax 466-5161; e-mail info .scbm@sc.com; internet www.standardchartered.com/mu; wholly owned subsidiary of Standard Chartered Bank PLC; 'offshore' banking unit.

State Bank of Mauritius Ltd: State Bank Tower, 1 Queen Elizabeth II Ave, POB 152, Port Louis; tel. 202-1111; fax 202-1234; e-mail sbm@sbmgroup.mu; internet www.sbmgroup.mu; f. 1973; cap. 303.7m., res 2,975.1m., dep. 61,252.9m. (June 2010); Chair. MUNI KRISHNA REDDY; CEO GAUTAM VIR; 48 brs.

Development Bank

Development Bank of Mauritius Ltd: rue La Chaussée, POB 157, Port Louis; tel. 203-3600; fax 208-8498; e-mail dbm@intnet.mu; internet www.dbm.mu; f. 1964; name changed as above in 1991; 85% govt-owned; cap. 225m., res 1,646.5m., dep. 4,155.9m. (June 2009); Chair. ERIC N. G. PING CHEUN; Man. Dir IQBAL CARRIM (acting); 6 brs.

Principal 'Offshore' Banks

Banque des Mascareignes Ltd: 1 Cathedral Sq., Level 8, 16 Jules Koenig St, POB 43, Port Louis; tel. and fax 207-8600; fax 210-2300; e-mail serviceclient@bm.mu; internet www.banquedesmascareignes .mu; f. 2004; name changed as above 2005; 100% owned by BPCE-IOM (France); cap. 838.7m., res 597.7m., dep. 11,793.0m. (Dec. 2011); Chair. PHILIPPE GARSUAULT; CEO HUY HOANG DANG.

Bank of Baroda, Barclays Bank PLC, AfrAsia Bank Ltd, PT Bank International Indonesia, Investec Bank (Mauritius), Standard Chartered Bank (Mauritius) and HSBC Bank PLC also operate 'offshore' banking units.

Islamic Bank

Century Banking Corpn Ltd: Suite 405, Barkly Wharf, 4th Floor, Le Caudan Waterfront, Port Louis; tel. 213-3400; fax 213-9200; internet cbc.com.mu; f. 2010; Pres. JEAN MARC RIEGEL; CEO NIK JOHARRIS NIK AHMAD.

Banking Organization

Mauritius Bankers Association Ltd (MBA): Newton Tower, Level 15, Sir William Newton St, Port Louis; tel. 213-2390; fax 213-0968; e-mail mba@mba.mu; internet www.mba.mu; f. 1967; Chair. JAIRAJ SONOO; CEO AISHA C. TIMOL; 21 mems.

STOCK EXCHANGE

Financial Services Commission: FSC House, 54 Cyber City, Ebene; tel. 403-7000; fax 467-7172; e-mail fscmauritius@intnet .mu; internet www.fscmauritius.org; f. 2001; regulatory authority for securities, insurance and global business activities; Chair. SAID LALLOO; Chief Exec. (vacant).

Stock Exchange of Mauritius Ltd: 1 Cathedral Sq., 4th Floor, 16 Jules Koenig St, Port Louis; tel. 212-9541; fax 208-8409; e-mail stockex@sem.intnet.mu; internet www.stockexchangeofmauritius .com; f. 1989; 11 mems; Chair. GAETAN LAN HUN KUEN; CEO SUNIL BENIMADHU.

INSURANCE

Albatross Insurance Co Ltd: 22 St George St, POB 116, Port Louis; tel. 207-9007; fax 208-4800; e-mail headoffice@ albatross-insurance.com; internet www.albatross-insurance.com; f. 1975; Chair. VAUGHAN HEBERDEN.

Anglo-Mauritius Assurance Society Ltd: Swan Group Centre, 10 Intendance St, POB 837, Port Louis; tel. 202-8600; fax 208-8956; e-mail anglo@intnet.mu; internet www.anglo.mu; f. 1951; Chair. CYRIL MAYER; CEO LOUIS RIVALLAND.

BAI Co (Mauritius) Ltd: BAI Centre, 217 Royal Rd, Curepipe; tel. 602-3000; fax 670-3384; e-mail bai@bai.intnet.mu; internet www.bai .mu; f. 1988 as British American Insurance Co (Mauritius) Ltd; renamed as above in 2010; Pres. and CEO RISHI SOOKDAWOOR.

Indian Ocean General Assurance Ltd: 35 Corderie St, POB 865, Port Louis; tel. 212-4125; fax 212-5850; e-mail info@iogaltd.com; internet iogaltd.com; f. 1971; total assets 221m. (June 2007); Gen. Man. R. L. MATHUR.

Jubilee Insurance (Mauritius) Ltd: Cathedral Sq., Pope Hennessy St, Port Louis; tel. 210-3678; fax 212-7970; e-mail sarah .hossen@jubileemauritius.com; f. 1998; Admin. Officer SARAH HOSSEN.

Lamco International Insurance Ltd: Lamco Bldg, 12 Barracks St, Port Louis; tel. 212-4494; fax 208-0612; e-mail lamco@intnet.mu; internet www.lamcoinsurance.com; f. 1978; Chair. ABOO BAKAR YACOOB ATCHIA; Gen. Man. NAJEEB C. ADIA.

Life Insurance Corpn of India: LIC Centre, John F. Kennedy St, POB 310, Port Louis; tel. 212-5316; fax 208-6392; e-mail liccmm@ intnet.mu; f. 1956; Chief Man. NAVIN PRAKASH SINHA.

Mauritian Eagle Insurance Co Ltd: IBL House, 1st Floor, Caudan Waterfront, POB 854, Port Louis; tel. 203-2200; fax 203-2299; e-mail caudan@mauritianeagle.com; internet www .mauritianeagle.com; f. 1973; Chair. PATRICE D'HOTMAN DE VILLIERS; Man. Dir ERIC A. VENPIN.

Mauritius Union Assurance Co Ltd: 4 Léoville l'Homme St, POB 233, Port Louis; tel. 207-5500; fax 212-2962; e-mail info@ mauritiusunion.com; internet www.mauritiusuniongroup.com; f. 1948; Chair. DOMINIQUE GALEA; Group Man. Dir KRIS LUTCHME-NARRAIDOO.

Mauritius Union Group: 4 Léoville l'Homme St, Port Louis; tel. 207-5500; fax 212-2962; e-mail info@mauritiusunion.com; internet www.mauritiusuniongroup.com; f. 1948; CEO KRIS LUTCHMENARRAIDOO.

New India Assurance Co Ltd: Bank of Baroda Bldg, 3rd Floor, 15 Sir William Newton St, POB 398, Port Louis; tel. 208-1442; fax 208-2160; e-mail niasurance@intnet.mu; internet www.niacl.com; f. 1935; general insurance; Chief Man. S. VAIDESWARAN.

Phoenix Insurance (Mauritius) Co Ltd: 36 Sir William Newton St, POB 852, Port Louis; tel. 208-0056; fax 213-3882; e-mail tilakf@ intnet.mu; f. 1977; CEO TILAK FERNANDO (acting).

Rainbow Insurance Co Ltd: 23 Edith Cavell St, POB 389, Port Louis; tel. 202-8800; fax 208-8750; e-mail raininsu@intnet.mu; internet www.rainbowinsurance.mu; f. 1976; Chair. B. GOKULSING; Gen. Man. PRAVIN RAMBURN.

State Insurance Co of Mauritius Ltd (SICOM): SICOM Bldg, Sir Celicourt Antelme St, Port Louis; tel. 203-8400; fax 208-7662; e-mail email@sicom.intnet.mu; internet www.sicom.mu; f. 1975; Man. Dir K. G. BHOOJEDHUR-OBEEGADOO.

Sun Insurance Co Ltd: 2 St George St, Port Louis; tel. 208-0769; fax 208-2052; e-mail suninsco@intnet.mu; f. 1981; Chair. Sir KAILASH RAMDANEE; Man. Dir A. MUSBALLY.

Swan Insurance Co Ltd: Swan Group Centre, 10 Intendance St, POB 364, Port Louis; tel. 207-3500; fax 208-6898; e-mail swan@ intnet.mu; f. 1955; Chair. J. M. ANTOINE HAREL; CEO M. E. CYRIL MAYER.

Trade and Industry

GOVERNMENT AGENCIES

Agricultural Marketing Board (AMB): Dr G. Leclézio Ave, Moka; tel. 433-4025; fax 433-4837; e-mail agbd@intnet.mu; internet amb .intnet.mu; f. 1964; operates under the aegis of the Ministry of Agro-industry and Food Security; markets certain locally produced and imported food products (such as potatoes, onions, garlic, spices and seeds); provides storage facilities to importers and exporters; Gen. Man. RODNEY RAMA.

Mauritius Meat Authority: Abattoir Rd, Roche Bois, POB 612, Port Louis; tel. 242-5884; fax 217-1077; e-mail mauritiusmeat@ intnet.mu; f. 1974; licensing authority; controls and regulates sale of meat and meat products; also purchases and imports livestock and markets meat products; Gen. Man. A. BALGOBIN.

Mauritius Sugar Authority: Ken Lee Bldg, 2nd Floor, Edith Cavell St, Port Louis; tel. 208-7466; fax 208-7470; e-mail msa@ intnet.mu; regulatory body for the sugar industry; Chair. S. HANOOMANJEE; Exec. Dir Dr G. RAJPATI.

Mauritius Tea Board: Wooton St, Curepipe Rd, Curepipe; POB 28, Eau Coulée; tel. 675-3497; fax 676-1445; e-mail teaboard@intnet.mu; internet www.gov.mu/portal/site/teaboard; f. 1975; regulates and controls the activities of the tea industry; Chair. V. GONDEEA; Gen. Man. ATMARAMSINGH SEEPERGAUTH.

Mauritius Tobacco Board: Plaine Lauzun, Port Louis; tel. 212-2323; fax 208-6426; e-mail tobaco@intnet.mu; internet tobaccoboard .intnet.mu; Gen. Man. HEMRAJSINGH RAMAHOTAR.

DEVELOPMENT ORGANIZATIONS

Board of Investment—Mauritius (BOI): 1 Cathedral Sq., 10th Floor, 16 Jules Koenig St, Port Louis; tel. 211-4190; fax 208-2924; e-mail invest@boi.intnet.mu; internet www.boimauritius.com; f. 2001 to promote international investment, business and services; Chair. of Bd MAURICE LAM; Man. Dir KEN POONOOSAMY.

Enterprise Mauritius: Saint James Court, 7th Floor, Saint Denis St, Port Louis; tel. 212-9760; fax 212-9767; e-mail info@em.intnet .mu; internet www.enterprisemauritius.biz; f. 2005 from parts of the Mauritius Industrial Development Authority, the Export Processing Zones Development Authority and the Sub-contracting and Partnership Exchange—Mauritius; operates under the aegis of the Ministry of Industry, Commerce and Consumer Protection; Chair. LOUIS AMÉDÉE DARGA; CEO DEV CHAMROO.

Joint Economic Council (JEC): Plantation House, 3rd Floor, pl. d'Armes, Port Louis; tel. 211-2980; fax 211-3141; e-mail jec@intnet .mu; internet www.jec-mauritius.org; f. 1970; the co-ordinating body of the private sector of Mauritius, including the main business orgs of the country; Pres. LOUIS RIVALLAND; Dir RAJ MAKOOND.

Mauritius Freeport Authority (MFA): 1 Cathedral Sq., Level 10, 16 Jules Koenig St, Port Louis; tel. 203-3800; fax 208-2924; e-mail contact@investmauritius.com; internet www.efreeport.com; f. 1990; Asst Dir NANDA NARRAINEN.

National Productivity and Competitiveness Council (NPCC): Alexander House, 4th Floor, Cyber City, Ebene; tel. 467-7700; fax

467-3838; e-mail natpro@intnet.mu; internet www.npccmauritius .com; f. 2000; represents the Govt, the private sector and trade unions; Chair. KEVIN LEERAJSINGH CHUTTUR; Exec. Dir Dr KRISHNA-LALL COONJAN.

Small Enterprises and Handicraft Development Authority (SEHDA): Industrial Zone, Coromandel; tel. 233-0500; fax 233-5545; e-mail sehda@intnet.mu; internet www.sehda.org; f. 2006 following the merger of the Small and Medium Industries Development Organization and the National Handicraft Promotion Agency; provides support to potential and existing small entrepreneurs; Man. Dir INDIRA SEEBURN.

State Investment Corpn Ltd (SIC): Air Mauritius Centre, 15th Floor, John F. Kennedy St, Port Louis; tel. 202-8900; fax 208-8948; e-mail contactsic@stateinvestment.com; internet www .stateinvestment.com; f. 1984; provides support for new investment and transfer of technology, in agriculture, industry and tourism; Man. Dir MUHAMMAD IQBAL MALLAM-HASHAM; Chair. RAJ DIREVIUM NAGAYA RINGADOO.

CHAMBERS OF COMMERCE

Chinese Chamber of Commerce: Jade Court, Suite 206, Jummah Mosque St, Port Louis; tel. and fax 242-0156; e-mail admin@ cccmauritius.org; internet www.cccmauritius.org; f. 1908; Pres. ARMAND AH-KONG.

Mauritius Chamber of Commerce and Industry: 3 Royal St, Port Louis; tel. 208-3301; fax 208-0076; e-mail mcci@intnet.mu; internet www.mcci.org; f. 1850; 400 mems; Pres. CÉDRIC DE SPEVILLE; Sec.-Gen. MAHMOOD CHEEROO.

INDUSTRIAL ASSOCIATIONS

Association of Mauritian Manufacturers (AMM): c/o The Mauritius Chamber of Commerce and Industry, 3 Royal St, Port Louis; tel. 208-3301; fax 208-0076; e-mail amm@mcci.intnet.mu; f. 1995; Pres. VINCENT DE LABAUVE D'ARIFAT.

Mauritius Export Processing Zone Association (MEPZA): Unicorn House, 6th Floor, 5 Royal St, Port Louis; tel. 208-5216; fax 212-1853; f. 1976; consultative and advisory body; Chair. GUIL-LAUME SUGNIN.

Mauritius Sugar Producers' Association (MSPA): Plantation House, 2nd Floor, Edinburgh Ave, Port Louis; tel. 212-0295; fax 212-5727; e-mail mspa@mspa.intnet.mu; internet www.mspa.mu; f. 1947; Chair. CYRIL MAYER; Dir JEAN LI YUEN FONG.

EMPLOYERS' ORGANIZATION

Mauritius Employers' Federation: MEF-MCCI Bldg, Cyber City, Ebene; tel. 466-3600; fax 465-8200; e-mail mef@intnet.mu; internet www.mef-online.org; f. 1962; Chair. CLENCY APPAVOO; Dir Dr AZAD JEETUN.

UTILITIES
Electricity

Central Electricity Board: Royal Rd, POB 40, Curepipe; tel. 601-1100; fax 675-7958; e-mail ceb@intnet.mu; internet ceb.intnet.mu; f. 1952; state-operated; Chair. BALRAJ NARROO; Gen. Man. SHIAM KRISHT THANNOO.

Water

Central Water Authority: Royal Rd, St Paul, Phoenix; tel. 601-5000; fax 686-6264; e-mail cwa@intnet.mu; corporate body; scheduled for privatization; f. 1973; Gen. Man. HARRY KISSOON BOOLUCK; Chair. MEGHDUTH CHUMROO.

Waste Water Management Authority: Sir Celicourt Antelme St, Port Louis; tel. 206-3000; fax 211-7007; e-mail wma@intnet.mu; internet wma.gov.mu; f. 2000; Chair. KHUSHAL LOBINE; Gen. Man. MOUSSA ELIAS ALLYBOCUS.

TRADE UNIONS
Federations

Federation of Civil Service and Other Unions (FCSOU): Jade Court, Rm 308, 3rd Floor, 33 Jummah Mosque St, Port Louis; tel. 216-1977; fax 216-1475; e-mail f.c.s.u@intnet.mu; internet www .fcsou.org; f. 1957; 72 affiliated unions with 30,000 mems (2006); Pres. NARENDRANATH GOPEE; Gen. Sec. VIDIANAND NAUGLOO.

General Workers' Federation: 7 Impasse Ruisseau des Creoles, Port Louis; tel. 213-1771; Pres. SERGE JAUFFRET; Sec.-Gen. DEVIA-NAND NARRAIN.

Mauritius Labour Congress (MLC): 8 Louis Victor de la Faye St, Port Louis; tel. 212-4343; fax 208-8945; e-mail mlcongress@intnet .mu; f. 1963; Pres. HANIFF PEERUN; Gen. Sec. BHOLANATH JEEWUTH.

Mauritius Trade Union Congress (MTUC): Emmanuel Anquetil Labour Centre, James Smith St, Port Louis; tel. 210-8567; f. 1946; Pres. DEWAN QUEDOU.

Transport

RAILWAYS

There are no operational railways in Mauritius.

ROADS

In 2009 there were 2,066 km of paved roads, of which 75 km were motorways, 1,000 km were other main roads, and 593 km were secondary roads. An urban highway links the motorways approaching Port Louis. A motorway connects Port Louis with Plaisance airport.

National Transport Corpn: Bonne Terre Vacoas; tel. 426-2938; fax 426-5489; e-mail cnt.bus@intnet.mu; internet ntc.intnet.mu; Chair. CHETAN RAMBANS DOOKUN; Gen. Man. PRADEEP KUMAR DASH.

SHIPPING

Mauritius is served by numerous foreign shipping lines. In 1990 Port Louis was established as a free port to expedite the development of Mauritius as an entrepôt centre. At 31 December 2012 Mauritius had a merchant fleet of 116 vessels, with a combined displacement of 192,439 grt.

Mauritius Ports Authority: H. Ramnarain Bldg, Mer Rouge, Port Louis; tel. 206-5400; fax 240-0856; e-mail info@mauport.com; internet www.mauport.com; f. 1976; Chair. MAURICE ALLET; Dir-Gen. SHEKUR SUNTAH.

Ireland Blyth Ltd: IBL House, Caudan, Port Louis; tel. 203-2000; fax 203-2001; e-mail iblinfo@iblgroup.com; internet www.iblgroup .com; Chair. THIERRY LAGESSE; CEO NICOLAS MAIGROT.

Mauritius Freeport Development Co Ltd: Freeport Zone 5, Mer Rouge, Port Louis; tel. 206-2000; fax 206-2025; e-mail info@mfd.mu; internet www.mfd.mu; f. 1997; manages and operates Freeport Zone 5, more than 40,000 sq m of storage facility; facilities include dry warehouses, cold warehouses, processing and transformation units, open storage container parks and a container freight station; largest logistics centre in the Indian Ocean region; Chair. RENÉ LECLÉZIO; CEO DOMINIQUE DE FROBERVILLE.

Mauritius Shipping Corpn Ltd: St James Court, Suite 417/418, St Denis St, Port Louis; tel. 208-5900; fax 210-5176; internet www .mauritiusshipping.mu; f. 1985; state-owned; operates two passenger-cargo vessels between Mauritius, Rodrigues, Réunion and Madagascar; Man. Dir Capt. J. PATRICK RAULT.

CIVIL AVIATION

Sir Seewoosagur Ramgoolam International Airport is at Plaisance, 4 km from Mahébourg. From 2006 air routes with France and the United Kingdom were liberalized, allowing new carriers to operate on the routes.

Civil Aviation Department: Sir Seewoosagur Ramgoolam International Airport, Plaine Magnien; tel. 603-2000; fax 637-3164; e-mail civil-aviation@mail.gov.mu; internet civil-aviation.gov.mu; under the aegis of the Prime Minister's Office (External Communications Division); Dir SARUPANAND KINNOO.

Air Mauritius: Air Mauritius Centre, John F. Kennedy St, POB 441, Port Louis; tel. 207-7070; fax 208-8331; e-mail contact@airmauritius .com; internet www.airmauritius.com; f. 1967; 51% state-owned; services to 18 destinations in Europe, Asia, Australia and Africa; Chair. APPALSAMY THOMAS; CEO ANDRÉ VILJOEN.

Tourism

Tourists are attracted to Mauritius by its scenery and beaches, the pleasant climate and the blend of cultures. Accommodation capacity totalled 21,072 beds in 2005. The number of visitors increased from 300,670 in 1990 to 964,642 in 2011, when the greatest numbers of visitors were from France (31.3%), Réunion (11.7%) and the United Kingdom (9.1%). Gross revenue from tourism in 2011 was estimated at MRs 42,717m. The Government sought to increase the volume of tourists visiting the country (to some 2m. people by 2015) by improving the jetty facilities in the port in order to welcome cruise ships and by liberalizing air transit routes.

Mauritius Tourism Promotion Authority: Victoria House, 4th and 5th Floor, St Louis St, Port Louis; tel. 210-1545; fax 212-5142; e-mail mtpa@intnet.mu; internet www.tourism-mauritius.mu; f. 1996; Man. Dir KARL MOOTOOSAMY.

Tourism Authority (TA): Victoria House, 1st and 2nd Floor, St Louis St, Port Louis; tel. 213-1740; fax 213-1738; e-mail contact@

tourismauthority.mu; internet www.tourismauthority.mu; f. 2003; parastatal; responsible for licensing, regulating and supervising the activities of tourist enterprises; Dir NIVEN MUNEESAMY.

Defence

The country has no standing defence forces, although as assessed at November 2012 paramilitary forces were estimated to number 2,500, comprising a special 1,700-strong mobile police unit, to ensure internal security, and a coast-guard of 800.

Defence Expenditure: Budgeted at Rs 2,590m. in 2013.

Education

Education is officially compulsory and free of charge for 11 years between the ages of five and 16. Primary education begins at five years of age and lasts for six years. Secondary education, beginning at the age of 11, lasts for up to seven years, comprising a first cycle of five years and a second of two years. At March 2005 up to 77% of pre-primary schools were privately run institutions. Primary and secondary education are available free of charge and became compulsory in 2005. According to UNESCO estimates, in 2009/10 enrolment at primary schools included 93% of pupils in the relevant age-group (males 92%; females 94%), while the comparable ratio for secondary schools in 2003/04 was 74% (males 74%; females 74%). The education system provides for instruction in seven Asian languages (71% of primary school children and 30% of secondary school children were studying at least one of these in 2005). The Government exercises indirect control of the large private sector in secondary education (in 2005 only 70 of 188 schools were state administered). The University of Mauritius had 7,531 students in 2006/07 (34.3% of whom were part-time students); in addition, many students receive further education abroad. A total of 7,221 students were enrolled in technical and vocational education in 2012. Of total expenditure by the central Government in 2011, Rs 10,329.3m. (12.9%) was for education.

MEXICO

Introductory Survey

LOCATION, CLIMATE, LANGUAGE, RELIGION, FLAG, CAPITAL

The United Mexican States is bordered to the north by the USA, and to the south by Guatemala and Belize. The Gulf of Mexico and the Caribbean Sea lie to the east, and the Pacific Ocean and Gulf of California to the west. The climate varies with altitude. The tropical southern region and the coastal lowlands are hot and wet, with an average annual temperature of 18°C (64°F), while the highlands of the central plateau are temperate. Much of the north and west is arid desert. In Mexico City, which lies at about 2,250 m (nearly 7,400 ft) above sea-level, temperatures are generally between 5°C (42°F) and 25°C (78°F). The country's highest recorded temperature is 58°C (136°F). The principal language is Spanish, spoken by more than 90% of the population, while about 8% speak indigenous languages, of which Náhuatl is the most widely spoken. Almost all of Mexico's inhabitants profess Christianity, and about 85% are adherents of the Roman Catholic Church. The national flag (proportions 4 by 7) has three equal vertical stripes from hoist to fly, of green, white and red, with the state emblem (a brown eagle, holding a snake in its beak, on a green cactus, with a wreath of oak and laurel beneath) in the centre of the white stripe. The capital is Mexico City.

CONTEMPORARY POLITICAL HISTORY

Historical Context

Conquered by Hernán Cortés in the 16th century, Mexico was ruled by Spain until the wars of independence of 1810–21. After the war of 1846, Mexico ceded about one-half of its territory to the USA. Attempts at political and social reform by the anti-clerical Benito Juárez precipitated civil war in 1857–60, and the repudiation of Mexico's external debts by Juárez in 1860 led to war with the United Kingdom, the USA and France. The Austrian Archduke Maximilian, whom France tried to install as Emperor of Mexico, was executed, on the orders of Juárez, in 1867. Order was restored during the dictatorship of Porfirio Díaz, which lasted from 1876 until the Revolution of 1910. The Constitution of 1917 embodied the aims of the Revolution by revising land ownership, drafting a labour code and curtailing the power of the Roman Catholic Church. From 1929–2000 the country was dominated by the Partido Revolucionario Institucional (PRI), for much of that time in an effective one-party system, although a democratic form of election was maintained. However, allegations of widespread electoral malpractice persistently arose in connection with PRI victories.

Domestic Political Affairs

In a presidential election held in 1976 the PRI candidate, José López Portillo, was elected with almost 95% of the votes cast. López Portillo initiated reforms to increase minority party representation in the legislature and to widen democratic participation. The high level of political participation in the presidential election of 1982 was without precedent, with left-wing groups taking part for the first time; however, the PRI's candidate, Miguel de la Madrid Hurtado, was successful. The concurrent elections to the Cámara Federal de Diputados (Federal Chamber of Deputies) resulted in another overwhelming victory for the PRI. The new President embarked on a programme of major economic reform, giving precedence to the repayment of Mexico's debts, a policy that imposed severe financial constraints upon the middle and lower classes, leading to growing disaffection among traditional PRI supporters. The opposition Partido Acción Nacional (PAN) made important gains at municipal elections in 1983. The PRI's effective response ensured success at the remaining elections, but provoked opposition allegations of electoral fraud. At elections in July 1985, the PRI secured all seven of the available state governorships and 288 of the 300 directly elective seats in the Cámara Federal de Diputados.

The formation of a six-party left-wing alliance, the Partido Mexicano Socialista (PMS), in 1987 and, in particular, the emergence of a dissident faction, the Corriente Democrática (CD), within the PRI were disturbing political developments for the ruling party. In 1988 the CD and four left-wing parties (including the PMS coalition) formed an electoral alliance, the Frente Democrático Nacional (FDN), headed by CD leader Cuauhtémoc Cárdenas Solórzano. The legitimacy of the PRI victory at the presidential and congressional elections in July was fiercely challenged by the opposition, following reports of widespread electoral fraud. For the first time ever, the opposition secured seats in the Senado (Senate).

The new Congreso de la Unión (Congress) immediately assumed the function of an electoral college, in order to investigate the claims of both sides. In September 1988 the allocation of 200 seats in the Cámara Federal de Diputados by proportional representation afforded the PRI a congressional majority and effective control of the electoral college. Opposition members withdrew from the Cámara in protest at the PRI's obstruction of the investigation, enabling the ruling party to ratify Carlos Salinas de Gortari as the new President. The results, although widely regarded as having been manipulated by the PRI, revealed a considerable erosion in support for the party.

Agreements on rescheduling Mexico's vast foreign debts were reached with the 'Paris Club' of official creditors in 1989, and with some 450 commercial banks in early 1990. An economic stability pact was also implemented, with the agreement of employers' organizations and trade unions. None the less, the country experienced severe labour unrest in 1989 in support of greater pay increases and in protest at the Government's divestment programme. In October proposed constitutional amendments were approved with the unexpected support of the PAN. A 'governability clause', whereby an absolute majority of seats in the Cámara Federal de Diputados would be awarded to the leading party, should it receive at least 35% of the votes at a general election, was criticized by the Partido de la Revolución Democrática (PRD), the successor party to the FDN.

In July 1991 the Federal Electoral Code was approved by the Cámara Federal de Diputados with support from all represented parties, except the PRD. The legislation contained provisions for the compilation of a new electoral roll, the issue of more detailed identification cards for voters, the modification of the Instituto Federal Electoral (IFE—Federal Electoral Institute), and the creation of a Tribunal Federal Electoral (Federal Electoral Tribunal, which, in 1996, became the Tribunal Electoral del Poder Judicial de la Federación).

At mid-term congressional elections in August 1991 the PRI won almost all of the 300 directly elective seats in the Cámara Federal de Diputados (plus 30 of the 200 seats awarded by proportional representation) and 31 of the 32 contested seats in the Senado. The return to the level of support that the PRI had enjoyed prior to the 1988 elections was largely attributed to the success of the Government's programme of economic reform. PRI victories at gubernatorial and legislative elections in several states during 1993 were again denounced by the opposition as fraudulent.

The Zedillo presidency, 1994–2000

In March 1994 Luis Donaldo Colosio, the PRI's presidential candidate, was assassinated at a campaign rally. Mario Aburto Martínez was identified as the apparently motiveless assassin. However, speculation that Colosio had been the victim of a conspiracy within the PRI establishment increased following the arrest of a number of party members associated with police and intelligence agencies in connection with the incident. The PRI subsequently named Ernesto Zedillo Ponce de León, a former cabinet minister and Colosio's campaign manager, as the party's presidential candidate. Zedillo was elected President on 21 August, ahead of the PAN candidate, Diego Fernández de Cevallos, and the PRD candidate, Cuauhtémoc Cárdenas. The PRI was also successful at the concurrent congressional elections. However, numerous incidents of electoral malpractice were reported.

The report of a special investigation into Colosio's murder, published in July 1994, concluded that Aburto Martínez had acted alone in the assassination, reversing the findings of a preliminary investigation, which had suggested the existence of a number of conspirators. Nevertheless, speculation that Colosio had been the first victim of a politically motivated campaign of violence, conducted by a cabal of senior PRI traditionalists in order to check the advance of the party's reformist wing, intensified following the murder, in September, of the PRI Secretary-General, José Francisco Ruiz Massieu. In November Ruiz Massieu's brother, Mario, resigned as Deputy Attorney-General, claiming that senior PRI officials, including the party's President and Secretary-General, had impeded his investigation into his brother's death. In February 1995 a report by the Attorney-General was highly critical of all previous investigations of the Colosio assassination, concluding that the murder had involved at least two gunmen. In the same month Raúl Salinas de Gortari, brother of former President Salinas, was arrested on charges of complicity in Ruiz Massieu's murder, and in April several new conspirators, including five state Governors, were implicated. In October two men were each sentenced to 18 years' imprisonment for the murder of the PRI Secretary-General. In October 1996 the case against Raúl Salinas was prejudiced further by the discovery of a body buried in the grounds of his property in Mexico City. Raúl Salinas was convicted of murder and, in January 1999, sentenced to 50 years' imprisonment (later reduced to almost 28 years); in August 2002 he was additionally charged with the embezzlement of up to 209m. new pesos from a secret presidential fund under his brother's control. In September 1999 Mario Ruiz Massieu committed suicide in the USA while awaiting trial on charges of laundering money gained from drugs-trafficking; he left a note repeating his earlier accusations against the PRI and blaming Zedillo and other senior officials for his own death and the assassination of Colosio.

In July 1996 the PRI, the PAN, the PRD and the Partido del Trabajo (PT, a labour party) reached consensus on reforms that would include introducing a directly elected governor of the Distrito Federal, increasing and regulating public financing for political parties, employing proportional representation in elections to the Senado, granting a right of vote to Mexican citizens resident abroad, and allowing the IFE greater independence. The reforms received congressional approval in August. However, in November, in apparent response to their diminishing share of the vote in recent municipal elections, PRI traditionalists secured the adoption by the Cámara Federal de Diputados of a series of amendments to the electoral reform bill, increasing public funding in 1997 for political parties by some 476%, pronouncing that to exceed campaign finance limits would no longer be a criminal or electoral offence, expanding the Government's access to the media, and restricting the right of opposition parties to form coalitions.

Meanwhile, in May 1996 President Zedillo dismissed Mexico City's chief of police following public outcry at the violent tactics employed by his officers to disperse a group of striking teachers in the capital. In the following months hundreds of police employees throughout the country were dismissed for incompetence or corruption, while army officers were increasingly appointed to positions within the police force. In March 1997 some 2,500 members of Mexico City's police force were replaced by army personnel, and in October an élite police unit was disbanded after accusations that as many as 35 of its members were implicated in the torture and murder of three youths in September. Several officers at the anti-abduction unit in the state of Morelos were also accused of torture and murder in early 1998, precipitating the resignation of the state's PRI Governor in May.

The PRI lost its overall majority for the first time at elections to the Cámara Federal de Diputados in July 1997, while the PRD and the PAN made substantial gains. The PRI retained its overall majority, albeit significantly reduced, at concurrent elections to the Senado, while the PAN and the PRD increased their representation. An informal congressional alliance between the PAN, the PRD, the Partido Verde Ecologista de México (PVEM) and the PT meant that opposition parties were able to take control of important legislative committees.

The Fox presidency, 2000–06

A presidential election was held on 2 July 2000. The PRI's candidate was the former Secretary of the Interior, Francisco Labastida Ochoa, while the former Governor of Guanajuato state, Vicente Fox Quesada, represented a PAN-PVEM alliance known as the Alianza por el Cambio (AC), and Cárdenas was once again the PRD's nominee (officially he stood for the PRD-dominated Alianza por México—AM). Fox secured 43% of the votes cast, while Labastida attracted 37% and Cárdenas 17%. Fox was thus elected President, ending the PRI's 71-year hegemony in Mexican government. In the concurrent elections to the

Congreso, the AC secured 223 of the 500 seats, compared with 209 won by the PRI and 68 by the AM. The PRI remained the largest grouping in the Senado, however. Fox took office as President on 1 December, stating that his priorities were a reduction in poverty, improved relations with the USA, and peace and reconciliation within Mexico.

In January 2002 the Government announced that an investigation was to be held into allegations that the state petroleum company, Petróleos Mexicanos (PEMEX), had covertly funded Labastida's presidential election campaign. A former director of PEMEX, Manuel Gómez-Peralta, was detained in connection with the allegations in May, and a former PEMEX President, Rogelio Montemayor, was arrested in Houston, Texas, USA, in October. In that month opposition parties demanded the reopening of investigations into allegations that Fox's presidential campaign had received substantial illegal foreign funding. In October 2003 the IFE fined both the PAN and the PVEM for accepting illegal campaign funding.

In November 2003 the Supreme Court ruled that prosecution for murder could proceed even in cases where no body had been found. The ruling enabled prosecutions to proceed for human rights abuses committed during the 'guerra sucia' ('dirty war') of the late 1970s; in February 2004 Miguel Nazar Haro, former director of the covert Dirección General de Seguridad, was arrested in connection with the disappearance of left-wing activist Jesús Piedra Ibarra in 1975. In mid-2004 the Supreme Court made a further ruling that cases concerning disappearance could be brought in connection with the suppression of dissent in the 1970s and 1980s. Meanwhile, a special prosecutor, Ignacio Carrillo, was appointed to investigate the role of, among others, former President Luis Echeverría in the 'guerra sucia'. In February 2005 the Supreme Court ruled that the Vienna Convention on genocide (which came into force in 2002) could not be applied retrospectively, and in July the case against Echeverría was dismissed on the grounds that there was no evidence of genocide. This dismissal, however, was itself overruled on appeal in November 2006, thereby reopening the possibility of a prosecution.

In March 2004 a scandal emerged surrounding the PRD Head of Government of the Distrito Federal, Andrés Manuel López Obrador, a likely candidate in the 2006 presidential election. A videotape appeared to show López Obrador's finance chief, Gustavo Ponce Meléndez, gambling large amounts at a casino in the USA (Ponce was arrested in October 2004). A further video recording came to light that apparently showed the Head of Government's former private secretary accepting money from a prominent Argentine businessman, Carlos Ahumada, who was accused of corruption. López Obrador denied any knowledge of either incident and claimed that a 'dirty tricks' campaign was being waged against him. Following a request by the Attorney-General's office the Cámara Federal de Diputados voted in April 2005 to remove López Obrador's immunity. Later that month as many as 1.2m. people participated in a demonstration in Mexico City in support of their mayor, who returned to his post the following day. The Attorney-General was subsequently dismissed and in May the new Attorney-General rejected all charges against López Obrador. In July he secured the PRD's presidential nomination.

Discord continued within the PRI during 2005 between the supporters of Elba Esther Gordillo Morales, the party's Secretary-General, and party President Roberto Madrazo Pintado in their respective campaigns to secure the nomination for the presidential election. In January Gordillo and the powerful teachers' union, the Sindicato Nacional de Trabajadores de la Educación (SNTE), of which she was President, launched the Nueva Alianza (NA) in order to consolidate support for her candidacy. In August a third faction, Unidad Democrática, more commonly known as Todos Unidos Contra Madrazo (TUCOM—Everyone United against Madrazo), elected Arturo Montiel, the outgoing Governor of the Estado de México, as its nominee for the PRI's presidential candidate. However, in October, following allegations of corruption, Montiel withdrew from the primary contest. It was widely assumed that Madrazo had been behind the allegations. A series of defections in late 2005 by prominent members of the PRI opposed to Madrazo further highlighted the divisions within the party. None the less, in November Madrazo won an overwhelming victory in the election for the PRI's presidential nomination.

Meanwhile, in October 2005 the former Secretary of Energy, Felipe Calderón Hinojosa, from the traditional, clericist wing of the PAN, unexpectedly won that party's 2006 presidential nomination. In December the PRI and the PVEM announced an alliance, Alianza por México, to contest the 2006 elections. The PRD and two smaller left-wing parties, Convergencia and the PT, also formed an alliance, Por el Bien de Todos (For the Good of Everyone), which later became the Frente Amplio Progresista (FAP).

The Calderón presidency, 2006–12

At the presidential election, held on 2 July 2006, the PAN's Calderón secured an extremely narrow margin of victory, of just 0.6% (243,934 votes out of almost 42m. cast), over López Obrador. According to official results, Calderón polled 35.9% of the total votes cast, compared with López Obrador's 35.3%. Madrazo, the PRI nominee, trailed in third place with 22.2%, a historic low for the party. López Obrador did not accept the results, alleging that electoral irregularities, combined with the narrow margin of defeat, undermined their legitimacy. Calderón was inaugurated as President on 1 December in a ceremony notable for its lack of celebration and ostentation. A week earlier López Obrador had held a ceremony in Mexico City's main square, declaring himself to be Mexico's legitimate President in front of a large crowd.

Results of concurrent elections to the Congreso were evenly distributed among the three leading parties, ensuring that the new President would face a legislature dominated by the opposition. The PAN secured 206 of the 500 seats in the Cámara Federal de Diputados, with the PRD-led Por el Bien de Todos alliance winning 158 seats and the PRI's Alianza por México garnering 123 seats. In the 128-seat Senado, the PAN won 52 seats, the Alianza por México 39 seats and Por el Bien de Todos 36 seats. Political obstacles in the Congreso threatened to undermine the new Government's ability to introduce reforms to the state sector, just as they had during President Fox's administration.

One of the first major challenges that the new Government faced was the increasing unrest in Oaxaca. In June 2006 some 70,000 teachers had begun industrial action in support of salary increases. Indigenous Indian rights activists and local farmers' co-operatives joined the accompanying demonstrations, which became violent when police and protesters clashed. President-elect Calderón dispatched 5,000 security personnel supported by armoured trucks and helicopters to retake control of the centre of the city. More than 150 people were subsequently arrested for their part in the protests, and many more were injured during violent confrontations. In total, 14 people were killed during the disturbances.

A law to reform the electoral system by reducing the influence of money in elections was approved with the votes of all three main parties in the Senado in September 2007 and entered into law in November. The provisions of the reform, *inter alia*, reduced the amount that a party could spend on an election campaign from 270m. to 40m. new pesos, granted each party a limited amount of publicity in the broadcast media, and prohibited the diffusion of propaganda that denigrated parties or candidates; the latter provision was in response to the negative campaign conducted by opponents of López Obrador that had preceded the 2006 presidential election.

Rapidly declining oil production, apparently owing to a lack of investment in exploration and refineries, led the PAN to propose energy reforms in early 2008 aimed at liberalizing the oil sector and allowing PEMEX to form alliances with foreign companies. The reforms were strongly opposed by the PRD, and facilitated the political revival of López Obrador, who led the protests, arguing that any private investment in PEMEX would threaten national sovereignty. However, the Congreso approved the energy reforms in October.

Meanwhile, in March 2008 an election to choose the President of the PRD highlighted the divisions in the party between a faction that supported López Obrador's continued claim to the presidency and refused to deal with what it considered to be an illegitimate Government, and those who favoured a more pragmatic approach. Initially, Alejandro Encinas, representing the pro-López Obrador faction, appeared to have defeated the moderate candidate, Jesús Ortega Martínez; however, both sides alleged that irregularities had occurred in the poll. In November the Tribunal Electoral del Poder Judicial de la Federación (TEPJF) ruled that Ortega was the rightful winner of the election, causing López Obrador to threaten to split away from the PRD.

Mid-term and gubernatorial elections

At the mid-term congressional elections on 5 July 2009, the PAN suffered a major defeat, securing only 143 seats in the Cámara Federal de Diputados (compared with its previous 206 seats), while the PRI won 237 seats (compared with its previous total of 108). The PVEM won a total of 22 seats, which, owing to the party's allegiance to the PRI, gave the PRI the necessary representation to have an absolute majority in the lower house. Participation in the election was low, estimated at some 44% of eligible voters. The PAN also suffered electoral losses in many of the state and municipal elections that took place concurrently. The scale of its defeat prompted the resignation of the party's President.

Gubernatorial, state and municipal elections took place in 12 states on 4 July 2010. The PRI retained six of the state governorships and secured control of an additional three (in Aguascalientes, Tlaxcala and Zacatecas), but lost the other three contested (in Oaxaca, Puebla and Sinaloa) to 'anti-PRI' alliances led by the PAN and the PRD. Meanwhile, six days before polling, the PRI candidate for the governorship of Tamaulipas, Rodolfo Torre Cantú, was assassinated, the killing being attributed to members of a drugs gang; his brother, Egidio Torre Cantú, was selected as the party's new candidate and retained the state governorship for the PRI.

The three main parties elected new leaders in late 2010 and early 2011: Gustavo Enrique Madero Muñoz, a senator from Chihuahua and the candidate preferred by Calderón, became President of the PAN; Humberto Moreira Valdés, hitherto Governor of Coahuila, was chosen as President of the PRI; and the PRD elected Jesús Zambrano Grijalva, who came from the same moderate faction of the party as his predecessor, Ortega, and supported the electoral alliances with the PAN.

A package of constitutional reforms, including proposed amendments that would allow members of the legislature to seek re-election for a second term of office and citizens to run for any office as independent candidates, was approved by the Senado in April 2011. Most of the measures were approved by the Congreso in April 2012, although it did not endorse re-election of deputies.

In November 2011 the Secretary of the Interior José Francisco Blake Mora was killed, together with seven other people, when a government-owned helicopter in which they were travelling crashed near Mexico City. Blake Mora's efforts to tackle the drugs cartels in Mexico led to some speculation that the incident had not been accidental, although no evidence emerged to substantiate these suspicions. Alejandro Poiré Romero, who had previously served as a government spokesperson on national security, was appointed as his successor.

The worst drought experienced in Mexico in 71 years led to crop failure and serious hardship in the north of the country during 2011. In January 2012 hundreds of farmers and indigenous Tarahumara Indians marched to Mexico City from Chihuahua state to demand increased assistance from the Government.

Recent developments: victory for Peña Nieto

The domestic political scene in early 2012 was dominated by the nomination and selection of the main parties' candidates for the presidential election scheduled for 1 July. The PRD once again selected Andrés Manuel López Obrador as its candidate, while the PRI chose former Governor of Mexico state Enrique Peña Nieto as their presidential nominee. After considerable internal disagreement, in early February the PAN finally selected Josefina Vásquez Mota as its candidate, the first time a woman had represented the party. In January the PRI announced its decision to separate from the electoral alliance it had formed with the NA. This was widely seen as an indication that the PRI wanted to distance itself from the NA's controversial leader Elba Esther Gordillo Morales who, as leader of the powerful teachers' union, the SNTE, was believed by many to have had undue influence over the political process. The electoral campaign was dominated by economic issues, particularly the high rates of poverty in the country, and the ongoing violence associated with the illegal drugs trade. Some commentators noted a lack of emphasis on the so-called 'war on drugs' in the PAN candidate's campaign, and suggested that the 60,000 people estimated to have been killed in drugs-related violence during the ruling party's six-year presidential term was likely to be a negative factor for many voters.

At the presidential election on 1 July 2012 Peña Nieto was successful for the PRI, securing some 39.2% of the votes cast, while López Obrador garnered 32.4% for the PRD-led alliance; Vásquez Mota of the ruling PAN was third-placed with just 26.1% of the votes. Both the PRD and PAN candidates alleged that the election had not been fair and that irregularities had included illegal levels of campaign spending, bribery and manipulation of media coverage. López Obrador refused to concede defeat, lodging a formal complaint over the allegations and demanding a full recount. The IFE ordered a partial recount, and on 7 July some 60,000 people marched through Mexico City in support of López Obrador. A further demonstration by some 30,000 people organized by a new student movement, Yo Soy 132, took place later that month. On 30 August the electoral tribunal announced the dismissal of all legal challenges against the results of the elections and ruled that no evidence had been found of 'vote-buying' or coercion. López Obrador, who continued to denounce the elections as fraudulent, urged his supporters to engage in 'peaceful, civil resistance' to the new Government, and in September announced the formation of a new political group, aimed predominantly at young people, the Movimiento de Regeneración Nacional (Morena—National Regeneration Movement).

Meanwhile, at concurrent congressional elections the PRI won the largest number of seats, with 213 in the Cámara Federal de Diputados and 54 in the Senado, but not sufficient to secure a legislative majority. The PAN secured 114 Cámara and 38 Senado seats, while the PRD garnered 104 and 22 seats, respectively.

At his inauguration on 1 December 2012 President Peña Nieto announced that the priorities of his Government would include securing peace within the country, reducing poverty and inequality, and reforming the education system. As part of his planned crime prevention programme, a new national police force of some 10,000 officers in 15 units was launched in mid-December, with the particular aim of reducing rates of kidnapping and extortion. In a gesture of co-operation the three main parties signed a 'Pact for Mexico' on the new Government's reform programme, which included 95 commitments focusing on social inclusion, security, accountability and democratic governance.

A series of reforms aimed at modernizing the education system and addressing corrupt practices in the sector was approved by the legislature in late February 2013. The measures included the establishment of a new independent body to oversee the profession and the introduction of regular assessments for teachers and schools. The changes proved controversial among some members of the profession, owing to fears that they signalled the onset of privatization, although the Government strongly denied this. The day after the approval of the reforms Elba Esther Gordillo Morales, the controversial leader of the powerful teachers' union, the SNTE, was arrested on suspicion of embezzling some US $200m. of union funds. Gordillo, who had led the union for some 20 years and had wielded considerable political influence in the role, was alleged to have spent millions of dollars on luxury property in the USA, a private aeroplane, and cosmetic surgery.

In March 2013, as part of the Pact for Mexico, Peña Nieto announced proposed reforms to the country's telecommunications sector. As well as liberalization of the sector to allow for foreign participation (of up to 49%), the plans presented to the Cámara de Diputados included the establishment of a new independent regulatory body, in charge of granting or rescinding licences, and the creation of two new national television channels. The proposals received federal congressional approval in April.

Human Rights and the Illegal Drugs Trade

Amnesty International published a report in 2003 that accused the Government of inefficiency and negligence in investigating the rape and murder of an estimated 307 women (and the disappearance of a further 500) in Ciudad Juárez over the previous 10 years. In 2004 some 130 government officials were investigated for negligence in the ongoing murder investigations. A further report by Amnesty International in that year alleged that the police and military routinely abused peasants, and that torture was commonly practised by police and in the justice system. In December 2004 President Fox announced a National Plan for Human Rights, aimed at eliminating torture and abuse. A subsequent report, commissioned by Fox acknowledged government responsibility in the massacres, torture and 'disappearances' of the 1970s.

In November 2002 the investigation into the 'guerra sucia' of the late 1970s resulted in the convictions of Brig.-Gen. Mario Acosta and Gen. Francisco Quirós on charges of protecting the operations of the Juárez cartel; they also faced charges over the disappearance of 143 activists. Despite efforts by President Fox to address the crime problem, drugs-related crime continued to escalate as the amount of narcotics crossing the Mexican–US border increased. It appeared that an internecine war between

the Tijuana, Golfo and Sinaloa cartels was taking place in the north of Mexico. During 2005 more than 180 people were killed in Nuevo Laredo, Tamaulipas, in what appeared to be an ongoing conflict between two drugs cartels.

Upon his election in 2006 President Calderón announced that law enforcement would form one of his priorities in office. A major offensive was subsequently launched in December against the activities of the drugs cartels in Michoacán state with the deployment of 7,000 troops and federal police officers. A second major operation was launched in Tijuana, Baja California, in January 2007, while later in the same month some 9,000 troops were sent into the states of Sinaloa, Durango and Chihuahua. Meanwhile, Calderón was highly commended by the US authorities for his decision in January to allow the extradition of 15 drugs-trafficking suspects to the USA. The extradition of the individuals (who included the head of the Golfo cartel and senior figures from the Sinaloa and Tijuana cartels) represented a significant change in policy from previous administrations, which had refused to allow extradition until suspects had faced a Mexican court. In January 2008 the arrest, in Culiacán, Sinaloa, of Alfredo Beltrán Leyva, a senior leader of the Sinaloa cartel, was one of a number of important successes in the offensive. The arrest, however, provoked further battles between rival factions of the Sinaloa-based Arellano Félix cartel, one loyal to Beltrán Leyva and the other to the notorious drugs-trafficker Joaquín Guzmán ('El Chapo'). Drugs-related violence escalated in 2008, with a reported 6,837 killings, more than twice the murder toll of the previous year. As previously, the violence was particularly, but not exclusively, concentrated in the states of Baja California, Chihuahua and Sinaloa, with 12 decapitated bodies also discovered in Yucatán in August, and a further dozen found in Chilpancingo, Guerrero, in December.

Confronted by widespread insecurity about the increasing crime rate, Calderón held a summit in August 2008, which led to a three-year plan to introduce 75 anti-crime measures, including the construction of maximum-security gaols and a national database to track mobile telephone usage. Nevertheless, the Government failed to inspire confidence about the security situation in many Mexicans. In late August more than 200,000 people filled the capital's main square in a night-time demonstration to denounce not only murders, kidnappings and drugs-trafficking, but also alleged police and government complicity and corruption. The arrest of one of the Arellano Félix brothers, Eduardo, in October, was followed by the revelation that two senior officials in the government unit for the investigation of organized crime, the Subprocuraduría de Investigación Especializada en Delincuencia Organizada (SIEDO), were in the pay of the Beltrán Leyva cartel. The SIEDO's reputation was damaged further in November when its former head, Noé Ramírez, was accused of having accepted US $450,000 from the Sinaloa cartel in exchange for supplying information about police investigations.

Despite the deployment of some 40,000 troops in the war against the drugs cartels, army incursions into the problem areas had little impact and tended to exacerbate violence. In a renewed campaign against drugs gangs in Ciudad Juárez in March 2009, 7,000 troops and police were deployed in the city, but persistent fears about the role of corrupt officials continued to hamper progress. In May a judge, 10 mayors and 17 other senior officials from Michoacán state were arrested and charged with drugs-related offences. Moreover, in July 29 state police officers were arrested in connection with the massacre of 12 federal agents whose bodies were dumped by a road in Michoacán in that month.

Ongoing violence in the country was brought to international attention in March 2010. First, 13 people were killed in Acapulco, a southern Mexican beach resort popular with US tourists. Some of the decapitated victims' bodies were dumped in scenic areas frequented by tourists. Second, three people associated with the US consulate in Ciudad Juárez (two of whom were US citizens) were murdered, provoking expressions of outrage from the US authorities. The security situation continued to deteriorate throughout 2010, amid signs that the violence was spreading to states that had previously been less affected, such as Tamaulipas and Nuevo León. In July the director of a prison in Durango was arrested and accused of allowing prisoners to carry out contract killings at night, using prison weapons and vehicles, for gangs involved in organized crime; the prisoners were alleged to have perpetrated three massacres in the city of Torreón. The murders, in August and September, of four mayors (bringing the total number of mayors killed that year to 10) followed that of the

PRI candidate for the governorship of Tamaulipas in June. In August the bodies of 72 migrants from various Central and South American countries were discovered in Tamaulipas; the massacre was attributed to members of the Zetas gang and prompted the resignation of the head of the National Institute of Migration. A leading member of the Zetas gang was arrested in October 2012 on suspicion of ordering the massacre and of organizing the escape of 131 inmates from the Piedras Negras prison in Coahuila, during the same period.

The Government released official statistics on drugs-related killings for the first time in January 2011: the number of deaths rose to 15,273 in 2010 from 9,614 in 2009 (6,837 in 2008 and 2,826 in 2007). The number of drugs-related murders in 2011 fell to 12,284. In January 2013 a national newspaper reported that 12,394 people died in violence related to organized crime in 2012. The total number of murders carried out during Calderón's six-year term was estimated at more than 60,000.

In January 2011, in response to escalating violence in Nuevo León, particularly around its capital, Monterrey (where more than 120 people, including 20 police officers, had reportedly been killed that month), the Government deployed troops to conduct joint patrols with police officers in the state. According to unofficial figures, drugs-related killings in Nuevo León had increased from some 99 in 2009 to 610 in 2010. In the first week of January 38 people were killed in drugs-related violence in the state of Guerrero shortly before gubernatorial elections. In the same month three mayors were assassinated in Coahuila, Morelos and Oaxaca states. In March 2011 the municipal government in Ciudad Juárez, where more than 3,100 people had been killed in 2010, announced the closure of more than 2,000 of the city's streets. A series of marches held in some 20 cities and towns nation-wide in April 2011 in protest against drugs-related violence coincided with the discovery in San Fernando, Tamaulipas, of several mass graves, containing a total of 145 bodies. The local leader of the Zetas gang, Omar Martín Estrada Luna, was arrested in connection with the murders and was also accused of involvement in the massacre of the 72 migrants whose bodies were found in the same area in 2010. Further mass graves containing about 40 bodies were found in Sinaloa and Durango states in April and were believed to be the result of a struggle between the Zetas and Sinaloa cartels to control territory in that part of the country. A further 20 members of the Zetas gang were arrested that month, together with 16 police officers accused of protecting the criminals. Targeted attacks against prominent public figures continued in mid-2011 with the assassination of a senior anti-drugs investigator in Chihuahua state, a mayor in Michoacán, a union leader in Morelos and a prison governor in Durango. A prominent crime journalist, his wife and son and a newspaper editor were also among those assassinated by the gangs. Twelve suspected members of the Zetas gang were killed in an armed confrontation with security forces in Tamaulipas and 11 members of the La Familia gang were shot dead in a similar operation in May. High-profile arrests continued in mid-2011 with the capture of senior members of the Sinaloa, La Familia and Zetas gangs. In August some 80 members of the Zetas gang were arrested following an arson attack on a casino in Monterrey in which 53 people were killed. The Government declared three days of national mourning after the attack, which was thought to have been carried out as part of an extortion operation by the Zetas gang. In late 2011 there was a marked increase in violence in Veracruz in the east of the country as the Zetas gang became involved in a territorial battle with the Nueva Generación gang. In one incident in November 35 bodies were dumped across the Boca del Rio–Veracruz highway. The Government responded by replacing the municipal police force with armed troops, but the violence continued, including on the day that troops began operations, when 16 bus passengers were killed in the city of Veracruz. Further arrests of senior gang members during 2012, including those of the leaders of the Golfo and Acapulco cartels, did not appear to have any immediate impact on the murder rate. The highly significant shooting of Heriberto Lazcano, the leader of the Zetas gang, by security forces in October, was somewhat undermined when a group of Lazcano's armed associates stole his body from the mortuary where it had been taken after his death. The capture and arrest of Jonathan Salas, known to be the security chief of Mexico's most notorious drugs-trafficker, Joaquín Guzmán ('El Chapo'), in February 2013 was seen as a considerable success for the new Government of President Peña Nieto. However, the ongoing problems of corruption and official complicity, illustrated in January 2013 by the arrest of more than 150 police officers

suspected of having links with the cartels in northern Mexico, continued to undermine popular confidence in the Government's ability to tackle drugs-related crime. One of the most visible symptoms of this lack of confidence was the increase in vigilante groups establishing self-styled security and policing operations in the areas of the country most affected by drugs violence.

In February 2012 a total of 44 inmates were killed and 29 escaped during a riot at a high security prison near Monterrey, Nuevo León. According to reports the prison governor, deputy governor and head of security were all affiliated to the Zetas cartel and the deaths were largely caused by fighting between rival gangs inside the prison. The incident illustrated the ongoing problem of high-level institutional corruption, which continued to impede efforts to combat drugs-related violent crime in the country. As similar incidents continued during the year, a total of 132 prisoners escaped from a prison near the US border in September, by means of a hand-dug tunnel, while in December 24 people were killed in a gun battle inside a prison in Durango state during an attempted mass escape.

In November 2011 Mexican human rights activists filed an official complaint at the International Criminal Court in The Hague, Netherlands, urging the institution to investigate a potential link between the Government's anti-drugs policies and the increasing number of civilian deaths. In the same month the US-based human rights organization Human Rights Watch published a report which alleged that the Mexican authorities had committed widespread human rights abuses in its efforts to curb the illegal drugs trade.

Zapatista Insurgency

On 1 January 1994 armed Indian groups numbering 1,000–3,000 took control of four municipalities of the southern state of Chiapas. The rebels issued the Declaration of the Lacandona Jungle, identifying themselves as the Ejército Zapatista de Liberación Nacional—EZLN (after Emiliano Zapata, who championed the land rights of Mexican peasants during the 1910–17 Revolution), and detailed a series of demands for economic and social change in the region, culminating in a declaration of war against the Government and a statement of intent to depose the 'dictator', President Salinas. A charismatic rebel spokesman, identified as 'subcomandante Marcos' (later tentatively identified as Rafael Sebastián Guillén Vicente, a former professor at the Universidad Autónoma Metropolitana), stated that the insurgency had been timed to coincide with the implementation of the North American Free Trade Agreement (NAFTA), which the rebels considered to be the latest in a series of segregative government initiatives adopted at the expense of indigenous groups. Negotiations between the Zapatistas and government representatives concluded with the publication of a document detailing 34 demands of the EZLN, and the Government's response to them. A preliminary accord was reached following the Government's broad acceptance of many of the rebels' stipulations, including an acceleration of the wide-ranging anti-poverty programme in the region, the incorporation of traditional Indian structures of justice and political organization, and a commitment from the Government to investigate the impact of NAFTA and recent land reform legislation on Indian communities. Official figures suggested that 100–150 guerrillas, soldiers and civilians had been killed during the conflict, while the Roman Catholic Church estimated that there had been as many as 400 casualties. Tensions, however, continued over the following years, with attempts to reach a definitive accord between the Zapatistas and the Government proving unsuccessful. In 1997 several thousand Zapatistas and their sympathizers staged a peaceful demonstration in Mexico City, during which the EZLN inaugurated the Frente Zapatista de Liberación Nacional, a political movement that embodied the Zapatistas' ideology. In December there was widespread disquiet at the killing of 45 Indians in a church in the village of Acteal, in the municipality of Chenalhó, Chiapas. Emilio Chuayffet, the Secretary of the Interior, and Julio César Ruiz Ferro, the Governor of Chiapas, were forced to resign, and April 1998 Gen. Julio César Santiago Díaz, acting chief of staff of Chiapas state police at the time of the massacre, was charged with failing to intervene to prevent the bloodshed. In September 1999 Jacinto Arias, mayor of Chenalhó at the time of the massacre, was convicted on charges of supplying the weapons used in the massacre and sentenced to 35 years' imprisonment. In November 2002 18 people were each sentenced to 36 years' imprisonment for their involvement in the deaths as part of a paramilitary group with links to the PRI; they joined 70 others previously convicted.

In February 2001 subcomandante Marcos and other Zapatista leaders began a tour of Mexico, culminating in a rally in Mexico City attended by some 150,000 people, in support of indigenous rights legislation. In March, the EZLN announced that formal dialogue with the Government would recommence and subcomandante Marcos successfully negotiated the dismantling of the remaining three garrisons in Chiapas. In April the Congreso approved amendments to six articles of the Constitution, which recognized and guaranteed indigenous political, legal, social and economic rights, and prohibited discrimination against Indians based on race and tribal affiliation. However, the legislation fell short of granting indigenous peoples the right to autonomy over land and natural resources; in response, the EZLN suspended all contact with the Government.

Foreign Affairs

Relations with the USA

Mexico's foreign policy has been determined largely by relations with the USA. The rapid expansion of petroleum production from the mid-1970s gave Mexico a new independence, empowering it to favour the left-wing regimes in Cuba and Nicaragua, opposed by the USA, during the 1980s. In February 1985 relations between Mexico and the USA deteriorated following the murder of an agent of the US Drug Enforcement Administration (DEA) by Mexican drugs-traffickers. The situation worsened in 1990, when a Mexican physician was abducted, by DEA agents in Mexico, and taken to the USA to be arrested on charges relating to the murder. Meanwhile, relations between Mexico and the USA remained tense, largely because of disagreement over the problem of illegal immigration from Mexico into the USA and Mexico's failure to take effective action against the illegal drugs trade. This situation improved following the deportation to the USA in 1996 of Juan García Abrego, the alleged head of the Golfo drugs cartel, and in the following year the USA 'certified' Mexico as a country co-operating in its campaign against drugs-trafficking. Bilateral relations were strained in 1998, when a major US counter-narcotics operation was conducted in Mexico, without Mexican authorization.

NAFTA, comprising Mexico, the USA and Canada, took effect from 1 January 1994. Among the Agreement's provisions were the gradual reduction of tariffs on 50% of products over a period of 10–15 years (some 57% of tariffs on agricultural trade between the USA and Mexico were removed immediately), and the establishment, by Mexico and the USA, of a North American Development Bank (NADBank) charged with the funding of initiatives for the rehabilitation of the two countries' common border. From January 2003 tariffs on a number of agricultural products were reduced or removed entirely, provoking widespread discontent among Mexico's 25m.-strong rural community. In particular, they pointed to the greater subsidies received by US farmers and to a poor transport infrastructure, which resulted in higher costs. Following the collapse, in September 2003, of the fifth Ministerial Conference of the World Trade Organization (WTO) in Cancún, Mexico joined the group of developing countries led by Brazil that opposed US-European Union (EU, see p. 281) subsidies of agricultural products.

The Fox Government sought to persuade the US Administration of George W. Bush, which took office in 2001, to adopt a more liberal position on Mexican immigrants to the USA. However, progress on immigration policy was suspended following the terrorist attacks in the USA on 11 September 2001, and proposals to tighten security on the US–Mexican border were approved by the US Congress in 2002. In March of that year, following a summit meeting in Monterrey, the two Presidents announced a 'smart border' partnership agreement, intended to facilitate the legal entry of Mexican people and goods into the USA while, at the same time, securing the frontier against possible acts of terrorism. In September, however, Fox requested that the emphasis in US-Mexican relations be shifted back to bilateral issues, which had been neglected in favour of border security. In the same month Mexico unilaterally withdrew from the Inter-American Treaty of Reciprocal Assistance (the Rio Treaty), the defence pact linking Mexico to the USA, resulting in a deterioration in relations with the USA.

In March 2003, with Mexican public opinion strongly against armed intervention to remove the regime of Saddam Hussain in Iraq, President Fox risked harming relations with both the USA and Spain by stating his opposition to war. His stance was all the more significant owing to Mexico's place as one of the 10 non-permanent members of the UN Security Council. In January 2004 the announcement of a revised US immigration initiative,

which offered significantly less to Mexican immigrants in the USA than had been hoped, was met with disappointment by the Mexican Government. In the same month US officials began managing the security arrangements for US-bound flights leaving Mexico City's airport.

Throughout 2005 tensions remained high between Mexico and the USA over border security and escalating drugs-related violence in Mexico (see Human Rights and the Illegal Drugs Trade). The Mexican Government expressed strong opposition to the USA's Secure Border Initiative, which was announced in late 2005 and envisaged the construction of security fences along some 1,130 km of the most accessible sections of the border in order to deter illegal immigrants. Despite the objections of the Mexican authorities, the proposal, involving the construction of a triple barrier, monitored by look-out towers, sensors and cameras, was approved by the US Congress in 2006. The Mexican Government appealed directly to President Bush to veto the bill, claiming that it would harm bilateral relations and be contrary to the spirit of co-operation necessary in guaranteeing the security of the common border. Various indigenous groups with territories that straddled the border also expressed concern at the proposal and others speculated that, by forcing Mexicans to take more dangerous routes into US territory, there would be an increase in the death rate of migrants. By early 2010 some 1,035 km of the border fencing had been constructed. In August 2010 US President Barack Obama enacted legislation providing for the deployment of an additional 1,500 agents to patrol the US–Mexican border, as well as unmanned surveillance drones. In late 2012, in a further attempt to increase border security, the US authorities announced new plans to install six towers equipped with highly sophisticated camera and radar technology capable of detecting a person at a distance of up to 8 km.

US-Mexican relations had deteriorated somewhat following Calderón's accession to the presidency in 2006, partly as a result not only of the USA's continued uncompromising stance on border security but also of Mexico's improved relations with Cuba and Venezuela. None the less, as a result of negotiations in March 2007 between Presidents Bush and Calderón, Bush promised the Mexican Government some US $500m. per year in order to combat drugs-related crime. The Mérida Initiative, as it became known, was signed into law in July 2008, although was subsequently reduced. In 2009, however, the US Senate voted to reduce the Mérida Initiative budget to $300m. None the less, the new US Administration of President Obama pledged to increase border security and to assist Mexico in fighting the drugs cartels, including the provision of $700m. for helicopters and law enforcement equipment. The move reflected concerns that drugs-related violence was increasingly affecting US border towns. President Calderón addressed the US Congress during a state visit in May 2010, notably urging legislators to introduce measures to restrict the flow of weapons from the USA to drugs gangs in Mexico.

The killing, in February 2011, of a US immigration and customs enforcement agent in the central state of San Luis Potosí, allegedly by members of the Zetas drugs gang, was strongly condemned by the US authorities, which subsequently announced that they would seek the extradition of suspects who had been detained in Mexico in connection with the murder. Tensions arose between Calderón and US officials that month, following the publication of leaked diplomatic cables in which US ambassador to Mexico Carlos Pascual had questioned the abilities of Mexico's intelligence and security services. Pascual resigned as ambassador in March. Meanwhile, revelations that the US Bureau of Alcohol, Tobacco, Firearms and Explosives, an agency of the Department of Justice, had allowed thousands of weapons to be smuggled into Mexico from the USA in 2009 and 2010, under an operation apparently intended to monitor the movement of arms from US smugglers to Mexican drugs-traffickers, provoked outrage in Mexico. In January 2012 the USA Government admitted that serious mistakes had been made under the operation, known as 'Fast and Furious', which was to be investigated by the US House of Representatives' Oversight Committee. The Chair of the committee, Darrell Issa, claimed that at least 200 Mexicans had been killed by weapons brought into their country from the USA under the operation.

Relations between the two countries were jeopardized in August 2012 when a diplomatic car carrying two US government officials was repeatedly shot at by a large group of Mexican police officers. The US officials were unhurt, owing to the fact that they had been travelling in an armoured vehicle. In November a total of 14 police officers, who had together fired more than 150 bullets at the car, were charged with attempted murder.

The fundamental difference of viewpoint between Mexico and the USA regarding the illegal drugs trade was starkly illustrated in late 2011 when Calderón urged the US Government to combat the 'insatiable appetite for drugs' in the USA, which had led to such violence in Mexico. Former President Fox joined the debate by appealing to the US Government to legalize drug use, claiming that the consumption of illegal drugs in the USA was responsible for prolonged and horrifying violence in his country. In addition, Calderón alleged that violence near the border with the USA was exacerbated by the US policy of deporting rather than prosecuting illegal immigrants. In 2010 some 50% of the estimated 400,000 illegal Mexican immigrants deported from the USA had criminal records, and many of these were believed to join gangs upon their return to Mexico. In late 2011 President Obama reiterated his country's commitment to 'unprecedented co-operation' between the two countries in fighting criminal organizations, although US Vice-President Joe Biden stated, during an official visit to Mexico in March 2012, that there would be no change in US policy on the illegal drugs trade, and particularly the issue of decriminalization.

Other external relations

During the 1990s Mexico concluded agreements for greater economic co-operation and increased bilateral trade with Colombia and Venezuela (as the Group of Three, see p. 461), and with Bolivia, Costa Rica and the EU. A free trade accord with Nicaragua came into force in 1998; a similar accord with Chile was signed in that year and came into force in 1999. A trade agreement with Guatemala, Honduras and El Salvador (the Northern Triangle) was concluded in 2000. In March of that year Mexico and the EU signed a free trade agreement, the first to be signed between the EU and a Latin American country. The accord provided for the gradual elimination of tariffs on industrial and agricultural products, the progressive liberalization of trade in services, and preferential access to public procurement; it also obliged the signatories to respect democratic principles and human rights. In 2003 Mexico signed an Organization of American States agreement on regional security, which was also aimed at increasing co-operation on social and environmental issues. In 2004 the Secretary of Foreign Affairs, Luis Ernesto Derbez, announced Mexico's aim of seeking permanent representation on the UN Security Council. In December 2011 Mexico concluded a free trade agreement with Peru which aimed to double bilateral trade between the two countries over the next five years. The agreement was also established with the aim of increasing both countries' participation in a proposed trade accord between Asia and the Latin American Pacific Rim nations. A free trade agreement between Mexico, Nicaragua, El Salvador, Honduras, Guatemala and Costa Rica, designed to improve the integration and efficiency of production chains between the countries, became operational in September 2012.

CONSTITUTION AND GOVERNMENT

The present Mexican Constitution was proclaimed on 5 February 1917, at the end of the Revolution, which began in 1910, against the regime of Porfirio Díaz. Its provisions regarding religion, education, and the ownership and exploitation of mineral wealth reflect the long revolutionary struggle against the concentration of power in the hands of the Roman Catholic Church and the large landowners, and the struggle that culminated, in the 1930s, in the expropriation of the properties of foreign petroleum companies. It has been amended from time to time.

Mexico is a federal republic comprising 31 states and a Distrito Federal (Federal District, comprising the capital). Under the 1917 Constitution, legislative power is vested in the bicameral Congreso de la Unión (Congress), elected by universal adult suffrage. The Senado (Senate) has 128 members (four from each state and the Distrito Federal), serving a six-year term. The Cámara Federal de Diputados (Federal Chamber of Deputies), directly elected for three years, has 500 seats, of which 300 are filled from single-member constituencies. The remaining 200 seats, allocated so as to achieve proportional representation, are filled from parties' lists of candidates. Executive power is held by the President, directly elected for six years at the same time as the Senado. He governs with the assistance of an appointed Cabinet. Each state has its own constitution and is administered by a Governor (elected for six years) and an elected Chamber of Deputies. The Distrito Federal is administered by a Head of Government.

REGIONAL AND INTERNATIONAL CO-OPERATION

Mexico is a signatory nation to the North American Free Trade Agreement (NAFTA, see p. 378). The country is a member of the Inter-American Development Bank (IDB, see p. 341), of the Latin American Integration Association (ALADI, see p. 370), and of the Community of Latin American and Caribbean States (see p. 475), which was formally inaugurated in December 2011. In June 2012 the Presidents of Mexico, Chile, Colombia and Peru signed a framework agreement in Antofagasta, Chile, creating a new regional economic bloc, the Pacific Alliance (see p. 463). Mexico has observer status at the Southern Common Market (Mercado Común del Sur—Mercosur, see p. 439), and in 2004 announced its intention of seeking full membership of the group.

Mexico became a member of the UN in 1945. As a contracting party to the General Agreement on Tariffs and Trade, Mexico joined the World Trade Organization (see p. 444) on its establishment in 1995. Mexico was admitted to the Asia-Pacific Economic Co-operation group (APEC, see p. 208) in 1993, and joined the Organisation for Economic Co-operation and Development (OECD, see p. 388) in 1994. The country is a member of the Group of 15 (G15, see p. 461) and of the Group of 20 (G20, see p. 466).

ECONOMIC AFFAIRS

In 2011, according to estimates by the World Bank, Mexico's gross national income (GNI), measured at average 2009–11 prices, was US $1,060,221m., equivalent to $9,240 per head (or $15,060 per head on an international purchasing-power parity basis). During 2002–11, it was estimated, the population increased at an average annual rate of 1.3%, while gross domestic product (GDP) per head increased, in real terms, by an average of 1.1% per year. Overall GDP increased, in real terms, at an average annual rate of 2.3% in 2002–11; GDP increased by 3.9% in 2011.

Agriculture (including forestry and fishing) contributed 3.8% of GDP in 2011 and engaged 13.9% of the employed labour force in 2012. The staple food crops are maize, wheat, sorghum, barley, rice, beans and potatoes. The principal cash crops are coffee, cotton, sugar cane, and fruit and vegetables (particularly tomatoes). Livestock-raising and fisheries are also important. During 2002–11 agricultural GDP increased at an average annual rate of 1.1%; agricultural GDP increased by 2.9% in 2010, but decreased by 2.6% in 2011.

Industry (including mining, manufacturing, construction and power) engaged 23.8% of the employed labour force in 2012 and provided 35.6% of GDP in 2011. During 2002–11 industrial GDP increased by an average of 1.8% per year; industrial GDP increased by 4.0% in 2011.

Mining contributed 10.2% of GDP in 2011, and, together with electricity production and distribution, engaged 0.9% of the employed labour force in 2012. During 2002–11 the GDP of the mining sector increased by an average of 0.3% per year; mining GDP increased by 1.2% in 2010, but decreased by 1.0% in 2011. Mexico has large reserves of petroleum and natural gas (mineral products accounted for an estimated 17.1% of total export earnings in 2011). Zinc, salt, silver, copper, celestite and fluorite are also major mineral exports. In addition, mercury, bismuth, antimony, cadmium, manganese and phosphates are mined, and there are significant reserves of uranium.

Manufacturing provided 17.7% of GDP in 2011 and engaged 15.3% of the employed labour force in 2012. Manufacturing GDP decreased at an average annual rate of 1.8% in 2002–11; the sector's GDP increased by 4.9% in 2011. The *maquila* sector (where intermediate materials produced on US territory are processed or assembled on the Mexican side of the border) is an important contributor to the economy. *Maquila* exports were valued at an estimated 111,823.8m. new pesos in 2006, equivalent to 45% of total revenue from manufacturing exports. An estimated 1.4m. people were employed in the *maquila* sector in 2010.

Construction engaged 7.5% of the employed labour force in 2012 and provided 6.5% of GDP in 2011. During 2002–11 construction GDP increased by an average annual rate of 2.6% per year; construction GDP declined by 0.6% in 2010, but increased by 4.6% in 2011

Energy is derived principally from hydrocarbons, coal and hydroelectric power. In 2010, according to the World Bank, some 52.2% of total output of electricity production was derived from natural gas, 16.1% came from petroleum, 13.8% came from hydroelectric plants and 12.1% was generated from coal-powered plants. In 2012, according to Petróleos Mexicanos, oil production was an estimated 2.5m. barrels per day, roughly the same level as the previous year. However, production of natural gas was estimated to have decreased to 6,380m. cu ft per day, a 3.2% decrease on the previous year. In 2010 mineral imports were estimated at 8.0% of total merchandise imports.

The services sector contributed 60.7% of GDP in 2011 and engaged 62.3% of the employed labour force in 2012. The GDP of the sector increased by an average of 3.0% per year in 2002–11; the sector expanded by 4.8% in 2011. Tourism is one of Mexico's principal sources of foreign exchange. In 2011 there were an estimated 23.4m. foreign visitors to Mexico (mostly from the USA and Canada). Revenue from the sector totalled US $10,006m. in the same year.

In 2011 Mexico recorded a visible merchandise trade deficit of an estimated US $1,171m., and there was a deficit of $11,086m. on the current account of the balance of payments. In 2011 the principal source of imports (49.7%) was the USA, which was also the principal market for exports (78.5%). The People's Republic of China was also an increasingly important trading partner. The principal exports in 2011 were mechanical and electrical appliances, transport equipment, and mineral products; the principal imports in 2011 were mechanical and electrical appliances, mineral products, transport equipment, base metals, chemical products, plastics and rubber articles.

In 2011 there was an estimated budgetary deficit of 365,414m. new pesos, equivalent to 2.5% of GDP. Mexico's general government gross debt was 6,285,472m. new pesos in 2011, equivalent to 43.1% of GDP. Mexico's external debt totalled US $200,081m. at the end of 2010, of which $111,467m. was public and publicly guaranteed debt. In that year, the cost of debt-servicing long-term public and publicly guaranteed debt and repayments to the IMF was equivalent to 9.8% of the value of exports of goods, services and income (excluding workers' remittances). The average annual rate of inflation was 4.3% in 2002–11. Consumer prices increased by an average of 3.4% in 2011. An estimated 5.2% of the total labour force were unemployed in 2012. It was estimated that remittances were Mexico's second largest source of foreign income, after petroleum exports. In 2012 remittances from Mexicans abroad totalled $22,446m.

The Mexican economy has been vulnerable to economic repercussions associated with its reliance on oil revenues and its excessive dependence on exports to the USA. Following the global financial crisis of 2009 Mexico's business sector suffered from the serious depreciation of the peso. In an attempt to counter this the Banco de México undertook a large-scale purchase of Mexican pesos, which drew on a significant portion of the country's international reserves. Inflows of remittances continued to decline in 2011, owing to stricter US anti-immigration legislation and high unemployment in the USA, particularly in the construction sector, which had engaged a large section of the migrant labour force. However, during 2012 several foreign manufacturers announced plans to increase their operations in Mexico, creating a total of 500,000 new jobs. Car manufacturers were the most significant among these, with Japan's Nissan announcing US $2,000m. of new investment in the country. It was hoped that efforts by the new Government of President Enrique Peña Nieto to increase trade links within Latin America, together with the elimination of tariffs on traded goods within the Pacific Alliance bloc in early 2013, would reduce the country's reliance on the US market. Although the dramatic upsurge in drugs-related violence in 2012 had a negative impact on both foreign investment in Mexico and the important tourist industry, investment was expected to increase significantly in 2013, owing, in large part, to the new Government's reform agenda, which included commitments on transparency and accountability in the business sector and the liberalization of the energy sector. GDP growth was forecast to decline from 4.0% in 2012 to 3.6% in 2013, before increasing slightly to a predicted 3.8% in 2014.

PUBLIC HOLIDAYS

2014: 1 January (New Year's Day), 3 February (Constitution Day), 17 March (Birthday of Benito Juárez), 17 April (Maundy Thursday)*, 18 April (Good Friday)*, 1 May (Labour Day), 5 May (Anniversary of the Battle of Puebla)*, 16 September (Independence Day), 2 November (All Souls' Day)*, 17 November (Anniversary of the Revolution), 12 December (Day of Our Lady of Guadalupe)*, 25 December (Christmas).

* Widely celebrated unofficial holidays.

Statistical Survey

Sources (unless otherwise stated): Instituto Nacional de Estadística, Geografía e Informática (INEGI), Edif. Sede, Avda Patriotismo 711, Torre A, 10°, Col. San Juan Mixcoac, Del. Benito Juárez, 03730 México, DF; tel. (55) 5278-1000 (ext. 1282); fax (55) 5278-1000 (ext. 1523); e-mail comunicacionsocial@inegi.org.mx; internet www.inegi.org.mx; Banco de México, Avda 5 de Mayo 1, Col. Centro, Del. Cuauhtémoc, 06059 México, DF; tel. (55) 5237-2000; fax (55) 5237-2370; internet www.banxico.org.mx.

Area and Population

AREA, POPULATION AND DENSITY

Area (sq km)	
Continental	1,959,248
Islands	5,127
Total	1,964,375*
Population (census and by-census results)	
29 October 2005	103,263,388
12 June 2010	
Males	54,855,231
Females	57,481,307
Total	112,336,538
Population (official estimates at mid-year)	
2011	115,618,330
2012	116,901,761
2013	118,129,240
Density (per sq km) at mid-2013	60.1

* 758,449 sq miles.
† Source: Consejo Nacional de Población (CONAPO), México, DF.

POPULATION BY AGE AND SEX
(official estimates at mid-2013)

	Males	Females	Total
0–14	17,135,993	16,418,076	33,554,069
15–64	36,965,861	39,871,710	76,837,571
65 and over	3,551,773	4,185,827	7,737,600
Total	57,653,627	60,475,613	118,129,240

Source: Consejo Nacional de Población (CONAPO), México, DF.

ADMINISTRATIVE DIVISIONS
(official estimates at mid-2013)

States	Area (sq km)*	Population†	Density (per sq km)	Capital
Aguascalientes (Ags) . .	5,623	1,248,015	221.9	Aguascalientes
Baja California (BC) . .	71,540	3,375,913	47.2	Mexicali
Baja California Sur (BCS) .	73,937	717,667	9.7	La Paz
Campeche (Camp.) .	57,718	879,811	15.2	Campeche
Chiapas (Chis) .	73,680	5,116,489	69.4	Tuxtla Gutiérrez
Chihuahua (Chih.) . .	247,490	3,627,811	14.7	Chihuahua
Coahuila (de Zaragoza) (Coah.) . .	151,447	2,886,614	19.1	Saltillo
Colima (Col.) .	5,629	696,221	123.7	Colima
Distrito Federal (DF) . . .	1,485	8,884,713	5,983.0	Mexico City
Durango (Dgo) .	123,364	1,722,681	14.0	Victoria de Durango
Guanajuato (Gto).	30,617	5,690,462	185.9	Guanajuato
Guerrero (Gro) .	63,618	3,511,268	55.2	Chilpancingo de los Bravos
Hidalgo (Hgo) .	20,855	2,795,766	134.1	Pachuca de Soto
Jalisco (Jal.) .	78,624	7,718,019	98.2	Guadalajara
México (Méx.) .	22,332	16,341,453	731.8	Toluca de Lerdo
Michoacán (de Ocampo) (Mich.) . .	58,672	4,505,937	76.8	Morelia
Morelos (Mor.) .	4,894	1,867,250	381.5	Cuernavaca
Nayarit (Nay.) .	27,861	1,174,770	42.2	Tepic
Nuevo León (NL).	64,206	4,936,466	76.9	Monterrey
Oaxaca (Oax.) .	93,348	3,946,853	42.3	Oaxaca de Juárez
Puebla (Pue.) .	34,246	6,051,533	176.7	Heroica Puebla de Zaragoza
Querétaro (de Arteaga) (Qro) .	11,659	1,938,372	166.3	Querétaro
Quintana Roo (Q.Roo) .	42,544	1,483,968	34.9	Ciudad Chetumal
San Luis Potosí (SLP) . .	61,165	2,692,221	44.0	San Luis Potosí
Sinaloa (Sin.) .	57,334	2,927,843	51.1	Culiacán Rosales
Sonora (Son.) .	179,527	2,848,307	15.9	Hermosillo
Tabasco (Tab.) .	24,747	2,333,646	94.3	Villahermosa
Tamaulipas (Tamps) . .	80,155	3,455,570	43.1	Ciudad Victoria
Tlaxcala (Tlax.) .	3,988	1,240,439	311.0	Tlaxcala de Xicohténcatl
Veracruz-Llave (Ver.) . .	71,856	7,908,973	110.1	Jalapa Enríquez
Yucatán (Yuc.) .	39,675	2,062,815	52.0	Mérida
Zacatecas (Zac.) .	75,412	1,541,374	20.4	Zacatecas
Total . .	1,959,248	118,129,140	60.3	—

* Excluding islands.
† Source: Consejo Nacional de Población (CONAPO), México, DF.

PRINCIPAL TOWNS
(population at census of June 2010)

Ciudad de México (Mexico City, capital) . .	8,851,080	Tlalnepantla de Baz (Tlalnepantla) .	664,225
Ecatepec de Morelos (Ecatepec) .	1,656,107	Benito Juárez (Cancún) . .	661,176
Tijuana . . .	1,559,683	Torreón . .	639,629
Heroica Puebla de Zaragoza (Puebla)	1,539,819	Santa María Chimalhuacán (Chimalhuacán) .	614,453
Guadalajara .	1,495,189	Reynosa . .	608,891
León	1,436,480	Tlaquepaque . .	608,114
Ciudad Juárez .	1,332,131	Victoria de Durango (Durango) . .	582,267
Zapopan . .	1,243,756	Tuxtla Gutiérrez .	553,374
Monterrey . .	1,135,550	Veracruz Llave (Veracruz) . .	552,156
Nezahualcóyotl .	1,110,565	Irapuato . . .	529,440
Mexicali . .	936,826	Tultitlán . . .	524,074
Culiacán Rosales (Culiacán) . .	858,638	Cuautitlán Izcalli .	511,675

Naucalpan de Juárez (Naucalpan) . .	833,779	Atizapán de Zaragoza . . .	489,937
Mérida	830,732	Matamoros . . .	489,193
Toluca de Lerdo (Toluca) . .	819,561	Tonalá . . .	478,689
Chihuahua . .	819,543	Iztapaluca . . .	467,361
Querétaro . .	801,940	Ensenada . .	466,814
Aguascalientes . .	797,010	Jalapa Enríquez (Xalapa) . . .	457,928
Acapulco de Juárez (Acapulco) . .	789,971	San Nicolás de los Garzas . .	443,273
Hermosillo . .	784,342	Mazatlán . . .	438,434
San Luis Potosí .	772,604	Nuevo Laredo . .	384,033
Morelia . . .	729,279	Cuernavaca . .	365,168
Saltillo . . .	725,123	Valle de Chalco (Xico)	357,645
Guadalupe . . .	678,006		

BIRTHS, MARRIAGES AND DEATHS

	Registered live births		Registered marriages		Registered deaths	
	Number	Rate (per 1,000)	Number	Rate (per 1,000)	Number	Rate (per 1,000)
2004 . .	2,625,056	19.8	600,563	5.8	473,417	4.8
2005 . .	2,567,906	19.3	595,713	5.7	495,240	4.8
2006 . .	2,505,939	19.0	586,978	5.6	494,471	4.8
2007 . .	2,655,083	18.6	595,209	5.6	514,420	4.9
2008 . .	2,636,110	18.3	589,352	5.5	539,530	4.9
2009 . .	2,577,214	18.0	558,913	5.2	564,673	4.9
2010 . .	2,643,908	17.8	568,632	5.2	592,018	5.0
2011 . .	2,586,287	n.a.	570,954	n.a.	590,693	n.a.

2011 (official projections): Crude birth rate 17.5 per 1,000; Crude death rate 5.0 per 1,000.

2012 (official projections): Crude birth rate 17.3 per 1,000; Crude death rate 5.1 per 1,000.

Life expectancy (years at birth): 76.7 (males 74.3; females 79.2) in 2010 (Source: World Bank, World Development Indicators database).

ECONOMICALLY ACTIVE POPULATION
(sample surveys, '000 persons aged 14 years and over, July–September)

	2010	2011*	2012*
Agriculture, hunting, forestry and fishing	5,903.3	6,680.1	6,737.9
Mining, quarrying and electricity.	319.7	384.7	446.3
Manufacturing	6,914.3	7,096.0	7,413.5
Construction	3,430.1	3,618.3	3,644.8
Trade	8,908.3	9,131.8	9,710.5
Hotels and restaurants . . .	2,944.3	3,139.5	3,318.4
Transport and communications .	2,183.6	2,247.7	2,259.0
Finance and business services .	2,908.7	3,118.0	3,410.6
Social services	3,746.4	3,759.8	3,947.4
Other services	4,651.5	4,985.1	5,200.6
Public sector	2,272.4	2,317.9	2,324.6
Sub-total	44,182.6	46,478.9	48,413.6
Activities not adequately defined .	298.0	337.0	318.7
Total employed	44,480.6	46,815.9	48,732.3
Unemployed	2,651.0	2,761.8	2,646.7
Total labour force	47,131.6	49,577.7	51,379.0
Males	29,308.6	30,952.9	31,749.8
Females	17,823.0	18,624.8	19,629.1

* Preliminary estimates.

Health and Welfare

KEY INDICATORS

Total fertility rate (children per woman, 2010) . . .	2.3
Under-5 mortality rate (per 1,000 live births, 2010) . . .	17
HIV/AIDS (% of persons aged 15–49, 2009)	0.3
Physicians (per 1,000 head, 2002)	1.5
Hospital beds (per 1,000 head, 2004)	1.0
Health expenditure (2009): US $ per head (PPP) . . .	922
Health expenditure (2009): % of GDP	6.5
Health expenditure (2009): public (% of total)	48.3
Access to water (% of persons, 2009)	96
Access to sanitation (% of persons, 2009)	85
Total carbon dioxide emissions ('000 metric tons, 2008) .	475,833.6
Carbon dioxide emissions per head (metric tons, 2008) .	4.3
Human Development Index (2011): ranking	57
Human Development Index (2011): value	0.770

For sources and definitions, see explanatory note on p. vi.

Agriculture

PRINCIPAL CROPS
('000 metric tons)

	2009	2010	2011
Wheat	4,116	3,677	3,628
Rice, paddy	263	217	173
Barley	519	672	487
Maize	20,143	23,302	17,635
Oats	130	111	51
Sorghum	6,108	6,940	6,429
Potatoes	1,501	1,537	1,433
Sugar cane	49,493	50,422	49,735
Beans, dry	1,041	1,156	568
Chick peas	132	132	72
Soybeans (Soya beans) . .	121	168	205
Groundnuts, with shell . . .	86	81	80
Coconuts*	1,191	1,157	1,017
Safflower seed	77	97	131
Cabbages	191	222	239
Lettuce and chicory . . .	318	341	370
Tomatoes	2,691	2,998	2,436
Cauliflower and broccoli . .	415	386	428
Pumpkins, squash and gourds .	577	522	525
Cucumbers and gherkins . .	540*	477	425
Chillies and peppers, green . .	1,942	2,336	2,132
Onions, dry	1,196	1,266	1,399
Carrots and turnips . . .	369	346	405
Bananas	2,232	2,103	2,139
Oranges	4,193	4,052	4,080
Tangerines, mandarins, clementines and satsumas . .	442	409	406
Lemons and limes	1,987	1,891	2,148
Grapefruit and pomelos . . .	432	401	397
Apples	561	585	631
Peaches and nectarines . . .	198	227	167
Strawberries	233	227	229
Grapes	275	307	281
Watermelons	1,007	1,037	1,002
Cantaloupes and other melons .	552	562	564
Guavas, mangoes and mangosteens	1,509	1,633	1,827
Avocados	1,231	1,107	1,264
Pineapples	749	702	743
Papayas	707	616	634
Coffee, green	264	245	237
Cocoa beans	60*	27	21
Tobacco, unmanufactured . . .	8	7	10

* FAO estimate(s).

Aggregate production ('000 metric tons, may include official, semi-official or estimated data): Total cereals 31,282.2 in 2009, 34,922.5 in 2010, 28,405.9 in 2011; Total fruits (excl. melons) 15,890.2 in 2009, 15,368.1 in 2010, 16,117.1 in 2011; Total vegetables (incl. melons) 11,726.8 in 2009, 12,514.8 in 2010, 11,908.1 in 2011.

Source: FAO.

LIVESTOCK
('000 head, year ending September)

	2009	2010	2011
Horses*	6,350	6,350	6,350
Asses*	3,260	3,260	3,260
Mules*	3,280	3,280	3,280
Cattle	32,307	32,642	32,936
Pigs	15,268	15,435	15,547
Sheep	8,018	8,106	8,219
Goats	8,989	8,993	9,004
Chickens	500,703	506,256	510,133
Ducks*	8,200	8,300	8,350
Turkeys	4,080	4,030	4,078

* FAO estimates.

Source: FAO.

LIVESTOCK PRODUCTS
('000 metric tons)

	2009	2010	2011
Cattle meat	1,705	1,745	1,804
Sheep meat	54	55	57
Goat meat	43	44	44
Pig meat	1,162	1,175	1,202
Horse meat*	82	83	83
Chicken meat	2,636	2,681	2,765
Cows' milk	10,549	10,677	10,724
Goats' milk	165	162	162
Hen eggs	2,360	2,381	2,459
Honey	56	56	58

* FAO estimates.

Source: FAO.

Forestry

ROUNDWOOD REMOVALS
('000 cubic metres, excl. bark)

	2009	2010	2011
Sawlogs, veneer logs and logs for sleepers	4,295	4,470	4,123
Pulpwood	628	423	417
Other industrial wood	203	148	330
Fuel wood*	38,752	38,829	38,834
Total	43,878	43,870	43,704

* FAO estimates.

Source: FAO.

SAWNWOOD PRODUCTION
('000 cubic metres, incl. railway sleepers)

	2009*	2010	2011
Coniferous (softwood)	2,409	2,136	2,068
Broadleaved (hardwood) . . .	405	295	276
Total	2,814	2,431	2,344

* FAO estimates.

Source: FAO.

Fishing

('000 metric tons, live weight)

	2008	2009	2010
Capture	1,581.2	1,611.1	1,523.8
Tilapias	61.8	62.9	62.4
California pilchard (sardine) .	655.4	691.7	630.2
Yellowfin tuna	82.8	105.8	94.2
American cupped oyster . .	40.5	36.9	46.7
Jumbo flying squid	84.4	57.9	42.9
Aquaculture	159.3	157.0*	126.2
Whiteleg shrimp	130.2	125.8	104.6
Total catch	**1,740.5**	**1,768.1***	**1,650.1**

* FAO estimate.

Note: Figures exclude aquatic plants ('000 metric tons, capture only): 4.9 in 2008; 5.2 in 2009; 1.1 in 2010. Also excluded are aquatic mammals and crocodiles (recorded by number rather than by weight), shells and corals. The number of bottlenose dolphins caught was 9 in 2008; nil in 2009; nil in 2010. The number of Morelet's crocodiles caught was: 724 in 2008; 485 in 2009; n.a. in 2010. The catch of marine shells and corals (metric tons) was: 325 in 2008; 429 in 2009; 647 in 2010.

Source: FAO.

Mining

(metric tons unless otherwise indicated)

	2009	2010	2011
Antimony*	74	71	5
Barytes	151,791	143,225	134,727
Bismuth*	854	982	935
Cadmium*	1,510	1,464	1,485
Celestite	36,127	31,429	40,669
Coal	9,496,189	11,246,639	13,718,159
Coke	1,315,444	2,105,000	2,121,866
Copper*	227,750	237,609	402,430
Crude petroleum ('000 barrels per day)†	2,601	2,576	2,550
Diatomite	808,07	91,710	84,231
Dolomite	982,650	1,499,744	2,785,314
Feldspar	347,510	398,849	382,497
Flourite	1,045,940	1,067,386	1,206,907
Gas (million cu ft per day)† . .	7,031	7,020	6,594
Gold (kg)*	51,393	72,596	84,118
Graphite	5,105	6,628	7,348
Gypsum	5,756,936	3,559,579	3,838,348
Iron*	7,073,440	7,931,194	7,763,048
Kaolin	78,086	120,094	120,003
Lead*	100,361	158,206	182,202
Manganese*	118,578	174,761	170,935
Molybdenum*	10,167	10,849	10,787
Salt	7,445,025	8,430,562	8,769,140
Silica	2,483,605	2,607,650	2,542,143
Silver*	2,693,265	3,499,470	4,150,347
Sulphur	1,114,028	991,802	959,488
Wollastonite	29,728	46,548	47,523
Zinc*	384,478	518,429	447,948

* Figures for metallic minerals refer to metal content of ores.
† Source: Petróleos Mexicanos, México, DF.

Industry

SELECTED PRODUCTS
('000 metric tons unless otherwise indicated)

	2006	2007	2008
Wheat flour	2,646	2,658	2,612
Maize (corn) flour	1,664	1,670	1,716
Raw sugar	3,198	3,224	3,293
Beer ('000 hl)	78,456	81,226	81,940
Soft drinks ('000 hl) . . .	143,764	151,517	149,895
Cigarettes (million units) . . .	42,762	39,474	42,213
Cotton yarn (pure and mixed) .	43	44	40
Tyres ('000 units)*	10,284	9,985	9,089
Cement	40,038	40,787	39,890
Non-electric, cooking or heating appliances—household ('000 units)	4,024	4,228	4,075
Refrigerators—household ('000 units)	3,026	2,668	2,547
Washing machines—household ('000 units)	1,033	937	675
Lorries, buses, tractors, etc. ('000 units)	549	547	438
Passenger cars ('000 units) . .	1,385	1,490	1,632
Electric energy (million kWh) .	252,014	263,465	258,913

* Tyres for road motor vehicles.

2009 (million kWh): Electric energy 261,018.

Source: UN Industrial Commodity Statistics Database.

Finance

CURRENCY AND EXCHANGE RATES

Monetary Units
100 centavos = 1 Mexican nuevo peso.

Sterling, Dollar and Euro Equivalents (31 December 2012)
£1 sterling = 20.530 nuevos pesos;
US $1 = 13.010 nuevos pesos;
€1 = 17.166 nuevos pesos;
1,000 Mexican nuevos pesos = £48.71 = $76.86 = €58.26.

Average Exchange Rate (nuevos pesos per US $)
2010   12.636
2011   12.423
2012   13.169

Note: Figures are given in terms of the nuevo (new) peso, introduced on 1 January 1993 and equivalent to 1,000 former pesos.

BUDGET*
(million new pesos)

Revenue	2009	2010	2011
Taxation	1,129,552.6	1,260,425.0	1,294,054.1
Income taxes	534,190.5	626,530.4	720,401.7
Value-added tax	407,795.1	504,509.3	537,142.5
Excise tax	50,567.4	4,463.8	−76,433.5
Import duties	30,197.1	24,531.3	26,883.0
Other revenue	870,895.5	819,588.0	1,026,187.6
Total revenue	**2,000,448.1**	**2,080,013.0**	**2,320,241.7**

Expenditure	2009	2010	2011
Programmable expenditure .	1,639,602.7	1,762,880.1	1,948,209.1
Current expenditure . .	345,275.5	365,481.0	400,215.6
Wages and salaries . .	205,441.7	217,574.1	229,627.3
Acquisitions	17,945.4	18,706.6	21,196.4
Other current expenditure .	121,888.4	129,200.3	149,391.9
Capital expenditure	101,524.5	136,051.3	163,268.7
Transfers	1,192,802.7	1,261,347.8	1,384,724.8
Non-programmable expenditure .	622,908.7	675,176.0	737,446.6
Interest and fees	231,265.4	216,270.7	240,537.6
Revenue sharing	375,717.3	437,327.6	477,256.2
Total expenditure	**2,262,511.4**	**2,438,056.1**	**2,685,655.7**

* Figures refer to the consolidated accounts of the central Government, including government agencies and the national social security system. The budgets of state and local governments are excluded.

INTERNATIONAL RESERVES
(excl. gold, US $ million at 31 December)

	2009	2010	2011
IMF special drawing rights . .	4,525	4,325	4,084
Reserve position in the Fund . .	961	1,057	2,422
Foreign exchange	94,103	114,884	137,485
Total	99,589	120,265	143,991

Source: IMF, *International Financial Statistics*.

MONEY SUPPLY
(million new pesos at 31 December)

	2009	2010	2011
Currency outside depository corporations	536,824	599,070	665,520
Transferable deposits . . .	1,079,230	1,261,669	1,452,298
Other deposits	1,999,716	2,217,835	2,372,420
Securities other than shares . .	14,513	15,181	11,791
Broad money	3,630,283	4,093,755	4,502,029

Source: IMF, *International Financial Statistics*.

COST OF LIVING
(Consumer Price Index; base: 2000 = 100)

	2006	2007	2008
Food, beverages and tobacco . .	134.1	142.6	154.1
Clothing and footwear . . .	113.5	115.0	117.0
Electricity, gas and other fuel .	173.1	178.2	190.7
Rent	133.2	137.2	141.4
All items (incl. others) . . .	131.8	137.0	144.0

2009: Food, beverages and tobacco 167.5; All items (incl. others) 151.6.

2010: Food, beverages and tobacco 174.0; All items (incl. others) 157.9.

2011: Food, beverages and tobacco 183.0; All items (incl. others) 163.3.
Source: ILO.

NATIONAL ACCOUNTS
('000 million new pesos at current prices, preliminary)
Expenditure on the Gross Domestic Product

	2009	2010	2011
Government final consumption expenditure	1,426.0	1,541.8	1,689.2
Private final consumption expenditure	7,850.2	8,562.7	9,278.2
Increase in stocks	296.4	541.6	729.2
Gross fixed capital formation . .	2,539.3	2,583.8	2,880.8
Total domestic expenditure .	12,111.8	13,229.9	14,577.4
Exports of goods and services . .	3,297.7	3,965.4	4,544.4
Less Imports of goods and services	3,472.2	4,123.7	4,725.9
GDP in purchasers' values .	11,937.2	13,071.6	14,395.8
GDP at constant 2003 prices .	8,384.2	8,827.0	9,170.2

Gross Domestic Product by Economic Activity

	2009	2010	2011
Agriculture, forestry and fishing .	448.9	490.4	522.2
Mining and quarrying	898.7	1,082.0	1,441.5
Manufacturing	2,035.9	2,269.3	2,510.3
Construction	815.1	836.1	929.0
Electricity, gas and water . .	139.2	155.9	171.0
Trade	1,730.0	1,997.4	2,280.6
Restaurants and hotels . .	263.5	283.4	304.3
Transport, storage and communications	1,160.1	1,284.3	1,357.8
Finance, insurance, real estate and business services	2,370.2	2,465.8	2,620.5
Public administration	504.8	547.5	591.2
Community, social and personal services	397.5	425.5	459.2
Education	593.1	630.2	678.3
Other activities	288.2	304.7	323.9
Sub-total	11,645.1	12,772.6	14,189.6
Less Financial intermediation services indirectly measured	206.9	244.6	301.5
GDP at factor cost	11,438.2	12,528.0	13,888.1
Indirect taxes, *less* subsidies . .	499.0	543.6	507.7
GDP in purchasers' values .	11,937.2	13,071.6	14,395.8

BALANCE OF PAYMENTS
(US $ million)

	2009	2010	2011
Exports of goods	229,975	298,860	349,946
Imports of goods	−234,901	−301,744	−351,116
Balance on goods	−4,926	−2,884	−1,171
Exports of services	14,730	15,167	15,298
Imports of services	−23,188	−25,295	−29,497
Balance on goods and services	−13,384	−13,012	−15,370
Primary income received . . .	6,934	7,583	9,165
Primary income paid	−20,208	−20,564	−27,841
Balance on goods, services and primary income	−26,657	−25,993	−34,047
Secondary income received . .	21,639	21,609	23,139
Secondary income paid . . .	−60	−86	−178
Current balance	−5,078	−4,469	−11,086
Direct investment assets . .	−8,464	−16,217	−10,685
Direct investment liabilities . .	16,316	20,868	20,357
Portfolio investment assets . .	−24,839	−7,330	1,525
Portfolio investment liabilities .	15,275	37,604	40,944
Financial derivatives and employee stock options (net)	4,271	−546	−725
Other investment assets . . .	14,967	−28,358	−5,186
Other investment liabilities . .	12,564	36,789	−4,527
Net errors and omissions . . .	−20,189	−17,546	−1,031
Reserves and related items .	4,821	20,795	29,585

Source: IMF, *International Financial Statistics*.

External Trade

PRINCIPAL COMMODITIES
(distribution by HS, US $ million)

Imports f.o.b.	2009	2010	2011
Live animals and products thereof	4,342.5	5,208.3	5,912.9
Vegetable products	7,449.1	8,109.7	11,097.1
Animal and vegetable oils and fats	1,073.6	1,283.5	1,720.4
Prepared food, beverages, spirits and tobacco	5,105.5	5,700.9	6,683.6
Mineral products	16,558.5	25,262.0	36,660.2
Chemicals and related industries .	19,786.6	23,605.7	27,325.4
Plastics, rubber and articles thereof	15,817.4	21,823.2	24,050.1
Raw hides, skins, leather and furs	856.2	1,124.2	1,413.0
Wood, charcoal, cork, straw, etc. .	1,022.6	1,206.5	1,299.0
Paper-making material; paper and paperboard and articles thereof .	5,474.4	6,612.3	6,898.9
Textiles and textile articles . .	6,718.6	8,089.7	9,501.9

Imports f.o.b.—*continued*	2009	2010	2011
Footwear, headgear, umbrellas, etc.	601.8	775.4	925.0
Articles of stone, plaster, cement, asbestos, etc.; glass and glassware	1,596.6	2,090.2	2,439.8
Pearls, precious stones and metals and articles thereof; imitation jewellery and coins	881.7	1,075.6	1,269.3
Base metals and articles thereof	18,235.9	24,998.3	29,417.1
Machinery and mechanical appliances; electrical equipment, parts and accessories	91,881.9	117,655.9	129,688.1
Vehicles, aircraft, vessels and associated transport equipment	19,078.4	25,405.9	30,102.2
Optical, photographic, measuring, precision and medical apparatus; clocks and watches; musical instruments	8,827.9	10,554.5	11,630.8
Arms and ammunitions, parts and accessories	60.9	81.3	66.2
Miscellaneous manufactured articles	4,540.7	5,033.1	5,411.0
Works of art, collectors' pieces, antiques	12.3	8.6	18.3
Total (incl. others)	234,385.0	301,481.8	350,842.9

Exports f.o.b.	2009	2010	2011
Live animals and products thereof	1,726.3	2,054.1	2,780.6
Vegetable products	7,033.6	7,828.0	9,212.8
Animal and vegetable oils and fats	127.2	134.0	202.2
Prepared food, beverages, spirits and tobacco	7,137.0	8,091.6	9,519.9
Mineral products	31,941.5	43,546.0	59,741.0
Chemicals and related industries	7,805.9	8,880.2	10,268.9
Plastics, rubber and articles thereof	5,780.0	7,336.0	8,780.0
Raw hides, skins, leather and furs	414.9	479.6	577.8
Wood, charcoal, cork, straw, etc.	303.5	300.4	313.4
Paper-making material; paper and paperboard and articles thereof	1,665.7	1,959.7	2,119.1
Textiles and textile articles	5,664.6	6,265.5	6,842.6
Footwear, headgear, umbrellas, etc.	367.9	459.2	555.7
Articles of stone, plaster, cement, asbestos, etc.; glass and glassware	2,342.8	2,863.9	2,970.2
Pearls, precious stones and metals and articles thereof; imitation jewellery and coins	6,198.1	9,214.9	13,313.8
Base metals and articles thereof	10,640.5	13,740.5	16,831.8
Machinery and mechanical appliances; electrical equipment, parts and accessories	89,361.7	113,105.7	118,955.4
Vehicles, aircraft, vessels and associated transport equipment	34,835.5	52,885.9	64,983.9
Optical, photographic, measuring, precision and medical apparatus; clocks and watches; musical instruments	8,694.6	10,336.6	11,077.8
Arms and ammunitions, parts and accessories	22.4	25.2	24.2
Miscellaneous manufactured articles	6,344.7	7,359.3	7,901.1
Works of art, collectors' pieces, antiques	7.5	8.6	7.9
Total (incl. others)	229,703.6	298,473.1	349,375.0

Note: The *maquila* sector is responsible for a large percentage of both merchandise imports and exports, but official figures on the value of the sector were last published in 2006, when imports were valued at US $86,527.3m. (equivalent to some 34% of total imports) and exports were valued at $111,823.8m. (almost 45% of total exports).

PRINCIPAL TRADING PARTNERS*
(US $ million)

Imports c.i.f.	2009	2010	2011
Brazil	3,495.3	4,327.5	4,561.9
Canada	7,303.7	8,607.5	9,645.5
China, People's Republic	32,529.0	45,607.6	52,248.0
France	2,502.5	3,024.4	3,359.6
Germany	9,727.3	11,076.8	12,862.6
Italy	3,146.7	3,996.9	4,982.7
Japan	11,397.1	15,014.7	16,493.5
Korea, Republic	10,958.7	12,776.6	13,690.4
Malaysia	4,035.5	5,276.2	5,609.9
Spain	3,004.0	3,232.3	3,843.2
Taiwan	4,592.1	5,620.7	5,769.9
United Kingdom	1,837.8	2,005.0	2,141.9
USA	112,433.8	145,007.4	174,356.0
Total (incl. others)	234,385.0	301,481.8	350,842.9

Exports f.o.b.	2009	2010	2011
Brazil	2,438.2	3,781.0	4,891.2
Canada	8,244.3	10,685.7	10,694.6
China, People's Republic	2,207.8	4,182.8	5,964.2
Colombia	2,490.5	3,757.1	5,632.6
Germany	3,210.2	3,571.7	4,343.0
Japan	1,600.6	1,923.2	2,252.3
Spain	2,507.8	3,838.1	4,870.1
United Kingdom	1,243.1	1,733.7	2,158.7
USA	185,101.2	238,684.4	274,431.0
Total (incl. others)	229,703.6	298,473.1	349,375.0

* Imports by country of origin; exports by country of destination.

Transport

RAILWAYS
(traffic)

	2008	2009	2010
Passengers carried ('000)*	8,915	28,000	40,399
Passenger-km (million)	178	449	843
Freight carried ('000 tons)	99,692	90,321	104,565
Freight ton-km (million)	74,582	69,185	78,770

* Including passengers carried on Linea 1 of the Ferrocarril Suburbano de la Zona Metropolitana del Valle de México.

Source: Dirección General de Planeación, Secretaría de Comunicaciones y Transportes.

ROAD TRAFFIC
('000 vehicles in use at 31 December, estimates)

	2008	2009	2010
Passenger cars	19,248	20,524	21,640
Lorries and vans	8,453	8,843	9,183
Buses and coaches	334	337	359
Motorcycles and mopeds	1,079	1,201	1,157

Source: IRF, *World Road Statistics*.

SHIPPING

Flag Registered Fleet
(at 31 December)

	2010	2011	2012
Number of vessels	584	608	628
Total displacement ('000 grt)	1,523.8	1,585.5	1,650.7

Source: Lloyd's List Intelligence (www.lloydslistintelligence.com).

Sea-borne Shipping
(domestic and international freight traffic, '000 metric tons)

	2009	2010	2011
Goods loaded	147,330	160,198	164,067
Goods unloaded	94,594	112,613	118,836

Source: Coordinación General de Puertos y Marina Mercante.

CIVIL AVIATION
(traffic on scheduled services)

	2008	2009	2010*
Passengers carried ('000) . .	53,293	46,971	48,698
Freight carried ('000 tons) . .	525	466	571

* Preliminary.

Source: Dirección General de Planeación, Secretaría de Comunicaciones y Transportes.

Tourism

VISITOR ARRIVALS BY COUNTRY OF ORIGIN
(including cross-border visitors)

	2008	2009	2010
Argentina	126,130	127,107	170,467
Brazil	76,491	68,211	117,658
Canada	1,136,305	1,222,634	1,460,418
Chile	59,634	54,179	67,661
Colombia	67,378	68,493	102,177
France	208,284	164,236	170,250
Germany	158,050	140,754	163,266
Guatemala	43,881	52,736	50,274
Italy	167,415	108,547	133,292
Japan	69,716	52,229	66,164
Korea, Republic	35,696	26,178	34,965
Netherlands	75,864	58,317	68,964
Spain	284,512	215,669	287,163
United Kingdom	311,113	257,367	295,831
USA	18,034,158	17,561,752	17,871,635
Venezuela	82,453	83,467	84,868
Total (incl. others)	22,637,405	21,454,117	22,260,352

Total tourist arrivals ('000): 23,403 in 2011.

Tourism receipts (excluding excursionists, US $ million): 9,431 in 2009; 9,991 in 2010; 10,006 in 2011.

Source: mainly World Tourism Organization.

Communications Media

	2009	2010*	2011*
Telephones ('000 main lines in use)	19,336.6	19,891.5	19,683.9
Mobile cellular telephones ('000 subscribers)	83,527.9	91,362.8	94,565.3
Internet subscribers ('000) . .	9,744.4	11,628.7	11,992.1
Broadband subscribers ('000) .	9,348.8	11,352.0	11,723.3

* Preliminary.

Source: International Telecommunication Union.

Education

(2009/10, preliminary)

	Institutions	Teachers	Students ('000)
Pre-primary	90,411	220,154	4,608.3
Primary	99,202	570,169	14,860.7
Secondary (incl. technical) . .	35,155	374,363	6,127.9
Intermediate: professional/ technical	1,408	28,146	372.9
Intermediate: Baccalaureate . .	13,019	241,155	3,681.8
Higher	5,501	294,617	2,718.6

Pupil-teacher ratio (primary education, UNESCO estimate): 28.1 in 2009/10 (Source: UNESCO Institute for Statistics).

Adult literacy rate (UNESCO estimates): 93.1% (males 94.4%; females 91.9%) in 2010 (Source: UNESCO Institute for Statistics).

Directory

The Government

HEAD OF STATE

President: ENRIQUE PEÑA NIETO (took office 1 December 2012).

CABINET
(May 2013)

The Government is formed by the Partido Revolucionario Institucional (PRI).

Secretary of the Interior: MIGUEL ANGEL OSORIO CHONG.

Secretary of Foreign Affairs: JOSÉ ANTONIO MEADE KURIBREÑA.

Secretary of Finance and Public Credit: LUIS VIDEGARAY CASO.

Secretary of National Defence: Gen. SALVADOR CIENFUEGOS ZEPEDA.

Secretary of the Navy: Adm. VIDAL FRANCISCO SOBERÓN SANZ.

Secretary of the Economy: ILDEFONSO GUAJARDO VILLARREAL.

Secretary of Social Development: ROSARIO ROBLES BERLANGA.

Secretary of Communications and Transport: GERARDO RUIZ ESPARZA.

Secretary of Labour and Social Welfare: ALFONSO NAVARRETE PRIDA.

Secretary of the Environment and Natural Resources: JUAN JOSÉ GUERRA ABUD.

Secretary of Energy: PEDRO JOAQUÍN COLDWELL.

Secretary of Agriculture, Livestock, Rural Development, Fisheries and Food: ENRIQUE MARTÍNEZ Y MARTÍNEZ.

Secretary of Public Education: EMILIO CHUAYFFET CHEMOR.

Secretary of Health: MERCEDES JUAN LÓPEZ.

Secretary of Tourism: CLAUDIA RUIZ MASSIEU SALINAS.

Secretary of Territorial and Urban Agrarian Development: JORGE CARLOS RAMÍREZ MARÍN.

Under-Secretary of Planning and Institutional Protection (Public Security): MANUEL MONDRAGÓN Y KALB.

Under-Secretary for Administrative and Procurement Responsibilities (Public Function): JULIÁN ALFONSO OLIVAS UGALDE.

Attorney-General: JESÚS MURILLO KARAM.

Legal Counsel to the President: HUMBERTO CASTILLEJOS CERVANTES.

SECRETARIATS OF STATE

Office of the President: Los Pinos, Col. San Miguel Chapultepec, 11850 México, DF; tel. (55) 5093-5300; fax (55) 5277-2376; e-mail enrique.penanieto@presidencia.gob.mx; internet www.presidencia.gob.mx.

Secretariat of State for Agriculture, Livestock, Rural Development, Fisheries and Food: Avda Municipio Libre 377, Col. Santa Cruz Atoyac, Del. Benito Juárez, 03310 México, DF; tel. (55) 3871-1000; fax (55) 9183-1018; e-mail contacto@sagarpa.gob.mx; internet www.sagarpa.gob.mx.

Secretariat of State for Communications and Transport: Avda Xola, esq. con Ejercito Central, Col. Narvarte, Del. Benito Juárez, 03020 México, DF; tel. (55) 5723-9300; fax (55) 5530-0093; e-mail webmaster@sct.gob.mx; internet www.sct.gob.mx.

Secretariat of State for the Economy: Alfonso Reyes 30, Col. Hipódromo Condesa, Del. Cuauhtémoc, 06140 México, DF; tel. (55) 5729-9100; fax (55) 5729-9320; e-mail primercontacto@economia.gob.mx; internet www.economia.gob.mx.

Secretariat of State for Energy: Insurgentes Sur 890, 17°, Col. del Valle, Del. Benito Juárez, 03100 México, DF; tel. (55) 5000-6000; fax (55) 5000-6222; e-mail calidad@energia.gob.mx; internet www.energia.gob.mx.

Secretariat of State for the Environment and Natural Resources: Blvd Adolfo Ruíz Cortines 4209, Col. Jardines en la Montaña, Del. Tlalpan, 14210 México, DF; tel. (55) 5490-0900; fax (55) 5628-0643; e-mail contactodgeia@semarnat.gob.mx; internet www.semarnat.gob.mx.

Secretariat of State for Finance and Public Credit: Palacio Nacional, Plaza de la Constitución, Col. Centro, Del. Cuauhtémoc, 06000 México, DF; tel. (55) 9158-2000; fax (55) 9158-1142; e-mail secretario@hacienda.gob.mx; internet www.hacienda.gob.mx.

Secretariat of State for Foreign Affairs: Plaza Juárez 20, Col. Centro, Del. Cuauhtémoc, 06010 México, DF; tel. (55) 3686-5100; fax (55) 3686-5582; e-mail atencionciudadanasre@sre.gob.mx; internet www.sre.gob.mx.

Secretariat of State for Health: Lieja 7, 1°, Col. Juárez, Del. Cuauhtémoc, 06600 México, DF; tel. (55) 5286-2383; fax (55) 5553-7917; e-mail portalesweb@salud.gob.mx; internet www.salud.gob.mx.

Secretariat of State for the Interior: Abraham González 48, Col. Juárez, Del. Cuauhtémoc, 06600 México, DF; tel. (55) 5728-7400; fax (55) 5728-7300; e-mail contacto@segob.gob.mx; internet www.gobernacion.gob.mx.

Secretariat of State for Labour and Social Welfare: Periférico Sur 4271, Col. Fuentes del Pedregal, Del. Tlalpan, 14149 México, DF; tel. (55) 3000-2100; fax (55) 5645-5594; e-mail webmaster1@stps.gob.mx; internet www.stps.gob.mx.

Secretariat of State for National Defence: Blvd Manuel Avila Camacho, esq. Avda Industria Militar, 3°, Col. Lomas de Sotelo, Del. Miguel Hidalgo, 11640 México, DF; tel. (55) 2122-8800; fax (55) 5395-2935; e-mail ggalvang@mail.sedena.gob.mx; internet www.sedena.gob.mx.

Secretariat of State for the Navy: Eje 2 oriente, Tramo Heroica, Escuela Naval Militar 861, Col. Los Cipreses, Del. Coyoacán, 04830 México, DF; tel. (55) 5624-6500; e-mail srio@semar.gob.mx; internet www.semar.gob.mx.

Secretariat of State for Public Education: Argentina 28, Col. Centro Histórico, Del. Cuauhtémoc, 06029 México, DF; tel. (55) 3601-1000; fax (55) 5329-6873; e-mail educa@sep.gob.mx; internet www.sep.gob.mx.

Secretariat of State for Public Function: Insurgentes Sur 1735, 10°, Col. Guadalupe Inn, Del. Alvaro Obregón, 01020 México, DF; tel. (55) 2000-3000; e-mail contactociudadano@funcionpublica.gob.mx; internet www.funcionpublica.gob.mx.

Secretariat of State for Social Development: Avda Paseo de la Reforma 116, Col. Juárez, Del. Cuauhtémoc, 06600 México, DF; tel. (55) 5328-5000; e-mail demandasocial@sedesol.gob.mx; internet www.sedesol.gob.mx.

Secretariat of State for Territorial and Urban Agrarian Development: Avda Heroica Escuela Naval Militar 669, Col. Presidentes Ejidales, 2 Sección, Del. Coyoacán, 04470 México, DF; tel. (55) 5624-0000; fax (55) 5695-6368; e-mail uenlace@sra.gob.mx; internet www.sedatu.gob.mx.

Secretariat of State for Tourism: Avda Presidente Masaryk 172, Col. Bosques de Chapultepec, Del. Miguel Hidalgo, 11580 México, DF; tel. (55) 3002-6300; fax (55) 1036-0789; e-mail atencion@sectur.gob.mx; internet www.sectur.gob.mx.

Office of the Attorney-General: Avda Paseo de la Reforma 211–213, Col. Cuauhtémoc, Del. Cuauhtémoc, 06500 México, DF; tel. (55) 5346-0000; fax (55) 5346-0908; e-mail ofproc@pgr.gob.mx; internet www.pgr.gob.mx.

Commission of Public Security: Avda Constituyentes 947, Col. Belén de las Flores, Del. Alvaro Obregón, 01110 México, DF; tel. (55)1103-6000; internet www.ssp.gob.mx.

State Governors
(May 2013)

Aguascalientes: CARLOS LOZANO DE LA TORRE (PRI).

Baja California: JOSÉ GUADALUPE OSUNA MILLÁN (PAN).

Baja California Sur: MARCOS COVARRUBIAS VILLASEÑOR (PAN).

Campeche: FERNANDO EUTIMIO ORTEGA BERNÉS (PRI).

Chiapas: MANUEL VELASCO COELLO (PVEM).

Chihuahua: CÉSAR HORATIO DUARTE JÁQUEZ (PRI).

Coahuila (de Zaragoza): RUBÉN IGNACIO MOREIRA VALDÉS (PRI).

Colima: MARIO ANGUIANO MORENO (PRI).

Durango: JORGE HERRERA CALDERA (PRI).

Guanajuato: MIGUEL MÁRQUEZ MÁRQUEZ (PAN).

Guerrero: ANGEL HELADIO AGUIRRE RIVERO (PRD).

Hidalgo: JOSÉ FRANCISCO OLVERA RUIZ (PRI).

Jalisco: JORGE ARISTÓTELES SANDOVAL DÍAZ (PRI).

México: ERUVIEL AVILA VILLEGAS (PRI).

Michoacán (de Ocampo): FAUSTO VALLEJO FIGUEROA (PRI).

Morelos: GRACO LUIS RAMÍREZ GARRIDO ABREU (PRD).

Nayarit: ROBERTO SANDOVAL CASTAÑEDA (PRI).

Nuevo León: RODRIGO MEDINA DE LA CRUZ (PRI).

Oaxaca: GABINO CUÉ MONTEAGUDO (Convergencia).

Puebla: RAFAEL MORENO VALLE (PAN).

Querétaro (de Arteaga): JOSÉ CALZADA ROVIROSA (PRI).

Quintana Roo: ROBERTO BORGE ANGULO (PRI).

San Luis Potosí: FERNANDO TORANZO FERNÁNDEZ (PRI).

Sinaloa: MARIO LÓPEZ VALDEZ (PAN).

Sonora: GUILLERMO PADRÉS ELÍAS (PAN).

Tabasco: ARTURO NÚÑEZ JIMÉNEZ (PRD).

Tamaulipas: EGIDIO TORRE CANTÚ (PRI).

Tlaxcala: MARIANO GONZÁLEZ ZARUR (PRI).

Veracruz-Llave: JAVIER DUARTE DE OCHOA (PRI).

Yucatán: ROLANDO ZAPATA BELLO (PRI).

Zacatecas: MIGUEL ALONSO REYES (PRI).

Head of Government of the Distrito Federal: MIGUEL ANGEL MANCERA ESPINOSA (PRD).

President and Legislature

PRESIDENT

Election, 1 July 2012

Candidate	Number of valid votes	% of valid votes
Enrique Peña Nieto (PRI-PVEM) . .	19,226,784	39.19
Andrés Manuel López Obrador (Movimiento Progresista*) . . .	15,896,999	32.40
Josefina Eugenia Vázquez Mota (PAN)	12,786,647	26.06
Gabriel Ricardo Quadri de la Torre (NA)	1,150,662	2.35
Total valid votes†	49,061,092	100.00

* An alliance of the PRD, the PT and Movimiento Ciudadano.
† In addition, there were 1,241,154 invalid votes and 20,907 votes for unregistered candidates.

CONGRESO DE LA UNIÓN

Senado

Senate: Avda Paseo de la Reforma 135, esq. Insurgentes Centro, Col. Tabacalera, Del. Cuauhtémoc, 06030 México, DF; tel. (55) 5130-2200; internet www.senado.gob.mx.

President: ERNESTO JAVIER CORDERO ARROYO (PAN).

Elections, 1 July 2012

Party	Seats
Partido Revolucionario Institucional (PRI) . .	54
Partido Acción Nacional (PAN)	38
Partido de la Revolución Democrática (PRD) . .	22
Partido Verde Ecologista de México (PVEM) . .	7
Partido del Trabajo (PT)	5
Nueva Alianza (NA)	1
Movimiento Ciudadano (MC)	1
Total	128

Cámara Federal de Diputados

Federal Chamber of Deputies: Avda Congreso de la Unión 66, Col. El Parque, Del. Venustiano Carranza, 15969 México, DF; tel. (55) 5628-1300; internet www.diputados.gob.mx.

President: FRANCISCO AGUSTÍN ARROYO VIEYRA (PRI).

Elections, 1 July 2012

Party	Seats
Partido Revolucionario Institucional (PRI) . .	213
Partido Acción Nacional (PAN)	114
Partido de la Revolución Democrática (PRD) . .	104
Partido Verde Ecologista de México (PVEM) . .	28
Movimiento Ciudadano (MC)	16
Partido del Trabajo (PT)	15
Nueva Alianza (NA)	10
Total	500

Election Commission

Instituto Federal Electoral (IFE): Viaducto Tlalpan 100, Col. Arenal Tepepan, Del. Tlalpan, 14610 México, DF; e-mail info@ife.org.mx; internet www.ife.org.mx; f. 1990; independent; Pres. LEONARDO VALDÉS ZURITA; Sec. EDMUNDO JACOBO MOLINA.

Political Organizations

To retain legal political registration, parties must secure at least 1.5% of total votes at two consecutive federal elections.

Movimiento Ciudadano (MC): Louisiana 113, esq. Nueva York, Col. Nápoles, Del. Benito Juárez, 03810 México, DF; tel. (55) 1167-6767; e-mail gestionsocial@convergencia.org.mx; internet www.movimientociudadano.org.mx; f. 1999 as Convergencia por la Democracia; changed name to Convergencia in 2002; restructured and adopted present name in 2011; contested the 2012 elections as part of the Movimiento Progresista; Co-ordinator DANTE ALFONSO DELGADO RANNAURO; Sec. MARÍA ELENA ORANTES LÓPEZ.

Movimiento Regeneración Nacional (Morena): San Luis Potosí 64, esq. Córdoba, Col. Roma, Del. Cuauhtémoc, 06700 México, DF; tel. (55) 4212-4758; internet www.amlo.org.mx; f. 2012; created by dissidents from the Partido de la Revolución Democrática (PRD); left-wing; Leader ANDRÉS MANUEL LÓPEZ OBRADOR.

Nueva Alianza (NA): Durango 199, Col. Roma, Del. Cuauhtémoc, 06700 México, DF; tel. (55) 3685-8485; fax (55) 3685-8455; e-mail monica.arriola@nueva-alianza.org.mx; internet www.nueva-alianza.org.mx; f. 2005 by dissident faction of the PRI; includes mems of the Sindicato Nacional de Trabajadores de la Educación and supporters of Elba Esther Gordillo Morales; Pres. LUIS CASTRO OBREGÓN; Sec.-Gen. MÓNICA ARRIOLA GORDILLO.

Partido Acción Nacional (PAN): Avda Coyoacán 1546, Col. del Valle, Del. Benito Juárez, 03100 México, DF; tel. (55) 5200-4000; e-mail correo@cen.pan.org.mx; internet www.pan.org.mx; f. 1939; democratic party; 150,000 mems; Pres. GUSTAVO ENRIQUE MADERO MUÑOZ; Sec.-Gen. GUADALUPE INÉS CRUZ AVILA.

Partido Popular Socialista (PPS): Avda Alvaro Obregón 185, Col. Roma, Del. Cuauhtémoc, 06797 México, DF; tel. (55) 5208-5063; fax (55) 2454-6593; e-mail info@ppsm.org.mx; internet www.ppsm.org.mx; f. 1948; Marxist-Leninist, Lombardist; Sec.-Gen. CUAUHTÉMOC AMEZCUA DROMUNDO.

Partido de la Revolución Democrática (PRD): Avda Benjamín Franklin 84, Col. Escandón, Del. Miguel Hidalgo, 11800 México, DF; tel. (55) 1085-8000; fax (55) 1085-8144; e-mail comunicacion@prd.org.mx; internet www.prd.org.mx; f. 1989; centre-left; contested the 2012 elections as part of the Movimiento Progresista; Pres. JESÚS ZAMBRANO GRIJALVA; Sec.-Gen. ALEJANDRO SÁNCHEZ CAMACHO.

Partido Revolucionario Institucional (PRI): Edif. 2, Insurgentes Norte 59, Col. Buenavista, Del. Cuauhtémoc, 06359 México, DF; tel. (55) 5729-9600; internet www.pri.org.mx; f. 1929 as the Partido Nacional Revolucionario; regarded as the natural successor to the victorious parties of the revolutionary period; broadly based and centrist; Pres. Dr CÉSAR CAMACHO QUIROZ; Sec.-Gen. IVONNE ORTEGA PACHECO; groups within the PRI include: the Corriente Crítica Progresista, the Corriente Crítica del Partido, the Corriente Constitucionalista Democratizadora, Corriente Nuevo PRI XIV Asamblea, Democracia 2000, México Nuevo and Galileo.

Partido del Trabajo (PT): Avda Cuauhtémoc 47, Col. Roma Norte, Del. Miguel Hidalgo, 06700 México, DF; tel. and fax (55) 5525-2727; internet www.partidodeltrabajo.org.mx; f. 1990; labour party; contested the 2012 elections as part of the Movimiento Progresista; Leader ALBERTO ANAYA GUTIÉRREZ.

Partido Verde Ecologista de México (PVEM): Loma Bonita 18, Col. Lomas Altas, Del. Miguel Hidalgo, 11950 México, DF; tel. and fax (55) 5257-0188; internet www.partidoverde.org.mx; f. 1987; ecologist party; Spokesman ARTURO ESCOBAR Y VEGA; Sec.-Gen. MARCO ANTONIO DE LA MORA TORREBLANCA.

The following parties are not officially registered but continue to be politically active:

Fuerza Ciudadana: Rochester 94, Col. Nápoles, 03810 México, DF; tel. (55) 5534-4628; e-mail info@fuerzaciudadana.org.mx; internet www.fuerzaciudadana.org.mx; f. 2002; citizens' asscn; Pres. JORGE ALCOCER VILLANUEVA; Sec. ALBERTO CONSEJO VARGAS.

Partido Democrático Popular Revolucionario: internet pdpr-epr.blogspot.in; f. 1996; political grouping representing the causes of 14 armed peasant orgs, including the EPR and the PROCUP; Commdr-Gen. FLORENCIA ELODIA CANSECO RUÍZ.

Partido Socialdemócrata (PSD): Tejocotes 164, Col. Tlacoquemécatl del Valle, Del. Benito Juárez, 03200 México, DF; tel. (55) 5488-1520; fax (55) 5488-1598; internet psdmexico.blogspot.in; f. 2005 as Partido Alternativa Socialdemócrata y Campesina; adopted current name 2008; progressive and peasants' rights; lost political registration following 2009 mid-term elections; Pres. JORGE CARLOS DÍAZ CUERVO.

Illegal organizations active in Mexico include the following:

Ejército Revolucionario Popular Insurgente (ERPI): internet www.enlace-erpi.org; f. 1996; left-wing guerrilla group active in Guerrero, Morelos and Oaxaca; Leader OMAR GUERRERO SOLÍS (alias Comandante Ramiro).

Ejército Zapatista de Liberación Nacional (EZLN): e-mail laotra@ezln.org.mx; internet www.ezln.org.mx; f. 1993; left-wing guerrilla group active in the Chiapas region; Leader Subcomandante MARCOS.

Diplomatic Representation

EMBASSIES IN MEXICO

Algeria: Sierra Madre 540, Col. Lomas de Chapultepec, Del. Miguel Hidalgo, 11000 México, DF; tel. (55) 5520-6950; fax (55) 5540-7579; e-mail embajadadeargelia@yahoo.com.mx; Ambassador ABDELHAMID ABROUS.

Angola: Gaspar de Zúñiga 226, Col. Lomas de Chapultepec, Sección Virreyes, Del. Miguel Hidalgo, 11000 México, DF; tel. (55) 5202-4421; fax (55) 5540-5928; e-mail info@embangolamex.org; Ambassador LEOVIGILDO DA COSTA E SILVA.

Argentina: Avda Palmas 910, Col. Lomas de Chapultepec, Del. Miguel Hidalgo, 11000 México, DF; tel. (55) 5520-9430; fax (55) 5540-5011; e-mail embajadaargentina@prodigy.net.mx; Ambassador PATRICIA VACA NARVAJA.

Australia: Rubén Darío 55, Col. Polanco, Del. Miguel Hidalgo, 11580 México, DF; tel. (55) 1101-2200; fax (55) 1101-2201; e-mail embaustmex@yahoo.com.mx; internet www.mexico.embassy.gov.au; Ambassador TIM GEORGE.

Austria: Sierra Tarahumara 420, Col. Lomas de Chapultepec, Del. Miguel Hidalgo, 11000 México, DF; tel. (55) 5251-0806; fax (55) 5245-0198; e-mail mexiko-ob@bmaa.gv.at; internet www.embajadadeaustria.com.mx; Ambassador ALFRED LANGLE.

Azerbaijan: Avda Virreyes 1015, Col. Lomas de Chapultepec, Del. Miguel Hidalgo, 11000 México, DF; tel. (55) 5540-4109; fax (55) 5540-1366; e-mail oficina@azembassy.mx; internet www.azembassy.mx; Ambassador ILGAR MUKHTAROV.

Belgium: Alfredo Musset 41, Col. Polanco, Del. Miguel Hidalgo, 11550 México, DF; tel. (55) 5280-0758; fax (55) 5280-0208; e-mail mexico@diplobel.org; internet www.diplomatie.be/mexico; Ambassador BOUDEWIJN E. G. DEREYMAEKAR.

Belize: Bernardo de Gálvez 215, Col. Lomas de Chapultepec, Del. Miguel Hidalgo, 11000 México, DF; tel. (55) 5520-1274; fax (55) 5520-6089; e-mail embelize@prodigy.net.mx; Ambassador OLIVER DEL CID.

Bolivia: Goethe 104, Col. Anzures, Del. Miguel Hidalgo, 11590 México, DF; tel. and fax (55) 5255-3620; e-mail embajada@embol .org.mx; internet www.embol.org.mx; Ambassador MARCOS DOMIC RUÍZ.

Brazil: Lope de Armendáriz 130, Col. Lomas Virreyes, Del. Miguel Hidalgo, 11000 México, DF; tel. (55) 5201-4531; fax (55) 5520-4929; e-mail brasemb.mexico@itamaraty.gov.br; internet mexico .itamaraty.gov.br; Ambassador MARCOS LEAL RAPOSO LOPES.

Bulgaria: Paseo de la Reforma 1990, Col. Lomas de Chapultepec, Del. Miguel Hidalgo, 11000 México, DF; tel. (55) 5596-3283; fax (55) 5596-1012; e-mail Embassy.Mexico@mfa.bg; internet www.mfa.bg/en/51; Ambassador HRISTO GEORGIEV GUDJEV.

Canada: Schiller 529, Col. Polanco, Del. Miguel Hidalgo, 11560 México, DF; tel. (55) 5724-7900; fax (55) 5724-7980; e-mail mxico@ international.gc.ca; internet www.canadainternational.gc.ca/ mexico-mexique; Ambassador SARA HRADECKY.

Chile: Andrés Bello 10, 18°, Col. Polanco, Del. Miguel Hidalgo, 11560 México, DF; tel. (55) 5280-9681; fax (55) 5280-9703; e-mail echilmex@ prodigy.net.mx; internet chileabroad.gov.cl/mexico; Ambassador ROBERTO AMPUERO ESPINOZA.

China, People's Republic: Avda San Jerónimo 217B, Del. Alvaro Obregón, 01090 México, DF; tel. (55) 5616-0609; fax (55) 5616-0460; e-mail embchina@data.net.mx; internet www.embajadachina.org .mx; Ambassador ZENG GANG.

Colombia: Paseo de la Reforma 379, 1° y 5°–6°, Col. Cuauhtémoc, Del. Cuauhtémoc, 06500 México, DF; tel. (55) 5525-0277; fax (55) 5208-2876; e-mail emexico@cancilleria.gov.co; internet www .embajadaenmexico.gov.co; Ambassador JOSÉ GABRIEL ORTIZ ROBLEDO.

Costa Rica: Río Po 113, Col. Cuauhtémoc, Del. Cuauhtémoc, 06500 México, DF; tel. (55) 5525-7764; fax (55) 5511-9240; e-mail embajada@embajada.decostaricaenmexico.org; internet www .embajada.decostaricaenmexico.org; Ambassador GABRIELA JIMÉNEZ CRUZ.

Côte d'Ivoire: Tennyson 67, Col. Polanco, Del. Miguel Hidalgo, 11560 México, DF; tel. 5280-8573; fax 5282-2954; e-mail ambacimex@cotedivoiremx.org; internet cotedivoiremx.org; Ambassador OBOU MARCELLIN ABIE.

Cuba: Presidente Masaryk 554, Col. Polanco, Del. Miguel Hidalgo, 11560 México, DF; tel. (55) 5280-8039; fax (55) 5280-0839; e-mail embajada@embacuba.com.mx; internet www.cubadiplomatica.cu/ mexico; Ambassador DAGOBERTO RODRÍGUEZ BARRERA.

Cyprus: Sierra Gorda 370, Col. Lomas de Chapultepec, Del. Miguel Hidalgo, 11000 México, DF; tel. (55) 5202-7600; fax (55) 5520-2693; e-mail limassol@prodigy.net.mx; internet www.mfa.gov.cy/ embassymexico; Chargé d'affaires a.i. ELEFTHERIOS PILAVAKIS.

Czech Republic: Cuvier 22, esq. Kepler, Col. Nueva Anzures, Del. Miguel Hidalgo, 11590 México, DF; tel. (55) 5531-2777; fax (55) 5531-1837; e-mail mexico@embassy.mzv.cz; internet www.mzv.cz/mexico; Ambassador JIŘÍ HAVLÍK.

Denmark: Tres Picos 43, Col. Chapultepec Morales, Del. Miguel Hidalgo, 11580 México, DF; tel. (55) 5255-3405; fax (55) 5545-5797; e-mail mexamb@um.dk; internet www.ambmexicocity.um.dk; Ambassador SUSANNE RUMOHR HÆKKERUP.

Dominican Republic: Prado Sur 755 (entre Monte Blanco y Monte Everest), Col. Lomas de Chapultepec, Del. Miguel Hidalgo, 11000 México, DF; tel. (55) 5540-3841; fax (55) 5520-0779; e-mail embajada@embadom.org.mx; internet www.embadom.org.mx; Ambassador FERNANDO ANTONIO PÉREZ MEMÉN.

Ecuador: Tennyson 217, Col. Polanco, Del. Miguel Hidalgo, 11560 México, DF; tel. (55) 5545-3141; fax (55) 5254-2442; e-mail mecuamex@prodigy.net.mx; Ambassador PATRICIO ALFONSO LÓPEZ ARAUJO.

Egypt: Alejandro Dumas 131, Col. Polanco, Del. Miguel Hidalgo, 11560 México, DF; tel. (55) 5281-0823; fax (55) 5282-1294; e-mail embassy.mexicocity@mfa.gov.eg; internet www.mfa.gov.eg/ Mexico_Emb; Ambassador IBRAHIM AHDY KHAIRAT.

El Salvador: Temístocles 88, Col. Polanco, Del. Miguel Hidalgo, 11560 México, DF; tel. (55) 5281-5725; fax (55) 5280-0657; e-mail embesmex@webtelmex.net.mx; Ambassador CARLOS ANTONIO ASCENCIO GIRÓN.

Finland: Monte Pelvoux 111, 4°, Col. Lomas de Chapultepec, Del. Miguel Hidalgo, 11000 México, DF; tel. (55) 5540-6036; fax (55) 5540-0114; e-mail finmex@prodigy.net.mx; internet www.finlandia.org .mx; Ambassador ANNE LAMMILA.

France: Campos Elíseos 339, Col. Polanco, Del. Miguel Hidalgo, 11560 México, DF; tel. (55) 9171-9893; fax (55) 9171-9703; e-mail prensa@ambafrance-mx.org; internet www.ambafrance-mx.org; Ambassador ELISABETH BETON DELÈGUE.

Georgia: Blvd de Los Virreyes 610, Col. Lomas de Virreyes, Del. Miguel Hidalgo, CP 11000 México, DF; tel. (55) 5520-0118; e-mail mexico.emb@mfa.gov.ge; Ambassador MALKHAZ MIKELADZE.

Germany: Horacio 1506, Col. Los Morales, Del. Miguel Hidalgo, 11530 México, DF; tel. (55) 5283-2200; fax (55) 5281-2588; e-mail info@mexi.diplo.de; internet www.mexiko.diplo.de; Ambassador EDMUND DUCKWITZ.

Greece: Sierra Gorda 505, Col. Lomas de Chapultepec, Del. Miguel Hidalgo, 11010 México, DF; tel. (55) 5520-2070; fax (55) 5202-4080; e-mail grem.mex@mfa.gr; Ambassador DIMITRIOS ANNINOS.

Guatemala: Explanada 1025, Col. Lomas de Chapultepec, Del. Miguel Hidalgo, 11000 México, DF; tel. (55) 5540-7520; fax (55) 5202-1142; e-mail embaguatemx@minex.gob.gt; Ambassador FERNANDO ANDRADE DIÁZ-DURÁN.

Haiti: Presa Don Martín 53, Col. Irrigación, Del. Miguel Hidalgo, 11500 México, DF; tel. (55) 5557-2065; fax (55) 5395-1654; e-mail ambadh@mail.internet.com.mx; Ambassador MARIE JOSEPH GUY LAMOTHE.

Holy See: Juan Pablo II 118, Col. Guadalupe Inn, Del. Alvaro Obregón, 01020 México, DF; tel. (55) 5663-3999; fax (55) 5663-5308; Apostolic Nuncio Most Rev. CHRISTOPHE PIERRE (Titular Archbishop of Gunela).

Honduras: Alfonso Reyes 220, Col. Condesa, Del. Cuauhtémoc, 06170 México, DF; tel. (55) 5211-5747; fax (55) 5211-5425; e-mail emhonmex@prodigy.net.mx; Ambassador JOSÉ MARIANO CASTILLO MERCADO.

Hungary: Paseo de las Palmas 2005, Col. Lomas de Chapultepec, Del. Miguel Hidalgo, 11000 México, DF; tel. (55) 5596-0523; fax (55) 5596-2378; internet www.mfa.gov.hu/kulkepviselet/MX/hu; Ambassador TEREZ DÖRÖMBÖZI DE DEHELAN.

India: Musset 325, Col. Polanco, Del. Miguel Hidalgo, 11550 México, DF; tel. (55) 5531-1050; fax (55) 5254-2349; e-mail indembmx@ prodigy.net.mx; internet www.indembassy.org; Ambassador SUJAN R. CHINOY.

Indonesia: Julio Verne 27, Col. Polanco, Del. Miguel Hidalgo, 11560 México, DF; tel. (55) 5280-6363; fax (55) 5280-7062; e-mail kbrimex@ prodigy.net.mx; internet mexicocity.kemlu.go.id; Ambassador HAMDANI DJAFAR.

Iran: Paseo de la Reforma 2350, Col. Lomas Altas, Del. Miguel Hidalgo, 11950 México, DF; tel. (55) 9172-2691; fax (55) 9172-2694; e-mail iranembmex@hotmail.com; internet mexicocity.mfa.ir; Ambassador JALAL KALANTARI.

Iraq: Paseo de la Reforma 1875, Col. Lomas de Chapultepec, Del. Miguel Hidalgo, 11000 México, DF; tel. (55) 5596-0933; fax (55) 5596-0254; e-mail mxcemb@iraqfamail.com; Chargé d'affaires a.i. ALI HASAN MUHAMMED.

Ireland: Cerrada Blvd Manuel Avila Camacho 76, 3°, Col. Lomas de Chapultepec, Del. Miguel Hidalgo, 11000 México, DF; tel. (55) 5520-5803; fax (55) 5520-5892; e-mail emexicoembassy@dfa.ie; internet www.irishembassy.com.mx; Ambassador SONJA HYLAND (designate).

Israel: Sierra Madre 215, Col. Lomas de Chapultepec, Del. Miguel Hidalgo, 11000 México, DF; tel. (55) 5201-1500; fax (55) 5201-1555; e-mail ambassadorsec@mexico.mfa.gov.il; internet mexico-city.mfa .gov.il; Ambassador RODICA RADIAN-GORDON.

Italy: Paseo de las Palmas 1994, Col. Lomas de Chapultepec, Del. Miguel Hidalgo, 11000 México, DF; tel. (55) 5596-3655; fax (55) 5596-2472; e-mail segreteria.messico@esteri.it; internet www .ambcittadelmessico.esteri.it; Ambassador ROBERTO SPINELLI.

Jamaica: Avda Paseo de las Palmas 1340, Col. Lomas de Chapultepec, 11000 México, DF; tel. (55) 5250-6804; fax (55) 5250-6160; e-mail embajadadejamaica@prodigy.net.mx; Ambassador DELROSE MONTAGUE.

Japan: Paseo de la Reforma 395, Apdo 5-101, Col. Cuauhtémoc, Del. Cuauhtémoc, 06500 México, DF; tel. (55) 5211-0028; fax (55) 5207-7743; e-mail embjapmx@mail.internet.com.mx; internet www.mx .emb-japan.go.jp; Ambassador SHUICHIRO MEGATA.

Korea, Democratic People's Republic: Calle Halley 12, Col. Anzures, Del. Miguel Hidalgo, 11590 México, DF; tel. (55) 5250-0263; fax (55) 5545-8775; e-mail dpkoreaemb@prodigy.net.mx; Ambassador AN KUN SONG.

Korea, Republic: Lope de Armendáriz 110, Col. Lomas Virreyes, Del. Miguel Hidalgo, 11000 México, DF; tel. (55) 5202-9866; fax (55) 5540-7446; e-mail embcoreamx@mofat.go.kr; internet mex.mofat.go .kr; Ambassador HONG SEONG-HOA.

Kuwait: Paseo de la Reforma 500, Col. Juárez, Del. Cuauhtémoc, 06500 México, DF; tel. (55) 5230-1870; fax (55) 5230-1808; e-mail kuwaitembsmexico@aol.com; Ambassador SAMEEH ESSA JOHAR HAYAT.

Lebanon: Julio Verne 8, Col. Polanco, Del. Miguel Hidalgo, 11560 México, DF; tel. (55) 5280-5614; fax (55) 5280-8870; e-mail embalibano@embajadelibano.org.mx; internet www .embajadadelibano.org.mx; Ambassador HICHAM HAMDAN.

Libya: Horacio 1003, Col. Polanco, Del. Miguel Hidalgo, 11550 México, DF; tel. (55) 5545-5725; fax (55) 5545-5677; e-mail libia.mexico@yahoo.com; Chargé d'affaires a.i. YOUSEF HADADA.

Malaysia: Sierra Nevada 435, Col. Lomas de Chapultepec, Del. Miguel Hidalgo, 11000 México, DF; tel. (55) 5282-5166; fax (55) 5282-4910; e-mail mwmexico@prodigy.net.mx; Ambassador Dato' JAMAIYAH MOHAMED YUSOF.

Morocco: Paseo de las Palmas 2020, Col. Lomas de Chapultepec, Del. Miguel Hidalgo, 11000 México, DF; tel. (55) 5245-1786; fax (55) 5245-1791; e-mail sifamex@infosel.net.mx; internet www.marruecos.org.mx; Ambassador ABDERRAHMAN LEIBEK.

Netherlands: Edif. Calakmul, 7°, Avda Vasco de Quiroga 3000, Col. Santa Fe, Del. Alvaro Obregón, 01210 México, DF; tel. (55) 1105-6550; fax (55) 5258-8138; e-mail mex-info@minbuza.nl; internet mexico.nlembajada.org; Ambassador COENRAAD HENDRIK ADOLPH HOGEWONING.

New Zealand: Edif. Corporativo Polanco, 4°, Jaime Balmes 8, Col. Los Morales Polanco, Del. Miguel Hidalgo, 11510 México, DF; tel. (55) 5283-9460; fax (55) 5283-9480; e-mail kiwimexico@prodigy.net.mx; internet www.nzembassy.com/mexico; Ambassador CLARE KELLY (designate).

Nicaragua: Prado Norte 470, Col. Lomas de Chapultepec, Del. Miguel Hidalgo, 11000 México, DF; tel. (55) 5540-5625; fax (55) 5520-6961; e-mail embanic@prodigy.net.mx; Ambassador TAMARA HAWKINS DE BRENES.

Nigeria: Paseo de las Palmas 1880, Col. Lomas de Chapultepec, Del. Miguel Hidalgo, 11000 México, DF; tel. (55) 5245-1487; fax (55) 5245-0105; e-mail nigembmx@att.net.mx; Ambassador ZHIRI JAMES GANA.

Norway: Avda de los Virreyes 1460, Col. Lomas Virreyes, Del. Miguel Hidalgo, 11000 México, DF; tel. (55) 5540-3486; fax (55) 5202-3019; e-mail emb.mexico@mfa.no; internet www.noruega.org.mx; Ambassador ARNE AASHEIM.

Pakistan: Hegel 512, Col. Chapultepec Morales, Del. Miguel Hidalgo, 11570 México, DF; tel. (55) 5203-3636; fax (55) 5203-9907; e-mail parepmex@hotmail.com; Ambassador MUHAMMAD MASOOD ASLAM.

Panama: Sócrates 339, Col. Polanco, Del. Miguel Hidalgo, 11560 México, DF; tel. (55) 5280-7857; fax (55) 5280-7586; e-mail informes@embpanamamexico.com; internet www.embpanamamexico.com; Ambassador FRANCISCO TROYA AGUIRRE.

Paraguay: Homero 415, 1°, esq. Hegel, Col. Polanco, Del. Miguel Hidalgo, 11570 México, DF; tel. (55) 5545-0405; fax (55) 5531-9905; e-mail embapar@prodigy.net.mx; Ambassador CARLOS HERIBERTO RIVEROS SALCEDO.

Peru: Paseo de la Reforma 2601, Col. Lomas Reforma, Del. Miguel Hidalgo, 11000 México, DF; tel. (55) 1105-2270; fax (55) 1105-2279; e-mail embaperu@prodigy.net.mx; internet www.embajadadelperu.com.mx; Ambassador ESTHER ELIZABETH ASTETE RODRÍGUEZ.

Philippines: Río Rhin 56, Cuauhtémoc, Del. Cuauhtémoc, 06500 México, DF; tel. (55) 5202-8456; fax (55) 5202-8403; e-mail mexico.pi@dfa.gov.ph; Ambassador GEORGE BELLO.

Poland: Cracovia 40, Col. San Angel, Del. Alvaro Obregón, 01000 México, DF; tel. (55) 5481-2051; fax (55) 5481-2056; e-mail embajadadepolonia@prodigy.net.mx; internet www.meksyk.polemb.net; Ambassador ANNA ELZBIETA NIEWIADOMSKA.

Portugal: Avda Alpes 1370, Lomas de Chapultepec, Del. Miguel Hidalgo, 11000 México, DF; tel. (55) 5520-7897; fax (55) 5520-4688; e-mail embpomex@prodigy.net.mx; internet embpomex.wordpress.com; Ambassador JOÃO JOSÉ GOMES CAETANO DA SILVA.

Romania: Sófocles 311, Col. Polanco, Del. Miguel Hidalgo, 11560 México, DF; tel. (55) 5280-0197; fax (55) 5280-0343; e-mail secretariat@rumania.org.mx; internet www.rumania.org.mx; Ambassador ANA VOICU.

Russia: José Vasconcelos 204, Col. Hipódromo Condesa, Del. Cuauhtémoc, 06140 México, DF; tel. (55) 5273-1305; fax (55) 5273-1545; e-mail embrumex@hotmail.com; internet www.embrumex.org; Ambassador EDUARD MALAYÁN.

Saudi Arabia: Paseo de las Palmas 2075, Col. Lomas de Chapultepec, Del. Miguel Hidalgo, 11000 México, DF; tel. (55) 5596-0173; fax (55) 5020-3160; e-mail saudiemb@prodigy.net.mx; Ambassador HUSSEIN MOHAMMAD ABDULFATAH AL-ASSIRI.

Serbia: Montañas Rocallosas Oeste 515, Col. Lomas de Chapultepec, Del. Miguel Hidalgo, 11000 México, DF; tel. (55) 5520-0524; fax (55) 5520-9927; e-mail embajadaserbia@alestra.net.mx; Chargé d'affaires a.i. TATJANA CONIĆ.

Slovakia: Julio Verne 35, Col. Polanco, Del. Miguel Hidalgo, 11560 México, DF; tel. (55) 5280-6669; fax (55) 5280-6294; e-mail emb.mexico@mzv.sk; internet www.mzv.sk/mexico; Ambassador JAROSLAV BLAŠKO.

South Africa: Edif. Forum, 9°, Andrés Bello 10, Col. Polanco, Del. Miguel Hidalgo, 11560 México, DF; tel. (55) 1100-4970; fax (55) 5282-9259; e-mail safrica@prodigy.net.mx; Ambassador SANDILE NOGXINA.

Spain: Galileo 114, esq. Horacio, Col. Polanco, Del. Miguel Hidalgo, 11550 México, DF; tel. (55) 5282-2271; fax (55) 5282-1520; e-mail emb.mexico@maec.es; internet www.maec.es/embajadas/mexico; Ambassador MANUEL ALABART FERNÁNDEZ-CAVADA.

Sweden: Paseo de las Palmas 1375, Col. Lomas de Chapultepec, Del. Miguel Hidalgo, 11000 México, DF; tel. (55) 9178-5010; fax (55) 5540-3253; e-mail suecia@prodigy.net.mx; internet www.suecia.com.mx; Ambassador JÖRGEN HANS PERSSON.

Switzerland: Paseo de las Palmas 405, 11°, Torre Óptima, Col. Lomas de Chapultepec, Del. Miguel Hidalgo, 11000 México, DF; tel. (55) 9178-4370; fax (55) 5520-8685; e-mail vertretung@mex.rep.admin.ch; internet www.eda.admin.ch/mexico; Ambassador RUDOLF KNOBLAUCH.

Thailand: Paseo de las Palmas 1610, Col. Lomas de Chapultepec, Del. Miguel Hidalgo, 11000 México, DF; tel. (55) 5540-4551; fax (55) 5540-4817; e-mail thaimex@prodigy.net.mx; internet www.thaiembmexico.co.nr; Ambassador CHIRACHAI PUNKRASIN.

Turkey: Monte Líbano 885, Col. Lomas de Chapultepec, Del. Miguel Hidalgo, 11000 México, DF; tel. (55) 5282-4277; fax (55) 5282-4894; e-mail embajada.mexico@mfa.gov.tr; internet mexico.emb.mfa.gov.tr; Ambassador ALI AHMET ACET.

Ukraine: Paseo de la Reforma 730, Col. Lomas de Chapultepec, Del. Miguel Hidalgo, 11000 México, DF; tel. (55) 5282-4085; fax (55) 5282-4768; e-mail emb_mx@mfa.gov.ua; internet www.mfa.gov.ua/mexico; Ambassador RUSLAN SPIRIN.

United Arab Emirates: Paseo de La Reforma 505, Col. Lomas de Chapultepec, Del. Miguel Hidalgo, 11000 México, DF; tel. (55) 5207-0025; fax (55) 5282-4387; e-mail mexico@mofa.gov.ae; Ambassador SAEED RASHAD OBAID SAIF ALZAABI.

United Kingdom: Río Lerma 71, Col. Cuauhtémoc, Del. Cuauhtémoc, 06500 México, DF; tel. (55) 5242-8500; fax (55) 5242-8517; e-mail ukinmex@att.net.mx; internet www.embajadabritanica.com.mx; Ambassador JUDITH ANNE MACGREGOR (until Aug. 2013), DUNCAN TAYLOR (from Aug. 2013).

USA: Paseo de la Reforma 305, Del. Cuauhtémoc, 06500 México, DF; tel. (55) 5080-2000; fax (55) 5080-2005; internet mexico.usembassy.gov; Ambassador EARL ANTHONY WAYNE.

Uruguay: Hegel 149, 1°, Col. Chapultepec Morales, Del. Miguel Hidalgo, 11560 México, DF; tel. (55) 5531-0880; fax (55) 5545-3342; e-mail uruguaymex@prodigy.net.mx; Ambassador JOSÉ RODOLFO CAMAROSANO BERSANI.

Venezuela: Schiller 326, Col. Chapultepec Morales, Del. Miguel Hidalgo, 11570 México, DF; tel. (55) 5203-4233; fax (55) 5254-1457; e-mail venezmex@prodigy.net.mx; Ambassador HUGO JOSÉ GARCÍA HERNÁNDEZ.

Viet Nam: Sierra Ventana 255, Col. Lomas de Chapultepec, Del. Miguel Hidalgo, 11000 México, DF; tel. (55) 5540-1632; fax (55) 5540-1612; e-mail vietnam.mx@mofa.gov.vn; internet www.vietnamembassy-mexico.org/vi; Ambassador LE THANH TUNG.

Judicial System

The principle of the separation of the judiciary from the legislative and executive powers is embodied in the 1917 Constitution. The judicial system is divided into two areas: the federal, dealing with federal law, and the local, dealing only with state law within each state.

The federal judicial system has both ordinary and constitutional jurisdiction, and judicial power is exercised by the Supreme Court of Justice, the Electoral Court, Collegiate and Unitary Circuit Courts and District Courts. The Supreme Court comprises two separate chambers: Civil and Criminal Affairs, and Administrative and Labour Affairs. The Federal Judicature Council is responsible for the administration, surveillance and discipline of the federal judiciary, except for the Supreme Court of Justice.

Mexico is divided into 29 judicial circuits. The Circuit Courts may be collegiate, when dealing with the *derecho de amparo* (protection of constitutional rights of an individual), or unitary, when dealing with appeal cases. The Collegiate Circuit Courts comprise three magistrates with residence in 38 cities around the country. The Unitary Circuit Courts comprise one magistrate with residence mostly in the same cities.

Suprema Corte de Justicia de la Nación: Pino Suárez 2, Col. Centro, Del. Cuauhtémoc, 06065 México, DF; tel. (55) 4113-1000; fax (55) 4195-0913; e-mail scjn_presidencia@scjn.gob.mx; internet www.scjn.gob.mx; Pres. and Chief Justice JUAN NEPOMUCENO SILVA MEZA.

President of the First Chamber—Civil and Criminal Affairs: JORGE MARIO PARDO REBOLLEDO.

President of the Second Chamber—Administrative and Labour Affairs: SERGIO ARMANDO VALLS HERNÁNDEZ.

Tribunal Electoral del Poder Judicial de la Federación (TEPJF): Carlota Amero 5000, Col. Culhuacán, Del. Coyoacán, 04480 México, DF; tel. (55) 5728-2300; fax (55) 5728-2400; e-mail contactoweb@te.gob.mx; internet www.te.gob.mx; Pres. JOSÉ ALEJANDRO LUNA RAMOS.

Religion

CHRISTIANITY

The Roman Catholic Church

The prevailing religion is Roman Catholicism, but the Church, disestablished in 1857, was for many years, under the Constitution of 1917, subject to state control. For ecclesiastical purposes, Mexico comprises 18 archdioceses, 68 dioceses, five territorial prelatures and two eparchies (both directly subject to the Holy See). According to the latest available census figures (2010), some 84% of the population are Roman Catholics.

Bishops' Conference

Conferencia del Episcopado Mexicano (CEM), Edif. S. S. Juan Pablo II, Prolongación Ministerios 26, Col. Tepeyac Insurgentes, Apdo 118-055, 07020 México, DF; tel. (55) 5781-8462; fax (55) 5577-5489; e-mail segcem@cem.org.mx; internet www.cem.org.mx; Pres. CARLOS AGUIAR RETES (Archbishop of Tlalnepantla); Sec.-Gen. JOSÉ LEOPOLDO GONZÁLEZ GONZÁLEZ.

Archbishop of Acapulco: CARLOS GARFIAS MERLOS, Arzobispado, Quebrada 16, Apdo 201, Centro, 39300 Acapulco, Gro; tel. and fax (744) 482-0763; e-mail arzobispadoaca@aca.cableonline.com.mx; internet www.arquidiocesisacapulco.org.mx.

Archbishop of Antequera, Oaxaca: JOSÉ LUIS CHÁVEZ BOTELLO, García Virgil 600, Anexos de Catedral, Col. Centro, 68000 Oaxaca, Oax.; tel. (951) 516-4822; fax (951) 514-1348; e-mail arzobispadooaxaca@hotmail.com; internet arquidiocesisoaxaca.org .mx.

Archbishop of Chihuahua: CONSTANCIO MIRANDA WECKMANN, Arzobispado, Avda Cuauhtémoc 1828, Apdo 7, Col. Cuauhtémoc, 31020 Chihuahua, Chih.; tel. (614) 410-3202; fax (614) 410-5621; e-mail ferar@megalink.com.mx; internet www.arquichi.org.mx.

Archbishop of Durango: HÉCTOR GONZÁLEZ MARTÍNEZ, Arzobispado, 20 de Noviembre 306, Poniente Centro, 34000 Durango, Dgo; tel. (618) 811-4242; fax (618) 812-8881; e-mail arqdgo@prodigy.net .mx.

Archbishop of Guadalajara: Cardinal JOSÉ FRANCISCO ROBLES ORTEGA, Arzobispado, Liceo 17, Apdo 1-331, Col. Centro, 44100 Guadalajara, Jal.; tel. (33) 3614-5504; fax (33) 3658-2300; e-mail arzgdl@arquinet.com.mx; internet www.arquidiocesisgdl.org.mx.

Archbishop of Hermosillo: JOSÉ ULISES MACÍAS SALCEDO, Arzobispado, Dr Paliza y Ocampo, Ala Sur de la Catedral, Col. Centenario, 83260 Hermosillo, Son.; tel. (662) 213-2138; fax (662) 213-1327; e-mail arzohmo@hotmail.com; internet www.iglesiahermosillo.com .mx.

Archbishop of Jalapa: HIPÓLITO REYES LARIOS, Arzobispado, Avda Manuel Avila Camacho 73, Apdo 359, Col. Centro, 91000 Jalapa, Ver.; tel. (228) 812-0579; fax (228) 817-5578; e-mail arzobispadoalxal@prodigy.net.mx.

Archbishop of León: JOSÉ GUADALUPE MARTÍN RÁBAGO, Arzobispado, Pedro Moreno 312, Apdo 108, 37000 León, Gto; tel. (477) 713-2747; fax (477) 713-1286; e-mail canciller@arquidiocesisleon.org.mx; internet www.arquidiocesisdeleon.org.mx.

Archbishop of Mexico City: Cardinal NORBERTO RIVERA CARRERA, Curia del Arzobispado de México, Durango 90, 5°, Col. Roma, Apdo 24433, 06700 México, DF; tel. (55) 5208-3200; fax (55) 5208-5350; e-mail arzobisp@arquidiocesismexico.org.mx; internet www .arzobispadomexico.org.mx.

Archbishop of Monterrey: Cardinal FRANCISCO ROBLES ORTEGA, Zuazua 1100 Sur con Ocampo Centro, Apdo 7, 64000 Monterrey, NL; tel. (81) 1158-2450; fax (81) 1158-2488; e-mail cancilleria@ arquidiocesismty.org; internet www.arquidiocesismty.org.mx.

Archbishop of Morelia: ALBERTO SUÁREZ INDA, Arzobispado, Costado Catedral, Frente Avda Madero, Apdo 17, 58000 Morelia, Mich.; tel. (443) 313-2493; fax (443) 312-0919; e-mail asuarexi@prodigy.net .mx; internet www.arquimorelia.org.mx.

Archbishop of Puebla de los Angeles: VÍCTOR SÁNCHEZ ESPINOSA, Avda 2 Sur 305, Apdo 235, Col. Centro, 72000 Puebla, Pue.; tel. (222) 232-4591; fax (222) 246-2277; e-mail rhuesca@mail.cem.org.mx.

Archbishop of San Luis Potosí: CARLOS CABRERO ROMERO, Arzobispado, Francisco Madero 300, Apdo 1, Col. Centro, 78000 San Luis Potosí, SLP; tel. (444) 812-4555; fax (444) 812-7979; e-mail arqsanluis@iglesiapotosina.org; internet www.iglesiapotosina.org.

Archbishop of Tijuana: RAFAEL ROMO MUÑOZ, Arzobispado, Calle Décima y Avda Ocampo 8525, Apdo 226, 22000 Tijuana, BC; tel. (664) 684-8411; fax (664) 684-7683; internet www.iglesiatijuana.org.

Archbishop of Tlalnepantla: CARLOS AGUIAR RETES, Arzobispado, Avda Juárez 42, Apdo 268, Col. Centro, 54000 Tlalnepantla, Méx.; tel. (55) 5565-3944; fax (55) 5565-2751; e-mail curia@arqtlalnepantla .org; internet www.arqtlalnepantla.org.

Archbishop of Tulancingo: DOMINGO DÍAZ MARTÍNEZ, Arzobispado, Plaza de la Constitución, Apdo 14, 43600 Tulancingo, Hgo; e-mail sgamitra@netpac.net.mx.

Archbishop of Tuxtla Gutiérrez: ROGELIO CABRERA LÓPEZ, Uruguay 500A, Col. El Retiro, Apdo 365, 29040 Tuxtla Gutiérrez, Chis; e-mail casaepiscopal@prodigy.net.mx.

Archbishop of Yucatán: EMILIO CARLOS BERLIE BELAUNZARÁN, Arzobispado, Calle 58 501, Col. Centro, 97000 Mérida, Yuc.; tel. (999) 924-7777; fax (999) 923-7983; e-mail aryu@prodigy.net.mx; internet www.arquidiocesisdeyucatan.org.

The Anglican Communion

Mexico is divided into five dioceses, which form the Province of the Anglican Church in Mexico, established in 1995.

Bishop of Cuernavaca: RAMIRO DELGADO VERA, Minerva 1, Col. Delicias, 62431 Cuernavaca, Mor.; tel. and fax (777) 315-2870; e-mail adoc@cableonline.com.mx; internet www.cuernavaca-anglican.org.

Bishop of Mexico City and Primate of the Anglican Church in Mexico: CARLOS TOUCHÉ PORTER, La Otra Banda 40, Avda San Jerónimo 117, Col. San Angel, 01000 México, DF; tel. and fax (55) 5616-2205; e-mail contacto@iglesiaanglicanademexico.org; internet www.iglesiaanglicanademexico.org.

Bishop of Northern Mexico: MARCELINO RIVERA DELGADO, Simón Bolívar 2005 Nte, Col. Mitras Centro, 64460 Monterrey, NL; tel. (81) 8333-0922; fax (81) 8348-7362; e-mail diocesisdelnorte@att.net.mx.

Bishop of South-Eastern Mexico: BENITO JUÁREZ MARTÍNEZ, Avda de las Américas 73, Col. Aguacatl, 91130 Jalapa, Ver.; tel. and fax (228) 814-6951; e-mail dioste99@aol.com.

Bishop of Western Mexico: LINO RODRÍGUEZ-AMARO, Francisco Javier Gamboa 255, Col. Barrera, 45150 Guadalajara, Jal.; tel. (33) 3615-5070; fax (33) 3615-4413; e-mail iamoccidente@prodigy.net.mx; internet www.iamoccidente.org.mx.

Protestant Churches

According to the 2010 census, some 8% of the population are Protestant or Evangelical Christians.

Iglesia Evangélica Luterana de México: Mina 5808 Poniente, Nuevo Laredo, Tamaulipas; 3,000 mems (2010); Pres. ENCARNACIÓN ESTRADA.

Iglesia Luterana Mexicana: POB 1-1034, 44101 Guadalajara, Jal.; tel. (33) 3639-7253; e-mail dtrejocoria@gmail.com; f. 1951; Pres. DANIEL TREJO CORIA; 1,500 mems.

Iglesia Metodista de México, Asociación Religiosa: Miravelle 209, Col. Albert, 03570 México, DF; tel. (55) 5539-3674; e-mail prenapro@iglesia-metodista.org.mx; internet www.iglesia -metodista.org.mx; f. 1873; 55,000 mems; Pres. Rev. RAÚL GARCÍA DE OCHOA; 700 congregations; comprises six episcopal areas.

National Baptist Convention of Mexico: Tlalpan 1035A, Col. Américas Unidas, 03610 México, DF; tel. (55) 5539-7720; fax (55) 5539-2302; e-mail comunicacion@cnbm.org.mx; internet www.cnbm .org.mx; f. 1903; Pres. Rev. JOSÉ TRINIDAD BONILLA MORALES.

BAHÁ'Í FAITH

National Spiritual Assembly of the Bahá'ís of Mexico: Emerson 421, Col. Bosque de Chapultepec, 11580 México, DF; tel. (55) 5545-2155; fax (55) 5255-5972; e-mail secretariado@bahai.mx; internet www.bahai.mx; mems resident in 1,065 localities.

JUDAISM

According to the 2000 census, the Jewish community numbers 45,260 (less than 1% of the population).

Comité Central de la Comunidad Judía de México: Cofre de Perote 115, Lomas Barrilaco, 11010 México, DF; tel. (55) 5520-9393; fax (55) 5540-3050; e-mail comitecentral@prodigy.net.mx; internet www.tribuna.org.mx; f. 1938; Pres. RAFAEL ZAGA.

The Press

DAILY NEWSPAPERS

México, DF

La Afición: Ignacio Mariscal 23, Apdo 64 bis, Col. Tabacalera, 06030 México, DF; tel. (55) 5140-4900; fax (55) 5546-5852; internet www

.laaficion.com; f. 1930; sport; Pres. FRANCISCO A. GONZÁLEZ; Exec. Editor CARLOS MARÍN; circ. 85,000.

La Crónica de Hoy: Londres 38, Col. Juárez, 06600 México, DF; tel. and fax (52) 5512-3429; e-mail cronica@cronica.com.mx; internet www.cronica.com.mx; Pres. JORGE KAHWAGI GASTINE; Editorial Dir FRANCISCO BAEZ RODRÍGUEZ.

Diario de México: Chimalpopoca 38, Col. Obrera, 06800 México, DF; tel. (55) 5442-6526; fax (55) 5442-6520; e-mail redaccionddm@ diariodemexico.com.mx; internet www.diariodemexico.com.mx; f. 1949; morning; Dir-Gen. FEDERICO BRACAMONTES BAZ; Editorial Dir LUIS RODRÍGUEZ MUNGUIA; circ. 76,000.

Diario Oficial de la Federación: Río Amazonas 62, Col. Cuauhtémoc, 06500 México, DF; tel. (55) 5093-3200; e-mail dof@segob.gob.mx; internet www.dof.gob.mx; f. 1867; govt gazette; Dir-Gen. ALEJANDRO LÓPEZ GONZÁLEZ.

El Economista: Avda Coyoacán 515, Col. del Valle, 03100 México, DF; tel. (55) 5237-0766; fax (55) 5687-3821; e-mail internet@ eleconomista.com.mx; internet www.economista.com.mx; f. 1988; financial; Pres. JOSÉ NACER GOBERA; Editor-in-Chief LUIS MIGUEL GONZÁLEZ; circ. 37,448.

Esto: Guillermo Prieto 7, 1°, Col. San Rafael, Del. Cuauhtémoc, 06470 México, DF; tel. and fax (55) 5566-1511; fax (55) 5591-0866; e-mail esto@oem.com.mx; internet www.esto.com.mx; f. 1941; published by Organización Editorial Mexicana; morning; sport; Dir SALVADOR AGUILERA GONZÁLEZ; Editor-in-Chief CARLOS GABINO CU UC; circ. 400,000, Mon. 450,000.

Excélsior: Bucareli 1, Apdo 120 bis, Col. Centro, 06600 México, DF; tel. (55) 5128-3000; fax (55) 5566-0223; e-mail foro@excelsior.com.mx; internet www.excelsior.com.mx; f. 1917; morning; independent; Pres. OLEGARIO VÁZQUEX RAÑA; Editorial Dir PASCAL BELTRÁN DEL RÍO; circ. 200,000.

El Financiero: Lago Bolsena 176, Col. Anáhuac (Pensil), entre Lago Peypus y Lago Onega, 11320 México, DF; tel. (55) 5227-7600; fax (55) 5254-6427; e-mail contacto@elfinanciero.com.mx; internet www.elfinanciero.com.mx; f. 1981; financial; Dir-Gen. MARÍA DEL PILAR ESTANDÍA GONZÁLEZ LUNA; Editor-Gen. GENARO MEJÍA; circ. 119,000.

La Jornada: Avda Cuauhtémoc 1236, Col. Santa Cruz Atoyac, Del. Benito Juárez, 03310 México, DF; tel. (55) 9183-0300; internet www.jornada.unam.mx; f. 1984; morning; Dir-Gen. CARMEN LIRA SAADE; Gen. Man. JORGE MARTÍNEZ JIMÉNEZ; circ. 86,275.

Milenio Diario: México, DF; tel. (55) 5140-4900; internet www.milenio.com; publishes Mexico City and regional edns, and a weekly news magazine, *Milenio Semanal*; Pres. FRANCISCO A. GONZÁLEZ; Dir-Gen. FRANCISCO D. GONZÁLEZ A.

Ovaciones: Lago Zirahuén 279, 20°, Col. Anáhuac, 11320 México, DF; tel. (55) 5328-0700; fax (55) 5260-2219; e-mail bjonofre@ova.com.mx; internet www.ovaciones.com; f. 1947; morning and evening editions; Pres. and Dir-Gen. MAURICIO VÁZQUEZ RAMOS; circ. 130,000; evening circ. 100,000.

La Prensa: Basilio Vadillo 40, Col. Tabacalera, 06030 México, DF; tel. (55) 5228-9977; fax (55) 5521-8209; e-mail oemenlinea@oem.com.mx; internet www.la-prensa.com.mx; f. 1928; published by Organización Editorial Mexicana; morning; Pres. and Dir-Gen. MARIO VÁZQUEZ RAÑA; Editor-in-Chief JESÚS SÁNCHEZ RAMÍREZ; circ. 270,000.

Reforma: Avda México Coyoacán 40, Col. Santa Cruz Atoyac, 03310 México, DF; tel. (55) 5628-7100; fax (55) 5628-7188; internet www.reforma.com; f. 1993; morning; Pres. and Dir-Gen. ALEJANDRO JUNCO DE LA VEGA ELIZONDO; Editorial Dir LÁZARO RÍOS; circ. 94,000.

El Sol de México: Guillermo Prieto 7, 20°, Col. San Rafael, 06470 México, DF; tel. (55) 5566-1511; fax (55) 5535-5560; e-mail enlinea@ elsoldemexico.com.mx; internet www.elsoldemexico.com.mx; f. 1965; published by Organización Editorial Mexicana; morning and midday; Pres. and Dir-Gen. MARIO VÁZQUEZ RAÑA; Man. RUBÉN PÉREZ GARCÍA; circ. 76,000.

El Universal: Bucareli 8, Apdo 909, Col. Centro, Del. Cuauhtémoc, 06040 México, DF; tel. (55) 5709-1313; fax (55) 5510-1269; e-mail rdirgral@eluniversal.com.mx; internet www.eluniversal.com.mx; f. 1916; morning; independent; centre-left; Pres. JUAN FRANCISCO EALY ORTIZ; Editorial Dir ROBERTO ROCKL; circ. 165,629, Sun. 181,615.

Unomásuno: Gabino Barreda 86, Col. San Rafael, México, DF; tel. (55) 1055-5500; fax (55) 5598-8821; e-mail cduran@servidor.unam.mx; internet www.unomasuno.com.mx; f. 1977; morning; left-wing; Pres. NAIM LIBIEN KAUI; circ. 40,000.

PROVINCIAL DAILY NEWSPAPERS

Baja California

El Sol de Tijuana: Rufino Tamayo 4, Zona del Río, 22320 Tijuana, BC; tel. (664) 634-3232; fax (664) 634-2234; e-mail jesparza@ elsoldetijuana.com.mx; internet www.oem.com.mx/elsoldetijuana; f. 1989; published by Organización Editorial Mexicana; morning;

Dir-Gen. MARIO VALDÉS HERNÁNDEZ; Editor-in-Chief JORGE ALCALÁ ALVARE; circ. 50,000.

La Voz de la Frontera: Avda Francisco I. Madero 1545, Col. Nueva, Apdo 946, 21100 Mexicali, BC; tel. (686) 533-4545; fax (686) 552-4243; e-mail ramondiaz@lavozdelafrontera.com.mx; internet www.oem.com.mx/lavozdelafrontera; f. 1964; morning; published by Organización Editorial Mexicana; Dir-Gen. FRANCISCO EDGARDO LEAL CORRALES; Dir JUAN GREGORIO AVILÉS TARÍN; circ. 65,000.

Chihuahua

El Diario: Publicaciones Paso del Norte, Avda Paseo Triunfo de la República 2505, Zona Pronaf, 32310 Ciudad Juárez, Chih.; tel. (656) 629-6900; e-mail gcruz@redaccion.diario.com.mx; internet www.diario.com.mx; f. 1976; Pres. OSVALDO RODRÍGUEZ BORUNDA; Editor GENARO CRUZ GARCÍA.

El Heraldo de Chihuahua: Avda Universidad 2507, Apdo 1515, 31240 Chihuahua, Chih.; tel. (614) 432-3800; fax (614) 413-9339; e-mail heraldo@elheraldodechihuahua.com.mx; internet www.elheraldodechihuahua.com.mx; f. 1927; published by Organización Editorial Mexicana; morning; Dir Dr JAVIER H. CONTRERAS; circ. 27,520, Sun. 31,223.

El Mexicano: Ramón Corona y Galeana 301, 32000 Ciudad Juárez, Chih.; e-mail publicidad@periodicoelmexicano.com.mx; internet www.oem.com.mx/elmexicano; f. 1959; published by Organización Editorial Mexicana; morning; Dir RAFAEL NAVARRO BARRÓN; Editor-in-Chief JAIME SALVADOR NÚÑEZ ÁNGEL; circ. 80,000.

Coahuila

El Siglo de Torreón: Avda Matamoros 1056 Poniente, Col. Centro, 27000 Torreón, Coah.; tel. (871) 759-1200; e-mail cartas@ elsiglodetorreon.com.mx; internet www.elsiglodetorreon.com.mx; f. 1922; morning; Pres. OLGA DE JUAMBELZ Y HORCASITAS; circ. 38,611, Sun. 38,526.

Vanguardia: Blvd Venustiano Carranza 1918, esq. con Chiapas, República Oriente, 25280 Saltillo, Coah.; tel. (844) 450-1000; e-mail vanlider@vanguardia.com.mx; internet www.vanguardia.com.mx; Dir-Gen. DIANA MARÍA GALINDO DE CASTILLA; Editorial Dir ARMANDO CASTILLA GALINDO.

Colima

Diario de Colima: Avda 20 de Noviembre 580, 28060 Colima, Col.; tel. (312) 312-5688; internet www.diariodecolima.com; f. 1953; Dir-Gen. HÉCTOR SÁNCHEZ DE LA MADRID; Editorial Dir ALBERTO MAGALLÓN ESTRADA.

Guanajuato

Correo de Guanajuato: Carreterra Guanajuato—Juventino Rosas Km 9.5, Apdo 32, 36260 Guanajuato, Gto; tel. (477) 733-1253; fax (477) 733-0057; e-mail correo@correo-gto.com.mx; internet www.correo-gto.com.mx; Dir-Gen. PABLO VILLANUEVA MARTÍNEZ; Editorial Dir MARTHA CELIA CAMACHO LEDESMA.

El Sol de Salamanca: Faro de Oro 800, 36700 Salamanca, Gto; tel. (464) 647-0144; e-mail publicidad@elsoldesalamanca.com.mx; internet www.elsoldesalamanca.com.mx; published by Organización Editorial Mexicana; Dir-Gen. ALEJANDRO HERRERA SÁNCHEZ; Editor-in-Chief JORGE CAUDILLO ELÍAS.

Guerrero

Novedades de Acapulco: Avda Costera Miguel Aléman 258, Fraccionamiento Hornos, 39355 Acapulco, Gro; tel. (744) 485-1155; e-mail informa@aca-novenet.com.mx; internet www.novedadesacapulco.mx; f. 1969; daily; Editorial Dir MARIO BUSTOS GARCÍA.

Jalisco

El Informador: Independencia 300, Apdo 3 bis, 44100 Guadalajara, Jal.; tel. (33) 3678-7700; e-mail sistemas@informador.com.mx; internet www.informador.com.mx; f. 1917; morning; Editor CARLOS ÁLVAREZ DEL CASTILLO; circ. 50,000.

El Occidental: Calzada Independencia Sur 324, Apdo 1-699, 44100 Guadalajara, Jal.; tel. (33) 3613-0690; fax (33) 3613-6796; e-mail publicidad@eloccidental.com.mx; internet www.eloccidental.com.mx; f. 1942; published by Organización Editorial Mexicana; morning; Dir JAVIER VALLE CHÁVEZ; Editor ANSELMO EDUARDO VÁZQUEZ M.; circ. 49,400.

México

ABC: Avda Hidalgo Oriente 1339, Centro Comercial, Col. Ferrocarriles Nacionales, 50070 Toluca, Méx.; tel. (722) 217-9646; fax (722) 217-8868; e-mail miled@abctoluca.com.mx; internet www.miled.com; f. 1984; morning; Pres. and Editor MILED LIBIEN KAUI; circ. 65,000.

El Heraldo de Toluca: Salvador Díaz Mirón 700, Col. Sánchez Colín, 50150 Toluca, Méx.; tel. (722) 217-3542; fax (722) 212-2535; e-mail heraldotoluca@prodigy.net.mx; internet www.heraldotoluca.com; f. 1955; morning; Editor JORGE MENA GARCÍA; circ. 90,000.

Portal–Diario de Toluca: Sebastián Lerdo de Tejada Poniente 864, esq. Agustín Millán, Col. Electricistas Locales, 50040 Toluca, Méx.; tel. (722) 214-5477; fax (722) 214-5463; e-mail portal@portaldigital.com.mx; internet diarioportal.com; f. 1980; morning; Dir-Gen. ESTEBAN RIVERA RIVERA; Editorial Dir FELIPE GONZÁLEZ LÓPEZ; circ. 22,200.

El Sol de Toluca: Santos Degollado 105, Apdo 54, Col. Centro, 50050 Toluca, Méx.; tel. (722) 214-7077; fax (722) 215-2564; e-mail publicidad@elsoldetoluca.com.mx; internet www.oem.com.mx/elsoldetoluca; f. 1947; published by Organización Editorial Mexicana; morning; Dir FIDEL RODRÍGUEZ GÓMEZ; Editor-in-Chief RODRIGO MIRANDA TORRES; circ. 42,000.

Michoacán

La Voz de Michoacán: Blvd del Periodismo 1270, Col. Arriaga Rivera, Apdo 121, 58190 Morelia, Mich.; tel. (443) 327-5600; fax (443) 327-3728; e-mail redaccilavoz@voznet.com.mx; internet www.vozdemichoacan.com.mx; f. 1948; morning; Dir-Gen. MIGUEL MEDINA ROBLES; circ. 50,000.

Morelos

El Diario de Morelos: Avda Morelos Sur 132, Col. Las Palmas, 62050 Cuernavaca, Mor.; tel. (777) 362-0220; fax (777) 362-0225; e-mail redaccion@diariodemorelos.com; internet www.diariodemorelos.com; f. 1978; morning; Propr Grupo BRACA de Comunicación; Pres. MIGUEL ANGEL BRACAMONTES BAZ; Editor-in-Chief MIRIAM ESTRADA DORANTES; circ. 35,000.

Nayarit

Meridiano de Nayarit: Independencia 335, Fracc. Las Aves, Tepic, Nay.; tel. (311) 210-3211; e-mail ventas@meridiano.com.mx; internet meridiano.nayaritpuntocom.com; f. 1942; morning; Dir Dr DAVID ALFARO; circ. 60,000.

Nuevo León

ABC: Platón Sánchez Sur 411, 64000 Monterrey, NL; tel. (81) 8344-2510; fax (81) 8344-2666; e-mail ventas@periodicoabc.mx; internet www.periodicoabc.mx; f. 1985; morning; Dir-Gen. GONZALO ESTRADO TORRES; Editorial Dir JUAN ANTONIO MARTÍNEZ; circ. 40,000, Sun. 45,000.

El Norte: Washington 629 Oeste, Apdo 186, 64000 Monterrey, NL; tel. (81) 8150-8100; fax (81) 8343-2476; internet www.elnorte.com.mx; f. 1938; morning; Man. Dir ALEJANDRO JUNCO DE LA VEGA; Editorial Dir MARTHA ALICIA TREVIÑO; circ. 133,872, Sun. 154,951.

El Porvenir: Galeana Sur 344, Apdo 218, 64000 Monterrey, NL; tel. (81) 8345-4080; fax (81) 8345-7795; internet www.elporvenir.com.mx; f. 1919; morning; Dir-Gen. JOSÉ GERARDO CANTÚ ESCALANTE; Editorial Dir JOSÉ MANUEL RODRÍGUEZ ARROYO; circ. 75,000.

Oaxaca

El Imparcial: Armenta y López 312, Apdo 322, 68000 Oaxaca, Oax.; tel. (951) 516-2812; fax (951) 514-7020; e-mail subdireccion@imparcialenlinea.com; internet www.imparoax.com.mx; f. 1951; morning; Dir-Gen. BENJAMÍN FERNÁNDEZ PICHARDO; circ. 17,000, Sun. 20,000.

Puebla

La Opinión: 3 Oriente 1207, Barrio del Analco, 238 Puebla, Pue.; tel. (222) 246-4358; fax (222) 232-7772; e-mail director@opinion.com.mx; internet www.opinion.com.mx; f. 1924; morning; Dir-Gen. OSCAR LÓPEZ MORALES; Editor-in-Chief NANCY ALONSO; circ. 40,000.

El Sol de Puebla: Avda 3 Oriente 201, Col. Centro, 72000 Puebla, Pue.; tel. (222) 514-3300; fax (222) 246-0869; e-mail elsoldepuebla@elsoldepuebla.com.mx; internet www.oem.com.mx/elsoldepuebla; f. 1944; published by Organización Editorial Mexicana; morning; Dir RUBÉN PÉREZ GARCÍA; circ. 67,000.

San Luis Potosí

El Heraldo: Villerías 305, 78000 San Luis Potosí, SLP; tel. (444) 812-3312; fax (444) 812-2081; e-mail redaccion@elheraldoslp.com.mx; internet www.elheraldoslp.com.mx; f. 1954; morning; Dir-Gen. ALEJANDRO VILLASANA MENA; circ. 60,620.

Pulso: Galeana 485, Centro Histórico, 78000 San Luis Potosí, SLP; tel. (444) 812-7575; fax (444) 812-3525; internet www.pulsoslp.com.mx; f. 1988; morning; Dir-Gen. PABLO VALLADARES GARCÍA; circ. 60,000.

El Sol de San Luis: Avda Universidad 565, Apdo 342, 78000 San Luis Potosí, SLP; tel. and fax (444) 812-4412; internet www.oem.com.mx/elsoldesanluis; f. 1952; published by Organización Editorial Mexicana; morning; Dir JOSÉ ANGEL MARTÍNEZ LIMÓN; Editor-in-Chief ALFONSO ALVAREZ TERRONES; circ. 60,000.

Sinaloa

El Debate de Culiacán: Madero 556 Poniente, 80000 Culiacán, Sin.; tel. (667) 716-6353; fax (667) 715-7131; e-mail andrea.miranda@debate.com.mx; internet www.debate.com.mx; f. 1972; morning; Dir ROSARIO I. OROPEZA; Editor ANDREA MIRANDA; circ. 23,603, Sun. 23,838.

Noroeste Culiacán: Grupo Periódicos Noroeste, Angel Flores 282 Oeste, Apdo 90, 80000 Culiacán, Sin.; tel. (667) 759-8100; fax (667) 712-8006; e-mail direccion@noroeste.com.mx; internet www.noroeste.com.mx; f. 1973; morning; Dir-Gen. MANUEL BECERRA GONZÁLEZ; Editor RODOLFO DIAZ FONSECA; circ. 35,000.

El Sol de Sinaloa: Blvd Gabriel Leyva Lozano y Corona 320, Apdo 412, 80000 Culiacán, Sin.; tel. (667) 713-1621; fax (667) 713-1800; e-mail publicidad@elsoldesinaloa.com.mx; internet www.elsoldesinaloa.com.mx; f. 1956; published by Organización Editorial Mexicana; morning; Dir JAVIER LÓPEZ LÓPEZ; Editor-in-Chief ARNOLDO ORTEGA MOLINA; circ. 30,000.

Sonora

Expreso: Blvd Abelardo L Rodirquez 16, Col. San Benito, 83190 Hermosillo, Son.; tel. (662) 108-3000; fax (662) 108-3006; e-mail romandia@expreso.com.mx; internet www.expreso.com.mx; f. 2005; Dir-Gen. LUIS ROMANDIA; circ. 17,000, Sun. 18,000.

El Imparcial: Sufragio Efectivo y Mina 71, Col. Centro, Apdo 66, 83000 Hermosillo, Son.; tel. (662) 259-4700; fax (662) 217-4483; e-mail lector@elimparcial.com; internet www.elimparcial.com; f. 1937; morning; Pres. and Dir-Gen. JUAN F. HEALY; Editor LOURDES LUGO; circ. 32,083, Sun. 32,444.

Tabasco

Tabasco Hoy: Avda de los Ríos 206, Col. Tabasco 2000, 86035 Villahermosa, Tab.; tel. (993) 316-2135; internet www.tabascohoy.com.mx; f. 1987; morning; Dir-Gen. MIGUEL CANTÓN ZETINA; Editorial Dir HÉCTOR TAPIA MARTÍNEZ DE ESCOBAR; circ. 50,000.

Tamaulipas

El Bravo: Morelos y Primera 129, Apdo 483, 87300 Matamoros, Tamps; tel. (871) 816-0100; fax (871) 816-2007; e-mail comenta@elbravo.com.mx; internet www.elbravo.com.mx; f. 1951; morning; Dir-Gen. JOSÉ CARRETERO BALBOA; Editorial Dir JESÚS CRUZ MEDRANO; circ. 60,000.

El Diario de Nuevo Laredo: González 2409, Apdo 101, 88000 Nuevo Laredo, Tamps; tel. (867) 712-8444; fax (867) 712-8221; e-mail publicidad@diario.net; internet www.diario.net; f. 1948; morning; Dir-Gen. RUPERTO VILLARREAL MONTEMAYOR; Editor MARCO GUILLERMO VILLARREAL MARROQUÍN; circ. 68,130, Sun. 73,495.

El Mañana: Juárez y Perú, Col. Juárez, Nuevo Laredo, Tamps; tel. (867) 711-9900; fax (867) 715-0405; e-mail mauricio.deleon@elmanana.com.mx; internet www.elmanana.com.mx; f. 1932; morning; Pres. NINFA DEÁNDAR MARTÍNEZ; Editor HERIBERTO CANTÚ DEÁNDAR; circ. 16,473, Sun. 20,957.

El Mañana de Reynosa: Calle Matías Canales 504, Apdo 14, Col. Ribereña, 88620 Ciudad Reynosa, Tamps; tel. (899) 921-9950; fax (899) 924-9348; internet www.elmanana.com; f. 1949; morning; Chief Editors HERIBERTO DEÁNDAR ROBINSON, HILDEBRANDO DEÁNDAR AYALA; circ. 52,000.

Prensa de Reynosa: Matamoros y González Ortega, Zona Centro, 88500 Reynosa, Tamps; tel. (899) 922-0299; fax (899) 922-2412; e-mail prensa_88500@yahoo.com; internet www.prensadereynosa.com; f. 1963; morning; Dir-Gen. and Editor FÉLIX GARZA ELIZONDO; circ. 60,000.

El Sol de Tampico: Altamira 311 Poniente, Apdo 434, 89000 Tampico, Tamps; tel. (833) 212-1067; fax (833) 212-6821; e-mail publicidad@elsoldetampico.com.mx; internet www.oem.com.mx/elsoldetampico; f. 1950; published by Organización Editorial Mexicana; morning; Dir-Gen. AGUSTÍN F. JIMÉNEZ HERNÁNDEZ; Editor-in-Chief MARIO ALBERTO FERNÁNDEZ AVALOS; circ. 77,000.

Veracruz

Diario del Istmo: Avda Hidalgo 1115, Col. Centro, 96400 Coatzacoalcos, Ver.; tel. (921) 211-8000; e-mail info@istmo.com.mx; internet www.diariodelistmo.com; f. 1979; morning; Dir-Gen. HÉCTOR ROBLES BARAJAS; Editor MIGUEL EDUARDO JIMÉNEZ; circ. 64,600.

El Dictamen: 16 de Septiembre y Arista, 91709 Veracruz, Ver.; tel. (229) 931-1745; fax (229) 931-5804; e-mail owar@eldictamen.org;

internet www.eldictamen.mx; f. 1898; morning; Pres. BERTHA ROSALIA MALPICA DE AHUED; circ. 25,000, Sun. 28,000.

La Opinión: Poza Rica de Hidalgo, Ver.; e-mail publicidad@laopinion.com.mx; internet www.laopinion.com.mx; Dir RAÚL GIBB.

Yucatán

Diario del Istmo: Avda Hidalgo 1115, Col. Centro, 96400 Coatzacoalcos, Ver.; tel. (921) 211-8000; e-mail info@istmo.com.mx; internet www.diariodelistmo.com; f. 1979; morning; Dir-Gen. HÉCTOR ROBLES BARAJAS; Editor MIGUEL EDUARDO JIMÉNEZ; circ. 64,600.

Por Esto!: Calle 60, No 576 entre 73 y 71, 97000 Mérida, Yuc.; tel. (999) 24-7613; fax (999) 28-6514; e-mail redaccion@poresto.net; internet www.poresto.net; f. 1991; morning; Dir-Gen. MARIO RENATO MENÉNDEZ RODRÍGUEZ; circ. 26,985, Sun. 28,727.

Zacatecas

Imagen: Calzada Revolución 24, Col. Tierra y Libertad, 98600 Guadalupe, Zac.; tel. and fax (492) 923-8898; e-mail buzon@imagenzac.com.mx; internet www.imagenzac.com.mx; Dir-Gen. PATRICIA MERCADO SÁNCHEZ; Editorial Dir MARÍA DEL CARMEN SALAZAR.

SELECTED WEEKLY NEWSPAPERS

El Heraldo Bajio: Hermanos Aldama 222, Apdo 299, Zona Centro, 37000 León, Gto; tel. (477) 719-8800; e-mail heraldo@el-heraldo-bajio.com.mx; internet www.el-heraldo-bajio.com.mx; f. 1957; Pres. and Dir-Gen. LEÓN MAURICIO BERCÚN LÓPEZ; circ. 85,000.

Zeta: Avda las Américas 4633, Fraccionamiento El Paraíso, Tijuana, BC; tel. (664) 681-6913; fax (664) 621-0065; e-mail asistente@zetatijuana.com; internet www.zetatijuana.com; f. 1980; news magazine; Editor ROSARIO MOSSO CASTRO.

SELECTED PERIODICALS

Boletín Industrial: Luis Khune 55-B, Col. Las Águilas, 01710 México, DF; tel. (55) 5337-2200; fax (55) 5337-2230; e-mail hvalades@boletinindustrial.com; internet www.boletinindustrial.com; f. 1983; publ. by Editorial Nova SA de CV; monthly; Pres. HUMBERTO VALADÉS; circ. 37,100.

Casas y Gente: Tapachula 31, Col. Roma, 06700 México, DF; tel. (55) 5286-7794; fax (55) 5211-7112; e-mail informac@casasgente.com; internet www.casasgente.com; 10 a year; interior design; Dir-Gen. ANNE SÁNCHEZ OSORIO; Editor DONATELLA LOCKHART.

Contenido: Darwin 101, Col. Anzures, 11590 México, DF; tel. (55) 5531-3162; fax (55) 5545-7478; e-mail contenido@contenido.com.mx; internet www.contenido.com.mx; f. 1963; monthly; popular appeal; Editor-in-Chief MARIANA CHAVEZ RODRÍGUEZ; circ. 124,190.

Cosmopolitan México: Vasco de Quiroga 2000, Col. Santa Fe, Del. Alvaro Obregón, 01210 México, DF; tel. (55) 5261-2600; fax (55) 5261-2704; internet www.cosmoenespanol.com; f. 1973; fortnightly; women's magazine; Dir SARA MARÍA CASTANY; circ. 300,000.

Expansión: Avda Constituyentes 956, Col. Lomas Altas, 11950 México, DF; tel. and fax (55) 9177-4100; e-mail adortega@expansion.com.mx; internet www.expansion.com.mx; fortnightly; business and financial; Editor ADOLFO ORTEGA; circ. 54,000.

Fama: Avda Eugenio Garza Sada 2245 Sur, Col. Roma, Apdo 3128, 64700 Monterrey, NL; tel. (81) 8359-2525; internet www.famaweb.com; fortnightly; show business; Pres. JESÚS D. GONZÁLEZ; Dir-Gen. RAÚL MARTÍNEZ GONZÁLEZ; circ. 350,000.

Fortuna: Avda Río Churubusco 590, Col. del Carmen, Del. Coyoacán, 04100 México, DF; tel. (55) 5554-9194; e-mail info@revistafortuna.com.mx; internet www.revistafortuna.com.mx; business; monthly; Dir CLAUDIA VILLEGAS.

Gaceta Médica de México: Academia Nacional de Medicina, Unidad de Congresos del Centro Médico Nacional Siglo XXI, Bloque B, Avda Cuauhtémoc 330, Col. Doctores, 06725 México, DF; tel. (55) 5578-2044; fax (55) 5578-4271; e-mail medigraphic@medigraphic.com; internet www.medigraphic.com; f. 1864; every 2 months; journal of the Academia Nacional de Medicina de México; Editor ALFREDO ULLOA AGUIRRE; circ. 20,000.

Kena Mensual: Río Balsas 101, Col. Cuauhtémoc, 06500 México, DF; tel. (55) 5442-9600; e-mail ginaum@grupoarmonia.com.mx; f. 1977; fortnightly; women's interest; Editor GINA URETA; circ. 80,000.

Manufactura: Avda Chapultepec 230, esq. Córdoba, Col. Roma Norte, Del. Cuauhtemoc, México, DF; tel. (55) 9177-4369; e-mail mramo@expansion.com.mx; internet www.manufactura.mx; f. 1994; monthly; industrial; Editor-Gen. MILDRED RAMO; circ. 30,000.

Marie Claire: Editorial Televisa, SA de CV, Avda Vasco de Quiroga 2000, Edif. E, 3°, Col. Santa Fe, 01210 México, DF; tel. (55) 5261-2622; fax (55) 5261-2733; e-mail mmartinezgom@editorial.televisa

.com.mx; internet www.esmas.com/editorialtelevisa; f. 1990; monthly; women's interest; Editor ARIADNE GRANT; circ. 145,000.

Men's Health: Avda Vasco de Quiroga 2000, Col. Santa Fe, Del. Alvaro Obregón, 01210 México, DF; tel. (55) 5265-0990; fax (55) 5261-2733; internet www.menshealthlatam.com; f. 1994; monthly; health; Editor JUAN ANTONIO SEMPERE; circ. 130,000.

Muy Interesante: Vasco de Quiroga 2000, Col. Santa Fe, Del. Alvaro Obregón, 01210 México, DF; tel. (55) 5261-2600; fax (55) 5261-2707; e-mail gsifuentesm@editorial.televisa.com.mx; internet www.esmas.com/editorialtelevisa; f. 1984; monthly; publ. by Editorial Televisa; scientific devt; Dir FRANCISCO VILLASEÑOR; circ. 250,000.

Negocios y Bancos: Insurgentes Sur 1442, Apdo 2, Col. Actpan, Del. Benito Juárez, 03230 México, DF; tel. (55) 5524-0871; fax (55) 5512-9411; e-mail negociosybancos@yahoo.com.mx; internet www.revistanegociosybancos.com; f. 1951; fortnightly; business, economics; Dir SALVADOR MARQUÉZ SANDÍN; circ. 10,000.

Nexos: Mazatlán 119, Col. Condesa, Del. Cuauhtémoc, 06140 México, DF; tel. (55) 5241-2510; fax (55) 5241-6930; e-mail bortigoza@nexos.com.mx; internet www.nexos.com.mx; f. 1978; current affairs; monthly; Dir HÉCTOR AGUILAR CAMÍN.

Proceso: Fresas 13, Col. del Valle, 03100 México, DF; tel. (55) 5636-2028; e-mail buzon@proceso.com.mx; internet www.proceso.com.mx; f. 1976; weekly; news analysis; Dir RAFAEL RODRÍGUEZ CASTAÑEDA; circ. 98,784.

Quién: Avda Constituyentes 956, Col. Lomas Altas, CP 11950, México, DF; tel. (55) 9177-4342; e-mail quien.com@expansion.com.mx; internet www.quien.com; fortnightly; celebrity news, TV, radio, films; Publr ADRIÁN VILLALBA; Editor LUIS NEREO BUENO.

La Revista Peninsular: Calle 35, 489 x 52 y 54, Zona Centro, Mérida, Yuc.; tel. and fax (999) 926-3014; e-mail direccion@larevista.com.mx; internet www.larevista.com.mx; f. 1988; weekly; news and politics; Dir-Gen. RODRIGO MENÉNDEZ CÁMARA.

Selecciones del Reader's Digest: Avda Lomas de Sotelo 1102, Col. Loma Hermosa, Del. Miguel Hidalgo, 11200 México, DF; tel. (55) 5351-2500; fax (55) 5395-6691; e-mail servicio.clientes@rd.com; internet www.selecciones.com.mx; f. 1940; monthly; Editor AUDÓN CORIA; circ. 611,660.

Siempre: Vallarta 20, Col. Tabacalera, 06030 México, DF; tel. and fax (55) 5566-9355; e-mail suscripciones@siempre.com.mx; internet www.siempre.com.mx; f. 1953; weekly; left of centre; Dir BEATRIZ PAGÉS REBOLLAR DE NIETO; Editor ENRIQUE MONTES GARCÍA; circ. 100,000.

Tiempo Libre: Holbein 75 bis, Col. Nochebuena Mixcoac, Del. Benito Juárez, 03720 México, DF; tel. (55) 5611-2884; fax (55) 5611-3982; e-mail buzon@tiempolibre.com.mx; internet www.tiempolibre.com.mx; f. 1980; weekly; entertainment guide; Dir JUAN ALBERTO BECERRA; Editor ALICIA LABRA GÓMEZ; circ. 95,000.

Tú: Vasco de Quiroga 2000, Col. Santa Fe, Del. Alvaro Obregón, 01210 México, DF; tel. (55) 5261-2600; fax (55) 5261-2730; e-mail tu@editorial.televisa.com.mx; internet tuenlinea.esmas.com; f. 1980; monthly; teenage; Editor MARÍA ANTONIETA SALAMANCA; circ. 250,000.

TV y Novelas: Vasco de Quiroga 2000, Col. Santa Fe, Del. Alvaro Obregón, 01210 México, DF; tel. (55) 5261-2600; fax (55) 5261-2704; internet www.tvynovelas.com; f. 1982; weekly; television guide and short stories; Dir JESÚS GALLEGOS; circ. 460,000.

Vanidades: Vasco de Quiroga 2000, Col. Santa Fe, Del. Alvaro Obregón, 01210 México, DF; tel. (55) 5261-2600; fax (55) 5261-2704; e-mail vanidades@editorialtelevisa.com; internet www.vanidades.com; f. 1961; fortnightly; women's magazine; Dir JAQUELINE BLANCO; circ. 290,000.

Vogue (México): Condé Nast México, Montes Urales 415, 4°, Col. Lomas de Chapultepec, 11000 México, DF; tel. (55) 5062-3736; fax (55) 5540-5639; internet www.vogue.mx; f. 1999; monthly; women's fashion; Editorial Dir KELLY TALAMAS; circ. 208,180.

ASSOCIATIONS

Federación de Asociaciones de Periodistas Mexicanos (Fapermex): Humboldt 5, Col. Centro, 06030 México, DF; tel. (55) 5510-2679; e-mail boletin@fapermex.mx; internet www.fapermex.mx; Pres. HILDA LUISA VALDEMAR Y LIMA; 88 mem. asscns; c. 9,000 mems.

Federación Latinoamericana de Periodistas (FELAP): Nuevo Leon 144, 1°, Col. Hipódromo Condesa, 06170 México, DF; tel. (55) 5286-6055; fax (55) 5286-6085; e-mail webmaster@felap.org; internet www.felap.org; Pres. JUAN CARLOS CAMAÑO; Sec.-Gen. JOSÉ RAFAEL VARGAS.

Fraternidad de Reporteros de México (FREMAC): Avda Juárez 88, Col. Centro, Del. Cuauhtémoc, México, DF; e-mail info@fremac.org.mx; internet www.fremac.org.mx; f. 1995; Pres. JAIME GUERRERO.

NEWS AGENCIES

Agencia de Información Integral Periodística (AIIP): Tabasco 263, Col. Roma, Del. Cuauhtémoc, 06700 México, DF; tel. and fax (55) 5514-7389; e-mail aiipmx@aiip.com.mx; internet www.aiip.com.mx; f. 1987; Dir-Gen. MIGUEL HERRERA LÓPEZ.

Agencia Mexicana de Información (AMI): Avda Cuauhtémoc 16, Col. Doctores, 06720 México, DF; tel. (55) 5761-9933; e-mail info@red-ami.com; internet www.ami.com.mx; f. 1971; Dir-Gen. JOSÉ LUIS BECERRA LÓPEZ; Gen. Man. EVA VÁZQUEZ LÓPEZ.

Notimex, SA de CV: Morena 110, 3°, Col. del Valle, 03100 México, DF; tel. (55) 5420-1163; fax (55) 5420-1188; e-mail ventas@notimex.com.mx; internet www.notimex.com.mx; f. 1968; services to press, radio and television in Mexico and throughout the world; Dir-Gen. HÉCTOR VILLARREAL.

Publishers

MÉXICO, DF

Alfaomega Grupo Editor, SA de CV: Pitágoras 1139, Col. Del Valle, Del. Benito Juárez, 03100 México, DF; tel. (55) 5575-5022; fax (55) 5575-2420; e-mail atencionalcliente@alfaomega.com.mx; internet www.alfaomega.com.mx; engineering, management, technology and computing; Dir ALBERTO UMAÑA CARRIZOSA.

Artes de México y del Mundo, SA de CV: Córdoba 69, Col. Roma, 06700 México, DF; tel. (55) 5525-5905; fax (55) 5525-5925; e-mail artesdemexico@artesdemexico.com; internet www.artesdemexico.com; f. 1988; art, design, poetry; Dir-Gen. ALBERTO RUY SÁNCHEZ LACY.

Cengage Learning Editores, SA. de CV: Avda Santa Fe 505, 12°, Col. Cruz Manca, Del. Cuajimalpa, 05349 México, DF; tel. (55) 1500-6000; fax (55) 1500-6019; e-mail clientes.ca@cengage.com; internet www.cengage.com.mx; educational; Country Man. PEDRO TURBAY GARRIDO.

Cidcli, SC (Centro de Información y Desarrollo de la Comunicación y la Literatura Infantiles): Avda México 145-601, Col. Coyoacán, 04100 México, DF; tel. (55) 5659-7524; fax (55) 5659-3186; e-mail elisa@cidcli.com.mx; internet www.cidcli.com.mx; f. 1980; children's literature; Dir PATRICIA VAN RHIJN ARMIDA.

Círculo Editorial Azteca, SA: Calle de la Luna 225–227, Col. Guerrero, 06300 México, DF; tel. (55) 5526-1157; fax (55) 5526-2557; e-mail info@circuloeditorialazteca.com.mx; internet www.circuloeditorialazteca.com.mx; f. 1956; part of Grupo Salinas; religion, literature and technical; Man. Dir JOSEFINA LARRAGOITI.

Ediciones B México, SA de CV: Bradley 52, Anzures, Del. Miguel Hidalgo, 11590 México, DF; tel. (55) 1101-0660; fax (55) 5254-0569; e-mail info@edicionesb.com; internet www.edicionesb.com.mx; general fiction; Dir CARLOS GRAEF SÁNCHEZ.

Ediciones Era, SA de CV: Calle del Trabajo 31, Col. La Fama, Tlalpan, 14269 México, DF; tel. (55) 5528-1221; fax (55) 5606-2904; e-mail info@edicionesera.com.mx; internet www.edicionesera.com.mx; f. 1960; general and social science, art and literature; Gen. Man. NIEVES ESPRESATE XIRAU.

Ediciones Larousse, SA de CV: Londres 247, Col. Juárez, Del. Cuauhtémoc, 06600 México, DF; tel. (55) 1102-1300; fax (55) 5208-6225; e-mail larousse@larousse.com.mx; internet www.larousse.com.mx; f. 1965; Dir-Gen. GERARDO GUILLERMO GUERRERO IBARRA.

Editorial Avante, SA de CV: Luis G. Obregón 9, 1°, Apdo 45-796, Col. Centro, 06020 México, DF; tel. (55) 5510-8804; fax (55) 5521-5245; e-mail didactips@editorialavante.com.mx; internet www.editorialavante.com.mx; f. 1948; educational, drama, linguistics; Man. Dir Lic. MARIO ALBERTO HINOJOSA SAENZ.

Editorial Everest Mexicana, SA: Calzada Ermita Iztapalapa 1681, Col. Barrio San Miguel del Iztapalapa, Apdo 55-570, 09360 México, DF; tel. (55) 5685-3704; fax (55) 5685-3433; e-mail editevem@prodigy.net.mx; f. 1980; general textbooks; Dir JOSÉ LUIS HUIDOBRO LEÓN.

Editorial Herder: Tehuantepec 50, esq. con Ures, Col. Roma Sur, Del. Cuauhtemoc, 06760 México, DF; tel. (55) 5523-0105; fax (55) 5669-2387; e-mail herder@herder.com.mx; internet www.herder.com.mx; social sciences; Dir JAN-CORNELIUS SCHULZ SAWADE.

Editorial Iztaccíhuatl, SA de CV: Miguel E. Schultz, No 21 y 25, Col. San Rafael, 06470 México, DF; tel. (55) 5705-0938; fax (55) 5535-2321; e-mail iztagerencia@editorializtaccihuatl.com.mx; internet www.editorializtaccihuatl.com.mx; Dir NORA MARÍA VIEYRA SICILIA.

Editorial Jus, SA de CV: Donceles 66, Centro Histórico, México, DF; tel. (55) 9150-1400; fax (55) 5529-0951; e-mail aramos@jus.com.mx; internet www.jus.com.mx; f. 1938; history of Mexico, law, philosophy, economy, religion; Dir FELIPE GARRIDO.

Editorial Lectorum, SA de CV: Calle Centeno 79A, Col. Granjas Esmeralda, México, DF; tel. (55) 5581-3202; fax (55) 5646-6892;

e-mail direccion@lectorum.com.mx; internet www.lectorum.com.mx; humanities, literature and sciences; Dir-Gen. Porfirio Rom LIZARRAGA.

Editorial Limusa, SA de CV: Balderas 95, 1°, Col. Centro, Del. Cuauhtémoc, 06040 México, DF; tel. (55) 5130-0700; fax (55) 5510-9415; e-mail limusa@noriegaeditores.com; internet www.noriega.com.mx; f. 1962; part of Grupo Noriega Editores; science, technical, textbooks; Dir-Gen. CARLOS BERNARDO NORIEGA ARIAS.

Editorial Orión: Calle Sierra Mojada 325, Lomas de Chapultepec, 11000 México, DF; tel. (55) 5520-0224; f. 1942; archaeology, philosophy, psychology, literature, fiction; Man. Dir SILVIA HERNÁNDEZ BALTAZAR.

Editorial Planeta Mexicana, SA de CV: Avda Presidente Masarik 111, 2°, Col. Chapultepec Morales, Del. Miguel Hidalgo, 11570 México, DF; tel. (55) 3000-6200; fax 3000-6257; e-mail rrodriguez@planeta.com.mx; internet www.editorialplaneta.com.mx; general literature, non-fiction; part of Grupo Planeta (Spain); Grupo Planeta incorporates Destino, Editorial Diana, Editorial Joaquín Mortiz, Emecé, Espasa Calpe, Lunwerg Editores, Martínez Roca, Seix Barral, Temas de Hoy and Timun Mas; Man. Dir JOSE CALAFELL.

Editorial Porrúa Hnos, SA: Argentina 15, 5°, Col. Centro, 06020 México, DF; tel. (55) 5704-7500; fax (55) 5704-7502; e-mail editorial@porrua.com; internet www.porrua.com; f. 1944; general literature; Dir JOSÉ ANTONIO PÉREZ-PORRÚA SUÁREZ.

Editorial Progreso, SA de CV: Sabino 275, Col. Santa María la Ribera, Del. Cuauhtémoc, 06400 México, DF; tel. (55) 1946-0620; fax (55) 1946-0649; e-mail dirgeneral@editorialprogreso.com.mx; internet www.editorialprogreso.com.mx; f. 1899; educational; Dir JOAQUÍN FLORES SEGURA.

Editorial Serpentina, SA de CV: Santa Margarita 430, Col. Del Valle, 03100 Mexico, DF; tel. (55) 5559-8338; fax (55) 5575-8362; e-mail editorial@editorialserpentina.com; internet www.editorialserpentina.com; f. 2004; cultural, adolescent and children's literature; Dir ALEJANDRA CANALES UCHA.

Editorial Trillas, SA: Avda Río Churubusco 385 Pte, Col. Xoco, Apdo 10534, 03330 México, DF; tel. (55) 5688-4233; fax (55) 5604-1364; e-mail fernando@trillas.com.mx; internet www.etrillas.com.mx; f. 1954; science, technical, textbooks, children's books; Man. Dir FERNANDO TRILLAS SALAZAR.

Fernández Editores, SA de CV: Eje 1 Pte México-Coyoacán 321, Col. Xoco, 03330 México, DF; tel. (55) 5090-7700; fax (55) 5688-9173; e-mail sfernandez@feduca.com.mx; internet www.fernandezeditores.com.mx; f. 1943; children's literature, textbooks, educational toys; Man. Dir SOFÍA FERNÁNDEZ PEÑA.

Fondo de Cultura Económica: Carretera Picacho-Ajusco 227, Col. Bosques del Pedregal, Tlalpan, 14200 México, DF; tel. (55) 5227-4672; fax (55) 5227-4659; e-mail director.general@fondodeculturaeconomica.com; internet www.fondodeculturaeconomica.com; f. 1934; economics, history, philosophy, children's books, science, politics, psychology, sociology, literature; state-owned; CEO JOAQUÍN DÍEZ-CANEDO.

Grupo Editorial Patria, SA de CV: Renacimiento 180, Col. San Juan Tlihuaca, Del. Azcapotzalco, 02400 México, DF; tel. (55) 5354-9100; fax (55) 5354-9109; e-mail info@editorialpatria.com.mx; internet www.editorialpatria.com.mx; f. 1933; fiction, general trade, children's books; Pres. CARLOS FRIGOLET LERMA.

McGraw-Hill Interamericana de México, SA de CV: Torre A, 17°, Paseo de la Reforma 1015, Col. Santa Fé, 01376 México, DF; tel. (55) 1500-5000; fax (55) 1500-5159; e-mail adriana_velazquez@mcgraw-hill.com; internet www.mcgraw-hill.com.mx; education, business, science; Man. Dir ANDRÉS RODRÍGUEZ.

Medios Publicitarios Mexicanos, SA de CV: Eugenia 811, Eje 5 Sur, Col. del Valle, 03100 México, DF; tel. (55) 5523-3342; fax (55) 5523-3379; e-mail editorial@mpm.com.mx; internet www.mpm.com.mx; f. 1958; advertising media rates and data; Gen. Man. FERNANDO VILLAMIL ÁVILA.

Ocean Sur Editorial México, SA de CV: 2ª Cerrada de Corola 17, Col. El Reloj, Del. Coyoacán, 04640 México, DF; tel. (55) 5421-4165; fax (55) 5553-5512; e-mail mexico@oceansur.com; internet www.oceansur.com; Ibero-American cultural literature; Dir MIGUEL ÁNGEL ÁGUILAR.

Petra Ediciones, SA de CV: Calle El Carmen 268, Col. Camino Real, 45040 México, DF; tel. (55) 3629-0832; fax (55) 3629-3376; e-mail petra@petraediciones.com; internet www.petraediciones.com; art, literature, photography and theatre; Dir MARÍA ESPERANZA ESPINOSA BARRAGÁN.

Random House Mondadori, SA de CV: Homero 544, Col. Chapultepec Morales, 11570, México, DF; tel. (55) 3067-8400; e-mail rbanchik@rhmx.com.mx; internet www.randomhousemondadori.com.mx; f. 1954; owned by Mondadori (Italy); general fiction, history, sciences, philosophy, children's books; Man. Dir ROBERTO BANCHIK.

Reverté Ediciones, SA de CV: Río Pánuco 141A, Col. Cuauhtémoc, 06500 México, DF; tel. (55) 5533-5658; fax (55) 5514-6799; e-mail reverte@reverte.com.mx; internet www.reverte.com; f. 1955; science, technical, architecture; Man. RAMÓN REVERTÉ MASCÓ.

Siglo XXI Editores, SA de CV: Avda Cerro del Agua 248, Col. Romero de Terreros, Del. Coyoacán, 04310 México, DF; tel. (55) 5658-7999; fax (55) 5658-7588; e-mail informes@sigloxxieditores.com.mx; internet www.sigloxxieditores.com.mx; f. 1966; art, economics, education, history, social sciences, literature, philology and linguistics, philosophy and political science; Dir-Gen. Dr JAIME LABASTIDA OCHOA; Gen. Man. JOSÉ MARÍA CASTRO MUSSOT.

Universidad Nacional Autónoma de México: Dirección General de Publicaciones y Fomento Editorial, Avda del Imán 5, Ciudad Universitaria, 04510 México, DF; tel. (55) 5622-6572; e-mail corbolgg@libros.unam.mx; internet www.unam.mx; f. 1935; publications in all fields; Dir-Gen. JULIA TAGÜEÑA PARGA.

ESTADO DE MÉXICO

Editorial Gustavo Gili de México, SA: Valle de Bravo 21, Naucalpan, 53050 Méx.; tel. (55) 5560-6011; fax (55) 5360-1453; e-mail info@ggili.com.mx; internet www.ggili.com.mx; f. 1902 in Spain; architecture, design, fashion, art and photography; Dir CARLOS LERMA.

Pearson Educación de México, SA de CV: Atlacomulco 500, 4°, Industrial Atoto, Naucalpan de Juárez, 53519 Méx.; tel. (55) 5387-0700; fax (55) 5358-0808; e-mail alma.vallejo@pearsoned.com; internet www.pearsoneducacion.net; f. 1984; educational books under the imprints Addison-Wesley, Prentice Hall, Allyn & Bacon, Longman and Scott Foresman; Pres. STEVE MARBAN; Dir JAIME ANDRÉS EDUARDO VALENZUELA SOLAR.

ASSOCIATIONS

Cámara Nacional de la Industria Editorial Mexicana: Holanda 13, Col. San Diego Churubusco, Del. Coyoacán, 04120 México, DF; tel. (55) 5688-2011; fax (55) 5604-3147; e-mail contacto@caniem.com; internet www.caniem.com; f. 1964; Pres. VÍCTORICO ALBORES SANTIAGO; Dir-Gen. CARLOS M. ESPINO GAYTÁN.

Centro Mexicano de Protección y Fomento de los Derechos de Autor, SGC: Avda Cuauhtémoc 1486, Despacho 601A, Col. Santa Cruz Atoyac, Del. Benito Juárez, 03310 México, DF; tel. (55) 5601-3528; fax (55) 5604-9856; e-mail info@cempro.com.mx; internet www.cempro.com.mx; f. 1998; manages intellectual property rights of authors and publrs; Pres. JULIO SANZ; Dir-Gen. VALERIA LEILANI SÁNCHEZ AGUIÑAGA.

Broadcasting and Communications

TELECOMMUNICATIONS

Alestra: Optima II, Paseo de las Palmas 275, 8°, Col. Lomas de Chapultepec, 11000 México, DF; tel. (55) 8503-5000; internet www.alestra.com.mx; 49% owned by AT&T; Chair. ARMANDO GARZA SADA; Dir-Gen. ROLANDO ZUBIRÁN SHETLER.

América Móvil, SA de CV: Edif. Telcel 2, Lago Alberto 366, Col. Anáhuac, 11320 México, DF; tel. (55) 2581-4449; fax (55) 2581-3948; e-mail daniela.lacuna@americamovil.com; internet www.americamovil.com; f. 2000 as a spin off from Telmex; subsidiaries operate mobile telephone services in 18 countries in the Americas; Chair. PATRICK SLIM DOMIT; CEO DANIEL HAJJ ABOUMRAD.

Telcel: tel. (55) 2581-3333; internet www.telcel.com; f. 1978, present name adopted 1989; subsidiary of above, providing mobile services in Mexico; COO PATRICIA RAQUEL HEVIA COTO.

Teléfonos de México, SA de CV (Telmex): Parque Vía 190, Col. Cuauhtémoc, 06599 México, DF; tel. (55) 5222-1212; fax (55) 5545-5500; e-mail ri@telmex.com; internet www.telmex.com.mx; majority-owned by América Móvil since 2010; Pres. CARLOS SLIM DOMIT; Dir-Gen. HÉCTOR SLIM SEADE.

AT&T México: Montes Urales 470, Col. Lomas de Chapultepec, 11000 México, DF; internet www.att.com; Pres. (México) JEFFREY MCELFRESH.

Axtel: Blvd Díaz Ordáz Km 3.33, Zona Industrial, 66215 San Pedro Garza García, NL; tel. (81) 8114-0000; e-mail contacto@axtel.com.mx; internet www.axtel.com.mx; f. 1993; fixed-line operator; Chair. and CEO TOMÁS MILMO SANTOS.

Comunicaciones Nextel de México, SA de CV: Paseo de los Tamarindos 90, 29°, Col. Bosques de las Lomas, Del. Cuajimalpa, CP 05120, México, DF; tel. (55) 1018-4000; internet www.nextel.com.mx; f. 1998; fourth largest mobile telephone operator in Mexico; owned by NII Holdings, Inc (USA); Pres. PETER FOYO.

Iusacell, SA de CV: Montes Urales No 460, Col. Lomas de Chapultepec, Del. Miguel Hidalgo, 11000 México, DF; tel. (55) 5109-4400; e-mail ateclientes@iusacell.com.mx; internet www.iusacell.com.mx;

f. 1992; operates third largest mobile cellular telephone network in Mexico; 74% owned by Móvil Access; Pres. RICARDO BENJAMÍN SALINAS PLIEGO.

Maxcom Telecomunicaciones, SAB de CV: Guillermo González Camarena 2000, Col. Centro Ciudad Santa Fe, Del. Álvaro Obregón, 01210 México, DF; tel. (55) 5147-1111; internet www.maxcom.com; f. 1996; fixed-line operator; Chair. and Exec. Pres. JACQUES GILKSBERG; CEO SALVADOR ALVAREZ.

Telecomunicaciones de México (TELECOMM): Torre Central de Telecomunicaciones, Eje Central Lázaro Cárdenas 567, 11°, Ala Norte, Col. Narvarte, Del. Benito Juárez, 03020 México, DF; tel. (55) 5090-1166; fax (55) 1035-2408; e-mail muycerca@telecomm.net.mx; internet www.telecomm.net.mx; govt-owned; Dir-Gen. JORGE A. JURAIDINI RUMILLA.

Telefónica México (Movistar México): Prolongación Paseo de la Reforma 1200, Lote B-2, Col. Santa Fe, Col. Cruz Manca, Del. Cuajimalpa de Morelos, 05348 México, DF; tel. (55) 1616-5000; e-mail francisco.caballero@telefonica.com; internet www.telefonica.com.mx; f. 1924 (in Spain); owned by Telefónica, SA (Spain); fixed, mobile and broadband services; operates telephone service Telefónica Móviles México (movistar), call centre co Atento, and research and devt co Telefónica I+D; Pres. FRANCISCO GIL DÍAZ.

Unefon: Periférico Sur 4119, Col. Fuentes del Pedregal, 14141 México, DF; tel. (55) 8582-5000; e-mail ainfante@unefon.com.mx; internet www.unefon.com.mx; mobile operator; Pres. RICARDO SALINAS.

Regulatory Authorities

Comisión Federal de Telecomunicaciones (Cofetel): Insurgentes Sur 1143, Col. Noche Buena, Del. Benito Juárez, 03720 México, DF; tel. and fax (55) 5015-4000; e-mail nuevaimagen@cft.gob.mx; internet www.cofetel.gob.mx; Pres. MONY DE SWANN ADDATI.

Dirección General de Política de Telecomunicaciones y de Radiodifusión: Centro Nacional SCT, Cuerpo C, 1°, Avda Xola y Universidad s/n, Col. Narvarte, Del. Benito Juárez, 03020 México, DF; tel. (55) 5723-9369; fax (55) 5723-9300; e-mail adelacru@sct.gob.mx; internet dgpt.sct.gob.mx; part of Secretariat of State for Communications and Transport; Dir-Gen. ANDRÉS DE LA CRUZ VIELMA.

BROADCASTING
Radio

ABC Radio (XEABC): Basilio Badillo 29,Col. Tabacalera, Del. Cuauhtémoc, 06030 México, DF; tel. (55) 3640-5210; fax (55) 3640-5277; e-mail rita@abcradio.com.mx; internet www.abcradio.com.mx; Pres. JAVIER MEDINA; Gen. Man. JOSÉ ANTONIO MARTÍNEZ RAMÍREZ.

Corporación Mexicana de Radiodifusión (CMR): Calle Tetitla 23, esq. Calle Coapa, Col. Toriello Guerra, Del. Tlalpan, 14050 México, DF; tel. (55) 5424-6380; fax (55) 5666-5422; e-mail comentarios@cmr.com.mx; internet www.cmr.com.mx; f. 1962; Pres. ENRIQUE BERNAL SERVÍN; Dir-Gen. OSCAR BELTRÁN MARTÍNEZ DE CASTRO.

Firme, SA (Funcionamiento Íntegro de Radiodifusoras Mexicanas Enlazadas, SA): Ejército Nacional 552, Col. Polanco Reforma, 11550 México, DF; tel. (55) 5250-7788; fax (55) 5250-7906; e-mail radiodifusion@firmesa.com.mx; internet www.firmesa.com.mx; f. 1972; Dir-Gen. LUIS IGNACIO SANTIBÁÑEZ FLORES.

Grupo Acir, SA: Monte Pirineos 770, Col. Lomas de Chapultepec, Del. Miguel Hidalgo, 11000 México, DF; tel. (55) 5201-1700; fax (55) 5201-1771; e-mail servicio@grupoacir.com.mx; internet www.grupoacir.com.mx; f. 1965; comprises 140 stations; Exec. Pres. FRANCISCO IBARRA LÓPEZ.

Grupo Imagen Radio: Mariano Escobedo 700, Col Anzures, 11590 México, DF; tel. (55) 5089-9000; fax (55) 5089-9139; e-mail rfml@imagen.com.mx; internet www.imagen.com.mx; Dir-Gen. ERNESTO RIVERA AGUILAR.

Grupo Radio Capital: Montes Urales 425, Col. Lomas de Chapultepec, 1000 México, DF; tel. (55) 3099-3000; fax (55) 5202-3370; e-mail hckaram@gmail.com; internet gruporadiocapital.com.mx; f. 1968; operates 12 radio stations; Dir-Gen. LUÍS MACCISE URIBE.

Grupo Radio Centro, SA de CV: Constituyentes 1154, Col. Lomas Atlas, Del. Miguel Hidalgo, 11950 México, DF; tel. (55) 5728-4800; fax (55) 5728-4900; e-mail rcentro@grc.com.mx; internet radiocentro.com.mx; f. 1965; comprises 100 radio stations; Pres. FRANCISCO AGUIRRE GÓMEZ; Dir-Gen. CARLOS AGUIRRE GÓMEZ.

Grupo Radio Digital del Sureste: Avda Chapultepec 473, 7°, Col. Juárez, Del. Cuauhtémoc, 06600 México, DF; tel. (55) 5211-1734; fax (55) 5211-7534; e-mail info@gruporadiodigital.com.mx; internet www.gruporadiodigital.com.mx; f. 1946; operates 8 radio stations in 4 provinces; Dir-Gen. SIMÓN VALANCI BUZALI.

Grupo Siete Comunicación: Montecito 38, 31°, Of. 33, Col. Nápoles, Del. Benito Juárez, 03810 México, DF; tel. (55) 9000-

0787; fax (55) 9000-0747; e-mail info@gruposiete.com.mx; internet www.gruposiete.com.mx; f. 1997; Pres. Lic. FRANCISCO JAVIER SÁNCHEZ CAMPUZANO; Dir-Gen. PEDRO MOGOYÁN SOLANO.

Instituto Mexicano de la Radio (IMER): Mayorazgo 83, 2°, Col. Xoco, Del. Benito Juárez, 03330 México, DF; tel. (55) 5628-1704; fax (55) 5628-1738; e-mail general@imer.com.mx; internet www.imer .com.mx; f. 1983; Dir-Gen. ANA CECILIA TERRAZAS VALDÉS.

MVS Radio: Copérnico 183, Col. Anzures, 11590 México, DF; tel. (55) 5263-2156; fax (55) 5263-2189; e-mail eahumada@mvs.com; internet www.mvsradio.com; f. 1968; operates four stations, EXA FM, La Mejor FM, FM Globo and Noticias MVS; Pres. JOAQUIN VARGAS.

Núcleo Radio Mil (NRM): Prolongación Paseo de la Reforma 115, Col. Paseo de las Lomas, Santa Fe, 01330 México, DF; tel. (55) 5258-1200; e-mail radiomil@nrm.com.mx; internet www.nrm.com.mx; f. 1942; comprises seven radio stations; Pres. and Dir-Gen. EDILBERTO HUESCA PERROTÍN.

Radio Cadena Nacional, SA (RCN): Lago Victoria 78, Col. Granada, 11520 México, DF; tel. (55) 5250-0324; fax (55) 2624-0052; e-mail rcnmex@prodigy.net.mx; internet www.rcn.com.mx; f. 1948; Pres. SERGIO FAJARDO ORTIZ; Gen. Man. GUADALUPE CAMPUZANO.

Radio Educación: Angel Urraza 622, Col. del Valle, 03100 México, DF; tel. (55) 4155-1050; e-mail direccion@radioeducacion.edu.mx; internet www.radioeducacion.edu.mx; f. 1968; Dir-Gen. CARLOS ANTONIO TENORIO MUÑOZ COTA.

Radio Fórmula, SA: Privada de Horacio 10, Col. Polanco, 11560 México, DF; tel. (55) 5282-1016; e-mail jcoello@grupoformula.com .mx; internet www.radioformula.com.mx; f. 1968 as Radio Distrito Federal; Pres. ROGERIO AZCARRAGA MADERO.

Radio Universidad Nacional Autónoma de México: Adolfo Prieto 133, Col. del Valle, Del. Benito Juárez, 03100 México, DF; tel. (55) 5536-8989; fax (55) 5687-3989; e-mail contacto@radiounam .unam.mx; internet www.radiounam.unam.mx; Pres. ROGERIO AZCÁRRAGA MADERO; Dir-Gen. FERNANDO CHAMIZO GUERRERO.

Radiodifusoras Asociadas, SA de CV (RASA): Durango 341, 2°, Col. Roma, 06700 México, DF; tel. (55) 5286-1222; fax (55) 5211-6159; e-mail rasa@rasa.com.mx; internet www.rasa.com.mx; f. 1956; Exec. Pres. JOSÉ LARIS RODRÍGUEZ; Dir-Gen. SARA LARIS RODRÍGUEZ.

Radiópolis, SA de CV: Tlalpan 3000, Col. Espartaco, Del. Coyoacán, 04870 México, DF; tel. (55) 5327-2000; fax (55) 5679-9710; e-mail rrodriguezg@televisa.com.mx; owned by Televisa, SA de CV and Grupo Prisa; owns 5 radio stations; affiliated to Radiorama, SA de CV (q.v.) in 2004; Dir-Gen. RAÚL RODRÍGUEZ GONZÁLEZ.

Radiorama, SA de CV: Reforma 2620, 2°, Col. Lomas Altas, Del. Miguel Hidalgo, 11950 México, DF; tel. (55) 1105-0000; fax (55) 1105-0002; e-mail grupo@radiorama.com.mx; internet www.radiorama .com.mx; Pres. JAVIER PÉREZ DE ANDA.

Sociedad Mexicana de Radio, SA de CV (SOMER): Paseo de la Reforma 115, 4°, Col. Lomas, Santa Fé, 01330 México, DF; tel. (55) 9177-6660; fax (55) 9177-6677; e-mail somer@somer.com.mx; internet www.somer.com.mx; Dir-Gen. HUMBERTO HUESCA BUSTAMENTE.

El Universal Radio: Bucareli 8, Col. Centro, Del. Cuauhtémoc, 06040 México, DF; tel. (55) 5709-1313; e-mail radio@eluniversal.com .mx; internet www.eluniversalradio.com.mx; Man. ROGELIO ARIAS DÍAZ DE LEÓN.

Television

Canal 22: Edif. Pedro Infante, Atletas 2, Col. Country Club, Del. Coyoacán, 04220 México, DF; tel. (55) 2122-9680; fax (55) 5549-1647; e-mail correo@canal22.org.mx; internet www.canal22.org.mx; f. 1993; part of Consejo Nacional para la Cultura y las Artes of the Govt; Dir-Gen. RAÚL CREMOUX.

MVS (Multivisión): Blvd Manuel Ávila Camacho 147, Col. Chapultepec Morales, 11510 México, DF; tel. (55) 5283-4300; fax (55) 5283-4314; e-mail jvargas@mvs.com; internet www.mvs.com; subscriber-funded; Pres. JOAQUÍN VARGAS GUAJARDO; Vice-Pres. ERNESTO VARGAS.

Once TV: Carpio 475, Col. Casco de Santo Tomás, 11340 México, DF; tel. (55) 5166-4000; fax (55) 5396-8001; e-mail info@oncetvmexico.ipn .mx; internet www.oncetv.ipn.mx; f. 1959; Dir-Gen. MARÍA ENRIQUETA CABRERA CUARÓN.

Televisa, SA de CV: Edif. Televicentro, 8°, Avda Chapultepec 28, Col. Doctores, 06724 México, DF; tel. (55) 5709-3333; fax (55) 5709-3021; e-mail imagencorporativa2@televisa.com.mx; internet www .televisa.com; f. 1973; commercial; 406 affiliated stations; Chair. and CEO EMILIO AZCÁRRAGA JEAN.

Televisión Azteca, SA de CV: Anillo Periférico Sur 4121, Col. Fuentes del Pedregal, 14141 México, DF; tel. (55) 5447-8844; fax (55) 5645-4258; e-mail contacto@tvazteca.com; internet www.tvazteca .com; f. 1992; assumed responsibility for fmr state-owned channels

7 and 13; Pres. RICARDO B. SALINAS PLIEGO; Dir-Gen. MARIO SAN ROMÁN.

Regulatory Authority

Dirección General de Radio, Televisión y Cinematografía (RTC): Roma 41, Col. Juaréz, Del. Cuauhtémoc, 06600 México, DF; tel. (55) 5140-8000; fax (55) 5530-4315; e-mail buzonrtc@segob .gob.mx; internet www.rtc.gob.mx; f. 1977; Dir-Gen. JOSÉ IGNACIO JUÁREZ SÁNCHEZ.

Association

Cámara Nacional de la Industria de Radio y Televisión (CIRT): Avda Horacio 1013, Col. Polanco Reforma, Del. Miguel Hidalgo, 11550 México, DF; tel. (55) 5726-9909; fax (55) 5545-6767; e-mail cirt@cirt.com.mx; internet www.cirt.com.mx; f. 1942; Pres. TRISTÁN CANALES NAJJAR; Dir-Gen. MIGUEL OROZCO GÓMEZ.

Finance

(cap. = capital; res = reserves; dep. = deposits; m. = million;
brs = branches; amounts in new pesos)

BANKING

Banking activity is regulated by the federal Government. Commercial banking institutions are constituted as *Sociedades Anónimas*, with wholly private social capital. Development banking institutions exist as *Sociedades Nacionales de Crédito*; participation in their capital is exclusive to the Federal Government, notwithstanding the possibility of accepting limited amounts of private capital.

Supervisory Authority

Comisión Nacional Bancaria y de Valores (CNBV) (National Banking and Securities Commission): Avda Insurgentes Sur 1971, Torre Norte, Sur y III, Col. Guadalupe Inn, Del. Alvaro Obregón, 01020 México, DF; tel. and fax (55) 1454-6000; e-mail info@cnbv.gob .mx; internet www.cnbv.gob.mx; f. 1924; govt commission controlling all credit institutions in Mexico; Pres. JAIME GONZÁLEZ AGUADÉ.

Central Bank

Banco de México (BANXICO): Avda 5 de Mayo 2, Col. Centro, Del. Cuauhtémoc, 06059 México, DF; tel. (55) 5237-2000; fax (55) 5237-2070; e-mail comsoc@banxico.org.mx; internet www.banxico.org.mx; f. 1925; currency issuing authority; became autonomous on 1 April 1994; cap. 7.1m., res –66,040m., dep. 878,727m. (Dec. 2009); Gov. AGUSTÍN GUILLERMO CARSTENS CARSTENS; 6 brs.

Commercial Banks

Banco del Bajío, SA: Avda Manuel J. Clouthier 508, Col. Jardines del Campestre, 37128 León, Gto; tel. (477) 710-4600; fax (477) 710-4693; e-mail internacional@bancobajio.com.mx; internet www .bancobajio.com.mx; f. 1994; cap. 2,427.1m., res 6,576.6m., dep. 52,555.5m. (Dec. 2011); Pres. SALVADOR OÑATE ASCENCIO.

Banco Mercantil del Norte, SA (BANORTE): Avda Revolución 3000, Col. Primavera, 64830 Monterrey, NL; tel. (81) 8319-7200; fax (81) 8319-5216; internet www.banorte.com; f. 1899; merged with Banco Regional del Norte in 1985; cap. 11,488m., res 5,379m., dep. 332,333m. (Dec. 2011); Pres. GUILLERMO ORTIZ MARTÍNEZ; Dir-Gen. ALEJANDRO VALENZUELA DEL RÍO; 970 brs.

Banco Nacional de México, SA (Banamex): Avda Isabel la Católica 44, 06089 México, DF; tel. (55) 5720-7091; fax (55) 5920-7323; e-mail prensa@banamex.com; internet www.banamex.com; f. 1884; transferred to private ownership in 1991; merged with Citibank México, SA in 2001; cap. 35,319m., res 81,863m., dep. 511,927m. (Dec. 2011); CEO MANUEL MEDINA MORA; 1,260 brs.

Banco Santander (Mexico), SA: Mod 401, 4°, Prolongación Paseo de la Reforma 500, Col. Lomas de Santa Fe, Del. Alvaro Obregon, 01219 México, DF; tel. (55) 5261-1543; fax (55) 5261-5549; internet www.santander.com.mx; f. 1864 as Banco Serfin; acquired by Banco Santander Central Hispano (Spain) in Dec. 2000; adopted current name 2006; cap. 11,091m., res 31,698m., dep. 315,643m. (Dec. 2011); Exec. Pres. and Dir-Gen. MARCOS MARTÍNEZ GAVICA; 554 brs.

BBVA Bancomer, SA: Centro Bancomer, Avda Universidad 1200, Col. Xoco, 03339 México, DF; tel. (55) 5621-3434; fax (55) 5621-3230; internet www.bancomer.com.mx; f. 2000 by merger of Bancomer (f. 1864) and Mexican operations of Banco Bilbao Vizcaya Argentaria (Spain); privatized in 2002; cap. 24,138.2m., res 27,330.6m., dep. 572,715.8m. (Dec. 2010); Pres. IGNACIO DESCHAMPS GONZÁLEZ.

HSBC México: Paseo de la Reforma 156, Col. Juárez, Del. Cuauhtémoc, 06600 México, DF; tel. (55) 5721-2222; fax (55) 5721-2393; e-mail contacto@hsbc.com.mx; internet www.hsbc.com.mx; f. 1941; bought by HSBC (United Kingdom) in 2002; name changed from Banco Internacional, SA (BITAL) in 2004; cap. 5,261.1m., res

33,719m., dep. 293,877.4m. (Dec. 2011); Dir-Gen. Luis Javier Peña Kegel; 1,400 brs.

Scotiabank Inverlat, SA: Blvd Miguel Avila Camacho 1, 18°, Col. Lomas de Chapultepec, Del. Miguel Hidalgo, 11009 México, DF; tel. (55) 5728-1000; fax (55) 5229-2019; internet www .scotiabankinverlat.com; f. 1977 as Multibanco Comermex, SA; changed name to Banco Inverlat, SA in 1995; 55% holding acquired by Scotiabank Group (Canada) and adopted current name 2001; cap. 7,451m., res 3,307m., dep. 116,852m. (Dec. 2011); Pres. Troy Wright; 476 brs.

Development Banks

Banco Nacional de Comercio Exterior, SNC (BANCOMEXT): Periférico Sur 4333, Col. Jardines en la Montaña, Del. Tlalpan, 14210 México, DF; tel. (55) 5449-9100; fax (55) 5652-9342; e-mail bancomext@bancomext.gob.mx; internet www.bancomext.com; f. 1937; cap. 14,959m., res 406m., dep. 50,919m. (Dec. 2011); Dir-Gen. Enrique de la Madrid Cordero.

Banco Nacional del Ejército, Fuerza Aérea y Armada, SNC (BANJERCITO): Avda Industria Militar 1055, Col. Lomas de Sotelo, Del. Miguel Hidalgo, 11200 México, DF; tel. and fax (55) 5626-0500; e-mail info@banjercito.com.mx; internet www.banjercito .com.mx; f. 1947; cap. 2,460m., res 3,045m., dep. 21,884m. (Dec. 2011); Dir-Gen. Gen. Carlos Demetrio Gaytán Ochoa.

Banco Nacional de Obras y Servicios Públicos, SNC (BANO-BRAS): Avda Javier Barros Sierra 515, Col. Lomas de Santa Fe, Del. Álvaro Obregón, 01219 México, DF; tel. (55) 5270-1552; fax (55) 5270-1564; internet www.banobras.gob.mx; f. 1933; govt-owned; cap. 11,765m., res 3,350m., dep. 245,896m. (Dec. 2009); Dir-Gen. Georgina Kessel Martínez.

Compartamos, SAB de CV: Insurgentes Sur 552, Col. Escandón, 11800 México, DF; tel. (55) 5276-7250; fax (55) 5276-7299; e-mail contacto@compartamos.com; internet www.compartamos.com; f. 1990; Dir-Gen. Alvaro Rodríquez Arregui.

Financiera Rural: Agrarismo 227, Col. Escandón, Del. Miguel Hidalgo, CP 11800, México, DF; tel. (55) 5230-1600; internet www .financierarural.gob.mx; f. 2004; state-run devt bank, concerned with agricultural, forestry and fishing sectors; Dir-Gen. Carlos Alberto Treviño Medina.

Nacional Financiera, SNC (NAFIN): Insurgentes Sur 1971, Torre IV, 13°, Col. Guadalupe Inn, 01020 México, DF; tel. (55) 5325-6700; fax (55) 5661-8418; e-mail info@nafin.gob.mx; internet www.nafin .com; f. 1934; cap. 8,805m., res 14,732m., dep. 106,420m. (Dec. 2011); Dir-Gen. Jacques Rogozinski; 32 brs.

BANKERS' ASSOCIATION

Asociación de Bancos de México: 16 de Setiembre 27, 3°, Col. Centro Histórico, 06000 México, DF; tel. (55) 5722-4300; internet www.abm.org.mx; f. 1928; Pres. Jaime Ruíz Sacristán; Dir-Gen. Juan Carlos Jiménez Rojas; 52 mems.

STOCK EXCHANGE

Bolsa Mexicana de Valores, SA de CV: Paseo de la Reforma 255, Col. Cuauhtémoc, 06500 México, DF; tel. (55) 5726-6000; fax (55) 5726-6836; e-mail cinforma@bmv.com.mx; internet www.bmv.com .mx; f. 1894; Pres. and CEO Luis Téllez Kuenzler.

INSURANCE

Supervisory Authority

Comisión Nacional de Seguros y Fianzas: Avda Insurgentes Sur 1971, Torre I Sur, 2°, Col. Guadalupe Inn, Del. Álvaro Obregón, CP 01020, México, DF; tel. 57247489; e-mail cdiaz@cnsf.gob.mx; internet www.cnsf.gob.mx; Pres. Manuel Sergio Aguilera Verduzco.

Principal Companies

ACE Seguros: Bosques de Alisos, 47A, 1°, Col. Bosques de las Lomas, Del. Cuajimalpa, 05120 México, DF; tel. (5) 5258-5800; fax (5) 5258-5899; e-mail info@acelatinamerica.com; internet www .acelatinamerica.com/ACELatinAmericaRoot/Mexico; f. 1990; fmrly Seguros Cigna; Pres. and Gen. Man. Roberto Flores.

Aseguradora Cuauhtémoc, SA: Manuel Avila Camacho 164, 11570 México, DF; tel. (55) 5250-9800; fax (55) 5540-3204; f. 1944; general; Exec. Pres. Juan B. Riveroll; Dir-Gen. Javier Compeán Amezcua.

Aseguradora Interacciones: Paseo de la Reforma 383, México, DF; e-mail on-line@interacciones.com; internet www.interacciones .com; f. 1966; general; 43% owned by Commercial Union (United Kingdom); Deputy Dir-Gen. Eduardo Citalán Juan.

Grupo Nacional Provincial, SAB: Avda Cerro de las Torres 395, Col. Campestre Churubusco, Del. Coyoacán, 04200 México, DF; tel.

(55) 5227-3999; internet www.gnp.com.mx; f. 1936; member of Grupo BAL; general; Chair. Alberto Baillères; CEO Alejandro Baillères.

MetLife: Blvd Manuel Avila Camacho 32, SKY 14–20 y PH, Col. Lomas de Chapultepec, Del. Miguel Hidalgo, 11000 México, DF; tel. (55) 5328-9000; e-mail contacto@metlife.com.mx; internet www .metlife.com.mx; f. 1931 as Aseguradora Hidalgo, acquired by MetLife Inc in 2002; life; CEO Alberto Vilar.

Quálitas, Cía de seguros: José María Castorena 426, Col. San José de los Cedros, Cuajimalpa, CP 05200, México, DF; e-mail qualitas@ qualitas.com.mx; internet www.qualitas.com.mx; Pres. Joaquín Brockman Lozano.

Royal & SunAlliance Mexico: Blvd Adolfo López Mateos 2448, Col. Altavista, 01060 México, DF; tel. (55) 5723-7999; fax (55) 5723-7941; e-mail direccion.general@mx.rsagroup.com; internet www .royalsun.com.mx; f. 1941; acquired Seguros BBV-Probursa in 2001; general, except life; Chair. John Napier.

Seguros Azteca, SA: Insurgentes Sur 3579, Tlalpan La Joya, 14000 México, DF; tel. (55) 1720-9854; e-mail infoseguros@segurosazteca .com.mx; internet www.segurosazteca.com.mx; f. 1933, renamed as above in 2003; general, incl. life; Dir-Gen. Alfredo Honsberg.

Seguros Banorte Generali: Avda Ceylán, esq. Privada Ceylán, Col. Industrial Vallejo, Del. Azcapotzalco, CP 02300, México DF; tel. (55) 5141-1414; e-mail privacidad.sbg@banorte.com; internet www .banorte-generali.com.mx; Dir-Gen. Fernando Solís Soberón.

Seguros BBVA Bancomer: tel. (5) 52262660; e-mail servicioaclientes@segurosbancomer.com.mx; internet www .segurosbancomer.com.mx; Dir-Gen. Juan Pablo Ávila Palafox.

Seguros Banamex, SA: Venustiano Carranza 63, Col. Centro Histórico, Del. Cuauhtémoc, 06000 México, DF; tel. (55) 1226-8100; e-mail sbainternet@banamex.com; internet www .segurosbanamex.com; f. 1994; life, accident and health; Dir-Gen. Daniel Garduño Gutiérrez.

Seguros Monterrey New York Life: Presidente Mazaryk 8, Bosques de Chapultepec, Del. Miguel Hidalgo, México, DF; tel. (55) 5326-9000; fax (55) 5536-9610; e-mail clientes@ monterrey-newyorklife.com.mx; internet www.monterrey -newyorklife.com.mx; f. 1940 as Monterrey Cía de Seguros; acquired by New York Life in 2000; casualty, life, etc.; Dir-Gen. Mario Vela Berrondo.

Skandia Vida: Bosque de Ciruelos 162, 1°, Col. Bosques de las Lomas, 11700, México, DF; tel. (55) 5093-0220; e-mail servicio@ skandia.com.mx; internet www.skandia.com.mx; CEO Othon de la Garza.

Insurance Association

Asociación Mexicana de Instituciones de Seguros, AC (AMIS): Francisco I Madero 21, Col. Tlacopac, San Angel, 01040 México, DF; tel. (55) 5480-0646; fax (55) 5662-8036; e-mail amis@ mail.internet.com.mx; internet www.amis.com.mx; f. 1946; all insurance cos operating in Mexico are mems; Pres. Juan Ignacio Gil Antón; Dir-Gen. Recaredo Arias Jiménez.

Trade and Industry

GOVERNMENT AGENCIES

Comisión Federal de Protección Contra Riesgos Sanitarios (COFEPRIS): Monterrey 33, esq. Oaxaca, Col. Roma, Del. Cuauhtémoc, 06700 México, DF; tel. (55) 5080-5200; fax (55) 5207-5521; e-mail mdiosdado@salud.gob.mx; internet www.cofepris.gob.mx; f. 2003; pharmaceutical regulatory authority; Sec.-Gen. Erwin Roeniger Servín.

Comisión Nacional Forestal (CONAFOR): Carretera a Nogales s/n, esq. Periférico Poniente 5360, 5°, San Juan de Ocotán, 45019 Zapopan, Jal.; tel. (33) 3777-7000; fax (33) 3777-7012; e-mail conafor@conafor.gob.mx; internet www.conafor.gob.mx; f. 2001; Dir-Gen. Juan Manuel Torres Rojo.

Comisión Nacional de Inversiones Extranjeras (CNIE): Dirección General de Inversión Extranjera, Insurgentes Sur 1940, 8°, Col. Florida, 01030 México, DF; tel. (55) 5229-6100; fax (55) 5229-6507; e-mail gcanales@economia.gob.mx; f. 1973; govt commission to coordinate foreign investment; Pres. Bruno Francisco Ferrari García de Alba.

Comisión Nacional de los Salarios Mínimos (CNSM): Avda Cuauhtémoc 14, 2°, Col. Doctores, Del. Cuauhtémoc, 06720 México 7, DF; tel. (55) 5998-3800; fax (55) 5578-5775; e-mail cnsm1@conasami .gob.mx; internet www.conasami.gob.mx; f. 1962, in accordance with Section VI of Article 123 of the Constitution; national commission on minimum salaries; Pres. Lic. Basilio González Núñez.

Instituto Nacional de Investigaciones Nucleares (ININ): Centro Nuclear de México, Carretera México–Toluca Km 36.5, La

Marquesa, 52750 Ocoyoacac, Méx.; tel. (55) 5329-7200; fax (55) 5329-7296; e-mail hernan.rico@inin.gob.mx; internet www.inin.gob.mx; f. 1979 to plan research and devt of nuclear science and technology; 2 nuclear reactors, each with a generating capacity of 654 MW; Dir-Gen. JOSÉ RAÚL ORTÍZ MAGAÑA.

Instituto Nacional de Pesca (INAPESCA) (National Fishery Institute): Pitágoras 1320, Col. Santa Cruz Atoyac, Del. Benito Juárez, 03310 México, DF; tel. (55) 3871-9517; fax (55) 5604-9169; e-mail gerardo.garcia@inapesca.sagarpa.gob.mx; internet www.inapesca.gob.mx; f. 1962; Dir-in-Chief RAÚL ADÁN ROMO TRUJILLO.

Procuraduría Federal del Consumidor (Profeco): Avda José Vasconcelos 208, Col. Condesa, Del. Cuauhtémoc, 06140 México, DF; tel. (55) 5625-6700; internet www.profeco.gob.mx; f. 1975; consumer protection; Procurator BERNARDO ALTAMIRANO RODRÍGUEZ.

Servicio Geológico Mexicano (SGM): Blvd Felipe Angeles, Carretera México–Pachuca, Km 93.50-4, Col. Venta Prieta, 42080 Pachuca de Soto, Hgo; tel. (771) 711-4266; fax (771) 711-4204; e-mail gintproc@sgm.gob.mx; internet www.sgm.gob.mx; f. 1957; govt agency for the devt of mineral resources; Dir-Gen. RAFAEL ALEXANDRI RIONDA.

DEVELOPMENT ORGANIZATIONS

Centro de Investigación para el Desarrollo, AC (CIDAC) (Centre of Research for Development): Jaime Balmes 11, Edif. D, 2°, Col. Los Morales Polanco, 11510 México, DF; tel. (55) 5985-1010; fax (55) 5985-1030; e-mail info@cidac.org.mx; internet www.cidac.org; f. 1984; researches economic and political devt; Dir-Gen. VERÓNICA BAZ.

Comisión Nacional de las Zonas Aridas (CONAZA): Blvd Isidro López Zertuche 2513, Col. Los Maestros, 25260 Saltillo, Coah.; tel. and fax (844) 450-5200; e-mail contacto@conaza.gob.mx; internet www.conaza.gob.mx; f. 1970; commission to co-ordinate the devt and use of arid areas; Dir-Gen. LUIS CARLOS FIERRO GARCÍA.

Fideicomiso de Fomento Mineiro (FIFOMI): Puente de Tecamachalco 26, 2°, Col. Lomas de Chapultepec, Del. Miguel Hidalgo, 11000 México, DF; tel. (55) 5249-9500; e-mail pguerra@fifomi.gob.mx; internet www.fifomi.gob.mx; trust for the devt of the mineral industries; Dir-Gen. ALBERTO ORTIZ TRILLO.

Fideicomisos Instituídos en Relación con la Agricultura (FIRA): Km 8, Antigua Carretera Pátzcuaro 8555, 58341 Morelia, Mich.; tel. (443) 322-2399; fax (443) 327-6338; e-mail webmaster@correo.fira.gob.mx; internet www.fira.gob.mx; a group of devt funds to aid agricultural financing, under the Banco de México, comprising Fondo de Garantía y Fomento para la Agricultura, Ganadería y Avicultura (FOGAGA); Fondo Especial para Financiamientos Agropecuarios (FEFA); Fondo Especial de Asistencia Técnica y Garantía para Créditos Agropecuarios (FEGA); Fondo de Garantía y Fomento para las Actividades Pesqueras (FOPESCA); Dir RODRIGO SÁNCHEZ MÚJICA.

Fondo de Operación y Financiamiento Bancario a la Vivienda (FOVI): Ejército Nacional 180, Col. Anzures, 11590 México, DF; tel. (55) 5263-4500; fax (55) 5263-4541; e-mail jmartinez@fovi.gob.mx; internet www.fovi.gob.mx; f. 1963 to promote the construction of low-cost housing through savings and credit schemes; devt fund under the Banco de México; Dir-Gen. MANUEL ZEPEDA PAYERAS.

Instituto Mexicano del Petróleo (IMP): Eje Central Lázaro Cárdenas 152, Col. San Bartolo Atepehuacan, Del. Gustavo A. Madero, 07730 México, DF; tel. (55) 9175-6000; fax (55) 9175-8000; e-mail gdgarcia@imp.mx; internet www.imp.mx; f. 1965 to foster devt of the petroleum, chemical and petrochemical industries; Dir EFRÉN PARADA ARIAS.

CHAMBERS OF COMMERCE

American Chamber of Commerce of Mexico (Amcham): Lucerna 78, Col. Juárez, 06600 México, DF; tel. (55) 5141-3800; fax (55) 5141-3833; e-mail amchammx@amcham.com.mx; internet www.amcham.com.mx; f. 1917; brs in Guadalajara and Monterrey; Pres. JOSÉ ZOZAYA; Exec. Vice-Pres. and Dir-Gen. GUILLERMO WOLF.

Cámara de Comercio, Servicios y Turismo Ciudad de México (CANACO) (Chamber of Commerce, Services and Tourism of Mexico City): Paseo de la Reforma 42, 3°, Col. Centro, Apdo 32005, Del. Cuauhtémoc, 06048 México, DF; tel. (55) 3685-2269; fax (55) 5592-2279; e-mail sos@ccmexico.com.mx; internet www.camaradecomerciodemexico.com.mx; f. 1874; 50,000 mems; Pres. RICARDO NAVARRO BENÍTEZ.

Cámara Nacional de la Industria de Transformación (CANACINTRA): Avda San Antonio 256, Col. Ampliación Nápoles, Del. Benito Juárez, 06849 México, DF; tel. (55) 5482-3000; fax (55) 5598-8044; e-mail direcciongeneral@canacintra.org.mx; internet www.canacintra.org.mx; represents majority of smaller manufacturing businesses; Pres. SERGIO ENRIQUE CERVANTES RODILES; Dir-Gen. LINO LANDEROS SANTOS.

Confederación de Cámaras Nacionales de Comercio, Servicios y Turismo (CONCANACO-SERVYTUR) (Confederation of National Chambers of Commerce, Services and Tourism): Balderas 144, 3°, Col. Centro, 06070 México, DF; tel. (55) 5722-9300; e-mail comentarios@concanaco.com.mx; internet www.concanaco.com.mx; f. 1917; Pres. JORGE E. DÁVILA FLORES; Dir-Gen. EDUARDO GARCÍA VILLASEÑOR; comprises 283 regional chambers.

CHAMBERS OF INDUSTRY

Central Confederation

Confederación de Cámaras Industriales de los Estados Unidos Mexicanos (CONCAMIN) (Confed. of Industrial Chambers): Manuel María Contreras 133, 4°, Col. Cuauhtémoc, Del. Cuauhtémoc, 06500 México, DF; tel. (55) 5140-7800; fax (55) 5140-7831; e-mail webmaster@concamin.org.mx; internet www.concamin.org.mx; f. 1918; represents and promotes the activities of the entire industrial sector; Pres. SALOMÓN PRESBURGER SLOVIK; Dir-Gen. MÓNICA GARDUÑO CALDERÓN; 108 mem. orgs.

INDUSTRIAL AND TRADE ASSOCIATIONS

Asociación Nacional de Importadores y Exportadores de la República Mexicana (ANIERM) (National Association of Importers and Exporters): Monterrey 130, Col. Roma, Del. Cuauhtémoc, 06700 México, DF; tel. (55) 5584-9522; fax (55) 5584-5317; e-mail anierm@anierm.org.mx; internet www.anierm.org.mx; f. 1944; Pres. FERNANDO TAMEZ MURGUÍA; Exec. Vice-Pres. LUIS ENRIQUE ZAVALA GALLEGOS.

Asociación Nacional de la Industria Química (ANIQ): Angel Urraza 505, Col. del Valle, 03100 México, DF; tel. (55) 5230-5100; internet www.aniq.org.mx; f. 1959; chemicals asscn; Dir-Gen. MIGUEL BENEDETTO; c. 200 mem. cos.

Comisión Nacional de Seguridad Nuclear y Salvaguardias (CNSNS): Dr José María Barragán 779, Col. Narvarte, Del. Benito Juárez, 03020 México, DF; tel. (55) 5095-3200; fax (55) 5095-3295; e-mail je@cnsns.gob.mx; internet www.cnsns.gob.mx; f. 1979; nuclear regulatory authority; Dir-Gen. JUAN EIBENSCHUTZ HARTMAN.

Consejo Empresarial Mexicano de Comercio Exterior, Inversión y Tecnología (COMCE): Lancaster 15, 2° y 3°, Col. Juárez, 06600 México, DF; tel. (52) 5231-7100; fax (55) 5321-7109; e-mail direccion@comce.org.mx; internet www.comce.org.mx; f. 1999 to promote international trade; Pres. VALENTÍN DIEZ MORODO; Dir-Gen. LORENZO YSASI MARTÍNEZ.

Consejo Mexicano de Asuntos Internacionales (COMEXI): Of. 502, Torre Magnum, Sierra Mojada 620, Col. Lomas de Chapultepec, 11000 México, DF; tel. (55) 5202-3776; e-mail info@consejomexicano.org; internet www.consejomexicano.org; Pres. ENRIQUE BERRUGA.

Consejo Nacional de la Industria Maquiladora y Manufacturera de Exportación (INDEX): Ejército Nacional 418, 12°, Of. 1204, Col. Chapultepec Morales, Del. Miguel Hidalgo, 11570 México, DF; tel. (55) 2282-9900; fax (55) 2282-9902; e-mail dirgral@index.org.mx; internet www.index.org.mx; f. 1973; Pres. LUIS AGUIRRE; Dir-Gen. CARLOS PALENCIA.

Instituto Nacional de Investigaciones Forestales, Agrícolas y Pecuarias (INIFAP) (National Research Institute for Forestry, Agriculture and Livestock): Avda Progreso No 5, Col. Barrio de Santa Catarina, Del. Coyoacán, 04010 México, DF; tel. (55) 3871-8700; fax (55) 3626-8639; e-mail brajcich.pedro@inifap.gob.mx; internet www.inifap.gob.mx; f. 1985; forestry conservation and management; plant and animal genetics and management; Dir-Gen. PEDRO BRAJCICH GALLEGOS.

EMPLOYERS' ORGANIZATIONS

Consejo Coordinador Empresarial (CCE): Lancaster 15, Col. Juárez, 06600 México, DF; tel. (55) 5229-1100; fax (55) 5592-3857; e-mail sistemas@cce.org.mx; internet www.cce.org.mx; f. 1976; co-ordinating body of private sector; Pres. MARIO SÁNCHEZ RUIZ; Dir-Gen. LUIS MIGUEL PANDO LEYVA.

STATE HYDROCARBONS COMPANY

Petróleos Mexicanos (PEMEX): Avda Marina Nacional 329, Col. Petróleos Mexicanos, 11311 México, DF; tel. (55) 1944-2500; fax (55) 5531-6354; e-mail petroleosmexicanos@pemex.com; internet www.pemex.com; f. 1938; govt agency for the exploitation of Mexico's petroleum and natural gas resources; Dir-Gen. EMILIO LOZOYA AUSTIN; 131,000 employees.

UTILITIES

Regulatory Authorities

Comisión Nacional del Agua (CONAGUA): Avda Insurgentes Sur 2416, Col. Copilco el Bajo, Del. Coyoacán, 04340 México, DF; tel. (55) 5174-4000; fax (55) 5550-6721; e-mail direccion@cna.gob.mx;

internet www.cna.gob.mx; commission to administer national water resources; Dir-Gen. DAVID KORENFELD FEDERMAN.

Comisión Reguladora de Energía (CRE): Avda Horacio 1750, Col. Los Morales Polanco, Del. Miguel Hidalgo, 11510 México, DF; tel. (55) 5283-1500; e-mail calidad@cre.gob.mx; internet www.cre .gob.mx; f. 1994; commission to control energy policy and planning; Pres. FRANCISCO XAVIER SALAZAR DIEZ DE SOLLANO; Exec. Sec. LUIS ALONSO GONZÁLEZ DE ALBA.

Secretariat of State for Energy: see section on The Government (Secretariats of State).

Electricity

Comisión Federal de Electricidad (CFE): Avda Reforma 64, Col. Juárez México, México, DF; tel. (55) 5229-4400; fax (55) 5553-5321; e-mail servicioalcliente@cfe.gob.mx; internet www.cfe.gob.mx; state-owned power utility; Dir-Gen. FRANCISCO ROJAS GUTIÉRREZ.

Gas

Gas Natural México (GNM): Jaime Blames 8-703, Col. Los Morales Polanco, 11510 México, DF; e-mail sugerencias@gnm.com.mx; internet www.gasnaturalmexico.com.mx; f. 1994 in Mexico; distributes natural gas in the states of Tamaulipas, Aguascalientes, Coahuila, San Luis Potosí, Guanajuato, Nuevo León and México and in the Distrito Federal; subsidiary of Gas Natural (Spain); Pres. ANGEL LARRAGA.

Petróleos Mexicanos (PEMEX): see State Hydrocarbons Company; distributes natural gas.

TRADE UNIONS

Confederación Regional Obrera Mexicana (CROM) (Regional Confederation of Mexican Workers): República de Cuba 60, México, DF; f. 1918; Sec.-Gen. LEONARDO CONTRERAS CISNEROS; 120,000 mems, 900 affiliated syndicates.

Confederación Revolucionaria de Obreros y Campesinos de México (CROC) (Revolutionary Confederation of Workers and Farmers): Hamburgo 250, Col. Juárez, Del. Cuauhtémoc, 06600 México, DF; tel. (55) 5208-5444; e-mail crocmodel@hotmail.com; internet www.croc.org.mx; f. 1952; Sec.-Gen. ISIAS GONZÁLEZ CUEVAS; 4.5m. mems in 32 state federations and 17 national unions.

Confederación de Trabajadores de México (CTM) (Confederation of Mexican Workers): Vallarta 8, Col. Tabacalera, Del. Cuauhtémoc, 06030 México, DF; tel. (55) 5141-1730; e-mail ctmorganizacion@prodigy.net.mx; internet ctmorganizacion.org .mx; f. 1936; admitted to ICFTU; Sec.-Gen. JOAQUÍN GAMBOA; 5.5m. mems.

Congreso del Trabajo (CT): Avda Ricardo Flores Magón 44, Col. Guerrero, 06300 México 37, DF; tel. (55) 5583-3817; internet www .congresodeltrabajo.org.mx; f. 1966; trade union congress comprising trade union federations, confederations, etc.; Pres. ANTONINO BAXZI MATA.

Federación Nacional de Sindicatos Independientes (National Federation of Independent Trade Unions): Isaac Garza 311 Oeste, 64000 Monterrey, NL; tel. (81) 8375-6677; e-mail fnsi@prodigy.net .mx; internet www.fnsi.org.mx/esp; f. 1936; Sec.-Gen. JACINTO PADILLA VALDEZ; 230,000 mems.

Federación de Sindicatos de Trabajadores al Servicio del Estado (FSTSE) (Federation of Unions of Government Workers): Gómez Farías 40, Col. San Rafael, 06470 México, DF; tel. (33) 5128-1600; e-mail contacto@fstse.com; internet www.fstse.com; f. 1938; Sec.-Gen. JOEL AYALA ALMEIDA; 2.5m. mems; 80 unions.

A number of major unions are non-affiliated, including:

Federación Democrática de Sindicatos de Servidores Públicos (Fedessp) (Democratic Federation of Public Servants): Vallarta 321, frente al Hotel Corinto, Col. Tabacalera, 06030 México, DF; tel. (55) 5546-2755; e-mail ser60gluz@hotmail.com; internet www .fedessp.org; f. 2005; Nat. Sec. JUAN MANUEL ESPINOZA ZAVALA.

Sindicato Nacional de Trabajadores de la Educación (SNTE) (Education Workers): Venezuela 44, Col. Centro, México, DF; tel. (55) 5702-0005; fax (55) 5702-6303; e-mail info@snte.org.mx; internet www.snte.org.mx; f. 1943; Pres. JUAN DIAZ DE LA TORRE; 1.4m. mems.

The major agricultural unions are:

Confederación Nacional Campesina (CNC) (National Peasant Confederation): Mariano Azuela 121, Col. Santa María de la Ribera, México, DF; tel. (55) 5547-8042; internet www.cnc.org.mx; Pres. GERARDO SÁNCHEZ GARCÍA.

Confederación Nacional de Organizaciones Ganaderas (National Confederation of Stockbreeding Organizations): Calzada Mariano Escobedo 714, Col. Anzures, México, DF; tel. (55) 5254-3118; e-mail teresa.hernandez@cnog.com.mx; internet www.cnog.com.mx; Pres. OSWALDO CHÁZARO MONTALVO; 300,000 mems.

Transport

Secretariat of State for Communications and Transport: see section on The Government (Secretariats of State).

Caminos y Puentes Federales (CAPUFE): Calzada de los Reyes 24, Col. Tetela del Monte, 62130 Cuernavaca, Mor.; tel. (55) 5200-2000; e-mail contacto@capufe.gob.mx; internet www.capufe.gob.mx; Dir-Gen. GUILLERMO CASTILLO CABALLERO.

RAILWAYS

In 2010 there were 26,717 km of main line track. A 300-km railway link across the isthmus of Tehuantepec connects the Caribbean port of Coatzacoalcos with the Pacific port of Salina Cruz. In 2013 the federal Government announced a project, at a cost of an estimated US $18,000m., to build a cross-country railway line linking major Mayan historical sites.

Ferrocarril Mexicano, SA de CV (Ferromex): Bosque de Ciruelos 99, Col. Bosques de la Loma, 11700 México, DF; tel. (55) 5246-3700; e-mail info@ferromex.com.mx; internet www.ferromex.com .mx; 50-year concession awarded to Grupo Ferroviario Mexicano, SA, (GFM) commencing in 1998; owned by Grupo México, SA de CV; 8,500 km of track and Mexico's largest rail fleet; links from Mexico City to Guadalajara, Hermosillo, Monterrey, Chihuahua and Pacific ports; Exec. Pres. ALFREDO CASAR PÉREZ; Dir-Gen. ROGELIO VÉLEZ LÓPEZ DE LA CERDA.

Ferrocarril del Sureste (Ferrosur): Bosque de Ciruelos 180, 1°, Col. Bosques de las Lomas, 11700 México, DF; tel. (55) 5387-6500; e-mail magarcia@ferrosur.com.mx; internet www.ferrosur.com.mx; 50-year concession awarded to Grupo Tribasa in 1998; 66.7% sold to Empresas Frisco, SA de CV, in 1999, owned by Grupos Carso, SA de CV; Dir-Gen. HUGO GÓMEZ DÍAZ.

Kansas City Southern de México (KCSM): Avda Manuel L. Barragán 4850, Col. Hidalgo, 64420 Monterrey, NL; tel. (81) 8305-7800; fax (81) 8305-7766; e-mail werdman@kcsouthern.com; internet www.kcsouthern.com; fmrly Ferrocarril del Noreste; 4,242 km of line, linking Mexico City with the ports of Lázaro Cárdenas, Veracruz, Tampico/Altamira and north-east Mexico; Chair. MICHAEL R. HAVERTY; Pres. and CEO DAVID L. STARLING.

Servicio de Transportes Eléctricos del Distrito Federal (STE): Avda Municipio Libre 402, 3°, Col. San Andrés Tetepilco, Del. Iztapalapa, 09440 México, DF; tel. (55) 2595-0000; fax (55) 5672-4758; e-mail sugiere@ste.df.gob.mx; internet www.ste.df.gob.mx; suburban tram route with 17 stops upgraded to light rail standard to act as a feeder to the metro; also operates bus and trolleybus networks; Pres. MIGUEL ANGEL MANCERA (Head of Govt of the Distrito Federal); Dir-Gen. RUFINO H. LEÓN TOVAR.

Sistema de Transporte Colectivo (Metro) (STC): Delicias 67, 06070 México, DF; tel. (55) 5709-1133; fax (55) 5512-3601; internet www.metro.df.gob.mx; f. 1967; the first stage of a combined underground and surface railway system in Mexico City was opened in 1969; 12 lines, covering 226 km, were operating in 2013; the system is wholly state-owned and the fares are partially subsidized; Dir-Gen. JOEL ORTEGA CUEVAS.

ROADS

Road transport accounts for about 98% of all public passenger traffic and for about 80% of freight traffic. Mexico's terrain is difficult for overland travel. In 2010 there were 371,936 km of roads, of which 36.4% were paved. Long-distance buses form one of the principal methods of transport in Mexico, and there are some 600 lines operating services throughout the country. In 2010 the Inter-American Development Bank (IDB) approved an amount of US $2.6m. for the Pacific Corridor project (Corredor Pacifico), a highway system connecting Mexico with Panama.

Dirección General de Autotransporte Federal: Calzada de las Bombas 411, Col. Los Girasoles, Del. Coyoacán, 04920 México, DF; tel. (55) 5011-9202; e-mail elizalde@sct.gob.mx; internet dgaf.sct.gob .mx; Dir Dr MIGUEL HERBERTO ELIZALDE LIZARRAGA.

SHIPPING

Mexico has 140 seaports, 29 river docks and a further 29 lake shelters. More than 85% of Mexico's foreign trade is conducted through maritime transport. At the end of 2012 the flag registered fleet comprised 628 vessels, totalling 1,650,684 grt. The Government operates the facilities of seaports.

Coordinación General de Puertos y Marina Mercante (CGPMM): Avda Nuevo León 210, Col. Hipódromo, 06100 México, DF; tel. (55) 5723-9300; fax (55) 5265-3108; e-mail egarciai@sct.gob .mx; internet cgpmm.sct.gob.mx; Co-ordinator ALEJANDRO CHACÓN DOMÍNGUEZ; Dir-Gen. de Puertos ALEJANDRO HERNÁNDEZ CERVANTES; Dir-Gen. de Marina Mercante MARCO ANTONIO VINAZA MARTÍNEZ.

Port of Acapulco: Administración Portuaria Integral Acapulco, Avda Costera Miguel Alemán s/n, Malecón Fiscal s/n, Col. Centro, CP

39300 Acapulco, Gro; tel. (744) 434-1710; fax (744) 483-1648; e-mail marketing@apiacapulco.com; internet www.apiacapulcoport.com; f. 1996; Dir-Gen. OCTAVIO GONZÁLEZ FLORES; Harbour Master Capt. ALEJANDRO MARCHENA.

Port of Coatzacoalcos: Administración Portuaria Integral de Coatzacoalcos, SA de CV, Interior Recinto Portuario s/n, Col. Centro, 96400 Coatzacoalcos, Ver.; tel. (921) 211-0270; fax (921) 211-0272; e-mail dirgral@puertocoatzacoalcos.com.mx; internet www .puertocoatzacoalcos.com.mx; Dir-Gen. GILBERTO RIOS RUÍZ; Harbour Master Capt. DELFINO CRUZ SANTOS.

Port of Dos Bocas: Administración Portuaria Integral de Dos Bocas, SA de CV, Carretera Federal Puerto Ceiba–Paraíso 414, Col. Quintín Arzuz, 86600 Paraíso, Tab.; tel. (933) 333-2744; e-mail ventanilla@puertodosbocas.com.mx; internet www .puertodosbocas.com; Dir-Gen. ROBERTO DE LA GARZA LICÓN; Harbour Master Capt. RAFAEL DURÁN LÓPEZ.

Port of Manzanillo: Administración Portuaria Integral de Manzanillo, SA de CV, Avda Teniente Azueta 9, Col. Burócrata, 28250 Manzanillo, Col.; tel. and fax (314) 331-1400; e-mail gcomercial@ puertomanzanillo.com.mx; internet www.puertomanzanillo.com .mx; Dir-Gen. FLOR DE MARIA CAÑAVERAL PEDRERO; Harbour Master Capt. JORGE ARTURO CASTAÑEDA USCANGA.

Port of Tampico: Administración Portuaria Integral de Tampico, SA de CV, Edif. API de Tampico, Zona Centro, 89000 Tampico, Tamps; tel. (833) 241-1400; fax (833) 212-5744; e-mail contacto@ puertodetampico.com.mx; internet www.puertodetampico.com.mx; Gen. Dir MANUEL FLORES GUERRA; Harbour Master Capt. MANUEL ACEITUNO RODRÍGUEZ.

Port of Veracruz: Administración Porturia Integral de Veracruz, SA de CV, Avda Marina Mercante 210, 7°, Col. Centro, 91700 Veracruz, Ver.; tel. (229) 932-2170; fax (229) 932-3040; e-mail mespinosa@puertodeveracruz.com; internet www.puertodeveracruz .com.mx; privatized in 1994; Dir-Gen. JUAN IGNACIO FERNÁNDEZ CARBAJAL; Harbour Master Capt. ENRIQUE CASARRUBIAS GARCÍA.

Transportación Marítima Mexicana, SA de CV (TMM): Avda de la Cúspide 4755, Col. Parque del Pedregal, Del. Tlalpan, 14010 México, DF; tel. (55) 5629-8866; fax (55) 5629-8899; e-mail grupotmm@tmm.com.mx; internet www.tmm.com.mx; f. 1955; cargo services to Europe, the Mediterranean, Scandinavia, the USA, South and Central America, the Caribbean and the Far East; Pres. JOSÉ F. SERRANO SEGOVIA; Sec. IGNACIO RODRÍGUEZ PULLEN.

CIVIL AVIATION

There were 62 international airports in Mexico in 2012. Of these, México, Cancún, Guadalajara, Monterrey and Tijuana registered the highest number of operations.

Aeropuertos y Servicios Auxiliares (ASA): Edif. B, Avda 602 161, Col. San Juan de Aragón, Del. Venustiano Carranza, 15620 México, DF; tel. (55) 5133-1000; fax (55) 5133-2985; e-mail quejasydenuncias@asa.gob.mx; internet www.asa.gob.mx; f. 1965; oversees airport management and devt; Gen. Man. GILBERTO LÓPEZ MEYER.

Dirección General de Aeronáutica Civil (DGAC): Avda Providencia No 807, 6°, Col. Del Valle, 03100 México, DF; tel. (55) 5523-6642; fax (55) 5523-7207; e-mail hgonzalw@sct.gob.m; internet dgac .sct.gob.mx; subdivision of Secretariat of State for Communications and Transport; regulates civil aviation; Dir-Gen. HECTOR GONZALEZ WEEKS.

Aeromar, Transportes Aeromar: Hotel María Isabel Sheraton, Paseo de la Reforma 325, Local 10, México, DF; tel. (55) 5514-2248; e-mail web.aeromar@aeromar.com.mx; internet www.aeromar.com .mx; f. 1987; scheduled domestic passenger and cargo services; Dir-Gen. AMI LINDENBERG.

Aeroméxico Cargo: Avda Texococo s/n, esq. Avda Tahel, Col. Peñón de los Baños, 15520 México, DF; tel. (55) 5133-0203; internet www .aeromexicocargo.com.mx; owned by state holding co Consorcio Aeroméxico, SA; cargo airline; Dir-Gen. MAURICIO NIETO.

Aerovías de México (Aeroméxico): Paseo de la Reforma 445, 3°, Torre B, Col. Cuauhtémoc, 06500 México, DF; tel. (55) 5133-4000; fax (55) 5133-4619; internet www.aeromexico.com; f. 1934 as Aeronaves de México, nationalized 1959; sold by state holding co Consorcio Aeroméxico, SA, to private investors in 2007; services between most principal cities of Mexico and the USA, Chile, Brazil, Peru, France and Spain; Pres. JOSÉ LUIS BARRAZA; Dir-Gen. ANDRÉS CONESA LABASTIDA.

Aviacsa: Aeropuerto Internacional, Zona C, Hangar 1, Col. Aviación General, 15520 México, DF; tel. (55) 5716-9005; fax (55) 5758-3823; internet www.aviacsa.com; f. 1990; operates internal flights, and flights to the USA; Dir-Gen. ANDRÉS FABRE.

Interjet (ABC Aerolíneas, SA de CV): Aeropuerto Internacional de Toluca, Toluca, Méx.; tel. (55) 1102-5555; e-mail atencionaclientes@

interjet.com.mx; internet www.interjet.com.mx; f. 2005; budget airline operating internal flights; Pres. JOSÉ LUIS GARZA.

Magnicharters (Grupo Aereo Monterrey SA. de CV): Calle Donato Guerra No 9, Col. Juarez, México, DF; tel. (55) 5141-1351; internet magnicharters.com.mx; f. 1994; services the domestic tourism market; Dir-Gen. GABRIEL BOJÓRQUEZ.

VivaAerobus: Aeropuerto de Monterrey, Terminal C, Zona de Carga, Carretera Miguel Alemán Km. 24, Apodaca, 66600 Nuevo León; tel. (81) 8215-0150; e-mail publicidad@vivaaerobus.com; internet www.vivaaerobus.com; f. 2006; low-cost domestic airline; Dir-Gen JUAN CARLOS ZUAZUA COSÍO.

Volaris: Aeropuerto Internacional de la Ciudad de Toluca, 50500 Toluca, Méx.; tel. (55) 1102-8000; e-mail comentarios@volaris.com .mx; internet www.volaris.com.mx; f. 2006; operated by Vuela Compañía de Aviación; budget airline operating internal flights; Pres. GILBERTO PÉREZALONSO CIFUENTES; Dir-Gen. ENRIQUE BELTRANENA.

Tourism

Tourism remains one of Mexico's principal sources of foreign exchange. Mexico received 23.4m. foreign visitors in 2011, and receipts from tourism in that year were US $10,006m. More than 90% of visitors come from the USA and Canada. The relics of the Mayan and Aztec civilizations and of Spanish Colonial Mexico are of historic and artistic interest. Zihuatanejo, on the Pacific coast, and Cancún, on the Caribbean, have been developed as tourist resorts.

Secretariat of State for Tourism: see section on The Government (Secretariats of State).

Asociación Mexicana de Agencias de Viajes (AMAV): Guanajuato 128, Col. Roma, Del. Cuauhtemoc, 06700 México, DF; tel. (55) 5584-9300; fax (55) 5584-9933; e-mail contacto@amavnacional.com; internet www.ofertasdeviajesmexico.com; f. 1945; asscn of travel agencies; Pres. JORGE HERNÁNDEZ DELGADO; Exec. Vice-Pres. JOSÉ LUIS MONTERO HERNÁNDEZ.

Fondo Nacional de Fomento al Turismo (FONATUR): Tecoyotitla 100, Col. Florida, 01030 México, DF; tel. (55) 5090-4200; fax (55) 5090-4469; e-mail fonatur-dg@fonatur.gob.mx; internet www .fonatur.gob.mx; f. 1956 to finance and promote the devt of tourism; Dir-Gen. ENRIQUE CARRILLO LAVAT.

Defence

As assessed at November 2012, Mexico's regular armed forces numbered 270,250: army 200,000, navy 58,500 (including naval air force, 1,250; marines, 21,500) and air force 11,750. There were also 87,350 reserves. Paramilitary forces numbered 59,500, comprising a federal preventive police force of 37,000, a federal ministerial police force of 4,500 and a rural defence militia numbering 18,000. Military service, on a part-time basis, is by lottery and lasts for one year.

Defence Budget: 68,900m. new pesos in 2012.

Chief of Staff of National Defence: Brig.-Gen. ROBLE ARTURO GRANADOS GALLARDO.

Superintendent and Comptroller of the Army and Air Force: Gen. GUILLERMO MORENO SERRANO.

Commander of the Air Force: Gen. LEONARDO GONZÁLEZ GARCÍA.

Chief of Staff of the Navy: Vice-Adm. JOAQUIN ZETINA ANGULO.

Education

State education in Mexico is free and compulsory at primary and secondary level. Primary education lasts for six years between the ages of six and 11. Secondary education lasts for up to six years. In 2009/10 enrolment at primary schools included 98% of pupils in the relevant age-group, while in 2009/10 enrolment at secondary schools included 71% of pupils in the relevant age-group. According to preliminary figures, in 2009/10 nursery schools numbered 90,411 and there were 99,202 primary schools. There were 35,155 secondary schools in the same year, attended by 6.1m. pupils. In spite of the existence of more than 80 indigenous languages in Mexico, there were few bilingual secondary schools. In 2009/10 there were an estimated 5,501 institutes of higher education, attended by some 2.7m. students. The 2011 federal budget allocated an estimated 23,000m. new pesos to the Secretariat of State for Public Education.

THE FEDERATED STATES OF MICRONESIA

Introductory Survey

LOCATION, CLIMATE, LANGUAGE, RELIGION, FLAG, CAPITAL

The Federated States of Micronesia forms (with Palau, q.v.) the archipelago of the Caroline Islands, about 800 km east of the Philippines. The Federated States of Micronesia comprises 607 islands and includes (from west to east) the states of Yap, Chuuk (formerly Truk), Pohnpei (formerly Ponape) and Kosrae. The islands are subject to heavy rainfall, although precipitation decreases from east to west. January, February and March are the driest months, although seasonal variations in rainfall and temperature are generally small. The annual average temperature is 27°C (81°F). The native population consists of various ethno-linguistic groups, but English is widely understood. The principal religion is Christianity, much of the population being Roman Catholic. The national flag (proportions 10 by 19) consists of four five-pointed white stars, arranged as a circle, situated centrally on a light blue field. The capital is Palikir, on Pohnpei.

CONTEMPORARY POLITICAL HISTORY

Historical Context

The Federated States of Micronesia was formerly part of the US-administered Trust Territory of the Pacific Islands (for history up to 1965, see the Marshall Islands).

From 1965 there were increasing demands for local autonomy within the Trust Territory of the Pacific Islands. In that year the Congress of Micronesia was formed, and in 1967 a commission was established to examine the future political status of the islands. In 1970 the commission declared Micronesians' rights to sovereignty over their own lands, to self-determination, to devise their own constitution and to revoke any form of free association with the USA. In May 1977, after eight years of negotiations, US President Jimmy Carter announced that his administration intended to adopt measures to terminate the trusteeship agreement by 1981. Until 1979 the four districts of Yap, Truk (Chuuk since 1990), Ponape (Pohnpei since 1984) and Kosrae were governed by a local Administrator, appointed by the President of the USA. However, on 10 May 1979 the four districts ratified a new Constitution to become the Federated States of Micronesia. The Constitution was promulgated in 1980.

The USA signed a Compact of Free Association with the Republic of Palau in August 1982, and reached agreement with the Marshall Islands and the Federated States of Micronesia in October. The trusteeship of the Pacific territory was due to end after the principle and terms of Compacts of Free Association had been approved by the respective peoples and legislatures of the new countries, by the US Congress and by the UN Security Council. Under the Compacts, the four countries (including the Northern Mariana Islands) would be independent of each other and would manage both their internal and foreign affairs separately, while the USA would remain responsible for defence and security. The Federated States of Micronesia approved its Compact by plebiscite in June 1983, and it was ratified by the islands' Congress in September.

US administration of the Federated States of Micronesia was formally ended in November 1986, and the UN Security Council ratified the termination of the trusteeship agreement in December 1990. Ponape was renamed Pohnpei in November 1984, when its Constitution came into effect, and Truk was renamed Chuuk in January 1990, when its new Constitution was proposed (being later adopted).

Domestic Political Affairs

The incumbent President (since 1987), John Haglelgam, was replaced by Bailey Olter, a former Vice-President, in May 1991. At congressional elections in March 1995 Olter was re-elected to the Pohnpei senator-at-large seat (each of the four Micronesian states choosing a senator-at-large to serve a four-year term). In May Olter was re-elected to the presidency unopposed. In July 1996 Olter suffered a stroke. Vice-President Jacob Nena served as acting President during Olter's subsequent absence from office, and in May 1997 was sworn in as President of the country. (Olter died in February 1999.)

Congressional elections took place in March 1997 for the 10 senators elected on a two-yearly basis, at which all of the incumbents were returned to office. A referendum held concurrently on a proposed amendment to the Constitution (which envisaged increasing the allocation of national revenue to the state legislatures from 50% to 80% of the total budget) was approved in Chuuk and Yap, but rejected in Pohnpei and Kosrae.

At the congressional elections held in March 1999, President Nena was re-elected to the Kosrae senator-at-large seat and Vice-President Leo Falcam to the Pohnpei senator-at-large seat. In May Congress elected Falcam as President and the Chuuk senator-at-large, Redley Killion, as Vice-President.

A first round of renegotiations of the Compact of Free Association (certain terms of which were due to expire in 2001) was completed in late 1999. The USA and the Federated States of Micronesia pledged to maintain defence and security relations, and the USA agreed to continue to provide economic aid to the islands. In July 2001 the USA offered annual assistance of US $61m. and a trust fund of $13m., while expressing concern that the $2,600m. that it had given to Micronesia and the Marshall Islands since 1986 had been mismanaged. Upon the expiry on 3 November 2001 of the Compact's funding terms for Micronesia, funding was continued at the Compact's 15-year average level while negotiations proceeded. Following a proposal by the USA in April 2002 to extend economic assistance for a period of 20 years, a new draft funding structure was agreed, and in March 2003 the US budget projections for 2004 granted Micronesian citizens access to private health care resources in the USA as part of the Federated States' continued entitlement to US federal programmes. On 1 May 2003 the amended Compact of Free Association was signed by representatives of the two countries in Pohnpei. The revised Compact envisaged direct annual grants of $76.2m. from 2004, in addition to a further $16m. annually, which was to be paid into a trust fund for Micronesia. From 2007 direct grants were to decrease by some $800,000, with this amount being transferred to the trust fund. (The total amount to be paid prior to the expected termination of US assistance in 2023 amounted, in 2004 terms, to some $1,760m.) Furthermore, the Micronesian Government also undertook to provide frequent, strictly monitored audit information on all US funding in order to ensure greater accountability. In October 2003 final agreement was reached on some outstanding security and immigration issues, and the US Congress approved the amended Compact in November. President George W. Bush signed the pact in December, and representatives of both Governments signed a document of implementation in June 2004.

Nevertheless, there remained widespread concern in the Federated States of Micronesia that the new Compact represented a substantial overall reduction in annual income over the long term. Moreover, the formula for the distribution of Compact funds to each of Micronesia's states and the removal of certain US subsidies remained the subject of considerable controversy. In August 2008 these concerns were renewed when the US Department of the Interior partly suspended Compact funding for the state of Chuuk, citing financial management problems. In March the US Office of Insular Affairs had confirmed that in 2008/09 the sum of almost US $20.3m. was to be allocated to the country's trust fund, in addition to the annual operating grants.

Meanwhile, in September 2002 a referendum was held on a number of proposed amendments to the Constitution, including a provision for the direct election of presidential candidates, the extension of the right of islanders to hold dual citizenship and changes to the distribution formula for Compact of Free Association funds. However, the measures did not receive the constitutionally required three-quarters' majority of votes and were thus rejected.

At the congressional elections of March 2003 President Leo Falcam unexpectedly failed to achieve re-election to a further four-year term as senator-at-large for Pohnpei. In May Congress appointed the senator-at-large for Yap, Joseph J. Urusemal, to the presidency. The elections were the subject of some controversy, as it appeared that elected officials had disbursed a portion of the 2002 US funding for Micronesia in order to enhance their electoral prospects. The alleged misallocation of funds was reportedly a significant factor in the worsening fiscal positions of Chuuk, Pohnpei and Kosrae. Perceptions of official accountability continued to deteriorate in 2003; in November three serving congressmen were indicted for their role in an alleged fraud involving some US $1.2m. in public funds. In January 2004 Congress approved a resolution to dismiss the judge assigned to the case. In August the Supreme Court ruled in favour of a petition lodged by President Urusemal against the judge's dismissal, on the grounds that it infringed the constitutionally guaranteed separation of powers. Also in January 2004, members of Congress attempted to introduce legislation effectively absolving public officials from corruption allegations relating to Compact of Free Association funds. The proposals aroused widespread public hostility, and several representatives of state legislatures threatened to secede from the federation unless the proposed bill were withdrawn. In March the so-called 'amnesty bill' was returned to a congressional sub-committee for further discussion; however, at March 2013 no subsequent developments had been reported.

At congressional elections held on 7 March 2005 all but one of the four incumbent senators-at-large were re-elected. On the following day eight of the 10 incumbent senators with two-year mandates were re-elected in separate polls. (Results from Chuuk were annulled, owing to alleged voting irregularities, and in late April a new round of voting was held in this state.) Concurrent with the second round of congressional elections, a referendum was held on three proposed constitutional amendments, including the question of whether each state should recognize and uphold the laws and judicial rulings of other states, and whether to allow dual citizenship. Although a majority of voters favoured the proposed amendments, the measures did not receive the required three-quarters' majority of votes and were thus rejected.

At congressional elections held in March 2007 for all 14 seats of the chamber, the incumbent senators-at-large for Kosrae, Pohnpei and Yap were re-elected, while Immanuel Mori defeated Vice-President Redley Killion to become senator-at-large for Chuuk. In May, in a congressional vote, Mori was elected President, while Alik L. Alik of Kosrae succeeded Killion as Vice-President. 'Special' congressional elections were conducted in July to fill the seats vacated by Mori and Alik. In a protracted confirmation process, members of Mori's Government were individually nominated and sworn in during the latter half of 2007 and early 2008. A reorganization of ministries was also instigated, including the creation of a Department of Education.

In April 2007 a memorandum of understanding (MOU) was signed between Congress and the state legislatures of Chuuk and Kosrae, under the terms of which Congress assumed the disbursement, accounting and reporting responsibilities for all US federal programme grants on behalf of the two states. The MOU was intended to assist the two states address various fiscal difficulties, including cash supply and long-term structural issues. In December 2011 Congress informed the respective Governors of Chuuk and Kosrae of its intention to terminate the MOU within six months, deeming the two state legislatures now capable of administering their own federal grants.

Meanwhile, in March 2008 Roosevelt D. Kansou, a senator from Chuuk, was convicted of conspiracy and was consequently removed from his seat in Congress. Tesime Kofot was elected to succeed Kansou in a special ballot in May, assuming the seat in September.

In March 2009 elections were conducted for 10 of the 14 seats in Congress. Elections were also held to determine the Governor and Lieutenant-Governor of Chuuk; following a run-off poll in April, incumbent Governor Wesley Simina and Lieutenant-Governor Johnson Elimo were both re-elected. In October Peter M. Christian was elected as senator-at-large for Pohnpei, following the death in June of the incumbent, Resio S. Moses; Christian was inaugurated in December.

Alongside gubernatorial and municipal elections held in Yap in November 2010, at which the incumbent Governor and Lieutenant-Governor—Sebastian Anefal and Anthony Tareg, respectively—were re-elected, a referendum on a proposed amendment to the state Constitution was held. The proposal, which would grant the state legislature the power to present for a popular vote, at a future election, the question of whether Yap should review its political status as a state, was approved by a sizeable majority. Gubernatorial and municipal elections also took place in Kosrae in November, but no candidate secured the 50% of votes required for a first-round victory. Lyndon Jackson, who had won the largest number of votes in the first round, was elected Governor in a run-off poll in January 2011; he was inaugurated later that month, together with Carson Sigrah, the new Lieutenant-Governor.

Recent developments

At elections for all 14 seats in Congress on 8 March 2011, President Mori, Vice-President Alik and six other incumbent senators retained their seats. On 11 May Mori and Alik were re-elected to a further four-year term by the newly installed Congress, which also re-elected Isaac Figir as Speaker. Special congressional elections were subsequently conducted to fill the seats vacated by Mori and Alik. Wesley Simina's election as Mori's replacement as Chuuk's senator-at-large led to his resignation as Governor of Chuuk; incumbent Lieutenant-Governor Johnson Elimo was elected to succeed Simina as Governor in August, being succeeded himself by Ritis Heldart. At a joint inauguration ceremony for the new national Government and Congress held that month, President Mori identified climate change, education, health, infrastructural development and private sector development as priority areas of concern for his administration, and also pledged to increase national revenue and foreign investment levels.

In July 2011 Kurt Campbell, the US Assistant Secretary of State for East Asian and Pacific Affairs, announced that the existing visa-free provision whereby citizens of Micronesia, the Marshall Islands and Palau could travel to the USA to live, work or study without restriction was currently under review, owing to mounting objections from US congressional and state government leaders with regard to the cost of health, education and social services provision to such visitors. In October senator-at-large Peter Christian introduced a resolution to Congress urging the termination of the Compact of Free Association with the USA by 2018 at the latest, in response to the perceived hardening in the stance of the US Administration of President Barack Obama in its relations with the Federated States of Micronesia. In the resolution, Christian accused the US Government of regarding the Compact as an 'act of charity' rather than as a treaty providing for a mutually beneficial relationship between two sovereign states.

At gubernatorial and municipal elections held in Pohnpei in November 2011, John Ehsa was re-elected as Governor and Marcelo Peterson was elected as Lieutenant-Governor. Ehsa and Peterson were formally inaugurated, together with the new state legislature, in January 2012.

On 5 March 2013 elections were conducted for 10 of the 14 seats in Congress. Elections were also held to determine the Governor and Lieutenant-Governor of Chuuk; following a run-off poll on 2 April, the incumbents Elimo and Heldart were re-elected to their respective posts, according to preliminary results.

Environmental Concerns and Human Development

Periodic extreme weather formations have caused loss of life and severe damage to crops, property and infrastructure in Micronesia. Following a severe typhoon in December 2002, President George W. Bush of the USA declared Micronesia a federal disaster area and ordered emergency US funding and resources to be allocated to the relief effort. A further typhoon that struck Yap in April 2004 left 1,200 people homeless; the US Government offered to assume 75% of the cost of the recovery effort.

In 2000 marine biologists issued a warning regarding the erosion of the islands' coastlines, caused by the destruction of the coral reefs by pollution, overfishing and increasing sea temperatures. Furthermore, in 2003 concerns over environmental pollution increased, owing to the damage caused by former US and Japanese military equipment submerged in Micronesian waters.

In September 2003 President Joseph Urusemal urged the UN General Assembly to work towards halting climate change and its consequent effects on sea levels and weather patterns. At a US congressional hearing in March 2008, the Federated States of Micronesia's Permanent Representative to the UN, Masao Nakayama, argued that climate change was directly affecting Micronesia and urged the USA to take action to alleviate the problem. In October 2009 President Immanuel Mori addressed

European and other world leaders on the issue of climate change at the European Development Days conference, held in Stockholm, Sweden. Declaring that Micronesia's water supplies, agricultural productivity and very existence were threatened by climate change, Mori appealed to developed nations to establish an Adaptation Fund to assist poorer nations in their efforts to mitigate and adapt to the effects of climate change.

At a conference held in Geneva, Switzerland, in June 2010 of Parties to the Montreal Protocol on Substances that Deplete the Ozone Layer—a multilateral treaty implemented in 1989 with the objective of phasing out the production of substances believed to be responsible for ozone depletion—the head of the Micronesian delegation emphasized the importance of taking 'urgent action' more effectively to control the release into the atmosphere of hydrofluorocarbons (HFCs—substances introduced to replace the use of ozone-depleting gases, some of which are believed nevertheless to contribute to climate change). At the annual UN Climate Change Conference held in Cancún, Mexico, in November–December 2010, Micronesia resubmitted a proposal that it had made in the previous year urging governments to take immediate action on the 50% of global warming thought to be caused by gases other than carbon dioxide, including methane and some HFCs. Micronesia also proposed transferring control of HFC emissions, currently under the remit of the Kyoto Protocol, to the Montreal Protocol, a strategy also propounded by the USA, Canada and Mexico in a separate, though similar, North American proposal.

In May 2011 Micronesia, with the support of the environmental action group Greenpeace, launched an unprecedented transboundary legal challenge against plans by the Czech Republic to expand a coal-fired power station, claiming that the potential environmental damage from what would be one of Europe's largest such stations could threaten the survival of the islands.

The *Human Development Report 2010*, published by the UN Development Programme (UNDP) in November of that year, included the Federated States of Micronesia in its Human Development Index for the first time. Micronesia was ranked 103rd out of 169 countries, its overall score falling below both the regional and global average. Micronesia fared similarly poorly in subsequent UNDP reports, ranking 117th out of 186 countries in the *Human Development Report 2013*.

In its *2011 Trafficking in Persons Report*, published in June of that year, the US Department of State downgraded the Federated States of Micronesia to its list of countries of particular concern with regard to human-trafficking ('Tier Three'). The report noted that, while there was a lack of data available as the Micronesian authorities had not conducted any investigations into human-trafficking, the forcing into prostitution of Micronesian women lured to the USA and its territories with promises of well-paid employment was a prevalent problem, as was the prostitution of women and children to crew members on fishing vessels within Micronesia's territorial waters. The report further stated that Micronesia did not fully comply with the minimum standards for the elimination of trafficking and 'was not making significant efforts to do so'. Confronted by the possibility of a withdrawal of US funding over the issue, in November a meeting of the Micronesian Legislative Conference—bringing together representatives of Congress and each of the four state legislatures—adopted a resolution accepting the obligation of the national and state legislatures comprehensively to address the problem of human-trafficking and to consider adopting a legal regime suitable to their respective jurisdictions. Consequently, in the 2012 human-trafficking report of the US Department of State Micronesia was reinstated on the list of 'Tier Two' countries in acknowledgement of its stated efforts to eliminate trafficking.

Regional Affairs

In February 2003 Pohnpei hosted the first summit of Micronesian leaders (the Micronesian Chief Executives' Summit—MCES) and regular such meetings have been held since to discuss co-operation among the states of Micronesia, Palau, the Northern Mariana Islands, the Marshall Islands and Guam in areas such as tourism, telecommunications, the environment, health, the economy, climate change and rising fuel prices. At the MCES held in Pohnpei in July 2011, a resolution was signed on the development of a strategic framework to implement a marine-based conservation programme that would establish the world's first regional shark sanctuary in the territorial waters of the Micronesian islands; the resolution also provided for the imposition of a ban on the possession of and trade in shark fins within the sanctuary area. During the summit meeting the Pacific leaders also discussed the establishment in

Guam of the Micronesian Center for a Sustainable Future. In August 2012 the first Micronesian Regional Women's Summit was held in Koror, Palau.

Relations between the Federated States of Micronesia and the People's Republic of China have become increasingly close during the early 21st century. In July 2006 the Chinese Minister of Foreign Affairs, Li Zhaoxing, became the most senior Chinese official ever to visit Micronesia, meeting President Urusemal and Sebastian Anefal, then the Secretary of the Department of Foreign Affairs. In September residences built by the Chinese for the Micronesian President, Vice-President, Speaker of Congress and Chief Justice were presented to the Government at a ceremony that highlighted the strong links between the two countries. Bilateral relations were further bolstered by the opening of a Micronesian embassy in the Chinese capital of Beijing in May 2007; Micronesia's first resident ambassador in Beijing, Akillino Susaia, assumed the post in April 2010. Meanwhile, Vice-President Alik made a six-day official visit to Beijing, at the invitation of his Chinese counterpart, Xi Jinping, in July 2009, during which he affirmed the island state's continued adherence to the 'one China' policy and pledged further to increase bilateral co-operation. Alik returned to the Chinese capital in November to mark the 20th anniversary of the formal establishment of diplomatic relations between Micronesia and China. In May 2010 President Immanuel Mori met with Chinese President Hu Jintao in the Chinese city of Shanghai. Hu appealed for greater co-operation in the fields of new energy, infrastructure, construction and the fisheries industry, and pledged a continuation of Chinese economic and technological aid to the Federated States of Micronesia and of encouragement and support to Chinese businesses looking to invest in the island state. A bilateral economic and technical co-operation agreement was signed between Micronesia and China in February 2011, under the terms of which China was to provide US $1.5m. in development aid to the Micronesian Government. In October a proposal was mooted by a private Chinese company, Exhibit and Travel Group (ETG), to construct a major tourism resort in Yap; the plans included the construction of between eight and 10 hotel complexes, providing a total of some 20,000 hotel rooms, as well as convention and entertainment centres, casinos and other leisure facilities. In January 2012 the state government of Yap and the ETG signed an MOU regarding the development of the state's tourism industry and infrastructure.

In the early years of the 21st century, Japan was the second largest donor to the Federated States of Micronesia, behind only the USA. Bilateral relations were further enhanced in June 2008 when the Japanese embassy in Kolonia, Pohnpei, welcomed its first resident ambassador, Shoji Sato. President Mori made an official visit to Japan in November to mark the 20th anniversary of the establishment of diplomatic relations between the two states. During another visit to Japan, in November 2010, Mori expressed gratitude for Japanese economic co-operation and assistance in Micronesia, while Japanese Prime Minister Naoto Kan thanked Micronesia for its support of Japan's bid to secure a permanent seat on the UN Security Council. During his visit, Mori also met with the Japanese Minister for Foreign Affairs, Seiji Maehara, who confirmed Japan's commitment to enhanced bilateral co-operation in a number of fields, including tourism and the fisheries industry.

CONSTITUTION AND GOVERNMENT

On 10 May 1979 the locally drafted Constitution of the Federated States of Micronesia, incorporating the four states of Kosrae, Yap, Ponape (later Pohnpei) and Truk (later Chuuk), became effective. The federal legislature, the Congress, comprises 14 members (senators). The four states each elect one senator-at-large, for a four-year term. The remaining 10 senators are elected for two-year terms: their seats are distributed in proportion to the population of each state. Each of the four states also has its own Constitution, Governor and legislature. The federal President and Vice-President are elected by the Congress from among the four senators-at-large; the offices rotate among the four states. (By-elections are then held for the seats to which the President and Vice-President had been elected.) In November 1986 the Compact of Free Association was signed by the Governments of the Federated States of Micronesia and the USA. Certain of its terms, due to expire in 2001, were renegotiated in late 1999, and an amended Compact was signed by the Governments of both countries on 1 May 2003. By the terms of the Compact, the Federated States of Micronesia is a sovereign, self-governing state.

Local government units are the municipalities and villages. Elected Magistrates and Councils govern the municipalities. Village government is largely traditional.

REGIONAL AND INTERNATIONAL CO-OPERATION

The Federated States of Micronesia is a member of the Pacific Community (see p. 422), the Pacific Islands Forum (see p. 426), the South Pacific Regional Trade and Economic Co-operation Agreement (SPARTECA, see p. 427), the UN's Economic and Social Commission for Asia and the Pacific (ESCAP, see p. 31) and the Asian Development Bank (ADB, see p. 214). The Federated States of Micronesia hosts the Western and Central Pacific Fisheries Commission, a multilateral agency established in 2004 to manage migratory fish stocks in the region.

The Federated States of Micronesia became a member of the UN in 1991.

ECONOMIC AFFAIRS

In 2011, according to estimates by the World Bank, gross national income (GNI) in the Federated States of Micronesia, measured at average 2009–11 prices, was US $323m., equivalent to $2,900 per head (or $3,610 per head on an international purchasing-power parity basis). During 2002–11, it was estimated, the population increased at an average annual rate of 0.4%, while gross domestic product (GDP) per head decreased, in real terms, by an average of 0.2% per year. According to UN figures, overall GDP increased, in real terms, at an average annual rate of 0.1% during 2002–11; real GDP increased by 1.0% in 2011. The Asian Development Bank (ADB) estimated GDP growth at 2.1% in the year ending September 2011 and at 1.4% in 2011/12.

The agricultural sector (including forestry and fishing) contributed 26.5% of GDP in 2011. According to FAO, the sector engaged about 21.4% of the total labour force in mid-2013. Agriculture is mainly on a subsistence level, although its importance is diminishing. The principal crops are coconuts, bananas, betel nuts, cassava and sweet potatoes. White peppercorns are produced on Pohnpei. In the year to September 2011 fishing access fees, mainly from Japanese fleets, totalled US $18.8m. (some 27.8% of total consolidated general government revenue). Exports of fish are a major source of revenue. The islands' tuna-processing facilities were upgraded in 2009/10, funded with Chinese assistance. According to UN figures, agricultural GDP increased, in real terms, at an average annual rate of 0.7% during 2002–11; sectoral GDP expanded by 2.9% in 2011.

Industry (including mining, manufacturing, utilities and construction) provided 6.5% of GDP in 2011. There is little manufacturing, other than the production of buttons using trochus shells, and the mining sector is negligible. Industrial GDP decreased, in real terms, at an average annual rate of 0.9% during 2002–11; the sector's GDP increased by 15.8% in 2010, but contracted by 13.4% in 2011.

Manufacturing contributed just 0.5% of GDP in 2011. Manufacturing GDP decreased, in real terms, at an average annual rate of 15.4% during 2002–11; the sector's GDP increased by 12.6% in 2010, but decreased by 2.6% in 2011.

Construction contributed 4.6% of GDP in 2011. The sector's GDP increased, in real terms, at an average annual rate of 4.2% during 2002–11; construction GDP expanded by 23.1% in 2010, but decreased by 20.3% in 2011.

The islands are heavily dependent on imported fuels. Purchases of petroleum products accounted for 26.2% of the costs of total imports in the year to September 2011. In April 2009 a new bio-gas project was initiated in Pohnpei, the first of four schemes financed by the Chinese province of Zhejiang.

The services sector provided 67.0% of GDP in 2011. A total of 14,788 people were employed in services in 2006/07, equivalent to some 90% of total employment in the formal sector. Tourism is an important industry, with receipts for 2006 totalling some US $18.3m. The number of tourist arrivals increased from 21,146 in 2007 to 25,627 in 2008. Remittances from overseas emigrants are a significant source of income support. The GDP of the services sector decreased, in real terms, at an average annual rate of 0.3% during 2002–11; the sector's GDP increased by 2.3% in 2011.

According to the IMF, in the financial year ending September 2011 there was a visible merchandise trade deficit of US $134.2m., with a deficit of $58.6m. on the current account of the balance of payments. The principal sources of imports in 2007 were the USA (which supplied 41.2% of the total), Guam and Japan. Guam was the principal market for exports in 2007, purchasing 22.5% of the total, followed by the USA. The principal imports in 2007 were mineral products (22.1% of the total), prepared foodstuffs, beverages and tobacco and machinery, mechanical appliances and electrical equipment. Fish is the major export commodity; marine products accounted for 76.0% of total exports in 2007. Other exports in that year included betel nuts and kava.

An estimated budget surplus of US $1.3m., equivalent to 0.4% of GDP, was recorded in the financial year ending September 2011. The Federated States of Micronesia relies heavily on financial assistance, particularly from the USA, with funding made available under the Compact of Free Association (see Contemporary Political History). In 2011/12 the USA was to provide a total of $105.5m. in Compact funding to Micronesia. Bilateral grants have been provided by Japan, a major donor, and the People's Republic of China. At the end of 2012, according to the ADB, the islands' total external debt stood at $87m. In that year the cost of debt-servicing was equivalent to 6.6% of the value of exports of goods and services. The annual rate of inflation averaged 4.1% in 2002–11. According to the ADB, consumer prices increased by an annual average of 5.6% in 2011/12. Some 16.2% of the labour force were unemployed in 2010.

Constraints upon the islands' economic development have included their remote location and the high rate of emigration. It was hoped that the Federated States of Micronesia would be in a position to achieve financial self-sufficiency by 2023, upon the scheduled expiry of the Compact of Free Association (see Contemporary Political History). Under the amended Compact, instead of general budgetary grants, US aid was to be targeted mainly towards specific projects, was to be conditional upon the efficiency of its management and use, and was to be reviewed annually. Meanwhile, the trust fund established to support the Micronesian economy in the longer term remained vulnerable to the volatility of international financial markets. Inflationary pressures rose from early 2011, largely owing to increases in the costs of imports of essential commodities, particularly fuel and foodstuffs, with inflation rising to 5.6% in 2011/12, according to the ADB. Remittances from emigrant workers were sustained in 2010. Following five years of budgetary deficits, small surpluses were achieved in the four years from 2008/09 as a result of fiscal consolidation (including improved rates of tax collection). Rising capital expenditure (on infrastructural development and public works projects) in 2011/12 was to be financed primarily by grants provided by the US Government. Meanwhile, the number of tourist arrivals increased in 2008/09, and receipts from tourism were reported to have improved in the following fiscal year. The extension of the runway at Pohnpei airport to accommodate larger aircraft, which was funded by the Japanese Government, was completed in June 2012. Along with improved flight connections, it was envisaged that the upgrading of the airport would bring major benefits to the tourism sector. The ADB estimated that Micronesia's GDP growth rate slowed to 1.4% in 2011/12, forecasting a further deceleration, to 1.0%, for 2012/13, partly owing to the completion of a number of construction projects. Although a modest budgetary surplus was forecast for 2012/13, in October 2011 the IMF identified the implementation of tax reforms, targeted expenditure reductions and structural reforms in order to foster private sector growth as being essential to Micronesia's long-term fiscal and economic sustainability. In December 2012 the Government announced that the USA had issued seven grants totalling US $50.7m. for 2012/13 (in addition to a supplementary educational grant of $11.8m. received in October).

PUBLIC HOLIDAYS

2014: 1 January (New Year's Day), 31 March (Micronesian Culture and Traditions Day), 18 April (Good Friday), 9 May (for Constitution Day), 24 October (United Nations Day), 3 November (Independence Day), 11 November (Veterans of Foreign Wars Day), 25 December (Christmas Day).

Statistical Survey

Source (unless otherwise indicated): Statistics Unit, Office of Statistics, Budget and Economic Management, Overseas Development Assistance and Compact Management (SBOC), POB PS-12, Palikir, Pohnpei, FM 96941; tel. 320-2820; fax 320-5854; e-mail fsmstat@sboc.fm; internet www.sboc.fm/index.php.

AREA AND POPULATION

Area: 700.8 sq km (270.6 sq miles): Chuuk (Truk, 294 islands) 127.4 sq km; Kosrae (5 islands) 109.6 sq km; Pohnpei (Ponape, 163 islands) 345.2 sq km; Yap (145 islands) 118.6 sq km.

Population: 107,008 at census of 1 April 2000; 102,624 (males 52,055, females 50,569) at census of 4 April 2010. *By State* (2010): Chuuk 48,651; Kosrae 6,616; Pohnpei 35,981; Yap 11,376. *2013* (UN estimate at mid-year): 112,725 (Source: UN, *World Population Prospects: The 2010 Revision*).

Density (at mid-2013): 160.9 per sq km.

Population by Age and Sex (UN estimates at mid-2013): *0–14:* 39,642 (males 20,500, females 19,142); *15–64:* 68,702 (males 35,136, females 33,566); *65 and over:* 4,381 (males 1,958, females 2,423); *Total* 112,725 (males 57,594, females 55,131). Source: UN, *World Population Prospects: The 2010 Revision*.

Principal Towns (population of municipalities at 2010 census): Weno (Moen) 13,700; Palikir (capital) 6,640; Nett 6,542; Kitti 6,470. Source: Thomas Brinkhoff, *City Population* (internet: www.citypopulation.de).

Births and Deaths (2003, official estimates): Registered live births 2,568 (birth rate 23.9 per 1,000); Deaths 442 (death rate 4.1 per 1,000). *2006:* Registered live births 2,147. *2005–10* (annual averages, UN estimates): Birth rate 25.5 per 1,000; Death rate 6.2 per 1,000 (Source: UN, *World Population Prospects: The 2010 Revision*).

Life Expectancy (years at birth): 68.9 (males 68.1; females 69.8) in 2011. Source: World Bank, World Development Indicators database.

Economically Active Population (persons aged 15 years and over, 2000 census): Agriculture, forestry and fishing 15,216; *Total employed* (incl. others) 29,175 (males 16,957, females 12,218); Unemployed 8,239 (males 4,419, females 3,820); *Total labour force* 37,414 (males 21,376, females 16,038). *Mid-2013* (estimates in '000): Agriculture, etc. 12; Total labour force 56 (Source: FAO).

HEALTH AND WELFARE

Key Indicators

Total Fertility Rate (children per woman, 2010): 3.5.

Under-5 Mortality Rate (per 1,000 live births, 2010): 42.

Physicians (per 1,000 head, 2009): 0.2.

Hospital Beds (per 1,000 head, 2009): 3.2.

Health Expenditure (2009): US $ per head (PPP): 424.

Health Expenditure (2009): % of GDP: 13.4.

Health Expenditure (2009): public (% of total): 90.7.

For sources and definitions, see explanatory note on p. vi.

AGRICULTURE, ETC.

Principal Crops ('000 metric tons, 2011, FAO estimates): Coconuts 52; Cassava 9; Sweet potatoes 3; Vegetables 3; Bananas 2.

Livestock ('000 head, year ending September 2011, FAO estimates): Pigs 33; Cattle 14; Goats 4; Chickens 190.

Livestock Products (metric tons, 2011, FAO estimates): Cattle meat 258; Pig meat 876; Chicken meat 140; Hen eggs 207.

Fishing ('000 metric tons, live weight, 2010, FAO estimates): Skipjack tuna 18.0; Yellowfin tuna 2.9; Bigeye tuna 2.9; Total catch (incl. others) 30.9.

Source: FAO.

FINANCE

Currency and Exchange Rates: United States currency is used: 100 cents = 1 United States dollar (US $). *Sterling and Euro Equivalents* (31 December 2012): £1 sterling = US $1.5780; €1 = US $1.3194; US $100 = £63.37 = €75.79.

Budget (US $ million, year ending 30 September 2011, preliminary): *Revenue:* Current 65.0; Grants 131.7; Total 196.7. *Expenditure:* Current 145.4; Capital 50.1; Total 195.4. Note: Figures represent a consolidation of the accounts of the national Government and the four state governments. Source: Asian Development Bank.

International Reserves (US $ '000 at 31 December 2011): IMF special drawing rights 9,535; Reserve position in IMF 0; Foreign exchange 65,527; *Total* 75,062. Source: IMF, *International Financial Statistics*.

Money Supply (US $ '000 at 31 December 2011): Demand deposits at banking institutions 27,224. Source: IMF, *International Financial Statistics*.

Cost of Living (Consumer Price Index, average of quarterly figures; base: April–June 2008 = 100): All items 109.4 in 2009; 114.1 in 2010; 119.3 in 2011. Source: Asian Development Bank.

Gross Domestic Product (US $ million at constant 2005 prices): 239.2 in 2008; 240.8 in 2009; 248.3 in 2010. Source: UN National Accounts Main Aggregates Database.

Expenditure on the Gross Domestic Product (US $ million at current prices, 2011): Final consumption expenditure 399.8; Gross fixed capital formation 99.7; Changes in inventories 6.3; *Total domestic expenditure* 505.8; Exports of goods and services 67.1; *Less* Imports of goods and services 254.5; *GDP in purchasers' values* 318.5. Source: UN National Accounts Main Aggregates Database.

Gross Domestic Product by Economic Activity (US $ million at current prices, 2011): Agriculture, hunting, forestry and fishing 79.2; Mining, electricity, gas and water 4.0; Manufacturing 1.4; Construction 13.9; Trade, restaurants and hotels 47.8; Transport, storage and communications 19.4; Other activities 132.8; *Sub-total* 298.5; Net of indirect taxes 20.0 (obtained as a residual); *GDP in purchasers' values* 318.5. Source: UN National Accounts Main Aggregates Database.

Balance of Payments (US $ million, year ending 30 September 2006, estimates): Merchandise exports f.o.b. 17.0; Merchandise imports f.o.b. −145.9; *Trade balance* −128.9; Exports of services 20.1; Imports of services −57.5; *Balance on goods and services* −166.2; Other income received 20.5; Other income paid −5.3; *Balance on goods, services and income* −151.0; Private unrequited transfers (net) 5.3; Official unrequited transfers (net) 107.3; *Current balance* −38.4; Capital account (net) 12.0; Other long-term capital (net) 1.9; Other short-term capital (net) 0.8; *Overall balance* (incl. errors and omissions) −23.6. *2010:* Exports of goods 30.1; Imports of goods −157.6; Trade balance −127.6; Exports of services and income 63.2; Imports of services and income −93.6; Balance on goods, services and income −158.0; Current transfers received 127.1; Current transfers paid −15.3; Current balance −46.2; Capital account (net) 85.7; Direct investment (net) 0.8; Portfolio investment (net) −17.9; Other investment (net) −12.3; Overall balance 10.1. Source: Asian Development Bank.

EXTERNAL TRADE

Principal Commodities (US $ '000, 2007): *Imports c.i.f.:* Mineral products 31,476; Prepared foodstuffs, beverages and tobacco 24,390; Machinery, mechanical appliances and electrical equipment 20,553; Vegetable products 8,538; Animals and animal products 8,755; Transportation equipment 8,480; Chemicals 7,660; Base metals and articles thereof 6,216; Total (incl. others) 142,658. *Exports f.o.b.:* Marine products 12,301; Betel nuts 2,224; Citrus 416; Kava 2,224; Total (incl. others) 16,190.

Principal Trading Partners (US $ '000, 2007): *Imports:* Australia 5,844; China, People's Republic 5,444; Guam 20,512; Hong Kong 8,955; Japan 12,067; Korea, Republic 5,820; Philippines 5,083; Singapore 12,413; USA 58,785; Total (incl. others) 142,658. *Exports:* Guam 3,641; Japan 660; USA (mainland only) 2,790; Total (incl. others) 16,190.

TRANSPORT

Shipping: *Flag Registered Fleet* (at 31 December 2012): Vessels 16; Total displacement (grt) 13,163. Source: Lloyd's List Intelligence (www.lloydslistintelligence.com).

TOURISM

Foreign Tourist Arrivals: 19,136 in 2006; 21,146 in 2007; 25,627 in 2008.

Tourist Arrivals by Country or Region of Residence (2008): Europe 2,788; Japan 2,949; Philippines 2,168; Other Asia 4,121; USA 8,732; Total (incl. others) 25,627.

Tourism Receipts (US $ million, incl. passenger transport): 16.5 in 2004; 17.1 in 2005; 18.3 in 2006.

Source: World Tourism Organization.

COMMUNICATIONS MEDIA

Telephones (main lines in use, 2010): 8,500.

Mobile Cellular Telephones (2010): 27,500 subscribers.

Internet Users (2009): 17,000.

Broadband Subscribers (2010): 100.

Personal Computers: 6,000 (54.8 per 1,000 persons) in 2005.

Radio Receivers (1996): 22,000 in use.

Television Receivers (1996): 19,800 in use.

Source: partly International Telecommunication Union.

EDUCATION

Primary (2006/07 unless otherwise indicated): 174 schools (1995); 1,113 teachers; 18,512 pupils (Sources: UN, *Statistical Yearbook for Asia and the Pacific* and UNESCO Institute for Statistics).

Secondary (2006/07 unless otherwise indicated): 24 schools (1995); 829 teachers; 14,742 pupils (Sources: UN, *Statistical Yearbook for Asia and the Pacific* and UNESCO Institute for Statistics).

Tertiary (1998/99): 1,510 students (Sources: UN, *Statistical Yearbook for Asia and the Pacific* and UNESCO Institute for Statistics).

Pupil-teacher Ratio (primary education, UNESCO estimate): 16.6 in 2006/07 (Source: UNESCO Institute for Statistics).

Adult Literacy Rate (population aged 10 years and over, 2000 census): 92.4% (males 92.9%; females 91.9%).

Directory

The Government

HEAD OF STATE

President: IMMANUEL (MANNY) MORI (took office 11 May 2007; re-elected 11 May 2011).

Vice-President: ALIK L. ALIK.

CABINET
(May 2013)

Secretary of the Department of Finance and Administration: KENSLEY IKOSIA.

Secretary of the Department of Foreign Affairs: LORIN S. ROBERT.

Secretary of the Department of Resources and Development: MARION HENRY.

Secretary of the Department of Health and Social Affairs: Dr VITA AKAPITO SKILLING.

Secretary of the Department of Justice: APRIL DAWN SKILLING.

Secretary of the Department of Transportation, Communication and Infrastructure: FRANCIS I. ITIMAI.

Secretary of the Department of Education: Dr RUFINO MAURICIO.

Public Defender: JULIUS JOEY SAPELALUT.

Postmaster-General: GINGER PORTER MIDA.

GOVERNMENT OFFICES

Office of the President: POB PS-53, Palikir, Pohnpei, FM 96941; tel. 320-2228; fax 320-2785; e-mail ppetrus@mail.fm; internet www.fsmpio.fm.

Department of Education: POB PS-87, Palikir, Pohnpei, FM 96941; tel. 320-2609; fax 320-5500; internet www.fsmed.fm.

Department of Finance and Administration: POB PS-158, Palikir, Pohnpei, FM 96941; tel. 320-2640; fax 320-7728; e-mail fsmsofa@mail.fm.

Department of Foreign Affairs: POB PS-123, Palikir, Pohnpei, FM 96941; tel. 320-2641; fax 320-2933; e-mail foreignaffairs@mail.fm; internet www.fsmgov.org/ovmis.html.

Department of Health and Social Affairs: POB PS-70, Palikir, Pohnpei, FM 96941; tel. 320-2872; fax 320-5263; e-mail fsmhealth@mail.fm.

Department of Justice: POB PS-105, Palikir, Pohnpei, FM 96941; tel. 320-2628; fax 320-3243; e-mail nphq@mail.fm.

Department of Resources and Development: POB PS-12, Palikir, Pohnpei, FM 96941; tel. 320-2646; fax 320-5854; e-mail fsmrd@dea.fm; internet www.fsminvest.fm.

Department of Transportation, Communication and Infrastructure: POB PS-2, Palikir, Pohnpei, FM 96941; tel. 320-2865; fax 320-5853; e-mail transcom@mail.fm; internet www.ict.fm.

Office of the Public Defender: POB PS-174, Palikir, Pohnpei, FM 96941; tel. 320-2648; fax 320-5775.

Public Information Office: POB PS-34, Palikir, Pohnpei, FM 96941; tel. 320-2548; fax 320-4356; e-mail fsmpio@mail.fm.

Legislature

CONGRESS OF THE FEDERATED STATES OF MICRONESIA

The Congress comprises 14 members (senators): four senators-at-large (one for each of the four states), who are elected for a four-year term; and 10 senators who serve a two-year term. The most recent election was held on 5 March 2013, when 10 senators were elected. There are no formal political parties.

Speaker: ISAAC V. FIGIR.

STATE LEGISLATURES

Chuuk State Legislature: POB 189, Weno, Chuuk, FM 96942; tel. 330-4284; fax 330-4282; e-mail speakeroffice@yahoo.com; internet www.chuukstatelegislature.fm; Senate of 10 mems and House of Representatives of 28 mems elected for 4 years; Gov. JOHNSON ELIMO.

Kosrae State Legislature: POB 187, Tofol, Kosrae, FM 96944; tel. 370-3019; fax 370-2177; e-mail Kenkenzmike@kosraelegislature.org; internet kosraestatelegislature.webs.com; unicameral body of 14 mems serving for 4 years; Gov. LYNDON H. JACKSON.

Pohnpei State Legislature: POB 114, Kolonia, Pohnpei, FM 96941; tel. 320-2753; fax 320-2754; e-mail legislature@mail.fm; internet www.fm/pohnpeileg; 27 representatives elected for 4 years (terms staggered); Gov. JOHN EHSA.

Yap State Legislature: POB 39, Colonia, Yap, FM 96943; tel. 350-2108; fax 350-4113; internet www.fsmlaw.org/yap; 10 mems, 6 elected from the Yap Islands proper and 4 elected from the Outer Islands of Ulithi and Woleai, for a 4 year term; Gov. SEBASTIAN L. ANEFAL.

Election Commission

National Election Commission: POB 1685, Kolonia, Pohnpei 96941; tel. 320-4283; fax 320-7805; e-mail ned@mail.fm; Dir ALBERT T. WELLY.

Political Organizations

There are no formal political parties in the Federated States of Micronesia.

Diplomatic Representation

EMBASSIES IN THE FEDERATED STATES OF MICRONESIA

Australia: POB S, Kolonia, Pohnpei, FM 96941; tel. 320-5448; fax 320-5449; e-mail australia@mail.fm; internet www.fsm.embassy.gov.au; Ambassador MARTIN QUINN.

China, People's Republic: POB 1530, Kolonia, Pohnpei, FM 96941; tel. 320-5575; fax 320-5578; e-mail chinaemb@mail.fm; internet fm.chineseembassy.org/eng; Ambassador ZHANG WEIDONG.

Japan: Pami Bldg, 3rd Floor, POB 1837, Kolonia, Pohnpei, FM 96941; tel. 320-5465; fax 320-5470; internet www.micronesia.emb-japan.go.jp; Ambassador EIICHI SUZUKI.

USA: POB 1286, Kolonia, Pohnpei, FM 96941; tel. 320-2187; fax 320-2186; e-mail usembassy@mail.fm; internet kolonia.usembassy.gov; Ambassador DOROTHEA-MARIA ROSEN.

Judicial System

Supreme Court of the Federated States of Micronesia: POB PS-J, Palikir Station, Pohnpei, FM 96941; tel. 320-2357; fax 320-2756; e-mail fsmsupcourt@mail.fm; internet www.fsmlaw.org; Chief Justice MARTIN G. YINUG.

State Courts and Appellate Courts have been established in Yap, Chuuk, Kosrae and Pohnpei.

Religion

The population is predominantly Christian, mainly Roman Catholic. The Assembly of God, Jehovah's Witnesses, Seventh-day Adventists, the Church of Jesus Christ of Latter-day Saints (Mormons), the United Church of Christ, Baptists and the Bahá'í faith are also represented.

CHRISTIANITY

The Roman Catholic Church

The Federated States of Micronesia forms a part of the diocese of the Caroline Islands, suffragan to the archdiocese of Agaña (Guam). The Bishop participates in the Catholic Bishops' Conference of the Pacific, based in Fiji. At 31 December 2007 there were 79,199 adherents in the diocese.

Bishop of the Caroline Islands: Most Rev. AMANDO SAMO, Bishop's House, POB 939, Weno, Chuuk, FM 96942; tel. 330-2399; fax 330-4585; e-mail diocese@mail.fm.

Other Churches

Calvary Baptist Church: Kolonia, Pohnpei, POB 2179, FM 96941; tel. 320-2830; fax 320-3887; e-mail cca_pohnpei@yahoo.com; Pastor ISAMO WELLES.

Liebenzell Mission USA: POB 66, Schooleys Mountain, NJ 07870; tel. 852-3044; e-mail missions@liebenzellusa.org; internet www.liebenzellusa.org; f. 1942; Global Ministries Dir BILL SCHUIT.

Truth Independent Baptist Church: Kolonia, Pohnpei, POB 65, FM 96941; tel. 320-3643; fax 320-6769; Pastor RICARDO P. VERACRUZ.

United Church of Christ in Pohnpei: Kolonia, Pohnpei, POB 864, FM 96941; tel. 320-2271; fax 320-4404; Pres. BERNELL EDWARD.

The Press

Da Rohng: Jano News Service, POB 510, Kolonia, Pohnpei FM 96941; tel. 320-6494; fax 320-4200; e-mail darohng2005@yahoo.com; Editor MARTIN JANO.

The Island Tribune: Pohnpei, FM 96941; f. 1997; fortnightly.

Kaselehlie Press: POB 2222, Pohnpei, FM 96941; tel. 320-6547; fax 320-6571; e-mail kpress@mail.fm; internet www.kpress.info; f. 2001; fortnightly; Man. Editor BILL JAYNES.

Micronesian Alliance: POB 543, Tofol, Kosrae, FM 96944; tel. 370-6131; e-mail equatormedia@yahoo.com.

Broadcasting and Communications

TELECOMMUNICATIONS

FSM Telecommunication Corporation: POB 1210, Kolonia, Pohnpei, FM 96941; tel. 320-2740; fax 320-2745; e-mail customerservice@telecom.fm; internet www.telecom.fm; provides domestic, international and internet services; Pres. and CEO JOHN D. SOHL.

BROADCASTING

Radio

Federated States of Micronesia Public Information Office: POB PS-34, Palikir, Pohnpei, FM 96941; tel. 320-2548; fax 320-4356; e-mail fsmpio@mail.fm; internet www.fsmpio.fm/pio.html; govt-operated; 4 regional stations, each broadcasting 18 hours daily; Information Officer PATRICK BLANK.

Station V6AH: POB 1086, Kolonia, Pohnpei, FM 96941; programmes in English and Pohnpeian; Man. WEIDEN MANUEL.

Station V6AI: POB 117, Colonia, Yap, FM 96943; tel. 350-2174; fax 350-4426; programmes in English, Yapese, Ulithian and Satawalese; Man. SEBASTIAN F. TAMAGKEN.

Station V6AJ: POB 147, Tofol, Kosrae, FM 96944; tel. 370-3040; fax 370-3880; e-mail kosraebroadcast@yahoo.com; programmes in English and Kosraean; Man. McDONALD ITTU.

Station V6AK: Wenn, Chuuk, FM 96942; tel. 330-2596; programmes in Chuukese and English; Man. JOE COMMOR.

WSZA Yap: Dept of Youth and Civic Affairs, POB 30, Colonia, Yap 96943; tel. 350-2174; Media Dir PETER GARAMFEL.

WSZD Pohnpei: POB 1086, Kolonia, Pohnpei 96941; tel. 320-2296; programmes in English and Pohnpeian; Man. FRANCIS ZARRED.

Television

Island Cable TV—Pohnpei: POB 1628, Pohnpei, FM 96941; tel. 320-2671; fax 320-2444; e-mail ictv@mail.fm; f. 1991; Gen. Man. DAVID O. CLIFFE.

TV Station Chuuk (TTTK): Wenn, Chuuk, FM 96942; tel. 330-4475; commercial.

TV Station Pohnpei (KPON): Central Micronesia Communications, POB 460, Kolonia, Pohnpei, FM 96941; f. 1977; commercial; Tech. Dir DAVID CLIFFE.

TV Station Yap (WAAB): Colonia, Yap, FM 96943; tel. 350-2160; fax 350-4113; govt-owned; Man. LOU DEFNGIN.

Finance

BANKING

Regulatory Authority

Federated States of Micronesia Banking Board: POB 1887, Kolonia, Pohnpei, FM 96941; tel. 320-2015; fax 320-5433; e-mail fmbb@mail.fm; f. 1980; Chair. ALEXANDER NARRUHN; Commissioner WILSON F. WAGUK.

Banks are also supervised by the US Federal Deposit Insurance Corporation.

Commercial Banks

Bank of the Federated States of Micronesia: POB 98, Kolonia, Pohnpei, FM 96941; tel. 320-2838; fax 320-5359; cap. US $4.6m., dep. US $70.4m. (Dec. 2011); brs in Kosrae, Yap, Pohnpei and Chuuk.

Bank of Guam (USA): POB 367, Kolonia, Pohnpei, FM 96941; tel. 320-2550; fax 320-2562; e-mail bogpohn@mail.fm; internet www.bankofguam.com; Br. Man. CHRISTOPHER CRUZ; brs in Chuuk, Kosrae and Yap.

Yap Credit Union: POB 610, Colonia, Yap; tel. 350-2142.

Development Bank

Federated States of Micronesia Development Bank: POB M, Kolonia, Pohnpei, FM 96941; tel. 320-2840; fax 320-2842; e-mail info@fsmdb.fm; internet www.fsmdb.fm; f. 1979; total assets US $38.2m. (2010); Chair. JOHN SOHL; Pres. ANNA MENDIOLA; 4 brs.

Banking services for the rest of the islands are available in Guam, Hawaii and on the US mainland.

INSURANCE

Actouka Executive Insurance: POB 55, Kolonia, Pohnpei; tel. 320-5331; fax 320-2331; e-mail mlamar@mail.fm.

Caroline Insurance Underwriters: POB 37, Chuuk; tel. 330-2705; fax 330-2207.

FSM Insurance Group: Kosrae; tel. 370-3788; fax 370-2120.

Islands Insurance: POB K, Kolonia, Pohnpei; tel. 320-3422.

Moylan's Insurance Underwriters: POB 1448, Kolonia, Pohnpei, FM 96941; tel. 320-2118; fax 320-2519; e-mail pohnpei@moylans.net; Pres. and Gen. Man. MELNER ISAAC.

Oceania Insurance Co: POB 1202, Weno, Chuuk, FM 96942; tel. 330-3036; fax 330-3764; e-mail oceanpac@mail.fm; also owns and manages Pacific Basin Insurance; Region Man. ERICSON MARAR.

Pacific Islands Insurance Underwriters: POB 386, Colonia, Yap; tel. 350-2340; fax 350-2341.

Transpacific Insurance: POB 510, Kolonia, Pohnpei; tel. 320-5525; fax 320-5524.

Yap Insurance Agency: POB 386, Colonia, Yap; tel. 350-2340; fax 350-2341; e-mail tachelioyap@mail.fm.

Trade and Industry

GOVERNMENT AGENCIES

Coconut Development Authority: POB 297, Kolonia, Pohnpei, FM 96941; tel. 320-2892; fax 320-5383; e-mail fsmcda@mail.fm; f. 1981; responsible for all purchasing, processing and exporting of copra and copra by-products in the islands; Gen. Man. NAMIO NANPEI.

FSM National Fisheries Corporation: POB R, Kolonia, Pohnpei, FM 96941; tel. 320-2529; fax 320-2239; e-mail nfcairfreight@mail.fm; internet www.fsmgov.org/nfc; f. 1984; established in 1990, with the Economic Devt Authority and an Australian co, the Caroline Fishing Corpn (3 vessels); promotes fisheries development; Pres. NICK SOLOMON.

National Oceanic Resource Management Authority (NORMA): POB PS-122, Palikir, Pohnpei, FM 96941; tel. 320-2700; fax 320-2383; e-mail info@norma.fm; internet norma.fm; fmrly Micronesian Fisheries Authority; name changed 2002; responsible for conservation, management and development of tuna resources and for issue of fishing licences; Exec. Dir PATRICK MACKENZIE; Deputy Dir EUGENE PANGELINAN.

Office of Compact Management: 253 Palikir Station, Pohnpei FM 96941; tel. 320-8375; fax 320-8377; Exec. Dir EHPEL ILON.

Pohnpei Economic Development Authority: POB 738, Kolonia, Pohnpei, FM 96941; tel. 320-2298; fax 320-2775; e-mail eda@mail.fm; chaired by the President of the Federated States of Micronesia; Exec. Dir SHELTEN NETH.

CHAMBERS OF COMMERCE

Chuuk Chamber of Commerce: POB 700, Weno, Chuuk, FM 96941; tel. 330-2318; fax 330-2314; e-mail larry.bruton@mail.fm; Pres. WILLIAM STINNETT.

Kosrae Chamber of Commerce: POB 877, Tofol, Kosrae, FM 96944; tel. 370-3483; e-mail info@kosraechamberofcommerce.org; internet www.kosraechamberofcommerce.org; Chair. SMITH SIGRAH.

Pohnpei Chamber of Commerce: POB 405, Kolonia, Pohnpei, FM 96941; tel. 320-2452; fax 320-5277; e-mail amc@mail.fm; Pres. LEON SENDA.

Yap Chamber of Commerce: Colonia, Yap, FM 96943; tel. 350-2298; Pres. PHILLIP RANGANBAY.

UTILITIES

Chuuk Public Works (CPW): POB 248, Weno, Chuuk, FM 96942; tel. 330-2242; fax 320-4815; Chief HERSIN RUBEN.

Kosrae Utility Authority: POB 277, Tofol, Kosrae, FM 96944; tel. 370-3799; fax 370-3798; e-mail info@kosraepower.com; internet kosraepower.com; corporatized in 1994; Gen. Man. FRED N. SKILLING.

Pohnpei Utilities Corporation: POB C, Kolonia, Pohnpei, FM 96941; tel. 320-2374; fax 320-2422; e-mail info@puc.fm; internet www.puc.fm; f. 1992; provides electricity, water and sewerage services; Gen. Man. FELICIANO PERMAN.

Yap State Public Service Corpn (YSPSC): POB 621, Colonia, Yap, FM 96943; tel. 350-2175; fax 350-2331; f. 1996; provides electricity, water and sewerage services; Gen. Man. FAUSTINO R. YANGMOG.

CO-OPERATIVES

Chuuk: Chuuk Co-operative, Faichuk Cacao and Copra Co-operative Asscn, Pis Fishermen's Co-operative, Fefan Women's Co-operative.

Pohnpei: Pohnpei Federation of Co-operative Asscns (POB 100, Pohnpei, FM 96941), Kapingamarangi Copra Producers' Asscn, Kitti Minimum Co-operative Asscn, Kolonia Consumers' and Producers' Co-operative Asscn, Kosrae Island Co-operative Asscn, Metalanim Copra Co-operative Asscn, Mokil Island Co-operative Asscn, Ngatik Island Co-operative Asscn, Nukuoro Island Co-operative Asscn, PICS Co-operative Asscn, Pingelap Consumers' Co-operative Asscn, Pohnpei Fishermen's Co-operative, Pohnpei Handicraft Co-operative, Uh Soumwet Co-operative Asscn.

Yap Co-operative Association Inc: POB 159, Colonia, Yap, FM 96943; tel. 350-2209; fax 350-4114; e-mail yca@mail.fm; internet yapcoop.com; f. 1952; Pres. FAUSTINO YANGMOG; Gen. Man. TONY GANNGIYAN; 1,832 mems.

Transport

ROADS

In 2004 the Federated States of Micronesia had a total road network of 240 km. Tarmac and concrete roads are found in the more important islands. Other islands have stone- and coral-surfaced roads and tracks.

SHIPPING

Pohnpei, Chuuk, Yap and Kosrae have deep-draught harbours for commercial shipping. The ports provide warehousing and transshipment facilities.

Caroline Fisheries Corporation (CFC): POB 7, Kolonia, Pohnpei, FM 96941; tel. 320-3926; fax 320-4733; e-mail cfc@mail.fm; Gen. Man. MILAN KAMBER.

Pacific Shipping Agency: POB 154, Lelu, Kosrae FM 96944; tel. 370-3956; fax 370-2912; e-mail KosraeAce@mail.fm; f. 1990; Gen. Man. SMITH SIGRAH.

Pohnpei Transfer & Storage, Inc: POB 340, Kolonia, Pohnpei FM 96941; tel. 320-2552; fax 320-2389; e-mail fsmlinejv@mail.fm; Gen. Man. JOE VITT.

Truk Transportation Company (TRANSCO): POB 99, Weno, Chuuk FM 96942; tel. 330-2143; fax 330-2726; e-mail transco@mail.fm; f. 1964; Pres. MYRON HASHIGUCHI; Gen. Man. GIDEON BISALEN.

Waab Transportation Company: POB 177, Colonia, Yap FM 96943; tel. 350-2301; fax 350-4110; e-mail waabtrans@mail.fm; agents for PM & O Lines (USA); Gen. Man. WILLIAM FITZSIMMONS.

CIVIL AVIATION

The Federated States of Micronesia is served by Continental Micronesia, Our Airline (formerly Air Nauru) and Continental Airlines (USA). Pacific Missionary Aviation, based in Pohnpei and Yap, provides domestic air services. There are international airports on Pohnpei, Chuuk, Yap and Kosrae, and airstrips on the outer islands of Onoun and Ta in Chuuk. The extension of the runway at Pohnpei airport, to accommodate larger aircraft, was completed in June 2012.

Tourism

The tourist industry is a significant source of revenue, although it has been hampered by the lack of infrastructure. Visitor attractions include excellent conditions for scuba-diving (notably in Chuuk Lagoon), Second World War battle sites and relics (many underwater) and the ancient ruined city of Nan Madol on Pohnpei. The number of tourist arrivals was estimated to total 25,627 in 2008. Tourism receipts totalled an estimated US $18.3m. in 2006.

Federated States of Micronesia Visitors Board: National Government, PO Box PS-12, Palikir, Pohnpei, FM 96941; tel. 320-5133; fax 320-3251; e-mail fsminfo@visit-fsm.org; internet www.visit-micronesia.fm.

Chuuk Visitors Bureau: POB FQ, Weno, Chuuk, FM 96942; tel. 330-4133; fax 330-4194; e-mail cvb@mail.fm.

Kosrae Visitors Bureau: POB 659, Tofol, Kosrae, FM 96944; tel. 370-2228; fax 370-3000; e-mail kosrae@mail.fm; internet www.kosrae.com; Administrator GRANT ISMAEL.

Pohnpei Department of Tourism and Parks: POB 66, Kolonia, Pohnpei, FM 96941; tel. 320-2421; fax 320-6019; e-mail tourismparks@mail.fm; Deputy Chief BUMIO SILBANUZ.

Pohnpei Visitors Bureau: POB 1949, Kolonia, Pohnpei, FM 96941; tel. 320-4851; fax 320-4868; e-mail pohnpeiVB@mail.fm; internet www.visit-pohnpei.fm.

Yap Visitors Bureau: POB 988, Colonia, Yap, FM 96943; tel. 350-2298; fax 350-7015; e-mail yvb@mail.fm; internet www.visityap.com; Man. VINCENT TAFILELUW; Sec. ABELYNN TAMAN.

Defence

Defence and security are the responsibility of the USA. The US Pacific Command is based in Hawaii, USA.

Education

Primary education, which begins at six years of age and lasts for eight years, is compulsory. Secondary education, beginning at 14 years of age, comprises two cycles, each of two years. The education system is based on the US pattern of eight years' attendance at an elementary school and four years' enrolment at a high school. The Micronesia Maritime and Fisheries Academy, which was opened in Yap in 1990, provides education and training in fisheries technology at secondary and tertiary levels. The College of Micronesia offers two- and three-year programmes leading to a degree qualification. In 2006/07 there were 18,512 pupils enrolled in primary education and 14,742 pupils enrolled in secondary education. In 2005/06 approximately 2,283 pupils were studying at college level.

MOLDOVA

Introductory Survey

LOCATION, CLIMATE, LANGUAGE, RELIGION, FLAG, CAPITAL

The Republic of Moldova is a small, landlocked country situated in south-eastern Europe. The republic is bounded to the north, east and south by Ukraine. To the west it borders Romania. The climate is favourable for agriculture, with long, warm summers and relatively mild winters. Average temperatures in Chişinău range from 21°C (70°F) in July to –4°C (24°F) in January. The 1994 Constitution describes the official language as Moldovan, a Romance language that is widely considered to be identical to Romanian. Most of the inhabitants of Moldova profess Orthodox Christianity. The national flag (proportions 1 by 2) consists of three equal vertical stripes, of light blue, yellow and red; the yellow stripe has at its centre the arms of Moldova (a shield bearing a stylized bull's head in yellow, set between an eight-pointed yellow star, a five-petalled yellow flower, and a yellow crescent, the shield being set on the breast of an eagle, in gold and red, which holds a green olive branch in its dexter talons, a yellow sceptre in its sinister talons, and a yellow cross in its beak). The capital is Chişinău.

CONTEMPORARY POLITICAL HISTORY

Historical Context

The area of the present-day Republic of Moldova corresponds to only part of the medieval principality of Moldova (Moldavia), which emerged as an important regional power in the 15th century. In the following century the principality came under Turkish Ottoman (Osmanlı) domination. Following a period of conflict between the Ottoman and Russian Empires, Moldova was divided into two parts in 1812: the eastern territory of Bessarabia, situated between the Prut and Dniester (Dnestr or Nistru) rivers—which roughly corresponds to the modern Republic of Moldova—was ceded to Russia, while the Ottomans retained control of western Moldova. A Romanian nationalist movement evolved in western Moldova and the neighbouring region of Wallachia during the 19th century, culminating in the proclamation of a Romanian state in 1877. In June 1918, after the collapse of the Russian Empire, Bessarabia was proclaimed an independent republic, although in November it voted to become part of Romania. This union was recognized in the Treaty of Paris (1920). However, the USSR (established in 1922) refused to recognize Romania's claims to the territory, and in October 1924 formed a Moldovan Autonomous Soviet Socialist Republic (ASSR) on the eastern side of the Dniester, within the Ukrainian Soviet Socialist Republic (SSR). In June 1940 Romania was forced to cede Bessarabia and northern Bucovina to the USSR, under the terms of the Treaty of Non-Aggression, concluded with Nazi Germany in August 1939. Northern Bucovina, southern Bessarabia and the Kotovsk-Balta region of the Moldovan ASSR were incorporated into the Ukrainian SSR. The remaining parts of the Moldovan ASSR and of Bessarabia were merged to form the Moldovan SSR, which formally joined the USSR on 2 August 1940.

Between July 1941 and 1944 the Moldovan SSR was reunited with Romania, forming (along with territories in present-day Romania and Ukraine) part of a Transnistria Governorate. However, the Soviet Army reannexed the region in 1944, and the Moldovan SSR was re-established. Soviet policy concentrated on isolating the region from its historical links with Romania: cross-border traffic virtually ceased, the Cyrillic script was imposed on the Romanian language (which was referred to as Moldovan) and Russian and Ukrainian immigration was encouraged. In the 1950s thousands of ethnic Romanians were deported to Central Asia.

Domestic Political Affairs

In May 1989 a number of cultural and political groups, which were denied legal status, allied to form the Popular Front (PF). In June some 70,000 people attended a protest demonstration, organized by the PF, on the anniversary of the Soviet annexation of Bessarabia in 1940. In August 1989 mass demonstrations were convened in the capital, Chişinău, in support of proposals by the Moldovan Supreme Soviet (Supreme Council—legislature) to declare Romanian the official language of the republic. Following protests by members of non-Romanian ethnic groups, the proposals were amended: legislation was enacted providing for Russian to be retained as a 'language of inter-ethnic communication', but the official language was to be Romanian, written in the Latin script. Following disturbances in Chişinău, during the celebrations of the anniversary of the Bolshevik Revolution on 7 November, the First Secretary of the ruling Communist Party of Moldova (CPM), Semion Grossu, was dismissed. He was replaced by Petru Lucinschi.

The increasing influence of the Romanian-speaking population was strongly opposed by other inhabitants of the republic (who, at the 1989 census, comprised some 35% of the total population). In the areas east of the Dniester, Transnistria or Pridnestrovie, where Russians and Ukrainians predominated (and which had mostly constituted the Moldovan ASSR in 1924–40), the local authorities refused to implement the language law. Opposition to growing Moldovan nationalism was led by the Unity Movement (dominated by leading CPM members) and the Slav-dominated United Work Collectives. Both organizations had links with Gagauz People, the most prominent of the political groups representing the 150,000-strong Gagauz minority (a Turkic, Orthodox Christian people, resident mostly in southern regions of Moldova). In January 1990 a referendum took place in the eastern town of Tiraspol, in which the predominantly Russian-speaking population voted to seek greater autonomy for Transnistria.

None of the independent political groups was officially allowed to endorse candidates in elections to the Moldovan Supreme Soviet in February 1990. About 80% of the 380 deputies elected were members of the CPM, but many were also sympathetic to the aims of the PF. The new Supreme Soviet convened in April, whereupon Mircea Snegur, a CPM member supported by the PF, was elected Chairman. In the following month the Government resigned after losing a vote of no confidence. A new Council of Ministers, chaired by an economist, Mircea Druc, implemented far-reaching political changes, revoking the CPM's constitutional right to power. On 23 June the Supreme Soviet adopted a declaration of sovereignty asserting the supremacy of Moldova's Constitution and law. In September Snegur was elected to the new post of President of the Republic.

The actions of the increasingly radical Romanian majority in the legislature provoked further anxiety among minority ethnic groups. In August 1990 a separate 'Gagauz SSR' was proclaimed in the southern region around Comrat (Komrat), and in September east-bank Slavs proclaimed their secession from Moldova and the establishment of the 'Transdnistrian SSR', with its self-styled capital at Tiraspol (this territory contained much of Moldova's industry, as well as three of the republic's five largest cities). The Moldovan Supreme Soviet immediately annulled both declarations. In October Moldovan nationalists sought to thwart elections to a Gagauz Supreme Soviet, sending 50,000 armed volunteers to the area. Violence was prevented only by the dispatch of Soviet troops to the region. The new Gagauz Supreme Soviet convened in Comrat and elected Stepan Topal as its President. Inter-ethnic violence occurred east of the Dniester in November, when elections were announced to a Transnistrian Supreme Soviet. Negotiations in Moscow, the Russian and Soviet capital, involving the Moldovan Government, the east-bank Slavs and the Gagauz, failed to resolve the crisis, but the elections proceeded without further violence.

In December 1990 around 800,000 people, attending a 'Grand National Assembly', voted to reject any new union treaty (which was being negotiated by other Soviet republics); in February 1991 the Moldovan Supreme Soviet resolved not to participate in the all-Union referendum on the future of the USSR. Despite the official boycott, in March some 650,000 people (mostly ethnic Russians, Ukrainians and Gagauz) did take part, voting almost unanimously for the preservation of the USSR. Nevertheless, the Moldovan Government and legislature continued the process of de facto secession. In May the designation 'Soviet Socialist' was removed from the republic's name and the Supreme Soviet was renamed Parlamentul (the Parliament). In the same month, following a vote of no confidence by the legislature, Druc was removed as Prime Minister.

Independence

Following the attempted coup by conservative communists in Moscow in August 1991, the republican leadership immediately announced its support for the Russian President, Boris Yeltsin. On 27 August, after the coup had collapsed, Moldova proclaimed its independence. In September President Snegur ordered the creation of national armed forces and proscribed the CPM.

At the election to the republican presidency on 8 December 1991, Snegur, the sole candidate, received 98.2% of the votes cast. On 21 December Moldova was among the 11 signatories to the Almaty (Alma-Ata) Declaration establishing the Commonwealth of Independent States (CIS, see p. 251). Moldovan affairs during the first half of 1992 were dominated by the armed conflict in Transnistria (see p. 3123) and by the question of possible unification with Romania, as advocated by the ruling PF (which in February was re-formed as the Christian Democratic Popular Front—CDPF). However, popular support for unification remained insubstantial. In June 1992 the CDPF-dominated Government announced its resignation. Andrei Sangheli was appointed Prime Minister, and a new Government was formed, led by the Agrarian Democratic Party (ADP), which largely comprised members of the former communist leadership. The CDPF became the main opposition party. The ADP declared its commitment to consolidating Moldovan statehood and rejected union with Romania. These policies were strongly supported by President Snegur.

During 1993 the ADP made substantial progress with the drafting of a new constitution, providing for a reduced, 104-member legislature. Multi-party elections were held on 27 February 1994, in which 73% of the electorate participated. Polling stations were not opened in Transnistria. In all, 13 parties and blocs contested the elections. The ADP obtained an overall majority in Parlamentul, with 56 seats. The Socialist Party (SP), the successor to the CPM won 28 seats in alliance with the Unity Movement. Two groups that favoured unification with Romania shared the remaining 20 seats: the Peasants' Party of Moldova/Congress of Intelligentsia alliance, with 11 and the CDPF, with nine. In a referendum held on 6 March, more than 95% of the votes cast (by 75% of the electorate) supported continued independence. A new Council of Ministers led by Sangheli, solely comprising members of the ADP, was appointed in April. In May the CPM was permitted to re-form, as the Party of Communists of the Republic of Moldova (PCRM).

The new Constitution, adopted by Parlamentul in July 1994, entered into force in August. As well as establishing the country's permanent neutrality, the Constitution provided for a 'special autonomous status' for Transnistria and Gagauz-Yeri (Gagauzia, the Gagauz-majority areas) within Moldova. The state language was specified as Moldovan (rather than Romanian).

At the presidential election, held on 17 November 1996, Snegur received 39% of the votes cast, more than any other candidate, with Lucinschi being placed second. In the 'run-off' election held on 1 December Lucinschi was elected President, with 54% of the votes cast. No polling took place in Transnistria. Lucinschi was inaugurated as President on 15 January 1997, and a new Government was announced later that month, headed by Ion Ciubuc, a non-party economist.

Parliamentary elections, which took place on 22 March 1998, were won by the PCRM, led by Vladimir Voronin, with 30.1% of the votes cast (40 seats). The Democratic Convention of Moldova (CDM), an alliance led by Snegur, took 19.2% (26 seats), while the Movement for a Democratic and Prosperous Moldova (MDPM) received 18.2% (24 seats) and the Moldovan Party of Democratic Forces 8.8% (11 seats). The ADP failed to secure the 4% of the votes required for representation.

At the first session of the new legislature, convened in April 1998, Dumitru Diacov was elected Chairman. The Government resigned shortly afterwards. The new Government, appointed in May (with Ciubuc retaining his post as Prime Minister), comprised members of the Alliance for Democracy and Reforms coalition led within Parlamentul by Snegur, including members of the MDPM, the CDM and the Moldovan Party of Democratic Forces.

Ciubuc resigned as Prime Minister in February 1999. Snegur resigned as parliamentary leader of the government coalition one day later, after his nominee for the premiership was rejected. Lucinschi subsequently nominated Ion Sturza, the Deputy Prime Minister and Minister of the Economy and Reforms, as premier. Although Parlamentul twice failed to endorse the appointment, confronted with a choice between acceptance or the constitutional requirement to hold an early general election, it narrowly approved Sturza's Government in March.

Local elections were held on 23 May 1999, after which the country was reorganized into nine provinces and two autonomous entities (Gagauz-Yeri and Transnistria). A referendum, held on the same day, provided for an increase in presidential powers; the Constitutional Court later deemed it to be valid (despite the rate of participation being below the stipulated threshold of 60%), but not binding.

In November 1999 Sturza lost a vote of confidence in the legislature. Following the failure of two candidates for the premiership (including Voronin) to secure the necessary support in the legislature, the President's nomination of Dumitru Braghiş, hitherto Deputy Minister of the Economy and Reform, as Prime Minister was approved in December.

In July 2000 Parlamentul voted in favour of amending the Constitution to permit the legislature to elect the Head of State, and swiftly overturned President Lucinschi's veto of the amendment, which duly took effect. In October Parlamentul announced that a presidential election would be contested within the legislature in December. However, neither of the two candidates in the presidential election—Voronin, for the PCRM, and Pavel Barbalat, the Chairman of the Constitutional Court, who had been proposed by a coalition of the Democratic Party of Moldova (PDM, as the MDPM had been renamed in April), the CDM, the Christian Democratic People's Party (PPCD, formerly the CDPF) and the Moldovan Party of Democratic Forces—obtained the requisite number of votes to secure an overall victory after three rounds of voting. After the PDM, the CDM, the PPCD and the Moldovan Party of Democratic Forces boycotted a fourth round of voting on 21 December, Lucinschi dissolved the legislature and scheduled early parliamentary elections.

Communists return to power

At the legislative elections, held on 25 February 2001, the PCRM won an overall majority in Parlamentul, securing 49.9% of the votes cast and 71 seats. The Braghiş Alliance of the incumbent Prime Minister, obtained 19 seats, while the PPCD obtained 11 seats. Organization for Security and Co-operation in Europe (OSCE, see p. 397) observers described the elections, in which 70% of the electorate participated, as free and fair. The rate of voter participation was some 70%. In the presidential election, which took place on 4 April, Voronin secured 71 votes, defeating Braghiş and another communist candidate. Following his inauguration as President on 7 April, Voronin nominated Vasile Tarlev, a former businessman without party affiliation, as premier.

Demonstrations took place in Chişinău in January 2002, organized by the PPCD, against the proposed introduction of the compulsory teaching of Russian language and history at schools. In late January the Ministry of Justice temporarily suspended the PPCD from participation in political activities, preventing it from organizing further protests. In February the Deputy Prime Minister and Minister of the Economy, Andrei Cucu, and the reformist Minister of Finance, Mihai Manole, the only two non-PCRM members of the Council of Ministers, tendered their resignations. Following further protests, the proposed educational reforms were retracted and the Minister of Education was dismissed on 26 February. On the following day Vasile Draganel resigned as Minister of the Interior, amid reports that he had been unwilling to dispel protesters by force. Despite a ruling by the Supreme Court declaring the ongoing protests to be illegal, further demonstrations were staged outside the headquarters of the national television company against state censorship and misinformation. In March the Deputy Chairman of the PPCD, Vlad Cubreacov, who had been involved in organizing the anti-Government demonstrations, was kidnapped; he was discovered alive in May.

At the local elections, held on 25 May and 8 June 2003, the PCRM won the majority of seats, followed by the newly formed Our Moldova Alliance (AMN). Following the elections, new legislation on administrative reform, approved by the Government in January, came into effect, according to which the provinces and autonomous regions were replaced with 33 districts and two municipalities. In July the AMN was formally constituted as a party, with Braghiş, a former Mayor of Chişinău, Serafim Urechean, and Veaceslav Untilă as its co-leaders. New legislation, approved on 19 December, which sought to promote the use of Russian as a 'language of inter-ethnic communication', while retaining Moldovan as an official language, was a further cause of demonstrations.

In February 2004 Parlamentul withdrew the immunity from prosecution of the PPCD Chairman, Iurie Roşca, and two other deputies of the party, to permit their prosecution on charges of organizing and participating in unauthorized protests. From April 2004 the PDM and the Social Liberal Party agreed to co-operate with the AMN, forming the Democratic Moldova bloc, in preparation for parliamentary elections. In December Andrei Strătan, Minister of Foreign Affairs since February, was also appointed as Deputy Prime Minister. In the legislative elections, held on 6 March 2005, the PCRM won 46.0% of the votes cast and 56 seats, the Democratic Moldova bloc 28.5% (34 seats) and the PPCD 9.1% (11 seats). Although the PCRM held a majority of seats in Parlamentul, it did not hold the quorum of 61 necessary for the election of a president. At the inaugural session of Parlamentul, the PDM and Social Liberal Party deputies withdrew from the Democratic Moldova bloc, which renamed itself the AMN faction. On 4 April Voronin was re-elected by 75 of the 101 deputies; the other candidate, Gheorghe Duca, who had also been nominated by the PCRM, received only one vote. Voronin was inaugurated as President on 7 April; on 19 April Parlamentul approved a new Government, again led by Tarlev and retaining many members of the previous Council of Ministers.

In October 2005 members of the PCRM voted in Parlamentul to remove the parliamentary immunity of Urechean and two other deputies, following allegations against them of abuse of office. In the same month Mihai Pop was appointed Minister of Finance, in succession to Zinaida Grecianîi, who became First Deputy Prime Minister. In November Braghiş left the AMN, leaving Urechean as the party's sole leader. In January 2006 a former Minister of Defence, Valeriu Pasat, was sentenced to 10 years' imprisonment, having been convicted of defrauding the state when selling redundant fighter aircraft to the USA in 1997. In February 2006 Pasat was indicted on further charges of having organized protests during the 2005 legislative elections in an attempt to overthrow Voronin and of conspiring to murder Roşca. (In July 2007 Pasat was released by the Court of Appeal and in July 2009 all remaining charges against him were withdrawn.)

In June 2007 local elections were conducted throughout Moldova; voter turn-out was recorded at 52.3% (and only 37.2% in Chişinău). Although the PCRM was the most successful party overall, both nationally and in the capital, Chirtoacă of the Liberal Party (PL) was elected Mayor of Chişinău.

In January 2008 Voronin appointed a prominent member of the PCRM, Victor Stepaniuc, as a Deputy Prime Minister. On 19 March Tarlev and his Government resigned. Voronin subsequently nominated Grecianîi to the premiership. On 31 March Parlamentul voted to approve a new Government by 56 votes, with opposition deputies abstaining from voting; Igor Dodon, the Minister of Economy and Trade, succeeded Grecianîi as First Deputy Prime Minister. In October the hitherto Minister of Internal Affairs, Valentin Mejinschi, became Deputy Prime Minister.

The April and July 2009 legislative elections

Elections to Parlamentul on 5 April 2009 resulted in a majority for the PCRM, which, according to preliminary results, secured about 49.5% of votes cast, while the PL won 13.1%, the Liberal Democratic Party of Moldova (PLDM) obtained 12.4% and the AMN received 9.8% of the votes cast. Despite a positive assessment of the conduct of the elections by the OSCE and other international observers, protests at alleged electoral malpractice began on 6 April. On the following day anti-Government demonstrations degenerated into rioting, including attacks on parliamentary and presidential buildings. The protests were suppressed by police, and some 200 demonstrators were arrested. Voronin accused the Romanian Government of organizing a coup attempt (many of the protesters had exhibited pro-Romanian sentiments), and immediately undertook diplomatic reprisals (see Regional relations). Romania denied the allegations of involvement and demanded that the European Union (EU, see p. 281) investigate alleged abuses by the Moldovan authorities. On 12 April the Constitutional Court ordered a recount of the preliminary results. Human rights groups corroborated claims that demonstrators in custody were subjected to assaults by police, and it was reported that at least three protesters had died following the arrests. Following negotiations with opposition leaders, mediated by the EU Special Representative to Moldova, Voronin announced an amnesty for all suspects in detention or under investigation for involvement in the riots, excepting those with criminal records. On 20 April the Electoral Commission announced that the recount had not resulted in a significant change to the results of the poll: the PCRM had secured 60 seats in Parlamentul, while the PL and PLDM had each received 15 seats, and the AMN 11 seats. On 23 April the Constitutional Court endorsed the election results, and Voronin was elected legislative Chairman on 12 May.

Grecianîi and a further candidate nominated by the PCRM, Stanislav Gropa, contested a presidential election within Parlamentul on 20 May 2009. Although all 60 PCRM deputies voted for the candidacy of Grecianîi, this was one too few for her election to be constitutionally valid, and the PL, PLDM and AMN deputies all boycotted the election. The three opposition parties boycotted a second ballot on 3 June, which was again inconclusive. On 10 June Parlamentul approved an acting, largely unchanged, Council of Ministers, headed by Grecianîi. Meanwhile, the PCRM suffered a reverse when a senior party member (also Voronin's predecessor as Chairman of Parlamentul), Marian Lupu, announced his departure from the party. Lupu joined the PDM (which had failed to obtain legislative representation at the elections in April) later in the month, becoming its Chairman. In early June Parlamentul approved several amendments to the electoral code, reducing the threshold required for a party to secure parliamentary representation from 6% of the votes cast to 5% and reducing the minimum rate of voter participation required to validate elections from 50% of the electorate plus one vote to 33% plus one vote. On 15 June Voronin issued a decree dissolving Parlamentul and scheduled new elections for 29 July. On 16 June Voronin appointed Roşca as a Deputy Prime Minister.

Although the PCRM lost its majority at the elections to Parlamentul conducted on 29 July 2009, it remained the largest party in the legislature, securing 44.7% of the votes cast and 48 of the 101 seats. The PLDM increased its share of the votes cast to 16.6%, receiving 18 seats; the PL obtained 14.7% and 15 seats. The PDM increased its support substantially, obtaining 12.5% of the votes cast and 13 seats, while support for the AMN decreased, to 7.4% and seven seats. A turn-out of 58.8% was recorded. OSCE observers reported that there was some evidence of voter intimidation and media bias, but concluded that major electoral fraud did not occur. On 8 August the PLDM, the PL, the PDM and the AMN announced the formation of a coalition, the Alliance for European Integration (AIE), with the intention of establishing a reformist government that would be committed to seeking eventual EU membership for Moldova. With a combined total of 53 seats in Parlamentul, the Alliance would require the support of at least eight PCRM deputies to secure the election of its presidential candidate. On 28 August Mihai Ghimpu, the Chairman of the PL, was elected as the parliamentary Chairman. On 9 September Grecianîi resigned as Prime Minister. Two days later Voronin resigned as President; Ghimpu, as Chairman of Parlamentul, succeeded Voronin in an acting capacity. On 17 September Ghimpu signed a decree nominating Vladimir Filat, the President of the PLDM, as Prime Minister. He also abolished the visa requirements imposed in April on Romanians entering the country. On 25 September a new Council of Ministers assumed office. Seven posts in the new administration (including that of Prime Minister) were allocated to the PLDM, five to the PL and four to each of the PDM and the AMN. One Deputy Prime Minister was appointed from each of the four coalition parties. Lupu was nominated as the AIE candidate in the forthcoming presidential election.

Constitutional impasse and further elections

Two attempts by the new legislature to elect a President, on 10 November and 7 December 2009, failed. On both occasions the PCRM boycotted the vote, and all 53 deputies from the AIE voted in support of Lupu's candidacy, eight too few for the election to be validated. Consequently, in accordance with constitutional norms, the legislature was to be dissolved, and further elections held. However, constitutional law dictated that a sitting of Parlamentul could not be dissolved less than one year after the most recent legislative dissolution. In an attempt to resolve this contradiction, in December the Constitutional Court requested that the Venice Commission of the Council of Europe provide its legal opinion. In January 2010 a left-wing and pro-Russian faction of the PCRM, including five legislative deputies, announced the formation of a new party, United Moldova, under the leadership of Vladimir Ţurcan, a former Minister of Internal Affairs and ambassador to Russia.

In March 2010 the Venice Commission provided its legal opinion on the constitutional impasse, stating that the demand that Parlamentul be dissolved no more than once a year should take precedence over the requirement that parliamentary dissolution take place when the election of a President by a three-fifths' legislative majority has proved impossible on two successive occasions. The Commission also recommended that Moldova adopt constitutional reforms in order to prevent any recurrence of the prolonged inability to elect a President. On 16 March the Constitutional Court confirmed that Parlamentul could only be dissolved after 16 June (one year after its previous dissolution). Ghimpu, as acting President, stated that he would not permit the dissolution of Parlamentul until the constitutional provisions on electing the head of state had been amended.

Meanwhile, rival political factions developed alternative proposals for constitutional reform that would permit the election of a President. On 18 June 2010 Parlamentul approved a number of amendments to the electoral code, which had been proposed by the AIE: the number of deputies required for a quorum was reduced from 52 to 51; the minimum requirement for a party to secure parliamentary representation was reduced from 5% to 4%, and for independent candidates from 3% to 2%; and the minimum required rate of participation in referendums was reduced from 60% to 33% of the electorate.

On 7 July 2010 Parlamentul approved the scheduling of a referendum, to be held on 5 September, on a new constitutional text, including provisions for a direct presidential election. Although 87.8% of the votes in the referendum supported the proposals, the rate of participation, at 30.3%, was insufficient for the reforms to be approved. (The PCRM and other opposition parties had urged a boycott of the plebiscite). On 28 September Ghimpu announced the dissolution of Parlamentul, and scheduled legislative elections for 28 November. It was subsequently announced that the parties of the AIE would contest the election separately.

The legislative elections on 28 November 2010 were contested by 20 political parties. According to the final results, announced by the Central Electoral Commission on 6 December, neither the PCRM nor the combined parties of the AIE had secured the 61 legislative seats required to elect a new President. The PCRM again won the largest share of votes cast, with 39.3%, obtaining a reduced representation of 42 seats; the PLDM, with 29.4% of votes, substantially increased its representation from 14 to 32 seats, the PDM, with 12.7%, obtained 15 seats, and the PL, with 10%, won 12 seats. A participation rate of 63.4% of the electorate was recorded. Although the PCRM claimed electoral violations had occurred, observers from the OSCE and the Council of Europe stated that the conduct of the elections had generally met democratic standards. On 30 December a reconstituted AIE coalition in the new Parlamentul elected Lupu as its Chairman, and consequently as acting President, with 57 votes. On 14 January 2011 the formation of a new AIE coalition Government, again under the premiership of Filat, was approved in Parlamentul. Nevertheless, the ruling coalition's lack of the parliamentary majority required to elect a President or revise the Constitution presented a continued cause of concern. In February, in response to a request for clarification by PCRM deputies, the Constitutional Court ruled that, as more than two months had passed since the expiry of the mandate of an elected President, Parlamentul had the right to decide when a presidential election should be held. In April the AMN merged with the PLDM.

In September 2011 the Constitutional Court rejected a request by Parlamentul that a simple majority of deputies be permitted to elect the President. In October Alexandru Tănase (Minister of Justice until the election of Oleg Efrim to that post in May) was elected Chairman of the Constitutional Court to replace Dumitru Pulbere, who had demanded that Parlamentul be dissolved if it failed to elect a President by 28 September. In November Grecianîi, Dodon and a further parliamentary deputy defected from the PCRM to the Social Democratic Party (PSD—a small party with hitherto no parliamentary representation), prompting renewed hopes that the impasse would be resolved; however, the main political parties subsequently failed to agree on a consensus candidate. On 16 December a further attempt by the AIE to elect Lupu as President was unsuccessful, when he secured only 58 votes (three fewer than necessary).

From January 2012 the PCRM (which had renewed a boycott of parliamentary sessions) organized weekly protests in Chişinău to demand the resignation of the Government and the organization of further legislative elections. The AIE subsequently entered into negotiations with the PSD, and on 12 March the nomination of a single presidential candidate, an independent judge, Nicolae Timofti, was announced. On 16 March Timofti

was elected President, with the support of the three PSD deputies, by 62 votes in Parlamentul. The PCRM contested the legitimacy of Timofti's election, on the grounds that the term of Parlamentul had been extended beyond the one-year period allowed to elect a President. In June a further three parliamentary deputies left the PCRM faction and became independents; later that month the PCRM ended its parliamentary boycott. In July Dorin Recean of the PLDM was appointed as Minister of Internal Affairs, replacing Alexei Roibu.

Recent developments: collapse of the AIE Government

In August 2012 the Central Electoral Commission rejected an initiative, instigated by the PSD and supported by the PCRM, calling for a referendum be held on Moldovan accession to a Russian-led customs union (also comprising Belarus and Kazakhstan), on the grounds that insufficient valid signatures had been presented in support of the demands. Lupu also denied a request by the PCRM than an extraordinary parliamentary session be convened to discuss the proposal. New legislation, supported by the Government, which had been adopted by Parlamentul in July, condemning crimes committed under the former communist regime and prohibiting the use of communist symbols officially entered into force on 1 October; the PCRM appealed to the Constitutional Court against the ban on communist symbols, and Voronin maintained that the party would not comply with the requirement. Following protests by radio journalists at continued state censorship, amendments to the criminal code, which were approved by the Government in December, provided for the introduction of punitive measures, including fines, for contravention of a ban on public media censorship and the obstruction of media activity.

Meanwhile, in December 2012 the death of a businessman, Sorin Paciu, after he had been accidentally shot during a hunting party attended by senior members of the judiciary, including the Prosecutor-General, Valeriu Zubco (a member of the PDM), precipitated considerable political controversy, including allegations that elements in the Government had sought to prevent an investigation into the circumstances of the shooting. Although Zubco ceded to pressure for his resignation in January 2013, charges relating to the incident were subsequently brought against another member of the hunting party, Andrei Usatov of the PLDM. The affair exacerbated conflict within the constituent parties of the coalition Government, in particular between the PDM (supported by the PL) and Filat's PLDM. In mid-February Filat effected the removal of a senior member of the PDM, Vladimir Plahotniuc, as First Vice-Chairman of Parlamentul, on grounds of corrupt business practices. The DP-controlled National Anti-Corruption Centre subsequently initiated corruption investigations against Recean and two other PLDM ministers, prompting Filat to accuse Plahotniuc of orchestrating a campaign of denigration against his party members, while PDM Chairman Lupu issued demands for Filat's resignation. On 28 February the PCRM proposed a vote of no confidence in the Government; with the support of the PDM deputies, the motion was adopted in Parlamentul on 5 March, effecting the collapse of Filat's administration. Failure to form a new government with parliamentary approval by the stipulated period of 45 days would result in further legislative elections. The Government formally resigned on 8 March, although Filat remained as acting Prime Minister until late April, when he resigned, in response to a Constitutional Court ruling that the loss of the vote of no confidence meant that he was not eligible to serve as premier; he was succeeded, also in an acting capacity, by the hitherto Deputy Prime Minister and Minister of Foreign Affairs, Iurie Leancă, as attempts to form a new administration continued.

Gagauz-Yeri

During the Transnistrian conflict in 1991–92 (see Transnistria, p. 3123), the situation in Gagauz-Yeri—which constitutes several non-contiguous territories—remained peaceful, although the region continued to demand full statehood. The 1994 Moldovan Constitution provides for a 'special autonomous status' for Gagauz-Yeri, as for Transnistria, and negotiations duly commenced on the details of this status. Agreement was quickly reached between the Government and the Gagauz authorities, and in December Parlamentul adopted legislation on the status of Gagauz-Yeri. The regions of southern Moldova populated by the Gagauz were to enjoy broad self-administrative powers, and Gagauz was to be one of three official languages (with Moldovan and Russian). Legislative power was to be vested in a regional assembly, and a directly elected başkan (governor) was to hold a quasi-presidential position, with an Executive Committee to serve as the regional government. The law entered into force in February 1995, and in March a local referendum was held to determine which settlements would form part of the region. Elections to the 35-seat Halk Toplusu (Popular Assembly) took place in May–June. Concurrent elections held to the post of Başkan were won by Gheorghe Tabunscic, the First Secretary of the branch of the PCRM in the principal Gagauz-inhabited city, Comrat. Under the new Constitution, the Başkan became a member of the Council of Ministers of Moldova. In May 1999 Gagauz-Yeri, like Transnistria, was designated an autonomous entity within Moldova. Elections to the Halk Toplusu and to the post of Başkan were held in late August. Following a second round of voting in September, Dumitru Croitor was elected as Başkan, with 61.5% of the votes cast. In mid-February 2002 the Halk Toplusu adopted a vote of no confidence in Croitor, and scheduled a referendum in the hope of securing his dismissal. On 24 February, when the referendum was scheduled to take place, the regional security forces reportedly seized the offices of the regional electoral commission, declaring its mandate to have expired and the plebiscite to be illegal. President Voronin subsequently visited the region and demanded the resignations of both Croitor and the Chairman of the Halk Toplusu. Croitor finally resigned at the end of June. At a second round of voting in an election held on 11 October, Tabunscic regained the post of Başkan. On 25 July 2003 Parlamentul officially recognized the autonomous status of Gagauz-Yeri through an amendment to the national Constitution. Legislative elections were held in the region in November–December, in which the PCRM and independent candidates each won almost one-half of the seats contested. On 17 December 2006 an independent candidate, Mihail Formuzal, was elected Başkan at a second round of voting. Further elections to the Halk Toplusu took place in March 2008, with voter turn-out estimated at 60.5%. A coalition formed by the PCRM with independent candidates commanded the greatest parliamentary representation, with 14 seats, while supporters of Formuzal won eight seats. In July an independent deputy and prominent journalist, Ana Harlamenco, was elected Chairman of the Halk Toplusu. On 22 September the Halk Toplusu narrowly approved a resolution formally recognizing the separatist regions of Abkhazia and South Ossetia as independent from Georgia, following Russian recognition of those territories as independent states, and declaring support for Russia's military action in Georgia in August (see Georgia).

In elections to the Moldovan Parlamentul in November 2010, the PCRM received about 60.0% of votes cast in Gagauz-Yeri, representing a decline in popular support for the party in that territory. The election to the post of Başkan was held on 12 December, when Formuzal (with around 37% of the votes cast) defeated the Mayor of Comrat, Nicolai Duduglo (who received 32%) and Irina Vlah of the PCRM, with 31%. The rate of participation was around 57%. In a second round of voting on 26 December, Formuzal, with 51.4% of the votes cast, narrowly defeated Dudoglo, with 48.6%. The Court of Appeal in Comrat rejected an appeal by Dudoglo against the election results, and monitors from the Council of Europe upheld the conduct of the elections (while noting certain irregularities). Formuzal was formally inaugurated to a further term as Başkan on 14 February 2011. At the end of March 2012 the Halk Toplusu signed protocols of co-operation with the Supreme Council of Transnistria. The dismissal, in late June, by the Gagauz Executive Committee, of the autonomy's representative to Transnistria, Ivan Burguji (who was regarded as a close ally of the separatist authorities in Transnitria), was criticized by the Halk Toplusu, which maintained that proper procedures had not been followed, and that such an act required its approval. Elections to the Halk Toplusu were conducted, in two rounds, on 9 and 23 September. Some 25 independent candidates were elected, together with seven representatives of the PCRM, two of the PLDM and one of the Party of Socialists of the Republic of Moldova.

In mid-January 2013 a group of deputies in the Halk Toplusu, led by Burguji, announced that they intended to commence impeachment proceedings against Formuzal, on the grounds of alleged abuse of office, including his failure to consult with the Halk Toplusu or the regional chief of police, and also claimed that the Başkan had been involved in criminal activities.

Foreign Affairs
Regional relations

Owing to the changing domestic situation, Moldova's membership of the CIS was equivocal until early 1994. In August 1993 Parlamentul failed by four votes to ratify the Almaty Declaration, largely owing to the influence of deputies favouring unification with Romania. However, in September President Snegur signed a treaty to join the new CIS economic union. Following Moldova's parliamentary elections of February 1994 and the referendum in March, which strongly endorsed continued independence, Parlamentul reversed its earlier decision, and in April it finally ratified membership of the CIS.

The communist Government elected in 2001 initially undertook a policy of rapprochement with Russia, and in December Parlamentul ratified a treaty on friendship and co-operation, which had been signed by the two countries' respective Presidents in the previous month. However, in 2004 relations deteriorated, largely owing to developments associated with Transnistria. From the beginning of 2006 Russia attempted to increase the price charged to Moldova for supplies of natural gas. In January a compromise agreement was reached, covering the first three months of the year; in return for agreeing to relinquish the Transnistrian assets of the joint-venture company MoldovaGaz to the Russian state-controlled gas supplier, Gazprom (which already held a majority stake in the company), Moldova was to be charged a concessionary price for its gas supplies from Russia. Leading officials of MoldovaGaz and Gazprom signed a five-year agreement, providing for staged increases in the price of gas supplied to Moldova, while the Moldovan Government was to transfer control of its gas distribution system to Gazprom. In March Russia suspended the import of Moldovan wine and other agricultural products, ostensibly owing to hygiene concerns. In early 2007 the Russian authorities announced that the import of fruit and vegetables from Moldova had resumed. In October the Russian Government announced that Moldovan wineries that had passed safety assessments were permitted to resume exports to Russia. Relations with Russia became strained after the reformist Government of the AIE assumed office in September 2009. In June 2010 Russia again suspended imports of Moldovan wine on grounds of poor quality; the Moldovan Government claimed that the decision was in reprisal for a decree issued by acting President Ghimpu designating 28 June as the 'Day of Soviet Occupation'. In early 2011 Gazprom increased the price of gas supplied to Moldova by about 12% (in accordance with the existing agreement). In September 2012 Prime Minister Filat made an official visit to Russia with the aim of negotiating a new gas supply contract; during his discussions with government leaders in Moscow and Sochi, the Russian Minister of Energy, Aleksandr Novak, offered a number of concessions, including the waiver of part of US $4,100m. in debt owed by Moldova for Russian gas supplies, a reduction in the price of gas, and increased investment in the country, on condition that the Moldovan Government renounced plans to enter into the EU's Third Energy Package (which would disallow Gazprom's control of Moldova's gas distribution network) in 2015. However, the Moldovan authorities failed to accept the Russian offer; an initiative by some political parties (with the encouragement of the Russian ambassador) for Moldova to join a Russian-led customs union had also been rejected (see Domestic Political Affairs).

In December 2005 Moldova attended a meeting in Kyiv, Ukraine, to launch the new Community of Democratic Choice, originally conceived by Ukraine and Georgia. The nine-member alliance aimed to remove divisions and resolve conflicts in the Baltic, Black Sea and Caspian regions. In May 2006 the leaders of Georgia, Ukraine, Azerbaijan and Moldova met in Kyiv, to revive the regional GUAM organization, renaming it the Organization for Democracy and Economic Development—GUAM (see p. 477).

Relations with Romania were subject to several tensions. A basic political treaty, agreed in 1999 and initialled in 2000 was not signed, and in 2003 the Romanian Prime Minister, Adrian Năstase, indicated that the country no longer considered the treaty to be relevant. In February 2000 many Moldovans applied to obtain Romanian citizenship as formal negotiations on Romania's accession to the EU commenced. Romania subsequently introduced measures to simplify the application process, angering the Moldovan authorities, since the Moldovan Constitution prohibited dual citizenship. The situation was resolved later in the year when Moldova approved legislation permitting its citizens to hold dual citizenship with Israel, Romania or Russia.

In March 2007 Moldova strongly criticized Romania for granting Romanian citizenship to large numbers of Moldovans (with an estimated 800,000 applications pending), on the grounds that the policy undermined Moldova's statehood. Romania's accession to full EU membership, which took effect in January, resulted in Moldovan citizens being required to possess entry visas to enter that country; in protest against this, the Moldovan authorities reversed a decision to allow Romania to open two new consulates in the country. In December Moldova expelled two Romanian diplomats, who had allegedly supplied funds to opposition newspapers, for activities 'incompatible with their status'.

The civil disturbances that followed Moldovan legislative elections in early April 2009, which led the Government to accuse Romania of organizing an attempted coup, prompted the imposition of a number of sanctions against Romania: most notably, the expulsion of the Romanian ambassador; the recall of the Moldovan envoy in Bucharest, Romania; and the immediate introduction of visa requirements for Romanians entering Moldova. The Romanian President, Traian Băsescu, subsequently pledged that the Romanian Government would expedite the process of granting Romanian citizenship to Moldovans, claiming that some 1m. applications had been received. The visa requirements for Romanian citizens wishing to visit Moldova were rescinded in September by the reformist Government led by Vladimir Filat. On 8 November 2010 Prime Minister Filat and the Romanian Minister of Foreign Affairs, on the occasion of a regional summit meeting in the Romanian capital, Bucharest, signed the bilateral treaty confirming the border between the two states and providing for closer co-operation.

Other external relations

Following the approval of the European Commission's Eastern Partnership initiative (which provided the framework for a closer relationship between the EU and Armenia, Azerbaijan, Belarus, Georgia, Moldova and Ukraine) in March 2009, the acting Prime Minister of the Czech Republic, Mirek Topolánek, in his capacity as President of the EU Council, visited Moldova in late April, and extended an invitation to the Moldovan authorities for a forthcoming Eastern Partnership summit meeting. In May Moldova was included in the EU's Eastern Partnership programme, which was officially inaugurated at the summit in Prague, Czech Republic. In March 2011, following the installation of a new AIE coalition Government, US Vice-President Joe Biden made an official visit to Chişinău (becoming the most senior US official to have visited the country), where he met government leaders and declared US support for reform efforts. After the EU announced in December that Moldova had made satisfactory progress in implementing reforms preparatory to EU integration, negotiations on the establishment of a free trade area for Moldova under the framework of the Eastern Partnership began in February 2012. An official visit to Moldova by German Chancellor Angela Merkel on 22 August, during which she commended the country's progress within the Eastern Partnership, was widely viewed as an endorsement of Moldova's European integration aspirations. In November European Commission President José Manuel Barroso met government leaders for discussions in Chişinău. Following negotiations on co-operation with the EU in the area of Common Security and Defence Policy, on 13 December a Framework Agreement for the participation of Moldova in EU crisis management operations was signed; it was envisaged that Moldova would contribute to an EU civilian mission in the Horn of Africa. Meanwhile, in October Moldova joined the US-led Global Peace Operations Initiative, and was to receive US funding of US $1.6m. for the development of its peace-keeping training. In December the US Senate endorsed a vote by the lower House of Representatives to end long-standing trade restrictions (imposed against the USSR in 1974) on Moldova.

CONSTITUTION AND GOVERNMENT

Under the Constitution of 1994, as subsequently amended, supreme legislative power is held by the unicameral Parlamentul (the Parliament), which is directly elected every four years. Parlamentul comprises 101 members. The President is Head of State and holds executive power in conjunction with the Council of Ministers, led by the Prime Minister. The President is elected by the legislature for a four-year term. Judicial power is exercised by the Supreme Court of Justice, the Court of Appeal, tribunals and courts of law. Judges sitting in the courts of law and the Supreme Court of Justice are appointed by the President following proposals by the Higher Magistrates' Council. The country is divided into 33 districts (rayons), two municipalities, and two autonomous entities—Gagauz-Yeri and Transnistria (the latter of which remained outside government control in mid-2012).

REGIONAL AND INTERNATIONAL CO-OPERATION

Moldova is a member of the Commonwealth of Independent States (CIS, see p. 251), the Council of Europe (see p. 260), the Organization for Security and Co-operation in Europe (OSCE, see p. 397) and the Organization of the Black Sea Economic Co-operation (BSEC, see p. 411).

Moldova joined the UN in 1992 and became a member of the World Trade Organization (WTO, see p. 444) in 2001.

ECONOMIC AFFAIRS

In 2011, according to estimates by the World Bank, Moldova's gross national income (GNI), measured at average 2009–11 prices, was US $7,055m., equivalent to $1,980 per head (or $3,670 per head on an international purchasing-power parity basis). During 2002–11, it was estimated, the population decreased at an average annual rate of 0.2%, while gross domestic product (GDP) per head increased, in real terms, at an average annual rate of 5.1%. Overall GDP increased, in real terms, at an average annual rate of 4.9% in 2002–11; GDP increased by 6.4% in 2011.

As a result of its extremely fertile land and temperate climate, Moldova's economy is dominated by agriculture and related industries. Some 85% of the country's terrain is cultivated. Agriculture (including hunting, forestry and fishing) contributed 14.4% of GDP and engaged 27.5% of the employed labour force in 2011. Principal crops include wine grapes and other fruit, tobacco, vegetables and grain. The wine industry has traditionally occupied a central role in the economy. The private ownership of land was legalized in 1991, although the sale of agricultural land was not permitted until 2001. In 2004 some 73.1% of agricultural land was privately owned and the private sector accounted for some 99% of production. According to the World Bank, the GDP of the agricultural sector, in real terms, declined by an average annual rate of 1.1% during 2002–11. Agricultural GDP increased, in real terms, by 7.2% in 2010, and remained constant in 2011, according to World Bank estimates.

Industry (including mining, manufacturing, power and construction) contributed 20.3% of GDP and engaged 18.7% of the employed labour force in 2011. In 2002–11, according to the World Bank, industrial GDP decreased at an average rate of 2.2% per year. Industrial GDP increased by 9.5% in 2010 and remained constant in 2011, according to World Bank estimates.

Mining and quarrying contributed 0.5% of GDP in 2011, according to official figures, and employed just 0.3% of the employed labour force in 2008. Moldova has extremely limited mineral resources. Activity is focused primarily on the extraction and processing of industrial minerals such as gypsum, limestone, sand and gravel. Deposits of petroleum and natural gas were discovered in southern Moldova in the early 1990s; total reserves of natural gas have been estimated at 22,000m. cu m.

The manufacturing sector contributed 13.3% of GDP in 2011 and engaged 10.9% of the employed labour force in 2008. The sector is dominated by food-processing, wine and tobacco production, machine-building and metal-working, and light industry. According to the World Bank, manufacturing GDP increased, in real terms, by an annual average of 0.1% in 2002–11. Manufacturing GDP increased by 9.6% in 2010 and remained constant in 2011.

Construction contributed 3.9% of GDP and engaged 5.7% of the employed labour force in 2011.

Moldova relies heavily on imported energy—primarily natural gas and petroleum products—from Russia, Romania and Ukraine (such imports accounted for 76.7% of consumption in 2004). In the mid-2000s Moldova announced its intention to diversify its gas suppliers, and to increase domestic energy production substantially; domestic production represented 23.3% of consumption in 2004. A large proportion of natural gas imports supply the Moldoveneasca power station, located in Transnistria, which contributes much of the country's electricity-generating capacity. The growing importance of natural gas to the generation of electricity has been paralleled by the rapid decline, from the mid-1990s, in the importance of coal-fired power sources; whereas in 1995 some 31.5% of electricity generated in Moldova was of coal origin, by 2004 the contribution of coal to electricity generation was negligible. In February 2005 an Azerbaijani company purchased the unfinished Giurgiulesti petroleum terminal in southern Moldova; the terminal commenced operations in September 2007. Natural gas accounted for 95.0% of electricity production in 2009, when hydroelectric power accounted for 1.5%. Mineral products comprised 23.4% of the value of total merchandise imports in 2012, according to preliminary official figures.

Services accounted for 65.3% of GDP and engaged 53.7% of the employed labour force in 2011. The GDP of the services sector increased, in real terms, at an annual average rate of 7.1% in 2002–11. Services GDP increased by 4.8% in 2010, but decreased by 13.1% in 2011.

In 2011 Moldova recorded a visible merchandise trade deficit of US $2,966.5m., while there was a deficit of $880.4m. on the current account of the balance of payments. In 2012, according to preliminary figures, the principal source of imports was Russia (accounting for 15.7% of the value of total imports). Other major suppliers were Romania, Ukraine, the People's Republic of China, Turkey, Germany and Italy. The main market for exports in that year was Russia (accounting for 30.3% of the value of total exports). Other important purchasers were Romania, Italy and Ukraine. In 2012 the principal imports were mineral products machinery and mechanical appliances, chemicals and related products, textiles and textile articles, foodstuffs, beverages and tobacco, vehicles and associated transport equipment, plastics, rubber and articles thereof, and base metals. The main exports in that year were foodstuffs, beverages and tobacco, vegetable products, textiles and textile articles, machinery and mechanical appliances, chemicals and related products, and miscellaneous manufactured articles.

In 2011, the consolidated state budget recorded a deficit of 1,961m, equivalent to 2.4% of GDP. Moldova's general government gross debt was 19,044m. Moldovan lei in 2011, equivalent to 23.2% of GDP. At the end of 2010 Moldova's total external debt totalled US $4,615m., of which $817m. was public and publicly guaranteed debt. In that year, the cost of servicing long-term public and publicly guaranteed debt and repayments to the IMF was equivalent to 12.8% of the value of exports of goods, services and income (excluding workers' remittances). Consumer prices decreased at an annual average rate of 0.1% during 2002–12. The average rate of inflation was 4.6% in 2012. The average rate of unemployment was 6.7% in 2011.

Although the economy recorded continued growth from 2000, in the mid-2000s Moldova was the poorest country in Europe. In the second half of the 2000s the reorganization of the taxation system and a programme of privatization were undertaken.

After a sharp economic contraction in 2009, related to the global economic crisis, GDP growth resumed in 2010 (strengthened by a substantial increase in exports) and continued in 2011. In January 2010 the IMF approved the release of funds worth US $574.4m. over a period of three years, under its Extended Credit Facility and Extended Fund Facility. In October 2011 Moldova and seven other member states of the Commonwealth of Independent States (CIS, see p. 251) signed a free trade agreement (although its enactment, initially scheduled for 2012, was delayed pending ratification by all signatory states). In December the European Union (EU, see p. 281) announced that Moldova had made satisfactory progress in implementing reforms preparatory to EU integration, and approved the opening of negotiations on the establishment of a free trade area as part of a future Association Agreement; these began in February 2012 and it was envisaged that they would be completed by November 2013. During 2012 the Government continued EU integration efforts, effectively precluding the negotiation of more advantageous gas supply arrangements with Russia (see Regional relations), while Moldova was expected to benefit from the decision of the US legislature in December to end longstanding trade restrictions against the country. Real GDP growth was projected to have slowed to 0.3% in 2012, owing to the impact of adverse weather conditions upon agriculture and continued economic weaknesses in Europe; it was anticipated that economic growth would recover to about 4.0% in 2013. The IMF urged the authorities, in addition to continued rationalization efforts, to increase support for the majority state-owned Banca de Economii, and generally to improve the transparency of the banking system. However, the collapse of the ruling coalition Government, following dissension between the main political parties, in March 2013 (see Domestic Political Affairs) prompted concerns that further progress, and signature of the EU Association Agreement, would be delayed.

PUBLIC HOLIDAYS

2014: 1 January (New Year's Day), 7–8 January (Russian Orthodox Christmas), 8 March (International Women's Day), 20–21 April (Orthodox Easter), 28 April ('Paștele Blajinilor', Parents' Day), 1 May (Labour Day), 9 May (Victory and Commemoration Day), 27 August (Independence Day), 31 August ('Limbă Noastră', National Language Day), 24–25 December (Romanian Orthodox Christmas).

Statistical Survey

Principal source (unless otherwise indicated): State Department for Statistics and Sociology, 2028 Chișinău, șos. Hîncești 53D; tel. (22) 73-37-74; fax (22) 22-61-46; e-mail dass@statistica.md; internet www.statistica.md.

Note: Most of the figures from 1993 onwards exclude the Transnistria (Pridnestrovie) region, which remained outside central government control.

Area and Population

AREA, POPULATION AND DENSITY

Area (sq km)	33,800*
Population (census results)†	
12 January 1989	4,335,360
5–12 October 2004	
Males	1,627,689
Females	1,755,643
Total	3,383,332
Population (official estimates at 1 January)‡	
2010	3,563,695
2011	3,560,430
2012	3,559,541
Density (per sq km) at 1 January 2012‡	105.3

* 13,050 sq miles.
† Figures refer to the *de jure* population. The *de facto* total at the 1989 census was 4,337,592 (males 2,058,160, females 2,279,432).
‡ Excluding Transnistria.

POPULATION BY AGE AND SEX
(official estimates at 1 January 2012)

	Males	Females	Total
0–14	297,024	280,266	577,290
15–64	1,282,226	1,346,416	2,628,642
65 and over	132,475	221,134	353,609
Total	1,711,725	1,847,816	3,559,541

POPULATION BY ETHNIC GROUP*
(permanent inhabitants, 2004 census)

	Number	%
Moldovan	2,564,849	75.8
Ukrainian	282,406	8.4
Russian	201,218	5.9
Gagauz	147,500	4.4
Romanian	73,276	2.2
Bulgarian	65,662	1.9
Others and unknown	48,421	1.4
Total	3,383,332	100.0

* According to official declaration of nationality.

ADMINISTRATIVE DIVISIONS
('000, official estimates of population at 1 January 2012)

Districts (raione)

Anenii Noi	83.1	Nisporeni	66.6
Basarabeasca	29.0	Ocniţa	55.8
Briceni	74.7	Orhei	125.8
Cahul	124.9	Rezina	52.3
Cantemir	62.5	Rîşcani	69.5
Călăraşi	78.8	Sîngerei	93.2
Căuşeni	92.0	Soroca	100.1
Cimişlia	61.3	Străşeni	91.5
Criuleni	73.3	Şoldăneşti	43.0
Donduşeni	44.8	Ştefan Vodă	71.5
Drochia	89.5	Taraclia	44.1
Dubăsari	35.2	Teleneşti	73.9
Edineţ	82.5	Ungheni	117.2
Făleşti	92.4	*Municipalities*	
Floreşti	89.5	Bălţi	149.2
Glodeni	61.4	Chişinău	794.8
		Autonomous	
Hînceşti	121.6	*Territory*	
Ialoveni	99.7	Gagauz-Yeri	161.2
Leova	53.6	**Total**	3,559.5

Population of Transnistria (Pridnestrovie) (estimated figure obtained as residual from total country population estimates at 1 January 2003): 601,088.

PRINCIPAL TOWNS
(population at census of 5–12 October 2004)

Chişinău (capital)	589,455	Soroca	28,362
Bălţi	122,669	Orhei	25,641
Cahul	35,488	Comrat	23,327
Ungheni	32,530	Ceadîr-Lunga	19,401

Population at 1 January 2012 (official estimates): Chişinău 667,600, Bălţi 144,300, Cahul 39,800, Ungheni 38,100, Soroca 37,500, Orhei 33,500, Comrat 25,600, Ceadir-Lunga 22,800.

Principal Towns within Transnistria (estimated population at Moldovan census of 1 January 1996): Tiraspol 187,000; Tighina (Bender) 128,000; Râbnita (Rybnitsa) 62,900.

IMMIGRATION AND EMIGRATION

	2009	2010	2011
Immigrants	2,010	2,512	2,704
Emigrants	6,663	4,714	3,920

BIRTHS, MARRIAGES AND DEATHS

	Registered live births		Registered marriages		Registered deaths	
	Number	Rate (per 1,000)	Number	Rate (per 1,000)	Number	Rate (per 1,000)
2004	38,272	10.6	25,164	7.0	41,668	11.6
2005	37,695	10.5	27,187	7.6	44,689	12.4
2006	37,587	10.5	27,128	7.6	43,137	12.0
2007	37,973	10.6	29,213	8.2	43,050	12.0
2008	39,018	10.9	26,666	7.5	41,948	11.8
2009	40,803	11.4	26,781	7.5	42,139	11.8
2010	40,474	11.4	26,483	7.4	43,631	12.2
2011	39,182	11.0	25,900	7.3	39,249	11.0

Life expectancy (years at birth): 70.9 (males 66.8; females 74.9) in 2011.

ECONOMICALLY ACTIVE POPULATION
(labour force survey, '000 persons aged 15 years and over)

	2009	2010	2011
Agriculture, hunting, forestry and fishing	333.7	314.7	323.0
Industry	155.4	145.8	153.2
Construction	72.9	67.5	66.8
Wholesale and retail trade; repair of motor vehicles, motorcycles and personal and household goods; hotels and restaurants	217.4	213.4	223.0
Transport, storage and communications	68.0	63.7	67.0
Public administration and defence; compulsory social security; education; health and social work	248.6	250.7	250.2
Other community, social and personal service activities	88.4	87.6	90.4
Total employed	1,184.4	1,143.4	1,173.5
Unemployed	81.0	92.0	84.0
Total labour force	1,265.3	1,235.4	1,257.5
Males	648.5	630.6	642.3
Females	616.8	604.8	615.3

Health and Welfare

KEY INDICATORS

Total fertility rate (children per woman, 2010)	1.5
Under-5 mortality rate (per 1,000 live births, 2010)	19
HIV/AIDS (% of persons aged 15–49, 2009)	0.4
Physicians (per 1,000 head, 2009)	2.7
Hospital beds (per 1,000 head, 2009)	6.2
Health expenditure (2009): US $ per head (PPP)	357
Health expenditure (2009): % of GDP	12.5
Health expenditure (2009): public (% of total)	48.5
Access to water (% of persons, 2010)	96
Access to sanitation (% of persons, 2010)	85
Total carbon dioxide emissions ('000 metric tons, 2008)	4,774.4
Carbon dioxide emissions per head (metric tons, 2008)	1.3
Human Development Index (2011): ranking	111
Human Development Index (2011): value	0.649

For sources and definitions, see explanatory note on p. vi.

Agriculture

PRINCIPAL CROPS
('000 metric tons)

	2009	2010	2011
Wheat	736.7	744.2	794.8
Barley	261.4	208.4	194.0
Maize	1,141.1	1,419.9	1,468.3
Potatoes	260.9	279.7	350.8
Sugar beet	337.4	837.6	588.6
Beans, dry	9.9	13.3	17.0
Peas, dry	15.4	21.5	13.3
Sunflower seed	284.2	382.3	427.4
Cabbages and other brassicas	32.8	36.2	35.1
Tomatoes	84.1	57.2	83.4
Cucumbers and gherkins	22.8	20.8	26.0
Chillies and peppers, green	23.8	18.9	24.0
Aubergines (Eggplants)	4.9	7.0	7.1
Onions, dry	40.9	56.2	58.3
Carrots and turnips	10.3	17.7	14.3
Watermelons	96.6	100.8	81.8
Apples	209.6	207.9	268.8
Plums and sloes	31.4	53.8	35.0
Grapes	685.1	481.6	594.8
Tobacco, unmanufactured	4.4	7.6	5.4

Aggregate production ('000 metric tons, may include official, semi-official or estimated data): Total cereals 2,149.2 in 2009, 2,386.0 in 2010, 2,466.4 in 2011; Total vegetables (incl. melons) 413.7 in 2009, 447.6 in 2010, 446.2 in 2011; Total fruits (excl. melons) 983.2 in 2009, 792.4 in 2010, 959.0 in 2011.

Source: FAO.

LIVESTOCK
('000 head at 1 January)

	2009	2010	2011
Horses	55.5	54.4	52.2
Cattle	217.7	221.6	216.0
Pigs	283.5	337.1	478.5
Sheep	761.9	803.7	787.9
Goats	103.8	111.2	117.6
Chickens*	18,220	22,340	34,000

* Unofficial figures.
Source: FAO.

LIVESTOCK PRODUCTS
('000 metric tons)

	2009	2010	2011
Cattle meat	11.0	10.2	9.7
Sheep meat	2.2	2.1	2.1
Pig meat	42.2	56.9	63.9
Chicken meat	34.5	41.0	41.3
Cows' milk	538.9	554.1	525.8
Sheep's milk	23.2	23.6	22.4
Goats' milk	12.6	13.4	11.9
Hen eggs*	35.8	40.2	39.3
Honey	2.6	2.6	2.7
Wool, greasy	2.0	2.1	2.0

* Unofficial figures.
Source: FAO.

Forestry

ROUNDWOOD REMOVALS
('000 cubic metres, excl. bark)

	2005*	2006	2007
Sawlogs, veneer logs and logs for sleepers	19	27	26
Other industrial wood	75	18	17
Fuel wood	94	334	309
Total	188	379	352

* FAO estimates.

2008–11: Production assumed to be unchanged from 2007 (FAO estimates).
Source: FAO.

SAWNWOOD PRODUCTION
('000 cubic metres, incl. railway sleepers)

	2005*	2006	2007
Coniferous (softwood)	—	14	16
Broadleaved (hardwood)	31	17	18
Total	31	31	34

* FAO estimates.

2008–11: Production assumed to be unchanged from 2007 (FAO estimates).
Source: FAO.

Fishing

(metric tons, live weight)

	2008	2009	2010
Capture	1,407	1,607	1,633
Common carp	580	715	738
Crucian carp	420	380	365
Aquaculture*	7,200	7,820	8,370
Common carp*	2,400	2,700	2,900
Silver carp*	3,900	4,200	4,500
Total catch*	8,607	9,427	10,003

* FAO estimates.
Source: FAO.

Mining

('000 metric tons unless otherwise indicated)

	2008	2009	2010
Limestone*†	165	150	170
Gypsum†	701	164	300*
Sand and gravel ('000 cu m)	2,846.8	1,929.5	2,326.2
Peat*†	475	475	475

* Estimated production.
† Source: US Geological Survey.

2011 ('000 cu m): Sand and gravel 2,994.6.

Industry

SELECTED PRODUCTS
('000 metric tons unless otherwise indicated)

	2009	2010	2011
Fruit and vegetable preserves .	58.2	68.8	67.0
Flour	115.6	108.0	116.9
Raw sugar	38.4	103.2	88.4
Wine ('000 hectolitres) . . .	1,250	1,270	1,250
Mineral water ('000 hectolitres)	1,110	1,160	1,080
Soft drinks ('000 hectolitres) . .	600	650	720
Footwear ('000 pairs, excl. rubber)	2,221	2,717	2,845
Glasses and bottles (million) . .	201.3	246.2	326.4
Electric energy (million kWh) .	1,028	1,054	1,011

Cigars and cigarettes (million): 4,975 in 2007.

Carpets and rugs ('000 sq m): 5,246 in 2007.

Plaster ('000 metric tons): 311,900 in 2007.

Cement ('000 metric tons, estimates): 750.0 in 2008; 700.0 in 2009; 900 in 2010 (Source: US Geological Survey).

Finance

CURRENCY AND EXCHANGE RATES

Monetary Units
100 bani (singular: ban) = 1 Moldovan leu (plural: lei).

Sterling, Dollar and Euro Equivalents (31 December 2012)
£1 sterling = 19.036 lei;
US $1 = 12.063 lei;
€1 = 15.916 lei;
1,000 Moldovan lei = £52.53 = $82.90 = €62.83.

Average Exchange Rate (Moldovan lei per US$)
2010   12.369
2011   11.739
2012   12.111

STATE BUDGET
(million lei)

Revenue	2009	2010	2011
Tax revenue	19,532	22,541	25,580
Taxes on personal incomes . .	1,908	2,029	2,341
Domestic taxes on goods and services	9,492	11,679	13,581
Taxes on ownership	253	281	281
Taxes on international trade .	908	1,080	1,179
Social Fund contributions . .	5,595	5,985	6,563
Health Fund contributions . .	1,377	1,487	1,636
Non-tax revenue	839	1,416	1,179
Other revenue	3,147	3,583	3,381
Total	23,518	27,540	30,140

Expenditure	2009	2010	2011
Economic services	2,619	3,197	3,616
Social and cultural services . .	19,191	21,407	22,946
Education	5,666	6,575	6,869
Health	3,847	3,997	4,260
Social assistance and security .	9,092	10,246	11,066
Recreational and cultural services	586	590	751
Defence services	2,080	1,880	2,156
General state services	1,413	1,362	1,457
External trade	201	211	229
State debt service	834	548	662
Other expenditures	1,017	722	1,035
Total	27,354	29,326	32,101

INTERNATIONAL RESERVES
(excluding gold, US $ million at 31 December)

	2009	2010	2011
IMF special drawing rights . .	3.57	0.35	0.89
Reserve position in IMF . . .	0.01	0.01	0.01
Foreign exchange	1,476.68	1,717.33	1,964.08
Total	1,480.27	1,717.69	1,964.98

Source: IMF, *International Financial Statistics*.

MONEY SUPPLY
(million lei at 31 December)

	2009	2010	2011
Currency outside depository corporations	8,848.98	10,107.57	10,864.51
Transferable deposits . . .	7,157.21	8,533.62	9,958.16
Other deposits	16,676.94	18,408.85	20,153.93
Securities other than shares . .	1.34	1.28	0.52
Broad money	32,684.46	37,051.32	40,977.12

Source: IMF, *International Financial Statistics*.

COST OF LIVING
(Consumer Price Index; base: previous year = 100)

	2010	2011	2012
Food and beverages	105.7	108.4	103.8
Other consumer goods . . .	107.3	105.8	104.2
Services	109.1	108.8	106.2
All items (incl. others) . . .	107.4	107.6	104.6

NATIONAL ACCOUNTS
(million lei at current prices, excl. Transnistria)

Expenditure on the Gross Domestic Product

	2009	2010	2011
Final consumption expenditure .	68,574.1	83,240.3	96,090.5
Households	53,352.6	66,051.8	78,104.1
Non-profit institutions serving households	15,221.5	17,188.5	17,986.4
Gross capital formation . . .	13,984.7	16,910.7	19,904.0
Gross fixed capital formation . Acquisitions, less disposals, of valuables	13,655.0	16,262.6	19,178.8
Changes in inventories . .	329.7	648.1	725.2
Total domestic expenditure .	82,558.8	100,151.0	115,994.5
Exports of goods and services .	22,281.8	28,197.2	37,033.6
Less Imports of goods and services	44,410.6	56,462.7	70,679.4
GDP in market prices . .	60,429.8	71,885.5	82,348.7

Gross Domestic Product by Economic Activity

	2009	2010	2011
Agriculture, hunting, forestry and fishing	5,134.5	8,657.4	10,095.2
Mining and quarrying	241.2	270.0	348.8
Manufacturing	6,390.8	7,618.9	9,354.7
Electricity, gas and water supply	1,398.8	1,645.8	1,814.8
Construction	2,108.7	2,437.5	2,719.9
Wholesale and retail trade; repair of motor vehicles, motorcycles and personal and household goods	7,954.1	9,212.9	11,119.2
Hotels and restaurants	809.7	911.3	1,006.5
Transport, storage and communications	7,226.0	8,099.2	9,001.6
Financial intermediation	3,850.9	4,105.6	4,135.6
Real estate, renting and business activities	5,183.9	5,826.7	6,841.9
Public administration and defence; compulsory social security	2,857.0	2,740.4	3,038.4
Education	4,250.4	4,837.1	5,184.0
Health and social work	2,685.4	3,007.5	3,310.7
Other community, social and personal services	1,702.6	2,049.1	2,192.5
Sub-total	51,794.0	61,419.5	70,164.0
Less Financial intermediation services indirectly measured	984.8	1,498.8	1,774.5
Gross value added in basic prices	50,809.2	59,920.7	68,389.6
Taxes, less subsidies, on products and imports	9,620.6	11,964.8	13,959.1
GDP in market prices	60,429.8	71,885.5	82,348.7

BALANCE OF PAYMENTS
(US $ million)

	2009	2010	2011
Exports of goods	929.8	1,175.0	1,749.0
Imports of goods	−2,986.6	−3,491.8	−4,715.4
Balance on goods	−2,056.8	−2,316.8	−2,966.5
Exports of services	785.7	804.0	972.6
Imports of services	−717.5	−776.5	−896.7
Balance on goods and services	−1,988.6	−2,289.3	−2,890.5
Primary income received	590.0	761.4	927.1
Primary income paid	−287.1	−262.6	−358.9
Balance on goods, services and primary income	−1,685.6	−1,790.5	−2,322.3
Secondary income received	1,254.6	1,312.1	1,542.0
Secondary income paid	−103.4	−89.5	−100.1
Current balance	−534.4	−567.9	−880.4
Capital account (net)	−17.5	−28.4	−29.7
Direct investment assets	3.4	−7.6	−33.8
Direct investment liabilities	135.2	201.5	287.2
Portfolio investment assets	−0.3	−0.2	−0.4
Portfolio investment liabilities	−5.6	5.8	5.1
Financial derivatives and employee stock options assets	−0.1	−0.6	—
Financial derivatives and employee stock options liabilities	0.4	—	0.2
Other investment assets	−210.6	75.5	91.1
Other investment liabilities	185.5	140.2	430.7
Net errors and omissions	49.9	39.1	87.7
Reserves and related items	−393.9	−142.6	−42.2

Source: IMF, *International Financial Statistics*.

External Trade

PRINCIPAL COMMODITIES
(distribution by Harmonized System, US $ million)

Imports c.i.f.	2010	2011	2012*
Vegetable products	168.9	199.1	204.6
Foodstuffs, beverages and tobacco	308.6	355.8	380.0
Mineral products	807.1	1,179.6	1,217.6
Mineral fuels, mineral oils and related materials	791.1	1,165.4	1,198.1
Chemicals and related products	404.3	529.7	558.2
Pharmaceutical products	178.8	214.3	220.4
Plastics, rubber and articles thereof	227.7	304.1	304.2
Plastics	171.7	217.9	220.2
Textiles and textile articles	282.3	383.5	384.8
Base metals and articles of base metals	242.4	312.4	284.5
Machinery and mechanical appliances	576.5	827.8	786.4
Apparatus such as nuclear reactors, boilers, machinery and mechanical appliances, and parts thereof	279.5	409.6	380.2
Electrical machinery and equipment and parts thereof; sound recorders and reproducers, television image and sound recorders and reproducers, and parts and accessories thereof	297.0	418.2	406.2
Vehicles and associated transport equipment	237.9	332.6	304.9
Vehicles other than railway or tramway rolling stock, and parts and accessories thereof	194.8	323.7	275.1
Total (incl. others)	3,855.3	5,191.3	5,213.1

Exports f.o.b.	2010	2011	2012*
Vegetable products	340.7	471.0	360.5
Edible fruit	167.6	187.0	202.3
Cereals	71.0	72.0	36.5
Oil seeds and oleaginous fruits, etc	90.4	181.5	99.9
Animal or vegetable fats	47.6	77.5	89.7
Foodstuffs, beverages and tobacco	316.9	330.6	390.9
Preparations of vegetables or fruits	52.3	68.8	60.4
Beverages, spirits and vinegar	178.2	181.3	215.0
Chemicals and related products	74.1	111.6	145.8
Pharmaceutical products	60.5	77.1	94.0

Exports f.o.b.—*continued*	2010	2011	2012*
Textiles and textile articles .	267.7	354.7	343.4
Articles of apparel and clothing accessories, knitted	102.6	115.5	103.8
Articles of apparel and clothing accessories, not knitted . .	126.5	157.4	145.8
Base metals and articles of base metals	58.3	112.9	73.4
Machinery and mechanical appliances	171.6	283.3	278.6
Apparatus such as nuclear reactors, boilers, machinery and mechanical appliances, and parts thereof	59.5	103.9	77.1
Electrical machinery and equipment and parts thereof; sound recorders and reproducers, television image and sound recorders and reproducers, and parts and accessories thereof . . .	112.1	179.4	201.5
Miscellaneous manufactured items	51.7	97.8	108.2
Furniture; bedding, mattresses, mattress supports, cushions and similar stuffed furnishings; lamps and lighting fittings, not elsewhere specified or included; illuminated signs, illuminated nameplates etc.; prefabricated buildings . . .	40.9	87.6	95.1
Total (incl. others)	1,541.5	2,216.8	2,161.8

* Preliminary data.

PRINCIPAL TRADING PARTNERS
(US $ million)

Imports c.i.f.	2010	2011	2012*
Austria	59.3	85.4	123.0
Belarus	119.1	194.7	172.2
Bulgaria	48.9	66.7	78.2
China, People's Republic . . .	320.2	399.8	415.7
Czech Republic	42.7	59.7	65.0
France	68.3	87.0	103.7
Germany	294.7	395.8	386.9
Greece	93.3	68.7	50.0
Hungary	63.8	100.0	89.0
Italy	270.7	348.1	327.6
Poland	105.1	134.6	152.1
Romania	386.7	574.2	620.6
Russia	586.5	823.0	816.9
Turkey	205.8	366.9	388.2
Ukraine	528.5	641.1	594.3
United Kingdom	52.6	64.9	58.0
USA	61.8	79.7	79.1
Total (incl. others)	3,855.3	5,191.3	5,213.1

Exports f.o.b.	2010	2011	2012*
Belarus	80.3	75.6	80.7
Bulgaria	18.8	33.8	33.8
France	23.3	24.0	30.2
Germany	75.4	106.5	70.2
Greece	17.7	24.0	13.3
Hungary	8.1	23.3	28.7
Italy	147.4	215.1	202.4
Kazakhstan	30.5	45.5	50.3
Poland	46.7	85.9	74.2
Romania	246.4	376.4	356.7
Russia	404.0	625.5	655.0
Switzerland	17.4	8.0	5.1
Turkey	67.5	73.4	56.1
Ukraine	91.6	153.0	122.4
United Kingdom	82.1	101.8	83.9
USA	22.0	24.9	30.0
Total (incl. others)	1,541.5	2,216.8	2,161.8

* Preliminary data.

Transport

RAILWAYS
(traffic)

	2010	2011	2012*
Passenger journeys (million) . .	5.0	4.7	4.3
Passenger-km (million) . . .	399	363	347
Freight transported (million metric tons)	3.9	4.6	4.1
Freight ton-km (million) . . .	959	1,196	961

* Provisional figures.

ROAD TRAFFIC
(motor vehicles in use)

	2009	2010	2011
Passenger cars	386,365	404,290	426,973
Buses and minibuses . . .	21,346	21,395	21,349
Lorries and vans	120,174	131,243	141,696

INLAND WATERWAYS
(traffic)

	2010	2011	2012*
Passenger journeys (million) . .	0.1	0.1	0.1
Passenger-km (million) . . .	0.2	0.2	0.5
Freight transported ('000 metric tons) . . .	127.2	149.1	115.7
Freight ton-km (million) . . .	0.4	0.5	0.2

* Provisional figures.

CIVIL AVIATION
(traffic)

	2010	2011	2012*
Passengers carried ('000) . . .	649.2	700.4	673.0
Passenger-km (million) . .	751	837	875
Freight transported ('000 metric tons) . . .	1.30	1.60	1.57
Freight ton-km (million) . . .	1.7	1.7	1.7

* Provisional figures.

Tourism

FOREIGN VISITOR ARRIVALS
(incl. excursionists)

Country of origin	2009	2010	2011
Bulgaria	380	324	289
France	196	283	248
Germany	460	482	1,001
Israel	156	225	138
Italy	258	474	445
Japan	76	93	258
Netherlands	154	311	219
Poland	291	204	371
Romania	765	1,698	1,600
Russia	1,713	1,327	1,404
Switzerland	291	108	78
Turkey	1,002	526	477
Ukraine	979	730	1,189
United Kingdom	744	405	350
USA	194	451	558
Total (incl. others)	9,189	8,956	10,788

Receipts from tourism (US $ million, excl. passenger transport): 173 in 2009; 174 in 2010; 194 in 2011 (provisional) (Source: World Tourism Organization).

Communications Media

	2009	2010	2011
Telephones ('000 main lines in use)	1,138.7	1,161.1	1,180.0
Mobile cellular telephones ('000 subscribers)	2,784.8	3,165.1	3,715.0
Internet subscribers ('000) . .	203.5	269.1	355.1
Broadband subscribers ('000) . .	187.0	269.1	350.5

Personal computers: 423,950 (114.3 per 1,000 persons) in 2006.

Source: International Telecommunication Union.

Education

(2011/12)

	Institutions	Teachers	Students
Pre-primary	1,400	12,330	135,427
Primary and Secondary: general	1,460	36,203	381,418
Secondary: vocational . . .	70	2,200	20,320
Higher: colleges	48	2,543	31,442
Higher: universities	34	6,147	103,956

Pupil-teacher ratio (primary education, UNESCO estimate): 15.6 in 2009/10 (Source: UNESCO Institute for Statistics).

Adult literacy rate (UNESCO estimates): 98.5% (males 99.1%; females 98.1%) in 2010 (Source: UNESCO Institute for Statistics).

Directory

The Government

HEAD OF STATE

President: NICOLAE TIMOFTI.

COUNCIL OF MINISTERS
(May 2013)

On 5 March 2013 the coalition Government listed below and led by Vladimir Filat, principally comprising representatives of the Liberal Democratic Party of Moldova (PLDM), the Liberal Party (PL) and the Democratic Party of Moldova (PDM), collapsed, following a legislative vote of no confidence. The Government resigned on 8 March, although Filat remained in office in an acting capacity, while attempts to form a new ruling coalition proceeded. Filat resigned as Prime Minister on 22 April, and was succeeded in an acting capacity, three days later, by the hitherto Deputy Prime Minister and Minister of Foreign Affairs, Iurie Leancă.

Prime Minister, and Minister of Foreign Affairs and European Integration: IURIE LEANCĂ (acting) (PLDM).

Deputy Prime Minister and Minister of the Economy: VALERIU LAZĂR (PDM).

Deputy Prime Minister: EUGEN CARPOV (Independent).

Deputy Prime Minister: MIHAI MOLDOVANU (PL).

Minister of Finance: VEACESLAV NEGRUȚA (PLDM).

Minister of Justice: OLEG EFRIM (PLDM).

Minister of Internal Affairs: DORIN RECEAN (PLDM).

Minister of Defence: VITALIE MARINUȚA (PL).

Minister of Regional Development and Construction: MARCEL RĂDUCAN (PDM).

Minister of Agriculture and the Food Industry: VASILE BUMACOV (PLDM).

Minister of Transport and Road Infrastructure: ANATOLIE ȘALARU (PL).

Minister of the Environment: GHEORGHE ȘALARU (PL).

Minister of Education: MAIA SANDU (PLDM).

Minister of Culture: BORIS FOCȘA (PDM).

Minister of Labour, Social Protection and the Family: VALENTINA BULIGA (PDM).

Minister of Health: ANDREI USATÎI (PLDM).

Minister of Youth and Sport: OCTAVIAN ȚÎCU (PL).

Minister of Information and Communications Technologies: PAVEL FILIP (PDM).

Note: the President of the Moldovan Academy of Sciences, GHEORGHE DUCA, and the Bașkan (Governor) of the Autonomous Territory of Gagauz-Yeri (Gagauzia), MIHAIL FORMUZAL, are also members of the Government.

MINISTRIES

Office of the President: 2073 Chișinău, bd. Ștefan cel Mare 154; tel. (22) 25-02-44; internet www.prezident.md.

Office of the Council of Ministers: 2033 Chișinău, Piața Marii Adunări Naționale 1; tel. (22) 25-01-01; fax (22) 23-38-72; e-mail petitii@gov.md; internet www.gov.md.

Ministry of Agriculture and the Food Industry: 2004 Chișinău, bd. Ștefan cel Mare 162; tel. (22) 23-34-27; fax (22) 21-02-04; e-mail adm_maia@moldova.md; internet www.maia.gov.md.

Ministry of Culture: 2033 Chișinău, Piața Marii Adunări Naționale 1; tel. (22) 22-76-20; fax (22) 23-23-88; e-mail office@mc.gov.md; internet www.mc.gov.md.

Ministry of Defence: 2021 Chișinău, șos. Hîncești 84; tel. (22) 25-22-22; fax (22) 25-24-00; e-mail ministru@army.md; internet www.army.md.

Ministry of the Economy: 2033 Chișinău, Piața Marii Adunări Naționale 1; tel. (22) 23-74-48; fax (22) 23-40-64; e-mail mineconcom@mec.gov.md; internet www.mec.gov.md.

Ministry of Education: 2033 Chișinău, Piața Marii Adunări Naționale 1; tel. (22) 23-33-48; fax (22) 23-35-15; e-mail viceministra@edu.md; internet www.edu.md.

Ministry of the Environment: 2005 Chișinău, str. Cosmonauților 9; tel. (22) 20-45-07; fax (22) 22-68-58; e-mail egreta@mediu.gov.md; internet www.mediu.gov.md.

Ministry of Finance: 2005 Chișinău, str. Cosmonauților 7; tel. (22) 22-66-29; fax (22) 24-00-55; e-mail cancelaria@minfin.moldova.md; internet www.minfin.md.

Ministry of Foreign Affairs and European Integration: 2012 Chișinău, str. 31 August 1989 80; tel. (22) 57-82-07; fax (22) 23-23-02; e-mail secdep@mfa.md; internet www.mfa.gov.md.

Ministry of Health: 2009 Chișinău, str. Vasile Alecsandri 2; tel. (22) 72-99-07; fax (22) 73-87-81; e-mail office@ms.gov.md; internet www.ms.md.

Ministry of Information and Communications Technologies: 2012 Chișinău, bd. Ștefan cel Mare și Sfînt 134; tel. and fax (22) 23-84-76; e-mail mtic@mtic.gov.md; internet www.mtic.gov.md.

Ministry of Internal Affairs: 2012 Chișinău, bd. Ștefan cel Mare 75; tel. (22) 25-53-46; e-mail mai@mai.md; internet www.mai.md.

Ministry of Justice: 2012 Chișinău, str. 31 August 1989 82; tel. (22) 23-47-95; fax (22) 23-47-97; e-mail secretariat@justice.gov.md; internet www.justice.gov.md.

Ministry of Labour, Social Protection and the Family: 2009 Chișinău, str. Vasile Alecsandri 1; tel. (22) 26-93-01; fax (22) 26-93-10; e-mail secretariat@mmpsf.gov.md; internet www.mpsfc.gov.md.

Ministry of Regional Development and Construction: 2005 Chișinău, str Cosmonauților 9; tel. (22) 20-45-69; fax (22) 22-07-48; e-mail mcdr@mcdr.gov.md; internet www.mcdt.gov.md.

Ministry of Transport and Road Infrastructure: 2004 Chișinău, bd. Ștefan cel Mare 162; tel. (22) 82-07-12; fax (22) 54-65-64; e-mail secretariat@mtid.gov.md; internet www.mtid.gov.md.

Ministry of Youth and Sport: 2004 Chișinău, bd. Ștefan cel Mare 162; tel. and fax (22) 82-08-61; e-mail ministru@mts.gov.md; internet www.mts.gov.md.

President

In voting by the members of Parlamentul (the Parliament) on 16 December 2011 the sole candidate for the presidency, the Chairman of Parlamentul (and acting President) MARIAN LUPU, failed to secure sufficient votes (of at least 61 deputies) to be elected. A further election was conducted in Parlamentul on 16 March 2012. The sole candidate, NICOLAE TIMOFTI, an independent, was elected, having received the votes of 62 of the 101 legislative deputies. Timofti assumed office on 23 March.

Legislature

Parlamentul
(The Parliament)
2073 Chişinău, bd. Ştefan cel Mare 105; tel. (22) 26-82-44; fax (22) 23-30-12; e-mail inform@parlament.md; internet www.parlament.md.

Chairman: MARIAN LUPU.

General Election, 28 November 2010

Parties and alliances	Votes	%	Seats
Party of Communists of the Republic of Moldova	676,671	39.32	42
Liberal Democratic Party of Moldova	506,365	29.42	32
Democratic Party of Moldova	218,847	12.72	15
Liberal Party	171,434	9.96	12
Others	147,630	8.58	—
Total	**1,720,947**	**100.00**	**101**

Election Commission

Comisia Electorală Centrală a Republicii Moldova (Central Electoral Commission of the Republic of Moldova): 2012 Chişinău, str. Vasile Alecsandri 119; tel. (22) 25-14-51; fax (22) 23-40-47; e-mail info@cec.md; internet www.cec.md; Pres. Dr IURIE CIOCAN.

Political Organizations

In January 2009 some 28 political parties were registered with the Ministry of Justice; the following were among the most important of those registered in mid-2011.

Christian Democratic People's Party (PPCD) (Partidul Popular Creştin Democrat): 2009 Chişinău, str. N. Iorga 5; tel. and fax (22) 23-44-80; fax (22) 23-86-66; e-mail echipa@ppcd.md; internet ppcd.md; f. 1989 as the People's Front of Moldova, renamed 1992, and as above 1999; advocates Moldova's entry into the European Union and the North Atlantic Treaty Organization; Chair. VICTOR CIOBANU.

Democratic Party of Moldova (PDM) (Partidul Democrat din Moldova): 2001 Chişinău, str. Tighina 32; tel. (22) 27-82-29; fax (22) 27-82-30; e-mail pdm@mtc.md; internet www.pdm.md; f. 1997; centrist; fmrly Movement for a Democratic and Prosperous Moldova, name changed in April 2000; contested 2005 legislative elections as mem. of the Democratic Moldova bloc; merged with Social Liberal Party in Feb. 2008; Chair. MARIAN LUPU.

European Action Movement (Mişcarea Acţiunea Europeană—MAE): 2012 Chişinău, str. Bucureşti 88; tel. (22) 24-36-56; e-mail office@ae.md; f. 2006; supports closer integration of Moldova with the European Union; Pres. VEACESLAV UNTILĂ.

Green Alliance Ecological Party of Moldova (Alianţa Verde Ecolojist—AVE): 2001 Chişinău, str. Bolgară 31A; tel. (22) 84-48-06; fax (69) 11-48-21; e-mail pve.moldova@gmail.com; internet www.greenparty.md; f. 1992; Pres. ANATOLIE PROHNITCHI.

Liberal Democratic Party of Moldova (PLDM) (Partidul Liberal Democrat din Moldova): 2012 Chişinău, str. Bucureşti 88; tel. (22) 81-51-54; fax (22) 81-51-63; e-mail info@pldm.md; internet www.pldm.md; f. 2007; absorbed Our Moldova Alliance Apr. 2011; Pres. VLADIMIR FILAT.

Liberal Party (PL) (Partidul Liberal): Chişinău, str. Bucureşti 87; tel. (22) 23-26-89; fax (22) 22-80-97; e-mail liberal@pl.md; internet www.pl.md; f. 1993 as Party of Reform; renamed as above 2005; Chair. MIHAI GHIMPU; 12,000 mems.

National Liberal Party (Partidul Naţional Liberal—PNL): 2069 Chişinău, Calea Ieşilor 6; tel. (22) 21-18-18; fax (22) 21-16-77; e-mail contacts@pnl.md; internet www.pnl.md; f. 2007; right-of-centre liberal party; Pres. VITALIA PAVLICENCO.

Party of Communists of the Republic of Moldova (PCRM) (Partidul Comuniştilor din Republica Moldova): 2012 Chişinău, str. N. Iorga 11; tel. (22) 23-46-14; fax (22) 23-36-73; e-mail pcrmcc@gmail.com; internet www.pcrm.md; fmrly the Communist Party of Moldova (banned Aug. 1991); revived as above April 1994; First Sec. VLADIMIR VORONIN.

Party of Socialists of the Republic of Moldova (PSRM): 2005 Chişinău, bd. Grigore Vieru 16/29; tel. (22); tel. and fax 22-96-46; e-mail verval@mail.ru; internet socialistii.md; f. 1996 by fmr mems of Socialist Party of Moldova; democratic socialist; Pres. IGOR DODON.

People's Democratic Party of Moldova (PPDM) (Partidul Popular Democrat din Moldova): 2011 Chişinău, or. Codru, str. Sf. Gheorghe 12; tel. (22) 23-41-51; e-mail presa.pasat@gmail.com; f. 2005 as Humanist Party of Moldova; present name adopted 2011; Christian humanist party, associated with the Moldovan Orthodox Church, supports closer relations with Russia; Pres. VALERIU PASAT.

Social Democratic Party (PSD) (Partidul Social Democrat): 2012 Chişinău, str. Nicolae Iorga 14; tel. and fax (22) 20-10-22; fax (22) 85-57-33; e-mail info@psdm.md; internet www.psdm.md; f. 1990; merged with Party of Social Democracy in 2007; Pres. VICTOR ŞELIN.

United Moldova Party (MU) (Partidul Moldova Unită): 2069 Chişinău, Calea Ieşilor 14/2; tel. (22) 26-81-10; fax (22) 74-68-20; e-mail mail@moldovaunita.md; f. 2010 by fmr members of Communist Party of Republic of Moldova and fmr Centrist Union of Moldova; leftist, supportive of closer relations with Russia; Leader VLADIMIR ŢURCAN.

Diplomatic Representation

EMBASSIES IN MOLDOVA

Azerbaijan: 2012 Chişinău, str. Kogelnichanu 64; tel. (22) 23-22-77; fax (22) 22-75-58; e-mail chisinau@mission.mfa.gov.az; internet www.azembassy.md; Ambassador NAMIK HASAN ALIYEV.

Belarus: 2009 Chişinău, str. Mateevici 83/1; tel. (22) 60-29-86; fax (22) 23-83-00; e-mail moldova@mfa.gov.by; internet moldova.mfa.gov.by; Ambassador VYACHESLAV A. OSIPENKO.

Bulgaria: 2012 Chişinău, str. Bucureşti 92; tel. (22) 23-79-83; fax (22) 23-79-78; e-mail embassy.chisinau@mfa.bg; internet www.mfa.bg/embassies/moldova; Ambassador GEORGI PANAYOTOV.

China, People's Republic: 2004 Chişinău, str. Mitropolit Dosoftei 124; tel. (22) 21-07-12; fax (22) 29-59-60; e-mail chinaemb@mtc.md; internet md.chineseembassy.org; Ambassador TONG MINGTAO.

Czech Republic: 2005 Chişinău, str. Moara Roşie 23; tel. (22) 20-99-42; fax (22) 29-64-37; e-mail chisinau@embassy.mzv.cz; internet www.mzv.cz/chisinau; Ambassador JAROMÍR KVAPIL.

France: 2012 Chişinău, str. V. Pîrcălab 6; tel. (22) 20-04-00; fax (22) 20-04-01; e-mail infos.chisinau-amba@diplomatie.gouv.fr; internet www.ambafrance-md.org; Ambassador GÉRARD GUILLONNEAU.

Germany: 2012 Chişinău, str. Maria Cibotari 35; tel. (22) 20-06-00; fax (22) 23-46-80; e-mail info@chisinau.diplo.de; internet www.chisinau.diplo.de; Ambassador MATTHIAS MEYER.

Hungary: 2004 Chişinău, bd. Ştefan cel Mare 131; tel. (22) 23-29-34; fax (22) 22-45-13; e-mail mission.kiv@mfa.gov.hu; internet www.mfa.gov.hu/emb/chisinau; Ambassador MÁTYÁS SZILÁGYI.

Israel: 2001 Chişinău, str. Tighina 12; tel. (22) 54-42-84; fax (22) 54-42-80; Ambassador OREN DAVID (resident in Jerusalem, Israel).

Lithuania: 2001 Chişinău, str. I. Valilenco 24/1; tel. (22) 54-31-94; fax (22) 23-42-87; e-mail amb.md@urm.lt; internet md.mfa.lt; Ambassador VIOLETA MOTULAITĖ.

Poland: 2019 Chişinău, str. Grenoble 126 A; tel. (22) 28-59-50; fax (22) 28-90-00; e-mail kiszyniow.amb.sekretariat@msz.gov.pl; internet www.kiszyniow.polemb.net; Ambassador ARTUR MICHALSKI.

Romania: 2001 Chişinău, str. Bucureşti 66/1; tel. (22) 21-30-37; fax (22) 22-81-29; e-mail secretariat@ambasadaromaniei.md; internet chisinau.mae.ro; Ambassador MARIUS LAZURCA.

Russia: 2004 Chişinău, bd. Ştefan cel Mare 153; tel. (22) 23-49-43; fax (22) 23-51-07; e-mail domino@mtc.md; internet www.moldova.mid.ru; Ambassador FARIT M. MUKHAMETSHIN.

Sweden: 2004 Chişinău, str. Toma Ciorba 12; tel. (22) 26-73-20; fax (22) 26-73-30; e-mail ambassaden.chisinau@gov.se; internet www.swedenabroad.com/chisinau; Ambassador INGRID TERSMAN.

Turkey: Chişinău, str. Valeriu Cupcea 60; tel. (22) 50-91-00; fax (22) 22-55-28; e-mail embassy.kishinev@mfa.gov.tr; internet www.chisinau.emb.mfa.gov.tr; Ambassador MAHMET SELIM KARTAL.

Ukraine: 2008 Chişinău, bd. Vasile Lupu 17; tel. (22) 58-21-51; fax (22) 58-51-08; e-mail emb_md@mfa.gov.ua; internet www.mfa.gov.ua/moldova; Ambassador SERHIY I. PYROZHKOV.

United Kingdom: 2012 Chişinău, str. N. Iorga 18; tel. (22) 22-59-02; fax (22) 25-18-59; e-mail enquiries.chisinau@fco.gov.uk; internet ukinmoldova.fco.gov.uk; Ambassador KEITH SHANNON.

USA: 2009 Chişinău, str. Mateevici 103; tel. (22) 40-83-00; fax (22) 23-30-44; e-mail chisinau-ca@state.gov; internet moldova .usembassy.gov; Ambassador WILLIAM H. MOSER.

Judicial System

Supreme Court of Justice of the Republic of Moldova (Curtea Supremă de Justiţie a Republicii Moldova): 2009 Chişinău, str. M. Kogălniceanu 70; tel. and fax (22) 22-31-69; e-mail info@csj.md; internet www.csj.md; comprises penal, economic, and civil and administrative chambers; Pres. MIHAI POALELUNGI.

Constitutional Court of the Republic of Moldova (Curtea Constitutionala a Republicii Moldova): 2004 Chişinău, str. A. Lăpuşneanu 28; tel. (22) 25-37-08; fax (22) 25-37-46; e-mail curtea@constcourt.md; internet www.constcourt.md; f. 1994; Chair. ALEXANDRU TĂNASE.

Prosecutor-General: (vacant), 2005 Chişinău, str. Mitropolit Bănulescu-Bodoni 26; tel. (22) 22-50-75; fax (22) 21-20-32; internet www.procuratura.md.

Religion

The majority of the inhabitants of Moldova profess Christianity, the largest denomination being the Eastern Orthodox Church. The Gagauz, of Turkic descent, are also adherents of Orthodox Christianity.

CHRISTIANITY

Eastern Orthodox Church

In December 1992 the Patriarch of Moscow and All Russia issued a decree altering the status of the Eparchy of Chişinău and Moldova to that of a Metropolitan See, which later became known as the Moldovan Orthodox Church (distinct from the Metropolitanate of Moldova and Bucovina of the Romanian Orthodox Church). In 2002 the Government permitted the registration of an Autonomous Metropolitate of Bessarabia. The recognition of the church, an exarchate of the Romanian Orthodox Church, was confirmed by the Supreme Court in late 2004. In late 2007 the Romanian Orthodox Church announced that three dioceses in Moldova, which had been abolished in 1944 following the Soviet occupation of the territory, were to be reactivated.

Metropolitanate of Bessarabia, Archbishop of Chişinău: 2004 Chişinău, str. 31 August 161; e-mail gbadea2006@yahoo.com; internet www.mitropoliabasarabiei.ro; Metropolitan of Bessarabia PETRU (PĂDURARU).

Moldovan Orthodox Church (Moscow Patriarchate): 2004 Chişinău, str. Bucureşti 119; tel. (22) 23-78-78; e-mail sec@ mitropolia.md; internet www.mitropolia.md; 1,520 parishes (2004); Metropolitan of Chişinău and all-Moldova VLADIMIR (CANTAREAN).

Roman Catholic Church

In October 2001 the diocese of Chişinău, covering the whole country, was established. At 31 December 2007 there were an estimated 20,000 Catholics in the Republic of Moldova.

Bishop of Chişinău: Rt Rev. ANTON COŞA, 2012 Chişinău, str. Mitropolit Dosoftei 85; tel. (22) 22-34-70; fax (22) 22-52-10; e-mail episcopia@starnet.md.

The Press

The publications listed below are in Moldovan, except where otherwise indicated.

PRINCIPAL NEWSPAPERS

Analytique Moldpresa: 2200 Chişinău, str. 31 August 85; tel. (22) 22-19-20; fax (22) 22-67-04; e-mail analytique@analytique.md; internet www.analytique.md; f. 2006; weekly; in Russian; Chief Editor NATALIA UZUN; circ. 8,000 (2008).

Argumenty i Fakty v Moldove (Arguments and Facts in Moldova): 2000 Chişinău, str. Armenească 55/101; tel. (22) 27-89-28; fax (22) 54-65-80; e-mail info@aif.md; internet www.aif.md; f. 1978; Moldovan version of *Argumenty i Fakty* (Russia); in Russian; weekly; Chief Editor YEVGENIYA ANOKHINA; circ. 25,000 (2008).

Curierul Agricol (The Agricultural Courier): 2012 Chişinău, str. Puşkin 22/214; tel. (22) 23-39-64; fax (22) 23-43-93; e-mail curier06@ mail.md; f. 2006; weekly; Chief Editor DUMITRU ŢIRA; circ. 4,000 (2008).

Curierul Economic (The Economic Courier): 2005 Chişinău, str. Bănulescu Bodoni 61/103; tel. (22) 40-28-33; fax (22) 24-52-57; e-mail curierul@ase.md; internet www.curier.ase.md; f. 1999; weekly; Dir TATIANA ROŞCA; circ. 4,000 (2008).

Ekonomicheskoye Obozreniye (Economic Review): 2000 Chişinău, str. S. Lazo 40; tel. (22) 88-77-77; fax (22) 88-77-89; e-mail red@logos.press.md; internet logos.press.md; f. 1990; weekly; in Russian; Chief Editor SERGEI MIŞIN; circ. 9,500 (2008).

Flux Continu: 2004 Chişinău, str. N. Iorga 8; tel. (22) 23-50-91; fax (22) 23-74-75; e-mail ap@flux.md; internet www.flux.md; f. 1995; 5 a week; Chief Editor SERGIU PRAPORŞCIC; circ. 35,000 (Fri.), 3,000 (Mon.–Thur.) (2008).

Glasul Naţiunii (The Voice of the Nation): 2001 Chişinău, str. 31 August 15; tel. (22) 54-27-82; fax (22) 54-31-37; e-mail glasul_natiunii@yahoo.com; f. 1989 as Glasul; 4 a week; culture, arts, literature, sport, politics; circ. 10,000 (2008).

Jurnal de Chişinău (Chişinău Journal): 2012 Chişinău, str. Vlaicu Pârcălab 63/3; tel. (22) 23-83-31; fax (22) 23-42-30; e-mail cotidian@ jurnal.md; internet www.jurnal.md; f. 1999; 3 a week; Chief Editor RODICA MAHU; circ. 26,000 (2008).

Kishinevskii Obozrevatel (Chişinău Correspondent): Chişinău, str. Calea Ieşilor 10; tel. and fax (22) 21-02-27; e-mail red@ko.md; internet www.ko.md; f. 1993; weekly; in Russian; Chief Editor IRINA ASTAKHOVA.

Kishinevskiye Novosti (Chişinău News): 2012 Chişinău, str. Puşkin 22; tel. and fax (22) 23-39-18; e-mail kn@kn.md; internet www.kn.md; f. 1991; weekly; in Russian; Chief Editor SERGHEI DROBOT; circ. 9,000 (2008).

Kommersant Plus (Businessman Plus): 2012 Chişinău, str. Puşkin 22/601; tel. and fax (22) 23-36-94; e-mail inform@commert.press.md; internet www.km.press.md; weekly; in Russian; politics and economics, incl. coverage of Gagauz-Yeri and Transnistria; Chief Editor ARTEM VARENIŢA; circ. 11,000 (2008).

Komsomolskaya Pravda v Moldove (Young Communist League Truth in Moldova): 2012 Chişinău, str. Vlaicu Pîrcălab 45; tel. (22) 22-45-12; fax (22) 22-12-74; e-mail kp@kp.md; internet www.kp.md; f. 1996; daily; in Russian; Moldovan edition of *Komsomolskaya Pravda* (Russia); Editor-in-Chief V. N. SUNGORKIN; circ. 9,000 (2008).

Moldavskiye Vedomosti (Moldovan Gazette): 2012 Chişinău, str. Vlaicu Pîrcălab 63; tel. and fax (22) 23-86-18; e-mail editor@ vedomosti.md; internet vedomosti.md; f. 1995; three a week; in Russian; Editor-in-Chief NATALIYA UZUN; circ. 9,000 (2010).

Moldova Suverană (Sovereign Moldova): 2012 Chişinău, str. Puşkin 22, 3rd Floor; tel. and fax (22) 23-35-38; e-mail cotidian@ moldova-suverana.md; internet www.moldova-suverana.md; f. 2005; daily; state-owned; Editor ION BERLINSKI; circ. 20,000 (per week).

Nezavisimaya Moldova (Independent Moldova): 2012 Chişinău, str. Puşkin 22; tel. (22) 23-36-08; fax (22) 23-31-41; e-mail mail@nm .md; internet www.nm.md; f. 2005; state-owned; daily; in Russian; Chief Editor IURII TIŞCENCO; circ. 92,700 (per month).

Timpul de Dimineaţa (The Morning Times): 2005 Chişinău, bd. Grigore Vieru 22/2; tel. (22) 22-56-70; e-mail secretariat@timpul.md; internet www.timpul.md; f. 2001; daily; Dir CONSTANTIN TANASE; Chief Editor SORINA ŞTEFÎRŢA; circ. 46,750 (2008).

Unimedia: 2012 Chişinău, bd. Ştefan cel Mare 180; tel. and fax (22) 23-54-75; tel. (22) 99-93-30; e-mail info@unimedia.md; internet www .unimedia.info; f. 2005; online only.

Vremya (Time): 2000 Chişinău, str. Ştefan cel Mare 13; tel. (22) 54-44-46; e-mail nata@vremea.md; f. 1998; daily; in Russian; Chief Editor EVGHENII PASCARI; circ. 8,800 (2008).

Gagauz-Yeri

Stolitsa Komrat (Capital City Comrat): 3805 Comrat, str. Tretiakov 36; tel. (298) 2-42-61; e-mail capitala@mail.ru; f. 2005; in Russian and Gagauz; Chief Editor ANA HARLAMENKO; circ. 8,000 (2008).

Vesti Gagauzii (Gagauz-Yeri News): 3800 Comrat, str. Lenin 200; tel. (298) 2-28-93; e-mail vesti@mtc-co.md; f. 1996; weekly; in Russian and Gagauz; publ. by the Halk Toplusu (People's Assembly) of Gagauz-Yeri; politics, culture, language; Chief Editor DMITRII MARINOV; circ. 4,500 (2008).

PRINCIPAL PERIODICALS

Alunelul (Little Hazelnut Tree): 2612 Chişinău, str. Puşkin 22; tel. (22) 22-26-41; f. 1982; for children aged 5–10 years; 10 a year; Chief Editor ŞTEFAN MELNIC; circ. 20,000 (2008).

Aquarelle: 2012 Chişinău, str. Puşkin 47/1A/3; tel. and fax (22) 22-07-73; e-mail aquarelle@aquarelle.md; internet www.aquarelle.md

f. 2003; in Russian; monthly; general women's interest; Chief Editor ANGELA SÎRBU; circ. 3,500 (2008).

Chipăruș Plus (Sharp Peppercorn): 2000 Chişinău, str. Ion Creangă 66/45; tel. and fax (22) 74-48-82; e-mail chiparusplus@yahoo.com; f. 2007; monthly; satirical; Dir MARGARETA CHIȚCATÎI; circ. 10,000 (2008).

Curierul Ortodox (The Orthodox Courier): 2060 Chişinău, bd. Traian 3, Biserica Sfîntul Dumitru; tel. (22) 77-25-33; e-mail fustei_nicolae@yahoo.com; internet curierulortodox.info; f. 1995; monthly; publ. of the Orthodox Church in the Republic of Moldova (Moscow Patriarchate); Chief Editor NICOLAE FUŞTEI; circ. 1,200 (2008).

Democraţia (Democracy): 2012 Chişinău, str. Puşkin 22/518; tel. (22) 24-32-53; fax (22) 24-35-85; e-mail democratiasaptaminal@yahoo.com; f. 2001; monthly; economics, politics, sport; Editor-in-Chief CORNEL CIUREA; circ. 11,000 (2008).

Florile Dalbe (The White Flowers): 2012 Chişinău, str. Puşkin 22; tel. and fax (22) 23-37-78; e-mail florile_d@mtc.md; f. 1941; weekly; education; Dir ION ANTON; circ. 15,000 (2008).

Legea şi Viaţa (The Law and Life): 2012 Chişinău, str. Puşkin 22/512; tel. and fax (22) 23-37-90; e-mail legea_zakon@mail.ru; f. 1990; monthly; in Moldovan and Russian; Chief Editor LEONTIE ARSENE; circ. 5,000 (2008).

Moldova (Moldova): 2012 Chişinău, str. Puşkin 22/539; tel. (22) 23-31-46; fax (22) 23-74-63; e-mail revistamoldova@list.ru; internet www.revista.md; f. 2004; monthly; in Moldovan, Russian and English; the arts; Editor NICOLAE ROŞCA; circ. 3,000 (2008).

Natura (Nature): 2004 Chişinău, str. S. Lazo 13; tel. and fax (22) 23-71-49; e-mail natura@natura.md; internet www.natura.md; f. 1990; monthly; nature, culture, and the environment; Chief Editor ALECU RENIŢĂ; circ. 10,000 (2012).

Noi (Us): 2012 Chişinău, str. Puşkin 22; tel. (22) 23-31-91; e-mail revistanoi@mail.md; f. 1935; for adolescents; Chief Editor VALERIU VOLONTIR; circ. 5,000 (2008).

Omnibus: 2000 Chişinău, str. V. Alecsandri 35A; tel. (22) 73-39-72; e-mail omnibus@hotbox.ru; f. 1993; in Russian; agriculture; Chief Editor MIHAIL BEREZICOV; circ. 5,500 (2008).

Profit/ Banky i Finansy (Profit/ Banks and Finance): 2014 Chişinău, str. Kogălniceanu 76; tel. (22) 23-49-30; fax (22) 23-49-33; e-mail office@profit.md; internet www.profit.md; f. 1995; monthly; in Romanian, Russian and English; economics and finance; Dir ALEXANDER TANAS; total circ. 4,800 (2009).

Puls (Pulse): 2001 Chişinău, str. Dosoftei 118; tel. (22) 83-81-86; fax (22) 29-59-54; e-mail red@puls.md; internet www.puls.md; f. 2004; weekly; in Russian; politics and economics; Chief Editor DMITRII KAVRUK; circ. 5,000 (2008).

Săptămína (The Week): 2012 Chişinău, str. 31 August 107; tel. (22) 22-62-51; fax (22) 22-44-61; e-mail saptamin@mdl.net; internet www.saptamina.md; f. 1992; weekly; politics, economics, social and cultural affairs; Chief Editor VIOREL MIHAIL; circ. 12,722 (2008).

Siesta: 2000 Chişinău, str. Kogălniceanu 88; tel. (22) 20-79-31; fax (22) 28-87-73; e-mail info@siesta.md; internet www.siesta.md; f. 2003; monthly; in Russian, Moldovan and English; coverage of cultural events in Chişinău; Chief Editor VLADIMIR GLADUN; circ. 6,000 (2008).

Vănătorul şi Pescarul Moldovei (Okhotnik i rybalov v Moldove) (The Hunter and Fisherman in Moldova): 2005 Chişinău, str. Şipotelor 2; tel. and fax (22) 24-20-27; e-mail svpm@mail.md; internet www.oxoma.md; f. 2006; monthly; in Moldovan and Russian; hunting, shooting, fishing; Chief Editor IONEL CĂPIŢĂ; circ. 3,000 (2010).

VIP Magazin (VIP Magazine): 2012 Chişinău, str. Puşkin 22/426-432; tel. and fax (22) 23-40-01; e-mail vip_magazin@mld.net; internet www.vipmagazin.md; f. 2004; monthly; politics, business, entertainment; Chief Editor SERGIU GAVRILIŢĂ; circ. 3,000.

NEWS AGENCIES

Infotag News Agency: 2014 Chişinău, str. Kogâlniceanu 76; tel. (22) 23-49-31; fax (22) 23-49-33; e-mail office@infotag.md; internet www.infotag.md; f. 1993; Dir ALEXANDRU TANAS.

State Information Agency—Moldpres: 2012 Chişinău, str. Puşkin 22; tel. (22) 23-23-72; fax (22) 23-26-98; e-mail inform@moldpres.md; internet www.moldpres.md; f. 1940 as ATEM, reorganized 1990 and 1994; Dir VALERIU RENITA.

PRESS ASSOCIATIONS

Association of Independent Press (API): 2005 Chişinău, str. Romană 2/2; tel. (22) 22-09-96; fax (22) 20-36-86; e-mail api@api.md; internet www.api.md; f. 1997; Pres. LUCIA JARDAN; Exec. Dir PETRU MACOVEI.

Independent Journalism Centre (IJC): 2012 Chişinău, str. Şciusev 53; tel. (22) 21-36-52; fax (22) 22-66-81; e-mail editor@ijc.md; internet www.ijc.md; f. 1994; non-governmental org.

Publishers

Editura Cartea Moldovei: 2004 Chişinău, bd. Ştefan cel Mare 180; tel. and fax (22) 29-59-35; f. 1996; fiction, non-fiction, poetry, art books; Dir RAISA SUVEICĂ.

Editura Hyperion: 2004 Chişinău, bd. Ştefan cel Mare 180; tel. (22) 24-40-22; f. 1976; fiction, literature, arts; Dir VALERIU MATEI.

Editura Lumina (Light): 2004 Chişinău, bd. Ştefan cel Mare 180; tel. and fax (22) 29-58-64; e-mail luminamd@mail.ru; internet www.edituralumina.md; f. 1966; educational textbooks; Dir ALEXANDRU STIROVICI; Editor-in-Chief ANATOL MALEV.

Editura Ştiinţa (Science): 2028 Chişinău, str. Academiei 3; tel. (22) 73-96-16; fax (22) 73-96-27; e-mail prini@stiinta.asm.md; internet www.stiinta.asm.md; f. 1959; textbooks, encyclopedias, dictionaries, children's books and fiction in various languages; Dir GHEORGHE PRINI.

Technica-Info: 2004 Chişinău, bd. Ştefan cel Mare 168; tel. (22) 23-78-61; fax (22) 23-85-04; e-mail bostan@utm.md; internet www.utm.md; f. 1993; technology; educational textbooks; Dir of Bd ION BOSTAN.

Univers Pedagogic: 2020 Chişinău, str. Socoleni 16/1, Centrul Ştiinţific; tel. (22) 24-32-79; e-mail univers_ped@yahoo.com; f. 1991; part of Ministry of Education; textbooks, guide books, children's literature; Dir I. SCUTELNICIUC.

Broadcasting and Communications
TELECOMMUNICATIONS

Moldcell: 2060 Chişinău, str. Belgrad 3; tel. (22) 20-62-06; fax (22) 20-62-07; e-mail moldcell@moldcell.md; internet www.moldcell.md; f. 1999; mobile telecommunications; owned by Fintur Holdings b.v. (Netherlands); Gen. Man. CHIRIL GABURICI.

Moldtelecom: 2001 Chişinău, bd. Ştefan cel Mare 10; tel. (22) 57-01-01; fax (22) 57-01-11; e-mail office@moldtelecom.md; internet www.moldtelecom.md; f. 1993; telephone communication and internet service provider; scheduled for partial privatization; Gen. Dir VLADIMIR DIDILICA.

Orange Moldova: 2071 Chişinău, str. Alba-Iulia 75; tel. (22) 57-50-10; e-mail orange@orange.md; internet www.orange.md; f. 1998 as Voxtel SA; present name adopted 2007; mobile cellular telecommunications; 56.7% owned by France Telecom Mobiles (France), 33.4% by MMT-BIS; Dir-Gen. LIUDMILA CLIMOC.

Sun Communications: 2001 Chişinău, bd. Ştefan cel Mare 134; tel. (22) 86-00-00; e-mail info@suntv.com; internet www.suncommunications.md; f. 1993; internet and fixed-line telecommunication services.

Unité: 2001 Chişinău, bd. Ştefan cel Mare 10; e-mail marketing@unite.md; internet www.unite.md; f. 2007; mobile cellular communications; 100% owned by Moldtelecom (q.v.).

Regulatory Authority

National Regulatory Agency in Electronic Communications and Information Technology (ANRCETI) (Agenţia Naţională pentru Reglementare în Comunicaţii Electronice şi Tehnologia Informatiei): 2012 Chişinău, bd. Ştefan cel Mare 134; tel. (22) 25-13-17; fax (22) 22-28-85; e-mail office@anrceti.md; internet www.anrceti.md; f. 2000; Dir SERGIU SITNIC.

BROADCASTING
Regulatory Authorities

National Radio Frequencies Centre (Centrul National pentru Frecvente Radio): 2021 Chişinău, str. Drumul Viilor 28/2; tel. (22) 73-53-64; fax (22) 73-39-41; e-mail cnfr@cnfr.md; internet www.cnfr.md; f. 1993; responsible for frequency allocations and monitoring, certification of post and communications equipment and services; Gen. Dir TEODOR CICLICCI.

Radio and Television Co-ordinating Council (Consiliul Coordonator al Audiovizualului): 2012 Chişinău, str. Vlaicu Parcalab 46; tel. (22) 27-75-51; fax (22) 27-74-71; e-mail office@cca.md; internet www.cca.md; f. 1995; state-owned; regulatory and licensing body; Pres. MARIAN POCAZNOI.

Radio

Radio Moldova: 2028 Chişinău, str. Mioriţa 1; tel. (22) 22-82-84; fax (22) 72-33-52; e-mail a.dorogan@yahoo.fr; internet www.trm.md;

f. 1930; subsidiary of Teleradio Moldova (q.v.); broadcasts in Romanian, Russian, Ukrainian, Gagauz and Yiddish; Dir-Gen. ALEXANDRU DOROGAN.

Radio Vocea Basarabiei (Radio Voice of Bessarabia): 2012 Chişinău, str. Puşkin 20A; tel. (22) 84-41-61; e-mail voceabasarabiei@yahoo.com; internet www.voceabasarabiei.net; f. 2000; Dir VEACESLAV TIBULEAC.

Television

Teleradio Moldova: 2028 Chişinău, str. Miorița 1; tel. (22) 22-82-84; fax (22) 72-33-52; e-mail trm@trm.md; internet www.trm.md; f. 1958; state-owned; Pres. CONSTANTIN MARIN; Exec. Dir (TV) ANGELA SIRBU.

Finance

(cap. = capital; res = reserves; dep. = deposits; m. = million; brs = branches; amounts in Moldovan lei)

BANKING

The National Bank of Moldova, established in 1991, is independent of the Government (but responsible to Parlamentul) and has the power to regulate monetary policy and the financial system. At February 2012 there were 14 authorized commercial banks in operation.

Central Bank

National Bank of Moldova (Banca Națională a Moldovei): 2005 Chişinău, bd. Grigore Vieru 1; tel. (22) 40-90-06; fax (22) 22-05-91; e-mail official@bnm.org; internet www.bnm.org; f. 1991; cap. 288.9m., res –957.7m., dep. 9,899.4m. (Dec. 2008); Gov. DORIN DRĂGUȚANU.

Commercial Banks

Banca de Economii: 2012 Chişinău, str. Columna 115; tel. (22) 21-80-05; fax (22) 21-80-06; e-mail bem@bem.md; internet www.bem.md; f. 1992; cap. 117.3m., res 18.8m., dep. 4,496.8m. (Dec. 2011); 56.1% owned by Ministry of Economy and Trade; Pres. CORINA BURLACU (acting); 37 brs.

Banca de Finanțe și Comerț (FinComBank SA—Finance and Trade Bank JSC): 2012 Chişinău, str. Puşkin 26; tel. (22) 26-99-00; fax (22) 23-73-08; e-mail fincom@fincombank.com; internet www.fincombank.com; f. 1993; cap. 131.5m., res 155.7m., dep. 1,050.1m. (June 2011); Chair. OLEG VORONIN; 13 brs.

Banca Socială: 2005 Chişinău, str. Bănulescu-Bodoni 61; tel. (22) 22-14-94; fax (22) 22-42-30; e-mail office@socbank.md; internet www.socbank.md; f. 1991; jt-stock commercial bank; cap. 100.0m., res 97.3m., dep. 2,170.3m. (Dec. 2011); Chair. VLADIMIR SUETNOV; Pres. VALENTIN CUNEV; 20 brs.

Energbank: 2012 Chişinău, str. Tighina 23/3; tel. (22) 54-43-87; fax (22) 85-80-80; e-mail office@energbank.com; internet www.energbank.com; f. 1997; cap. 100.0m., res 23.3m., dep. 1,151.0m. (Dec. 2011); Chair. IURII VASILACHI; 68 brs.

EuroCreditBank: 2001 Chişinău, str. Ismail 33; tel. (22) 50-02-00; fax (22) 54-88-27; e-mail telebank@eurocreditBank.md; internet www.telebank.md; f. 1992; jt-stock co; commercial investment bank; cap. 108.0m., res 26.5m., dep. 253.3m. (Dec. 2011); Pres. AURELIU CINCILEI; 3 brs.

Eximbank: 2004 Chişinău, bd. Ştefan cel Mare şi Sfânt 171/1; tel. (22) 11-02-30; fax (22) 60-16-11; e-mail info@eximbank.com; internet www.eximbank.com; f. 1994; cap. 635.0m., res 11.2m., dep. 1,927.7m. (Dec. 2011); Gen. Dir MARCEL CHIRCĂ.

Mobiasbanca: 2012 Chişinău, bd. Ştefan cel Mare şi Sfânt 81A; tel. (22) 25-64-56; fax (22) 54-19-74; e-mail contactell@mobiasbanca.md; internet www.mobiasbanca.md; f. 1990; 67.9% owned by Société Générale (France); acquired Bancoop in 2001; commercial bank; cap. 100.0m., res 162.0m., dep. 1,889.3m. (Dec. 2011); Pres. RIDHA TEKAIA; 11 brs.

Moldova Agroindbank: 2006 Chişinău, str. Cosmonauților 9; tel. (22) 85-65-65; fax (22) 22-80-58; e-mail aib@maib.md; internet www.maib.md; f. 1991; jt-stock commercial bank; cap. 207.5m., res 224.3m., dep. 5,853.8m. (Dec. 2011); Chair. of Bd VICTOR MICULEȚ; Chair. NATALIA VRABIE; 45 brs.

Unibank: 2012 Chişinău, str. Mitropolit G. Bănulescu-Bodoni 45; tel. (22) 25-38-01; fax (22) 22-05-30; e-mail welcome@unibank.md; internet www.unibank.md; f. 1993; jt-stock commercial bank; cap. 122.0m., res 18.7m., dep. 371.3m. (Dec. 2011); Pres. DUMITRU TUGULSCHI; 5 brs.

Victoriabank: 2004 Chişinău, str. 31 August 1989 141; tel. (22) 57-61-00; fax (22) 23-45-33; e-mail office@victoriabank.md; internet www.victoriabank.md; f. 1990; cap. 250.0m., res 52.9m., dep. 6,802.9m. (Dec. 2011); Pres. NATALIA POLITOV-CANGAS; 103 brs.

STOCK EXCHANGE

Moldovan Stock Exchange (Bursa de Valori a Moldovei SA): 2001 Chişinău, bd. Ştefan cel Mare 73; tel. (22) 27-75-94; fax (22) 27-73-56; e-mail postmaster@moldse.md; internet www.moldse.md; f. 1994; Chair. SERGIU CEBOTARI.

INSURANCE

In March 2010 there were 24 insurance companies operating in Moldova.

Acord Grup: 2038 Chişinău, str. Decebal 80/1; tel. (22) 26-44-44; fax (22) 53-88-33; e-mail office@acordgrup.md; f. 2002; Dir VICTOR GAICIUC.

Alianța Modocoop: 2001 Chişinău, bd. Ştefan cel Mare 67; tel. and fax (22) 27-21-63; f. 2001; life and non-life; Dir NICOLAE RODEANU.

Artas: 2009 Chişinău, str. Puşkin 4; tel. (22) 22-84-74; fax (22) 22-96-49; e-mail asigurari.artas@gmail.com; internet www.artas.md; f. 1993; non-life; Dir EUGENIA GOHBERG.

Asito: 2005 Chişinău, str. Bănulescu-Bodoni 57/1; tel. (22) 22-62-12; fax (22) 22-11-79; e-mail asito@asito.md; internet www.asito.md; f. 1991; 48.3% owned by Moldova Investment Group (United Kingdom); fmrly QBE Asito; Gen. Man. EUGEN ŞLOPAC.

Asterra Grup: 2005 Chişinău, O. Goga 26; tel. (22) 21-17-58; fax (22) 21-17-59; internet www.asterra.md; life and non-life; Dir ANATOLII BANTAŞ.

Donaris Group: 2012 Chişinău, str. 31 August 1989, 108/1; tel. (22) 26-57-10; fax (22) 27-83-94; e-mail d.gherasim@dg.md; internet www.donaris.md; life and non-life, insurance and reinsurance; Dir DINU GHERASIM.

Galas: 2012 Chişinău, str. Diordița 2; tel. (22) 21-34-50; fax (22) 22-39-54; e-mail galas@dnt.md; internet www.galas.md; Dir VERA VIERU.

Garantie: 2005 Chişinău, str. Puşkin 47/1; tel. (22) 27-00-50; fax (22) 27-00-55; e-mail office@garantie.md; internet www.garantie.md; f. 1993; life and non-life; Pres. ALEXEI TOPOROV.

Grawe Carat Asigurări: 2012 Chişinău, str. Alexandru cel Bun 51; tel. (22) 27-93-32; fax (22) 27-93-56; e-mail office@grawe.md; internet www.grawe.md; f. 1972; life and non-life; Dir PETER KASYK.

Klassika Asigurări: 2001 Chişinău, str. Tighina 12; tel. (22) 85-09-50; fax (22) 22-32-43; e-mail office@klassikaasig.md; internet www.klassikaasig.md; life and non-life; Dir NIKOLAI DIYAKONU.

Moldasig: 2009 Chişinău, str. M. Eminescu 2; tel. (22) 23-81-61; fax (22) 23-83-46; e-mail moldasig@dnt.md; internet www.moldasig.md; f. 2002; 51% owned by Banca de Economii SA, 25% owned by Calea Ferată din Moldova, 24% owned by Poşta Moldovei; Gen. Dir VITALI I. BODYA.

Moldcargo: 2012 Chişinău, str. V. Alecsandri 97; tel. (22) 24-55-67; fax (22) 27-92-93; e-mail office@moldcargo.md; internet www.moldcargo.md; f. 1999; life and non-life; Dir CRISTINA DOLGHI.

Sigur-Asigur: 2009 Chişinău, str. M. Kogălniceanu 73/2; tel. (22) 25-60-00; fax (22) 27-82-62; e-mail info@sigur-asigur.md; internet www.sigur-asigur.md; f. 2003; life and non-life; Dir SERGIU CERTAN.

Victoria Asigurări: 2005 Chişinău, str. Romană 8; tel. (22) 22-83-50; fax (22) 22-83-52; e-mail office@victoria-asiguari.md; internet www.victoria-asigurari.md; fmrly Orateh, name changed as above in Oct. 2006; life and non-life; Dir-Gen. OCTAVIAN LUNGU.

Regulatory Commission

National Commission for Financial Market (Comisia Națională a Pieței Financiare): 2012 Chişinău, str. Stefan cel Mare, 77; tel. (22) 85-94-01; fax (22) 85-95-04; e-mail cnpf@cnpf.md; internet www.cnpf.md; f. 2007; regulates non-banking financial market; Dep. Chair. VICTOR CAPTARI, ARTUR GHERMAN.

Trade and Industry

GOVERNMENT AGENCIES

Agency for Energy Efficiency (AEE) (Agenția pentru Eficiență Energetică): 2033 Chişinău, Piața Marii Adunări Naționale 1; tel. (22) 23-74-48; fax (22) 23-40-64; e-mail mihail.stratan@aee.md; f. 2010; forms part of the Ministry of the Economy (q.v.); Dir-Gen. MIHAIL STRATAN.

State Department for Privatization (Departamentul Privatizarii al Republicii Moldova): 2012 Chişinău, str. Puşkin 26; tel. and fax (22) 23-43-50; e-mail privatization@dnt.md; f. 1991; Dir-Gen. ALEKSANDR BANNICOV.

Moldovan Investment and Export Promotion Organization (MEPO) (Organizația de Atragere a Investițiilor și Promovare a Exportului din Moldova): 2009 Chişinău, str. Mateevici 65; tel. (22) 27-36-54; fax (22) 22-43-10; e-mail office@miepo.md; internet www

.miepo.md; f. 1999; assists enterprises in increasing exports and improving business environment; Exec. Dir DENIS JELIMALAI.

CHAMBER OF COMMERCE

Chamber of Commerce and Industry of the Republic of Moldova (Camera de Comerţ şi Industrie a Republicii Moldova): 2004 Chişinău, str. Ştefan cel Mare 151; tel. (22) 22-15-52; fax (22) 23-44-25; e-mail camera@chamber.md; internet www.chamber.md; f. 1991; brs in Bălţi, Cahul, Ceadir-Lunga (Gagauz-Yeri), Edineţ, Lapusna, Orhei, Soroca, Tighina (Bendery—Transnistria), Ungheni; 16 sub-brs; Pres. GHEORGHE CUCU.

UTILITIES

Regulatory Authority

National Agency for Energy Regulation (ANRE) (Agentia Nationala pentru Reglementare in Energetica): 2012 Chişinău, str. Columna 90; tel. (22) 54-13-84; fax (22) 85-29-00; e-mail anre@anre.md; internet www.anre.md; f. 1997; autonomous public institution; Gen. Dir VICTOR PARLICOV.

Electricity

The sector comprises one transmission company, five distribution companies and four power generation plants.

MoldElectrica IS: 2012 Chişinău, str. V. Alecsandri 78; tel. (22) 25-35-48; fax (22) 25-31-42; e-mail cancelar@moldelectrica.md; internet www.moldelectrica.md; f. 2000 to assume the transmission and distribution functions of Moldtranselectro; Dir GENNADII DIMOV.

Red Union Fenosa: 2024 Chişinău, str. A. Doga 4; tel. (24) 43-11-11; fax (22) 43-12-05; e-mail ot24@ufmoldova.com; internet www.ufmoldova.com; privatized in 2000; wholly owned by Unión Eléctrica Fenosa (Spain); distribution co supplying electricity to Chişinău; Pres. RADU SILVIA.

Gas

MoldovaGaz SA: 2005 Chişinău, str. Albişoara 38; tel. (22) 57-80-02; fax (22) 22-00-02; e-mail office@moldovagaz.md; internet www.moldovagaz.md; f. 1999; national gas pipeline and distribution networks; comprises two transmission companies and 18 distribution companies; 50% owned by Gazprom (Russia) (q.v.), 35% owned by Govt of Moldova, and 13% owned by Property Committee of Transnistria; Pres. ALEKSANDR GUSEV.

TRADE UNIONS

National Trade Union Confederation of Moldova (Confederaţia Naţională a Sindicatelor din Moldova): 2012 Chişinău, str. 31 August 129; tel. (22) 26-65-02; fax (22) 23-45-08; e-mail office@cnsm.md; internet www.cnsm.md; f. 2007 by merger of Confederation of Trade Unions of Moldova and the Moldovan Confederation of Free Trade Unions Solidarity; Pres. OLEG BUDZA; 500,000 union mems.

Transport

RAILWAYS

In 2010 the total length of railway lines in use was around 1,156 km. Railways connect Chişinău with Odesa (Ukraine) and the Romanian cities of Iaşi and Galaţi.

Calea Ferată din Moldova: 2012 Chişinău, str. Vlaicu Pîrcălab 48; tel. (22) 25-44-08; fax (22) 22-13-80; e-mail secr@railway.md; internet www.railway.md; f. 1992; total network 1,075 km; Dir-Gen. VITALIE STRUNA.

ROADS

In 2010 Moldova's network of roads totalled 12,835 km (86.2% of which was hard-surfaced), including 3,336 km of main roads.

INLAND WATERWAYS

In 2005 the total length of navigable waterways in Moldova was 424 km. The main river ports are located within the separatist territory of Transnistria, at Tighina (Bender) and at Rābniţa.

CIVIL AVIATION

Moldova has four civilian airports, in Chişinău, Tiraspol, Bălţi and Mărculeşti.

Civil Aviation Administration (Administraţia de stat a Aviaţiei Civile): 2026 Chişinău, Aeroportul Chişinău; tel. (22) 52-40-64; fax (22) 52-91-18; e-mail dgasac@caa.md; internet www.caa.md; f. 1993; Dir-Gen. IURIE ZIDU (acting).

Air Moldova (Compania Aeriana Moldova): 2026 Chişinău, bd. Dacia 80/2, Aeroportul Chişinău; tel. (22) 52-55-02; fax (22) 52-60-09; e-mail info@airmoldova.md; internet www.airmoldova.md; f. 1993; wholly state-owned; scheduled and charter passenger and cargo flights to destinations in Europe and the CIS; Gen. Dir IULIAN SCORPAN.

Moldavian Airlines: 2026 Chişinău, Aeroportul Chişinău; tel. (22) 52-93-56; fax (22) 52-50-64; e-mail secretary@mdv.md; internet www.mdv.md; f. 1994; scheduled flights to Budapest (Hungary), İstanbul (Turkey) and Timisoara (Romania); also charter passenger and cargo flights; Pres. and Chief Exec. NICOLAE PETROV.

Tourism

There were 10,788 tourist arrivals, including excursionists, in 2011, when receipts from tourism (including passenger transport) totalled US $194m, according to provisional figures.

Department of Tourism Development: 2004 Chişinău, bd. Ştefan cel Mare şi Sfânt 180, bir. 901; tel. (22) 21-07-74; fax (22) 23-26-26; e-mail dept@turism.md; internet www.turism.md.

Defence

Following independence from the USSR, Moldova initiated the creation of national armed forces. As assessed at November 2012, these numbered 5,350, with an army of 3,250, an air force of 800 and a logistic support force of 1,300. In addition, there were 58,000 reserves. Paramilitary forces attached to the Ministry of Internal Affairs number 2,400, including 900 riot police. The term of conscription is 12 months.

Under an agreement concluded in late 1994, the former Soviet 14th Army (under Russian jurisdiction) was to have been withdrawn from Transnistria within three years, but in March 1998 it was announced that Russian forces would remain in Transnistria until a political settlement for the region was reached. Despite subsequent agreements providing for a withdrawal, some 1,500 Russian troops (including 355 peace-keeping troops) remained in Transnistria at November 2012. There were also 12 Organization for Security and Co-operation in Europe troops and 10 Ukrainian military observers in Moldova at that time.

In early 1994 Moldova joined the North Atlantic Treaty Organization's 'Partnership for Peace' programme, although the country's Constitution guarantees a neutral status.

Defence Expenditure: Budgeted at 221m. lei in 2013.

Chief of General Staff and Commander of the National Army: VITALIE STOIAN.

Education

Primary education begins at seven years of age and lasts for four years. Secondary education lasts for a maximum of seven years, comprising a first cycle of five years and a second of two years. In 2009/10 enrolment at primary schools included 88% of children in the relevant age-group, while the comparable figure for secondary schools was 79%. In 2007/08 some 79.8% of those enrolled in primary and secondary schools were taught in Moldovan and 20.0% in Russian. In 2011/12 some 381,418 students were enrolled at Moldova's 1,460 primary and secondary schools, while 135,398 students were enrolled at the 82 higher education institutions. In 2011 general government expenditure on education amounted to 6,869m. lei, according to preliminary figures (equivalent to 21.4% of total general spending).

MOLDOVAN SECESSIONIST TERRITORY

The self-styled 'Transnistrian Moldovan Republic' (formerly 'Transnistrian Moldovan Soviet Socialist Republic')—Transnistria or Pridnestrovie—inhabited by principally ethnic Russians, Ukrainians and Moldovans, was proclaimed in September 1990. After the dissolution of the USSR at the end of 1991, a military conflict with the authorities of the newly independent Republic of Moldova, in which the Transnistrian authorities enjoyed the de facto support of elements of the Russian military based in the territory, ensued. Although a peace agreement was reached in July 1992, the status of Transnistria remained unresolved, and the territory remained beyond the control of the Moldovan authorities. While the separatist authorities have enjoyed de facto support from Russia, the self-proclaimed 'Republic' is not formally recognized by any state.

TRANSNISTRIA

Introductory Survey

LOCATION, CLIMATE, LANGUAGE, RELIGION, FLAG, CAPITAL

Transnistria comprises the eastern region of Moldova, including all territories on the east ('left') bank of the Nistru (Dniester) river, and also certain districts of the city of Tighina (Bender) on the west bank. The eastern boundary of the territory is with Ukraine. The territory has hot summers and cold winters, with moderate rainfall. The average summer temperature is 21°C (70°F) and the winter average is −3°C (27°F), and precipitation averages 495mm (19 ins) per year. The separatist authorities use a flag (proportions 1 by 2) with horizontal stripes of red, green, and red, with, on the obverse side only, a gold hammer and sickle in the canton, surmounted by the gold outline of a five-pointed red star. The principal city and capital of the self-proclaimed 'Republic' is Tiraspol.

CONTEMPORARY POLITICAL HISTORY

In October 1924 the USSR, which refused to recognize Romania's claims to the territory of Bessarabia (constituting most of the present day Republic of Moldova, and which had formed part of the Russian Empire until 1917), established a Moldavian (Moldovan) Autonomous Soviet Socialist Republic (ASSR) to the east of the Dniester, within and subordinated to the Ukrainian Soviet Socialist Republic (SSR). The town of Balta (now in Ukraine) was the first capital of this ASSR, but in 1929 the administrative centre of the territory become Tiraspol. At this time the area was subject to agricultural collectivization and industrialization. Following Soviet territorial gains early in the Second World War the Moldavian ASSR was abolished and its western territories amalgamated with formerly Romanian-controlled lands in Bessarabia and Bukovina to form the Moldovan SSR—a Union Republic in its own right—in 1940, while eastern territories remained part of the Ukrainian SSR. Although the entire territory came under wartime Romanian control in July 1941, when, with neighbouring territories in Ukraine, it formed part of a Governorate of Transnistria, after its recapture by the USSR in August 1944 the Moldovan SSR was re-established. Subsequently, Russian and Ukrainian immigration was encouraged, and the territories of Transnistria became the industrial heartland of the Moldovan SSR.

As the reformist policies favoured by Soviet leader Mikhail Gorbachev took effect in the late 1980s, Romanian nationalism—including calls for reunification with Romania—became increasingly popular in Moldova, despite opposition from the Slavic population. This opposition was a prominent factor behind the proclamation, in August 1990, of Transnistria's secession from Moldova, as the 'Transnistrian Moldovan Soviet Socialist Republic'. The separatists were dominated by conservative communist elements largely opposed to the dissolution of the USSR.

Armed conflict broke out in December 1991, as the Transnistrian leadership, opposed to the Moldovan Government's objective of reunification with Romania, launched a campaign to gain control of all the territories on the east bank of the Dniester, with the ultimate aim of unity with Russia. Over six months of military conflict with Moldovan troops ensued. The situation was complicated by the presence (and involvement in support of the east-bank Slavs) of the former Soviet 14th Army, which was still stationed in the region and jurisdiction over which had been transferred to Russia. By June 1992 some 700 people were believed to have been killed in the conflict. On 21 July, however, a peace agreement was finally negotiated by President Mircea Snegur of Moldova and his Russian counterpart, Boris Yeltsin, whereby Transnistria was to be accorded 'special status' within Moldova, the terms of which were to be formulated later. Later in July Russian, Moldovan and Transnis-trian peace-keeping troops were deployed in the region to monitor the cease-fire.

Transnistria continued to demand full statehood, and in January 1994 the Moldovan Government accepted proposals by the Conference on Security and Co-operation in Europe (CSCE—later OSCE) for greater autonomy for Transnistria. In April Snegur and the Transnistrian leader, Igor Smirnov, pledged their commitment to a peaceful resolution of the conflict. In July, following the adoption of the new Moldovan Constitution, which provided for a 'special autonomous status' for Transnistria, negotiations commenced on the details of the region's future status. Progress was obstructed by disagreement over the future of the 15,000-strong 14th Army, the continued presence of which the Transnistrian leadership demanded as a guarantor of security. In October Moldova and Russia reached an agreement on the gradual withdrawal of the 14th Army, whereupon Transnistria's 'special autonomous status' would take effect. A referendum (declared illegal by President Snegur) was held in Transnistria in March 1995, in which 91% of participants voted against the withdrawal of the 14th Army. In December two further referendums were held in Transnistria: 82.7% of the electorate endorsed a new constitution that proclaimed the region's independence, while 89.7% voted for Transnistria to join the Commonwealth of Independent States (CIS, see p. 251) as a sovereign state. In February 1996, however, the CIS rejected admittance for Transnistria.

Smirnov was re-elected as President of Transnistria in December 1996. In May 1997 Smirnov and the new Moldovan President, Petru Lucinschi, meeting in the Russian capital, Moscow, signed the memorandum, with Russia and Ukraine acting as guarantors. In March 1998 a further agreement (the Odesa Accords) was signed by Lucinschi, Smirnov, Russian premier Viktor Chernomyrdin and President Leonid Kuchma of Ukraine, which envisaged that Russian troops would remain in Transnistria until a final political settlement was reached, while Moldova's peace-keeping troops were to be gradually reduced in number. In late May 1999 Transnistria was formally designated an autonomous entity.

In June 2000 the 'Transnistrian Supreme Council (Soviet)' was converted to a unicameral legislature, and in July Smirnov introduced a form of presidential rule. Moldova's relations with the Transnistrian authorities deteriorated in September, following the Moldovan Government's introduction of new customs procedures, in accordance with the requirements of the World Trade Organization (WTO, see p. 444), leading to Transnistria alleging that Moldova was attempting to impose an 'economic blockade' on the region. Smirnov was re-elected to a second presidential term in December in a poll that was recognized by neither Moldova nor the international community.

In July 2002 mediators from Russia, Ukraine and the OSCE submitted a new draft agreement (the 'Kyiv agreement') according to which Moldova would become a federal state, in which the autonomous territories would maintain their own legislatures and constitutions. In February 2003 the European Union (EU) and the USA imposed a travel ban on those Transnistrian officials considered to be 'primarily responsible for a lack of co-operation in promoting a political settlement'. In November Russian President Vladimir Putin announced new proposals for a settlement. Drafted by the deputy head of the Russian presidential administration, Dmitrii Kozak, the plan envisaged the establishment of an 'asymmetrical federation'. The leaders of both Transnistria and Moldova initially responded positively to the proposals, but the Moldovan President, Vladimir Voronin, withdrew his support later in the month. In mid-2004 controversy arose over the closure by the Transnistrian authorities of Moldovan-language schools teaching a Moldovan syllabus, in the Latin script. The Moldovan Government responded by withdrawing from the OSCE-mediated negotiation process and imposing economic sanctions on Transnistria, which retaliated in kind. The EU and the

USA condemned the closure of the schools and added a further 10 Transnistrian officials to the list of those prohibited from travelling to their countries. (Several schools in the territory subsequently submitted appeals to the European Court of Human Rights.)

In December 2004, at an OSCE meeting held in Sofia, Bulgaria, the Russian delegation obstructed the adoption of a final statement containing a reference to the Russian commitment to withdraw troops and ammunition from Moldova. In April 2005 President Viktor Yushchenko of Ukraine, during a summit meeting in Chișinău, presented a plan for the resolution of the Transnistrian conflict, which envisaged that Transnistria would be awarded special status within Moldova, and would, moreover, be permitted to participate in foreign-policy decisions that were determined to affect its interests. In June Parlamentul endorsed the Yushchenko Plan, while noting that it made no mention of either the withdrawal of Russian troops or the establishment of border controls along the Transnistrian–Ukrainian border. In July Moldova removed the trade sanctions imposed against Transnistria in the previous year. In September all five parties to the negotiations on the status of Transnistria agreed to invite the EU and the USA to participate in the process as observers; however, subsequent meetings failed to record any substantive progress. Legislative elections (recognized by neither Moldova nor the international community) were held in Transnistria in December, at which the reformist Renewal bloc won the most seats in the region's Supreme Council.

At the end of November 2005 the EU launched a mission to assist in securing the Transnistrian–Ukrainian border. In March 2006, following an agreement reached with Moldova, Ukraine refused to recognize Transnistria's customs regime and agreed henceforth to deal only in goods processed through the Moldovan customs system. In response, the Transnistrian authorities withdrew from the internationally mediated negotiations and introduced legislation banning all foreign-financed non-governmental organizations.

On 17 September 2006 the Transnistrian authorities conducted an internationally unrecognized referendum on the territory's future status, at which some 97% voted for a continuation of de facto independence from Moldova and an objective of eventual unification with Russia, while some 95% voted against the territory being ruled as part of Moldova. On 10 December Smirnov won a presidential election in Transnistria (again unrecognized by the international community), with 82.4% of votes cast. Shortly after the unilateral declaration of independence by Kosovo (hitherto a UN-administered province within Serbia) in February 2008, Transnistria formally requested that the Russian legislature, the UN and other organizations recognize its independence, although in the event no party did so. In April Smirnov and Moldovan President Vladimir Voronin met for the first time since 2001, in Tighina (Bender), Transnistria

On 18 March 2009 a meeting between Voronin and Smirnov was convened in Moscow, under the aegis of Russian President Dmitrii Medvedev. The three leaders signed a declaration providing for the conversion of the existing peace-keeping force in Transnistria into an OSCE-supervised operation, and reiterated commitments to return to the '5 + 2' negotiating format (comprising Moldova, Transnistria, Russia, Ukraine and the OSCE, together with the USA and the EU). However, Voronin subsequently accused the Transnistrian authorities of failing to respect their obligations to continue dialogue and abandoned a planned meeting with Smirnov in Tiraspol later in March. On 8 July Yevgenii Shevchuk announced his resignation as President of the Transnistrian Supreme Council, citing 'deep disagreements' with Smirnov. The deputy leader of the Renewal parliamentary faction, Anatolii Kaminskii, was elected to the post unopposed later in the month. Internationally unrecognized legislative elections took place in Transnistria on 12 December; it was reported that the Renewal bloc had won 25 of the 43 seats in the Supreme Council, with about 42% of the electorate participating. Following the installation of a new reformist Government in Transnistria in January 2011, an OSCE initiative for the resumption of negotiations on the status of the territory began. In September Filat and Smirnov met, under OSCE auspices, in Bad Reichenhall, Germany, and again in Moscow. At the end of November negotiations under the '5+2' format formally resumed in the Lithuanian capital, Vilnius, with the mediation of Lithuania (which at that time chaired the OSCE).

Recent developments: Yevgenii Shevchuk elected as President

Prior to the election to the Transnistrian presidency due to be held in late 2011, Smirnov was subject to significant pressure from the Russian authorities to withdraw his candidacy, rather than seeking a fifth term of office. Notably, in late October it was announced that criminal proceedings had commenced in Russia against Smirnov's son, Oleg, who was accused of the embezzlement of humanitarian aid funds that Russia had supplied to Transnistria. Smirnov was, nevertheless, among six candidates to contest the first round of the election on 11 December, but he was only placed third, with 24.7% of the votes cast, behind Shevchuk, who, contesting the election as an

independent candidate, secured 38.6% of votes cast, and Kaminskii, with 26.3%. At the run-off poll between the two leading candidates held on 25 December, Shevchuk was overwhelmingly elected President, securing 73.9% of votes cast; Kaminskii received 19.7%, while 4.5% of the votes were against all candidates. Voter turnout was reported to be 58.9% in the first round, and 52.5% in the run-off. While Kaminskii had been the Russian administration's preferred candidate, Shevchuk was widely regarded as a Russian-orientated reformist.

On 10 January 2012 Shevchuk appointed Petr Stepanov, the General Director of the Transnistrian state controlled gas-import firm, Tiraspoltransgaz-Pridestroviye, and the hitherto Minister of Industry, as Chairman of the Government; a substantially reorganized administration, comprising mostly new ministers, was formed later in the month. Also in January a young Moldovan was shot dead by a Russian officer at a checkpoint on Transnistria's de facto border with Moldova, causing the Moldovan Government to renew demands for the Russian military mission to be reconstituted on a civilian basis. Following Shevchuk's election, official negotiations under the '5+2' format were convened in Dublin, Ireland, in February; however, these ended without conclusion, after the Russian and Moldovan delegations presented further procedural demands. On 21 March President Medvedev appointed a Deputy Chairman of the Russian Government (and prominent Russian nationalist), Dmitrii Rogozin, to the new post of his Special Representative to Transnistria. (Similar positions were created for the two Georgian secessionist territories of Abkhazia and South Ossetia, both of which, unlike Transnistria, Russia formally recognized as independent states.) At the end of March Shevchuk and Filat, meeting in Tiraspol, signed a protocol for the resumption of full train services across Transnistria. In the same month the Supreme Council of Transnistria signed protocols of co-operation with the legislature of Gagauz-Yeri (similar agreements had earlier been signed with the separatist parliaments of Abkhazia and South Ossetia). Further negotiations under the '5+2' format, convened in Vienna, Austria, in April and July, again resulted in little progress, apparently after the Russian government representative objected to new draft provisions establishing equal status for all the '5+2' participants.

In April 2012 it was reported that the Russian Minister of Defence had conducted an inspection of Russian troops in Transnistria, prompting an official protest from the Moldovan authorities. Shortly afterwards, during his first visit to Chișinău and Tiraspol in his new capacity, Rogozin announced, *inter alia*, the intention of the Russian Government to rearm and re-equip its troops in Transnistria as part of the modernization of its army. An official statement issued upon the 20th anniversary of the deployment of Russian troops in Transnistria in July indicated that Russia planned to maintain its military presence in the territory indefinitely until the agreement of a permanent settlement (despite Moldova's demands that it be replaced with an international civilian mission); it was also implied that the only resolution acceptable to Russia would be based on the 'federalization' of Moldova. During a press interview at the end of that month, Russian President Vladimir Putin declared his support for Transnistria's self-determination. On 2 August Shevchuk visited Moscow to meet Rogozin; Russia's state flag and Transnistria's flag (depicting the Soviet symbols) were displayed together at a public appearance of the two officials, implying that Russia regarded Transnistria as constituting a state, despite having refused to formally grant formal recognition of the territory's statehood.

In September 2012 the EU ended its travel restrictions on former Transnistrian government officials, in recognition of progress in negotiations to resolve the conflict (following the resumption of the '5+2' discussions), but stipulated that further developments, including with respect to the rights of Latin-script Moldovan-language schools to operate in the territory, would be closely monitored. Nevertheless, any advance in negotiations was hampered by tensions surrounding Russia's strenuous objections to Moldova's admission to US and EU defence agreements in late 2012. Following proposed EU cross-border initiatives for economic co-operation, in early November the Russian Government offered 3,000m. roubles to fund the establishment of a 'Eurasian economic region' in Transnistria and to strengthen Russia's military presence in the region. Later that month the new Moldovan President, Nicolae Timofti, strongly rejected a proposal by the Russian Government to establish a representative office in Transnistria of the Russian consulate in Chișinău. Discussions under the '5+2' format were convened in Lviv, Ukraine, in February 2013, after which the OSCE announced that negotiation efforts were to continue in Odesa in May. However, a political crisis in Moldova following the collapse of the pro-EU coalition Government in March presented a further obstacle to the peace process. Tensions between the Moldovan and Transnistrian authorities intensified in April, as a consequence of a number of disputes in and around Tighina, the only area on the west bank of the Nistru controlled by the separatist authorities. The town's authorities announced that, henceforth, any Moldovan police officers in the town (which was jointly patrolled by Moldovan and Transnistrian police, in accordance with a 1992 agreement) would not be permitted to wear uniform. In response, the Moldovan authorities announced that they were to establish new checkpoints in the security zone that separates the areas controlled by Transnistria from the territories controlled by the Moldovan Government. Subsequently, the Transnistrian authorities began constructing checkpoints around the village of Varniţa, near Tighina, which remained under Moldovan control. In late April fighting broke out between residents of the village and Transnistrian special forces, after the residents dismantled the checkpoints. Meanwhile, the Transnistrian authorities claimed that the presence of heavily armed guards at two Moldovan prisons in Tighina constituted the creation of a military base in the city, and demanded the withdrawal of the armed personnel from the prisons.

PUBLIC HOLIDAYS

2014: 1–2 January (New Year), 7 January (Christmas—Julian Calendar), 23 February (Defenders of the Fatherland Day), 8 March (International Women's Day), 1–2 May (Days of Solidarity with Workers), 9 May (Republic Day), 2 September (Liberation Day), 7 November (Great October Socialist Revolution), 24 December (Constitution Day), 25 December (Christmas—Gregorian Calendar).

Directory

The Government of the 'Transnistrian Moldovan Republic'

President: YEVGENII SHEVCHUK.

CABINET OF MINISTERS
(May 2013)

Chairman: PETR P. STEPANOV.

Deputy Chairman, responsible for Social Policy: NATALIYA G. NIKIFOROVA.

Deputy Chairman, responsible for Economic Development and Finance, Minister of Economic Development: MAIYA I. PARNAS.

Deputy Chairman, responsible for International Co-operation, Minister of Foreign Affairs: NINA V. SHTANSKI.

Deputy Chairman: ALEKSANDR V. SVIDERSKII.

Minister of Internal Affairs: SERGEI N. MONUL.

Minister of Defence: Maj.-Gen. ALEKSANDR A. LUKYANENKO.

Minister of Justice: OLGA S. DUBROVINA.

Minister of Finance: YELENA G. GIRZHUL.

Minister of Agriculture and Natural Resources: NIKOLAI I. NEDELKOV.

Minister of Social Protection and Labour: OKSANA V. BULANOVA (acting).

Minister of Health: VASILII F. GUMENNYI.

Minister of Education: SVETLANA I. FADEYEVA.

Note: the Chairmen of the State Administrations of the seven primary territorial subdivisions are also members of the Government.

MINISTRIES

Office of the President: 3300 Tiraspol, ul. Gorkogo 53; tel. (533) 6-27-20; fax (533) 8-05-02; e-mail psp.pmr@mail.ru; internet president .gospmr.ru.

Office of the Chairman of the Government: 3300 Tiraspol, ul. 25 Oktyabrya 45; tel. (533) 6-24-55; e-mail people@gov-pmr.org; internet gov-pmr.org.

Ministry of Agriculture and Natural Resources: 3300 Tiraspol, ul. Yunosti 58/3; tel. (533) 2-67-45; fax (533) 2-78-96; e-mail ecopmr@mail.ru; internet ecology-pmr.org.

Ministry of Defence: 3300 Tiraspol, per. K. Tsetkin 6A; tel. (533) 9-70-78; internet www.mopmr.idknet.com.

Ministry of Economic Development: 3300 Tiraspol, ul. Sverdlova 57; tel. (533) 9-63-66; fax (533) 9-74-10; e-mail economy.pmr@gmail .com; internet www.mepmr.org.

Ministry of Education: 3300 Tiraspol, ul. Mira 27; tel. (533) 2-22-29; fax (533) 2-34-97; e-mail prosveshenie@minpros.info; internet www.minpros.info.

Ministry of Finance: 3300 Tiraspol, ul. Karla Marksa 187; tel. and fax (533) 7-86-03; e-mail info@minfin-pmr.org; internet www .minfin-pmr.org.

Ministry of Foreign Affairs: 3300 Tiraspol, ul. Sverdlova 45; tel. and fax (533) 7-43-46; e-mail office@mfa-pmr.org; internet www .mfa-pmr.org.

Ministry of Health: 3300 Tiraspol, per. Dnestrovskii 3; tel. (533) 8-05-25; internet www.minzdravpmr.org.

Ministry of Internal Affairs: 3300 Tiraspol, ul. Manoilova 68; tel. (533) 8-15-29; e-mail shtab-mvd-pmr@rambler.ru; internet www .mvdpmr.org.

Ministry of Justice: 3300 Tiraspol, ul. Lenina 26; tel. (533) 8-18-18; fax (533) 8-17-53; e-mail inbox@justice.idknet.com; internet justice .idknet.com.

Ministry of Social Protection and Labour: 3300 Tiraspol, ul. 25 Oktyabrya 114; tel. (533) 8-18-44; internet www.minsoctrud.org.

President

Presidential Election, First Round, 11 December 2011

Candidates	Votes	% of votes
Yevgenii Shevchuk (Independent) . .	95,765	38.55
Anatolii Kaminskii (Renewal Republican Party)	65,330	26.30
Igor Smirnov (Independent)	61,248	24.66
Oleg Khorzhan (Transnistrian Communist Party)	12,646	5.09
Dmitrii Soin (Breakthrough People's Democratic Party)	1,441	0.58
Andrei Safanov (Independent)	1,303	0.52
Against all candidates	4,667	1.88
Total*	248,386	100.00

* Including 5,986 invalid votes (2.41% of total votes).

Second Round, 25 December 2011

Candidates	Votes	% of votes
Yevgenii Shevchuk (Independent) . . .	165,502	73.88
Anatolii Kaminskii (Renewal Republican Party)	44,071	19.67
Against all candidates	9,977	4.45
Total*	224,010	100.00

* Including 4,460 invalid votes (1.99% of total votes).

Legislature

Elections were held to the 43-member Supreme Council on 12 December 2010. It was reported that the Renewal bloc had won 25 of the 43 seats in the Supreme Council, and that the majority of the remaining deputies had no formal party allegiance.

Supreme Council
3300 Tiraspol, ul. 25 Oktyabrya 45; tel. (533) 9-44-49; e-mail kav@vspmr.org; internet vspmr.org.

Chairman: ANATOLII V. KAMINSKII.

Election Commission

Central Electoral Commission: 3300 Tiraspol, ul. Shevchenko 12; tel. (533) 72022; fax (533) 73136; e-mail izbircom@cikpmr.idknet .com; internet www.cikpmr.idknet.com; Chair. PETR G. DENISENKO.

Political Organizations

The following are among the principal political parties operating in the 'Transnistrian Moldovan Republic'.

Breakthrough People's Democratic Party (Proryv) (Narodno-demokratiheskaya partiya 'Proryv'): 2069 Tiraspol, per. Naberezhnyi 1A; tel. (533) 5-66-78; e-mail psproriv@gmail.com; internet www .proriv.wordpress.com; f. 2006; Chair. ALEKSANDR GORELOVSKII.

Liberal Democratic Party of the Transnistrian Republic (LDPR-P) (Liberalno-demokraticheskaya partiya Respubliki Pridnestrovye): Tiraspol, ul. 25 Oktyabrya 37A; tel. and fax (533) 95-370; e-mail ldprpr@gmail.com; internet ldprpmr.com; f. 2006; affiliated to the Russian nationalist Liberal Democratic Party of Russia; Leader ROMAN KHUDYAKOV.

Renewal Republican Party (Obnovleniye) (Respublikanskaya partiya 'Obnovleniye'): 3300 Tiraspol, ul. 25 Oktyabrya 118; tel. (533) 4-57-44; internet www.obnovlenie.info; f. 2000; allied with the de facto ruling party of Russia, United Russia; Chair. ANATOLIY V. KAMINSKI.

Transnistrian Communist Party (Pridnestrovskaya Kommunis-ticheskaya Partiya): 2069 Tiraspol, bulv. Gagarina 1 B; tel. and fax (533) 9-77-76; internet www.pkp.ucoz.ru; f. 1991 as successor to the local branch of the Communist Party of the Soviet Union; allied with the Communist Party of Ukraine and the Communist Party of the Russian Federation; Chair. OLEG O. KHORZHAN.

The Press

In January 2012 some 14 principal newspapers were published in Transnistria, and three news agencies were operating.

PRINCIPAL NEWSPAPERS AND PERIODICALS

Chelovek i ego prava (Man and his Rights): Tiraspol; f. 2003; in Russian; published by the Foundation for the Defence of Human Rights and Effective Politics; human rights, social and political; 48 a year; Editor-in-Chief NICOLAE BUCEACCHI.

Dnestrovskaya Pravda/Adevărul Nistrean (Dniestr/Nistru Truth): 3300 Tiraspol, str. 25 Octombrie 101/236–237; tel. (533) 3-46-86; fax (233) 3-46-86; e-mail tiraspol@dn_prav.mldnet.com; internet www.tiraspol.tripod.com; f. 1941; Russian and Moldovan (Cyrillic script) editions; funded by the authorities of the 'Transnistrian Moldovan Republic'; daily; Editors TATYANA RUDENKO (Russian edn), VLADIMIR COVALI (Moldovan edn).

Dobrâi Deni (Good Afternoon): Rîbniţa; independent; pro-opposition; in Romanian.

Gomin (The Echo): Rîbniţa, str. Kirov, 130; tel. (555) 3-08-61; fax (555) 4-26-27; e-mail gomin130@mail.ru; f. 1996; weekly; in Ukrainian; Chief Editor DMITRII CERNEGA; circ. 2,460 (2008).

Novaya Gazeta (New Gazette): Bendery; f. 2000; in Russian; Editor ANDREI SAFONOV.

Obnovleniye (Renewal): 3300 Tiraspol, str. 25 Octombrie 118; tel. (533) 9–04-19; fax (533) 5-00-10; e-mail obnovlenie@idknet.com; internet www.obnovlenie.info; f. 2000; monthly; in Russian; politics and economics; circ. 80,000 (2008); Chair. ANATOLII V. KAMINSKII.

Partner (Partner): 3300 Tiraspol, ul. Lenina 48; tel. (533) 9-64-80; e-mail makireeva@yandex.ru; internet www.tiraspol.ru/partner; f. 2004; monthly; in Russian; publ. by the Chamber of Trade and Industry of the 'Transnistrian Moldovan Republic'; Chief Editor MARINA KIREYEVA; circ. 999 (2008).

Pridnestrovye (Transnistria): 3300 Tiraspol, str. Lunacearski 13; tel. (533) 9-30-24; fax (533) 7-47-00; e-mail pridnestr@idknet.com; internet www.pridnestrovie-daily.net; f. 1994; owned by the author-ities of the 'Transnistrian Moldovan Republic'; in Russian; politics, economics, culture; 5 a week; Editor-in-Chief NATALIYA VOROBIYEVA; circ. 4,241 (2008).

NEWS AGENCIES

Dniester: Tiraspol; e-mail dniester.post@gmail.com; internet www .dniester.ru; f. 2009; Russian; online only; Man. ROMAN KONOPLEV.

Lenta PMR (Newswire of the 'Transnistrian Moldovan Republic'): Tiraspol; tel. (533) 8-44-46; e-mail tiras.ru@gmail.com; internet www .tiras.ru; Russian; Editor-in-Chief ROMAN KONOPLEV.

Olvia-Press: 3300 Tiraspol, ul. Rozy Lyuksemburga 10; tel. (533) 8-24-97; fax (533) 8-20-04; e-mail olvia@idknet.com; internet www .olvia.idknet.com; f. 1992; Russian; owned by the authorities of the 'Transnistrian Moldovan Republic'; reports political, economic and cultural devts in the region; Editor-in-Chief OLEG A. YELKOV.

PRESS ASSOCIATION

Media Center Transnistria: 3300 Tiraspol, ul. Kuchurganskaya 38; tel. (777) 5-84-81; e-mail smi.pridnestrovie@gmail.com; f. 2009; fmrly the Creative Union of Young Journalists of Transnistria; promoting the independence of mass media and the development of civil society.

Finance

BANKING

Central Bank

Republican Bank of Transnistria (PRB) (Pridnestrovskii Respu-blikanskii Bank): 3300 Tiraspol, ul. 25 Oktyabya 71; tel. (533) 5-98-70; fax (533) 5-99-07; e-mail info@cbpmr.net; internet www.cbpmr .net; f. 1992; Chair. EDUARD A. KOSOVSKII.

Trade and Industry

CHAMBER OF COMMERCE

Chamber of Commerce and Industry of the 'Transnistrian Moldovan Republic' (Pridnestrovie) (TPP PMR): 3300 Tiraspol, ul. Lenina 48; tel. (533) 9-54-36; fax (533) 9-42-03; e-mail tpp@ tiraspol.ru; internet www.tiraspol.ru; f. 1996; non-commercial partnership; brs in Tighina (Bender), Râbniţa and Dubăsari; Pres. VASILY KOZHAN.

MONACO

Introductory Survey

LOCATION, CLIMATE, LANGUAGE, RELIGION, FLAG

The Principality of Monaco lies in Western Europe. The country is a small enclave in south-eastern France, about 15 km east of Nice. It has a coastline on the Mediterranean Sea but is otherwise surrounded by French territory. The climate is Mediterranean, with warm summers and very mild winters. The official language is French, but Monégasque (a mixture of the French Provençal and Italian Ligurian dialects), Italian and English are also spoken. Most of the population profess Christianity, with about 91% belonging to the Roman Catholic Church. The national flag (proportions 4 by 5) has two equal horizontal stripes, of red and white. The state flag (proportions 4 by 5) displays the princely arms of Monaco (a white shield, held by two monks and superimposed on a pavilion of ermine) on a white background.

CONTEMPORARY POLITICAL HISTORY

Historical Context

The Principality of Monaco is a hereditary monarchy, which has been ruled by the Grimaldi dynasty since 1297. It was abolished during the French Revolution but re-established in 1814. In 1861 Monaco became an independent state under the protection of France. The first Constitution, promulgated in January 1911, vested legislative power jointly in the Prince and a 12-member Conseil national (National Council), selected for a term of five years by a panel comprising nine delegates of the municipality and 21 members elected by universal suffrage. Agreements in 1918 and 1919 between France and Monaco provided that, should the reigning prince die without leaving a male heir, Monaco would become an autonomous state under French sovereignty. Prince Louis II, the ruler of Monaco from 1922, died in May 1949, and was succeeded by his grandson, Prince Rainier III. A new Constitution, introduced in December 1962, abolished the principle of the divine right of the monarch, gave women the franchise and stipulated that the Conseil national (enlarged to 18 members) was to be elected solely by universal adult suffrage. Executive power was to be exercised, under the authority of the Prince, by the Council of Government, led by a Minister of State appointed by the Prince.

Domestic Political Affairs

Supporters of Prince Rainier, grouped in the Union Nationale et Démocratique (UND), dominated at five-yearly elections in 1963–88, on all but two occasions taking all 18 seats on the Conseil national. A UND list of candidates was not formed for the 1993 general election, although an electoral list headed by Jean-Louis Campora (the President of the Principality's football team, AS Monaco) secured 15 seats. At legislative elections in 1998 the UND list, now headed by Campora, secured all 18 seats.

In the first half of 2002 the Conseil national approved a number of measures that were partly intended to expedite Monaco's application for full membership of the Council of Europe (see p. 260), which had been submitted in 1998. The age of majority was lowered from 21 to 18 years, and several executive powers of the Prince were transferred to the Conseil national, which was to be increased to 24 members (of whom eight were to be elected on the basis of a form of proportional representation) following the elections in 2003. Additionally, the law of succession was modified, to permit succession through the female line.

In late 2002 discontent was reported at a proposal, supported by Campora, to sell AS Monaco to a Russian investment company based in the Principality, Fedcominvest. Following allegations that Fedcominvest was involved in money-laundering, Prince Rainier, who, on behalf of the Principality, retained ultimate control over the club, prohibited the sale. The scandal appeared to be a significant factor in appreciably reducing support for Campora's UND at the legislative elections held in February 2003, when the UND secured only three seats on the enlarged Conseil national; the remaining 21 seats were awarded to the list of the Union pour Monaco (UpM), a coalition comprising mainly members of the Union pour la Principauté (UP) and the Union Nationale pour l'Avenir de Monaco (UNAM) and led by a former member of the UND, Stéphane Valeri.

In April 2004 the Council of Europe ruled that further reforms were required before Monaco could be considered for full membership; among the principal requirements were the extension of eligibility for several senior government positions, including the Minister of State (who, under the terms of a 1930 treaty, was required to be a French civil servant), to Monégasque citizens, and an enhancement of fiscal regulation. Following the decision of the Council of Europe that talks between France and Monaco had demonstrated significant progress towards the eventual reform of the 1930 convention, Monaco was admitted as a full member in October. A convention on administrative co-operation between France and Monaco was duly signed in November 2005, allowing Monégasque citizens to be appointed to senior government positions, subject to consultation with the French authorities. Agreements on financial regulation and judicial co-operation were signed concurrently.

On 6 April 2005 Prince Rainier died at the age of 81. He was succeeded by his son, Prince Albert II, who had acted as Regent of the Principality since 31 March. In July, several days before his formal inauguration as Head of State, it was confirmed that Prince Albert, who was unmarried and had no legal heir, had fathered a son in 2003. It was announced, however, that the child would not be eligible to inherit the throne. (In June 2006 Prince Albert formally acknowledged paternity of a second child—a daughter born to another woman in 1992—who would also not be eligible to inherit the throne.) Albert II was formally enthroned as the Ruling Prince on 19 November 2005. Prince Albert married Charlene Wittstock, a South African citizen, in July 2011.

At legislative elections held on 3 February 2008, the UpM retained its 21 seats in the Conseil national. The remaining three seats were won by the Rassemblement et Enjeux pour Monaco list.

In December 2008 Prince Albert announced that a plan to extend the Principality (by some 5%) into the sea, by creating an artificial peninsula, had been abandoned due to funding constraints as a result of the international financial crisis and unresolved environmental concerns. In May 2013 the Government invited bids for a similar development, with the potential to extend Monaco's land area by some 3%, which was planned for construction by 2024.

In January 2010 Valeri, the President of the Conseil national, replaced Jean-Jacques Campana as Government Councillor for Social Affairs and Health. Valeri was the first President of the Conseil national to be appointed to the Council of Government, in a move that was widely held to indicate the growing importance of the legislative body under Prince Albert's reign. Jean-François Robillon was subsequently elected to the presidency of the Conseil national. In March Michel Roger, a French civil servant, replaced Jean-Paul Proust as Minister of State; Prince Albert had declined to exercise his new authority, under the Franco-Monégasque treaty of 2005, to appoint a Monégasque citizen to the post. In the following month divisions within the UpM prompted the withdrawal from the coalition of the UNAM, which held four seats in the legislature.

Two electoral alliances and one political group contested the legislative elections held on 10 February 2013—Horizon Monaco (comprising Rassemblement et Enjeux pour Monaco, the UP and Synergie Monégasque, and headed by Laurent Nouvion) secured 20 seats, Union Monégasque (comprising the Union des Monégasques and the UNAM, and led by the incumbent President of the Conseil national, Robillon) won three seats, and the remaining seat was taken by Renaissance (a new party composed solely of employees of the Principality's largest employer, Société des Bains de Mer). Nouvion was subsequently elected President of the Conseil national.

Foreign Affairs

Monaco participates in the work of a number of international organizations, becoming a member of the UN in 1993 and the Council of Europe in 2004. In October 2002 Monaco and France signed a treaty of friendship and co-operation to replace the Franco-Monégasque Treaty of 1918. Under its terms, France guaranteed Monaco's full sovereignty and territorial integrity and recognized the law of succession as established by the recent constitutional amendments; the possibility that France might assume sovereignty over Monaco in the event of the throne becoming vacant was thus eliminated. In addition, the treaty provided for the establishment of diplomatic-level relations between the two states, while Monaco agreed to conduct its foreign relations in accordance with France's fundamental interests. In 2006 France upgraded the status of its diplomatic representation in Monaco from consular to ambassadorial level in accordance with the treaty, becoming the first country to operate an embassy in the Principality. Italy also opened an embassy in Monaco later in the year.

Controversy surrounding the use of Monaco's financial sector for the transfer of funds derived from criminal activities intensified in 1998 with the culmination of an investigation into the deposit of US $5.5m. in cash, suspected of originating from the illegal drugs trade, at a bank in Monaco in 1995. The affair led to a crisis in relations between France and the Principality, with the French Government overruling Prince Rainier by refusing to extend the mandate of Monaco's Chief Prosecutor, whom it suspected of not conducting a sufficiently thorough investigation of the scandal. Following further criticisms of Monégasque banking practice in a report by the Organisation for Economic Co-operation and Development (OECD, see p. 388) in 2000, the French Government recommended a rapid revision of the bilateral treaties between Monaco and France, proposing that Monégasque institutions be brought into greater conformity with French excise, fiscal and banking regulations. In a list published in April 2002, OECD defined Monaco as an 'unco-operative tax haven'; in early 2009 Monaco was removed from the list (see Economic Affairs). In December 2004 the EU signed an agreement with Monaco on the taxation of savings income. Under the agreement, savings income, in the form of interest payments made in Monaco to residents of the European Union (EU, see p. 281) was to be subject to a withholding tax from 1 July 2005. Monaco also agreed to exchange information on request with EU member states in criminal or civil cases of tax fraud or comparable offences.

In December 2012 the Commission of the EU published a report outlining options for the further integration of the European microstates, Andorra, Monaco and San Marino, into the EU. The report dismissed EU membership for the three states in the near future, but recommended either membership of the European Economic Area or the drawing up of a comprehensive, multilateral Framework Association Agreement with each of the states.

CONSTITUTION AND GOVERNMENT

Under the Constitution of 17 December 1962, as amended on 2 April 2002, legislative power is vested jointly in the Prince, a hereditary ruler, and the 24-member Conseil national (National Council), which is elected by universal adult suffrage, partly under a system of proportional representation, for a term of five years. The electorate comprises only Monégasque citizens aged 18 years or over. Executive power is exercised, under the authority of the Prince, by the five-member Council of Government, headed by the Minister of State (a Monégasque or French civil servant appointed by the Prince after consultation with the French Government). The Prince represents the Principality in its relations with foreign powers, and signs and ratifies treaties. For the purposes of local administration there is, additionally, a consultative Conseil communal (Municipal Council), comprising 15 members elected for a term of four years, headed by a mayor.

REGIONAL AND INTERNATIONAL CO-OPERATION

Monaco is a member of the Council of Europe (see p. 260) and the Organization for Security and Co-operation in Europe (OSCE, see p. 397). By virtue of its customs union and open border with France, it forms part of the customs territory of the European Union (EU, see p. 281) and participates in the EU's Schengen Agreement on border controls; it also uses the euro as its currency. Monaco joined the UN in 1993.

ECONOMIC AFFAIRS

In 2009, according to World Bank estimates, Monaco's gross national income (GNI), measured at average 2007–09 prices, was US $6,479m., equivalent to US $183,150 per head. According to UN estimates, Monaco's gross domestic product (GDP) was

$5,917m. in 2011 (equivalent to $167,021 per head). The annual rate of population growth remained unchanged during 2002–11. Monaco has the highest population density of all the independent states in the world. According to the World Bank, GDP increased, in real terms, at an average annual rate of 4.5% during 2002–09. GDP declined by 11.5% in 2009, but increased by 2.5% in 2010.

There is no agricultural land in Monaco. In 1990 a Belgian enterprise established an offshore fish farm for sea bass and sea bream. In December 2011 there were just 50 private sector employees working in the primary sector.

Industry contributed 6.6% of the Principality's turnover in 2011. The sector engaged 14.8% of those employed in the private sector in December 2011. Industry is mainly light in Monaco. The principal sectors are chemicals, pharmaceuticals and cosmetics (which together accounted for 40.5% of all industrial turnover in 2010), plastics (30.4%), electrical and electronic goods (9.5%), machine goods and paper and textile production.

Service industries represent the most significant sector of the economy in Monaco, contributing 93.9% of total turnover in 2010, and providing employment to 85.1% of those working in the private sector in December 2011. Banking and finance accounted for more than 24.6% of the services sector and employed some 1,400 people in the late 1990s. At the end of 2009 the total value of deposits in Monaco's private banking sector was estimated at €24,970m. Wholesale and retail trade accounted for 45.3% of national turnover in 2011, while banking and financial activities accounted for 12.5%.

Tourism is also an important source of income; it engaged some 20% of the employed labour force in the late 1990s, while the hotel business alone contributed 3.6% of the Principality's total turnover in 2011, and (together with restaurants and associated activities) engaged 8.5% of those employed in the private sector in December 2011. In 2011 a total of 294,901 tourists (excluding excursionists) visited Monaco, representing an increase of 5.6% compared with 2010. The greatest number of visitors (excluding excursionists) in 2011 were from France (22.3%), Italy (18.0%), the United Kingdom (10.6%) and the USA (7.6%).

Monaco's external trade is included in the figures for France. Excluding trade within the association with France, in 2011 Monaco's principal merchandise imports were consumer goods and semi-finished non-metallic goods. The most significant exports were semi-finished non-metallic goods, consumer goods and processed agricultural manufactures. Excluding France, the most important sources of imports in 2011 were Italy and Germany (15.9% and 13.2% of the total value, respectively), followed by the United Kingdom and the People's Republic of China. Italy and Germany were also the most important market for exports (excluding France), contributing 9.3% and 8.6% of total export earnings, respectively. The United Kingdom, Spain and Switzerland were also important markets for exports.

In 2011 there was a budgetary deficit of €51.8m.; expenditure amounted to €861.1m. Value-added tax (VAT) contributes about one-half of total government revenue.

Monaco is a prosperous state, which attracts wealthy residents through its tax regime; there is no income or inheritance tax and business rates are favourable. Monaco is largely dependent on imports from France, owing to its lack of natural resources. The economy is reliant on migrant workers (many of whom remain resident in France and Italy). Following the establishment of a casino in the 1860s, tourism became the dominant sector in the economy. In particular, the Principality has sought to establish itself as a major centre of the conference industry. An 18.3% decline in tourist arrivals in 2009 was attributed to recessionary conditions in the countries that provide the majority of Monaco's visitors, and contributed to an 11.5% decline in GDP that year. There was some recovery in the tourism sector in 2010 and 2011, when arrivals increased by 5.5% and 5.6%, respectively. GDP rose by 2.5% in 2010 and by an estimated 6.6% in 2011, owing in part to a recovery in tax revenues and an increase in corporate profits; however, continued recovery depended very much on global economic performance. The profits of the hotel, casino and leisure group, Société des Bains de Mer, which is 69% state-owned, generally constitute an important source of government income. However, the company recorded a net loss in 2010/11 (its first since 1996/97), prompting it to announce a three-year recovery plan in February 2012, which included an aim to attract more customers from China and Russia. Following several years of fiscal deficits, the Government aimed to balance its budget by 2014. Partly as a result of cuts in public expenditure on cultural institutions, the budget deficit decreased by 33.7% in 2011, compared with 2010. From the 1980s the industry and real estate sectors expanded, as a series of land reclamation projects increased Monaco's area by 20%. A number of foreign companies and banks are registered in Monaco in order to take advantage of the low rates of taxation on company profits. In March 2009 Monaco announced that it would adopt Organisation for Economic Co-operation and Development (OECD, see p. 388) standards on transparency and information exchange with regards to bank data, in an effort to combat tax evasion. Consequently, in May Monaco was removed from the OECD list of 'unco-operative tax havens'.

PUBLIC HOLIDAYS

2014: 1 January (New Year's Day), 27 January (St Devota's Day), 21 April (Easter Monday), 1 May (Labour Day), 29 May (Ascension Day), 9 June (Whit Monday), 15 August (Assumption), 1 November (All Saints' Day), 19 November (National Day/Fête du Prince), 8 December (Immaculate Conception), 25–26 December (Christmas).

Statistical Survey

Source (unless otherwise stated): Direction de l'expansion économique, Division des statistiques et des études économiques, 9 rue du Gabian, MC 98000; tel. 93-15-41-59; fax 93-15-87-59.

AREA AND POPULATION

Area: 2.02 sq km.

Population: 32,020 at census of July 2000; 31,109 (males 15,076, females 15,914) at census of June–July 2008. Note: Total includes 119 persons with gender not declared. *2011* (official estimate at 31 December): 36,371.

Density (at 31 December 2011): 18,005 per sq km.

Population by Age and Sex (at 2008 census): *0–14:* 3,965 (males 2,010, females 1,955); *15–64:* 19,063 (males 9,502, females 9,561); *65 and over:* 7,366 (males 3,276, females 4,090); *Total* 31,109 (males 15,076, females 15,914). Note: Total includes 715 persons of unknown age-group, and 119 persons with gender not declared.

Population by Nationality (at 2008 census): French 8,785; Monégasque 6,687; Italian 5,778; Other 9,859.

Districts (population at 2008 census): Monte-Carlo 14,586; La Condamine 11,946; Fontvieille 3,602; Monaco-Ville 975.

Births, Marriages and Deaths (2011 unless otherwise indicated): Live births 1,028; Marriages 171 (2004); Deaths 499.

Life expectancy (years at birth, WHO estimates): 82 (males 78; females 85) in 2009. Source: WHO, *World Health Statistics*.

Employment (private sector only, December 2011): Agriculture, hunting, forestry and fishing 50; Mining and quarrying 2; Manufacturing 2,819; Construction 4,097; Electricity and gas 166; Services 40,827 (Hotels, restaurants and associated activities 4,053; Real estate, renting and business services 12,900); *Total* 47,961.

HEALTH AND WELFARE

Key Indicators

Total Fertility Rate (children per woman, 2010): 1.5.

Under-5 Mortality Rate (per 1,000 live births, 2010): 4.

Physicians (per 1,000 head, 1995): 5.80.

Hospital Beds (per 1,000 head, 1995): 19.6.

Health Expenditure (2009): US $ per head (PPP): 5,932.

Health Expenditure (2009): % of GDP: 4.2.

Health Expenditure (2009): public (% of total): 88.0.

For sources and definitions, see explanatory note on p. vi.

FINANCE

Currency and Exchange Rates: French currency: 100 cent = 1 euro (€). *Sterling and Dollar Equivalents* (31 December 2012): £1 sterling = 1.196 euros; US $1 = 0.758 euros; €10 = £8.36 = $13.19. *Average Exchange Rate* (euros per US dollar): 0.7550 in 2010; 0.7194 in 2011; 0.7779 in 2012. Note: The local currency was formerly the French franc, although some Monégasque currency, at par with the French franc, also circulated. From the introduction of the euro, with French participation, on 1 January 1999, a fixed exchange rate of €1 = 6.55957 French francs was in operation. Euro notes and coins were introduced on 1 January 2002. The euro and local currency circulated alongside each other until 17 February, after which the euro became the sole legal tender.

Budget (€ million, 2011): Revenue 809.3; Expenditure 861.1 (Current expenditure 654.5, Capital expenditure 206.6).

Turnover of the Principality (official figures, private sector only, € million, 2011): Industry 1,009.6; Public works and real estate 923.0; Hotel business 548.7; Banking and finance 1,902.3; Wholesale and retail trade 6,882.9; Transport 333.4; Other activities 3,610.4; *Total* 15,210.2.

Gross Domestic Product (€ million at constant 2000 prices): 3,785.0 in 2008; 3,704.0 in 2009; 3,795.5 in 2010.

National Income and Product (€ million at current prices, 2010): Compensation of employees 2,271.7; Gross operating surplus 1,609.3; Taxes, less subsidies, on production 248.5; *Gross domestic product* 4,129.5.

Gross Domestic Product by Economic Activity (€ million at constant 2000 prices, 2010): Industry 428.8; Finance 594.1; Other services 2,772.6; *Total* 3,795.5.

EXTERNAL TRADE

Note: Monaco's imports and exports are included in the figures for France, and separate figures for Monaco's trade with France are not included here.

Principal Commodities (€ million, 2011): *Imports:* 609.7 (Jewellery and musical instruments 84.9; Plastic products 30.4; Road vehicles and trailers 30.0; Ships and boats 49.6; Clothing 49.4). *Exports:* 621.8 (Soaps, cleaning products and perfumes 138.8; Plastic products 23.4; Automobiles 24.6; Pharmaceutical products and preparations 25.1; Electrical equipment 40.6; Clothing 30.5).

Principal Trading Partners (€ million, 2011): *Imports:* Belgium 9.3; China, People's Republic 58.9; Dominican Republic 10.5; Germany 80.5; Hong Kong 26.4; Indonesia 11.3; Ireland 25.7; Italy 97.0; Japan 8.5; Madagascar 8.5; Spain 10.4; Switzerland 9.1; Taiwan 20.6; Turkey 33.1; Tunisia 19.9; United Kingdom 60.0; USA 17.7; Viet Nam 22.1; Total (incl. others) 609.7. *Exports:* Algeria 10.0; Belgium 43.0; Brazil 13.0; China, People's Republic 16.7; Côte d'Ivoire 7.0; Gabon 13.4; Germany 53.2; Greece 25.6; Italy 57.8; Netherlands 14.6; Nigeria 11.2; Portugal 8.6; Russia 7.5; Senegal 8.0; Spain 47.2; Switzerland 31.2; Tunisia 18.4; United Kingdom 47.9; USA 19.0; Total (incl. others) 621.8.

TRANSPORT

Road Traffic (vehicles in use at 31 December 2010): Passenger cars 25,929; Buses and coaches 115; Lorries and vans 4,831; Motorcycles and mopeds 8,733.

Shipping: *Flag Registered Fleet* (at 31 December 2012): Vessels registered 9; Displacement: 1,379 grt. Source: Lloyd's List Intelligence (www.lloydslistintelligence.com).

TOURISM

Tourist Arrivals (excluding excursionists): 264,540 in 2009; 279,166 in 2010; 294,901 in 2011. Figures refer to arrivals of foreign visitors at hotels and similar establishments.

Tourist Arrivals by Country (2011): France 65,659; Germany 13,002; Italy 53,081; Japan 4,997; Russia 17,229; Spain 5,803; Switzerland 8,841; United Kingdom 31,351; USA 22,331; Total (incl. others) 294,901.

COMMUNICATIONS MEDIA

Telephones (2011): 44,500 main lines in use.

Mobile Cellular Telephones (2011): 31,800 subscribers.

Internet Subscribers (2011): 15,900.

Broadband Subscribers (2011): 15,700.

Source: mostly International Telecommunication Union.

EDUCATION

(2009/10 unless otherwise indicated)

Pre-primary: 40 teachers (33 public, 7 private) (2004/05); 857 pupils (683 public, 174 private).

Elementary: 172 teachers (149 public, 23 private); 1,820 pupils (1,412 public, 408 private).

Secondary: 337 teachers (298 public, 39 private); 2,999 pupils (2,347 public, 652 private).

Note: Educational establishments in Monaco in 2004/05 comprised the following: three public pre-primary schools; four primary schools (three public, one private), which integrate pre-primary and elementary age-groups; one public elementary school; three public secondary schools, comprising one lower secondary school, one general upper secondary school, and one vocational secondary school; and one private school integrating primary and secondary age-groups. There was also one private higher educational establishment, the International University of Monaco, a business school where instruction is conducted in English.

Source: Direction de l'éducation nationale, de la jeunesse et des sports.

Directory

The Government

HEAD OF STATE

Ruling Prince: HSH Prince ALBERT II (succeeded 6 April 2005).

COUNCIL OF GOVERNMENT
(May 2013)

Minister of State: MICHEL ROGER.

Government Councillor for Finance and the Economy: JEAN CASTELLINI.

Government Councillor for the Interior: PAUL MASSERON.

Minister of Public Works, the Environment and Urban Development: MARIE-PIERRE GRAMAGLIA.

Government Councillor for Health and Social Affairs: STÉPHANE VALERI.

Government Councillor for External Relations: JOSÉ BADIA.

MINISTRY OF STATE AND DEPARTMENTS

Ministry of State: place de la Visitation, MC 98000; tel. 98-98-80-00; fax 98-98-82-17; e-mail sgme@gouv.mc; internet www.gouv.mc.

Department of External Relations: Ministère d'Etat, place de la Visitation, BP 522, MC 98000 Cedex; tel. 98-98-89-04; fax 98-98-85-54; e-mail relext@gouv.mc.

Department of Finance and the Economy: Ministère d'Etat, place de la Visitation, MC 98000; tel. 98-98-82-56.

Department of Health and Social Affairs: Ministère d'Etat, place de la Visitation, MC 98000; tel. and fax 98-98-19-19; e-mail afss@gouv.mc.

Department of the Interior: Ministère d'Etat, place de la Visitation, MC 98000; tel. 98-98-84-56; fax 93-50-82-45.

Department of Public Works, the Environment and Urban Development: Ministère d'Etat, place de la Visitation, MC 98000; tel. 98-98-81-92.

Legislature

Conseil national
(National Council)

2 place de la Visitation, MC 98000; tel. 93-30-41-15; fax 93-25-31-90; e-mail vviora@conseil-national.mc; internet www.conseilnational .mc.

President: LAURENT NOUVION.

Vice-President: CHRISTOPHER STEINER.

Election, 10 February 2013

	% of votes	Seats
Horizon Monaco*	50.34	20
Union Monégasque†	38.99	3
Renaissance‡	10.67	1
Total	100.00	24

* Alliance of Rassemblement et Enjeux pour Monaco (REM), Union pour Monaco (UpM), and Synergie Monégasque.
† Alliance of Union des Monégasques (UDM) and Union Nationale pour l'Avenir de Monaco (UNAM).
‡ Candidates comprise employees of Société des Bains de Mer (SBM).

Advisory Councils

Conseil d'Etat (Council of State): Palais de Justice, Monte-Carlo; advises on proposed laws or ordinances submitted for its approval by the Ruling Prince or by the Government, or on any other matter; 12 mems, appointed by the Ruling Prince, following the advice of the Minister of State and the Director of Judicial Services; Pres. PHILIPPE NARMINO; Sec. BRIGITTE GRINDA-GAMBARINI.

Conseil de la Couronne (Crown Council): Monte-Carlo; f. 1942; advises the Ruling Prince on matters of state, and must be consulted by the Ruling Prince prior to the implementation of certain constitutional matters, including the signature or ratification of treaties, the dissolution of the Conseil national, questions of naturalization or reintegration, the issuing of pardons or amnesties; 7 mems, appointed for renewable terms of 3 years; Pres. and 3 mems are appointed by free choice of the Ruling Prince, the remaining 3 mems are nominated by the Ruling Prince on the recommendation of the Conseil national; all mems must hold Monégasque nationality; Pres. MICHEL-YVES MOUROU; Sec. RICHARD MILANESIO.

Conseil économique et social (Economic and Social Council): Centre Administratif, 8 rue Louis-Notari, MC 98000; tel. 97-97-77-91; fax 93-50-05-96; f. 1945; advises on economic matters; 36 mems, appointed for a term of 3 years; 12 mems directly appointed by Govt, 12 appointed by Govt from list prepared by Union des Syndicats de Monaco, 12 appointed by Govt from list prepared by the Fédération Patronale Monégasque; the Ruling Prince appoints Pres. and 2 Vice-Pres from among the mems; Pres. ANDRÉ GARINO; Vice-Pres PIERRE-YVES REICHNECKER, HENRI LEIZE.

Political Organizations

There were traditionally no political parties as such in Monaco; instead, candidates were generally grouped into lists to contest elections to the Conseil national. However, since 2003 political groupings have begun to establish a more permanent presence.

Rassemblement et Enjeux pour Monaco (REM) (Rally and Issues for Monaco): 1 rue de Vedel, MC 98000; tel. 92-16-20-13; fax 93-25-20-09; e-mail info@rassemblement-enjeux.org; internet www .rassemblement-enjeux.org; coalition comprising members of the Rassemblement pour Monaco and Valeurs et Enjeux; contested the 2013 parliamentary election as part of Horizon Monaco; Pres. LAURENT NOUVION.

Synergie Monégasque: 41 ave Hector Otto, MC 98000; e-mail synergie@monaco.mc; internet www.synergie-mc.org; contested the 2013 parliamentary election as part of Horizon Monaco.

Union pour Monaco (UpM) (Union for Monaco): 11 rue du Gabian, MC 98000 Monaco; coalition comprising members of the Union pour la Principauté and the Union Nationale pour l'Avenir de Monaco; contested the 2013 parliamentary election as part of Horizon Monaco; Pres. STÉPHANE VALERI.

Union des Monégasques (UDM): BP 524, MC 98015 Monaco; tel. 93-25-23-02; e-mail info@unionmonegasque.mc; internet www .unionmonegasque.mc; f. 2011; contested the 2013 parliamentary election as part of Union Monégasque; Leader JEAN-FRANÇOIS ROBILLON.

Union Nationale pour l'Avenir de Monaco (UNAM) (National Union for the Future of Monaco): Monaco; contested the 2013 parliamentary election as part of Union Monégasque; Pres. ERIC GUAZZONE.

Diplomatic Representation

In February 2006 France opened an embassy in Monaco, becoming the first country to institute ambassadorial-level diplomatic relations with the Principality. Italy opened an embassy in Monaco later in the year. By December 2011 ambassadors from 83 countries were accredited to Monaco; most were resident in France, Spain or Belgium.

France: Le Roc fleuri, 1 rue du Tenao, BP 45, MC 98006 Cedex; tel. 92-16-54-60; fax 92-16-54-64; e-mail courrier@ambafrance-mc.org; Ambassador HUGUES MORET.

Italy: L'Annonciade, 17 ave de l'Annonciade, MC 98000; tel. 93-50-22-71; fax 93-50-06-89; e-mail ambasciata.montecarlo@esteri.it; internet www.ambprincipatomonaco.esteri.it; Ambassador ANTONIO MORABITO.

Judicial System

The organization of the legal system is similar to that of France. There is one Justice of the Peace, a Tribunal de Première Instance (Tribunal of First Instance), a Cour d'Appel (Court of Appeal), a Cour de Révision (High Court of Appeal), a Tribunal Criminel (Criminal Tribunal) and finally the Tribunal Suprême (Supreme Tribunal), which deals with infringements of the rights and liberties provided by the Constitution, and also with legal actions aiming at the annulment of administrative decisions for abusive exercise of power.

Palais de Justice: 5 rue Col Bellando de Castro, MC 98000; tel. 98-98-88-11; fax 98-98-85-89.

Director of Judicial Services: PHILIPPE NARMINO.

President of the Supreme Tribunal: HUBERT CHARLES.

President of the Court of Revision: JEAN APOLLIS.

First President of the Court of Appeal: BRIGITTE GRINDA-GAMBARINI.

President of the Tribunal of First Instance: MARTINE COULET-CASTOLDI.

Attorney-General: JEAN-PIERRE DRÉNO.

Religion

CHRISTIANITY

The Roman Catholic Church

Monaco comprises a single archdiocese, directly responsible to the Holy See. At 31 December 2006 there were an estimated 29,000 adherents in the Principality, representing about 90.6% of the total population.

Archbishop of Monaco: Most Rev. BERNARD BARSI, Archevêché, 1 rue de l'Abbaye, BP 517, MC 98015 Cedex; tel. 93-30-77-86; fax 92-16-39-31; e-mail info@eglise-catholique.mc; internet www.diocese.mc.

The Anglican Communion

Within the Church of England, Monaco forms part of the diocese of Gibraltar in Europe.

Chaplain: Fr WALTER H. RAYMOND, St Paul's Church House, 22 ave de Grande Bretagne, Monte-Carlo, MC 98000; tel. 93-30-71-06; fax 93-30-50-39; e-mail chaplain@stpaulsmonaco.com; internet www.stpaulsmonaco.com.

The Principality also has two Protestant churches and a synagogue.

The Press

La Gazette de Monaco: BP 130, MC 98003 Cedex; tel. 93-25-56-83; fax 97-98-01-41; e-mail rédaction@lagazette.mc; internet www.lagazettedemonaco.com; f. 1926; monthly; regional information; Dir-Gen. NOËL METTEY; Editor-in-Chief GEOGES OLIVIER KALIFA; circ. 10,000.

Journal de Monaco: Ministère d'Etat, place de la Visitation, BP 522, MC 98015; tel. 98-98-80-00; fax 93-15-82-17; e-mail journaldemonaco@gouv.mc; internet www.gouv.mc/dataweb/jourmon.nsf; f. 1858; edited at the Ministry of State; official weekly; contains texts of laws and decrees; Editor ROBERT COLLE.

Monaco Hebdo: 27 blvd d'Italie, MC 98000; tel. 93-50-56-52; fax 93-50-19-22; e-mail monacohebdo@free.fr; internet monacohebdo.free.fr; Man. Editor ROBERTO TESTA.

Monte-Carlo Méditerranée: 46, blvd des Moulins, 98000 Monaco; tel. and fax 93-25-10-00; Editor-in-Chief CAROLE CHABRIER.

French newspapers are widely read, and a special Monaco edition of the daily *Nice-Matin* is published in Nice, France.

NEWS AGENCY

Monte-Carlo Press: Le Beverly Palace, 13 blvd de Belgique, MC 98000; tel. 97-70-74-24; e-mail mcpress@mcpress.mc; internet www.mcpress.mc; f. 1987.

Publishers

Editions Alphée: 28 rue Comte Félix Gastaldi, BP 524, MC 98015; tel. 93-30-40-06; fax 97-70-37-00; e-mail contact@editions-alphee.com; internet www.editions-alphee.com; f. 1972; spirituality, personal devt; Dir JEAN-PAUL BERTRAND.

Editions EGC: 9 ave Albert II, BP 438, MC 98011 Cedex; e-mail multiprint@multiprintmc.com; economics, history, literature; Gen. Man. GÉRARD COMMAN.

Editions Victor Gadoury: 57 rue Grimaldi, MC 98000; tel. 93-25-12-96; fax 93-50-13-39; e-mail contact@gadoury.com; internet www.gadoury.com; f. 1967; numismatics.

Marsu Productions: 9 ave des Castelans, MC 98000; tel. 92-05-61-11; fax 92-05-76-60; e-mail contact@marsupilami.com; internet www.marsupilami.com; comic strips, children's entertainment.

Editions de l'Oiseau-Lyre: Les Remparts, BP 515, MC 98015 Cedex; tel. 93-30-09-44; fax 93-30-19-15; e-mail oiseaulyre@monaco.mc; internet www.oiseaulyre.com; f. 1932; owned by The Lyrebird Trust; classical music publishers; Pres. and Man. Dir KENNETH GILBERT.

Editions du Rocher: 28 rue Comte Félix Gastaldi, BP 521, MC 98015; tel. 99-99-67-17; fax 99-99-67-18; internet www.editionsdurocher.fr; f. 1943; fiction, history, sciences; Pres. ERNESTO ROSSI DI MONTELERA; Man. Dirs MARC LARIVÉ, SERGE BÉRARD; Dir-Gen. PATRICK MAHÉ.

Editions André Sauret SAM: Monte-Carlo; tel. 93-50-67-94; fax 93-30-71-04; art, fiction; Dir RAYMOND LEVY.

Broadcasting and Communications

TELECOMMUNICATIONS

Direction des Commmunications Electroniques: 23 ave Albert II, MC 98000; tel. 98-98-88-00; fax 97-98-56-57; e-mail nic@gouv.mc; internet www.nic.mc; Dir MARIE-PIERRE GRAMAGLIA.

Monaco Telecom: 9 rue du Gabian Fontvieille, MC 98000 Cedex; tel. 99-66-33-00; fax 99-66-33-33; e-mail communication@monaco-telecom.mc; internet www.monaco-telecom.mc; f. 1997; 49% owned by Cable & Wireless (United Kingdom), 45% by the Société Nationale de Financement (wholly owned by Govt of Monaco), 6% by the Compagnie Monégasque de Banque; incorporates the wholly owned subsidiaries Monaco Telecom International, Société Monégasque de Services de Telecoms (SMST), Société Monégasque de Télédistribution (SMT) and Divona; Pres. ETIENNE FRANZI; Dir-Gen. MARTIN PERONNET.

BROADCASTING

Radio

Monte-Carlo Doualiya: 1 ave Henri Dunant, MC 98000; internet www.mc-doualiya.com; fmr subsidiary of RMC, transferred to Radio-France Internationale in 1996; in French and Arabic; Pres. ANTOINE SCHWARZ; Man. Dir PHILIPPE BEAUVILLARD.

Radio Monaco: 7 rue du Gabian, MC 98000; tel. 702707; e-mail info@radio-monaco.com; internet www.radio-monaco.com; Dir-Gen. GILDO PASTOR.

Riviera Radio: 10 quai Antoine 1er, MC 98000; tel. 97-97-94-94; fax 97-97-94-95; e-mail info@rivieraradio.mc; internet www.rivieraradio.mc; owned by Morris Communications Co (USA); broadcasts in English; Man. Dir PAUL KAVANAGH.

Trans World Radio SC: c/o Courtin Global Assistance, BP 349, MC 98007; tel. 97-77-70-04; fax 92-05-92-32; e-mail cdetwiler@twr.org; internet www.twr.org; f. 1955; Evangelical Christian broadcaster; Pres. LAUREN LIBBY.

Television

Monaco switched from analogue to digital broadcasting in 2011.

TMC Monte-Carlo: 6 bis Antoine 1er, MC 98000; tel. 92-16-54-80; fax 92-16-54-81; e-mail contact@tmc.mc; internet www.tmc.tv; f. 1954; Dir-Gen. CAROLINE GOT.

TVI Monte-Carlo: 8 quai Antoine 1er, MC 98000; tel. 92-16-88-20; fax 93-25-46-39; e-mail tvimc@frateschi.mc; programmes in Italian; CEO LUIGI FRATESCHI.

Finance

(cap. = capital, res = reserves, dep. = deposits, m. = million,
br(s) = branch(es), amounts in euros)

BANKING

In 2011 a total of 36 banks, including major British, French, Italian and US banks, were represented in the Principality.

Banque de Gestion Edmond de Rothschild: Les Terrasses, 2 ave de Monte-Carlo, BP 317, MC 98000; tel. 93-10-47-47; fax 93-25-75-57; e-mail bger@lcf-rothschild.mc; internet www.lcf-rothschild.mc; f. 1986; present name adopted 1993; cap. 12.0m., res 27.4m., dep. 682.3m. (Dec. 2011); Chair. LEONARDO P. A. POGGI; Gen. Man. GIAMPAOLO BERNINI.

Banque J. Safra (Monaco): La Belle Epoque, 15–17 bis ave d'Ostende, MC 98000; tel. 93-10-66-55; fax 93-50-60-71; internet www.safra.com; f. 1994 as Banque du Gothard (Monaco); present name adopted 2006; 100% owned by Banque Jacob Safra (Switzerland); cap. 40.0m., res 6.7m., dep. 1,267.1m. (Dec. 2010); Pres. JOSEPH SAFRA; Gen. Man. YVES BRACCALENTI.

BNP Paribas Wealth Management Monaco: 15–17 ave d'Ostende, MC 98000; tel. 93-15-68-00; fax 93-15-68-01; e-mail wealthmanagement.monaco@bnpparibas.com; internet www .privatebank.bnpparibas.mc; f. 2003 by merger of United European Bank—Monaco and BNP Paribas Private Bank Monaco; acquired Société Monégasque de Banque Privée and Bank Von Ernst (Monaco) 2005; name changed as above in 2009; private banking; cap. 13.0m. (April 2007); Dir-Gen. ERIC GEORGES.

Compagnie Monégasque de Banque: 23 ave de la Costa, BP 149, MC 98007; tel. 93-15-77-77; fax 93-25-08-69; e-mail cmb@cmb.mc; internet www.cmb.mc; f. 1976; 100% owned by Mediobanca—Banca di Credito Finanziario SpA (Italy); cap. 111.1m., res 347m., dep. 1,543.9m. (Dec. 2011); Chair. ETIENNE FRANZI; Vice Chair. ALDO CIVASCHI; 2 brs.

Crédit Foncier de Monaco (CFM Monaco): 11 blvd Albert 1er, BP 499, MC 98012 Cedex; tel. 93-10-20-00; fax 93-10-23-50; internet www.cfm.mc; f. 1922; 77.1% owned by Calyon (France); cap. 35.0m., res 83m., dep. 3,278.8m. (Dec. 2011); Chair. YVES BARSALOU; CEO GILLES MARTINENGO.

Crédit Suisse (Monaco): 27 ave de la Costa, BP 155, MC 98003; tel. 93-15-27-27; fax 93-25-27-99; e-mail alain.ucari@credit-suisse.com; f. 1987; cap. 12.0m., res 1.4m., dep. 1,880.5m. (Dec. 2011); Chair. FRANCO MULLER; Man ALAIN UCARI.

EFG Bank (Monaco) SAM: Villa Les Aigles, 15 ave d'Ostende, MC 98000; tel. 93-15-11-11; fax 93-15-11-12; e-mail enquiries_mco@ efgbank.com; internet www.efggroup.com; f. 1990; merged with Banque Monegasque de Gestion SA in 2007; name changed as above in 2009; owned by EFG Bank (Switzerland); private banking; cap. 26.9m., res 3.2m., dep. 761.8m. (Dec. 2011); Dir-Gen. GEORGE CATSIAPIS.

HSBC Private Bank (Monaco): 17 ave d'Ostende, MC 98000; tel. 93-15-25-25; fax 93-15-25-00; internet www.hsbcprivatebank.com; f. 1997 as Republic National Bank of New York (Monaco) SA; present name adopted 2004; owned by HSBC Private Banking Holdings (Suisse) SA (Switzerland); private banking; cap. 151.0m., res 4.4m., dep. 5,771.2m. (Dec. 2011); Chief Exec. and Dir-Gen. GÉRARD COHEN.

KBL Monaco Private Bankers: 8 ave de Grande Bretagne, BP 262, MC 98005; tel. 92-16-55-55; fax 92-16-55-99; internet www .europeanprivatebankers.com; f. 1996; owned by KBL European Private Bankers S.A; cap. 8.5m., res 3.9m., dep. 345m. (Dec. 2011); Chair. PAUL MARIE JACQUES; Man. Dir STEPHEN BARBALACO.

UBS (Monaco) SA: 2 ave de Grande Bretagne, BP 189, MC 98007; tel. 93-15-58-15; fax 93-15-58-00; e-mail antonio.mancino@ubs.com; internet www.ubs.com/monaco; f. 1956; present name adopted 1998; owned by UBS AG (Switzerland); cap. 9.2m., res 38.1m., dep. 1,191.3m. (Dec. 2009); Chair. AXEL A. WEBER; CEO SERGIO P. ERMOTTI.

INSURANCE

Assurances J.P. et C. Sassi AXA: Le Suffren, 7 rue Suffren-Reymond, BP 25, MC 98001; tel. 93-30-45-88; fax 93-25-86-07; e-mail agence.sassi@axa.fr; f. 1968; Dir JEAN-PIERRE SASSI.

The Eric Blair Network: 11 ave St Michael, 98000 Monaco; tel. 93-50-99-66; fax 97-70-72-00; e-mail info@ericblairnet.com; internet www.ericblairnet.com; Chief Exec. ERIC BLAIR.

Gramaglia Assurances: 14 blvd des Moulins, BP 153, MC 98003 Cedex; tel. 92-16-59-00; fax 92-16-59-01; internet www.gramaglia .mc; f. 1948; Dir PHILIPPE VERDIER.

Mourenon et Giannotti: 22 blvd Princesse Charlotte, MC 98000; tel. 97-97-08-88; fax 97-97-08-80; e-mail monacometg@agence .generali.fr; internet mgassurances.com; f. 1975; Dirs JEAN-PHILIPPE MOURENON, JOSÉ GIANNOTTI.

Trade and Industry

GOVERNMENT AGENCIES

Direction de l'Environnement: 3 ave de Fontvieille, MC 98013; tel. 98-98-80-00; fax 92-05-28-91; e-mail environnement@gouv.mc; Dir CYRIL GOMEZ.

Direction de l'Expansion Economique: 9 rue du Gabian, MC 98000; tel. 98-98-98-00; fax 92-05-75-20; e-mail expansion@gouv.mc; comprises 3 divisions: Monaco Welcome and Business Office, General Administration and Intellectual Property; Dir SERGE PIERRYVES.

Direction de la Prospective, de l'Urbanisme et de la Mobilité: 23 ave Albert II, MC 98000; tel. 98-98-22-99; fax 98-98-88-02; e-mail prospective@gouv.mc; Dir JEAN-MICHEL MANZONE.

Direction des Services Fiscaux: 'Le Panorama', 57 rue Grimaldi, BP 475, MC 98000; tel. 98-98-80-00; fax 93-15-81-55; Dir ANTOINE DINKEL.

CHAMBER OF COMMERCE

Jeune Chambre Economique de Monaco: 1 ave des Castelans, MC 98000; tel. 92-05-20-19; fax 92-05-31-29; e-mail jcemonaco@ jcemonaco.mc; internet www.jcemonaco.mc; f. 1963; Pres. MARINA MAZZA.

EMPLOYERS' ASSOCIATION

Fédération Patronale Monégasque (FPM) (Employers' Fed. of Monaco): 'Le Coronado', 20 ave de Fontvieille, MC 98000; tel. 92-05-38-92; fax 92-05-20-04; e-mail info@federation-patronale.mc; internet www.federation-patronale.mc; f. 1944; Pres. PHILIPPE ORTELLI; Sec.-Gen. CORINNE BERTANI; 27 mem. orgs, with 1,200 individual mems.

UTILITIES

Electricity and Gas

Société Monégasque de l'Electricité et du Gaz (SMEG): 10 ave de Fontvieille, BP 633, MC 98013 Cedex; tel. 92-05-05-00; fax 92-05-05-92; e-mail smeg@smeg.mc; internet www.smeg.mc; f. 1890; 64% owned by GDF SUEZ (France); 20% owned by the Govt of Monaco; Dir-Gen. GUY MAGNAN.

Water

Société Monégasque des Eaux (SME): 5 ave de Fontvieille, MC 98000; tel. 97-98-51-00; fax 92-05-23-83; e-mail sme@sme.mc; internet www.sme.mc; f. 1983; Pres. STÉPHANE GIACCARDI.

TRADE UNION FEDERATION

Union des Syndicats de Monaco (USM): 28 blvd Rainier III, BP 113, MC 98000; tel. 93-30-19-30; fax 93-25-06-73; e-mail usm@usm .mc; internet www.usm.mc; f. 1944; Pres. BETTY TAMBUSCIO; Sec.-Gen. MONIQUE FERRETE; 41 mem. unions.

Transport

RAILWAYS

The 1.7 km of railway track in Monaco, running from France to Monte-Carlo on the Nice-Menton-Ventimiglia railway line is operated by the French state railway, the Société Nationale des Chemins de fer Français (SNCF). As part of the Government's policy of land reclamation, an underground railway station was opened in 1999.

ROADS

In 2010 there were an estimated 77 km of major roads in the Principality.

SHIPPING

The two main ports in Monaco are Port Hercules and Port Fontvieille. The former is a deep-water port, which provides an anchorage for up to 700 vessels. The latter accommodates up to 275 boats with a maximum draught of three metres. At 31 December 2012 the flag registered fleet comprised 9 vessels, totalling 1,379 grt.

Direction des Affaires Maritimes: quai Jean-Charles Rey, BP 468, MC 98012 Cedex; tel. 98-98-22-80; fax 98-98-22-81; Dir ARMELLE ROUDAUT-LAFON.

Société d'Exploitation des Ports de Monaco (SEPM): 6 quai Antoine 1er, BP 453, MC 98011 Cedex; tel. 97-77-30-00; fax 97-77-30-01; e-mail info@ports-monaco.com; internet www.ports-monaco .com; f. 2002; state-owned; responsible for management and devt of the 2 principal ports in Monaco, at La Condamine (Port Hercule) and Fontvieille; Pres. ALECO KEUSSEOGLOU; Gen. Man. GIANBATTISTA BOREA D'OLMO.

Shipping Companies

d'Amico Dry Ltd: 20 blvd de Suisse, MC 98000 Cedex; tel. 93-10-52-70; fax 93-25-41-62; e-mail info@damicoship.com; internet www.damicoship.com; f. 2002; owned by d'Amico Società di Navigazione SpA (Italy); Pres. PAOLO D'AMICO; Group CEO CESARE D'AMICO.

MC Shipping Inc.: Gildo Pastor Center, 7 rue du Gabian, MC 98000; tel. 97-97-49-90; fax 97-97-49-99; e-mail operations@mcshipping.com; f. 1989; CEO ANTON U. PARDINI.

Société Anonyme Monégasque d'Administration Maritime et Aérienne (SAMAMA): Villa Saint Jean, 3 ruelle Saint Jean, MC 98000; tel. 99-99-51-00; fax 99-99-51-09; e-mail general@samama-monaco.com; f. 1975; Pres. FRANK O. WALTERS; Dir-Gen. J.F. MEGGINSON.

CIVIL AVIATION

There is a helicopter shuttle service between the international airport at Nice, France, and Monaco's heliport at Fontvieille.

Héli Air Monaco SAM: Héliport de Monaco, MC 98000; tel. 92-05-00-50; fax 92-05-00-51; e-mail helico@heliairmonaco.com; internet www.heliairmonaco.com; f. 1976; CEO JACQUES CROVETTO.

Tourism

Tourists are attracted to Monaco by the Mediterranean climate, dramatic scenery and numerous entertainment facilities, including a casino. In 2011 294,901 tourists (excluding excursionists) visited Monaco.

Direction du Tourisme et des Congrès: 2A blvd des Moulins, MC 98030 Cedex; tel. 92-16-61-16; fax 92-16-60-00; e-mail dtc@gouv.mc; internet www.visitmonaco.com; Pres. GUILLAUME ROSE.

Société des Bains de Mer (SBM): place du Casino, BP 139, MC 98000; tel. 92-16-25-25; fax 92-16-26-26; e-mail resort@sbm.mc; internet www.montecarloresort.com; f. 1863; corpn in which the Govt holds a 69.5% interest; controls the entertainment facilities of Monaco, including the casino and numerous hotels, clubs, restaurants and sporting facilities; Chair. JEAN-LUC BIAMONTI; Gen. Man. BERNARD LAMBERT.

Defence

France is responsible for the Principality's defence.

Education

Education follows the French system. Compulsory education lasts for 10 years for children aged six to 16 years. Primary education begins at six years of age and lasts for five years. Secondary education begins at 11 years of age and lasts for seven years. There is one public institution of higher education, the Académie de Musique et de Théâtre Fondation Prince Rainier III de Monaco (founded 1933), and one private higher educational institution, the International University of Monaco (founded 1986), a business school where instruction is conducted in English and where US-style Bachelors, Masters and Doctoral degree courses are offered. In 2010 expenditure on education was equivalent to 6.4% of total government expenditure.

MONGOLIA

Introductory Survey

LOCATION, CLIMATE, LANGUAGE, RELIGION, FLAG, CAPITAL

Mongolia is a land-locked country in central Asia, with the Russian Federation to the north and the People's Republic of China to the south, east and west. The climate is dry, with generally mild summers but very cold winters. Temperatures in Ulan Bator (traditional spelling; Ulaanbaatar in transcription from Mongolian Cyrillic) range between $-32°C$ ($-26°F$) and $22°C$ ($71°F$). The principal language is Khalkha Mongolian. Kazakh is spoken in the province of Bayan-Ölgii. There is no state religion, but Buddhist Lamaism is being encouraged once again. The national flag (proportions 1 by 2) has three equal vertical stripes, of red, blue and red, with the 'soyombo' symbol (a combination of abstract devices) in gold on the red stripe at the hoist. The capital is Ulan Bator (Ulaanbaatar).

CONTEMPORARY POLITICAL HISTORY

Historical Context

The country was formerly the Manchu province of Outer Mongolia. In 1911, following the republican revolution in China, Mongolian princes declared the province's independence. With support from Tsarist Russia, Outer Mongolia gained autonomy, as a feudal Buddhist monarchy, but Russia accepted Chinese suzerainty over the province in 1915. Following the Russian revolution of 1917, China began to re-establish control in Mongolia in 1919. In 1920 Mongol nationalists appealed to the new Soviet regime for assistance, and in March 1921 they met on Soviet territory to found the Mongolian People's Party (renamed the Mongolian People's Revolutionary Party—MPRP—in 1924) and established a Provisional People's Government. After nationalist forces, with Soviet help, drove anti-Bolshevik troops from the Mongolian capital, the People's Government was proclaimed on 11 July 1921. Soviet Russia recognized the People's Government in November of that year. In November 1924, after the death of Bogd Khan (King) Javzandamba Khutagt VIII, the Mongolian People's Republic was proclaimed.

The Mongolian People's Republic became increasingly dependent on the USSR's support. The Government conducted campaigns to collectivize the economy and to destroy the power of the nobility and Buddhist priests. In 1932 an armed uprising was suppressed with Soviet assistance. Following his reorganization of the MPRP and army leadership in 1936–39, power was held by Marshal Khorloogiin Choibalsan as Prime Minister and MPRP leader. The dictatorship of Choibalsan closely followed the model of the regime of Stalin (Iosif Dzhugashvili, 1924–53) in the USSR. Many thousands of victims included eminent politicians, military officers, religious leaders and intellectuals. In 1939 a Japanese invasion from Manchuria was repelled by Soviet and Mongolian forces at Khalkhyn Gol (Nomonhan). In accordance with the Yalta agreement to preserve the status quo in Mongolia, war was declared on Japan in August 1945, four days before the Japanese surrender, and northern China was invaded. In a Mongolian plebiscite in October, it was reported that 100% of the votes were cast in favour of independence, and this was recognized by China in January 1946.

Domestic Political Affairs

Choibalsan died in January 1952 and was succeeded as Prime Minister by Yumjaagiin Tsedenbal, who had been the MPRP's First Secretary since 1940. Tsedenbal reassumed responsibility for his former post in November 1958, and a new Constitution was adopted in July 1960.

Jamsrangiin Sambuu, head of state since July 1954, died in May 1972. He was replaced in June 1974 by Tsedenbal, who remained First Secretary of the MPRP (restyled General Secretary in 1981) but relinquished the post of Chairman of the Council of Ministers to Jambyn Batmönkh. In August 1984 Tsedenbal was removed from the party leadership and from his position as head of state, apparently owing to ill health, and Batmönkh replaced him as General Secretary of the MPRP. In December Batmönkh also became head of state, while Dumaagiin Sodnom, hitherto a Deputy Chairman of the Council of

Ministers and the Chairman of the State Planning Commission, was appointed Chairman of the Council of Ministers.

Between December 1989 and March 1990 there was a great increase in public political activity. Several newly formed opposition movements—the most prominent of which was the Mongolian Democratic Union (MDU; founded in December 1989 and led by Sanjaasürengiin Zorig)—organized a series of peaceful demonstrations, involving as many as 20,000 people, in Ulan Bator, demanding political and economic reforms, and precipitating a crisis of confidence within the MPRP. At a party plenum in mid-March 1990 Batmönkh announced the resignation of the entire Political Bureau as well as of the Secretariat of the Central Committee. Gombojavyn Ochirbat was elected to replace Batmönkh as General Secretary, Yumjaagiin Tsedenbal was expelled from the party, and a new five-member Political Bureau was formed.

At a session of the People's Great Khural (legislature), held shortly after the MPRP plenum, Punsalmaagiin Ochirbat, hitherto the Minister of Foreign Economic Relations and Supply, was elected Chairman of the Presidium (head of state), replacing Batmönkh, and other senior positions in the Presidium were reallocated. Dumaagiin Sodnom was dismissed from his post as Chairman of the Council of Ministers and was replaced by Sharavyn Gungaadorj, a Deputy Chairman and Minister of Agriculture and the Food Industry. The Khural also adopted amendments to the Constitution, including the deletion of references to the MPRP as the 'guiding force' in Mongolian society, and approved a new electoral law, with early legislative elections scheduled for mid-1990. In late March an estimated 13,000 disenchanted citizens demonstrated in Ulan Bator to demand the dissolution of the Khural. Opposition leaders called for the introduction of a multi-party electoral law. In May the People's Great Khural adopted a law on political parties, which legalized the new 'informal' parties through official registration, and also adopted further amendments to the Constitution, introducing a presidential system with a standing legislature, the State Little Khural, which was to be elected by proportional representation of parties.

At the July 1990 legislative elections and consequent re-elections, 430 deputies were elected to serve a five-year term: 357 from the MPRP (in some instances unopposed), 16 from the Mongolian Democratic Party (MDP, the political wing of the MDU), 19 shared among the Mongolian Revolutionary Youth League, the Mongolian National Progress Party (MNPP), and the Mongolian Social-Democratic Party (MSDP), and 39 without party affiliation. Under constitutional amendments adopted in May, the People's Great Khural was required to convene at least four times during its five-year term.

In September 1990 the People's Great Khural elected Punsalmaagiin Ochirbat to be the country's first President, with a five-year term of office; the post of Chairman of the Presidium (as the Political Bureau had been renamed in April) was abolished. Dashiin Byambasüren was appointed Prime Minister (equivalent to the former post of Chairman of the Council of Ministers) and began consultations on the formation of a multi-party government. The newly restyled Cabinet was elected by the State Little Khural in September and October. Under the amended Constitution, the President, Vice-President and ministers were not permitted to remain concurrently deputies of the People's Great Khural; therefore, re-elections of deputies to the legislature were held in November. Büdragchaagiin Dash-Yondon, the Chairman of the Ulan Bator City Party Committee, was elected Chairman of the MPRP Central Committee in February 1991.

A new Constitution was adopted by the Great Khural in January 1992. It provided for a unicameral Mongolian Great Khural, comprising 76 members, to replace the People's Great Khural, following elections to be held in June. (The State Little Khural was abolished.) The country's official name was changed from the Mongolian People's Republic to Mongolia, and the communist gold star was removed from the national flag.

The elections to the Mongolian Great Khural of June 1992 were contested by the MPRP, an alliance of the MDP, the MNPP and the United Party (UP), the MSDP, six other parties and another alliance. Some 95.6% of the electorate participated in the poll. Candidates were elected by a simple majority, provided that they obtained the support of at least 50% of the electorate in their constituency. The MPRP candidates received some 57% of the total votes, but won 70 (71 including a pro-MPRP independent) of the 76 seats in 26 constituencies. The remaining seats were taken by the MDP (two, including an independent), the MSDP, MNPP and UP (one each).

In the first session of the Mongolian Great Khural, which opened in July 1992, Puntsagiin Jasrai (who had served as a Deputy Chairman of the Council of Ministers in the late 1980s) was appointed Prime Minister, and his Cabinet was approved. Natsagiin Bagabandi, a Vice-Chairman of the MPRP Central Committee, was elected Chairman of the Great Khural (Speaker). Meanwhile, a National Security Council was established, with the country's President as its Chairman, and the Prime Minister and Chairman of the Great Khural as its members.

In October 1992 the MDP, MNPP, UP and the Mongolian Renewal Party amalgamated to form the Mongolian National Democratic Party (MNDP), with a General Council headed by the MNPP leader, Davaadorjiin Ganbold, and including Sanjaasürengiin Zorig and other prominent opposition politicians. In the same month the MPRP Central Committee was renamed the MPRP Little Khural, and its membership was increased to 169 (and subsequently to 198). The MPRP Presidium was replaced by a nine-member party Leadership Council, headed by Büdragchaagiin Dash-Yondon as its General Secretary.

Following the adoption by the Great Khural of a Presidential Election Law in March 1993, direct elections to the presidency were held in June. President Ochirbat, nominated by a coalition of the MNDP and the MSDP, secured a convincing victory, winning 57.8% of the votes cast, compared with 38.7% for the MPRP's candidate, Lodongiin Tüdev.

In early 1996 the MPRP forced through the Great Khural the passage of amendments that increased the number of constituencies from 26 to 76, making them all single-seat constituencies, while preserving the majority vote system. To be declared elected, a candidate was required to have received a minimum of 25% of the constituency votes. In response, opposition parties formed an electoral coalition, the Democratic Alliance, which enjoyed the support of the Mongolian Green Party and the MDU.

The end of MPRP rule

At the legislative elections held in June 1996, a resounding victory was achieved by the opposition Democratic Alliance, which won 50 of the 76 seats in the Great Khural, receiving some 46.7% of the total votes cast. The MPRP took only 25 seats (40.6%), while one seat was won by a candidate of the United Heritage Party (UHP—subsequently also known as the Mongolian Traditional United Party). Electoral turn-out was 92.2%. At the legislature's inaugural session in July the leader of the MSDP, Radnaasümbereliin Gonchigdorj, was elected to the post of Chairman of the Great Khural, while Mendsaikhany Enkhsaikhan, the leader of the Democratic Alliance, was elected as Prime Minister. Following the conclusion of a three-day boycott of the Great Khural by the MPRP over a dispute concerning the allocation of positions in the legislature, the leader of the MNDP, Tsakhiagiin Elbegdorj, was elected Vice-Chairman of the Great Khural, and a new Government was formed at the end of July.

Following their election defeat, and amid growing evidence of a rift between supporters of tradition and advocates of the reform process, in July 1996 the MPRP Little Khural elected a new Leadership Council and General Secretary of the party, Nambaryn Enkhbayar. In February 1997 several prominent dissenting members resigned from the MPRP, and Natsagiin Bagabandi, who had been Chairman of the Great Khural in 1992–96, was elected Chairman of the party.

At the presidential election held in May 1997, the MPRP's candidate, Bagabandi, secured a convincing victory with some 60.8% of the total votes cast. In a severe set-back to the democratic movement, the incumbent Ochirbat received only 29.8%, a reflection of popular dissatisfaction at the rigorous economic reform policies implemented by the ruling Democratic Alliance. The UHP's candidate, Jambyn Gombojav, a former Vice-Chairman of the Great Khural, obtained 6.6% of the votes. Enkhbayar was subsequently elected to replace Bagabandi as Chairman of the MPRP and in August he won a by-election for Bagabandi's former seat in the Great Khural.

In April 1998 the Democratic Alliance decided that, henceforth, the Cabinet was to comprise members of the Great Khural,

headed by the leader of the Alliance. Tsakhiagiin Elbegdorj, leader of the MNDP, was thus appointed Prime Minister, and a new Cabinet was formed in May. The Government became embroiled in a dispute over the amalgamation of the state-owned Reconstruction Bank, declared bankrupt after over-extending its credit, with the private Golomt Bank. Amid accusations that Democratic Alliance leaders had obtained loans from the bank shortly before its failure, the MPRP effected a boycott of the Great Khural. The opposition party rejected the Government's reinstatement of Reconstruction Bank and returned to the Great Khural in late July to pursue a motion of no confidence in the Government. The vote was carried by 42 votes to 33, with the support of 15 members of the Democratic Alliance.

Following a protracted dispute during the latter half of 1998 between the Democratic Alliance, President Bagabandi and the Great Khural over suitable candidates for the position of Prime Minister, the Democratic Alliance finally nominated Bagabandi's candidate, the Mayor of Ulan Bator, Janlavyn Narantsatsralt, who was appointed Prime Minister in December. The formation of his Government was completed in January 1999, but it remained in power for just over six months. In July Narantsatsralt lost a vote of confidence, in which MSDP members of the Great Khural voted with the opposition MPRP, following the emergence of a letter that the premier had written in January to a Russian government official, in which he seemingly acknowledged Russia's right to privatize its share in the Erdenet copper-mining joint venture without reference to Mongolia. Rinchinnyamyn Amarjargal was elected as the new Prime Minister at the end of July, and all but one of the ministers of Narantsatsralt's Government were reappointed. In November Amarjargal assumed the presidency of the MNDP, replacing Narantsatsralt.

The 1992 Constitution was amended for the first time in December 1999 by a Great Khural decree supported by all three parliamentary parties, which simplified the procedure for the appointment of the Prime Minister and allowed members of the Great Khural to serve as government ministers while retaining their seats in the legislature. An attempt by the President to veto the decree was defeated by the Great Khural in January 2000, but the Constitutional Court ruled in March that the decree had been illegal. When the Great Khural reconvened in April, members rejected the ruling and refused to discuss it, despite the Constitutional Court's demand for a statement on the issue.

As the legislative elections approached, a breakaway grouping of the MNDP re-established the Mongolian Democratic Party, and a faction of the MSDP founded the Mongolian New Social Democratic Party. Sanjaasürengiin Oyuun (the sister of Sanjaasürengiin Zorig, former Minister of Infrastructure Development and founder of the Mongolian Democratic Movement, who had been murdered in October 1998) established the Civil Courage Party (CCP—Irgenii Zorig Nam, subsequently also known as Citizens' Will). The CCP drew away from the MNDP several more members of the Great Khural, and formed an electoral alliance with the Mongolian Green Party. The MNDP, unable to reconstitute the previously successful Democratic Alliance with the MSDP, therefore formed a new Democratic Alliance with the Mongolian Believers' Democratic Party.

The MPRP's return to power

At the elections held in early July 2000, the MPRP won 72 of the 76 seats in the Great Khural, with 50.2% of the votes cast; Prime Minister Rinchinnyamyn Amarjargal and his entire Cabinet lost their seats. The level of participation was 82.4% of the electorate. The MPRP's main support lay in rural constituencies, where it was widely seen as willing and able to halt the economic and social stagnation of the countryside. The Democratic Alliance won 13% of the votes cast, while the Mongolian Democratic New Socialist Party (MDNSP, which had amalgamated with the Mongolian Workers' Party in 1999) received 10.7% of the votes; each of them won one seat, and the remaining one seat was taken by an independent candidate. When the legislature opened in mid-July 2000, Lkhamsürengiin Enebish, the MPRP General Secretary, was elected Chairman of the Great Khural, and the MPRP Chairman, Nambaryn Enkhbayar, was elected Prime Minister; Enkhbayar's Cabinet was approved in August.

At a conference in early December 2000 five parties—the MNDP, the MSDP, the Mongolian Democratic Party, the Mongolian Believers' Democratic Party and the Democratic Renewal Party—dissolved themselves and formed a new Democratic Party (DP). Dambyn Dorligjav, a former Minister of Defence and director of the Erdenet copper enterprise, was elected Chairman of the new party, while Narantsatsralt and the former

Minister of the Environment, Sonomtserengiin Mendsaikhan, were elected as Vice-Chairmen.

In mid-December 2000 the Great Khural readopted, unchanged and for immediate implementation, the decree of December 1999 amending the 1992 Constitution. His veto of the decree having been rejected, President Bagabandi finally approved the amendments in May 2001. Meanwhile, in February the 23rd Congress of the ruling MPRP re-elected the Prime Minister, Enkhbayar, as its Chairman, approved the establishment of a new Little Khural of 244 members and enlarged the party Leadership Council from 11 to 15 members. In September Lkhamsürengiin Enebish, Chairman of the Great Khural and recently re-elected as General Secretary of the MPRP, died; he was succeeded in the latter post by Doloonjingiin Idevkhten and as Chairman of the Great Khural by Sanjbegziin Tömör-Ochir, hitherto MPRP Secretary.

At the presidential election of May 2001, the incumbent Natsagiin Bagabandi, the MPRP candidate, was re-elected, having received nearly 58.0% of the votes cast. Radnaasümbereliin Gonchigdorj of the DP won 36.6% of the votes; Luvsandambyn Dashnyam, the candidate of the CCP, received 3.5%.

In March 2002 Sanjaasürengiin Oyuun's CCP merged with Bazarsadyn Jargalsaikhan's Mongolian Republican Party to form the Civil Courage Republican Party, under Oyuun's leadership. However, in June 2003 Jargalsaikhan withdrew from the merger after disagreement about the formation of a coalition with the DP. Attempts in December to oust Oyuun from the party leadership failed, and in March 2004 she agreed to join the Motherland Democracy (MD) coalition comprising Badarchiin Erdenebat's MDNSP and the DP.

In June 2002 the Great Khural approved the Law on Land and the Law on Land Privatization. Although less than 1% of the country's total territory was to be available for privatization, the laws generated much controversy. From November farmers took part in several demonstrations in Ulan Bator. The demonstrators, led by DP leader Erdeniin Bat-Üül, protested that the poor would be denied land by the 'oligarchy'. The privatization law duly entered into force in May 2003.

The National Human Rights Programme was adopted in December 2003, following the publication earlier in the year of the National Human Rights Commission's annual report, which was highly critical of bureaucracy, corruption and cronyism, and accused the police of numerous cases of brutality. Also in 2003, Damirangiin Enkhbat, who had been suspected of the murder of Sanjaasürengiin Zorig in 1998 and had since been resident in France, was reported to have been abducted by Mongolian secret agents and subsequently imprisoned in Mongolia. In early 2004 reports from the human rights organization Amnesty International suggested that Enkhbat had been tortured during interrogation. In December 2005 the UN's Special Rapporteur charged with investigating such allegations, Manfred Nowak, published a report condemning torture in Mongolian prisons and criticizing the provisions of the Law on State Secrets for preventing dissemination of information about death sentences. (Enkhbat was released from prison in February 2006 on the grounds of ill health, and subsequently died.)

Meanwhile, campaigning began for the next elections to the Mongolian Great Khural, which were scheduled for mid-2004. The new General Election Committee (GEC) incorporated many MPRP nominees. The opposition MD election pact, formed by Mendsaikhany Enkhsaikhan's DP and Erdenebat's MDNSP, was joined by Sanjaasürengiin Oyuun's Civil Courage Republican Party, minus the followers of Bazarsadyn Jargalsaikhan, who left to re-establish the Republican Party. After the registration of participating political parties and coalitions, the GEC examined the official lists, rejecting all Mongolian Youth Party candidates.

The initial results of the legislative elections of 27 June 2004 (compiled as percentages of the total ballot in each constituency) left the political scene in disarray: the MPRP and the MD coalition won 36 seats and 34 seats, respectively, leaving neither with the necessary majority of 39 (one-half of the Great Khural seats plus one seat). The three independents elected, although all DP members, were discounted. The Republican Party won one seat and two seats remained vacant owing to the results being contested. The rate of participation was 82.2% of registered voters. Amid mutual accusations of bribery and fraud in several constituencies, efforts to form a government became embroiled in disputes at the GEC and the recently established City Administrative Court.

The GEC submitted the results in 74 of the 76 constituencies to President Bagabandi in early July 2004, at the first session of the newly elected Great Khural, which was boycotted by the MPRP. The MD members were not allowed to take the oath. Meeting separately, 70 of the MPRP members elected in 2000 filed a lawsuit against the President on the grounds that he had contravened the Constitution and allowed the Great Khural to meet without a quorum (57 members being present) before the final session of the outgoing Great Khural had taken place. The closing session of the previous legislature was held in late July 2004. Among other decisions, it released the Great Khural's Deputy Chairman Jamsrangiin Byambadorj (who had lost his parliamentary seat in the recent elections) to take up a vacant seat in the Constitutional Court and accused the President of acting unconstitutionally in convening the first session of the incoming legislature. All these decisions were vetoed by President Bagabandi in late July as unconstitutional. (Byambadorj was elected a member, then the Chairman, of the Constitutional Court in January 2005.)

Postponed after another MPRP boycott, the first plenary session of the new Great Khural was held in late July 2004, when 74 members were sworn in. Following several weeks of discussions, at the end of August former Prime Minister Nambaryn Enkhbayar of the MPRP was appointed Chairman of the Great Khural, and Tsakhiagiin Elbegdorj of the MD coalition became Prime Minister. Although the newly elected members of the Mongolian Great Khural agreed on the formation, chairmanship and membership of the Khural's standing committees and sub-committees, discussion of the basic principles for the establishment of a coalition government were protracted. The new Cabinet was finally appointed in September. The deputy ministers, one-half nominated by the MD coalition and one-half by the MPRP, were appointed in November and December, respectively.

Coalition government

Radnaasümbereliin Gonchigdorj assumed the chairmanship of the DP at the end of December 2004 and installed his supporters in other senior party posts. His predecessor, Mendsaikhany Enkhsaikhan, appeared to retain the backing of the DP's National Assembly. Although a court ruled that the leadership change was contrary to the party's regulations, it declined to intervene. Badarchiin Erdenebat, the Minister of Defence and leader of the MDNSP, then withdrew from the MD coalition, which collapsed. The Civil Courage Republican Party leader, Sanjaasürengiin Oyuun, was obliged to relinquish her post of Deputy Chairwoman of the Great Khural in January 2005. Prime Minister Elbegdorj took over the defence portfolio from Erdenebat in February, and a new Minister of Defence, Tserenkhüügiin Sharavdorj, was appointed in March. The parliamentary group of the erstwhile MD coalition disbanded, and many DP legislators, including Gonchigdorj (but not Enkhsaikhan), joined the Khural's MPRP group to form a parliamentary 'combined group', of which Gonchigdorj was elected Deputy Chairman. Meanwhile, Doloonjingiin Idevkhten was replaced as General Secretary of the MPRP by Sanjaagiin (Sanjiin) Bayar, the Mongolian ambassador to Russia. In February Jügderdemidiin Gürragchaa (of the MPRP) and in September Zandaakhüügiin Enkhbold (of the MD) were declared the winners in the two constituencies where the results of the 2004 elections to the Great Khural had been contested. Gürragchaa was duly sworn in, but Enkhbold had already accepted the post of Chairman of the State Property Committee in December 2004.

At the presidential election held on 22 May 2005, Nambaryn Enkhbayar (of the MPRP) emerged victorious with more than 53% of the votes cast, defeating Bazarsadyn Jargalsaikhan (of the Republican Party), Badarchiin Erdenebat (of the Motherland Party, as the MDNSP had recently been renamed) and Mendsaikhany Enkhsaikhan (of the DP). At the MPRP's congress in June, the Mayor of Ulan Bator, Miyeegombyn Enkhbold, was chosen to replace Enkhbayar as party Chairman, while the party Leadership Council was enlarged to 21 members. Enkhbayar was inaugurated as President of Mongolia on 24 June. In July the Great Khural elected the Minister of Justice and Home Affairs, Tsendiin Nyamdorj (of the MPRP), to replace Enkhbayar as its Chairman.

After an attempt by the MPRP to force the Prime Minister to resign, including the expulsion of DP members from the 'combined' MPRP parliamentary group (the 'group of 62'), and shortly before the closing of its spring 2005 session, the Great Khural voted in favour of the formation of a DP parliamentary group, which 25 party members (headed by Gonchigdorj) joined. The by-election in Enkhbayar's former constituency in August was won by the MPRP Chairman, Miyeegombyn Enkhbold.

In January 2006 a Motherland Party deputy defected to the MPRP, thereby increasing the parliamentary representation of the latter to 38 seats. Following demands by the MPRP for Prime Minister Elbegdorj's resignation, the 10 MPRP ministers in his Cabinet resigned and the 'grand coalition' Government was voted out of office. Miyeegombyn Enkhbold, MPRP Chairman and Mayor of Ulan Bator, was elected Prime Minister. He formed a new 'national solidarity' Government which included the Motherland and Republican Party leaders Erdenebat and Jargalsaikhan, ex-DP member Lamjavyn Gündalai, who had recently established a new party, the Party of the People, and three DP members—Enkhsaikhan, Narantsatsralt and Mishigiin Sonompil—who were subsequently expelled from the remnant DP, now excluded from the MPRP's new coalition. (Narantsatsralt was killed in a car accident in November 2007.)

Following his appointment in January 2006 to the post of Deputy Prime Minister, Mendsaikhany Enkhsaikhan and his supporters formed a new party, which was named the National New Party at its first congress in May. After the death of legislator Onomoogiin Enkhsaikhan in March, the resultant by-election was delayed until September, when it was won by the Minister of Education, Culture and Science, Ölziisaikhany Enkhtüvshin (of the MPRP).

Meanwhile, the high levels of corruption in Mongolia had become a major concern among international partners. Furthermore, the political upheaval of early 2006 delayed a decision on amendments to the 1997 Minerals Law, introduced at the end of December 2005, which caused disquiet among foreign investors in Mongolia's mining industry. Amid much public debate about the merits of state control of the country's resources and various protests, the Great Khural discussed the amendments, consolidated them in committee and finally adopted a new redaction of the 1997 law in July 2006. According to initial reports, mining licences were to be granted only to companies, not to individuals; foreign and domestic investors in mining were to be taxed at the same rate; stability agreements were to be replaced by investment contracts; and local people in proposed mining areas would be granted greater rights with regard to decisions on exploitation licences. Also, the Government would have the right to acquire up to 50% of the resources of deposits discovered with the help of state funds and to control up to 34% of resources obtained from privately funded deposits. Royalties were to be raised from 2.5% to 5.0%, severe penalties were envisaged for serious environmental damage and the size of foreign work-forces would be limited to 10%.

In October 2006 a parliamentary motion of no confidence was submitted against the Government: Prime Minister Enkhbold was accused of misconduct in relation to land sales during his tenure of the post of Mayor of Ulan Bator, while the Government was criticized for alleged incompetence and its failure to improve the living standards of the population. However, the motion failed to garner sufficient votes to succeed. Meanwhile, in preparation for the legislative elections of mid-2008, the Great Khural approved amendments to the electoral law, restoring 26 large multi-candidate constituencies (similar to those prevailing at the time of the 1992 legislative elections) and introducing a quota of 30% for female members.

In early 2007 it emerged that Tsendiin Nyamdorj, the Chairman of the Great Khural, had re-edited legislation, including the Election Law and the Minerals Law, after the final texts had been approved by the Great Khural. Following a Constitutional Court ruling that his actions were unconstitutional, Nyamdorj was obliged to resign from his post in June. He was replaced by the Deputy Chairman, Danzangiin Lündeejantsan.

At the MPRP's 25th Congress in October 2007, delegates voted to remove Miyeegombyn Enkhbold from the chairmanship of the party, in favour of General Secretary Sanjaagiin Bayar. The members of a new 255-member MPRP Little Khural and 21-member Leadership Council were later announced. Former MPRP secretary Yondongiin Otgonbayar was elected General Secretary and six new secretaries were approved, including Enkhbold and Nyamdorj. For the first time, intra-party political movements and factions were represented by three Leadership Council members; also of note was the inclusion of four women, one of them a Mongolian Kazakh.

An important consequence of these events was Miyeegombyn Enkhbold's resignation as Prime Minister in November 2007, thus allowing Sanjaagiin Bayar's election to the position later in the month. Bayar's first acts included the appointment of

Ravdangiin Bold, ambassador to the USA, to the post of head of the Main Directorate of Intelligence and the dismissal of the ministers responsible for disaster reduction and professional inspection, their portfolios passing to the new Deputy Prime Minister, Enkhbold. After signing co-operation agreements with the CCP and the National New Party, Bayar formed a new Cabinet in December. Among three female appointees was CCP leader Sanjaasürengiin Oyuun, who assumed the role of Minister of Foreign Affairs.

In preparation for the next elections, in December 2007 the electoral law was amended to dispense with the recently introduced requirement for a 30% quota of female members in the legislature. President Enkhbayar unsuccessfully attempted to veto the Great Khural's revision of the law. The level of participation in the legislative elections held on 29 June 2008 was reported to be 74.3%. Amid allegations of widespread irregularities, the Chairman of the DP, Tsakhiagiin Elbegdorj, demanded that the votes be recounted. The Citizens' Alliance (CA, a grouping that represented the Citizens' Movement Party, the Mongolian Green Party and the MSDP) accused both the MPRP and the DP of malpractice. Following the publication of provisional results awarding a narrow parliamentary majority to the MPRP, thousands of demonstrators took to the streets of Ulan Bator to protest against the perceived electoral fraud. Several people were killed in the rioting that ensued, mostly from gunshot wounds, and hundreds were injured. About 700 demonstrators were reported to have been detained. The headquarters of the MPRP were damaged by arson, and the GEC building was also attacked. On 1 July a state of emergency was declared, which remained in place for four days.

It was reported in mid-July 2008 that the GEC had allocated 39 seats in the Great Khural to the MPRP, 25 to the DP, one to the CCP and one to an independent candidate. The winners of 10 of the 76 seats were yet to be declared. Nevertheless, the legislature was instructed by President Enkhbayar to convene its first session. The session duly opened but was swiftly abandoned by DP members, who refused to be inaugurated pending the announcement of the final election results. The withdrawal of the DP from the proceedings thus removed the quorum required for the registration of legislators. Furthermore, the DP demanded an investigation into the conduct of the elections by the Chairman of the GEC, Bataagiin Battulga. After several unsuccessful attempts, the Great Khural finally convened at the end of August, with the participation of the DP and with 67 legislators in attendance. Damdingiin Demberel of the MPRP was appointed as the chamber's Chairman.

On 11 September 2008 the Great Khural re-elected Sanjaagiin Bayar as Prime Minister. Negotiations between the MPRP and the DP, which had encompassed the contentious issue of the development of the country's mineral resources, resulted in an agreement on the formation of a coalition Government, whereby 60% of the ministerial positions were to be allocated to the MPRP and 40% to the DP. Norovyn Altankhuyag, who in late August had replaced Elbegdorj as Chairman of the DP following the latter's resignation, became First Deputy Prime Minister. Miyeegombyn Enkhbold of the MPRP was appointed as Deputy Prime Minister. Sükhbaataryn Batbold (also of the MPRP) was allocated responsibility for external relations, formerly the portfolio of foreign affairs, which had been modified to incorporate economic matters. The Ministry of Trade and Industry was abolished and a new Ministry of Mining and Energy was established.

As the GEC continued its investigations into the disputed results in six constituencies, the DP resumed its boycott of the Great Khural. Following the eventual declaration of the outstanding results, the MPRP held a total of 45 seats in the Great Khural and the DP 27; one seat was occupied by a representative of the CCP, one by a member of the Mongolian Green Party and another by an independent parliamentarian.

The presidential election of 2009 and other events

At the presidential election held on 24 May 2009, the incumbent Nambaryn Enkhbayar of the MPRP was defeated by Tsakhiagiin Elbegdorj, the former Prime Minister and candidate of the DP, whose campaign had focused on the issues of corruption and the need for a more equitable distribution of the country's mineral wealth. Elbegdorj, who had served as Prime Minister in 1998 and again in 2004–06, received 51.2% of the votes cast. His candidacy was supported by the Mongolian Green Party and the CCP. The level of voter participation was 73.6% of the registered electorate. Enkhbayar swiftly conceded defeat, and in a smooth transition Elbegdorj was inaugurated on 18 June 2009.

In October 2009 Prime Minister Sanjaagiin Bayar resigned owing to ill health and was replaced by Sükhbaataryn Batbold, hitherto the Minister of External Relations. In the following month Gombojavyn Zandanshatar of the MPRP was allocated the portfolio of external relations, and Chimediin Khürelbaatar, also of the MPRP, was appointed to head the Government Affairs Directorate. Batbold replaced Bayar as Chairman of the MPRP in April 2010.

One of Bayar's last official duties, in October 2009, was to attend the signing of a highly significant agreement with representatives of international mining companies for the development of the Oyu Tolgoi copper and gold deposits. The exploitation of these resources, located in the Gobi region and to be developed in collaboration with Ivanhoe Mines of Canada and Rio Tinto of Australia, was expected to transform the Mongolian economy (see Economic Affairs). However, considerable discontent was expressed within Mongolia regarding the large share of the deposits given away to foreign interests, with the Mongolian Government retaining only a 34% stake (although this would increase to 50% after 30 years).

Mongolia experienced its most severe winter conditions for several decades in 2009/10. The exceptionally low temperatures and persistent snowfalls resulted in the loss of millions of livestock and extreme hardship for many Mongolians. In February 2010, in return for payments to herders, the UN Development Programme initiated a scheme for the collection of animal carcasses, the accumulation of which posed a serious health risk upon the return of milder weather. Humanitarian assistance was provided by the International Committee of the Red Cross, which in March launched a global appeal for emergency funding, and by other relief agencies.

In April 2010 about 5,000 demonstrators rallied in Ulan Bator to protest against the inequalities in Mongolian society arising from the perceived inequitable distribution of the benefits of the country's substantial mineral wealth. The protesters demanded the dissolution of the Great Khural and the release of government aid to impoverished Mongolians, upon whom the unusually harsh winter conditions had had a serious impact.

Meanwhile, in a development that was welcomed by human rights groups, in January 2010 the President announced that there was to be a moratorium on the implementation of the death penalty. It was hoped that the formal abolition of the death penalty would follow, although many opposition members of the Great Khural were reported to favour its retention.

In November 2010 the delegates attending the MPRP's 26th party congress in Ulan Bator voted, by an overwhelming majority, to change the name of the party back to the Mongolian People's Party (MPP), as it had been called from its foundation in 1921 until 1925, when, under Soviet influence, the word 'revolutionary' had been added—a word that Prime Minister Batbold claimed had confrontational connotations that were no longer appropriate for the more pragmatic environment of modern-day Mongolia. Also during the congress, Batbold was re-elected as party Chairman. At the first conference of the renamed party, the Leadership Council was enlarged from 21 to 31 members. In January 2011 former President Nambaryn Enkhbayar was elected as leader of a new Mongolian People's Revolutionary Party formed by those who had rejected the change in the party's name in November 2010.

In March 2011 the CCP and the Mongolian Green Party merged to form the Civil Courage-Green Party (CC-GP). The new party was finally registered by the Supreme Court in March 2012, with Dangaasürengiin Enkhbat of the Mongolian Green Party and Sanjaasürengiin Oyuun of the CCP as Joint Chairmen.

In April 2011 a group of approximately 200 herdsmen gathered in the central square of Ulan Bator to demand the resignation of the Government and the dissolution of the Great Khural, accusing the Mongolian authorities of having become pawns to foreign mining interests. The protesters appealed for a popular referendum to be staged on the question of conducting parliamentary elections without the participation of political parties. In June around 50 protesters, led by Tsetsgeegiin Mönkhbayar, leader of the Gal Undesten (Fire Nation) association, a coalition of environmental and political groups, set up a makeshift camp in Ulan Bator's central square and fired arrows at the parliamentary building, in protest at the Government's refusal to acquiesce to the demands for a referendum.

Under considerable pressure from the Great Khural, in September 2011 the Mongolian Government announced its intention to renegotiate the terms of the agreement signed with

Ivanhoe Mines and Rio Tinto in October 2009 for the development of the Oyu Tolgoi copper and gold deposits, seeking to increase its stake from 34% to 50%. However, following severe resistance from the Canadian and Australian firms, the Government agreed to maintain the original terms of agreement, with its stake scheduled to increase to 50% only after 30 years. Meanwhile, in October 2010 the Government had announced the establishment of Erdenes Tavan Tolgoi, a state-owned company that would retain 100% ownership of the Tavan Tolgoi coal deposits, with the company authorized to award development contracts only, in an apparent acknowledgement of the increasing public consternation regarding the extent of foreign ownership of Mongolia's mining industry. Furthermore, in mid-2011 the Government announced its intention to give away 10% of Erdenes Tavan Tolgoi's shares to the Mongolian population; each Mongolian citizen was to receive more than 500 shares in early 2012, shortly prior to the company's initial public offering.

Parliamentary discussions during the course of 2011 over the adoption of new electoral legislation in advance of the forthcoming legislative elections, scheduled to be held in June 2012, were widely seen as a response to the widespread unpopularity of the new electoral system that had been adopted prior to the 2008 elections. However, disagreements between the MPP and the DP concerning the proposed nature of the changes—with the former in favour of a majority system of voting, while the latter preferred a system of proportional representation—led to a protracted impasse between the two coalition parties, and precipitated the resignations in June 2011 of both the Chairman and Deputy Chairman of the MPP parliamentary group. Finally, however, a compromise agreement was reached between the two parties, and in December the Great Khural approved the new legislation, which was to take effect from the 2012 elections. Voters would be able to vote for an individual candidate in one of 48 single-seat constituencies, and also for a political party, with 28 members to be indirectly elected in the latter vote on the basis of proportional representation. Parties would be required to obtain at least 5% of the total number of votes nation-wide in order to secure parliamentary representation. The legislation also reintroduced the quota for female members that had been introduced prior to the 2008 elections (but which had then been repealed in December 2007), although the percentage of seats to be reserved henceforth for women was set at the lower level of 20%.

However, political tensions within the Government soon re-emerged and in early January 2012 the DP announced its withdrawal from the coalition, precipitating the resignation from the Cabinet later that month of the six DP ministers. Prime Minister Batbold submitted a list of MPP nominees to replace the outgoing ministers in mid-January, but this was rejected by President Elbegdorj on the grounds that legislative arrangements formally to end the coalition had not yet been made. However, after further consultations, Batbold resubmitted his list, and five of the six proposed appointments were approved by the Great Khural in late January, including those of Jadambaagiin Enkhbayar as Minister of Defence, Damdingiin Khayankhyarvaa as Minister of Finance and Nyamdavaagiin Khürelbaatar as Minister of Health. Batbold had nominated Ukhnaagiin Khürelsükh, General Secretary of the MPP, for the role of Chief Deputy Prime Minister, but in the event the post was abolished on the grounds that it had been created purely for the purposes of the coalition and was no longer required.

In mid-April 2012 former President Nambaryn Enkhbayar was detained, following a raid on his home by the security forces. The authorities claimed that he had failed to respond to requests to appear for questioning in connection with a corruption investigation into his alleged misuse of public assets while in power. Amnesty International expressed concern about his treatment, while protests were staged by his supporters in Ulan Bator. Following an 11-day hunger strike protesting his innocence, Enkhbayar was released on bail in mid-May and received hospital treatment. He had intended to contest the legislative elections scheduled for June as the leader of the new Mongolian People's Revolutionary Party. Supporters contended that his arrest had been politically motivated to prevent his participation in the elections.

In May 2012 the Great Khural passed new legislation limiting the size of foreign investments in the country's 'strategic' industries, including mining, banking and telecommunications, without both government and parliamentary prior approval. The law provided for the capping of foreign ownership at 49%, but was applicable only to stakes valued at more than US $76m. or to investments by foreign state-owned companies. The

Government admitted that the passage of the new legislation had been prompted by a recent unsuccessful bid by the Chinese state-owned company Aluminium Corporation of China (CHALCO) to purchase a majority stake in the Mongolian coal company SouthGobi Resources.

Recent developments: the legislative elections of 2012

In the run-up to the legislative elections, which were scheduled to be held (under the new electoral system) on 28 June 2012, the main contenders attempted to win public support by pledging better wealth distribution. The MPP asserted that, if elected, it would establish a national sovereign wealth fund and increase spending in the health and education sectors, while the DP promised to complete a decade-old programme of free allocation of state-owned agricultural land to the populace. In the event, following challenges to the results in some constituencies that ended in the initial results being overturned, the DP won 36 of the 76 seats in the Great Khural, the MPP secured 24 seats, the newly established Justice Coalition, which comprised the MNDP and the Mongolian People's Revolutionary Party of Nambaryn Enkhbayar (who had himself been barred from contesting the elections by the GEC owing to his impending trial), obtained 11 seats, the CC-GP took 2 seats and three seats were won by independent candidates. Electoral turn-out was relatively low, at 65.2%. Owing to the legal challenges to the results, the final two members of the Great Khural were not sworn in until May 2013.

Outgoing Prime Minister Sükhbaataryn Batbold, who blamed his party's defeat on the loss of votes to Enkhbayar's breakaway party, resigned as Chairman of the MPP at a party conference on 25 July 2012; he was replaced by former Minister of Education, Culture and Science, Ölziisaikhany Enkhtüvshin. Following lengthy negotiations and weeks of uncertainty, on 10 August the Great Khural finally approved the nomination of the Chairman of the DP, Norovyn Altankhuyag, as Prime Minister. A coalition Cabinet, composed of members of the DP, the Justice Coalition and the CC-GP was endorsed by the legislature on 20 August. Among the notable appointments were those of Dendeviin Terbishdagva, the Deputy Chairman of the Mongolian People's Revolutionary Party, as Deputy Prime Minister and of Luvsanvdangiin Bold of the DP as Minister of External Relations.

Meanwhile, on 2 August 2012 Enkhbayar, having delayed his trial until after the elections, was convicted of corruption and received a prison sentence of seven years (of which three years were commuted) as well as a sizeable fine; the former President stated that he intended to launch an appeal against his conviction.

In April 2013 the Deputy Speaker of the Great Khural, Sangajavyn Bayartsogt, resigned following the emergence of evidence that from 2008 he had owned an offshore company and held a Swiss bank account that he had failed to declare on the disclosure documents required to assume public office. Bayartsogt, who had been the Minister of Finance in 2008–12, stepped down after an overwhelming vote in favour of his resignation took place in the Great Khural.

Foreign Affairs

Following its admission to the UN in 1961, Mongolia was accorded diplomatic recognition by the United Kingdom (in 1963) and other Western European states, as well as by many developing countries. By January 1987, when Mongolia was finally granted diplomatic recognition by the USA, it maintained diplomatic relations with more than 100 states.

Regional relations

Relations with the People's Republic of China were good until the onset of the Sino–Soviet dispute in the 1960s. However, Sino-Mongolian relations improved significantly from 1986 when the Chinese Vice-Minister of Foreign Affairs visited Ulan Bator, and the two countries signed agreements on consular relations and trade. A new Treaty of Friendship and Co-operation was concluded during a visit to Ulan Bator by Chinese Premier Li Peng in April 1994. None the less, Mongolia continued to protest in 1995 at the series of nuclear tests being carried out in the Xinjiang Uygur (Sinkiang Uighur) autonomous region of China, while Mongolian human rights groups and the Ulan Bator press supported protests in the northern Chinese autonomous region of Nei Monggol (Inner Mongolia) against the arrest by the Chinese authorities of human rights activists in December. However, relations were consolidated by a series of senior-level bilateral visits during the late 1990s and early 2000s, including

that of Prime Minister Jasrai to the Chinese capital, Beijing, in March 1996; reciprocal visits by Chinese President Jiang Zemin and Mongolian Prime Minister Amarjargal in July and November 1999, respectively; and a visit to Ulan Bator by Chinese President Hu Jintao in June 2003.

In August 2006 the Dalai Lama, the head of the Buddhist clergy of Tibet (Xizang), undertook his seventh visit to Mongolia, at the invitation of local Buddhists, and presided over religious ceremonies in Ulan Bator, to the consternation of the Chinese Government. In November Miyeegombyn Enkhbold signed a trade and economic co-operation agreement with China, during his first official visit to that country since becoming Prime Minister in January. In April 2008 President Enkhbayar travelled to China to attend the Bo'ao Forum for Asia, at which he had discussions with President Hu Jintao.

President Elbegdorj embarked upon a six-day state visit to China in April 2010, hoping to strengthen bilateral co-operation in areas such as the formulation of measures to combat desertification. In the same month Prime Minister Batbold attended the Bo'ao conference in China, and in June of that year the Chinese Premier, Wen Jiabao, paid an official visit to Mongolia (the first by a Chinese premier for 16 years), during which the two sides signed an intergovernmental border regime agreement (renewing an accord of 1998). In addition, the two countries agreed to enhance bilateral co-operation in areas such as energy, trade and environmental protection, and Premier Wen proposed the arrangement of an early date for a feasibility study of the establishment of a Sino-Mongolian free trade area. In June 2011 Mongolia and China upgraded their relations to a strategic partnership, during a visit to Ulan Bator by Premier Wen, during which he met with Prime Minister Batbold. However, tensions arose in November when the Dalai Lama made another visit to Mongolia, again at the request of local Buddhists. The Chinese Government remained staunchly opposed to any country affording a political platform to the Dalai Lama; however, the Mongolian Government insisted that the visit had been exclusively religious in nature.

Diplomatic relations between Mongolia and Japan were established in 1972, and were consolidated by a number of high-level meetings during the 1990s and 2000s. In July 2006 Mongolia received Japanese Prime Minister Junichiro Koizumi, who discussed joint efforts to develop energy resources in Mongolia, as well as issues relating to the Democratic People's Republic of Korea (North Korea). In February 2007 President Enkhbayar visited Japan and signed a joint agreement with Japanese Prime Minister Shinzo Abe pledging to expand bilateral relations, including plans to utilize mineral resources in Mongolia. The two leaders agreed to co-operate in resolving tensions caused by the North Korean nuclear dispute and to collaborate in Japan's quest to attain a permanent seat on the UN Security Council. During a visit to the Japanese capital of Tokyo in July 2009, Prime Minister Bayar had discussions with his counterpart, Taro Aso, during which Bayar expressed his desire for much closer relations with Japan. In November 2010, during a state visit by President Elbegdorj to Japan, the two countries signed a Mongolia-Japan Joint Declaration aimed at strengthening strategic relations. However, reports in mid-2011 that the Mongolian, Japanese and US Governments had provisionally reached an agreement providing for Mongolia to host a regional facility for the storage of nuclear waste, potentially with technical support from the UN's International Atomic Energy Agency, prompted significant popular resentment within Mongolia, although all three Governments denied the existence of any such proposal. In March 2013 the recently re-elected Prime Minister Abe visited Mongolia, where he held discussions with President Elbegdorj and the new Mongolian Prime Minister, Norovyn Altankhuyag, on the establishment of closer trade and energy ties. The two sides also discussed the worrying nuclear ambitions and recent bellicose posturing of North Korea.

In May 1999 Mongolia received South Korean President Kim Dae-Jung, marking the first such visit by a Korean head of state. Following talks with the Mongolian Minister of Defence, Sharavdorj Tuvdendorj, President Kim obtained the Mongolian Government's support for his policy of political engagement with the North Korean regime. In November Mongolian Prime Minister Amarjargal made a reciprocal visit to the Republic of Korea. In May 2006 the South Korean President, Roh Moo-Hyun, undertook a state visit to Mongolia, where he discussed a range of issues with President Enkhbayar, including trade and environmental co-operation. In March 2011 Prime Minister Batbold paid an official visit to South Korea, during which the two sides held talks on co-operation in the development of coal and other mineral resources in Mongolia. South Korean President Lee Myung-bak made a reciprocal visit to Mongolia in August, where he met with President Elbegdorj. The two heads of state agreed to elevate relations to a 'comprehensive partnership', and pledged to expand co-operation in a wide range of fields, including national and regional defence, energy and mining, infrastructural development, construction, transport, health care, agriculture and the environment. Elbegdorj reaffirmed Mongolian support for South Korea's efforts to resolve the North Korean nuclear issue, stressing that a complete and irreversible denuclearization of North Korea was essential to hopes of regional peace and stability.

In November 1999 Prime Minister Amarjargal visited the North Korean capital of Pyongang and exchanged views with Premier Hong Song Nam on the development of bilateral relations. Amarjargal also met with, Kim Yong Nam, President of the Presidium of the North Korean Supreme People's Assembly. President Bagabandi visited Pyongyang in December 2005 to promote joint co-operation. In July 2007 Mongolia received Kim Yong Nam, and a bilateral agreement to co-operate in the areas of public health, medical science and marine transport was signed. In November 2010 the close nature of relations between Mongolia and North Korea was revealed following the online release by WikiLeaks, an organization publishing leaked private and classified content, of a series of US diplomatic cables; in one such communiqué a Mongolian diplomat divulged that during a meeting between Mongolian and North Korean officials in August 2009 a North Korean government minister had proposed that Mongolia host disarmament talks between the USA and North Korea. In April 2013 it was reported that the Mongolian Independent Agency against Corruption was investigating allegations that the recently resigned head of the Mongolian air force, Brig.-Gen. Tojoon Dashdeleg, had arranged in 2011 to sell salvaged parts from about 20 disused fighter aircraft to North Korea; the North Korean authorities claimed to have paid for but not to have received the parts.

Other external relations

For many years foreign affairs were dominated by Mongolia's relations with the Soviet Union. Following the dissolution of the USSR in 1991, co-operation with Russia, the largest of the successor states, continued. During an official visit to Russia in January 1993, President Ochirbat and the Russian President, Boris Yeltsin, issued a joint statement expressing regret at the execution and imprisonment of Mongolian citizens in the USSR during the Stalinist period. Ochirbat and Yeltsin also signed a new 20-year Mongolian-Russian Treaty of Friendship and Co-operation to replace the defunct Mongolian-Soviet treaty of 1986. In November 2000 the Russian President, Vladimir Putin, made a brief stop in Ulan Bator en route to a conference in Brunei, thus becoming the most senior Russian or Soviet visitor to Mongolia since 1974. Russia affirmed its commitment to guaranteeing Mongolia's security in connection with its nuclear weapons-free status. Russian Prime Minister Mikhail Kasyanov undertook an official visit to Mongolia in late March 2002 to discuss economic and military co-operation, and also the issue of Mongolia's outstanding debt of 11,400m. transferable roubles that the Russian Government claimed it was owed for Soviet aid granted during 1947–91; the Mongolian Government referred to this as the 'big debt'. The two countries had been unable to agree terms for the previous 10 years. Mongolia disagreed with Russia's position that the debt should be paid in full at par value with the US dollar, and there was also Mongolian opposition pressure to offset the cost of damage inflicted on the environment by Soviet military activity.

When the two Prime Ministers met in the Russian capital of Moscow in July 2003, a new five-year agreement on the operation of the Erdenet copper enterprise was reached, preserving Mongolia's 51% ownership of stock. In December Russia announced that it had received Mongolia's payment in settlement of the 'big debt'. Russia had waived 98% of the total debt and accepted US $250m. Prime Minister Nambaryn Enkhbayar celebrated a political and diplomatic victory for the MPRP Government, but the full details of the settlement remained unclear.

Several high-level meetings took place in 2006–08, including a state visit to Moscow by the Mongolian President in December 2006 and a further presidential visit in May 2008. Prime Minister Sanjaagiin Bayar visited Moscow in March 2009, when the Russian Government announced the offer of a loan of US $300m. to support the Mongolian agricultural sector. The proposed financing was linked to Mongolia's purchase of Russian equip-

ment and other agricultural supplies. The Russian President Dimitrii Medvedev's visit to Mongolia in August resulted in the signing of various agreements relating to mining ventures and providing for greater Russian participation in the management of railway operations in Mongolia. The question of the settlement of Mongolia's long-standing debt to Russia was also raised, when Medvedev stated that certain issues remained unresolved. Mongolia's strengthening links with Russia were underlined in early 2011 by the Mongolian Government's approval of plans to construct a 1,500-km rail link to the north-east of the country where it was to connect with the Russian Trans-Siberian network; however, at April 2013 construction work on the proposed railway had not yet commenced. At the end of May 2011 President Elbegdorj embarked upon a week-long state visit to Russia, during which he held discussions with Medvedev on a range of issues that was reported to include proposals for a bilateral free trade agreement as well as measures further to enhance defence co-operation.

During an official visit to the USA in November 2001, Prime Minister Enkhbayar addressed the UN General Assembly in New York; he also had a meeting with President George W. Bush. Enkhbayar reaffirmed his country's strategic partnership with the USA and urged greater US investment in Mongolia. Having condemned the attacks of 11 September against the USA, he informed President Bush of Mongolia's readiness to allow the use of its air space to help combat terrorism. Following the US military intervention in Iraq in March 2003, members of the Mongolian army's élite battalion were dispatched to Iraq. (The Mongolian deployment remained in Iraq until September 2008.) In July 2004 President Bagabandi met President Bush in Washington, DC, USA, and signed a Trade and Investment Framework Agreement. In 2005 the USA provided Mongolia with US $18m. in military assistance, including regular training exchanges and peace-keeping exercises. In November 2005 President Bush made the first visit to Mongolia by an incumbent US President.

In February 2006, following a closed meeting in Ulan Bator with foreign donors (the World Bank, the Asian Development Bank, the IMF, the UN, Japan, the USA and Germany), which urged greater accountability, the US Administration issued a statement noting that the US Agency for International Development had found that corruption in Mongolia was increasing at all levels. Mongolia was to be required to draw up lists of specific actions to combat corruption and to detail all the changes needed within existing law in order that it might comply with the UN Convention Against Corruption (UNCAC). A new Anti-Corruption Law was adopted by the Mongolian legislature in July.

President Elbegdorj made an official visit to Washington, DC, in June 2011, during which he met with the US President, Barack Obama, and in August the US Vice-President, Joseph Biden, made a state visit to Ulan Bator, where he met with Batbold (now Prime Minister) and Elbegdorj. Biden's visit, during which he commended Mongolia's transition to democracy, was widely welcomed in Mongolia; however, a small group of demonstrators gathered in the capital to protest against an alleged informal agreement between the Mongolian, US and Japanese Governments for Mongolia to host a regional facility for the storage of nuclear waste (see Regional relations). During a visit to Mongolia by US Secretary of State Hillary Clinton in July 2012, when she met President Elbegdorj, the US official praised Mongolia as a model of democracy and freedom of expression.

CONSTITUTION AND GOVERNMENT

Supreme legislative power is vested in the 76-member Mongolian Great Khural (Assembly), elected by universal adult suffrage for four years. The Great Khural recognizes the President on his election and appoints the Prime Minister and members of the Cabinet, which is the highest executive body. The President, who is directly elected for a term of four years, is head of state and Commander-in-Chief of the Armed Forces. Under the terms of a revision to the electoral law approved in December 2011, which took effect from the June 2012 elections, voters can vote for an individual candidate in one of 48 single-seat constituencies, and for a political party, with 28 members to be indirectly elected on the basis of proportional representation.

Mongolia is divided into 21 provinces (*aimag*) and one municipality (Ulan Bator), with appointed governors and elected local assemblies.

REGIONAL AND INTERNATIONAL CO-OPERATION

Mongolia is a member of the Asian Development Bank (ADB, see p. 214), of the Association of Southeast Asian Nations (ASEAN) Regional Forum (ARF, see p. 221) and of the UN's Economic and Social Commission for Asia and the Pacific (ESCAP, see p. 31).

Mongolia became a member of the UN in 1961. It was admitted to the World Trade Organization (WTO, see p. 444) in 1997. Mongolia is also a member of the European Bank for Reconstruction and Development (EBRD, see p. 276), and Mongolbank, the country's central bank, has joined the Bank for International Settlements (see p. 228). In November 2012 the country acceded to the Organization for Security and Co-operation in Europe (OSCE, see p. 397) as a full participating state; Mongolia had been an OSCE Partner for Co-operation since 2004.

ECONOMIC AFFAIRS

In 2011, according to estimates by the World Bank, Mongolia's gross national income (GNI), measured at average 2009–11 prices, was US $6,488m., equivalent to $2,320 per head (or $4,360 per head on an international purchasing-power parity basis). During 2002–11, it was estimated, the population increased at an average annual rate of 1.5%, while gross domestic product (GDP) per head increased, in real terms, at an average of 6.7% per year. Overall GDP increased, in real terms, at an average annual rate of 8.2% in 2002–11. According to Asian Development Bank (ADB) estimates, real GDP increased by 17.5% in 2011 and by 12.3% in 2012.

Agriculture (including forestry and fishing) contributed 15.3% of GDP in 2011 and engaged 33.0% of the employed labour force. Animal herding is the main economic activity and is practised throughout the country. Most livestock is privately owned. A summer drought in 2009 was followed by unusually low winter temperatures, as a result of which a total of 8.2m. livestock (sheep, goats, horses, cattle and camels) were reported to have died by May 2010; more than one-half of these losses were goats. By the end of 2010 livestock numbers had dwindled, to 32.5m., although a substantial recovery in numbers was recorded over the following two years. The principal crops are wheat, potatoes and vegetables. Production of cereals rose from 446,100 metric tons in 2011 to 479,300 tons in 2012. During 2002–11, according to figures from the World Bank, the GDP of the agricultural sector increased, in real terms, at an average annual rate of 4.6%. According to the ADB, agricultural GDP contracted by 0.5% in 2011, but grew by 21.3% in 2012.

Industry (comprising mining, manufacturing, construction and utilities) provided 36.3% of GDP in 2011 and the sector (excluding printing and publishing) engaged 17.3% of the employed labour force. According to the World Bank, during 2002–11 industrial GDP increased, in real terms, at an average rate of 5.7% per year. According to the ADB, the industrial sector's GDP increased by 9.1% in 2011 and by 10.1% in 2012.

Mining contributed 23.9% of GDP in 2011, and employed less than 2% of the work-force in 2012, according to the ADB. Mongolia has significant, largely unexplored, mineral resources and is a leading producer and exporter of copper, gold, molybdenum and fluorspar concentrates. Mining contributed 89.2% of exports in 2012, according to the ADB. The value of exports of copper concentrate totalled around US $770.6m. in both 2010 and 2011. In addition to the major copper-molybdenum works at Erdenet, a Mongolian-Russian joint venture, the sites of other mineral deposits are being developed in collaboration with various foreign enterprises, notably the Oyu Tolgoi copper and gold deposits. Production of copper concentrate commenced at Oyu Tolgoi in early 2013. There were delays, however, in reaching agreement with foreign enterprises regarding the exploitation of the Tavan Tolgoi coalfield and the proposed partial privatization of Erdenes Tavan Tolgoi, the state-owned company established to supervise the development of the coking coal deposits. Meanwhile, gold production declined from some 22,600 kg in 2006 to 5,703 kg in 2011. Output of coal rose from 8.1m. metric tons in 2006 to 32.0m. tons in 2011. Other mineral resources include tungsten, tin, uranium and lead. Mongolia's production of crude petroleum has increased rapidly, from 366,800 barrels in 2006 to 2,548,900 barrels in 2011. According to the ADB, the GDP of the mining sector expanded at an average annual rate of 8.4% in 2003–11; the sector's GDP increased, in real terms, by 8.9% in 2012.

The manufacturing sector accounted for 8.3% of GDP in 2011. Manufacturing industries are based largely on the products of the agricultural and animal husbandry sector. The principal branches of manufacturing include food products, beverages, textiles and garments. Mongolia is one of the world's foremost producers of cashmere, and the country also manufactures garments, leather goods and carpets. According to figures from the World Bank, manufacturing GDP increased at an average annual rate of 5.9% in 2001–10. The sector's GDP grew by 16.8% in 2011 and by 13.4% in 2012, according to ADB data.

Construction accounted for just 1.5% of GDP in 2011 and engaged 5.0% of the employed population. According to figures from the ADB, the sector's GDP decreased by an average of 3.0% per year in 2003–11. The sector expanded by 14.3% in 2011.

Energy is derived principally from thermal power stations, fuelled by coal. Most provincial centres have thermal power stations or diesel generators, while minor rural centres generally rely on small diesel generators. In more isolated areas wood, roots, bushes and dried animal dung are used for domestic fuel. In August 2011 the Mongolian Government revealed proposals to build and commission the country's first nuclear power plant by 2017. There is also much potential for the development of renewable energy resources. Construction of the country's first wind farm, located at Salkhit, around 70 km from Ulan Bator, was expected to be completed by the end of 2013 and was forecast to provide some 5% of Mongolia's electricity requirements while reducing carbon dioxide emissions. Mongolia imports from Russia electricity and petroleum products, including liquid petroleum gas. In 2010 the cost of Mongolia's imports of fuels and lubricants rose to US $713.8m., thus accounting for 22.3% of the total cost of merchandise imports, but this share decreased to 18.0% in 2011, although the total cost of these imports increased to $1,188.3m.

The services sector contributed 48.3% of GDP in 2011 and engaged 40.2% of the employed labour force. During 2002–11, according to figures from the World Bank, the GDP of the sector increased, in real terms, by an average of 9.4% annually. Receipts from tourism were estimated to have reached US $222.4m. in 2010. The number of visitor arrivals increased from 456,090 in 2009 to 460,360 in 2011, when about 43% of visitors came from the People's Republic of China. According to the ADB, the GDP of the services sector grew by 9.8% in 2010 and by 17.1% in 2011.

According to IMF figures, Mongolia's visible merchandise trade deficit was US $990.1m. in 2011 and there was a deficit of $2,760.4m. on the current account of the balance of payments. In 2011 the principal source of imports was China, supplying 30.8% of the total, followed by Russia, the USA, Japan and the Republic of Korea. China was also the principal market for exports in that year, purchasing 92.1% of the total. The principal imports in 2011 were machinery and electrical goods, followed by motor vehicles and aircraft, fuels and lubricants, and food and live animals. The leading export was minerals, and specifically coal and copper concentrate. Other significant exports included gold and textiles.

In 2012 there was a cash budget deficit (as opposed to a structural budget deficit) equivalent to 7.7% of GDP, according to the ADB, compared with a deficit equivalent to 4.8% of GDP in 2011. Mongolia's total external debt was US $15,260m. at the end of 2012. In that year, the cost of debt-servicing was equivalent to 9.3% of the value of exports of goods and services. According to figures from the ADB, the annual rate of inflation averaged 11.3% during 2005–11. Consumer prices rose by 9.1% in 2011 and by 14.3% in 2012, according to the ADB. The number of registered unemployed persons decreased from 57,200 in 2011 to 35,800 in 2012. However, the number of unregistered unemployed persons was believed to be far greater. According to the ADB, the official rate of unemployment was higher than 5% in 2011, but labour surveys indicated a rate of about 8%.

The reduction in the value of the country's exports, notably copper, as well as a substantial decrease in cashmere prices, as a result of the international financial crisis of 2008–09 had a serious impact on the Mongolian economy. However, in a major advance, in October 2009 the Government concluded an agreement with Canadian and British-Australian interests for the development of the Oyu Tolgoi copper and gold deposits. Commercial production was expected to commence in June 2013 and was forecast to reach full operating capacity—an annual 450,000 metric tons of copper and 330,000 oz of gold—in 2020. According to some estimates, the mine could potentially generate annual revenue of more than US $8,000m. for the next 40–50 years. However, in February 2013 the Mongolian authorities revoked the gold-mining licences for a key section of the Oyu Tolgoi mine amid a mounting dispute with the British-Australian Rio Tinto Group over project financing. In the same month, following multiple financing problems, bureaucratic delays and political opposition to initial plans to include foreign investors, it was announced that production would commence later that year at the West Tsankhi block of the vast Tavan Tolgoi coalfield (the world's largest coking coal deposit). Operations would be under the management of Erdenes Tavan Tolgoi (a state-owned company established in 2010 to supervise the development of the coalfield). Negotiations with foreign interests for the development of the West Tsankhi block had been conducted during 2011–12, but no contract had been finalized. Despite Mongolia's vast wealth of mineral resources, development of the national economy has been obstructed by, *inter alia*, severe infrastructural deficiencies. Poor transport links—both within Mongolia and to neighbouring China and Russia, and beyond—have impeded trade and investment, as well as prohibiting access to employment opportunities for those living in more remote regions. Unemployment was unofficially estimated to have fallen from about 13% in 2010 to 8% in 2011, although in some more remote districts it was reported to exceed 60%. It was hoped that an ADB-funded road improvement project in western Mongolia, completion of which was scheduled for 2020, would reduce the isolation of and encourage development in one of the country's most impoverished regions. Meanwhile, economic recovery in 2010, with GDP growth of 6.4%, was due mainly to an increase in international prices of minerals, to high levels of investment in the mining sector and to a robust economic revival in China. The rapidly expanding mining sector and swiftly increasing government expenditure led to the growth rate increasing to 17.5% in

2011, before moderating to 12.3% in 2012, according to the ADB. The high rate of growth of GDP was projected by the ADB to continue, at 16.5% and 14.0% for 2013 and 2014, respectively. However, the rapid rise in fiscal expenditure in 2010–12 led to high rates of inflation (at times exceeding the official target ceiling of 10%) with consumer prices increasing by 10.1% in 2010, by 9.1% in 2011 and by 14.3% in 2012. According to ADB projections, inflation was expected to fall to 13.0% in 2013 and to 10.0% in 2014, assuming the introduction of more stringent monetary policies (including lower off-budget expenditure). The Government, aware of the risks implicit in its highly expansionary fiscal policies, as well as the insecurities inherent in mineral-based economies, established a Fiscal Stability Fund in early 2011 to be used during periods of economic downturn; a proportion of the fund was also intended to help finance measures to address the country's long-term infrastructural needs. By December 2012 the Fund held 328,000m. tögrög, equivalent to around 2.4% of GDP. Other ongoing concerns of the Government included the need to promote economic diversification (to avoid over-reliance on the mining sector) and the persistent levels of poverty (around one-third of the population still lived below the poverty line).

PUBLIC HOLIDAYS

2014: 1 January (New Year), 31 January–2 February (Tsagaan Sar, lunar new year), 8 March (International Women's Day), 1 June (Children's Day), 11–13 July (Anniversary of the People's Revolution and Naadam, national sports festival), November (Genghis Khan Day), 29 December (National Freedom Day).

Statistical Survey

Unless otherwise indicated, revised by Alan J. K. Sanders

Area and Population

AREA, POPULATION AND DENSITY

Area (sq km)	1,564,116*
Population (census results)	
5 January 2000	2,373,493
19 November 2010†	2,754,685
Population (official estimate at 31 December)	
2011	2,811,600
Density (per sq km) at 31 December 2011	1.8

* 603,909 sq miles.
† Including foreign nationals (16,320), stateless persons (108) and Mongolian citizens resident abroad (107,140).

POPULATION BY AGE AND SEX
(UN estimates at mid-2013)

	Males	Females	Total
0–14	403,111	394,463	797,574
15–64	972,371	999,715	1,972,086
65 and over	49,537	68,666	118,203
Total	1,425,019	1,462,844	2,887,863

Note: Estimates not adjusted to take account of 2010 census.

Source: UN, *World Population Prospects: The 2010 Revision.*

ADMINISTRATIVE DIVISIONS
(official population estimates at 31 December 2011)

Province (Aimag)	Area ('000 sq km)	Estimated population ('000)	Provincial centre
Arkhangai	55.3	84.3	Tsetserleg
Bayankhongor	116.0	76.7	Bayankhongor
Bayan-Ölgii	45.7	88.8	Ölgii
Bulgan	48.7	54.1	Bulgan
Darkhan-Uul	3.3	96.0	Darkhan
Dornod (Eastern) . .	123.6	70.2	Choibalsan
Dornogobi (East Gobi) . .	109.5	60.2	Sainshand
Dundgobi (Central Gobi) .	74.7	37.7	Mandalgobi
Gobi-Altai	141.4	53.0	Altai
Gobi-Sümber	5.5	13.9	Choir
Khentii	80.3	66.4	Öndörkhaan
Khovd	76.1	77.2	Khovd
Khövsgöl	100.6	115.9	Mörön
Orkhon	0.8	91.5	Erdenet
Ömnögobi (South Gobi) .	165.4	63.4	Dalanzadgad
Övörkhangai	62.9	101.2	Arvaikheer
Selenge	41.2	99.2	Sükhbaatar
Sükhbaatar	82.3	51.8	Baruun Urt
Töv (Central)	74.0	85.7	Zuun mod
Ulan Bator (Ulaanbaatar)*	4.7	1,287.1	(capital city)
Uvs	69.6	73.0	Ulaangom
Zavkhan	82.5	64.2	Uliastai
Total	1,564.1	2,811.6	

* Ulan Bator, including Nalaikh, and Bagakhangai and Baganuur districts beyond the urban boundary, has special status as the capital city.

ETHNIC GROUPS
(resident Mongolian citizens at 2010 census)

	Number	%
Khalkh (Khalkha)	2,168,141	82.4
Kazakh (Khasag)	101,526	3.9
Dörvöd (Durbet)	72,403	2.8
Bayad (Bayat)	56,573	2.2
Buryat (Buriat)	45,087	1.7
Zakhchin	32,845	1.2
Dariganga	27,412	1.0
Uriankhai	26,654	1.0
Other ethnic groups	100,476	3.8
Total	2,631,117	100.0

Note: Data exclude foreign nationals (16,320), stateless persons (108) and Mongolian citizens resident abroad (107,140).

PRINCIPAL TOWNS
(estimated population at December)

Ulan Bator (capital)	1,287,100*	Erdenet	74,300†

* 2011.
† 2007.

BIRTHS, MARRIAGES AND DEATHS

	Registered births		Registered marriages*		Registered deaths	
	Number	Rate (per 1,000)	Number	Rate (per 1,000)	Number	Rate (per 1,000)
2004	45,501	18.1	11,242	7.2	16,404	6.5
2005	45,326	17.8	14,993	9.3	16,480	6.5
2006	49,092	19.0	48,996	19.0	16,682	6.5
2007	56,636	21.7	40,965	15.7	16,259	6.2
2008	63,768	24.0	32,982	12.4	15,413	5.8
2009	69,167	25.5	34,071	12.6	16,911	6.2
2010	63,270	22.9	9,349	3.4	18,293	6.6
2011	68,853	25.1	11,869	4.3	19,155	6.9

* Persons aged 18 years and over.

2012: 74,778 registered births; 16,923 registered deaths.

Source: Mongolian Statistical Office.

Life expectancy (years at birth): 68.32 (males 64.68; females 73.76) in 2011 (Source: *Mongolian Statistical Yearbook*).

EMPLOYMENT
('000 employees at 31 December)

	2009	2010	2011
Agriculture, forestry and fishing .	348.8	346.6	342.8
Industry*	113.1	119.1	127.9
Construction	49.6	48.8	52.0
Transport and storage	78.9	91.0	75.8
Trade	160.3	146.2	152.5
Public administration	56.1	61.0	55.6
Education	74.9	85.3	85.5
Science, research and development	10.9	9.5	11.4
Health	35.7	40.3	36.4
Total (incl. others)	1,006.3	1,033.7	1,037.7

* Comprising manufacturing (except printing and publishing), mining and quarrying, electricity and water.

Source: *Mongolian Statistical Yearbook*.

Mongolians working abroad ('000 in 2009, official estimates): 182.5 (Kazakhstan 90.0; Republic of Korea 31.0) (Source: Montsame—Mongolian News Agency).

Registered unemployed ('000 at 31 December): 38.3 in 2010; 57.2 (Ulan Bator 29.3) in 2011; 35.8 in 2012   (Sources: Asian Development Bank; Mongolian Statistical Office).

Total unemployed ('000 in 2011): 87.1 (Ulan Bator 21.4) (Source: *Mongolian Statistical Yearbook*).

Health and Welfare

KEY INDICATORS

Total fertility rate (children per woman, 2010)	2.5
Under-5 mortality rate (per 1,000 live births, 2010) . . .	32
HIV/AIDS (% of persons aged 15–49, 2009)	<0.1
Physicians (per 1,000 head, 2008)	2.8
Hospital beds (per 1,000 head, 2010)	5.8
Health expenditure (2009): US $ per head (PPP) . . .	217
Health expenditure (2009): % of GDP	5.7
Health expenditure (2009): public (% of total)	54.8
Access to water (% of persons, 2010)	82
Access to sanitation (% of persons, 2010)	51
Total carbon dioxide emissions ('000 metric tons, 2008) . .	10,894.7
Carbon dioxide emissions per head (metric tons, 2008) . .	4.1
Human Development Index (2011): ranking	110
Human Development Index (2011): value	0.653

For sources and definitions, see explanatory note on p. vi.

Agriculture

PRINCIPAL CROPS
(metric tons)

	2010	2011	2012
Cereals*	355,061	446,050	479,300
Potatoes	167,956	201,638	245,900
Other vegetables	82,266	98,973	98,900
Hay	1,137,300	1,195,238	1,001,175

* Mostly wheat (461,600 metric tons in 2012), but also small quantities of barley and oats.

Note: In addition, fodder crops were grown amounting to 34,800 metric tons in 2010, 40,400 tons in 2011 and 45,000 tons in 2012.

LIVESTOCK
(at mid-December census)

	2010	2011	2012
Sheep	14,480,400	15,668,500	17,908,700
Goats	13,883,200	15,934,600	17,369,300
Horses	1,920,300	2,112,900	2,298,900
Cattle	2,176,000	2,339,700	2,551,900
Camels	269,600	280,100	304,200
Pigs	24,842	30,397	n.a.
Poultry	425,800	596,800	n.a.

LIVESTOCK PRODUCTS
('000 metric tons, unless otherwise indicated)

	2009	2010	2011
Meat	269.1	204.4	208.0
Beef	58.6	47.5	53.6
Mutton and goat meat . . .	168.9	126.4	124.3
Sheep's wool	22.4	23.5	17.6
Cashmere	6.4	6.3	4.4
Hides and skins ('000)	13,076.3	16,784.7	8,793.3
Milk	493.7	338.4	458.6
Eggs (million)	30.8	47.9	53.6

Source: *Mongolian Statistical Yearbook*.

Forestry

ROUNDWOOD REMOVALS
('000 cubic metres)

	2006	2007	2008
Total	574.8	580.5	612.0

Source: *Mongolian Statistical Yearbook*.

SAWNWOOD PRODUCTION
('000 cubic metres, incl. railway sleepers)

	2009	2010	2011
Total	28.8	32.7	26.8

Source: Mongolian Statistical Office.

Fishing

(metric tons, live weight)

	2007	2008	2009
Total catch (freshwater fishes)	185	88	90

2010: Catch for 2010 assumed to be unchanged from 2009 (FAO estimate).
Source: FAO.

Mining

(metric tons unless otherwise indicated)

	2009	2010	2011
Coal ('000 metric tons)	13,164	25,246	32,030
Fluorspar concentrate	115,300	140,700	116,400
Copper concentrate*	370,900	357,100	347,400
Molybdenum concentrate*	5,125	4,677	4,163
Zinc concentrate*	141,500	112,600	104,700
Tungsten concentrate*	38.6	19.9	12.6
Iron ore	1,379,000	3,203,200	5,678,300
Gold (kilograms)	9,803	6,037	5,703
Crude petroleum (barrels)	1,870,000	2,181,400	2,548,900

* Figures refer to the gross weight of concentrates. Copper concentrate has an estimated copper content of 35%, while the metal content of molybdenum concentrate is 47% and that of zinc is 50%; the metal content of tungsten concentrate was not indicated.

Source: Mongolian Statistical Office.

Industry

SELECTED PRODUCTS

	2009	2010	2011
Flour ('000 metric tons)	105.3	143.5	105.3
Bread ('000 metric tons)	23.5	21.7	23.8
Confectionery ('000 metric tons)	12.8	12.9	13.1
Salt (metric tons)	1,402	1,862	2,182
Sheep's guts ('000 bunches)	1,057.1	1,288.5	1,250.8
Vodka ('000 litres)	17,410.9	20,396.7	25,596.1
Beer ('000 litres)	32,445.1	44,878.5	57,133.6
Soft drinks ('000 litres)	69,909.7	110,967.0	130,275.0
Bottled water ('000 litres)	17,058.2	24,405.0	32,861.0
Cashmere (combed) (metric tons)	1,586.7	824.7	874.3
Felt ('000 metres)	128.7	134.9	263.2
Camelhair blankets ('000 metres)	36.9	15.3	25.8
Knitwear ('000 garments)	639.2	801.1	853.5
Sheepskin coats	12,094	16,558	22,520
Carpets ('000 sq metres)	542.2	609.6	850.8

—*continued*	2009	2010	2011
Leather footwear ('000)	5.3	9.9	9.1
Felt footwear ('000 pairs)	13.0	27.9	42.6
Surgical syringes (million)	10.3	4.0	0.8
Briquettes (metric tons)	3,656.1	3,528.8	4,244.4
Lime ('000 metric tons)	43.1	50.2	45.3
Cement ('000 metric tons)	234.8	322.5	425.8
Bricks (million)	18.0	27.7	31.9
Copper (metric tons)	2,470.1	2,746.2	2,388.7
Copper wire (metric tons)	298.5	147.3	1,263.0
Electricity (million kWh)	4,038.8	4,312.8	4,536.4

Source: Mongolian Statistical Office.

Finance

CURRENCY AND EXCHANGE RATES

Monetary Units
100 möngö = 1 tögrög (tughrik).

Sterling, Dollar and Euro Equivalents (31 December 2012)

£1 sterling = 2,196.7 tögrög;
US $1 = 1,392.1 tögrög;
€1 = 1,836.7 tögrög;
10,000 tögrög = £4.55 = $7.18 = €5.44.

Average Exchange Rate (tögrög per US $)
2009   1,437.80
2010   1,357.06
2011   1,265.52

BUDGET
(million tögrög)

Revenue	2009	2010	2011
Tax revenue	1,620,549.6	2,688,236.3	3,636,866.0
Income tax	520,170.6	974,970.8	831,827.7
Excise duty	166,743.3	268,526.7	293,952.2
Taxes on goods and services	508,808.2	865,325.8	1,428,556.2
Value-added tax	325,956.4	579,119.6	1,108,325.9
Other current revenue	352,069.7	390,053.6	504,407.9
Social insurance	263,563.4	331,309.0	450,427.0
Grants and transfers	19,067.7	38,487.6	1,541.8
Stabilization fund	—	—	241,019.9
Other revenue	2,308.6	5,686.6	16,786.2
Total	1,993,995.6	3,122,464.2	4,400,621.8

Expenditure	2009	2010	2011
Current expenditure	1,788,157.6	2,256,282.6	3,234,411.2
Goods and services	970,143.8	1,166,323.4	1,528,097.1
Wages and salaries	575,912.4	648,105.8	801,243.0
Interest payments	29,621.6	42,327.8	37,329.0
Subsidies and transfers	788,392.2	1,047,631.4	1,668,985.1
Capital expenditure	460,564.5	591,039.5	1,067,167.7
Foreign financed	26,657.3	49,132.7	12,955.2
Lending (net)	87,907.6	233,363.0	490,452.0
Total	2,336,629.7	3,080,685.1	4,792,030.9

2012: Total revenue 4,880,900; Total expenditure 6,043,900.
Source: Mongolian Statistical Office.

2013 (million tögrög, forecasts): Total revenue 7,088,300; Total expenditure 7,444,600 (Source: *Mongol Messenger*).

INTERNATIONAL RESERVES
(US $ million at 31 December)

	2010	2011	2012
Gold (national valuation) . .	91.56	175.86	195.32
IMF special drawing rights . .	72.73	69.80	67.79
Reserve position in IMF . . .	0.21	0.21	0.21
Foreign exchange	2,123.76	2,205.16	3,862.30
Total	2,288.26	2,451.03	4,125.62

Source: IMF, *International Financial Statistics*.

MONEY SUPPLY
(million tögrög at 31 December)

	2010	2011	2012
Currency outside depository corporations	388,203	517,494	603,884
Transferable deposits . . .	1,535,555	2,004,421	2,090,631
Other deposits	2,728,573	3,837,067	4,787,388
Securities other than shares . .	27,651	53,277	135,369
Broad money	4,679,981	6,412,259	7,617,272

Source: IMF, *International Financial Statistics*.

COST OF LIVING
(Consumer Price Index at December; base: December 2005 = 100)

	2009	2010	2011
Foods	166.9	197.9	214.1
Clothing and footwear . . .	146.0	161.4	183.8
Rent and utilities	152.5	171.8	196.0
All items (incl. others) . . .	159.1	179.7	198.1

Source: *Mongolian Statistical Yearbook*.

NATIONAL ACCOUNTS

Expenditure on the Gross Domestic Product
('000 million tögrög at current prices)

	2009	2010	2011
Government final consumption expenditure	971.9	1,155.1	1,516.1
Private final consumption expenditure	3,809.6	4,515.6	5,505.4
Increase in stocks	361.3	694.4	1,069.4
Gross fixed capital formation . .	1,904.0	2,738.3	5,262.9
Total domestic expenditure .	7,046.8	9,103.4	13,353.8
Exports of goods and services . .	3,313.6	4,602.7	6,873.7
Less Imports of goods and services	3,792.0	5,246.6	9,327.8
Statistical discrepancy* . . .	22.2	−45.1	−70.2
GDP in purchasers' values .	6,590.6	8,414.5	10,829.7
GDP at constant 2005 prices .	3,913.7	4,162.8	4,881.4

* Referring to the difference between the sum of the expenditure components and official estimates of GDP, compiled from the production approach.

Source: Asian Development Bank.

Gross Domestic Product by Economic Activity
(million tögrög at current prices)

	2009	2010	2011
Agriculture, forestry and fishing .	1,177,380.3	1,202,155.6	1,405,504.7
Mining and quarrying	1,285,899.7	1,913,040.1	2,191,239.1
Manufacturing	425,000.6	539,836.0	764,729.4
Construction	86,238.7	107,201.6	137,716.0
Electricity, gas, etc.	157,422.9	190,211.6	205,173.9
Water supply, sewerage and waste management	26,356.8	30,200.2	32,751.4
Wholesale and retail trade; repair of motor vehicles and motorcycles	432,646.2	696,502.6	1,051,804.4
Transport and storage . . .	546,745.5	645,747.5	774,702.3
Hotels and restaurants . . .	43,680.8	47,522.9	58,313.1
Information and communications .	215,504.0	245,884.3	284,856.3
Finance and insurance . . .	212,724.0	239,607.2	287,528.6
Real estate and renting . . .	479,635.3	554,498.9	711,151.8

—*continued*	2009	2010	2011
Professional, scientific and technical	65,655.8	69,976.0	84,172.1
Administrative and support services	88,804.4	88,090.4	106,761.2
Public administration and defence; compulsory social security . .	267,246.3	303,036.1	373,799.9
Education	312,138.4	336,646.3	436,293.6
Health and social work . . .	123,042.0	143,194.3	189,961.5
Arts, entertainment and recreation	27,876.2	31,064.1	39,482.5
Other service activities . . .	24,871.5	26,473.7	31,777.8
Sub-total	5,998,869.3	7,410,889.5	9,167,719.6
Taxes, less subsidies, on products .	591,767.8	1,003,615.1	1,661,969.9
GDP in market prices . . .	6,590,637.1	8,414,504.6	10,829,689.5

2012: GDP in market prices 13,944,200.

Source: Mongolian Statistical Office.

BALANCE OF PAYMENTS
(US $ million)

	2009	2010	2011
Exports of goods	1,880.9	2,907.9	4,816.4
Imports of goods	−2,059.1	−3,079.9	−5,806.6
Balance on goods	−178.2	−172.0	−990.1
Exports of services	417.2	485.9	621.3
Imports of services	−571.0	−788.7	−1,784.6
Balance on goods and services .	−332.0	−474.9	−2,153.4
Primary income received . . .	24.3	28.9	43.7
Primary income paid	−219.8	−627.0	−888.8
Balance on goods, services and primary income	−527.4	−1,072.9	−2,998.5
Secondary income received . .	260.3	309.4	452.4
Secondary income paid . . .	−74.6	−122.4	−214.3
Current balance	−341.8	−885.9	−2,760.4
Capital account (net)	160.5	152.2	113.9
Direct investment assets . . .	−53.8	−61.7	−94.5
Direct investment liabilities . .	623.6	1,691.4	4,714.6
Portfolio investment assets . .	−138.8	143.3	20.9
Portfolio investment liabilities .	56.7	751.0	56.0
Other investment assets . . .	−144.8	−1,040.2	−2,383.8
Other investment liabilities . .	265.6	107.8	437.1
Net errors and omissions . . .	127.6	17.0	−76.0
Reserves and related items .	554.7	874.8	27.9

Source: IMF, *International Financial Statistics*.

External Trade

PRINCIPAL COMMODITIES
(US $ million)

Imports c.i.f.	2009	2010	2011
Food and live animals . . .	240.4	295.4	354.8
Animal and vegetable oils . .	16.7	22.8	29.7
Raw materials	15.6	20.8	42.2
Fuels and lubricants	544.4	713.8	1,188.3
Chemicals	143.1	195.1	321.7
Basic manufactures	321.7	414.4	980.2
Machinery and vehicles . . .	689.7	1,261.7	3,260.6
Manufactured articles . . .	114.5	211.1	323.8
Total (incl. others)	2,137.7	3,200.1	6,598.4

Exports f.o.b.		2009	2010	2011
Food and live animals	. . .	42.7	60.2	29.6
Raw materials	. . . .	1,005.4	1,505.0	1,977.9
Copper concentrate	. .	501.9	770.6	770.6
Fuels and lubricants	. .	437.5	1,055.6	2,544.6
Machinery and vehicles	. .	23.7	22.8	23.6
Manufactured articles	. . .	46.3	53.9	78.0
Gold, unwrought or in semi-manufactured forms		308.5	178.3	109.8
Total (incl. others)	. . . .	1,885.4	2,908.5	4,817.5

2012: Total imports 6,738.9; Total exports 4,384.6.

Source: Mongolian Statistical Office.

PRINCIPAL TRADING PARTNERS
(US $ million)

Imports c.i.f.		2009	2010	2011
China, People's Republic	. . .	538.6	971.0	2,023.9
Germany	. . . . . .	70.3	87.2	273.6
Japan	. . . . . .	97.0	196.5	490.2
Korea, Republic	. . . .	155.1	181.8	356.7
Russia	. . . . . .	772.8	1,046.7	1,624.7
USA	. . . . . .	103.7	158.9	536.8
Total (incl. others)	. . . .	2,137.7	3,200.0	6,598.4

Exports f.o.b.		2009	2010	2011
Canada	. . . .	147.5	141.6	90.8
China, People's Republic	. .	1,393.9	2,466.3	4,439.9
Italy	. . . . . .	31.4	31.8	49.8
Korea, Republic	. . . .	15.5	30.5	37.9
Russia	. . . .	68.2	82.7	96.3
United Kingdom	. . . .	126.9	67.4	20.0
Total (incl. others)	. . .	1,885.4	2,908.5	4,817.5

2012: Total imports 6,738.9; Total exports 4,384.6.

Source: Mongolian Statistical Office.

Transport

FREIGHT CARRIED
('000 metric tons)

		2009	2010	2011
Rail	. . . .	14,171.5	16,804.0	18,447.7
Road	. . . .	10,563.8	12,610.2	25,635.3
Air	. . . .	1.4	1.6	2.9
Total (incl. other)	. . . .	24,736.7	29,415.9	44,086.0

2012: Total 53,000.

Source: Mongolian Statistical Office.

PASSENGERS CARRIED
(million)

		2009	2010	2011
Rail	. . . .	3.1	3.5	3.8
Road	. . . .	229.0	246.7	291.8
Air*	. . . .	0.3	0.4	0.6
Total	. . . .	232.5	250.7	296.2

* MIAT only.

2012: Total 318.7.

Source: Mongolian Statistical Office.

RAILWAYS
(traffic)

	2009	2010	2011
Passengers carried ('000) . . .	3,118.3	3,516.3	3,832.1
Freight carried ('000 metric tons) .	14,171.5	16,804.0	18,447.7
Freight ton-km (million) . . .	7,852.1	10,286.7	11,418.7

Source: Mongolian Statistical Office.

ROAD TRAFFIC
(motor vehicles in use)

	2009	2010	2011
Passenger cars	153,906	172,583	208,514
Buses and coaches	16,136	16,366	22,547
Lorries, special vehicles and tankers	54,026	65,537	81,481

Source: Mongolian Statistical Office.

SHIPPING
Flag Registered Fleet
(at 31 December)

	2010	2011	2012
Number of vessels	206	207	221
Total displacement ('000 grt) . .	734	688	608

Source: Lloyd's List Intelligence (www.lloydslistintelligence.com).

CIVIL AVIATION
(traffic on scheduled services)

	2009	2010	2011
Passengers carried ('000) . . .	309.3	398.2	574.0
International passengers ('000) .	235.9	277.1	379.2
Freight carried (tons)	1,369.1	1,642.9	2,930.9

Source: Mongolian Statistical Office.

Tourism

FOREIGN TOURIST ARRIVALS BY NATIONALITY

Country	2009	2010	2011
China, People's Republic . . .	229,451	193,370	200,010
France	6,706	7,527	7,570
Germany	6,867	8,095	8,545
Japan	11,401	14,140	14,988
Korea, Republic	38,273	42,231	43,994
Russia	108,105	121,647	102,738
United Kingdom	5,872	6,209	7,120
USA	11,344	12,808	15,423
Total (incl. others)	492,836	456,090	460,360

Source: Mongolian Statistical Office.

Tourism receipts (US $ million): 213.3 in 2009; 222.4 in 2010 (Source: Ministry of Environment and Tourism, Ulan Bator).

Communications Media

	2009	2010	2011
Television receivers ('000 in use) .	489.5	554.5	708.1
Cable television subscribers ('000).	112.9	120.5	180.1
Telephones ('000 main lines in use)	142.9	143.2	131.8
Mobile cellular telephones ('000 subscribers)	2,208.7	2,532.9	2,942.3
Internet users ('000)	106.0	199.8	457.6
Personal computers ('000 in use) .	189.5	373.1	421.9
Books (million printers' sheets) .	49.7	55.5	47.5
Newspapers (million printers' sheets)	37.5	42.2	40.8

Newspapers (titles): 126 in 2012.

Periodicals (titles): 93 in 2012.

Sources: mainly *Mongolian Statistical Yearbook*.

Education

(2011/12)

	Institutions	Teachers	Students ('000)
General education schools:			
Primary (grades 1–3) . .	62		256.6
Incomplete secondary (grades 4–9)	144	26,500	169.2
Complete secondary (grades 10–11)	546		79.6
Vocational schools			
State-owned	49	2,100	37.2
Private	22		10.9
Universities			
State-owned	10		88.8
Private	4	7,300	17.1
Other higher education			
State-owned	5		15.3
Private	77		51.2

Note: In addition, 700 students were studying abroad through inter-governmental agreements.

Pre-school institutions (2011/12): 879 kindergartens attended by 164,300 infants, with 4,907 pre-school teachers.

Source: Mongolian Statistical Office.

Pupil-teacher ratio (primary education, UNESCO estimate): 30.2 in 2009/10 (Source: UNESCO Institute for Statistics).

Adult literacy rate (15 years and over, 2010 census): 98.3% in urban areas, 96.3% in rural areas.

Directory

The Government

PRESIDENCY

President and Commander-in-Chief of the Armed Forces: TSAKHIAGIIN ELBEGDORJ (elected 24 May 2009; inaugurated 18 June 2009).

Head of Presidential Secretariat: PUNTSAGIIN TSAGAAN.

NATIONAL SECURITY COUNCIL

The President heads the National Security Council; the Prime Minister and the Chairman of the Mongolian Great Khural are its members.

National Security Council: State Palace, Sükhbaataryn Talbai 6, Ulan Bator; tel. (11) 263959; e-mail info@nsc.gov.mn; internet www .nsc.gov.mn.

Chairman: TSAKHIAGIIN ELBEGDORJ.

Members: ZANDAAKHÜÜGIIN ENKHBOLD, NOROVYN ALTANKHUYAG.

Secretary: TSAGAANDARIIN ENKHTÜVSHIN.

CABINET
(May 2013)

The Government is formed by members of the Democratic Party (DP), the Justice Coalition, comprising the Mongolian National Democratic Party (MNDP) and the Mongolian People's Revolutionary Party (MPRP), and the Civil Courage-Green Party (CC-GP).

Prime Minister: NOROVYN ALTANKHUYAG (DP).

Deputy Prime Minister: DENDEVIIN TERBISHDAGVA (Justice/MPRP).

General Ministries

Minister of Environment and Green Development: SANJAASÜR-ENGIIN OYUUN (CC-GP).

Minister of External Relations: LUVSANVANDANGIIN BOLD (DP).

Minister of Finance: CHÜLTEMIIN ULAAN (Justice/MPRP).

Minister of Law: KHISHIGDEMBERELIIN TEMÜÜJIN (DP).

Sectoral Ministries

Minister of Construction and Urban Development: TSEVEL-MAAGIIN BAYARSAIKHAN (DP).

Minister of Culture, Sport and Tourism: TSEDEVDAMBYN OYUUN-GEREL (DP).

Minister of Defence: DASHDEMBERELIIN BAT-ERDENE (DP).

Minister of Economic Development: NYAMJAVYN BATBAYAR (DP).

Minister of Education and Science: LUVSANNYAMYN GANTÖMÖR (DP).

Minister of Energy: MISHIGIIN SONOMPIL (Justice/MNDP).

Minister of Health: NATSAGIIN UDVAL (Justice/MPRP).

Minister of Industry and Agriculture: KHALTMAAGIIN BATTULGA (DP).

Minister of Labour: YADAMSÜRENGIIN SANJMYATAV (DP).

Minister of Mining: DAVAAJAVYN GANKHUYAG (DP).

Minister of Population Development and Social Welfare: SODNOMZUNDUIN ERDENE (DP).

Minister of Roads and Transport: AMARJARGALYN GANSÜKH (DP).

Head, Government Affairs Directorate: CHIMEDIIN SAIKHANBILEG (DP).

MINISTRIES AND GOVERNMENT DEPARTMENTS

Prime Minister's Office: State Palace, Sükhbaataryn Talbai 6, Ulan Bator; tel. (11) 322356; fax (11) 328329; internet www.pmis.gov .mn.

Ministry of Construction and Urban Development: Ulan Bator; tel. (51) 263319.

Ministry of Culture, Sport and Tourism: Ulan Bator; tel. (11) 322269.

Ministry of Defence: Government Bldg 7, Dandaryn Gudamj 51, Bayanzürkh District, Ulan Bator; tel. (51) 263448; e-mail mdef@ mdef.pmis.gov.mn; internet www.mdef.pmis.gov.mn.

Ministry of Economic Development: Government Bldg 2, Negdsen Ündestnii Gudamj 5/1, Chingeltei District, Ulan Bator; tel. and fax (51) 265912; fax (51) 263569; e-mail info@med.gov.mn.

Ministry of Education and Science: Government Bldg 3, Baga Toiruu 44, Sükhbaatar District, Ulan Bator; tel. (51) 265912; fax (51) 323158; e-mail info@mecs.gov.mn; internet www.mecs.gov.mn.

Ministry of Energy: Government Bldg 14, Chingisiin Örgön Chölöö, 3rd Sub-District, Khan-Uul District, Ulan Bator; fax 70043479; e-mail info@energy.gov.mn; internet www.energy.gov.mn.

Ministry of External Relations: Enkhtaivny Örgön Chölöö 7A, Sükhbaatar District, Ulan Bator; tel. (51) 262788; fax (11) 322127; e-mail info@mfat.gov.mn; internet www.mfat.gov.mn.

Ministry of Finance: Block D, Soliin Danzangiin Gudamj, Ulan Bator; tel. and fax (51) 267468; e-mail support@mof.gov.mn; internet www.mof.gov.mn.

Ministry of Health: Government Bldg 8, Olimpiin Gudamj 2, Sükhbaatar District, Ulan Bator; tel. (51) 263913; fax (11) 320916; e-mail admin@moh.mn; internet www.moh.mn.

Ministry of Industry and Agriculture: Government Bldg 9, Enkhtaivny Örgön Chölöö 16A, Bayanzürkh District, Ulan Bator; tel. 262271; fax 453121; e-mail mofa@mofa.gov.mn; internet www.mofa.gov.mn.

Ministry of Labour: Ulan Bator; tel. 99041959.

Ministry of Law: Government Bldg 5, Khudaldaany Gudamj 6/1, Chingeltei District, Ulan Bator; tel. and fax (51) 267533; e-mail foreign@moj.gov.mn.

Ministry of Mining: Ulan Bator; tel. (51) 263253.

Ministry of Population Development and Social Welfare: Negdsen Ündestnii Gudamj 5, Chingeltei District, Ulan Bator; tel. () 264197; fax (11) 328634; e-mail mpdsp@mongolnet.mn; internet www.mpdsp.mn.

Ministry of Roads and Transport: Government Bldg 13, Chingisiin Örgön Chölöö, Sükhbaatar District, Ulan Bator; tel. (11) 322406; fax (11) 312315; e-mail info@mrt.gov.mn; internet www.mrt.gov.mn.

Government Affairs Directorate (Cabinet Secretariat): State Palace, Sükhbaataryn Talbai 6, Ulan Bator; tel. and fax (51) 262408; e-mail info@cabinet.gov.mn; internet www.pmis.gov.mn/cabinet.

President and Legislature

PRESIDENT

Office of the President: State Palace, Sükhbaataryn Talbai 6, Ulan Bator; fax (11) 311121; internet www.president.mn.

Election, 24 May 2009

Candidate	Votes	%
Tsakhiagiin Elbegdorj (Democratic Party)	562,718	51.21
Nambaryn Enkhbayar (MPRP)	520,948	47.41

MONGOLIAN GREAT KHURAL

Under the fourth Constitution, which came into force in February 1992, the single-chamber Mongolian Great Khural is the State's supreme legislative body. With 76 members elected for a four-year term, the Great Khural must meet for at least 50 working days in every six months. Its Chairman may act as President of Mongolia when the President is indisposed.

The revised Law on Elections to the Mongolian Great Khural, approved in December 2011, introduced an element of proportional representation at the June 2012 general election. While 48 seats were filled in 28 constituencies by a simple majority vote, the remaining 28 seats were allocated proportionately to parties receiving at least 5% of the total ballot.

Mongolian Great Khural: State Palace, Sükhbaataryn Talbai, Ulan Bator; e-mail secretariat@parliament.mn; internet www.parliament.mn.

Speaker (Chairman): ZANDAAKHÜÜGIIN ENKHBOLD.

Deputy Speakers (Vice-Chairmen): LOGIIN TSOG (Justice/MPRP), MIYEEGOMBYN ENKHBOLD (MPP), RADNAASÜMBERELIIN GONCHIGDORJ (DP).

Secretary-General: BYAMBADORJIIN BOLDBAATAR.

General Election, 28 June 2012

Party	Seats
Democratic Party (DP)	36
Mongolian People's Party (MPP)	24
Justice Coalition*	11
Civil Courage-Green Party (CC-GP)	2
Independents	3
Total	76†

* Comprising the Mongolian National Democratic Party (MNDP), which won six seats, and the Mongolian People's Revolutionary Party (MPRP), which won five.

† The 48 seats won by direct election in the 26 constituencies were: DP 22, MPP 19, Justice Coalition 4 and Independents 3. The balance made up from party lists increased these totals to DP 32, MPP 28, Justice 11 and CC-GP 2. Subsequently the results in some constituencies were challenged and overturned, and it was only after several court cases that in May 2013 the last of the 76 members were sworn in.

Election Commission

General Election Committee: Government Bldg 11, Sambuugiin Gudamj 11, Ulan Bator; tel. (11) 263383; fax (11) 326975; e-mail gecm@mongol.net; internet www.gec.gov.mn; f. 1992; Chair. CHOIN-ZONGIIN SODNOMTSEREN.

Political Organizations

Citizens' Movement Party: Rm 304, National Information and Technology Park, Baga Toiruu 49, Sükhbaatar District, Ulan Bator; tel. (11) 321900; f. 2007; 815 mems; Chair. NYAMAAGIIN DAVAA.

Civil Courage-Green Party (CC-GP): internet www.greenparty.mn; amalgamation of the Civil Courage Party and the Mongolian Green Party was agreed in January 2011 and began in March; registration approved March 2012; Jt Chairs. SANJAASÜRENGIIN OYUUN, SAMBUUGIIN DEMBEREL, DANGAASÜRENGIIN ENKHBAT.

Democratic Party (DP): CPOB 578, Sükhbaatar District, Ulan Bator; tel. (11) 320355; fax (11) 323755; e-mail info@demparty.mn; internet www.demparty.mn; f. 2000; est. by amalgamation of the Mongolian National Democratic Party, Mongolian Social-Democratic Party, Mongolian Democratic Party, Mongolian Democratic Renewal Party and the Mongolian Believers' Democratic Party; Mongolian Social-Democratic Party re-est. as independent party in 2004; c. 150,000 mems. (2008); Chair. NOROVYN ALTANKHUYAG; Sec.-Gen. TSAGAANY OYUUNDARI.

Development Programme Party: Rm 2, Poverty Reduction Programme Foundation Bldg, 14th Sub-District, Sükhbaatar District, Ulan Bator; tel. 96019222; f. 2007; 933 mems (2008); Chair. O. ZAYAA.

Freedom Implementer Party: Varyeta Centre, 1st Sub-District, Bayangol District, Ulan Bator (POB 48/117); tel. 88113439; fax (11) 327899; e-mail freedom_ofmn@yahoo.com; 1,600 mems; f. 2006; Chair. SHOOVDORYN TÖMÖRSÜKH.

Justice Coalition: Mongolian Great Khural, State Palace, Sükhbaatar Sq., Ulan Bator; f. 2012; electoral pact of the Mongolian People's Revolutionary Party (MPRP) and the Mongolian National Democratic Party (MNDP); in January 2012 the MPRP and MNDP signed a nine-year agreement on the formation of the MPRP-MNDP Political Association, which published a joint list of election candidates of the MPRP-MNDP Third Force Coalition for Establishing Justice; Chair. (MPRP) NAMBARYN ENKHBAYAR; Chair. (MNDP) MENDSAIKHANY ENKHSAIKHAN.

Mongolian Democratic Movement Party: Rm 306, Ikh Surguuliin Gudamj 3/2, 6th Sub-District, Sükhbaatar District, Ulan Bator (POB 20A/158); tel. 99009093; f. 2008; 850 mems (2008); Chair. TÖGSMAAGIIN OYUUNAA.

Mongolian Green Party: Internom Block B, Amaryn Gudamj 2, Sükhbaatar District, Ulan Bator; tel. 314560; e-mail info@greenparty.mn; internet www.greenparty.mn; f. 1990; political wing of Alliance of Greens; majority of mems joined Civil Courage-Green Party in 2011; Chair. O. BUM-YALAGCH; Sec.-Gen. CH. MÖNKHBAYAR.

Mongolian Liberal Party: Ulan Bator Higher School of Intellect, 4th Sub-District, Chingeltei District, Ulan Bator (POB 23/320); tel. 99852957; fax (11) 328198; f. 1999 as Mongolian Civil Democratic New Liberal Party, renamed 2004; ruling body Little Khural of 90 mems with Leadership Council of nine; 1,300 mems (2008); Chair. B. DASHZEVEG.

Mongolian National Democratic Party (MNDP): No. 2 Bldg, Enkh Taivny Örgön Chölöö 12, 1st Sub-District, Sükhbaatar District, Ulan Bator; tel. (11) 260535; fax (11) 312596; f. 2006; registered under above name in Oct. 2011; est. after a split in the leadership of the Democratic Party upon formation of the national solidarity govt; fmrly National New Democratic Party (previously National New Party); 2,400 mems (2008); Chair. MENDSAIKHANY ENKHSAIKHAN; Sec.-Gen. NAMDAGIIN BATTSEREG.

Mongolian People's Party (MPP): Palace of Independence, Ulan Bator; tel. and fax 77444167; e-mail contact@mpp.mn; internet www.mpp.mn; f. 1920; est. as Mongolian People's Party; renamed as Mongolian People's Revolutionary Party (MPRP) in 1925; reorganized in the 1990s; reverted to Mongolian People's Party in Nov. 2010; 200,196 mems (May 2012); ruling body Baga Khural or Conference (310 mems at March 2012), which elects the Leadership (Steering) Council (31 mems, incl. Sec.-Gen. and nine secretaries); Chair. OLZIISAIKHANY ENKHTÜVSHIN; Gen. Sec. GOMBOJAVYN ZANDANSHATAR.

Mongolian People's Revolutionary Party (MPRP): Ulan Bator; f. 2011; breakaway faction of the Mongolian People's Party; registered in June 2011; 20,000 mems; Chair. NAMBARYN ENKHBAYAR (sentenced to four years' imprisonment in Aug. 2012); Sec.-Gen. NATSAGIIN UDVAL.

Mongolian Social-Democratic Party (MSDP): Room 12, No. 5 Bldg, 1st Sub-District, Sükhbaatar District, Ulan Bator (CPOB 680); tel. 99114273; fax (11) 323828; f. 1990; merged in Dec. 2000 to form part of Democratic Party; refounded Jan. 2005; c. 3,000 mems (2008); Chair. ARYAAGIIN GANBAATAR; Deputy Chair. D. ENKHZAYAA.

Mongolian Traditional United Party (MTUP): Room 3, Mika Hotel, Elchingiin Gudamj, 1st Sub-District, Sükhbaatar District, Ulan Bator (POB 44/5240); tel. (11) 327690; fax (11) 310133; also known as the United Heritage (conservative) Party; f. 1994; est. as an amalgamation of the United Private Owners' Party and the Independence Party; 1,503 mems (2008); ruling body General Political Council; Chair. BATDELGERIIN BATBOLD.

Motherland Party: Motherland Party Central Bldg, Jukovyn Örgön Chölöö 7a, Ulan Bator (POB 49/404); tel. 90150268; fax (11) 453178; f. 1998; amalgamated with Mongolian Workers' Party 1999; fmrly Mongolian Democratic New Socialist Party, name changed as above in 2005; reported to be disbanding in 2009; c. 160,000 mems (2008); Chair. BADARCHIIN ERDENEBAT; Sec. I. ERDENEBAATAR.

National Labour Party: Ulan Bator; registration denied by Supreme Court Feb. 2011; Chair. T. ENKHBAYAR; Sec.-Gen. G. BAYARSAIKHAN.

Republican Party (RP): Rm 106, Buyan Holding Co Bldg, 3rd Sub-District, Bayangol District, Ulan Bator; tel. (11) 344844; fax (11) 344843; f. 2004; 50,000 mems (2008); Chair. BAZARSADYN JARGALSAIKHAN; Sec.-Gen. TS. GANKHUYAG.

Diplomatic Representation

EMBASSIES IN MONGOLIA

Bulgaria: Olimpiin Gudamj 8, Ulan Bator (CPOB 702); tel. (11) 322841; fax (11) 324841; e-mail posolstvob@magicnet.mn; Ambassador (vacant).

Canada: Central Tower, 6th Floor, Sükhbaataryn Talbai 2, Sükhbaatar District, Ulan Bator (CPOB 1028); tel. (11) 332500; fax (11) 332515; e-mail ulan@international.gc.ca; internet www.canadainternational.gc.ca/mongolia-mongolie; Ambassador GREGORY GOLDHAWK.

China, People's Republic: Zaluuchuudyn Örgön Chölöö 10, Sükhbaatar District, Ulan Bator (CPOB 672); tel. (11) 320955; fax (11) 311943; internet mn.chineseembassy.org; Ambassador WANG XIAOLONG.

Cuba: Negdsen Ündestnii Gudamj 5, Ulan Bator (CPOB 710); tel. (11) 323778; fax (11) 327709; Ambassador (vacant).

Czech Republic: Olimpiin Gudamj 14, Ulan Bator (CPOB 665); tel. (11) 321886; fax (11) 323791; e-mail czechemb@magicnet.mn; internet www.mzv.cz/ulaanbaatar; Ambassador IVANA GROLLOVA.

France: Enkhtaivny Örgön Chölöö 3, Chingeltei District, Ulan Bator (CPOB 687); tel. (11) 324519; fax (11) 319176; e-mail ambafrance@magicnet.mn; internet www.ambafrance-mn.org; Ambassador YVES DELAUNAY.

Germany: Negdsen Ündestnii Gudamj 7, Ulan Bator (CPOB 708); tel. (11) 323325; fax (11) 323905; e-mail info@ulan.diplo.de; internet www.ulan-bator.diplo.de; Ambassador PETER SCHALLER.

India: Zaluuchuudyn Örgön Chölöö 10, Sükhbaatar District, Ulan Bator (CPOB 691); tel. (11) 329522; fax (11) 329532; e-mail indembmongolia@magicnet.mn; internet www.indianembassy.mn; Ambassador SATBIR SINGH.

Japan: Olimpiin Gudamj 8, Sükhbaatar District, Ulan Bator (CPOB 1011); tel. (11) 320777; fax (11) 313332; e-mail jpemb@mongol.net; internet www.mn.emb-japan.go.jp; Ambassador TAKENORI SHIMIZU.

Kazakhstan: Zaisangiin Gudamj 31-6, 1st Sub-District, Khan-Uul District, Ulan Bator (CPOB 291); tel. (11) 315408; fax (11) 341707; e-mail kzemby@mbox.mn; Ambassador ORMAN NURBAYEV.

Korea, Democratic People's Republic: Khuvisgalchdyn Gudamj, Ulan Bator; tel. (11) 326153; fax (11) 330529; Ambassador HONG GYU.

Korea, Republic: Olimpiin Gudamj 10, Ulan Bator (CPOB 1039); tel. (11) 321548; fax (11) 311157; e-mail kormg@mofat.go.kr; internet mng.mofat.go.kr; Ambassador LEE TAE-RO.

Kuwait: Town House No. 1, Villa Vesta Town, 11th Sub-District, Khan-Uul District, Ulan Bator; tel. 77444441; fax 77444443; e-mail ulaanbaatar@mofa.gov.kw; Ambassador MUBARAK M. F. AL-SEHAIJAN.

Laos: Ikh Toiruu 59, Sükhbaatar District, Ulan Bator (CPOB 1030); tel. (11) 326440; fax (11) 321048; e-mail emblao@magicnet.mn; Ambassador BUNNYAN SAISSANAVONG.

Russia: Enkhtaivny Gudamj 6-A, Ulan Bator (CPOB 661); tel. (11) 327191; fax (11) 327018; e-mail embassy_ru@mongol.net; internet www.mongolia.mid.ru; Ambassador VIKTOR V. SAMOILENKO.

San Marino: Diplomatic Bldg 95 1-5, 4th Sub-District, Chingeltei District, Ulan Bator; tel. 70113998; fax 70113997; Ambassador ROBERTO DI SERIO.

Turkey: Enkhtaivny Gudamj 5, Ulan Bator (CPOB 1009); tel. (11) 311200; fax (11) 313992; e-mail embassy.ulaanbaatar@mfa.gov.tr; internet ulaanbaatar.emb.mfa.gov.tr; Ambassador MUSTAFA SARNIC.

United Kingdom: Enkhtaivny Gudamj 30, Ulan Bator 13 (CPOB 703); tel. (11) 458133; fax (11) 458036; e-mail britemb@mongol.net; internet ukinmongolia.fco.gov.uk; Ambassador CHRISTOPHER STUART.

USA: Ikh Toiruu 59/1, Ulan Bator (CPOB 1021); tel. (11) 329095; fax (11) 320776; e-mail UlaanbaatarACS@state.gov; internet mongolia.usembassy.gov; Ambassador PIPER A. W. CAMPBELL.

Viet Nam: Enkh Taivny Örgön Chölöö 47, Ulan Bator (CPOB 670); tel. (11) 458917; fax (11) 458923; e-mail vinaemba@magicnet.mn; internet www.vietnamembassy-mongolia.org; Ambassador HOANG TUAN THINH.

Judicial System

The Chief Justice is chosen from among the members of the Supreme Court and approved by the President for a six-year term. Routine civil, criminal and administrative cases are handled by 30 rural district and inter-district courts and eight urban district courts. There are 22 appellate courts at provincial and capital city level. Some legal cases are required by law to be dealt with by the Supreme Court, appellate courts or special courts (military, railway, etc.). Under the fourth Constitution, judicial independence is protected by the General Council of Courts, consisting by presidential decree in May 2013 of three representatives of the assemblies of judges of supervisory, appellate and ordinary levels and chaired by a representative of the Ministry of Law, Professor Nanzaddorjiin Lündendorj. The Procurator General and his deputies, who play an investigatory role, are nominated by the President and approved by the Great Khural for six-year terms.

Supreme Court: Sambuugiin Gudamj, 40 and 50 Myangat-1, Ulan Bator; tel. (11) 320622; e-mail contact@supremecourt.gov.mn; internet www.supremecourt.mn; Chief Justice TSEVEGMIDIIN ZORIG.

State Procurator's Office: Baga Toiruu 15/1, Chingeltei District, Ulan Bator; tel. (11) 264374; internet www.gpo.gov.mn; Procurator General DAMBYN DORLIGJAV.

Religion

The 1992 Constitution maintains the separation of Church and State. The Law on State-Church Relations (of November 1993) sought to make Buddhism the predominant religion and restricted the dissemination of beliefs other than Buddhism, Islam and shamanism. During the early years of communist rule Mongolia's traditional Mahayana Buddhism was virtually destroyed. In the early 1990s some 2,000 lamas (monks) established small communities at the sites of 120 former monasteries, temples and religious schools, some of which were being restored. The Kazakhs of western Mongolia are nominally Sunni Muslims. Mosques, also destroyed in the 1930s or closed subsequently, are only now being rebuilt or reopened. Traces of shamanism from the pre-Buddhist period still survive. In recent years there has been an increase in Christian missionary activity in Mongolia. According to the November 2010 population census, of those aged over 15 years, 53% were Buddhists, 3.0% Muslims, 2.9% shamanic and 2.2% Christians.

BUDDHISM

At the end of 2011 there were 142 Buddhist temples and monasteries in Mongolia, including 41 in Ulan Bator, with 1,571 lamas, including 715 in Ulan Bator, 2,760 employees and 837 students in religious schools. According to the 2010 population census, Mongolia has more than 1,010,100 Buddhist believers.

Living Buddha: The Ninth Javzandamba Khutagt (Ninth Bogd), Jambalnamdolchoijinjaltsan died on 1 March 2012. The search for his reincarnation in Mongolia is being organized.

Asian Buddhist Conference For Peace: Gandan, Ulan Bator (CPOB 38); tel. and fax (11) 360069; e-mail blgn_abcp@yahoo.com; Sec.-Gen. Dr T. BULGAN.

Gandantegchinlen Monastery: Zanabazaryn Gudamj, Bayangol District, Ulan Bator; tel. (11) 360354; Centre of Mongolian Buddhists; Khamba Lama (Abbot) DEMBERELIIN CHOIJAMTS.

'Good Merit' Buddhist Society: Ulan Bator; Pres. Lama A. ERDENEBAT.

Karmapa Monastery: Khamba Lama (Abbot) DAVAASAMBUUGIIN TAIVANSAIKHAN.

Pethub Buddhist Institute: Ikh Toiruu, Chingeltei District, Ulan Bator (POB 38/105); tel. (11) 321867; fax (11) 320676; e-mail pethubmongolia@magicnet.mn; internet www.pethubmonastery.com; f. 2001 by Ven. Kushok Bakula Rinpoche (Indian Ambassador to Mongolia 1990–2000).

CHRISTIANITY

At the end of 2011 there were 161 Christian congregations in Mongolia, including 110 in Ulan Bator, with 191 priests and ministers, including 112 in Ulan Bator, 666 employees and 108 students attending Christian studies. According to the November 2010 population census, Mongolia has 41,900 Christian believers.

Roman Catholic Church

The Church is represented in Mongolia by a single mission. At June 2012, according to Vatican sources, there were 800 Roman Catholics, a bishop, 21 priests and 49 missionaries in the country. The main place of worship is the Cathedral of St Peter and St Paul in Ulan Bator.

Catholic Mission: 18th Sub-District, Bayanzürkh District, Ulan Bator (CPOB 694); tel. (11) 458825; fax (11) 458027; f. 1992; Apostolic Prefect Bishop WENCESLAO PADILLA.

Protestant Church

Association of Mongolian Protestants: f. 1990; Pastor M. BOLD-BAATAR.

Mongolian Evangelical Alliance: Jijig Ür Bldg, 3rd Sub-District, Bayanzürkh District, Ulan Bator; tel. 70152040; e-mail mea@magicnet.mn; internet www.mea.mn; f. 1998; a branch of the World Evangelical Alliance.

Other Christian Churches

Church of Jesus Christ of Latter-Day Saints (Mormon): Khudaldaany Gudamj, Chingeltei District, Ulan Bator; tel. (11) 312761.

Jesus Reigns Assembly: Ulan Bator; Pastor D. NARANMANDAKH.

Russian Orthodox Church: Holy Trinity Church, Jukovyn Gudamj 55, Bayanzürkh District, Ulan Bator; tel. 99256732; fax (11)454425; e-mail fateraleksei@hotmail.com; internet www.pravoslavie.mn; opened in 1864, closed in 1927; services recommenced 1997 for Russian community; new Holy Trinity Church consecrated in June 2009; Head Father ALEKSEI TRUBACH.

Seventh-day Adventist Church: 5th Sub-District, Bayangol District, Ulan Bator; tel. (11) 688031; fax (11) 688032.

ISLAM

At the end of 2011 there were 18 Muslim congregations (none in Ulan Bator), with 20 clergy, 90 employees and 417 students. A mosque was due to be built in Ulan Bator. It was stated in March 2005 that Mongolia had 32 mosques in Bayan-Ölgii and Khovd provinces and in the towns of Darkhan and Nalaikh. Mongolia has 57,180 Muslim believers, according to the population census of November 2010.

Chief Imam (Ölgii): KH. BATYRBEK.

Imam of Gümyr shrine (Ölgii): DÖITENGIIN SHERKHAN.

Association of Mongolian Muslim Societies: f. 2009; Exec. Dir KH. BATYRBEK.

BAHÁ'Í FAITH

Bahá'í Society: Ulan Bator; tel. (11) 321867; f. 1989; Leader A. ARIUNAA.

SHAMANISM

There are 55,200 believers in Shamanism, according to the population census of November 2010.

Darkhad Shamanic Study Centre: Ulan Bator; Leader CH. TSERENBAAVAI.

Tengeriin Süld Shamanic Union: Ulan Bator; Pres. CH. CHINBAT.

The Press

PRINCIPAL NATIONAL NEWSPAPERS

State-owned publications in Mongolia were denationalized with effect from 1 January 1999, although full privatization could not proceed immediately. As of January 2012, Mongolia had 126 newspapers and 93 periodicals. A total of 31 provincial and town newspapers were published 36 times a year, with four appearing 48 times a year.

Ardchilal (Democracy): Democracy Palace, 7th Sub-District, Sükhbaatar District, Ulan Bator (POB 20/360); tel. and fax 70110187; e-mail info@ardchilal.com; internet www.ardchilal.com; f. 1990; 260 a year; Editor-in-Chief TSEND-AYUUSHIIN TSOLMON; circ. 3,000.

Ardyn Erkh (People's Power): Ardyn Erkh Bldg, West of Mongolkino Studio, 5th Sub-District, Bayanzürkh District, Ulan Bator; tel. and fax 99098705; e-mail info@news.mn; e-mail ardiin_erkh@mongolnet.mn; f. 2005; original title ceased publication in 1999 (see *Ödriin Sonin*, below); subsequently assumed by new publr; 256 a year; Exec. Dir BAYARMAGNAIN TEMÜÜLEN; circ. 3,000.

Mongolyn Medee (Mongolian News): Free Press Foundation, Sükhbaatar District, Ulan Bator; tel. and fax 70113551; e-mail mongoliin_medee@yahoo.com; f. 1998; 256 a year; Editor-in-Chief S. GANTOGOO; Sec. B. OYUUNGEREL; circ. 2,900.

Mongolyn Ünen (Mongolian Truth): Mongolyn Ünen Newspaper Bldg, Amaryn Gudamj, Sükhbaatar District, Ulan Bator; tel. (11) 321877; fax (11) 323223; e-mail unen@mongol.net; internet www.unen.imedia.mn; f. 1920; publ. 1925–2010 by MPRP as Ünen; 256 a year; Editor-in-Chief J. MÖNKHBAT; circ. 8,330.

Montsame Medee (Montsame News): Montsame News Agency, Jigjidjavyn Gudamj 8, Ulan Bator (CPOB 1514); tel. (11) 314511; e-mail localnews@montsame.mn; internet www.montsame.mn; daily news digest primarily for govt depts; 248 a year; Editor B. NOMINCHIMED.

Ödriin Shuudan (Daily Mail): Central Cultural Palace, Amaryn Gudamj, 8th Sub-District, Sükhbaatar District, Ulan Bator; tel. 50001001; fax (11) 330383; e-mail info@udriinshuudan.mn; 256 a year; Editor-in-Chief BIBISHIIN OYUUN-ERDENE.

Ödriin Sonin (Daily News): Ödriin Sonin Bldg, Ikh Toiruu, Sükhbaatar District, Ulan Bator; tel. 99193519; fax 70134164; e-mail info@dailynews.mn; internet www.dailynews.mn; f. 1924; restored 1990; fmrly Ardyn Erkh, Ardyn Ündesnii Erkh, Ündesnii Erkh and Ödriin Toli; 312 a year; Editor-in-Chief J. MYAGMARSÜREN; circ. 14,200.

Öglöönii Sonin (Morning News): 1st Sub-District, Bayanzürkh District, Ulan Bator (POB 46/411); tel. and fax (11) 450640; e-mail ugluuniisonin@yahoo.com; f. 2006; 252 a year; Editor-in-Chief L. NINJJAMTS; circ. 7,000.

Önöödör (Today): Mongol News Co Bldg, Juulchny Gudamj 40, Chingeltei District, Ulan Bator; tel. 70111096; fax (11) 330798; e-mail today@mongolnews.mn; internet www.mongolnews.mn; f. 1996; 300 a year; Editor-in-Chief B. NANDINTÜSHIG; circ. 10,000.

Ulaanbaatar Taims (Ulan Bator Times): Lucky Times Bldg, Ard Ayuushiin Örgön Chölöö, 18th Sub-District, Bayangol District, Ulan Bator; tel. 70123989; fax 70123989; e-mail zulaab2000@yahoo.com; internet www.ubtimes.mn; f. 1929; est. as Ulaanbaatar Khotyn Medee; renamed Ulaanbaataryn Medee in 1955, Ulaanbaatar in 1990, and Ulaanbaatar Taims in 1999; publ. by Ulan Bator City Govt; 244 a year; Editor-in-Chief DAGIIMAAGIIN ERDENECHIMEG; circ. 3,500.

Uls Töriin Sonin (Political Newspaper): Delta Centre, Juulchny Gudamj, Chingeltei District, Ulan Bator (POB 46/796); tel. 99095040; fax (11) 312608; f. 2005 following closure of the *Mongol Times*; 48 a year; Editor GANTÖMÖRIIN UYANGA.

Uls Töriin Toim (Political Review): Central Sports Palace Ext., 8th Sub-District, Sükhbaatar District, Ulan Bator; tel. 99149788; e-mail ulstoriintoim@yahoo.com; 256 a year; Editor-in-Chief A. MÖN-KHBAYASGALAN.

Ündesnii Shuudan (National Post): fmr Ardyn Erkh Bldg, Ikh Toiruu, Sükhbaataryn District, Ulan Bator; tel. (11) 354632; fax (11) 354631; e-mail undesniishuudan@yahoo.com; internet www.undesniishuudan.mn; f. 2007; 312 a year; Editor-in-Chief BAASAN-JAVYN GANBOLD; circ. 9,000.

Zuuny Medee (Century's News): Amaryn Gudamj 1, Ulan Bator; tel. 70116004; fax (11) 321279; e-mail zuuniimedee@yahoo.com;

internet www.zuuniimedee.imedia.mn; f. 1991; previously titled Zasgiin Gazryn Medee; 312 a year; Editor-in-Chief DEMCHIGJAVYN OTGONBAYAR; circ 8,000.

OTHER NEWSPAPERS AND PERIODICALS

4 dekh Zasaglal (Fourth Estate): Mongol Sonin Co, Gazar Holding Bldg, Variete Centre, Ulan Bator (POB 46A/81); tel. 99188125; e-mail dorovdekhzasaglal@yahoo.com; 36 a year; Editor A. ENKHBAYAR.

81-r Suvag (Channel 81): Söüliin Gudamj, Bayangol District, Ulan Bator (POB 46A/81); tel. 96003992; fax (11) 460718; publishes views of the Mongolian Newspaper Asscn; 36 a year; Editor-in-Chief T. TSOGT-ERDENE.

Altangadas (Pole Star): AG Töv, Söüliin Gudamj, Bayanzürkh District, Ulan Bator (CPOB 430); tel. (11) 319411; fax (11) 319414; e-mail info@altangadas.mn; internet www.altangadas.mn; monthly political magazine; Editor NOROVYN ALTANKHUYAG.

Anagaakh Arga Bilig (The Healthy Way of Yin and Yang): Negdsen Ündesunii Baiguullagyn Gudamj 44, Sükhbaatar District, Ulan Bator (CPOB 1053); tel. 88554491; 24 a year; Editor YA. ARSLAN.

Bagsh (Teacher): Rm 106, Teachers' College, Sükhbaatar District, Ulan Bator; tel. 99183398; f. 1989; est. by Ministry of Education; 24 a year.

Biznesiin Medee (Business News): East of Wrestlers Palace, 6th Sub-District, Bayanzürkh District, Ulan Bator (POB 20/335); tel. and fax 70155513; e-mail biznesiin_medee@yahoo.com; 36 a year; Editor-in-Chief S. KHÜREL.

Bolson Yavdal (Events): Söüliin Gudamj, Sükhbaatar District, Ulan Bator (POB 36/346); tel. 96664409; e-mail bolsonyavdal@yahoo.com; 36 a year; Editor T. SANGAA.

Business Times: Business Times Bldg, 1st Sub-District, Khan-Uul District, Ulan Bator; tel. and fax (11) 325374; internet www .businesstimes.mn; 48 a year; Editor BATSÜKHIIN SARANTUYAA.

Deedsiin Amidral (Elite's Life): Bldg 4, Rm 514, A. Amaryn Gudamj, Ulan Bator (CPOB 356); tel. 91189699; fax (11) 323847; e-mail deedsiinamidral@mongol.mn; 36 a year; Editor-in-Chief B. OTGONBAYAR.

Deedsiin Khüreelen (Elite's Forum): Ulan Bator (CPOB 1114); tel. and fax (11) 450602; e-mail deed_huree@yahoo.com; 48 a year; Publr M. SÜKHBAATAR; Editor KH. UYANGA; circ. 12,000.

Ekh Orny Manaa (Guard of the Motherland): Main Directorate of Border Defence, Ulan Bator; internet bpo.gov.mn; 36 a year.

Emiin Medeelel (Medicine Information): National Health Development Centre, Ministry of Health, Ulan Bator; tel. (11) 321485; fax (11) 320633; e-mail zorig@nchd.mn; bimonthly magazine published by the National Health Development Centre; Editor T. ZORIG.

Erüül Mend (Health): Super Zuun Co, Ulan Bator (POB 20/412); tel. 99192239; fax (11) 321278; e-mail dr_jargal_d@yahoo.com; publ. by Ministry of Health; monthly; Editor D. JARGALSAIKHAN; circ. 5,600.

Gan Zam (Steel Road): Railway Printing House, Magsarjavyn Gudamj, Bayangol District, Ulan Bator; tel. (21) 244560; internet www.railcom.mn/ganzam; weekly; Sec. I. NARANCHIMEG.

Khani (Spouse): National Agricultural Co-operative Members' Association Bldg 12, Khiimor Khotkhon, Bayanzürkh District, Ulan Bator (POB 49/600); tel. (11) 460698; fax (11) 458550; e-mail khani_sonin@yahoo.com; women and family issues; 20 a year; Editor-in-Chief DEMBERELIIN BATSÜKH; circ. 64,920.

Khiimori (Wind-Horse): Ödriin Sonin Bldg, Ikh Toiruu 20, Sükhbaatar District, Ulan Bator; tel. (11) 354565; monthly; Editor-in-Chief A. ERDENETUYAA.

Khödölmör (Labour): Sükhbaataryn Talbai 3, Ulan Bator; tel. (11) 323026; f. 1928; publ. by Confederation of Mongolian Trade Unions; 48 a year; Editor-in-Chief TSOODOLYN KHULAN; circ. 64,920.

Khökh Tolbo (Blue Spot): Mon-Azi Co Bldg 54, 4th Sub-District, Chingeltei District, Ulan Bator (POB 24/306); tel. (11) 312405; fax (11) 312794; 36 a year; Publr BATYN ERDENEBAATAR; Editor-in-Chief E. ENKHTSOLMON; circ. 3,500.

Khöröngiin Zakh Zeel (Capital Market): Mongolian Stock Exchange, Sükhbaataryn Talbai 2, Ulan Bator (POB) tel. (11) 313511; fax (11) 325170; e-mail info@mse.mn; monthly; Editor (vacant).

Khuuli Züin Medeelel (Legal Information): National Legal Centre, Chingeltei District, Ulan Bator; tel. (11) 322094; fax (11) 315735; e-mail altantuya.s@legalinstitute.mn; internet www.legalinstitute .mn; f. 1990; 36 a year; publ. by National Legal Institute.

Khuviin Soyol (Personal Culture): Rm 2, Block 39, behind No. 5 School, Baga Toiruu, Ulan Bator (CPOB 1254); 24 a year; Editor BEKHBAZARYN BEKHSÜREN.

Khümüün Bichig (People and Script): Montsame News Agency, Jigjidjavyn Gudamj 8, Ulan Bator (CPOB 1514); tel. (11) 329486; fax (11) 327857; e-mail khumuun@montsame.mn; current affairs in Mongolian classical script; 48 a year; Editor S. ALTANTSETSEG; circ. 15,000.

Khümüüs (People): Khümüüs Bldg, 1st Sub-District, Bayanzürkh District, Ulan Bator (POB 46/411); tel. 70168363; fax (11) 450323; internet www.humuus.mn; 48 a year; Editor O. MÖNKH-ERDENE.

Khümüüsiin Amidral (People's Lives): Central Palace of Culture, Ulan Bator (POB 46/411); 48 a year; Editor B. AMGALAN.

Mash Nuuts (Top Secret): Mongol Shaazan Bldg, 2nd Sub-District, Sükhbaatar District, Ulan Bator (POB 49/113); tel. and fax (11) 328673; e-mail tsecret@mongolnet.mn; 32 a year; Editor-in-Chief ONONGIIN CHINZORIG.

Mongoljin Goo (Mongolian Beauty): Mongolian Women's Federation, Ulan Bator (POB 44/717); tel. and fax 70118336; e-mail monwofed@magicnet.mn; internet www.mwf.mn; f. 1990; monthly; Editor J. ERDENECHIMEG; circ. 3,000.

Mongolyn Anagaakh Ukhaan (Mongolian Medicine): Ulan Bator (CPOB 696); tel. (11) 112306; fax (11) 451807; e-mail nymadawa@ hotmail.com; publ. by Scientific Society of Mongolian Physicians and Mongolian Academy of Sciences; quarterly; Editor-in-Chief Prof. PAGVAJAVYN NYAMDAVAA.

Mongolyn Khödöö (Mongolian Countryside): Agricultural University, Zaisan, 11th Sub-District, Khan-Uul District, Ulan Bator; tel. (11) 345211; publ. by Mongolian State University of Agriculture and Academy of Agricultural Sciences; 36 a year; Editor-in-Chief Prof. BEGZIIN DORJ.

Mongolyn Neg Ödör (One Day of Mongolia): Bldg 31, Bayanzürkh District, Ulan Bator (POB 44/764); tel. (11) 450103; fax (11) 460718; e-mail oneday@mongolmedia.com; 48 a year; Editor-in-Chief SH. OTGONSETSEG.

Mongolyn Tör Erkh Züi Setgüül (Mongolian State and Law Journal): Mongolian Supreme Court, 3rd Sub-District, Chingeltei District, Ulan Bator; tel. (11) 261465; internet www.supremecourt .mn; quarterly.

Myangany Zuuch (Millennium Messenger): Mönkh Press Co, West side of Choijin Lama Temple, Sükbataar District, Ulan Bator (POB 46/390); tel. and fax (11) 319745; e-mail monkh@mobinet.mn; 36 a year; Deputy Editor G. ENKHJARGAL.

Niigmiin Toli (Mirror of Society): Monkord Bldg, 4th Sub-District, Chingeltei District, Ulan Bator; tel. 99049531; e-mail enkhtaivan_987@yahoo.com; 264 a year; Editor-in-Chief SANDAGDORJIIN ENKHTUUL.

Notstoi Medee (Important News): Maximus Press Co, Ulan Bator (POB 20/359); tel. 99113322; 36 a year; Editor B. GALSANSÜKH.

Nyam Garig (Sunday): Mongol News Co Bldg, Juulchny Gudamj, Ulan Bator; tel. (11) 330797; fax (11) 330798; e-mail weekend@ mongolnews.mn; weekly supplement of *Önöödör*; Editor-in-Chief B. BOLDKHÜÜ.

Onigoo (Jokes): Konsulyn Gudamj 5-13, Bayanzürkh District, Ulan Bator (POB Sky Post 46/50); tel. 70150001; e-mail onigoosonin@ yahoo.com; 32 a year; Editor S. SARANCHIMEG.

Sankhüügiin Medee (Financial News): Ulan Bator; 36 a year; Editor L. DONDOG.

Serüüleg (Alarm Clock): Business Plaza, Enkhtaivny Örgön Chölöö, Bayanzürkh District, Ulan Bator (CPOB 1094); tel. 99114341; fax 70151401; e-mail seruuleg1996@yahoo.com; 48 a year; Editor-in-Chief BAYANMÖNKHIIN TSOOJCHULUUNTSETSEG; circ. 28,600.

Setgüülch (Journalist): Ulan Bator (POB 46/600); tel. (11) 325388; fax (11) 313912; f. 1982; publ. by Union of Journalists; journalism, politics, literature, art, economy; quarterly; Editor TSENDIIN ENKHBAT.

Shar Sonin (Yellow Newspaper): Ulan Bator (POB 46A/225); tel. (11) 313984; e-mail thesharsonin@yahoo.com; 36 a year; Editor B. NAMUUN.

Shine Erkh Chölöö (New Freedom): Ödriin Sonin Bldg, Ikh Toiruu, Ulan Bator (CPOB 2590); tel. and fax 70137010; e-mail erkhcholoo2007@yahoo.com; monthly; social and political affairs; Editor-in-Chief TS. OYUUNCHIMEG.

Shine Yörtönts (New Universe): Empathy Centre, Zaluuchuud Hotel, 6th Sub-District, Sükhbaatar District, Ulan Bator; tel. (11) 313019; fax (11) 321520; e-mail info@empathy.mn; internet www .empathypress.mn; quarterly; popular science magazine; Dir ELCI MEHMET.

Shinjlekh Ukhaany Akademiin Medee (Academy of Sciences News): Yörönkhii Said Amaryn Gudamj 1, Ulan Bator (POB 20A/34); tel. and fax (11) 262247; e-mail mas@mas.ac.mn; internet www.mas .ac.mn; f. 1961; publ. by Academy of Sciences; quarterly; Editor-in-Chief T. GALBAATAR.

Shuurkhai Zar (Quick Advertisement): Enkhtaivny Örgön Chölöö 62, 4th Sub-District, Sükhbaatar District, Ulan Bator (POB 46A/ 151); tel. and fax (11) 318787; e-mail shzar@mongol.mn; 100 a year; Editor E. TSEYENKHORLOO.

Soyombo: Ministry of Defence, Ulan Bator; tel. 91177221; f. 1924; est. as *Ardyn Tsereg* (People's Soldier); renamed *Ekh Orny Tölöö* (For the Motherland), then *Ulaan Od* (Red Star); weekly; Dep. Editor-in-Chief Lt-Col G. NYAMDORJ.

Strategi Sudlal (Strategic Studies): Institute of Strategic Studies, National Security Council, Ulan Bator (CPOB 870); tel. (11) 260710; fax (11) 324055; f. 1991; 4 a year; Editor DAMBYN GANBAT.

Tavan Tsagarig (Five Rings): Mongol News Co Bldg, Juulchny Gudamj, Chingeltei District, Ulan Bator; tel. (11) 70111095; internet www.mongolnews.mn/tavantsagarig; f. 1995; 100 a year; Editor-in-Chief TSAGAANBAATARYN BYAMBAA.

Tengerleg Khümüüs (Heavenly People): Soyombo Press Co, Partizany Gudamj 17, Sükhbaatar District, Ulan Bator (POB 44/716); tel. (11) 325250; fax (11) 330383; 36 a year; Dir-Gen. D. AMBARBAYASGALAN; Editor P. JARGALSAIKHAN.

Tonshuul (Woodpecker): Enkhtaivny Örgön Chölöö 4, Rm 148, Bayanzürkh District (CPOB 322), Ulan Bator; tel. 99191474; fax (11) 459265; e-mail ariun_tonshuul@yahoo.com; fortnightly magazine of cartoons, humour and satire; Editor TS. ARIUNAA.

Töriin Medeelel (State Information): Editorial Office, Rm 124, State Palace, Ulan Bator; tel. (11) 329612; fax (11) 322866; e-mail turiin_medeelel@parliament.mn; internet www.parl.gov.mn; f. 1990; presidential and governmental decrees, state laws; 48 a year; circ. 5,000.

Tsog (Ember): Mongolian Union of Writers, Ulan Bator; literary; quarterly.

Tsonkh (Window): Chingisiin Örgön Chölöö 1, Ulan Bator (CPOB 1085); tel. (11) 310717; publ. by the Democratic Party's Political Department; 6 a year.

Utga Zokhiol Urlag (Literature and Art): Mongolian Union of Writers, Sükhbaataryn Gudamj 11, Ulan Bator (POB 46A/555); tel. 99294530; e-mail info@utgazokhiol.mn; internet www.utgazokhiol.mn; f. 1955; 36 a year; Editor JAMSRANGIIN BAYARJARGAL; circ. 3,000.

Üg (The Word): Bldg 86, Chingeltei District, Ulan Bator; tel. 55152675; fax (11) 329795; e-mail ugsonin@mol.mn; journal of the Mongolian Social-Democratic Party (from 2005); Editor-in-Chief ARYAAGIIN GANBAATAR.

Zar Medee (Advertisement News): Arvit 20 Ail, 4th Sub-District, Chingeltei District, Ulan Bator; tel. 70110008; fax 70110009; e-mail zar_sonin@yahoo.com; internet zarsonin.mn; personal and company adverts; 100 a year; Editor D. BAYASGALAN.

Zindaa (Ranking): Kyokshüyu Tower, 6th Sub-District, Bayangol District, Ulan Bator; tel. 70151619; fax (11) 354555; wrestling news; 36 a year; Editor-in-Chief KH. MANDAKHBAYAR.

FOREIGN LANGUAGE PUBLICATIONS

Inspiring Mongolia: Mongolian National Chamber of Commerce and Industry, Mahatma Gandhi Gudamj, 1st Sub-District, Khan-Uul District, Ulan Bator; tel. (11) 327176; fax (11) 324620; e-mail marketing@mongolchamber.mn; internet www.mongolchamber.mn; magazine in English, publ. twice a year; Editor-in-Chief SAMBUUGIIN DEMBEREL.

Menggu Xiaoxi Bao (News of Mongolia): Montsame News Agency, Ulan Bator (CPOB 1514); tel. (11) 320077; e-mail mgxxbao@chinggis.com; f. 1929; weekly; in Chinese; Sec. P. OYUUNTSETSEG.

The Mongol Messenger: Montsame News Agency, Jigjidjavyn Gudamj 8, Ulan Bator (CPOB 1514); tel. (51) 266740; fax (11) 325512; e-mail monmessenger@magicnet.mn; f. 1991; weekly newspaper in English; owned by Montsame national news agency; Editor-in-Chief GIVAANDONDOGIIN PÜREVSAMBUU; circ. 2,000.

Mongolian Magazine: Interpress Publishers, Ulan Bator; f. 2004; English-language monthly illustrated magazine about Mongolian history, culture, nature, life and customs.

Mongolia This Week: Ulan Bator; tel. and fax (11) 318339; e-mail mongoliathisweek@mobinet.mn; weekly in English, online daily; Editor-in-Chief D. NARANTUYAA; English Editor ERIC MUSTAFA.

Mongolia Today: Montsame News Agency, Jigjidjavyn Gudamj 8, Ulan Bator (CPOB 1514); quarterly; in English; Editor-in-Chief G. PÜREVSAMBUU.

Mongoliya Segodnya (Mongolia Today): Undruul Hotel, Rm 5, 5th Sub-District, Bayanzürkh District, Ulan Bator (POB 51/404); tel. 88871402; fax (11) 457968; e-mail ms@mongoliyasegodnya.mn; weekly; in Russian; Editor-in-Chief DÜNGER-YAICHILIIN SOLONGO.

Mongoru Tsushin (Mongolia News): Montsame News Agency, Jigjidjavyn Gudamj 8, Ulan Bator (CPOB 1514); 48 a year; in Japanese.

Montsame Daily News: Montsame News Agency, Jigjidjavyn Gudamj 8, Ulan Bator (CPOB 1514); tel. (11) 99188684; fax (11) 327857; e-mail paula_jlo@yahoo.com; f. 1921; daily English news digest for embassies, etc.

Novosti Mongolii (News of Mongolia): Montsame News Agency, Jigjidjavyn Gudamj 8, Ulan Bator (CPOB 1514); tel. (11) 310157; fax

(11) 327857; e-mail novosty_mongolii@yahoo.co.uk; f. 1942; weekly; in Russian; Editor-in-Chief DÜGERSÜRENGIIN ARIUNBOLD.

Solongo (Rainbow): Green House, 6th Sub-District, Sükhbaatar District, Ulan Bator (POB 23/628); tel. 91887376; internet www.solonggo.net; f. 1992; monthly; about relations with China; in Mongolian and Chinese; Deputy Editor-in-Chief T. BAYANJARGAL.

The UB Post: Mongol News Co, Juulchny Gudamj, Ulan Bator; tel. 70111095; fax (11) 330798; e-mail ubpost@mongolnews.mn; internet ubpost.mongolnews.mn; f. 1996; 144 a year; in English; Editor-in-Chief G. ÖLZIISAIKHAN; circ. 4,000.

NEWS AGENCIES

Khurd: OMRT TV Centre, Khuvisgalchdyn Gudamj, Ulan Bator; tel. (11) 321832; fax (11) 328334; e-mail info@khurdagency.mn; internet www.khurdagency.mn; information agency of Mongolian National Public Radio.

Montsame (Mongol Tsakhilgaan Medeenii Agentlag) (Mongolian News Agency): Jigjidjavyn Gudamj 8, Ulan Bator (CPOB 1514); tel. (11) 266904; fax (11) 327857; e-mail montsame@magicnet.mn; internet www.montsame.mn; f. 1921; govt-controlled; Gen. Dir A. BAATARKHUYAG; Editor-in-Chief TS. SÜRENJAV.

Mongolyn Medee (Mongolian News): Public Radio and Television, Khuvisgalyn Zam, Ulan Bator; Dir S. BATZAYAA.

News: Ardyn Erkh Sonin, 5th Sub-District, Bayanzürkh District, Ulan Bator; e-mail info@news.mn; internet www.news.mn; services in Mongolian and English.

PRESS ASSOCIATIONS

Daily Newspaper Association: c/o Önöödör, Mongol News Co, Juulchny Gudamj, Ulan Bator; f. 2006; Pres. S. GANTOGOO.

Mongolian Newspaper Association: Ulan Bator; Pres. RADNAAGIIN KHADBAATAR.

Press Institute: Ulan Bator; internet www.pressinst.org.mn; f. 1995; Dir M. MÖNKHMANDAKH.

Publishers

The ending of the state monopoly has led to the establishment of several small commercial publishers, including Shuvuun Saaral (Ministry of Defence), Mongol Khevlel and Soyombo Co, Mongolpress (Montsame), Erdem (Academy of Sciences), Süülenkhüü children's publishers, Sudaryn Chuulgan, Interpress, Sükhbaatar Co, Öngöt Khevlel, Admon, Odsar, Khee Khas Co, etc.

Admon Co: Amaryn Gudamj 2, Sükhbaatar District, Ulan Bator (CPOB 92); tel. (11) 329253; fax (11) 327251; e-mail admon@magicnet.mn; Dir R. ENKHBAT.

Darkhan Sergelen Co: Naadamchdyn Gudamj, Darkhan; tel. (7037) 23049; fax (7037) 24741; internet www.munkhiin-useg.mn.

Khevleliin Khüreelen (Press Institute NGO): Ikh Toiruu 11, Sükhbaatar District, Ulan Bator; tel. and fax (11) 350012; e-mail ts_byambaa12@yahoo.com; internet www.owc.org.mn/pressinstitute; Chair. TS. ENKHBAT.

Mon Sudar: Admon Bldg, Amaryn Gudamj, Sükhbaatar District, Ulan Bator; tel. (11) 314244; fax (11) 327251.

Mongol Khevlel: Mongol Khevlel Bldg, 8th Sub-District, Sükhbaatar District, Ulan Bator; tel. (11) 323636; fax (11) 329180; e-mail monprint@hotmail.com.

Mongol News Group: Mongol News Group Bldg, Juulchny Gudamj, Ulan Bator; tel. (11) 330797; fax (11) 330798; e-mail mntoday@mobinet.mn; f. 1996; owns newspapers *MN-Önöödör*, *Tavan Tsagarig*, *Nyam Garig* and *The UB Post*, TV Channel 25 and ABM Co printers; Pres. B. NANDINTÜSHIG.

Mönkhiin Üseg Group: Teeverchdiin Gudamj 27, Sükhbaatar District, Ulan Bator; tel. (11) 319658; fax (11) 321316; e-mail munuseg@mbox.mn; internet www.munkhiin-useg.mn; Chair. G. BATMÖNKH.

Öngöt Khevlel Co: Amaryn Gudamj 2, Sükhbaatar District, Ulan Bator; tel. (11) 329519; fax (11) 321579; e-mail ungutkhevlel1912@yahoo.com.

Sükhbaatarprint Co: Amaryn Gudamj 2, Sükhbaatar District, Ulan Bator; tel. and fax (11) 320504; e-mail sukhprint@magicnet.mn.

Zurag Züi Co (Cartography): Ikh Toiruu 15, Ulan Bator; tel. (11) 322164; e-mail cart@magicnet.mn; publr and retailer of maps and atlases.

PUBLISHERS' ASSOCIATIONS

Local Press and Information Association: Ulan Bator; f. 2006; Pres. S. SHARAVDORJ.

Mongolian Book Publishers' Association: Ulan Bator; Exec. Dir S. Tserendorj.

Mongolian Free Press Publishers' Association: Ulan Bator (POB 24/306); tel. and fax (11) 313405; Pres. Batyn Erdenebaatar.

Broadcasting and Communications

TELECOMMUNICATIONS

Digital exchanges have been installed in Ulan Bator, Darkhan, Erdenet, Sükhbaatar, Bulgan and Arvaikheer, while radio relay lines have been digitalized between: Ulan Bator–Darkhan–Sükhbaatar; Ulan Bator–Darkhan–Erdenet; and Dashinchilen–Arvaikheer. Mobile telephone companies operate in Ulan Bator and other central towns, in addition to Arvaikheer, Sainshand and Zamyn-Üüd.

Bodicom: Ulan Bator; tel. (11) 325144; fax (11) 318486; e-mail bodicom@mongolnet.mn.

Datacom: San Business Centre, 8th Sub-District, Sükhbaatar District, Ulan Bator; tel. (11) 327309; e-mail support@datacom.mn; internet www.datacom.mn; service provider for MagicNet connection to internet; domain registration; Dir Dangaasürengiin Enkhbat.

G-Mobile: Gem International Co, 1st Sub-District, Chingeltei District, Ulan Bator; tel. (11) 333636; e-mail info@g-mobile.mn; internet www.g-mobile.mn; Dir-Gen. Ts. Tserenpuntsag.

Incomnet: Enkhtaivny Örgön Chölöö, Bayanzürkh District, Ulan Bator (CPOB 582); tel. and fax (11) 480808; e-mail info@incomnet .mn; internet www.incomnet.mn; internet service provider, satellite communications; Deputy Dir D. Yöröölt.

MagicNet: Rm 222, Ground Floor, Science and Technology Information Centre, Ulan Bator; tel. (11) 312061; fax (11) 311496; e-mail info@magicnet.mn; internet www.magicnet.mn; internet service provider.

MCSCom: MCS Plaza, 3rd Floor, Baga Toiruu 49, Ulan Bator; tel. (11) 327854; fax (11) 311323; e-mail sales@mcscom.mn; internet www.mcscom.mn; internet service provider.

Medeelel Kholboo: Central Post Office Bldg, Sükhbaataryn Talbai 1, Chingeltei District, Ulan Bator; tel. and fax 70112519; internet www.icnc.mn; installation of digital radio relays and fibre optic cables for communications and internet, television and radio.

Micom: Central Post Office Bldg, Sükhbaataryn Talbai 1, Chingeltei District, Ulan Bator (CPOB 1124); tel. (11) 313229; fax (11) 322473; e-mail info@micom.mng.mn; internet www.micom.mn; Dir Ch. Narantungalag.

MobiCom: MobiCom Corpn Central Bldg, Sambuugiin Gudamj 7-1, 5th Sub-District, Chingeltei District, Ulan Bator; tel. 95070202; fax (11) 310411; e-mail feedback@mobicom.mn; internet www.mobicom .mn; mobile telephone service provider; Exec. Dir Fumiaki Shiga; Dir-Gen. R. Ariuntsogt.

Moncom: Ulan Bator (POB 51/207); tel. (11) 329409; e-mail ch .enkhmend@hotmail.com; pager services.

Mongolia Telecom: Central Post Office Bldg, Sükhbaataryn Talbai 1, Ulan Bator (CPOB 1166); tel. 70102390; fax 70102247; e-mail hr@ mtcom.net; internet www.telecommongolia.mn; 54.6% state-owned, 40.0% owned by Korea Telecom; Pres. and CEO Oonoigiin Shaaluu; Exec. Dir O. Batchuluun.

MonSat: New Horizon Bldg, Olimpiin Gudamj 6, 1st Sub-District, Sükhbaatar District, Ulan Bator; tel. (11) 323705; fax (11) 312699; e-mail monsat@mcs.mn; internet www.monsat.mcs.mn; satellite communications, mobile telephone and internet services.

Newcom: Naiman Zovkhis Bldg, Sööliin Gudamj 21, Sükhbaatar District, Ulan Bator; tel. (11) 313183; fax (11) 318521; e-mail secretary@newcom.mn; internet www.newcom.mn; Chair. Ts. Boldbaatar; Exec. Dir B. Byambasaikhan.

Newtel: TEDY Centre, Sambuugiin Gudamj 18, Chingeltei District, Ulan Bator (CPOB 425); e-mail marketing@ntc.mn; internet www .ntc.mn; Exec. Dir D. Bolor.

Orbitnet: Central Tower Bldg, Sükhbaataryn Talbai 2, Sükhbaatar District, Ulan Bator; tel. (11) 323705; fax (11) 312699; e-mail orbitnet@mcs.mn; internet www.orbitnet.mcs.mn; Dir P. Sükhbaatar.

Railcom: Mongolian Railways (MTZ), Teeverchdiin Gudamj, 3rd Sub-District, Bayangol District, Ulan Bator (CPOB 376); tel. (11) 242601; e-mail info@railcom.mn; internet www.railcom.mn; telephone, TV and internet service provider.

Skynetcom: 1st Sub-District, Chingeltei District, Ulan Bator; tel. (11) 318840; fax (11) 318841; e-mail info@skynetcom.mn; internet www.skynetcom.mn; mobile telephone service provider.

Skytel: Skytel Plaza Centre, Chingisiin Örgön Chölöö 9, Ulan Bator (CPOB 811); tel. (11) 319191; fax (11) 318487; e-mail skytel_comment@yahoo.com; internet www.skytel.mn; mobile telephone and voice mail service provider; Mongolia-Republic of Korea jt venture; Dir-Gen. D. Bolor; Marketing Man. G. Tüvshintögs.

Ulusnet: Zovkhis Bldg, Sööliin Gudamj 21, Sükhbaatar District, Ulan Bator; tel. (11) 321434; fax (11) 322686; e-mail service@ulusnet .mn; internet www.ulusnet.mn; Mongolia's first Wimax service provider.

Unitel: Central Tower, Sükhbaataryn Talbai 2, Sükhbaatar District, Ulan Bator; tel. (11) 328888; fax (11) 330708; e-mail info@unitel .mn; internet www.unitel.mn; f. 2005 by MBSB Telecom, Uangel Corpn (Republic of Korea) and Dream Choice Co (Canada); mobile telephone service provider; Dir-Gen. B. Bilgüün.

Univision: Unitel Corpn, Ulan Bator; tel. 77118811; e-mail info@ univision.mn; internet www.univision.mn; IPTV, HD cable TV, internet, mobile telephone service provider; CEO N. Naranbat.

BROADCASTING

A 1,900-km radio relay line from Ulan Bator to Altai and Ölgii provides direct-dialling telephone links as well as television services for western Mongolia. New radio relay lines have been built from Ulan Bator to Choibalsan, and from Ulan Bator to Sükhbaatar and Sainshand. Most of the population is in the zone of television reception, following the inauguration of relays via satellites operated by the International Telecommunications Satellite Organization (INTELSAT). At January 2012 Mongolia had 72 radio stations and 149 television stations.

In 2009 Mongolia had 373 television transmitters and relay stations. However, over 54,600 households continued to receive radio broadcasts by the old wired networks

All provincial centres receive two channels of Mongolian national television, and all district centres can receive television. At the beginning of 2005 the first legislative measures were taken to end state control, with the approval of the Law on Public Broadcasting, the provisions of which entered into force on 1 July 2005, creating an independent public service broadcaster to be known as Public Radio and Television. In 2009 Mongolia's first internet television station, Mongol TV, was launched.

Mongolian National Public Radio and Television (ONRT): Mongolian National Public Radio and Television Central Bldg, Khuvisgalyn Zam 3, Bayangol District, Ulan Bator; tel. (11) 322580; f. 2006; replaced the govt-run Directorate of Radio and Television Affairs; budgetary expenditure on ONRT amounted to 5,428.5m. tögrög in 2011; Chair. of National Council Khaidavyn Chilaajav; Dir-Gen. Myanganbuugiin Naranbaatar; Editor-in-Chief Demberetiin Erdenetsetseg.

Radio

Mongolian National Public Radio (Mongolradio): Mongolian National Public Radio and Television Central Bldg, Khuvisgalyn Zam 3, Bayangol District, Ulan Bator; tel. (11) 323096; f. 1934; operates for 17 hours daily on three long-wave and one medium-wave frequency, and VHF; programmes in Mongolian (two); part of Public Radio and Television; Dir L. Tseren-Ochir; Dep. Dir B. Khanddolgor.

> **Voice of Mongolia:** Ulan Bator (CPOB 365); tel. and fax (11) 325468; fax (11) 328234; e-mail densmaa9@yahoo.com; internet www.vom.mn; f. 1964; external service of Mongolradio; broadcasts in Russian, Chinese, English and Japanese on short wave; Dir Zorigtyn Densmaa.

AE and JAAG Co: Ikh Toiruu, Sükhbaatar District, Ulan Bator (POB 20/126); tel. 99118563; fax (11) 352463; e-mail aejaag@ magicnet.mn; f. 1996; broadcasts for 4.5–5 hours daily; CEO Z. Altai.

FM 95.1 Khamag Mongol (All Mongolia): Sonor Plaza, Sükhbaatar District, Ulan Bator; tel. 96648002; e-mail micky_adiya@yahoo.com.

FM 96.3 Avtoradio: 4th Sub-District, Chingeltei District, Ulan Bator; tel. 98189655; e-mail mongol_media@yahoo.com.

FM 96.9 Elgen Nutag (Homeland): 12th Sub-District, Bayanzürkh District, Ulan Bator; tel. 70160096.

FM 98.1 Formula: 5th Sub-District, Chingeltei District, Ulan Bator; tel. 70110981.

FM 98.5 Best: Ulan Bator Bank Bldg, 4th Sub-District, Chingeltei District, Ulan Bator; tel. (11) 339917.

FM 98.9 Royal Radio: Royal Academy, Bayanzürkh District, Ulan Bator; tel. 50006633; e-mail royalradio989@yahoo.com.

FM 99.3 Ineemseglel (Smile): Central Palace of Culture, Sükhbaatar District, Ulan Bator; tel. 99093713; fax (11) 319789; Dir Kh. Ikhbayar.

FM 99.7 Ikh Mongol (Great Mongolia): Grand Plaza, Enkhtaivny Örgön Chölöö, Bayangol District, Ulan Bator; tel. 70121444.

FM 100.1 Kiss: Ulan Bator Bank, Chingeltei District, Ulan Bator; tel. (11) 312334; e-mail kiss100_1@yahoo.com.

FM 100.5 Minii Mongol (My Mongolia): Central Palace of Culture, Sükhbaatar District, Ulan Bator; tel. (11) 322199.

FM 100.9 Khökh Tenger (Blue Sky Radio): Mongolian National Television Bldg, Chingeltei District, Ulan Bator; tel. (11) 320522; broadcasts for 12 hours Mon. to Sat. and shorter hours on Sun; short-wave transmitter on 4,850 kHz; Dir L. AMARZAYAA.

FM 101.7 Niisleliin Radio: Narny Titem, 5th Sub-District, Chingeltei District, Ulan Bator; tel. 70110981; fax (11) 322472; Dir U. BULGAN.

FM 102.1 Ekh Oron (Homeland): Central Palace of Culture, Sükhbaatar District, Ulan Bator; tel. (11) 327383; fax (11) 322472; operated by the Open Information Foundation.

FM 102.5 Radio Ulan Bator: Grand Plaza, Enkhtaivny Örgön Chölöö, Bayangol District, Ulan Bator; tel. 70121025; fax 70137388; e-mail FMub102.5@yahoo.com.

FM 103.1: Ulan Bator; BBC World Service Relay.

FM 103.6: TV9 Bldg, Amaryn Gudamj, Sükhbaatar District, Ulan Bator; tel. 70121036; TV-9's radio station; Dir M. BAYANZUL.

FM 104 Life: Business Plaza, Enkhtaivny Örgön Chölöö, 15th Sub-District, Bayanzürkh District, Ulan Bator; tel. and fax (11) 463782; e-mail life_fm104@yahoo.com.

FM 104.5 Ger Büliin Radio (Family Radio): Bldg 10, 2nd Sub-District, Bayanzürkh District, Ulan Bator; tel. (11) 461045; fax (11) 452987.

FM 105 Tany Derged (Near You): Central Palace of Culture, Sükhbaatar District, Ulan Bator; tel. (11) 319789.

FM 105.5 Necktie: Central Palace of Culture, Sükhbaatar District, Ulan Bator; tel. and fax 70114440; Dir B. TÜVSHINTÖGS.

FM 106.6: Democratic Party Bldg, Chingisiin Örgön Chölöö, Ulan Bator; tel. (11) 329353; Voice of America news and information in Mongolian, English lessons and music.

FM 107.5 Shine Dolgion (New Wave): Namyanjügiin Gudamj 40, Bayanzürkh District, Ulan Bator; tel. and fax (11) 452444; relays of Voice of America broadcasts in English and Russian, entertainment programmes; Dir TS. ARIUNAA.

There are seven long- and short-wave radio transmitters and 49 FM stations in 23 towns. Some rural districts have set up their own small FM radio stations to broadcast local information.

Television

Mongolian Television Association: Ulan Bator; mems: BTV, Channel 25, Eagle, Education, NTV, SBN, TM, TV5, TV8, TV9 and UBS.

Mongolian National Public Television (MNTV): Mongolian National Public Radio and Television Central Bldg, Khuvisgalyn Zam 3, Bayangol District, Ulan Bator (CPOB 365); tel. (11) 327214; fax (11) 328939; e-mail mrtv@magicnet.mn; f. 1967; daily 16-hour transmissions, except Mon; short news bulletins in English Mon., Wed. and Fri; part of Public Radio and Television; Dir CH. DAVAABAYAR.

Bolovsrol (Education) TV Channel: Bayangol District, Behind Mongolian National Public TV Bldg, Ulan Bator; tel. (11) 300722; fax (11) 300710; e-mail develop@edutv.mn; f. 2005; broadcasts 20–22 hours a day; Gen. Dir NATSAGDORJIIN SANJ.

C-1: Supermarket No. 1, Tömörchnii Gudamj, Chingeltei District, Ulan Bator; tel. (11) 312126; fax (11) 325438; e-mail info@c1.mn; internet www.c1.mn; f. 2006; daily 17-hour transmissions; news link with Reuters; Dir BEN MOYLE.

Channel 25: Mongol News Bldg, Juulchny Gudamj, Chingeltei District, Ulan Bator; tel. and fax (11) 321989; daily 18-hour transmissions; Dir ZORIGIIN ALTAI; Gen. Man. AYUUSHIIN AVIRMED.

Eagle Broadcasting Co: Erkhüüd Centre, Lkhagvasürengiin Gudamj, Ulan Bator; tel. (11) 463088; fax (11) 463087; internet www.eagle-tv.mn; f. 1994; several news bulletins a day; Christian message; commenced operations in 1996; broadcasts restarted 2005 after two years off air; Pres. THOMAS TERRY; Dir BALJINNYAMYN BAYARSAIKHAN.

Khiimori Co: Bldg 3A, No. 2 Combined Clinical General Hospital, Ulan Bator; tel. (11) 458531; fax (11) 458569; f. 1995; cable TV service provider.

National Times News: NTN HD Media Group, Ritz House, Ikh Toiruu 180, Bayanzürkh District, Ulan Bator; tel. (11) 483790; fax (11) 483789; internet www.ntn.mn.

New TV (NTV): Capital House, Chingisiin Örgön Chölöö 14, 2nd Sub-District, Khan-Uul District, Ulan Bator; tel. 77117777; fax 77110002; internet www.ntv.mn; Dir M. ULAMBADRAKH.

Sansar KATV: Sansar Bldg, 3rd Sub-District, Chingeltei District, Ulan Bator; tel. (11) 322813; internet www.sansar.mn.

SBN (Supervision Broadcasting Network): Khuvisgalchdyn Gudamj, Bayangol District, Ulan Bator; tel. (11) 301641; fax (11) 301643; e-mail contact@sbn.mn; internet www.sbn.mn; Exec. Dir N. BOLORKHUU.

Supervision KATV: SBN TV Bldg, Khuvisgalchdyn Gudamj, Bayangol District, Ulan Bator; tel. (11) 363616; internet www.supervision.mn.

TV-5: Sapporo Centre, 1st Sub-District, Songinokhairkhan District; tel. (11) 680327; fax (11) 680326; e-mail feedback@tv5.mn; internet www.tv5.mn; daily 18-hour transmissions; Editor-in-Chief E. DAGIIMAA.

TV-9: Amaryn Gudamj 3, Sükhbaatar District, Ulan Bator; tel. 70110630; e-mail info@tv9.mn; internet www.tv9.mn; f. 2003; 24-hour broadcaster; Dir TS. ENKHBAT.

UBS (Ulaanbaatar Broadcasting System): Khuvisgalchdyn Gudamj 3, Bayangol District, Ulan Bator; tel. 70140434; fax (11) 300435; e-mail info@ubs.mn; internet www.ubs.mn; f. 1992; fmrly state-owned; privatized in 2005; three channels; Dir-Gen. LKHAGVADORJIIN BALKHJAV.

Cable television companies (29 in total) operate in 19 towns. There are local television stations in Ulan Bator (three), Darkhan, Sükhbaatar and Baganuur. Chinese, Kazakh, Russian, German and French television services are among those that can also be received.

Finance

(cap. = capital; res = reserves; dep. = deposits; m. = million; brs = branches; amounts in tögrög, unless otherwise stated)

BANKING

Central Bank

Bank of Mongolia (Mongolbank): Baga Toiruu 9, Ulan Bator; tel. (11) 310413; fax (11) 311471; e-mail ad@mongolbank.mn; internet www.mongolbank.mn; f. 1924; est. as the State Bank of the Mongolian People's Republic; cap. 5,000m., res 103,504m., dep. 2,369,433m. (Dec. 2009); Pres. NAIDANSÜRENGIIN ZOLJARGAL; Chief Vice-Pres. BOLDYN JAVKHLAN.

Other Banks

Capital Bank: Sambuugiin Gudamj 43, Chingeltei District, Ulan Bator; tel. 50115040; fax (11) 310833; e-mail info@capitalbank.mn; internet www.capitalbank.mn; cap. 8,007m., res 16.5m., dep. 66,751.1m. (Dec. 2009); f. 1990; 99% owned by Bishrelt Holding Co; CEO AGVAANJAMBYN ARIUNBOLD; Dep. CEO S. ALTANGEREL; 24 brs.

Capitron Bank: Capitron Bank Bldg, Usny Gudamj 4, Sükhbaatar District, Ulan Bator; tel. (11) 328373; fax (11) 328372; e-mail info@capitronbank.mn; internet www.capitronbank.mn; f. 2001; cap. 8,000.5m., res 333m., dep. 58,530.3m. (Dec. 2009); 49% owned by B. Medree, 46% by P. Mönkhsaikhan; CEO PÜREVJAVYN MÖNKHSAIKHAN.

Chinggis Khaan Bank: New Century Plaza, Chingisiin Örgön Chölöö 15, Sükhbaatar District, Ulan Bator (POB 28/418); tel. (11) 318367; fax (11) 318373; internet www.chinggiskhaanbank.com; f. 2001; est. by Millennium Securities Management Ltd and Coral Sea Holdings Ltd (British Virgin Islands); cap. 39,373m., dep. 98,820m. (Dec. 2009); Chair. SERGEI GROMOV; CEO L. ARIUNAA.

Credit Bank: Cnr Sambuugiin Gudamj and Ikh Surguuliin Gudamj, East of State Palace, Sükhbaatar District, Ulan Bator; tel. (11) 319038; fax (11) 310853; f. 1997; owned by Basic Element Finance Ltd, Cyprus; cap. 8,090m., res 20,594m., dep. 12,363m. (July 2006); Propr OLEG DERIPASKA; Exec. Dir B. TSENGEL.

Development Bank: Government Bldg 2, Negsden Ündestnii Gudamj 5/1, Chingeltei District, Ulan Bator; tel. 70130516; fax 70130602; Chair. BEGZSÜRENGIIN SHINEBAATAR.

Erel Bank: Erel Bank Bldg, Chingisiin Örgön Chölöö, Khan-Uul District, Ulan Bator; tel. (11) 344550; fax (11) 343387; e-mail info@erelbank.mn; internet www.erelbank.mn; f. 1997; privately owned; cap. 4,000m., res 45.9m., dep. 3,163.4m. (Dec. 2005); CEO DAVAAKHÜÜGIIN TÖMÖRKHÜÜ.

Golomt Bank of Mongolia: Golomt Bank Central Bldg, Sükhbaataryn Talbai, Ulan Bator; tel. (11) 311530; fax (11) 311958; e-mail mail@golomtbank.com; internet www.golomtbank.com; f. 1995; est. by Mongolian-Portuguese IBH Bodi International Co Ltd; cap. 189,087m., dep. 1,840,136m. (Dec. 2011); Chair. DANZANDORJIIN BAYASGALAN; CEO JOHN FINIGAN; 14 brs.

Khadgalamjiin Bank (Savings Bank): Kholboochdyn Gudamj 4, Chingeltei District, Ulan Bator; tel. (11) 310103; fax (11) 327467; e-mail contact@savingsbank.mn; internet www.savingsbank.mn; f. 1996; est. as Ardyn Bank; owned by MD Securities Co, a consortium of Chinggis Khaan Bank, Mongol Daatgal Consortium and Bratsk People's Bank (Russian Federation); took over Mongol Shuudan Bank (Post Bank) 2010; cap. 8,031.0m., res 2,544.5m., dep.

65,986.0m. (Dec. 2007); Chair. SH. BATKHÜÜ; Dir L. BADAMTSETSEG; 60 brs.

Khan Bank (KhAAN or Agricultural Bank): Söуliin Gudamj 25, Sükhbaatar District, Ulan Bator (POB 44/192); tel. (11) 332333; fax 70117023; e-mail info@khanbank.com; internet www.khanbank .com; f. 1991; purchased by H and S Securities (Japan) in Feb. 2003; cap. 12,994m., res 14,591.7m., dep. 869,790m. (Dec. 2009); owned by Itochu Corpn and Tavan Bogd Group; Chair. HIDEO SAWADA; Dir YOSHIAKI MISHIMA; 380 brs.

National Investment Bank: NI Bank Bldg, Usny Gudamj 1, Sükhbaatar District, Ulan Bator; tel. (11) 321995; fax (11) 330434; e-mail info@nibank.mn; internet www.nibank.mn; f. 2006; 55% owned by D. Dagvadorj, 22% by UB Diversified Ltd, and 22% by Firebird Funds; f. 2006; Chair. SUMYAABAZAR; CEO BANZRAGCHIIN BAYARSAIKHAN.

State Bank (Töriin Bank): Baga Toiruu 7/1, 1st Sub-District, Chingeltei District, Ulan Bator (POB 44/304); tel. (11) 312107; fax (11) 330595; e-mail contact@statebank.mn; internet www.statebank .mn; f. 1999; cap. 14,666.7m., res 11,971m., dep. 159,806m. (Dec. 2008); fmrly Zoos Bank; name changed as above when nationalized in 2009; Exec. Dir JALBUUGIIN OTGONBILEG.

Trade and Development Bank of Mongolia (Khudaldaa Khögjliin Bank): Cnr of Juulchny Gudamj 7 and Baga Toiruu 12, Chingeltei District, Ulan Bator; tel. (11) 312362; fax (11) 331155; e-mail hqbranch@tdbm.mn; internet www.tdbm.mn; f. 1991; carries out Mongolbank's foreign operations; cap. 6,610.1m., res 14,619.2m., dep. 670,631.5m. (Dec. 2009); 76% equity bought by Banca Commerciale (Lugano) and Gerald Metals (Stanford, CT), May 2002; Chair. D. ERDENEBILEG; Pres. RANDOLPH KOPPA; CEO BALBARYN MEDREE.

Transport and Development Bank (Trans Bank): Juulchny Gudamj 35, 1st Sub-District, Chingeltei District, Ulan Bator; tel. and fax 70110202; e-mail info@transbank.mn; internet www .transbank.mn; owned by Russian interests; CEO K. ZEINESH (acting).

Ulaanbaatar City Bank: Sükhbaataryn Gudamj 16, Chingeltei District, Ulan Bator (POB 46/370); tel. (11) 319041; fax (11) 330508; e-mail info@ubcbank.mn; internet www.ubcbank.mn; f. 1998; est. by Capital City with assistance from the Bank of Taipei (Taiwan); cap. 5,349m., dep. 50,064m. (June 2005); Chair. D. BATJARGAL; CEO A. ENKHMEND.

XacBank: Yörönkhii Said Amaryn Gudamj, Sükhbaatar District, Ulan Bator (POB 20A/721); tel. (11) 318185; fax (11) 328701; e-mail bank@xacbank.mn; internet www.xacbank.org; f. 2001; cap. 13,290.6m., res 13,605.4m., dep. 148,804.1m. (Dec. 2009); owned by Mercy Corps; Chair. CHULUUNY GANBOLD; Exec. Dir DÜGERSÜRENGIIN BAT-OCHIR.

Bankers' Association

Mongolian Bank Association: Vista Office, Chingisiin Örgön Chölöö 17, Sükhbaatar District, Ulan Bator (CPOB 101); tel. (11) 323581; fax (11) 314105; e-mail monba@mongolnet.mn; internet www.mba.mn; f. 2000; Pres. B. NAIDALAA; Exec. Dir ZUUNAIN SHAGDARSÜREN.

STOCK EXCHANGE

Under a co-operation agreement with the London Stock Exchange, the Millennium IT system was being installed at the Mongolian Stock Exchange at a cost of some US $14m. to raise operations to international standards. Business was interrupted in July 2012 during installation of the system's T+3 add-on, whose purpose was to restrict low-turnover local buying and selling and prepare the exchange for large-scale international trading.

Stock Exchange: Sükhbaataryn Talbai 2, Ulan Bator; tel. (11) 313511; fax (11) 325170; e-mail info@mse.mn; internet www.mse .mn; f. 1991; Exec. Dir KHANGAIN ALTAI; Chair. LKHAGVAGIIN GANBAT.

INSURANCE

Ard Daatgal: Central Tower, Sükhbaatar Sq. 2, Ulan Bator; tel. 77200088; fax 77200089; e-mail daatgal@arddaatgal.mn; internet www.arddaatgal.mn; f. 1994; est. with Omni Whittington Guernsey; Chair. TSEVGEENII TOGTOKHBAYAR; CEO DAGVABALJIRYN CHULUUNTSETSEG.

Bodi Daatgal Co: Bodi Tower, Jigjidjavyn Gudamj, Ulan Bator; tel. (11) 323444; fax (11) 326535; e-mail bodi@bodiinsurance.mn; internet www.bodiinsurance.mn; Dir L. BOLDKHUYAG.

Ganzam Insurance: Mongolian Railways (MTZ), Zamchdyn Gudamj, Ulan Bator; tel. and fax (11) 242643.

MIG Daatgal: MIG Bldg, Enkhtaivny Örgön Chölöö, 1st Sub-District, Chingeltei District, Ulan Bator (CPOB 200); tel. (11) 330131; fax (11) 330132; e-mail mig@magicnet.mn; internet www .mig.mn; f. 1997; privately owned; CEO JANDAVYN BAT-ORSHIKH.

Mongol Daatgal: Enkhtaivny Örgön Chölöö 13, Sükhbaatar District, Ulan Bator; tel. (11) 313697; fax (11) 310347; e-mail insurance@ mongoldaatgal.mn; internet www.mongoldaatgal.mn; f. 1934; sold Dec. 2003 to consortium formed by Angara-SKB and Chinggis Khan Bank; Chair. BADARCHIIN ENKHBAT; CEO T. BATZÜL.

National Life Daatgal: Financial Service Corpn, Ambassador Bldg, Enkhtaivny Örgön Chölöö 17A/5, 1st Sub-District, Sükhbaatar District, Ulan Bator (POB 48/35); tel. 70110784; fax 70110781; e-mail national.life@fscomongolia.mn; internet www.fscomongolia.mn; Exec. Dir B. BATBAYAR.

Nomin Daatgal: State Department Store, Enkhtaivny Örgön Chölöö, Chingeltei District, Ulan Bator; tel. (11) 330023; fax (11) 325528; e-mail insurance@nomin.net; internet www.insurance.nomin.net; CEO SANJAAGIIN GANCHIMEG.

Ochir Undraa Daatgal: Söуliin Gudamj 15/2, 4th Sub-District, Sükhbaatar District, Ulan Bator (POB 44/398); tel. (11) 324248; fax (11) 326466; e-mail insurance@ochir-undraa.com; internet www .ochir-undraa.com.

Tüshig Daatgal Co: Zoos Bank Bldg, Baga Toiruu, Chingeltei District, Ulan Bator; tel. (11) 316119; fax (11) 330578; e-mail insurance@tushigdaatgal.mn; internet www.tushigdaatgal.mn; Exec. Dir M. JALAVDORJ.

UB Daatgal Co: Monre-Impex Bldg, Sükbataar District, Ulan Bator (POB 46/385); tel. (11) 324828; fax (11) 322362; e-mail sanal_huselt@ ubdaatgal.mn; internet www.ubdaatgal.mn.

Insurers' Association

Mongolian Insurers' Association: Ulan Bator; Pres. PÜREVJAVYN GANZORIG.

Trade and Industry

GOVERNMENT AGENCIES

Mineral Resources Directorate: Government Bldg 12, Barilgachdyn Talbai 3, Chingeltei District, Ulan Bator; tel. (11) 263701; fax (11) 310370; internet mram.gov.mn; f. 2008; subordinate to Minister of Mining; Head GALSANGIIN ALTANSÜKH.

Nuclear Energy Directorate: Ulan Bator; f. 2008; subordinate to Prime Minister; Head N. TEGSHBAYAR.

Petroleum Directorate: Ulan Bator; f. 2008; subordinate to Minister of Mining; Head G. ÖLZIIBÜREN.

DEVELOPMENT ORGANIZATIONS

Agricultural Equipment, Science and Technology Production Association: Zaisan 53, Khan-Uul District, Ulan Bator; tel. (11) 341155; fax (11) 327099; e-mail agrtechcor@magicnet.mn; f. 1997; devt of farm machinery, including biogas plants; 100% state-owned; Exec. Dir J. TÜMEN.

Business Council of Mongolia: Express Tower, Enkhtaivny Örgön Chölöö, Ulan Bator; tel. and fax (11) 317027; e-mail info@ bcmongolia.org; internet www.bcmongolia.org; f. 2007; promotes international trade and business links, working with companies, government departments, embassies and NGOs; Chair. LAURENZ MELCHERS; CEO JIM DWYER.

Economics and Market Research Centre: Government Bldg 1, J. Sambuugiin Gudamj 11, Ulan Bator; tel. (11) 324258; fax (11) 324620; e-mail emrc@mongolchamber.mn; internet www .mongolchamber.mn; Dir J. BOZKHÜÜKHEN.

Mongolian Business Development Agency: Yörönkhii Said Amaryn Gudamj, Ulan Bator (CPOB 458); tel. (11) 311094; fax (11) 311092; internet www.mbda-mongolia.org; f. 1994; Gen. Man. D. BAYARBAT.

Mongolian Development Research Centre: Rm 50, Baga Toiruu 13, Chingeltei District, Ulan Bator (POB 20A/63); tel. and fax (11) 315686; internet www.mdrc.mn; f. 1998; Chair. TSEDENDAMBYN BATBAYAR.

National Centre for Renewable Energy: Ulan Bator; Dir N. ENEBISH.

CHAMBERS OF COMMERCE

Mongolian Franchising Council of the Mongolian National Chamber of Commerce and Industry: MNCCI Bldg, Makhatma Gandiin Gudamj, Khan-Uul District, Ulan Bator; tel. (11) 327176; fax (11) 324620; e-mail munkhnast@mongolchamber.mn; internet www.mongolchamber.mn; Chair. SAMBUUGIIN DEMBEREL.

Mongolian National Chamber of Commerce and Industry: Makhatma Gandiin Gudamj 11, 1st Sub-District, Khan-Uul District, Ulan Bator 38; tel. (11) 327176; fax (11) 324620; e-mail chamber@ mongolchamber.mn; internet www.mongolchamber.mn; f. 1960; responsible for establishing economic and trading relations, contacts between trade and industrial organizations, both at home and abroad, and for generating foreign trade; organizes commodity inspection, press information, and international exhibitions and fairs at home and abroad; registration of trademarks and patents; issues certificates of origin and of quality; Chair. SAMBUUGIIN DEMBEREL.

INDUSTRIAL AND TRADE ASSOCIATIONS

Association of Exporters of Livestock, Raw Materials and Semi-Processed Products: Ulan Bator; Exec. Dir B. TÖRMÖNKH.

Association of Mongolian Sewn Goods and Knitwear Products Manufacturers: Ulan Bator; Pres. N. DASH-ÖLZII.

Association of Window and Door Makers: Ulan Bator; Chair. L. GANTÖMÖR.

Building Materials Industry Association: Ulan Bator; Exec. Dir O. LKHAGVADORJ.

Financial Market Association: Ulan Bator; Pres. Ö. GANZORIG.

Funeral Services Association: Ulan Bator; f. 2008; Pres. G. IDERMAA.

Grain Producers' Association: Ulan Bator; Pres. TSEVEENJAVYN ÖÖLD.

Mineral Concentration Association: Ulan Bator; Pres. G. SHARKHÜÜ.

Mongolian Accountants' Association: Ulan Bator; Pres. LAMJAVYN ENKH-AMGALAN.

Mongolian Air Traffic Controllers' Association: National Air Traffic Services, Chinggis Khaan International Airport, Buyant-Ukhaa, Ulan Bator; tel. (11) 282008; fax (11) 282108; e-mail monatca@mcaa.gov.mn.

Mongolian Association of Container and Packaging Makers and Users: Ulan Bator; Pres. DEMBERELIIN OTGONBAATAR.

Mongolian Builders' Association: Block 3, Urt Tsagaan, Chingeltei District, Ulan Bator; tel. 99112636; fax (11) 318685; Pres. MÖNKHBAYARYN BATBAATAR.

Mongolian Coal Association: Ulan Bator; tel. and fax (11) 328582; e-mail coalasso@yahoo.com; Exec. Dir TÜVDENGIIN NARAN.

Mongolian Energy Association: Ulan Bator; Pres. G. PÜREVDORJ.

Mongolian Entrepreneurs' Association: Ulan Bator; Chair. B. GARMAASÜREN.

Mongolian Exporters' Association: Macro Centre, Erkhüügiin Gudamj 7/1, Sükhbaatar District, Ulan Bator (POB 20/352); tel. 99119356; fax (11) 354533; e-mail info@exportmongolia.mn; f. 2006; Pres. DAMBYN GALSANDORJ.

Mongolian Farmers' and Flour Producers' Association: Agro-Pro Business Centre, 19th Sub-District, Bayangol District, Ulan Bator; tel. (11) 300114; fax (11) 362875; e-mail agropro@magicnet .mn; f. 1997; research and quality inspection services in domestic farming and flour industry; Pres. SHARAVYN GUNGAADORJ.

Mongolian Felt Producers' Association: Ulan Bator; Vice-Pres. G. ALZAKHGÜI.

Mongolian Food and Agriculture Association: Ulan Bator; Pres. R. MÖNKHBAT.

Mongolian Food Producers' Association: Ulan Bator; Pres. L. DAMDINSÜREN.

Mongolian Forest Industries Association: Teeverchdiin 32, 1st Sub-District, Bayangol District, Ulan Bator (POB 36/51); tel. 91111191; fax (11) 321500; e-mail tsogoots@gmail.com; f. 1996; Chair. TSEDENPUNTSAGIIN TSOGOO.

Mongolian Foresters' United Association: Ulan Bator; Pres. L. LUVSANTSEREN.

Mongolian Heating Supply Association: Ulan Bator; Chair. D. BYAMBA-OCHIR.

Mongolian Industrial Geologists' Association: Ulan Bator; Pres. D. BAT-ERDENE.

Mongolian Institute of Internal Auditors: Ulan Bator; tel. (11) 70119107; e-mail miia@bizcon.mn; internet www.bizcon.mn; Pres. L. OTGONBAYAR.

Mongolian Insurers' Association: Ulan Bator; Pres. PÜREVJAVYN GANZORIG.

Mongolian International Financial Market Association: Ulan Bator; Pres. Ö. GANZORIG.

Mongolian Logistics Association: Ulan Bator; Pres. A. MÖNKHBOLD.

Mongolian Marketing Association: Ulan Bator; tel. 99096400; fax 70113756; e-mail bold_dag@yahoo.com; Pres. B. DAVAASÜREN; Exec. Dir D. BOLD.

Mongolian Meat Association: B 303, Zaisan 8, Khan-Uul District, Ulan Bator (POB 1322); tel. 99176995; fax (11) 343117; e-mail meat@

mobinet.mn; internet www.monmeat.mn; f. 1999; Pres. L. GANPÜREV; Exec. Dir M. LKHACHINBAL.

Mongolian Metallurgists' Association: School of Technology, Darkhan-Uul Province; tel. (37) 24723; Pres. TS. MÖNKHJARGAL.

Mongolian Mining Engineers' Association: Ulan Bator; Pres. KH. VLADIMIR.

Mongolian Motor Road Companies Consortium: Ulan Bator; Exec. Dir Ü. BATMÖNKH.

Mongolian Motor Transporters' United Association: Ulan Bator; f. 1996; est. as Mongolian National Society of Motor Transport Owners, amalgamated 2005 with the Mongoltrans Transporters' Asscn; 39 mem. businesses and orgs incl. the Private Bus Owners' Asscn, Taxi Owners' Asscn and Large & Small Bus Asscn; Pres. GAVAAGIIN BATKHÜÜ.

Mongolian National Construction Association: Ulan Bator; Vice-Pres. TS. ERDENECHULUUN.

Mongolian National Metal and Machine Industry Association: Ulan Bator; Pres. GAVAAGIIN BATKHÜÜ.

Mongolian National Mining Association: 501 Geosan Company Bldg, Ikh Surguuliin Gudamj 8, Ulan Bator; tel. (11) 314877; fax (11) 330032; e-mail info@miningmongolia.mn; internet www .miningmongolia.mn; f. 1994; provides legal protection and represents views of mining interests in govt policy and devt of mineral sector; Pres. DAMJINY DAMBA; Exec. Dir NAMGARYN ALGAA.

Mongolian Oil Shale Association: Ambassador Office Center, Enkhtaivny Örgön Chölöö 15A/5, Sükhbaatar District, Ulan Bator; tel. 70149971; fax 70149972; e-mail da.ganbold@gmail.com; Pres. DAVAADORJIIN GANBOLD.

Mongolian Pig Farmers' Association: Ulan Bator; Exec. Dir M. ZOLZAYAA.

Mongolian Power Development Association: Ulan Bator; Pres. B. JIGJID.

Mongolian Power Engineers' Association: Ulan Bator; Pres. R. GANJUUR; Exec. Dir B. BADRAL.

Mongolian PR Association: Ulan Bator; Chair. D. BOLDKHUYAG.

Mongolian Printing Works Association: Ulan Bator; Pres. E. MYAGMARPÜREV.

Mongolian Rare Earths Association: Ulan Bator; Pres. L. BAYARMANDAL.

Mongolian Refining Association: Ulan Bator; Chair. G. SHARKHÜÜ.

Mongolian Skins and Hides Production Association: Ulan Bator; Pres. B. ENKH-AMGALAN.

Mongolian Surveyors' Association: Ulan Bator; Pres. D. DONDOV.

Mongolian Wool and Cashmere Federation: Eermel Co Bldg, Khan-Uul District, Ulan Bator; tel. (11) 342950; fax (11) 342814; Pres. D. GANKHUYAG.

Mongolian Woollen Goods Producers' Association: Ulan Bator; Dep. Chair. G. AYUULGÜI.

National Information and Communications Association: Ulan Bator; Pres. D. BOLOR.

National Motor Roads Association: Ulan Bator; Pres. B. GARAMGAIBAATAR.

Petroleum Gas Association: Ulan Bator; f. 2005; Chair. R. BATBAYAR.

Pharmacology Organizations United Association: Ulan Bator; Pres. B. TUYAA.

EMPLOYERS' ORGANIZATIONS

Employers' and Owners' United Association: Rm 401, 4th Floor, Mongolian Youth Association 'B' Bldg, Ulan Bator; tel. (11) 326513; Exec. Dir B. SEMBEEJAV.

Federation of Professional Business Women of Mongolia: Ulan Bator; tel. and fax (11) 315638; e-mail mbpw@mongolnet.mn; f. 1992; provides education, training, and opportunities for women to achieve economic independence; Pres. OCHIRBATYN ZAYAA; 7,000 mems, 14 brs.

Forestry and Timber Production Managers' Association: Ulan Bator; tel. (11) 341310; e-mail info@fmwa.mn; internet fmwa .mn; f. 2010; Head D. BAASANBYAMBA.

Immovable Property (Real Estate) Business Managers' Association: Ulan Bator; Pres. J. BYAMBADORJ.

Mongolian Employers' Federation: Tavan Bogd Bldg, Sükhbaataryn Talbai 18, Ulan Bator; tel. and fax (11) 325635; fax (11) 325635; e-mail monef@magicnet.mn; internet www.monef.mn; f. 1990; fmrly Private Industry Owners' Association; 8,600 mems; Vice-Pres. KH. GANBAATAR.

Mongolian Food Trade Managers' Association: Ulan Bator; Dir D. NAMSRAI.

Mongolian Liquefied Gas Managers' Association: Ulan Bator; Chair. N. BAATARJAV.

Mongolian Management Association: 102 and 202, Bldg B, The Academy of Management, Chingisiin Örgön Chölöö, Khan Uul District, Ulan Bator; tel. (11) 341570; e-mail info@mamo.mn; internet www.eng.mamo.mn; Pres. DAGVADORJIIN TSERENDORJ.

Private Business Owners' Association: Tsatsral Mon Bldg, 1st Sub-District, Songinokhairkhan District, Ulan Bator; tel. (11) 682905; Pres. T. NYAMDORJ.

Refuse Disposal Business Managers' Association: Ulan Bator; Chair. SH. BAASANJAV.

Scrap Business Managers' Association: Ulan Bator; Dir S. ALTANTSETSEG.

Securities Exchange Managers' Association: Ulan Bator; Exec. Dir TS. BÜRENJARGAL.

Small and Medium Business Directors' United Association: Ulan Bator; Pres. P. ALTAN-ERDENE.

UTILITIES
Electricity

Central Zone Power Distribution Network: Chingisiin Örgön Chölöö 45, Khan-Uul District, Ulan Bator; tel. (11) 341674; fax (11) 343061; e-mail info@ubedn.mn; internet www.ubedn.mn; Exec. Dir E. TÜVSHINCHULUUN.

Dulaan Tsakhilgaan Stants-IV Co: 20th Sub-District, Bayangol District, Ulan Bator; tel. (11) 631768; Mongolia's biggest power station; Exec. Dir B. TSEVEEN.

Water

Dulaany Süljee Co: Ulan Bator; tel. (11) 343047; e-mail engineer@dhc.mn; internet www.dhc.mn; supervision of hot water district heating network in Ulan Bator; Exec. Dir DAGVASHADAVYN BYAMBA-OCHIR.

USUG (Water Management Office): Tokiogiin Gudamj 5, Bayanzürkh District, Ulan Bator; tel. (11) 455055; fax (11) 450120; e-mail usag@magicnet.mn; supervision of water supply network in Ulan Bator; Chair. OSORYN ERDENEBAATAR.

IMPORT AND EXPORT ORGANIZATIONS

Agrotekhimpeks: Ulan Bator; tel. 99119840; imports agricultural machinery and implements, seed, fertilizer, veterinary medicines and irrigation equipment.

Altjin: Ulan Bator; company imports and distributes oil and oil products; manages distilleries; fmrly part of APU; Dir G. ALTAN.

Arisimpex: Ulan Bator; tel. (11) 343007; fax (11) 343008; exports hides and skins, fur and leather goods; imports machinery, chemicals and accessories for leather, fur and shoe industries; Pres. A. TSERENBALJID.

Avtoimpeks: Ulan Bator; f. 1934; state-owned; international trader in motor vehicles; Exec. Dir S. CHULUUNBAT.

Barter and Border: Khuvisgalchdyn Gudamj, Ulan Bator; tel. (11) 324848; barter and border trade operations.

Khorshoololimpeks: Tolgoit, Ulan Bator (CPOB 262); tel. (11) 332926; fax (11) 331128; f. 1964; exports skins, hides, wool and furs, handicrafts and finished products; imports equipment and materials for housing, and for clothing and leather goods; Dir L. ÖLZIIBUYAN.

Kompleksimport: Enkhtaivny Örgön Chölöö 7, Ulan Bator; tel. and fax (11) 688948; f. 1963; imports consumer goods, foodstuffs, sets of equipment and turnkey projects; training of Mongolians abroad; state-owned pending planned privatization; cap. 3,500m. tögrög.

Makhimpeks: 4th Sub-District, Songinokhairkhan District, Ulan Bator; tel. (11) 632471; fax (11) 632517; f. 1946; abattoir, meat-processing, canning, meat imports and exports; 51% share privatized in 1999; cap. 7,800m. tögrög; Exec. Dir N. ODGEREL.

Materialimpex: Teeverchdiin Gudamj 2B, Bayangol District, Ulan Bator; tel. (11) 365143; fax (11) 367904; e-mail matimpex@mongolnet.mn; internet www.materialimpex.com; f. 1957; exports cashmere, wool products, animal skins; imports glass, roofing material, dyes, sanitary ware, metals and metalware, wallpaper, bitumen, wall and floor tiles; partially privatized Feb. 1999, but most shares still state-owned; Gen. Dir B. ZORIG; 126 employees.

Medimpex International: New Horizon Bldg, Olimpiin Gudamj 6, 1st Sub-District, Sükhbaatar District, Ulan Bator; tel. (11) 319680; fax (11) 318254; e-mail medimpex@mcs.mn; internet www.medimpex.mcs.mn.

Metallimpeks (Metalimpex): Ulan Bator; tel. 70111203; Dir D. GANBAT.

Monfa Trade: Monfarma Trade Co, Khudaldaany Gudamj, 4th Sub-District, Chingeltei District, Ulan Bator; tel. and fax (11) 324420; e-mail monfatrade@mongol.net; procurement and distribution of pharmaceuticals.

Mongoleksport Co Ltd: Government Bldg 7, 8th Fl., Erkh Chölöönii Talbai, Ulan Bator; tel. (11) 327884; exports wool, hair, cashmere, mining products, antlers, skins and hides; Dir-Gen. D. CHIMEDDAMBAA.

Mongolemimpex: Teeverchdiin Gudamj 39, Ulan Bator; tel. (11) 322695; fax (11) 323877; e-mail info@meic.mn; internet www.meic.mn; f. 1923; procurement and distribution to hospitals and pharmacies of drugs and surgical appliances; Dir-Gen. BATBAYARYN BOLORMAA.

Mongolimpeks: Khuvisgalchdyn Örgön Chölöö, Ulan Bator; tel. (11) 326081; exports cashmere, camels' wool, hair, fur, casings, powdered blood and horn, antlers, wheat gluten, alcoholic drinks, cashmere and camels' wool knitwear, blankets, copper concentrate, souvenirs, stamps and coins; imports light and mining industry machinery, scientific instruments, chemicals, pharmaceuticals and consumer goods; state-owned; Dir-Gen. DORJPALAMYN DÖKHÖMBAYAR.

Monnis International: Monnis Tower, Chingisiin Örgön Chölöö 15, Ulan Bator; tel. (11) 311687; fax (11) 323248; e-mail info@monnis.com; internet www.monnis.com; f. 1998; est. as distributor for Nissan Motor Co Ltd; other commercial interests incl. geology, mining, energy, construction, freight-forwarding, foreign trade, communications, banking and aviation; CEO B. CHULUUNBAATAR; 700 employees, 8 subsidiaries.

Monnoos: Ulan Bator (POB 36/450); tel. (11) 343201; fax (11) 342591; e-mail monnoos@mongolnet.mn; wool trade enterprise; Dir SANJIIN BAT-OYUUN.

Monos Cosmetics: Sonsgolongiin Toiruu 5, 20th Sub-District, Songinokhairkhan District, Ulan Bator; tel. and fax (11) 633257; e-mail cosmetics@monos.mn; internet www.monoscosmetics.mn; f. 1990; production, export and import of cosmetics; Chair. and CEO BALDANDORJIIN ERDENEKHISHIG; Exec. Dir KH. SOLONGO; 90 employees.

Monos Pharm Trade: Monos Group, Namyanjügiin Gudamj 23, 18th Sub-District, Bayanzürkh District, Ulan Bator; tel. and fax 70114567; fax (11) 463158; internet www.monos.mn; f. 1990; production, export and import of medicine, medical equipment and health food; Dir-Gen. LUVSANGIIN ERDENECHIMEG; 280 employees.

NIK (Neft Import Kontsern): Petrovis Co Bldg, Yörönkhii Said Amaryn Gudamj, Sükhbaatar District, Ulan Bator; tel. (11) 323656; fax (11) 327001; e-mail nic@nic.com.mn; internet www.nic.com.mn; Chair. CH. DAVAANYAM; Exec. Dir M. KHALIUNBAT.

Noosimpeks: Ulan Bator; tel. (11) 341577; exports scoured sheep's wool, yarn, carpets, fabrics, blankets, mohair and felt boots; imports machinery and chemicals for wool industry.

Packaging: Tolgoit, Ulan Bator; tel. (11) 31053; exports raw materials of agricultural origin, sawn timber, consumer goods, unused spare parts and equipment, and non-ferrous scrap; imports machinery and materials for packaging industry, and consumer goods.

Petrovis: Petrovis Co Bldg, Yörönkhii Said Amaryn Gudamj 7, Sükhbaatar District, Ulan Bator; tel. (11) 327051; fax (11) 327288; e-mail info@petrovis.mn; internet www.petrovis.mn; oil products importer and distributor; in Feb. 2004 acquired the 80% state-owned shares in the country's biggest distributor NIK (Neft Import Kontsern) for US $8.5m; Chair. J. OYUUNGEREL; Exec. Dir M. KHALIUNBAT.

Raznoimpeks: 3rd Sub-District, Bayangol District, Ulan Bator; tel. (11) 329465; fax (11) 329901; f. 1933; exports wool, cashmere, hides, canned meat, powdered bone, alcoholic drinks, macaroni and confectionery; imports cotton and woollen fabrics, silk, knitwear, shoes, fresh and canned fruit, vegetables, tea, milk powder, acids, paints, safety equipment, protective clothing, printing and packaging paper; state-owned pending planned privatization; cap. 6,100m. tögrög; Exec. Dir TS. BAT-ENKH.

Tekhnikimport: Ulan Bator; tel. (11) 685190; imports machinery, instruments and spare parts for light, food, wood, building, power and mining industries, road-building and communications; state-owned; Dir-Gen. D. GANTSETSEG.

Tüshig Trade Co Ltd: Enkhtaivny Örgön Chölöö, Ulan Bator (POB 44/481); tel. (11) 323206; fax (11) 314052; exports sheep and camel wool, and cashmere goods; imports machinery for small enterprises, foodstuffs and consumer goods; Dir-Gen. D. GANBAATAR.

Whole Sale: Songinokhairkhan District, Ulan Bator; tel. 99112100; fax (11) 632119; e-mail boch30@mobinet.mn; f. 1952; wholesale trader; privately owned; Dir-Gen. OCHBADRAKHYN BALJINNYAM.

YuniGaz: Midtown Centre, Enkhtaivny Gudamj 15/2, Ulan Bator; tel. (11) 314018; fax (11) 327051; e-mail info@unigas.mn; internet www.unigas.mn; petrol, diesel and LPG distributor; Dir-Gen. B. TÜMENTSOGT.

CO-OPERATIVES

Association of Private Herders' Co-operatives: Ulan Bator (POB 21/787); tel. (11) 633601; fax (11) 325935; e-mail mongolherder@magicnet.mn; f. 1991; Pres. R. ERDENE; Exec. Dir Ts. MYAGMAR-OCHIR.

Central Association of Consumer Co-operatives: Ulan Bator; tel. and fax (11) 329025; f. 1990; wholesale and retail trade; exports animal raw materials; imports foodstuffs and consumer goods; Chair. G. MYANGANBAYAR.

Mongolian Association of Production Co-operatives: Urt Tsagaan, Khudaldaany Gudamj 12, Chingeltei District, Ulan Bator; tel. (11) 310956; e-mail cumic@mol.mn.

Mongolian Association of Savings and Credit Co-operatives: Bldg 2, State Property Committee, Chingeltei District, Ulan Bator; tel. (11) 313665; Pres. SH. GOOKHÜÜ.

Mongolian Co-operatives Development Centre: Ulan Bator; Dir DANZANGIIN RADNAARAGCHAA.

National Association of Mongolian Agricultural Co-operatives: Enkhtaivny Örgön Chölöö 18A/1, Bayanzürkh District, Ulan Bator; fax (11) 458899; e-mail info@namac.coop; internet www.namac.coop; f. 1992; Pres. NADMIDYN BAYARTSAIKHAN.

National United Association of Mongolian Co-operatives: Ulan Bator; Dir. N. ENKHBOLD.

Union of Mongolian Production and Services Co-operatives: Bldg 16, 2nd 40,000, 3rd Sub-District, Chingeltei District, Ulan Bator (POB 46/470); tel. (11) 327583; fax (11) 328446; e-mail umpscoop@hotmail.com; f. 1990; Pres. SAMDANY ENKHTUYAA.

TRADE UNIONS

Confederation of Mongolian Trade Unions: Sükhbaataryn Talbai 7, Chingeltei District, Ulan Bator; tel. 70112125; fax (11) 322128; e-mail info@cmtu.mn; internet www.cmtu.mn; brs throughout the country; Chair. SAINKHÜÜGIIN GANBAATAR; Sec.-Gen. M. GANAA.

Transport

MTT (Mongol Transport Team): MTT Bldg, 5th Sub-District, Bayangol District, Ulan Bator; tel. (11) 689000; fax (11) 684953; e-mail mtt@mtteam.mn; internet www.mtteam.mn; international freight-forwarding by air, sea, rail and road; offices in Beijing, Berlin, Moscow and Prague.

Tuushin Co Ltd: Tuushin Bldg, Yörönkhii Said Amaryn Gudamj, Sükhbaatar District, Ulan Bator; tel. (11) 312092; fax (11) 325570; e-mail tuushin@magicnet.mn; internet www.tuushin.mn; f. 1990; international freight forwarders; transport and forwarding policy and services, warehousing, customs agent; tourism; offices in Beijing, Moscow and Prague; Dir-Gen. N. ZORIGT.

RAILWAYS

Mongolyn Tömör Zam (Mongolian Railways): Finance Center, 9th Floor, Jigjidjav Gudamj 8, Ulan Bator; tel. (11) 336611; fax (11) 336644; e-mail info@mtz.mn; internet www.mtz.mn; f. 2009; state-owned limited co, est. by Erdenes Mongol and Russian Railways (50% each) to modernize Ulan Bator Railway; CEO PÜREVDORJIIN BAT-ERDENE.

Ulan Bator Railway: Söüliin Gudamj 42, Bayangol District, Ulan Bator (CPOB 376); tel. and fax (21) 243012; internet www.ubtz.mn; f. 1949; jt-stock co (equal shares) with Russia; Dir G. SEREENENDORJ; Chairs O. N. MOROZOV, AMARJARGALYN GANSÜKH.

External Lines: from the Russian frontier at Naushki/Sükhbaatar (connecting with the Trans-Siberian Railway) to Ulan Bator and on to the Chinese frontier at Zamyn-Üüd/Erenhot, connecting with Beijing (total length 1,110 km).

Branches: from Darkhan to Sharyn Gol coalfield (length 63 km); branch from Salkhit near Darkhan, westwards to Erdenet (Erdenetiin-ovoo open-cast copper mine) in Bulgan Province (164 km); from Bagakhangai to Baganuur coal-mine, south-east of Ulan Bator (96 km); from Khar Airag to Bor-Öndör fluorspar mines (60 km); from Sainshand to Züünbayan oilfield (63 km).

Eastern Railway, linking Mongolia with the Trans-Siberian and Chita via Borzya; from the Russian frontier at Solovyevsk to Choibalsan (238 km), with branch from Chingis Dalan to Mardai uranium mine near Dashbalbar (110 km), possibly inactive.

Planned railway construction: broad-gauge lines (1,040 km) from Tavan Tolgoi coal mine to Züünbayan, and from Sainshand to Baruun-Urt and Choibalsan (existing link with the Trans-Siberian).

IFFC (International Freight-forwarding Centre of Mongolian Railways): Mongolian Railways, Söüliin Gudamj 42, Bayangol District, Ulan Bator (CPOB 376); tel. (21) 244845; fax (11) 313165; e-mail iffc@railcom.mn; internet www.iffc.mn; international freight-forwarding.

ROADS

Mongolia divides its road system into state-grade and country-grade roads. State-grade roads (of which there were 12,722 km in 2012) run from Ulan Bator to provincial centres and from provincial centres to the border. Country-grade roads account for the remaining roads, but they are mostly rough cross-country tracks. The length of 'improved roads' reached 7,633 km in 2011, of which 4,063 km were hard-surfaced. To mark the millennium, the Government announced its decision to construct a new east–west road, linking the Chinese and Russian border regions via Ulan Bator. In 2011 some sections of the Millennium Road were to be realigned to avoid areas of permafrost.

SHIPPING

Maritime Administration: Ulan Bator; state-owned co, operating until 2010 with Singapore-based Maritime Chain as its agent; Dir KH. ENHBATAAR.

CIVIL AVIATION

Civil aviation in Mongolia, including the provision of air traffic control and airport management, is the responsibility of the Main Directorate of Civil Aviation, which provides air traffic and airport management services. It also supervises the Mongolian national airline (MIAT) and smaller operators such as Khangarid and Tengeriin Ulaach, which operate local flights. Aeroflot (Russia) and Air China operate flights to Ulan Bator (Chinggis Khaan International Airport). Mongolia has 14 airfields with surfaced runways, and 31 with dirt strips.

In 2013 Khanbumbat airport was under construction at Oyu Tolgoi copper mine, with a runway suitable for C-130 and Boeing 737 aircraft.

Ulan Bator's new international airport, with a 3,600m runway, was under construction in 2013 at Khöshigiin Khöndii, south of the capital; it will have a 37-km motorway link. Due to enter into service in 2015, the airport will have twice the capacity of Chinggis Khaan (Buyant-Ukhaa) airport, where high ground to the south limits the use of the single runway to take-offs and landings to and from the north.

Main Directorate of Civil Aviation: Chinggis Khaan International Airport, Buyant-Ukhaa, Ulan Bator; tel. (11) 282025; fax (11) 282102; e-mail webmaster@mcaa.gov.mn; internet www.mcaa.gov.mn; Dir-Gen. SENGEEGIIN BUYANDALAI.

A-Jet Aviation: Olimpiin Gudamj, 1st Sub-District, Sükhbaatar District, Ulan Bator (POB 46/202); tel. (11) 318480; fax (11) 319780; e-mail aviation@ajet.mn; internet www.ajetaviation.mn; f. 2000; fmrly Central Mongolia Airways; helicopter services for tourists, aerial surveys and photography; Exec. Dir NYAMBARYN LKHAMJAV.

Aero Mongolia Co Ltd: Chinggis Khaan International Airport, Buyant-Ukhaa, Ulan Bator (POB 34/105); tel. (11) 379616; fax (11) 379943; e-mail management@aeromongolia.mn; internet www.aeromongolia.mn; f. 2001; began operations in 2003; operates scheduled international flights to Irkutsk (Russia), and Hohhot (China), and scheduled internal flights to five provincial centres and Juulchin's South Gobi tourist camp; twice-weekly flights to the Republic of Korea; Dir B. JARGALSAIKHAN.

Blue Sky Aviation: Door 2, Apt S-61, 1st Sub-District, Sükhbaatar District, Ulan Bator (CPOB 932); tel. (11) 312085; fax (11) 322857; e-mail bsa@maf-europe.org; internet www.blueskyaviation.mn; jt venture of Mission Aviation Fellowship and Exodus International; operates charter flights and medical emergency services; f. 1999; Dir TOM MASON; Operations Man. BATSUURIIN BAYARJIN.

Eznis (Easiness) Airways: Naiman Zovkhis Bldg, Söüliin Gudamj, Sükhbaatar District, Ulan Bator; tel. (11) 333311; fax (11) 331514; e-mail feedback@eznis.com; internet www.eznisairways.com; f. 2006; fleet of seven aircraft, incl. Q400 and Boeing 737-700; operates internal routes and twice-weekly flights to Hailar (northern China) via Choibalsan; CEO SÜKHBAATARYN MÖNKHSÜKH.

Khangarid: Room 210, MPRP Bldg, Baga Toiruu 37/1, Ulan Bator; tel. (11) 320138; fax (11) 311333; e-mail hangard_air_co@magicnet.mn; domestic and international passenger and freight services; Dir L. SERGELEN.

Khünnü Airlines: Narny Zam 15, Sükhbaatar District, Ulan Bator; tel. 70001111; fax (11) 328025; e-mail info@mongolianairlines.com; internet www.mongolianairlines.com; f. 2011; fmrly Mongolian Airlines Group, renamed as above in 2013; flights to Mörön, Khovd, Choibalsan, Dalanzadgad and Bayankhongor; seasonal operator of Airbus A-319 aircraft to Tokyo and Hong Kong, and Fokker 50 aircraft on internal routes; Dir. Gen. B. BAYAR.

Mongolian Civil Air Transport (MIAT): MIAT Bldg, Chinggis Khaan International Airport, Buyant-Ukhaa, Khan-Uul District, Ulan Bator; tel. 70049935; fax 70049919; e-mail contact@miat.com;

internet www.miat.com; f. 1956; operates two Boeing 767-300ER and two Boeing 737-800 aircraft; scheduled services to Moscow, Beijing, Seoul, Osaka, Berlin and Tokyo; internal flights to Mörön and Khovd resumed in July 2009; Chair. D. MAKHBAL; Exec. Dir GUNGAAGIIN. JARGALSAIKHAN.

MIAT Cargo: MIAT Bldg, Chinggis Khaan International Airport, Buyant-Ukhaa, Khan-Uul District, Ulan Bator; tel. 70049956; fax 70049645; e-mail cargo@miat.com.

Tengeriin Ulaach (Sky Horse Aviation): Chinggis Khaan International Airport, Buyant-Ukhaa, Khan-Uul District, Ulan Bator (POB 34/17); tel. (11) 282023; fax (11) 379765; e-mail skyhorsenew@mbox.mn; internal helicopter transport for tourists and business passengers; Exec. Dir U. GALBADRAKH.

Thomas Air: Ulan Bator; tel. 94101911; e-mail info@thomasair.mn; internet www.thomasair.mn; leasing of Air Tractor AT-602 aircraft for agricultural and environmental protection work; cargo charters, medical evacuation, crop-dusting, surveys, tourism, flying school; CEO KH. BÜREN-ERDENE.

Trans-Ölgii: Ölgii, Bayan-Ölgii Province; f. 2006; operates on Ölgii–Ulan Bator route twice a week.

Tourism

The country's main attractions are its scenery, wildlife and historical relics. A foreign tourist service bureau was established in 1954, but the tourism sector remained undeveloped. At March 2008 there were 248 tour operators, 326 hotels (with 8,000 beds) and 30 tourist camps (with 6,400 beds). Of the 30 or more hotels in Ulan Bator, all but four are relatively small, and in the peak summer season there is a shortage of rooms. The outlying tourist centres (Terelj, South Gobi, Öndör-Dov and Khujirt) have basic facilities. Tourist arrivals totalled 460,360 in 2011; Chinese and Russian tourists remained the most numerous. Tourism revenue reached US $222.4m. in 2010.

Mongolian Tourism Association: Room 309, Üildverchnii Evleliin Kholboony Bldg, Sükhbaataryn Talbai 11, Ulan Bator; tel. and fax (11) 327820; e-mail info@travelmongolia.org; internet www.travelmongolia.org; Pres. TS. BAYARSAIKHAN.

Mongolian Tourism Board: Government Bldg 2, Negdsen Ündesnii Gudamj 5/2, Chingeltei District, Ulan Bator; tel. (51) 267545; fax (51) 264447; e-mail tourism@mne.gov.mn; internet www.mongoliatourism.gov.mn; part of the Ministry of Culture, Sport and Tourism.

Defence

As assessed at November 2012, according to the International Institute for Strategic Studies, Mongolia's defence forces numbered 10,000, comprising an army of 8,900 (of whom 3,300 were thought to be conscripts), 800 air defence personnel and 300 construction troops. There was a paramilitary force of about 7,200, comprising 1,200 internal security troops and 6,000 border guards under the Ministry of Law. Army reserves numbered an estimated 137,000. Each year a small quota of men can purchase exemption from conscription; in 2010 a total of 1,709 men paid 2.3m. tögrög each. Military service is for 12 months (for males aged 18–25 years), but only about 40% of conscripts are found fit for service. There are financial inducements for regular service soldiers, especially those in the best trained and equipped 'élite' battalions, some of whom have served with coalition forces in Iraq and on UN peace-keeping operations elsewhere. In 2012 men of the Main Directorate for Emergency Relief were sent abroad for the first time, to serve as peace-keepers in South Sudan.

Mongolia has restarted annual military exercises with the Russian army, during which its Soviet-made equipment is serviced and updated. In 2009 Russia began to supply Mongolia with new military

technology under a bilateral agreement. In 2011 Russia was reported to have supplied small numbers of Mi-8, Mi-24 and Mi-171 helicopters and YaK-130 jet combat trainers. Paired surface-to-air missiles of the Pechora type were paraded in mobile launchers. In July that year it was reported that the Mongolian Ministry of Defence was planning to purchase four or five MiG-29 fighter aircraft and a flight simulator; a subsequent plan to acquire a new military transport aircraft was also reported. By the beginning of 2012 Mongolia's ground forces had in military service the following (all Soviet–manufactured) equipment: 370 T-54/55 tanks, BMP-1 infantry combat vehicles, 120 BRDM-2 reconnaissance vehicles, 150 BTR-60 armoured transporters, 130 Grad rocket launchers and 150 D-30 and ML-20 artillery guns. In mid-2012 Russia reportedly additionally supplied Mongolia with up to 50 T-72A tanks, 40 BTR-70M armoured transporters and a number of Ural vehicles.

Defence Expenditure: Defence spending for 2013 was projected at 176,988.8m. tögrög (some 2.5% of total planned government expenditure in that year). Defence expenditure for 2011 totalled 106,000m. tögrög (about 2.4% of total budgetary expenditure).

Chief of Staff of the Mongolian Armed Forces: Lt-Gen. TSER-ENDEJIDIIN BYAMBAJAV.

Deputy Chief of Staff, Commander General Purpose Troops: Brig.-Gen. RADNAABAZARYN SÜKHBAT.

Deputy Chief of Staff, Director of Peacekeeping: Brig.-Gen. BYAMBAASÜRENGIIN BAYARMAGNAI.

Commander of Air Defence Troops: Col N. BATKHÜREL.

Education

General education is state-administered. Eleven-year education is compulsory, and 12-year education is being introduced. In the 2011/12 school year there were an estimated 505,400 pupils receiving general education in 752 schools, whose teaching staff totalled 26,492. The 49 state and 22 private vocational schools, with a total of 48,100 students in 2011/12, train personnel for the service industries, including electricians, drivers and machine operators.

The Mongolian State University has three faculties (biology; chemistry; geography and geology) and nine schools (including foreign languages, mathematics, computer science, law, economics and social sciences). The School of Foreign Service provides diplomatic training. There were 104,101 students enrolled in state universities and colleges, and 68,302 enrolled in private universities and colleges in 2011/12.

In 2011/12 there were five state-owned and 77 private institutes of other higher education; 15,300 students were enrolled at the state institutes and 51,200 at the private institutes of higher education, excluding those studying in Russia, Germany, Turkey, the USA and elsewhere. The student enrolment abroad was estimated at 9,550 in 2009/10.

In July 2010 the Government approved a project for reform of higher education during 2010–12, which included structural change such as the consolidation of some colleges and institutes (e.g. the merger of Ulaanbaatar University and the Higher School of Trade and Industry with the Mongolian State University) and an improved admissions policy in order to raise teaching and research standards to international levels.

In general education schools, the first steps were taken to introduce a Cambridge assessment-type curriculum. The news agency Montsame reported in August 2012 that some 70% of private universities and colleges had undergone certification since the process began in May and about 10% were expected to fail and close.

The state budget allocation to the Ministry of Education and Science for 2013 was 1,234,087.5m. tögrög (17.9% of planned budgetary expenditure). The amount spent in 2012 was 1,100,421.4m. tögrög (about 22.6% of total budgetary expenditure).

MONTENEGRO

Introductory Survey

LOCATION, CLIMATE, LANGUAGE, RELIGION, FLAG, CAPITAL

Montenegro is situated in the central Balkan peninsula, in south-eastern Europe. Montenegro has frontiers with Bosnia and Herzegovina to the west and north-west, Serbia to the north, Kosovo to the east, and Albania to the south-east, and a short frontier with Croatia in the south-west. There is a western coastline along the Adriatic Sea (part of the Mediterranean). Montenegro has a rugged mountainous terrain, being dominated by the Black Mountains (Crna Gora), from which the country takes its name. The climate is Mediterranean near the coast, and continental inland. Mountainous areas have a colder climate with heavy snowfall in winter. Average temperatures range from between $-7°C$ ($19.4°F$) and $23°C$ ($73.4°F$) inland, and between $11°C$ ($51.8°F$) and $28°C$ ($84.2°F$) on the coast. Montenegro's mountainous regions receive some of the highest amounts of rainfall in Europe. The 2007 Constitution describes the principal language as Montenegrin, with the Cyrillic and Latin alphabets of equal status. Serbian, Bosnian, and Croatian (all of which, in common with Montenegrin, were formerly described as variants of Serbo-Croat) and Albanian are also in official use. The principal religion is Orthodox Christianity, and there are significant Roman Catholic and Muslim communities. The national flag (proportions 1 by 2) is red, with a golden coat of arms depicting a double-headed eagle. Podgorica is the capital of Montenegro. The historical capital is Cetinje.

CONTEMPORARY POLITICAL HISTORY

Historical Context

After the Second World War, Montenegro became one of the six constituent republics of the federal Yugoslavia established by the Communist Party of Yugoslavia (later the League of Communists of Yugoslavia—LCY) under Josip Broz (Tito). Montenegro generally supported the Serbian reassertion of dominance within Yugoslavia after the death of Tito in the 1980s. Institutionally, this was helped by the installation of a new party leadership in the republic, following demonstrations during 1988 in favour of the Serbian leader, Slobodan Milošević. Subsequent reforms reconstituted the Skupština Crne Gore (Assembly of Montenegro) as a unicameral body of 125 members and replaced Montenegro's collective presidency with a directly elected state President. The elections, in December 1990, represented a victory for the ruling League of Communists of Montenegro (later renamed the Democratic Party of Socialists of Montenegro—DPS), which secured 83 seats in the new legislature, while its presidential candidate, Momir Bulatović, became President. In February 1991 Bulatović invited Milo Đukanović, also of the DPS, to head the republican Government, while Svetozar Marović became the Chairman of the Skupština.

The onset of armed conflict in Yugoslavia prompted Montenegro to adopt a pragmatic response to the disintegration of the federation. Although Montenegro adopted a declaration of state sovereignty on 18 October 1991 and a new Constitution in November, its continued commitment to the federation with Serbia was confirmed in a referendum in March 1992. The two republics announced a new federal Constitution, creating the Federal Republic of Yugoslavia (FRY), which came into effect on 27 April. A new Montenegrin Constitution was introduced on 12 October and in early 1993 Bulatović was re-elected Montenegrin President, while Đukanović remained premier. Meanwhile, another Montenegrin, Radoje Kontić, became the Yugoslav Prime Minister.

Relations between Montenegro and Serbia deteriorated from the mid-1990s, particular in response to the attempts of Serbian leader Slobodan Milošević to disassemble Montenegro's separate defence and foreign policy structures. However, the principal division in Montenegrin politics was between the republican presidency and premiership. Đukanović, in early 1997, publicly declared Milošević unfit to hold public office, and resisted the demands of Bulatović that he dismiss all anti-Milošević ministers in the Montenegrin Government. The ruling DPS (which again won the Montenegrin legislative elections in November

1996) subsequently split into two factions, as a result of Bulatović's support for Milošević (who became the Yugoslav President in July 1997). Bulatović and Đukanović, who by then led separate factions within the DPS, became the leading candidates in the Montenegrin presidential election of October. Đukanović won the second round of voting, with 50.8% of the votes cast.

Đukanović was inaugurated as the President of Montenegro in January 1998, amid violent protests from supporters of Bulatović. A compromise agreement on early legislative elections in May was reached, pending which a transitional Government, led by the Đukanović faction of the DPS, was formed in February. Bulatović's faction refused to participate and renamed itself the Socialist People's Party of Montenegro (SPPM). In the elections, held in May, the DPS won an outright majority, and a coalition Government, led by Filip Vujanović, was formed in July. Bulatović, who was appointed as Yugoslav Prime Minister in May, proceeded to purge many Montenegrin officials from federal institutions. Montenegro refused to acknowledge the administration of Bulatović, and suspended all links with his Government in August.

Relations with Serbia continued to deteriorate during 1999. Continued military action by Serbian forces against the ethnic Albanian population in the Serbian province of Kosovo led to the aerial bombardment of Yugoslavia by forces of the North Atlantic Treaty Organization (NATO, see p. 380) in March–June, during which Montenegro suffered damage. Montenegro refused to recognize the state of war declared by the Yugoslav Government in March, and Đukanović subsequently refused to place Montenegrin security forces under federal military command, as ordered by President Milošević.

In the aftermath of the open conflict in Kosovo, the Yugoslav federation became increasingly unstable. The Government of Montenegro proposed the replacement of the federal system with an association of two states, threatening a referendum on full independence if Milošević did not agree, and in October 1999 the Skupština enacted a citizenship law. Attempting to separate itself from the isolated Serbian economy, in November Montenegro replaced the depreciating Yugoslav dinar with the German Deutsche Mark as its official currency (the federal Constitutional Court declared the measure illegal in January 2000, to little effect). Serbia responded by imposing a full economic embargo against Montenegro in March. While most of the Montenegrin Government preferred a looser confederation with Serbia, fears of Milošević increasing his political influence or of Serbian military action (such as the federal army's seizure of control over Montenegro's main airport in December 1999) further escalated tensions.

Following elections in September, Milošević was ousted as Yugoslav President in October, and Bulatović subsequently resigned as premier. Đukanović began to advocate full independence for Montenegro, urging a referendum on the issue. This prompted the pro-federation People's Party of Montenegro to withdraw from the ruling Montenegrin coalition. At the ensuing legislative elections, held on 22 April 2001, the DPS-led coalition won 36 of the 77 seats, the SPPM-led alliance 33 and the pro-independence Liberal Alliance of Montenegro (LAM) six. Vujanović was reappointed as premier. Meanwhile, negotiations about a new form of association with Serbia were ongoing, which, from November, were mediated by the European Union (EU, see p. 281). The federal Yugoslav leadership and that of both republics signed a framework agreement on confederation on 14 March 2002, providing for a shared presidency and legislature, which would be responsible for foreign and defence policies, and for separate republican economic and other state structu. Crucially, Montenegro had the right to refer the issue of independence to a referendum after three years. Later in March the LAM resigned from the Government in protest at the agreement. The Skupština approved the accord on 9 April; however, unable to form a new coalition administration, Vujanović dissolved the legislature in July and scheduled further elections.

On 20 October 2002 the DPS-led, pro-independence ruling coalition, the Democratic List for a European Montenegro, won 39 of the 75 seats in the republican legislature. Together for

Changes, which had opposed a looser union with Serbia and was led by the SPPM (under a new leadership), retained 30 seats. Vujanović was elected Speaker of the Skupština on 5 November, and became acting President of Montenegro 20 days later, when Đukanović resigned from that post. A dispute over the allocation of ministerial portfolios with the DPS's ally, the Social Democratic Party of Montenegro (SDP), delayed the formalization of a governing coalition, and the Skupština approved the new Government, headed by Đukanović as Prime Minister, on 8 January 2003. Meanwhile, both the SPPM and the LAM boycotted of the presidential election, held on 22 December 2002, which was consequently won by Vujanović, with 83.7% of the votes cast, but with those votes amounting to less than the one-half of the total electorate legally required to validate the result. Vujanović won 82.0% of votes in the repeated poll held on 9 February 2003, but this poll, too, was declared invalid, as only 47% of the electorate voted, prompting the Skupština to abolish the regulation on minimum participation. Vujanović was duly elected President on 11 May, with 62.9% of the votes cast (and about 48% of the electorate participating). Following his election, Vujanović pledged to schedule a referendum on independence for Montenegro after a period of three years.

Domestic Political Affairs

Meanwhile, on 29 January 2003 the Skupština approved the new arrangements for confederation with Serbia. On 4 February the federal parliament formally adopted a Constitutional Charter, thereby transforming Yugoslavia into the State Union of Serbia and Montenegro. A Skupština, President (the former Montenegrin parliamentary Speaker and DPS leader, Marović) and Prime Minister of the State Union were elected in late February and March. In July the Skupština adopted a new Montenegrin flag and anthem, and declared 13 July (the anniversary of the 1878 recognition of Montenegrin independence by the Congress of Berlin and of the 1941 start of a popular revolt against the occupying Axis powers) a national holiday.

After it was agreed that the EU should set the conditions for and supervise the conduct of any referendum on Montenegrin independence, in February 2006, amid much controversy, the EU announced that a proposal of Montenegrin independence would require the approval of 55% of those voting (with a minimum rate of participation of 50% of the registered electorate), in order to secure international recognition. Legislation providing for a referendum to be held on 21 May was duly enacted on 1 March. In April the Government formally presented to the Serbian Government a guarantee of equal status for Serbian citizens within Montenegro in the event of independence.

Independence

Two days after the referendum of 21 May 2006, the electoral authorities declared Montenegro to have voted in favour of independence. With a participation rate of over 86%, some 55.5% of the votes cast at the referendum were in favour of independence, thereby narrowly fulfilling the EU criteria. The EU and other international organizations declared the vote to have been free and fair. The Skupština duly declared Montenegro independent on 3 June. Serbia, which declared itself to be the successor state to the State Union of Serbia and Montenegro on 5 June, officially recognized Montenegro's independence in mid-June and established diplomatic relations one week later. Montenegro was admitted to the Organization for Security and Cooperation in Europe (see p. 397) on 22 June and to the UN on 28 June, and acceded to the Geneva Conventions on 2 August. A new Ministry of Defence formally assumed responsibility for all military units of the State Union on Montenegrin territory, while in July agreement was reached on the division of the financial rights and obligations of the former State Union (of which Montenegro was to receive 5.9% of the convertible currency and gold reserves).

The ruling coalition of the DPS and the SDP won outright legislative elections held on 10 September 2006, securing 41 of the 81 seats in an expanded Skupština. The SPPM-led alliance only obtained 11 seats (eight for the SPPM itself), being displaced as the largest opposition grouping by the Serbian List, led by Andrija Mandić of the Serb People's Party, which took 12 seats. A new, pro-European party, the Movement for Changes (MFC), also obtained 11 seats. The Liberal Party of Montenegro (the successor organization to the LAM), in alliance with the Bosniak Party, secured three seats. In October 2006 Đukanović announced that he would not seek to continue his premiership, as he wished to develop his business interests. (He had been accused of involvement with organized crime, and was under

investigation by the Italian authorities, mainly in connection with large-scale illicit tobacco trade in the Balkans.) The appointment of a new Government, headed by the hitherto Minister of Justice, Željko Šturanović, was approved by the Skupština on 10 November.

The Government declared its aspirations to join NATO and the EU. (The EU had agreed to continue negotiations on a Stabilization and Association Agreement—SAA—that had commenced with the former State Union with the two independent states.) Montenegro was admitted to NATO's 'Partnership for Peace' (see p. 383) programme on 14 December 2007, and officially became a member of the World Bank in the following month, also joining the IMF and the other associated institutions. Montenegro initialled the SAA with the EU on 15 March 2007. On 11 May Montenegro was admitted to the Council of Europe (see p. 260).

After acrimonious debate (particularly on the questions of state symbols, and the designation of the official language and religious communities), a new Constitution was approved by 55 of the 76 deputies present in the Skupština on 19 October 2007, narrowly achieving the requisite two-thirds' majority of the vote; the Constitution was officially promulgated on 22 October. Serb parties in Montenegro denounced the new Constitution, taking particular exeption to the description of the main official language as Montenegrin. The adoption of the Constitution (which was deemed to be in accordance with EU standards) allowed the official signature of the SAA at a meeting of EU foreign ministers in the same month.

On 31 January 2008 Šturanović resigned as Prime Minister, on grounds of ill health. On 29 February the appointment of Đukanović as premier and of his Government (which remained unchanged from the previous administration) was narrowly approved, with 41 votes cast, in the Skupština. (Although the Italian investigation into organized crime allegations continued, Đukanović's immunity from prosecution was restored by his return to office.)

Vujanović was re-elected to the presidency on 6 April 2008, with 51.9% of the votes cast, thereby further consolidating the strength of the DPS. Mandić was placed second, with 19.6% of the vote, while the reformist leader of the MFC, Nebojša Medojević, was third, with 16.7%. The rate of voter participation was estimated at about 69%. Vujanović was inaugurated for a second term on 21 May. In October Montenegro's recognition of Kosovo as a sovereign state prompted pro-Serbian opposition parties to organize a protest in Podgorica, to demand the calling of a referendum on the matter. On 15 December 2008 Montenegro submitted an official application for EU membership (see Foreign Affairs).

The 2009 legislative elections

In January 2009 the governing coalition (which had already agreed that legislative elections, due in 2010, be brought forward to September 2009) submitted a proposal to the Skupština that the elections take place that March in order to allow the administration a stronger mandate to fulfil Montenegro's commitments in the EU integration process. On 26 January the Skupština voted in favour of ending its mandate to allow an early poll, which were duly scheduled for 29 March. Later in January Mandić merged his Serb People's Party of Montenegro with the People's Socialist Party to form a new party, New Serbian Democracy.

The elections to the Skupština on 29 March 2009 were contested by a total of 16 parties and alliances; Đukanović's Coalition for a European Montenegro secured a decisive victory, with 51.9% of the votes cast and 48 seats in the chamber, while the SPPM won 16.8% of the vote and 16 seats, New Serbian Democracy (formed recently by the merger of Mandić's Serb People's Party of Montenegro and the People's Socialist Party) 9.2% of the vote and eight seats, and the MFC 6.0% of the votes and five seats. Four other groups each obtained one seat. A participation rate of 66.2% was recorded. The EU praised the democratic organization of the poll, but urged the Government to reform electoral legislation. Following endorsement of Đukanović's premiership, a new Government was approved in the Skupština Crne Gore in early June; the six new ministers included Marović as a Deputy Prime Minister.

In March 2010 Vujanović announced that local elections would be conducted to 14 municipal councils on 23 May, despite opposition demands for a later date. A motion of no confidence in the Government, proposed by the Movement for Changes, was defeated in the Skupština on 13 April. At the local elections on 23 May, the DPS won a majority in seven of the contested 14 municipal councils, and was to form a coalition, mostly with the SDP, in five others, including in Podgorica.

The 2012 legislative elections

In October 2010 the mandate of the Governor of the Central Bank, Ljubiša Krgović, was ended, after he criticized the provision of state assistance for the loss-making Prva Banka, in which the brother of Prime Minister Đukanović held a majority share; the Skupština approved Vujanović's nomination of Radoje Žugić (hitherto Director of the Pension and Disability Insurance Fund) to replace Krgović. On 21 December Đukanović tendered his resignation as premier (but was to remain DPS Chairman); Deputy Prime Minister and Minister of Finance Igor Lukšić was nominated by the DPS as his successor. On the same day Marović also resigned his government post, following the initiation of an investigation into the illegal construction of a tourist complex in Budva. Later in December the Mayor of Budva municipality, Rajko Kuljaca, his deputy Dragan Marović (the brother of former Svetozar Marović) and eight other officials were arrested and subsequently charged with abuse of office in connection with the investigation. (In June 2012 Kuljaca and the nine other defendants were sentenced to five years' imprisonment.) On 29 December 2010 the Skupština endorsed the nomination of Lukšić and the establishment of a new Government (comprising the same coalition parties as previously) under his premiership. Milorad Katnić replaced Lukšić as Minister of Finance in the new administration.

In May 2011 the Montenegrin Orthodox Church presented four cases against Montenegro at the European Court of Human Rights, seeking the restitution of church properties and monuments that had been nationalized when Montenegro was part of Yugoslavia. In September, following protracted negotiations between Lukšić and opposition leaders, the Skupština adopted a new electoral law and amendments to education legislation providing for equality between the Serbian and Montenegrin languages in schools, in accordance with EU criteria for the opening of accession negotiations. In March 2012 an assault against a journalist, Olivera Lakić, working for the daily newspaper *Vijesti*, who had previously been threatened after reporting on the illegal labelling of tobacco products, was condemned by the OSCE, amid increased concerns that media freedom in Montenegro was being undermined. In July Lakić's assailant was sentenced to nine months' imprisonment.

At the elections to the Skupština Crne Gore on 14 October 2012, the Coalition for a European Montenegro, again led by Đukanović, secured the most substantial representation, with 46.3% of the votes cast and 39 seats (this none the less representing a loss of support compared with the 2009 elections). An alliance formed by the MFC and the New Serbian Democracy, the Democratic Front, obtained 23.2% of the vote and 20 seats, and the SPPM obtained 11.2% of the vote and nine seats. A participation rate of 70.6% was recorded, and OSCE observers endorsed the conduct of the elections. Local elections were held concurrently in the municipalities of Budva, Nikšić and Kotor, which resulted in an opposition coalition securing control of the Nikšić municipal council. In early November Đukanović negotiated an agreement with the minority parties represented in the Skupština that enabled him to command a parliamentary majority, and was designated Prime Minister by Vujanović. On 4 December the Skupština approved Đukanović's return to the premiership and the formation of his coalition Government; the new administration included four Deputy Prime Ministers, among them Lukšić, who also held the foreign affairs and European integration portfolio. It was subsequently announced that Svetozar Marović would replace Đukanović as leader of the DPMS.

Recent developments: the 2013 presidential election

In January 2013 the next presidential election was officially scheduled for 7 April; Vujanović declared his intention to seek a further term in office, although the SDP opposed his candidacy on the grounds that he had already served two terms (including during the period prior to independence). Following the failure of the opposition parties in Nikšić to agree on the formation of a municipal administration, a poll was repeated there on 7 March, which was won by the DPS. Meanwhile, the leader of the Democratic Front, Miodrag Lekić, was registered as the consensus opposition candidate in the forthcoming presidential election.

Vujanović and Lekić both claimed victory, based on partial results, shortly after the presidential election was conducted on 7 April 2013. The EU, following the recommendations of OSCE

observers, urged the adoption of measures to strengthen confidence in public institutions and the judiciary. On 8 April the official preliminary results were released, according to which Vujanović had been narrowly re-elected, with 51.2% of the votes cast. Although the Election Commission subsequently rejected all complaints of irregularities submitted by Lekić, the Democratic Front continued to accuse the authorities of malpractice.

Foreign Affairs

Regional relations

In March 2008 Prime Minister Đukanović and his Croatian counterpart, meeting in Zagreb, Croatia, declared that the demarcation of the maritime boundary between the two countries around the Prevlaka peninsula (which was regulated by a 2002 interim agreement) would be referred to the International Court of Justice (ICJ, see p. 26) at The Hague, Netherlands. In October 2008 Montenegro announced official recognition of Kosovo as a sovereign state, following its declaration of independence on 17 February; the decision prompted Serbia to expel the Montenegrin ambassador. In May 2009 President Vujanović visited the Serbian capital, Belgrade, in an effort to improve bilateral relations; Serbian President Boris Tadić made a reciprocal visit to Montenegro in June. In October Serbia finally accepted the Montenegrin Government's nomination of a new ambassador. In December 2011 the Governments of Montenegro, Albania and the former Yugoslav republic of Macedonia signed an agreement providing for the abolition of border controls for citizens of their respective states. In January 2013 the Serbian President, Tomislav Nikolić, made an official visit to Montenegro.

Other external relations

Following independence in June 2006, Montenegro's admission to international organizations proceeded rapidly. At a NATO summit meeting, held in Bucharest, Romania, in April 2008, Montenegro (together with Bosnia and Herzegovina) was invited to enter into an intensified dialogue towards membership. (According to a subsequent opinion poll, however, only around one-quarter of Montenegrins supported NATO membership for the country.) In April 2009 the EU Council of Ministers approved consideration of Montenegro's EU membership application (which was submitted in December 2008). At the end of November 2009 it was announced that Montenegro had met EU requirements for the abolition of visa requirements, which were thereby removed from the citizens of these countries with effect from late December. Also in December Montenegro was granted a NATO Membership Action Plan. The Stabilization and Association Agreement that Montenegro signed with the EU in October 2007 (see above) entered into effect on 1 May 2010, following its ratification by all member states. The European Council granted Montenegro candidate status for EU membership on 17 December. In a report issued in October 2011, the European Commission recommended that accession negotiations be opened with Montenegro, stating that the Government had made satisfactory progress towards meeting the criteria for EU membership. On 29 April 2012 Montenegro became a full member of the World Trade Organization (WTO, see p. 444). Following a decision by EU foreign ministers, accession negotiations with Montenegro were officially opened on 29 June. A favourable European Parliament report, which was issued in January 2013, commended the progress of the Montenegrin authorities in combating corruption and organized crime, but emphasized the necessity of strengthening the independence of the judiciary, improving media freedom and equal representation in decision-making bodies, and reforming administrative structures.

CONSTITUTION AND GOVERNMENT

Montenegro became independent of the former State Union of Serbia and Montenegro on 3 June 2006, following a national referendum held on 21 May. The Constitution of Montenegro was adopted by the legislature on 19 October 2007 and was officially promulgated on 22 October. Legislative power is vested in the 81-member Skupština Crne Gore (Assembly of Montenegro), which is directly elected for a period of four years. Executive power is vested in the Government and judicial power in the courts of law. The President is directly elected for a term of five years, and is restricted to two terms in office. Constitutionality and legality are protected by the Constitutional Court. The President nominates the Prime Minister for approval by the Skupština. The Prime Minister proposes the composition of the Government to the Skupština. The Supreme Court is the highest court in Montenegro. For administrative purposes, Montenegro is divided into 21 municipalities.

REGIONAL AND INTERNATIONAL CO-OPERATION

Montenegro is a member of the Organization for Security and Co-operation in Europe (OSCE, see p. 397), the Council of Europe (see p. 260), and the Central European Free Trade Agreement (CEFTA, see p. 459).

Montenegro joined the UN on 28 June 2006.

ECONOMIC AFFAIRS

In 2011, according to estimates by the World Bank, Montenegro's gross national income (GNI), measured at average 2009–11 prices, was US \$4,461m., equivalent to \$7,060 per head (or \$13,720 per head on an international purchasing-power parity basis). During 2002–11, it was estimated, the population increased at an average annual rate of 0.1%, while gross domestic product (GDP) per head increased, in real terms, by an average annual rate of 3.9%. Overall GDP increased, in real terms, at an average annual rate of 4.0% in 2002–11; real GDP increased by 2.5% in 2011.

Agriculture (including hunting, forestry and fishing) contributed 9.5% of GDP and engaged 1.4% of the employed labour force in 2011. The principal crops are potatoes, maize and wheat. The cultivation of fruit (particularly grapes, plums, oranges and tangerines) and vegetables is also important. According to the World Bank, agricultural output increased by an annual average of 2.4% during 2002–11; output declined by 3.9% in 2010, and increased by 12.1% in 2011.

Industry (including mining, manufacturing, construction and power) contributed 19.5% of GDP and engaged 19.5% of the employed labour force in 2011. According to the World Bank, industrial production increased by an average annual rate of 2.9% during 2002–11; sectoral output increased by 5.8% in 2011.

The mining and quarrying sector contributed 1.3% of GDP and engaged 1.2% of the employed labour force in 2011. The principal minerals extracted are lignite, red bauxite and sea salt. Production in the sector declined by an annual average rate of 2.0% during 2002–06. Output increased by 1.5% in 2011.

The manufacturing sector contributed 6.0% of GDP and engaged 8.8% of the employed labour force in 2011. In 2005 the principal branches of manufacturing were metals, building materials, chemicals, woodworking, and food and tobacco products. Production in the sector decreased by an annual average rate of 2.3% during 2002–11, according to the World Bank; output decreased by 3.6% in 2010, and increased by 13.7% in 2011.

The construction sector contributed 5.8% of GDP and engaged 4.9% of the employed labour force in 2011. The real GDP of the sector increased by 15.8% in 2011.

Energy in Montenegro is derived principally from hydroelectric power (which provided about 65.2% of total electricity generated in 2005) and thermoelectric power (34.8%). Imports of mineral fuels accounted for 18.1% of the value of total imports in 2011.

Services contributed 71.0% of GDP and engaged 79.1% of the employed labour force in 2011. There were 1,201,099 foreign tourist arrivals in 2011. According to the World Bank, services GDP increased by an average annual rate of 4.8% during 2002–11; the sector grew by 0.8% in 2011.

In 2011 Montenegro recorded a merchandise trade deficit of €1,306.1m., and there was a deficit of €633.8m. on the current account of the balance of payments. In 2011 the principal source of imports was Serbia (accounting for 28.4% of imports); other major sources were Greece, Italy, Germany and the People's Republic of China. Serbia was also the principal market for exports in that year (taking 17.6% of the total); other important purchasers were Greece, Italy and Slovenia. The principal imports in 2011 were miscellaneous manufactured articles, food and live animals, mineral fuels and lubricants, machinery and transport equipment, and chemical products. The main exports in that year were miscellaneous manufactured articles, crude materials except fuels, mineral fuels and lubricants, and machinery and transport equipment.

In 2011, the overall budgetary surplus was €87.3m., which was equivalent to 2.7% of GDP. Montenegro's general government gross debt was €1,316m. in 2010, equivalent to 42.4% of GDP. The total external debt of the country was US \$1,554m. in 2010, of which \$1,350m. was public and publicly guaranteed debt. In that year, the cost of servicing long-term public and publicly guaranteed debt and repayments to the IMF was equivalent to 5.9% of the value of exports of goods, services and income (excluding workers' remittances). Consumer prices declined by 2.8% in 2010, but increased by 2.6% in 2011. The rate of unemployment was 15.9% in 2011.

In November 2006 the EU issued a progress report on Montenegro's first months of independence, which emphasized the need for economic reform to combat a continuing over-reliance on certain sectors of the economy, high unemployment and regulatory obstacles. Agreements on bilateral economic relations were signed with neighbouring and other European countries. High levels of growth followed, based largely on capital growth and massive inflows of foreign direct investment, particularly in the tourism, banking and construction sectors, and a reduction in the rate of unemployment. In October 2007 Montenegro signed a Stabilization and Association Agreement (SAA) with the EU, which entered into effect in May 2010. On 29 April 2012 Montenegro officially joined the World Trade Organization (WTO, see p. 444). In accordance with the recommendation of the European Commission, accession negotiations with the EU were opened in June. Following his return to government in December (see Domestic Political History), premier Milo Đukanović pledged to continue EU integration efforts, particularly in combating corruption and organized crime, and to generate employment. As a result of stabilization measures implemented by the authorities, in accordance with IMF recommendations, Montenegro's economy had by 2011 demonstrated a gradual recovery from the impact of the 2008–09 international financial crisis, with a rise to an almost pre-crisis level of growth, assisted by the tourism sector. Following continued difficulties in the euro area, however, the IMF estimated a GDP increase of only 0.2% in 2012, while the fiscal deficit had exceeded the revised target and public debt also remained high. In early 2013 government plans to introduce an austerity tax rise in response to the widening budget deficit prompted trade union protests, after which the authorities compromised with the adoption, in February, of a 6% tax increase on salaries higher than the national average. In March Đukanović announced that the Government would continue measures to reduce public expenditure and illicit economic activities. Meanwhile, in January an EU report commended the Government's anti-corruption efforts, but emphasized the necessity of progress in a number of political reforms.

PUBLIC HOLIDAYS

2014: 1–2 January (New Year), 7–8 January (Orthodox Christmas), 18–21 April (Orthodox Easter), 1–2 May (Labour Day), 21 May (Independence Day), 13 July (National Day).

Statistical Survey

Source: Statistical Office of Montenegro, 81000 Podgorica, IV Proleterske 2; tel. (20) 241206; fax (20) 241270; e-mail statistika@cg.yu; internet www.monstat.org.

AREA AND POPULATION

Area: 13,812 sq km (5,333 sq miles). *By Municipality* (sq km): Andrijevica 283; Bar 598; Berane 717; Bijelo Polje 924; Budva 122; Cetinje 910; Danilovgrad 501; Herceg Novi 235; Kolašin 897; Kotor 335; Mojkovac 367; Nikšić 2,065; Plav 486; Pljevlja 1,346; Plužine 854; Podgorica 1,441; Rožaje 432; Šavnik 553; Tivat 46; Ulcinj 255; Žabljak 445.

Population: 620,145 at census of 31 October 2003; 620,029 at census of 1 April 2011.

Density (at 2011 census): 44.9 per sq km.

Population by Age and Sex (population at 2011 census): *0–14:* 118,751 (males 61,766, females 56,985); *15–64:* 421,693 (males 210,713, females 210,980); *65 and over:* 79,585 (males 33,757, females 45,828); *Total* 620,029 (males 306,236, females 313,793).

Population by Municipality (population at 2011 census): Andrijevica 5,071; Bar 42,048; Berane 33,970; Bijelo Polje 46,051; Budva 19,218; Cetinje 16,657; Danilovgrad 18,472; Herceg Novi 30,864; Kolašin 8,380; Kotor 22,601; Mojkovac 8,622; Nikšić 72,443; Plav 13,108; Pljevlja 30,786; Plužine 3,246; Podgorica 185,937; Rožaje 22,964; Šavnik 2,070; Tivat 14,031; Ulcinj 19,921; Žabljak 3,569; *Total* 620,029.

Ethnicity (population as declared at 2011 census): Montenegrin 278,865; Serb 178,110; Bosniak 53,605; Albanian 30,439; Muslim 20,537; Croat 6,021.

Principal Towns (population at 2011 census): Podgorica 150,977; Nikšić 56,970; Pljevlja 19,136; Cetinje 13,918; Bar 13,503; Budva 13,338; Bijelo Polje 12,900; Berane 11,073; Herceg Novi 11,059; Ulcinj 10,707.

Births, Marriages and Deaths (2011, preliminary): Live births 7,215 (birth rate 11.6 per 1,000); Marriages 3,814 (marriage rate 6.2 per 1,000); Deaths 5,847 (death rate 9.4 per 1,000).

Life Expectancy (years at birth): 74.5 (males 72.1; females 77.0) in 2011 (Source: World Bank, World Development Indicators database).

Economically Active Population (persons aged 15 years and over, annual averages, 2011): Agriculture, hunting, forestry and fishing 2,292; Mining and quarrying 1,975; Manufacturing 14,368; Electricity, gas and water supply 7,422; Construction 8,049; Wholesale and retail trade, repair of motor vehicles, motorcycles, and personal and household goods 37,820; Hotels and restaurants 12,429; Transport, storage and communications 13,906; Financial intermediation 4,183; Real estate, renting and business activities 10,988; Public administration and defence, and compulsory social security 19,195; Education 12,223; Health and social work 10,565; Other community, social and personal service activities 7,667; *Total employed* 163,082; Unemployed 30,875; *Total labour force* 193,957.

HEALTH AND WELFARE

Key Indicators

Total Fertility Rate (children per woman, 2010): 1.7.

Under-5 Mortality Rate (per 1,000 live births, 2010): 8.

Physicians (per 1,000 head, 2006): 2.0.

Hospital Beds (per 1,000 head, 2006): 4.1.

Health Expenditure (2009): US $ per head (PPP): 1,215.

Health Expenditure (2009): % of GDP: 9.4.

Health Expenditure (2009): public (% of total): 71.3.

Access to Water (% of persons, 2010): 98.

Access to Sanitation (% of persons, 2010): 90.

Human Development Index (2011): ranking: 54.

Human Development Index (2011): value: 0.771.

AGRICULTURE, ETC.

Principal Crops (metric tons, 2011): Wheat 2,446; Maize 11,688; Barley 1,955; Potatoes 180,126; Tobacco 258; Plums 12,145; Olives 1,557; Oranges and tangerines 7,912; Grapes 32,815. Source: FAO.

Livestock ('000 head, 2011): Cattle 87.2; Horses 4.0; Pigs 21.4; Sheep 208.8; Poultry 470. Source: FAO.

Livestock Products (metric tons, 2011): Cattle meat 3,850 (FAO estimate); Pig meat 1,900 (FAO estimate); Sheep meat 1,000 (FAO estimate); Cows' milk ('000 metric tons) 197; Eggs 3,790 (unofficial figure). Source: FAO.

Forestry ('000 cu m, 2011, unless otherwise indicated): *Timber removals:* 542.7 (broadleaved 236.1, coniferous 306.6); *Assortments* (2008 figures): 485.0 (broadleaved 201.9, coniferous 283.1).

Fishing (metric tons, 2011): Total catch 1,516 (marine 716, freshwater 800).

MINING

Selected Products ('000 metric tons, 2011): Lignite 1,973.0; Red bauxite 158.6; Sea salt 10.0.

INDUSTRY

Selected Products ('000 metric tons, 2011, unless otherwise indicated): Wheat flour 34.3; Wines ('000 hl) 104.4; Beer ('000 hl) 404.4; Spruce and fir lumber ('000 cu m) 62.9; Oxygen, nitrogen and acetylene 1.8; Cut marble panels ('000 sq m) 32.8; Steel ingots 42.3; Steel castings 15.1 (2010); Aluminium oxide 58.5 (2009); Aluminium ingots 92.8; Electric energy (kWh) 4,403.0m.

FINANCE

Currency and Exchange Rates: 100 cent = 1 euro (€). *Sterling and Dollar Equivalents* (31 December 2012): £1 sterling = 1.196 euros; US $1 = 0.758 euros; €10 = £8.36 = $13.19. *Average Exchange Rate* (euros per US dollar): 0.7550 in 2010; 0.7194 in 2011; 0.7779 in 2012.

Budget (€ million, 2011): *Revenue:* Total current revenues 1,118.6 (Taxes 699.1, Contributions 349.6, Duties 15.9, Reimbursements 25.7, Other current revenues 24.3, Loan repayments 4.0); Property disbursements 3.3; Grants and loans 220.9; Total revenue 1,342.7. *Expenditure:* Gross wages and salaries 371.3; Other personal income and fringe benefits 12.8; Expenditure for materials and services 104.1; Maintenance 23.6; Interest rates 45.4; Rent 7.5; Subsidies 45.4; Transfers to individuals and institutions 87.9; Social protection transfers 454.8; Other current expenses 5.5; Capital expenses 83.3; Total loans and loan repayments 2.1; Total reserves 11.8; Total expenditure 1,255.4. Source: Central Bank of Montenegro.

International Reserves (US $ million at 31 December 2011, excl. gold): IMF special drawing rights 40.20; Reserve position in IMF 10.13; Foreign exchange 342.36; *Total* 392.69. Source: IMF, *International Financial Statistics*.

Money Supply (€ million at 31 December 2011): Demand deposits at banking institutions 578.7. Source: IMF, *International Financial Statistics*.

Cost of Living (Consumer Price Index; base: 2008 = 100): All items 103.4 in 2009; 100.5 in 2010; 103.1 in 2011.

Expenditure on the Gross Domestic Product (€ million at current prices, 2011): Government final consumption expenditure 714.7; Private final consumption expenditure 2,728.5; Gross fixed capital formation 596.5; Changes in inventories 35.3; *Total domestic expenditure* 4,075.0; Exports of goods and services 1,299.3; *Less* Imports of goods and services 2,140.1; *GDP in purchasers' values* 3,234.1.

Gross Domestic Product by Economic Activity (€ million at current prices, 2011): Agriculture, hunting, forestry and fishing 256.7; Mining and quarrying 35.7; Manufacturing 162.5; Electricity, gas and water supply 170.4; Construction 158.1; Wholesale and retail trade, repair of motor vehicles, motorcycles, and personal and household goods 391.7; Hotels and restaurants 161.2; Transport, storage and communications 315.8; Financial intermediation 131.8; Real estate, renting and business activities 334.8; Public administration and defence, and compulsory social security 255.5; Education 139.3; Health and social work 131.7; Other community, social and personal service activities 59.4; *Sub-total* 2,704.7; Taxes, less subsidies, on products 529.4; *GDP in purchasers' values* 3,234.1.

Balance of Payments (€ million, 2011): Exports of goods 476.5; Imports of goods −1,782.6; *Trade balance* −1,306.1; Exports of services 847.2; Imports of services −316.8; *Balance on goods and services* −775.7; Other income received 192.3; Other income paid −166.6; *Balance on goods, services and income* −750.0; Current transfers received 154.7; Current transfers paid −38.5; *Current balance* −633.8; Capital account (net) −3.0; Direct investments (net) 389.1; Portfolio investments (net) 163.6; Other investments (net) −383.4; Net errors and omissions 353.2; *Overall balance* −114.3. Source: Central Bank of Montenegro.

EXTERNAL TRADE

Principal Commodities (€ million, 2011): *Imports:* Food and live animals 417.6; Mineral fuels, lubricants, etc. 330.7; Chemical products 169.6; Machinery and transport equipment 315.8; Miscellaneous manufactured articles 489.5; Total (incl. others) 1,823.2. *Exports:* Crude materials (except fuels) 65.6; Mineral fuels, lubricants, etc. 63.0; Machinery and transport equipment 23.9; Miscellaneous manufactured articles 236.4; Total (incl. others) 454.4.

Principal Trading Partners (€ million, 2011): *Imports:* Austria 33.9; Brazil 25.1; China, People's Republic 103.0; Croatia 90.0; Germany 104.3; Greece 144.1; Italy 107.3; Russia 8.2; Serbia 518.5; Switzerland 14.3; Total (incl. others) 1,823.2. *Exports:* Bosnia and Herzegovina 22.4; Greece 39.3; Italy 31.1; Serbia 79.8; Slovenia 30.3; Total (incl. others) 454.4.

TRANSPORT

Road Transport (2010): 164,653 passenger cars in use.

Railways (traffic, 2011): Passengers carried ('000) 692; Passenger-km ('000) 65,100; Freight carried ('000 metric tons) 1,050; Total ton-km ('000) 135,522.

Shipping (freight handled, '000 metric tons, 2011): Goods loaded 758.2; Goods unloaded 960.4.

Civil Aviation (2011): Passenger movements 1,258,835; Freight carried 1,074 metric tons.

TOURISM

Total Foreign Tourist Arrivals: 1,044,014 in 2009; 1,087,794 in 2010; 1,201,099 in 2011.

Overnight Stays by Nationality (foreign tourists, 2011): Albania 153,850; Bosnia and Herzegovina 743,591; Czech Republic 164,979; France 145,058; Germany 176,055; Italy 136,039; Russia 1,782,295; Serbia 2,069,863; Slovenia 128,910; USA 40,130; Total (incl. others) 7,634,207.

COMMUNICATIONS MEDIA

Telephones (main lines in use, 2011): 170,856.

Mobile Cellular Telephones (subscribers, 2010): 1,393,297.

EDUCATION

Pre-primary (2011/12 unless otherwise indicated): Schools 108 (2010/11); Pupils 13,885; Teaching staff 1,439.

Primary (2011/12 unless otherwise indicated): Schools 442 (2008/09); Pupils 69,461; Teaching staff 5,048.

Secondary (2008/09 unless otherwise indicated): Schools 47; Students 31,914 (2011/12); Teaching staff 2,243.

Higher (incl. faculties, art academies and private institutions, 2008/09, unless otherwise indicated): Schools 38; Students 22,163 (2010/11); Teaching staff 1,405.

Adult Literacy Rate: 97.65% (males 99.63%; females 95.70%) at 2003 census.

Directory

The Government

HEAD OF STATE

President: FILIP VUJANOVIĆ (elected 11 May 2003; took office 13 June 2003; re-elected 6 April 2008).

COUNCIL OF MINISTERS
(May 2013)

The Government comprises members of the Democratic Party of Socialists of Montenegro (DPS), the Social Democratic Party of Montenegro (SDP), the Bosniak Party (BP) and the Croatian Civic Initiative (HGI).

Chairman of the Government: MILO ĐUKANOVIĆ (DPS).

Deputy Chairman of the Government and Minister of Foreign Affairs and European Integration: IGOR LUKŠIĆ (DPS).

Deputy Chairman of the Government, responsible for the Political System and Internal and Foreign Affairs, and Minister of Justice: DUŠKO MARKOVIĆ (BP).

Deputy Prime Minister, responsible for Economic Policy and the Financial System, and Minister of Information Society and Telecommunications: VUJICA LAZOVIĆ (SDP).

Deputy Prime Minister: RAFET HUSOVIĆ (BP).

General Secretary of the Government: ŽARKO ŠTURANOVIĆ (DPS).

Minister of Internal Affairs: RAŠKO KONJEVIĆ (SDP).

Minister of Defence: MILICA PEJANOVIĆ-ĐURIŠIĆ (DPS).

Minister of Finance: RADOJE ŽUGIĆ (Independent).

Minister of Education: SLAVOLJUB STJEPOVIĆ (DPS).

Minister of Culture: BRANISLAV MIĆUNOVIĆ (DPS).

Minister of the Economy: VLADIMIR KAVARIĆ (DPS).

Minister of Transport and Maritime Affairs: IVAN BRAJOVIĆ (SDP).

Minister of Agriculture and Rural Development: PETAR IVANOVIĆ (DPS).

Minister of Sustainable Development and Tourism: BRANIMIR GVOZDENOVIĆ (DPS).

Minister of Health: MIODRAG RADUNOVIĆ (DPS).

Minister for Human and Minority Rights: SUAD NUMANOVIĆ (DPS).

Minister of Labour and Social Welfare: PREDRAG BOŠKOVIĆ (DPS).

Minister of Science: SANJA VLAHOVIĆ (DPS).

Minister without Portfolio: MARIJA VUČINOVIĆ (HGI).

MINISTRIES

Office of the President: 81000 Podgorica, Sveti Petra Cetinjskog 3; tel. (20) 241410; fax (20) 245849; e-mail filip.vujanovic@predsjednik.me; internet www.predsjednik.me.

Office of the Chairman of the Government: 81000 Podgorica, Karađorđeva bb; tel. (20) 242530; fax (20) 242329; e-mail vojin.vlahovic@gov.me; internet www.gov.me.

Ministry of Agriculture and Rural Development: 81000 Podgorica, Rimski trg 46; tel. (20) 482109; fax (20) 482364; e-mail kabinet.mpsv@gov.me; internet www.minpolj.gov.me.

Ministry of Culture: 81250 Cetinje, ul. Njegoševa; tel. (41) 232571; fax (41) 232572; e-mail kabinet.kultura@mku.gov.me; internet www.ministarstvokulture.gov.me.

Ministry of Defence: 81000 Podgorica, ul. Jovana Tomaševića 29; tel. (20) 242042; fax (20) 224702; e-mail kabinet@mod.gov.me; internet www.odbrana.gov.me.

Ministry of the Economy: 81000 Podgorica, Rimski trg 46; tel. (20) 482119; fax (20) 234027; e-mail masa.vukotic@mek.gov.me; internet www.minekon.gov.me.

Ministry of Education: 81000 Podgorica, Vaka Đurovića bb; tel. (20) 410100; fax (20) 410101; e-mail mps@mps.gov.me; internet www.mpin.gov.me.

Ministry of Finance: 81000 Podgorica, Stanka Dragojevića 2; tel. (20) 242835; fax (20) 224450; e-mail mf@mif.gov.me; internet www.mf.gov.me.

Ministry of Foreign Affairs and European Integration: 81000 Podgorica, Stanka Dragojevića 2; tel. (20) 246357; fax (20) 224670; e-mail kabinet@mfa.gov.me; internet www.mip.gov.me.

Ministry of Health: 81000 Podgorica, Rimski trg 46; tel. (20) 242276; fax (20) 242762; e-mail mzdravlja@gov.me; internet www.mzdravlja.gov.me.

Ministry for Human and Minority Rights: 81000 Podgorica, Rimski trg bb; tel. (20) 482129; fax (20) 234198; e-mail min.manj@t-com.me; internet www.minmanj.gov.me.

Ministry of Information Society and Telecommunications: 81000 Podgorica, Rimski trg 45; tel. (20) 241412; fax (20) 241790; e-mail kabinet@mid.gov.me; internet www.mid.gov.me.

Ministry of Internal Affairs: 81000 Podgorica, bul. Svetog Petra Cetinjskog 22; tel. (20) 241590; fax (20) 246779; e-mail kabinet@mup.gov.me; internet www.mup.gov.me.

Ministry of Justice: 81000 Podgorica, Vuka Karadžića 3; tel. (20) 407501; fax (20) 407515; e-mail minpravde@t-com.me; internet www.pravda.gov.me.

Ministry of Labour and Social Welfare: 81000 Podgorica, Rimski trg 46; tel. (20) 482148; fax (20) 234227; e-mail ministar.mrss@mrss.gov.me; internet www.minradiss.gov.me.

Ministry of Science: 81000 Podgorica, Rimski trg 46; tel. (20) 482145; fax (20) 234168; e-mail kabinet@mna.gov.me; internet www.mna.gov.me.

Ministry of Sustainable Development and Tourism: 81000 Podgorica, IV proleterske brigade 19; tel. (20) 446200; fax (20) 446215; e-mail zoran.tomic@mrt.gov.me; internet www.mrt.gov.me.

Ministry of Transport and Maritime Affairs: 81000 Podgorica, Rimski trg 46; tel. (20) 482196; fax (20) 234342; e-mail jelena.raspopovic@msp.gov.me; internet www.minsaob.gov.me.

President

Presidential Election, 7 April 2013

Candidate	Votes	%
Filip Vujanović (Democratic Party of Socialists of Montenegro)	161,940	51.21
Miodrag Lekić (Democratic Front*)	154,290	48.79
Total	316,230	100.00

*Comprising the Movement for Changes and the New Serbian Democracy.

Legislature

Skupština Crne Gore
(Assembly of Montenegro)

81000 Podgorica, bul. Svetog Petra Cetinjskog 10; tel. (20) 404565; fax (20) 245125; e-mail press@skupstina.me; internet www .skupstina.me.

Speaker: RANKO KRIVOKAPIĆ.

Election, 14 October 2012

Party	Votes	%	Seats
Coalition for a European Montenegro* .	165,380	46.33	39
Democratic Front†	82,773	23.19	20
Socialist People's Party of Montenegro .	40,131	11.24	9
Positive Montenegro	29,881	8.37	7
Bosniak Party	15,124	4.24	3
New Democratic Power	5,244	1.47	1
Albanian Coalition‡	3,824	1.07	1
Croatian Civic Initiative	1,470	0.41	1
Others	13,123	3.68	—
Total	**356,950**	**100.00**	**81**

* Comprising the Democratic Party of Socialists of Montenegro, the Social Democratic Party of Montenegro, and the Liberal Party of Montenegro.
† Comprising New Serbian Democracy and the Movement for Changes.
‡ Comprising the Democratic League of Montenegro, the Democratic Party and the Albanian Alternative.

Political Organizations

Bosniak Party (BP) (Bošnjačka Stranka): 84310 Rožaje; tel. (51) 270164; fax (51) 270165; e-mail info@bscg.me; internet www.bscg .me; f. 2006; Pres. RAFET HUSOVIĆ.

Croatian Civic Initiative (Hrvatska građanska inicijativa—HGI): 85320 Tivat, Luke Tomanovića bb; tel. and fax (32) 660348; e-mail hgicg@t-com.me; internet www.hgi.co.me; f. 2003; joined Democratic Party of Socialists of Montenegro coalition 2006; Pres. MARIJA VUČINOVIĆ.

Democratic Party: Podgorica.

Democratic Party of Socialists of Montenegro (DPS) (Demokratska Partija Socijalista Crne Gore): 81000 Podgorica, Jovana Tomaševića bb; tel. (20) 245292; fax (20) 245282; e-mail portparol@ dps.me; internet www.dps.me; fmrly League of Communists of Montenegro, present name adopted 1991; contested 2012 legislative elections as mem. of the Coalition for a European Montenegro; Chair. MILO ĐUKANOVIĆ.

Democratic Serbian Party of Montenegro (DSP) (Demokratska Srpska Stranka Crne Gore—DSS): 81000 Podgorica, Radnička 33; tel. (20) 206120; fax (20) 206121; internet www.dsscg.com; f. 2003; centre-right; Leader RANKO KADIĆ.

Democratic Union of Albanians (DUA) (Demokratska Unija Albanaca): c/o Skupština Crne Gore, 81000 Podgorica, bul. Svetog Petra Cetinjskog 10; tel. (20) 404565; e-mail press@skupstina.me; f. 1993; Leader FERHAT DINOŠA.

Liberal Party of Montenegro (LPM) (Liberalna Partija Crne Gore—LPCG): 81000 Podgorica, Miljana Vukova 51; tel. and fax (67) 500884; e-mail liberalnapartija@t-com.me; internet www.lpcg.me; f. 2004; contested 2012 legislative elections as mem. of the Coalition for a European Montenegro; Pres. ANDRIJA POPOVIĆ.

Movement for Changes (MFC) (Pokret za Promjene—PZP): 81000 Podgorica, Dalmatinska 130 D; tel. and fax (20) 269337; e-mail pzp@ promjene.org; internet www.promjene.org; f. 2002 as nongovernmental org.; became political party in 2006; supports European integration; contested 2012 legislative elections as mem. of the Democratic Front coalition; Pres. NEBOJŠA MEDOJEVIĆ.

New Democratic Power (Nova Demokratska Snaga—FORCA): 85360 Ulcinj, Skenderbeu; tel. (30) 401760; fax (30) 401761; e-mail info@forca.me; internet www.forca.me; f. 2005; principally ethnic Albanian party; Chair. NAZIF CUNGU.

New Serbian Democracy (Nova Srpska Demokratija—NOVA): 81000 Podgorica, Vojislava Grujića 4; tel. (20) 651903; fax (20) 652147; e-mail centar@nova.org.me; internet www.nova.org.me; f. 2009 by merger of Serb People's Party with People's Socialist Party and other small groups; contested 2012 legislative elections as mem. of the Democratic Front coalition; Pres. ANDRIJA MANDIĆ.

Social Democratic Party of Montenegro (SDP) (Socijaldemokratska Partija Crne Gore): 81000 Podgorica, Jovana Tomaševića bb; tel. (20) 248648; fax (20) 612133; e-mail sdp@sdp.co.me; internet www.sdp.co.me; f. 1990; contested 2012 legislative elections as mem. of the Coalition for a European Montenegro; Pres. RANKO KRIVOKAPIĆ.

Socialist People's Party of Montenegro (SPPM) (Socijalistička Narodna Partija Crne Gore—SNP): 81000 Podgorica, Vaka Đurovića 5; tel. (20) 272421; fax (20) 272420; e-mail snp@t-com.me; internet www.snp.co.me; f. 1997; Pres. SRĐAN MILIĆ.

Diplomatic Representation

Albania: 81000 Podgorica, Stanka Dragojevića 14; tel. (20) 667380; fax (20) 667381; e-mail embassy.potgorica@mfa.gov.al; Ambassador TONIN BECI.

Austria: 81000 Podgorica, bul. Svetog Petra Cetinjskog 1A; tel. (20) 201135; fax (20) 624344; e-mail podgorica-ob@bmaa.gv.at; Ambassador MARTIN PAMMER.

Bosnia and Herzegovina: 81000 Podgorica, Atinska 58; tel. (20) 618015; fax (20) 618016; e-mail amb.podgorica@mvp.gov.ba; Ambassador IZMIR TALIĆ.

Bulgaria: 81000 Podgorica, Vukice Mitrovića 10; tel. (20) 655009; fax (20) 655008; e-mail embassy.podgorica@mfa.bg; internet www .mfa.bg/embassies/montenegro; Ambassador MAYA N. DOBREVA.

China, People's Republic: 81000 Podgorica, Radosava Burića 4A; tel. and fax (20) 609275; e-mail chinaemb_me@hotmail.com; Ambassador ZHI SHAOLIN.

Croatia: 81000 Podgorica, Vladimira Ćetkovića 2; tel. (20) 269760; fax (20) 269810; e-mail croemb.podgorica@mvep.hr; Ambassador IVANA PERIĆ.

France: 81000 Podgorica, Atinska 35; tel. (20) 665348; fax (20) 655643; e-mail ambafrance@ambafrance.co.me; internet www .ambafrance-me.org; Ambassador DOMINIQUE GAZUY.

Germany: 81000 Podgorica, Hercegovačka 10; tel. and fax (20) 441000; internet www.podgorica.diplo.de; Ambassador PIUS FISCHER.

Greece: 81000 Podgorica, Atinska 4C; tel. (20) 655544; fax (20) 655543; e-mail gremb.pod@mfa.gr; Ambassador EMMANUEL PAPADO-GIORGAKIS.

Hungary: 81000 Podgorica, Kralja Nikole 104; tel. (20) 602910; fax (20) 625243; e-mail mission.pdg@mfa.gov.hu; internet www.mfa.gov .hu/emb/podgorica; Ambassador TIBOR CSÁSZÁR.

Italy: 81000 Podgorica, Džordža Vašingtona 26; tel. (20) 234661; fax (20) 234663; e-mail segreteria.podgorica@esteri.it; internet www .ambpodgorica.esteri.it; Ambassador SERGIO BARBANTI.

Macedonia, former Yugoslav republic: 81000 Podgorica, Hercegovačka 49/3; tel. (20) 667415; fax (20) 667205; e-mail podgorica@mfa .gov.mk; Ambassador ALEKSANDAR VASILEVSKI.

Poland: 20000 Podgorica, Kozaračka 79; tel. (20) 608320; fax (20) 658581; e-mail podgorica.amb.sekretariat@msz.gov.pl; internet www.podgorica.polemb.net; Ambassador GRAŻYNA SIKORSKA.

Romania: 81000 Podgorica, Vukice Mitrovića 40; tel. (20) 618040; fax (20) 655081; e-mail ambs.romania.mne@t-com.me; Ambassador MIHAIL FLOROVICI.

Russia: 81000 Podgorica, Veliše Mugoše 1; tel. (20) 272460; fax (20) 272317; e-mail info@ambrus.me; internet www.ambrus.me; Ambassador ANDREI NESTERENKO.

Serbia: 81000 Podgorica, Hercegovačka 18; tel. (20) 667305; fax (20) 664301; e-mail embassy.podgorica@mfa.rs; Ambassador ZORAN LUTOVAC.

Slovenia: 81000 Podgorica, Atinska 41; tel. (20) 618150; fax (20) 655671; e-mail kpg@gov.si; internet podgorica.embassy.si; Ambassador VLADIMIR GASPARIČ.

Turkey: 81000 Podgorica, Radosava Burica bb; tel. (20) 445700; fax (20) 445777; e-mail podgorica.be@mfa.gov.tr; Ambassador MEHMET NIYAZI TANILIR.

Ukraine: 81000 Podgorica, ul. Serdara Jola Piletica 15; tel. (20) 227521; fax (20) 227181; e-mail emb_me@mfa.gov.ua; internet www .mfa.gov.ua/montenegro; Ambassador OKSANA SLYUSARENKO.

United Arab Emirates: 81000 Podgorica, bul. Svetog Petra Cetinjskog 147; tel. (20) 411401; fax (20) 411402; e-mail montenegro@mofa .gov.ae; Ambassador HAFSA ABDULLAH MUHAMMAD SHARIF AL-ULAMA.

United Kingdom: 81000 Podgorica, Ulcinjska 8, Gorica C; tel. (20) 618010; fax (20) 618020; e-mail podgorica@fco.gov.uk; internet ukinmontenegro.fco.gov.uk; Ambassador CATHERINE KNIGHT-SANDS.

USA: 81000 Podgorica, Dzona Dzeksona 2; tel. (20) 410500; fax (20) 241358; e-mail podgoricaprot@state.gov; internet podgorica .usembassy.gov; Ambassador SUE KATHRINE BROWN.

Judicial System

Constitutional Court (Ustavni Sud Crne Gore): 81000 Podgorica, Njegoševa 2; tel. and fax (20) 665410; e-mail ustavni.sud@ustavnisud .me; internet www.ustavnisudcg.co.me; comprises a President and five judges; Pres. Dr MILAN MARKOVIĆ.

Supreme Court (Vrhovni Sud Crne Gore): 81000 Podgorica, Njegoševa 10; tel. (20) 665390; fax (20) 665405; e-mail vrhsud@t-com.me; internet www.sudovi.me; comprises a President and 17 judges; incorporates criminal, civil and administrative divisions; Pres. VESNA MEDENICA.

Office of the Supreme State Prosecutor (Vrhovni državni tužilac): 81000 Podgorica, Slobode 20; tel. and fax (20) 230624; e-mail vdtcg@tuzilastvo.me; internet www.tuzilastvocg.co.me; Public Prosecutor RANKA ČARAPIĆ.

Religion

CHRISTIANITY

The Eastern Orthodox Church

Montenegrin Orthodox Church (Crnogorska Pravoslavna Crkva): 81250 Cetinje, Gruda bb; tel. and fax (41) 31310; e-mail crkva@moc-cpc.org; internet www.moc-cpc.org; autocephalous until 1920, when it was dissolved and annexed to the Serbian Orthodox Church; restored 1993; Archbishop of Cetinje and Metropolitan of Montenegro MIHAILO (DEDEIĆ).

Orthodox Metropolitanate of Montenegro and the Littoral— Serbian Orthodox Church (Pravoslavna Mitropolija Crnogorsko Primorska—Srpska Pravoslavna Crkva): 81250 Cetinje; tel. (41) 231273; fax (41) 231273; e-mail mitropolija@t-com.me; internet www.mitropolija.me; Metropolitan of Montenegro and the Littoral AMFILOHIJE (RADOVIĆ).

The Roman Catholic Church

At 31 December 2008 there were an estimated 12,475 adherents in the archdiocese of Bar (which is directly answerable to the Holy See) and an estimated 10,000 adherents in the Diocese of Kotor (which is suffragan to the archdiocese of Split-Makarska, based in Croatia). There is also an Apostolic Exarchate for adherents of the Byzantine Rite in Serbia and Montenegro, based in Belgrade, Serbia.

Archbishop of Bar: Most Rev. ZEF GASHI, 85000 Bar, Popovići 98; tel. (30) 344236; fax (30) 344233.

Bishop of Kotor: Most Rev. ILIJA JANJIĆ, 85330 Kotor, Stari grad 336; tel. (32) 322315; fax (32) 322175.

ISLAM

Almost 20% of the population of Montenegro profess Islam, many being ethnic Slav Muslims (Bosniaks) of the Sandžak region (which was partitioned between Montenegro and Serbia in 1913).

The Press

PRINCIPAL DAILIES

Dan (The Day): 81000 Podgorica, 13 Jula 10; tel. (20) 481520; fax (20) 481522; e-mail dan@t-com.me; internet www.dan.co.me; f. 1999; Chief Editor MLADEN MILUTINOVIĆ.

Pobjeda (Victory): 81000 Podgorica, bul. Revolucije 15, POB 101; tel. (20) 244474; fax (20) 202455; e-mail urednik@pobjeda.co.me; internet www.pobjeda.me; f. 1944; morning; Editor-in-Chief SRĐAN KUSOVAC; circ. 18,000 (2003).

Republika (The Republic): 81000 Podgorica, trg Republike bb; tel. (20) 215260; fax (20) 215270; Editor-in-Chief VELIZAR BRAJOVIĆ.

Vijesti (The News): 81000 Podgorica, bul. Revolucije 9; tel. (20) 406901; fax (20) 242306; e-mail mihailo.jovovic@vijesti.me; internet www.vijesti.me; f. 1997; Editor-in-Chief MIHAILO JOVOVIĆ.

PERIODICALS

Koha Javore: 81000 Podgorica, bul. Revolucije 9; tel. (20) 247799; fax (20) 247674; e-mail kohajavore@t-com.me; internet www .kohajavore.co.me; weekly; f. 2002; science and culture; in Albanian; Editor-in-Chief ALI SALAJ.

Monitor: 81000 Podgorica, Vuka Karadžića 11; tel. (20) 231955; fax (20) 231944; e-mail monitor@t-com.me; internet www.monitor.co .me; f. 1990; weekly; independent; politics, general; Editor-in-Chief ESAD KOČAN.

NEWS AGENCY

Montenegrin News Agency (MINA): Podgorica; tel. (81) 264363; e-mail mnnews@mnnews.net; internet www.mnnews.net; f. 2002; commercial; Montenegrin, Albanian and English; Exec. Dir JAŠA JOVIĆEVIĆ.

PRESS ASSOCIATION

Asscn of Journalists of Montenegro (UNCG) (Udruženja novinara Crne Gore): 81000 Podgorica; Pres VLATKO VUJOVIĆ.

Publishers

Obod: 81250 Cetinje, Njegoševa 3; tel. (41) 21331; fax (41) 21953; general literature; Dir VASKO JANKOVIĆ.

Pobjeda (Victory) Publishing House: 81000 Podgorica, Južni bul. bb; tel. (20) 44433; f. 1974; poetry, fiction, lexicography and scientific works.

Broadcasting and Communications

TELECOMMUNICATIONS

Despite the liberalization of the sector, the formerly state-owned company, Crnogorski Telekom, continues to dominate the provision of fixed-line telephones, while the rate of subscription to mobile telecommunications services is among the highest in Central and South-Eastern Europe. In 2010 there were 167,720 fixed telephone lines and 1.5m. subscriptions to mobile telephone services in Montenegro.

Crnogorski Telekom: 81000 Podgorica, Moskovska 29; tel. (20) 433433; fax (20) 225752; e-mail office@telekom.me; internet www .telekom.me; 76.53% owned by Magyar Telekom (Hungary); Exec. Dir DANIEL SZASZ.

m:tel: 81000 Podgorica, Kralja Nikole 27A; e-mail kabinet@mtel.me; internet www.mtel-cg.com; f. 2007; owned by Telekom Srbija (Serbia) and Ogalar (Netherlands); mobile cellular telecommunications services; Exec. Dir LJUBOMIR RAJŠIĆ.

T-Mobile Crna Gora: 81000 Podgorica, bul. Svetog Petra Cetinjskog bb; tel. (20) 400801; fax (20) 225752; e-mail office@monetcg.com; internet www.t-mobile.me; f. 2000; fmrly Monet; present name adopted 2006; subsidiary of Crnogorski Telekom; mobile cellular telecommunications services.

Telenor Montenegro: 81000 Podgorica, bul. Džordža Vašingtona 83; tel. (20) 235000; fax (20) 235035; e-mail info@telenor.me; internet www.telenor.me; f. 1996; fmrly offered services under the brand Promonte; rebranded as above in 2010; 100% owned by Telenor (Norway); mobile cellular telecommunications services; Exec. Dir KAAREN HILSEN.

Regulatory Agency

Agency for Electronic Communications and Postal Services (Agencija za elektronske komunikacije i poštansku djelatnost— EKIP): 81000 Podgorica, bul. Džordža Vašingtona bb; tel. (20) 406711; fax (20) 406702; e-mail ekip@ekip.me; internet www.ekip .me; f. 2001 as Agency for Telecommunications; renamed as above in 2008; independent regulatory body; Exec. Dir ZORAN SEKULIĆ.

BROADCASTING

There are 15 public (one national and 14 local) and 34 commercial radio stations operating in Montenegro. In addition to four publicly owned (one national and three local) television stations there are 15 main licensed commercial television stations active in the country.

Regulatory Agency

Montenegro Broadcasting Agency (Agencija za radio-diffuziu Crne Gore): 81000 Podgorica, bul. Svetog Petra Cetinjskog 9; tel. (20) 201430; fax (20) 201440; internet www.ardcg.org; CEO ABAZ BELI DŽAFIĆ.

Television and Radio

Radiotelevizija Crne Gore (Radio and Television of Montenegro): 81000 Podgorica, Cetinjski put bb; tel. (20) 225602; fax (20) 225108; internet www.rtcg.org; f. 1944 (radio) and 1971 (television); two terrestrial television channels and one satellite channel; two radio channels; Dir-Gen. BRANKO VOJIČIĆ; Dir of Television RADOJKA RUTOVIĆ; Dir of Radio BUDIMIR RAIČEVIĆ.

Radio D: 81000 Podgorica, Vasa Raičkovića 18A; tel. (20) 238909; internet www.radioddplus.com; f. 2000; independent; also Radio D Plus; Chief Editor DRAGANA KUKRIĆ.

RTV Corona: 85000 Bar, Jovana Tomaševica, Poslovni centar G-9; tel. and fax (30) 317727; e-mail mcorona@t-com.me; f. 2000; comprises Radio Corona (f. 2000) and TV Corona (f. 2008); information and entertainment programming; Exec. Dir DRAGAN DESPOTOVIĆ.

TV Vijesti: 81000 Podgorica, Trg Republike bb; tel. (20) 404601; fax (20) 232065; e-mail tvvijesti@t-com.me; f. 2007; broadcasts 24 hours a day; information, news, politics, economics, culture, entertainment, sport; Exec. Dir SLAVOLJUB ŠĆEKIĆ.

Finance

(cap. = capital; res = reserves; dep. = deposits; m. = million; amounts in euros; brs = branches)

BANKING

Central Bank

Central Bank of Montenegro (Centralna Banka Crne Gore—CBCG): 81000 Podgorica, bul. Petra Cetinjskog 6; tel. and fax (20) 403105; e-mail pristup.informacijama@cb-cg.org; internet www.cb-mn.org; f. 2001; cap. 2.5m., res 41.9m., dep. 438.9m. (Dec. 2007); Gov. (vacant).

Selected Banks

At December 2011 11 banks were operating in Montenegro, nine of which were foreign-owned.

Crnogorska komercijalna banka a.d. Podgorica (CKB): 81000 Podgorica, Moskovska bb; tel. (20) 404232; fax (20) 235757; e-mail info@ckb.me; internet www.ckb.me; f. 1997; 100% owned by OTP Bank (Hungary) (q.v.); cap. 106.9m., res 0.9m., dep. 561.6m. (Dec. 2011); Pres. JÓZSEF WINDHEIM; 40 brs.

Erste Bank a.d. Podgorica: 81000 Podgorica, Marka Miljanova 46; tel. (20) 440440; fax (20) 440432; e-mail info@erstebank.me; internet www.erstebank.me; f. 2002; fmrly Opportunity Bank; present name adopted 2009; subsidiary of Erste Bank der Oesterreichischen Sparkassen AG (Austria); cap. 5.3m., res 1.5m., dep. 164.6m. (Dec. 2011); Chief Exec. ALEKSA LUKIĆ.

NLB Montenegrobanka a.d. Podgorica: 81000 Podgorica, Dragojevića 46; tel. (20) 402000; fax (20) 402212; e-mail info@montenegro-banka.com; internet www.montenegrobanka.com; f. 1905; fmrly MNB Crnogorska banka—Banque de Montenegro; present name adopted Jan. 2006; 97.4% owned by Nova Ljubljanska Banka d.d. (Slovenia); cap. 12.9m., res 12.8m., dep. 382.9m. (Dec. 2011); Pres. MATEJ NARAT; CEO CRTOMIR MESARIĆ.

Prva Banka: 81000 Podgorica, bul. Svetog Petra Cetinjskog 141; tel. (20) 409174; fax (20) 409124; e-mail info@prvabankacg.com; internet www.prvabankacg.com; f. 1901 as Prva Nikšićka štedionica; current name adopted in 2007; CEO MILAN PEROVIĆ.

STOCK EXCHANGE

Montenegro Stock Exchange (Montenegroberza): 81000 Podgorica, Moskovska 77; tel. (20) 229710; fax (20) 229711; e-mail info@mnse.me; internet www.mnse.me; f. 1993; CEO GOJKO MAKSIMOVIĆ.

INSURANCE

Lovćen Osiguranje a.d. Podgorica (Lovćen Insurance Co Podgorica): 81000 Podgorica, ul. Slobode 13 A; tel. (20) 404400; fax (20) 665281; e-mail lovosig@co.me; internet www.lovcenosiguranje.co.me; majority stake owned by Zavarovalnica Triglav d.d. (Slovenia); insurance and reinsurance; Exec. Dir PURIĆ RADENKO.

Sava Montenegro Osiguranje: 81000 Podgorica, Rimski trg 70, PC 'Kruševac'; tel. (20) 234008; fax (20) 234407; e-mail info@sava.co.me; internet www.sava.co.me; wholly owned by Sava Re (Slovenia); fmrly Montenegro Osiguranje; life and non-life, insurance and reinsurance; Chief Exec. NEBOJŠA ŠĆEKIĆ.

Swiss Osiguranje a.d. Podgorica (Swiss Insurance Co Podgorica): 81000 Podgorica, Novaka Miloševa 6/II; tel. (20) 230734; e-mail info@swiss-osiguranje.com; internet www.swiss-osiguranje.com/swiss; fmrly Agroosiguranje a.d. Podgorica; life and non-life, insurance and reinsurance; Exec. Dir DRAGAN IVANOVIĆ.

Trade and Industry

CHAMBER OF COMMERCE

Chamber of Commerce of Montenegro (Privredna Komora Crne Gore): 81000 Podgorica, Novaka Miloševa 29; tel. (20) 230545; fax (20) 230493; e-mail predsjednik@pkcg.org; internet www.pkcg.org; Pres. VELIMIR MIJUSKOVIĆ.

UTILITIES

Electricity

Elektroprivreda Crne Gore a.d. Nikšić (EPCG) (Montenegro Electricity Co): 81400 Nikšić, Vuka Karadžića 2; tel. (40) 204137; fax (40) 214329; e-mail milvujacic@epcg.co.me; internet www.epcg.co.me; production, transmission and distribution of electric power; Exec. Dir ENRICO MALERBA.

Transport

RAILWAYS

The total length of the railway network was 250 km in 2009. The 167-km line between Bar and Vrbnica is electrified.

Željeznica Crne Gore: 81000 Podgorica, trg Golootočkih žrtava 13; tel. (20) 441302; fax (20) 633957; internet www.zcg-prevoz.me; 60.1% state-owned; Chair. of Bd of Dirs RANKO MEDENIĆA; Gen. Man. REŠAD NUHODŽIĆ.

SHIPPING

The principal coastal outlet is the port of Bar, which is linked to the Italian ports of Ancona and Bari by a regular ferry service. At 31 December 2012 Montenegro's flag registered fleet comprised seven vessels, totalling 49,066 grt.

Port of Bar (Luka Bar): 85000 Bar, Luka Bar; tel. (30) 312409; fax (30) 312409; e-mail lukabar@t-com.me; internet www.lukabar.me; f. 1906; Chair. of Bd Prof. Dr PREDRAG IVANOVIĆ.

CIVIL AVIATION

Montenegro Airlines: 81000 Podgorica, Beogradska 10; tel. (20) 405501; fax (20) 405548; internet www.montenegroairlines.com; f. 1994; operations commenced 1997; direct flights between Podgorica and Tivat (Montenegro), Belgrade and Niš (Serbia), Frankfurt (Germany), Ljubljana (Slovenia), Paris (France), Rome (Italy), Vienna (Austria), and Zurich (Switzerland); Pres. ZORAN DURIŠIĆ; CEO PETAR GLOMAZIĆ.

Tourism

There were 1,201,099 foreign tourist arrivals in 2011, when receipts from tourism totalled US $777m.

National Tourism Organization of Montenegro: 81000 Podgorica, bul. Svetog Petra Cetinjskog 130; tel. (77) 100001; fax (77) 100009; e-mail info@montenegro.travel; internet www.montenegro.travel; Man. Dir SAŠA RADOVIĆ.

Defence

Following Montenegro's declaration of independence on 3 June 2006, the Montenegrin Government established a Ministry of Defence and revoked compulsory military service. In December Montenegro was admitted to the 'Partnership for Peace' programme of the North Atlantic Treaty Organization (NATO). As assessed at November 2012, Montenegro's total armed forces numbered 2,080, comprising an army of an estimated 1,500, a navy of 350 and an air force of 230. There was, in addition, a paramilitary force of an estimated 10,100, comprising 6,000 Ministry of Internal Affairs personnel and 4,100 members of special police units.

Defence Expenditure: Budgeted at €47m. in 2013.

Chief of Staff: Vice-Adm. DRAGAN SAMARDŽIĆ.

Education

Primary education is free and compulsory for all children between the ages of seven and 15 years. A new system of primary education, beginning at the age of six years and lasting for 9 years, was gradually introduced from 2004/05. Secondary education comprises gymnasia (grammar schools) and art schools that offer four-year programmes, as well as vocational education schools that offer two-, three- or four-year courses. In 2009/10 the primary education enrolment ratio included 83% of children in the relevant age-group, while the enrolment ratio for secondary education was equivalent to 98% of children in the relevant age-group in 2008/09. Higher education is offered at the University of Montenegro, Podgorica, which was established in 1974, and at post-secondary schools. Some 22,163 students were enrolled in higher education in 2010/11.

MOROCCO

Introductory Survey

LOCATION, CLIMATE, LANGUAGE, RELIGION, FLAG, CAPITAL

The Kingdom of Morocco is situated in the extreme north-west of Africa. It has a long coastline on the shores of the Atlantic Ocean and, east of the Strait of Gibraltar, on the Mediterranean Sea, facing southern Spain. Morocco's eastern frontier is with Algeria, while to the south lies the disputed territory of Western Sahara (under Moroccan occupation), which has a lengthy Atlantic coastline and borders Mauritania to the east and south. The Spanish External Territories, Ceuta and Melilla, lie within Moroccan territory on the Mediterranean coast. Morocco's climate is semi-tropical. It is warm and sunny on the coast, while the plains of the interior are intensely hot in summer. Average temperatures are 27°C (81°F) in summer and 7°C (45°F) in winter for Rabat, and 38°C (101°F) and 4°C (40°F), respectively, for Marrakesh. The rainy season in the north is from November to April. The official language is Arabic, but a large minority speak Berber. Spanish is widely spoken in the northern regions, and French in the rest of Morocco. The established religion is Islam, and most of the country's inhabitants are Muslims. There are small minorities of Christians and Jews. The national flag (proportions 2 by 3) is red, with a green pentagram (intersecting lines in the form of a five-pointed star), known as 'Solomon's Seal', in the centre. The capital is Rabat.

CONTEMPORARY POLITICAL HISTORY

Historical Context

In 1912, under the terms of the Treaty of Fez, most of Morocco became a French protectorate, while a smaller Spanish protectorate was instituted in the north and far south of the country. Spain also retained control of Spanish Sahara (now Western Sahara), and Tangier became an international zone in 1923. A nationalist movement developed in Morocco during the 1930s and 1940s, led by the Istiqlal (Independence) grouping, and on 2 March 1956 the French protectorate achieved independence as the Sultanate of Morocco. Sultan Muhammad V, who had reigned since 1927 (although he had been temporarily removed from office by the French authorities between 1953 and 1955), became the first head of state. The northern zone of the Spanish protectorate joined the new state in April 1956, and Tangier's international status was abolished in October. The southern zone of the Spanish protectorate was ceded to Morocco in 1958, but no agreement was reached on the enclaves of Ceuta and Melilla, in the north, the Ifni region in the south, or the Saharan territories to the south of Morocco, which all remained under Spanish control. The Sultan was restyled King of Morocco in August 1957, and became Prime Minister in May 1960. He died in February 1961, and was succeeded by his son, Moulay Hassan, who took the title of Hassan II.

Elections to Morocco's first House of Representatives took place in May 1963, and King Hassan relinquished the post of Prime Minister six months later. In June 1965, however, increasing political fragmentation prompted Hassan to declare a 'state of exception', and to resume full legislative and executive powers. The emergency provisions remained in force until July 1970, when a new Constitution was approved. Elections in the following month resulted in a pro-Government majority in the new Majlis al-Nuab (Chamber of Representatives).

Domestic Political Affairs

In July 1971 an attempted *coup d'état* was suppressed by forces loyal to the King. Among those subsequently arrested were numerous members of the left-wing Union nationale des forces populaires (UNFP), five of whom were sentenced to death. Although a revised Constitution was approved in March 1972 by popular referendum, a general election did not take place until June 1977. Two-thirds of the deputies in the Chamber of Representatives were directly elected, the remainder being elected by local government councils, professional associations and labour organizations. Supporters of the King's policies won a majority of seats in the new legislature. A Government of national unity was formed, including opposition representatives

from Istiqlal and the Mouvement populaire (MP) in addition to the pro-monarchist independents.

All 14 deputies belonging to the Union socialiste des forces populaires (USFP) withdrew from the Chamber of Representatives in October 1981, when it was announced that the legislative term was to be extended from four to six years. Elections were postponed, and an interim Government of national unity was appointed under Muhammad Karim Lamrani (Prime Minister in 1971–72). The new Government included members of the six main political parties: Istiqlal, the MP, the Parti national démocrate (PND), the Rassemblement national des indépendants (RNI), the Union constitutionnelle (UC) and the USFP. The deferred elections took place in September–October 1984. The USFP made significant gains, but the Chamber of Representatives remained dominated by the centre-right parties. A new Cabinet, appointed in April 1985, included members of the MP, the PND, the RNI and the UC. Lamrani resigned in September 1986, on health grounds, and was replaced by Azzeddine Laraki.

King Hassan announced in March 1992 that the Constitution was to be revised and submitted for approval in a national referendum, in preparation for legislative elections (which had been postponed since 1990, pending settlement of the Western Sahara dispute). The King indicated in July that the elections would take place in November, and that voting would be extended to include Western Sahara—irrespective of the UN's progress in organizing a referendum on the territory's status (see Western Sahara). In August the King dissolved the Government, and named Lamrani as Prime Minister in an interim, non-partisan Government. According to official results of the referendum, which proceeded in September, the revised Constitution was endorsed by 99.96% of voters. Under the terms of the new Constitution, the King would retain strong executive powers, including the right to appoint the Prime Minister, but government members would henceforth be nominated by the latter. The Government would be required to reflect the composition of the Chamber of Representatives, and was obliged to submit its legislative programme for the Chamber's approval; new legislation would automatically be promulgated one month after having been endorsed by parliament, regardless of whether royal assent had been received. Provision was also made for the establishment of a constitutional council and of an economic and social council, and guarantees of human rights were enshrined in the Constitution.

Legislative elections eventually took place in June 1993. Parties of the Bloc démocratique (also called the Koutla démocratique)—grouping Istiqlal, the USFP, the Parti du progrès et du socialisme (PPS), the Organisation de l'action démocratique et populaire (OADP) and the UNFP—won a combined total of 99 of the 222 directly elective seats in the enlarged Chamber. The MP won 33 seats, the RNI 28 and the UC 27. The indirect election (by electoral college) of the remaining 111 members, which followed on 17 September, was less favourable to the Bloc démocratique, which won only 21 further seats. Of the 333 seats in the Chamber, the USFP now controlled 56, the UC 54, Istiqlal 52, the MP 51 and the RNI 41. Lamrani was reappointed as Prime Minister in November, but in May 1994 King Hassan replaced him with Abdellatif Filali, who retained his post as Minister of State for Foreign Affairs and Co-operation. In July the King appealed to all political parties to particpate in a government of national unity, and in October he announced his intention to select a premier from the ranks of the opposition. However, negotiations on the formation of a coalition government failed, apparently owing to the Bloc démocratique's refusal to join an administration in which Driss Basri (a long-serving government member and close associate of the King) remained as Minister of the Interior and Information, and in January 1995 Hassan instructed Filali to form a new cabinet.

Muhammad Basri, a prominent opposition figure (sentenced to death *in absentia* in 1974) and founder member of both the UNFP and the USFP, returned to Morocco from France in June 1995, after 28 years in exile. It was widely believed that his rehabilitation had been precipitated by the royal amnesty of July

1994 and by the return to Morocco (also from France) in May 1995 of the First Secretary of the USFP, Abd al-Rahman el-Youssoufi. Despite King Hassan's assertion that there were no longer any political detainees in Morocco, a report published by the Association marocaine des droits humains (AMDH) in February 1996 claimed that 58 political prisoners (mainly radical Islamists, supporters of independence for Western Sahara and left-wing activists) remained in detention.

In August 1996 the King presented further constitutional amendments, including the creation of an indirectly elected second parliamentary assembly, the Majlis al-Mustasharin (Chamber of Advisers), and the introduction of direct elections for all members of the Chamber of Representatives. Most political parties supported the reforms; however, an appeal by the OADP leadership for a boycott of a planned referendum on the amendments led to a split in the party and the subsequent establishment of the Parti socialiste démocratique (PSD). According to official results of the referendum, held in September, the reforms were approved by 99.6% of voters. Legislation regarding the new bicameral parliament was promulgated in August 1997: the Chamber of Representatives was to comprise 325 members, directly elected for a five-year term; the 270 members of the Chamber of Advisers would be indirectly elected, for a nine-year term, by local councils (which would choose 162 members), chambers of commerce (81) and trade unions (27).

At the subsequent elections to the Chamber of Representatives, held in November 1997, the Bloc démocratique won a combined total of 102 seats (of which the USFP took 57 and Istiqlal 32); the centre-right Entente nationale took 100 seats (the UC 50 and the MP 40), and centrist parties 97 (including 46 won by the RNI). The Mouvement populaire constitutionnel et démocratique (MPCD), which earlier in the year had formally absorbed members of the Islamist Al Islah wa Attajdid, secured parliamentary representation for the first time, with nine seats. At indirect elections to the Chamber of Advisers, which followed in December, centrist parties won 90 seats (the RNI 42 and the Mouvement démocratique et social 33), the Entente nationale 76 (the UC 28 and the MP 27) and the Bloc démocratique 44 (Istiqlal 21). In February 1998 the King appointed el-Youssoufi as Morocco's first Socialist Prime Minister. In October the MPCD was renamed the Parti de la justice et du développement—PJD.

The accession of King Muhammad VI

King Hassan died on 23 July 1999, and was succeeded by his eldest son, Crown Prince Sidi Muhammad, as King Muhammad VI. Some 8,000 prisoners were freed, and more than 38,000 had their sentences reduced, under the terms of an amnesty decreed by the new King. In August the King ordered the creation within the Conseil Consultatif des Droits de l'Homme (CCDH)—established by King Hassan in April 1990—of an independent commission to determine levels of compensation for families of missing political activists and for those subjected to arbitrary detention. In April 1999 the CCDH had announced that it had been agreed to compensate the families of 112 people who were now officially acknowledged as having 'disappeared' between 1960 and 1990. However, Morocco's independent human rights organizations asserted that the number of missing persons amounted to almost 600. In November 1999 King Muhammad approved the return to Morocco of the family of former opposition activist and UNFP leader Mehdi Ben Barka, who had been abducted and apparently murdered in Paris, France, in 1965.

King Muhammad dismissed the influential Minister of State for the Interior, Driss Basri, in November 1999, apparently in response to the violent suppression of protests in Western Sahara in September. The new Minister of the Interior, Ahmed Midaoui (a former Director of National Security), immediately pledged to work towards the strengthening of democracy and national reconciliation. Victims of repression and their families, together with left-wing political parties and non-governmental organizations, subsequently formed a 'Justice and Trust' organization, with the stated aim of investigating human rights abuses in Morocco since independence. In April 2000 the Government commenced payments, reportedly totalling 40m. dirhams, in respect of the cases of an initial 40 victims of arbitrary detention, from the fund established the previous year. In September the King appointed Driss Jettou, a former Minister of Finance and Industry, as Minister of the Interior. A royal institute was established in October, charged with preserving the language and culture of the country's Berber population.

In June 2001 the Moroccan authorities granted the French judge leading the inquiry into the disappearance of Mehdi Ben Barka, permission to visit Morocco as part of his investigation.

Later that month a former member of the Moroccan special services, Ahmed Boukhari, alleged that Ben Barka had been had been tortured to death by Morocco's then Minister of the Interior, Gen. Muhammad Oufkir, having been kidnapped in Paris by French police officers working for the Moroccan secret service. Boukhari was subsequently summoned to appear before the French investigation into Ben Barka's disappearance; however, the Moroccan authorities refused to grant him a passport, and in August he was arrested on charges of financial irregularity. Human rights organizations protested that the Moroccan Government was attempting to prevent Boukhari from testifying at the inquiry. In December 2002 Morocco announced that it would co-operate fully with the French investigation, and in January 2003 a French judge travelled to Rabat to interview Boukhari about the disappearance of the former UNFP leader. In October 2007 the French investigating magistrate in the case issued warrants for the arrest of five Moroccan officials suspected of involvement in the case. However, the release of the warrants was deferred, and in October 2009 it was announced that the release was to be suspended to allow the French authorities to obtain more details on the suspects as required by the International Criminal Police Commission (Interpol). The warrants subsequently lapsed, although in August 2012 it was reported that the French magistrate had made a request to the British police for the arrest of one of the officials, Gen. Hosni Benslimane, the head of the Moroccan royal gendarmerie, who was visiting London in his capacity as chief of Morocco's national committee for the Olympic Games.

In March 2002 the Government agreed a number of changes to the electoral system, including the introduction of proportional representation and a guarantee that at least 10% of the 325 seats in the lower house would be reserved for women. At the election to the Chamber of Representatives in September, the USFP again won the largest number of seats, although its representation was reduced to 50 seats. The UC, by contrast, fared poorly, retaining just 16 seats. Istiqlal performed strongly, winning 48 seats, as did the PJD, which took 42 seats; the RNI returned 41 members, the MP 27, and the Mouvement national populaire (MNP) 18. In October King Muhammad appointed Driss Jettou as Prime Minister, and a new Government was announced the following month. The new Cabinet, which included three women, comprised members of the USFP, Istiqlal, the RNI, the MNP, the MP and the PPS, as well as a number of non-affiliated technocrats.

In May 2003 King Muhammad marked the occasion of the birth of a son and heir to the throne, Prince Moulay Hassan, by ordering the release of an estimated 9,000 prisoners and reducing the gaol terms of a further 38,000.

Suicide attacks in Casablanca

In May 2003 45 people died and more than 100 others were injured in a series of suicide bomb attacks in central Casablanca, which targeted the Belgian consulate, a Spanish restaurant and a Jewish cultural centre. Among those killed were reported to be 12 suicide bombers. Two further presumed attackers were detained by the security forces, along with some 30 others suspected of involvment in the bombings. The Moroccan authorities believed that the bombers were linked to a small Moroccan-based militant Islamist group, al-Assirat al-Moustaquim (Righteous Path), but that the attacks had been orchestrated by an international terrorist network operating in Europe, possibly al-Qa'ida. In late May the suspected co-ordinator of the attacks, who had been arrested in Fez, died in police custody as a result of ill health. At the end of the month stricter anti-terrorism measures were approved by the legislature, including an increase in the number of offences punishable by the death sentence.

In July 2003 10 of 31 alleged members of the radical Islamist group Salafia Jihadia, who had been arrested during police operations against Islamist networks the previous year, were sentenced to death by a court in Casablanca, having been convicted of murder and attempted murder. The remainder of the accused received lengthy prison terms. Later in July it was announced that more than 700 people would be tried in connection with the May bomb attacks; 52 defendants subsequently appeared before Casablanca's criminal court. In August four men, including the two surviving alleged suicide bombers, received death sentences for their part in the violence; 39 others were sentenced to life imprisonment for plotting further attacks in Agadir, Marrakesh and Essaouira. In February 2005 10 men were imprisoned for eight years for membership of Salafia Jihadia, and in July two members of Salafia Jihadia were sentenced to death, having been convicted of the murders of five people in Casablanca. In April 2008 nine of the men convicted for their links to the suicide bombings in Casablanca escaped from prison in Kénitra, north of Rabat. Seven of the fugitives were reportedly serving life sentences, while the other two were serving terms of 20 years. It was reported that seven of the fugitives had been rearrested by the Moroccan security forces by January 2009.

Meanwhile, King Muhammad continued to pursue his policies of reform and modernization of Moroccan society, including provision for the teaching of the Berber language in schools. In October 2003 the King announced major revisions to the *mudawana* (family code), which he claimed would promote female equality and protect children's rights. The reforms (originally outlined in 2000) would raise the legal age of marriage for women from 15 to 18 years, and simplify the procedure for women seeking a divorce from their husband. Although polygamy would not be outlawed under the new legislation, a woman would be able to prevent her husband from taking a second wife, and would also be provided with equal authority and property rights within the marriage. The changes to the *mudawana* were approved by the legislature in January 2004.

In May–June 2006 police arrested more than 500 members of Al-Adl wal-Ihsan (Justice and Charity), an unauthorized but previously tolerated Islamist movement, after unconfirmed reports that it was planning an uprising; most of those detained were quickly released. Al-Adl wal-Ihsan had launched an 'open doors' campaign earlier in 2006 to disseminate information among the general public and recruit new members outside its traditional areas of support such as mosques and universities. In July–August 56 members of the militant Islamist group Ansar al-Mahdi (Helpers of the Mahdi) were arrested on suspicion of planning a campaign of violence against the monarchy. Among those detained were several members of the police and armed forces. In January 2008 the leader of Ansar al-Mahdi, Hassan Khattab, was sentenced to 25 years' imprisonment, while 49 other members of the group received prison terms of between two and 20 years, having been convicted of various crimes, including plotting to attack government buildings and stealing funds to enable them to pursue militant activities.

In March 2007 three people were injured in a suicide bomb attack at an internet café in Casablanca. In April, during a police operation in the city in connection with the recent bombing, three suspected Islamist militants detonated explosive belts; a fourth was shot dead by police as he attempted to do so. Four days later two suicide bombers targeted the US consulate and a US cultural centre in the city. The series of attacks coincided with two large explosions in Algiers, Algeria, that were claimed by the al-Qa'ida Organization in the Land of the Islamic Maghreb (AQIM, formerly the Groupe salafiste pour la prédication et le combat—see the chapter on Algeria). Although an online statement purporting to be from al-Qa'ida claimed responsibility for the explosions in Casablanca, Moroccan police insisted that they were the work of a group with no links to external organizations. In October 2008 more than 40 people received prison sentences, ranging from two to 30 years, for their involvement in the bombings. In February, meanwhile, 32 members of the small Islamist party al-Badil al-Hadari (Alternative Civilization)—including its Secretary-General, Mustapha Moatassim—were arrested on suspicion of plotting to carry out politically motivated attacks. The party was subsequently banned, following the discovery of weapons and in response to allegations of links with international terrorist networks, including al-Qa'ida in Afghanistan. By this time Moroccan police claimed to have dismantled at least 50 terrorist cells and to have made almost 3,000 arrests since the Casablanca suicide bombings in 2003. Extensive anti-terrorism operations continued, with 32 people being imprisoned in October 2008 on charges of recruiting militants to fight in Iraq. In April 2009 43 people were convicted of belonging to terrorist organizations, including AQIM; 29 received prison sentences of between two and 20 years, and the remainder were fined.

At the general election of September 2007, Istiqlal secured the largest number of seats in the Chamber of Representatives, winning 52. The PJD took 46 seats, the MP (which had merged with the MNP and the Union démocratique in 2006) 41, and the RNI 39. The USFP, which previously had the largest number of deputies, retained only 38 seats, while the UC's representation recovered somewhat, to 27 seats. The rate of participation by voters was a record low of 37% of eligible participants. King Muhammad subsequently appointed Abbas el-Fassi, the leader of Istiqlal and Minister of State in the outgoing administration, was as the new Prime Minister, and in October a new

Government comprising Istiqlal, the RNI, the USFP and the PPS, along with several independent ministers, was sworn into office.

A new political organization, the Parti de l'authenticité et de la modernité (PAM), was established in August 2008 by Fouad Ali el-Himma, a former Deputy Minister of the Interior and close ally of King Muhammad. Several existing parties, including the Parti Al Ahd, the Parti de l'environnement et du développement and the PND, joined the new grouping; however, differences quickly emerged, and the former leaders of those parties left the PAM to re-form their previous organizations in 2008–09. In May 2009 the PAM announced that it was to withdraw its support from the governing coalition and align itself with the opposition. It thus presented itself as a viable alternative, despite close links to the King. At the municipal elections in June the PAM won 21.7% of the votes cast, replacing Istiqlal (which took 19.1%) as the major party at municipal level. The RNI obtained 14.8% of the vote and the USFP 11.6%, while the PJD, which secured just 5.5% of the vote, blamed its poor results on vote-buying by its rivals. In June 2010 Abdelilah Benkirane succeeded Saâdeddine el-Othmani as Secretary-General of the PJD.

In early 2010 King Muhammad announced plans to devolve certain powers from central government to local councils. The programme, under the supervision of a newly created Advisory Committee on Regionalization, aimed to provide regional authorities with greater powers to determine their own development plans; it was ongoing in early 2013.

King Muhammad announces political and economic reforms

In February 2011 thousands of Moroccans joined street protests in Rabat and a number of other cities to demand improved living conditions, an end to state corruption, and reform of the country's political system—in particular reduced powers for the monarch. Some youths set themselves alight, in imitation of an act of self-immolation by a Tunisian man in December 2010, which had prompted the popular unrest across the Middle East and North Africa that came to be known as the 'Arab spring'. In Morocco the protesters, including left-wing activists, students and Islamists, coalesced in the February 20 Movement for Change, named after the largest pro-reform demonstrations held in around 20 cities on that date. Although the protests were generally peaceful, five people were reported to have died in a fire started by rioters in al-Hoceima.

On 21 February 2011 King Muhammad inaugurated a new Economic and Social Council (Conseil économique et social—CES—provision for which had been enshrined in the 1992 Constitution), chaired by a former Minister of the Interior, Chakib Benmoussa. The CES was to formulate a new social chapter and to advise the Government on a wide range of socio-economic issues, including the demands of the labour market. In an address to the nation in early March, King Muhammad pledged to implement a review of the Constitution and to introduce other political reforms, notably an independent judiciary, a strengthened role for parliament, provision for the leader of the party with the largest representation in the Chamber of Representatives to form a government, and implementation of the plan to devolve certain powers to Morocco's regional authorities. A constitutional reform committee was subsequently appointed—including among its members representatives of political parties, civil society organizations and trade unions—under the chairmanship of a lawyer, Prof. Abdellatif Menouni, and requested to issue its proposals on possible constitutional amendments by June. Proposed reforms would then be subject to approval in a national referendum. None the less, some members of the February 20 Movement began to demand the dismissal of the Cabinet, and complained that King Muhammad retained excessive influence over the committee's work.

Meanwhile, at the beginning of March increased powers were granted to the Advisory Council on Human Rights, which was renamed the National Human Rights Council and was to investigate alleged human rights violations. Largely peaceful rallies in support of political, social and economic reforms continued during March and April in cities including Rabat, Casablanca and Marrakesh.

From mid-March 2011 many Islamists held in Moroccan prisons on terrorism-related charges joined hunger strikes in protest against what they deemed to be their unfair detention, leading the Ministry of Justice to initiate a dialogue with representatives of the prisoners in order to address their grievances. In April the King ordered the immediate release of 96 prisoners, many of whom were political detainees—among them Mustapha Moatassim, Secretary-General of the banned Islamist organization al-Badil al-Hadari; the prison terms of a further 94 prisoners were reduced.

In late April 2011 17 people were killed (including three Moroccans and eight French nationals) in a bombing at a café known to be popular with foreign tourists in the centre of Marrakesh. AQIM denied responsibility, and the Moroccan authorities stated that they believed the bombing to have been perpetrated by an independent Islamist organization inspired by al-Qa'ida. Trial proceedings against nine Moroccans accused of crimes including committing terrorist acts, the possession and manufacture of explosives, and premeditated murder began in Salé in June. In late October one of the defendants, Adel Othmani, was sentenced to death, having been found guilty of carrying out the Marrakesh bombing; a second defendant convicted of playing a leading role received a life sentence, while the remaining seven—found to have assisted Othmani in carrying out the attack—were given prison terms of between two and four years. In early March 2012, however, an appeals court converted the second defendant's life sentence to a death sentence, increased the prison terms of six of the remaining seven to between six and 10 years, and also confirmed Othmani's death sentence. It was, nevertheless, deemed unlikely that the two death sentences would be carried out, since the 'gradual abolition' of the death penalty was one of the changes being implemented under the King's reform programme.

King Muhammad formally announced his proposed changes to the Constitution in June, having received the findings of the reform committee. These included a notable strengthening of the powers of the Prime Minister, who was to replace the King as head of government and who would henceforth appoint the Cabinet and dissolve the legislature. The King would, however, retain the right to chair meetings of an inner 'royal cabinet', and cabinet appointments would still need his approval. Moreover, he would also retain charge of military, security and religious affairs. As amended, the Constitution would provide for, *inter alia*, the appointment as Prime Minister of the leader of the largest party in the Chamber of Representatives; the designation of Berber as an official language of the state; an increase in the rights of women, who would be granted 'civic and social' as well as 'political' equality; and the creation of a Supreme Security Council, as part of efforts to reduce corruption.

The national referendum on the proposed constitutional changes followed on 1 July 2011. Official results, published on 19 July, showed that 98.5% of participating voters approved the amended Constitution, which was to come into effect after the next parliamentary elections. Voter turn-out was officially recorded at 73.5%. Although all the main political parties had campaigned in favour of the constitutional changes, the amendments failed to satisfy pro-reform activists, who continued to demand a further easing of the King's still far-reaching powers. Moreover, there was some scepticism—particularly among the constituent parties of the February 20 Movement, which had urged voters to boycott the referendum—regarding both the validity of the overwhelming result in favour of the King's reforms, and the high rate of voter participation. Further opposition demonstrations followed the announcement of the outcome of the referendum, with protesters urging the Government to improve its human rights record and to bring corrupt officials to account. Supporters of the monarchy joined large counter-demonstrations.

Recent developments: Morocco's first Islamist-led Government

In August 2011 the Government confirmed that elections to the Chamber of Representatives would be held one year early, on 25 November, in order to allow the newly amended Constitution to take effect. The number of seats in the legislature was to increase from 325 to 395—with 305 seats to be reserved for candidates from local party lists, and the remainder to be allocated to candidates on national lists. Each party would be required to allocate two-thirds of its share of those 90 seats to women and the remaining one-third to men 40 years of age. In October the formally barred Al-Adl wal-Ihsan movement joined other opposition parties in declaring that it would boycott the forthcoming polls, which it expected to be 'fraudulent'. At the elections, the moderate Islamist PJD secured the highest number of seats, winning 107 overall, ahead of Istiqlal, with 60 seats, and the RNI, with 52. The PAM also performed strongly, taking

47 seats. The USFP returned 39 deputies, the MP 32, the UC 23 and the PPS 18. Voter turn-out was recorded at 45.4%.

At the end of November 2011, in accordance with the terms of the revised Constitution, Abdelilah Benkirane, as the leader of the largest party in the Chamber of Representatives, was appointed as Prime Minister-designate. The PJD leader swiftly began discussions with other parties regarding the formation of a broad coalition government, and in mid-December a coalition agreement was signed with Istiqlal, the MP and the PPS (the USFP having declined to join an Islamist-led administration). The new Cabinet was sworn in before the Chamber of Representatives in early January 2012, the PJD becoming the first Islamist party to lead Morocco's Government. Saâdeddine el-Othmani, the former PJD leader, was named as Minister of Foreign Affairs and Co-operation; Nizar Baraka, of Istiqlal, as Minister of the Economy and Finance, and Mohand Laenser, of the MP, as Minister of the Interior. The independent Minister-delegate in charge of National Defence, Abdellatif Loudiyi, retained his post. Among the stated key aims of Benkirane's Government, which won a parliamentary vote of confidence at the end of the month, were measures to tackle poverty and corruption, reduce unemployment, particularly high rates of joblessness among young people, and stimulate economic growth. Meanwhile, also in December 2011 Karim Ghellab, of Istiqlal, had been appointed to succeed the USFP's Abdelwahed Radi as President of the Chamber of Representatives.

Social issues continued to dominate the domestic political agenda under the new administration. At the end of May 2012 trade unions organized a mass demonstration in Casablanca to protest against the Government's perceived inaction in implementing substantive reforms, and to demand higher salaries and improved social conditions. The number of demonstrators was officially stated to be 15,000–20,000, although the organizers put the total at 50,000. The February 20 Movement led a protest March in Rabat in late July, involving some 3,000 demonstrators. At the end of July, in a speech marking the anniversary of his accession, King Muhammad pledged to continue to pursue the programme of political and social reform; he also emphasized the moderate identity of Islam in Morocco. In the same month three prominent ultra-conservative Salafist clerics announced their support for an edict (*fatwa*), issued by an imam in Oujda, seeking the death of Mokhtar el-Ghzioui, the editor of *Al-Ahdath al-Maghribia* newspaper; el-Ghzioui had, in a televised debate in June, expressed support for the decriminalization of pre-marital sex. In January 2013 the Ministry of Justice and Liberties announced its support for proposals to amend a provision of the penal code whereby, in the case of rape of a minor, the perpetrator could in effect evade prosecution by marrying the victim under 'special circumstances'; the ministry also indicated that it would consider amending the code to require longer prison sentences for the rape of a minor. Article 475 of the penal code had come to prominence following the suicide, in March 2012, of a 16-year-old girl who had been coerced into marriage following rape. Women's and human rights groups welcomed the proposed changes, but stated that further reforms of the code were needed to protect women against discrimination and violence.

Meanwhile, addressing the opening session of the legislature in October 2012, King Muhammad emphasized the importance of the parliament's role in pursuing democratic reform through measures to promote good governance, the independence of the judiciary, regionalization and the granting of offial status to the Berber language. Earlier in October, more than 2,000 members of the judiciary had joined an unauthorized protest in Rabat to demand guarantees of an independent judicial system and an end to official interference in the profession.

A mass protest took place in Rabat at the end of March 2013, led by trade unionists, human rights activists, members of the February 20 Movement and representatives of civil society, to demand economic and social reforms, and to protest against continuing high rates of unemployment and living costs; some demonstrators demanded the removal from office of Prime Minister Benkirane. Unofficial reports put the number of demonstrators at 30,000, while police stated that 3,000 people had taken part in a peaceful march to the parliament building. The Government's announcement, in early April, that it was to defer some 15,000m. dirhams in investment spending, in an effort to address the public deficit, drew immediate criticism from its opponents, despite assurances by the Minister of the Economy and Finance, Nizar Baraka, that employment and social measures would not be affected. In early May Istiqlal announced its withdrawal from the coalition Government, criticizing

Benkirane for monopolizing decisions within the Cabinet and his Government for pursuing policies that raised consumer prices. However, following a subsequent intervention by King Muhammad, the party revoked its decision, citing a desire to maintain stability and to serve the interests of the country.

Western Sahara

Following the cession of the Spanish enclave of Ifni to Morocco in 1969, political opinion in Morocco was united in opposing the continued occupation by Spain of areas considered to be historically parts of Moroccan territory: namely Spanish Sahara and Spanish North Africa (q.v.)—a number of small enclaves on Morocco's Mediterranean coast. A campaign to annex Spanish Sahara, initiated in 1974, received active support from all Moroccan political parties. In October 1975 King Hassan ordered a 'Green March' by more than 300,000 unarmed Moroccans to occupy the territory. The marchers were stopped by the Spanish authorities when they had barely crossed the border, but in November Spain agreed to cede the territory to Morocco and Mauritania, to be apportioned equally between them. Spain formally relinquished sovereignty of Spanish Sahara in February 1976. Moroccan troops moved into the territory to confront a guerrilla uprising led by the Frente Popular para la Liberación de Saguia el-Hamra y Río de Oro (the Polisario Front), a national liberation movement supported by Algeria and (later) Libya, which aimed to achieve an independent Western Saharan state. Polisario declared the 'Sahrawi Arab Democratic Republic' (SADR) on 27 February, and shortly afterwards established a 'Government-in-exile' in Algeria. In protest, Morocco severed diplomatic relations with Algeria.

Moroccan troops inflicted heavy casualties on the insurgents, but failed to prevent constant infiltration, harassment and sabotage by Polisario forces. After Mauritania renounced its claim to Saharan territory and signed a peace treaty with the Polisario Front in August 1979, Morocco immediately asserted its claim to the whole of Western Sahara and annexed the region.

In July 1980 the SADR applied to join the Organization of African Unity (OAU, now African Union—AU, see p. 191) as a sovereign state. Although 26 of the 50 members then recognized the Polisario Front as the rightful government of Western Sahara, Morocco insisted that a two-thirds' majority was needed to confer membership. Morocco rejected an OAU proposal for a cease-fire and a referendum on the territory, and heavy fighting resumed in the region in 1981. The SADR was accepted as the OAU's 51st member in early 1982, but a threat by 18 members to leave the organization in protest necessitated a compromise whereby the SADR remained as a member but agreed not to attend meetings. In late 1984 a SADR delegation did attend a summit meeting of the OAU with little opposition from other states, causing Morocco to resign from the organization. Meanwhile, Morocco constructed a 2,500-km defensive wall of sand, equipped with electronic detectors, to surround the territory of Western Sahara.

In October 1985 Morocco announced a unilateral cease-fire in Western Sahara, and invited the UN to supervise a referendum (then scheduled to be held in the territory in the following January). A series of indirect talks between the two sides in 1986–87 failed to make progress, and in January 1988 Polisario forces renewed their offensive against Moroccan positions in Western Sahara. In August, however, it was announced that the Polisario Front and Morocco had provisionally accepted a UN-proposed peace plan, which envisaged the conclusion of a formal cease-fire, a reduction in Moroccan military forces in Western Sahara and the withdrawal of Polisario forces to their bases, to be followed by a referendum on self-determination in Western Sahara. A list of eligible voters was to be based on the Spanish census of 1974. A meeting in Marrakesh in January 1989 between King Hassan and officials of the Polisario Front and the SADR—the first direct contact for 13 years—was followed, in February, by the announcement of a unilateral cease-fire by Polisario. In September, however, Hassan rejected the possibility of official negotiations with the SADR, and Polisario subsequently renewed attacks on Moroccan positions.

UN Security Council Resolution 690, of April 1991, established a peace-keeping force, the UN Mission for the Referendum in Western Sahara (MINURSO, see p. 89), which was to implement the 1988 plan for a referendum on self-determination. In June 1991 Polisario agreed to a formal cease-fire, with effect from September, whereupon the MINURSO force, with an initial envisaged strength of 2,000 troops, would deploy in the region. Morocco, for its part, would withdraw one-half of its 130,000 troops from Western Sahara by mid-September. Reports that

month suggested that some 30,000 people had entered Western Sahara from Morocco, prompting claims that the Moroccan authorities were attempting to alter the region's demography in advance of the referendum. It was also reported that more than 170,000 Sahrawis who had fled the region since 1976 were being repatriated in order that they might participate in the referendum. By November 1991 only 200 MINURSO personnel had been deployed in Western Sahara, while Morocco had not withdrawn any of its forces from the region. In May 1992 the UN Secretary-General, Dr Boutros Boutros-Ghali, announced that Morocco and Polisario representatives were to begin indirect talks under his auspices. In the same month, however, Morocco appeared to prejudge the result of the proposed referendum by including the population of Western Sahara in the voting lists for its own regional and local elections. In June the SADR Government, which by this time was recognized by 75 countries, appealed to the international community and the UN to condemn alleged Moroccan violations of the cease-fire and to exert pressure for the implementation of the UN peace plan.

In July 1993 the first direct negotiations took place between the Moroccan Government and Polisario, although little progress was achieved. In April 1994 Polisario accepted the UN programme for the registration of voters. However, the work of a UN voter identification commission, which had been due to commence in June, was delayed by the Moroccan Government's objection to the inclusion of OAU observers in the process. In mid-1995 Polisario withdrew from the voter identification process, in protest against the severity of sentences placed upon pro-independence Sahrawi protesters by the Moroccan authorities and against alleged Moroccan violations of the cease-fire. In September the SADR announced the formation of a new 14-member Government, headed by Mahfoud Ali Beïba, and in October the first elected Sahrawi national council was inaugurated at a refugee camp in Tindouf, Algeria. In May 1996 the UN Security Council voted to suspend the registration of voters in Western Sahara until 'convincing proof' was offered by the Moroccan Government and the Sahrawi leadership that they would not further obstruct preparations for the referendum.

In March 1997 the new UN Secretary-General, Kofi Annan, appointed James Baker (a former US Secretary of State) as his Personal Envoy for Western Sahara. By September 1998 a total of 147,350 voters had been identified since the commencement of the process of identification in August 1994, but the issue of disputed tribes remained unresolved. In June 1998, meanwhile, as Morocco intensified its efforts to rejoin the OAU, several member states debated the expulsion from the organization of the SADR; only a minority of OAU member countries continued to recognize its independent status at this time.

During talks with Moroccan and SADR officials in November 1998, the UN Secretary-General warned that the UN would withdraw from Western Sahara if the two parties failed to show political will towards resolving the conflict. Annan presented proposals regarding the disputed tribes, the publication of a list of voters not contested by either party, and the repatriation of refugees under the auspices of the UN High Commissioner for Refugees (UNHCR). Although the proposals were accepted by Polisario, the Moroccan authorities expressed reservations. In July 1999 MINURSO published a list of 84,251 people provisionally entitled to vote in the referendum, which was scheduled to be held on 31 July 2000.

In February 1999, meanwhile, the SADR announced the formation of a new Government, led by Beïba's predecessor, Bouchraya Hammoudi Bayoune. In September the Polisario Front congress re-elected the President of the SADR, Muhammad Abd al-Aziz, as its Secretary-General. In September King Muhammad established a royal commission to monitor affairs in Western Sahara, and in October, at the King's behest, a Moroccan Government delegation was dispatched to el-Aaiún (Laâyoune), the principal city in Western Sahara, for consultations. Polisario released 191 Moroccan prisoners in November. In January 2000 it was announced that 86,381 of a total of 198,481 people identified in Western Sahara would be eligible to vote in the referendum. However, in February the UN Secretary-General postponed the referendum indefinitely: Annan warned that persistent differences regarding criteria for eligibility to vote it meant that the referendum might never take place. By March the number of appeals lodged by those deemed ineligible to vote exceeded 130,000. In October Annan urged Morocco partially to devolve authority in Western Sahara, stating that if no concessions were granted in this regard, the UN would reactivate referendum plans. In February 2001 he further announced that if Morocco failed to offer or support some devolution of governmental authority, MINURSO would be directed to begin the process of hearing appeals regarding eligibility to vote.

In June 2001 the UN Security Council unanimously approved a compromise resolution (No. 1359), that encouraged Polisario and Morocco to discuss an autonomy plan for Western Sahara without abandoning the postponed referendum. Under the autonomy proposal, formulated by Baker, the inhabitants of Western Sahara would have the right to elect their own legislative and executive bodies; the territory would control most areas of local government for a period of at least five years, during which Morocco would retain control over defence and foreign affairs. A referendum on final status would take place within this five-year period. Representatives of Polisario, Mauritania and Algeria attended talks hosted by Baker in Wyoming, USA, in August; however, Polisario subsequently accused the UN of ceding to Moroccan pressure, and in September Polisario announced its formal rejection of Baker's proposal. King Muhammad visited Western Sahara in October, for the first time since his accession to the throne, and in November granted an amnesty to 56 prisoners there.

Following exploratory negotiations held between Baker and government officials in Mauritania and Algeria, as well as with Abd al-Aziz and King Muhammad, in May 2003 Kofi Annan formally released details of a new peace plan for Western Sahara. Baker Plan II proposed immediate self-government for Western Sahara for a period of four to five years, after which time a referendum would be held in order to give all bona fide residents the opportunity to decide the long-term future of the territory. The UN Security Council approved the proposals in June. Polisario, under strong pressure from Algeria, accepted the plan as a basis for negotiation, but Morocco refused to accept any 'imposed decision' on Western Sahara. At the end of July the Security Council unanimously adopted Resolution 1495, which supported Baker Plan II and urged the parties and states of the region to co-operate fully with the Secretary-General and his Personal Envoy towards its implementation. (Notably, however, following strong opposition from France, the resolution did not demand that Morocco and Polisario comply with the plan.) The resolution also called on Polisario to release without further delay all remaining Moroccan prisoners of war, and for both sides to co-operate with the International Committee of the Red Cross to resolve the fate of persons unaccounted for since the beginning of the conflict. Polisario released 243 Moroccan prisoners of war in September, 300 in November, and a further 100 in February 2004.

In April 2004 the UN Security Council unanimously adopted Resolution 1541, which urged the two sides to accept the UN plan to grant Western Sahara immediate self-government. Morocco, however, continued to reject this proposal, maintaining that it could not accept a referendum plan that included independence as an option; instead, it insisted on granting the territory 'autonomy within the framework of Moroccan sovereignty'. In June James Baker resigned as Annan's Personal Envoy for Western Sahara; his responsibilities were taken on by Álvaro de Soto, of Peru, who had hitherto been the Secretary-General's Special Representative for Western Sahar. In September de Soto commenced talks with the Moroccan authorities and Polisario, and a resolution (No. 1570) adopted by the Security Council in October calling for an advancement towards a political solution was welcomed by the Moroccan authorities. In July 2005 Annan appointed Peter van Walsum, of the Netherlands, as his new Personal Envoy for Western Sahara, and in August it was announced that Francesco Bastagli, of Italy, would replace de Soto as Special Representative of the Secretary-General and MINURSO Chief of Mission. Later that month Polisario released the remaining 408 Moroccan prisoners of war, some of whom had been held in Tindouf for more than 20 years. In a televised address to mark the 30th anniversary of the Green March, King Muhammad announced his intention to consult with Morocco's political parties on the issue of autonomy for Western Sahara 'within the sovereignty of the kingdom'. However, Polisario immediately rejected the plan, and stated that a referendum was the only viable solution.

During a visit to Western Sahara in March 2006, King Muhammad announced the appointment of a revised Royal Advisory Council for Saharan Affairs (CORCAS—originally established by his father in 1981). The 140 newly appointed members were to assist with the formulation of draft proposals for Sahrawi autonomy. Royal pardons were granted to 216

Sahrawi prisoners, and in April the King ordered the release of all the remaining 48 Sahrawi prisoners held by Morocco. In a report submitted to the UN Security Council in that month, Annan noted the demise of Baker Plan II, which had not been mentioned in any of the pertinent Security Council resolutions since Morocco rejected the proposal in 2004, and called on all parties in the dispute, including Algeria, to engage in direct negotiations without preconditions in order to reach a consensual solution to the impasse. In February 2007 the new UN Secretary-General, Ban Ki-Moon, appointed Julian Harston, of the United Kingdom, as his Special Representative in Western Sahara and MINURSO Chief of Mission.

The 'Moroccan initiative for negotiating an autonomy statute for the Sahara region' was finally presented to the UN Security Council in April 2007. It proposed the granting of extensive legislative, executive and judicial autonomy to the region, with Morocco retaining sovereignty and control of borders, as well as responsibility for national security, and foreign and religious affairs, among other areas. The plan was rejected as 'null and void' by Polisario, which immediately offered the UN a rival plan for a referendum with three options—full independence, autonomy within Morocco or full integration—including proposals for a special political and economic relationship with Morocco in the event of a vote for independence. At the end of April the Security Council unanimously adopted Resolution 1754, which described Morocco's plan as 'serious and credible', while also noting the Polisario proposal, and again called on both sides to enter into direct negotiations, without preconditions, under the aegis of the Secretary-General. UN-mediated talks between Morocco and Polisario (attended by representatives of Algeria and Mauritania) took place in June and August in Manhasset, New York, USA; these were followed by two further rounds of negotiations in January and March 2008. While the talks failed to achieve any significant progress, Moroccan officials and Polisario agreed to consider relaxing restrictions on people travelling by road to visit families in the disputed territory. Resolution 1813, adopted by the Security Council in April 2008, emphasized the legitimacy of the Moroccan autonomy proposal.

A renewed UN effort to facilitate another round of peace talks began in January 2009 with the appointment of Christopher Ross, of the USA, as Personal Envoy to the Secretary-General for Western Sahara. In April the Security Council approved Resolution 1871, reiterating the principles of the previous year's resolution. In July Ban Ki-Moon appointed Hany Abd al-Aziz, of Egypt, as Special Representative for Western Sahara and MINURSO Chief of Mission, in succession to Harston. Informal talks took place between representatives of Polisario and the Moroccan Government in Vienna, Austria, in August. However, tensions arose in October when seven Sahrawi human rights activists were arrested in Casablanca and charged with making contact with parties hostile to Morocco after they had visited Sahrawi refugee camps in Tindouf. In November a prominent Sahrawi activist, Aminatou Haidar, was expelled to the Canary Islands, Spain, having refused to declare Moroccan nationality upon returning to Western Sahara from the USA. Following a 32-day hunger strike by Haidar, the Moroccan authorities reversed their decision and allowed her to return to el-Aaiún.

Informal discussions between representatives of the Moroccan Government and Polisario were held under UN auspices in Armonk, USA, in February 2010, but ended without substantive agreement. UN Security Council 1920, adopted in April, welcomed progress towards direct negotiations. In May Polisario officials announced that they were suspending contact with MINURSO, because of its failure to implement the referendum on self-determination, and accused the UN mission of supporting Morocco's occupation of Western Sahara. The Moroccan Government, in contrast, expressed its satisfaction that the UN continued to place the focus of bilateral negotiations on Morocco's autonomy proposal. Another round of informal talks (with Algerian and Mauritanian participation) was held in Manhasset in November. Despite a negative assessment of the talks by Polisario representatives, there had reportedly been agreement on the convening of future talks and on ways to resume confidence-building measures. Meanwhile, there were violent demonstrations in el-Aaiún, after Moroccan security forces forcibly entered a camp close to the city, where a large group of displaced Sahrawis had for several weeks been protesting against social and economic conditions in the territory. According to UN reporting, 11 members of the Moroccan security forces and two Sahrawis (one a minor) were killed, and corpses were mutilated. (In February 2013 a military tribunal in Rabat sentenced nine Sahrawi civilians to life imprisonment for their part in the violence.)

A sixth round of UN-sponsored informal talks took place in Valletta, Malta, in March 2011. UN Security Council Resolution 1979, adopted in April, notably emphasized the importance of improving the human rights situation in Western Sahara and the Tindouf camps, and welcomed Morocco's establishment of its National Human Rights Council (see King Muhammad announces political and economic reforms) with a proposed component concerning Western Sahara. It was reported that further discussions held under UN auspices in June and July 2011 had failed to break the deadlock between Morocco and Polisario. Meanwhile, in June there were reports that a group of young Sahrawis had formed a rival movement to the Polisario Front, to be based in Spain, amid frustration over the failure of the Front to further the negotiations. Muhammad Abd al-Aziz was re-elected as Secretary-General of the Polisario Front and a new SADR Government was formed in January 2012. In mid-February voting took place in refugee camps in western Algeria and in what Polisario termed 'liberated' territories of Western Sahara for the SADR national council; when the council convened in Tifariti at the end of the month, Khatri Adduh was elected as its speaker for a second term.

A ninth round of informal talks was held in Manhasset in early March 2012. The UN Secretary-General's report to the Security Council, published in early April, expressed some frustration at the perceived obstruction of MINURSO's operations by Morocco. At the end of the month the Security Council adopted Resolution 2044, which, among other remarks, welcomed the commencement of operations by commissions of the Moroccan National Council on Human Rights in el-Aaiún and Dakhla, and anticipated the inauguration—as part of confidence-building measures adopted under UNHCR auspices in Geneva, Switzerland, in January—of family visits by land, the continuation and expansion of the existing programme of visits by air, and the facilitation of advanced communication links between families. In mid-June Wolfgang Weisbrod-Weber, of Germany, was appointed to succeed Abd al-Aziz as Special Representative of the UN Secretary-General and MINURSO Chief of Mission.

Progress towards further UN-sponsored talks, planned for June and July 2012, was impeded after the Moroccan Government, in May, withdrew confidence in Christopher Ross, accusing the Secretary-General's Personal Envoy of bias, and holding him responsible for the impasse in negotiations. A third meeting of representatives of Morocco, Polisario, Algeria and Mauritania to discuss confidence-building measures was, meanwhile, convened in Geneva in September. Eventually—and following intervention by Ban Ki-Moon, who spoke via telephone with King Muhammad in August—Ross resumed mediation, and, during a visit to the region in October–November, made his first visit to Western Sahara. In early April 2013, in his annual report to the UN Security Council regarding Western Sahara, Ban noted that Ross had secured the continued commitment of both the Moroccan Government and Polisario, as well as neighbouring states, to remain engaged in the UN-sponsored effort. However, it had been agreed that, since Morocco and Polisario remained 'strongly attached' to their respective proposals, and had yet to consider possible compromises, to convene further informal talks in the near future would not advance the negotiating process. Ross made a second visit in March–April 2013, and further visits were envisaged, with a view to the commencement of bilateral consultations. In mid-April, prior to the annual Security Council vote to extend the MINURSO mission, Morocco cancelled scheduled joint military exercises involving some 1,400 US and 900 Moroccan personnel, following a proposal by the USA to expand the mandate of the peace-keeping force to encompass monitoring and investigation of human rights issues in Western Sahara. The Moroccan Government stated that such an extension of MINURSO's remit would represent an attack on Morocco's national sovereignty, and would have 'negative consequences' for regional stability. The final text of Resolution 2099, adopted unanimously in late April, included a compromise wording that encouraged parties to the conflict to continue their respective efforts to enhance the promotion and protection of human rights in Western Sahara and the refugee camps; and recognized and welcomed steps taken by Morocco to strengthen operations of the commissions of the National Council on Human Rights in this regard, together with Morocco's ongoing interaction with the UN Human Rights Council. With the adoption of the resolution, MINURSO's mandate was extended for a further year.

Foreign Affairs
Regional relations

Relations with other North African states, which had been strained by the situation in Western Sahara, improved significantly in the late 1980s. Morocco re-established diplomatic relations with Mauritania in April 1985 (they had been suspended in 1981) and with Algeria in May 1988. In February 1989 North African heads of state, meeting in Marrakesh, signed a treaty establishing the Union du Maghreb arabe (UMA—Union of the Arab Maghreb, see p. 464). The new body, grouping Morocco, Algeria, Libya, Mauritania and Tunisia, aimed to promote trade by allowing the free movement of goods, services and workers. However, there were political disagreements particularly concerning Algeria's continued support for the Polisario Front, and over Moroccan condemnation of Iraq's invasion of Kuwait in August 1990. In early 1993 the five UMA members decided that there should be a 'pause' in the development of a closer union; of 15 conventions signed since the inauguration of the UMA, none had been fully applied. However, the organization continued to hold meetings on an annual basis. In December 1995 King Hassan expressed disapproval at Algeria's continued support for the independence of Western Sahara, and demanded that UMA activities be suspended.

During 1999 and 2000 both President Zine al-Abidine Ben Ali of Tunisia and King Muhammad pledged to take measures to reactivate the UMA. A summit meeting of ministers responsible for foreign affairs of the five UMA states proceeded in the Algerian capital in March 2001. However, the meeting, which was to have made preparations for the first summit meeting of UMA heads of state since 1995, quickly broke down following disagreements between Moroccan and Algerian representatives. Libya assumed the chairmanship of the UMA in December 2003, and a summit meeting of the UMA heads of state was planned to take place in Tripoli, Libya, in May 2005. However, a statement of renewed support for the Polisario Front by the Algerian President, Abdelaziz Bouteflika, provoked a fresh dispute between Morocco and Algeria days before the meeting was due to begin, and King Muhammad declined to attend. Despite the ongoing failure to convene an official UMA summit, a meeting was held in Tangier in April 2008 to celebrate the 50th anniversary of the first proposal of a union of Arab states in the Maghreb; this was attended by both the Prime Ministers of both Morocco and Algeria, along with delegates from the three other UMA member states. The meeting ended amicably, with renewed appeals for regional political and economic co-operation. Ministers responsible for foreign affairs from the UMA member states met again in Tripoli a year later.

The developments arising from the mass protests across the region from the end of 2010 and subsequent changes of government apparently led to the furthering of co-operation between the countries of the Maghreb. Following the ousting of President Ben Ali in January 2011, the new Tunisian Government offered to host a UMA summit meeting in Tunis; and representatives of the five member states attended what was reported as the first meeting for 18 years of the UMA Monitoring Committee of ministers responsible for foreign affairs, which took place in Rabat in February 2012. A meeting of central bank governors and ministers of the UMA countries was held in Nouakchott, Mauritania, in January 2013, attended by the Managing Director of the IMF, Christine Lagarde, at which the establishment was announced of a UMA investment bank to finance, in partnership with the private sector, infrastructural development projects for the region. UMA ministers of the interior met in Rabat in April for discussions on regional security.

Efforts were made to normalize relations between Morocco and Algeria from the late 1990s, although the Western Sahara issue continued to be a particular source of tension, and the border, closed in 1994, remained unopened. Algeria's President, Abdelaziz Bouteflika, was vocal in opposing the UN proposals for Western Sahara in mid-2001, which he claimed unduly favoured Morocco. Morocco asserted that Algerian support for the partition of Western Sahara risked destabilizing the region; for its part, Algeria accused Morocco of blocking a UN-sponsored solution to the Western Sahara issue. During a visit to Algiers by the Moroccan Minister of Foreign Affairs and Co-operation in June 2003, it was agreed to establish three bilateral commissions to consider political, economic and social matters. Following talks in July 2004 between the Moroccan Minister of the Interior and his Algerian counterpart, the two countries signalled their desire to improve diplomatic relations. In May 2005, however, Bouteflika issued a statement renewing Algeria's support for the

Polisario Front, and in October allegations by Polisario that Morocco had abandoned African migrants in the Western Saharan desert further increased tensions between the two countries. Prime Minister Driss Jettou accused Algeria of instigating the allegations, and claimed that Algeria had exacerbated the problem by allowing some illegal immigrants to establish camps close to their joint border. In April 2009, at the Tripoli meeting of UMA ministers of foreign affairs, the Moroccan minister declared his country's readiness to renew bilateral relations with Algeria. In July 2010 King Muhammad sent a senior Moroccan delegation to the Algerian capital to express his nation's condolences following the death of President Bouteflika's brother; he also pledged to seek 'reconciliation and solidarity' between the two countries. During 2011 officials from both countries continued to express their hopes for a swift normalization of relations. Morocco's newly appointed Minister of Foreign Affairs and Co-operation, Saâdeddine el-Othmani, visited Algiers in January 2012 for talks with his Algerian counterpart, Mourad Medelci, and with President Bouteflika. In April it was reported that the new Moroccan Prime Minister, Abdelilah Benkirane, had left the funeral of the first President of independent Algeria, Ahmed Ben Bella, on the instruction of King Muhammad, after discovering that the Polisario leader, Muhammad Abd al-Aziz, was also present. None the less, relations in general continued to improve throughout the year. In April 2013 Morocco's Minister of the Interior, Mohand Laenser, visited Algiers for talks with his counterpart, Dahou Ould Kablia; and, following the Rabat meeting of UMA interior ministers later in the month, Kablia stated that the issue of the two countries' joint border could soon be resolved.

Morocco participated in the international coalition force, led by the North Atlantic Treaty Organisation (NATO, see p. 380), established in March 2011 to protect Libyan civilians from attack by armed forces loyal to Libyan leader Col Muammar al-Qaddafi. Following the ousting of Qaddafi in August, and the capture and killing of the Libyan leader by opposition fighters in October, the Moroccan Government offered its support to the National Transitional Council that assumed power in Libya.

From the late 1990s Morocco was actively involved in wider regional integration efforts, as a member of the Community of Sahel-Saharan States (CEN-SAD, see p. 460), and also through bilateral and multilateral free trade arrangements; in May 2001, notably, the Governments of Morocco, Iraq, Jordan and Tunisia agreed, at a meeting in Agadir, to establish a free trade zone.

In September 1994 Morocco became only the second Arab country (after Egypt) to establish direct links with Israel; liaison offices were subsequently opened in Rabat and Tel-Aviv, Israel. In March 1997, however, in condemnation of recent Israeli settlement policy, ministers of foreign affairs of the League of Arab States (the Arab League, see p. 372) recommended a number of sanctions against Israel, including the closure of representative missions. Although in January 2000 Morocco and Israel agreed in principle to upgrade diplomatic relations to ambassadorial level, in October, as the crisis in Israeli–Palestinian relations deepened, Morocco announced that it had closed down Israel's liaison office in Rabat and its own representative office in Tel-Aviv. There was widespread outrage in Morocco in response to the Israeli military offensive in Palestinian-controlled areas of the West Bank from March 2002. Public demonstrations also took place in January 2009 in response to the military campaign launched by Israel against Islamic Resistance Movement (Hamas) targets in the Gaza Strip in December 2008. In October 2010 King Muhammad declined the possibility of holding discussions with the Israeli President, Shimon Peres, who was visiting Morocco to attend a meeting of the World Economic Forum. As Israeli-Palestinian talks within the context of the Middle East peace process remained at an impasse, the King cited his frustration over the Israeli Government's continued refusal to halt its settlement expansion programme.

Morocco's relations with Iran deteriorated abruptly in February 2009, after King Muhammad joined regional and international leaders in condemning a speech by Ali Akbar Nateq Nouri, a senior political figure in Iran, in which he described Bahrain as a former province of Iran; the remark was widely interpreted as an attack on Bahrain's sovereignty. Morocco's chargé d'affaires was recalled from Iran in late February—having apparently been the only diplomat to be summoned by the Iranian authorities to explain their country's response to the incident—and in March Morocco announced the suspension of diplomatic relations with Iran. Furthermore, Iran was also accused of interfering in the religious unity of Morocco through its promotion of Shi'a Islam in the mainly Sunni country. Bilateral relations had not been re-established by April 2013.

In May 2011, amid unprecedented political and social unrest occurring across large parts of the Middle East and North Africa, Morocco was formally, and apparently unexpectedly, invited (with Jordan) to apply to join the Cooperation Council of the Arab States of the Gulf (Gulf Cooperation Council—GCC, see p. 255). It remained uncertain thereafter whether Morocco would proceed with an application for membership. In December GCC member states created a development fund, offering both Morocco and Jordan an initial aid payment of US $2,500m.

Other external relations

Morocco signed an association agreement with the European Union (EU, see p. 281) in 1996, which provided for greater political and economic co-operation, financial aid, and the eventual establishment of a free trade zone. In October 2008, following more than eight years of negotiations, and in recognition of the Government's programme of social and political reforms, Morocco became the first Maghreb country to be accorded 'advanced status' relations with the EU. The new status was expected to enable Morocco to attract more European investment and financial aid, as well as allow Moroccan participation in some EU agencies and committees.

In 2007 Nicolas Sarkozy, during his election campaign for the French presidency, proposed the establishment of a Mediterranean Union to foster economic, political and cultural links between Mediterranean states. The initiative was described by Sarkozy as building on the Barcelona Process launched by Euro-Mediterranean ministers responsible for foreign affairs in November 1995. The project—by now renamed the Union for the Mediterranean, and encompassing 43 countries, including all 27 EU member states—was formally inaugurated in Paris, France, in July 2008. In April, meanwhile, Morocco and France signed a number of agreements aimed at consolidating bilateral economic and social co-operation. A further 11 co-operation accords were signed in July 2010, including an agreement concerning French assistance to Morocco in the field of nuclear energy. France also pledged €600m. in financial assistance for 2010–12, in support of Morocco's ongoing reform programme. Addressing the Moroccan parliament during a visit to Morocco in early April 2013—in the course of which he met with King Muhammad and Prime Minister Benkirane—President François Hollande of France commended what he termed Morocco's 'decisive steps' towards democracy, noting the country's stability and the tolerance guaranteed by the constitutional amendments of 2011. With particular reference to the Islamist-led revolt in northern Mali (q.v.), Hollande emphasized the importance of achieving a resolution of the Western Sahara issue, stating that the situation was detrimental to families separated by the conflict, to its refugees, and to relations within the Maghreb. King Muhammad, for his part, expressed support for the French military intervention in Mali. Bilateral investment accords signed during Hollande's visit were valued at an estimated €300m. Later in the month France supported Morocco in its opposition to US-led efforts within the UN Security Council to extend the MINURSO mandate to including monitoring of human rights issues (see Western Sahara).

Following the approval by the Spanish parliament of statutes of autonomy for the enclaves of Ceuta and Melilla, in February 1995 Morocco intensified its diplomatic campaign to obtain sovereignty over the territories. In January 1998 the two countries established a joint commission to examine security issues, including illegal immigration (to Spain) and drugs-trafficking. In August 1999 Prime Minister el-Youssoufi urged a review of the statutes of Ceuta and Melilla; however, Spain asserted that no Moroccan sovereignty claims with regard to this issue would be considered. The Spanish premier, José María Aznar, visited Morocco in May 2000, and in September, during King Muhammad's first visit to Spain since his accession, two economic co-operation agreements were signed. Nevertheless, relations remained strained owing to lack of progress in negotiations with the EU regarding a new fisheries accord and attacks by Spanish fishermen on lorries carrying Moroccan products through Spanish ports.

In July 2001, in an attempt to limit the increasing number of Moroccans entering Spain illegally, the two countries signed an agreement that would allow as many as 20,000 Moroccans to enter Spain each year in search of employment. In September, however, Spain refuted allegations made by King Muhammad that Spanish criminal associations were responsible for the large increase in numbers of Moroccan economic migrants attempting illegally to cross the Strait of Gibraltar, asserting that collusion between Moroccan police and the smugglers was ongoing. Morocco subsequently recalled its ambassador from Spain. Moroccan–Spanish relations were further strained in July 2002, when a small detachment of Moroccan troops occupied the uninhabited rocky islet of Perejil (called Leila by Morocco), west of the Spanish enclave of Ceuta and close to the Moroccan coastline. Morocco claimed that it was establishing a surveillance post on the island as part of its campaign against illegal emigration and drugs-smuggling. However, Spain insisted that there had been an agreement since 1990 that neither country would occupy Perejil, and, with the support of the EU and NATO, demanded the immediate evacuation of Moroccan troops from the island. Spain's ambassador to Morocco was recalled, and Spanish special forces intervened and forcibly removed Moroccan troops from Perejil. Spanish forces withdrew from the island following US mediation, and talks in Rabat later that month between the Moroccan and Spanish ministers responsible for foreign affairs resulted in an agreement to return to the *status quo ante*. In January 2003 King Muhammad temporarily allowed Spanish boats to fish in Moroccan waters, and in the following month the two countries agreed to the return of their respective ambassadors.

In December 2003 Morocco and Spain announced plans to construct a 39-km underwater rail tunnel between the two countries. However, although the feasibility study for the project—the scheduled completion date of which was 2025—was concluded by late 2010, no final decision on whether or not to proceed with the plans had been made by early 2013. Meanwhile, in December 2011 the Moroccan Government responded to a decision by the EU not to renew the annual agreement whereby member states paid Morocco for licences to fish in its waters by announcing that EU fishing vessels were no longer permitted to fish off the Moroccan coast. The EU claimed that the current arrangement did not take into consideration the population of Western Sahara, from where most of the fishing took place. Negotiations for a new fisheries protocol were ongoing in early 2013.

In March 2004 a series of bomb attacks on commuter trains in the Spanish capital, Madrid, killed 191 people. A number of Moroccans from the Groupe islamique combattant marocain, who had also been linked with the Casablanca bombings of 2003, were among a group of suspected militant Islamists detained by the Spanish authorities in connection with the attacks, and in December 2004 a Moroccan man, Hassan al-Haski, was charged with having planned the bombings. (Al-Haski was sentenced to 14 years' imprisonment in Spain for his involvement in the Madrid bombings, and, following his extradition to Morocco in 2008, was also convicted of involvement in the Casablanca bombings and sentenced to 10 years' imprisonment.) In May 2004 Morocco and Spain announced plans to establish a joint task force to tackle terrorism and organized crime. However, relations were again strained in mid-2005, after several delegations of Spanish politicians and journalists, seeking to conduct investigations following demonstrations in Western Sahara, were accused by Morocco of supporting Sahrawi independence and were permission to enter the disputed territory.

In September–October 2005 at least 11 African migrants were reported to have died while attempting to enter Ceuta and Melilla illegally. Four were shot dead by Moroccan troops as the migrants scaled fences constructed to protect the borders between Morocco and the Spanish enclaves. Spain urged Morocco to increase its efforts to prevent illegal border crossings, and later suspended the return of unsuccessful migrants to Morocco, amid claims by human rights organizations that migrants had been taken to the southern Moroccan desert and abandoned by the authorities. At a bilateral summit meeting in March 2007, attended by the Spanish Prime Minister, José Luis Rodríguez Zapatero, the two countries reached an agreement on the prevention of unaccompanied child migrants. Zapatero also welcomed Morocco's plan for autonomy in Western Sahara as a means to the opening of dialogue within the framework of the UN, while maintaining that Spain was committed to a consensual solution. The Moroccan Government temporarily recalled its ambassador to Spain in November, when it was announced that King Juan Carlos of Spain would pay his first royal visit to Ceuta and Melilla. Nevertheless, bilateral relations improved markedly in late 2008, and Prime Ministers Zapatero and Abbas el-Fassi attended a summit meeting in Madrid in December. Talks at the summit encompassed bilateral relations,

immigration, the issue of Western Sahara, and economic and security co-operation. A Spanish investment fund of more than €520m. for infrastructure projects in Morocco was subsequently announced. In January 2009 agreements between the two countries on increased co-operation in security and law enforcement were finalized. The first EU-Morocco summit (a product of Morocco's 'advanced status' relations with the EU) was hosted by Spain during its presidency of the EU in March 2010.

There were renewed difficulties between Spain and Morocco in August 2010, after Moroccan demonstrators blockaded the country's border crossing with Melilla to assert their claims of sovereignty over the enclave. The protest followed official complaints by the Moroccan authorities that its citizens who entered the two Spanish enclaves on a daily basis had suffered mistreatment at the hands of the Spanish police. In November, following Spanish criticism of Morocco regarding the deaths of protesters at a camp in Western Sahara, Morocco's Chamber of Representatives voted in favour of referring the status of Ceuta and Melilla to the UN Special Committee on Decolonization. Relations eased somewhat following the attendance of the Spanish Crown Prince at a bilateral economic conference held in Morocco in June 2012. In July, however, it was reported that Morocco had sought clarification of remarks made during a visit to Melilla by the Spanish Minister of Home Affairs suggesting that Spain intended to reinforce its presence in the Chafarinas Islands (administered by Spain as part of Melilla) in order to counter illegal immigration and drugs-trafficking.

The Moroccan Government was swift to condemn the September 2001 attacks on the USA, for which the al-Qa'ida network was held responsible. In June 2002 the Moroccan authorities announced that they had arrested three Saudi nationals alleged to be members of an Islamist cell linked to al-Qa'ida that was preparing terrorist attacks on US and British warships in the Strait of Gibraltar. Seven Moroccans had also been arrested for allegedly acting as couriers between the suspects in Morocco and al-Qa'ida, which had provided them with funds and logistical support. In February 2003 the three Saudi Arabians were sentenced to 10 years' imprisonment by a court in Casablanca; six of the Moroccans received lesser sentences. Also in February a Moroccan student, Mounir al-Motassadek, who was alleged to have been a member of the cell that had planned and executed the September 2001 attacks, was convicted by a court in Hamburg, Germany, of belonging to a terrorist group and of aiding and abetting the murder of 3,066 people. He was sentenced to 15 years' imprisonment. In March 2004 al-Motassadek's conviction was quashed by the German Federal Criminal Court, and he was released from detention in April. A retrial began in August, and al-Motassadek was acquitted in August 2005 of involvement in the September 2001 attacks; he was nevertheless convicted of belonging to a terrorist organization and sentenced to seven years' imprisonment. In November 2006 the German Federal Court of Justice overturned al-Motassadek's acquittal on charges of accessory to murder, and he was again sentenced to 15 years' imprisonment in January 2007. A final appeal was rejected by the Federal Court of Justice in May.

In June 2004 Morocco became the second Arab country (after Jordan in 2001) to sign a free trade agreement with the USA; the accord was ratified by both chambers of the Moroccan parliament in January 2005. In recent years the US Administration has praised Morocco for its strong leadership and its efforts against militant Islamist groups. During 2011 US officials also commended the Moroccan Government for the manner in which it responded to the opposition-led pro-democracy protests. Issues of human rights have, none the less, been the cause of some tension, most recently in April 2013, when Morocco opposed US-led efforts at the UN Security Council to include monitoring of human rights within the mandate of MINURSO (see Western Sahara).

CONSTITUTION AND GOVERNMENT

The 2011 Constitution provides for a modified constitutional monarchy, with a hereditary King as head of state. Legislative power is vested in the Majlis al-Nuab (Chamber of Representatives), with 395 members directly elected, on the basis of universal adult suffrage, for five years, and in the Majlis al-Mustasharin (Chamber of Advisers), with no fewer than 90 and no more than 120 members, three-fifths of whom are elected by electoral colleges of local councils; the remainder are elected by electoral colleges representing chambers of commerce and trade unions. Members of the Chamber of Advisers are elected for a six-year term. Executive power is vested in the King, who must appoint as Prime Minister the leader of the party with the largest representation in the Chamber of Representatives. Upon the Prime Minister's recommendation, the King appoints the other members of the Cabinet. The Government must gain an absolute majority in a vote by the members of the Chamber of Representatives prior to taking office. Both the King and the Prime Minister may dissolve the legislature after consultation.

REGIONAL AND INTERNATIONAL CO-OPERATION

Morocco is a founder member of the Union du Maghreb arabe (UMA—Union of the Arab Maghreb, see p. 464). The permanent headquarters of the organization are located in Rabat. The country also participates in the League of Arab States (the Arab League, see p. 372) and the Community of Sahel-Saharan States (CEN-SAD, see p. 460).

Morocco became a member of the UN in November 1956, having gained independence in March of that year. As a contracting party to the General Agreement on Trade and Tariffs, Morocco joined the World Trade Organization (WTO, see p. 444) on its establishment in 1995. The country also adheres to the Organization of Islamic Cooperation (OIC, see p. 413).

ECONOMIC AFFAIRS

In 2011, according to estimates by the World Bank, Morocco's gross national income (GNI), measured at average 2009–11 prices, was US $97,619m., equivalent to $2,970 per head (or $4,910 per head on an international purchasing-power parity basis). During 2002–11, it was estimated, the population increased at an average annual rate of 1.0%, while gross domestic product (GDP) per head increased, in real terms, by an average of 3.7% per year. Overall GDP increased, in real terms, at an average annual rate of 4.8% in 2002–11; it increased by 4.5% in 2011.

Agriculture (including forestry and fishing) contributed 15.5% of GDP in 2011, according to provisional figures, and engaged 39.8% of the employed labour force in 2011. The principal crops are cereals (mainly wheat and barley), sugar beet and sugar cane, potatoes, tomatoes, melons, and citrus fruit. Almost all of Morocco's meat requirements are produced within the country. The sale of licences to foreign fishing fleets is an important source of revenue. According to provisional figures, seafoods and seafood products accounted for 5.4% of total exports in 2011. According to the World Bank, during 2002–11 agricultural GDP increased at an average annual rate of 5.9%; after a prolonged period of drought in 2007, sectoral GDP declined by 1.9% in 2010, before increasing, by 2.8%, in 2011.

Industry (including mining, manufacturing, construction and power) provided 30.2% of GDP in 2011, according to provisional figures, and engaged 21.9% of the employed labour force in 2011. According to the World Bank, during 2002–11 industrial GDP increased by an average of 3.7% per year; sectoral GDP grew by 3.5% in 2011.

Mining and quarrying contributed 5.6% of GDP in 2011, according to provisional figures, and engaged only 0.5% of the employed labour force in that year. The major mineral exports are phosphate rock and phosphoric acid, which together earned 7.4% of export revenues in 2011, according to provisional figures. Morocco is the world's largest exporter of phosphate rock. Petroleum exploration activity was revived at the end of the 1990s, and the discovery of major oil and natural gas reserves in the Talsinnt region of eastern Morocco was announced in 2000. Coal, salt, iron ore, barytes, lead, copper, zinc, silver, gold and manganese are mined. Deposits of nickel, cobalt and bauxite have been discovered. During 1990–2002 mining GDP increased at an average annual rate of 1.3%. According to official estimates, mining GDP increased by 1.8% in 2006.

Manufacturing, together with oil-refining, contributed 15.7% of GDP in 2011, according to provisional figures. The manufacturing sector engaged 10.9% of the employed labour force in 2011. The most important branches, measured by gross value of output, are oil-refining and energy products, food-processing, textiles, and chemicals. According to provisional figures, manufactured garments accounted for 10.5% of export revenues in 2011. According to the World Bank, during 2002–11 manufacturing GDP increased at an average annual rate of 2.6%; the sector's GDP expanded by 2.1% in 2011.

Construction contributed 6.5% of GDP in 2011, according to provisional figures. The sector engaged 10.1% of the employed labour force in 2011.

In 2009 electric energy was derived principally from coal (52.4%), petroleum (20.3%), natural gas (13.3%) and hydroelectric power stations (12.1%). Facilities for generating wind power have also been developed. In 2009 the Government detailed a US $9,000m. project to develop five solar power plants; the project was due for completion by 2020, and was expected to have a capacity of 2,000 MW, equivalent to some 38% of Morocco's installed energy capacity. In November 2011 the World Bank agreed to part-finance construction of one of the plants, to be located in Ouarzazate, near Marrakesh, which was expected to begin electricity production by 2014. According to provisional figures, imports of energy and lubricants comprised an estimated 25.3% of the value of total merchandise imports in 2011.

The services sector contributed an estimated 54.3% of GDP in 2011, according to provisional figures, and engaged 38.3% of the employed labour force. The tourism industry is generally a major source of revenue (accounting for some 9% of GDP in 2011), and foreign tourist arrivals totalled some 4.9m. in 2010. According to a 10-year strategy for the tourism industry announced in November 2010, 177,000m. dirhams would be invested in an attempt to raise the number of visitors to 18.6m. per year by 2020. The GDP of the services sector increased by an average of 5.2% per year during 2002–11, and by 9.1% in 2011, according to the World Bank.

In 2011 Morocco recorded a visible merchandise trade deficit of US $21,387m., and there was a deficit of $8,337m. on the current account of the balance of payments. According to provisional figures, in 2011 the principal source of imports was France (which provided 14.3% of merchandise imports); other major suppliers in that year included Spain, the USA, the People's Republic of China and Italy. France was also the principal market for exports (20.5%) in 2011; Spain, India and Brazil were also important purchasers of Moroccan exports. The principal exports in 2011 were semi-finished products (including phosphoric acid and electronic components), finished consumer products (notably manufactured garments and hosiery), finished industrial capital goods, and foodstuffs, beverages and tobacco (particularly seafoods and seafood products). The principal imports in that year were fuel and energy products (notably crude petroleum), semi-finished products, finished capital goods, finished consumer products, and foodstuffs, beverages and tobacco.

In 2011 Morocco recorded an overall budget deficit of 18,680m. dirhams. The country's general government gross debt was 436,479m. dirhams in 2011, equivalent to 54.4% of GDP. Morocco's total external debt in 2010 was US $25,403m., of which $21,015m. was public and publicly guaranteed debt. In that year, the cost of servicing long-term public and publicly guaranteed debt and repayments to the IMF was equivalent to 10.7% of the value of exports of goods, services and income (excluding workers' remittances). The annual rate of inflation averaged 1.8% in 2006–11; consumer prices increased by an average of 0.9% in both 2010 and 2011. According to official figures, some 8.9% of the labour force were unemployed in 2011.

Morocco has generally seen sustained growth since the mid-2000s, and initially showed some resilience to the effects of the global economic slowdown from 2008. However, slower GDP growth in 2012, estimated at 3.2%, was attributed to lower-than-average production in the agricultural sector, owing to poor rainfall, together with the impact of unfavourable external conditions, in particular the ongoing difficulties in the eurozone—which notably affected tourism, export earnings and remittances from abroad—and high prices for oil and other commodities. These factors contributed to a widening of the external current account deficit (in surplus until 2008) to 8.8% of GDP, from 8.0% in 2011. Recovery in the agricultural sector was projected to contribute to GDP growth of 4.5% in 2013, and, together with lower world energy prices and higher exports, to a narrowing of the current account deficit to 6.3% of GDP. In June 2012 the new Government implemented measures to increase the domestic prices of some subsidized energy products. The IMF estimated in early 2013 that this would contribute to a reduction in the fiscal deficit to 6.1% of GDP in 2012, from 6.8% in 2011; the Government's objective was to reduce the deficit to 4.7% of GDP in 2013. Reflecting the adjustment to subsidies, annual inflation was expected to increase to 1.3% in 2012 and to a projected 2.2% in 2013—still a low level. However, the aim of substantially reducing subsidies on fuel and staple foods was likely to conflict with popular pressure on the Government to alleviate deteriorating conditions, including rising living costs. The high rate of unemployment, particularly youth and urban unemployment, remained a particular concern: government figures in early 2013 put joblessness among 25–34-year-olds at some 18%, and urban unemployment at more than 13%. In April 2013 the Government announced that it was to defer 15,000m. dirhams in planned investment spending, in an effort to reduce the public deficit. Although assurances were given that spending on employment and social measures would not be affected, there was wider speculation regarding the likely negative impact of reduced public expenditure on job creation.

PUBLIC HOLIDAYS

2014: 1 January (New Year), 11 January (Independence Manifesto), 13–14 January* (Mouloud, Birth of the Prophet), 1 May (Labour Day), 30 July (Festival of the Throne, anniversary of King Muhammad's accession), 28–29 July* (Eid el-Seghir—Id al-Fitr, end of Ramadan), 14 August (Oued el-Dahab Day, anniversary of the 1979 annexation), 20 August (The King and People's Revolution), 21 August (Festival of Youth—King Muhammad's Birthday), 4–5 October* (Eid el-Kebir—Id al-Adha, Feast of the Sacrifice), 24 October* (Muharram, Islamic New Year), 6 November (Anniversary of the Green March), 18 November (Independence Day).

* These holidays are dependent on the Islamic lunar calendar and may vary by one or two days from the dates given.

Statistical Survey

Sources (unless otherwise stated): Haut Commissariat au Plan, Direction de la Statistique, rue Muhammad Belhassan el-Ouazzani, BP 178, Rabat 10001; tel. (53) 7773606; fax (53) 7773217; e-mail statguichet@statistic.gov.ma; internet www.hcp.ma; Bank Al-Maghrib, 277 ave Muhammad V, BP 445, Rabat; tel. (53) 7702626; fax (53) 7706667; e-mail webmaster@bkam.ma; internet www.bkam.ma.

Note: Unless otherwise indicated, the data exclude Western (formerly Spanish) Sahara, a disputed territory under Moroccan occupation.

Area and Population

AREA, POPULATION AND DENSITY

Area (sq km)	710,850*
Population (census results)†	
2 September 1994	
Males	12,944,517
Females	13,074,763
Total	26,019,280
2 September 2004	29,891,708
Population (UN estimates at mid-year)‡	
2011	32,272,973
2012	32,598,538
2013	32,925,555
Density (per sq km) at mid-2013 . . .	46.3

* 274,461 sq miles. This area includes the disputed territory of Western Sahara, which covers 252,120 sq km (97,344 sq miles).
† Including Western Sahara, with an estimated population of 417,000 at the 2004 census.
‡ Source: UN, *World Population Prospects: The 2010 Revision.*

POPULATION BY AGE AND SEX
(UN estimates at mid-2013)

	Males	Females	Total
0–14	4,534,725	4,341,173	8,875,898
15–64	10,712,832	11,437,693	22,150,525
65 and over	855,440	1,043,692	1,899,132
Total	16,102,997	16,822,558	32,925,555

Source: UN, *World Population Prospects: The 2010 Revision.*

REGIONS
(population at 2004 census)

	Population
Oued el-Dahab Lagouira*	99,367
El-Aaiún Boujdour*	256,152
Guelmim el-Semara†	462,410
Souss Massa-Draa	3,113,653
Gharb Chrarda Beni-Hsen	1,859,540
Chaouia Ouardigha	1,655,660
Marrakech Tensift al-Haou	3,102,652
Oriental	1,918,094
Grand Casablanca	3,631,061
Rabat Salé Zemmour Zaer	2,366,494

—continued	Population
Doukkala Abda	1,984,039
Tadla Azilal	1,450,519
Meknès Tafilalet	2,141,527
Fès Boulemane	1,573,055
Taza al-Hoceima Taounate	1,807,113
Tanger Tétouan	2,470,372
Total	29,891,708

* Regions situated in Western Sahara.
† Region partly situated in Western Sahara.

PRINCIPAL TOWNS
(population at 2004 census)

Casablanca . .	2,933,684	Tétouan	320,539
Rabat (capital)*	1,622,860	Safi	284,750
Fès (Fez) . .	946,815	Mohammedia . .	188,619
Marrakech			
(Marrakesh) . .	823,154	El-Aaiún† . . .	183,691
Agadir . . .	678,596	Khouribga . . .	166,397
Tanger (Tangier) .	669,685	Beni-Mellal . .	163,286
Meknès . . .	536,232	El-Jadida . . .	144,440
Oujda . . .	400,738	Taza	139,686
Kénitra . . .	359,142		

* Including Salé and Temara.
† Town situated in Western Sahara.

Source: Thomas Brinkhoff, *City Population* (internet www.citypopulation.de).

Mid-2011 (incl. suburbs, UN estimate): Rabat 1,842,850 (Source: UN, *World Urbanization Prospects: The 2011 Revision*).

BIRTHS AND DEATHS
(annual averages, UN estimates)

	1995–2000	2000–05	2005–10
Birth rate (per 1,000)	23.4	20.9	20.2
Death rate (per 1,000)	6.4	6.0	5.8

Source: UN, *World Population Prospects: The 2010 Revision.*

Life expectancy (years at birth): 72.1 (males 69.9; females 74.5) in 2011 (Source: World Bank, World Development Indicators database).

ECONOMICALLY ACTIVE POPULATION
('000 persons aged 15 years and over)

	2009	2010	2011
Agriculture, hunting, forestry and fishing	4,311.3	4,188.1	4,179.0
Mining and quarrying	42.5	41.8	50.2
Manufacturing	1,190.9	1,182.7	1,148.4
Electricity, gas and water	45.5	42.9	37.3
Construction	967.6	1,029.1	1,059.0
Wholesale and retail trade; repairs	1,503.9	1,522.7	1,555.9
Hotels and restaurants	225.5	248.2	266.8
Transport, storage and communications	442.4	464.6	493.5
General administration and community services	1,042.5	1,005.1	1,020.4
Financial intermediation, real estate and business services	669.4	665.2	683.9
Sub-total	10,441.4	10,390.5	10,494.3
Activities not adequately defined	13.4	14.2	15.0
Total employed	10,454.8	10,404.7	10,509.3
Unemployed	1,029.4	1,037.1	1,028.3
Total labour force	11,484.1	11,441.8	11,537.6

Health and Welfare

KEY INDICATORS

Total fertility rate (children per woman, 2010)	2.3
Under-5 mortality rate (per 1,000 live births, 2010)	36
HIV/AIDS (% of persons aged 15–49, 2009)	0.1
Physicians (per 1,000 head, 2009)	0.62
Hospital beds (per 1,000 head, 2009)	1.1
Health expenditure (2009): US $ per head (PPP)	241
Health expenditure (2009): % of GDP	5.2
Health expenditure (2009): public (% of total)	38.8
Access to water (% of persons, 2010)	83
Access to sanitation (% of persons, 2010)	70
Total carbon dioxide emissions ('000 metric tons, 2008)	47,905.7
Carbon dioxide emissions per head (metric tons, 2008)	1.5
Human Development Index (2011): ranking	130
Human Development Index (2011): value	0.582

For sources and definitions, see explanatory note on p. vi.

Agriculture

PRINCIPAL CROPS
('000 metric tons)

	2009	2010	2011
Wheat	6,371	4,876	3,400*
Rice, paddy	50	51	40
Barley	3,770	2,566	2,340*
Maize	205	279	200*
Potatoes	1,234	1,605	1,948†
Sugar cane	813	632	632†
Sugar beet	2,753	2,436	2,436†
Broad beans, dry	153	149	134†
Peas, dry	28	26	28†
Chick peas	52	57	62†
Lentils	23	28	31†
Almonds, with shell	115	102	131†
Groundnuts, with shell	52	50	45†
Olives	850	1,484	1,365†
Sunflower seeds	50	59	55*
Cabbages and other brassicas	39	65	59†
Artichokes	57	45	44†
Tomatoes	1,230	1,278	1,236†
Cauliflowers and broccoli	51	70	93†
Pumpkins, squash and gourds	238	208	212†
Cucumbers and gherkins	35	115	125†
Aubergines (Eggplants)	30	38	38†
Chillies and peppers, green	203	225	224†
Onions, dry	802	1,131	1,196†
Peas, green	144	140	123†
String beans†	90	160	157

—continued	2009	2010	2011
Carrots and turnips	239	253	288†
Carobs†	20	20	20
Watermelons	747	453	449†
Cantaloupes and other melons	887	567	558†
Figs†	70	74	74
Grapes	338	316	317†
Dates	85	119	119†
Apples	423	506	506†
Pears	39	41	41†
Quinces	39	46	46†
Peaches and nectarines	87	93	93†
Plums and sloes	74	83	83†
Strawberries	355	141	141†
Oranges	715	849	850*
Tangerines, mandarins, clementines and satsumas	353	473	473†
Apricots	134	132	133†
Bananas†	240	280	290
Anise, badian, fennel and coriander†	23	29	29

* Unofficial figure.
† FAO estimate(s).

Aggregate production ('000 metric tons, may include official, semi-official or estimated data): Total cereals 10,444 in 2009, 7,834 in 2010, 6,039 in 2011; Total pulses 276 in 2009, 282 in 2010, 281 in 2011; Total roots and tubers 1,246 in 2009, 1,615 in 2010, 1,956 in 2011; Total vegetables (incl. melons) 5,256 in 2009, 5,487 in 2010, 5,657 in 2011; Total fruits (excl. melons) 3,088 in 2009, 3,292 in 2010, 3,307 in 2011.

Source: FAO.

LIVESTOCK
('000 head, year ending September)

	2009	2010	2011*
Cattle	2,788	2,896	2,900
Sheep	17,006	18,023	18,500
Goats	5,293	5,686	5,900
Camels*	50	52	55
Horses	147	155	160
Asses	963	955*	955
Mules	505	500*	500
Chickens*	165,000	170,000	175,000

* FAO estimate(s).

Source: FAO.

LIVESTOCK PRODUCTS
('000 metric tons)

	2009	2010	2011*
Cattle meat	190	192	200
Sheep meat	134	139	142
Goat meat	22	23	25†
Chicken meat	490	560	591
Cows' milk	1,800	1,900	1,900
Sheep's milk*	33	38	38
Goats' milk*	40	58	58
Hen eggs*	200	230	230
Honey	3	4	4
Wool, greasy*	55	55	55

* FAO estimates.

Source: FAO.

Forestry

ROUNDWOOD REMOVALS
('000 cubic metres, excl. bark)

	2009	2010	2011
Sawlogs, veneer logs and logs for sleepers	190	113*	113*
Pulpwood	305	259	259*
Fuel wood*	6,802	6,786	6,762
Total*	7,297	7,158	7,134

* FAO estimate(s).

Source: FAO.

SAWNWOOD PRODUCTION
('000 cubic metres, incl. railway sleepers)

	1987*	1988	1989
Coniferous (softwood)	40	26*	43*
Broadleaved (hardwood)	40	27	40
Total	80	53	83

* FAO estimate(s).

1990–2011: Production assumed to be unchanged from 1989 (FAO estimates).

Source: FAO.

Fishing

('000 metric tons, live weight)

	2008	2009	2010
Capture	997.1	1,165.1	1,136.2
European pilchard (sardine)	647.0	790.6	771.5
Chub mackerel	106.5	83.8	76.0
Jack and horse mackerels	26.3	23.4	23.2
Octopuses	56.4	60.2	32.0
Aquaculture*	1.4	1.5	1.5
Total catch (incl. others)*	998.5	1,166.5	1,137.8

* FAO estimates.

Note: Figures exclude aquatic plants ('000 metric tons, all capture): 9.0 in 2008; 10.4 in 2009; 7.4 in 2010. Also excluded are corals (metric tons, all capture): 3.7 in 2008; 6.5 in 2009; 7.1 in 2010.

Source: FAO.

Mining

('000 metric tons)

	2009	2010	2011
Iron ore*	30.5	44.7	78.9
Copper concentrates*	42.1	53.3	43.0
Lead concentrates*	49.0	46.4	43.8
Manganese ore*	51.8	75.6	58.0
Zinc concentrates*	88.4	87.4	90.1
Phosphate rock†	18,307.0	26,603.0	28,052.0
Fluorspar (acid grade)	72.1	89.7	79.2
Barytes	586.9	572.4	769.5
Salt (unrefined)	310.4	503.4	720.8
Bentonite	84.1	110.7	97.1

* Figures refer to the gross weight of ores and concentrates.

† Including production in Western Sahara.

Source: Ministère de l'Energie, des Mines, de l'Eau et de l'Environnement.

Industry

SELECTED PRODUCTS
('000 metric tons unless otherwise indicated)

	2007	2008	2009
Wine*	37	35	29
Olive oil (crude)	75	95	112†
Motor spirit—petrol	365	404	313
Naphthas	596	455	335
Distillate fuel oils	1,996	1,819	1,385
Residual fuel oils	2,269	1,880	1,492
Jet fuel	292	262	257
Petroleum bitumen—asphalt	257	275	307
Liquefied petroleum gas ('000 barrels)	2,500*	2,500	2,500
Cement	12,792	14,048	14,519
Carpets and rugs ('000 sq m)	226	n.a.	n.a.
Electric energy (million kWh)	19,670	20,345	21,191

* Estimated figure(s).
† Unofficial figure.

2010 (estimates unless otherwise indicated): Wine 33; Olive oil (crude) 148 (unofficial figure); Liquefied petroleum gas ('000 barrels) 2,500; Cement 14,000.

2011: Wine 33 (estimate); Olive oil (crude) 130 (unofficial figure).

Sources: FAO, US Geological Survey, UN Industrial Commodity Statistics Database.

Finance

CURRENCY AND EXCHANGE RATES

Monetary Units:
100 centimes (santimat) = 1 Moroccan dirham.

Sterling, Dollar and Euro Equivalents (30 November 2012):
£1 sterling = 13.744 dirhams;
US $1 = 8.559 dirhams;
€1 = 11.115 dirhams;
100 Moroccan dirhams = £7.28 = $11.68 = €9.00.

Average Exchange Rate (dirhams per US $):
2009   8.057
2010   8.417
2011   8.090

GENERAL BUDGET
(million dirhams)

Revenue*†	2011	2012‡	2013‡
Tax revenue	189,711	205,290	219,880
Taxes on income and profits	68,460	72,363	78,050
Taxes on property	9,231	10,522	11,222
Taxes on goods and services	93,717	100,124	107,406
Taxes on international trade	13,653	13,173	14,249
Other tax revenues	4,651	9,109	8,953
Non-tax revenue	30,631	29,366	26,525
Total	220,342	234,656	246,405

Expenditure§	2011	2012‡	2013‡
Wages and salaries	98,038	106,188	110,548
Use of goods and services	22,742	24,049	30,233
Interest	18,234	20,244	22,003
Subsidies	48,830	51,550	39,422
Grants	27,623	29,713	32,956
Other expense	24,865	16,897	16,897
Total	240,332	248,640	252,060

* Excluding grants (million dirhams): 1,310 in 2011; 4,940 in 2012 (budget projection); 10,890 in 2013 (budget projection).
† Includes tariffs destined for food subsidies and road fund revenues.
‡ Projections.
§ Excluding net lending.

Source: IMF, *Morocco: Request for an Arrangement Under the Precautionary and Liquidity Line—Staff Report; Press Release on the Executive Board Discussion; and Statement by the Executive Director for Morocco* (August 2012).

INTERNATIONAL RESERVES
(US $ million at 31 December)

	2009	2010	2011
Gold (national valuation) . .	783	1,000	1,116
IMF special drawing rights . .	763	743	616
Reserve position in IMF . . .	110	108	108
Foreign exchange	21,924	21,762	18,802
Total	23,580	23,613	20,642

Source: IMF, *International Financial Statistics*.

MONEY SUPPLY
(million dirhams at 31 December)

	2009	2010	2011
Currency outside depository corporations	136,664	144,660	158,288
Transferable deposits . . .	341,668	366,450	393,110
Other deposits	301,016	322,311	329,675
Securities other than shares . .	13,526	21,996	30,480
Broad money	792,875	855,417	911,553

Source: IMF, *International Financial Statistics*.

COST OF LIVING
(Consumer Price Index for urban areas; base: 2006 = 100)

	2009	2010	2011
Food and non-alcoholic beverages .	113.3	114.7	116.3
Alcoholic beverages and tobacco .	108.2	108.3	108.3
Clothing	103.8	104.3	106.0
Shelter	103.8	104.3	104.8
Household equipment . . .	105.4	106.2	107.1
All items (incl. others) . . .	107.4	108.4	109.4

NATIONAL ACCOUNTS
(million dirhams at current prices)

Expenditure on the Gross Domestic Product

	2009	2010	2011*
Government final consumption expenditure	133,397	133,938	146,332
Private final consumption expenditure	418,461	437,547	472,938
Change in inventories . . .	34,898	33,251	42,168
Gross fixed capital formation .	226,177	234,407	246,394
Total domestic expenditure .	812,933	839,143	907,832
Exports of goods and services .	210,241	253,941	285,530
Less Imports of goods and services	290,725	329,053	390,755
GDP in purchasers' values .	732,449	764,031	802,607

Gross Domestic Product by Economic Activity

	2009	2010	2011*
Agriculture, hunting and forestry	100,757	98,991	106,342
Fishing and aquaculture . . .	6,293	6,543	8,524
Mining and quarrying	16,925	29,579	41,355
Manufacturing	104,004	105,250	114,338
Oil refining and energy products .	1,084	2,799	1,960
Electricity and water . . .	18,953	19,362	18,962
Construction	45,776	47,085	47,941
Commerce	72,054	72,815	76,977
Hotels and restaurants . . .	16,775	19,446	18,852
Transport	25,795	27,480	28,424
Post and communications . .	22,097	23,065	22,473
Public administration and social security	59,875	62,600	69,611
Other services	162,769	172,707	186,660
Sub-total	653,157	687,722	742,419
Taxes, less subsidies, on imports .	79,292	76,309	60,188
GDP in purchasers' values .	732,449	764,031	802,607

* Provisional figures.

BALANCE OF PAYMENTS
(US $ million)

	2009	2010	2011
Exports of goods	9,166	12,309	15,946
Imports of goods	−28,027	−29,627	−37,333
Balance on goods	−18,861	−17,318	−21,387
Exports of services	14,833	14,736	15,899
Imports of services	−6,898	−7,372	−8,574
Balance on goods and services	−10,927	−9,953	−14,063
Primary income received . .	925	868	804
Primary income paid . . .	−2,421	−2,110	−2,856
Balance on goods, services and primary income	−12,422	−11,196	−16,115
Secondary income received . .	7,278	7,240	8,071
Secondary income paid . . .	−218	−254	−293
Current balance	−5,362	−4,209	−8,337
Direct investment assets . .	−479	−580	−248
Direct investment liabilities . .	1,970	1,241	2,521
Portfolio investment assets . .	−12	−22	−400
Portfolio investment liabilities .	−4	132	166
Other investment assets . .	−56	880	−536
Other investment liabilities . .	63	−287	791
Net errors and omissions . . .	−523	−167	−370
Reserves and related items .	−4,404	−3,012	−6,413

Source: IMF, *International Financial Statistics*.

External Trade

PRINCIPAL COMMODITIES
(million dirhams)

Imports c.i.f.	2009	2010	2011*
Foodstuffs, beverages and tobacco	24,213	29,100	38,755
Wheat	5,483	7,397	11,524
Energy and lubricants . . .	54,136	68,479	90,686
Crude petroleum . . .	17,166	25,090	31,423
Crude products	13,776	15,915	22,425
Semi-finished products . . .	52,813	62,266	76,428
Chemical products . . .	10,039	12,454	15,456
Finished capital goods . .	66,136	65,939	68,213
Finished consumer products . .	52,908	55,753	61,459
Pharmaceutical products . .	4,069	4,554	4,907
Textile and cotton fabrics . .	6,501	6,611	7,721
Total (incl. others)	263,982	297,963	357,987

Exports f.o.b.	2009	2010	2011*
Foodstuffs, beverages and tobacco	25,193	26,796	26,335
Crustaceans and molluscs . .	4,439	4,564	5,080
Prepared and preserved fish .	4,837	5,154	4,271
Energy and lubricants . . .	2,628	1,589	7,166
Crude mineral products . .	7,376	14,322	19,830
Phosphates	4,453	8,984	12,950
Semi-finished products . . .	25,962	43,420	52,801
Finished industrial capital goods .	16,326	23,133	26,204
Electric wire and cable . . .	9,087	13,737	15,547
Finished consumer products . .	32,829	35,078	37,905
Manufactured garments . .	17,796	18,041	18,259
Hosiery	6,461	6,973	7,727
Total (incl. others)	113,020	149,583	173,977

* Provisional figures.

PRINCIPAL TRADING PARTNERS
(million dirhams)*

Imports c.i.f.	2009	2010†	2011†
Algeria	5,772	7,055	8,687
Belgium-Luxembourg	4,183	4,283	7,029
Brazil	6,046	6,443	8,423
Canada	3,165	1,867	2,942
China, People's Republic	20,610	24,993	23,331
France	41,584	41,080	51,146
Germany	14,394	14,394	16,007
India	3,198	4,875	4,760
Italy	17,290	17,717	18,614
Japan	4,049	3,766	3,378
Netherlands	6,337	5,195	6,141
Spain	32,141	31,404	39,174
United Kingdom	4,800	6,331	7,175
USA	18,289	20,981	28,953
Total (incl. others)	263,982	297,963	357,987

Exports f.o.b.	2009	2010†	2011†
Belgium-Luxembourg	2,010	3,985	3,435
Brazil	2,339	5,645	9,016
France	27,464	33,558	35,743
Germany	3,827	4,685	4,823
India	5,852	9,056	11,786
Italy	5,286	6,725	7,249
Netherlands	2,925	4,219	5,001
Spain	23,574	25,297	31,618
United Kingdom	3,764	4,341	4,413
USA	3,560	5,640	7,558
Total (incl. others)	113,020	149,583	173,977

* Imports by country of production; exports by country of last consignment.
† Provisional figures.

Transport

RAILWAYS
(traffic)*

	2009	2010	2011†
Passengers carried ('000)	29,599	30,910	33,879
Freight ('000 metric tons)	25,722	35,669	37,178

* Figures refer to principal railways only.
† Provisional.

2008: Passenger-km (million) 3,836; Freight ton-km (million) 4,985).

ROAD TRAFFIC
('000 motor vehicles in use at 31 December)

	1999	2000	2001
Passenger cars	1,161.9	1,211.1	1,253.0
Commercial vehicles	400.3	415.7	431.0

Motorcycles and scooters: 20,388 in 2000; 20,569 in 2001.

Passenger cars: 1,326,108 in 2003.

2007: Passenger cars 1,644,523; Buses and coaches 22,841; Vans and lorries 525,334; Motorcycles and mopeds 22,841.

2010: Passenger cars 1,976,172; Motorcycles and mopeds 31,353.

Sources: IRF, *World Road Statistics*; UN, *Statistical Yearbook*.

SHIPPING
Flag Registered Fleet
(at 31 December)

	2010	2011	2012
Number of vessels	412	409	409
Total displacement ('000 grt)	383.7	374.9	364.6

Source: Lloyd's List Intelligence (www.lloydslistintelligence.com).

International Sea-borne Freight Traffic
('000 metric tons)

	2008	2009	2010*
Goods loaded	26,158	20,341	26,123
Goods unloaded	41,557	39,395	43,113

* Provisional figures.

CIVIL AVIATION
(traffic on scheduled services)

	2007	2008	2009
Kilometres flown (million)	120	110	111
Passengers carried ('000)	4,624	4,927	4,931
Passenger-km (million)	9,073	9,901	9,582
Total ton-km (million)	861	947	947

Source: UN, *Statistical Yearbook*.

2010: Aircraft movements 196,538; Passengers carried ('000) 15,499; Freight carried (metric tons) 55,558.

2011 (provisional): Aircraft movements 192,553; Passengers carried ('000) 15,802; Freight carried (metric tons) 55,297.

Tourism

FOREIGN TOURIST ARRIVALS*

Country of nationality	2008	2009	2010
France	1,707,055	1,699,201	1,827,453
Germany	179,037	174,384	205,417
Italy	163,315	177,915	233,224
Spain	595,279	642,817	726,540
United Kingdom	274,762	252,945	338,060
Other European countries	205,746	209,153	255,076
Maghreb countries	135,820	135,766	155,550
USA	110,778	121,144	135,376
Total (incl. others)	4,211,855	4,292,958	4,928,572

* Excluding Moroccans resident abroad (3,376,719 in 2007; 3,666,784 in 2008; 4,048,279 in 2009).

Cruise-ship passengers: 329,920 in 2008; 319,353 in 2009; 320,000 in 2010.

Receipts from tourism (US $ million, excl. passenger transport): 6,703 in 2010; 7,307 in 2011 (provisional) (Source: World Tourism Organization).

Communications Media

	2009	2010	2011
Telephones ('000 main lines in use)	3,516.3	3,749.4	3,566.1
Mobile cellular telephones ('000 subscribers)	25,310.8	31,982.3	36,553.9
Internet subscribers ('000) . .	479.8	500.5	591.6
Broadband subscribers ('000) . .	475.8	498.7	589.0

Personal computers: 1,800,000 (57.0 per 1,000 persons) in 2008.

Source: International Telecommunication Union.

Education

(2010/11 unless otherwise indicated)

	Institutions	Teachers	Pupils/Students		
			Males	Females	Total
Pre-primary . .	33,577*	36,736	438,041	302,155	740,196
Primary . . .	6,565†	151,477	2,103,914	1,897,399	4,001,313
public† . .	5,940	n.a.	1,884,457	1,647,604	3,532,061
private† . .	625	n.a.	183,285	163,294	346,579
Secondary (public and private) .	1,664†	100,367‡	1,184,132§	989,322§	2,173,454§
Tertiary . . .	68*	19,598‡	222,568‡	196,315‡	418,883‡

* 1997/98 figure.
† 1999/2000 figure.
‡ 2003/04 figure.
§ 2006/07 figure.

Pupils/Students (2008/09): Primary 3,863,838 (public 3,492,312, private 371,526); Secondary 2,232,289 (public 2,103,768, private 128,521).

Teachers: Primary 144,722 in 2008/09.
Source: Ministry of National Education, Higher Education, Staff Training and Scientific Research; UNESCO Institute for Statistics.

Pupil-teacher ratio (primary education, UNESCO estimate): 26.4 in 2010/11 (Source: UNESCO Institute for Statistics).

Adult literacy rate (UNESCO estimates): 56.1% (males 68.9%, females 43.9%) in 2009 (Source: UNESCO Institute for Statistics).

Directory

The Government

HEAD OF STATE

Monarch: HM King MUHAMMAD VI (acceded 23 July 1999).

CABINET
(May 2013)

A coalition of the Parti de la justice et du développement (PJD), Istiqlal, the Mouvement populaire (MP), the Parti du progrès et du socialisme (PPS) and independents (Ind.).

Prime Minister: ABDELILAH BENKIRANE (PJD).

Minister of State: ABDELLAH BAHA (PJD).

Minister of the Interior: MOHAND LAENSER (MP).

Minister of Foreign Affairs and Co-operation: SAÂDEDDINE EL-OTHMANI (PJD).

Minister of Justice and Liberties: MUSTAFA RAMID (PJD).

Minister of Habous (Religious Endowments) and Islamic Affairs: AHMED TOUFIQ (Ind.).

Secretary-General of the Government: DRISS DAHAK (Ind.).

Minister of the Economy and Finance: NIZAR BARAKA (Istiqlal).

Minister of Housing, Town Planning and Development: MUHAMMAD NABIL BENABDELLAH (PPS).

Minister of Agriculture and Fisheries: AZIZ AKHANNOUCH (Ind.).

Minister of National Education: MUHAMMAD EL-OUAFA (Istiqlal).

Minister of Higher Education, Staff Training and Scientific Research: LAHCEN DAOUDI (PJD).

Minister of Youth and Sports: MUHAMMAD OUZZINE (MP).

Minister of Equipment and Transport: AZIZ RABBAH (PJD).

Minister of Health: EL-HOSSEIN EL-OUARDI (PPS).

Minister of Communication and Government Spokesperson: MUSTAPHA EL-KHALFI (PJD).

Minister of Energy, Mining, Water and the Environment: FOUAD DOUIRI (Istiqlal).

Minister of Employment and Vocational Training: ABDEL-OUAHED SOUHAIL (PPS).

Minister of Industry, Trade and New Technologies: ABDEL-KADER AÂMARA (PJD).

Minister of Tourism: LAHCEN HADDAD (MP).

Minister of Solidarity, Women, Family and Social Development: BASSIMA HAKKAOUI (PJD).

Minister of Culture: MUHAMMAD AMINE SBIHI (PPS).

Minister of Handicrafts: ABDESSAMAD QAIOUH (Istiqlal).

Minister in charge of Relations with Parliament and Civil Society: LAHBIB CHOUBANI (PJD).

Minister-delegate to the Prime Minister, in charge of the Administration of National Defence: ABDELLATIF LOUDIYI (Ind.).

Minister-delegate to the Prime Minister, in charge of Moroccans Resident Abroad: ABDELLATIF MAÂZOUZ (Istiqlal).

Minister-delegate to the Minister of the Interior: CHARKI DRAISS (Ind.).

Minister-delegate to the Minister of Foreign Affairs and Co-operation: YOUSSEF AMRANI (Ind.).

Minister-delegate to the Prime Minister, in charge of General Affairs and Governance: MUHAMMAD NAJIB BOULIF (PJD).

Minister-delegate to the Prime Minister, in charge of Civil Service and the Modernization of the Public Sector: ABDELÂDIM GUERROUJ (MP).

Minister-delegate to the Minister of the Economy and Finance, in Charge of the Budget: DRISS EL-AZAMI EL-IDRISSI (PJD).

MINISTRIES

Office of the Prime Minister: Palais Royal, Touarga, Rabat; tel. (53) 7219400; fax (53) 7768656; e-mail courrier@pm.gov.ma; internet www.pm.gov.ma.

Ministry in charge of the Administration of National Defence: Rabat.

Ministry of Agriculture and Fisheries: ave Muhammad V, Quartier Administratif, pl. Abdellah Chefchaouni, BP 607, Rabat; tel. (53) 7760933; fax (53) 7776411; internet www.agriculture.gov .ma.

Ministry of Civil Service and the Modernization of the Public Sector: Quartier Administratif, rue Ahmed Cherkaoui, Agdal, BP 1076, Rabat; tel. (53) 7773106; fax (53) 7778438; e-mail info@mmsp .gov.ma; internet www.mmsp.gov.ma.

Ministry of Communication: ave Allal el-Fassi, Madinat al-Irfane Souissi, 10000 Rabat; tel. (53) 7678112; fax (53) 7680178; e-mail ministre@mincom.gov.ma; internet www.mincom.gov.ma.

Ministry of Culture: 1 rue Ghandi, Rabat; tel. (53) 7209494; fax (53) 7209400; e-mail webmaster@minculture.gov.ma; internet www .minculture.gov.ma.

Ministry of the Economy and Finance: blvd Muhammad V, Quartier Administratif, Chellah, Rabat; tel. (53) 7677501; fax (53) 7677526; e-mail internet@finances.gov.ma; internet www.finances.gov.ma.

Ministry of Employment and Vocational Training: ave Muhammad V, Hassan, BP 5015, Rabat; tel. (53) 7760521; fax (53) 7750192; e-mail communication@emploi.gov.ma; internet www.emploi.gov.ma.

Ministry of Energy, Mining, Water and the Environment: rue Abou Marouane Essaadi, BP 6208, Agdal, Rabat; tel. (53) 7688857; fax (53) 7688863; e-mail dsi@mem.gov.ma; internet www.mem.gov.ma.

Ministry of Equipment and Transport: Quartier Administratif, Chellah, Rabat; tel. (53) 7684151; fax (53) 7764825; internet www.mtpnet.gov.ma.

Ministry of Foreign Affairs and Co-operation: ave Franklin Roosevelt, Rabat; tel. (53) 7761583; fax (53) 7765508; e-mail mail@maec.gov.ma; internet www.maec.gov.ma.

Ministry in charge of General Affairs and Governance: Quartier Administratif, Agdal, BP 412, Rabat; tel. (53) 7687300; fax (53) 7771697; e-mail sec-sg@affaires-generales.gov.ma; internet www.affaires-generales.gov.ma.

Ministry of Habous (Religious Endowments) and Islamic Affairs: al-Mechouar Essaid, Rabat; tel. (53) 7766801; fax (53) 7666037; e-mail infos@islam-maroc.ma; internet www.habous.gov.ma.

Ministry of Handicrafts: Rabat; internet www.artesnet.gov.ma.

Ministry of Health: 335 ave Muhammad V, Rabat; tel. (53) 7761121; fax (53) 7763895; e-mail information@sante.gov.ma; internet srvweb.sante.gov.ma.

Ministry of Higher Education, Staff Training and Scientific Research: rue Idriss Al Akbar-Hassan, BP 4500, Rabat; tel. (53) 7217501; fax (53) 7217547; internet www.enssup.gov.ma.

Ministry of Housing, Town Planning and Development: rues al-Jouaze and al-Joumaize, Hay Riad, Secteur 16, 10000 Rabat; tel. (53) 7577000; fax (53) 7577373; e-mail mhuae@mhuae.gov.ma; internet www.mhu.gov.ma.

Ministry of Industry, Trade and New Technologies: 1 ave el-Hassan, Rabat; tel. (53) 7761878; fax (53) 7766265; e-mail ministre@mcinet.gov.ma; internet www.mcinet.gov.ma.

Ministry of the Interior: Quartier Administratif, Chellah, Rabat; tel. (53) 7761868; fax (53) 7762056.

Ministry of Justice and Liberties: pl. Mamounia, Rabat; tel. (53) 7732941; fax (53) 7730772; e-mail kourout@justice.gov.ma; internet www.justice.gov.ma.

Ministry in charge of Moroccans Resident Abroad: 59 rue Moulouya, Agdal 10000, Rabat; tel. (53) 7737573; fax (53) 7770006; e-mail info@mcmre.gov.ma; internet www.marocainsdumonde.gov.ma.

Ministry of National Education: Bab Rouah, Rabat; tel. (53) 7771822; fax (53) 7687255; internet www.men.gov.ma.

Ministry in charge of Relations with Parliament and Civil Society: Nouveau Quartier Administratif, Agdal, Rabat; tel. (53) 7775170; fax (53) 7777719; e-mail mirepa@mcrp.gov.ma; internet www.mcrp.gov.ma.

Ministry of Solidarity, Women, Family and Social Development: 47 ave ibn Sina, Agdal, Rabat; tel. (53) 7684060; fax (53) 7671967; e-mail mdsfs@mdsfs.ma; internet www.social.gov.ma.

Ministry of Tourism: Centre d'Affaires-Aile Sud, Lot 1 C17, ave Ennakhil-Hay Riad, Rabat; tel. (53) 7563729; fax (53) 7716923; e-mail webmaster@tourisme.gov.ma; internet www.tourisme.gov.ma.

Ministry of Youth and Sports: ave ibn Sina, Agdal, Rabat; tel. (53) 7680028; e-mail masterweb@mjs.gov.ma; internet www.mjs.gov.ma.

Legislature

Majlis al-Nuab
(Chamber of Representatives)

POB 431, Rabat; tel. (53) 7760960; fax (53) 7767726; e-mail parlement@parlement.ma; internet www.parlement.ma.

President: KARIM GHELLAB.

General Election, 25 November 2011

			Seats
Parti de la justice et du développement (PJD)	.	.	107
Istiqlal	.	.	60
Rassemblement national des indépendants (RNI)	.		52
Parti de l'authenticité et de la modernité (PAM)	.	.	47
Union socialiste des forces populaires (USFP)	.	.	39
Mouvement populaire (MP)	.	.	32
Union constitutionnelle (UC)	.	.	23
Parti du progrès et du socialisme (PPS)	.	.	18
Parti travailliste (PT)	.	.	4
Mouvement démocratique et social (MDS)	.	.	2
Parti du renouveau et de l'équité (PRE)	.	.	2
Parti de l'environnement et du développement durable (PEDD)	.	.	2
Parti Al Ahd Démocratique	.	.	2
Others	.	.	5
Total	.	.	**395***

* Of the total number of seats, 305 seats are reserved for candidates from local party lists, while the remaining 90 seats are allocated to candidates from national lists. Each party must allocate two-thirds of its share of those 90 seats to women and the remaining one-third to men under 40 years of age.

Majlis al-Mustasharin
(Chamber of Advisers)

POB 432, Rabat; tel. (53) 7218304; fax (53) 7733192; e-mail info@conseiller.ma; internet www.conseiller.ma.

President: MUHAMMAD CHEIKH BIADILLAH.

Election, 5 December 1997*

			Seats
Rassemblement national des indépendants (RNI)	.	.	42
Mouvement démocratique et social (MDS)	.	.	33
Union constitutionnelle (UC)	.	.	28
Mouvement populaire (MP)	.	.	27
Parti national démocrate (PND)	.	.	21
Istiqlal	.	.	21
Union socialiste des forces populaires (USFP)	.	.	16
Mouvement national populaire (MNP)	.	.	15
Parti de l'action (PA)	.	.	13
Front des forces démocratiques (FFD)	.	.	12
Parti du progrès et du socialisme (PPS)	.	.	7
Parti socialiste démocratique (PSD)	.	.	4
Parti démocratique et de l'indépendance (PDI)	.	.	4
Trade unions			
Confédération démocratique du travail (CDT)	.	.	11
Union marocaine du travail (UMT)	.	.	8
Union générale des travailleurs du Maroc (UGTM)	.	.	3
Others	.	.	5
Total	.	.	**270**

* Of the chamber's 270 members, 162 were elected by local councils, 81 by chambers of commerce and 27 by trade unions. Further elections were held on 15 September 2000, 6 October 2003, 8 September 2006 and 3 October 2009. According to the provisions of the 2011 Constitution, the number of seats in the Chamber was to be reduced to no more than 120.

Political Organizations

Congrès national ittihadi (CNI): 209 blvd Strasbourg, Résidence C, 2ème étage, Casablanca; tel. and fax (52) 2447664; e-mail onittihadi@caramail.com; f. 2001 by dissident mems of USFP; Sec.-Gen. ABDESSALAM ELAZIZ.

Front des forces démocratiques (FFD): 13 ave Tariq ibn Ziad, Hassan, Rabat; tel. (53) 7661625; fax (53) 7660621; e-mail forces@menara.ma; internet www.ffd.ma; f. 1997 after split from PPS; Sec.-Gen. THAMI EL-KHYARI.

Istiqlal (Independence): 4 ave Ibn Toumert, Bab el-Had, 50020 Rabat; tel. (53) 7730951; fax (53) 7725417; e-mail p.istiqlal2009@hotmail.com; internet www.partistiqlal.org; f. 1944; aims to raise living standards and to confer equal rights on all; emphasizes the Moroccan claim to Western Sahara; Sec.-Gen. HAMID CHABAT.

Mouvement démocratique et social (MDS): 4 ave Imam Malik, route des Zaêrs, Rabat; tel. (57) 7631552; fax (53) 7658253; f. 1996 as Mouvement national démocratique et social after split from Mouvement national populaire (MNP); adopted current name in Nov. 1996; Sec.-Gen. MAHMOUD ARCHANE.

Mouvement populaire (MP): 66 rue Patrice Lumumba, Rabat; tel. (53) 7766431; fax (53) 7767537; e-mail parti_mp@hotmail.fr; internet www.alharaka.ma; f. 1958; merged with the MNP and Union démocratique in 2006; liberal; Sec.-Gen. MOHAND LAENSER.

Parti de l'action (PA): 113 ave Allal Ben Abdallah, Rabat; tel. (53) 7206661; f. 1974; advocates democracy and progress; Sec.-Gen. MUHAMMAD EL-IDRISSI.

Parti Al Ahd Démocratique: 14 rue Idriss al-Akbar, rue Tafraout, Hassan, Rabat; tel. (53) 7204816; fax (53) 7204786; e-mail alhakika@iam.net.ma; f. 2002; Chair. NAJIB EL-OUAZZANI.

Parti de l'authenticité et de la modernité (PAM): internet www.pam.ma; f. 2008; Founder FOUAD ALI EL-HIMMA; Sec.-Gen. MUSTAPHA BAKKOURI.

Parti de l'avant-garde démocratique socialiste (PADS): 54 ave de la Résistance Océan, Rabat 10000; tel. and fax (53) 7200559; e-mail pads.pads@gmail.com; an offshoot of USFP; legalized in April 1992; Sec.-Gen. ABDERRAHMAN BENAMEUR.

Parti démocrate national (PDN): f. May 2009 by fmr members of Parti national démocrate, following that party's merger into the PAM; Sec.-Gen. ABDULLAH KADIRI.

Parti démocratique et de l'indépendance (PDI): 9 Lalla Yakout, rue Araar, Apt 11, 2ème étage, blvd d'Anfa, Casablanca; tel. (52) 2200949; fax (52) 2200928; f. 1946; Sec.-Gen. ABDELWAHID MAÂCH.

Parti de l'environnement et du développement durable (PEDD): 3 rue Azilal, Hassan, Rabat; tel. and fax (53) 7670620; e-mail pedmaroc@menara.ma; internet www.pedmaroc.ma; f. 2002 as Parti de l'environnement et du développement; merged with PAM in 2008; relaunched as above in 2009; environmentalist; Sec.-Gen. Dr AHMAD AL-ALAMI.

Parti des forces citoyennes (PFC): 353 blvd Muhammad V, 9ème étage, Casablanca; tel. (52) 2400608; fax (52) 2400613; e-mail citoyennes@menara.ma; f. 2001; Sec.-Gen. ABDERRAHIM LAHJOUJI.

Parti de la justice et du développement (PJD): ave Abdelwahed Elmorakechi, rue Elyafrani, 4 les Orangers, Rabat; tel. (53) 7208862; fax (53) 7208854; e-mail info@pjd.ma; internet www.pjd.ma; f. 1967 as Mouvement populaire constitutionnel et démocratique; breakaway party from MP; formally absorbed mems of the Islamic asscn Al Islah wa Attajdid in June 1996; adopted current name in Oct. 1998; Sec.-Gen. ABDELILAH BENKIRANE.

Parti marocain libéral (PML): 114 ave Allal Ben Abdellah, 2ème étage, Rabat; tel. (53) 7733670; fax (53) 7733611; e-mail pml@menara.ma; f. 2002; Nat. Co-ordinator MUHAMMAD ZIANE.

Parti du progrès et du socialisme (PPS): 29 ave Muhammad VI, Youssoufia, Rabat; tel. (53) 7759464; fax (53) 7759476; e-mail sg@pps.maroc.org; internet www.ppsmaroc.com; f. 1974; successor to Parti communiste marocain (banned in 1952) and Parti de la libération et du socialisme (banned in 1969); left-wing; advocates modernization, social progress, nationalization and democracy; 35,000 mems; Sec.-Gen. MUHAMMAD NABIL BENABDELLAH.

Parti de la réforme et du développement (PRD): 34 ave Pasteur, Rabat; tel. and fax (53) 7703801; f. 2001 by fmr mems of RNI; Sec.-Gen. MUHAMMAD GOUMANI.

Parti de la renaissance et de la vertu: Bouznika; f. 2005; national democratic party based on the principles of Islam; Sec.-Gen. MUHAMMAD KHALIDI.

Parti du renouveau et de l'équité (PRE): 16 rue Sebou, Apt 5, Agdal, Rabat; tel. (53) 7777266; fax (53) 7777452; e-mail partipre@yahoo.fr; internet www.pre.ma; f. 2002; Pres. CHAKIR ACHEHBAR.

Parti socialiste unifié (PSU): 9 rue d'Agadir, Immeuble Maréchal Ameziane, Casablanca; tel. (52) 2485902; fax (52) 2278442; e-mail psumaroc@yahoo.fr; f. 2005 by merger of Parti de la gauche socialiste unifieé and Fidélité à la démocratie; Sec.-Gen. NABILA MOUNIB.

Parti travailliste (PT): 9 rue Ksar Essouk, Hassan, Rabat; f. 2005; centre-left; Sec.-Gen. ABDELKRIM BENATIQ.

Rassemblement national des indépendants (RNI): 6 rue Laos, ave Hassan II, Rabat; tel. (53) 7721420; fax (53) 7733824; internet www.rni.ma; f. 1978 from the pro-Govt independents' group that then formed the majority in the Chamber of Representatives; Pres. SALAHEDDINE MEZOUAR.

Union constitutionnelle (UC): 158 ave des Forces Armées Royales, Casablanca; tel. (52) 2441144; fax (52) 2441141; e-mail union_constit@menara.ma; f. 1983; 51-mem. Political Bureau; Sec.-Gen. MUHAMMAD ABIED.

Union Marocaine pour la démocratie (UMD): Rabat; f. 2006; Sec.-Gen. JAMAL MANDRI.

Union socialiste des forces populaires (USFP): 9 ave al-Araâr, Hay Riad, Rabat; tel. (53) 7565511; fax (53) 7565510; e-mail usfp@usfp.ma; internet www.usfp.ma; f. 1959 as Union nationale des forces populaires (UNFP); became USFP in 1974 after UNFP split into 2 separate entities; merged with Parti socialiste démocratique in 2005; democratic socialist and progressive party; 260,000 mems; First Sec. DRISS LACHGAR.

The following movement is not authorized as a political party by the Government, but is generally tolerated:

Al-Adl wal-Ihsan (Justice and Charity): internet www.aljamaa.net; advocates an Islamic state based on *Shari'a* law; rejects violence; Sec.-Gen. MUHAMMAD ABBADI.

The following group is active in the disputed territory of Western Sahara:

Frente Popular para la Liberación de Saguia el-Hamra y Río de Oro (Frente Polisario) (Polisario Front): BP 10, el-Mouradia, Algiers, Algeria; fax (2) 747206; e-mail dgmae@mail.wissal.dz; f. 1973 to gain independence for Western Sahara, first from Spain and then from Morocco and Mauritania; signed peace treaty with Mauritanian Govt in 1979; supported by Algerian Govt; in February 1976 proclaimed the Sahrawi Arab Democratic Republic (SADR); admitted as the 51st mem. of the OAU in Feb. 1982 and currently recognized by more than 75 countries world-wide; its main organs are a 33-mem. Nat. Secretariat, a 101-mem. Sahrawi Nat. Assembly (Parliament) and a 13-mem. Govt; Sec.-Gen. of the Polisario Front and Pres. of the SADR MUHAMMAD ABD AL-AZIZ; Prime Minister of the SADR ABDELKADER TALEB OUMAR.

Diplomatic Representation

EMBASSIES IN MOROCCO

Algeria: Angle ave Muhammad VI, Rue Ghiyata, Soulssi, BP 448, 10001 Rabat; tel. (537) 756931; fax (537) 756918; Ambassador AHMED BENYAMINA.

Angola: km 5, 53 Ahmed Rifaï, BP 1318, Souissi, Rabat; tel. (53) 7659239; fax (53) 7659238; e-mail amb.angola@menara.ma; Ambassador MANUEL MIGUEL DA COSTA ARAGÃO.

Argentina: 4 ave Mehdi Ben Barka, Souissi, 10000 Rabat; tel. (53) 7755120; fax (53) 7755410; e-mail emarr@mrecic.gov.ar; Ambassador JOSÉ PEDRO PICO.

Austria: 2 rue Tiddas, BP 135, 10000 Rabat; tel. (53) 7761698; fax (53) 7765425; e-mail rabat-ob@bmeia.gv.at; internet www.aussenministerium.at/rabat; Ambassador Dr WOLFGANG ANGERHOLZER.

Azerbaijan: rue 3 Abu Hanifa, Aqdal, Rabat; tel. (53) 7671915; fax (53) 7671918; e-mail azembma@menara.ma; Ambassador TAREK ISMAEIL ALIEV.

Bahrain: rue Béni Hassan, km 6.5, route des Zaêrs, Villa 318, POB 1470, Souissi, Rabat; tel. (53) 7633500; fax (53) 7630732; e-mail rabat.mission@mofa.gov.bh; Ambassador KHALID BIN SALMAN AL KHALIFA.

Bangladesh: 25 ave Tarek ibn Ziad, BP 1468, Rabat; tel. (53) 7766731; fax (53) 7766729; e-mail bangladoot@menara.ma; internet bangladeshembassy-morocco.webs.com; Ambassador NUR MUHAMMAD.

Belgium: 6 ave de Muhammad el-Fassi, Tour Hassan, Rabat; tel. (53) 7268060; fax (53) 7767003; e-mail rabat@diplobel.fed.be; internet www.diplomatie.be/rabat; Ambassador JEAN-LUC BODSON.

Benin: 30 ave Mehdi Ben Barka, BP 5187, Souissi, 10105 Rabat; tel. (53) 7754158; fax (53) 7754156; e-mail benin@menara.ma; Ambassador BIO TORO OROUGUIWA.

Brazil: 10 ave el-Jacaranda, Secteur 2, Hay Riad, 10000 Rabat; tel. (53) 7714613; fax (53) 7714808; e-mail ambassadedubresil@menara.ma; internet rabat.itamaraty.gov.br; Ambassador FREDERICO SALOMÃO DUQUE ESTRADA MEYER.

Bulgaria: 4 ave Ahmed el-Yazidi, BP 1301, 10000 Rabat; tel. (53) 7765477; fax (53) 7763201; e-mail embassy.rabat@mfa.bg; internet www.mfa.bg/embassies/morocco; Ambassador BORIANA SIMEONOVA.

Burkina Faso: 7 rue al-Bouziri, BP 6484, Agdal, 10101 Rabat; tel. (53) 7675512; fax (53) 7675517; e-mail ambfrba@smirt.net.ma; Ambassador YERO BOLY.

Cameroon: 20 rue du Rif, BP 1790, Souissi, Rabat; tel. (53) 7758818; fax (53) 7750540; e-mail ambacam@iam.net.com; Ambassador MOUHAMADOU YOUSSIFOU.

Canada: 13 bis rue Jaâfar al-Sadik, BP 709, Agdal, Rabat; tel. (53) 7687400; fax (53) 7687430; e-mail rabat@international.gc.ca; internet www.morocco.gc.ca; Ambassador SANDRA McCARDELL.

Central African Republic: 65, rue 29 Youssoufia est-ext. de l'etat, BP 770, Agdal, 10000 Rabat; tel. (53) 7658970; fax (53) 7659216; e-mail centreafriquemaghreb1@menara.ma; Ambassador ISMAÏLA NIMAGA.

Chile: 35 ave Ahmed Balafrej, Souissi, Rabat; tel. (53) 7636065; fax (53) 7636067; e-mail echilema@mtds.com; Ambassador CARLOS CHARME SILVA.

China, People's Republic: 16 ave Ahmed Balafrej, 10000 Rabat; tel. (53) 7754056; fax (53) 7757519; e-mail chinaemb_ma@mfa.gov.cn; internet ma.china-embassy.org; Ambassador XU JINGHU.

Congo, Democratic Republic: 34 ave de la Victoire, BP 553, 10000 Rabat; tel. (53) 7262280; fax (53)7207407; e-mail ambardcrabat60@yahoo.fr; Chargé d'affaires a.i. WAWA BAMIALY.

Congo, Republic: 197 ave Général Abdendi Britel, Souissi II, Rabat; tel. (53) 7659966; fax (53) 7659959; Ambassador VALENTIN OLLESSONGO.

Côte d'Ivoire: 21 rue de Tiddas, BP 192, 10001 Rabat; tel. (53) 7763151; fax (53) 7762792; e-mail ambcim@clam.net.ma; Ambassador IDRISSA TRAORE.

Croatia: 73 rue Marnissa, Souissi, Rabat; tel. (53) 7638824; fax (53) 7638827; e-mail croemb.rabat@mvpei.hr; Chargé d'affaires a.i. JASNA MILETA.

Czech Republic: Villa Merzaa, km 4.5, ave Muhammad VI, BP 410, rue Zankat Aït Melloul, Souissi, 10000 Rabat; tel. (53) 7755421; fax (53) 7754393; e-mail rabat@embassy.mzv.cz; internet www.mzv.cz/rabat; Ambassador MICHAELA FROŇKOVÁ.

Denmark: 14 rue Tiddas angle rue Roudana, Quartier Hassan, 10020 Rabat; tel. (53) 7665020; fax (53) 7665021; e-mail rbaamb@um.dk; internet www.rabat.um.dk; Ambassador LARS VISSING.

Dominican Republic: 3 ave Mehdi Ben Barka, Secteur 6, Bloc E, Hay Riad, 10000 Rabat; tel. (53) 7715905; fax (53) 7715957; Ambassador FRANCISCO A. CARABALLO.

Egypt: 31 rue al-Jazair, 10000 Rabat; tel. (53) 7731833; fax (53) 7706821; e-mail embegypt@mtds.com; Ambassador ABU BAKR HEFNI.

Equatorial Guinea: ave President Roosevelt, angle rue d'Agadir 9, Rabat; tel. and fax (53) 7660337; Chargé d'affaires a.i. LUCRECIA SIPACO.

Finland: 145 rue Soufiane Ben Wahb, BP 590, 10002 Rabat; tel. (53) 7658775; fax (53) 7658904; e-mail sanomat.rab@formin.fi; internet www.finlande.ma; Ambassador CHRISTINA HARTTILA.

France: 1 rue Aguelmane Sidi Ali, BP 577, Agdal, 10190 Rabat; tel. (53) 7276600; fax (53) 7276711; internet www.ambafrance-ma.org; Ambassador CHARLES FRIES.

Gabon: 72 ave Mehdi Ben Barka, BP 10170, Souissi, 10105 Rabat; tel. (53) 7751950; fax (53) 7757550; e-mail chancellerie@ambagabon.ma; internet www.ambagabon.ma; Chargé d'affaires a.i. FRANÇOIS BANGA EBOUMI.

The Gambia: 11 rue Cadi Ben Hammadi Senhadji, Souissi, 10000 Rabat; tel. (53) 7638045; fax (53) 7752908; Ambassador LAMIN KABBA BAJO.

Germany: 7 Zankat Madnine, BP 235, 10000 Rabat; tel. (53) 7218600; fax (53) 706851; e-mail info@rabat.diplo.de; internet www.rabat.diplo.de; Ambassador MICHAEL WITTER.

Ghana: 27 rue Ghomara, La Pinede, Souissi, Rabat; tel. (53) 7757620; fax (53) 7757630; e-mail ghanaemb@menara.ma; Ambassador CLIFFORD AKOTEY.

Greece: km 5.5, ave Muhammad VI, Villa Chems, Souissi, 10000 Rabat; tel. (53) 7638964; fax (53) 7638990; e-mail gremb.rab@mfa.gr; internet www.mfa.gr/missionsabroad/morocco; Ambassador PANAYOTIS STOURNARAS.

Guinea: 15 rue Hamzah, Agdal, 10000 Rabat; tel. and fax (53) 7674148; fax (53) 7675070; e-mail ambaguirabat@mae.gov.gn; Ambassador ABOUBACAR KABA.

Holy See: rue Béni M'tir, BP 1303, Souissi, Rabat (Apostolic Nunciature); tel. (53) 7772277; fax (53) 7756213; e-mail nuntius@iam.net.ma; Apostolic Nuncio Most Rev. ANTONIO SOZZO (Titular Archbishop of Concordia).

Hungary: route des Zaêrs, 17 Zankat Aït Melloul, BP 5026, Souissi, Rabat; tel. (53) 7750757; fax (53) 7754123; e-mail mission.rba@kum.hu; internet www.mfa.gov.hu/emb/rabat; Ambassador JÁNOS PERÉNYI.

India: 88, rue Oulad Tidrarine, Souissi, Rabat; tel. (53) 7635801; fax (53) 7634733; e-mail amb.rabat@mea.gov.in; internet www.indianembassyrabat.com; Ambassador KRISHAN KUMAR.

Indonesia: 63 rue Béni Boufrah, km 6, route des Zaêrs, BP 576, 10000 Rabat; tel. (53) 7757860; fax (53) 7757859; e-mail kbrirabat@iam.net.ma; internet www.indonesie.ma; Ambassador TOSARI WIDJAJA.

Iran: ave Imam Malik, rue Kadi Muhammad Achour, BP 490, Souissi, 10001 Rabat; tel. (53) 7752167; fax (53) 7659118; e-mail ambassadiran@gmail.com; Ambassador (vacant).

Iraq: 39 blvd Mehdi Ben Barka, 10100 Rabat; tel. (53) 7754466; fax (53) 7759749; e-mail rbtemb@iraqmofamail.net; Ambassador HAZEM AHMED MAHMOUD AL-YOUSOFI.

Italy: 2 rue Idriss al-Azhar, BP 111, 10001 Rabat; tel. (53) 7219730; fax (53) 7706882; e-mail ambassade.rabat@esteri.it; internet www.ambrabat.esteri.it; Ambassador PIERGIORGIO CHERUBINI.

Japan: 39 ave Ahmed Balafrej, Souissi, 10170 Rabat; tel. (53) 7631782; fax (53) 7750078; e-mail amb-japon@fusion.net.ma; internet www.ma.emb-japan.go.jp; Ambassador TOSHINORI YANAGIYA.

Jordan: 65 Villa Wafaa Lodgement Militaire, Souissi II, Rabat; tel. (53) 7751125; fax (53) 7758722; e-mail jo.am@iam.net.ma; Ambassador ALI HASSAN EL-KAID.

Korea, Republic: 41 ave Mehdi Ben Barka, Souissi, 10100 Rabat; tel. (53) 7756791; fax (53) 7750189; e-mail morocco@mofat.go.kr; internet mar.mofat.go.kr; Ambassador LEE TAE-HO.

Kuwait: km 4.3, ave Imam Malik, Souissi, Rabat; tel. (53) 7631111; fax (53) 7753591; e-mail alrabat@mofa.gov.kw; Ambassador SHAMLAN ABD AL-AZIZ AL-ROUMI.

Lebanon: 114 ave Abd el-Malek Ben Marouane, Rabat; tel. (53) 7656949; fax (53) 7657195; Chargé d'affaires a.i. YOUSSEF RAJJI.

Liberia: 23 rue Qadi Ben Hamadi Senhaji, Souissi, Rabat; tel. and fax (53) 7638426; e-mail liberanmissioninrabat@yahoo.fr; Chargé d'affaires MORIEBA K. SANOE.

Libya: km 5.5, route de Zaêrs, ave Imam Malik, Souissi, Rabat; tel. (53) 7631871; fax (53) 7631877; Ambassador ABUBAKR ALI SHAKLAWOON.

Malaysia: 17 ave Bir Kacem, Souissi, Rabat; tel. (53) 7658324; fax (53) 7658363; e-mail malrabat@kln.gov.my; internet www.kln.gov.my/perwakilan/rabat; Ambassador JAMAL BIN HASSAN.

Mali: 7 rue Thami Lamdouar, Souissi, Rabat; tel. (53) 7759121; fax (53) 7754742; Ambassador TOUMANI DJIMÉ DIALLO.

Mauritania: 6 rue Thami Lamdouar, BP 207, Souissi, 10000 Rabat; tel. (53) 7656678; fax (53) 7656680; e-mail ambarim-rabat@menara.com; internet www.ambarimrabat.ma; Ambassador MOHAMED OULD MAAOUYA.

Mexico: 6 rue Kadi Mohamed Brebri, BP 1789, Souissi, 10100 Rabat; tel. (53) 7631969; fax (53) 7631971; e-mail embamexmar@smirt.net.ma; internet embamex.sre.gob.mx/marruecos; Ambassador PORFIRIO THIERRY MUÑOZ-LEDO CHEVANNIER.

Netherlands: 40 rue de Tunis, BP 329, Hassan, 10001 Rabat; tel. (53) 7219600; fax (53) 7219665; e-mail rab@minbuza.nl; internet www.mfa.nl/rab; Ambassador RON STRIKKER.

Niger: 14 bis, rue Jabal al-Ayachi, Agdal, Rabat; tel. (53) 7674615; fax (53) 7674629; Ambassador ABDOULAYE MOUMOUNI DJERMAKOYE.

Nigeria: 70 ave Omar ibn al-Khattab, BP 347, Agdal, Rabat; tel. (53) 7671857; fax (53) 7672739; e-mail nigerianrabat@menara.ma; Ambassador ABDULLAH MUHAMMAD WALI.

Norway: 6 rue Beni Ritoune, BP 757, Agdal, Souissi, 10106 Rabat; tel. (53) 7664200; fax (53) 7664299; e-mail emb.rabat@mfa.no; internet www.norvege.ma; Ambassador FRED HARALD NOMME.

Oman: 21 rue Hamza, Agdal, 10000 Rabat; tel. (53) 7673788; fax (53) 7674567; Ambassador MOUSA HAMDAN MOUSA AL-TAEI.

Pakistan: 37 ave Ahmed Balafrej, Souissi, Rabat; tel. (53) 7631192; fax (53) 7631243; e-mail pareprabat@menara.ma; internet www.mofa.gov.pk/morocco/mission.aspx; Ambassador (vacant).

Peru: 16 rue d'Ifrane, 10000 Rabat; tel. (53) 7723236; fax (53) 7702803; e-mail leprurabat@menara.ma; Ambassador (vacant).

Poland: 23 rue Oqbah, Agdal, BP 425, 10000 Rabat; tel. (53) 7771173; fax (53) 7775320; e-mail apologne@menara.ma; internet www.rabat.polemb.net; Ambassador WITOLD SPIRYDOWICZ.

Portugal: 5 rue Thami Lamdouar, Souissi, 10100 Rabat; tel. (53) 7756446; fax (53) 7756445; e-mail ambassade.portugal@menara.ma; Ambassador FRANCISCO XAVIER ESTEVES.

Qatar: 4 ave Tarik ibn Ziad, BP 1220, 10001 Rabat; tel. (53) 7765681; fax (53) 7765774; e-mail rabat@mofa.gov.qa; Ambassador SAQR MUBARAK AL-MANSOURI.

Romania: 10 rue d'Ouezzane, Hassan, 10000 Rabat; tel. (53) 7724694; fax (53) 7700196; e-mail amb.roumanie@menara.ma; internet rabat.mae.ro; Ambassador SIMONA MARIANA IOAN.

Russia: km 4, ave Muhammad VI, Souissi, Rabat; tel. (53) 7753509; fax (53) 7753590; e-mail ambrusmaroc@inbox.ru; internet www.marocco.mid.ru; Ambassador BORIS BOLOTIN.

Saudi Arabia: 322 ave Imam Malik, km 3.5, route des Zaêrs, Rabat; tel. (53) 7657454; fax (53) 7639696; e-mail maemb@mofa.gov.sa; Ambassador Dr MUHAMMAD ABD AL-RAHMAN IBN ABD AL-AZIZ BACHAR.

Senegal: 17 rue Cadi Ben Hamadi Senhaji, Souissi, BP 365, 10000 Rabat; tel. (53) 7754171; fax (53) 7754149; e-mail ambassene@menara.ma; Ambassador AMADOU HABIBOU NDIAYE.

Serbia: BP 5014, 23 ave Mehdi Ben Barka, Souissi, 10105 Rabat; tel. (53) 7752201; fax (53) 7753258; e-mail sermont@menara.ma; Ambassador STANISLAV STAKIC.

South Africa: 34 rue Saâdiens, Rabat; tel. (53) 7706760; fax (53) 7706756; e-mail sudaf@mtds.com; Chargé d'affaires N. K. M. SELEKA.

Spain: 3 rue Aïn Khalouiya, ave Muhammad VI, km 5.3, route des Zaêrs, Souissi, 10000 Rabat; tel. (53) 7633900; fax (53) 7630600; e-mail emb.rabat@maec.es; internet www.maec.es/subwebs/embajadas/rabat; Ambassador ALBERTO JOSÉ NAVARRO GONZÁLEZ.

Sudan: 5 ave Ghomara, Souissi, 10000 Rabat; tel. (53) 7752863; fax (53) 7752865; e-mail sudanirab@menara.com; Ambassador TAYEB ALI AHMED.

Sweden: 159 ave Muhammad VI, BP 428, Souissi, 10001 Rabat; tel. (53) 7633210; fax (53) 7758048; e-mail ambassaden.rabat@gov.se; internet www.swedenabroad.com/rabat; Ambassador ANNA HAMMARGREN.

Switzerland: sq. de Berkane, BP 169, 10020 Rabat; tel. (53) 7268030; fax (53) 7268040; e-mail rab.vertretung@eda.admin.ch; internet www.eda.admin.ch/rabat; Ambassador LOUIS BERTRAND.

Syria: km 5.2, route des Zaërs, BP 5158, Souissi, Rabat; tel. (53) 7757521; fax (53) 7757522; e-mail syriaembassy@menara.ma; Ambassador (vacant).

Thailand: 33 ave Lalla Meriem, Souissi, 10170, Rabat; tel. (53) 7634603; fax (53) 7634607; e-mail thaima@menara.ma; internet www.thaiembassy.org/rabat; Ambassador KUNDALEE PRACHIMDHIT.

Tunisia: 6 ave de Fès et 1 rue d'Ifrane, 10000 Rabat; tel. (53) 7730636; fax (53) 7730637; Ambassador RAFA BEN ACHOUR.

Turkey: 7 ave Abdelkrim Benjelloun, 10010 Rabat; tel. (53) 7661522; fax (53) 7660476; e-mail ambassade.rabat@mfa.gov.tr; internet rabat.emb.mfa.gov.tr; Ambassador UĞUR ARINER.

Ukraine: 222, rue Mouaouya Ben Houdaig, Cité OLM, Souissi II, 10020 Rabat; tel. (53) 7657840; fax (53) 7754679; e-mail emb_ma@mfa.gov.ua; internet www.mfa.gov.ua/morocco; Ambassador YAROSLAV KOVAL.

United Arab Emirates: 11 ave des Alaouines, 10000 Rabat; tel. (53) 7702085; fax (53) 7724145; e-mail rabat@mofa.gov.ae; internet uae-embassy.ae/embassies/ma; Ambassador AL-ASRI SAID AHMAD AL-DAHIRI.

United Kingdom: 28 ave S. A. R. Sidi Muhammad, BP 45, Souissi, 10105 Rabat; tel. (53) 7633333; fax (53) 7758709; e-mail generalenquiries.rabat@fco.gov.uk; internet ukinmorocco.fco.gov.uk; Ambassador TIMOTHY MORRIS.

USA: 2 ave de Muhammad el-Fassi, Rabat; tel. (53) 7762265; fax (53) 7765661; e-mail ircrabat@usembassy.ma; internet morocco.usembassy.gov; Ambassador SAMUEL L. KAPLAN.

Venezuela: 58 Lot OLM, Villa Yasmine, rue Capitaine Abdeslam el-Moudden el-Alami, Souissi, Rabat; tel. (53) 7650315; fax (53) 7650372; e-mail emvenez@menara.ma; Chargé d'affaires a.i. AHMED ABUSAID.

Yemen: ave Imam Malik, km 6.6, rue Beni Tajit, Quartier des Ambassadeurs, Souissi, Rabat; tel. (53) 7631220; fax (53) 7631267; e-mail yemen@menara.ma; Chargé d'affaires a.i. AHMAD MUHAMMAD SALEM HAIDRAH.

Judicial System

Supreme Court (Al-Majlis al-Aala): Hay Riad, Ave al-Nakhil, Rabat; tel. (53) 7714931; fax (53) 7715106; e-mail coursupreme@coursupreme.ma; internet www.coursupreme.ma; responsible for the interpretation of the law and regulates the jurisprudence of the courts and tribunals of the Kingdom. The Supreme Court sits at Rabat and is divided into 6 Chambers; First Pres. MUSTAPHA FARÈS.

Courts of Appeal: The 21 courts hear appeals from lower courts and also comprise a criminal division.

Courts of First Instance: The 65 courts pass judgment on offences punishable by up to five years' imprisonment. These courts also pass judgment, without possibility of appeal, in personal and civil cases involving up to 3,000 dirhams.

Communal and District Courts: composed of one judge, who is assisted by a clerk or secretary, and hear only civil and criminal cases.

Administrative Courts: The seven courts pass judgment, subject to appeal before the Supreme Court pending the establishment of administrative appeal courts, on litigation with government departments.

Commercial Courts: The nine courts pass judgment, without the possibility of appeal, on all commercial litigations involving up to 9,000 dirhams. They also pass judgment on claims involving more than 9,000 dirhams, which can be appealed against in the commercial appeal courts.

Permanent Royal Armed Forces' Court: tries offences committed by the armed forces and military officers.

Attorney-General: MUSTAPHA MEDDAH.

Religion

ISLAM

About 99% of Moroccans are Muslims (of whom about 90% are of the Sunni sect), and Islam is the state religion.

CHRISTIANITY

There are about 69,000 Christians, mostly Roman Catholics.

The Roman Catholic Church

Morocco (excluding the disputed territory of Western Sahara) comprises two archdioceses, directly responsible to the Holy See. The Moroccan archbishops participate in the Conférence Episcopale Régionale du Nord de l'Afrique (f. 1985).

Bishops' Conference: Conférence Episcopale Régionale du Nord de l'Afrique, 1 rue Hadj Muhammad Riffaï, BP 258, 10001 Rabat; tel. (53) 7709239; fax (53) 7706282; e-mail archev.rabat@wanadoo.net.ma; f. 1985; Pres. Most Rev. VINCENT LANDEL (Archbishop of Rabat).

Archbishop of Rabat: Most Rev. VINCENT LANDEL, Archevêché, 1 rue Hadj Muhammad Riffaï, BP 258, 10001 Rabat; tel. (53) 7709239; fax (53) 7706282; e-mail landel@wanadoo.net.ma.

Archbishop of Tangier: Most Rev. SANTIAGO AGRELO MARTÍNEZ, Archevêché, 55 rue Sidi Bouabid, BP 2116, 9000 Tangier; tel. (53) 9932762; fax (53) 9949117; e-mail agrelomar@hotmail.com.

Western Sahara comprises a single Apostolic Prefecture, with an estimated 80 Catholics (2007).

Prefect Apostolic of Western Sahara: Fr ACACIO VALBUENA RODRÍGUEZ, Misión Católica, BP 31, 70001 el-Aaiún; e-mail omisahara@menara.ma.

The Anglican Communion

Within the Church of England, Morocco forms part of the diocese of Gibraltar in Europe. There are Anglican churches in Casablanca and Tangier.

Protestant Church

Evangelical Church: 33 rue d'Azilal, 20000 Casablanca; tel. (52) 2302151; fax (52) 2444768; e-mail eeam@lesblancs.com; f. 1920; established in 8 towns; Pres. Pastor JEAN-LUC BLANC; 1,000 mems.

JUDAISM

It is estimated that there are fewer than 7,000 Jews in Morocco, of whom approximately 5,000 reside in Casablanca, with smaller communities in Rabat and other cities.

Conseil des Communautés Israélites du Maroc: 52 Béni Snassen, Souissi, Rabat; tel. (53) 222861; fax (53) 266953; Pres. SERGE BERDUGO.

The Press

DAILIES

Casablanca

Al-Ahdath al-Maghribia (Moroccan Events): 5 rue Saint-Emilion, Casablanca; tel. (52) 2443038; fax (52) 2442976; e-mail elberini@ahdath.info; f. 1998; Arabic; Dir MUHAMMAD EL-BERINI; circ. 19,811 (2008/09).

Assabah (The Morning): Groupe Ecomedia, 70 blvd al-Massira al-Khadra, Casablanca; tel. (52) 2953660; fax (52) 2364358; e-mail assabahcasa@leconomiste.com; internet www.assabah.press.ma; f. 2000; Arabic; sister publication of *l'Economiste*; Pres. ABDELMOUNAÏM DILAMI; Dir-Gen. KHALID BELYAZID; circ. 71,935 (2008/09).

Assahra al-Maghribia: 17 rue Othman Ben Affan, Casablanca; tel. (52) 2489120; fax (52) 2203935; e-mail web.master@almaghribia.ma; internet www.almaghribia.ma; f. 1989; Arabic; Dir AHMED NACHATTI.

Aujourd'hui le Maroc: 213 Rond-Point d'Europe, 20490 Casablanca; tel. (52) 2262674; fax (52) 2262443; e-mail alm@aujourdhui.ma; internet www.aujourdhui.ma; f. 2001; French; Dir KHALIL HACHIMI IDRISSI; Editor-in-Chief OMAR DAHBI; circ. 5,435 (2008/09).

Al-Bayane (The Manifesto): 119 blvd Emile Zola, 8ème étage, BP 13152, Casablanca; tel. (52) 2307882; fax (52) 2308080; internet www.casanet.net.ma/albayane; f. 1971; Arabic and French; organ of the Parti du progrès et du socialisme; Dir ALLAL EL-MALEH; Editor AHMED ZAKI; circ. 2,364 (2008/09).

L'Economiste: Groupe Ecomedia, 70 blvd al-Massira al-Khadra, Casablanca; tel. (52) 2953600; fax (52) 2365926; e-mail info@leconomiste.com; internet www.leconomiste.com; f. 1991; French; Pres. ABDELMOUNAÏM DILAMI; Dir-Gen. KHALID BELYAZID; Editor-in-Chief NADIA SALAH; circ. 19,937 (2008/09).

Al-Ittihad al-Ichtiraki (Socialist Unity): 33 rue Amir Abdelkader, BP 2165, Casablanca; tel. (52) 2407385; fax (52) 2619405; e-mail ail@menara.ma; internet www.alittihad.press.ma; Arabic; f. 1983; organ of the Union socialiste des forces populaires; Dir ABD AL-HADI DATE; Editor MUSTAPHA LAÂRAKI; circ. 9,513 (2008).

Libération: 33 rue Amir Abdelkader, BP 2165, Casablanca; tel. (52) 2619400; fax (52) 2620972; e-mail liberation@usfp.ma; internet www.liberation.press.ma; f. 1964; French; organ of the Union socialiste des forces populaires; Dir ABDELHADI KHAÏRAT; circ. 2,719 (2008).

Al-Massae (The Evening): 10 ave des Forces Armées Royales, 2ème étage, Casablanca; tel. (52) 2275918; fax (52) 2275597; e-mail contact@almassae.press.ma; internet www.almassae.press.ma; f. 2006; Arabic; independent; Dir RACHID NINI; circ. 113,849 (2008/09).

Le Matin du Sahara et du Maghreb: 17 rue Othman Ben Affane, Casablanca; tel. (52) 2489100; fax (52) 2203048; e-mail m.jouahri@lematin.ma; internet www.lematin.ma; f. 1971; French; royalist; Dir-Gen. MUHAMMAD JOUAHRI; Editor-in-Chief ABDELHADI GADI; circ. 24,816 (2008/09).

Rissalat al-Oumma (The Message of the Nation): 152 ave des Forces Armées Royales, BP 20005, Casablanca; tel. (52) 2901925; fax (52) 2901926; Arabic; weekly edn in French; organ of the Union constitutionnelle; Dir MUHAMMAD TAMALDOU.

Rabat

Al-Alam (The Flag): ave Hassan II, Lot Vita, BP 141, Rabat; tel. (53) 7294832; fax (53) 7291784; e-mail alalam@alalam.ma; internet www.alalam.ma; f. 1946; Arabic; literary supplement on Sat; organ of the Istiqlal party; Dir ABD AL-JABBAR SUHEIMAT; Editor-in-Chief HASSAN ABDELKHALEK; circ. 10,274 (2008/09).

Annahar Al Maghribia (The Moroccan Day): 12 pl. des Alaouites, 2ème étage, Rabat; tel. (53) 7737568; fax (53) 7737547; e-mail annahar21@yahoo.fr; internet www.annahar.ma; f. 2002; Arabic; Dir and Editor-in-Chief ABD EL-HAKIM BADI; circ. 6,953 (2008).

Attajdid (Reform): 3 blvd al-Moukawama, BP 9173, Rabat; tel. (53) 7705854; fax (53) 7705852; e-mail attajdid@attajdid.ma; internet www.attajdid.ma; f. 1999; Arabic; associated with the Parti de la justice et du développement; Dir ABDELILAH BENKIRANE; circ. 2,903 (2008/09).

Al-Haraka (Progress): 66 rue Patrice Lumumba, BP 1317, Rabat; tel. (53) 7768667; fax (53) 7767537; e-mail harakamp@menara.ma; internet www.harakamp.ma; Arabic; organ of the Mouvement populaire; Dir ALI ALAOUI; circ. 1,002 (2008).

L'Opinion: ave Hassan II, Lot Vita, Rabat; tel. (53) 7293002; fax (53) 7292639; e-mail lopinion@lopinion.ma; internet www.lopinion.ma; f. 1962; French; organ of Istiqlal; Dir MUHAMMAD IDRISSI KAÏTOUNI; Editor-in-Chief JAMAL HAJJAM; circ. 18,347 (2008/09).

SELECTED PERIODICALS

Casablanca

actuel: 1 blvd Abdellatif Ben Kaddour, 20050 Casablanca; tel. (52) 2951815; fax (52) 2951814; e-mail courrier@actuel.ma; internet www.actuel.ma; f. 2009; weekly; French; publ. by Logique Presse; Dir and Editor HENRI LOIZEAU.

Al-Ayam (The Days): Espace Paquet, 508 rue Muhammad Smiha, Casablanca; tel. (52) 2442694; fax (52) 2441173; e-mail alayams75@yahoo.fr; f. 2001; Arabic; weekly; Editor NOUREDDINE MIFTAH; circ. 22,163 (2008).

CGEM Mag: 23 blvd Muhammad Abdou, Palmiers, 20340 Casablanca; tel. (52) 2997000; fax (52) 2983971; e-mail mustaphamoulay@cgem.ma; internet www.cgem.ma; monthly; French; organ of the Confédération Générale des Entreprises du Maroc; Dir MIRIEM BENSALAH-CHAQROUN; Editor-in-Chief MUSTAPHA MOULAY.

Challenge Hebdo: 58 ave des Forces Armées Royales, Tour des Habous, 13ème étage, Casablanca; tel. (52) 2548150; fax (52) 2318094; e-mail redaction@challengehebdo.com; internet www.challengehebdo.com; weekly; French; business; Dir ADIL LAHLOU; Editor-in-Chief KHALID TRITKI; circ. 8,410 (2008/09).

Construire: 744 rue Boukrâa (angle rue Ouled Said), Résidence Hanane Jassim I, Bourgogne, Casablanca; tel. (52) 2220271; fax (52) 2273627; e-mail nlleconstruire@yahoo.fr; internet www.nouvelleconstruire.com; f. 1940; weekly; French; building and architecture magazine; Dir ABDELKRIM TALAL.

Femmes du Maroc: Immeuble Zénith I, Lot Attaoufik, route de Nouaceur, Sidi Maârouf, Casablanca; tel. (52) 2973949; fax (52) 2973929; internet www.femmesdumaroc.com; monthly; French; lifestyle magazine for women; Dir AÏCHA ZAÏMI SAKHRI; Editor-in-Chief GÉRALDINE DULAT; circ. 12,029 (2008/09).

La Gazette du Maroc: ave des Forces Armées Royales, Tour des Habous, 13ème étage, Casablanca; tel. (52) 2548150; fax (52) 2318094; e-mail info@lagazettedumaroc.com; internet www.lagazettedumaroc.com; weekly; French; Dir KAMAL LAHLOU; Editor-in-Chief ABD AL-LATIF EL-AZIZI; circ. 8,969 (2008).

Le Journal Hebdomadaire: 61 ave des Forces Armées Royales, BP 20000, Casablanca; tel. (52) 2546670; fax (52) 2446185; e-mail courrier@lejournal-press.com; internet www.lejournal-press.com; weekly; French; news, politics, economics; Dir ALI AMAR; Editor-in-Chief ABOUBAKR JAMAÏ; circ. 11,895 (2008/09).

Maroc Hebdo International: 4 rue des Flamants, Casablanca; tel. (52) 2238176; fax (52) 2981346; e-mail mhi@maroc-hebdo.press.ma; internet www.maroc-hebdo.com; f. 1991; weekly; French; Editor-in-Chief MUHAMMAD SELHAMI; circ. 10,510 (2008).

Nissae min al-Maghrib (Women of Morocco): Immeuble Zénith I, Lot Attaoufik, route de Nouaceur, Sidi Maârouf, Casablanca; tel. (52) 2973949; fax (52) 2973929; e-mail y.guennoun@akwagroup.com; monthly; Arabic edn of *Femmes du Maroc*; Editor-in-Chief KHADIJA SABIL; circ. 30,703 (2008/09).

La Nouvelle Tribune: 320 blvd Zerktouni, angle rue Bouardel, Casablanca; tel. (52) 2424670; fax (52) 2200031; e-mail courrier@lanouvelletribune.com; internet www.lanouvelletribune.com; f. 1996; weekly (Thur.); French; Dir FAHD YATA; circ. 6,741 (2007).

Parade: Immeuble Zénith I, Lot Attaoufik, route de Nouaceur, Sidi Maârouf, Casablanca; tel. (52) 2973949; fax (52) 2973929; e-mail y.guennoun@akwagroup.com; monthly; French; Editor-in-Chief MARIA DAIF; circ. 4,716 (2006).

Perspectives du Maghreb: 8 blvd Yacoub el Mansour, 31 Maârif, Casablanca; tel. (52) 2257844; fax (52) 2257738; e-mail popmedia@menara.ma; f. 2005; monthly; French; circ. 6,531 (2007).

La Quinzaine du Maroc: 53 rue el-Bakri, Casablanca; tel. (52) 2440033; fax (52) 2440426; e-mail mauro@editionsmauro.ma; internet www.quinzainedumaroc.com; f. 1951; fortnightly; English and French; visitors' guide; Dir HUBERT MAURO.

Le Reporter: 1 Sahat al-Istiqlal, 2ème étage, 20000 Casablanca; tel. (52) 2541103; fax (52) 2541105; e-mail lereporter@gmail.com; internet www.lereporter.ma; f. 1998; weekly; French; Dir BAHIA AMRANI.

TelQuel: 28 ave des Forces Armées Royales, Casablanca; tel. (52) 2220951; fax (52) 2220563; e-mail courrier@telquel.info; internet www.telquel-online.com; f. 2001; weekly; French; Dir AHMED BENCHEMSI; Editor-in-Chief KARIM BOUKHARI; circ. 23,172 (2008/09).

Version Homme: ave des Forces Armées Royales, Tour des Habous, 13ème étage, Casablanca; tel. (52) 2450089; fax (52) 2442213; e-mail redaction@versionhomme.com; internet www.versionhomme.com; monthly; lifestyle magazine for men; Dir ADIL LAHLOU; circ. 6,051 (2008/09).

La Vie éco: 5 blvd Abdallah Ben Yacine, 20300 Casablanca; tel. (52) 2450555; fax (52) 2304542; e-mail vieeco@marocnet.net.ma; internet www.lavieeco.com; f. 1921; weekly; French; economics; Dir FADEL AGOUMI; Editor-in-Chief SAÂD BEN MANSOUR; circ. 16,426 (2008/09).

La Vie Touristique Africaine: 17 rue El Houcine Ben Ali, Casablanca; tel. (52) 2227643; fax (52) 2275319; e-mail vietouristique@wanadoo.net.ma; internet www.vietouristique.com; fortnightly; French; tourist information; Dir AHMED ZEGHARI.

Al-Watan al-An (The Nation Now): 33 rue Muhammad Bahi, Casablanca; tel. (52) 2251295; fax (52) 2251325; e-mail alwatanpress@menara.ma; internet www.alwatan.press.ma; weekly; Arabic; news; Editor ABDERRAHIM ARIRI; circ. 5,982 (2008).

Rabat

Al-Alam al-Amazighi: Éditions Amazigh, 5 rue Dakar, BP 477, Rabat; tel. 66-1767073 (mobile); fax (53) 7727283; e-mail lemondeamazigh@hotmail.com; weekly; Berber.

Asdae (Echoes): 30 ave Okba, Rabat; tel. (53) 7773706; e-mail asdae@menara.ma; internet www.asdae.com; weekly; Arabic; Dir and Editor-in-Chief EL-HASSAN ARBAI; circ. 1,415 (2008/09).

Da'ouat al-Haqq (Call of the Truth): al-Michwar al-Said, Rabat; tel. (53) 7766851; e-mail direction_haq@habous.gov.ma; internet www.daouatalhaq.ma; publ. by Ministry of Habous (Religious Endowments) and Islamic Affairs; f. 1957; monthly; Arabic.

Al-Mountakhab (The Team): 42 bis rue de Madagascar, Rabat; tel. (53) 7201774; fax (53) 7201776; e-mail contact@almountakhab.com; internet www.almountakhab.com; f. 1986; fortnightly; Arabic; sport; Dir MUSTAFA BADRI; Editor-in-Chief BADREDDINE IDRISSI; circ. 25,137 (2008/09).

Al-Tadamoun (Solidarity): Apt 1, Immeuble 6, rue Aguensous, ave Hassan II, Les Orangers, BP 1740, Rabat; tel. (53) 7730961; fax (53) 7738851; e-mail amdh1@mtds.com; internet www.amdh.org.ma; monthly; Arabic; organ of the Association marocaine des droits humains; Dir ABD AL-MAJID SEMLALI EL-HASANI.

Tangier

Achamal 2000: 137 blvd Prince Héritier, 1, Tangier; tel. (53) 9940391; fax (53) 9944216; e-mail ashamal@menara.ma; weekly; Arabic; Editor-in-Chief KHALID MECHBAL; circ. 7,912 (2008/09).

Le Journal de Tanger: 7 bis, rue Omar Ben Abdelaziz, Tangier; tel. (53) 9943008; fax (53) 9945709; e-mail direct@lejournaldetanger .com; internet www.lejournaldetanger.com; f. 1904; weekly; French, English, Spanish and Arabic; Dir ABDELHAK BAKHAT; Editor-in-Chief MUHAMMAD ABOUABDILLAH; circ. 8,776 (2008/09).

NEWS AGENCY

Maghreb Arabe Presse (MAP): 122 ave Allal Ben Abdallah, BP 1049, 10000 Rabat; tel. (53) 7279464; fax (53) 7279465; e-mail mapweb@map.co.ma; internet www.map.ma; f. 1959; Arabic, French, English and Spanish; state-owned; Dir-Gen. KHALIL HACHIMI IDRISSI.

PRESS ASSOCIATIONS

Fédération Marocaine des Editeurs de Journaux (FMEJ): Groupe Ecomedia, 70 blvd al-Massira al-Khadra, Casablanca; tel. (52) 2953600; fax (52) 2365926; f. 2005; Pres. ABDELMOUNAIM DILAMI.

Organisme de Justification de la Diffusion (OJD Maroc): 4 rue des Flamants, Casablanca; tel. (52) 2238176; fax (52) 2981346; e-mail asmae@maroc-hebdo.press.ma; internet www.ojd.ma; f. 2004; compiles circ. statistics; Pres. AISSAM FATHYA; Dir ASMAE HASSANI.

Publishers

Afrique Orient: 159 bis blvd Yacoub el-Mansour, Casablanca; tel. (52) 2259813; fax (52) 2440080; f. 1983; sociology, philosophy and translations; Dir MUSTAPHA CHAJII.

Belvisi: 17 rue Abbas Ibnou Farnass, BP 8044, Casablanca; tel. (52) 2250973; fax (52) 2986258; f. 1986.

Dar el-Kitab: place de la Mosquée, Quartier des Habous, BP 4018, Casablanca; tel. (52) 2305419; fax (52) 3026630; f. 1948; Arabic and French; philosophy, history, Africana, general and social sciences; state-controlled; Dir BOUTALEB ABDOU ABD AL-HAY; Gen. Man. KHADIJA EL-KASSIMI.

Editions Le Fennec: 89B blvd d'Anfa, 14ème étage, Casablanca; tel. (52) 2209314; fax (52) 2277702; e-mail info@lefennec.com; internet www.lefennec.com; f. 1987; fiction, social sciences; Dir LAYLA B. CHAOUNI.

Editions La Porte: 281 blvd Muhammad V, BP 331, Rabat; tel. (53) 7709958; fax (53) 7706476; e-mail la_porte@meganet.net.ma; law, guides, economics, educational books.

Les Editions Maghrébines: Quartier Industriel, blvd E, N 15, Sin Sebaâ, Casablanca; tel. (52) 2351797; fax (52) 2357892; f. 1962; general non-fiction.

Les Editions Toubkal: Immeuble I. G. A, pl. de la Gare Voyageurs, Bélvèdere, 20300 Casablanca; tel. and fax (52) 22342323; e-mail contact@toubkal.ma; internet www.toubkal.ma; f. 1985; economy, history, social sciences, literature, educational books; Dir ABDELJALIL NADEM.

Malika Editions: 60 blvd Yacoub el-Mansour, 20100 Casablanca; tel. (52) 2235688; fax (52) 2251651; e-mail edmalika@connectcom.net .ma; internet www.malikaedition.com; art publications.

Tarik Editions: 321 route el-Jadida, 20390 Casablanca; tel. (52) 2259007; fax (52) 2232550; e-mail tarik.edition@gmail.com; internet www.tarikeditions.com; f. 2000; history and social sciences; Dir BICHR BENNANI.

Yomad: 4 rue Melouiya, Apt 7, Agdal, Rabat; tel. (53) 7686430; fax (53) 7686431; e-mail yomadeditions@yahoo.com; internet www .yomadeditions.net; f. 1998; children's literature; Dir NADIA ESSALMI.

GOVERNMENT PUBLISHING HOUSE

Imprimerie Officielle: ave Yacoub el-Mansour, Rabat-Chellah; tel. (53) 7765024; fax (53) 7765179.

Broadcasting and Communications

TELECOMMUNICATIONS

inwi: Lot la Colline II, Sidi Maârouf, 20190 Casablanca; tel. (52) 2900000; internet www.inwi.ma; f. 2009 as Wana following award of third GSM licence; mobile telephone and internet services launched Feb. 2010; Dir-Gen. FRÉDÉRIC DEBORD.

Itissalat al-Maghrib—Maroc Télécom: ave Annakhil Hay Riad, Rabat; tel. (53) 7719000; fax (53) 7714860; e-mail webmaster@iam .ma; internet www.iam.ma; f. 1998; privatized in 2004; Vivendi SA (France) holds a 53% stake; Chair. ABDESLAM AHIZOUNE.

Méditel: Twin Centre, angle blvd Zerktouni et blvd Massira al-Khadra, Casablanca; e-mail hassan.bouchachia@meditel.ma; internet www.meditel.ma; f. 1999; Caisse de Dépôt et de Gestion (CDG) and FinanceCom hold a 64.4% stake; provides national mobile telecommunications services; Dir-Gen. MUHAMMAD EL-MANDJRA; Chair. OTHMAN BENJELLOUN; 8.63m. subscribers (June 2009).

Regulatory Authority

Agence Nationale de Réglementation des Télécommunications (ANRT): Centre d'Affaires, blvd al-Riad, BP 2939, Hay Riad, 10100 Rabat; tel. (53) 7718400; fax (53) 7203862; e-mail com@anrt.ma; internet www.anrt.ma; f. 1998; Dir-Gen. AZDIR EL-MOUNTASSIR BILLAH.

BROADCASTING

Morocco can receive broadcasts from Spanish radio stations, and the main Spanish television channels can also be received in northern Morocco.

Radio

Radio Casablanca: c/o Loukt s.a.r.l, BP 16011, Casa Principal, 20001 Casablanca; e-mail i-rc@maroc.net; internet www.maroc.net/ rc; f. 1996; Gen. Man. AMINE ZARY.

Radio Méditerranée Internationale: 3 rue M'sallah, BP 2055, 9000 Tangier; tel. (53) 9936363; fax (53) 9935755; e-mail medi1@ medi1.com; internet www.medi1.com; Arabic and French; Man. Dir PIERRE CASALTA.

Voice of America Radio Station in Tangier: c/o US Consulate-General, chemin des Amoureux, Tangier.

Television

Société Nationale de Radiodiffusion et de Télévision: 1 rue el-Brihi, BP 1042, 1000 Rabat; tel. (53) 7685100; fax (53) 7733733; internet www.snrt.ma; govt station; transmission commenced 1962; 45 hours weekly; French and Arabic; carries commercial advertising; Dir-Gen. and Dir Television FAIÇAL LARAICHI.

SOREAD 2M: Société d'études et de réalisations audiovisuelles, km 7.3, route de Rabat, Aïn-Sebaâ, Casablanca; tel. (52) 2667373; fax (52) 2677856; e-mail portail@tv2m.co.ma; internet www.2m.tv; f. 1988; transmission commenced 1989; public television channel; owned by Moroccan Govt (72%) and by private national foreign concerns; broadcasting in French and Arabic; Man. Dir SAMI EL-JAI.

Finance

(cap. = capital; res = reserves; dep. = deposits; m. = million; br(s) = branch(es); amounts in dirhams)

BANKING

Central Bank

Bank Al-Maghrib: 277 ave Muhammad V, BP 445, Rabat; tel. (53) 7702626; fax (53) 7706667; e-mail webmaster@bkam.ma; internet www.bkam.ma; f. 1959 as Banque du Maroc; name changed as above in 1987; bank of issue; cap. 500m., res 5,033m., dep. 47,366m. (Dec. 2009); Gov. ABDELLATIF JOUAHRI; Gen. Man. ABDELLATIF FAOUZI; 20 brs.

Other Banks

Attijariwafa Bank: 2 blvd Moulay Youssef, BP 11141, 20000 Casablanca; tel. (52) 2298888; fax (52) 2294125; e-mail contact@ attijariwafa.com; internet www.attijariwafabank.com; f. 2004 by merger between Banque Commerciale du Maroc SA and Wafabank; 33.2% owned by Groupe ONA, 14.6% by Grupo Santander (Spain); cap. 1,929m., res 4,152m., dep. 222,003m. (Dec. 2010); Pres. and Dir-Gen. MUHAMMAD EL-KETTANI.

Banque Centrale Populaire (Crédit Populaire du Maroc): 101 blvd Muhammad Zerktouni, BP 10622, 21100 Casablanca; tel. (52) 2202533; fax (52) 2229699; e-mail bcp@banquepopulairemorocco .ma; internet www.cpm.co.ma; f. 1961; 51% state-owned, 49% privately owned; merged with Société Marocaine de Dépôt et Crédit in 2003; cap. 6,111m., res 12,605m., dep. 171,335m. (Dec. 2010); Pres. and Man. Dir MUHAMMAD BENCHAÂBOUNE; 530 brs.

Banque Marocaine du Commerce Extérieur SA (BMCE): 140 ave Hassan II, BP 13425, 20000 Casablanca; tel. (52) 2200325; fax (52) 2200512; e-mail communicationfinanciere@bmcebank.co.ma; internet www.bmcebank.ma; f. 1959; transferred to majority private ownership in 1995; cap. 1,719m., res 8,813m., dep. 149,906m. (Dec. 2011); Pres. and Dir-Gen. OTHMAN BENJELLOUN; 310 domestic brs and 3 brs abroad.

Banque Marocaine pour le Commerce et l'Industrie SA (BMCI): 26 pl. des Nations Unies, BP 15573, Casablanca; tel. (52) 22461000; fax (52) 22299406; e-mail adiba.lahbabi@africa.bnpparibas.com; internet www.bmci.ma; f. 1964; 65.05% owned by BNP Paribas (France); cap. 1,281m., res 5,625m., dep. 59,728m. (Dec. 2011); Chair. MOURAD CHERIF; 260 brs.

Citibank-Maghreb: Zénith Millenium, Immeuble 1, Lot Attaoufik, Sidi Maârouf, BP 13362, Casablanca; tel. (52) 2489600; fax (52) 2974197; f. 1967; cap. and res 194.0m., total assets 1,211.0m. (Dec. 2003); Pres. NUHAD SALIBA; 2 brs.

Crédit Agricole du Maroc SA: 29 rue Abou Faris al-Marini, BP 49, 10000 Rabat; tel. (53) 7208219; fax (53) 7445063; e-mail m_kettani@creditagricole.ma; internet www.creditagricole.ma; f. 1961 as Caisse Nationale de Crédit Agricole; became a limited co and adopted present name in 2003; 78% owned by Ministry of the Economy and Finance; cap. 2,820m., res –1,197m., dep. 60,843m. (Dec. 2009); Chair. TARIQ SIJILMASSI.

Crédit Immobilier et Hôtelier: 187 ave Hassan II, Casablanca; tel. (52) 2479000; fax (52) 2479363; e-mail info-client@cih.co.ma; internet www.cih.co.ma; f. 1920; transferred to majority private ownership in 1995; cap. 2,660m., res 5m., dep. 20,112m. (Dec. 2011); Pres. and CEO AHMAD RAHHOU; 91 brs.

Crédit du Maroc SA: 48–58 blvd Muhammad V, BP 13579, 20000 Casablanca; tel. (52) 2477477; fax (52) 2477127; e-mail mohammadine.menjra@ca-cdm.ma; internet www.cdm.co.ma; f. 1963 as Crédit Lyonnais Maroc; name changed as above in 1966; 52.6% owned by Crédit Agricole (France); cap. 2,586m., res 382m., dep. 40,014m. (Dec. 2011); Chair. PIERRE-LOUIS BOISSIERE; 264 domestic brs, 1 br. abroad.

Société Générale Marocaine de Banques SA: 55 blvd Abdelmoumen, BP 13090, 21100 Casablanca; tel. (52) 2438888; fax (52) 2234931; e-mail contact@sgmaroc.com; internet www.sgmaroc.com; f. 1962; cap. 2,050m., res 3,414m., dep. 54,878m. (Dec. 2010); Pres. ALBERT LE DIRAC'H; 300 brs.

STOCK EXCHANGE

Bourse de Casablanca: angle ave des Forces Armées Royales et rue Muhammad Errachid, Casablanca; tel. (52) 2452626; fax (52) 2452625; e-mail contact@casablanca-bourse.com; internet www.casablanca-bourse.com; f. 1929; Chair. AOMAR YIDAR; CEO K. HAJJI.

INSURANCE

Atlanta Assurances: 181 blvd d'Anfa, BP 13685, 20001 Casablanca; tel. (52) 2957676; fax (52) 2369812; e-mail info@atlanta.ma; internet www.atlanta.ma; f. 1947; cap. 591.6m.; Dir-Gen. MUHAMMAD HASSAN BENSALAH.

AXA Assurance Maroc: 120–122 ave Hassan II, 20000 Casablanca; tel. (52) 2889292; fax (52) 2889189; e-mail communication@axa.ma; internet www.axa.ma; cap. 900m.; Pres. and Dir-Gen. MICHEL HASCOET.

CNIA Saada Assurance: 216 blvd Muhammad Zerktouni, 20000 Casablanca; tel. (52) 2474040; fax (52) 2206081; internet www.cniasaada.ma; f. 2009 by merger of CNIA Assurance and Es-Saada; 53% owned by Groupe Saham; Pres. and Dir-Gen. MOULAY HAFID ELALAMY.

Compagnie d'Assurances et de Réassurances SANAD: 181 blvd d'Anfa, Tours Balzac, Casablanca; tel. (52) 2957878; fax (52) 2360406; e-mail webmaster@sanad.ma; internet www.sanad.ma; f. 1946; cap. 125m.; Chair. MUHAMMAD HASSAN BENSALAH; Dir-Gen. ABDELTIF TAHIRI.

La Marocaine Vie: 37 blvd Moulay Youssef, Casablanca; tel. (52) 2206320; fax (52) 2297307; f. 1978; 83% owned by Société Générale Marocaine de Banques SA; Pres. MARC DUVAL; Gen. Man. KARIM MOULTAKI.

Mutuelle Centrale Marocaine d'Assurances (MCMA): 16 rue Abou Inane, BP 27, Rabat; tel. (53) 7767800; fax (53) 7766440; f. 1968; part of the MAMDA-MCMA group; CEO HICHAM BELMRAH.

Mutuelle d'Assurances des Transporteurs Unis (MATU): 215 blvd Muhammad Zerktouni, Casablanca; tel. (52) 2954500; fax (52) 2367721; e-mail info@matu.ma; Pres. HADJ OMAR BENNOUNA; Dir-Gen. AHMAD MAZOUZ.

RMA Watanya: 83 ave des Forces Armées Royales, 20000 Casablanca; tel. (52) 2312163; fax (52) 2313137; e-mail contact@rmawatanya.com; internet www.rmawatanya.com; f. 2005 by merger of Al-Wataniya and La Royale Marocaine d'Assurances; cap. 1,774m.; Pres. OTHMAN BENJELLOUN.

Société Centrale de Réassurance (SCR): Tour Atlas, pl. Zallaqa, BP 13183, Casablanca; tel. (52) 2460400; fax (52) 2460460; e-mail scr@scrmaroc.com; internet www.scrmaroc.com; f. 1960; cap. 30m.; Chair. AHMAD ZINOUN; Man. Dir MUHAMMAD LARBI NALI.

Société Marocaine d'Assurance à l'Exportation (SMAEX): 24 rue Ali Abderrazak, BP 15953, Casablanca; tel. (52) 2982000; fax (52)
2252070; e-mail smaex@smaex.com; internet www.smaex.com; f. 1988; insurance for exporters in the public and private sectors; assistance for export promotion; Pres. and Dir-Gen. NEZHA LAHRICHI; Asst Dir-Gen. ABDERRAZZAK M'HAIMDAT.

WAFA Assurance: 1–3 blvd Abd al-Moumen, BP 13420, 20001 Casablanca; tel. (52) 2224575; fax (52) 2209103; e-mail webmaster@wafaassurance.com; internet www.attijariwafabank.com; subsidiary of Attijariwafa Bank; Pres. ABDELAZIZ ALAMI; CEO MUHAMMAD EL-KETTANI.

Zurich Assurances Maroc: 166 angle Zerktouni et rue Hafid Ibrahim, 20000 Casablanca; tel. (52) 22499808; fax (52) 22491733; e-mail customerservice@zurich.com; f. 1954; cap. 90m.; all kinds of insurance; Pres. and Dir-Gen. BERTO FISLER.

Insurance Association

Fédération Marocaine des Sociétés d'Assurances et de Réassurances: 154 blvd d'Anfa, Casablanca; tel. (52) 2391850; fax (52) 2391854; e-mail contact@fmsar.ma; internet www.fmsar.org.ma; f. 1958; 15 mem. cos; Pres. MUHAMMAD HASSAN BENSALAH.

Trade and Industry

GOVERNMENT AGENCIES

Agence National pour la Promotion de Petite et Moyenne Entreprise (ANPME): 10 rue Gandhi, BP 211, 10001 Rabat; tel. (53) 7708460; fax (53) 7707695; e-mail info@anpme.ma; internet www.anpme.ma; f. 1973 as the Office pour le Développement Industriel; name changed as above in 2002; state agency to develop industry; Dir-Gen. LATIFA ECHIHABI.

Centre Marocain de Promotion des Exportations (CMPE): 23 rue Ibnou Majed el-Bahar, BP 10937, 20000 Casablanca; tel. (52) 2302210; fax (52) 2301793; e-mail info@marocexport.ma; internet www.cmpe.org.ma; f. 1980; state org. for promotion of exports; Man. Dir SAAD BEN ABDALLAH.

Direction des Entreprises Publiques et de la Privatisation (DEPP): rue Haj Ahmed Cherkaoui, Quartier Administratif, Agdal, Rabat; tel. (53) 7689303; fax (53) 7689347; e-mail talbi@depp.finances.gov.ma; part of the Ministry of the Economy and Finance; in charge of regulation, restructuring and privatization of state enterprises; Dir ABDELAZIZ TALBI.

Office National des Hydrocarbures et des Mines (ONHYM): 5 ave Moulay Hassan, BP 99, 10050 Rabat; tel. (53) 7239898; fax (53) 7709411; e-mail presse@onhym.com; internet www.onhym.com; f. 2003 to succeed Bureau de Recherches et de Participations Minières and Office National de Recherches et d'Exploitations Pétrolières; state agency conducting exploration, valorization and exploitation of hydrocarbons and mineral resources; Dir-Gen. AMINA BENKHADRA.

Société de Gestion des Terres Agricoles (SOGETA): 35 rue Daïet-Erroumi, BP 731, Agdal, Rabat; tel. (53) 7772778; fax (53) 7772765; f. 1973; oversees use of agricultural land; Man. Dir BACHIR SAOUD.

DEVELOPMENT ORGANIZATIONS

Caisse de Dépôt et de Gestion: pl. Moulay el-Hassan, BP 408, 10001 Rabat; tel. (53) 7669000; fax (53) 7763849; e-mail cdg@cdg.ma; internet www.cdg.ma; f. 1959; finances small-scale projects; Dir-Gen. ANASS ALAMI; Sec.-Gen. SAÏD LAFTIT.

Caisse Marocaine des Marchés (Marketing Fund): 101 blvd Abdelmoumen, 4e étage, 20100 Casablanca; tel. (52) 22472683; fax (52) 22472554; e-mail s.benbrahim@cmm.ma; internet www.cmm.ma; f. 1950; cap. 70m. dirhams.

Société de Développement Agricole (SODEA): ave Hadj Ahmed Cherkaoui, BP 6280, Rabat; tel. (53) 7677953; fax (53) 7771514; internet www.sodea.com; f. 1972; state agricultural devt org.; Man. Dir AHMED HAJJAJI.

Société Nationale d'Investissement (SNI): 60 rue d'Alger, BP 38, 20000 Casablanca; tel. (52) 2224102; fax (52) 2484303; f. 1966; transferred to majority private ownership in 1994; cap. 10,900m. dirhams; Pres. HASSAN BOUHEMOU; Sec.-Gen. SAÂD BENDIDI.

CHAMBERS OF COMMERCE

Fédération des Chambres Marocaines de Commerce, d'Industrie et de Services (FCMCIS): 6 rue Erfoud, BP 218, Hassan, Rabat; tel. (53) 7767078; fax (53) 7767896; e-mail fcmcis@menara.ma; internet www.fcmcis.ma; f. 1962; groups the 28 Chambers of Commerce and Industry; Pres. DRISS HOUAT; Dir-Gen. MUHAMMAD LARBI EL-HARRAS.

Chambre de Commerce, d'Industrie et de Services de la Wilaya de Rabat-Salé: 1 rue Gandhi, BP 131, Rabat; tel. (53)

7706444; fax (53) 7706768; e-mail info@rabat.cci.ma; internet www
.ccirabat.ma; Pres. OMAR DERRAJI.

**Chambre de Commerce, d'Industrie et de Services de la
Wilaya du Grand Casablanca:** 98 blvd Muhammad V, BP 423,
Casablanca; tel. (52) 2264327; fax (52) 2268436; e-mail ccisc@ccisc
.gov.ma; internet www.ccisc.gov.ma; Pres. HASSAN BERKANI.

INDUSTRIAL AND TRADE ASSOCIATIONS

**Office National Interprofessionnel des Céréales et des Légu-
mineuses (ONICL):** 3 ave Moulay Hassan, BP 154, Rabat; tel. (53)
7217300; fax (53) 7709626; e-mail directeur@onicl.org.ma; internet
www.onicl.org.ma; f. 1937; Dir-Gen. ABDELLATIF GUEDIRA.

Office National des Pêches: 15 rue Lieutenant Mahroud, BP
16243, 20300 Casablanca; tel. (52) 2242084; fax (52) 2242305;
e-mail onp@onp.co.ma; internet www.onp.co.ma; f. 1969; state
fishing org.; Man. Dir MAJID KAISSAR EL-GHAIB.

EMPLOYERS' ORGANIZATIONS

Association Marocaine des Exporteurs (ASMEX): 36B blvd
Anfa, Casablanca; tel. (52) 2261033; fax (52) 2484191; e-mail
asmex@asmex.org; internet www.asmex.org; f. 1982; Pres. ABDEL-
LATIF BEN MADANI.

**Association Marocaine des Industries du Textile et de l'Habil-
lement (AMITH):** 92 blvd Moulay Rachid, Casablanca; tel. (52)
2942086; fax (52) 2940587; e-mail amith@amith.org.ma; internet
www.textile.ma; f. 1960; 850 mems; textiles, knitwear and ready-
made garment mfrs; Pres. MUSTAPHA SAJID; Dir-Gen. MUHAMMAD
TAZI.

Association des Producteurs d'Agrumes du Maroc (ASPAM):
283 blvd Zerktouni, Casablanca; tel. (52) 2363946; fax (52) 2364041;
e-mail aspam@menara.ma; f. 1958; links Moroccan citrus growers;
has its own processing plants; Pres. HASSAN LYOUSSI.

**Association Professionnelle des Agents Maritimes, Consign-
ataires de Navires, et Courtiers d'Affrètement du Maroc
(APRAM):** 219 blvd des Forces Armées Royales, 5ème étage,
20000 Casablanca; tel. (52) 2541112; fax (52) 2541415; e-mail
apram@wanadoopro.ma; internet www.apram.ma; f. 1999; 37 mems;
Pres. ABDELAZIZ MANTRACH.

Association Professionnelle des Cimentiers (APC): Villa APC,
Lot Allaymoune 1, 476 Hay Almatar, Casablanca; tel. (52) 2936660;
fax (52) 2904491; e-mail apc@menara.ma; internet www.apc.ma; 4
mems; cement mfrs; Pres. JEAN-MARIE SCHMITZ.

Confédération Générale des Entreprises du Maroc (CGEM):
23 blvd Muhammad Abdou, Quartier Palmiers, 20100 Casablanca;
tel. (52) 2997000; fax (52) 2983971; e-mail cgem@cgem.ma; internet
www.cgem.ma; 25 affiliated feds; Pres. MUHAMMAD HORANI.

UTILITIES

Electricity and Water

Office National de l'Eau Potable (ONEP): Station de Traitement
ONEP, ave Muhammad Belhassan El Ouazzani, BP 10002 Rabat-
Chellah, Rabat; tel. (53) 7759600; fax (53) 7759106; e-mail onepbo@
onep.ma; internet www.onep.ma; f. 1972; responsible for drinking-
water supply; Dir-Gen. ALI FASSI FIHRI.

Office National de l'Electricité (ONE): 65 rue Othman Ben Affan,
BP 13498, 20001 Casablanca; tel. (52) 2668080; fax (52) 2220038;
e-mail offelec@one.org.ma; internet www.one.org.ma; f. 1963; state
electricity authority; Dir-Gen. ALI FASSI FIHRI.

Gas

Afriquia Gaz: 139 blvd Moulay Ismail, Aïn Sebaâ, 20700 Casablanca; tel. (52) 22639600; fax (52) 22639666; e-mail r.idrissi@
akwagroup.com; internet www.afriquiagaz.com; f. 1992; Morocco's
leading gas distributor; Pres. ALI WAKRIM; Dir-Gen. TAWFIK
HAMOUMI.

TRADE UNIONS

Confédération Démocratique du Travail (CDT): 64 rue al-
Mourtada, Quartier Palmier, BP 13576, Casablanca; tel. (52)
2994470; fax (52) 2994473; e-mail cdtmaroc@cdt.ma; internet www
.cdt.ma; f. 1978; Sec.-Gen. NOUBIR EL-AMAOUI.

Fédération Démocratique du Travail (FDT): 12 rue Muhammad Diouri, Sidi Belyoute, Casablanca; tel. (52) 2446362; fax (52)
2446365; e-mail fdt@menara.ma; internet www.fdt.ma; f. 2003 by
fmr mems of CDT associated with USFP; Sec.-Gen. ABD EL-HAMID
FATIHI.

Transport

Société Nationale des Transports et de la Logistique (SNTL):
rue al-Fadila, Quartier Industriel, BP 114, Chellah, Rabat; tel. (53)
7289300; fax (53) 7797850; e-mail ahachemi@sntl.ma; internet www
.sntl.ma; f. 1958; Dir-Gen. OUSSAMA LOUDGHIRI.

RAILWAYS

In 2010 the total length of Moroccan railways was 2,109 route-km. All
services are nationalized. Plans for a four-line, 76-km tram system in
Casablanca were approved in 2008; Line One, comprising 50 stations
on a 29-km route, was scheduled for completion by late 2012.
Meanwhile, a feasibility study into plans for a 39-km railway tunnel
under the Strait of Gibraltar linking Morocco and Spain commenced
in 2007; however, by mid-2013 the project had yet to receive formal
approval. In December 2010 Morocco and France signed an agreement whereby France would provide rolling stock and equipment for
the first African high-speed train link; the new line was scheduled to
run between Casablanca and Tangier by the end of 2015, and
subsequently to be extended to other major Moroccan cities.

Office National des Chemins de Fer (ONCF): 8 bis rue Abderrahmane el-Ghafiki, Rabat-Agdal; tel. (53) 7774747; fax (53)
7774480; e-mail ketary@oncf.ma; internet www.oncf.ma; f. 1963;
administers all Morocco's railways; Dir-Gen. MUHAMMAD RABIE
KHLIE.

ROADS

In 2010 there were 58,395 km of roads, of which 1,096 km were
motorways, 11,364 km were highways, main or national roads, and
10,091 km were secondary or regional roads.

Autoroutes du Maroc (ADM): Hay Riad, Rabat; tel. (53) 7711056;
fax (53) 7711059; e-mail naitbrahim.ismail@adm.co.ma; internet
www.adm.co.ma; responsible for the construction and upkeep of
Morocco's motorway network; Dir-Gen. OTMANE FASSI FIHRI.

Compagnie de Transports au Maroc (CTM—SA): km 13.5,
autoroute Casablanca–Rabat, Casablanca; tel. (52) 2762100; fax
(52) 2765428; internet www.ctm.ma; f. 1919; 18 agencies nation-
wide; privatized in 1993, with 40% of shares reserved for Moroccan
citizens; Pres. and Dir-Gen. MUHAMMAD BOUDA.

SHIPPING

According to official figures, Morocco's ports handled 96m. metric
tons of goods in 2011. The most important ports, in terms of the
volume of goods handled, are Casablanca, Jorf Lasfar, Safi and
Mohammedia. Tangier is the principal port for passenger services.
The first phase of a new container port, Tangier-Med, which had an
initial annual capacity of 3.5m. containers, became operational in
2007. Construction work on a second phase began in 2009, which was
expected to increase capacity to 8.5m. containers per year on its
completion in 2015. At 31 December 2012 Morocco's flag registered
fleet consisted of 409 vessels, with a combined displacement of
364,598 grt, of which 297 were fish carriers and six were general
cargo ships.

Port Authorities

Agence Nationale des Ports (ANP): f. 2006, following division of
Office d'Exploitation des Ports; regulator of port activity; also respon-
sible for development and maintenance of port facilities; Dir-Gen.
MUHAMMAD JAMAL BENJELLOUN.

Société d'Exploitation des Ports (Marsa Maroc): 175 blvd Zerktouni, 20100 Casablanca; tel. (52) 2258258; fax (52) 2995217; internet
www.sodep.co.ma; f. 2006, following division of Office d'Exploitation
des Ports; responsible for management of port terminals and
quayside facilities; Pres. MUHAMMAD ABDELJALIL.

Principal Shipping Companies

Agence Med SARL: 3 rue ibn Rochd, 90000 Tangier; tel. (53)
9935875; fax (53) 9933239; e-mail agencemed@menara.ma; f. 1904;
owned by the Bland Group; also at Agadir, Casablanca, Jorf Lasfar,
Nador and Safi; Operations Man. MUHAMMAD CHATT.

Compagnie Chérifienne d'Armement: 5 blvd Abdallah Ben
Yacine, 21700 Casablanca; tel. (52) 2309455; fax (52) 2301186;
f. 1929; regular services to Europe; Man. Dir MAX KADOCH.

Compagnie Marocaine d'Agences Maritimes (COMARINE):
45 ave des Forces Armées Royales, BP 60, 20000 Casablanca; tel. (52)
2548510; fax (52) 2548570; e-mail comarine@comarine.co.ma.

Compagnie Marocaine de Navigation (COMANAV): 7 blvd de la
Résistance, BP 628, Casablanca 20300; tel. (52) 2303012; fax (52)
2302006; e-mail comanav@comanav.co.ma; internet www.comanav
.ma; f. 1946 as Cie Franco-Chérifienne de Navigation; name changed
as above in 1959; privatization pending; regular services to European, Middle Eastern and West African ports; tramping; Pres. and
Dir-Gen. TOUFIQ IBRAHIMI; Sec.-Gen. MEHDI BELGHITI; 12 agencies.

Intercona: 6 rue Méditérranée, Edifici Coficom, Tangier 90000; tel. (53) 9945907; fax (53) 9945909; e-mail intercona-sa@menara.ma; internet intercona.com; f. 1943; shipping agent; Pres. VICENTE JORRO.

Limadet-ferry: 3 rue ibn Rochd, Tangier; tel. (53) 933639; fax (53) 937173; e-mail headoffice@limadet.com; f. 1966; daily services between Algeciras (Spain) and Tangier; Dir-Gen. RACHID BEN MANSOUR.

Société Marocaine de Navigation Atlas: 81 ave Houmane el-Fatouaki, 21000 Casablanca; tel. (52) 2224190; fax (52) 2200164; e-mail atlas@marbar.co.ma; f. 1976; Chair. HASSAN CHAMI; Man. Dir MUHAMMAD SLAOUI.

Voyages Paquet: 65 ave des Forces Armées Royales, 20000 Casablanca; tel. (52) 2761941; fax (52) 2442108; f. 1970; Pres. MUHAMMAD ELOUALI ELALAMI; Dir-Gen. NAÏMA BAKALI ELOUALI ELALAMI.

CIVIL AVIATION

The main international airports are at Casablanca (King Muhammad V), Rabat, Tangier, Marrakesh, Agadir Inezgane, Fez, Oujda, al-Hocima, el-Aaiún, Ouarzazate, Agadir al-Massira and Nador. The completion of a second runway at King Muhammad V airport was followed by the inauguration, in September 2007, of a second terminal, which increased the airport's annual passenger capacity from 5m. to 11m. Plans were under way to increase the capacity at Marrakesh International airport from 4.5m. passengers a year to 10m. by 2013.

Jet4you: 4 Lot la Colline, Sidi Maarouf, 20270 Casablanca; fax (52) 2584228; internet www.jet4you.com; f. 2006; wholly owned by TUI Travel PLC (United Kingdom); low-cost airline; services to destinations in 5 European countries; CEO JAWAD ZIYAT.

Office National des Aéroports (ONDA): Siège Social Nouasseur, BP 8101, Casablanca; tel. (52) 2539040; fax (52) 2539901; e-mail onda@onda.ma; internet www.onda.ma; f. 1990; Dir-Gen. DALIL GUENDOUZ.

Royal Air Maroc (RAM): Aéroport de Casablanca-Anfa; tel. (52) 2912000; fax (52) 2912087; e-mail callcenter@royalairmaroc.com; internet www.royalairmaroc.com; f. 1953; 94.4% state-owned; scheduled for partial privatization; domestic flights and services to Western Europe, Scandinavia, the Americas, North and West Africa, the Middle East; Chair. and CEO DRISS BENHIMA.

Tourism

Tourism is Morocco's second main source of convertible currency. The country's tourist attractions include its sunny climate, ancient sites (notably the cities of Fez, Marrakesh, Meknès and Rabat) and spectacular scenery. There are popular holiday resorts on the Atlantic and Mediterranean coasts. In 2010 foreign tourist arrivals totalled 4.93m., compared with 1.63m. in 1996. Tourism receipts, excluding passenger transport, were estimated at US $7,307m. in 2011.

Office National Marocain du Tourisme: angle rue Oued el-Makhazine et rue Zalaga, BP 19, Agdal, Rabat; tel. (53) 7674013; fax (53) 7674015; e-mail contact@onmt.org.ma; internet www.tourisme-marocain.com/onmt; f. 1918; Dir-Gen. FATHIA BENNIS.

Defence

Commander-in-Chief of the Armed Forces: HM King MUHAMMAD VI.

Defence Budget (2012): 29,400m. dirhams.

Military Service: 18 months.

Total Armed Forces (as assessed at November 2012): 195,800 (army 175,000—including some 100,000 conscripts; navy 7,800—including 1,500 marines; air force 13,000). Reserves 150,000.

Paramilitary Forces (as assessed at November 2012): 50,000: royal guard 20,000; auxiliary force 30,000.

Education

Since independence in 1956, Morocco has tried to resolve a number of educational problems: a youthful and fast-growing population, an urgent need for skilled workers and executives, a great diversity of teaching methods between French, Spanish, Muslim and Moroccan government schools (syllabuses have been standardized since 1967), and, above all, a high degree of adult illiteracy. In recent years increasing attention has been given to education for girls. There are now a number of mixed and girls' schools, notably in urban areas.

In 2010/11 there were an estimated 4,001,313 pupils in primary schools. A decree of November 1963 made education compulsory for children between the ages of seven and 13 years, and this has now been applied in most urban areas; from September 2002 children were to be educated from six years of age. In 2010/11, according to UNESCO estimates, enrolment at primary level included 96% of the relevant age-group. Instruction is given in Arabic for the first two years and in Arabic and French for the next four years, with English as the first additional language. Teaching in the principal Berber language, Tamazight, began in primary schools in the 2003/04 academic year.

Secondary education, beginning at the age of 13, lasts for up to six years (comprising two cycles of three years), and in 2008/09 provided for an estimated 2,232,289 pupils. In 1988 the secondary school graduation examination, the *baccalauréat*, was replaced by a system of continuous assessment. Secondary enrolment in 2006/07 was equivalent to 56% of the relevant age-group. Under the 2009 budget, expenditure on education by the central Government was projected at 47,269m. dirhams (21.7% of total spending).

There are eight universities in Morocco, including the Islamic University of al-Quarawiyin at Fez (founded in 859), the Muhammad V University at Rabat (opened in 1957), and an English-language university, inaugurated in Ifrane in 1995. In addition, there are institutes of higher education in business studies, agriculture, mining, law, and statistics and advanced economics. In 2003/04 there were some 418,883 students enrolled in tertiary education.

MOZAMBIQUE

Introductory Survey

LOCATION, CLIMATE, LANGUAGE, RELIGION, FLAG, CAPITAL

The Republic of Mozambique lies on the east coast of Africa, bordered to the north by Tanzania, to the west by Malawi, Zambia and Zimbabwe, and to the south by South Africa and Swaziland. The country has a coastline of about 2,470 km (1,535 miles) on the shores of the Indian Ocean, and is separated from Madagascar, to the east, by the Mozambique Channel. Except in a few upland areas, the climate varies from tropical to sub-tropical. Rainfall is irregular, but the rainy season is usually from November to March, when average temperatures in Maputo are between 26°C (79°F) and 30°C (86°F). In the cooler dry season, in June and July, the average temperatures are 18°C (64°F) to 20°C (68°F). Portuguese is the official language, while there are 39 indigenous languages, the most widely spoken being Makhuwa, Tsonga, Sema and Lomwe. Many of the inhabitants follow traditional beliefs. There are about 5m. Christians, the majority of whom are Roman Catholics, and 4m. Muslims. The national flag (proportions 2 by 3) has three equal horizontal stripes, of green, black and yellow, separated by narrow white stripes. At the hoist is a red triangle containing a five-pointed yellow star, on which are superimposed an open book, a hoe and a rifle. The capital is Maputo (formerly Lourenço Marques).

CONTEMPORARY POLITICAL HISTORY

Historical Context

Mozambique became a Portuguese colony in the 19th century and an overseas province in 1951. Nationalist groups began to form in the 1960s. The Frente de Libertação de Moçambique (Frelimo—Mozambique Liberation Front) was formed in 1962 and launched a military campaign for independence in 1964. After the coup in Portugal (q.v.) in April 1974, negotiations between Frelimo and the new Portuguese Government resulted in a period of rule in Mozambique by a transitional Government, followed by full independence on 25 June 1975. The leader of Frelimo, Samora Machel, became the first President of Mozambique. Between September and December 1977 elections took place to local, district and provincial assemblies and, at national level, to the Assembleia Popular (People's Assembly).

In March 1976 Mozambique closed its border with Rhodesia (now Zimbabwe) and applied economic sanctions against that country. Mozambique was the principal base for Rhodesian nationalist guerrillas, and consequently suffered considerable devastation as a result of offensives launched by Rhodesian government forces against guerrilla camps. The border was reopened in January 1980.

After Zimbabwean independence in April 1980, South Africa adopted Rhodesia's role as supporter of the Mozambican opposition guerrilla group, Resistência Nacional Moçambicana (Renamo), also known as the Movimento Nacional da Resistência de Moçambique. The activities of Renamo subsequently increased, causing persistent disruption to road, rail and petroleum pipeline links from Mozambican ports, which were vital to the economic independence of southern African nations from South Africa. In March 1984 Mozambique and South Africa signed a formal joint non-aggression pact, the Nkomati Accord, whereby each Government undertook to prevent opposition forces on its territory from launching attacks against the other, and a Joint Security Commission was established. The Accord effectively implied that South Africa would withdraw its covert support for Renamo in return for a guarantee by Mozambique that it would prevent any further use of its territory by the then banned African National Congress of South Africa (ANC). However, following an intensification of Renamo activity, in 1985 the Frelimo Government appealed to foreign powers for increased military assistance, and in June it was agreed that Zimbabwe would augment its military presence in Mozambique. A major military offensive against Renamo in July resulted in the capture, in August, of the rebels' national operational command centre. Mozambique subsequently alleged that South Africa had repeatedly violated the Nkomati Accord by providing material support for the rebels. The Joint Security Commission ceased to meet in 1985.

President Machel died in an air crash in South Africa in October 1986. The causes of the incident were unclear, and the Mozambican Ministry of Information declared that it did not exclude the possibility of South African sabotage. (In May 1998 it was announced that South Africa's Truth and Reconciliation Commission—TRC—was to examine evidence relating to the crash. The TRC's final report stated that the evidence was inconclusive, but a number of questions merited further investigation and in early 2006 the South African Government announced that it was to reopen the inquiry into Machel's death.) In November 1986 the Central Committee of Frelimo appointed Joaquim Alberto Chissano, hitherto Minister for Foreign Affairs, as President. At a Frelimo congress in July 1989, the party's exclusively Marxist-Leninist orientation was renounced, and party membership was opened to Mozambicans from all sectors of society.

Meanwhile, in May 1998 Mozambican and South African officials agreed to reactivate the Nkomati Accord and to re-establish the Joint Security Commission; subsequently a joint commission for co-operation and development was established.

Domestic Political Affairs

The introduction, on 30 November 1990, of a new Mozambican Constitution, formally ended Frelimo's single-party rule and committed the State to political pluralism and a free-market economy; it also enshrined private property rights and guarantees of press freedom. The official name of the country was changed from the People's Republic of Mozambique to the Republic of Mozambique. Renamo refused to recognize the new Constitution, declaring that it had been drafted without democratic consultation. The President was henceforth to be elected by direct universal suffrage, and the legislature was renamed the Assembleia da República (Assembly of the Republic). A new law concerning the formation, structure and function of political parties came into effect in February 1991. In accordance with the Constitution, Renamo would not be recognized as a legitimate political party until it had renounced violence completely.

In October 1991 Renamo and the Government signed a protocol agreeing fundamental principles and containing a set of mutual guarantees as a basis for a peace accord. Throughout the discussions (held in Rome, Italy) Renamo continued guerrilla attacks, many of which were launched (despite the Nkomati Accord) from South Africa. Under the terms of the protocol, Renamo effectively recognized the legitimacy of the Government and agreed to enter the multi-party political framework. In return, the Government pledged not to legislate on any of the points under negotiation until a general peace accord had been signed. In November a second protocol was signed by both parties, enabling Renamo to begin functioning as a political party immediately after the signing of a general peace accord.

In March 1992 a third protocol was signed establishing the principles for the country's future electoral system. Under its terms, the elections, to be held under a system of proportional representation, were to be supervised by international observers. An electoral commission was to be established, with one-third of its members to be appointed by Renamo. On 7 August, following three days of discussions in Rome, Chissano and the Renamo leader, Afonso Macacho Marceta Dhlakama, signed a joint declaration committing the two sides to a total cease-fire by 1 October, as part of an Acordo Geral de Paz (AGP—General Peace Agreement). In September Chissano and Dhlakama met in Gaborone, Botswana, to attempt to resolve the deadlocked military and security issues. Chissano offered to establish an independent commission to monitor and guarantee the impartiality of the Serviço de Informação e Segurança do Estado (SISE—State Information and Security Service). In addition, the figure of 30,000 was agreed upon as the number of troops to comprise the joint national defence force.

The AGP was finally signed on 4 October 1992. Under the terms of the agreement, a general cease-fire was to come into force immediately after ratification of the treaty by the legislature. Both the Renamo troops and the government forces were to withdraw to assembly points within seven days of ratification. The new national defence force, the Forças Armadas de Defesa de Moçambique (FADM), would then be created, drawing on equal numbers from each side, with the remaining troops surrendering their weapons to a UN peace-keeping force within six months. A Cease-fire Commission, incorporating representatives from the Government, Renamo and the UN, was to supervise the implementation of the truce regulations. Overall political control of the peace process was to be vested in a Comissão de Supervisão e Controle (CSC—Supervision and Control Commission), comprising representatives of the Government, Renamo and the UN. In addition, Chissano was to appoint a Comissão Nacional de Informação (COMINFO—National Information Commission), with responsibilities including supervision of the SISE. Presidential and legislative elections were to take place, under UN supervision, one year after the signing of the AGP, provided that it had been fully implemented and the demobilization process completed. The AGP was duly ratified by the Assembleia da República and came into force on 15 October. On that day UN observers arrived in Maputo to supervise the first phase of the cease-fire. However, shortly afterwards the Government accused Renamo of systematically violating the accord. Dhlakama subsequently claimed that Renamo's actions had been defensive manoeuvres and, in turn, accused government forces of violating the accord by advancing into Renamo territory.

In November 1992, owing to considerable delays in the formation of the various peace commissions envisaged in the AGP, the timetable for the cease-fire operations was redrafted. In December the UN Security Council finally approved a plan for the establishment of the UN Operation in Mozambique (ONUMOZ), providing for the deployment of some 7,500 troops, police and civilian observers to oversee the process of demobilization and formation of the FADM, and to supervise the forthcoming elections. However, there were continued delays in the deployment of ONUMOZ. In March 1993 the peace process was effectively halted when Renamo withdrew from the CSC and the Cease-fire Commission, protesting that proper provisions had not been made to accommodate its officials. In April Dhlakama announced that his forces would begin to report to assembly points only when Renamo received US $15m. to finance its transition into a political party. Meanwhile, the first UN troops became operational on 1 April.

In June 1993 Renamo rejoined the CSC. The commission subsequently agreed to a formal postponement of the election date to October 1994. A meeting in Maputo of international aid donors, also in June 1993, produced promises of additional support for the peace process, bringing the total pledged by donors to US $520m., including support for the repatriation of 1.5m. refugees from neighbouring countries, the resettlement of 4m.–5m. displaced people and the reintegration of some 80,000 former combatants into civilian life. The UN also agreed to establish a trust fund of $10m. to finance Renamo's transformation into a political party. In November the UN Security Council renewed the mandate of ONUMOZ for a further six months. In addition, it acceded to the joint request by the Government and Renamo for a UN police corps. In the same month consensus was finally reached on the text of the electoral law, which was promulgated at the end of December. At a meeting of the CSC in mid-November an agreement was signed providing for the confinement of troops, to be concluded by the end of the year.

In February 1994 the UN Security Council announced that, in response to demands made by Renamo, it would be increasing the membership of the UN police corps monitoring the confinement areas from 128 to 1,144. By the end of February only 50% of troops had entered designated assembly points, and none had officially been demobilized. In March, in an effort to expedite the confinement process, the Government announced that it was to commence the unilateral demobilization of its troops. Renamo began the demobilization of its troops shortly afterwards. In April Lt-Gen. Lagos Lidimo, the nominee of the Government, and the former Renamo guerrilla commander, Lt-Gen. Mateus Ngonhamo, were inaugurated as the high command of the FADM. In the same month Chissano issued a decree scheduling the presidential and legislative elections for October, and in May the UN Security Council renewed the mandate of ONUMOZ for the final period, ending on 15 November.

On 16 August 1994, in accordance with the provisions of the AGP, the government Forças Armadas de Moçambique were formally dissolved and their assets transferred to the FADM,

which was inaugurated as the country's official armed forces on the same day. In December the Cease-fire Commission issued its final report, according to which ONUMOZ had registered a combined total of 91,691 government and Renamo troops during the confinement process, of whom 11,579 had enlisted in the FADM (compared with the 30,000 envisaged in the AGP).

The 1994 elections

In August 1994 Renamo formally registered as a political party. In the same month the Partido Liberal e Democrático de Moçambique, the Partido Nacional Democrático and the Partido Nacional de Moçambique formed an electoral coalition, the União Democrática (UD). The presidential and legislative elections took place on 27–29 October. In the presidential election Chissano secured an outright majority (53.3%) of the votes. His closest rival was Dhlakama, who received 33.7% of the votes. In the legislative elections Frelimo also secured an overall majority, winning 129 of the 250 seats in the Assembleia da República; Renamo obtained 112 seats, and the UD the remaining nine. Later in November the UN Security Council extended the mandate of ONUMOZ until the end of January 1995. Chissano was inaugurated as President on 9 December 1994, and the new Government, in which all portfolios were assigned to members of Frelimo, was sworn in on 23 December.

By the end of March 1995 only a small unit of ONUMOZ officials remained in the country. In February 1996 the Government proposed that municipal elections, which the Constitution stipulated must be conducted no later than October 1996, be held in 1997. Delays in the election process had resulted from a dispute between the opposition, which demanded local elections throughout Mozambique, and the Government, which sought to hold elections only in those areas that had attained municipal status. In October 1996 the Assembleia da República approved a constitutional amendment differentiating between municipalities and administrative posts. In August 1997 the Government postponed the elections until 1998, owing to funding shortfalls. In April Renamo was among 16 opposition parties that officially withdrew from the elections, alleging that the voter registration process had been fraudulent. Renamo subsequently campaigned vigorously to dissuade the electorate from participating in the ballot. At the elections, which took place on 30 June, Frelimo won control of all the municipal authorities contested, its main competition coming from independent candidates. The voter turn-out was only 14.6%, prompting Renamo to demand the annulment of the elections.

Presidential and legislative elections took place on 3–5 December 1999. In the presidential contest, Chissano defeated Dhlakama (his sole challenger), taking 52.3% of the valid votes cast. Frelimo secured 133 of the 250 seats in the Assembleia da República; Renamo—União Eleitoral, a Renamo-led coalition of 11 opposition parties, obtained the remaining seats, although Renamo rejected the outcome, claiming that the vote had been fraudulent. On 15 January 2000 Chissano was sworn in for a further five-year presidential term.

In December 2000 Dhlakama and President Chissano held talks in an attempt to resolve the growing tension between their two parties. Dhlakama stated that he was prepared to accept the results of the 1999 elections, while Chissano pledged to consult Renamo about future state appointments. In a second meeting between the two leaders, in January 2001, it was agreed that a number of working groups (including groups on defence and security, constitutional and parliamentary affairs, and the media) would be established in February. At a further meeting, in March, Chissano referred Dhlakama's demand for the appointment of Renamo state governors to the Assembleia da República, whose Frelimo representatives were strongly opposed to accommodating Renamo demands. In protest, Dhlakama ceased negotiations in April.

President Chissano announced in May 2001 that he would not stand for re-election on the expiry of his term in 2004. At the long-postponed Renamo congress, held in October 2001, Dhlakama was re-elected party President; Joaquim Vaz was elected Secretary-General. The holding of a party congress by Renamo for the first time since the end of the civil war, as well as the establishment of a 10-member Political Committee, were regarded as confirmation of the movement's decision to establish itself as a full political party, and to decentralize the party leadership and structure.

In June 2002 Frelimo elected Armando Guebuza as its Secretary-General, and thus also its candidate for the 2004 presidential election. During July Renamo's attempt to establish itself as a legitimate opposition party was threatened after Dhlakama dismissed Vaz as Secretary-General, assuming the position himself, and dissolved the party's Political Committee. Nevertheless, in November the party regained some stability with the appointment of Viana Magalhaes as Secretary-General.

The Conselho Constitucional (CC—Constitutional Council), which was to supervise elections and determine the constitutionality of new legislation, was inaugurated in early November 2003. Municipal elections were held on 19 November. Despite allegations by Renamo of irregularities, the elections proceeded smoothly, and their conduct was later commended by an observer mission from the European Union (EU, see p. 281), although voter turn-out, at 24.2%, was low. Frelimo won a majority in 29 municipalities, while Renamo won a majority in four. Luísa Dias Diogo was appointed as Prime Minister in February 2004 following the resignation of Pascoal Mocumbi.

In November 2004 the Assembleia da República approved changes to the Constitution, which were to take effect on the day following the declaration of the results of the forthcoming presidential and legislative elections. Notably, the President would no longer be afforded immunity from prosecution and a Conselho de Estado (Council of State) was to be created, which would act as an advisory body to the President.

Guebuza elected to the presidency

The presidential and legislative elections took place as scheduled on 1–2 December 2004, and proceeded without notable incident, although 37 voting stations did not open, reportedly owing to bad weather. For the first time Mozambicans living abroad were able to vote. Although national and international observers stated that the elections had been generally free and fair, they did express concern at the lack of access that they had been granted to the counting process and about the low rate of voter participation, which was recorded at just 36.3%. Renamo, later joined by other opposition parties, announced that it would not recognize the results, owing to alleged irregularities produced by the computer system used to tabulate the votes and demanded that the elections be re-run. Official results, which were released on 21 December, revealed that Guebuza had won 63.7% of the votes cast at the presidential election, while Dhlakama had taken 31.7%. In the legislative elections, Frelimo secured 160 of the available 250 seats, while Renamo took the remaining 90 seats. Protests lodged by Renamo with the Comissão Nacional de Eleicões (CNE—National Elections Commission) and the CC were rejected in January 2005, and Renamo announced that it would accept the election results and participate in the new legislature.

The new Assembleia da República was inaugurated on 31 January 2005, and Eduardo Mulémbue was re-elected to the post of Chairman. Guebuza was sworn in as President on 2 February. The new Government, featuring a number of new appointees, was announced the following day. Diogo retained her position as Prime Minister; however, in a reorganization of ministerial functions, Manuel Chang became Minister of Finance, while Aiuba Cuereneia headed the newly created Ministry of Planning and Development. In March Chissano resigned as President of Frelimo and was replaced by Guebuza.

Meanwhile, in February 2005 it was reported that members of Dhlakama's guard, protesting against the non-payment of wages and poor living conditions, had taken five Renamo officials hostage. The following month the Government announced plans to integrate the guards (estimated to number 100–150), who had been maintained by Dhlakama as his personal defence force following the end of the civil war in 1992, into the state security forces; however, such attempts were consistently stalled by Dhlakama. In September 2005 conflict between Frelimo and Renamo supporters led to the deaths of 12 people in Mocímboa da Praia, in Cabo Delgado province, following a disputed by-election earlier in the year.

In November 2005 the Assembleia da República adopted legislation providing for the formation of the Conselho de Estado, as envisaged in changes to the Constitution approved in late 2004. Members of the Conselho, including Dhlakama, were subsequently appointed by Guebuza and the Assembleia da República, and took office in December 2005.

In December 2006 the Assembleia da República approved amendments to the electoral legislation. Among the changes were provisions for the restructuring of the CNE, which had been reduced in size to 13 members. Five members were henceforth to be nominated by the Assembleia in proportion to the number of seats held by each political party, while the remaining eight members were to be nominated by legally constituted civil society bodies. A 14th member was to be appointed by the Government, but would not have the right to vote. Also approved was a requirement that the electorate re-register every five years and the abolition of the 5% 'barrier clause', whereby only parties that won at least 5% of votes cast had secured representation in the Assembleia.

In March 2007 an explosion at a munitions storage facility in a residential area of Maputo resulted in the deaths of more than 100 people and left over 500 others injured. A commission of inquiry was established in April to investigate the incident. The Government admitted that it had been storing equipment since the end of the civil war and weapons experts were later deployed to dispose of obsolete military equipment. In June a munitions expert from South Africa was killed in an explosion while assisting with the destruction of unexploded missiles. Following a further explosion in October, the Government agreed to relocate weapons stores away from residential areas. In March 2008 Minister of National Defence Gen. (retd) Tobias Joaquim Dai was dismissed and replaced by Filipe Nhussi; no official reason was given for the change, although Dai had been severely criticized for the military's negligence with regard to the armaments explosions.

In February 2008 riots broke out in Maputo, as people took to the streets in protest against rising fuel prices and government plans to increase fares on public transport. Some 12 people were killed and hundreds more injured when the police opened fire on the demonstration. The Government subsequently reduced fuel costs for privately operated taxis and minibuses, and cancelled the increase in transport fares. Human rights organization Amnesty International accused the police of acting with impunity and excessive violence in response to rising crime rates.

Frelimo secured a resounding victory in municipal elections in November 2008, winning a majority in 42 of the 43 municipal assemblies, while Renamo lost four of the five municipalities it had gained in the elections in 2003. International observers stated that, despite some minor problems, the elections had been conducted in a transparent and fair manner.

Recent developments: the 2009 elections

In April 2009 the Assembleia da República adopted electoral legislation under which the presidential, legislative and provincial elections would henceforth be held on the same ballot, and later that month President Guebuza confirmed that the elections would take place concurrently on 28 October. At the presidential election, Guebuza secured an overwhelming victory, taking 75.0% of the valid votes cast. His nearest challenger, Dhlakama, won 16.4%, while Daviz Simango of the newly founded Movimento Democrático de Moçambique (MDM) took 8.6%. Members of the opposition alleged that the vote was compromised by fraudulent activity. The CC acknowledged that certain irregularities had taken place, notably the deliberate invalidation of votes by polling station staff, but that such incidents had not been on a sufficient scale to alter the election results. The CC also confirmed that Guebuza's Frelimo party had increased its majority in the legislature, winning 74.5% of the votes cast and 191 of the 250 seats. Renamo took 17.7% and 51 seats. The MDM was the only other party to gain representation in the Assembleia da República, securing eight seats. Frelimo was also declared to have won 704 of the 812 provincial assembly seats, thus consolidating its power at all three levels of government.

Guebuza was inaugurated for a second term as President on 14 January 2010, appointing a new Government five days later. Aires Bonifácio Ali was selected as the new Prime Minister, vacating his former position as Minister of Education and Culture. This portfolio was divided between two ministers: Zeferino de Alexandre Martins became Minister of Education, while Armando Artur João assumed responsibility for culture. The key portfolios within the new administration were little altered from the outgoing Government. In late January Veronica Macamo was elected as the first female Chairperson of the Assembleia da República. A Renamo boycott of the legislature, in protest against the conduct of the 2009 elections, was inconsistently observed by the party's 51 deputies and ended fairly rapidly. Meanwhile, legislation on the Assembleia decreed that only parties with at least 11 deputies could form an official parliamentary group, meaning that the MDM, with just eight deputies, was not authorized to participate fully in the legislature. With Frelimo support, however, this legislation was amended in April 2010, and the MDM was officially designated as the third parliamentary group in the Assembleia in May.

Antonio Munguambe, Minister of Transport and Communications in Guebuza's Council of Ministers during 2005–08, was sentenced to 20 years' imprisonment in February 2010 for his involvement in the embezzlement of some US $1.7m. from the state-owned airport management body, Aeroportos de Moçambique. (After launching a successful appeal, in May 2011 Munguambe's sentence was reduced to four years and five months.) Munguambe was the first former or serving government minister to have been imprisoned since the country gained its independence in 1975. In March 2011 Almerino Manhenje was convicted of financial malpractice and abuse of office during his tenure as Minister of the Interior (1995–2005) and received a two-year prison sentence, although he subsequently appealed against this ruling.

Violent demonstrations in protest against rising prices, particularly the cost of bread and other essential foodstuffs, erupted in Maputo, Matola, Chimoio and Beira during early September 2010. The Government had implemented an increase in electricity and water rates, while a global decline in wheat production, combined with the country's depreciating currency, had made wheat imports (upon which Mozambique is heavily dependent) less affordable, resulting in higher bread prices. Protesters erected barricades and clashed with police officers, and widespread looting was reported. The police, who claimed that the protest action was illegal since a permit had not been procured, fired tear gas and live ammunition at the demonstrators, causing the deaths of 13 people and more than 600 injuries. Military units were subsequently deployed to reinforce police patrols and dismantle the roadblocks, and more than 400 protesters were arrested. The authorities also allegedly disrupted mobile cellular telephone text-messaging services, which had reportedly been the main method used by the demonstrators to organize the protests. In response to the unrest, the Government announced on 7 September that it would subsidize bread prices, reduce the duties payable on certain imported foodstuffs, lower electricity and water tariffs, and freeze the salaries of senior officials in the Government and public bodies. Although these measures pacified the protesters, they were financially unsustainable and hence only a temporary solution to the long-standing problems of poverty and unemployment.

Guebuza effected a reorganization of the Council of Ministers in October 2010. Soares Nhaca, the Minister of Agriculture, was replaced by hitherto Minister of the Interior José Condungua Pacheco, who had been widely criticized for supporting the repressive measures employed by the police in response to the food riots. Alberto Mondlane was assigned the interior portfolio, while Alexandre Manguele and Armando Inroga were appointed as Minister of Health and Minister of Industry and Trade, respectively.

In December 2010 the Assembleia da República approved the establishment of a commission to draft unspecified modifications to the Constitution. Amid suspicions that the Frelimo-dominated commission would propose the removal of presidential term limits, thereby allowing Guebuza to contest a third term in office, Renamo announced in January 2011 that it was boycotting the body. Frelimo officials maintained that the aim of the commission was merely to 'consolidate' the Constitution and rejected claims that it would alter the term-limit clauses. (Guebuza had frequently stated that he would not seek re-election.) The commission was officially inaugurated in October. Frelimo presented its constitutional proposals later that month, which included plans for the establishment of a Constitutional Court (with a broader mandate than the existing CC) and other minor reforms; no mention was made of amending the presidential term limits. Renamo and the MDM denounced Frelimo's proposals as superficial, claiming that they did not warrant the implementation of an expensive and time-consuming constitutional review process. Nevertheless, public consultations commenced in February 2013, and the Assembleia da República was expected to vote on the reforms by early 2014.

Legislation was approved in May 2011 authorizing the provision of 'bonus' payments and other financial benefits to veterans of the country's civil conflicts. Although the benefits applied to ex-combatants from both Frelimo and Renamo, they were ostensibly weighted in favour of the former, prompting strong criticism from Renamo. By-elections were held on 7 December following the resignation of three Frelimo mayors earlier in the year. While Frelimo retained control of two of the municipalities, the MDM won the important mayoralty of Quelimane, a result that was regarded by analysts as an indication of the declining popularity of the incumbent administration. Renamo boycotted the elections, dismissing them as illegitimate.

In March 2012 two deaths were reported following a violent altercation between the police and armed Dhlakama loyalists at

Renamo's headquarters in Nampula. It was suspected that members of Dhlakama's controversial guard had been involved in the incident. Dhlakama and President Guebuza held a meeting in the following month to discuss this matter and other Renamo grievances, and both parties reaffirmed their commitment to maintaining peace within the country. None the less, in October Dhlakama and several hundred of his allies relocated to Gorongosa, Renamo's base of operations during the civil war, and began military training exercises in an apparent attempt to intimidate the Government into making concessions. Dhlakama issued a series of demands, including the formation of a transitional administration, the integration of Renamo combatants into the country's security apparatus and a greater opposition presence on the CNE. A government contingent met with Renamo representatives on three occasions in December, but the talks soon foundered. Under legislation adopted during that month, Frelimo, as the largest party in the Assembleia da República, was granted the right to designate five appointees to a new CNE (compared with two for Renamo and one for the MDM). Renamo, reiterating earlier threats, declared its intention to boycott and disrupt the upcoming municipal elections (due to take place in November 2013) in protest against the CNE legislation. Some commentators argued that Renamo's frequent ultimatums, boycotts and aggressive posturing were acts of frustration by an organization lacking the necessary popular support to influence policy via normal democratic channels.

Meanwhile, in October 2012 Guebuza appointed Alberto Clementino António Vaquina as Prime Minister and also replaced the heads of the education, tourism, youth, and science ministries. A public probity law came into force in November, requiring public officials to reveal their financial assets and detailing new regulations on potential conflicts of interest. In accordance with the law, a Central Public Ethics Commission was inaugurated in January 2013.

Foreign Affairs

After independence, Mozambique developed strong international links with the USSR and other countries of the communist bloc, and with neighbouring African states: it is a member of the Southern African Development Community (SADC, see p. 434), founded in 1979 as the Southern African Development Co-ordination Conference, then with the aim of reducing the region's economic dependence on South Africa, principally by developing trade routes through Mozambique. In December 1996 Mozambique, Malawi, Zambia and Zimbabwe (also SADC members) formally agreed to establish the Beira Development Corridor as a trading route avoiding South Africa's ports. In 1993 full diplomatic relations were established with South Africa. In July 1994 Mozambique and South Africa established a new Joint Defence and Security Commission, replacing the Joint Security Commission originally established in 1984.

During 1995 the activities, principally in the border province of Manica, of a group of mainly Zimbabwean dissidents, known as Chimwenje, came under increasing scrutiny. The group, which was alleged to have links with Renamo, was believed to be preparing for military incursions into Zimbabwe, where it sought the overthrow of President Robert Mugabe. In early 1996 the Chissano Government announced its intention to expel the dissidents from Mozambique. In June, following a series of armed attacks on both sides of the Mozambique–Zimbabwe border, which were believed to have been perpetrated by Chimwenje, the Governments of Mozambique and Zimbabwe agreed to combine and intensify efforts to combat the activities of the dissidents. The group was suppressed in late 1996. During late 2002 and early 2003 Mozambique resettled a number of white Zimbabwean farmers whose land had been appropriated by the Mugabe regime.

Following widespread xenophobic violence in South African townships in May 2008, at least 23 Mozambicans were believed to have been killed and around 40,000 were forced to return home. Refugee camps were established on the common border and near Maputo to manage the influx of refugees. In June 2011 Mozambique and South Africa concluded an anti-piracy accord, under the terms of which a South African patrol vessel was deployed in the Mozambican Channel to bolster Mozambique's efforts to combat the growing problem of piracy in its territorial waters. A further counter-piracy agreement was signed by Mozambique, South Africa and Tanzania in February 2012. Meanwhile, in December 2011 Mozambique, Tanzania and the Comoros formally delineated their maritime boundaries.

Relations between Mozambique and land-locked Malawi were strained during late 2010, after the Malawian Government opened a port at Nsanje on the Shire river in October, in an attempt to create a new trade route to the Indian Ocean via the Zambezi river (which passes through Mozambique). The Mozambican authorities seized a barge that was making the inaugural journey to Nsanje, claiming that permission had not been granted for the vessel to travel through Mozambique's waters. Guebuza insisted that a number of technical studies had to be completed before expanded commercial shipping activities on the Zambezi river would be authorized, and Malawi finally conceded to this demand in February 2012. However, commentators suspected that the Mozambican Government's actions were mainly motivated by concerns that the new trade route would be financially detrimental to Mozambique's coastal ports.

CONSTITUTION AND GOVERNMENT

The Constitution of 30 November 1990 (amended in 1996 and 2004) provides for a multi-party political system. Legislative power is vested in the Assembleia da República, with 250 members, who are elected for a five-year term. Members are elected by universal, direct adult suffrage in a secret ballot, according to a system of proportional representation. The President of the Republic, who is Head of State, is directly elected for a five-year term; the President holds executive power and governs with the assistance of an appointed Council of Ministers. A Council of State advises the President, who, however, has no obligation to follow its advice. Judicial functions are exercised through the Supreme Court and other courts provided for in the law on the judiciary, which also subordinates them to the Assembleia da República. Judges are independent, subject only to the law. Provincial governors, appointed by the President, have overall responsibility for the functions of government within each of the 11 provinces. For the purposes of local government, Mozambique is divided into 33 municipalities.

REGIONAL AND INTERNATIONAL CO-OPERATION

Mozambique is a member of the African Union (see p. 191) and of the Southern African Development Community (SADC, see p. 434).

Mozambique became a member of the UN in 1975 and was admitted to the World Trade Organization (WTO, see p. 444) in 1995. Mozambique participates in the Group of 77 (G77, see p. 461) developing countries. Mozambique was admitted, by special dispensation, as a full member of the Commonwealth (see p. 244) in 1995 and became an observer member of the Organisation Internationale de la Francophonie (see p. 477) in 2006.

ECONOMIC AFFAIRS

In 2011, according to estimates by the World Bank, Mozambique's gross national income (GNI), measured at average 2009–11 prices, was US $11,240m., equivalent to $470 per head (or $980 per head on an international purchasing-power parity basis). During 2002–11, it was estimated, the population increased at an average annual rate of 2.5%, while gross domestic product (GDP) per head grew, in real terms, by an average of 4.6% per year. Overall GDP increased, in real terms, at an average annual rate of 7.5% in 2003–11; growth in 2011 was 7.3%.

Agriculture (including forestry and fishing) contributed 30.8% of GDP in 2011. In mid-2013 the sector employed an estimated 79.8% of the economically active population, according to FAO. Fishing is a significant export activity: fish, crustaceans and molluscs accounted for 1.2% of total export earnings in 2011. The principal cash crops are fruit and nuts, cotton, sugar cane and copra. After production of cashews fell sharply in the 1990s, the Government attempted to increase revenue from the crop by promoting production and improving processing facilities. The main subsistence crop is cassava. During 2003–11, according to official figures, agricultural GDP increased by an average of 7.2% per year; growth in 2011 was 6.7%.

Industry (including mining, manufacturing, construction and power) provided 21.7% of GDP in 2011, and employed 5.6% of the economically active population in 1997. During 2003–11, according to official figures, industrial GDP increased at an average annual rate of 6.1%; the sector grew by 4.8% in 2011.

Mining contributed 1.5% of GDP in 2011, and employed 0.5% of the economically active population in 1997. Only coal, bauxite, marble, gold and salt are exploited in significant quantities, although gravel and crushed rocks are also mined. In November 2004 the Companhia Vale do Rio Doce (Brazil) was granted a coal-mining concession in Moatize; the mine commenced

production in May 2011, with forecast annual production of 11m. metric tons (doubling to 22m. tons from 2014). There are reserves of other minerals, including high-grade iron ore, precious and semi-precious stones, and natural gas. Plans were launched in 1994 to exploit natural gas reserves at Pande, in the province of Inhambane, which were estimated at 55,000m. cu m. A South African company, SASOL Ltd, was granted a 25-year concession to develop gasfields at Pande and Temane (also in Inhambane province); it was anticipated that the Government would receive revenues of some US $900m. from the project, and the construction of a pipeline to transport the gas to South Africa was completed in early 2004. A gas-processing centre opened in Temane in early 2004. In 1999 reportedly one of the largest reserves of titanium in the world (estimated at 75m. tons) was discovered in the district of Chibuto, in the province of Gaza; at early 2013, after several licences had been revoked, the Government was still seeking a company to explore the titanium-bearing heavy sands at Chibuto. Meanwhile, from 2002 the British company Pan African Resources plc undertook a project to investigate the viability of developing a new gold mine in Manica province. Preliminary estimates suggested that gold reserves totalled some 3m. oz. In August 2012 the Manica Gold Project was sold to the Australian company Terranova Minerals (subsequently renamed Auroch Minerals). According to official figures, mining GDP increased at an average annual rate of 18.2% in 2003–11; growth in 2011 was 16.1%.

Manufacturing contributed 12.8% of GDP in 2011, and employed 3.0% of the economically active population in 1997. A large aluminium smelter, Mozal, was opened in 2000 and expanded in 2003, with the completion of Mozal II, which more than doubled capacity, to some 580,000 metric tons of aluminium ingots per year. Aluminium production was valued at 19,067,000m. meticais in 2003, equivalent to 16.8% of GDP. Aluminium accounted for 54.7% of total export earnings in 2008, but earnings declined sharply in 2009 owing to low international prices, weak demand resulting from the global economic downturn and electricity shortages; prices recovered strongly in 2010. During 2003–11, according to official figures, manufacturing GDP increased at an average annual rate of 4.5%; manufacturing GDP grew by 3.0% in 2011.

Construction contributed 3.1% of GDP in 2011, and employed 0.8% of the economically active population according to the census of 1980. According to official figures, construction GDP increased at an average annual rate of 6.9% in 2003–11. Growth in 2011 was 4.6%.

Electrical energy is derived almost exclusively from hydroelectric power, which provided some 99.9% of total electricity production in 2009. Mozambique's important Cahora Bassa hydroelectric plant on the Zambezi river supplies electricity to South Africa and Zimbabwe. By 2004 an extended power supply from Cahora Bassa to Zambézia, Manica and Sofala was in operation. In early 2011 an environmental impact study for the construction of a hydroelectric dam at Mepanda Uncua, some 70 km downstream of Cahora Bassa, was under way. It was envisaged that power from the Mepanda Uncua plant, which would have an initial generating capacity of 1,500 MW (to be expanded to 2,500 MW in a second phase), would also be exported to South Africa. Mozambique currently imports all of its petroleum requirements. Imports of mineral fuels and lubricants comprised 23.6% of the value of total imports in 2011.

The services sector contributed 47.5% of GDP in 2011, and engaged 12.3% of the economically active population in 1997. By the end of the 1990s tourism was the fastest growing sector of the economy. It was hoped that the formal opening, in April 2002, of the Great Limpopo Transfrontier Park, comprising South Africa's Kruger National Park, Zimbabwe's Gonarezhou National Park and Mozambique's Limpopo National Park, would attract additional tourists. In 2010 some 1.8m. tourists visited Mozambique, compared with about 711,000 in 2004, and receipts from tourism totalled US $197m. in 2010 and an estimated $231m. in 2011. The GDP of the services sector increased by an average of 8.3% per year in 2003–11, according to official figures; services GDP grew by 7.0% in 2011.

In 2011 Mozambique recorded a merchandise trade deficit of US $2,249.3m. and there was a deficit of $2,438.3m. on the current account of the balance of payments. In 2011 the principal source of imports was South Africa (providing 33.6% of total imports); other major suppliers were the Netherlands, the United Arab Emirates and the People's Republic of China. In 2011 the Netherlands was the principal market for exports (receiving 38.9% of the total); South Africa and the United

Kingdom were the other significant purchaser. The principal exports in 2011 were electrical energy and tobacco. (However, aluminium is generally the most significant export.) The main imports in 2011 were mineral fuels and lubricants (particularly petroleum oils), nuclear reactors, boilers and machinery, and road vehicles.

In 2011 there was an overall budgetary deficit of 18,530m. meticais, equivalent to 0.01% of GDP. Mozambique's general government gross debt was 134,395m. meticais in 2011, equivalent to 42.0% of GDP. Total external debt was US $4,124m. in 2010, of which $2,960m. was public and publicly guaranteed debt. In that year, the cost of servicing long-term public and publicly guaranteed debt and repayments to the IMF was equivalent to 2.9% of the value of exports of goods, services and income (excluding workers' remittances). According to the ILO, the average annual rate of inflation was 10.3% in 2003–11; consumer prices increased by an average of 10.4% in 2011, according to the IMF. An unemployment rate of 18.7% was recorded in 2004/05.

During the 1990s Mozambique's economy was one of the fastest growing in the world and in the early 2000s a significant amount of the country's foreign debt was deferred and subsequently cancelled. The country possesses considerable mineral resources, including aluminium, gold, natural gas, petroleum and coal. Mozambique is, however, prone to drought, while flooding is a frequent problem during the rainy season. The economy withstood the turmoil caused by the global financial crisis, and the rate of real GDP growth accelerated to 7.1% in 2010, driven by rising demand for the country's commodities. However, an upsurge in the cost of food and fuel during 2010–11 led to persistently high levels of inflation. Strong performances in the extractive sector (as well as in agriculture and services) contributed to further economic expansion, of 7.3%, in 2011, with a number of large-scale mining projects commencing operations in that year and investment inflows rising sharply. An upturn in coal production supported a 7.5% increase in GDP during 2012, according to IMF estimates. Robust export and investment levels were recorded in that year, and the stability of the local currency underpinned a marked reduction in inflation. During 2011–12 several major natural gas discoveries were announced, leaving Mozambique with some of the largest reserves in Africa. With production expected to begin in 2016 and the broader mining sector continuing to attract strong interest from foreign investors, Mozambique's medium-term economic outlook appeared positive. The country's substandard infrastructure continued to be regarded as a potential obstacle to future growth, but numerous development projects aimed at addressing this problem were under way in 2013. The IMF forecast economic growth of 8.4% in that year.

PUBLIC HOLIDAYS

2014: 1 January (New Year's Day), 3 February (Heroes' Day, anniversary of the assassination of Eduardo Mondlane), 7 April (Day of the Mozambican Woman), 1 May (Workers' Day), 25 June (Independence Day), 7 September (Victory Day—anniversary of the end of the Armed Struggle), 25 September (Anniversary of the launching of the Armed Struggle for National Liberation, and Day of the Armed Forces of Mozambique), 4 October (Peace and National Reconciliation Day), 25 December (National Family Day).

Statistical Survey

Source (unless otherwise stated): Instituto Nacional de Estatística, Comissão Nacional do Plano, Av. Ahmed Sekou Touré 21, CP 493, Maputo; tel. 21491054; fax 21490384; e-mail webmaster@ine.gov.mz; internet www.ine.gov.mz.

Area and Population

AREA, POPULATION AND DENSITY

Area (sq km)	799,380*
Land	786,380
Inland waters	13,000
Population (census results)	
1 August 1997	15,278,334
1 August 2007	
Males	9,734,678
Females	10,491,618
Total	20,226,296
Population (UN estimates at mid-year)† . . .	
2011	23,929,710
2012	24,475,184
2013	25,028,314
Density (per sq km) at mid-2013	31.3

* 308,641 sq miles.
† Source: UN, *World Population Prospects: The 2010 Revision.*

POPULATION BY AGE AND SEX
(UN estimates at mid-2013)

	Males	Females	Total
0–14	5,471,767	5,424,313	10,896,080
15–64	6,389,887	6,899,913	13,289,800
65 and over	358,118	484,316	842,434
Total	**12,219,772**	**12,808,542**	**25,028,314**

Source: UN, *World Population Prospects: The 2010 Revision.*

PROVINCES
(at census of 1 August 2007)

Province	Area (sq km)	Population	Density (per sq km)
Cabo Delgado	82,625	1,605,649	19.4
Gaza	75,709	1,226,272	16.2
Inhambane	68,615	1,252,479	18.3
Manica	61,661	1,412,029	22.9
City of Maputo . . .	300	1,094,315	3,647.7
Maputo Province . . .	26,058	1,205,553	46.3
Nampula	81,606	3,985,285	48.8
Niassa	129,056	1,169,837	9.1
Sofala	68,018	1,642,636	24.2
Tete	100,724	1,783,967	17.7
Zambézia	105,008	3,848,274	36.6
Total	**799,380**	**20,226,296**	**25.3**

PRINCIPAL TOWNS
(at 2007 census, preliminary)

Maputo (capital) .	1,099,102	Nacala-Porto . .	207,894
Matola	675,422	Quelimane . . .	192,876
Nampula . . .	477,900	Tete	152,909
Beira	436,240	Xai-Xai	116,343
Chimoio	238,976		

Mid-2011 (incl. suburbs, UN estimate): Maputo 1,150,030 (Source: UN, *World Urbanization Prospects: The 2011 Revision*).

BIRTHS AND DEATHS

	2009	2010	2011
Crude birth rate (per 1,000) . .	41.8	41.6	41.4
Crude death rate (per 1,000) . .	14.0	13.7	13.5

Source: African Development Bank.

Life expectancy (years at birth): 50.2 (males 49.2; females 51.1) in 2011 (Source: World Bank, World Development Indicators database).

ECONOMICALLY ACTIVE POPULATION
(persons aged 12 years and over, 1980 census)

	Males	Females	Total
Agriculture, forestry, hunting and fishing	1,887,779	2,867,052	4,754,831
Mining and quarrying . . . }			
Manufacturing . . . . }	323,730	23,064	346,794
Construction	41,611	510	42,121
Commerce	90,654	21,590	112,244
Transport, storage and communications . . .	74,817	2,208	77,025
Other services*	203,629	39,820	243,449
Total employed . . .	2,622,220	2,954,244	5,576,464
Unemployed	75,505	19,321	94,826
Total labour force . . .	2,697,725	2,973,565	5,671,290

* Including electricity, gas and water.

Source: ILO, *Yearbook of Labour Statistics*.

1997 (percentage distribution of economically active population at census of 1 August): Agriculture, forestry and hunting: 91.3% of females, 69.6% of males; Mining: 0.0% of females, 1.0% of males; Manufacturing: 0.8% of females, 5.5% of males; Energy: 0.0% of females, 0.3% of males; Construction: 0.3% of females, 3.9% of males; Transport and communications: 0.1% of females, 2.3% of males; Commerce and finance: 4.3% of females, 9.7% of males; Services: 2.2% of females, 3.4% of males; Unknown: 0.9% of females, 1.4% of males.

Mid-2013 ('000 persons, estimates): Agriculture, etc. 9,250; Total labour force 11,596 (Source: FAO).

Health and Welfare

KEY INDICATORS

Total fertility rate (children per woman, 2010)	4.9
Under-5 mortality rate (per 1,000 live births, 2010) . . .	135
HIV/AIDS (% of persons aged 15–49, 2009)	11.5
Physicians (per 1,000 head, 2008)	0.03
Hospital beds (per 1,000 head, 2007)	0.8
Health expenditure (2009): US $ per head (PPP) . . .	47
Health expenditure (2009): % of GDP	5.4
Health expenditure (2009): public (% of total)	73.1
Access to water (% of persons, 2010)	47
Access to sanitation (% of persons, 2010)	18
Total carbon dioxide emissions ('000 metric tons, 2008) . .	2,313.9
Carbon dioxide emissions per head (metric tons, 2008) . .	0.1
Human Development Index (2011): ranking	184
Human Development Index (2011): value	0.322

For sources and definitions, see explanatory note on p. vi.

Agriculture

PRINCIPAL CROPS
('000 metric tons)

	2009	2010	2011
Rice, paddy	179*	180†	193†
Maize	1,932*	1,878*	2,091†
Millet	49*	50†	57†
Sorghum	384*	395†	503†
Potatoes†	110	111	102
Sweet potatoes†	900	920	861
Cassava (Manioc)†	5,670	5,700	6,267
Cashew nuts, with shell . . .	64	61†	72†
Groundnuts, with shell* . . .	68	70	67
Coconuts†	270	278	266
Sunflower seed†	7	7	6
Tomatoes†	15	16	12
Bananas†	113	115	100
Oranges†	21	21	26
Grapefruits and pomelos† . .	11	11	11
Guavas, mangoes and mangosteens†	19	19	20
Pineapples†	8	10	11
Papayas†	42	44	43
Tobacco, unmanufactured . .	63	57†	58†

* Unofficial figure.
† FAO estimate(s).

Aggregate production ('000 metric tons, may include official, semi-official or estimated data): Total cereals 2,547 in 2009, 2,506 in 2010, 2,846 in 2011; Total roots and tubers 6,689 in 2009, 6,739 in 2010, 7,239 in 2011; Total vegetables (incl. melons) 255 in 2009, 216 in 2010, 244 in 2011; Total fruits (excl. melons) 375 in 2009, 369 in 2010, 358 in 2011.

Source: FAO.

LIVESTOCK
('000 head, year ending September)

	2009	2010*	2011*
Asses*	45	45	45
Cattle	1,277	1,250	1,265
Pigs	1,341	1,350	1,375
Sheep	220	200	205
Goats	3,907	4,800	5,000
Chickens	23,922	24,500	25,000

* Estimates.

Source: FAO.

LIVESTOCK PRODUCTS
('000 metric tons, FAO estimates)

	2009	2010	2011
Cattle meat	19	19	19
Goat meat	22	24	24
Pig meat	94	97	98
Chicken meat	22	23	27
Cows' milk	67	67	67
Goats' milk	8	9	9
Hen eggs	14	15	15

Source: FAO.

Forestry

ROUNDWOOD REMOVALS
('000 cubic metres, excl. bark, FAO estimates)

	2008	2009	2010
Sawlogs, veneer logs and logs for sleepers	113	136	225
Other industrial wood	1,191	1,191	1,191
Fuel wood	16,724	16,724	16,724
Total	18,028	18,051	18,140

2011: Production assumed to be unchanged from 2010 (FAO estimates).

Source: FAO.

SAWNWOOD PRODUCTION
('000 cubic metres, incl. railway sleepers, FAO estimates)

	2008	2009	2010
Coniferous (softwood)	6	6	6
Broadleaved (hardwood)	51	114	192
Total	57	120	198

2011: Production assumed to be unchanged from 2010 (FAO estimates).

Source: FAO.

Fishing

(metric tons, live weight)

	2008	2009	2010
Dagaas	10,055	13,131	11,018
Penaeus shrimps	7,482	7,349	7,313
Knife shrimp	1,448	1,163	1,243
Marine fishes	78,457	101,134	105,092
Total catch (incl. others)	119,646	148,049	150,634

Note: Figures exclude crocodiles, recorded by number rather than by weight. The number of Nile crocodiles caught was: 566 in 2008; n.a. in 2009; 2,448 in 2010.

Source: FAO.

Mining

('000 metric tons unless otherwise indicated)

	2008	2009	2010*
Bauxite	5.4	3.6	11.0
Coal	37.7	25.9	50.0
Gold (kilograms)†	298	511	80
Quartz (metric tons)	157.3	140.6	700.0
Gravel and crushed rock ('000 cubic metres)	115.5	1,200.0*	1200.0
Marble (slab) ('000 square metres)	7.9	0.3	n.a.
Salt (marine)*	110	110	110
Natural gas (million cu m)	3,037	2,803	3,100

* Estimate(s).
† Figures exclude unreported gold production; total gold output is estimated at 600 kg–900 kg per year.

Source: US Geological Survey.

Industry

SELECTED PRODUCTS
('000 metric tons unless otherwise indicated)

	2005	2006	2007
Wheat flour	204	193	182
Raw sugar	164	172	183
Groundnut oil ('000 metric tons)*	14.4	11.8	10.1
Beer ('000 hl)	1,412	n.a.	n.a.
Soft drinks ('000 hl)	1,149	1,170	1,170
Cigarettes (metric tons)	1,735	2,543	2,571
Footwear (excl. rubber, '000 pairs)	37	37	40
Cement	564	774	771
Electric energy (million kWh)	13,285	14,737	16,076

* FAO estimates.

2008: Groundnut oil 11,090 metric tons (FAO estimate); Cement 744,000 metric tons; Electric energy (million kWh) 15,127.

2009: Groundnut oil 7,214 metric tons (FAO estimate); Cement 777,000 metric tons; Electric energy (million kWh) 16,963.

2010: Groundnut oil 3,883 metric tons (FAO estimate); Cement 884,000 metric tons.

2011: Groundnut oil 3,300 metric tons (FAO estimate).

Sources: FAO; UN Industrial Commodity Statistics Database; US Geological Survey.

Finance

CURRENCY AND EXCHANGE RATES

Monetary Units
100 centavos = 1 metical (plural: meticais).

Sterling, Dollar and Euro Equivalents (30 November 2012)
£1 sterling = 48.15 meticais;
US $1 = 29.99 meticais;
€1 = 38.95 meticais;
1,000 meticais = £20.77 = $33.34 = €25.68.

Average Exchange Rate (meticais per US $)
2009	27.52
2010	33.96
2011	29.07

Note: Between April 1992 and October 2000 the market exchange rate was the rate at which commercial banks purchased from and sold to the public. Since October 2000 it has been the weighted average of buying and selling rates of all transactions of commercial banks and stock exchanges with the public. A devaluation of the metical, with 1 new currency unit becoming equivalent to 1,000 of the former currency, was implemented on 1 July 2006.

BUDGET
('000 million meticais)

Revenue*	2009	2010†	2011†
Taxation	41.47	56.54	71.54
Taxes on income and profits	13.72	18.48	24.89
Domestic taxes on goods and services	22.89	31.69	38.42
Taxes on international trade	4.08	5.26	6.73
Other taxes	0.78	1.10	1.51
Non-tax revenue	5.26	7.94	9.58
Total	46.73	64.48	81.12

Expenditure‡	2009	2010†	2011†
Current expenditure . . .	47.87	59.56	71.50
Compensation of employees .	23.62	29.11	35.66
Goods and services . . .	11.72	13.09	15.57
Interest on public debt . . .	1.36	2.67	3.58
Transfer payments . . .	11.17	14.69	16.46
Capital expenditure	34.41	43.70	50.60
Total	82.28	103.30	122.09

* Excluding grants received ('000 million meticais): 25.30 in 2009; 28.34 in 2010 (estimate); 28.63 in 2011 (estimate).

† Estimates.

‡ Excluding net lending ('000 million meticais): 4.42 in 2009; 1.93 in 2010 (estimate); 6.17 in 2011 (estimate).

Source: IMF, *Republic of Mozambique: Fourth Review Under the Policy Support Instrument and Request for Modification of Assessment Criteria— Staff Report; Debt Sustainability Analysis; Press Release on the Executive Board Discussion; and Statement by the Executive Director for Mozambique.* (June 2012).

INTERNATIONAL RESERVES
(US $ million at 31 December)

	2009	2010	2011
IMF special drawing rights . .	170.34	167.07	165.05
Reserve position in IMF . . .	0.01	0.01	0.01
Foreign exchange	1,928.91	1,992.32	2,303.71
Total	2,099.27	2,159.39	2,468.77

Source: IMF, *International Financial Statistics.*

MONEY SUPPLY
('000 million meticais at 31 December)

	2009	2010	2011
Currency outside depository corporations	13,053.6	17,393.6	17,475.6
Transferable deposits . . .	60,847.7	73,744.5	80,162.5
Other deposits	33,173.7	42,273.7	46,223.3
Broad money	107,075.0	133,411.8	143,861.4

Source: IMF, *International Financial Statistics.*

COST OF LIVING
(Consumer Price Index; base: 1998 = 100)

	2002	2003	2004
Food, beverages and tobacco . .	151	175	187
Clothing and footwear . . .	126	122	125
Firewood and furniture . . .	190	215	263
Health	119	133	134
Transportation and communications	205	232	234
Education, recreation and culture .	145	150	151
Other goods and services . . .	136	154	159
All items	157	179	195

Source: IMF, *Republic of Mozambique: Selected Issues and Statistical Appendix* (August 2005).

All items (Consumer Price Index; base: 2005 = 100): 139.5 in 2009; 157.2 in 2010; 173.5 in 2011 (Source: IMF, *International Financial Statistics*).

NATIONAL ACCOUNTS
('000 million meticais at current prices)

Expenditure on the Gross Domestic Product

	2009	2010	2011
Government final consumption expenditure	34,368	44,020	48,896
Private final consumption expenditure	214,369	241,073	277,007
Change in stocks	−4,164	4,774	2,577
Gross fixed capital formation . .	43,959	51,862	64,701
Total domestic expenditure .	288,532	341,729	393,181
Exports of goods and services . .	73,799	89,565	98,372
Less Imports of goods and services	96,119	115,354	134,826
Statistical discrepancy* . . .	—	−979	8,607
GDP in purchasers' values .	266,213	314,961	365,334
GDP at constant 2003 prices .	171,873	184,050	197,524

* Referring to the difference between the sum of the expenditure components and official estimates of GDP, compiled from the production approach.

Gross Domestic Product by Economic Activity

	2009	2010	2011
Agriculture, livestock and forestry	67,425	83,974	98,600
Fishing	4,227	5,255	5,714
Mining	3,566	4,074	5,086
Manufacturing	34,449	39,880	43,168
Electricity and water . . .	11,586	13,277	14,828
Construction	7,533	8,855	10,337
Wholesale and retail trade; repairs	37,735	46,400	56,486
Restaurants and hotels . . .	3,904	4,837	6,200
Transport and communications .	24,913	28,666	33,030
Financial services	10,508	12,034	12,813
Real estate and business services	14,254	14,883	15,726
Public administration and defence	9,848	11,250	13,421
Education	10,888	12,244	13,356
Health	4,015	4,615	5,028
Other services	3,874	4,176	4,564
Sub-total	248,725	294,420	338,357
Less Financial services indirectly measured . . .	6,403	6,946	7,406
Gross value added in basic prices	242,322	287,474	330,951
Taxes on products	23,891	27,487	34,384
Less Subsidies on products . .			
GDP in market prices . .	266,213	314,961	365,334

BALANCE OF PAYMENTS
(US $ million)

	2009	2010	2011
Exports of goods	2,147.2	2,333.3	3,118.3
Imports of goods	−3,422.0	−3,512.4	−5,367.6
Balance on goods	−1,274.8	−1,179.2	−2,249.3
Exports of services	611.7	599.1	716.0
Imports of services	−1,069.0	−1,317.7	−1,510.2
Balance on goods and services	−1,732.1	−1,897.8	−3,043.5
Primary income received . . .	150.3	151.4	155.1
Primary income paid	−427.2	−475.9	−345.0
Balance on goods, services and primary income	−2,009.1	−2,222.4	−3,233.4
Secondary income received . .	931.7	817.2	954.9
Secondary income paid . . .	−168.6	−179.9	−159.7
Current balance	−1,246.0	−1,585.1	−2,438.3
Capital account (net) . . .	422.3	345.5	379.0
Direct investment assets . . .	−6.0	−15.6	10.8
Direct investment liabilities . .	895.7	1,005.4	2,079.3
Portfolio investment assets . .	4.4	0.3	−34.3
Portfolio investment liabilities .	0.1	1.1	0.2
Other investment assets . . .	−118.6	−265.0	−229.8
Other investment liabilities . .	260.0	404.7	5.6
Errors and omissions (net) . .	−16.9	153.1	549.5
Reserves and related items .	195.0	44.4	321.9

Source: IMF, *International Financial Statistics.*

External Trade

PRINCIPAL COMMODITIES
(US $ million)

Imports c.i.f.	2009	2010	2011
Cereals	275.6	149.2	308.3
Rice	152.3	74.1	135.4
Vegetables, fruits and food preparations	14.5	10.5	16.7
Tomatoes, prepared or preserved	0.7	0.6	0.8
Cucumbers, gherkins and onions preserved by vinegar	0.0	0.0	1.0
Mineral fuels, lubricants, etc.	582.8	711.0	1,487.8
Petroleum oils	411.5	520.6	1,097.4
Iron and steel and products thereof	104.9	102.5	229.4
Nuclear reactors, boilers, machinery, etc.	397.7	360.8	882.2
Electrical and electronic equipment	191.8	152.6	230.5
Road vehicles	452.6	368.6	643.2
Trucks and motor vehicles for transport of goods	180.9	146.6	272.3
Total (incl. others)	3,764.2	3,564.2	6,305.6

Exports f.o.b.	2009	2010	2011
Fish, crustaceans, molluscs and preparations thereof	65.4	56.6	51.8
Crustaceans	60.3	52.3	45.0
Tobacco and manufactured tobacco substitutes	180.6	144.5	179.5
Tobacco, unmanufactured	179.3	142.6	178.4
Mineral fuels, lubricants, etc.	374.2	447.4	586.7
Electrical energy	274.4	276.5	297.2
Aluminium and articles thereof	n.a.	1,160.0	1,625.7
Nuclear reactors, boilers, machinery, etc.	78.6	23.6	55.8
Total (incl. others)	2,147.2	2,243.1	3,604.1

Source: Trade Map-Trade Competitiveness Map, International Trade Centre, www.intracen.org/marketanalysis.

PRINCIPAL TRADING PARTNERS
(US $ million)

Imports c.i.f.	2009	2010	2011
Argentina	26.6	2.6	36.0
Bahrain	14.9	94.7	108.4
China, People's Republic	173.1	130.0	373.8
Germany	66.4	79.5	34.1
India	244.7	201.7	300.5
Indonesia	16.0	14.5	41.1
Italy	56.9	74.7	45.7
Japan	141.6	126.3	185.4
Malaysia	46.3	34.9	63.4
Netherlands	488.2	642.9	676.1
Pakistan	55.1	49.2	61.5
Portugal	142.0	154.2	225.6
Saudi Arabia	49.3	7.1	20.4
Singapore	67.2	7.9	37.1
South Africa	1,333.8	1,226.8	2,121.4
Spain	24.7	10.2	26.8
Taiwan	7.2	7.6	14.3
Thailand	127.6	52.2	119.6
United Arab Emirates	75.6	47.6	401.1
United Kingdom	28.4	57.4	222.8
USA	134.8	74.4	292.3
Yemen	0.7	—	—
Total (incl. others)	3,764.2	3,564.2	6,305.6

Exports f.o.b.	2009	2010	2011
China, People's Republic	74.5	79.6	167.7
Germany	24.8	20.4	75.4
India	56.5	30.4	87.2
Malawi	46.7	27.0	46.5
Netherlands	893.9	1,181.9	1,402.1
Poland	24.3	7.9	8.0
Portugal	32.2	108.3	42.7
Russia	29.5	13.6	24.7
Singapore	28.4	11.0	9.6
South Africa	460.3	467.2	584.0
Spain	31.4	30.6	83.4
United Kingdom	28.7	1.4	198.7
USA	41.4	16.4	25.7
Zimbabwe	73.8	72.1	127.3
Total (incl. others)	2,147.2	2,243.1	3,604.1

Source: Trade Map-Trade Competitiveness Map, International Trade Centre, www.intracen.org/marketanalysis.

Transport

RAILWAYS
(traffic)

	2009	2010	2011
Passenger-km (million)	164.0	239.4	248.0
Freight ton-km (million)	771.8	936.4	1,166.0

ROAD TRAFFIC
(motor vehicles in use)

	2009	2010	2011
Light vehicles	203,799	233,086	270,762
Heavy vehicles	72,550	82,389	92,828
Trailers	8,584	10,004	8,562
Tractors	3,422	4,724	3,800
Motorbikes	46,822	50,141	54,091
Total	335,177	380,344	430,043

SHIPPING

Flag Registered Fleet
(at 31 December)

	2010	2011	2012
Number of vessels	71	72	75
Total displacement ('000 grt)	35.0	35.7	35.9

Source: Lloyd's List Intelligence (www.lloydslistintelligence.com).

Freight Handled
('000 metric tons)

	2009	2010	2011
Goods loaded and unloaded	12,652	14,316	18,796

International Sea-borne Freight Traffic
('000 metric tons)

	2001	2002	2003
Goods loaded	2,962	2,780	2,982
Goods unloaded	3,144	4,062	3,837

CIVIL AVIATION
(traffic on scheduled services)

	2007	2008	2009
Kilometres flown (million) . .	8	8	8
Passengers carried ('000) . . .	443	463	490
Passenger-km (million) . . .	471	505	552
Total ton-km (million)	48	52	56

Source: UN, *Statistical Yearbook*.

2010: Passengers carried ('000) 553.3 (Source: World Bank, World Development Indicators database).

Tourism

TOURIST ARRIVALS BY COUNTRY OF RESIDENCE

Country	2008	2009	2010
Malawi	96,562	114,849	228,092
Portugal	31,406	37,353	25,810
South Africa	675,745	803,720	946,583
Swaziland	157,703	187,570	39,016
United Kingdom	27,900	33,184	50,420
USA	21,682	25,788	21,292
Zimbabwe	238,825	284,084	149,060
Total (incl. others)	1,438,684	1,711,147	1,836,143

Tourism receipts (US $ million, excl. passenger transport): 196 in 2009; 197 in 2010 (provisional); 231 in 2011 (provisional).

Source: World Tourism Organization.

Communications Media

	2009	2010	2011
Telephones ('000 main lines in use)	82.4	88.1	88.1
Mobile cellular telephones ('000 subscribers)	5,970.8	7,224.2	7,855.3
Internet subscribers ('000) . .	13.5	n.a.	16.3
Broadband subscribers ('000) . .	12.5	14.6	16.3

Source: International Telecommunication Union.

Education

(2005, unless otherwise indicated)

	Institutions	Teachers	Students
Pre-primary*†	5,689	28,705	1,745,049
Primary‡			
First level	8,696	45,887	3,393,677
Second level	1,320	11,011	452,888
Secondary§			
First level	156	210,128	5,004
Second level	35	25,737	861
Technical	41	1,028	21,752
Teacher training‖	18	n.a.	9,314

* Public education only.
† 1997 figures.
‡ Primary education is divided into two cycles of five years followed by two years.
§ Secondary education is divided into two cycles of three years.
‖ 2002 figures.

Source: mainly Ministry of Education.

Students (2010/11 unless otherwise indicated): Primary 5,253,670; Secondary 716,289; Tertiary 28,298 (2004/05) (Source: UNESCO Institute for Statistics).

Teachers (2010/11 unless otherwise indicated): Primary 94,798; Secondary 20,902; Tertiary 3,009 (2004/05) (Source: UNESCO Institute for Statistics).

Pupil-teacher ratio (primary education, UNESCO estimate): 55.4 in 2010/11 (Source: UNESCO Institute for Statistics).

Adult literacy rate (UNESCO estimates): 56.1% (males 70.8%; females 42.8%) in 2010 (Source: UNESCO Institute for Statistics).

Directory

The Government

HEAD OF STATE

President of the Republic and Commander-in-Chief of the Armed Forces: ARMANDO EMÍLIO GUEBUZA (took office 2 February 2005; re-elected 28 October 2009).

COUNCIL OF MINISTERS
(May 2013)

Prime Minister: ALBERTO CLEMENTINO ANTÓNIO VAQUINA.

Minister of the Interior: ALBERTO RICARDO MONDLANE.

Minister of Finance: MANUEL CHANG.

Minister of Planning and Development: AIÚBA CUERENEIA.

Minister of Foreign Affairs and Co-operation: OLDEMIRO JÚLIO MARQUES BALOI.

Minister of National Defence: FILIPE JACINTO NHUSSI.

Minister of Justice: MARIA BENVINDA LEVI.

Minister of Environmental Co-ordination: ALCINDA ANTÓNIO DE ABREU.

Minister of Agriculture: JOSÉ CONDUNGUA PACHECO.

Minister of Health: ALEXANDRE MANGUELE.

Minister of Industry and Trade: ARMANDO INROGA.

Minister of Science and Technology: LOUIS AUGUSTO PELEMBE.

Minister of Labour: MARIA HELENA TAÍPO.

Minister of Transport and Communications: PAULO FRANCISCO ZUCULA.

Minister of Public Works and Housing: CADMIEL FILIANE MUTHEMBA.

Minister of Public Service: VITÓRIA DIAS DIOGO.

Minister of Tourism: CARVALHO MUÁRIA.

Minister of State Administration: CARMELITA RITA NAMASHULUA.

Minister of Mineral Resources: ESPERANÇA LAURINDA FRANCISCO NHIUANE BIAS.

Minister of Energy: SALVADOR NAMBURETE.

Minister of Veterans' Affairs: MATEUS ÓSCAR KIDA.

Minister of Education: AUGUSTO JONE.

Minister of Culture: ARMANDO ARTUR JOÃO.

Minister of Fisheries: VICTOR MANUEL BORGES.

Minister of Women's Affairs and Social Welfare Co-ordination: IOLANDA MARIA PEDRO CAMPOS CINTURA.

Minister of Youth and Sport: FERNANDO SUMBANA.

Minister of Presidential Affairs: ANTÓNIO CORREIA FERNANDES SUMBANA.

Minister in the Presidency with responsibility for Social Affairs: FELICIANO SALOMÃO GUNDANA.

Minister in the Presidency with responsibility for Parliamentary, Municipal and Provincial Assembly Affairs: ADELAIDE ANCHIA AMURANE.

There were also 26 Deputy Ministers.

MINISTRIES

Office of the President: Av. Julius Nyerere 1780, Maputo; tel. 21491121; fax 21492065; e-mail gabimprensa@teldata.mz; internet www.presidencia.gov.mz.

Office of the Prime Minister: Praça da Marinha Popular, Maputo; tel. 21426861; fax 21426881; internet www.portaldogoverno.gov.mz.

Ministry of Agriculture: Praça dos Heróis Moçambicanos, CP 1406, Maputo; tel. 21460011; fax 21460055; internet www.minag.gov .mz.

Ministry of Culture: Rua de Tchamba 86, Maputo; tel. 21492582; fax 21498040.

Ministry of Education: Av. 24 de Julho 167, CP 34, Maputo; tel. 21492006; fax 21492196; internet www.mec.gov.mz.

Ministry of Energy: Av. 25 de Setembro, 1218 3° andar, CP 1831, Maputo; tel. 21303265; fax 21313971; e-mail asi@me.gov.mz; internet www.me.gov.mz.

Ministry of Environmental Co-ordination: Rua Kassoende 167, Maputo; tel. 21492403; e-mail jwkacha@virconn.com; internet www .micoa.gov.mz.

Ministry of Finance: Praça da Marinha Popular, CP 272, Maputo; tel. 21315000; fax 21306261.

Ministry of Fisheries: Rua Consiglieri Pedroso 347, CP 1723, Maputo; tel. 21431266; fax 21425087; internet www.mozpesca.gov .mz.

Ministry of Foreign Affairs and Co-operation: Av. 10 de Novembro 620–640, Maputo; tel. 21327000; fax 21327020; e-mail minec@minec.gov.mz; internet www.minec.gov.mz.

Ministry of Health: Avs Eduardo Mondlane e Salvador Allende 1008, CP 264, Maputo; tel. 21427131; fax 21427133; e-mail mdgedge@dnsdee.misau.gov.mz; internet www.misau.gov.mz.

Ministry of Industry and Trade: Praça 25 de Junho 300, CP 1831, Maputo; tel. 21352600; fax 214262301; e-mail infomic@mic.gov.mz; internet www.mic.gov.mz.

Ministry of the Interior: Av. Olof Palme 46/48, CP 290, Maputo; tel. 21303510; fax 21420084.

Ministry of Justice: Av. Julius Nyerere 33, Maputo; tel. 21491613; fax 21494264.

Ministry of Labour: Av. 24 de Julho 2351, CP 281, Maputo; tel. 21428301; fax 21421881; internet www.mitrab.gov.mz.

Ministry of Mineral Resources: Av. Fernão de Magalhães 34, 1° andar, CP 294, Maputo; tel. 21314843; fax 320618; e-mail msithole .mirem@tvcabo.co.mz; internet www.mirem.gov.mz.

Ministry of National Defence: Av. Mártires de Mueda 280, CP 3216, Maputo; tel. 21492081; fax 21491619.

Ministry of Planning and Development: Av. Ahmed Sekou Touré 21, CP 4087, Maputo; tel. 21490006; fax 21495477; internet www.mpd.gov.mz.

Ministry of Public Service: Av. Julius Nyerere 3, CP 1225, Maputo; tel. 21485558; fax 21485683; internet www.mfp.gov.mz.

Ministry of Public Works and Housing: Av. Karl Marx 606, CP 268, Maputo; tel. 21430028; fax 21421369; internet www.moph.gov .mz.

Ministry of Science and Technology: Av. Patrice Lumumba 770, Maputo; tel. 21352800; fax 21352860; e-mail secretariado@mct.gov .mz; internet www.mct.gov.mz.

Ministry of State Administration: Rua da Rádio Moçambique 112, CP 4116, Maputo; tel. 21426666; fax 21428565; internet www .mae.gov.mz.

Ministry of Tourism: Av. 25 de Setembro 1018, CP 4101, Maputo; tel. 21306210; fax 21306212; internet www.mitur.gov.mz.

Ministry of Transport and Communications: Av. Mártires de Inhaminga 336, CP 276, Maputo; tel. 21430152; fax 21431028; internet www.mtc.gov.mz.

Ministry of Veterans' Affairs: Rua General Pereira d'Eça 35, CP 3697, Maputo; tel. 21490601.

Ministry of Women's Affairs and Social Welfare Co-ordination: Rua de Tchamba 86, CP 516, Maputo; tel. 21490921; fax 21492757; internet www.mmas.gov.mz.

Ministry of Youth and Sport: Av. 25 de Setembro 529, CP 2080, Maputo; tel. 21312172; fax 21300040; e-mail mjd@tvcabo.co.mz; internet www.mjd.gov.mz.

PROVINCIAL GOVERNORS
(May 2013)

Cabo Delgado Province: ELISEU JOAQUIM MACHAVA.

Gaza Province: RAIMUNDO MAICO DIOMBA.

Inhambane Province: AGOSTINHO ABACAR TRINTA.

Manica Province: ANA COMOANA SOFALA.

Maputo Province: MARIA ELIAS JONAS.

Nampula Province: CIDÁLIA CHAÚQUE.

Niassa Province: DAVID NGOANE MARIZANE.

Sofala Province: FÉLIX PAULO.

Tete Province: RATXIDE GOGO.

Zambézia Province: JOAQUIM VERÍSSIMO.

City of Maputo: LUCÍLIA JOSÉ MANUEL NOTA HAMA.

President and Legislature

PRESIDENT

Presidential Election, 28 October 2009

Candidate	Votes	% of votes
Armando Guebuza (Frelimo)	2,974,627	75.01
Afonso Macacho Marceta Dhlakama (Renamo)	650,679	16.41
Daviz Simango (MDM)	340,579	8.59
Total*	3,965,885	100.00

* Excluding 175,553 invalid votes and 264,655 blank votes.

LEGISLATURE

Assembleia da República: CP 1516, Maputo; tel. 21400826; fax 21400711; e-mail cdi@sortmoz.com; internet www.parlamento.org .mz.

Chair.: VERÓNICA NATANIEL MACAMO DLHOVO.

General Election, 28 October 2009

Party	Votes	% of votes	Seats
Frelimo	2,907,335	74.66	191
Renamo	688,782	17.69	51
MDM	152,836	3.93	8
PLD	26,929	0.69	—
PDD	22,410	0.58	—
PVM	19,577	0.50	—
Others	75,989	1.95	—
Total*	3,893,858	100.00	250

* Excluding 143,893 invalid votes and 349,499 blank votes.

Election Commission

Comissão Nacional de Eleições (CNE): Rua Almeida Ribeiro, Maputo; tel. 21300626; fax 214274360; internet www.stae.org.mz; f. 1997; 13 mems; Pres. JOÃO LEOPOLDO DA COSTA.

Political Organizations

The following political organizations were successful in gaining approval from the Comissão Nacional de Eleições to contest the November 2009 legislative and presidential elections.

Aliança Democrática de Antigos Combatentes para o Desenvolvimento (ADACD): Maputo; f. 2009; coalition comprising the Partido do Progresso do Povo de Moçambique (PPPM), the Partido Socialisa de Moçambique (PSM), the Partido do Congresso Democrático (PACODE) and the Partido da União para a Reconciliação (PUR); Leader JOÃO LIKALAMBA.

Aliança Independente de Moçambique (ALIMO): f. 1998; Leader KHALID HUSSEIN SIDAT.

Coligação União Eleitoral (UE): f. 1999; Co-ordinator MANECA DANIEL.

    Partido Ecologista de Moçambique (PEMO): Maputo.

    Partido de Unidade Nacional (PUN): TV Sado 9, Maputo; tel. 21419204; Pres. HIPOLITO COUTO.

Frente de Libertação de Moçambique (Frelimo): Rua Pereira do Lago 10, Bairro de Sommerschield, Maputo; tel. 21490181; fax

21490008; e-mail info@frelimo.org.mz; internet www.frelimo.org
.mz; f. 1962 by merger of three nationalist parties; reorg. 1977 as a
'Marxist-Leninist vanguard movement'; in 1989 abandoned its
exclusive Marxist-Leninist orientation; Pres. ARMANDO EMÍLIO
GUEBUZA; Sec.-Gen. FILIPE CHIMOIO PAÚNDE.

Movimento Democrático de Moçambique (MDM): Maputo;
f. 2009; Pres. DAVIZ SIMANGO; Sec.-Gen. LUÍS BOAVIDA.

Movimento Patriótico para Democracia (MPD): f. 2009; Leader
MATIAS DIANHANE BANZE.

**Partido Ecologista—Movimento da Terra (ECOLOGISTA—
MT):** Leader JOÃO PEDRO MASSANGO.

Partido Humanitário de Moçambique (Pahumo): Nampula;
f. 2010 by fmr mems of the Frente de Libertação de Moçambique
(Frelimo), Resistência Nacional Moçambicana (Renamo) and Partido
para a Paz, Democracia e Desenvolvimento (PDD); Pres. CORNÉLIO
QUIVELA; Sec.-Gen. JOSÉ HENRIQUE LOPES.

Partido de Liberdade e Desenvolvimento (PLD): f. 2009; Pres.
CAETANO SABILE.

Partido Nacional dos Operários e Camponeses (PANAOC):
f. 1998; Leader ARMANDO GIL SUEIA.

Partido para a Paz, Democracia e Desenvolvimento (PDD):
Av. Amilcar Cabral 570, Maputo; tel. 21486759; fax 21486765; e-mail
pdd@tvcabo.co.mz; internet www.pdd.org.mz; f. 2003; liberal; Leader
RAÚL MANUEL DOMINGOS.

Partido Popular Democrático (PPD): f. 2004; Leader MARCIANO
FIJAMA.

Partido de Reconciliação Democrática Social (PRDS): f. 1998;
Leader ARMANDO GIL SUEIA.

Partido de Reconciliação Nacional (PARENA): Maputo; f. 2004;
Leader ANDRÉ BALATE.

Partido de Solidariedade e Liberdade (PAZS): f. 2004; Leader
CARLOS INÁCIO COELHO.

Partido Trabalhista (PT): f. 1993; Pres. MIGUEL MABOTE; Sec.-
Gen. LUÍS MUCHANGA.

Partido os Verdes de Moçambique (PVM): f. 1997; Leader BRUNO
SAPEMBA.

Resistência Nacional Moçambicana (Renamo): Av. Julius
Nyerere 2541, Maputo; tel. 21493107; internet www.renamo.org
.mz; also known as Movimento Nacional da Resistência de
Moçambique (MNR); f. 1976; fmr guerrilla group, in conflict with
the Govt between 1976 and Oct. 1992; obtained legal status in 1994;
Pres. AFONSO MACACHO MARCETA DHLAKAMA; Sec.-Gen. OSSUFO
MOMADE.

**União dos Democratas de Moçambique—Partido Popular
(UDM—PP):** f. 2009; Leader JOSÉ RICARDO VIANA.

União Nacional de Moçambique (UNAMO): f. 1987; breakaway
faction of Renamo; social democratic; obtained legal status 1992;
Pres. CARLOS ALEXANDRE DOS REIS.

União para a Mudança (UM): f. 1993; Leader FRANCISCO MAIN-
DANE MUARIVA.

Diplomatic Representation

EMBASSIES AND HIGH COMMISSIONS IN MOZAMBIQUE

Algeria: Rua de Mukumbura 121–125, CP 1709, Maputo; tel.
21492070; fax 21490582; e-mail ambalgmaputo@tvcabo.co.mz;
Ambassador AHMED LAKHDAR TAZIR.

Angola: Av. Kenneth Kaunda 783, CP 2954, Maputo; tel. 21493139;
fax 21493930; Ambassador ISAÍAS JAIME VILINGA.

Brazil: Av. Kenneth Kaunda 296, CP 1167, Sommerschield, Maputo;
tel. 21484800; fax 21484806; e-mail ebrasil@teledata.mz; internet
maputo.itamaraty.gov.br/pt-br; Ambassador ANTONIO JOSÉ MARIA DE
SOUZA E SILVA.

Canada: Av. Kenneth Kaunda 1138, CP 1578, Maputo; tel.
21492623; fax 21492667; e-mail mputo@international.gc.ca; High
Commissioner ALAIN LATULIPPE.

China, People's Republic: Av. Julius Nyerere 3142, CP 4668,
Maputo; tel. 21491560; fax 21491196; e-mail chinaemb_mz@mfa.gov
.cn; Ambassador LI CHUNHUA.

Congo, Democratic Republic: Av. Kenneth Kaunda 127, CP 2407,
Maputo; tel. 21497154; fax 21494929; Ambassador ANTOINE KOLA
MASALA NE BEBY.

Congo, Republic: Av. Kenneth Kaunda 783, CP 4743, Maputo; tel.
21490142; Chargé d'affaires a.i. MONSEGNO BASHA OSHEFWA.

Cuba: Av. Kenneth Kaunda 492, CP 387, Maputo; tel. 21492444; fax
21491905; e-mail embacuba.mozambique@tvcabo.co.mz; internet
emba.cubaminrex.cu/mozambique; Ambassador RAFAEL ARÍSTIDES
JIMENO LÓPEZ.

Denmark: Av. Julius Nyerere 1162, CP 4588, Maputo; tel.
21480000; fax 21480010; e-mail mpmamb@um.dk; internet www
.ambmaputo.um.dk; Ambassador JOHNNY FLENTØ.

Egypt: Av. Mao Tse Tung 851, CP 4662, Maputo; tel. 21491118; fax
21491489; e-mail egypt@tvcabo.co.mz; Ambassador FAWZY MOHAMED
EL-ASHMAWY.

Finland: Av. Julius Nyerere 1128, CP 1663, Maputo; tel. 21482400;
fax 21491662; e-mail sanomat.map@formin.fi; internet www.finland
.org.mz; Ambassador MATTI KÄÄRIÄINEN.

France: Av. Julius Nyerere 2361, CP 4781, Maputo; tel. 21484600;
fax 21491727; e-mail ambafrancemz@tvcabo.co.mz; internet www
.ambafrance-mz.org; Ambassador SERGE SEGURA.

Germany: Rua Damião de Góis 506, CP 1595, Maputo; tel.
21482700; fax 21492888; e-mail info@maputo.diplo.de; internet
www.maputo.diplo.de; Ambassador ULRICH KLÖCKNER.

Holy See: Av. Kwame Nkrumah 224, CP 2738, Maputo; tel.
21491144; fax 21492217; Apostolic Nuncio Most Rev. ANTONIO ARCARI
(Titular Archbishop of Caeciri).

Iceland: Av. do Zimbabwe 1694, Maputo; tel. 21483509; fax
21483511; e-mail mozambique@iceida.is; internet www.iceland
.org/mo; Chargé d'affaires a.i. AGÚSTA GÍSLADÓTTIR.

India: Av. Kenneth Kaunda 167, CP 4751, Maputo; tel. 21492437;
fax 21492364; e-mail hicomind@tvcabo.co.mz; internet www
.hicomind-maputo.org; High Commissioner ASHOK KUMAR AMROHI.

Ireland: Av. Julius Nyerere 3332, Maputo; tel. 21491440; fax
21493023; e-mail maputoembassy@dfa.ie; Ambassador RUAIRÍ DE
BURCA.

Italy: Av. Kenneth Kaunda 387, CP 976, Maputo; tel. 21492229; fax
21490503; e-mail ambasciata.maputo@esteri.it; internet www
.ambmaputo.esteri.it; Ambassador ROBERTO VELLANO.

Japan: Av. Julius Nyerere 2832, CP 2494, Maputo; tel. 21499819;
fax 21498957; internet www.mz.emb-japan.go.jp; Ambassador EJI
HASHIMOTO.

Korea, Democratic People's Republic: Rua da Kaswende 167,
Maputo; tel. 21491482; Ambassador PAK KUN GWANG.

Malawi: Av. Kenneth Kaunda 75, CP 4148, Maputo; tel. 21492676;
fax 21490224; High Commissioner MARTIN O. KANSICHI.

Mauritius: Rua Dom Carlos 42, Av. do Zimbabwe, Sommerschield,
Maputo; tel. 21494624; fax 21494729; e-mail maputo@mail.gov.mu;
High Commissioner JEAN HAREL LAMVOHEE.

Netherlands: Av. Kwame Nkrumah 324, CP 1163, Maputo; tel.
21484200; fax 21484248; e-mail map@minbuza.nl; internet www
.hollandinmozambique.org; Ambassador FRÉDÉRIQUE DE MAN.

Nigeria: Av. Kenneth Kaunda 821, CP 4693, Maputo; tel. and fax
21490991; High Commissioner TOYE OLOFINTUYI.

Norway: Av. Julius Nyerere 1162, CP 828, Maputo; tel. 21480100;
fax 21480107; e-mail emb.maputo@mfa.no; internet www.norway
.org.mz; Ambassador TOVE BRUVIK WESTBERG.

Portugal: Av. Julius Nyerere 720, CP 4696, Maputo; tel. 21490316;
fax 21491172; e-mail embaixada@embpormaputo.org.mz; Ambassador MÁRIO GODINHO DE MATOS.

Russia: Av. Vladimir I. Lénine 2445, CP 4666, Maputo; tel.
21417372; fax 21417515; e-mail embrus@tvcabo.co.mz; internet
www.mozambique.mid.ru; Ambassador IGOR V. POPOV.

South Africa: Av. Eduardo Mondlane 41, CP 1120, Maputo; tel.
21243000; fax 21493029; e-mail ritterb@dirco.gov.za; High Commissioner CHARLES NQAKULA.

Spain: Rua Damião de Góis 347, CP 1331, Maputo; tel. 21492025; fax
21494769; e-mail emb.maputo@maec.es; Ambassador SANTIAGO
MIRALLES HUETE.

Swaziland: Av. Kwame Nkrumah, CP 4711, Maputo; tel. 21491601;
fax 21492117; High Commissioner Prince TSHEKEDI.

Sweden: Av. Julius Nyerere 1128, CP 338, Maputo; tel. 21480300;
fax 21480390; e-mail ambassaden.maputo@gov.se; internet www
.swedenabroad.se/maputo; Ambassador ULLA ANDRÉN.

Switzerland: Av. Ahmed Sekou Touré 637, CP 135, Maputo; tel.
21315275; fax 21315276; e-mail map.vertretung@eda.admin.ch;
internet www.eda.admin.ch/maputo; Ambassador THERESA ADAM.

Tanzania: Ujamaa House, Av. dos Mártires da Machava 852, CP
4515, Maputo; tel. 21490110; fax 21494782; e-mail ujamaa@zebra
.eum.mz; High Commissioner ISSA MOHAMED ISSA.

Timor-Leste: Av. do Zimbabwe 1586, Maputo; tel. 21493644; fax
21493544; e-mail embrdtl@tvcabo.co.mz; Ambassador MARINA
RIBEIRO ALKATIRI.

United Kingdom: Av. Vladimir I. Lénine 310, CP 55, Maputo; tel.
21356000; fax 21356060; e-mail bhcgeneral@gmail.com; internet
ukinmozambique.fco.gov.uk/en; High Commissioner ANTHONY
SHAUN CLEARY.

USA: Av. Kenneth Kaunda 193, CP 783, Maputo; tel. 21492797; fax 21490114; e-mail maputoirc@state.gov; internet maputo.usembassy .gov; Ambassador DOUGLAS M. GRIFFITHS.

Zambia: Av. Kenneth Kaunda 1286, CP 4655, Maputo; tel. 21492452; fax 21491893; e-mail zhcmmap@zebra.uem.mz; High Commissioner SIMON GABRIEL MWILA.

Zimbabwe: Av. Kenneth Kaunda 816, CP 743, Maputo; tel. 21490404; fax 21492237; e-mail maro@isl.co.mz; Ambassador AGRIPA MUTAMBARA.

Judicial System

The Constitution of November 1990 provides for a Supreme Court and other judicial courts, a Constitutional Council, an Administrative Court, courts-martial, customs courts, maritime courts and labour courts. The Supreme Court consists of professional judges, appointed by the President of the Republic, and judges elected by the Assembleia da República. It acts in sections, as a trial court of primary and appellate jurisdiction, and, in plenary session, as a court of final appeal. The Administrative Court controls the legality of administrative acts and supervises public expenditure.

Tribunal Supremo: Av. Vladimir I. Lénine 103, CP 278, Maputo; tel. 1321037; fax 1310674; Pres. OSIAS PONDJA.

Conselho Constitucional: Rua Mateus Sansão Muthemba 493, CP 2372, Maputo; tel. 21487431; fax 21487432; e-mail correiocc@ cconstitucional.org.mz; internet www.cconstitucional.org.mz; f. 1990; Pres. HERMENEGILDO GAMITO.

Tribunal Administrativo: Rua Mateus S. Muthemba 65, CP 254, Maputo; tel. 21490170; fax 21498890; e-mail ta@ta.gov.mz; internet www.ta.gov.mz; Pres. MACHATINE PAULO MARRENGANE MUNGUAMBE.

Attorney-General: AUGUSTO PAULINO.

Religion

There are an estimated 5m. Christians and 4m. Muslims, as well as small Hindu, Jewish and Bahá'í communities. In 2004 over 100 religious groups were officially registered.

CHRISTIANITY

There are many Christian organizations registered in Mozambique.

Conselho Cristão de Moçambique (CCM) (Christian Council of Mozambique): Av. Agostino Neto 1584, CP 108, Maputo; tel. 21322836; fax 21321968; f. 1948; 22 mems; Pres. Rt Rev. ARÃO MATSOLO; Gen. Sec. Rev. DINIS MATSOLO.

The Roman Catholic Church

Mozambique comprises three archdioceses and nine dioceses. The number of adherents represents some 22% of the total population.

Bishops' Conference

Conferência Episcopal de Moçambique (CEM), Secretariado Geral da CEM, Av. Paulo Samuel Kankhomba 188/RC, CP 286, Maputo; tel. 21490766; fax 21492174.

f. 1982; Pres. Most Rev. LÚCIO ANDRICE MUANDULA (Bishop of Xai-Xai).

Archbishop of Beira: Most Rev. CLAUDIO DALLA ZUANNA, Cúria Arquiepiscopal, Rua Correia de Brito 613, CP 544, Beira; tel. 23322313; fax 23327639; e-mail arquidbeira@teledata.mz.

Archbishop of Maputo: Most Rev. FRANCISCO CHIMOIO, Paço Arquiepiscopal, Av. Eduardo Mondlane 1448, CP 258, Maputo; tel. 21326240; fax 21321873.

Archbishop of Nampula: Most Rev. TOMÉ MAKHWELIHA, Paço Arquiepiscopal, CP 84, 70100 Nampula; tel. 26213024; fax 26214194; e-mail arquidiocesenpl@teledata.mz.

The Anglican Communion

Anglicans in Mozambique are adherents of the Anglican Church of Southern Africa (formerly the Church of the Province of Southern Africa). There are two dioceses in Mozambique. The Metropolitan of the Province is the Archbishop of Cape Town, South Africa.

Bishop of Lebombo: Rt Rev. DINIS SALOMÃO SENGULANE, CP 120, Maputo; tel. 21734364; fax 21401093; e-mail bispo_sengulane@ virconn.com.

Bishop of Niassa: Rev. MARK VAN KOEVERING, CP 264, Lichinga, Niassa; tel. 27112735; fax 27112336; e-mail bishop.niassa@gmail .com.

Other Churches

Baptist Convention of Mozambique: Av. Maguiguane 386, CP 852, Maputo; tel. 2126852; Pres. Rev. BENTO BARTOLOMEU MATUSSE; 78 churches, 25,000 adherents.

The Church of Jesus Christ of the Latter-Day Saints: Maputo; 9 congregations, 1,975 mems.

Evangelical Lutheran Church in Mozambique: Av Kim II Song 520, CP 1488, Sommerschield, Maputo; tel. 212489200; fax 212489201; e-mail mabasso.ielm@tvcabo.co.mz; Sen. Pastor JOSE MABASSO; 12,606 mems (2010).

Free Methodist Church: Pres. Rev. FRANISSE SANDO MUVILE; 214 churches, 21,231 mems.

Igreja Congregational Unida de Moçambique: Rua 4 Bairro 25 de Junho, CP 930, Maputo; tel. 21475820; Pres., Sec. of the Synod A. A. LITSURE.

Igreja Maná: Rua Francisco Orlando Magumbwe 528, Maputo; tel. 21491760; fax 21490896; e-mail adm_mocambique@igrejamana .com; Bishop DOMINGOS COSTA.

Igreja Reformada em Moçambique (IRM) (Reformed Church in Mozambique): CP 3, Vila Ulongue, Anogonia-Tete; f. 1908; Gen. Sec. Rev. SAMUEL M. BESSITALA; 60,000 mems.

Presbyterian Church of Mozambique: Av. Ahmed Sekou Touré 1822, CP 21, Maputo; tel. 21421790; fax 21428623; e-mail ipmoc@ zebra.uem.mz; f. 1887; 100,000 adherents; Pres. of Synodal Council Rev. ORIENTE SIBANE.

Seventh-Day Adventist Church: Av. Maguiguana 300, CP 1468, Maputo; tel. and fax 21427200; e-mail victormiconde@teledata.co .mz; 937 churches, 186,724 mems (2004).

Other denominations active in Mozambique include the Church of Christ, the Church of the Nazarene, the Greek Orthodox Church, the United Methodist Church of Mozambique, the Wesleyan Methodist Church, the Zion Christian Church, and Jehovah's Witnesses.

ISLAM

Comunidade Mahometana: Av. Albert Luthuli 291, Maputo; tel. 21425181; fax 21300880; internet www.paginaislamica.8m.com/pg1 .htm; Pres. SALEEM AHMED.

Congresso Islâmico de Moçambique (Islamic Congress of Mozambique): represents Sunni Muslims; Chair. ASSANE ISMAEL MAQBUL.

Conselho Islâmico de Moçambique (Islamic Council of Mozambique): Pres. ABDUL CARIMO.

The Press

DAILIES

Correio da Manha: Av. Filipe Samuel Magaia 528, CP 1756, Maputo; tel. 21305322; fax 21305321; e-mail refi@virconn.com; f. 1997; published by Sojornal, Lda; also publishes weekly Correio Semanal; Dir REFINALDO CHILENGUE.

Diário de Moçambique: Av. 25 de Setembro 1509, 2° andar, CP 2491, Beira; tel. and fax 23427312; f. 1981; under state management since 1991; Dir EZEQUIEL AMBRÓSIO; Editor FARUCO SADIQUE; circ. 5,000 (2003).

Expresso da Tarde: Av. Patrice Lumumba 511, 1° andar, Maputo; tel. 21314912; subscription only; distribution by fax; Dir SALVADOR RAIMUNDO HONWANA.

Mediafax: Av. Amílcar Cabral 1049, CP 73, Maputo; tel. 21301737; fax 21302402; e-mail mediafax@tvcabo.co.mz; f. 1992 by co-operative of independent journalists Mediacoop; news-sheet by subscription only, distribution by fax and internet; Editor BENEDITO NGOMANE.

Notícias de Moçambique: Rua Joaquim Lapa 55, CP 327, Maputo; tel. 21420119; fax 21320120; internet www.jornalnoticias.co.mz; f. 1926; morning; f. 1906; under state management since 1991; Pres. ESSELINA MACOME; Dir ROGÉRIO SITOE; circ. 12,793 (2003).

Further newspapers available solely in e-mail or fax format include Diário de Notícias and Matinal.

WEEKLIES

Campeão: Av. 24 de Julho 3706, CP 2610, Maputo; tel. and fax 21401810; sports newspaper; Dir RENATO CALDÉIRA; Editor ALEXANDRE ZANDAMELA.

Correio Semanal: Av. Filipe Samuel Magaia 528, CP 1756, Maputo; tel. 21305322; fax 21305312; Dir REFINALDO CHILENGUE.

Desafio: Rua Joaquim Lapa 55, Maputo; tel. 21305437; fax 21305431; Dir ALMIRO SANTOS; Editor BOAVIDA FUNJUA; circ. 3,890 (2003).

Domingo: Rua Joaquim Lapa 55, CP 327, Maputo; tel. 21431026; fax 21431027; f. 1981; Sun.; Dir JORGE MATINE; circ. 15,000 (2007).

Fim de Semana: Rua da Resistência 1642, 1° andar, Maputo; tel. and fax 21417012; e-mail fimdomes@tvcabo.co.mz; internet www.fimdesemana.co.mz; f. 1997; independent.

Jornal@Verdade: Av. Mártires da Machava 905, Maputo; tel. 843998624; e-mail averdademz@gmail.com; internet www.verdade.co.mz; f. 2008; CEO ERIK CHARAS; Editor-in-Chief ADÉRITO CALDEIRA.

Savana: Av. Amílcar Cabral 1049, CP 73, Maputo; tel. 21301737; fax 21302402; e-mail savana@mediacoop.co.mz; internet www.savana.co.mz; f. 1994; owned by mediacoop, SA; CEO FERNANDO LIMA; Publr KOK NAM; Editor FERNANDO GONÇALVES; circ. 15,000 (2009).

Tempo: Av. Ahmed Sekou Touré 1078, CP 2917, Maputo; tel. 21426191; f. 1970; magazine; under state management since 1991; Dir ROBERTO UAENE; Editor ARLINDO LANGA; circ. 40,000.

Zambeze: Rua José Sidumo, Maputo; tel. 21302019; Dir ANGELO MUNGUAMBE; circ. 2,000 (2003).

PERIODICALS

Agora: Afrisurvey, Lda, Rua General Pereira d'Eça 200, 1° andar, CP 1335, Maputo; tel. 21494147; fax 21494204; internet www.agora.co.mz; f. 2000; monthly; economics, politics, society; Pres. MARIA DE LOURDES TORCATO; Dir JOVITO NUNES; Editor-in-Chief ERCÍLIA SANTOS; circ. 5,000.

Agricultura: Instituto Nacional de Investigação Agronómica, CP 3658, Maputo; tel. 2130091; f. 1982; quarterly; publ. by Centro de Documentação de Agricultura, Silvicultura, Pecuária e Pescas.

Aro: Av. 24 de Julho 1420, CP 4187, Maputo; f. 1995; monthly; Dir POLICARTO TAMELE; Editor BRUNO MACAME, Jr.

Arquivo Histórico: Av. Filipe Samuel Magaia 715, CP 2033, Maputo; tel. 21421177; fax 21423428; f. 1934; Editor JOEL DAS NEVES TEMBE.

Boletim da República: Av. Vladimir I. Lénine, CP 275, Maputo; govt and official notices; publ. by Imprensa Nacional da Moçambique.

Moçambique–Novos Tempos: Av. Ahmed Sekou Touré 657, Maputo; tel. 21493564; fax 21493590; f. 1992; Dir J. MASCARENHAS.

Mozambiquefile: c/o AIM, Rua da Radio Moçambique, CP 896, Maputo; tel. 21313225; fax 21313196; e-mail aim@aim.org.mz; internet www.sortmoz.com/aimnews; monthly; Dir GUSTAVO MAVIZ; Editor PAUL FAUVET.

Mozambique Inview: c/o Mediacoop, Av. Amílcar Cabral 1049, CP 73, Maputo; tel. 21430722; fax 21302402; e-mail inview@savana.co.mz; internet www.mediacoop.odline.com; f. 1994; 2 a month; economic bulletin in English; Dir KOK NAM.

Portos e Caminhos de Ferro: CP 276, Maputo; English and Portuguese; ports and railways; quarterly.

Revista Maderazinco: CP 477, Maputo; tel. 823004770; e-mail maderazinco@yahoo.com; internet www.tropical.maderazinco.co.mz; f. 2002; quarterly; literature; Editor ROGÉRIO MANJATE.

Revista Médica de Moçambique: Instituto Nacional de Saúde, Ministério da Saúde e Faculdade de Medicina, Universidade Eduardo Mondlane, CP 264, Maputo; tel. 21420368; fax 21431103; e-mail mdgedge@malarins.uem.mz; f. 1982; 4 a year; medical journal; Editor MARTINHO DGEDGE.

NEWS AGENCY

Agência de Informação de Moçambique (AIM): Rua da Rádio Moçambique, CP 896, Maputo; tel. 21313225; fax 21313196; e-mail aim@aim.org.mz; f. 1975; daily reports in Portuguese and English; Dir GUSTAVO LISSETIANE MAVIE.

Publishers

Arquivo Histórico de Moçambique (AHM): Av. Filipe Samuel Magaia 715, CP 2033, Maputo; tel. 21421177; fax 21423428; internet www.ahm.uem.mz; Dir JOEL DAS NEVES TEMBE.

Central Impressora: c/o Ministério da Saúde, Avs Eduardo Mondlane e Salvador Allende 1008, CP 264, Maputo; tel. 21427131; fax 21427133; owned by the Ministry of Health.

Centro de Estudos Africanos: Universidade Eduardo Mondlane, CP 1993, Maputo; tel. 21490828; fax 21491896; f. 1976; social and political science, regional history, economics; Dir Col SERGIO VIEIRA.

Editora Minerva Central: Rua Consiglieri Pedroso 84, CP 212, Maputo; tel. 2122092; fax 21328816; e-mail geral@minerva.co.mz; internet www.minerva.co.mz; f. 1908; stationers and printers, educational, technical and medical textbooks; Man. Dir J. F. CARVALHO.

Editorial Ndjira, Lda: Av. Ho Chi Minh 85, Maputo; tel. 21300180; fax 21308745; f. 1996.

Empresa Moderna, Lda: Av. 25 de Setembro, CP 473, Maputo; tel. 21424594; f. 1937; fiction, history, textbooks; Man. Dir LOUIS GALLOTI.

Fundo Bibliográfico de Língua Portuguesa: Av. 25 de Setembro 1230, 7° andar, Maputo; tel. 21429531; fax 21429530; e-mail palop@zebra.uem.mz; f. 1990; state owned; Pres. LOURENÇO ROSÁRIO.

Imprensa Universitária: Universidade Eduardo Mondlane, Praça 19 de Maio, Maputo; internet www.uem.mz/imprensa_universitaris; university press.

Instituto Nacional do Livro e do Disco: Av. 24 de Julho 1921, CP 4030, Maputo; tel. 21434870; govt publishing and purchasing agency; Dir ARMÉNIO CORREIA.

Moçambique Editora: Rua Armando Tivane 1430, Bairro de Polana, Maputo; tel. 21495017; fax 21499071; e-mail info@me.co.mz; internet www.me.co.mz; f. 1996; educational textbooks, dictionaries.

Plural Editores: Av. Patrice Lumumba 765, Maputo; tel. 21360900; fax 21308868; e-mail plural@pluraleditores.co.mz; internet www.pluraleditores.co.mz; f. 2003; educational textbooks; part of the Porto Editora Group.

GOVERNMENT PUBLISHING HOUSE

Imprensa Nacional de Moçambique: Rua da Imprensa, CP 275, Maputo; tel. 21427021; fax 21424858; internet www.imprensanac.gov.mz; part of Ministry of State Administration; Dir VENÂNCIO T. MANJATE.

Broadcasting and Communications

TELECOMMUNICATIONS

The monopoly of Telecomunicações de Moçambique on the provision of fixed-line services was ended in December 2007, although it remained the sole fixed-line operator at early 2012. There were also three mobile telephone operators in early 2012.

Moçambique Celular (mCel): Rua Belmiro Obadias Muianga 384, CP 1483, Maputo; tel. 21351100; fax 21351117; internet www.mcel.co.mz; f. 1997 as a subsidiary of TDM; separated from TDM in 2003; mobile cellular telephone provider; Pres. SALVADOR ADRIANO.

Telecomunicações de Moçambique, SARL (TDM): Rua da Sé 2, CP 25, Maputo; tel. 21431921; fax 21431944; e-mail scatdm@tdm.mz; internet www.tdm.mz; f. 1993; Chair. JOAQUIM RIBEIRO PEREIRA DE CARVALHO; Man. Dir MAMUDO IBRAIMO.

Vodacom Moçambique (VM): Time Square Complex, Bloco 3, Av. 25 de Setembro, Maputo; tel. 840900000; fax 840901775; e-mail yumna.bhikha@vm.co.mz; internet www.vm.co.mz; f. 2002; mobile cellular telephone provider; owned by Vodacom Group (South Africa) and local shareholders; Chair. SALIMO ABDULA; Man. Dir JOSÉ DOS SANTOS.

Regulatory Authority

Instituto Nacional das Comunicações de Moçambique (INCM): Av. Eduardo Mondlane 123–127, CP 848, Maputo; tel. 21490131; fax 21494435; e-mail info@incm.gov.mz; internet www.incm.gov.mz; regulates post and telecommunications systems; Pres. ISIDORO PEDRO DA SILVA.

BROADCASTING

Radio

Rádio Encontro: Av. Francisco Manyanga, CP 366, Nampula; tel. 26215588; fax 26215878; e-mail radioencontro@teledata.mz.

Rádio Feba Moçambique: Av. Julius Nyerere 441A, CP 1648, Maputo; tel. 21440002; fax 21440009; e-mail febamoz@org.ue.mz; internet febamoz.go.co.mz.

Rádio Maria: Rua Igreja 156A, Machava Sede, Matola, Maputo; tel. 21750505; fax 21752124; e-mail info.moz@radiomaria.org; internet www.radiomaria.org.mz; f. 1995; evangelical radio broadcasts; Dir Fr JOÃO CARLOS H. NUNES.

Rádio Miramar: Rede de Comunicação, Av. Julius Nyerere 1555, Maputo; tel. 21486311; fax 21486813; e-mail jose.guerra@tvcabo.co.mz; owned by Brazilian religious sect, the Universal Church of the Kingdom of God.

Rádio Moçambique: Rua da Rádio 2, CP 2000, Maputo; tel. 21431687; fax 21321816; e-mail sepca_mz@yahoo.com.br; internet www.rm.co.mz; f. 1975; programmes in Portuguese, English and vernacular languages; Chair. RICARDO MADAUANE MALATE.

Rádio Terra Verde: Av. Eduardo Mondlane 2623, 5° andar, Maputo; tel. and fax 21302083; fmrly Voz da Renamo; owned by former rebel movement Renamo; transmitters in Maputo and Gorongosa, Sofala province.

Rádio Trans Mundial Moçambique: Av. Eduardo Mondlane 2998, CP 1526, Maputo; tel. 21440003; fax 21440004; e-mail rtransmundial@isl.co.mz.

Television

Rádio Televisão Klint (RTK): Av. Agostinho Neto 946, Maputo; tel. 21422956; fax 21493306; Dir CARLOS KLINT.

RTP África: Rua Pero de Anaia 248, Maputo; tel. (21) 497344; fax (21) 487347; e-mail rtp.a.moc@teledata.mz.

Televisão Miramar: Rua Pereira Lago 221, Maputo; tel. 21486311; fax 21486813; owned by Brazilian religious sect, the Igrega Universal do Reino de Deus (Universal Church of the Kingdom of God).

Televisão de Moçambique, EP (TVM): Av. 25 de Setembro 154, CP 2675, Maputo; tel. 21308117; fax 21308122; e-mail tvm@tvm.co .mz; internet www.tvm.co.mz; f. 1981; Pres. of Administrative Council ARMINDO CHAVANA.

TV Cabo Moçambique: Av. dos Presidentes 68, CP 1750, Maputo; tel. 21480550; fax 21480501; e-mail tvcabo@tvcabo.co.mz; internet www.tvcabo.co.mz; cable television and internet services in Maputo.

Finance

(cap. = capital; res = reserves; dep. = deposits; m. = million; brs = branches; amounts in meticais, unless otherwise stated)

BANKING

In 2009 there were 14 banks and three microfinance institutions in Mozambique.

Central Bank

Banco de Moçambique: Av. 25 de Setembro 1695, CP 423, Maputo; tel. 21354600; fax 21323247; e-mail gpi@bancomoc.mz; internet www.bancomoc.mz; f. 1975; bank of issue; cap. 248.9m., res 845.2m., dep. 43,260.2m. (Dec. 2009); Gov. ERNESTO GOUVEIA GOVE; 4 brs.

National Banks

Banco de Desenvolvimento e de Comércio de Moçambique, SARL (BDCM): Av. 25 de Setembro 420, 1° andar, sala 8, Maputo; tel. 21313040; fax 21313047; f. 2000; 42% owned by Montepio Geral (Portugal).

Banco Mercantil e de Investimento, SARL (BMI): Av. 24 de Julho 3549, Maputo; tel. 21407979; fax 21408887.

Banco Nacional de Investimentos (BNI): Maputo; f. 2010; 49.5% owned by the Govt of Mozambique, 49.5% owned by the Govt of Portugal, 1% owned by Banco Comercial e de Investimentos, SARL; cap. US $500,000m.; Exec. Dir ADRIANO MALEIANE.

Banco Terra: Av. Samora Machel 341 R/C, CP 69, Maputo; tel. 21359300; fax 21316120; internet www.bancoterra.co.mz; f. 2008; provides access to a full range of financial services to the rural and peri urban population in Mozambique; cap. 185m., dep. 100.3m. (Dec. 2007); 30.7% owned by Rabobank (Netherlands); Pres. H. MERTENS; CEO KARL MOURSOND.

Barclays Bank Mozambique SA: Av. 25 de Setembro 1184, CP 757, Maputo; tel. 21351700; fax 21323470; internet www .bancoaustral.co.mz; f. 1995 as Banco Popular de Desenvolvimento (BPD); name changed to Banco Austral SARL in 1998; name changed as above in 2007; 80% owned by Amalgamated Banks of South Africa, 20% owned by União, Sociedade e Participacões, SARL, which represents employees of the bank; cap. 315m., res 311.7m., dep. 5,347.5m. (Dec. 2008); Chair. CASIMIRO FRANCISCO; Man. Dir PAUL NICE; 58 brs and agencies.

BCI Fomento (BCI) (Banco Comercial e de Investimentos, SARL): Edif. John Orr's, Av. 25 de Setembro 1465, CP 4745, Maputo; tel. 21353700; fax 21309831; e-mail bci@bci.co.mz; internet www.bci.co .mz; f. 1996; renamed as above following 2003 merger between Banco Comercial e de Investimentos and Banco de Fomento; 51% owned by Caixa Geral de Depósitos (Portugal), 30% Banco Português de Investimento, 18% owned by INSITEC; cap. 319.8m., res 516.7m., dep. 11,996.4m. (Dec. 2006); Chair. CELSO ISMAEL CORREIA; CEO IBRAIMO IBRAIMO; 68 brs.

ICB-Banco Internacional de Comércio, SARL: Av. 25 de Setembro 1915, Maputo; tel. 21311111; fax 21314797; e-mail icbm@ icbank-mz.com; internet www.icbank-mz.com; f. 1998; cap. and res 44,923,748m., total assets 164,773,569m. (Dec. 2003); Chair. JOSEPHINE SIVARETNAM; CEO LEE SANG HUAT; 4 brs.

Millennium bim: Av. 25 de Setembro 1800, CP 865, Maputo; tel. 21354496; fax 21354415; e-mail scheman@millenniumbim.co.mz; internet www.millenniumbim.co.mz; f. 1995; name changed from Banco Internacional de Moçambique in 2005; 66.7% owned by Banco Comercial Português, 17.4% by the state; cap. 741.0m., res 2,291.0m.,

dep. 29,744.7m. (Dec. 2008); Pres. MÁRIO FERNANDES DA GRAÇA MACHUNGO; CEO JOÃO FILIPE DE FIGUEIREDO JÚNIOR; 86 brs.

Moza Banco: Av. Kwame Nkrumah 97, CP 1012, Maputo; tel. 21480800; fax 21480801; e-mail info@mozabanco.co.mz; internet www.mozabanco.co.mz; f. 2008; cap. US $15m.; Chair. PRAKASH RATILAL.

Novo Banco, SARL: Av. do Trabalho 750, Maputo; tel. and fax 21407705; f. 2000; cap. and res 51,995m., total assets 108,847m. (Dec. 2003).

Standard Bank, SARL (Moçambique): Praça 25 de Junho 1, CP 2086, Maputo; tel. 21352500; fax 21426967; e-mail camal.daude@ standardbank.co.mz; internet www.standardbank.co.mz; f. 1966 as Banco Standard Totta de Mozambique; 98.14% owned by Stanbic Africa Holdings, UK; cap. 1,294.0m., res 430.6m., dep. 14,362.1m. (Dec. 2011); Man. Dir ANTONIO COUTINHO; 24 brs.

Foreign Banks

African Banking Corporation (Moçambique), SA: ABC House, Av. Julius Nyerere 99, Polana, CP 1445, Maputo; tel. 21482100; fax 21487474; e-mail abcmoz@africanbankingcorp.com; internet www .africanbankingcorp.com; f. 1999; 100% owned by African Banking Corpn Holdings Ltd (Botswana); fmrly BNP Nedbank (Moçambique), SARL; changed name as above after acquisition in 2002; cap. 148m., res 101m., dep. 3,598.9m. (Dec. 2009); Chair. BENJAMIM ALFREDO; Man. Dir JOSEPH SIBANDA; 2 brs.

African Banking Corporation Leasing, SARL: Rua da Imprensa 256, 7° andar, CP 4447, Maputo; tel. 21300451; fax 21431290; e-mail ulcmoz@mail.tropical.co.mz; 66% owned by African Banking Corpn Holdings Ltd (Botswana); fmrly ULC (Moçambique); changed name as above in 2002; Chair. ANTÓNIO BRANCO; Gen. Man. VICTOR VISEU.

Mauritius Commercial Bank (Moçambique) SA: Av. Friedrich Engels 400, Maputo; tel. 21481900; fax 21498675; e-mail contact@ mcbmozambique.com; internet www.mcbmozambique.com; f. 1999; name changed as above in June 2007; 81% owned by Mauritius Commercial Bank Group; total assets US $46,777m. (Dec. 2006); Chair. PIERRE GUY NOEL; Gen. Man. PETER HIGGINS.

DEVELOPMENT FUND

Fundo de Desenvolvimento Agrário: Rua Joaquim Lapa 192, 2° andar, Maputo; tel. 21302814; fax 21430044; e-mail antonio.andre@ ffa.org.mz; f. 2006 to provide credit for small farmers and rural co-operatives; promotes agricultural and rural devt; Sec. ANTÓNIO ANDRÉ.

STOCK EXCHANGE

Bolsa de Valores de Moçambique: Av. 25 de Setembro 1230, Prédio 33, 5° andar, Maputo; tel. 21308826; fax 21310559; e-mail bvm@bvm.co.mz; internet www.bolsadevalores.co.mz; f. 1999; Chair. ANABELA CHAMBUCA.

INSURANCE

In December 1991 the Assembleia da República approved legislation terminating the state monopoly of insurance and reinsurance activities. In 2005 five insurance companies were operating in Mozambique.

Companhia de Seguros de Moçambique, IMPAR: Rua da Imprensa 625, Prédio 33, Maputo; tel. 21429695; fax 21430640; f. 1992; Pres. INOCÊNCIO A. MATAVEL; Gen. Man. MANUEL BALANCHO.

Empresa Moçambicana de Seguros, EE (EMOSE): Av. 25 de Setembro 1383, CP 1165, Maputo; tel. 21356300; fax 21424526; e-mail comercial@emose.co.mz; internet www.emose.co.mz; f. 1977 as state insurance monopoly; took over business of 24 fmr cos; 80% govt-owned, 20% private; cap. 150m.; Chair. VENÂNCIO MONDLANE.

Seguradora Internacional de Moçambique: Av. 25 Setembro 1800, Maputo; tel. 21430959; fax 21430241; e-mail simseg@zebra .uem.mz; Pres. MÁRIO FERNANDES DA GRAÇA MACHUNGO.

Trade and Industry

GOVERNMENT AGENCIES

Centro de Promoção de Investimentos (CPI) (Investment Promotion Centre): Rua da Imprensa 332, CP 4635, Maputo; tel. 21313295; fax 21313325; e-mail cpi@cpi.co.mz; internet www.cpi .co.mz; f. 1987; encourages domestic and foreign investment and IT ventures with foreign firms; evaluates and negotiates investment proposals; Dir LOURENÇO SAMBO.

Instituto do Algodão de Moçambique (IAM): Av. Eduardo Mondlane 2221, 1° andar, CP 806, Maputo; tel. 21424264; fax 21430679; e-mail iampab@zebra.uem.mz; internet www.iam.gov

.mz; responsible for promotion and devt of the cotton industry; Dir NORBERTO MAHALAMBE.

Instituto do Fomento do Cajú (INCAJU): Maputo; internet incaju.gov.mz; national cashew institute; Dir FILOMENA MAIOPUE.

Instituto Nacional de Açúcar (INA): Rua da Gávea 33, CP 1772, Maputo; tel. 21326550; fax 21427436; e-mail gpsca.ina@tvcabo.co.mz; Chair. ARNALDO RIBEIRO.

Instituto Nacional de Petróleo (INP): Av. Fernão de Magalhães 34, 1º/2ºandar, CP 4724, Maputo; tel. 21320935; fax 21320932; e-mail info@inp.gov.mz; internet www.inp.gov.mz; f. 2005; regulates energy sector; Pres. ARSÉNIO MABOTE.

Instituto para a Promoção de Exportações (IPEX): Av. 25 de Setembro 1008, 2° andar, CP 4487, Maputo; tel. 21307257; fax 21307256; e-mail ipex@tvcabo.co.mz; internet www.ipex.gov.mz; f. 1990 to promote and co-ordinate national exports abroad; Pres. Dr JOÃO MACARINGUE.

Unidade Técnica para a Reestruturação de Empresas (UTRE): Rua da Imprensa 256, 7° andar, CP 4350, Maputo; tel. 21426514; fax 21421541; implements restructuring of state enterprises; Dir MOMADE JUMAS.

CHAMBERS OF COMMERCE

Câmara de Comércio de Moçambique (CCM): Rua Mateus Sansão Muthemba 452, CP 1836, Maputo; tel. 21491970; fax 21490428; e-mail ccm@tvcabo.co.mz; internet www.ccmoz.org.mz; f. 1980; Pres. JOÃO AMÉRICO MPFUMO; Sec.-Gen. MANUEL NOTIÇO.

Mozambique-USA Chamber of Commerce: Rua Matheus Sansão Muthemba 452, Maputo; tel. 21492904; fax 21492739; e-mail ccmusa@tvcabo.co.mz; internet www.ccmusa.co.mz; f. 1993; Sec. PETER MUCHIRI.

South Africa-Mozambique Chamber of Commerce (SAMO-ZACC): tel. 768548303; fax 866049050; e-mail info@samozacc.co.za; internet www.samozacc.co.za; f. 2005; Chair. (Mozambique) DAVID ROBBETZE.

TRADE ASSOCIATIONS

Associação das Indústrias do Cajú (AICAJU): Maputo; cashew processing industry asscn; Chair. CARLOS COSTA; 12 mem. cos.

Confederação das Associações Económicas de Moçambique (CTA): Rua de Fernando Ganhão 120, CP 2975, Maputo; tel. 21491914; fax 21493094; internet www.cta.org.mz; Pres. SALIMO ABDULA; Sec. OLGA TIMBA; 58 mem. cos.

STATE INDUSTRIAL ENTERPRISES

Empresa Nacional de Hidrocarbonetos de Moçambique (ENH): Av. Fernão de Magalhães 34, CP 4787, Maputo; tel. 21429456; fax 21421608; controls concessions for petroleum exploration and production; Dir MÁRIO MARQUES.

Petróleos de Moçambique (PETROMOC): Praça dos Trabalhadores 9, CP 417, Maputo; tel. 21427191; fax 21430181; internet www.petromoc.co.mz; f. 1977 to take over the Sonarep oil refinery and its associated distribution co; formerly Empresa Nacional de Petróleos de Moçambique; state directorate for liquid fuels within Mozambique, incl. petroleum products passing through Mozambique to inland countries; CEO JOSÉ MATEUS MUÁRIA KATHUPA.

UTILITIES
Electricity

Electricidade de Moçambique (EDM): Av. Agostinho Neto 70, CP 2447, Maputo; tel. 21490636; fax 21491048; e-mail ligacaoexpresso@edm.co.mz; internet www.edm.co.mz; f. 1977; 100% state-owned; production and distribution of electric energy; in 2004 plans were announced to extend the EDM grid to the entire country by 2020, at an estimated cost of US $700m; Pres. MANUEL JOÃO CUAMBE; Dir PASCOAL BACELA; 2,700 employees.

Companhia de Transmissão de Moçambique, SARL (MOTRACO) (Mozambique Transmission Co): Av. 25 de Setembro 420, Prédio JAT, 4° andar, Maputo; tel. 21313427; fax 21313447; e-mail asimao@motraco.co.mz; internet www.motraco.co.mz; f. 1998; jt venture between power utilities of Mozambique, South Africa and Swaziland; electricity distribution; Gen. Man. FRANCIS MASAWI.

Water

Direcção Nacional de Águas: Av. 25 de Setembro 942, 9° andar, CP 1611, Maputo; tel. 21420469; fax 21421403; e-mail watco@zebra.uem.mz; internet www.dnaguas.gov.mz; Dir AMÉRICO MUIANGA.

TRADE UNIONS

Freedom to form trade unions, and the right to strike, are guaranteed under the 1990 Constitution.

Confederação de Sindicatos Livres e Independentes de Moçambique (CONSILMO): Sec.-Gen. JEREMIAS TIMANE.

Organização dos Trabalhadores de Moçambique—Central Sindical (OTM—CS) (Mozambique Workers' Organization—Trade Union Headquarters): Rua Manuel António de Sousa 36, Maputo; tel. 21426786; fax 21421671; internet www.otm.org.mz; f. 1983; 15 affiliated unions with over 94,000 mems; Pres. CARLOS MUCAREIA; Sec.-Gen. ALEXANDRE MUNGUAMBE.

Transport

Improvements to the transport infrastructure since the signing of the Acordo Geral de Paz (General Peace Agreement) in 1992 have focused on the development of 'transport corridors', which include both rail and road links and promote industrial development in their environs. The Beira Corridor, with rail and road links and a petroleum pipeline, runs from Manica, on the Zimbabwean border, to the Mozambican port of Beira, while the Limpopo Corridor joins southern Zimbabwe and Maputo. Both corridors form a vital outlet for the land-locked southern African countries, particularly Zimbabwe. The Maputo Corridor links Ressano Garcia in South Africa to the port at Maputo, and the Nacala Corridor runs from Malawi to the port of Nacala. Two further corridors were planned: the Mtwara Corridor was to link Mozambique, Malawi, Tanzania and Zambia, while the Zambezi Corridor was to link Zambézia province with Malawi.

RAILWAYS

In 2010 the total length of track was 3,116 km, of which 2,072 km was operational. There are both internal routes and rail links between Mozambican ports and South Africa, Swaziland, Zimbabwe and Malawi. During the hostilities many lines and services were disrupted. In the early 2000s work commenced on upgrading the railway system and private companies were granted non-permanent concessions to rehabilitate and operate the railways. In mid—2012 the Government awarded the tender for the construction of a line connecting Moatize with the Malawian railway south of Blantyre; work on the line was expected to commence at the end of the year and be finished within three years. There were also plans for a line to connect Mutarara with Malema. Rehabilitation work on the 670-km Sena railway line linking Beira with Moatize was expected to be completed in 2013.

Beira Railway Co: Dondo; f. 2004; 51% owned by Rites & Ircon (India), 49% owned by CFM; rehabilitating and managing Sena and Zimbabwe railway lines.

Portos e Caminhos de Ferro de Moçambique (CFM): Praça dos Trabalhadores 2158, Maputo; tel. 21327173; fax 21427746; e-mail cfmnet@cfmnet.co.mz; internet www.cfmnet.co.mz; fmrly Empresa Nacional dos Portos e Caminhos de Ferro de Moçambique; privatized and restructured in 2002; Chair. ROSÁRIO MUALEIA; comprises four separate systems linking Mozambican ports with the country's hinterland, and with other southern African countries, including South Africa, Swaziland, Zimbabwe and Malawi:

CFM—Centro (CFM—C): Largo dos CFM, CP 236, Beira; tel. 23321000; fax 23329290; lines totalling 994 km linking Beira with Zimbabwe and Malawi, as well as link to Moatize (undergoing rehabilitation); Exec. Dir JOAQUIM VERÍSSIMO.

CFM—Norte: Av. do Trabalho, CP 16, Nampula; tel. 26214320; fax 26212034; lines totalling 872 km, including link between port of Nacala with Malawi; management concession awarded to Nacala Corridor Development Co (a consortium 67% owned by South African, Portuguese and US cos) in January 2000; Dir of Railways MANUEL MANICA.

CFM—Sul: Praça dos Trabalhadores, CP 2158, Maputo; tel. and fax 21430894; lines totalling 1,070 km linking Maputo with South Africa, Swaziland and Zimbabwe, as well as Inhambane–Inharrime and Xai-Xai systems; Exec. Dir JOAQUIM ZUCULE.

CFM—Zambézia: CP 73, Quelimane; tel. 24212502; fax 24213123; 145-km line linking Quelimane and Mocuba; Dir ORLANDO J. JAIME.

ROADS

In 2009 there were an estimated 30,331 km of roads in Mozambique, of which 6,309 km were paved.

Administração Nacional de Estradas (ANE): Av. de Moçambique 1225, CP 1294, Maputo; tel. 21475157; fax 21475290; internet www.ane.gov.mz; f. 1999 to replace the Direcção Nacional de Estradas e Pontes; implements government road policy through the Direcção de Estradas Nacionais (DEN) and the Direcção de Estradas Regionais (DER); Pres. Eng. LUCIANO DE CASTRO; Dir-Gen. CECÍLIO GRACHANE.

SHIPPING

Mozambique has three main sea ports, at Nacala, Beira and Maputo, while inland shipping on Lake Niassa and the river system remain underdeveloped. At 31 December 2012 Mozambique's flag registered fleet consisted of 75 vessels, totalling 35,900 grt.

Portos e Caminhos de Ferro de Moçambique (CFM-EP): Praça dos Trabalhadores, CP 2159, Maputo; tel. 21427173; fax 21427746; e-mail cfmnet@cfmnet.co.mz; internet www.cfmnet.co.mz; fmrly Empresa Nacional dos Portos e Caminhos de Ferro de Moçambique; privatized and restructured in 2002; Chair. ROSÁRIO MUALEIA; Port Dir CFM-Sul Eng. ANTÓNIO FRANCISCO MANUEL BIÉ; Port Dir CFM-Norte Eng. FRANCO CATUTULA; Port Dir CFM-Centro Dr CÂNDIDO JONE.

Agência Nacional de Frete e Navegação (ANFRENA): Rua Consiglieri Pedroso 396, CP 492, Maputo; tel. 21427064; fax 21427822; Dir FERDINAND WILSON.

Empresa Moçambicana de Cargas, SARL (MOCARGO): Rua Consiglieri Pedroso 430, 1°–4° andares, CP 888, Maputo; tel. 21428318; fax 21302067; e-mail msamaral@mocargo.com; internet www.mocargo.co.mz; f. 1982; shipping, chartering and road transport; Man. Dir MANUEL DE SOUSA AMARAL.

Manica Freight Services, SARL: Praça dos Trabalhadores 51, CP 557, Maputo; tel. 21356500; fax 21431084; e-mail fdimande@manica.co.mz; internet www.manica.co.mz; international shipping agents; Man. Dir AHMAD Y. CHOTHIA.

Maputo Port Development Co, SARL (MPDC): Port Director's Building, Porto de Maputo, CP 2841, Maputo; tel. 21313920; fax 21313921; e-mail info@portmaputo.com; internet www.portmaputo.com; f. 2002; private sector international consortium with concession (awarded 2003) to develop and run port of Maputo until 2018; Pres. DAVE RENNIE; CEO OSÓRIO LUCAS.

Mozline, SARL: Av. Karl Marx 478, 2° andar, Maputo; tel. 21303078; fax 21303073; e-mail mozline1@virconn.com; shipping and road freight services.

Navique, SARL: Av. Mártires de Inhaminga 125, CP 145, Maputo; tel. 21312705; fax 21426310; e-mail smazoi@navique.co.mz; internet www.navique.com; f. 1985; Chair. J. A. CARVALHO; Man. Dir PEDRO VIRTUOSO.

CIVIL AVIATION

In 2010 there were eight international airports in Mozambique. In that year expansion work on Maputo International Airport was completed at an estimated cost of US $75m. to increase annual capacity to 900,000 passengers. In February 2012 Aeroportos de Moçambique announced that it was to invest $500m. over the following three years in the modernization and rehabilitation of the airports at Maputo, Pemba, Nacala-Porto and Tete.

Aeroportos de Moçambique: Av. Acordos de Lusaka 3267, CP 2631, Maputo; tel. 21465375; fax 21465359; internet www.aeroportos.co.mz; under Ministry of Transport and Communications; Chair. MANUEL VETERANO.

Instituto de Aviação Civil de Moçambique (IACM): Maputo; civil aviation institute; Dir ALBERTO MABJAIA.

Air Corridor, SARL: Av. Eduardo Mondlane 945, Nampula; tel. 26213333; fax 26213355; e-mail fagadit@aircorridor.com.mz; internet www.aircorridor.co.mz; f. 2004; domestic carrier and cargo transport; Chair. MOMADE AQUI RAJAHUSSEN; Commercial Dir FARUK ALY GADIT.

Linhas Aéreas de Moçambique, SARL (LAM): Aeroporto Internacional de Maputo, CP 2060, Maputo; tel. 21465137; fax 21422936; e-mail jrviegas@lam.co.mz; internet www.lam.co.mz; f. 1980; 80% state-owned; operates domestic services and international services to South Africa, Tanzania, Mayotte, Zimbabwe and Portugal; CEO MARLENE MENDES MANAVE.

Sociedade de Transportes Aéreos/Sociedade de Transporte e Trabalho Aéreo, SARL (STA/TTA): Rua da Tchamba 405, CP 665, Maputo; tel. 21491765; fax 21491763; e-mail sta.tta@sta.co.mz; f. 1991; domestic airline and aircraft charter transport services; acquired Empresa Nacional de Transporte e Trabalho Aéreo in 1997; Chair. JOSÉ CARVALHEIRA; Dir of Operations FERNANDO CARREIRA.

Other airlines operating in Mozambique include Serviço Aéreo Regional, South African Airlines, Moçambique Expresso, SA—Airlink International, Transairways (owned by LAM) and TAP Air Portugal.

Tourism

Tourism, formerly a significant source of foreign exchange, ceased completely following independence, and was resumed on a limited scale in 1980. There were only 1,000 visitors in 1981 (compared with 292,000 in 1972 and 69,000 in 1974). With the successful conduct of multi-party elections in 1994 and the prospect of continued peace, there was considerable scope for development of this sector. By the late 1990s tourism was the fastest growing sector of the Mozambique economy, and in 2000 it was announced that a comprehensive tourism development plan was to be devised, assisted by funding from the European Union. In 2005 there were 5,030 hotels in Mozambique. The formal opening of the Great Limpopo Transfrontier Park in 2002, linking territories in Mozambique with South Africa and Zimbabwe, was expected to attract additional tourists. Further national parks were planned. There were 1.8m. foreign tourist arrivals in 2010 and tourism receipts in 2011 totalled an estimated US $231m.

Fundo Nacional do Turismo: Av. 25 de Setembro 1203, CP 4758, Maputo; tel. 21307320; fax 21307324; internet www.futur.org.mz; f. 1993; hotels and tourism; CEO Dr ZACARIAS SUMBANA.

Defence

As assessed at November 2012, total active armed forces were estimated at 11,200 (army 10,000, navy 200, air force 1,000).

Defence Expenditure: Budgeted at an estimated 2,020m. meticais in 2011.

Commander-in-Chief of the Armed Forces: Pres. ARMANDO EMÍLIO GUEBUZA.

Chief of General Staff: Brig. PAULO MACARINGUE.

Deputy Chief of General Staff: Gen. OLIMPIO CAMBONA.

Education

Primary education is officially compulsory for seven years from the age of six. It is divided into two cycles, of five and two years. Secondary schooling, from 13 years of age, lasts for five years and comprises a first cycle of three years and a second of two years. According to UNESCO estimates, in 2010/11 90% of children in the relevant age-group were enrolled at primary schools (males 92%; females 87%), while secondary enrolment included only 17% of children in the relevant age-group (males 18%; females 17%). There were 28,298 students in tertiary education in 2004/05. Two privately owned higher education institutions, the Catholic University and the Higher Polytechnic Institute, were inaugurated in 1996. In 2003 it was announced that education would no longer take place solely in Portuguese, but also in some Mozambican dialects. In 2006 some US $39m. was granted by international donors to develop educational resources. Education was allocated 20.2% of total current expenditure in that year.

MYANMAR

Introductory Survey

LOCATION, CLIMATE, LANGUAGE, RELIGION, FLAG, CAPITAL

The Republic of the Union of Myanmar (Pyidaungsu Thammada Myanmar Naingngandaw—formerly Burma) lies in the north-west region of South-East Asia, between the Tibetan plateau and the Malay peninsula. The country is bordered by Bangladesh and India to the north-west, by the People's Republic of China and Laos to the north-east and by Thailand to the south-east. The climate is tropical, with an average temperature of 27°C (80°F) and monsoon rains from May to October. Average annual rainfall is between 2,500 mm and 5,000 mm in the coastal and mountainous regions of the north and east, but reaches a maximum of only 1,000 mm in the lowlands of the interior. Temperatures in Yangon (Rangoon) are generally between 18°C (65°F) and 36°C (97°F). The official language is Myanmar (Burmese), and there are also a number of tribal languages. About 87% of the population are Buddhists. There are animist, Muslim, Hindu and Christian minorities. A new national flag (proportions 2 by 3), which was officially introduced in October 2010, consists of three equal horizontal stripes, of yellow, green and red, with a large, five-pointed white star in the centre. In 2006 the functions of the capital city were transferred from Yangon to the new administrative centre of Nay Pyi Taw.

CONTEMPORARY POLITICAL HISTORY

Historical Context

Burma (now Myanmar) was annexed to British India during the 19th century, and became a separate British dependency, with a limited measure of self-government, in 1937. Japanese forces invaded and occupied the country in 1942, and Japan granted nominal independence under a Government of anti-British nationalists. The Burmese nationalists later turned against Japan and aided Allied forces to reoccupy the country in 1945. They formed a resistance movement, the Anti-Fascist People's Freedom League (AFPFL), led by Gen. Aung San, which became the main political force after the defeat of Japan. Aung San was assassinated in July 1947 and was succeeded by U Nu. On 4 January 1948 the Union of Burma became independent, outside the Commonwealth, with U Nu as the first Prime Minister.

Domestic Political Affairs

During the first decade of independence Burma was a parliamentary democracy, and the Government successfully resisted revolts by communists and other insurgent groups. In 1958 the ruling AFPFL split into two wings—the 'Clean' AFPFL and the 'Stable' AFPFL—and U Nu invited the army chief of staff, Gen. Ne Win, to head a caretaker Government. Elections to the Chamber of Deputies in February 1960 gave an overwhelming majority to U Nu, leading the 'Clean' AFPFL (which was renamed the Union Party in March), and he resumed office in April. Despite its popularity, the U Nu administration proved ineffective, and in March 1962 Gen. Ne Win staged a coup to depose U Nu (who was subsequently detained until 1966). The new Revolutionary Council suspended the Constitution and instituted authoritarian control through the government-sponsored Burma Socialist Programme Party (BSPP). All other political parties were outlawed in March 1964.

During the next decade a more centralized system of government was created, in an attempt to win popular support and to nationalize important sectors of the economy. A new Constitution, aiming to transform Burma into a democratic socialist state, was approved in a national referendum in December 1973. The Constitution of the renamed Socialist Republic of the Union of Burma, which came into force in January 1974, confirmed the BSPP as the sole authorized political party, and provided for the establishment of new organs of state. Elections to a legislative People's Assembly took place in January 1974, and in March the Revolutionary Council was dissolved. Ne Win (who, together with other senior army officers, had become a civilian in 1972) was elected President by the newly created State Council. However, Burma's economic problems increased, and in 1974 there were riots over food shortages and social injustices. Stu-

dent demonstrations took place in 1976, as social problems mounted. Following an attempted coup by members of the armed forces in July, the BSPP adopted a new economic programme in 1977 in an effort to quell unrest.

An election in January 1978 gave Ne Win a mandate to rule for a further four years, and in March he was re-elected Chairman of the State Council. In May 1980 a general amnesty was declared for political dissidents, including exiles (as a result of which U Nu, who had been living abroad since 1969, returned to Burma). Gen. San Yu, formerly the army Chief of Staff, was elected Chairman of the State Council in November 1981. In August 1985 Ne Win was re-elected Chairman of the BSPP. Elections for a new People's Assembly were held in November.

In August 1987, owing to the country's increasing economic problems, an unprecedented extraordinary meeting, comprising the BSPP Central Committee, the organs of the State Council and other state bodies, was convened. Ne Win proposed a review of the policies of the past 25 years. In September the announcement of the withdrawal from circulation of high-denomination banknotes, coupled with rice shortages, provoked student riots (the first civil disturbances since 1976). Owing to continued economic deprivation, further student unrest in Rangoon (now Yangon) in March 1988 culminated in major protests, which were violently suppressed by riot police under the direct command of Sein Lwin, the BSPP Joint General Secretary. Further demonstrations were staged in June. The Government's response was again extremely brutal, and many demonstrators were killed. In July vain attempts were made to counter the growing unpopularity of the Government, including the removal from office of the Minister of Home and Religious Affairs and the head of the People's Police Force in Rangoon. (The Prime Minister, also, was subsequently dismissed.) Finally, at an extraordinary meeting of the BSPP Congress, Ne Win resigned as party Chairman and asked the Congress to approve the holding of a national referendum on the issue of a multi-party political system. The Congress rejected the referendum proposal and the resignation of four other senior members of the BSPP, including that of Sein Lwin, but accepted the resignation of San Yu, the BSPP Vice-Chairman.

The subsequent election of Sein Lwin to the chairmanship of the BSPP, and his appointment as Chairman of the State Council and as state President, provoked further student-led riots. In August 1988 martial law was imposed on Rangoon, and thousands of unarmed demonstrators were reportedly massacred by the armed forces throughout the country. Sein Lwin was forced to resign after only 17 days in office. He was replaced by the more moderate Dr Maung Maung, hitherto the Attorney-General, whose response to the continued rioting was conciliatory. Martial law was revoked; Brig.-Gen. Aung Gyi (formerly a close colleague of Ne Win, now an outspoken critic of the regime), who had been detained under Sein Lwin, was released; and permission was given for the formation of the All Burma Students' Union. However, demonstrations continued, and by September students and Buddhist monks had assumed control of the municipal government of many towns. In that month U Nu requested foreign support for his formation of an 'alternative government'. The emerging opposition leaders, Aung Gyi, Aung San Suu Kyi (daughter of Gen. Aung San) and Gen. (retd) Tin Oo (a former army Chief of Staff and Minister of Defence), then formed the National United Front for Democracy, which was subsequently renamed the League for Democracy and later the National League for Democracy (NLD).

At an emergency meeting of the BSPP Congress in September 1988 it was decided that free elections would be held within three months and that members of the armed forces, police and civil service could no longer be affiliated to a political party. Now distanced from the BSPP, the armed forces, led by Gen. (later Senior Gen.) Saw Maung, seized power on 18 September, ostensibly to maintain order until multi-party elections could be arranged. A State Law and Order Restoration Council (SLORC) was formed, all state organs (including the People's Assembly, the State Council and the Council of Ministers) were abolished, demonstrations were banned and a night-time curfew was imposed nation-wide. Despite these measures, opposition movements demonstrated in favour of an interim civilian government, and it was estimated that more than 1,000 demonstrators were killed in the first few days following the coup. The SLORC announced the formation of a nine-member Government, with Saw Maung as Minister of Defence and of Foreign Affairs and subsequently also Prime Minister. Although ostensibly in retirement, it was widely believed that Ne Win retained a controlling influence over the new leaders. The new Government changed the official name of the country to the Union of Burma (as it had been before 1973). The law maintaining the BSPP as the sole party was abrogated, and new parties were encouraged to register for the forthcoming elections. The BSPP registered as the National Unity Party (NUP). In December 1988, owing to disagreements with Suu Kyi, Aung Gyi was expelled from the NLD after he had founded the Union National Democracy Party. Tin Oo was elected as the new NLD Chairman. U Nu returned to prominence as the leader of a new party, the League for Democracy and Peace (LDP), and also commanded the support of the new Democracy Party.

From October 1988 to January 1989 Suu Kyi campaigned across the nation, and elicited much popular support, despite martial law regulations banning public gatherings of five or more people. In March 1989 there were anti-Government demonstrations in many cities, in protest at the increasing harassment of Suu Kyi and the arrest of many NLD supporters and activists. In July Suu Kyi cancelled a rally to commemorate the anniversary of the assassination of her father, owing to the threat of government violence; two days later, both she and Tin Oo were placed under house arrest.

In May 1989 electoral legislation was ratified, providing for multi-party elections to be held on 27 May 1990. In June 1989 the SLORC changed the official name of the country to the Union of Myanmar (Pyidaungsu Myanmar Naingngandaw), on the grounds that the previous title conveyed the impression that the population consisted solely of ethnic Burmans. The transliteration to the Roman alphabet of many other place names was changed, to correspond more closely with pronunciation.

In December 1989 Tin Oo of the NLD was sentenced by a military tribunal to three years' imprisonment, with hard labour, for his part in the anti-Government uprising in 1988. U Nu was disqualified from contesting the forthcoming general election, owing to his refusal to dissolve the 'alternative government' that he had proclaimed in September 1988. In January 1990 U Nu and other members of the 'alternative government' were placed under house arrest. Later in January Suu Kyi was barred from contesting the election, owing to her 'entitlement to the privileges of a foreigner' (a reference to her marriage to a British citizen) and her alleged involvement with insurgents. Tens of thousands of residents were reported to have been forcibly evicted from densely populated areas in major cities, where anti-Government demonstrations had received much support, and resettled in rural areas during 1989. By February 1990 martial law had been revoked in 18 townships.

In May 1990 93 parties presented a total of 2,296 candidates to contest 492 seats at the general election for the new assembly; there were also 87 independent candidates. The voting was reported to be free and orderly. The NLD received 59.9% of the total votes and won 396 of the 485 seats that were, in the event, contested; the NUP obtained 21.2% of the votes, but secured only 10 seats. The NLD demanded the immediate opening of negotiations with the SLORC, and progress towards popular rule. However, the SLORC announced that the election had been intended to provide not a legislature but a Constituent Assembly. The resulting draft constitution would require endorsement by referendum and subsequent approval by the SLORC. In July the SLORC announced Order 1/90, stating that the SLORC would continue as the de facto Government until a new constitution was drafted. In response, elected members of the NLD urged (independently of their leadership) that an assembly of all elected representatives be convened by September.

In September 1990 the SLORC arrested six members of the NLD, including the acting Chairman, Kyi Maung, and acting Secretary-General, Chit Hlaing, on charges of passing state secrets to unauthorized persons. Kyi Maung was replaced as acting NLD Chairman by Aung Shwe. Influential monks agreed to support the proposed declaration of a provisional government in Mandalay, but the plan was abandoned after government troops surrounded monasteries. The SLORC subsequently ordered the dissolution of all Buddhist organizations involved

in anti-Government activities (all except nine sects) and empowered military commanders to impose death sentences on rebellious monks. More than 50 senior members of the NLD were arrested, and members of all political parties were required to endorse Order 1/90: in acquiescing, the NLD effectively nullified its demand for an immediate transfer of power.

In December 1990 a group of candidates who had been elected to the Constituent Assembly fled to Manerplaw, on the Thai border, and announced a 'parallel government', the National Coalition Government of the Union of Burma (NCGUB), with the support of the Democratic Alliance of Burma (DAB), a broadly based organization uniting ethnic rebel forces with student dissidents and monks. The self-styled Prime Minister of the NCGUB was Sein Win, the leader of the Party for National Democracy (PND) and a cousin of Suu Kyi. The NLD leadership expelled members who had taken part in the formation of the 'parallel government', despite broad support within the NLD. The SLORC subsequently deregistered the PND, the LDP and two other parties and annulled the elected status of the eight members of the NCGUB. In April 1991 Gen. (later Senior Gen. or Field Marshal) Than Shwe, the Vice-Chairman of the SLORC and the Deputy Chief of Staff of the armed forces, officially announced that the SLORC would not transfer power to the Constituent Assembly, as the political parties involved were 'subversive' and 'unfit to rule'. In response to continued pressure from the SLORC, the NLD carried out a complete reorganization of the party's Central Executive Committee, replacing Suu Kyi as General Secretary with the previously unknown U Lwin, and Tin Oo with the former acting Chairman, Aung Shwe.

In July 1991 the SLORC retroactively amended electoral legislation adopted in May 1989, extending the grounds on which representatives of the Constituent Assembly could be disqualified or debarred from contesting future elections to include convictions for breaches of law and order. More than 80 elected representatives had already died, been imprisoned or been forced into exile since the election in May 1990. In September 1991 Ohn Gyaw was appointed Minister of Foreign Affairs in place of Saw Maung, becoming the first civilian in the Cabinet.

In October 1991 Suu Kyi was awarded the Nobel Peace Prize. In December Sein Win attended the presentation of the award to Suu Kyi's family in Norway. In Myanmar students who staged demonstrations (the first since 1989) to coincide with the ceremony were dispersed by security forces. It was subsequently announced that Suu Kyi and Tin Oo had been expelled from the NLD.

Three additional members were appointed to the SLORC in January 1992, and the Cabinet was expanded to include seven new ministers, four of whom were civilians. The changes, together with a reorganization of senior ministers in February, were perceived to benefit the Chief of Military Intelligence, Maj.-Gen. (later Lt-Gen.) Khin Nyunt (First Secretary of the SLORC). Khin Nyunt was widely regarded as the most powerful member of the SLORC, owing to Ne Win's continued patronage. Divisions within the ruling junta between Khin Nyunt and the more senior officers were becoming increasingly evident. In March Than Shwe replaced Saw Maung as Minister of Defence, and in April Saw Maung retired as Chairman of the SLORC and Prime Minister for reasons of ill health. Than Shwe was subsequently appointed to both these posts. The SLORC promptly ordered the release of several political prisoners, including U Nu, and announced that Suu Kyi could receive a visit from her family. In June the first meeting took place between members of the SLORC and opposition representatives from the remaining 10 legal parties, in preparation for the holding of a national convention to draft a new constitution.

In January 1993 the National Convention finally assembled, but was adjourned several times during the year, owing to the objections of the opposition members to SLORC demands for a leading role in government for the armed forces. Towards the end of the year the Chairman of the National Convention's Convening Committee, Aung Toe (the Chief Justice), announced (seemingly without grounds) that a consensus existed in favour of the SLORC's demands, which comprised: the inclusion, in both the lower and upper chambers of a proposed parliament, of military personnel (to be appointed by the Commander-in-Chief of the Armed Forces); the election of the President by an electoral college; the independent self-administration of the armed forces; and the right of the Commander-in-Chief to exercise state power in an emergency (effectively granting legitimate status to a future coup).

In September 1993 an alternative mass movement to the NUP (which had lost credibility through its election defeat in 1990) was formed to establish a civilian front through which the armed forces could exercise control. The Union Solidarity and Development Association (USDA), the aims of which were indistinguishable from those of the SLORC, was not officially registered as a political party, thus enabling civil servants to join the organization, with the incentive of considerable privileges.

In January 1994 the National Convention reconvened, and in April it was adjourned, having adopted guidelines for three significant chapters of the future Constitution. The changes envisaged Myanmar being renamed the Republic of the Union of Myanmar, comprising seven states (associated with some of the country's minority ethnic groups) and seven regions in central and southern Myanmar (largely representing the areas populated by the ethnic Bamars—Burmans). The Republic would be headed by an executive President, elected by the legislature for five years; proposals for the disqualification of any candidate with a foreign spouse or children would prevent Suu Kyi from entering any future presidential election. Reconvening in September, the Convention again stressed that the central role of the military (as 'permanent representatives of the people') be enshrined in the new Constitution. It was proposed that legislative power be shared between a bicameral Pyidaungsu Hluttaw (Union Assembly) and divisional and state assemblies, all of which were to include representatives of the military. The Pyidaungsu Hluttaw was to comprise the Pyithu Hluttaw (House of Representatives) and the Amyotha Hluttaw (House of Nationalities): the former would comprise 330 elected deputies and 110 members of the armed forces, and would be elected for five years. The latter would be composed of equal numbers of representatives from the proposed seven regions and seven states of the Republic, as well as members of the military, and was to comprise a maximum of 224 deputies. A general election was scheduled for September 1997 (but never held).

In September 1994, following mediation by a senior Buddhist monk, Suu Kyi was permitted to leave her home to meet Than Shwe and Khin Nyunt. In October Suu Kyi held a second meeting with senior SLORC members. In November it was reported that Suu Kyi had met other detained members of the NLD, including Tin Oo. In January 1995 the SLORC announced that Suu Kyi would be freed only when the new Constitution had been completed; Suu Kyi simultaneously rejected suggestions that she might reach a compromise with the SLORC on the terms for her release. In February leading members of the SLORC held talks in Yangon with an envoy of the UN Secretary-General. In March the Government released 31 political prisoners, including Tin Oo and Kyi Maung.

In July 1995 Suu Kyi was unexpectedly granted an unconditional release from house arrest, whereupon she made a conciliatory speech, urging negotiations with the SLORC and a spirit of compromise. Suu Kyi swiftly reconciled the early leaders of the NLD with the new leadership, which had compromised with the SLORC. Hundreds of supporters gathered daily to hear Suu Kyi speak outside her house in Yangon. Suu Kyi was reinstated as General Secretary of the NLD in October, in a reorganization of the party's executive committee; Tin Oo and Kyi Maung were named Vice-Chairmen. Aung Shwe, who had led the 'legal' NLD and represented the party at the National Convention, was retained as party Chairman. Meanwhile, in August Win Htein, Suu Kyi's personal assistant, was arrested and sentenced to seven years' imprisonment (subsequently doubled) for allegedly conspiring with groups in India to destabilize the country.

In November 1995 the National Convention reconvened. The NLD attended the opening session, but later withdrew when the SLORC ignored its requests to expand the Convention to make it truly representative. Denouncing the Convention as illegitimate and undemocratic, the NLD for the first time appealed for international support for its cause. The SLORC, which had already begun to imprison NLD supporters for petty crimes, reacted strongly to the NLD boycott, officially expelling the party from the Convention.

In May 1996 more than 260 members of the NLD (mostly delegates elected to the Constituent Assembly in 1990) were arrested prior to the party's first congress. The majority were detained for the duration of the congress, which only 18 NLD members were able to attend. The congress resolved to draft an alternative constitution. In June the SLORC intensified its action against the NLD with an order banning any organization that held illegal gatherings or obstructed the drafting of the new Constitution by the National Convention; members of a pro-

scribed party could be liable to between five and 20 years' imprisonment. In September police erected road-blocks around Suu Kyi's house, and again detained NLD activists, in order to prevent the holding of a further congress. Suu Kyi's telephone line was disconnected, and she was unable to deliver her regular weekend speech for the first time since her release from house arrest. From October the road-block was set up each week to prevent access to Suu Kyi's speech. The SLORC recommenced talks with NLD officials later that month, but relations quickly deteriorated following an attack on vehicles in which Suu Kyi and other NLD leaders were travelling.

In October 1996 student action in Yangon, in protest against the detention and brutal treatment of fellow students, prompted further repression and numerous arrests (among those detained was Kyi Maung). This was followed in early December by the largest pro-democracy demonstration since 1988, involving more than 2,000 students. The gathering was dispersed peacefully, although some 600 demonstrators were temporarily detained. Smaller student demonstrations continued sporadically until mid-December, when Suu Kyi was briefly confined to her home, and tanks were deployed in Yangon; university establishments were closed indefinitely. At the end of December 1996 some 50 members of the Communist Party of Burma (CPB) and of the NLD were arrested in connection with the protests.

In January 1997 Suu Kyi was allowed to deliver her weekly speech for the first time in three months. However, the SLORC imposed new restrictions on media access to Suu Kyi, and barricades remained outside her home. In March a series of attacks on Muslim targets by Buddhist monks took place across the country. The attacks were rumoured to have been perpetrated by opponents within the regime of Myanmar's bid to join the Association of Southeast Asian Nations (ASEAN, see p. 218), in an attempt to alienate the organization's Muslim-dominated countries.

In April 1997 a bomb attack at the home of the Second Secretary of the SLORC, Lt-Gen. Tin Oo (as distinct from Tin Oo of the NLD), resulted in the death of his daughter. The Government attributed the bombing to anti-Government groups based in Japan. The attack was rumoured to be related to a power struggle between Khin Nyunt, who was increasingly regarded as a moderate, and the more conservative Commander-in-Chief of the Army and Vice-Chairman of the SLORC, Gen. Maung Aye, who commanded the support of Tin Oo. The detention of NLD members increased during 1997, while government propaganda vilifying the opposition grew more frequent and Suu Kyi's freedom of movement and association remained restricted. In July, however, Khin Nyunt invited the NLD Chairman, Aung Shwe, to a meeting, which constituted the first senior-level contact between the SLORC and the NLD since the release of Suu Kyi from house arrest in July 1995. The SLORC granted permission for an NLD congress to be held in September 1997.

The State Peace and Development Council

On 15 November 1997 the ruling junta unexpectedly announced the dissolution of the SLORC and its replacement with the State Peace and Development Council (SPDC). The 19-member SPDC comprised exclusively military personnel; the four most senior members of the SLORC retained their positions at the head of the new junta: Than Shwe was appointed Chairman, Maung Aye Vice-Chairman, Khin Nyunt First Secretary and Tin Oo Second Secretary. A number of former members of the SLORC were ostensibly promoted to an 'Advisory Group', which was subsequently abolished; five members of this group, who had also held positions in the Cabinet, were placed under house arrest in December, pending investigations into allegations of corruption. The SPDC immediately implemented a reorganization of the Cabinet. The new 40-member Cabinet included 25 former ministers, but, in contrast to the SLORC (the members of which had virtually all held cabinet portfolios), only one member of the SPDC, Than Shwe, was appointed to serve concurrently as a cabinet minister. In December the SPDC announced a further cabinet reorganization and the appointment of a new Chairman (the Minister of Hotels and Tourism, Maj.-Gen. Saw Lwin) and Vice-Chairmen of the National Convention Convening Commission; however, the Convention, which had adjourned in March 1996, remained in recess.

Harassment and persecution of members of the NLD and other opposition movements continued. In March 1998 40 people were arrested on charges of complicity in a conspiracy allegedly led by the exiled All-Burma Students Democratic Front (ABSDF, an armed movement formed in 1988 by students within the DAB, which had officially renounced its armed struggle in 1997) to assassinate leaders of the military junta and perpetrate terrorist attacks on government offices and foreign embassies. The ABSDF, which rejected the allegations, was accused of complicity with the NLD. Six of the accused were sentenced to death in April 1998. However, the SPDC unexpectedly authorized an NLD party congress, attended by 400 delegates, in May to celebrate the eighth anniversary of the general election. In June the NLD demanded that the SPDC reconvene the Pyithu Hluttaw, in accordance with the results of the 1990 election, by 21 August. Some 40 elected NLD representatives were detained at the end of June, and others were forced to sign pledges restricting their freedom of movement. In July the SPDC ordered NLD elected representatives to report to their local police station twice a day and confined them to their townships. Suu Kyi attempted to visit NLD members outside the city, but was repeatedly obstructed by road-blocks. She was forcibly returned to her home by security personnel after a six-day protest in her car in July, following government refusals to comply with her demands for the release of detained opposition members and the commencement of substantive dialogue with the NLD. In a further incident, in August, Suu Kyi was returned to her home by ambulance after spending 13 days in her car.

Shortly before the NLD's prescribed deadline of 21 August 1998 for convening the Pyithu Hluttaw, the SPDC published an official rejection of the NLD's demands. The NLD responded by declaring its intention unilaterally to convene a 'People's Parliament', which would include elected representatives of all the ethnic minority groups. Student demonstrations took place in Yangon (for the first time since December 1996), in support of the NLD's demands. In September 1998 thousands of students staged anti-Government demonstrations, which were dispersed by security forces. Arrests of opposition activists increased dramatically, and by early September 193 elected NLD members of the Pyithu Hluttaw and hundreds of party supporters had been detained. In the same month a 10-member Representative Committee, led by Suu Kyi and Aung Shwe, was established by the NLD to act on behalf of the 'People's Parliament' until a legislature could be convened under the 1990 election law. The Committee asserted that no laws enacted by the military junta over the previous 10 years had legal authority, and also demanded the immediate and unconditional release of all political prisoners. Four parties representing Shan, Mon, Arakanese and Zomi ethnic groups expressed their support for the 'People's Parliament', together with the ABSDF. Also in September 1998, 15 senior military officers were reportedly arrested for allegedly planning to meet with Suu Kyi, and a number of large pro-Government rallies were held in Yangon. The NLD condemned the alleged use of coercion, intimidation and threats by government military intelligence units to secure the involuntary resignations of vast numbers of NLD members and the closure of a number of regional party headquarters. Following the death in custody in October of one of its members, the NLD formally denounced the junta's treatment of detained opposition party members in a letter to Than Shwe. In the same month UN Assistant Secretary-General Alvaro de Soto met with SPDC leaders and also with Suu Kyi during a visit to Myanmar. He reportedly offered large-scale financial and humanitarian aid to the junta in exchange for the initiation of substantive dialogue with the NLD. During October and November about 300 opposition members were released by the Government; however, a further 500 were believed to remain in detention.

In March 1999, despite requests from several foreign Governments, the ruling junta refused to grant a visa to Suu Kyi's terminally ill husband, Michael Aris. The junta instead encouraged Suu Kyi to visit Aris in the United Kingdom; however, Suu Kyi declined to leave Myanmar for fear that she would not be allowed to return. Following Aris's death later that month, more than 1,000 supporters of Suu Kyi were permitted to attend a Buddhist ceremony at her home to mark her husband's demise. In April 1999 the UN adopted a unanimous resolution deploring the escalation in the persecution of the democratic opposition in Myanmar. Nevertheless, the harassment and intimidation of NLD members continued, and several hundred members were reported to have been forced to resign from the party over the course of the year. In August a series of protests was staged by opposition supporters to mark the anniversary of the massacre of thousands of pro-democracy demonstrators by the military Government in 1988. In October 1999 the Supreme Court rejected a claim by the NLD that its activities had been 'continuously disrupted, prevented and destroyed' and that hundreds of its members had been illegally detained.

In August 2000 Suu Kyi and 14 NLD colleagues attempted to visit members of the party in Kunyangon, a town just outside Yangon. The group was stopped by a military road-block, but refused to return home. A nine-day confrontation finally ended with Suu Kyi and her party colleagues being forcibly returned to Yangon. Suu Kyi and eight others were kept under house arrest for the next two weeks. Undeterred, the NLD announced in September that it was to draft a new constitution for the country, an act declared illegal in 1996 and punishable by 20 years' imprisonment. Later in the month Suu Kyi attempted to leave Yangon again, this time by train to Mandalay, only to be told that all trains were full. The NLD leader was once again returned home and placed under house arrest, while NLD Vice-Chairman Tin Oo and eight other party workers were taken to a government 'guest house'. Pressure on the NLD increased in October 2000, when a deadline for an eviction order for the party to vacate its headquarters expired.

Despite the sustained suppression of the opposition party, Razali Ismail, the newly appointed UN Secretary-General's Special Envoy to Myanmar, was allowed access to Suu Kyi during a four-day visit in October 2000. A degree of conciliation between the SPDC and the NLD was confirmed in January 2001, when it was announced that the two parties had been holding secret talks since the previous October, the first senior-level discussions between the opponents since 1994. Lt-Gen. Khin Nyunt met with Suu Kyi several times. At the end of January 2001 the SPDC released NLD Vice-Chairman Tin Oo and 84 other party supporters, who had been detained since Suu Kyi's attempted train journey in September 2000. A few days later a delegation of the European Union (EU, see p. 281) was permitted to meet with Suu Kyi, as was the UN Special Rapporteur on the situation of human rights in Myanmar, Dr Paulo Sérgio Pinheiro, in April 2001.

A bomb explosion in May 2001 reportedly killed 12 people and injured eight others in a market in Mandalay. In the same month it was reported that religious riots in Toungoo, Bago Division, had led to the deaths of 24 Buddhist monks. The disturbances spread to other towns, prompting allegations that the SPDC had instigated the riots in an attempt to divert public attention from political and economic problems.

In February 2001 SPDC Second Secretary Lt-Gen. Tin Oo, the Council's fourth most powerful member, was killed in a helicopter crash, amid rumours of assassination. In November SPDC Third Secretary Lt-Gen. Win Myint and Deputy Prime Minister Tin Hla were dismissed, and two days later the SPDC announced that five government ministers were to retire, including two other Deputy Prime Ministers. Meanwhile, in mid-2001, as conciliatory discussions continued, the Government ordered the release of a number of NLD members from prison and permitted the reopening of the NLD headquarters in Yangon. In August the release of NLD Chairman Aung Shwe and Vice-Chairman Tin Oo was hailed as an indication of progress. Shortly afterwards Razali Ismail held further talks with Suu Kyi during a visit to Yangon. Ismail revisited the country in November, and expressed satisfaction with the progress that had been made.

In January 2002 it was reported that Suu Kyi had met privately with Gen. Than Shwe for the first time since 1994, raising hopes that the two sides might be close to reaching a breakthrough. In March 2002 the son-in-law and three grandsons of Ne Win were arrested on charges of plotting to overthrow the Government. It was alleged that they had intended to abduct three government leaders and force them to form a figurehead government under Ne Win's influence. Four senior military officials—the Commander-in-Chief of the Air Force, Maj.-Gen. Myint Swe, the Chief of Police, Maj.-Gen. Soe Win, and two regional commanders—were dismissed and questioned in connection with the attempted coup. Ne Win and his daughter, Sandar Win, were placed under house arrest. Despite suspicions that the coup allegations were linked to internal conflicts within the military, owing to the insubstantial nature of the evidence gathered to support the charges, in September Ne Win's four relatives were convicted of high treason and sentenced to death. In December Ne Win himself died while under house arrest.

In May 2002 Suu Kyi was released from house arrest. The SPDC stated that her release was unconditional and that it would not attempt to impose any restrictions upon her travel. Suu Kyi travelled to Mandalay without incident in June. An EU delegation visited Myanmar in September and met with Suu Kyi. In November the junta announced the release of 115 prisoners, the largest number to date. In early 2003 representatives from the human rights organization Amnesty International were permitted to enter Myanmar for the first time and to hold talks with Suu Kyi. In February it was reported that Suu Kyi wanted existing economic sanctions to be upheld against the Myanma Government until it began a meaningful dialogue with the opposition. In the same month it was announced that Lt-Gen. Soe Win would assume the still vacant post of Second Secretary of the SPDC. In March Paulo Sérgio Pinheiro restated a UN demand that the junta release all remaining political prisoners, estimated to number 1,200, and enter into serious dialogue with the opposition.

In April 2003 Suu Kyi issued a rare public criticism of the SPDC for refusing to enter into any substantive dialogue with the opposition. In May the political situation deteriorated further when violent confrontations took place in the northern town of Ye-u, between government supporters and opposition members travelling with an entourage conveying Suu Kyi. While the SPDC insisted that the violence had been provoked by the opposition, it was subsequently reported that Suu Kyi and her supporters had been ambushed and attacked by pro-Government forces. Around 80 members of the entourage were believed to have been killed. On the following day it was reported that Suu Kyi had been taken into 'protective custody' by the SPDC; meanwhile, the headquarters of the NLD, together with NLD offices across the country, were closed down, and all universities under the control of the Ministry of Education were shut indefinitely. Razali Ismail proceeded with a planned visit to Myanmar in June, when he was permitted to meet with Suu Kyi. The junta's detention of Suu Kyi prompted widespread international criticism. At a meeting of ASEAN ministers of foreign affairs held in mid-June the organization departed from its traditional policy of non-interference in the affairs of other member states, urging Suu Kyi's release and a peaceful transition to democracy. Later in June, following the failure of its appeal to the SPDC for the release of Suu Kyi, the country's largest aid donor, Japan, suspended all economic aid to Myanmar. In July the Government announced that it had freed 91 of the NLD activists detained after the violence of May and permitted a delegation from the International Committee of the Red Cross (ICRC) to visit Suu Kyi; the delegates subsequently confirmed that she was in good health.

In July 2003 it was reported that three cabinet ministers, including Minister of Industry (No. 1) Aung Thaung, had been dismissed. In August a major reorganization of the Government was announced, in which the former First Secretary of the SPDC, Lt-Gen. Khin Nyunt, replaced Senior-Gen. Than Shwe as Prime Minister. However, Than Shwe remained Chairman of the SPDC and retained the defence portfolio. Lt-Gen. Soe Win became First Secretary and was replaced as Second Secretary by Lt-Gen. Thein Sein.

In September 2003 it was announced that Suu Kyi had returned to her home and was being held under house arrest, having undergone major surgery in hospital. In November five members of the NLD's Central Executive Committee, who had been held in connection with the violence in May, were released. In December nine people were sentenced to death, having been convicted of high treason; they were among 12 people arrested in July for allegedly plotting to overthrow the ruling junta. (All nine of the death sentences were subsequently commuted to lesser sentences on appeal.) In January 2004 the release of a further 26 members of the NLD was announced; in February NLD Vice-Chairman Tin Oo was placed under house arrest, having been imprisoned since May 2003. Also in January 2004, following a meeting with government officials, representatives from 25 ethnic groups and alliances rejected the proposed 'road map' to democracy outlined by the Prime Minister in August 2003 and reiterated demands for the Government to begin talks with the opposition. In April 2004 the SPDC released the NLD's Chairman, Aung Shwe, and its Secretary, U Lwin, who had both been under house arrest since May 2003, and allowed the party's headquarters to reopen.

The National Convention (which had been in recess since 1996) was reconvened in May 2004, despite a boycott by some ethnic minority groups and the NLD. More than 1,000 delegates attended the opening session, which was chaired by SPDC Second Secretary Lt-Gen. Thein Sein. It was stressed that the Convention was to be a continuation of the discussions held between 1993 and 1996, at which a number of constitutional provisions had already been drafted. The Convention was adjourned in July 2004. In August courts in Yangon and Mandalay refused to accept petitions from the NLD for the release of Suu Kyi and Tin Oo, and for the reopening of the party's branch offices. Shortly afterwards the UN Secretary-General, Kofi Annan, urged the Myanma Government to free Suu Kyi and to hold substantive talks with the NLD and other political parties, noting that the National Convention would otherwise lack credibility.

In September 2004 the civilian Minister of Foreign Affairs, Win Aung, and his deputy, Khin Maung Win, were replaced by senior military officers, Maj.-Gen. Nyan Win and Col Maung Myint, respectively. Amid reports of a power struggle within the SPDC, Khin Nyunt was removed from the premiership and from his position as Chief of Military Intelligence in October, and was placed under house arrest, apparently owing to his alleged involvement in smuggling by military intelligence staff. Lt-Gen. Soe Win was appointed as Prime Minister, while Lt-Gen. Thein Sein replaced Soe Win as First Secretary of the SPDC. The National Intelligence Bureau was abolished, and many associates of Khin Nyunt were subsequently arrested. In November it was reported that three senior military intelligence officers had been convicted of corruption charges and sentenced to 22 years' imprisonment, and that 12 senior judicial officials, who were either linked to Khin Nyunt or had resisted the removal of those loyal to the former Prime Minister, had been dismissed.

In November 2004 the SPDC ordered the release of 9,248 prisoners who, it claimed, had been wrongly imprisoned by the dissolved National Intelligence Bureau. However, according to the opposition, the mass amnesty included only 43 political prisoners. In December the SPDC freed a further 5,070 prisoners, 11 of whom were reported to be political prisoners, including the Chairman of the Democracy Party, Thu Wai. In January 2005 speculation about tension within the leadership continued. In the same month it was reported that four associates of Khin Nyunt who had been arrested in October 2004 had died in detention, while the closed trials of some 300 others on corruption charges had commenced in a prison in Yangon. The National Convention resumed in February 2005, again without the participation of the NLD and several ethnic minority groups, amid criticism from the EU, the UN and the USA. Meanwhile, the detention under house arrest of both Suu Kyi and Tin Oo was extended for a further year.

In July 2005 Khin Nyunt was convicted on eight charges, including corruption and bribery, and was given a suspended prison sentence of 44 years. In the same month the Government authorized the release of dozens of political prisoners; however, approximately 1,100 dissidents were believed to remain in detention in Myanmar at that time.

In November 2005 the Government announced that it had initiated the first phase of a relocation of the country's administrative capital from Yangon to Pyinmana, a sparsely populated mountainous region about 400 km (nearly 250 miles) to the north of Yangon. According to a government statement, the decision to move to Pyinmana had been made owing to its central location and resultant ease of access to and from other parts of the country. The new administrative centre was officially named Nay Pyi Taw in March 2006. Also in November 2005 the NLD announced that Suu Kyi's detention under house arrest had again been extended for a further year.

Having being refused access to the country for almost two years, Razali Ismail resigned as the UN Secretary-General's Special Envoy to Myanmar in January 2006. Later that month the SPDC adjourned a session of the National Convention, with a view to reconvening towards the end of the year. In April former Minister of Foreign Affairs Win Aung was convicted on corruption and bribery charges, and sentenced to seven years' imprisonment. Meanwhile, in February the detention under house arrest of Tin Oo was again extended by a further year. In May UN envoy Ibrahim Gambari was permitted to enter the country, whereupon he held discussions with Than Shwe and briefly met with Suu Kyi. Later in the month UN Secretary-General Kofi Annan urged Than Shwe to free Suu Kyi; on the following day, however, her term of house arrest was extended for a further year. In September the UN Security Council reviewed the human rights situation in Myanmar for the first time. Gambari paid a second visit to Myanmar in November and was again allowed to hold a brief meeting with Suu Kyi. In January 2007 a draft resolution urging the Myanma Government to release all political prisoners and end its violation of human rights was submitted to the UN Security Council, sponsored by the USA and the United Kingdom. However, the resolution was defeated when the People's Republic of China and Russia, two of the five permanent members of the Security Council, exercised their right of veto.

Meanwhile, in April 2006 the ABSDF, the Federation of Trade Unions—Burma (FTUB), the NCGUB and the National League for Democracy—Liberated Area (NLD—LA) were denounced as terrorist organizations by the Government, in relation to a series of bomb attacks and attempted bombings in 2000–06. The admission of the foreign press to the proceedings of the reconvened National Convention in October 2006 represented progress to some observers, but the absence of the NLD and the relatively small number of delegates from other political parties did not bode well for democratic reform. In January 2007 it was reported that the SPDC had released 2,831 prisoners in an amnesty to mark Independence Day, although only 30 were political prisoners. The detention under house arrest of Tin Oo was extended for a further year in February, as was that of Suu Kyi in May, despite ongoing international pressure for their release.

In May 2007 Lt-Gen. Thein Sein, the First Secretary of the SPDC, assumed the role of Prime Minister in an acting capacity, amid conjecture about Lt-Gen. Soe Win's health. During the final session of the National Convention, in July–September, detailed principles for a new constitution were adopted; a 54-member commission, chaired by Chief Justice Aung Toe, was appointed by the SPDC in October to draft the new Constitution and commenced work in December without the participation of the opposition.

The protests of September 2007

Substantial unexpected increases in fuel prices in August 2007 provoked a series of anti-Government protests in Yangon and other towns. More than 60 demonstrators had been arrested by the end of the month, including leaders of the '88 Generation' students' group who had participated in the 1988 pro-democracy uprising. The protests escalated in September 2007 with the involvement of Buddhist monks. During two days of demonstrations in Pakokku, in central Myanmar, monks held some 20 government officials captive for several hours after the security forces had forcibly dispersed some 300–400 monks, detaining around 10 and injuring several. The Alliance of All Burmese Buddhist Monks, a previously unknown group, made a series of demands to the SPDC—an apology for the force used in Pakokku, a reduction in commodity and fuel prices, the release of all political prisoners and those detained for participating in the recent protests, and the initiation of a dialogue with pro-democracy forces—threatening to withdraw all religious services from the authorities if they did not comply by 17 September. The SPDC accused the NLD and 'external groups' of instigating the unrest. Some of the marches were allowed to proceed peacefully, but tear gas was used to disperse a rally of some 1,000 monks and other citizens in the western town of Sittwe. Meanwhile, with the monks' demands unfulfilled, daily marches commenced in Yangon. The Alliance of All Burmese Buddhist Monks issued a statement describing the military Government as 'the enemy of the people' and pledging to continue protesting until the Government was removed from office. On the sixth consecutive day of demonstrations in Yangon, Suu Kyi made a brief public appearance when the monks were permitted to pass her residence. On the same day up to 10,000 monks were reported to have marched in Mandalay. Around 150 Buddhist nuns joined some 5,000 monks in Yangon, and a mass protest in the capital was attended by an estimated 50,000–100,000 monks and civilians, including NLD leaders, while demonstrations also took place in more than 20 other towns.

The SPDC imposed a night-time curfew in Yangon and Mandalay, banned gatherings of more than five people and deployed armed troops on the streets. When up to 10,000 monks and other protesters defied government warnings to halt the marches, troops fired live ammunition, reportedly killing five people. Some 200 monks were later reported to have been detained in overnight operations against several monasteries, during which many were allegedly beaten. The Government claimed that 10 people had died in the violence (later raising this figure to 15), but diplomats and witnesses reported that the death toll was much higher, with some estimating that up to 200 had been killed. The UN Security Council expressed concern at the situation in an emergency meeting, but China, Myanmar's closest ally, rejected a US proposal to consider the imposition of sanctions against the Myanma authorities. By the end of the month the uprising had been largely quashed, with many monks in detention. During October the security forces continued to arrest those suspected of involvement in the street protests, and reports emerged of ill-treatment in detention centres, including claims that an NLD member had died as a result of being tortured in custody. In December the UN Special Rapporteur on the situation of human rights in Myanmar, Paulo Sérgio Pinheiro, reported that at least 31 people had died during the unrest and that 3,000–4,000 people had been arrested in September and October, 500–1,000 of whom were still in detention; according to the security forces, only 80 people, including 21 monks, remained in custody at this time. Meanwhile, the curfew in Yangon and Mandalay was removed.

UN envoy Ibrahim Gambari visited Myanmar in late September 2007, initially holding discussions with acting Prime Minister Thein Sein and other government ministers, as well as with Suu Kyi, and in early October he was finally permitted to meet Than Shwe and Maung Aye. The SPDC agreed to Gambari's recommendation that a government official be appointed to enter into dialogue with Suu Kyi, assigning this role (Minister of Relations with Aung San Suu Kyi) to the Deputy Minister of Labour, Aung Kyi. In mid-October the UN Security Council unanimously adopted a statement deploring the use of violence against peaceful demonstrators in Myanmar, and calling for the early release of all political prisoners and remaining detainees.

Thein Sein was formally appointed Prime Minister in October 2007, following Soe Win's death earlier that month, and was replaced as First Secretary of the SPDC by Lt-Gen. Thiha Thura Tin Aung Myint Oo. At the same time Aung Kyi was promoted to the position of Minister of Labour, while retaining responsibility for liaising with Suu Kyi. On the following day Aung Kyi and Suu Kyi held their first talks.

In early November 2007 the Myanma Government announced the expulsion of Charles Petrie, the most senior UN official resident in the country. Petrie had recently publicly linked the pro-democracy protests to economic hardship and a 'deteriorating humanitarian situation'. Shortly afterwards Gambari arrived for a further visit, during which he held discussions with Thein Sein and Suu Kyi, although not with Than Shwe. It was reported by the Myanma state media that the SPDC had rejected an offer by Gambari to mediate in the dialogue between Suu Kyi and Aung Kyi. However, following the visit, Gambari issued a statement on behalf of Suu Kyi, in which she declared her willingness to co-operate with the SPDC 'in the interest of the nation'. A second meeting subsequently took place between Aung Kyi and Suu Kyi, who was also permitted to meet other members of the NLD for the first time in more than three years. In December the Government announced that it had granted amnesty to 8,585 prisoners since mid-November to mark the conclusion of the National Convention, although it was reported that only 10 were political detainees. Suu Kyi held two rounds of talks with Aung Kyi in January 2008, and was also permitted to meet NLD colleagues again at the end of the month. Meanwhile, in mid-January the UN Security Council expressed regret at the slow rate of progress towards meeting the objectives outlined in its statement of October 2007 (i.e. the release of political prisoners and meaningful dialogue with Suu Kyi), and urged Myanmar to allow another visit by Gambari. In late January 2008 Amnesty International claimed that 96 pro-democracy activists had been arrested since November 2007, increasing the total number in detention to 1,850, of whom 700 were accused of participating in the August and September protests.

In February 2008 the SPDC unexpectedly announced that a constitutional referendum would be held in May, followed by multi-party elections in 2010. Chief Justice Aung Toe subsequently confirmed that his commission had completed the draft constitution. A few days later the detention under house arrest of Tin Oo was again extended by a further year; Suu Kyi's house arrest was similarly extended in May. Ibrahim Gambari returned to Myanmar in March 2008, meeting Suu Kyi and several government officials. However, no apparent progress was made during the visit, with the Government rejecting Gambari's proposal that independent observers be allowed to monitor the forthcoming referendum and refusing to consider amending the draft constitution to allow Suu Kyi to contest elections. Suu Kyi reportedly refused to meet with Gambari during the envoy's visit to Myanmar in August, arousing speculation about her dissatisfaction with the pace of developments. The newly appointed UN Special Rapporteur on the situation of human rights in Myanmar, Tomás Ojea Quintana, also paid a visit in that month.

In May 2008 the devastating Cyclone Nargis struck southern Myanmar. Yangon and four other regions, including the Ayeyarwady (Irrawaddy) Delta, were declared disaster areas. The Government's restrictions on international aid efforts exacerbated the difficulties confronting the survivors, many of whom had no access to clean drinking water, food or shelter. Although some provisions supplied by the UN and foreign donors were eventually allowed into the country, the Government continued to refuse entry to foreign aid workers and Ban Ki-Moon criticized the Government's reaction to the disaster as 'unacceptably slow'. By late June the official death toll had risen to more than 84,500. However, the ICRC reckoned that the number of fatalities might be as high as 128,000, while the UN estimated that 2.5m. people had been affected by the cyclone.

Meanwhile, the text of the draft constitution, which was published in April 2008, included the changing of the country's official name to the 'Republic of the Union of Myanmar'. Also enshrined in the draft was the ultimate establishment of a multi-party democracy. Nevertheless, as proposed in the 1994 sessions of the National Convention, legislative power was to be vested in a bicameral Pyidaungsu Hluttaw, comprising the Pyithu Hluttaw (lower house) and the Amyotha Hluttaw (upper house), with 25% of the seats to be allocated to representatives of the military nominated by the Commander-in-Chief of the Armed Forces. Furthermore, the Commander-in-Chief of the Armed Forces was to designate the government ministers responsible for defence, security, home affairs and border affairs, and was to assume executive, legislative and judicial power in the event of a state of emergency being declared, while Suu Kyi's marriage to a foreign citizen would disqualify her from contesting elections. Despite the widespread destruction caused by Cyclone Nargis, which prompted the Government to postpone the constitutional referendum in the affected regions, the poll proceeded as scheduled in other areas on 10 May 2008. According to official reports, turn-out was high, at 99%, with 92.4% of voters endorsing the new Constitution, thereby completing the ratification process; observers remained sceptical.

In August 2008, on the 20th anniversary of the 1988 pro-democracy uprising, several protesters were arrested in Taunggok. Tensions rose in Yangon and surrounding areas as the anniversary of the September 2007 protests approached, with bomb explosions resulting in several fatalities in September 2008. Also in September, the junta announced a large-scale amnesty involving as many as 9,000 detainees. Among those released was Win Tin, a senior political activist and founding member of the NLD who had been imprisoned for 19 years; however, in October Ohn Kyaing, another veteran NLD member, was detained. This was followed by the culmination of dozens of trials that had begun in July, with the sentencing of more than 100 activists and dissidents in November. Many defendants received substantial prison terms, some as long as 65 years. Those convicted included senior members of the '88 Generation', the NLD and monks' groups who were accused of involvement in the September 2007 uprising.

In May 2009, shortly before her term of house arrest was due to expire, Suu Kyi was taken to Insein Prison, following an unauthorized visit to her home by an uninvited US citizen, John Yettaw, who had gained access by swimming across the adjacent lake. She was tried on charges of violating the conditions of her house arrest, and in August was convicted and sentenced to three years' imprisonment with hard labour, although this was commuted to 18 months' house arrest. The verdict was widely criticized by the international community. Yettaw, meanwhile, was sentenced to seven years' imprisonment, including four years' hard labour; however, he was subsequently released and allowed to return to the USA, following negotiations between Than Shwe and US Senator Jim Webb—the first time that a senior US official had been allowed to meet with the reclusive Myanma leader. Webb was also granted rare access to Suu Kyi, whose supporters claimed that the Yettaw incident had been exploited by the military junta as a pretext for further prolonging the opposition leader's detention. Opposition leader Tin Oo was finally released from house arrest in February 2010.

The 2010 legislative elections

In March 2010 the junta approved new electoral laws in advance of the forthcoming legislative elections, which, *inter alia*, prohibited anyone with a criminal conviction from belonging to a political party, a rule that was widely interpreted as being intended to force the NLD to expel Suu Kyi from its ranks; Suu Kyi was already barred from standing for political office by the new Constitution. The junta formally annulled the NLD's victory in the 1990 general election, stating that the result was invalid since the poll had been conducted under legislation repealed by the newly enacted laws. Divisions emerged within the NLD regarding whether the party should expel Suu Kyi, Tin

Oo and other members with criminal convictions in order to be able to contest the elections. Despite some members contending that the NLD's absence from the polling would effectively lead to a one-party political system in which the policies of the military junta would remain unchecked, at the end of March the NLD announced that it would not be registering for the elections, a decision that served severely to compromise the credibility of the poll from the perspective of the international community.

In April 2010 about 20 senior members of the ruling junta, including Prime Minister Thein Sein, resigned from their military positions in what was widely interpreted as a move to circumvent the restriction, to 25% of the total, of the number of legislative seats that were to be allocated to representatives of the military in the forthcoming elections. Thein Sein applied to register a new political party, the Union Solidarity and Development Party (USDP), which was headed by the premier.

In July 2010 it was announced that the USDA, the mass movement formed in September 1993 to establish a civilian front through which the armed forces could exercise control, had disbanded and that its assets had been transferred to the USDP, prompting widespread criticism from critics of the Government, who argued that the assets belonged to the State and that their transfer to the USDP afforded the party an unfair advantage. Also in July 2010 Suu Kyi's former assistant, Win Htein, was released from prison, having served his sentence of 14 years' imprisonment for conspiracy to destabilize the country.

A date for the elections was finally announced by the junta in August 2010: the first legislative poll in 20 years was to be held on 7 November, one week prior to the scheduled expiry of the detention under house arrest of Suu Kyi. In September the Union Election Commission (UEC—created in March and chaired by a retired army major-general, Thein Soe) announced that 37 parties had successfully registered to participate in the forthcoming elections. Not unexpectedly, the USDP was among those approved, as were the NUP (which had contested the 1990 elections) and the National Democratic Force (a splinter group established in April by a group of 25 former NLD members who did wish to participate in the elections and chaired by Than Nyein); many of the remainder were small, ethnic-based parties contesting a limited number of regional seats. The UEC also announced the formal dissolution of 10 parties, five of which had been dissolved owing to non-registration, including the NLD (the first public confirmation of its suspected dissolution), the Shan Nationalities League for Democracy, which had also performed well in the 1990 elections, and the Union Pa-O National Organization; the remaining five (predominantly ethnic-based) parties were disbanded owing to their alleged non-compliance with regulations governing the registration of candidates. The application of the Kachin State Progressive Party (KSPP) to register for the polls was rejected by the UEC on the grounds that the KSPP was allegedly affiliated to the Kachin Independence Organization (see Insurgency and Dissidence), and the applications of 14 KSPP members who had applied to contest the elections as individuals were also rejected. Also in mid-September the UEC announced the cancellation of voting in about 300 villages across five states that were deemed to be 'troubled', claiming that voting in those areas would not be free or fair; at least 1.5m. people were thus excluded from voting, leading to speculation that the SPDC was endeavouring to disenfranchise Myanmar's ethnic population.

Strict campaigning restrictions governed the official electoral campaign period, which began on 25 September 2010. Registered parties were each granted 15 minutes of broadcasting time in which to make known their electoral platforms on state television and radio (although full scripts were required to be submitted to the UEC for prior approval). In October the SPDC announced the introduction of a new national flag and anthem, and changed the country's official name from the Union of Myanmar to the Republic of the Union of Myanmar, in accordance with the provisions of the 2008 Constitution.

The elections to both chambers of the Pyidaungsu Hluttaw, and to 14 state and regional assemblies, were held, as scheduled, on 7 November 2010. A total of 3,069 candidates from the 37 registered parties contested more than 1,100 seats. There were widespread allegations of voting irregularities committed by supporters of the USDP. The UEC subsequently claimed that voter turn-out had totalled 77% of the electorate; however, many independent sources suggested that the actual figure was considerably lower than this, with some claiming a turn-out of only 30%. According to official results released by the UEC on 17 November, the USDP secured 259 seats of the 330 contested seats in the 440-member Pyithu Hluttaw; the USDP's closest rival, the Shan Nationalities Democratic Party (SNDP), won just 18, while the NUP garnered 12, the Rakhine Nationalities Development Party (RNDP) nine and the National Democratic Force won eight. Other, mostly ethnic-based, parties collectively accounted for a further 19 seats, with one seat won by an independent; the four remaining seats were unfilled at this time. There was a similar pattern evident in the electoral results for the Amyotha Hluttaw, as well as for the seven state and seven regional assemblies. Of the 168 contested seats in the Amyotha Hluttaw, the USDP won 129 seats; the RNDP took seven and the NUP five, while the National Democratic Force, the All Mon Region Democracy Party (AMRDP) and the Chin Progressive Party each won four seats, and the SNDP and the Phalon-Sawaw Democratic Party obtained three seats each. In total, the USDP took 882 of the 1,154 contested seats, while the second-placed NUP won 63. The National Democratic Force was placed joint sixth overall—tied with the AMRDP—with just 16 seats, and Chairman Than Nyein denounced the elections as 'absolutely not free and fair'. Many losing opposition candidates subsequently claimed that the UEC-sanctioned procedures to file a challenge against the results, including a substantial payment for each individual challenge, were designed to confuse and discourage would-be complainants.

On 13 November 2010, two days after her (largely symbolic) final appeal against her detention under house arrest had been rejected, Suu Kyi was finally released, her latest detention order having expired. Thousands of supporters gathered outside the NLD party headquarters in Yangon to hear Suu Kyi's first public address since her release. At a press conference, which foreign journalists were allowed to attend, Suu Kyi questioned the legitimacy of the recent elections. The dissolution of the NLD was upheld on appeal by the Supreme Court in January 2011. Meanwhile, in November 2010 new legislation was introduced allowing the Government to draft men (between the ages of 18 and 45) and women (between the ages of 18 and 35) into the armed forces for a period of two to three years, or for five years during times of national crisis.

In mid-January 2011 Gen. Than Shwe appointed 110 military representatives to the Pyithu Hluttaw, 56 to the Amyotha Hluttaw and 222 to the state and regional assemblies, in accordance with the constitutional quotas. On 31 January Myanmar's new bicameral Pyidaungsu Hluttaw convened for the first time, marking the formal completion of the transfer of power from the military junta to an elected parliament under the new Constitution. Legislation announced by state media in November 2010 imposed strict regulations on legislators' conduct during parliamentary sessions: although freedom of speech was to be allowed, words deemed to represent a risk to 'national security and unity' were prohibited while protests within parliament were to be punishable by up to two years' imprisonment; legislators were required to submit parliamentary questions 10 days in advance of a meeting; and media reporting (other than by state media) on parliamentary proceedings was banned. During the first parliamentary session Shwe Mann, formerly army Chief of Staff, was elected Speaker of the Pyithu Hluttaw, while Khin Aung Myint, a former Minister of Culture, was elected Speaker of the Amyotha Hluttaw.

On 1 February 2011 the Pyidaungsu Hluttaw nominated five legislators for three vice-presidential positions; the three candidates selected would become presidential candidates. Among the five nominees were the outgoing Prime Minister, Thein Sein, and former First Secretary of the SPDC Lt-Gen. Tin Aung Myint Oo; the remaining three nominees were members of ethnic minorities, which was widely interpreted as a conciliatory gesture on the part of the USDP legislators, amid increased tensions in the ethnic border areas in the aftermath of the elections (see Insurgency and Dissidence). On 3 February the Pyithu Hluttaw voted for Thein Sein as its presidential candidate, while the Amyotha Hluttaw elected Dr Sai Mauk Kham, a little-known USDP member of the Shan ethnic minority group; Tin Aung Myint Oo, as the vice-presidential nominee of the military representatives in parliament, was automatically approved as the military's presidential candidate. Thein Sein was elected President of Myanmar on 4 February, garnering 408 votes; Tin Aung Myint Oo, who won 171 votes, and Sai Mauk Kham, with 75 votes, were confirmed as Vice-Presidents.

Recent developments: reform under President Thein Sein

On 30 March 2011 Thein Sein was inaugurated as the country's President, the first session of the Pyithu Hluttaw was formally concluded, and the SPDC was dissolved, signalling the formal completion of the transfer of power from the military junta to an elected parliament and President. Than Shwe was replaced as Commander-in-Chief of the Armed Forces by Gen. Min Aung Hlaing. The incoming Cabinet comprised 30 members and was dominated by former military officers who had retired in order to contest the 2010 legislative elections, including about a dozen who had been ministers in the outgoing Cabinet. The defence portfolio was allocated to Maj.-Gen. Hla Min and that of home affairs to Lt-Gen. Ko Ko. Wunna Maung Lwin was appointed as Minister of Foreign Affairs, while Maj.-Gen. Thein Htay became Minister of Border Affairs and of Myanma Industrial Development. On 31 March 2011 state media formally announced the creation of an 11-member National Defence and Security Council (NDSC), the establishment of which was provided for under the terms of the 2008 Constitution. Membership of the NDSC comprised the President, the two Vice-Presidents, the Commander-in-Chief and Vice-Commander-in-Chief of the Armed Forces, the Ministers of Defence, of Foreign Affairs, of Home Affairs and of Border Affairs, and the Speakers of the two legislative chambers.

Meanwhile, in February 2011 Than Shwe announced the creation of an eight-member State Supreme Council (SSC), which he himself was to head, appearing to cast doubt on the commitment to genuine democratic reform within Myanmar. Unlike the NDSC, the SSC was not mandated by the 2008 Constitution, and was to be charged with advising the new legislature on all matters of national importance, including defence and national security. The development appeared to answer ongoing speculation as to the future role of Than Shwe, who many observers had expected to be named President; as head of the SSC, Than Shwe was expected effectively to remain the most powerful figure within the country. Other members of the SSC included former Vice-Chairman of the SPDC Maung Aye and former army Chief of Staff Shwe Mann.

President Thein Sein signed a general amnesty 'on humanitarian grounds' in May 2011, providing for the release of nearly 15,000 prisoners. However, human rights groups roundly condemned the limited scope of the amnesty, under the terms of which death sentences were commuted to life imprisonment and prison terms were reduced by one year, noting that very few of the country's estimated 2,200 political prisoners were among those being released. Critics contested that the amnesty was merely a ploy calculated to improve the image of the new administration of Thein Sein without making any real civil liberties concessions.

In June 2011 the Government ordered the NLD, which remained an outlawed organization, to desist from all political activities, stating that it should apply to register as a social organization if it wished to engage in social affairs. In early July Suu Kyi made her first trip outside of Yangon since her release from house arrest, visiting the city of Bagan, in Mandalay, with one of her sons. The trip, which, although non-political in nature, was widely perceived as a test of the limits on Suu Kyi's freedom, passed off without incident, and later in July Suu Kyi was granted her first formal audience with a member of the new Cabinet, meeting with her erstwhile dialogue partner Aung Kyi, who had retained the labour portfolio while concurrently being appointed Minister of Social Welfare, Relief and Resettlement.

Signs of a relaxation in the Government's stance towards Suu Kyi became further evident in August 2011, when she was allowed to make her first political trip outside of Yangon. During her visit to Bago (50 miles north of Yangon), hundreds of supporters gathered to listen as Suu Kyi appealed for national unity and many thousands more lined the streets to cheer her passing convoy. Later in the month Suu Kyi made her first visit to Nay Pyi Taw, at the invitation of the Government, in order to attend a government workshop on economic development. During Suu Kyi's visit she also held talks with Thein Sein at the presidential palace—the first time that the two had met in person; in an unexpected and highly symbolic gesture, the President received her underneath a large portrait of her assassinated father, Gen. Aung San. In a subsequent radio interview, Suu Kyi declared her belief that Thein Sein was sincere in wanting to implement reform, but warned that it remained too early to ascertain how far the reforms would go and to what extent they would bring about real, tangible change in the lives of the Myanma population.

The Myanma Government's commitment to genuine democratic reform was further called into question in September 2011, following the conviction of a journalist employed by the dissident broadcasting station, the Democratic Voice of Burma, on the charge of disseminating material online that could threaten the security of the Government. Sithu Zeya, who was already serving an eight-year prison term after photographing the scene of a minor bomb attack in Yangon in April 2010, was sentenced to a further 10 years' imprisonment. According to the Democratic Voice of Burma, 16 other journalists employed by the station, which remained fiercely critical of the Government, were in detention in Myanmar at mid-2011.

Amid criticism of Sithu Zeya's conviction from human rights groups, legislation providing for greater media freedom and the establishment of a self-regulating Press Council—the Printing Press and Publications Bill—was drafted by early 2012, although there were delays in presenting it to the legislature. Nevertheless, increased access to the internet was reported during the latter half of 2011, and journalists did appear to have been afforded greater scope to cover formerly prohibited subjects, including the activities of Suu Kyi, reporting on which had hitherto been strictly forbidden. In November legislation providing for the right to protest received parliamentary approval, although permission would need to be requested at least five days in advance of planned demonstrations, which remained banned at government offices, factories and hospitals, and staging a protest without permission would be punishable by one year's imprisonment. Meanwhile, in September the Government announced the creation of a 15-member National Human Rights Commission, in a development that was cautiously welcomed by domestic and international rights groups.

A presidential amnesty providing for the release of a further 6,359 prisoners, thought to include around 200 political prisoners, was announced in October 2011. However, the NLD urged the authorities to release all remaining political prisoners. Another presidential amnesty was announced in January 2012, providing for the release of an additional 651 prisoners, including, significantly, Sithu Zeya and others of the country's most prominent political prisoners. Upon his release, Sithu Zeya claimed to have been physically assaulted by prison guards during his detention in prison, as well as being forced to forgo food and water for days at a time. Sithu Zeya also questioned the intent behind the recent series of reforms implemented by the Thein Sein administration, claiming that the authorities sought only to placate external powers and secure foreign investment and an easing of international sanctions.

In its annual report published in January 2012, US-based organization Human Rights Watch acknowledged that the Myanma Government had made 'some significant moves' towards democratization, but stated that the human rights situation in the country had nevertheless remained 'dire' during 2011. Although welcoming the release of a number of political prisoners during the year, the report noted that many more remained in detention, while freedom of expression, association and assembly continued to be 'severely curtailed'. The report also indicated that ethnic violence had escalated, with a number of cease-fires agreed between the Myanma army and ethnic armed groups being broken during the year, and claimed that the army continued to be responsible for indiscriminate attacks and other abuses against civilians in conflict areas, including forced labour, extrajudicial killings, sexual violence and the use of 'human shields'.

Meanwhile, in mid-November 2011 the NLD announced that it was to seek re-registration as a political party with a view to contesting by-elections (subsequently called for 1 April 2012) for 45 seats, including those that had been left vacant by ministerial appointments. The announcement followed the adoption by parliament earlier in the month of a number of amendments to the electoral law, including, crucially, the removal of the clause barring anyone convicted of a crime from membership of a political organization. Furthermore, in an unexpected development, in an interview conducted by *The Yangon Times* in early November, the Speaker of the Amyotha Hluttaw, Khin Aung Myint, had made a rare public acknowledgement by a government official of the NLD's victory in the 1990 elections, conceding that the party had won 'with a vast majority'. The Speaker of the upper chamber had also stated that the Government would welcome an application by the NLD to re-register as a political party. The NLD's application was formally approved in mid-December 2011 and in the same month Suu Kyi confirmed her intention to stand as a candidate in the forthcoming by-elections.

In January 2012 Suu Kyi was appointed as the NLD's new Chairman, while Tin Oo, hitherto NLD Vice-Chairman, was appointed Chairman of the party's newly formed Patron Committee, which was expected to serve in a primarily advisory capacity.

The NLD won a comprehensive victory in the parliamentary by-elections to 45 seats in the legislature on 1 April 2012, winning 43 of the 44 seats it contested, including 37 seats in the 440-member lower chamber, according to official results. International observers approved the conduct of the by-elections, which were regarded by many as a vital test of the Government's commitment to democratic reform, although parliament remained dominated by the military and its allies. Parliament convened with its newly elected members at the end of April, although the NLD deputies, including Suu Kyi, initially refused to take their seats in protest at the wording of the parliamentary oath, which included a commitment to 'safeguard' the Constitution. The NLD had campaigned for constitutional reform, contending that the Constitution, drafted under military rule, was undemocratic since it effectively preserved power for the armed forces. The NLD requested that the wording of the parliamentary oath be altered, substituting 'respect' for 'safeguard'. However, the NLD deputies subsequently agreed to swear the existing parliamentary oath, taking their seats in early May. Tin Aung Myint Oo, who was regarded as an opponent of political reform, submitted his resignation from the post of Vice-President the following day, citing health reasons; he actually stood down as Vice-President on 1 July and was replaced by the hardline former navy chief, Nyan Tun, on 15 August.

Meanwhile, having been given a passport in early May 2012 for the first time in 24 years, Suu Kyi, in her new de facto role as ambassador for Myanmar, visited a number of countries during that year, including Thailand, Switzerland, Ireland, France, Norway (where she accepted the Nobel Peace Prize awarded to her in 1991), the United Kingdom, India and the USA. Her willingness to leave Myanmar indicated the confidence that she now appeared to hold in the administration of Thein Sein that she would be permitted to return. In each country that she visited Suu Kyi requested assistance in the furtherance of democratic reform in Myanmar and the genuine empowerment of its people, and warned against complacency and 'reckless optimism'. In her first parliamentary statement, in late July, Suu Kyi demanded the introduction of legislation to protect the rights of Myanmar's ethnic minorities, although she did not specifically mention the Muslim Rohingyas in her speech.

A further sign of increasing democratization within Myanmar was the series of street demonstrations that were conducted in Mandalay and a number of other towns in late May 2012 in protest at chronic electricity shortages. The demonstrations were the largest to be held since those organized by the Buddhist monks in 2007. While not acting forcibly to suppress the demonstrations, the authorities warned the protesters to remain within the law and stated that permission should be sought prior to the staging of any public gatherings. In August 2012 the Government announced the abolition of pre-publication censorship of the media (excluding films), although strict regulations remained in place over what could be included in reports. In the following month the chief editor and publisher of the independent journal *The Voice Weekly* were charged with libel after publishing an article regarding alleged corruption within the Ministry of Mines. In late December the Government announced that from April 2013 the publication of privately owned newspapers would be permitted for the first time in nearly 50 years.

President Thein Sein carried out a cabinet reorganization in late August/early September 2012; among the notable changes was the appointment of the first female cabinet minister (Dr Daw Myat Ohn Khin, as Minister of Social Welfare, Relief and Resettlement) since 1948 and the replacement of the prominent hardliner, Kyaw Hsan, as Minister of Information by the more moderate Aung Kyi, who had acted as the representative of the military regime in negotiations with Suu Kyi during her years under house arrest. A few days later the Government appeared further to distance itself from the repressive policies of the past by removing the names of more than 2,000 people from a blacklist drawn up over the preceding decades by the military authorities of those banned from entering or leaving the country on the grounds that they were deemed to pose a security threat. Among those taken off the list (which had consequently been reduced in size to around 4,000 names) were former US Secretary of State Madeleine Albright, the late Philippine President Corazon Aquino, Suu Kyi's two sons, human rights officials and numerous foreign journalists. In a sign of the growing authority of parliament, in early September the Pyithu Hluttaw approved the impeachment of all nine judges of the Constitutional Tribunal (a move that had been approved by the upper house the previous month), following an attempt by the court earlier that year to limit the power of parliamentary committees and commissions. President Thein Sein accepted the subsequent resignations of the judges. A few days before the President's scheduled visit to the UN in New York, USA, where he was to seek international support for his programme of reforms, in mid-September the authorities announced the release under a presidential amnesty of more than 500 prisoners, including, it was believed, more than 50 political detainees. However, the exact number of political prisoners who remained in custody was still not known (although estimates put it at around 240–300 individuals). A further 452 prisoners were released in mid-November, shortly before the historic visit to Myanmar of US President Barack Obama, yet there were no reports of any political detainees being among those set free. On the actual day of Obama's arrival in Myanmar, however, the authorities announced the release of around 40 political prisoners.

In the wake of its overwhelming defeat at the hands of the NLD in the by-elections in April 2012, the USDP held its first ever conference in mid-October with the aim of regrouping and drawing up new strategies to prepare for the next general election (due to be held in 2015). Although many had expected the Speaker of the lower house, Shwe Mann, to be assigned the role, Thein Sein was reappointed as Chairman of the governing party. A few days later Thein Sein broke new ground by giving his first news conference in Myanmar. The process of political liberalization continued in January 2013 when the Government abolished a 25-year-old ban on public gatherings of more than five people. Moreover, in February the Government announced plans to further national reconciliation by establishing a committee to review the detention of all remaining political prisoners. Meanwhile, in January President Thein Sein accepted the resignations of Minister of Communications and Information Technology Thein Tun and Minister of Religious Affairs Thura Myint Maung, with no reason cited except that the resignations were voluntary. The following month the vacant posts were assigned, respectively, to the erstwhile air force chief, Gen. Myat Hein, and to Hsan Hsint. Another former senior military officer, Lt-Gen. Thet Naing Win, was appointed to head the Ministry of Border Affairs.

At the NLD's congress held in Yangon in March 2013, Suu Kyi was unanimously re-elected as the party's leader and the executive committee was enlarged from seven to 15 members. Later that month, in what was viewed as a sign of the growing rapprochement between the opposition and the military, Suu Kyi attended Armed Forces' Day in Nay Pyi Taw for the first time.

Meanwhile, as the process of liberalization and the easing of restrictive legislation advanced so too did the concepts of political mobilization and public protest. A major grievance that came increasingly to the fore during 2011–12 was public anger over land seizures carried out under military rule. In late November 2012 more than 50 demonstrators were reportedly injured when security forces used water cannon and tear gas to break up a sit-in protest (launched earlier that year) against the planned expansion of a huge Chinese-funded copper mine in Monywa in the north-west region of Sagaing. The protesters, who included Buddhist monks, environmentalists and political activists, claimed that local farmers had been forced to accept an agreement in 2010 according to which they were obliged to give up their land in exchange for financial compensation and new housing. In response, the Government asserted that the deal had been voluntary and that only a small minority of farmers had rejected it. Following the staging of rallies across the country in December 2012 by Buddhist monks in protest at the authorities' crackdown at the mine the previous month, Suu Kyi was appointed to head an official inquiry into the Government's actions and the future of the mine. In February 2013 a report compiled by Myanma lawyers and the US-based Justice Trust claimed that the police had fired military-issue white phosphorous grenades to disperse the protest at the mine in November 2012; these allegations appeared to be corroborated by the fact that many of those injured in the clampdown suffered serious burns. In March 2013 the findings of the investigative commission headed by Suu Kyi confirmed that smoke bombs containing phosphorus had been used against the protesters, but recommended that work on the mine expansion project proceed as planned. However, fur-

ther protests by farmers who refused to surrender their land took place in late April. An amnesty providing for the release of 93 prisoners, reported to include around 56 political prisoners, was announced that month.

Insurgency and Dissidence

After Burma gained independence in 1948, various groups conducted armed insurgency campaigns against government forces. The most effective of the ethnic-based insurgency groups was the Karen (Kayin) National Union (KNU), founded in 1948, which led a protracted campaign for the establishment of an independent state for the Karen ethnic group (restyled Kayin in the transliteration changes of 1989), partly through the activities of its military wing, the Karen (Kayin) National Liberation Army (KNLA). The KNU was a member of the National Democratic Front (NDF), an anti-Government organization that at one time comprised 11 ethnic minority groups—including Kachin, Karenni (Kayinni), Mon, Shan, Pa-O, Palaung, Wa, Arakanese (Rakhine) and Lahu parties—formed in 1975 (by five groups, originally) with the aim of making Burma a federal union. By May 1986 the various minority groups in the NDF had agreed to relinquish their individual demands for autonomy, in favour of a unified demand for a federal system of government. At the same time, the CPB, which had gained control of significant areas in northern Burma, withdrew its demand for a 'one-party' government and entered into an alliance with the NDF. At the second NDF Congress in June 1987, various leadership changes removed all KNU representatives from senior NDF positions. The new NDF leaders advocated the establishment of autonomous, ethnic-based states within a Burmese union. In November 1988 22 anti-Government groups, led by members of the NDF, formed the Democratic Alliance of Burma (DAB); the KNU leader, Gen. Bo Mya, was elected President.

In April 1989 dissatisfaction with the CPB leadership led to a mutiny by Wa tribespeople, who captured the CPB headquarters, and the party's leaders were forced into exile in the People's Republic of China. The leaders of the mutiny subsequently accepted SLORC proposals for the erstwhile forces of the CPB army to become government-controlled militia forces in exchange for supplies of rice, financial support and development aid. The former CPB troops agreed to use their main forces against the 25,000-strong rebel separatist Mong Tai Army (formerly the Shan United Army), whose leader, Khun Sa, controlled much of the drug trade in the 'Golden Triangle', the world's major opium-producing area, where the borders of Myanmar, Laos and Thailand meet. The SLORC also approached members of the NDF, and was successful in securing agreements with the Shan State Progressive Party in September 1989, and with the Pa-O National Organization and the Palaung State Liberation Organization in March and May 1991, respectively. At the third NDF Congress in July, these three movements were expelled, reducing the NDF's membership to eight organizations; Nai Shwe Kyin was elected as its new President.

Meanwhile, intense fighting between government and rebel forces continued throughout 1989–92. The Kachin Independence Organization (KIO) appeared to have signed a peace agreement with the Government in April 1993 but, owing to its attempts to persuade other members of the DAB to enter discussions with the SLORC, the cease-fire was not announced until October. The agreement was ratified in Yangon in February 1994. The KIO was suspended from the DAB in October 1993 for negotiating separately with the SLORC; however, under Thai pressure, the DAB policy of negotiating as a front was subsequently unofficially abandoned.

In May 1994 the Karenni (Kayinni) National People's Liberation Front concluded a cease-fire agreement with the SLORC, reportedly the 11th insurgent group to do so. This was followed by the declaration of cease-fires by the Kayan New Land Party and the Shan State Nationalities Liberation Organization in July and October, respectively. In December government forces launched a new offensive against the KNU, capturing its headquarters at Manerplaw in January 1995 (and forcing many hundreds of KNU fighters across the border into Thailand). The virtual defeat of the KNU forces was attributed to their reportedly severe lack of ammunition and funds and also to the recent defection from the Christian-led KNU of a mainly Buddhist faction, which established itself as the Democratic Karen (Kayin) Buddhist Army (DKBA). The DKBA, which had comprised about 10% of the strength of the KNLA, allegedly supported the government forces in their offensive. In February the Myanma army captured the KNU's last stronghold, and in the following month Bo Mya resigned as the Commander-in-Chief of the KNLA (although he remained the leader of the KNU). In March the KNU declared a unilateral cease-fire, with the aim of initiating negotiations with the SLORC. Earlier in the month the Karenni (Kayinni) National Progress Party (KNPP) reportedly became the 14th ethnic insurgent group to abandon its armed struggle against the SLORC. This agreement collapsed in June, however, as government troops entered areas designated in the accord to be under KNPP control. In August 5,000 troops were dispatched to suppress the KNPP rebellion. However, the KNPP continued its armed struggle, with support from the All-Burma Students Democratic Front.

In 1997–98 the DKBA, allegedly supported by government forces, launched a number of attacks on Kayin refugee camps in Thailand, prompting renewed fighting between the KNU and government forces, and leading to the forcible relocation of Kayin away from KNU bases in Myanmar and across the border into Thailand. The Thai armed forces denied collusion with the Myanma troops in the process of forced repatriations of Kayin refugees. In April 1999 the KNU confirmed the deaths of seven members of a group of 13 government officials whom they had abducted in February; the remaining six were said to have been released unharmed. In January 2000 Bo Mya resigned as KNU Chairman owing to ailing health, and was replaced by the former General Secretary of the organization, Saw Ba Thin; Bo Mya assumed the vice-chairmanship. Talks were held between the KNU and the State Peace and Development Council (SPDC) in February–March but proved inconclusive. However, in late 2000 the Government began to use 'scorched-earth' tactics to deprive the KNU of its support base, displacing up to 30,000 people in eastern Myanmar.

Meanwhile, in December 1993 the SLORC initiated a major offensive against Khun Sa's Mong Tai Army encampments on the Thai border. In May 1994 Khun Sa proclaimed an independent Shan State, of which he declared himself 'President'. In the same month fighting intensified between government forces and the Mong Tai Army near the Thai border, with heavy losses reported on both sides. In March 1995 government forces launched an intensive campaign, lasting several months, against the Mong Tai Army. In August a faction calling itself the Shan State National Army (SSNA) broke away from the Mong Tai Army, accusing Khun Sa of using Shan nationalism as a 'front' for drugs-trafficking. Khun Sa subsequently offered to relinquish areas under his control to an international force that could ensure the safety of the Shan while eradicating illicit drugs. Khun Sa's position was considerably weakened in September, as improving relations between Thailand and Myanmar led to a Thai pledge to close the common border, thus obstructing his supply routes, and cease-fires with neighbouring ethnic groups allowed the Government to deploy troops in hitherto inaccessible areas. Certain ethnic groups, notably the Wa, were also actively engaged in fighting the Mong Tai Army to gain control of the opium trade. In November Khun Sa announced his retirement from all political and military positions, citing his betrayal by the breakaway group. In January 1996 government troops entered Homong without resistance, and thousands of his former supporters surrendered. Although no formal agreement with the SLORC was announced, it was widely believed that Khun Sa had previously negotiated a settlement with the authorities since he was not detained and it was officially announced that he would not be extradited to the USA on drugs-trafficking charges. (Khun Sa was, moreover, later accorded the status of an honoured elder. He died in Yangon in October 2007.) The Mong Tai Army was subsequently transformed into a militia volunteer unit under the command of the armed forces.

Between November 1996 and February 1997 there were reports of clashes between the Shan United Revolutionary Party (a faction of the Mong Tai Army that had not surrendered in January 1996) and government forces. In September 1997 the alliance between three of the major Shan groups who continued their resistance—including the SSNA, remnants of the Mong Tai Army, and the Shan State Peace-keeping Council (SSPC) and its military wing, the Shan State Army (SSA)—was formalized, and the groups joined together in an enlarged SSA. Shan separatist groups launched a further offensive against government troops in November. In May 1999 it was reported that at least 300,000 Shan had been forced from their villages into resettlement camps by government troops. In May 2000 several senior army officers died in an SSA ambush. In the following month more than 60 Shan and hill tribespeople, who had been forcibly relocated and had then attempted to return to their village, were reportedly

killed by the Myanma military in a retaliatory attack. In similar incidents in the region in June, as many as 50 other villagers were believed to have been murdered. In 2001 the Government launched several offensives against SSA border camps, causing hundreds more Shan to flee the area. In September the SSA stated that it would be willing to enter into peace talks with the SPDC.

In January 2000 it was reported that the SPDC was to launch an operation to relocate 50,000 people from opium-growing areas controlled by the United Wa State Army (UWSA—which reached an accommodation with the SLORC in 1989), with the alleged intention of eradicating the production of drugs in the areas by 2005. The relocation programme began to cause ethnic tension in early 2001, as the Shan complained that the Wa tribespeople were occupying land that they had previously owned. It was also claimed that the Wa were still growing opium, in spite of the fact that the scheme had been introduced supposedly to prevent heroin production. Some 300,000 Shan were reported to have fled to Thailand owing to the Wa influx by February.

In April 2003 the KNU claimed responsibility for a series of explosions that had destroyed sections of a gas pipeline in Kayin State over the previous two months. Several bombings along the border with Thailand in the following month were also attributed to the KNU. In January 2004 Bo Mya and other KNU officials held talks with government representatives in Yangon, which resulted in the conclusion of an informal cease-fire arrangement between the two sides. However, sporadic fighting continued between government troops and the KNLA. Bo Mya retired as Vice-Chairman of the KNU in December because of ill health; he was replaced by Gen. Tamalabaw. In January 2005 10 government troops were reportedly killed in clashes with the KNU after attacking one of the group's bases near the border with Thailand. Later in that month the KNU demanded a resumption of the peace talks, which had been curtailed at the Government's request in October 2004 following the dismissal of Prime Minister Khin Nyunt. Government offensives in Kayin State in early 2006 were reported to have forced an estimated 15,000 Kayin people to flee from the violence. Bo Mya died in a Thai hospital in December 2006. In February 2007 a relatively small breakaway faction of the KNU led by Htain Maung negotiated a peace agreement with the Government, but the goals of the KNU itself remained unaffected and its armed campaign continued unabated. Meanwhile, in February 2008 the General Secretary of the KNU, Pado Mahn Sha, was killed by two unidentified gunmen at his home in the Thai border town of Mae Sot; it was speculated that the DKBA was responsible for the assassination. The Chairman of the KNU, Saw Ba Thin, died in May; in October Vice-Chairman Gen. Tamalabaw was appointed as his replacement, while Tamalabaw's daughter, Zipporah Sein, succeeded Mahn Sha as General Secretary.

Following the referendum in 2008 in favour of the new Constitution (see Domestic Political Affairs), the SPDC requested that all ethnic minority groups form political parties to enable their participation in the legislative elections scheduled for 2010. However, many were reluctant to do so owing to the reservation of one-quarter of seats in the national and local legislatures for members of the national army. In April 2009 the SPDC demanded that all ethnic cease-fire groups transform into new 'Border Guard Force' (BGF) battalions, which were to include a unit of 30 government soldiers and one government officer. Although most of the cease-fire groups initially resisted the order, some—including the DKBA—were gradually coerced into acquiescing. The introduction of the BGFs was widely regarded as an attempt to reduce the risk of ethnic uprisings prior to the 2010 elections. The forthcoming polls were a divisive subject among the ethnic-based groups: some were adamantly opposed to any participation, which, they argued, would lend a false impression of legitimacy to the proceedings, while others contended that a refusal to participate would ensure their total exclusion from the legislative process.

As the elections approached, with the SPDC's rejection of a number of ethnic parties and individual candidates, along with its apparent endeavours to disenfranchise a large number of ethnic voters (see Domestic Political Affairs), tensions in the ethnic border areas intensified. In October 2010 the Kachin Independence Army (KIA—the military wing of the KIO, which continued to refuse to become a BGF) was reported to be engaged in a tense stand-off with government troops, following the arrest of three of its members; meanwhile, members of the SSA were reported to have been attacked by government forces in several separate incidents. At the beginning of November six ethnic groups reportedly reached an agreement to join forces in the event of a government attack; a spokesperson for the KIO contested that the ethnic groups had 'no real option but to unite, politically and militarily'. Heavy fighting broke out in Myawaddy on 8 November, immediately following the legislative elections, after a breakaway faction of the DKBA—led by Na Kham Mwe and comprising those opposed to the DKBA leadership's decision to agree to become a BGF—seized control of government buildings in the Kayin town, where they encountered armed opposition from government troops. At least three civilians were killed during the clashes, and an estimated 20,000 Kayin were reported to have fled into neighbouring Thailand to escape the violence. Government troops regained control of Myawaddy a few days later, and issued an ultimatum to the renegade faction, threatening to annihilate it if it did not surrender its weapons and agree to become a BGF by the end of December. However, sporadic fighting continued. In mid-November the DKBA faction and the KNLA agreed to unite in their common pursuit of autonomy.

Intermittent violent clashes in Kayin State and other border areas continued in 2011. Four KIA fighters and 16 government soldiers were reported to have been killed during fierce fighting in Kachin State in June, while thousands of civilians were reported to have been displaced by the violence, many of them fleeing across the border into China. The Government subsequently accused the KIA of instigating the clashes (which had officially ended the 17-year cease-fire agreement between the KIA and the Myanma authorities), claiming that the rebel troops had ignored an order to withdraw from an area close to the construction site of two Chinese-financed dams in Momauk, the Tarpein 1 and Tarpein 2 dams. Later in June three apparently co-ordinated bomb explosions, in Nay Pyi Taw, Mandalay and Pyin Oo Lwin, were attributed by the authorities to ethnic rebel groups; three people were reported to have been injured in the attacks. Sporadic clashes continued into July, and in August seven people were reported to have been killed when KIA rebels ambushed a vehicle carrying workers from the Tarpein power plant. Meanwhile, in March 2011 the KIO had sent an open letter to the Chinese Government urging it to cancel a hydropower plant and dam project at Myitsone, an area within Kachin State of considerable cultural and ecological significance, and warning that it would not be held responsible if 'civil war' broke out as a result of continued construction. The KIO argued that the Myitsone dam and other Chinese-financed power projects were wreaking severe environmental and social disruption, including the displacement of local communities. (In April 2010 three bombs had been detonated at the Myitsone dam project, killing three people and injuring at least 20 others; around 60 people were arrested in Kachin State in May in connection with the explosions.) In an apparent acknowledgment of the concerns expressed by the KIO and many members of the international community, the Myanma Government unexpectedly announced the suspension of the Myitsone project in September 2011 (see Foreign Affairs).

In a statement broadcast on national television in August 2011, the Government invited rebel groups to enter into formal dialogue aimed at resolving the ongoing ethnic conflicts. A series of meetings was subsequently held between the Government and the KIO, and in December the Government ordered the military to halt all offensive operations against the KIA; however, intermittent clashes between government troops and KIA rebels continued to be reported in early 2012. Meanwhile, cease-fire agreements were concluded with the SSA and the KNU, in December 2011 and January 2012, respectively. The Government's unconditional release in March of Mahn Nyein Maung, a KNU leader who had been convicted of unlawful association and violating immigration laws and sentenced to 17 years' imprisonment in December 2011, gave new impetus to the peace process. A second round of negotiations with the Government took place in the Kayin State capital of Pa-an in April 2012 and KNU leaders attended a meeting with President Thein Sein in Nay Pyi Taw. A preliminary cease-fire agreement was concluded with the New Mon State Party in February and with the KNPP in March, providing for an end to the fighting pending discussions on a permanent accord. A further cease-fire agreement was signed with the KNPP in June. The Kachins remained the only armed ethnic group yet to sign a cease-fire agreement. Fighting intensified in December when government forces launched a new offensive (including airborne attacks) on KIA strongholds in Kachin State; by early February 2013, despite international condemnation of the escalation in violence and the resultant civilian casualties, the army had captured several key rebel positions around the town of Laiza.

The Rohingyas and Inter-communal Unrest

In late 1989 the SLORC began resettling Bamar (Burman) Buddhists in the predominantly Muslim areas of Arakan (renamed Rakhine), displacing the local Rohingya Muslims. In April 1991 Rohingya refugees were forced over the border into Bangladesh, as a result of the brutal operations of the Myanma armed forces, including the destruction of villages, widespread killings and pillaging. The Rohingyas had been similarly persecuted in 1976–78, when more than 200,000 of them had sought refuge in Bangladesh. The Rohingyas had finally been repatriated, only to lose their citizenship following the introduction of new nationality legislation in 1982. In November 1991 the SLORC pledged to repatriate genuine Myanma citizens, but claimed that many of the refugees were illegal Bengali immigrants. In April 1992 the Myanma and Bangladeshi Governments signed an agreement providing for the repatriation of those Rohingya refugees in possession of official documentation. However, the repatriation programme was delayed, owing to the continuing flow of refugees to Bangladesh (reaching an estimated 270,000 by the end of June). The first Rohingya refugees were returned to Myanmar in September, and by May 1995 more than 216,000 refugees had been repatriated.

In April 2000 the International Federation of Human Rights Leagues (FIDH) issued a report condemning the treatment of Rohingya Muslims by the Myanma Government, including forced labour, punitive taxes and extrajudicial killings. The FIDH claimed that the Myanma regime was attempting to force the exodus of Rohingyas from their native Rakhine and criticized the office of the UN High Commissioner for Refugees (UNHCR) for its effective complicity with the regime in designating the more recent refugees as economic migrants. In February 2001 violence between Buddhist and Muslim communities in the state capital, Sittwe, was reported to have resulted in at least 12 deaths, prompting the Government to regulate further the movement of Rohingya and other Muslims in and out of Rakhine.

In December 2009 it was announced that Myanmar had agreed to repatriate about 9,000 Rohingyas living in Bangladeshi camps following a meeting between the two countries' respective ministers responsible for foreign affairs. Nevertheless, at August 2012 an estimated 29,000 Rohingyas were reported to be living in official refugee camps in Bangladesh, many of whom appeared to be unwilling to return to Myanmar. In addition, it was estimated that some 270,000 Rohingyas were residing in Bangladesh without refugee status.

In a report published in January 2012, the non-governmental organization Arakan Project claimed that, although representatives in Myanmar's new legislature had been able to submit questions during parliamentary sessions on discriminatory policies and restrictions targeting the Rohingya population in Rakhine, replies provided by the Government in August and September 2011 had reaffirmed its commitment to those policies, including the denial of citizenship and marriage rights, and stringent restrictions on movement, justifying their implementation on the grounds of national population growth control and 'illegal migration management'.

Sectarian tension between the Muslim and Buddhist populations in Rakhine heightened from mid-2012, as the number of violent incidents across the state between members of the two communities increased considerably (prompted by the killing, in early June, of 10 Muslim men travelling on a bus in the town of Taungup by a group of Buddhists; it was reported that the victims were mistakenly identified by the mob as having carried out the rape and murder of a Buddhist woman in the town of Ramree in May). President Thein Sein declared a state of emergency and imposed a curfew in Rakhine on 10 June in an attempt to curb the growing unrest. However, within a week the total number of people killed in the violence had reached around 50, tens of thousands (mainly Rohingya Muslims) had been displaced by the fighting and hundreds of Rohingyas were attempting to flee to Bangladesh by boat. Bangladesh's subsequent decision to close its border was criticized by human rights organizations as a violation of international law. Although the communal violence had abated somewhat by mid-July, there were reports of continuing attacks on the Muslim population and their property by both the Buddhist community and the security forces. There were also reports of hundreds of arbitrary arrests being carried out by the security forces in Rohingya areas of the state. Having rejected a UN proposal to set up an independent inquiry, in mid-August the Government announced the establishment of a commission, incorporating members from different political and religious groups of Myanmar, which was to identify and then attempt to address the reasons behind the resurgence in sectarian violence in Rakhine. In October President Thein Sein blocked plans by the Organization of Islamic Cooperation to open a support office in Myanmar for the country's Muslims. Another series of violent clashes between Muslims and Buddhists broke out in Rakhine in late October, leading to at least another 80 deaths, the destruction of hundreds of houses and the displacement of thousands of people into makeshift camps. In a report released in April 2013, the government commission established in August 2012 proposed doubling the number of security forces in Rakhine and improving their training and equipment. It also recommended that Muslim Rohingyas and Buddhists should be continue to be segregated, while acknowledging that this did not represent an appropriate long-term solution, and that Rohingya citizenship claims should be addressed.

In March 2013 it appeared that inter-communal tension had spread elsewhere in Myanmar when clashes erupted between the Muslim and Buddhist communities of the town of Meiktila in Mandalay Division. Despite the imposition by the Government of a state of emergency in the town and the dispatch of hundreds of riot police to the area, by the end of the month more than 40 people were reported to have been killed in the violence and thousands (mainly Muslims) forced from their homes. In a worrying development, there were also reports that anti-Muslim violence had broken out in a number of towns further south in the division. There was widespread concern that sectarian unrest would be aggravated following the deaths of 13 young Muslim students in a fire at a mosque in Yangon in early April, despite assurances by the authorities that the fire had been caused by an electrical fault. In mid-April three Muslims were sentenced to 14 years' imprisonment for their role in provoking the violence in Meiktila; further prosecutions, of both Muslims and Buddhists, were expected. In a further incident in late April, one person was killed when a group of Buddhists reportedly attacked several Muslim properties and a mosque in the town of Oakkan, near Yangon.

Foreign Affairs

Following the seizure of power by the military junta under Gen. Ne Win in 1962, Myanmar's foreign relations were characterized by international mistrust and condemnation. As repression by the Myanma military junta increased, in July 1996 opposition leader Aung San Suu Kyi for the first time advocated the imposition of international economic sanctions against the regime. There followed a period of increased economic and diplomatic isolation. After the staging of legislative elections in November 2010, and the transition to an at least nominally democratic, civilian system of governance in early 2011, there were signs of a significant shift in the international community's attitudes towards Myanmar, which appeared increasingly keen to re-engage with both its regional neighbours and those further afield. However, at early 2013 it still remained to be seen whether concessions announced by the Thein Sein administration following its inauguration at the end of March 2011 merely constituted, as some critics alleged, a calculated ploy to expedite the lifting of international sanctions and attract foreign investment, or whether such measures represented a genuine desire to initiate a process of sustained democratic reform and to co-operate fully with the demands of the international community.

Regional relations

The People's Republic of China restored diplomatic relations with Burma in 1978. From 1988, as Burma's international isolation deepened, China assumed an increasingly important role, becoming Myanmar's principal aid donor, supplier of weapons and source of consumer goods. In December 2001 the Chinese President, Jiang Zemin, travelled to Myanmar, becoming the first Chinese head of state to visit the country since 1985. Before his arrival the Myanma Government announced that it had ordered the release of more than 200 Chinese prisoners as a gesture of goodwill. Following successful discussions, the two Governments signed a series of bilateral agreements intended to enhance co-operative ties. Relations were further strengthened in March 2004, during a visit to Yangon by Chinese Vice-Premier Wu Yi, by the signing of 24 agreements on economic and technical co-operation. Another series of bilateral co-operation agreements, pertaining to energy and development aid, among other fields, was signed during a visit to Myanmar in June 2010 by Chinese Premier Wen Jiabao. During a reciprocal visit to China

by Than Shwe in September, a Chinese government spokesperson stressed that the forthcoming legislative elections in Myanmar were an internal matter for that country, but expressed China's hope that the international community would seek constructive engagement with Myanmar. However, one of a series of US diplomatic cables released at the end of 2010 by WikiLeaks, an organization publishing leaked private and classified content, revealed that the Chinese Government was becoming increasingly frustrated with the 'footdragging' of Than Shwe and the general recalcitrance of the Myanma Government.

Ongoing unrest in the Myanmar ethnic border areas close to China was a further source of tensions between the two countries in 2010–12. Some 5,000 Chinese troops were deployed to the border in mid-2010. Following an outbreak of fighting between ethnic Kachin rebels and government troops in June 2011, in part fuelled by Kachin opposition to Chinese-funded dam projects in the northern Myanma state, thousands of civilians fled across the border into China, with some 7,000–10,000 reported to remain there in early 2013. (In August 2012 Human Rights Watch alleged that China was flouting international law by forcibly returning Kachin refugees across the border into Myanmar.) The decision by the new administration of President Thein Sein in September 2011 to suspend construction of a controversial US $3,600m. Chinese-financed hydroelectric dam for the duration of his tenure (i.e. until at least 2015) was a source of considerable annoyance to the Chinese Government, but was widely welcomed by ethnic and environmentalist groups in Myanmar. Some 90% of the electricity expected to have been generated by the 3,600-MW Myitsone dam was to have been exported to China. Announcing the decision, Thein Sein declared that the project was 'contrary to the will of the people'. However, many analysts suggested that the project's suspension was more a response to international than domestic pressures, with the Myanma Government appearing eager to appease Western (and particularly US) concerns over its heavy reliance on China.

In an attempt to end its isolation, accelerate economic growth and gain protection from Western criticism of its internal affairs, Myanmar applied to join ASEAN and was admitted as a full member of the organization in July 1997. In May 2000 Myanmar hosted a meeting of the economic ministers of the ASEAN member countries. Myanmar enjoyed particularly cordial relations with Indonesia, and the military regime aspired to Indonesia's internationally accepted political system, in which the dominant role of the armed forces was enshrined in the Constitution. In July 2005 it was announced at the ASEAN Ministerial Meeting held in Laos that Myanmar would not assume the chair of ASEAN in 2006 as had been scheduled. Myanmar had recently come under increasing pressure from the international community, and in particular from the other member states of ASEAN, to forgo its turn to assume the rotating chair in order to enable the Myanma Government instead to focus its attention on addressing the country's human rights situation.

In September 2007, in a rare departure from the Association's policy of non-interference in member states' internal affairs, ASEAN ministers responsible for foreign affairs, meeting in New York, issued a statement in which they declared that they had expressed their 'revulsion' to their Myanma counterpart over reports that anti-Government protests were being violently suppressed, and had urged the Myanma Government to resume efforts at national reconciliation and to release all political detainees. ASEAN came under pressure to take action against Myanmar in advance of its summit meeting in November, at which member states signed a new charter committing themselves, *inter alia*, to strengthening democracy and promoting and protecting human rights. By the end of October 2008 all 10 member nations had ratified the new charter, despite the continued detention of Suu Kyi.

Following the holding of legislative elections in Myanmar (and the release from house arrest of Suu Kyi) in November 2010, Viet Nam, in its capacity as ASEAN chair for that year, hailed the polls as 'a significant step forward'. Furthermore, in January 2011 ASEAN urged the USA and other Western nations to remove economic sanctions against Myanmar, stating that the sanctions were impeding the country's development, and appealing for dialogue with Myanmar in order to ensure further progress towards democracy in that country. At the ASEAN summit meeting held in Jakarta, Indonesia, in May 2011, President Thein Sein requested that Myanmar be allowed to assume the chair of ASEAN in 2014, in a move interpreted as an attempt to gain domestic and international legitimacy for the new Myanma Government. Following the enactment of domestic reforms by the Myanma Government in the latter half of 2011 (see Domestic Political Affairs), at the ASEAN summit meeting held on Bali, Indonesia, in November, the bloc unanimously voted to award Myanmar the chair in 2014. However, the outcome of the vote was not universally popular, with critics citing Myanmar's poor human rights record and the continued detention of hundreds of political prisoners. At the summit meeting held in Cambodia in April 2012, ASEAN formally demanded that all sanctions against Myanmar be lifted immediately in order to support the processes of democratic reform and economic development in that country.

Meanwhile, following the release of Suu Kyi from house arrest in July 1995, Japan resumed substantial economic aid to Myanmar, which had been halted in 1988. The international community criticized Japan's decision to resume aid as being premature in the light of Myanmar's failure to end forced labour and other human rights abuses in the country. In November 1999 the Japanese Prime Minister met with Than Shwe during an ASEAN summit meeting in the Philippine capital, Manila; the meeting was the first between the leader of a major world power and a senior member of the military Government since the junta's suppression of the democratic opposition in 1988. In June 2003, following the junta's reimprisonment of Suu Kyi in May of that year, the Japanese Government once again suspended all economic aid to Myanmar. However, in early 2004 it was announced that Japan was to resume aid, having been satisfied that the release of some political prisoners by the SPDC constituted adequate progress towards democracy in the country. In January 2012 the Japanese Ministry of Foreign Affairs commended the Myanma Government for its release of a number of prominent political prisoners and pledged a continuance of Japanese support for the Thein Sein administration's efforts to 'further advance democratization'. In April, following the by-elections at which 43 NLD candidates were elected to parliament, President Thein Sein paid an official visit to Japan, during which it was announced that Japan would cancel debts owed by Myanmar of more than US $3,700m. and would resume development aid. Agreement was also reached on a plan to establish a special economic zone near Yangon. In March 2013 it was reported that Myanmar was to resume exports of rice to Japan in May, the first such transaction between the two nations since 1968. Suu Kyi held discussions with Japanese Prime Minister Shinzo Abe in April 2013, during her first visit to Japan in 27 years.

Relations with Thailand, which had often been strained during the 1990s and early 2000s, deteriorated sharply in mid-2002 when fighting broke out on the bilateral border between government troops, allied with the United Wa State Army, and the Shan State Army (SSA). It was alleged that Thai troops had fired shells into Myanmar, in the belief that the fighting had encroached upon Thai territory. In response, the Myanma Government repeated previous claims that Thailand was providing support to the SSA. The border was closed shortly afterwards, as border incursions continued, but reopened in October. Following the adoption of a policy of 'soft engagement' by the Thai Government, in early 2003 the two countries signed an unprecedented agreement pledging that future military exercises would be conducted at a suitable distance from the border. In December Thailand hosted an international forum, the 'Bangkok Process', at which the Myanma Minister of Foreign Affairs, Win Aung, presented the 'road map' on democratic reform (see Domestic Political Affairs) to government representatives from 10 other Asian and European countries. A second round of talks in the 'Bangkok Process', scheduled for April 2004, was postponed indefinitely at Myanmar's request. A second 'Friendship Bridge' linking the two countries opened in January 2006.

A decision by the Myanmar junta in July 2010 to close a border crossing at Myawaddy, adjacent to the Thai border town of Mae Sot, was a source of considerable irritation to the Thai Government. The escalation of tensions in Myanmar's ethnic border areas in the immediate aftermath of the November legislative elections (see Insurgency and Dissidence) was reported to have forced more than 20,000 Myanma nationals to flee into Thailand to escape the violence. Three Thai nationals were injured when mortar and grenade attacks strayed across the Myanma–Thai border during fighting between the Democratic Karen (Kayin) Buddhist Army and Myanma government troops, causing Mae Sot to be evacuated. Thai Prime Minister Abhisit Vejjajiva announced the deployment of additional troops to the area in order to reinforce border security, and offered assurances that

Kayin and other Myanma refugees into Thailand would be treated humanely. According to UNHCR, at early 2013 there were around 84,900 registered and an estimated 62,000 unregistered Myanma refugees resident in nine camps in Thailand. More than 70,000 refugees were resettled in third countries between January 2005 and December 2011, a large proportion of whom had been accepted by the USA. Meanwhile, following a meeting between the Myanma and Thai Ministers of Foreign Affairs in the Myanma border town of Tachilek in December 2010, the Three Pagodas Pass border crossing, a principal 'black market' trade route between Thailand and Myanmar, was reopened after a three-year closure. In January 2011 Myanmar eased border control restrictions between Myawaddy and Mae Sot, allowing the transit of goods via cross-border trading ports to resume. During a visit to Myanmar in October, the new Thai Prime Minister, Yingluck Shinawatra, urged the Myanma authorities fully to reopen the land border crossing between Myawaddy and Mae Sot, the closure of which had significantly restricted cross-border trade. The Myanma authorities complied, and the border crossing duly reopened in December. On her first trip outside Myanmar since 1988, opposition leader Aung San Suu Kyi visited Thailand to attend the World Economic Forum in May 2012; during her visit Suu Kyi vowed to help the thousands of Myanma migrant workers in Thailand and held talks with Yingluck. President Thein Sein undertook his first official visit to Thailand in July.

In October 2002 the Australian Minister for Foreign Affairs, Alexander Downer, became the most senior Australian politician to visit Myanmar for 20 years. During his stay he met with senior members of the SPDC and with Suu Kyi. In October 2007 the Australian Government imposed financial sanctions on more than 400 Myanma leaders and associates. In October 2010 the Australian Minister for Foreign Affairs, Kevin Rudd, released a statement expressing 'grave reservations' about the validity of the legislative elections due to be held in Myanmar in the following month. Nevertheless, in June–July 2011 Rudd became the first Australian government minister to visit Myanmar since Downer in 2002, meeting with members of the new Myanma Government as well as members of the political opposition, including Suu Kyi. Following the election to parliament of Suu Kyi and other members of the NLD in April 2012, the Australian Government eased sanctions against Myanmar and announced its intention to normalize trading relations, although an embargo on arms sales remained in place. Following his visit to Myanmar in June 2012, the Australian Minister for Foreign Affairs, Robert Carr, pledged to double aid to Myanmar to almost US $100m. per year by 2015. In March 2013 Thein Sein became the first Myanma head of state to visit Australia since 1974; following his visit, it was announced that Australia, in further recognition of Myanmar's ongoing programme of reforms, was to relax restrictions on defence co-operation (involving military humanitarian aid and peace-keeping) with Myanmar.

Relations with the USA

Following the military junta's refusal to honour the results of the legislative elections in May 1990, and its violent suppression of the opposition, the US Government withdrew its ambassador from Myanmar. In May 1997 the USA imposed trade sanctions in protest at persistent and large-scale repression by the SLORC, prohibiting further investment in Myanmar, although existing US interests in the country remained unaffected. The sanctions were subsequently renewed annually. Following the detention of Suu Kyi in May 2003, in July US President George W. Bush approved the Burmese Freedom and Democracy Act, already adopted by Congress, banning all imports from Myanmar for three years and extending visa sanctions already imposed on SPDC officials. The Burmese Freedom and Democracy Act was renewed for a further three years in August 2006. In September 2007 the US Department of State expanded its visa ban to more than 35 additional government and military officials; the assets of a further 14 senior officials were also frozen. In October Bush announced the imposition of stricter controls on imports from Myanmar, as well as sanctions affecting the property interests of senior Myanma leaders. In May 2008, furthermore, the US Treasury was ordered to freeze the assets of all state-owned companies in Myanmar.

Following its inauguration in January 2009, the Administration of US President Barack Obama swiftly adopted a policy of 'pragmatic engagement' with those countries with which the USA did not have cordial relations (rejecting the policy of isolation to which the Bush Administration had adhered). However, the new Government stressed that sanctions would remain in place until tangible progress towards democratic change had been achieved by Myanmar. In July Obama renewed the Burmese Freedom and Democracy Act for a further three years, following its approval by the US Congress. In November 2009 Obama attended the ASEAN-US Leaders' Meeting, hosted by Singapore, at which Prime Minister Thein Sein was also present, demonstrating the Obama Administration's stated commitment to re-engaging with Myanmar; previously the USA had boycotted those meetings with ASEAN at which Myanma officials were present. Following Obama's inauguration, the military junta appeared more amenable to requests from US officials to meet with Suu Kyi and vice versa. As well as Senator Jim Webb, who met with Suu Kyi after securing the release of John Yettaw in August 2009 (see Domestic Political Affairs), several Western diplomats were allowed to meet with the opposition leader in late 2009 and early 2010. The US Assistant Secretary of State for East Asian and Pacific Affairs, Kurt Campbell, was permitted to meet with Suu Kyi when he led a fact-finding mission to Myanmar in November 2009, during which he also met with senior members of the military leadership. However, Campbell stated that the USA was 'very disappointed and concerned' by the electoral legislation enacted by the junta in March 2010 (see Domestic Political Affairs), which he described as a 'set-back' for US-Myanma relations, as well as for political dialogue within Myanmar. US economic sanctions against Myanmar were extended for a further year in July. One of the leaked US diplomatic cables published at the end of 2010 by WikiLeaks revealed that the US Government was deeply concerned by rumours, based on satellite images and other evidence, that Myanmar was developing a covert nuclear weapons programme in remote locations with the assistance of the Democratic People's Republic of Korea (North Korea). Myanmar and North Korea both denied the claims, with the Myanma Government denouncing such allegations as the result of a politically motivated plot orchestrated by 'anti-Government elements' to undermine its efforts to re-engage with the international community. During a visit to Myanmar in May 2011—the first by a senior US official following the inauguration of the Thein Sein administration at the end of March—Joseph Yun, the US Deputy Assistant Secretary for East Asian and Pacific Affairs, underscored US concerns about Myanma-North Korean military ties and urged the Myanma Government to abide by its public commitments to uphold UN Security Council resolutions on the issue of nuclear proliferation. In June 2012, while addressing a security forum in Singapore, the Myanma Minister of Defence, Lt-Gen. Hla Min, asserted that Myanmar had never pursued the development of nuclear weapons and, moreover, had now abandoned research into nuclear power generation, for reasons of cost.

Rejecting appeals by ASEAN for a lifting of sanctions against Myanmar following the staging of legislative elections in November 2010, President Obama announced the renewal of sanctions for a further year in May 2011, and urged the Thein Sein Government more fervently to pursue democratic reforms and to end its 'large-scale oppression' of the political opposition. In an indication of the US Administration's commitment to enhanced engagement with the Myanma Government, in mid-2011 President Obama appointed a special envoy for Myanmar, Derek Mitchell. Mitchell twice visited Myanmar in the latter half of the year for talks with the Government that were reported to have been constructive. The announcement in mid-November that US Secretary of State Hillary Clinton was to visit Myanmar at the end of the month—the most senior US visit since the military junta seized power in 1962—was widely construed as an acknowledgement of reforms announced by the Thein Sein administration in October, and followed an announcement on the previous day that the opposition NLD was to apply to re-register as a political party, thereby bestowing greater legitimacy on the political process within Myanmar. Some observers suggested that the US Government was keen to foster closer relations with Myanmar also as a means of countering increasing Chinese dominance in the Asia-Pacific region. During her visit, Clinton met with senior government leaders, including President Thein Sein, as well as with Suu Kyi and other senior NLD leaders, and announced a series of modest measures in recognition of recent progress demonstrated by the Government: the measures included a pledge to support proposals for enhanced co-operation between Myanmar and the World Bank and the IMF; an assurance that the USA would no longer object to Myanmar participation in the Mekong River Commission, for which the US Government provided funding; and US support for

UN-managed health-care, micro-finance and anti-narcotics programmes within Myanmar. However, she reiterated the need for the Myanma Government to effect further reforms, and urged the Government to sever military ties with North Korea and to resolve the country's ongoing ethnic conflicts (see Insurgency and Dissidence). Following the release of some of Myanmar's most prominent political prisoners in January 2012 (see Domestic Political Affairs), Clinton announced that the USA and Myanmar were to begin the process of exchanging ambassadors.

In February 2012 the Obama Administration announced the easing of one of the sanctions imposed against the Myanma Government as a reward for the latter's progress towards democratic governance. Following the successful conduct of parliamentary by-elections in April, the USA relaxed sanctions further, allowing limited US investment in a number of project areas. It was also announced that an office of the US Agency for International Development would be established in the country and Derek Mitchell, the former special envoy for Myanmar, was subsequently named as the new US ambassador to Myanmar.

Relations between Myanmar and the USA were further strengthened in the latter half of 2012: in July the US Administration announced that US companies were now allowed to 'responsibly do business' in Myanmar (excluding military or financial ventures) and a number of high-profile visits were conducted by leaders of both countries. During her visit to the USA in September, Suu Kyi met both Obama and Clinton and received the US Congressional Gold Medal that she had been awarded in 2008. The following week President Thein Sein became the first Myanma head of state to visit the USA in 46 years. During his visit, the President addressed the UN General Assembly and was informed by Clinton that the USA would ease its import ban on goods from Myanmar. In a reciprocal visit in November, Obama became the first ever incumbent US President to visit Myanmar, where he held talks with Thein Sein and Suu Kyi. Critics of this symbolic visit claimed that it was premature, given the ongoing ethnic unrest in Rakhine and Kayin State, the continued incarceration of political prisoners and the need for further reform. During his visit, however, Obama made a speech at the University of Yangon in which he demanded an end to communal violence between Muslims and Buddhists. In a further significant development, at the invitation of the USA, Myanmar sent observers to participate in the annual US-led military exercises—'Cobra Gold'—in Thailand in February 2013.

Relations with the UN

In June 1999 a resolution condemning Myanmar for its widespread use of forced labour was adopted by the member countries of the UN's International Labour Organization (ILO), and the country was barred from participating in any ILO activities. Following the failure of the ruling junta to carry out ILO recommendations regarding the use of forced labour and the suppression of trade unions in Myanmar, in November 2000 the ILO voted to proceed with sanctions against Myanmar. This was the first time such action had been undertaken in the UN labour body's 81-year history. The ILO subsequently requested its members to review their relations with Myanmar and to adopt sanctions. China, India, Malaysia and Russia voted against the action.

In September 2001 an ILO contingent visited Myanmar to ascertain whether the military junta had honoured its promise to bring about the abolition of forced labour. In November the ILO issued a report concluding that, while some progress had been made, the practice was still endemic in many parts of the country. In March 2002 the ILO agreed to establish a liaison office in Myanmar and, in October, an ILO mission visited the country to assist further in the development of good labour practices. In early 2004, following a visit by an ILO envoy, the SPDC agreed to allow ILO representatives to work freely towards the elimination of forced labour practices in the country. In February 2007 the ILO announced that the Myanma authorities had tentatively agreed to allow investigations into submitted forced labour cases without negative repercussions for alleged victims. However, in June 2009 the ILO denounced the Myanma Government's actions to end forced labour thus far as 'totally inadequate', and insisted that it must amend the new Constitution to include an explicit ban on forced labour and must be committed to punishing those found to be employing forced labour. The adoption of new labour legislation in October 2011 granting Myanma workers the right to form trade unions and to strike (with the exception of those working in essential services) was cautiously welcomed by the ILO. During an extensive European tour undertaken in June 2012, Suu Kyi addressed the ILO in Geneva, Switzerland, requesting that the international community aid economic development in Myanmar that benefited the whole population and not just an élite minority.

Meanwhile, in October 2007 the UN Human Rights Council adopted a resolution deploring the violent repression of peaceful demonstrations in the previous month and urging the release of peaceful protesters and all other political detainees. In November, during his first visit to Myanmar since March 2003, the UN Special Rapporteur on the situation of human rights in Myanmar, Dr Paulo Sérgio Pinheiro, held talks with government ministers and several prominent political prisoners, although he was not permitted to meet Suu Kyi. Following his visit, Pinheiro stated that the Myanma authorities had admitted that 15 people had been killed during the suppression of the anti-Government protests in September 2007 (five more than previously acknowledged), and in the following month he reported that his investigations indicated that at least a further 16 people had died, that 500–1,000 people were still being detained by the authorities (far more than claimed by the Government) and that 74 people were missing. Pinheiro also reported that the ill-treatment of detainees and the poor conditions in which they were being held had resulted in several deaths in custody.

Tomás Ojea Quintana, who replaced Pinheiro in April 2008, undertook visits to Myanmar in August 2008, February 2009 and February 2010. In a report presented to the UN Human Rights Council following his third visit to Myanmar, Ojea Quintana noted 'a pattern of gross and systematic violation of human rights', which, he argued, appeared to be 'the result of a state policy'. In March UN Secretary-General Ban Ki-Moon urged the Myanma Government to create suitable conditions for credible, inclusive elections, which would necessitate the release of political prisoners, including Suu Kyi; he also admitted to frustration at the 'disappointing' progress achieved as a result of UN engagement with the junta, and described the latter's efforts to ensure free and fair elections thus far as 'frustrating'. Shortly after the elections in November, Ibrahim Gambari's replacement as UN Special Envoy to Myanmar, Vijay Nambiar, visited the country, where he met with senior government officials in the outgoing junta, and insisted that they address the widespread concerns about the polls.

An amelioration in relations between the UN and Myanmar became evident following the transfer from military rule to a nominally civilian Government in January 2011. Ojea Quintana was allowed to visit Myanmar in August, his first visit to the country since February 2010, during which he welcomed the Government's 'stated commitments to reform', but urged it to address the long-standing social, economic and development challenges confronting Myanmar. Following a five-day visit in January–February 2012, Ojea Quintana commended the Myanma Government for the 'continuing wave of reforms' since his previous visit, including the establishment of the National Human Rights Commission, but expressed concerns regarding, *inter alia*, the continued detention of a number of political prisoners, and ongoing tensions and conflict with armed ethnic groups in border areas—particularly in Kachin State—noting persistent reports of extrajudicial killings, attacks against civilians, sexual violence, internal displacement, land confiscations, forced labour and the recruitment of child soldiers. At the end of April, at the invitation of President Thein Sein, UN Secretary-General Ban Ki-Moon visited Myanmar, where he met Suu Kyi, as well as the President, and became the first foreigner to address parliament, urging its members to accelerate the pace of reform. In his historic speech to the UN General Assembly in New York in September, President Thein Sein asserted that the democratic reforms being carried out in Myanmar were irreversible and paid tribute to Suu Kyi (referring to her, for the first time, as a Nobel laureate). In March 2013 Ojea Quintana expressed his serious concern over the recent spread of inter-communal violence in Myanmar and urged the Government to take steps to counteract this worrying development.

Relations with the European Union

From March 1997 the EU withdrew Myanmar's special trading status, in response to concerns over the country's human rights record; two scheduled meetings between the EU and ASEAN, due to take place in late 1997 and early 1999, respectively, were cancelled by the EU, owing to its objection to the representation of Myanmar at the talks. However, an agreement was subsequently reached by the two sides to allow Myanmar to take a 'passive role' in the Joint Co-operation Committee meeting between the EU and ASEAN.

In January 2003 the Myanma Deputy Minister of Foreign Affairs, Khin Maung Win, was permitted to attend an EU-ASEAN summit meeting for the first time since Myanmar's suspension from the meetings in 1997. However, in April 2003 the EU elected to extend its sanctions against the country and to increase the list of SPDC officials subject to visa sanctions and freezing of their assets. These sanctions were subsequently renewed annually. In October 2004 EU ministers responsible for foreign affairs implemented an earlier threat to broaden sanctions against Myanmar if the country did not make progress towards democratization in time for an Asia-Europe Meeting of heads of government (ASEM) held in Viet Nam earlier in the month. The ministers agreed to widen the list of Myanma officials subject to visa sanctions and to co-ordinate international bans on investment in the country (although the bans excluded European countries that had already invested in Myanmar).

In November 2007, in response to the violent suppression of anti-Government protests in Myanmar in September, the EU formally increased the number of officials subject to visa sanctions and asset freezing, expanded the scope of an investment ban on state-owned enterprises and imposed a new ban on some Myanma exports, including timber, metals and gemstones. However, in response to the programme of political reform undertaken by the Myanma Government following the inauguration of President Thein Sein in March 2011, in January 2012 the EU agreed to suspend the bloc's imposition of visa sanctions on senior Myanma officials—including the President, the two Vice-Presidents, the two parliamentary Speakers and members of the Cabinet. In April, following the successful conduct of parliamentary by-elections, the EU opened an embassy-level office in Yangon and announced the suspension of sanctions for a period of one year, allowing trade and investment in Myanmar and ending travel bans on nearly 500 individuals; an embargo on the sale of arms remained in place. In April 2013 the EU decided to make the removal of sanctions permanent, again with exception of the embargo on arms sales.

Other external relations

In May 1999 the ICRC, which had withdrawn from Myanmar in 1995 but reopened its offices there in October 1998, regained permission from the ruling junta to visit a limited number of prisons in the country. In January 2006 the ICRC suspended its prison visits, claiming that it was unable to fulfil its independent and impartial mandate owing to interference by the Myanma Government, and in October the SPDC ordered the organization to close its offices in Myanmar. In June 2007, in an unusual departure from its policy of neutrality, the ICRC issued a statement severely criticizing the Myanma authorities, claiming that human rights violations in Myanmar were causing 'immense suffering'. The ICRC resumed its monitoring of Myanma prisons in July 2011. In January 2013 the President of the ICRC, Peter Maurer, became the first head of that body to visit Myanmar. During his visit Maurer held talks with President Thein Sein and the head of the Myanmar Red Cross Society.

Despite the killing of three Indian soldiers in a clash with Myanma troops in October 2000, relations between India and Myanmar subsequently improved. Gen. Maung Aye visited India in November, meeting both the country's President and the Prime Minister. In February 2001 India's Minister of External Affairs, Jaswant Singh, visited Myanmar, the first Indian cabinet minister to do so since the SLORC's assumption of power in 1988. While there, Singh officially opened the Tamu–Kalewa highway, a road built by India to increase bilateral trade with Myanmar. In January 2003 Minister of Foreign Affairs Win Aung paid a visit to India, during which he met with the Prime Minister and several cabinet ministers. The two Governments agreed to hold regular consultations and to co-operate in counter-terrorism activities. In October 2004 the Chairman of the SPDC, Than Shwe, paid the first visit to India by a Myanma head of state in 24 years, agreeing at meetings with the Indian President and Prime Minister to further bilateral co-operation. In March 2006 President Aavul Pakkiri Jainulabidin Abdul Kalam visited Yangon, the first ever state visit to Myanmar by an Indian President. Than Shwe visited India for a second time in July 2010, meeting with Indian President Pratibha Patil and Prime Minister Dr Manmohan Singh; during his visit bilateral agreements were signed on enhancing co-operation in the fields of energy, anti-terrorism measures and defence, as well as boosting joint efforts to combat transnational drugs-trafficking, money-laundering and weapons-smuggling. During a visit to India in

October 2011, President Thein Sein met with Prime Minister Singh, whereupon a series of agreements intended to bolster bilateral trade and investment, including the provision by India of a grant for infrastructural development projects, was signed. The two leaders also pledged to enhance co-operation in the field of oil and gas exploration. In May 2012 Prime Minister Singh became the first Indian premier to visit Myanmar since 1987; during his visit the two countries agreed to establish a joint trade and investment forum. Singh also held a brief meeting with Suu Kyi (who herself visited India in November).

A protocol agreement signed between Myanmar and Russia in 1999 provided for the holding of regular consultation meetings between the two countries' respective ministers responsible for foreign affairs, to facilitate co-operation on regional and international issues; the most recent such meeting was held in Moscow in May 2012. Meanwhile, in May 2007 it was announced that Russia was to assist with the construction of a 10-MW nuclear research reactor in Myanmar. The two countries were reported in December 2009 to have signed a US $570m. agreement whereby Russia would provide Myanmar with 20 fighter aircraft, and in June 2011 an agreement providing for the export of Myanma rice to Russia was signed. During a visit to Myanmar in January 2013 the Russian Minister of Foreign Affairs, Sergei Lavrov, expressed his country's support for the lifting of all remaining sanctions against Myanmar, claiming that they were no longer justified. In March the Russian Minister of Defence, Col-Gen. Sergei Shoigu, paid an official visit to Myanmar in the course of which he stated that the Russian Government wished to extend military co-operation with Myanmar and to increase arms sales to that country.

CONSTITUTION AND GOVERNMENT

A new Constitution was approved in a national referendum in May 2008 and entered into force on 31 January 2011. Multi-party elections, the first for more than 20 years, were held in November 2010; 25% of seats in the bicameral national legislature, which was responsible for choosing the country's President, were reserved for representatives of the military. Following the inauguration in March 2011 of the new President, the State Peace and Development Council (SPDC), which had been established by the ruling military junta in November 1997, was dissolved. The incoming Cabinet comprised 30 members and was dominated by former military officers, as were the new eight-member State Supreme Council and 11-member National Defence and Security Council, created in February and March 2011, respectively.

REGIONAL AND INTERNATIONAL CO-OPERATION

Myanmar is a member of the Association of Southeast Asian Nations (ASEAN, see p. 218), the Asian Development Bank (ADB, see p. 214), the UN's Economic and Social Commission for Asia and the Pacific (ESCAP, see p. 31) and the Colombo Plan (see p. 460).

Myanmar became a member of the UN in 1948. As a contracting party to the General Agreement on Tariffs and Trade, Myanmar joined the World Trade Organization (WTO, see p. 444) on its establishment in 1995. Myanmar participates in the Non-aligned Movement (see p. 477), and is a member of the International Labour Organization (ILO, see p. 142).

ECONOMIC AFFAIRS

In 1986, according to estimates by the World Bank, Myanmar's gross national income (GNI), measured at average 1984–86 prices, was US $7,450m., equivalent to $200 per head. During 2002–11, it was estimated, the population rose at an average annual rate of 0.6%, while gross domestic product (GDP) per head increased, in real terms, by an average of 7.3% per year. Overall GDP increased at an average annual rate of 9.4% in 2002–11, according to the IMF. The Asian Development Bank (ADB) estimated real GDP growth at 5.5% in the financial year 2011/12 and at 6.3% in 2012/13.

According to the ADB, agriculture (including forestry and fishing) contributed 36.4% of GDP in 2010/11. The sector engaged an estimated 66.1% of the employed labour force at mid-2013, according to FAO. Rice is the staple crop, and production reached an estimated 32.8m. metric tons in 2011. In 2010/11 pulses and beans accounted for an estimated 9.1% of total exports. Other crops include sugar cane, maize, groundnuts, sesame seed, plantains and rubber. The fishing sector is also important. The total catch reached an estimated 3.9m. metric tons in 2010. Sales of teak and other hardwood provided

an estimated 6.5% of total export revenue in 2010/11. Myanmar is currently the world's second largest source of illicit opium (after Afghanistan). After several consecutive years of decline, the area under opium poppy cultivation reportedly began to rise in 2007. According to a survey conducted by the UN Office on Drugs and Crime (UNODC, see p. 80), the area under poppy cultivation expanded by an estimated 17% in 2012 to reach 51,000 ha. The potential production of dry opium was thought likely to have increased from 610 tons in 2011 to 690 tons in 2012. According to the ADB, following yearly growth rates that in 2000/01–05/06 ranged between 6.0% (recorded in 2002/03) and a high point of 12.1% (2005/06), the real GDP of the agricultural sector increased at an average annual rate of 6.0% in 2006/07–10/11. Agricultural GDP reportedly increased by 4.7% in 2010/11.

Industry (including mining, manufacturing, construction and utilities) provided 26.0% of GDP in 2010/11, according to the ADB. The industrial sector engaged 22.0% of the employed labour force (excluding activities not adequately defined) in 2005. According to the ADB, during 2000/01–05/06 yearly GDP growth rates ranged between 19.9% (in 2005/06) and 35.0% (2002/03). Between 2006/07 and 2010/11 industrial GDP increased at an average annual rate of 18.5%. The GDP of the industrial sector reportedly expanded by 18.6% in 2010/11.

Mining and quarrying contributed only 0.9% of GDP in 2010/11, according to the ADB. The sector engaged 0.7% of the employed labour force in 1997/98. Significant new onshore and offshore discoveries of natural gas and petroleum resulted from exploration and production-sharing agreements with foreign companies, the first of which was signed in 1989. In 2005, however, the Government announced that henceforth all onshore oil and gas blocks would be operated exclusively by a state enterprise. Other important minerals that are commercially exploited include tin, copper, coal, lead, jade, gemstones, silver and gold; some of Myanmar's potentially lucrative mineral resources remain largely unexploited. According to ADB data, the GDP of the mining sector increased at an average annual rate of 11.2% between 2006/07 and 2010/11, rising by 13.4% in the latter year.

Manufacturing contributed 19.5% of GDP in 2010/11, according to the ADB, and the sector engaged 9.1% of the employed labour force in 1998. The most important branches are food- and beverage-processing, the production of industrial raw materials (cement, plywood and fertilizers), petroleum refining and textiles. Revenue from garment exports rose from 1,543.7m. kyats in 2009/10 to an estimated 1,876.0m. kyats in 2010/11, equivalent to 3.8% of total exports in the latter year. The real GDP of the manufacturing sector expanded, according to ADB data, at an average annual rate of 19.7% between 2006/07 and 2010/11, increasing by 20.3% in 2010/11.

Construction provided 4.5% of GDP in 2010/11, according to the ADB. The sector engaged only 2.2% of the employed labour force (excluding activities not adequately defined) in 1998. Between 2006/07 and 2010/11, according to ADB figures, construction GDP increased at an average annual rate of 15.4%; the sector's GDP reportedly grew by 12.5% in 2010/11.

Energy is derived principally from hydroelectric power, which contributed 71.5% of total electricity production in 2009; natural gas accounted for 19.6% and petroleum 8.9%. China has provided considerable assistance in the development of hydropower resources. Myanmar's hydropower potential is estimated at around 30,000 MW. Imports of mineral oils accounted for around 14.2% of total imports in 2010/11.

The services sector contributed 37.6% of GDP in 2010/11, according to the ADB, and engaged 25.1% of the employed labour force in 1997/98. Tourism revenue is an important source of foreign exchange. Revenue from this sector rose from US $56m. in 2009 to $73m. in 2010. The number of tourist arrivals increased from 310,688 in 2010 to a provisional 391,000 in 2011. In 2000/01–05/06, according to ADB data, the services sector's yearly rates of GDP growth ranged between 12.9% (in 2001/02) and 14.8% (2002/03). Services GDP increased at an average annual rate of 12.1% in 2006/07–10/11. GDP growth in the sector was reported at 11.6% in 2010/11.

In 2011 Myanmar recorded a visible merchandise trade surplus of US $208.0m., while there was a deficit of $1,423.8m. on the current account of the balance of payments. In 2010/11 the principal sources of imports were the People's Republic of China (which supplied 33.8% of the total), Singapore and Thailand. The principal market for exports (32.7%) was Thailand; other significant purchasers were Hong Kong, China, India and Singapore. The principal imports in 2010/11 were refined mineral oils, machinery and transport equipment, and base metals and manufactures. The principal exports in that year included gas (which accounted for 32.6% of total export earnings) and dried pulses.

An overall budget deficit of 1,813,600m. kyats, equivalent to 4.5% of GDP, was recorded in 2010/11, according to the ADB. Myanmar's general government gross debt was 19,307,010m. kyats in 2010, equivalent to 53.0% of GDP. According to the ADB, the outstanding external debt at the end of 2012 totalled US $12,251m.; the cost of servicing external debt in that year was equivalent to 5.1% of exports of goods and services. The annual rate of inflation averaged 18.4% in 2001–10. According to the ADB, the rate of inflation was 3.5% in 2012. The rate of unemployment in 2011 was estimated by the ADB at 4.0% of the labour force.

Weaknesses in data have impeded accurate assessments of Myanmar's economy. Progress towards democratic reform by the new Government that came into office in March 2011, headed by President Thein Sein, led to an increase in foreign direct investment (FDI) and tourism revenues as Myanmar began gradually to re-engage with the rest of the international community after many years of almost total economic isolation. In the fiscal year ending March 2012 FDI, almost all of which was in the hydropower and oil and gas sectors, increased to an estimated US $2,800m. However, in September 2011 the Myanma Government suspended construction of the $3,600m. Chinese-funded Myitsone dam project, citing environmental concerns. Plans for the establishment of special economic zones (SEZs) included the development of a major maritime hub and industrial estate in the southern coastal town of Dawei, and two other zones, in Thilawa near Yangon, and Kyaukphyu on the west coast. The Government hoped to attract foreign investment to these zones by means of tax incentives. However, at early 2013 progress with the Dawei SEZ had stalled owing to a lack of funding, the 5,000 villagers who were to be relocated from Thilawa were refusing to leave without adequate compensation, and international environmental groups had expressed concerns over the potential damage to people's health and the natural habitat that the development of the Kyaukphyu SEZ would entail. The easing of international sanctions, in recognition of progress towards political and economic reform, was expected to have a positive impact on trade and investment, as well as providing renewed access to concessionary finance and aid assistance. In February 2012 the Myanma Government revealed that its total foreign debt stood at $11,023m. and stated that it had commenced negotiations on debt repayments with multilateral institutions and donor nations, including Japan (which accounted for $6,390m. of the total debt). Following the successful conduct of parliamentary by-elections in April, Japan agreed to cancel Myanma debt worth $3,700m. In January 2013 the Paris Club of creditor nations agreed to cancel about $6,000m. of Myanmar's debt (some 60% of the total owed). In August 2012 the World Bank opened an office in Yangon (shared with the ADB) to begin a process of re-engagement by offering an initial aid sum of $85m.; the World Bank had ceased funding to Myanmar in 1987, when the Government had halted debt repayments. Following Myanmar's clearance of its arrears with the two institutions, in January 2013 the ADB and the World Bank approved loans of $512m. and $440m., respectively, to aid social and economic development in the country; the ADB loan was that institution's first such credit to Myanmar for 30 years. Among economic reforms implemented by the new Government was the introduction on 1 April 2012 of a unified exchange rate, ending the dual exchange rate (an official rate and a black market rate) that had existed for decades, with the aim of eliminating the informal currency market. In addition, a group of 11 private banks in Myanmar were authorized by the Central Bank of Myanmar to trade in three foreign currencies, the US dollar, the euro and the Singapore dollar, facilitating trade and business transactions. In response to the notable rise in foreign interest in investment, legislation approved in November 2012 reportedly removed the 50% cap on foreign holdings. The ADB forecast that GDP would expand by 6.5% in 2013/14, supported by investment in the oil and gas industries, as well as increased tourism revenues and foreign remittances, while the rate of inflation would rise to 5.1% in 2013.

PUBLIC HOLIDAYS

2014: 4 January (Independence Day), 12 February (Union Day), 2 March (Peasants' Day, anniversary of the 1962 coup), 7 March* (Full Moon of Tabaung), 27 March (Armed Forces' Day), 13–16 April* (Maha Thingyan—Water Festival), 17 April* (Myanma New Year), 1 May (Workers' Day), 5 May* (Full Moon of Kason), 19 July (Martyrs' Day), 2 August* (Full Moon of Waso and beginning of Buddhist Lent), 30 October* (Full Moon of Thadingyut and end of Buddhist Lent), 28 November* (Tazaungdaing Festival), 8 December* (National Day), 25 December (Christmas Day).

* A number of holidays depend on lunar sightings.

Statistical Survey

Source (unless otherwise stated): Central Statistical Organization, Ministry of National Planning and Economic Development, Building 32, Nay Pyi Taw; tel. (67) 406325; fax (67) 407265; e-mail cso.stat@mptmail.net.mm; internet www.csostat.gov.mm.

Area and Population

AREA, POPULATION AND DENSITY

Area (sq km)	676,552*
Population (census results)	
31 March 1973	28,885,867
31 March 1983	
Males	17,518,255
Females	17,789,658
Total	35,307,913
Population (UN estimates at mid-year)†	
2011	48,336,764
2012	48,724,385
2013	49,119,647
Density (per sq km) at mid-2012	72.6

* 261,218 sq miles.
† Source: UN, *World Population Prospects: The 2010 Revision.*

POPULATION BY AGE AND SEX
(UN estimates at mid-2013)

	Males	Females	Total
0–14	6,034,301	5,916,275	11,950,576
15–64	17,001,987	17,544,056	34,546,043
65 and over	1,163,647	1,459,381	2,623,028
Total	24,199,935	24,919,712	49,119,647

Source: UN, *World Population Prospects: The 2010 Revision.*

PRINCIPAL TOWNS
(population at census of 31 March 1983)

Yangon (Rangoon, capital) . .	2,513,023	Pathein (Bassein) .	144,096
Mandalay . .	532,949	Taunggyi . . .	108,231
Mawlamyine (Moulmein) . .	219,961	Sittwe (Akyab) . .	107,621
Bago (Pegu) . .	150,528	Manywa	106,843

Note: In 2006 the functions of the capital city were transferred from Yangon to the new administrative centre of Nay Pyi Taw.

Source: UN, *Demographic Yearbook.*

Mid-2011 (incl. suburbs, UN estimates): Nay Pyi Taw (capital) 1,059,530 (Source: UN, *World Urbanization Prospects: The 2011 Revision*).

BIRTHS AND DEATHS
(annual averages, UN estimates)

	1995–2000	2000–05	2005–10
Birth rate (per 1,000)	22.3	19.3	17.9
Death rate (per 1,000)	9.3	8.9	8.9

Source: UN, *World Population Prospects: The 2010 Revision*.

Life expectancy (years at birth): 65.2 (males 63.5; females 66.9) in 2011 (Source: World Bank, World Development Indicators database).

ECONOMICALLY ACTIVE POPULATION*
('000 persons, official estimates)

	1997	1998
Agriculture, hunting, forestry and fishing	11,381	11,507
Mining and quarrying	132	121
Manufacturing	1,573	1,666
Electricity, gas and water	21	48
Construction	378	400
Trade, restaurants and hotels	1,746	1,781
Transport, storage and communications	470	495
Financing, insurance, real estate and business services	577	597
Community, social and personal services†	1,686	1,744
Total employed	17,964	18,359
Unemployed‡	535	452
Total labour force	18,499	18,811

* Excludes members of the armed forces.
† Includes activities not adequately defined.
‡ Persons aged 18 years and over.

Unemployed ('000 persons aged 18 years and over): 183.4 in 2006; 118.7 in 2007; 137.8 in 2008 (Source: ILO).

Mid-2013 ('000 persons, estimates): Agriculture, etc. 19,318; Total labour force 29,245 (Source: FAO).

Health and Welfare

KEY INDICATORS

Total fertility rate (children per woman, 2010)	2.0
Under-5 mortality rate (per 1,000 live births, 2010)	66
HIV/AIDS (% of persons aged 15–49, 2009)	0.6
Physicians (per 1,000 head, 2008)	0.5
Hospital beds (per 1,000 head, 2006)	0.6
Health expenditure (2009): US $ per head (PPP)	36
Health expenditure (2009): % of GDP	2.1
Health expenditure (2009): public (% of total)	11.3
Access to water (% of persons, 2010)	83
Access to sanitation (% of persons, 2010)	76
Total carbon dioxide emissions ('000 metric tons, 2008)	12,775.8
Carbon dioxide emissions per head (metric tons, 2008)	0.3
Human Development Index (2011): ranking	149
Human Development Index (2011): value	0.483

For sources and definitions, see explanatory note on p. vi.

Agriculture

PRINCIPAL CROPS
('000 metric tons)

	2009	2010	2011
Wheat	182	184	185*
Rice, paddy	32,682	32,580	32,800*
Maize	1,245	1,376	1,370*
Millet*	185	185	187
Potatoes	563	573	573*
Sweet potatoes*	59	50	48
Cassava (Manioc)	478	607	615*
Sugar cane	9,715	9,398	9,400*
Beans, dry	3,375	3,000*	3,722*
Peas, dry	58	61	65*
Chick peas	404	441	467
Cow peas, dry	213	215	218

—*continued*	2009	2010	2011
Pigeon peas	765	773	837
Arecanuts	116	122*	121*
Soybeans (Soya beans)	244	258	259
Groundnuts, with shell	1,305	1,362	1,392
Coconuts	420	407†	420*
Sunflower seed	780	782	790
Sesame seed	853	868	862
Onions, dry	1,040	1,109	1,131
Garlic	181	201	209
Plantains	770	842	951
Tea†	30	31	32
Jute	1	1	2
Tobacco, unmanufactured	28	29	29†
Natural rubber	93	112	128

* FAO estimate(s).
† Unofficial figure(s).

Aggregate production ('000 metric tons, may include official, semi-official or estimated data): Total cereals 34,521 in 2009, 34,555 in 2010, 34,764 in 2011; Total roots and tubers 1,100 in 2009, 1,230 in 2010, 1,236 in 2011; Total vegetables (incl. melons) 4,841 in 2009, 5,195 in 2010, 5,317 in 2011; Total fruits (excl. melons) 2,185 in 2009, 2,192 in 2010, 2,476 in 2011.

Source: FAO.

LIVESTOCK
('000 head, year ending September)

	2009*	2010	2011
Horses*	120	115	114
Cattle	13,000	13,186	13,609
Buffaloes	2,900	2,875	2,977
Pigs	8,000	8,496	9,416
Sheep	584	664	700*
Goats	3,025	3,421	3,500*
Chickens	124,993	138,938	156,407
Ducks	12,835	14,051	14,500
Geese	1,565	1,748	1,800*

* FAO estimate(s).

Source: FAO.

LIVESTOCK PRODUCTS
('000 metric tons)

	2009	2010	2011
Cattle meat*†	145.0	175.0	200.0
Buffalo meat*	32.9	34.6	34.3
Goat meat	32.0*	36.0*	38.0†
Pig meat	470.6	534.7	585.3
Chicken meat	797.8	923.1	1,015.9
Cows' milk*	1,070.0	1,200.0	1,300.0
Buffaloes' milk*	244.7	265.1	303.0
Goats' milk†	12.8	13.0	13.0
Hen eggs	265.0†	318.3	342.0
Other poultry eggs	34.5*	38.6*	40.0†

* Unofficial figure(s).
† FAO estimate(s).

Source: FAO.

Forestry

ROUNDWOOD REMOVALS
('000 cubic metres, excl. bark)

	2003	2004	2005
Sawlogs, veneer logs and logs for sleepers	2,885	2,816	2,849
Other industrial wood	1,353	1,380	1,413
Fuel wood	37,954	37,560	38,286
Total	42,191	41,756	42,548

2006–11: Figures assumed to be unchanged from 2005 (FAO estimates).

Source: FAO.

SAWNWOOD PRODUCTION
('000 cubic metres, incl. railway sleepers, unofficial figures)

	2004	2005	2006
Coniferous (softwood) . . .	77	61	80
Broadleaved (hardwood) . . .	1,056	1,530	1,530
Total	1,133	1,591	1,610

2007–11: Production assumed to be unchanged from 2006 (unofficial figures).

Source: FAO.

Fishing

('000 metric tons, live weight)

	2008	2009	2010
Capture*	2,493.8	2,766.9	3,063.2
Freshwater fishes . . .	814.7	899.4	1,002.4
Marine fishes	1,643.6	1,827.5	2,016.6
Aquaculture*	674.8	778.1	850.7
Common carp	18.6	20.9	23.4
Roho labeo	433.1	488.0	546.3
Total catch*	3,168.5	3,545.0	3,913.9

* FAO estimate(s).

Source: FAO.

Mining

(metric tons unless otherwise indicated)

	2008	2009	2010
Coal and lignite	249,442	245,418	217,650
Crude petroleum ('000 barrels) .	7,242	6,881	6,806
Natural gas (million cu m)* . .	12,445	11,555	12,425
Copper ore††	—	3,500	12,000‡
Lead ore†‡	3,000	7,500	7,000
Zinc ore†	7,000	6,000	7,000
Tin concentrates†	800	1,000	4,000
Silver ore (kilograms)† . .	—	249	—
Gold ore (kilograms)†§‡ . . .	100	100	100
Feldspar‡§	10,000	10,000	10,000
Barite (Barytes)	5,679	7,623	8,975
Salt (unrefined, excl. brine)‡ . .	35,000	35,000	35,000
Gypsum (crude)	82,224	97,518	81,051
Rubies, sapphires and spinel ('000 metric carats)§	3,570	2,767	3,542
Jade	30,896	25,427	38,990

* Marketed production.
† Figures refer to the metal content of ores and concentrates (including mixed concentrates).
‡ Estimated production.
§ Twelve months beginning 1 April of year stated.

Source: US Geological Survey.

Industry

SELECTED PRODUCTS OF STATE-OWNED ENTERPRISES
('000 metric tons unless otherwise indicated)

	2008/09	2009/10	2010/11
Sugar	28.4	20.3	21.4
Beer ('000 gallons) . . .	1,514.4	441.2	n.a.
Cigarettes (million) . . .	2,351.8	n.a.	n.a.
Cotton fabrics ('000 yards) . .	19.1	20.0	18.5
Cotton yarn ('000 lbs) . . .	13.9	15.1	18.2
Plywood ('000 sq ft) . . .	135.6	160.2	204.8
Fertilizers	106.1	69.8	35.3
Diesel oil ('000 gallons) . . .	50,582	32,843	63,044
Furnace oil ('000 gallons) . . .	17,078	14,243	11,517
Liquefied petroleum gas ('000 gallons) . . .	3,566	3,199	3,291
Motor spirit (petrol, '000 gallons) .	103,854	112,615	129,292
Cement	690.8	628.2	547.6
Paper	19.9	13.3	14.7
Soap	76.9	67.4	44.7
Electric energy (million kWh) .	6,621.8	6,964.3	7,543.1*

* Provisional figure.

Finance

CURRENCY AND EXCHANGE RATES

Monetary Units
100 pyas = 1 kyat.

Sterling, Dollar and Euro Equivalents (30 November 2012)
£1 sterling = 1,362.436 kyats;
US $1 = 848.500 kyats;
€1 = 1,101.862 kyats;
100 kyats = £73.40 = $117.86 = €90.76.

Average Exchange Rate (kyats per US $)
2009   5.576
2010   5.635
2011   5.444

Note: In April 2012, in an attempt gradually to unify the disparate official and unofficial exchange rates which had prevailed in the country for decades, the Government initiated a 'managed float' of the kyat on the open market; an initial daily reference exchange rate of US $1 = 818 kyats was published by the central bank on 1 April.

CENTRAL GOVERNMENT BUDGET
(million kyats, year ending 31 March, excl. capital account)

Current revenue and grants	2003/04	2004/05	2005/06
Tax revenue	170,569	297,104	476,945
Taxes on income, profits and capital gains	91,860	138,866	206,676
Domestic taxes on goods and services	74,107	136,626	251,821
General sales, turnover or value-added tax	58,214	112,543	225,121
Taxes on international trade and transactions	4,602	21,613	18,448
Other revenue	213,542	290,190	342,273
Grants	111	171	316
Total	384,222	587,465	819,534

Current expenditure	2003/04	2004/05	2005/06
General public services, incl. public order	114,195	206,848	354,848
Defence	172,633	173,558	197,792
Education	71,665	101,936	68,676
Health	18,808	26,545	21,963
Social security and welfare	7,865	9,933	8,406
Recreational, cultural and religious affairs	4,112	5,863	4,511
Economic affairs and services	194,354	234,513	346,361
Agriculture, forestry, fishing and hunting	61,056	71,028	93,300
Transportation	119,190	131,839	198,261
Housing and community amenities	7,397	8,622	6,228
Total	591,029	767,818	1,008,785

Source: IMF, *Government Finance Statistics Yearbook.*

INTERNATIONAL RESERVES
(US $ million at 31 December)

	2009	2010	2011
Gold (national valuation)	12.8	12.6	12.6
IMF special drawing rights	113.3	2.6	1.0
Foreign exchange	5,138.4	5,714.3	7,003.0
Total	5,264.5	5,729.5	7,016.6

Source: IMF, *International Financial Statistics.*

MONEY SUPPLY
('000 million kyats at 31 December)

	2009	2010	2011
Currency outside depository corporations	3,568.55	4,278.93	5,132.60
Transferable deposits	630.61	1,269.95	1,556.05
Other deposits	2,380.64	3,827.33	5,542.64
Broad money	6,579.81	9,376.21	12,231.29

Source: IMF, *International Financial Statistics.*

COST OF LIVING
(Consumer Price Index; base: 2000 = 100)

	2008	2009	2010
Food (incl. beverages)	638.3	524.0	562.0
Fuel and light	561.9	432.9	448.9
Clothing (incl. footwear)	583.4	577.8	599.9
Rent	658.6	787.0	902.8
All items (incl. others)	610.3	515.3	555.1

Source: ILO.

NATIONAL ACCOUNTS
(million kyats at current prices, year ending 31 March)

Expenditure on the Gross Domestic Product

	2008/09	2009/10	2010/11
Final consumption expenditure	24,141,260	28,542,971	31,731,871
Increase in stocks	−29,231	−43,199	106,080
Gross fixed capital formation	4,599,845	6,436,829	9,073,444
Total domestic expenditure	28,711,874	34,936,601	40,911,395
Exports of goods and services	32,214	38,673	46,150
Less Imports of goods and services	24,874	22,837	35,508
Statistical discrepancy	514,074	−1,046,771	−414,095
GDP in purchasers' values	29,233,288	33,905,666	40,507,942
GDP at constant 2005/06 prices	17,155,078	18,970,327	20,946,337

Gross Domestic Product by Economic Activity

	2008/09	2009/10	2010/11
Agriculture, hunting, forestry and fishing	11,773,735	12,916,382	14,729,014
Mining and quarrying	254,409	331,351	367,042
Manufacturing	4,917,322	6,136,416	7,905,155
Electricity, gas and water	218,167	337,675	418,532
Construction	1,236,065	1,518,309	1,839,335
Wholesale and retail trade	6,175,062	6,890,046	8,037,819
Transport, storage and communications	3,731,536	4,586,601	5,577,546
Finance	20,938	27,392	31,417
Government services	399,679	551,654	866,630
Other services	506,375	609,840	735,452
GDP in purchasers' values	29,233,288	33,905,666	40,507,942

Source: Asian Development Bank.

BALANCE OF PAYMENTS
(US $ million)

	2009	2010	2011
Exports of goods	5,903.4	7,334.7	7,699.0
Imports of goods	−3,315.3	−3,857.5	−7,491.0
Balance on goods	2,588.1	3,477.2	208.0
Exports of services	349.2	369.2	671.8
Imports of services	−617.2	−789.0	−1,090.2
Balance on goods and services	2,320.1	3,057.5	−210.4
Primary income received	94.7	147.5	195.2
Primary income paid	−1,861.9	−1,869.5	−1,797.7
Balance on goods, services and primary income	552.9	1,335.5	−1,812.9
Secondary income received	496.6	345.7	493.0
Secondary income paid	−63.4	−107.1	−103.9
Current balance	986.0	1,574.2	−1,423.8
Direct investment liabilities	1,079.0	901.1	1,000.6
Other investment liabilities	459.5	216.2	706.1
Net errors and omissions	−1,324.6	−2,132.9	987.8
Reserves and related items	1,199.9	558.5	1,270.7

Source: IMF, *International Financial Statistics.*

External Trade

PRINCIPAL COMMODITIES
(distribution by SITC, million kyats, year ending 31 March)

Imports c.i.f.	2008/09	2009/10	2010/11
Edible vegetable oil and other hydrogenated oils	1,610.0	975.9	934.2
Pharmaceutical products	679.0	797.7	905.3
Base metals and manufactures	1,818.3	1,992.9	2,469.7
Machinery and transport equipment	7,240.2	4,908.2	4,600.5
Electrical machinery and apparatus	948.6	977.1	1,421.5
Paper, paperboard and manufactures	391.7	318.1	309.0
Refined mineral oils	3,192.2	3,674.3	5,046.1
Fabric of artificial materials and synthetics	817.4	780.2	1,053.9
Plastic	908.8	859.2	1,182.0
Total (incl. others)	24,873.8	22,837.4	35,508.4

Exports f.o.b.	2008/09	2009/10	2010/11
Dried beans, peas, etc. (shelled) .	4,068.8	5,062.9	4,449.8
Fresh and dried prawns . . .	472.1	346.2	371.3
Fish and fish products	972.3	1,053.3	1,270.9
Teak	1,146.3	1,171.7	1,689.3
Other hardwood	1,065.7	1,518.9	1,499.7
Base metals and ores	176.5	182.7	305.1
Gas	12,995.7	15,853.8	16,020.7
Garments	1,593.9	1,543.7	1,876.0
Total (incl. others)	37,027.8	41,289.1	49,106.8

PRINCIPAL TRADING PARTNERS
(million kyats, year ending 31 March)

Imports	2008/09	2009/10	2010/11
China, People's Republic . . .	6,578.1	6,854.9	12,005.1
Hong Kong	177.7	59.8	46.5
India	796.8	1,058.5	1,079.9
Indonesia	1,139.5	760.4	1,526.1
Japan	908.4	1,412.4	1,417.1
Korea, Republic	1,027.3	1,221.5	1,683.4
Malaysia	1,972.1	871.3	805.0
Singapore	5,712.7	6,593.0	9,116.9
Thailand	2,150.7	2,069.6	3,938.6
Total (incl. others)	24,873.8	22,837.4	35,508.4

Exports	2008/09	2009/10	2010/11
China, People's Republic . . .	3,352.3	3,359.0	6,662.9
Hong Kong	3,611.0	5,162.9	10,530.6
India	4,387.8	5,512.9	4,858.1
Indonesia	155.1	205.3	228.0
Japan	1,005.8	966.1	1,314.0
Malaysia	1,716.0	832.2	2,445.9
Singapore	4,638.4	3,690.9	2,499.9
Thailand	14,340.6	17,431.0	16,065.2
United Kingdom	284.4	202.6	193.0
Total (incl. others)	37,027.8	41,289.1	49,106.8

Transport

RAILWAYS
(traffic, million)

	2008/09	2009/10	2010/11
Passenger-miles	3,405	3,338	3,329
Freight ton-miles	581	658	698

ROAD TRAFFIC
(registered motor vehicles at 31 March)

	2008/09	2009/10	2010/11
Passenger cars	239,895	254,797	279,066
Trucks	58,857	61,132	64,888
Buses	19,683	19,807	20,944
Motorcycles	1,612,423	1,749,083	1,883,958
Others	68,102	62,585	59,665
Total	1,998,960	2,147,404	2,308,521

INLAND WATERWAYS
(traffic by state-owned vessels)

	2008/09	2009/10	2010/11
Passenger-miles (million) . . .	783	820	902
Freight ton-miles (million) . .	639	687	754

SHIPPING

Flag Registered Fleet
(at 31 December)

	2010	2011	2012
Number of vessels	62	60	62
Displacement ('000 grt) . . .	179.5	163.1	166.0

Source: Lloyd's List Intelligence (www.lloydslistintelligence.com).

International Sea-borne Traffic
('000 metric tons)

	2008/09	2009/10	2010/11
Goods loaded	2,955	4,539	3,256
Goods unloaded	4,123	6,883	8,601

CIVIL AVIATION
(traffic on scheduled services)

	2007	2008	2009
Kilometres flown (million) . .	23	23	22
Passengers carried ('000) . .	1,663	1,638	1,527
Passenger-km (million) . . .	1,609	1,585	1,470
Total ton-km (million) . . .	148	145	134

Source: UN, *Statistical Yearbook*.

Passenger-miles (million): 75.3 in 2006/07; 77.6 in 2007/08; 81.9 in 2008/09; 71.9 in 2009/10; 105.6 in 2010/11.

Tourism

TOURIST ARRIVALS BY COUNTRY OF NATIONALITY

	2008	2009	2010
Australia	5,374	7,163	7,693
China, People's Republic . . .	30,792	36,341	46,141
France	8,217	10,458	13,143
Germany	8,947	9,608	11,082
India	7,173	8,609	9,849
Italy	3,030	5,975	7,169
Japan	10,881	13,809	16,186
Korea, Republic	12,369	12,508	18,930
Malaysia	8,268	9,668	16,186
Singapore	8,599	10,712	12,114
Taiwan	11,472	12,276	14,170
Thailand	27,311	43,254	59,692
United Kingdom	5,397	6,171	7,340
USA	13,195	15,053	16,504
Total (incl. others)	193,319	243,278	310,688

Tourist arrivals ('000): 391 in 2011 (provisional). **Tourism receipts** (US $ million, excl. passenger transport): 56 in 2009; 73 in 2010.

Source: World Tourism Organization.

Communications Media

	2009	2010	2011
Telephones ('000 main lines in use)	444.3	493.3	523.9
Mobile cellular telephones ('000 subscribers)	502.0	594.0	1,243.6
Internet subscribers ('000)	n.a.	n.a.	15.3
Broadband subscribers ('000)	20.4	23.0	11.1

Source: International Telecommunication Union.

Education

(2009/10 unless otherwise indicated)

	Institutions*	Teachers	Students
Pre-primary schools	n.a.	9,194	159,270
Primary schools	35,856	181,666	5,125,942
Middle schools	2,058	} 83,703	2,852,447
High schools	858		
Vocational schools	86	1,847*	21,343*
Teacher training	17	615*	4,031*
Higher education	45	6,246*	247,348*
Universities	6	2,901*	62,098*

* Data for 1994/95; figure for primary schools excludes 1,152 monastic primary schools with an enrolment of 45,360 in 1994/95.

Source: mainly UNESCO Institute for Statistics.

Pupil-teacher ratio (primary education, UNESCO estimate): 28.2 in 2009/10 (Source: UNESCO Institute for Statistics).

Adult literacy rate (UNESCO estimates): 92.3% (males 94.8%; females 89.9%) in 2010 (Source: UNESCO Institute for Statistics).

Directory

The Government

HEAD OF STATE

President: THEIN SEIN (took office 30 March 2011).
Vice-Presidents: Dr SAI MAUK KHAM, Adm. NYAN TUN.

CABINET
(May 2013)

Ministers of the President's Office: THEIN NYUNT, SOE MAUNG, SOE THEIN, AUNG MIN, HLA TUN, TIN NAING THEIN.
Minister of Defence: Lt-Gen. WAI LWIN.
Minister of Home Affairs: Lt-Gen. KO KO.
Minister of Border Affairs: Lt-Gen. THET NAING WIN.
Minister of Foreign Affairs: WUNNA MAUNG LWIN.
Minister of Information: AUNG KYI.
Minister of Culture: AYE MYINT KYU.
Minister of Agriculture and Irrigation: MYINT HLAING.
Minister of Environmental Conservation and Forestry: WIN TUN.
Minister of Finance and Revenue: WIN SHEIN.
Minister of Construction: KYAW LWIN.
Minister of National Planning and Economic Development: Dr KAN ZAW.
Minister of Livestock and Fisheries: OHN MYINT.
Minister of Commerce: WIN MYINT.
Minister of Communications and Information Technology: Gen. MYAT HEIN.
Minister of Labour, Employment and Social Security: MAUNG MYINT.
Minister of Social Welfare, Relief and Resettlement: Dr DAW MYAT OHN KHIN.
Minister of Mines: Dr MYINT AUNG.
Minister of Co-operatives: KYAW HSAN.
Minister of Transportation: NYAN TUN AUNG.
Minister of Sports: TINT HSAN.
Minister of Industry (No. 1 and No. 2): AYE MYINT.
Minister of Rail Transportation: Maj.-Gen. ZEYAR AUNG.
Minister of Energy: THAN HTAY.
Minister of Electric Power: KHIN MAUNG SOE.
Minister of Hotels and Tourism: HTAY AUNG.
Minister of Education: Dr MYA AYE.
Minister of Health: Dr PE THET KHIN.
Minister of Religious Affairs: HSAN HSINT.
Minister of Science and Technology: Dr KO KO OO.
Minister of Immigration and Manpower: KHIN YI.

MINISTRIES

Ministry of President Office: Bldg 18, Nay Pyi Taw; internet www.president-office.gov.mm.
Ministry of Agriculture and Irrigation: Bldg 15, Nay Pyi Taw; tel. (67) 410004; fax (67) 140130; e-mail dg-dap@myanmar.com.mm; internet www.moai.gov.mm.
Ministry of Border Affairs: Bldg 14, Nay Pyi Taw; tel. (67) 409022.
Ministry of Commerce: Bldg 3, Nay Pyi Taw; tel. (67) 408002; fax (67) 408004; e-mail moc@commerce.gov.mm; internet www.commerce.gov.mm.
Ministry of Construction: Bldg 11, Nay Pyi Taw; tel. (67) 407073; fax (67) 407181; internet www.construction.gov.mm.
Ministry of Co-operatives: Bldg 16, Nay Pyi Taw; tel. (67) 410033; fax (67) 410036; e-mail mocoop@mptmail.net.mm; internet www.myancoop.gov.mm.
Ministry of Culture: Bldg 35, Nay Pyi Taw; tel. (67) 408023.
Ministry of Defence: Bldg 20, Nay Pyi Taw.
Ministry of Education: Bldg 13, Nay Pyi Taw; tel. (67) 407131; internet www.myanmar-education.edu.mm.
Ministry of Electric Power: Bldg 27 and 38, Nay Pyi Taw; tel. (67) 411083.
Ministry of Energy: Bldg 6, Nay Pyi Taw; tel. (67) 411060; fax (67) 411012; e-mail moe.ho@energy.gov.mm; internet www.energy.gov.mm.
Ministry of Environmental Conservation and Forestry: Bldg 28, Nay Pyi Taw; tel. (67) 405004; e-mail ofpma@mptmail.net.mm; internet www.myanmarteak.gov.mm.
Ministry of Finance and Revenue: Bldg 26, Nay Pyi Taw; tel. (67) 410046; fax (67) 410189; e-mail ho.mofr@mptmail.net.mm; internet www.mofr.gov.mm.
Ministry of Foreign Affairs: Bldg 9, Nay Pyi Taw; tel. (67) 412359; e-mail mofa.aung@mptmail.net.mm; internet www.mofa.gov.mm.
Ministry of Health: Bldg 4, Nay Pyi Taw; tel. (67) 411358; internet www.moh.gov.mm.
Ministry of Home Affairs: Bldg 10, Nay Pyi Taw; tel. (67) 412079.
Ministry of Hotels and Tourism: Bldg 33, Nay Pyi Taw; tel. (67) 406406; fax (67) 406057; e-mail mo.moht@mptmail.net.mm; internet www.myanmartourism.org.
Ministry of Immigration and Manpower: Bldg 23, Nay Pyi Taw; tel. (67) 404026.
Ministry of Industry (No. 1): Bldg 37, Nay Pyi Taw; tel. (67) 408063; fax (67) 408080; e-mail moi1@myanmar.com.mm; internet www.industry1myanmar.com.
Ministry of Industry (No. 2): Bldg 30, Nay Pyi Taw; tel. (67) 405135; e-mail ministryofindustry@gmail.com; internet www.industry2.gov.mm.
Ministry of Information: Bldg 7, Nay Pyi Taw; tel. (67) 412321; e-mail contact@ministryofinformation.gov.mm; internet www.ministryofinformation.gov.mm.

Ministry of Labour, Employment and Social Security: Bldg 51, Nay Pyi Taw; tel. (67) 404339; e-mail mol@mptmail.net.mm; internet www.mol.gov.mm.

Ministry of Livestock and Fisheries: Bldg 36, Nay Pyi Taw; tel. (67) 408045; e-mail molf@livestock-fisheries.gov.mm; internet www.livestock-fisheries.gov.mm.

Ministry of Mines: Bldg 19, Nay Pyi Taw; tel. (67) 409019; fax (67) 409010; internet www.mining.com.mm.

Ministry of National Planning and Economic Development: Bldg 1, Nay Pyi Taw; tel. (67) 407023; fax (67) 407004; e-mail ministry.nped@mptmail.net.mm; internet www.mnped.gov.mm.

Ministry of Communications and Information Technology: Bldg 2, Nay Pyi Taw; tel. (67) 407037; e-mail dg.ptd@mptmail.net .mm; internet www.mcpt.gov.mm.

Ministry of Rail Transportation: Bldg 29, Nay Pyi Taw; tel. (67) 405034; internet www.mrt.gov.mm.

Ministry of Religious Affairs: Bldg 31, Nay Pyi Taw; tel. (67) 406008; internet www.mora.gov.mm.

Ministry of Science and Technology: Bldg 21, Nay Pyi Taw; tel. (67) 404004; fax (67) 404011; internet www.most.gov.mm.

Ministry of Social Welfare, Relief and Resettlement: Bldg 23, Nay Pyi Taw; tel. (67) 404021; e-mail social-wel-myan@mptmail.net .mm; internet www.myanmar.gov.mm/ministry/MSWRR/index .html.

Ministry of Sports: Bldg 31, Nay Pyi Taw; tel. (67) 406028; e-mail info@myasoc.org; internet www.mosports.gov.mm.

Ministry of Transportation: Bldg 5, Nay Pyi Taw; tel. (67) 411033; fax (67) 411038; e-mail minotran@mptmail.net.mm; internet www .mot.gov.mm.

Legislature

PYIDAUNGSU HLUTTAW (UNION ASSEMBLY)

The bicameral Pyidaungsu Hluttaw (Union Assembly or National Parliament) comprises the lower chamber of the Pyithu Hluttaw (House of Representatives or People's Assembly), which has 440 seats, and the Amyotha Hluttaw (House of Nationalities or National Assembly), with 224 seats. Under a constitutional provision, 25% of seats in both chambers are reserved for appointed representatives of the armed forces. Elections for 14 state and regional assemblies, were held concurrently with the polls for the Pyidaungsu Hluttaw on 7 November 2010.

Amyotha Hluttaw (House of Nationalities)

The Amyotha Hluttaw comprises 168 civilian representatives (12 from each of the seven states and seven regions) and 56 military representatives, who are appointed by the Commander-in-Chief of the Armed Forces.

Speaker: KHIN AUNG MYINT.
General Election, 7 November 2010

Party	Seats
Union Solidarity and Development Party	129
Rakhine Nationalities Development Party	7
National Unity Party	5
Chin Progressive Party	4
National Democratic Force	4
All Mon Region Democracy Party	3
Phalon-Sawaw Democratic Party	3
Shan Nationalities Democratic Party	3
China National Party	2
Wa Democratic Party	1
Others	7
Appointed members*	56
Total	224

* Military representatives appointed by the Commander-in-Chief of the Armed Forces.
Note: At by-elections held on 1 April 2012, the National League for Democracy won four seats in the Amyotha Hluttaw, the Shan Nationalities Democratic Party one seat and the Union Solidarity and Development Party (USDP) one seat (a net loss of five seats for the USDP).

Pyithu Hluttaw (House of Representatives)

Speaker: SHWE MANN.
General Election, 7 November 2010

Party	Seats
Union Solidarity and Development Party	259
Shan Nationalities Democratic Party	18
National Unity Party	12
Rakhine Nationalities Development Party	9
National Democratic Force	8
All Mon Region Democracy Party	3
Pa-O National Organization	3
Chin National Party	2
Chin Progressive Party	2
Phalon-Sawaw Democratic Party	2
Wa Democratic Party	2
Others	10
Appointed members*	110
Total	440

* Military representatives appointed by the Commander-in-Chief of the Armed Forces.

Note: At by-elections held on 1 April 2012, the National League for Democracy won 37 seats in the Pyithu Hluttaw.

Election Commission

Union Election Commission (UEC): Nay Pyi Taw; f. 2010; Chair. Lt-Gen. (retd) TIN AYE; Sec. WIN KO.

Political Organizations

Registered political parties include:

88 Generation Students and Youth Organization: Rm 301, Bldg F, Pearl Condominium, Kaba Aye Pagoda Rd, Bahan, Yangon; f. 2010; Leader YE HTUN; Gen. Sec. SAN OO.

All Mon Region Democracy Party: Lot 7, Holdings Kha 23, 20th St, Myinethaya Ward, Mawlamyine, Mon State; f. 2010; sole party registered for 2010 election representing the Mon ethnic group; advocates democracy and a free-market economy; Chair. NAI NGWE THEIN.

Arakan (Rakhine) League for Democracy: Yangon; f. 1989, reregistered as a political party in 2012; Pres. AYE THAR AUNG; Sec. SAW MAUNG.

Chin National Party: 277 BPI Rd, West Gyogon Ward, Insein Township, Yangon; tel. (1) 5030870; f. 2010; Chair. PU ZOZAM; Gen. Sec. CEU BIK THAWNG.

Chin Progressive Party: Rm 22, Bldg 2, Pyi Yeik Mon Housing Estate, Narnattaw Rd, Ward 8, Kamayut Township, Yangon; f. 2010; promotes equal rights and economic opportunities for Chin people; Pres. PU NOTHANKAP.

Democratic Party: 6 Kwat Thit St, Yegyaw, Pazundaung Township, Yangon; f. 1988; re-formed 2010; Chair. THU WAI.

Ethnic National Development Party: Lailinpi, Matupi Township, Chin State; Chair. PU HIPA; Gen. Sec. NI LYIN.

Kaman National Progressive Party: Mya Lay Yone St, Tamwe Township, Yangon; f. 2010; Chair. ZAW WIN; Gen. Sec. TIN HLAING WIN.

Kayin People's Party (KPP): 51 Tawwin Rd, Ward 3, Shwe Pyi Tha, Yangon; f. 2001; Leader SIMON THA; Chair. TUN AUNG MYINT.

Lahu National Development Party: 43 Fourth Lane, Parami Rd, Ward 1, Lashio, Shan State; f. 1988; deregistered 1994; reregistered 2010; Chair. KYA HAR SHE.

Mon Democracy Party: Mawlamyine, Mon State; f. 2012; fmrly the Mon National Democratic Front; Chair. NAI NGWE THEIN.

Mro (or) Khami National Solidarity Organization (MKNSO): 202 Sartaik Rd, Pyitawtha Ward, Kyauktaw, Rakhine State; f. 1988; Chair. and Leader SAN THA AUNG.

National Democratic Force: Rm 103, Bldg 3, Dagonlwin Rd, Mittanyunt Ward, Tamway, Yangon; tel. (1) 551654; e-mail info@ ndfmyanmar.com; f. 2010; est. by fmr mems of the National League for Democracy; Chair. Dr THAN NYEIN.

National Democratic Party for Development: Bo Sun Pek Rd, Pabedan Township, Yangon; f. 2010; Chair. MAUNG MAUNG NI.

National League for Democracy (NLD): 97B West Shwegondine Rd, Bahan Township, Yangon; e-mail contact@nldburma.org; internet www.nldburma.org; f. 1988; est. as Nat. United Front for

Democracy; name subsequently changed to League for Democracy; above name adopted 1988; cen. exec. cttee of 20 mems; cen. cttee of 108 mems; Chair. AUNG SAN SUU KYI.

National Political Alliances League: 49 16th St, Lanmadaw Township, Yangon; f. 2010; membership includes breakaway factions from the National League for Democracy; Leader OHN LWIN; Chair. TIN WIN.

National Unity Party (NUP): 24 Aung Zeya St, Shwe Taung Gyar Ward 1, Bahan, Yangon; tel. (1) 278180; f. 1962; est. as the Burma Socialist Programme Party; sole legal political party until Sept. 1988, when present name was adopted; 15-mem. cen. exec. cttee and 280-mem. cen. cttee; Leader TUN YI; Sec.-Gen. THAN TIN.

Pa-O National Organization: 18 West Circular Rd, Zaypaing Ward, Taunggyi, Shan State; signed a cease-fire agreement with the military junta in April 1991; est. by the merger of the Union Pa-O National Organization and the cease-fire group; controls Special Region 6 in southern Shan State; 1,235 mems; Patron AUNG KHAM HTI; Chair. KHUN SAN LWIN; military wing: Pa-O National Army.

Peace and Diversity Party (PDP): 2/2/232 Mahawgani Rd, Htaukkyant, Mingaladon Township, Yangon; tel. 98610719 (mobile); f. 2010; also known as the Difference and Peace Party; Leader NYO MIN LWIN; Gen. Sec. NAY MYO WAI.

Phalon-Sawaw Democratic Party: Ward 7, Hpa-an Township, Karen State; f. 2010; represents the Karen ethnic group; Chair. KHIN MAUNG MYINT.

Rakhine Nationalities Development Party: Khaung Laung Kyaung Rd, Lanmadaw (South) Ward, Sittwe Township, Rakhine State; f. 2010; Chair. Dr AYE MAUNG.

Shan Nationalities Democratic Party (SNDP): 9 Thitsar Uyin Housing, Thitsar Rd, Ward 8, South Okkalapa, Yangon; tel. (9) 5018229; f. 2010; also known as the White Tiger Party; Chair. SAI AIK PAUNG; Vice-Chair. SAI SAUNG SI.

Shan State Kokang Democratic Party: Laukkaing, Shan State; registered 2012; Chair. ANTONI SU.

Taaung (Palaung) National Party: 110 Bogyoke Aung San Rd, Mingala Ward, Namhsan Township, Shan State; f. 2010; 3,300 mems; Gen. Sec. MAI OHN KHAING.

Union Democratic Party: 123 U Chit Maung Rd, North-West Saya San Ward, Bahan, Yangon; f. 2010, following a merger between the Public Democracy Party and the Union Democracy Alliance Party; espouses support for democracy, human rights and national reconciliation; Chair. THEIN HTAY; Gen. Sec THEIN THIN AUNG.

Union of Myanmar Federation of National Politics (UMFNP): Bldg F, Rm 301, Pearl Condominium, Kaba Aye Rd, Bahan Township, Yangon; tel. (1) 556554; f. 2010; broadly pro-govt group; Leader AYE LWIN; Gen. Sec. KHIN MAUNG OO.

Union Solidarity and Development Party (USDP): Plot 5, cnr of Yazathingaha Rd and C Rd, Dekkhinathiri Township, Nay Pyi Taw; f. 2010; est. as successor to the Union Solidarity and Development Asscn (USDA—formed in 1993 as civil society group intrinsically linked to the military regime); Chair. THEIN SEIN; Gen. Sec. HTAY OO.

Unity and Democracy Party of Kachin State: Myothit Ward, Myitkyina; est. and backed by the military junta; Chair. KHET HTEIN NAN.

Wa Democratic Party: tel. 4/7 Hsenwi Rd, Ward 8, Lashio, Shan State; f. 2010; Chair. TUN LU.

Wunthanu Democratic Party: NanU Lwin Village, Pathein Gyi, Mandalay; f. 2010; fmrly Wunthanu NLD; Leader YE MIN.

Deregistered parties include:

Democratic Party for a New Society (DPNS): based in Thailand; e-mail hq@dpns.org; internet www.dpns.org; f. 1988; 8-mem. cen. exec. cttee; Chair. AUNG MOE ZAW; Gen. Sec. NGWE LIN.

Kachin State Progressive Party (KSPP): Myothit Quarter, Myitkyina; f. 2009; 150-mem. cen. cttee; registration for 2010 elections withdrawn due to alleged links with the Kachin Independence Organisation; Leader Dr MANAN TUJA.

Union Pa-O National Organization: f. 1988; Leader KHUN SEIN WIN HLA.

United Nationalities League for Democracy: Yangon; f. 1988; an alliance of parties representing non-Bamar nationalities; won a combined total of 65 seats at the 1990 election.

Wa National Unity Party: Lashio, Shan; fmrly Wa National Development Party; Chair. LOAP PAUNG; Leader SAW PHILIP SAM.

The following groups are, or have been, in armed conflict with the Government:

Chin National Front: e-mail chinlandweb@gmail.com; internet www.chinland.org; f. 1988; forces trained by Kachin Independence Army 1989–91; first party congress 1993; carried out an active bombing campaign in 1996–97, mainly in Chin State; joined the Democratic Alliance of Burma (1988), the National Democratic

(1989) and the Chin National Council (2006); Leader ZING CUNG; military wing: Chin National Army (Leader Col RAL HNIN).

Communist Party of Burma (CPB): internet www.cpburma.org; f. 1939; reorg. 1946; operated clandestinely after 1948; participated after 1986 in jt military operations with sections of the NDF; in 1989 internal dissent resulted in the rebellion of about 80% of CPB members, mostly Wa hill tribesmen and Kokang Chinese; the CPB's military efficacy was thus completely destroyed; leadership exiled in the People's Republic of China; Sec.-Gen. KYIN MAUNG.

Democratic Alliance of Burma (DAB): Manerplaw; f. 1988; formed by members of the NDF to incorporate dissident students, monks and expatriates; Pres. Maj.-Gen. BO MYA; Gen. Sec. TIN MAUNG WIN; remaining organizations include:

All-Burma Student Democratic Front (ABSDF): Dagwin; e-mail absdfhq@csloxinfo.com; internet www.absdf8888.org; f. 1988; in 1990 split into two factions, under MOE THI ZUN and NAING AUNG; the two factions reunited in 1993; Chair. THAN KHE; Sec.-Gen. M. SONNY.

Karen (Kayin) National Union (KNU): internet www.karennationalunion.net; f. 1948; Chair. Gen. TAMALA BAW; Vice-Chair. DAVID TAKAPAW; Gen. Sec. ZIPPORAH SEIN; military wing: Karen (Kayin) National Liberation Army (KNLA); c. 6,000 troops; Chief of Staff MU TU; preliminary cease-fire agreement with the Government concluded in January 2012.

Karenni (Kayinni) National Progressive Party: agreement with the State Law and Order Restoration Council (SLORC) signed in March 1995 but subsequently collapsed; resumed fighting in June 1996; cease-fire agreement with the Government concluded in June 2012; Sec. KHU OO REH; military wing: Karenni (Kayinni) Revolutionary Army.

National Democratic Front (NDF): POB 101, Mae Sot, Tak 63110, Thailand; e-mail ndf.burma@gmail.com; f. 1975; alliance of eight ethnic resistance groups incl. KNU, CNF, NMSP, PSLF; aims to establish a federal union based on national self-determination; Chair., Cen. Exec. Cttee DAVID TAKAPAW.

Palaung State Liberation Front (PSLF): POB 368, Chiang Mai 50000, Thailand; e-mail palaungpslf@gmail.com; f. 1992; est. by mems of Palaung State Liberation Organization opposed to 1991 cease-fire agreement; Sec.-Gen. MAI AIK PHONE.

Shan State Army (SSA): formed in 1964, the original SSA was engaged in an armed rebellion against the military regime until the signing of a cease-fire agreement in 1989; elements led by Sao Sai Lek rejected the cease-fire and came to be known as the **Shan State Army—South (SSA—S)**; following the dissolution of the separatist Mong Tai Army (MTA), in 1997 the SSA—S formed an alliance with the Shan State National Army (Leader KARN YORD), the Shan United Revolutionary Army and other MTA remnants; both wings were reunified May 2011; operates five bases close to the Thai–Myanma border; preliminary cease-fire agreement with the Government concluded in December 2011; Chair. Col YAWD SERK; political wing: **Restoration Council of Shan State** (300 mems; cen. cttee of 21 elected mems).

Most of the following groups signed cease-fire agreements, or reached other means of accommodation, with the military junta prior to 2009. In April 2009 the junta declared that all ethnic cease-fire groups would have to transform into new 'Border Guard Force' (BGF) battalions, including a component of 30 soldiers and one officer from the Myanmar Armed Forces; however, many groups resisted the order.

Democratic Karen (Kayin) Benevolent Army: f. 1994, fmrly Democratic Karen Buddhist Army; breakaway group from the Karen (Kayin) National Union; political wing: Klo Htoo Baw Karen (Kayin) Organization (Founder MAHN ROBERT KA ZAN); military wing: Klo Htoo Baw Karen (Kayin) Battalion; a cease-fire agreement with the govt was effected Nov. 2011; Leader THUZANA.

Kachin Defence Army: agreement with junta reached in Jan. 1991; fmrly the 4th Brigade of the Kachin Independence Army; adopted BGF status in Jan. 2010; Leader MAHTU NAW.

Kachin Independence Organization (KIO): agreement with junta reached in Feb. 1994, ended in 2011 with the resumption of violence; based in Laiza, Kachin State; rejected the junta's BGF proposal; Chair. LANYAW ZAWNG HRA; military wing: Kachin Independence Army (8,000 regular troops in 2012).

Karenni (Kayinni) National People's Liberation Front: agreement with junta reached in May 1994; transformed into a BGF in Nov. 2009; Leader TUN KYAW.

Kayan National Guard: agreement with junta reached in Feb. 1992breakaway faction from the KNLP.

Kayan New Land Party (KNLP): agreement with junta reached in July 1994; rejected the junta's BGF proposal; Jt-Sec. Col SAW LWIN.

Myanmar National Democratic Alliance Army (MNDAA): agreement with junta reached in March 1989; est. by fmr mems of the CPB; based in Kokang region of northern Shan State; forced into exile by the occupation of its cease-fire zone by govt forces in late 2009; Leader PENG JIASHENG.

National Democratic Alliance Army (NDAA): agreement with junta reached in June 1989; est. by splinter group of the CPB; based in eastern Shan State; Leader SAI LEUN.

New Mon State Party (NMSP): POB 1 Sangkhlaburi, Kanchanaburi 71240, Thailand; e-mail nmsp2006@yahoo.com; internet www .nmsp.info; f. 1958; preliminary cease-fire agreement with the Government concluded in Feb. 2012; Chair. NAI HTAW MON; military wing: Mon National Liberation Army, f. 1971.

Palaung State Liberation Organization: (April 1991); military wing: Palaung State Liberation Army; 7,000–8,000 men.

Shan State Nationalities People's Liberation Organization: re-est. 2012; agreement with junta reached in Oct. 1994; Leaders KHUN SEIN SHWE, SOE AUNG LWIN.

United Wa State Party: (May 1989); fmrly part of the CPB; rejected the junta's BGF proposal; seeks the establishment of an autonomous Wa state; military wing: United Wa State Army (20,000–30,000 men); Leaders CHAO NGI LAI, PAO YU CHANG.

Since 1991 the National Coalition Government of the Union of Burma, constituted by representatives elected in the general election of 1990, has served as a government-in-exile:

National Coalition Government of the Union of Burma (NCGUB): POB 693, Rockville, MD 20848, USA; tel. (202) 705-6262; e-mail ncgub@ncgub.net; internet www.ncgub.net; Prime Minister Dr SEIN WIN.

Diplomatic Representation

EMBASSIES IN MYANMAR

Australia: 88 Strand Rd, Yangon; tel. (1) 251810; fax (1) 246159; e-mail austembassy.yangon@dfat.gov.au; internet www.burma .embassy.gov.au; Ambassador BRONTE MOULES.

Bangladesh: 11B Than Lwin Rd, Yangon; tel. (1) 515275; fax (1) 515273; e-mail bdootygn@mptmail.net.mm; Ambassador (vacant).

Brazil: 56 Pyay Rd, Yangon; tel. (1) 507225; fax (1) 507483; e-mail administ.yangon@itamaraty.gov.br; internet yangon.itamaraty.gov .br; Ambassador (vacant).

Brunei: 317–319 U Wisara Rd, Sanchaung Township, Yangon; tel. (1) 524285; fax (1) 512854; e-mail myangon.myanmar@mfa.gov.bn; Ambassador Dato' Paduka Haji ABDUR RAHMANI BIN Haji BASIR.

Canada: Yangon; Ambassador MARK MCDOWELL.

Cambodia: 34 Kaba Aye Pagoda Rd, Bahan Township, Yangon; tel. (1) 549609; fax (1) 541462; e-mail recyangon@myanmar.com.mm; Ambassador CHHONG TOEUN.

China, People's Republic: 1 Pyidaungsu Yeiktha Rd, Yangon; tel. (1) 221281; fax (1) 227019; e-mail chinaemb_mm@mfa.gov.cn; internet mm.china-embassy.org; Ambassador YANG HOULAN.

Denmark: 7 Pyithu Rd, Mayangon Township, Yangon; tel. (1) 663887; Chargé d'affaires a.i. ULRICH SØRENSEN.

Egypt: 81 Pyidaungsu Yeiktha Rd, POB 1131, Dagon Township, Yangon; tel. (1) 222886; fax (1) 222865; e-mail embassy.yangon@ mofa.gov.eg; internet www.mfa.gov.eg/yangon_emb; Ambassador HANY RIAD MOAWAD.

France: 102 Pyidaungsu Yeiktha Rd, POB 858, Yangon; tel. (1) 212520; fax (1) 212527; e-mail ambafrance.rangoun@diplomatie .gouv.fr; internet www.ambafrance-mm.org; Ambassador THIERRY MATHOU.

Germany: 9 Bogyoke Aung San Museum Rd, POB 12, Yangon; tel. (1) 548951; fax (1) 548899; e-mail info@rangun.diplo.de; internet www.rangun.diplo.de; Ambassador CHRISTIAN-LUDWIG WEBER-LORTSCH.

India: 545–547 Merchant St, POB 751, Kyauktada Township, Yangon; tel. (1) 243972; fax (1) 254086; e-mail indiaembassy@ mptmail.net.mm; internet www.indiaembassy.net.mm; Chargé d'affaires a.i. Y. K. SAILAS THANGAL.

Indonesia: 100 Pyidaungsu Yeiktha Rd, POB 1401, Yangon; tel. (1) 254465; fax (1) 254468; e-mail info@kbriyangon.org; internet www .deplu.go.id/yangon; Ambassador SEBASTIANUS SUMARSONO.

Israel: 15 Khabaung Rd, Hlaing Township, Yangon; tel. (1) 515115; fax (1) 515116; e-mail info@yangon.mfa.gov.il; internet yangon.mfa .gov.il; Ambassador HAGAY MOSHE BEHAR.

Italy: 3 Inya Myaing Rd, Golden Valley, Bahan Township, Yangon 11201; tel. (1) 527100; fax (1) 514565; e-mail ambyang.mail@esteri.it; internet www.ambyangon.esteri.it; Ambassador PAOLO ANDREA BARTORELLI.

Japan: 100 Natmauk Rd, Bahan Township, Yangon 11021; tel. (1) 549644; fax (1) 549643; e-mail info.cul@yn.mofa.go.jp; internet www .mm.emb-japan.go.jp; Ambassador MIKIO NUMATA.

Korea, Republic: 97 University Ave, Bahan Township, POB 1408, Yangon; tel. (1) 527142; fax (1) 513286; e-mail myanmar@mofat.go .kr; internet mmr.mofat.go.kr; Ambassador KIM HAE-YONG.

Laos: A1 Diplomatic Quarters, Franser Rd, Yangon; tel. (1) 222482; fax (1) 227446; Ambassador KOUILY A. SOUPHAKHET.

Malaysia: 82 Pyidaungsu Yeiktha Rd, Dagon Township, Yangon; tel. (1) 220249; fax (1) 221840; e-mail malyangon@kln.gov.my; internet www.kln.gov.my/web/mmr_yangon; Ambassador Dr AHMAD FAISAL MUHAMMAD.

Nepal: 16 Natmauk Yeiktha Rd, Tamwe, Yangon; tel. (1) 545880; fax (1) 549803; Ambassador PARAS GHIMIRE.

Norway: 7 Pyithu Rd, Mayangon Township, Yangon; tel. (1) 663887; e-mail emb.office.yangon@mfa.no; Chargé d'affaires a.i. ARNE JAN FLØLO.

Pakistan: A4 Diplomatic Quarters, Pyay Rd, Dagon Township, POB 581, Yangon; tel. (1) 222881; fax (1) 221147; e-mail pakembyangon@ gmail.com; internet www.mofa.gov.pk/myanmar; Ambassador AMJAD MAJID ABBASI.

Philippines: 50 Saya San Rd, Bahan Township, Yangon; tel. (1) 558149; fax (1) 558154; e-mail p.e.yangon@gmail.com; internet www .philembassy-yangon.com; Ambassador ALEX G. CHUA.

Russia: 38 Sagawa Rd, Dagon Township, Yangon; tel. (1) 241955; fax (1) 241953; e-mail rusinmyan@mptmail.net.mm; internet www .myanmar.mid.ru; Ambassador VASILY BORISOVICH POSPELOV.

Saudi Arabia: 287–289 U Wisara Rd, Sanchaung Township, Yangon; tel. (1) 516952; fax (1) 516951; e-mail biemb@mofa.gov.sa; Ambassador TALA M. S. ABDULSALAM.

Serbia: 114A Inya Rd, Kamayut Township, POB 943, Yangon; tel. (1) 515282; fax (1) 504274; e-mail serbemb@yangon.net.mn; Chargé d'affaires a.i. NINO MALJEVIĆ.

Singapore: 238 Dhamazedi Rd, Bahan Township, Yangon; tel. (1) 559001; fax (1) 559002; e-mail singemb_ygn@sgmfa.gov.sg; internet www.mfa.gov.sg/yangon; Ambassador ROBERT CHUA.

Sri Lanka: 34 Taw Win Rd, POB 1150, Yangon; tel. (1) 222812; fax (1) 221509; e-mail srilankaemb@myanmar.com.mm; internet www .slembyangon.org; Ambassador H. R. PIYASIRI.

Switzerland: 11 Kabaung Lane, Pyay Rd, Hlaing Township, Yangon; tel. (1) 534754; e-mail ygn.vertretung@eda.admin.ch; Ambassador CHRISTOPH BURGENER.

Thailand: 94 Pyay Rd, Dagon Township, Yangon; tel. (1) 222784; fax (1) 221713; e-mail thaiembassyygn@gmail.com; internet www .thaiembassy.org/yangon; Ambassador PISANU SUVANAJATA.

Turkey: Chatrium Hotel, 40 Natmauk Rd, Tamwe Township, Yangon; tel. (1) 544500; fax (1) 544400; e-mail naypidav.be@mfa .gov.tr; Ambassador MURAT YAVUZ ATES.

United Kingdom: 80 Strand Rd, Kyauktada Township, POB 638, Yangon; tel. (1) 380322; fax (1) 370866; e-mail BE.Rangoon@fco.gov .uk; internet ukinburma.fco.gov.uk; Ambassador ANDREW HEYN.

USA: 110 University Ave, Kamayut Township, Yangon; tel. (1) 536509; fax (1) 511069; e-mail consularrangoon@state.gov; internet burma.usembassy.gov; Ambassador DEREK MITCHELL.

Viet Nam: 70–72 Than Lwin Rd, Bahan Township, Yangon; tel. (1) 511305; fax (1) 514897; e-mail vnembmyr@cybertech.net.mm; internet www.vietnamembassy-myanmar.org; Ambassador CHU CONG PHUNG.

Judicial System

The Union Judiciary Law establishing the current judicial system of Myanmar under the 2008 Constitution came into force in October 2010, following which the Supreme Court, the High Courts of the regions and states, the Courts of the self-administered divisions and zones, the District Courts, the Township Courts and other courts were inaugurated.

Supreme Court: Bldg 24, Nay Pyi Taw; tel. (67) 404140; the highest appellate court; has original jurisdiction enabling it to hear cases in the first instance and revisionary power against a judgment or order delivered by a lower court; comprises seven to 11 sitting justices and a Chief Justice; Chief Justice TUN TUN OO.

Office of the Union Attorney-General: ; tel. (67) 404089; fax (67) 404106; Attorney-General Dr TUN SHIN.

Religion

Freedom of religious belief and practice is guaranteed. In 1992 an estimated 87.2% of the population were Buddhists, 5.6% Christians, 3.6% Muslims, 1.0% Hindus and 2.6% animists or adherents of other religions.

BUDDHISM

State Sangha Maha Nayaka Committee: c/o Dept of Promotion and Propagation of the Sasana, Kaba Aye Pagoda Precinct, Mayangone Township, Yangon; tel. (1) 660759.

CHRISTIANITY

Myanmar Naing-ngan Khrityan Athin-dawmyar Kaung-si (Myanmar Council of Churches): 601 Pyay Rd, University PO, Kamayut, Yangon 11041; tel. (1) 537957; fax (1) 296848; e-mail raymond@gmail.com; internet mcc-mm.org; f. 1914; est. as Burma Representative Council of Mission; reconstituted as Burma Council of Churches in 1974; 13 mem. nat. churches, 9 mem. nat. Christian orgs; Pres. Rev. SAW MAR GAY GYI; Gen. Sec. Rt Rev. SMITH N. ZA THAWNG.

The Roman Catholic Church

Myanmar comprises three archdioceses and 11 dioceses. At 31 December 2007 an estimated 1.2% of the total population were adherents.

Catholic Bishops' Conference of Myanmar

292 Pyay Rd, Sanchaung PO, Yangon 11111; tel. (1) 525868; fax (1) 527198; e-mail secrcbcm@myanmar.com.mm.

f. 1982; Pres. Most Rev. PAUL ZINGHTUNG GRAWNG (Archbishop of Mandalay).

Archbishop of Mandalay: Most Rev. PAUL ZINGHTUNG GRAWNG, Archbishop's House, cnr of 82nd and 25th Sts, Mandalay 06011; tel. and fax (2) 33916; e-mail info@mandalayarchdiocese.com; internet www.mandalayarchdiocese.com.

Archbishop of Taunggyi: Most Rev. MATTHIAS U SHWE, Archbishop's Office, Bayint Naung Rd, Taunggyi 06011; tel. (81) 21689; fax (81) 22164; e-mail ushwe1@gmail.com.

Archbishop of Yangon: Most Rev. CHARLES MAUNG BO, Archbishop's House, 289 Theinbyu Rd, Botahtaung PO, Yangon 11161; tel. (1) 246710; fax (1) 379059; e-mail archdygn@myanmar.com.mm.

The Anglican Communion

Anglicans are adherents of the Church of the Province of Myanmar, comprising six dioceses. The Province was formed in February 1970, and contained an estimated 45,000 adherents in 1985.

Archbishop of Myanmar and Bishop of Yangon: Most Rev. STEPHEN THAN MYINT OO, Bishopscourt, 140 Pyidaungsu Yeiktha Rd, Dagon PO, Yangon 11191; tel. (1) 246813; fax (1) 251405; e-mail abcpm@myanmar.com.mm.

Protestant Churches

Lutheran Bethlehem Church: 181–183 Theinbyu St, Mingala Taung Nyunt PO, Yangon 11221; tel. and fax (1) 246585; e-mail jenson-lbc@mail4u.com.mm; Pres. Rev. JENSON RAJAN ANDREWS.

Lutheran Church of Myanmar: 247 Bogkoye St, Kyauktada Township, POB 526, 11182 Yangon; tel. (1) 245626; e-mail lcmyanmar@gmail.com; f. 1995; Pres. Rev. Dr LAL SAWI THANGA.

Mara Evangelical Church: Evangelical Mission, 7/86 Chinpyan Rd, Sittaway, Rakhine State; tel. (1) 645955; e-mail mec1907@gmail.com; f. 1907; 21,573 mems; Gen. Sec. VICTOR VE-U.

Myanmar Baptist Convention: 143 Minye Kyawswa Rd, POB 506, Yangon; tel. (1) 223231; fax (1) 221465; e-mail mbc@mptmail.net.mm; f. 1865; est. as Burma Baptist Missionary Convention; present name adopted 1954; 650,293 mems (2003); Pres. Rev. Dr HONOR NYO; Gen. Sec. Rev. K. D. TU LOM.

Myanmar Lutheran Church: 38D Thar Yar Aye, 1st St, Taung Thu Gone Ward, Insein, Yangon; tel. (1) 642550; e-mail myanmarle@mttmail.net.mm; 2,150 mems; Pres. Rev. ANDREW MANG LONE.

Myanmar Methodist Church: 47 Baho Rd, Thazin Lane, Ah Lone Township 65, Alanpya Pagoda Rd, Dagon, Yangon; Pres. Bishop ZOTHAN MAWIA.

Presbyterian Church of Myanmar: Synod Office, Falam, Chin State; 22,000 mems; Pres. Rev. SUN KANGLO.

Other denominations active in Myanmar include the Lisu Christian Church and the Salvation Army.

The Press

From April 2013 private companies were permitted to publish and circulate daily newspapers, ending a state monopoly on the daily press.

DAILIES

Botahtaung (The Vanguard): 22–30 Strand Rd, Botahtaung PO, POB 539, Yangon; tel. (1) 274310; Myanmar.

The Daily Eleven: 22 South Horse Racing Rd, Tamwe Township, Yangon; internet www.thedailyeleven.com; owned by the Eleven Media Group; f. 2013; Man. Editor Dr THEIN MYINT.

Guardian: 392–396 Merchant St, Botahtaung PO, POB 1522, Yangon; tel. (1) 270150; English.

Kyahmon (The Mirror): 77 52nd St, Dazundaung PO, POB 819, Yangon; tel. (1) 282777; internet www.myanmar.com/newspaper/kyaymon/index.html; Myanmar.

Myanmar Ahlin (New Light of Myanmar): 58 Komin Kochin Rd, Bahan PO, POB 21, Yangon; tel. (1) 544309; internet www.myanmar.com/newspaper/myanmarahlin/index.html; f. 1963; fmrly Loktha Pyithu Nezin (Working People's Daily); organ of the SPDC; morning; Myanmar; Chief Editor WIN TIN; circ. 400,000.

New Light of Myanmar: 22–30 Strand Rd, Yangon; tel. (1) 297028; e-mail webmaster@myanmar.com; internet www.myanmar.com/newspaper/nlm/index.html; f. 1963; fmrly Working People's Daily; organ of the SPDC; morning; English; Chief Editor KYAW MIN; circ. 14,000.

The Voice: 458–460, 4th Floor, cnr of 31 St and Manabandula Rd, Pabedan Township, Yangon; tel. (1) 242424; e-mail newsroom@thevoiceweekly.net; internet www.thevoicemyanmar.com; est. as The Voice Weekly; launched a daily version in April 2013; Chief Editor KYAW MIN SWE.

Other dailies published in 2013 were Shwe Naing Ngan Thit (Golden Fresh Land), Pyidaungsu (The Union) and San Taw Chein.

PERIODICALS

A Hla Thit (New Beauty): 46 90th St, Yangon; tel. (1) 287106; international news.

Dana Business Magazine: 72 8th St, Lanmadaw Township, Yangon; tel. and fax (1) 224010; e-mail dana@mptmail.net.mm; economic; Editor-in-Chief WILLIAM CHEN.

Do Kyaung Tha: Myawaddy Press, 184 32nd St, Yangon; tel. (1) 274655; f. 1965; monthly; Myanmar and English; circ. 17,000.

Gita Padetha: Yangon; journal of Myanma Music Council; circ. 10,000.

Guardian Magazine: 392–396 Merchant St, Botahtaung PO, POB 1522, Yangon; tel. (1) 296510; f. 1953; nationalized 1964; monthly; English; literary; circ. 11,600.

Kyee Pwar Yay (Prosperity): 296 Bo Sun Pat St, Yangon; tel. (1) 278100; economic; Editor-in-Chief MYAT KHINE.

Moethaukpan (Aurora): Myawaddy Press, 184 32nd St, Yangon; tel. (1) 274655; f. 1980; monthly; Myanmar and English; circ. 27,500.

Myanma Dana (Myanmar's Economy): 210A 36th St, Kyauktada Post Office, Yangon; tel. (1) 284660; economic; Editor-in-Chief THIHA SAW.

Myanmar Morning Post: Yangon; f. 1998; weekly; Chinese; news; circ. 5,000.

Myanmar Times & Business Review: 379–383 Bo Aung Kyaw St, Kyauktada Township, Yangon; tel. (1) 392928; fax (1) 254158; e-mail management@myanmartimes.com.mm; internet www.mmtimes.com; f. 2000; CEO Dr TIN TUN OO ; Man. Dir BILL CLOUGH (acting).

Myawaddy Journal: Myawaddy Press, 184 32nd St, Yangon; tel. (1) 274655; f. 1989; fortnightly; news; circ. 8,700.

Myawaddy Magazine: Myawaddy Press, 184 32nd St, Yangon; tel. (1) 274655; f. 1952; monthly; literary magazine; circ. 4,200.

Ngwetaryi Magazine: Myawaddy Press, 184 32nd St, Yangon; tel. (1) 274655; f. 1961; monthly; cultural; circ. 3,400.

Pyinnya Lawka Journal: 529 Merchant St, Yangon; tel. (1) 283611; publ. by Sarpay Beikman Management Board; quarterly; circ. 18,000.

Shwe Thwe: 529 Merchant St, Yangon; tel. (1) 283611; weekly; bilingual children's journal; publ. by Sarpay Beikman Management Board; circ. 100,000.

Taw Win Journal (Royal Journal): 149 37th St, Yangon; news; Editor-in-Chief SOE THEIN.

Teza: Myawaddy Press, 184 32nd St, Yangon; tel. (1) 274655; f. 1965; monthly; English and Myanmar; pictorial publ. for children; circ. 29,500.

Thwe Thauk Magazine: Myawaddy Press, 184 32nd St, Yangon; f. 1946; monthly; literary.

Ya Nant Thit (New Fragrance): 186 39th St, Yangon; tel. (1) 276799; international news; Editor-in-Chief CHIT WIN MG.

Yangon Times: Yangon Media Group Ltd, 101, 1st Floor, Mahabandoola Condo, Mahabandoola Rd, Pazaungdaung, Yangon; tel. (1)

9010072; fax (1) 9010075; e-mail yangonmediagroup.ltd@gmail.com; internet www.theyangontimes.com; 2 a week; Exec. Dir DAW MYAT MYAT SOE.

NEWS AGENCY

Myanmar News Agency (MNA): 212 Theinbyu Rd, Botahtaung, Yangon; tel. (1) 270893; f. 1963; govt-controlled; Chief Editors ZAW MIN THEIN (domestic section), KYAW MIN (external section).

Publishers

Hanthawaddy Press: 157 Bo Aung Kyaw St, Yangon; f. 1889; textbooks, multilingual dictionaries; Man. Editor ZAW WIN.

Knowledge Publishing House: 130 Bo Gyoke Aung San St, Yegyaw, Yangon; art, education, religion, politics and social sciences.

Kyipwaye Press: 84th St, Letsaigan, Mandalay; tel. (2) 21003; arts, travel, religion, fiction and children's.

Myawaddy Press: 184 32nd St, Yangon; tel. (1) 276889; journals and magazines; CEO THEIN SEIN.

Sarpay Beikman Management Board: 529 Merchant St, Yangon; tel. (1) 283611; f. 1947; encyclopaedias, literature, fine arts and general; also magazines and translations; Chair. AUNG HTAY.

Shumawa Press: 146 West Wing, Bogyoke Aung San Market, Yangon; mechanical engineering.

Shwepyidan: 12A Haiaban, Yegwaw Quarter, Yangon; politics, religion, law.

Smart and Mookerdum: 221 Sule Pagoda Rd, Yangon; arts, cookery, popular science.

Thu Dhama Wadi Press: 55–56 Maung Khine St, POB 419, Yangon; f. 1903; religious; Propr TIN HTOO; Man. PAN MAUNG.

GOVERNMENT PUBLISHING HOUSE

Printing and Publishing Enterprise: 365–367 Bo Aung Kyaw St, Kyauktada Township, Yangon; tel. (1) 294645; f. 1880; est. as Govt Printing Office; Man. Dir AUNG NYEIN.

PUBLISHERS' ASSOCIATION

Myanma Publishers' Union: 146 Bogyoke Market, Yangon.

Broadcasting and Communications

TELECOMMUNICATIONS

In January 2013 the Ministry of Communications and Information Technology announced the planned development of telecommunications services in Myanmar; two nation-wide licences were to be granted by June that year.

Myanma Posts and Telecommunications (MPT): No. 2 Office Bldg, Special Development Zone, Nay Pyi Taw; tel. (1) 407333; fax (1) 407008; internet www.mpt.net.mm; fmrly the Posts and Telecommunications Corpn; Man. Dir AUNG MAW.

Yatanarpon Teleport: Yatanarpon Cyber City, Mandalay; tel. (2) 5178116; fax (2) 5178004; e-mail helpdesk@teleport.net.mm; internet www.yatanarpon.net.mm; f. 2002; internet and data network services.

Regulatory Authority

Posts and Telecommunications Department: Blk 68, Ayeyar Wun Rd, South Dagon Township, Yangon; tel. (1) 591388; fax (1) 591383; e-mail dg.ptd@mptmail.net.mm; internet www.mcpt.gov .mm/ptd/index.htm; regulatory authority responsible for supervising radio communication, telephone, telegraph and post operations; Dir-Gen. TIN HTWE.

BROADCASTING

Radio

Radio broadcasting is largely state-controlled, although several private radio stations have emerged since early 2001.

Myanma Radio and Television (MRTV): Tatkone, Nay Pyi Taw; tel. (67) 79475; fax (67) 79205; e-mail mrtv@mptmail.net.mm; internet www.mrtv3.net.mm; govt-owned; frmly Burma Broadcasting Service; broadcasts in Myanmar, Kachin, Shan, Rakhine, Chin (Falan), Chin (Mindat), Wa, Kokant, Kayin (Sagaw), Kayin (Poe), Mon, Kayah, Cayan, Gaykho, Gaybar and English; Dir-Gen. TIN SWE; Dir of Radio Broadcasting WIN AUNG.

Television

Digital television broadcasting began in Myanmar in 2005, with coverage extending to more than one-half of the population by 2010. The removal of analogue service was not envisaged until at least 2025.

Myanma Radio and Television; see Radio; colour television transmission began in 1980.

TV Myawaddy: Hmawbi, Hmawbi Township, Yangon; tel. (1) 620270; f. 1995; military broadcasting station transmitting public information, education and entertainment programmes via satellite.

In 2005 the Democratic Voice of Burma (DVB) began broadcasting Myanmar-language news and educational programmes via satellite from Norway.

Finance

(cap. = capital; res = reserves; dep. = deposits; m. = million; br(s) = branch(es); amounts in kyats unless otherwise stated)

BANKING

Central Bank

Central Bank of Myanmar: Office 55, Nay Pyi Taw; tel. (67) 418203; fax (67) 418270; e-mail director.admin.cbm@mptmail.net .mm; internet www.cbm.gov.mm; f. 1947; est. as People's Bank of the Union of Burma; present name adopted 1990; bank of issue; cap. 350m., dep. 13,545m.; Gov. THAN NYEIN; 37 brs.

State Banks

Myanma Economic Bank (MEB): 26, Myat Pan Thazin Rd, Nay Pyi Taw; tel. (67) 420441; fax (67) 420988; e-mail mebhoadmin@mpt .net.mm; internet www.mebank.com.mm; f. 1975; provides domestic banking network throughout the country; Man. Dir MYAT MAW.

Myanma Foreign Trade Bank: 80–86 Maha Bandoola Garden St, Kyauktada Township, Yangon; tel. (1) 284911; fax (1) 289585; e-mail mftb-hoygn@mptmail-net.mm; f. 1976; handles all foreign exchange and international banking transactions; Chair. and Man. Dir THAN YE; Man. and Sec. HTIN KYAW THEIN.

Myanma Investment and Commercial Bank (MICB): 170–176 Bo Aung Kyaw St, Botahtaung Township, Yangon; tel. (1) 250515; fax (1) 256871; e-mail micb.hoygn@mptmail.net.mm; f. 1989; state-owned; cap. 940m., res 890,75m., dep. 25,040m. (March 2007); Chair. and Man. Dir SOE MIN; 1 br.

Private Banks

In 2012 there were 19 private banks operating in Myanmar.

Asia Green Development Bank Ltd (AGD): 168 Thiri Yadanar Market, Nay Pyi Taw; tel. (67) 414622; internet www.agdbank.com; f. 2010; Chair. THAN YI.

Asian Yangon Bank Ltd: 319–321 Maha Bandoola St, Botahtaung Township, Yangon; tel. (1) 245825; fax (1) 245865; f. 1994; est. as Asian Yangon Int. Bank Ltd; name changed as above in 2000; Gen. Man. MYO MYINT.

Ayeyarwady Bank (AYA): 1 Ywama Curve, Ba Yint Naung Rd, Block 2, Hlaing Township, Yangon; tel. (1) 531067; fax (1) 531045; e-mail info@ayabank.com.mm; internet www.ayabank.com; f. 2010; Exec. Chair. ZAW ZAW; Man. Dir THAN ZAW.

Co-operative Bank Ltd: 334–336, cnr of Strand Rd and 23rd St, Latha Township, Yangon; tel. (1) 371848; fax (1) 371851; e-mail contact@cbbankmm.com; internet www.cbbankmm.com; f. 1992; Chair. KHIN MAUNG AYE; Exec. Vice-Chair. KYAW LYNN; 36 brs.

First Private Bank Ltd (FPB): 619–621, cnr of Merchant St and Bo Soon Pat St, Pabedan Township, Yangon; tel. (1) 251750; fax (1) 242320; e-mail fpb.hq@mptmail.net.mm; internet www .fpbbank-myanmar.com; f. 1992; est. as the first publicly subscribed bank; fmrly Commercial and Devt Bank Ltd; provides loans to private business and small-scale industrial sectors; cap. 5,000m. (March 2008); Chair. Dr SEIN MAUNG; 16 brs.

Innwa Bank Ltd: 554–556 Merchant St, cnr of 35th and 36th Sts, Kyauktada Township, Yangon; tel. (1) 254642; fax (1) 254431; f. 1997; Gen. Man. YIN SEIN.

Kanbawza Bank Ltd: 615/1 Pyay Rd, Kamayut Township, Yangon; tel. (1) 538075; fax (1) 538069; e-mail kbzhr@kbzbank.com; internet www.kbzbank.asia; f. 1994; Chair. AUNG KO WIN; Gen. Man. YE HTUN OO; 39 brs.

Myanma Citizens Bank Ltd (MCB): 383 Maha Bandoola St, Kyauktada Township, Yangon; tel. (1) 379176; fax (1) 245932; e-mail mcbankygn@mptmail.net.mm; f. 1991; Chair. MYO OO; Man. Dir AUNG THIN WIN.

Myanma Oriental Bank Ltd (MOB): 166–168 Pansodan St, Kyauktada Township, Yangon; tel. (1) 246594; fax (1) 253217;

e-mail mobl.ygn@mptmail.net.mm; f. 1993; Chair. MYA THAN; Man. Dir and CEO WIN MYINT.

Myanmar Industrial Development Bank Ltd: Plot 2, Oktayathiri Quarter, Nay Pyi Taw; f. 1996; cap. US $335m.

Myawaddy Bank Ltd: Plot B-1, near Thiriyadana Super Market, Hotel Zone, Nay Pyi Taw; e-mail mwdbankygn@mtpt400.stems.com; f. 1993; Gen. Mans TUN KYI, MYA MIN.

Tun Foundation Bank Ltd: 165–167 Bo Aung Kyaw St, Yangon; tel. (1) 240710; e-mail tfbbank@mptmail.net.mm; f. 1997; Chair. THEIN TUN.

Yadanabon Bank Ltd: 58A, 26th St, cnr of 84th and 85th Sts, Aung Myay Thar Zan Township, Mandalay; tel. (2) 23577; f. 1992.

Yangon City Bank Ltd: cnr of Settyon St and Banyerdala St, Mingalar Taung Nyunt Township, Yangon; tel. (1) 289256; fax (1) 289231; f. 1993; auth. cap. 500m.; 100% owned by Yangon City Devt Cttee; Chair. Col MYINT AUNG.

Yoma Bank Ltd: 1 Kungyan St, Mingala Taung Nyunt Township, Yangon; tel. (1) 242138; fax (1) 246548; f. 1993; Chair. SERGE PUN.

Foreign Banks

By November 2010 13 foreign banks had opened representative offices in Yangon.

STOCK EXCHANGE

Myanmar Securities Exchange Centre: 1st Floor, 21–25 Sule Pagoda Rd, Yangon; tel. (1) 283984; f. 1996; jt venture between MEB and Japan's Daiwa Institute of Research; Man. Dir EIJI SUZUKI.

INSURANCE

At the end of November 2003 there were three representative offices of foreign insurance companies in Myanmar.

Myanma Insurance: 627–635 Merchant St, Yangon; tel. (1) 252373; fax (1) 250275; e-mail myansure@mptmail.net.com; internet www.soft-comm.com/myanma_insurance/index.html; f. 1976; govt-controlled; Man. Dir Col THEIN LWIN.

Trade and Industry

GOVERNMENT AGENCIES

Inspection and Agency Services: 383 Maha Bandoola St, Yangon; tel. (1) 284821; fax (1) 284823; promotes business with foreign cos on behalf of state-owned enterprises; Man. Dir OHN KHIN.

Myanmar Economic Corpn (MEC): 74–76 Shwedagon Pagoda Rd, Dagon Township, Yangon; tel. (1) 254738; (retd) Brig.-Gen. Thura MYINT THIEN.

Myanmar Investment Commission (MIC): Ministry of National Planning and Economic Development, Bldg 32, Nay Pyi Taw; tel. (67) 406334; fax (67) 406333; f. 1994; Chair. MAUNG MAUNG THEIN.

Union of Myanmar Economic Holdings: 72–74 Shwadagon Pagoda Rd, Yangon; tel. (1) 78905; f. 1990; public holding co; auth. cap. 10,000m. kyats; 40% of share capital subscribed by the Ministry of Defence and 60% by members of the armed forces.

CHAMBER OF COMMERCE

Union of Myanmar Federation of Chambers of Commerce and Industry (UMFCCI): 29 Min Ye Kyawswa Rd, Lanmadaw Township, Yangon; tel. (1) 214344; fax (1) 214484; e-mail umfcci@mptmail .net.mm; internet www.umfcci.com.mm; f. 1919; est. as Burmese Chamber of Commerce; present name adopted 1999; Pres. WIN AUNG; Sec.-Gen. Dr MYO THET.

INDUSTRIAL AND TRADE ASSOCIATIONS

Myanmar Aquaculture and Fisheries Association: 74–86 Bo Sun Pat St, Pabedan Township, Yangon; tel. (1) 243150; fax (1) 248177.

Myanmar Computer Industry Association: Myanmar Info-Tech, Main Bldg, Hlaing University Campus, Hlaing Township, Yangon; tel. (1) 652238; e-mail mcia@mail4u.com.mm; internet www.mcia.org.mm; Pres. WAH WAH HTUN.

Myanmar Construction Entrepreneurs' Association: Thanthumar Rd, cnr Thuwunna Rd, Thingankyun Township, Yangon; tel. (1) 579547; fax (1) 575947.

Myanmar Edible Oil Dealers' Association: 81–82 Kantgaw St, Bayint Naung Warehouse, Mayangon Township, Yangon; tel. (1) 680910; Chair. KO KO GYI.

Myanmar Engineers' Association: Bldg 6, Rm 5, MICT Park, Hlaing Township, Yangon; tel. (1) 652294.

Myanmar Fisheries Federation (MFF): cnr Bayint Naung Rd and Say War Sat Yone St, West Gyo Gone, Insein Township, Yangon;

tel. (1) 683652; fax (1) 683662; e-mail fish-fed@mff.com.mm; internet www.fishfedmyanmar.com; six mem. asscns; Pres. HTAY MYINT.

Myanmar Garment Manufacturers' Association (MGMA): J V-2 Bldg, between Lanthit St and Wardan St, Seikkan Township, Yangon; tel. (1) 220879; fax (1) 222706; Chair. MYINT SOE.

Myanmar Industries Association: 504–506 Merchant St, Kyauktada Township, Yangon; tel. and fax (1) 241919; f. 1993; Chair. PAW HEIN.

Myanmar Livestock Federation: Livestock Breeding and Veterinary Department Compound, Insein Rd, Insein Township, Yangon; tel. (1) 640820; fax (1) 225955.

Myanmar Rice and Paddy Wholesalers' Association: 504–506 Merchant St, Kyauktada Township, Yangon; tel. (1) 241920.

Myanmar Rice Industry Association: f. 2010; est. to co-ordinate the rice industry, promote private investment and develop the export potential of the sector; provides low-interest loans and improved seeds, fertilizers and technology; 40 exec. mems; Chair. CHIT KHAING.

Myanmar Rice Millers' Association: 69 Theinbyu St, Botahtaung Township, Yangon; tel. (1) 296284; Pres. TIN WIN.

Myanmar Timber Merchants Association: 29 Min Ye Kyaw Swa St, Lanmadaw Township, Yangon; tel. (1) 214838; fax (1) 214840; e-mail mfptma@mptmail.net.mm; internet www .myanmartimberassociation.org; f. 1993; Chair. SEIN LWIN; Sec.-Gen. Dr MYO THET.

Myanmar Women Entrepreneurs' Association: 288–290 Shwedagon Pagoda Rd, Dagon Township, Yangon; tel. (1) 254400; fax (1) 254566; e-mail mwea2008@gmail.com; internet www.mweamm.org; f. 1995; Pres. YI YI MYINT (acting).

UTILITIES

Electricity

Myanma Electric Power Enterprise (MEPE): 197–199 Lower Kyimyindine Rd, Yangon; tel. (1) 410066; fax (1) 440392; e-mail mepe@mptmail.net.mm; Man. Dir KHIN MAUNG ZAW.

Water

Mandalay City Development Committee (Water and Sanitation Dept): cnr of 26th and 72nd Sts, Mandalay; tel. (2) 70431; f. 1992; Head of Water and Sanitation Dept TINT LWIN.

Water Resources Utilization Department (WRUD): Ministry of Agriculture and Irrigation, Office 50, Nay Pyi Taw; tel. (67) 431291; internet wrud.moai.gov.mm; f. 1995; Dir-Gen. KYI HTUT WIN.

Yangon City Development Committee (Water and Sanitation Dept): City Hall, cnr of Maha Bandoola Rd and Sule Pagoda Rd, Kyauktada Township, Yangon; tel. (1) 248112; fax (1) 246016; e-mail priycdc@mptmail.net.mm; internet www.yangoncity.com.mm/ycdc/index.asp; f. 1992; Head of Water and Sanitation Dept ZAW WIN.

CO-OPERATIVES

In 2003, according to official reports, there were 18,041 co-operative societies.

Central Co-operative Society Ltd: Saya San Plaza, cnr Saya Rd and New University Ave, Bahan Township, Yangon; tel. (1) 557640; fax (1) 553894; e-mail ccscencoop@gmail.com; internet www .ccsmyanmar.com; Chair. KHIN MAUNG AYE.

Co-operative Department: Ministry of Co-operatives, Bldg 16, Nay Pyi Taw; tel. (1) 410339; fax (1) 410024; e-mail coopdeptdg@mptmail.net.mm; internet www.myancoop.gov.mm/co-department .htm; Dir-Gen. MAUNG HTI.

WORKERS' AND PEASANTS' COUNCILS

Peasants' Asiayone (Organization): Yangon; tel. (1) 82819; f. 1977; Chair. Brig.-Gen. THAN NYUNT; Sec. SAN TUN.

Workers' Unity Organization: Central Organizing Committee, 61 Theinbyu St, Yangon; tel. (1) 284043; f. 1968; workers' representative org.; Chair. OHN KYAW; Sec. NYUNT THEIN.

Transport

All railways, domestic air services, passenger and freight road transport services, and inland water facilities are owned and operated by state-controlled enterprises.

RAILWAYS

The railway network comprised 5,726 km of track in 2012, with a further 2,844 km under construction.

Myanma Railways: 361 Theinbyu St, Botahtaung Township, Yangon; tel. (1) 298585; fax (1) 284220; e-mail webmaster@

myanmarailways.com; internet www.myanmarailways.com; f. 1877; govt-operated; Man. Dir MIN SWE; Gen. Man. HLA YI.

ROADS

In 2010 the total length of the road network in Myanmar was 34,377 km. The construction of a highway linking Yangon to the Thai border in Kayin State was scheduled to be completed in 2014.

Road Transportation Department: 375 Bogyoke Aung San St, Yangon; tel. (1) 284426; fax (1) 289716; f. 1963; controls passenger and freight road transport; Man. Dir OHN MYINT.

INLAND WATERWAYS

The principal artery of traffic is the River Ayeyarwady (Irrawaddy), which is navigable as far as Bhamo, about 1,450 km inland, while parts of the Thanlwin and Chindwinn rivers are also navigable.

Inland Water Transport: 50 Pansodan St, Kyauktada Township, Yangon; tel. (1) 380753; fax (1) 380752; e-mail iwt@mpt.net.mm; internet www.iwt.gov.mm; f. 1865; govt-owned; operates cargo and passenger services throughout Myanmar with a fleet of 476 vessels; Man. Dir SOE TINT.

SHIPPING

Yangon is the chief port. Vessels with a displacement of up to 15,000 grt can be accommodated. In December 2012 the Myanma flag registered fleet comprised 62 vessels, with a total displacement of 166,029 grt.

Myanma Port Authority: 10 Pansodan St, POB 1, Yangon; tel. (1) 382722; fax (1) 295134; e-mail mpa@mptmail.net.mm; internet www .myanmaportauthority.com; f. 1880; general port and harbour duties; Man. Dir HTIEN HTAY; Gen. Man. HLAING SOON.

Myanma Five Star Line: 132–136 Theinbyu St, POB 1221, Yangon; tel. (1) 295279; fax (1) 297669; e-mail mfslhq@mptmail.net.mm; internet www.mfsl-shipping.com; f. 1959; cargo services to the Far East and Australia; Man. Dir MAUNG MAUNG NYEIN; Gen. Man. WIN PE; fleet of 26 coastal and ocean-going vessels.

CIVIL AVIATION

Mingaladon Airport, near Yangon, is equipped to international standards. Mandalay International Airport was inaugurated in September 2000, and Nay Pyi Taw International Airport commenced services in 2011. The construction of a fourth international airport (Hanthawaddy) in Bago was scheduled to be resumed in June 2013 for completion in 2016.

Department of Civil Aviation: Yangon International Airport, Yangon 11021; tel. (1) 533000; fax (1) 533016; e-mail dgdca@dca .gov.mm; internet www.dca.gov.mm; Dir-Gen. TIN NAING TUN.

Air Bagan Ltd: 56 Shwe Taung Gyar St, Bahan Township, Yangon; tel. (1) 514861; fax (1) 515102; e-mail info@airbagan.com.mm; internet www.airbagan.com; f. 2004; domestic services to 17 destinations; Chair. TAY ZA; Man. Dir HTOO THET HTWE.

Air Mandalay: 146 Dhammazedi Rd, Bahan Township, Yangon; tel. (1) 501520; fax (1) 525937; e-mail info@airmandalay.com; internet www.airmandalay.com; f. 1994; jt venture between Air Mandalay Holding, Premier Airlines and Myanma Airways; operates domestic services and regional services to Thailand and Cambodia; Chair. MAUNG MAUNG OHN; Man. Dir ADAM HTOON.

Myanmar Airways (MA): 104 Kanna Rd, Yangon; tel. (1) 246452; fax (1) 371120; e-mail myanmaairways@mptmail.net.mm; internet myanmaairways.aero; f. 1993; govt-controlled; internal network operates services to 21 airports; Man. Dir TIN MAUNG TUN.

Myanmar Airways International (MAI): 08-02 Sakura Tower, 339 Bogyoke Aung San Rd, Yangon; tel. (1) 255260; fax (1) 255305; e-mail management@maiair.com; internet www.maiair.com; f. 1993; est. by Myanmar Airways in jt venture with RMT company for international schedule services; operates services to Bangkok, Guangzhou, Hong Kong, Kuala Lumpur, Seoul and Singapore; Man. Dir SI THU.

United Myanmar Air: Summit Parkview Hotel, Yangon; internet www.unitedmyanmar.com; f. 2003; jt venture between Myanmar Airways and Sunshine Strategic Investments Holdings of Hong Kong; international services to Bangkok, Hong Kong, Kuala Lumpur and Singapore; CEO EDWARD TAN.

Yangon Airways: MMB Tower, 5th Floor, 166 Upper Pansodan Rd, Mingalar Taungnyunt Township, Yangon; tel. (1) 383100; fax (1) 383109; e-mail marketing@mmb.com.mm; internet www.yangonair .com; f. 1996; domestic services to 13 destinations; Gen. Man. TIN MAUNG AYE.

Tourism

Yangon, Mandalay, Taunggyi and Pagan possess outstanding palaces, Buddhist temples and shrines. Myanmar was to host the Southeast Asian Games in 2013. In 2011 there were a provisional 391,000 foreign tourist arrivals. Revenue from tourism (including passenger transport) totalled an estimated US $73m. in 2010.

Myanmar Hotels and Tourism Services: 77–91 Sule Pagoda Rd, Yangon 11141; tel. (1) 282013; fax (1) 254417; e-mail mtt.mht@ mptmail.net.mm; govt-controlled; manages all hotels, tourist offices, tourist dept stores and duty-free shops; Man. Dir HLA HTAY.

Myanmar Tourism Promotion Board: Business Centre, 3rd Floor, 223 Signal Pagoda Rd, Yangon; tel. (1) 242828; fax (1) 242800; e-mail mtpb@mptmail.net.mm; internet www .myanmar-tourism.com; Chair. AUNG MYAT KYAW.

Myanmar Travels and Tours: 118–120 Mahabandoola St, Kyauktada Township, Yangon; tel. (1) 371286; fax (1) 254417; e-mail mtt .mht@mptmail.net.mm; internet www.myanmartravelsandtours .com; f. 1964; govt tour operator and travel agent; handles all travel arrangements for groups and individuals; Gen. Man. HTAY AUNG.

Union of Myanmar Travel Association (UMTA): 29 Min Ye Kyawswa Rd, Lanmadaw Township, Yangon; tel. (1) 214941; fax (1) 214945; e-mail UMTA@mptmail.net.mm; internet www.umtanet .org; f. 2002; organizes private travel agencies and tour operators; Chair. MAUNG MAUNG SWE.

Defence

As assessed at November 2012, the total strength of the armed forces was an estimated 406,000 (army 375,000, navy 16,000, air force 15,000). Military service is compulsory for men (between the ages of 18 and 45) and women (between the ages of 18 and 35) for a period of two to three years, or for five years during times of national crisis. Paramilitary forces include a people's police force (72,000 men) and a people's militia (35,000 men). The 11-member National Defence and Security Council was established in March 2011.

Defence Expenditure: Budgeted at US $2,270m. for 2012.

Commander-in-Chief of the Armed Forces: Sr Gen. MIN AUNG HLAING.

Commander-in-Chief of the Army: Vice-Sr Gen. SOE WIN.

Commander-in-Chief of the Navy: Vice-Adm. Thura THET SWE.

Commander-in-Chief of the Air Force: Maj.-Gen. KHIN AUNG MYINT.

Education

The organization and administration of education is the responsibility of the Ministry of Education. Pre-school education begins at four years of age. Primary education, which is compulsory, lasts for five years between the ages of five and 10. Secondary education, beginning at 10 years of age, comprises a first cycle of four years and a second of two years. In 2009/10 enrolment at the pre-primary level included 10% (both male and female) of children in the relevant age-group, and in 2007/08 enrolment at primary schools was equivalent to 82% of children in the relevant age-group. In 2009/10 enrolment in secondary schools included 51% (males 49%, females 52%) of students in the relevant age-group.

In 2001/02 there were 958 tertiary-level institutions, at which an estimated 587,300 students were enrolled. According to provisional estimates, 507,660 students were enrolled in tertiary-level institutions in 2007/08.

In 2012/13 government expenditure on education was forecast at 617,214m. kyats (4.9% of total budgeted spending).

NAMIBIA

Introductory Survey

LOCATION, CLIMATE, LANGUAGE, RELIGION, FLAG, CAPITAL

The Republic of Namibia (formerly known as South West Africa) lies in south-western Africa, with South Africa to the south and south-east, Botswana to the east and Angola to the north. The country has a long coastline on the Atlantic Ocean. The narrow Caprivi Strip, between Angola and Botswana in the north-east, extends Namibia to the Zambezi river, giving it a border with Zambia. The climate is generally hot, although coastal areas have relatively mild temperatures. Most of the country is subject to drought and unreliable rainfall. The average annual rainfall varies from about 50 mm (2 ins) on the coast to 550 mm (22 ins) in the north. The arid Namib Desert stretches along the west coast, while the easternmost area is part of the Kalahari Desert. The official language is English; however, most of the African ethnic groups have their own languages. At the 2001 census the most widely spoken African languages were Oshiwambo (used in 48% of households), Nama/Damara (11%), Rukavango (10%) and Otjiherero (8%). In addition, Afrikaans is spoken (11%) and German is also used. About 90% of the population are Christians. The national flag (proportions 2 by 3) comprises a blue triangle in the upper hoist corner, bearing a yellow sun (a blue-bordered disc, surrounded by 12 triangular rays), separated from a green triangle in the lower fly corner by a white-bordered, broad red stripe. The capital is Windhoek.

CONTEMPORARY POLITICAL HISTORY

Historical Context

South West Africa became a German possession in 1884. The territory excluded the port of Walvis Bay and 12 small offshore islands, previously annexed by the United Kingdom and subsequently incorporated into South Africa. During the First World War South African forces occupied South West Africa in 1914, and in 1915 Germany surrendered the territory. In 1920 the League of Nations entrusted South Africa with a mandate to administer South West Africa. In 1925 South Africa granted a Constitution giving limited self-government to European (white) inhabitants only. No trusteeship agreement was concluded with the UN after the Second World War, and in 1946 the UN refused South Africa's request for permission to annex South West Africa. In 1949 the territory's European voters were granted representation in the South African Parliament. The following year the International Court of Justice (ICJ, see p. 26) issued a ruling that the area should remain under international mandate and that South Africa should submit it to UN control. South Africa refused to comply with this judgment. In October 1966 South Africa's security and apartheid laws were extended to South West Africa, retrospective to 1950.

Opposition within South West Africa to South African rule led to the establishment of two African nationalist organizations, the South West Africa People's Organisation (SWAPO—founded in 1957 as the Ovamboland People's Congress) and the South West African National Union (SWANU—formed in 1959). During 1966 SWAPO's military wing, the People's Liberation Army of Namibia (PLAN), launched an armed struggle for the liberation of the territory. PLAN operated from bases in Angola and Zambia, and was controlled by the external wing of SWAPO (led by Sam Nujoma—the organization's President from 1959). SWAPO also had a legal wing, which was tolerated in South West Africa.

South Africa was consistently criticized at the UN over its extension of apartheid to the territory. The UN General Assembly voted to terminate South Africa's mandate in October 1966, established a UN Council for South West Africa in May 1967, and changed the name of the territory to Namibia in June 1968. In 1971 the ICJ ruled that South Africa's presence was illegal. In 1973 the UN General Assembly recognized SWAPO as 'the authentic representative of the Namibian people', and appointed a UN Commissioner for Namibia to undertake 'executive and administrative tasks'.

A multiracial constitutional conference on the territory's future, organized by the all-white South West Africa Legislative Assembly, was convened in Windhoek in September 1975, attended by representatives of the territory's 11 main ethnic groups. However, neither the UN nor the Organization of African Unity (OAU, now the African Union, see p. 191) recognized this so-called Turnhalle Conference, owing to its ethnic and non-democratic basis. In 1976 and 1977 proposals for procedures whereby Namibia was to achieve independence and formulate a constitution were made by the Turnhalle Conference, but rejected by SWAPO, the UN and the OAU. In September 1977 South Africa appointed an Administrator-General to govern the territory. In November the Turnhalle Conference was dissolved, and the Democratic Turnhalle Alliance (DTA), a coalition of conservative political groups representing the ethnic groups involved in the Turnhalle Conference, was formed.

In early 1978 talks were held between South Africa, SWAPO and a 'contact group' comprising Canada, France, the Federal Republic of Germany, the United Kingdom and the USA. In September the contact group's proposals for a Namibian settlement, including the holding of UN-supervised elections, were conditionally accepted by both South Africa and SWAPO and were incorporated in UN Security Council Resolution 435. However, South Africa continued to implement its own internal solution for Namibia with an election for a Constituent Assembly in December. The election was contested by five parties, but boycotted notably by SWAPO. Of the 50 seats in the Assembly, 41 were won by the DTA. In May 1979 South Africa unilaterally established a legislative National Assembly, without executive powers, from the existing Constituent Assembly.

All-party negotiations, held under UN auspices in Geneva, Switzerland, in January 1981, failed in their aim of arranging a cease-fire and eventual UN-supervised elections. Later in 1981 the contact group attempted to secure support for a three-phase independence plan. However, South Africa's insistence (supported by the USA) that any withdrawal of South African forces must be linked to the withdrawal of Cuban troops from Angola was rejected by Angola and the UN. Meanwhile, the Ministerial Council, formed in 1980 and chaired by Dirk Mudge (also Chairman of the DTA), assumed much of the Administrator-General's executive power in September 1981. However, the Ministerial Council was dissolved in January 1983, when, after several months of disagreement with the South African Government regarding the future role of the DTA in the territory, Mudge resigned as Council Chairman. South Africa disbanded the National Assembly and resumed direct rule of Namibia, with Willem van Niekerk as Administrator-General.

The Multi-Party Conference (MPC) was established in November 1983, grouping, initially, seven internal political parties. Boycotted by SWAPO, it appeared to be promoted by South Africa as a means of settling the independence issue outside the framework of Resolution 435, and of reducing SWAPO's dominance in any future post-independence government for Namibia. None the less, South Africa continued to negotiate on the independence issue with SWAPO and Angola. In February 1984 South Africa and Angola agreed to a cease-fire on the Angola–Namibia border, and set up a joint commission to monitor the withdrawal of all South African troops from Angola. Angola undertook to ensure that neither Cuban nor SWAPO forces would move into the areas vacated by the South African troops. Discussions on the independence issue in mid-1984, involving van Niekerk, SWAPO and the MPC, ended inconclusively, as did negotiations in 1984–86 between the South African Government and the US Assistant Secretary of State for African Affairs.

In April 1985 the South African Government accepted a proposal by the MPC for a 'Transitional Government of National Unity' (TGNU) in Namibia. This was formally established in Windhoek in June, although the arrangement was condemned in advance by the contact group and was declared 'null and void' by the UN Secretary-General. The TGNU consisted of an executive Cabinet, drawn from a National Assembly of 62 members who were appointed from among the parties constituting the MPC. Its establishment was accompanied by the proclamation of a 'bill of rights', drafted by the MPC, which prohibited racial discrimination. A Constitutional Council was also established to prepare a constitution for an independent Namibia. The South African Government retained responsibility for foreign affairs, defence and internal security, and all legislation was to be subject to approval by the Administrator-General. Louis Pienaar replaced van Niekerk in this post in July.

During 1987, following the liberalization of labour laws and the legalization of trade unions for black workers in 1986, the trade union movement became increasingly active. In mid-1987 the Constitutional Council published a draft document; however, South Africa indicated that it could not accept the lack of a guarantee of minority rights in the proposal. In March 1988 the Namibian Supreme Court declared the 'AG8' law of 1980 (providing for the election of 'second-tier' legislative assemblies and for the administration of education and health facilities on an ethnic, rather than a geographical, basis) to be in conflict with the 1985 'bill of rights'.

Both Angola and Cuba were reported in January 1988 to have accepted, in principle, the US demand for a complete withdrawal of Cuban troops from Angola, but they reiterated that this would be conditional on the cessation of South African support for the insurgent União Nacional para a Independência Total de Angola (UNITA). In July Angola, Cuba and South Africa reached agreement on 14 'essential principles' for a peaceful settlement, and in August it was agreed that the implementation of Resolution 435 would begin on 1 November. However, it was not until December that Angola, Cuba and South Africa signed a formal treaty designating 1 April 1989 as the implementation date for Resolution 435 and establishing a joint commission to monitor the treaty's implementation. (A further agreement was signed by Angola and Cuba, requiring the evacuation of all Cuban troops from Angola by July 1991.) A Constituent Assembly was to be elected in Namibia on 1 November 1989. South African forces in Namibia were to be confined to their bases, and their numbers reduced to 1,500 by July 1989; all South African troops were to have been withdrawn from Namibia one week after the November election. SWAPO forces were to be confined to bases in Angola in April, before being disarmed and repatriated. A multinational military observer force, the UN Transition Assistance Group (UNTAG), was to monitor the South African withdrawal, and civilian administrators and an international police force were to supervise the election. At the end of February the TGNU was formally disbanded, and on 1 March the National Assembly voted to dissolve itself; until independence the territory was governed by the Administrator-General, in consultation with a Special Representative of the UN Secretary-General, Martti Ahtisaari. Pienaar and Ahtisaari were to be jointly responsible for arranging the November election. In June most racially discriminatory legislation was repealed, and an amnesty was granted to Namibian refugees and exiles: by late September nearly 42,000 people, including Nujoma, had returned to Namibia. Meanwhile, South Africa completed its troop reduction ahead of schedule.

Voting proceeded peacefully on 7–11 November 1989, with the participation of more than 95% of the electorate. SWAPO received 57.3% of all votes cast and won 41 of the Constituent Assembly's 72 seats, while the DTA, with 28.6% of the votes, secured 21 seats. Following the election, South Africa's remaining troops were evacuated from Namibia, while SWAPO's bases in Angola were decommissioned. The SWAPO Government subsequently reached an agreement with South Africa that no legal action would be taken for atrocities committed by either side. The agreement also precluded the establishment of a truth and reconciliation commission.

In February 1990 the Constituent Assembly adopted a draft Constitution, providing for a multi-party democracy based on universal adult suffrage. Later in the month the Constituent Assembly elected Nujoma as Namibia's first President. On 21 March Namibia finally achieved independence; the Constituent Assembly was redesignated the National Assembly, and Nujoma assumed executive power. A Cabinet, headed by the Constituent Assembly Chairman, Hage Geingob (a long-serving SWAPO activist), was also sworn in.

Domestic Political Affairs

Following Namibia's independence, the port of Walvis Bay, its surrounding territory of 1,124 sq km and the 12 offshore Penguin Islands remained under South African jurisdiction. In September 1991 the Namibian and South African Governments agreed to administer the disputed territories jointly, pending a final settlement on sovereignty, and in August 1992 the two countries announced the forthcoming establishment of a joint administration authority. In August 1993, however, South Africa's multi-

party constitutional negotiating committee instructed the Government to prepare legislation for the transfer of sovereignty over Walvis Bay to Namibia. Accordingly, negotiations between Namibia and South Africa resulted in bilateral agreements regarding the future of South African interests in the Walvis Bay area. Namibia formally took control of Walvis Bay and its islands from 1 March 1994.

Namibia's first post-independence presidential and legislative elections in December 1994 resulted in overwhelming victories for Nujoma and SWAPO. Nujoma was elected for a second term as President, securing 76.3% of the votes cast, while SWAPO secured 53 of the elective seats in the National Assembly, with 73.9% of the valid votes cast. The DTA won 15 seats (with 20.8% of the votes), and the United Democratic Front (UDF) two. The remaining two seats were won by the Democratic Coalition of Namibia (an alliance of the National Patriotic Front and the German Union) and the Monitor Action Group (MAG).

At the SWAPO Congress in May 1997 Nujoma was re-elected unopposed as party President. Among the resolutions endorsed by the Congress was a proposal that Nujoma should seek re-election for a third term as national President. It was agreed that the Constitution, which stipulated that a President may serve no more than two consecutive terms, could be exceptionally amended to allow Nujoma to seek a further mandate, since the incumbent had initially been appointed by the Constituent Assembly, and had only once been elected President on a popular mandate. In August 1998 a senior SWAPO official, Ben Ulenga, resigned as Namibia's High Commissioner to the United Kingdom, in protest at the proposed arrangement to allow Nujoma to seek a renewed mandate. The exceptional constitutional amendment was approved by the requisite two-thirds' majority in the National Assembly in October and by the National Council in November. In March 1999 it was reported that Ulenga was to establish a new political party, the Congress of Democrats (CoD).

In August 1998 the DTA's executive announced the suspension of Mishake Muyongo as party President, and dissociated the party from Muyongo's overt support for the secession of the Caprivi Strip—a narrow area of land extending in the north-east, between Angola and Botswana, as far as the Zambezi river (Namibia's border with Zambia). In November it emerged that Muyongo, leading the so-called Caprivi Liberation Movement (CLM), was among more than 100 people who, apparently armed, had crossed into Botswana in October, and who were now seeking asylum in that country. The Namibian Government stated that it had discovered plans for a secessionist rebellion, led by Muyongo and a chief of the Mafwe tribe, Boniface Mamili, in Caprivi. Representatives of the office of the UN High Commissioner for Refugees (UNHCR) subsequently advised the Botswana authorities that the secessionists' fears of persecution, should they be returned to Namibia, were 'plausible'. In subsequent weeks many more people crossed into Botswana, claiming to be fleeing harassment and persecution by the Namibian security forces. During a visit to Botswana in March 1999 Nujoma reached an agreement with President Festus Mogae of that country, whereby the separatist leaders (whose extradition had hitherto been sought by Namibia in order that they could be tried on terrorist charges) would be accorded refugee status, on condition that they be resettled in a third country. Muyongo and Mamili were subsequently granted asylum in Denmark. The agreement also provided for the return to Namibia, under the auspices of UNHCR and without fear of prosecution or persecution, of the estimated 2,500 refugees who had crossed into Botswana since late 1998.

A period of apparent calm in the Caprivi region ended abruptly in early August 1999 with an armed attack by members of an organization styling itself the Caprivi Liberation Army (CLA), who targeted a military base at Mpacha airport and the police headquarters and offices of the Namibian Broadcasting Corporation in the regional capital, Katima Mulilo. At least eight members of the Namibian security forces and five CLA fighters were killed during the attack and its suppression. Nujoma responded by declaring a state of emergency in the region. While there was support within Namibia for the declaration, the CoD, as well as church leaders and human rights organizations, expressed concern at evidence of the ill-treatment of detainees. Visiting Katima Mulilo in late August, Nujoma announced an end to the state of emergency, although army and police reinforcements were to remain in Caprivi. Initially, 12 alleged rebels were remanded on charges of high treason, murder, public violence and illegal possession of firearms; the prosecution asserted that 17 known leaders of the CLA remained at large.

Meanwhile, a further 47 suspects were charged with aiding and abetting the rebels. Repatriations of refugees from Botswana were halted following the attack on Katima Mulilo. In September 2001, in response to a request from the Namibian Government, the Gaborone Magistrates' Court in Botswana ordered the extradition of a group of suspected Caprivi separatists who were wanted to stand trial for high treason in connection with the attack on Katima Mulilo. The Namibian Government was also seeking to extradite Muyongo from Denmark to answer similar charges. In October 2003, after numerous delays, the trial commenced of 121 Namibians charged with offences related to the attack on Katima Mulilo. In February 2004 the trial judge ruled that 13 of the defendants were 'irregularly before the court', as a result of a process of 'disguised extradition' whereby they had been removed from Zambia and Botswana, and ordered their release. It was reported that the 13 defendants thus acquitted had been immediately rearrested on their release. In August 2007 10 individuals were convicted in relation to the rebellion and sentenced to up to 32 years' imprisonment, while in February 2013 43 of the accused men were cleared of any wrongdoing. The trial of the remaining defendants was ongoing in early 2013, marking almost 14 years since the suspects had been detained.

Meanwhile, presidential and legislative elections, which were held on 30 November and 1 December 1999, resulted in an overwhelming victory for Nujoma and SWAPO, with Ulenga and the CoD apparently winning support at the expense of the DTA. In the presidential election Nujoma was returned for a third (and final) term of office, with 76.8% of the votes cast, while Ulenga took 10.5% and Katuutire Kaura (Muyongo's successor as President of the DTA) 9.6%. SWAPO won 55 of the elective seats in the National Assembly, with 76.1% of the votes cast (thus ensuring that it retained the two-thirds' majority required to amend the Constitution); the CoD and the DTA each won seven seats (taking, respectively, 9.9% and 9.5% of the total votes cast).

In August 2002 Nujoma reorganized his Cabinet; Theo-Ben Gurirab was appointed Prime Minister, replacing Geingob. Hidipo Hamutenya became Minister of Foreign Affairs, Information and Broadcasting, but was dismissed without explanation in May 2004: many observers regarded the decision as part of a plan by the President to manoeuvre his own choice of successor, the Minister of Lands, Resettlement and Rehabilitation, Hifikepunye Pohamba, into a stronger position. Pohamba was duly selected as SWAPO's presidential candidate later that month.

The Pohamba presidency

At national elections held on 15–16 November 2004 Pohamba was elected President with 76.4% of the votes cast; his nearest rival, Ulenga, secured 7.3%. SWAPO also recorded a decisive victory in the elections to the National Assembly, retaining 55 of the 72 seats with 76.1% of the national vote. The CoD increased its share of the vote but won only five seats, compared with seven in the 1999 elections. The DTA took four seats, the UDF three and the MAG one seat, while two newly reactivated parties, the National Unity Democratic Organization (NUDO) and the Republican Party (RP), won three seats and one seat, respectively. Turn-out was 85%. (Following claims of electoral irregularities by members of the opposition, a recount was held in March 2005: with the exception of the CoD, all parties received fewer votes, although the overall allocation of seats remained the same.)

Nujoma stood down as President on 21 March 2005, but remained leader of SWAPO. Following his inauguration as President that day, Pohamba announced his Cabinet, which included six new appointees. The former Minister of Higher Education, Training and Employment Creation, Nahas Angula, and the former Minister of Health and Social Services, Dr Libertina Amathila, were appointed as Prime Minister and Deputy Prime Minister, respectively.

Meanwhile, in April 2001 the Government announced that it had allocated N $100m. to acquire land for redistribution on a voluntary basis over a five-year period. At that time approximately 4,000 (mainly white-owned) farms occupied 52% of the total land area, while the Government had acquired only some 6% of the land required for resettlement. In October 2002 the Government announced that it was considering the seizure of white-owned farms for redistribution to the landless black population, and criticized white farmers for taking advantage of the voluntary basis for land redistribution by charging excessively high prices for their land. In March 2004 the Government estimated that it would cost more than US $150m. over a five-

year period to redistribute some 9m. ha of land among an estimated 243,000 applicants. (It was reported that land prices had increased three-fold between 1990 and 2005.) By September 2004 the Government had bought just over 140 farms at a cost of N $131m.—under the 'willing buyer, willing seller' scheme—and resettled 9,156 people. The expropriation of the first white-owned commercial farm was carried out in November 2005; a further 19 farms were listed for expropriation under compulsory purchase orders.

In December 2005 the National Assembly approved legislation granting former President Nujoma the title of 'Founding Father'. Pohamba was elected as SWAPO leader in November 2007, following Nujoma's retirement. In the same month a new political party, the Rally for Democracy and Progress (RDP), was registered under the leadership of two former cabinet ministers and members of SWAPO. Jesaya Nyamu, who was named as acting Chairman of the party, had been Minister of Trade and Industry until 2004 and Hidipo Hamutenya, acting President of the RDP, was formerly Minister of Foreign Affairs.

In April 2008 President Pohamba announced a major reorganization of the Cabinet. The most notable appointment was that of former Prime Minister Geingob to the post of Minister of Trade and Industry.

In May 2008 workers at the Skorpion Zinc Mine in southern Namibia commenced industrial action following a wage dispute. The strike lasted for 19 days before a 12% pay increase was agreed. There was further industrial action in September, when more than 1,900 workers at TransNamib Holdings, a transport services company, went on strike, paralysing the country's rail network. The strike, which lasted for seven days, was estimated by the Government to have cost the Namibian economy some N $180m.

Recent developments: the 2009 elections

Presidential and legislative elections were held concurrently on 27–28 November 2009. In the former poll Pohamba was overwhelmingly re-elected to serve a second presidential term, securing 76.4% of the valid votes cast. Of his 11 challengers, only Hamutenya, representing the RDP, took more than 4% of the vote, winning 11.1%. SWAPO retained its majority in the National Assembly, taking 54 of the 72 seats in the legislative elections, with 75.3% of the national vote. The RDP won eight seats, while the DTA, NUDO and the UDF all secured two seats. Several African election observer missions declared the polls to have been transparent, free and fair; however, eight of the opposition parties that contested the elections criticized the delay in vote counting and the release of the results, and alleged that numerous irregularities had taken place during the voting process. In March 2010 the Namibian High Court dismissed, owing to 'technical' reasons, a challenge to the results brought by a number of the defeated parties. In response to this ruling, the opposition parties appealed to the Supreme Court, while the RDP, RP and DTA announced a boycott of the National Assembly.

In late March 2010 President Pohamba announced the formation of a new Government, again headed by Prime Minister Angula. Dr Marco Hausiku, hitherto Minister of Foreign Affairs, became Deputy Prime Minister in place of Amathila, while Utoni Nujoma—the son of Sam Nujoma—who was among five new ministers appointed to the Cabinet, assumed responsibility for the foreign affairs portfolio. In September the Supreme Court overruled the High Court's earlier judgment and declared that the opposition challenge to the 2009 election results was valid, prompting the RDP and the RP to end their six-month boycott of the National Assembly. (The DTA had ended its boycott in June 2010.) However, after hearing their case, in February 2011 the High Court ruled against the opposition parties, concluding that there was insufficient evidence to support their claims of electoral misconduct. Shortly afterwards the opposition grouping announced its intention to appeal once again to the Supreme Court. In October 2012, however, the Supreme Court rejected the opposition's petition, although it did acknowledge that the electoral process had been imperfect.

Meanwhile, leaked documents emerged in mid-2010 relating to the Development Capital Portfolio (DCP), an investment arm of the Government Institutions Pension Fund (GIPF) that had ceased operating in 2002 after suffering huge financial losses due to the collapse of a number of companies to which the GIPF had lent large sums of DCP funds. Among the files was a previously unpublished audit report produced by the country's financial regulator, the Namibia Financial Institutions Supervisory Authority (NAMFISA), which in 2006 had conducted an independent investigation into the DCP's losses. The report described the DCP as being 'deeply flawed' and criticized the weak regulations governing the allocation of DCP funding, while media reports alleged that most of the businessmen awarded DCP loans had close ties with the Government or with senior members of the GIPF. NAMFISA had recommended an overhaul of the GIPF, including the removal of senior management, and that measures be taken to recover the lost money from the receivers of the loans; however, the report's recipient, Prime Minister Angula, had failed to act on this guidance. The Government was criticized by trade unions and opposition parties for failing to bring to account those responsible for the DCP's losses, which amounted to over N $650m. according to NAMFISA, and there was widespread outrage among the general public. In response, in October 2010 the Government initiated another audit into the DCP's finances and suspended the DCP's successor scheme, the Unlisted Investment Policy. The results of the second audit, presented to the President in February 2011, corroborated the findings from NAMFISA's earlier investigation, and the reform of the GIPF and the introduction of new lending regulations were recommended. Following a protest march in the capital by hundreds of government workers, Pohamba announced that those who had borrowed DCP funds would be pursued for repayment under threat of prosecution, although he seemed reluctant to hold high-ranking GIPF members responsible for the scandal.

After the failure of negotiations on the formation of an opposition electoral alliance, the RDP merged with the RP in October 2010 (retaining the former's name) in an attempt to present SWAPO with a more robust challenge in the local and regional elections scheduled for the following month. Nevertheless, the elections, held on 26–27 November, resulted in another convincing victory for SWAPO, which secured the overwhelming majority of local and regional council seats. The rate of participation by the electorate, at 39%, was the lowest on record. Shortly before the elections the SWAPO-dominated National Assembly had approved controversial legislation granting the President the power to appoint regional governors, who had hitherto been elected by the regional councillors. Opposition parties had strongly criticized the bill, arguing that it would weaken democracy and that it contradicted the Government's declared adherence to decentralization. The Government, however, claimed that the new law would enhance national unity and deter potential tribal conflict, while providing governors with a direct channel of communication to the central authorities. In December Pohamba duly appointed the 13 regional governors, all of whom were SWAPO members.

In July 2011 President Pohamba suffered what was described as a mild stroke, raising doubts that he would be able to complete the remainder of his second presidential term, which was due to expire in 2015, and leading to speculation regarding the identity of his successor. The country's Constitution is at odds with SWAPO's own constitution, with the former dictating that the Prime Minister would take over in the event of the President being unable to continue; however, it is the party's prerogative to appoint its Vice-President as the country's next presidential candidate. The ambiguities in the succession process were seemingly resolved in December 2012, when Geingob was re-elected as SWAPO Vice-President and then appointed as Prime Minister. In the same cabinet reorganization, erstwhile premier Angula was named as Minister of Defence, Pendukeni Ivula-Ithana received the home affairs portfolio and Neitumbo Nandi-Ndeitwah became Minister of Foreign Affairs.

Foreign Affairs
Regional relations
Following independence, Namibia became a member of the UN, the Commonwealth, the OAU and the Southern African Development Co-ordination Conference—now the Southern African Development Community (SADC, see p. 434). Despite expressed concerns at South African dominance of the regional economy, the Nujoma regime forged close links with post-apartheid South Africa, and in 1994 SWAPO contributed funds to the electoral campaigns of the African National Congress of South Africa and the Pan-Africanist Congress. In February 1997 legislation providing for the cancellation of Namibia's debt (now amounting to N $1,200m.) was formally approved by the South African Parliament. In August 2001 the foreign ministers of Namibia and South Africa held talks regarding their 400-km border; Namibia claimed its southern border extended to the middle of the Orange river, while South Africa claimed that its territory stretched to

the northern bank. (When South Africa's borders were reassessed in 1994, following its first democratic elections, the Surveyors-General of both Namibia and South Africa had agreed to place the border in the middle of the river, but the agreement was never signed.) The confusion over the location of the border has led to differences over mineral and fishing rights in the river, as well as grazing rights on its islands. In November 2012 Namibia and South Africa agreed to form a bilateral commission to facilitate greater co-operation between the two countries with respect to economic, diplomatic and security matters.

In March 1993 UNITA alleged that members of the Namibia Defence Force (NDF) had crossed the border into southern Angola to assist Angolan government forces in offensives against UNITA, and subsequently claimed that some 2,000 Cuban troops had landed at Namibia's southern port of Lüderitz, from where they had been transferred to Angola to assist government forces. The Namibian authorities denied any involvement in the Angolan conflict, however. A 550-km stretch of the Okavango river border was closed from September 1994, following the deaths of three Namibians in an attack attributed by the Namibian authorities to UNITA. In September 1995 the Namibian Government announced the formation of a border control unit to assist police and NDF troops deployed along the Okavango. In November the two countries' joint defence and security commission agreed new measures aimed at facilitating the work of border patrols. Namibia subsequently announced that the Government was to contribute 200 NDF troops to the UN peace-keeping mission in Angola.

Following the attack on Katima Mulilo by Caprivi separatists in August 1999, the Namibian Government alleged that UNITA was lending military and logistical support to the CLA. There was considerable speculation that not only was Caprivi an important supply route for UNITA, but also that the Angolan rebel movement was attempting to divert resources of the Namibian armed forces away from the conflict in the Democratic Republic of the Congo (DRC).

Tensions in the region of the Namibia–Angola border escalated from late 1999, after the two countries began joint patrols targeting UNITA, and the Namibian Government authorized the Angolan armed forces to launch attacks against UNITA from Namibian territory. In February 2000 it was announced that Nujoma and President José Eduardo dos Santos of Angola had agreed to implement measures to restore security in the border region; by June, when a curfew was imposed on the north-eastern border with Angola, more than 50 Namibians had been killed in cross-border raids by the Angolan rebels. Continuing conflict in southern Angola resulted in a large number of refugees entering Namibia (some 6,000 arrived from Angola between November 1999 and August 2000, although increased border security subsequently reduced the flow). In March 2001 President Nujoma ordered a further reinforcement of the Namibian military presence in Caprivi. In October UNITA rebels were reported to have destroyed an electricity substation in the Kavango region, and in November a group of unidentified gunmen killed four people in western Caprivi before escaping to Angola.

In April 2002 the Namibian Government welcomed the signing of a formal cease-fire agreement by the Angolan Government and UNITA. Some stability was restored in the Kavango and Caprivi regions in mid-2002, and in August a number of Angolan refugees were repatriated; the majority of them, estimated at around 20,000, were due to return home in mid-2003, under the auspices of UNHCR. In February 2005 Namibia and Angola reached agreement on a maritime border; negotiations had begun in 1993 but were not formalized until 2003 when a joint commission for delimitation and demarcation was established. In September 2008 Namibia's National Society for Human Rights (NSHR) reported that it had discovered what were believed to be unmarked mass graves near the border with Angola. The organization claimed that it had 'reasonable cause' to believe the remains it had discovered belonged to victims of the Namibian security forces, who were killed between 1994 and 2003. According to the NSHR, in 1994 the Namibian authorities ordered that all illegal immigrants be cleared from the northern border area, some of whom were accused of being members of UNITA. This allegedly resulted in systematic attacks on local people, who were subject to summary executions and 'forced disappearances': the Namibian Government, however, strongly denied these claims.

In mid-1996 Namibia and Botswana referred a dispute regarding the demarcation of their joint border on the Chobe river (specifically, the issue of the sovereignty of the small, uninhabited island of Kasikili-Sedudu) for adjudication by the ICJ. The Court ruled in December 1999 that the island formed part of the territory of Botswana; the judgment further ruled that nationals of (and vessels flying the flags of) Botswana and Namibia should enjoy equal treatment in the two channels around the island. In January 1998 the two countries' Joint Commission on Defence and Security held an emergency meeting, following allegations by Namibia that troops from Botswana had taken control of a further island in disputed border territory—Situngu Island in the Caprivi Strip. The Joint Commission agreed to expedite the establishment of a Joint Technical Commission for the demarcation of the border. Relations were complicated by the issue of Caprivi secessionism (see above). Situngu is claimed as Mafwe land; furthermore, Namibia's representative in discussions regarding the island, said to be a member of the secessionist movement, was reported to have fled to Angola. In 2003 Botswana and Namibia accepted the demarcation by a joint commission of their joint border along the Kwando, Linyanti and Chobe rivers.

Other external relations

Germany has been a major aid donor to Namibia since independence, and relations are generally close. In September 1995, none the less, during a visit by the German Chancellor, Helmut Kohl, some 300 members of the Herero ethnic group staged a demonstration outside the German embassy in Windhoek to demand compensation for suffering inflicted on the Herero under German rule. In June 2001 the Herero filed a lawsuit in Washington, DC, USA, against three German companies (Deutsche Bank AG, Woermann Line and Terex Corporation), claiming US $2,000m. in reparation for the alleged exploitation and eventual extermination of some 65,000 Herero in 1904–07; a second lawsuit, for a further US $2,000m., was filed against the German Government in September 2001. The case against Terex Corporation was subsequently withdrawn, after the company claimed that it was under different management at the time of the atrocities. In October 2003 it was reported that the Federal Court in Washington, DC, had ruled that it did not have jurisdiction over the Herero case, and that the Herero were consequently considering filing a lawsuit in New York, USA. In January 2004, at a commemoration of the Herero uprising against German rule in 1904, the Government of Germany expressed its regret for the extermination of Herero, but declared itself unwilling to pay compensation to descendants of the victims. During a visit to Namibia in August 2004 the German Minister of Economic Co-operation and Development, Heidemarie Wieczorek-Zeul, apologized to the Herero community for the atrocities carried out during 1904–07. During a visit to Germany in December 2005 President Pohamba rejected an offer of reparations valued at N $160m. Bilateral consultations took place in May 2006 and included a German proposal to invest N $150m., over a 10-year period, in regions inhabited by descendants of populations that had suffered during the colonial occupation. The money would be made available in addition to existing aid commitments, which were reported to amount to some €11m. per year. However, the German Government denied that the additional money was intended as war reparations. Germany has also provided Namibia with military assistance in the form of training and equipment donation. In September 2008 it was reported that the German Advisory Group in Namibia had supplied the Namibian Defence Force with an Integrated Logistics System, completing a N $16.5m. project to establish a communications network linking all military bases in the country. In October 2011 it was reported that Germany had returned to Namibia 20 Herero skulls that had been taken some 100 years ago. However, the gesture was met with hostility, with many Namibians once more demanding reparations for the atrocities committed by Germany at the beginning of the 20th century.

CONSTITUTION AND GOVERNMENT

On 21 March 1990 Namibia became independent, and the Constitution took effect. Executive authority is held by the President, who is the Head of State. According to the Constitution, the President shall be directly elected by universal adult suffrage for a term of five years, and permitted to hold office for a maximum of two terms. (In late 1998 legislation was approved whereby the Constitution was to be exceptionally amended to allow the incumbent President to seek a third term of office.) Legislative power is vested in the National Assembly, comprising 72 members directly elected by universal adult suffrage and as many as six non-voting members nominated by the President.

The National Assembly has a maximum term of five years. An advisory National Council, comprising two representatives from each of the country's 13 Regional Councils, elected for a six-year period, operates as the second chamber of parliament. Each region has its own Governor.

REGIONAL AND INTERNATIONAL CO-OPERATION

Namibia is a member of the African Union (see p. 191), of the Common Market for Eastern and Southern Africa (see p. 241), of the Southern African Development Community (see p. 434), and of the Southern African Customs Union (with Botswana, Lesotho, South Africa and Swaziland); and is also a signatory to the Cotonou Agreement with the European Union.

Namibia became a member of the UN in 1990. As a contracting party to the General Agreement on Tariffs and Trade, Namibia joined the World Trade Organization (WTO, see p. 444) on its establishment in 1995. Namibia participates in the Group of 77 (G77, see p. 461) developing countries.

ECONOMIC AFFAIRS

In 2011, according to estimates by the World Bank, Namibia's gross national income (GNI), measured at average 2009–11 prices, was US $10,934m., equivalent to US $4,700 per head (or US $6,600 per head on an international purchasing-power parity basis). During 2002–11, it was estimated, the population increased at an average annual rate of 1.8%, while gross domestic product (GDP) per head increased, in real terms, by an average of 3.0% per year. Overall GDP increased, in real terms, at an average annual rate of 4.9% in 2002–11. According to the Bank of Namibia, real GDP increased by 4.8% in 2011.

Agriculture (including hunting, forestry and fishing) contributed 7.8% of GDP in 2011, according to the Bank of Namibia. An estimated 31.4% of the labour force were employed in the sector in mid-2013, according to FAO. The principal agricultural activity is beef production; the production of karakul sheepskins is also important. In addition, seal hunting and ostrich farming are practised on a commercial basis. The main subsistence crops are root crops, millet and maize, although Namibia remains highly dependent on imports of basic foods, especially in drought years. Plantations of seedless grapes were developed on the banks of the Orange river in the late 1990s, and projected growth in production was expected to increase significantly their contribution to export revenue. In recent years Namibia's traditionally rich fisheries have suffered a reverse, and in February 2006 fishing quotas were further lowered and a five-year moratorium was declared on new fishing rights. Nevertheless, exports of fish and fish products provided 11.2% of total export earnings in 2008. Legislation aimed at developing aquaculture was adopted in 2003 and a number of fish farms were established. Agricultural GDP decreased at an average annual rate of 1.8% in 2007–11; sectoral GDP declined by 1.1% in 2010, but increased by 7.7% in 2011.

Industry (including mining, manufacturing, construction and power) contributed 30.5% of GDP in 2011, and engaged 14.8% of the employed labour force in 2004. During 2007–11 industrial GDP increased by an average of 0.3% per year. The GDP of the industry sector grew by 14.4% in 2010, driven mainly by the rapid expansion of the construction industry, and by 1.0% in 2011.

Mining and quarrying contributed 10.4% of GDP in 2011, and engaged 2.0% of the employed labour force in 2004. Namibia has rich deposits of many minerals, and is among the world's leading producers of gem diamonds (some 98% of diamonds mined in Namibia are of gem quality). Diamond-mining contributed 75.8% of the sector's GDP in 2011, and diamonds are the principal mineral export, accounting for 16.5% of export earnings in 2008. Total production was 2.4m. carats in 2008, but declined to an estimated 1.2m. carats in 2009, before recovering to 1.7m. carats in 2010. In July 2004 the Israeli company Lev Leviev Diamonds established a diamond-cutting and -polishing factory in Windhoek, the first in Namibia and the largest of its kind in Africa. Copper production, which ceased in 1998, following the liquidation of the Tsumeb Corporation, resumed at the former Tsumeb sites in September 2000, but was suspended again in late 2008 owing to declining international prices. The smelter at Tsumeb, operated by Ongopolo, continued operations, however, processing imported ore. The Skorpion zinc mine and refinery near Rosh Pinah, opened in 2003 by Anglo American plc and owned since November 2010 by Vedanta Resources plc, produces around 150,000 metric tons of zinc per year. Despite health and environmental concerns, a new uranium mine began production at Langer Heinrich in 2007; Namibia was the fifth largest uranium producer in the world in 2011. In addition, lead, gold, salt, fluorspar, marble and semi-precious stones are extracted, and there are also considerable deposits of hydrocarbons, lithium, manganese, tungsten, cadmium and vanadium. Furthermore, Namibia is believed to have substantial reserves of coal, iron ore and platinum. Mining GDP decreased at an average annual rate of 9.1% in 2007–11; the sector's GDP increased by 32.7% in 2010, but declined by 8.5% in 2011.

Manufacturing contributed 13.3% of GDP in 2011, and engaged 6.2% of the employed labour force in 2004. The sector has hitherto remained underdeveloped, largely owing to Namibia's economic dependence on South Africa. The principal manufacturing activities are the processing of fish and minerals for export; brewing, meat-processing and the production of chemicals are also significant. Manufacturing GDP increased by an average of 4.9% per year in 2007–11; the sector's GDP increased by 10.8% in 2010 and by 1.2% in 2011.

Construction contributed 3.9% of GDP in 2011, and engaged 5.1% of the employed labour force in 2004. During 2007–11 construction GDP increased by an average of 3.1% per year. The sector's GDP grew by 16.2% in 2011.

In 2009 82.0% of Namibia's electricity production was derived from hydroelectric power, while coal accounted for 17.5% of total production. There is a hydroelectric station at Ruacana, on the Cunene river at the border with Angola, and a second hydroelectric power station was planned at Divundu on the Okavango river. Final agreement was reached on developing the Kudu offshore gasfield in early 2006. An 800-MW 'gas-to-power' plant would supply the domestic market and the surplus would be exported to South Africa under an agreement with that country's Electricity Supply Commission. However, the project subsequently suffered repeated delays. The construction of another 400-MW gas-fired plant, at Walvis Bay, was also envisaged. Imports of mineral fuels and lubricants accounted for 13.6% of the value of total merchandise imports in 2008. South Africa supplies all of Namibia's petroleum requirements.

The services sector contributed 61.7% of GDP in 2011. Tourism is expanding rapidly, and has been the focus of a major privatization initiative. The acquisition of Walvis Bay in March 1994, and subsequent establishment there of a free-trade zone, was expected to enhance Namibia's status as an entrepôt for regional trade. By March 2004 it was estimated that the free-trade zone had attracted some N $80m. of foreign direct investment. The GDP of the services sector increased at an average annual rate of 4.7% in 2007–11. Services GDP increased by 4.3% in 2011.

In 2011 Namibia recorded a visible merchandise trade deficit of US $1,212.4m. and there was a deficit of US $584.7m. on the current account of the balance of payments. South Africa was the dominant source of imports in 2008, providing 67.8% of the total, followed by the United Kingdom. In that year South Africa was also the principal market for Namibian exports (31.8%), followed by the United Kingdom, Angola, Canada, the USA and Spain. The principal exports were printed matter, diamonds, uranium and thorium ores and concentrates, and fresh or frozen fish. The principal import groups in that year included machinery and transport equipment (notably road vehicles), basic manufac-

tures, mineral fuels and lubricants, chemicals and related products, and food and live animals.

In the financial year ending 31 March 2010 Namibia recorded an overall budget deficit of N $862.3m., equivalent to 1.1% of GDP. An estimated budget deficit of N $4,761.6m. was recorded in the financial year ending 31 March 2013. Namibia's general government gross debt was N $12,477m. in 2009, equivalent to 15.6% of GDP. In 1997 South Africa officially cancelled the external public debt inherited by Namibia at independence. Namibia's external debt was estimated at US $716m. in 2003. The annual rate of inflation averaged 6.0% in 2002–11; consumer prices increased by 5.1% in 2011. According to the 2001 census, some 31% of the labour force were unemployed.

Namibia's potential for economic prosperity remains high, given its abundant mineral reserves and well-developed infrastructure, both of which were enhanced in 1994 by the acquisition of sovereignty over Walvis Bay and of important diamond-mining rights. The mining of offshore diamond deposits is of increasing importance, the leading diamond producer being Namdeb (a joint venture between the Government and De Beers). However, tackling poverty and unemployment remain the main challenges for the Government. Unemployment stood at 34% in 2009/10, while Namibia's reclassification as an upper middle-income country in 2009 belies the reality of large income inequality. Moreover, Namibia's economic progress continues to be largely influenced by its dependence on South Africa—the Namibian dollar, introduced in 1993, is at par with the rand—while adverse market conditions, resulting from the global financial crisis, impeded Namibia's valuable minerals sector in 2008–09. More positively, several uranium-mining projects were established in 2009, with the potential to create some 5,000 new jobs and Namibia aimed to be the world's third largest supplier of uranium by 2015. Real GDP grew by 6.6% in 2010, as the diamond and uranium sectors recovered, although a slowdown in mining activity during 2011 resulted in growth moderating to 4.8% in that year. The Government used its expansionary spending policies in early 2012 to encourage domestic demand. However, the IMF, in its largely positive assessment of the Namibian economy in February, noted the country's growing public debt as an area for concern, urging the Government to reduce spending and continue to check the progress of its stimulus programme—worth some US $14,900m.—which is targeting the creation of 104,000 new jobs annually. According to the IMF, real GDP expanded by an estimated 4.0% in 2012, driven by an upturn in diamond and uranium output. The Fund projected that the economy would grow by a further 4.2% in 2013, and, with the mining industry continuing to attract investment, the medium-term outlook appeared favourable.

PUBLIC HOLIDAYS

2014: 1 January (New Year's Day), 21 March (Independence Day), 18 April–21 April (Easter), 1 May (Workers' Day), 4 May (Cassinga Day), 25 May (Africa Day, anniversary of the OAU's foundation), 29 May (Ascension Day), 26 August (Heroes' Day), 10 December (Human Rights Day), 25–26 December (Christmas), 26 December (Family Day).

Statistical Survey

Source (unless otherwise indicated): Central Bureau of Statistics, National Planning Commission, Government Office Park, Block D2, Luther St, Windhoek; PMB 13356, Windhoek; tel. (61) 2834056; fax (61) 237620; e-mail info@npc.gov.na; internet www.npc.gov.na.

Area and Population

AREA, POPULATION AND DENSITY

Area (sq km)	825,615*
Population (census results)	
28 October 2001	1,830,330
28 August 2011 (preliminary)†	
Males	1,021,600
Females	1,083,300
Total	2,104,900
Population (UN estimates at mid-year)	
2012	2,364,431
2013	2,404,478
Density (per sq km) at mid-2013	2.9

* 318,772 sq miles.

† Data rounded to nearest 100 persons.

‡ Source: UN, *World Population Prospects: The 2010 Revision*; estimates not adjusted to take account of 2011 census.

POPULATION BY AGE AND SEX
(UN estimates at mid-2013)

	Males	Females	Total
0–14	425,007	417,514	842,521
15–64	731,619	737,357	1,468,976
65 and over	39,766	53,215	92,981
Total	1,196,392	1,208,086	2,404,478

Note: Estimates not adjusted to take account of results of 2011 census.

Source: UN, *World Population Prospects: The 2010 Revision*.

ETHNIC GROUPS
(population, 1988 estimates)

Ovambo . . .	623,000	Caprivian . . .	47,000
Kavango . . .	117,000	Bushmen . . .	36,000
Damara . . .	94,000	Baster	31,000
Herero . . .	94,000	Tswana	7,000
White . . .	80,000	Others	12,000
Nama . . .	60,000	**Total** . . .	1,252,000
Coloured . . .	51,000		

REGIONS
(population at 2011 census, preliminary)

	Area (sq km)	Population*	Density (per sq km)
Caprivi	14,785	90,100	6.1
Erongo	63,539	150,400	2.4
Hardap	109,781	79,000	0.7
Karas	161,514	76,000	0.5
Kavango	48,742	222,500	4.6
Khomas	36,964	340,900	9.2
Kunene	115,260	88,300	0.8
Ohangwena	10,706	245,100	22.9
Omaheke	84,981	70,800	0.8
Omusati	26,551	242,900	9.1
Oshana	8,647	174,900	20.2
Oshikoto	38,685	181,600	4.7
Otjozondjupa	105,460	142,400	1.4
Total	825,615	2,104,900	2.5

* Data are rounded to nearest 100 persons.

PRINCIPAL TOWNS
(population at 2011 census, preliminary)

Windhoek . . .	322,500	Rehoboth . . .	28,800
Rundu . . .	61,900	Katima Mulilo . .	28,200
Walvis Bay . .	61,300	Otjiwarongo . .	28,000
Swakopmund . .	44,700	Okahandja . .	22,500
Oshakati . . .	35,600	Ondangwa . . .	21,100

Note: Data are rounded to nearest 100 persons.

BIRTHS AND DEATHS
(annual averages, UN estimates)

	1995–2000	2000–05	2005–10
Birth rate (per 1,000)	32.9	29.9	27.4
Death rate (per 1,000)	9.3	10.6	8.6

Source: UN, *World Population Prospects: The 2010 Revision*.

Life expectancy (years at birth): 62.3 (males 61.8; females 62.9) in 2011 (Source: World Bank, World Development Indicators database).

EMPLOYMENT
(persons aged 15 to 69 years, 2004 labour force survey)

	Males	Females	Total
Agriculture, hunting and forestry .	64,991	37,645	102,636
Fishing	7,933	4,787	12,720
Mining and quarrying	5,909	1,653	7,562
Manufacturing	12,082	11,673	23,755
Electricity, gas and water . . .	5,031	1,120	6,151
Construction	18,296	1,309	19,605
Wholesale and retail trade, repair of motor vehicles, motorcycles and personal and household goods	27,004	26,891	53,895
Restaurants and hotels . . .	5,889	7,243	13,132
Transport, storage and communications	12,744	3,117	15,861
Financial intermediation . . .	3,506	4,076	7,582
Real estate, renting and business activities	5,280	4,095	9,375
Public administration and defence; compulsory social security . .	20,216	10,469	30,685
Education	12,313	18,855	31,168
Health and social work . . .	3,533	10,477	14,010
Other community, social and personal services	7,480	5,152	12,632
Private households with employed persons	4,067	20,014	24,081
Extra-territorial organizations and bodies	72	—	72
Sub-total	216,346	168,576	384,922
Not classifiable by economic activity	305	102	407
Total employed	216,651	168,678	385,329

Source: ILO.

Mid-2013 ('000 persons, FAO estimates): Agriculture, etc. 272; Total labour force 866 (Source: FAO).

Health and Welfare

KEY INDICATORS

Total fertility rate (children per woman, 2010) . . .	3.2
Under-5 mortality rate (per 1,000 live births, 2010) . .	40
HIV/AIDS (% of persons aged 15–49, 2009)	31.1
Physicians (per 1,000 head, 2004)	0.3
Hospital beds (per 1,000 head, 2006)	3.3
Health expenditure (2009): US $ per head (PPP) . . .	448
Health expenditure (2009): % of GDP	7.2
Health expenditure (2009): public (% of total)	55.0
Access to water (% of persons, 2010)	93
Access to sanitation (% of persons, 2010)	32
Total carbon dioxide emissions ('000 metric tons, 2008) . .	3,967.7
Carbon dioxide emissions per head (metric tons, 2008) . .	1.8
Human Development Index (2011): ranking	120
Human Development Index (2011): value	0.625

For sources and definitions, see explanatory note on p. vi.

Agriculture

PRINCIPAL CROPS
('000 metric tons)

	2009	2010*	2011*
Wheat	12.4	12.5	13.0
Maize	57.3	58.0	60.0
Millet . . . . . . † .	37.3	40.0	24.2
Sorghum	4.7	5.0	4.1
Grapes	20.0*	21.5	22.0

* FAO estimate(s).

Aggregate production ('000 metric tons, may include official, semi-official or estimated data): Total cereals 111.7 in 2009, 115.5 in 2010, 101.3 in 2011; Total roots and tubers 327.1 in 2009, 342.5 in 2010, 357.6 in 2011; Total vegetables (incl. melons) 55.7 in 2009, 60.0 in 2010, 59.9 in 2011; Total fruits (excl. melons) 33.3 in 2009, 34.3 in 2010, 35.8 in 2011.

Source: FAO.

LIVESTOCK
('000 head, year ending September, FAO estimates unless otherwise indicated)

	2009	2010	2011
Horses	46	47	47
Asses	140	140	140
Cattle	2,471*	2,400	2,350
Sheep	2,700	2,800	2,850
Goats	2,000	2,100	2,150
Pigs	60	65	70
Chickens	4,900	5,100	5,250

* Unofficial figure.

Source: FAO.

LIVESTOCK PRODUCTS
('000 metric tons)

	2009	2010	2011
Cattle meat	36.0	35.0*	34.3*
Sheep meat*	12.1	12.2	12.3
Chicken meat*	11.2	11.6	12.0
Cows' milk*	110.0	115.0	115.0
Hen eggs*	3.3	3.4	3.4
Wool, greasy*	1.3	1.4	1.4

* FAO estimate(s).

Source: FAO.

Forestry

Separate figures are not yet available. Data for Namibia are included in those for South Africa.

Fishing

('000 metric tons, live weight)*

	2008	2009	2010†
Capture†	372.8	370.3	370.0
Cape hakes (Stokvisse) . . .	126.3	136.9	140.0
Kingklip	3.7	4.5	4.4
Devil anglerfish	8.6	n.a.	n.a.
Southern African pilchard . .	20.7	13.7	14.0
Cape horse mackerel (Maasbanker)	192.7	198.3	198.0
Aquaculture†	0.5	0.5	0.5
Total catch†	373.3	370.9	370.5

* Figures include quantities caught by licensed foreign vessels in Namibian waters and processed in Lüderitz and Walvis Bay. The data exclude aquatic mammals (whales, seals, etc.). The number of South African fur seals caught was: 47,115 in 2008; 47,403 in 2009; n.a. in 2010.
† FAO estimate(s).

Source: FAO.

Mining

(metric tons unless otherwise indicated)

	2008	2009	2010
Copper ore†	7,471	—	—
Lead concentrates†	14,062	10,129	10,140
Zinc concentrates†	38,319	48,856	53,624
Silver ore (kilograms)*† . . .	30,000	30,000	30,000
Uranium oxide	4,838	5,600	5,473
Gold ore (kilograms)† . . .	2,126	2,057	2,683
Fluorspar (Fluorite)‡	118,263	80,857	104,494
Salt (unrefined)	732,000	807,348	770,636
Diamonds ('000 metric carats) .	2,435	1,192	1,693

* Estimate.
† Figures refer to the metal content of ores and concentrates.
‡ Figures (on a wet-weight basis) refer to acid-grade material.

Source: US Geological Survey.

Industry

SELECTED PRODUCTS
(metric tons)

	2007	2008	2009
Unrefined (blister) copper (unwrought)	20,600*	16,271	21,543
Electrical energy (million kWh) .	1,694	2,097	1,742

* Estimate.

2010: Unrefined (blister) copper (unwrought) 25,019.

Sources: US Geological Survey; UN Industrial Commodity Statistics Database.

Finance

CURRENCY AND EXCHANGE RATES

Monetary Units
100 cents = 1 Namibian dollar (N $).

Sterling, US Dollar and Euro Equivalents (31 December 2012)
£1 sterling = N $13.415;
US $1 = N $8.501;
€1 = N $11.216;
N $100 = £7.45 = US $11.76 = €8.92.

Average Exchange Rate (N $ per US $)
2010   7.3212
2011   7.2611
2012   8.2100

Note: The Namibian dollar was introduced in September 1993, replacing (at par) the South African rand. The rand remained legal tender in Namibia.

CENTRAL GOVERNMENT BUDGET
(N $ million, year ending 31 March)

Revenue*	2008/09	2009/10	2010/11†
Taxation	19,884.8	22,272.7	21,055.8
Taxes on income and profits .	7,354.0	8,136.6	9,357.6
Taxes on property . . .	167.0	221.9	238.0
Domestic taxes on goods and services	3,712.0	5,162.3	5,286.3
Taxes on international trade and transactions	8,501.8	8,585.2	5,975.3
Other taxes	150.0	166.7	198.6
Non-tax revenue	1,348.6	1,568.5	1,377.8
Entrepreneurial and property income	815.6	1,112.0	895.6
Fines and forfeitures . .	24.0	35.1	40.4
Administrative fees and charges	475.5	421.4	430.9
Return on capital from lending and equity	33.5	4.6	10.9
Total	21,233.4	23,845.8	22,433.6

Expenditure	2008/09	2009/10	2010/11†
Current expenditure . . .	17,401.0	19,499.8	22,552.6
Personnel expenditure . .	7,709.0	9,045.0	10,963.7
Expenditure on goods and other services	3,731.0	4,064.9	4,318.3
Interest payments . . .	1,331.0	1,427.1	1,316.9
Subsidies and other current transfers	4,630.0	4,962.8	5,953.7
Capital expenditure . . .	5,064.1	4,337.8	5,605.9
Capital investment . . .	3,775.4	2,763.1	4,507.6
Capital transfers . . .	159.4	900.0	561.5
Total lending and equity participation	1,129.3	674.7	536.8
Statistical discrepancy . . .	—	1,071.3	–414.3
Total	22,465.1	24,908.9	27,744.2

* Excluding grants received from abroad (N $ million): 141.0 in 2008/09; 200.8 in 2009/10; 265.1 in 2010/11 (estimate).
† Estimates.

2010/11 (N $ million, year ending 31 March, revised estimates): *Revenue:* Taxation 21,518.0 (Taxes on income and profits 9,910.4, Taxes on property 138.5, Domestic taxes on goods and services 5,284.7, Taxes on international trade and transactions 5,975.9, Other taxes 208.4); Non-tax revenue 1,697.9; Return on capital from lending and equity 4.2; Total revenue 23,220.1 (excl. grants 23.5). *Expenditure:* Current expenditure 22,411.0; Capital expenditure 4,143.1; Interest payments 965.5; Total expenditure (incl. others) 27,552.7.

2011/12 (N $ million, year ending 31 March, estimates): *Revenue:* Taxation 25,405.8 (Taxes on income and profits 10,412.1, Taxes on property 233.1, Domestic taxes on goods and services 7,393.9, Taxes on international trade and transactions 7,137.0, Other taxes 229.8); Non-tax revenue 1,402.4; Return on capital from lending and equity 20.4; Total revenue 26,828.6 (excl. grants 24.2). *Expenditure:* Current expenditure 27,801.1; Capital expenditure 8,070.0; Interest payments 1,279.8; Total expenditure (incl. others) 37,165.8.

2012/13 (N $ million, year ending 31 March, estimates): *Revenue:* Taxation 33,811.2 (Taxes on income and profits 11,593.8, Taxes on property 282.4, Domestic taxes on goods and services 7,850.7, Taxes on international trade and transactions 13,795.8, Other taxes 288.5); Non-tax revenue 1,564.5; Return on capital from lending and equity 19.7; Total revenue 35,395.4 (excl. grants 24.9). *Expenditure:* Current expenditure 31,045.0; Capital expenditure 6,715.7; Interest payments 2,194.3; Total expenditure (incl. others) 40,157.0.

Source: Bank of Namibia, *Annual Report*.

INTERNATIONAL RESERVES
(excluding gold, US $ million at 31 December)

	2009	2010	2011
IMF special drawing rights . .	204.44	200.83	8.09
Reserve position in IMF . . .	0.12	0.12	0.12
Foreign exchange	1,846.37	1,494.74	1,778.48
Total	2,050.93	1,695.69	1,786.69

Source: IMF, *International Financial Statistics*.

MONEY SUPPLY
(N $ million at 31 December)

	2009	2010	2011
Currency outside depository corporations	1,156.7	1,292.7	1,697.7
Transferable deposits	19,741.5	22,760.4	26,152.8
Other deposits	27,642.1	29,141.9	32,678.7
Securities other than shares . .	3.9	—	—
Broad money	48,544.2	53,194.9	60,529.2

Source: IMF, *International Financial Statistics*.

COST OF LIVING
(Consumer Price Index; base: December 2001 = 100)

	2009	2010	2011
Food and non-alcoholic beverages .	192.6	198.9	209.0
Alcoholic beverages and tobacco .	187.2	205.8	218.8
Clothing and footwear	122.6	126.7	127.9
Housing, fuel and power . . .	148.8	157.4	172.8
Health	124.5	130.4	137.8
Transport	181.2	192.0	202.1
Communications	123.5	125.1	126.7
Recreation and culture . . .	139.4	144.0	149.5
Education	174.6	183.8	193.2
All items (incl. others) . . .	165.4	172.7	181.5

NATIONAL ACCOUNTS
(N $ million at current prices)

National Income and Product

	2009	2010	2011
Compensation of employees . .	31,065	35,661	37,811
Operating surplus	28,018	27,864	32,588
Domestic factor incomes . .	59,083	63,525	70,399
Consumption of fixed capital . .	9,713	10,604	11,597
Gross domestic product (GDP) at factor cost	68,795	74,130	81,996
Taxes, less subsidies, on production and imports	6,275	7,006	8,846
GDP in purchasers' values .	75,070	81,136	90,842
Primary income received from abroad	2,112	1,524	1,658
Less Primary income paid abroad .	3,937	5,237	5,456
Gross national income . . .	73,245	77,422	87,045
Less Consumption of fixed capital .	9,713	10,604	11,597
National income in market prices	63,532	66,818	75,448
Other current transfers from abroad	11,245	9,659	10,169
Less Other current transfers paid abroad	632	640	579
National disposable income .	74,146	75,836	85,038

Expenditure on the Gross Domestic Product

	2009	2010	2011
Government final consumption expenditure	17,277	19,714	22,469
Private final consumption expenditure	48,069	52,944	57,675
Change in stocks	168	–1,303	–1,095
Gross fixed capital formation . .	16,609	18,531	19,115
Total domestic expenditure .	82,123	89,886	98,164
Exports of goods and services . .	35,511	38,483	40,644
Less Imports of goods and services	42,116	44,419	47,610
Statistical discrepancy . . .	–448	–2,814	–356
GDP in purchasers' values .	75,070	81,136	90,842
GDP in constant 2004 prices .	50,482	53,802	56,407

Gross Domestic Product by Economic Activity

	2009	2010	2011
Agriculture and forestry . . .	2,989	3,360	3,770
Fishing	2,428	2,539	2,709
Mining and quarrying . . .	8,002	6,882	8,659
Diamond mining	2,749	4,042	6,567
Manufacturing	10,142	10,582	11,034
Electricity and water . . .	1,850	2,077	2,509
Construction	2,465	2,712	3,229
Wholesale and retail trade, repairs, etc.	8,610	9,711	10,538
Hotels and restaurants . . .	1,399	1,467	1,593
Transport, storage and communications	3,800	4,526	4,533
Financial intermediation . . .	3,648	4,262	4,717
Real estate and business services .	5,987	6,363	7,164
Public administration and defence	7,100	8,182	9,268
Education	5,948	6,826	7,297
Health	2,437	2,721	2,853
Community, social and personal services	2,446	2,503	2,740
Private households with employed person	559	597	643
Sub-total	69,809	75,309	83,258
Less Financial services indirectly measured	1,014	1,180	1,261
GDP at basic prices . . .	68,795	74,130	81,996
Taxes, less subsidies, on products .	6,275	7,006	8,846
GDP in purchasers' values .	75,070	81,136	90,842

Source: Bank of Namibia, *Quarterly Bulletin*.

BALANCE OF PAYMENTS
(US $ million)

	2009	2010	2011
Exports of goods	3,146.3	4,025.7	4,373.0
Imports of goods	−4,396.6	−4,914.7	−5,585.5
Balance on goods	−1,250.3	−889.0	−1,212.4
Exports of services	653.9	897.1	944.4
Imports of services	−575.5	−701.3	−724.1
Balance on goods and services	−1,172.3	−693.2	−992.0
Primary income received . . .	263.0	293.2	321.6
Primary income paid	−481.5	−726.4	−799.8
Balance on goods, services and primary income	−1,390.8	−1,126.4	−1,470.2
Secondary income received . .	1,063.9	974.8	965.7
Secondary income paid . . .	−76.1	−87.5	−80.2
Current balance	−403.0	−239.1	−584.7
Capital account (net) . . .	66.7	112.5	186.8
Direct investment assets . . .	12.8	26.0	−20.0
Direct investment liabilites . .	514.9	675.0	936.7
Portfolio investment assets . .	−586.8	−717.2	−881.5
Portfolio investment liabilities .	4.0	4.4	488.5
Other investment assets . . .	−376.0	−473.1	−399.0
Other investment liabilities . .	−173.7	−149.5	−112.0
Net errors and omissions . . .	262.1	−317.2	72.6
Reserves and related items .	−678.7	−1,078.3	−312.7

Source: IMF, *International Financial Statistics*.

External Trade

PRINCIPAL COMMODITIES
(US $ million)

Imports c.i.f.	2006	2007	2008
Food and live animals	335.7	502.8	506.1
Mineral fuels and lubricants . .	86.7	416.4	637.7
Petroleum and petroleum products . .	83.1	399.4	610.0
Chemicals and related products .	294.4	368.4	510.7
Basic manufactures	472.3	671.1	876.5
Non-metallic mineral manufactures .	80.7	133.2	254.6
Metal products	152.6	247.5	267.2
Machinery and transport equipment	1,082.0	1,383.5	1,456.5
Machinery specialized for particular industries	135.0	167.2	225.4
General industrial machinery, equipment and parts	106.2	119.6	167.6
Telecommunications and sound equipment	104.4	111.2	108.8
Telecommunications equipment, parts and accessories . . .	80.4	80.3	77.1
Electrical machinery, apparatus, etc. .	124.8	143.1	156.6
Road vehicles	413.4	485.2	597.5
Passenger motor vehicles (excl. buses)	243.7	286.9	287.1
Other transport equipment . . .	92.4	169.0	38.0
Miscellaneous manufactured articles	366.7	513.4	477.5
Clothing and accessories . . .	86.8	130.6	115.8
Total (incl. others)	2,798.5	4,026.0	4,688.6

Exports f.o.b.	2006	2007	2008
Food and live animals	746.2	807.9	852.5
Fish, shellfish and preparations thereof.	434.7	458.9	527.7
Fresh or frozen fish	415.4	431.7	493.2
Beverages and tobacco	111.9	137.7	195.8
Beverages	107.1	135.6	149.6
Alcoholic beverages	100.7	126.4	136.7
Beer made from malt	85.4	110.5	114.8
Crude materials (inedible) except fuels	336.1	647.9	1,042.5
Metal ores and scrap	188.6	474.5	840.0
Ores and concentrates of uranium and thorium	163.0	350.3	741.7
Basic manufactures	1,516.8	1,556.5	1,314.7
Non-metallic mineral manufactures .	911.7	723.0	798.8
Pearl, precious and semi-precious stones	900.8	705.0	780.6
Diamonds	900.4	704.6	780.0
Machinery and transport equipment	121.0	280.3	288.6
Miscellaneous manufactured articles	362.0	422.1	890.7
Printed matter	292.7	357.0	807.3
Total (incl. others)	3,375.9	4,040.3	4,729.3

Source: UN, *International Trade Statistics Yearbook*.

PRINCIPAL TRADING PARTNERS
(US $ million)

Imports c.i.f.	2006	2007	2008
China, People's Repub.	96.8	101.5	153.3
Germany	62.4	83.9	96.6
South Africa	2,305.3	3,143.0	3,179.8
Spain	19.8	91.4	22.3
United Kingdom	23.6	45.2	373.3
USA	41.6	54.8	94.9
Total (incl. others)	2,798.5	4,026.0	4,688.6

Exports f.o.b.	2006	2007	2008
Angola	192.9	260.9	405.6
Belgium	12.2	12.9	50.8
Canada	127.6	199.3	334.2
Congo, Democratic Republic of	45.4	43.1	51.2
France	53.7	106.4	126.7
Germany	109.0	99.8	48.9
Italy	243.5	570.9	63.9
Netherlands	36.7	74.8	76.0
South Africa	829.2	1,172.3	1,505.0
Spain	202.0	242.8	242.4
United Kingdom	865.2	682.9	709.7
USA	81.7	102.1	260.8
Total (incl. others)	3,375.9	4,040.3	4,729.3

Source: UN, *International Trade Statistics Yearbook*.

Transport

RAILWAYS

	2002/03	2003/04
Freight (million net ton-km)	1,244.6	1,247.4
Passengers carried	125,656	112,033

Source: TransNamib Holdings Ltd, *2004 Annual Report*.

ROAD TRAFFIC
(motor vehicles in use at 31 December)

	2008	2009	2010
Passenger cars	107,825	100,460	108,467
Buses and coaches	2,396	3,012	3,452
Lorries and vans	117,410	120,978	131,909
Motorcycles and mopeds	4,792	5,356	5,593

Source: IRF, *World Road Statistics*.

SHIPPING
Flag Registered Fleet
(at 31 December)

	2010	2011	2012
Number of vessels	118	117	122
Displacement (gross registered tons)	104,620	102,717	108,203

Source: Lloyd's List Intelligence (www.lloydslistintelligence.com).

Sea-borne Freight Traffic
('000 freight tons*, year ending 30 August, unless otherwise indicated)

	2007/08	2008/09	2009/10
Port of Lüderitz:			
Goods loaded	56.8	26.0	120.1
Goods unloaded	126.5	124.9	138.7
Goods transshipped (freight tons)	29	—	—
Containers handled (total TEUs)	13,019	15,401	8,576
Port of Walvis Bay:			
Goods loaded	1,251.3	1,219.8	1,239.5
Goods unloaded	2,702.4	2,994.3	2,638.2
Goods transshipped	439.0	824.0	1,023.5
Containers handled (total TEUs)	170,586	250,262	247,743

* One freight ton = 40 cu ft (1.133 cu m) of cargo capacity.

Source: Namibian Ports Authority.

CIVIL AVIATION
(traffic on scheduled services)

	2007	2008	2009
Kilometres flown (million)	12	12	12
Passengers carried ('000)	431	452	455
Passenger-km (million)	1,683	1,723	1,668
Total ton-km (million)	164	175	171

Source: UN, *Statistical Yearbook*.

Passengers carried ('000): 488 in 2010 (Source: World Bank, World Development Indicators database).

Tourism

FOREIGN TOURIST ARRIVALS

Country of origin	2008	2009	2010
Angola	310,395	309,127	296,825
Botswana	26,378	26,918	31,503
Germany	81,543	81,974	87,072
South Africa	243,038	285,779	277,655
United Kingdom	28,111	28,039	25,717
USA	20,856	20,080	17,826
Zambia	50,248	54,333	54,229
Zimbabwe	29,281	31,842	37,667
Total (incl. others)	931,110	980,178	984,098

Tourism receipts (US $ million, excl. passenger transport): 398 in 2009; 438 in 2010; 517 in 2011 (provisional).

Source: World Tourism Organization.

Communications Media

	2009	2010	2011
Telephones ('000 main lines in use)	148.7	157.0	159.1
Mobile cellular telephones ('000 subscribers)	1,217.0	1,534.5	2,240.2
Internet users ('000)	127.5	n.a.	n.a.
Broadband subscribers ('000)	0.4	9.6	18.5

Personal computers: 500,000 (239.4 per 1,000 persons) in 2007.

Source: International Telecommunication Union.

Education

(2008/09 unless otherwise indicated)

	Teachers	Students		Total
		Males	Females	
Pre-primary	1,314*	16,414†	16,322†	32,736†
Primary	13,516	206,011	200,909	406,920
Secondary	7,031	78,414	90,976	169,390
Tertiary‡	1,204	8,506	11,201	19,707

* Estimate for 1999/2000.
† 2005/06.
‡ 2007/08.

Source: UNESCO, Institute for Statistics.

Pupil-teacher ratio (primary education, UNESCO estimate): 30.1 in 2008/09 (Source: UNESCO Institute for Statistics).

Adult literacy rate (UNESCO estimates): 88.8% (males 89.0%; females 88.5%) in 2010 (Source: UNESCO Institute for Statistics).

Directory

The Government

HEAD OF STATE

President and Commander-in-Chief of the Defence Force: HIFIKEPUNYE POHAMBA (elected by direct suffrage 15–16 November 2004; took office 21 March 2005; re-elected 27–28 November 2009).

THE CABINET
(May 2013)

President: HIFIKEPUNYE POHAMBA.

Prime Minister: Dr HAGE GEINGOB.

Deputy Prime Minister: Dr MARCO HAUSIKU.

Minister of Presidential Affairs and Attorney-General: ALBERT KAWANA.

Minister of Home Affairs: PENDUKENI IVULA-ITHANA.

Minister of Safety and Security: IMMANUEL NGATJIZEKO.

Minister of Defence: NAHAS ANGULA.

Minister of Foreign Affairs: NEITUMBO NANDI-NDEITWAH.

Minister of Information and Communication Technology: JOEL KAAPANDA.

Minister of Education: Dr ABRAHAM IYAMBO.

Minister of Mines and Energy: ISAK KATALI.

Minister of Justice: UTONI NUJOMA.

Minister of Trade and Industry: CALLE SCHLETTWEIN.

Minister of Agriculture, Water and Forestry: JOHN MUTORWA.

Minister of Finance: SAARA KUUGONGELWA-AMADHILA.

Minister of Health and Social Services: Dr RICHARD KAMWI.

Minister of Labour and Social Welfare: DOREEN SIOKA.

Minister of Regional and Local Government and Housing and Rural Development: CHARLES NAMOLOH.

Minister of Environment and Tourism: UAHEKUA HERUNGUA.

Minister of Works, Transport and Communications: ERRKI NGHINTINA.

Minister of Lands, Resettlement and Rehabilitation: ALPHEUS NARUSEB.

Minister of Fisheries and Marine Resources: BEN ESAU.

Minister of Gender Equality and Child Welfare: ROSALIA NGHIDINWA.

Minister of Youth, National Service, Sport and Culture: JERRY EKANDJO.

Minister of Veteran Affairs: Dr NICKEY IYAMBO.

Also attending Cabinet

Dir-Gen. of the Namibia Central Intelligence Agency: Lt-Gen. (retd) LUCAS HANGULA.

Dir-Gen. of the National Planning Commission: TOM K. ALWEENDO.

MINISTRIES

Office of the President: State House, Robert Mugabe Ave, PMB 13339, Windhoek; tel. (61) 2707111; fax (61) 221780; e-mail angolo@op.gov.na; internet www.op.gov.na.

Office of the Prime Minister: Robert Mugabe Ave, PMB 13338, Windhoek; tel. (61) 2879111; fax (61) 226189; internet www.opm.gov.na.

Ministry of Agriculture, Water and Forestry: Government Office Park, PMB 13184, Windhoek; tel. (61) 2087111; fax (61) 221733; internet www.mawf.gov.na.

Ministry of Defence: PMB 13307, Windhoek; tel. (61) 2049111; fax (61) 232518; e-mail psecretary@mod.gov.na; internet www.mod.gov.na.

Ministry of Education: Government Office Park, PMB 13186, Windhoek; tel. (61) 2933358; fax (61) 2933368; internet www.mec.gov.na.

Ministry of Environment and Tourism: 2nd Floor, FGI House, Post St Mall, PMB 13346, Windhoek; tel. (61) 2842111; fax (61) 2842216; e-mail kshangula@met.gov.na; internet www.met.gov.na.

Ministry of Finance: Fiscus Bldg, John Meinert St, PMB 13295, Windhoek; tel. (61) 2099111; fax (61) 227702; internet www.mof.gov.na.

Ministry of Fisheries and Marine Resources: Uhland and Goethe Sts, PMB 13355, Windhoek; tel. (61) 2059111; fax (61) 233286; e-mail mfmr@mfmr.gov.na; internet www.mfmr.gov.na.

Ministry of Foreign Affairs: Govt Bldgs, Robert Mugabe Ave, PMB 13347, Windhoek; tel. (61) 2829111; fax (61) 223937; e-mail headquarters@mfa.gov.na; internet www.mfa.gov.na.

Ministry of Gender Equality and Child Welfare: Juvenis Bldg, Independence Ave, PMG 13359, Windhoek; tel. (61) 2833111; fax (61) 221304; e-mail genderequality@mgecw.gov.na; internet www.mgecw.gov.na.

Ministry of Health and Social Services: Old State Hospital, Harvey St, PMB 13198, Windhoek; tel. (61) 2032000; fax (61) 227607; e-mail doccentre@mhss.gov.na; internet www.healthnet.org.na.

Ministry of Home Affairs: Cohen Bldg, Kasino St, PMB 13200, Windhoek; tel. (61) 2922111; fax (61) 2922185; internet www.mha.gov.na.

Ministry of Information and Communication Technology: PMB 13344, Windhoek; tel. (61) 2839111; fax (61) 222343; internet www.mict.gov.na.

Ministry of Justice: Justitia Bldg, Independence Ave, PMB 13248, Windhoek; tel. (61) 2805111; fax (61) 221615.

Ministry of Labour and Social Welfare: 32 Mercedes St, Khomasdal, PMB 19005, Windhoek; tel. (61) 2066111; fax (61) 212323; internet www.mol.gov.na.

Ministry of Lands, Resettlement and Rehabilitation: Brendan Simbwaye Bldg, Goethe St, PMB 13343, Windhoek; tel. (61) 2852111; fax (61) 254240.

Ministry of Mines and Energy: 1st Aviation Rd, PMB 13297, Windhoek; tel. (61) 2848111; fax (61) 238643; e-mail info@mme.gov.na; internet www.mme.gov.na.

Ministry of Presidential Affairs: Windhoek.

Ministry of Regional and Local Government and Housing and Rural Development: PMB 13289, Windhoek; tel. (61) 2975111; fax (61) 226049; internet www.mrlgh.gov.na.

Ministry of Safety and Security: Brendan Simbwaye Bldg, Goethe St, PMB 13323, Windhoek; tel. (61) 2846111; fax (61) 233879.

Ministry of Trade and Industry: Block B, Brendan Simbwaye Sq., Goethe St, PMB 13340, Windhoek; tel. (61) 2837111; fax (61) 220227; e-mail tic@mti.gov.na; internet www.mti.gov.na.

Ministry of Veteran Affairs: PMB 13407, Windhoek; tel. (61) 222330; fax (61) 221615.

Ministry of Works, Transport and Communications: 6719 Bell St, Snyman Circle, PMB 13341, Windhoek; tel. (61) 2088111; fax (61) 224381; e-mail jngweda@mwtc.gov.na; internet www.mwtc.gov.na.

Ministry of Youth, National Service, Sport and Culture: NDC Bldg, Goethe St, PMB 13391, Windhoek; tel. (61) 270611; fax (61) 2706303.

President and Legislature

PRESIDENT

Presidential Election, 27–28 November 2009

Candidate			Votes	% of votes
Hifikepunye Pohamba (SWAPO)	.	.	611,241	76.42
Hidipo Hamutenya (RDP)	.	.	88,640	11.08
Katuutire Kaura (DTA)	.	.	24,186	3.02
Kuaima Riruako (NUDO)	.	.	23,735	2.97
Justus Garoeb (UDF)	.	.	19,258	2.41
Others	.	.	32,810	4.10
Total	.	.	799,870*	100.00

* Excluding 12,363 invalid votes.

NATIONAL ASSEMBLY

Speaker: THEO-BEN GURIRAB.

General Election, 27–28 November 2009

Party								Votes	% of votes	Seats
SWAPO	.	.	.	.	.	.	.	602,580	75.27	54
RDP	.	.	.	.	.	.	.	90,556	11.31	8
DTA	.	.	.	.	.	.	.	25,393	3.17	2
NUDO	.	.	.	.	.	.	.	24,422	3.05	2
UDF	.	.	.	.	.	.	.	19,489	2.43	2
APP	.	.	.	.	.	.	.	10,795	1.35	1
RP	.	.	.	.	.	.	.	6,541	0.82	1
CoD	.	.	.	.	.	.	.	5,375	0.67	1
SWANU	.	.	.	.	.	.	.	4,989	0.62	1
Others	.	.	.	.	.	.	.	10,427	1.30	—
Total	.	.	.	.	.	.	.	800,567*	100.00	72†

* Excluding 10,576 invalid votes.

† In addition to the 72 directly elected members, the President of the Republic is empowered to nominate as many as six non-voting members.

NATIONAL COUNCIL

Chairman: ASSER KUVERI KAPERE.

The second chamber of parliament is the advisory National Council, comprising two representatives from each of the country's 13 Regional Councils, elected for a period of six years.

Election Commission

Electoral Commission of Namibia (ECN): 11 Goethe St, POB 13352, Windhoek; tel. (61) 220337; fax (61) 249348; e-mail mndjarakana@opm.gov.na; internet www.ecn.na; f. 1992; independent; Chair. NOTEMBA TJIPUEJA; Dir of Elections and CEO MOSES K. NDJARAKANA.

Political Organizations

All People's Party of Namibia (APP): f. 2008 in Kavango region; splinter group of the CoD, which split in late 2007; Pres. IGNATIUS SHIXWAMENI.

Congress of Democrats (CoD): 8 Storch St, POB 40905, Windhoek; tel. (61) 256954; fax (61) 256980; internet www.cod.org.na; f. 1999 after split from SWAPO; Pres. BEN ULENGA; Nat. Chair. ARNOLD LOSPER; Sec.-Gen. TSUDAO GURIRAB.

Democratic Party of Namibia (DPN): Windhoek; f. 2008; Interim Pres. SALOMON DAWID ISAACKS; Sec.-Gen. ADAM ISAAK.

Democratic Turnhalle Alliance of Namibia (DTA): Rand St, Khomasdal, POB 173, Windhoek; tel. (61) 238530; fax (61) 226494; e-mail m.venaani@parliament.gov.na; internet www.dtaofnamibia.org.na; f. 1977 as a coalition of 11 ethnically based political groupings; reorg. in 1991 to allow dual membership of coalition groupings and the main party; Pres. KATUUTIRE KAURA; Chair. JOHAN DE WAAL; Sec.-Gen. McHENRY VENAANI.

Monitor Action Group (MAG): POB 80808, Olympia, Windhoek; tel. (61) 252008; fax (61) 229242; e-mail mag@iway.na; f. 1991 by mems of the National Party of South West Africa alliance; Leader and Chair. J. W. F. (KOSIE) PRETORIUS.

National Democratic Party of Namibia (NDP): Daily Park, POB 2438, Ngweze, Katima Mulilo; f. 2004; Pres. MARTIN LUKATO.

National Unity Democratic Organization (NUDO): Clemence Kapuuo St, Plot 1881, POB 62691, Soweto, Katutura; tel. and fax (61) 211550; e-mail nudoparty@iway.na; internet www.nudoofnamibia.org.na; f. 1964 by the Herero Chiefs' Council; joined the DTA in 1977; broke away from the DTA in 2003; Pres. Chief KUAIMA RIRUAKO; Sec.-Gen. ASSER MBAI.

Rally for Democracy and Progress (RDP): POB 83141, Olympia, Windhoek; tel. (61) 255973; e-mail info@rdp.org.na; internet www.rdp.org.na; f. 2007 by fmr mems of ruling SWAPO party; absorbed the Republican Party in Oct. 2010; Pres. HIDIPO HAMUTENYA; Sec.-Gen. JESAYA NYAMU.

SWAPO Party of Namibia (SWAPO): Hans-Dietrich Genscher St, Plot 2464, Katutura, POB 1071, Windhoek; tel. (61) 238364; fax (61) 232368; internet www.swapoparty.org; f. 1957 as the Ovamboland People's Congress; renamed South West Africa People's Organization in 1960; Pres. HIFIKEPUNYE POHAMBA; Vice-Pres. HAGE GEINGOB; Sec.-Gen. PENDUKENI IIVULA-ITHANA.

South West African National Union (SWANU): POB 2976, Windhoek; e-mail swanu@swanu.org.na; internet www.swanu.org.na; f. 1959 by mems of the Herero Chiefs' Council; formed alliance with the Workers' Revolutionary Party in 1999; Pres. USUTUAIJE MAAMBERUA; Vice-Pres. B. B. DE CLERK.

United Democratic Front (UDF): POB 20037, Windhoek; tel. (61) 230683; fax (61) 237175; f. 1989 as a centrist coalition of eight parties; reorg. as a single party in 1999; Nat. Chair. ERIC BIWA; Pres. JUSTUS GAROEB.

The **Caprivi Liberation Army (CLA)**, f. 1998 as the Caprivi Liberation Movement, seeks secession of the Caprivi Strip; conducts military operations from bases in Zambia and Angola; political wing operates from Denmark as the **Caprivi National Union**, led by MISHAKE MUYONGO and BONIFACE MAMILI.

Diplomatic Representation

EMBASSIES AND HIGH COMMISSIONS IN NAMIBIA

Algeria: 96 Gloudina St, Ludwigsdorf, POB 3079, Windhoek; tel. (61) 221507; fax (61) 236376; e-mail Ambalg.w@mweb.com; Ambassador LAHCENE KAID-SLIMANE.

Angola: Angola House, 3 Dr Agostinho Neto St, Ausspannplatz, Private Bag 1220, Windhoek; tel. (61) 227535; fax (61) 221498; Ambassador MANUEL ALEXANDRE DUARTE RODRIGUES.

Botswana: 101 Nelson Mandela Ave, POB 20359, Windhoek; tel. (61) 221941; fax (61) 236034; internet www.botnam.com.na; High Commissioner GOBOPANG DUKE LEFHOKO.

Brazil: 52 Bismarck St, POB 24166, Windhoek; tel. (61) 237368; fax (61) 233389; e-mail brasemb@mweb.com.na; internet windhoek.itamaraty.gov.br/pt-br; Ambassador JOSÉ VICENTE DA SILVA LESSA.

China, People's Republic: 13 Wecke St, POB 22777, Windhoek; tel. (61) 372800; fax (61) 225544; e-mail chinaemb_na@mfa.gov.cn; internet na.chineseembassy.org; Ambassador XIN SHUNKANG.

Congo, Democratic Republic: 56 Bismarck St, POB 9064, Windhoek; tel. (61) 256287; fax (61) 256286; Ambassador ANASTAS KABOBA KASONGO WA-KIMBA.

Congo, Republic: 9 Körner St, POB 22970, Windhoek; tel. (61) 257517; fax (61) 240796; Ambassador MARIE THÉRÈSE AVEMEKA.

Cuba: 37 Quenta St, Ludwigsdorf, POB 23866, Windhoek; tel. (61) 227072; fax (61) 231584; e-mail embajada@cubanembassy.net; internet www.cubadiplomatica.cu/namibia; Ambassador CARLOS MANUEL ROJAS LAGO.

Egypt: 10 Berg St, POB 11853, Windhoek; tel. (61) 221501; fax (61) 228856; e-mail embassy.windhoek@mfa.gov.eg; internet www.mfa.gov.eg/windhoek_emb; Ambassador HAZEM RAMADAN.

Finland: 2 Crohn St (cnr Bahnhof St), POB 3649, Windhoek; tel. (61) 221355; fax (61) 221349; e-mail sanomat.win@formin.fi; internet www.finland.org.na; Chargé d'affaires a.i. ANNE SALORANTA.

France: 1 Goethe St, POB 20484, Windhoek; tel. (61) 276700; fax (61) 276710; e-mail contact@ambafrance-na.org; internet www.ambafrance-na.org; Ambassador JEAN-LOUIS ZOËL.

Germany: Sanlam Centre, 6th Floor, 154 Independence Ave, POB 231, Windhoek; tel. (61) 273100; fax (61) 222981; e-mail reg1@wind.diplo.de; internet www.windhuk.diplo.de; Ambassador ONNO HÜCKMANN.

Ghana: 5 Nelson Mandela Ave, POB 24165, Windhoek; tel. (61) 221341; fax (61) 221343; e-mail ghanahc@iwwn.com.na; High Commissioner Maj.-Gen. SAMUEL ANUM ODOTEI.

India: 97 Nelson Mandela Ave, POB 1209, Windhoek; tel. (61) 226037; fax (61) 237320; e-mail hicomind@mweb.com.na; internet www.highcommissionofindia.web.na; High Commissioner SATYA PAL MANN.

Indonesia: 103 Nelson Mandela Ave, POB 20691, Windhoek; tel. (61) 2851000; fax (61) 2851231; e-mail kbri@iafrica.com.na; internet www.kemlu.go.id/windhoek; Ambassador AGUSTINUS SUMARTONO.

Kenya: Kenya House, 5th Floor, 134 Robert Mugabe Ave, POB 2889, Windhoek; tel. (61) 226836; fax (61) 221409; e-mail kenyanet@mweb.com.na; High Commissioner PETER GITAU.

Libya: 69 Burg St, Luxury Hill, POB 124, Windhoek; tel. (61) 234454; fax (61) 234471; Chargé d'affaires a.i. ENNAS A. A. ENAAS.

Malaysia: 63 Joseph Mukwayu Ithana St, Ludwigsdorf, POB 312, Windhoek; tel. (61) 259342; fax (61) 259343; e-mail malwdhoek@kln.gov.my; internet www.kln.gov.my/perwakilan/windhoek; Chargé d'affaires MUSTAFA HJ MANSOR.

Nigeria: 4 Gen. Murtala Muhammed Ave, Eros Park, POB 23547, Windhoek; tel. (61) 232103; fax (61) 221639; e-mail nhcnam@mweb.com.na; internet www.nhcwindhoek.org; High Commissioner BIODUN NATHANIEL OLORUNFEMI.

Portugal: 4 Karin St, Ludwigsdorf, POB 443, Windhoek; tel. (61) 259791; fax (61) 259792; e-mail ambassaden.windhoek@sida.se; Ambassador HELENA ALEXANDRA ANDRADE FURTADO DE PAIVA.

Russia: 4 Christian St, POB 3826, Windhoek; tel. (61) 228671; fax (61) 229061; e-mail rusemnam@mweb.com.na; internet www.rusemwhk.mid.ru; Ambassador ALEXANDER KHUDIN.

South Africa: RSA House, cnr Jan Jonker St and Nelson Mandela Ave, POB 23100, Windhoek; tel. (61) 2057111; fax (61) 224140; e-mail dibem@foreign.gov.za; High Commissioner YVETTE LILLIAN MAVIVI MYAKAYAKA-MANZINI.

Spain: 58 Bismarck St, POB 21811, Windhoek-West; tel. (61) 223066; fax (61) 227209; e-mail emb.windhoek@mae.es; Ambassador MARÍA DEL CARMEN DÍEZ OREJAS.

Turkey: 14 Cathy St, Ludwigsdorf, POB 090998, Windhoek; tel. (61) 2962929; fax (61) 2962931; e-mail emaral@mfa.gov.tr; Ambassador MURAT AHMET YÖRÜK.

United Kingdom: 116 Robert Mugabe Ave, POB 22202, Windhoek; tel. (61) 274800; fax (61) 228895; e-mail general.windhoek@fco.gov.uk; internet www.ukinnamibia.fco.gov.uk; High Commissioner MARIANNE YOUNG.

USA: 14 Lossen St, PMB 12029, Windhoek; tel. (61) 2958500; fax (61) 2958603; internet windhoek.usembassy.gov; Ambassador WANDA L. NESBITT.

Venezuela: 12 Nelson Mandela Ave, 39 Post St Mall, Private Bag 13353, Windhoek; tel. (61) 227905; fax (61) 227804; Ambassador JUAN CARLOS BARRIOS HURTADO.

Zambia: 22 Sam Nujoma Dr, cnr Mandume Ndemufayo Ave, POB 22882, Windhoek; tel. (61) 237610; fax (61) 228162; e-mail zahico@iway.na; internet www.zahico.iway.na; High Commissioner WENDY SINKALA.

Zimbabwe: cnr Independence Ave and Grimm St, POB 23056, Windhoek; tel. (61) 228134; fax (61) 226859; e-mail zimbabwe@mweb.com.na; Ambassador CHIPO ZINDOGA.

Judicial System

Judicial power is exercised by the Supreme Court, the High Court, and a number of Magistrate and Lower Courts. The Constitution provides for the appointment of an Ombudsman.

The Supreme Court: Private Bag 13398, Windhoek; tel. (61) 279900; fax (61) 224979; e-mail cjudge@iway.na; internet www.superiorcourts.org.na/supreme; f. 1990; Chief Justice PETER SHIVUTE; Additional Judge JOHANNES DAWID GERHARDUS MARITZ.

The High Court: Private Bag 13179, Windhoek; tel. (61) 2921111; fax (61) 221686; e-mail chiefregistrar@mtcmobile.com.na; internet www.superiorcourts.org.na/high; Judge Pres. PETRUS DAMASEB.

Religion

It is estimated that about 90% of the population are Christians.

CHRISTIANITY

Council of Churches in Namibia: 8 Mont Blanc St, POB 41, Windhoek; tel. (61) 374054; fax (61) 62786; e-mail ccn.gensec@mweb.com.na; f. 1978; eight mem. churches; Pres. Bishop ERICH HERTEL; Gen. Sec. Rev. MARIA KAPERE.

The Anglican Communion

Namibia comprises a single diocese in the Anglican Church of Southern Africa (formerly the Church of the Province of Southern Africa). The Metropolitan of the Province is the Archbishop of Cape Town, South Africa. In 2006 there were an estimated 110,000 Anglicans in the country.

Bishop of Namibia: Rt Rev. NATHANIEL NDAXUMA NAKWATUMBAH, POB 57, Windhoek; tel. (61) 238920; fax (61) 225903; e-mail shirley@mweb.com.na.

Dutch Reformed Church

Dutch Reformed Church in Namibia (Nederduitse Gereformeerde Kerk in Namibië): 46A Schanzen Rd, POB 389, Windhoek; tel. (61) 374350; fax (61) 227287; e-mail clem@ngkn.com.na; internet www.ngkerk.org.za/namibie; f. 1898; Sec. Rev. CLEM MARAIS; 22,368 mems in 44 congregations (2012).

Evangelical Lutheran

Evangelical Lutheran Church in Namibia (ELCIN): POB 2018, Ondangwa; tel. (65) 240241; fax (65) 240472; e-mail gen.sec@elcin.org.na; internet www.elcin.org.na; f. 1870; became autonomous in 1954; Presiding Bishop Dr SHEKUTAAMBA V. V. NAMBALA; Gen. Sec. Rev. ELIKAIM N. K. SHAANIKA; 703,893 mems (2010).

Evangelical Lutheran Church in the Republic of Namibia (ELCRN) (Rhenish Mission Church): POB 5069, 6 Church St, Ausspanplatz, 9000 Windhoek; tel. (61) 224531; fax (61) 226775; e-mail bishop@elcrnam.org; f. 1957; became autonomous in 1972; Pres. Bishop Dr ZEPHANIA KAMEETA; 420,000 mems (2010).

German Evangelical-Lutheran Church in Namibia (ELCIN—GELC): POB 233, 12 Fidel Castro St, Windhoek; tel. (61) 224294; fax (61) 221470; e-mail bishop-office@elcin-gelc.org; internet www.elcin-gelc.org; Pres. Bishop ERICH HERTEL; 5,100 mems (2010).

Methodist

African Methodist Episcopal Church: POB 798, Keetmanshoop; tel. (63) 222347; fax (63) 223026; e-mail erikke5@hotmail.com; bishop resident in Cape Town, South Africa; Rep. Rev. Dr ANDREAS BIWA; c. 8,000 mems in 33 churches.

Methodist Church of Southern Africa: POB 143, Windhoek; tel. (61) 228921; fax (61) 229202; e-mail central@iway.na; internet www.methodist.org.za; Rep. Rev. KEVIN ENDRES.

The Roman Catholic Church

Namibia comprises one archdiocese, one diocese and one apostolic vicariate. Some 18% of the population are Roman Catholics.

Bishops' Conference

Namibian Catholic Bishops' Conference, POB 11525, Windhoek 9000; tel. (61) 224798; fax (61) 228126; e-mail ncbc@windhoek.org.na.

f. 1996; Pres. LIBORIUS NDUMBUKUTI NASHENDA (Archbishop of Windhoek).

Archbishop of Windhoek: LIBORIUS NDUMBUKUTI NASHENDA, POB 272, Windhoek 9000; tel. (61) 227595; fax (61) 229836; e-mail rcarch@iafrica.com.na; internet www.rcchurch.na.

Other Christian Churches

Among other denominations active in Namibia are the Evangelical Reformed Church in Africa, the Presbyterian Church of Southern Africa, Seventh Day Adventists and the United Congregational Church of Southern Africa. At mid-2000 there were an estimated 820,000 Protestants and 192,000 adherents professing other forms of Christianity.

JUDAISM

Windhoek Hebrew Congregation: POB 563, Windhoek; tel. (61) 221990; fax (61) 226444.

BAHÁ'Í FAITH

National Spiritual Assembly: POB 20372, Windhoek; tel. (61) 302663; e-mail bahainamibia@iway.na; Sec. ROSI STEVENSON; mems resident in 215 localities.

The Press

The African Magazine: NCCI, 2 Jenner St, POB 1770, Windhoek; tel. and fax (61) 255018; e-mail info@theafricanmagazin.org; internet www.theafricanmagazin.org.

AgriForum: 114A Robert Mugabe Ave, Private Bag 86641, Eros, Windhoek; tel. (61) 256023; fax (61) 256035; e-mail agriforum@agrinamibia.com.na; internet www.agriforum.com.na; f. 1978; monthly; Afrikaans and English; publ. by the Namibia Agricultural Union; Editor MARIETJIE VAN STADEN; circ. 5,000.

Allgemeine Zeitung: 11 Gen. Murtala Muhammed Ave, POB 86695, Eros, Windhoek; tel. (61) 225822; fax (61) 220225; e-mail azinfo@az.com.na; internet www.az.com.na; f. 1916; publ. by Newsprint Namibia; daily; German; Editor-in-Chief STEFAN FISCHER; circ. 5,000.

Caprivi Vision: Windhoek; tel. (61) 253162; monthly; Editor VISCO LUMAMEZI.

Informanté: POB 11363, Windhoek; tel. (61) 2754000; fax (61) 2754090; e-mail informante1@tqi.na; internet www.informante.web.na; weekly; Editor NGHIDIPO NANGOLO.

Insight Namibia: IMLT Bldg, 70–72 Dr Frans Indongo St, POB 86058, Windhoek; tel. (61) 301438; fax (61) 240385; e-mail editor@insight.com.na; internet www.insight.com.na; f. 2004; monthly; business and current affairs; Editor ROBIN SHERBOURNE.

Namib Times: 8 Sam Nujoma Ave, POB 706, Walvis Bay; tel. (64) 205854; fax (64) 204813; e-mail ntimes@iway.na; internet www.namibtimes.net; f. 1958; 2 a week; Afrikaans, English, German and Portuguese; Editor FLORIS STEENKAMP; circ. 4,300.

Namibia Brief: Independence Ave, POB 2123, Windhoek; tel. (61) 251044; fax (61) 237251; e-mail cblatt@iafrica.com.na; 2 a year; English; Editor CATHY BLATT; circ. 7,500.

Namibia Economist: 7 Schuster St, POB 49, Windhoek 9000; tel. (61) 221925; fax (61) 220615; e-mail info@economist.com.na; internet www.economist.com.na; f. 1986; weekly; English; business, finance and economics; Editor DANIEL STEINMANN; circ. 7,000.

Namibiamagazin: Sudetenland-Str. 18, 37085 Goettingen, Germany; tel. and fax (551) 7076870; e-mail redaktion@namibia-magazin.info; publ. by Klaus Hess Verlag; German; politics, tourism, culture, economics, and German-Namibian relations; Rep. KLAUS A. HESS.

Namibia Review: Directorate Print Media and Regional Offices, Regular Publications, Turnhalle Bldg, Bahnhof St, PMB 13344, Windhoek; tel. (61) 2839111; fax (61) 224937; e-mail bupe@webmail.co.za; f. 1992; publ. by the Ministry of Information and Communication Technology; monthly; information on govt policy and developmental issues; Editor ELIZABETH KALAMBO-M'ULE; circ. 5,000.

Namibia Sport: Unit 3, 14 Liliencron St, POB 1246, Windhoek; tel. (61) 224132; fax (61) 224613; e-mail editor@namibiasport.com.na; internet www.namibiasport.com.na; f. 2002; monthly; Editor HELGE SCHUTZ; circ. 2,000.

Namibia Today: 21 Johan Albrecht St, POB 24669, Windhoek; tel. (61) 276730; fax (61) 276381; e-mail editor@namibiatoday.com.na; 2 a week; Afrikaans, English, Otjiherero and Oshiwambo; publ. by SWAPO; Editor ASSER NTINDA; circ. 5,000.

The Namibian: 42 John Meinert St, POB 20783, Windhoek; tel. (61) 279600; fax (61) 279602; e-mail editor@namibian.com.na; internet www.namibian.com.na; daily; English; Editor TANGENI AMUPADHI; circ. 23,000 (Mon.–Thur.), 32,000 (Fri.).

Namibian Sun: 11B Gen. Murtala Muhammad Ave, Eros, POB 86829, Windhoek; tel. (61) 383400; fax (61) 306853; e-mail sun@namibiansun.com; internet www.namibiansun.com; Mon. to Fri.; English; Editor TABBY MOYO.

NCCI Namibia Business Journal: NCCI Head Office, 2 Jenner St, POB 9355, Windhoek; tel. (61) 228809; fax (61) 228009; publ. by the Namibia Chamber of Commerce and Industry; 6 a year; English; CEO TARAH SHAANIKA; Editor CHARITY MWIYA; circ. 4,000.

New Era: Daniel Tjongarero House, cnr Kerby and W. Kulz Sts, PMB 13364, Windhoek; tel. (61) 273300; fax (61) 220584; e-mail editor@newera.com.na; internet www.newera.com.na; f. 1991; daily; publ. by the Ministry of Information and Communication Technology; English; Chair. MATTHEW GOWASEB; CEO SYLVESTER BLACK; Editor RAJAH MUNAMAVA; circ. 10,000.

Plus Weekly: POB 21506, Windhoek; tel. (61) 233635; fax (61) 230478; e-mail info@namibiaplus.com; publ. by Feddersen Publications; Afrikaans, English and German.

Republikein: 11 Gen. Murtala Muhammed Ave, POB 3436, Eros, Windhoek; tel. (61) 2972000; fax (61) 223721; e-mail republikein@republikein.com.na; internet www.republikein.com.na; f. 1977; daily; Afrikaans and English; owned by Democratic Media Holdings; Editor DANI BOOYSEN; circ. 21,000.

Sister Namibia: 163 Nelson Mandela Ave, POB 86753, Windhoek; tel. (61) 230618; fax (61) 236371; e-mail director@sisternamibia.org; internet www.sisternamibia.org; f. 1989; 4 a year; publ. by Sister Namibia human rights org.; women's rights and gender equality issues; Dir LAURA SASMAN; circ. 6,000.

The Southern Times: cnr Dr W. Külz and Kerby Sts, POB 32235, Windhoek; tel. (61) 301094; fax (61) 301095; internet www.southerntimesafrica.com; f. 2004; weekly (Sun.); owned by New Era and Zimpapers, Zimbabwe; printed in Namibia and Zimbabwe; regional; CEO PETER MIETZNER.

Space Magazine: Sanlam Centre, 3rd Floor, POB 3717, Windhoek; tel. (61) 225155; e-mail space@mweb.com.na; monthly; English; family life; Publr ESTER SMITH; Editor YANNA SMITH.

Windhoek Observer: 6 Schuster St, POB 2255, Windhoek; tel. (61) 221737; fax (61) 226098; e-mail whkob@africaonline.com.na; f. 1978; weekly; English; Editor KUVEE KANGUEEHI; circ. 14,000.

NEWS AGENCY

Namibia Press Agency (Nampa): cnr Keller and Eugene Marais Sts, POB 26185, Windhoek 9000; tel. (61) 374000; fax (61) 221713; e-mail admin@nampa.org; internet www.nampa.org; f. 1991; Chair. REGGIE DIERGAARDT; CEO NGHIDINUA HAMUNIME.

PRESS ASSOCIATION

Press Club Windhoek: POB 2032, Windhoek; tel. (61) 2796000; fax (61) 279602; e-mail carmen@namibian.com.na; Chair. CARMEN HONEY.

Publishers

ELOC Printing Press: PMB 2013, Oniipa, Ondangwa; tel. (65) 240211; fax (65) 240536; e-mail elocbook@iway.na; internet www.elocbook.iway.na; f. 1901; Exec. Dir JOEL AKUDHENGA.

Gamsberg Macmillan Publishers (Pty) Ltd: 19 Faraday St, POB 22830, Windhoek; tel. (61) 232165; fax (61) 233538; e-mail gmp@iafrica.com.na; internet www.macmillan-africa.com; imprints incl. New Namibia Books and Out of Africa; Man. Dir HERMAN VAN WYK.

Longman Namibia: POB 9251, Eros, Windhoek; tel. (61) 231124; fax (61) 224019; Publr LINDA BREDENKAMP.

National Archives of Namibia: 1–9 Eugène Marais St, PMB 13250, Windhoek; tel. (61) 2935211; fax (61) 2935217; e-mail natarch@mec.gov.na; f. 1939; Chief Archivist WERNER HILLEBRECHT.

PUBLISHERS' ASSOCIATION

Association of Namibian Publishers: POB 40219, Windhoek; tel. (61) 228284; fax (61) 231496; f. 1991; Chair. Dr H. MELBER.

Broadcasting and Communications

REGULATORY AUTHORITY

Communications Regulatory Authority of Namibia (CRAN): Communication House, 56 Robert Mugabe Ave, Windhoek; Private Bag, 13309, Windhoek; tel. (61) 222666; fax (61) 238646; e-mail cran@cran.na; internet www.cran.na; f. 2011; issues broadcasting licences, supervises broadcasting activities and programme content; Chair. LAZARUS JACOBS; CEO STANLEY SHANAPINDA.

TELECOMMUNICATIONS

State-owned Telecom Namibia Ltd (Telecom) has a monopoly on the provision of fixed-line services.

Leo Namibia: POB 40799, Windhoek; tel. 0855550000 (mobile); e-mail info@leo.na; internet www.leo.na; f. 2007; fmrly Cell One, name changed as above in 2009; CEO GERHARD MAY.

Mobile Telecommunications Ltd (MTC): cnr Mosé Tjitendero and Hamutenya Wanahepo Ndadi Sts, Olympia, Windhoek; POB 23051, Windhoek; tel. (61) 2802000; fax (61) 2802124; e-mail feedback@mtc.com.na; internet www.mtc.com.na; f. 1995 as jt venture between Namibia Post and Telecommunications Holdings (NPTH), Telia and Swedfund; 34% owned by Portugal Telecom, 64% by NPTH; Chair. DIRK CONRADIE; Man. Dir MIGUEL GERALDES.

Telecom Namibia Ltd (Telecom): 9 Lüderitz St, POB 297, Windhoek; tel. (61) 2012221; fax (61) 239844; e-mail ndoromaaf@telecom.na; internet www.telecom.na; f. 1992; operates fixed-line and fixed wireless network; state-owned; Chair. J. IITA; Man. Dir FRANS NDOROMA.

BROADCASTING
Radio

In 2007 there were a total of 14 radio stations broadcasting from Windhoek, including:

Namibian Broadcasting Corpn (NBC): Pettenkofer St, Windhoek West, POB 321, Windhoek; tel. (61) 2919111; fax (61) 215767; e-mail tnandjaa@nbc.com.na; internet www.nbc.com.na; f. 1990; runs 10 radio stations, broadcasting daily to 90% of the population in English (24 hours), Afrikaans, German and eight indigenous languages (10 hours); Chair. SVEN THIEM; Dir-Gen. ALBERTUS AOCHAMUB.

Channel 7/Kanaal 7: POB 20500, Windhoek; tel. (61) 235815; fax (61) 240190; e-mail channel7@k7.com.na; internet www.k7.com.na; Christian community radio station; English and Afrikaans; Man. NEAL VAN DEN BERGH.

Katutura Community Radio: Clemence Kapuuo St, POB 70448, KHD, Katutura, Windhoek; tel. (61) 263726; fax (61) 236371; f. 1995 by non-governmental orgs; Dir FREDERICK GOWASEB.

Kudu FM: 158 Jan Jonker St, POB 5369, Windhoek; tel. (61) 247262; fax (61) 247259; e-mail radiokudu@radiokudu.com.na; internet www.radiokudu.com.na; f. 1998; commercial station affiliated to Omulunga Radio; English, Afrikaans and German.

Ninety Nine FM (Pty) Ltd (99 FM): POB 11849, Klein-Windhoek, Windhoek; tel. (61) 383450; fax (61) 230964; e-mail 99@99fm.com.na; f. 1994; CEO CHRISNA GREEFF.

Omulunga Radio: POB 40789, Windhoek; tel. (61) 239706; fax (61) 247259; e-mail omulunga@omulunga.com.na; internet www.omulunga.com.na; f. 2002; Ovambo interest station affiliated to Kudu FM; Oshiwambo and English.

Radio Energy (Radio 100): Energy House 17, cnr Bismark and Church Sts, Windhoek West; POB 676, Windhoek; tel. (61) 256380;

fax (61) 256379; e-mail energy@iway.na; internet www.energy100fm
.com; f. 1996; commercial radio station; Man. Dir JOHN WALENGA.

Other radio stations included: Kosmos Radio, Radio France International (via relay), Radio 99 and Radio Wave. There were six community radio stations including: Radio Ecclesia (Catholic), Live FM (in Rehoboth), Ohangwenga Community Radio, and UNAM Radio (University of Namibia). A further four community stations were planned in 2005 at Oshakti, Gobabis, Keetmanshoop and Swakopmund.

Television

Namibian Broadcasting Corpn (NBC): Cullinan St, Northern Industrial, POB 321, Windhoek; tel. (61) 2913111; fax (61) 216209; internet www.nbc.com.na; f. 1990; broadcasts television programmes in English to 45% of the population, 18 hours daily; Chair. SVEN THIEME; Dir-Gen. ALBERTUS AOCHAMUB.

Multi-Choice Namibia: Kenya House, Robert Mugabe Ave, POB 2662, Windhoek; tel. (61) 2705261; fax (61) 2705247; commercial television channels; Gen. Man. KOBUS BEZUIDENHOUT.

One Africa TV: 79 Hosea Kutako Dr., POB 21593, Windhoek; tel. (61) 2891500; fax (61) 259450; internet www.oneafrica.tv.

Trinity Broadcasting Namibia: POB 1587, Swakopmund; tel. (64) 401100; fax (64) 403752; e-mail comments@tbnnamibia.tv; internet www.tbnnamibia.tv; f. 2002; CEO COENIE BOTHA.

Finance

(cap. = capital; res = reserves; dep. = deposits; m. = million;
brs = branches; amounts in Namibian dollars)

BANKING

In 2010 there were five commercial banks in Namibia.

Central Bank

Bank of Namibia: 71 Robert Mugabe Ave, POB 2882, Windhoek; tel. (61) 2835111; fax (61) 2835067; e-mail jerome.mutumba@bon .com.na; internet www.bon.com.na; f. 1990; cap. 40.0m., res 1,662.9m., dep. 10,930.5m. (Dec. 2009); Gov. IPUMBU WENDELINUS SHIIMI; Dep. Gov. P. HARTMAN.

Commercial Banks

Bank Windhoek Ltd: Bank Windhoek Bldg, 262 Independence Ave, POB 15, Windhoek; tel. (61) 2991223; fax (61) 223188; e-mail info@bankwindhoek.com.na; internet www.bankwindhoek.com.na; f. 1982; cap. 4.8m., res 1,229.4m., dep. 4,182.2m. (June 2010); Chair. J. C. 'KOOS' BRANDT; Man. Dir JAMES HILL; 32 brs.

FIDES Bank Namibia: Windhoek; internet www.fidesbank.co.na; Chair. MARIA GAOMAS.

First National Bank of Namibia Ltd: 209–211 Independence Ave, POB 195, Windhoek; tel. (61) 2992111; fax (61) 2220979; e-mail info@ fnbnamibia.com.na; internet www.fnbnamibia.com.na; f. 1987 as First Nat. Bank of Southern Africa Ltd; present name adopted 1990; res 1,703.6m., dep. 12,179.3m. (June 2010); Chair. H. DIETER VOIGTS; CEO L. J. HAYNES; 28 brs and 12 agencies.

Nedbank Namibia Ltd: 12–20 Dr Frans Indongo St, POB 1, Windhoek; tel. (61) 2959111; fax (61) 2952046; e-mail service@ nedbank.com; internet www.nedbank.com.na; f. 1973; fmrly Commercial Bank of Namibia Ltd; subsidiary of Nedbank Ltd, South Africa; cap. 16m., res 110m., dep. 4,436m. (Dec. 2007); Chair. T. J. FRANK; Man. Dir ERASTUS HOVEKA; 16 brs and 3 agencies.

Standard Bank Namibia Ltd: Standard Bank Centre, cnr Werner List St and Post St Mall, POB 3327, Windhoek; tel. (61) 2942126; fax (61) 2942583; e-mail info@standardbank.com.na; internet www .standardbank.com.na; f. 1915; controlled by Standard Bank Africa; cap. 2.0m., res 1,137.7m., dep. 10,969.5m. (Dec. 2009); Chair. LEAKE S. HANGALA; Man. Dir MPUMZI PUPUMA; 23 brs.

Agricultural Bank

Agricultural Bank of Namibia (AgriBank): 10 Post St Mall, POB 13208, Windhoek; tel. (61) 2074111; fax (61) 2074289; e-mail info@ agribank.com.na; internet www.agribank.com.na; f. 1922; state-owned; total assets 739.1m. (March 2001); Chair. HANS-GUENTHER STIER; CEO LEONARD N. IIPUMBU.

Development Bank

Development Bank of Namibia (DBN): 12 Daniel Munamava St, POB 235, Windhoek; tel. (61) 2908000; fax (61) 2908049; e-mail info@ dbn.com.na; internet www.dbn.com.na; f. 2004; Chair. SVEN THIEME; CEO DAVID NUYOMA.

SME Bank: Jan Jonker Rd, Windhoek; f. 2012; Man. Dir TAWANA MUMVUMA; Chair. FRANS KAPOFI.

STOCK EXCHANGE

Namibian Stock Exchange (NSX): Robert Mugabe Ave 4, POB 2401, Windhoek; tel. (61) 227647; fax (61) 248531; e-mail info@nsx .com.na; internet www.nsx.com.na; f. 1992; CEO JOHN D. MANDY; Operations Man. MANDA STEYNBERG.

INSURANCE

In 2010 there were 18 long-term and 13 short-term insurance companies operating in Namibia.

Corporate Guarantee and Insurance Co of Namibia Ltd (CGI): Corporate House, Ground Floor, 17 Lüderitz St, POB 416, Windhoek; tel. (61) 259525; fax (61) 255213; e-mail info@ corporateguarantee.com; internet www.corporateguarantee.com; f. 1996; wholly owned subsidiary of Nictus Group Ltd since 2001; Chair. F. R. VAN STADEN; Man. Dir and Principal Officer P. J. DE W. TROMP.

Insurance Co of Namibia (INSCON): POB 2877, Windhoek; tel. (61) 275900; fax (61) 233808; f. 1990; short-term insurance; Chair. CHARLES KAURAISA; Man. Dir FERDINAND OTTO.

Legal Shield: 140–142 Robert Mugabe Ave, POB 11363, Windhoek; tel. (61) 2754200; fax (61) 2754090; internet www.legalshield.na; f. 2000; legal, funeral and medical insurance; Man. Dir SANDRA MILLER.

Metropolitan Namibia: Metropolitan Pl., 1st Floor, cnr Bülow and Stubel Sts, POB 3785, Windhoek; tel. (61) 2973000; fax (61) 248191; internet www.metropolitan.com.na; f. 1996; subsidiary of Metropolitan Group, South Africa; acquired Channel Life in 2004; Chair. M.L. SMITH; Man. Dir JASON NANDAGO.

Mutual and Federal Insurance Co Ltd: Mutual and Federal Centre, 5th–7th Floors, 227 Independence Ave, POB 151, Windhoek; tel. (61) 2077111; fax (61) 2077205; f. 1990; subsidiary of Mutual and Federal, South Africa; acquired CGU Holdings Ltd in 2000 and FGI Namibia Ltd in 2001; Man. Dir G. KATJIMUNE; Gen. Man. J. W. B. LE ROUX.

Namibia National Reinsurance Corpn Ltd (NamibRE): Capital Centre, 2nd Floor, Levinson Arcade, POB 716, Windhoek; tel. (61) 256905; fax (61) 256904; e-mail info@namibre.com; internet www.namibre.com; f. 2001; 100% state-owned; Man. Dir ANNA NAKALE-KAWANA.

Old Mutual Life Assurance Co (Namibia) Ltd: Mutual Platz, 5th Floor, Post St Mall, POB 165, Windhoek; tel. (61) 2993999; fax (61) 2993520; e-mail infonamibia@oldmutual.com; internet www .oldmutual.com.na; Chair. G. S. VAN NIEKERK; Chief Exec. BERTIE VAN DER WALT.

Sanlam Namibia: 154 Independence Ave, POB 317, Windhoek; tel. (61) 2947418; fax (61) 2947416; e-mail marketing@sanlam.com.na; internet www.sanlam.com.na; f. 1928; subsidiary of Sanlam Ltd, South Africa; merged with Regent Life Namibia, Capricorn Investments and Nam-Mic Financial Services in Dec. 2004; Chair. KOOS BRANDT; CEO TERTIUS STEARS.

Santam Namibia Ltd: Ausspannplaza Complex, Ausspannplatz, POB 204, Windhoek; tel. (61) 2928000; fax (61) 235225; 60% owned by Santam, South Africa; 33.3% owned by Bank Windhoek Holdings Ltd; acquired Allianz Insurance of Namibia Ltd in 2001; Chief Exec. RIAAN LOUW.

Swabou Insurance Co Ltd: Swabou Bldg, Post St Mall, POB 79, Windhoek; tel. (61) 2997528; fax (61) 2997551; internet www .fnbnamibia.com.na; f. 1990; acquired by FNB Namibia Holdings Ltd in 2004; short-term insurance; Man. Dir RENIER TALJAARD.

Swabou Life Assurance Co Ltd: 209–211 Independence Ave, POB 79, Windhoek; tel. (61) 2997502; fax (61) 2997550; e-mail tgurirab@ fnbnamibia.com.na; internet www.fnbnamibia.com.na; f. 1990; acquired by FNB Namibia Holdings Ltd in 2004; life assurance; CEO GERHARD MANS.

Trade and Industry

GOVERNMENT AGENCIES

Karakul Board of Namibia—Swakara Fur Producers and Exporters: PMB 13300, Windhoek; tel. (61) 237750; fax (61) 231990; e-mail swakara@agra.com.na; internet www.swakara.net; f. 1982; promotes development of karakul wool and the pelt industry; Chair. RAIMAR VAN HASE; Man. WESSEL H. VISSER.

Meat Board of Namibia: POB 38, Windhoek; tel. (61) 275830; fax (61) 228310; e-mail info@nammic.com.na; internet www.nammic .com.na; f. 1935; facilitates export of livestock, meat and processed meat products; Chair. POENA POTGIETER; Gen. Man. PAUL STRYDOM.

Meat Corpn of Namibia (Meatco Namibia): POB 3881, Windhoek; tel. (61) 3216400; fax (61) 3217045; e-mail hoffice@meatco.com .na; internet www.meatco.com.na; f. 1986; processors of meat and meat products at four abattoirs and one tannery; CEO Kobus du Plessis.

Namibian Agronomic Board: 30 David Merero St, POB 5096, Ausspannplatz, Windhoek; tel. (61) 379500; fax (61) 225371; e-mail nabdesk@nammic.com.na; internet www.nab.com.na; f. 1985; Chair. Gernot Eggert; CEO Christof Brock.

National Petroleum Corpn of Namibia (NAMCOR): Petroleum House, 1 Aviation Rd, PMB 13196, Windhoek; tel. (61) 2045000; fax (61) 2045061; e-mail info@namcor.com.na; internet www.namcor.com.na; f. 1965 as Southern Oil Exploration Corpn (South-West Africa) (Pty) Ltd—SWAKOR; present name adopted 1990; state petroleum co; responsible for importing 50% of national oil requirements; Chair. F. Kisting; Man. Dir Samuel Beukes.

DEVELOPMENT ORGANIZATIONS

Namibia Investment Centre (NIC): Ministry of Trade and Industry, Brendan Simbwaye Sq., Block B, 6th Floor, Goethe St, PMB 13340, Windhoek; tel. (61) 2837335; fax (61) 220278; e-mail nic@mti.gov.na; f. 1990; promotes foreign and domestic investment; Exec. Dir Bernadette Artivor.

Namibia Non-Governmental Organisations' Forum Trust (NANGOF Trust): 9 Strauss St, off Beethoven St, POB 70433, Khomasdal, Windhoek; tel. (61) 212503; fax (61) 211306; e-mail info@nangoftrust.org.na; internet www.nangoftrust.org.na; f. 1991 as NANGOF; renamed NANGOF Trust in July 2007; CEO Ivin Lombardt.

National Housing Enterprise: 7 Gen. Murtala Muhammed Ave, Eros, POB 20192, Windhoek; tel. (61) 2927111; fax (61) 222301; internet www.nhe.com.na; f. 1993; replaced Nat. Building and Investment Corpn; provides low-cost housing; manages Housing Trust Fund; 100% state-owned; Chair. V. R. Rukoro; CEO Vincent Hailulu.

CHAMBERS OF COMMERCE

Chamber of Mines of Namibia (CoM): Channel Life Tower, 4th Floor, Post St Mall, POB 2895, Windhoek; tel. (61) 237925; fax (61) 222638; e-mail dmeyer@chamberofmines.org.na; internet www.chamberofmines.org.na; f. 1979; Pres. Mike Leech; Gen. Man. Veston Malango; 60 mems (2009).

Namibia Chamber of Commerce and Industry (NCCI): 2 Jenner St, cnr Simpson and Jenner Sts, POB 9355, Windhoek; tel. (61) 228809; fax (61) 228009; e-mail ncciinfo@ncci.org.na; internet www.ncci.org.na; f. 1990; Chair. John Endjala; CEO Tarah Shaanika; c. 3,000 mems (2008).

EMPLOYERS' ORGANIZATIONS

Construction Industries Federation of Namibia: cnr Stein and Schwabe Sts, POB 1479, Klein Windhoek; tel. (61) 230028; fax (61) 224534; e-mail info@cif.namibia.na; internet www.cifnamibia.com; Pres. Karl Heinz Schulz; Gen. Man. Bärbel Kirchner; 71 contracting mems, 21 small and medium enterprises members, 17 trade mems, 7 affiliated mems.

Namibia Agricultural Union (NAU): PMB 13255, Windhoek; tel. (61) 237838; fax (61) 220193; e-mail nau@agrinamibia.com.na; internet www.agrinamibia.com.na; f. 1947; represents commercial farmers; Pres. Ryno van der Merwe; Exec. Man. Sakkie Coetzee.

Namibia National Farmers' Union (NNFU): 4 Axalie Doeseb St, Windhoek West; POB 3117, Windhoek; tel. (61) 271117; fax (61) 271155; e-mail info@nnfu.org.na; internet www.nnfu.org.na; f. 1992; represents communal farmers; Pres. Pintile Davids.

Namibia Professional Hunting Association (NAPHA): 318 Sam Nujoma Dr., Klein Windhoek; POB 11291, Windhoek; tel. (61) 234455; fax (61) 222567; e-mail napha@mweb.com.na; internet www.napha.com.na; f. 1974; represents hunting guides and professional hunters; Pres. Johannes Brand; c. 470 mems.

UTILITIES

Electricity

Electricity Control Board: 8 Bismarck St, ECB House, POB 2923, Windhoek; tel. (61) 374300; fax (61) 374304; e-mail info@ecb.org.na; internet www.ecb.org.na; f. 2000; CEO Siseho C. Simasiku.

Namibia Power Corpn (Pty) Ltd (NamPower): NamPower Centre, 15 Luther St, POB 2864, Windhoek; tel. (61) 2054111; fax (61) 232805; e-mail paulinus.shilamba@nampower.com.na; internet www.nampower.com.na; f. 1964; state-owned; Chair. Andries Leevi Hungamo; Man. Dir Paulinus Shilamba.

Water

Namibia Water Corporation Ltd (NamWater): 176 Iscor St, Northern Industrial Area, POB 13389, Windhoek; tel. (61) 710000; fax (61) 713000; e-mail shigwedhaj@namwater.com.na; internet www.namwater.com.na; f. 1997; state-owned; CEO Dr Vaino Shivute.

TRADE UNIONS

In 2004 there were 27 unions representing more than 100,000 workers.

Trade Union Federations

National Union of Namibian Workers (NUNW): Mungunda St, Katutura; POB 50034, Windhoek; tel. (61) 215037; fax (61) 215589; f. 1972; affiliated to the SWAPO party; Pres. Elias Manga; Sec.-Gen. Evilastus Kaaronda; c. 70,000 mems.

Trade Union Congress of Namibia (TUCNA): POB 2111, Windhoek; tel. (61) 246143; fax (61) 212828; f. 2002 following the merger of the Namibia People's Social Movement (f. 1992 as the Namibia Christian Social Trade Unions) and the Namibia Fed. of Trade Unions (f. 1998); Pres. Paulus Hango; c. 45,000 mems (2005).

Transport

RAILWAYS

The main line runs from Nakop, at the border with South Africa, via Keetmanshoop to Windhoek, Kranzberg, Tsumeb, Swakopmund and Walvis Bay. There are three branch lines, from Windhoek to Gobabis, Otavi to Grootfontein and Keetmanshoop to Lüderitz. The total rail network covers 2,382 route-km. Under phase one of the Northern Railway Line Extension Project, the Kranzberg–Tsumeb line was extended by 248 km to Ondangwa in 2006. Phase two of the project, a further 60-km extension of this line to Oshikango, was officially opened in July 2012, and phase three was to involve the eventual construction of a 58-km international link with Oshakati, Angola. In early 2013 plans were under way for the construction of a trans-Kalahari railway linking Walvis Bay with the Mmamabula coal deposits in Botswana. There were also plans for a railway line connecting the Namibian railway system with Mulobezi, Zambia.

TransNamib Holdings Ltd: TransNamib Bldg, cnr Independence Ave and Bahnhof St, PMB 13204, Windhoek; tel. (61) 2982437; fax (61) 2982386; e-mail pubrelation@transnamib.com.na; internet www.transnamib.com.na; f. 1998; state-owned; Chair. Foibe Jacobs; CEO Titus Haimbili.

ROADS

Between 2000 and 2002 the total road network decreased from 66,467 km to 42,237 km of roads, of which 12.8% was paved in 2002. In 2010 there were an estimated 44,138 km of roads, of which 14.5% were paved. A major road link from Walvis Bay to Jwaneng, northern Botswana, the Trans-Kalahari Highway, was completed in 1998, along with the Trans-Caprivi Highway, linking Namibia with northern Botswana, Zambia and Zimbabwe. The Government is also upgrading and expanding the road network in northern Namibia.

Roads Authority: Snyman Circle, Ausspannplatz, Windhoek; tel. (61) 2847000; fax (61) 2847158; e-mail pr@ra.org.na; internet www.ra.org.na; Chair. Hileni Kaifanua; CEO Conrad Lutombi (acting).

SHIPPING

The ports of Walvis Bay and Lüderitz are linked to the main overseas shipping routes and handle almost one-half of Namibia's external trade. Walvis Bay has a container terminal, built in 1999, and eight berths; it is a hub port for the region, serving landlocked countries such as Botswana, Zambia and Zimbabwe. In 2005 NAMPORT added a N $30m. floating dock to the Walvis Bay facilities with a view to servicing vessels used in the region's expanding petroleum industry. Traditionally a fishing port, a new quay was completed at Lüderitz in 2000, with two berths, in response to growing demand from the offshore diamond industry. At 31 December 2012 Namibia's flag registered fleet comprised 122 vessels, with a combined displacement of 108,203 gross registered tons.

African Portland Industrial Holdings (APIH): Huvest Bldg, 1st Floor, AE/Gams Centre, Sam Nujoma Dr., POB 40047, Windhoek; tel. (61) 248744; fax (61) 239485; e-mail jacques@apiholdings.com; f. 1994; 80% owned by Grindrod (South Africa); bulk port terminal operator; Man. Dir Athol Emerton; Sec. Jacques Conradie.

Namibian Ports Authority (NAMPORT): 17 Rikumbi Kandanga Rd, POB 361, Walvis Bay; tel. (64) 2082207; fax (64) 2082320; e-mail jerome@namport.com.na; internet www.namport.com; f. 1994; Chair. Mike van der Meer; Man. Dir Gerson Adolf Bisey Uirab.

CIVIL AVIATION

There are international airports at Windhoek (Hosea Kutako) and Walvis Bay (Rooikop), as well as a number of other airports throughout Namibia and numerous landing strips.

Directorate of Civil Aviation: POB 12003, Windhoek; tel. (61) 702212; fax (61) 702244; e-mail director@dca.com.na; internet www .dca.com.na; Dir ANGELINE SIMANA PAULO.

Air Namibia: TransNamib Bldg, cnr Independence Ave and Bahnhof St, POB 731, Windhoek; tel. (61) 2996000; fax (61) 2996101; e-mail aarickerts@airnamibia.com.na; internet www.airnamibia .com.na; f. 1946 as South West Air Transport; present name adopted in 1991; state-owned; part-privatization postponed indefinitely in 2003; services to Angola, Botswana, Ghana, South Africa, Zimbabwe, Germany and the United Kingdom; Chair. HINYANGERWA PIUS ASHEEKE; Man. Dir THEO NAMASES.

Kalahari Express Airlines (KEA): POB 40179, Windhoek; tel. (61) 245665; fax (61) 245612; f. 1995; domestic and regional flights; Exec. Dir PEINGONDJABI SHIPOH.

Namibia Airports Company (NAC) Limited: 5th Floor, Sanlam Centre Independence Ave, POB 23061, Windhoek; tel. (61) 2955000; fax (61) 2955022; e-mail pr@airports.com.na; internet www.airports .com.na; f. 1998; Chair. NDEUHALA KATONYALA; CEO TAMER EL-KALLAWI (acting).

Tourism

Namibia's principal tourist attractions are its game parks and nature reserves, and the development of 'eco-tourism' is being promoted. Tourist arrivals in Namibia in 2010 totalled 984,098. In 2011 tourism receipts (excluding passenger transport) amounted to an estimated US $517m.

Namibia Tourism Board: 1st Floor, Channel Life Towers, 39 Post Street Mall, Private Bag 13244, Windhoek; tel. (61) 2906000; fax (61) 254848; e-mail info@namibiatourism.com.na; internet www .namibiatourism.com.na; Chair. ERICKA AKUENJE; CEO DIGU NAOBEB.

Defence

As assessed at November 2012, the Namibian Defence Force numbered an estimated 9,000 men; there was also a 200-strong navy, operating as part of the Ministry of Fisheries and Marine Resources, and a paramilitary force of 6,000.

Defence Expenditure: Budgeted at N $3,130m. for 2012.

Commander-in-Chief of the Defence Force: Pres. HIFIKEPUNYE POHAMBA.

Chief of Staff of the Defence Force: Lt-Gen. EPAPHRAS DENGA NDAITWAH.

Commander of the Army: Maj.-Gen. JOHN MUTWA.

Commander of the Air Force: Air Vice-Marshal MARTIN PHINEHAS.

Commander of the Navy: Rear Adm. PETER VILHO.

Education

Education is officially compulsory and free of charge for 10 years between the ages of six and 16 years, or until primary education has been completed (whichever is the sooner). Under the Education Act of 2001, free basic education was extended to grade 12, although it is not compulsory beyond the limits set in the Constitution. Primary education begins at six years of age and lasts for seven years. Secondary education, beginning at the age of 13, lasts for up to five years, comprising a first cycle of three years and a second of two. According to UNESCO estimates, in 2008/09 enrolment at primary schools included 85% of children in the relevant age-group (males 83%; females 88%), while the comparable ratio for secondary enrolment in 2006/07 was 51% (males 44%; females 57%). Higher education is provided by the University of Namibia, the Technicon of Namibia, a vocational college and four teacher-training colleges. In 2007/08 19,707 students were enrolled in tertiary education. Various schemes for informal adult education are also in operation in an effort to combat illiteracy. In 2009/10 education received an estimated 18.6% of total government expenditure.

NAURU

Introductory Survey

LOCATION, CLIMATE, LANGUAGE, RELIGION, FLAG, CAPITAL

The Republic of Nauru is a small island in the central Pacific Ocean, lying about 40 km (25 miles) south of the Equator and about 4,000 km (2,500 miles) north-east of Sydney, Australia. Its nearest neighbour is Banaba (formerly Ocean Island), in Kiribati, about 300 km (186 miles) to the east. The climate is tropical, with a westerly monsoon season from November to February. Average annual rainfall is about 2,060 mm (80 ins), but actual rainfall is extremely variable. Day temperatures vary between 24°C and 34°C (75°–93°F). Of the total resident population in 2002, 77% were indigenous Nauruans. Their language is Nauruan, but English is also widely understood. The majority of Nauruans are Christians, mostly adherents of the Nauruan Protestant Church. The national flag (proportions 1 by 2) is royal blue, divided by a narrow horizontal yellow stripe, with a 12-pointed white star at the lower hoist. The island state has no official capital, but the seat of the legislature and most government offices are in Yaren district.

CONTEMPORARY POLITICAL HISTORY

Historical Context

Nauru, inhabited by a predominantly Polynesian people, organized in 12 clans, was annexed by Germany in 1888. In 1914, shortly after the outbreak of the First World War, the island was captured by Australian forces. It continued to be administered by Australia under a League of Nations mandate (granted in 1920), which also named the United Kingdom and New Zealand as co-trustees. During 1942–45 Nauru was occupied by the Japanese, who deported 1,200 islanders to Truk (now Chuuk), Micronesia, where many died in bombing raids or from starvation. In 1947 the island was placed under UN Trusteeship, with Australia as the administering power on behalf of the Governments of Australia, New Zealand and the United Kingdom. The UN Trusteeship Council proposed in 1964 that the indigenous people of Nauru be resettled on Curtis Island, off the Queensland coast. This offer was made in anticipation of the progressive exhaustion of the island's phosphate deposits, and because of the environmental devastation resulting from the mining operations. However, the Nauruans elected to remain on the island. Nauru was accorded a considerable measure of self-government in January 1966, with the establishment of Legislative and Executive Councils, and proceeded to independence on 31 January 1968 (exactly 22 years after the surviving Nauruans returned to the island from exile in Micronesia). Nauru became a full member of the Commonwealth in May 1999, and a member of the UN in September of that year. (In 2005, after falling behind on its subscription payments, Nauru was relegated to special membership of the Commonwealth, designated by the title 'member in arrears'. Following an improvement in state finances, however, Nauru was reinstated to full membership in mid-2011.)

Domestic Political Affairs

The Head Chief of Nauru, Hammer DeRoburt, was elected President in May 1968 and re-elected in 1971 and 1973. Dissatisfaction with his increasingly personal rule led to the election of Bernard Dowiyogo (leader of the recently established, informal Nauru Party) to the presidency in 1976. Dowiyogo was re-elected President after a general election in late 1977. However, DeRoburt's supporters adopted tactics of obstruction in Parliament, and in December 1977 Dowiyogo resigned, in response to Parliament's refusal to approve budgetary legislation; he was re-elected shortly afterwards, but was again forced to resign in April 1978, following the defeat of a legislative proposal concerning phosphate royalties. Lagumot Harris, another member of the Nauru Party, succeeded him, but resigned three weeks later when Parliament rejected a finance measure, and DeRoburt was again elected President. He was re-elected in December of that year, in December 1980 and in May and December 1983.

In September 1986 DeRoburt resigned, following the defeat of a government budget proposal; he was replaced as President by Kennan Adeang. However, after holding office for only 14 days,

Adeang was defeated in a parliamentary vote of no confidence, and DeRoburt subsequently resumed the presidency. Following a general election in December, Adeang was again narrowly elected President, but he was subsequently ousted by another vote of no confidence; DeRoburt was reinstated as President. The atmosphere of political uncertainty generated by the absence of a clear majority in Parliament led DeRoburt to dissolve Parliament in preparation for another general election in January 1987, following which the incumbent was re-elected to the presidency. In February Adeang announced the establishment of the Democratic Party of Nauru, essentially a revival of the Nauru Party. Eight members of Parliament joined the new party, which declared that its aim was to curtail the extension of presidential powers and to promote democracy. In August 1989 a parliamentary motion of no confidence in DeRoburt (proposed by Adeang) was approved, and Kenas Aroi, a former Minister of Finance, was subsequently elected President. Aroi resigned in December, owing to ill health, and after a general election in the same month Dowiyogo was re-elected President, defeating DeRoburt. At the next presidential election, held shortly after a general election in November 1992, Dowiyogo defeated Buraro Detudamo.

At a general election held in November 1995, when a total of 67 candidates contested the 18 parliamentary seats, all cabinet members were re-elected. A subsequent presidential election resulted in Lagumot Harris's defeat of the incumbent Dowiyogo. The resignation of the Chairman of Air Nauru, following allegations of misconduct, prompted Parliament to vote on a motion of no confidence in the Government in November 1996. The motion was narrowly approved and Harris was replaced by Dowiyogo as President. Later that month, however, Dowiyogo's new Government was itself defeated in a parliamentary vote of no confidence, and Adeang was elected to the presidency. A further motion of no confidence was approved in December, when Adeang was similarly removed from office. At a subsequent presidential contest Reuben Kun, a former Minister of Finance, defeated Adeang, on the understanding that his administration would organize a general election. An election duly took place in February 1997, at which four new members were elected to Parliament, following an apparent agreement between the supporters of Harris and those of Dowiyogo to end the political manoeuvring that had resulted in several months of instability in Nauru. At the subsequent election to the presidency Kinza Clodumar (nominated by Dowiyogo) defeated Harris by nine parliamentary votes to eight.

In early 1998 five members of Parliament (including former President Lagumot Harris) were dismissed by Adeang, the Speaker, for refusing to apologize for personal remarks about him that had been published in an opposition newsletter. At the resultant by-elections, held in February, three of the five members were re-elected. A motion expressing no confidence in the President was approved in June, and Dowiyogo was consequently elected to replace Clodumar. In April 1999 Dowiyogo was himself defeated in a further vote of no confidence; his replacement was Rene Harris, previously Chairman of the Nauru Phosphate Corporation.

Following the legislative elections held in April 2000, Rene Harris was re-elected President, narrowly defeating Dowiyogo. Ludwig Scotty was elected Speaker of Parliament. However, Scotty and his deputy, Ross Cairn, subsequently resigned, stating only that they were unable to continue under the 'current political circumstances'. Harris therefore tendered his resignation and was replaced by Dowiyogo, whereupon Scotty and Cairn were re-elected to their posts in the legislature.

In early 2001 Anthony Audoa, the Minister of Home Affairs, Culture, Health and Women's Affairs, resigned, claiming that Dowiyogo had squandered Nauru's wealth during his various tenures as President and that in promoting the island as a tax haven he had allowed Nauru to be used by Russian criminal gangs to launder their illegal funds. In March Dowiyogo was ousted from the presidency in a parliamentary vote of no confidence while he was undergoing hospital treatment in Australia. The motion led to Rene Harris regaining the presidency.

Allegations that Nauru's 'offshore' financial centre was being used extensively by Russian criminal organizations for laundering the proceeds of their illegal activities had led Dowiyogo to order a full review of the industry in March 1999. In early 2000 President Rene Harris announced that Nauru was to suspend its 'offshore' banking services and improve the accountability of existing banks on the island, as part of the Government's efforts to bring Nauru's financial services regulations into conformity with international standards. Dowiyogo similarly reaffirmed his commitment to reform the 'offshore' sector, following his election in April 2000. However, in February 2001 11 members of Nauru's 18-member legislature signed a petition requesting that Dowiyogo attend a special parliamentary session to answer questions relating to the island's alleged role in laundering significant funds from Russian criminal organizations. The allegations originated in claims by Russia's central bank that some US $70,000m. of illegal funds had been processed in 'offshore' banks in Nauru. It was estimated that more than 400 such banks existed on the island in early 2001. The Government subsequently approved an Anti-Money Laundering Act in August 2001, but the Paris-based Financial Action Task Force (FATF, see p. 465) found that the new legislation contained several deficiencies and imposed sanctions in December. The Government announced revised anti-moneylaundering legislation in the same month. Meanwhile, following the Islamist attacks in the USA on 11 September 2001, Nauru's financial system was subject to international scrutiny, amid suspicion that it might have been used as a conduit for the terrorists' funds.

As a result of continued US pressure, Nauru's Parliament approved a new law in February 2004 to address the problem of money-laundering, along with legislation to close down the country's 'offshore' banks. In October the FATF withdrew counter-measures against the country, and in October 2005, following the implementation of the requisite legislation, Nauru became the last of the Pacific islands to be removed from the FATF list of non-co-operative countries and territories. Furthermore, in December 2003, following the island's commitment to improve transparency and to exchange information on tax matters with other countries, Nauru had been removed from a list of unco-operative tax havens, issued in April 2002 by the Organisation for Economic Co-operation and Development (see p. 388).

In early January 2003, meanwhile, President Rene Harris was defeated in a motion of no confidence and was replaced by Bernard Dowiyogo. The vote followed the defeat of the Government's budget proposals, amid reports of increasing dissatisfaction with Harris's management of the economy. Nauru's deteriorating financial situation, in addition to the Government's decision to accept more than 1,000 asylum seekers in return for aid from Australia (see Processing of Asylum Seekers), were believed to be major factors in the loss of confidence in Harris. However, Harris applied to the Supreme Court, and on 10 January 2003 an injunction was issued against Dowiyogo accepting the presidency, on the grounds that only 11 of the 18 members of Parliament had attended the session when the vote took place, thus rendering it invalid. Despite the injunction, Dowiyogo maintained his position and appointed a new Cabinet. Following several days of confusion, Harris was reinstated as President, after the intervention of Nauru's Chief Justice (based in Melbourne, Australia), but he resigned from the presidency on the following day. In the resultant contest Dowiyogo narrowly defeated Kinza Clodumar to become the new President on 20 January. However, a lack of support for Dowiyogo within Parliament continued to create problems, amid appeals for an early election to resolve the impasse.

Meanwhile, a complete collapse of Nauru's telecommunications system in January 2003 effectively cut the island off from the rest of the world. A speech by Dowiyogo claiming that Nauru was on the verge of bankruptcy, unable to pay its public servants or to send its sick citizens to Australia for treatment, and appealing to donor countries for emergency assistance, could not be transmitted for almost a month. Telecommunications services were finally restored in March.

In early March 2003 Dowiyogo travelled to Washington, DC, USA, at the request of the US Government, which had threatened to impose harsh economic sanctions on the island and to repossess Air Nauru's only aircraft, if Nauru did not discontinue its 'offshore' banking services. The Administration of George W. Bush was reported to be concerned over the possibility that individuals with links to terrorist organizations might have used the island's financial services to launder their funds. Consequently, Dowiyogo agreed to sign executive orders not to renew any banking licences or to issue any further so-called 'investor passports'. However, shortly after the meeting, Dowiyogo collapsed and, following emergency heart surgery, died on 9 March. Derog Gioura was appointed acting head of state and on 20 March was elected President by nine parliamentary votes to seven. Legislation providing for the expiry of most 'offshore' banking licences within 30 days (and for the remainder within six months) was approved by Parliament in late March. At the end of the month President Derog Gioura himself suffered a heart attack and was flown to Australia for treatment.

Legislative elections took place on 3 May 2003. However, the new Speaker resigned one day after his election, and with no further nominations for the position, Parliament was unable to proceed to a presidential election. The impasse was resolved when a Speaker was finally elected in late May and Ludwig Scotty won the subsequent presidential election, defeating Kinza Clodumar. However, on 8 August Scotty was ousted from office by a no-confidence motion and was replaced by Rene Harris, who thus became the fourth individual to hold the presidency in 2003. The reasons for Scotty's removal were not clear, although concerns had been expressed about his plans to close the recently opened embassies in Washington, DC, and in the capital of the People's Republic of China, Beijing (see Foreign Affairs).

In February 2004 the Minister of Justice resigned, precipitating a vote of no confidence in the President. A further political crisis arose when the motion received an equal number of votes in favour and against. Moreover, when Parliament was unable to agree on the election of a new Speaker, following the resignation of the incumbent in early April, the resulting impasse meant that Parliament could not be formally convened. As the country's financial crisis deepened, President Rene Harris travelled to Australia in mid-April to request assistance in averting imminent bankruptcy for the island. On his return to Nauru, Harris was confronted by angry demonstrations by hundreds of government employees (who constituted the majority of paid employees on the island) protesting at the considerable hardship imposed on them as a result of their salaries having been unpaid for 12 months. In the same month receivers were appointed to manage the assets of the Nauru Phosphate Royalties Trust (including Nauru's extensive property portfolio in Australia), with the company unable to pay off debts of some $A230m. to US interests. Nauruans working in government-owned buildings in the Australian cities of Melbourne and Sydney were served with eviction notices. Meanwhile, with neither the Government nor the opposition willing to nominate a Speaker from among its members (thereby giving the other side a majority in Parliament), the legislature was unable to draw up a budget. In May, however, during another of Harris's overseas trips, the opposition elected one of its members as Speaker and immediately approved legislation making it illegal for a government to operate without a budget. In the following month, and before the Supreme Court had ruled on the matter, Kinza Clodumar, the Minister of Finance, crossed the floor, thereby allowing the opposition to approve a motion of no confidence in Harris. Ludwig Scotty was subsequently elected to the presidency. In July Australian Treasury official Peter Depta arrived in Nauru to take up the post of Financial Secretary, effectively assuming control of the island's finances.

Nauru's precarious political situation deteriorated during September 2004, and by the end of the month President Ludwig Scotty had dissolved Parliament and declared a state of emergency. His action had been prompted by the suspension by the Speaker, Russell Kun, of the Minister of Health, Dr Kieren Keke, on the grounds that he held dual Nauruan and Australian nationality. Keke's suspension had resulted in the loss of the Government's one-seat majority and a consequent stalemate in Parliament, during which budget legislation could not be approved. Scotty assumed sole responsibility over the government of the country until a general election took place on 23 October. At the election all nine members of Scotty's Government retained their seats in the legislature, while seven of the nine opposition members of Parliament were not re-elected. The result thus gave President Scotty an ample majority in Parliament. Within days of its election the new Government approved a budget that included a reduction in public sector salaries and increased import duties. In the following month legislation aimed at discouraging criminals, particularly terrorists, from using the country's financial sector was approved, in addition to the establishment of a procedure for conducting possible future referendums and for reviewing the Constitution. The sudden death of the Speaker, Vassal Gadoengin, in December 2004 led to the election of Valdon Dowiyogo, a son of the former President, as his replacement in the following month.

Meanwhile, in July 2004 President Ludwig Scotty held emergency discussions with the Presidents of Kiribati and Tuvalu regarding at least US $2m. in outstanding salary payments owed to their nationals employed in Nauru by the Nauru Phosphate Corporation. Nauru's financial crisis led it to appeal for assistance from the Pacific region and the international community. In September the Pacific Islands Forum (see p. 426) offered to help pay the salaries of Nauruan government employees, who had been unpaid for many months (see above). The Government of Cuba responded to an appeal for health care workers by sending 11 doctors to Nauru to alleviate an increasingly serious situation, in which only three doctors were available to administer to sick Nauruans.

In January 2005 a committee of members of Parliament began a review of Nauru's Constitution, motivated by a desire to achieve greater political stability in the country and to improve the accountability of public institutions. In 2006 the committee formed an independent Constitutional Review Commission, which analysed and considered public suggestions, and in mid-2007 a Constitutional Convention met to discuss the Commission's conclusions.

A few days after the legislative elections on 25 August 2007 Ludwig Scotty was re-elected as President, defeating Marcus Stephen. Scotty's new Cabinet retained all the ministers of the previous Government. In December, however, Scotty was removed from office in a vote of no confidence, amid allegations of corruption made against the Minister of Foreign Affairs and of Finance, David Adeang, and the withdrawal of support of several government members. Marcus Stephen was subsequently elected to replace Scotty.

The new Government's progress was hampered by increasing discord and its lack of a majority in the legislature. In April 2008 David Adeang, now Speaker as well as a member of the opposition, announced the suspension of all nine government members of Parliament. President Stephen subsequently declared a state of emergency and dissolved Parliament. At an early election conducted on 26 April, the incumbent Government increased its parliamentary representation to 12 of the 18 legislators. Riddell Akua was elected Speaker. Parliament re-elected Stephen as President and confirmed the membership of the Cabinet, which remained largely unchanged. Three of Stephen's supporters subsequently defected to the opposition, amid allegations that Getax, an Australian company which apparently hoped to secure greater control of Nauru's phosphate resources, had attempted to influence the island's politics. Getax had financed a trip to Singapore by 11 of the 18 members of the Nauruan Parliament, including the three government supporters who then joined the opposition.

The political impasse of 2010

In February 2010 President Stephen survived a parliamentary vote of no confidence relating to alleged irregularities in the use of overseas loans. In Nauru's first ever referendum, which was conducted at the end of the month, various proposals for constitutional change, including the direct election of the country's President, were rejected by voters; 78% of the electorate participated in the poll. Parliament was dissolved in March, in preparation for an early election the following month, when President Stephen hoped to secure wider support.

However, at the election, held on 24 April 2010, all 18 incumbent members of Parliament were returned to office, thus resulting in no change to the composition of the legislature and again leaving Parliament evenly divided between the two sides (with nine seats each). In mid-May, at its sixth attempt, Parliament chose Godfrey Thoma as Speaker. However, having declared that he would resign if a fresh election were not called within four days, Thoma duly resigned when this condition was not met. Meanwhile, President Stephen indicated that he favoured the amendment of the Constitution to permit the selection of the Speaker from outside Parliament, effectively proposing the addition of a 19th member to the legislature, in order to prevent any recurrence of the impasse that had rendered Parliament unable to function. The incumbent Government's candidate for the position of Speaker, Dominic Tabuna, was elected in early June, after reportedly receiving the support of two opposition legislators. However, just three days after taking office, Tabuna resigned in unclear circumstances.

On 11 June 2010, citing the need to approve the national budget, President Stephen declared a state of emergency and called fresh elections for 19 June. However, the poll failed to produce a clear majority for either side: all but one of the 18 incumbent members were returned to office. The sole newcomer, Milton Dube, an independent who won a seat previously held by the opposition, thus held the balance of power. Stephen contended that the results of the second poll indicated a 'rallying' behind his grouping by Nauruans, and urged Dube to lend his support to the interim Government. However, in late June Aloysius Amwano (one of the three opposition members who had withdrawn his support for the Government following the Getax-sponsored trip to Singapore) was elected Speaker; upon taking office, Amwano urged Stephen to resign. The President indicated his willingness to do so, on the condition that a replacement be selected from within his grouping. In early July the interim Government announced that it had secured the support of an opposition member, thereby affording it the majority that it required to form a new government and elect a President. However, Amwano refused to allow the motion to elect a President to be presented to Parliament, prompting Stephen to issue a presidential order demanding the Speaker's removal from office on the grounds that Amwano was in contravention of his constitutional requirements.

In August 2010 it emerged that the opposition was considering initiating a legal challenge to President Stephen's dismissal of the Speaker and the declaration of a state of emergency in June, claiming that his actions had been unconstitutional. In an attempt to answer claims of autocracy, in September Stephen amended the emergency powers in order to allow challenges to be lodged against the measure with the Supreme Court. The opposition formally presented its challenge to the Court in early October. In mid-October the Court ruled that the President had acted within his constitutional rights, noting that the Constitution explicitly stated that it was the right of the President, not the Supreme Court, to declare a state of emergency.

In late October 2010 it was revealed that, at the request of President Stephen, Australian federal police had begun investigating allegations of bribery by Getax of members of the Nauruan opposition. Documents allegedly pertaining to unusual financial transactions and the possibility of electoral irregularities were reported to have been handed over to the Australian High Commissioner in Nauru. The police investigation was reportedly terminated in September 2011 owing to a 'lack of jurisdiction'.

Former President Ludwig Scotty accepted a nomination for the post of Speaker, while reaffirming his position as an opposition legislator, and was duly elected in November 2010. Parliament swiftly re-elected Stephen as President, who removed the state of emergency, thereby appearing finally to have resolved the six-month impasse. The national budget was quickly approved, almost four months after it was scheduled to have been implemented.

2011 presidential changes

In October 2011 opposition member David Adeang divulged to Parliament some correspondence between Stephen and a phosphate dealer in Thailand that, Adeang claimed, proved that Stephen had requested supplementary payments to himself to enable phosphate sales. Adeang tabled a vote of no confidence in the President, but Stephen resigned on 10 November, the day on which the vote was due to take place. On the same day Parliament elected as his successor Freddy Pitcher, who had served as Minister of Commerce, Industry and the Environment prior to his resignation from the Cabinet earlier in the year. On 15 November, however, Pitcher was in turn removed from the presidency by a vote of no confidence, once more tabled by Adeang, and was replaced by Sprent Dabwido, a former Minister of Telecommunications, who had defected from the Government to the opposition for the vote against Pitcher. Dabwido subsequently stated that he had backed the vote of no confidence in an attempt to gain opposition support for the passage of previously mooted constitutional reforms (the Parliamentary Amendments Bill, which had been provisionally approved by the legislature in August 2009 pending further amendments) that could avert future political instability and avoid future elections resulting in another hung Parliament. The main proposals of the bill were the election of the Speaker from outside the legislature, the appointment of an Ombudsman, a code of ethics for legislators, and the addition of a 19th member of Parliament. In Dabwido's new Cabinet, Adeang was reinstated to the post of Minister of Finance—a position that he had lost in 2007 following allegations of corruption—and was also allocated the justice and sustainable development portfolios, while the President himself assumed responsibility for several portfolios, including foreign affairs.

Recent developments: political unrest

On 11 June 2012 President Dabwido unexpectedly dismissed his whole Cabinet, citing his frustration over the legislature's failure to approve the final draft of the Parliamentary Amendments Bill. However, according to some sources, Dabwido ousted the ministers in order to avoid the possibility of a parliamentary no-confidence vote. A new, five-member Cabinet was appointed on the following day. Dr Kieren Keke and former President Marcus Stephen notably returned to office, as Minister for Foreign Affairs and Trade, Health and Sport and Minister of Commerce, Industry and Environment, Nauru Phosphate Royalties Trust, and Fisheries, respectively, while Adeang left the Government, with the finance portfolio being assigned to Roland Kun (along with the portfolios of sustainable development and education).

Following the opposition's unsuccessful introduction of a vote of no confidence in the Government on 7 February 2013, Keke resigned from the Cabinet without any reason being given. In the following week the Government was thrown into further disarray by Dabwido's unexplained dismissal of Stephen and a few days later by the resignation of Kun. The former portfolios of Keke, Stephen and Kun were divided between the President and his remaining two ministers, Dominic Tabuna and Riddell Akua. Later that month, in an attempt to re-establish functional and constitutional government, the President appointed two new cabinet members: Aloysius Amwano was allocated the education portfolio and Shadlog Bernicke the health portfolio. Nonetheless, on 1 March, at the request of President Dabwido, the Speaker, Ludwig Scotty, adjourned Parliament indefinitely, citing the continuing unruly behaviour of the legislators. On 9 March Scotty officially announced the dissolution of Parliament and gave notice of the holding of a general election on 6 April. However, following the launching of a legal challenge led by Keke, on 15 March the Supreme Court ruled that the adjournment of Parliament had been unconstitutional (since the legislators had not been given the opportunity to debate the measure) and that it was consequently null and void (as was the writ issued for the general election). The Court ordered the Speaker to reconvene Parliament within 28 days. In order to avoid the need to meet this deadline, on 11 April Dabwido withdrew his original request for the dissolution of Parliament, issuing a new notice for dissolution on 15 April. Two attempts to reconvene Parliament in the following week to discuss the proposed dissolution failed, however, as a boycott by some members resulted in a lack of quorum. The next scheduled sitting of Parliament, on 23 April, was attended by a sufficient number of deputies, but ended swiftly owing to a failure to elect a new Speaker, following Scotty's resignation on 18 April. Although Godfrey Thoma was elected Speaker on 25 April, the political impasse continued at early May, as several subsequent sittings of Parliament were again adjourned in the absence of a significant number of legislators. Meanwhile, Tabuna was removed from the Government in mid-April, being replaced by Kun, who was additionally allocated the foreign affairs and trade portfolio, which Dabwido had occupied since Keke's resignation in February.

Processing of Asylum Seekers

In September 2001 Nauru agreed to accept 310 of 460 predominantly Afghan asylum seekers who were on board a Norwegian freighter, unable to disembark on Christmas Island, in the Indian Ocean, as Australia refused to grant them entry into its territory (see Christmas Island). The Australian Government agreed to fund the processing of the asylum seekers and to pay an undisclosed sum to Nauru, which was to accommodate the asylum seekers, initially for three months, while their claims for asylum were assessed. Following the interception of several other boats carrying asylum seekers in Australian waters later the same month, Nauru received a pledge of $A20m. from the Australian Government for agreeing to host 800 asylum seekers. In December Nauru signed an agreement with Australia's Minister for Foreign Affairs to accommodate a total of 1,200 at any one time, in return for a further $A10m. of aid. Local residents and owners of the land upon which the camps were located expressed concern over the delays in processing the asylum seekers' claims, which were due to be completed by July 2002. In December some 700 people remained in the camps. In the same month the President signed a new agreement with the Australian Government to extend the duration of the camps' operations and to accommodate up to 1,500 asylum seekers.

In mid-2003 the Australian Government was criticized for its detention of some 100 children in the camps on Nauru and for failing to reunite families held in separate camps for extended periods. Concerns about the conditions at the camps and the welfare of the detainees increased during 2003, and in December a reported 40 of those held began a hunger strike in order to attract attention to their situation. The Nauruan Government's subsequent appeals for assistance from Australia to care for the hunger strikers, many of whom required hospital treatment during the following weeks, were refused. The hunger strike ended after about a month, and in January 2004 the Australian Government sent a delegation to inspect medical facilities available to asylum seekers on the island. However, the resultant report, which found services for those held in detention to be adequate, was widely regarded as flawed, as it had failed to examine any of the detainees and had been compiled solely by Australian government officials. In June the first of 146 Afghan asylum seekers, approved for entry to Australia, left the detention centre. In November 2005, after four years of detention on the island, a total of 25 asylum seekers were transferred to Melbourne. It was reported that only two detainees, who had failed to meet security requirements, remained on Nauru; their departure from the centre was finally arranged in late 2006. In early 2007 the claims of 82 Sri Lankan asylum seekers, who had been intercepted by the Australian navy in February, were being processed on Nauru, along with those of seven detainees from Myanmar. In February 2008 the 21 remaining detainees left Nauru, marking the end of Australia's policy of accommodating asylum seekers on the island. The Australian Government's decision was not welcomed by all Nauruans, in view of its anticipated impact on the island's economy. In July 2010 President Marcus Stephen expressed Nauru's willingness to reopen the detention centre if approached by Australia. However, the Australian Government of Prime Minister Julia Gillard, which had taken office in the previous month, stated its refusal to consider any such reopening while Nauru remained a non-signatory to the UN's 1951 Convention relating to the Status of Refugees. In June 2011, following a visit to the island by Australian opposition politician Tony Abbott, who voiced his support for the reopening of the detention centre in preference to an exchange arrangement under negotiation between Australia and Malaysia, President Stephen officially signed the UN Convention.

The sinking of two boats carrying asylum seekers near Christmas Island in two separate incidents in June 2012 (with the subsequent loss of more than 100 lives) and a sharp increase in the number of asylum seekers led to renewed demands by the opposition in Australia for the reopening of the detention centres on Nauru and on Manus Island in Papua New Guinea. Following the recommendations of an expert panel, the Government abruptly reversed its policy and legislation was approved by the Australian Parliament in August to reopen the centres; the first asylum seekers arrived on Nauru in the following month. By early February 2013 there were some 450 asylum seekers (mostly from Sri Lanka) in the rudimentary processing camps. As previously, the detainees protested against their poor living conditions and the uncertainty surrounding the length of their detention (which could reportedly last up to five years), and many of them undertook hunger strikes or self-harmed in an attempt to have their concerns addressed. Conditions in the camps were described as 'cruel' and 'degrading' by human rights organization Amnesty International, which had sent a team to assess the detention centre in late November 2012, and a report published by a monitoring mission of the office of the UN High Commissioner for Refugees in the following month concluded that the centre did not meet international protection standards. Although accommodation at the centre initially consisted of basic tents, by February 2013 some more permanent structures had been erected to house the inmates. The processing of the asylum seekers' claims was reported to have commenced in March.

Phosphate-mining Issues

In February 1987 representatives of the British, Australian and New Zealand Governments signed documents effecting the official demise of the British Phosphate Commissioners, who from 1919 until 1970 had overseen the mining of Nauru's phosphate deposits. President DeRoburt subsequently expressed concern about the distribution of the Commissioners' accumulated assets, which were estimated to be worth $55m. His proposal that part of this sum be spent on the rehabilitation of areas of the island that had been mined before independence was rejected by the three Governments involved. DeRoburt subsequently established a commission of inquiry to investigate proposals for rehabilitation. The commission proposed that the three Governments provide one-third ($A72m.) of the estimated rehabilitation costs. In 1989 Australia's refusal to contribute to the rehabilitation of former phosphate-mining areas prompted Nauru to institute proceedings, claiming compensation from Australia for damage to its environment, at the International Court of Justice in The Hague, Netherlands. However, in August 1993, following negotiations between President Dowiyogo and the Australian Prime Minister, Paul Keating, a Compact of Settlement was signed, under which the Australian Government was to pay Nauru a lump sum of $A57m., followed by $A50m. in instalments over a period of 20 years. New Zealand and the United Kingdom subsequently agreed to contribute $A12m. each towards the settlement. An investigation into methods for the rehabilitation of the damaged areas of the island included plans to use landfill to encourage the restoration of vegetation to the mined areas, and the re-establishment of many of the species of flora and fauna that had previously been abundant on the island. In mid-1995 a report commissioned by the Government published details of a rehabilitation programme extending over the next 20–25 years and costing $A230m. However, the success of the rehabilitation scheme was dependent on the co-operation of landowners, some of whom were expected to continue to allow areas to be mined for residual ore once phosphate reserves had been exhausted. In mid-1997 Parliament approved the Nauru Rehabilitation Corporation (NRC) Act, providing for the establishment of a corporate body to manage the rehabilitation programme. The NRC held its inaugural meeting in May 1999. The rehabilitation programme (which was to be partly financed from the Compact of Settlement) was expected to transform the mined areas into sites suitable for agriculture, new housing and industrial units, but the project was hampered considerably by delays. Results published in September 2004 from a series of test sites on the island indicated that the potential for residual phosphate mining might be greater than had been previously thought (with reported mineable reserves of an estimated 20m. metric tons remaining). A major refurbishment of the island's mining plant was subsequently undertaken, and exports of phosphates resumed in 2006 (see Economic Affairs). In March 2008 protests reportedly related to the export of phosphates escalated into violence, with a group of approximately 100 demonstrators setting fire to a police station. Intense foreign competition for greater control of Nauru's remaining phosphate resources led to the emergence in 2010 of claims of bribery of local parliamentarians, while in 2011 allegations of corruption related to phosphate sales resulted in the resignation of President Stephen (see Domestic Political Affairs).

Foreign Affairs

In 1989 a UN report on the greenhouse effect (the heating of the earth's atmosphere and a resultant rise in sea-level) listed Nauru as one of the countries that might disappear beneath the sea in the 21st century, unless drastic action were taken. The Government of Nauru strongly criticized Australia's refusal, at the December 1997 Conference of the Parties to the Framework Convention on Climate Change (see UN Environment Programme, see p. 61), in Kyoto, Japan, to reduce its emissions of pollutant gases known to contribute to the greenhouse effect. Following a change of government in Australia, the country signed the Kyoto Protocol in December 2007.

Despite such tensions, Nauru maintained generally good relations with Australia, which continued to provide substantial development aid. In August 2009 the two countries signed the Australia-Nauru Partnership for Development. Priority areas included the improvement of the education system and of health facilities in Nauru. In early 2010 the Australian consulate-general in Nauru was upgraded to a full high commission.

In August 2001 Nauru hosted a summit meeting of the Pacific Islands Forum. In September 2010 the UN opened a bureau on Nauru combining offices of the UN Development Programme, the UN Population Fund and the UN Children's Fund (UNICEF), which was welcomed by President Marcus Stephen as an opportunity to forge closer co-operation with the organization.

In 2011 Nauru began a three-year chairmanship of the Alliance of Small Island States, a position that it was expected to use to advocate the extension of the Kyoto Protocol and to encourage awareness of the threat posed to island nations by climate change. Nevertheless, an appeal by President Stephen to the UN Security Council in July of that year, seeking a range of specific actions aimed at preparing for the threat of rising sea levels, failed to gain the Council's approval.

In mid-2002 President Rene Harris announced Nauru's recognition of the People's Republic of China, thus ending 22 years of diplomatic relations with Taiwan. The President swiftly accepted US $60m. in aid and $77m. in debt annulment from China. In February 2003 Nauru opened two diplomatic missions, in Washington, DC, and in Beijing. However, suspicions regarding the use of Nauru's facilities by international terrorists were confirmed in the same month when two members of the Islamist al-Qa'ida organization were found to be travelling on Nauruan passports. In March, at the request of the US Government, which had threatened to impose harsh economic sanctions and to repossess Air Nauru's only aircraft if the country did not discontinue its 'offshore' banking services, President Dowiyogo flew to the USA for discussions. The Administration of George W. Bush was reported to have been particularly concerned by the possibility that individuals with links to terrorist organizations might have used the island's financial services in order to launder their funds. In July President Scotty announced plans to close the newly opened diplomatic missions, citing economic constraints and his belief that they were not serving their intended purpose. Representatives in China and the USA expressed surprise at the announcement and queried the President's motives, questioning in particular his commitment to ending the lucrative sale of Nauruan passports.

In March 2005 President Scotty made an official visit to mainland China, where he took part in discussions on bilateral aid and economic and technical co-operation. However, in May the Chinese Government revealed that Nauru had severed its diplomatic relations with the People's Republic by restoring recognition to Taiwan. In March 2006 it was announced that Taiwan was providing US $3m. in overdue salary payments to some 1,000 former phosphate miners from Kiribati and Tuvalu, who had remained stranded on Nauru since the island's financial crisis had resulted in the Government's inability to pay their wages. In the same month Nauru's national carrier recovered its sole aircraft, which had been repossessed in December 2005 owing to unpaid debt, with the help of Taiwanese funding. In March 2010 Taiwanese President Ma Ying-jeou undertook an official visit to Nauru, where discussions focused on the topics of agricultural co-operation and food safety. In October the Nauruan Minister of Foreign Affairs and Trade, Dr Kieren Keke, visited Taiwan, whereupon he met with President Ma. During Keke's visit, a bilateral agreement was signed exempting visa requirements for travel between Nauru and Taiwan by diplomatic and government officials. Proposals regarding 'green energy' projects were also discussed. By mid-2011 aid from Taiwan had enabled the installation of some 155 solar-powered street lights in Nauru, and in November of that year it was announced that Taiwan's health aid to Nauru was to be doubled.

Nauru was persistently critical of France's use of the South Pacific region for the testing of nuclear weapons, and was one of the most vociferous opponents of the French Government's decision in mid-1995 to resume its testing programme. Diplomatic relations, suspended between the two countries in 1995, were formally resumed in December 1997. In February 2010 Nauru was included on a list of 18 countries and territories deemed unco-operative by the French Government with regard to the issues of transparency in the financial sector and compliance with international tax reporting standards. Nauru remained on updated lists released in April 2011 and 2012.

Nauru attracted considerable controversy in June 2005 when, at a meeting of the International Whaling Commission (IWC) in the Republic of Korea, it voted with Japan to remove the moratorium on commercial whaling introduced in 1986. Japan was accused by some observers of encouraging small, developing countries to join the IWC and of then attempting to influence their voting with financial incentives. Nauru denied that it had been subjected to any form of manipulation by the Japanese Government, stating that it had voted to remove the ban on whaling in order to preserve its tuna stocks.

Further international controversy ensued in December 2009 when it was revealed that, in exchange for a commitment of Russian aid reportedly totalling US $50m., Nauru had accorded diplomatic recognition to the secessionist republics of Abkhazia and South Ossetia. Nauru's recognition of these separatist regions of Georgia drew widespread criticism. The Nauruan Minister of Foreign Affairs, Dr Kieren Keke, visited South Ossetia, as well as the Russian capital of Moscow, for discussions. As part of the agreement, Russia released funding of $9m. in mid-2010, to be disbursed on vital repair work on Nauru's port and moorings.

CONSTITUTION AND GOVERNMENT

Under the Constitution of 1968, legislative power is vested in the unicameral Parliament, with 18 members elected by universal adult suffrage for a term of three years. Executive authority is vested in a Cabinet, which consists of the President of the Republic, elected by Parliament, and ministers appointed by him. The Cabinet is collectively responsible to Parliament. For administrative purposes the country is divided into 14 districts, which are themselves grouped into eight electoral constituencies.

REGIONAL AND INTERNATIONAL CO-OPERATION

Nauru is a member of the Pacific Community (see p. 422), of the Pacific Islands Forum (see p. 426) and of the Asian Development Bank (ADB, see p. 214), all of which aim to promote regional development. The country is also a member of the UN's Economic and Social Commission for Asia and the Pacific (ESCAP, see p. 31), having joined the UN in 1999.

ECONOMIC AFFAIRS

In 2011, according to the UN, Nauru's gross domestic product (GDP), measured at current prices, was US $71.7m., equivalent to US $6,954 per head. In 2002–11, it was estimated, GDP increased, in real terms, at an average annual rate of 0.8%, while the population increased by an average of 0.3% per year. Having shown no discernible growth in 2010, real GDP increased by 4.0% in 2011. According to the Asian Development Bank (ADB), real GDP rose by 4.9% in 2011/12.

Agricultural activity comprises mainly the small-scale production of tropical fruit, vegetables and livestock, although the production of coffee and copra for export is increasingly significant. According to FAO estimates, agriculture and fishing engaged some 20% of the economically active population in mid-2013. The sector provided 5.9% of GDP in 2011. Coconuts are the principal crop. Bananas, pineapples and the screw-pine (*Pandanus*) are also cultivated as food crops, while the islanders keep pigs and chickens. Almost all of Nauru's requirements are imported. Increased exploitation of the island's marine resources was envisaged following the approval by Parliament of new fisheries legislation in the late 1990s. However, the sector failed to develop as hoped, and in early 2009 it was reported that a fisheries adviser, funded by Australia, had been engaged. Meanwhile, revenue from fishing licence fees issued to foreign fleets totalled an estimated $A7m. in 2005/06. According to the UN, agricultural GDP decreased, in real terms, at an average annual rate of 3.8% during 2002–11. Sectoral GDP increased by 52.3% in 2010, but decreased by 13.2% in 2011.

Industrial activity (mining, manufacturing, construction and utilities) accounted for 47.3% of GDP in 2011. In real terms, according to UN figures, industrial GDP increased at an average annual rate of 26.1% during 2002–11. Sectoral GDP declined by 30.3% in 2010, but rose by 21.5% in 2011.

Mining and utilities contributed 22.8% of GDP in 2011. Nauru's economy has traditionally been based on the mining of phosphate rock, which constituted four-fifths of the island's surface area. Phosphate extraction was conducted largely by indentured labour, notably by I-Kiribati and Tuvaluan workers. Revenue from phosphate sales was invested in a long-term trust fund, the Nauru Phosphate Royalties Trust (NPRT—see below), and the (now defunct) Nauru Local Government Council. As the depletion of primary (surface) deposits continued, in 2004 an Australian company undertook a survey of the island's potential for secondary phosphate mining. The discovery of substantial new reserves of high-grade phosphate was announced in 2005. In September 2006, following the upgrading of processing facilities, the first major shipment of phosphate for nearly 10 years was exported to India. However, subsequent operations were intermittently disrupted when the island's port facilities were damaged in recurrent storms. In 2011 Nauru Ocean Resources was granted a contract by the International Seabed Authority to explore for deep sea minerals in an area of the north-eastern Pacific Ocean reserved for developing states. According to UN figures, the combined GDP of the mining and utilities sectors declined by 20.6% in 2010, but rose by 15.2% in 2011.

Manufacturing accounted for 19.9% of GDP in 2011, while the construction sector contributed 4.6%. In real terms, according to UN figures, manufacturing GDP increased by 21.4% during 2002–11; sectoral GDP decreased by 46.5% in 2010, before expanding by 36.9% in 2011. During 2002–11, according to UN figures, the GDP of the construction sector contracted at an average annual rate of 0.9%; sectoral GDP rose by 23.1% in 2010, but declined by 0.1% in 2011.

Energy is derived principally from imported petroleum. Output of electrical energy totalled 35.0m. kWh in 2008. Electricity supplies remained intermittent for some years until August 2009, when the upgrading of the island's generators was completed.

The services sector, accounting for 46.8% of Nauru's GDP in 2011, comprises mainly those employed in public service. There is no real tourism sector, and banking services are not widely available. In real terms, the GDP of the services sector decreased at an average annual rate of 4.6% during 2002–11, according to UN figures. The sector's GDP increased by 29.9% in 2010, but declined by 4.9% in 2011.

According to the ADB, a merchandise trade surplus of US $36.9m. was recorded in 2011. The deficit on the current account of the balance of payments was estimated at 10.3% of GDP in 2006/07. According to the ADB, in 2008 the value of Nauru's exports rose by an estimated 570.7% (owing to strong phosphate sales). Exports increased by 26.1% in 2011, in comparison with the previous year, while the cost of imports grew by 46.6%. The principal imports in 2005 were manufactured goods and other manufactured articles (40.4% of total imports), along with machinery and transport equipment, food and live animals. The main exports in 2005 included manufactured goods and crude materials. Phosphate has traditionally been the most important export. The principal export market in 2011 was the Republic of Korea (which purchased 64.8% of the total); Australia, New Zealand and India were also important purchasers. The principal source of Nauru's imports in that year was Australia (providing 54.5% of the total); the Republic of Korea was also a significant supplier.

The 2011/12 budget envisaged government expenditure of $A32.5m. (excluding donor-finded development projects). The ADB estimated a budget deficit equivalent to 1.2% of GDP in that year. Development assistance from Australia was projected at $A31.8m. for 2012/13. Under the Australia-Nauru Partnership for Development signed in 2009, aid was to be directed to five priority areas, including infrastructure and services, improvements in the public sector and the promotion of the private sector. Nauru's external debt was estimated by the ADB at US $63m. in 2010. In 2009 the cost of servicing external debt was equivalent to 2.1% of the value of exports of goods and services. The Government's domestic debt was estimated at $A481m. in September 2010. Consumer prices increased by 17.9% in 2000, but inflation subsequently moderated. Consumer prices declined by 3.5% in 2010/11 and by 0.5% in 2011/12. The rate of unemployment in 2002 was estimated at 22.7% of the labour force.

After gaining independence in 1968, Nauru benefited from sole control of earnings from phosphate mining, and as a result its income per head was among the highest in the world. However, through a combination of profligate spending and poor investment choices, the assets of the NPRT were estimated to have decreased from $A1,300m. in 1991 to only $A300m. in 2003, and in 2004 the portfolio was placed into receivership. In November 2005 Nauru hosted an international donor meeting, at which it requested support for its National Sustainable Development Strategy (2005–25). The aims of this long-term programme included greater revenue from phosphate production, better use of fisheries resources and the encouragement of agricultural activities, with particular emphasis on local food production. In August 2009 the Pacific Islands Forum agreed that its Pacific Regional Assistance to Nauru initiative, which had commenced in 2004, could be concluded, owing to the economic progress made by Nauru. However, Australia's closure in 2008 of an offshore processing centre for asylum seekers, from which Nauru had derived substantial revenue, had a major impact on the island's economy. The reopening of the centre in September 2012 meant that the island would once again benefit from the considerable payments made by the Australian authorities; there were reports that the Nauruan Government could expect to receive as much as $A90m. over a five-year period for housing up to 1,500 asylum seekers. Nauru remained heavily dependent on external support, with budgetary expenditure funded by foreign donors totalling $A33.6m. in 2011/12. Furthermore, the high level of public debt continued to be a major concern. The economy was impeded by the suspension of Parliament for much of 2010, as a result of which the enactment of the annual budget was delayed by four months. The political upheaval in early 2013 was also expected to have an adverse effect on the economy. Nevertheless, following a sharp contraction in 2008/09 and stagnation in 2009/10, GDP increased by 3.8% in 2010/11 and by 4.9% in 2011/12, according to the ADB, mainly owing to increased revenue from phosphate exports. The ADB anticipated GDP growth of 8.0% for 2012/13. In 2011 the ADB agreed to assist Nauru in the estab-lishment of a new trust fund; the Nauruan Parliament approved the Nauru Trust Fund Bill in February 2012.

PUBLIC HOLIDAYS

2014: 1 January (New Year's Day), 31 January (Independence Day), 18 April (Good Friday), 21–22 April (Easter), 19 May (for Constitution Day), 27 October (for Angam Day), 25–26 December (Christmas).

Statistical Survey

Source (unless otherwise indicated): Bureau of Statistics, Ministry of Finance, Government Offices, Yaren District; tel. 444-3142; fax 444-3125; e-mail statistics@naurugov.nr; internet www.spc.int/prism/country/nr/stats.

AREA AND POPULATION

Area: 21.3 sq km (8.2 sq miles).

Population: 8,042 (Nauruan 4,964, Other Pacific Islanders 2,134, Asians 682, Caucasians—mainly Australians and New Zealanders—262) at census of 13 May 1983; 9,919 at census of 17 April 1992; 10,065 (males 5,136, females 4,929) at census of 23 September 2002; 9,945 (males 5,031, females 4,914) at census of 30 October 2011 (preliminary).

Density (at 2011 census): 466.9 per sq km.

Population by Age and Sex (Secretariat of the Pacific Community estimates at mid-2012): *0–14:* 3,657 (males 1,864, females 1,793); *15–64:* 6,592 (males 3,349, females 3,243); *65 and over:* 144 (males 69, females 75); *Total* 10,393 (males 5,282, females 5,111). Note: Estimates not adjusted to take account of 2011 census results (Source: Pacific Regional Information System).

Principal Districts (population at 2011 census): Meneng 1,380; Aiwo 1,220; Boe 851; Yaren (capital) 747; Buada 739.

Births, Marriages and Deaths (Secretariat of the Pacific Community estimates, 2010, unless otherwise indicated): Registered live births 294 (birth rate 29.8 per 1,000); Marriages (registrations, 1995) 57 (marriage rate 5.3 per 1,000); Registered deaths 88 (death rate 8.9 per 1,000).

Life Expectancy (years at birth, WHO estimates): 60 (males 56; females 65) in 2009. Source: WHO, *World Health Statistics.*

Economically Active Population (census of 17 April 1992): 2,007 (Elementary occupations 401, Clerks and office workers 355, Craft and related workers 299, Service, shop and market sales workers 250, Professionals 208, Plant, machine operators and assemblers 136, Technicians and associate professionals 115, Legislators, senior officials and managers 18, Agriculture and related workers 2, Not classified 223). *2002* (census of 23 September): Total employed 2,534; Unemployed 746; Total labour force 3,280. *Mid-2013* (estimates): Agriculture, etc. 1,000; Total labour force 5,000 (Source: FAO).

HEALTH AND WELFARE

Key Indicators

Total Fertility Rate (children per woman, 2010): 3.1.

Under-5 Mortality Rate (per 1,000 live births, 2010): 40.

Physicians (per 1,000 head, 2010): 0.7.

Hospital Beds (per 1,000 head, 2010): 5.0.

Health Expenditure (2009): US $ per head (PPP): 256.

Health Expenditure (2009): % of GDP: 11.2.

Health Expenditure (2009): public (% of total): 68.5.

For sources and definitions, see explanatory note on p. vi.

AGRICULTURE, ETC.

Principal Crop and Livestock (2011, FAO estimates): Coconuts 2,579 metric tons; Pigs 3,000 head; Chickens 5,000 head.

Livestock Products (metric tons, 2011, FAO estimates): Pig meat 72; Chicken meat 4; Hen eggs 16.

Fishing (metric tons, live weight of capture, 2010, FAO estimates): Yellowfin tuna 8; Bigeye tuna 2; Skipjack tuna 10; Total catch (incl. other marine fishes) 200.

Source: FAO.

MINING

Phosphate Rock ('000 metric tons, estimates): 84 in 2003; 22 in 2004; 11 in 2005. The phosphoric acid content ('000 metric tons, estimates) was: 26 in 2003; 7 in 2004; 3 in 2005. Source: US Geological Survey.

INDUSTRY

Electric Energy (million kWh): 33 in 2006; 34 in 2007; 35 in 2008. Source: UN Industrial Commodity Statistics Database.

FINANCE

Currency and Exchange Rates: Australian currency: 100 cents = 1 Australian dollar ($A). *Sterling, US Dollar and Euro Equivalents* (31 December 2012): £1 sterling = $A1.5166; US $1 = $A0.9611; €1 = $A1.2680; $A100 = £65.94 = US $104.05 = €78.86. *Average Exchange Rate* (Australian dollars per US $): 1.0902 in 2010; 0.9695 in 2011; 0.9658 in 2012.

Budget ($A '000, year ending 30 June 2007, budget forecasts): *Total Revenue:* 22,288 (Tax revenue 8,646, Non-tax revenue 13,643); *Total Expenditure:* 22,226 (Employee expenses 5,890, Operating expenses 8,543, Property expenses 505, Current transfers 2,150, Gross fixed capital formation 4,682, Other 457). *2010:* Total revenue (incl. grants) 57,800; Total expenditure (incl. net lending) 57,800 (Source: Asian Development Bank).

Gross Domestic Product ($A '000, year ending 30 June at current prices): 69,540 in 2009; 69,114 in 2010; 69,493 in 2011. Source: Asian Development Bank.

Expenditure on the Gross Domestic Product ($A million at current prices, 2011): Government final consumption expenditure 26.1; Private final consumption expenditure 68.0; Increase in stocks 0.2; Gross fixed capital formation 29.3; *Total domestic expenditure* 123.6; Exports of goods and services 9.0; *Less* Imports of goods and services 63.1; *GDP in purchasers' values* 69.5 (Source: UN, National Accounts Main Aggregates Database).

Gross Domestic Product by Economic Activity ($A million at current prices, 2011): Agriculture, hunting and fishing 3.6; Mining and utilities 14.0; Manufacturing 12.2 Construction 2.8; Retail trade and hotel and restaurants 11.8; Transport, storage and communications 6.6 Other services 10.3; *Sub-total* 61.3; Net indirect taxes (obtained as residual) 8.2; *GDP in market prices* 69.5 (Source: UN, National Accounts Main Aggregates Database).

EXTERNAL TRADE

Principal Commodities (US $ '000, year ending 30 June 2005): *Imports:* Food and live animals 4,548; Beverages and tobacco 1,891; Crude materials (except food and fuel) 1,741; Mineral fuels and lubricants 1,528; Animal fats and vegetable oils 1,698; Chemical products 3,300; Manufactured goods 11,898; Machinery and transport equipment 5,375; Miscellaneous manufactured articles 1,705; Total (incl. others) 33,683. *Exports:* Food and live animals 293; Crude materials (except food and fuel) 1,489; Chemical products 408; Manufactured goods 2,039; Machinery and transport equipment 616; Miscellaneous manufactured articles 113; Total (incl. others) 4,959.

Principal Trading Partners (US $ million, year ending 31 December 2011): *Imports:* Australia 17.5; Fiji 1.3; Korea, Republic of 9.4; USA 0.4; Total (incl. others) 32.1. *Exports:* Australia 10.0; India 5.1; Korea, Republic 44.7; New Zealand 5.9; Total (incl. others) 69.0. Source: Asian Development Bank.

Trade Totals (US $ million, year ending 31 December): *Imports c.i.f.:* 102.5 in 2009; 21.9 in 2010; 32.1 in 2011. *Exports f.o.b.:* 24.9 in 2009; 54.7 in 2010; 69.0 in 2011. Source: Asian Development Bank.

TRANSPORT

Road Traffic (1989): 1,448 registered motor vehicles.

Shipping: *Flag Registered Fleet* (at 31 December 2012): Vessel 1; Displacement 948 grt. Source: Lloyd's List Intelligence (www.lloyd-slistintelligence.com). *International Freight Traffic* (estimates, '000 metric tons, 1990): Goods loaded 1,650; Goods unloaded 59. Source: UN, *Monthly Bulletin of Statistics*.

Civil Aviation (traffic on scheduled services, 2009): Kilometres flown (million) 4; Passengers carried ('000) 210; Passenger-km (million) 354; Total ton-km (million) 35. Source: UN, *Statistical Yearbook*.

COMMUNICATIONS MEDIA

Telephones (main lines, 2009): 1,900 in use.

Mobile Cellular Telephones (2011): 6,700 subscribers.

Internet Users: 300 in 2005.

Broadband Subscribers (2010): 400.

Source: International Telecommunication Union.

EDUCATION

Pre-primary (2008 unless otherwise indicated): 4 schools (2007); 42 teachers; 663 pupils.

Primary (2008 unless otherwise indicated): 2 schools (2007); 56 teachers; 1,254 pupils.

Secondary (2008 unless otherwise indicated): 4 schools (2007); 57 teachers; 816 pupils.

Vocational (2003 unless otherwise indicated): 2 schools (2004); 4 teachers; 38 students.

Pupil-teacher Ratio (primary education, UNESCO estimate): 22.4 in 2007/08 (Source: UNESCO Institute for Statistics).

Note: Nauruans studying at secondary and tertiary levels overseas in 2001 numbered 85.

Source: Department of Education, Yaren, Nauru.

Directory

The Government

HEAD OF STATE

President: SPRENT DABWIDO (elected 15 November 2011).

CABINET
(May 2013)

President and Minister of Public Service, Home Affairs, Police and Emergency Services, Climate Change and Nauru Phosphate Royalties Trust: SPRENT DABWIDO.

Minister for Transport, Telecommunications, Utilities, Nauru Air Corporation, and Commerce, Industry and Environment: RIDDELL AKUA.

Minister for Justice, Republic of Nauru Phosphate (RONPHOS), Nauru Rehabilitation Corporation, Finance and Sustainable Development, Sport, Fisheries, and Foreign Affairs and Trade: ROLAND KUN.

Minister for Education: ALOYSIUS AMWANO.

Minister for Health: SHADLOG BERNICKE.

MINISTRIES

Office of the President: Yaren; tel. 557-3133; fax 444-3776; e-mail andromeda.amram@naurugov.nr.

Ministry of Commerce, Industry and Resources: Yaren; tel. 444-3133; fax 444-3188; e-mail minister.cir@naurugov.nr.

Ministry of Education: Yaren; tel. 444-3130; fax 444-3718; e-mail minister.education@naurugov.nr.

Ministry of Finance: Government Offices, Yaren; tel. 557-3133; e-mail minister.finance@naurugov.nr.

Ministry of Fisheries: e-mail minister.fisheries@naurugov.nr.

Ministry of Foreign Affairs and Trade: Government Offices, Yaren; tel. 444-3133; e-mail minister.foreignaffairs@naurugov.nr.

Ministry of Health: Yaren; tel. 444-3133; fax 444-3188; e-mail minister.health@naurugov.nr.

Ministry of Home Affairs: Yaren; fax 444-3891; e-mail minister.homeaffairs@naurugov.nr.

Ministry of Justice: Yaren; tel. 444-3160; fax 444-3108; e-mail minister.justice@naurugov.nr.

Ministry for the Nauru Phosphate Royalties Trust: Yaren; e-mail minister.nprt@naurugov.nr.

Ministry of Police: e-mail minister.police@naurugov.nr.

Ministry of Public Service: e-mail minister.publicservice@naurugov.nr.

Ministry of Sport: Yaren; e-mail minister.sport@naurugov.nr.

Ministry of Telecommunications: Yaren; e-mail minister.telecommunications@naurugov.nr.

Ministry of Transport: Yaren; tel. 444-3133; fax 444-3136; e-mail minister.transport@naurugov.nr.

Ministry of Utilities: e-mail minister.utilities@naurugov.nr.

Legislature

PARLIAMENT

Parliament comprises 18 members. The general election held on 24 April 2010 failed to produce a conclusive result, with all 18 incumbent legislators being returned to office. A fresh election was therefore conducted on 19 June, when one of the nine opposition members was defeated. On 9 March 2013 the Speaker dissolved Parliament and announced that a general election would take place on 6 April. However, on 15 March the Supreme Court ruled that the adjournment of Parliament had been unconstitutional and that it was consequently null and void (as was the writ issued for the general election), ordering the Speaker to reconvene Parliament within 28 days. The two subsequent sittings of Parliament were boycotted by a number of legislators and could not reach a quorum. At a sitting on 23 April there were sufficient legislators present, but there were no candidates to replace the Speaker who had resigned the previous week. (A debate on the proposed dissolution of Parliament could not take place without a Speaker.) Although a new Speaker was elected on 25 April, the impasse continued at early May, as several subsequent sittings of Parliament were adjourned owing to a repeated failure to achieve a quorum.

Speaker: GODFREY THOMA.

Political Organizations

Democratic Party of Nauru: c/o Parliament House, Yaren; f. 1987; revival of Nauru Party (f. 1975); Leader KENNAN ADEANG.

Naoero Amo (Nauru First): c/o Parliament House, Yaren; e-mail visionary@naoeroamo.com; f. 2001; Co-Leaders DAVID ADEANG, Dr KIEREN KEKE.

Diplomatic Representation

EMBASSY AND HIGH COMMISSION IN NAURU

Australia: MQ45 NPC OE, Aiwo; tel. 557-3380; fax 557-3382; e-mail george.fraser@dfat.gov.au; High Commissioner BRUCE COWLED.

Taiwan (Republic of China): Civic Centre, 1st Floor, Aiwo; tel. 557-3333; e-mail nru@mofa.gov.tw; internet www.taiwanembassy.org/nr; Ambassador TIMOTHY HSIANG.

Judicial System

The Chief Justice presides over the Supreme Court, which exercises original, appellate and advisory jurisdiction. The Resident Magistrate presides over the District Court, and he also acts as Coroner under the Inquests Act 1977. The Supreme Court is a court of record. The Family Court consists of three members, one being the Resident Magistrate as Chairman, and two other members drawn from a panel of Nauruans. The Chief Justice is Chairman of the Public Services Appeals Board and of the Police Appeals Board.

Supreme Court: Yaren; tel. 444-3163; fax 444-3104; Chief Justice GEOFFREY EAMES (non-resident).

Resident Magistrate of the District Court and Chairman of the Family Court: PETER LAW.

Religion

Nauruans are predominantly Christians, adhering either to the Nauruan Protestant Church or to the Roman Catholic Church.

Nauruan Protestant Church: Head Office, Nauru; Moderator (vacant).

Roman Catholic Church: POB 224, Nauru; tel. and fax 444-3708; e-mail taewenteangmsc@gmail.com; Nauru forms part of the diocese of Tarawa and Nauru, comprising Kiribati and Nauru. The Bishop resides on Tarawa Atoll, Kiribati.

The Press

Mwinen Ko: Nauru; f. 2010; fortnightly; est. with assistance from AusAID (the Australian Govt's aid agency); Editor SANDRA BILL.

Broadcasting and Communications

TELECOMMUNICATIONS

Digicel Nauru Ltd: Ground Floor, Aiwo Civic Centre, Aiwo; e-mail Nauru_CC_Agents@digicelgroup.com; internet www.digicelnauru.com; f. 2009; a joint venture between Digicel Group and the Nauru Govt; mobile services.

Nauru Telecommunications Service: ICT Centre, Civic Centre Complex, Aiwo, Nauru; tel. 444-3324; fax 444-3111; e-mail director.ict@naurugov.nr.

BROADCASTING

Radio

Nauru Broadcasting Service: Information and Broadcasting Services, Chief Secretary's Department, POB 77, Nauru; tel. 444-3133; fax 444-3153; f. 1968; state-owned and non-commercial; broadcasts in the mornings in English and Nauruan; operates Radio Nauru; Station Man. RIN TSITSI; Man. Dir GARY TURNER.

Television

Nauru Television (NTV): Nauru; tel. 444-3133; fax 444-3153; began operations in June 1991; govt-owned; broadcasts 24 hrs per day on 3 channels; most of the programmes are supplied by foreign TV companies via satellite or on videotape; a weekly current affairs programme is produced locally; Man. MICHAEL DEKARUBE; Dir of Media ROD HENSHAW (acting).

Finance

BANKING

Nauru's only bank, the state-owned Bank of Nauru, ceased operations in 2006, owing to insolvency. A liquidator was appointed in 2011 to finalize its formal closure.

INSURANCE

Nauru Insurance Corporation: POB 82, Nauru; tel. 444-3346; fax 444-3731; f. 1974; sole licensed insurer and reinsurer in Nauru; Chair. NIMES EKWONA.

Trade and Industry

GOVERNMENT AGENCIES

Nauru Agency Corporation: Civic Centre, 1st Floor, POB 300, Aiwo; tel. 558-7301; e-mail info@nauruoffshore.com; internet www.nauruoffshore.com; f. 1972; management service to assist entrepreneurs in the incorporation of holding and trading corpns and the procurement of trust and insurance licences; CEO R. MOSES.

Nauru Corporation: Civic Centre, Yaren; f. 1925; operated by the Nauru Council; the major retailer in Nauru; Gen. Man. A. EPHRAIM.

Nauru Fisheries and Marine Resources Authority: POB 449, Aiwo; tel. 444-3733; fax 444-3812; e-mail nfmra@cenpac.net.nr; f. 1997; CEO CHARLESTON DEIYE.

Nauru Phosphate Royalties Trust (NPRT): Nauru; statutory corpn; invests phosphate royalties to provide govt revenue; extensive int. interests, incl. hotels and real estate; assets put into receivership in 2004; legislation providing for the establishment of a new Nauru trust fund was adopted in Feb. 2012; Sec. NIRAL FERNANDO.

Nauru Rehabilitation Corporation (NRC): Camp Ibaganiquane, Meneng; tel. and fax 444-3200; e-mail nrcadmin8464@gmail.com; internet www.nrurehab.org.nr; f. 1999; manages and devises programmes for the rehabilitation of those parts of the island damaged by the over-mining of phosphate; CEO REYNOLD DAVID.

UTILITIES

Eigigu Holding Corporation: Civic Centre, Aiwo; tel. 557-8011; public works, water and waste management; also has interests in supermarket retail and television broadcast distribution; Chair. DAVID AINGIMEA.

Nauru Central Utilities (Nauru Utilities Authority): Aiwo; tel. 444-3247; fax 444-3521; e-mail apisake.soakai@naurugov.nr; f. 1968; sole electricity provider; CEO APISAKE SOAKAI.

RONPhos Corporation (Republic of Nauru Phosphate Company): Aiwo; tel. 444-3839; fax 444-2752; f. 1967; est. as Nauru Phosphate Corpn; has operated the phosphate industry and several public services of the Republic of Nauru (including provision of electricity) on behalf of the Nauruan people; present name adopted in 2005 following reorganization; Chair. RIDDELL AKUA; Gen. Man. LESI OLSSON.

Transport

RAILWAYS

There are 5.2 km of 0.9-m gauge railway serving the phosphate workings.

ROADS

A sealed road, 16 km long, circles the island, and another serves Buada District.

SHIPPING

In 1998 finance was secured from the Japanese Government for the construction of a harbour in Anibare district, which was opened in 2000.

Nauru Pacific: Government Bldg, Yaren; tel. 444-3133; f. 1969; operates cargo charter services to ports in Australia, New Zealand, Asia, the Pacific and the west coast of the USA; Man. Dir (vacant).

CIVIL AVIATION

There is one airport, Nauru International Airport, which is served solely by Our Airlines.

Our Airline: Directorate of Civil Aviation, Government Offices, POB 40, Yaren; tel. and fax 557-7000; e-mail info@ourairline.com.au; internet www.ourairline.com.au; f. 1970; fmrly Air Nauru; name changed as above in 2006; operates passenger and cargo services to Kiribati, Fiji, Solomon Islands and Australia; Chair. Capt. KEVIN POWER; CEO KARAM CHAND.

Tourism

There is no tourism industry on the island.

Defence

Nauru has no defence forces. Under an informal agreement, Australia is responsible for the defence of the island.

Education

Education is free and compulsory for children between the ages of six and 16. In 2007 the island had four pre-primary schools, with 663 pupils and 42 teachers in 2008. In 2007 the island had two primary schools and four secondary schools. In 2008 a total of 1,254 pupils were enrolled in primary education with 56 teachers, and 816 pupils in secondary education with 57 teachers. In addition, there were two vocational training schools in 2004. An extension centre of the University of the South Pacific, based in Suva, Fiji, was opened in Nauru in the late 1980s.

NEPAL

Introductory Survey

LOCATION, CLIMATE, LANGUAGE, RELIGION, FLAG, CAPITAL

The Federal Democratic Republic of Nepal is a land-locked Asian country in the Himalaya mountain range, with India to the east, south and west, and Tibet (the Xizang Autonomous Region), in the People's Republic of China, to the north. The climate varies sharply with altitude, from arctic on the higher peaks of the Himalaya mountains (where the air temperature is permanently below freezing point) to humid subtropical in the central valley of Kathmandu, which is warm and sunny in summer. Temperatures in Kathmandu, which is 1,337 m (4,386 ft) above sea-level, are generally between 2°C (35°F) and 30°C (86°F), with an annual average of 11°C (52°F). The rainy season is between June and October. Average annual rainfall varies from about 1,000 mm (40 ins) in western Nepal to about 2,500 mm (100 ins) in the east. The official language is Nepali, which was spoken by 48.6% of the population in 2001. Other languages include Maithir (12.3% in 2001) and Bhojpuri (7.5%). Some 80.6% of the population were Hindus in 2001, with 10.7% Buddhists and 4.2% Muslims. The national flag (proportions 4 by 3) is composed of two crimson pennants, each with a blue border. The upper section contains a white crescent moon (horns upwards and surmounted by a disc with eight rays) and the lower section a white sun in splendour. The capital is Kathmandu.

CONTEMPORARY POLITICAL HISTORY

Historical Context

Although Nepal was an hereditary monarchy, for more than 100 years, until 1951, effective control over the country was wielded by the Rana family, who created the post of hereditary Prime Minister. A popular revolution, led by the Nepali Congress Party (NCP), ousted the Ranas and restored King Tribhuvan to power. A limited constitutional monarchy was established in 1951. During most of the 1950s government was controlled by the monarchy, initially under Tribhuvan and then, after his death in 1955, under his son, Mahendra. In February 1959 King Mahendra promulgated Nepal's first Constitution, providing for a bicameral parliament, including a popularly elected lower house. Elections held later that month resulted in victory for the NCP, led by Bisweswor Prasad (B. P.) Koirala, who became Prime Minister. However, the King retained a certain degree of power, and persistent differences between the King and the Prime Minister led to a royal coup in December 1960: Nepal's first brief period of democracy was thus brought to an abrupt end. The King dismissed the Council of Ministers and dissolved Parliament. A royal decree of January 1961 banned political parties. King Mahendra accused the Koirala administration of corruption, and in December 1962 he introduced a new Constitution, reasserting absolute royal power and providing for a 'partyless' system of government, based on the Panchayat (village council), with a Prime Minister appointed by the King. In January 1972 King Mahendra died and was succeeded by his son, Birendra. In December 1975 the Government made major changes to the Constitution, which allowed for a widening of the franchise and more frequent elections to the Rashtriya Panchayat (National Assembly), but in no way were the King's powers eroded.

Domestic Political Affairs

B. P. Koirala, the former Prime Minister and an advocate of parliamentary democracy, was acquitted of treason in February 1978. Returning from abroad a year later, he was placed under house arrest in April 1979, but was subsequently released, partly to appease students who had been demonstrating for reforms. National unrest grew and, after King Birendra announced in May that there would be a national referendum on whether to restore multi-party democracy, Prime Minister Kirti Nidhi Bista resigned and was succeeded by Surya Bahadur Thapa. In the referendum, held in May 1980, 54.8% of the voters supported the Panchayat system with reforms. As a result, the King formed a Constitutional Reforms Commission, and in December he issued a decree under which amendments to the Constitution were made, including the proviso that the appointment of the Prime Minister by the King would henceforth be on the recommendation of the Rashtriya Panchayat. In accordance with the new provisions, direct legislative elections were held in May 1981, the first of their kind since 1959, although still on a non-party basis. Thapa was re-elected by the Rashtriya Panchayat as Prime Minister in June 1981, and the King installed a new Council of Ministers (on the recommendation of the Prime Minister). An extensive ministerial reorganization took place in October 1982, but this failed to stem increasing official corruption and economic mismanagement. In July 1983, for the first time in the 23-year history of the Panchayat system, the incumbent Prime Minister, Thapa, was ousted, and a new Council of Ministers was formed by a former Chairman of the Rashtriya Panchayat, Lokendra Bahadur Chand, who had successfully introduced a motion expressing no confidence in Thapa.

The rise of the Nepali Congress Party and the restoration of multi-party democracy

In May 1985 the NCP embarked upon a campaign of civil disobedience, aimed at restoring a multi-party political system and parliamentary rule under a constitutional monarchy. In June there was a series of bomb explosions, resulting in loss of life. The explosions were apparently co-ordinated by two newly formed anti-monarchist and anti-Government groups, the Janawadi Morcha (Democratic Front) and the Samyukta Mukti Bahini (United Liberation Torch-bearers). These bombings united an otherwise seriously divided legislature against the terrorists, and forced the predominantly moderate opposition to abandon the campaign of civil disobedience and to disclaim any responsibility for the explosions. In August the Rashtriya Panchayat approved a stringent anti-terrorist law, and more than 1,000 people were arrested in connection with the unrest.

In May 1986 about 64% of the electorate voted in a general election, despite appeals by the NCP and the pro-China faction of the Communist Party of Nepal (CPN) (neither of which presented candidates) for a boycott of the polls. All the candidates in the election were nominally independents, but it was reported that among the 72 new entrants to the Rashtriya Panchayat were at least 16 members of the Marxist-Leninist faction of the CPN. In June the King nominated 25 additional members of the new Rashtriya Panchayat, and Marich Man Singh Shrestha (previously Chairman of the Rashtriya Panchayat) was elected unopposed by the Assembly as the new Prime Minister. In late 1986, to counter the growing influence of the communist faction in the Rashtriya Panchayat, several senior figures established a 'Democratic Panchayat Forum', which expressed full support for the non-party system.

In November 1989 several political groups dissatisfied with the country's non-party system convened to discuss the formation of a country-wide, peaceful 'movement for the restoration of democracy' to work towards the alleviation of Nepal's severe economic problems, the transfer from absolute to constitutional monarchy, the immediate replacement of the Panchayat Government by an interim national government, the removal of the ban on political activities, and the introduction of a multi-party system. The so-called Jana Andolan (People's Movement) was formalized in January 1990 by the NCP and the newly formed United Left Front (ULF—which was led by Sahana Pradhan and comprised six factions of the CPN and a labour group). The Government responded to the new movement with a campaign of arrests and censorship; violent demonstrations, strikes and mass arrests ensued. The Government's aggressive approach to the Jana Andolan reportedly prompted criticism within its ranks and resulted in an extensive ministerial reorganization. In an effort to end the political unrest, the King dismissed Shrestha's Government on 6 April and nominated a restricted four-member Council of Ministers, under the leadership of the more moderate Chand. The Government initiated talks with the opposition, and on 8 April the King announced that the 30-year ban on political parties was to be ended, thus enabling the future holding of multi-party elections, and that a commission to study constitutional reform was to be established. The Jana Andolan suspended its campaign of demonstrations, but many political activists continued to agitate, demanding the removal of the formal structure of the Panchayat system. A week later, the King accepted Prime Minister Chand's resignation, dismissed the Council of Ministers and announced the dissolution of the Rashtriya Panchayat. King Birendra then invited the opposition alliance of the NCP and the ULF to form an interim government. On 19 April a new coalition Council of Ministers (including two ministers nominated by the King and two independents), under the premiership of the President of the NCP, Krishna Prasad (K. P.) Bhattarai, was sworn in. The new Prime Minister announced that a general election would be held, on a multi-party basis, within a year. The principal task of the interim Government was to prepare a new constitution in accordance with the spirit of multi-party democracy and constitutional monarchy. King Birendra stated that he was committed to transforming his role into that of a constitutional monarch.

In May 1990 the King delegated the legislative powers of the dissolved Rashtriya Panchayat to the new Council of Ministers, empowering it to enact, amend and repeal legislation in order to facilitate the introduction of multi-party democracy. A Constitutional Recommendation Commission was established to prepare a draft constitution within three months. A general amnesty for all political prisoners was announced in May, and in July the death sentence was abolished and the laws restricting freedom of the press and freedom of association were repealed. The draft of the new Constitution, which was published at the end of August, recommended the introduction of a constitutional monarchy; a democratic multi-party system and a bicameral legislature, composed of a 205-member House of Representatives (Pratinidhi Sabha) and a 60-member National Assembly (Rashtriya Sabha); the official guarantee of fundamental rights (including freedom of expression); an independent judiciary; and the placing of the army under the control of a National Defence Council, headed by the Prime Minister. Under the draft Constitution, the King would be allowed to declare a state of emergency on the advice of the Council of Ministers, but such declarations would have to be approved by the House of Representatives within three months. A crucial clause under consideration required the King 'to obey and protect' the Constitution: under the old regime, the King was considered to be above the Constitution. The draft Constitution was approved by the Council of Ministers on 15 October and sent to the King for his endorsement. However, King Birendra amended the draft in a final effort to retain sovereign authority and full emergency powers. This retrograde action provoked violent protests. The Council of Ministers rejected most of the proposed amendments in the royal counter-draft, but agreed to the King's proposal to establish a Council of State (Raj Parishad), with a standing committee headed by a royal appointee; Bhattarai stressed that the committee would not function as a parallel body to the Council of Ministers. He also emphasized that the King would only be permitted to act on judicial, executive and legislative matters on the advice of the Council of Ministers. The new Constitution was officially promulgated by the King on 9 November.

The communist movement in Nepal suffered a set-back in December 1990, when four of the seven constituent members of the ULF broke away from the front, citing their lack of representation in the interim coalition Council of Ministers; the three remaining factions continued to operate as the ULF. In January 1991 two major factions of the CPN (the Marxist and Marxist-Leninist factions) merged to form the CPN (Unified Marxist-Leninist—UML).

The general election was held on 12 May 1991. The NCP contested the election alone rather than aligning itself with its former Jana Andolan partners, a move interpreted by the communists as indicative of an increased consensus between the monarchy and the NCP that the rise of communism in the country needed to be forestalled. Consequently, relations between the NCP and the UML became strained and competitive. The general election proceeded peacefully and was characterized by a high turn-out (65.2% of the electorate). The NCP won a comfortable overall majority, but it was soundly defeated by the UML in the eastern hill districts and in some parts of the Terai. In Kathmandu, supposedly an NCP stronghold, the party lost all of the seats but one. The UML established itself as the second largest party in the House of Representatives, followed by the United People's Front (UPF), an amalgam of radical, Maoist groups. The two pro-monarchy parties, the Rashtriya Prajatantra Party (Chand) and the Rashtriya Prajatantra Party (Thapa),

led by the former Prime Ministers of those names, managed only four seats between them. Acting Prime Minister Bhattarai lost his seat in the capital, and was replaced in the premiership by Girija Prasad (G. P.) Koirala, the General Secretary of the NCP and brother of the late B. P. Koirala.

The Government came under pressure in April 1992 when a *bandh* (general strike), organized by communist and other opposition parties in Kathmandu in protest against price rises, water shortages and alleged government corruption, resulted in the deaths of at least seven demonstrators following violent clashes with the police. The opposition staged a number of anti-Government protest marches and demonstrations during the following week. The success of a second general strike, which was held in May and brought Kathmandu to a standstill, demonstrated the continuing strength of the radical left.

Meanwhile, by the end of 1991 unity within the ruling NCP was threatened by growing internal dissent among its leadership, particularly between the senior leader, Ganesh Man Singh, and G. P. Koirala. Under Koirala's leadership the centrist NCP Government shifted to the right. The public image of the monarchy and leading members of the former Panchayat regime were rehabilitated and no charges were brought against senior officials of the former administration for corruption or human rights violations. Replicating the patronage system of the Panchayat regime, the NCP rapidly began to dominate the public administration structure. The ruling party's persistent failure to democratize its internal bodies and the absence of open election to posts in the party leadership met with criticism both within and outside the NCP. In addition to dissent from within the NCP leadership, G. P. Koirala was confronted with demands from the opposition to resign for proceeding with a water access agreement with India in the absence of a parliamentary vote.

In early 1993 the national UML congress abandoned much of the party's Marxist dogma and tacitly acknowledged its commitment to working within a democratic multi-party system. However, the untimely deaths of the party's General Secretary, Madan Bhandari, and Politburo member Jiv Raj Ashrit, in a road accident in May, threw the UML into disarray. The party's rejection of the findings of a government inquiry, which concluded that the deaths had been accidental, provoked nation-wide protests in support of demands for an independent inquiry into the so-called 'Dasdhunga incident'. In late May Madhav Kumar (M. K.) Nepal was appointed as the new General Secretary of the UML.

In the mean time, the rehabilitation of officials of the former Panchayat regime continued. In January 1993 the King appointed senior figures of the old administration, including former Prime Ministers Chand and Shrestha, to the 121-member Council of State. In June the right-wing Rashtriya Prajatantra Party (RPP, formed in February 1992, following a merger of the Chand and Thapa factions) held its first national conference in Kathmandu, an event that would have been inconceivable three years previously, when its leaders were forced into hiding by the democracy movement.

In August 1993 the UML signed an agreement with the NCP, providing for the permanent withdrawal of the UML from anti-Government agitation in return for the ruling party's pledge to establish an independent commission to investigate the Dasdhunga incident. However, the UPF and other left-wing groups continued their campaign of nation-wide general strikes and demonstrations. Further serious rifts became apparent within the NCP when the party's President, K. P. Bhattarai, lost a legislative by-election to the UML candidate in Kathmandu in February 1994; his defeat was widely attributed to G. P. Koirala's public opposition to his candidature. In March the Government survived a vote of no confidence (by 113 votes to 81) presented to the House of Representatives by the UML. The crisis within the NCP culminated on 10 July when followers of Ganesh Man Singh withdrew their support for Koirala, who thereby lost his parliamentary majority. Consequently, the Prime Minister offered his resignation, and on the following day the King dissolved the House of Representatives. Koirala was appointed as interim Prime Minister pending the holding of a general election, which was brought forward from mid-1996 to 15 November 1994. At the general election, which attracted a turn-out of 58%, the UML unexpectedly emerged as the single largest party, winning 88 of the 205 seats in the House of Representatives, while the NCP took 85 seats. At the end of the month the UML formed a minority Government under the premiership of its moderate Chairman, Man Mohan Adhikari. Following an attempt to avert a parliamentary no-confidence motion registered by the NCP in June 1995 (by ordering a dissolution of the legislature), the short-lived UML Government was brought down in a vote of no confidence in September, and swiftly replaced by a coalition Government composed of members of the NCP, RPP and NSP, and headed by the NCP's parliamentary leader, Sher Bahadur Deuba.

Political instability and the Maoist insurgency

In March 1996 the Government introduced a number of security measures following a series of violent clashes between a group of Maoist activists and the police in western Nepal, which resulted in the deaths of at least 11 people (by the end of the year more than 100 people had been killed as a result of the insurgency). The left-wing extremists (many of whom were members of the underground Communist Party of Nepal (Maoist)—CPN (M)—and the UPF) had launched a 'people's revolutionary war' in the hills of Nepal in February, demanding the abolition of the constitutional monarchy and the establishment of a republic. In May G. P. Koirala was elected to replace Bhattarai as President of the NCP; for the first time since its foundation, the party elected its leader by ballot. The Government suffered a set-back at the end of January 1997 when the UML, already the largest party in the House of Representatives, increased its strength from 87 to 90 deputies, following its success in three by-elections. Deuba's administration collapsed in March when it lost a vote of confidence in the House of Representatives. Chand was appointed as the new Prime Minister (for the fourth time) at the head of a coalition Government composed of members of the RPP, the UML, the NSP and the Nepal Workers' and Peasants' Party. However, the new Government seemed unstable from the outset, since the members of the Thapa faction of the RPP refused to support Prime Minister Chand and the ideological differences between the communists and the former pro-monarchists appeared insuperable. Although Chand held the premiership, the UML, as the largest component of the coalition, was responsible for more ministerial posts than the RPP. In May and June the communists replaced the NCP as the country's dominant force in local government, following resounding successes in local elections. However, about 30 people were killed in violent clashes between supporters of the main political parties, and in mid-June there were large demonstrations in protest against alleged electoral irregularities on the part of the UML.

In October 1997 the Government lost a parliamentary vote of no confidence tabled by the NCP. King Birendra appointed Thapa, the President of the RPP, to replace Chand as Prime Minister. A new coalition Government, comprising members of the RPP and the NSP, took office on the following day. In December Prime Minister Thapa expanded the Council of Ministers in a reorganization that introduced members of the NCP and a number of independents into the coalition. In February 1998 the Government survived, by a narrow margin, a no-confidence vote introduced by the UML and dissident members of the RPP (including Chand). In January Chand and nine other rebel deputies had been expelled from the RPP, forming a breakaway faction known as the RPP (Chand). In March the UML suffered a serious reverse when about one-half of the party's parliamentary deputies formed a breakaway faction entitled the Communist Party of Nepal (Marxist-Leninist) (ML), with Bam Dev Gautam as its leader.

Under an agreement reached in October 1997 when Thapa assumed power, the Prime Minister was to transfer the leadership of the coalition Government to the NCP within an agreed time frame. Although Thapa initially appeared reluctant to relinquish his post, the President of the NCP, G. P. Koirala, replaced him as Prime Minister in April 1998 at the head of an NCP Council of Ministers. In August, in a seeming attempt to strengthen his own precarious administration and to encourage the UML's communist rivals, the Prime Minister invited the ML to enter an alliance with the NCP. A new coalition administration was subsequently established on 26 August (with the NCP retaining the most important ministries), giving Prime Minister Koirala an adequate parliamentary majority. Meanwhile, the 'people's war' waged by the Maoist activists in the hills of west Nepal was gathering momentum.

In December 1998 the ML withdrew from the coalition Government, alleging that the NCP had failed to implement a number of agreements drawn up between the two parties and other political groups in August. Prime Minister G. P. Koirala tendered his resignation, but was asked to head a new coalition Council of Ministers, which was to hold power in an acting capacity pending the holding of a general election the following year. On the recommendation of the Prime Minister, the King appointed a caretaker administration, comprising members of the NCP, the UML and the NSP, and, for the first time in eight years, a nominee of the King, on 25 December.

In May 1999 the NCP won an outright majority in the general election, securing 110 of the 205 seats in the lower house; the UML obtained 68 seats and the RPP (Thapa) took 11 seats, while the ML and the RPP (Chand) both failed to win a single seat. Voting was conducted relatively peacefully, according to government sources, despite threats by the Maoist insurgents to disrupt the electoral process. A new Council of Ministers, headed by the veteran NCP leader K. P. Bhattarai and composed solely of NCP members, was appointed at the end of the month.

In November 1999, in an effort to resolve the Maoist insurgency, which, according to government sources, now affected (moderately to severely) 31 of Nepal's 75 districts and had led to the deaths of more than 1,000 people, the Prime Minister offered to grant the guerrillas an amnesty and various rehabilitation measures if they surrendered their arms and entered into negotiations with the Government. In response, the insurgents (who were estimated to number 5,000–6,000 and to have the support of about 8,000 sympathizers) stated that they were not prepared to enter into peace talks until arrest warrants issued against their leaders were withdrawn, official investigations were carried out into alleged extrajudicial killings of suspected militants by the police, and imprisoned activists were released.

Koirala had initially been supportive of Bhattarai's premiership, but had subsequently become a vociferous critic of his rival's administration, particularly with regard to the Government's perceived mismanagement of the Maoist crisis. In February 2000, following a number of internal disagreements and ministerial resignations, the political unrest culminated in the registration of two successive votes of no confidence by dissident NCP legislators against Prime Minister Bhattarai; although neither took place, the pressure led to his resignation. It was announced that G. P. Koirala was to be the new Prime Minister (for the fourth time), following his election as parliamentary party leader of the NCP. Koirala and a new Council of Ministers were sworn in by the King on 22 March. In May a Human Rights Commission was formed following accusations that both the security forces and the Maoist guerrillas had committed human rights violations, including murder and torture.

In April 2000 Prime Minister Koirala activated the National Defence Council, which, according to the Constitution, comprised the Prime Minister, the Minister of Defence and the Commander-in-Chief of the Royal Nepal Army, to resolve the Maoist crisis. In comparison to the inadequately trained and poorly armed police force, which had suffered numerous casualties, the army was much better equipped to deal with the insurgency, and Koirala expressed his wish to mobilize the armed forces in the ongoing fight against militant activity. At the end of August the Maoist crisis worsened: during two Maoist attacks in Dolpa and Lamjung, 24 police officers were killed and 44 were injured. The Royal Nepal Army was criticized for failing to intervene to protect the police from insurgents, and the Minister of Home Affairs, Govinda Raj Joshi, resigned after admitting his failure to 'maintain law and order in the country'. It was subsequently decided that the Government would employ the dual approach of using the army, while simultaneously encouraging negotiations, in order to resolve the Maoist crisis. At the end of October the first direct, unofficial negotiations began between the Government and the CPN (M); however, they were short-lived, and the violence resumed in early November.

In February 2001 leading opposition parties issued a memorandum to the Prime Minister, demanding his resignation over his alleged involvement in a corrupt aircraft deal and also over the worsening security situation. In March Koirala was confronted by increasing opposition from within and outside his party and a number of ministers resigned. The opposition continued to disrupt parliamentary proceedings, and, as a result, the King prorogued the National Assembly and House of Representatives in early April. At the end of the month the anti-corruption commission cleared the Prime Minister of involvement in the controversial aircraft agreement, but, at the same time, Koirala was accused of accepting bribes in another aircraft deal. The opposition continued to demand his resignation and organized a nation-wide strike in protest against the Government's alleged misuse of power.

The royal family massacre; the Maoist insurgency escalates

On 1 June 2001 King Birendra, Queen Aishwarya and six other members of the royal family were shot dead; the heir to the throne, Crown Prince Dipendra, was gravely wounded. Another family member, Dhirendra Shah, died later in hospital. Initial reports suggested that Prince Dipendra had shot members of his family before shooting himself, following a dispute between himself and his mother regarding his intentions to marry a woman of whom the Queen disapproved. Immediately after the incident Prince Dipendra was pronounced King, and Prince Gyanendra, the brother of the deceased King Birendra, was appointed regent. On 4 June King Dipendra died and was succeeded by Prince Gyanendra. These events caused considerable unrest in Kathmandu, and a curfew was imposed. Following his accession, King Gyanendra established a commission to investigate the royal deaths. The commission, comprising the Chief Justice and the Speaker of the House of Representatives, duly concluded that Dipendra had been responsible for the shootings and that at the time had been under the influence of drugs and alcohol. King Gyanendra bestowed the title of Queen on his wife, Princess Komal, but did not declare his son, Paras Shah, the Crown Prince until the end of October, owing to the latter's unpopularity among the public, caused by his profligate behaviour.

In June–July 2001 Maoist leaders, taking advantage of the unrest in Nepal, intensified their activities. On 13 July the Deputy Prime Minister, Ram Chandra Poudel, resigned, owing to disagreements with the Prime Minister over government policy towards the insurgency. Several days later a senior Maoist leader declared that he would enter negotiations with the Government on the condition that the Prime Minister resigned. On 19 July Prime Minister Koirala stood down, citing long-standing corruption allegations against him and his failure to curb the Maoist insurgency; former premier Sher Bahadur Deuba succeeded Koirala as leader of the NCP and Prime Minister.

Immediately after his appointment Prime Minister Deuba persuaded the Maoist leaders to reciprocate his offer of a cease-fire and agree to enter into dialogue. Prior to the negotiations, both sides took part in a series of confidence-building measures, including the reciprocal release of kidnapped police officers and imprisoned Maoist activists. At the same time Parliament adopted legislation to establish a new Armed Police Force and to develop the co-ordination of regional development and security. However, despite the cease-fire, Maoist insurgents continued to carry out violent acts. During the peace talks, which had commenced in August 2001, tens of thousands of people held demonstrations against the fighting. The third round of negotiations, which took place in November, ended in failure, owing to the Maoists' continued demand for the dissolution of the Constitution, the establishment of an interim government, the election of a constituent assembly and, ultimately, a republic. Two days later the leader of the CPN (M), Pushpa Kamal Dahal (better known under his pseudonym, 'Prachanda'—'The Fierce One'), announced the end of the cease-fire. The Maoists established a parallel central government, the 'United People's Revolutionary Government', with parallel local administrations in 40 of the country's 75 districts, and direct rule in 22 districts in western Nepal. Following an escalation in the violence, on 26 November the King declared a state of emergency. The King termed the Maoists as 'terrorists' and promulgated the Terrorist and Disruptive Activities Ordinance 2001, which sanctioned a number of counter-terrorist measures, including the suspension of civil liberties and the imposition of media restrictions.

In January 2002 the Nepal Rastra Bank froze the bank accounts of individuals and organizations associated with Maoist militants. In mid-February Maoist insurgents launched their heaviest offensive to date against government outposts; more than 150 people, mainly soldiers and police officers, were killed in the fighting. The army was subsequently instructed to use offensive as well as defensive measures to combat the insurgency. On 21 February the legislature voted to extend the state of emergency for three months. Although the opposition criticized the Government for its handling of the insurgency and for failing to react to warnings that major attacks were imminent, it voted for the extension after the Prime Minister agreed to establish social and economic development programmes in poor rural areas where Maoists were active, and ensured the fair use of the emergency powers.

In the mean time, in February 2002 the UML and its breakaway faction, the ML, merged. The amalgamation of the more moderate communist parties was regarded largely as a move to counter the influence of the Maoist insurgents. In its first annual report, the Human Rights Commission of Nepal accused both the Maoist insurgents and the Government of committing serious human rights abuses. The violent insurgency escalated in April, and in early May the army launched an intensive attack against Maoist insurgents in Rolpa district, resulting in the deaths of more than 500 guerrillas, according to government sources. A series of counter-attacks and attacks ensued, leading to further hundreds of fatalities. Deuba tabled a parliamentary motion proposing an extension of the six-month state of emergency (which was due to expire on 25 May), prompting strong opposition from within and outside his party. Growing rifts in the NCP led King Gyanendra to dissolve unexpectedly the House of Representatives on 22 May, on the recommendation of the Prime Minister. A general election was scheduled to take place on 13 November, and the incumbent Government was instructed to rule the country in the interim. Political leaders of all affiliations strongly condemned this decision. On 23 May Deuba was suspended from his party and three days later was expelled from the NCP for three years. In the mean time, three ministers, including the Minister of Finance, resigned in protest against the calling of early elections. In late May King Gyanendra extended the state of emergency by three months.

In June 2002 the NCP officially split during a 'general convention' held by the Deuba faction. Eventually, in September the Election Commission recognized the faction led by G. P. Koirala as the official NCP. Several days later Deuba's minority breakaway faction registered as a new political party, the Nepali Congress Party—Democratic (NCP—D). Meanwhile, in April the NSP split into two factions and in July two communist parties, the National People's Front and the UPF, merged to form the People's Front Nepal (Janamorcha Nepal).

The state of emergency expired in August 2002 and the Maoists consequently intensified their violent campaign. In October Deuba requested King Gyanendra to postpone the general election (scheduled for November) by one year, citing the deteriorating law and order situation. The King responded by dismissing the Prime Minister and the acting Council of Ministers for reportedly failing to organize the election. He appointed a nine-member interim Government, headed by former premier and monarchist Lokendra Bahadur Chand, and postponed the general election indefinitely. The NCP, UML and legal experts condemned the dismissal of Deuba and his Government and the establishment of a new Council of Ministers as unconstitutional. In December the human rights organization Amnesty International issued a damning report on the human rights situation in Nepal since the collapse of peace talks in November 2001. The army and Armed Police Force were severely criticized for the alleged 'unprecedented levels' of human rights abuses, including torture, arbitrary detention and deaths in custody. In addition, the report accused Maoist insurgents of torturing and killing captives, taking hostages and recruiting children. The report claimed that nearly one-half of the 4,366 people who had died in the conflict since late 2001 were civilians, killed by both security forces and Maoists.

In January 2003 suspected Maoist militants shot dead the chief of the Armed Police Force in Kathmandu. Three days later the CPN (M) and the Government announced an immediate cease-fire and agreed to resume peace negotiations after the Government agreed to declassify Maoist activists as terrorists, to withdraw rewards offered for the arrest of Maoist leaders and to cancel international police warrants issued for the guerrilla leaders. Informal talks and formal negotiations from February resulted in some progress, with the interim Government agreeing to release several Maoist detainees and to restrict the movement of army troops; however, the third round of negotiations in mid-August ended in impasse over the Maoists' demand for an elected assembly to draft a new constitution. In late August Prachanda ended the seven-month cease-fire and withdrew from the peace process, while the Government reclassified the insurgents as 'terrorists'. A few days later thousands of people marched in Kathmandu to demand the resumption of peace talks.

In the mean time, at the end of May 2003 Prime Minister Chand resigned in response to pressure from leaders of the major political parties. On 4 June the King appointed monarchist and former premier Surya Bahadur Thapa as Prime Minister, rejecting the nomination by the five opposition parties of M. K. Nepal, the General Secretary of the UML. One week later the King appointed a new interim Council of Ministers, which was composed entirely of members of the monarchist RPP. Opposition parties held a large demonstration in Kathmandu, demanding Thapa's resignation, the reinstatement of the legislature and the establishment of an all-party government. On 1 September the Government banned all demonstrations or public gatherings of five or more people in the Kathmandu valley, citing fears of infiltration by Maoist guerrillas. None the less, about a week later more than 1,000 pro-democracy protesters, including former premier G. P. Koirala, were arrested for defying the ban and taking part in a demonstration.

The CPN (M) fully resumed its violent campaign in September 2003. In January 2004 the Maoists announced the formation of autonomous people's governments in 10 districts under their control. At the end of the month the CPN (M) stated that it would give priority to development in these areas, and that representatives of the King and the USA (which had proscribed the Maoist party in October 2003 as a threat to national security and which was providing the Nepalese army with military assistance for its campaign against the insurgents) were banned from operating in districts under Maoist control. The violence increased, meanwhile, and the Maoists organized a series of disruptive nation-wide general strikes. The number of people killed in the eight-year 'people's war' had risen sharply to more than 9,130 by mid-March 2004, of whom more than 1,500 had died since the collapse of the cease-fire in August 2003.

In January 2004 there were almost daily student-led, pro-republic protests held in Kathmandu. At the end of the month the five main opposition parties issued a joint statement offering formal support to the student movement, indicating that the NCP, hitherto a committed supporter of the constitutional monarchy, and the UML were reconsidering their views towards the monarchy. In March the five main opposition parties announced that a constitutional monarchy had not been successful and that, henceforth, their movement would be directed at achieving the establishment of a republic. In May the Prime Minister tendered his resignation as a result of the continuing political impasse. The resignation prompted the collapse of the entire Government; King Gyanendra authorized Thapa to remain in office in an acting capacity pending the formation of a new administration. In June King Gyanendra appointed Sher Bahadur Deuba as Prime Minister for the third time. Several days later the King appointed two members of the NCP (D) to the new Council of Ministers, in which Deuba held the majority of portfolios. The Council was expanded to 31 members in the following month and incorporated ministers from the four-party coalition (comprising the NCP (D), the UML, the RPP and the NSP) that had been formed following the resignation of Prime Minister Thapa.

In November 2004 Prime Minister Deuba set the Maoist rebels a deadline of 13 January 2005 to commence peace talks with the Government; however, Prachanda rejected the proposed deadline. The rejection reportedly led to disagreement within the Government over the feasibility of holding elections amid the ongoing insurgency. The Government was destabilized further in November when the founding President of the RPP, former Prime Minister Thapa, announced that he intended to launch a new political party, effectively creating a split once again within the RPP (the Chand and Thapa factions had reunited in 2000).

King Gyanendra imposes direct rule (2005–06)
In February 2005 King Gyanendra abruptly dismissed Prime Minister Deuba and his Government, declared an indefinite state of emergency and announced that, henceforth, he would rule Nepal directly. All communications links into and out of Nepal were severed temporarily, censorship was imposed on the media and former ministers were placed under house arrest. The King claimed that his actions were a result of the Prime Minister's failure to halt the Maoist insurgency and to hold legislative elections in the country. In an attempt to prevent protests, the King ordered the detention of large numbers of political activists. Maoist rebels subsequently instigated a two-week blockade of national highways in protest against the King's actions. Shortly after he had assumed supreme power, the King appointed a new, 10-member Council of Ministers, under his chairmanship. Former Prime Ministers Dr Tulsi Giri and Kirti Nidhi Bista were selected to serve as Vice-Chairmen. King Gyanendra's assumption of power met with an unfavourable international response, with Nepal's key allies, India and the United Kingdom, suspending military aid to the country and several nations recalling their ambassadors from Nepal in protest.

In March 2005 Thapa announced the foundation of his new political party, the Rashtriya Janashakti Party (RJP—National People's Power Party). Meanwhile, the Maoist insurgency intensified, with several clashes taking place between rebels and government troops. The state of emergency was lifted at the end of April, although public meetings and demonstrations continued to be prohibited, and police powers of arrest and detention were extended. In July former Prime Minister Deuba was convicted by the newly established Royal Commission for Corruption Control (RCCC)—a body Deuba refused to recognize—of charges of embezzlement relating to the issuing of a water contract and sentenced to a two-year prison term. (Deuba was released when the RCCC was outlawed in January 2006.)

Meanwhile, in May 2005 an alliance of seven political parties, including the NCP, announced a joint agenda for the restoration of democracy in Nepal, demanding that King Gyanendra end his period of direct rule and that the House of Representatives, which had been dissolved in 2002, be recalled. Moreover, the seven-party alliance subsequently established a dialogue with the CPN (M). In September 2005 the Maoists announced a three-month, unilateral cease-fire, an offer to which the Government responded cautiously. In November the seven-party alliance announced that it had reached a 12-point agreement with the Maoist rebels intended to restore democracy to Nepal. The agreement included a boycott of the February 2006 municipal elections and the election of a constituent assembly, the latter being a long-standing Maoist demand.

In December 2005 an extensive reorganization of the Council of Ministers took place, in which eight ministers were dismissed and several ministers from the RPP and RJP were appointed. In January 2006 the CPN (M) stated that the cease-fire had come to an end, owing to the Government continuing to authorize offensive operations against them. The insurgency subsequently intensified. In the following month the municipal elections were held, taking place in only 36 of the 58 municipal councils owing to an insufficient number of candidates and against the background of a four-day general strike co-ordinated by the Maoists. Turn-out reached an estimated 20% of registered voters, according to official figures, although the major opposition parties, which boycotted the polls, claimed that the figure was significantly lower. In March the Maoists instigated an indefinite blockade of Kathmandu in another attempt to force King Gyanendra to end his direct rule.

The reinstatement of Parliament
In April 2006 the opposition alliance called a nation-wide general strike. Mass demonstrations followed, in response to which the Government announced the imposition of a 'shoot-on-sight' curfew. As thousands of protesters defied the curfew and violent clashes ensued, King Gyanendra's position appeared increasingly untenable. Following almost three weeks of demonstrations, the King offered to permit the opposition alliance to name a new Prime Minister. However, this offer was rejected and the protests continued to escalate. Several days later, in accordance with opposition demands, the King announced that he would reinstate Parliament, thus quelling the unrest. The CPN (M), however, vowed to continue its insurgency, accusing the political parties of betraying the 12-point agreement. It did, none the less, agree to observe a three-month cease-fire, which was extended periodically. The opposition alliance subsequently nominated former Prime Minister G. P. Koirala to lead a new Government. The House of Representatives formally convened at the end of April and approved legislation enabling the establishment of a constituent assembly to redraft the country's Constitution. By June all of the seven-party alliance members were represented in the Government, with the exception of the Nepal Workers' and Peasants' Party.

On 3 May 2006 the Council of Ministers had announced a cease-fire with the CPN (M), offering to declassify the group as a terrorist organization in exchange for the holding of peace talks; numerous Maoist prisoners were also released. While the Maoists insisted on the release of all their prisoners, as well as the abolition of the existing Constitution, legislature and monarchy, they attended preliminary discussions with the Government on 26 May. Meanwhile, on 18 May the House of Representatives approved a resolution divesting the King of his role as Commander-in-Chief of the Army, his authority to make military appointments and nominate an heir, and his legal immunity and exemption from taxes. Nepal was officially transformed from a Hindu state into a secular state in an attempt to extricate the concept of a divinely instituted monarchy from the national ideology. The transfer of power away from the monarchy continued in June: the King was no longer able to veto legislation, he was not required to open and close parliamentary sessions, and he lost the authority to announce government policy.

In June 2006 talks between Koirala and Prachanda in Kathmandu led to the announcement that the CPN (M) would be included in a new interim government, which was to oversee elections for a constituent assembly. At Koirala's request, a UN team arrived in Nepal at the end of July to determine weapons management strategies for the Nepalese army and the People's Liberation Army (PLA) of the Maoists; Koirala reportedly deemed the decommissioning of weapons as a prerequisite of the entry of the CPN (M) into government. In August it was agreed that the movement of both government and rebel forces would be restricted. In October further negotiations produced a tentative schedule for elections to the constituent assembly, with a deadline of the end of June 2007 for the assembly's first session. Prachanda reiterated his demand for the declaration of a republic, stating that an agreement to this effect would ensure the disarmament of Maoist forces. The Comprehensive Peace Agreement (CPA), which was signed by Koirala and Prachanda on 21 November, provided for the establishment of an interim constitution, assembly and council of ministers by 1 December, and was hailed as the end of a civil war that had claimed the lives of more than 13,000 people. A disarmament agreement soon followed, the terms of which included the complete cessation of hostilities by both sides. The Maoist military forces were to be contained in cantonments and their weapons registered and impounded under UN supervision, while the Nepalese army, which was to remain in barracks, would also have its arms locked away. With the signing of an Interim Constitution in December, constitutional powers of governance were reassigned from the monarchy to the Prime Minister. The National Assembly and House of Representatives were dissolved with the promulgation of the Interim Constitution in mid-January 2007. In their place, an Interim Parliament, or 'Legislature-Parliament', was established; this body included members of the original 1999 Parliament as well as appointees selected by the seven-party alliance and the CPN (M). A few days later the Maoists announced the closure of their 'People's Governments' and 'People's Courts'. The UN Mission in Nepal (UNMIN) was established in January 2007, at the request of the seven-party alliance and the CPN (M). UNMIN's main task was to help in overseeing fair and free elections to the constituent assembly and to monitor the proper enactment of the CPA (including the disarmament and integration of the PLA into the regular army).

Meanwhile, in 2007 groups representing the Madhesi people of southern Nepal, which were demanding increased independence for their region and greater representation in government, organized demonstrations and strikes to draw attention to their campaign. The protests were at times violent and clashes with police resulted in several fatalities. Following negotiations between Madhesi groups and the Government, constitutional amendments approved by the Interim Parliament in March provided for proportional representation and a federal style of government, and the revision of constituency boundaries to grant one-half of parliamentary seats to the southern plains, where an estimated 50% of the population resided. Despite these concessions, an element of dissatisfaction remained, with the Madhesi Jana Adhikar Forum Nepal (Madhesi People's Rights Forum Nepal—MPRFN) demanding total autonomy.

In April 2007 an Interim Council of Ministers was approved by the Interim Parliament. G. P. Koirala was reappointed interim Prime Minister, heading an administration that included five members of the CPN (M). The UML was assigned responsibility for foreign affairs and the newly created peace and reconstruction portfolio. In May the Government announced the postponement of elections to the constituent assembly until November, and in July the CPN (M) registered itself as a political party with the Election Commission of Nepal.

Although it had been agreed that the fate of the monarchy lay with the constituent assembly, demands for the declaration of a republic continued to be made. Seven royal palaces were nationalized by the Government in August 2007. In September the NCP and the NCP (D) announced their merger. In the same month the CPN (M) withdrew from the Government, citing the continuing existence of the monarchy and disagreement over the composition of the constituent assembly as major obstacles to co-operation with its coalition partners. A period of intense negotiation ensued, during which the constituent assembly elections were postponed indefinitely and the future of the peace process itself appeared to hang in the balance. However, in December the CPN (M) returned to government after the Interim Parliament approved constitutional amendments ensuring the abolition of the monarchy upon the approval of the constituent assembly. More than one-half of the assembly was to be determined by a system of proportional representation, with the bulk of the remainder to be directly elected, in addition to several appointed deputies; elections were scheduled for April 2008.

Meanwhile, in the latter half of 2007 the security situation deteriorated in the Terai region, where the MPRFN and other Madhesi groups continued to campaign for autonomy. In December the Minister of Environment, Science and Technology, Mahantha Thakur, resigned, together with several Madhesi members of the Interim Parliament, citing the Government's unwillingness to address the ongoing unrest in the Terai. Shortly after these resignations, the Samyukta Loktantrik Madhesi Morcha (SLMM—United Democratic Madhesi Front), an alliance of three political organizations—the MPRFN, the Sadbhavana Party (a breakaway faction of the NSP) and the Terai Madhes Loktantrik Party (Terai Madhes Democratic Party)—was established. In February 2008 blockades orchestrated by the SLMM caused widespread disruption in the south of the country and led to fuel shortages in Kathmandu and elsewhere. Later in the month the Government and the SLMM signed an agreement ending the blockades and allowing for increased autonomy and representation of Madhesis on party lists and in institutions such as the Nepalese army. However, concerns remained regarding the campaigns of more hard-line Madhesi groups operating outside the negotiations.

The Maoists take power and the monarchy is abolished

At the constituent assembly elections, which were held on 10 April 2008, the CPN (M) won 220 out of a total of 575 elected seats under the mixed electoral system, twice as many as the NCP, which came second with 110 seats. The UML secured only 103 seats, putting it in third place and prompting the resignation of the party's General Secretary, M. K. Nepal, while the MPRFN won 52. Although the period leading up to the polls had been marked by bombings and violent clashes, the day of the elections was largely peaceful, with a relatively sizeable proportion of the electorate participating (around 60%). Prachanda declared victory on behalf of the CPN (M) and indicated that he would lead a coalition government. The CPN (M) also urged the King to abdicate voluntarily in advance of the inevitable declaration of a republic. This declaration was duly made following overwhelming approval at the inaugural session of the Constituent Assembly on 28 May, when the monarchy was abolished; King Gyanendra voluntarily vacated the royal palace in Kathmandu in June, opting to move to his summer residence outside the city.

Meanwhile, the CPN (M)'s lack of a parliamentary majority proved to be an obstacle in the formation of a new government, with a lack of consensus between the three major parties over the mandate of the new post of president, a position Prachanda was keen to assume. Although by early June 2008 the CPN (M) had accepted the notion of a civilian president, the impasse continued, with the CPN (M) ministers of the interim Government tendering their resignations over a dispute with Prime Minister Koirala and the NCP. In June Koirala stated that his resignation would come into effect upon the election of somebody to the presidency, which, it was decided, would be a largely ceremonial role. In a separate development, the seven-party alliance had reportedly been dissolved. A presidential election finally took place in the Constituent Assembly on 19 July, but the leading candidate, Ram Baran Yadav, who was supported by the NCP, was unable to secure a majority. Paramananda Jha, who had been nominated by the MPRFN, was elected Vice-President. At a second round of voting two days later, Yadav defeated the CPN (M) candidate, Ramraja Prasad Singh, securing the support of the UML as well as the MPRFN. Notably, Yadav, Singh and Jha were all Madhesis.

The CPN (M), disgruntled with the alliance between the NCP, the UML and the MPRFN and the resulting failure of its presidential candidate, initially warned that it would decline to form a government. However, with the support of the UML and MPRFN, in August 2008 Prachanda defeated NCP candidate and former Prime Minister Sher Bahadur Deuba in a vote held in the Constituent Assembly for the post of prime minister. Prachanda appointed a new Council of Ministers, comprising members of the CPN (M), the MPRFN, the Sadbhavana Party, the UML, the People's Front Nepal and the Communist Party of Nepal (United) (CPN—U). The NCP remained outside the Government, forming the opposition. On 30 October the Kingdom of Nepal officially became the Federal Democratic Republic of

Nepal. In November the Constituent Assembly approved a timetable for the new constitution, with a deadline of May 2010 for its promulgation. The first draft of the constitution was expected to be made public in September 2009. A constitutional committee appointed by the Constituent Assembly began drafting the document in December 2008. However, ongoing disputes between the Government and the opposition, and the unresolved issue of the integration of some 19,000 former Maoist fighters into the army—which strained relations between the Government and the military in early 2009—continued to hamper progress in other areas. In January 2009 the CPN (M) was restyled the Unified Communist Party of Nepal (Maoist)—UCPN (M)—following a merger with the CPN (Unity Centre-Masal).

The collapse of the Maoist Government

On 4 May 2009 Nepal was confronted with a serious political crisis following the resignation of Prime Minister Prachanda and the withdrawal of the UCPN (M) from the ruling coalition. This dramatic development resulted from President Yadav's refusal to accept Prachanda's earlier dismissal of the Chief of Army Staff, Lt-Gen. Rukmangad Katuwal, who was allegedly defying government orders to integrate former rebel fighters into the national army (claiming that they were politically indoctrinated) and was actively recruiting new personnel into the army (in contravention of the peace agreement). A series of protests by Maoist activists demanding the removal of the reinstated army chief subsequently took place in the capital, and a number of clashes occurred between the protesters and riot police. The President set a deadline of 9 May for the formation of a new coalition government, but this date passed without any resolution to the political impasse. The UCPN (M) refused to participate in negotiations unless the President reversed his decision on the reinstatement of Lt-Gen. Katuwal. On 10 May President Yadav directed the Constituent Assembly to elect a new Prime Minister by a majority vote in an attempt to end the political crisis. On 17 May an alliance of 22 political parties, including the NCP and the UML, filed a claim to form a new coalition government and appealed for a parliamentary vote to elect their candidate, the veteran communist leader M. K. Nepal, as the new prime minister. In response, Prachanda stated that the move to form a new administration that excluded that Maoists was a conspiracy to derail the peace process. None the less, M. K. Nepal was elected to the premiership and was sworn in at the end of May at the head of a new, small coalition Government (expanded over the following few weeks).

The Maoists promptly launched a series of anti-Government street protests and strikes in Kathmandu and elsewhere in the country and threatened to renew their revolutionary insurgency. Their demand for the holding of a parliamentary debate on the reinstatement of Lt-Gen. Katuwal (who had since retired) was rejected by Prime Minister Nepal in September 2009. The UCPN (M) responded by continuing to boycott and disrupt the proceedings of the Constituent Assembly; the Maoists succeeded in delaying the approval of the 2009/10 budget for four months, and it was not adopted until November 2009. In December the UCPN (M) led a mass rally in the capital and organized a three-day national strike, which paralysed the country. The political impasse continued into 2010, and in late April, with only weeks to go before the deadline for the introduction of a new constitution (28 May), the Maoists intensified their protest campaign with the convergence of thousands of their supporters in Kathmandu to attend a mass May Day rally. In an attempt to force the Government to resign, the UCPN (M) announced the enforcement of an indefinite general strike. However, the strike was suspended after less than a week to alleviate the hardships being suffered by the Nepalese people and to recommence negotiations with the Government.

On 28 May 2010, following threats by President Yadav to impose emergency or presidential rule if the political impasse were not resolved, the NCP, the UML and the Maoists agreed to extend the tenure of the Constituent Assembly by one year, on the condition that Prime Minister Nepal resigned to enable the formation of a national consensus government. Accordingly, M. K. Nepal announced his resignation from the premiership on 30 June; however, he and his Government were to remain in their posts in an acting capacity pending the appointment of a consensus administration by 7 July. When the formation of a new government failed to materialize by this deadline, owing to lack of agreement between the three main parties, the President declared that the Constituent Assembly would elect a new prime minister by majority vote. This proved an extremely lengthy

process: between July and November the Assembly made 16 unsuccessful attempts to elect a new premier. The main candidates in the first seven rounds of voting were Prachanda of the UCPN (M) and Ram Chandra Poudel of the NCP; the UML's candidate, Jhala Nath Khanal, withdrew from the process following his failure to win a majority of votes in the first two rounds of voting in July. On each of the seven occasions that he participated in the poll, Prachanda received more votes than his rival, but failed to achieve the requisite 301 votes (constituting a majority in the 601-seat Assembly). The deadlock in the voting process was caused by the persistent abstention of the UML and smaller parliamentary parties (notably the various Madhesi organizations), which claimed that neither candidate was acceptable. The prolonged stalemate led to economic instability (with delays in the implementation of the budget) and widespread public disillusionment with the political parties and their leaders. The peace process also came to a virtual halt, with thousands of former Maoist militants remaining in UN-monitored holding camps. In late September Sushil Koirala was elected as the new President of the NCP, defeating his closest rival, Sher Bahadur Deuba, by more than 300 votes. At the end of the month, prior to the eighth attempt by the Constituent Assembly to elect a new prime minister, Prachanda withdrew from the contest following a pact with the UML. With the UCPN (M) now abstaining from the voting process, the sole remaining candidate, Poudel, failed to garner the required majority in the nine further polls that were held in 2010 (only 101 legislators participated in the 16th round, which was conducted on 4 November).

Meanwhile, in an effort to resolve numerous outstanding issues over the drafting of the new constitution, a seven-member multi-party task force, headed by Prachanda, was established in October 2010. Following the failure of the Constitutional Council to convene for several months, a number of constitutional bodies, including the Office of the Auditor-General and the Election Commission, lacked permanent office heads and risked becoming dysfunctional. In November the three main parties held a series of crisis talks to discuss the stalled peace process (the stated priority of the NCP and the UML) and power-sharing and government formation (the Maoists' primary concern). To prevent a political vacuum, the Supreme Court ruled in December that no legislators would henceforth be permitted to abstain from voting in the prime ministerial election process. In January 2011, the NCP having withdrawn its candidacy from the scheduled 17th round of prime ministerial elections, President Yadav gave the three main parties a week-long deadline to attempt once again to form a government of national consensus. However, this approach too proved unsuccessful owing to the persistent intransigence of the three parties regarding their respective claims to the leadership of the new government.

On 15 January 2011 UNMIN commenced its withdrawal from Nepal following the decision of the NCP and the UML not to request an extension of the mission's mandate (despite the Maoists' requests to do so). A few days later Prachanda formally handed responsibility for the 19,000 former PLA troops remaining in the holding camps to a special government committee (headed by the Prime Minister), which was to supervise the disarmament, integration and rehabilitation of the ex-militants.

The seven-month political stalemate finally came to an end on 3 February 2011 when the Chairman of the UML, Jhala Nath Khanal, with the support of the UCPN (M) (Prachanda having withdrawn his candidacy at the last minute), was elected as the new Prime Minister by the Constituent Assembly. Khanal won a clear majority, with 368 of the votes cast; Poudel received 122 votes and Bijaya Kumar Gachchhadar of the MPRFN (Democratic) took 67. Khanal was sworn in on 6 February, but appointments to the new Council of Ministers were delayed by several weeks of protracted negotiations with the Maoists over power-sharing arrangements (notably the question of the allocation of the home affairs portfolio). A few days after the inauguration of the new Prime Minister it emerged that, prior to Khanal's election, the UCPN (M) and the UML had signed a secret seven-point agreement regarding their future co-operation in government. Of some controversy were allegations that the agreement had included plans to establish a military body of former Maoist combatants that was to be separate from the country's regular army. The NCP, which had decided to stay in opposition in protest against the secret pact between the UML and the Maoists, claimed that the formation of such a body would prove highly detrimental to the peace process. In March Khanal expanded his core three-member UML Council of Ministers to include representatives of the UCPN (M); Krishna Bahadur Mahara was assigned one of the deputy premierships, but Khanal himself retained control of the home affairs post. The UML and the Maoists expressed concern at the NCP's refusal to join the Government, claiming that the party's absence would jeopardize the drafting of the constitution (scheduled to be completed by 28 May) and the peace process. In April the Council of Ministers was further enlarged to incorporate 12 new UML ministers and state ministers.

In early May 2011, following protracted negotiations with the Maoists, Prime Minister Khanal announced a further expansion of the Council of Ministers, appointing 12 new UCPN (M) ministers and state ministers. In a major concession to the Maoists, Mahara was accorded the disputed home affairs portfolio, in addition to his existing role as Deputy Prime Minister. The appointment, which effectively gave the UCPN (M) control over Nepal's internal security, was strongly criticized by the opposition and by some members of the UML. The coalition Government was further broadened with the addition of three members of the regional MPRFN—party leader Upendra Yadav was appointed Deputy Prime Minister and Minister of Foreign Affairs—and one representative from both the CPN (U) and the ML. The distribution of ministerial posts among the Maoists, especially the allocation of the home affairs portfolio, appeared further to exacerbate internal schisms within the UCPN (M). Barshaman Pun, a leading Maoist candidate for the home affairs position, resigned as Minister of Peace and Reconstruction, a post to which he had been appointed in March; furthermore, by mid-May, as a result of factional disagreements, four Maoist ministerial nominees had refused to take their oaths of office. With the latest deadline for the drafting of a new constitution about to expire, at the end of May the Government and the main opposition parties signed a five-point agreement that provided for a further three-month extension of the Constituent Assembly, during which the preliminary draft of the new constitution would have to be completed and a national unity government formed. Furthermore, Prime Minister Khanal was to resign once consensus had been reached on the composition of a new government.

The Maoists return to power

Following threats made by the UCPN (M) that it would withdraw from government unless a reorganization of the Council of Ministers were carried out, Prime Minister Khanal appointed nine new UCPN (M) ministers and one MPRFN minister on 1 August 2011. However, on 14 August, Khanal tendered his resignation, citing his failure to forge political unity and to make any real progress in the peace process (including the drafting of a new constitution). President Yadav requested the formation of a new government of national consensus within a week. This deadline was not met, but on 28 August the Constituent Assembly elected Dr Baburam Bhattarai, a Vice-Chairman of the UCPN (M) and former Minister of Finance under Prachanda, as the new Prime Minister. Bhattarai, who was supported by various Madhesi-based parties, won 340 votes, while his only rival, Ram Chandra Poudel of the NCP, received 235 votes. Bhattarai appointed the leader of the MPRFN (Democratic), Bijaya Kumar Gachchhadar, as Deputy Prime Minister and Minister of Home Affairs, but both the NCP and the UML refused to participate in the new Government. Not surprisingly, given the political instability, the deadline of 31 August for drawing up the draft constitution was not met, and on 29 August the Interim Parliament extended the term of the Constituent Assembly by another three months. In early September Prime Minister Bhattarai appointed 12 more ministers to his coalition Government, which now comprised members of the UCPN (M), two factions of the MPRFN, two factions of the Terai Madhes Loktantrik Party and two factions of the Sadbhavana Party. Of especial note was the appointment of Narayan Kaji Shrestha of the UCPN (M) as Deputy Prime Minister and Minister of Foreign Affairs. In October the Prime Minister dismissed Minister of Defence Sarat Singh Bhandari and Minister of Land Reform and Management Prabhu Sah; the former—a senior member of the MPRFN (Democratic)—had made controversial remarks in public regarding the possible future secession of Terai districts from Nepal, while the latter was implicated in a murder case. Deputy Prime Minister Gachchhadar assumed responsibility for the defence portfolio and Bhim Prasad Gautam was appointed as the new Minister of Land Reform and Management the following month.

Meanwhile, following their party's return to power, in September 2011 the Maoist commanders in the seven largest

cantonments around the country commenced their official hand-over of weapons (which had been stored in locked containers under UN supervision) to a special multi-party committee which was charged with the supervision, integration and rehabilitation of the former PLA combatants. Despite opposition from a hard-line faction within the UCPN (M) led by one of the party's Vice-Chairmen, Mohan Baidya, there was a major breakthrough in the peace process on 1 November when the country's main political parties signed a seven-point agreement, according to which around one-third of the former Maoist fighters (some 6,500 men and women) were to be integrated into the regular forces to form a new unit and the remainder were to be offered either a voluntary retirement payment or a rehabilitation package including vocational training. In addition, it was agreed that a truth and reconciliation commission and a missing persons commission would be established, that the Young Communist League (a paramilitary group within the UCPN—M) would be disbanded, that land captured or confiscated by the PLA would be returned to its original owners, and that a cross-party state restructuring commission would be created to oversee the transition of the country into a federal system.

In the mean time, in the course of November 2011 Prime Minister Bhattarai further expanded his Council of Ministers, bringing the total number of government members to 49 (the largest in Nepal's history). As expected, on 29 November the Interim Parliament extended the term of the Constituent Assembly by another six months; the deadline to complete the draft constitution was now 27 May 2012. The Government was faced with a minor set-back in February 2012 when the Minister of Information and Communications and Chairman of the MPRFN (Republican), Jaya Prakash Prasad Gupta, was convicted on charges of accumulating wealth beyond his income and abuse of power, and was sentenced to 18 months' imprisonment. The following week a bomb explosion in the centre of Kathmandu killed three people; an obscure militant group called the Unified National Liberation Front claimed responsibility, citing government corruption and fuel price rises as its main motivation.

In April 2012, following an agreement between the Government and the main opposition parties, all 15 Maoist cantonments, and the arms caches therein, were brought under the direct control of the Nepalese national army. It was anticipated that this development would expedite the integration of the former Maoist fighters into the regular army and give new impetus to the peace process. Nevertheless, significant disagreements between the main parties regarding the drafting of the new constitution remained; notably, over the formation of the proposed federal administrative units. In May, in an effort to expedite an agreement on the constitution, Prime Minister Bhattarai forged an agreement with the main opposition parties on the establishment of a Government of national unity. The Council of Ministers was duly dissolved and a new cabinet, comprising members of the UCPN (M), the NCP, the UML, the SLMM bloc and a number of smaller parties, was appointed. Bhattarai remained as Prime Minister, while Deputy Prime Ministers Shrestha and Gachchhadar were reappointed to their posts; Krishna Prasad Sitaula of the NCP and Ishwar Pokharel of the UML were also appointed as Deputy Prime Ministers.

At the same time, the main parties were involved in intensive negotiations on the key outstanding constitutional questions, namely the federal divisions and the constitutional status of the President and the Prime Minister. The latter appeared to have been partially resolved in May 2012, when the parties reportedly agreed that the position of President would be directly elected, while the Prime Minister would be elected by parliament; the extent of the president's powers was not confirmed. The federalism issue remained a major obstacle to the finalization of the constitution, with the UCPN (M) and Madhesi parties advocating provincial demarcation according to ethnicity and the NCP and the UML concerned that this approach was divisive; there was further disagreement over the number of provinces. The prospects for a conclusive political solution were placed in considerable doubt when, on 24 May, the Supreme Court rejected a parliamentary bill tabled by the Government proposing to extend the tenure of the Constituent Assembly by a further three months. The NC had criticized the proposal and withdrew from the Government on the same day, submitting the resignations of Deputy Prime Minister Krishna Prasad Sitaula and Minister of Federal Affairs Surya Man Gurung. Pointing to his limited options within the existing political framework, Bhattarai opted to call fresh constituent assembly elections for

22 November. There was little support for his decision, which other parties in the Government claimed was unconstitutional and had been taken unilaterally. The UML and two other parties withdrew from the coalition Government, and the UML joined the NC and other parties in demanding Bhattarai's resignation. At the end of May President Yadav gave the Government caretaker status pending the formation of a new administration, in light of the dissolution of the Constituent Assembly and the consequent expiry of Bhattarai's parliamentary membership.

In June 2012 a splinter group of the UCPN (M) loyal to one of its senior members, Mohan Baidya, announced the formation of the Communist Party of Nepal (Maoist) (CPN—M), its primary purpose being to attain the original objectives of the Maoists' 'people's war', which, it claimed, the UCPN (M) leaders had abandoned. More than a quarter of the UCPN (M)'s central committee was said to have joined the CPN—M. In July former king Gyanendra returned to the public eye with a television interview, during which he expressed a desire to return to the throne, albeit in no more than a ceremonial capacity. There was speculation that Gyanendra was exploiting the fragile political situation in the country.

Recent developments: preparations for elections to a new Constituent Assembly

In July 2012 there were increasing concerns about an impending crisis when the failure of the major parties to agree on elections forced the UCPN (M) to postpone the planned November poll. The NC and the UML continued to insist on the formation of a coalition government consisting of all the main parties as a precondition for their participation in elections. The Election Commission also maintained that the proposed November elections were unviable, owing to the absence of appropriate constitutional provisions with respect to the current the political circumstances. By September some consensus had been reached by the principal parties over the holding of a constituent assembly election in April 2013, with a national unity government presiding over the pre-election period. Perhaps inevitably, there was much wrangling over which party would lead the interim government: the NC and the UML continued to demand Bhattarai's resignation, while the UCPN (M) urged the NC and the UML to join the current Government. In addition, the continuing lack of a constitutional provision for a second constituent assembly election needed to be addressed, perhaps with President Yadav's intervention.

In November 2012 the Government announced that the election would take place by mid-May 2013. In January 2013, after violent protests staged by the opposition parties to force his resignation, Bhattarai reiterated that the election would be held in May. Earlier in the month, as the political stalemate continued, Prachanda had threatened to cancel the CPA if the various parties were unable to come to an agreement. In February the main parties agreed to a postponement of the election date to 21 June and the formation of an interim government led by the Chief Justice of the Supreme Court. The hardline CPN—M refused to support the decision and organized a nation-wide strike in protest. Nevertheless, a formal agreement between the UCPN (M), the NC, the UML and the SLMM was signed in March, declaring the establishment of an 'Interim Election Council', comprising former civil servants and headed by a chairman (the Chief Justice) rather than a prime minister. The newly elected constituent assembly would comprise 491 members. Progress was also made on the constitutional hindrances to an election, with a plan to be submitted to the President. Chief Justice Khil Raj Regmi was sworn in as Chairman soon after, taking charge of the defence, co-operatives and poverty alleviation portfolios. Madhav Prasad Ghimire was allocated the foreign affairs and home affairs portfolios, and Hari Prasad Neupane assumed responsibility for law, justice, constituent assembly and parliamentary affairs, and for labour and employment. Eight further appointments followed, including that of Shankar Prasad Koirala as Minister of Finance, of Industry, and of Commerce and Supplies. By the beginning of May the Election Commission had yet to announce a date for the forthcoming election, and it was widely expected that the caretaker administration would activate a clause contained in the March agreement that provided for a deferment of the poll, if necessary, until mid-November 2013.

Meanwhile, in August 2012 Khum Bahadur Khadka became the fourth former minister of the post-1990 NC government era to be convicted of corruption. Others convicted previously were Chiranjivi Wagley, Govinda Raj Goshi and Jaya Prakash Prasad Gupta—the latter had left the NC for the Madhesi Janadhikar Forum in 2007 and had been acquitted of corruption charges in the same year, but was convicted in February 2012, while serving as Minister of Information and Communications, and given an 18-month prison term. Khadka, a former minister of the interior, was also sentenced to 18 months' imprisonment.

Attempts by the interim election cabinet to establish a truth and reconciliation commission, a previously agreed component of the peace process, were blocked by the Supreme Court in April 2013 amid fears of an amnesty for those who had committed major crimes during the civil war. Proposals for an amnesty had previously prompted criticism from the UN in August 2012.

Regional Affairs

In 1978 the old Trade and Transit Treaty between Nepal and India was replaced by two treaties, one concerning bilateral trade between the two countries, the other allowing Nepal to develop trade with other countries via India. Relations with India deteriorated considerably in March 1989, however, when India decided not to renew the treaties, insisting that a common treaty covering both issues be negotiated. Nepal refused, stressing the importance of keeping the treaties separate, on the grounds that trade issues are negotiable, whereas the right of transit is a recognized basic right of land-locked countries. In response, India closed 13 of the 15 transit points through which most of Nepal's trade was conducted, causing severe shortages of food and fuel. It was widely believed that a major issue aggravating the dispute was Nepal's purchase of weapons from the People's Republic of China in 1988, which, according to India, violated the Treaty of Peace and Friendship concluded by India and Nepal in 1950. A joint communiqué was signed by the two countries in June 1990, restoring trade relations and reopening the transit points, and assuring mutual consultations on matters of security. A few days earlier, as an apparent gesture of goodwill to India, the Nepalese Government deferred indefinitely the delivery of the final consignment of Chinese weapons destined for Nepal. The visit to Kathmandu by the Indian Prime Minister in February 1991 (the first official visit to Nepal by an Indian head of government since 1977) helped to reaffirm the traditionally amicable ties between the two countries. Separate trade and transit treaties were signed during a visit by Prime Minister Koirala to India in December 1991. A major breakthrough in Indo-Nepalese relations was achieved in February 1996, when the Prime Ministers of the two countries formally signed a treaty in New Delhi, India, regarding the shared utilization of the waters of the Mahakali River basin (for irrigation, general consumption and the production of hydroelectric power). The costs and benefits of the project, which involved the construction of a massive hydroelectric power plant, were to be divided between Nepal and India, although not, some critics claimed, to Nepal's benefit. During a visit to Nepal by the Indian Prime Minister in June 1997, the Mahakali Treaty was formally endorsed, and India granted Nepal access to Bangladeshi ports through a new transit facility across Indian territory via the Karkavita-Phulbari road. Some tension in Indo-Nepalese relations, nevertheless, remained; this centred on border demarcation disputes and, in particular, on the Indian border police's use of territory that Nepal claimed as its own in the far west of the country (namely the strategically situated Kalapani junction between India, Nepal and China, which covers an area of about 35 sq km). In late 2001 India supplied Nepal with two helicopters and arms to assist its neighbour in its campaign against the Maoist insurgency. In early 2002 the Nepalese and Indian Governments held talks on the civil disorder problem in Nepal and India repeated its offer of financial assistance. From early 2003, however, the Indian Government became increasingly concerned about King Gyanendra's perceived disregard for democracy. India condemned the King's assumption of executive power in February 2005 and suspended military aid to Nepal. It also intensified security along the shared border, owing to increased fears of infiltration by Maoist insurgents and their possible co-operation with rebels operating in India's fractious north-eastern states. In July India resumed non-lethal military aid to Nepal. During the Maoists' tenure of power in Nepal in 2008–09 there was growing apprehension among certain sectors of the Indian authorities regarding the Nepalese Maoists' perceived anti-India stance as well as their links with China and with India's own Maoist insurgencies. In August 2009 the new Prime Minister, M. K. Nepal, made an official visit to India during which the two countries signed a trade treaty and India pledged to assist its neighbour with development projects such as road and rail links (notably the Terai Roads Project, which envisaged the construction of more than 1,450 km of asphalted roads in the Terai region) and the establishment of a police academy. In August 2010, following the resignation of M. K. Nepal's Government, the former Indian foreign secretary and ambassador to Nepal, Shyam Saran, was dispatched by the Indian authorities as a special envoy to Nepal with the aim of persuading the Nepalese parties to reach consensus on the formation of a new administration. The Indian delegation was viewed with suspicion by the Maoists, who believed that India did not wish to see them regain power and was exerting pressure on other parties not to support them. In January 2011 President Yadav undertook a 10-day official visit to India, during which he held discussions with the Indian Government regarding Nepal's ongoing attempts to break the political deadlock. The Maoist leader Dr Baburam Bhattarai, who was appointed as the new Nepalese Prime Minister in August, attempted to strengthen relations with India and to reassure the Indian authorities that they could trust and work effectively with a Maoist-led Government in Nepal. During an official visit to India in October Bhattarai signed a Bilateral Investment Promotion and Protection Agreement (BIPPA) with his Indian counterpart; the BIPPA was criticized by certain hard-line Maoist politicians as being biased in favour of Indian companies. In December 2012 President Yadav paid an official visit to India, meeting with his Indian counterpart, Pranab Mukherjee, the Indian Prime Minister, Manmohan Singh, and other high-ranking Indian officials. Yadav was reportedly encouraged to work towards the settlement of the enduring political impasse in Nepal (see Domestic Political Affairs), about which the Indian Government expressed concern.

The People's Republic of China has contributed a considerable amount to the Nepalese economy. The first meeting of a joint committee on economic co-operation took place in 1984. This committee met for a second time (and thenceforth annually) in Kathmandu in 1986, when China agreed to increase its imports from Nepal in order to minimize trade imbalances. Relations between Nepal and China improved further during the late 1980s and 1990s, as indicated by reciprocal visits made by high-ranking Nepalese and Chinese officials (notably, a state visit to Nepal was conducted by the Chinese President, Jiang Zemin, in 1996). In May 2001 the leaders of Nepal and China signed a six-point co-operation agreement to improve cross-border trade, increase road and aviation links, and promote tourism. China subsequently continued to expand its investments in Nepal, particularly in the areas of hydroelectricity, telecommunications and road construction. In August 2011, during a visit to Kathmandu by a high-ranking Chinese delegation, the two countries signed four agreements on bilateral co-operation worth some NRs 1,000m. Relations between Nepal and China were further strengthened by a short, but politically significant, visit made to the Nepalese capital by the Chinese Premier, Wen Jiabao, in January 2012. In March the Nepalese Government signed an agreement with the Chinese Three Gorges Corporation for a US $1,600m. hydroelectricity project, with 75% Chinese investment, constituting the largest foreign investment project in the country.

In 1985 it was agreed that Nepal's border with Tibet (the Xizang Autonomous Region) should be opened. Following the outbreak of ethnic violence in Tibet in 1989, however, the border between Nepal and Tibet was closed indefinitely. The Nepalese authorities have been consistent in their commitment to the 'One China' policy and in their efforts to repatriate refugees fleeing from Tibet. In 1993 G. P. Koirala paid an informal visit to Tibet—the first visit to the region by a Nepalese premier since the 1950s. In 1995, however, the Nepalese authorities banned a proposed peace march by Tibetans through Nepalese territory. During a visit to China by the Nepalese Minister of Foreign Affairs in August 2000 an agreement was reached to allow Nepal increased use of a new road in Tibet. Greater technological and economic co-operation was also achieved, therefore noticeably increasing bilateral trade. Nepal provoked strong criticism from the UN and Western governments in May 2003, after it helped Chinese officials to deport 18 Tibetan refugees from Kathmandu to Tibet (Nepal's usual policy was to transfer Tibetan refugees to officials of the UN High Commissioner for Refugees—UNHCR). It was reported in June that a further 19 Tibetans had been arrested in the western Nepalese district of Accham. In 2008 a series of demonstrations was held by Tibetan refugees in Kathmandu, as the approach of the Beijing Olympic Games in China drew international attention to the Tibet issue. The Nepalese police force was widely criticized for its reportedly violent suppression of the protests and the arrests of hundreds of activists; at the same time, China urged the Nepalese Government to control the demonstrations more stringently.

Ties with Bangladesh are also significant, particularly regarding the utilization of joint water resources. Large-scale migration from Bangladesh has resulted in a notable demographic transformation in Nepal, with the Muslim population increasing from around 4% of the total in the early 1990s to, unofficially, about 10% by the end of the decade. In 1998 the Phulbari Treaty drawn up between India and Bangladesh allowed Nepalese goods access to Bangladesh (and Bangladesh ports) through a transit route in India across the Siliguri Corridor (the narrow strip of territory linking India's north-eastern states with the rest of the country). At a summit meeting of South Asian Association for Regional Cooperation (SAARC, see p. 430) finance ministers in early 2012, Nepalese proposals for the establishment of a major hydroelectric power plant, under a Nepalese-Bangladeshi joint-venture agreement, were discussed. At the same time, the Nepalese authorities requested an expansion of their transit rights within Bangladesh, in order to gain direct access for Nepalese goods to Bangladesh's Mongla Port.

In December 1982 Nepal and Pakistan strengthened their trade links by renewing a 1962 agreement, and in 1983 they established a joint economic commission and a regular air link. In March 2005 the joint economic commission met for the first time in 10 years, when a delegation of Pakistani economic officials visited Nepal. In April 2010 the Pakistani Prime Minister, Yousaf Raza Gilani, met Prime Minister M. K. Nepal during a visit to Kathmandu; the two leaders pledged further to enhance bilateral relations and to work together to ensure peace and security in South Asia.

In late 1991 thousands of Bhutanese of Nepalese origin began to arrive at refugee camps in eastern Nepal, following the outbreak of political and ethnic unrest in Bhutan. Talks held between Bhutanese and Nepalese government officials in 1993 were inconclusive, with both countries denying responsibility for the refugees: the Nepalese Government refused to consider any solution that did not include the resettlement in Bhutan of all ethnic Nepalese refugees living in the camps; the Bhutanese Government rejected the Nepalese proposal, claiming that the majority of the camp population were not actually Bhutanese, had absconded from Bhutan (thus forfeiting their citizenship) or had departed voluntarily. By early 1996 nearly 100,000 refugees were living in eight camps in the districts of Jhapa and Morang. In April 1997 more than 10,000 Bhutanese refugees gathered at a mass demonstration in eastern Nepal to demand UN intervention in the crisis. A breakthrough was achieved during negotiations in December 2000, when both countries reached agreement on a formula for verifying the nationality of the refugees, and a Joint Verification Team (JVT) was subsequently established to inspect the camps and classify the inhabitants. However, the process was hindered by frequent technical disagreements. In January 2003 Nepal and Bhutan finally harmonized their positions on the categorization of the refugees into four different groups: Bhutanese nationals who had been forcefully evicted (Category I); Bhutanese nationals who had left Bhutan voluntarily (Category II); non-Bhutanese (Category III); and Bhutanese who had committed criminal acts (Category IV). The joint verification process continued. The two countries later decided that Bhutan would be fully responsible for any Category I persons, while Category II people could apply for either Bhutanese or Nepalese citizenship, in accordance with the respective national laws. However, talks between the two countries were suspended after Bhutanese members of the JVT were attacked in December in the Khudanabari camp by several thousand refugees protesting against the terms of the agreement. In October 2006 the US Government offered to resettle as many as 60,000 of the refugees (who by now totalled around 106,000); similar offers followed from Australia, Canada and New Zealand. In late 2007 it was reported that the refugees were facing 'severe intimidation' from political leaders who were opposed to the offers of resettlement abroad on the grounds that this would undermine their political struggle to settle all the 'camp people' in Bhutan. Nevertheless, in March 2008 the resettlement of refugees in the USA and New Zealand began. In April 2011 the Bhutanese Prime Minister, Jigmi Yozer Thinley, in his capacity of Chairman of the SAARC, paid a three-day official visit to Nepal, during which he held talks with his Nepalese counterpart, Jhala Nath Khanal; the two leaders agreed to resume talks on the refugee issue (stalled since 2003). According to UNHCR, by mid-2012 about 69,000 persons claiming Bhutanese refugee status had been resettled in third countries since November 2007: the USA had taken the majority of these, followed by Canada, Australia, New Zealand, Denmark, Norway, the Netherlands and the United Kingdom. By 2012 an estimated 44,000 persons remained in camps in Nepal, the majority of whom were reported to have expressed an interest in third-country resettlement; the number of camps in eastern Nepal had been reduced from seven to two in that year. In late 2012, during a meeting with Prime Minister Thinley, the Nepali Deputy Prime Minister and Minister of Foreign Affairs, Narayan Kaji Shrestha, urged Bhutan to work towards a solution for those refugees, reportedly 14,000 in number, who had rejected third-country resettlement.

CONSTITUTION AND GOVERNMENT

On 15 January 2007 the bicameral legislature instituted by the 1990 Constitution was dissolved upon the promulgation of a new Interim Constitution, and a 330-member Interim Parliament, or 'Legislature-Parliament', was convened by agreement of the seven-party alliance and the Maoists. In accordance with articles stipulated in the Interim Constitution, constitutional powers of governance were reassigned from the monarchy to the acting Prime Minister and the temporary legislature was to facilitate preparations for the democratic election of a constituent assembly by the end of June of that year. The constituent assembly, with a term of two years, would be responsible for drawing up a new permanent constitution. According to the Interim Constitution, the future of the monarchy was to be decided at the first official sitting of the constituent assembly. In December 2007 a parliamentary resolution declaring Nepal a republic received the requisite two-thirds' majority for a constitutional amendment, but this decision did not come into effect until the inaugural session of the Constituent Assembly, held in May 2008. At this stage, the Interim Parliament was dissolved. In mid-2008 the Constituent Assembly elected a new President, Vice-President and Prime Minister; the presidency was a largely ceremonial position. Owing to the ongoing political instability, the deadline for the introduction of a new constitution—28 May 2010—was not met, and on that date the Government and the main opposition parties agreed to extend the tenure of the Constituent Assembly by one year. With the process of drafting a new constitution still incomplete, the tenure of the Constituent Assembly was subsequently extended on several further occasions. When the latest deadline of May 2012 expired, the Constituent Assembly was dissolved. In March 2013 a non-partisan interim government was established, under the leadership of the Chief Justice, in preparation for elections to a new 491-member Constituent Assembly, scheduled for June.

For the purposes of local administration, Nepal is divided into 14 zones, 75 districts, 3,754 village development committees and 99 municipalities, which are together grouped into five development regions. Each of the districts is headed by a permanent chief district officer, who is responsible for maintaining law and order and for co-ordinating the work of field agencies of the various government ministries.

REGIONAL AND INTERNATIONAL CO-OPERATION

Nepal is a member of the Asian Development Bank (ADB, see p. 214), the Colombo Plan (see p. 460) and the South Asian Association for Regional Cooperation (SAARC, see p. 430), all of which seek to encourage regional economic development.

Having joined the UN in 1955, Nepal is a member of the Economic and Social Commission for Asia and the Pacific (ESCAP, see p. 31). Nepal became a member of the World Trade Organization (WTO, see p. 444) in 2004.

ECONOMIC AFFAIRS

In 2011, according to estimates by the World Bank, Nepal's gross national income (GNI), measured at average 2009–11 prices, was US $16,601m., equivalent to $540 per head (or $1,260 per head on an international purchasing-power parity basis). During 2002–11, it was estimated, the population increased at an average annual rate of 2.0%, while gross domestic product (GDP) per head increased, in real terms, by an average of 2.2% per year. According to the official figures, overall GDP increased, in real terms, at an average annual rate of 4.2% in 2000/01–2011/12; real GDP grew by 4.6% in 2011/12.

Agriculture (including forestry and fishing) contributed a preliminary 35.1% of GDP in the fiscal year ending 15 July 2012. The sector was projected to engage an estimated 92.8% of the economically active population at mid-2013, according to

FAO figures. The principal crops are rice, sugar cane, potatoes, maize, wheat, millet, and vegetables and melons. During 2000/01–2011/12 agricultural GDP increased by an average of 3.4% per year; the sector grew by 4.9% in 2011/12.

Industry (comprising mining, manufacturing, construction and utilities) employed 10.8% of the labour force in 2008, and provided a preliminary 14.6% of GDP in 2011/12, according to official figures. About 60% of Nepal's industrial output derives from traditional cottage industries, and the remainder from modern industries. During 2000/01–2011/12 industrial GDP increased at an average annual rate of 2.4%; industrial production rose by 1.7% in 2011/12.

Mining employed only 0.2% of the labour force in 2008, and contributed a preliminary 0.6% of GDP in 2011/12. During 2000/01–2011/12 mining GDP increased by an average of 3.9% per year. The sector's GDP rose by 2.0% in 2010/11 and by 5.0% in 2011/12. Mica is mined east of Kathmandu, and there are also small deposits of lignite, copper, talc, limestone, cobalt and iron ore. Geophysical investigations have indicated that the Siwalik range and the Terai belt are potential prospective areas for petroleum.

Manufacturing contributed a preliminary 6.2% of GDP in 2011/12, and employed about 6.6% of the labour force in 2008. Manufacturing GDP increased at an average annual rate of 0.8% in 2000/01–2011/12. Manufacturing production rose by 1.3% in 2011/12. The principal branches of the sector include textiles (particularly carpets and rugs), food products, wearing apparel and tobacco products. Traditional cottage industries include basket-making and the production of cotton fabrics and edible oils.

Construction contributed a preliminary 6.7% of GDP in 2011/12, and employed about 3.1% of the labour force in 2008. Construction GDP increased at an average annual rate of 3.4% in 2000/01–2011/12; it rose by 4.8% in 2010/11, but fell by 0.1% in 2011/12.

Energy is derived principally from traditional sources (particularly fuelwood). However, imports of mineral fuel and lubricants (mainly for the transport sector) comprised an estimated 22.3% of the cost of total imports in 2011/12. In addition, Nepal's rivers are exploited for hydroelectric power (HEP) production: the country has a huge potential generating capacity (estimated at 83,000 MW), but only about 1% of Nepal's energy needs are supplied by hydropower. In January 2004 the 144-MW Kali Gandaki A HEP plant, the country's largest to date, was officially inaugurated. The country's generating capacity will be boosted considerably by scheduled completion in 2016 of the 456-MW Upper Tamakoshi HEP project, construction of which commenced in 2011 with assistance from People's Republic of China. In August 2004 Cairn Energy Co of the United Kingdom signed an agreement with the Nepalese Government to explore for petroleum and gas in a 22,000-sq km area in the Terai plain, near the border with India. However, in 2012 Cairn Energy was reported to have suspended its operations in Nepal.

The services sector employed 15.3% of the labour force in 2008. The sector contributed a preliminary 50.3% of GDP in 2011/12. The GDP of the services sector increased at an average annual rate of 4.5% in 2000/01–2011/12. Sectoral GDP grew by 5.1% in 2011/12. By 1996 tourism had emerged as Nepal's major source of foreign exchange; in 1999/2000 revenue from tourism amounted to 12.9% of total foreign exchange earnings. The Maoist insurgency adversely affected visitor levels in the first half of the 2000s. The cessation of hostilities in 2006—combined with the introduction of additional airline services between Nepal and other Asian countries—led to a significant recovery in the tourism sector. In 2011 tourist arrivals increased by 22.1%, compared with the previous year, to 736,215; in the same year, revenue from tourism increased by 12.2% to an estimated US $386m.

In 2011 Nepal recorded a visible merchandise trade deficit of US $4,666.1m., while there was a surplus of $49.0m. on the current account of the balance of payments. In 2011/12 India was the principal source of imports (supplying 64.8% of the total) and the principal market for exports (66.8%). In 2009/10, other major trading partners were China, the USA, Indonesia, Thailand, the United Kingdom and Japan. In 2011/12 the principal exports were basic manufactures and manufactured goods (particularly woven articles and garments), and food and live animals. The principal imports were basic manufactures, machinery and transport equipment, and mineral fuels and lubricants.

In 2010/11 there was an estimated overall budget deficit of NRs 48,456.7m. Foreign aid plays a vital role in the Nepalese economy. According to the Asian Development Bank (ADB),

Nepal's total external debt was an estimated US $3,863m. at the end of 2012. In that year the cost of debt-servicing was equivalent to 11.1% of receipts from exports of goods and services. According to figures by the International Labour Organization, the average annual rate of inflation was 8.1% in 2002–12; according to the ADB, consumer prices rose by 8.3% in 2012. During the first decade of the 2000s it was estimated that more than 40% of Nepalese workers were underemployed, while urban unemployment, a major problem, particularly among educated youths, stood at around 7%. The national unemployment rate was estimated at 2.1% in 2008.

With an inhospitable terrain and high rates of poverty, Nepal is among the least developed countries in the world. Successive administrations since 1991 have pursued a policy of economic liberalization: many state enterprises have been privatized (although there have been numerous delays in the process), and there have been attempts to reduce the fiscal deficit, to increase revenue mobilization, to restructure and improve the financial sector, and to institute and operate open trade and investment policies. Nepal's accession to the World Trade Organization in 2004 was expected to lead to the country's further integration into the global economy. However, foreign investment has remained negligible, with significant reforms needed if Nepal's attractiveness as an investment destination is to increase. The instability caused by the country's transition from a monarchy to a republic in 2008 and the ensuing political upheaval and general unrest over the following five years has hindered the country's economic development. A protracted political stalemate in 2012 prompted the Government to introduce an emergency short-term budget in July; the delayed annual budget was finally announced in November. A deceleration in the rate of growth of remittances, together with a widening trade deficit and worsening power outages, all contributed to a fall in the GDP growth rate from 4.6% in 2009/10 to 3.5% in 2010/11. GDP growth was on the increase again in 2011/12, at 4.6%, but the IMF's forecast for 2012/13 was more pessimistic, with growth slowing to 3.8%. On a more positive note, Nepal has enjoyed considerable success in recent years in tackling poverty: the number of those living below the poverty line (about US $160 a year) was estimated to have decreased to 25% of the population in 2011, compared with 31% in 2004. Tourism has been identified as a vital sector for driving economic growth. Although the Government's target of 1m. tourist arrivals in 2011 was not achieved, according to the Nepal Tourism Board, the total number of foreign visitors grew by some 22%, compared with the previous year, to reach 736,215. Reflecting recent improvements in air links between Nepal and its neighbours, there were particularly large increases in the number of tourists from India and China. In January 2012 the Prime Minister announced an ambitious action plan, which focused on infrastructure development (including Chinese-financed hydroelectric power projects and the construction of a second international airport outside Kathmandu) and envisaged the creation of some 677,000 new jobs. In September the UN Development Assistance Framework was published by the National Planning Commission and the UN Country Team in Nepal, which planned for $685m. to be spent on development and international co-operation during 2013–2017. However, the ongoing delay to the drafting of the constitution and ensuing political instability in 2012–13 were unlikely to improve Nepal's image as a viable business destination for foreign direct investment.

PUBLIC HOLIDAYS

The Nepalese year (Bikram Sambat) 2070 runs from 14 April 2013 to 13 April 2014, and the year 2071 from 14 April 2014 to 13 April 2015. The public holidays observed in Nepal vary locally. The dates given below apply to Kathmandu.

2014: 15 January (Maghi Sankranti/Maghi Parba), 30 January (Martyrs' Day), 31 January (Sonam Lhosar, Tibetan New Year), 19 February (Rashtriya Prajatantra Divas—National Democracy Day), 27 February (Maha Shivaratri—in honour of Lord Shiva), 2 March (Ghyalbo Lhosar, Sherpa New Year), 8 March (International Women's Day), 16 March (Phagu Purnima/Holi), 14 April (Navabarsha—New Year's Day), 1 May (Labour Day), 14 May (Buddha Purnima—Lord Buddha's Birthday), 28 May (Republic Day), 28 July (Id al-Fitr—end of Ramadan), 10 August (Janai Purnima/Raksha Bandhan—Sacred Thread Ceremony), 17 August (Janmashtami—Lord Krishna's Birthday), 25 September (Ghatasthapana), 3 October* (Vijaya Dashain), 4 October (Id al-Adha—Feast of the Sacrifice), October* (Kojagrat Purnima—End of Dashain), 23 October (Laxmi Puja and Diwali—Festival of Lights, over three days), 24 October (Gobhardhan Puja), 27 October (Bhai Tika—Brothers' Day), 25 December (Christmas Day).

* Forms part of the extended Dashain holiday, which generally involves up to five days of official holidays.

Note: A number of Hindu, Muslim and Buddhist holidays depend on lunar sightings.

Statistical Survey

Sources (unless otherwise stated): Central Bureau of Statistics, Thapathali, Kathmandu; tel. (1) 4229406; fax (1) 4227720; e-mail info@cbs.gov.np; internet www.cbs.gov.np; Federation of Nepalese Chambers of Commerce and Industry (FNCCI), Pachali Shahid Shukra FNCCI Milan Marg, Teku, POB 269, Kathmandu; tel. (1) 4262061; fax (1) 4261022; e-mail fncci@mos.com.np; internet www.fncci.org.

Area and Population

AREA, POPULATION AND DENSITY

Area (sq km)	147,181*
Population (census results)	
22 June 2001†‡	23,151,423
22 June 2011	
Males	12,849,041
Females	13,645,463
Total	26,494,504
Density (per sq km) at 2011 census	180.0

* 56,827 sq miles.
† Population is *de jure*.
‡ Includes estimates for certain areas in 12 districts where the census could not be conducted, owing to violence and disruption.

POPULATION BY AGE AND SEX
(at 2011 census)

	Males	Females	Total
0–14	4,714,763	4,533,483	9,248,246
15–64	7,437,790	8,410,885	15,848,675
65 and over	696,488	701,095	1,397,583
Total	12,849,041	13,645,463	26,494,504

PRINCIPAL TOWNS
(population at 2011 census)

Kathmandu* . .	1,003,285	Butwal	120,982
Pokhara . . .	264,991	Dharan . . .	119,915
Lalitpur . . .	226,728	Mahendranagar .	106,666
Biratnagar . . .	204,949	Dhangadhi . . .	104,047
Bharatpur . . .	147,777	Janakpur . . .	98,446
Birgunj	139,068		

* Total for urban agglomeration 1,744,240.

BIRTHS AND DEATHS
(annual averages, UN estimates)

	1995–2000	2000–05	2005–10
Birth rate (per 1,000)	35.0	30.9	25.6
Death rate (per 1,000)	9.7	7.8	6.2

Source: UN, *World Population Prospects: The 2010 Revision.*

2011 (estimates): Birth rate 24.0 per 1,000; Death rate 7.7 per 1,000.

Life expectancy (years at birth): 68.7 (males 67.9; females 69.6) in 2011 (Source: World Bank, World Development Indicators database).

ECONOMICALLY ACTIVE POPULATION
(labour force survey, '000 persons aged 15 years and over, 2008)

	Males	Females	Total
Agriculture, hunting, forestry and fishing	3,429	5,275	8,704
Mining and quarrying	19	8	27
Manufacturing	469	305	773
Electricity, gas and water . .	39	70	109
Construction	326	41	367
Wholesale and retail trade; repair of motor vehicles, motorcycles and personal and household goods	447	245	692
Hotels and restaurants . . .	94	103	197
Transport, storage and communications	191	8	198
Financial intermediation . . .	22	10	32
Real estate, renting and business activities	57	13	71
Public administration and defence; compulsory social security . .	96	13	109
Education	189	96	285
Health and social work . . .	46	31	77
Other community, social and personal services	77	23	99
Private households with employed persons	14	19	33
Extra-territorial organizations and bodies	4	1	5
Total employed	5,519	6,260	11,779
Unemployed	127	126	253
Total labour force	5,646	6,386	12,032

Note: Totals may not be equal to the sum of components, owing to rounding.

Source: ILO.

Mid-2013 (estimates in '000): Agriculture, etc. 13,097; Total labour force 14,112 (Source: FAO).

Health and Welfare

KEY INDICATORS

Total fertility rate (children per woman, 2010)	2.7
Under-5 mortality rate (per 1,000 live births, 2010) . . .	50
HIV/AIDS (% of persons aged 15–49, 2009)	0.4
Physicians (per 1,000 head, 2004)	0.21
Hospital beds (per 1,000 head, 2006)	0.5
Health expenditure (2009): US $ per head (PPP)	63
Health expenditure (2009): % of GDP	5.5
Health expenditure (2009): public (% of total)	32.0
Access to water (% of persons, 2010)	89
Access to sanitation (% of persons, 2010)	31
Total carbon dioxide emissions ('000 metric tons, 2008) . .	3,542.3
Carbon dioxide emissions per head (metric tons, 2008) . .	0.1
Human Development Index (2011): ranking	157
Human Development Index (2011): value	0.458

For sources and definitions, see explanatory note on p. vi.

Agriculture

PRINCIPAL CROPS
('000 metric tons)

	2009	2010	2011
Wheat	1,344	1,557	1,746
Rice, paddy	4,524	4,024	4,460
Barley	23	28	30
Maize	1,931	1,855	2,068
Millet	293	300	303
Potatoes	2,424	2,518	2,508
Sugar cane	2,354	2,593	2,718
Beans, dry*	26	27	34
Pigeon peas	18	19	14
Lentils	148	152	207
Mustard seed	135	155	176
Garlic	34	39	41
Oranges	49	51	51
Apples	39	42	43
Ginger	179	211	216
Jute	18	21	14
Tobacco, unmanufactured . . .	2	2	1

* FAO estimates.

Aggregate production ('000 metric tons, may include official, semi-official or estimated data): Total cereals 8,114 in 2009, 7,763 in 2010, 8,607 in 2011; Total roots and tubers 2,579 in 2009, 2,679 in 2010, 2,668 in 2011; Total vegetables (incl. melons) 2,819 in 2009, 3,077 in 2010, 3,320 in 2011; Total fruits (excl. melons) 1,284 in 2009, 1,327 in 2010, 1,456 in 2011.

Source: FAO.

LIVESTOCK
('000 head, year ending September)

	2009	2010	2011
Cattle	7,175	7,199	7,226
Buffaloes	4,680	4,837	4,994
Pigs	1,045	1,065	1,108
Sheep	803	801	805
Goats	8,473	8,844	9,186*
Chickens	24,481	25,760	39,531

* Unofficial figure.

Source: FAO.

LIVESTOCK PRODUCTS
('000 metric tons)

	2009	2010	2011
Cattle meat*	50.2	50.2	51.0
Buffalo meat	156.6	162.2	167.9
Sheep meat	2.7	2.7	2.7
Goat meat	48.5	49.9	52.8
Pig meat	17.0	17.1	17.9
Chicken meat	16.7	16.5	36.1
Cows' milk	413.9	429.0	447.2
Buffaloes' milk	1,031.5	1,066.9	1,109.3
Goats' milk*	71.2	73.3	73.3
Hen eggs†	30.8	31.7	34.5

* FAO estimates.
† Unofficial figures.

Source: FAO.

Forestry

ROUNDWOOD REMOVALS
('000 cubic metres, excl. bark, FAO estimates)

	2009	2010	2011
Sawlogs, veneer logs and logs for sleepers	1,260	1,260	1,260
Fuel wood	12,555	12,526	12,464
Total	13,815	13,786	13,724

Source: FAO.

SAWNWOOD PRODUCTION
('000 cubic metres, incl. railway sleepers)

	1999	2000	2001
Coniferous (softwood)*	20	20	20
Broadleaved (hardwood) . . .	610	610	610
Total	630	630	630

* FAO estimates.

2002–11: Production as in 2001 (FAO estimates).

Source: FAO.

Fishing

('000 metric tons, live weight)

	2008	2009	2010
Capture	21.5	21.5	21.5
Aquaculture	27.3	26.7	28.2
Common carp	5.5	4.1	4.2
Bighead carp	2.9	3.3	3.5
Silver carp	8.2	9.3	10.0
Total catch	48.8	48.2	49.7

Source: FAO.

Industry

SELECTED PRODUCTS
('000 metric tons unless otherwise indicated, year ending 15 July)

	2005/06	2006/07	2007/08
Cement	613.6	644.3	670.1*
Raw sugar	98.5	103.4	107.5*
Tea	11.6	12.2	12.7*
Vegetable ghee	179.2	188.2	195.7*
Noodles	32.3	35.6	37.0*
Paper	29.9	31.4	32.7*
Cigarettes ('000 million) . . .	9.5	10.0	10.4*
Soap	44.8	47.1	48.9*
Electric energy (million kWh) .	2,514.7	2,723.0	2,768.3

* Annual estimate based on data for first eight months.

Finance

CURRENCY AND EXCHANGE RATES

Monetary Units:
  100 paisa (pice) = 1 Nepalese rupee (NR).

Sterling, Dollar and Euro Equivalents (31 December 2012):
  £1 sterling = NRs 138.50;
  US $1 = NRs 87.77;
  €1 = NRs 115.80;
  1,000 Nepalese rupees = £7.22 = $11.39 = €8.64.

Average Exchange Rate (rupees per US $):
  2010   73.156
  2011   74.020
  2012   85.197

BUDGET
(NRs million, year ending 15 July)*

Revenue†	2008/09	2009/10	2010/11
Taxation	117,051.9	156,294.9	172,777.6
Taxes on external trade . . .	26,792.9	35,150.8	35,711.6
Value-added tax	39,700.9	54,920.9	61,663.6
Excise duties	16,237.4	24,473.2	26,747.4
Income and property transfer tax	34,320.7	41,750.0	48,655.1
Non-tax revenue	26,422.6	23,650.9	27,041.1
Interest	4,616.9	2,401.1	2,632.9
Civil administration	11,435.7	10,572.6	11,802.3
Dividend	7,197.4	7,352.0	8,624.7
Royalty and sale of fixed assets .	2,541.7	2,948.4	2,660.1
Miscellaneous	630.9	376.8	1,321.2
Total	143,474.5	179,945.8	199,819.0

Expenditure‡	2008/09	2009/10	2010/11
Recurrent expenditure . . .	127,738.9	151,019.1	168,824.2
General administration . . .	21,832.4	25,540.6	29,336.0
Defence	13,748.4	16,576.0	17,410.3
Social services	47,437.9	62,394.7	70,541.7
Education	32,141.8	42,490.0	48,945.3
Health	10,491.0	13,578.3	14,387.1
Economic services	12,052.6	14,927.3	17,789.2
Agriculture-related . . .	5,589.3	7,314.7	9,502.9
Forestry	2,441.4	2,753.8	3,246.6
Interest payments	8,154.2	9,981.3	12,737.1
Other purposes	24,513.2	21,599.2	21,009.8
Capital expenditure	73,089.0	90,237.7	108,153.2
Administration and defence . .	3,094.7	3,891.0	4,466.8
Social services	34,056.8	36,495.2	45,591.1
Education	3,520.2	3,903.9	6,258.4
Health	2,677.4	3,170.7	4,566.0
Provision of drinking water . .	5,657.7	5,335.0	4,838.6
Economic services	31,999.9	42,968.0	45,615.3
Irrigation	5,695.8	7,974.6	7,352.0
Transport	9,893.7	17,016.6	20,184.4
Electricity	6,073.3	12,503.4	11,291.2
Interest payments	934.6	3,319.8	8,984.6
Miscellaneous	3,002.9	3,563.7	3,495.6
Total	200,827.9	241,256.8	276,977.4

* Figures refer to the recurrent and capital budgets of the central Government.

† Excluding grants received (NRs million): 26,382.8 in 2008/09; 38,545.9 in 2009/10; 45,922.2 in 2010/11.

‡ Excluding re-payments (NRs million): 18,834.1 in 2008/09; 18,432.3 in 2009/10; 17,220.5 in 2010/11.

Source: Ministry of Finance, Kathmandu.

INTERNATIONAL RESERVES
(US $ million at mid-December)

	2003	2004	2005
Gold*	6.5	6.5	5.4
IMF special drawing rights . .	0.8	9.7	8.8
Reserve position in IMF . . .	8.6	—	—
Foreign exchange	1,213.1	1,452.5	1,490.2
Total	1,229.0	1,468.7	1,504.4

* Valued at US $42.5 per troy ounce in 2003 and 2004, and at $41.9 in 2005.

IMF special drawing rights (US $ million at mid-December): 99.9 in 2009; 93.7 in 2010; 89.0 in 2011.

Foreign exchange (US $ million at mid-December): 2,661.2 in 2009; 2,831.3 in 2010; 3,541.8 in 2011.

Source: IMF, *International Financial Statistics*.

MONEY SUPPLY
(NRs million at mid-December)*

	2009	2010	2011
Currency outside depository corporations	128,974	137,392	155,282
Transferable deposits	72,075	70,107	75,288
Other deposits	596,122	666,115	806,149
Broad money	797,171	873,613	1,036,719

* Excluding Indian currency in circulation.

Source: IMF, *International Financial Statistics*.

COST OF LIVING
(Consumer Price Index; base: 2000 = 100)

	2010	2011	2012
Food (incl. beverages) . . .	211.3	236.1	256.1
All items (incl. others) . . .	192.8	209.8	230.2

Source: ILO.

NATIONAL ACCOUNTS
(NRs million at current prices, year ending 15 July)

Expenditure on the Gross Domestic Product

	2009/10	2010/11	2011/12*
Final consumption expenditure .	1,056,185	1,251,421	1,402,707
Households	916,993	1,096,653	1,216,333
Non-profit institutions serving households	20,002	23,104	26,697
General government . . .	119,189	131,664	159,677
Gross capital formation . .	457,395	445,322	510,590
Gross fixed capital formation .	264,888	290,693	305,682
Increase in stocks† . . .	192,507	154,629	204,908
Total domestic expenditure .	1,513,580	1,696,743	1,913,297
Exports of goods and services .	114,298	121,886	152,369
Less Imports of goods and services	434,198	449,199	507,492
GDP in purchasers' values .	1,193,679	1,369,430	1,558,174
GDP at constant 2000/01 prices	618,529	642,553	672,326

* Preliminary figures.
† Including statistical discrepancy.

Gross Domestic Product by Economic Activity

	2009/10	2010/11	2011/12*
Agriculture and forestry . . .	391,519	470,850	510,760
Fishing	4,236	4,524	5,007
Mining and quarrying	5,926	6,956	8,166
Manufacturing	70,924	79,489	90,547
Electricity, gas and water . .	15,244	15,288	16,565
Construction	77,289	89,356	98,772
Wholesale and retail trade . .	161,067	182,465	209,095
Restaurants and hotels . . .	17,347	21,866	26,164
Transport, storage and communications	95,304	102,724	122,406
Financial intermediation . .	46,083	55,431	68,403
Real estate, renting and business.	93,747	106,236	119,991
Public administration and defence	21,695	24,819	31,087
Education	61,384	62,631	80,840
Health and social work . . .	15,382	16,469	22,712
Other community and social services	41,423	49,412	58,102
Sub-total	1,118,571	1,288,517	1,468,617
Less Financial intermediation services indirectly measured (FISIM)	35,156	42,094	50,401
GDP at basic prices . . .	1,083,415	1,246,423	1,418,216
Indirect taxes, *less* subsidies . .	109,358	121,997	138,809
Statistical discrepancy . . .	906	1,010	1,149
GDP in market prices . .	1,193,679	1,369,430	1,558,174

* Preliminary figures.

BALANCE OF PAYMENTS
(US $ million)

	2009	2010	2011
Exports of goods	837.4	901.8	999.0
Imports of goods	−4,265.4	−5,016.4	−5,665.1
Balance on goods	−3,428.1	−4,114.6	−4,666.1
Exports of services	705.3	671.8	863.5
Imports of services	−842.2	−871.0	−782.2
Balance on goods and services	−3,564.9	−4,313.7	−4,584.8
Primary income received . .	210.1	209.8	287.7
Primary income paid . . .	−52.4	−116.2	−140.3
Balance on goods, services and primary income	−3,407.2	−4,220.2	−4,437.4
Secondary income received . .	3,289.5	3,835.8	4,538.5
Secondary income paid . . .	−109.8	−53.4	−52.1
Current balance	−227.5	−437.8	49.0
Capital account (net) . . .	132.4	185.4	189.5
Direct investment liabilities . .	38.2	87.8	94.0
Other investment assets . .	−306.2	−355.6	−300.1
Other investment liabilities . .	83.7	435.9	253.1
Net errors and omissions . . .	−72.6	−186.1	283.0
Reserves and related items .	−352.1	−270.3	568.6

Source: IMF, *International Financial Statistics.*

External Trade

PRINCIPAL COMMODITIES
(NRs million, year ending 15 July)

Imports from India

	2009/10	2010/11	2011/12*
Rice	1,256.5	1,954.3	4,267.0
Textiles	2,440.7	1,966.1	2,410.5
Thread	3,022.7	2,855.3	4,132.5
Medicines	7,962.8	9,807.8	10,383.4
Chemicals	3,133.4	3,123.5	4,072.9
Coal	2,126.0	3,118.7	5,550.4
Cement	4,414.5	4,372.8	3,300.1
Petroleum products	51,610.4	75,080.8	92,255.6
Coldrolled sheet (in coil) . . .	6,802.6	8,235.5	7,507.9
Hotrolled sheet (in coil) . . .	4,111.3	5,459.4	5,542.6
Mild steel (MS) billet	13,720.7	18,337.2	19,437.3
Mild steel (MS) wire rod . . .	6,107.6	5,003.8	6,761.0
Transport vehicles and parts . .	23,776.6	20,681.4	17,051.0
Other machine equipment and parts	8,416.9	9,793.1	8,342.0
Electrical equipment	6,089.5	7,223.7	7,009.8
Agricultural equipment and parts	3,372.8	3,162.3	4,145.8
Total (incl. others)	217,114.3	261,925.2	299,389.6

* Provisional.

Imports from Other Countries

	2009/10	2010/11	2011/12*
Crude palm oil	2,026.4	6,096.6	4,210.6
Betel nut	3,324.1	1,965.3	1,639.2
Crude soybean oil	4,337.5	6,507.6	9,962.3
Ready-made garments . .	3,736.3	4,256.1	1,047.3
Textile dyes	3,25.5	1,896.0	88.0
Textiles	1,910.5	2,609.1	1,275.2
Threads	2,735.2	1,942.9	1,854.9
Medicines	3,358.0	2,135.4	1,976.1
Gold	41,635.8	11,357.6	25,770.4
Silver	3,250.9	3,725.6	4,370.9
Copper wire rod, scrapes and sheets	1,776.2	1,312.8	1,875.2
Polyethylene granules . .	5,787.6	4,701.2	5,786.7
Electrical equipment . .	6,837.7	6,505.5	7,311.6
Computer parts . . .	5,341.1	6,178.3	6,150.3
Transport equipment and parts .	4,235.9	4,215.2	2,859.3
Other machine equipment and parts	7,656.1	6,409.2	7,197.5
Telecommunications equipment and parts	8,521.9	9,493.2	8,459.0
Aircraft and parts . . .	2,218.2	2,472.4	1,406.1
Total (incl. others) . .	157,220.9	134,250.3	162,278.1

* Provisional.

Exports to India

	2009/10	2010/11	2011/12*
Juice	1,750.1	2,363.1	3,027.1
Catechu (extract of Acacia) .	1,682.0	1,114.0	1,002.5
Cardamom	1,316.0	1,914.5	3,275.5
Polyester yarn	3,397.9	2,640.7	3,657.2
Thread	2,771.5	3,351.1	2,628.2
Textiles (cotton, synthetic and others)	3,361.9	3,733.5	5,130.3
Jute goods	2,896.7	3,998.1	4,064.7
Toothpaste	673.2	972.7	1,099.0
Galvanized iron sheet . . .	1,794.8	3,894.8	3,343.4
Other wire	1,200.1	1,637.7	1,809.6
Steel pipes	695.1	943.1	797.8
Total (incl. others) . . .	39,993.7	43,360.4	49,616.3

* Provisional.

Exports to Other Countries

	2009/10	2010/11	2011/12*
Pulses	3,952.0	3,357.9	2,497.0
Herbs	239.4	125.7	197.7
Animal hides and skins . .	307.0	434.2	723.5
Woollen carpet . . .	4,078.7	4,860.4	6,938.0
Ready-made garments . .	3,890.7	3,062.7	4,006.3
Pashmina goods . . .	1,267.6	2,273.1	3,230.3
Nepalese paper and paper products	553.3	399.0	587.3
Handicraft goods (of metal and wood)	1,082.8	457.5	510.1
Silverware and jewellery . .	126.6	90.5	110.0
Total (incl. others) . . .	20,830.3	20,978.1	24,644.7

* Provisional.

PRINCIPAL TRADING PARTNERS
(NRs million, year ending 15 July)

Imports	2007/08	2008/09	2009/10
Australia	1,751.0	2,283.2	4,950.3
China, People's Republic . . .	22,255.8	32,852.9	39,218.2
Germany	3,430.3	2,244.4	2,321.8
Hong Kong	1,177.4	1,612.8	4,227.4
India	142,376.5	165,119.0	214,261.1
Indonesia	9,913.5	8,307.2	8,093.8
Japan	6,148.1	6,111.2	6,267.6
Korea, Republic	2,077.0	2,955.3	5,885.3
Malaysia	3,833.7	4,888.9	4,207.3
New Zealand	817.9	887.8	1,091.6
Saudi Arabia	2,677.7	8,683.7	1,832.9
Singapore	5,268.7	7,047.1	5,007.3
Taiwan	1,232.0	1,752.8	1,519.8
Thailand	4,983.5	6,638.0	7,504.7
United Kingdom . . .	1,643.4	6,499.9	7,298.8
USA	3,718.1	3,808.6	5,384.8
Total (incl. others)	221,937.7	284,469.6	378,795.6

Exports	2007/08	2008/09	2009/10
China, People's Republic . . .	736.4	1,847.9	1,008.7
France	1,001.2	1,144.7	1,152.9
Germany	2,332.1	2,785.0	2,391.0
India	38,555.7	43,574.5	39,902.8
Italy	583.8	851.5	716.2
United Kingdom	1,066.3	1,429.7	1,228.2
USA	4,598.9	4,878.6	3,867.2
Total (incl. others)	59,266.5	67,697.5	61,126.8

Imports: *2009/10* (revised figures): India 217,114.3; Other countries 157,220.9; Total 374,335.2. *2010/11:* India 261,925.2; Other countries 134,250.3; Total 396,175.5. *2011/12* (provisional figures): India 299,389.6; Other countries 162,278.1; Total 461,667.7. **Exports:** *2009/10* (revised figures): India 39,993.7; Other countries 20,830.3; Total 60,824.0. *2010/11:* India 43,360.4; Other countries 20,978.1; Total 64,338.5. *2011/12* (provisional figures): India 49,616.3; Other countries 24,644.7; Total 74,261.0.

Transport

ROAD TRAFFIC
(vehicles registered)

	2009/10	2010/11	2011/12
Cars, jeeps and vans	12,268	8,510	5,403
Buses and minibuses	2,668	2,980	1,618
Tractors	11,460	7,937	2,512
Other agro-industrial vehicles .	4,524	1,969	593
Motorcycles	168,707	138,907	90,305
Total (incl. others)	201,787	163,640	101,779

Source: Department of Transport Management, Kathmandu.

CIVIL AVIATION
(traffic on scheduled services of Royal Nepal Airlines Corporation)

	2007	2008	2009
Kilometres flown (million) . .	11	11	10
Passengers carried ('000) . .	528	520	484
Passenger-km (million) . . .	947	931	858
Total ton-km (million)	90	88	80

Source: UN, *Statistical Yearbook*.

2010: Passengers carried ('000) 288 (Source: World Bank, World Development Indicators database).

Tourism

FOREIGN TOURIST ARRIVALS

Nationality	2009	2010	2011
Australia	15,461	16,243	19,824
Bangladesh	15,385	16,470	17,563
China, People's Republic . . .	32,272	46,360	61,917
France	22,155	24,550	26,720
Germany	19,247	22,583	27,472
India	93,885	120,898	149,504
Italy	7,983	10,226	12,621
Japan	22,446	23,332	26,283
Korea, Republic	16,145	20,320	24,488
Netherlands	11,148	13,471	16,836
Sri Lanka	36,363	45,531	59,884
Thailand	27,397	21,528	33,541
United Kingdom	35,383	35,091	39,091
USA	32,044	36,425	42,875
Total (incl. others)	509,972	602,867	736,215

Tourism receipts (US $ million, excl. passenger transport): 412 in 2009; 344 in 2010; 386 in 2011 (provisional).

Source: partly World Tourism Organization.

Communications Media

	2009	2010	2011*
Telephones ('000 main lines in use)	812.6	841.7*	845.5
Mobile cellular telephones ('000 subscribers)	5,597.9	9,195.6	13,354.5
Internet subscribers ('000) . .	n.a.	128.4*	n.a.
Broadband subscribers ('000) .	15.6	58.4*	94.7

* At December.

Personal computers: 132,000 (4.8 per 1,000 persons) in 2005.

Source: International Telecommunication Union.

Education

(2010/11 unless otherwise indicated)

	Teachers	Students ('000)		
		Males	Females	Total
Pre-primary	40,980	529.6	488.9	1,018.5
Primary	167,216	2,457.5	2,494.5	4,952.0
Secondary	95,292	1,228.0*	1,077.2*	2,305.2*
Tertiary	9,932†	223.7‡	153.2‡	376.9‡

* 2007/08.
† 2006/07.
‡ 2009/10.

Source: UNESCO Institute for Statistics.

Institutions (2004): Primary 24,746; Lower secondary 7,436; Secondary 4,547. Note: Many schools offer education at more than one level. The total number of primary, lower secondary and secondary institutions was 26,277 (Source: Ministry of Education and Sports, Kathmandu).

Pupil-teacher ratio (primary education, UNESCO estimate): 29.6 in 2010/11 (Source: UNESCO Institute for Statistics).

Adult literacy rate (UNESCO estimates): 60.3% (males 73.0%; females 48.3%) in 2010 (Source: UNESCO Institute for Statistics).

Directory

The Government

HEAD OF STATE

President: Dr RAM BARAN YADAV (assumed office 23 July 2008).
Vice-President: PARAMANANDA JHA.

COUNCIL OF MINISTERS
(May 2013)

On 13 March 2013 the leaders of the main political parties signed an agreement providing for the establishment of a non-partisan interim government (known as the Interim Election Council), under the leadership of the Chief Justice, in preparation for elections to a new Constituent Assembly. Consequently, Prime Minister Baburam Bhattarai and the members of his national coalition Government stood down. On 14 March Chief Justice Khil Raj Regmi was sworn in as Chairman of the Interim Election Council; Regmi subsequently appointed a cabinet comprised of former bureaucrats.

Chairman of the Interim Election Council, and Minister of Defence, and of Co-operatives and Poverty Alleviation: KHIL RAJ REGMI.

Minister of Home Affairs and of Foreign Affairs: MADHAV PRASAD GHIMIRE.

Minister of Law, Justice, Constituent Assembly and Parliamentary Affairs, and of Labour and Employment: HARI PRASAD NEUPANE.

Minister of General Administration, Information and Communications, and of Education: MADHAV PAUDEL.

Minister of Women, Children and Social Welfare, and of Land Reform and Management: RIDHI BABA PRADHAN.

Minister of Federal Affairs and Local Development, and of Health Population: BIDHYADHAR MALLIK.

Minister of Finance, of Industry, and of Commerce and Supplies: SHANKAR PRASAD KOIRALA.

Minister of Physical Infrastructure and Transport, and of Urban Development: CHHABI RAJ PANTA.

Minister of Agricultural Development, and of Forest and Soil Conservation: TEK BAHADUR THAPA.

Minister of Youth and Sports, of Peace and Reconstruction, and of Culture, Tourism and Civil Aviation: RAM KUMAR SHRESTHA.

Minister of Science, Technology and Environment, of Irrigation, and of Energy: UMA KANTA JHA.

MINISTRIES

Prime Minister's Office: Singha Durbar, POB 23312, Kathmandu; tel. (1) 4211000; e-mail info@opmcm.gov.np; internet www.opmcm.gov.np.

Ministry of Agriculture and Co-operatives: Singha Durbar, Kathmandu; tel. (1) 4211706; fax (1) 4211935; e-mail memoad@moad.gov.np; internet www.moad.gov.np.

Ministry of Commerce and Supplies: Singha Durbar, Kathmandu; tel. (1) 4211631; fax (1) 4211167; e-mail info@mocs.gov.np; internet www.mocs.gov.np.

Ministry of Defence: Singha Durbar, Kathmandu; tel. (1) 4211289; fax (1) 4211294; e-mail mod@mos.com.np; internet www.mod.gov.np.

Ministry of Education: Singha Durbar, Kathmandu; tel. (1) 4412804; fax (1) 4418191; e-mail infomoe@moe.gov.np; internet www.moe.gov.np.

Ministry of Energy: Singha Durbar, Kathmandu; tel. (1) 4211516; fax (1) 4211510; e-mail info@moen.gov.np; internet www.moen.gov.np.

Ministry of Federal Affairs and Local Development: Shree-mahal Pulchwok, Lalitpur; tel. (1) 5523329; fax (1) 5522045; e-mail secretary@mld.gov.np; internet www.mofald.gov.np.

Ministry of Finance: Singha Durbar, Kathmandu; tel. (1) 4211809; fax (1) 4211831; e-mail admindivision@mof.gov.np; internet www.mof.gov.np.

Ministry of Foreign Affairs: Narayanhiti, Kathmandu; tel. (1) 4200182; fax (1) 4200061; e-mail adm@mofa.gov.np; internet www.mofa.gov.np.

Ministry of Forests and Soil Conservation: Singha Durbar, Kathmandu; tel. (1) 4211567; fax (1) 4211868; e-mail info@mfsc.gov.np; internet www.mfsc.gov.np.

Ministry of General Administration: Singha Durbar, Kathmandu; tel. (1) 4245367; fax (1) 4200238; e-mail info@moga.gov.np; internet www.moga.gov.np.

Ministry of Health and Population: Singha Durbar Plaza, Ramshah Path, Kathmandu; tel. (1) 4262862; fax (1) 4262896; e-mail info@mohp.gov.np; internet www.mohp.gov.np.

Ministry of Home Affairs: Singha Durbar, Kathmandu; tel. (1) 4211204; fax (1) 4211246; e-mail info@moha.gov.np; internet www.moha.gov.np.

Ministry of Industry: Singha Durbar, Kathmandu; tel. (1) 4211579; fax (1) 4211619; e-mail info@moi.gov.np; internet www.moi.gov.np.

Ministry of Information and Communications: Singha Durbar, Kathmandu; tel. (1) 4211556; fax (1) 4211729; e-mail moicppme@ntc.net.np; internet www.moic.gov.np.

Ministry of Irrigation: Singha Durbar, Kathmandu; tel. (1) 4211426; fax (1) 4200026; e-mail info@moir.gov.np; internet www.moir.gov.np.

Ministry of Labour and Employment: Singha Durbar, Kathmandu; tel. (1) 4211889; fax (1) 4211877; e-mail info@moltm.gov.np; internet www.moltm.gov.np.

Ministry of Land Reform and Management: Singha Durbar, Kathmandu; tel. (1) 4211833; fax (1) 4211708; e-mail info@molrm.gov.np; internet www.molrm.gov.np.

Ministry of Law, Justice, Constituent Assembly and Parliamentary Affairs: Singha Durbar, Kathmandu; tel. (1) 4211987; fax (1) 4211684; e-mail info@moljpa.gov.np; internet www.moljpa.gov.np.

Ministry of Peace and Reconstruction: Singha Durbar, Kathmandu; tel. (1) 4211189; fax (1) 4211186; e-mail info@peace.gov.np; internet www.peace.gov.np.

Ministry of Physical Planning and Works: Singha Durbar, Kathmandu; tel. (1) 4211782; fax (1) 4211720; e-mail info@moppw.gov.np; internet www.moppw.gov.np.

Ministry of Science, Technology and Environment: Singha Durbar, Kathmandu; tel. (1) 4211637; fax (1) 4211754; e-mail info@moste.gov.np; internet www.moste.gov.np.

Ministry of Culture, Tourism and Civil Aviation: Singha Durbar, Kathmandu; tel. (1) 4211870; fax (1) 4211758; e-mail info@tourism.gov.np; internet www.tourism.gov.np.

Ministry of Women, Children and Social Welfare: Singha Durbar, Kathmandu; tel. (1) 4200408; fax (1) 4200116; e-mail mail@mowcsw.gov.np; internet www.mowcsw.gov.np.

Ministry of Youth and Sports: Kamalpokhari, Kathmandu; tel. (1) 4416788; fax (1) 4416489; e-mail info@moys.gov.np; internet www.moys.gov.np.

Legislature

CONSTITUENT ASSEMBLY

The Constituent Assembly, which was responsible for drafting a new constitution, comprised 601 members, of whom 575 were elected (using the mixed electoral system) and 26 nominated by the incumbent Interim Parliament. The term of office of its members was initially two years, but on 28 May 2010, following the failure of the Assembly to finalize a new constitution, the term of office was extended by one year. Following three further extensions, the Assembly's term of office expired on 27 May 2012.

Election, 10 April 2008

Party	Seats*
Communist Party of Nepal (Maoist)†	220
Nepali Congress Party (NCP)	110
Communist Party of Nepal (Unified Marxist-Leninist)	103
Madhesi People's Rights Forum Nepal	52
Terai Madhes Loktantrik Party	20
Sadbhavana Party	9
Communist Party of Nepal (Marxist-Leninist)	8
Rashtriya Prajatantra Party‡	8
Janamorcha Nepal	7
Communist Party of Nepal (United)	5
Nepal Workers' and Peasants' Party	4
Rashtriya Prajatantra Party Nepal	4
Rastriya Janamorcha	4
Rashtriya Janashakti Party‡	3
Communist Party of Nepal (Unified)	2
Nepali Janata Dal	2
Nepali Sadbhavana Party (Anandi Devi)	2
Rastriya Janamukti Party	2
Sanghiya Loktantrik Rastriya Manch	2
Churevawar Rastriya Ekata Party Nepal	1
Dalit Janajati Party	1
Nepal Loktantrik Samajbadi Dal	1
Nepal Pariwar Dal	1
Nepal Rastriya Party	1
Samajwadi Prajatantrik Janata Party Nepal	1
Independents	2
Nominated	26
Total	**601**

* Includes seats determined by proportional representation and 'first-past-the-post' systems.
† Name changed to Unified Communist Party of Nepal (Maoist) in January 2009, following a series of mergers.
‡ Merged to form Rastriya Shakti Prajatantra Party in January 2010.

Election Commission

Election Commission of Nepal: Bahadur Bhawan, Kantipath, Kathmandu; tel. (1) 4228663; fax (1) 4229227; e-mail info@election.gov.np; internet www.election.gov.np; independent; appointed by the Prime Minister, on recommendation of a Constitutional Council, for a six-year term; Chief Election Commr NEEL KANTHA UPRETY.

Political Organizations

In 2012 there were about 80 parties registered with the Election Commission.

Communist Party of Nepal (Maoist) (CPN—M): Kathmandu; est. after split in the Unified Communist Party of Nepal (Maoist) in Jun. 2012; 44-mem. cen. cttee; Chair. MOHAN BAIDYA.

Communist Party of Nepal (Marxist-Leninist) (CPN—ML): Maitidevi, Kathmandu; tel. (1) 4443589; e-mail cpnml.cc@gmail.com; internet www.cpnml.org.np; re-formed in 2002 following the reunification of the Communist Party of Nepal (Marxist-Leninist) with the Communist Party of Nepal (Unified Marxist-Leninist); C. P. Mainali, co-founder of the original CPN—ML as a breakaway faction of the CPN (UML) in 1998, had opposed the merger and formed a separate party under the CPN—ML title; Leader C. P. MAINALI.

Communist Party of Nepal (Unified): Kathmandu; internet cpnunified.org.np; f. 2007; Gen. Sec. RAJ SINGH SHRIS.

Communist Party of Nepal (Unified Marxist-Leninist) (UML): Madan Nagar, Balkhu, POB 5471, Kathmandu; tel. (1) 4278081; fax (1) 4278084; e-mail uml@ntc.net.np; internet www.cpnuml.org; f. 1991 when two major factions of the Communist Party of Nepal (CPN; f. 1949; banned 1960; legalized 1990)—the Marxist and Marxist-Leninist factions—merged; the Communist Party of Nepal (Marxist-Leninist—ML) seceded in 1998 and rejoined the UML in 2002; the Communist Party of Nepal (Verma) merged with the UML in 2001; Chair. JHALA NATH KHANAL; Gen. Sec. ISHWAR POKHAREL.

Communist Party of Nepal (United): Kathmandu; f. 2007 following a split in the Communist Party of Nepal (United Marxist); Chair. CHANDRA DEV JOSHI; Gen. Sec. GANESH SHAH.

Madhesi Jana Adhikar Forum Nepal (Madhesi People's Rights Forum Nepal, MPRFN): f. 2006; Chair. UPENDRA YADAV; Gen. Sec. RAM SAHAYA YADAV; in addition, there are two breakaway factions: the Madhesi Jana Adhikar Forum Nepal—Loktantrik (MPRFN—Democratic), headed by BIJAYA KUMAR GACHCHHADAR; and the Madhesi Jana Adhikar Forum Nepal—Ganatantrik (MPRFN—Republican), headed by JAYA PRAKASH GUPTA.

Nepal Workers' and Peasants' Party: Golmadhi Tole-7, Bhaktapur, Kathmandu; tel. (1) 6610974; fax (1) 6613207; e-mail nwpp@ntc .net.np; Chair. NARAYAN MAN BIJUKCHHEN (Comrade Rohit); Gen. Sec. SUNIL PRAJAPATI.

Nepali Congress Party (NCP): B. P. Smriti Bhavan, B. P. Nagar, Sanepa, Lalitpur; tel. (1) 5555263; fax (1) 5555188; e-mail ncparty@ wlink.com.np; internet www.nepalicongress.org; f. 1947; banned 1960; legalized 1990; Nepali Congress Party—Democratic formed as breakaway faction in 2002, rejoined Sept. 2007; 317,000 active mems, 1,000,000 ordinary mems; Pres. SUSHIL KOIRALA; Leader SHER BAHADUR DEUBA; Vice-Pres. RAM CHANDRA POUDEL; Gen. Secs PRAKASH MAN SINGH, KRISHNA PRASAD SITAULA.

Nepali Janata Dal: Tripureshwor, Kathmandu; tel. (1) 4212389; f. 1990; advocates the consolidation of the multi-party democratic system and supports the campaign against corruption; Chair. HARI CHARAN SHAH.

Nepal Sadbhavana Party (NSP) (Nepal Goodwill Party): Shantinagar, New Baneshwor, Kathmandu; tel. (1) 4488068; fax (1) 4470797; f. 1990; promotes the rights of the Madhesi community, who are of Indian origin and reside in the Terai; demands that the Government recognizes Hindi as an official language, that constituencies in the Terai be allocated on the basis of population, and that the Government grant citizenship to those who settled in Nepal before April 1990; in 2003 the party split into two factions, one led by Badri Prasad Mandal, known as the Mandal Group, and the other led by Anandi Devi Singh, known as the Anandi Devi group.

People's Front Nepal (Janamorcha Nepal): Kathmandu; f. 2002 following merger of Rashtriya Jana Morcha (National People's Front) and United People's Front; split into three factions in Dec. 2006; Chair. LILAMANI POKHAREL (acting).

Rastriya Janamorcha: Kathmandu; tel. (1) 4420226; internet www.rajamo.org; Hindu; pro-royalist; Chair. CHITRA BAHADUR K. C.

Rastriya Janamukti Party: Maha Laxmisthan, Lagan Khel, POB 5569, Kathmandu; tel. (1) 5542212; fax (1) 5525531; e-mail zhedi43@ yahoo.com; internet www.janamuktiparty.com; f. 1990; Pres. MALBAR SINGH THAPA; Gen. Sec. SURYA RAJBANSI.

Rastriya Prajatantra Party (RPP): Central Office, Charumati, Chabahil Kathmandu; tel. (1) 4471071; fax (1) 4460324; e-mail rppnepal@enet.com.np; internet rppnepal.org; f. 1990; fmrly divided into two factions led by former Prime Ministers Lokendra Bahadur Chand and Surya Bahadur Thapa, respectively; centre-right, with origins as a monarchist party; Leader LOKENDRA BAHADUR CHAND; Chair. PASHUPATI S. J. B. RANA.

Rastriya Prajatantra Party Nepal: Ichchhumati Marga, Baluwatar; tel. and fax (1) 4430635; internet rppn.org.np; f. 2008 as splinter group of RPP; monarchist; Chair. KAMAL THAPA.

Rastriya Shakti Prajatantra Party (RSPP): Kathmandu; est. February 2010 to facilitate the reunification of Surya Bahadur Thapa's Rastriya Janashakti Party and the Rastriya Prajatantra Party.

Sadbhavana Party (SP): Kathmandu; Chair. RAJENDRA MAHATO; Gen. Sec. MANISH SUMAN; there is also a breakaway faction entitled the Federal Sadbhavana Party.

Samajwadi Prajatantrik Janata Party Nepal: Kathmandu; f. 2008; Chair. PREM BAHADUR SINGH.

Sanghiya Loktantrik Rastriya Manch: Kathmandu; f. 2007; Pres. KAMAL CHARAHANG.

Terai Madhes Loktantrik Party (Terai Madhes Democratic Party—TMDP): 657/21 Bhakti Thapa Marg, Bijulibazaar, Kathmandu; tel. (1) 4462398; 9 members of the party separated to form a faction called Terai Madhes Loktantrik Party (Nepal) in Dec. 2010; Pres. MAHANTHA THAKUR.

Unified Communist Party of Nepal (Maoist) (UCPN—M): Central Office, Perishdanda, Koteshwor, Kathmandu; tel. (1) 4602290; fax (1) 4602289; e-mail ucpnminfo69@gmail.com; internet ucpnmaoist.org; f. 1990 as Communist Party of Nepal (Unity Centre), renamed as CPN (Maoist) in 1995; fmr underground political movement, represented in Interim Parliament in 2007; orchestrated 'people's war' in hills of western Nepal (1996–2006); merged with CPN (Unified Marxist-Leninist-Maoist) in Sept. 2007; merged with CPN (Marxist) in Feb. 2008; merged with CPN (Unity Centre-Masal) in Jan. 2009 and name changed as above; 175-mem. cen. cttee; Chair. PUSHPA KAMAL DAHAL ('Prachanda'); Vice-Chair. Dr BABURAM BHATTARAI, NARYANKAJI SHRESTHA.

Other parties elected to the Constituent Assembly in April 2008 were Churevawar Rastriya Ekata Party Nepal, Dalit Janajati Party, Nepal Loktantrik Samajbadi Dal, Nepal Pariwar Dal and Nepa Rastriya Party.

Diplomatic Representation
EMBASSIES IN NEPAL

Australia: Suraj Niwas, Bansbari, POB 879, Kathmandu; tel. (1) 4371678; fax (1) 4371533; internet www.nepal.embassy.gov.au; Ambassador GLENN WHITE (designate).

Brazil: POB 19299, Chundevi Marg, Mahargunj, Kathmandu; tel. 9801032381; e-mail marcos.dupart@itamaraty.br; Ambassador MARCOS BORGES D. RIBEIRO.

Bangladesh: Bashundhara, Chakrapath, Ward 4, Kathmandu; tel. (1) 4390130; fax (1) 4390132; e-mail mission.kathmandu@mofa.gov .bd; internet bangladoot.org.np; Ambassador (vacant).

China, People's Republic: Baluwatar, POB 4234, Kathmandu; tel. (1) 4411740; fax (1) 4414045; e-mail chinaemb_np@mfa.gov.cn; internet np.chineseembassy.org/; Ambassador WU CHUNTAI.

Denmark: 761 Neel Saraswati Marg, Lazimpat, POB 6332, Kathmandu; tel. (1) 4413010; fax (1) 4411409; e-mail ktmamb@um.dk; internet www.ambkathmandu.um.dk; Ambassador MORTEN JESPERSEN.

Egypt: Naya Bazar Chowk, Saibu Bhaisepati, Lalitpur, POB 792, Kathmandu; tel. (1) 5590544; fax (1) 5592661; e-mail embassy .kathmandu@mfa.gov.eg; Ambassador Dr MOUSTAFA ABDELHAMID MOHAMED GENDY.

Finland: Bishalnagar, POB 2126, Kathmandu; tel. (1) 4416636; fax (1) 4416703; e-mail sanomat.kat@formin.fi; internet www.finland .org.np; Ambassador ASKO LUUKKAINEN.

France: Lazimpat, POB 452, Kathmandu; tel. (1) 4412332; fax (1) 4419968; e-mail ambassade@ambafrance-np.org; internet www .ambafrance-np.org; Ambassador JEAN-CHARLES DEMARQUIS.

Germany: 690 Gyaneshwar Marg, POB 226, Kathmandu; tel. (1) 4412786; fax (1) 4416899; e-mail info@kathmandu.diplo.de; internet www.kathmandu.diplo.de; Ambassador FRANK MEYKE.

India: 336 Kapurdhara Marg, POB 292, Kathmandu; tel. (1) 4410900; fax (1) 4428279; e-mail pic@eoiktm.org; internet www .indianembassy.org.np; Ambassador JAYANT PRASAD.

Israel: Bishramalaya House, Lazimpat St, POB 371, Kathmandu; tel. (1) 4411811; fax (1) 4413920; e-mail info@kathmandu.mfa.gov.il; internet kathmandu.mfa.gov.il; Ambassador HANAN GODAR.

Japan: Panipokhari, POB 264, Kathmandu; tel. (1) 4426680; fax (1) 4414101; e-mail comjpn@mos.com.np; internet www.np.emb-japan .go.jp; Ambassador KUNIO TAKAHASHI.

Korea, Democratic People's Republic: Jhamsikhel, Lalitpur, Kathmandu; tel. (1) 5521855; fax (1) 5525394; e-mail rimnine@ wlink.com.np; Ambassador KIM YOUNG SU.

Korea, Republic: Ravibhawan, Kathmandu; tel. (1) 4270172; fax (1) 4272041; e-mail konepemb@gmail.com; internet npl.mofat.go.kr; Ambassador ILDOO KIM.

Malaysia: Blk B, 2nd Floor, Karmachari Sanchaya Kosh Bldg, Pulchowk, POB 24372, Lalitpur, Kathmandu; tel. (1) 5010004; fax (1) 5010492; e-mail malkatmandu@kln.gov.my; internet www.kln .gov.my/perwakilan/kathmandu; Chargé d'affaires a. i. FADLI ADILAH.

Myanmar: Nakhhu Height, Bhaisepati, Lalitpur, POB 2437, Kathmandu; tel. (1) 5592774; fax (1) 5592776; e-mail myanmaremb@ wlink.com.np; internet www.mofa.gov.mm/myanmarmissions/ nepal.html; Ambassador THET OO.

Norway: Surya Court, Pulchowk, Lalitpur, POB 20765, Kathmandu; tel. (1) 5545307; fax (1) 5545226; e-mail emb.kathmandu@ mfa.no; internet www.norway.org.np; Ambassador ALF ARNE RAMSLIEN.

Pakistan: Pushpanjali, Maharajgunj, Chakrapath, POB 202, Kathmandu; tel. (1) 4374024; fax (1) 4374012; e-mail pakembktm@gmail .com; internet www.mofa.gov.pk/nepal; Ambassador ARSHED SAUD KHOSA.

Russia: Baluwatar, POB 123, Kathmandu; tel. (1) 4412155; fax (1) 4416571; e-mail ruspos@info.com.np; internet www.nepal.mid.ru; Ambassador Dr SERGEI V. VELICHKIN.

Saudi Arabia: Soaltee Crowne Plaza, Kathmandu; tel. (1) 4302705; fax (1) 4302707; e-mail saudikaemb@mofa.gov.sa; Ambassador ABDUL NASSER BIN HUSSAIN AL-HARTHY.

Sri Lanka: 'Shah Villa', Chundevi Rd, Maharajgunj, POB 8802, Kathmandu; tel. (1) 4720623; fax (1) 4720128; e-mail info@slembktm .com; internet www.slembktm.com; Ambassador W. M. SENEVIRATHNA.

Switzerland: Jawalakhel, Ekanta Kuna, SDC-Compound, Lalitpur, POB 113, Kathmandu; tel. (1) 5524927; fax (1) 5525358; e-mail kat.vertretung@eda.admin.ch; internet www.eda.admin.ch/ kathmandu; Ambassador THOMAS GASS.

Thailand: 167/4 Ward 3, Maharajgunj-Bansbari Rd, POB 3333, Kathmandu; tel. (1) 4371410; fax (1) 4371409; e-mail thaiemb@wlink

.com.np; internet www.thaiembnepal.org.np; Ambassador KANTHONG UNAKUL.

United Kingdom: Lainchaur, POB 106, Kathmandu; tel. (1) 4410583; fax (1) 4411789; e-mail bekathmandu@fco.gov.uk; internet ukinnepal.fco.gov.uk; Ambassador ANDREW JAMES SPARKES.

USA: Maharajgunj, POB 295, Kathmandu; tel. (1) 4007200; fax (1) 4007272; e-mail usembktm@state.gov; internet nepal.usembassy .gov; Ambassador PETER W. BODDE.

Judicial System

According to the Interim Constitution (which was officially endorsed in January 2007), the judicial system has three tiers: the Supreme Court (which is also a Court of Record), the Appellate Courts and the District Courts. The Supreme Court consists of a Chief Justice and a maximum of 14 other judges. The Chief Justice is appointed by the Prime Minister on the recommendation of the Constitutional Council; other Supreme Court, Appellate Court and District Court judges are nominated by the Chief Justice on the recommendation of the Judicial Council. A Constituent Assembly Court was established in February 2008 to deal with election matters.

On 14 March 2013 Chief Justice Khil Raj Regmi was sworn in as Chairman of an interim Government (Acting Prime Minister, effectively), in preparation for fresh elections to Nepal's Constituent Assembly. Regmi's judicial authority was transferred to Justice Damodar Prasad Sharma in the interim period.

Supreme Court: Ramashah Path, Kathmandu; tel. (1) 4262895; e-mail info@supremecourt.gov.np; internet www.supremecourt.gov .np; Chief Justice KHIL RAJ REGMI; Acting Chief Justice DAMODAR PRASAD SHARMA; Registrar LOHIT CHANDRA SHAH.

Office of the Attorney-General: Ramshah Path, Kathmandu; tel. (1) 4240210; fax (1) 4262582; e-mail info@attorneygeneral.gov.np; internet www.attorneygeneral.gov.np; Attorney-General DRONA RAJ REGMI.

Religion

At the 2001 census, an estimated 80.6% of the population professed Hinduism, while 10.7% were Buddhists and 4.2% Muslims. The actual number of Muslims in the country was considered to be much higher, owing to immigration from Bangladesh. There were an estimated 101,976 Christians in Nepal in 2001.

BUDDHISM

All Nepal Bhikkhu Association: Vishwa Shanti Vihara (World Peace Temple), 465 Ekadantamarga, Minbhavan, New Baneshwor, POB 8973 NPC-327, Kathmandu; tel. (1) 4622984; fax (1) 4622250; e-mail anbanepal@gmail.com; internet www.anba.org.np; f. 1950; Sec. Gen BHIKSHU KONDANYA.

Nepal Buddhist Council: Nahtole, Lalitpur 20; tel. (1) 5534277; e-mail nepalbuddhistcouncil@gmail.com; f. 1977; Chair. MAHISWOR RAJ BAJRACHARYA.

United Trungram Buddhist Foundation: Hattigauda, Bansbari, POB 3157, Kathmandu; tel. (1) 4370089; fax (1) 4370292; internet www.utbf.org; Spiritual Dir GYALTRUL RINPOCHE.

CHRISTIANITY

Protestant Church

Nepal Northern Evangelical Lutheran Church: AT Laxmipur, POB 3, Babiya Birta, Morang Dist.; tel. 9842045726 (mobile); e-mail josephsoren@hotmail.com; Pres. Rev. JOSEPH SOREN.

Presbyterian Church of the Kingdom of Nepal: POB 3237, Kathmandu; tel. and fax (1) 4524450.

The Roman Catholic Church

The Church is represented in Nepal by a single apostolic prefecture. At 31 December 2007 there were an estimated 6,115 adherents in the country.

Apostolic Vicariate: Church of the Assumption, GPOB 8975, EPC-343, Kathmandu; tel. (1) 5542802; fax (1) 5521710; e-mail anath@ wlink.com.np; f. 1983 as Catholic Mission; Vicar Apostolic Bishop ANTHONY FRANCIS SHARMA.

The Press

PRINCIPAL DAILIES

The Commoner: Naradevi, POB 203, Kathmandu; tel. (1) 4228236; f. 1956; English; Publr and Chief Editor GOPAL DASS SHRESTHA; circ. 7,000.

Daily News: Bhimsensthan, POB 171, Kathmandu; tel. (1) 4279147; e-mail manju_sakya@hotmail.com; f. 1983; Nepali and English; Chief Editor MANJU RATNA SAKYA; Publr SUBHA LAXMI SAKYA; circ. 20,000.

Gorkhapatra: Dharma Path, POB 23, Kathmandu; tel. (1) 4244437; fax (1) 4222921; e-mail gopa@gorkhapatra.org.np; internet www .gorkhapatra.org.np; f. 1901; Nepali; govt-owned; Chair. RAM KISHORE SINGH; Gen. Man. KAPIL GHIMIRE (acting); circ. 75,000.

The Himalayan Times: International Media Network Nepal (Pvt) Ltd, APCA House, Baidya Khana Rd, Anam Nagar, POB 11651, Kathmandu; tel. (1) 4771489; fax (1) 4770701; e-mail editorial@ thehimalayantimes.com; internet www.thehimalayantimes.com; f. 2001; English; Editor AJAYA BHADRA KHANAL.

Kantipur: Kantipur Complex, Subhidhanagar, POB 8559, Kathmandu; tel. (1) 4480100; fax (1) 4466320; e-mail khimghale@ kantipur.com.np; internet www.ekantipur.com; f. 1993; Nepali; Chair. and Man. Dir KAILASH SIROHIYA; Editor KHIM GHALE; circ. 210,000.

Kathmandu Post: Kantipur Complex, Subhidhanagar, POB 8559, Kathmandu; tel. (1) 4480100; fax (1) 4466320; e-mail au@kantipur .com.np; internet www.kantipuronline.com; f. 1993; English; Editor AKHILESH UPADHYAY; circ. 40,000.

Nepal Samacharpatra: Red Cross Marg, Kalimati, POB 2045, Kathmandu; tel. (1) 4287777; fax 4288700; e-mail pushkarlal@ newsofnepal.com; internet newsofnepal.com; f. 1945; Nepali; Editor-in-Chief PUSHKAR LAL SHRESTHA; circ. 1,000.

Nepali Hindi Daily: 72 Kalinchok Marg, Maitidevi, POB 49, Kathmandu; tel. (1) 4436374; fax (1) 4435931; e-mail das@ntc.net .np; f. 1954; evening; Hindi; Publr UMA KANT DAS; Chief Editor VIJOY KUMAR DAS; circ. 100,000.

Rajdhani: Kathmandu; internet www.rajdhani.com.np; Editor KAPIL KAFLE; circ. 50,000.

Rising Nepal: Dharma Path, POB 1623, Kathmandu; tel. (1) 4244437; fax (1) 4224381; e-mail trn@gorkhapatra.org.np; internet www.gorkhapatra.org.np; f. 1965; English; Editor-in-Chief PUSKAR MATHEMA; circ. 20,000.

Swatantra Samachar: Kathmandu; f. 1957; Editor MADAN DEV SHARMA; circ. 2,000.

SELECTED PERIODICALS

Agricultural Credit: Agricultural Training and Research Institute, Agricultural Development Bank, Head Office, Ramshah Path, Panchayat Plaza, Kathmandu; tel. (1) 4220756; fax (1) 4225329; 2 a year; publ. by the Agricultural Development Bank; Chair. Dr NARAYAN N. KHATRI; Editor RUDRA PD DAHAL.

Arpan: Bhimsensthan, POB 285, Kathmandu; tel. (1) 4244450; e-mail manju_sakya@hotmail.com; internet www.nepalnews.com/ arpan.php; f. 1964; weekly; Nepali; Publr and Chief Editor MANJU RATNA SAKYA; circ. 18,000.

Awake Weekly Chronicle: Kathmandu; English.

Commerce: Bhimsensthan, POB 171, Kathmandu; tel. (1) 4279636; e-mail manju_sakya@hotmail.com; f. 1971; monthly; English; Publr and Chief Editor MANJU RATNA SAKYA; Editor SUBHA LAXMI SAKYA; circ. 12,000.

Current: Gautam Marg, Kamalpokhari, Kathmandu; tel. (1) 4419484; fax (1) 4445406; f. 1982; weekly; Nepali; publ. by private limited co; Man. Editor KIRAN GAUTAM; Chief Editor DEVENDRA GAUTAM; circ. 10,000.

Foreign Affairs Journal: 5/287 Lagon, Kathmandu; f. 1976; 3 a year; articles on Nepalese foreign relations and diary of main news events; Publr and Editor BHOLA BIKRUM RANA; circ. 5,000.

Himal Southasian: Patan Dhoka, Lalitpur, POB 24393; tel. (1) 5547279; fax (1) 5552141; e-mail info@himalmag.com; internet www .himalmag.com; f. 1987; monthly; political, business, social and environmental issues throughout South Asia; Editor-in-Chief KANAK MANI DIXIT.

Janadharana (People's Opinion): Kathmandu; e-mail janadharana@gmail.com; weekly; independent; Editor NIMKANT PANDEY.

Janmabhumi: Janmabhumi Press, Tahachal, Kathmandu; tel. (1) 4280979; fax (1) 4274795; e-mail sirishnp@hotmail.com; f. 1970; weekly; Nepali; Publr and Editor SHIRISH BALLABH PRADHAN.

Koseli: Kathmandu; e-mail koseli@kantipur.com.np; weekly; Nepali.

Madhuparka: Dharmapath, POB 23, Kathmandu; tel. (1) 4222278; f. 1986; monthly; Nepali; literary; Editor BIJAYA CHALISE; circ. 20,000.

Mulyankan: Kathmandu; monthly, left-wing; Editor JHALAK SUBEDI.

Nepal National Weekly: Kantipur Publications Pvt Ltd, Kantipur Complex, Subhidhanagar, POB 8559, Kathmandu; tel. (1) 4480100; fax (1) 4466320; e-mail prashanta@kantipur.com.np; internet www

.ekantipur.com/nepal; f. 2000; fortnightly; Nepali; Editor PRASHANT ARYAL; circ. 40,000.

Nepal Overseas Trade Statistics: Trade and Export Promotion Centre, Pulchowk, Lalitpur, POB 825, Kathmandu; tel. (1) 5532642; fax (1) 5525464; e-mail info@tepc.gov.np; internet www.tepc.gov.np; f. 2006; annual; English; Chair. LAL MANI JOSHI; Dir TEJ SINGH BISTA (acting).

Nepal Trade and Export Bulletin: Trade and Export Promotion Centre, Pulchowk, Lalitpur, POB 825, Kathmandu; tel. (1) 5532642; fax (1) 5525464; e-mail info@tepc.gov.np; internet www.tepc.gov.np; f. 2006; 3 a year; English; Chair. LAL MANI JOSHI.

Nepali Times: Himalmedia Pvt Ltd, POB 7251, Kathmandu; tel. (1) 5250333; fax (1) 5251013; e-mail editors@nepalitimes.com; internet www.nepalitimes.com; f. 2000; weekly; English; publ. by Himalmedia Pvt Ltd; Publr KUNDA DIXIT; Editor TRISHNA RANA; circ. 15,000.

People's Review: Pipalbot, Dillibazar, POB 3052, Kathmandu; tel. (1) 4417352; fax (1) 4438797; e-mail preview@ntc.net.np; internet www.peoplesreview.com.np; f. 1991; weekly; English; Chief Editor and Publr PUSHPA RAJ PRADHAN; circ. 15,000.

Rastrabani: Kathmandu; tel. (1) 4410339; weekly; Nepali; Chief Editor HARI LAMSAL.

Samaya: Kamal Press, Ramshah Path, Kathmandu; f. 1954; Nepali; Editor MANIK LALL SHRESTHA; circ. 18,000.

Sanghu Weekly: Kathmandu; weekly; Editor GOPAL BUDHATHOKI.

Saptahik Weekly: Kantipur Complex, Subhidhanagar, POB 8559, Kathmandu; tel. (1) 4480100; fax (1) 4466320; e-mail subas@kantipur.com.np; internet www.kantipuronline.com/saptahik; f. 1997; weekly; Nepali; news and entertainment; Editor SUBASH DHAKAL.

Swatantra Manch Weekly: POB 49, Ghattekulo, Kathmandu; tel. (1) 4436374; fax (1) 4435931; e-mail das@ntc.net.np; f. 1985; independent; weekly; Nepali; Publr and Chief Editor VIJOY KUMAR DAS; circ. 40,000.

The Telegraph: Ghattekulo, Laligurans Marg, POB 4063, Kathmandu; tel. (1) 4770370; e-mail tgw@ntc.net.np; internet www.telegraphnepal.com; f. 2007; weekly; English; Chief Editor NARENDRA P. UPADHYAYA.

NEWS AGENCY

Rastriya Samachar Samiti (RSS): Bhadrakali Plaza, POB 220, Kathmandu; tel. (1) 4262912; fax (1) 4262744; e-mail info@rss.com.np; internet www.rss.com.np; f. 1962; state-operated; Chair. KAMAL NATH BARAL; Gen. Man. BASUDEV SHRESTHA.

PRESS ASSOCIATIONS

Federation of Nepalese Journalists (FNJ): Media Village, Tilganga, Kathmandu; tel. (1) 4112763; fax (1) 4112785; e-mail fnjnepal@mail.com.np; internet www.fnjnepal.org; f. 1956; Pres. SHIVA GAUNLE; Gen. Sec. OM SHARMA.

Nepal Journalists' Association (NJA): Maitighar, POB 285, Kathmandu; tel. (1) 4262426; e-mail manju_sakya@hotmail.com; internet www.nja.org.np; 5,400 mems; Pres. MANJU RATNA SAKYA; Gen. Sec. NIRMAL KUMAR ARYAL.

Press Council: Sanchargram, Tilganga, POB 3077, Kathmandu; tel. (1) 4469799; fax (1) 4112694; e-mail prescoun_mdf@wlink.com.np; internet www.presscouncilnepal.org; f. 1970; Chair. BORNA BAHADUR KARKI; Sec. LAXMI BILASH KOIRALA.

Publishers

Educational Publishing House: POB 5178, Kathmandu; tel. (1) 4241255; e-mail eph.nepal@gmail.com; f. 1962; educational and technical; Dir JYOTSNA SHRESTHA.

Himal Books: Himal Association, 540 Lazimpat, Narayangopal Sadak, Kathmandu; tel. (1) 5542544; fax (1) 5541196; e-mail info@himalbooks.com; internet www.himalbooks.com; f. 1992; subsidiary operation of Himal Association; general interest and academic publications in English and Nepali; Exec. Dir BASANTA THAPA.

Pilgrims Book House: Thamel, POB 3872, Kathmandu; tel. (1) 4700942; fax (1) 4700943; e-mail pilgrims@wlink.com.np; internet www.pilgrimsbooks.com; f. 1986; Asian studies, religion and travel; Propr PUSHPA TIWARI.

Pilgrims Publishing Nepal (Pvt) Ltd: Goldhunga 4, POB 21646, Kathmandu; tel. (1) 4356764; fax (1) 4700544; internet www.pilgrimsbooks.com; f. 2000; Exec. Dir JOHN SNYDER; Man. Dir BISHOW BHATTA.

Ratna Pustak Bhandar: 71 Ga Bank Marg, POB 98, Kathmandu; tel. (1) 4223026; fax (1) 4248421; e-mail rpb@wlink.com.np; internet ratnabooks.com; f. 1945; textbooks, general, non-fiction and fiction; Propr GOVINDA PRASAD SHRESTHA.

Royal Nepal Academy: Kamaladi, Kathmandu; tel. (1) 4221241; fax (1) 4221175; f. 1957; languages, literature, social sciences, art and philosophy; Dep. Admin. Chief T. D. BHANDARI.

Sajha Prakashan: Pulchowk, Lalitpur, POB 20259, Kathmandu; tel. (1) 5521118; fax (1) 5544236; e-mail sajhap@wlink.com.np; internet www.sajha.org.np; f. 1964; educational, literary and general; Chair. and Gen. Man. MAMTA JHA.

Sunbird Publishers: POB 13363, Kathmandu; tel. (1) 4412799; e-mail sunbirdpublishers@gmail.com; internet www.sunbird.org.np; comprises two separate imprints: *Ramailo Kitaab* for children and *Yuwa Pushtak* for teenagers.

Trans Asian Media Pvt Ltd: Thapathali Crossing, POB 5320, Kathmandu; tel. (1) 4242895; fax (1) 4223889; Man. Editor SHYAM GOENKA.

GOVERNMENT PUBLISHING HOUSE

Department of Information: Ministry of Information and Communications, Singha Durbar, Kathmandu; tel. (1) 483254; fax (1) 483252; e-mail info@doinepal.gov.np; internet www.doinepal.gov.np.

Broadcasting and Communications

TELECOMMUNICATIONS

According to the Nepal Telecommunications Authority, in November 2012 there were 16.4m. mobile telephone subscribers, representing a mobile penetration rate of 62% of the population. There were 834,352 fixed-line telephone subscribers at this time.

Nepal Telecommunications Authority: Bluestar Office Complex, Tripureswor, POB 9754, Kathmandu; tel. (1) 4101030; fax (1) 4101034; e-mail info@nta.gov.np; internet www.nta.gov.np; telecommunications regulatory body; f. 1998; Chair. BHESH RAJ KANEL.

Nepal Telecom (Nepal Doorsanchar Co Ltd): Bhadrakali Plaza, POB 11803, Kathmandu; tel. (1) 4210202; fax (1) 4222424; e-mail rkt@ntc.net.np; internet www.ntc.net.np; f. 1975; operates fixed-line and mobile services; 85% state-owned, 10% owned by Nepalese public, 5% owned by Nepal Telecom employees; Chair. AVANINDRA KUMAR SHRESTHA; Sec. BUDDHI PRASAD ACHARYA.

Spice Nepal (Pvt) Ltd (Ncell): Krishna Tower, Buddhanagar, New Baneshwor, Kathmandu 10; tel. (980) 5554444; fax (980) 5554442; e-mail info@ncell.com.np; internet www.ncell.com.np; f. 2004; subsidiary of Telia Sonera Group (Sweden); launched Nepal's first privately owned GSM mobile network under Mero Mobile brand in 2005; services rebranded as Ncell in 2010; CEO PASI KOISTINEN; 4.8m. subscribers (2010).

STM Telecom Sanchar (Gramintel): 768/47 Thirbam Sadak, Baluwatar, Kathmandu; tel. (1) 4445981; fax (1) 4419366; e-mail info@stmtelecom.com; internet www.gramintel.com; f. 2003 as jt venture between the USA, Thailand and Nepal; awarded World Bank-funded project to provide rural telecommunication services to eastern region of Nepal; CEO ABHINAV PURI; 5,336 subscribers (Jan. 2012).

United Telecom Ltd: Fourth Floor, Triveni Complex, Putali Sadak, Kathmandu; tel. (1) 2222222; fax (1) 2499999; e-mail info@utlnepal.com; internet www.utlnepal.com; f. 2003; jt venture between Indian-owned Mahanagar Telephone Nigam Ltd, Telecommunications Consultants India Ltd, Tata Communications Ltd, and Nepal Ventures Pvt Ltd; Chair. R. S. P. SINHA.

BROADCASTING

Radio

In August 2009 there were an estimated 186 FM radio stations in operation.

Radio Nepal: Radio Broadcasting Service, Government of Nepal, Singha Durbar, POB 634, Kathmandu; tel. (1) 4211910; fax (1) 4211952; e-mail radio@engg.wlink.com.np; internet www.radionepal.org; f. 1951; broadcasts on short-wave, medium-wave and FM frequencies in 20 regional languages, incl. Nepali and English, for 18 hours daily (incl. two hours of regional broadcasting in the morning and evening); short-wave station at Khumaltar and medium-wave stations at Bhainsepati, Pokhara, Surkhet, Dipayal, Bardibas and Dharan; FM stations at Kathmandu, Kanchanpur, Rupandhi, Chitwan, Makawanpur, Bara, Jumla, Mustang, Ilam, Simikot and Humla; Exec. Dir TAPANATH SHUKLA.

Hits FM: POB 21912, Baneshwor, Kathmandu; tel. (1) 4780534; fax (1) 4780543; e-mail info@hitsfm.com.np; internet www.hitsfm.com.np; f. 1996; broadcasts 24 hrs daily; Chair. RAJIB RAJ BHANDARI; CEO JEEVAN LAL SHRESTHA.

Image FM (Kath FM): POB 5566, Panipokhari, Kathmandu; tel. (1) 4433141; fax (1) 4427262; e-mail imagefm@wlink.com.np; internet www.imagechannels.com; f. 1999; Station Man. BHARAT SHAKYA.

Janaki FM: Janakpurdham, Nepal; tel. (41) 5527430; fax (41) 5527432; e-mail info@janakifm.org.np; internet www.janakifm.org.np; f. 2007.

Kalika FM: Bharatpur 10, Chitwan; tel. (56) 527158; fax (56) 527161; e-mail info@kalikafm.com.np; internet www.kalikafm.com.np; f. 2002.

Kantipur FM: Kantipur Complex, Subhidhanagar, POB 8559, Kathmandu; tel. (1) 4480100; fax (1) 4470178; e-mail kfm@kanti.mos.com.np; internet www.radiokantipur.com; f. 1998; broadcasts 24 hrs daily; Man. Dir KAILASH SIROHIYA; Station Man. PRABHAT RIMAL.

Radio Lumbini: Aanandabane VDC, Ward No. 3, Manigram, Rupandehi, Lumbini; tel. (71) 561003; fax (71) 561545; e-mail info@radiolumbini.org; internet www.radiolumbini.org; f. 2000; CEO KRISHNA PRASAD NEPAL.

Radio Sagarmatha: Bakhundol, Lalitpur, GPOB 6958, Kathmandu; tel. (1) 5528091; fax (1) 5530227; e-mail stationmanager@radiosagarmatha.org; internet www.radiosagarmatha.org; f. 1997; independent; Chair. LAXMAN UPRETI; Station Man. GHAMA RAJ LUITEL.

Times FM: GPOB 8975, EPC 906, Chabahil Ganesthan, Kathmandu; tel. and fax (1) 4462465; e-mail info@timesfm906.com; internet www.timesfm906.com; Man. Dir R. K. SHRESTHA.

Television

Nepal Television Corpn: Singha Durbar, POB 3826, Kathmandu; tel. (1) 4220348; fax (1) 4200212; internet www.ntv.org.np; f. 1985; operates NTV and NTV2; programmes in Nepali (50%), English (25%) and Hindi/Urdu (25%); regional station at Kohalpur; Exec. Chair. KUNDAN ARYAL; Gen. Man. DEEPAK MANI DHITAL (acting).

Avenues TV: 11 Avenues Plaza, Teku Rd, Ganeshman Marga, Kathmandu; tel. (1) 4227222; fax (1) 4248811; e-mail atv@avenues.tv; internet www.avenues.tv; f. 2003; news service.

Image Channel: POB 5566, Panipokhari, Kathmandu; tel. (1) 4006555; fax (1) 4427262; e-mail ichannel@wlink.com.np; internet www.imagechannels.com; f. 2003; privately owned; Chair. R. K. MANANDHAR.

Kantipur Television Network (KTV): Kantipur Complex, Subhidhanagar, POB 8559, Kathmandu; tel. (1) 4466300; fax (1) 4466321; e-mail info@kantipurtv.com; internet www.kantipurtv.com; f. 2003; Chair. HEM RAJ GYAWALI; Man. Dir KAILASH SIROHIYA.

Sagarmatha Television (STV): POB 10537, Rudramati Marg, Dhobikhola, Babarmahal, Kathmandu; tel. (1) 4233071; fax (1) 4233073; e-mail info@sagarmatha.tv; internet www.sagarmatha.tv; f. 2007; news channel; broadcasts in more than five dialects.

Space-Time Network: Minbhavan, New Baneshwor, Kathmandu; tel. (1) 4487228; fax (1) 4492261; e-mail info@spacetimenetwork.com.np; internet www.spacetimenetwork.com.np; f. 1994; satellite transmission services; launched Channel Nepal, the country's first satellite channel, in 2001; Man. Dir (vacant).

Finance

(auth. = authorized; cap. = capital; m. = million; dep. = deposits; res = reserves; brs = branches; amounts in Nepalese rupees)

BANKING

Central Bank

Nepal Rastra Bank: Central Office, Baluwatar, POB 73, Kathmandu; tel. (1) 4410158; fax (1) 4410159; e-mail fxm@nrb.org.np; internet www.nrb.org.np; f. 1956; bank of issue; 100% state-owned; cap. 3,000m., res 43,930m., dep. 75,703m. (July 2009); Gov. and Chair. Dr YUBA RAJ KHATIWADA; 9 brs.

Domestic Commercial Banks

Kumari Bank Ltd: Durbarmarg, POB 21128, Kathmandu; tel. (1) 4221312; fax (1) 4231960; e-mail info@kbl.com.np; internet www.kumaribank.com; f. 2001; auth. cap. 1,603.8m., res 607m., dep. 16,986m. (July 2011); Chair. MIN BAHADUR GURUNG; CEO RADHESH PANT; 8 brs.

Nepal Bank Ltd: Nepal Bank Bldg, Dharmapath, New Rd, POB 36, Kathmandu; tel. (1) 4222397; fax (1) 4220414; e-mail info@nepalbank.com.np; internet www.nepalbank.com.np; f. 1937; 40% state-owned, 60% owned by Nepalese public; cap. 380m., res 2,333.8m., dep. 46,808.4m. (July 2011); CEO MAHESWOR LAL SHRESTHA; 105 brs.

Nepal Industrial and Commercial Bank Ltd (NIC Bank): Kamaladi, Ganeshthan, POB 7367, Kathmandu; tel. (1) 4262277; fax (1) 4241865; e-mail kamaladi@nicbank.com.np; internet www.nicbank.com.np; f. 1998; privately owned; cap. 1,311m., res 618m.,

dep. 19,167.7m. (July 2011); Chair. JAGDISH PRASAD AGRAWAL; CEO SASHIN JOSHI; 36 brs.

Rastriya Banijya Bank (National Commercial Bank): POB 8368, Singha Durbar Plaza, Kathmandu; tel. (1) 4252595; fax (1) 4252931; e-mail rbb.info@rbb.com.np; internet www.rbb.com.np; f. 1966; 100% state-owned; cap. 5,497.6m., dep. 87,775m. (July 2012); Chair. NARAHARI DHAKAL; CEO KRISHNA PD. SHARMA; 129 brs, 5 regional offices.

Joint-venture Banks

Bank of Kathmandu Ltd: Kamal Pokhari, POB 9044, Kathmandu; tel. (1) 4414541; fax (1) 4418990; e-mail info@bok.com.np; internet www.bok.com.np; f. 1993; 58% owned by Nepalese public, 42% by local promoters; cap. 1,604m., res 976m., dep. 24,991.4m. (July 2012); Chair. NARENDRA KUMAR BASNYAT; CEO AJAY SHRESTHA; 37 brs.

Everest Bank Ltd (EBL): POB 13384, EBL House, Lazimpath, Kathmandu; tel. (1) 4443377; fax (1) 4443160; e-mail ebl@mos.com.np; internet www.everestbankltd.com; f. 1994; 50% owned by directors, 20% by Punjab National Bank (India) and 30% by the Nepalese public; cap. 1,767.1m., res 1,978.6m., dep. 50,006.1m. (July 2011); Chair. BISHNU KRISHNA SHRESTHA; CEO P. K. MOHAPATRA; 35 brs.

Global Bank Ltd: Adarshanagar, Birgunj 13, POB 45, Parsa; tel. (1) 530337; fax (1) 530338; e-mail info@globalbank.com.np; internet www.globalbanknepal.com; f. 2006; cap. 2,250.3m., res 281.5m., dep. 26,913.7m. (July 2012); Chair. CHANDRA PRASAD DHAKAL; CEO RATNA RAJ BAJRACHARYA.

Himalayan Bank Ltd: Karmachari Sanchaya Kosh Bldg, Tridevi Marg, Thamel, POB 20590, Kathmandu; tel. (1) 4246218; fax (1) 4222800; e-mail hbl@himalayanbank.com; internet www.himalayanbank.com; f. 1993; 20% owned by Habib Bank Ltd (Pakistan); cap. 2,400m., res 1,562.5m., dep. 40,920.6m. (July 2011); Chair. MANOJ BAHADUR SHRESTHA; CEO ASOKE S. J. B. RANA; 12 brs.

Laxmi Bank Ltd: Hattisar, POB 19593, Kathmandu; tel. (1) 4444684; fax (1) 4444640; e-mail info@laxmibank.com; internet www.laxmibank.com; f. 2001; cap. 1,694m., res 537m., dep. 22,715.6m. (July 2012); Chair. RAJENDRA K. KHETAN; CEO SUMAN JOSHI.

Nabil Bank Ltd (Nabil): Nabil House, Kamaladi, POB 3729, Kathmandu; tel. (1) 4429546; fax (1) 4429548; e-mail nabil@nabilbank.com; internet www.nabilbank.com; f. 1984 as Nepal Arab Bank Ltd; name changed as above Jan. 2000; 50% owned by National Bank of Bangladesh, 30% by the Nepalese public and 20% by Nepalese govt financial institutions; cap. 2,435.7m., res 1,324.4m., dep. 54,905.6m. (July 2012); Chair. SATYENDRA PYARA SHRESTHA; CEO ANIL GYAWALI; 48 brs.

Nepal Bangladesh Bank Ltd (NB Bank): Bijuli Bazar, New Baneshwor, POB 9062, Kathmandu; tel. (1) 4783976; fax (1) 4780826; e-mail nbblho@nbbl.com.np; internet www.nbbl.com.np; f. 1994; 50% owned by International Finance Investment and Commerce Bank Ltd (Bangladesh), 20% by Nepalese promoters and 30% public issue; cap. 2,009.4m., res 1,290.5m., dep. 16,952.7m. (July 2012); CEO GYANENDRA PRASAD DHUNGANA; Chair. PUSHPARAJ RAJ KARNIKAR; 19 brs.

Nepal Credit and Commerce Bank Ltd: NB Bldg, Bagh Bazar, Kathmandu; tel. (1) 4246991; fax (1) 4244610; e-mail corporate@nccbank.com.np; internet www.nccbank.com.np; est. as Nepal Bank of Ceylon; reconstituted as above in Sept. 2002 after Bank of Ceylon (Sri Lanka) sold its shares to NB Group (Nepal); cap. 1,399.7m., res 331.9m., dep. 10,824.7m. (July 2010); Chair. PRITHIVI RAJ LIGAL; CEO RATNA RAJ BAJRACHARYA; 17 brs.

Nepal Investment Bank Ltd (NIBL): Durbar Marg, POB 3412, Kathmandu; tel. (1) 4228229; fax (1) 4226349; e-mail nibl@nibl.com.np; internet www.nibl.com.np; f. 1986 as Nepal Indosuez Bank Ltd, name changed as above in June 2002; 50% owned by a consortium of Nepalese investors, 20% by general public, 15% by Rastriya Banijya Bank and 15% by Rastriya Beema Sansthan; cap. 3,766.1m., res 2,264.1m., dep. 57,010.6m. (July 2012); Chair. and Chief Exec. PRITHIVI BAHADUR PANDE; 40 brs.

Nepal SBI Bank Ltd: Corporate Office, Hattisar, POB 6049, Kathmandu; tel. (1) 4435516; fax (1) 4435612; e-mail nsblco@nsbl.com.np; internet www.nepalsbi.com.np; f. 1993; 50% owned by State Bank of India, 30% by Nepalese public, 15% by Employees' Provident Fund (Nepal) and 5% by Agricultural Devt Bank (Nepal); cap. 2,355.7m., res 839.5m., dep. 53,337.2m. (July 2012); Chair. HASANA SHARMA; Man. Dir ALOK KUMAR SHARMA.

Standard Chartered Bank Nepal Ltd: Grindlays Bhavan, Naya Baneshwor, POB 3990, Kathmandu; tel. (1) 4246753; fax (1) 4226762; e-mail outserve.nepal@standardchartered.com; internet www.standardchartered.com/np; f. 1986 as Nepal Grindlays Bank; name changed in July 2001; 75% owned by Standard Chartered Bank (United Kingdom) and 25% by the Nepalese public; cap. 1,851.7m., res 2,261.5m., dep. 35,965.6m. (July 2012); Chair. SUNIL KAUSHAL; CEO JOSEPH SILVANUS; 14 brs.

Banking Organization

Nepal Bankers' Association (NBA): Heritage Plaza, Blk C & D, 2nd Floor, Kamaladi, Kathmandu; tel. (1) 4169114; fax (1) 4169113; e-mail nepalbankers@mail.com.np; internet www.nepalbankers .com; Pres. ASHOKE SUMSHER J. B. RANA.

Development Finance Organizations

Agricultural Development Bank Ltd: Ramshah Path, Kathmandu; tel. (1) 4262885; fax (1) 4262616; e-mail info@adbn.gov.np; internet www.adbl.gov.np; f. 1968; 93.6% state-owned, 2.1% owned by the Nepal Rastra Bank, and 4.3% by co-operatives and private individuals; specialized agricultural credit institution providing credit for agricultural development to co-operatives, individuals and asscns; receives deposits from individuals, co-operatives and other asscns to generate savings in the agricultural sector; operational networks include 10 regional offices, 37 brs, 92 sub-brs, 52 depots and 160 small farmers' development projects and 5 regional training centres; Chair. GAJA NAND AGRAWAL; CEO TEJ BAHADUR BUDHATHOKI.

Gurkha Development Bank Ltd (GDB): Triveni Complex, Putalisadak, POB 5617, Kathmandu; tel. (1) 4255650; fax (1) 4242829; e-mail info@gdbl.com.np; internet www.gurkhabank.com; Man. Dir AMOD DOMZAN.

Nepal Aawas Finance Ltd: New Baneshwor, POB 5624, Kathmandu; tel. (1) 4780259; fax (1) 4782753; Chair. JITENDRA NATH RIMAL.

STOCK EXCHANGE

Nepal Stock Exchange Ltd (NEPSE): Singha Durbar Plaza, POB 1550, Kathmandu; tel. (1) 4250755; fax (1) 4262538; e-mail info@ nepalstock.com; internet www.nepalstock.com; f. 1976; reorg. 1984; converted in 1993 from Securities Exchange Centre Ltd to Nepal Stock Exchange Ltd; 147 listed cos, 139 scripts; Chair. Dr JIBA NATH DHITAL; Gen. Man. SHANKER MAN SINGH.

INSURANCE

Alliance Insurance Co Ltd: POB 10811, Tinkune, Kathmandu; tel. (1) 4499220; fax (1) 4499647; e-mail info@allianceinsurance.com .np; internet www.allianceinsurance.com.np; f. 1996; Chair. GOVINDA DAS SHRESTHA; CEO YUGESH BHAKTA BADE SHRESTHA.

Everest Insurance Co Ltd: Hattisar, POB 10675, Kathmandu; tel. (1) 4444717; fax (1) 4444366; e-mail info@eic.com.np; internet www .everestinsurance.com; f. 1994; Chair. RAJENDRA K. KHETAN; CEO KEWAL K. SHRESTHA.

Himalayan General Insurance Co Ltd: Babar Mahal, POB 148, Kathmandu; tel. (1) 4231788; fax (1) 4241517; e-mail ktm@hgi.com .np; internet www.hgi.com.np; f. 1993; Chair. RAJ KRISHNA SHRESTHA; CEO MAHENDRA KRISHNA SHRESTHA.

Neco Insurance Ltd: Star Mall, 7th Floor, Putalisadak, POB 12271, Kathmandu; tel. (1) 4427354; fax (1) 4418761; e-mail info@ necoins.com.np; internet www.necoins.com.np; f. 1994; CEO BHOJ RAJ SHARMA; Sec. RABINDRA LAL JOSHI.

Nepal Insurance Co Ltd: NIC Bldg, Kulratna Marg, Kamaladi, POB 3623, Kathmandu; tel. (1) 4221353; fax (1) 4225446; e-mail nic@ wlink.com.np; internet www.nepalinsurance.com.np; f. 1947 as Nepal Malchalani Tatha Beema Co; name changed as above in 1991; Chair. Dr DEVRAJ ADHIKARI; Gen. Man. KESHAB DUBADI.

NLG Insurance Co Ltd: Panipokhari, Lazimpat, POB 20600, Kathmandu; tel. (1) 4442646; fax (1) 4416427; e-mail info@nlgi .com.np; internet www.nlg.com.np; 70% owned by National Life Insurance Co Ltd; Chair. KRISHNA PRASAD SHARMA; CEO VIJAYA BAHADUR SHAH.

Premier Insurance Co (Nepal) Ltd: Tripureswor, POB 9183, Kathmandu; tel. (1) 4413543; fax (1) 4413442; e-mail premier@picl .com.np; internet www.premier-insurance.com.np; f. 1994; Chair. RAM LAL SHRESHTHA; Man. Dir SURESH LAL SHRESTHA.

Rastriya Beema Sansthan (National Insurance Corpn): POB 527, Kathmandu; tel. (1) 4262520; fax (1) 4262610; e-mail beema@wlink .com.np; internet www.beema.com.np; f. 1967; Chair. RAJENDRA PRAKASH LOHANI.

Sagarmatha Insurance Co Ltd: Surakshan Bhavan, Bhagawati Marg, Naxal, POB 12211, Kathmandu; tel. (1) 4412367; fax (1) 4412378; e-mail sagarmatha@insurance.wlink.com.np; internet www.sagarmathainsurance.com.np; f. 1996; Chair. RAM KRISHNA MANANDHAR; Exec. Dir KRISHNA BAHADUR BASNYAT.

United Insurance Co (Nepal) Ltd: POB 9075, Trade Tower, Thapathali, Kathmandu; tel. (1) 4246686; fax (1) 5111112; e-mail uic@mail.com.np; internet www.unitedinsurance.com.np; f. 1993; Chair. RAVI BHAKTA SHRESTHA.

Trade and Industry
GOVERNMENT AGENCIES

National Planning Commission (NPC): Singha Durbar, POB 1284, Kathmandu; tel. (1) 4225879; fax (1) 4226500; e-mail npcs@ npcnepal.gov.np; internet www.npc.gov.np; Sec. YUVRAJ BHUSAL.

National Trading Ltd: Teku, POB 128, Kathmandu; tel. (1) 4225799; fax (1) 4225151; e-mail info@nationaltrading.com.np; internet www.nationaltrading.com.np; f. 1962; state trading org.; imports and distributes construction materials and raw materials for industry; also machinery, vehicles and consumer goods; operates bonded warehouse, duty-free shop and related activities; brs in all major towns; Chair. L. P. AGRAWAL.

Trade and Export Promotion Centre (TEPC): Na Tole, Pulchowk, Lalitpur, POB 825, Kathmandu; tel. (1) 5525898; fax (1) 5525464; e-mail info@tepc.gov.np; internet www.tepc.gov.np; f. 1971; govt-owned; Chair. LAL MANI JOSHI; Exec. Dir ISHWARI PRASAD GHIMIRE.

DEVELOPMENT ORGANIZATIONS

National Productivity and Economic Development Centre: Balaju Industrial District, POB 1318, Kathmandu; tel. (1) 4350566; fax (1) 4350530; e-mail npedc@wlink.com.np; internet www .npedc-nepal.org; functions as secretariat of National Productivity Council; provides services for industrial promotion and productivity improvement through planning research, consultancy, training, seminars and information services; Gen. Man. YUDDHA BHADUR PANT (acting).

National Tea and Coffee Development Board (NTCDB): New Baneshwor, POB 9683, Kathmandu; tel. (1) 4495792; fax (1) 4497941; e-mail ntcdboard@wlink.com.np; internet teacoffee.gov .np; f. 1992 to promote and expand the Nepalese tea industry; Exec. Dir BINAY KUMAR MISHRA.

Nepal Tea Development Corpn Ltd: Triveni Complex, Putali Sadak, Kathmandu; tel. (1) 4224074; fax (1) 4266133; e-mail ntdc@ trivenionline.com; internet www.ntdcltd.com; f. 1966; privatized in early 2000s; commercial production of tea; Contact SUBHASH C. SHANGHAI.

CHAMBERS OF COMMERCE

Federation of Nepalese Chambers of Commerce and Industry (FNCCI): Pachali Shahid Shukra FNCCI Milan Marg, Teku, POB 269, Kathmandu; tel. (1) 4262061; fax (1) 4261022; e-mail fncci@mos .com.np; internet www.fncci.org; f. 1965; comprises 92 District Municipality Chambers (DCCIs), 80 Commodity Associations, 453 leading industrial and commercial undertakings in both the public and private sector, and 10 Bi-national Chambers; publishes annual *Nepal and the World: A Statistical Profile*; Pres. SURAJ VAIDYA; Dir Dr HEMANT DABADI.

Birganj Chamber of Commerce and Industries: Hospital Rd, Birganj; tel. (51) 522290; fax (51) 526049; e-mail bicci@bicci.org.np; internet www.bicci.org.np; 605 mems; Pres. ASHOK KUMAR TEMANI.

Lalitpur Chamber of Commerce and Industry: Mangal Bazar, Patan Durbar Sq., POB 26, Lalitpur; tel. (1) 5530663; fax (1) 5530661; e-mail lcci@mos.com.np; internet www.lcci.org.np; f. 1967; Pres. AJAR MAN JOSHI; Sec.-Gen. KRISHNA LAL MAHARJAN.

Nepal Chamber of Commerce: Chamber Bhavan, Kantipath, POB 198, Kathmandu; tel. (1) 4230947; fax (1) 4229998; e-mail chamber@wlink.com.np; internet www.nepalchamber.org; f. 1952; non-profit org. promoting industrial and commercial development; 8,000 regd cos and 1,600 ordinary mems; Pres. SURESH KUMAR BASNET; Sec.-Gen. KAMLESH KUMAR AGRAWAL.

INDUSTRIAL AND TRADE ASSOCIATIONS

Association of Craft Producers: Ravi Bhavan Mode, POB 3701, Kathmandu; tel. (1) 4275108; fax (1) 4272676; e-mail export@ craftacp.org.np; internet acp.org.np; f. 1984; local non-profit org. providing technical, marketing and management services for craft producers; manufacturer, exporter and retailer of handicraft goods; Exec. Dir MEERA BHATTARAI; Programme Dir REVITA SHRESTHA.

Association of Nepalese Rice, Oil and Pulses Industries: POB 20782, Radha Bhavan, Tripureswor, Kathmandu; tel. (1) 4215676; e-mail nfma@mcmail.com.np; Pres. KUMUD KUMAR DUGAD; Gen. Sec. CHANDRA KRISHNA KARMACHARYA.

Association of Pharmaceutical Producers of Nepal (APPON): 4th Floor, Bagmati Chamber, Teku, Kathmandu; tel. (1) 4100024; fax (1) 4231871; e-mail appoappon123@gmail.com; internet www.appon .org; Pres. MAHESH GORKHALI; Sec.-Gen. JEEVAN LAL AMATYA.

Cargo Agents' Association of Nepal: Thamel, POB 5355, Kathmandu; tel. (1) 4419019; fax (1) 4419858.

Central Carpet Industries Association of Nepal: POB 2419, Narayanhiti Lazimpat (N), Kathmandu; tel. and fax (1) 4415793;

e-mail ccia@enet.com.np; internet www.nepalcarpet.org; Pres. LANK MAN ROKA; Gen. Sec. CHHIRING SHERPA.

Computer Association of Nepal: POB 4982, 235/39 Maitidevi Marga, Kathmandu; tel. (1) 4432700; fax (1) 4441998; e-mail info@can.org.np; internet www.can.org.np; f. 1992; asscn of the IT Businessmen's Organization; Pres. BINOD DHAKAL.

Confederation of Nepalese Industries: 5th Floor, Trade Tower, Thapathali, Kathmandu; tel. (1) 5111122; fax (1) 5111125; e-mail cni@wlink.com.np; internet www.cnind.org; f. 2000; Pres. NARENDRA KUMAR BASNYAT.

Federation of Handicraft Associations of Nepal: Upma Marg, Thapathali, POB 784, Kathmandu; tel. (1) 4244231; fax (1) 4222940; e-mail han@wlink.com.np; internet www.nepalhandicraft.org.np; f. 1972; Pres. BIKASH RATNA DHAKHWA.

Federation of Nepal Cottage and Small Industries (FNCSI): Maitighar Height, POB 6530, Kathmandu; tel. (1) 4222751; fax (1) 4215602; e-mail fncsi@ntc.net.np; internet www.fncsi.org; f. 1990; business networks in 74 districts; represents interests and promotes development of nation's micro-, cottage and small industries; 30,000 general mems (2007); Pres. SURESH PRADHAN.

Garment Association of Nepal: Shankhamul Rd, New Baneshwor, POB 21332, Kathmandu; tel. (1) 4780691; fax (1) 4780173; e-mail gan@ntc.net.np; internet www.ganasso.org; Pres. UDAY RAJ PANDEY.

Himalayan Orthodox Tea Producers' Association of Nepal: Bakhundole, Lalitpur; tel. (1) 2041036; e-mail hotpa@mail.com.np; internet www.nepaltea.com.np; f. 1998; non-profit org.; represents and promotes the Himalayan tea sector; Chair. UDAYA CHAPAGAIN.

Leather Footwear and Goods Manufacturers' Association of Nepal: Bag Bazar, POB 19732, Kathmandu; tel. (1) 4219349; e-mail lfgman@ntc.net.np; Pres. HOM NATH UPADHYAYA.

Nepal Foreign Trade Association: Bagmati Chamber, 1st Floor, Milan Marg, Teku, POB 541, Kathmandu; tel. (1) 4223784; fax (1) 4247159; e-mail nfta@mos.com.np; f. 1972; Pres. ASHOK KUMAR AGRAWAL; 431 mems.

Nepal Forest Industries Association: Naxal, Nag Pokhari, POB 5623, Kathmandu; tel. (1) 4411865; fax (1) 4413838; e-mail padmasri@ccsl.com.np; Pres. HARI PRASAD GIRI; Sec.-Gen. ROHINI THAPALIYA.

Nepal Leather Industries Association: POB 9944, Anamnagar, Kathmandu; tel. (1) 4265248; fax (1) 4228978; e-mail giris@atcnet .com.np; Pres. SANJAY GIRI; Sec.-Gen. RAMESH RAJ POKHAREL.

Nepal Plastic Manufacturers' Association: Kandevsthan, Kupandol, POB 2350, Lalitpur; tel. and fax (1) 5528185; Pres. SHAILENDRA LAL PRADHAN; Sec.-Gen. RAJESWOR LAL JOSHI.

Nepal Trans-Himalayan Trade Association: Jyoti Bhavan, Kantipath, POB 133, Kathmandu; tel. (1) 4225490; fax (1) 4254048; e-mail syamukapu@unilever.wlink.com.np; Pres. DURGA BAHADUR SHRESTHA; Gen. Sec. MAHESH TULADHAR.

Silk Association of Nepal: Tripureshwor, Kathmandu; tel. (1) 4254093; e-mail san@nepsilk.wlink.com.np; internet www.nepalsilk .org.np; f. 1992; organizes and promotes sericulture and silk devt activities; Pres. SHANKAR P. PANDEYA.

UTILITIES

Electricity

Nepal Electricity Authority: Durbar Marga, POB 10020, Kathmandu; tel. (1) 4153052; fax (1) 4153067; e-mail info@nea.org.np; internet www.nea.org.np; f. 1985 following merger; govt-owned; Man. Dir RAMESHWAR YADAV.

Butwal Power Co Ltd: 313 Ganga Devi Marga, Buddha Nagar, POB 11728, Kathmandu; tel. (1) 4784026; fax (1) 4780994; e-mail info@bpc.com.np; internet www.bpc.com.np; f. 1966; partially privatized in 2003; principal shareholders: 68.95% owned by Shangri-La Energy Ltd, 9.09% by Govt and 6.05% by Interkraft Norway; 5.91% divided between Nepalese energy orgs and employees; public sector retains 10% ownership; owns and operates Jhimruk and Andhi Khola Hydropower Plants; supplies electricity to the national grid; 326 employees; Chair. PADMA JYOTI.

Chilime Hydropower Co Ltd: Lazimpat, Kathmandu; tel. (1) 4439163; fax (1) 4443077; e-mail chpcl@wlink.com.np; internet www.chilime.com.np; 51% owned by Nepal Electricity Authority; Chair. TEEKA RAM B. C.

Department of Electricity Development: 576 Bhakti Thapa Sadak-4, POB 2507, Anamnagar, Kathmandu; tel. (1) 4480326; fax (1) 4480257; e-mail info@doed.gov.np; internet www.doed.gov.np; f. 1993; fmrly Electricity Development Centre; name changed as above 1999; Dir-Gen. DILLI BAHADUR SINGH.

Water

Nepal Water Supply Corpn: Tripureshwor Marg, POB 5349, Kathmandu; tel. (1) 4259857; fax (1) 4262229; e-mail nwsc@mos .com.np; internet www.nwsc.gov.np; f. 1990; govt-owned; Chair. MAHESH DUTTA.

TRADE UNIONS

Nepal Trade Union Congress—Independent (NTUC—I): POB 5507, Kathmandu; tel. (1) 4107754; fax (1) 4107759; e-mail ntuc@ wlink.com.np; internet www.ntuci.org.np; f. 1947 as the Nepal Trade Union Congress; 28 affiliated unions; affiliated to ICFTU; operates in association with Nepali Congress Party; merged with Democratic Confederation of Nepalese Trade Unions in March 2008 and name changed to the above; Pres. LAXMAN BAHADUR BASNET; Gen. Sec. ACHAYUT RAJ PANDEY; 192,000 mems.

General Federation of Nepalese Trade Unions (GEFONT): Man Mohan Labour Bldg, GEFONT Plaza, Putali Sadak, POB 10652, Kathmandu; tel. (1) 4168000; fax (1) 4168012; e-mail dfa@ gefont.org; internet www.gefont.org; f. 1989; 19 affiliated unions; Pres. BISHNU RIMAL.

Transport

Department of Transport Management: Ministry of Labour and Transport Management, Singha Durbar, Kathmandu; tel. (1) 4602126; fax (1) 4602440; e-mail info@dotm.gov.np; internet www .dotm.gov.np; Dir-Gen. CHANDRA MAN SHRESTHA.

RAILWAYS

A short narrow-gauge line in Janakpur district is the sole railway in operation. However, a feasibility study into plans for a 1,318-km electric rail network was completed in mid-2010. In addition to a 945-km east–west line, linking the districts of Mechi and Mahakali, the proposed network included a 185-km Kathmandu–Pokhara section and up to six branch lines connecting with the rail network of India.

Nepal Railways Corpn Ltd (NRC): Khajuri, Janakpur; tel. (41) 52082; HQ Jaynagar, India; f. 1937 as Janakpur-Jaynagar Railways; name changed as above June 2004; 53 km open, linking Jaynagar in India with Janakpur and Bijalpura; narrow gauge; 11 steam engines, 25 coaches and vans, and 20 wagons; Gen. Man. MADAN SINGH MAHAT.

ROADS

In 2010 Nepal had 19,875 km of roads, of which 53.9% had paved surfaces. A 190-km mountain road, Tribhuwana Rajpath, links the capital, Kathmandu, with the Indian railhead at Raxaul. The Siddhartha Highway, constructed with Indian assistance, connects the Pokhara valley, in mid-west Nepal, with Sonauli, on the Indian border in Uttar Pradesh. The 114-km Arniko Highway, constructed with Chinese help, connects Kathmandu with Kodari, on the Chinese border. In the early 1990s the final section of the 1,030-km East–West Highway (Mahendra Highway) was constructed.

Roads Board Nepal: POB 11406, Arnico Bldg, Minbhavan, Kathmandu; tel. (1) 4493515; fax (1) 4493542; e-mail roadsboard@wlink .com.np; internet www.roadsboardnepal.org; f. 2002; maintenance and devt of the road network; Exec. Dir DIPAK NATH CHALISE.

ROPEWAY

A 42-km ropeway links Hetauda and Kathmandu and can carry 22 metric tons of freight per hour throughout the year. Foodgrains, construction goods and heavy goods on this route are transported by the ropeway.

CIVIL AVIATION

Tribhuvan International Airport (TIR) is situated about 6 km from Kathmandu. Work to upgrade facilities and expand capacity at TIR, including extension of the runway and construction of a new international terminal, commenced in 2011. Gautam Buddha Airport in Lumbini was also scheduled for development. In 2011 there were 35 airports, of various standards, in operation.

The monopoly of the Royal Nepal Airlines Corporation in domestic air services came to an end in 1992. By 2007 there were about 16 private airlines in Nepal providing domestic cargo and passenger services.

Civil Aviation Authority of Nepal (CAAN): Babar Mahal, Kathmandu; tel. (1) 4262387; fax (1) 4262516; e-mail dgca@caanepal.org .np; internet www.caanepal.org.np; f. 1998; chaired by the Minister of Tourism and Civil Aviation; Dir-Gen. TRIRATNA MANANDHAR.

Nepal Airlines Corpn (NAC): NAC Bldg, Kantipath, Kathmandu; tel. (1) 4220757; fax (1) 4225348; e-mail info@nac.com.np; internet nepalairlines.com.np; f. 1958; fmrly Royal Nepal Airlines Corpn; 100% state-owned (scheduled for transfer to private ownership); scheduled services to 19 domestic airfields, international scheduled flights to five destinations in the Middle East and the Far East, charter flights; Chair. MANARUP SHAHI.

Agni Air: POB 23650, Prayag Marg, Shantinagar, Kathmandu; tel. (1) 4489386; fax (1) 4107655; e-mail info@agniair.com; internet www .agniair.com; f. 2006; scheduled passenger flights to domestic destinations; 5 aircraft; Chair. SUDHIR BASNYAT.

Buddha Air: Jawalakhal, Lalitpur, POB 2167, Kathmandu; tel. (1) 5521015; fax (1) 5537726; e-mail buddhaair@buddhaair.com; internet www.buddhaair.com; f. 1997; domestic passenger services; services to Paro, Bhutan, commenced in 2010; services to Varanasi, India, commenced in 2012; Man. Dir BIRENDRA B. BASNET; Chair. SURENDRA B. BASNET.

Cosmic Air: Kalimatidole, Sinamangal, POB 3488, Kathmandu; tel. (1) 4490146; fax (1) 4497569; e-mail soi@wlink.com.np; internet www .cosmicair.com; f. 1997; operates domestic cargo, passenger and mountain flights; began operating flights to a limited no. of Indian destinations in 2004; Exec. Chair. SANJAYA PRADHAM; Man. Dir M. B. MATHEMA; 179 employees.

Gorkha Airlines: Maharajgunj, POB 9451, Kathmandu; tel. (1) 4435122; fax (1) 4444525; e-mail gorkha@mos.com.np; internet www .gorkhaairlines.com; f. 1996; scheduled and charter passenger and cargo flights to domestic destinations; Gen. Man. RABINDRA SILWAL.

Yeti Airlines: Tilganga, POB 20011, Kathmandu; tel. (1) 4465888; fax (1) 4464977; e-mail yetiair@wlink.com.np; internet www .yetiairlines.com; f. 1998; operates scheduled and chartered domestic flights; Chair. LHAKPA SONAM SHERPA; Man. Dir ANG TSHERING SHERPA.

Tourism

Major tourist attractions include: Lumbini, the birthplace of Buddha; the lake city of Pokhara; and the Himalaya mountain range, including Mt Everest, the world's highest peak. Since 1989, in an effort to increase tourism, the Government has abolished travel restrictions in remote areas of Nepal that had previously been inaccessible to foreigners. Following the restoration of parliamentary democracy in 1990, tourist arrivals in Nepal rose considerably. However, the insurgency in the west hindered development in the early and mid-2000s. Since 2005 access has been granted to an additional 175 mountains, raising the total number of mountains open to climbers to 326. The cessation of Maoist hostilities in 2006 and the subsequent peace agreement—combined with the introduction of additional airline services between Nepal and other Asian countries—led to a significant recovery in the tourism sector. Tourism arrivals witnessed massive growth, from 383,926 in 2006 to 526,633 in 2007. In 2011 tourist arrivals reached an estimated 736,000; in the same year, revenue from tourism totalled US $386.0m.

Nepal Tourism Board (NTB): Tourist Service Centre, Bhrikuti Mandap, POB 11018, Kathmandu; tel. (1) 4256909; fax (1) 4256910; e-mail info@ntb.org.np; internet www.welcomenepal.com; f. 1998; Chair. SUSHIL GHIMIRE; CEO SUBASH NIROLA.

Hotel Association Nepal (HAN): Subarna Shamsher Marg, Gairidhara, POB 2151, Kathmandu; tel. (1) 4412705; fax (1) 4424914; e-mail info@hotelassociation.org.np; internet www .hotelassociationnepal.org; f. 1966; Pres. NARENDRA BAJRACHARYA.

Nepal Association of Tour and Travel Agents (NATTA): Gairidhara Rd, Goma Ganesh, Naxal, POB 362, Kathmandu; tel. (1) 4419409; fax (1) 4418684; e-mail info@natta.org.np; internet www .natta.org.np; f. 1966 to promote and regulate development in the

tourism industry; non-governmental org.; more than 500 mems; Pres. PAVITRA KUMAR KARKI; Sec.-Gen. ACHYUT GURAGAIN.

Nepal Mountaineering Association (NMA): Nagpokhari, Naxal, POB 1435, Kathmandu; tel. (1) 4434525; fax (1) 4434578; e-mail office@nepalmountaineering.org; internet www .nepalmountaineering.org; f. 1973; promotes mountaineering and mountain tourism; Pres. ZIMBA ZANGBU SHERPA.

Tourist Guide Association of Nepal (TURGAN): POB 5344, Kamaladi, Kathmandu; tel. and fax (1) 4225102; e-mail turgan@ wlink.com.np; internet www.turgannepal.com; Pres. HARE RAM BARAL.

Trekking Agencies' Association of Nepal (TAAN): Maligaun Ganesthan, POB 3612, Kathmandu; tel. (1) 4427473; fax (1) 4419245; e-mail taan@wlink.com.np; internet www.taan.org.np; f. 1979; Pres. MAHENDRA SINGH THAPA; Gen. Sec. MOHAN LAMSAL.

Defence

As assessed at November 2012, Nepal's total armed forces numbered 95,750 men. Paramilitary forces comprised 62,000 men. Military service is voluntary. There was a 15,000-strong Armed Police Force under the Ministry of Home Affairs.

Defence Budget: NRs 19,100m. in 2012.

Chief of Army Staff: Gen. GAURAV SHAMSHER JUNG BAHADUR RANA.

Education

Primary education, beginning at six years of age and lasting for five years, is officially compulsory and is provided free of charge in government schools. Secondary education, beginning at the age of 11, lasts for a further five years, comprising a first cycle of three years (lower secondary) and a second of two years (secondary). In 2006/07 enrolment at primary schools included 76.1% of children in the relevant age group (boys 77.9%; girls 74.2%), while the ratio for secondary enrolment in 2005/06 was equivalent to 43.2% of pupils in the relevant age-group (boys 45.7%; girls 40.5%). Some 8,000 pupils attended the country's 321 primary schools in 1950; by 2004 there were an estimated 24,746 primary schools, and in 2010 there were 4.9m. primary pupils. The number of secondary schools rose from two in 1950 to 11,983 in 2004. In 2008 there were an estimated 2.3m. pupils enrolled at secondary schools.

The oldest of the colleges of higher education in Nepal is Tri Chandra School in Kathmandu, founded in 1918, which provides four-year arts courses. The only other advanced college in existence before the 1951 Revolution was the Sanskrit College in Kathmandu, founded in 1948. There are four state universities and one privately funded university. The Tribhuvan University in Kathmandu had 115,608 students in 2001/02. The second state university, the Mahendra Sanskrit Viswavidyalaya in Beljhundi, Dang, was founded in 1986. In 2000/01 the university had an enrolment of 3,252 students. The Purbanchal University, which was opened in 1995, had 2,840 students in 2001/02, and the Pokhara University, which was opened in 1997, had 2,946 students. In addition, there is one private university—the Kathmandu University in Banepa, Kavrepalanchok, which was opened in 1992. In 2001/02 the university had an enrolment of 1,783 students.

Proposed expenditure on education by the central Government in the 2010/11 budget was NRs 57,827m. (17.1% of total spending). According to UNESCO, literacy among the adult population of Nepal was only 60.3% in 2009 (males 73.0%; females 48.3%); it was hoped that an adult literacy rate of 70% would be achieved by the conclusion of the 12th Five-Year Plan in 2017.

THE NETHERLANDS

Introductory Survey

LOCATION, CLIMATE, LANGUAGE, RELIGION, FLAG, CAPITAL

The Kingdom of the Netherlands is situated in Western Europe, bordered to the east by Germany and to the south by Belgium. Its northern and western shores face the North Sea. The Caribbean islands of Bonaire, Saba and Sint (St) Eustatius have the status of *bijzondere gemeente* (special municipalities), while Aruba, Curaçao and Sint (St) Maarten are independent countries within the Kingdom of the Netherlands. The climate is temperate: the average temperature in January is 0°C (32°F), while the average in summer is 21°C (70°F). The national language is Dutch. There is a Frisian-speaking minority (numbering about 400,000). About one-third of the inhabitants are Roman Catholics and about one-quarter are Protestants, while most of the remainder do not profess any religion. The national flag (proportions 2 by 3) has three equal horizontal stripes, of red, white and blue. The capital is Amsterdam, but the seat of government is The Hague (Den Haag or 's-Gravenhage).

CONTEMPORARY POLITICAL HISTORY

Historical Context

The Netherlands remained neutral throughout the First World War. During the Second World War the Netherlands was occupied by Germany. Following its liberation in 1945, it became a founder member of the UN. In 1948 the Netherlands formed the Brussels Treaty Organization with Belgium and Luxembourg. The Treaty establishing the Benelux Economic Union (see p. 459) between these three countries was signed in 1958 and came into force in 1960, and a single customs area was established in 1970. The Netherlands was a founder member of the European Community (EC, now European Union—EU, see p. 281). Queen Juliana, who had reigned since 1948, abdicated in favour of her eldest daughter, Beatrix, in April 1980, following the adoption in February of a constitutional amendment that allowed for the accession of the reigning monarch's eldest child, regardless of gender.

Domestic Political Affairs

After the Second World War successive administrations were formed by various coalitions between the several 'confessional' Roman Catholic and Protestant and 'progressive' Socialist and Liberal parties. At a general election held in 1971 left-wing parties made substantial gains. In July 1972 the Government was forced to resign after losing its working majority in the Second Chamber (Tweede Kamer) of the States-General. Another general election took place in November, at which the 'confessional' parties suffered a major reverse, and in May 1973 a new Government was formed by a left-of-centre coalition under the leadership of Dr Joop den Uyl of the Partij van de Arbeid (PvdA—Labour Party).

The coalition collapsed in March 1977; a general election followed in May. Attempts to form a left-of-centre coalition between the PvdA, the Christen Democratisch Appèl (CDA—Christian Democratic Appeal)—an alliance of 'confessional' groupings, which united in 1980 to form a single party—and Democraten '66 were unsuccessful, and in December 1977 Andries van Agt, of the CDA, formed a centre-right coalition Government of the CDA and the right-wing Volkspartij voor Vrijheid en Democratie (VVD—People's Party for Freedom and Democracy). Despite retaining only a narrow majority in the Second Chamber and several ministerial disagreements, the Government survived its full term in office. A general election was held in May 1981, and a centre-left coalition Government was formed in September, led by van Agt and comprising the CDA, the PvdA and Democraten '66. The Council of Ministers resigned after only five weeks in office, owing to its failure to agree on economic strategy. In November the coalition partners accepted a compromise economic programme, but deep divisions within the Government continued. The coalition collapsed again in May 1982, when all six PvdA ministers resigned, after which van Agt led a minority interim Government of the CDA and Democraten '66.

Although at a general election held in September 1982 the PvdA became the largest party in the Second Chamber (with 47 of 150 deputies), the election produced a significant swing to the right. In November a centre-right CDA-VVD coalition was established under the leadership of Ruud Lubbers, who had recently succeeded van Agt as Chairman of the CDA. The CDA-VVD coalition was returned to power at a general election in May 1986, having retained its majority in the Second Chamber. A loss of nine seats by the VVD was offset by a corresponding gain by the CDA, which, with 54 seats, became the party with the largest representation in the Second Chamber. The election did, none the less, produce a shift towards the centrist parties, with the PvdA and Democraten '66 (D66, as the party was restyled) both gaining seats at the expense of smaller radical groups. Following the election, Wim Kok replaced den Uyl as parliamentary leader of the PvdA. A new CDA-VVD coalition was formed in July.

In May 1989 the VVD caused the collapse of the Government by refusing to support Lubbers' proposals for the financing of a 20-year National Environment Policy (NEP), which was to involve a reduction in government spending in sectors such as defence and housing, an increase in taxes on motor fuels and the abolition of tax concessions for commuters using private transport. A general election was called for September, at which the CDA again secured 54 seats in the Second Chamber, while the PvdA took 49 seats. The VVD lost five seats. An alliance of left-wing organizations, GroenLinks, won six. In October negotiations between the CDA and the PvdA culminated in the formation of a centre-left coalition, again led by Lubbers. The coalition accord envisaged increased welfare provision, to be funded by a reduction in defence expenditure, as well as a programme of job creation and reductions in certain categories of taxation. Kok was appointed Deputy Prime Minister and Minister of Finance. In August 1990 the Government introduced an amended version of the NEP, designated the National Environment Policy Plus (NEPP), which placed strong emphasis on energy conservation and improvements in waste disposal and recycling.

In November 1992 the Second Chamber ratified the Treaty on European Union, which had been signed by EC Heads of Government at Maastricht in December 1991; the First Chamber (Eerste Kamer) similarly approved the Treaty in December 1992.

The CDA performed poorly at the May 1994 general election, winning only 34 seats in the Second Chamber. The PvdA became the party with the largest representation in the Chamber, with 37 seats. Both the VVD and D66 improved upon their performances at the previous general election, securing 31 and 24 seats respectively. The remaining 24 seats were distributed among eight smaller parties and special issue groups. Negotiations on a three-party coalition agreement between the PvdA, the VVD and D66 were initially retarded by deeply entrenched disagreement between the VVD and PvdA over the latter's reluctance to sanction severe reductions in social welfare spending. Following several concessions by the PvdA, a tripartite coalition, with Kok as Prime Minister, was eventually agreed in August.

The PvdA won increased representation at the general election to the Second Chamber held on 6 May 1998, taking 45 seats. The VVD secured 38 seats, while the CDA's representation was further reduced, to 29 seats. D66 won only 14 seats, having lost votes to GroenLinks and the Socialistische Partij (SP—Socialist Party). None the less, the PvdA, VVD and D66 agreed to renew their coalition (it was considered that D66 would be useful as an intermediary in conflicts of policy between the two leading partners), and a new Government, led by Kok, was inaugurated in August.

In May 1999 the Senate rejected the Government's proposal to allow the use of referendums on policy issues, a key demand of D66, after the refusal of a prominent member of the VVD to support the measure. D66 subsequently announced that it could no longer work with the VVD, and withdrew from the ruling coalition, prompting the resignation of the Council of Ministers. However, following a series of talks between the three parties, in June the Government formally withdrew its resignation. In January 2001 the three coalition parties reached a new agreement on the use of referendums. The new proposals were for a judicially non-binding referendum and would not require a change to the Constitution. The temporary referendum law entered into force on 1 January 2002 and expired three years later. Legislation was subsequently adopted to allow a national referendum to be held exceptionally on the proposed EU constitutional treaty in June 2005.

In August 2001 Kok announced that he would not seek re-election for a further term in office at the general election, scheduled for May 2002. He also announced that he would step down as party leader of the PvdA and subsequently endorsed the appointment of Ad Melkert, the parliamentary leader of the party, as his successor. Jaap de Hoop Scheffer, the parliamentary leader of the CDA, resigned in September 2001. He was replaced by Jan Peter Balkenende in the following month.

Report on the Srebrenica massacre; the 2002 election

In April 2002 the entire Council of Ministers resigned following the publication of a report by the Netherlands Institute for War Documentation into the massacre of some 7,000 Bosnian Muslims by Bosnian Serb troops in Srebrenica, Bosnia and Herzegovina, in July 1995. The report blamed the Dutch Government, the Dutch military and the UN for their respective roles in failing to prevent the atrocity and claimed that the 100 lightly armed Dutch peace-keeping troops who had been stationed in the town at the time had been ill-trained and had no clear mandate (see Foreign Affairs). At the request of Queen Beatrix, the Government agreed to remain in office in a caretaker capacity pending the forthcoming general election, which was scheduled to be held on 15 May 2002.

On 6 May 2002 the controversial politician Pim Fortuyn was shot dead in Hilversum, in the central Netherlands, a few days before the general election, in which his newly established party, the populist and anti-immigration Lijst Pim Fortuyn (LPF—Pim Fortuyn List), was expected to secure a substantial proportion of the vote. Fortuyn had formed the movement following his dismissal in January as leader of the Leefbaar Nederland (LN—Livable Netherlands) party for his anti-immigration rhetoric. In April 2003 Volkert van der Graaf, an animal-rights activist who claimed that he believed Fortuyn had presented a threat to vulnerable members of society, was convicted of the murder.

At the general election of 15 May 2002 the CDA won 43 of the 150 seats in the Second Chamber. The LPF took 26 seats, the VVD 24 and the PvdA 23. In the light of their electoral defeats, both the PvdA and the VVD changed their parliamentary leaders, to Jeltje van Nieuwenhoven and Gerrit Zalm, respectively.

Balkenende becomes Prime Minister: 2002–06

Jan Peter Balkenende was inaugurated as Prime Minister on 21 July 2002, leading a coalition Government comprising the CDA, the LPF and the VVD. Allegations were made by a newspaper that the LPF's new leader, Mat Herben, had tried unfairly to influence the selection procedure for the LN's electoral candidates when Fortuyn was still leader and Herben a party member. Herben resigned at the end of July and was subsequently replaced as party leader by Harry Wijnschenk. The new Government detailed policies to reform the health insurance and social security system and reduce the number of illegal immigrants to the Netherlands, and introduced compulsory instruction for Muslim religious leaders (imams) in Dutch values and social conventions.

Meanwhile, the LPF was riven by factionalism and personal acrimony, including, in October 2002, a dispute over the deputy premiership between Herman Heinsbroek, the Minister of Economic Affairs, and the incumbent Deputy Prime Minister and Minister of Public Health, Welfare and Sport, Dr Eduard Bomhoff. Despite the subsequent resignations of Heinsbroek and Bomhoff from the Council of Ministers, the LPF's coalition partners refused to co-operate further with the party and the Government resigned on 16 October. Balkenende presided over a minority Government, comprising the CDA and the VVD, pending a general election, which was scheduled for January 2003.

At the general election of 22 January 2003 the CDA won 44 seats in the Second Chamber, while the PvdA increased its number of seats from 23 to 42, under its new leader, Wouter Bos. The LPF, again led by Herben, following the resignation of Wijnschenk in late 2002, secured only eight seats, while D66 obtained six. Although the popularity of the right-wing LPF had declined sharply, immigration became a prominent subject of debate, the VVD echoing Fortuyn's statement that the Netherlands was already 'full'. In late January 2003 negotiations began

regarding the formation of a coalition administration under Balkenende. Disagreements between the CDA and the PvdA over Dutch support for an impending US-led military campaign to remove the regime of Saddam Hussein in Iraq hindered progress. In March, in his capacity as Prime Minister of the interim administration, Balkenende announced that, while Dutch troops would not assist in the campaign, some units of the armed forces and weapons would be supplied to help defend Turkey, should the conflict escalate. Negotiations resumed in late March and, as the US-led coalition entered Iraq, both parties expressed their support for the military operation. After the CDA and the PvdA failed to agree on reductions in budgetary expenditure necessary to revive the stagnant economy, in May the CDA negotiated the formation of a centre-right coalition with the VVD and D66, thereby gaining a majority of six in the 150-seat Second Chamber. The coalition Government, under the renewed premiership of Balkenende, was formally sworn in on 27 May.

In late May 2003 the Provincial Councils elected a new Senate in which the CDA-VVD-D66 coalition also obtained a majority, securing 41 of the 75 seats. The new Council of Ministers largely resembled the caretaker administration formed in October 2002. The CDA held eight portfolios, the VVD six and D66 two. Two new Deputy Prime Ministers were appointed: Zalm of the VVD, who was also assigned the post of Minister of Finance, and Thom de Graaf of D66, who was also named as Minister of Government Reform and Kingdom Relations.

The Government introduced a number of stringent new policies regarding immigrants and asylum seekers. In late January 2004 the Government announced that, in order to prevent the destabilization of the employment market, a maximum of 22,000 immigrants from the 10 new EU member states (which were scheduled to join the EU on 1 May) would be permitted to settle in the Netherlands. In February parliament approved a bill authorizing the provision of a repatriation payment and a free flight to their country of origin to failed asylum seekers. The law was condemned by human rights groups, but was welcomed by certain sectors of society that felt threatened by the rising level of unemployment. The 'voluntary returns' policy came into effect in June 2004.

In September 2004 the Government announced proposals for an austerity budget for 2005, in an attempt to reduce the budget deficit and prepare for the economic effects of an ageing population, including reforms to unemployment and disability benefits, reductions in health care expenditure and the elimination of tax benefits for those saving for early retirement. The proposals provoked widespread industrial action and protests in September and October. A compromise was reached in November whereby the trade union leaders accepted the proposed disincentive to early retirement and the restriction of eligibility for disability benefits, and agreed to demand only minimal wage increases over the forthcoming year.In March 2005 de Graaf tendered his resignation as Deputy Prime Minister and Minister of Government Reform, after the rejection by parliament of an electoral reform bill that would have introduced the direct election of mayors. The two remaining D66 cabinet members announced that they were also reconsidering their positions, but an agreement was reached that ensured the continuance of the incumbent Government. Pechtold, the Chairman of D66 and the Mayor of Wageningen, was appointed Minister of Government Reform and Kingdom Relations, while the D66 Minister of Economic Affairs, Laurens Jans Brinkhorst, assumed the additional role of Deputy Prime Minister.

In January 2005, meanwhile, legislation was adopted requiring all citizens and foreigners to carry official identification, in an attempt to improve security after the leader of militant Islamist organization had been convicted of murder, and other members of the group had been convicted in connection with threats to kill prominent politicians who were critical of Islam. In October the Minister of Immigration and Integration, Rita Verdonk, announced proposals that would prohibit the wearing of traditional Islamic dress, such as the burka and other face veils, in certain public places. Despite criticism by Muslim and human rights organizations, a motion in support of such measures was narrowly approved by the Second Chamber in December. In March 2006, however, following an investigation into the implications of human rights law on such a ban, the Government failed to reach agreement on the issue, and the proposals were to be reconsidered. In the same month further measures to control immigration were introduced, requiring potential immigrants from the majority of non-EU countries to pass an examination in their country of origin on their knowledge of Dutch culture and language.

In May 2006 the Secretary of State for Education, Culture and Science, Mark Rutte, defeated Verdonk in a contest for the VVD leadership, which had emphasized deep divisions within the party, particularly regarding immigration. During the leadership election campaign, Verdonk had publicly questioned the right to Dutch citizenship of her Somali-born parliamentary colleague, Ayaan Hirsi Ali. Hirsi Ali admitted to falsifying elements of her application for citizenship and announced that she would resign as a member of the Second Chamber. In June, however, Verdonk announced that an inquiry into Hirsi Ali's original application for citizenship had found that her claim was legitimate. Two days later Verdonk survived a motion of censure in the Second Chamber urging her departure from office. The motion had been supported by the D66, the three Government members of which subsequently resigned. On 30 June the remaining members of the Government followed suit. A minority interim administration comprising the CDA and the VVD was sworn in on 7 July, with a general election scheduled for November.

The 2006 election and nationalist controversy

A general election was held on 22 November 2006. The three largest parties all suffered a reduction in support among the electorate (80.1% of whom voted). The CDA emerged as the largest party in the Second Chamber, with 41 of the 150 seats, three fewer than in 2003. The PvdA won 33 seats, down from 42 in 2003) and the VVD 22 seats, down from 28). The SP achieved the largest electoral gain, winning 25 seats, compared with eight previously) and the 'confessional' ChristenUnie (CU—Christian Union) party also increased its representation, achieving six seats, from three in the previous parliament). The nationalist Partij voor de Vrijheid (PVV—Freedom Party), which was formed in February 2006 by a former VVD parliamentarian, Geert Wilders, won nine seats.

Following protracted negotiations between the main parties, in late February 2007 a centre-left coalition of the CDA, the PvdA and the CU was formed under the renewed premiership of Balkenende. The PvdA leader, Bos, became Deputy Prime Minister and Minister of Finance, and the CU leader, André Rouvoet, Deputy Prime Minister and Minister of Youth and the Family. In total, the CDA held eight portfolios, the PvdA six and the CU two. The appointment of two foreign-born Muslim Secretaries of State, Ahmed Aboutaleb and Nebahat Albayrak, both of the PvdA, was criticized by Wilders after it was revealed that, in addition to their Dutch citizenship, they retained Moroccan and Turkish nationality, respectively. The PVV and some VVD representatives, including Verdonk, demanded that the two ministers renounce their foreign nationality—despite the fact that this was not legally possible—and proposed legislation to prevent government members from holding dual nationality. The proposal was later withdrawn. The new coalition agreement included a slowing in the reduction of disability payments and a relaxation of restrictions on immigration. In June the Second Chamber approved a government-proposed amnesty for asylum seekers whose applications had been rejected, reversing legislation approved in February 2004 that allowed for their voluntary repatriation.

The limited progress of the Government in implementing its reform programme allowed nationalist groups to dominate the political agenda in late 2007. In October Verdonk resigned her membership of the VVD, following her expulsion from the party's parliamentary group in September for criticizing the leadership. None the less, Verdonk retained her seat in the Second Chamber and a week later she announced the formation of a new political movement, Trots op Nederland (Proud of the Netherlands), under her leadership; Trots op Nederland was formally inaugurated in April 2008. Meanwhile, in March 2008 Wilders provoked controversy when a film he had produced, which was critical of the Islamic religion, was broadcast on an internet site. Following the broadcast, the Government accused Wilders of attempting deliberately to cause offence, and in January 2009 the Amsterdam Court of Appeal ordered that Wilders should be prosecuted for 'initiating hatred and discrimination'. The ruling, which took into account not only Wilders' controversial film, but also a letter that had been published by the Dutch daily *De Volkskrant* in August 2007, in which Wilders described the Koran as 'fascist', reversed an earlier decision by the Dutch prosecution service. Nevertheless, Wilders' PVV enjoyed significant success in elections to the European Parliament in June, securing 17.0% of the votes cast and four seats, second only to the CDA (with 20.1% and

five seats). Wilders' trial for fomenting hatred and discrimination against the Muslim community began in January 2010 in Amsterdam, and a concurrent demonstration was held outside the court in support of Wilders and freedom of speech; after the completion of the preliminary hearings, the trial was adjourned until later in the year.

Government collapse and the general election of 2010

By late 2008 the Netherlands began to suffer the effects of the global financial crisis. In early October the Government was forced to nationalize the Dutch operations of the Belgian-Dutch financial services group, Fortis. It was also announced later in October that the Dutch Government was to acquire a minority stake in the country's largest bank, ING. By February 2009 the Prime Minister, Balkenende, acknowledged that the Netherlands had entered a deep recession. Following negotiations between the coalition parties, along with business representatives and trade unions, in March the Government announced fiscal stimulus measures valued at some €6,000m., most notably including a reduction in expenditure on health care, increased spending on public infrastructure projects and an extension of the retirement age to 67 years.

Following long-standing tensions within the governing coalition regarding reductions in government spending, particularly on defence, and proposals to raise the retirement age, the PvdA withdrew from the coalition in February 2010 after a disagreement over Dutch involvement in the conflict in Afghanistan, precipitating the collapse of the Government. The PvdA had argued in favour of a withdrawal of Dutch troops from Afghanistan by August, while the CDA was supportive of a NATO request to extend the duration of the Dutch presence, despite a parliamentary vote in October 2009 in favour of an August 2010 withdrawal (which the Government had not endorsed). The CDA and the CU remained in power in a caretaker capacity pending a general election, scheduled for 9 June; all major policy decisions were consequently placed on hold, and the Council of Ministers was reorganized, with the positions vacated by the PvdA being reassigned to CDA and CU members. Notably, Jan Kees de Jager of the CDA, hitherto Secretary of State for Finance, became Minister of Finance, while the Minister of Justice, Ernst Hirsch Ballin, also of the CDA, was additionally allocated the interior portfolio.

The CDA and the PvdA suffered significant losses at the March 2010 local elections; D66 and the VVD were the main beneficiaries. The PVV achieved its first representation at local level: it won a majority of seats in Almere and became the second largest party in The Hague. Following the PvdA's poor results, Bos resigned as leader of the party and was replaced by Job Cohen; the SP leader, Agnes Kant, also resigned in March after similarly disappointing results in the local elections, and was replaced by Emile Roemer.

At the general election on 9 June 2010 (in which 75.4% of the registered electorate participated) the VVD became the largest party in the Second Chamber, with 31 seats, compared with 22 seats at the previous general election in 2006. The PvdA won 30 seats, a loss of three. The number of seats held by the PVV increased from nine to 24, making Wilders' party the third largest in the Second Chamber. The CDA secured only 21 seats, down from 41 at the previous election. The SP won 15 seats, compared with 25 previously, while D66 and GroenLinks increased their representation to 10 seats each (from three and seven, respectively), and the CU won five, a loss of one seat. On the day of his party's severe defeat, Balkenende resigned as party leader of the CDA, although he remained as Prime Minister in an interim capacity; the parliamentary leadership of the CDA was assumed by Maxime Verhagen, the interim Minister of Foreign Affairs and of Development Cooperation.

Recent developments: the Governments led by Mark Rutte

Negotiations between the various parties on the formation of a new Government began immediately after the June 2010 election and continued for almost four months. Initially, discussions were held between the VVD, the CDA and the PVV, but many members of the CDA (including Ballin, the interim Minister of Justice and of the Interior, and Ab Klink, the interim Minister of Health, Welfare and Sport) were reluctant to share power with the controversial PVV, and there was disagreement concerning both economic policy and the controls on immigration and Islamic practice demanded by the PVV. Discussions between the VVD and three left-wing parties, the PvdA, D66 and Groen-

Links, also failed to reach agreement, particularly on the reductions in government spending proposed by the VVD. Eventually, in October, an agreement was reached whereby the VVD and the CDA would form a minority administration, led by Mark Rutte of the VVD, which would rely on the support of the PVV in the legislature, although no ministerial posts were to be allocated to the PVV. Together the three parties commanded 76 of the 150 seats in the Second Chamber, a majority of only one. The new administration undertook, among other things, to make considerable reductions in public spending by 2015, to increase the police force, impose new limits on immigration, and ban the wearing of the Islamic burka in public. Posts in Rutte's Council of Ministers, announced in mid-October 2010, were shared equally between the VVD and the CDA, each party controlling six ministries and four junior ministries. Appointments included Maxime Verhagen, the acting leader of the CDA, as Deputy Prime Minister and Minister of Economic Affairs, Agriculture and Innovation (an amalgamation of two former portfolios), and Uri Rosenthal (VVD) as Minister of Foreign Affairs, while Jan Kees de Jager (CDA) retained the post of Minister of Finance. Two ministries were amalgamated to form a Ministry of Infrastructure and the Environment.

The trial of Geert Wilders on charges of inciting hatred and discrimination, which had been adjourned in January 2010, resumed in October, but at the end of the month a retrial was ordered after Wilders' defence lawyer successfully argued that the judges in the case had given the impression of bias against the defendant. In November revelations were published concerning PVV members of the legislature, several of whom, it was reported, had criminal convictions or were under investigation following allegations of misconduct. Wilders' new trial began in March 2011, and in June he was acquitted; the court ruled that his statements, while offensive, had been permissible within the context of public debate. In early 2012 the PVV provoked fresh controversy by establishing a website on which members of the public were invited to make complaints about the behaviour of immigrants from Central and Eastern Europe.

Meanwhile, provincial elections took place on 2 March 2011, when the VVD became the largest party in the legislatures of seven provinces (six of which had previously been led by the CDA), the PvdA in three and the CDA in one; in one province, Limburg, the CDA and the PVV led with equal numbers of seats. At the indirect election to the Senate by the Provincial Councils on 23 May, the ruling coalition of the VVD and the CDA, with the support of the PVV, were one seat short of an overall majority, and would therefore need to solicit support from a fundamentalist Christian party, the Staatkundig Gereformeerde Partij (SGP), which effectively held the balance of power in the Senate with one seat, in order to pass controversial legislation.

During 2011 there was widespread domestic opposition (particularly by the PVV) to the Netherlands' participation in emergency assistance for Greece as part of the response to the sovereign debt crisis in the eurozone (see Regional relations). In October the Dutch legislature was one of the last in the eurozone to approve the expansion of the European Financial Stability Facility (EFSF), under which the Netherlands was obliged to increase the amount of its guarantees to the EFSF from €56,000m. to €98,000m. The PVV opposed the expansion, and the ruling coalition depended on the support of the PvdA, D66 and GroenLinks for the measure to be adopted. In March 2012 the Government was obliged to begin inter-party negotiations on controversial extra reductions in budgetary spending over the next three years, in order to comply with the EU's recently concluded Treaty on Stability, Co-ordination and Governance (the 'fiscal compact'), which imposed legally binding limits on national budget deficits. The reductions were opposed not only by the PVV, which unsuccessfully demanded a national referendum on quitting the euro area, but also by the PvdA and the SP, which declared that the planned reductions would be too fast and would damage the economy. (In February the leader of the PvdA, Job Cohen, had resigned after accusations that his opposition to the reductions was not forceful enough: he was replaced by Diederik Samsom.) Negotiations on the austerity measures broke down in April when the PVV refused to support the budget proposals, and Rutte tendered the Government's resignation. It was announced that an early general election would be held in September. Later in April, however, the VVD/CDA coalition, now governing in a 'caretaker' capacity, succeeded in gaining the support of D66, GroenLinks and the CU for the 2013 budget (although it was not to be submitted for parliamentary approval until after the general election). In May the

CDA elected Sybrand van Haersma Buma (the party's leader in the legislature) to the vacant party leadership.

At the general election on 12 September 2012 (when 74.6% of the registered electorate took part) the VVD and the PvdA both increased their support in the Second Chamber, winning 41 and 38 of the 150 seats, respectively (compared with 31 and 30, respectively, at the 2010 election). The CDA won only 13 seats (21 previously), and the PVV also lost support, winning 15 seats (24 previously). The SP, whose anti-austerity campaign had initially won it a leading place in pre-election opinion polls, also won only 15 seats (the same number as previously). After nearly seven weeks of negotiations, in early November 2012 the VVD and the PvdA formed a coalition Government, with Mark Rutte retaining the post of Prime Minister: the new Council of Ministers comprised seven VVD members and six PvdA members, and included several previous holders of ministerial posts. Lodewijk Asscher (PvdA) became Deputy Prime Minister with responsibility for social affairs and employment, while Frans Timmermans (PvdA) was appointed Minister of Foreign Affairs, Jeanine Hennis-Plasschaert (VVD) Minister of Defence and Jeroen Dijsselbloem (PvdA) Minister of Finance. The coalition agreement (involving concessions on both sides) envisaged savings amounting to €16,000m. by 2017 in order to balance the budget, including reductions in unemployment benefits and health-care benefits, the replacement of student loans by grants, and a reduction in overseas aid; following a public outcry, however, particularly from middle-income citizens, the new Government was forced to abandon the introduction of income-related health insurance premiums, instead increasing income tax for higher earners. Elements of the new Government's programme also encountered challenges in the Senate, where the ruling coalition was eight seats short of a majority; in February 2013 the Government was obliged to modify proposed reforms of social housing, in order to gain the support of D66, the CU and the SGP in the upper house. During March and April the Government held discussions with trade unions and employers' organizations in an effort to achieve consensus on proposed reforms to redundancy law, pensions and unemployment benefit, before submitting budget plans for 2014 to the European Commission.

In December 2012 the Government announced plans to merge three of the country's 12 provinces, namely Noord-Holland, Utrecht and Flevoland, into a single entity by 2015, with the eventual aim of reducing the number of provinces to five.

In January 2013 Queen Beatrix announced, shortly before her 75th birthday, that she intended to abdicate at the end of April, after 33 years as reigning monarch. Her son, Prince Willem-Alexander, succeeded her on the throne on 30 April.

Dutch Dependencies

The Netherlands East Indies (except West New Guinea, now Papua, which remained under Dutch control until 1963) formally seceded from the Union of the Netherlands, to form the United States of Indonesia in December 1949. In 1975 Suriname became independent, leaving the Netherlands Antilles as the only remaining Dutch dependency. Aruba, formerly part of the Netherlands Antilles, was granted separate status within the Kingdom of the Netherlands in 1986. A commission, established jointly by the Governments of the Netherlands and the Netherlands Antilles, recommended in October 2004 that the islands of Curaçao and St Maarten (in the Netherlands Antilles) should be given autonomous status within the Kingdom of the Netherlands (i.e. have *status aparte*, like that of Aruba), while the three other islands of the dependency, Saba, Bonaire and Sint (St) Eustatius, should be placed under direct rule. In a series of non-binding referendums between 2000 and 2005 a majority of voters in Sint (St) Maarten and Curaçao favoured obtaining *status aparte*, while the electorates of both Bonaire and Saba strongly favoured direct rule. St Eustatius was the only island to favour remaining part of the Netherlands Antilles. None the less, in late October 2005 the Dutch Government concluded an outline agreement on constitutional reform with all five islands. Curaçao and St Maarten were to be granted *status aparte*, while Bonaire, Saba and St Eustatius would become *koninkrijkseilanden* (kingdom islands) with direct ties to the Netherlands. The future status of Bonaire, Saba and St Eustatius was subsequently refined to that of *bijzondere gemeente* (special municipalities), similar in most ways to other metropolitan Netherlands municipalities, although with separate social security and currency arrangements, for example. However, the populations of the Antillean municipalities would be able to vote in Dutch and European elections (the province of Noord-Holland offered to include the three territories). Following the negotiation of further details, the Dutch Prime Minister, Jan Peter Balkenende, and the Antillean premier, Emily de Jongh-Elhage, signed an agreement confirming the new status of the five islands at a meeting in Curaçao on 15 December 2008. The agreement entered into effect on 10 October 2010.

Foreign Affairs

Regional relations

The Netherlands was a founder member of the North Atlantic Treaty Organization (NATO, see p. 380) in 1949, abandoning its previous policy of neutrality. The treaty establishing the Benelux Economic Union (see p. 459) between the Netherlands, Belgium and Luxembourg was signed in 1958 and came into force in 1960. In June 2008 Balkenende, along with the Prime Ministers of Belgium and Luxembourg, signed a new Benelux Treaty on political and economic co-operation, providing for greater co-operation between the three Governments on justice and home affairs, as well as customs and cross-border trade. In recognition of this, the official title of the organization was to change from the Benelux Economic Union to the Benelux Union. The treaty was ratified by the legislatures of the three countries and by the parliaments of the five Belgian federal units by May 2011, and entered into force on 1 January 2012.

The Netherlands was a founder member of the European Community (EC, now European Union—EU, see p. 281). The EU Treaty establishing a Constitution for Europe was signed by the EU heads of state and of government in October 2004. It required ratification by all 25 EU member countries, either through a referendum or by a vote in the national legislature, before it could come into force. A non-binding referendum on the treaty took place in the Netherlands on 1 June 2005, when 61.6% of those who voted (63% of the electorate) were opposed to the treaty's ratification. On the following day the Government formally withdrew the proposed legislation. This decisive rejection of the treaty by Dutch voters, and by French voters a few days earlier, prompted several other member countries to postpone indefinitely their own referendums. In March 2007 Balkenende expressed his new coalition Government's opposition to proposals by Germany and some other EU member countries to introduce a new treaty that would contain some of the main elements of the constitutional treaty, instead favouring a new treaty similar to those signed in Maastricht in 1992 and Amsterdam in 1997. In late June 2007 EU heads of state and of government reached a preliminary agreement for a comprehensive reform treaty. In September Balkenende announced that the new treaty would be submitted to the legislature, thus avoiding the prospect of a further defeat at a national referendum. The Treaty of Lisbon was formally signed by EU leaders on 13 December at a summit meeting in Lisbon, Portugal. The treaty was ratified by parliamentary vote in the Netherlands in July 2008. It came into force on 1 December 2009.

The Netherlands Government supported the creation of the European Financial Stability Facility (EFSF) in 2010, to safeguard the financial stability of the eurozone after the onset of the sovereign debt crisis afflicting some member states, and in July 2011 approved the expansion of the facility, together with a second instalment of emergency assistance for Greece. It supported the German Government in insisting that private creditors should participate in the assistance programme by accepting losses on their loans, and that strict conditions should be attached to emergency assistance for heavily indebted member states, particularly Greece. The Netherlands Government was firmly in favour of the adoption of the Treaty on Stability, Co-ordination and Governance (the 'fiscal compact'), signed in March 2012 by all EU member governments except those of the Czech Republic and the United Kingdom; the treaty made legally binding the previously stipulated limit (of 3% of gross domestic product) on the budgetary deficits of participating countries. In order to comply with the treaty the Netherlands Government was subsequently obliged (despite domestic opposition) to introduce new restrictions on its own expenditure. During 2012 the Netherlands Government, like that of Germany, opposed the issuing of 'eurobonds' (whereby all eurozone members would guarantee individual states' debts) and the use of EU funds for direct support of banks. With Germany and other members, the Netherlands successfully urged a reduction in EU budget spending under the Multiannual Financial Framework (MFF) for 2014–20, negotiations for which were concluded in February 2013 (subject to approval by the European Parliament).

Other external relations

In January 2003 a parliamentary commission concluded that the Netherlands Government bore responsibility for the massacre by Bosnian Serbs of some 7,000 Bosnian Muslims who had taken shelter in a UN compound at Srebrenica (Bosnia and Herzegovina) in July 1995, but had been ordered to leave by Dutch members of the UN peace-keeping force there. In September 2008 a Netherlands court ruled that the Government could not be held responsible for the actions of the peace-keeping force, as they had been operating under a UN mandate. In July 2011, however, a court of appeal ordered the Netherlands Government to pay damages to two of the families whose relatives had been killed: the decision was expected to strengthen the case of thousands of other families who were currently undertaking legal action against the UN and the Netherlands Government in connection with the massacre. In March 2013 the Netherlands public prosecution department concluded that the officer who had been in charge of the Dutch peace-keeping force should not face charges of facilitating genocide and war crimes.

Government plans to commit troops to a NATO peace-keeping mission to southern Afghanistan prompted fierce opposition in late 2005. (Some 350 soldiers from the Netherlands were already stationed in the north and east of Afghanistan, while a further 250 were engaged in counter-terrorism operations.) Opponents of further participation in the International Security Assistance Force referred to events in Srebrenica in 1995, and claimed that Afghanistan's southern provinces were not sufficiently stable for peace-keeping exercises. However, following a debate in the Second Chamber, in February 2006 the Minister of Defence, Henk Kamp, announced that 1,200 military personnel were to join the mission in the province of Uruzgan, in central Afghanistan, from August. (Dutch troops had been withdrawn from Iraq in March 2005.) In December 2007 the Second Chamber voted to extend the mandate of Dutch troops in Uruzgan province until December 2010. Despite a NATO request for an extension of the Dutch presence and the collapse of the governing coalition over the issue (see Domestic Political Affairs), the Netherlands forces were withdrawn from Afghanistan in July. In January 2011, however, the Government agreed to provide personnel, numbering 545, to train police officers in northern Afghanistan, and this was approved by a small majority in the legislature, after assurances that the mission would be civilian in nature; in March 2013 it was announced that the mission was to be concluded in July. During 2012 four Netherlands naval vessels were operating off the coast of Somalia as part of efforts by the EU and NATO to combat piracy.

CONSTITUTION AND GOVERNMENT

The Netherlands is a constitutional and hereditary monarchy. Legislative power is held by the bicameral States-General (Staten-Generaal). The First Chamber (Eerste Kamer) or Senate (Senaat) has 75 members and is indirectly elected for four years by members of the 12 Provincial Councils. The Second Chamber (Tweede Kamer) comprises 150 members and is directly elected by universal adult suffrage for four years (subject to dissolution), on the basis of proportional representation. The head of state has mainly formal prerogatives, and executive power is exercised by the Council of Ministers, which is led by the Prime Minister and is responsible to the States-General. The monarch appoints the Prime Minister and, on the latter's recommendation, other ministers. Each of the 12 provinces is administered by a directly elected Provincial Council, a Provincial Executive and a Sovereign Commissioner, who is appointed by Royal Decree.

REGIONAL AND INTERNATIONAL CO-OPERATION

The Netherlands was a founder member of the European Community, now the European Union (EU, see p. 281), the Benelux Economic Union (see p. 459), the Organization for Security and Co-operation in Europe (OSCE, see p. 397) and the Council of Europe (see p. 260).

The Netherlands was a founder member of the UN in 1945. As a contracting party to the General Agreement on Tariffs and Trade, it joined the World Trade Organization (WTO, see p. 444) on its establishment in 1995. The Netherlands was also a founder member of the North Atlantic Treaty Organization (NATO, see p. 380) and the Organisation for Economic Co-operation and Development (OECD, see p. 388).

ECONOMIC AFFAIRS

In 2011, according to estimates by the World Bank, the Netherlands' gross national income (GNI), measured at average 2009–

11 prices, was US $830,219m., equivalent to $49,730 per head (or $43,260 per head on an international purchasing-power parity basis). During 2002–11, it was estimated, the population grew at an average annual rate of 0.4%, while gross domestic product (GDP) per head increased, in real terms, at an average annual rate of 1.1% over the same period. According to official figures, overall GDP increased, in real terms, at an average annual rate of 1.4% in 2002–11; real GDP increased by 1.0% in 2011.

Agriculture (including hunting, forestry and fishing) contributed an estimated 1.6% of GDP in 2011, and 2.6% of the employed labour force were engaged in the sector in that year. In mid-2013, according to FAO, the sector was expected to engage an estimated 2.2% of the labour force. The Netherlands is a net exporter of agricultural products: in 2011 exports of food and live animals provided 11.7% of total export earnings. The principal crops are potatoes, sugar beet, wheat and onions. The main agricultural activity is horticulture; market gardening is highly developed, and the production of cut flowers and bulbs has traditionally been a significant industry, although its contribution to export earnings showed some decline in the early years of the 21st century (partly compensated for by re-exports from other growers to European markets). Livestock farming is also an important activity. According to the Central Bureau of Statistics, during 2002–11 agricultural GDP increased, in real terms, at an average annual rate of 2.1%; the sector's GDP declined by 1.1% in 2010, but rose by 1.6% in 2011.

Industry (including mining, manufacturing, construction and power) contributed an estimated 24.8% of GDP in 2011 and engaged 15.9% of the employed labour force in 2011. The Central Bureau of Statistics put the increase in industrial GDP, in real terms, at an average annual rate of 0.7% in 2002–11; real industrial GDP grew by 1.7% in 2011.

Mining and quarrying provided an estimated 3.7% of GDP in 2011 and engaged 0.1% of the employed labour force in the same year. The principal mineral resource is natural gas. Total production in 2011 was an estimated 64,196m. cu m. Reserves of petroleum and salts are also exploited. The GDP of the mining sector declined, in real terms, at an average annual rate of 0.9% in 2002–11; it grew by 12.9% in 2010, but declined by 7.6% in 2011.

Manufacturing contributed an estimated 12.9% of GDP in 2011, and accounted for 9.6% of the employed labour force in 2011. Several multinational companies are domiciled in the Netherlands, including the electrical firm Philips, the brewer Heineken, and two British-Dutch firms, the food industry company Unilever and the petroleum firm Royal Dutch Shell. According to the Central Bureau of Statistics, manufacturing GDP increased at an average annual rate of 1.5% in 2002–11; it grew by 3.5% in 2011.

The construction sector contributed an estimated 5.3% of GDP in 2011, and engaged 5.5% of the employed labour force in that year. According to the Central Bureau of Statistics, construction GDP decreased at an average annual rate of 0.7% in 2002–11; it decreased by 11.1% in 2010, but increased by 4.5% in 2011.

In 2010 natural gas provided 62.2% of total electricity production and coal 22.0%. Imports of mineral fuels and lubricants comprised 10.4% of the value of total imports in 2003; by 2011 this figure had increased to 21.9%. In recent years the gradual depletion of the Groningen natural gas field has prompted the exploration of investment possibilities in smaller fields, while successive Governments have sought to promote the utilization of renewable energy resources.

The services sector contributed an estimated 73.6% of GDP and engaged 81.5% of the employed labour force in 2011. Within the sector, financial services, tourism and transport are of considerable importance. The GDP of the services sector increased, in real terms, at an average annual rate of 1.8% in 2002–11; it increased by 1.2% in 2011.

In 2011 the Netherlands recorded a visible merchandise trade surplus of €63,597m. and there was a surplus of €81,323m. on the current account of the balance of payments. The principal source of imports in 2011 was Germany (contributing 16.7% of the total); other major suppliers were Belgium, the People's Republic of China, the United Kingdom and the USA. Germany was also the principal market for exports in that year (accounting for 24.2% of the total); other major purchasers in 2011 were Belgium, France and the United Kingdom. The principal exports in 2011 were machinery and transport equipment, chemicals and related products, mineral fuels and lubricants, food and live animals, basic manufactures, miscellaneous manufactured articles, and crude materials (except fuels). The principal imports in that year were also machinery and transport equipment, followed by mineral fuels, lubricants, chemicals and related products, miscellaneous manufactured articles, and basic manufactures.

In 2011, according to official estimates, the Netherlands recorded an overall budgetary deficit of €27,711m., equivalent to 4.6% of GDP. Netherlands's general government gross debt was €392,500m. in 2011, equivalent to 65.2% of GDP. In 2002–11 the annual rate of inflation averaged 1.7%. Consumer prices increased by 2.3% in 2011. The rate of unemployment in December 2012 was 7.2%.

The Netherlands' small size and dependence on external trade make it particularly vulnerable to external economic conditions. Decreasing industrial production and increasing labour costs in the 2000s, combined with an ageing population and rising levels of unemployment, led to increased demand for state-funded pensions, health care and welfare benefits. In an attempt to reduce the budget deficit to comply with the limit of 3% of GDP imposed by the EU's Stability and Growth Pact, the Government undertook a comprehensive reform of the health system and restricted access to unemployment and disability payments, thereby reducing the budget deficit to the equivalent of 0.2% of GDP in 2005; small surpluses, of 0.8% and 0.6%, were recorded in 2006 and 2007, respectively. However, the global economic crisis in 2008–09 had a detrimental effect on the economy: exports and investment declined sharply in the second half of 2008, while banks suffered severe losses that required significant state intervention. Following the introduction of necessary fiscal stimulus measures, government finances deteriorated substantially, with a budget deficit equivalent to 4.5% of GDP in 2009 and a large increase in the levels of government indebtedness. GDP declined by 3.5% in 2009, but the swift introduction of the stimulus measures limited the negative impact of the global financial crisis on the country, with real GDP growth of 1.7% in 2010. The Government that took office in October 2010 introduced further reductions in expenditure (particularly on health and social care and public sector salaries) in order to reduce the budgetary deficit, which in 2011 was equivalent to 65.2% of GDP; De Nederlandsche Bank, the central bank, recorded growth of 1.0% in GDP for that year. During 2012 and early 2013 controversial further reductions in expenditure and tax increases were proposed by the Government in order to comply with the recently adopted EU treaty on fiscal discipline. The central bank reported a contraction in GDP of 1.0% in 2012, reflecting reductions in investment, house prices and consumer spending, while the budget deficit diminished slightly to 4.1% of GDP; inflation increased to 2.8% in that year, largely as a result of high energy prices and an increase in value-added tax. The bank predicted that the constraints imposed by fiscal consolidation would lead to a further decline in GDP of some 0.6% for 2013, and an increase in unemployment to an average of just over 6%, but expected that strengthening world trade would lead to a moderate recovery, with GDP growth of around 1% in 2014.

PUBLIC HOLIDAYS

2014: 1 January (New Year's Day), 18 April (Good Friday), 21 April (Easter Monday), 27 April (King's Day), 29 May (Ascension Day), 9 June (Whit Monday), 25–26 December (Christmas).

Statistical Survey

Source (unless otherwise stated): Netherlands Central Bureau of Statistics, Prinses Beatrixlaan 428, POB 959, 2270 AZ Voorburg; tel. (70) 3373800; fax (70) 3877429; e-mail infoservice@cbs.nl; internet www.cbs.nl.

Area and Population

AREA, POPULATION AND DENSITY

Area (sq km)	
Land	33,718
Inland waters	3,635
Coastal water	4,187
Total	41,540*
Population (census results)†	
1 January 2001‡	15,987,075
1 January 2012‡	
Males	8,282,871
Females	8,447,477
Total	16,730,348
Density (per sq km of land) at 1 January 2012	496.2§

* 16,039 sq miles.
† Population is *de jure*.
‡ Based on a compilation of continuous accounting and sample surveys.
§ Land area only.

POPULATION BY AGE AND SEX
(official estimates at 1 January 2011)

	Males	Females	Total
0–14	1,487,164	1,419,911	2,907,075
15–64	5,615,630	5,538,148	11,153,778
65 and over	1,140,688	1,454,258	2,594,946
Total	8,243,482	8,412,317	16,655,799

PROVINCES
(population at 1 January 2012)

	Land area (sq km)	Population	Density (per sq km)
Groningen	2,325	580,875	249.8
Friesland	3,340	647,214	193.8
Drenthe	2,639	490,807	186.0
Overijssel	3,324	1,137,668	342.3
Flevoland	1,415	395,525	279.5
Gelderland	4,970	2,010,745	404.6
Utrecht	1,383	1,237,117	894.5
Noord-Holland	2,665	2,709,822	1,016.8
Zuid-Holland	2,808	3,552,407	1,016.8
Zeeland	1,784	381,407	213.8
Noord-Brabant	4,914	2,463,686	501.4
Limburg	2,150	1,123,075	522.4
Total	33,718	16,730,348	496.2

PRINCIPAL TOWNS
(population of municipalities at 1 January 2012)

Amsterdam (capital)*	790,110	Haarlem	151,818
Rotterdam	616,260	Arnhem	149,271
's-Gravenhage/Den			
Haag (The Hague)*	502,055	Zaanstad	148,281
Utrecht	316,275	Amersfoort	148,250
Eindhoven	217,225	Haarlemmermeer	143,943
		's-Hertogenbosch/Den	
Tilburg	207,580	Bosch	141,893
Almere	193,163	Zoetermeer	122,331
Groningen	193,127	Zwolle	121,527
Breda	176,401	Maastricht	121,050
Nijmegen	165,182	Dordrecht	118,862
Enschede	158,048	Leiden	118,748
Apeldoorn	156,961		

* Amsterdam is the capital, while The Hague is the seat of government.

BIRTHS, MARRIAGES AND DEATHS

	Live births*		Marriages		Deaths*	
	Number	Rate (per 1,000)	Number	Rate (per 1,000)	Number	Rate (per 1,000)
2004	194,007	11.9	72,231	4.5	136,553	8.4
2005	187,910	11.5	72,263	4.4	136,402	8.4
2006	185,057	11.3	72,369	4.4	135,372	8.3
2007	181,336	11.1	72,485	4.4	133,022	8.1
2008	184,634	11.2	75,438	4.6	135,136	8.2
2009	184,915	11.2	73,477	4.4	134,235	8.1
2010	184,397	11.1	75,399	4.5	136,058	8.2
2011	180,060	10.8	71,572	4.3	135,741	8.1

* Including residents outside the country if listed in a Netherlands population register.

Life expectancy (years at birth): 80.7 (males 78.8; females 82.7) in 2010 (Source: World Bank, World Development Indicators database).

IMMIGRATION AND EMIGRATION

	2009	2010	2011
Immigrants	146,378	154,432	162,962
Emigrants	111,897	121,351	133,194

EMPLOYMENT
('000 persons, incl. self–employed, 15 years and over)

	2009	2010*	2011*
Agriculture, hunting, forestry and fishing	228	226	225
Mining and quarrying	8	8	8
Manufacturing	869	843	836
Electricity, gas and water supply	63	64	65
Construction	497	485	476
Wholesale and retail trade and repair	1,421	1,421	1,442
Hotels and restaurants	312	318	328
Transport, storage and communications	669	653	661
Financial intermediation	278	269	264
Real estate, renting and business activities	1,485	1,421	1,439
Public administration, social security and defence	496	510	499
Education	484	486	485
Health and social work	1,251	1,315	1,353
Other community, social and personal service activities	332	338	337
Private households with employed persons	278	279	280
Total employed	8,671	8,636	8,698

* Provisional figures.

Unemployment ('000 persons): 327 in 2009; 390 in 2010; 389 in 2011; 469 in 2012.

Health and Welfare

KEY INDICATORS

Total fertility rate (children per woman, 2010)	1.8
Under-5 mortality rate (per 1,000 live births, 2010) . . .	4
HIV/AIDS (% of persons aged 15–49, 2007)	0.2
Physicians (per 1,000 head, 2008)	2.9
Hospital beds (per 1,000 head, 2009)	4.7
Health expenditure (2009): US $ per head (PPP) . . .	4,881
Health expenditure (2009): % of GDP	12.0
Health expenditure (2009): public (% of total)	79.0
Total carbon dioxide emissions ('000 metric tons, 2008) . .	173,749.8
Carbon dioxide emissions per head (metric tons, 2008) . .	10.6
Human Development Index (2011): ranking	3
Human Development Index (2011): value	0.910

For sources and definitions, see explanatory note on p. vi.

Agriculture

PRINCIPAL CROPS
('000 metric tons)

	2009	2010	2011
Wheat	1,402	1,370	1,175
Barley	310	204	205
Maize	245	197	204
Rye	11	10	6
Triticale (wheat-rye hybrid) . .	17	14	10
Potatoes	7,181	6,844	7,333
Sugar beet	5,735	5,280	5,858
Cabbages and other brassicas .	282	277	249
Lettuce and chicory	86	83	84
Spinach	32	30	34
Tomatoes	800	815	815
Cauliflowers and broccoli . .	59	61	57
Cucumbers and gherkins . .	435	435	430
Aubergines (eggplants) . . .	46	46	46
Chillies and green peppers . .	370	365	365
Onions and shallots, green* . .	35	35	37
Onions, dry	1,269	1,302	1,541
Leeks and other alliaceous vegetables	96	100	90
Beans, green	49	47	44
Peas, green	31	21	21
Carrots and turnips	561	481	482
Mushrooms and truffles . . .	230	266	304
Apples	407	334	418
Pears	295	274	336
Strawberries	43	43	47

* FAO estimates.

Aggregate production ('000 metric tons, may include official, semi-official or estimated data): Total cereals 1,994 in 2009, 1,803 in 2010, 1,610 in 2011; Total roots and tubers 7,181 in 2009, 6,844 in 2010, 7,333 in 2011; Total vegetables (incl. melons) 4,746 in 2009, 4,788 in 2010, 5,050 in 2011; Total fruits (excl. melons) 763 in 2009, 667 in 2010, 821 in 2011.

Source: FAO.

LIVESTOCK
('000 head, year ending September)

	2009	2010	2011
Horses*	134	135	136
Cattle	3,968	3,975	3,885
Chickens	96,860	101,248	96,919
Sheep	1,117	1,130	1,088
Goats	374	353	380
Pigs	12,187	12,255	12,429

* FAO estimates.

Source: FAO.

LIVESTOCK PRODUCTS
('000 metric tons)

	2009	2010	2011
Cattle meat	402	389	382
Sheep meat	14	13	13
Pig meat	1,275	1,288	1,347
Chicken meat	764	781	841
Turkey meat*	58	57	58
Cows' milk	11,469	11,626	11,627
Hen eggs	638	670	692

* FAO estimates.

Source: FAO.

Forestry

ROUNDWOOD REMOVALS
('000 cubic metres, excl. bark)

	2009	2010	2011
Sawlogs, veneer logs and logs for sleepers	354	385	326
Pulpwood	324	353	301
Other industrial wood	48	52	62
Fuel wood	290	290	290
Total	**1,016**	**1,081**	**979**

Source: FAO.

SAWNWOOD PRODUCTION
('000 cubic metres, incl. railway sleepers)

	2009	2010	2011
Coniferous (softwood)	144	152	169
Broadleaved (hardwood) . . .	66	79	69
Total	**210**	**231**	**238**

Source: FAO.

Fishing

('000 metric tons, live weight)

	2008	2009	2010
Capture*	416.7	382.1	389.4
European plaice	20.8	23.5	28.3
Blue whiting	78.8	35.8	35.0
Atlantic herring	56.7	56.9	55.8
Round sardinella	67.5	42.2	57.0
European pilchard	9.6	33.9	27.9
Atlantic horse mackerel . .	63.0	61.5	79.2
Atlantic mackerel	20.4	23.4	24.9
Aquaculture*	46.6	55.6	66.9
Blue mussel	36.1	45.6	56.2
Total catch*	**463.4**	**437.7**	**456.3**

* FAO estimates.

Note: Figures exclude aquatic mammals, recorded by number rather than by weight.

Source: FAO.

Mining

	2008	2009	2010*
Crude petroleum ('000 barrels) .	12,231	9,300	9,000
Salt ('000 metric tons)	6,000*	6,000	6,000

* Estimated production.

Source: US Geological Survey.

Natural gas (million cu m, excl. gas flared or recycled): 62,709 in 2009; 70,508 in 2010; 64,196 in 2011 (Source: BP, *Statistical Review of World Energy*).

Industry

SELECTED PRODUCTS
('000 metric tons unless otherwise indicated)

	2007	2008	2009
Mechanical wood pulp* . . .	133	142	72
Newsprint*	421	462	273
Printing and writing paper* . .	924	708	653
Wrapping and packaging paper and paperboard*	1,764	1,690	1,563
Synthetic rubber†	194	177	n.a.
Jet fuels	6,597	6,136	5,526
Kerosene	430	337	373
Motor spirit (petrol) . . .	6,905	6,903	n.a.
Naphthas	8,457	9,052	n.a.
Gas-diesel (distillate fuel) oil . .	19,253	20,438	n.a.
White spirit	38	40	39
Residual fuel (Mazout) oils . .	9,526	8,647	8,496
Lubricating oils	583	794	n.a.
Petroleum bitumen (asphalt) . .	362	275	291
Liquefied petroleum gas . . .	1,312	1,313	1,403
Coke	2,273	2,204	n.a.
Coke-oven gas (terajoules) . .	19,582	19,469	n.a.
Cement‡§	2,400	2,700	2,700
Pig-iron‖	6,412	6,130	4,601
Crude steel‖	7,368	6,853	5,194
Aluminium (unwrought): primary‡	301	317	300
Refined lead: secondary‡§ . .	16	16	16
Zinc (unwrought): primary‡ . .	232	240	224
Electricity (million kWh) . . .	105,162	107,645	113,502

* Source: FAO.

† Refers to amounts sold by establishments employing 20 persons or more.

‡ Data from US Geological Survey.

§ Estimates.

‖ Source: World Steel Association (Brussels).

Source: unless otherwise indicated, UN Industrial Commodity Statistics Database.

2010 ('000 metric tons): Mechanical wood pulp 97; Newsprint 242; Printing and writing paper 725; Wrapping and packaging paper and paperboard 1,774; Crude steel 6,651; Pig-iron 5,799; Cement 2,700 (estimate); Aluminium (unwrought—primary) 300 (estimate); Zinc (unwrought—primary) 220 (estimate); Refined lead (secondary) 16 (estimate) (Sources: World Steel Association—Brussels; FAO; US Geological Survey).

2011 ('000 metric tons): Mechanical wood pulp 34; Newsprint 253; Printing and writing paper 693; Wrapping and packaging paper and paperboard 1,681; Crude steel 6,937; Pig-iron 5,943 (Sources: World Steel Association—Brussels; FAO).

2012 ('000 metric tons, estimates): Crude steel 6,866; Pig-iron 5,909 (Source: World Steel Association—Brussels).

Finance

CURRENCY AND EXCHANGE RATES
Monetary Units
  100 cent = 1 euro (€).

Sterling and Dollar Equivalents (31 December 2012)
  £1 sterling = 1.196 euros;
  US $1 = 0.758 euros;
  €10 = £8.36 = $13.19.

Average Exchange Rate (euros per US $)
  2010   0.7550
  2011   0.7194
  2012   0.7779

Note: The national currency was formerly the guilder. From the introduction of the euro, with the Netherlands' participation, on 1 January 1999, a fixed exchange rate of €1 = 2.20371 guilders was in operation. Euro notes and coins were introduced on 1 January 2002. The euro and local currency circulated alongside each other until 28 January, after which the euro became the sole legal tender.

GOVERNMENT FINANCE
(general government transactions, non-cash basis, € million)*
Summary of Balances

	2008	2009	2010
Revenue	277,684	262,721	271,827
Less Expense	270,512	287,861	296,576
Net operating balance . . .	7,172	−25,140	−24,749
Less Net acquisition of non-financial assets	4,269	6,563	4,660
Net lending/borrowing . . .	2,903	−31,703	−29,409

Revenue

	2008	2009	2010
Tax revenue	143,575	137,576	143,100
Taxes on income, profits and capital gains	63,418	61,489	63,581
Taxes on goods and services .	70,455	67,822	71,269
Taxes on property	9,175	7,649	7,658
Social contributions	90,442	83,466	86,901
Grants	267	273	392
Other revenue	43,400	41,406	41,434
Total	277,684	262,721	271,827

Expense/Outlays

Expense by economic type†	2008	2009	2010
Compensation of employees . .	54,691	57,670	59,088
Use of goods and services . .	44,004	47,636	47,684
Consumption of fixed capital . .	15,092	15,697	16,224
Interest	13,202	12,416	11,256
Subsidies	7,191	8,891	8,853
Grants	8,504	6,654	9,521
Social benefits	120,866	129,148	135,331
Other expense	6,962	9,749	8,619
Total	270,512	287,861	296,576

Outlays by function of government	2008	2009	2010
General public services . . .	34,423	32,725	34,865
Defence	8,184	8,627	8,315
Public order and safety . . .	11,833	12,450	12,466
Economic affairs	30,508	35,639	35,219
Environment protection . . .	9,928	10,641	10,447
Housing and community amenities	3,432	5,152	3,852
Health	43,331	46,905	49,114
Recreation, culture and religion .	10,035	10,726	10,782
Education	32,404	34,086	34,640
Social protection	90,703	97,473	101,536
Total	274,781	294,424	301,236

* Figures represent a consolidation of the operations of the Government, comprising all central and local government accounts.
† Including net acquisition of non-financial assets.

Source: IMF, *Government Finance Statistics Yearbook*.

2011 (general government transactions, € million, preliminary): *Revenue:* Total 274,045 (Tax revenue 139,448, Social security contributions 89,174, Sales of goods and services 20,347, Other 25,076). *Expenditure:* Total 301,756 (Compensation of employees 58,866, Use of goods and services 46,450, Gross investments in fixed assets 21,040, Social benefits 136,100, Other 39,300).

INTERNATIONAL RESERVES
(US $ million at 31 December)

	2009	2010	2011
Gold (Eurosystem valuation) . .	21,739	27,769	31,003
IMF special drawing rights . .	7,660	7,502	7,276
Reserve position in IMF . . .	1,597	2,068	3,828
Foreign exchange	8,613	8,902	9,160
Total	39,609	46,241	51,267

Source: IMF, *International Financial Statistics*.

MONEY SUPPLY
(incl. shares, depository corporations, national residency criteria, € '000 million at 31 December)

	2009	2010	2011
Currency issued	42.91	44.60	46.99
De Nederlandsche Bank . .	23.04	21.66	19.71
Demand deposits	209.52	235.81	236.78
Other deposits	560.71	532.14	557.46
Securities other than shares . .	460.76	512.67	553.32
Shares and other equity . . .	126.23	130.52	142.55
Other items (net)	33.12	−3.37	−1.96
Total	1,433.26	1,452.36	1,535.14

Source: IMF, *International Financial Statistics*.

COST OF LIVING
(Consumer Price Index; base: 2000 = 100)

	2008	2009	2010
Food (incl. non-alcoholic beverages)	115.6	116.8	116.7
Electricity, gas and other fuels .	180.5	181.9	167.4
Clothing (incl. footwear) . . .	99.3	98.9	98.4
Rent	122.1	125.0	127.7
All items (incl. others) . . .	119.1	120.6	122.1

2011: Food 104.0; All items (incl. others) 125.0.

Source: ILO.

NATIONAL ACCOUNTS
(€ million at current prices)
National Income and Product

	2009	2010*	2011*
Compensation of employees . .	298,488	300,434	306,609
Net operating surplus/mixed income	126,603	135,621	144,102
Domestic primary incomes	425,091	436,055	450,711
Consumption of fixed capital . .	87,974	89,212	88,726
Gross domestic product (GDP) at factor cost	513,065	525,267	539,437
Taxes on production and imports .	70,147	73,568	72,038
Less Subsidies	9,977	10,095	9,502
GDP in market prices . . .	573,235	588,740	601,973
Net primary income from the rest of the world	−13,850	−9,423	5,207
Gross national income (GNI) .	559,385	579,317	607,180
Less Consumption of fixed capital	87,974	89,212	88,726
Net national income . . .	471,411	490,105	518,454
Net current transfers from the rest of the world	−8,267	−8,871	−9,248
Net national disposable income	463,144	481,234	509,206

Expenditure on the Gross Domestic Product

	2009	2010*	2011*
Government final consumption expenditure	164,140	167,065	168,157
Private final consumption expenditure	263,537	267,810	271,111
Changes in inventories . . .	−3,283	3,828	2,221
Gross fixed capital formation . .	108,774	102,031	106,690
Total domestic expenditure .	533,168	540,734	548,179
Exports of goods and services .	393,050	460,493	499,620
Less Imports of goods and services	352,983	412,487	445,826
GDP in purchasers' values .	573,235	588,740	601,973
GDP at constant 2005 prices .	541,000	549,814	555,271

Gross Domestic Product by Economic Activity

	2009	2010*	2011*
Agriculture, hunting, forestry and fishing	7,898	9,297	8,663
Mining and quarrying	15,556	17,039	19,708
Manufacturing	60,025	65,086	69,626
Electricity, gas and water supply .	17,259	16,877	15,699
Construction	30,678	27,985	28,727
Wholesale and retail trade; transport; repair of motor vehicles, motorcycles and personal household goods; hotels and restaurants	94,259	98,004	101,201
Information and communications .	25,022	25,333	25,351
Finance, insurance, real estate and other business activities . .	132,934	135,453	137,394
General government; education; health; social work activities .	114,103	117,736	119,377
Care and other service activities .	13,118	13,366	13,629
GDP at basic prices	510,852	526,176	539,375
Taxes, less subsidies, on imports .	59,608	62,815	61,575
Value-added tax, less imputed bank service charge	2,775	−251	1,023
GDP in purchasers' values .	573,235	588,740	601,973

* Provisional.

BALANCE OF PAYMENTS
(€ million)

	2009	2010	2011
Exports of goods	406,983	469,164	544,175
Imports of goods	−358,915	−412,838	−480,578
Balance on goods	48,068	56,326	63,597
Exports of services	94,274	96,826	107,943
Imports of services	−86,474	−86,070	−94,443
Balance on goods and services	55,867	67,082	77,097
Primary income received	92,429	100,198	116,983
Primary income paid	−94,764	−92,497	−97,694
Balance on goods, services and primary income	53,532	74,784	96,386
Secondary income received	15,595	12,329	14,234
Secondary income paid	−27,552	−26,919	−29,297
Current balance	41,575	60,194	81,323
Capital account (net)	−284	−1,317	−159
Direct investment assets	−28,286	−55,663	−35,534
Direct investment liabilities	34,271	−10,271	13,886
Portfolio investment assets	−72,349	12,064	−12,223
Portfolio investment liabilities	36,705	44,127	39,736
Financial derivatives and employee stock options assets	206,464	437,499	689,721
Financial derivatives and employee stock options liabilities	−179,368	−452,314	−698,906
Other investment assets	98,858	−40,101	−160,562
Other investment liabilities	−146,028	37,814	93,784
Net errors and omissions	15,401	−31,539	−7,802
Reserves and related items	6,959	493	3,263

Source: IMF, *International Financial Statistics*.

External Trade

PRINCIPAL COMMODITIES
(distribution by SITC, € million)

Imports c.i.f.	2009	2010	2011
Food and live animals	25,721	28,323	32,062
Crude materials (inedible) except fuels	9,831	13,343	15,875
Mineral fuels, lubricants, etc.	42,970	60,048	80,037
Petroleum, petroleum products, etc.	34,534	51,324	69,589
Crude petroleum	18,565	27,104	32,961
Chemicals and related products	43,960	51,036	46,936
Organic chemicals	9,173	11,712	14,331
Medicinal and pharmaceutical products	19,072	21,537	12,258
Basic manufactures	28,288	33,616	38,287
Machinery and transport equipment	82,967	100,146	103,038
Office machines and automatic data-processing equipment	21,660	27,536	26,090
Telecommunications and sound equipment	16,637	20,436	19,239
Other electrical machinery, apparatus, etc.	12,329	15,712	15,857
Road vehicles (incl. air-cushion vehicles) and parts (excl. tyres, engines, and electrical parts)	12,894	15,644	18,533
Miscellaneous manufactured articles	33,829	37,822	39,412
Total (incl. others)	274,025	331,914	364,922

Exports f.o.b.	2009	2010	2011
Food and live animals	40,157	45,214	48,044
Vegetables and fruit	11,084	12,493	12,323
Crude materials (inedible) except fuels	15,436	19,078	20,841
Mineral fuels, lubricants, etc.	38,309	50,963	67,812
Petroleum, petroleum products, etc.	24,643	36,104	n.a.
Chemicals and related products	59,255	70,644	73,462
Organic chemicals	13,266	17,329	19,500
Medicinal and pharmaceutical products	20,187	n.a.	18,451
Plastics in primary form	8,839	11,279	12,828
Basic manufactures	26,733	33,191	36,662
Machinery and transport equipment	88,254	106,478	111,812
Office machines and automatic data-processing equipment	24,710	28,095	27,350
Automatic data-processing machines	10,316	12,902	11,817
Telecommunications and sound equipment	15,408	19,216	18,592
Other electrical machinery, apparatus, etc.	14,018	17,594	17,672
Road vehicles (incl. air-cushion vehicles) and parts (excl. tyres, engines, and electrical parts)	9,063	10,980	13,772
Miscellaneous manufactured articles	30,512	34,642	36,883
Total (incl. others)*	309,359	371,549	409,358

* Including victuals and stores supplied to foreign ships and aircraft.

PRINCIPAL TRADING PARTNERS
(€ million)

Imports c.i.f.	2009	2010	2011
Belgium	27,452	31,864	36,420
Brazil	3,893	4,397	5,612
China, People's Republic	21,967	30,997	30,874
Denmark	2,975	2,725	3,303
Finland	2,640	3,177	3,887
France	13,591	14,438	16,785
Germany	52,537	58,913	60,943
Ireland	3,154	3,994	4,604
Italy	6,322	7,163	7,786
Japan	7,251	9,274	10,100
Malaysia	4,309	5,564	5,577
Norway	6,787	8,430	10,343
Poland	3,595	4,624	5,094
Russia	9,628	14,023	16,959
Saudi Arabia	1,415	2,376	3,890
Spain	4,799	7,037	6,564
Sweden	3,992	5,281	6,238
United Kingdom	17,648	22,130	24,505
USA	22,995	25,055	23,541
Total (incl. others)	274,025	331,914	364,922

Exports f.o.b.	2009	2010	2011
Austria	4,102	4,885	5,160
Belgium	34,619	41,265	48,678
China, People's Republic	4,589	5,391	6,696
Denmark	4,076	4,716	5,176
Finland	2,888	3,913	4,326
France	27,484	32,489	36,245
Germany	75,225	90,269	99,189
Italy	16,007	18,596	19,528
Poland	5,948	7,378	8,411
Russia	4,419	5,641	6,405
Spain	10,512	12,604	12,234
Sweden	5,185	6,649	7,194
Switzerland	4,781	5,381	5,132
Turkey	3,482	4,487	4,749
United Kingdom	25,879	29,651	32,326
USA	13,928	16,875	19,632
Total (incl. others)	309,359	371,549	409,358

Transport

RAILWAYS
(traffic)

	1996	1997	1998
Passenger-km (million)	14,131	14,485	14,879
Freight ton-km (million)	3,123	3,406	3,778

Passenger-km (million): 16,180 in 2008; 16,315 in 2009; 16,359 in 2010 (Source: Nederlandse Spoorwegen NV, *Annual Report 2010*).

ROAD TRAFFIC
('000 motor vehicles)

	2009	2010	2011
Passenger cars	7,542	7,622	7,736
Vans and lorries	951	946	933
Buses and coaches	11	12	11
Trailers and semi-trailers	1,039	1,057	1,071
Tractors	75	72	71
Special purpose vehicles	64	65	65
Motorcycles	606	623	636

SHIPPING

Inland Waterways
(transport fleet at 1 January)

	1997	1998	1999
Number of vessels	5,067	5,003	4,577
Carrying capacity ('000 metric tons)	5,859	5,589	5,212

Inland Waterways
(freight traffic, million metric tons)

	1996	1997	1998
Internal transport: Commercial	61.2	75.7	79.3
Internal transport: Private	28.2	20.9	19.3
International transport	201.1	224.5	219.7

Merchant Fleet
(at 31 December)

	2007	2008	2009
Number of vessels	1,258	1,296	1332
Displacement ('000 grt)	6,139.4	6,684.2	6,966.2

Source: IHS Fairplay, *World Fleet Statistics*.

Sea-borne Freight Traffic
('000 metric tons)

	1997	1998	1999
Goods loaded	88,667	85,137	92,000
Goods unloaded	312,864	319,684	305,000

CIVIL AVIATION*
(Netherlands scheduled air services)

	2007	2008	2009
Kilometres flown (million)	521	573	537
Passengers carried ('000)	28,857	30,946	29,109
Passenger-km (million)	90,915	95,190	90,185
Total ton-km (million)	14,108	14,306	13,112

* Figures include data for airlines based in the territories and dependencies of the Netherlands.

Source: UN, *Statistical Yearbook*.

2010: Passengers carried ('000) 48,592; Freight carried ('000 metric tons) 1,575; Mail (metric tons) 25,878.

2011: Passengers carried ('000) 53,868; Freight carried ('000 metric tons) 1,589; Mail (metric tons) 25,880.

Tourism

FOREIGN TOURIST ARRIVALS
('000)*

Country of origin	2009	2010	2011
Belgium	1,170	1,260	1,350
France	570	670	670
Germany	2,740	2,850	2,980
Italy	370	440	440
Spain	350	440	430
United Kingdom	1,410	1,560	1,510
Total (incl. others)	9,920	10,880	11,300

* Arrivals at all accommodation establishments.

Total tourist arrivals ('000): 11,300 in 2011 (provisional).

Tourism receipts (US $ million, excl. passenger transport): 12,368 in 2009; 12,883 in 2010; 14,445 in 2011 (provisional). (Source: World Tourism Organization).

Communications Media

	2009	2010	2011
Telephones ('000 main lines in use)	7,256	7,232	7,135
Mobile cellular telephones ('000 subscribers)	20,149	19,179*	19,835
Internet subscribers ('000)	6,130	6,330	n.a.
Broadband subscribers ('000)	6,130	6,330	6,456

* At July.

Source: International Telecommunication Union.

Education

(2011/12, provisional)

	Institutions	Students ('000)
Primary	7,112	1,559.3
Secondary	659	948.9
Higher vocational	39	423.7
University	13	245.3

Directory

The Government

HEAD OF STATE

King of the Netherlands: HM King WILLEM-ALEXANDER (succeeded to the throne 30 April 2013).

COUNCIL OF MINISTERS
(May 2013)

A coalition of the Volkspartij voor Vrijheid en Democratie (VVD—People's Party for Freedom and Democracy) and the Partij van de Arbeid (PvdA—Labour Party).

Prime Minister, Minister of General Affairs: MARK RUTTE (VVD).

Deputy Prime Minister, Minister of Social Affairs and Employment: LODEWIJK ASSCHER (PvdA).

Minister of Foreign Affairs: FRANS TIMMERMANS (PvdA).

Minister of Security and Justice: IVO OPSTELTEN (VVD).

Minister of the Interior and Kingdom Relations: RONALD PLASTERK (PvdA).

Minister of Education, Culture and Science: JET BUSSEMAKER (PvdA).

Minister of Finance: JEROEN DIJSSELBLOEM (PvdA).

Minister of Defence: JEANINE HENNIS-PLASSCHAERT (VVD).

Minister of Infrastructure and the Environment: MELANIE SCHULTZ VAN HAEGEN-MAAS GEESTERANUS (VVD).

Minister of Economic Affairs: HENK KAMP (VVD).

Minister of Health, Welfare and Sport: EDITH SCHIPPERS (VVD).

Minister for Foreign Trade and Development Co-operation: LILIANNE PLOUMEN (PvdA).

Minister for Housing and the Central Government Sector: STEF BLOK (VVD).

State Secretary for Security and Justice: FRED TEEVEN (VVD).

State Secretary for Education, Culture and Science: SANDER DEKKER (VVD).

State Secretary for Finance: FRANS WEEKERS (VVD).

State Secretary for Infrastructure and the Environment: WILMA MANSVELD (PvdA).

State Secretary for Economic Affairs: SHARON DIJKSMA (PvdA).

State Secretary for Social Affairs and Employment: JETTA KLIJNSMA (PvdA).

State Secretary for Health, Welfare and Sport: MARTIN VAN RIJN (PvdA).

MINISTRIES

Office of the Prime Minister, Ministry of General Affairs: Binnenhof 19, POB 20001, 2500 EA The Hague; tel. (70) 3564100; fax (70) 3564683; internet www.rijksoverheid.nl/ministeries/az.

Ministry of Defence: Plein 4, POB 20701, 2500 ES The Hague; tel. (70) 3188188; fax (70) 3187888; e-mail defensievoorlichting@mindef.nl; internet www.rijksoverheid.nl/ministeries/def.

Ministry of Economic Affairs: Bezuidenhoutseweg 30, POB 20401, 2500 EC The Hague; tel. (70) 3796868; internet www.rijksoverheid.nl/ministeries/eleni.

Ministry of Education, Culture and Science: Rijnstraat 50, POB 16375, 2500 BJ The Hague; tel. (70) 4123456; fax (70) 4123450; internet www.rijksoverheid.nl/ministeries/ocw.

Ministry of Finance: Korte Voorhout 7, POB 20201, 2500 EE The Hague; tel. (70) 3428000; fax (70) 3427900; e-mail webmaster@minfin.nl; internet www.rijksoverheid.nl/ministeries/fin.

Ministry of Foreign Affairs: Bezuidenhoutseweg 67, POB 20061, 2500 EB The Hague; tel. (70) 3486486; fax (70) 3484848; internet www.rijksoverheid.nl/ministeries/bz.

Ministry of Health, Welfare and Sport: Rijnstraat 50, POB 20350, 2500 EJ The Hague; tel. (70) 3407911; fax (70) 3407834; internet www.rijksoverheid.nl/ministeries/vws.

Ministry of Infrastructure and the Environment: Plesmanweg 1–6, POB 20901, 2500 EX The Hague; tel. (70) 4560000; fax (70) 4561111; internet www.rijksoverheid.nl/ministeries/ienm.

Ministry of the Interior and Kingdom Relations: Schedeldoekshaven 200, POB 20011, 2500 EA The Hague; tel. (70) 4266426; fax (70) 3639153; internet www.rijksoverheid.nl/ministeries/bzk.

Ministry of Security and Justice: Turfmarkt 147, POB 20301, 2500 EH The Hague; tel. (70) 3707911; fax (70) 3707900; e-mail voorlichting@minjus.nl; internet www.rijksoverheid.nl/ministeries/venj.

Ministry of Social Affairs and Employment: Anna van Hannoverstraat 4, POB 90801, 2509 LV The Hague; tel. (70) 3334444; fax (70) 3334033; internet www.rijksoverheid.nl/ministeries/szw.

Legislature

STATEN-GENERAAL
(States-General)

Eerste Kamer
(First Chamber)

Binnenhof 22, 2513 AA The Hague; POB 20017, 2513 AA The Hague; tel. (70) 3129200; fax (70) 3129390; e-mail postbus@eerstekamer.nl; internet www.eerstekamer.nl.

President: G. J. DE GRAAF (CDA).

Election, 23 May 2011

Party	Seats
Volkspartij voor Vrijheid en Democratie (VVD) . .	16
Partij van de Arbeid (PvdA)	14
Christen Democratisch Appèl (CDA) . . .	11
Partij voor de Vrijheid (PVV) . . .	10
Socialistische Partij (SP)	8
Democraten 66 (D66)	5
GroenLinks (GL)	5
ChristenUnie (CU)	2
50Plus	1
Staatkundig Gereformeerde Partij (SGP) . . .	1
Partij voor de Dieren	1
Independent	1
Total	**75**

Tweede Kamer
(Second Chamber)

Binnenhof 4, 2513 AA The Hague; POB 20018, 2500 EA The Hague; tel. (70) 3182211; internet www.tweedekamer.nl.

President: ANOUCHKA VAN MILTENBURG (VVD).

General Election, 12 September 2012

Party	Votes	%	Seats
Volkspartij voor Vrijheid en Democratie (VVD) . . .	2,504,948	26.58	41
Partij van de Arbeid (PvdA) .	2,340,750	24.84	38
Partij voor de Vrijheid (PVV) .	950,263	10.08	15
Socialistische Partij (SP) .	909,853	9.65	15
Christen Democratisch Appèl (CDA)	801,620	8.51	13
Democraten 66 (D66) . . .	757,091	8.03	12
ChristenUnie (CU) . . .	294,586	3.13	5
GroenLinks (GL) . . .	219,896	2.33	4
Staatkundig Gereformeerde Partij (SGP)	196,780	2.09	3
Partij voor de Dieren . . .	182,162	1.93	2
50Plus	177,631	1.88	2
Others	88,655	0.93	—
Total	**9,424,235**	**100.00**	**150**

Election Commission

Kiesraad (Dutch Electoral Council): Herengracht 21, POB 20011, 2511 EG The Hague; POB 20011, 2500 EA The Hague; tel. (70) 4266266; fax (70) 4266089; e-mail kiesraad@kiesraad.nl; internet www.kiesraad.nl; f. 1917; independent; Chair. Prof. HENK KUMMELING; Sec.-Dir MELLE BAKKER.

Advisory Councils

Raad van State (Council of State): Kneuterdijk 22, POB 20019, 2500 EA The Hague; tel. (70) 4264426; fax (70) 3651380; e-mail voorlichting@raadvanstate.nl; internet www.raadvanstate.nl; comprises a Vice-Pres. and up to 60 mems nominated by the Sovereign, who formally presides over the Council; advises on legislation, constitutional issues, international treaties and all matters of national importance; Vice-Pres. J. PIET HEIN DONNER; Sec. H. H. C. VISSER.

Sociaal-Economische Raad (SER) (Social and Economic Council): Bezuidenhoutseweg 60, POB 90405, 2509 LK The Hague; tel. (70) 3499499; fax (70) 3832535; e-mail m.vander.burg@ser.nl; internet www.ser.nl; f. 1950; tripartite advisory body; advises Govt on social and economic policy; monitors commodity and industrial boards; 33 mems, of whom 11 belong to trade union federations, 11 belong to the employers' organizations, and 11 are independent experts in social and economic affairs appointed by the Crown; Chair. Dr WIEBE DRAIJER; Sec.-Gen. Dr VÉRONIQUE TIMMERHUIS.

Political Organizations

Christen Democratisch Appèl (CDA) (Christian Democratic Appeal): Buitenom 18, POB 30453, 2500 GL The Hague; tel. (70) 3424888; fax (70) 3643417; e-mail cda@cda.nl; internet www.cda.nl; f. 1980 by merger of 3 'confessional' parties; Party Pres. RUTH PEETOOM; 69,000 mems.

ChristenUnie (CU) (Christian Union): Johan van Oldenbarneveltlaan 46, POB 439, 3800 AK Amersfoort; tel. (33) 4226969; fax (33) 4226968; e-mail bureau@christenunie.nl; internet www .christenunie.nl; f. 2000 by merger of 2 'evangelical' parties, the Gereformeerd Politiek Verbond and the Reformatorische Politieke Federatie; interdenominational, based on biblical precepts; mem. of European Christian Political Movement; Chair. PIET ADEMA; Parliamentary Leader ARIE SLOB; c. 27,500 mems (2008).

Democraten 66 (D66) (Democrats 66): Hoge Nieuwstraat 30, 2514 EL The Hague; POB 660, 2501 CR The Hague; tel. (70) 3566066; fax (70) 3641917; e-mail info@d66.nl; internet www.parlement.com/ D66; f. 1966; Chair. INGRID VAN ENGELSHOVEN; Parliamentary Leader ALEXANDER PECHTOLD; 21,985 mems.

Fryske Nasjonale Partij (FNP) (Frisian National Party): Obrechtstrjitte 32, 8916 EN Ljouwert; tel. (58) 2131422; e-mail fnphus@fnp.nl; internet www.fnp.nl; f. 1962; promotes federalism and greater regional autonomy; Leader ANNIGJE TOERING-SCHUURMANS; c. 1,300 mems.

De Groenen (The Greens): POB 1251, 3500 BG Utrecht; tel. (30) 2341545; e-mail info@degroenen.nl; internet www.degroenen.nl; f. 1983; founding mem. of the European Green Party; Acting Pres. and Sec. OTTO TER HAAR.

GroenLinks (GL) (Green Left): Oudegracht 312, POB 8008, 3503 RA Utrecht; tel. (30) 2399900; fax (30) 2300342; e-mail info@ groenlinks.nl; internet www.groenlinks.nl; f. 1990 by merger of Communistische Partij van Nederland, Evangelische Volkspartij, Pacifistisch-Socialistische Partij and Politieke Partij Radicalen; Chair. RIK GRASHOFF; Parliamentary Leader BRAM VAN OJIK; c. 20,000 mems.

Nieuwe Communistische Partij Nederland (NCPN) (New Communist Party of the Netherlands): Haarlemmerweg 177, 1051 LB Amsterdam; tel. (20) 6825019; fax (20) 6828276; e-mail manifest@ ziggo.nl; internet www.ncpn.nl; f. 1992; Chair. JOB PRUIJSER.

Nieuwe Midden Partij (NMP) (New Centre Party): POB 2087, 8203 AB Lelijstad; tel. and fax (320) 281412; e-mail info@nmp.nl; internet www.sdnl.nl/nmp.htm; f. 1970; campaigns on economic issues; Leader JOS BRON.

Partij van de Arbeid (PvdA) (Labour Party): Herengracht 54, 1015 BN Amsterdam; tel. (20) 5512155; fax (20) 5512250; e-mail voorzitter@pvda.nl; internet www.pvda.nl; f. 1946 by merger of progressive and liberal organizations; social democratic; Chair. HANS SPEKMAN; Party Leader DIEDERIK SAMSOM; c. 55,000 mems.

Partij voor de Dieren (Party for the Animals): POB 17622, 1001 JM Amsterdam; tel. (20) 5203870; e-mail administratie@ partijvoordedieren.nl; internet www.partijvoordedieren.nl; f. 2002; promotes animal rights and animal welfare; Chair. MARIANNE THIEME.

Partij voor de Vrijheid (PVV) (Freedom Party): POB 20018, 2500 EA The Hague; internet www.pvv.nl; f. 2004 as Groep Wilders; present name adopted 2006; populist, anti-immigration; Leader GEERT WILDERS.

Socialistische Alternatieve Politiek (SAP) (Socialist Political Alternative): Postbus 2096, 3000 CB Rotterdam; tel. (20) 6259272; e-mail redactie@grenzeloos.nl; internet www.grenzeloos.org; f. 1974; Trotskyist.

Socialistische Partij (SP) (Socialist Party): Vijverhofstraat 65, 3032 SC Rotterdam; tel. (10) 2435555; fax (10) 2435566; e-mail onderzoek@sp.nl; internet www.sp.nl; f. 1972; Chair. JAN MARIJNISSEN; Parliamentary Leader EMILE ROEMER; Gen. Sec. HANS VAN HEIJNINGEN; 46,000 mems.

Staatkundig Gereformeerde Partij (SGP) (Political Reformed Party): Dinkel 7, 3068 HB Rotterdam; tel. (82) 7200770; fax (82) 7200784; e-mail voorlichting@sgp.nl; internet www.sgp.nl; f. 1918; Calvinist; female membership banned until 2006; Chair. Rev. A. VAN HETEREN; Parliamentary Leader KEES VAN DER STAAIJ; Gen. Sec. V. A. SMIT; 29,648 mems (2013).

Verenigde Senioren Partij (VSP) (United Senior Citizens' Party): Israëlslaan 37, 3431 AS Nieuwegein; tel. (30) 6300208; fax (30) 6300209; e-mail secretariaat@verenigdeseniorenpartij.nl; internet www.verenigdeseniorenpartij.nl; Chair. H. J. (HERMAN) TROOST; Sec. JACK KOEHORST.

Volkspartij voor Vrijheid en Democratie (VVD) (People's Party for Freedom and Democracy): Laan Copes van Cattenburch 52, POB 30836, 2500 GV The Hague; tel. (70) 3613061; fax (70) 3608276; e-mail info@vvd.nl; internet www.vvd.nl; f. 1948; advocates free enterprise, individual freedom and responsibility, but its programme also supports social security and recommends the participation of workers in profits and management; Chair. BENK KORTHALS; Parliamentary Leader MARK RUTTE; 38,000 mems.

50Plus: Lange Poten 4, The Hague; e-mail info@50pluspartij.nl; internet 50pluspartij.nl; pursuing pensioners' interests; f. 2009; Chair. WILLEM HOLTHUIZEN.

Diplomatic Representation

EMBASSIES IN THE NETHERLANDS

Afghanistan: Laan van Meerdervoort 51, POB 10630, 2501 HP The Hague; tel. (70) 4278771; fax (70) 4272540; e-mail contact@ afghanistanembassy.nl; internet www.afghanistanembassy.nl; Ambassador ENAYATULLAH NABIEL.

Albania: Anna Paulownastraat 109B, 2518 BD The Hague; tel. (70) 4272101; fax (70) 4272083; e-mail embalba@xs4all.nl; Ambassador GAZMEND BARBULLUSHI.

Algeria: Van Stolklaan 1–3, 2585 JS The Hague; tel. (70) 3522954; fax (70) 3061961; e-mail ambalg4@ziggo.nl; internet www .embalgeria.nl; Ambassador NASSIMA BAGHLI.

Argentina: Javastraat 20, 2585 AN The Hague; tel. (70) 3118411; fax (70) 3118410; e-mail argentina@xs4all.nl; internet www.epbaj .mrecic.gov.ar; Ambassador HÉCTOR HORACIO SALVADOR.

Armenia: Laan van Meerdervoort 90, 2517 AP The Hague; tel. and fax (70) 3311002; e-mail armembnl@mfa.am; internet netherlands .mfa.am/en; Ambassador DZIUNIK AGHAJANIAN.

Australia: Carnegielaan 4, 2517 KH The Hague; tel. (70) 3108200; fax (70) 3107863; e-mail austemb_thehague@dfat.gov.au; internet www.netherlands.embassy.gov.au; Ambassador NEIL ALLAN MULES.

Austria: Van Alkemadelaan 342, 2597 AS The Hague; tel. (70) 3245470; fax (70) 3282066; e-mail den-haag-ob@bmeia.gv.at; internet www.bmeia.gv.at/denhaag; Ambassador Dr JOHANNES WERNER DRUML.

Azerbaijan: Andries Bickerweg 6, 2517 JP The Hague; tel. (70) 3921939; fax (70) 3469604; e-mail info@azembassy.nl; internet www .azembassy.nl; Ambassador MIR-HAMZA EFENDIYEV.

Bangladesh: Wassenaarseweg 39, 2596 CG The Hague; tel. (70) 3283722; fax (70) 3283524; e-mail amb.thehague@mofa.gov.bd; internet www.bangladeshembassy.nl; Ambassador MUHAMMAD ALI SORCAR.

Belarus: Anna Paulownastraat 34, 2518 BE The Hague; tel. (70) 3631566; fax (70) 3640555; e-mail netherlands@mfa.gov.by; internet www.netherlands.mfa.gov.by; Ambassador ELENA GRITSENKO.

Belgium: Alexanderveld 97, 2585 DB The Hague; tel. (70) 3123456; fax (70) 3645579; e-mail thehague@diplobel.fed.be; internet www .diplomatie.be/thehague; Ambassador FRANK GEERKENS.

Bolivia: Nassaulaan 5, 2514 JS The Hague; tel. (70) 3616707; fax (70) 3620039; e-mail embolned@embassyofbolivia.nl; Ambassador ROBERTO CALZADILLA SARMIENTO.

Bosnia and Herzegovina: Bezuidenhoutseweg 223, 2594 AL The Hague; tel. (70) 3588505; fax (70) 3584367; e-mail info@bhembassy .nl; Ambassador AHMET HALILOVIC.

Brazil: Mauritskade 19, 2514 HD The Hague; tel. (70) 3023959; fax (70) 3023950; e-mail brasil@brazilianembassy.nl; internet haia .itamaraty.gov.br; Ambassador JOSÉ ARTUR DENOT MEDEIROS.

Bulgaria: Duinrooseweg 9, 2597 KJ The Hague; tel. (70) 3503051; fax (70) 3584688; e-mail embassy.hague@mfa.bg; Ambassador NIKOLA IVANOV KOLEV.

Cameroon: Amaliastraat 14, 2514 JC The Hague; tel. (70) 3469715; fax (70) 3652979; e-mail ambacam-la-haye@planet.nl; internet www .cameroon-embassy.nl; Ambassador ODETTE MELONO.

Canada: Sophialaan 7, POB 30820, 2500 JP The Hague; tel. (70) 3111600; fax (70) 3111620; e-mail info@canada.nl; internet www

.canadainternational.gc.ca/netherlands-pays_bas; Ambassador JAMES LAMBERT.

Chile: Mauritskade 51, 2514 HG The Hague; tel. (70) 3123640; fax (70) 3452109; e-mail echilenl@echile.nl; internet www.echile.nl; Ambassador JUAN ANTONIO MARTABIT SCAFF.

China, People's Republic: William Lodewijklaan 10, 2517 JT The Hague; tel. (70) 3065091; fax (70) 3551651; e-mail chinaemb_nl@mfa .gov.cn; internet nl.china-embassy.org; Ambassador CHEN XU.

Colombia: Groot Hertoginnelaan 14, 2517 EG The Hague; tel. (70) 3614545; fax (70) 3614636; e-mail info@colombiaemb.nl; internet www.colombiaemb.nl; Ambassador EDUARDO PIZARRO LEONGÓMEZ.

Congo, Democratic Republic: Violenweg 2, 2597 KL The Hague; tel. (70) 3547904; fax (70) 3541373; Ambassador HENRI SAKANYI MOVA.

Costa Rica: Laan Copes van Cattenburch 46, 2585 GB The Hague; tel. (70) 3540780; fax (70) 3584754; e-mail embajada@embacrica .demon.nl; Ambassador JORGE ANTONIO URBINA ORTEGA.

Côte d'Ivoire: Laan van Meerdervoort 16, 2517 AK The Hague; tel. (70) 3117878; fax (70) 3924017; e-mail ambacoti.paysbas@yahoo .com; Ambassador SALLAH BEN ABD EL-KADER HAMZA.

Croatia: Amaliastraat 16, 2514 JC The Hague; tel. (70) 3623638; fax (70) 3623195; e-mail vrhhaag@mvep.hr; internet nl.mfa.hr; Ambassador VESELA MRĐEN KORAĆ.

Cuba: Scheveningseweg 9, 2517 KS The Hague; tel. (70) 3606061; fax (70) 3647586; e-mail embacuba@xs4all.nl; internet www .cubadiplomatica.cu/holanda; Ambassador ZELMYS MARIA DOMINGUEZ CORTINA.

Cyprus: Surinamestraat 15, 2585 GG The Hague; tel. (70) 3466499; fax (70) 3924024; e-mail hagueembassy@mfa.gov.cy; internet www .mfa.gov.cy/embassythehague; Ambassador KYRIACOS KOUROS.

Czech Republic: Paleisstraat 4, 2514 JA The Hague; tel. (70) 3130031; fax (70) 3563349; e-mail hague@embassy.mzv.cz; internet www.mfa.cz/hague; Ambassador JAROSLAV HORÁK.

Denmark: Koninginnegracht 30, 2514 AB The Hague; tel. (70) 3025959; fax (70) 3025950; e-mail haaamb@um.dk; internet www .ambhaag.um.dk; Ambassador REIMER REINHOLDT NIELSEN.

Dominican Republic: Raamweg 21–22, 2596 HL The Hague; tel. (70) 3317553; fax (70) 4049890; e-mail embajadadominicananl@ gmail.com; internet www.embajadadominicana.nl; Ambassador LUIS ARIAS NÚÑEZ.

Ecuador: Koninginnegracht 84, 2514 AJ The Hague; tel. (70) 3469563; fax (70) 3658910; e-mail info@embassyecuador.eu; internet www.embassyecuador.eu; Ambassador MIGUEL CALAHORRANO CAMINO.

Egypt: Badhuisweg 92, 2587 CL The Hague; tel. (70) 3542000; fax (70) 3543304; e-mail info@ambeg.nl; Ambassador MAHMOUD AHMED SAMIR SAMY.

El Salvador: Riouwstraat 137, 2585 HP The Hague; tel. (70) 3249855; fax (70) 3247842; Ambassador VLADIMIRO P. VILLALTA.

Eritrea: Nassauplein 13, 2585 EB The Hague; tel. (70) 4276812; fax (70) 4277236; e-mail eritrea@xs4all.nl; Ambassador (vacant).

Estonia: Zeestraat 92, 2518 AD The Hague; tel. (70) 3029050; fax (70) 3029051; e-mail embassy.haag@mfa.ee; internet www.estemb .nl; Ambassador PEEP JAHILO.

Finland: Groot Hertoginnelaan 16, 2517 EG The Hague; tel. (70) 3469754; fax (70) 3107174; e-mail info.haa@formin.fi; internet www .finlande.nl; Ambassador KLAUS KORHONEN.

France: Anna Paulownastraat 76, 2518 BJ The Hague; tel. (70) 3125800; fax (70) 3125824; e-mail info@ambafrance-nl.org; internet www.ambafrance-nl.org; Ambassador PIERRE HENRI MÉNAT.

Georgia: Groot Hertoginnelaan 28, 2517 EG The Hague; tel. (70) 3029080; fax (70) 3029081; e-mail thehague.emb@mfa.gov.ge; internet www.netherlands.mfa.gov.ge; Ambassador SHOTA GVINERIA.

Germany: Groot Hertoginnelaan 18–20, 2517 EG The Hague; tel. (70) 3420600; fax (70) 3651957; e-mail ambduits@euronet.nl; internet www.den-haag.diplo.de; Ambassador FRANZ JOSEF KREMP.

Ghana: Laan Copes van Cattenburch 70, 2585 GD The Hague; tel. (70) 3384384; fax (70) 3062800; e-mail mission@ghanaembassy.nl; internet www.ghanaembassy.nl; Ambassador AANAA NAAMUA ENIN.

Greece: Amaliastraat 1, 2514 JC The Hague; tel. (70) 3638700; fax (70) 3563040; e-mail gremb.hag@mfa.gr; internet www .greekembassy.nl; Ambassador JOHN ECONOMIDES.

Guatemala: Javastraat 44, 2585 AP The Hague; tel. (70) 3020253; fax (70) 3602270; e-mail embpaisesbajos@minex.gob.gt; Ambassador JORGE ALFREDO LEMCKE AREVALO.

Holy See: Carnegielaan 5, 2517 KH The Hague; tel. (70) 3503363; fax (70) 3521461; e-mail apost.nuntiatuur@inter.nl.net; Apostolic Nuncio Most Rev. ANDRÉ DUPUY (Titular Archbishop of Selsea).

Honduras: Burgemeester Patijnlaan 1932, 2585 CB The Hague; tel. (70) 3641684; fax (70) 3649134; e-mail info@embassyofhonduras.nl; internet www.embassyofhonduras.nl; Ambassador MAURICIO R. AGUILAR ROBLES.

Hungary: Hogeweg 14, 2585 JD The Hague; tel. (70) 3500404; fax (70) 3521749; e-mail mission.hga@kum.hu; internet www .hungarianembassy.nl; Ambassador GYULA SÜMEGHY.

India: Buitenrustweg 2, 2517 KD The Hague; tel. (70) 3469771; fax (70) 3617072; e-mail ambassador@indianembassy.nl; internet www .indianembassy.nl; Ambassador BHASWATI MUKHERJEE.

Indonesia: Tobias Asserlaan 8, 2517 KC The Hague; tel. (70) 3108100; fax (70) 3643331; e-mail bidpen@indonesia.nl; internet www.indonesia.nl; Ambassador RETNO LESTARI PRIANSARI MARSUDI.

Iran: Duinweg 20, 2585 JX The Hague; tel. (70) 3384001; fax (70) 3503224; e-mail info@iranembassy.nl; internet www .iranianembassy.nl; Ambassador KAZEM QARIBABADI.

Iraq: Johan de Wittlaan 16, 2517 JR The Hague; tel. (70) 3101260; fax (70) 3924958; e-mail info@embassyofiraq.nl; internet www .embassyofiraq.nl; Ambassador SAAD ABD AL-MAJEED IBRAHIM IBRAHIM.

Ireland: Scheveningseweg 112, 2584 AE The Hague; tel. (70) 3630993; fax (70) 3617604; e-mail thehagueembassy@dfa.ie; internet www.embassyofireland.nl; Ambassador MARY WHELAN.

Israel: Buitenhof 47, 2513 AH The Hague; tel. (70) 3760500; fax (70) 3760555; e-mail info@hague.mfa.gov.il; internet thehague.mfa.gov .il; Ambassador HAIM DIVON.

Italy: Alexanderstraat 12, 2514 JL The Hague; tel. (70) 3021030; fax (70) 3614932; e-mail embitaly.denhaag@esteri.it; internet www .amblaja.esteri.it; Ambassador FRANCESCO AZZARELLO.

Japan: Tobias Asserlaan 2, 2517 KC The Hague; tel. (70) 3469544; fax (70) 3106341; e-mail info@hg.mofa.go.jp; internet www.nl .emb-japan.go.jp; Ambassador YASUMASA NAGAMINE.

Jordan: Badhuisweg 79, 2587 CD The Hague; tel. (70) 4167200; fax (70) 4167209; e-mail info@jordanembassy.nl; internet www .jordanembassy.nl; Ambassador KHALDOUN TALHOUNI.

Kazakhstan: Nieuwe Parklaan 69, 2597 LB The Hague; tel. (70) 3634757; fax (70) 3657600; e-mail hague@mfa.kz; Ambassador MAINURA S. MURZAMADIYEVA.

Kenya: Nieuwe Parklaan 21, 2597 LA The Hague; tel. (70) 3504215; fax (70) 3553594; e-mail info@kenyanembassy-nl.com; Ambassador ROSE MAKENA MUCHIRI.

Korea, Republic: Verlengde Tolweg 8, 2517 JV The Hague; tel. (70) 3586076; fax (70) 3504712; e-mail koreanemb@koreanembassy.nl; internet nld.mofat.go.kr; Ambassador LEE KEY-CHEOL.

Kosovo: Anna Paulownastraat 56A, 2518 BG The Hague; tel. (70) 3020025; fax (70) 3644473; e-mail embassy.netherlands@ks-gov.net; Ambassador NEXHMI REXHEPI.

Kuwait: Carnegielaan 9, 2517 KH The Hague; tel. (70) 3123400; fax (70) 3924588; e-mail info@kuwaitembassy.nl; Ambassador HAFEEZ MUHAMMAD SALIM AL-AJMI.

Latvia: Balistraat 88, 2585 XX The Hague; tel. (70) 3065000; fax (70) 3065009; e-mail embassy.netherlands@mfa.gov.lv; Ambassador MARIS KLISANS.

Lebanon: Frederikstraat 2, 2514 LK The Hague; tel. (70) 3658906; fax (70) 3620779; e-mail info@lebanonembassy.nl; internet www .lebanonembassy.nl; Chargé d'affaires MOHAMED HAJJAR.

Libya: Parkweg 15, 2585 JH The Hague; tel. (70) 355886; fax (70) 3559075; e-mail embassylibia@ziggo.nl; Chargé d'affaires a.i. AHMED M. TABULI.

Lithuania: Laan van Meerdervoort 20, 2517 AK The Hague; tel. (70) 3855418; fax (70) 3853940; e-mail amb.nl@urm.lt; internet nl.mfa.lt; Ambassador DARIUS JONAS SEMAŠKA.

Luxembourg: Nassaulaan 8, 2514 JS The Hague; tel. (70) 3607516; fax (70) 3462000; e-mail lahaye.amb@mae.etat.lu; internet lahaye .mae.lu; Ambassador PIERRE-LOUIS LORENZ.

Macedonia, former Yugoslav republic: Laan van Meerdervoort 50C, 2517 AM The Hague; tel. (70) 4274464; fax (70) 4274469; e-mail hague@mfa.gov.mk; internet www.missions.gov.mk/hague; Ambassador NIKOLA DIMITROV.

Malaysia: Rustenburgweg 2, 2517 KE The Hague; tel. (70) 3506506; fax (70) 3506536; e-mail malaysia@euronet.nl; internet www.kln.gov .my/perwakilan/thehague; Ambassador Dr FAUZIAH MOHD TAIB.

Malta: Carnegielaan 4–14, 2517 KH The Hague; tel. (70) 3561252; fax (70) 3464796; e-mail maltaembassy.thehague@gov.mt; Ambassador MARTIN VALENTINO.

Mexico: Nassauplein 28, 2585 EC The Hague; tel. (70) 3602900; fax (70) 3560543; e-mail embamex@embamex-nl.com; internet www .embamex-nl.com; Ambassador EDUARDO IBARROLA-NICOLÍN.

Morocco: Oranjestraat 9, 2514 JB The Hague; tel. (70) 3469617; fax (70) 3562829; e-mail ambamar.lahaye@wanadoo.nl; Ambassador ABD EL-OUAHAB BELLOUKI.

New Zealand: Eisenhowerlaan 77N, 2517 KK The Hague; tel. (70) 3469324; fax (70) 3632983; e-mail hague.info@mfat.govt.nz; internet www.nzembassy.com/netherlands; Ambassador GEORGE TROUP.

Nicaragua: Statenlaan 52, 2582 GE, The Hague; tel. (70) 3225063; fax (70) 3508331; e-mail info@embanic.nl; Ambassador CARLOS ARGÜELLO GÓMEZ.

Nigeria: Wagenaarweg 5, 2597 LL The Hague; tel. (70) 3501703; fax (70) 3551110; e-mail nigembassy@nigerianembassy.nl; internet www.nigerianembassy.nl; Ambassador Dr NIMOTA NIHINLOLA AKANBI.

Norway: Lange Vijverberg 11, 2513 AC The Hague; tel. (70) 3117611; fax (70) 3659630; e-mail emb.hague@mfa.no; internet www.noorwegen.nl; Ambassador ANNIKEN RAMBERG KRUTNES.

Oman: Nieuwe Parklaan 9, 2597 LA The Hague; tel. (70) 3615800; fax (70) 3605364; e-mail s.vanderborden@embassyofoman.nl; Ambassador SAYYID MUHAMMAD BIN HARIB BIN ABDULLAH AL-SAID.

Pakistan: Amaliastraat 8, 2514 JC The Hague; tel. (70) 3648948; fax (70) 3106047; e-mail info@pakembassy.nl; internet www.embassyofpakistan.com; Ambassador FAUZIA MAZHAR SANA.

Peru: Nassauplein 4, 2585 EA The Hague; tel. (70) 3653500; fax (70) 3651929; e-mail info@embassyofperu.nl; Ambassador ALLAN WAGNER TIZÓN.

Philippines: Laan Copes van Cattenburch 125, 2585 EZ The Hague; tel. (70) 3604820; fax (70) 3560030; e-mail thehague@philembassy.nl; internet www.philembassy.nl; Ambassador LOURDES G. MORALES.

Poland: Alexanderstraat 25, 2514 JM The Hague; tel. (70) 7990100; fax (70) 7990137; e-mail haga.amb.sekretariat@msz.gov.pl; internet haga.msz.gov.pl; Ambassador JAN BORKOWSKI.

Portugal: Zeestraat 74, 2518 AD The Hague; tel. (70) 3630217; fax (70) 3615589; e-mail info@portembassy.nl; Ambassador JOSÉ DE BOUZA SERRANO.

Qatar: Borweg 7, 2597 LR The Hague; tel. (70) 4166666; fax (70) 4166660; e-mail hague@mofa.gov.qa; internet www.embassyofqatar.nl; Ambassador HAMAD BIN ALI JABIR AL-HENZAB.

Romania: Catsheuvel 55, 2517 KA The Hague; tel. (70) 3543796; fax (70) 3541587; e-mail roembnl@xs4all.nl; internet haga.mae.ro; Ambassador IRENY COMAROSCHI.

Russia: Andries Bickerweg 2, 2517 JP The Hague; tel. (70) 3468888; fax (70) 3617960; e-mail ambrusnl@euronet.nl; internet www.netherlands.mid.ru; Ambassador ROMAN KOLODKIN.

Rwanda: Johan van Oldenbarneveltlaan 9B, 2582 NE The Hague; tel. 3926571; fax 4275326; e-mail ambalahaye@gmail.com; internet www.ambalahaye.nl; Ambassador IMMACULEE UWANYILIGIRA.

Saudi Arabia: Alexanderstraat 19, 2514 JM The Hague; tel. (70) 3614391; fax (70) 3561452; e-mail saudiembassy@casema.nl; internet www.saudiembassy.nl; Ambassador ABDULLAH A. Z. AL-SHAGHROOD.

Serbia: Burgemeester van Karnebeeklaan 19, 2585 The Hague; tel. (70) 3636800; fax (70) 3602421; e-mail embassy.hague@mfa.rs; Ambassador ČEDOMIR RADOJKOVIĆ.

Slovakia: Parkweg 1, 2585 JG The Hague; tel. (70) 4167777; fax (70) 4167783; e-mail emb.hague@mzv.sk; internet www.mzv.sk/haag; Ambassador JAROSLAV CHLEBO.

Slovenia: Anna Paulownastraat 11, 2518 BA The Hague; tel. (70) 3108690; fax (70) 3626608; e-mail vhg@gov.si; internet www.haag.veleposlanistvo.si; Ambassador LEON MARC.

South Africa: Wassenaarseweg 40, 2596 CJ The Hague; tel. (70) 3924501; fax (70) 3460669; e-mail info@zuidafrika.nl; internet www.zuidafrika.nl; Ambassador PETER GOOSEN.

Spain: Lange Voorhout 50, 2514 EG The Hague; tel. (70) 3024999; fax (70) 3617959; e-mail ambassade.spanje@worldonline.nl; Ambassador FRANCISCO JAVIER VALLAURE DE ACHA.

Sri Lanka: Jacob de Graefflaan 2, 2517 JM The Hague; tel. (70) 3655910; fax (70) 3465596; e-mail mission@srilankaembassy.nl; Ambassador BUDDHI K. ATHAUDA.

Sudan: Koninginnegracht 63–64, 2514 AG The Hague; tel. (70) 3605300; fax (70) 3617975; e-mail info@sudanembassy.nl; Ambassador SIRAJUDDIN HAMID YOUSIF.

Suriname: Alexander Gogelweg 2, 2517 JH The Hague; tel. (70) 3650844; fax (70) 3617445; e-mail ambassade.suriname@wxs.nl; Chargé d'affaires a.i. CHANTAL RACHIEDA DOEKHIE.

Sweden: Jan Willem Frisolaan 3, 2517, JS The Hague; tel. (70) 4120200; fax (70) 4120211; e-mail ambassaden.haag@gov.se; internet www.swedenabroad.com/thehague; Ambassador HÅKAN EMSGÅRD.

Switzerland: Lange Voorhout 42, POB 30913, 2500 GX The Hague; tel. (70) 3642831; fax (70) 3561238; e-mail hay.vertretung@eda.admin.ch; internet www.eda.admin.ch/denhaag; Ambassador MARKUS BÖRLIN.

Thailand: Laan Copes van Cattenburch 123, 2585 EZ The Hague; tel. (70) 3450766; fax (70) 3451929; e-mail thaiembassy.thehague@gmail.com; Ambassador VIRACHAI PLASAI.

Tunisia: Gentsestraat 98, 2587 HX The Hague; tel. (70) 3512251; fax (70) 3514323; e-mail ambassadetunisie@ziggo.nl; Ambassador MUHAMMAD KARIM BEN BECHER.

Turkey: Jan Evertstraat 15, 2514 BS The Hague; tel. (70) 3023100; fax (70) 3617969; e-mail embassy.thehague@mfa.gov.tr; internet www.lahey.be.mfa.gov.tr; Ambassador UĞUR DOĞAN.

Ukraine: Zeestraat 78, 2518 AD The Hague; tel. (70) 3626095; fax (70) 3615565; e-mail embukr@wxs.nl; Ambassador ALEKSANDR HORIN.

United Arab Emirates: Eisenhowerlaan 130, 2517 KN The Hague; tel. (70) 3384370; fax (70) 3384373; e-mail info.lahaye@mofa.gov.ae; internet www.uae-embassy.nl; Ambassador ABDULLAH HAMDAN AL NAQBI.

United Kingdom: Lange Voorhout 10, 2514 ED The Hague; tel. (70) 4270427; fax (70) 4270345; e-mail ukinnl@fco.gov.uk; internet www.britain.nl; Ambassador PAUL ARKWRIGHT.

USA: Lange Voorhout 102, 2514 EJ The Hague; tel. (70) 3102209; fax (70) 3102207; e-mail ircthehague@state.gov; internet thehague.usembassy.gov; Chargé d'affaires a.i. EDWIN R. NOLAN.

Uruguay: Mauritskade 33, 2514 HD The Hague; tel. (70) 3609815; fax (70) 3562826; e-mail uruholan@wxs.nl; Ambassador Dr ALVARO MARCELO MOERZINGER PAGANI.

Venezuela: Nassaulaan 2, 2514 JS The Hague; tel. (70) 3633805; fax (70) 3656954; e-mail embve.nlhya@mppre.gob.ve; internet paisesbajos.embajada.gob.ve; Ambassador HAIFA AISSAMI MADAH.

Viet Nam: Nassauplein 12, 2585 EB The Hague; tel. (70) 3648917; fax (70) 3648656; e-mail vnembassy.nl@mofa.gov.vn; internet www.vietnamembassy.nl; Ambassador HUYNH MINH CHÍNH.

Yemen: Nassaulaan 2A, 2514 JS The Hague; tel. (70) 3653936; fax (70) 3563312; e-mail yemenembassy@planet.nl; internet www.yemen-embassy.nl; Ambassador (vacant).

Judicial System

Justices and judges must have graduated in law at a Dutch university, and are nominated for life by the Crown. The justices of the Supreme Court are nominated from a list of three compiled by the Second Chamber of the States-General.

SUPREME COURT

De Hoge Raad der Nederlanden: POB 20303, 2500 EH The Hague; Kazernestraat 52, 2514 CV The Hague; tel. (70) 3611311; fax (70) 3611451; e-mail info@hogeraad.nl; internet www.rechtspraak.nl/gerechten/hogeraad; for appeals in cassation against decisions of courts of lower jurisdiction; the Supreme Court, as a court of first instance, tries offences committed in their official capacity by members of the States-General and ministers; when dealing with appeals in cassation, the court is composed of five or, in more straightforward cases, of three justices (Raadsheren); Pres. G. J. M. CORSTENS; Procurator-Gen. J. W. FOKKENS; Sec. of the Court E. HARTOGS.

COURTS OF APPEAL

Gerechtshoven: Five courts: Amsterdam, Arnhem, 's-Hertogenbosch, Leeuwarden, The Hague. A court is composed of three judges (Raadsheren); appeal is from decisions of the District Courts of Justice. Fiscal Divisions (Belastingkamers) of the Courts of Appeal deal with appeals against decisions relating to the enforcement of the fiscal laws (administrative jurisdiction). The court of Arnhem has a Tenancy Division (Pachtkamer), composed of three judges and two assessors (a tenant and a landlord), and a Penitentiary Division (Penitentiaire Kamer), composed of three judges and two experts. The Tenancy Division hears appeals from decisions of all Canton Tenancy Divisions. The Penitentiary Division hears appeals against refusals of release on license, which is usually granted after two-thirds of a prison sentence longer than one year, unless there are special objections from the Minister of Justice. A Companies Division (Ondernemingskamer) is attached to the court at Amsterdam, consisting of three judges and two experts as assessors.

DISTRICT COURTS OF JUSTICE

Arrondissementsrechtbanken: There are 19 courts for important civil and penal cases and for appeals from decisions of the Canton Judges. A court is composed of three judges (Rechter); no jury;

summary jurisdiction in civil cases by the President of the Court; simple penal cases, including economic offences, generally by a single judge (Politierechter). Offences committed by juveniles are (with certain exceptions) tried by a specialized judge (Kinderrechter), who is also competent to take certain legal steps when the upbringing of a juvenile is endangered. Economic offences, and in particular environmental offences, are also dealt with by a specialized judge sitting alone.

CANTON COURTS

Kantongerechten: There are 62 courts for civil and penal cases of minor importance. A court consists of a single judge, the Canton Judge (Kantonrechter). Each Canton Court has a Tenancy Division (Pachtkamer), presided over by the Canton Judge who is assisted by two assessors (a landlord and a tenant).

ADMINISTRATIVE COURTS

The administrative courts regulate relations between the authorities and citizens according to the provisions of the General Administrative Law Act. The majority of cases are heard by the Administrative Law Sections of the District Courts, while appeals are heard by the Administrative Law Division of the Council of State (Afdeling Bestuursrechtspraak van de Raad van State), which also acts as the court of sole and last instance in the majority of cases concerning education, the environment and spatial planning. In addition, cases relating to certain areas of administrative law are heard by the following bodies:

Centrale Raad van Beroep (Central Appeals Council): POB 16002, 3500 DA Utrecht; Graadt van Roggenweg 200–250, 3531 AH Utrecht; tel. (30) 8502100; fax (30) 8502198; e-mail crvb@rechtspraak.nl; internet www.rechtspraak.nl/organisatie/crvb; hears appeals against decisions of the District Courts in matters concerning the public service and social security; Pres. T. G. M. SIMONS.

College van Beroep voor het Bedrijfsleven (Trade and Industry Appeals Tribunal): POB 20021, 2500 EA The Hague; Prins Clauslaan 60, 2595 AJ The Hague; tel. (70) 3813910; fax (70) 3813999; e-mail cbb@rechtspraak.nl; internet www.rechtspraak.nl/gerechten/cbb; hears in first and last instance appeals against decisions enforcing socio-economic and agricultural legislation made by certain bodies, such as regulatory bodies and Chambers of Commerce, and by certain ministers; Pres. T. G. M. SIMONS.

Administration Law Section, Aliens Division, District Court of The Hague: court of sole and last instance in cases involving immigration; brs in Zwolle, 's-Hertogenbosch, Amsterdam and Haarlem. The introduction of a limited right of further appeal is pending.

Tariefcommissie (Tariff Commission): court of sole and last instance for all customs and excise disputes.

Religion

CHRISTIANITY

Raad van Kerken in Nederland (Council of Churches in the Netherlands): Koningin Wilhelminalaan 5, 3818 HN Amersfoort; tel. (33) 4633844; e-mail rvk@raadvankerken.nl; internet www.raadvankerken.nl; f. 1968; 18 mem. churches; Pres. Drs H. J. VAN HOUT; Gen. Sec. Drs K. VAN DER KAMP.

The Roman Catholic Church

The Netherlands comprises one archdiocese and six dioceses. At 31 December 2006 there were an estimated 4,647,300 adherents in the country (28.6% of the population).

Bishops' Conference

Nederlandse Bisschoppenconferentie, Biltstraat 121, POB 13049, 3507 LA Utrecht; tel. (30) 2326900; fax (30) 2334601; e-mail secrbk@rkk.nl; internet rkkerk.nl.

f. 1986; Pres. Cardinal WILLEM JACOBUS EIJK (Archbishop of Utrecht).

Archbishop of Utrecht: Most Rev. WILLEM JACOBUS (WIM) EIJK, Aartsbisdom, Maliebaan 38–40, 3581 CR Utrecht; tel. (30) 2338030; e-mail secretariaat@aartsbisdom.nl; internet www.aartsbisdom.nl.

Protestant Churches

Christelijke Gereformeerde Kerken in Nederland (Christian Reformed Churches in the Netherlands): POB 334, 3900 AH Veenendaal; Ghandistr. 2, 3902 KD Veenendaal; tel. (318) 582350; e-mail lkb@cgk.nl; internet www.cgk.nl; f. 1834; Relations Dir Rev. J. G. H. VAN DER VINNE; c. 73,400 mems; 180 churches.

Deutsche Evangelische Gemeinde (German Evangelical Church): Bleijenburg 3B, 2511 VC, The Hague; tel. (70) 3465727;

e-mail deg.haag@tiscali.nl; internet www.evangelischekirche-denhaag.nl; f. 1857; Leaders Pastor ECKHARD BENZ-WENZLAFF, Pastor BARBARA WENZLAFF.

Dutch Mennonites: Algemene Doopsgezinde Sociëteit, Singel 454, 1017 AW Amsterdam; tel. (20) 6230914; fax (20) 6278919; e-mail ads@doopsgezind.nl; internet www.doopsgezind.nl; f. 1811; Pres. OTTO BLEKER; Sec.-Gen. H. W. STENVERS; 9,000 mems; 118 parishes.

Evangelische Broedergemeente (Hernhutters): Zusterpl. 20, 3703 CB Zeist; tel. (30) 6924833; internet www.ebg.nl; f. 1746; Pres. RITA HARRY; 10,000 mems in the Netherlands; 7 parishes.

First Church of Christ, Scientist: Winschoterweg 9, 9723 CG Groningen; e-mail peter.faas@hccnet.nl; churches in Amsterdam, Haarlem and The Hague.

Hersteld Apostolische Zendingkerk (Restored Apostolic Missionary Church): Hogerbeetsstraat 32, 2242 TR Wassenaar; tel. and fax (318) 438149; e-mail s.de.jong.hazk@hazknederland.org; internet www.hazknederland.org; f. 1863; Pres. Apostle for the Netherlands H. F. RIJNDERS; Sec. J. L. M. STRAETEMANS; 500 mems; 10 parishes.

Protestante Kerk in Nederland (Protestant Church in the Netherlands): POB 8504, 3503 RM Utrecht; tel. (30) 8801880; fax (30) 8801447; e-mail servicedesk@pkn.nl; internet www.pkn.nl; f. 2004; unification of the Nederlandse Hervormde Kerk with the Gereformeerde Kerken in Nederland and the Evangelisch-Lutherse Kerk; 2m. mems, 3,000 parishes in 77 districts; Pres. G. J. KRAMER; Sec.-Gen. Rev. Dr B. PLAISIER.

Remonstrantse Broederschap (Remonstrant Church): Nieuwe Gracht 27A, 3512 LC Utrecht; tel. (30) 2316970; fax (30) 2311055; e-mail info@remonstranten.org; internet www.remonstranten.org; f. 1619; Pres. CEES DE MONCHY; Gen. Sec. TOM MIKKERS; 5,800 mems; 44 parishes.

Unie van Baptistengemeenten in Nederland (Union of Baptist Churches in The Netherlands): Raadhuisplein 6–8, NL 3771 ER Barneveld; tel. (342) 712457; e-mail info@baptisten.nl; internet www.baptisten.nl; f. 1881; Pres. ELS LEEUW-VERMEULEN; 12,000 mems.

Other Christian Churches

Anglikaans Kerkgenootschap (Anglican Church): Ary van der Spuyweg 1, 2585 JA The Hague; tel. (70) 3555359; e-mail churchoffice@stjohn-stphilip.org; internet www.stjohn-stphilip.org; f. 1698; Chaplain Rev. ANDREW GREADY.

Katholiek Apostolische Gemeenten (Catholic Apostolic Church): 1E De Riemerstraat 3, 2513 CT The Hague; tel. (70) 3555018; f. 1867; 7 parishes in the Netherlands and 3 in Belgium.

Oud-Katholieke Kerk van Nederland (Old Catholic Church): Koningin Wilhelminalaan 3, 3818 HN Amersfoort; tel. (33) 4620875; e-mail buro@okkn.nl; internet www.okkn.nl; f. 1723 in the Netherlands with Jansenist influence; refuses to accept papal infallibility and other 'new' dogmas of the Roman Catholic Church; in full communion with the Anglican Churches since 1931; Leader and Archbishop of Utrecht Mgr Dr JORIS A. O. L. VERCAMMEN (18 parishes); Bishop of Haarlem Mgr Dr DICK JAN SCHOON (10 parishes); 10,000 mems.

ISLAM

At 1 January 2004 there were around 944,000 Muslims in the Netherlands, representing some 5.8% of the total population. (Some 4% of the population were Muslims in 2011.)

Contactorgaan Moslims en Overheid (CMO) (Contact Group for Muslims and the Government): Beeklaan 207, 2562 AE The Hague; tel. (70) 3921123; e-mail info@contactorgaanmoslimsenoverheid.nl; internet www.cmoweb.nl; f. 2004; promotes dialogue between Muslim community and the Government; includes 19 Muslim groups; Pres. R. BAL.

JUDAISM

Nederlands Israëlitisch Kerkgenootschap (Organization of Jewish Communities in the Netherlands): Postbus 7967, 1008 AD Amsterdam; tel. (20) 3018484; fax (20) 3018485; e-mail nik@nik.nl; internet www.nik.nl; f. 1814; 36 communities with around 5,000 mems; Rabbi RAPHAEL EVERS.

Portugees-Israëlietische Gemeente (Portuguese Synagogue): Mr. Visserplein 3, 1011 RD Amsterdam; tel. (20) 6245351; e-mail info@esnoga.com; internet portugesegemeente.nl; f. 1675; Gen. Sec. NATHAN MOKED.

BAHÁ'Í FAITH

National Spiritual Assembly (Bahá'í Community of the Netherlands): Riouwstraat 27, 2585 GR The Hague; tel. (70) 3554017; e-mail secretariaat@bahai.nl; internet www.bahai.nl; f. 1962; mems resident in 180 locations.

The Press

PRINCIPAL DAILIES
(All circulation figures as at March 2011, unless otherwise stated)

Alkmaar

Noordhollands Dagblad: Edisonweg 10, POB 2, 1800 AA Alkmaar; tel. (72) 5196196; fax (72) 5124152; e-mail redactiesecretariaat@ hdcmedia.nl; internet www.noordhollandsdagblad.nl; f. 1799; owned by Telegraaf Media Groep NV; morning; 9 regional edns; Editor MIKE ACKERMANS; circ. 135,257.

Amersfoort

AD Amersfoortse Courant: Grote Koppel 8, POB 43, 3800 AA Amersfoort; tel. (33) 4647911; fax (33) 4647334; e-mail ac.redactie@ ad.nl; internet www.ad.nl; f. 1887; publ. by AD NieuwsMedia; evening; Editor-in-Chief CHRISTIAAN RUESINK.

Amsterdam

Het Financieele Dagblad (Dutch Financial Daily): FD Mediagroep, Prins Bernhardplein 173, POB 216, 1000 AE Amsterdam; tel. (20) 5928888; fax (20) 5928800; e-mail redsec@fd.nl; internet www.fd.nl; f. 1796; morning; Mon.–Sat.; Editor JAN BONJER; circ. 62,685.

Metro: Metro Holland BV, Nachtwachtlaan 20, POB 90009, 1006 BA Amsterdam; tel. (20) 5114000; fax (20) 5114090; e-mail info@ metronieuws.nl; internet www.metronieuws.nl; f. 2004 in Rotterdam; separate Amsterdam edn since 2005; morning; owned by Metro International SA; Editor ROBERT VAN BRANDWIJK; circ. 480,916.

Het Parool: Jacob Bontiusplaats 9, POB 433, 1000 AK Amsterdam; tel. (20) 5584444; fax (88) 5725095; e-mail redactie@parool.nl; internet www.parool.nl; f. 1940; evening; Editor BARBARA VAN BEUKERING; circ. 85,388.

Sp!ts: POB 2620, 1000 CP Amsterdam; tel. (20) 5853045; fax (20) 5853065; e-mail redactie@spitsnieuws.nl; internet www.spitsnieuws.nl; f. 1998; owned by Telegraaf Media Groep NV; morning; distributed free of charge; Editor JAN-JAAP DE KLOET; circ. 391,178.

De Telegraaf: POB 376, 1000 EB Amsterdam; tel. (20) 5852329; fax (20) 5852435; e-mail redactie@telegraaf.nl; internet www.telegraaf.nl; f. 1893; morning; Editor SJUUL PARADIJS; circ. 609,930.

Trouw (Loyalty): Jacob Bontiusplaats 9, POB 859, 1000 AW Amsterdam; tel. (20) 5629444; fax (88) 5725082; e-mail secretariaat@trouw.nl; internet www.trouw.nl; f. 1943; morning; Editor WILLEM SCHOONEN; circ. 105,440.

De Volkskrant (The People's Journal): Jacob Bontiusplaats 9, 1018 LL Amsterdam; tel. (88) 561555; fax (88) 561561; e-mail redactie@ volkskrant.nl; internet www.volkskrant.nl; f. 1919; morning; Editor PHILIPPE REMARQUE; circ. 264,890.

Apeldoorn

Reformatorisch Dagblad: Laan van Westenenk 12, POB 670, 7300 AR Apeldoorn; tel. (55) 5390222; fax (55) 5412288; e-mail redactie@ refdag.nl; internet www.refdag.nl; f. 1971; evening; publ. by Erdee Media Groep; Editor-in-Chief WIM B. KRANENDONK; circ. 52,268.

De Stentor: Laan van Westenenk 6, POB 99, 7336 AZ Apeldoorn; tel. (55) 5388388; fax (55) 5388200; e-mail redactiesecretariaat@ destentor.nl; internet www.destentor.nl/regio/apeldoorn; f. 2003; evening; publishes 9 regional versions; Editor ALEX ENGBERS; circ. 129,550.

Barneveld

Nederlands Dagblad: Hermesweg 20, POB 111, 3770 AC Barneveld; tel. (342) 411711; fax (342) 411611; e-mail redactie@nd.nl; internet www.nd.nl; f. 1944; morning; Editor-in-Chief PETER BERGWERFF; circ. 29,505.

Breda

BN/De Stem (The Voice): Spinveld 55, POB 3229, 4800 MB Breda; tel. (76) 5312311; fax (76) 5312355; e-mail redactie@bndestem.nl; internet www.bndestem.nl; f. 1998 by merger of *Brabants Nieuwsblad* and *De Stem*; owned by Koninklijke Wegener NV; morning; Editor JOHAN VAN UFFELEN; circ. 113,073.

Dordrecht

AD De Dordtenaar: POB 54, 3300 AB Dordrecht; tel. (78) 6324711; e-mail dd.redactie@ad.nl; internet www.ad.nl; f. 1946; morning; Group Editor CHRISTIAAN RUESINK.

Eindhoven

Eindhovens Dagblad (ED): Begijnenhof 4–6, POB 534, 5600 AM Eindhoven; tel. (40) 2336336; fax (40) 2436954; e-mail redactie@ed .nl; internet www.ed.nl; owned by Wegener; Editor JOHN VAN DEN OETELAAR; circ. 109,378.

Enschede

De Twentsche Courant Tubantia: Getfertsingel 41, POB 28, 7500 AA Enschede; tel. (53) 4842842; fax (53) 4842200; e-mail enschede@ tctubantia.nl; internet www.tctubantia.nl; f. 1844; publ. by Koninklijke Wegener NV; Editor ANDRÉ VIS; circ. 112,599.

's-Gravenhage/Den Haag
(The Hague)

AD Haagsche Courant: Verrijn Stuartlaan, First Floor, Rijswijk, POB 16050, 2500 AA The Hague; tel. (70) 3190911; fax (70) 3954783; e-mail hc.redactie@ad.nl; internet www.ad.nl/denhaag; evening; Group Editor CHRISTIAAN RUESINK.

Nederlandse Staatscourant: Prinses Margrietplantsoen 88, POB 20020, 2500 EA The Hague; tel. (70) 3789639; fax (70) 3855505; e-mail staatscourant@sdu.nl; internet www.staatscourant.nl; f. 1814; morning; Editor W. M. C. DE JONG; circ. 5,913 (2006).

Groningen

Dagblad van het Noorden: Lübeckweg 2, POB 60, 9700 MC Groningen; tel. (50) 5844444; fax (50) 5844209; e-mail redactie@ dvhn.nl; internet www.dvhn.nl; f. 1888; morning; Editor PIETER SIJPERSMA; circ. 130,000 (2012).

Haarlem

Haarlems Dagblad: Stationsplein 86, POB 507, 2003 PA Haarlem; tel. (88) 8241111; e-mail starsredactie@haarlemdagblad.nl; internet www.haarlemsdagblad.nl; f. 1656; evening; Editors MIKE ACKERMANS, JAN GEERT MAJOOR; combined circ. 39,046.

IJmuider Courant: Kennemerlaan 56, 1972 EP IJmuiden; tel. (255) 561800; fax (255) 561888; e-mail redactie@ijmuidercourant.nl; internet www.ijmuidercourant.nl; daily; Editors MIKE ACKERMANS, JAN GEERT MAJOOR.

's-Hertogenbosch/Den Bosch

Brabants Dagblad: Emmaplein 25, POB 235, 5201 HB 's-Hertogenbosch; tel. (73) 6157115; e-mail redactiesecretariaat@ brabantsdagblad.nl; internet www.brabantsdagblad.nl; f. 1771; morning; publ. by Koninklijke Wegener NV; Editor ANNEMIEKE BESSELING; circ. 130,127.

Hilversum

De Gooi- en Eemlander: Seinstraat 14, 1223 DA Hilversum; tel. (35) 6477000; fax (35) 6477108; e-mail redactie@gooieneemlander.nl; internet www.gooieneemlander.nl; f. 1871; evening; Editors GEERT TEN DAM, JAN-GEERT MAJOOR; circ. 26,549.

Leeuwarden

Leeuwarder Courant: Sixmastraat 15, POB 394, 8901 BD Leeuwarden; tel. (58) 2845655; fax (58) 2845419; e-mail redactie@lc.nl; internet www.lc.nl; f. 1752; evening; Editor HANS SNIJDER; circ. 89.942 (2012).

Leiden

Leidsch Dagblad: 3e Binnenvestgracht 23, POB 54, 2300 AB Leiden; tel. (71) 5356356; fax (71) 5356415; e-mail stadsredactie@ leidschdagblad.nl; internet www.leidschdagblad.nl; f. 1860; publ. by HDC Media; morning; Editors MIKE ACKERMANS, JAN-GEERT MAJOOR; circ. 31,923.

Nijmegen

De Gelderlander: Winselingseweg 10, POB 36, 6500 DA Nijmegen; tel. (24) 3650611; fax (24) 3650479; e-mail redactie@gelderlander.nl; internet www.gelderlander.nl; f. 1848; owned by Koninklijke Wegener NV; morning; Editor KEES PIJNAPPELS; circ. 147,771.

Rotterdam

AD: Marten Meesweg 35, POB 8983, 3009 TC Rotterdam; tel. (10) 4066077; e-mail redactie@ad.nl; internet www.ad.nl; f. 1946; fmrly *Algemeen Dagblad*; morning; Group Editor CHRISTIAAN RUESINK; circ. 433,013.

AD Rotterdams Dagblad: Westblaak 180, POB 2999, 3000 CZ Rotterdam; tel. (10) 4004400; e-mail rd.redactie@ad.nl; internet www.ad.nl/rotterdam; f. 1991; evening; Group Editor CHRISTIAAN RUESINK.

NRC Handelsblad: Marten Meesweg 35, POB 8987, 3009 TH Rotterdam; tel. (10) 4066333; fax (10) 4066306; e-mail nrc@nrc.nl; internet www.nrc.nl; f. 1970; evening; Editor PETER VANDERMEERSCH; circ. 198,513.

Sittard

Dagblad De Limburger: Mercator 3, POB 5111, 6130 PC Sittard; tel. (46) 4116300; e-mail lezersservice@mgl.nl; internet www .limburger.nl; f. 1845; morning; Editor-in-Chief Jos ADRIAENS; circ. 124,180.

Limburgs Dagblad: Mercator 3, 6135 KW Sittard; tel. (46) 4116000; fax (46) 4116471; e-mail marketing@mgl.nl; internet www.limburger.nl; f. 1918; morning; Editor Jos ADRIAENS; circ. 40,963.

Utrecht

AD Utrechts Nieuwsblad: Vredenburg 24, POB 210, 3500 AE Utrecht; tel. (30) 2360300; e-mail un.brieven@ad.nl; internet www .ad.nl; f. 1993; evening; Group Editor CHRISTIAAN RUESINK.

Vlissingen

Provinciale Zeeuwse Courant: Park Veldzigt 35, POB 91, 4330 AB Middelburg; tel. (118) 434 010; fax (118) 434019; e-mail redactie@ pzc.nl; internet www.pzc.nl; f. 1758; morning; Editor PETER JANSEN; circ. 54,871.

SELECTED WEEKLIES

Adformatie: Heemstedeveste, Poeldijkstraat 4, POB 75462, 1070 AL Amsterdam; tel. (20) 5733644; e-mail redactie@adformatie.nl; internet www.adformatie.nl; advertising, marketing and media; Editor-in-Chief THEO VAN VUGT; circ. 40,000.

Avrobode: 's-Gravelandseweg 52, 1217 ET Hilversum; tel. (35) 6717911; fax (35) 717443; e-mail redactie@avrobode.nl; internet www.avrobode.nl; publ. by Algemene Omroepvereniging; radio and TV guide; Editor REIN VAN ROOIJ; circ. 271,113 (2011).

Boerderij: Hanzestraat 1, POB 4, 7000 BA Doetinchem; tel. (314) 349446; fax (314) 344397; e-mail redactie@boerderij.nl; internet www.boerderij.nl; f. 1915; farming; Editor-in-Chief GEERT HEKKERT; circ. 65,000.

Donald Duck: POB 1680, 2130 JB Hoofddorp; internet www .donaldduck.nl; f. 1952; children's interest; weekly; Publr SUZAN SCHOUTEN HAAGMANS; Editor THOM ROEP; circ. 296,179.

Elsevier: Radarweg 29, POB 152, 1000 AD Amsterdam; tel. (20) 5159944; fax (20) 5159900; e-mail redactie.elsevier@elsevier.nl; internet www.elsevier.nl; f. 1945; current affairs; Chief Editor ARENDO JOUSTRA; circ. 158,303 (2011).

Fashionista: POB 1680, 2130 JB Hoofddorp; tel. (23) 5565117; fax (23) 5565116; e-mail redactie@fashionistamagazine.nl; internet www.fashionistamagazine.nl; teenage girls' interest; Editor MIES DE VRIES; circ. 120,000.

Libelle: POB 1742, 2130 JC Hoofddorp; tel. (88) 5500221; e-mail redactie@libelle.nl; internet www.libelle.nl; f. 1934; women's interest; Editor-in-Chief FRANSKA STUY; circ. 427,110 (2011).

Margriet: POB 1650, 2130 JB Hoofddorp; tel. (88) 5500222; e-mail redactie@margriet.nl; internet www.margriet.nl; f. 1938; women's interest; Editor-in-Chief LEONTINE VAN DEN BOS; circ. 251,230 (2011).

Mikro Gids: POB 10050, 1201 DB Hilversum; tel. (35) 6726880; fax (35) 6726878; internet www.mikrogids.nl; f. 1974; radio and TV guide; Editor-in-Chief HANS SANDERS; circ. 364,261 (2011).

NCRV-Gids: POB 25900, 1202 HW Hilversum; tel. (35) 6726890; internet www.ncrvgids.nl; f. 1966; publ. by Nederlandse Christelijke Radio Vereniging; radio and TV guide; Dir SASKIA DE JONG; Editor MARJOLEINE TEPE; circ. 228,359 (2011).

Nederlands Tijdschrift voor Geneeskunde (Dutch Journal of Medicine): POB 75971, 1070 AZ Amsterdam; tel. (20) 6620150; fax (20) 6735481; e-mail redactie@ntvg.nl; internet www.ntvg.nl; f. 1856; Editor Prof. Dr PETER DE LEEUW; circ. 30,000.

Nieuwe Revu: Capellalaan 65, POB 41006, 2130 MK Hoofddorp; tel. (88) 7518380; e-mail redactie@revu.nl; internet www.revu.nl; f. 1953; general interest; Editor-in-Chief ERIK NOOMEN; circ. 41,140 (2011).

Panorama: Ceylonpoort 5–25, POB 4028, 2037 AA Haarlem; tel. (23) 5304304; fax (23) 5361624; e-mail panorama@smm.nl; internet www.panorama.nl; f. 1913; general interest; Editor FRANS LOMANS; circ. 55,938 (2011).

Privé: POB 1980, 1000 BZ Amsterdam; tel. (20) 5853375; fax (20) 5854225; e-mail redactie@prive.nl; internet www.prive.nl; f. 1977; owned by Telegraaf Media Groep NV; women's interest; Editor EVERT SANTEGOEDS; circ. 167,326 (2011).

Story: Capellalaan 65, POB 1652, 2130 JB Hoofddorp; tel. (23) 5564894; fax (23) 5564911; internet www.story.nl; f. 1974; women's interest; Editor MATTHIEU SLEE; circ. 98,564 (2011).

TeleVizier: POB 580, 1200 AN Hilversum; tel. (35) 6726850; fax (35) 6726878; e-mail redactie@televizier.nl; internet www.televizier.nl; publ. by Algemene Omroepvereniging; radio and TV guide; Editor JEROEN DE GOEIJ; circ. 141,308 (2011).

Tina: Ceylonpoort 5–25, 2037 AA Haarlem; tel. (23) 5304304; fax (23) 5352554; f. 1967; teenage girls' interest; circ. 51,919.

TrosKompas: POB 1431, 1000 BK Amsterdam; tel. (35) 6728798; fax (35) 6728631; e-mail info@troskompas.nl; internet www .troskompas.nl; f. 1966; owned by Hilversumse Media Compagnie; radio and TV guide; Editor EDGER HAMER; circ. 372,286 (2011).

TV Krant: POB 28600, 1202 LR Hilversum; tel. (35) 6728798; fax (35) 6728631; internet www.tvkrant.nl; f. 1990; radio and TV guide; Editor EDGER HAMER; circ. 158,814 (2011).

Vara TV Magazine: Sumatralaan 49, POB 175, 1200 AD Hilversum; tel. (35) 6711445; fax (35) 6711429; e-mail tv.magazine@vara .nl; internet vara.nl; radio and TV guide; Editor RUTGER VERHOEVEN; circ. 500,000.

Veronica: 2a Olympia, POB 22000, 1202 CA Hilversum; tel. (35) 6463333; fax (35) 6463300; e-mail bladredactie@veronicapublishing .nl; internet www.veronicamagazine.nl; f. 1971; radio and TV guide; Editor JOHN LUKKEN; circ. 797,787 (2011).

Viva: POB 1630, 2130 JA Hoofddorp; tel. (23) 5565165; fax (23) 5565200; e-mail redactie@viva.nl; internet www.viva.nl; women's interest; Editor KARIN VAN GILST; circ. 73,003 (2011).

VPRO-Gids: POB 11, 1200 JC Hilversum; tel. (35) 6712665; fax (35) 6712552; e-mail gids@vpro.nl; internet www.gids.vpro.nl; radio and TV guide; Editor HUGO BLOM; circ. 221,237 (2011).

Vrij Nederland: Raamgracht 4, POB 1254, 1000 BG Amsterdam; tel. (20) 5518711; fax (20) 6247476; e-mail redactie@vn.nl; internet www.vn.nl; f. 1940; current affairs; Dir. KARIN VAN GILST; Editor FRITS VAN EXTER; circ. 49,752 (2011).

SELECTED PERIODICALS

Art, History and Literature

De Architect: POB 20025, 2501 AG The Hague; tel. (70) 3789911; fax (70) 3854321; e-mail architect@wkths.nl; internet www .dearchitect.nl; Dir HARM TILMAN; circ. 4,859 (2010).

Geschiedenis Magazine: Molukkenstraat 200, 1098 TW Amsterdam; tel. (20) 6652759; fax (20) 6657831; e-mail redactie@ geschiedenismagazine.nl; internet www.geschiedenismagazine.nl; f. 1966; monthly; history and archaeology; Editor-in-Chief MARTIJN VAN LIESHOUT; circ. 8,000.

Kunstbeeld: POB 256, 1110 AG Diemen; tel. (20) 5310900; fax (20) 5310971; e-mail redactie@kunstbeeld.nl; internet www.kunstbeeld .nl; monthly; art, sculpture; Editor ROBBERT ROOS; circ. 11,000 (2007).

Tableau Fine Arts Magazine: POB 71197, 1008 BD Amsterdam; tel. (20) 6648543; e-mail tableaumedia@kpnplanet.nl; internet www .tableaumagazine.nl; f. 1978; every 2 months; publ. by Tableau Fine Arts Media BV; Editor-in-Chief ANJA FRENKEL; circ. 18,000.

Economics and Business

Computable: POB 37109, 1030 BA Haarlem; tel. (23) 2042925; e-mail computable@vnumedia.nl; internet www.computable.nl; Editor ALEX BESHUIZEN; circ. 39,914 (2010).

Elektronica + Embedded Systems: POB 58, 7400 AB Deventer; tel. (570) 504381; fax (570) 504399; e-mail h.vries@mybusinessmedia .nl; internet www.engineersonline.nl; f. 1953; 8 a year; electronics design; Editor HENK DE VRIES; circ. 5,000.

Intermediair: POB 1900, 2003 BA Haarlem; tel. (23) 5463455; fax (23) 5465530; e-mail redactie@intermediair.nl; internet www .intermediair.nl; f. 1965; weekly; business recruitment; Editor ALEX BEISHUIZEN; circ. 240,678.

Management Team: Paul van Vlissingenstr. 10, 1096 BK Amsterdam; tel. (20) 2620701; e-mail redactie@mt.nl; internet www.mt.nl; f. 1980; monthly; management; Editor EWALD SMITS.

PCM (Personal Computer Magazine): Ceylonpoort 5–25, 2037 AA Haarlem; tel. (23) 5463704; fax (23) 5465524; internet www.pcmweb .nl; f. 1982; monthly; computing; Editor-in-Chief EDWIN AMMERLAAN; circ. 94,997.

Trade Channel: Nieuw Guineastraat 30, 2022 PA Haarlem; tel. (23) 5319022; fax (23) 5317974; e-mail pvroom@tradechannel.com; internet www.tradechannel.com; f. 1945; monthly; 2 edns: *Trade Channel Consumer Goods* and *Trade Channel Industrial & Technical Products*; promote imports and exports; Editor HENK VAN CAPELLE; circ. 13,286 (consumer edn), 55,000 (technical edn).

Home, Fashion and General

Ariadne at Home: Capellalaan 65, POB 1722, 2130 JC Hoofddorp; tel. (88) 5564435; e-mail redactie@ariadneathome.nl; internet www .ariadneathome.nl; f. 1946; monthly; home decoration; Editor ATY LUITZE; circ. 169,198.

Cosmopolitan: Capellalaan 65, POB 1730, 2132 JL Hoofddorp; fax (23) 5565259; e-mail c.straatmans@sanoma-uitgevers.nl; internet www.cosmopolitan.nl; f. 1982; monthly; women's interest; Editor CLAUDIA STRAATMANS; circ. 152,659 (2010).

Delicious: Capellalaan 65, POB 1632, 2130 JA Hoofddorp; tel. (23) 5565466; fax (23) 5565488; e-mail deliciousmagazine@ sanoma-uitgevers.nl; internet www.deliciousmagazine.nl; f. 1977; monthly; cookery; Editor-in-Chief MAKKIE MULDER; circ. 62,218 (2010).

HP/De Tijd (The Times): POB 95044, 1090 HA Amsterdam; tel. (20) 5979400; fax (20) 5979490; e-mail redactie@hpdetijd.nl; internet www.hpdetijd.nl; f. 1845 as daily; owned by Audax; changed to weekly in 1974, and to monthly in 2012; progressive; current affairs; Editor-in-Chief FRANK POORTHUIS; circ. 30,000.

KIJK: POB 40091, 2130 KZ Hoofddorp; tel. (88) 7518328; e-mail info@kijk.nl; internet www.kijk.nl; science, technology, history and current events; Editor VIVIANNE BENDERMACHER; circ. 60,023 (2010).

Knipmode: Capellalaan 65, POB 1900, 2130 JL Hoofddorp; tel. and fax (23) 5565006; internet www.knipmode.nl; monthly; DIY fashion; Editor-in-Chief ELLEN DE JONG; Publr WOUTER VERKENNIS; circ. 124,000.

Nouveau: Capellalaan 65, POB 1710, 2132 JC Hoofddorp; tel. (23) 304304; fax (23) 350621; internet www.nouveau.nl; f. 1986; women's interest; Dir K. P. M. VAN DE PAS; circ. 62,708 (2010).

Opzij: Raamgracht 4, POB 2748, 1000 CS Amsterdam; tel. (20) 5518525; fax (20) 5518638; e-mail redactie@opzij.nl; internet www .opzij.nl; f. 1972; monthly; owned by Weekbladpers Media; feminist themes; Editor MARGRIET VAN DER LINDEN; circ. 77,540 (2010).

Ouders van Nu: POB 740, 2400 AS Alphen Aan Den Ryn; tel. (23) 5565066; fax (23) 5565095; e-mail ouders@jongezinnen.nl; internet www.oudersvannu.nl; f. 1967; monthly; childcare; Editor K. KROON-STUIVER; circ. 68,029 (2010).

Reader's Digest: POB 23330, 1100 DV Amsterdam; tel. (20) 5678911; fax (20) 6976422; e-mail hetbeste@readersdigest.nl; internet www.readersdigest.nl; f. 1957; monthly; general interest; Country Man. JOOST MARTENS; circ. 304,453.

SEN: Mathenesserlaan 179, 3014 HA Rotterdam; fax (102) 092629; e-mail info@senmagazine.com; internet www.senmagazine.com; f. 2004; monthly; women's interest; Publr SENAY OZDEMIR; circ. 20,000.

VT-Wonen: Maassluisstraat 2, POB 1900, 2130 JH Hoofddorp; tel. (30) 822511; fax (30) 898388; e-mail vtwonen@sanoma-utigevers.nl; internet www.vtwonen.nl; f. 1964; monthly; home-owning and decorating; Editors MONIQUE WIEMEYER, FRANCIEN DE VET; circ. 130,640 (2010).

101 Woonideeën: POB 1702, 2130 JC Hoofddorp; tel. (23) 5564590; fax (23) 5564505; e-mail 101woonideeen@sanoma-uitgevers.nl; internet www.101woonideeen.nl; f. 1957; monthly; home ideas; Editor ANNET NITERINK; circ. 72,622 (2010).

Leisure Interests and Sport

Autokampioen: POB 93200, 2509 BA The Hague; tel. (88) 2696039; e-mail autokampioen@anwb.nl; internet www.anwb.nl/auto; f. 1908; publ. by Royal Dutch Touring Club (ANWB); motoring; fortnightly; Chief Editor JOS VROOMANS; circ. 36,826 (2010).

Grasduinen (Browsing): POB 41000, 2130 2130 MK Hoofddorp; tel. (20) 7518110; fax (20) 7510111; e-mail info@grasduinen.nl; internet www.grasduinen.nl; monthly; leisure, healthy living, art; Editor FANNY GLAZENBURG; circ. 23,661 (2010).

Kampeer en Caravankampioen: POB 93200, 2509 BA The Hague; tel. (88) 2692222; e-mail kck@anwb.nl; internet www .kck-online.nl; f. 1941; monthly; camping and caravanning; publ. by Royal Dutch Touring Club (ANWB); Editor-in-Chief F. VOORBERGEN; circ. 98,892 (2010).

Kampioen: POB 93200, 2509 BA The Hague; tel. (80) 2692222; fax (70) 3146983; e-mail kampioen@anwb.nl; internet www.kampioen .nl; f. 1885; monthly; recreation and tourism; publ. by Royal Dutch Touring Club (ANWB); Editor E. LODEWYKS; circ. 3,608,835 (2010).

Reizen Magazine: POB 93200, 2509 BA The Hague; tel. (88) 2696670; fax (88) 2697610; e-mail reizen@anwb.nl; internet www .reizen.nl; 11 issues a year; tourism, travel; publ. by Royal Dutch Touring Club (ANWB); Editor-in-Chief HARRI THEIRLYNCK; circ. 55,788 (2010).

Voetbal International: WP Sport Media BV, POB 764, 1000 AT Amsterdam; tel. (20) 5518510; e-mail webmaster@vi.nl; internet www.vi.nl; weekly; football; Editor-in-Chief JOHAN DERKSEN; circ. 166,723 (2010).

Waterkampioen: POB 93200, 2509 BA The Hague; tel. (88) 2697049; fax (88) 2697359; e-mail waterkampioen@anwb.nl; internet lwww.anwbwatersport.nl; f. 1927; monthly; water sports and yachting; publ. by Royal Dutch Touring Club (ANWB); Editor JAN BRIEK; circ. 38,710 (2010).

Scientific and Medical

Huisarts en Wetenschap: Nederlands Huisartsen Genootschap, POB 3231, 3502 GE Utrecht; tel. (30) 2823500; fax (30) 2823501;

e-mail redactie@nhg.org; internet www.henw.org; monthly; medical; Editor Dr JUST EEKHOF; circ. 12,463 (2010).

Natuur & Techniek: POB 256, 1110 AG Diemen; tel. (46) 4389444; fax (46) 4370161; e-mail redactie@natutech.nl; internet www .natutech.nl; f. 1932; monthly; Editor R. DOBBELAER; circ. 47,360.

Technische Revue: POB 4, 7000 BA Doetinchem; tel. (314) 349968; fax (314) 361522; internet www.reedbusiness.nl; monthly; review of new products; Chief Editor M. L. MATSER; circ. 28,000.

NEWS AGENCY

Algemeen Nederlands Persbureau (ANP) (Netherlands News Agency): POB 1, 2501 AA The Hague; tel. (70) 4141414; fax (70) 4140560; e-mail redactie@anp.nl; internet www.anp.nl; f. 1934; official agency of the Netherlands Daily Press Asscn; Man. Dir ERIK VAN GRUIJTHUIJSEN; Editor-in-Chief MARCEL VAN LINGEN.

PRESS ORGANIZATIONS

Buitenlandse Persvereniging in Nederland (Foreign Press Asscn in the Netherlands): Oudezijds Voorburgwal 129, 1012 EP Amsterdam; tel. (20) 4221209; e-mail ccorder@ap.org; internet www .bpv-fpa.nl; f. 1925; Pres. KERSTIN SCHWEIGHÖFER; 120 mems.

Nederlandse Dagbladpers (NDP) (Dutch Asscn of Daily Newspaper Publrs): Hogehilweg 6, POB 12040, 1100 AA Amsterdam-Zuidoost; tel. (20) 4309171; fax (20) 4309199; e-mail ndp@nuv.nl; internet www.nuv.nl; f. 1908; affiliated to Nederlands Uitgevers-verbond; Chair. C. G. G. SPAAN; Gen. Sec. T. NAUTA; 31 mems.

De Nederlandse Nieuwsbladpers (NNP) (Organization of Local News Media in the Netherlands): Hogebrinkerweg 23C, 3871 KM Hoevelaken; tel. (33) 4481650; fax (33) 4481652; e-mail nnpnl@nnp .nl; internet www.nnp.nl; f. 1945; asscn of publrs of non-daily local newspapers and other local news media; Pres. P. V. J. H. (PAUL) JANSSEN; Dir J. P. (PAUL) BOS; 131 mems.

Nederlandse Vereniging van Journalisten (Netherlands Association of Journalists): Johannes Vermeerstraat 22, POB 75997, 1070 AZ Amsterdam; tel. (20) 6766771; fax (20) 6624901; e-mail vereniging@nvj.nl; internet www.nvj.nl; f. 1884; publ. *De Journalist* (fortnightly); Chair. H. LIEFTING; Gen. Sec. T. BRUNING; 8,000 mems.

Publishers

Uitgeverij Altamira BV: Zijlweg 308, 2000 AH Haarlem; tel. (23) 5286882; e-mail info@gottmer.nl; internet www.altamira-becht.nl; f. 1985; philosophy, psychology, New Age, health and spirituality.

Uitgeverij Ankh-Hermes BV: Smyrnastraat 5, POB 125, 7400 AC Deventer; tel. (57) 0678900; fax (57) 0624632; e-mail info@ ankh-hermes.nl; internet www.ankh-hermes.nl; f. 1972; health, Eastern and Western religions, astrology, alternative medicine, psychology, esoterics; part of VBK-media since 2011; Dir A. STEENBERGEN; Publrs E. TEN SELDAM, W. DE VEER.

Ambo Anthos: Herengracht 499, 1017 BR Amsterdam; tel. (20) 5245411; fax (20) 4200422; e-mail info@amboanthos.nl; internet www.amboanthos.nl; literature, cultural history, biographies, history, politics; Dir R. AMMERLAAN.

APA (Academic Publishers Associated): Voorburgwal 286, 1012 RT Amsterdam; tel. (20) 6265544; fax (20) 5285298; e-mail apa@ apa-publishers.com; internet www.apa-publishers.com; f. 1966; subsidiaries: Apantiqua, Holland University Press, Fontes Pers, Oriental Press, Philo Press, van Heusden, Hissink & Co; old, new and reprint edns in the arts, humanities and science; Man. Dir G. VAN HEUSDEN.

BV Uitgeverij De Arbeiderspers: Franz Lisztpl. 200, 3533 JG Utrecht; tel. (30) 2470411; fax (30) 2410018; e-mail info@ arbeiderspers.nl; internet www.arbeiderspers.nl; participant in Weekbladpers holdings group; general, fiction and non-fiction; Dir LEX JANSEN.

A. Asher & Co BV: Zeeweg 264, POB 258, 1971 AG IJmuiden; tel. (25) 5523839; fax (25) 5510352; e-mail info@asherbooks.com; internet www.asherbooks.com; f. 1830; natural history; Dirs M. J. ROOS, J. W. STEINER.

Bert Bakker BV: Herengracht 540, POB 1662, 1000 BR Amsterdam; tel. (20) 6241934; fax (20) 6225461; e-mail info@pbo.nl; internet www.uitgeverijprometheus.nl/bb; f. 1893; Dutch and international literature, sociology, history, politics, science; Editor JOB LISMAN.

John Benjamins BV: Klaprozenweg 75G, POB 36224, 1020 ME Amsterdam; tel. (20) 6304747; fax (20) 6739773; e-mail customer .services@benjamins.nl; internet www.benjamins.com; f. 1964; linguistics, philology, psychology and art history; antiquarian scholarly periodicals; Man. Dir SELINE BENJAMINS.

Uitgeverij De Bezige Bij BV: Van Miereveldstraat 1, POB 75184, 1070 AD Amsterdam; tel. (20) 3059810; fax (20) 3059824; e-mail info@debezigebij.nl; internet www.debezigebij.nl; f. 1945; Publr MICHIEL GAAF.

Erven J. Bijleveld: Janskerkhof 7, 3512 BK Utrecht, POB 1238, 3500 BE Utrecht; tel. (30) 2317008; fax (30) 2368675; e-mail bijleveld .publishers@wxs.nl; internet www.bijleveldbooks.nl; f. 1865; psychology, sociology, philosophy, religion and history; computer books (as Bijleveld Press); Mans J. B. BOMMELJÉ, L. S. BOMMELJÉ.

Boekencentrum Uitgevers: Goudstraat 50, POB 29, 2700 AA Zoetermeer; tel. (79) 3615481; fax (79) 3615489; e-mail info@ boekencentrum.nl; internet www.boekencentrum.nl; bibles, books and magazines; Dir N. A. DE WAAL.

Bohn Stafleu Van Hoghum BV: Het Spoor 2, POB 246, 3990 GA Houten; tel. (30) 6383736; fax (30) 6383999; e-mail klachten@bsl.nl; internet www.bsl.nl; mem. of Wolters Kluwer NV holdings group; social sciences, humanities, medical, dental and nursing; Dir P. J. A. SNAKKERS.

Boom Uitgevers Amsterdam BV: Prinsengracht 747–751, POB 15970, 1001 JX Amsterdam; tel. (20) 6226107; fax (20) 6253327; e-mail info@boomamsterdam.nl; internet www.boomamsterdam.nl; f. 1842; fmrly Boom Pers BV, Meppel; philosophy, educational and social sciences, environment, history; Man. Dir DRIES VAN INGEN.

Brill: Plantijnstraat 2, POB 9000, 2300 PA Leiden; tel. (71) 5353500; fax (71) 5317532; e-mail marketing@brill.com; internet www.brill .com; f. 1683; academic books and periodicals (mainly in English); classics, medieval, renaissance and oriental studies, comparative religion, biology, law; CEO HERMAN PABBRUWE.

A. W. Bruna Uitgevers BV: Kobaltweg 23–25, POB 40203, 3504 AA Utrecht; tel. (30) 2470411; fax (30) 2410018; e-mail info@awbruna.nl; internet www.awbruna.nl; f. 1868; general fiction and non-fiction; Dir J. A. A. BOEZEMAN.

CRC Press/Balkema–Taylor & Francis Group (CRC Press/ Balkema): Schipholweg 107c, 2316 XC Leiden; POB 447, 2301 AK Leiden; tel. (71) 5243080; fax (71) 5234571; e-mail pub.nl@tandf.co .uk; internet www.crcpress.com; f. 1901 as Swets & Zeitlinger Publishers; acquired by Taylor & Francis (UK) in 2003; publr of books on civil engineering, water, geosciences and earth sciences; Sr Publr JANJAAP BLOM.

Uitgeverij Cantecleer BV: Julianalaan 11, POB 309, 3740 AM Baarn; tel. (35) 5486600; fax (35) 5486645; e-mail cantecleer@ worldonline.nl; internet www.cantecleer.nl; f. 1948; mem. of Bosch & Keuning Uitgevers group; Man. Dir H. SCHWURMANS.

Uitgeverij De Fontein BV: Herculesplein 20, POB 13288, 3507 LG Utrecht; tel. (35) 5486311; fax (35) 5423855; internet www .defonteinkinderboeken.nl; f. 1981; mem. of NDC/VBK; commercial fiction, non-fiction and children's books; Dir T. AKVELD.

Uitgeverij van Gennep BV: Nieuwezijds Voorburgwal 330, 1012 RW Amsterdam; tel. (20) 6247033; fax (20) 6247035; e-mail info@ vangennep-boeken.nl; internet vangennep-boeken.nl; history, social theory, political science, biographies, literature; Dir CHRISTEN KATE.

Gottmer Uitgevers Groep: Zijlweg 308, POB 317, 2000 CN Haarlem; tel. (23) 5411190; fax (23) 5274404; e-mail info@gottmer .nl; internet www.gottmer.nl; f. 1937; fiction, non-fiction, children's books, religion, spirituality, travel guides; imprints incl. Aramith, Becht, Dominicus and Hollandia; Dir C. G. A. VAN WIJK.

Uitgeverij Holland BV: Spaarne 110, 2011 CM Haarlem; tel. (23) 5323061; fax (23) 5342908; e-mail info@uitgeverijholland.nl; internet www.uitgeverijholland.nl; f. 1922; literature, reference, science, children's books; Publr J. B. VAN ULZEN.

Uitgeverij J. H. Kok: KCC VBK Media, POB 13288, 3507 LG Utrecht; tel. (88) 8002062; e-mail info@kok.nl; internet www.kok.nl; f. 1894; theology, belles-lettres, science, periodicals; mem. of Veen Bosch & Keuning Uitgevers; 9 subsidiaries; Dir B. A. ENDEDIJK.

Ten Have BV: IJsseldijk 31, POB 5018, 8260 GA Kampen; tel. (38) 3328912; fax (38) 3392500; e-mail info@uitgeverijtenhave.nl; internet www.uitgeverijtenhave.nl; f. 1831; imprint of Uitgeefmaatschappij J. H. Kok; religious; Dir B. A. ENDEDIJK; Editor P. DE BOER.

Uitgeverij Voorhoeve: POB 13288, 3507 LG Utrecht; tel. (35) 5418855; fax (35) 5413174; f. 1876; imprint of Uitgeversmaatschappij J. H. Kok; general non-fiction, children's books; Dir B. A. ENDEDIJK.

Kosmos Uitgevers: Herculespl. 20, POB 13288, LG Utrecht; tel. (30) 2528500; fax (30) 2528598; e-mail info@kosmosuitgevers.nl; internet www.kosmosuitgevers.nl; f. 1992; mem. of Veen Bosch & Keuning Uitgevers; Dir GENEVIÈVE WALDMANN.

Lemniscaat BV: Vijverlaan 48, POB 4066, 3006 AB Rotterdam; tel. (10) 2062929; fax (10) 4141560; e-mail info@lemniscaat.nl; internet www.lemniscaat.nl; f. 1963; philosophy, psychology, care of the disabled and mentally handicapped, books for juveniles and young adults, picture books; Dir J. C. BOELE VAN HENSBROEK.

Uitgeverij Leopold BV: Singel 262, POB 3879, 1001 AR Amsterdam; tel. (20) 5511250; fax (20) 4204699; e-mail info@leopold.nl;

internet www.leopold.nl; f. 1923; mem. of Weekbladpers BV; children's books; Dir ANNETTE PORTEGIES.

Uitgeverij Luitingh-Sijthoff BV: Leidsegracht 105A, POB 289, 1000 AG Amsterdam; tel. (20) 5307340; fax (20) 626251; e-mail info@ luitingh-sijthoff.nl; internet www.luitinghsijthoff.nl; f. 1989 following the merger of Sijthoff (f. 1851) and Luitingh (f. 1947); mem. of Veen Bosch & Keuning Uitgevers publishing group; fiction and popular non-fiction; Man. Dir HANCA LEPPINK.

Malmberg BV: Leeghwaterlaan 16, POB 233, 5201 AE Den Bosch; tel. (73) 6288811; fax (73) 6210512; e-mail malmberg@malmberg.nl; internet www.malmberg.nl; f. 1885; part of SanomaWSOY Group (Finland); educational; Dir J. DRIESSEN.

J. M. Meulenhoff BV: Nieuwe Herengracht 507, 1017 BV Amsterdam; tel. (20) 5353135; fax (20) 5353130; e-mail info@meulenhoff.nl; internet www.meulenhoff.nl; f. 1895; literature, historical, political, social/cultural, art, paperbacks and pocket books; Dir ROB HOGENES.

NDC/VBK de Uitgevers BV: Sixmastraat 15, POB 394, 8932 PA Leeuwarden; tel. (30) 2845245; e-mail communicatie@ndcvbk.nl; internet www.ndcvbk.nl; f. 2005; merger between NDC Holding BV and Veen Bosch & Keuning Uitgevers NV; Chair. JAN K. W. DE ROOS.

Nienhuis Montessori International BV: Industriepark 14, 7021 AA Zelhem; tel. (314) 627110; fax (314) 627128; e-mail info@nienhuis .nl; internet www.nienhuis.nl; f. 1800; holdings group; publrs and printers specializing in scientific books and periodicals; Dir A. J. NIENHUIS.

Noordhoff Uitgevers: Winschoterdiep 70A, POB 58, 9700 MB Groningen; tel. (50) 5226922; fax (50) 5277599; e-mail info@ wolters.nl; internet www.wolters-noordhoff.nl; f. 1836; educational and scientific books, educational software, geographical and historical atlases and maps; Man. Dir Dr A. M. W. HOLL.

Uitgeverij Ploegsma BV: Singel 262, 1016 AC Amsterdam; tel. (20) 5511250; fax (20) 6203509; e-mail info@ploegsma.nl; internet www .ploegsma.nl; subsidiary: Uitgeverij De Brink.

Em. Querido's Uitgeverij BV: Singel 262, POB 3879, 1001 AR Amsterdam; tel. (20) 5511262; fax (20) 6391968; e-mail info@querido .nl; internet www.querido.nl; f. 1915; subsidiary: Uitgeverij Nijgh & van Ditmar; participant in 'Singel 262' holdings group; general fiction, history, children's books, translations from Latin and Greek texts; Dir ARY T. LANGBROEK.

Reed Elsevier NV: Radarweg 29, POB 152, 1043 NX Amsterdam; tel. (20) 5159944; fax (20) 5159900; e-mail redactie.elsevier@elsevier .nl; internet www.elsevier.nl; f. 1979 by merger; subholdings include some 60 subsidiaries in the Netherlands and abroad specializing in reference works, handbooks, weekly magazines, newspapers, trade and technical publs, (postgraduate) scientific books and journals, audiovisual materials, further education study courses, databases; CEO ERIK ENGSTROM.

Elsevier BV Excerpta Medica: Radarweg 29, 1043 NX Amsterdam; tel. (20) 4853975; fax (20) 4853188; e-mail excerptamedica@ elsevier.com; internet www.excerptamedica.com; Man. Dir EDWARD ROOS.

Editions Rodopi BV: Tijnmuiden 7, 1046 AK Amsterdam; tel. (20) 6114821; fax (20) 4472979; e-mail info@rodopi.nl; internet www .rodopi.nl; f. 1966; Dir Y. L. SCHIPPERS.

SDU: Prinses Beatrixlaan 116, POB 20025, 2500 EA The Hague; tel. (70) 3789911; fax (70) 3854321; e-mail sdu@sdu.nl; internet www.sdu .nl; Chair. Dr L. JONGSMA.

Springer: Van Godewijckstraat 30, POB 989, 3311 GX Dordrecht; tel. (78) 6576050; fax (78) 6576467; internet www.springeronline .com; merged with Kluwer Academic Publrs in 2004; publrs of books and journals in the fields of science, technology and medicine, incl., *inter alia*, natural sciences, mathematics, engineering, computer science and psychology; CEO DERK HAANK.

Strengholt United Media: Hofstede Oud-Bussem, Flevolaan 41, POB 338, 1400 AH Bussum; tel. (35) 6958430; fax (35) 6958440; e-mail info@utigeverijstrengholt.nl; internet www .uitgeverijstrengholt.nl; f. 1928; health, biography, music, current affairs, psychology, parapsychology, sports, cookery; Dir T. M. JANSEN.

Uitgeverij De Tijdstroom BV: Janskerkhof 26, POB 775, 3500 AT Utrecht; tel. (30) 2364450; fax (30) 2699354; e-mail info@tijdstroom .nl; internet www.tijdstroom.nl; f. 1921; educational and professional publications on health and welfare, periodicals in these fields; Dir N. F. VAN 'T ZET.

Unieboek BV: Papiermolen 14–24, POB 97, 3990 DB Houten; tel. (30) 7998300; fax (30) 7998398; e-mail info@unieboek.nl; internet www.unieboek.nl; f. 1890; holding group incorporating 10 publishing houses; general and juvenile literature, fiction, popular science, history, art, social, economics, religion, textbooks, etc.; Dir W. VAN GILS.

VNU Business Publications BV: Lincolnweg 40, POB 37040, 1030 AA Amsterdam; tel. (20) 2042000; fax (20) 2042001; e-mail info@bp

.vnu.com; internet www.vnubp.nl; trade and fashion, careers, IT, personal computer, management, training.

Wolters Kluwer NV: Zuidpoolsingel 2, POB 1030, 2400 BA, Alphen aan den Rijn; tel. (172) 641400; fax (172) 474889; e-mail info@ wolterskluwer.com; internet www.wolterskluwer.com; operates in legal, tax, accounting, health, risk and compliance, regulatory and financial services; CEO and Chair., Exec. Bd NANCY MCKINSTRY; CFO BOUDEWIJN BEERKENS.

PUBLISHERS' ASSOCIATIONS

Koninklijke Vereniging van het Boekenvak (KVB) (Royal Asscn for the Book Trade): Herengracht 166, 1016 BP Amsterdam; tel. (20) 6240212; fax (20) 6208871; e-mail info@kvb.nl; internet www .kvb.nl; f. 1815; Chair. L. C. BRINKMAN; Dir ANNA BAKKER; 1,500 mems.

Nederlands Uitgeversverbond (NUV) (Dutch Publrs' Asscn): Hogehilweg 6, POB 12040, 1100 AA Amsterdam Zuidoost; tel. (20) 4309150; fax (20) 4309199; e-mail info@nuv.nl; internet www.nuv.nl; Chair. LOEK HERMANS; Dir G. NOORMAN; 250 mems.

Broadcasting and Communications

TELECOMMUNICATIONS

Koninklijke KPN NV: POB 30000, 2500 The Hague; Maanplein 55, 2516CK The Hague; tel. (70) 3434343; fax (70) 3436568; e-mail webmaster@kpn.com; internet www.kpn.com; privatized 1989; fmrly Koninklijke PTT NV, present name adopted 1998; operates KPN Mobile; acquired Telfort BV in 2005, Enertel NV in 2006 and debitel Nederland BV in 2008; fixed-line operator and internet access provider; Chair. and CEO EELCO BLOK.

Telfort BV: POB 23079, 1100 DN Amsterdam Zuid-Oost; tel. 0800-1771; internet www.telfort.com; f. 1996; mobile cellular telecommunications and internet access; Man. Dir ROBIN CLEMENTS.

Online: POB 10241, 1001 EE Amsterdam; Muiderstr. 1, 1011 PZ Amsterdam; tel. (20) 5355555; e-mail info@dutchtone.nl; internet www.online.nl; mobile cellular telecommunications and internet access; fmrly Orange Nederland NV; name changed to present in 2008; owned by Deutsche Telekom; CEO DAVID HOLLIDAY.

T-Mobile: Waldorpstr. 60, 2521 CC The Hague; tel. (61) 4095000; internet www.t-mobile.nl; owned by Deutsche Telekom; mobile telephone operator.

UPC Nederland NV: POB 80900, 1005 DA Amsterdam; Kabelweg 51, 1014 BA Amsterdam; tel. (20) 7755000; fax (20) 7756724; e-mail mediarelations@upc.nl; internet www.upc.nl; subsidiary of UPC Broadband; broadband internet, telephone, digital television and radio service provider; Man. Dir ROBERT DUNNE.

Vodafone: Simon Carmiggelstraat 6, POB 2251, 1000 CG Amsterdam; tel. (43) 3555555; e-mail press.nl@vodafone.com; internet www .vodafone.nl; f. 1999; owned by Vodafone Group PLC (UK); CEO ROB SHUTER.

BROADCASTING

Under the Netherlands public broadcasting system the two co-ordinating bodies work with the seven licensed broadcasters to provide a complete range of programmes.

Co-ordinating Bodies

Nederlandse Publieke Omroep (NPO) (Netherlands Public Broadcasting): POB 26444, 1202 JJ Hilversum; Sumatralaan 45, 1217 GP Hilversum; tel. (35) 6779222; fax (35) 6772649; e-mail npo .communicatie@omroep.nl; internet www.publiekeomroep.nl; f. 1969; co-ordination of Dutch national public broadcasting and news, sports and teletext programmes on 6 national public radio and 3 television channels; fmrly Nederlandse Omroep Stichting; Chair. HENK N. HAGOORT.

NTR (Dutch Public Broadcaster for Information, Education and Culture): POB 29000, 1202 MA Hilversum; tel. (88) 1003100; fax (88) 1004464; e-mail info@ntr.nl; internet www.ntr.nl; f. 2010 by the merger of national broadcasters Nederlandse Programma Stichting (NPS), Teleac and RVU; Dir PAUL RÖMER.

Broadcasting Associations

Algemene Omroepvereniging AVRO: POB 2, 1200 JA Hilversum; 's-Gravelandseweg 80, 1217 EW Hilversum; tel. (35) 6717911; fax (35) 6717439; e-mail info@avro.nl; internet www.avro.nl; f. 1923; independent; general broadcaster; 800,000 mems; Chair. PAUL SMITS; Dir. WILLEMIJN MAAS.

Evangelische Omroep (EO): POB 21000, 1202 BA Hilversum; Oude Amersfoortseweg 79, 1213 AC Hilversum; tel. (35) 6474747; fax

(35) 6474727; e-mail eo@eo.nl; internet www.eo.nl; f. 1967; Protestant; Chair., Supervisory Bd AD DE BOER; Man. Dir ARJAN LOCK.

Katholieke Radio Omroep (KRO): POB 23000, 1202 EA Hilversum; 's-Gravelandseweg 80, 1217 EW Hilversum; tel. (35) 6713911; fax (35) 6713666; e-mail infolijn@kro.nl; internet www.kro.nl; f. 1925; Catholic; 615,000 mems; Pres. Dr KOEN BECKING; Man. Dir Dr YVONNE DE HAAN.

Nederlandse Christelijke Radio Vereniging (NCRV): POB 25000, 1202 HB Hilversum; 's-Gravelandseweg 80, 1217 EW Hilversum; tel. (35) 6719911; fax (35) 6719285; e-mail info@ncrv.nl; internet www.ncrv.nl; f. 1924; Protestant; more than 550,000 mems; Chair. Dr E. P. DE JONG; Dir COEN ABBENHUIS.

Omroepvereniging VARA: POB 175, 1200 AD Hilversum; Sumatralaan 49, 1217 GP Hilversum; tel. (35) 6711911; fax (35) 6711333; e-mail vara@vara.nl; internet www.vara.nl; f. 1925; social democratic and progressive; 515,000 mems; Chair. RUUD KOOLE.

Omroepvereniging VPRO: POB 11, 1200 JC Hilversum; Villa VPRO, Mediapark, Sumatralaan 49, 1217 GP Hilversum; tel. (35) 6712911; fax (35) 6712100; e-mail info@vpro.nl; internet www.vpro .nl; f. 1926; progressive; 380,000 mems; Pres. PETER VAN LIESHOUT; Dir of Radio GERARD WALHOF; Dirs of Television KAREN DE BOK, FRANK WIERING.

Televisie en Radio Omroep Stichting (TROS): POB 28450, 1202 LL Hilversum; Lage Naarderweg 45–47, 1217 GN Hilversum; tel. (35) 6715715; fax (35) 6715236; e-mail publiekservice@tros.nl; internet www.tros.nl; f. 1964; independent; general broadcaster; 573,664 mems; Chair. and CEO PETER KUIPERS.

Radio

There are six privately owned national radio stations that are operated on a public service basis, as well as 13 regional stations and about 330 local stations.

Radio 1: internet www.radio1.nl; 24-hour news and sports programming.

Radio 2: Sumatralaan 45, POB 26444, 1202 JJ Hilversum; tel. (35) 6775052; fax (35) 6773311; e-mail info@radio2.nl; internet www .radio2.nl; broadcasts popular music.

3FM: POB 26444, 1202 JJ Hilversume-mail redactie@3fm.nl; internet www.3fm.nl; broadcasts contemporary music.

Radio 4: internet www.radio4.nl; broadcasts popular classical music.

Radio 5: Sumatralaan 45, POB 26444, 1202 JJ Hilversum; tel. (35) 6775052; e-mail info@radio5nostalgia.nl; internet www.radio5.nl; broadcasts popular music, current affairs and cultural programmes; aimed at people aged over 55 years.

Radio 6: POB 26444, 1202 JJ Hilversume-mail radio6@omroep.nl; internet www.radio6.nl; broadcasts Americana, electronica, folk, jazz and 'world' music.

Television

Television programmes are transmitted on three public channels, each of which is allocated to a different combination of broadcasting associations and other organizations, and on the commercially funded channels operated by RTL Nederland.

RTL Nederland: Postbus 15016, 1200 TV Hilversum; Sumatralaan 47, 1217 GP Hilversum; tel. (35) 6718718; fax (35) 6236892; e-mail info@rtl.nl; internet www.rtl.nl; f. 1996 as Holland Media Groep; present name adopted 2004; operates 5 television channels: RTL 4, RTL 5, RTL 7, RTL 8 and RTL Lounge; subsidiary of RTL Group (Luxembourg); CEO BERT HABETS.

SBS 6/NET5: Plantage Rietlandpark 333, POB 18179, 1001 ZB Amsterdam; tel. (20) 8007000; fax (20) 8007001; e-mail sbs6@ publieksservice.sbs.nl; internet www.sbs6.nl; private broadcaster; Man. PASCAL VAN MEERTEN.

United Pan-Europe Communications NV: POB 80900, 1005 DA Amsterdam; Kabelweg 51, 1014 BA Amsterdam; tel. (20) 7755000; fax (20) 7729988; e-mail service@upc.nl; internet www.upc.nl; cable broadcaster.

Overseas Broadcasting

BVN TV: POB 222, 1200 JG Hilversum; Witte Kruislaan 55, 1217 AM Hilversum; tel. (35) 6724333; fax (35) 6724343; internet www .bvn.tv; f. 1998; by Radio Nederland Wereldomroep, VRT and Nederlandse Publieke Omroep (NPO); daily international transmissions of news and cultural programmes from public service broadcasters in Flanders and the Netherlands; Channel Man. R. VAN BAAREN.

Radio Nederland Wereldomroep (Radio Netherlands Worldwide): Witte Kruislaan 55, POB 222, 1200 JG Hilversum; tel. (35) 6724211; fax (35) 6724343; e-mail wereldomroep@rnw.nl; internet www.rnw.nl; f. 1947; public service broadcaster; daily transmissions in Arabic, Dutch, English, Indonesian, Papiamento, Portuguese,

Sarnami Hindi and Spanish; programme and transcription services for foreign radio and TV stations; Radio Nederland Training Centre (for students from developing countries); Chair. Dr B. R. BOT; Dir-Gen. JAN HOEK.

Finance

(cap. = capital; res = reserves; dep. = deposits; m. = million; br(s). = branch(es); amounts in euros)

BANKING

Central Bank

De Nederlandsche Bank NV: Westeinde 1, POB 98, 1000 AB Amsterdam; tel. (20) 5249111; fax (20) 5242500; e-mail info@dnb.nl; internet www.dnb.nl; f. 1815; nationalized 1948; merged with Pensioen- en Verzekeringskamer (Chamber of Insurance and Pensions) in 2004; cap. 500m., res 17,253m., dep. 26,290m. (Dec. 2007); Pres. Prof. KLAAS KNOT; Exec. Dirs HENK BROUWER, Prof. LEX H. HOOGDUIN, JOANNE KELLERMANN.

Principal Commercial Banks

ABN AMRO Bank NV: Gustav Mahlerlaan 10, POB 283, 1082 PP Amsterdam; tel. (20) 6289898; fax (20) 6287740; internet www .abnamro.com; f. 1991 by merger of Algemene Bank Nederland NV and Amsterdam-Rotterdam Bank NV; acquisition by consortium comprising Royal Bank of Scotland PLC (UK), Grupo Santander (Spain) and Fortis agreed in Oct. 2007; Dutch Govt replaced Fortis as stakeholder in Oct. 2008; cap. 1,015m., res 11,322m., dep. 247,310m. (Dec. 2012); Chair., Management Bd GERRIT ZALM; 915 brs nationally.

Amsterdam Trade Bank NV: Herengracht 469, 1017 BS Amsterdam; tel. (20) 5209429; fax (20) 5209219; e-mail info@atbank.nl; internet www.atbank.nl; f. 1994 as Stolichny Bank International NV; present name adopted 1999; 100% owned by Alfa-Bank (Russia); cap. 117.3m., res 5.2m., dep. 2,416.4m. (Dec. 2011); Chair., Supervisory Bd P. SMIDA; Man. Dirs ALEXEI V. DROVOSSEKOV, J. P. J. KONIJN, ANTON H. den HELD.

Bank Nederlandse Gemeenten NV (BNG): Koninginnegracht 2, POB 30305, 2500 GH The Hague; tel. (70) 3750750; fax (70) 3454743; e-mail info@bng.nl; internet www.bng.nl; f. 1914 as NV Gemeentelijke Crediebank; present name adopted 1992; 50% Govt-owned, 50% by provincial and municipal authorities; cap. 139m., res 1,502m., dep. 33,161m. (Dec. 2011); Chair. C. VAN EYKELENBURG.

Dexia Nederland BV: Piet Heinkade 55, POB 808, 1000 AV Amsterdam; tel. (20) 3485000; fax (20) 5571414; e-mail klantenservie@dexiabank.nl; internet www.dexiabank.nl; f. 2001; owned by Dexia banking group; name changed as above in 2010; Chair. B. F. M. KNÜPPE; 1 br.

Friesland Bank NV: Beursplein 1, POB 1, 8900 AA Leeuwarden; tel. (58) 2994499; fax (58) 2994591; e-mail service@frieslandbank.nl; internet www.frieslandbank.nl; f. 1913 as Coöperatieve Zuivel-Bank; present name adopted 1995; cap. 141.9m., res 653.9m., dep. 6,839.8m. (Dec. 2011); Chair. Dr ROBBERT KLAASMAN; Dir A. VLASKAMP; 33 brs.

GE Artesia Bank: Herengracht 539–543, POB 274, 1000 AG Amsterdam; tel. (20) 5204911; fax (20) 6247502; e-mail info@ artesia.nl; internet www.geartesiabank.nl; f. 1863 as the Nederlandsche Credit & Depositobank; became Banque Paribas Nederland in 1984; acquired by GE Commercial Finance (USA) in 2006; cap. 73.7m., res 193.1m., dep. 44.4m. (Dec. 2011); CEO STEVEN PRINS; mems, Exec. Bd JOHAN BENNING, JOHN-HAROLD EVERY; 9 brs.

ING Bank NV: Amstelveenseweg 500, 1081 KL Amsterdam; tel. (20) 5415411; fax (20) 5415444; e-mail ing@ing.com; internet www.ing .com; f. 1990 by merger of Nationale-Nederlanden and NMB Postbank Groep; Govt acquired an 8.5% stake in Oct. 2008; cap. 525m., res 18,696m., dep. 601,053m. (Dec. 2011); Chair., Supervisory Bd PETER A. F. W. ELVERDING; more than 400 brs.

KAS BANK NV: Spuistraat 172, POB 24001, 1000 DB Amsterdam; tel. (20) 5575911; fax (20) 5576100; e-mail info@kasbank.com; internet www.kasbank.com; f. 1806 by merger; present name adopted 2002; cap. 15.7m., res 146.9m., dep. 4,934.5m. (Dec. 2011); Chair., Management Bd ALBERT A. RÖELL.

F. van Lanschot Bankiers NV: Hooge Steenweg 29, POB 289, 5200 HC 's-Hertogenbosch; tel. (73) 5483548; fax (73) 5483648; e-mail vanlanschot@vanlanschot.nl; internet www.vanlanschot.nl; f. 1737; merger with CenE Bankiers NV completed 2005; cap. 41m., res 1,431.7m., dep. 13,700.1m. (Dec. 2011); Chair. KARL GUHA; 28 brs.

Mizuho Corporate Bank Nederland NV: Apollolaan 171, POB 7075, 1007 JB Amsterdam; tel. (20) 5734343; fax (20) 5734372; f. 2000 by merger of Dai Ichi Kangyo Bank Europe NV and Fuji Bank Nederland NV; cap. 141.8m., res 95.6m., dep. 2,108.2m. (Dec. 2011); Man. Dir TETSUO HIRAMATSU.

NIBC Bank NV: Carnegieplein 4, POB 380, 2501 BH The Hague; tel. (70) 3425625; fax (70) 3459129; e-mail info@nibc.com; internet www .nibc.com; f. 1945 as Herstelbank; present name adopted 2005; cap. 80m., res 300m., dep. 11,077m. (Dec. 2011); Chair., Management Bd and CEO JEROEN DROST; 1 br.

Rabobank Nederland (Coöperatieve Centrale Raiffeisen-Boerenleenbank BA): Croeselaan 18, POB 17100, 3500 HG Utrecht; tel. (30) 2160000; fax (30) 2162672; e-mail rabocomm@rn .rabobank.nl; internet www.rabobank.nl; f. 1972 by merger of Coöperatieve Centrale Raiffeisenbank of Utrecht and Coöperatieve Centrale Boerenleenbank of Eindhoven; cap. 8,013m., res 7,945m., dep. 561,176m. (Dec. 2011); Chair. PIET MOERLAND; 1,727 brs.

SNS Bank NV: Croeselaan 1, 3503 BJ Utrecht; tel. (30) 2915100; fax (30) 2915300; e-mail info@snsbank.nl; internet www.sns.nl; f. 1971 as Bank der Bondsspaarbanken NV; present name adopted 2002; cap. 381m., res 1,460m., dep. 45,436m. (Dec. 2011); Group Chair. and CEO S. VAN KEULEN; 256 brs.

Staalbankiers NV: Lange Houtstraat 8, POB 327, 2501 CH The Hague; tel. (70) 3101510; fax (70) 3396515; e-mail info@ staalbankiers.nl; internet www.staalbankiers.nl; f. 1916 as Bankierskantoor Staal & Co NV; present name adopted 2005; mem. of Achmea Groep; cap. 6.5m., res 171.5m., dep. 1,961.5m. (Dec. 2011); Chair. and CEO P. A. DE RUIJTER; Man. Dirs P. J. HUURMAN, D. BECK.

Bankers' Association

Nederlandse Vereniging van Banken (NVB) (Netherlands Bankers' Asscn): Singel 236, POB 3543, 1001 AH Amsterdam; tel. (20) 5502888; fax (20) 6239748; e-mail info@nvb.nl; internet www .nvb.nl; f. 1989; Chair. B. STAAL; Dir HEIN G. M. BLOCKS; 93 mems.

STOCK EXCHANGE

A supervisory authority, the Netherlands Securities Board, commenced activities in 1989.

Euronext Amsterdam: Beursplein 5, POB 19163, 1000 GD Amsterdam; tel. (20) 5504444; fax (20) 5504899; e-mail info@euronext.nl; internet www.euronext.com; subsidiary of NYSE Euronext; Euronext NV was formed by merger of Amsterdam, Paris and Brussels stock exchanges and joined in 2002 by the London futures exchange, LIFFE and the Lisbon stock exchange; merged with New York Stock Exchange in 2007 to form NYSE Euronext; unitary stock and options exchange; Chair. JOOST VAN DER DOES DE WILLEBOIS.

There are also financial futures, grain, citrus fruits and insurance bourses in the Netherlands; a 'spot' market for petroleum operates from Rotterdam.

INSURANCE

Principal Companies

AEGON Nederland: AEGONplein 50, POB 202, 2501 CE The Hague; tel. (70) 3443210; fax (70) 3475238; internet www.aegon .nl; f. 1983 by merger; life, accident, health, general and linked activities; Chair. MARCO B. A. KEIM.

ASR: Archimedeslaan 10, POB 2072, 3500 HB Utrecht; tel. (30) 2579111; f. 2000 by merger of ASR Verzekeringsgroep NV (f. 1720) and AMEV Nederland NV (f. 1883); state owned; fmrly Fortis ASR Verzekeringsgroep NV; name changed as above in 2008; Chair. JOS BAETEN.

Delta Lloyd Verzekeringen NV: Spaklerweg 4, POB 1000, 1000 BA Amsterdam; tel. (20) 5949111; fax (20) 6937968; internet www .deltalloyd.nl; f. 1807; Chair. NIEK HOEK.

Duinrand Makelaars in Assurantiën: Ruysdaelplein 42, 2282 BJ Rijswijk; tel. (70) 3246788; fax (70) 4150507; e-mail info@duinrand .nl; internet www.duinrand.nl; f. 1990; formed by merger of Stalpert CV and Fiducia Assurantiën BV in 2009; home, vehicle, non-life; Man. Dir MARCEL DE WIT.

Generali Verzekeringsgroep: Diemerhof 42, 1112 XN Diemen; tel. (20) 6680000; fax (20) 3983000; e-mail uwgenerali@generali.nl; internet www.generali.nl; f. 1870; life and non-life; Gen. Dir FREEK WANSINK.

ING Groep NV: Amstelveenseweg 500, 1081 KL Amsterdam; tel. (20) 5415411; fax (20) 5760950; e-mail nanne.bos@ing.com; internet www.ing.com; f. 1963; Chair., Management Bd JAN H. M. HOMMEN.

Nationale-Nederlanden NV: Kantoor Delftse Poort, Weena 505, 3013 AL Rotterdam; tel. (10) 5130303; internet www.nn.nl; f. 1863; CEO TOM KLIPHUIS.

RVS: Loevestein 33, 6714 BS Ede; tel. (318) 662054; e-mail rvs@rvs .nl; internet www.rvs.nl; f. 1838; subsidiary of ING Groep NV; mem. of Internationale-Nederlanden group; life and non-life; Chair. MARC VAN DER PLOEG.

SNS REAAL: Croeselaan 1, 3521 BJ Utrecht; tel. (30) 2915200; e-mail info@snsreaal.nl; internet www.snsreaal.nl; f. 1997; by the merger of SNS group and REAAL group; banking and insurance; life and non-life; Chair. PIERO OVERMARS (acting); CEO GERARD VAN OLPHEN.

Regulatory Authority

Autoriteit Financiële Markten (AFM): Vijzelgracht 50, 1017 HS, Amsterdam; tel. (20) 7972000; fax (20) 7973800; internet www.afm.nl; Chair. RONALD GERRITSE.

Insurance Association

Verbond van Verzekeraars (Asscn of Insurers): Bordewijklaan 2, POB 93450, 2509 AL The Hague; tel. (70) 3338500; fax (70) 3338510; e-mail info@verzekeraars.nl; internet www.verzekeraars.nl; f. 1978; Chair. MARCO KEIM; Gen. Man. R. WEURDING.

Trade and Industry

GOVERNMENT AGENCY

Autoriteit Consument & Markt (ACM) (Authority for Consumers and Markets): Muzenstraat 41, 2511 WB The Hague; POB 16326, 2500 BH The Hague; tel. (70) 7222000; fax (70) 7222355; e-mail info@acm.nl; internet www.acm.nl; f. 2013; formed by the merger of the Independent Postal and Telecommunications Authority of Netherlands (OPTA), Netherlands Competition Authority (NMA) and the Netherlands Consumers Authority; regulation, competition, consumer protection, market analyses; Chair. CHRIS A. FONTEIJN.

Netherlands Foreign Investment Agency: Prinses Beatrixlaan 2, 2595 AL The Hague; tel. (88) 6028818; e-mail info@nfia.nl; internet www.nfia.nl; f. 1978; govt agency; facilitates foreign direct investment.

CHAMBERS OF COMMERCE

There are 12 autonomous Chambers of Commerce and Industry in the Netherlands. The most important are:

Kamer van Koophandel Amsterdam (Chamber of Commerce and Industry for Amsterdam): De Ruyterkade 5, 1013 AA Amsterdam; POB 2852, 1000 CW Amsterdam; tel. (20) 5314000; fax (20) 5314799; e-mail info@amsterdam.kvk.nl; internet www.amsterdam.kvk.nl; f. 1811; Dir-Gen. H. E. VAN BAARSBANK.

Kamer van Koophandel Rotterdam (Chamber of Commerce for Rotterdam): Blaak 40, POB 450, 3000 AL Rotterdam; tel. (10) 4027777; fax (10) 4145754; e-mail info@rotterdam.kvk.nl; internet www.rotterdam.kvk.nl; f. 1803; Pres. G. J. H. VAN DER VEGT.

EMPLOYERS' ORGANIZATIONS

De Maatschappij—Nederlandsche Maatschappij voor Nijverheid en Handel (NMNH) (Netherlands Society for Industry and Trade): Jan van Nassaustraat 75, 2596 BP The Hague; tel. (70) 3141940; fax (70) 3247515; e-mail info@de-maatschappij.nl; internet www.de-maatschappij.nl; f. 1777; Pres. LUUC MANNAERTS; more than 3,000 mems.

LTO-Nederland (Netherlands Agricultural Organization): Bezuidenhoutseweg 225, POB 29773, 2502 LT The Hague; tel. (70) 3382700; fax (70) 3382710; e-mail info@lto.nl; internet www.lto.nl; f. 1995; Chair. A. J. MAAT; 50,000 mems.

Nederlands Centrum voor Handelsbevordering (NCH) (Netherlands Council for Trade Promotion): Prinses Beatrixlaan 712, POB 10, 2501 CA The Hague; tel. (70) 3441544; fax (70) 3853531; e-mail info@nchnl.nl; internet www.handelsbevordering.nl; f. 1946 as Centraal Instituut voor Handelsvoorlichting; name changed as above 1975; Man. Dir JOCHUM HAAKMA; 800 mem. cos.

De Nederlandse Tuinbouwraad (NTR) (Netherlands Horticultural Council): POB 1000, 1430 BA Aalsmeer; tel. (297) 395005; fax (297) 395012; e-mail informatie@tuinbouwraad.nl; internet www.tuinbouwraad.nl; f. 1908; Chair. Dr NICO KOOMEN; Sec. GEORGE FRANKE.

NERG (Nederlands Elektronica- en Radiogenootschap): POB 39, 2260 AA Leidschendam; tel. (70) 3325112; fax (70) 3326477; e-mail secretariaat@nerg.nl; internet www.nerg.nl; f. 1920; Chair. Dr A. VAN OTTERLO; Sec. D. VAN MEETEREN; c. 400 mems.

Vereniging VNO-NCW (Confederation of Netherlands Industry and Employers): Bezuidenhoutseweg 12, POB 93002, 2509 AA The Hague; tel. (70) 3490349; fax (70) 3490300; internet www.vno-ncw.nl; f. 1997 as merger of Verbond van Nederlandse Ondernemingen (VNO) and Nederlands Christelijk Werkgeversverbond (NCW); represents almost all sectors of the Dutch economy; Pres. B. E. M. (BERNARD) WIENTJES; mems: 160 asscns representing more than 115,000 enterprises.

UTILITIES

Electricity

ENECO: Marten Meesweg 5, 3068 AV Rotterdam; tel. (10) 8889511111; e-mail corporatecommunicatie@eneco.com; internet www.eneco.nl; Chair. J. F. (JEROEN) DE HAAS; 7,000 employees.

E.ON Benelux BV: Capelseweg 400, POB 8642, 3009 AP Rotterdam; tel. (10) 2895711; internet www.eon.nl; f. 2000; replaced Electriciteitsbedrijf Zuid Holland (f. 1941); supplies energy to large-volume customers and distributors; CEO ROLF FOUCHIER.

Essent: Nieuwe Stationsstraat 20, 6811 KS Arnhem; internet www.essent.nl; f. 1999 by merger of Edon Group and Pnem Mega Group; electricity generation and supply, also supplier of gas; CEO ERWIN LAETHEM.

Nuon NV: Spaklerweg 20, POB 41920, 1009 DC Amsterdam; tel. (26) 8450271; fax (88) 0983199; internet www.nuon.com; f. 1999; energy and water; Chair., Supervisory Bd ØYSTEIN LØSETH; CEO HUIB MORELISSE.

TenneT BV: Utrechtseweg 310, POB 718, 6800 AS Arnhem; tel. (26) 3731111; fax (26) 3731112; e-mail servicecentre@tennet.org; internet www.tennet.org; f. 1999; independent; Dutch Transmission System operator; manages 220/380-kW national grid and supplies electricity to direct suppliers; Pres. and CEO J. M. (MEL) KROON.

Gas

Full liberalization of the gas market in the Netherlands took effect from the beginning of July 2004. Although retaining ownership of the main transport network, NV Nederlandse Gasunie passed the legal tasks of the national transmission system operator to a new, state-owned organization, Gas Transport Services BV, founded in July 2004.

ENECO: see Electricity.

Essent: see Electricity.

Gas Transport Services BV: Concourslaan 17, POB 181, 9700 AD Groningen; tel. (50) 5212250; fax (50) 3603036; e-mail customerdesk@gastransport.nl; internet www.gastransportservices.nl; f. 2006; independent; transmission system operator; Dir-Gen. A. J. KRIST.

NV Nederlandse Gasunie: Concourslaan 17, POB 19, 9700 MA Groningen; tel. (50) 5219111; fax (50) 5211999; e-mail communicatie@gasunie.nl; internet www.gasunie.nl; f. 2005; Chair. and CEO PAUL C. VAN GELDER.

RWE Obragas NV: POB 300, 5700 AH Helmond; tel. (49) 2594888; fax (49) 2594990; internet www.rwe.nl.

Water

Nuon NV: see Electricity.

Vewin: Sir Winston Churchilllaan 273, POB 1019, 2280 CA Rijswijk; tel. (70) 4144750; fax (70) 4144420; e-mail info@vewin.nl; internet www.vewin.nl; f. 1952; Chair Dr C. P. VEERMAN; Dir J. J. SCHMITZ.

TRADE UNIONS

Central federations and affiliated unions are mainly organized on a religious, political or economic basis. The most important unions are those of the transport, metal, building and textile industries, the civil service and agriculture.

Central Federations

Christelijk Nationaal Vakverbond in Nederland (CNV) (Christian National Federation of Trade Unions): Tiberdreef 4, POB 2475, 3500 GL Utrecht; tel. (30) 7511001; fax (30) 7511109; e-mail cnvinfo@cnv.nl; internet www.cnv.nl; f. 1909; affiliated to ITUC and European Trade Union Confederation; Pres. JAAP SMIT; 350,000 mems.

Federatie Nederlandse Vakbeweging (FNV) (Netherlands Trade Union Confederation): Naritaweg 10, POB 8456, 1005 AL Amsterdam; tel. (20) 5816300; fax (20) 5816319; e-mail persvoorlichting@vc.fnv.nl; internet www.fnv.nl; f. 1975 as confederation of the Netherlands Federation of Trade Unions (f. 1906) and the Netherlands Catholic Trade Union Federation (f. 1909); Pres. TON HEERTS; 1,367,848 mems (Dec. 2011).

Vakcentrale voor Middengroepen en Hoger Personeel (MHP) (Federation for Professional and Managerial Staff): Bezuidenhoutseweg 60, 2594 AW The Hague; tel. (70) 3499740; e-mail info@vc-mhp.nl; internet www.vakcentralemhp.nl; f. 1974; mem. of the European Trade Union Confederation; Pres. REGINALD VISSER; 125,000 mems.

Consultative Organization

Stichting van de Arbeid (Labour Foundation): Bezuidenhoutseweg 60, POB 90405, 2509 LK The Hague; tel. (70) 3499577; fax (70) 3499796; e-mail info@stvda.nl; internet www.stvda.nl; f. 1945; central organ of co-operation and consultation between employers and employees; 16 bd mems; Jt Pres B. E. M. WIENTJES, A. J. M. HEERTS.

Land Reclamation and Development

Without intensive land-protection schemes, nearly the whole of the north and west of the Netherlands (about one-half of the total area of the country) would be inundated by sea water twice a day. A large part of the country (including a section of the former Zuiderzee, now the IJsselmeer) has already been drained.

The Delta Plan, which was adopted in 1958 and provided for the construction of eight dams, a major canal, several locks and a system of dykes, aimed to shorten the southern coastline by 700 km and to protect the estuaries of Zeeland and Southern Holland. The final cost of the delta works project, which had originally been projected at 2,500m. guilders, totalled around 14,000m. guilders, as the result of a complex adaptation to ensure the preservation of the delta's ecological balance.

Transport

RAILWAYS

At the end of 2011 there was a total track network of 3,013 km, of which 2,266 km were electrified. The infrastructure of the Dutch railway network remains wholly under public ownership. Until early 2002 the main railway operator, Nederlandse Spoorwegen (NS), was partially privatized, but, following a sharp deterioration in the quality of service, it was taken back under government control. NS retains a majority of the passenger and freight rolling stock, and station premises, while there is a small number of additional, privately owned network service providers.

NS (Nederlandse Spoorwegen NV—Dutch Rail): POB 2025, 3500 HA Utrecht; Laan van Puntenberg 100, 3511 ER Utrecht; tel. (30) 2359111; fax (30) 2332458; internet www.ns.nl; f. 1937; partially privatized until early 2002, when the Govt reasserted management control; operates passenger services on most railway lines in the Netherlands; Pres. and Man. Dir BERT MEERSTADT.

Arriva Nederland: Trambaan 3, POB 626, 8440 AP Heerenveen; tel. (51) 36558511; fax (51) 3655808; internet www.arriva.nl; f. 1999; operates 100 trains and 1,000 buses, including cross-border rail services into Germany; Man. Dir ANNE HETTINGA.

ProRail: POB 2038, 3500 GA Utrecht; Moreelsepark 3, 3511 EP Utrecht; tel. (30) 2357104; fax (30) 2359056; internet www.prorail.nl; f. 2003; manages and maintains railway infrastructure, and controls passenger and freight traffic; independent; Chair. MARION GOUT-VAN SINDEREN.

DB Schenker Rail Nederland NV: Moreelspark 1, 3511 Utrecht; tel. (30) 2358347; fax (30) 2353666; e-mail jelle.rebbers@dbschenker.com; internet www.rail.dbschenker.nl; fmrly Railion Nederland; international goods transport by rail; Man. Dir Dr AART KLOMPE.

ROADS

In 2010 there were 2,646 km of motorways, 2,463 km of main roads, 7,861 km of secondary roads and 124,377 km of other roads in the Netherlands.

INLAND WATERWAYS

An extensive network of rivers and canals navigable for ships of 50 metric tons and over, totalling 6,104 km in 2010, has led to the outstanding development of Dutch inland shipping. About one-third of goods transported inside the Netherlands are carried on the canals and waterways. The main commercial waterways have a total length of 2,200 km, and account for about 40% of international freight movements in the country. Dutch inland shipping has access to Germany and France along the Rhine and its branch rivers, and to France and Belgium along the Meuse and Scheldt (including the Rhine-Scheldt link). Ocean traffic reaches Rotterdam via the New Waterway, and the 21-km long North Sea Canal connects Amsterdam to the North Sea.

SHIPPING

The Netherlands is one of the world's leading shipping countries. At the end of 2012 the flag registered fleet comprised 2,262 vessels, with a combined displacement of 8.1m. grt. of which 287 were tanks and 666 were general cargo ships The Port of Rotterdam complex, incorporating Europoort (for large oil tankers and bulk carriers), is the main European Union port and the busiest in the world.

Principal Companies

Amasus Shipping BV Delfzijl: Zijlvest 22–26, Farmsum, POB 250, 9930 Delfzijl; tel. (596) 649800; fax (596) 649801; e-mail agency@amasus.nl; internet www.amasus.nl; shipowners, managers and operators.

Koninklijke Wagenborg BV: Marktstraat 10, POB 14, 9930 AA Delfzyl; tel. (596) 636911; fax (596) 636250; e-mail info@wagenborg.com; internet www.wagenborg.com; shipowners, managers and operators; Man. Dirs Dr E. VUURSTEEN, Dr G. R. WAGENBORG.

Seatrade Groningen BV: Laan Corpus den Hoorn 200, POB 858, 9700 AW Groningen; tel. (50) 5215300; fax (50) 5215399; e-mail info@seatrade.nl; internet www.seatrade.nl; shipowners, managers and operators; Man. Dir Capt. MARK JANSEN.

Spliethoff's Bevrachtingskantoor BV: POB 409, 1000 AK Amsterdam; Radarweg 36, 1042 AA Amsterdam; tel. (20) 4488400; fax (20) 4488500; e-mail gogracht@spliethoff.com; internet www.spliethoff.com; f. 1921; shipowners, managers and operators.

Stena Line: POB 2, 3150 AA Hoek van Holland; Stationsweg 10, 3151 HS oek van Holland; tel. (17) 4389333; fax (17) 4389389; e-mail info.nl@stenaline.com; internet www.stenaline.nl; operates daily (day and night) ferry services for accompanied private cars, commercial freight vehicles and trailers between Hoek van Holland and Harwich (UK); Man. Dir CARL-JOHAN HAGMAN.

Van der Helm–Hudig: Orionweg 6-8, 4782 SC Moerdijk; tel. (10) 2995750; fax (10) 5069126; e-mail info@hudig.nl; internet www.hudig.com; f. 1795; international freight services; Van der Helm Transport Group took over Hudig Freight Services in 2007; Mems, Managing Bd GERARD VAN DER HELM, RICHARD VAN DER HELM, GERARD VAN DER WERFF.

Van Uden Maritime BV: POB 1123, 3000 BC, Rotterdam; Brielselaan 85, 3081 AB Rotterdam; tel. (10) 2973100; fax (10) 4851044; e-mail group@van-uden.nl; internet www.van-uden.nl; f. 1848; agencies in Rotterdam, Amsterdam; liner operators and representatives; international chartering; Man. Dir JASPER BROCADES ZAALBERG.

Vopak: Westerlaan 10, POB 863, 3000 AW Rotterdam; tel. (10) 4002911; fax (10) 4139829; internet www.vopak.com; f. 1999; Chair. EELCO HOEKSTRA.

Vroon BV: POB 28, 4510 AA Breskens; Haven Westzijde 21, 4511 AR Breskens; tel. (117) 384910; fax (117) 384218; e-mail info@vroon.nl; internet www.vroon.nl; shipowners, managers and operators; Man. Dir COCO VROON.

Wijnne & Barends' Cargadoors- en Agentuurkantonen BV: POB 123, 9930 AC Delfzijl; Handelskade Oost 5, 9934 AR Delfzijl; tel. (596) 637777; fax (596) 637790; e-mail info@wijnne-barends.nl; internet www.wijnne-barends.nl; f. 1855; became part of Spliethoff Group in 2003; shipowners, managers and operators; cargo services and agents.

Shipping Associations

Federatie van Werknemers in de Zeevaart (Dutch Seafarers' Federation): Heemraadssingel 323, POB 25131, 3001 HC Rotterdam; tel. (10) 4771188; fax (10) 4773846; e-mail fwz.nl@wxs.nl; f. 1967.

Koninklijke Vereniging van Nederlandse Reders (KVNR) (Royal Asscn of Netherlands' Shipowners): Bldg Willemswerf, 15th Floor, Boompjes 40, 3011 XB Rotterdam; tel. (10) 4146001; fax (10) 2330081; e-mail info@kvnr.nl; internet www.kvnr.nl; f. 1905; Chair. T. NETELENBOS; Dir MARTIN DORSMAN; 400 mems.

Vereniging Nederlandse Scheepsbouw Industrie (VNSI) (Netherlands Shipbuilding Industry Asscn): Boompjes 40, 3011 XB Rotterdam; tel. (10) 4444333; fax (10) 2130700; e-mail info@scheepsbouw.nl; internet www.vnsi.nl; promotes Dutch shipbuilding on a national basis; Chair J. J. C. M. VAN DOOREMALEN; 95 mems.

CIVIL AVIATION

The main Dutch airport is at Schiphol, near Amsterdam. There are also international airports at Zestienhoven for Rotterdam, Beek for Maastricht, Eelde for Groningen, and at Eindhoven.

KLM (Koninklijke Luchtvaart Maatschappij) NV (Royal Dutch Airlines): POB 7700, 1117 ZL Schiphol; Amsterdamseweg 55, 1182 GP Amstelveen; tel. (20) 6499123; fax (20) 6488069; internet www.klm.com; f. 1919; merged with Air France in 2004 to form holding co Air France–KLM; regular international air services; subsidiaries: KLM Cityhopper, transavia.com; Pres. and CEO PETER F. HARTMAN.

Martinair Holland NV: Piet Guilonardweg 17, 1117 EE Schiphol; tel. (20) 6011100; fax (20) 6011303; internet www.martinair.nl; f. 1958; world-wide passenger and cargo services; Pres. and CEO PAUL GREGOROWITSCH.

transavia.com: Piet Guilonardweg 15, POB 7777, 1118 ZM Schiphol Airport; tel. (20) 6046555; internet transavia.com; f. 1965 as Transavia Limburg NV; scheduled and charter services to leisure destinations; subsidiary of KLM; Chair., Supervisory Bd HANS BAKKER; CEO BRAM GRÄBER.

Tourism

The principal tourist attractions in the Netherlands are the cosmopolitan city of Amsterdam (which receives nearly one-half of all tourist visits), the historic towns, the canals, the cultivated fields of spring flowers, the outlying islands, the art galleries and modern architecture. Some 11.3m. foreign tourists stayed in hotels and boarding houses in the Netherlands in 2011. Receipts from tourism (excluding passenger transport) totalled a provisional US $14,445m. in 2011.

Nederlands Bureau voor Toerisme & Congressen (NBTC) (Netherlands Board for Tourism & Conventions): Prinses Catharina Amaliastraat 5, POB 63470, 2496 XD The Hague; tel. (70) 3705705; fax (70) 3705343; e-mail info@holland.com; internet www.holland .com; f. 1968; Man. Dir JOS VRANKEN.

Royal Dutch Touring Club ANWB: POB 93200, 2596 EC The Hague; tel. (70) 3147147; fax (70) 3146969; e-mail info@anwb.nl; internet www.anwb.nl; f. 1883; CEO GUIDO H. N. L. VAN WOERKOM; 55 brs in Europe; 4m. mems.

Defence

The Netherlands is a member of the North Atlantic Treaty Organization (NATO). Conscription to the armed forces was ended in August 1996, and a gradual reduction in the number of military personnel is ongoing. The total strength of the armed forces, as assessed at November 2012, was 37,400: army 20,850; navy 8,500; air force 8,050. In addition, the Royal Military Constabulary numbered 5,900. Total reserves stood at 3,200 (army 2,700; air force 420; navy 80; military police 80). In August 1995 a joint Dutch-German army corps, numbering 28,000 troops, was inaugurated, and in January 1996 the operational units of the Royal Netherlands Navy merged with the Belgian navy under the command of the Admiral of the Benelux. In November 2004 the European Union agreed to create a number of 'battlegroups' (each comprising about 1,500 men), which could be deployed at short notice to carry out peace-keeping activities at crisis points around the world. The battlegroups, two of which were to be ready for deployment at any one time, following a rotational schedule, reached full operational capacity from 1 January 2007. The Netherlands was committed to contributing troops to two of the battlegroups; one with the participation of Germany and Finland, and one with the United Kingdom.

General Government Defence Expenditure: €7,870m. in 2013.

Chief of Defence Staff: Gen. TOM MIDDENDORP.

Secretary-General of Defence Staff: ANTONIUS HERMANUS CHRISTOFFEL (TON) ANNINK.

Education

There are two types of school in the Netherlands: public schools, which are maintained by municipalities, and attended by about one-third of all school children; and private schools, which are, for the most part, denominational and are attended by almost two-thirds of the school-going population. Both types of school are fully subsidized by the state. Schools are administered by school boards, responsible to the local authorities or to the private organizations that operate them, thus providing teachers with considerable freedom. The Ministry of Education, Culture and Science, advised by an education council, is responsible for educational legislation and its enforcement.

Full-time education is compulsory in the Netherlands from five to 16 years of age, and part-time education is compulsory for a further two years. Pre-primary education, also known as early childhood education, is offered to educationally disadvantaged children between the ages of two and five years. Almost 99% of children of four years of age attend *Basisschool*, although it is not compulsory until the age of five years. Primary education lasts for eight years and is followed by various types of secondary education. Secondary education lasts to the age of 18 years, and is provided free of charge. In 2010/11 total enrolment in primary education included 100% of children in the relevant age-group, while total enrolment in secondary education included 87% of children in the relevant age-group. Pre-university schools provide various six-year courses that prepare pupils for university education. General secondary education comprises senior and junior secondary schools, providing five- and four-year courses that prepare pupils for higher vocational institutes and senior secondary vocational education, respectively. In all types there is latitude in the choice of subjects taken. Higher education comprises higher professional education (*hoger beroepsonderwijs*—HBO) and university education (*wetenschappelijk onderwijs*—WO). In 2010/11 some 241,700 students were enrolled at the Netherlands' 13 universities, while some 416,900 students were enrolled at the 50 institutes of higher vocational education. In addition, students can register with the Open Universiteit Nederland (Open University).

Total government expenditure on education was an estimated €33,243m. in 2011.

NETHERLANDS DEPENDENCIES

Ministry of the Interior and Kingdom Relations: Schedeldoekshaven 200, POB 20011, 2500 EA The Hague; tel. (70) 4266426; fax (70) 3639153; internet www.rijksoverheid.nl/ministeries/bzk.
Minister of the Interior and Kingdom Relations: RONALD PLASTERK.

Netherlands Special Municipalities

Following the dissolution of the Netherlands Antilles on 10 October 2010, Bonaire, Saba and Sint (St) Eustatius adopted the status of *bijzondere gemeente* (special municipalities) within the Kingdom of the Netherlands.

BONAIRE

Introductory Survey

Bonaire lies about 80 km (50 miles) off the coast of Venezuela. The territory, some 288 sq km (111 sq miles), consists of Bonaire and, nestled in its western crescent, the uninhabited islet of Klein Bonaire. Together with Aruba and Curaçao, Bonaire forms the Benedenwindse Eilands or Leeward Islands. The climate is tropical, moderated by the sea, with an average annual temperature of 27.5°C (81°F) and little rainfall. The official languages are Dutch and Papiamento (a mixture of Dutch, Spanish, Portuguese, English, Arawak Indian and several West African dialects), which is the dominant language of the Leeward Islands. Almost all of the inhabitants, which numbered 13,389 at 1 January 2010, profess Christianity, predominantly Roman Catholicism. The population density of the territory was 46.5 per sq km in January 2010. The state flag (proportions 2 by 3) has a large blue triangle in the lower right corner and a smaller yellow triangle in the upper left corner. The triangles are separated by a white strip, inside of which is a black compass and a red six-pointed star (each point represents one of the original six villages of Bonaire). The capital is Kralendijk, on the western coast of the island.

The Leeward Islands, already settled by communities of Arawak Indians, were discovered by the Spanish in 1499 and were seized by the Dutch in the 1630s. After frequent changes in possession, the islands (including Aruba) were finally confirmed as Dutch territory in 1816. Together with the Windward Islands (comprising Sint (St) Eustatius, Saba and Sint (St) Maarten), Bonaire was administered as Curaçao and Dependencies between 1845 and 1948. Slavery was abolished in 1863. During the Second World War Queen Wilhelmina of the Netherlands promised independence, and in 1954 a Charter gave the federation of six islands full autonomy in domestic affairs, and declared it to be an integral part of the Kingdom of the Netherlands.

From 1954 until 2010 Bonaire was a constituent part of the Netherlands Antilles (a six-member federation until 1986 when Aruba gained separate status). Political allegiances were generally divided along island, rather than policy, lines. This led to a series of unstable coalitions governing the federation. By the early 1990s it had become clear that although the metropolitan Dutch Government was unwilling to allow the complete disintegration of the federation, it would consider a less centralized system, or the creation of two federations in the separate island groups.

A referendum on status was conducted on Bonaire in October 1994 (simultaneous plebiscites were also held on St Maarten, St Eustatius and Saba). Some 88% of voters favoured continued federation with the Netherlands.

On 8 October 2004 the Jesurun Commission, established by the Dutch and Antillean Governments and headed by Edsel Jesurun (a former Governor of the Netherlands Antilles), recommended the dissolution of the Netherlands Antilles. The Commission proposed that Bonaire, along with Saba and St Eustatius, should be directly administered by the Dutch Government. In September, in an official referendum, a majority of voters (59%) on Bonaire strongly favoured becoming part of the Netherlands. On 3 December 2005 a preliminary agreement with the Dutch Government that the extant federation be dissolved by 1 July 2007 was duly signed in Curaçao. Under the new structure, Bonaire was to become a *koninkrijseilande*, or 'kingdom island', with direct ties to the Netherlands, a status equivalent to that of a Dutch province. The future status of Bonaire was subsequently refined to that of a *bijzondere gemeete*, or 'special municipality', similar in most ways to other metropolitan Dutch municipalities, although with separate social security and currency arrangements.

An agreement confirming Bonaire's impending accession to 'special municipality' status was signed in The Hague, Netherlands, on 12 October 2006, and included provisions for citizens of the island to participate in Dutch national and local elections and in the election of candidates to the European Parliament. A further 'transition accord' was signed by the Netherlands Antilles central Government, the Island Council of Bonaire, and the Netherlands on 12 February 2007, envisaging Bonaire's complete secession from the federation. Under the terms of this covenant, the Netherlands was to pledge over NA Fl. 1,000m. (in addition to existing financial assistance) to facilitate the process of disintegration, with each participating island receiving individual allocations. The metropolitan administration also agreed to write off almost three-quarters of the Antilles' debt.

Following further negotiations, a meeting was held in Curaçao on 15 December 2008 at which the Dutch Prime Minister, Jan Peter Balkenende, and the Antillean premier, Emily de Jongh-Elhage, signed an agreement confirming the new status of the island. At the end of September 2009, at a meeting of the Dutch State Secretary for the Interior and Kingdom Relations, Ank Bijleveld-Schouten, and representatives of the Netherlands Antilles, it was agreed that the target date for dissolution of the federation would be 10 October 2010.

The Dutch Government postponed the payment of Bonaire's debt in October 2009, after the island's recently formed Executive Council, led by the Partido Demokrátiko Boneriano (PDB), proposed a 'free association' status with the Netherlands, involving greater independence, rather than the planned integration as a municipality. The Dutch Government asserted the island could adopt municipality status, as planned, or assume full self-governance. None the less, the Executive Council proceeded to schedule a referendum on its proposal. Acting on the advice of Bonaire's Lieutenant-Governor, in February 2010 Goedgedrag cancelled the referendum due to be conducted in March, on the grounds that it contravened international law, as Dutch nationals who had only resided on Bonaire since January 2007 would have been barred from voting. Nevertheless, the referendum was held in December 2010, although the low turn-out meant the result was declared invalid. The Unión Patriótico Boneriano (UPB), which had taken office in September, had urged the electorate to boycott the plebiscite.

On 10 October 2010, following the formal dissolution of the Netherlands Antilles, Bonaire officially became a special municipality of the Netherlands. The US dollar was formally adopted as the island's currency from 1 January 2011, replacing the Netherlands Antilles guilder; the Island Council had opposed the introduction of the euro, the currency of the Netherlands.

At elections to the Island Council on 2 March 2011, the UPB secured four of the nine seats available. The PDB won three seats and the recently formed Movementu Boneiru Liber and Partido Pro Hustisia & Union each won one seat. A coalition government was subsequently formed. Lydia Emerencia was sworn in as the island's new Lieutenant-Governor in March 2012.

Owing to Bonaire's change in administrative status, the island's residents were henceforth entitled to vote in Dutch polls. The islanders first opportunity to exercise this right came on 12 September 2012, when elections to the Tweede Kamer (Second Chamber—the lower house of the Dutch parliament) were conducted. The Partij van de Arbeid received 23.9% of the valid votes cast in Bonaire, while the Volkspartij voor Vrijheid en Democratie garnered 20.9%, the Christen Democratisch Appèl 19.3% and Democraten 66 11.5%. The rate of participation by the electorate was just 24.8% (compared with 74.6% nation-wide). Commentators attributed this very low turn-out to a lack of campaigning on the island.

Bonaire's economy is dependent on tourism and petroleum transfers. There was a 9.9% decrease in visitor numbers in 2009, following a fall in tourist arrivals from the lucrative North American market.

Although no refining takes place on the island, the Bonaire Petroleum Corporation stores oil for transfer from large tankers to smaller ones and is a significant contributor to the economy. Bonaire has reserves of limestone and salt, which are mined; salt production averaged 400,000 metric tons per year. There is also a textile factory. Bonaire is a major exporter of aloes. In 2012 the annual inflation rate was 2.9%.

PUBLIC HOLIDAYS

In addition to the holidays of the metropolitan Netherlands, Bonaire celebrates the following public holidays.

2014: 1 January (New Year's Day), 3 March (Carnival), 1 May (Labour Day), 29 May (Ascension Day), 6 September (Flag Day), 15 December (Kingdom Day).

For statistical information on Bonaire, see the Statistical Survey in Curaçao.

Directory

The Government

HEAD OF STATE

King of the Netherlands: HM King WILLEM-ALEXANDER.

Lieutenant-Governor: LYDIA EMERENCIA, Bestuurskantoor, Wilhelminaplein 1, Kralendijk; tel. 717-5330; fax 717-2824; e-mail gezag@bonairelive.com; internet www.bonairegov.an.

ISLAND COUNCIL
(May 2013)

The Government is formed by a coalition of the Unión Patriótico Boneriano (UPB), Partido Demokrátiko Boneriano (PDB), Partido Pro Hustisia & Union (PHU) and Movementu Boneiru Liber (MBL).

Island Council: CLARK ABRAHAM (PDB), ROBERT BEUKENBOOM (PDB), NOLLY OLEANA (PDB), MELENA WINKLAAR (UPB), EVELINA BETANCOURT-ANTHONY (UPB), JEFFERY LEVENSTONE (UPB), MARITZA SILBERIE (UPB), BENITO DIRKSZ (MBL), RAFAEL SANTANA (PHU).

Island Secretary: NEREIDA M. GONZALES.

Election, 2 March 2011

Party	Seats
Unión Patriótico Boneriano (UPB)	4
Partido Democrátiko Boneriano (PDB) . . .	3
Movementu Boneiru Liber (MBL)	1
Partido Pro Hustisia & Unio (PHU)	1
Total	**9**

Executive Council: PABLO JAMES KROON, BURNEY EL HAGE, SILVANA SERFILIA.

MINISTRY

National Office for the Caribbean Netherlands Bonaire (Rijksdienst Caribisch Nederland Bonaire): Kaya International z/n, POB 357, Kralendijk; tel. 715-8303; fax 715-8330; e-mail info@rijksvertegenwoordiger.nl; internet www.rijksdienstcn.com; Kingdom Rep. WILBERT STOLTE.

Political Organizations

Movementu Boneiru Liber (MBL) (Free Bonaire Movement): Passangrahan, Plasa Reina Wilhelmina, Kralendijk; tel. 717-4008; fax 717-6125; e-mail movementu@gmail.com; internet www.vota-mbl.com; f. 2010; Leader BENITO DIRKSZ; Sec. JOSÉ A. E. CAPELLA.

Partido Demokrátiko Boneriano (PDB) (Bonaire Democratic Party): Kaya America 13A, POB 294, Kralendijk; tel. 717-8903; fax 717-5923; e-mail info@partido-demokrat.org; internet partido-demokrat.org; f. 1954; also known as Democratische Partij—Bonaire (DPB); liberal, promotes self-governance for Bonaire; known as the Aliansa Demokratika Bonairiana in 2009–10; Leader ROBBY BEUKENBOOM.

Partido Pro Hustisia & Union (PHU): Kralendijk; tel. 796-2650; e-mail m.bijkerk@telbonet.an; f. 2010; Pres. RAFAEL A. SANTANA.

Unión Patriótico Boneriano (UPB) (Patriotic Union of Bonaire): Kaya Sabana 22, Kralendijk; tel. 717-8906; fax 717-5552; internet votaupb.com; f. 1969; 2,134 mems; Christian democratic; Leader RAMOSITO T. BOOI; Sec.-Gen. C. V. WINKLAAR.

Religion

Almost all of the inhabitants profess Christianity, predominantly Roman Catholicism.

The Press

Arco Bonaire: Kaya Isabel 1, Kralendijk; tel. 717-2427; e-mail info@arcocarib.com; internet www.arcocarib.com; magazine; Editor M. BIJKERK L. M.

Bonaire Reporter: Kaya Gob. Debrot 200-6, POB 407, Kralendijk; tel. and fax 786-6125; fax 786-6518; e-mail info@bonairenews.com; internet www.bonairereporter.com; English; weekly; Publ. GEORGE DESALVO; Editor-in-Chief LAURA DESALVO.

Broadcasting and Communications

TELECOMMUNICATIONS

Chippie Bonaire: Kaya Caracas 2, Kralendijk; tel. 717-0117; fax 717-0119; e-mail info@uts.an; internet www.chippie.an; mobile telecommunication provider; subsidiary of UTS Group, Curaçao.

Digicel Bonaire: Kaya Grandi 26, Kralendijk; tel. 717-4400; fax 717-4466; e-mail customercare@digicelcuracao.com; internet www.digicelbonaire.com; f. 1999; bought majority shareholding of Antilliano Por NV in April 2006; Digicel acquired mobile business of TELBO (Bonaire) in Dec. 2006; Chair. DENIS O'BRIEN; CEO (Dutch Caribbean) SANDER GIELEN.

Telbo NV (Telefonia Bonairiano NV): Kaya Libertador Simon Bolivar 8, Kralendijk; tel. 715-7000; fax 717-5007; e-mail info@telbo.an; internet www.telbo.an; f. 1983; owned by Bonaire Holding Maatschappij (govt-controlled holding co); fixed-line telecommunications and internet service provider; Gen. Man. GILBERT DE BREE.

BROADCASTING

Radio

Radiodifusión Boneriana NV: Kaya Gobernador Nicolaas Debrot 2, Kralendijk; tel. 717-5947; fax 717-8220; e-mail vozdibonaire@gmail.com; internet www.vozdibonaire.com; f. 1962; Owner FELICIANO DA SILVA PILOTO.

Alpha FM: broadcasts in Spanish.

Mega FM: internet www.megahitfm.com; broadcasts in Dutch.

Voz di Bonaire (PJB2) (Voice of Bonaire): broadcasts in Papiamento.

Trans World Radio (TWR): Kaya Gobernador N. Debrot 64, Kralendijk; tel. 717-8800; fax 717-8808; e-mail 800am@twr.org; internet www.twr.org; f. 1964; religious, educational and cultural station; programmes to South, Central and North America, and Caribbean in five languages; Pres. LAUREN LIBBY; Station Dir JOSEPH BARKER.

Television

Relay stations provide Bonaire with television programmes from Curaçao.

Finance

BANKING

Regulatory Authority

College Financieel Toezicht (CFT): De Rouvilleweg 39, Willemstad, Curaçao; tel. (9) 461–9081; e-mail info@cft.an; internet www.cft.an; f. 2007; bd of financial supervision; oversees financial administration in Bonaire, Sint Eustatius and Saba; Age BAKKER; Rep. of Bonaire, Saba and St Eustatius THEODORE M. PANDT.

Commercial Banks

Girobank, NV: 12 Kaya L.D. Gerharts, Kralendijk; tel. 717-8115; e-mail info@gironet.com; internet www.girobank.net; f. 1965; Pres. and CEO ERIC GARCIA; Man. JOAN SILIE.

Maduro & Curiel's Bank (Bonaire), NV: 1 Kaya L. D. Gerharts, Kralendijk; tel. 715-5520; e-mail info@mcbbonaire.com; internet www.mcbbonaire.com; Man. Dir EVERT PIAR.

Banking Associations

Bonaire Bankers' Association: Maduro & Curiel's Bank (Bonaire) NV, Kaya L. D. Gerharts 1, POB 366, Kralendijk; tel. 717-5520; fax 717-5884; Man. Dir RUDY GOMEZ.

INSURANCE

ENNIA Bonaire: Centrumgebied z/n, POB 349, Kralendijk; tel. 717-8546; fax 717-7546; e-mail mail@ennia.com; internet www.ennia-bonaire.com; f. 1948; part of ENNIA Caribe Holding, NV; Man. PATRICK THISSEN.

NAGICO Bonaire (National General Insurance Corpn): Kaya Gilberto F. Betico Croes 2, Kralendijk; tel. 717-3022; fax 717-3029; e-mail info.bonaire@nagico.com; internet www.nagico.com; Exec. Dir DETLEF HOOYBOER; Man. UNDINE POURIER.

RSA Bonaire: Bonaire District Plaza, Unit 4, Kaya Gobernador Debrot, Kralendijk; tel. 717-2080; fax 717-2112; e-mail insurance@an.rsagroup.com; internet www.rsa-abc.com; f. 1889; Man. NORMIGIA ILARIO.

Trade and Industry

CHAMBER OF COMMERCE

Bonaire Chamber of Commerce and Industry: Kaya Grandi 67, POB 52, Kralendijk; tel. 717-5595; fax 717-8995; e-mail office@kvkbonaire.com; internet www.bonairechamber.com; Chair. EVERT PIAR.

UTILITIES

EcoPower Bonaire BV: Kaminda Turistiko 1000, Postbus 281, Kralendijk; tel. 701-8323; e-mail info@ecopowerbonaire-bv.com; internet www.ecopowerbonaire-bv.com; f. 2007; consortium of Econcern (Germany), MAN (Germany) and Enercon (Netherlands); sustainable energy producer; Plant Man. VINCENT KOOIJ.

Water & Energiebedrijf Bonaire (WEB) NV: Kaya Carlos A. Nicolaas 3, POB 381, Kralendijk; tel. 715-8244; fax 717-8756; e-mail web@web.an; internet webbonaire.com; f. 1978; Gen. Man. PEDRO HUBERT DE PALM.

TRADE UNIONS

Algemene Federatie van Bonaireaanse Werknemers (AFBW): Kaya Korona 13, Kralendijk; tel. 717-5437; Pres. NILCO ROLLAN.

Federashon Bonaireana di Trabou (FEDEBON): Kaya Krabè 6, POB 324, Nikiboko; tel. and fax 717-8845; e-mail geroldbernabela@bonairelive.com; Pres. GEROLD BERNABELA.

Transport

There are no railways, but Bonaire has a network of all-weather roads. There is public transportation on the island in the form of buses, mini-vans and taxis.

SHIPPING

There are no ferry services between Bonaire and neighbouring islands; however, there are chartered boats. The port of Kralendijk has piers for dry cargo transfer and cruise vessels. At 31 December 2012 the flag registered fleet comprised two vessels, totalling 1,573 grt.

Bonaire Port Authority, NV: Fort Oranje, Harbour Office, Kralendijk; tel. 717-8151; fax 717-8797.

Rocargo Services Bonaire, NV: Kaya Industria No. 12, POB 20, Kralendijk; tel. 717-8922; fax 717-8524; e-mail rocargobonaire@rocargo.com; internet www.rocargo.com; f. 1982; ship and liner agency, cargo and freight handlers; Man. MARIELA GOELOE DORTALINA.

CIVIL AVIATION

Bonaire International Airport, NV (Flamingo Airport) at Kralendijk has a runway of 2,880 m (9,449 ft). Bonaire is served by numerous airlines (including KLM, Air Berlin and United Airlines), linking the island with destinations in the Caribbean, Europe, the USA and South America.

Bonaire International Airport, NV (Flamingo Airport): Plasa Medardo SV Thielman 1, Kralendijk; tel. 717-5600; fax 717-5607; e-mail info@flamingoairport.com; internet www.flamingoairport.com; f. 1945; Man. Dir GEORGE SOLIANA.

Tourism

Bonaire's attractions include scuba-diving and snorkelling facilities, flamingo and donkey sanctuaries, Bonaire National Marine Park, the historic rock paintings of Caquieto Indians and the white, sandy beaches. In 2009 visitor arrivals to the island totalled 67,000 and tourism receipts totalled an estimated US $106m.

Bonaire Hotel and Tourism Association (BONHATA): Kaya Soeur Bartola 15B, POB 358, Kralendijk; tel. 717-5134; fax 717-8534; e-mail info@bonhata.org; internet www.ilovebonaire.com; f. 1980; Pres. CRAIG DEWEY; CEO IRENE DINGJAN.

Tourism Corporation Bonaire (TCB): Kaya Grandi 2, Kralendijk; tel. 717-8322; fax 717-8408; e-mail info@tourismbonaire.com; internet www.tourismbonaire.com; Dir ETHSEL PIETERNELLA.

Defence

The Netherlands is responsible for the defence of Bonaire.

Education

The education system is the same as that of the Netherlands. Dutch is the principal language of instruction, although instruction in Papiamento is also used in primary schools. Education was made compulsory on Bonaire in 1992.

SABA

The small, volcanic island of Saba lies in the north-eastern Caribbean Sea, about 27 km (17 miles) north-west of Sint (St) Eustatius. With Sint (St) Maarten, 45 km (28 miles) north of Saba, these three islands comprise the Bovenwindse Eilands, or Windward Islands, although actually in the Leeward group of the Lesser Antilles. Saba is 13 sq km (5 sq miles) in area. The climate is tropical, moderated by the sea, with an average annual temperature of 27.5°C (81°F) and little rainfall. English is the official and principal language, although Dutch is also spoken. Almost all of the inhabitants, of which there were 1,737 in January 2010, profess Christianity, predominantly Roman Catholicism. The population density of the territory was 133.6 in January 2010. The state flag (proportions 2 by 3) is divided into four triangles, two red at the top, two blue at the bottom. In the centre of the flag is a white diamond, with a yellow five-pointed star in the centre. The capital is The Bottom.

The Dutch captured Saba, once settled by Carib Indians, in 1640. After frequent changes in possession, the islands were finally confirmed as Dutch territory in 1816, administered by the Dutch West Indian Company (WIC). Owing to its difficult terrain, Saba remained sparsely populated. In 1845 Saba was ceded to the Dutch Crown and administered as Curaçao and Dependencies, comprising the Windward Islands and the three territories of the Leeward Islands—Aruba, Bonaire and Curaçao. During the Second World War Queen Wilhelmina of the Netherlands promised independence, and in 1954 a Charter gave the federation of six islands full autonomy in domestic affairs, and declared the Netherlands Antilles to be an integral part of the Kingdom of the Netherlands.

Despite the 1954 Charter, there were demands for further self-government from elements within the federation for most of the latter half of the 20th century. A referendum on the status issue was held on Saba in October 1994; 91% of voters opted for continued membership of the Antillean federation. Nevertheless, similar plebiscites in the other constituent members of the Netherlands Antilles produced differing results and in October 2004 the Jesurun Commission, established by the Dutch and Antillean Governments and headed by Edsel Jesurun (a former Governor of the Netherlands Antilles), recommended the dissolution of the federation. The Commission proposed that Saba (as well as Bonaire and St Eustatius) should be directly administered by the Dutch Government. In November, in another official referendum, a majority of voters (86%) on Saba again voted in favour of becoming part of the Netherlands. On 3 December 2005 a preliminary agreement with the Dutch Government that the extant federation be dissolved by 1 July 2007 was duly signed in Curaçao. Under the new structure, Saba was to become *koninkrijkseilande*, or 'kingdom island', with direct ties to the Netherlands, a status equivalent to that of a Dutch province. The future status of Saba was subsequently refined to that of a *bijzondere gemeete*, or 'special municipality', similar in most ways to other metropolitan Dutch municipalities, although with separate social security and currency arrangements.

An agreement confirming Saba's impending accession to 'special municipality' status was signed in The Hague, Netherlands, on 12 October 2006, and included provisions for citizens of the island to participate in Dutch national and local elections and in the election of candidates to the European Parliament. A further 'transition accord' was signed by the Netherlands Antilles central Government, the Island Council, and the Netherlands on 12 February 2007, envisaging the island's complete secession from the federation. Under the terms of this covenant, the Netherlands was to pledge over NA Fl. 1,000m. (in addition to existing financial assistance) to facilitate the process of disintegration, with Saba, Bonaire and St Eustatius receiving individual allocations. The metropolitan administration also agreed to write off almost three-quarters of the Antilles' debt. Following further negotiations, a meeting was held in Curaçao on 15 December 2008 at which the Dutch Prime Minister, Jan Peter Balkenende, and the Antillean premier, Emily de Jongh-Elhage, signed an agreement confirming the new status of the island.

The Antilles Government's announcement in August 2009 that a general election would be held in January 2010, despite plans for the dissolution of the Netherlands Antilles to take place later that year, prompted the Executive Council of Saba to declare its intention to become independent from the Netherlands Antilles. The Island Council argued that the central Government lacked the political will to complete the transition process. However, it was generally agreed that Saba's secession from the federation at this stage would not be legally feasible. In September 2009 it was agreed that the target date for dissolution of the Netherlands Antilles would be 10 October 2010, at which date Saba would become a special municipality of the Netherlands. The US dollar was formally adopted as the island's currency from 1 January 2011, replacing the Nether-lands Antilles guilder; the Island Council had opposed the introduction of the euro, the currency of the Netherlands.

Elections to Saba's Island Council were held on 2 March 2011. The Windward Islands People's Movement won four of the five available seats, while the Saba Labour Party secured the remaining seat. The new Council was sworn into office on 11 March.

Owing to Saba's change in administrative status, the island's residents were henceforth entitled to vote in Dutch polls. The islanders first opportunity to exercise this right came on 12 September 2012, when elections to the Tweede Kamer (Second Chamber—the lower house of the Dutch parliament) were conducted. Democraten 66 received 54.5% of the valid votes cast in Saba, while the Partij van de Arbeid garnered 19.8% and the Socialistische Partij 9.0%. The rate of participation by the electorate was just 28.4% (compared with 74.6% nation-wide). Commentators attributed this very low turn-out to a lack of campaigning on the island.

Lieutenant-Governor: JONATHAN JOHNSON, 1 Power St, The Bottom; tel. 416-3311; fax 416-3274; e-mail governor@sabagov.nl; internet www.sabagovernment.com.

Island Council: ROLANDO R. W. WILSON, CARL BUNCAMPER, ISHMAEL LEVENSTONE, EVITON HEYLIGER, SHAMARA NICHOLSON.

Island Secretary: MENNO VAN DER VELDE.

Executive Council: BRUCE ZAGERS, CHRIS JOHNSON.

National Office for the Caribbean Netherlands Saba (Rijksdienst Caribisch Nederland Saba): Captain Mathew Levenstone St, Old Antique Inn, The Bottom; tel. 416-3934; e-mail info@rijksdienstcn.com; internet www.rijksdienstcn.com; Kingdom Rep. WILBERT STOLTE (resident in Bonaire).

SINT EUSTATIUS

Sint (St) Eustatius (also known as Statia—from the original Spanish name St Anastasia) is a volcanic island, some 21 sq km (8 sq miles) in area, in the north-eastern Caribbean Sea, about 20 km north-east of Saint Christopher (St Kitts) and Nevis. Together with Saba and St Maarten, St Eustatius comprises the Bovenwindse Eilands or Windward Islands (although actually in the Leeward group of the Lesser Antilles). The climate is tropical, moderated by the sea, with an average annual temperature of 27.5°C (81°F) and little rainfall. English is the official and principal language, although Dutch is also spoken. There were 2,886 inhabitants of St Eustatius in January 2010, giving a population density of 137.4. Almost all of the inhabitants profess Christianity, predominantly Protestantism. The state flag (proportions 2 by 3) is divided into four five-sided blue squares with red borders. In the centre of the flag is a white diamond, in which an outline of the island appears. At the top of the diamond is a five-pointed gold star. The capital is Oranjestad.

The Dutch settled the Windward Islands, once settled by Carib Indians, in the mid-17th century. St Eustatius came under Dutch control in 1635. After frequent changes in possession, the islands were finally confirmed as Dutch territory in 1816. Together with the Leeward Islands (comprising Aruba, Bonaire and Curaçao), the Windward islands were administered as Curaçao and Dependencies between 1845 and 1948. In the early 18th century St Eustatius prospered as a trading centre and transshipment centre for African slaves. During the Second World War Queen Wilhelmina of the Netherlands promised independence, and in 1954 a Charter gave the federation of six islands full autonomy in domestic affairs, and declared it to be an integral part of the Kingdom of the Netherlands.

Political allegiance within the federation was traditionally along island, rather than party lines. These divisions increased following Aruba's secession from the federation in 1986. Calls for further autonomy increased in Curaçao and St Maarten, although the population of St Eustatius remained broadly in favour of maintaining the status quo. In a referendum on status held in October 1994 some 86% of voters opted for continued membership of the Antillean federation. Nevertheless, plebiscites in the other constituent parts of the federation produced differing results, and in the 1990s and early 2000s movements to obtain autonomy in Curaçao and St Maarten increased. In October 2004 the Jesurun Commission, established by the Dutch and Antillean Governments and headed by Edsel Jesurun (a former Governor of the Netherlands Antilles), recommended the dissolution of the federation; support for the continued union had, it was argued, virtually disintegrated on most of the islands. The Commission proposed that Curaçao and St Maarten should become autonomous states within the Netherlands (i.e. have *status aparte*), while Saba, Bonaire and St Eustatius should be directly administered by the Dutch Government. A further referendum on the constitutional futures of St Eustatius took place on 8 April 2005: from a voter turn-out of 55%, 76% of the electorate favoured remaining part of the Netherlands Antilles, while 20% voted for closer ties with the Netherlands and 1% preferred to seek complete independence for the tiny island. On 3 December 2005 a preliminary agreement with the Dutch Government that the extant federation be dissolved by 1 July 2007 was duly signed in Curaçao. Under the new structure, St Eustatius was to become a *koninkrijseilande*, or 'kingdom island', with direct ties to the Netherlands, a status equivalent to that of a Dutch province. The future status of St Eustatius was subsequently refined to that of a *bijzondere gemeete*, or 'special municipality', similar in most ways to other metropolitan Dutch municipalities, although with separate social security and currency arrangements.

An agreement confirming St Eustatius's impending accession to 'special municipality' status was signed in The Hague, Netherlands, on 12 October 2006, and included provisions for citizens of the island to participate in Dutch national and local elections and in the election of candidates to the European Parliament. A further 'transition accord' was signed by the Netherlands Antilles central Government, the Island Council of St Eustatius, and the Netherlands on 12 February 2007, envisaging the island's complete secession from the federation. Under the terms of this covenant, the Netherlands was to pledge over NA Fl. 1,000m. (in addition to existing financial assistance) to facilitate the process of disintegration, with St Eustatius, Saba and Bonaire receiving individual allocations. The metropolitan administration also agreed to write off almost three-quarters of the Antilles' debt.

Following further negotiations, a meeting was held in Curaçao on 15 December 2008 at which the Dutch Prime Minister, Jan Peter Balkenende, and the Antillean premier, Emily de Jongh-Elhage, signed an agreement confirming the new status of the island. At the end of September 2009, at a meeting of the Dutch State Secretary for the Interior and Kingdom Relations, Ank Bijleveld-Schouten, and representatives of the Netherlands Antilles, it was agreed that the target date for dissolution of the federation would be 10 October 2010, at which date St Eustatius would become a special municipality of the Netherlands. The US dollar was formally adopted as the island's currency from 1 January 2011, replacing the Netherlands Antilles guilder; the Island Council had opposed the introduction of the euro, the currency of the Netherlands.

In elections to the new five-member Island Council held on 2 March 2011, the Democratic Party of St Eustatius won two seats, while the Progressive Labour Party, the United People's Coalition and the St Eustatius Empowerment Party each won one seat. The new members of the Council were sworn into office on 11 March.

Owing to St Eustatius's change in administrative status, the island's residents were henceforth entitled to vote in Dutch polls. The islanders first opportunity to exercise this right came on 12 September 2012, when elections to the Tweede Kamer (Second Chamber—the lower house of the Dutch parliament) were conducted. The Partij van de Arbeid received 28.2% of the valid votes cast in St Eustatius, while Democraten 66 garnered 27.9% and the Socialistische Partij 21.8%. The rate of participation by the electorate was just 15.6% (compared with 74.6% nation-wide). Commentators attributed this very low turn-out to a lack of campaigning on the island.

Lieutenant-Governor: GERARD BERKEL, Govt Bldg, Oranjestad; tel. 318-2552; fax 318-2324; e-mail lt.governor@statiagovernment .com; internet www.statiagovernment.com.

Island Council: REUBEN MERKMAN, FRANKLIN BROWN, REGINALD C. ZAANDAM, MILLICENT LIJFROCK-MARSDIN, F. A. SPANNER.

Island Secretary: JAN HELMOND.

Executive Council: Commr NICOLAAS SNEEK, Commr C. TEARR.

National Office for the Caribbean Netherlands Sint Eustatius (Rijksdienst Caribisch Nederland Sint-Eustatius): Mazinga Complex A and B, Fort Oranjestraat, POB 26, Oranjestad; tel. 318-3370; e-mail info@rijksvertegenwoordiger.nl; internet www.rijksdienstcn .com; Kingdom Rep. WILBERT STOLTE (resident in Bonaire).

Netherlands Autonomous Countries

Under the 1983 Constitution, the Kingdom of the Netherlands comprises territories in Europe (the Netherlands) and in the Caribbean (Aruba, Curaçao and Sint (St) Maarten). The Charter for the Kingdom of the Netherlands, signed by Queen Juliana in 1954, designates these territories as a single realm, ruled by the House of Orange-Nassau. Aruba gained *status aparte* (separate status) within the Kingdom on 1 January 1986. Following further constitutional amendments, on 10 October 2010 Curaçao and St Maarten, formerly part of the Netherlands Antilles, also became independent countries within the Kingdom of the Netherlands.

ARUBA

Introductory Survey

LOCATION, CLIMATE, LANGUAGE, RELIGION, FLAG, CAPITAL

Aruba is one of the group of Benedenwinse Eilands or Leeward Islands, which it forms with Bonaire and Curaçao, and lies in the southern Caribbean Sea, 25 km (16 miles) north of Venezuela and 68 km (42 miles) west of Curaçao. The climate is tropical, with an average annual temperature of 28°C (82°F), but is tempered by north-easterly winds. Rainfall is very low, averaging only about 426 mm (16.8 ins) annually. The official language is Dutch, but the dominant language is Papiamento (a mixture of Dutch, Spanish, English, Arawak Indian and several West African dialects). Spanish and English are also spoken. Most of the inhabitants profess Christianity and belong to the Roman Catholic Church, although a wide variety of other denominations are represented. The national flag (proportions 2 by 3) is blue, with two narrow yellow horizontal stripes in the lower section and a white-bordered four-pointed red star in the upper hoist. The capital is Oranjestad.

CONTEMPORARY POLITICAL HISTORY

Historical Context

The Caribbean island of Aruba was claimed for Spain in 1499, but was first colonized by the Dutch in 1636 and subsequently formed part of the Dutch possessions in the West Indies. Administered from Curaçao after 1845, in 1954 Aruba became a member of the autonomous federation of the Netherlands Antilles. The establishment in 1929 of a large petroleum refinery on the island, at Sint (St) Nicolaas, led to the rapid expansion of the economy and a high standard of living for the islanders. However, many Arubans resented the administrative dominance of Curaçao, and what they regarded as the excessive demands made upon Aruban wealth and resources by the other five islands within the Netherlands Antilles. The island's principal political party, the Movimentu Electoral di Pueblo (MEP), campaigned, from its foundation in 1971 onwards, for Aruban independence and separation from the other islands. In a referendum held in Aruba in 1977 82% of voters supported independence and withdrawal from the Antillean federation. The MEP used its position in the coalition Government of the Netherlands Antilles, formed in 1979, to press for concessions from the other islands towards early independence for Aruba. In 1981 (after the MEP had withdrawn from the Government of the Netherlands Antilles) a provisional agreement regarding Aruba's future was reached between the Dutch and Antillean Governments. Following further discussions, it was agreed in 1983 that Aruba should receive *status aparte* (separate status), within the Kingdom of the Netherlands, from 1 January 1986. The Dutch Government would remain responsible for defence and external relations until independence, while Aruba was to form a co-operative union with the Netherlands Antilles (the Antilles of the Five) in economic and monetary affairs.

Domestic Political Affairs

At local elections in 1983 the MEP increased its representation to 13 of the 21 seats in the Staten (parliament), and the leader of the MEP, Gilberto F. (Betico) Croes, remained as leader of the island Government. Austerity measures introduced in late 1984 provoked a series of strikes and demonstrations by civil servants in protest at wage reductions and price rises. The MEP consequently lost popular support and, following elections to the Staten in 1985, was succeeded in government by a coalition of four opposition parties led by the Arubaanse Volkspartij (AVP). Aruba achieved *status aparte*, as planned, on 1 January 1986, and Jan Hendrik Albert (Henny) Eman, leader of the AVP, became its first Prime Minister.

From 1988 Aruba began to enjoy an economic recovery, based on tourism. However, the MEP claimed that the benefits to the whole community were limited, and also criticized Eman's stated reservations about independence in 1996 and his refusal to negotiate with the Netherlands about transitional arrangements. At a general election in January 1989 the MEP came within 28 votes of securing an absolute majority in the Staten. The MEP leader Nelson Oduber formed a Government in coalition with the Partido Patriótico Arubano (PPA) and the Acción Democrático Nacional (ADN). (Both these parties had been in the previous Government, and retained one seat each at the election.)

The MEP and the AVP each secured nine seats in the Staten at the January 1993 general election. Despite gaining fewer votes than the AVP, the MEP administration remained in office, renewing the coalition with the ADN and the PPA. In April 1994, however, Oduber announced the Government's resignation, following the withdrawal of the two smaller parties from the coalition. Following a fresh general election in July, the AVP held 10 seats, while the MEP won nine seats and the Organisacion Liberal Arubano (OLA) the remaining two. In August Eman formed a Government in coalition with the OLA.

In March 1994 the Governments of Aruba, the Netherlands and the Netherlands Antilles cancelled plans for Aruba's transition to full independence, due to take place in 1996. The possibility of a transition to full independence at a later date was not excluded, but was not considered a priority, and would, moreover, require the approval of the Aruban people, by referendum, as well as the support of a two-thirds' majority in the Staten.

In September 1997 the Staten was dissolved after the OLA withdrew from the coalition. A general election was thus held in December which resulted in a political composition identical to that of the 1993 polls. Following protracted negotiations, the AVP and the OLA renewed their coalition in mid-1998, and a new Council of Ministers, headed by Eman, was appointed.

In June 2001 the governing coalition collapsed, following the withdrawal of the OLA's support for the AVP's plan to privatize the Aruba Tourism Authority. In a general election held in September, the MEP comfortably defeated the incumbent AVP, securing 12 seats in the Staten. The AVP legislative representation was reduced to six seats. The three remaining seats were shared between the PPA and the OLA. Oduber was once again appointed Prime Minister and a new single-party Government took office in November.

At a general election in September 2005 the MEP again won a majority of seats (11) in the Staten. The victory came in spite of broad public criticism of the Government's unwillingness to defend wage levels from the downward pressure caused by large-scale immigration from South America. Notably, the minimum wage had not been adjusted for five years. The AVP won eight seats, while the Movimento Patriotico Arubano and RED Democratico each secured one. The electoral turn-out among those eligible to vote was 85%. Oduber continued as Prime Minister.

The AVP, led since 2003 by Michiel Eman (the brother of former Prime Minister Henny Eman), defeated the governing MEP in a general election held on 25 September 2009, winning 12 of the Staten's 21 seats, with 48% of the votes cast. The MEP obtained eight seats and Democracia Real secured the remaining seat. A voter participation rate of 86% was recorded. Oduber attributed his party's loss to Dutch interference in Aruba's affairs (see Foreign Affairs) and to the recent closure of the petroleum refinery at St Nicolaas (see Economic Affairs).

Recent developments: refinery closure

The Eman Government's early policies focused on the economy, including reviving the important tourism industry and reopening the Valero refinery. In January 2010 the administration succeeded in resolving a long-running dispute over tax with the refinery owners; the refinery finally resumed operations in January 2011. However, in December Valero revealed that, owing to the challenging global economic climate, the refinery was operating at a loss, and in March 2012 the facility was closed again. Valero held talks with other oil companies to discuss a potential takeover of the refinery, but no firm offers were received. Thus, in September Valero announced its intention to convert the plant into an oil depot, resulting in many refinery workers losing their jobs.

Foreign Affairs

Aruba's relations with the Antilles of the Five improved after 1986. Aruba's relations with the 'metropolitan' Netherlands were dominated at this time by the latter's pressure for more control to be exercised over the large amount of aid that it gave to Aruba, and by the issue of independence, in particular the future arrangements for the island's security: Aruba's strategic position, close to the South American mainland, and the possibility of it being used as a base for drugs-trafficking, were matters of particular concern. In 1990 Aruba adopted the 1988 UN Convention on measures to combat trade in illegal drugs. In 1996, however, the USA included Aruba on its list of major drugs-producing or transit countries. New legislation to facilitate the extradition of suspected drugs-traffickers and money-launderers took effect in the following year and in 1999 US naval and air force patrols began operating from a base in Aruba in an effort to counter the transport of illicit drugs. In 2001 the Caribbean Financial Action Task Force commended the Government on its efforts in combating money-laundering. In the same year the territory was removed from the list of so-called 'unco-operative tax havens' drawn up by the Organisation for Economic Co-operation and Development (OECD, based in Paris, France), after the Government pledged to reform the territory's financial sector. In 2003 Aruba signed an agreement with the USA to exchange tax information in order to combat illegal financial activities, such as money-laundering, that are associated with international terrorism and drugs-trafficking. However, in April 2009 Aruba was included in OECD's so-called 'grey list' of territories that had committed to improving financial transparency, but had yet substantially to implement reform. Following efforts to conclude further bilateral agreements on the exchange of tax information in the second half of the year, Aruba was removed from the list. Tensions between Aruba and the Netherlands rose in 2008–09 as a result of persistent allegations made by Dutch politicians of corruption on Aruba. The AVP Government that took office in Aruba in October 2009 pledged to improve relations with the Netherlands.

After acquiring *status aparte*, Aruba fostered relations with some of its Caribbean neighbours and with countries in Latin America. This included the development of ties with Venezuela, which had traditionally laid claim to the Dutch Leeward Islands, including Aruba, and the signing of a memorandum of understanding with Brazil in 2006, which sought to promote more extensive air transport links. In 2009 the Dutch Minister of Foreign Affairs refuted allegations by the Venezuelan Government that the US military was being permitted to use airbases on Aruba and Curaçao to launch reconnaissance flights over Venezuelan territory.

CONSTITUTION AND GOVERNMENT

Aruba has separate status (*status aparte*) within the Kingdom of the Netherlands. Legislative power is held by the unicameral Staten (parliament) of 21 members, elected by universal adult suffrage for four years (subject to dissolution). Executive power in all domestic affairs is vested in the Council of Ministers (led by the Prime Minister), responsible to the Staten. The Governor, appointed by the Dutch Crown for a term of six years, represents the monarch of the Netherlands on Aruba and holds responsibility for external affairs and defence. The Governor is assisted by an advisory council. The Government of Aruba appoints a minister plenipotentiary to represent it in the Government of the Kingdom.

REGIONAL AND INTERNATIONAL CO-OPERATION

Aruba forms a co-operative union with Curaçao and Sint (St) Maarten in monetary and economic affairs, and has observer status with the Caribbean Community and Common Market (CARICOM, see p. 231). As part of the Kingdom of the Netherlands, Aruba is classed as an Overseas Territory in association with the European Union (EU, see p. 281).

ECONOMIC AFFAIRS

In 2010, according to the UN, Aruba's gross national income (GNI) was US $2,516m. During 2002–11 the population increased at an average annual rate of 1.5%. According to the central bank, gross domestic product (GDP) per head decreased, in real terms, by an average of 0.3% per year in 2002–11. Overall GDP decreased, in real terms, at an average annual rate of 0.8% in 2002–11. Real GDP decreased by 3.2% in 2010, but increased by 8.9% in 2011.

The agricultural sector engaged 0.6% of the employed labour force in 2010 and contributed 0.4% of total GDP in 2011. Owing to the poor quality of the soil and the prohibitive cost of desalinated water, the only significant agricultural activity is the cultivation of aloes (used in the manufacture of cosmetics and pharmaceuticals); aloe-based products are exported. Some livestock is raised, and there is a small fishing industry. According to the UN estimates, during 2002–11 agricultural GDP increased, in real terms, at an average annual rate of 0.6%; the sector's GDP decreased by 12.4% in 2010, but grew by 9.2% in 2011.

The industrial sector contributed an estimated 19.1% of GDP in 2011, and engaged 14.6% of the employed labour force in 2010. The industrial sector, and the island's economy, was based on the refining and transshipment of imported petroleum and petroleum products. The petroleum refinery at St Nicolaas, owned by the US-based Valero Energy Corporation, refined 52.9m. barrels of crude petroleum in 2011 before its closure in March 2012. Imports of crude petroleum were valued at A Fl. 558m. in 2010 (when the refinery was closed), before increasing to A Fl. 8,405m. in the following year. Exports of refined petroleum were valued at only A Fl. 56m. in 2010, before increasing to A Fl. 8,284m. in 2011 (total exports excluding mineral fuels and free trade zone transactions amounted to just A Fl. 54.9m. in 2011). There is a large petroleum transshipment terminal on Aruba, and a small petrochemicals industry. An advanced-technology coker plant supplies liquefied petroleum gas, largely for export to the USA. There are believed to be exploitable reserves of hydrocarbons within Aruban territory, and Aruba also has reserves of salt. During 2002–11, according to the UN estimates, industrial GDP increased at an average annual rate of 2.3%; the sector's GDP increased by 6.3% in 2011.

Manufacturing contributed an estimated 4.0% of GDP in 2011 and engaged 5.0% of the employed labour force in 2010. Light industry is engaged in the production of beverages, building materials, paints and solvents, paper and plastic products, candles, detergents, disinfectants, soaps and aloe-based cosmetics. There is a 'free zone', and the ports of Oranjestad and Barcadera provide bunkering and repair facilities for ships. According to the UN estimates, during 2002–11 manufacturing GDP increased, in real terms, at an average annual rate of 0.3%; the sector's GDP decreased by 9.6% in 2010, but increased by 8.5% in 2011.

The construction sector contributed an estimated 6.1% of GDP in 2011 and employed 8.3% of the active work-force in 2010. In 2005–07 some US $150m. was allocated to the renovation and expansion of existing hotels and resorts in an attempt to reinvigorate the sector. During 2002–11, according to the UN estimates, sectoral GDP increased at an average annual rate of 1.7%; construction GDP increased by 15.3% in 2010 and by only 2.0% in 2011.

Services are Aruba's principal economic activity, employing 84.8% of the active labour force in 2010, and contributing an estimated 80.4% of the island's GDP in 2011. Aruba's principal source of income is tourism; the sector was estimated directly to provide 26.5% of Aruba's GDP in 2012. The number of visitor arrivals fluctuates from year to year. The number of stop-over arrivals increased by 1.5% in 2010, to 824,702 and by a further 5.7% in 2011, to 871,316. Conversely, the number of cruise ship passengers decreased in 2010 (to 569,424, from 606,768 in the previous year), but then increased in 2011 (to 599,893). Receipts from tourism decreased to A Fl. 2,176.5m. in 2009, but recovered significantly, to A Fl. 2,413.5m., in 2011. Financial services are well established in Aruba, particularly the data-processing sector, an important service to US companies in particular. According to the UN estimates, during 2002–11 services GDP decreased, in real terms, at an average annual rate of 0.4%; the sector's GDP decreased by 7.7% in 2010, but increased by 9.4% in 2011.

Aruba is obliged to import most of its requirements, particularly machinery and electrical equipment (which accounted for 18.1% of the total value of imports in 2011), foodstuffs and chemical products; in 2011 the island recorded a merchandise trade deficit of US $712.0m. There was a deficit on the current account of the balance of payments of US $234.9m. in the same year. In 2011 the principal source of imports, excluding the petroleum sector and the free zone, was the USA (51.4% of the total value); another major source was the Netherlands. The principal export commodity was refined petroleum (see above). Excluding the petroleum sector and the free zone, the principal market for exports in 2011 was also the USA (accounting for 32.8% of the total value of exports), followed by Aruba's fellow members of the Kingdom of the Netherlands.

In 2011 Aruba recorded a budget deficit of A Fl. 311.4m., equivalent to 6.5% of GDP in that year. At the end of 2011 total government debt was A Fl. 2,771.9m. (equivalent to 57.8% of GDP), much of which was owed to the Government of the Netherlands. The average annual rate of inflation was 1.3% in 2002–11; consumer prices fell by 0.7% in 2010, but rose by 6.1% in 2011. Some 10.6% of the labour force were unemployed at the 2010 census.

Aruba was considered one of the most prosperous islands in the Caribbean. Concern, however, was expressed that its high public sector wage bill and the generous nature of the island's social welfare system, combined with its ageing population, would threaten the future stability of public finances, already hindered by a narrow taxation base and poor revenue collection. A decline in tourist arrivals following the onset of the global economic downturn in 2008, coupled with the closure of the petroleum refinery in 2009 (see above), resulted in a sharp economic contraction in 2009, of 10.5%. The recession extended into 2010, with the economy contracting by a further 3.2%. Internal demand, exports and investment declined during the year, activity in the tourism sector remained slow, and the unemployment rate continued to rise. Nevertheless, real GDP grew by an estimated 8.9% in 2011, driven by a recovery in tourist arrivals, increasing domestic consumption, and a strong rise in exports and investment. The reopening of the petroleum refinery also contributed to economic growth. However, production at the facility was suspended again in March 2012, leading to a decline in exports and an increase in unemployment. The negative economic repercussions of the closure were partially offset by the strong performance of the tourism industry during 2012, but a 1.2% contraction in real GDP was registered in that year, none the less. The Central Bank forecast economic growth of 5.1% in 2013. An agreement signed by the Government in January 2013 with Spanish company Repsol for offshore oil exploration could, if fruitful, provide a much-needed boost for the economy.

PUBLIC HOLIDAYS

2014: 1 January (New Year's Day), 25 January (Gilberto F. Croes's Birthday), 3 March (Lenten Carnival), 18 March (National Anthem and Flag Day), 18–21 April (Easter), 26 April (King's Day), 1 May (Labour Day), 29 May (Ascension Day), 25–26 December (Christmas).

Statistical Survey

Sources (unless otherwise stated): Central Bureau of Statistics, Ministry of Finance, Communications, Utilities and Energy, Sun Plaza Bldg, 3rd Floor, L. G. Smith Blvd 160, Oranjestad; tel. 5837433; fax 5838057; internet www.cbs.aw; Centrale Bank van Aruba, J. E. Irausquin Blvd 8, POB 18, Oranjestad; tel. 5252100; fax 5252101; e-mail cbaua@setarnet.aw; internet www.cbaruba.org.

AREA AND POPULATION

Area: 180 sq km (69.5 sq miles).

Population: 90,506 at census of 14 October 2000; 101,484 (males 48,241, females 53,243) at census of 29 September 2010. *Mid-2013* (UN estimate): 108,884 Source: UN, *World Population Prospects: The 2010 Revision*.

Density (at mid-2013): 604.9 per sq km.

Population by Age and Sex (UN estimates at mid-2013): *0–14:* 19,404 (males 9,816, females 9,588); *15–64:* 78,084 (males 37,032, females 41,052); *65 and over:* 11,396 (males 4,820, females 6,576); *Total* 108,884 (males 51,668, females 57,216). Source: UN, *World Population Prospects: The 2010 Revision*.

Principal Town (population at 2010 census): Oranjestad (capital) 28,294.

Births, Marriages and Deaths (2011): Live births 1,092 (birth rate 10.6 per 1,000); Marriages 768 (marriage rate 7.5 per 1,000); Deaths 633 (death rate 6.2 per 1,000).

Life Expectancy (years at birth, 2011): 75.7 (males 72.7; females 78.8). Source: Pan American Health Organization.

Immigration and Emigration (2011): Immigration 3,466; Emigration 2,339.

Economically Active Population (persons aged 14 years and over, 2010 census): Agriculture, hunting and forestry 297; Mining and quarrying 24; Manufacturing 2,334; Electricity, gas and water 529; Construction 3,851; Wholesale and retail trade, repairs 7,523; Hotels and restaurants 9,526; Transport, storage and communications 2,475; Financial intermediation 1,593; Real estate, renting and business activities 4,224; Public administration, defence and social security 4,570; Education 2,078; Health and social work 2,526; Other community, social and personal services 3,492; Private households with employed persons 1,242; Extra-territorial organizations and bodies 14; *Sub-total* 46,299; Activities not adequately defined 227; *Total employed* 46,526; Unemployed 5,519; *Total labour force* 52,045 (males 26,184, females 25,861).

HEALTH AND WELFARE

Total Fertility Rate (children per woman, 2011): 1.8.

Under-5 Mortality Rate (per 1,000 live births, 2010): 16.8.

Physicians (per 1,000 head, 2008): 1.51.

Hospital Beds (per 1,000 head, 2009): 2.8.

Health Expenditure (% of GDP, 2010): 10.0.

Total Carbon Dioxide Emissions ('000 metric tons, 2008): 2,288.2.

Carbon Dioxide Emissions Per Head (metric tons, 2008): 21.7.

Source: partly Pan American Health Organization.

For definitions, see explanatory note on p. vi.

FISHING

Total catch (metric tons, live weight, 2010): 153 (Groupers 15, Snappers and jobfishes 45, Wahoo 45, Other marine fishes 48). Source: FAO.

INDUSTRY

Electric Energy (million kWh, 2011): 930.5.

FINANCE

Currency and Exchange Rates: 100 cents = 1 Aruban gulden (guilder) or florin (A Fl.). *Sterling, Dollar and Euro Equivalents* (31 December 2012): £1 sterling = A Fl. 2.825; US $1 = A Fl. 1.790; €1 = A Fl. 2.362; A Fl. 100 = £35.40 = $55.87 = €42.34. Note: the Aruban florin was introduced in January 1986, replacing (at par) the Netherlands Antilles guilder or florin (NA Fl.). Since its introduction, the currency has had a fixed exchange rate of US $1 = A Fl. 1.79.

Budget (A Fl. million, 2011): *Revenue:* Tax revenue 856.9; Non-tax revenue 121.5; Total 978.4. *Expenditure:* Wages 356.0; Wage subsidies 157.3; Goods and services 217.4; Interest payments 137.4; Investments 35.6; Transfer to the General Health Insurance (AZV) 110.8; Total (incl. others) 1,289.8.

International Reserves (US $ million at 31 December 2011): Gold 175.2; Foreign exchange 536.7; *Total* 711.9. Source: IMF, *International Financial Statistics*.

Money Supply (A Fl. million at 31 December 2011): Currency outside banks 182.9; Demand deposits at commercial banks 1,371.6; Total money (incl. others) 1,554.8. Source: IMF, *International Financial Statistics*.

Cost of Living (Consumer Price Index; base: 2006 = 100): All items 107.9 in 2008; 115.2 in 2009; 114.4 in 2010; 121.4 in 2011.

Gross Domestic Product (A Fl. million at constant 2000 prices): 2,014.8 in 2007; 2,029.1 in 2008; 1,875.0 in 2009.

Expenditure on the Gross Domestic Product (A Fl. million at current prices, 2011): Final consumption expenditure 4,087; Gross capital formation 1,374; *Total domestic expenditure* 5,461; Exports of goods and services 3,299; *Less* Imports of goods and services 3,968; *GDP in purchasers' values* 4,791.

Gross Domestic Product by Economic Activity (A Fl. million at current prices, 2011): Agriculture, hunting, forestry and fishing 20; Mining and utilities 407; Manufacturing 184; Construction 279; Wholesale, retail trade, restaurants and hotels 904; Transport, storage and communications 392; Other activities 2,362; *Total gross value added* 4,547; Net taxes on products 244 (figure obtained as a residual); *GDP in purchasers' values* 4,791. Source: UN National Accounts Main Aggregates Database.

Balance of Payments (US $ million, 2011): Exports of goods f.o.b. 5,179.4; Imports of goods f.o.b. –5,891.5; *Balance on goods* –712.0; Exports of services 1,676.7; Imports of services –857.0; *Balance on goods and services* 107.7; Primary income received 40.6; Primary income paid –269.3; *Balance on goods, services and primary income* –121.1; Secondary income received 75.2; Secondary income paid –189.0; *Current balance* –234.9; Capital account (net) 3.2; Direct investment assets –3.1; Direct investment from liabilities 543.8; Portfolio investment assets –19.4; Portfolio investment liabilities 22.3; Other investment assets –537.3; Other investment liabilities 193.7; Net errors and omissions –4.6; *Reserves and related items* –36.3. Source: IMF, *International Financial Statistics*.

EXTERNAL TRADE

Principal Commodities (A Fl. million, 2011): *Imports c.i.f.:* Live animals and animal products 146.4; Food products 223.0; Chemical products 206.5; Base metals and articles thereof 117.4; Machinery and electrical equipment 379.2; Transport equipment 121.8; Total (incl. others) 2,091.9. *Exports f.o.b.:* Live animals and animal products 0.7; Machinery and electrical equipment 5.7; Transport equipment 5.5; Art objects and collectors' items 8.7; Total (incl. others) 54.9. Note: Figures exclude transactions involving mineral fuels and those of the Free Trade Zone of Aruba.

Principal Trading Partners (A Fl. million, 2011): *Imports c.i.f.:* Brazil 25.4; Colombia 33.2; Japan 24.3; Netherlands 247.2; Netherlands Antilles 53.8; Panama 72.3; USA 1,075.4; Venezuela 39.0; Total (incl. others) 2,091.9. *Exports f.o.b.:* Colombia 0.8; Netherlands 10.7; Netherlands Antilles 11.9; USA 18.0; Venezuela 1.7; Total (incl. others) 54.9. Note: Figures exclude transactions of the petroleum sector and those of the Free Trade Zone of Aruba.

TRANSPORT

Road Traffic (motor vehicles registered, December 2011): Passenger cars 49,984; Lorries 901; Buses 289; Taxis 373; Rental cars

3,620; Government cars 448; Motorcycles 1,791; Total (incl. others) 57,555.

Shipping: *Arrivals* (2011): 2,098 vessels. *Flag Registered Fleet* (31 December 2012): Number of vessels 1; Total displacement 221 grt (Source: Lloyd's List Intelligence—www.lloydslistintelligence .com).

Civil Aviation: *Aircraft Landings:* 18,939 in 2009; 19,097 in 2010; 19,225 in 2011. *Passenger Arrivals:* 906,644 in 2009; 919,281 in 2010; 980,544 in 2011.

TOURISM

Tourist Arrivals: 1,419,391 (812,623 stop-over visitors, 606,768 cruise ship passengers) in 2009; 1,394,126 (824,702 stop-over visitors, 569,424 cruise ship passengers) in 2010; 1,471,209 (871,316 stop-over visitors, 599,893 cruise ship passengers) in 2011.

Tourism Receipts (A Fl. million): 2,176.5 in 2009; 2,222.7 in 2010; 2,413.5 in 2011.

COMMUNICATIONS MEDIA

Telephones (2010): 35,000 main lines in use.

Mobile Cellular Telephones (2010): 131,800 subscribers.

Internet Subscribers (2008): 18,400.

Broadband Subscribers (2010): 19,200.

Personal Computers: 10,000 (97.4 per 1,000 persons) in 2006.

Source: International Telecommunication Union.

EDUCATION

Pre-primary (September 2010 unless otherwise indicated): 28 schools (provisional); 2,809 pupils (2009/10); 144 teachers (2009/10).

Primary (September 2010 unless otherwise indicated): 39 schools (provisional); 9,792 pupils (2009/10); 579 teachers (2009/10).

General Secondary (September 2010 unless otherwise indicated): 12 schools (provisional); 7,592 pupils (2009/10); 544 teachers (2009/ 10).

Technical-Vocational (September 2010, provisional): 2 schools; 1,751 pupils; 173 teachers.

Community College (1999/2000): 1 school; 1,187 pupils; 106 teachers.

University (September 2010, provisional): 1 university; 183 students; 8 tutors.

Teacher Training (September 2010, provisional, unless otherwise indicated): 1 institution; 105 students; 59 teachers (2008).

Special Education (September 2008 unless otherwise indicated): 5 schools (2010, provisional); 524 pupils; 75 teachers.

Private, Non-aided (September 2008): 7 schools; 530 pupils; 47 teachers.

International School (2000/01): 1 school; 154 pupils; 25 teachers.

Pupil-teacher Ratio (primary education, UNESCO estimate): 16.8 in 2009/10 (Source: UNESCO Institute for Statistics).

Adult Literacy Rate (UNESCO estimates, 2010): 96.7% (males 96.9%; females 96.8%) (Source: UNESCO Institute for Statistics).

Directory

The Government

HEAD OF STATE

King of the Netherlands: HM King WILLEM-ALEXANDER.

Governor: FREDIS J. REFUNJOL (took office 7 May 2004).

COUNCIL OF MINISTERS
(May 2013)

The Government is formed by the Arubaanse Volkspartij.

Prime Minister and Minister of General Affairs: MICHIEL GOD-FRIED EMAN.

Minister of Integration, Infrastructure and the Environment: OSLIN BENITO SEVINGER.

Minister of Finance, Communications, Utilities and Energy: MIKE ERIC DE MEZA.

Minister of Tourism, Transport and Labour: OTMAR ENRIQUE ODUBER.

Minister of Justice and Education: ARTHUR LAWRENCE DOWERS.

Minister of the Economy, Social Affairs and Culture: MICHELLE JANICE HOOYBOER-WINKLAAR.

Minister of Public Health and Sports: RICHARD WAYNE MILTON VISSER.

Minister Plenipotentiary and Member of the Council of Ministers of the Realm for Aruba in the Netherlands: EDWIN BIBIANO ABATH.

Minister Plenipotentiary of the Realm for Aruba in Washington, DC (USA): JOCELYNE CROES.

Secretary to the Council of Ministers: NICOLE HOEVERTSZ.

MINISTRIES

Office of the Governor: Plaza Henny Eman 3, POB 53, Oranjestad; tel. 5834445; fax 5820730; e-mail info@kabga.aw; internet www .kabga.aw.

Office of the Prime Minister: Government Offices, L. G. Smith Blvd 76, Oranjestad; tel. 5880300; fax 5880024.

Ministry of the Economy, Social Affairs and Culture: L. G. Smith Blvd 76, Oranjestad; tel. 5885455; fax 5827526.

Ministry of Finance, Communications, Utilities and Energy: L. G. Smith Blvd 76, Oranjestad; tel. 5833457; fax 5827538.

Ministry of General Affairs: L. G. Smith Blvd 76, Oranjestad; tel. 5830001; fax 5827513; e-mail rekenkamer@aruba.gov.aw.

Ministry of Integration, Infrastructure and the Environment: L. G. Smith Blvd 76, Oranjestad; tel. 5828368; fax 5827564.

Ministry of Justice and Education: L. G. Smith Blvd 76, Oranjestad; tel. 5830004; fax 5827518.

Ministry of Public Health and Sports: L. G. Smith Blvd 76, Oranjestad; tel. 5825751; fax 5827569.

Ministry of Tourism, Transport and Labour: L. G. Smith Blvd 76, Oranjestad; tel. 5827718; fax 5827556.

Office of the Minister Plenipotentiary for Aruba in the Netherlands: R. J. Schimmelpennincklaan 1, 2517 JN The Hague, Netherlands; tel. (70) 3566200; fax (70) 3451446; e-mail info@ arubahuis.nl; internet www.arubahuis.nl.

Office of the Minister Plenipotentiary for Aruba in Washington, DC (USA): 4200 Linnean Ave, NW, Washington, DC 20008, USA; tel. (202) 274-2601; fax (202) 237-8303; e-mail was-plvcdp@ minbuza.nl.

Legislature

STATEN

President: PAULDRICK FRANÇOIS TEODORIC CROES.

General Election, 25 September 2009

Party	Seats at election	Seats at May 2013
Arubaanse Volkspartij (AVP) . .	12	12
Movimentu Electoral di Pueblo (MEP)	8	5
Democracia Real	1	1
Independents	—	3
Total	**21**	**21**

Political Organizations

Arubaanse Volkspartij (AVP) (Aruba People's Party): Avda Alo Tromp 56, Oranjestad; tel. 5830911; fax 5837963; e-mail info@ avparuba.net; f. 1942; advocates Aruba's separate status; Leader MICHIEL GODFRIED EMAN.

Democracia Real (Real Democracy): Oranjestad; tel. 5941900; e-mail andin.bikker@gmail.com; f. 2004; Leader AINDIN BIKKER.

Movimento Patriotico Arubano (MPA) (Aruban Patriotic Movement): Oranjestad; Leader MONICA KOCK ARENDS.

Movimentu Electoral di Pueblo (MEP) (People's Electoral Movement): Santa Cruz 74D, Oranjestad; tel. 5854495; fax 5850768; e-mail mep@setarnet.aw; internet www.mep.aw; f. 1971; socialist; 1,200 mems; Pres. and Leader EVELYN WEVER-CROES.

Organisacion Liberal Arubano (OLA) (Aruban Liberal Organization): Oranjestad; f. 1991; Leader GLENBERT FRANCOIS CROES.

Partido Patriotico di Arubà (PPA) (Patriotic Party of Aruba): Clavelstraat 5, Sint Nicolaas; tel. 5844609; e-mail nisbet@ppa-aruba

.org; internet www.ppa-aruba.org; f. 1949; social democratic; opposed to complete independence for Aruba; Leader BENEDICT (BENNY) JOCELYN MONTGOMERY NISBET.

RED Democratico (RED Democratic Network): Belgiestraat 14, Oranjestad; tel. 5820213; e-mail info@red.aw; f. 2003; Leader ARMANDO (RUDY) LAMPE.

Judicial System

Legal authority is exercised by the Court of First Instance. Appeals are heard by the Joint High Court of Justice of Aruba, Curaçao and St Maarten.

Attorney-General of Aruba: ROBERT PIETERSZ.

Solicitor-General of Aruba: TACO STEIN.

Courts of Justice: J. G. Emanstraat 51, Oranjestad; tel. 5822294; fax 5821241; e-mail griffiekopie@setarnet.aw.

Religion

CHRISTIANITY

The Roman Catholic Church

Roman Catholics form the largest religious community, numbering more than 75% of the population. Aruba forms part of the diocese of Willemstad, comprising Aruba and the former constituent parts of the Netherlands Antilles. The Bishop resides in Willemstad (Curaçao).

Roman Catholic Church: J. Yrausquin Plein 3, POB 445, Oranjestad; tel. 5821434; fax 5821276; e-mail parokiasanfrancisco@yahoo.com.

The Anglican Communion

Within the Church in the Province of the West Indies, Aruba forms part of the diocese of the North Eastern Caribbean and Aruba. The Bishop is resident in The Valley, Anguilla.

Anglican Church: Holy Cross, Weg Seroe Pretoe 31, Sint Nicolaas; tel. 5845142; fax 5843394; e-mail holycross@setarnet.aw.

Protestant Churches

Baptist Church: Aruba Baptist Mission, SBC, Paradera 98-C; tel. 5883893.

Church of Christ: Pastoor Hendrikstraat 107, POB 2206, Sint Nicolaas; tel. 5848172; e-mail lwaymire@setarnet.aw; Minister LARRY WAYMIRE.

Church of Jesus Christ of Latter Day Saints: Dadelstraat 16, Oranjestad; tel. 5823507.

Dutch Protestant Church: Wilhelminastraat 1, Oranjestad; tel. 5821435.

Evangelical Church of San Nicolas: Jasmijnstraat 7, Sint Nicolaas; tel. 5848973; e-mail ecsnaua@gmail.com; f. 1970; Pastor NORMAN BROWNE.

Faith Revival Center: Rooi Afo 10, Paradera; tel. 5831010; fax 5833070; e-mail frc_aruba@yahoo.com; internet faithrevival.googlepages.com.

Iglesia Evangelica Pentecostal: Asamblea di Dios, Reamurstraat 2, Oranjestad; tel. 5831940.

Jehovah's Witnesses: Guyabastraat 3, Oranjestad; tel. 5828963.

Methodist Church: Bernhardstraat 245, Sint Nicolaas; tel. 5845243; fax 5934810; e-mail relismartinriley@yahoo.com; Supt Rev. RELIS F. MARTIN-RILEY.

New Apostolic Church: Goletstraat 5A, Oranjestad; tel. 5833762.

Pentecostal Apostolic Assembly: Bernhardstraat 185; tel. 5848710; fax 5845699.

Seventh-day Adventist: Weststraat, Oranjestad; tel. 5845896; Pastor K. LUIS.

JUDAISM

Beth Israel Synagogue: Adriaan Laclé Blvd 2, Oranjestad; tel. 5823272; fax 5823534; e-mail jcommaruba@gmail.com; internet bethisrael-aruba.blogspot.com; Rabbi MARIO GUREVICH.

BAHÁ'Í FAITH

Spiritual Assembly: Bucutiweg 19, Oranjestad; tel. 5823104; Contact M. CHRISTIAN.

The Press

DAILIES

Amigoe di Aruba: Bilderdijkstraat 16-2, POB 323, Oranjestad; tel. 5824333; fax 5822368; e-mail web@amigoe.com; internet www.amigoe.com; f. 1884; Dutch; Dir WILLEM DA COSTA GOMEZ; Editor JEAN MENTENS; circ. 12,000.

Aruba Today: Weststraat 22, Oranjestad; tel. 5827800; fax 5827093; e-mail info@arubatoday.com; internet www.arubatoday.com; English; Editor-in-Chief JULIA C. RENFRO.

Bon Dia Aruba: Weststraat 22, Oranjestad; tel. 5827800; fax 5827044; e-mail infor@bondia.com; internet www.bondia.com; Papiamento; Dirs JOHN CHEMALY, JOHN CHEMALY, Jr.

Diario: Engelandstraat 29, POB 577, Oranjestad; tel. 5826747; fax 5828551; e-mail noticia@diario.aw; internet www.diarioaruba.com; f. 1980; Papiamento; morning; Editor and Man. JOSSY M. MANSUR; circ. 15,000.

The News: Italiestraat 5, POB 300, Oranjestad; tel. 5824725; fax 5889430; e-mail thenewsaruba@setarnet.aw; f. 1951; English; Dir SONIA WEVER-SCHOUTEN; Editor-in-Chief MARGARET BONARRIVA-WEVER; circ. 6,900.

NEWS AGENCIES

Algemeen Nederlands Persbureau (ANP) (The Netherlands): Caya G. F. (Betico) Croes 110, POB 323, Oranjestad; tel. 5824333; fax 5822368; internet www.anp.nl.

Aruba News Agencies: Bachstraat 6, Oranjestad; tel. 5821243.

Publishers

Aruba Experience Publications NV: Verbindingsweg 2, POB 634, Oranjestad; tel. 5834467; fax 5384520; e-mail info@arubaexperience.com; internet www.arubaexperience.com; f. 1985; Gen. Man. FRANCO SNEEK.

Caribbean Publishing Co Ltd (CPC): L. G. Smith Blvd 116, Oranjestad; tel. 5820485; fax 5820484.

De Wit Stores NV: L. G. Smith Blvd 110, POB 386, Oranjestad; tel. 5823500; fax 5821575; e-mail info@dewitvandorp.com; f. 1948; Gen. Man. LYANNE BEAUJON.

Editorial Charuba: Beatrixstraat 23, Oranjestad; tel. 7301512; fax 5827526; e-mail alivaro@hotmail.com; f. 1982; Pres. ALICE VAN ROMONDT.

Gold Book Publishing: L. G. Smith Blvd 116, Oranjestad; tel. 5820485; fax 5820484; internet www.caribbeanhotelassociation.com; a division of the Caribbean Hotel and Tourism Asscn, based in Miami, FL, USA; Chair. WARREN BINDER.

Oranjestad Printing NV: Italiestraat 5, POB 300, Oranjestad; Man. Dir GERARDUS J. SCHOUTEN.

ProGraphics Inc: Italiestraat 5, POB 201, Oranjestad; tel. 5824550; fax 5833072; e-mail prographics@setarnet.aw; f. 2001; fmrly VAD Printers Inc; Publr H. VAN DER PUTTEN.

Broadcasting and Communications

TELECOMMUNICATIONS

Digicel Aruba: Marisol Bldg, L. G. Smith Blvd 60, POB 662, Oranjestad; tel. 5222222; fax 5222223; e-mail customercarearuba@digicelgroup.com; internet www.digicelaruba.com; f. 2003; owned by an Irish consortium; established a mobile cellular telephone network connecting Aruba with Bonaire and Curaçao in July 2006; Chair. DENIS O'BRIEN; CEO (Dutch Caribbean) SANDER GIELEN; Gen. Man. (Aruba) REMKO VAN DER VELDT.

Servicio di Telecomunicacion di Aruba NV (SETAR): Seroe Blanco z/n, POB 13, Oranjestad; tel. 5251000; fax 5251515; e-mail sysop@setarnet.aw; internet www.setar.aw; f. 1986; Man. Dir ROLAND CROES.

BROADCASTING

Radio

Canal 90 FM Stereo: Van Leeuwenhoekstraat 26, Oranjestad; tel. 5821601; fax 837340; e-mail canal90fm@gmail.com; internet www.canal90fm.aw/index2.htm; Producer M. GRAVENHORST.

Cool FM 98.9: Caya Betico Croes 23, Oranjestad; tel. 5833100; fax 5833101; e-mail publica@coolaruba.com; internet www.coolaruba.com; part of A & K Broadcasting Corpn NV; Dir ALEXANDER PONSON.

Hit 94 FM: Caya Ernesto Petronia 68, Oranjestad; tel. 5820694; fax 5820494; e-mail hit94@setarnet.aw; internet www.hit94fm.com; f. 1993; Dir JOHNNY HABIBE.

Magic 96.5 FM: Caya G. F. (Betico) Croes 164, Oranjestad; tel. 5865353; fax 5835354; internet www.magic965.com; Owner and Dir ERIN J. CROES.

Power FM 101.7: Piedra Plat 44 C-D, Lok 12, Paradera; tel. 5851017; e-mail info@blizz.aw; internet blizz.aw; fmrly Blizz FM; name changed as above in 2012; Man. RUBEN (SCORPIO) GARCIA.

Radio 1270 AM: Bernardstraat 138, POB 28, Sint Nicolaas; tel. 5845602; fax 5827753; commercial station; programmes in Dutch, English, Spanish and Papiamento; Dir F. A. LEAUER; Station Man. J. A. C. ALDERS.

Radio Carina FM: Datustraat 10A, Oranjestad; tel. 5821450; fax 5831955; commercial station; programmes in Dutch, English, Spanish and Papiamento; Dir-Gen. ALBERT R. DIEFFENTHALER.

Radio Caruso Booy FM: G. M. de Bruynewijk 49, Savaneta; tel. 5847752; fax 5843351; e-mail radiocarusobooy@hotmail.com; commercial station; broadcasts for 24 hrs a day; programmes in Dutch, English, Spanish and Papiamento; Gen. Man. SIRA BOOY.

Radio Kelkboom: Bloemond 14, POB 146, Oranjestad; tel. 5821899; fax 5834825; e-mail radiokelkboom@setarnet.aw; internet www.watapana-aruba.com; f. 1954; commercial radio station; affiliated with Radio Nederland Wereldomroep (Netherlands) and Voice of America (USA); programmes in Papiamento, Dutch, English and Spanish; Man. Dir EMILE A. M. KELKBOOM.

Radio Victoria: Washington 23A, POB 5291, Oranjestad; tel. and fax 5873444; e-mail radiovictoria@setarnet.aw; internet www .radiovictoriaaruba.org; f. 1958; religious and cultural FM radio station owned by the Radio Victoria Foundation; programmes in Dutch, English, Spanish, Papiamento, Dutch, Tagalog, Creole and Mandarin; Pres. N. J. F. ARTS.

Voz di Aruba (Voice of Aruba): Van Leeuwenhoekstraat 26, POB 219, Oranjestad; tel. 5823355; fax 5837340; commercial radio station; programmes in Dutch, English, Spanish and Papiamento; also operates Canal 90 on FM; Dir A. M. ARENDS, Jr.

Television

ABC Aruba Broadcasting Co NV (ATV): Royal Plaza Suite 223, POB 5040, Oranjestad; tel. 5838150; fax 5838434; e-mail emily@ 15atv.com; internet www.15atv.com; Rep. EMILY HUDSON.

Telearuba NV: Pos Chiquito 1A, POB 392, Oranjestad; tel. 5851000; fax 5851111; e-mail info@telearuba.aw; internet www.telearuba.aw; f. 1963; fmrly operated by Netherlands Antilles Television Co; commercial; acquired by SETAR in March 2005; Gen. Man. M. MARCHENA.

Finance

(cap. = capital; res = reserves; dep. = deposits; m. = million;
brs = branches; amounts in Aruban florin, unless otherwise stated)

BANKING

Central Bank

Centrale Bank van Aruba: J. E. Irausquin Blvd 8, POB 18, Oranjestad; tel. 5252100; fax 5252101; e-mail cbaua@setarnet.aw; internet www.cbaruba.org; f. 1986; cap. 10.0m., res 174.8m., dep. 884.7m. (Dec. 2009); Chair. C. G. MADURO; Pres. JEANETTE R. FIGAROA-SEMELEER.

Commercial Banks

Aruba Bank NV: Camacuri 12, POB 192, Oranjestad; tel. 5277777; fax 5277715; e-mail info@arubabank.com; internet www.arubabank .com; f. 1925; acquired Interbank Aruba NV in Dec. 2003; total assets US $260m. (Dec. 2004); Chair. B. W. H. GUIS; Man. Dir and CEO EDWIN TROMP; 5 brs.

Banco di Caribe NV: Vondellaan 31, POB 493, Oranjestad; tel. 5232000; fax 5832422; e-mail management@bancodicaribe.com; internet www.bancodicaribe.com; f. 1987; Gen. Man. and CEO IDEFONS D. SIMON; Man. (Aruba) EDUARDO DE KORT; 1 br.

Caribbean Mercantile Bank NV: Caya G. F. (Betico) Croes 53, POB 28, Oranjestad; tel. 5823118; fax 5830919; e-mail executive_office@cmbnv.com; internet www.cmbnv.com; f. 1963; cap. 4.0m., dep. 1,140.6m. (Dec. 2011); Chair. LIONEL CAPRILES, II; Gen. Man. J. E. WOLTER; 6 brs.

RBC Royal Bank (Aruba) NV: Italiestraat 36, Sasakiweg, Oranjestad; tel. 5233100; fax 58821576; e-mail tt-info@rbc.com; internet www.rbtt.com; f. 2001; fmrly First National Bank of Aruba NV (f. 1985 and acquired by Royal Bank of Trinidad and Tobago Ltd in 1998); name changed as above Mar. 2012; cap. 114.4m., res 139.2m., dep. 3,549.7m. (Dec. 2009); Chair. PETER J. JULY; 4 brs.

Investment Bank

AIB Bank NV: Wilhelminastraat 34–36, POB 1011, Oranjestad; tel. 5827327; fax 5827461; e-mail info@aib-bank.com; internet www

.aib-bank.com; f. 1987 as Aruban Investment Bank; name changed as above in April 2004; total assets 149.0m. (Dec. 2005); Man. Dir FRENDSEL W. GIEL; Asst Man. Dir HERRY M. KOOLMAN.

Mortgage Bank

Fundacion Cas pa Comunidad Arubano (FCCA): Sabana Blanco 66, Oranjestad; tel. 5238800; fax 5836272; e-mail info@fcca .com; internet www.fcca.com; f. 1979; Man. Dir PETER VAN POPPEL.

INSURANCE

There were seven life insurance companies and 13 non-life insurance companies active in Aruba in July 2011.

Association

Insurance Association of Aruba (IAA): Sun Plaza 202, Oranjestad; tel. 5825500; fax 5822126; e-mail prakash.gupta@aig.com; Pres. PRAKASH GUPTA; 17 mems.

Trade and Industry

DEVELOPMENT ORGANIZATIONS

Department of Agriculture, Husbandry and Fisheries (DLVV): Piedra Plat 114A, Oranjestad; tel. 5858102; fax 5855639; e-mail dlvv@aruba.gov.aw; internet www.overheid.aw; f. 1976; Dir T. G. DAMIAN.

Department of Economic Affairs, Commerce and Industry (Directie Economische Zaken, Handel en Industrie): Sun Plaza Bldg, L. G. Smith Blvd 160, Oranjestad; tel. 5821181; fax 5834494; e-mail deaci@setarnet.aw; internet www.arubaeconomicaffairs.aw; f. 1986; Dir MARIA DIJKHOFF-PITA.

CHAMBERS OF COMMERCE AND INDUSTRY

Aruba Chamber of Commerce and Industry: J. E. Irausquin Blvd 10, POB 140, Oranjestad; tel. 5821566; fax 5883962; e-mail Secretariat@arubachamber.com; internet www.arubachamber.com; f. 1930; Pres. JAMAL MAHAWAT KHAN; Exec. Dir LEONICIO J. MADURO.

Association of Dutch Caribbean Chambers of Commerce & Industry: J. E. Irausquin Blvd 10, POB 140, Oranjestad; tel. 5821566; fax 5883962; e-mail secretariat@arubachamber.com; f. 2011; asscn of chambers of commerce in Aruba, Bonaire, Curaçao, Saba, Sint Eustatius and Sint Maarten.

TRADE ASSOCIATION

Aruba Trade and Industry Association (ATIA): ATIA Bldg, Pedro Gallegostraat 6, Dakota, POB 562, Oranjestad; tel. 5827593; fax 5833068; e-mail atiaruba@setarnet.aw; internet www.atiaruba .org; f. 1945; Chair. RONALD VAN TRIGT; Sec. MICHEL HENRIQUEZ; 250 mems.

UTILITIES

Electricity and Water

Utilities Aruba NV: Arulex Center, Punta Brabo z/n; tel. 5828277; fax 5828682; e-mail utilities.aruba.hhenriquez@gmail.com; govt-owned holding co; Man. Dir HAROLD HENRIQUEZ.

Electriciteit-Maatschappij Aruba (ELMAR) NV: Wilhelminastraat 110, POB 202, Oranjestad; tel. 5237100; fax 5828991; e-mail info@elmar.aw; internet www.elmar.aw; independently managed co, residing under Utilities Aruba NV; electricity distribution; Man. Dir A. O. RAFINÉ; 160 employees.

Water en Energiebedrijf Aruba (WEB) NV: Balashi 76, POB 575, Oranjestad; tel. 5254600; fax 5857681; e-mail info@webaruba .com; internet www.webaruba.com; f. 1991; independently managed co, residing under Utilities Aruba NV; production and distribution of industrial and potable water, and electricity generation; Man. Dir OSLIN J. BOEKHOUDT.

Gas

Aruba Gas Supply Company Ltd (ARUGAS): Barcadera z/n, POB 190, Oranjestad; tel. 5851198; fax 5852187; e-mail webmaster@ arugas.com; internet www.arugas.com; f. 1940; Man. R. P. GEERMAN.

BOC Gases Aruba NV: Balashi z/n, POB 387, Oranjestad; tel. 5852624; fax 5852823; e-mail bocaruba@setarnet.aw; internet www .boc-gases.com; acquired by the Linde Group global industrial gases and engineering org. in 2006; Man. Dir J. KENT MASTERS (responsible for Americas, South Pacific and Africa).

TRADE UNION

Federacion di Trahadornan di Aruba (FTA) (Aruban Workers' Federation): Bernhardstraat 23, Sint Nicolaas; tel. 5845448; fax 5845504; e-mail info@fta.aw; internet www.fta.aw; f. 1964; independent; affiliated with the International Trade Union Confed;

Pres. José Rudolf (Rudy) Geerman; Vice-Pres. Hubert Mariano Dirksz.

Transport

There are no railways, but Aruba has a network of all-weather roads.

Arubus NV: Sabana Blanco 67, Oranjestad; tel. 5882300; fax 5828633; e-mail info@arubus.com; internet www.arubus.com; f. 1979; state-owned company providing public transport services; runs a fleet of 48 buses; Man. Dir Teo Croes.

SHIPPING

The island's principal seaport is Oranjestad, whose harbour can accommodate ocean-going vessels. There are also ports at Barcadera and Sint Nicolaas.

Aruba Ports Authority NV: Port Administration Bldg, L. G. Smith Blvd 23, Oranjestad; tel. 5826633; fax 5832896; e-mail info@arubaports.com; internet www.arubaports.com; f. 1981; responsible for the administration of the ports of Oranjestad and Barcadera; Man. Dir Juan Alfonso Boekhoudt.

Valero Aruba Refining Co NV: Lagoweg 5, POB 2150, Sint Nicolaas; tel. 5894904; fax 5849087; internet www.valero.com; f. 1989; acquired by Valero in 2004; petroleum refinery, responsible for the administration of the port of Sint Nicolaas; closed in 2012; plans to convert plant into oil depot ongoing in mid-2013; Gen. Man. Raymond A. Buckley.

Principal Shipping Companies

Aruba Stevedoring Co (ASTEC), NV: Port Administration Bldg, L. G. Smith Blvd 23, Oranjestad; tel. 5822558; fax 5834570; e-mail astec_admin@setarnet.aw; f. 1983; Man. Dir Ernand Mike de L'Isle.

Global Marine Services NV: De la Sallestraat 71-D, Oranjestad; tel. 5887212; fax 5887210; e-mail info@globalmarineservicesnv.co; internet www.globalmarineservicesnv.com; f. 2004; ship agent, liner shipping services, STS operations and freight services; Man. Maria Winkel.

Rocargo Services Aruba, NV: Lago Heightstraat 28, Lago Heights, POB 2527, San Nicolas; tel. 5844900; fax 5844880; e-mail rocargoaruba@rocargo.com; internet www.rocargo.com; f. 1994; shipping and port agents, cargo handling and transportation; Man. Joop Kraaijeveld.

SEL Maduro & Sons (Aruba) Inc: Rockefellerstraat 1, Oranjestad; tel. 55826039; fax 5826136; e-mail Vessel_coll@selmaduro.com; internet www.selmaduro.com; ship husbandry and port agent; also provides container services, cargo services, moving services, real estate and travel services; Man. Dir Hans Beaujon (acting); Man. Graceo Dunlock (Shipping and Container Services).

VR Shipping NV: Executive Bldg, Frankrijkstraat 1, POB 633, Oranjestad; tel. 5821953; fax 5825988; e-mail bronswinkelh@vrshipping.com; internet www.vrshipping.com; f. 1975 as Anthony Veder & Co; name changed as above 2000; Man. Hanley Bronswinkel.

CIVIL AVIATION

The Queen Beatrix International Airport (Aeropuerto Internacional Reina Beatrix), about 2.5 km from Oranjestad, is served by numerous airlines (including Dutch Antilles Express, based in Curaçao), linking the island with destinations in the Caribbean, Europe, the USA, and Central and South America. The airport handles an estimated 2.6m. passengers per year and in 2011 a three-stage expansion project, estimated to cost between US $18m.–$29m., was begun.

Aruba Airport Authority NV: Queen Beatrix International Airport, Wayaca z/n, Oranjestad; tel. 5242424; fax 5834229; e-mail p.steinmetz@airportaruba.com; internet www.airportaruba.com; Man. Dir Peter Steinmetz.

Tiara Air: Sabana Blanco 70E, Suite 11, Oranjestad; tel. 5884272; fax 5885002; e-mail sales@tiara-air.com; internet www.tiara-air.com; daily flights to Colombia and Venezuela, scheduled flights to Bonaire, Curaçao; Pres. Alejandro Muyale.

Tourism

Aruba's white sandy beaches, particularly along the southern coast, are an attraction for foreign visitors, and tourism is a major industry. The number of hotel rooms totalled 7,441 in 2009. In 2011 some 1,471,209 tourists visited Aruba, of which 871,316 were stop-over visitors and 599,893 were cruise ship passengers. Most stop-over visitors came from the USA (65% in 2010), Venezuela (11%) and the Netherlands (5.0%). Receipts from tourism totalled A Fl. 2,413.5m. in 2011.

Aruba Cruise Tourism: Royal Plaza Mall, Suite 230, L. G. Smith Blvd 94, POB 5254, Oranjestad; tel. 5833648; fax 5835088; e-mail info@arubabycruise.com; internet www.arubabycruise.com; f. 1995 as the Cruise Tourism Authority—Aruba; name changed as above in 2005; non-profit government organization; Exec. Dir Tamara Waldron.

Aruba Hotel and Tourism Association (AHATA): L. G. Smith Blvd 174, POB 542, Oranjestad; tel. 5822607; fax 5824202; e-mail info@ahata.com; internet www.ahata.com; f. 1965; 101 mems; Chair. Alex Nieuwmeyer; Pres. and CEO James Hepple.

Aruba Tourism Authority (ATA): L. G. Smith Blvd 172, Eagle, Oranjestad; tel. 5823777; fax 5834702; e-mail ata.pr@aruba.com; internet www.aruba.com; f. 1953; CEO Ronella Tjin Asjoe-Croeswill.

Defence

The Netherlands is responsible for Aruba's defence, and military service is compulsory. The Dutch-appointed Governor is Commander-in-Chief of the armed forces on the island. A Dutch naval contingent is stationed in Curaçao and Aruba.

Education

A Compulsory Education Act was introduced in 1999 for those aged between four and 16 years. Kindergarten begins at four years of age. Primary education begins at six years of age and lasts for six years. Secondary education, beginning at the age of 12, lasts for up to six years. In 2009/10 enrolment at primary schools included 100% of pupils in the relevant age-group, while the comparable ratio at secondary schools was 73%. The main language of instruction is Dutch, but Papiamento (using a different spelling system from that of Bonaire and Curaçao) is used in kindergarten and primary education, and is also being introduced into the curriculum in all schools. Aruba has two institutes of higher education: the University of Aruba, comprising the School of Law and the School of Business Administration, and the Teachers' College. There is also a community college. However, the majority of students continue their studies abroad, generally in the Netherlands. General government expenditure on education in 2009 was equivalent to 20.5% of total expenditure.

CURAÇAO

Introductory Survey

LOCATION, CLIMATE, LANGUAGE, RELIGION, FLAG, CAPITAL

Curaçao, a dependency of the Netherlands, lies about 55 km (34 miles) off the coast of Venezuela in the Caribbean Sea. Together with Aruba and Bonaire, the island forms the Benedenwindse Eilanden or Leeward Islands. The climate is tropical, moderated by the sea, with an average annual temperature of 27.5°C (81°F) and little rainfall. The official languages are Dutch and Papiamento (a mixture of Dutch, Spanish, Portuguese, English, Arawak Indian and several West African dialects). Almost all of the inhabitants profess Christianity, predominantly Roman Catholicism. The state flag (propor-

tions 2 by 3) is blue, with a yellow horizontal stripe just below the midline and two white, five-pointed stars in the canton. The capital is Willemstad.

Until October 2010 Curaçao formed part of the Netherlands Antilles, with Bonaire, Sint (St) Maarten, Saba and Sint (St) Eustatius. On 10 October 2010 the Netherlands Antilles was formally dissolved as a federation and Curaçao assumed the new status of an autonomous country within the Kingdom of the Netherlands.

CONTEMPORARY POLITICAL HISTORY
Historical Context

The Leeward Islands, already settled by communities of Arawak Indians, were discovered by the Spanish in 1499 and were seized by the Dutch in the 1630s. Curaçao became prosperous in the late 17th and 18th centuries as an entrepôt for trade in the Caribbean. After frequent changes in possession, the Leeward Islands were finally confirmed as Dutch territory in 1816. The islands (including Aruba and the Windward Islands—comprising St Eustatius, Saba and St Maarten) were administered as Curaçao and Dependencies between 1845 and 1948. Slavery was abolished in 1863, and the islands suffered from an economic decline until the establishment of a petroleum refinery on Curaçao in 1918. During the Second World War Queen Wilhelmina of the Netherlands promised independence, and in 1954 a Charter gave the federation of six islands full autonomy in domestic affairs, and declared it to be an integral part of the Kingdom of the Netherlands.

Domestic Political Affairs

Divisions of political allegiance within the Netherlands Antilles were along island, rather than policy, lines, and Curaçao traditionally dominated administrative affairs. Following Aruba's secession from the federation to assume *status aparte* (separate status) within the Kingdom in 1986, the Antilles of the Five was ruled by a series of unstable coalition Governments. By the early 1990s the 'metropolitan' Government in the Netherlands indicated that it was willing to consider the creation of two federations in separate island groups. A referendum was held on Curaçao in November 1993 regarding its constitutional status; 74% of the electorate voted for a continuance of the island's status as a member of the Antillean federation. The option of *status aparte*, favoured by the Government, received only 18% of the votes cast. As a result of this defeat, the Government collapsed. A general election took place in February 1994, at which a new, Curaçao-based party, the Partido Antía Restrukturá (PAR), led by Miguel A. Pourier, became the largest single party in the Staten. Pourier assumed the leadership of a broadly based coalition Government, which was inaugurated in March.

The PAR lost four of its eight seats in the Staten at a general election in January 1998 and Pourier lacked the support needed to form a new administration. Dissatisfaction with the new Government's attempts to reduce the fiscal deficit in October 1999 led to its collapse and that of the island Government of Curaçao. In the following month former Prime Minister Pourier formed a new broad-based coalition Government, which had the support of 18 of the 22 members of the Staten. The general election of 18 January 2002 was won by the Curaçao-based Frente Obrero i Liberashon 30 di mei (FOL), led by Anthony Godett, which had campaigned against the stringent measures imposed by the IMF. However, the FOL was unable to form a government because of allegations of corruption and mismanagement of funds by party leaders. Eventually, in June, a coalition Government under the leadership of the new PAR leader, Etienne Ys, replaced Pourier's caretaker administration.

The Ys Government ruled until April 2003, when the cabinet resigned to allow a fresh governing coalition to be established. Ys was eventually replaced by Mirna Luisa Godett, the sister of Anthony, in August, who formed a FOL-dominated coalition. The dominance of the FOL heralded a deterioration of the island's political relationship with the Netherlands, which had improved under the PAR leadership. The new Prime Minister immediately announced that a delegation of Dutch MPs would not be officially received when they visited the territory. Relations continued to worsen, and in January 2004 Godett accused Dutch officials of spying on her Government after it emerged that local justice officials had met two visiting Dutch ministers without her knowledge. Godett was forced to resign in April 2004 amid allegations of corruption among FOL members. The next federal Government was formed by a seven-party coalition, once again led by Ys.

In October 2004 the Jesurun Commission, established by the Dutch and Antillean Governments and headed by Edsel Jesurun (a former Governor of the territory), recommended the dissolution of the Netherlands Antilles; support for the federation had, it was argued, virtually disintegrated on most of the islands. The Commission proposed that Curaçao and St Maarten should become autonomous states within the Netherlands (i.e. have *status aparte*). A further referendum on the constitutional future of Curaçao took place on 8 April 2005: 68% of participants in Curaçao favoured *status aparte*, in line with the recommendations of the Commission, 23% voted for closer ties with the Netherlands and 5% voted for complete independence—there was a 54% voter turn-out. On 3 December 2005 a preliminary agreement with the Dutch Government that the extant federation be dissolved by 1 July 2007 was duly signed in Curaçao. Under the new structure, Curaçao was, as expected, to become an autonomous member of the Kingdom of the Netherlands.

On 2 November 2006 the Dutch Government granted Curaçao independent governance within the Kingdom of the Netherlands; endorsement of this latter agreement was contingent upon the island ceding authority for the administration of defence, foreign policy and law enforcement matters to the Dutch Government. However, on 28 November, Curaçao's Island Council voted by a decisive 13–6 majority against the accord, averring that further negotiations were required in order to safeguard the interests of the island's citizens, specifically over the administration of justice (over which they regarded the Dutch Government as having too great an influence). Particular concern had been expressed by the detractors with regard to stipulations for the management of the islands' respective budgets—entailing submission to a joint central bank—and the supervision of their judicial and police departments by the Dutch Government; furthermore, potential deficiencies had been identified within the Dutch system regarding the regulation of political practices, freedom of expression, the synthesis of European Union (EU, see p. 281) directives with national democratic tenets, and the integration of foreign nationals into Dutch society. Representatives of the PAR and conservative Partido Nashonal di Pueblo (PNP), who had voted in favour of the final agreement, left the Island Council in protest at the decision. Their departure left Curaçao without a legitimate government. Furthermore, in January 2007 the Netherlands Government rejected the island's request for a renegotiation of the 2 November accord. Curaçao's abstention was regarded as having jeopardized certain provisions of the agreement that were dependent upon all five islands becoming signatories and provoked polarized responses from the island's people. The urgency of addressing Curaçao's already burdensome public debt was rendered more acute in light of the fact that the island would no longer benefit from the debt relief awarded by the Netherlands to signatories of the 2 November agreement.

Curaçao was also conspicuously absent from the provisions of a further 'transition accord' signed by the Netherlands Antilles central Government and the other four Island Councils on 12 February 2007, envisaging the islands' complete secession from the federation. The Netherlands was to provide over NA Fl. 1,000m. to facilitate the process of disintegration. Curaçao's exclusion from the restructured Netherlands Antilles precipitated serious concerns for the island's pursuit of autonomy and its future status and relations with the Dutch Government, and, consequently, on 9 July the Curaçao Island Council signed the November accord's 'closing statement', although its late accession to the arrangement precluded the island from the Netherlands Government's debt-restructuring provisions. Opposition-led protests took place in late 2007 in Curaçao in response to the continuing constitutional negotiations with the Dutch Government. The demonstrators objected to the Dutch Government having the power to intervene in the island's future financial and legal affairs. One week later the Island Council formally ratified the results of the 2005 referendum: at a second peaceful demonstration held in December and attended by several thousand people, opposition parties demanded an end to the negotiations and for the Government to seek to achieve the autonomous status of Curaçao, in accordance with the results of the ballot.

A round table conference was held in Curaçao's capital, Willemstad, on 14–16 December 2008, at which it was established that Curaçao (and St Maarten) would gain autonomy, while the other three islands would become Dutch municipalities. Agreement was reached on the extent of the administrative powers of the Netherlands Government within the two seceding territories. In return for retaining some legal and financial controls over Curaçao and St Maarten, the Netherlands agreed to write off almost three-quarters of the Antilles' debt. The agreement was narrowly endorsed, by 52% of participants, in a referendum in Curaçao on 15 May 2009.

Autonomy

In September 2009, at a meeting of the Dutch State Secretary for the Interior and Kingdom Relations, Ank Bijleveld-Schouten, and representatives of the Netherlands Antilles, Curaçao and St Maarten, it was agreed that the target date for dissolution of the Netherlands Antilles would be 10 October 2010. Prior to securing autonomy, Curaçao (and St Maarten) would be required to introduce an appropriate legislative framework and to prepare their public authorities for the additional tasks entailed in administering an independent state.

An election to Curaçao's new designated legislature, the Estates of Curaçao, was held on 27 August 2010. The PAR won eight of the 21 seats, followed by the newly formed Movementu Futuro Korsou (MFK), led by Gerrit Schotte, which gained five seats, and the Pueblo Soberano (PS) with four seats. The Movementu Antia Nobo (MAN) garnered two seats while the FOL and the PNP each secured one seat each. The MFK subsequently formed a coalition with the Pueblo Soberano and the MAN and on 10 October Schotte was sworn in as Curaçao's first Prime Minister. On the same day Fritz Goedgedrag took office as the autonomous territory's Governor.

The Schotte Government came under scrutiny in October 2011 after the Prime Minister and two fellow MFK members, Minister of Finance George Jamaloodin and Minister of Economic Development Abdul Nasser El Hakim, were accused by Central Bank Governor, Emsley Tromp, of corruption. In response, the Government announced that the international anti-corruption organization Transparency International would conduct an independent investigation into the government of the island. The inquiry was expected to be published in 2013.

In May 2012 Prime Minister Schotte unexpectedly announced the suspension of the island's intelligence service, the Veiligheidsdienst

Curaçao (VDC). He accused VDC agents of plotting a coup against the Government in 2010 and announced that the Netherlands secret service would restructure the agency. In April the VDC had been accused by a parliamentary committee of disclosing information to third parties, although the security of the country had not been compromised.

Recent developments: political instability

Irreconcilable disputes between the constituent parties of the governing coalition led to the collapse of the administration in August 2012. Schotte and the Council of Ministers resigned on 3 August, and an interim Government, headed by Stanley Betrian, was inaugurated on 29 September, with a general election scheduled to take place on 19 October. The Netherlands recognized the interim authorities, although Schotte argued that he was entitled to remain in power until a new government was elected, claiming that his replacement by Betrian constituted a 'coup'. The PS attracted the most votes in the general election and gained control of five seats in the legislature. The MFK also won five seats, while the PAR (which had been renamed the Partido Alternativo Real in late 2010) and the Partido pa Adelanto i Inovashon Soshal (PAIS) each secured four seats, the MAN two, and the PNP one. Voter turn-out was recorded at 74.5%. Following lengthy discussions, in mid-December the PS, the PAIS, the PNP and an independent deputy (formerly of the PAR) agreed that, after a transitional period of three–six months, they would form a coalition government. Daniel Hodge was sworn in as transitional Prime Minister on 31 December, and his administration of 'professionals' assumed office on 2 January 2013. Meanwhile, Goedgedrag resigned as Governor in November 2012 owing to health problems; he was succeeded by Adele van der Pluijm-Vrede.

Hodge announced in late March 2013 that his transitional Council of Ministers would resign, in preparation for negotiations to form a new coalition government, under the supervision of a Governor-appointed formateur. In early May Helmin Wiels, the leader of the PS, the largest party in the Staten, was shot dead in Willemstad.

CONSTITUTION AND GOVERNMENT

The Constitution of Curaçao was approved by the Island Council in September 2010 and came into effect on 10 October. The Governor of Curaçao, appointed by the Dutch Government for a term of six years, represents the monarch of the Netherlands in the territory. The Governor is assisted by an advisory council. Executive power in internal affairs is invested in the Council of Ministers. The Council of Ministers is responsible to the Estates of Curaçao, the 21-seat parliament, elected by universal adult suffrage.

ECONOMIC AFFAIRS

In 2011 the gross national income (GNI) of Curaçao, measured at current prices, was an estimated US $4,095m., equivalent to some $20,187 per head. Gross domestic product (GDP) was some $4,138m. in 2011 (equivalent to $20,401 per head), according to UN estimates. In 2002–11 the population increased at an average annual rate of 1.3%, while GDP per head increased, in real terms, by an average of 2.5% per year. According to UN estimates, the GDP of the Netherlands Antilles increased, in real terms, at an average annual rate of 1.2% in 2002–11. According to the Central Bank, real GDP grew by 0.4% in 2011.

Agriculture, together with forestry, fishing and mining, contributed only 0.7% of GDP in 2010. The sector employed an average of 1.2% of the working population in 2007–09. Some 8% of the total land area is cultivated. The chief products are sorghum, divi-divi, groundnuts, beans, fresh vegetables and tropical fruit. A bitter variety of orange is used in the production of Curaçao liqueur. There is also some fishing.

Industry (comprising manufacturing, construction, utilities and mining) contributed 17.5% of GDP in 2010, and employed an average of 18.3% of the working population in 2007–09.

The mining and quarrying sector employed only 0.3% of the working population on Curaçao in 2000. Curaçao has few significant mineral reserves.

Manufacturing contributed 8.2% of GDP in 2010, and employed an average of 6.9% of the working population in 2007–09; activities include food-processing, production of Curaçao liqueur, and the manufacture of paint, paper, soap and cigarettes. Curaçao's free trade zone is of considerable importance in the economy, but there are very few manufacturing activities. Petroleum-refining (using petroleum imported from Venezuela) is the principal industrial activity, with the Isla refinery leased to the Venezuelan state petroleum company, Petróleos de Venezuela (PDVSA). Production capacity at the refinery was about 335,000 barrels per day. An oil spill at the refinery in August 2012 caused considerable environmental damage. Petroleum transshipment is also important, and ship repairs at the Curaçao dry dock make a significant contribution to the economy.

Construction contributed 5.8% of GDP in 2010, and employed an average of 8.7% of the working population on Curaçao in 2007–09.

The services sector contributed 81.8% of GDP in 2010 and engaged an average of 81.7% of the employed labour force in 2007–09. Curaçao was a major 'offshore' financial centre. In September 2011 the Organisation for Economic Co-operation and Development's (based in Paris, France) urged Curaçao to improve financial transparency by accelerating implementation of bilateral agreements on the exchange of tax information and making available information on foreign companies on the island. The financial and business services sector contributed 31.2% of GDP in Curaçao in 2010, and employed an average of 18.1% of the Curaçao working population in 2007–09. A major industry is tourism, which is the largest employer after the public sector. The number of stop-over tourists to the Netherlands Antilles as a whole reached 411,179 in 2008, but declined thereafter, standing at 390,082 in 2011. In addition to tourism, Curaçao has sought to establish itself as a centre for regional trade, exploiting its excellent harbours. In 1998 a free trade zone was established at the island's airport, which further enhanced Curaçao's entrepôt status.

In 2011 Curaçao recorded a visible merchandise trade deficit (excluding oil products) of NA Fl. 1,969m. Petroleum is the principal commodity for both import and export and, according to unofficial figures compiled from partner countries, accounted for 45.9% of imports and 66.0% of exports in 2009. In 2010 the principal source of imports was the USA (36.7%), the Netherlands and Puerto Rico; the USA was also the principal market for exports (39.8% of the total exports).

In 2011 the central Government recorded a budgetary deficit of NA Fl. 169.3m. At the end of 2008 total domestic debt amounted to NA Fl. 4,998.1m. (70.6% of GDP), while total foreign debt stood at NA Fl. 805.2m. (11.4% of GDP). The average annual rate of inflation was 3.0% in 2002–11; consumer prices increased by an average of 2.4% in 2011. Some 9.8% of the Curaçao work-force were unemployed in 2011.

Curaçao faced substantial economic challenges upon gaining autonomy. Recent years have witnessed a progressive weakening of the economy, leading to high unemployment and increasing rates of emigration. Despite receiving substantial debt relief from the Netherlands, Curaçao's current account deficit was equivalent to 25.5% of GDP in 2010, according to the IMF. The island was closely linked to Venezuela, which meant it was vulnerable to fluctuations in that country's economy. Owing to the favourable fixed exchange rate and a limit to how much US currency Venezuelans can buy, many Venezuelan visitors travel to Curaçao in order to purchase dollars, which are then sold on the 'black' market at an inflated exchange rate. A devaluation of the Venezuelan currency in 2010 led to a fall in exchange rate revenues in that year. Curaçao's free trade zone had also been boosted by Venezuelan custom, which decreased in 2010. The important tourism sector, however, withstood the worst of the global economic downturn from 2008, focused as it was on the higher-end market. The sector has made significant efforts to diversify arrivals; North American tourists increased by 29% in 2011 alone, although almost one-half of arrivals still came from Europe. The number of stay-over tourists rose by around 5% in 2012, and there was a marked increase in visitors from South America. The Central Bank put real GDP growth at 0.6% in 2011, while the Government estimated that the economy registered zero growth in 2012 and would expand by a maximum of 0.7% in 2013. The continuing political instability in Curaçao in 2012–13 meant that necessary structural reforms were not able to be implemented. Nevertheless, austerity measures, including an increase in the retirement age and reductions in health care expenditure, were adopted in early 2013 by the transitional Government of Daniel Hodge in an attempt to stabilize the island's public finances; a rise in property tax was also introduced in April.

PUBLIC HOLIDAYS

2014: 1 January (New Year's Day), 3 March (Lenten Carnival), 18–21 April (Easter), 26 April (King's Day), 1 May (Labour Day), 29 May (Ascension Day), 2 July (National Flag and Anthem Day), 10 October (Curaçao Day), 25–26 December (Christmas).

Statistical Survey

Note: The Netherlands Antilles was officially dissolved on 10 October 2010. The figures in this Statistical Survey refer to Curaçao only, unless otherwise indicated.

Sources (unless otherwise stated): Centraal Bureau voor de Statistiek, Fort Amsterdam, Willemstad, Curaçao; tel. (9) 461-1031; fax (9) 461-1696; internet www.cbs.cw/; Centrale Bank van Curaçao en Sint Maarten, Simon Bolivar Plein 1, Willemstad, Curaçao; tel. (9) 434-5500; fax (9) 461-5004; e-mail info@centralbank.an; internet www.centralbank.an.

AREA AND POPULATION

Area: 444 sq km (171.4 sq miles).

Population: 150,563 (males 68,848, females 81,715) at census of 26 March 2011.

Density (at 2011 census): 339.1 per sq km.

Population by Age and Sex (official estimates at 1 January 2011): *0–14:* 30,307 (males 15,550, females 14,757); *15–64:* 97,177 (males 43,890, females 53,287); *65 and over:* 17,922 (males 7,142, females 10,780); *Total* 145,406 (males 66,582, females 78,824).

Principal Town: Willemstad (capital), population (incl. suburbs, UN estimate) 114,831 at mid-2011. Source: UN, *World Urbanization Prospects: The 2011 Revision.*

Births, Marriages and Deaths (2011): Registered live births 1,974 (birth rate 13.1 per 1,000); Registered marriages 859 (marriage rate 5.7 per 1,000); Registered deaths 1,276 (death rate 8.5 per 1,000).

Life Expectancy (years at birth): Males 73.3; Females 80.3 in 2010 (Source: IMF, *2011 Article IV Consultation—Staff Report; Informational Annex; and Public Information Notice on the Executive Board Discussion* (December 2011)).

Immigration and Emigration (2011): *Immigration:* Aruba 101; China, People's Republic 59; Colombia 150; Dominican Republic 181; Netherlands 3,465; Venezuela 221; Total (incl. others) 5,276. *Emigration:* Aruba 75; Netherlands 3,804; USA 79; Total (incl. others) 4,900.

Economically Active Population (sample survey, persons aged 15 years and over, average 2007–09): Agriculture, forestry, fishing and mining 705; Manufacturing 3,914; Electricity, gas and water 806; Construction 4,911; Wholesale and retail trade, repairs 9,993; Hotels and restaurants 4,247; Transport, storage and communications 3,894; Financial intermediation 4,132; Real estate, renting and business activities 6,118; Public administration, defence and social security 4,307; Education 2,739; Health and social work 5,071; Other community, social and personal services 3,383; Private households with employed persons 2,176; Extra-territorial organizations and bodies 186; *Total employed* 56,582; Unemployed 6,045; *Total labour force* 62,627 (males 30,193, females 32,434). *2011* (labour force survey, persons aged 15 years and over): Total employed 62,042; Unemployed 6,721; Total labour force 68,763 (males 32,421, females 36,342).

HEALTH AND WELFARE

(Data refer to Netherlands Antilles)

Total Fertility Rate (children per woman, 2010): 2.0.

Under-5 Mortality Rate (per 1,000 live births, 2010): 13.5.

Physicians (per 1,000 head, 1999): 1.4.

Hospital Beds (per 1,000 head, 2002): 7.24.

Health Expenditure (% of GDP, 2005): 4.8.

Total Carbon Dioxide Emissions ('000 metric tons, 2007): 6,232.5.

Total Carbon Dioxide Emissions Per Head (metric tons, 2007): 32.4.

Source: mostly Pan American Health Organization.

For other sources and definitions, see explanatory note on p. vi.

AGRICULTURE, ETC.

(Data refer to Netherlands Antilles)

Livestock ('000 head, year ending September 2010, FAO estimates): Cattle 0.7; Pigs 2.7; Goats 13.7; Sheep 9.3; Chickens 165.

Livestock Products (metric tons, 2010, FAO estimates): Pig meat 203; Chicken meat 380; Cows' milk 460; Hen eggs 630.

Fishing (metric tons, live weight, 2010): Skipjack tuna 9,179; Yellowfin tuna 5,302; Bigeye tuna 2,688; Total catch (incl. others) 18,455 (FAO estimate).

Source: FAO.

MINING

(Data refer to Netherlands Antilles)

Production ('000 metric tons, estimate): Salt 500 in 2003–08. Source: US Geological Survey.

INDUSTRY

(Data refer to Netherlands Antilles unless otherwise indicated)

Production ('000 metric tons, 2008, unless otherwise indicated): Jet fuel 731; Kerosene 46 (2004); Residual fuel oils 3,789; Lubricating oils 327 (2007); Petroleum bitumen (asphalt) 1,128 (2007); Liquefied petroleum gas, refined 78; Motor spirit (petrol) 1,856; Aviation gasoline 17; Distillate fuel oils (gas-diesel oil) 2,195; Sulphur (recovered) 23; Electric energy (Curaçao only, million kWh, 2011) 902.2.

FINANCE

Currency and Exchange Rates: 100 cents = 1 Netherlands Antilles gulden (guilder) or florin (NA Fl.). *Sterling, Dollar and Euro Equivalents* (31 December 2012): £1 sterling = NA Fl. 2.825; US $1 = NA Fl. 1.790; €1 = NA Fl. 2.362; NA Fl. 100 = £35.40 = $55.87 = €42.34. *Exchange Rate:* In December 1971 the central bank's mid-point rate was fixed at US $1 = NA Fl. 1.80. In 1989 this was adjusted to $1 = NA Fl. 1.79. In December 2009 it was announced that the US dollar would replace the Netherlands Antilles guilder and florin in Bonaire, St Eustatius and Saba from 1 January 2011, following the dissolution of the previous federation of the Netherlands Antilles in October 2010. In Curaçao and St Maarten, the Netherlands Antilles guilder was expected to be replaced with a newly created Caribbean guilder from 2013.

Central Government Budget (NA Fl. million, 2011): *Revenue:* Tax revenue 1,414.6 (Taxes on income 701.3, Taxes on property 47.7, Taxes on goods and services 478.9, Taxes on international trade and transactions 181.3, Other taxes 5.3); Non-tax revenue 142.3; Total 1,556.9. *Expenditure:* Current expenditure 1,694.5 (Wages and salaries 566.7; Other goods and services 400.8; Interest payments 49.8; Subsidies 46.5; Current transfers 583.2); Capital expenditure (incl. transfers and net lending) 31.7; Total 1,726.2.

International Reserves (Netherlands Antilles, US $ million at 31 December 2009): Gold (national valuation) 356; Foreign exchange 867; Total 1,223. Source: IMF, *International Financial Statistics.*

Money Supply (Curaçao and Sint Maarten, NA Fl. million at 31 December 2010): Currency outside banks 326; Demand deposits at commercial banks 2,811; Total (incl. others) 3,137 (Source: IMF, *2011 Article IV Consultation—Staff Report; Informational Annex; and Public Information Notice on the Executive Board Discussion* (December 2011)).

Cost of Living (Consumer Price Index; base: October 2006 = 100): All items 111.2 in 2009; 114.3 in 2010; 117.0 in 2011.

Gross Domestic Product (million NA Fl. at current prices): 5,071.8 in 2008; 5,135.8 in 2009; 5,282.9 in 2010.

Gross Domestic Product by Economic Activity (million NA Fl. at current prices, 2010): Agriculture, fishing and mining 32.4; Electricity, gas and water 170.5; Manufacturing 403.2; Construction 284.2; Trade, restaurants and hotels 861.8; Transport, storage and communications 543.4; Real estate, renting and business activities 760.7; Financial services 768.1; Public administration and defence 391.2; Education 116.3; Health and social welfare 313.7; Other activities 247.1; *Sub-total* 4,892.4; Net of indirect taxes 390.5; *GDP in purchasers' values* 5,282.9.

Balance of Payments (NA Fl. million, 2011): Exports of goods f.o.b. 1,661.3; Imports of goods f.o.b. –3,812.3; *Trade balance* –2,151.0; Services (net) 775.5; *Balance on goods and services* –1,375.7; Income (net) –24.8; *Balance on goods, services and income* –1,400.3; Current transfers (net) –131.4; *Current balance* –1,531.7; Capital account (net) 95.8; Direct investment (net) 177.4; Portfolio investment (net) 265.0; Other investment (net) 1,010.6; Net errors and omissions 18.6; *Overall balance* 35.8.

EXTERNAL TRADE

(Note: Although the import and export of petroleum and petroleum products, largely for refinery, transshipment and storage purposes, made a significant contribution to the economy of Curaçao, such transactions are not included in official trade statistics.)

Principal Commodities (NA Fl. million, 2010, excl. petroleum): *Imports c.i.f.* (Free Zone only): Food and live animals 5; Beverages and tobacco 81; Chemical products 34; Manufactured goods 18; Machinery and transport equipment 195; Miscellaneous articles 501; Total (incl. others) 947. Note: Data exclude non-free zone imports (1,319). *Exports f.o.b.:* Food and live animals 25; Beverages and tobacco 12; Chemical products 22; Manufactured goods 24; Machinery and transport equipment 146; Miscellaneous articles 20; Total (incl. others) 259.

Principal Trading Partners (NA Fl. million, 2010, excl. petroleum): *Imports c.i.f.:* Aruba 48; Brazil 43; China, People's Republic 50; Colombia 63; Japan 57; Netherlands 442; Panama 91; Puerto Rico 122; USA 831; Venezuela 109; Total (incl. others) 2,266.

Exports f.o.b.: Aruba 26; Bonaire 28; Netherlands 37; USA 103; Total (incl. others) 259.

TRANSPORT

Road Traffic (motor vehicles registered, excl. government-owned vehicles, 2011): Passenger cars 61,578; Lorries 12,021; Buses 379; Taxis 179; Other cars 163; Motorcycles 1,117.

Shipping: *International Sea-borne Freight Traffic* (TEUs moved, 2010): 93,603. *Flag Registered Fleet* at 31 December 2012): Number of vessels 164; Total displacement 1,427,949 grt (Source: Lloyd's List Intelligence—www.lloydslistintelligence.com).

Civil Aviation (2011): Aircraft landings 22,634 (Commercial 16,512); Passenger movements 1,629,106.

TOURISM

Tourist Arrivals: *Stop-overs:* 366,679 (Netherlands 126,952; USA 36,716; Venezuela 105,635) in 2009; 341,651 (Netherlands 140,189; USA 49,487; Venezuela 44,353) in 2010; 390,082 (Netherlands 141,547; USA 63,334; Venezuela 61,564) in 2011. *Cruise ship passengers:* 417,324 in 2009; 382,697 in 2010; 400,596 in 2011.

Tourism Receipts (Netherlands Antilles, NA Fl. million, incl. passenger transport): 1,683.5 in 2002; 1,761.0 in 2003; 1,906.5 in 2004.

COMMUNICATIONS MEDIA

(Data refer to Netherlands Antilles)

Telephones (December 2011): 68,070 main lines in use.

Mobile Cellular Telephones (December 2011): 206,294 subscribers.

EDUCATION

Students: Secondary 2,012 (2007/08); University 222 (2009/10).

Pupil-teacher Ratio (Netherlands Antilles, primary education, UNESCO estimate): 19.8 in 2002/03.

Adult Literacy Rate (Netherlands Antilles, 2009, UNESCO estimates): 96.5% (males 96.5%; females 96.4%).

Source: partly UNESCO Institute for Statistics.

Directory

The Government

HEAD OF STATE

King of the Netherlands: HM King WILLEM-ALEXANDER.

Governor: ADELE VAN DER PLUIJM-VREDE.

COUNCIL OF MINISTERS
(May 2013)

The transitional Government was formed by the Pueblo Soberano, the Partido Adelanto i Inovashon Soshal, the Partido Nashonal di Pueblo, and an Independent. In March 2013 Prime Minister Hodge announced the resignation of the transitional Council of Ministers in preparation for negotiations on the formation of a new, permanent Government, which were under way in May.

Prime Minister: Dr DANIEL ROBERT HODGE.

First Vice Prime Minister and Minister of Economic Development: Dr IVAN STEVE MARTINA.

Second Vice Prime Minister and Minister of Finance: Dr JOSÉ MANUEL NORBERTO JARDIM.

Minister of Health and Environment: Dr BERNARD DENZIL WHITEMAN.

Minister of Social Affairs and Labour: SHERWIN RICHINÉ FRANSISCUS JOSEPHA.

Minister of Justice: NELSON GENARO NAVARRO.

Minister of Education, Science and Sports: Dr RUBINA LUCIA BITORINA.

Minister of Traffic, Communication and Urban Planning: EARL WINSTON BALBORDA.

Minister of Administration, Planning and Service Provision: ETIENNE VAN DER HORST.

Minister Plenipotentiary of Curaçao in the Netherlands: RODERICK (ROY) PIETERS.

MINISTRIES

Office of the Governor: Fort Amsterdam 2, Willemstad; tel. (9) 461-2148; fax (9) 461-2045; e-mail adjudant@kgcur.org; internet www.gouverneurvancuracao.org.

Office of the Prime Minister: Fort Amsterdam 17, Willemstad; tel. (9) 463-0495; fax (9) 461-7199.

Ministry of Administration, Planning and Service Provision: Willemstad.

Ministry of Economic Development: Dienst Economische Zaken, Pietermaai 25B, Willemstad; tel. (9) 462-1444; fax (9) 462-7590; e-mail info.meo@gobiernu.cw.

Ministry of Education, Science and Sports: Schouwburgweg 102, Willemstad; tel. (9) 461-5133; fax (9) 461-5133; e-mail info.sae@gobiernu.cw.

Ministry of Finance: Pietermaai 17, Willemstad; tel. (9) 432-8000; fax (9) 461-3339; e-mail directie.financien@gobiernu.cw.

Ministry of Health and Environment: LVV, Klein Kwartier 33, Willemstad; tel. (9) 738-1466; fax (9) 738-1467; e-mail info.gmn@gobiernu.cw.

Ministry of Justice: Wilhelminaplein z/n, Willemstad; tel. (9) 463-0628; fax (9) 461-0598; e-mail Ministerie.Justitie@gobiernu.cw.

Ministry of Social Affairs and Labour: Concordiastraat 24, Willemstad; tel. (9) 461-0017; fax (9) 465-8738; e-mail info.dwi@gobiernu.cw.

Ministry of Traffic, Communication and Urban Planning: Berg Arrarat Perceel C, Willemstad; tel. (9) 465-1477; fax (9) 461-465-1474; e-mail info.vvrp@gobiernu.cw.

Office of the Minister Plenipotentiary for Curaçao in the Netherlands: Kabinet van de Gevolmachtigde Minister van de Curaçao, Badhuisweg 173–175, POB 90706, 2509 LS The Hague, Netherlands; tel. (70) 306-6111; fax (70) 306-6110; internet www.vertegenwoordigingcuracao.nl.

Legislature

STATEN

President: MARCOLINO (MIKE) FRANCO (PAIS).

Vice-President: JAIME CORDOBA (PS).

Election, 19 October 2012

Party	Votes	% of votes	Seats
Pueblo Soberano (PS) .	19,716	22.65	5
Movementu Futuro Korsou (MFK) . . .	18,441	21.18	5
Partido Alternativo Real (PAR)*	17,149	19.70	4
Partido pa Adelanto I Inovashon Soshal (PAIS)	15,395	17.68	4
Movementu Antia Nobo (MAN)	8,297	9.53	2
Partido Nashonal di Pueblo (PNP)	5,136	5.89	1
Others	2,924	3.36	—
Total†	87,058	100.00	21

* A PAR deputy, Glenn Sulvaran, subsequently declared he would sit in the Staten as an Independent, reducing the PAR's parliamentary representation to three.

† In addition, there were 370 invalid/blank votes.

Election Commission

Konseho Supremo Elektoral (KSE): Roodeweg 42, Willemstad; tel. (9) 434-1600; fax (9) 461-8166; e-mail info@kse.cw; internet www.kse.cw; Chair. GEOMALY MARTES.

Political Organizations

Democratische Partij—Curaçao (DP—C) (Democratic Party—Curaçao): Neptunusweg 28, Willemstad; f. 1944; Leader NORBERTO VIERA RIBEIRO.

Frente Obrero i Liberashon 30 di mei (FOL) (Workers' Liberation Front of 30 May): Mayaguanaweg 16, Willemstad; tel. (9) 461-8105; f. 1969; socialist; Leader ANTHONY GODETT.

Lista di Kambio (LdK) (List of Change): Willemstad; electoral alliance; Leader CHARLES F. COOPER.

Forsa Kòrsou: F. D. Rooseveltweg 347, Willemstad; tel. (9) 888-3041; fax (9) 888-3504; e-mail forsakorsou@onenet.an; internet www.forsakorsou.com; Pres. NELSON NAVARRO; Leader GREGORY DAMOEN.

Movementu Antia Nobo (MAN) (Movement for a New Antilles): Landhuis Morgenster, Willemstad; tel. (9) 468-4781; internet www.new.partidoman.org; f. 1971; socialist; Pres. EUGENE CLEOPA; Leader EUNICE EISDEN.

Niun Paso Atras: Willemstad; Leader CARLOS MONK.

Movementu Futuro Korsou (MFK) (Movement for the Future of Curaçao): Willemstad; internet www.gerritschotte.com; f. 2010; Leader GERRIT F. SCHOTTE.

Partido Adelanto i Inovashon Soshal (PAIS): Rozenweg 1, Willemstad; tel. (9) 518-8802; internet www.partidopais.com; f. 2010; Leader ALEX ROSARIA.

Partido Alternativo Real (PAR) (Real Alternative Party): Fokkerweg 26, Unit 3, Willemstad; tel. (9) 465-2566; fax (9) 465-2622; internet www.partido-par.com; f. 1993 as the Partido Antiá Restrukturá, renamed as above following the dissolution of the Netherlands Antilles in 2010; social-Christian ideology; Leader (vacant); Pres. ZITA JESUS-LEITO.

Partido Nashonal di Pueblo (PNP) (National People's Party): Winston Churchillweg 133, Willemstad; tel. (9) 869-6777; fax (9) 869-6688; f. 1958; also known as Nationale Volkspartij; social-Christian party; Leader HUMPHREY DAVELAAR.

Pueblo Soberano (PS): Willemstad; internet www.pueblosoberano .org; pro-independence; Leader (vacant).

Judicial System

Legal authority is exercised by the Court of First Instance and in appeal by the Joint High Court of Justice of Curaçao, St Maarten and Aruba. The members of the Joint High Court of Justice sit singly as judges in the Courts of First Instance. The Chief Justice of the Joint High Court of Justice, its members and the Attorney-General of Curaçao are appointed for life by the Dutch monarch, after consultation with the Government of Curaçao. The Supreme Court of the Netherlands (based in The Hague) is the court of Final Instance for any appeal.

Joint High Court of Justice: Wilhelminaplein 4, Willemstad; tel. (9) 463-4111; fax (9) 461-8341; e-mail hofcur@cura.net; Chief Justice LISBETH HOEFDRAAD.

Religion

CHRISTIANITY

Most of the population are Christian, the predominant denomination being Roman Catholicism. There are also small communities of Jews, Muslims and Bahá'ís.

Curaçaose Raad van Kerken (Curaçao Council of Churches): Periclesstraat 6, Willemstad; tel. (9) 465-3207; fax (9) 461-0733; e-mail ddtic@yahoo.com; f. 1958; six mem. churches; Chair. IDA VISSER; Exec. Sec. PAUL VAN DER WAAL.

The Roman Catholic Church

Roman Catholics form the largest single group on Curaçao. Curaçao and the other former constituent territories of the Netherlands Antilles, as well as Aruba, together form the diocese of Willemstad, suffragan to the archdiocese of Port of Spain (Trinidad and Tobago). The Bishop participates in the Antilles Episcopal Conference, currently based in Trinidad and Tobago.

Bishop of Willemstad: Rt Rev. LUIGI ANTONIO SECCO, Bisdom, Breedestraat 31, Otrobanda, Willemstad; tel. (9) 462-5857; fax (9) 462-7437; e-mail bisdomwstad@curinfo.an.

Other Churches

The largest of the other churches in the Netherlands Antilles, according to the 2001 census, were the Pentecostal (5% of the population), Protestant (3%), Seventh-day Adventist (3%) and Methodist (3%). According to the 2001 census, around 1% of the population of the Netherlands Antilles were Anglicans. Other denominations included the Moravian, Apostolic Faith, Wesleyan Holiness and Norwegian Seamen's Churches, the Baptists, Calvinists, Jehovah's Witnesses, Evangelists, the Church of Christ, and the New Testament Church of God.

Iglesia Protestant Uni (United Protestant Church): Fortkerk, Fort Amsterdam, Willemstad; tel. (9) 461-1139; fax (9) 465-7481; e-mail vpg-cur@curlink.com; internet www.vpg-curacao.com; f. 1825 by union of Dutch Reformed and Evangelical Lutheran Churches; associated with the World Council of Churches and the Caribbean and North American Council for Mission (CANACOM); Pres. JOHANNES (HANCO) DE LIJSTER; 3 congregations; 11,280 adherents; 3,200 mems.

JUDAISM

According to the 2001 census, around 1% of the population of the Netherlands Antilles were Jews.

Congregation 'Shaarei Tsedek' Ashkenazi Orthodox Jewish Community: 37 Magdalenaweg, Willemstad; tel. and fax (9) 738-5949; e-mail rel_yes@yahoo.com; 140 mems; Rabbi ARIEL YESHURUN.

Reconstructionist Shephardi Congregation Mikvé Israel-Emanuel: Hanchi di Snoa 29, POB 322, Willemstad; tel. (9) 461-1067; fax (9) 465-4141; e-mail information@snoa.com; internet www .snoa.com; f. 1732 on present site; Pres. RENÉ LEVY MADURO; about 150 mems.

The Press

Amigoe: Kaya Fraternan di Skèrpènè z/n, POB 577; tel. (9) 767-2000; fax (9) 767-4084; e-mail directie@amigoe.com; internet www .amigoe.com; f. 1884; Christian; daily; evening; Dutch; Dir ERNEST VOGES; Editor-in-Chief GINO BERNADINA; circ. 12,000.

Antilliaans Dagblad: ABCourant NV, Prof. Kernkampweg z/n, POB 725; tel. (9) 747-2200; fax (9) 747-2257; e-mail algemeen@ antilliaansdagblad.com; internet www.antilliaansdagblad.com; f. 2003; daily; Dutch; privately owned; Publr MIKE WILLEMSE.

Bala: Noord Zapateer nst 13, Willemstad; tel. (9) 467-1646; fax (9) 467-1041; e-mail bala@cura.net; daily; Papiamento.

Curaçao Holiday: POB 569, Willemstad; tel. (9) 461-1211; fax (9) 461-8087; f. 1960; tourist guide; English; 3 a year; circ. 300,000.

De Curaçaosche Courant: Salinja 147, Willemstad; tel. (9) 461-2766; fax (9) 461-6302; e-mail info@curcourant.com; f. 1812; weekly; Dutch; Editor J. KORIDON.

Extra: W. I. Compagniestraat 41, Willemstad; tel. (9) 462-4595; fax (9) 462-7575; e-mail redactie@extra.cw; internet extra.cw; daily; morning; Papiamento; Man. R. YRAUSQUIN; Editor MIKE OEHLERS; circ. 20,000.

Nobo: Scherpenheuvel w/n, POB 323, Willemstad; tel. (9) 767-3500; fax (9) 767-3550; daily; evening; Papiamento; Editor CARLOS DAANTJE; circ. 15,000.

La Prensa: W. I. Compagniestraat 41, Willemstad; tel. (9) 462-3850; fax (9) 462-5983; e-mail webmaster@laprensacur.com; f. 1929; daily; evening; Papiamento; Man. R. YRAUSQUIN; Editor SIGFRIED RIGAUD; circ. 10,750.

De Telegraaf (Caribische Editie): ABCourant NV, Prof. Kernkampweg z/n, Willemstad; tel. (9) 747-2200; fax (9) 747-2257; e-mail algemeen@antilliaansdagblad.com; internet www.antilliaans dagblad.com; Caribbean edn of Dutch daily.

Ultimo Noticia: Frederikstraat 100, Willemstad; tel. (9) 462-3446; fax (9) 462-6535; e-mail redakshon@ultimo.cw; daily; morning; Papiamento; Editor CHICHO JONCKHEER.

NEWS AGENCY

Algemeen Nederlands Persbureau (ANP) (Netherlands): Panoramaweg 5, POB 439, Willemstad; tel. (9) 461-2233; fax (9) 461-7431; Representative RONNIE RENS.

Publishers

Drukkerij Scherpenheuvel NV: Lindberghweg 28A, Willemstad; tel. (9) 465-6801.

Drukkerij de Stad NV: W. I. Compagniestraat 41, POB 3011, Willemstad; tel. (9) 462-3566; fax (9) 462-2175; e-mail management@ destad.an; internet www.drukkerijdestad.com; f. 1929; Dir KENRICK A. YRAUSQUIN.

Broadcasting and Communications

TELECOMMUNICATIONS

Digicel Curaçao: Biesheuvel 24–25; tel. (9) 736-1056; fax (9) 736-1057; e-mail customercare@digicelcuracao.com; internet www .digicelcuracao.com; f. 1999 as Curaçao Telecom; bought by Digicel (Ireland) in 2005, present name adopted 2006; telephone and internet services; Chair. DENIS O'BRIEN; CEO (Dutch Caribbean) SANDER GIELEN.

Scarlet: Fokkerweg 26, Suite 106, Willemstad; tel. (9) 766-0000; fax (9) 461-8301; internet www.scarlet.an; telecommunications provider in Curaçao and St Maarten; CEO ERIC E. STAKLAND.

United Telecommunication Services, NV (UTS): UTS Headquarters, Rigelweg 2, Willemstad; tel. (9) 777-0101; fax (9) 777-1284; e-mail info@uts.cw; internet www.uts.cw; f. 1999 following merger of Antelecom NV (f. 1908) and SETEL (f. 1979); Antelecom and SETEL still operate under own names; CEO PAUL DE GEUS.

Servicio de Telekomunikashon (UTS Wireless Curaçao) (SETEL): UTS Headquarters, Rigelweg 2, Willemstad; tel. (9) 777-0101; fax (9) 777-1284; e-mail info@uts.cw; internet www.uts .cw; f. 1979; forms part of UTS; state-owned, privatization pending; telecommunications equipment and network provider; Pres. ANGEL R. KOOK; Man. Dir JULIO CONSTANCIA; 400 employees.

BROADCASTING
Radio

Curom Broadcasting Inc: Roodeweg 64, POB 2169, Willemstad; tel. (9) 462-2020; fax (9) 462-5796; e-mail z86@curom.com; internet www.curom.com; f. 1933; broadcasts in English, Papiamento, Dutch and Spanish; Dir ORLANDO CUALES.

Mi 95: f. 1988; FM; music station, aimed at adults.

Z-86: news station.

88 Ròckòrsou: rock music station, aimed at young people.

Easy 97.9 FM: Arikokweg 19A, Willemstad; tel. (9) 462-3162; fax (9) 462-8712; e-mail radio@easyfm.com; internet www.easyfm.com; f. 1995; Dir KEVIN CARTHY.

Gold 91.5 FM Curaçao: De Rouvilleweg 7, Ingang Klipstraat, POB 6103, Willemstad; tel. (9) 426-1803; fax (9) 461-9103; e-mail info@gold915.com; internet www.gold915.com; music station.

Paradise FM: De Rouvilleweg 7, Ingang Klipstraat, POB 6103, Willemstad; tel. (9) 426-1803; fax (9) 461-9103; e-mail studio@paradisefm.an; internet paradisefm.an; news station.

Radio Caribe: Ledaweg 35, Brievengat, Willemstad; tel. (9) 736-9564; fax (9) 736-9569; f. 1955; commercial station; programmes in Dutch, English, Spanish and Papiamento; Dir-Gen. C. R. HEILLEGGER.

Radio Exito: Julianaplein 39, Willemstad; tel. (9) 462-5577; fax (9) 462-5580.

Radio Hoyer NV: Plasa Horacio Hoyer 21, Willemstad; tel. (9) 461-1678; fax (9) 461-6528; e-mail hoyer1@radiohoyer.com; internet www.radiohoyer.com; f. 1954; commercial; two stations: Radio Hoyer I (mainly Papiamento, also Spanish) and II (mainly Dutch, also English) in Curaçao; Man. Dir HELEN HOYER.

Radio Korsou FM: Bataljonweg 7, POB 3250, Willemstad; tel. (9) 737-3012; fax (9) 737-2888; e-mail studio@korsou.com; internet www .korsou.com; f. 1976; 24 hrs a day; programmes in Papiamento and Dutch; Gen. Man. ALAN H. EVERTSZ.

Radio Tropical: Kaya W. F. G. Mensing, Willemstad; tel. (9) 465-0190; fax (9) 465-2470; e-mail tropi@cura.net; Dir DWIGHT RUDOLPHINA.

Television

Antilliaanse Televisie Maatschappij NV (TeleCuraçao): Berg Ararat z/n, POB 415, Willemstad; tel. (9) 461-1288; fax (9) 461-4138; e-mail web@telecuracao.com; internet www.telecuracao.com; f. 1960; fmrly operated Tele-Aruba; commercial; owned by United Telecommunication Services; also operates cable service, offering programmes from US satellite television and two Venezuelan channels; Dir PAUL DE GEUS; Gen. Man. HUGO LEW JEN TAI.

Five television channels can be received on Curaçao in total. Curaçao has a publicly owned cable television service, TDS.

Finance

(cap. = capital; res = reserves; dep. = deposits; m. = million; br.(s) = branch(es); amounts in Netherlands Antilles guilders unless otherwise indicated)

BANKING
Regulatory Authority

College Financieel Toezicht (CFT): De Rouvilleweg 39, Willemstad; tel. (9) 461-9081; e-mail info@cft.an; internet www.cft.an; f. 2008; board of financial supervision; office on Sint Maarten (q.v.); Chair. AGE BAKKER.

Central Bank

Centrale Bank van Curaçao en Sint Maarten: Simon Bolivar Plein 1, Willemstad; tel. (9) 434-5500; fax (9) 461-5004; e-mail info@centralbank.cw; internet centralbank.cw; f. 1828 as Curaçaosche Bank, renamed Bank van de Nederlandse Antillen in 1962, present name adopted in 2010; cap. 30.0m., res 610.5m., dep. 2,520.9m. (Dec. 2009); Pres. Dr EMSLEY D. TROMP; br. on St Maarten.

Commercial Banks

Banco di Caribe NV: Schottegatweg Oost 205, POB 3785, Saliña, Willemstad; tel. (9) 432-3000; fax (9) 461-5220; e-mail info@bancodicaribe.com; internet www.bancodicaribe.com; f. 1973;

cap. 96.4m., res 37.6m., dep. 1,424.3m. (Dec. 2011); Chair. R. GIBSON; CEO and Gen. Man. Dir IDEFONS D. SIMON; 5 brs.

CITCO Banking Corporation NV: De Ruyterkade 62, POB 707, Willemstad; tel. (9) 732-2322; fax (9) 732-2330; e-mail curacao-bank@citco.com; internet www.citco.com; f. 1980 as Curaçao Banking Corpn NV; Man. Dir and Gen. Man. RONALD IRAUSQUIN; Man. Dirs GLENDA E. C. LALLJEE-TRAPENBERG, NIHAILA TH FANEYTE.

FirstCaribbean International Bank (Curaçao) NV: De Ruyterkade 61, POB 3144, Willemstad; tel. (9) 433-8338; fax (9) 433-8198; e-mail bank.curacao@firstcaribbeanbank.com; internet www .firstcaribbeanbank.com/curacao; f. 1964 as ABN AMRO Bank NV; part of FirstCaribbean Group, based in Barbados; 91.5% owned by CIBC, Canada; Exec. Chair. MICHAEL MANSOOR; Man. Dir (Dutch Caribbean) W. M. (PIM) VAN DER BERG; 6 brs.

Girobank NV: Scharlooweg 35, Willemstad; tel. (9) 433-9999; fax (9) 461-7861; e-mail info@gironet.com; internet www.girobank.net; cap. 46.5m., res 49.2m., dep. 1,236m. (Dec. 2011); Pres. ERIC GARCIA; Man. Dirs STEPHAN CAPELLA, RICHARD RAJACK.

Maduro & Curiel's Bank NV: Plaza Jojo Correa 2–4, POB 305, Willemstad; tel. (9) 466-1100; fax (9) 466-1122; e-mail info@mcb-bank.com; internet www.mcb-bank.com; f. 1916 as NV Maduro's Bank; merged with Curiel's Bank in 1931; affiliated with Bank of Nova Scotia NV, Toronto, Canada; br. in Bonaire; cap. 51m., res 195.5m., dep. 5,001.6m. (Dec. 2011); Pres. and CEO LIONEL CAPRILES; Man. Dirs MICHAEL DE SOLA, JOE VAN DONGEN; 15 brs.

Meespierson (Curaçao) NV: Berg Arrarat 1, POB 3889, Willemstad; tel. (9) 463-9200; fax (9) 461-3769; e-mail privatebanking_curacao@meespierson.com; internet www .meespierson.cw; f. 1952 as Pierson, Heldring and Pierson (Curaçao) NV; became Meespierson (Curaçao) NV in 1993; name change to Fortis Bank (Curaçao) NV in 2000, and reverted to Meespierson (Curaçao) NV in 2009; international banking/trust co; Man. Dir VICTOR DEN HOEDT.

Orco Bank NV: Dr Henry Fergusonweg 10, POB 4928, Willemstad; tel. (9) 737-2000; fax (9) 737-6741; e-mail info@orcobank.com; internet www.orcobank.com; f. 1986; cap. 7.8m., res 17.4m., dep. 600.1m. (Dec. 2011); Man. Dirs M. N. S. SPROCK, K. R. CANWORD, M. M. S. BOSKALJON-ROMER; 3 brs.

Rabobank Curaçao NV: Zeelandia Office Park, Kaya W. F. G. (Jombi), Mensing 14, POB 3876, Willemstad; tel. (9) 465-2011; fax (9) 465-2066; e-mail l.an.curacao.ops@rabobank.com; internet www .rabobank.com; f. 1978; cap. US $53.0m., res $17.8m., dep. $4,535.2m. (Dec. 2003); Chair. GUILLERMO BILBAO; Gen. Man. T. STEVENS.

RBC Royal Bank NV: Kaya Flamboyan 1, Rooi Catootje, POB 763, Willemstad; tel. (9) 763-8438; fax (9) 737-0620; e-mail tt-info@rbc .com; internet www.rbc.com/caribbean; f. 1997 as Antilles Banking Corpn; name changed to RBTT Bank NV in 2002; name changed as above in 2012; cap. 114.5m., res 139m., dep. 3,553.2m. (Dec. 2010); Pres. and Country Head (Curaçao) ROBERT DA SILVA; 4 brs.

SFT Bank NV: Schottegatweg Oost 44, POB 707, Willemstad, Curaçao; tel. (9) 732-2900; fax (9) 732-2905; e-mail info@sftbank .com; internet www.sftbank.com; f. 1982 as Curaçao Banking Corpn; restructured as CITCO Bank Antilles in 1984; changed name as above in 1995; total assets 453.2m. (Dec. 2011); Man. Dir LEO RIGAUD.

'Offshore' Banks

Abu Dhabi International Bank NV: Kaya W. F. G. (Jombi), Mensing 36, POB 3141, Willemstad; tel. (9) 461-1299; fax (9) 461-5392; e-mail info@ant-trust.com; internet www.nbad.com; f. 1981; cap. US $20.0m., res $30.0m., dep. $112.2m. (Dec. 2006); Pres. NAGY KOLTA.

DVB Bank America NV: Zeelandia Office Park, Kaya W. F. G. (Jombi) Mensing 14, POB 3107, Willemstad; tel. (9) 431-8700; fax (9) 465-2366; e-mail sandra.sponselee@dvbbank.com; internet www .dvbbank.com; Gen. Man. SANDRA SPONSELEE.

Van Lanschot Bankiers (Curaçao) NV: Schottegatweg Oost 32, POB 4799, Willemstad; tel. (9) 737-1011; fax (9) 737-1086; e-mail info@vanlanschot.com; internet www.vanlanschot.com; f. 1962; wholly owned by F. Van Lanschot Bankiers NV (Netherlands); Man. A. VAN GEEST.

Savings Bank

Curaçaose Postspaarbank (PSB Bank): Schottegatweg Noord 24 Units M-N-O, Willemstad; tel. (9) 432-2000; fax (9) 737-2969; e-mail info@psbbanknv.com; internet www.psbbanknv.com; f. 1905; post office savings bank; Man. Dir GUIVERON WEERT; cap. 21m.; 20 brs.

Banking Associations

Association of International Bankers (IBA): A. M. Chumaceiro Blvd 3, POB 3369, Willemstad; tel. (9) 461-5367; fax (9) 461-5369; e-mail info@ibna.an; internet www.ibna.an; f. 1980; supervisory body for banks operating in Curaçao and Sint Maarten; 32 mems; Pres. ARTHUR ADAMS; Sec. ANTONIO TORRES.

Curaçao Bankers' Association (CBA): Girobank NV, Scharlooweg 35, Willemstad; tel. (9) 433-9999; fax (9) 461-7861; e-mail florisela.bentoera@an.rbtt.com; f. 1972; Pres. LIONEL CAPRILES; Sec. FLORISELA BENTOERA.

Curaçao International Financial Services Association (CIFA): A. M. Chumaceiro Blvd 3, Willemstad; tel. (9) 461-5371; fax (9) 461-5378; e-mail info@cifa-curacao.com; internet www .cifa-curacao.com; representative association for the international financial services sector; Chair. ETIENNE YS.

INSURANCE

ASKA Holding NV (ASKA Levenverzekering NV / ASKA Schadeverzekering NV): Scharlooweg Oost 19, POB 3778, Willemstad; tel. (9) 734-5566; fax (9) 766-5577; e-mail info@askanv.com; internet www.askanv.com; f. 1995; accident and health, motor vehicle, property.

ENNIA Caribe Holding NV: J.B. Gorsiraweg 6, POB 581, Willemstad; tel. (9) 434-3800; fax (9) 434-3873; e-mail mail@ennia.com; internet www.ennia.com; f. 1948 as Nieuw Eerste Nederlandse Insurance Co; changed name as above in 1974; part of the Parman International BV (USA) since Jan. 2006; Pres. DONALD BAKHUIS; Man. Dir ALBARTUS WILLEMSEN.

> **Ennia Caribe Schaden NV:** J. B. Gorsiraweg 6, POB 581, Willemstad; tel. (9) 434-3800; fax (9) 434-3873; e-mail mail@ennia.com; f. 1948; general; life insurance as Ennia Caribe Leven NV.

> **Ennia Caribe Zorg NV:** John B. Gorsiraweg 6, POB 581, Willemstad; tel. (9) 461-6399; fax (9) 461-6709; fmrly De Amersfoortse Antillen NV; name changed as above in 2002; health care.

Fatum: Cas Coraweg 2, Roi Katochi, Willemstad; tel. (9) 777-7777; fax (9) 737-0176; internet fatum.com; f. 1904; owned by Guardian Holdings Ltd; bought Royal & Sun Alliance (Antilles) N.V. in Dec. 2012; Pres. and CEO STEVEN MARTINA.

Maduro & Curiel's Insurance Services NV: Lio Capriles Banking Center, Rooi Catootje, POB 305, Willemstad; tel. (9) 466-1855; fax (9) 466-1611; e-mail mcis@mcb-bank.com; internet www .mcb-insurance.com; Man. KENNETH ISIDORA.

NAA-Citizens Curaçao NV: Salinja 170, Willemstad; tel. (9) 465-7144; fax (9) 461-6269; e-mail rwawoe@citizens-ins.net; internet www.naa-curacao.com; fmrly Netherlands Antilles and Aruba Assurance Company (NA&A) NV; accident and health, motor vehicle, property.

United Insurance Company Ltd: c/o UNIRISK, Schottegatweg Oost 60, POB 609, Willemstad; tel. (9) 737-4005; fax (9) 737-4006; e-mail info@united.cw; internet www.united.cw.

Trade and Industry

DEVELOPMENT ORGANIZATIONS

Curaçao Industrial and International Trade Development Company NV (CURINDE): Emancipatie Blvd 7, Landhuis Koningsplein; tel. (9) 737-6000; fax (9) 737-1336; e-mail info@ curinde.com; internet www.curinde.com; f. 1980; state-owned; manages the harbour free zone, the airport free zone and the industrial zone; Man. Dir ERIC R. SMEULDERS.

World Trade Center Curaçao (WTCC): POB 6005, Piscadera Bay; tel. (9) 463-6132; fax (9) 463-6573; e-mail ceo@wtccuracao.com; internet www.worldtradecentercuracao.com; CEO CARMELO DE STEFANO.

CHAMBER OF COMMERCE

Curaçao Chamber of Commerce and Industry: Kaya Junior Salas 1, Pietermaai, World Trade Centre Bldg, POB 10, Piscadera Bay; tel. (9) 461-1451; fax (9) 461-5652; e-mail management@ curacao-chamber.cw; internet www.curacao-chamber.cw; f. 1884; Chair. WILLIAM JONCKHEER; Exec. Dir JOHN H. JACOBS.

INDUSTRIAL AND TRADE ASSOCIATIONS

Curaçao Exporters' Association (CEA): c/o Seawings NV, Maduro Plaza z/n CEA, POB 6049, Willemstad; tel. (9) 733-1585; fax (9) 733-1599; e-mail seawings@madurosons.com; f. 1993; Dir ALBERT ELENS.

Curaçao International Financial Services Association (CIFA): Chumaceiro Blvd 3, POB 220, Willemstad; tel. (9) 461-5371; fax (9) 461-5378; e-mail info@cifa-curacao.com; internet www .cifa-curacao.com; f. 1980; represents financial services companies, over 100 mems; Chair. ETIENNE YS.

Curaçao Trade and Industry Association (Vereniging Bedrijfsleven Curaçao—VBC): Kaya Junior Salas 1, POB 49, Willemstad;

tel. (9) 461-1410; fax (9) 461-5422; e-mail info@vbcuracao.com; internet www.vbcuracao.com; f. 1944; Pres. BASTIAN KOOYMAN; Exec. Dir JOHAN LIEUW.

STATE HYDROCARBON COMPANY

Refinería di Korsou NV: Ara Hilltop Office Complex, Pletterijweg 1, POB 3627, Willemstad; tel. (9) 461-1050; fax (9) 461-3377; internet info@refineriadikorsou.com; internet www.refineriadikorsou.com; f. 1915 by Royal Dutch Shell Co, taken over by Govt and leased to PDVSA of Venezuela in 1985; Man. (vacant); Pres. OSWALD VAN DER DIJS.

UTILITY

Electricity and Water

Aqualectra Production NV (KAE): Rector Zwijsenstraat 1, POB 2097; tel. (9) 463-2200; fax (9) 463-2228; e-mail info@aqualectra.com; internet www.aqualectra.com; present name adopted in 2001 following the restructuring of Curaçao's energy sector; CEO ANTHON CASPERSON.

TRADE UNIONS

Central General di Trahadonan di Corsow (CGTC) (General Headquarters for Workers of Curaçao): POB 2078, Otrobanda, Willemstad; tel. (9) 737-6097; fax (9) 737-3145; e-mail cgtc.curacao@ gmail.com; f. 1949; Sec.-Gen. ROLAND (NACHO) IGNACIO.

Curaçaosche Federatie van Werknemers (Curaçao Federation of Workers): Schouwburgweg 44, POB 4327, Willemstad; tel. (9) 737-0390; fax (9) 737-1403; e-mail curafed@yahoo.com; f. 1964; Pres. WILFRED SPENCER; Sec.-Gen. GILBERT POULINA; 204 affiliated unions; about 2,000 mems.

Sentral di Sindikatonan di Korsou (SSK) (Central Trade Unions of Curaçao): Schouwburgweg 44, POB 3036, Willemstad; tel. (9) 737-0255; fax (9) 737-5250; e-mail ssk@cura.net; Pres. ALCIDES COVA; 6,000 mems.

Transport

RAILWAYS

There are no railways.

ROADS

Curaçao has a good system of all-weather roads.

SHIPPING

Curaçao is an important centre for the refining and transshipment of Venezuelan and Middle Eastern petroleum. Willemstad is served by the Schottegat harbour, set in a wide bay with a long channel and deep water. There are a further six ports on the island. A 'mega cruise' facility, with capacity for the largest cruise ships, has been constructed on the Otrobanda side of St Anna Bay. Ports at Bullen Bay and Caracas Bay also serve Curaçao. At December 2012 the flag registered fleet comprised 164 vessels, totalling 1,427,949 grt.

Curaçao Ports Authority: Werf de Wilde z/n, POB 689, Willemstad; tel. (9) 434-5999; fax (9) 461-3907; e-mail info@curports.com; internet curports.com; Man. Dir AGUSTÍN DÍAZ.

Principal Shipping Companies

Caribbean Cargo Services NV: Caracasbaaiweg 328, POB 442, Willemstad; tel. (9) 767-2588; fax 747-1155; internet www.ccs.an; Man. Dir LOES VAN DER WOUDE.

Curaçao Drydock Company (CDM): POB 3012; tel. (9) 733-0000; fax (9) 736-5580; f. 1958; state-owned; ship repair yard.

Dammers Ship Agencies Inc: Dammers Bldg, Kaya Flamboyan 11, POB 3018, Willemstad; tel. (9) 737-0600; fax (9) 737-3875; e-mail directorate@dammers-curacao.com; internet www.dammers -curacao.com; f. 1964; fmrly Dammers & van der Heide, Shipping and Trading (Antilles) Inc; Man. Dir (Finance) PETER GOVERS; Man. Dir (Marketing and Sales) ROBERT VAN HEULEN.

Gomez Shipping NV: Landhuis Zeelandia z/n, Willemstad; tel. (9) 461-5900; fax (9) 461-3358; e-mail info@gomezshipping.ibm.net; Man. FERNANDO DA COSTA GÓMEZ.

S. E. L. Maduro Shipping: Dokweg 19, Maduro Plaza, POB 3304, Willemstad; tel. (9) 733-1510; fax (9) 733-1538; e-mail maduroship@ madurosons.com; internet www.madurosons.com; f. 1837; Man. Dir H. MEIJER.

VR Shipping NV: Scarlet Bldg, Fokkerweg 26, POB 3677, Willemstad; tel. (9) 461-4700; fax (9) 461-2576; e-mail info@vrshipping .com; internet vrops@vrshipping.com; f. 1975 as Anthony Veder & Co NV; brs in Aruba and Bonaire.

CIVIL AVIATION

Curaçao International Airport is located at Hato, 12 km from Willemstad. In 2006 a new passenger terminal building was opened.

Curaçao Airline Association (CAA): Curaçao International Airport, Hato; tel. (9) 839-1111; fax (9) 839-1112; internet curacaoairlinesassociation.org; f. 2003; 42 mems; Pres. GERMAINE RICHIE; Sec. GERHARD GOSELINK.

Dutch Antilles Express: Pietermaai 33–35, POB 4101, Willemstad; tel. (9) 461-2502; fax (9) 461-2508; e-mail curacao@flydae.com; internet www.flydae.com; f. 2005; scheduled passenger flights within the Caribbean and South America.

InselAir: Curaçao International Airport, Hato; tel. (9) 737-0444; e-mail customerrelations@fly-inselair.com; internet www.fly-inselair.com; f. 2006; flights within Caribbean, to Venezuela and to USA (Charlotte, NC); CEO ALBERT J. KLUIJVER.

Tourism

Tourism is a major industry on Curaçao. The principal attractions for tourists are the white, sandy beaches, marine wildlife and diving facilities. Visitor arrivals to Curaçao totalled 390,000 in 2011, when tourism receipts totalled US \$453m. The majority of visitors were from the Netherlands (36%) and the USA (16%).

Curaçao Hospitality and Tourism Association (CHATA): Kaya Junior Salas 01, Willemstad; tel. (9) 465-1005; fax (9) 465-1052; e-mail info@chata.org; internet www.chata.org; f. 1967 as Curaçao Hotel Asscn; Pres. and CEO LIZANNE DINDIAL.

Curaçao Tourist Board: Pietermaai 19, POB 3266, Willemstad; tel. (9) 434-8200; fax (9) 461-5017; e-mail info@curacao.com; internet www.curacao.com; f. 1989; supervised by the Curaçao Tourism Development Bureau; CEO GHATIM KABBARA.

Defence

Although defence is the responsibility of the Netherlands, compulsory military service is laid down in an Antilles Ordinance. The Governor is the Commander-in-Chief of the armed forces, and a Dutch contingent is stationed in Willemstad.

Commander of the Navy: Brig.-Gen. DICK SWIJGMAN.

Education

Education was made compulsory in 1992. The island's educational facilities are generally of a high standard. The education system is the same as that of the Netherlands. Dutch is the principal language of instruction, although lessons in Papiamento have been introduced in primary schools. Primary education begins at six years of age and lasts for six years. Secondary education lasts for a further five years. There were 2,211 university students in 2011/12.

SINT MAARTEN

Introductory Survey

Sint (St) Maarten lies in the north-eastern Caribbean Sea, 20 km (12 miles) to the north of Saint-Barthélemy, a French Overseas Collectivity. St Maarten shares a land border with Saint-Martin, the northern half of the island and another Overseas Collectivity of France. St Maarten, as well as Saba (45 km to the south) and Sint (St) Eustatius (56 km south) are known as the Bovenwindse Eilands or Windward Islands (although actually in the Leeward group of the Lesser Antilles). The climate is tropical, moderated by the sea, with an average annual temperature of 27.5°C (81°F) and little rainfall. The official language is English, although Dutch is also spoken. Almost all of the inhabitants profess Christianity, predominantly Protestantism. The state flag (proportions 2 by 3) comprises two equal horizontal stripes, red over blue, with a white triangle at the hoist. In the centre of the triangle is the territory's coat of arms. The capital is Philipsburg.

The Dutch settled the Windward Islands, once inhabited by Carib Indians, in the mid-17th century. The island of St Maarten was divided between the Dutch and the French in 1648, but conflicts over ownership continued for many decades before finally, in 1817, the current partition line between the Dutch and French territories was established. The Dutch part of the island then prospered as a slave-based plantation economy and a major exporter of salt. Together with the Leeward Islands (comprising Aruba, Bonaire and Curaçao), the Windward islands were administered as Curaçao and Dependencies between 1845 and 1948. The territory attracted immigration from Europe, particularly Dutch Protestants but also some French. During the Second World War Queen Wilhelmina of the Netherlands promised independence, and following the end of the war calls for independence became more persistent in St Maarten (as well as in Curaçao—see separate chapter). In 1954 the Dutch Government gave the federation of six islands full autonomy in domestic affairs, and declared it to be an integral part of the Kingdom of the Netherlands.

Political allegiance within the federation was traditionally along island, rather than party lines. These divisions increased following Aruba's secession from the federation in 1986. Calls for further autonomy increased in Curaçao and St Maarten. By the early 1990s it appeared that, while the 'metropolitan' Government was unwilling to allow the complete disintegration of the federation, it was prepared to consider a less centralized system or the creation of two federations in the separate island groups. Nevertheless, in a referendum on the status issue held in St Maarten in October 1994, 60% of the electorate voted to remain within the Antillean federation, while the option of *status aparte* (separate status) received 32% of the vote.

A further referendum on the constitutional future of St Maarten took place on 23 June 2000. Only 4% of participants favoured maintaining the status quo. Some 69% favoured obtaining *status aparte* within the Kingdom of the Netherlands, 14% favoured complete independence and 12% preferred a restructuring of the Antilles of the Five. However, the Dutch Government indicated that it would not support a request by St Maarten to receive *status aparte*. In February 2003 the Dutch Minister of Interior and Kingdom Relations confirmed that the Netherlands would not permit St Maarten to leave the federation. Despite this setback, St Maarten had signed an agreement with the central Antilles Government in August 2002, which would permit the island's Executive Council to take out loans on its own initiative, without seeking permission from the central bank.

The Jesurun Commission, established by the Dutch and Antillean Governments and headed by Edsel Jesurun (a former Governor of the territory), on 8 October 2004 recommended the dissolution of the Netherlands Antilles; support for the federation had, it was argued, virtually disintegrated on most of the islands. The Commission proposed that St Maarten (and Curaçao) should become an autonomous state within the Netherlands (i.e. have *status aparte*), while Saba, Bonaire and St Eustatius should be directly administered by the Dutch Government. A preliminary agreement with the Dutch Government was signed in Curaçao on 3 December 2005; the accord set out that the extant federation be dissolved by 1 July 2007 and that St Maarten would become an autonomous member of the Kingdom of the Netherlands.

On 2 November 2006 the Dutch Government granted St Maarten (and Curaçao) independent governance within the Kingdom of the Netherlands, with the exception of matters of defence, foreign policy and law enforcement matters to the Dutch Government. The Common Court of Justice of the Netherlands Antilles and Aruba was to be retained as the islands' principal judicial authority. The metropolitan administration would assume responsibility for the Netherlands Antilles' substantial collective debt, estimated at NA Fl. 5,000m. St Maarten's Island Council acceded to the proposed agreement on 28 November; however, progress towards dissolving the federation was delayed by the Curaçao Island Council's voting against ratification of the accord, citing concern over provisions relating to judicial matters, policing and debt relief (for further details see the Curaçao chapter). The Dutch Government refused to countenance renegotiation of the terms of the agreement. Nevertheless, on 12 February 2007, at a meeting in Philipsburg, a further 'transition accord' was signed by the Island Councils of Saba, Bonaire, St Eustatius and St Maarten, and the Netherlands, establishing a target date of 15 December 2008 for the dissolution of the federation.

In January 2007 draft legislation was submitted to the Island Council of St Maarten for the proposed repatriation of persons who had assumed illegal residence on the island since 2005. The measure appeared to coincide with requirements for immigration and security reforms ahead of the proposed redesignation of the territory within the Kingdom of the Netherlands. In late 2009 a six-week programme was implemented to grant residency and working rights to illegal immigrants who could prove that they had been living in the territory since the end of 2006, or who possessed a valid contract from an employer.

During 2008 it became increasingly clear that the December deadline for constitutional change would not be met. Negotiations continued throughout that year and at a round-table conference in

Willemstad, Curaçao, on 14–16 December 2008, representatives of all five islands of the federation and the Dutch Prime Minister, Jan Pieter Balkenende, agreed on the new political structure of the Netherlands Antilles. St Maarten would become self-governing except in matters of defence, foreign policy, justice and finance. In return for retaining some legal and financial controls over St Maarten, the Dutch Government agreed to write off almost three-quarters of the Antilles' debt, beginning in 2009. Negotiations stalled, however, other matters, particularly policing and sound financial management (the latter despite the establishment of a financial supervision body, the College financieel toezicht). In September 2009 it was agreed that a second proposed dissolution date of January 2010 was unattainable, and that constitutional change would be set for 10 October of that year. Prior to securing autonomy, St Maarten would be required to introduce an appropriate legislative framework and to prepare its public authorities for the additional tasks entailed in administering an independent state. If the criteria was not met, a strategic plan to implement necessary changes would be devised, with developments to be monitored by a progress committee.

An election was held on 17 September 2010 to St Maarten's new 15-seat legislature. The National Alliance (NA), comprising the Sint Maarten Patriotic Alliance and the National Progressive Party, gained seven seats, while the United People's Party (UP) won six seats and the Democratic Party (DP) the remaining two seats. Following the ballot, the UP and the DP agreed to form a coalition government following the introduction of the new Constitution. The DP's leader, Sarah Wescott-Williams took office as the autonomous territory's first Prime Minister on 10 October, on the same day that the first meeting of parliament was convened. Eugene Holiday assumed the office of Governor.

The newly autonomous St Maarten faced many challenges, in particular a rising rate of crime. The deterioration in the security situation had adverse effects on tourism, the country's major economic activity. Tourism officials expressed concerns that the country would lose vital cruise ship business if the Government did not improve domestic security.

The UP and DP coalition administration collapsed at the end of April 2012 after the UP parliamentary leader, Romain Laville, resigned from the party in protest at what he perceived to be a lack of progress with the legislative agenda. He and two other deputies then withdrew their support for the coalition. Following the loss of the coalition's majority, the Council of Ministers submitted its resignation on 8 May. An agreement on the formation of a new administration was signed by the NA, the DP and three independents (including Laville) on 11 May. The new coalition Government, which was again headed by Wescott-Williams, took office on 21 May. Legislative elections were due to be held in 2014.

In addition to tourism, aggregate is also quarried and consumed primarily by the local construction industry, which contributed 10.1% of gross domestic product (GDP) in 2008. In 2012 the rate of unemployment stood at 11.8% and annual inflation averaged 3.5%. According to the central bank, real GDP contracted by 1.5% in 2011 and there was only negligible growth in 2012.

PUBLIC HOLIDAYS

2014: 1 January (New Year's Day), 18 April (Good Friday), 21 April (Easter Monday), 26 April (King's Day), 29 April (Carnival Day—Jouvert Jump Up), 1 May (Labour Day), 29 May (Ascension Day), 9 June (Whit Monday), 1 July (Emancipation Day), 11 November (St Maarten Day), 15 December (Kingdom Day), 25–26 December (Christmas).

Statistical Survey

(Note: The Netherlands Antilles was officially dissolved on 10 October 2010. The figures in this Statistical Survey refer to Sint Maarten only, unless otherwise indicated.)

Sources (unless otherwise stated): Department of Statistics (STAT), Ministry of Tourism, Economic Affairs, Traffic & Telecommunications (TEZVT), Juancho Yrausquin Blvd 6, Units 7/8, Philipsburg; tel. 542-2151; fax 542-9907; internet www.sintmaartengov.org; Centrale Bank van Curaçao en Sint Maarten, Walter Nisbeth Rd 25, Philipsburg; tel. 542-3529; fax 542-4307; e-mail info@centralbank.an; internet www.centralbank.an.

AREA AND POPULATION

Area: 34 sq km (13.1 sq miles).

Population (official estimate at 1 January 2010): 37,429 (males 17,960, females 19,469).

Density (at 1 January 2010): 1,100.9 per sq km.

Population by Age and Sex (official estimates at 1 January 2010): *0–14:* 8,754 (males 4,299, females 4,455); *15–64:* 27,312 (males 13,053, females 14,259); *65 and over:* 1,363 (males 608, females 755); *Total* 37,429 (males 17,960, females 19,469).

Births, Marriages and Deaths (2008 unless otherwise indicated): Births 462 (2007, provisional); Registered marriages 232 (marriage rate 5.7 per 1,000); Death rate 3.7 per 1,000.

Life Expectancy (years at birth, 2010): Males 73.1; females 78.2 (Source: IMF, *Kingdom of the Netherlands—Curaçao and Sint Maarten: 2011 Article IV Consultation—Staff Report; Informational Annex; and Public Information Notice on the Executive Board Discussion* (December 2011)).

Immigration and Emigration (2009): *Immigration:* Dominican Republic 160; Guadeloupe 79; Guyana 128; India 84; Netherlands 297; Total (incl. others) 2,170. *Emigration:* Aruba 40; Netherlands 365; USA 10; Total (incl. others) 827.

Economically Active Population (labour force survey at March, persons aged 15 years and over, 2007): Agriculture, fishing and mining 227; Manufacturing 622; Electricity, gas and water 285; Construction 2,248; Wholesale and retail trade, repairs 4,315; Hotels and restaurants 2,876; Transport, storage and communications 1,784; Financial intermediation 604; Real estate, renting and business activities 2,034; Public administration, defence and social security 1,658; Education 782; Health and social work 573; Other community, social and personal services 1,893; Private households with employed persons 685; Extra-territorial organizations and bodies 183; Unallocated 1; *Total employed* 20,770. *2009* (labour force survey at June, persons aged 15 years and over): Total employed 21,378; Unemployed 2,966; Total labour force 24,344 (males 12,545, females 11,799). Source: Netherlands Antilles Central Bureau of Statistics.

FINANCE

Currency and Exchange Rates: 100 cents = 1 Netherlands Antilles gulden (guilder) or florin (NA Fl.). *Sterling, Dollar and Euro Equivalents* (31 December 2012): £1 sterling = NA Fl. 2.825; US $1 = NA Fl. 1.790; €1 = NA Fl. 2.362; NA Fl. 100 = £35.40 = $55.87 = €42.34. *Exchange Rate:* In December 1971 the Netherlands Antilles' central bank's mid-point rate was fixed at US $1 = NA Fl. 1.80. In 1989 this was adjusted to $1 = NA Fl. 1.79. In December 2009 it was announced that the US dollar would replace the Netherlands Antilles guilder and florin in Bonaire, St Eustatius and Saba from 1 January 2011, following the dissolution of the previous federation of the Netherlands Antilles in October 2010. In Curaçao and St Maarten, the Netherlands Antilles guilder was expected to be replaced with a newly created Caribbean guilder from 2013.

Budget (NA Fl. million, 2011): *Revenue:* Tax revenue 343.9 (Taxes on income and profits 156.6, Taxes on goods and services 166.8, Taxes on property 20.5); Non-tax revenue 60.7; Total 404.6. *Expenditure:* Total 403.5.

Cost of Living (Consumer Price Index at October; base: October 2006 = 100): All items 111.2 in 2010; 117.8 in 2011; 121.9 in 2012.

Gross Domestic Product (million NA Fl. at current prices): 1,258.7 in 2006; 1,340.5 in 2007; 1,422.5 in 2008.

Gross Domestic Product by Economic Activity (million NA Fl. at current prices, 2008): Agriculture, fishing and mining 6.1; Electricity, gas and water 77.2; Manufacturing 31.6; Construction 137.4; Trade, restaurants and hotels 372.0; Transport, storage and communications 144.5; Real estate, renting and business activities 100.4; Financial services 114.8; Public administration and defence; compulsory social security 71.0; Education 13.7; Health and social welfare 35.2; Households and non-profit institutions serving households 166.8; Other community, social and personal services 91.5; *Sub-total* 1,362.3; Net of indirect taxes 60.2; *GDP in purchasers' values* 1,422.5.

Balance of Payments (NA Fl. million, 2011): Exports of goods f.o.b. 227.2; Imports of goods f.o.b. –1,313.2; *Trade balance* –1,086.0; Services (net) 1,191.9; *Balance on goods and services* 105.9; Income (net) –61.7; *Balance on goods, services and income* 44.2; Current transfers (net) –48.8; *Current balance* –4.6; Capital account (net) 27.3; Direct investment (net) –88.9; Portfolio investment (net) –75.2; Other investment (net) 137.8; Net errors and omissions 16.1; *Overall balance* 12.6.

EXTERNAL TRADE

Principal Commodities (distribution by SITC, NA Fl. million, 2008): *Imports:* Food and live animals 92.4; Beverages and tobacco 38.3; Mineral fuels, lubricants, etc. 165.6; Manufactured goods classified chiefly by material 116.1; Machinery and transport equipment 86.5; Miscellaneous manufactured articles 277.0; Total (incl. others) 813.2. *Exports f.o.b.:* Food and live animals 15.8; Beverages and tobacco 33.3; Manufactured goods classified chiefly by material 7.1; Machinery and transport equipment 9.3; Miscellaneous manufactured articles 46.0; Total (incl. others) 116.1.

TRANSPORT

Road Traffic (motor vehicles registered as 31 December 2008, excl. government-owned vehicles): Passenger cars 17,882; Lorries 2,950; Buses 135; Taxis 249; Rental cars 2,496; Motorcycles and mopeds 828.

Shipping (Netherlands Antilles unless otherwise indicated): *Cruise Ship Arrivals* (Sint Maarten only): 500 in 2009; 551 in 2010; 596 in 2011. *Merchant Fleet* (registered at 31 December 2009): Number of vessels 171; Total displacement 1,406,987 grt (Source: IHS Fairplay, *World Fleet Statistics*).

Civil Aviation (Princess Juliana International Airport traffic, 2008): Commercial landings 62,757; Passenger movements 1,714,987.

TOURISM

Tourist Arrivals: *Stop-overs:* 440,185 (Canada 32,277; Netherlands 15,216; USA 240,431) in 2009; 443,136 (Canada 33,498; Netherlands 16,497; USA 236,379) in 2010; 424,340 (Canada 33,256; Netherlands 16,607; USA 219,204) in 2011. *Cruise ship passengers:* 1,215,146 in 2009; 1,512,618 in 2010; 1,656,159 in 2011.

COMMUNICATIONS MEDIA

Telephones (2008): 12,779 main lines in use.

Mobile Cellular Telephones (2008): 68,749 subscribers.

EDUCATION

University of Sint Maarten (2006/07): 217 students (males 64, females 153).

Directory

The Government

HEAD OF STATE

King of the Netherlands: HM King WILLEM-ALEXANDER.
Governor: EUGENE HOLIDAY.

COUNCIL OF MINISTERS
(May 2013)

The Government was formed by a coalition of the Democratische Partij, the National Alliance and Independents.

Prime Minister and Minister of General Affairs: SARAH WESCOT-WILLIAMS.
Deputy Prime Minister and Minister of Housing and Spatial Planning, Environment and Infrastructure: WILLIAM V. MARLIN.
Minister of Finance: ROLAND S. TUITT.
Minister of Justice: ROLAND E. DUNCAN.
Minister of Education, Culture, Youth and Sports: SILVERIA JACOBS.
Minister of Public Health, Social Development and Labour: VAN HUGH CORNELIUS DE WEEVER.
Minister of Tourism, Economic Affairs, Transport and Tele-communication: ROMEO F. PANTOPHLET.
Minister Plenipotentiary of Sint Maarten in the Netherlands: MATHIAS S. VOGES.

MINISTRIES

Office of the Governor: 3 Falcon Dr., Harbour View, Philipsburg; tel. 542-1160; fax 542-1187; e-mail kabinet@kabgsxm.com; internet www.kabgsxm.com.
Office of the Prime Minister: Clem Labega Sq., POB 943, Philipsburg; tel. 542-2233; fax 542-4300; internet www.sintmaartengov.org.
All government offices are located in Philipsburg.

Legislature

STATEN

President: RODOLPHE E. SAMUEL.
General Election, 17 September 2010

Party	Votes	% of votes	Seats
National Alliance (NA) . .	6,298	45.94	7
United People's Party (UP) . .	4,943	36.06	6
Democratische Partij (DP) . .	2,339	17.06	2
Others	128	0.94	—
Total	**13,708**	**100.00**	**15**

Political Organizations

Democratische Partij (DP): Tamarind Tree Dr. 4, Union Rd, Cole Bay; tel. 543-1166; fax 542-4296; Leader SARAH WESCOTT-WILLIAMS.
National Alliance (NA): Philipsburg; comprises the Sint Maarten Patriotic Alliance and the National Progressive Party; Leader WILLIAM MARLIN.
United People's Party (UP): Philipsburg; f. 2010; Leader THEO HEYLIGER.

Judicial System

Legal authority is exercised by the Court of First Instance, the Constitutional Court and the Joint Court of Justice of Aruba, Curacao, St Maarten, and Bonaire, St Eustatius and Saba. The jurisdiction of the Supreme Court of the Netherlands is the court of Final Instance for any appeal.

Joint Court of Justice: The Courthouse, Frontstreet 58, Philipsburg; tel. 542-3205; fax 542-5451; e-mail sintmaarten@caribjustitia.org; internet www.gemhofvanjustitie.org; Chief Justice LISBETH HOEFDRAAD.
Constitutional Court: Philipsburg; Pres. JACOB (BOB) WIT; Registrar MARITZA JAMES-CHRISTINA.
Court of First Instance: The Courthouse, Frontstreet 58, Philipsburg; tel. 542-3205; fax 542-5451; Chief Judge RENÉ VAN VEEN.

Religion

Almost all of Sint (St) Maarten's population profess Christianity. Roman Catholicism forms the largest single group on St Maarten. St Maarten and the other former constituent territories of the Netherlands Antilles, as well as Aruba, together form the diocese of Willemstad, suffragan to the archdiocese of Port of Spain (Trinidad and Tobago). The Bishop participates in the Antilles Episcopal Conference, currently based in Trinidad and Tobago. Within the Anglican Communion, St Maarten forms part of the diocese of the North Eastern Caribbean and Aruba, within the Church in the Province of the West Indies. The Bishop is resident in The Valley, Anguilla.

The Press

Daily Herald: Bush Rd 22, POB 828, Philipsburg; tel. 542-5253; fax 542-5913; e-mail editorial@thedailyherald.com; internet www.thedailyherald.com; daily; English.
Teen Times: Bush Rd 22, POB 828, Philipsburg; tel. 542-5597; e-mail info@teentimes.com; for teenagers by teenagers; sponsored by *The Daily Herald*; English; Editor-in-Chief MICHAEL GRANGER.

Publisher

House of Nehesi Publishers (HNP): POB 460, Philipsburg; tel. 554-7089; e-mail nehesi@sintmaarten.net; internet www.houseofnehesipublish.com; f. 1986; fiction and non-fiction; Pres. JACQUELINE SAMPLE.

Broadcasting and Communications

TELECOMMUNICATIONS

Caribserve (New Technologies Group, NV): Harbor View Corporate Park, Brooks Tower, Suite 5A/B, Philipsburg; tel. 542-4233; fax 542-4229; e-mail info@caribserve.net; internet www.caribserve.net; internet service provider; subsidiary of UTS, NV; Gen. Man. ROY RICHARDSON.
Scarlet, BV: Three Palms Plaza, 60 Welfare Rd, Colebay; tel. 544-5529; fax 544-2336; e-mail info@scarlet-sxm.com; internet www.scarlet-sxm.com.
St Maarten Telecommunications Group: Soualiga Blvd 5, Philipsburg; tel. 542-0200; fax 543-0101; e-mail info@telemgroup.an; internet www.telemgroup.an; f. 1975; comprises TelEm (providing local services), TelCell NV (digital mobile services), TelNet Communications NV (internet services) and SMITCOMS NV (international services); 15,000 subscribers (TelEm); Chair. RAFAEL BOASMAN; CEO BRIAN MINGO.
UTS St Maarten: Codville Webster Rd 2, Philipsburg; tel. 542-0101; fax 542-4922; e-mail infosxm@uts.an; internet www.sxm.uts.an; Man. CHRISTINA SPROCK.

Regulatory Authority

Bureau Telecommunications en Post St Maarten (BTP): Sparrow Rd 1-D, Harbour View, Philipsburg; tel. 542-4699; fax 542-4817; e-mail info@sxmregulator.sx; internet www.sxmregulator.sx;

f. 2010; regulatory authority; Chair. BRENDA BROOKS; CEO PEGGY ANN BRANDON.

BROADCASTING
Radio

Philipsburg Broadcasting: 106 A. T. Illidge Rd, Philipsburg; tel. 543-2200; fax 543-2229; owns and operates three radio stations; Man. Dir FRANCIS CARTY.

Laser 101 FM: e-mail master@laser101.com; internet www.laser101.fm; 24 hours a day; music; English and Papiamento.

Oasis 96.3 FM: tel. 543-7963; internet www.oasis963.fm.

Tropixx 105.5FM: tel. 543-7960; internet www.tropixx.fm.

Voice of St Maarten (PJD2 Radio): 187 Backstreet, POB 366, Philipsburg; tel. 542-2580; fax 542-2356; internet www.pjd2radio.com; f. 1959; also operates PJD3 on FM (24 hrs); commercial; programmes in English; Gen. Man. DONALD R. HUGHES.

Television

Leeward Broadcasting Corporation—Television: POB 375, Philipsburg; tel. 525-3491; transmissions for approx. 10 hours daily.

TV 15 (Sint Maarten Cable TV Channel 15): 4 Johan Vermeer St, POB 515, Madame Estate; tel. 542-4361; fax 542-5284; e-mail info@sxmtv15.com; internet www.sxmtv15.com; local programming; Station Man. DAVEY WOODS.

WTN TV (Channel 10): Obersi Bldg, Sparrow Rd 1B, Harbour View, Philipsburg; tel. 542-2785; e-mail info@wtntv.com; internet www.wtntv.com; f. 2010; subsidiary of Obersi Group of Cos; CEO ALVIN OBERSI; Gen. Man. ROBERTO GIBBS.

Relay stations provide St Maarten with programmes from Puerto Rico.

Finance

(cap. = capital; res = reserves; dep. = deposits; m. = million)

BANKING
Regulatory Authority

College Financieel Toezicht (CFT): Convent Bldg, 26 Front St, Philipsburg; tel. 543-0331; e-mail info@cft.an; internet www.cft.an; f. 2008; board of financial supervision; office on Curaçao (q.v.); Chair. AGE BAKKER; Mem. (St Maarten) RICHARD GIBSON.

Central Bank

Centrale Bank van Curaçao en Sint Maarten: 25 Walter Nisbeth Rd, Pondfill, Philipsburg; tel. 542-3520; fax 542-4307; e-mail info@centralbank.cw; internet centralbank.cw; Br. Man. L. HASSELL.

Commercial Bank

Windward Islands Bank Ltd: Clem Labega Sq., POB 220, Philipsburg; tel. 542-2313; fax 542-4761; e-mail info@wib-bank.net; internet www.wib-bank.net; affiliated to Maduro & Curiel's Bank NV; f. 1960; cap. and res 53.2m. NA Fl., dep. 662.2m. NA Fl. (Dec. 2006); Chair. LEONEL CAPRILES, III; Man. Dir JAN J. BEAUJON.

Banking Association

St Maarten Bankers' Association: Clem Labega Sq. 7, Philipsburg; tel. 542-2313; fax 542-6355; Pres. J. BEAUJON.

Trade and Industry
CHAMBER OF COMMERCE

St Maarten Chamber of Commerce and Industry: Cannegieterstraat 11, POB 454, Philipsburg; tel. 542-3590; fax 542-3512; e-mail info@sxmcoci.org; internet www.sxmcoci.org; f. 1979; Pres. GLEN CARTY; Exec. Dir CLARET CONNOR.

INDUSTRIAL AND TRADE ASSOCIATION

St Maarten Hospitality and Trade Association: W. J. A. Nisbeth Rd 33A, POB 486, Philipsburg; tel. 542-0108; fax 542-0107; e-mail info@shta.com; internet www.shta.com; Pres. EMIL LEE; Exec. Dir VALYA PANTOPHLET.

UTILITY

GEBE NV: W. J. A. Nisbeth Rd 35, Pond Fill, POB 123, Philipsburg; tel. 542-2213; fax 542-4810; e-mail gebesxm@nvgebe.com; internet www.nvgebe.com; f. 1961; generates and distributes electricity via island network; operates island water supply system on St Maarten and St Eustatius; in Oct. 2011 it was decided to dissolve GEBE to allow for new utilities to be established on St Maarten, Saba and St Eustatius; Dir PAUL MARSHALL (acting).

TRADE UNION

Windward Islands Chamber of Labour Unions (WIFOL): Walter Nisbett Rd 89, POB 1097, Pondfill, Philipsburg; tel. 542-2797; fax 542-6631; e-mail wifol@sintmaarten.net; comprises six unions: Windward Islands Federation of Labour (WIFOL); Windward Islands Civil Servants Union/Private Sector Union (WICSU/PSU); Windward Islands Teachers' Union (WITU); St Maarten Communications Union; Windward Islands Health Care Union Asscn (WIHCUA); and the Asscn of Staff Employees of GEBE; Pres. THEOPHILUS THOMPSON.

Transport
SHIPPING

St Maarten is one of the Caribbean's leading ports for visits by cruise ships, and in 2001 new pier facilities were opened in Philipsburg that could accommodate up to six cruise ships and add more cargo space.

Intermar, SA: 1 Intermar Dr., 2 Groundove Rd, POB 497, Philipsburg; tel. 542-4734; fax 542-5895; e-mail bvdmark@intermar-sxm.com; internet www.intermar-sxm.com; Gen. Man. BOB VAN DER MARK.

SEL Maduro & Sons (WWI) Inc.: 1 Emmaplein Bldg, POB 63, Philipsburg; tel. 542-3407; fax 542-2958; e-mail madops@maduro.org; internet www.maduro-sxm.com; f. 1837; Man. Dir H. L. CHANCE.

St Maarten Ports Authority (SMPA): J. Yrausquin Blvd, POB 146, Philipsburg; tel. 542-2307; fax 542-5048; e-mail comments@portofstmaarten.com; internet www.portofstmaarten.com; f. 1989; Chair. JOSEPH RICHARDSON; Man. Dir MARK MINGO.

CIVIL AVIATION

Princess Juliana International Airport is located 16 km from Philipsburg. The second phase of a US $118m. project to expand the airport was completed in 2006. The development comprised a new terminal, enhancing the airport's annual passenger-handling capacity by 2.5m.

Windward Express Airways: Princess Juliana International Airport; tel. 545-2001; fax 545-2224; e-mail reservations@windwardexpress.com; internet www.windwardexpress.com; f. 2000; domestic and limited Caribbean island charter flights, incl. destinations with restricted access; passenger and cargo flights; Pres. JEAN HALLEY; Man. Dir CURLETTA HALLEY.

Windward Islands Airways International (WIA—Winair) NV: POB 2088, Princess Juliana International Airport; tel. 545-4237; fax 545-2002; e-mail info@fly-winair.com; internet www.fly-winair.com; f. 1961; govt-owned since 1974; scheduled and charter flights throughout north-eastern Caribbean; Man. Dir EDWIN HODGE.

Tourism

The island is famous for its diving and snorkelling locations, and hiking trails to Mount Concordia and to the cliffs of Cupecoy. The annual Heineken Regatta and the St Maarten Carnival also attract visitors. There were 424,340 stop-over arrivals in 2011, while tourism receipts were estimated at US $719m.

St Maarten Tourism Bureau: Krippa Bldg, Unit 10, Juancho Yrausquin Blvd 6, Philipsburg; tel. 542-2337; fax 542-2734; e-mail info@e-stmaarten.com; internet www.vacationstmaarten.com; Dir EDWARD DEST (acting).

Defence

The Netherlands is responsible for the defence of St Maarten. Military service is compulsory. The Governor is Commander-in-Chief of the armed forces in the territory. A Coast Guard Force operates from St Maarten.

Education

Education was made compulsory in 1992. The education system is the same as that of the Netherlands, and is generally of a high standard. English is the official language of instruction. Primary education begins at six years of age and lasts for six years. Secondary education lasts for a further five years.

NEW ZEALAND

Introductory Survey

LOCATION, CLIMATE, LANGUAGE, RELIGION, FLAG, CAPITAL

The Dominion of New Zealand lies in the South Pacific Ocean, about 1,750 km (1,100 miles) south-east of Australia. It consists of North Island and South Island, separated by the narrow Cook Strait, and several smaller islands, including Stewart Island (or Rakiura) in the south. The climate is temperate and moist, with an average temperature of 12°C (52°F), except in the far north, where higher temperatures are reached. The official languages are English and Maori. At the 2001 census, 15.7% of respondents professed adherence to the Anglican Church, 13.0% to Roman Catholicism and 11.5% to Presbyterianism. At the 2006 census, 55.6% of respondents professed adherence to Christianity. The national flag (proportions 1 by 2) is dark blue, with a representation of the United Kingdom flag as a canton in the upper hoist. In the fly are four five-pointed red stars, edged in white, in the form of the Southern Cross constellation. The capital is Wellington, on North Island.

CONTEMPORARY POLITICAL HISTORY

Historical Context

New Zealand is a former British colony. It became a dominion, under the British Crown, in 1907 and achieved full independence by the Statute of Westminster, adopted by the British Parliament in 1931 and accepted by New Zealand in 1947. With Australia and the USA, New Zealand signed the ANZUS Security Treaty (see p. 474) in 1951. In 1962 Western Samoa (now Samoa, q.v.), formerly administered by New Zealand, achieved independence, and in 1965 the Cook Islands attained full internal self-government, but retained many links, including common citizenship, with New Zealand. In October 1974 Niue, one of New Zealand's island territories, obtained similar status 'in free association with New Zealand'. New Zealand retains two Dependent Territories, Ross Dependency and Tokelau (see New Zealand's Dependent Territories).

Domestic Political Affairs

In December 1972 the first Labour Government for more than 12 years came to power, under the leadership of Norman Kirk, after a succession of New Zealand National Party administrations, most recently led by John Marshall, who had replaced Sir Keith Holyoake upon his retirement in February of that year. The New Zealand Labour Party took office at a time when the economy was thriving, mainly as a result of a sharp increase in international prices for agricultural commodities. However, this prosperity was accompanied by inflation, and the international energy crisis of 1973–74 led to a rapid deterioration in the country's economy.

Kirk died in August 1974, and Wallace Rowling, hitherto Minister of Finance, became Prime Minister in September. The economic recession worsened, and in November 1975 a general election resulted in victory for the National Party, which won 55 of the 87 seats in the House of Representatives, while the Labour Party took the remaining 32 seats. The new Government, under Robert (later Sir Robert) Muldoon, who had led the National Party since July 1974, introduced austere economic policies, and in 1976 reduced the annual intake of migrants from 30,000 to 5,000, while conducting a campaign against illegal immigrants.

The National Party retained power at the general election in November 1978, with 50 of the 92 seats in the enlarged House of Representatives, but its share of the vote decreased markedly. Labour won 41 seats, and the Social Credit Party obtained the remaining seat. In the November 1981 election Muldoon's majority was further reduced. The National Party won 47 seats in the House, while Labour, which again received more votes, secured 43 seats and Social Credit (despite obtaining 20.6% of votes cast) only two.

In February 1984 Muldoon's Government antagonized New Zealand's trade unions by effecting legislation to ban 'closed shop' agreements with employers, thus giving employees the right to choose whether or not to join a trade union. Further legislation was used in June to compel striking construction workers to return to work. In the same month, owing to dissent within his own party, Muldoon called an early general election for July. The Labour Party secured 56 of the 95 seats in an enlarged House of Representatives, while the National Party took 37 seats. David Lange (the leader of the Labour Party since February 1983) became Prime Minister. James McLay defeated Muldoon in an election for the leadership of the National Party in November 1984, but he was replaced as party leader by his deputy, James (Jim) Bolger, in March 1986.

The Labour Government introduced controversial deregulatory measures to improve the country's economic situation. The initial success of these measures, together with widespread popular support for the Government's anti-nuclear policy (see below), contributed to another victory for the Labour Party in a general election in August 1987. Of the 97 seats in the expanded House of Representatives, the Labour Party secured 58 and the National Party 39. (The Democratic Party lost both the seats that its predecessor, the Social Credit Party, had won at the 1984 election.)

In 1987 Lange's Government initiated a controversial policy of privatization of state-owned enterprises. In November 1988 policy disagreements prompted Lange to dismiss the minister responsible for the privatization programme, Richard Prebble. Lange was accused by cabinet colleagues of acting without consultation, and in December Roger (later Sir Roger) Douglas, the Minister of Finance, declared that he would not serve another term under Lange. Douglas was dismissed from office, and later that month unsuccessfully challenged Lange for the leadership of the Labour Party. In May 1989 the formation of the NewLabour Party (led by a former president of the Labour Party, Jim Anderton) was announced: the party aimed to appeal to disillusioned Labour supporters. In August Douglas was elected by Labour Members of Parliament (MPs) to a vacant cabinet post, prompting Lange to resign. Shortly afterwards, Geoffrey Palmer, hitherto the deputy leader of the Labour Party, was elected the party's parliamentary leader and Prime Minister.

In January 1990 Palmer effected an extensive government reorganization. The return of Prebble to the Cabinet, in his former post as Minister for State-owned Enterprises, provoked anger within the Labour Party. The Government aroused further hostility by its introduction of a substantial fee for tertiary-level students and by the continued sale of state assets, especially that of the telecommunications company Telecom. In September, less than eight weeks before the next general election, Palmer resigned as Prime Minister. Michael Moore, the Minister of External Relations and Trade (who had also contested the August 1989 leadership election), replaced Palmer as Prime Minister and Labour Party leader. At the general election of October 1990, the National Party took 67 of the 97 seats in the House of Representatives. The Labour Party won 29 seats, while the NewLabour Party retained its sole seat. Jim Bolger, as leader of the National Party, thus became Prime Minister.

The new Government's first economic proposals included the repeal of legislation on equal pay for women, and envisaged reductions in public spending, particularly on social welfare. In December 1990 the Government proposed reductions in unemployment benefit, family benefits, and in medical and sickness payments, in preparation for the introduction of a system whereby users of medical and educational services (hitherto provided free of charge) would be required to pay, according to a means test. These measures prompted an angry response from social and church groups. Protest marches took place in April 1991, and plans for a freeze in the levels of old-age pensions led to groups representing the elderly unsuccessfully to petition the British monarch (through the Governor-General) to dismiss the Government. Two National Party MPs resigned from the party in August, in protest against the proposals, and the Minister of Maori Affairs, Winston Peters, who had openly criticized the Government's economic strategy, was dismissed in October. In November Sir Robert Muldoon announced that he would resign from the legislature in early 1992, in protest against the Government's economic policies. Earlier in the month criticism had prompted the Government to withdraw its stringent means-testing measures for the allocation of state pensions, but the overall level of payments remained lower than previously.

In December 1991 a coalition was formed by minor parties as a challenge to the two main parties. The grouping, known as the Alliance, consisted of the NewLabour Party, the New Zealand Democratic Party, the Green Party of Aotearoa—New Zealand and Mana Motuhake. In September 1992 a preliminary referendum on proposed electoral reform was held. The electorate voted overwhelmingly in favour of the replacement of the 'first-past-the-post' system by a form of proportional representation; of the four alternatives offered, the mixed member proportional (MMP) system (similar to that used in Germany) received the greatest support. The new rules were to be implemented at the 1996 election, following a second, binding referendum.

In March 1993 the outspoken Winston Peters resigned from his parliamentary seat in order to stand for re-election as an independent candidate. The by-election in April resulted in an overwhelming victory for Peters, the major political parties having declined to present candidates. In July Peters established a new party, New Zealand First.

At the general election held in November 1993, the National Party, which had campaigned mainly on the Government's record of economic recovery, was narrowly returned to office, securing 50 of the 99 seats in the enlarged House of Representatives. The Labour Party won 45 seats, the Alliance two and New Zealand First two. At a concurrent, second referendum on electoral reform, 54% of voters favoured the adoption of the MMP system.

In October 1994 Peter Dunne, a former cabinet minister, resigned from the Labour Party, following differences over the party's policy on taxation, and declared his intention to remain in the House of Representatives as an independent member. He subsequently established a new party, Future New Zealand. The traditional two-party system was further challenged in early 1995, when support for ACT New Zealand, co-founded by Sir Roger Douglas (Minister of Finance in 1984–88), began to increase rapidly. In June 1995, however, the position of the ruling party was strengthened by the formation of United New Zealand by seven members of the House of Representatives (four National, two Labour and Future New Zealand leader Dunne). The new grouping pledged its support for the Government on issues of confidence. In February 1996, for the first time since the early 1930s, a formal coalition Government was established when the National Party formed an official alliance with United New Zealand. In the ensuing government reorganization, Dunne joined the Cabinet as Minister of Revenue and Internal Affairs. In March 1996 Sir Michael Hardie Boys replaced Dame Catherine Tizard as Governor-General.

At the first general election under the MMP system, held in October 1996, no party achieved an outright majority. The National Party received 34.1% of the votes cast and took 44 of the 120 seats in the expanded House of Representatives, the Labour Party (28.3%) secured 37 seats and New Zealand First (13.1%) garnered 17 seats, while the Alliance won 13 seats, ACT New Zealand eight and United New Zealand one. A notable development was the increase in the number of Maori MPs from six to 15, a figure almost equivalent to the proportion of Maori (the country's aboriginal inhabitants) in the population as a whole. Following protracted negotiations, an alliance was formed in December between the National Party and Winston Peter's New Zealand First. Jim Bolger thus continued as Prime Minister, while Peters was appointed Deputy Prime Minister and Treasurer. Although Peters had previously discounted the possibility of entering into a coalition with the National Party, he had altered his stance in exchange for concessions on economic policy. The incoming Cabinet incorporated five members of New Zealand First.

In September 1997 proposals for the introduction of a compulsory retirement savings scheme were overwhelmingly rejected in a national referendum. The holding of the referendum had been a condition of New Zealand First's participation in the ruling coalition, but the Prime Minister had also actively supported the proposed pension reforms. In the following month thousands of protesters took to the streets to demand the resignation of the Government, its policies on health and education having drawn particular criticism.

In November 1997, following a leadership challenge from cabinet minister Jenny Shipley, the Prime Minister announced his intention to resign. Shipley was thus sworn in as New Zealand's first female Prime Minister in December. In the ensuing government reorganization, most supporters of Jim Bolger retained their portfolios, Winston Peters continued as Deputy Prime Minister, and the other members of New Zealand First also remained in the Cabinet.

In August 1998, following an acrimonious dispute regarding the sale of the Government's stake in Wellington airport, Winston Peters was dismissed from the post of Deputy Prime Minister and Treasurer, and the dissolution of the coalition Government was announced. Rejecting demands for an early general election, Jenny Shipley reallocated many cabinet portfolios. Although Minister of Maori Affairs Tau Henare (who in late 1998 founded a new party, Mauri Pacific, having been removed as deputy leader of New Zealand First in July) was the only former New Zealand First minister to retain his cabinet post, three other erstwhile members of the party remained as ministers outside the Cabinet. Despite the defection of Peters to the opposition, Shipley was able to secure the support of eight of the 16 New Zealand First MPs, and in September she secured a vote of confidence in the House.

In December 1998 the minority Government's position was further weakened by the unexpected resignation of a supporting independent (and former New Zealand First) MP, following the administration's decision to proceed with its acquisition of 28 F-16 fighter aircraft from the USA. The Prime Minister was placed under further pressure in early 1999, when it was alleged that the Minister of Tourism, Murray McCully, had acted inappropriately regarding the handling of a major contract for the advertising business of the New Zealand Tourism Board. In February, as the Prime Minister became personally implicated in the affair and as opposition MPs accused her of deliberately misleading the legislature over her association with the head of the advertising agency in question, the Government narrowly survived a motion of no confidence. Claiming that the ruling party had intended to exploit its links with the agency during the next general election campaign, the Labour Party demanded an inquiry into the Government's alleged payments to departing members of the New Zealand Tourism Board and into the Board's expenditure on overseas promotions. In March the marketing contract with the agency was terminated, and McCully relinquished the tourism portfolio the following month.

The Labour Party's return to power

At the general election of November 1999, the Labour Party, having secured 38.7% of the votes cast, was allocated 49 of the 120 seats in the House of Representatives, while the National Party, with 30.5% of the votes, received 39 seats. The Alliance (which had absorbed the Liberal Party in 1998) was allocated 10 seats and ACT New Zealand nine seats. Under the system of proportional representation, the victory in one constituency of the Green Party (which was no longer a member of the Alliance) automatically entitled the movement to a further six seats in the legislature. New Zealand First's representation declined to five seats, and United New Zealand took the one remaining seat. Having previously discounted any co-operation with the Green Party, the Labour Party was thus obliged to seek the support not only of the Alliance but also of the seven Green MPs.

The leader of the Labour Party, Helen Clark (who had served as Deputy Prime Minister in 1989–90), thus became Prime Minister. The minority Government, which incorporated several members of the Alliance, took office in December 1999. Jim Anderton, the leader of the Alliance, was appointed Deputy Prime Minister, Minister for Economic Development and Minister for Industry and Regional Development. The treasury and finance portfolios were assigned to Dr Michael Cullen, while Phil Goff became Minister of Foreign Affairs and Trade and also assumed responsibility for the justice portfolio. One of the new Government's stated priorities was the 'Closing the Gaps' initiative, which aimed to address the socio-economic disparities between the Maori and non-Maori communities, particularly in health, housing, education, income and the incidence of crime. Among its first actions were the repeal of the 1991 Employment Contracts Act and the cancellation of the contract to lease 28 F-16 fighter aircraft from the USA.

In June 2000 the Prime Minister was obliged to dismiss the Minister of Maori Affairs, Dover Samuels, following allegations of sexual misconduct. In April 2001 Dame Silvia Cartwright (New Zealand's first female High Court Judge) took office as Governor-General. Her appointment represented a significant achievement for women in New Zealand public life, and created an unprecedented situation in which the five most important public roles in the country (those of Prime Minister, Leader of the

Opposition, Attorney-General and Chief Justice, along with that of Governor-General) were all occupied by women.

In October 2001 Jenny Shipley resigned as leader of the National Party and was replaced by Bill English, a former Minister of Health. In December Jim Anderton was placed under considerable pressure from left-wing members of the Alliance to withdraw his support for the Government's involvement in the US-led military campaign in Afghanistan. In early April 2002, after months of discord, the Alliance split. Anderton and six other members of the party agreed to form a breakaway party, later named the Progressive Coalition, but continued to support the ruling coalition. The seven MPs were expelled from the Alliance in late April. Laila Harré, Minister of Women's Affairs, Youth Affairs and Statistics, succeeded Anderton as leader of the Alliance and confirmed her party's support for the Government until the next legislative elections.

Some 77% of registered voters participated in the general election, which took place earlier than planned (partly owing to the disintegration of the Alliance), on 27 July 2002. The Labour Party received 41% of the votes cast, but failed to secure an overall majority in the House of Representatives, winning 52 of the 120 seats. The National Party performed badly, winning only 21% of the votes; its representation declined by 12 seats to 27. New Zealand First secured 13 seats, ACT New Zealand nine, the Greens nine and United Future New Zealand (UFNZ, which had been formed in 2000 by the merger of United New Zealand and Future New Zealand) eight. The Progressive Coalition took two seats, while the Alliance failed to secure any parliamentary representation. Clark formed a minority coalition Government with the Progressive Coalition, and also secured the support of UFNZ.

In June 2003 Clark announced that the Government intended to draw up new legislation to ensure that the country's coastline and seabed were owned by the Crown, following a ruling by the Court of Appeal that Maori tribes could pursue their own claims to ownership of the Marlborough Sands foreshore and seabed in South Island. Maori condemned the Government's actions as 'draconian' and 'colonialist'. In October the legislature voted overwhelmingly in favour of the Anti-Terrorism Act (an extension of the 2002 Terrorism Suppression Act), which widened the powers of the police force and created various new offences. The Green Party opposed the legislation, claiming that it infringed upon civil liberties. Legislation providing for the replacement of the monarch's Privy Council (based in London, United Kingdom) as New Zealand's court of final appeal by an independent Supreme Court, consisting of five judges headed by the Chief Justice, was approved in October 2003; the new court began functioning in July 2004.

The Minister of Commerce and of Immigration, Lianne Dalziel, was forced to resign in February 2004, after it transpired that she had lied over the disclosure to the media of a confidential legal document relating to the deportation of a Sri Lankan youth. In the same month the new leader of the opposition National Party, Don Brash, a former governor of the central bank, announced that if he won power he would discontinue all forms of positive discrimination for Maori, considering 'special privileges' to be unnecessary and divisive. Brash also pledged to abolish the parliamentary seats reserved for Maori and to repeal 'divisive, race-based' legislation. Clark accused Brash of creating disharmony by breaking the national consensus on dealing with Maori affairs; nevertheless, two days later she promised a review of state assistance for Maori, agreeing that policies should be based on need and not on any perceived privilege. In a government reorganization effected later in February, Clark also created the post of Co-ordinating Minister for Race Relations after opinion polls indicated a decline in support for her administration over its policies towards the Maori. The portfolio was assigned to the Minister of Education, of State Services, and for Sport and Recreation, Trevor Mallard; he was given the immediate responsibility of conducting a full review of government policy.

In April 2004 the Progressive Coalition was renamed the Progressive Party. In the same month Clark dismissed the Associate Minister of Maori Affairs, Tariana Turia, after Turia stated that she intended to vote against the Government's Foreshore and Seabed Bill, which would ensure that coastal areas were owned by the Crown, on the grounds that the proposed legislation was in contravention of the rights of indigenous Maori. Turia resigned from the Labour Party and the House of Representatives in May. The Prime Minister secured a narrow victory in a vote of no confidence precipitated by Turia's resignation. Meanwhile, a two-week *hikoi* (protest march) against the planned legislation arrived outside the Parliament building in Wellington.

In July 2004 Tariana Turia, running as a candidate of the newly formed Maori Party, secured victory in a by-election to the seat of Te Tai Hauauru on North Island, necessitated by her resignation from the House of Representatives. In November the controversial Foreshore and Seabed Bill was narrowly approved by the legislature, after the Government secured the support of New Zealand First. (However, the legislation was repealed following the adoption in March 2011 of the Marine and Coastal Area (Takutai Moana) Act 2011—see Maori Land Rights and the Waitangi Tribunal Process.) Also in November 2004 the Minister of Youth Affairs, for Land Information and of Statistics, John Tamihere, resigned following allegations of fraud. A major government reorganization took effect in February 2005, including the departure of Attorney-General Margaret Wilson from the Cabinet in order to succeed Jonathan Hunt as Speaker of the House of Representatives. Deputy Prime Minister Michael Cullen became the new Attorney-General, while retaining his existing portfolios. In March the Serious Fraud Office announced that, following an investigation, it would not charge Tamihere with any offence. In May David Benson-Pope resigned as Minister of Fisheries, following the commencement of a police inquiry into allegations that he had abused children during his former career as a teacher; however, he was reinstated to the Cabinet in the following month.

At the general election held on 17 September 2005, the Labour Party secured victory by a narrow margin, winning 41.1% of the votes cast and 50 seats. The National Party won 39.1% of the votes and 48 seats, a significant improvement in comparison with its performance at the 2002 election. The Maori Party secured 2.1% of the vote, winning four of the seven seats reserved for Maoris. As the Labour Party had failed to gain an overall majority, it subsequently entered into a coalition with the Progressive Party, which had won only one seat. With the more informal support of New Zealand First and UFNZ, this brought the total number of seats controlled by the Government in the new legislature to 61.

The new Government took office in October 2005. New Zealand First leader Winston Peters was appointed Minister of Foreign Affairs, and Peter Dunne of UFNZ was allocated the revenue portfolio, but with the unusual provision that both would remain outside the Cabinet. The appointment of Peters drew widespread criticism, owing to his anti-immigration views. In March 2006 David Parker resigned as Attorney-General, having admitted that he had made an error while filing an annual return for a company with which he was involved. However, he retained the cabinet portfolios of energy and transport. Deputy Prime Minister Michael Cullen subsequently became Attorney-General for the second time, holding the post concurrently with the finance and tertiary education portfolios.

In May 2006 Maj.-Gen. Jerry (later Lt-Gen. Sir Jerry) Mateparae, hitherto Chief of the Army, became the first Maori to assume the role of Chief of the New Zealand Defence Force. In August Te Arikinui (Dame Te Atairangikaahu, the Maori Queen) died, bringing to an end her 40-year reign, and her son, Tuheitia Paki, took the throne. Also in August Anand (later Sir Anand) Satyanand, a retired judge of Indo-Fijian descent, replaced Dame Silvia Cartwright as Governor-General upon the expiry of her term of office.

In October 2006 the Auditor-General, Kevin Brady, published a report on an investigation into campaign funding during the 2005 legislative elections. Brady found that the Labour Party had improperly spent $NZ768,000 of taxpayers' money on its election campaign; several other parties, including New Zealand First and the Green Party, were similarly implicated in breaches of regulations, albeit for smaller sums. Labour promptly announced that it was to reimburse the funds. Legislation retrospectively validating the relevant election campaign expenditure was swiftly enacted by the House of Representatives, but controversy persisted. In November 2006 Don Brash resigned as leader of the National Party, citing concerns that increased speculation about his position was having a negative effect on the party. Brash had applied for an injunction against the publication of his e-mails in a book that attempted to prove a link between himself and the Exclusive Brethren, a business-orientated Christian group that had allegedly been involved in improperly influencing the outcome of the 2005 election; he denied allegations of irregular campaign practices and maintained that his resignation was not related to the impending publication of the book. John Key was subsequently elected unopposed to the leadership of the National Party.

In July 2007 David Benson-Pope, the Minister for Social Development and Employment and for the Environment, resigned in connection with the allegedly unfair dismissal of an employee of the Ministry for the Environment. Amid opinion poll results suggesting an increase in support for the National Party, Prime Minister Clark announced a ministerial reorganization in October.

In October 2007 a nation-wide police operation resulted in the arrest of 17 people under the Terrorism Suppression Act. Some of the detainees were reported to be activists for causes including Maori independence and the environment, and were alleged to have been involved in illegal training camps where firearms and other weapons were found. Tame Iti, a well-known Maori campaigner, was among those arrested. Hundreds of people took part in demonstrations to protest against the police action, and in November the Solicitor-General concluded that the detainees could not be charged under the Terrorism Suppression Act.

In August 2008 Winston Peters relinquished the foreign affairs and racing portfolios, following the commencement of an investigation by the Serious Fraud Office into allegations of irregularities with regard to donations intended for his New Zealand First party. Prime Minister Clark assumed responsibility for the portfolios, pending the outcome of the inquiry. In October the investigation concluded that Peters had not committed any fraud. However, he did not resume his ministerial role, owing to the imminence of the general election, which was scheduled for November.

The National Party-led coalition Government

At the election held on 8 November 2008, the National Party won 58 seats in the House of Representatives, having received 44.9% of the votes cast. The Labour Party took 43 seats, with 34.0% of the votes, and nine seats were won by the Green Party. Turn-out was almost 79.5% of the registered electorate. In the absence of an overall majority for the National Party, John Key established an informal coalition administration, having secured the support of members of ACT New Zealand (which had won five seats), the Maori Party (also below) and UFNZ (one seat). The total number of seats in the legislature expanded to 122, as two of the five seats taken by the Maori Party were 'overhang' seats, which are awarded under the MMP electoral system in the case of a party winning more constituency seats than it would be entitled to based on its proportion of party list votes. The Maori Party had won 2.4% of the party list vote (thus entitling it to three seats in the House), but had secured five constituency seats. Following the defeat of the Labour Party, Helen Clark resigned as party leader, and was replaced by Phil Goff, whose portfolios in the outgoing Government had included that of defence.

On 19 November 2008 John Key was sworn in as Prime Minister, and also assumed the tourism portfolio. Bill English was appointed as Deputy Prime Minister and Minister of Finance. Other notable appointments to the new Cabinet included Murray McCully as Minister of Foreign Affairs, who was additionally allocated responsibility for sport and recreation, and New Zealand's first minister of Asian origin, Pansy Wong, who was appointed as Minister for Ethnic and Women's Affairs. Five 'support party ministers' included Dr Pita Sharples as Minister of Maori Affairs; Tariana Turia, also a member of the Maori Party, as Minister for the Community and Voluntary Sector; and Peter Dunne of UFNZ as Minister of Revenue. As global financial conditions rapidly deteriorated and New Zealand entered recession, the incoming Government underlined that its immediate priority was to address the country's economic difficulties.

In June 2009 the Prime Minister accepted the resignation of John Worth, Minister for Land Information, Archives New Zealand and the National Library, and Associate Minister for Justice, following a series of allegations of inappropriate behaviour and a police investigation into accusations of harassment. Taito Phillip Field, a former Labour cabinet member and New Zealand's first legislator of Pacific island descent, was sentenced to a six-year prison term in October after being found guilty in August of corruption, bribery and perverting the course of justice; he thus became the first senior New Zealand politician to be convicted of such charges. Field was found to have given favourable treatment to eight Thai immigrants in exchange for free labour on his properties in Auckland and Samoa. (Field was released on parole, having served two years of his prison term, in October 2011; however, a final appeal against his conviction was dismissed by the Supreme Court later that

month.) Meanwhile, in February 2010 the Minister of Fisheries and of Housing, Phil Heatley, submitted his resignation in response to allegations of irregularities relating to claims for parliamentary expenses. However, he was subsequently exonerated, following an investigation by the Auditor-General, and reinstated in his cabinet position.

In November 2009 parliamentary approval was narrowly secured for the Government's contentious emissions trading scheme (ETS), intended to encourage the reduction of greenhouse gas emissions. The opposition Labour Party regarded the ETS as a weaker version of a similar initiative that it had proposed in 2008 and argued that insufficient incentives were being offered to polluters to curtail their carbon emissions. Labour and the Greens also expressed concern at the cost of the ETS. Nevertheless, the trading scheme entered into effect during the latter half of 2010.

Following the Government's announcement in March 2010 of proposals to replace the divisive Foreshore and Seabed Act (see Maori Land Rights and the Waitangi Tribunal Process), in April the Government unexpectedly declared its support for the controversial UN Declaration on the Rights of Indigenous Peoples, thereby officially acknowledging the Maori right to self-determination (within the boundaries of New Zealand law). Labour had refused to support the non-binding Declaration in 2007, owing to fears that it would conflict with the Waitangi Tribunal process and the Constitution by potentially prompting further Maori land claims, while bestowing additional rights upon the Maori but excluding the remainder of the country's population.

In April 2010 the Government launched a new welfare initiative, Whanau Ora ('family wellness'). By providing social services through a single consolidated agency, the programme was primarily intended to redress the consistently low social indicators of Maori, although it was emphasized that the scheme was open to all. Tariana Turia, the co-leader of the Maori Party, was appointed to head the programme, the portfolio being added to her existing responsibilities. Amid criticism of the Whanau Ora initiative by the opposition parties for its lack of clarity, the Government announced funding for the scheme of $NZ134m. over a four-year period, well short of the $NZ1,000m. initially envisaged.

Some 20,000 demonstrators converged in Auckland in May 2010 (reportedly the largest demonstration in the country for some 20 years) to protest against controversial government plans to initiate mining operations in protected conservation zones.

In November 2010 Pansy Wong resigned as Minister for Ethnic Affairs and of Women's Affairs, following allegations of misuse of a parliamentary travel allowance, a claim that related to an internal flight in China taken by her husband in 2008; she was replaced by Hekia Parata, of the National Party. Prime Minister Key subsequently announced that the Government was to introduce legislation that would provide for ministerial allowances to be controlled by the independent Remuneration Authority; hitherto, all ministerial entitlements were determined by the Prime Minister and Speaker, with the Remuneration Authority responsible only for setting ministers' base salaries. In mid-December Wong resigned from the House of Representatives, stating that the ongoing debate over her misuse of travel entitlements was causing 'unnecessary distractions' to the Government. Jami-Lee Ross retained the parliamentary seat vacated by Wong for the National Party in a by-election in March 2011.

Meanwhile, legislation to reform the electoral finance system prior to the holding of the next general election, due in late 2011, was adopted by Parliament in December 2010. The legislation, which, *inter alia*, clarified regulations governing matters such as donations to political parties, replaced the complex, and unpopular, 2007 Electoral Finance Act, which had been repealed in late 2009.

Following an earthquake 10 km south-east of Christchurch in mid-February 2011, which claimed the lives of 185 people and caused widespread damage to buildings and infrastructure, Key effected a minor reallocation of ministerial portfolios, in order to allow the Minister for Economic Development and of Energy and Resources, and Leader of the House of Representatives, Gerry Brownlee, who had also been appointed Minister for Earthquake Recovery following an earlier earthquake that had struck about 40 km west of Christchurch in September 2010, to focus exclusively on recovery efforts in the aftermath of the second, more serious disaster. The economic development portfolio was transferred, on an interim basis, to David Carter, while Hekia Parata became acting Minister of Energy and Resources; the Minister of Justice, for State-owned Enterprises and of Commerce, Simon Power, was appointed acting Leader of the House of Representatives. A state of national emergency was declared in Christchurch, which remained in force for nearly 10 weeks. Insurance estimates suggested that the total cost of the damages arising from the second earthquake would amount to around $NZ17,000m.

Recent developments: the 2011 general election

In early February 2011 Prime Minister John Key announced that the general election was to be held on 26 November. A nonbinding referendum on the issue of the MMP system was to be held concurrently with the election, at which voters were to be asked two questions: first, if they favoured the retention of the current system; and, second, which alternative system they preferred from a range of options.

Maori Party legislator Hone Harawira was expelled from the Maori Party's parliamentary caucus in mid-February 2011 owing to his outspoken criticism of the party's support for the National-led Government despite the latter pursuing what he argued was anti-Maori legislation—a reference to the Marine and Coastal Area (Takutai Moana) Bill (see Maori Land Rights and the Waitangi Tribunal Process). Harawira resigned from the Maori Party in late February, after the party's disciplinary committee was reported to have recommended his expulsion from the organization. In April Harawira announced the formation of a new, left-leaning political party, Mana, and in the following month he resigned from the House of Representatives in order to seek re-election in the Te Tai Tokerau constituency as leader of the new party. Harawira duly secured re-election by a comfortable margin at the ensuing by-election in June. In July Harawira was expelled from a parliamentary session by the Speaker, after refusing to read the oath of allegiance to Queen Elizabeth II, as required of newly elected legislators under New Zealand law, instead electing to swear allegiance—in Maori—to the 1840 Treaty of Waitangi, generally perceived to be the founding document of modern-day New Zealand (see Maori Land Rights and the Waitangi Tribunal Process). The Mana leader was finally inaugurated in August 2011, after agreeing to read the oath of allegiance to the Queen. In November 2012 the Maori Party proposed legislation to allow new MPs the option to uphold the Treaty of Waitangi when they swore the oath of allegiance; the draft bill was supported by the Greens, Mana and the Labour Party, but was defeated by 69 votes to 52.

Meanwhile, in March 2011 Lt-Gen. Sir Jerry Mateparae, who had relinquished the post of Chief of the New Zealand Defence Force in January (whereupon he had been replaced by Lt-Gen. Richard Rhys Jones), was named as the new Governor-General of New Zealand. He was formally inaugurated at the end of August, upon the expiry of Sir Anand Satyanand's term of office.

In mid-April 2011 the Minister of Justice, for State-owned Enterprises and of Commerce, Simon Power, relinquished responsibility for state-owned enterprises, citing his desire to avoid a potential conflict of interest prior to a planned transition into the business sector following the forthcoming general election. The Minister of Health and of State Services, Tony Ryall, was awarded concurrent responsibility for the state-owned enterprises portfolio. In June Craig Foss was appointed as a minister outside the Cabinet, assuming responsibility for the racing, civil defence and senior citizens portfolios, in place of John Carter, who had been appointed as the new high commissioner to the Cook Islands. The Ministry of Agriculture and Forestry and the Ministry of Fisheries officially merged in July, although they retained separate identities until the creation of the Ministry for Primary Industries in April 2012.

Meanwhile, in an unexpected development, in late April 2011 Don Brash, who had remained a member of the National Party following his resignation as party leader in 2006 (see The Labour Party's return to power), announced his wish to assume the leadership of ACT New Zealand, claiming that the latter party would perform better under his direction than that of Rodney Hide, who had served as party leader since 2004. Having received the endorsement of ACT New Zealand's parliamentary caucus, Brash's leadership application was ratified by the party's board of trustees at the end of April 2011, with ACT New Zealand's President, Chris Simmons, expressing the hope that the change of leadership would reinvigorate the party ahead of the general election.

The general election was held, as scheduled, on 26 November 2011. As in 2008, the National Party narrowly failed to secure an overall majority, winning 59 seats, having received 47.3% of the vote. The Labour Party's representation continued to decline, to just 34 seats (27.5% of the vote), while the Green Party garnered 14 seats, New Zealand First eight and the Maori Party three (including one 'overhang' seat); ACT New Zealand, Mana and UFNZ each secured one seat. With only one 'overhang' seat awarded, the size of the legislature was reduced from 122 seats following the 2008 election to 121 seats. Turn-out was recorded at 74% of the registered electorate. In the concurrent referendum on the voting system, 57.8% of voters favoured the retention of the MMP system. In response to the question on which system would be preferable if New Zealand were to change to another voting system, the 'first-past-the post' system received the greatest support (46.7% of the valid votes cast). Following negotiations, John Key secured the support of all three of the National Party's coalition partners in the outgoing administration—ACT New Zealand, UFNZ and the Maori Party, which was sufficient to form a coalition Government with control of 64 seats in the House of Representatives.

The new Government, again led by Prime Minister John Key, who also retained the tourism portfolio, was inaugurated in mid-December 2011. Bill English remained Deputy Prime Minister and Minister of Finance. Steven Joyce relinquished the transport portfolio and was appointed Minister of Economic Development and of Science and Innovation, while remaining Minister for Tertiary Education, Skills and Employment. Gerry Brownlee retained the Canterbury earthquake recovery portfolio and was awarded concurrent responsibility for transport. Other notable appointments included that of Dr Jonathan Coleman, hitherto Minister of Immigration and of Broadcasting, as the new Minister of Defence and of State Services, while ACT New Zealand's sole MP, John Banks, was appointed Minister for Regulatory Reform and for Small Business, and UFNZ leader Peter Dunne retained the revenue portfolio.

Meanwhile, Labour Party leader Phil Goff and deputy leader Annette King tendered their resignations three days after the election, citing their wish to allow the party to rebuild following its disappointing results. David Shearer and Grant Robertson were subsequently elected by the Labour Party parliamentary caucus to replace Goff and King, respectively. Don Brash had also resigned as leader of ACT New Zealand, declaring that he accepted full responsibility for the party's worst ever electoral performance; John Banks was elected as the party's new leader in February 2012.

Dr Nick Smith resigned as Minister for Climate Change Issues, for the Environment and of Local Government in March 2012, after it was revealed that, while serving as Minister for ACC (Accident Compensation Corporation, a government agency that provides insurance for personal injuries), he had intervened in a friend's claim for compensation without declaring a conflict of interest. Prime Minister Key consequently effected a government reshuffle in early April, redistributing Smith's portfolios among existing ministers. A new Ministry of Business, Innovation and Employment was established in July, from the merger of the functions of the Ministry of Economic Development, the Ministry of Science and Innovation, the Ministry of Consumer Affairs, the Department of Labour and the Department of Building and Housing. In November Kate Wilkinson resigned as Minister of Labour after a royal commission concluded that her office had failed to prevent a disaster at Pike River coal mine in November 2010 in which 29 people had lost their lives. She initially retained responsibility for several other portfolios, but was removed from the Government in January 2013, when Prime Minister Key announced several further cabinet changes, including the unexpected return of Nick Smith, as Minister of Conservation and of Housing, and the appointment of a number of newcomers to government. In addition, National Party stalwart David Carter vacated the primary industries portfolio and replaced the outgoing Alexander Lockwood Smith, who had been appointed as the new high commissioner to the United Kingdom, as Speaker of the House of Representatives.

New Zealand became the first country in the Asia-Pacific region to legalize same-sex marriage in April 2013, when the House of Representatives approved the measure by 77 votes to 44.

Maori Land Rights and the Waitangi Tribunal Process

During 1987 there were protests by the Maori concerning their cultural and economic rights and, in particular, their claims to land in accordance with the Treaty of Waitangi, concluded in 1840 by the British Government and Maori leaders, whereby sovereignty had been ceded to the United Kingdom in return for the Maori people's retention of hunting and fishing grounds. In November 1987 a ruling by the Waitangi Tribunal, reconvened in 1975 to consider retrospectively the claims of Maori land rights activists, recommended the restoration of an Auckland harbour headland to the Maori people. By 1994 about 75% of the country was subject to land claims by Maori groups. In December of that year the Government offered the sum of $NZ1,000m., payable over a 10-year period, in full and final settlement of outstanding claims for compensation. However, the condition that all future land claims be renounced was rejected by most Maori groups. In the same month an historic agreement between the Government and the Tainui people of Waikato provided for the return of land confiscated in 1863 and for the deposit over a period of five years of $NZ65m. in a land acquisition trust.

In May 1995 the Prime Minister and the Queen of the Tainui people signed an agreement relating to a full and final settlement, valued at $NZ170m., of land grievances dating back to 1863. However, increasing ethnic tension was demonstrated by the destruction in September 1995 of an old school building by Maori protesters involved in a land dispute and by the burning down in October of an historic church, the 'Maori Cathedral', at Otaki, in an apparent retaliatory arson attack by white extremists. In November, in a highly significant ceremony in Wellington, Queen Elizabeth II gave her personal assent to the legislation ending the Tainui grievances when she signed the Waikato Raupatu Claims Settlement Act: this implemented the $NZ170m. agreement, including the return of 15,780 ha of land, and incorporated an apology from the Crown for the loss of lives and for the confiscation of property. A final settlement payment of $NZ13m. was made to the Tainui tribe in late 2000.

In July 1997 a Maori tribe that had been driven off its land in the 1840s lodged a claim to the site of the Parliament building in Wellington. The Ngati Tama also presented claims to other areas of the capital, while declaring their willingness to negotiate. At a ceremony in Wellington in September, following six years of negotiations, the Government and South Island's Ngai Tahu (one of New Zealand's smallest Maori tribes) reached a formal agreement regarding a $NZ170m. settlement. The Government's offer also included the right to name mountains and rivers, often in combination with the English equivalents, and incorporated a full apology from the Crown. In November the historic deed of full and final settlement was signed by the Prime Minister and representatives of the Ngai Tahu. In March 1998 the Ngai Tahu Claims Settlement Bill was duly submitted to the House of Representatives, where it received approval six months later. In July, exercising for the first time its power of compulsory recommendation, the Waitangi Tribunal ordered the Government to return to the Ngati Turangitukua land (now valued at $NZ6.1m.) that had been confiscated from its Maori owners more than 30 years previously to permit the construction of housing for workers engaged on an electric power project in the central North Island.

In March 2001 the Ngati Ruanui became the first Taranaki tribe to conclude a deed of settlement with the Government, amounting to $NZ41m. In early 2003 the Ngati Awa voted in favour of a treaty settlement with the Government, which included an apology from the Crown, the return of 64 ha of land and $NZ42m. In August 2005 Prime Minister Helen Clark announced that all historical Maori land claims under the Treaty of Waitangi would have to be filed by 1 September 2008, in order that they could be settled by 2020 (contemporary claims could be filed beyond this deadline). By 2007 the Waitangi Tribunal had reportedly been able to settle only about 20 claims. On the closing date for registration the Waitangi Tribunal received more than 1,000 new historical grievance claims from Maori communities. In October 2007 the Government instigated a campaign to persuade Maoris living in Australia to return to New Zealand.

In June 2008, in a settlement valued at $NZ418m., the New Zealand Government signed an agreement with seven Maori tribes to transfer ownership of 176,000 ha of Crown forestry land in the central North Island, originally ceded under the Treaty of Waitangi. The Maori tribes, which represented approximately 100,000 people, also stood to receive backdated forest rental payments of $NZ223m., in addition to future annual rental income and carbon credits. In February 2009 the Government awarded $NZ300m. in compensation to eight Maori tribes, comprising more than 12,000 members, in recognition of historic injustices arising from violations of the Treaty of Waitangi and illegal seizures of land. Furthermore, in the first such decision relating to an issue of intellectual property, the Government recognized that the Ka Mate haka, the 'war dance' traditionally

performed by the New Zealand rugby team at international games but increasingly being used for commercial exploitation, had been written in the 1820s by Maori chief Te Rauparaha, an ancestor of the Ngati Toa tribe. A $NZ25m. settlement encompassing the greater Wellington region was agreed in July 2009; significantly, the *iwi* (tribe) involved in the agreement issued an unprecedented formal statement of forgiveness to the Crown.

The Ngati Kuia concluded a deed of settlement with the Crown in October 2010, the first such agreement in South Island since 1997; the settlement included an apology from the Crown, the return of culturally sensitive land and $NZ24m. in compensation. The Ngati Porou, New Zealand's second largest *iwi*, comprising about 72,000 members, signed a deed of settlement with the Crown in December 2010, which included the return of approximately 5,900 ha of land and $NZ110m. in compensation. The Ngai Tamanuhiri became the first Turanga *iwi* to conclude a deed of settlement with the Crown, in March 2011, which included the return of culturally sensitive land, together with the payment of $NZ11.1m. in compensation. A deed of settlement was also concluded between the Crown and another of New Zealand's three Turanga *iwi*, the Rongowhakaata, in September, which similarly provided for the return of culturally sensitive land and the payment of compensation, amounting to $NZ22m., as well as a formal apology from the Crown for, *inter alia*, the unjustified use of military force in Turanga, the detention without trial of Rongowhakaata prisoners on the Chatham Islands and the summary executions of prisoners at Ngatapa in 1869. Further deeds of settlement were signed between the Crown and the Ngati Makino, the Ngati Manuhiri and the Ngati Whatua o Kaipara in April, May and September 2011, respectively, each of which provided for the return to the tribes of culturally sensitive land, together with compensation of $NZ11.9m., $NZ9.0m. and $NZ22.1m., respectively.

In December 2012 the High Court ruled against an application by the New Zealand Maori Council filed earlier that year requesting a judicial review of the Government's planned partial divestment of its assets in a number of energy companies; the Council argued that such sales would prejudice any future recognition of Maori rights over the country's water and geothermal resources.

Maori fishing rights

In response to Maori grievances over fishing rights, in 1989, in an interim agreement, the Crown transferred 10% of the country's fishing quota, together with $NZ50m. and shareholdings in fishing companies, to the Maori Fisheries Commission, which had been established to resolve the issue of the allocation among Maori of fisheries resources. In 1992 the Treaty of Waitangi (Fisheries Claims) Settlement Act (or so-called Sealord deal) was adopted, marking the full and final settlement of Maori fishing claims under the Treaty. According to the agreement, the *iwi* would receive a 50% share in Sealord products (Sealord being New Zealand's largest fishing company), 20% of all new species brought under the quota management system and a further $NZ18m.

The allocation of fisheries assets among the tribes proved the subject of much litigation. In April 1997, despite having no coastline, urban Maori were outraged at a proposal by the Treaty of Waitangi Fisheries Commission (as the Maori Fisheries Commission had now become) to allocate fishery assets on a tribal basis, rather than according to *iwi* size as the populous northern tribes demanded. The Ngai Tahu and other *iwi*, meanwhile, argued that the length of coastline and traditional fishing grounds should determine the allocation of assets. In early 1998 it was announced that new regulations were to govern the management of 'customary' fishing by *tangata whenua* (people of the land), whereby Maori were permitted to take an unlimited amount of seafood provided that it was not for pecuniary gain.

In mid-1998 the Waitangi Tribunal ruled that urban Maori without blood ties should be accorded similar negotiating rights to those of traditional *iwi*. The historic decision thus acknowledged urban Maori trusts as modern tribes. In August, however, a High Court judge ruled in favour of traditional Maori tribes, effectively declaring that urban Maori groups had no claim to fishery assets. In October 1999, furthermore, the urban Maori claim was rejected by the Court of Appeal. In September 2004 the final version of the Maori Fisheries Act was approved by the House of Representatives. The new legislation transferred control to Maori tribes of some $NZ750m. in fisheries assets; around one-half of these assets was to be allocated directly to the *iwi* and the other half was to be managed centrally, with the creation of the country's largest fishing group, Aotearoa Fisheries Ltd, which would have an interest in approximately one-third of New Zealand's lucrative commercial fishing industry.

In March 2010 the Government announced proposals to replace the Foreshore and Seabed Act with new legislation, following a ministerial review in 2009, which had advised repealing the legislation, concluding that it failed to balance the interests of all New Zealanders and was discriminatory against Maori. In June 2010 Prime Minister John Key announced that the Government, the Maori Party and *iwi* leaders had reached an agreement providing for the repeal of the Act and its replacement with new legislation that would abrogate Crown ownership of the coastal areas in question and place them in the public domain, thereby also preventing Maori ownership claims, while allowing Maori groups to seek recognition of their customary rights from the Government or by application to the High Court—a right that had been denied to them under the Foreshore and Seabed Act. The Marine and Coastal Area (Takutai Moana) Bill was introduced to Parliament in August, whereupon it encountered significant opposition from some quarters, including Maori Party legislator Hone Harawira, who argued that the draft legislation was 'a fraud' since Maori seeking to claim customary rights over foreshore and seabed areas would be required to prove unbroken tenure of the areas in question since 1840, which, he contended, 98% of Maori would be unable to do. Conversely, the Coastal Coalition, an umbrella organization comprising those who believed the foreshore and seabed to be 'the birthright and common heritage of all New Zealanders equally' and should remain under the ownership of the Crown, opposed the bill as a 'massive coastal land grab for the Maori'. An opinion poll conducted in February indicated that just 11% of Maori approved of the Marine and Coastal Area (Takutai Moana) Bill. Nevertheless, in March 2011 the legislation was narrowly approved by the House of Representatives (by 63 votes to 56), having been supported by the National Party, the Maori Party and UFNZ. In the previous month Harawira had resigned from the Maori Party (see Domestic Political Affairs).

Foreign Affairs

The Labour Government that took office at the end of 1972 adopted a more independent policy than that of its predecessors. It phased out New Zealand's military commitments under the South-East Asia Treaty Organization and established diplomatic relations with the People's Republic of China. New Zealand became committed to the objective of the global elimination of all nuclear weapons, and in November 1996 was a co-sponsor of a UN resolution, overwhelmingly adopted by the General Assembly, to promote the establishment of a nuclear-weapons-free southern hemisphere. In October 2000 New Zealand ratified the Waigani Convention, which banned the export of hazardous and radioactive waste to the Pacific islands.

Regional relations

New Zealand has played an active role in Pacific island affairs. In 1997, in the quest for peace in Papua New Guinea, it participated in a peace-keeping force on the secessionist island of Bougainville. New Zealand hosted discussions between the Papua New Guinea Government and representatives of the secessionist movement, and in January 1998 a permanent ceasefire agreement was signed in Christchurch. New Zealand strongly condemned the coup in Fiji in May 2000. New Zealand's Minister of Foreign Affairs and Trade, Phil Goff, led a Commonwealth delegation, together with his Australian counterpart, to negotiate with the ethnic militias involved in a coup in Solomon Islands in June 2000. A New Zealand naval frigate was dispatched to the islands to serve as a venue for peace talks, and a cease-fire agreement was signed in October. In mid-2003 New Zealand troops joined forces from Australia and several Pacific islands to provide a peace-keeping force in Solomon Islands (the last of the remaining New Zealand troops withdrew from the islands in November 2012). New Zealand, together with Australia, deployed security forces to Tonga in November 2006 to restore stability following violent demonstrations. Tonga established a high commission in Wellington in 2009, but this was closed in September 2011, as part of efforts by the Tongan Government to reduce public spending.

In December 2006 Prime Minister Clark condemned the military coup in Fiji as an 'outrage'; the Government subsequently imposed defence, travel and development sanctions. Further sanctions were announced in June 2007 after New Zealand's high commissioner to Fiji was expelled because of his alleged interference in the country's internal affairs. In

December 2008, as the restoration of democracy in Fiji appeared increasingly unlikely, the acting high commissioner of New Zealand in Fiji was expelled, in response to which her Fijian counterpart was asked to leave New Zealand. Nevertheless, New Zealand was one of several nations swiftly to offer, via non-governmental agencies, aid to the emergency flood relief effort in Fiji in January 2009. In April New Zealand was particularly critical of the abrogation of the Fijian Constitution and subsequent developments in the country (see Fiji). The country's high commissioner to Fiji was expelled again in November in response to the New Zealand Government's continuing firm stance towards the Fijian regime. A reciprocal expulsion by New Zealand followed soon afterwards. Although senior diplomats returned to the respective missions in early 2010, the exchange was not at ambassadorial level. None the less, New Zealand continued to supply relief aid to Fiji. In January 2012 New Zealand's Minister of Foreign Affairs, Murray McCully, expressed his disappointment at the imposition by the Fijian regime of repressive new legislation, which was widely condemned as a set-back for hopes of a restoration of democracy in the country. However, following progress made by Fiji towards the drafting of a new constitution and the organization of elections in 2014, in July 2012 New Zealand agreed to restore full diplomatic relations (at ambassadorial level) with Fiji.

Meanwhile, in June 2008 the New Zealand Government released details of its Pacific Development Strategy Plan, which envisaged expenditure of $NZ2,000m. in official development assistance to the Pacific region over an eight-year period. This new initiative aimed to improve health services and education facilities, to strengthen governance, to reduce poverty and to promote economic growth in the Pacific islands. Minister of Foreign Affairs McCully visited Vanuatu and Solomon Islands in June 2011, and Tonga, Samoa, the Cook Islands and Niue in July, to discuss regional issues and priorities for the Pacific Islands Forum, the 42nd summit meeting of which was hosted by New Zealand in Auckland in September.

Although New Zealand's trade with the People's Republic of China assumed increasing significance from the 1990s, relations were strained by the issue of China's nuclear-testing programme. Relations were further tested in September 1996 when the Dalai Lama, the exiled spiritual leader of Tibet, visited New Zealand, where he was welcomed by the Prime Minister. In September 1997, however, the New Zealand Deputy Prime Minister expressed support for China's application to join the World Trade Organization (WTO, see p. 444). In November 1998 New Zealand's decision to accord Taiwanese government officials similar privileges to those granted to representatives of the People's Republic of China provoked serious concern in China. During a visit to China in July 1999, however, the Prime Minister of New Zealand reaffirmed her country's support for the 'one China' policy. An official visit to China by the Prime Minister in April 2001 was intended to improve New Zealand's trading position with the country, prior to its accession to the WTO. The Chinese Premier, Wen Jiabao, paid an official visit to New Zealand in April 2006. In March 2008 it was reported that China had agreed to grant 'most favoured nation' status to New Zealand as part of a free trade agreement between the two countries, which was signed in the following month. The signature of this accord, the provisions of which were to be phased in gradually over 12 years, represented the first time that China had entered into a comprehensive free trade agreement with a developed country. During his first official visit to China in April 2009 Prime Minister John Key expressed his commitment to the consolidation of the bilateral trading relationship and also urged an expansion in cultural exchanges with China, which had become the largest source of New Zealand's students from overseas. In February 2011 the New Zealand Government announced that total bilateral trade between China and New Zealand had increased by more than one-third since the implementation of the free trade agreement; China was New Zealand's second largest trading partner in 2011 (after Australia). In late 2010 Key and Wen Jiabao pledged their commitment to effecting a doubling of bilateral trade by 2015, a commitment that was reaffirmed by both countries during a visit to Beijing by New Zealand's Deputy Prime Minister and Minister of Finance, Bill English, in April 2011. Five agreements were signed during a visit to Wellington in September by Chinese Vice-Premier Hui Liangyu, including a memorandum of understanding providing for greater co-operation between New Zealand and the state-run China Development Bank on infrastructural development projects, including in the earthquake-struck Canterbury region (see

Domestic Political Affairs). Meanwhile, a Closer Economic Partnership Agreement was signed with Hong Kong in March 2010 and entered into force in January 2011.

Relations with the countries of South-East Asia continued to assume greater significance. In June 2001 President Abdurrahman Wahid undertook an official visit to New Zealand, the first by an Indonesian head of state for 26 years. In July 2005 New Zealand signed the Treaty of Amity and Co-operation of the Association of Southeast Asian Nations (ASEAN, see p. 218). In December New Zealand was represented at the inaugural East Asia Summit meeting, convened in Malaysia and attended by leaders of ASEAN members and various other countries of the Asia-Pacific region. In February 2009 (along with Australia) New Zealand signed a free trade agreement with ASEAN, which entered into force in January 2010. A separate free trade agreement with Malaysia, a significant export market for New Zealand, was signed in October 2009 and entered into force in July 2010; the agreement provided for the elimination of trade tariffs on 99.5% of New Zealand's exports to Malaysia within seven years. Minister of Foreign Affairs Murray McCully visited Indonesia and Malaysia in October 2010; during his visit to the former, the Indonesia-New Zealand Friendship Council was established, with the aim of fostering closer co-operation.

New Zealand's foreign policy has continued to be influenced by the country's need to diversify its export markets, particularly within Asia; the Republic of Korea (South Korea), for example, has become a significant trading partner—New Zealand's fifth largest in 2011—and at early 2013 negotiations over a New Zealand-South Korean free trade agreement were ongoing. Closer relations with Singapore and Thailand have also been developed.

About 3,500 New Zealand soldiers served in Viet Nam between 1964 and 1971. However, New Zealand's decision to contribute troops in support of the US war effort was not popular, and it was only in May 2008 that the New Zealand Prime Minister issued a public apology to the veterans for their lack of recognition.

Relations with Japan, which was New Zealand's fourth largest trading partner in 2011, continued to be strained by New Zealand's opposition to the East Asian country's controversial whaling programme. Japan caught an estimated 1,000 whales each year, which the New Zealand Government, along with many others within the international community, contended was in direct breech of a ban on commercial whaling introduced by the International Whaling Commission (see p. 453) in 1986, while the Japanese Government maintained that its whaling activities were for scientific-based research programmes. In October 2011 Minister of Foreign Affairs McCully denounced an announcement by the Japanese Government that it was to resume whaling in the Antarctic Ocean later in the year (having abandoned its whaling season in 2010 owing to ongoing disruptions posed by anti-whaling activists), and argued that Japan was at risk of isolating itself from the rest of the international community over the issue.

Within the ANZUS pact, from 1984 New Zealand's relations with both Australia and the USA were severely tested by the issue of the nuclear ban (see The ANZUS Treaty and other relations with the USA). In 1982 New Zealand signed an agreement for a 'closer economic relationship' with Australia; trade barriers between the two countries were eliminated in 1990. In September 2001 relations with Australia were strained by the failure of Ansett, the Melbourne-based airline. Ansett's owner, Air New Zealand, had been unable to find a purchaser for the loss-making company, which was therefore placed in receivership. Nevertheless, in the same month the New Zealand Government helped Australia to resolve an international crisis, when it agreed to accept up to 150 of the refugees stranded aboard a Norwegian vessel (see Christmas Island). During her first state visit to New Zealand since acceding to the Australian premiership in June 2010, Prime Minister Julia Gillard met with her New Zealand counterpart, John Key, in Wellington, whereupon the two leaders pledged to hold bilateral prime ministerial discussions on an annual basis thenceforth.

The ANZUS Treaty and other relations with the USA

In 1984 the Lange Government's pledge to ban from New Zealand's ports all vessels believed to be carrying nuclear weapons, or powered by nuclear energy, placed considerable strain on the country's relations with Australia and the USA, its partners in ANZUS. The ban was duly imposed in February 1985. In July 1986 the US Government announced its intention to devise new, bilateral defence arrangements with Australia, and in August the USA's military obligations to New Zealand under the ANZUS

Treaty were formally suspended. In February 1987 the US Government announced its decision not to renew a 1982 memorandum of understanding, whereby New Zealand was able to purchase military equipment from the USA at favourable prices. The Lange Government subsequently defined a new defence strategy, based on increased self-reliance for the country's military forces. In June 1987 legislation banning nuclear-armed ships was formally enacted by the New Zealand House of Representatives, despite opposition from the National Party. In September 1989 New Zealand agreed the terms for a joint venture with Australia to build as many as 12 naval frigates to patrol the South Pacific. The decision proved to be very contentious because of the high costs and because of allegations that the Government was succumbing to political pressure from Australia to return to the ANZUS alliance and abandon its independent anti-nuclear stance. In March 1990 the National Party announced its support for the anti-nuclear policy, a position that it retained after its election to office in October.

The US Government's decision, in September 1991, to remove nuclear weapons from surface naval vessels and the announcement, in July 1992, that its warships no longer carried tactical nuclear weapons were welcomed by the New Zealand Government, and in February 1994 the USA resumed senior-level contacts with New Zealand, suspended since 1985. After attending the summit meeting of the Asia-Pacific Economic Cooperation (APEC, see p. 208) forum held in Auckland in September 1999, US President Bill Clinton announced the end of the 14-year ban on New Zealand's participation in military exercises with the USA, in preparation for the dispatch of a multinational peace-keeping force to East Timor (now Timor-Leste—q.v.), of which New Zealand troops were to form part.

The Government was quick to express support for the USA following the suicide attacks in that country of 11 September 2001 and offered to share intelligence in the effort to combat terrorism. In October New Zealand provided troops from the Special Air Service (SAS) for the US-led military campaign against the al-Qa'ida organization, held principally responsible for the attacks, and its Taliban hosts in Afghanistan. However, US policy in the 'war on terror' was a source of concern in New Zealand. In 2003, during preparations for the US-led military campaign to remove the regime of Saddam Hussein in Iraq, the Government stated that it would favour action in Iraq only through the UN, a stance that was popularly supported in New Zealand. In May Prime Minister Clark warned the USA and the United Kingdom that they had set a dangerous precedent by invading Iraq without the endorsement of a UN resolution. None the less, New Zealand provided humanitarian support for Iraq and assistance in the rehabilitation of the country once the UN had authorized reconstruction efforts following the ousting of Saddam Hussein.

In March 2004 the New Zealand Government, which had already sent members of the New Zealand Defence Force to Afghanistan to assist in reconstruction efforts in the province of Bamian (Bamyan), agreed to send SAS troops back to that country to take part in the search for senior al-Qa'ida leaders. A further SAS deployment in Afghanistan was effected in September 2009, following a US request for additional military assistance; in February 2011 it was announced that the deployment was to be extended for 12 months, effective from April, but with a reduction in the number of personnel, from 70 to 35 troops. The SAS deployment was concluded, as scheduled, at the end of March 2012. Having suffered 10 military fatalities since commencing its mission in Afghanistan a decade earlier, in April 2013 the New Zealand Defence Force withdrew its remaining contingent of around 140 troops from Bamyan, some five months earlier than initially scheduled. A small group of 27 planning and intelligence personnel from New Zealand remained in the Afghan capital of Kabul.

An improvement in relations with the USA was indicated in July 2008 by the visit to New Zealand of Condoleezza Rice, the US Secretary of State and thus the most senior representative of the US Government to visit the country since the late 1990s. Rice's discussions with Prime Minister Clark and with the Minister of Foreign Affairs focused on trade issues, renewing hopes that a free trade agreement between the two countries might be negotiated. Further discussions on a free trade agreement were held between Prime Minister Key and US Vice-President Joseph Biden in April 2010, although no substantive progress was reported. US Secretary of State Hillary Clinton visited Wellington in November, whereupon she and the New Zealand Minister of Foreign Affairs, Murray McCully, signed a strategic co-operation agreement, which effectively formalized the amelioration in bilateral relations and greater engagement between the two countries in recent years. The so-called Wellington Declaration focused on enhancing dialogue and practical co-operation between New Zealand and the USA across a wide range of bilateral, Pacific and international issues, including combating the effects of climate change, the pursuit of renewable energy initiatives, and the co-ordination of disaster recovery initiatives. The Wellington Declaration also committed the two countries to regular diplomatic, trade and defence discussions. Improved bilateral relations were further cemented in 2011 by visits to Washington, DC, USA, by McCully in May, during which he held 'very positive' discussions with Secretary of State Clinton, and by Prime Minister John Key in July, when he met with President Barack Obama. In June 2012, in Washington, DC, the New Zealand Minister of Defence, Dr Jonathan Coleman, and his US counterpart, Leon Panetta, signed an agreement (the so-called Washington Declaration) to expand defence co-operation between their two countries, including in the areas of maritime security and disaster relief. Following a visit to New Zealand by Panetta in September (the first visit to New Zealand by a US Secretary of Defense since 1986), the USA lifted the ban imposed in 1986 that prevented New Zealand naval ships from docking at its ports.

Other external relations

In July 1985 the *Rainbow Warrior*, the flagship of the anti-nuclear environmentalist group Greenpeace (which was to have led a flotilla to Mururoa Atoll, in French Polynesia, to protest against France's testing of nuclear weapons in the South Pacific), was blown up and sunk in Auckland Harbour. One member of the crew was killed as a result of the explosion. Two agents of the French secret service were tried for manslaughter in November and sentenced to 10 years' imprisonment. Following requests by the French Government for the release or repatriation of the agents, in July 1986 New Zealand and France reached an agreement whereby the agents were to be transferred to detention on Hao Atoll, in French Polynesia, for three years. The French Government made a formal apology for its part in the sabotage operation, and paid the New Zealand Government $NZ7m. in compensation. By May 1988, however, both the agents had been taken back to France, ostensibly for medical reasons. When neither agent was returned to the atoll, Lange referred the matter to the UN: in May 1990 an arbitration panel ruled that France's repatriation of the agents constituted a substantial violation of the 1986 agreement, but it announced that the agents would not be required to return to Hao Atoll. France agreed to pay an initial US $2m. into a joint fund intended to foster close and friendly relations between the two countries. In April 1991 the French Prime Minister, Michel Rocard, visited New Zealand and again apologized for the sinking of the *Rainbow Warrior*, while reiterating that French testing of nuclear weapons in the Pacific was to continue. Relations between the two countries deteriorated in July, following the French Government's announcement that it had conferred an honour for distinguished service on one of the two agents responsible for the sabotage of the *Rainbow Warrior*. In July 2005 an article in a French newspaper confirmed that the sinking of the *Rainbow Warrior* had been authorized by the then French President, François Mitterrand. Meanwhile, France announced the suspension of its nuclear testing in the South Pacific in April 1992.

President Jacques Chirac's announcement in June 1995 that France was to resume its nuclear-testing programme in the South Pacific aroused international condemnation. New Zealand suspended military relations with France, and the New Zealand ambassador to Paris was recalled. The first in the new series of tests was carried out in September. Later in the month the International Court of Justice ruled that it could not reopen New Zealand's case against France, brought in 1973. France's continuation of its testing programme was a major issue at the Commonwealth heads of government meeting held in Auckland in November 1995. In March 1996 (the French tests having been concluded) France, the United Kingdom and the USA finally acceded to the South Pacific Nuclear-Free Zone Treaty (Treaty of Rarotonga—Pacific Islands Forum, see p. 426), thus opening the way to improved relations with New Zealand and other Pacific nations. In October 1997, following an official visit to Paris by the New Zealand Prime Minister, the resumption of normal relations with France was declared, and a number of senior-level bilateral visits took place in subsequent years, including, most recently, a state visit to France by Prime Minister John Key in April 2011, during which he held discussions with French

President Nicolas Sarkozy, Prime Minister François Fillon and other high-ranking government officials.

In December 1996 the New Zealand Government announced that it was to finance a lawsuit against the United Kingdom that was being prepared by former servicemen (and veterans' widows) who had long campaigned for compensation for their exposure to the effects of British hydrogen bomb tests conducted in the South Pacific region in the late 1950s. As part of her golden jubilee tour of the Commonwealth, Queen Elizabeth II visited New Zealand in February 2002. Having previously stated that New Zealand's eventual transition to a republic was inevitable, Prime Minister Helen Clark attracted some criticism for her absence from the country on the day of the Queen's arrival. During a state visit to London to attend the royal wedding of Prince William and Catherine Middleton in April 2012, Prime Minister John Key met with the Queen, Prime Minister David Cameron and a number of senior business leaders.

Negotiations between New Zealand and India on a bilateral free trade agreement commenced in Wellington in April 2010, with an eighth round of negotiations being held in New Delhi in June 2012. Meanwhile, during a state visit to Delhi in June 2011, Prime Minister John Key and his Indian counterpart, Manmohan Singh, reaffirmed the commitment of their respective countries to resolving all outstanding points of contention pertaining to the trade pact, which was expected to be wide-ranging, with agricultural produce, biotechnology, education, health care, technology and tourism considered likely to be among the areas covered. Bilateral trade amounted to $NZ985m. in 2009, representing an increase of 180% on that recorded in 2001, and was reported to have risen further, to around $NZ1,300m., in 2011.

CONSTITUTION AND GOVERNMENT

New Zealand has no written Constitution. Executive power is vested in the British monarch, as head of state, and is exercisable by an appointed representative, the Governor-General, who must be guided by the advice of the Executive Council (Cabinet), led by the Prime Minister. Legislative power is vested in the unicameral Parliament; the House of Representatives is elected for three years by universal adult suffrage. A system of mixed member proportional (MMP) representation was introduced in 1996. The legislature comprises 120 seats (70 electorate members, including seven seats reserved for Maori, and 50 being chosen from party lists). However, under the MMP system, the awarding of 'overhang' seats is allowed in the case of a party winning more constituency seats than it would be entitled to based on its proportion of party list votes; as a result, the legislature comprised a total of 121 seats following the 2011 elections. The Governor-General appoints the Prime Minister and, on the latter's recommendation, other Ministers. The Cabinet is responsible to the House.

REGIONAL AND INTERNATIONAL CO-OPERATION

New Zealand is a member of Asia-Pacific Economic Cooperation (APEC, see p. 208), the Pacific Community (see p. 422), the Pacific Islands Forum (see p. 426) and the Cairns Group (see p. 517). The country is also a member of the Colombo Plan (see p. 460) and of the UN's Economic and Social Commission for Asia and the Pacific (ESCAP, see p. 31).

New Zealand joined the UN in 1945. As a contracting party to the General Agreement on Tariffs and Trade (GATT), the country joined the World Trade Organization (WTO, see p. 444) upon its establishment in 1995. New Zealand is also a member of the Organisation for Economic Co-operation and Development (OECD, see p. 388).

ECONOMIC AFFAIRS

In 2010, according to estimates by the World Bank, New Zealand's gross national income (GNI), measured at average 2008–10 prices, was US $128,200m., equivalent to US $29,350 per head (or US $28,970 per head on an international purchasing-power parity basis). During 2002–11, it was estimated, the population increased at an average annual rate of 1.2%, while gross domestic product (GDP) per head increased, in real terms, by an average of 0.6% per year during 2002–10. According to the UN, overall GDP increased, in real terms, at an average annual rate of 1.8% in 2002–11. According to chain linked methodologies, GDP increased by 1.9% in the year ending March 2012.

Agriculture (including fishing, forestry and logging) contributed 6.6% of GDP in the year ending March 2010. About 6.9% of the employed labour force were engaged in the sector in 2011. The principal crops are potatoes, wheat, barley and maize. Fruit (particularly kiwi fruit, apples and pears) and vegetables are also cultivated. New Zealand is a major producer of wool, although its significance as a source of export earnings has declined in recent years. Meat and dairy products are important, contributing 11.6% and 25.2% of export earnings, respectively, in 2011. A severe drought on the North Island in early 2013 (described as the worst to occur in some 30 years) led to substantial losses in the agricultural sector, which were expected to reduce overall economic growth by around 1%. The forestry industry expanded strongly in the early 1990s. In 2011 exports of logs, wood and wood articles totalled $NZ3,197m. (equivalent to 6.7% of total export earnings). The fisheries sector is of increasing significance, with exports worth $NZ1,361m. (equivalent to 2.9% of total export earnings) in 2011. According to UN figures, agricultural GDP (including fishing and forestry) increased at an average annual rate of 1.7% in 2002–11. The GDP of the sector decreased by 5.2% in the year ending March 2011, but grew by 23.0% in 2011/12, according to chain linked methodologies.

Industry (including mining, manufacturing, construction and utilities) provided 24.1% of GDP in the year ending March 2010. The sector engaged 20.2% of the employed labour force in 2011. In 2002–11 industrial GDP increased at an average annual rate of 0.1%, according to the UN; industrial GDP, measured at constant prices, grew by 1.0% in 2010, but declined by 1.1% in 2011.

Mining contributed only 2.4% of GDP in the year ending March 2010; the sector engaged just 0.3% of the employed labour force in 2011. New Zealand has substantial coal reserves; petroleum, natural gas, iron, gold and silica are also exploited. A considerable amount of natural gas is used to produce synthetic petrol. According to the UN, the combined GDP of the mining and utilities sectors increased at an average annual rate of 0.8% in 2002–11. According to chain linked methodologies, the GDP of the mining sector (excluding utilities) declined by 14.5% in the year ending March 2012.

Manufacturing contributed 12.4% of GDP in the year ending March 2010. The sector engaged 11.3% of the employed labour force in 2011. The principal branches of manufacturing are food products, printing and publishing, wood and paper products, chemicals, metals and metal products, machinery and transport equipment. According to the UN, in 2002–11 manufacturing GDP decreased by an average of 0.5% per year. Manufacturing GDP increased by 2.1% in the year ending March 2012, according to chain linked methodologies.

Construction contributed 5.9% of GDP in the year ending March 2010. The sector engaged 7.8% of the employed labour force in 2011. According to the UN, the GDP of the construction sector grew at an average annual rate of 1.1% in 2002–11. According to chain linked methodologies, sectoral GDP increased by 2.7% in the year ending March 2011, but declined by 8.2% in 2011/12.

Energy is derived mainly from domestic supplies of hydro-electric power, natural gas and coal. Hydroelectric power supplied 55.1% of total electricity output in 2010 and gas 22.0%. Imports of petroleum and its products comprised 17.2% of the total value of merchandise imports in 2011.

The services sector provided 69.3% of GDP in the year ending March 2010. The sector engaged 72.9% of the employed labour force in 2011. Tourism became the single largest source of foreign exchange in the late 1980s. Visitor arrivals decreased to 2.56m. in 2012 from 2.60m. in 2011, in which year tourism receipts rose to $NZ5,763m. In 2002–11 the GDP of the services sector increased at an average annual rate of 2.4%, according to the UN. Services GDP expanded by 1.7% in the year ending March 2012, according to chain linked methodologies.

New Zealand's visible merchandise trade balance moved into surplus in 2009. In 2011 a surplus of US $2,739m. was recorded, although there was a deficit of US $6,763m. on the current account of the balance of payments. In 2011 the principal sources of imports were the People's Republic of China (15.9%), Australia, the USA and Japan. Australia was the principal market for exports in that year (purchasing 22.8%), followed by China, the USA and Japan. The main exports in 2011 were dairy products,

meat, logs, wood and wood articles, boilers, machinery and mechanical appliances, and fruit. The main imports were petroleum and petroleum products, boilers, machinery and mechanical appliances, vehicles, parts and accessories, and electrical machinery and equipment.

In the year ending June 2013 a budgetary deficit of $NZ7,383m. was forecast. In December 2012 total overseas debt was estimated by the central bank at $NZ252,553m. (comprising $NZ200,072m. owed by the corporate sector and $NZ52,481m. of official government debt), equivalent to 120.7% of GDP. New Zealand's general government gross debt was $NZ76.641m. in 2011, equivalent to 38.2% of GDP. Annual inflation averaged 2.8% in 2002–11. Consumer prices increased by 4.0% in 2011. The average rate of unemployment increased from 6.5% of the labour force in 2011 to 6.9% in 2012.

In mid-2008, for the first time in nine years, New Zealand entered economic recession. In order to address the repercussions of the global economic crisis, in December 2008 the new Government of Prime Minister John Key announced a financial stimulus programme. By April 2009 the Reserve Bank of New Zealand had lowered the interest rate to a record low level of 2.5%, where it remained until April 2010 when it was raised to 3.0%. In March 2011, however, with the objective of mitigating the economic impact of the Christchurch earthquake in February, the rate was again reduced to 2.5%, at which level it remained in early 2013. Meanwhile, following two successive years of recession, the economy returned to positive growth in the ending March 2011, expanding by 1.5% in that year and by 1.9% in 2011/12, according to chain linked methodologies. The Treasury forecast a further acceleration in the rate of expansion, to 2.3% in 2012/13 and to 2.9% in 2013/14, with reconstruction activities following the earthquakes in the Canterbury region in 2010–11 and rapidly increasing trade with China expected to stimulate growth. Inflationary pressures increased from late 2010, and by the second quarter of 2011 the annual rate of inflation had reached 5.3%. However, in the year ending March 2012 inflation eased to just 1.6%, owing to declining food prices, the early effects of an increase (in October 2010) in the rate of the goods and services tax, from 12.5% to 15.0%, and the strength of the New Zealand dollar: at early April 2013 the value of the New Zealand dollar had risen to some US $0.85, from a nadir of US $0.50 in March 2009, prompting some concern that, if sustained, the strength of the currency would lead to increasing difficulties for the country's exporters. Inflation was projected to decrease to 1.5% in the year ending March 2013, while the rate of unemployment was forecast to rise slightly from 6.7% in 2011/12 to 6.9% in 2012/13, before falling to 6.2% in 2013/14. Youth unemployment was of considerable concern, with some 17.1% of those in the labour force aged between 15 and 24 years registered as unemployed in the year ending March 2012. The 2011/12 budget provided funding of $NZ1,600m. (over a four-year period) for the purposes of infrastructural improvements. By reducing expenditure in other areas, including welfare payments, and by further reforming the tax system, the Government envisaged that the budget would return to a modest operating surplus (of around $NZ66m.) by 2014/15. The Government planned to reduce its stake in Air New Zealand and to dispose of other state assets, including 49% of its shareholding in the state electricity company Mighty River Power. New Zealand's growing trade and investment links with China, India and other Asian developing countries were expected to help to offset the downturn in trade with Europe caused by the continuing sovereign debt crisis in the eurozone.

PUBLIC HOLIDAYS

2014: 1–2 January (New Year), 6 February (Waitangi Day, anniversary of 1840 treaty), 18 March (Good Friday), 21 April (Easter Monday), 25 April (ANZAC Day, anniversary of 1915 landing at Gallipoli), 2 June (Queen's Official Birthday), 27 October (Labour Day), 25–26 December (Christmas).

In addition to these national holidays, each region celebrates an anniversary day.

Statistical Survey

Source (unless otherwise stated): Statistics New Zealand, Aorangi House, 85 Molesworth St, POB 2922, Wellington 1; tel. (4) 931-4600; fax (4) 931-9135; e-mail info@stats.govt.nz; internet www.stats.govt.nz.

Area and Population

AREA, POPULATION AND DENSITY

Area (sq km)	270,534*
Population (census results)†	
6 March 2001	3,737,277
7 March 2006	
Males	1,965,618
Females	2,062,329
Total	4,027,947
Population (official estimates at mid-year)	
2010	4,367,800
2011	4,405,200
2012	4,433,000
Density (per sq km) at mid-2012	16.4

* 104,454 sq miles.
† Figures refer to the population usually resident. The total population (including foreign visitors) was: 3,820,749 in 2001; 4,143,282 in 2006.

POPULATION BY AGE AND SEX
(official estimates at mid-2012)

	Males	Females	Total
0–14	457,400	434,900	892,300
15–64	1,442,000	1,487,400	2,929,300
65 and over	280,700	330,700	611,400
Total	**2,180,100**	**2,253,000**	**4,433,000**

Note: Totals may not be equal to the sum of components, owing to rounding.

ADMINISTRATIVE REGIONS
(census of March 2006)

	Area (sq km)	Population	Density (per sq km)
North Island			
Northland	13,296	148,470	11.2
Auckland	5,048	1,303,068	258.1
Waikato	26,170	382,713	14.6
Bay of Plenty . . .	11,428	257,379	22.5
Gisborne	8,355	44,499	5.3
Hawke's Bay Region . .	13,764	147,783	10.7
Taranaki	7,227	104,124	14.4
Manawatu-Wanganui . .	22,687	222,423	9.8
Wellington	8,056	448,959	55.7
Total North Island . . .	**116,031**	**3,059,418**	**26.4**
South Island			
Tasman	14,538	44,625	3.1
Nelson	444	42,891	96.6
Marlborough	12,493	42,558	3.4
West Coast	23,351	31,326	1.3
Canterbury	45,845	521,832	11.4
Otago	31,476	193,800	6.2
Southland	25,392	90,876	3.6
Total South Island . .	**153,540**	**967,908**	**38.1**
Area outside regions . . .	963	618	0.6
Total	**270,534**	**4,027,947**	**14.9**

Note: Totals may not be equal to the sum of components, owing to rounding.

PRINCIPAL CENTRES OF POPULATION
(census of March 2006, enumerated totals, incl. visitors)

Auckland city . .	404,658	Palmerston North .	75,543
Christchurch . .	348,435	Hastings district .	70,842
Wellington (capital).	179,466	Rotorua district .	65,901
Hamilton . . .	129,249	Napier	55,359
Dunedin . . .	118,683	Nelson	42,888
Tauranga . . .	103,635		

BIRTHS, MARRIAGES AND DEATHS

	Live births*		Marriages†		Deaths*	
	Number	Rate (per '000)	Number	Rate (per '000)	Number	Rate (per '000)
2004 . .	58,073	14.2	21,006	5.1	28,419	7.0
2005 . .	57,745	14.0	20,470	5.0	27,034	6.5
2006 . .	59,193	14.1	21,423	5.1	28,245	6.8
2007 . .	64,044	15.1	21,494	5.1	28,522	6.7
2008 . .	64,343	15.1	21,948	5.1	29,188	6.8
2009 . .	62,543	14.5	21,628	5.0	28,964	6.7
2010 . .	63,897	14.6	20,940	4.8	28,438	6.5
2011 . .	61,403	13.9‡	20,231	4.6	30,082	6.8‡

* Data for births and deaths are tabulated by year of registration rather than by year of occurrence.
† Based on the resident population concept, replacing the previous de facto concept.
‡ Provisional.

Life expectancy (years at birth): 80.7 (males 78.8; females 82.7) in 2010 (Source: World Bank, World Development Indicators database).

IMMIGRATION AND EMIGRATION

	2009	2010	2011
Long-term immigrants* . . .	86,410	82,469	84,187
Long-term emigrants†	65,157	72,018	86,042

* Figures refer to persons intending to remain in New Zealand for 12 months or more, and New Zealand citizens returning after an absence of 12 months or more.
† Figures refer to New Zealand citizens intending to remain abroad for 12 months or more, and overseas migrants departing after a stay of 12 months or more.

ECONOMICALLY ACTIVE POPULATION
(annual averages, labour force sample survey, '000 persons aged 15 years and over, excl. armed forces)

	2009	2010	2011
Agriculture, forestry and fishing	143.0	149.2	153.0
Mining and quarrying	6.8	7.0	7.2
Manufacturing	249.5	247.5	249.5
Electricity, gas and water . . .	14.6	16.8	16.6
Construction	181.0	179.1	172.1
Wholesale and retail trade; repair of motor vehicles, motorcycles and personal and household goods; restaurants and hotels .	436.3	440.3	443.0
Transport, storage and communications	134.4	134.7	139.8
Financial intermediation . . .	68.5	62.5	66.6
Real estate, renting and business activities	278.9	273.8	279.0
Public administration and defence; compulsory social security . .	118.2	123.9	125.1
Education and training . . .	184.0	189.8	201.7
Health and social work . . .	220.6	223.5	230.4
Other community, social and personal service activities . .	119.7	124.6	125.1
Sub-total	**2,155.5**	**2,172.7**	**2,209.1**
Activities not adequately defined	8.7	7.6	6.4
Total employed	**2,164.4**	**2,180.3**	**2,215.4**
Unemployed	141.5	152.2	154.6
Total labour force	**2,305.9**	**2,332.5**	**2,370.0**
Males	1,223.5	1,238.7	1,257.4
Females	1,082.5	1,093.7	1,112.6

Health and Welfare

KEY INDICATORS

Total fertility rate (children per woman, 2010)	2.2
Under-5 mortality rate (per 1,000 live births, 2010) . . .	6
HIV/AIDS (% of persons aged 15–49, 2009)	0.1
Physicians (per 1,000 head, 2010)	2.7
Hospital beds (per 1,000 head, 2002)	6.2
Health expenditure (2009): US $ per head (PPP) . . .	2,907
Health expenditure (2009): % of GDP	10.0
Health expenditure (2009): public (% of total) . . .	83.0
Total carbon dioxide emissions ('000 metric tons, 2008) . .	33,094.7
Carbon dioxide emissions per head (metric tons, 2008) . .	7.8
Human Development Index (2011): ranking	5
Human Development Index (2011): value	0.908

For sources and definitions, see explanatory note on p. vi.

Agriculture

PRINCIPAL CROPS
('000 metric tons)

	2009	2010	2011
Wheat	403	445	383
Barley	435	308	368
Maize	238	189	210
Oats	34	48	28
Potatoes*	545	591	522
Peas, dry	21	37	32
Cabbages and other brassicas* .	42	43	37
Lettuce and chicory* . . .	32	32	28
Tomatoes*	92	99	63
Cauliflowers and broccoli* . .	42	42	37
Pumpkins, squash and gourds* .	160	161	141
Onions and shallots, green* . .	203	205	179
Peas, green*	43	43	38
Carrots and turnips* . . .	65	66	55
Maize, green*	90	91	79
Grapes*	250	230	234
Apples	431	386*	438*
Pears*	32	25	33
Kiwi fruit*	390	379	365

* FAO estimate(s).

Aggregate production ('000 metric tons, may include official, semi-official or estimated data): Total cereals 1,124 in 2009, 1,001 in 2010, 999 in 2011; Total roots and tubers 557 in 2009, 604 in 2010, 534 in 2011; Total vegetables (incl. melons) 958 in 2009, 972 in 2010, 825 in 2011; Total fruits (excl. melons) 1,220 in 2009, 1,136 in 2010, 1,181 in 2011.

Source: FAO.

LIVESTOCK
('000 head at 30 June)

	2009	2010	2011
Cattle	9,961	9,864	10,021
Sheep	32,384	32,563	31,132
Goats	82	95	85
Pigs	323	335	327
Horses	65	64	56
Chickens	13,147	13,505	13,800
Ducks*	180	180	180
Geese and guinea fowls* . . .	80	80	80
Turkeys*	76	76	76

* FAO estimates.

Source: FAO.

LIVESTOCK PRODUCTS
('000 metric tons)

	2009	2010	2011
Cattle meat	637.0	635.3	622.6
Sheep meat	478.4	470.9	465.3
Pig meat	46.7	47.1	50.2
Chicken meat	135.0	143.1	158.3
Game meat	27.2	21.3	22.7
Cows' milk	16,483	17,011	17,894
Hen eggs*	51.8	52.3	52.3
Other poultry eggs*	3.1	3.2	3.2
Honey	12.6	12.6	12.6
Wool, greasy*	179.2	165.8	165.8

* FAO estimates.

Source: FAO.

Forestry

ROUNDWOOD REMOVALS
('000 cubic metres, FAO estimates)

	2009	2010	2011
Sawlogs, veneer logs and logs for sleepers	8,966	7,474	8,328
Pulpwood	3,119	3,461	3,681
Other industrial roundwood . .	8,125	11,021	13,114
Total	**20,210**	**21,956**	**25,123**

Source: FAO.

SAWNWOOD PRODUCTION
('000 cubic metres, year ending 31 March)

Species	2008/09	2009/10	2010/11
Radiata pine	3,435	3,551	3,841
Other introduced pines . . .	2	0	0
Douglas fir	138	115	100
Rimu and miro	3	2	1
Total (incl. others)	**3,610**	**3,695**	**3,971**

Source: Forestry Statistics Section, Ministry of Agriculture and Forestry, Wellington.

Fishing

('000 metric tons, live weight)

	2008	2009	2010
Capture*	452.3	439.4	436.2
Southern blue whiting . . .	29.3	39.4	38.6
Blue grenadier (Hoki) . . .	96.0	91.5	110.0
Oreo dories	15.6	16.0	20.4
Jack and horse mackerels . .	47.3	40.2	41.0
Snoek (Barracouta)	27.4	27.8	26.4
Skipjack tuna	26.1	25.1	12.4
Wellington flying squid . . .	55.6	46.3	32.6
Aquaculture	112.4†	105.0	110.6
New Zealand mussel . . .	100.1	89.9	95.2
Total catch	**564.7†**	**544.3**	**546.8**

* Excluding catches made by chartered vessels and landed outside New Zealand.
† FAO estimate.

Note: Figures exclude aquatic plants (metric tons, all capture); 196 in 2008; 366 in 2009; 396 in 2010. Also excluded are aquatic mammals (recorded by number rather than by weight). The number of whales and dolphins caught was: 5 in 2008; 21 in 2009; 22 in 2010.

Source: FAO.

Mining

('000 metric tons unless otherwise indicated)

	2008	2009	2010
Coal (incl. lignite)	4,909	4,563	5,330
Gold (kg)	13,403	13,442	13,469
Crude petroleum ('000 barrels) .	21,436	20,026	19,302
Gross natural gas (million cu m) .	4,484	4,644	5,052
Liquid petroleum gas ('000 barrels)	979	857	900*
Ironsands	2,020	2,092	2,439
Silica sand	48.6	43.5	113.2
Limestone	4,810	4,572	4,540

* Estimate.

Source: US Geological Survey.

Industry

SELECTED PRODUCTS
(metric tons unless otherwise indicated)

	2007	2008	2009
Wine (million litres) . . .	147.6	205.2	205.2
Chemical wood pulp* . . .	205,743	191,253	207,107
Mechanical wood pulp* . .	186,020	183,724	191,102
Newsprint*	66,533	74,172	79,253
Other paper and paperboard* .	149,555	142,853	151,297
Fibre board (cu m)*	193,708	153,933	172,453
Particle board (cu m)* . . .	57,480	54,107	33,080
Veneer (cu m)*	121,566	118,468	120,454
Plywood (cu m)*	96,678	85,683	68,647
Jet fuels ('000 metric tons) . .	837	891	867
Motor spirit—petrol ('000 metric tons) . . .	1,423	1,503	1,416
Gas-diesel (Distillate fuel) oils ('000 metric tons)	1,731	1,778	n.a.
Residual fuel oils ('000 metric tons)	400	509	558
Cement ('000 metric tons) . . .	1,200	1,200	1,200
Aluminium—unwrought ('000 metric tons):			
primary	351.1	315.5	271.9
secondary†	22.0	22.0	22.0
Electric energy (million kWh) .	43,750	43,850	43,472

* Source: Ministry of Agriculture and Forestry, Wellington.
† Estimates.

Sources (unless otherwise stated): UN, *Industrial Commodity Statistics Yearbook* and *Monthly Bulletin of Statistics*; US Geological Survey; New Zealand Wine Online.

2010: Wine (million litres) 190.0; Chemical wood pulp (metric tons) 232,665; Mechanical wood pulp (metric tons) 189,842; Newsprint (metric tons) 297,822; Other paper and paperboard (metric tons) 631,588; Fibre board (cu m) 161,906; Particle board (cu m) 34,317; Veneer (cu m) 169,302; Plywood (cu m) 94,098 (Sources: New Zealand Wine Online; Ministry of Agriculture and Forestry, Wellington).

2011: Wine (million litres) 235.0; Chemical wood pulp (metric tons) 204,328; Mechanical wood pulp (metric tons) 177,251; Newsprint (metric tons) 293,068; Other paper and paperboard (metric tons) 615,881; Fibre board (cu m) 176,473; Particle board (cu m) 34,317; Veneer (cu m) 173,288; Plywood (cu m) 98,557 (Sources: New Zealand Wine Online; Ministry of Agriculture and Forestry, Wellington).

2012: Wine (million litres) 194.0; (Sources: New Zealand Wine Online).

Finance

CURRENCY AND EXCHANGE RATES

Monetary Units
100 cents = 1 New Zealand dollar ($NZ).

Sterling, US Dollar and Euro Equivalents (31 December 2012)
£1 sterling = $NZ1.924;
US $1 = $NZ1.219;
€1 = $NZ1.608;
$NZ100 = £51.98 = US $82.03 = €62.17.

Average Exchange Rate (New Zealand dollars per US $)
2010   1.3874
2011   1.2658
2012   1.2342

BUDGET
($NZ million, year ending 30 June)

Revenue	2006/07	2007/08*	2008/09*
Taxation	53,064	56,186	55,911
Compulsory fees, fines, penalties and levies	3,496	3,851	4,037
Sales of goods and services . .	12,613	13,682	14,222
Interest revenue and dividends .	2,995	3,203	3,358
Other	2,421	2,891	2,591
Total	74,589	79,813	80,119

Expenditure	2006/07	2007/08*	2008/09*
Social security and welfare . .	19,829	22,274	22,843
GSF pension expenses . . .	645	714	652
Health	10,661	10,765	12,024
Education	9,853	10,803	11,017
Core government services . .	4,628	3,163	3,412
Law and order	2,822	3,192	3,341
Defence	1,478	1,524	1,697
Transport and communications .	6,990	7,185	8,027
Economic and industrial services .	4,723	7,433	7,918
Primary services	1,233	1,404	1,364
Heritage, culture and recreation .	2,043	2,366	3,130
Housing and community development . . .	865	965	1,036
Other	74	84	83
Finance costs	2,885	2,954	2,503
Future spending forecast . . .	—	—	249
Adjustment	—	–240	–495
Total (incl. others)	68,729	74,586	78,801

* Forecasts.

2010/11: *Revenue:* Tax revenue 58,595; Non-tax revenue 7,326; Capital receipts 1,763; Total 67,684. *Expenditure:* Education 11,788; Health 13,158; Social development 21,110; Total (incl. others) 80,307.

2011/12 (estimates): *Revenue:* Tax revenue 61,459; Non-tax revenue 7,016; Capital receipts 1,824; Total 70,299. *Expenditure:* Education 9,276; Health 13,522; Social development 21,549; Total (incl. others) 79,499.

2012/13 (estimates): *Revenue:* Tax revenue 65,384; Non-tax revenue 7,070; Capital receipts 1,828; Total 74,282. *Expenditure:* Education 9,605; Health 14,125; Social development 21,638; Total (incl. others) 81,665.
Source: New Zealand Treasury, Wellington.

INTERNATIONAL RESERVES
(excl. gold, US $ million at 31 December)

	2009	2010	2011
IMF special drawing rights . .	1,340	1,317	1,272
Reserve position in IMF . . .	273	273	499
Foreign exchange	13,982	15,133	15,242
Total	15,594	16,723	17,012

Source: IMF, *International Financial Statistics*.

MONEY SUPPLY
($NZ million at 31 December)

	2008	2009	2010
Currency outside banks . . .	3,526	3,580	3,720
Demand deposits at banking institutions	31,361	31,316	32,760
Total money	34,888	34,896	36,480

Source: IMF, *International Financial Statistics.*

COST OF LIVING
(Consumer Price Index; base: 2000 = 100)

	2007	2008	2009
Food (incl. beverages) . . .	118.8	129.0	137.0
Fuel and light	149.5	160.2	167.0
Clothing (incl. footwear) . .	101.6	101.5	104.0
Rent	105.2	108.5	110.0
All items (incl. others) . . .	119.6	124.4	127.0

2010: Food (incl. beverages) 138.1; All items (incl. others) 129.9.

2011: Food (incl. beverages) 145.5; All items (incl. others) 135.1.

Source: ILO.

NATIONAL ACCOUNTS
($NZ million at current prices, year ending 31 March)

Expenditure on the Gross Domestic Product

	2009/10	2010/11	2011/12
Government final consumption expenditure	38,437	39,862	41,548
Private final consumption expenditure	112,878	117,571	123,493
Change in inventories . . .	−897	1,037	1,959
Gross fixed capital formation . .	36,246	37,021	37,281
Total domestic expenditure .	186,664	195,491	204,281
Exports of goods and services . .	53,770	59,331	62,521
Less Imports of goods and services	50,716	56,318	60,633
GDP in market prices . . .	189,718	198,504	206,170

Gross Domestic Product by Economic Activity

	2007/08	2008/09	2009/10
Agriculture	9,222	6,765	9,112
Fishing	1,454	1,359	1,416
Forestry and logging . . .	900	896	1,022
Mining and quarrying . . .	3,922	4,286	4,154
Manufacturing	22,653	23,939	21,736
Electricity, gas and water . .	5,376	5,868	6,090
Construction	10,693	10,397	10,381
Wholesale and retail trade . .	17,819	17,313	17,511
Hotels and restaurants . .	3,670	3,606	3,727
Transport, storage and communications	14,337	13,210	13,590
Financial intermediation (incl. insurance)	8,201	9,277	11,060
Property and business activities .	23,929	24,635	25,219
Ownership of dwellings . . .	12,126	11,924	10,907
Public administration and defence	11,335	12,171	12,316
Education	7,609	8,227	8,749
Health and community services .	10,302	11,242	11,898
Cultural and recreational services	2,762	2,701	2,783
Personal and other services . .	3,520	3,685	3,750
Statistical discrepancy . . .	−2	−3	−2
Gross value added at basic prices	169,828	171,498	175,419
Goods and services tax on production	12,268	12,206	12,440
Import duties	1,901	1,850	1,859
GDP in market prices . . .	183,997	185,555	189,718

BALANCE OF PAYMENTS
(US $ million)

	2009	2010	2011
Exports of goods	25,336	31,883	38,345
Imports of goods	−24,029	−29,539	−35,606
Balance on goods	1,307	2,344	2,739
Exports of services	8,164	9,033	10,089
Imports of services	−8,065	−9,343	−10,965
Balance on goods and services	1,406	2,034	1,862
Primary income received . . .	2,968	3,771	4,038
Primary income paid	−7,856	−10,771	−12,382
Balance on goods, services and primary income	−3,482	−4,965	−6,482
Secondary income received . .	1,205	1,014	1,039
Secondary income paid . . .	−972	−1,043	−1,320
Current balance	−3,248	−4,994	−6,763
Capital account (net)	275	2,797	8,337
Direct investment assets . . .	1,399	−573	−2,795
Direct investment liabilities . .	−719	701	3,580
Portfolio investment assets . .	−4,086	−2,331	−2,533
Portfolio investment liabilities .	6,128	4,685	4,333
Other investment assets . . .	−993	−1,601	−2,965
Other investment liabilities . .	3,033	1,332	−455
Net errors and omissions . . .	1,866	832	−320
Reserves and related items .	3,654	848	420

Source: IMF, *International Financial Statistics.*

External Trade

PRINCIPAL COMMODITIES
($NZ million)

Imports c.i.f.	2009	2010	2011
Vehicles, parts and accessories .	3,226	4,267	4,359
Boilers, machinery and mechanical appliances	5,024	5,195	5,654
Petroleum, petroleum products, etc.	5,855	6,487	8,074
Electrical machinery and equipment	3,975	3,633	4,015
Paper and paperboard . . .	955	1,032	1,038
Plastic and plastic articles . .	1,488	1,612	1,657
Iron and steel and articles . .	1,127	1,189	1,254
Optical, medical and measuring equipment	1,371	1,327	1,358
Total (incl. others)	40,221	42,360	46,895

Exports f.o.b.	2009	2010	2011
Dairy produce; birds' eggs; natural honey; edible products of animal origin, not elsewhere specified or included	8,116	10,415	12,021
Meat and edible offal	5,142	5,089	5,529
Logs, wood and wood articles . .	2,319	2,949	3,197
Boilers, machinery and mechanical appliances; parts thereof . .	1,658	1,722	1,823
Fruit and nuts; peel of citrus fruit or melons	1,601	1,471	1,593
Fish, crustaceans and molluscs .	1,262	1,307	1,361
Aluminium and aluminium articles	883	1,213	1,242
Electrical machinery and equipment	982	1,029	1,109
Total (incl. others)*	39,672	43,532	47,701

* Including re-exports.

PRINCIPAL TRADING PARTNERS
($NZ million)

Imports (c.i.f.)*	2009	2010	2011
Australia	7,397	7,697	7,369
Canada	538	521	630
China, People's Republic	6,066	6,762	7,439
France	1,331	595	946
Germany	1,684	1,739	1,994
Indonesia	720	647	729
Italy	728	701	837
Japan	2,981	3,107	2,921
Korea, Republic	1,357	1,387	1,454
Malaysia	1,085	1,524	1,478
Qatar	945	825	1,041
Russia	185	425	1,204
Saudi Arabia	272	305	919
Singapore	1,625	1,622	2,163
Taiwan	607	732	692
Thailand	1,062	1,372	1,330
United Arab Emirates	466	885	778
United Kingdom	937	955	1,267
USA	4,328	4,393	5,026
Total (incl. others)	40,221	42,360	46,895

* Excluding specie and gold.

Exports*	2009	2010	2011
Algeria	261	232	500
Australia	9,132	10,025	10,848
Belgium	490	360	404
Canada	501	497	597
China, People's Republic	3,628	4,826	5,887
France	508	457	426
Germany	765	658	775
Hong Kong	794	866	798
India	630	901	938
Indonesia	963	930	856
Italy	404	437	459
Japan	2,821	3,375	3,441
Korea, Republic	1,240	1,414	1,675
Malaysia	705	776	875
Netherlands	480	494	625
Philippines	570	729	757
Saudi Arabia	475	615	691
Singapore	1,100	826	813
Taiwan	756	843	899
Thailand	453	679	732
United Kingdom	1,696	1,528	1,545
USA	3,953	3,759	3,997
Venezuela	362	463	486
Total (incl. others)	39,672	43,532	47,701

* Including re-exports, but excluding specie and gold.

Transport

RAILWAYS
(traffic, year ending 30 June)

	2000/01	2001/02	2002/03
Freight ('000 metric tons)	14,461	14,330	14,822
Passengers ('000)	12,714	12,521	12,300*

* Excludes passengers on the Tranz Scenic network.

Source: Tranz Rail Ltd, Wellington.

ROAD TRAFFIC
(vehicles licensed at June)

	2009	2010	2011
Passenger cars	2,330,312	2,337,934	2,344,864
Taxis	7,855	7,575	7,362
Buses and service coaches	19,067	19,388	19,653
Trailers and caravans	453,488	459,912	465,104
Motorcycles and mopeds	78,217	76,548	64,070
Tractors	28,703	29,030	29,223
Trucks	427,525	426,491	422,452

Source: New Zealand Transport Agency.

SHIPPING
Flag Registered Fleet
(at 31 December)

	2010	2011	2012
Number of vessels	151	150	150
Displacement (grt)	255,121	245,210	237,148

Source: Lloyd's List Intelligence (www.lloydslistintelligence.com).

Vessels Handled
(international, '000 grt)

	1993	1994	1995
Entered	37,603	39,700	48,827
Cleared	35,128	37,421	42,985

Source: UN, *Statistical Yearbook*.

International Sea-borne Freight Traffic
('000 metric tons, year ending 30 June)

	2004/05	2005/06	2006/07*
Goods loaded	21,894	21,840	22,986
Goods unloaded	19,164	18,119	18,499

* Provisional.

CIVIL AVIATION
(domestic and international traffic on scheduled services)

	2007	2008	2009
Kilometres flown (million)	208	212	203
Passengers carried ('000)	12,598	12,951	12,104
Passenger-km (million)	27,281	28,045	25,924
Total metric ton-km (million)	3,679	3,772	3,429

Source: UN, *Statistical Yearbook*.

2010: Passengers carried ('000) 10,128 (Source: World Bank, World Development Indicators database).

Tourism

VISITOR ARRIVALS

Country of residence	2009	2010	2011
Australia	1,082,680	1,119,879	1,156,426
China, People's Republic	102,259	122,712	145,524
Germany	64,564	64,648	63,719
Japan	78,426	87,735	68,963
Korea, Republic	52,921	67,309	52,787
United Kingdom	258,438	234,314	230,316
USA	197,792	189,709	184,714
Total (incl. others)	2,447,346	2,525,044	2,601,444

Tourism receipts ($NZ million): 6,187 in 2009; 5,595 in 2010; 5,763 in 2011.

Source: Tourism Research Council, Wellington.

Communications Media

	2009	2010	2011
Telephones ('000 main lines in use)	1,870	1,870	1,880
Mobile cellular telephones ('000 subscribers)	4,700	5,020	4,820
Internet subscribers ('000) . .	1,415	1,400	1,400
Broadband subscribers ('000) . .	981	1,050	1,140

Source: International Telecommunication Union.

Education

(July 2011 unless otherwise indicated)

	Institutions	Teachers (full-time equivalent)	Students
Early childhood services . .	5,258	14,271	194,101[1]
Primary schools[2]	2,007	24,698[3]	433,524
Composite schools[4] . . .	155	2,672[3]	50,753
Secondary schools[5] . . .	342	18,864[3]	275,011
Special schools	44	1,060[3]	2,882
Polytechnics	20[6]	4,194[7]	174,964[8]
Colleges of education . . .	4[6]	301[9]	65,005[8]
Universities	8[6]	7,869[7]	156,069[8]
Wananga[10]	3[6]	572[7]	42,293[8]
Private training establishments receiving government grants . . .	522[6]	4,177[6]	59,158[11]

[1] Includes children on the regular roll of kindergartens, playcentres, the Correspondence School, Te Kohanga Reo, Early Childhood Development Unit funded playgroups, Early Childhood Development Unit funded Pacific Islands language groups, education and care centres (including home-based child care).
[2] Primary schools include Full Primary Years 1–8, Contributing Years 1–6, Intermediate Years 7–8.
[3] Teachers employed in state schools at 1 April 2012.
[4] Composite schools provide both primary and secondary education (includes area schools and the Correspondence School).
[5] Secondary schools include Years 7–15, Years 9–15.
[6] 2003 figure.
[7] 2009 figure.
[8] 2010 figure.
[9] 2006 figure.
[10] Tertiary institutions providing polytechnic and university level programmes specifically for Maori students, with an emphasis on Maori language and culture.
[11] 2004 figure.

Source: Ministry of Education, Wellington.

Pupil-teacher ratio (primary education, UNESCO estimate): 14.5 in 2009/10 (Source: UNESCO Institute for Statistics).

Directory

The Government

Head of State: HM Queen ELIZABETH II (acceded to the throne 6 February 1952).

Governor-General and Commander-in-Chief: Lt-Gen. Sir JERRY MATEPARAE (assumed office 31 August 2011).

CABINET
(May 2013)

The Government is formed by the National Party, in coalition with ACT New Zealand, the Maori Party and UnitedFuture New Zealand.

Prime Minister and Minister of Tourism: JOHN KEY.

Deputy Prime Minister and Minister of Finance: BILL ENGLISH.

Minister of Transport and for Canterbury Earthquake Recovery: GERRY BROWNLEE.

Minister for Economic Development, of Science and Innovation, and for Tertiary Education, Skills and Employment: STEVEN JOYCE.

Minister of Justice, for ACC and for Ethnic Affairs: JUDITH COLLINS.

Minister of Health and for State-owned Enterprises: TONY RYALL.

Minister of Education and of Pacific Island Affairs: HEKIA PARATA.

Attorney-General and Minister for Treaty of Waitangi Negotiations, and for Arts, Culture and Heritage: CHRISTOPHER FINLAYSON.

Minister for Social Development: PAULA BENNETT.

Minister of Defence and of State Services: Dr JONATHAN COLEMAN.

Minister of Foreign Affairs and for Sport and Recreation: MURRAY MCCULLY.

Minister of Police and of Corrections: ANNE TOLLEY.

Minister of Conservation and of Housing: Dr NICK SMITH.

Minister of Trade and for Climate Change Issues: TIM GROSER.

Minister for the Environment, and for Communications and Information Technology: AMY ADAMS.

Minister for Primary Industries and for Racing: NATHAN GUY.

Minister of Commerce, of Broadcasting and for Consumer Affairs: CRAIG FOSS.

Minister of Internal Affairs and of Local Government: CHRIS TREMAIN.

Minister of Energy and Resources and of Labour: SIMON BRIDGES.

Minister of Civil Defence, of Youth Affairs and for Food Safety: NIKKI KAYE.

MINISTERS OUTSIDE CABINET

Minister for Building and Construction, of Customs, for Land Information and of Statistics: MAURICE WILLIAMSON.

Minister for the Community and Voluntary Sector, for Senior Citizens and of Women's Affairs: JO GOODHEW.

Minister for Courts: CHESTER BORROWS.

Minister of Immigration and of Veterans' Affairs: MICHAEL WOODHOUSE.

SUPPORT PARTY MINISTERS

Minister of Revenue: PETER DUNNE.

Minister for Regulatory Reform and for Small Business: JOHN BANKS.

Minister of Maori Affairs: Dr PITA SHARPLES.

Minister for Whanau Ora and for Disability Issues: TARIANA TURIA.

MINISTRIES AND GOVERNMENT DEPARTMENTS

Department of the Prime Minister and Cabinet: Executive Wing, Parliament Bldgs, Wellington 6011; tel. (4) 817-9682; fax (4) 472-3181; e-mail dpmc.information@dpmc.govt.nz; internet www .dpmc.govt.nz.

Ministry of Business, Innovation and Employment: Level 8, 33 Bowen St, POB 5488, Wellington 6011; tel. (4) 901-1499; fax (4) 917-0190; e-mail info@mbie.govt.nz; internet www.mbie.govt.nz.

Ministry of Civil Defence and Emergency Management: Level 9, 22 The Terrace, POB 5010, Wellington; tel. (4) 473-7363; fax (4) 473-7369; e-mail emergency.management@dia.govt.nz; internet www.civildefence.govt.nz.

Department of Conservation: POB 10-420, Wellington 6143; tel. (4) 471-0726; fax (4) 381-3057; e-mail enquiries@doc.govt.nz; internet www.doc.govt.nz.

Department of Corrections: POB 1206, Wellington 6140; tel. (4) 460-3000; fax (4) 460-3208; e-mail info@corrections.govt.nz; internet www.corrections.govt.nz.

Ministry for Culture and Heritage: ASB House, Level 4, 101 The Terrace, POB 5364, Wellington 6011; tel. (4) 499-4229; fax (4) 499-4490; e-mail info@mch.govt.nz; internet www.mch.govt.nz.

Ministry of Defence: Defence House, Level 4, 2–12 Aitken St, POB 12-703, Wellington; tel. (4) 496-0999; fax (4) 496-0859; e-mail info@defence.govt.nz; internet www.defence.govt.nz.

Ministry of Education: 45–47 Pipitea St, Level 3, POB 1666, Thorndon, Wellington 6140; tel. (4) 463-8000; fax (4) 463-8001; e-mail info@minedu.govt.nz; internet www.minedu.govt.nz.

Ministry for the Environment: Environment House, 23 Kate Sheppard Pl., POB 10-362, Thorndon, Wellington 6143; tel. (4) 439-7400; fax (4) 439-7700; e-mail info@mfe.govt.nz; internet www.mfe .govt.nz.

Ministry of Foreign Affairs and Trade: 195 Lambton Quay, Private Bag 18901, Wellington 5045; tel. (4) 439-8000; fax (4) 4392-8505; e-mail enquiries@mfat.govt.nz; internet www.mfat.govt.nz.

Ministry of Health: 133 Molesworth St, POB 5013, Wellington 6011; tel. (4) 496-2000; fax (4) 496-2340; e-mail info@health.govt.nz; internet www.health.govt.nz.

Department of Inland Revenue: POB 39010, Wellington Mail Centre, Lower Hutt 5045; tel. (4) 978-0779; e-mail nonres@ird.govt .nz; internet www.ird.govt.nz.

Department of Internal Affairs: 46 Waring Taylor St, POB 805, Wellington 6011; tel. (4) 495-7200; e-mail info@dia.govt.nz; internet www.dia.govt.nz.

Ministry of Justice: Vogel Centre, 19 Aitken St, DX 10088, Wellington; tel. (4) 918-8800; fax (4) 918-8820; e-mail info@justice.govt .nz; internet www.justice.govt.nz.

Ministry of Maori Development (Te Puni Kokiri): Te Puni Kokiri House, 143 Lambton Quay, POB 3943, Wellington 6011; tel. (4) 819-6000; fax (4) 819-6299; e-mail info@tpk.govt.nz; internet www.tpk .govt.nz.

Ministry of Pacific Island Affairs: ASB Bldg, Level 2, 101–103 The Terrace, POB 833, Wellington 6011; tel. (4) 473-4493; fax (4) 473-4301; e-mail contact@mpia.govt.nz; internet www.mpia.govt.nz.

Ministry for Primary Industries: Pastoral House, 25 The Terrace, POB 2526, Wellington; tel. (4) 894-0100; fax (4) 894-0720; internet www.mpi.govt.nz.

Ministry of Social Development: Bowen State Bldg, Bowen St, POB 1556, Wellington 6011; tel. (4) 916-3300; fax (4) 918-0099; e-mail information@msd.govt.nz; internet www.msd.govt.nz.

State Services Commission: Reserve Bank Bldg, Level 10, 2 The Terrace, POB 329, Wellington 6140; tel. (4) 495-6600; fax (4) 495-6686; e-mail commission@ssc.govt.nz; internet www.ssc.govt.nz.

Statistics New Zealand (Tatauranga Aotearoa): Statistics House, The Boulevard, Harbour Quays, POB 2922, Wellington 6140; tel. (4) 931-4600; fax (4) 931-4030; e-mail info@stats.govt.nz; internet www .stats.govt.nz.

Ministry of Tourism: 33 Bowen St, POB 5640, Wellington; tel. (4) 498-7440; fax (4) 498-7445; e-mail info@tourism.govt.nz; internet www.tourism.govt.nz.

Ministry of Transport: SAS House, Level 6, 89 The Terrace, POB 3175, Wellington 6140; tel. (4) 439-9000; fax (4) 439-9001; e-mail info@transport.govt.nz; internet www.transport.govt.nz.

Treasury: Level 5, 1 The Terrace, POB 3724, Wellington 6011; tel. (4) 472-2733; fax (4) 473-0982; e-mail info@treasury.govt.nz; internet www.treasury.govt.nz.

Ministry of Women's Affairs: Revera House, Level 2, 48 Mulgrave St, POB 10-049, Wellington 6011; tel. (4) 915-7112; fax (4) 916-1604; e-mail mwa@mwa.govt.nz; internet www.mwa.govt.nz.

Ministry of Youth Development: Bowen State Bldg, Level 7, Bowen St, POB 1556, Wellington; tel. (4) 916-3300; fax (4) 918-0091; e-mail mydinfo@myd.govt.nz; internet www.myd.govt.nz.

Legislature

PARLIAMENT

Parliament comprises the Crown and the elected House of Representatives.

House of Representatives

Speaker: DAVID CARTER.

General Election, 26 November 2011

Party	Number of party votes	% of votes	Elect-orate seats	List seats	Total seats
NZ National Party	1,058,638	47.31	42	17	59
NZ Labour Party	614,936	27.48	22	12	34
Green Party	247,370	11.06	—	14	14
New Zealand First	147,544	6.59	—	8	8
Maori Party	31,982	1.43	3	—	3
Mana	24,168	1.08	1	—	1
ACT New Zealand	23,889	1.07	1	—	1
UnitedFuture NZ	13,443	0.61	1	—	1
Total (incl. others)	2,237,462	100.00	70	51	121

Election Commission

Electoral Commission of New Zealand: 34–42 Manners St, POB 3220, Wellington; tel. (4) 474-0670; fax (4) 474-0674; e-mail enquiries@elections.govt.nz; internet www.elections.org.nz; f. 2010; independent Crown entity; assumed responsibilities of Chief Electoral Office and previous Electoral Commission in Oct. 2010; Chair. Sir HUGH WILLIAMS; Chief Electoral Officer ROBERT PEDEN.

Political Organizations

At October 2012 13 political parties were registered.

ACT New Zealand: Level 2, 27 Gillies Ave, Newmarket, Auckland; tel. (9) 523-0470; fax (9) 523-0472; e-mail info@act.org.nz; internet www.act.org.nz; f. 1994; supports free enterprise, tax reform and choice in education and health; Pres. JOHN BOSCAWEN; Leader JOHN BANKS.

Green Party of Aotearoa—New Zealand: Level 2, 17 Garrett St, Te Aro, POB 11-652, Wellington; tel. (4) 801-5102; fax (4) 801-5104; e-mail greenparty@greens.org.nz; internet www.greens.org.nz; f. 1989; fmrly Values Party, f. 1972; Co-Leaders RUSSEL NORMAN, METIRIA TUREI.

Mana: 515 Taikorea Rd, Palmerston North 4473; e-mail info@mana .net.nz; internet www.mana.net.nz; f. 2011; advocates development and equality of income for local people; Pres. ANNETTE SYKES; Leader HONE HARAWIRA.

Maori Party: POB 50-271, Porirua; tel. (4) 471-9900; fax (4) 499-7269; e-mail hekeretari2@maoriparty.com; internet www .maoriparty.org; f. 2004; Co-Leaders Dr PITA SHARPLES, TARIANA TURIA; Pres. PEM BIRD.

New Zealand Democratic Party for Social Credit: POB 5164, Waikiwi, Invercargill 9843; tel. and fax (3) 215-7170; e-mail democrats@democrats.org.nz; internet www.democrats.org.nz; f. 1953; est. as Social Credit Political League; subsequently known as New Zealand Democratic Party Inc; liberal; Pres. DAVID WILSON; Leader STEPHNIE DE RUYTER.

New Zealand First: Albany, North Shore City, POB 301158, Auckland 0752; tel. and fax (9) 422-2370; e-mail nzfirstparty@ nzfirstparty.org.nz; internet nzfirst.org.nz; f. 1993; Leader WINSTON PETERS; Pres. KEVIN GARDENER.

New Zealand Labour Party: Fraser House, Level 1, 160–162 Willis St, POB 784, Wellington; tel. (4) 384-7649; fax (4) 384-8060; e-mail office@labourparty.org.nz; internet labour.org.nz; f. 1916; advocates an organized economy guaranteeing an adequate standard of living to every person able and willing to work; Pres. MOIRA COATSWORTH; Leader DAVID SHEARER; Gen. Sec. TIM BARNETT.

New Zealand National Party: Willbank House, Level 14, 57 Willis St, POB 1155, Wellington 6001; tel. (4) 472-5211; fax (4) 478-1622; e-mail hq@national.org.nz; internet www.national.org.nz; f. 1936; centre-right; supports private enterprise and competitive business, together with maximum personal freedom; Pres. PETER GOODFELLOW; Leader JOHN KEY.

UnitedFuture New Zealand (UFNZ): Bowen House, Parliament Bldgs, Wellington; tel. (4) 471-9410; e-mail garrod@xtra.co.nz; internet www.unitedfuture.org.nz; f. 2000 by merger of Future New Zealand (f. 1994 by Peter Dunne, a fmr Labour minister) and United New Zealand (f. 1995 by four mems of Nat. Party, two mems of Labour Party and Dunne); Leader PETER DUNNE; Pres. ROBIN GUNSTON.

Other registered parties included the Alliance, the Aotearoa Legalise Cannabis Party, Libertarianz and the Conservative Party of New Zealand.

Diplomatic Representation

EMBASSIES AND HIGH COMMISSIONS IN NEW ZEALAND

Argentina: Prime Finance Tower, Level 14, 142 Lambton Quay, POB 5430, Wellington; tel. (4) 472-8330; fax (4) 472-8331; e-mail enzel@mrecic.gov.ar; internet www.enzel.mrecic.gob.ar; Ambassador FERNANDO ESCALONA.

Australia: 72–76 Hobson St, Thorndon, POB 4036, Wellington; tel. (4) 473-6411; fax (4) 498-7135; e-mail nzinbox@dfat.gov.au; internet www.australia.org.nz; High Commissioner MICHAEL POTTS.

Brazil: Deloitte House, Level 9, 10 Brandon St, POB 5432, Wellington 6011; tel. (4) 473-3516; fax (4) 473-3517; e-mail brasemb@brazil.org.nz; internet www.brazil.org.nz; Ambassador EDUARDO GRADILONE.

Canada: 125 The Terrace, Level 11, POB 8047, Wellington; tel. (4) 473-9577; fax (4) 471-2082; e-mail wlgtn@international.gc.ca; internet www.canadainternational.gc.ca/new_zealand-nouvelle_zelande; High Commissioner CAROLINE CHRÉTIEN.

Chile: 19 Bolton St, POB 3861, Wellington; tel. (4) 471-6270; fax (4) 472-5324; e-mail echile@embchile.co.nz; internet chileabroad.gov.cl/nueva-zelanda/en; Ambassador ISAURO TORRES.

China, People's Republic: 2–6 Glenmore St, Kelburn, Wellington; tel. (4) 472-1382; fax (4) 499-0419; e-mail administration@chinaembassy.org.nz; internet www.chinaembassy.org.nz; Ambassador XU JIANGUO.

Cuba: 76 Messines Rd, Karori, Wellington; tel. (4) 464-2210; fax (4) 464-2207; e-mail embajada@xtra.co.nz; Ambassador MARÍA DEL CARMEN HERRERA CASEIRO.

Fiji: 31 Pipitea St, Thorndon, POB 3940, Wellington; tel. (4) 473-5401; fax (4) 499-1011; e-mail viti@paradise.net.nz; internet www.fiji.org.nz; Head of Mission MERE TORA (acting).

France: Sovereign House, Levels 12 and 13, 34–42 Manners St, POB 11-343, Wellington 6142; tel. (4) 384-2555; fax (4) 384-2577; e-mail ambassade@ambafrance-nz.org; internet www.ambafrance-nz.org; Ambassador FRANCIS ETIENNE.

Germany: 90–92 Hobson St, POB 1687, Wellington; tel. (4) 473-6063; fax (4) 473-6069; e-mail info@wellington.diplo.de; internet www.wellington.diplo.de; Ambassador Dr ANNE-MARIE SCHLEICH.

Greece: Petherick Tower, Level 11, 38–42 Waring Taylor St, POB 24-066, Wellington; tel. (4) 473-7775; fax (4) 473-7441; e-mail gremb.wel@mfa.gr; internet www.mfa.gr/wellington; Chargé d'affaires a.i. VASILEIOS KOINI.

Holy See: Apostolic Nunciature, 112 Queens Dr., Lyall Bay, POB 14-044, Wellington 6241; tel. (4) 387-3470; fax (4) 387-8170; e-mail nuntius@ihug.co.nz; Apostolic Nuncio (vacant).

India: 180 Molesworth St, POB 4045, Wellington 6015; tel. (4) 473-6390; fax (4) 499-0665; e-mail hicomind@hicomind.org.nz; internet www.hicomind.org.nz; High Commissioner AVANINDRA KUMAR PANDEY.

Indonesia: 70 Glen Rd, Kelburn, POB 3543, Wellington; tel. (4) 475-8698; fax (4) 475-9374; e-mail info@indonesianembassy.org.nz; internet www.indonesianembassy.org.nz; Ambassador AMRIS HASSAN.

Iran: 151 Te Anau Rd, POB 14733, Wellington; tel. (4) 386-2983; fax (4) 939-8108; e-mail info@iranembassy.org.nz; internet www.iranembassy.org.nz; Ambassador SEYED MAJID TAFRESHI KHAMENEH.

Israel: Level 13, Bayley's Bldg, 36 Brandon St, Wellington; tel. (4) 439-9500; fax (4) 439-9555; e-mail info@wellington.mfa.gov.il; internet wellington.mfa.gov.il; Ambassador SHEMI TZUR.

Italy: 34–38 Grant Rd, Thorndon, POB 463, Wellington; tel. (4) 473-5339; fax (4) 472-7255; e-mail ambasciata.wellington@esteri.it; internet www.ambwellington.esteri.it/ambasciata_wellington; Ambassador ALESSANDRO LEVI SANDRI.

Japan: The Majestic Centre, Level 18, 100 Willis St, POB 6340, Wellington 6011; tel. (4) 473-1540; fax (4) 471-2951; e-mail enquiry@wl.mofa.go.jp; internet www.nz.emb-japan.go.jp; Ambassador YASUAKI NOGAWA.

Korea, Republic: ASB Bank Tower, Level 11, 2 Hunter St, POB 11-143, Wellington; tel. (4) 473-9073; fax (4) 472-3865; e-mail info-nz@mofat.go.kr; internet nzl-wellington.mofat.go.kr; Ambassador PARK YONG-KYU.

Malaysia: 10 Washington Ave, Brooklyn, POB 9422, Wellington; tel. (4) 385-2439; fax (4) 385-6973; e-mail mwwelton@xtra.co.nz; internet www.kln.gov.my/web/nzl_wellington; High Commissioner Datuk ROSMIDAH BINTI ZAHID.

Mexico: AMP Chambers, Level 2, 185–187 Featherston St, POB 11-510, Wellington; tel. (4) 472-0555; fax (4) 496-3559; e-mail embassy.of.mexico@actrix.co.nz; internet www.sre.gob.mx/nuevazelandia; Ambassador ROSAURA RUEDA GUTIÉRREZ.

Netherlands: POB 840, Wellington 6140; tel. (4) 471-6390; fax (4) 471-2923; e-mail wel-ca@minbuza.nl; internet www.netherlandsembassy.co.nz; Ambassador ARIE VAN DER WIEL.

Pakistan: 182 Onslow Rd, Khandallah, Wellington 6035; tel. (4) 479-0026; fax (4) 479-4315; e-mail pakhcwellington@xtra.co.nz; internet www.pakistanhc.org.nz; High Commissioner ZEHRA H. AKBARI.

Papua New Guinea: Goethe-Institut Bldg, Level 5, 148–150 Cuba St, POB 197, Wellington; tel. (4) 385-2474; fax (4) 385-2477; e-mail pngnz@globe.net.nz; High Commissioner WILLIAM DIHM.

Philippines: 50 Hobson St, Thorndon, Wellington 6011; tel. (4) 890-3741; fax (4) 890-3740; e-mail embassy@wellington-pe.co.nz; internet www.philembassy.org.nz; Ambassador Dr VIRGINIA HONRADO BENAVIDEZ.

Poland: City Chambers, Level 9, 142–144 Featherston St, POB 10211, Wellington; tel. (4) 499-7844; fax (4) 499-7846; e-mail wellington.amb.sekretariat@msz.gov.pl; internet www.wellington.mfa.gov.pl; Ambassador BEATA STOCZYŃSKA.

Russia: 57 Messines Rd, Karori, Wellington; tel. (4) 476-6113; fax (4) 476-3843; e-mail russia@clear.net.nz; internet www.newzealand.mid.ru; Ambassador VALERY TERESHCHENKO.

Samoa: 1A Wesley Rd, Kelburn, POB 1430, Wellington; tel. (4) 472-0953; fax (4) 471-2479; e-mail shc@paradise.net.nz; High Commissioner LEASI PAPALI'I SCANLAN.

Singapore: 17 Kabul St, Khandallah, POB 13140, Wellington; tel. (4) 470-0850; fax (4) 479-4066; e-mail singhc_wlg@sgmfa.gov.sg; internet www.mfa.gov.sg/wellington; High Commissioner PETER CHAN JER HING.

South Africa: State Insurance Bldg, Level 7, 1 Willis St, POB 25406, Wellington; tel. (4) 815-8484; fax (4) 472-5010; e-mail wellington@dirco.gov.za; High Commissioner NTOMBIZODWA MSUTHUKAZI LALLIE.

Spain: BNZ Trust House Bldg, Level 11, 50 Manners St, POB 24-150, Wellington 6142; tel. (4) 802-5665; fax (4) 801-7701; e-mail emb.wellington@maec.es; internet www.maec.es/subwebs/embajadas/wellington; Ambassador JESÚS MIGUEL SANZ ESCORIHUELA.

Switzerland: 10 Customhouse Quay, Level 12, POB 25004, Wellington 6011; tel. (4) 472-1593; fax (4) 499-6302; e-mail wel.vertretung@eda.admin.ch; internet www.eda.admin.ch/wellington; Ambassador Dr MARION WEICHELT KRUPSKI.

Thailand: 110 Molesworth St, POB 12-247, Wellington; tel. (4) 476-8619; fax (4) 476-8610; e-mail thailand@thaiembassynz.org.nz; internet www.thaiembassynz.org.nz; Ambassador NOPPADON THEPPITAK.

Turkey: 15–17 Murphy St, Level 8, POB 12-248, Thorndon, Wellington; tel. (4) 472-1292; fax (4) 472-1277; e-mail embassy.wellington@mfa.gov.tr; Ambassador DAMLA YESIM SAY.

United Kingdom: 44 Hill St, POB 1812, Wellington; tel. (4) 924-2888; fax (4) 473-4982; e-mail ppa.mailbox@fco.gov.uk; internet ukinnewzealand.fco.gov.uk; High Commissioner VICTORIA TREADELL.

USA: 29 Fitzherbert Terrace, POB 1190, Wellington; tel. (4) 462-6000; fax (4) 499-0490; internet newzealand.usembassy.gov; Ambassador Dr DAVID HUEBNER.

Viet Nam: Grand Plimmer Tower, Level 21, 2–6 Gilmer Terrace, POB 8042, Wellington; tel. (4) 473-5912; fax (4) 473-5913; e-mail embassyvn@clear.net.nz; internet www.vietnamembassy-newzealand.org; Ambassador NGUYEN HONG CUONG.

Judicial System

The Judicial System of New Zealand comprises a Supreme Court, a Court of Appeal, a High Court and District Courts, all of which have civil and criminal jurisdiction, and the specialist courts, the Employment Court, the Family Court, the Youth Court and the Maori Land Court.

The Ministry of Justice also administers tribunals to hear and resolve disputes over facts of law, including the Employment Tribunal (administered by the Department of Labour), Disputes Tribunal, Complaints Review Tribunal, Residential Tenancies Tribunal, Waitangi Tribunal, Environment Court, Deportation Review Tribunal and Motor Vehicles Disputes Tribunal.

Supreme Court: 85 Lambton Quay, Wellington; tel. (4) 918-8222; fax (4) 914-3560; e-mail supremecourt@justice.govt.nz; internet www.courtsofnz.govt.nz/about/supreme; f. 2004; replaced the Judicial Committee of the Privy Council in the United Kingdom as the final appellate court, following the Supreme Court Act 2003; the right to appeal to the Supreme Court is granted only if the Court is satisfied that the case involves a matter of general or public importance or commercial significance, or in order to correct or prevent a substantial miscarriage of justice; the Chief Justice is the head of the judiciary in New Zealand and is the Head of Bench of the Supreme Court, which consists of five other judges; Chief Justice Dame SIAN ELIAS.

Court of Appeal: cnr Molesworth and Aitken Sts, Wellington; tel. (4) 914-3540; fax (4) 914-3570; hears appeals from the High Court and from jury trials in the district courts, although it does have some original jurisdiction; its decisions are final, except in cases that may be appealed to the Supreme Court; appeals regarding convictions and sentences handed down by the High Court or District Trial Courts are by leave only; Pres. MARK O'REGAN.

High Court: internet www.courtsofnz.com/about/high; the High Court is the superior court for general jurisdiction in New Zealand; it is a single national court which sits in a number of courthouses; judges are permanently located in Wellington, Auckland and Christchurch and go on circuit to other locations as required; it hears appeals from lower courts and tribunals (excluding those that go directly to the Court of Appeal), and reviews administrative actions; Chief High Court Judge HELEN WINKELMANN.

District Courts: internet www.courtsofnz/district; have an extensive criminal and civil law jurisdiction, hearing civil cases, while Justices of the Peace can hear minor criminal and traffic matters; the Family Court, which is a division of the District Courts, has the jurisdiction to deal with dissolution of marriages, adoption, guardianship applications, domestic actions, matrimonial property, child support, care and protection applications regarding children and young persons, and similar matters; there are 145 District Court judges and a Chief District Court Judge; Chief District Court Judge JAN-MARIE DOOGUE.

Attorney-General: the senior Law Officer of the Crown with principal responsibility for the Government's administration of the law and a Minister of the Crown responsible for the Crown Law Office, the Serious Fraud Office and the Parliamentary Counsel Office CHRISTOPHER FINLAYSON.

Religion

CHRISTIANITY

Te Runanga Whakawhanaunga i Nga Hahi o Aotearoa (Maori Council of Churches in New Zealand): Private Bag 11903, Ellerslie, Auckland; tel. (9) 525-4179; fax (9) 525-4346; f. 1982; 4 mem. churches; Administrator TE RUA GRETHA.

The Anglican Communion

The Anglican Church in Aotearoa, New Zealand and Polynesia comprises Te Pihopatanga o Aotearoa and eight dioceses (one of which is Polynesia). In 1996 the Church had an estimated 631,764 members in New Zealand.

Primate of the Anglican Church in Aotearoa, New Zealand and Polynesia, and Bishop of Aotearoa: Rt Rev. WILLIAM BROWN TUREI, POB 568, Gisborne 4040; tel. (6) 867-8856; fax (9) 377-6962; e-mail browntmihi@xtra.co.nz.

General Secretary and Treasurer of the Anglican Church in Aotearoa, New Zealand and Polynesia: Rev. MICHAEL HUGHES, POB 87-188, Meadowbank, Auckland 1742; tel. (9) 521-4439; fax (9) 521-4490; e-mail gensec@ang.org.nz; internet www.anglican.org.nz.

The Roman Catholic Church

For ecclesiastical purposes, New Zealand comprises one archdiocese and five dioceses. At 31 December 2007 there were an estimated 524,645 adherents.

Bishops' Conference

New Zealand Catholic Bishops' Conference, Catholic Centre, 22–30 Hill St, POB 1937, Wellington 6140; tel. (4) 496-1747; fax (4) 496-17461; e-mail adickinson@nzcbc.org.nz; internet www.catholic.org.nz.

f. 1974; Pres. Most Rev. JOHN DEW (Archbishop of Wellington); Sec. Rev. PATRICK DUNN (Bishop of Auckland); Exec. Officer ANNE DICKINSON.

Archbishop of Wellington: Most Rev. JOHN A. DEW, Catholic Centre, 22–30 Hill St, POB 1937, Wellington 6140; tel. (4) 496-1766; fax (4) 496-1330; e-mail g.burns@wn.catholic.org.nz; internet www.wn.catholic.org.nz.

Other Christian Churches

Baptist Churches of New Zealand: 473 Great South Rd, POB 12149, Penrose, Auckland; tel. (9) 526-0333; fax (9) 526-0334; e-mail info@baptist.org.nz; internet www.baptist.org.nz; f. 1882; 22,274 mems; Pres. GARY COLVILLE; Nat. Leader CRAIG VERNALL.

Congregational Union of New Zealand: 8C Kirrie Dr., Te Atatu South, Auckland; tel. (9) 837-2220; fax (9) 620-8291; e-mail cunzsecretary@xtra.co.nz; internet www.congregational.org.nz; f. 1884; 600 mems, 13 churches; Chair. PETER ECCLES; Sec. LUISA FAITAUA.

Lutheran Church of New Zealand: POB 7606, Wellington 6242; tel. (4) 385-2540; e-mail lcnz@clear.net.nz; internet www.lcnz.org.nz; 1,130 mems (2010); Pres. Rev. MARK WHITFIELD.

Methodist Church of New Zealand: Connexional Office, POB 931, Christchurch 8140; tel. (3) 366-6049; fax (3) 358-7146; e-mail info@methodist.org.nz; internet www.methodist.org.nz; 18,548 mems; Gen. Sec. Rev. DAVID BUSH.

Presbyterian Church of Aotearoa New Zealand: Terralink House, Level 1, 275–283 Cuba St, POB 9049, Wellington; tel. (4) 801-6000; fax (4) 801-6001; e-mail info@presbyterian.org.nz; internet www.presbyterian.org.nz; f. 1840; 30,000 mems; Moderator Rev. PETER CHEYNE; Assembly Convenor Rev. EMMA KEOWN.

There are several Maori Churches in New Zealand, with a total membership of over 30,000. These include the Ratana Church of New Zealand, Ringatu Church, Church of Te Kooti Rikirangi, Absolute Maori Established Church, Destiny Church and United Maori Mission. The Antiochian Orthodox Church, the Assemblies of God, the Greek Orthodox Church of New Zealand, the Liberal Catholic Church and the Society of Friends (Quakers) are also active.

BAHÁ'Í FAITH

National Spiritual Assembly of the Bahá'ís of New Zealand: POB 21-551, Henderson, Auckland 1231; tel. (9) 837-4866; fax (9) 837-4898; e-mail nationaloffice@bahai.org.nz; internet www.bahai.org.nz; f. 1957; CEO BETH LEW.

The Press

NEWSPAPERS AND PERIODICALS

Principal Dailies

Ashburton Guardian: 161 Burnett St, POB 77, Ashburton; tel. (3) 307-7900; fax (3) 307-7980; e-mail enquiries@theguardian.co.nz; internet www.ashburtonguardian.co.nz; f. 1879; morning; Mon.–Sat.; Editor PETER O'NEILL; Man. Dir BRUCE BELL; circ. 5,243 (2010).

Bay of Plenty Times: 108 Durham St, Private Bag 12002, Tauranga; tel. (7) 577-7770; fax (7) 578-0047; e-mail editor@bopp.co.nz; internet www.bayofplentytimes.co.nz; f. 1872; evening; Mon.–Sat.; Gen. Man. DAVID MACKENZIE; Editor SCOTT INGLIS; circ. 20,352 (2010).

The Daily Post: 1143 Hinemoa St, POB 1442, Rotorua; tel. (7) 348-6199; fax (7) 348-0220; e-mail editor@dailypost.co.nz; internet www.dailypost.co.nz; f. 1885; evening; Gen. Man. GREG ALEXANDER; Editor KIM GILLESPIE; circ. 10,294 (2010).

Dominion Post: Dominion Post House, 40 Boulcott St, POB 3740, Wellington; tel. (4) 474-0000; fax (4) 474-0584; e-mail editor@dompost.co.nz; internet www.dompost.co.nz; f. 2002; est. by merger of *The Evening Post* and *The Dominion*; morning; Mon.–Sat.; Gen. Man. GERARD WATT; Editor BERNADETTE COURTNEY; circ. 79,438 (2012).

Gisborne Herald: 64 Gladstone Rd, POB 1143, Gisborne; tel. (6) 869-0600; fax (6) 869-0643; e-mail info@gisborneherald.co.nz; internet www.gisborneherald.co.nz; f. 1874; evening; Man. Dir MICHAEL MUIR; Editor JEREMY MUIR; circ. 7,064 (2012).

Greymouth Star: Werita St, POB 3, Greymouth; tel. (3) 768-7121; fax (3) 768-6205; internet www.greystar.co.nz; f. 1866; Mon.–Sat.

(evening); Gen. Man. JOHN GOULDING; Editor PAUL MADGWICK; circ. 4,284 (2010).

Hawke's Bay Today: 113 Karamu Rd, POB 180, Hastings; tel. (6) 873-0800; fax (6) 873-0812; e-mail editor@hbtoday.co.nz; internet www.hbtoday.co.nz; f. 1999; evening; conservative; Gen. Man. RUSSELL BROUGHTON; Editor ANTONY PHILLIPS; circ. 24,682 (2010).

Manuwatu Standard: 57–64 The Square, POB 3, Palmerston North; tel. (6) 356-9009; fax (6) 350-9545; e-mail editor@msl.co.nz; internet www.manawatustandard.co.nz; f. 1880; evening; Gen. Man. (vacant); Editor MICHAEL CUMMINGS; circ. 17,000 (2010).

Marlborough Express: 62–66 Arthur St, POB 242, Blenheim 7274; tel. (3) 520-8900; fax (3) 520-8911; e-mail smason@marlexpress.co .nz; internet www.marlboroughexpress.co.nz; f. 1866; Gen. Man. VANESSA WATSON; Editor STEVE MASON; circ. 8,986 (2010).

The Nelson Mail: 15 Bridge St, POB 244, Nelson; tel. (3) 548-7079; fax (3) 546-2802; e-mail mailbox@nelsonmail.co.nz; internet www .stuff.co.nz/nelsonmail; f. 1866; evening; Gen. Man. CRAIG DENNIS; Editor PAUL MCINTYRE; circ. 15,609 (2010).

New Zealand Herald: POB 32, Auckland; tel. (9) 379-5050; fax (9) 373-6421; internet www.nzherald.co.nz; f. 1863; morning; CEO MARTIN SIMONS; Editor-in-Chief TIM MURPHY; circ. 170,677 (2010).

The Northern Advocate: 88 Robert St, POB 210, Whangarei; tel. (9) 470-2899; fax (9) 470-2869; e-mail daily@northernadvocate.co.nz; internet www.northernadvocate.co.nz; f. 1875; evening; 6 a week; Gen. Man. ALEX LAWSON; Editor CRAIG COOPER; circ. 13,292 (2010).

The Oamaru Mail: 80 Thames St, POB 343, Oamaru; tel. (3) 434-9970; fax (3) 433-0549; e-mail news@oamarumail.co.nz; internet www.oamarumail.co.nz; f. 1876; Mon.–Fri.; morning; Gen. Man. TONY NIELSEN; Editor SALLY BROOKER; circ. 2,869 (2010).

Otago Daily Times: 52 Stuart St, POB 517, Dunedin; tel. (3) 477-4760; fax (3) 474-7422; e-mail odt.editorial@odt.co.nz; internet www.odt.co.nz; f. 1861; morning; 6 a week; Man. Dir JULIAN C. S. SMITH; Editor ROBIN CHARTERIS; circ. 39,097 (2010).

The Press: 22 Cathedral Sq., Private Bag 4722, Christchurch 8140; tel. (3) 379-0940; fax (3) 364-8492; e-mail letters@press.co.nz; internet www.press.co.nz; f. 1861; morning; Gen. Man. ANDREW BOYLE; Editor (vacant); circ. 81,017 (2010).

Southland Times: 67 Esk St, POB 805, Invercargill 9840; tel. (3) 211-1130; fax (3) 214-9905; e-mail letters@stl.co.nz; internet www .southlandtimes.co.nz; f. 1862; morning; Mon.–Sat.; Gen. Man. SUE GREGORY; Editor FRED TULETT; circ. 28,002 (2011).

Taranaki Daily News: 49–65 Currie St, POB 444, New Plymouth; tel. (6) 757-6862; fax (6) 758-4653; e-mail editor@dailynews.co.nz; internet www.stuff.co.nz/dailynews; f. 1857; morning; Gen. Man. MIKE BREWER; Editor ROY PILOTT; circ. 23,005 (2010).

Timaru Herald: POB 46, Timaru; tel. (3) 684-4129; fax (3) 688-1042; e-mail editor@timaruherald.co.nz; f. 1864; morning; Gen. Man. CHRIS MCAUSLIN; Editor DAVID KING; circ. 14,010 (2010).

Waikato Times: Private Bag 3086, Hamilton; tel. (7) 849-6180; fax (7) 849-9554; e-mail editor@waikatotimes.co.nz; internet www.stuff .co.nz/waikatotimes; f. 1872; morning; independent; Gen. Man. GARETH CODD; Editor JONATHAN MACKENZIE; circ. 40,096 (2010).

Wairarapa Times-Age: cnr Perry St and Chapel St, POB 445, Masterton; tel. (6) 378-9999; fax (6) 378-2371; internet www .times-age.co.nz; f. 1938; morning; 6 a week; Gen. Man. ANDREW DENHOLM; Editor HEATHER MCCRACKEN; circ. 6,566 (2010).

Wanganui Chronicle: 59 Taupo Quay, POB 433, Wanganui; tel. (6) 349-0710; fax (6) 349-0721; e-mail news@wanganuichronicle.co.nz; internet www.wanganuichronicle.co.nz; f. 1856; morning; Gen. Man. ANDY JARDEN; Editor ROSS PRINGLE; circ. 11,217 (2010).

Weeklies and Other Newspapers

Best Bets: 6 Mitchellson Ave, Greenlane, Auckland; tel. (9) 520-8208; e-mail alan.caddy@nzracingboard.co.nz; Mon. and Thur.; horse-racing, trotting and greyhounds; Editor ALAN CADDY; circ. 10,000.

Herald on Sunday: 58 Albert St, POB 32, Auckland; tel. (9) 373-9323; fax (9) 373-9372; internet www.heraldonsunday.co.nz; f. 2004; Editor BRYCE JOHNS; circ. 96,069 (2010).

MG Business: POB 20-034, Bishopdale, Christchurch 8543; tel. (3) 358-3219; fax (3) 358-4490; internet www.mgpublications.co.nz; f. 1876; fmrly Mercantile Gazette; fortnightly; economics, finance, management, stock market, politics; Editor BILL HORSLEY; circ. 16,300.

The National Business Review: POB 1734, Auckland 1140; tel. (9) 307-1629; fax (9) 373-3997; e-mail editor@nbr.co.nz; internet www .nbr.co.nz; f. 1970; weekly; Editor-in-Chief NEVIL GIBSON; circ. 9,093 (2010).

New Zealand Gazette: POB 805, Wellington 6140; tel. (4) 495-7200; fax (4) 470-2932; e-mail info@dia.govt.nz; internet www.gazette.govt

.nz; official govt publ; f. 1840; weekly; Chief Exec BRENDAN BOYLE; circ. 1,000.

New Zealand Truth Weekly: Truth Publications Ltd, POB 9613, Newmarket, Auckland 1149; tel. (9) 909-3660; fax (9) 373-5410; e-mail editor@truth.co.nz; internet www.truth.co.nz; f. 1905; Friday; local news and features, TV and entertainment, sports; owned by Truth Publs Ltd; Editor WAYNE BUTLER; circ. 24,000.

North Shore Times: POB 33-235, Takapuna, Auckland; tel. (9) 489-4189; fax (9) 486-6700; e-mail janet.ainsworth@snl.co.nz; 3 a week; Man. JANET AINSWORTH; Editor PETER ELEY; circ. 69,834 (2010).

The Star: POB 1467, Christchurch; tel. (3) 379-7100; fax (3) 366-0180; e-mail star.reporters@starcanterbury.co.nz; internet www .starcanterbury.co.nz; f. 1868; fmrly Christchurch Star; 2 a week; Editor BARRY CLARKE; circ. 118,170.

Sunday News: POB 1327, Auckland; tel. (9) 302-1300; fax (9) 358-3003; e-mail editor@sunday-news.co.nz; internet www.sundaynews .co.nz; Man. Editor MITCHELL MURPHY; circ. 51,740 (2010).

Sunday Star-Times: POB 1327, Auckland 1140; tel. (9) 302-1300; fax (9) 309-0258; e-mail letters@star-times.co.nz; internet www.stuff .co.nz/sunday-star-times; f. 1994 by merger; Editor DAVID KEMEYS; circ. 160,592 (2010).

Taieri Herald: 92 Gordon Rd, POB 105, Mosgiel; tel. (3) 489-7123; fax (3) 489-7668; e-mail katie.tucholski@stl.co.nz; f. 1962; weekly; morning; Editor DARYL HOLDEN; circ. 13,068 (2011).

Wairarapa News: Media House, 89 Chapel St, POB 902, Masterton; tel. (6) 370-5690; fax (6) 370-5699; e-mail editor@wainews.co.nz; f. 1869; weekly; Editor WALT DICKSON; circ. 21,019 (2010).

Other Periodicals

AA Directions: POB 5, Auckland 1010; tel. (9) 966-8800; fax (9) 966-8975; e-mail editor@aa.co.nz; internet www.aa.co.nz/Online; f. 1991; quarterly; official magazine of the New Zealand Automobile Asscn; Editor KATHRYN WEBSTER; circ. 542,242 (2010).

Architecture New Zealand: AGM Publishing Ltd, Private Bag 99-915, Newmarket, Auckland; tel. (9) 846-4068; fax (9) 846-8742; e-mail justine.harvey@agm.co.nz; internet www.agm.co.nz; f. 1987; every 2 months; Man. Dir IAN CLOSE; Editor JUSTINE HARVEY; circ. 5,609 (2010).

Australian Women's Weekly (NZ edition): Wellesley St, Private Bag 92-512, Auckland; tel. (9) 308-2945; fax (9) 302-0667; e-mail aww@acpmagazines.co.nz; f. 1987; monthly; Editor LEONIE BARLOW; circ. 80,032 (2010).

Dairying Today: Shortland St, POB 3855, Auckland 1140; tel. (9) 307-0399; fax (9) 307-0122; e-mail sudeshk@ruralnews.co.nz; internet www.ruralnews.co.nz; fortnightly; Editor SUDESH KISSUN; circ. 26,792 (2007).

Fashion Quarterly: ACP Media Centre, Private Bag 92-512, Auck-land; tel. (9) 308-2409; fax (9) 302-0667; e-mail fq@acpmagazines.co .nz; f. 1982; 6 a year; Editor FIONA HAWTIN; circ. 24,167 (2011).

Grapevine: Private Bag 92-124, Auckland; tel. (9) 813-4956; fax (9) 813-4957; e-mail info@grapevine.org.nz; internet www.grapevine .org.nz; f. 1981; 4 issues a year; family magazine; Editor MIKE COONEY; circ. 125,000.

Home New Zealand: ACP Media Centre, cnr Fanshawe and Beaumont Sts, Private Bag 92-512, Auckland; tel. (9) 308-2739; e-mail homenewzealand@acpmagazines.co.nz; f. 1936; fmrly NZ Home and Entertaining; bi-monthly; design, architecture, lifestyle; Editor JEREMY HANSEN; circ. 13,472 (2010).

Info-Link: AGM Publishing Ltd, 409 New North Rd, Kingsland, Auckland; tel. (9) 846-4068; fax (9) 846-8742; e-mail infolink@agm.co .nz; internet www.info-link.co.nz; quarterly; Publr PARUL SHEOPURI; Editor MARK LONGLEY; circ. 19,303 (2008).

Inwood Magazine: POB 17124, Greenlane, Auckland 1546; tel. (9) 269-4531; fax (9) 535-7295; e-mail info@inwoodmag.com; internet www.inwoodmag.com; f. 1993; monthly; forestry; Man. Dir TONY NEILSON; circ. 8,000.

Landfall: Otago University Press, POB 56, Dunedin; tel. (3) 479-4194; fax (3) 479-8385; e-mail rachel.scott@otago.ac.nz; internet www.otago.ac.nz/press/landfall; f. 1947; 2 a year; new fiction, poetry, biographical and critical essays, cultural commentary; Publr RACHEL SCOTT; Editor DAVID EGGLETON; circ. 1,200.

Mana Magazine: POB 1101, Rotorua; tel. (7) 349-0260; fax (7) 349-0258; e-mail editor@manaonline.co.nz; internet www.manaonline.co .nz; Maori news magazine; Editor DEREK FOX.

New Idea New Zealand: 48 Greys Ave, 4th Floor, Auckland; tel. (9) 979-2726; fax (9) 979-2721; f. 1992; weekly; women's interest; Editor HAYLEY MCLARIN; circ. 50,563 (2010).

New Zealand Dairy Exporter: 8 Weld St, POB 529, Feilding; tel. (6) 323-7104; fax (6) 323-7101; e-mail amelia.grant@nzx.com; internet www.dairymag.co.nz; f. 1925; monthly; Editor GLENYS CHRISTIAN; circ. 7,201 (2010).

New Zealand Gardener: Wellesley St, POB 6341, Auckland 1141; tel. (4) 909-6800; fax (4) 909-6802; e-mail mailbox@nzgardener.co.nz; internet www.nzgardener.co.nz; f. 1944; monthly; Editor LYNDA HALLIMAN; circ. 48,699 (2010).

New Zealand Horse and Pony: POB 12965, Penrose, Auckland; tel. (9) 634-1800; fax (9) 634-2948; e-mail rowan.dixon@horse-pony.co.nz; internet www.horse-pony.co.nz; f. 1959; monthly; Editor ROWAN DIXON; circ. 10,901 (2010).

New Zealand Management: Mediaweb, Wellesley St, POB 5544, Auckland 1141; tel. (9) 529-3000; fax (9) 529-30016; e-mail editor@management.co.nz; internet www.management.co.nz; f. 1955; monthly; business; Publr TONI MYERS; circ. 7,997 (2011).

New Zealand Medical Journal: POB 21306, Christchurch; tel. (3) 968-3451; fax (3) 968-3452; e-mail nzmj@nzma.org.nz; internet journal.nzma.org.nz; f. 1887; publ. by New Zealand Medical Asscn; online publ.; articles free to non-subscribers 6 months after publ; 20 a year; Editor Prof. FRANK A. FRIZELLE; circ. 5,000.

New Zealand Science Review: POB 1874, Wellington; tel. (021) 487-284; e-mail editor@scientists.org.nz; internet www.scientists.org.nz; f. 1942; 4 a year; reviews, policy and philosophy of science; Editor ALLEN PETREY.

New Zealand Woman's Day: Wellesley St, Private Bag 92-512, Auckland; tel. (9) 308-2718; fax (9) 357-0978; e-mail wdaynz@acpmagazines.co.nz; weekly; Editor SIDO KITCHIN; circ. 105,127 (2010).

New Zealand Woman's Weekly: Victoria St West, POB 90-119, Auckland 1142; tel. (9) 373-9400; fax (9) 373-9405; e-mail editor@nzww.co.nz; internet www.nzwomansweekly.co.nz; f. 1932; Mon.; women's issues and general interest; Editor LOUISE WRIGHT; circ. 80,439 (2010).

Next: Level 4, cnr Fanshawe and Beaumont Sts, Westhaven, Private Bag 92-512, Auckland 1036; tel. (9) 308-2775; fax (9) 377-6725; e-mail next@acpmagazines.co.nz; internet www.acpmedia.co.nz; f. 1991; monthly; home and lifestyle; owned by ACP Media; Editor CHRISTINA SAYERS WICKSTEAD; circ. 46,489 (2010).

North & South: Wellesley St, Private Bag 92-512, Auckland; tel. (9) 366-5337; fax (9) 308-9498; e-mail north&south@bauermedia.co.nz; f. 1986; monthly; current affairs and lifestyle; Editor VIRGINIA LARSON; circ. 27,596 (2012).

NZ Catholic: POB 147-000, Ponsonby, Auckland 1034; tel. (9) 360-3067; fax (9) 360-3065; e-mail contact@nzcatholic.org.nz; internet www.nzcatholic.org.nz; f. 1996; fortnightly; Roman Catholic; Man. Editor PETER GRACE; circ. 6,700.

NZ House and Garden: 317 New North Rd, Eden Terrace, Auckland; tel. (9) 909-6913; fax (9) 909-6802; e-mail sally.duggan@nzhouseandgarden.co.nz; internet www.nzhouseandgarden.co.nz; f. 1994; monthly; Editor KATE COUGHLAN; circ. 48,752 (2010).

NZ Listener: Victoria St West, POB 90-783, Auckland 1142; tel. (9) 373-9400; fax (9) 373-9406; e-mail submissions@listener.co.nz; internet www.listener.co.nz; f. 1939; weekly; current affairs and entertainment; Editor PAMELA STIRLING; Publr and Chief Exec. SARAH SANDLEY; circ. 73,404.

Otago Southland Farmer: POB 105, Mosgiel; tel. (3) 489-7123; fax (3) 489-7668; e-mail newspapersales@stl.co.nz; f. 1982; fortnightly; Editor TAM MATANGI; circ. 22,180 (2008).

Pacific Wings: POB 57163, Mana, Porirua 5247; tel. (4) 233-8368; e-mail editor@pacificwingsmagazine.com; internet www.pacificwingsmagazine.com; f. 1932; monthly; aviation; Editor and Publr ROB NEIL; circ. 20,000.

PC World: Wellesley St, POB 6813, Auckland; tel. (9) 926-9108; fax (9) 909-6989; e-mail ted.gibbons@ffxbusinessgroup.co.nz; internet pcworld.co.nz; f. 1988; monthly; Editor ZARA BAXTER; circ. 12,120 (2010).

Prodesign: AGM Publishing Ltd, Private Bag 99-915, Newmarket, Auckland; tel. (9) 846-2722; fax (9) 846-8742; e-mail michael.barrett@agm.co.nz; f. 1992; every 2 months; publ. of the Designers' Institute of New Zealand; Editor MICHAEL BARRETT; circ. 5,717 (2010).

PSA Journal: PSA House, 11 Aurora Terrace, POB 3817, Wellington 6140; tel. (4) 495-7633; fax (4) 917-2051; e-mail enquiries@psa.org.nz; internet www.psa.org.nz; f. 1913; 4 a year; journal of the NZ Public Service Asscn; Pres. PAULA SCHOLES; circ. 52,000.

Reader's Digest: POB 90-487, Mail Service Centre, Auckland; e-mail editor@readersdigest.co.nz; internet www.readersdigest.co.nz; f. 1950; monthly; Editor TONY SPENCER-SMITH; circ. 91,145 (2008).

RSA Review: RNZRSA National Headquarters, POB 27248, Wellington 6030; tel. (6) 384-7994; fax (6) 385-3325; e-mail subscribe@rnzrsa.org.nz; internet www.rsa.org.nz; quarterly; official magazine of the Royal New Zealand Returned and Services' Asscn; Editor BARRY ALLISON; circ. 95,000.

Rural News: POB 3855, Auckland; tel. (9) 307-0399; fax (9) 307-0122; e-mail editor@ruralnews.co.nz; internet www.ruralnews.co.nz; f. 1988; fortnightly; Gen. Man. ADAM FRICKER; circ. 80,767 (2012).

Spanz: POB 9049, Wellington; tel. (4) 801-6000; fax (4) 801-6001; e-mail amanda@presbyterian.org.nz; internet www.presbyterian.org.nz; f. 1987; bi-monthly; magazine of Presbyterian Church; circ. 21,500.

Straight Furrow: c/o Rural Press, POB 4233, Auckland; tel. (9) 524-1177; fax (9) 524-1170; e-mail straightfurrow@ruralpress.com; internet www.straightfurrow.co.nz; f. 1933; weekly; Group Editor JEFF SMITH; circ. 85,000.

Time New Zealand: POB 198, Auckland 1015; fax (9) 366-4706; internet www.time.com; weekly; circ. 23,970 (2008).

TV Guide (NZ): 317–319 New North Rd, Eden Terrace, POB 6341, Auckland; tel. (9) 909-6902; fax (9) 909-6912; e-mail julie.eley@tv-guide.co.nz; internet www.stuff.co.nz/entertainment/tv; f. 1986; weekly; Editor JULIE ELEY; circ. 139,520 (2011).

United Nations Association New Zealand: UNANZ, POB 24494, Wellington 6142; tel. (4) 496-9638; e-mail office@unanz.org.nz; internet unanz.org.nz; f. 1946; every 3 months; Pres. Prof. GRAHAM HASSALL.

NEWS AGENCY

South Pacific News Service Ltd (Sopacnews): Lambton Quay, POB 5026, Wellington; tel. and fax (3) 472-8329; e-mail farthing@deepsouth.co.nz; f. 1948; Man. Editor NEALE MCMILLAN.

PRESS COUNCIL

New Zealand Press Council: The Terrace, 79 Boulcott St, POB 10879, Wellington; tel. (4) 473-5220; fax (4) 471-1785; e-mail info@presscouncil.org.nz; internet www.presscouncil.org.nz; f. 1972; Chair. BARRY PATERSON; Exec. Dir M. E. MAJOR.

PRESS ASSOCIATIONS

Commonwealth Press Union (New Zealand Section): POB 1066, Wellington; tel. (4) 472-6223; fax (4) 471-0987; Sec. LINCOLN GOULD.

Newspaper Publishers' Association of New Zealand (Inc): Newspaper House, 93 Boulcott St, POB 1066, Wellington 6015; tel. (4) 472-6223; fax (4) 471-0987; e-mail npa@npa.co.nz; internet www.npa.co.nz; f. 1898; 31 mems; Pres. MICHAEL MUIR; CEO TIM PANKHURST.

Publishers

Auckland University Press: Private Bag 92019, University of Auckland, Auckland 1142; tel. (9) 373-7528; fax (9) 373-7465; e-mail press@auckland.ac.nz; internet www.press.auckland.ac.nz; f. 1966; scholarly press; Dir SAM ELWORTHY.

Canterbury University Press: University of Canterbury, Private Bag 4800, Christchurch 8140; tel. (3) 364-2914; e-mail mail@cup.canterbury.ac.nz; internet www.cup.canterbury.ac.nz; f. 1991; academic and general; Publr RACHEL SCOTT.

The Caxton Press Ltd: 113 Victoria St, POB 25-088, Christchurch 8013; tel. (3) 366-8516; fax (3) 365-7840; e-mail peter@caxton.co.nz; internet www.caxton.co.nz; f. 1935; human and general interest, local and NZ history, tourist publs; Man. Dir BRUCE BASCAND.

Dunmore Publishing Ltd: POB 250-80, Wellington 6146; tel. (4) 472-2705; fax (4) 471-0604; e-mail books@dunmore.co.nz; internet dunmore.circlesoft.net; f. 1975; non-fiction, educational; Publrs MURRAY GATENBY, SHARMIAN FIRTH.

Hachette New Zealand Ltd: POB 100-749, North Shore Mail Centre, Auckland 0745; tel. (9) 477-5550; fax (9) 477-5560; e-mail admin@hachette.co.nz; f. 1971; fmrly Hachette Livre NZ Ltd; Man. Dir KEVIN CHAPMAN.

HarperCollins Publishers (New Zealand) Ltd: POB 1, Shortland St, Auckland 1140; tel. (9) 443-9400; fax (9) 443-9403; e-mail editors@harpercollins.co.nz; internet www.harpercollins.co.nz; f. 1888; general and educational; CEO JAMES KELLOW; Man. Dir GRAHAM MITCHELL.

Huia Publishers: 39 Pipitea St, Thorndon, Wellington 6011; tel. (4) 473-9262; fax (4) 473-9265; internet www.huia.co.nz; f. 1991; books on Maori history and people, textbooks, translations; Publr ROBYN BARGH.

Learning Media Ltd: POB 3293, Wellington 6140; tel. (4) 472-5522; fax (4) 472-6444; e-mail info@learningmedia.co.nz; internet www.learningmedia.co.nz; f. 1947; est. as School Publs; state-owned enterprise; contract publishing, professional devt services, and educational products in a range of media and languages; Chief Exec. DAVID GLOVER.

Legislation Direct: POB 12357, Wellington 6144; tel. (4) 568-0005; fax (4) 568-0003; e-mail Ldorders@legislationdirect.co.nz; internet www.legislationdirect.co.nz; general publishers and leading distributor of government publs; fmrly Govt Printing Office/GP Publications; Publications Man. WENDY CAYLOR.

LexisNexis NZ Ltd: Level 1, 181 Wakefield St, POB 472, Wellington 6140; tel. (4) 385-1479; fax (4) 385-1598; internet www.lexisnexis.co.nz; legal; Man. Dir HUGO MAHONEY.

McGraw-Hill Book Co, New Zealand Ltd: Private Bag 11904, Ellerslie, Auckland 1005; tel. (9) 526-6200; fax (9) 526-6216; e-mail cservice_auckland@mcgraw-hill.com; internet www.mcgraw-hill.com.au; f. 1974; educational; Man. Dir MURRAY ST LEGER.

New Zealand Council for Educational Research: POB 3237, Wellington 6140; tel. (4) 384-7939; fax (4) 384-7933; e-mail sales@nzcer.org.nz; internet www.nzcer.org.nz; f. 1934; scholarly, research monographs, educational, academic, periodicals; Chair. ALISON GILMORE; Dir ROBYN BAKER.

Otago University Press: POB 56, Dunedin; tel. (3) 479-8807; fax (3) 479-8385; e-mail university.press@otago.ac.nz; internet www.otago.ac.nz/press; f. 1958; publishes titles on New Zealand, the Pacific and Asia, with special emphasis on history, literature, the arts and natural and social sciences; also educational titles and journals; Publr WENDY HARREX.

Pearson Education New Zealand Ltd: Private Bag 102-902, North Shore City, Auckland 0745; tel. (9) 442-7400; fax (9) 442-7401; e-mail customer.service@pearsonnz.co.nz; internet www.pearsoned.co.nz; f. 1968; fmrly Addison Wesley Longman; educational; Dirs ROSEMARY STAGG, P. FIELD.

Penguin Group (NZ) Ltd: Private Bag 102-902, North Shore Mail Centre, Auckland 0745; tel. (9) 442-7400; fax (9) 442-7401; e-mail publishing@penguin.co.nz; internet www.penguin.co.nz; f. 1973; Man. Dir MARGARET THOMPSON.

Wendy Pye Ltd: Sunshine Bookshop, 413 Great South Rd, Ellerslie, 1051 Auckland; tel. (9) 525-3575; fax (9) 525-4205; e-mail sales@sunshine.co.nz; internet www.sunshinebooks.com.au; children's fiction and educational; Man. Dir WENDY PYE.

Random House New Zealand Ltd: Private Bag 102-950, North Shore Mail Centre, Auckland; tel. (9) 444-7197; fax (9) 444-7524; e-mail admin@randomhouse.co.nz; internet www.randomhouse.co.nz; f. 1977; general; Chair. MICHAEL MOYNAHAN; Man. Dir KAREN FERNS.

Victoria University Press: POB 600, Wellington; tel. (4) 463-6580; fax (4) 463-6581; e-mail victoria-press@vuw.ac.nz; internet www.victoria.ac.nz/vup; f. 1970; Publr FERGUS BARROWMAN.

PUBLISHERS' ASSOCIATION

Publishers' Association of New Zealand Inc: Private Bag 102-006, North Shore, Auckland 0745; tel. (9) 477-5589; fax (9) 477-5570; e-mail admin@publishers.org.nz; internet www.publishers.org.nz; f. 1977; Dir ANNE DE LAUTOUR.

Broadcasting and Communications

In March 2012 50 telecommunications and broadcasting operators were registered.

TELECOMMUNICATIONS

CallPlus: Level 4, 110 Symonds St, POB 108-109, Auckland; tel. (9) 915-7575; e-mail support@callplus.co.nz; internet www.callplus.co.nz; f. 1996; 100% New Zealand owned; full-service telecommunications co; Gen. Man. KELVIN HUSSEY.

Compass Communications Ltd: Compass House, Level 2, 162 Grafton Rd, Grafton, POB 2533, Auckland; tel. (9) 965-2200; fax (9) 965-2270; internet www.compass.net.nz; f. 1995; CEO KARIM HUSSONA.

Kordia: Fidelity House, Level 4, 81 Carlton Gore Rd, Auckland 1023; tel. (9) 551-7000; fax (9) 916-6402; internet www.kordiasolutions.com; fmrly known as THL Group; name changed as above 2006; telecommunications, broadcasting and converged solutions; operates in New Zealand and Australia; Chair. DAVID CLARKE; CEO GEOFF HUNT.

Orcon Internet Ltd: POB 302362, North Harbour, Auckland 0751; tel. (9) 444-4414; e-mail support@orcon.net.nz; internet www.orcon.net.nz; state-owned; provides mobile and internet services; CEO SCOTT BARTLETT.

Telecom Corpn of New Zealand Ltd: Telecom Place, 167 Victoria St West, Auckland 1010; tel. (4) 801-9000; fax (4) 385-3469; internet www.telecom.co.nz; Chair. MARK VERBIEST; Chief Exec. SIMON MOUTTER.

TelstraClear: Private Bag 92-143, Auckland 1142; tel. (9) 913-9150; fax (9) 982-6232; internet www.telstraclear.co.nz; f. 1990; est. as Clear Communications Ltd; merged with TelstraSaturn Ltd 2001; owned by Australian telecommunications co Telstra; business solutions, local and toll services, enhanced internet, etc.; Chair. JOHN STANHOPE; CEO Dr ALLAN FREETH.

Two Degrees Mobile Ltd: Symonds St, POB 8355, Auckland 1150; tel. 222002000 (mobile); e-mail info@2degreesmobile.co.nz; internet www.2degreesmobile.co.nz; CEO ERIC HERTZ.

Vodafone New Zealand Ltd: 20 Viaduct Harbour Ave, Auckland 1030; tel. (9) 355-2007; fax (9) 962-9300; e-mail lee.maddox@vodafone.co.nz; internet www.vodafone.co.nz; fmrly Bell South; cellular network; over 2m. subscribers; CEO RUSSELL STANNERS.

Woosh Wireless Ltd: 11–15 Railway St, POB 9635, Newmarket, Auckland; tel. (9) 940-0111; fax (9) 520-3447; internet www.woosh.com; f. 1999 as Walker Wireless Ltd; name changed as above 2003; provides internet and telephony services; Craig Wireless Systems Ltd (USA) acquired a 51% stake in Woosh Wireless Holdings Ltd, the parent co of Woosh Wireless Ltd in 2011; Chair. ROD INGLIS; CEO KEVIN WILEY.

WorldxChange Communications Ltd: Tower Two, Level 9, 55–65 Shortland St, POB 3296, Auckland; tel. (9) 950-1300; fax (9) 950-1301; e-mail info@wxc.co.nz; internet www.wxc.co.nz; CEO CECIL ALEXANDER.

Regulatory Authority

Energy and Communications Branch, Ministry of Economic Development: 33 Bowen St, POB 1473, Wellington; tel. (4) 472-0030; fax (4) 473-4638; e-mail info@med.govt.nz; internet www.med.govt.nz.

BROADCASTING

Radio

Radio New Zealand Ltd: RNZ House, 155 The Terrace, POB 123, Wellington; tel. (4) 474-1999; fax (4) 474-1459; e-mail rnz@radionz.co.nz; internet www.radionz.co.nz; f. 1936; Crown-owned entity, operating non-commercial national networks: Radio New Zealand National and Radio New Zealand Concert; parliamentary broadcasts on AM Network; Radio New Zealand News and Current Affairs; short-wave service, Radio New Zealand International; Chair. RICHARD GRIFFIN; CEO PETER CAVANAGH.

The Radio Network of New Zealand Ltd: 54 Cook St, Private Bag 92-198, Auckland; tel. (9) 373-0000; fax (9) 367-4802; e-mail reception@radionetwork.co.nz; internet www.radionetwork.co.nz; operates 128 commercial stations, reaching 1.4m. people; CEO JANE HASTINGS.

Association

Radio Broadcasters' Association (NZ) Inc: POB 3762, Auckland; tel. (9) 378-0788; fax (9) 378-8180; e-mail janine@rba.co.nz; internet www.rba.co.nz; represents commercial radio industry; Exec. Council Chair. JOHN MCELHINNEY; Exec. Dir DAVID INNES; 13 mems.

Television

Television New Zealand (TVNZ) Ltd: Television Centre, 100 Victoria St West, POB 3819, Auckland; tel. (9) 916-7000; fax (9) 916-7934; e-mail news@tvnz.co.uk; internet www.tvnz.co.nz; f. 1960; the television service is responsible for the production of programmes for five TV networks: TV One, TV2, TVNZ Sport Extra, TVNZ 7 and U; networks are commercial all week and transmit in colour; channels broadcast 24 hours a day, seven days a week, and reach 99.9% of the population; Chair. WAYNE WALDEN; CEO KEVIN KENRICK.

Maori Television: 9–15 Davis Cres., POB 113-017, Newmarket, Auckland; tel. (9) 539-7000; fax (9) 539-7199; e-mail info@maoritelevision.com; internet www.maoritelevision.com; f. 2003; owned by the Crown and Te Putahi Paoho; operates two stations; Te Reo station, launched in early 2008, broadcasts Maori-language programmes daily; Maori Television channel broadcasts Maori- and English-language programmes; Chair. GARRY MURIWAI; CEO JIM MATHER.

Private Television

Auckland Independent Television Services Ltd: POB 1629, Auckland.

Sky Network Television Limited: 10 Panorama Rd, Mt Wellington, Auckland; tel. (9) 579-9999; fax (9) 579-0910; internet www.skytv.co.nz; f. 1990; UHF service on seven channels, satellite service; 829,421 subscribers (June 2011); Chair. PETER MACOURT; CEO JOHN FELLET.

TV3 Network Services Ltd: Symonds St, Private Bag 92-624, Auckland; tel. (9) 928-9000; fax (9) 366-5984; internet www.tv3.co.nz; f. 1989; operated by MediaWorks NZ; CEO PAUL MAHER.

Finance

(cap. = capital; res = reserves; dep. = deposits; m. = million; br(s). = branch(es); amounts in New Zealand dollars)

BANKING

Central Bank

Reserve Bank of New Zealand (RBNZ): 2 The Terrace, POB 2498, Wellington 6011; tel. (4) 472-2029; fax (4) 473-8554; e-mail rbnz-info@rbnz.govt.nz; internet www.rbnz.govt.nz; f. 1933; cap. 1,600m., res 1,085m., dep. 19,464m. (June 2010); Gov. GRAEME WHEELER; Chair. Dr ARTHUR GRIMES.

Regulatory Authority

Financial Markets Authority: Level 2, 1 Grey St, Wellington; tel. (4) 472-9830; fax (4) 472-8076; internet www.fma.govt.nz; f. 2011; regulatory body for securities exchanges, financial advisers and brokers, trustees and issuers, and auditors; Chair. SIMON ALLEN; CEO SEAN HUGHES.

Registered Banks

At July 2012 there were 21 registered banks in New Zealand.

ANZ National Bank Ltd: ANZ Tower, Level 14, 215–229 Lambton Quay, Wellington; tel. (4) 470-3142; fax (4) 494-4000; internet www.anz.co.nz; f. 1979; subsidiary of Australia and New Zealand Banking Group Ltd of Melbourne, Australia; fmrly ANZ Banking Group (New Zealand) Ltd; name changed as above 2004 following merger with Nat. Bank of New Zealand Ltd; cap. 6,943m., res 187m., dep. 79,245m. (Sept. 2011); Chair. JOHN JUDGE; CEO DAVID HISCO; 143 brs and sub-brs.

ASB Bank Ltd: ASB Tower, cnr Albert and Wellesley Sts, Auckland; tel. (9) 306-3000; fax (9) 302-1815; e-mail helpdesk@asbbank.co.nz; internet www.asbbank.co.nz; f. 1847; est. as Auckland Savings Bank, name changed 1988; cap. 2,798m., res 7m., dep. 55,559m. (June 2011); Chair. G. R. WALKER; Man. Dir BARBARA CHAPMAN; 138 brs.

Bank of India (New Zealand) Ltd: 10 Manukau Rd, Epsom, POB 99491, Auckland; tel. (9) 926-5797; fax (9) 526-9719; e-mail boinz.md@bankofindia.co.in; internet www.bankofindia.co.nz; Man. Dir P. N. RAO.

Bank of New Zealand (BNZ): Level 4, 80 Queen St, Auckland; tel. (4) 931-8209; internet www.bnz.co.nz; f. 1861; owned by Nat. Australia Bank; cap. 2,361m., res 144m., dep. 47,354m. (Sept. 2011); Chair. JOHN WALLER; Man. Dir and CEO ANDREW THORBURN; 179 domestic brs and 1 overseas br.

Citibank NA (USA): Citibank Centre, Level 11, 23 Customs St East, POB 3429, Auckland 1140; tel. (9) 307-1902; fax (9) 308-9928; e-mail citinewzealand@citi.com; internet www.citi.co.nz; Chief Country Officer DEREK SYME; 2 brs.

Deutsche Bank New Zealand: Vero Centre, Level 36, 48 Shortland St, Auckland; tel. (9) 351-1000; fax (9) 351-1001; e-mail deutsche-ausnz.press@db.com; internet www.deutsche-bank.co.nz; f. 1986; fmrly Bankers Trust New Zealand; Chair. Dr JOSEF ACKERMANN.

Hongkong and Shanghai Banking Corporation Ltd (Hong Kong): Level 19, HSBC House, 1 Queen St, Auckland 1010; tel. (9) 918-8688; fax (9) 918-8797; e-mail premier@hsbc.co.nz; internet www.hsbc.co.nz; CEO NOEL GERARD MCNAMARA; 6 brs.

Kiwibank Ltd: Private Bag 39888, Wellington Mail Centre, Lower Hutt 5045; tel. (4) 473-1133; fax (4) 462-7922; internet www.kiwibank.co.nz; f. 2002; 100% New Zealand-owned; savings bank for small depositors; cap. 310m., res –39m., dep. 11,461m. (June 2011); Chair. ROB MORRISON; Chief Exec. PAUL BROCK.

Rabobank (New Zealand): POB 38-396, Wellington Mail Centre, Wellington; tel. (4) 819-2700; fax (4) 819-2706; e-mail wellington.enquiry@rabobank.com; internet www.rabobank.co.nz; f. 1996; full subsidiary of Rabobank Nederland; Chair. JOHN PALMER; CEO BENJAMIN RUSSELL; 30 brs.

TSB Bank Ltd: POB 240, New Plymouth; tel. (6) 872-2265; fax (6) 968-3815; internet www.tsbbank.co.nz; f. 1850; cap. 10m., dep. 4,715.2m. (March 2012); Chair. ELAINE GILL; Man. Dir KEVIN MURPHY; 24 brs.

Westpac New Zealand: 16 Takutai St, Auckland 1010; tel. (9) 367-3999; e-mail westpacnz@westpac.co.nz; internet www.westpac.co.nz; acquired Trust Bank New Zealand; New Zealand division of Westpac Banking Corpn (Australia); Chair. PETER WILSON; CEO PETER CLARE; 200 brs.

Association

New Zealand Bankers' Association: 80 The Terrace, Level 15, POB 3043, Wellington 6140; tel. (4) 802-3358; fax (4) 473-1698; e-mail nzba@nzba.org.nz; internet www.nzba.org.nz; f. 1891; Chief Exec. KIRK HOPE.

STOCK EXCHANGES

Dunedin Stock Exchange: POB 298, Dunedin; tel. (3) 477-5900; Chair. E. S. EDGAR; Sec. R. P. LEWIS.

New Zealand Exchange Ltd (NZX): NZX Centre, Level 2, 11 Cable St, POB 2959, Wellington 6140; tel. (4) 472-7599; fax (4) 496-2893; e-mail info@nzx.com; internet www.nzx.com; Chair. ANDREW HARMOS; CEO TIM BENNETT.

INSURANCE

ACE Insurance NZ Ltd: POB 734, Auckland 1010; tel. (9) 377-1459; fax (9) 303-1909; e-mail michael.poole@ace-ina.com; internet www.aceinsurance.co.nz; CEO GILES WARD.

Atradius: POB 2404, Auckland 1140; tel. (9) 302-4560; fax (9) 353-1244; e-mail info.nz@atradius.com; internet www.atradius.co.nz; f. 1925; fmrly known as Gerling NCM; name changed as above following acquisition by Deutsche Bank and Swiss Re; trade credit insurance services.

AXA New Zealand Ltd: POB 1692, Wellington 6140; tel. (4) 474-4500; fax (4) 161-699; e-mail askus@axa.co.nz; internet www.axa.co.nz; Gen. Man. SID MILLER.

BNZ Life Insurance Ltd: POB 1299, Wellington; tel. (4) 382-2577; fax (4) 474-6883; internet www.bnz.co.nz; Chair. JOHN WALLER; Man. Dir and CEO ANDREW THORBURN.

Farmers' Mutual Group: POB 1943, Palmerston North Central, Palmerston North 4440; tel. (6) 356-9456; fax (6) 356-4603; e-mail contact@fimg.co.nz; internet fmg.co.nz; f. 1905; comprises Farmers' Mutual Finance Ltd and other cos; insurance investment and financial services for the New Zealand rural sector; Chair. GREG GENT.

ING Life (NZ) Ltd: Victoria St West, Private Bag 92131, Auckland 1142; tel. (9) 442-4800; fax (9) 442-4801; e-mail clientserviceslife@onepath.co.nz; internet www.inglife.co.nz; operates ANZ- and The Nat. Bank-branded insurance policies; CEO HELEN TROUP; Man. Dir, Insurance NAOMI BALLANTYNE.

New Zealand Insurance: NZI, Private Bag 92130, Auckland 1030; tel. (9) 969-6000; fax (9) 309-7097; internet www.nzi.co.nz; owned by Insurance Australia Group New Zealand Ltd; Exec. Gen. Man. KARL ARMSTRONG.

New Zealand Local Government Insurance Corporation Ltd (Civic Assurance): POB 5521, Wellington 6145; tel. (4) 978-1250; fax (4) 978-1260; e-mail info@civicassurance.co.nz; internet www.civicassurance.co.nz; f. 1960; local govt insurance provider; fire, motor, all risks, accident; Chief Exec. TIM SOLE.

QBE Insurance (International) Ltd: AMP Centre, Level 6, 29 Customs St West, Auckland; tel. (9) 366-9920; fax (9) 308-8526; internet www.qbe.co.nz/insurance.html; f. 1890; Gen. Man. ROSS CHAPMAN.

Sovereign Ltd: Private Bag Sovereign, Auckland Mail Centre 1142; tel. (9) 487-9000; fax (9) 487-8003; e-mail enquire@sovereign.co.nz; internet www.sovereign.co.nz; f. 1989; life insurance and investment; Chief Exec. CHARLES ANDERSON.

State Insurance Ltd: POB 3233, Wellington 6140; tel. (9) 969-1150; fax (4) 476-9664; internet www.state.co.nz; f. 1905; mem. NRMA Insurance Group; Man. Dir T. C. SOLE.

Tower Insurance Ltd: Tower Centre, Level 11, 22 Fanshawe St, POB 90347, Auckland; tel. (9) 369-2000; fax (9) 369-2040; e-mail contactus@tower.co.nz; internet www.tower.co.nz; f. 1869; fmrly Nat. Insurance Co of New Zealand; Chair. TONY GIBBS; Group Man. Dir ROB FLANNAGAN.

Associations

Insurance Council of New Zealand: Asteron House, Level 2, 139 The Terrace, POB 474, Wellington; tel. (4) 472-5230; fax (4) 473-3011; e-mail icnz@icnz.org.nz; internet www.icnz.org.nz; f. 1895; Chief Exec. TIM GRAFTON.

Investment Savings and Insurance Association of New Zealand Inc: City Chambers, cnr Johnston and Featherston Sts, POB 1514, Wellington, 6140; tel. (4) 473-8730; fax (4) 471-1881; e-mail isi@isi.org.nz; internet www.isi.org.nz; f. 1996 from Life Office Asscn and Investment Funds Asscn; represents cos that act as manager, trustee, issuer, insurer, etc. of managed funds, life insurance and superannuation; Chair. SEAN CARROLL; Chief Exec. PETER NEILSON.

Trade and Industry

GOVERNMENT AGENCY

New Zealand Trade and Enterprise (NZTE): POB 2878, Wellington 6140; tel. (4) 816-8100; fax (4) 816-8101; e-mail info@nzte.govt.nz; internet www.nzte.govt.nz; f. 2003; national govt devt agency, with global network of offices; provides businesses, organizations and investors with access to goods and services; facilitates partnerships with New Zealand businesses and investment opportunities; Chair. ANDREW FERRIER; CEO PETER CHRISP.

CHAMBERS OF COMMERCE

Auckland Regional Chamber of Commerce and Industry: POB 47, Auckland 1140; tel. (9) 309-6100; fax (9) 309-0081; e-mail auckland@chamber.co.nz; internet www.chamber.co.nz; CEO MICHAEL BARNETT; Chair. JOHN LINDSAY.

Canterbury Employers' Chamber of Commerce: 57 Kilmore St, POB 359, Christchurch 8140; tel. (3) 366-5096; fax (3) 379-5454; e-mail info@cecc.org.nz; internet www.cecc.org.nz; f. 1859; formed through merger of Employers' Fed. and Chamber of Commerce; employment and business support services, incl. legal consultancy and international trade advice, business performance and training, networking and advocacy; Chief Exec. PETER TOWNSEND; Pres. PETER DAVIES.

Employers' Chamber of Commerce Central: POB 1087, Wellington 6140; tel. (4) 473-7224; fax (4) 473-4501; e-mail ema@emacentral.org.nz; internet www.eccc.org.nz; f. 1997 as Employers' and Manufacturers' Association (Central Inc); renamed as above following merger with Wellington Regional Chamber of Commerce; CEO KEN HARRIS; 2,200 mems.

Otago Chamber of Commerce Inc: Level 3, 442 Moray Pl., POB 5173, Dunedin 9058; tel. (3) 479-0181; fax (3) 477-0341; e-mail office@otagochamber.co.nz; internet www.otagochamber.co.nz; f. 1861; CEO J. A. CHRISTIE; Pres. P. MCINTYRE.

Wellington Employers' Chamber of Commerce: POB 1590, Wellington 6140; tel. (4) 473-7224; fax (4) 473-4501; e-mail info@wecc.org.nz; internet www.wecc.org.nz; f. 1856; fmrly Wellington Regional Chamber of Commerce; Chief Exec. KEN HARRIS; Pres. RICHARD STONE; 1,000 mems.

INDUSTRIAL AND TRADE ASSOCIATIONS

Employers' and Manufacturers' Association (Northern Inc): 159 Khyber Pass Rd, Grafton, Private Bag 92066, Auckland; tel. (9) 367-0900; fax (9) 367-0902; e-mail ema@ema.co.nz; internet www.ema.co.nz; f. 1886; fmrly Auckland Manufacturers' Asscn; Chief Exec. ALASDAIR THOMPSON; Pres. GRAHAM MOUNTFORT; 5,000 mems.

ENZA: 405 Williams St, POB 279, Hastings; tel. (9) 878-1898; fax (9) 878-1850; e-mail info@enza.co.nz; internet www.enza.co.nz; f. 1956; owned by Turners and Growers Ltd; fmrly New Zealand Apple and Pear Marketing Bd; export apples, pears and kiwifruit; creates new apple varieties; Man. Dir JEFF WESLEY; Gen. Man. SNOW HARDY.

Federated Farmers of New Zealand (Inc): POB 715, Wellington; tel. (4) 473-7269; fax (4) 473-1081; e-mail receptionwgton@fedfarm.org.nz; internet www.fedfarm.org.nz; f. 1945; Pres. DON NICOLSON; CEO CONOR ENGLISH; 16,000 mems.

Horticulture New Zealand: POB 10232, The Terrace, Wellington 6143; tel. (4) 472-3795; fax (4) 471-2861; e-mail info@hortnz.co.nz; internet www.hortnz.co.nz; est. by merger of New Zealand Fruitgrowers' Fed., New Zealand Berryfruit Fed. and New Zealand Vegetable and Potato Growers' Fed; 7,000 mems; Pres. and Chair. ANDREW FENTON; CEO PETER SILCOCK.

Kiwifruit New Zealand (KNZ): POB 4683, Mt Maunganui South 3149; tel. (7) 572-3685; fax (7) 572-5934; e-mail richard.procter@knz.co.nz; f. 2000; Chair. Sir BRIAN ELWOOD.

Meat and Wool New Zealand: POB 121, Wellington 6140; tel. (4) 473-9150; fax (4) 474-0800; e-mail enquiries@beeflambnz.com; internet www.meatandwoolnz.com; Chair. MIKE PETERSEN; CEO Dr SCOTT CHAMPION.

Meat Industry Association of New Zealand (Inc) (MIA): Wellington Chambers, Level 5, 154 Featherston St, Wellington 6011; tel. (4) 473-6465; fax (4) 473-1731; e-mail info@mia.co.nz; internet www.mia.co.nz; Chair. W. J. (BILL) FALCONER; CEO TIM RITCHE.

National Beekeepers' Association of New Zealand (Inc): Adecco House, Level 6, 330 Lambton Quay, POB 10792, Wellington; tel. (6) 471-6254; fax (6) 499-0876; e-mail secretary@nba.org.nz; internet www.nba.org.nz; f. 1913; 400 mems; Pres. SETH BELSON; Secs JESSICA WILLIAMS, PAULINE DOWNIE.

New Zealand Animal By-Products Exporters' Association: 11 Longhurst Terrace, POB 12-222, Christchurch; tel. (3) 332-2895; fax (3) 332-2825; 25 mems; Sec. J. L. NAYSMITH.

New Zealand Council of Wool Exporters Inc: POB 2857, Christchurch; tel. (3) 353-1049; fax (3) 374-6925; e-mail cwe@woolexport.net; internet www.woolexport.net; f. 1893; Exec. Man. R. H. F. NICHOLSON; Pres. JOHN DAWSON.

The New Zealand Forest Owners' Association: POB 1208, Wellington 6140; tel. (4) 473-4769; fax (4) 499-8893; e-mail nzfoa@nzfoa.org.nz; internet www.nzfoa.org.nz; f. 1926; Pres. PETER BERG; Chief Exec. DAVID RHODES.

New Zealand Fruit Wine and Cider Makers Inc: POB 912, New Plymouth; tel. and fax (6) 769-9009; e-mail admin@fruitwines.co.nz; internet www.fruitwines.co.nz; f. 1985; 40 mems; represents all nongrape wine, cider, perry and mead makers in New Zealand; Chair. JUSTIN HALL; Exec. Officer CHRISTINE GARNHAM.

New Zealand Manufacturers' and Exporters' Association (MEA): POB 13152, Armagh, Christchurch 8141; tel. (3) 353-2540; fax (3) 353-2549; e-mail cma@cma.org.nz; internet www.mea.org.nz; f. 2007; est. by merger of Canterbury Manufacturers' Asscn and New Zealand Engineers' Fed; CEO JOHN L WALLEY; Pres. BRIAN WILLOUGHBY.

New Zealand Meat Board: POB 121, Wellington 6140; tel. (4) 473-9150; fax (4) 474-0801; e-mail info@nzmeatboard.org; internet www.nzmeatboard.org; f. 1922; Chair. MIKE PETERSEN; 10 mems.

New Zealand Pork Industry Board (NZ Pork): Level 4, 94 Dixon St, POB 4048, Wellington 6140; tel. (4) 917-4750; fax (4) 385-8522; e-mail info@pork.co.nz; internet www.pork.co.nz; f. 1937; Chair. IAN CARTER; CEO OWEN SYMMANS.

New Zealand Retailers' Association Inc: POB 12086, Wellington 6144; tel. (4) 805-0830; fax (4) 805-0831; e-mail helpline@retail.org.nz; internet www.retail.org.nz; 6,000 direct mems; Pres. RAY CLARKE; CEO JOHN ALBERTSON.

New Zealand Timber Industry Federation: POB 308, Wellington; tel. (4) 473-5200; fax (4) 473-6536; e-mail inquiries@nztif.co.nz; internet www.nztif.co.nz; f. 1983; 350 mems; Exec. Dir WAYNE. S. COFFEY.

Registered Master Builders' Federation (Inc): Level 6, 234 Wakefield St, POB 1796, Wellington; tel. (4) 385-8999; fax (4) 385-8995; e-mail mbfinfo@masterbuilder.org.nz; internet www.masterbuilder.org.nz; Chief Exec. WARWICK QUINN.

Seafood New Zealand: Private Bag 24901, Manners St, Wellington 6142; tel. (4) 385-4005; fax (4) 385-2727; e-mail info@seafood.org.nz; internet www.seafoodnewzealand.org.nz; fmrly New Zealand Seafood Industry Council; CEO TIM PANKHURST; Chair. ERIC BARRATT.

EMPLOYERS' ORGANIZATION

Business New Zealand: Lumley House, Level 6, 3–11 Hunter St, POB 1925, Wellington; tel. (4) 496-6555; fax (4) 496-6550; e-mail admin@businessnz.org.nz; internet www.businessnz.org.nz; f. 2001; Chief Exec. PHIL O'REILLY.

UTILITIES

Energy Efficiency and Conservation Authority (EECA): POB 388, Wellington 6140; tel. (4) 470-2200; fax (4) 499-5330; e-mail info@eeca.govt.nz; internet www.eeca.govt.nz; f. 2000; Chair. THOMAS CAMPBELL; Chief Exec. MIKE UNDERHILL.

Gas and Electricity

Following parliamentary approval of the Electricity Industry Bill in September 2010, the new Electricity Authority was established on 1 November in place of the Electricity Commission.

Electricity Authority: ASB Bank Tower, Level 7, 2 Hunter St, POB 10041, Wellington 6143; tel. (4) 460-8860; fax (4) 460-8879; e-mail info@ea.govt.nz; internet www.ea.govt.nz; f. 2010; replaced Electricity Commission; independent regulatory body supervising electricity sector; Chair. Dr BRENT LAYTON; Chief Exec. CARL HANSEN.

Contact Energy Ltd: Harbour City Tower, Level 1, 29 Brandon St, POB 10742, Wellington; tel. (4) 449-4001; fax (4) 499-4003; e-mail help@contact-energy.co.nz; internet www.contactenergy.co.nz; f. 1996; generation of electricity, wholesale and retail of energy; Chair. GRANT KING; CEO DENNIS BARNES.

Genesis Energy Ltd: Private Bag 3131, Hamilton 3240; tel. (9) 838-7863; fax (9) 580-4891; internet www.genesisenergy.co.nz; f. 1999; state-owned; generation and retail of electricity and gas; Chair. Dame JENNY SHIPLEY; Chief Exec. ALBERT BRANTLEY.

The Marketplace Co Ltd (M-CO): NZX Ltd, Level 2, NZX Center, 11 Cable St, POB 2959, Wellington 6140; tel. (4) 473-5240; fax (4) 473-5247; e-mail info@m-co.com; internet www.m-co.co.nz; f. 1993; administers wholesale electricity market; acquired by NZX Ltd in 2009; Chief Exec. CARL HANSEN.

Meridian Energy Ltd: POB 2128, Christchurch; tel. (3) 353-9500; fax (3) 353-9501; e-mail contactus@meridianenergy.co.nz; internet www.meridianenergy.co.nz; state-owned; generation and retail of electricity; Chair. CHRIS MOLLER; Chief Exec. MARK BINNS.

Mighty River Power Ltd: Level 14, 23–29 Albert St, POB 90-399, Auckland; tel. (9) 308-8200; fax (9) 308-8209; e-mail enquiries@mightyriver.co.nz; internet www.mightyriverpower.co.nz; f. 1998; electricity generation and retail; mems include Vector Electricity; Chair. JOAN WITHERS; Chief Exec. DOUG HEFFERMAN.

NGC Holdings Ltd: NGC Bldg, Level 8, 44 The Terrace, Private Bag 39-980, Wellington Mail Centre, Wellington; tel. (4) 462-8700; fax (4) 462-8600; internet www.ngc.co.nz; f. 1992; fmrly Natural Gas Corpn

Holdings Ltd; name changed as above 2002; purchase, processing and transport of natural gas; wholesale and retail sales; Chair. MICHAEL STIASSNY; Chief Exec. BRYAN CRAWFORD.

Nova Energy: 52 Commerce St, POB 404, Whakatane 3158; tel. (7) 922-2700; fax (7) 307-0922; e-mail info@novaenergy.co.nz; internet www.novaenergy.co.nz; fmrly Nova Gas Ltd, merged with Bay of Plenty Energy in 2012; generation, purchase and supply of electricity, LPG, natural gas and solar energy; owned by the Todd Corpn; CEO BABU BAHIRATHAN.

Orion New Zealand Ltd: POB 13896, Christchurch 8141; tel. (3) 363-9898; fax (3) 363-9899; e-mail info@oriongroup.co.nz; internet www.oriongroup.co.nz; f. 1998; electricity distribution network; Chair. CRAIG BOYCE; CEO ROB JAMIESON.

Todd Energy Ltd: 95 Customhouse Quay, POB 3141, Wellington; tel. (4) 471-6555; fax (4) 472-2474; e-mail energy@toddenergy.co.nz; internet www.toddenergy.co.nz; CEO PAUL MOORE.

Transpower New Zealand Ltd: Transpower House, Level 7, 96 The Terrace, POB 1021, Wellington; tel. (4) 495-7000; fax (4) 495-7100; internet www.transpower.co.nz; f. 1994; manages national grid; Chair. MARK VERBIEST; Chief Exec. PATRICK STRANGE.

TrustPower Ltd: Private Bag 12-023, Tauranga Mail Centre, Tauranga 3143, Auckland; tel. (7) 574-4754; fax (7) 574-4803; e-mail enquiries@trustpower.co.nz; internet www.trustpower.co.nz; f. 1920 as Tauranga Electric Power Board; independent generator; Chair. Dr BRUCE HARKER; CEO VINCE HAWKSWORTH.

Vector Electricity Ltd: 101 Carlton Gore Rd, Newmarket, Auckland 1023; tel. (9) 978-7788; fax (9) 978-7799; e-mail info@vector.co.nz; internet www.vector.co.nz; owned by Vector Ltd; fmrly Mercury Energy Ltd; operates power networks in Auckland, Manukau and Papakura; distributes natural gas in Auckland; Chair. MICHAEL STIASSNY; Group CEO SIMON MACKENZIE.

Wanganui Gas Ltd: 179 Hill St, POB 32, Wanganui; tel. (6) 349-0909; fax (6) 345-4931; e-mail enquiries@wanganuigas.co.nz; internet www.wanganuigas.co.nz; f. 1879; supplier of gas on North Island; Chair. MATTHEW J DOYLE; Chief Exec. TREVOR GOODWIN.

Water

Waste Management NZ Ltd: 86 Lunn Ave, Mt Wellington, Private Bag 14-919, Panmure, Auckland 1741; tel. (9) 527-1300; fax (9) 570-1417; internet www.wastemanagement.co.nz; f. 1985; waste collection, recovery and disposal; liquid waste collection and processing; recycling; subsidiary of Transpacific Industries Group; Chief Financial Officer KEVIN BUGDEN.

Watercare Services Ltd: Private Bag 92521, Wellesley St, Auckland 1141; tel. (9) 442-2222; fax (9) 970-1461; e-mail info@water.co.nz; internet www.watercare.co.nz; f. 1993; provides water and waste water services in the Auckland area; Chair. ROSS KEENAN; Chief Exec. MARK FORD.

TRADE UNIONS

New Zealand Council of Trade Unions: Education House, West Block, 178 Willis St, POB 6645, Wellington 6141; tel. (4) 385-1334; fax (4) 385-6051; e-mail helenk@nzctu.org.nz; internet www.union.org.nz; f. 1937; present name since 1987; affiliated to ITUC; 40 affiliated unions with more than 350,000 mems; Pres. HELEN KELLY; Sec. PETER CONWAY.

Transport

RAILWAYS

There were 4,128 km of railways in New Zealand in 2008, of which about 506 km were electrified.

New Zealand Railways Corporation (NZRC—KiwiRail): POB 593, Wellington 6140; tel. 800-801-070; fax (4) 473-1589; e-mail kiwirail@kiwirail.co.nz; internet www.kiwirail.co.nz; f. 2008; state-owned enterprise, est. following Govt's purchase of rail and inter-island ferry operations of Toll NZ Ltd; Chair. JOHN SPENCER; Chief Exec. JIM QUINN.

ROADS

In 2010 there were a total of 94,277 km of maintained roads in New Zealand, including 179 km of motorways. In 2009 there were 17,510 km of urban local roads and 65,492 km of rural and special purpose roads.

New Zealand Transport Agency: Victoria Arcade, 50 Victoria St, Private Bag 6995, Wellington 6141; tel. (4) 894-5400; fax (4) 894-6100; e-mail info@nzta.govt.nz; internet www.nzta.govt.nz; f. 2008; formed by merger of Land Transport NZ and Transit NZ; Crown entity charged with contributing to an integrated, safe, responsive and sustainable land transport system; Chair. CHRIS MOLLER; Chief Exec. GEOFF DANGERFIELD.

SHIPPING

There are 13 main seaports, of which the most important are Auckland, Tauranga, Wellington, Lyttleton (the port of Christchurch) and Port Chalmers (Dunedin). In December 2012 the New Zealand flag registered fleet comprised 150 vessels, with a total displacement of 237,148 grt.

Principal Companies

Maersk New Zealand: The CPO, Level 3, 12 Queen St, Auckland; tel. (9) 359-3499; fax (9) 359-3488; e-mail nezcsedir@maersk.com; internet www.maerskline.com; f. 1928; CEO SØREN SKOU.

Matson South Pacific Ltd: 68 Anzac Ave, Auckland; tel. (9) 302-2204; fax (9) 302-0096; e-mail info@matson.co.nz; internet www.reefship.co.nz; f. 2013, fmrly Reef Shipping Ltd, acquired by Matson Inc in 2012; operates services between New Zealand and the Pacific islands; Gen. Man. JASON WARD.

Sofrana Unilines NZ Ltd: 38 Ponsonby Rd, POB 3614, Auckland; tel. (9) 356-1400; fax (9) 356-1429; e-mail info@sofrana.co.nz; internet www.sofrana.co.nz; Chair. DIDIER LEROUX; Man. Dir BENOIT MARCENAC.

Other major shipping companies operating services to New Zealand include Blue Star Line (NZ) Ltd and Columbus Line, which link New Zealand with Australia, the Pacific islands, South-East Asia and the USA.

CIVIL AVIATION

There are long-distance international airports at Auckland and Christchurch. International airports at Dunedin, Queenstown, Rotorua and Wellington provide limited regional connectivity.

Civil Aviation Authority of New Zealand: Asteron Centre, 55 Featherston St, POB 3555, Wellington; tel. (4) 560-9400; fax (4) 569-2024; e-mail info@caa.govt.nz; internet www.caa.govt.nz; Dir of Civil Aviation GRAEME HARRIS.

Principal Airlines

Air Nelson: Private Bag 32, Nelson 7042; tel. (3) 547-8700; fax (3) 547-8788; e-mail airnelsonadmin@airnz.co.nz; internet www.airnelson.co.nz; f. 1979; owned by Air New Zealand, operates along with Mount Cook and Eagle Air as Air New Zealand Link; present name adopted 1986; operates services throughout New Zealand; Gen. Man. GRANT KERR.

Air New Zealand: Private Bag 92007, Auckland 1142; tel. (9) 336-2287; fax (9) 366-2664; e-mail investor@airnz.co.nz; internet www.airnewzealand.co.nz; f. 1942; privatized in 1989, recapitalized by the Govt in 2001; 73.7% govt-owned; services to and from Australia, the Pacific islands, Asia, Europe and North America, as well as regular daily services to regional New Zealand; Chair. JOHN PALMER; CEO CHRISTOPHER LUXON.

Virgin Australia (NZ) Ltd: internet www.virginaustralia.com; f. 2003 as Pacific Blue Airlines; renamed as above in 2011; wholly owned subsidiary of Virgin Australia; services to Australia and the Pacific Islands; CEO MARK PITT.

Tourism

New Zealand's principal tourist attractions are its mountains, lakes, forests, volcanoes, hot springs and beaches. The sector makes a substantial contribution to the country's economy. Visitor arrivals decreased to 2.56m. in 2012 from 2.60m. in 2011, in which year tourism receipts rose to $NZ5,763m. The majority of visitors are from Australia, the People's Republic of China, the United Kingdom and the USA.

Tourism New Zealand: Vodafone House, Level 22, 157 Lambton Quay, POB 95, Wellington; tel. (4) 462-8000; fax (4) 917-5495; e-mail enquiries@tnz.govt.nz; internet www.newzealand.com; f. 1901; responsible for marketing of New Zealand as a tourism destination; offices in Auckland, Wellington and Christchurch; 13 offices overseas; Chair. KERRY PRENDERGAST; Chief Exec. KEVIN BOWLER.

Defence

As assessed at November 2012, the total strength of the regular forces was 8,550: army 4,300, navy 1,900 and air force 2,350. In addition, there were approximately 2,290 regular reserves (army 1,800, navy 300, air force 190) and 1,800 territorial reserves. Military service is voluntary. New Zealand is a participant in the Five-Power Defence Arrangements with Australia, Malaysia, Singapore and the United Kingdom.

Defence Expenditure: Budgeted at $NZ2,910m. for 2012.

Chief of Defence Force: Lt-Gen. RICHARD RHYS JONES.

Chief of Army: Maj.-Gen. ARTHUR DAVID GAWN.
Chief of Navy: Rear-Adm. JACK STEER.
Chief of Air Force: Air Vice-Marshal PETER JAMES STOCKWELL.
Commander Joint Forces New Zealand: Air Vice-Marshal KEVIN SHORT.

Education

Education in New Zealand is free and secular in state schools. It is compulsory for all children aged six to 16 years, although in practice almost 100% start at the age of five years. Budgetary expenditure on education by the central Government in 2012/13 was forecast at $NZ9,605m., representing 11.8% of total spending.

In July 2011 there were 194,101 children enrolled in early childhood education services, while 433,524 pupils were enrolled in primary classes at 2,007 schools. A total of 275,011 pupils attended 342 secondary schools. Composite schools, which were attended by 50,753 pupils, provide education at both primary and secondary levels.

In 2010 enrolment at primary level included 99% of all students in the relevant age-group, while enrolment at secondary institutes included 95% of all students in the relevant age-group.

NEW ZEALAND'S DEPENDENT TERRITORIES

New Zealand's two Dependent Territories are the Ross Dependency, which is situated in Antarctica, and Tokelau, located in the Pacific Ocean.

ROSS DEPENDENCY

The Ross Dependency comprises the sector of Antarctica between 160°E and 150°W (moving eastward) and the islands lying between those degrees of longitude and south of latitude 60°S. It has been administered by New Zealand since 1923 and has a total area of 750,310 sq km (289,700 sq miles), comprising a land area of 413,540 sq km and an ice shelf of 336,770 sq km. The Territory rises to a height of 3,794 m above sea level at the peak of the volcano, Mount Erebus.

Scott Base was established by New Zealand in 1957 on Ross Island, and in the following year the Ross Dependency Research Committee was formed to supervise New Zealand activity on the Territory. In 1968 a new scientific station was set up by New Zealand at Lake Vanda, about 130 km (80 miles) west of Scott Base; owing to environmental concerns, the Vanda Station was closed down in 1995. In addition to Scott Base, there are currently three other stations located in the Territory: the US McMurdo Station, which, like the Scott Base, is permanently occupied; the seasonally occupied US Amundsen-Scott South Pole Station; and the summer-occupied Italian Zucchelli Station. In 1986 traces of petroleum were discovered in the Territory, more than 600 m below the seabed. The Ross Dependency Research Committee was disbanded in 1995. Legislation approved in the mid-1990s consolidated measures aimed at conserving the region's flora and fauna (which includes 18 species of penguin, six species of seal and several rare species of whale) included in the Antarctic Treaty (see p. 472), and reinforced the Convention for the Conservation of Antarctic Marine Living Resources. Since 1997 New Zealand has conducted exploratory fishing for toothfish in the Ross Sea; the fishing is conducted under strict supervision and quotas. In October 2012 the New Zealand and US Governments presented a joint proposal to the Commission for the Conservation of Antarctic Marine Living Resources (see p. 471) on the establishment of a marine protected area in the Ross Sea, which would allow for the continued fishing of toothfish. However, the Commission failed to reach agreement on the proposal, which was to be reconsidered at a meeting in July 2013. Following a visit by the New Zealand Minister of Research, Science and Technology in November 2006, new proposals, including emphasis on the provision of renewable energy resources and the encouragement of greater investment in scientific projects in the territory, were announced.

TOKELAU

Introductory Survey

LOCATION, CLIMATE, LANGUAGE, RELIGION, FLAG, CAPITAL

Tokelau consists of three atolls (Atafu, Nukunonu and Fakaofo), which lie about 480 km (300 miles) north of Samoa, in the Pacific Ocean. The annual average temperature is 28°C (82°F), July being the coolest month and May the warmest; rainfall is heavy but inconsistent. The principal language is Tokelauan (a Polynesian language), although English is also widely spoken. The population is almost entirely Christian, with 67% adhering to the Congregational Christian Church (a Protestant denomination) and 30% to the Roman Catholic Church. The national flag (proportions 1 by 2) is dark blue, with four five-pointed white stars in the form of the Southern Cross constellation in the upper hoist and a yellow canoe in full sail facing towards the hoist across the bottom. Tokelau has no capital, each atoll having its own administrative centre. However, the seat of government, the Office of the Council for the Ongoing Government of Tokelau (formerly the Council of Faipule), is recognized as 'the capital' and is rotated on a yearly basis among the three atolls.

CONTEMPORARY POLITICAL HISTORY

Historical Context

The Tokelau (formerly Union) Islands became a British protectorate in 1877. At the request of the inhabitants, the United Kingdom annexed the islands in 1916 and included them within the Gilbert and Ellice Islands Colony (now Kiribati and Tuvalu). The British Government transferred administrative control of the islands to New Zealand by legislation enacted in 1925, effective from February 1926. The group was officially designated the Tokelau Islands in 1946, and sovereignty was transferred to New Zealand by legislation of 1948, effective from January 1949. From 1962 until the end of 1971 the High Commissioner for New Zealand in Western Samoa (now Samoa) was also the Administrator of the Tokelau Islands. In November 1974 the administration of the Tokelau Islands was transferred to the Ministry of Foreign Affairs in New Zealand. In 1976 the Tokelau Islands were officially redesignated Tokelau.

Domestic Political Affairs

A programme of constitutional change, agreed in 1992 and formalized in January 1994, provided for a more defined role for Tokelau's political institutions, as well as for their expansion. A process of relocating the Tokelau Public Service (hitherto based in Apia, Western Samoa—now Samoa) to the Territory began in 1994, and by 1995 all government departments, except Transport and Communications and part of the Administration and Finance Department, had been transferred to Tokelauan soil. However, the Tokelau Apia Liaison Office (formerly the Office for Tokelau Affairs) was to remain in Western Samoa, owing to that country's more developed communications facilities.

The development of Tokelau's institutions at a national level prompted renewed interest in the islands' prospects for greater internal autonomy. In a statement to the UN Special Committee on Decolonization in June 1987, Tokelau had expressed a desire to achieve a greater degree of political autonomy, while maintaining its relationship with New Zealand. In June 1994 the General Fono, the Territory's highest advisory body, adopted a National Strategic Plan, which gave details of Tokelau's progression (over the next five to 10 years) towards increased self-determination and, possibly, free association with New Zealand. The executive and administrative powers of the Administrator were formally transferred, in that year, to the General Fono and, when the Fono was not in session, to the Council of Faipule (cabinet). A draft constitution was subsequently drawn up. In May 1996 the New Zealand House of Representatives approved the Tokelau Amendment Bill, granting the General Fono the power to enact legislation, to impose taxes and to declare public holidays, effective from 1 August 1996 (although New Zealand was to retain the right to legislate for Tokelau).

Following electoral reforms introduced in the latter half of the 1990s, delegates were, for the first time, elected to the General Fono for a three-year term in January 1999; they had previously been nominated by each Taupulega (Island Council or Council of Elders). As part of the same reform process, the number of delegates to the General Fono was reduced from 27 to 18. At the elections two of the Territory's Faipule (political leaders) were re-elected, while the third Faipule and all three Pulenuku (village mayor) posts were secured by new candidates. At elections in January 2002, when a population-based pattern of representation was adopted by the General Fono, all three incumbent Faipule and one Pulenuku were re-elected to office; two new Pulenuku were elected. In January 2005 the three Faipule were again re-elected, along with one of the Pulenuku; two new Pulenuku were chosen.

Meanwhile, mounting fears among islanders that, despite their wishes, New Zealand was seeking to loosen its ties with Tokelau, led the New Zealand Minister of Foreign Affairs and Trade to state in April 2000 that his country would not impose independence on the Territory and that any change in its political status would occur only with the consent of Tokelauans. In early 2001 the head of the Tokelau Public Service Commission, Aleki Silau, reiterated the islanders' reluctance to renounce New Zealand citizenship. A report by the UN Special Committee on Decolonization in 2002 listed Tokelau as one of 16 dependent territories that it was seeking to encourage towards independence. However, a UN decolonization mission, which visited the islands in September of that year, was informed that the majority of Tokelauans wanted to remain part of New Zealand and that the Territory was far too dependent on that country to change its status. Meanwhile, under legislation approved in 1999, management of the islands' Public Service was formally transferred to Tokelau in July 2001. In July 2003 responsibility for the islands' budget was transferred to the General Fono.

A number of constitutional changes were instituted in October 2003. The Council of Faipule was renamed the Council for the Ongoing Government of Tokelau, henceforth to comprise the three Faipule and the three Pulenuku. In November New Zealand's Governor-General, Dame Silvia Cartwright, made an official visit to Tokelau to sign the Principles of Partnership agreement. The document was described by New Zealand's Minister of Foreign Affairs, Phil Goff, as a step closer to decolonization for the islands. Goff reiterated that the final decision on Tokelau's future would be made by its inhabitants, although he also confirmed that he expected the islands to adopt a system of self-government in free association with New Zealand, similar to that existing in Niue and the Cook Islands. In March 2004 it was announced that new powers were to be granted to the three atolls' Taupulega, giving them greater control over local affairs. In June the Administrator's powers were formally transferred from the General Fono to the three Taupulega, as part of the Modern House of Tokelau Project.

In August 2004 New Zealand's Prime Minister, Helen Clark, made an official visit to Tokelau (the first such visit in more than 20 years). During the visit Clark announced the provision of a grant worth some US $300,000 towards improvements for boat access to the islands and a review of the islands' communications infrastructure. The Prime Minister also expressed her confidence that the islanders would vote in favour of free association with New Zealand when the issue was finally put to a referendum. In November leaders from Tokelau travelled to New Zealand for a series of meetings with the latter's Minister of Foreign Affairs, Phil Goff, following which certain elements to be included in a treaty of free association with New Zealand were agreed upon. However, contrary to the New Zealand Government's expectations, at a referendum on the issue of the future status of Tokelau held between 11 and 15 February 2006 the requisite two-thirds' majority in favour of the proposed change to free association with New Zealand was not received: 349 votes were cast in favour of greater self-government, while 232 voters wanted Tokelau to remain a Dependent Territory. In June it was announced that the General Fono had agreed to the holding of another referendum on the issue of Tokelau's status.

In October 2006 David Payton replaced Neil Walter as Tokelau's Administrator. The decision to appoint a New Zealand diplomat to the position was interpreted by some observers as a reflection of a lack of confidence in the people of Tokelau and their ability to manage their own affairs. At the second referendum on Tokelau's status, conducted in October 2007, the level of participation was reported to be almost 100%. However, support for self-government was again not sufficient to produce the requisite two-thirds' majority, with 246 out of 692 voters rejecting the proposal. There was speculation about the influence of Tokelauans living in New Zealand, although expatriates were not permitted to cast a vote. Prime Minister Clark pledged her Government's 'ongoing friendship and support'. Elections to the General Fono were held on 18–19 January 2008, when 20 delegates were elected; one new Faipule was elected to office and two incumbent Faipule were re-elected, while three new Pulenuku were also chosen.

In February 2005, meanwhile, all three atolls were struck by Cyclone Percy, which caused widespread damage to infrastructure, homes and crops. Nukunonu was subjected to severe flooding as a result of the storm. The New Zealand Government approved some $NZ500,000 in emergency aid in the form of food supplies and temporary shelters (shipped from Samoa) and the restoration of essential services.

Recent developments

On 7 September 2009, in a development regarded as important in advancing the islands' identity, the New Zealand Governor-General,

Sir Anand Satyanand, formally presented Tokelau with an official flag, in place of the New Zealand flag used hitherto.

The islands' isolation remained a significant issue for Tokelau, access being possible only by a boat journey of at least 24 hours from Apia, Samoa. Long-standing demands for a new ferry for the islands gained fresh impetus in mid-2009 following the sinking of a ferry in Tonga with the loss of 74 lives. Without an airstrip, the only means of transport to and from Tokelau was a single vessel donated to the islands by New Zealand in the 1970s, which had become unseaworthy, according to the Tokelauan authorities. New Zealand Prime Minister John Key undertook to review the issue, but expressed concern at the high cost of a replacement ferry. In June 2012 it was announced that New Zealand was to provide Tokelau with a new ferry (with passenger capacity of up to 50 persons), at an estimated cost of $NZ6m. for a two-year lease; the new vessel commenced services between Apia and Tokelau in July. The provision of the new ferry constituted part of a $NZ17m. transport package offered by the New Zealand Government. Other elements of the package included an investigation into the proposed construction of a small coral airstrip on Nukunonu and the development of safe and effective ship-to-shore operations.

In April 2010 Tokelau announced that it intended to ban whaling in its territorial waters. The New Zealand Ministry of Foreign Affairs was not consulted prior to this declaration, despite the fact that the implementation of such a whale sanctuary would require New Zealand's assistance. However, the New Zealand Government indicated that it would support Tokelau's bid to implement the ban on whaling. In September 2011 Tokelau announced that its entire exclusive economic zone (comprising some 319,031 sq km) was henceforth to be designated as a shark sanctuary.

Elections to the General Fono were held on 19–20 January 2011, when 20 delegates were elected; two new Faipule, on Atafu and Nukunonu, were elected to office, a new Pulenuku was chosen on Atafu, while the incumbent Pulenuku on Nukunonu and the incumbent Faipule and Pulenuku on Fakaofo were all re-elected. In February Jonathan Kings replaced John Allen as the islands' Administrator. Allen had replaced David Payton in an acting capacity in 2009.

Following the announcement in May 2011 by the authorities of Samoa that the country was to transfer from the eastern to the western side of the International Date Line, with effect from December, in October the Tokelauan authorities announced that Tokelau would also switch to the western side of the Date Line, in order to facilitate the conduct of business with Australia and New Zealand by being in a similar time zone. The transition duly took place at the end of 29 December, following which Tokelau and Samoa were both one hour ahead of (rather than 23 hours behind) the New Zealand capital, Wellington, and three hours ahead of (rather than 21 hours behind) the Australian business and financial hub of Sydney.

Meanwhile, a state of emergency was declared in early October 2011 in response to a severe shortage of fresh water in Tokelau, which led to significant pressures on food sources, with livestock and crops both affected, and underscored the need for the Tokelauan authorities to develop more effective water resource management policies. Later in the month the Secretariat of the Pacific Regional Environment Programme (SPREP) disbursed funding, through its Small Grants Scheme, to enable Tokelau urgently to address the challenges posed by the ongoing drought. New Zealand, the USA and Samoa also provided assistance, in the form of deliveries of desalinated water, and, following the first substantial rainfall in nearly six months, the state of emergency was rescinded in late October. SPREP also pledged to assist Tokelau in long-term water resource management planning, including increasing water storage capacity and improving water conservation.

Foreign Affairs

New Zealand is responsible for the external relations of Tokelau. Strong links are maintained with Samoa, to the people of which the Tokelauans are closely related. There is considerable co-operation in health and education matters.

In December 1980 New Zealand and the USA signed a treaty whereby a US claim to Tokelau, dating from 1856, was relinquished. At the same time New Zealand abandoned a claim, on behalf of Tokelau, to Swains Island, which had been administered by the USA since 1925 as part of American Samoa. The treaty was ratified in August 1983, although there was some dissent in Tokelau. In March 2007 the Faipule of Fakaofo, Kolouei O'Brien, declared that if the islands achieved greater autonomy then Tokelau would wish to enter immediate negotiations with the USA regarding the return of Swains Island.

In 1989 Tokelau supported efforts by the South Pacific Forum to impose a regional ban on drift-net fishing (which was believed to have resulted in a serious depletion in tuna stocks). In November New Zealand prohibited drift-net fishing within Tokelau's exclusive economic zone (which extends to 200 nautical miles—370 km—from the islands' coastline). Tokelau was one of the 15 signatories of the Convention for the Prohibition of Fishing with Long Drift Nets in the

South Pacific, which was drafted by the South Pacific Forum in 1989 and came into force in May 1991. At the annual meeting of the Pacific Islands Forum (formerly the South Pacific Forum) in August 2002, New Zealand endorsed Tokelau's membership of the Forum Fisheries Agency. Tokelau was granted observer status at the Pacific Islands Forum in October 2005.

A visit to the islands by the Prime Minister of Tuvalu in mid-1996, for the signing of a mutual co-operation agreement (covering shipping, trade and fisheries), was widely interpreted as an indication of Tokelau's increased autonomy. A further co-operation agreement was established in March 2003, following a five-day visit to the islands by the Prime Minister of Samoa. Tokelau's traditional leaders agreed a framework for annual meetings with the Samoan Government to discuss issues of concern and mutual benefit in what was regarded as a sign of their growing relationship.

In November 2011 Tokelau was one of eight Pacific states and territories that jointly established the Polynesian Leaders Group (see p. 478), which was widely viewed as being intended to provide a counterweight to the Melanesian Spearhead Group. The first formal meeting of the Group, which pledged to enhance co-operation among its members across a wide range of fields, including trade and investment, education, climate change and health, was held in the Cook Islands, on the sidelines of the annual Pacific Islands Forum summit, in August 2012.

CONSTITUTION AND GOVERNMENT

Tokelau is administered under the authority of the Tokelau Islands Act 1948, incorporating subsequent amendments and regulations. The administration of Tokelau is the responsibility of the Minister of Foreign Affairs of New Zealand, who is empowered to appoint an Administrator to the Territory. In practice, most of the Administrator's powers are delegated to the Official Secretary, who heads the Tokelau Apia Liaison Office, as well as to the General Fono and the Council for the Ongoing Government of Tokelau (formerly the Council of Faipule). Each atoll has its own Taupulega (Island Council or Council of Elders), which comprises the heads of family groups together with two elected members, the Faipule and the Pulenuku. The Faipule represents the atoll in its dealings with the administering power and the public service, and presides over the Council and the court. The Pulenuku is responsible for the administration of village affairs. The Faipule and the Pulenuku are democratically elected by universal adult suffrage every three years. The three Faipule, who hold ministerial portfolios and along with the three Pulenuku form the six-member Council for the Ongoing Government of Tokelau, choose one of their number to hold the title Ulu-O-Tokelau (Head of Tokelau) for a term of one year. The territorial assembly, the General Fono, is a meeting of 20 delegates, who are elected by universal adult suffrage for a three-year term (including the three Faipule and the three Pulenuku) and who represent the entire Territory. Members of the General Fono elect a Chairman, and hold three or four sessions a year on the atoll of the Ulu-O-Tokelau.

REGIONAL AND INTERNATIONAL CO-OPERATION

Tokelau is a member of the Pacific Community (see p. 422), and, as a Dependent Territory of New Zealand, has been represented by that country in the Pacific Islands Forum (see p. 426) and other international organizations. In October 2005 Tokelau was granted observer status at the Pacific Islands Forum. In November 2011 Tokelau was one of eight founding members of the Polynesian Leaders Group (see p. 478).

ECONOMIC AFFAIRS

According to estimates by the UN Development Programme (UNDP), in 1982 Tokelau's gross national product (GNP) was US $1.2m., equivalent to US $760 per head. Gross domestic product (GDP) was estimated at US $1.5m. in 1993. Between the censuses of 2001 and 2011 the population declined at an average rate of 0.9% per year.

Agriculture (including fishing) is, excluding copra production, of a basic subsistence nature. Coconuts (the source of copra) are the only cash crop, for which there is an increasingly limited market. Pulaka, breadfruit, papayas, the screw-pine (*Pandanus*) and bananas are cultivated as food crops. Livestock comprises pigs, ducks and other poultry. Ocean and lagoon fish and shellfish are staple constituents of the islanders' diet. The sale to foreign fleets of fishing licences permitting them to operate in Tokelau's exclusive economic zone (EEZ) provides an important, albeit fluctuating, source of income (see below).

The industrial sector has been constrained by a lack of resources. Manufacturing comprises mainly the production of handicrafts, notably woven items such as mats. However, the opening on Atafu, in 1990, of a factory processing highly priced yellowfin tuna provided another important source of income. The principal markets for the product were New Zealand and Japan.

Energy was traditionally provided by diesel-powered generators, the fuel for which was imported via Samoa at considerable expense. With funding from New Zealand, a major power project to supply all three atolls with a more reliable source of electricity was initiated in 2002. Over the following decade, greater emphasis was placed on the development of renewable forms of energy, particularly solar power. In conjunction with the Governments of New Zealand and France, UNDP and UNESCO, in 2003 Tokelau embarked on a programme aimed at utilizing the Territory's solar energy potential for grid-connected power generation. In October 2012, following the installation of 4,032 solar panels (totalling 1 MW) and 1,344 batteries by the New Zealand company PowerSmart, it was announced that Tokelau had become the world's first territory to have the capacity to meet its energy requirements solely through solar power. It was expected, however, that around 7% of the Territory's energy would continue to be provided by generators (for cloudy days, working by night and for emergencies), which would now be powered by locally produced coconut oil rather than diesel.

The services sector is dominated by village services and public administration. The tourism sector is limited, having remained undeveloped owing to the lack of air services and the difficulty of access. There is just one recognized hotel and one resort, both of which are located on the central atoll of Nukunonu. Fewer than 30 tourists visited the islands in 2001. Following the purchase by a Dutch entrepreneur of the islands' internet domain address '.tk' in 2001, more than 1.6m. names had been registered to the facility by 2007. Although the Government's precise earnings from Dot TK were not disclosed, the services of this joint venture with Teletok, the islands' communications company, were reported to be proving highly lucrative. The establishment of Dot TK was believed to have increased annual government revenue by about 10%. In 2012 revenue from Dot TK was reported to account for about one-sixth of Tokelau's GDP. Furthermore, the concomitant upgrading of Tokelau's communications infrastructure, including a broadband connection via satellite, greatly enhanced the islanders' own information technology facilities. In March 2007, however, a leading information technology publication reported that '.tk' was the most insecure web domain in the world. A content-filtering system was subsequently installed, in an attempt to reduce the risks. Furthermore, in March 2008 an international software security company reported that, along with Niue, in per caput terms Tokelau was one of the world's worst offenders with regard to the relaying of unsolicited e-mails.

Imports to the value of $NZ1.7m. were purchased in 2002. The principal imports in that year were food and live animals (accounting for 55.2% of the total cost of imports), mineral fuels (11.6%) and miscellaneous manufactured goods (11.0%).

In 1999/2000 there was a budgetary deficit of $NZ0.9m. Tokelau's budget for 2001/02 was to include at least $NZ4.2m. from New Zealand and an estimated $NZ1.7m. to be obtained from local revenues such as fisheries licensing, duty, taxes, philatelic sales, freight charges and interest earned. Tokelau assumed responsibility for the management of its own budgetary affairs in 2003. Since then most of New Zealand's bilateral assistance has been transferred directly to the Territory's budget, thereby enabling Tokelau to finance its recurrent expenditure on services such as transport, education and health. Local revenue was estimated to have reached about $NZ2m. in 2005. Receipts from EEZ fees rose from $NZ286,000 in 2004 to an estimated $NZ569,000 in 2005. Fees for shipping, radio excises and customs duties have provided another source of revenue; local receipts from such duties increased from $NZ372,000 in 2004 to an estimated $NZ388,000 in 2005. The sale of postage stamps and souvenir coins (which are legal tender, although New Zealand currency is in general use) also makes a significant contribution to the Territory's income. Receipts from this source increased from $NZ54,000 in 2004 to an estimated $NZ70,000 in 2005. Some revenue is provided by remittances from Tokelauans working abroad, mainly in New Zealand. Official development assistance from New Zealand increased from an estimated $NZ17.0m. in 2011/12 to a projected $NZ20.3m. in 2012/13. In addition to its links to New Zealand, Tokelau maintains a bilateral development assistance plan with Australia, focused upon human resource development. In 2012/13 Australia was to provide Tokelau with funding totalling $A600,000.

Tokelau's agricultural development has been constrained by the lack of suitable cultivable soil and by the adverse effects of inclement weather. In February 2005 Cyclone Percy caused serious destruction on the islands, coinciding with 'king tides' that flooded the Territory resulting in widespread damage. Moreover, the Territory's small size, remote location, lack of land-based resources and the population's continuing migration to New Zealand have severely hindered economic development. It was hoped that Tokelau would derive greater benefits from its fisheries resources as a result of a plan initiated by the Secretariat of the Pacific Community in 2004; the initiative focused on community-based activities and included the increased exploitation of the islands' giant clam resources. In that year the Tokelau International Trust Fund (TITF) was established, with assistance from New Zealand and with the objective of enhancing the Territory's prospects for long-term self-reliance. Australia and the United Kingdom also contributed to the TITF, along with Tokelau itself. Following New Zealand's contribution of $NZ15m. in

November 2008, the assets of the TITF totalled $NZ52m., and by the end of 2012 this figure had risen to $NZ70m. A four-year National Strategic Plan for Infrastructure and Development (entitled 'Healthy and Active Communities with Opportunities for All') was launched by Tokelau, in partnership with New Zealand, in 2010. Areas targeted for development included transport, renewable energy, fisheries, good governance, sustainability, human resources development, education and health. With Tokelau accessible only by sea (via Samoa), the maintenance of adequate shipping services remained a major focus in 2012; New Zealand's provision of a new ferry in that year was a very welcome development. The construction of an airstrip, to encourage tourism, has been intermittently considered. Under the Administrative Assistance scheme (part of the Principles of Partnership agreement—see Contemporary Political History), the limited capacity of the Tokelau Public Service is supplemented by the resources of various New Zealand government departments through short-term secondments of staff, training or mentoring.

PUBLIC HOLIDAYS

2014: 1 January (New Year's Day), 6 February (Waitangi Day, anniversary of 1840 treaty), 18 April (Good Friday), 21 April (Easter Monday), 25 April (ANZAC Day, anniversary of 1915 landing at Gallipoli), 2 June (Queen's Official Birthday), 27 October (Labour Day), 25–26 December (Christmas).

Statistical Survey

Source (unless otherwise indicated): Tokelau Apia Liaison Office, POB 805, Apia, Samoa; tel. 20822; fax 21761; e-mail f.aukuso@clear .net.nz; internet www.spc.int/prism/country/tk/stats/.

AREA AND POPULATION

Area: Atafu 3.5 sq km; Nukunonu 4.7 sq km; Fakaofo 4.0 sq km; Total 12.2 sq km (4.7 sq miles).

Population: 1,466 (males 736, females 730) at census of 19 October 2006; 1,411 (males 701, females 710) at census of 18 October 2011 (including 226 persons usually resident but absent on census night). *By Atoll* (2011 census): Atafu 482; Nukunonu 397; Fakaofo 490; Samoa 42; Total 1,411. Note: Data for census of 18 October 2011 refer to the usually resident population of Tokelau.

Density (at 2011 census): 115.7 per sq km.

Population by Age and Sex (2011 census): *0–14:* 465 (males 242, females 223); *15–64:* 836 (males 408, females 428); *65 and over:* 110 (males 51, females 59); *Total* 1,411 (males 701, females 710).

Births and Deaths (1996): Birth rate 33.1 per 1,000; Death rate 8.2 per 1,000. *2010* (Secretariat of the Pacific Community estimates): Live births 26 (birth rate 22.1 per 1,000); Registered deaths 9 (death rate 7.6 per 1,000) (Source: Pacific Regional Information System).

Life Expectancy (years at birth, 1996, official estimates): Males 68; Females 70. Source: Ministry of Foreign Affairs and Trade, Wellington.

Economically Active Population (2001 census, persons aged 15 years and over): Construction 78; Retail trade 12; Hotels and restaurants 4; Transport 7; Communications 20; Village services 182; Public administration 59; Education 53; Medical 23; Total 438. *2011 Census:* Total in paid employment 489 (males 287, females 202).

HEALTH AND WELFARE
Key Indicators

Access to Water (% of households, 2004): 88.

Access to Sanitation (% of households, 2004): 78.

For sources and definitions, see explanatory note on p. vi.

AGRICULTURE, ETC.

Crop Production (metric tons, 2011, FAO estimates): Coconuts 4,223; Roots and tubers 184; Bananas 14.

Livestock (year ending September 2011, FAO estimates): Pigs 1,000; Chickens 5,000.

Livestock Products (metric tons, 2011, FAO estimates): Pig meat 20; Chicken meat 5; Hen eggs 8.

Fishing (metric tons, live weight, 2010, FAO estimate): Total catch 54.

Source: FAO.

INDUSTRY

Production (1990, estimate): Electric energy 300,000 kWh.

FINANCE

Currency and Exchange Rates: New Zealand currency is legal tender. Tokelau souvenir coins have also been issued. New Zealand currency: 100 cents = 1 New Zealand dollar ($NZ); *Sterling, US Dollar and Euro Equivalents* (31 December 2012): £1 sterling = $NZ1.9237; US $1 = $NZ1.2191; €1 = $NZ1.6084; $NZ100 = £51.98 = US $82.03 = €62.17. *Average Exchange Rate* ($NZ per US $): 1.3874 in 2010; 1.2659 in 2011; 1.2342 in 2012.

Budget ($NZ, year ending 30 June 1998): *Revenue:* Local 734,950; New Zealand subsidy 4,600,000; Total 5,334,950. *Expenditure:* Total 5,208,449.

Overseas Aid (projection, $NZ '000, 2002/03): Official development assistance from New Zealand 8,100 (of which Budget support 4,750, Projects and training 2,650). *2010/11:* Total development assistance from New Zealand $NZ17.25m. *2011/12:* (estimate): Total development assistance from New Zealand $NZ17.00m. *2012/13:* (projection): Total development assistance from New Zealand $NZ20.300m.

EXTERNAL TRADE

Principal Commodities ($NZ, 2002): *Imports:* Food and live animals 923,766; Mineral fuels, lubricants, etc. 194,779; Animal and vegetable oils, fats and waxes 50,012; Chemicals and related products 45,429; Manufactured goods 183,488; Total (incl. others) 1,673,389.

COMMUNICATIONS MEDIA

Telephones (2010): 300 main lines in use.

Source: International Telecommunication Union.

EDUCATION

Schools (1999): 3 (one school for all levels on each atoll).

Teachers (2003): Primary 23; Secondary 17.

Pupils (2011 census): Pre-primary 16; Primary 267; Secondary 236; University 78; Other tertiary 48.

Students Overseas (1999): Secondary 22; Tertiary 20.

Pupil-teacher Ratio (primary education, UNESCO estimate): 5.8 in 2002/03 (Source: UNESCO Institute for Statistics).

Directory

The Government
(May 2013)

Administrator: JONATHAN KINGS (took office in Feb. 2011).

FAIPULE

The title of Ulu-O-Tokelau (Head of Tokelau) is held on a one-year rotational basis by each Faipule in turn. The Faipule of Nukunonu, Salesio Lui, is the Ulu-O-Tokelau for 2013. At elections held on 19–20 January 2011 new Faipule were chosen on Atafu and Nukunonu, while the incumbent Faipule was re-elected on Fakaofo.

Faipule of Fakaofo: FOUA TOLOA.

Faipule of Nukunonu: SALESIO LUI.

Faipule of Atafu: KELISIANO KALOLO.

PULENUKU

At elections held on 19–20 January 2011 a new Pulenuku (Village Mayor) was chosen on Atafu, while the two incumbent Pulenuku on Nukunonu and Fakaofo were re-elected.

Pulenuku of Fakaofo: OTINIELU TUUMULI.

Pulenuku of Nukunonu: PANAPA SAKARIA.

Pulenuku of Atafu: FAAFETAI TAUMANU.

GOVERNMENT OFFICES

Council for the Ongoing Government of Tokelau: POB 3298, Apia, Samoa; tel. 20822; fax 21761; e-mail jsuveinakama@yahoo .com; internet www.tokelau.org.nz; Gen. Man. JOVILISI SUVEINA-KAMA.

Tokelau Apia Liaison Office/Ofiha o Fehokotakiga Tokelau Ma Apia: POB 865, Savalalo, Apia, Samoa; tel. 20822; fax 21761;

e-mail maka@lesamoa.net; internet www.tokelau-govt.info; responsible for transport, accounting and consular functions; Gen. Man. FALANI AUKUSO.

The Tokelau Public Service has seven departments, divided among the three atolls, with a supervising administrative official located in each village. Two departments are established on each atoll, while the seventh department, the Council for the Ongoing Government of Tokelau (formerly the Council of Faipule), rotates on a yearly basis in conjunction with the position of Ulu-O-Tokelau. Management of the Tokelau Public Service was formally transferred to Tokelau in July 2001.

Legislature

GENERAL FONO

The General Fono, or territorial assembly, is a meeting of delegates representing the Territory, and includes the Faipule and Pulenuku; it is the highest advisory body and must be consulted by the administration about all policy affecting the Territory. The General Fono has responsibility for the territorial budget and has the power to enact legislation, impose taxes and declare public holidays. The assembly is elected by universal suffrage and, since the legislative elections of 2002, the number of representatives from each atoll has been determined by its proportion of the total population. Members of the General Fono elect a Chairman, and hold between three and four sessions a year on the Ulu-O-Tokelau's atoll.

Chairman: IOSUA ALENI.

Judicial System

Tokelau's legislative and judicial systems are based on the Tokelau Islands Act 1948 and subsequent amendments and regulations. The Act provided for a variety of British regulations to continue in force and, where no other legislation applies, the law of England and Wales in 1840 (the year in which British sovereignty over New Zealand was established) was to be applicable. New Zealand statute law applies in Tokelau only if specifically extended there. In 1986 legislation formalized the transfer of High Court civil and criminal jurisdiction from Niue to New Zealand. Most cases are judged by the Commissioner established on each atoll, who has limited jurisdiction in civil and criminal matters. Commissioners are appointed by the New Zealand Governor-General, after consultation with the elders of the atoll.

Commissioner of Fakaofo: PENEHE TULAFONO.

Commissioner of Nukunonu: IOANE TUMUA.

Commissioner of Atafu: SALASOPA SEMU IUPATI.

Religion

On Atafu almost all inhabitants are members of the Congregational Christian Church, on Nukunonu all are Roman Catholic, while both denominations are represented on Fakaofo. In the late 1990s some 70% of the total population adhered to the Congregational Christian Church, and 30% to the Roman Catholic Church.

CHRISTIANITY

Roman Catholic Church

The Church is represented in Tokelau by a Mission, established in 1992. There were an estimated 500 adherents at 31 December 2007.

Superior: Mgr OLIVER P. ARO, Catholic Mission, Nukunonu, Tokelau (via Apia, Samoa); tel. 4160; fax 4236; e-mail dr.tovite@clear.net.n3.

Broadcasting and Communications

Each atoll has a radio station to broadcast shipping and weather reports. Radio-telephone provided the main communications link with other areas until the late 1990s. A new telecommunications system established at a cost of US $2.76m. (US $1m. of which was provided by New Zealand) and operating through an earth station, linked to a communications satellite, on each atoll, became operational in 1997. A new weekly radio programme, called Vakai, broadcast by Samoa Broadcasting Service to Tokelau's three atolls, began in October 2004.

TELECOMMUNICATIONS

Telecommunications Tokelau Corporation (TeleTok): Fenuafala, Fakaofo; tel. 3100; fax 3108; e-mail apvitale@clear.net.nz; f. 1996; govt-owned; telephone and internet services; Gen. Man. AUKUSITINO VITALE.

Finance

There are no banks in operation in Tokelau; however, the Office of Tokelau Affairs provides a facility for deposits and withdrawals, and pays interest on accounts. Commercial and other banking facilities are available in Apia, Samoa.

Trade and Industry

A village co-operative store was established on each atoll in 1977. These stores are operated by village management committees, which work with the public service administration to reduce the costs of imported goods. Most imports are purchased from Samoa, with an increasing amount coming from New Zealand and Fiji. Local industries include copra production, woodwork and plaited craft goods, and the processing of tuna. In October 2012, following the installation of 4,032 solar panels (totalling 1 MW) and 1,344 batteries by the New Zealand company PowerSmart, it was announced that Tokelau had the capacity to meet its energy requirements solely through solar power. It was expected, however, that around 7% of the Territory's energy would continue to be provided by generators, which would be powered by locally produced coconut oil.

Transport

There are no roads or motor vehicles. Unscheduled inter-atoll voyages by sea are forbidden because the risk of missing landfall is too great. Passengers and cargo are transported by vessels that anchor off shore, as there are no harbour facilities. The vessel *Forum Tokelau*, operated by Pacific Forum Line, began a monthly service between Tokelau and Apia, Samoa, in 1997. A New Zealand-funded inter-atoll vessel commenced service in 1991, providing the first regular link between the atolls for 40 years. A new ferry, *PB Matua*, with a passenger capacity of up to 50 persons, commenced services between Apia and Tokelau in July 2012. The provision of the ferry by the New Zealand Government, at an estimated cost of $NZ6m. for a two-year lease, was part of a range of transport measures, worth a total of $NZ17m., which also included an investigation into the proposed construction of a small coral airstrip on Nukunonu and the development of safe and effective ship-to-shore operations.

Education

Education is provided free of charge, and attendance is virtually 100%. Kindergarten facilities are available for children from the age of three years, while primary education takes place between the ages of five and 14. The provision of an additional year of schooling, for those aged 15, is rotated among the territory's three schools every five years. In 2003 there were 23 primary school teachers and 17 secondary school teachers. Pupil enrolment recorded by the 2011 census totalled 16 at pre-primary level, 267 at primary level, 236 at secondary level, 78 at university level and 48 in other tertiary education. The New Zealand Department of Education provides advisory services and some educational equipment. The Education Department of Samoa organizes daily radio broadcasts. Scholarships are awarded for secondary and tertiary education, and for vocational training, in New Zealand, Australia and other Pacific countries. Link arrangements exist between Tokelau and the Fiji-based University of the South Pacific, which has an outpost on each atoll that is electronically connected. In 2004 a total of 53 Tokelauans over the age of 15 years were studying overseas under the Tokelau Sponsorship Scheme (34 in Samoa, 12 in New Zealand and seven in Fiji). In 2001 there were some 169 Tokelauan pupils enrolled at the Samoa Secondary School. Australia also provides scholarships.

NEW ZEALAND'S ASSOCIATED STATES

New Zealand's two Associated States are the self-governing Cook Islands and Niue, both of which are situated in the Pacific Ocean.

THE COOK ISLANDS

Introductory Survey

LOCATION, CLIMATE, LANGUAGE, RELIGION, FLAG, CAPITAL

The 13 inhabited and two uninhabited islands of the Cook Islands are located in the southern Pacific Ocean and lie between American Samoa, to the west, and French Polynesia, to the east. The islands extend over about 2m. sq km (more than 750,000 sq miles) of ocean, and form two groups: the Northern Cooks, which are all atolls and include Pukapuka, Rakahanga and Manihiki, and the Southern Cooks, including Aitutaki, Mangaia and Rarotonga, which are all volcanic islands. From December to March the climate is warm and humid, with the possibility of severe storms; from April to November the climate is mild and equable. The average annual rainfall on Rarotonga is 2,012 mm (79 ins). The official languages are English and Cook Islands Maori. The principal religion is Christianity, with the majority of the population adhering to the Congregationalist Cook Islands Christian Church. The islands' flag (proportions 1 by 2) displays 15 five-pointed white stars (representing the islands of the group) on a royal blue field, with the United Kingdom's Union Flag as a canton in the upper hoist. The capital is Avarua, on Rarotonga.

CONTEMPORARY POLITICAL HISTORY

Historical Context

The first Europeans to visit the islands were members of a British expedition, led by Capt. James Cook (after whom the islands are named), in 1773. The Cook Islands was proclaimed a British protectorate in 1888, and a part of New Zealand in 1901.

On 4 August 1965 the Cook Islands became a self-governing Territory in free association with New Zealand. The people are New Zealand citizens. Sir Albert Henry, leader of the Cook Islands Party (CIP), was elected Premier in 1965 and re-elected in 1971, 1974 and March 1978. However, in July 1978, following an inquiry into alleged electoral malpractice, the Chief Justice disallowed votes cast in the elections to the Legislative Assembly (later renamed Parliament) by Cook Islands expatriates who had been flown from New Zealand, with their fares paid from public funds. The amended ballot gave a majority to the Democratic Party (DP), and its leader, Dr (later Sir) Thomas Davis, was sworn in as Premier. In August 1979 Sir Albert Henry was convicted of conspiracy to defraud, and was formally stripped of his knighthood.

Domestic Political Affairs

In May 1981 the Cook Islands' Constitution was amended to increase the membership of Parliament from 22 to 24, and to extend the parliamentary term from four to five years. In March 1983 Sir Thomas Davis lost power to the CIP, under Geoffrey (later Sir Geoffrey) Henry, cousin of the former Premier. However, with one seat already subject to re-election, Henry's majority of three was reduced by the death of one CIP member of Parliament and the transfer of allegiance to the DP by another. Henry resigned in August, and a general election in November returned the DP to power under Davis. In August 1984 Davis formed a coalition Government with the CIP, with Henry as Deputy Prime Minister. In mid-1985, however, Davis dismissed Henry, who had endorsed an unsuccessful motion expressing no confidence in the Government, and Henry's supporters withdrew from the coalition. Henry's successor as Deputy Prime Minister was Dr (later Sir) Terepai Maoate, one of four CIP members who continued to support the Davis Government, in defiance of the CIP central committee.

Davis was forced to resign as Prime Minister in July 1987, after the approval of a parliamentary motion expressing no confidence in his administration. He was succeeded by Dr Pupuke Robati of the DP. Geoffrey Henry again became Prime Minister following a general election victory for the CIP in January 1989. The defection in mid-1990 of a member of Parliament from the DP to the CIP provided the latter with the minimum two-thirds' majority support necessary to amend the Constitution. In August 1991 a constitutional amendment was approved to increase the number of members of Parliament to 25, and at an election to the newly created seat a CIP candidate was successful.

At a general election in March 1994 the CIP increased its majority, winning 20 seats in Parliament; the DP secured three seats and the Alliance Party (established in 1992 by Norman George) two. Davis, who failed to win a seat, subsequently resigned as leader of the DP. A referendum held simultaneously revealed that a majority of the electorate favoured retaining the Territory's current name (69.8% of voters) and national anthem (80.2%), while 48.5% favoured the retention of its flag. (At subsequent by-elections the CIP lost two seats and the DP and Alliance Party each gained one seat.)

In August 1997 Parliament approved the Outer Islands Local Government Act, providing for a new budgetary system to allocate funds for projects in the outer islands and for increased powers for local authorities, with the aim of reducing significantly central government administration of the outer islands. As part of the plan, three new government bodies were elected in April 1998. Meanwhile, in December 1997 the Ministry of Public Works, Survey, Housing, Water Supply and Environment Services was closed for exceeding its budget. The minister responsible, Tihina Tom Marsters, resigned in protest against the closure, which resulted in the loss of more than 100 public servants' jobs, problems with the supply of utilities (particularly water) and the suspension of several development projects.

At the legislative elections of June 1999 the CIP won 11 of the 25 seats in Parliament, the Democratic Alliance Party (DAP, a grouping that included the DP) 10 seats and the New Alliance Party (NAP, formerly the Alliance Party) four seats. Sir Geoffrey Henry of the CIP was reappointed Prime Minister and formed a new Cabinet, following the establishment of a political coalition with the NAP, the leader of which, Norman George, became Deputy Prime Minister. However, three members of the CIP subsequently left the party to form a coalition with the DAP, in protest against the alliance with the NAP, and at the end of July Henry resigned and was replaced by a 'rebel' CIP member, Dr Joe Williams. Williams was confirmed as the new Prime Minister by 13 votes to 12 in a parliamentary vote of confidence. Williams' appointment provoked a public protest in Rarotonga, exacerbated by general discontent at the nomination of a Prime Minister whose parliamentary constituency was outside the Cook Islands (having been elected to the seat reserved for non-resident voters). The result of the contest for the Pukapuka seat, which had been won by former Prime Minister Inatio Akaruru by just one vote, was challenged by the DAP. The Court of Appeal subsequently declared the result invalid, stripping the Government of its one-seat majority. The result of a by-election held in September 1999 to decide the Pukapuka seat was again said to be invalid and a further by-election was scheduled. The Government became a minority administration in October when the Prime Minister dismissed Norman George and the Minister of Education, following their defection to the opposition. In November Williams resigned, shortly before a vote of no confidence was to be tabled against him by Dr Terepai Maoate, now the leader of the opposition DAP. Maoate won the vote by 14 votes to 11 and was appointed Prime Minister, forming a new coalition Government with the NAP. He subsequently reappointed Norman George to the post of Deputy Prime Minister.

In early 2000 the islands of Penrhyn, Pukapuka, Rakahanga and Manihiki expressed their desire to become fully devolved and to take sole control over areas such as administration, public expenditure and justice. In response, the Government pledged gradually to phase out the Ministry of Outer Islands Development, as well as the post of Government Representative in the outer islands.

In July 2001 Norman George was again dismissed from the position of Deputy Prime Minister, this time owing to Maoate's belief that George was attempting to undermine him. He was replaced by Dr Robert Woonton. However, Woonton was also highly critical of Maoate's leadership. In late 2001 the rift between the Prime Minister and his Cabinet widened. Woonton announced his resignation, which Maoate refused to accept. This led to a motion of no confidence in the Prime Minister, which he only narrowly survived. In February 2002 15 of the 25 members of Parliament voted against Maoate in a second motion of no confidence, and he was replaced by Woonton. In an extensive ministerial reorganization Sir Geoffrey Henry returned to the Cabinet as Deputy Prime Minister.

In November 2002 Parliament approved a constitutional amendment abolishing the requirement for electoral candidates to reside in the islands for a qualifying period of three months. This action was widely interpreted as a way of retaining the overseas voters' parliamentary seat for the CIP leader, Dr Joe Williams, who lived permanently in New Zealand. In the same month the CIP and the DP formed a coalition Government (the fifth such coalition since the previous election), which left Norman George, who had been recently dismissed from his position in the Cabinet, as the sole opposition member of Parliament. The Government's action prompted a demonstration outside the parliament building by some 150 people, organized by a recently formed organization, the Group for Political Change. The protesters claimed that the virtual absence of an opposition constituted an erosion of democracy and appealed to the Prime Minister to commit to an early general election. However, in January 2003 the CIP was ousted from the coalition. The continued political manoeuvring was widely denounced, particularly among the business community, for creating a climate of instability in the islands. Public dissatisfaction with the situation resulted in the presentation of a petition to the Government in March signed by a significant percentage of the population; the petition demanded a number of political reforms including a reduction in the number of members of Parliament, the introduction of a shorter parliamentary term and the abolition of the overseas seat. Moreover, businessman Teariki Heather announced the formation of a new political party, the Cook Islands National, in the same month. In September legislation was approved providing for the abolition of the overseas seat and for a referendum (to be held concurrently with the next general election) on a proposal to shorten the parliamentary term from five years to four. (An earlier referendum on this issue in 1999 had narrowly failed to receive the support of the two-thirds' majority required to amend the Constitution.) In November 2003 Dr Terepai Maoate, who had been appointed Deputy Prime Minister earlier in the year, and the Minister of Justice, Tangata Vavia, resigned following an unsuccessful attempt by Maoate to propose a motion of no confidence in the Government.

The elections of 2004 and 2006; other events

At a general election in September 2004 the DP won 14 of the 24 seats, the CIP secured nine and an independent candidate took the remaining seat. Prime Minister Robert Woonton regained his seat by only four votes, amid accusations that he had secured the support of some voters through bribery. In the concurrent referendum 82.3% of participating voters favoured the shortening of the parliamentary term from five years to four. The period immediately after the election was characterized by political manoeuvring and the initiation of several legal cases challenging the outcome in a number of constituencies. In November Woonton announced that the DP was to form a coalition government with the CIP. This decision was widely opposed within the DP, and prompted the resignation of the Deputy Prime Minister, Aunty Mau Munokoa. Further controversy was caused by the appointment of Norman George to the position of Speaker. In December, with the DP effectively divided over Woonton's actions, Jim Marurai, of the minority Democratic Tumu Party, was elected Prime Minister and a coalition was formed between his party and the CIP. It was understood that Marurai would serve as Prime Minister for the first two years of the parliamentary term and would then be replaced by Sir Geoffrey Henry of the CIP. However, in August 2005 Henry was dismissed and replaced by DP leader Dr Terepai Maoate. In September two further CIP cabinet ministers were dismissed and replaced by DP members. Marurai declared that the coalition had been dissolved, claiming that the action followed threats to his leadership.

The islands suffered considerable damage in February and March 2005 when five cyclones struck. The resultant damage to housing, infrastructure and crops was estimated at $NZ25m.

In October 2005 Peri Vaevae Pare, the Minister of Health and Internal Affairs, whose other portfolios included social services, was suspended from office following allegations of fraud. In November he was convicted on three charges of intent to defraud and gain pecuniary advantage, each conviction carrying a maximum sentence of five years' imprisonment. In early 2006 the Prime Minister requested the formal resignation of the suspended Minister, who was subsequently replaced. In March Woonton, who had previously been appointed as the islands' High Commissioner to New Zealand, was dismissed from that post, following allegations that he had been involved in an attempt to oust the islands' Government.

In July 2006 a by-election victory for the opposition CIP gave it a parliamentary majority, prompting the Queen's Representative, Sir Frederick Goodwin, to dissolve the legislature and to call an early election. Provisional results of the election, held on 26 September, indicated that the DP had secured 15 of the 24 parliamentary seats and the CIP seven, with one seat being taken by an independent candidate. Henry Puna, who had succeeded Sir Geoffrey Henry as leader of the CIP, failed to retain his seat. A by-election to resolve the tied result in the remaining constituency resulted in victory for the CIP candidate in November. In the following month it was announced that a by-election would also be held in Titikaveka after the eligibility of the winning candidate, Robert Wigmore of the DP, was called into question. Wigmore won the Titikaveka by-election in

February 2007, thus taking the final result of the 2006 election to 15 seats for the DP and eight for the CIP, along with one independent. Jim Marurai, who had returned to the DP, thus retained the position of Prime Minister, although Maoate continued as leader of the DP. In August 2007 Wilkie Rasmussen, the cabinet member responsible for foreign affairs among other portfolios, was elected deputy leader of the DP, having left the CIP prior to the 2006 election.

Preparations for the 2009 South Pacific Mini Games, which were to be hosted by the islands in September of that year, attracted considerable media attention in 2007–08, with the Ministry of Finance and Economic Management warning against the acceptance of a grant from the People's Republic of China to finance the construction of a sports complex, maintaining that it would neither be cost-effective nor serve the long-term economic interests of the islands (see Foreign Affairs). Preparations were marred by allegations of financial mismanagement, and in March 2009 the Government announced an audit into the finances of the Pacific Mini Games Company, the enterprise responsible for organizing the event, while the rising cost of the Mini Games forced the Government to allocate additional funding in a supplementary budget in April. Nevertheless, the Mini Games were staged successfully in September and provided a short-term increase in economic activity.

Recent developments: the election of 2010

Following the dismissal from the Cabinet of Wilkie Rasmussen in July 2009, on the grounds that he had allegedly colluded with members of the opposition in order to establish a new government (claims that were denied by Rasmussen), the foreign affairs portfolio was reassigned to the Deputy Prime Minister, Sir Terepai Maoate. However, in December Prime Minister Jim Marurai dismissed Maoate owing to his role in an abortive deal to purchase a fuel depot, which had lost the Government some $NZ2m. Three DP ministers resigned in protest against Maoate's dismissal. In the subsequent cabinet reorganization in January 2010, Robert Wigmore became Deputy Prime Minister and was also allocated responsibility for foreign affairs. Rasmussen was reappointed to the Cabinet, securing the finance portfolio, among other responsibilities, despite having denounced Marurai as 'totally incompetent' at the time of his dismissal in July 2009.

In February 2010 the island of Aitutaki was devastated by Cyclone Pat, which damaged up to 90% of the island's housing and disabled communications and electricity lines. Following the declaration of a state of disaster, the New Zealand Government pledged $NZ5.5m. in reconstruction aid in March. The Cook Islands Government was censured for the slow pace of the recovery effort, and, despite demands from the DP and the CIP for Marurai to recall Parliament so that official approval could be given to the New Zealand aid programme, the Prime Minister controversially refused to reconvene the legislature until September, apparently owing to a threat of a motion of no confidence being tabled by the opposition.

Following a lengthy trial on corruption charges dating back to 1999–2002, Norman George was found not guilty in May 2010. George alleged that the charges against him had been politically motivated and accused Maoate of having used his former position as Attorney-General to influence the police investigation.

In an escalating dispute within the DP regarding the dismissal of Sir Terepai Maoate, all six members of the Cabinet, including Marurai, were expelled from the party in March 2010. However, at a conference held in June, the six were readmitted to the party; Wigmore was elected party Leader in place of Maoate, with Rasmussen returned as his deputy; Sean Willis was elected as the new party President, replacing Makiuti Tonga. In September 2010 Maoate was defeated in his bid to secure election as the DP candidate for the Rarotonga seat of Ngatangiia; the former premier subsequently announced that he would be contesting the election as an independent candidate.

Meanwhile, in August 2010 Marurai announced that the next legislative elections were to be held in November, and that a popular referendum on parliamentary reform, comprising a proposal to reduce the number of parliamentary seats, was to take place concurrently. The participation in the elections of some 16 independents (12 more than in the 2006 poll), together with the emergence of, and the fielding of six candidates by, Te Kura O Te Au, represented a significant challenge to the traditional two-party contest between the CIP and the DP. Established earlier in the year, Te Kura O Te Au pledged to pursue political reform that remained 'in tune with spiritual and cultural values'.

However, in the event, the election held on 17 November 2010 was, as in previous polls, entirely dominated by the two main parties. Not unexpectedly, given the fractious past 12 months experienced by the incumbent DP, the CIP secured a commanding victory, winning 16 of the 24 seats, and thus a two-thirds' majority, while the DP garnered just eight seats. Turn-out, at about 78%, was considerably lower than in previous polls. According to the results of the referendum on parliamentary reform, 59.2% of voters cast their ballot in support of the proposal to reduce the number of seats, thus falling short of the two-thirds' majority required to force Parliament to take action. CIP

Leader Henry Puna, who regained the seat that he had lost in 2006, criticized the handling of the referendum, contending that many people, particularly those on the outer islands, had not been sufficiently apprised of the issues, with some remaining unaware even that a referendum was being held.

Henry Puna was inaugurated as Prime Minister on 1 December 2010. On the following day he announced the composition of his Cabinet, which included Tom Marsters as Deputy Prime Minister. Norman George, who had publicly questioned the competence of Puna shortly after the election, was not included. Ministerial portfolios were assigned to the cabinet ministers a few days later, with Puna taking, *inter alia*, the portfolios of justice and of energy and renewable energy, and Marsters being accorded additional responsibility for foreign affairs, immigration, transport, and mineral and natural resources. Puna identified the national economy as the main priority of the new Government. Sir Geoffrey Henry was appointed parliamentary Speaker in February 2011.

Petitions lodged by the DP challenging the election results in three constituencies were rejected by the Chief Justice in February 2011, although the DP's petition about the improper conduct of voting in a fourth constituency, Pukapuka, was upheld; however, at the resultant by-election held in Pukapuka in June, the disputed winning candidate in the November 2010 poll was again victorious, defeating the DP candidate by a comfortable margin.

Meanwhile, the Secretary of Justice, Mark Short, was suspended indefinitely in February 2011, pending an investigation into the apparent mismanagement of funds during the election; in his role as Chief Registrar of Elections, Short was alleged to have been responsible for significant overspending. Following Short's dismissal in May, former Solicitor-General Tingika Elikana was appointed as the new Secretary of Justice in October. Meanwhile, in May Prime Minister Puna announced the creation of three associate ministerial roles within the Cabinet.

Government targets announced in July 2011 envisaged 50% of the Cook Islands' energy needs being met by renewable sources (solar and wind power) by 2015, rising to 100% by 2020. Funding sources for the required renewable energy projects, which were presented as an effort to reduce carbon emissions and thereby to stem the pace of climate change, were to include China, Japan and the UN Development Programme. Further highlighting concerns about the environment and the effects of climate change, in October 2011 the Cook Islands authorities reported that potable water supplies were at a dangerously low level, following recent declarations of a state of emergency by the respective authorities in nearby Tokelau and Tuvalu owing to severe drought. However, the situation was ameliorated by heavy rainfall, the first in nearly six months, later in October.

In February 2012, as a result of the ill health of the DP Leader, Robert Wigmore, the party's Deputy Leader, Wilkie Rasmussen, was appointed leader of the opposition. Following Wigmore's death in April, a by-election was held in June to fill the vacant parliamentary seat; the poll was won by the DP candidate. Rasmussen succeeded Wigmore as Leader of the DP in April and was confirmed in this position at a party conference in August. Meanwhile, the Speaker, former Prime Minister Sir Geoffrey Henry, died in May and was replaced by the Secretary-General of the Cook Islands Red Cross, Niki Rattle. The appointment of Rattle was criticized by the opposition, which held that, although not stipulated by the Constitution, an elected member of Parliament should have been afforded the position.

The 'Offshore' Financial Sector

A reported increase in the number of Russian nationals opening accounts in the Cook Islands led to allegations in early 1999 that the islands' 'offshore' financial centre was being used extensively by criminal organizations for 'laundering' the proceeds of their activities. The claims were vigorously denied by banking officials. However, in June 2000 the naming of the islands by the Paris-based Financial Action Task Force (FATF, see p. 465) as one of a number of countries and territories that had failed to co-operate in regional efforts to combat money-laundering, along with the islands' identification by the Organisation for Economic Co-operation and Development (OECD, see p. 388) as a tax 'haven' that lacked financial transparency, led to increased international pressure on the Government to implement stricter controls over its 'offshore' financial centre. Consequently, legislation was approved in August of that year providing for the creation of the Money Laundering Authority and the introduction of new regulations aimed at reducing criminal activity in the sector. In February 2005 the Cook Islands was finally removed from the FATF list of non-co-operative countries and territories.

In February 2009 the Government introduced legislation into Parliament to abolish 'offshore' banks in the Cook Islands, arguing that the cost of regulating such organizations outweighed any financial benefits that they brought to the country. The Banking Amendment Bill, which provided for the closure of 'offshore' banks operating without the requisite domestic licence, was approved by

the islands' Parliament in August 2010. However, in April 2009 OECD had included the Cook Islands on its so-called 'grey list' of countries that, while committed to the internationally agreed tax standard, had yet to implement substantial measures to combat tax evasion. In response, the Government sought to negotiate agreements on tax information exchange with other nations, and in September 2010 the Cook Islands was removed from the 'grey list', having signed the requisite 12th such agreement, with France. In February 2010 the French Government had included the Cook Islands on a 'black list' (to be updated annually) of nations accused of a lack of transparency in tax reporting; a 50% tax was to be imposed upon transactions between France and the black-listed nations. Following the ratification of the bilateral tax information exchange agreement in the second half of 2011, the Cook Islands was not included on the updated 'black list' released in April 2012.

Meanwhile, the operating licence of the Wall Street Banking Corporation Bank (WSBC Bank) was revoked in April 2009. The WSBC Bank had links to a New Zealand financial services company, WSD Global Markets, which was being investigated by the New Zealand Serious Fraud Office in connection with suspected money-laundering activities. Further controversy ensued in the second half of 2010 when concerns were raised over the legitimacy of the transfer to WSD of assets worth an estimated $NZ20m. from former clients of WSBC Bank. However, the Office announced the closure of its investigation into WSD and related companies in April 2011, owing to a lack of evidence of any fraudulent activity; nevertheless, it noted that the decision not to file criminal charges was as a result of insufficient evidence pertaining to nine specific complaints that had been filed against the company and 'should not be interpreted as an approval or endorsement of the WSD businesses'.

Foreign Affairs

Since becoming a self-governing Territory in 1965, the Cooks Islands has developed a distinct identity in its external relations. Although not a sovereign state, by mid-2013 it had established diplomatic relations with more than 30 countries and international organizations, most latterly with the Republic of Korea in February 2013.

In August 1985 eight members of the South Pacific Forum (subsequently restyled the Pacific Islands Forum, see p. 426), including the Cook Islands, signed a treaty on Rarotonga, designating a 'nuclear-free' zone in the South Pacific. The treaty imposed a ban on the manufacture, testing, storage and use of nuclear weapons, and the dumping of nuclear waste, in the region.

In January 1986, following the rift between New Zealand and the USA in respect of the ANZUS (see p. 474) security arrangements, Sir Thomas Davis declared the Cook Islands a neutral party, because he considered that New Zealand (which has control over the Cook Islands' defence and foreign policy) was no longer in a position to defend the islands. The proclamation of neutrality meant that the Cook Islands would not enter into a military relationship with any foreign power, and, in particular, would prohibit visits by US warships. Visits by US naval vessels were allowed to resume by the Government of Geoffrey (later Sir Geoffrey) Henry. In November 2007 the Cook Islands and the USA signed agreements on maritime surveillance and anti-trafficking measures. In August 2012 Hillary Clinton became the first US Secretary of State to visit the Cook Islands when she attended the summit meeting of the Pacific Islands Forum in Rarotonga. Many observers held that the increased involvement of the USA in the Pacific region was an attempt to offset the growing diplomatic and economic influence of the People's Republic of China in that area of the world.

In October 1991 the Cook Islands signed a treaty of friendship and co-operation with France, covering economic development, trade and surveillance of the islands' exclusive economic zone (EEZ). The establishment of closer relations with France was widely regarded as an expression of the Cook Islands Government's dissatisfaction with existing arrangements with New Zealand. However, relations deteriorated when the French Government resumed its programme of nuclear weapons testing at Mururoa Atoll, French Polynesia, in September 1995. Henry was fiercely critical of the decision and dispatched a *vaka* (traditional voyaging canoe) with a crew of Cook Islands' traditional warriors to protest near the test site. The tests were concluded in January 1996. Full diplomatic relations with France were established in early 2000.

Meanwhile, the islands established diplomatic relations at ambassadorial level with the People's Republic of China in July 1997. In November 1998 Henry made an official visit to China, during which the two countries signed a bilateral trade agreement and each conferred the status of 'most favoured nation' on the other. Henry stated that the move constituted a further attempt by his Government to reduce the islands' dependence on New Zealand. In February 2008 the Government accepted a loan of US $10.2m. from China, the bulk of which was to fund preparations for the 2009 South Pacific Mini Games, which were to be hosted by the Cook Islands in September of that year; the decision resulted in threats of legal action from the local Chamber of Commerce. In March 2009 China agreed to provide a further loan of nearly US $28m., of which US $11m. was to be allocated to the construction of a sports stadium and the remainder was to finance infrastructure projects. The announcement prompted further demands for a public inquiry from the opposition, which claimed that the Cook Islands could not afford to repay such a large loan. The Deputy Prime Minister, Sir Terepai Maoate, who was also responsible for the finance portfolio, was alleged to have stated that repayments would be made with New Zealand aid; however, a New Zealand government official was reported as stating that such requests for aid were likely to be rejected. In March 2010 Minister of Finance Wilkie Rasmussen stated that the Government was extremely reluctant to accept a $NZ37.5m. Chinese loan for projects to upgrade the road and water systems in Rarotonga owing to the islands' already high external debt levels. In January 2011 it was announced that China had signed an agreement providing for a $NZ1.9m. grant to the islands, to be spent according to the Cook Islands Government's wishes. During a visit to China by Teina Bishop, the Minister of Marine Resources, in November, a fishing agreement was signed under the terms of which Chinese vessels would be allowed to conduct exploratory fishing for tuna and swordfish in the Cook Islands' EEZ for a period of three years. The Cook Islands was expected to earn a total of $NZ2.4m. from the agreement. The Cook Islands and China also signed an agreement providing for Chinese assistance, in the form of funding and labour, for the pearl-farming industry on the islands. In August 2012 a major infrastructure project to improve Rarotonga's water mains system was announced; of the project's total estimated cost of around $NZ60m., the majority was to be funded by a $NZ15m. grant from New Zealand and a $NZ32m. loan from China. The joint undertaking was particularly notable for the fact that it represented the first time that China had entered into partnership with a developed country to deliver an aid and development project.

During a visit to the islands in June 2001, Helen Clark, the New Zealand Prime Minister, stated that if the Cook Islands desired complete independence, and membership of international organizations, the process would not be obstructed by New Zealand. However, Cook Islanders would then be obliged to renounce their New Zealand citizenship. In December 2010 the New Zealand Minister of Foreign Affairs, Murray McCully, made an official four-day visit to the Cook Islands, where he met with incoming Prime Minister Henry Puna and his new Cabinet. During his stay, McCully was reported to have discussed a wide range of issues with the Puna Government, including New Zealand's programme of development assistance to the islands, with education, health care and tourism identified as the main priorities for assistance. Further bilateral talks were held in the Cook Islands in early and mid-2011, during which New Zealand budgetary support for the islands and infrastructure co-operation were among the issues discussed. In August 2012 New Zealand Prime Minister John Key and McCully both attended the Pacific Islands Forum summit in Rarotonga.

In September 2008 the Cook Islands became a member of the International Maritime Organization (IMO) after securing the approval of two-thirds of the organization's members, rendering it eligible for IMO funding and assistance. In April 2009 the Cook Islands Government submitted a claim, via the UN Secretary-General, to the Commission on the Limits of the Continental Shelf to extend its seabed boundaries by over 400,000 sq km. The application, the first such claim to be lodged by a Pacific island nation, was motivated by the Government's desire to gain access to potential reserves of petroleum, gas and manganese. A sub-commission was established, in mid-2011, to examine the application; as of early 2013, it had yet to issue its recommendations.

In November 2011 the Cook Islands was one of eight Pacific states and territories that jointly established the Polynesian Leaders Group (see p. 478), which was widely viewed as being intended to provide a counterweight to the Melanesian Spearhead Group. The first formal meeting of the Group, which pledged to enhance co-operation among its members across a wide range of fields, including trade and investment, education, climate change and health, was held in Rarotonga, on the sidelines of the Pacific Islands Forum summit, in August 2012. During the summit, Prime Minister Henry Puna announced the establishment of a shark sanctuary in the EEZ around the Cook Islands; the sanctuary, which was officially inaugurated in December, was contiguous with a sanctuary set up by French Polynesia in the same month.

CONSTITUTION AND GOVERNMENT

Under the Constitution of 1965, the Cook Islands is an internally self-governing state in free association with New Zealand, which is responsible for the Cook Islands' external affairs and defence (although the Territory has progressively assumed control over much of its foreign policy). Executive authority is vested in the British monarch, who is head of state, and is exercised through her official representative; a representative of the New Zealand Government (redesignated High Commissioner in 1994) resides on Rarotonga. Executive government is carried out by the Cabinet, consisting of the Prime Minister and between five and seven other ministers. The Cabinet is collectively responsible to the Parliament, which is formed of 24 members (decreased from 25 in 2004, following the abolition of the seat for a member chosen by non-resident voters) who are elected by universal adult suffrage every four years (reduced from five years by a referendum in 2004). The House of Ariki, which comprises up to 15 members who are hereditary chiefs, can advise the Government, but has no legislative powers. The Koutu Nui is a similar body, comprising sub-chiefs. Each of the main islands, except Rarotonga, has an elected island council, and a government representative who is appointed by the Prime Minister.

REGIONAL AND INTERNATIONAL CO-OPERATION

The Cook Islands has membership of the Pacific Community (see p. 422) and the Pacific Islands Forum (see p. 426) and is an associate member of the UN Economic and Social Commission for Asia and the Pacific (ESCAP, see p. 31). In 1999 the Cook Islands was granted observer status at the Lomé Conventions with the European Union (subsequently superseded by the Cotonou Agreement, see p. 334). In November 2011 the Cook Islands was one of eight founding members of the Polynesian Leaders Group (see p. 478).

ECONOMIC AFFAIRS

In 2010, according to provisional official figures, the Cook Islands' gross domestic product (GDP), measured at current prices, totalled $NZ334.8m., and GDP per head was $NZ14,188. During 2002–11, it was estimated, the population increased at an average annual rate of 3.7%, while GDP per head increased, in real terms, by an average of 1.2% per year during 2001–10. Overall GDP increased, in real terms, at an estimated average annual rate of 0.7% in 2001–10, declining by 3.6% in 2009, but rising by a provisional 0.2% in 2010. According to the Asian Development Bank (ADB), GDP grew by 1.0% in the year ending 30 June 2011 and by 3.3% in 2011/12.

According to provisional official figures, agriculture (including fishing) contributed 4.9% of GDP in 2010. The sector engaged 4.3% of the employed labour force in 2011, according to that year's census. Cash crops include coconuts and tropical fruits such as mangoes, pineapples, bananas and papayas. Cassava, sweet potatoes and vegetables are cultivated as food crops. Pigs and poultry are the main livestock kept. The sale of fishing licences to foreign fleets provides an important source of income. Revenue from the export of fresh and chilled fish reached an estimated $NZ2.4m. in 2011, providing 60.4% of export earnings. Pearl oyster farming is also an important industry. Receipts from pearl exports totalled an estimated $NZ0.4m. (equivalent to 9.3% of total export earnings) in 2011. The real GDP of the agricultural sector (including pearl farming) decreased by an average of 1.6% per year during 2001–10. The sector's GDP declined by 5.6% in 2009, but increased by a provisional 14.4% in 2010.

Industry (comprising mining and quarrying, manufacturing, construction and utilities) provided a provisional 9.1% of GDP in 2010. The sector engaged 11.7% of the employed labour force in 2011. Industrial GDP increased, in real terms, by an average of 1.8% per year during 2001–10; sectoral GDP declined by a provisional 2.7% in 2010.

The manufacturing sector engaged 3.4% of the employed labour force in 2011. The manufacturing and mining sectors together accounted for a provisional 3.4% of GDP in 2010. The real GDP of manufacturing and mining increased by an average of 0.4% per year during 2001–10. The combined GDP of the two sub-sectors declined by a provisional 8.4% in 2010.

Construction contributed a provisional 3.3% of GDP in 2010; the sector engaged 5.9% of the employed labour force in 2011. The GDP of the construction sector increased at an average annual rate of 2.9% during 2001–10; the sector's GDP declined by 10.6% in 2009, but increased by a provisional 0.5% in 2010.

The islands depend on imports for their energy requirements. Mineral fuels and lubricants accounted for 14.7% of total import costs in 2011. In July 2011 the Government announced targets of 50% of the Cook Islands' energy needs being met by renewable sources (solar and wind power) by 2015, and 100% by 2020.

Service industries contributed a provisional 86.0% of GDP in 2010. The sector engaged 84.0% of the employed labour force in 2011. The GDP of the services sector increased, in real terms, at an average annual rate of 1.1% in 2001–10; services GDP decreased by a provisional 0.4% in 2010. Tourism expanded considerably from the late 1980s, and generated revenue of an estimated US $110m. in 2010. Visitor arrivals rose from 104,265 in 2010 to a provisional 112,643 in 2011. The restaurants and hotels sector contributed a provisional 14.0% of GDP in 2010. 'Offshore' banking, introduced to the islands in 1982, expanded rapidly, with more than 2,000 international companies registered by 1987. In August 2010, however, legislation to abolish 'offshore' banks operating without a domestic licence was approved by Parliament; the banks concerned were given 12 months in which to cease their operations. The financial and business services sector provided a provisional 12.6% of GDP in 2010, and engaged 5.3% of the employed labour force (including persons occupied in the real estate sector) in 2011. Significant revenue is provided by remittances from emigrants (who outnumber the residents of the islands by more than three-fold).

In 2011 the cost of imports amounted to $NZ138.4m. (according to official estimates), while export revenue totalled some $NZ4.0m., resulting in a trade deficit of $NZ134.4m. The principal exports in 2011 were fresh and chilled fish, and pearls. The principal imports in that year were food and live animals, machinery and transport equipment, basic manufactures, mineral fuels and lubricants, and miscellaneous manufactured articles. The principal source of imports in 2011 was New Zealand (which supplied 77.1% of the total). Fiji and Australia were also significant sources of imports. Japan (which purchased 58.8%) was the principal market for exports in that year.

In the financial year ending June 2011 an overall budgetary surplus (including grants) of $NZ15.6m. was recorded. Development assistance is provided mainly by New Zealand and Australia. In 2004 New Zealand and Australia agreed to combine their programmes of aid to the Cook Islands in order to improve their effectiveness. Between 2009/10 and 2011/12 aid to the Cook Islands from New Zealand and Australia was expected to total $NZ51m. The islands were also to receive a total of €3.3m. between 2008 and 2013 (to be spent on improvements to the environment, water supply and sanitation, including waste disposal) under the Cotonou Agreement with the European Union. It was estimated by the ADB that at the end of 2011 the islands' external debt stood at US $85m. and that the cost of debt-servicing in that year was equivalent to 97.2% of the value of exports of goods and services. The annual rate of inflation in Rarotonga averaged 3.7% in 2006–11; consumer prices decreased by 0.3% in 2010, but rose by 2.2% in 2011. According to the census of 2011, the unemployment rate was 8.2% of the total labour force.

The National Sustainable Development Plan and the 20-year Infrastructure Master Plan, which were announced in 2007, envisaged substantial capital expenditure. In October 2009, following the deterioration in global economic conditions, an economic recovery programme, which included support for vulnerable families and funding for infrastructural projects, was implemented. Upon taking office in late 2010, Prime Minister Henry Puna declared the islands' economy to be his administration's main priority. The economy has become heavily dependent on tourism, despite concerns that the Cook Islands might be unable to sustain such rapid development in the longer term. The islands' Government continued to subsidize Air New Zealand flights on the route between Los Angeles, USA, and Rarotonga, and the capacity of the tourism sector was further enhanced by the inauguration of weekly flights from the Australian city of Sydney in July 2011; visitor arrivals from Australia were projected to increase by some 44% in the year ending 30 June 2012. Visitor arrivals rose by 8.0% in 2011. In late 2011 the Government announced a target of 150,000 arrivals per year within three to five years. Fisheries and pearls typically account for around three-quarters of total export earnings. The fisheries sector displayed strong growth in 2010–11, but the value of pearl exports continued to decline, although it was hoped that the downward trend might be stemmed by the implementation of Chinese-funded development programmes that aimed to double pearl output by 2015. Inflationary pressures re-emerged in 2011, mainly owing to the higher costs of food, clothing, energy and transport; according to the ADB, consumer prices rose by an annual average of 2.8% in 2011/12 (although they fell again during the latter half of calendar year 2012 as international commodity prices began to decline). The rate of GDP growth accelerated to 3.3% in 2011/12, fuelled by an increase in public spending on infrastructure projects and by the continuing strength of the tourism sector. The cost of infrastructure improvements was partly the reason for a budgetary deficit of 2.2% of GDP being recorded in 2011/12, although it was well below the 3% ceiling set by the Government. The ADB forecast that GDP growth would slow to around 3.0% in 2012/13 as project expenditure diminished.

PUBLIC HOLIDAYS

2014: 1 January (New Year's Day), 2 January (Second day of New Year), 18 April (Good Friday), 21 April (Easter Monday), 25 April (ANZAC Day, anniversary of 1915 landing at Gallipoli), 2 June (Queen's Official Birthday), 7 July (for Ra o te Ui Ariki—Anniversary of the Establishment of the House of Ariki), 4 August (Constitution Day), 27 October (for Cook Islands Gospel Day), 25–26 December (Christmas).

Statistical Survey

Sources (unless otherwise stated): Cook Islands Statistics Office, Ministry of Finance and Economic Management, POB 41, Rarotonga; tel. 29511; fax 21511; e-mail info@stats.gov.ck; internet www

.stats.gov.ck; Prime Minister's Department, Government of the Cook Islands, Avarua, Rarotonga; tel. 29300; fax 22856.

AREA AND POPULATION

Area: 236.7 sq km (91.4 sq miles).

Population: 19,342 at census of 1 December 2006; 17,794 (males 8,815, females 8,979) at census of 1 December 2011. *By Island* (2011 census): Rarotonga (including the capital, Avarua) 13,095; Aitutaki 2,038; Atiu 480; Mangaia 572; Manihiki 239; Mauke 307; Mitiaro 189; Nassau 73; Palmerston (Avarua) 60; Penrhyn (Tongareva) 213; Pukapuka 451; Rakahanga 77; Total 17,794.

Density (at 2011 census): 75.2 per sq km.

Population by Age and Sex (at 2011 census): *0–14:* 4,627 (males 2,368, females 2,259); *15–64:* 11,537 (males 5,645, females 5,892); *65 and over:* 1,630 (males 802, females 828); *Total* 17,794 (males 8,815, females 8,979).

Principal Town (UN population estimate at mid-2003, incl. suburbs): Rarotonga (capital) 15,007. Source: UN, *World Urbanization Prospects: The 2011 Revision.*

Births, Marriages and Deaths (2011, provisional): Registered live births 262 (birth rate 14.7 per 1,000); Registered marriages 921 (marriage rate 51.8 per 1,000); Registered deaths 77 (death rate 4.3 per 1,000).

Life Expectancy (years at birth, WHO estimates): 76 (males 72; females 80) in 2009. Source: WHO, *World Health Statistics.*

Economically Active Population (resident population aged 15 years and over, 2011 census): Agriculture, hunting, forestry and fishing 297; Mining and quarrying 70; Manufacturing 270; Electricity, gas and water 66; Construction 409; Trade, restaurants and hotels 2,539; Transport, storage and communications 524; Financing, insurance, real estate and business services 368; Community, social and personal services 2,395; *Total employed* 6,938 (males 3,708, females 3,230); Unemployed 616 (males 331, females 285); *Total labour force* 7,554 (males 4,039, females 3,515). *Mid-2013* (estimates): Agriculture, etc. 2,000; Total labour force 8,000. Source: FAO.

HEALTH AND WELFARE

Key Indicators

Total Fertility Rate (children per woman, 2010): 2.4.

Under-5 Mortality Rate (per 1,000 live births, 2010): 9.

Physicians (per 1,000 head, 2004): 1.2.

Hospital Beds (per 1,000 head, 2005): 6.3.

Health Expenditure (2009): US $ per head (PPP): 382.

Health Expenditure (2009): % of GDP: 4.3.

Health Expenditure (2009): public (% of total): 93.8.

Access to Water (% of persons, 2006): 95.

For sources and definitions, see explanatory note on p. vi.

AGRICULTURE, ETC.

Principal Crops (metric tons, 2011, FAO estimates): Cassava 989; Sweet potatoes 615; Coconuts 1,900; Tomatoes 167; Watermelons 55; Guavas, mangosteens and mangoes 189; Papayas 569; Bananas 57; Oranges 62. *Aggregate Production* (metric tons, may include official, semi-official or estimated data): Roots and tubers 3,143; Vegetables (incl. melons) 1,697; Fruits (excl. melons) 1,167.

Livestock (head, year ending September 2011, FAO estimates): Cattle 130; Pigs 32,200; Goats 1,010; Poultry 20,000; Horses 305.

Livestock Products (metric tons, 2011, FAO estimates): Hen eggs 36; Pig meat 555; Chicken meat 20.

Forestry ('000 cu m, 2011, FAO estimate): Roundwood removals (excl. bark) 5.

Fishing (metric tons, live weight, 2010): Albacore 2,523; Yellowfin tuna 361; Bigeye tuna 211; Total catch (incl. others) 10,021 (FAO estimate).

Source: FAO.

INDUSTRY

Electric Energy (production, million kWh): 32.7 in 2009; 33.7 in 2010; 33.6 in 2011.

FINANCE

Currency and Exchange Rates: New Zealand currency is legal tender. In mid-1995 it was announced that the Cook Islands dollar (formerly the local currency, at par with the New Zealand dollar)

was to be withdrawn from circulation. New Zealand currency: 100 cents = 1 New Zealand dollar ($NZ); for details of exchange rates, see Tokelau.

Budget ($NZ '000, year ending 30 June 2011): *Revenue:* Total revenue 102,687 (Tax 84,674, Other current 8,725, Capital 9,288). (Note: Revenue excludes grants of 34,560). *Expenditure:* Total expenditure 121,644 (Current 96,723, Capital 24,921).

Overseas Aid ($NZ '000): Official development assistance from New Zealand (incl. $A1.5m. annual contributions from Australia, but administered by New Zealand) 51,000 for 2009/10–2011/12. Source: Ministry of Foreign Affairs and Trade, Wellington.

Cost of Living (Consumer Price Index for Rarotonga, average of quarterly figures; base: December 2006 = 100): All items 117.7 in 2009; 117.4 in 2010; 120.0 in 2011.

Gross Domestic Product ($NZ '000 at constant 2006 prices): 278,937 in 2008; 268,977 in 2009; 269,554 in 2010 (provisional).

Gross Domestic Product by Economic Activity ($NZ '000 in current prices, 2010, provisional): Agriculture and fishing 17,114; Mining, quarrying and manufacturing 11,929; Electricity, gas and water 8,429; Construction 11,771; Wholesale and retail trade 80,795; Restaurants and hotels 49,419; Transport and communications 44,241; Finance and business services 44,209; Education and health services 18,510; Public administration 34,592; Other community, social and personal services 8,275; Ownership of dwellings 22,916; *Sub-total* 352,199; *Less* Imputed bank service charge 17,374; *GDP in purchasers' values* 334,825.

EXTERNAL TRADE

Principal Commodities ($NZ '000, 2011): *Imports c.i.f.:* Food and live animals 32,974; Mineral fuels, lubricants, etc. 20,342; Chemicals 8,489; Basic manufactures 23,451; Machinery and transport equipment 27,703; Miscellaneous manufactured articles 15,267; Total (incl. others) 138,379. *Exports f.o.b.:* Fish, fresh or chilled 2,390; Pearls 369; Total (incl. others) 3,956.

Principal Trading Partners ($NZ '000, 2011): *Imports:* Australia 7,336; Fiji 13,826; Japan 985; New Zealand 106,701; USA 2,912; Total (incl. others) 138,379. *Exports:* Australia 61; Japan 2,325; New Zealand 172; USA 115; Total (incl. others) 3,956.

TRANSPORT

Road Traffic (registered vehicles, April 1983): 6,555. *New Motor Vehicles Registered* (Rarotonga, 2011): Motorcycles 456; Cars and jeeps 145; Vans and pick-ups 70; Trucks and buses 17; Others 18; *Total* 706.

Shipping: *Flag Registered Fleet* (at 31 December 2012): 150 vessels, displacement 441,008 grt (Source: Lloyd's List Intelligence—www.lloydslistintelligence.com); *International Sea-borne Freight Traffic* ('000 metric tons, estimates): Goods unloaded 32.6 (2001); Goods loaded 9; Goods unloaded 32 (1990). Source: UN, *Monthly Bulletin of Statistics.*

Civil Aviation (2011): *Aircraft Movements:* 729 departures. *Freight Traffic* (metric tons): Goods loaded 67; Goods unloaded 1,326.

TOURISM

Foreign Tourist Arrivals: 101,229 in 2009; 104,265 in 2010; 112,643 in 2011.

Tourist Arrivals by Place of Residence (2011, provisional): Australia 18,466; Canada 2,030; Europe 10,261; New Zealand 74,857; USA 4,436; Total (incl. others) 112,643.

Tourism Revenue (US $ million, excl. passenger transport): 103 in 2009; 110 in 2010. Source: World Tourism Organization.

COMMUNICATIONS MEDIA

Telephones (main lines, 2010): 7,200 in use.

Mobile Cellular Telephones (2010): 7,800 subscribers.

Internet Subscribers (2009): 1,900.

Broadband Subscribers (2010): 1,700.

Source: International Telecommunication Union.

EDUCATION

Pre-primary (2011 unless otherwise indicated): 26 schools (1998); 33 teachers; 517 pupils.

Primary (2011 unless otherwise indicated): 28 schools (1998); 117 teachers; 1,861 pupils.

Secondary* (2011 unless otherwise indicated): 23 schools (1998); 130 teachers; 1,793 pupils.

Higher (1980): 41 teachers; 360 pupils†.

* Includes high school education.

† Source: UNESCO, *Statistical Yearbook.*

Pupil-teacher Ratio (primary education, UNESCO estimate): 15.9 in 2010/11. Source: UNESCO Institute for Statistics.

Directory

The Government

Queen's Representative: Sir FREDERICK GOODWIN.

New Zealand High Commissioner: JOHN CARTER.

CABINET
(May 2013)

The Government is formed by the Cook Islands Party.

Prime Minister and Minister for the Public Service Commission, Office of the Head of State, Attorney-General, Parliamentary Services, Police, Minister of Justice, Ombudsman, National Environment Service, Energy and Renewable Energy, and Emergency Management: HENRY PUNA.

Deputy Prime Minister and Minister of Foreign Affairs, Immigration, Transport, and Mineral and Natural Resources: TOM MARSTERS.

Minister of Finance and Economic Management, Business Trade and Investment Board, Cook Islands Investment Corporation, Internal Affairs, Commerce Commission, Financial Intelligence Unit, Telecommunication, Financial Services Development Authority, Financial Supervisory Commission, National Superannuation, and Public Expenditure and Review Committee Audit (PERCA): MARK BROWN.

Minister of Infrastructure and Planning, Cultural Development and House of Ariki: TEARIKI HEATHER.

Minister of Health and Agriculture: NANDI GLASSIE.

Minister of Education, Marine Resources, Tourism, and National Human Resource Development: TEINA BISHOP.

GOVERNMENT OFFICES

Office of the Queen's Representative: Titikaveka, POB 134, Rarotonga; tel. and fax 29311; fax 28311; e-mail queenrep@oyster.net.ck.

Office of the Prime Minister: Government of the Cook Islands, Private Bag, Avarua, Rarotonga; tel. 25494; fax 20856; e-mail coso@pmoffice.gov.ck; internet www.pmoffice.gov.ck.

Office of the Public Service Commissioner: POB 24, Rarotonga; tel. 29421; fax 21321; e-mail thomas@psc.gov.ck; internet www.psc.gov.ck.

New Zealand High Commission: Philatelic Bureau Bldg, 1st Floor, Takuvaine Rd, Avarua, POB 21, Rarotonga; tel. 22201; fax 21241; e-mail nzhcraro@oyster.net.ck.

Ministries

Ministry of Agriculture: POB 96, Rarotonga; tel. 28711; fax 21881; e-mail mat.purea@agriculture.gov.ck; internet www.agriculture.gov.ck.

Ministry of Cultural Development: POB 8, Rarotonga; tel. 20725; fax 23725; e-mail parts@culture.gov.ck; internet www.mocd.gov.ck.

Ministry of Education: POB 97, Rarotonga; tel. 29357; fax 28357; e-mail cieducat@oyster.net.ck; internet www.education.gov.ck.

Ministry of Energy: POB 72, Rarotonga; tel. 24484; fax 24483; e-mail punanga@energy.gov.ck.

Ministry of Finance and Economic Management: POB 120, Rarotonga; tel. 22878; fax 23877; e-mail cifinsec@mfem.gov.ck; internet www.mfem.gov.ck.

Ministry of Foreign Affairs and Immigration: POB 105, Rarotonga; tel. 29347; fax 21247; e-mail secfa@mfai.gov.ck.

Ministry of Health: POB 109, Rarotonga; tel. 29664; fax 22670; e-mail eiro@health.gov.ck; internet www.health.gov.ck.

Ministry of Infrastructure and Planning: POB 102, Rarotonga; tel. 20321; fax 21134; e-mail dnuma@moip.gov.ck; internet www.moip.gov.ck.

Ministry of Internal Affairs: POB 98, Rarotonga; tel. 29370; fax 23608; e-mail secintaff@intaff.gov.ck.

Ministry of Justice: POB 111, Rarotonga; tel. 29410; fax 29610; e-mail tingika@justice.gov.ck.

Ministry of Marine Resources: POB 85, Rarotonga; tel. 28721; fax 29721; e-mail rara@mmr.gov.ck.

Ministry of Transport: POB 61, Rarotonga; tel. 28810; fax 28816; e-mail ned@transport.gov.ck.

National Environment Service: POB 371, Rarotonga; tel. 21256; fax 22256; e-mail resources@environment.org.ck; internet www .environment.org.ck.

Advisory Chambers

House of Ariki: POB 13, Rarotonga; tel. 26500; fax 21260; Pres. TRAVEL TOU ARIKI.

Koutu Nui: POB 13, Rarotonga; tel. 29317; fax 21260; e-mail nvaloa@parliament.gov.ck; Pres. TURI MATAIAPO MARIA HENDERSON.

Legislature

PARLIAMENT

Parliamentary Service

POB 13, Rarotonga; tel. 26500; fax 21260; e-mail nvaloa@parliament .gov.ck.

Speaker: NIKI RATTLE.

General Election, 17 November 2010

Party	Seats
Cook Islands Party (CIP)	16
Democratic Party (DP)	8
Total	**24**

Political Organizations

Cook Islands Labour Party: Rarotonga; f. 1988; anti-nuclear; Leader RENA ARIKI JONASSEN.

Cook Islands Party (CIP): Rarotonga; f. 1965; Pres. RAU NGA; Leader HENRY PUNA.

Democratic Party (DP): POB 73, Rarotonga; tel. 21224; e-mail demo1@oyster.net.ck; f. 1972; Pres. SEAN WILLIS; Leader WILKIE RASMUSSEN.

Party Tumu: c/o Parliament, POB 13, Rarotonga; f. 2010; est. as Cook Islands Party Tumu; obliged to change name as above following court ruling; Leader ALBERT NICHOLAS.

Te Kura O Te Au: Rarotonga; f. 2010; based upon People's Movement; advocates reform in accordance with spiritual and cultural values; opposed to Sunday flights to Aitutaki; Leader TIM TEPAKI.

Judicial System

The judiciary comprises the Privy Council, the Court of Appeal and the High Court. The High Court exercises jurisdiction in respect of civil, criminal and land titles cases on all the islands, except for Mangaia, Pukapuka and Mitiaro, where disputes over land titles are settled according to custom. The Court of Appeal hears appeals against decisions of the High Court. The Privy Council, sitting in the United Kingdom, is the final appellate tribunal for the country in civil, criminal and land matters.

High Court: Avarua, Rarotonga; e-mail offices@justice.gov.ck; Chief Justice TOM WESTON.

Attorney-General: HENRY PUNA.

Solicitor-General: TINGIKA ELIKANA.

President of the Court of Appeal: Sir IAN BARKER.

Religion

CHRISTIANITY

The principal denomination is the Cook Islands (Congregational) Christian Church, to which the majority of islanders belong.

Religious Advisory Council of the Cook Islands: POB 763, Rarotonga; tel. 23778; fax 21767; e-mail tpere@oyster.net.ck; f. 1972; six mem. churches; Pres. Pastor TUTAI PERE.

The Roman Catholic Church

The Cook Islands form the diocese of Rarotonga, suffragan to the archdiocese of Suva (Fiji). At 31 December 2007 the diocese contained an estimated 2,471 adherents. The Bishop participates in the Catholic Bishops' Conference of the Pacific, based in Suva.

Bishop of Rarotonga: Rev. PAUL DONOGHUE, Catholic Diocese, Avarua, POB 147, Rarotonga; tel. 20817; fax 29817; e-mail sbish@ oyster.net.ck.

The Anglican Communion

The Cook Islands are within the diocese of Polynesia, part of the Church of the Province of New Zealand. The Bishop of Polynesia is resident in Fiji.

Protestant Churches

Cook Islands Christian Church: Takamoa, POB 93, Rarotonga; tel. 26452; 11,193 mems (1986); Pres. Rev. TANGIMETUA TANGATA-TUTA; Gen. Sec. WILLIE JOHN.

Seventh-day Adventists: POB 31, Rarotonga; tel. 22851; fax 22852; e-mail umakatu@oyster.net.ck; 732 mems (1998); Pres. UMA KATU.

Other churches active in the islands include the Assembly of God, the Church of Latter-day Saints (Mormons), the Apostolic Church, the Jehovah's Witnesses and the Baptist Church.

BAHÁ'Í FAITH

Administrative Committee of the Bahá'ís of Cook Islands: POB 1, Rarotonga; tel. 20658; e-mail nsacooks@bahai.org.ck; mems resident in 6 localities; Sec. JANE LAMB.

The Press

Cook Islands Herald: Tutakimoa, POB 126, Rarotonga; e-mail bestread@ciherald.co.ck; internet www.ciherald.co.ck; weekly; Publr GEORGE PITT; Editor CHARLES PITT.

Cook Islands News: POB 15, Rarotonga; tel. 22999; fax 25303; e-mail editor@cookislandsnews.com; internet www.cinews.co.ck; f. 1954; est. by Govt; transferred to private ownership in 1989; 6 a week; mainly English; Editor JOHN WOODS; circ. 2,100.

Cook Islands Star: POB 798, Rarotonga; tel. 29965; e-mail jason@ oyster.net.ck; fortnightly; Chief Reporter JASON BROWN.

Broadcasting and Communications

TELECOMMUNICATIONS

Telecom Cook Islands Ltd: Avarua, POB 106, Rarotonga; tel. 29680; fax 26174; e-mail sales@telecom.co.ck; internet www.telecom .co.ck; CEO JULES MAHER.

BROADCASTING

Radio

Cook Islands Broadcasting Corpn (CIBC): Avarua, POB 126, Rarotonga; tel. 29460; fax 21907; f. 1989; est. to operate new TV service, and radio service of former Broadcasting and Newspaper Corpn; state-owned; Gen. Man. EMILE KAIRUA.

Radio Cook Islands: tel. 20100; e-mail tunein@radio.co.ck; internet www.radio.co.ck; broadcasts in English and Maori 18 hours daily.

KC Radio: Avarua, POB 521, Rarotonga; tel. 23203; f. 1979; est. as Radio Ikurangi; commercial; operates station ZK1ZD; broadcasts 18 hours daily on FM; Man. Dir and Gen. Man. DAVID SCHMIDT.

Television

Cook Islands Broadcasting Corpn (CIBC): see Radio.

Cook Islands TV (CITV): Parekura, 00682 Avarua, Rarotonga; tel. 29461; fax 21907; e-mail newsteam@citv.co.ck; f. 1989; operated by Elijah Communications; broadcasts nightly, in English and Maori; 10 hours of local programmes per week; remainder provided by Television New Zealand.

Finance

(cap. = capital; dep. = deposits; m. = million; brs = branches)

Financial Supervisory Commission: Avarua, POB 594, Rarotonga; tel. 20798; fax 29183; e-mail Inquire@fsc.gov.ck; internet www.fsc.gov.ck; f. 1981; est. as Cook Islands Monetary Bd; present name adopted 2003; supervises banks and insurance cos; licenses trustee cos; registers international cos, limited liability cos, trusts, financial institutions, etc.; Commr JOHN HOBBS; Chair. RAYMOND NEWNHAM.

Trustee Companies Association (TCA): Rarotonga; controlling body for the 'offshore' financial sector; Sec. LOU COLVEY.

BANKING

Legislation was adopted in 1981 to facilitate the establishment of 'offshore' banking operations.

Development Bank

Bank of the Cook Islands (BCI): Avarua, POB 113, Rarotonga; tel. 29341; fax 29343; e-mail cash@bci.co.ck; internet www.bci.co.ck; f. 2003; est. by merger of Cook Islands Devt Bank and Cook Islands Savings Bank; 100% state-owned; finances devt projects in all areas of the economy and helps islanders to establish small businesses and industries by providing loans and management advisory assistance; Man. Dir TERUATU RINGI; 10 brs throughout the Cook Islands.

Commercial Banks

ANZ Cook Islands: ANZ House, Maire Nui Dr., Avarua, POB 907, Rarotonga; tel. 21750; fax 21760; e-mail murphyp@anz.co.uk; internet www.anz.com/cookislands; Gen. Man. DAVID DENNIS.

Capital Security Bank Ltd: ANZ House, Avarua, POB 906, Rarotonga; tel. 22505; fax 22506; e-mail info@csb.co.ck; internet www.capitalsecuritybank.com; cap. US $1.2m., dep. US $149m. (Dec. 2010); Chair. BRIAN MASON.

Westpac Banking Corpn (Australia): Main Rd, Avarua, POB 42, Rarotonga; tel. 22014; fax 20802; e-mail westpaccookislands@westpac.com.au; internet www.westpac.co.ck; Man. CARMEL BUTLER.

INSURANCE

Cook Islands Insurance: POB 44, Rarotonga.

International General Insurance (Cook Islands) Ltd: Avarua, POB 11, Rarotonga; tel. 20514; fax 20667; e-mail info@internationalgeneral.com; internet www.internationalgeneral.com; f. 1982.

Trade and Industry

GOVERNMENT AGENCIES

Business Trade Investment Board: Private Bag, Avarua, Rarotonga; tel. 24296; fax 24298; e-mail info@btib.gov.ck; internet www.btib.gov.ck; f. 1996; est. as replacement for Devt Investment Council; present name adopted 2009, following a merger between the Development Investment Board (DIB) and Small Business Enterprise Centre (SBEC); promotes, monitors and regulates foreign investment, promotes international trade, advises the private sector and Govt, and provides training in business skills; Chair. GRANT PRIEST; CEO TERRY RANGI.

Cook Islands Investment Corporation: Rarotonga; tel. 29391; fax 29381; e-mail ciic@oyster.net.ck; f. 1998; manages govt assets and shareholding interests; Chair. JULIAN DASHWOOD; CEO LLOYD MILES (acting).

Cook Islands Public Service Commission: POB 24, Rarotonga; tel. 29421; fax 21321; e-mail epati@psc.gov.ck; internet www.psc.gov.ck; Commr NAVY EPATI; CEO PRISCILLA MARUARIKI.

Cook Islands Trading Corporation (CITC): Private Bag 1, Avarua, Rarotonga; tel. 22000; fax 20857; e-mail directors@citc.co.ck; internet kiaorana.net/citc; f. 1891; principal importer, distributor, wholesaler and retailer of products in the Cook Islands; Exec. Chair. TREVOR CLARKE; Gen. Man. GAYE WHITTA.

CHAMBER OF COMMERCE

Chamber of Commerce: POB 242, Rarotonga; tel. 20925; e-mail chamber@commerce.co.ck; internet www.cookislandschamber.org; f. 1956; represents the private sector in the Cook Islands; Pres. TERESA MANARANGI-TROTT.

INDUSTRIAL AND TRADE ASSOCIATION

Pearl Guild of the Cook Islands: POB 257, Rarotonga; tel. 21902; fax 21903; e-mail trevon@oyster.net.ck; f. 1994; monitors standards of quality within the pearl industry and develops marketing strategies; Pres. TREVON BERGMAN.

UTILITIES

Electricity

Te Aponga Uira O Tumutevarovaro (TAUOT) (Rarotonga Electricity Authority): POB 112, Rarotonga; tel. 20054; fax 21944; e-mail atimoti@electricity.co.ck; internet www.teaponga.com; Chair. APII TIMOTI.

Water

Water Supply Department: Arorangi, POB 102, Rarotonga; tel. 20034; fax 21134.

TRADE UNIONS

Airport Workers' Association: Rarotonga Int. Airport, POB 90, Rarotonga; tel. 25890; fax 21890; e-mail jessie@airport.gov.ck; f. 1985; Pres. (vacant).

Cook Islands Industrial Union of Waterside Workers: Avarua, Rarotonga.

Cook Islands Workers' Association (CIWA): Avarua, POB 403, Rarotonga; tel. 24422; fax 24423; e-mail ciwa@oyster.net.ck; largest union in the Cook Islands; Pres. ANTHONY TURUA; Gen. Sec. TUAINE MAUNGA; 700 mems (2006).

Transport

ROADS

On Rarotonga a 33-km sealed road encircles the island's coastline. A partly sealed inland road, parallel to the coastal road and known as the Ara Metua, is also suitable for vehicles. In February 2006 it was announced that construction of a cyclone-proof road, which would encompass the flood-prone area west of Rarotonga airport, was to be initiated with aid from the People's Republic of China. Roads on the other islands are mainly unsealed.

SHIPPING

The main ports are on Rarotonga (Avatiu), Penrhyn, Mangaia and Aitutaki. The Cook Islands National Line operates a three-weekly cargo service between the Cook Islands, Tonga, Samoa and American Samoa. In August 2002 the Government approved proposals to enlarge Avatiu Harbour. The project received additional funding from the Ports Authority and from New Zealand. In October 2008 plans further to upgrade Avatiu Wharf, to enable large ships to berth in the harbour, were endorsed by the Government. The Asian Development Bank agreed to lend US $15.5m. for the three-year project. The Avatiu Port Development Project was expected to be completed by 2013.

Apex Maritime: POB 378, Rarotonga; tel. 27651; fax 21138.

Cook Islands National Line: POB 264, Rarotonga; tel. 20374; fax 20855; 30% govt-owned; operates 3 fleet cargo services between the Cook Islands, Niue, Samoa, Norfolk Island, Tonga and New Zealand; Dirs CHRIS VAILE, GEORGE ELLIS.

Cook Islands Shipping Ltd: Arorangi, POB 2001, Rarotonga; tel. 24905; fax 24906.

Ports Authority: POB 84, Rarotonga and Aitutaki; tel. 21921; fax 21191; e-mail info@ports.co.ck; internet www.ports.co.ck; Gen. Man. NOOROA TOU.

Reef Shipping Ltd: Rarotonga; tel. 25193; fax 25194; e-mail shipping@xcil.co.ck; operates services between New Zealand and the Pacific islands.

Taio Shipping Ltd: POB 2001, Rarotonga; tel. 24905; fax 24906; e-mail taio@oyster.net.ck; f. 1991; inter-island cargo shipping service; Dir TAPI TAIO.

Triad Maritime (1988) Ltd: Rarotonga; fax 20855.

CIVIL AVIATION

An international airport was opened on Rarotonga in 1974. An airport rebuilding project was completed in 2010. Air New Zealand is among the airlines operating services between Rarotonga and other airports in the region. Air Pacific (Fiji) began a twice-weekly service between Nadi and Rarotonga in June 2000, and in August of that year Air New Zealand began a direct service from Rarotonga to Los Angeles, USA. Direct weekly flights between Rarotonga and the Australian city of Sydney were inaugurated in July 2011, following a successful four-month trial in 2010.

Airport Authority, Cook Islands: POB 90, Rarotonga; tel. 25890; fax 21890; e-mail aaci@airport.gov.ck; f. 1986; CEO JOE NGAMATA.

Air Rarotonga: POB 79, Rarotonga; tel. 22888; fax 23288; e-mail admin@airraro.co.ck; internet www.airraro.com; f. 1978; privately owned; operates internal passenger and cargo services and charter services to Niue and French Polynesia; Man. Dir EWAN F. SMITH.

Tourism

Tourism is the most important industry in the Cook Islands. In 2011 the number of foreign tourist arrivals reached a provisional 112,643, the majority of whom came from New Zealand. Australia and Europe are also important sources of tourists. There were 1,874 beds available at hotels and similar establishments in the islands in 1999. Most of the tourist facilities are to be found on Rarotonga and Aitutaki, but the outer islands also offer attractive scenery. Revenue from tourism was estimated at some US $110m. in 2010.

Cook Islands Tourism Corporation: POB 14, Rarotonga; tel. 29435; fax 21435; e-mail tourism@cookislands.gov.ck; internet www.cookislands.travel; Chair. EWAN F. SMITH; CEO HALOTOA FUA.

Education

Free secular education is compulsory for all children between six and 15 years of age. In 1998 there were 26 pre-primary schools, 28 primary schools and 23 secondary schools. In 2011 there were 517 pupils enrolled in pre-primary education, 1,861 in primary education and 1,793 in secondary education. Enrolment at primary schools in 2010 included an estimated 94% of children in the relevant age-group, while the comparable ratio for secondary schools in 2011 was 78% (males 72%; females 84%). Under the New Zealand Training Scheme, the New Zealand Government offers overseas scholarships in New Zealand, Fiji, Papua New Guinea, Australia and Samoa for secondary and tertiary education, career-training and short-term in-service training. There is an extension centre of the University of the South Pacific (based in Fiji) in the Cook Islands. Budgetary expenditure on education was estimated at $NZ13m. in 2012/13.

NIUE

Introductory Survey

LOCATION, CLIMATE, LANGUAGE, RELIGION, FLAG, CAPITAL

Niue is a coral island, located in the Pacific Ocean, about 480 km (300 miles) east of Tonga and 930 km (580 miles) west of the southern Cook Islands. Rainfall occurs predominantly during the hottest months, from December to March, when the average temperature is 27°C (81°F). Average annual rainfall is 7,715 mm (298 ins). Niuean, a Polynesian language, and English are spoken. The population is predominantly Christian, with some 63% belonging to the Ekalesia Niue, a Protestant church, in 2001. Niue's flag (proportions 1 by 2) is yellow, bearing, in the upper hoist corner, the United Kingdom's Union Flag with a yellow five-pointed star on each arm of the cross of St George and a slightly larger yellow five-pointed star on a blue disc in the centre of the cross. Some 30% of the population resides in Alofi, which is the capital and administrative centre of Niue.

CONTEMPORARY POLITICAL HISTORY

Historical Context

The first Europeans to discover Niue were members of a British expedition, led by Capt. James Cook, in 1774. Missionaries visited the island throughout the 19th century, and in 1900 Niue was declared a British protectorate. In 1901 Niue was formally annexed to New Zealand as part of the Cook Islands, but in 1904 it was granted a separate administration.

In October 1974 Niue attained 'self-government in free association with New Zealand'. Niueans retain New Zealand citizenship, and the migration of Niueans to New Zealand has been a cause of concern, with many more Niueans living in New Zealand than on Niue. Robert (from 1982, Sir Robert) Rex, who had been the island's political leader since the early 1950s, was Niue's Premier when it became self-governing, and retained the post at three-yearly general elections during 1975–90.

Domestic Political Affairs

In December 1992 Sir Robert Rex died, and Young Vivian, the leader of the Niue People's Action Party (NPAP—Niue's sole political party), who had been serving as acting Premier at the time of Rex's death, was unanimously elected Premier by the Government. Legislative elections took place in February 1993, and in the following month the Niue Assembly elected Frank Lui, a former cabinet minister, as Premier. Lui, who defeated Young Vivian by 11 votes to nine, announced a new Cabinet following the election; among the new Premier's stated objectives were the development of tourism and a continuation of efforts to encourage Niueans resident in New Zealand to return to the island.

In March 1994 Vivian proposed an unsuccessful motion of no confidence in the Government, and a further attempt by the opposition to introduce a similar motion was invalidated in the High Court in October on a procedural matter. However, during the ensuing debate, the Minister of National Planning and Economic Development, Sani Lakatani, resigned in order to join the opposition as its deputy leader, thus leaving the Government with only 10 official supporters in the Niue Assembly. Subsequent opposition demands for the intervention of the Governor-General of New Zealand in dissolving the legislature, in preparation for a fresh general election, were rejected, and, despite Lui's assurance that an early election would take place in order to end the atmosphere of increasing political uncertainty, polls were not held until February 1996. The Premier and his three cabinet ministers were re-elected to their seats, although support among the electorate for candidates of the Niue People's Party (NPP, as the NPAP had been renamed in 1995) and independents appeared fairly equally divided; in one village the result was decided by the toss of a coin when both candidates received an equal number of votes. Lui was re-elected by the Niue Assembly as Premier, defeating Robert Rex, Jr, the son of Niue's first Premier, by 11 votes to nine.

At a general election on 19 March 1999 Lui lost his legislative seat and subsequently retired from politics. The Minister of Finance, Aukuso Pavihi, also failed to be re-elected. On 29 March Sani Lakatani, leader of the NPP, was elected Premier by the new Assembly, defeating O'Love Jacobsen by 14 votes to six. Lakatani's stated priority as Premier was to oversee an increase in Niue's population to at least 3,000; he claimed that the sharp decline in the number of residents constituted a threat to the island's self-governing status.

At the general election held on 20 April 2002 all 20 incumbent members were returned to the Niue Assembly. Independent candidate Toke Talagi polled the highest number of votes (445), but overall the NPP was victorious. However, despite having polled the second-highest number of votes (428), Sani Lakatani did not command the general support of his party, and a leadership challenge was mounted by his deputy, Young Vivian. Following several days of lobbying within the NPP, Vivian was chosen as Premier. Vivian announced that the party had the support of 10 elected members, having formed a coalition with several independents associated with Toke Talagi. Lakatani was appointed Deputy Premier later that year. The NPP was dissolved in July 2003 as a result of ongoing disagreement among its membership and the failure of several projects. Opposition member Terry Coe expressed satisfaction with the news, stating that he hoped that party politics would cease henceforth in Niue.

In September 2003 the opposition expressed concern that a significant amount of public money was being used to fund overseas trips by government members. At the time of the statement seven of the Niue Assembly's 20 members (including two cabinet ministers) were absent on engagements overseas. In the same month it was announced that Niue was to receive US $90,000 from the People's Republic of China in order to build new accommodation for the 300 delegates and visitors who were expected to visit the island for the Pacific Islands Forum (see p. 426) summit meeting in 2004. However, the meeting was relocated, following the widespread devastation of the island by Cyclone Heta in January 2004.

Cyclone Heta, which was described as the worst in the island's recent history, caused the deaths of two people and the destruction of many buildings, along with the loss of most food crops. In addition, there was extensive damage to Niue's infrastructure, communications and coral reef. Relief supplies were sent from New Zealand as part of an initial aid programme worth some US $3.5m. It was estimated that US $23m. would be needed for a rebuilding programme to be carried out over a five-year period.

The Government conducted a survey in September 2004 to assess the current population of the island. However, its apparent reluctance to release the information prompted speculation that more people had left Niue than official reports had previously indicated. When its findings were made public in October, some observers disputed the figure of 1,550 (which many believed was higher than the reality, in order to attract more favourable levels of economic assistance). A local newspaper conducted a similar survey and estimated a resident population of 1,300. In July 2005 the Premier announced that ongoing efforts to attract Niueans back to the island, notably by promoting the farming and fisheries sectors, were to be increased. The people of Niue were also to be granted better access to health care following an agreement concluded in November 2005 between the Niue Ministry for Health and the Counties Manukau District Health Board of New Zealand. The agreement was expected to facilitate the referral of Niuean patients to New Zealand.

In November 2004 Niue's High Commissioner to New Zealand, Hima Takelesi Douglas (hereafter referred to as Hima Takelesi), announced his intention to return to the island to stand for parliament in the forthcoming general election. His stated motivation was a desire to form a stronger partnership with the 20,000 Niueans resident in New Zealand, in an attempt to ensure that Niue retained its current status and did not become incorporated into New Zealand. At the election, held on 30 April 2005, Hima Takelesi succeeded in securing a seat in the Niue Assembly. Young Vivian was re-elected Premier several days later, defeating O'Love Jacobsen (who had founded the Alliance of Independents in December 1991) by 17 votes to three. Vivian's stated priorities for the new Assembly included ongoing efforts to increase Niue's population, the clearing of some 350 derelict homes and the introduction of measures to improve the island's economic prospects.

In February 2007, in an attempt to ease its financial difficulties, the Government announced a 10% decrease in public servants' salaries, along with a reduction in working hours for certain employees and decreases in local grants. In the following month a parliamentary motion of no confidence submitted by the opposition against Premier Vivian, in protest against the Government's alleged financial mismanagement, was defeated. Niue's financial problems were again highlighted in late 2007, when a member of the opposition reported that the island's financial secretary had admitted the Government's bankruptcy.

Recent developments: the 2008 and 2011 elections

On 7 June 2008 a general election was held, with 11 of the 20 parliamentary seats being contested. Three new members were elected to the Niue Assembly, including Togia Sioneholo, hitherto Secretary of Justice, who defeated Hima Takelesi. On 26 June Toke Talagi, a former Minister of Finance, was elected Premier by 14 parliamentary votes to five, thereby succeeding the incumbent Young Vivian. Talagi assumed responsibility for numerous ministerial portfolios, including planning, economic development, finance, external affairs and environment. O'Love Jacobsen was allocated the portfolios of health, public works, women's affairs and Niue Power Corporation. Togia Sioneholo received the justice portfolio, along with other responsibilities. Pokotoa Sipeli was appointed Minister of Agriculture, Forestry and Fisheries, Posts and Telecommunications, and Administrative Services. The new Premier declared that his immediate priority was to address the island's economic situation.

In February 2009, after a delay of almost two years, modified legislation providing for the introduction of a new consumption tax, which would be applicable to visitors to the island, was finally approved by the Niue Assembly. Owing to its likely impact on low-income families, the controversial tax had encountered widespread opposition within the Assembly, culminating in the filing of a motion of no confidence in Toke Talagi in early February (which had been defeated by 11 votes to six).

In December 2010 the Cabinet approved, in principle, a proposal mooted by Toke Talagi to construct a casino on Niue in a bid to expand the island's tourism industry. The proposal, if pursued, was expected to require the introduction of legislation to ensure the proper management and operation of the casino. O'Love Jacobsen resigned from the Cabinet in March 2011, following her appointment as High Commissioner to New Zealand.

A general election was held on 7 May 2011, following which Toke Talagi was re-elected as Premier, having secured the support of 12 of the 20 incoming assembly members. Following the subsequent reallocation of cabinet portfolios and a further reorganization in June, Joan Viliamu became Minister of Health, Community Affairs and Niue Broadcasting Corporation. Pokotoa Sipeli retained the agriculture, forestry and fisheries portfolio, while assuming concurrent responsibility for education and administrative services, and Kupa Magatogia was appointed Minister of Public Works, Niue Power Corporation, Justice, Lands and Survey, and Bulk Fuel. Two assistant ministers were also appointed: Billy Talagi, who assumed responsibility for Taoga Niue (an initiative aimed at preserving traditional customs and cultural practices on the island), religion and the environment, and Dalton Tagelagi, who was awarded the youth and sports development portfolio, together with that of meteorological services and climate change. Prior to the poll the parliamentary Speaker, Siakimotu Atapana, had announced his retirement after nine years in office; Ahohiva Levi was chosen as his replacement.

In May 2011 it was announced that a judicial code of conduct was being drafted for Niue, by members of the local judiciary in conjunction with a British magistrate serving as a consultant for the Pacific Judicial Development Programme. It was hoped that the code of conduct, which required all judges to remain independent and above influence, would reinforce public confidence in Niue's judiciary and better inform the public of the judiciary's responsibilities.

In November 2011 former Minister of Justice Togia Sioneholo alleged that the appointment of two assistant ministers within the Cabinet was in breach of the Constitution, which stated that the Cabinet should comprise four ministers only. Sioneholo argued that Tagelagi and Talagi were assistant ministers in nominal terms only, since they had been awarded responsibility for portfolios hitherto awarded to full ministers, and urged the Niue High Court to intervene. In the following month members of the Niue Assembly voted in favour of significant increases in parliamentary salaries, which were to be funded by interest accrued by the island's trust fund. However, some opposition legislators, including Terry Coe, argued that the funds would be better spent on development projects.

The 'Offshore' Financial Sector

In late 1999 allegations made by a foreign news agency that Niue was being used by criminal organizations for 'laundering' the proceeds of their illegal activities were strongly denied by Sani Lakatani, the island's Premier. However, the naming of the island in a report by the Financial Action Task Force (FATF, see p. 465) in June 2000 as one of a number of countries and territories that had failed to co-operate in regional efforts to combat money-laundering led the Government to suspend the issue of any further 'offshore' banking licences until stricter regulations governing the financial sector had been introduced. In early 2001 the USA imposed sanctions on Niue (including a ban on transactions with US banks), claiming that the island had not implemented all the recommendations of the report. Lakatani appealed directly to US President George W. Bush to end the embargo, which he described as having had a devastating effect on Niue's economy. The Government stressed its commitment to meeting international requirements in its financial sector but claimed that it was having difficulty in doing so, given its limited legal resources. Moreover, the Premier expressed strong disapproval that a nation as powerful as the USA should inflict such hardship on a small, economically vulnerable island, and he urged other Pacific islands targeted by the report to unite in protest against such impositions. In June 2001 the Government engaged a US law firm in an effort to persuade two banks, Chase Manhattan and Bank of New York, to remove their bans on the transfer of some $NZ1m. to Niue via the business registry in Panama that the Government used for its 'offshore' tax activity.

Having failed to meet an FATF deadline in August 2001, in February 2002 Niue pledged to repeal its 'offshore' banking legislation. Premier Sani Lakatani was also considering closing down international business registrations based in Niue. The FATF announced in April that, in view of the island's commitment to improving the transparency of its tax and regulatory systems, the organization was to remove Niue from its list of non-co-operative territories; the decision was duly implemented in October. The bank-licensing legislation was repealed in June.

Although by 2002 most 'offshore' financial activity had ostensibly ended, the sector once again became the focus of scrutiny in February 2010 after the French Government included Niue on a 'black list' (to be updated annually) of nations accused of a lack of transparency in tax reporting. Consequently, the French Government announced that it would impose a 50% tax upon transactions between France and the black-listed nations. Niue remained on updated 'black lists' released in April 2011 and 2012. Furthermore, in April 2009 Niue was placed on a 'grey list' of nations compiled by the Organisation for Economic Co-operation and Development (OECD, see p. 388) owing to the island's failure to have concluded the requisite number of tax information exchange agreements. Niue, having only signed one such agreement, with New Zealand, in August 2012, remained on the 'grey list' in early 2013.

Relations with New Zealand

In March 2000 a Niue-New Zealand joint consultative committee met, for the first time, in Alofi to consider the two sides' future constitutional relationship. Later that year the committee proposed to conduct a survey of islanders' views and to consider all options, from reintegration with New Zealand to full independence. A meeting of the joint committee took place in March 2001 in Wellington at which the issues of New Zealand aid and reciprocal immigration laws were discussed, as well as options for Niue's future constitutional status. In early 2001 Hima Takelesi was appointed Niue's first High Commissioner to New Zealand. New Zealand remained committed to annual assistance of $NZ6.3m. in the years 2001–03. A total of 20,148 Niueans were recorded as resident in New Zealand at New Zealand's 2001 census, increasing to 22,476 at New Zealand's 2006 census. Discussions took place in Wellington in March 2003 between the New Zealand Prime Minister, Helen Clark, and Niue's Premier, Young Vivian. Topics debated included budgetary assistance, a review of the island's development plan and the continued migration of islanders from the territory to New Zealand.

In October 2004 Helen Clark made an official visit to Niue to celebrate the 30-year anniversary of the island's attainment of self-governing status. She urged expatriate Niueans to return to the island and support efforts to regenerate its infrastructure and economy. She also announced a programme to introduce the Niuean language into the education curriculum from pre-school level onwards by 2006, as part of the Taoga Niue initiative. The Halavaka ke he Monuina Arrangement (HkhMA), a bilateral agreement signed in October 2004, which aimed to facilitate closer co-operation between the various government agencies of Niue and New Zealand, represented a major shift in New Zealand's approach to the management of its relationship with Niue. In addition, Clark confirmed that $NZ6m. was to be made available to rebuild the hospital destroyed by Cyclone Heta. The new hospital, located at Kaimiti, opened in March 2006. In April of that year New Zealand and France agreed jointly to finance the construction of a government administration building on Niue.

The New Zealand Minister of Foreign Affairs, Murray McCully, visited Niue in January 2009 and again in October. The Government of Niue hoped that New Zealand might provide financial assistance for the reopening of a fish-processing plant, a joint venture between the Niuean Government and the Auckland-based Reef Group, which had closed in 2007 and resulted in many job losses (see Economic Affairs). However, McCully was reluctant to support the reopening of the plant, since a similar operation in neighbouring American Samoa had closed in September 2009.

Premier Toke Talagi criticized the New Zealand Government in June 2009 for withholding investment funds pledged as part of the HkhMA, particularly a $NZ2m. tranche that had been allocated for the island's tourism industry. In the following month, during New Zealand Prime Minister John Key's first visit to Niue and amid rising tensions, Key emphasized that the tourism aid would not be dispensed without a more detailed plan of how it was to be spent. In late 2009 the New Zealand Government expressed a willingness to finance an expansion of the island's main hotel, Matavai Resort, alongside concurrent reforms to the taxation and property ownership laws in Niue. (A New Zealand-funded refurbishment and expansion project was under way at the hotel in 2012.) Meanwhile, in September 2010 Mark Blumsky was appointed as New Zealand High Commissioner to Niue.

A report published by a New Zealand parliamentary committee in December 2010 included a critical assessment of Niue, contending that 40 years of New Zealand aid to the island had yielded 'almost no return'. The report urged Niue to reduce the size of its parliament, arguing that a 20-member legislature for an electorate comprising just 600 voters was 'an abuse of trust and responsibility', and noted that the island was caught in a 'vicious cycle' in which its economic difficulties were both reflected in, and exacerbated by, its ongoing population decline. The committee concluded that Niue could never be a sustainable economic entity, and proposed that the island be redesignated as a retirement village in which inhabitants would be granted access to the same services as other New Zealand citizens. The proposals received a mixed response, with some, including the Niuean Minister of Health, Public Works, Women's Affairs and the Niue Power Corporation, O'Love Jacobsen, arguing that the proposal raised serious questions about the long-term constitutionality of Niue, while others contended that a harmonization of services between New Zealand and Niue would attract expatriate Niueans back to the island, which would provide a stimulus to its economy. In late December Premier Talagi contested that the island economy was viable and that the most significant impediment to economic growth and development was the New Zealand Government, which, he argued, was frustrating efforts to expand the Niuean tourism sector owing to a reluctance to release funds. Jacobsen was appointed High Commissioner to New Zealand in March 2011. In September a joint development aid agreement was signed providing for New Zealand funding of $NZ15m., over a three-year period, for tourism-related development projects on Niue.

Foreign Affairs

Following almost 10 years of technical and political consultations, Niue and the USA signed a maritime boundary treaty in May 1997, delineating the precise boundary between the territorial waters of Niue and American Samoa. In October 2003 Niue's Premier issued a statement inviting the residents of Tuvalu (whose continued existence on those islands was increasingly threatened by rising sea levels) to migrate to Niue. The Government of Tuvalu subsequently requested that Niue produce a memorandum of understanding giving formal details of this invitation and of the rights that Tuvaluans would enjoy on Niue. Further discussions between officials from the two Governments took place in June 2005. In October 2006 Niue agreed to join the Regional Assistance Mission to Solomon Islands (RAMSI), with the deployment of two Niuean police officers to Solomon Islands. In August 2008 Niue hosted the annual summit meeting of the Pacific Islands Forum, at which the Niue Declaration on Climate Change was endorsed. In May 2009 an FAO conference on Pacific food security, and a meeting of the Pacific Islands Forum Fisheries Agency, were convened in Niue. The island hosted a meeting of the Pacific Island Forum ministers responsible for economic affairs in October 2010 and the Pacific Climate Change Roundtable in March 2011. In November 2011 Niue was one of eight Pacific states and territories that jointly established the Polynesian Leaders Group (see p. 478), which was widely viewed as being intended to provide a counterweight to the Melanesian Spearhead Group. The first formal meeting of the Group, which pledged to enhance co-operation among its members across a wide range of fields, including trade and investment, education, climate change and health, was held in the Cook Islands, on the sidelines of the annual Pacific Islands Forum summit, in August 2012.

Niue established diplomatic relations with the People's Republic of China in December 2007. In February 2011 China was reported to have provided funding for an extension of Niue's airport terminal and

the erection of security fencing at the airport. Following a meeting with the Chinese ambassador in that month, Premier Toke Talagi hailed the burgeoning bilateral relationship and expressed his belief that closer co-operation would be forged between the two countries, particularly in the tourism and fisheries sectors. Speculation emerged in July that the Government was considering a proposal to allow up to 100 Chinese families to settle on Niue, reportedly as part of efforts to secure additional Chinese investment in the island's economy. There were also reports in October 2012 that Niue was seeking to reach a free trade agreement with China, despite the island having very little to offer in terms of export commodities apart from fish.

CONSTITUTION AND GOVERNMENT

Under the Niue Constitution Act 1974, the island enjoys self-government in free association with New Zealand. The New Zealand Government remains responsible for the island's defence and external affairs, although in practice Niue may conduct its own external relations. Executive government is carried out by the Premier and three other ministers. Legislation is the responsibility of the Niue Assembly, which has 20 members (14 village representatives and six elected on a common roll), but New Zealand, if called upon to do so by the Assembly, will also legislate for the island. There is a New Zealand representative in Niue, whose status was upgraded to that of High Commissioner in 1993. The Governor-General of New Zealand acts as the sovereign's representative for Niue.

REGIONAL AND INTERNATIONAL CO-OPERATION

Niue is a member of the Pacific Community (see p. 422) and of the Pacific Islands Forum (see p. 426). It is an associate member of the UN's Economic and Social Commission for Asia and the Pacific (ESCAP, see p. 31). In 2000 Niue became a signatory of the Cotonou Agreement (see p. 334) with the European Union (EU). In November 2011 Niue was one of eight founding members of the Polynesian Leaders Group (see p. 478).

ECONOMIC AFFAIRS

Niue's gross domestic product (GDP) was estimated at $NZ30.7m. in 2011, and GDP per head was estimated at $NZ16,575 in 2009. The population decreased at an average annual rate of 1.0% in 2001–2011, according to provisional census figures.

Agriculture, forestry and fishing contributed 16.3% of GDP in 2011. According to the census of 2006, the sector engaged 15.9% of the employed labour force. Two-thirds of the land surface is uncultivable, but many households practise subsistence gardening. The principal crops are coconuts, taro, yams, cassava and sweet potatoes. A taro export scheme was successfully introduced in the early 1990s, and production of the crop increased by more than 500% in 1993. Exports of taro, principally to New Zealand, contributed nearly 89% of total export earnings in 2008, being facilitated by a regular shipping service introduced in 2003. Plans to increase the production of vanilla as an export crop were discussed in 2003, but the promising crop was destroyed by the cyclone of early 2004. The reintroduction of vanilla cultivation, as well as that of organic nonu (or noni), a fruit renowned for its medicinal properties), for export was initiated during 2004 as part of the Government's post-cyclone recovery programme. Honey is also produced for export. Pigs, poultry, goats and beef cattle are raised, mainly for local consumption. An island development plan for 2003 included proposals to develop Niue's fishing industry by employing a fleet of used Korean fishing vessels. The construction of a fish-processing factory at Amanau was completed in 2004. It was estimated that the new plant, which was a joint project with the New Zealand shipping company Reef Group, might raise $NZ9m. annually in revenue. Fishing licences to five New Zealand vessels and four Samoan vessels were issued. However, a series of problems resulted in operational difficulties at the plant. Operations were suspended in 2007. Niue remained hopeful, none the less, that the plant, an important source of employment for islanders, might resume activities; however, Reef Group went into receivership in November 2012.

Industry (including mining, manufacturing, construction and utilities) contributed only 5.1% of GDP in 2011. In 2006 industry engaged 17.1% of the labour force. The manufacturing sector has been very limited, accounting for a mere 2.4% of GDP in 2011. A noni juice factory opened in October 2004. Exploration for deposits of uranium continued on the island in 2005, but in November it was announced that no commercially viable resources had been identified. The extensive damage caused by Cyclone Heta led to much activity in the construction sector from early 2004, as rebuilding programmes commenced.

The island remains dependent upon imported diesel fuel for its energy requirements. In collaboration with the international environmentalist group Greenpeace, in December 2005 Niue confirmed its commitment to the development of wind power, hoping to become one of the first locations in the world to be completely reliant on renewable energy sources. In April 2009 Niue signed a memorandum of understanding on the Pacific Petroleum Project, a regional initiative that aimed to reduce the energy costs of the Pacific islands through collective negotiations for the bulk procurement of petroleum supplies. In October 2012 Premier Talagi announced that work on a Japanese-funded solar power project would commence in 2013. The installation process was expected to take around 12 months, and it was forecast that the solar power grid would initially provide up to 30% of Niue's energy requirements, as well as substantially reducing the island's dependency on fuel imports.

The services sector contributed 78.6% of GDP in 2011. In 2006 the sector engaged 66.9% of the labour force. The Government is the most important employer, engaging 512 members of the paid labour force in December 2004, when an estimated 269 people were employed in the private sector. Tourism has begun to make a significant contribution to the economy, and arrivals by air reached a provisional 6,000 in 2011. Visitor arrivals doubled between 2006 and 2010. Receipts from tourism amounted to US $2.0m. in 2010. From the 1990s various attempts to secure new sources of revenue in Niue included the leasing of the island's telecommunications facilities to foreign companies for use in specialist telephone services. However, this enterprise (which earned the island an estimated $NZ1.5m. per year) caused considerable controversy when it was revealed that Niue's telephone code had been made available to companies offering personal services considered indecent by the majority of islanders. The sale of Niue's internet domain name '.nu' generated significant revenue but led to further controversy when a report published in July 2004 claimed that the island was hosting some 3m. pages of pornographic material via its '.nu' domain. In March 2008, furthermore, an international software security company reported that, along with Tokelau, Niue had become one of the world's worst offenders in per caput terms with regard to the relaying of unsolicited e-mails. Niue's inaugural mobile telephone service was launched in July 2011.

Niue records an annual trade deficit, with imports generally far exceeding exports. The value of Niue's exports totalled only $NZ346,000 in 2011, while the cost of the island's imports reached almost $NZ14.0m. New Zealand is the island's main trading partner, supplying more than 95% of its imports in 2008. The principal exports in 2008 were taro, coconut and vanilla. The principal imports were mineral products (which constituted 38.3% of the total cost of imports), base metals, machinery and prepared foodstuffs.

The budget for 2012/13 projected expenditure of $NZ44.05m. and revenue of $NZ44.06m. Official development assistance from New Zealand totalled $NZ14.0m. in 2011/12. Meanwhile, the Halavaka Arrangement announced in late 2004 (see Contemporary Political History) provided funding of $NZ20m. over a five-year period. Other donors include Australia, the People's Republic of China, Japan, France and various multilateral organizations. With the objective of providing Niue with an independent source of future revenue, in 2006 the Niue International Trust Fund was established, with a total contribution of $NZ10m. from New Zealand and Australia. By 2011 the trust fund's assets stood at $NZ41m. Revenue from the fund was not expected to be drawn before 2014. The annual rate of inflation averaged 5.2% in 2003–11. Consumer prices increased by 5.4% in 2010 and by 3.0% in 2011. The unemployment rate was estimated at 13.8% of the labour force in 2001.

Niue's economy was severely affected by Cyclone Heta, which struck the island in January 2004, causing extensive damage to housing, infrastructure and crops. New Zealand assisted in Niue's subsequent recovery programme, which emphasized rebuilding works and industrial projects. Upon taking office in June 2008, Premier Toke Talagi stated that his priority was to be the economy of Niue, with a particular focus on the control of government expenditure and the creation of new sources of revenue. In April 2009 a controversial new consumption tax entered into effect (see Contemporary Political History); levied at a rate of 12.5%, the tax on goods and services was expected to make a substantial contribution to government revenue. Talagi's Government identified the tourism sector as a potential source of higher income. However, constraints on development included the lack of business expertise and dearth of professional skills among the islanders. A US $6m. project, funded by aid from New Zealand, to refurbish and expand the Matavai Resort, Niue's main hotel, was under way in 2012. Meanwhile, the establishment of a casino was under consideration, and capacity on Air New Zealand's weekly flight to Niue was increased; in April 2013 the frequency of Air New Zealand's service was increased to twice weekly. Furthermore, the Chinese Government had provided funds for the expansion of Niue's airport terminal and plans were mooted for the construction of a new Chinese-financed hotel. Upon securing re-election in May 2011, Talagi pledged to continue efforts to stabilize Niue's economy, reaffirmed his commitment to expanding the tourism sector, and identified fisheries and mining as additional sources of potential revenue. Personal income tax was to be reduced, while the reach of the consumption tax introduced in April 2009 was to be extended, to apply to all businesses with an annual turnover in excess of $NZ75,000 (compared with a previous threshold of $NZ200,000). The Government hoped that the creation of a Niuean shipping registry, under the management of a Singaporean company, in 2012 would generate government revenue of US $100,000 in its first year of operation.

PUBLIC HOLIDAYS

2014: 1 January (New Year's Day), 2 January (Commission Day), 6 February (Waitangi Day, anniversary of 1840 treaty), 18 April (Good Friday), 21 April (Easter Monday), 25 April (ANZAC Day, anniversary of 1915 landing at Gallipoli), 2 June (Queen's Official Birthday), 19 October (Constitution Day celebrations), 27 October (Peniamina's Day), 25–26 December (Christmas).

Statistical Survey

Source (unless otherwise indicated): Statistics Unit, Economics, Planning, Development Office, Government of Niue, POB 95, Alofi; tel. 4219; fax 4148; e-mail statsniue@mail.gov.nu; internet www.spc .int/prism/country/nu/stats.

AREA AND POPULATION

Area: 261.5 sq km (100.9 sq miles).

Population: 1,625 (males 802, females 823) at census of September 2006 (an estimated 22,473 Niueans lived in New Zealand at the time of the 2006 census); 1,615 at census of 10 September 2011 (provisional result).

Density (at 2011 census): 6.2 per sq km.

Population by Age and Sex (official estimates at mid-2010, on-island residents): *0–14:* 383 (males 187, females 196); *15–64:* 929 (males 482, females 447); *65 and over:* 182 (males 85, females 97); *Total* 1,494 (males 754, females 740).

Ethnic Groups (2001 census, declared ethnicity): Niuean 1,399; Caucasian 81; Pacific Islander 182; Niuean/Caucasian 28; Niuean/Pacific Islander 42; Asian 4.

Principal Villages (population at mid-2010, official estimates): Alofi (capital) 540; Hakupu 138; Avatele 137; Tamakautoga 115; Tuapa 105.

Births, Marriages and Deaths: *2009* (including Niueans temporarily resident in New Zealand): Live births 31; Marriages 12; Deaths 12. *2010* (Secretariat of the Pacific Community estimate): Birth rate 14.8 per 1,000; Death rate 9.7 per 1,000 (Source: Pacific Regional Information System).

Life Expectancy (years at birth, WHO estimates): 72 (males 66; females 80) in 2009. Source: WHO, *World Health Statistics*.

Immigration and Emigration (2009): Arrivals 6,380; Departures 6,426.

Economically Active Population (2006 census, persons aged 15 years and over): Agriculture, forestry and fishing 119; Mining, electricity, gas, water and construction 61; Manufacturing 67; Trade, restaurants and hotels 84; Transport, storage and communications 43; Finance, real estate, business activities 33; Public administration 180; Education and health 117; Community, social and personal services 43; *Total employed* 747. Note: Figures exclude subsistence workers. *Paid Employment* (December 2004): Government sector 512 (males 294, females 218); Private sector (estimates) 269 (males 143, females 126).

HEALTH AND WELFARE

Key Indicators

Total Fertility Rate (children per woman, 2006): 2.6.

Under-5 Mortality Rate (per 1,000 live births, 2010): 22.

Physicians (per 1,000 head, 2008): 6.0.

Hospital Beds (per 1,000 head, 2006): 5.2.

Health Expenditure (2009): US $ per head (PPP): 3,280.

Health Expenditure (2009): % of GDP: 17.5.

Health Expenditure (2009): public (% of total): 99.3.

For sources and definitions, see explanatory note on p. vi.

AGRICULTURE, ETC.

Principal Crops (metric tons, 2011, FAO estimates): Taro 2,773; Sweet potatoes 228; Yams 135; Coconuts 3,174; Bananas 76; Lemons and limes 89. *Aggregate Production* ('000 metric tons, may include official, semi-official or estimated data): Vegetables (incl. melons) 127; Fruits (excl. melons) 715.

Livestock (year ending September 2011, FAO estimates): Cattle 115; Pigs 2,100; Chickens 15,000.

Livestock Products (metric tons, 2011, FAO estimates): Pig meat 60; Chicken meat 20; Cows' milk 60; Hen eggs 16; Honey 6.

Forestry (cu m, 1985): Roundwood removals 613; Sawnwood production 201.

Fishing (metric tons, live weight, 2010, FAO estimate): Total catch 113.

Source: FAO.

INDUSTRY

Production (2009, estimate): Electric energy 3 million kWh. Source: UN Industrial Commodity Statistics Database.

FINANCE

Currency and Exchange Rates: 100 cents = 1 New Zealand dollar ($NZ). For details, see Tokelau.

Budget ($NZ '000, year ending 30 June 2006, provisional): Internal revenue 14,206; New Zealand budgetary support 6,953; *Total revenue* 21,159; Recurrent expenditure 21,417; Capital 90; *Total Expenditure* 21,507. *2006/07* ($NZ '000, forecasts): Internal revenue 16,499; New Zealand budgetary support 6,915; Total revenue 23,414; Recurrent expenditure 23,364; Capital projects 50; Total expenditure 23,414. *2012/13* ($NZ '000, forecasts): Total revenue 44,055; Total expenditure 44,052.

Overseas Aid ($NZ '000, 2011/12, provisional): Official development assistance from New Zealand 14,000. Source: Ministry of Foreign Affairs and Trade, Wellington.

Cost of Living (Consumer Price Index, average of quarterly figures; base: July–Sept. 2003 = 100): All items 138.3 in 2009; 145.7 in 2010; 150.0 in 2011.

Gross Domestic Product ($NZ '000 in current prices): 17,771 in 2004; 19,441 in 2005; 20,541 in 2006. *2011* $NZ '000 in current prices, Secretariat of the Pacific Community estimate): Gross domestic product 30,724.1 (Source: Pacific Regional Information System).

Gross Domestic Product by Economic Activity ($NZ '000 in current prices, Secretariat of the Pacific Community estimates, 2011): Agriculture, forestry and fishing 4,807.3; Mining and quarrying 20.2; Manufacturing 704.6; Electricity, gas and water 552.7; Construction 217.2; Trade 3,336.2; Restaurants and hotels 1,588.7; Transport, storage and communications 1,310.9; Financial and business services, real estate, etc. 2,481.1; Public administration 13,400.4; Other community, social and personal services 1,082.0; *Sub-total* 29,501.2; *Less* Imputed bank service charge 351.2; *GDP at factor cost* 29,150.0; Indirect taxes, less subsidies 1,574.1; *GDP in purchasers' values* 30,724.1 Source: Pacific Regional Information System.

EXTERNAL TRADE

Principal Commodities ($NZ '000, 2008): *Imports c.i.f.:* Animals and animal products 679; Prepared foodstuffs 1,250; Mineral products 4,206; Chemical products 321; Plastics and rubber 195; Wood and wood products 403; Base metals and articles thereof 1,176; Machinery, mechanical appliances and electrical equipment 915; Miscellaneous manufactured articles 461; Total (incl. others) 10,968. *Exports f.o.b.:* Taro 24; Coconut 2; Vanilla 1; Total (incl. others) 27.

Principal Trading Partners ($NZ '000, 2008): *Imports c.i.f.:* China, People's Republic 113; Japan 296; New Zealand 10,478; Total (incl. others) 10,968. *Exports f.o.b.:* Total 27.

TRANSPORT

Road Traffic (2001 census): Passenger cars 323; Motorcycles 134; Vans 170; Trucks 74; Pick-ups 76; Buses 11.

International Shipping: *Ship Arrivals* (1989): Yachts 20; Merchant vessels 22; Total 42. *Freight Traffic* (metric tons, 1989, official estimates): Unloaded 3,410; Loaded 10. *Flag Registered Fleet* (at 31 December 2012): Vessel 1; Displacement 396 grt (Source: Lloyd's List Intelligence—www.lloydslistintelligence.com).

Civil Aviation: *Passengers* (1992): Arrivals 3,500; Departures 3,345. *Freight Traffic* (metric tons, 1992): Unloaded 41.6; Loaded 15.7.

TOURISM

Foreign Tourist Arrivals: 4,748 in 2008; 4,662 in 2009; 6,000 in 2010–11 (provisional).

Tourist Arrivals by Country of Residence (2010): Australia 539; Germany 1,043; New Zealand 2,935; United Kingdom 103; USA 230; Total (incl. others) 6,214. Source: World Tourism Organization.

Tourism Receipts (US $ million, excl. passenger transport): 2.0 in 2009; 2.0 in 2010. Source: World Tourism Organization.

COMMUNICATIONS MEDIA

Telephones (2010): 1,000 main lines in use.

Mobile Cellular Telephones (2009): 1,100 units in use.

Internet Users (2009): 1,100.

Source: International Telecommunication Union.

EDUCATION

Pre-primary and Primary (2006): 1 school; 212 pupils (males 104, females 108); 20 teachers (males 3, females 17).

Secondary (2006): 1 school; 191 pupils (males 102, females 89); 31 teachers (males 9, females 22).

Source: Department of Education, Niue.

Pupil-teacher Ratio (primary education, UNESCO estimate): 11.9 in 2004/05. Source: UNESCO Institute for Statistics.

Directory

The Government

New Zealand High Commissioner: MARK BLUMSKY.
Secretary to Government: RICHARD HIPA.

CABINET
(May 2013)

Premier, Chairman of the Cabinet and Minister responsible for Finance, Customs and Revenue and Government Assets, Premier's Department (Civil Aviation, Crown Law, External Affairs, Planning, Economic Development and Statistics), Infrastructure, Transport, Public Service Commission, Police and National Security, Tourism, Posts and Telecommunications, and Immigration and Population: TOKE TUFUKIA TALAGI.

Minister of Education, Agriculture, Forestry and Fisheries, and Administrative Services: POKOTOA SIPELI.

Minister of Public Works, Niue Power Corpn, Justice, Lands and Survey, and Bulk Fuel: KUPA MAGATOGIA.

Minister of Health, Community Affairs and Niue Broadcasting Corpn: JOAN VILIAMU.

GOVERNMENT OFFICES

All ministries are in Alofi.

Office of the New Zealand High Commissioner: Tapeu, POB 78, Alofi; tel. 4022; fax 4173; e-mail sog.hipa@mail.gov.nu; internet www .gov.nu.

Office of the Secretary to Government: POB 40, Alofi; tel. 4220; fax 4232; e-mail richard.hipa@mail.gov.nu.

Legislature

ASSEMBLY

The Niue Assembly or Fono Ekepule has 20 members (14 village representatives and six members elected on a common roll). The most recent general election was held on 7 May 2011.

Speaker: AHOHIVA LEVI.

Political Organizations

There have been no active political parties on Niue since the disbanding, in 2003, of the Niue People's Pary (f. 1987—Niue's sole political party to date). All politicians on the island are de facto independents.

Judicial System

The Chief Justice of the High Court, which exercises civil and criminal jurisdiction, and the Judge of the Land Court, which is concerned with litigation over land and titles, visit Niue quarterly. In addition, locally appointed lay justices exercise limited criminal and civil jurisdiction. Appeals against High Court judgments are heard in the Court of Appeal of Niue, while appeals against Land Court judgments are heard in the Land Appellate Court. Established in 1992, sessions of the Court of Appeal of Niue are usually held in the New Zealand capital of Wellington. In April 2009, however, for the first time the four New Zealand judges heard various cases, including several land disputes, on Niue itself. The final appellate tribunal in civil, criminal and land matters is the Privy Council, sitting in the United Kingdom.

Chief Justice of the High Court: PATRICK SAVAGE.
Registrar of the High Court: JUSTIN KAMUPALA.

Religion

About 63% of the population belong to the Ekalesia Niue, a Protestant Congregationalist organization, which had 1,093 adherents at the time of the 2001 census. Within the Roman Catholic Church, which had 128 adherents (equivalent to 7.4% of the population) in 2001, Niue forms part of the diocese of Tonga. The Church of Jesus Christ of Latter-day Saints (Mormon—which had 158 adherents in 2001), the Seventh-day Adventists, the Jehovah's Witnesses and the Church of God of Jerusalem are also represented.

Ekalesia Kerisiano Niue: Head Office, POB 25, Alofi; tel. 4195; fax 4352; e-mail ekalesia.niue@niue.nu; f. 1846; est. by London Missionary Society, became Ekalesia Niue in 1966; Pres. Rev. ARTHUR PIHIGIA; Gen. Sec. Rev. PETESA SIONETUATO.

The Press

Niue Business News: 20 Lautamina Rd, Mutalau 110175; tel. 3317; fax 4010; e-mail sioneholof@gmail.com; f. 2000; owned by Tropical Suppliers; electronic; previously publ. in print as *Niue Economic Review*; CEO FRANK SIONEHOLO.

Niue Star: weekly; Niuean and English; publ. in Alofi until destruction of office by Cyclone Heta in 2004; operations transferred to Auckland, New Zealand; Publr MIKE JACKSON; circ. 800.

Broadcasting and Communications

TELECOMMUNICATIONS

In 2003 Niue became the first location in the world to have a national wireless internet system allowing access from anywhere on the island by means of solar-powered aerials attached to coconut palms. A four-fold expansion of the island's internet capacity was announced in March 2010. A mobile telephone service was introduced in 2011.

Director of Posts and Telecommunications: POB 37, Alofi; tel. 4000; fax 4010.

Internet Niue: Rocket Systems Ltd, Fatalupe, POB 229, Alofi; tel. 4638; fax 4237; internet internetniue.nu; f. 1997; operated by Rocket Systems Ltd and upgraded by PacTel Int; Dir EMANI FAKAOTIMANAVA-LUI.

Telecom Niue: POB 37, Alofi; tel. 4000; e-mail telecom.callcentre@mail.gov.nu; internet www.telecomniue.com; Dir RICHARD HIPA.

BROADCASTING

Radio

Broadcasting Corporation of Niue: POB 68, Alofi; tel. 4026; fax 4217; operates radio and TV services; govt-owned; Chair. NEAL MORRISSEY; CEO TREVOR TIAKIA; Gen. Man. PATRICK LINO.

Radio Sunshine: broadcasts in English and Niuean between 6 a.m. and 10 p.m. Mon.–Sat.

Television

Broadcasting Corporation of Niue: see Radio.

Television Niue broadcasts in English and Niuean six days a week from 5 p.m. to 11 p.m.

Finance

DEVELOPMENT BANK

Niue Development Bank: POB 34, Alofi; tel. 4335; fax 4290; e-mail devbank@niue.nu; internet niuedevelopmentbank.nu; f. 1993; govt-owned; began operations July 1994; Chair. MISIATA TASMANIA; Gen. Man. VAINE PASISI.

COMMERCIAL BANK

The planned closure of Bank South Pacific's branch in Niue, and its replacement by a branch of Kiwibank Ltd (New Zealand), was reported in April 2013.

Bank South Pacific Ltd: Main St, POB 76, Alofi; tel. 4220; fax 4043; e-mail bsp@niue.nu; internet www.bsp.com.pg/niue; acquired from Westpac Banking Corpn in Sept. 2004; closure reportedly planned in mid-2013; Man. ANN PESAMINO.

Trade and Industry

GOVERNMENT AGENCIES

Business Advisory Service: Alofi; tel. 4228.

Office of Economic Affairs, Planning and Development, Statistics and Trade and Investment: POB 42, Alofi; tel. 4148; e-mail business.epdsu@mail.gov.nu; responsible for planning and financing activities in the agricultural, tourism, industrial sectors, business advisory and trade and investment.

CHAMBER OF COMMERCE

Niue Chamber of Commerce: POB 213, Alofi; tel. 4399; e-mail chamber@niue.nu; Chair. AVI RUBEN; Pres. ROSSALOFA REX.

UTILITIES

Niue Power Corporation: POB 198, Alofi; tel. 4119; fax 4385; e-mail gm.npc@mail.gov.nu; Gen. Man. SPEEDO HETUTU.

TRADE UNION

Public Service Association: Alofi.

Transport

ROADS

There are 123 km of all-weather roads and 106 km of access and plantation roads.

SHIPPING

The best anchorage is an open roadstead at Alofi, the largest of Niue's 14 villages. The New Zealand Shipping Corporation operates a monthly service between New Zealand, Nauru and Niue. Fuel supplies are delivered by a tanker (the *Pacific Explorer*) from Fiji. In December 2002 the Government signed an agreement with Reef Shipping Ltd to provide a service to New Zealand every three to four weeks. The Reef Group went into receivership in November 2012, but its primary shipping assets were acquired by US company Matson South Pacific Ltd, which relaunched the service from Niue to New Zealand in January 2013. Legislation providing for the creation of new registry permitting ships to sail under the Niuean flag was adopted in March 2012; the registry opened later that year, under the management of a Singaporean company.

CIVIL AVIATION

Hanan International Airport has a total sealed runway of 2,350 m, following the completion of a 700 m extension in 1995, with New Zealand assistance. In 2005 Air New Zealand began a weekly service between Auckland and Niue. The frequency of this service was increased to twice weekly from April 2013. Meanwhile, in early 2011 the provision of funding by the People's Republic of China, to finance improvements that included the extension of the airport terminal, was confirmed.

Tourism

Niue has a small but significant tourism industry (specializing in holidays based on activities such as diving, rock-climbing, caving and game fishing), which has benefited from an increase in the frequency of flights between the island and New Zealand. The Matavai Resort provides the main tourist facilities; the resort was in the process of being extended in 2012. In September 2011 it was announced that over a three-year period New Zealand was to provide a total of $NZ15m. for the purposes of tourism development projects. Tourism receipts (including passenger transport) totalled US $2m. in 2010. A provisional total of 6,000 people arrived by air to visit Niue in 2011. Most visitors are from New Zealand. Visitor arrivals doubled between 2006 and 2010.

Niue Tourism Office: POB 42, Alofi; tel. 4224; fax 4225; e-mail niuetourism@mail.gov.nu; internet www.niueisland.com; Dir of Tourism HAYDEN PORTER.

Education

Education is free and compulsory between six and 16 years of age (the school-leaving age having been raised from 14 in 1998). In 1987 the island's seven village primary schools were closed and a single national primary school was opened at Halamahaga. In 2006 this bilingual (Niuean/English) primary school had 20 teachers and an enrolment of 212 pupils. There was one secondary school at Paliati, with a teaching staff of 31 and a total enrolment of 191 pupils in 2006. Higher education takes place at the Niue Extension Centre of the University of the South Pacific (based in Fiji), on government training schemes or by correspondence. Some study overseas, in the Pacific region and New Zealand. A private medical school opened in Niue in 2000 but closed in the following year. A private university offering online business and information technology courses opened in late 2003.

NICARAGUA

Introductory Survey

LOCATION, CLIMATE, LANGUAGE, RELIGION, FLAG, CAPITAL

The Republic of Nicaragua lies in the Central American isthmus, bounded by the Pacific Ocean to the west and by the Caribbean Sea to the east. Its neighbours are Honduras, to the north, and Costa Rica, to the south. The climate is tropical, with an annual average temperature of 25.5°C (78°F). The rainy season extends from May to October. The national language is Spanish, although English is also spoken on the Caribbean coast. Almost all of the inhabitants profess Christianity, and a majority are Roman Catholics. The national flag (proportions 3 by 5) has three equal horizontal stripes, of blue, white and blue, with the state emblem (a triangle enclosing a dark blue sea from which rise five volcanoes, in green, surmounted by a Phrygian cap from which extend white rays and, at the top, a rainbow, all encircled by the words, in gold capitals, 'República de Nicaragua' and 'América Central') in the centre of the white stripe; the same flag without the state emblem is an alternative version of the civil flag. The capital is Managua.

CONTEMPORARY POLITICAL HISTORY

Historical Context

Nicaragua was under Spanish rule from the 16th century until 1821. It then became part of the Central American Federation until 1838. From 1927 US troops were based in Nicaragua at the request of the Government, which was opposed by a guerrilla group, led by Augusto César Sandino. In 1933, following the establishment of the National Guard (commanded by Gen. Anastasio Somoza García), the US troops left Nicaragua. Sandino was assassinated in 1934, but some of his followers ('Sandinistas') continued actively to oppose the new regime. Somoza seized power in a coup in 1935 and took office as President in 1936. Apart from a brief interlude in the late 1940s, Somoza remained as President until September 1956, when he was assassinated. However, the Somoza family continued to dominate Nicaraguan politics until 1979.

Domestic Political Affairs

In 1962 the left-wing Frente Sandinista de Liberación Nacional (FSLN—Sandinista National Liberation Front) was formed with the object of overthrowing the Somozas by revolution. Gen. Anastasio Somoza Debayle, son of the former dictator, became President in May 1967, holding office until 1972. The Congreso Nacional (National Congress) was dissolved, and a triumvirate ruled until Gen. Somoza was re-elected President in September 1974. In 1978 the murder of Pedro Joaquín Chamorro Cardenal, the leader of the opposition coalition and the editor of *La Prensa* (the country's only independent newspaper), provoked violent demonstrations against the Government.

In June 1979 the FSLN formed a provisional Junta of National Reconstruction. With the FSLN in command of many towns, President Somoza resigned and left the country. (He was assassinated in Paraguay in 1980.) After the Sandinistas had gained control of the capital, the Junta and its Provisional Governing Council took power in July 1979 as the Government of National Reconstruction. The 1974 Constitution was abrogated, and the bicameral Congreso Nacional dissolved. A Basic Statute, providing for the creation of an appointed Council of State to act as an interim legislature, was issued. The National Guard was disbanded and replaced by the Ejército Popular Sandinista (Sandinista People's Army). In August the Junta issued a 'Statute on Rights and Guarantees for the Citizens of Nicaragua', providing for basic personal freedoms and restoring freedom of the press and broadcasting. Civil rights were restored in January 1980. In March 1981 Commdr Daniel Ortega Saavedra was appointed Co-ordinator of the Junta and of its new consultative body, the Council of Government.

By 1981 discontent at the postponement of elections and the increasing hegemony of the Sandinistas had led to the creation of counter-revolutionary forces ('Contras'), who were mostly members of the former National Guard and operated from camps in Honduras. Meanwhile, relations between the US and Nicar-

aguan Governments had seriously deteriorated, culminating in the suspension of US economic aid. In the same year the US Government donated US $10m. in support of the Contras, while covert operations by the US Central Intelligence Agency (CIA) attempted to destabilize the Sandinista regime. The Sandinista Government declared a state of emergency in 1982. However, the intensity of attacks by the Fuerzas Democráticas Nicaragüenses, anti-Sandinista guerrillas based in Honduras, increased. A Contra group, the Alianza Revolucionaria Democrática, was also established in Costa Rica, led by Edén Pastora Gómez, a prominent figure in the revolution who had become disillusioned with the Sandinistas.

In 1984 talks commenced between the Nicaraguan and US Governments in order to foster peace negotiations proposed by the 'Contadora group' (Colombia, Mexico, Panama and Venezuela), which was attempting to find solutions to disputes involving Central America. However, although the Sandinistas agreed to sign a peace agreement, the USA rejected the agreement on the grounds that the forthcoming Nicaraguan elections would not be fairly conducted. In 1985 the US Congress voted to allocate US $27m. in non-military aid to the Contras. None the less, the Nicaraguan Government reaffirmed its desire to resume negotiations with the USA. Concurrently, however, the civil conflict escalated, and clashes along Nicaragua's borders with Costa Rica and Honduras became increasingly frequent.

A presidential election and elections to a constituent assembly were held in November 1984. The assembly was to draw up a constitution within two years of taking office. In August the Government had restored the majority of the civil rights that had been previously suspended. Ortega, the FSLN candidate, won the presidential ballot, and his party won a majority of seats in the National Constituent Assembly, which replaced the Council of State. Ortega's new Government and the National Constituent Assembly were inaugurated in January 1985.

In 1986 the US Congress approved assistance for the Contras worth US $100m. Later the same year the US Government disclosed that funds accruing from its clandestine sales of military equipment to Iran had been used to support the Contras.

In January 1987 a new Constitution was promulgated; on the same day, however, civil liberties, guaranteed in the Constitution, were again suspended by the renewal of the five-year-old state of emergency. In February the Governments of Costa Rica, El Salvador, Guatemala and Honduras approved a peace plan for Nicaragua, largely based on earlier Contadora proposals, but placing greater emphasis on democratization, including the ending of the state of emergency. Following some modification, in August the peace plan was signed by the Presidents of the five nations. In accordance with the plan, a four-member National Commission for Reconciliation was created, chaired by Cardinal Miguel Obando y Bravo, the Archbishop of Managua, a leading critic of the Government. In January 1988 the Government ended the state of emergency, and consented to participate directly in negotiations with the Contras. In March negotiations between representatives of the Government and the Contras resulted in agreement on a 60-day cease-fire (which was later unilaterally extended by the Government until November 1989). The Government agreed to the gradual release of political prisoners and to the participation of the Contras in domestic political dialogue and, eventually, in elections. In August 1988 the US Senate approved the provision of US $27m. in humanitarian aid for the Contras. As the hope of further military aid diminished, the Contras retreated into Honduras.

In February 1989, at a meeting of the five Central American Presidents in El Salvador, it was agreed that, in return for the dismantling of Contra bases in Honduras, there would be moves towards greater democracy in Nicaragua. These included a pledge to hold a general election, open to opposition parties, by February 1990. A number of electoral reforms were introduced: Contra rebels were to be permitted to return to vote, on condition that they relinquished their armed struggle under a proposed demobilization plan. In August 1989 the five Presidents signed an agreement in Tela, Honduras, providing for the voluntary demobilization, repatriation or relocation of the Contra forces within a 90-day period. An International Commission of Support and Verification (CIAV) was established by the UN and the Organization of American States (OAS, see p. 404). Following mediation, the Government concluded an agreement with the leaders of the Miskito Indians of the Caribbean coast. The rebels agreed to renounce their armed struggle and to join the political process.

In November 1989 President Ortega declared the ending of the cease-fire with the Contras, on the grounds that the rebels had made insufficient progress in implementing the Tela agreement and disbanding their forces stationed in Honduras. In response, the UN Security Council established the UN Observer Group in Central America (ONUCA) to monitor compliance with the Tela agreement, to prevent cross-border incursions by rebels and to assist in supervising the forthcoming Nicaraguan elections.

Chamorro in power

The general election of February 1990 resulted in an unexpected victory for Violeta Barrios de Chamorro (the widow of Pedro Chamorro), the presidential candidate of the recently formed Unión Nacional Opositora (UNO), comprising 14 opposition parties. After the election, the Sandinista Government decreed an immediate cease-fire. The President-elect pledged to 'depoliticize' the security forces, and urged the Contra rebels to disband and return to civilian life. However, the UNO had not secured a sufficient majority of seats in the Asamblea Nacional to make amendments to the Constitution. Before the transfer of power on 25 April, a General Amnesty and National Reconciliation Law was adopted: this was designed to pre-empt retaliatory measures against outgoing officials and to quash legal proceedings against those who had committed politically motivated crimes against the State since 1979.

On 19 April 1990 a cease-fire was agreed by the Contras and the Sandinista armed forces. The Contras agreed to surrender their weapons, and to assemble in 'security zones' supervised by UN troops. A transitional agreement between the outgoing Government and the UNO administration provided for a reduction in the strength of the security forces and their subordination to civilian authority. In return for a commitment from the Contras to sign the demobilization accords, the Government agreed to the establishment of a special police force, composed of former Contra rebels, in order to guarantee security within the demobilization zones. Demobilization of the Contra rebels was officially concluded on 27 June, signifying the end of 11 years of civil war in Nicaragua.

On assuming office, the UNO Government attempted to reverse much Sandinista policy. The suspension of the civil service law in May 1990 provoked a public sector strike. Chamorro was forced to concede wage increases of 100% and the establishment of a joint commission of trade union and government representatives to revise the civil service law. In July another general strike was held in support of demands for wage increases and also in protest at the implementation of legislation allowing the restoration to private ownership of land. Once again the Government made concessions. In October the Government formed a National Agrarian Commission to study problems of land distribution and illegal land seizures. In mid-1991, however, the emergence of groups of re-armed Contra rebels (known as Re-contras) became apparent. The Re-contras' stated aim was to publicize the grievances of thousands of demobilized Contras in the north of the country who had not received land and aid promised under the terms of the resettlement plan.

The phased disarmament of the Re-contras and the Re-compas (groups of rearmed Sandinistas) began in January 1992. However, in April groups of the former combatants began joining forces to form the Revueltos, demanding land and credit promised to them prior to demobilization. In May the Government allocated 800 plots of land outside the capital to the Revueltos. However, rebel activity continued. In February 1994 a peace agreement was signed that provided for the demobilization of a prominent Re-contra group, the Frente Norte 3-80, by April, in return for which the rebels were granted an amnesty and the right to be incorporated into the national police force. Nevertheless, violent incidents continued.

In June 1991 the FSLN withdrew its 39 deputies from the Asamblea Nacional in protest against the proposal to revoke two laws concerning redistribution of property. The so-called *piñata* laws had been introduced by the FSLN immediately prior to the transfer of power to the Chamorro administration. They guaranteed the property rights of the thousands of people who had benefited from the land expropriation that had been conducted by the Sandinistas. In August the legislature approved the abrogation of the *piñata* laws, but President Chamorro vetoed parts of the bill that she deemed to be unconstitutional. Disagreement over the property issue had by now led to the alienation by Chamorro of the majority of UNO deputies, and the legislature only narrowly failed to overturn the veto in December.

In May 1992 the US Congress suspended aid to Nicaragua, on the grounds that the Nicaraguan Government had failed to compensate US citizens for land expropriated under the Sandinista regime. In September Chamorro signed decrees establishing a property ombudsman's office and other provisions to expedite the processing of property claims. In addition, the President signed an agreement specifying that all unjustly confiscated property would be returned (or the rightful owners compensated).

A serious legislative crisis arose in September 1992, when the President of the Asamblea Nacional, Alfredo César, convened the legislature in the absence of the deputies of the FSLN and the Grupo de Centro (GC—dissident UNO deputies who had maintained their allegiance to the Government), recruiting substitute deputies in order to elect new legislative authorities. Chamorro announced that no laws approved by the legislature would be promulgated. In December Chamorro ordered the army to occupy the assembly building and appointed a provisional administration to manage parliamentary affairs pending the election of new legislative authorities.

In October 1993 the Alianza Política Opositora (APO—as the UNO had become) and the FSLN signed an agreement providing for the implementation of partial constitutional reforms. The Asamblea Nacional reconvened in January 1994, and a new working alliance elected new legislative authorities. In November the Asamblea Nacional approved amendments to some 67 of the Constitution's 202 articles, which adjusted the balance of authority in favour of the legislature. In particular, the Government would be required to seek legislative approval for external loans, debt negotiations and international trade agreements. Other reforms included a reduction in the presidential and legislative terms and the withdrawal of the absolute ban on presidential re-election, although consecutive terms remained prohibited. The amendments were deemed illegal by the FSLN leadership but won the support of FSLN deputies, reflecting the divisions within the party.

In February 1995 the constitutional amendments were signed. Following Chamorro's refusal to promulgate the reforms, the Asamblea Nacional enacted them. In June a resolution to the dispute was achieved by the signing of a political accord between the Government and the legislature. Under the terms of the agreement, many of the amendments intended to reduce presidential authority were to be moderated. Legislation defining the interpretation and implementation of the amendments was approved by the Asamblea Nacional in July, and was subsequently promulgated by Chamorro.

The Alemán and Bolaños administrations

Presidential and legislative elections were held in October 1996. Arnoldo Alemán Lacayo of the Partido Liberal Constitucionalista (PLC), the candidate of the Alianza Liberal, secured the presidency. The Alianza Liberal also won the largest number of seats in the Asamblea Nacional, although it failed to gain a majority.

In June 1999 the Government and the FSLN reached an agreement to begin negotiations on constitutional and electoral reform. In January 2000 a series of constitutional reforms came into force. The principal amendments included a reduction in the proportion of votes necessary for a President to be elected outright from 45% to 35%, thus increasing the likelihood of an FSLN victory. In return, Alemán, whose administration had been confronted by allegations of corruption, was guaranteed a seat in the Asamblea Nacional after leaving office, thus making him virtually immune from prosecution. Other reforms included the restructuring of the judiciary and the electoral authorities.

Presidential and legislative elections took place in November 2001. Former Vice-President and PLC candidate Enrique Bolaños Geyer was elected President, with 56% of votes cast, while Ortega, standing again for the FSLN, secured 42%. The PLC also won a majority of seats in the Asamblea Nacional.

Bolaños took office in January 2002. Almost immediately he encountered opposition from within his own party, when members of the PLC rejected his preferred candidate for President of the Asamblea Nacional, Jaime Cuadra, and voted in favour of former President Alemán. In March the Attorney-General announced that Alemán was to face charges of fraud and embezzlement. In the months that followed Bolaños made several unsuccessful attempts to remove Alemán's congressional immunity, as internal divisions within the PLC meant that he lacked the votes necessary to have the motion approved.

In September 2002 several of Alemán's relatives and former members of his Government were convicted of laundering some US $100m. from state communications, infrastructure, insurance and petroleum enterprises. One week later Alemán, who faced the same charges, suspended a parliamentary session at which the removal of his immunity was to be discussed. The following day FSLN members joined the Bolaños faction of the PLC to vote in favour of Alemán's dismissal. Cuadra was installed as President of the Asamblea. In December the Asamblea Nacional approved a motion revoking Alemán's immunity; the former President was immediately put under house arrest.

In October 2002 Bolaños himself became the subject of allegations of fraud. In response to charges filed with the Supreme Court, that he and his Vice-President, José Rizo Castellón, had used an illegal fund controlled by Alemán to finance his 2001 electoral campaign, Bolaños renounced his presidential immunity. In November Bolaños and Rizo were formally charged with embezzling US $4.1m. from public funds.

Alemán's arrest further deepened divisions within the PLC. In March 2003 the pro-Alemán faction of the PLC officially announced that it was in opposition to the Government, in protest at the Government's alliance with the FSLN. This left Bolaños with the unconditional support of only nine PLC members in the Asamblea (although six members of the Alemán faction later declared their allegiance to the President).

In December 2003 Alemán was found guilty of money-laundering, fraud and theft of state funds and was sentenced to 20 years' imprisonment. He was also fined US $17m. Owing to ill health, however, he was to serve his prison term under house arrest. In the same month the alliance between the FSLN and the pro-Bolaños PLC members collapsed, following the latter's insistence on the release of Alemán.

In March 2004 President Bolaños, Vice-President Rizo and 31 other senior members of the PLC were accused of illegal campaign-financing during the previous presidential election. Seven PLC members were arrested, including party President Jorge Castillo Quant. In October the Comptroller-General requested that President Bolaños be removed from power for withholding information regarding the financing of his 2001 election campaign. Supporters of the President claimed that the request was politically motivated, as the office of the Comptroller-General was controlled by the FSLN and the anti-Bolaños faction of the PLC. At the invitation of Bolaños, a delegation arrived from the OAS to investigate the Comptroller-General's findings. Following a meeting with the OAS representatives, Ortega agreed to withdraw FSLN support for the initiation of impeachment proceedings against the President until after the November municipal elections.

The FSLN won a decisive victory in the local elections of November 2004. The following day a two-thirds' majority in the Asamblea Nacional voted in support of constitutional reform legislation limiting presidential powers. The reforms would notably require the President to seek legislative ratification for key appointments and would enable the Asamblea to remove officials deemed to be incompetent. In December President Bolaños appealed to the Supreme Court, contending that the reforms, supported by the FSLN and the PLC, were unconstitutional. In January 2005 the Central American Court of Justice ruled that ratification of the controversial constitutional amendments should be suspended. None the less, one week later the Asamblea approved the legislation. Following further negotiations between factions supporting Bolaños, Ortega and Alemán, the President agreed to promulgate the controversial reforms in return for a pledge from the opposition that it would work towards a consensus with the executive on such matters as the budget and social security reform.

Meanwhile, accusations against Bolaños and his associates of illegal campaign-financing persisted. In September 2005 seven Central American heads of state gathered in Managua to demonstrate their support for Bolaños. None the less, later that month the Asamblea Nacional removed the immunity from prosecution of three ministers and three deputy ministers.

Dissent over the proposed constitutional reforms impeded the Government's legislative agenda in 2005, including efforts to gain approval for the proposed Dominican Republic-Central American Free Trade Agreement (DR-CAFTA, comprising Nicaragua, Costa Rica, the Dominican Republic, El Salvador,

Guatemala, Honduras and the USA). Following the intervention of the US Assistant Secretary of State, who publicly criticized the PLC-FSLN legislative pact and proposed the implementation of DR-CAFTA without Nicaragua, in October the FSLN withdrew its opposition to the trade agreement, which was swiftly approved by the Asamblea Nacional.

The return of Ortega

Presidential and legislative elections took place on 5 November 2006. Ortega, who had sought to distance himself from the more extreme Sandinista policies of the 1980s, was elected to the presidency with 38% of the votes cast. Eduardo Montealegre Rivas of the Alianza Liberal Nicaragüense (ALN), a recently founded party composed primarily of dissident former PLC members opposed to Alemán (who had been released on probation in 2005), secured 28%, while former Vice-President Rizo, a close ally of Alemán, took 27% on behalf of the PLC. The FSLN also became the largest party in the Asamblea Nacional. An estimated 69% of the electorate participated in the poll.

Ortega took office on 10 January 2007. His wife, Rosario Murillo Zambrana, was appointed to the newly created cabinet position of Co-ordinator of the Communication and Citizenship Council, in which role she was to be responsible for all government publicity. Later that month the President issued a decree more than halving his own salary and substantially lowering those of government ministers and other senior officials. The Asamblea Nacional adopted amendments to legislation on the organization and duties of the executive. Proposed by Ortega and supported by the PLC, these reforms gave the President greater control over the police force and the military and allowed the President to create 'Citizen Power Councils' by decree. Amid concerns regarding the potential power of these Councils, which were intended to encourage direct democracy by co-ordinating the work of non-governmental organizations and public institutions on a regional and local level, opposition parties insisted that they should be purely consultative and not assume any of the functions of government ministries.

Also in late January 2007 the legislature approved the further postponement, for one year, of the constitutional amendments limiting presidential powers that had been due to take effect that month. A special commission, comprising seven deputies, was charged in February with drafting new constitutional reform legislation. In January 2008 the Supreme Court annulled the law postponing the implementation of the constitutional reforms, although it also declared invalid the majority of the reforms themselves. However, it did not annul the law requiring the President to seek legislative approval of key appointments, with the result that this reform duly entered into force.

The Commission for Verification, Reconciliation, Peace and Justice was formally constituted in May 2007 under the chairmanship of Cardinal Obando y Bravo. Its stated remit was to continue the work of the commission established following the peace accords of 1987, ensuring that former combatants and victims of the war had received land and compensation as stipulated in the accords.

The 2008 municipal elections

Events surrounding the municipal elections of November 2008 caused substantial tension between the FSLN and its opponents. In April the Government postponed the elections in the Región Autónoma Atlántico Norte (RAAN) until 2009, owing to the damage caused by Hurricane Felix in 2007. Anti-Government protesters claimed that the FSLN was acting to avoid an electoral defeat in the autonomous region, and riots led to two deaths. In June 2008 the CSE, composed of seven magistrates, all of whom were aligned with either the FSLN or the PLC, revoked the legal status of the MRS and the Partido Conservador (PC) for administrative reasons, provoking criticism that the PLC-FSLN legislative pact remained in place and continued to pose a threat to multi-party democracy. In the elections, which were held on 9 November, the FSLN secured 105 of the 146 contested mayoralties, including that of Managua, while the PLC took 37. However, allegations of widespread fraud undermined the results. A recount in Managua was negotiated, but demands that it be monitored by independent observers were rejected, and the recount confirmed the victory of the FSLN candidate, Alexis Argüello. Standing in opposition to Argüello was former presidential candidate Eduardo Montealegre, whose movement, Vamos con Eduardo (VCE), had formed a political alliance with the PLC. The PLC-VCE alliance, supported by the monitoring organization Etica y Transparencia (EyT, which the Government had refused to accredit), maintained that Montealegre was the rightful mayor of Managua. The FSLN made significant gains in the delayed municipal elections held in the RAAN in January 2009. A report published in March by the non-governmental anti-corruption organization Transparency International alleged that fraud had occurred in at least 40 of the 146 municipalities contested in November 2008. Following the apparent suicide of Argüello in July 2009, his deputy, Daisy Torres, became mayor of Managua. At elections to the Atlantic Coast Regional Councils in March 2010, which were marked by a high rate of abstention, the FSLN remained the largest party in the RAAN, as did the PLC in the Región Autónoma Atlántico Sur (RAAS), although neither secured a majority of seats.

Judicial controversy

The Government continued to attract controversy during 2009, managing in October to secure the removal of the one-term limit on presidential tenure by means of a ruling by the constitutional panel of the highly politicized Supreme Court. The ruling, which was deemed illegal on the basis that only the Asamblea Nacional could effect constitutional change, was condemned by opposition parties and by the US authorities. Further tension was provoked in January 2010, when the President issued a decree extending the terms of incumbent electoral and judicial officials, defying a constitutional provision according the Asamblea Nacional responsibility for such appointments. An opposition boycott of the legislature ensued in protest against the decree. Following the refusal of two FSLN-aligned Supreme Court judges to leave their posts on the expiry of their terms in April, opposition deputies attempted to convene with the aim of overturning Ortega's controversial decree, but were forcibly prevented from doing so by government supporters. The crisis escalated in August, with the replacement of seven PLC-affiliated judges who had refused to participate in court sessions in protest against the continuance in office of the two FSLN judges whose terms had expired; five of the substitute judges were aligned with the ruling party and two with the opposition. In two contentious judgments in September, the Supreme Court upheld both the decree issued by Ortega extending the mandates of electoral and judicial officials and the ruling that revoked the constitutional provision prohibiting consecutive presidential re-election. In October, moreover, the Asamblea Nacional approved the publication in the previous month of a new version of the Constitution, incorporating Ortega's January decree.

In February 2011 the FSLN officially designated Ortega as its candidate for the forthcoming presidential election, which was scheduled to take place on 6 November, concurrently with legislative polls. In addition to Alemán, who had been endorsed as the PLC's candidate at a party congress in July 2010, Ortega's main rival for the presidency was former PLC member Fabio Gadea Mantilla, representing an alliance of the Partido Liberal Independiente (PLI) and the Unidad Nicaragüense por la Esperanza (UNE), which comprised various opposition parties and movements, including the VCE and the MRS. In April the CSE rejected a challenge by the PLI to the legitimacy of Ortega's candidacy.

The re-election of Ortega

Ortega was victorious in the presidential election of 6 November 2011, winning 62.5% of the valid votes cast, followed by Gadea, with 31.0%, and Alemán, with only 5.9%; two other candidates contested the ballot, but each attracted less than 0.5% of the vote. The FSLN also performed strongly in the concurrently held legislative elections, securing an unexpected two-thirds' majority in the Asamblea Nacional, with 62 of the 90 elective seats, while the PLI took 26 seats and the PLC two. Gadea and the outgoing Vice-President, Jaime René Morales Carazo of the FSLN, were both awarded supplementary legislative seats, in accordance with electoral rules. However, Gadea rejected the results, alleging widespread manipulation of the vote by the FSLN. International observers from the OAS and the European Union (EU) also expressed concern about the transparency of the vote, as well as the independence of the CSE, while domestic observers from the Nicaraguan civil society group Instituto para el Desarrollo y la Democracia (Ipade) and EyT, which had not been accredited by the Government, reported numerous irregularities. Three opposition supporters and one Sandinista were killed in post-election violence in the north of the country.

Notwithstanding the allegations of fraud in the 2011 elections and ongoing doubts concerning the legality of his candidacy, Ortega's overwhelming victory and that of his party could be attributed to the popularity and success of the Government's poverty reduction and other social programmes (largely funded by Venezuela) and the stability of the economy. In December 2011 Gadea announced that, despite continuing to maintain that the elections were fraudulent, the PLI would assume its seats in the Asamblea in order to provide opposition to Ortega's administration, but that he would not take up the supplementary seat to which he was entitled as second-placed presidential candidate, as he refused to accept defeat. President Ortega was inaugurated for a further term of office on 10 January 2012 in a ceremony boycotted by the main opposition parties.

In February 2012 Antenor Rosales was replaced as President of the central bank by Alberto Guevara Obregón, hitherto Minister of Finance and Public Credit. The resignation of Rosales, ostensibly for health reasons, was widely believed to be linked to his reluctance to implement Ortega's plan to use some US $17m. of Nicaragua's international reserves for the creation of a regional bank proposed by the Venezuela-led Bolivarian Alliance for the Peoples of our America (Alianza Bolivariana para las Pueblos de Nuestra América—ALBA, see p. 474). Obregón was succeeded at the finance ministry by his deputy, Iván Acosta. Meanwhile, FSLN supporters protested outside the party's headquarters in February against the imposition by the party leadership of candidates for municipal elections scheduled for November.

The confiscation, in February 2012, of land belonging to a Swiss-Nicaraguan investor, and its transferral to the ownership of former Sandinista guerrilla Edén Pastora (who had reconciled with Ortega since unsuccessfully contesting the 2006 presidential election), provoked consternation within the private sector regarding the Government's respect for property rights, with opposition members drawing comparisons with the land expropriation conducted by the Sandinistas towards the end of Ortega's first presidential mandate (1979–90). In the following month thousands of former Sandinista combatants blocked roads in several northern provinces for more than one week, demanding land, medical assistance, pensions and other benefits that they had been promised prior to demobilization in the early 1990s. The Government agreed to address their demands, but there was renewed unrest in mid-2012. Legislation on benefits for veterans was finally approved in January 2013.

In April 2012 the President of the Asamblea Nacional, René Núñez Téllez, announced that the long-awaited election by the legislature of 23 senior judicial and electoral officials was to take place. Although the mandates of the incumbents of these posts had expired, they had continued serving in accordance with the decree issued by Ortega in January 2010 (see Judicial controversy), when the FSLN notably lacked a legislative majority. It was noted, however, that several officials, including the President of the CSE, Ortega ally Roberto Rivas Reyes, were not among those to be replaced, despite their mandates also having expired.

Reforms to legislation on municipalities, which provided for an increase in the number of councillors from 2,178 to 6,534 and permitted the re-election of local officials, were adopted by the Asamblea Nacional in May 2012. Although the Government stated that the changes were intended to strengthen direct democracy, critics claimed that the Ortega administration was seeking to expand its control at municipal level.

In July 2012 the Asamblea Nacional approved a government proposal to create a new state body, chaired by the Deputy Minister of Foreign Affairs, Manuel Coronel Kautz, with responsibility for planning the construction of an inter-oceanic canal. It was estimated that the project would take 10 years to complete and cost some US $30,000m., around one-half of which would be sourced from foreign investors.

Recent developments: the 2012 municipal elections

The FSLN consolidated its power at the municipal elections of 4 November 2012, securing control of 134 of the 153 municipalities and 16 of the 17 departmental and regional capitals; the PLI won 13, the PLC two, the ALN one, and Yatama, which was allied to the FSLN, three. In Managua, the FSLN's Torres was re-elected as mayor with 83% of the votes cast. The MRS boycotted the polls on the grounds that conditions were not in place for transparent elections, while another opposition party, the Unión Demócrata Cristiana, was prevented from participating by the CSE, which claimed that it had failed to meet the legal requirement to present candidates in over 80% of municipalities. Monitors from the OAS noted some problems, notably with the voters' register, but were generally satisfied with the conduct of the elections. However, the EyT, which had not received official accreditation, claimed that fraud had been perpetrated in four municipalities and noted irregularities in a further 66, while

Ipade (also not accredited) expressed concerns regarding the process of issuing voter identity cards, and opposition parties claimed that some of the candidates registered were in fact dead. The CSE, which had refused to amend the ballot papers in response to these complaints prior to voting, rejected official opposition challenges to the results in four municipalities. Violence marred the period surrounding the elections: a PLC candidate was shot dead in Siuna, in the RAAN, in late October, and three people were killed the day after polling, as clashes broke out in several municipalities between government and opposition supporters.

Foreign Affairs

Relations with the USA

Full military relations between Nicaragua and the USA, suspended since 1980, were re-established in 2001. In 2004 the Government agreed to destroy one-half of its stockpile of surface-to-air missiles. However, dissatisfaction with a lack of progress on the issue prompted the US Administration to suspend military aid to Nicaragua in April–October 2005. In 2007 President Daniel Ortega proposed the destruction of 651 missiles, leaving 400 for the purposes of national defence, in exchange for military helicopters and medical equipment from the USA. Talks between the two countries concerning the destruction of the missiles took place during 2008, but did not result in agreement.

The dispute regarding the results of the municipal elections of November 2008 strained international relations: in that month the EU and the USA both suspended budgetary aid to Nicaragua owing to the country's failure to resolve the dispute. In June 2009 the US Government's Millennium Challenge Corporation announced the cancellation of US $62m. (of a total of $175m.) of funds to Nicaragua. Ortega criticized the decision and declared that the shortfall would in part be compensated by assistance from ALBA. The November 2011 general election also provoked international concern: the US Secretary of State, Hillary Clinton, in January 2012 described the election as a 'setback to democracy', while the US-based human rights group Freedom House removed Nicaragua from its list of electoral democracies, citing irregularities before and during the election. In June, moreover, citing Nicaragua's failure to account fully for finance provided by Venezuela, the USA decided not to renew its waiver for Nicaragua from restrictions on assistance to the governments of countries deemed not to be maintaining international standards of fiscal transparency. As a result, military and counternarcotics aid worth some $3m. was witheld. However, in July, by contrast, the USA opted to renew a separate annual waiver for Nicaragua from legislation prohibiting US support for assistance from international financial institutions for countries that had not compensated US citizens for confiscated property; the cancellation of this property waiver would potentially have been much more damaging financially to Nicaragua. Fears in Nicaragua that the fiscal transparency and property waivers would be cancelled had been raised in May, when the recently appointed US ambassador to the country, Phyllis Powers, had issued a warning suggesting that both were under threat owing to concerns regarding fiscal transparency, insufficient progress in resolving new and historic property seizures and the overall state of democracy. Following the municipal elections in November, the US Department of State again criticized the electoral process in Nicaragua, asserting that a range of irregularities had marred successive recent elections in the country.

Other regional relations

In December 1999, following confrontations with Honduras, Nicaragua initiated proceedings at the International Court of Justice (ICJ, see p. 26) in The Hague, Netherlands, to determine the maritime delimitation in the Gulf of Fonseca. In that month a dispute arose prompting Nicaragua to sever commercial ties with, and impose import taxes on, Honduras, in direct contravention of Central American free trade undertakings. Following mediation by the OAS, in 2000 Nicaragua ended its trade sanctions against Honduras, and both countries signed an accord committing them to observe a maritime exclusion zone in the Caribbean and to reduce troop numbers on their common border. However, following further illegal incursions by both sides, in 2001 Nicaragua submitted documentation to the ICJ contesting the treaty. Nicaragua also refused to participate in the joint patrol of the Gulf of Fonseca. In June, following OAS-sponsored discussions in March, Nicaragua and Honduras concluded a confidence-building agreement, which provided for OAS observers to monitor the actions of army and navy forces on both sides

of the common border. The ICJ ruled on a revised maritime border approximately mid-way between the two countries in 2007. Both the Nicaraguan and Honduran Governments declared themselves satisfied with the ruling.

In 1997 relations with Costa Rica became strained when the latter began deporting Nicaraguans who were residing illegally in the country. Remittances from Nicaraguans in Costa Rica represented a significant contribution to the Nicaraguan economy. Further antagonism had developed between the two countries in 1998 when Nicaragua prohibited Costa Rican civil guards from carrying arms while navigating the San Juan river, which forms the border between the two countries. According to a long-standing treaty, the river, which is Nicaraguan territory, was only to be used by Costa Rica for commercial purposes. Following protests by Costa Rica, agreement was reached allowing for that country's civil guard to carry arms on the river while under escort by the Nicaraguan authorities. In August, however, Nicaragua annulled the accord. In 2000 both Governments agreed a procedure that would allow armed Costa Rican police officers to patrol the river. However, following continued tensions over Costa Rica's use of the river, in 2002 the two countries agreed to attempt to resolve the dispute within three years. Failure to achieve this prompted Costa Rica to refer the matter to the ICJ in September 2005. In response, President Bolaños recalled the Nicaraguan ambassador to Costa Rica, ordered the troops patrolling the border area to prohibit the passage of armed Costa Rican police officers, and imposed a 35% tariff on Costa Rican imports. In July 2009 the ICJ upheld Nicaragua's right to regulate traffic on the river and ruled that, although Costa Rica had the right to navigate freely on the river for commercial purposes, Costa Rican vessels undertaking police functions were not permitted to use the river. Bilateral tensions were renewed in October 2010, however, when the Costa Rican Government deployed armed police officers to the joint border, alleging that Nicaraguan troops had violated Costa Rican territory while dredging the river. Costa Rica referred the matter to the ICJ. Pending a definitive ruling, in March 2011 the Court ordered both sides to withdraw police, security and civilian personnel from the disputed area, but did not accede to a Costa Rican demand that Nicaraguan dredging operations be suspended. Amid continued tensions, in December 2011 Nicaragua initiated new proceedings against Costa Rica at the ICJ, claiming that major works by the latter country in the border area, particularly the construction of a road parallel to the southern bank of the San Juan river, were in violation of Nicaragua's sovereignty and causing environmental damage to its territory. Laura Chinchilla, the President of Costa Rica, was notably absent from President Ortega's inauguration in January 2012. Relations deteriorated further in June, when the Costa Rican Ministry of Foreign Relations sent a formal letter of complaint to Nicaragua over its plans to build an inter-oceanic canal, one potential route for which would follow the course of the San Juan river. In the following month Costa Rica rejected a ruling by the Central American Court of Justice ordering it to halt the construction of the road parallel to the southern bank of the river, stating that it did not recognize the court's jurisdiction. The case against Costa Rica had been filed by two Nicaraguan non-governmental institutions, which cited environmental concerns. Tensions mounted in October, when Costa Rica accused Nicaragua of continuing to post personnel to the disputed area of the river, in contravention of the March 2011 interim ruling by the ICJ. In February 2013 it was reported that Nicaragua had requested that the ICJ grant it navigational rights on the Colorado river, which is Costa Rican territory, provoking condemnation from the Costa Rican Government.

In 2001 a dispute with Colombia arose after a Nicaraguan fishing vessel was captured, allegedly in Colombian waters. Nicaragua presented a request to the ICJ that its claim over territorial waters in the Caribbean Sea and around the islands of San Andrés and Providencia be recognized. The ICJ dismissed Nicaragua's claim to the San Andrés archipelago in December 2007, while continuing to consider the jurisdiction of the other disputed waters. The ICJ issued its final judgment in November 2012, confirming Colombian sovereignty over all seven disputed cays and smaller islands, but awarding Nicaragua control of an estimated 75,000 sq km of territorial waters hitherto considered Colombian. The binding ruling was generally interpreted as a victory for Nicaragua, with the Colombian Government rejecting the new maritime border delineated by the ICJ and ordering its naval forces to remain in the waters to be ceded to Nicaragua, while the Nicaraguan Government announced plans to commence oil explorations in its new waters. At a meeting of

President Ortega and his Colombian counterpart, Juan Manuel Santos, in Mexico at the beginning of December, both leaders sought to downplay bilateral tensions, insisting that the dispute would be resolved peacefully. Meanwhile, relations had been further strained in June, when a Colombian journalist, Luis Felipe Ríos Castaño, was charged with espionage in Nicaragua; having pleaded guilty, Ríos Castaño was convicted in July of seeking classified information on Nicaragua's defence and security on behalf of the Colombian intelligence forces, and sentenced to 16 years' imprisonment.

President Ortega sought to strengthen relations with other left-wing administrations in Latin America. In 2007 he confirmed Nicaragua's participation in ALBA, which had been devised by Venezuela as an alternative model to the US-promoted Free Trade Area of the Americas. Furthermore, Ortega signed a number of economic agreements with the Venezuelan President, Hugo Chávez, who pledged substantial financial assistance to Nicaragua, including the construction of a petroleum refinery and the provision of low-interest loans for impoverished Nicaraguans living in rural areas. In March a joint Nicaraguan-Venezuelan committee was formed to advance plans for bilateral co-operation, particularly in the energy sector. Under its Petrocaribe initiative, Venezuela was to supply Nicaragua with 10,000 barrels of petroleum per day at preferential rates and 32 electricity generators to alleviate severe energy shortages. Following a visit to Managua by Chávez, in 2010 Ortega announced that ALBA funds would be used to finance the provision of monthly bonuses of US $25 for some 120,000 (later increased to 147,500) public sector workers; the bonus was raised to $31 per month a year later. Following pressure from the IMF, in April 2011 the central bank published a report on foreign funds received by Nicaragua, which revealed that Venezuela had provided some $1,590m. during 2007–10. Financial co-operation from Venezuela continued to rise in 2011, reaching $609m. (more than 90% of which was related to subsidized petroleum), an increase of 14% from the $533m. received in 2010. Following Chávez's death in March 2013, concerns mounted in Nicaragua regarding the possibility of a future decline in financial assistance from Venezuela—particularly in the form of the amendment or abolition of the Petrocaribe arrangement—despite the election of Chávez's favoured successor, Nicolás Maduro, to the Venezuelan presidency in April.

CONSTITUTION AND GOVERNMENT

A new Constitution was promulgated in January 1987. Amendments to the Constitution were approved by the Asamblea Nacional (National Assembly) in 1995 and 2000. Executive power is vested in the President, who is elected by popular vote for a five-year term. The President is assisted by a Vice-President and an appointed Cabinet. Legislative power is held by the Asamblea Nacional, elected by universal adult suffrage, under a system of proportional representation, for a five-year term.

REGIONAL AND INTERNATIONAL CO-OPERATION

Nicaragua is a member of the Organization of American States (see p. 404), the Central American Common Market (CACM, see p. 237), the Inter-American Development Bank (see p. 341), the Association of Caribbean States (see p. 459), and of the Community of Latin American and Caribbean States (see p. 475), which was formally inaugurated in December 2011. Implementation of the Dominican Republic-Central American Free Trade Agreement (DR-CAFTA) with the USA, which entailed the gradual elimination of tariffs on most industrial and agricultural products over the following 10 and 20 years, respectively, took place in April 2006. A free trade agreement between Nicaragua, Costa Rica, El Salvador, Guatemala, Honduras and Mexico was signed in November 2011. Nicaragua is a founder member of the UN. As a contracting party to the General Agreement on Tariffs and Trade, Nicaragua joined the World Trade Organization (see p. 444) on its establishment in 1995. Nicaragua is a member of the Group of 77 (see p. 461).

ECONOMIC AFFAIRS

In 2011, according to estimates by the World Bank, Nicaragua's gross national income (GNI), measured at average 2009–11 prices, was US $6,842m., equivalent to $1,170 per head (or $2,840 per head on an international purchasing-power parity basis). During 2002–11 the population increased at an average annual rate of 1.3%, while gross domestic product (GDP) per head grew, in real terms, by an average of 2.0% per year.

Nicaragua's GDP increased, in real terms, by an average of 3.4% per year in 2002–11; GDP expanded by a preliminary 5.4% in 2011.

Agriculture (including forestry and fishing) contributed a preliminary 20.5% of GDP and engaged some 31.5% of the employed work-force in 2011. The principal cash crops are coffee (which accounted for 19.0% of export earnings in 2011), groundnuts, sugar cane and beans. Maize, rice and beans are the principal food crops. Meat and meat products accounted for 18.9% of export earnings in 2011. According to official estimates, agricultural GDP increased at an average annual rate of 3.3% during 2002–11; agricultural GDP increased by 2.5% in 2011.

Industry (including mining, manufacturing, construction and power) provided a preliminary 29.6% of GDP and engaged 18.5% of the employed labour force in 2011. According to official estimates, industrial GDP increased by an average of 3.9% per year during 2002–11; the sector expanded by 8.2% in 2011.

Mining contributed a preliminary 2.0% of GDP and engaged 0.7% of the employed labour force in 2011. Nicaragua has workable deposits of gold, silver, copper, lead, antimony, zinc and iron; its non-metallic minerals include limestone, gypsum, bentonite and marble. In 2011 gold accounted for 15.6% of export earnings. According to official estimates, the GDP of the mining sector increased at an average annual rate of 1.9% in 2002–11; the sector's GDP increased by 11.7% in 2011.

Manufacturing contributed some 19.5% of GDP and engaged 11.4% of the employed labour force in 2011. The principal branches of manufacturing were food products, beverages and tobacco. The *maquila* (or assembly) sector was important. The principal products were clothing, footwear, aluminium frames and jewellery. Manufacturing GDP increased, according to official figures, by an average of 4.9% per year in 2002–11; the sector's GDP grew by 7.6% in 2011.

Construction contributed some 5.2% of GDP and engaged 5.9% of the employed labour force in 2011. Construction GDP fell, according to official figures, by an average of 1.1% per year in 2002–11; the sector's GDP decreased by 12.5% in 2010, but increased by 17.0% in 2011.

Energy is derived principally from imported petroleum (about 69.1% in 2009), although two hydroelectric plants in the department of Jinotega accounted for some 8.6% of the electrical energy generated in the country in that year. Imports of crude petroleum comprised 11.8% of the total value of imports in 2011. In 2011 Nicaragua produced an estimated 3,824.2m. kWh of electrical energy.

The services sector contributed an estimated 49.9% of GDP and engaged 50.0% of the employed labour force in 2011. The tourism sector has become increasingly significant in recent years; in 2011 annual tourism income totalled US $377m., with arrivals put at 1,011,251, an increase of 8.5% on the previous year's figures. According to official figures, the GDP of the services sector increased by an average of 3.5% per year in 2002–11; the sector's GDP increased by 4.5% in 2011.

In 2011 Nicaragua recorded a visible merchandise trade deficit of US $2,180.8m., and there was a deficit of $1,302.1m. on the current account of the balance of payments. In 2011 the principal source of imports (21.9% of the total) was Venezuela; other major suppliers were the USA, Mexico and Nicaragua's partners in the Central American Common Market (CACM—Costa Rica, El Salvador, Guatemala and Honduras, see p. 237). The USA was the principal market for exports (28.7% of the total) in 2011; other notable purchasers were Venezuela, Canada and El Salvador. A free trade agreement with Mexico entered into force in September 2012. The principal exports in 2011 were coffee, meat, gold and sugar. The principal imports were non-durable consumer goods, primary materials and intermediate goods for industry, and crude petroleum.

In 2011 Nicaragua recorded a budgetary surplus of an estimated 1,011m. gold córdobas. Nicaragua's general government gross debt was 115,750m. gold córdobas in 2011, equivalent to 70.7% of GDP. At the end of 2010 Nicaragua's total external debt was US $4,786m., of which $2,668m. was public and publicly guaranteed debt. In that year, the cost of servicing long-term public and publicly guaranteed debt and repayments to the IMF was equivalent to 14.3% of the value of exports of goods, services and income (excluding workers' remittances). According to the ILO, in 2002–11 the average annual rate of increase in consumer prices was 8.9%. Consumer prices rose by an annual average of 8.1% in 2011. An estimated 6.3% of the labour force was unemployed in 2011.

A focus on social policies by the administration of Daniel Ortega, which took office in 2007, resulted in a reduction in maternal mortality and poverty rates, increased school enrolment and literacy, and improved access to safe water. In addition, programmes were initiated to stimulate agricultural productivity, and in 2011 FAO praised Nicaraguan efforts to attain self-sufficiency in crop production. Following disputed municipal elections in 2008 and criticism of the conduct of the general election of November 2011 (see Contemporary Political History), the USA, the EU and several European countries suspended or halted aid to Nicaragua, although contributions from Venezuela, which have been substantial during Ortega's presidency, continued to rise. The economy was adversely affected by the global financial crisis in 2009, not least because of the decline in income from exports (particularly textiles sales to the USA) and remittances from workers abroad. After a contraction in real GDP of 2.2% in 2009, a strong recovery in export earnings, remittances and investment contributed to robust GDP growth rates in 2010 and 2011 of 3.6% and 4.4%, respectively. Inflation also eased, declining from 9.2% in 2010 to 6.6% in 2012. Remittances grew by 11.2% in 2012, to US $1,014m., while foreign direct investment (FDI) declined by 16.3%, having increased by 90.5% in 2011, to a record $967.9m., partly owing to Nicaragua's low labour costs and relative security compared with other Central American countries. The energy and telecommunications sectors and free trade zones attracted 52% of total FDI in 2011, with renewable energy projects of particular interest to investors, in line with a government aim to increase the proportion of energy generated by renewable sources from some 40% currently to 80% by 2017. Official data put GDP growth at 5.2% in 2012, although the IMF estimated economic expansion to be lower, at 3.7%. The budget for 2013 forecast GDP growth in that year of 4.1%, amid an uncertain global economic outlook. Negotiations aimed at concluding a new agreement with the IMF commenced in November 2012, following the expiry in 2011 of an Extended Credit Facility approved in 2007. Tax reforms, including a gradual increase in the income tax threshold and measures to improve administration, were adopted that month, but civil society groups criticized a decision to retain certain tax exemptions for the private sector for a further two years.

PUBLIC HOLIDAYS

2014: 1 January (New Year's Day), 17 April (Maundy Thursday), 18 April (Good Friday), 1 May (Labour Day), 19 July (Liberation Day), 14 September (Battle of San Jacinto), 15 September (Independence Day), 2 November (All Souls' Day, afternoon only), 8 December (Immaculate Conception), 25 December (Christmas Day).

Various local holidays are also observed.

Statistical Survey

Sources (unless otherwise stated): Banco Central de Nicaragua, Carretera Sur, Km 7, Apdos 2252/3, Zona 5, Managua; tel. 265-0500; fax 265-2272; e-mail bcn@cabcn.gob.ni; internet www.bcn.gob.ni; Instituto Nacional de Información de Desarrollo, Los Arcos, Frente Hospital Fonseca, Managua; tel. 266-6178; e-mail webmaster@inide.gob.ni; internet www.inide.gob.ni.

Area and Population

AREA, POPULATION AND DENSITY

Area (sq km)	
Land	120,340
Inland water	10,034
Total	130,373*
Population (census results)	
25 April 1995	4,357,099
28 May–11 June 2005	
Males	2,534,491
Females	2,607,607
Total	5,142,098
Population (official estimates at mid-year)	
2010	5,815,524
2011	5,888,946
2012	6,071,045
Density (per sq km) at mid-2012	50.4†

* 50,337 sq miles.
† Land area only.

POPULATION BY AGE AND SEX
(official estimates at mid-2011)

	Males	Females	Total
0–14	1,021,153	981,415	2,002,568
15–64	1,768,451	1,852,436	3,620,887
65 and over	123,252	142,239	265,491
Total	**2,912,856**	**2,976,090**	**5,888,946**

ADMINISTRATIVE DIVISIONS
(land area only, population estimates at mid-2012)

	Area (sq km)	Population	Density (per sq km)	Capital
Departments:				
Chinandega . .	4,822.4	423,062	87.7	Chinandega
León	5,138.0	404,471	78.7	León
Managua . .	3,465.1	1,448,271	418.0	Managua
Masaya . . .	610.8	348,254	570.2	Masaya
Carazo . . .	1,081.4	186,898	172.8	Jinotepe
Granada . . .	1,039.7	200,991	193.3	Granada
Rivas . . .	2,161.8	174,589	80.8	Rivas
Estelí . . .	2,229.7	220,703	99.0	Estelí
Madriz . . .	1,708.2	158,020	92.5	Somoto
Nueva Segovia . .	3,491.3	243,014	69.6	Ocotal
Jinotega . .	9,222.4	417,372	45.3	Jinotega
Matagalpa . .	6,803.9	542,419	79.7	Matagalpa
Boaco . . .	4,176.7	174,682	41.8	Boaco
Chontales . .	6,481.3	182,838	28.2	Juigalpa
Río San Juan . .	7,540.9	122,666	16.3	San Carlos
Autonomous Regions:				
Atlántico Norte (RAAN) . .	32,819.7	453,541	13.8	Bilwi
Atlántico Sur (RAAS) . .	27,546.3	369,254	13.4	Bluefields
Total	**120,339.5**	**6,071,045**	**50.4**	—

PRINCIPAL TOWNS
(population at 2005 census)

Managua (capital) .	937,489	Chinandega . .	121,793
León	174,051	Estelí . .	112,084
Masaya . . .	139,582	Granada . .	105,171
Matagalpa . .	133,416	Tipitapa . .	101,685

Mid-2012 (official estimates): Managua (capital) 1,028,808; León 201,100; Masaya 166,588; Matagalpa 150,643; Chinandega 133,361; Tipitapa 130,627; Granada 123,697; Estelí 122,924.

BIRTHS, MARRIAGES AND DEATHS
(annual averages, UN estimates)

	1995–2000	2000–05	2005–10
Birth rate (per 1,000)	30.1	26.2	24.8
Death rate (per 1,000)	5.6	5.0	4.7

Source: UN, *World Population Prospects: The 2010 Revision.*

2007: Registered live births 128,171; Registered marriages 20,918; Registered deaths 17,288. Note: Registration believed to be incomplete.

Life expectancy (years at birth): 74.0 (males 71.0; females 77.1) in 2011 (Source: World Bank, World Development Indicators database).

ECONOMICALLY ACTIVE POPULATION
('000, population aged 10 years and over)

	2009	2010	2011
Agriculture, forestry and fishing	600.8	834.2	883.8
Mining and quarrying	5.7	10.9	19.3
Manufacturing	274.6	299.2	320.4
Electricity, gas and water	10.9	13.8	13.2
Construction	99.4	103.0	166.2
Trade, restaurants and hotels	485.9	638.9	688.0
Transport and communications	86.6	97.7	102.3
Financial services	82.7	80.8	93.3
Public administration	90.2	—	—
Social and personal services	359.6	513.3	520.6
Total employed	2,096.5	2,591.7	2,807.1
Unemployed	186.2	220.1	189.6
Total labour force	2,282.7	2,811.8	2,996.7

Health and Welfare

KEY INDICATORS

Total fertility rate (children per woman, 2010)	2.6
Under-5 mortality rate (per 1,000 live births, 2010)	27
HIV/AIDS (% of persons aged 15–49, 2009)	0.2
Physicians (per 1,000 head, 2003)	0.4
Hospital beds (per 1,000 head, 2008)	0.9
Health expenditure (2009): US $ per head (PPP)	254
Health expenditure (2009): % of GDP	9.6
Health expenditure (2009): public (% of total)	54.8
Access to water (% of persons, 2010)	85
Access to sanitation (% of persons, 2010)	52
Total carbon emissions ('000 metric tons, 2008)	4,330.7
Carbon dioxide emissions per head (metric tons, 2008)	0.8
Human Development Index (2011): ranking	129
Human Development Index (2011): value	0.589

For sources and definitions, see explanatory note on p. vi.

Agriculture

PRINCIPAL CROPS
('000 metric tons)

	2009	2010	2011
Rice, paddy	334.5	454.0	516.7*
Maize	522.0	457.0	441.6*
Sorghum	57.7	58.8	62.4*
Cassava (Manioc)	101.9	73.8	75.0*
Sugar cane	5,115.5	4,893.9	5,937.5
Beans, dry	213.5	138.4	130.3*
Groundnuts, in shell†	167.4	180.3	183.0
Oil palm fruit*	73.0	86.7	86.7
Bananas	46.6	35.2	39.6
Plantains*	60.1	45.4	64.4
Oranges*	111.7	84.4	95.1
Pineapples*	66.8	50.5	56.8
Coffee, green	92.2	78.7	103.7

* FAO estimates.
† Unofficial figures.

Aggregate production ('000 metric tons, may include official, semi-official or estimated data): Total cereals 914 in 2009, 970 in 2010, 1,021 in 2011; Total roots and tubers 154 in 2009, 111 in 2010, 113 in 2011; Total vegetables (incl. melons) 37 in 2009, 37 in 2010 39 in 2011; Total fruits (excl. melons) 319 in 2009, 241 in 2010, 271 in 2011.

Source: FAO.

LIVESTOCK
('000 head, year ending September, FAO estimates)

	2009	2010	2011
Cattle	3,650	3,700	3,750
Pigs	475	480	495
Goats	7	7	8
Horses	268	268	268
Asses	9	9	9
Mules	48	48	48
Poultry	18,500	19,000	19,500

Source: FAO.

LIVESTOCK PRODUCTS
('000 metric tons)

	2009	2010	2011*
Cattle meat	107.6	121.0	130.0
Pig meat	7.2	7.7	7.9
Horse meat*	2.5	2.5	2.5
Chicken meat	89.6	102.3	112.0
Cows' milk	747.8	753.3	753.3
Hen eggs	23.2	24.5	24.5

* FAO estimates.
Source: FAO.

Forestry

ROUNDWOOD REMOVALS
('000 cubic metres, excl. bark, FAO estimates)

	2009	2010	2011
Sawlogs, veneer logs and logs for sleepers	54	202	118
Fuel wood	6,064	6,097	6,110
Total	6,118	6,299	6,228

Source: FAO.

SAWNWOOD PRODUCTION
('000 cubic metres, incl. railway sleepers, FAO estimates)

	2009	2010	2011
Coniferous	12.0	29	29
Broadleaved	40.0	77	33
Total	52.0	106	62

Source: FAO.

Fishing

('000 metric tons, live weight)

	2008	2009	2010
Capture	29.8	35.7	37.4
Snooks	1.1	0.5	0.9
Snappers	1.6	1.7	1.3
Yellowfin tuna	5.5	8.3	9.9
Skipjack tuna	6.0	4.4	4.3
Common dolphinfish	0.4	0.5	0.2
Caribbean spiny lobsters	4.2	3.4	3.7
Penaeus shrimp	1.8	2.3	2.6
Aquaculture	16.1	18.9	17.0
Whiteleg shrimp	14.7	17.4	16.6
Total catch	45.9	54.6	54.4

Source: FAO.

Mining

	2008	2009	2010
Gold (kg)	2,965	2,590	4,900
Silver (kg)	3,440	4,492	6,995
Gypsum and anhydrite (metric tons)	49,930	37,400	20,330

Source: US Geological Survey.

Industry

SELECTED PRODUCTS
('000 barrels unless otherwise indicated)

	2009	2010*	2011†
Liquid gas	140	172	192
Motor spirit	825	818	828
Kerosene	229	225	275
Diesel	1,591	1,586	1,657
Fuel oil	2,630	2,519	2,361
Bitumen (asphalt)	64	53	74
Electric energy (million kWh)	3,445.5	3,659.1	3,824.2

* Preliminary figures.
† Estimates.

Cement ('000 metric tons, estimates): 530 in 2006–10 (Source: US Geological Survey).

Finance

CURRENCY AND EXCHANGE RATES

Monetary Units
100 centavos = 1 córdoba oro (gold córdoba).

Sterling, Dollar and Euro Equivalents (30 November 2012)
£1 sterling = 38.579 gold córdobas;
US $1 = 24.026 gold córdobas;
€1 = 31.200 gold córdobas;
1,000 gold córdobas = £25.92 = $41.62 = €32.05.

Average Exchange Rate (gold córdobas per US dollar)
2009   20.3395
2010   21.3564
2011   22.4243

Note: In February 1988 a new córdoba, equivalent to 1,000 of the former units, was introduced, and a uniform exchange rate of US$1 = 10 new córdobas was established. Subsequently, the exchange rate was frequently adjusted. A new currency, the córdoba oro (gold córdoba), was introduced as a unit of account in May 1990 and began to be circulated in August. The value of the gold córdoba was initially fixed at par with the US dollar, but in March 1991 the exchange rate was revised to $1 = 25,000,000 new córdobas (or 5 gold córdobas). On 30 April 1991 the gold córdoba became the sole legal tender.

BUDGET
(million gold córdobas)

Revenue*	2009	2010	2011
Taxation	22,175.2	25,585.7	31,824.3
Income tax	7,817.7	8,350.7	11,143.4
Value-added tax	8,285.6	10,213.9	12,492.6
Taxes on petroleum products	2,276.6	2,698.9	2,700.1
Taxes on imports	975.2	1,558.6	1,901.4
Other revenue	1,684.1	1,989.3	2,722.6
Total	23,859.3	27,575.0	34,546.9

Expenditure†	2009	2010	2011
Compensation of employees	10,177.9	10,661.2	11,957.1
Goods and services	3,313.1	3,522.7	5,536.7
Interest payments	1,711.3	1,990.6	2,261.9
Domestic	1,158.0	1,396.2	1,552.8
External	553.3	594.5	709.1
Current and capital transfers	8,097.9	8,980.9	10,333.9
Social security contributions	1,324.0	1,358.9	822.0
Other expenditure	1,534.0	1,530.9	1,904.4
Total	26,158.3	28,045.3	32,816.1

* Excluding grants received (million gold córdobas): 3,079.5 in 2009; 2,833.9 in 2010; 3,151.2 in 2011.
† Excluding net acquisition of non-financial assets (million gold córdobas): 3,634.4 in 2009; 3,715.0 in 2010; 3,871.0 in 2011.

INTERNATIONAL RESERVES
(excluding gold, US $ million at 31 December)

	2009	2010	2011
IMF special drawing rights	164.48	161.48	175.77
Foreign exchange	1,408.60	1,637.50	1,716.48
Total	1,573.08	1,798.98	1,892.25

Source: IMF, *International Financial Statistics*.

MONEY SUPPLY
(million gold córdobas at 31 December)

	2009	2010	2011
Currency outside depository corporations	6,157.7	8,224.8	9,686.4
Transferable deposits	13,967.4	18,674.5	17,622.2
Other deposits	32,463.8	37,087.5	44,754.4
Broad money	52,589.0	63,986.8	72,062.9

Source: IMF, *International Financial Statistics*.

COST OF LIVING
(Consumer Price Index; base: 1999 = 100)

	2008	2009	2010
Food	242.8	252.4	263.8
Clothing	140.0	149.5	156.0
Rent, fuel and light . . .	219.3	213.8	233.7
All items (incl. others) . . .	214.2	222.2	234.4

2011: Food 287.7; All items (incl. others) 253.2.

Source: ILO.

NATIONAL ACCOUNTS
(million gold córdobas at current prices, preliminary)

Expenditure on the Gross Domestic Product

	2009	2010	2011
Final consumption expenditure .	125,448.6	140,707.3	167,749.8
Gross capital formation . . .	34,373.2	38,098.3	48,699.1
Total domestic expenditure .	159,821.8	178,805.6	216,449.0
Exports of goods and services . .	45,752.0	60,009.3	75,031.4
Less Imports of goods and services	79,187.5	98,063.2	127,839.7
GDP in purchasers' values .	126,386.2	140,751.7	163,640.6
GDP at constant 2006 prices .	127,397.7	132,012.9	139,206.3

Gross Domestic Product by Economic Activity

	2009	2010	2011
Agriculture, hunting, forestry and fishing	22,283.1	25,688.2	30,759.9
Mining and quarrying . . .	1,352.6	2,208.0	2,948.8
Manufacturing	21,576.2	24,427.0	29,288.4
Electricity, gas and water . .	3,477.2	4,079.6	4,460.7
Construction	6,261.5	5,921.9	7,794.1
Wholesale and retail trade . .	17,234.0	18,837.1	21,145.9
Transport and communications .	6,799.2	7,278.4	7,946.6
Finance, insurance and business services	6,609.2	6,464.4	6,859.5
General government services . .	15,666.4	16,019.9	17,935.3
Other services	17,786.1	19,265.7	21,082.7
Sub-total	119,045.5	130,190.4	150,221.9
Net taxes on products . . .	14,370.9	17,177.3	20,569.4
Less Imputed bank service charge.	7,030.2	6,616.0	7,150.7
GDP in purchasers' values .	126,386.2	140,751.7	163,640.6

BALANCE OF PAYMENTS
(US $ million)

	2009	2010	2011
Exports of goods	2,131.4	2,801.0	3,655.1
Imports of goods	−3,742.6	−4,535.5	−5,835.9
Balance on goods	−1,611.2	−1,734.5	−2,180.8
Exports of services	632.4	672.8	771.9
Imports of services	−664.2	−719.2	−837.5
Balance on goods and services	−1,643.0	−1,780.9	−2,246.4
Primary income received . .	14.7	14.5	17.4
Primary income paid	−265.2	−289.4	−264.7
Balance on goods, services and primary income	−1,893.5	−2,055.8	−2,493.7
Secondary income (net) . . .	1,118.4	1,172.8	1,191.6
Current balance	−775.1	−883.0	−1,302.1
Capital (net)	394.0	271.3	250.2
Direct investment liabilities . .	434.2	508.0	967.9
Other investment assets . .	−189.1	−100.9	−232.2
Other investment liabilities . .	274.2	411.1	496.2
Net errors and omissions . .	−79.6	−300.4	−371.8
Reserves and related items .	58.5	−94.0	−191.8

Source: IMF, *International Financial Statistics*.

External Trade

PRINCIPAL COMMODITIES
(US $ million, preliminary)

Imports c.i.f.	2009	2010	2011
Consumer goods	1,250.1	1,497.4	1,654.8
Non-durable consumer goods .	1,041.1	1,211.5	1,339.3
Durable consumer goods . .	208.9	285.9	315.5
Petroleum, mineral fuels and lubricants	699.0	776.0	1,256.4
Crude petroleum	346.8	419.8	615.6
Mineral fuels and lubricants .	352.0	355.6	639.3
Intermediate goods	870.1	1,122.4	1,337.4
Primary materials and intermediate goods for agriculture and fishing . .	182.4	222.4	271.9
Primary materials and intermediate goods for industry	525.4	681.2	799.7
Construction materials . . .	162.3	218.8	265.8
Capital goods	658.1	768.6	947.2
For agriculture and fishing . .	32.7	58.6	64.7
For industry	403.6	440.7	532.1
For transport	221.7	269.3	350.4
Miscellaneous	11.7	8.8	8.0
Total	3,489.0	4,173.2	5,203.7

Exports f.o.b.	2009	2010	2011
Coffee	236.8	341.6	429.3
Groundnuts	65.9	61.8	96.1
Cattle on hoof	17.8	21.5	18.6
Beans	61.5	59.4	30.2
Bananas	11.7	6.6	2.4
Lobster	31.1	40.4	45.9
Fresh fish	13.4	17.1	16.3
Shrimp	44.5	57.9	62.2
Tobacco (leaf)	5.1	6.7	6.3
Gold	81.2	208.3	352.3
Meat and meat products . .	230.6	307.6	427.0
Refined sugars, etc.	50.0	126.8	156.3
Cheese	76.9	68.7	81.4
Wood products	4.7	8.9	13.3
Chemical products	66.9	28.3	27.9
Refined petroleum	11.3	22.3	15.2
Porcelain products	4.6	6.1	8.3
Total (incl. others)	1,393.8	1,851.1	2,264.0

PRINCIPAL TRADING PARTNERS
(US $ million, preliminary)

Imports c.i.f.	2009	2010	2011
Costa Rica	319.7	350.2	438.2
Ecuador	41.4	31.2	10.0
El Salvador	170.0	197.5	234.0
Germany	42.4	51.6	65.0
Guatemala	217.4	280.3	347.8
Honduras	125.4	137.8	169.7
Japan	80.2	120.8	145.0
Korea, Republic	123.9	64.6	90.8
Mexico	243.6	336.8	406.3
Russia	38.8	27.5	67.9
Spain	51.7	65.0	54.7
USA	692.9	908.6	905.4
Venezuela	601.6	669.4	1,139.8
Total (incl. others)	3,489.0	4,173.2	5,203.7

Exports f.o.b.		2009	2010	2011
Belgium	. . . .	15.7	22.0	34.1
Canada	. . . .	42.3	157.4	273.4
Costa Rica	. . . . .	86.0	82.9	98.8
El Salvador	. . . . .	199.4	206.3	206.6
France	. . . .	19.0	28.2	25.9
Germany	. . . . . .	14.8	22.2	32.9
Guatemala	. . . . .	61.7	68.3	71.0
Honduras	. . . . .	100.6	61.6	59.4
Italy	. . . .	18.3	24.5	33.4
Japan	. . . .	9.1	15.5	23.3
Mexico	. . . . . .	56.7	51.7	82.8
Puerto Rico	. . . .	40.7	40.1	45.3
Spain	. . . .	36.3	39.1	36.4
Taiwan	. . . . . .	16.8	29.2	38.4
United Kingdom	. . .	40.3	4.7	38.5
USA	. . . .	412.5	566.2	648.8
Venezuela	. . . .	119.2	248.6	302.6
Total (incl. others)	. . . .	1,393.8	1,851.1	2,264.0

Transport

RAILWAYS
(traffic)

		1990	1991	1992
Passenger-km (million)	. . .	3	3	6

Freight ton-km (million): 4 in 1985.

Source: UN, *Statistical Yearbook*.

ROAD TRAFFIC
(motor vehicles in use)

		2007	2009*	2010
Passenger cars	. . . . .	95,498	101,021	96,021
Buses and coaches	. . . .	38,602	38,665	36,291
Lorries and vans	. . . .	183,671	192,544	196,700
Motorcycles and mopeds	. .	56,525	87,247	112,632

* Data for 2008 were not available.

Source: IRF, *World Road Statistics*.

SHIPPING
Flag Registered fleet
(at 31 December)

		2010	2011	2012
Number of vessels	. . . .	8	8	7
Total displacement (grt)	. . .	4,814	4,814	3,949

Source: Lloyd's List Intelligence (www.lloydslistintelligence.com).

International Sea-Borne Freight Traffic
('000 metric tons)

		1997	1998	1999
Imports	. . . . . .	1,272.7	1,964.7	1,180.7
Exports	. . . . . .	329.3	204.5	183.6

Total international cargo movements ('000 metric tons): 2,832 in 2009; 3,009 in 2010; 3,436 in 2011.

CIVIL AVIATION
(traffic at Augusto César Sandino airport)

	2009	2010*	2011†
Passengers carried ('000) . . .	1,089.7	1,100.9	1,010.6
Freight carried (metric tons) . .	18,860	25,869	9,967

* Preliminary.
† Estimates.

Tourism

TOURIST ARRIVALS BY COUNTRY OF ORIGIN

		2008	2009	2010
Canada	. . . . . .	20,233	24,161	23,597
Costa Rica	. . . . .	70,733	111,861	125,811
El Salvador	. . . . .	123,501	121,069	135,455
Guatemala	. . . . .	68,819	67,317	76,695
Honduras	. . . . .	182,511	176,120	214,776
Panama	. . . . . .	14,924	17,147	20,174
USA	. . . .	196,602	212,648	210,479
Total (incl. others)	857,901	931,904	1,011,251

Total tourist arrivals ('000): 1,060 in 2011 (provisional).

Tourism receipts (US $ million, excl. passenger transport): 334 in 2009; 308 in 2010; 377 in 2011 (provisional).

Source: World Tourism Organization.

Communications Media

	2009	2010	2011
Telephones ('000 main lines in use)	254.7	258.3	287.6
Mobile cellular telephones ('000 subscribers)	3,344.6	3,962.2	4,822.2
Internet users ('000)	199.8	n.a.	n.a.
Broadband subscribers ('000) . .	59.6	73.3	85.1

Source: International Telecommunication Union.

Education

(2009/10 unless otherwise indicated)

	Institutions*	Teachers	Students		
			Males	Females	Total
Pre-primary .	5,980	10,289	109,836	108,226	218,062
Primary . . .	8,251	30,571	475,981	447,764	923,745
Secondary: general . .	1,249	15,089	221,894	236,427	458,321
Tertiary: university level	35	3,630†	47,683‡	51,222‡	98,905‡
Tertiary: other higher . . .	73	210†	1,902‡	2,770‡	4,672‡

* 2002/03 figures.
† 2001/02 figure.
‡ 2003/04 figure.

Sources: UNESCO, *Statistical Yearbook*; Ministry of Education.

Pupil-teacher ratio (primary education, UNESCO estimate): 30.2 in 2009/10 (Source: UNESCO Institute for Statistics).

Adult literacy rate (UNESCO estimates): 80.5% (males 79.7%; females 81.4%) in 2007 (Source: UNESCO Institute for Statistics).

Directory

The Government

HEAD OF STATE

President: José Daniel Ortega Saavedra (elected 5 November 2006; re-elected 6 November 2011).

Vice-President: Moises Omar Halleslevens Acevedo.

CABINET
(May 2013)

The Government is formed by the Frente Sandinista de Liberación Nacional.

Minister of Foreign Affairs: Samuel Santos López.

Minister of the Interior: Ana Isabel Morales Mazún.

Secretary-General of Defence with Ministerial Rank: Dr Martha Ruiz Sevilla.

Minister of Finance and Public Credit: Iván Acosta.

Minister of Development, Industry and Trade: Dr Orlando Solórzano Delgadillo.

Minister of Labour: Alba Luz Torres Briones.

Minister of the Environment and Natural Resources: Juana Argeñal Sandoval.

Minister of Transport and Infrastructure: Pablo Fernando Martínez Espinoza.

Minister of Agriculture and Forestry: Ariel Bucardo Rocha.

Minister of Health: Dr Sonia Castro González.

Minister of Education: Miriam Ráudez.

Minister of the Family, Adolescence and Childhood: Marcia Ramírez Mercado.

Minister of Energy and Mines: Emilio Rappaccioli Baltodano.

Secretary to the Presidency: Paul Oquist.

Co-ordinator of the Communication and Citizenship Council: Rosario Murillo Zambrana.

MINISTRIES

Office of the President: Casa Presidencial, Managua; fax 2266-3102; e-mail daniel@presidencia.gob.ni; internet www.presidencia.gob.ni.

Ministry of Agriculture and Forestry: Km 8½, Carretera a Masaya, Managua; tel. 2276-0512; fax 2276-0204; e-mail ministro@magfor.gob.ni; internet www.magfor.gob.ni.

Ministry of Defence: De los semáforos el Redentor, 4 c. arriba, donde fue la casa 'Ricardo Morales Aviles', Managua; tel. 2222-2201; fax 2222-5439; e-mail prensa.midef@midef.gob.ni; internet www.midef.gob.ni.

Ministry of Development, Industry and Trade: Edif. Central, Km 6, Carretera a Masaya, Apdo 8, frente a camino de oriente, Managua; tel. 2248-9300; fax 2270-095; e-mail acastilb@mific.gob.ni; internet www.mific.gob.ni.

Ministry of Education: Centro Cívico, Módulo K, Planta Alta, Apdo 505, Managua; tel. 2265-0046; fax 2265-0081; e-mail webmaster@mined.gob.ni; internet www.mined.gob.ni.

Ministry of Energy and Mines: Hospital Bautista, 1 c. al oeste, 1 c. al norte, Managua; tel. 2280-9500; fax 2280-9516; e-mail despacho@mem.gob.ni; internet www.mem.gob.ni.

Ministry of the Environment and Natural Resources: Km 12½, Carretera Norte, Apdo 5123, Managua; tel. 2233-1111; fax 2263-1274; e-mail jargenal@marena.gob.ni; internet www.marena.gob.ni.

Ministry of the Family, Adolescence and Childhood: De donde fue ENEL Central, 100 m al sur, Managua; tel. 2278-1620; e-mail mramirez@mifamilia.gob.ni; internet www.mifamilia.gob.ni.

Ministry of Finance and Public Credit: Frente a la Asamblea Nacional, Apdo 2170, Managua; tel. 2222-6530; fax 2222-6430; e-mail webmaster@mhcp.gob.ni; internet www.hacienda.gob.ni.

Ministry of Foreign Affairs: Del Antiguo Cine González, 1 c. al sur, sobre Avda Bolívar, Managua; tel. 2244-8000; fax 2228-5102; e-mail despacho.ministro@cancilleria.gob.ni; internet www.cancilleria.gob.ni.

Ministry of Health: Complejo Nacional de Salud 'Dra Concepción Palacios', costado oeste Colonia Primero de Mayo, Apdo 107, Managua; tel. 2289-7164; e-mail webmaster@minsa.gob.ni; internet www.minsa.gob.ni.

Ministry of the Interior: Edif. Silvio Mayorga, Costado oeste de la DGI Sajonia, Apdo 68, Managua; tel. 2222-7538; fax 2222-2789; e-mail relacionespublicas@migob.gob.ni; internet www.migob.gob.ni.

Ministry of Labour: Estadio Nacional, 400 m al norte, Apdo 487, Managua; tel. 2222-2115; fax 2228-2103; e-mail info@mitrab.gob.ni; internet www.mitrab.gob.ni.

Ministry of Transport and Infrastructure: Frente al Estadio Nacional Denis Martínez, Apdo 26, Managua; tel. 2222-5952; fax 2222-5111; e-mail webmaster@mti.gob.ni; internet www.mti.gob.ni.

President and Legislature

PRESIDENT

Election, 6 November 2011

Candidate	Votes	% of total
José Daniel Ortega Saavedra (FSLN)	1,569,287	62.46
Fabio Gadea Mantilla (PLI-UNE)	778,889	31.00
Arnoldo Alemán Lacayo (PLC)	148,507	5.91
Enrique Quiñónez (ALN)	10,003	0.40
Roger Guevara (APRE)	5,898	0.23
Total	**2,512,584**	**100.00**

ASAMBLEA NACIONAL

National Assembly: Complejo Legislativo Carlos Nuñez, Avda Peatonal Gen. Augusto C. Sandino, Apdo 4659, Managua; tel. 2276-8488; e-mail info@asamblea.gob.ni; internet www.asamblea.gob.ni.

President: Santos René Núñez Téllez.

First Vice-President: Irís Marina Montenegro Blandón.

Second Vice-President: Gladys de los Angeles Báez.

Third Vice-President: Carlos Wilfredo Navarro Moreira.

Election, 6 November 2011

Party	Valid votes cast	% of valid votes	Seats
Frente Sandinista de Liberación Nacional (FSLN)	3,178,669	60.75	62
Partido Liberal Independiente (PLI)*	1,646,203	31.45	26
Partido Liberal Constitucionalista (PLC)	340,945	6.51	2
Alianza Liberal Nicaragüense (ALN)	44,528	0.86	—
Alianza por la República (APRE)	22,380	0.43	—
Total	**5,232,725†**	**100.00**	**92‡**

* Supported by the Unidad Nicaragüense por la Esperanza (UNE).

† Each elector had two votes: one for representatives at regional level (for which there were 70 seats) and one for representatives at national level (20 seats). The total number of votes cast at regional level was 2,630,889, while at national level 2,601,836 votes were cast.

‡ Under the Constitution, one seat is reserved for the President of the Republic. Furthermore, another seat is given to the second-placed candidate in the presidential election. Thus, the FSLN's total number of seats increased to 63, while PLI's representation increased to 27.

Election Commission

Consejo Supremo Electoral (CSE): Iglesia Las Palmas, 1 c. al sur, Apdo 2241, Managua; tel. 2268-7948; e-mail info@cse.gob.ni; internet www.cse.gob.ni; Pres. Roberto José Rivas Reyes.

Political Organizations

Alianza Liberal Nicaragüense (ALN): del Hotel Mansión Teodolinda, 3c abajo, Managua; e-mail hebertaln@hotmail.com; fmrly Movimiento de Salvación Liberal; adopted current name in 2006; Pres. Alejandro Mejía Ferreti; Sec.-Gen. Carlos García.

Alianza por la República (APRE): Busto José Martí, 4 c. arriba, 3 y ½ c. al lago, Managua; tel. 2264-2446; e-mail partido.apre@gmail.com; f. 2004 by supporters of Pres. Enrique Bolaños Geyer; Pres. Carlos Canales.

Partido Social Cristiano Nicaragüense (PSC): Ciudad Jardín, Pizza María, 1 c. al lago, Managua; tel. 2249-3460; e-mail pscnicaragua@hotmail.com; f. 1957; 42,000 mems; Pres. ABEL REYES TÉLLEZ; Sec.-Gen. ANTONIO BENITO GÓMEZ.

Camino Cristiano Nicaragüense (CCN): Costado, 1 c. al sur, 1 c. arriba, Calle 27 de Mayo, Managua; tel. 2254-5411; fax 2254-5405; e-mail info@caminocristianonicaraguense.org; internet www.caminocristianonicaraguense.org; Pres. GUILLERMO ANTONIO OSORNO MOLINA; Sec. OSWALDO BONILLA.

Frente Sandinista de Liberación Nacional (FSLN): Costado oeste Parque El Carmen, Managua; tel. and fax 2266-8173; f. 1960; Gen. Sec. JOSÉ DANIEL ORTEGA SAAVEDRA.

Movimiento Renovador Sandinista (MRS): De los semáforos del Ministerio de Gobernación, ½ c. al norte, Managua; tel. 2250-9461; fax 2278-0268; e-mail info@partidomrs.com; internet www.partidomrs.com; f. 1995; fmr faction of Frente Sandinista de Liberación Nacional (q.v.); contested the 2011 elections in alliance with the Unidad Nicaragüense por la Esperanza (q.v.); Pres. ANA MARGARITA VIJIL.

Movimiento de Unidad Cristiana (MUC): Del Portón del Cementerio Periférico, 1 c. al norte, Avda América 505, Managua; tel. 2249-5672; e-mail paritdomuc@hotmail.com; Pres. Pastor DANIEL ORTEGA REYES.

Partido Conservador (PC): Colegio Centroamérica, 500 m al sur, Managua; tel. 2278-8430; fax 2270-6820; e-mail partido conservador1@hotmail.com; f. 1992 following merger between Partido Conservador Demócrata and Partido Socialconservadurismo; legal status annulled by the Consejo Supremo Electoral in 2008; Pres. ALFREDO CÉSAR AGUIRRE.

Partido Indígena Multiétnico (PIM): Residencial Los Robles, de Farmacentro 1 c. al este, 80 varas al sur, Managua; Pres. RAYFIELD HODGSON.

Partido Liberal Constitucionalista (PLC): Semáforos Country Club 100 m al este, Apdo 4569, Managua; tel. 2278-8705; fax 2278-1800; f. 1967; Pres. MARÍA HAYDÉE OSUNA; Nat. Sec. MIGUEL ROSALES ORTEGA.

Partido Liberal Independiente (PLI): Ciudad Jardín, H-4, Calle Principal, Managua; tel. 2249-5547; internet partidoliberal independiente.org; f. 1944; dormant between 1996 and 2011; contested the 2011 elections in alliance with the Unidad Nicaragüense por la Esperanza (q.v.); Pres. EDUARDO MONTEALEGRE.

Partido Liberal Nacionalista (PLN): Managua; f. 1913; Pres. CONSTANTINO VELÁSQUEZ ZEPEDA.

Partido Movimiento de Unidad Costeña (PAMUC): Bilwi Puerto Cabeza; Pres. KENNETH SERAPIO HUNTER.

Partido Neo-Liberal (Pali): Cine Dorado, 2 c. al sur, 50 m arriba, Managua; tel. 2266-5166; f. 1986; legal status suspended in April 2013; Pres. ADOLFO GARCÍA ESQUIVEL.

Partido Resistencia Nicaragüense (PRN): Edif. VINSA, frente a Autonica, Carretera Sur, Managua; tel. and fax 2270-6508; e-mail salvata@ibw.com.ni; f. 1993; nationalist; Pres. JULIO CÉSAR BLANDÓN SÁNCHEZ (KALIMÁN).

Partido Unionista Centroamericano (PUCA): Cine Cabrera, 1 c. al este, 20 m al norte, Managua; f. 1904; legal status suspended in April 2013; Pres. BLANCA ROJAS ECHAVERRY.

Unidad Nicaragüense por la Esperanza (UNE): Managua; f. 2010; contested the 2011 elections in alliance with the Partido Liberal Independiente (q.v.);.

Unión Demócrata Cristiana (UDC): De Iglesia Santa Ana, 2 c. abajo, Barrio Santa Ana, Apdo 3089, Managua; tel. 2266-2576; f. 1976 as Partido Popular Social Cristiano; present name adopted in 1993; legal status suspended in April 2013; Pres. AGUSTÍN JARQUÍN ANAYA.

Yatama (Yapti Tasba Masraka Nanih Aslatakanka): Of. de Odacan, Busto José Martí, 1 c. al este y ½ c. al norte, Managua; tel. 2228-1494; Atlantic coast Miskito org.; Leader BROOKLYN RIVERA BRYAN.

Diplomatic Representation

EMBASSIES IN NICARAGUA

Argentina: Reparto Las Colinas, Calle Prado Ecuestre 235B (intersección con Calle los Mangos), Apdo 703, Managua; tel. 2255-0062; fax 2276–2654; e-mail enica@mrecic.gov.ar; internet www.enica.mrecic.gov.ar; Ambassador MARCELO FELIPE VALLE FONROUGE.

Brazil: Km 7¾, Carretera Sur, Quinta los Pinos, Apdo 264, Managua; tel. 2265-0035; fax 2265-2206; e-mail ebrasil@ibw.com.ni; Ambassador LUIZ FELIPE MENDOÇA FILHO.

Chile: Entrada principal los Robles, Semáforos Hotel Milton Princess, 1 c. abajo, 1 c. al sur, Apdo 1289, Managua; tel. 2278-0619; fax 2270-4073; e-mail echileni@amnet.com.ni; internet chileabroad.gov

.cl/nicaragua; Ambassador HERNÁN JAVIER ALEJANDRO MENA TABOADA.

Colombia: 2a Entrada a Las Colinas, 1 c. arriba, ½ c. al lago, Casa 97, Apdo 1062, Managua; tel. 2276-2149; fax 2276-0644; e-mail emanagua@cancilleria.gov.co; internet www.embajadaennicaragua.gov.co; Ambassador LUZ STELLA JARA PORTILLA.

Costa Rica: Reparto Las Colinas, Calle Prado Ecuestre 304, 1°, Managua; tel. 2276-1352; fax 2276-0115; e-mail infembcr@cablenet.com.ni; Ambassador JAVIER SANCHO BONILLA.

Cuba: 3a Entrada a Las Colinas, 400 varas arriba, 75 al sur, Managua; tel. 2276-0742; fax 2276-0166; e-mail embacuba@embacuba.net.ni; internet www.cubadiplomatica.cu/nicaragua; Ambassador EDUARDO MARTÍNEZ BORBONET.

Dominican Republic: Reparto Las Colinas, Prado Ecuestre 100, con Curva de los Gallos, Apdo 614, Managua; tel. 2276-2029; fax 2276-0654; e-mail embdom@cablenet.com.ni; Ambassador LUIS JOSÉ GONZÁLEZ SÁNCHEZ.

Ecuador: Barrio Bolonia, Sede Central Los Pipitos, 1½ c. al oeste, Managua; tel. 2268-1098; fax 2266-8081; e-mail ecuador@ibw.com.ni; Ambassador ANTONIO EUTIMIO PRECIADO BEDOYA.

El Salvador: Reparto Las Colinas, Avda del Campo y Pasaje, Los Cerros 142, Apdo 149, Managua; tel. 2276-0712; fax 2276-0711; e-mail embajadanicaragua@rree.gob.sv; internet embajada nicaragua.rree.gob.sv; Ambassador JUAN JOSÉ FIGUEROA TENAS.

Finland: Sucursal Jorge Navarro, Apdo 2219, Managua; tel. 2278-1216; fax 2278-2840; e-mail sanomat.mgu@formin.fi; internet www.finlandia.org.ni; Chargé d'affaires a.i. EEVA-LIISA MYLLYMÄKI.

France: Iglesia el Carmen 1½ c. abajo, Apdo 1227, Managua; tel. 2222-6210; fax 2268-5630; e-mail info@ambafrance-ni.org; internet www.ambafrance-ni.org; Ambassador ANTOINE JOLY.

Germany: Bolonia, de la Rotonda El Güegüense, 1½ c. al lago, contiguo a Optica Nicaragüense, Apdo 29, Managua; tel. 2266-3917; fax 2266-7667; e-mail alemania@cablenet.com.ni; internet www.managua.diplo.de; Ambassador KARL-OTTO KÖNIG.

Guatemala: Km 11½, Carretera a Masaya, Apdo E-1, Managua; tel. 2279-9609; fax 2279-9610; e-mail embnic@minex.gob.gt; Ambassador HÉCTOR DARÍO GULARTE ESTRADA.

Holy See: Apostolic Nunciature, Km 10.8, Carretera Sur, Apdo 506, Managua; tel. 2265-8657; fax 2265-7416; e-mail nuntius@cablenet.com.ni; Apostolic Nuncio Most Rev. FORTUNATUS NWACHUKWU (Titular Archbishop of Aquaviva).

Honduras: Reparto Las Colinas, Prado Ecuestre 298, frente a Residencia de la Embajada de China (Taiwán), Apdo 321, Managua; tel. 2276-2406; fax 2276-1998; e-mail embhonduras@cablenet.com.ni; Ambassador LEDIN ORLANDO TORRES.

Iran: Del Club Terraza, 300 m al este, de la principal entrada de las Cumbres, 3 c. al sur, No E4, Managua; tel. 2270-0954; fax 2255-0565; e-mail embirannic@cablenet.com.ni; Ambassador MORTEZA KHALAJ.

Italy: Residencial Bolonia, Rotonda El Güegüense, 1 c. al norte, ½ c. al oeste, Apdo 2092, Managua 4; tel. 2266-2961; fax 2266-3987; e-mail ambasciata.managua@esteri.it; internet www.ambmanagua.esteri.it; Ambassador FABRIZIO MAZZA.

Japan: Plaza España, 1 c. abajo y 1 c. al lago, Bolonia, Apdo 1789, Managua; tel. 2266-8668; fax 2266-8566; e-mail embjpnic@ibw.com.ni; internet www.ni.emb-japan.go.jp; Ambassador MASAHARU SATO.

Korea, Republic: De la Rotonda El Güegüense 3. al oeste, ½ c. al sur, casa A-45, Apdo LV101, Managua; tel. 2254-8107; fax 2254-8131; e-mail nicaragua@mofat.go.kr; internet nic.mofat.go.kr; Ambassador SOON TAE KIM.

Libya: Del portón principal del Hospital Militar 1 c. al lago, 1 c. abajo y ½ al lago, Reparto Bolonia, Managua; tel. 2266-8540; fax 2266-8542; e-mail ofilibia@ibw.com.ni; Chargé d'affaires a.i. MOHAMED ABOHMEDA.

Luxembourg: Residencial Bolonia del Hospital Militar, 1 c. al lago y 1½ abajo, Contiguo al Hotel Maracas Inn, Apdo 969, Managua; tel. 2268-1881; fax 2266-7965; e-mail secretariat.managua@mae.etat.lu; Chargé d'affaires a.i. THIERRY RENÉ LIPPERT.

Mexico: Contiguo a Optica Matamoros, Km 4½, Carretera a Masaya, 25 varas Arriba, Altamira, Apdo 834, Managua; tel. 2278-4919; fax 2278-2886; e-mail embamex@turbonett.com.ni; internet embamex.sre.gob.mx/nicaragua; Ambassador JUAN RODRIGO LABARDINI FLORES.

Netherlands: Calle Erasmus de Rotterdam, Carretera a Masaya Km 5, del Colegio Teresiano 1 c. al sur, 1 c. abajo, Apdo 3688, Managua; tel. 2276-8630; fax 2276-0399; e-mail mng@minbuza.nl; internet nicaragua.nlambassade.org; Chargé d'affaires a.i. REINA BUIJS.

Panama: Casa 93, Reparto Mántica, del Cuartel General de Bomberos 1 c. abajo, Apdo 1, Managua; tel. 2266-8633; fax 2266-2224; e-mail embdpma@enitel.com.ni; Ambassador GABRIELA AROSEMENA DE ROUX.

Peru: Del Hospital Militar, 1 c. al norte, 2 c. hacia oeste, casa 325, Apdo 211, Managua; tel. 2266-8678; fax 2266-8679; e-mail embajada@peruennicaragua.com.ni; internet www .peruennicaragua.com.ni; Ambassador RUDECINDO VEGA CARREAZO.

Russia: Reparto Las Colinas, Calle Vista Alegre 214, Apdo 249, Managua; tel. 2276-0374; fax 2276-0179; e-mail rossia@cablenet.com .ni; internet www.nicaragua.mid.ru; Ambassador NIKOLAY M. VLA-DIMIR.

Spain: Avda Central 13, Las Colinas, Apdo 284, Managua; tel. 2276-0966; fax 2276-0937; e-mail emb.managua@maec.es; internet www .maec.es/embajadas/managua; Ambassador LEÓN DE LA TORRE KRAIS.

Taiwan (Republic of China): Optica Matamoros, 2 c. abajo, $\frac{1}{2}$ c. al lago, Carretera a Masaya, Planes de Altamira, Apdo 4653, Managua; tel. 2277-1333; fax 2267-4025; e-mail nic@mofa.gov.tw; internet www.roc-taiwan.org.ni; Ambassador YING-WHEI HSING.

USA: Km 5$\frac{1}{2}$, Carretera Sur, Apdo 327, Managua; tel. 2252-7100; fax 2252-7304; e-mail consularmanagua@state.gov; internet nicaragua .usembassy.gov; Ambassador PHYLLIS MARIE POWERS.

Venezuela: Costado norte de la Iglesia Santo Domingo, Las Sierritas, Casa 27, Apdo 406, Managua; tel. 2272-0267; fax 2272-2265; e-mail embaveznica@cablenet.com.ni; Ambassador JOSÉ FRANCISCO ARRÚE DE PABLO.

Judicial System

The Supreme Court deals with both civil and criminal cases, acts as a Court of Cassation, appoints Judges of First Instance, and generally supervises the legal administration of the country.

Corte Suprema de Justicia: Km 7 $\frac{1}{2}$ Carretera Norte, Managua; tel. 2233-2128; fax 2233-0004; e-mail webmaster@csj.gob.ni; internet www.poderjudicial.gob.ni; Pres. Dr ALBA LUZ RAMOS VANEGAS; Vice-Pres. MARVIN AGUILAR GARCÍA.

Attorney-General: Dr JOAQUÍN HERNÁN ESTRADA SANTAMARÍA.

Religion

All religions are tolerated. Almost all of Nicaragua's inhabitants profess Christianity, and the majority belong to the Roman Catholic Church. The Moravian Church predominates on the Caribbean coast.

CHRISTIANITY

The Roman Catholic Church

Nicaragua comprises one archdiocese, six dioceses and the Apostolic Vicariate of Bluefields. According to the latest available census figures (2005), some 58% of the population aged five years and above are Roman Catholics.

Bishops' Conference

Conferencia Episcopal de Nicaragua, Ferretería Lang 1 c. al norte, 1 c. al este, Zona 3, Las Piedrecitas, Apdo 2407, Managua; tel. 2266-6292; fax 2266-8069; e-mail cen@tmx.com.ni.

f. 1975; statute approved 1987; Pres. LEOPOLDO JOSÉ BRENES SOLÓRZANO (Archbishop of Managua).

Archbishop of Managua: LEOPOLDO JOSÉ BRENES SOLÓRZANO, Arzobispado, Apdo 2008, Managua; tel. 2276-0129; fax 2276-0130; e-mail mob@unica.edu.ni.

The Anglican Communion

Nicaragua comprises one of the five dioceses of the Iglesia Anglicana de la Región Central de América.

Bishop of Nicaragua: Rt Rev. STURDIE W. DOWNS, Apdo 1207, Managua; tel. 2222-5174; fax 2222-6701; e-mail episcnic@tmx.com .ni.

Protestant Churches

Some 22% of the population aged five years and above are members of evangelical churches, according to the last census (2005).

Baptist Convention of Nicaragua: Apdo 2593, Managua; f. 1917; 135 churches, 20,000 mems (2006); Pres. Rev. FÉLIX PEDRO RUIZ RIVERA; Sec. Rev. GUADALUPE ANTONIO GÓMEZ RÍOS.

The Moravian Church in Nicaragua: Iglesia Morava, Bilwi; tel. and fax 2282-2222; 199 churches, 83,000 mems; Leader Rt Rev. JOHN WILSON.

The Nicaraguan Lutheran Church of Faith and Hope: Apdo 151, Managua; tel. 2266-4467; fax 2268-2401; e-mail luterana@ turbonett.com.ni; f. 1994; 7,050 mems (2010); Pres. Rev. VICTORIA CORTEZ RODRÍGUEZ.

The Press

NEWSPAPERS AND PERIODICALS

Bolsa de Noticias: Col. Centroamérica, Grupo L 852, Apdo VF-90, Managua; tel. 2270-0546; fax 2277-4931; e-mail diseno@ bolsadenoticias.com.ni; internet www.bolsadenoticias.com.ni; f. 1974; daily; Dir MARÍA ELSA SUÁREZ GARCÍA; Editor-in-Chief MARÍA ELENA PALACIOS.

Confidencial: De Pharoahs Casino, 2 c. abajo, 2 c. al sur, Managua; tel. 2277-5134; fax 2270-7017; e-mail info@confidencial.com.ni; internet www.confidencial.com.ni; weekly; political analysis; Dir CARLOS F. CHAMORRO; Editors IVÁN OLIVARES, CARLOS SALINAS MALDONADO.

La Gaceta, Diario Oficial: De la Rotonda de Plaza Inter, 1 c. arriba, 2 c. al lago, Managua; tel. 2228-3791; fax 2228-4001; e-mail lagaceta@ presidencia.gob.ni; internet www.lagaceta.gob.ni; f. 1912; morning; daily; official; Dir Dr LEOPOLDO CASTRILLO.

Hoy: Km 4$\frac{1}{2}$, Carretera Norte, Apdo 192, Managua; tel. 2255-6767; fax 2255-6780; e-mail mario.mairena@hoy.com.ni; internet www .hoy.com.ni; Editor MARIO MAIRENA.

La Jornada: Entrada Principal de Villa Progreso, 3c al norte, Casa A-350, Managua; tel. 2251-8277; e-mail info@lajornadanet.com; internet www.lajornadanet.com; f. 1986; Dir and Editor RAÚL ARÉVALO ALEMÁN.

Nuevo Diario: Pista P. Joaquín Chamorro, Km 4, Carretera Norte, Apdo 4591, Managua; tel. 2249-0499; fax 2249-0700; e-mail info@ elnuevodiario.com.ni; internet www.elnuevodiario.com.ni; f. 1980; morning; daily; independent; Dir LEÓN NÚÑEZ; Editor-in-Chief ROBERTO COLLADO; circ. 45,000.

El Observador Económico: De Pricesmart, 2 c. al lago, Apdo 2074, Managua; tel. 2266-8708; fax 2266-8711; e-mail info@ elobservadoreconomico.com; internet www.elobservadoreconomico .com; Dir-Gen. ALEJANDRO MARTÍNEZ CUENCA.

La Prensa: Km 4$\frac{1}{2}$, Carretera Norte, Apdo 192, Managua; tel. 2249-8405; fax 2249-6926; e-mail info@laprensa.com.ni; internet www .laprensa.com.ni; f. 1926; morning; daily; independent; Pres. JAIME CHAMORRO CARDENAL; Editor-in-Chief EDUARDO ENRÍQUEZ; circ. 30,000.

Prensa Proletaria: Managua; e-mail agenciaapp@gmail.com; internet prensaproletaria.blogspot.com; fortnightly; official publ. of the Movimiento de Acción Popular Marxista-Leninista.

Revista Encuentro: Universidad Centroamericana, Apdo 69, Managua; tel. 2278-3923; fax 2267-0106; e-mail dirinv@ns.uca.edu.ni; internet encuentro.uca.edu.ni; f. 1968; termly; academic publ. of the Universidad Centroamericana; Dir JORGE ALBERTO HUETE PÉREZ; Editor WENDY BELLANGER.

Revista Envío: Edif. Nitlapán, 2°, Campus Universidad Centroamericana, Apdo A-194, Managua; tel. 2278-2557; fax 2278-1402; e-mail info@envio.org.ni; internet www.envio.org.ni; f. 1981; 11 a year; political, economic and social analysis; edns in Spanish, English and Italian; Dir JUAN RAMIRO MARTÍNEZ; Chief Editor MARÍA LÓPEZ VIGIL.

Revista Revelaciones: esq. suroeste del Colegio San Francisco, $\frac{1}{2}$ c al oeste, Estelí; tel. 2713-7578; e-mail info@revistarevelaciones.com; internet revistarevelaciones.com; monthly; Dir GEMA HERNÁNDEZ; Editor BRENDA ESTRADA.

Trinchera de la Noticia: Semáforos de la Tenderi, 1 c abajo, 10 vrs abajo, Ciudad Jardín, Managua; tel. 2240-0114; e-mail info@ trinchera.com.ni; internet www.trinchera.com.ni; daily; Dir XAVIER REYES ALBA; Man. EMILIO NÚÑEZ TENORIO.

Visión Sandinista: Costado este, Parque El Carmen, Managua; tel. and fax 2268-1565; e-mail vision@ibw.com.ni; internet www .visionsandinista.com; f. 1980; weekly; official publ. of the Frente Sandinista de Liberación Nacional; Dir MAYRA REYES SANDOVAL.

Association

Unión de Periodistas de Nicaragua (UPN): Apdo 4006, Managua; tel. 2271-2436; e-mail uperiodistasnic@yahoo.com; internet www.aquinicaragua.com/periodistas2.html; Pres. CÁNDIDA DÍAZ.

Publishers

Academia Nicaragüense de la Lengua: Avda del Campo, 42 Las Colinas, Apdo 2711, Managua; fax 2249-5389; e-mail pavsa@ munditel.com.ni; f. 1928; languages; Dir JORGE EDUARDO ARELLANO SANDINO.

Ediciones Océano, SA: Km. 7 $\frac{1}{2}$, Carretera a Masaya, Contiguo a Nitalsa, Managua; tel. 2276-1372; fax 2276-1443; e-mail edocanic@ ibw.com.ni; internet www.oceano.com; Spanish culture and language; Dir-Gen. ELVIN CANO.

Editora de Arte SA: Etapa 53, Col. Los Robles III, Managua; tel. 2278-5854; e-mail editarte@editarte.com.ni; internet www.editarte.com.ni.

Editorial Nueva Nicaragua: Paseo Salvador Allende, Km 3½, Carretera Sur, Apdo 073, Managua; fax 266-6520; f. 1981; Dr SERGIO RAMÍREZ MERCADO; Dir-Gen. ROBERTO DÍAZ CASTILLO.

Editorial Unión: Altagracia Rest Los Ranchos, 4 ½ c. al sur, Managua; tel. 2266-0019; travel.

Librería Hispanoamericana (HISPAMER): Costado este de la UCA, Apdo A-221, Managua; tel. 2278-1210; fax 2278-0825; e-mail hispamer@hispamer.com.ni; internet hispamer.com.ni; f. 1991; Man. JESÚS DE SANTIAGO.

UCA Publicaciónes: Avda Universitaria, Rotonda Rubén Darío 150 m al oeste, Apdo 69, Managua; tel. 2278-5951; fax 2278-5951; e-mail comsj@ns.uca.edu.ni; internet www.uca.edu.ni; academic publishing dept of the Universidad Centroamericana; Publ. Dir GUNTER GADEA BARBERENA.

Universidad Nacional Agraria: Km 12½ Carretera Norte, Apdo 453, Managua; tel. 233-1950; e-mail info@una.edu.ni; internet www.una.edu.ni; sciences.

Broadcasting and Communications

TELECOMMUNICATIONS

Claro: Villafontana, 2°, Apdo 232, Managua; tel. 2277-3057; fax 2270-2128; e-mail cliente@claro.com.ni; internet www.claro.com.ni; f. 2006 by merger of ALO PCS (f. 2002) and Empresa Nicaragüense de Telecomunicaciones (Enitel; f. 1925); subsidiary of América Móvil, SA de CV (Mexico); Chair. PATRICIO SLIM DOMIT; Gen. Man. ROBERTO SANSÓN.

Telefónica Celular de Nicaragua, SA (Movistar Nicaragua—TCN): Edif. Movistar, Km 6 ½, Carretera a Masaya, Managua; tel. 2277-0731; fax 2268-0389; e-mail gerardo.mena@telefonica.com.ni; internet www.movistar.com.ni; Gen. Man. JUAN MANUEL ARGÜELLO.

Regulatory Body

Instituto Nicaragüense de Telecomunicaciones y Correos (Telcor): Edif. Telcor, Avda Bolívar diagonal a Cancillería, Apdo 2264, Managua; tel. 2222-7350; fax 2222-7554; e-mail mgutierrez@telcor.gob.ni; internet www.telcor.gob.ni; Exec. Pres. ORLANDO CASTILLO.

BROADCASTING

Radio

La Nueva Radio YA: Pista de la Resistencia, Frente a la Universidad Centroamericana, Managua; tel. 2278-8336; fax 2278-8334; e-mail info@nuevaya.com.ni; internet nuevaya.com.ni; f. 1990 as Radio Ya; restyled as above in 1999; operated by Entretenimiento Digital, SA; Dir-Gen. DENNIS SCHWARTZ.

Radio Católica: Altamira D'Este 621, 3°, Apdo 2183, Managua; tel. 2278-0836; fax 2278-2544; e-mail oramos@radiocatolica.org; internet www.radiocatolica.org; f. 1961; controlled by Conferencia Episcopal de Nicaragua; Dir Fr ROLANDO ÁLVAREZ; Gen. Man. ALBERTO CARBALLO MADRIGAL.

Radio Corporación, Gadea y Cía: Avda Ponciano Lombillo, Ciudad Jardín Q-20, Apdo 24242, Managua; tel. 2249-1619; fax 2244-3824; e-mail rc540@radio-corporacion.com; internet www.radio-corporacion.com; f. 1995; Gen. Man. FABIO GADEA MANTILLA; Asst Man. CARLOS GADEA MANTILLA.

Radio Estrella: Sierritas de Santo Domingo, frente al Cementerio, Apdo UNICA 104, Managua; tel. 2276-0241; fax 2276-0062; e-mail radiosm@radioestrelladelmar.com; internet www.radioestrelladelmar.org; f. 1997; Catholic; Dir FRANCISCO VELÁSQUEZ.

Radio Nicaragua: Villa Fontana, Contiguo a Enitel, Apdo 4665, Managua; tel. 2227-2330; fax 2267-1448; e-mail director@radionicaragua.com.ni; internet www.radionicaragua.com.ni; f. 1960; govt station; Dir-Gen. ALBERTO CARBALLO MADRIGAL.

Radio Ondas de Luz: Costado Sur del Hospital Bautista, Apdo 607, Managua; tel. and fax 2249-7058; internet www.miradioondasdeluz.com; f. 1959; religious and cultural station; Pres. GUILLERMO OSORNO MOLINA.

Radio Sandino: Paseo Tiscapa Este, Contiguo al Restaurante Mirador, Apdo 4776, Managua; tel. 2228-1330; fax 2262-4052; internet www.radiosandino.com; f. 1977; station controlled by the Frente Sandinista de Liberación Nacional; Pres. RAFAEL ORTEGA MURILLO; Gen. Man. WILLIAM BURGOS.

Radio Segovia: Ocotal, Nueva Segovia; tel. 2732-2870; fax 2732-2271; e-mail info@radiosegovia.net; internet www.radiosegovia.net; f. 1980; commercial; Dir RÓGER SOLÍS COREA.

Radio Tiempo: Barrio San Judas, Supermercado Pali, 2 c. al Sur, Apdo 3337, Managua; tel. 8821-0258; e-mail radionuevotiempofm@yahoo.com; internet www.nuevotiempofm.com; f. 1976; Dir DAVID MURILLO.

Radio Universidad: Avda Card, 3 c. abajo, Apdo 2883, Managua; tel. 2278-4743; fax 2277-5057; internet radiouniversidadnica.com; f. 1984; Dir LUIS LÓPEZ RUIZ.

There are some 50 other radio stations.

Television

Canal 4: Montoya, 1 c. al sur, 2 c. arriba, Managua; tel. 2228-1310; fax 2222-4067; internet www.multinoticiastv4.com; owned by Radio y Televisión de Nicaragua, SA (RATENSA).

Canal 15: Lomas de Tiscapa, Frente al Hospital Militar, Managua; tel. 2266-9086; fax 2266-0318; internet www.canal15.com.ni; f. 1995; Dir VERÓNICA CHAVEZ.

Nicavisión, Canal 12: Bolonia Dual Card, 1 c. abajo, ½ c. al sur, Apdo 2766, Managua; tel. 2266-0691; fax 2266-1424; f. 1993; Dir MARIANO VALLE PETERS.

Televicentro de Nicaragua, SA, Canal 2: Casa del Obrero, 6½ c. al sur, Apdo 688, Managua; tel. 2268-2222; fax 2266-3688; e-mail tvnoticias@canal2.com.ni; internet www.canal2.com.ni; f. 1965; Pres. OCTAVIO SACASA RASKOSKY; Gen. Man. ALEJANDRO SACASA PASOS.

Televisora Nicaragüense, SA (Telenica 8): De la Mansión Teodolinda, 1 c. al sur, ½ c. abajo, Bolonia, Apdo 3611, Managua; tel. 2266-5021; fax 2266-5024; e-mail webmaster@tn8.tv; internet www.tn8.tv; f. 1989; sold to private buyer in 2010; Gen. Man. JOSÉ MOJICA MEJÍA.

TV Red (Canal 11): Hotel Mansión, Teodolinda, 2 c. abajo, Managua; tel. 2222-7788; e-mail veronica.rocha@tvred.com.ni; internet www.tvredcanal11.com.ni; Gen. Man. VERÓNICA ROCHA.

Finance

(cap. = capital; res = reserves; dep. = deposits; m. = million; amounts in gold córdobas)

BANKING

Supervisory Authority

Superintendencia de Bancos y de Otras Instituciones Financieras: Edif. SIBOIF, Km 7, Carretera Sur, Apdo 788, Managua; tel. 2265-1555; fax 2265-0965; e-mail correo@sibiof.gob.ni; internet www.siboif.gob.ni; f. 1991; Supt Dr VICTOR M. URCUYO VIDAURRE.

Central Bank

Banco Central de Nicaragua: Carretera Sur, Km 7, Apdos 2252/3, Zona 5, Managua; tel. 2255-7171; fax 2265-0495; e-mail info@bcn.gob.ni; internet www.bcn.gob.ni; f. 1961; bank of issue and govt fiscal agent; cap. and res 4,941m., dep. 42,721m. (Dec. 2009); Pres. ALBERTO JOSÉ GUEVARA OBREGÓN; Gen. Man. LEONARDO OVIDIO REYES RAMÍREZ.

Private Banks

Banco de América Central (BAC): Km 4½, Carretera a Masaya, Managua; tel. 2274-4444; fax 2274-4441; e-mail serviciocliente@bac.com.ni; internet www.bac.net/nicaragua; f. 1991; total assets 10,516m. (1999); Gen. Man. JUAN CARLOS SANSÓN CALDERA; 66 brs.

Banco Citibank de Nicaragua: Plaza España, Rotonda el Güegüense 20 m al oeste, Managua; tel. 2254-4848; fax 2266-8796; e-mail info@bancouno.com.ni; internet www.citi.com.ni; Gen. Man. AMALIA BARRIOS VELÁSQUEZ.

Banco Lafise Bancentro (BANCENTRO): Edif. BANCENTRO, Km 4½ Carretera a Masaya, Managua; tel. 2278-2777; fax 2278-6001; e-mail info@bancolafise.com.ni; internet www.lafise.com; f. 1991; frmly Banco de Crédito Centroamericano; name changed as above in 2010; cap. 1,144.4m., res 425.2m., dep. 22,191.7m. (Dec. 2011); Pres. ROBERTO JOSÉ ZAMORA LLANES; Gen. Man. CARLOS ALBERTO BRICEÑO RÍOS.

STOCK EXCHANGE

Bolsa de Valores de Nicaragua: Edif. Oscar Pérez Cassar, Centro BANIC, Km 5½, Carretera Masaya, Apdo 121, Managua; tel. 2278-3830; fax 2278-3836; e-mail info@bolsanic.com; internet bolsanic.com; f. 1993; Pres. Dr RAÚL A. LACAYO SOLÓRZANO.

INSURANCE
State Company

Instituto Nicaragüense de Seguros y Reaseguros (INISER): Centro Comercial Camino de Oriente, Km 6, Carretera a Masaya, Apdo 1147, Managua; tel. 2255-7575; e-mail iniser@iniser.com.ni; internet www.iniser.com.ni; f. 1979 to assume the activities of all the pre-revolution national private insurance cos; Exec. Pres. EDUARDO HALLESLEVENS; Vice-Pres GUILLERMO JIMÉNEZ, JUAN JOSÉ UBEDA.

Private Companies

ASSA Cía de Seguros, SA: Rotonda El Periodista, 400m al Norte, Edif. El Centro, MR-67, Managua, Nicaragua; internet www.assanet .com.ni; Pres. Dr LEONEL ARGÜELLO RAMÍREZ; Sec. HORACIO ARGÜELLO CARAZO.

Mapfre Nicaragua, SA: Edif. Invercasa, 1°, Managua; tel. 2276-8890; fax 2278-6358; e-mail lucia.ramirez@mapfre.com.ni; internet www.mapfre.com.ni; fmrly Aseguradora Mundial; changed name as above in 2010; Pres. JOSÉ ANTONIO ARIAS BERMÚDEZ; Gen. Man. LUCÍA RAMÍREZ.

Seguros América, SA: Centro BAC, Km $5\frac{1}{2}$ Carretera a Masaya, Apdo 6114, Managua; tel. 2274-4200; fax 2274-4202; e-mail info@ segurosamerica.com.ni; internet www.segurosamerica.com.ni; f. 1996; Pres. ADOLFO BENARD; Man. DANILO MANZANARES ENRIQUEZ.

Seguros Lafise, SA: Centro Financiero Lafise, Km $5\frac{1}{2}$, Carretera a Masaya, Managua; tel. 2270-3505; fax 2270-3558; e-mail seguros@ seguroslafise.com.ni; internet www.seguroslafise.com.ni; fmrly Seguros Centroamericanos (Segurossa); Pres. ROBERTO ZAMORA LLANES; Gen. Man. CLAUDIO TABOADA RODRÍGUEZ.

Trade and Industry
GOVERNMENT AGENCIES

Empresa Nicaragüense de Alimentos Básicos (ENABAS): Salida a Carretera Norte, Apdo 1041, Managua; tel. 2248-1640; e-mail direccion.administrativa@enabas.gob.ni; internet www .enabas.gob.ni; f. 1979; controls trading in basic foodstuffs; Exec. Dir HERMINIO ESCOTO GARCÍA.

Instituto de Desarrollo Rural (IDR) (Institute of Rural Development): B3, Camino de Oriente, Apdo 3593, Managua; tel. 2255-8777; e-mail divulgacion@idr.gob.ni; internet www.idr.gob.ni; f. 1995; Exec. Dir PEDRO HASLAM MENDOZA.

Instituto Nicaragüense de Apoyo a la Pequeña y Mediana Empresa (INPYME): De la Shell Plaza el Sol, 1 c. al sur, 300 m abajo, Apdo 449, Managua; tel. 2278-7836; e-mail bcantillo@inpyme .gob.ni; internet www.inpyme.gob.ni; supports small and medium-sized enterprises; Exec. Dir MARTHA LORENA BRIONES.

Instituto Nicaragüense de Tecnología Agropecuaria (INTA): Col. Centroamérica, contiguo al Distrito 5, Apdo 1247, Managua; tel. 2227-2290; fax 2278-0373; e-mail bayserfe@inta.gob.ni; internet www.inta.gob.ni; f. 1993; Dir-Gen. MARÍA ISABEL MARTÍNEZ.

Instituto de la Vivienda Urbana y Rural (INVUR): Km $4\frac{1}{2}$, Carretera Sur, contiguo a INISER, Managua; tel. 2226-6112; e-mail gmartinez@invur.gob.ni; internet www.invur.gob.ni; housing devt; Pres. JUDITH SILVA; Gen. Man. MARÍA EMILIA RIZO.

DEVELOPMENT ORGANIZATIONS

Asociación de Productores y Exportadores de Nicaragua (APEN): Del Hotel Intercontinental, 2 c. al sur y 2 c. abajo, Bolonia, Managua; tel. 2268-6053; fax 2266-5160; internet www.apen.org.ni; Pres. ENRIQUE ZAMORA LLANES; Gen. Man. AZUCENA CASTILLO.

Cámara de Industrias de Nicaragua: Rotonda el Güegüense, Plaza España 300 m al sur, Apdo 1436, Managua; tel. 2266-8847; fax 2266-1891; e-mail cadin@cadin.org.ni; internet www.cadin.org.ni; f. 1964; Pres. MARIO AMADOR RIVAS; Vice-Pres. ALFREDO MARÍN XÍMENEZ.

Cámara Nicaragüense de la Construcción (CNC): Bolonia de Aval Card, 2 c. abajo, 50 varas al sur, Managua; tel. 2226-3363; fax 2266-3327; e-mail info@construccion.org.ni; internet www .construccion.org.ni; f. 1961; construction industry; Pres. BENJAMÍN LANZAS SOMARRIBA; Gen. Man. BRUNO VIDAURRE.

Instituto Nicaragüense de Fomento Municipal (INIFOM): Edif. Central, Carretera a la Refinería, entrada principal residencial Los Arcos, Apdo 3097, Managua; tel. and fax 2266-6050; e-mail eduardo.centeno@inifom.gob.ni; internet www.inifom.gob.ni; Pres. EDUARDO CENTENO GADEA.

PRONicaragua: Edif. PRONicaragua, Restaurante TipTop, 1 c. al oeste, Km $4\frac{1}{2}$, Carretera a Masaya, Managua; tel. 2270-6400; fax 2277-3299; e-mail info@pronicaragua.org; internet www .pronicaragua.org; f. 2002; investment and export promotion agency; br. in Washington, DC (USA); Exec. Dir JAVIER CHAMORRO RUBIALES.

CHAMBERS OF COMMERCE

Cámara de Comercio Americana de Nicaragua: Plaza España, Rotonda el Güegüense, 400 m al sur, 75 m al este, detrás de American Airlines, Managua; tel. and fax 2266-2758; e-mail avil.ramirez@ amcham.org.ni; internet www.amcham.org.ni; f. 1974; Pres. YALI MOLINA PALACIOS.

Cámara de Comercio de Nicaragua (CACONIC): Rotonda el Güegüense 400 m al sur, 20 m al oeste, Managua; tel. 2268-3505; fax 2268-3600; e-mail comercio@caconic.org.ni; internet www.caconic .org.ni; f. 1892; 904 mems; Pres. MARIO GONZÁLES LACAYO; Exec. Dir EDUARDO FONSECA.

Cámara Oficial Española de Comercio de Nicaragua: Restaurante la Marseilleisa, $\frac{1}{2}$ c. arriba, Los Robles, Apdo 4103, Managua; tel. 2278-9047; fax 2278-9088; e-mail camacoesnic@cablenet.com.ni; internet www.camacoesnic.com.ni; Pres. JOSÉ DE LA JARA AHLERS; Sec.-Gen. MARÍA AUXILIADORA MIRANDA DE GUERRERO.

EMPLOYERS' ORGANIZATIONS

Asociación de Café Especiales de Nicaragua (ACEN): Oficentro Norte, Km 5, Carretera Panamericana Norte, Managua; tel. 2249-0180; fax 2249-0182; internet www.acen.org.ni; coffee producers and exporters; Pres. JUAN CARLOS MUNGUÍA; Exec. Dir EDWIN RUÍZ.

Consejo Superior de la Empresa Privada (COSEP): De Telcor Zacarías Guerra, 1 c. abajo, Apdo 5430, Managua; tel. 2276-3333; fax 2276-1666; e-mail cosep@cablenet.com.ni; internet www.cosep.org .ni; f. 1972; private businesses; consists of Cámara de Industrias de Nicaragua (CADIN), Unión de Productores Agropecuarios de Nicaragua (UPANIC), Cámara de Comercio, Cámara de la Construcción, Confederación Nacional de Profesionales (CONAPRO), Instituto Nicaragüense de Desarrollo (INDE); mem. of Coordinadora Democrática Nicaragüense; Pres. Dr JOSÉ ADÁN AGUERRI CHAMORRO; Exec. Dir MARÍA GERMANIA CARRIÓN SOTO.

Instituto Nicaragüense de Desarrollo (INDE): Col. Los Robles, del Hotel Colón 1 c. al sur, 1 c. abajo, mano izquierda, frente a Funeraria Reñazco, Managua; tel. 2252-5800; fax 2270-9866; e-mail inde@inde.org.ni; internet www.inde.org.ni; f. 1963; private business org.; 650 mems; Pres. SERGIO ARGUELLO; Vice-Pres. EDUARDO CALDERA.

Unión Nacional de Agricultores y Ganaderos (UNAG): Managua; tel. 2268-7429; fax 2266-1675; e-mail unag@unag.org.ni; internet www.unag.org.ni; f. 1981; Pres. ALVARO FIALLOS OYANGUREN; Sec. DOUGLAS ALEMÁN.

Unión de Productores Agropecuarios de Nicaragua (UPANIC): Edif. Jorge Salazar, Reparto Serrano, DGI Central, 1 c. al norte $\frac{1}{2}$ c. al este, Apdo 2351, Managua; tel. 2251-0340; fax 2251-0307; e-mail upanic@ibw.com.ni; internet www.upanic.org.ni; private agriculturalists' asscn; Pres. MANUEL ALVAREZ SOLÓRZANO; Sec. FERNANDO MANSELL VILLANUEVA.

UTILITIES
Regulatory Bodies

Comisión Nacional de Energía y Minas (CNEM): Hospital Bautista, 1 c. al oeste, 1 c. al norte, Managua; Pres. EMILIO RAPPACCIOLI BALTODANO (Minister of Energy and Mines).

Instituto Nicaragüense de Acueductos y Alcantarillados (INAA): De la Mansión Teodolinda, 3 c. al sur, Bolonia, Apdo 1084, Managua; tel. 2266-7882; fax 2266-7917; e-mail inaa@inaa .gob.ni; internet www.inaa.gob.ni; f. 1979; water regulator; Exec. Pres. CARLOS SCHUTZE SUGRAÑES.

Instituto Nicaragüense de Energía (INE): Edif. Petronic, 4°, Managua; tel. 2277-5317; fax 2228-3104; e-mail dac@ine.gob.ni; internet www.ine.gob.ni; Pres. JOSÉ DAVID CASTILLO SÁNCHEZ; Exec. Sec. MARIELA DEL CARMEN CERRATO VÁSQUEZ.

Electricity

Empresa Nicaragüense de Electricidad (ENEL): Ofs Centrales, Pista Juan Pablo II y Avda Bolívar, Managua; tel. 2277-4160; fax 2267-2683; e-mail relapub@ibw.com.ni; internet www.enel.gob.ni; responsible for planning, organization, management, administration, research and development of energy resources; Pres. EMILIO RAPPACCIOLI BALTODANO (Minister of Energy and Mines); Sec. RAÚL CASTRO CASCO.

Empresa Nacional de Transmisión Eléctrica, SA (ENATRÉL): Intersección Avda Bolívar y Pista Juan Pablo II, Apdo 283, Managua; tel. 2277-4159; fax 2267-4379; internet www .enatrel.gob.ni; operates the electricity transmission network; Exec. Pres. SALVADOR MANSELL CASTRILLO.

ORMAT Momotombo Power Co: Momotombo; internet www .ormat.com; f. 1999 on acquisition of 15-year concession to rehabilitate and operate Momotombo power plant; 30 MW capacity geothermal plant; subsidiary of ORMAT International, Inc; CEO YEHUDIT (DITA) BRONICKI; Gen. Man. RÓGER ARCIA LACAYO.

Unión Fenosa DISSUR y DISNORTE: Managua; tel. 2274-4700; e-mail comunicacion@ni.unionfenosa.com; internet www .disnorte-dissur.com.ni; electricity distribution co; privatized in 2000; distributes some 1,460 GWh (DISSUR 658 GWh, DISNORTE 802 GWh); Country Man. CARLOS HERNÁNDEZ.

Water

Empresa Nicaragüense de Acueductos y Alcantarillados Sanitarios (ENACAL): Km 5, Carretera sur 505, Asososca; tel. 2266-7875; e-mail ccomunicacion@enacal.com.ni; internet www .enacal.com.ni; Exec. Pres. EVERT ALEMÁN LARA.

TRADE UNIONS

Central Sandinista de Trabajadores (CST): Iglesia del Carmen, 1 c. al oeste, ½ c. al sur, Managua; tel. 2265-1096; fax 2240-1285; Sec.-Gen. ROBERTO GONZÁLEZ GAITÁN; 40,000 mems.

Central de Trabajadores de Nicaragua (CTN) (Nicaraguan Workers' Congress): De la Iglesia del Carmen, 1 c. al sur, ½ c. arriba y 75 varas al sur, Managua; tel. 2268-3061; fax 2265-2056; f. 1962; mem. of Coordinadora Democrática Nicaragüense; Sec.-Gen. ANTONIO JARQUÍN.

Confederación General de Trabajadores Independientes (CGT-i) (Independent General Confederation of Labour): Centro Comercial Nejapa, 1 c. arriba y 3 c. al lago, Managua; tel. 2222-5195; fax 2228-7505; e-mail salasara@yahoo.es; f. 1953; Sec.-Gen. NILO M. SALAZAR AGUILAR; 4,843 mems (est.) from 6 federations with 40 local unions, and 6 non-federated local unions.

Confederación de Unificación Sindical (CUS) (Confederation of United Trade Unions): Casa Q3, del Colegio la Tenderi 2½ c. arriba, Ciudad Jardín, Managua; tel. 8895-7221; e-mail cusorganizacion@ yahoo.com; internet cusnicaragua.org; f. 1972; affiliated to the Inter-American Regional Organization of Workers; mem. of Coordinadora Democrática Nicaragüense; Sec.-Gen. JOSÉ ESPINOZA NAVAS.

Frente Nacional de los Trabajadores (FNT) (National Workers' Front): Residencial Bolonia, de la Optica Nicaragüense, 2 c. arriba, 20 varas al sur, Managua; tel. 2266-3065; fax 2266-7457; e-mail prensa@fnt.org.ni; internet www.fnt.org.ni; f. 1979; affiliated to Frente Sandinista de Liberación Nacional; Sec.-Gen. Dr GUSTAVO PORRAS CORTÉS.

Transport

RAILWAYS

There are no functioning railways in Nicaragua. The state-owned rail operator, Ferrocarril de Nicaragua, ceased operations in 1994, and the only remaining private line closed in 2001.

ROADS

In 2010 there were an estimated 22,111 km of roads, of which 6,018 km were highways and 2,045 km were secondary roads. In 2010 the Inter-American Development Bank approved a $20m. loan for road improvements. The Pan-American Highway runs for 384 km in Nicaragua and links Managua with the Honduran and Costa Rican frontiers and the Atlantic and Pacific Highways, connecting Managua with the coastal regions.

Fondo de Mantenimiento Vial (FOMAV): 50 m al sur, Iglesia El Carmen, Managua; tel. 2268-6836; fax 2268-6831; internet www .fomav.gob.ni; devt and maintenance of the national road network; Pres. AMADEO SANTANA RODRÍGUEZ; Exec. Dir KAREN DEYANIRA MOLINA VALLE.

SHIPPING

Corinto, Puerto Sandino, San Juan del Sur and Potosí, on the Pacific, and Puerto Cabezas, El Bluff (Bluefields) and El Rama, on the Caribbean, are the principal ports. Corinto deals with about 60% of trade. In addition to sea ports, there are small ports on two inland lakes. At 31 December 2012 the flag registered fleet comprised seven vessels, totalling 3,949 grt.

Empresa Portuaria Nacional (EPN): Residencial Bolonia, de la Optica Nicaragüense 1 c. abajo, Managua; tel. 2266-3039; fax 2266-3488; e-mail epn_puertos@epn.com.ni; internet www.epn.com.ni; Pres. VIRGILIO SILVA MUNGÜIA.

CIVIL AVIATION

The principal airport is the Augusto Sandino International Airport in Managua. There are some 185 additional airports in Nicaragua.

Empresa Administradora de Aeropuertos Internacionales (EAAI): Km 11, Carretera Norte, POB 5179, Managua; tel. 2233-1624; fax 2263-1072; e-mail czamora@eaai.com.ni; internet www .eaai.com.ni; autonomous govt entity; operates Managua International Airport and 3 national airports: Bluefields, Puerto Cabezas and Corn Island; Pres. DANILO LACAYO RAPPACIOLI; Gen. Man. ORLANDO CASTILLO GUERRERO.

La Costeña: Managua International Airport, Km 11, Carretera Norte, Managua; tel. 2263-2142; fax 2263-1281; e-mail info@ lacostena.com.ni; internet www.lacostena.com.ni; Gen. Man. ALFREDO CABALLERO.

Tourism

Nicaragua attracts tourists for its landscapes, the twin volcanoes, Maderas and Concepción, and the lake Cocibolca. Other destinations of interest are the colonial cities of León and Granada, the Corn Islands, and ecological reserves such as the Indio Maíz Biological Reserve. In 2011 tourist arrivals totalled a provisional 1.06m. and receipts from tourism US $377m.

Asociación Nicaragüense de Agencias de Viajes y Turismo (ANAVYT): Edif. Policlínica Nicaragüense, Reparto Bolonia, Apdo 1045, Managua; tel. 2266-9742; fax 2266-4474; e-mail aeromund@ cablenet.com.ni; f. 1966; Pres. ANA MARÍA ROCHA C.

Cámara Nacional de Turismo (CANATUR): Edif. de la Camara Española Nicaraguense, Restaurante la Marseillaise, 50 m al este, Managua; tel. 2270-2587; fax 2278-9971; e-mail direccion@ canaturnicaragua.org; internet www.canatur-nicaragua.org; f. 1976; Pres. SYLVIA DE LEVY; Exec. Dir ZENAYDA LAGUNA.

Instituto Nicaragüense de Turismo (INTUR): Del Hotel Crowne Plaza, 1 c. al sur, 1 c. al oeste, Apdo 5088, Managua; tel. 2254-5191; fax 2222-6610; e-mail promocion@intur.gob.ni; internet www.intur .gob.ni; f. 1998; Exec. Pres. MARÍO SALINAS PASOS; Sec.-Gen. ELVIA ESTRADA ROSALES.

Defence

As assessed at November 2012, Nicaragua's professional armed forces numbered an estimated 12,000: army 10,000, navy 800 and air force 1,200. There is a voluntary military service which lasts 18–36 months.

Defence Budget: an estimated 1,550m. gold córdobas in 2012.

Commander-in-Chief: Gen. JULIO CÉSAR AVILÉS CASTILLO.

Education

Primary and secondary education in Nicaragua is provided free of charge. Primary education, which is officially compulsory, begins at seven years of age and lasts for six years. Secondary education, beginning at the age of 13, lasts for up to five years, comprising a first cycle of three years and a second of two years. In 2009/10 enrolment at primary schools included 92% of children in the relevant age-group. Secondary enrolment in that year included 46% of children in the relevant age-group, according to UNESCO estimates. There are many commercial schools and eight universities. In 2003/04 some 103,577 students attended universities and other higher education institutes. In 2011 budgetary expenditure on education was projected at US $3.8m, representing 23.0% of total government expenditure.

NIGER

Introductory Survey

LOCATION, CLIMATE, LANGUAGE, RELIGION, FLAG, CAPITAL

The Republic of Niger is a land-locked country in western Africa, with Algeria and Libya to the north, Nigeria and Benin to the south, Mali and Burkina Faso to the west, and Chad to the east. The climate is hot and dry, with an average temperature of 29°C (84°F). The official language is French, but numerous indigenous languages, including Hausa (spoken by about one-half of the population), Tuareg, Djerma and Fulani, are also used (the 1991 sovereign National Conference identified 10 'national' languages). Some 95% of the population are Muslims, the most influential Islamic groups being the Tijaniyya, the Senoussi and the Hamallists. Most of the remainder of the population follow traditional beliefs, and there is a small Christian minority. The national flag (proportions 6 by 7) has three equal horizontal stripes, of orange, white and green, with an orange disc in the centre of the white stripe. The capital is Niamey.

CONTEMPORARY POLITICAL HISTORY

Historical Context

Formerly a part of French West Africa, Niger became a self-governing member of the French Community in December 1958 and was granted independence on 3 August 1960. Hamani Diori, leader of the Parti Progressiste Nigérien (the local section of the Ivorian-dominated Rassemblement Démocratique Africain) and Prime Minister since December 1958, became Head of State. Diori was elected President in November 1960, and re-elected in 1965 and 1970. Close links were maintained with France.

The Sahelian drought of 1968–74 was particularly damaging to the Nigerien economy and was a major factor in precipitating a military coup in April 1974 following which Lt-Col (later Maj.-Gen.) Seyni Kountché, the armed forces Chief of Staff, became President. The new administration, headed by a Conseil Militaire Suprême (CMS), suspended the Constitution; the legislature was replaced by a consultative Conseil National de Développement (CND), and political activity was banned. Kountché obtained the withdrawal of French troops and reduced French influence over the exploitation of Niger's deposits of uranium (which France had initiated in 1968).

From 1977 the proportion of army officers in the Government was progressively reduced and in January 1983 a civilian, Oumarou Mamane, was appointed to the newly created post of Prime Minister. In November Mamane, who in August had been appointed President of the CND, was replaced as premier by Hamid Algabid.

Domestic Political Affairs

A draft 'national charter' was approved by a reported 99.6% of voters in a referendum in June 1987. In November Kountché died while undergoing medical treatment in France, and Col (later Brig.) Ali Saïbou, the army Chief of Staff, was inaugurated as Chairman of the CMS and Head of State. In July 1988 Mamane (who had been replaced as President of the CND in September 1987) was reinstated as Prime Minister, and the CND was given the task of drafting a new constitution. In August 1988 Saïbou formed a new ruling party, the Mouvement National pour la Société de Développement (MNSD).

In May 1989 an MNSD congress elected a Conseil Supérieur d'Orientation Nationale (CSON) to succeed the CMS. The draft Constitution was endorsed by a reported 99.3% of voters in a referendum in September. At elections in December Saïbou (as President of the CSON and the sole candidate) was confirmed as President of the Republic, for a seven-year term, by 99.6% of those who voted, while 99.5% of voters endorsed a single list of CSON-approved deputies to a new, 93-member Assemblée nationale. In March 1990 a prominent industrialist, Aliou Mahamidou, was appointed Prime Minister in an extensive government reorganization. In November Saïbou announced that a multi-party political system would be established. A national conference on political reform was to be convened in mid-1991, and multi-party national elections would take place in 1992.

In March 1991 the armed forces Chief of Staff announced that the armed forces were to distance themselves from the MNSD—Nassara (as the MNSD had been restyled) with immediate effect. In July Saïbou resigned as Chairman of the MNSD—Nassara, in preparation for the National Conference, which was convened in Niamey later that month and attended by about 1,200 delegates, including representatives of the organs of state, 24 political organizations, the military and civil society. It declared itself sovereign, voting to suspend the Constitution and dissolve the legislature. Saïbou would remain in office as Head of State on an interim basis, but the Conference would supervise the exercise of his (now largely ceremonial) powers. The Government was dissolved in September, and in October the Conference appointed Cheiffou Amadou to head a transitional Council of Ministers, which was intended to hold office until the inauguration of democratically elected institutions, now scheduled for early 1993. Prior to the conclusion of the Conference, in November 1991, its President, André Salifou, was designated Chairman of a 15-member interim legislative body, the Haut Conseil de la République (HCR), which was, inter alia, to supervise the drafting of a new constitution.

The new Constitution was approved by 89.8% of those who voted in a referendum held on 26 December 1992. The MNSD—Nassara won the greatest number of seats (29) at elections to the 83-member Assemblée nationale, held on 14 February 1993, but was prevented from resuming power by the rapid formation, following the elections, of the Alliance des Forces de Changement (AFC) by six parties with a total of 50 seats in the legislature. Principal members of the AFC were the Convention Démocratique et Sociale—Rahama (CDS), the Parti Nigérien pour la Démocratie et le Socialisme—Tarayya (PNDS), and the Alliance Nigérienne pour la Démocratie et le Progrès Social—Zaman Lahiya (ANDP). At the first round of the presidential election, held on 27 February, Col (retd) Mamadou Tandja, Saïbou's successor as leader of the MNSD—Nassara, won the greatest proportion of votes cast (34.2%). He and his nearest rival, Mahamane Ousmane (the leader of the CDS, with 26.6%), proceeded to a second round on 27 March, at which Ousmane was elected President by 55.4% of voters; his inauguration took place on 16 April. Ousmane appointed Mahamadou Issoufou of the PNDS as Prime Minister. Despite an attempt by the MNSD—Nassara to block the appointment, in May Moumouni Adamou Djermakoye of the ANDP became President of the Assemblée nationale.

The new regime's efforts to curb public expenditure, combined with the effects of the 50% devaluation of the CFA franc in January 1994, provoked considerable disquiet among workers and students. In September the PNDS withdrew from the AFC, and Issoufou resigned the premiership, in protest at the perceived transfer of certain prime ministerial powers to the President. A new minority Government, led by Souley Abdoulaye of the CDS, failed to withstand a parliamentary motion of no confidence proposed by the MNSD—Nassara and the PNDS in October. Ousmane therefore dissolved the Assemblée nationale.

At legislative elections held in mid-January 1995 the MNSD—Nassara won 29 seats and subsequently led a 43-strong majority group in the Assemblée nationale. Although the CDS increased its representation to 24 seats, the AFC secured only 40 seats. Ousmane declined to accept the new majority's nominee to the premiership, Hama Amadou (the Secretary-General of the MNSD—Nassara), instead appointing another member of that party, Amadou Aboubacar Cissé, a former official of the World Bank. The MNSD—Nassara and its allies announced that they would not co-operate with his administration, and Cissé was expelled from the party. Meanwhile, Issoufou was elected President of the Assemblée nationale. In February the legislature approved a motion of censure against Cissé, and Ousmane accepted the nomination of Amadou as Prime Minister. This political 'cohabitation' encountered serious difficulties, as the President and Prime Minister disputed their respective competencies, in particular with regard to a proposed programme for the reorganization and privatization of state enterprises, which Ousmane opposed. Following several months of industrial unrest, Ousmane's rejection of the Government's draft budget, in January 1996, resulted in a new impasse in relations.

Ousmane overthrown

On 27 January 1996 the elected organs of state were overthrown by the military. The coup leaders, who formed a Conseil de Salut National (CSN), chaired by Col (later Brig.-Gen.) Ibrahim Baré Maïnassara, armed forces Chief of Staff since March 1995 and a former aide-de-camp to Kountché, asserted that their seizure of power had been necessitated by Niger's descent into political chaos. The CSN annulled the Constitution and dissolved the Assemblée nationale, while political parties were suspended. A national forum was to be convened to consider the revision of the Constitution and the electoral code, and to determine a timetable for a return to civilian rule. The CSN appointed Boukary Adji, the Deputy Governor of the Banque Centrale des Etats de l'Afrique de l'Ouest, as Prime Minister. Adji's transitional Government, named in February 1996, was composed entirely of civilians.

Two consultative bodies were established to prepare for the restoration of civilian government, the advisory Conseil des Sages and the co-ordinating committee of the national forum. The National Forum for Democratic Renewal, which was convened in April 1996, adopted revisions to the Constitution which aimed to guarantee greater institutional stability, essentially by conferring executive power solely on the President.

The revised Constitution was approved by some 92.3% of the votes cast at a referendum on 12 May 1996 (about 35% of the electorate participated). The ban on political activity was lifted shortly afterwards. Voting in the presidential election commenced, as scheduled, on 7 July 1996, but was quickly halted in several areas where preparations were incomplete: polling took place in these areas on 8 July. According to the Supreme Court, Maïnassara won the election, with some 52.2% of the votes cast; Ousmane secured 19.8% and Tandja 15.7%. Maïnassara was installed as President on 7 August.

Legislative elections proceeded on 23 November 1996. According to official results, the pro-Maïnassara Union Nationale des Indépendants pour le Renouveau Démocratique (UNIRD) won 52 of the Assemblée nationale's 83 seats. International observers pronounced themselves satisfied with the organization and conduct of the election. (The Supreme Court later annulled the results in three constituencies won by the UNIRD, on the grounds of fraud.) A new Government was formed, with Cissé as Prime Minister. In November 1997 Maïnassara dismissed the entire Government and subsequently appointed Ibrahim Hassane Maiyaki, hitherto Minister of Foreign Affairs and Cooperation, as Prime Minister.

The death of Maïnassara

On 9 April 1999 Maiyaki made a broadcast to the nation, announcing the death of Maïnassara in an 'unfortunate accident' at a military airbase in Niamey. The Prime Minister stated that the defence and security forces would continue to be the guarantors of republican order and national unity, and announced the dissolution of the Assemblée nationale, as well as the temporary suspension of all party political activity. Despite the official explanation for his death, it was generally perceived that members of the presidential guard had assassinated Maïnassara in a *coup d'état*. Although members of the Assemblée nationale initially rejected its dissolution, on 11 April the Constitution was suspended and its institutions dissolved. A military Conseil de Réconciliation Nationale (CRN), under the chairmanship of Maj. Daouda Mallam Wanké (hitherto head of the presidential guard), was to exercise executive and legislative authority during a nine-month transitional period, prior to the restoration of elected civilian institutions. Wanké immediately signed an ordinance on interim political authority, which was to function as a constitutional document during the transitional period. Maiyaki was reappointed as Prime Minister of the transitional Government on 12 April; a new Council of Ministers was named shortly afterwards. Moussa Moumouni Djermakoye, who had been succeeded as armed forces Chief of Staff by Lt-Col Soumara Zanguina, became Minister of National Defence.

The new draft Constitution was submitted to referendum on 18 July 1999, when it was approved by 89.6% of those who voted (about one-third of the registered electorate). The Constitution envisaged a balance of powers between the President, the Government and the legislature, but, none the less, vested strong powers in the Head of State, who was to be politically liable only in the case of high treason. The Government, under a Prime Minister appointed by the President, was to be responsible to the

Assemblée nationale, which would be competent to remove the Prime Minister by vote of censure. A clause in the Constitution guaranteeing all those involved in the military take-overs of 1996 and 1999 immunity from prosecution provoked controversy and was condemned by the human rights organization Amnesty International, in a report in September, as undermining the rule of law. The report was regarded as particularly significant in that it published the testimony of a witness who alleged that Maïnassara had been killed by the presidential guard under Wanké's command. The Wanké regime continued to assert that Maïnassara's death had been accidental, and that a commission of inquiry into the death had been ordered in response to a complaint lodged by the late President's family.

Voting at the presidential election, which was contested by seven candidates, took place on 17 October 1999, and was considered both by the Commission Électorale Nationale Indépendante (CENI) and by independent observers to have been largely transparent and peaceful. Tandja, representing the MNSD—Nassara, won 32.3% of the votes cast, followed by Issoufou, of the PNDS, with 22.8%, and Ousmane, of the CDS, with 22.5%. The rate of participation by voters was 43.7%. Tandja and Issoufou proceeded to a second round on 24 November. Having secured the support of Ousmane, Tandja was elected President, with 59.9% of the votes cast. About 39% of the registered electorate voted. The MNSD—Nassara was similarly successful in the concurrent elections to the Assemblée nationale, winning 38 of the 83 seats; the CDS took 17, the PNDS 16, the pro-Maïnassara Rassemblement pour la Démocratie et le Progrès—Djamaa (RDP) eight and the ANDP four. Tandja, who had served in the CMS under Kountché and was Minister of the Interior in the early 1990s, was inaugurated as President on 22 December. Hama Amadou was subsequently appointed Prime Minister, and a new Council of Ministers was named in January 2000.

In January 2000 the Assemblée nationale adopted draft amnesty legislation, as provided for in the Constitution. The amnesty was opposed by the RDP, and many party activists joined a demonstration in February to denounce the legislation and to demand an international inquiry into the death of Maïnassara. In March 12 opposition parties, led by the PNDS, formed a coalition, the Coordination des Forces Démocratiques (CFD). Similarly, 17 parties loyal to the President, most notably the MNSD—Nassara and the CDS, formed the Alliance des Forces Démocratiques (AFD). In May Col Bourahima Moumouni was appointed armed forces Chief of Staff. None the less, rumours persisted of dissent within the army. In July the ANDP withdrew from the opposition CFD alliance and joined the AFD, thereby increasing the Government's parliamentary majority by four seats. Explaining his party's shift in allegiances, the leader of the ANDP, Moumouni Adamou Djermakoye, accused the CFD of intolerance and of failing to ease social tensions.

Tandja implemented a major government reorganization in November 2002, as a result of which the position of allies of Prime Minister Amadou was reportedly strengthened. At the end of December the Assemblée nationale approved legislation providing for the creation of a special military tribunal to try those accused of involvement in a rebellion earlier in the year (a total of 268 arrests were reported); elements within the opposition alleged that the legislation violated several articles of the Constitution. However, many soldiers were reportedly released during 2003, owing to a lack of evidence, and the three highest-ranking officers arrested were provisionally freed in February 2004. (Six of the mutineers were awarded custodial sentences at a military tribunal in early 2006.)

In mid-October 2003 the Council of Ministers announced proposals to increase the number of deputies in the Assemblée nationale from 83 to 113, in order to reflect the growth in the population recorded between the national censuses of 1988 and 2001.

The 2004 presidential election

In the first round of the presidential election, held on 16 November 2004, Tandja won 40.7% of votes cast, followed by Issoufou, who received 24.6%, and both, therefore, proceeded to a second round of voting, while the four eliminated candidates all urged their supporters to transfer their allegiance to Tandja. In the second round of voting, held on 4 December, Tandja was victorious, receiving 65.5% of votes cast. (Turn-out in the first round was reported to be 48.5% of registered voters, declining slightly, to 45.0%, in the second round.) At elections to the newly enlarged 113-seat Assemblée nationale, held concurrently with the second round of voting in the presidential election, the MNSD—Nassara won the largest number of seats, obtaining 47, while allied pro-presidential parties secured a further 41 seats. An opposition coalition formed around the PNDS, which also comprised the Parti Nigérien pour l'Autogestion (PNA), the Parti Progressiste Nigérien—Rassemblement Démocratique Africain (PPN—RDA), the Union pour la Démocratie et la République (UDR) and the Union des Nigériens Indépendants (UNI), won a total of 25 seats. Ousmane was subsequently re-elected as President of the Assemblée nationale, 13 seats in which, in accordance with legislation adopted in 2001, were reserved for women. Later in December President Tandja announced the formation of a new Government, in which Amadou remained as Prime Minister.

In May 2007 the Government was dissolved following a vote of no confidence in the Assemblée nationale, supported by 62 of the 113 deputies. The following month President Tandja named Seyni Oumarou as Prime Minister, an appointment which drew considerable criticism from opposition members. Oumarou was nevertheless sworn in and he later announced a new Council of Ministers in which many key portfolios remained unchanged.

Increased measures by the authorities against the independent media was reported, including the closure of the private radio station Sahara FM by the media regulatory authority in April 2008, after it had broadcast testimonies from victims of attacks by the Nigerien military. Despite being considered a potential candidate to succeed Tandja as President, former Prime Minister Hama Amadou was arrested and charged with corruption in June. Around 100 people protested outside the High Court of Justice in response to his arrest and were dispersed by police; in October several thousand demonstrators took to the streets of Niamey to call for his release. Amadou denied the charges against him, claiming that they were part of a campaign to prevent him contesting the presidential election, scheduled for December 2009.

Political crisis and Constitution of the Sixth Republic

A campaign to prolong Tandja's presidency gained momentum in December 2008, when a demonstration was staged in the capital in support of the extension of his term in office, and a change to the Constitution to allow the President to serve beyond the two-term limit stipulated therein. There were reports of similar rallies taking place elsewhere in the country, while counter-demonstrations by opponents of a third mandate for Tandja also followed. In March 2009 Tandja announced that, although he would be willing to remain in power after the end of his second term, he would not amend the Constitution in order to do so. An extraordinary congress of the MNSD—Nassara, held in Zinder in February, designated Oumarou as President of the party, replacing Amadou, whose supporters declared the change of leadership to be illegal, on the grounds that it contravened party regulations. Amadou was released from prison in April, owing to ill health, and subsequently fled abroad.

In early May 2009 Tandja declared his intention to conduct a constitutional referendum on the extension of his mandate. His announcement was widely criticized by opposition parties, non-governmental organizations and trade unions; the PNDS subsequently organized a large opposition protest in Niamey. On 26 May, after the Constitutional Court ruled in response to an appeal by opposition parliamentary deputies that a referendum on his retention of power would be illegal, the President dissolved the Assemblée nationale. In early June Tandja created a committee to draft a new constitution (of what was to be designated the Sixth Republic) that would enable him to remain in office for a transitional period of three years if endorsed at a national referendum (subsequently scheduled for 4 August). However, on 12 June the Constitutional Court annulled the decree on the organization of the referendum. Following denouncement of Tandja's plan, a large protest was staged by opposition supporters in Niamey. The CENI subsequently declared that legislative elections would take place on 20 August, while the CDS withdrew its eight ministers from the Government, in recognition of the ruling by the Constitutional Court.

Following the Constitutional Court's refusal to review its decision regarding the referendum, on 26 June 2009 Tandja assumed emergency powers to rule by decree, subsequently dissolving the Court and suspending the Constitution. Opposition leaders accused Tandja of staging a coup and trade unions organized a one-day general strike in protest, which was only partially observed. Amid mounting international concern, in early July the European Commission threatened to suspend aid to the country; the Economic Community of West African States (ECOWAS) had also earlier threatened economic and diplomatic

sanctions, while other international donors, including the UN, France and the USA, urged the Nigerien Government to respect the constitutional order. Nevertheless, Tandja appointed members to a new Constitutional Court, prompting condemnation from the opposition, and again decreed that a constitutional referendum would be held on 4 August. Later in July a joint delegation of the UN, the African Union (AU, see p. 191) and ECOWAS visited Niamey in an effort to resolve the political crisis; however, the referendum proceeded, as scheduled, on 4 August. According to results released by the CENI, 92.5% of those that participated in the vote (68.3% of the electorate) were in favour of the new Constitution, which, in addition to prolonging Tandja's mandate by three years, provided for the removal of the limit on presidential terms, the significant expansion of the powers of the President and the creation of a Senate. An opposition coalition of political parties, trade unions and human rights groups, known as Coordination des Forces pour la Démocratie et la République (CFDR), which had urged voters to boycott the referendum, disputed the results, and claimed that the overall turn-out was less than 5% of the electorate. Nevertheless, on 14 August the Constitutional Court endorsed the validity of the result. On 18 August the Constitution of the Sixth Republic entered into force by presidential decree. Oumarou's Government was reappointed by Tandja on 19 August. On the same day a presidential decree declared that early legislative elections would be held on 20 October. The CFDR condemned the arrest in early September of 30 former deputies on charges of embezzlement of public funds, maintaining that Tandja had ordered measures against opposition members. On 24 September it was announced that Oumarou and two ministers had resigned from their posts in order to contest the legislative elections. On 2 October Tandja appointed Ali Badjo Gamatié, hitherto Vice-Governor of the Central Bank of West African States, as the new Prime Minister.

Despite international pressure for a postponement of the poll and a further opposition boycott, the elections to the Assemblée nationale proceeded on 20 October 2009. ECOWAS announced the suspension of Niger's membership of the organization until the restoration of constitutional order, and announced that it would not recognize the outcome of the elections, while the European Union (EU, see p. 281) also warned of punitive measures. According to official results, which were released by the CENI, on 24 October, the MNSD—Nassara secured 76 seats (compared with 47 in 2004), while the remaining seats were won by parties or candidates allied to the MNSD—Nassara, with the Rassemblement Social-Démocratique—Gaskiya (RSD) receiving 15 seats and the RDP seven seats. In early November the Constitutional Court endorsed the validity of the election results. The EU suspended development aid to Niger and issued an ultimatum that discussions begin on a return to constitutional order. In December the CFDR organized a mass demonstration in Niamey demanding that Tandja relinquish power by 22 December, the date marking the expiry of his presidential mandate under the previous Constitution. Later that month negotiations began between government and opposition representatives, mediated by former Nigerian President Abdulsalami Abubakar on behalf of ECOWAS, in an effort to resolve the impasse. On 23 December the US State Department announced that the country had suspended non-humanitarian assistance to the Government and had imposed travel restrictions on members and supporters of Tandja's regime. In January 2010 Abubakar presented negotiating representatives with a plan to resolve the crisis, which would allow Tandja to retain power for a transitional period under a 'government of national reconciliation'. However, in early February the discussions, which had repeatedly been adjourned, were abandoned after government and opposition representatives failed to reach agreement on Abubakar's draft plan, prompting a large anti-Government demonstration outside the parliamentary building.

Military coup

On 18 February 2010 members of the armed forces stormed the presidential office during a cabinet meeting and captured Tandja, together with all the government members; it was reported that some 10 people had been killed. The coup leaders, the self-styled Conseil Suprême pour la Restauration de la Démocratie (CSRD), announced the suspension of the Constitution and dissolution of all state organs; following meetings with UN, AU and ECOWAS delegations, they pledged to restore democratic rule and oversee the drafting of a new constitution. The President of the Conseil, a senior army officer, Squadron Commdr Salou Djibo, was named as acting Head of State and

Head of Government. On the following day the AU suspended Niger's membership of the organization and demanded the restoration of constitutional rule; the UN and ECOWAS also condemned the military coup. Meanwhile, the CFDR organized a large rally in Niamey in support of the ousting of Tandja and intervention of the military junta. On 23 February Djibo appointed Mahamadou Danda, who was not a member of a political party and had served in the transitional administration after the April 1999 coup, as acting Prime Minister. On 2 March Djibo announced the appointment of a 20-member transitional Government, comprising 15, largely technocratic civilians and five military officers; Gen. Mamadou Ousseini, the former army chief of staff, became Minister of National Defence, while a further two senior army officers who had served under Tandja were allocated portfolios. Djibo declared that no member of the CSRD or of the transitional Government would be permitted to contest a pledged presidential election. Later in March Djibo replaced eight regional governors with army officers. Also in March Djibo appointed military officers to replace civilian regional governors who had been dismissed following the coup, and installed a 131-member advisory council for the transitional period, the Conseil Consultatif National, chaired by civil society activist Marou Amadou. In late March Oumarou and 13 other former ministers and officials loyal to Tandja (who remained in detention in the presidential buildings in Niamey) were arrested and accused of involvement in 'subversive activities' aimed at undermining the transitional process; they were released several days later.

In April 2010 Djibo appointed a 16-member committee to draft a new constitution, electoral law and charter governing political parties. In early May, in an announcement that was welcomed by ECOWAS, the CSRD declared that the transition to civilian rule would be completed by 18 February 2011, following a constitutional referendum and local, legislative and presidential elections. Later in May 2010 Djibo promulgated a new electoral code, based on the recommendations of the Conseil Consultatif National, which notably reduced the presidential term from five years to four (renewable only once) and required presidential candidates to be aged between 40 and 70 years and to possess a university degree. A new CENI was inaugurated in mid-June, under the chairmanship of a judge, Abdourahmane Ghousmane. On 3 July Ghousmane announced that a constitutional referendum would take place on 31 October, followed by legislative elections and the first round of a presidential election on 3 January 2011. Also on 3 July 2010 ECOWAS announced that Niger was to be reinstated as an observer member. In mid-July the leaders of 17 member parties of the CFDR, including the CDS, the PNDS and the Mouvement Démocratique Nigérien (Moden—established by supporters of former Prime Minister Hama Amadou), signed an accord in which they pledged to support whoever of their candidates succeeded in reaching the second round of the presidential election. In September the CENI announced a postponement of the elections owing to organizational difficulties; according to the revised timetable, local elections were to be conducted on 8 January 2011, followed by legislative elections and the first round of the presidential election on 31 January (with a second round scheduled for 12 March).

Recent developments: presidential and legislative elections

At the national referendum, which took place, as scheduled, on 31 October 2010, the Constitution of the Seventh Republic was endorsed by 90.2% of votes cast, with a recorded participation rate of about 52.0%. The new Constitution included provisions restricting the President to two five-year terms in office, prohibited members of the armed forces from seeking the presidency, and also granted an amnesty to the protagonists of the military coup in February. The Constitution was promulgated by Djibo on 26 November. At a CDS congress in November, Ousmane was re-elected unopposed as the party's President.

In January 2011, as campaigning for the forthcoming elections began, it was reported that Tandja had been transferred from house arrest to prison, after being formally charged with misappropriation of public funds. Local and regional elections were conducted on 11 January (after a delay of three days). The first round of the presidential election, which was contested by 10 candidates took place, concurrently with the legislative elections, on 31 January as scheduled. In the legislative elections, the PNDS secured 39 of the 113 seats, while the MNSD—Nassara took 26 and Moden 24 seats, according to provisional results. In the presidential poll, PNDS leader Issoufou secured the highest number of votes, with 36.2%, followed by former

premiers Oumarou (23.2%) and Amadou (19.8%), and former President Ousmane (8.3%). The second round of the presidential election between Issoufou and Oumarou took place on 12 March: the CENI announced that Issoufou had been elected to the presidency, with about 58% of votes cast, according to provisional results. ECOWAS and AU observers commended the successful organization of the presidential election. Issoufou's inauguration as President on 7 April officially marked the end of military rule. He immediately appointed a member of the Tuareg community and former minister, Brigi Rafini, as Prime Minister. Later that month a new, 24-member Government, comprising representatives of the PNDS and allied parties, was announced. Three senior ministers were appointed: Bazoum Mohamed, the Vice-President of the PNDS, as Minister of State, Minister of Foreign Affairs, African Integration and Nigeriens Abroad; former Prime Minister Cissé, the President of the Union pour la Démocratie et la République—Tabbat, as Minister of State, Minister of Planning, Land Settlement and Community Development; and Abdou Labo, a dissident member of the CDS, as Minister of State, Minister of the Interior, Public Security, Decentralization and Religious Affairs. Meanwhile, Amadou was elected as President of the Assemblée nationale. Former President Tandja was released from prison in May, after the Court of Appeal in Niamey overturned the charges against him. Later that month the Assemblée nationale approved legislation according an amnesty to those responsible for ousting Tandja from office in February 2010, as envisaged in the Constitution. In July 2011 it was reported that several soldiers and civilians had been arrested on charges of conspiring to assassinate President Issoufou. In September a minor government reorganization was effected.

In early April 2012 President Issoufou announced the removal of three ministers from the Government. The Minister of Finance, Ouhoumoudou Mahamadou, was replaced by Jules Bayé, while the equipment and transport portfolios were awarded to Sadi Soumaila and Ibrahim Yacouba, respectively.

Tuareg issues

Ethnic unrest followed the return to northern Niger, during the late 1980s, of large numbers of Tuareg nomads who had migrated to Libya and Algeria in the early 1980s to escape the Sahelian drought. It was widely believed that the perceived failure of the Saïbou administration to assist in the rehabilitation of returnees was a significant factor contributing to the subsequent Tuareg uprising. In January 1992 the transitional authorities intensified security measures in the north and, for the first time, formally acknowledged that there was a rebellion in the country. Rhissa Ag Boula, the leader of the rebel Front de Libération de l'Aïr et l'Azaouad (FLAA), subsequently stated that the Tuareg rebels were seeking to achieve the establishment of a federal system of governance. In August the security forces launched a major offensive against rebel Tuareg groups. Military authority was reinforced in October by the appointment of senior members of the security forces to northern administrative posts. In November, none the less, a commission that had been appointed by the transitional Government recommended a far-reaching programme of decentralization, according legal status and financial authority to local communities.

In mid-1993 a three-month truce agreement between representatives of the Government and the Tuaregs, which provided for the demilitarization of the north, and envisaged negotiations on the Tuaregs' political demands, was signed in Paris, France. However, a new group, the Armée Révolutionnaire de Libération du Nord-Niger (ARLN), emerged to denounce the truce, and supporters of the truce (led by Mano Dayak, the Tuareg signatory to the agreement) broke away from the FLAA to form the Front de Libération de Tamoust (FLT): Ag Boula and the remainder of the FLAA stated that they could not support any agreement that contained no specific commitment to discussion of federalism. In September the FLT and the Government agreed to extend the truce for a further three months. Although the FLAA and the ARLN refused to sign the accord, in October they joined with the FLT in a Coordination de la Résistance Armée (CRA), with the aim of presenting a cohesive programme in future negotiations.

Tentative agreement was reached in June 1994 on the creation of ethnically based autonomous regions, each of which was to have its own elected assembly and governor to function in parallel with the organs of central government. Despite renewed unrest, in September the CRA presented Nigerien government negotiators with a plan for the restoration of peace. Formal negotiations resumed, with mediation by the Burkinabè

President, Blaise Compaoré, as well as representatives of France and Algeria, in Ouagadougou (Burkina Faso) in October. A new peace accord resulted, emphasizing that Niger was 'unitary and indivisible', while proposing the establishment of elected assemblies or councils for territorial communities, which would be responsible for the implementation of economic, social and cultural policies. A renewable three-month truce was to take immediate effect, to be monitored by French and Burkinabè military units. A commission was established in January 1995 to consider the administrative reorganization of the country.

Ag Boula, who had withdrawn from the CRA, and refused to participate in the decentralization committee, in protest at alleged delays in the implementation of the provisions of the October 1994 agreement, emerged as the leader of the Tuareg delegation (now renamed the Organisation de la Résistance Armée—ORA) at negotiations in Ouagadougou in March 1995. In April it was announced that a lasting peace agreement had been reached. Demobilized rebels were to be integrated into the Nigerien military and public sector; particular emphasis was to be placed on the economic, social and cultural development of the north, and the Government undertook to support the decentralization process. There was to be a general amnesty for all parties involved in the Tuareg rebellion and its suppression. The peace agreement was formally signed by Ag Boula and a representative of the Nigerien Government on 24 April 1995, one day before the cease-fire took effect.

Meanwhile, there was increasing ethnic unrest in the Lake Chad region of south-east Niger, where several thousand (mainly Toubou) Chadian refugees had settled since the overthrow of President Hissène Habré in late 1990. The Front Démocratique du Renouveau (FDR) emerged in October 1994 to demand increased autonomy for the Toubou population of the south-east. In November, in compliance with a request by the UN, Niger established a committee to disarm militias and to combat arms-trafficking, which was reportedly prevalent in the Agadez and Lake Chad regions. A Comité Spécial de la Paix (CSP) was inaugurated in May 1995, and a military observer group, comprising representatives of Burkina and France, was deployed in the north in July. The Prime Minister approved an amnesty in that month, and all Tuareg prisoners were reported to have been released shortly afterwards. The peace process was undermined, however, by evidence that Dayak and other Tuareg groups in a revived CRA were making common cause with the FDR in demanding autonomy for their respective regions. In December Dayak was one of three leading CRA members to be killed in an air crash. In January 1996 the new leader of the FLT (and acting leader of the CRA), Mohamed Akotai, indicated that his movement favoured inter-Tuareg reconciliation and a dialogue with the Government.

Following the coup of January 1996, the CSN expressed its commitment to the peace process. Nevertheless, insecurity persisted, particularly in the east, and violent clashes were reported in March 1997, involving several hundred soldiers and Toubou rebels. In July the FDR announced its withdrawal from the peace process, stating that Nigerien and Chadian military units had attacked one of its bases; the FDR reported that 17 members of the armed forces had been killed in clashes with its fighters. In November a peace accord, known as the Algiers addendum protocol, providing for an immediate cease-fire, was signed in Algeria between the Nigerien Government and several opposition movements. In March 1998 the ORA and CRA surrendered their weapons stocks at Agadez. Meanwhile, Ag Boula was appointed as Minister-delegate responsible for Tourism in December 1997.

Following the death of President Maïnassara, in April 1999, the military CRN gave assurances that the peace process would be continued. Ag Boula was promoted to the rank of minister in the transitional Government and retained his ministerial post in the new Government of Hama Amadou, formed in January 2000. However, in February 2004 Ag Boula was dismissed from his ministerial post and detained on a charge of complicity in the murder of an MNSD—Nassara activist (in order to maintain Tuareg representation in the Government, Mohamed Anako was appointed as a Minister-delegate at the Ministry of the Economy and Finance). The Government subsequently denied rumours that elements of FLAA had resumed insurgent activities in the north; however, following a clash with government forces in October, in which five people were reported to have died, Ag Boula's brother, Mohamed Ag Boula, claimed responsibility for the attack, citing the failure of the Government to implement the 1995 peace agreements, and the continuing detention of certain

former insurgents, as motivation for the attack. In July 2008 Rhissa Ag Boula (who had fled to France following his release from detention in March 2005) was convicted for the murder of the MNSD—Nassara activist and sentenced to death *in absentia*.

Meanwhile, in February 2007 a lesser known Tuareg rebel group, the Mouvement des Nigériens pour la Justice (MNJ), claimed responsibility for an attack on a military base north of Niamey, prompting concerns that ethnic unrest was once again increasing. Further attacks were reported in mid-2007. Despite repeated demands from the rebel group for fairer distribution of revenue generated by mining the uranium resources of the northern region, the Government refused to enter into negotiations, insisting that the attacks were not considered to be a rebellion. However, by August the situation had worsened, with the number of Tuareg attacks increasing, and in that month President Tandja declared a three-month state of emergency in the region and granted additional powers of arrest to the security forces.

The MNJ claimed that it was responsible for an attack on the town of Tanhout in January 2008, in which seven soldiers were reported to have been killed and several more captured; the civilian administrator of the town was also taken prisoner. In March the Nigerien armed forces launched an offensive against the MNJ in the north. The MNJ denied army claims that 10 rebels had been killed. In May the army announced that it had killed a further 11 Tuareg rebels in a new operation against rebel bases in the north (the MNJ again denied this claim), while President Tandja issued a decree extending the state of emergency declared in August 2007. In July 2008 further clashes between government forces and the MNJ resulted in the death of a senior member of that organization, Mohamed Acherif.

In August 2008 a government spokesman falsely claimed that the Tuareg rebels had agreed to cease hostilities after holding peace talks with Libyan Revolutionary Leader Col Muammar al-Qaddafi. Nevertheless, a senior MNJ member stated that the rebels were willing to engage in peace talks with the Government, on the condition that they were conducted outside Niger. Despite this development there were reports in October that MNJ forces had attacked an army convoy near the town of Arlit, and in December another Tuareg rebel organization, the Front des Forces de Redressement (FFR), claimed responsibility for the kidnapping of a Canadian diplomat, Robert Fowler; the FFR, however, later retracted its claim. An Algerian-based rebel group styled al-Qa'ida Organization in the Islamic Maghreb (AQIM— previously known as the Groupe Salafiste pour la Prédication et le Combat) subsequently claimed that it had Fowler in captivity, and in March 2009 demanded the return of 20 of its members detained in Mali and elsewhere, as a condition for his release and that of several other Western hostages. Meanwhile, in the same month, numerous members of the MNJ split from the group to form the Front Patriotique du Niger (FPN), which sought to enter into negotiations with the Government to restore peace. Days later al-Qaddafi appealed to all Tuareg rebels in Niger and Mali to engage in a peace process, and in April the Government dispatched a senior security official to Libya for mediation with the rebels.

After two days of Libyan-sponsored talks held in early April 2009, delegates from the Nigerien Government, the MNJ, the FPN and the FFR reportedly committed themselves to restoring peace in the north. President Tandja held talks with representatives of the three Tuareg groups for the first time in early May in Agadez, offering an amnesty if the rebels disarmed; shortly beforehand, the MNJ announced the release of the last remaining hostage. In mid-May the MNJ and the FPN were reported to have agreed to a cease-fire during discussions with Prime Minister Oumarou, which were, however, boycotted by the FFR. In early October the MNJ symbolically surrendered its weapons at a ceremony in southern Libya, attended by al-Qaddafi. The leaders of the main Tuareg movements returned to Niamey after Tandja was overthrown in February to seek involvement in the transitional process and to apply pressure on the new military authorities to accelerate the reintegration of former rebels. However, Ag Boula was arrested in the capital in March in connection with his 2008 conviction.

In September 2010 five French nationals, together with one from Togo and one from Madagascar, were seized by an armed group in northern Niger; AQIM claimed responsibility for the kidnapping. The French Government subsequently announced that it had deployed 80 military personnel to Niamey to assist Niger's military forces in locating the hostages. In January 2011 a further two French nationals, who had been taken hostage by suspected AQIM militants in Niamey, were killed during a failed rescue operation by Nigerien troops and French special forces. In February three of the hostages who had been seized in the previous September (one French, one Togolese and one Malagasy) were released. In November 14 people (including one soldier) were killed, and a further 13 were arrested, when government forces were deployed to block a convoy of vehicles carrying a group of armed gunmen (believe to include ethnic Tuaregs returning from Libya) in northern Niger, near the border with Mali.

Foreign Affairs

Regional relations

In May 2000 a long-term dispute between Niger and Benin regarding the ownership of a number of small islands along their common border at the Niger river escalated, reportedly following the sabotage of a Beninois administrative building on the island of Lété, apparently by Nigerien soldiers. A meeting between representatives of the two Governments failed to resolve the dispute, which was subsequently referred to the Organization of African Unity (OAU, now the African Union, see p. 191) for arbitration. Further clashes between rival groups of farmers were reported on Lété in late August. In April 2002 the two Governments officially ratified an agreement (signed in 2001) to refer the issue of ownership of the islands to the International Court of Justice, ICJ (see p. 26) in The Hague, Netherlands, for arbitration. In November 2003 a five-member chamber formed to consider the case held its first public sitting. Both countries subsequently submitted counter-arguments, and a third written pleading was submitted by both parties in December of that year. Meanwhile, in late 2004 Nigerien traders and haulage contractors boycotted Cotonou port in Benin in reaction to the shooting of two Nigerien citizens by Beninois gendarmes in the city in September. The boycott was ended in January 2005 following a visit to Niamey by the Beninois Minister of Foreign Affairs and African Integration, Rogatien Biaou, during which he announced that the Beninois Government would compensate the victims' families. In July the ICJ issued a final ruling to the effect that 16 of the 25 disputed islands, including Lété, belonged to Niger; the Governments of both countries announced their acceptance of the ruling.

In June 2001 Niger and Nigeria announced that joint border patrols of their common frontier would be instigated, in order to combat increasing cross-border crime and smuggling in the region. It was reported that the introduction of *Shari'a* law in several northern Nigerian states, from 2000, had been instrumental in encouraging Nigerian criminal gangs to operate from within Niger. Further concerns regarding regional security were raised in early 2004, when Islamic militants reportedly attacked a group of tourists in northern Niger. Following clashes between the militants and Chadian and Nigerien troops in March, it was announced that the Governments of Algeria, Chad, Mali and Niger were to reinforce security co-operation in the regions of their common borders.

In October 2006 the Government announced that it was to forcibly remove some 150,000 Mahamid Arabs from eastern Niger and return them to their native Chad. Several thousand Chadians had crossed the border into Niger during the 1970s to escape widespread drought, which had caused outbreaks of violence in their homeland. During the 1980s thousands more fled to Niger when conflict escalated into civil war in Chad. Mahamid communities continued to establish themselves in the Diffa region, but there followed complaints of deteriorating relations between the Mahamids and the local population, and it was feared that the Chadians' presence posed a serious threat to national security. The Office of the UN High Commissioner for Refugees (UNHCR) responded with claims that the Mahamid communities did not hold refugee status and stipulated that it be ensured that those forced to leave would not become victims of discrimination on their return to Chad. The Niger authorities then reversed the earlier decision, stating instead that the Mahamids would be asked to move to land better suited to their agricultural needs. In late October several thousand Nigeriens protested against that ruling, threatening that they would be forced to take action to protect their land and property if the Mahamids were not returned to Chad. The Nigerien Government subsequently announced that only those who did not have the required documents would be sent back; according to the census of 2001, the majority of the Arab community held identity cards issued by the local authorities.

The Nigerien Government moved quickly to strengthen its border security arrangements after Tuareg and Islamist rebels seized control of large swathes of territory in northern Mali during early 2012. Fearing that the instability could spread into Niger, the Government agreed to contribute approximately 500 troops to the African-led International Support Mission in Mali (AFISMA), which was granted a one-year mandate in December 2012 under UN Security Council Resolution 2085. The Chief of General Staff of the Nigerien Armed Forces, Brig.-Gen. Seyni Garba, was appointed as AFISMA's Deputy Force Commander. Also in December, Libya closed most of its land borders, including its frontier with Niger, citing heightened security concerns. Nigerien soldiers entered Mali in January 2013, and, owing to a concomitant intervention by French forces, the insurgency was rapidly suppressed. UNHCR estimated that 50,000 Malians had fled to Niger by January, and a further 5,600 refugees arrived in late March–early April.

Other external relations

The EU suspended all assistance to Niger in the aftermath of the military take-over in April 1999 and made its resumption dependent on a full investigation into Maïnassara's death; the CRN subsequently stated that its report had been lodged with organizations including the EU, and EU aid recommenced in June 2000. France also suspended military and civilian co-operation with Niger in April 1999. Following a visit to France by Mamadou Tandja in January 2000, the resumption of French co-operation was formalized, with the announcement of exceptional assistance principally to allow payment of outstanding salaries in the public sector. In early November 2009 the EU suspended development aid to Niger, accusing President Tandja of violating the Constitution; the gradual resumption of EU development aid to Niger, concurrent with the transitional process, was approved by EU member governments in September 2010. With the security situation in the Sahel continuing to deteriorate, an EU anti-terrorism mission, involving the deployment to Niger of 50 security advisers, commenced in August 2012. The EU also pledged US $118m. in funding for the Nigerien Government's five-year security and development programme for northern regions, which was inaugurated in October. During early 2013, following a deadly attack on an Algerian natural gas facility by Islamist extremists, a contingent of French soldiers was deployed to Arlit, Niger, to guard a key uranium mine operated by the French company Areva.

Around 100 US military personnel were sent to Niger in February 2013 to support, in a non-combat capacity, the international efforts to quell the rebellion in neighbouring Mali. It was also reported that a US surveillance drone (unmanned aerial vehicle) base would be established in Niger to monitor the movements of militant Islamist groups in the region.

CONSTITUTION AND GOVERNMENT

The Constitution of the Seventh Republic was promulgated on 26 November 2010. The President of the Republic is the Head of State and is elected by direct, universal suffrage for a term of five years, renewable only once. Candidates for the presidency must be at least 35 years of age. The President appoints a Prime Minister, upon whose recommendation he appoints the members of the Government. The Prime Minister is the Head of Government. Legislative power is exercised by the Assemblée nationale, members of which are elected by direct, universal suffrage for terms of five years.

For the purposes of local administration, Niger comprises seven regions and the municipality of Niamey.

REGIONAL AND INTERNATIONAL CO-OPERATION

Niger is a member of numerous regional organizations, including the Economic Community of West African States (ECOWAS, see p. 268), the West African organs of the Franc Zone (see p. 339), the Conseil de l'Entente (see p. 460), the Lake Chad Basin Commission (see p. 462), the Liptako–Gourma Integrated Development Authority (see p. 462), the Niger Basin Authority (see p. 463) and the Permanent Inter-State Committee on Drought Control in the Sahel (see p. 463). On 20 October 2009 Niger's membership of ECOWAS was suspended (see Domestic Political Affairs), and on 19 February 2010 the African Union (see p. 191) also suspended Niger's membership, in response to a military coup. The country's membership to both bodies was reinstated in March 2011 following the organization of democratic elections.

Niger became a member of the UN in 1960 and was admitted to the World Trade Organization (WTO, see p. 444) in 1996. Niger participates in the Group of 77 (G77, see p. 461) developing countries.

ECONOMIC AFFAIRS

In 2011, according to estimates by the World Bank, Niger's gross national income (GNI), measured at average 2009–11 prices, was US $5,795m., equivalent to $360 per head (or $720 on an international purchasing-power parity basis). During 2002–11, it was estimated, the population increased at an average annual rate of 3.6%, while gross domestic product (GDP) per head increased, in real terms, by an average of 0.5% per year. Overall GDP increased, in real terms, at an average annual rate of 4.1% in 2002–11; GDP grew by 8.0% in 2010 and by 2.3% in 2011.

Agriculture (including hunting, forestry and fishing) contributed 42.6% of GDP in 2011. According to FAO, some 82.0% of the labour force were estimated to be employed in the sector in mid-2013. The principal cash crops are cow-peas, onions, groundnuts and cotton. The principal subsistence crops are millet and sorghum. Niger is able to achieve self-sufficiency in basic foodstuffs in non-drought years. The effects of drought and locust invasion in the mid-2000s were believed to have caused significant damage to pasture land: livestock-rearing in Niger is especially important among the nomadic population, and live animals intended chiefly for food accounted for 9.8% of total export earnings in 2010, constituting the second most important source of export revenue, after uranium. Major anti-desertification and re-afforestation programmes are in progress. Agricultural GDP increased by an average of 4.3% per year in 2007–11; agricultural GDP increased by 16.3% in 2010, but decreased by 3.1% in 2011.

Industry (including mining, manufacturing, construction and power) contributed 15.9% of GDP in 2011. Some 32.8% of the labour force were employed in industrial activities in 2010, according to official figures. Industrial GDP increased by an average of 6.9% per year in 2007–11; growth was 8.5% in 2010 and 4.3% in 2011.

Mining contributed 6.3% of GDP in 2011, but employed only 0.6% of the labour force in 2010, according to official figures. Niger is among the world's foremost producers of uranium (the fifth largest, after Kazakhstan, Canada, Australia and Namibia, in 2010), although the contribution of uranium-mining to the domestic economy has declined, as production costs have exceeded world prices for the mineral. In 2010 exports of uranium accounted for 50.2% of total export earnings. In addition, gypsum, coal, salt and cassiterite are also extracted, and commercial exploitation of gold (previously mined on a small scale) at the Samira Hill mine began in 2004, with production of 79,300 oz of gold in 2007. GDP of the mining sector increased at an average annual rate of 13.7% in 2007–2011; mining GDP increased by 21.9% in 2010 but by only 0.2% in 2011.

Manufacturing contributed 5.5% of GDP in 2011, and employed 18.1% of the labour force in 2010. The processing of agricultural products (groundnuts, cereals, cotton and rice) constitutes the principal activity. Some light industries, including a textiles plant, a brewery and a cement works, supply the internal market. Manufacturing GDP increased by an average of 4.3% per year in 2007–11; manufacturing GDP increased by 4.8% in 2011.

The construction sector contributed 2.8% of GDP in 2011, and employed 10.8% of the labour force in 2010. In 2007–11 construction GDP increased by an average of 5.7% per year; the sector recorded growth of 5.3% in 2011.

The domestic generation of electricity (almost entirely thermal) provides a little less than one-half of Niger's electrical energy requirements, much of the remainder being imported from Nigeria. Construction of a 130-MW hydroelectric installation at Kandadji, on the Niger, commenced in May 2011 and was scheduled to be completed by September 2015. Imports of mineral fuels accounted for 12.5% of the value of merchandise imports in 2010.

The services sector contributed 41.5% of GDP in 2011, and employed 64.4% of the labour force in 2010. The GDP of the sector

increased by an average of 3.9% per year in 2007–11; growth was 0.3% in 2010 and 6.0% in 2011.

In 2011 Niger recorded a visible merchandise trade deficit of an estimated 443,800m. francs CFA and there was a deficit of 803,800m. francs CFA on the current account of the balance of payments. The People's Republic of China was Niger's principal source of imports in 2010, supplying 43.8%; other major suppliers were France the USA and the United Kingdom. The principal markets for exports in that year were the USA (16.7%), Japan, Switzerland-Liechtenstein, Nigeria, France and China. The principal exports in 2010 were uranium, and food and live animals. The principal imports in that year were machinery and transport equipment, basic manufactures, food and live animals, mineral fuels, lubricants, and chemicals and related products.

Niger's overall budget deficit for 2012 was projected at 388,700m. francs CFA. Niger's general government gross debt was 472,184m. francs in 2011, equivalent to 16.6% of GDP. Niger's total external debt was US $1,127m. at the end of 2010, of which $972m. was public and publicly guaranteed debt. In 2009 the cost of servicing long-term public and publicly guaranteed debt and repayments to the IMF was equivalent to 3.0% of the value of exports of goods, services and income (excluding workers' remittances). According to the ILO, consumer prices increased by an average of 2.2% per year during 2002–12. Consumer prices increased by 3.0% in 2011 and by 0.5% in 2011. Some 64,987 people were registered as unemployed in 2001.

Niger is one of the world's poorest countries, and has consistently been among the lowest ranking countries in the UN Development Programme's Human Development Report. Niger's narrow export base, which is dominated by uranium, and political instability have adversely affected economic performance. In July 2005 Niger was among 18 countries to be granted 100% debt relief on multilateral debt by the Group of Eight leading industrialized nations (G8). However, a protracted political crisis from May 2009 (see Domestic Political Affairs) resulted in the virtual suspension of Niger's relations with international donor nations and organizations. Following a military coup on 18 February 2010, the international community demanded the restoration of democratic rule prior to the normalization of relations. By mid-2011 the transition to democratic rule had reached a successful conclusion, following legislative and presidential elections. Priorities identified by President Mahamadou Issoufou for the Government included the modernization of the agricultural and livestock sectors and an increase in expenditure on education. The EU confirmed the full resumption of development co-operation with Niger in June, while in March 2012 the IMF authorized a three-year Extended Credit Facility, valued at almost US $121m. After contracting in 2009, the economy grew by 8.0% in 2010, owing to a good harvest and the resumption of external donor financing. In 2011, despite the commencement of petroleum production and large-scale investments in uranium-mining projects, real GDP expanded by just 2.3%. None the less, according to IMF estimates, growth of 11.3% was registered in 2012, supported by strong performances in the agricultural and extractive sectors. The Fund forecast that real GDP would rise by a further 6.2% in 2013, and, with considerable potential still to be realized in the mining sector, Niger's medium-term economic outlook appeared favourable.

PUBLIC HOLIDAYS

2014: 1 January (New Year's Day), 13 January* (Mouloud, Birth of the Prophet), 21 April (Easter Monday), 24 April (National Concord Day), 1 May (Labour Day), 28 July* (Id al-Fitr, end of Ramadan), 3 August (Independence Day), 4 October* (Tabaski, Feast of the Sacrifice), 15 October* (Islamic New Year), 18 December (Republic Day).

* These holidays are dependent on the Islamic lunar calendar and may vary by one or two days from the dates given.

Statistical Survey

Source (unless otherwise stated): Institut national de la Statistique, Immeuble sis à la Rue Sirba, derrière la Présidence de la république, BP 720, Niamey; tel. 20-72-35-60; fax 20-72-21-74; e-mail insniger@ins.ne; internet www.stat-niger.org.

Area and Population

AREA, POPULATION AND DENSITY

Area (sq km)	1,267,000*
Population (census results)	
20 May 1988	7,248,100
20 May 2001	
Males	5,516,588
Females	5,543,703
Total	11,060,291
Population (UN estimates at mid-year)†	
2011	16,068,992
2012	16,644,338
2013	17,239,823
Density (per sq km) at mid-2013	13.6

* 489,191 sq miles.
† Source: UN, *World Population Prospects: The 2010 Revision.*

POPULATION BY AGE AND SEX
(UN estimates at mid-2013)

	Males	Females	Total
0–14	4,313,001	4,099,195	8,412,196
15–64	4,183,643	4,250,484	8,434,127
65 and over	184,002	209,498	393,500
Total	**8,680,646**	**8,559,177**	**17,239,823**

Source: UN, *World Population Prospects: The 2010 Revision.*

ETHNIC GROUPS
(2001 census, Nigerien citizens only)

	Population	%
Hausa	6,069,731	55.36
Djerma-Sonraï	2,300,874	20.99
Tuareg	1,016,883	9.27
Peulh	935,517	8.53
Kanouri-Manga	513,116	4.68
Toubou	42,172	0.38
Arab	40,085	0.37
Gourmantché	39,797	0.36
Others	5,951	0.05
Total	**10,964,126**	**100.00**

ADMINISTRATIVE DIVISIONS
(2011)

Agadez	. . .	511,188	Niamey (city) . .	1,302,910
Diffa	. . .	489,531	Tahoua	2,741,922
Dosso	. . .	2,078,339	Tillabéri . . .	2,572,125
Maradi	. . .	3,117,810	Zinder	2,916,929

PRINCIPAL TOWNS
(population at 2001 census)

Niamey (capital)	.	707,951	Agadez	78,289
Zinder	. . .	170,575	Tahoua . . .	73,002
Maradi	. . .	148,017	Arlit	69,435

Mid-2011 (incl. suburbs, UN estimate): Niamey 1,297,160 (Source: UN, *World Urbanization Prospects: The 2011 Revision*).

BIRTHS AND DEATHS
(annual averages, UN estimates)

	1995–2000	2000–05	2005–10
Birth rate (per 1,000)	53.5	51.3	49.5
Death rate (per 1,000)	19.3	16.2	13.8

Source: UN, *World Population Prospects: The 2010 Revision.*

2011: Birth rate 48.2 per 1,000; Death rate 12.6 per 1,000 (Source: African Development Bank).

Life expectancy (years at birth): 54.7 (males 54.2; females 55.2) in 2011 (Source: World Bank, World Development Indicators database).

EMPLOYMENT
('000 persons at 31 December)

	2008	2009	2010
Agriculture, hunting, forestry and fishing	157	128	158
Mining and quarrying . . .	86	29	31
Manufacturing	950	907	1,012
Electricity, gas and water . . .	112	161	181
Construction	433	490	603
Trade, restaurants and hotels .	871	704	1,419
Transport, storage and communications	369	502	635
Financing, insurance, real estate and business services . .	220	205	224
Community, social and personal services	963	1,096	1,315
Total	**4,161**	**4,222**	**5,578**

2001 census (persons aged 10 years and over): Total employed 4,015,951 (males 2,706,910, females 1,309,041), Unemployed 64,987 (males 49,437, females 15,550), Total labour force 4,080,938 (males 2,756,347, females 1,324,591).

Mid-2013 (estimates in '000): Agriculture, etc. 4,677; Total labour force 5,707 (Source: FAO).

Health and Welfare

KEY INDICATORS

Total fertility rate (children per woman, 2010)	7.1
Under-5 mortality rate (per 1,000 live births, 2010) . . .	143
HIV/AIDS (% of persons aged 15–49, 2009)	0.8
Physicians (per 1,000 head, 2008)	0.02
Hospital beds (per 1,000 head, 2005)	0.3
Health expenditure (2009): US $ per head (PPP) . . .	37
Health expenditure (2009): % of GDP	5.4
Health expenditure (2009): public (% of total)	50.3
Access to water (% of persons, 2010)	49
Access to sanitation (% of persons, 2010)	9
Total carbon dioxide emissions ('000 metric tons, 2008) . .	850.7
Carbon dioxide emissions per head (metric tons per, 2008) .	0.1
Human Development Index (2011): ranking	186
Human Development Index (2011): value	0.295

For sources and definitions, see explanatory note on p. vi.

Agriculture

PRINCIPAL CROPS
('000 metric tons)

	2009	2010	2011
Wheat*	8.6	8.7	6.3
Rice, paddy	20.1	30.0	21.7
Millet	2,678	3,843	2,926
Sorghum	739	1,305	807
Potatoes	34.0	35.0*	26.4
Sweet potatoes	49	36	56
Cassava (Manioc)	108	113	98
Sugar cane	212	222	177
Cow peas, dry	787.5	1,774.5	1,517.1
Groundnuts, with shell	253.5	406.2	395.7
Sesame seed	76	86	89
Cottonseed*	8	2	5
Cabbages and other brassicas	112	117	145
Lettuce and chicory	66	70	69
Tomatoes	56	54	109
Chillies and peppers, green	16	19*	21*
Onions, dry	384	367	372
Garlic	2	3	4
Beans, green*	25	30	34
Carrots and turnips	7	8	11
Dates	38	40	16
Tobacco, unmanufactured	2.3	2.3	2.4*

* FAO estimate(s).

Aggregate production ('000 metric tons, may include official, semi-official or estimated data): Total cereals 3,451 in 2009, 5,203 in 2010, 3,773 in 2011; Total roots and tubers 190 in 2009, 184 in 2010, 180 in 2011; Total vegetables (incl. melons) 790 in 2009, 797 in 2010, 899 in 2011; Total pulses 847 in 2009, 1,832 in 2010, 1,565 in 2011.

Source: FAO.

LIVESTOCK
('000 head, year ending September)

	2009	2010	2011
Cattle	9,262	9,817	9,552
Sheep	10,548	10,917	10,019
Goats	13,147	13,673	13,231
Pigs*	40	40	41
Horses	240	242	236
Asses	1,599	1,631	1,632
Camels	1,654	1,680	1,655
Chickens*	16,882	17,101	17,323

* FAO estimates.
Source: FAO.

LIVESTOCK PRODUCTS
('000 metric tons, FAO estimates)

	2009	2010	2011
Game meat	26	28	28
Horse meat	1	1	1
Goat meat	58.2	61.2	63.0
Sheep meat	44.8	48.0	46.4
Chicken meat	11.0	11.5	12.0
Hen eggs	8.5	7.5	7.9

Source: FAO.

Forestry

ROUNDWOOD REMOVALS
('000 cubic metres, excl. bark, FAO estimates)

	2004	2005	2006
Industrial wood	579	701	701
Fuel wood	2,857	2,857	2,857
Total	3,436	3,558	3,558

2007–11: Production assumed to be unchanged from 2006 (FAO estimates).
Source: FAO.

SAWNWOOD PRODUCTION
('000 cubic metres, incl. railway sleepers, FAO estimates)

	1991	1992	1993
Total (all broadleaved)	0	1	4

1994–2011: Figures assumed to be unchanged from 1993 (FAO estimates).
Source: FAO.

Fishing

(metric tons, live weight)

	2007	2008	2009
Capture (freshwater fishes)	29,728	29,960	29,884
Aquaculture	40	40	70*
Total catch	29,768	30,000	29,954*

* FAO estimate.
2010: Catch assumed to be unchanged from 2009 (FAO estimates).
Source: FAO.

Mining

('000 metric tons unless otherwise indicated)

	2008	2009	2010
Hard coal	182.9	225.1	246.6*
Tin (metric tons)*†‡	n.a.	5.9	5.7
Uranium (metric tons)	2,993	3,241	4,198*
Gold (kg)	2,314	2,067	1,929
Gypsum*	8.7	19.7	7.6

* Provisional.
† Data refer to the metal content of ore.
‡ Artisanal production only.

Industry

SELECTED PRODUCTS
('000 metric tons unless otherwise indicated)

	2007	2008	2009
Raw sugar	10	10	10
Cement	42.0	40.0	40.0
Electric energy (million kWh)	195	213	234

Sources: UN Industrial Commodity Statistics Database; US Geological Survey.

2007 ('000 metric tons unless otherwise indicated): Soap 9.4; Textile fabrics (million metres) 2.6; Beer ('000 bottles) 99.9 (Source: IMF, *Niger: Selected Issues and Statistical Appendix*—February 2009)).

Finance

CURRENCY AND EXCHANGE RATES

Monetary Units

100 centimes = 1 franc de la Communauté Financière Africaine (CFA).

Sterling, Dollar and Euro Equivalents (31 December 2012)

£1 sterling = 784.523 francs CFA;
US $1 = 497.163 francs CFA;
€1 = 655.957 francs CFA;
10,000 francs CFA = £12.75 = $20.11 = €15.24.

Average Exchange Rate (francs CFA per US $)

2010   495.277
2011   471.866
2012   510.290

Note: An exchange rate of 1 French franc = 50 francs CFA, established in 1948, remained in force until January 1994, when the CFA franc was devalued by 50%, with the exchange rate adjusted to 1 French franc = 100 francs CFA. This relationship to French currency remained in effect with the introduction of the euro on 1 January 1999. From that date, accordingly, a fixed exchange rate of €1 = 655.957 francs CFA has been in operation.

BUDGET

('000 million francs CFA)

Revenue*	2009	2010	2011
Tax revenue	343.0	361.7	485.9
Income and profits	102.3	86.9	96.5
Goods and services	99.0	109.9	162.1
International trade	116.6	135.0	192.4
Other taxes	25.1	29.9	34.9
Non-tax revenue	20.6	23.9	28.5
Total	363.6	385.6	514.4

Expenditure†	2009	2010	2011
Current expenditure	276.5	346.1	461.3
Wages and salaries	93.6	103.2	141.0
Materials and supplies	83.9	94.2	115.4
Subsidies and transfers	97.2	135.5	197.3
Other	1.8	13.2	7.6
Capital expenditure	309.1	217.8	206.0
Exceptional expenses	24.3	20.1	24.6
Total	609.9	584.0	691.9

* Excluding grants received ('000 million francs CFA): 110.9 in 2009; 130.2 in 2010; 113.5 in 2011.

† Excluding lending minus repayment ('000 million francs CFA): 0.0 in 2009–11.

2012 ('000 million francs CFA, budget projections): *Revenue:* Tax revenue 539.8, Non-tax revenue 66.2; Total 606.0. *Expenditure:* Current expenditure 412.2; Capital expenditure 582.4; Total 994.7 (Source: IMF, *Niger: Request for a New Three-Year Arrangement Under the Extended Credit Facility - Staff Report; Press Release on the Executive Board Discussion; and Statement by the Executive Director for Niger*—May 2012).

INTERNATIONAL RESERVES

(US $ million at 31 December, excl. gold)

	2009	2010	2011
IMF special drawing rights	85.1	83.6	83.3
Reserve position in IMF	13.5	13.3	13.3
Foreign exchange	556.9	663.4	576.5
Total	655.5	760.3	673.0

Source: IMF, *International Financial Statistics*.

MONEY SUPPLY

('000 million francs CFA at 31 December)

	2009	2010	2011
Currency outside banks	187.9	234.9	269.6
Demand deposits at deposit money banks*	166.6	214.1	204.7
Checking deposits at post office	1.7	1.4	1.8
Total money (incl. others)*	356.4	450.5	476.4

* Excluding the deposits of public enterprises of an administrative or social nature.

Source: IMF, *International Financial Statistics*.

COST OF LIVING

(Consumer Price Index for Niamey, annual averages; base: 2000 = 100 unless otherwise indicated)

	2009	2010	2011
Food*	132.1	132.5	137.0
Clothing	101.0	n.a.	n.a.
Rent	115.7	n.a.	n.a.
All items (incl. others)	131.9	128.2	132.0

* Base: 2006 = 100.

2012: All items 132.6.

Source: ILO.

NATIONAL ACCOUNTS

('000 million francs CFA at current prices)

Expenditure on the Gross Domestic Product

	2009	2010	2011
Government final consumption expenditure	423.2	422.2	510.7
Private final consumption expenditure	1,860.0	1,982.4	2,192.7
Gross fixed capital formation	923.2	1,146.4	1,128.0
Changes in inventories	1.5	33.5	0.6
Total domestic expenditure	3,207.9	3,584.4	3,832.0
Exports of goods and services	517.9	572.6	654.0
Less Imports of goods and services	1,192.3	1,348.0	1,481.6
GDP at purchasers' values	2,533.4	2,809.1	3,004.4

Gross Domestic Product by Economic Activity

	2009	2010	2011
Agriculture, hunting, forestry and fishing	987.0	1,182.1	1,179.3
Mining and quarrying	159.9	164.9	173.0
Manufacturing	128.3	137.6	150.7
Electricity, gas and water supply	28.6	32.7	37.2
Construction	64.1	71.5	78.3
Wholesale and retail trade; restaurants and hotels	384.2	396.6	431.8
Finance, insurance and real estate	131.0	137.8	149.0
Transport and communications	156.5	164.4	184.9
Public administration and defence	224.8	226.7	261.7
Other services	105.2	107.7	119.2
Sub-total	2,369.6	2,622.0	2,765.1
Less Imputed bank service charge	21.7	23.7	26.7
Indirect taxes (net)	185.5	210.9	266.0
GDP at purchasers' values	2,533.4	2,809.1	3,004.4

BALANCE OF PAYMENTS
('000 million francs CFA)

	2009	2010*	2011†
Exports of goods f.o.b.	470.7	508.7	605.4
Imports of goods f.o.b.	−847.2	−887.3	−1,049.3
Trade balance	−376.5	−378.6	−443.8
Services (net)	−299.7	−397.1	−483.2
Balance on goods and services	−676.2	−775.7	−927.1
Income (net)	−16.3	−15.8	−29.2
Balance on goods, services and income	−692.6	−791.5	−956.3
Private unrequited transfers (net)	53.9	72.9	36.5
Public unrequited transfers (net)	17.3	153.2	116.0
Current balance	−621.3	−565.5	−803.8
Capital account (net)	120.3	95.8	162.5
Direct investment (net)	345.4	495.3	478.3
Portfolio investment (net)	7.4	17.9	1.3
Other investment (net)	65.5	61.0	123.6
Net errors and omissions	−7.1	—	—
Overall balance	−89.8	104.5	−38.1

* Preliminary.
† Projections.

Source: IMF, *Niger: Request for a New Three-Year Arrangement Under the Extended Credit Facility - Staff Report; Press Release on the Executive Board Discussion; and Statement by the Executive Director for Niger* (May 2012).

External Trade

PRINCIPAL COMMODITIES
(distribution by SITC, US $ million)

Imports c.i.f.	2008	2009	2010
Food and live animals	247.8	187.0	272.0
Dairy products and birds' eggs	32.4	28.4	25.4
Milk and cream	31.9	28.0	24.9
Milk and cream, preserved, concentrated or sweetened	31.2	27.1	23.2
Cereals and cereal preparations	141.7	90.3	151.7
Rice, semi-milled or wholly milled	106.1	61.7	66.1
Rice, semi-milled or milled (unbroken)	89.5	49.8	55.8
Sugar, sugar preparations and honey	28.2	23.8	25.2
Beverages and tobacco	29.1	37.6	43.0
Cigarettes	25.5	32.3	38.1
Crude materials (inedible) except fuel	87.0	76.5	67.7
Textile fibres (not wool tops) and their wastes (not in yarn)	56.1	49.0	44.3
Bulk textile waste, old clothing, traded in bulk or in bales	55.4	49.0	44.3
Mineral fuels, lubricants, etc. (incl. electric current)	207.2	194.2	286.3
Petroleum, petroleum products, etc.	189.2	176.2	261.0
Petroleum products, refined	185.9	172.5	258.1
Animal and vegetable oils, fats and waxes	32.4	28.2	31.1
Fixed vegetable oils and fats	27.4	25.9	26.2
Palm oil	19.2	20.9	16.4
Chemicals and related products	175.1	145.8	142.6

Imports c.i.f.—*continued*	2008	2009	2010
Medicinal and pharmaceutical products	118.7	63.0	37.9
Basic manufactures	161.1	282.2	571.4
Textile yarn, fabrics, made-up articles, etc.	26.3	47.0	23.8
Cotton fabrics, woven (not incl. narrow or special fabrics)	18.0	22.3	12.8
Machinery and transport equipment	251.6	525.3	757.6
Telecommunications, sound recording and reproducing equipment	24.9	55.7	30.9
Road vehicles	76.4	149.6	209.6
Passenger motor vehicles (excl. buses)	29.7	31.5	34.0
Miscellaneous manufactured articles	56.2	150.3	118.3
Total (incl. others)	1,247.5	1,627.2	2,290.0

Exports f.o.b.	2008	2009	2010
Food and live animals	85.9	179.4	78.2
Live animals chiefly for food	46.3	132.7	47.2
Animals of the bovine species (incl. buffaloes), live	21.0	51.3	26.9
Sheep and goats, live	18.4	70.2	14.7
Fish, crustaceans and molluscs, and preparations thereof	0.4	n.a.	n.a.
Vegetables and fruit	17.8	37.8	15.0
Vegetables, fresh or simply preserved; roots and tubers	17.1	37.3	14.2
Other fresh or chilled vegetables	12.2	33.4	10.6
Beverages and tobacco	8.1	5.6	6.8
Cigarettes	7.8	5.4	6.5
Crude materials (inedible) except fuels	321.9	361.0	255.2
Textile fibres (not wool tops) and their wastes (not in yarn)	30.8	11.2	11.0
Ores and concentrates of uranium and thorium	289.4	348.7	242.9
Mineral fuels, lubricants, etc., (incl. electric current)	16.4	7.2	7.6
Petroleum, petroleum products, etc.	16.3	7.2	7.6
Basic manufactures	24.8	13.8	13.9
Fabrics, woven, 85% plus of cotton, bleached, dyed, etc., or otherwise finished	22.7	12.7	12.9
Total (incl. others)	503.1	628.0	483.5

Source: UN, *International Trade Statistics Yearbook*.

2011 (million francs CFA): Total imports 854,405; Total exports 424,586.

PRINCIPAL TRADING PARTNERS
(US $ million)

Imports c.i.f.	2008	2009	2010
Argentina	13.0	10.9	11.4
Belgium	31.1	19.7	32.1
Benin	12.0	5.9	19.7
Brazil	25.4	24.1	19.8
Burkina Faso	10.7	18.8	12.6
Cameroon	13.2	n.a.	n.a.
China, People's Republic	156.8	499.1	1,002.5
Côte d'Ivoire	62.5	62.6	51.5
France (incl. Monaco)	164.1	219.7	252.5
Germany	26.8	42.4	46.7
Ghana	17.7	13.2	17.7
India	29.0	26.2	11.1
Italy	14.2	19.5	16.8
Japan	44.5	70.4	75.4
Malaysia	26.0	21.0	21.9

Imports c.i.f.—*continued*	2008	2009	2010
Netherlands	89.4	70.2	73.4
Nigeria	58.1	82.0	88.4
Pakistan	42.3	22.1	13.0
South Africa	11.2	15.0	8.0
Thailand	43.7	n.a.	n.a.
Togo	49.4	42.0	52.0
United Kingdom	40.3	44.0	118.4
USA	95.4	79.2	138.9
Viet Nam	18.4	15.2	22.3
Total (incl. others)	1,247.5	1,627.2	2,290.0

Exports f.o.b.	2008	2009	2010
Belgium	3.8	1.3	1.6
Benin	0.9	2.5	1.2
Brazil	7.6	3.2	6.6
Burkina Faso	3.8	3.0	3.0
Cameroon	2.9	3.2	2.5
China, People's Republic	5.5	3.1	37.6
Côte d'Ivoire	17.9	11.5	8.9
France (incl. Monaco)	167.3	295.7	43.5
Germany	2.3	3.8	5.7
Ghana	7.1	24.1	6.6
Italy	3.7	n.a.	n.a.
Japan	49.8	0.6	80.0
Korea, Democratic People's Republic	6.4	3.2	3.0
Mali	0.1	n.a.	n.a.
Netherlands	8.7	0.8	3.7
Nigeria	59.2	139.1	53.6
South Africa	—	1.5	—
Spain	8.5	13.5	19.9
Switzerland-Liechtenstein	21.8	44.3	75.5
Thailand	10.0	3.6	5.8
Togo	0.3	1.1	0.3
United Kingdom	0.5	n.a.	n.a.
USA	88.7	49.2	80.6
Total (incl. others)	503.1	628.0	483.5

Source: UN, *International Trade Statistics Yearbook*.

2011 (million francs CFA): Total imports 854,405; Total exports 424,586.

Transport

ROAD TRAFFIC
(motor vehicles in use at 31 December, estimates)

	2007	2008	2009
Passenger cars	75,697	84,675	93,118
Buses and coaches	4,019	4,560	5,066
Tractors and semi-trailers	6,024	7,429	9,053

CIVIL AVIATION
(traffic on scheduled services)

	2008	2009	2010
Aircraft movements	4,556	5,647	5,022
Passengers carried ('000)	121.3	154.5	156.3
Freight carried (metric tons)	3,216	3,327	1,891
Mail (metric tons)	90	103	n.a.

Tourism

FOREIGN TOURIST ARRIVALS BY NATIONALITY*

	2008	2009	2010
Africa	46,981	42,312	44,702
America	4,528	4,078	4,589
East Asia and the Pacific	3,507	3,158	3,560
Europe	18,138	16,335	18,416
France	14,667	13,209	14,892
Total (incl. others)	73,154	65,883	74,278

* Figures refer to arrivals at national borders.

Receipts from tourism (US $ million, excl. passenger transport): 66.0 in 2009; 79.0 in 2010.

Source: World Tourism Organization.

Communications Media

	2009	2010	2011
Telephones ('000 main lines in use)	76.3	83.6	90.0
Mobile cellular telephones ('000 subscribers)	2,599.0	3,805.6	4,742.9
Internet users ('000)	115.9	3.7	15.8
Broadband subscribers	1,000	1,500	1,800

* Estimated figure.

Source: International Telecommunication Union.

Education

(2010/11 unless otherwise indicated)

	Institutions	Teachers	Students
Pre-primary	1,283	2,961	96,022
Primary	13,763	48,976	1,910,166
Secondary*	859	9,724	286,709
Tertiary†	7	278	4,953
University*	2	304	11,292

* 2009/10 figures.
† 2004/05 figures.

Pupil-teacher ratio (primary education, UNESCO estimate): 39.0 in 2010/11 (Source: UNESCO Institute for Statistics).

Adult literacy rate (UNESCO estimates): 30.4% (males 44.3%; females 16.4%) in 2007 (Source: UNESCO Institute for Statistics).

Directory

The Government

HEAD OF STATE

President: MAHAMADOU ISSOUFOU (inaugurated 7 April 2011).

COUNCIL OF MINISTERS
(May 2013)

Prime Minister: BRIGI RAFINI.

Minister of State, Minister of Foreign Affairs, African Integration and Nigeriens Abroad: BAZOUM MOHAMED.

Minister of State, Minister of Planning, Land Settlement and Community Development: AMADOU BOUBACAR CISSÉ.

Minister of State, Minister of the Interior, Public Security, Decentralization and Religious Affairs: ABDOU LABO.

Minister of State, Minister of Mines and Industrial Development: OMAR HAMIDOU TCHIANA.

Minister of Public Health: SOUMANA SANDA.

Minister of Petroleum and Energy: FOUMAKOYE GADO.

Minister of Justice, Keeper of the Seals and Government Spokesperson: MAROU AMADOU.

Minister of Equipment: SADI SOUMAILA.

Minister of Town Planning, Housing and Sanitation: MOUSSA BAKO ABDOULKARIM.

Minister of Trade and the Promotion of the Private Sector: SALEY SAIDOU.

Minister of Communication and New Information Technology: SALIFOU LABO BOUCHÉ.

Minister of Population, the Promotion of Women and the Protection of Children: MAIKIBI KADIDIATOU DAN DOBI.

Minister of National Defence: KARIDJO MAHAMADOU.

Minister of Finance: JULES BAYÉ.

Minister of Professional Training and Employment: NGADÉ NANA HADIZA NOMA KAKA.

Minister of Higher Education and Scientific Research: MAMADOU YOUBA DIALLO.

Minister of National Education, Literacy and the Promotion of National Languages: ALI MARIAMA ELHADJ IBRAHIM.

Minister of Agriculture: OUHA SAIDOU.

Minister of Water Resources and the Environment: ISSOUFOU ISSAKA.

Minister of Stockbreeding: MAHAMANE ELHADJ OUSMANE.

Minister of Transport: IBRAHIM YACOUBA.

Minister of Youth, Sports and Culture: HASSANE KOUNOU.

Minister of Handicrafts and Tourism: YAHAYA BAARÉ HAOUA ABDOU.

Minister of the Civil Service and Labour: SABO FATOUMA ZARA BOUBACAR.

Minister, in charge of Relations with the Institutions: ELHADJ LAOUALI CHAÏBOU.

MINISTRIES

Office of the President: BP 550, Niamey; tel. 20-72-23-80; fax 20-72-33-96; internet www.presidence.ne.

Office of the Prime Minister: BP 893, Niamey; tel. 20-72-26-99; fax 20-73-58-59.

Ministry of Agriculture: BP 12091, Niamey; tel. 20-73-35-41; fax 20-73-20-08.

Ministry of the Civil Service and Labour: BP 11107, Niamey; tel. 20-73-22-31; fax 20-73-61-69; e-mail sani.yakouba@caramail.com.

Ministry of Communication and New Information Technology: Niamey.

Ministry of Equipment: Niamey.

Ministry of Finance: BP 389, Niamey; tel. 20-72-23-74; fax 20-73-59-34.

Ministry of Foreign Affairs, African Integration and Nigeriens Abroad: BP 396, Niamey; tel. 20-72-29-07; fax 20-73-52-31.

Ministry of Handicrafts and Tourism: BP 480, Niamey; tel. 20-73-65-22; fax 20-72-23-87; internet www.niger-tourisme.com.

Ministry of Higher Education and Scientific Research: BP 628, Niamey; tel. 20-72-26-20; fax 20-72-40-40; e-mail mesnt@intnet.ne.

Ministry of the Interior, Public Security, Decentralization and Religious Affairs: BP 622, Niamey; tel. 20-72-32-62; fax 20-72-21-76.

Ministry of Justice: BP 466, Niamey; tel. 20-72-31-31; fax 20-72-37-77.

Ministry of Mines and Industrial Development: BP 11700, Niamey; tel. 20-73-45-82; fax 20-73-27-59.

Ministry of National Defence: BP 626, Niamey; tel. 20-72-20-76; fax 20-72-40-78.

Ministry of National Education, Literacy and the Promotion of National Languages: BP 557, Niamey; tel. 20-72-28-33; fax 20-72-21-05; e-mail scdameb@intnet.ne.

Ministry of Petroleum and Energy: Niamey.

Ministry of Planning, Land Settlement and Community Development: BP 403, Niamey; tel. 20-73-53-57; fax 20-72-21-71.

Ministry of Population, the Promotion of Women and the Protection of Children: BP 11286, Niamey; tel. 20-72-23-30; fax 20-73-61-65.

Ministry of Professional Training and Employment: Immeuble ex-HCCT, blvd Mali Béro, BP 628, Niamey; tel. 20-72-59-51; fax 20-73-67-81.

Ministry of Public Health: BP 623, Niamey; tel. 20-72-28-08; fax 20-73-35-70.

Ministry of Relations with the Institutions: Niamey.

Ministry of Stockbreeding: BP 12091, Niamey; tel. 20-73-79-59; fax 20-73-31-86.

Ministry of Town Planning, Housing and Sanitation: BP 403, Niamey; tel. 20-73-53-57; fax 20-72-21-71.

Ministry of Trade and the Promotion of the Private Sector: BP 480, Niamey; tel. 20-73-29-74; fax 20-73-21-50; e-mail nicom@intnet.ne.

Ministry of Transport: BP 12130, Niamey; tel. 20-72-28-21; fax 20-73-36-85.

Ministry of Water Resources and the Environment: BP 257, Niamey; tel. 20-73-47-22; fax 20-72-40-15.

Ministry of Youth, Sports and Culture: BP 215, Niamey; tel. 20-72-32-35; fax 20-72-23-36.

President and Legislature

PRESIDENT

Presidential Election, First Round, 31 January 2011

Candidate	Votes	% of votes
Mahamadou Issoufou (PNDS—Tarayya)	1,192,945	36.16
Seyni Oumarou (MNSD—Nassara)	766,215	23.23
Hama Amadou (Moden)	653,737	19.82
Mahamane Ousmane (CDS)	274,676	8.33
Cheiffou Amadou (RSD—Gaskiya)	134,732	4.08
Others*	276,336	8.38
Total	**3,298,641**	**100.00**

* There were five other candidates.

Second Round, 12 March 2011, provisional results

Candidate	Votes	% of votes
Mahamadou Issoufou (PNDS—Tarayya)	1,820,639	57.95
Seyni Oumarou (MNSD—Nassara)	1,321,248	42.05
Total	**3,141,887**	**100.00**

LEGISLATURE

Assemblée nationale

pl. de la Concertation, BP 12234, Niamey; tel. 20-72-27-38; fax 20-72-43-08; e-mail an@assemblee.ne; internet www.assemblee.ne.

President: HAMA AMADOU.

General Election, 31 January 2011, provisional results

Party	Votes	% of votes	Seats
PNDS—Tarayya	1,143,263	33.02	39
MNSD—Nassara	707,191	20.43	26
Moden	684,583	19.77	24
ANDP—Zaman Lahiya . .	252,857	7.30	8
RDP—Djamaa	232,105	6.70	7
UDR—Tabbat	185,473	5.36	6
CDS—Rahama	109,536	3.16	2
RSD—Gaskiya	60,048	1.73	—
UNI	32,277	0.93	1
Others	54,552	1.58	—
Total	**3,461,885**	**100.00**	**113***

* Including eight special seats, five of which were allocated to the PNDS—Tarayya, two to Moden and one to the MNSD—Nassara.

Election Commission

Commission Électorale Nationale Indépendante (CENI): Niamey; internet www.ceni-niger.net; Pres. ABDOURAHMANE GHOUSMANE.

Political Organizations

A total of 23 political parties contested the legislative elections of January 2011.

Alliance Nigérienne pour la Démocratie et le Progrès Social—Zaman Lahiya (ANDP—Zaman Lahiya): Quartier Abidjan, Niamey; tel. 20-74-07-50; Pres. MOUSSA MOUMOUNI DJERMAKOYE.

Alliance pour la Démocratie et le Progrès—Zumunci (ADP): Niamey; tel. 20-73-67-57; e-mail adp@zumunci.com; internet www.adpzumunci.com; f. 1992; Chair. ISSOUFOU BACHAR.

Convention Démocratique et Sociale—Rahama (CDS—Rahama): BP 11973, Niamey; tel. 20-74-19-85; f. 1991; mem. of Alliance des Forces Démocratiques (AFD); Pres. MAHAMANE OUSMANE.

Mouvement Démocratique Nigérien (Moden): Niamey; e-mail mdnloumana@gmail.com; f. 2009 by supporters of former Prime Minister Hama Amadou; Pres. HAMA AMADOU; Sec.-Gen. OMAR HAMIDOU TCHIANA.

Mouvement National pour la Société de Développement—Nassara (MNSD—Nassara): rue Issa Beri 30, cnr blvd de Zarmaganda, porte 72, BP 881, Niamey; tel. 20-73-39-07; fax 20-72-41-74; e-mail presi@mnsd-nassara.org; internet www.mnsd.ne; f. 1988; sole party 1988–90; restyled as MNSD—Nassara in 1991; Pres. SEYNI OUMAROU.

Mouvement des Nigériens pour la Justice (MNJ): e-mail mnj.contact@gmail.com; internet m-n-j.blogspot.com; f. 2007; Pres. (vacant); First Vice-Pres. Capt. ASHARIF MOHAMED-ALMOCTAR.

Parti des Masses pour le Travail—al Barka (PMT—al Barka): Niamey; tel. 20-74-02-15; Pres. MAMALO ABDOULKARIM.

Parti Nigérien pour la Démocratie et le Socialisme—Tarayya (PNDS—Tarayya): pl. Toumo, Niamey; tel. 20-74-48-78; internet pnds-tarayya.net; f. 1990; Pres. MAHAMADOU ISSOUFOU; Sec.-Gen. FOUMAKOYE GADO.

Parti Social-Démocrate Nigérien—Alheri (PSDN): tel. 20-72-28-52; Pres. LABO ISSAKA.

Rassemblement pour la Démocratie et le Progrès—Djamaa (RDP—Djamaa): pl. Toumo, Niamey; tel. 20-74-23-82; party of late Pres. Maïnassara; Chair. HAMID ALGABID; Sec.-Gen. MAHAMANE SOULEY LABI.

Rassemblement des Patriotes Nigériens—al Kalami (RPN—al Kalami): Niamey; f. 2009; Pres. OUSMANE ISSOUFOU OUBANDAWAKI.

Rassemblement Social-Démocratique—Gaskiya (RSD—Gaskiya): Quartier Poudrière, Niamey; tel. 20-74-00-90; f. 2004 following split in the CDS; Pres. CHEIFFOU AMADOU.

Rassemblement pour un Sahel Vert—Ni'ima (RSV): BP 12515, Niamey; tel. and fax 20-74-11-25; e-mail agarba_99@yahoo.com; f. 1991; Pres. ADAMOU GARBA.

Union pour la Démocratie et le Progrès Social—Amana (UDPS): internet www.udps-amana.com; represents interests of Tuaregs; Chair. RHISSA AG BOULA.

Union pour la Démocratie et la République—Tabbat (UDR—Tabbat): Quartier Plateau, Niamey; f. 2002; Pres. AMADOU BOUABACAR CISSÉ.

Union des Nigeriens Indépendants (UNI): Quartier Zabarkan, Niamey; tel. 20-74-23-81; Leader AMADOU DJIBO.

Union des Patriotes Démocratiques et Progressistes—Shamuwa (UPDP): Niamey; tel. 20-74-12-59; Chair. Prof. ANDRÉ SALIFOU.

Union des Socialistes Nigériens—Talaka (USN): f. 2001 by mems of the UFPDP; Leader ISSOUFOU ASSOUMANE.

Diplomatic Representation

EMBASSIES IN NIGER

Algeria: route des Ambassades-Goudel, BP 142, Niamey; tel. 20-72-35-83; fax 20-72-35-93; Ambassador HAMID BOUKRIF.

Benin: BP 11544, Niamey; tel. 20-72-28-60; Ambassador AWAHOU LABOUDA.

Chad: POB 12820, Niamey; tel. 20-75-34-64; fax 20-72-43-61; Ambassador MAHAMAT NOUR MALLAYE.

China, People's Republic: 4 blvd des Ambassades, Quartier Goudel, BP 873, Niamey; tel. 20-72-32-83; fax 20-72-32-85; e-mail chinaemb_ne@mfa.gov.cn; internet ne.china-embassy.org/chn; Ambassador SHI HU.

Cuba: rue Tillaberi, angle rue de la Cure Salée, face lycée Franco-Arabe, Plateau, BP 13886, Niamey; tel. 20-72-46-00; fax 20-72-39-32; e-mail embacuba@niger.cubaminrex.cu; internet emba.cubaminrex.cu/nigerfr; Ambassador ROBERTO RODRÍGUEZ PEÑA.

Egypt: Terminus Rond-Point Grand Hôtel, BP 254, Niamey; tel. 20-73-33-55; fax 20-73-38-91; Ambassador BELAL ELMASSRY.

France: route de Tondibia, Quartier Yantala, BP 10660, Niamey; tel. 20-72-24-32; fax 20-72-25-18; e-mail webmestre@mail.com; internet www.ambafrance-ne.org; Ambassador CHRISTOPHE BOUCHARD.

Germany: 71 ave du Général de Gaulle, BP 629, Niamey; tel. 20-72-35-10; fax 20-72-39-85; e-mail amb-all-ny@web.de; internet www.niamey.diplo.de; Ambassador Dr GORDON KRICKE.

India: BP 201, Niamey; tel. 20-37-00-29; fax 20-20-37-01; e-mail amb.niamey@mea.gov.in; Ambassador YOGENDRA PRATAP SINGH.

Iran: 11 rue de la Présidence, BP 10543, Niamey; tel. 20-72-21-98; fax 20-72-28-10; e-mail aliakbar_100@yahoo.com; Ambassador MOHAMAD NIKKHAH.

Korea, Democratic People's Republic: Niamey; Ambassador PAK SONG IL.

Libya: route de Goudel, BP 683, Niamey; tel. 20-72-40-19; fax 20-72-40-97; e-mail boukhari@intnet.ne; Ambassador (vacant).

Morocco: ave du Président Lubke, face Clinique Kaba, BP 12403, Niamey; tel. 20-73-40-84; fax 20-73-80-27; e-mail ambmang@intnet.ne; Ambassador TAYEB RAOUF.

Nigeria: rue Goudel, BP 11130, Niamey; tel. 20-73-24-10; fax 20-73-35-00; e-mail embnig@intnet.ne; Ambassador ALIYU ISA SOKOTO.

Pakistan: 90 rue YN 001, ave des Zarmakoye, Yantala Plateau, BP 10426, Niamey; tel. 20-75-32-57; fax 20-75-32-55; e-mail parepniamey@yahoo.com; Ambassador (vacant).

Saudi Arabia: route de Tillabery, BP 339, Niamey; tel. 20-75-32-15; fax 20-75-24-42; e-mail neemb@mofa.gov.sa; Ambassador SAOUD BIN ABDUL AZIZ AL-DAYIL.

Spain: 151 rue de la Radio, BP 11888, Niamey; tel. 20-75-59-61; e-mail emb.niamey@maec.es; Ambassador MARÍA SOLEDAD FUENTES GÓMEZ.

USA: rue des Ambassades, BP 11201, Niamey; tel. 20-73-31-69; fax 20-73-55-60; e-mail NiameyPASN@state.gov; internet niamey.usembassy.gov; Ambassador BISA WILLIAMS.

Judicial System

According to the Constitution of the Seventh Republic, promulgated on 25 November 2010, the judiciary is independent and consists of a Constitutional Court, a Court of Cassation, a Council of State, a Court of Auditors, and any other courts and tribunals instituted by law. However, at the end of December 2012 the Constitutional Court and the Court of Cassation had not yet been established, and their functions were being fulfilled by the Constitutional Council of Transition and the Court of State, respectively.

Constitutional Council of Transition (Conseil Constitutionnel de Transition du Niger): BP 10779, Niamey; internet cour-constitutionnelle-niger.org; 7 mems; replacement by Constitutional Court pending; Pres. FATIMATA SALIFOU BAZEYE.

High Court of Justice (Haute Cour de Justice): Niamey; mems elected by deputies of the Assemblée nationale from among themselves; competent to indict the members of the Government; Pres. HADIZATOU MOUSSA GROS.

Court of State: Niamey; division into a Court of Cassation and a Council of State pending; Pres. OUMAROU YAYÉ; Chief Prosecutor MANOU FASSOUMA MOUSSA.

Courts of Appeal: at Niamey and Zinder; Niamey: Pres. SÉKOU BOUKAR DIOP; Zinder: Pres. EMILIEN B. BONAVENTURE.

Audit Court: Niamey; Pres. ELIANE J. ALAGBADA.

There are also nine Tribunaux de Grande Instance (at Agadez, Arlit, Birni N'Konni, Diffa, Dosso, Maradi, Tillabéry and Zinder), one military court and 30 Tribunaux d'Instance (one in each department).

Religion

It is estimated that some 95% of the population are Muslims, 0.5% are Christians and the remainder follow traditional beliefs.

ISLAM

The most influential Islamic groups in Niger are the Tijaniyya, the Senoussi and the Hamallists.

Association Islamique du Niger: BP 2220, Niamey; tel. 20-74-08-90; Dir CHEIKH OUMAROU ISMAEL.

CHRISTIANITY

The Roman Catholic Church

Niger comprises one archdiocese and one diocese. The Archbishop and Bishop participate in the Bishops' Conference of Burkina Faso and Niger (based in Ouagadougou, Burkina Faso).

Archbishop of Niamey: Rt Rev. MICHEL CHRISTIAN CARTATÉGUY, Evêché, BP 10270, Niamey; tel. 20-73-32-59; fax 20-73-80-01; e-mail cartateguymi@voila.fr; internet eglisecatholiqueauniger.org.

Bishop of Maradi: Rt Rev. AMBROISE OUÉDRAOGO, Evêché, BP 447, Maradi; tel. and fax 20-41-03-30; fax 20-41-13-86; e-mail evechemi@intnet.ne.

The Press

The following were among those newspapers and periodicals believed to be appearing regularly in the early 2010s:

L'Action: Quartier Yantala, Niamey; tel. 96-96-92-22; e-mail action_ne@yahoo.fr; internet www.tamtaminfo.com/action.pdf; f. 2003; fortnightly; popular newspaper intended for youth audience; Dir of Publication BOUSSADA BEN ALI; circ. 2,000 (2003).

L'Actualité: Quartier Terminus, BP 383, Niamey; tel. 20-73-30-91; e-mail actualite98@yahoo.fr; internet lactualite-niger.com; f. 2010; weekly; Dir of Publication MAHAROU HABOU OUMAROU; circ. 1,500.

L'Alternative: BP 10948, Niamey; tel. 20-74-24-39; fax 20-74-24-82; e-mail alter@intnet.ne; internet www.alternative.ne; f. 1994; weekly; in French and Hausa; Dir MOUSSA TCHANGARI; Editor-in-Chief ABDRAMANE OUSMANE.

Anfani: Immeuble DMK, rue du Damagaram, BP 2096, Niamey; tel. 20-74-08-80; fax 20-74-00-52; e-mail anfani@intnet.ne; f. 1992; 2 a month; Editor-in-Chief IBBO DADDY ABDOULAYE; circ. 3,000.

Le Canard Déchaîné: BP 383, Niamey; tel. 93-92-66-64; satirical; weekly; Dir of Publication ABDOULAYE TIÉMOGO; Editor-in-Chief IBRAHIM MANZO.

Le Canard Libéré: BP 11631, Niamey; tel. 20-75-43-52; fax 20-75-39-89; e-mail canardlibere@caramail.com; satirical; weekly; Dir of Publication TRAORÉ DAOUDA AMADOU; Editorial Dir OUMAROU NALAN MOUSSA.

Le Démocrate: 21 rue 067, NB Terminus, BP 11064, Niamey; tel. 20-73-24-25; e-mail le_democrate@caramail.com; internet www.tamtaminfo.com/democrate.pdf; weekly; independent; f. 1992; Dir of Publication ALBERT CHAÏBOU; Editor-in-Chief OUSSEINI ISSA.

Les Echos du Sahel: Villa 4012, 105 Logements, BP 12750, Niamey; tel. and fax 20-74-32-17; e-mail ecosahel@intnet.ne; f. 1999; rural issues and devt; quarterly; Dir IBBO DADDY ABDOULAYE.

L'Enquêteur: BP 172, Niamey; tel. 93-90-18-74 (mobile); e-mail lenqueteur@yahoo.fr; fortnightly; Publr TAHIROU GOURO; Editor IBRAHIM SOULEY.

Haské: BP 297, Niamey; tel. 20-74-18-44; fax 20-73-20-06; e-mail webmaster@planetafrique.com; internet www.haske.uni.cc; f. 1990; weekly; also Haské Magazine, quarterly; Dir CHEIKH IBRAHIM DIOP.

Journal Officiel de la République du Niger: BP 116, Niamey; tel. 20-72-39-30; fax 20-72-39-43; f. 1960; fortnightly; govt bulletin; Man. Editor BONKOULA AMINATOU MAYAKI; circ. 800.

Libération: BP 10483, Niamey; tel. 96-97-96-22 (mobile); f. 1995; weekly; Dir BOUBACAR DIALLO; circ. 1,000 (2003).

Le Républicain: Nouvelle Imprimerie du Niger, pl. du Petit Marché, BP 12015, Niamey; tel. 20-73-47-98; fax 20-73-41-42; e-mail webmasters@republicain-niger.com; internet www.republicain-niger.com; f. 1991; weekly; independent; Dir of Publication MAMANE ABOU; circ. 2,500.

La Roue de l'Histoire: Zabarkan, rue du SNEN, BP 5005, Niamey; tel. 20-74-05-69; internet www.tamtaminfo.com/roue.pdf; weekly; Propr SANOUSSI JACKOU; Dir ABARAD MOUDOUR ZAKARA.

Le Sahel Quotidien: BP 13182, ONEP, Niamey; tel. 20-73-34-87; fax 20-73-30-90; e-mail onep@intnet.ne; internet www.lesahel.org; f. 1960; publ. by Office National d'Edition et de Presse; daily; Dir IBRAHIM MAMANE TANTAN; Editor-in-Chief ALASSANE ASOKOFARE; circ. 3,000; also Sahel-Dimanche, Sundays; circ. 5,000.

Sauyi: BP 10948, Niamey; tel. 20-74-24-39; fax 20-74-24-82; e-mail sarji@alternative.ne; fortnightly; Hausa; publ. by Groupe Alternative; Hausa; rural interest; Dir SAÏDOU ARJI.

La Source: Academie des Arts, BP 5320, Niamey; tel. 96-53-95-77 (mobile); e-mail amanimb9@yahoo.fr; weekly; Dir of Publication AMANI MOUNKAÏLA; circ. 1,000.

Stadium: BP 10948, Niamey; tel. 96-96-73-07 (mobile); e-mail abbarimi@gmail.com; sports; 2 a month; Editor ABBA KIARI.

Le Témoin: BP 10483, Niamey; tel. 96-96-58-51; e-mail istemoin@yahoo.fr; internet www.tamtaminfo.com/temoin.pdf; 2 a month; Dir of Publication IBRAHIM SOUMANA GAOH; Editors AMADOU TIÉMOGO, MOUSSA DAN TCHOUKOU, I. S. GAOH; circ. 1,000 (2005).

Ténéré Express: BP 13600, Niamey; tel. 20-73-35-76; fax 20-73-77-75; e-mail tenerefm@intnet.ne; daily; independent; current affairs; Dir ABDOULAYE MOUSSA MASSALATCHI.

Le Trophée: BP 2000, Niamey; tel. 20-74-12-79; e-mail strophee@caramail.com; sports; 2 a month; Dir ISSA HAMIDOU MAYAKI.

Le Visionnaire: quartier Plateau, Niamey; tel. 98-15-62-40; weekly; Dir of Publication SALIFOU SOUMAÏLA ABDOULKARIM; circ. 1,000.

NEWS AGENCIES

Agence Nigérienne de Presse (ANP): BP 11158, Niamey; tel. 20-74-08-09; e-mail anpniger@intnet.ne; f. 1987; state-owned; Dir YAYE HASSANE.

Sahel—Office National d'Edition et de Presse (ONEP): BP 13182, Niamey; tel. 20-73-34-86; f. 1989; Dir MAHAMADOU ADAMOU.

PRESS ASSOCIATION

Association Nigérienne des Editeurs de la Presse Indépendante (ANEPI): Niamey; Pres. IBRAHIM SOUMANA GAOH; Sec.-Gen. IBRAHIM MANZO DIALLO.

Publishers

La Nouvelle Imprimerie du Niger (NIN): pl. du Petit Marché, BP 61, Niamey; tel. 20-73-47-98; fax 20-73-41-42; e-mail imprim@intnet.ne; f. 1962 as Imprimerie Nationale du Niger; govt publishing house; brs in Agadez and Maradi; Dir MAMAN ABOU.

Réseau Sahélien de Recherche et de Publication: Niamey; tel. 20-73-36-90; fax 20-73-39-43; e-mail resadep@ilimi.uam.ne; press of the Université Abdou Moumouni; Co-ordinator BOUREIMA DIADIE.

Broadcasting and Communications

TELECOMMUNICATIONS

In 2011 there were five licensed providers of telecommunications services in Niger: three mobile cellular telephone operators, one fixed-line operator and one dual operator.

Airtel Niger: route de l'Aéroport, BP 11922, Niamey; tel. 20-73-23-46; fax 20-73-23-85; e-mail info.ne@zain.com; internet africa.airtel.com/niger; f. 2001 as Zain Niger; present name adopted in 2010; Dir-Gen. ALAIN KAHASHA.

Moov Niger: route de l'Aéroport, 720 blvd du 15 Avril, BP 13379, Niamey; tel. 20-74-19-54; fax 20-74-19-39; internet www.moov.ne; f. 2001; 68% owned by Orascom Telecom (Egypt); Dir CHEIKH BEN HAÏDARA.

Orange Niger: 1282 blvd Mali Bero, BP 2874, Niamey; tel. 90-22-22-22; e-mail service.client@orange-niger.ne; internet www.orange.ne; provides mobile, fixed-line and internet services; Dir-Gen. BRELOTTE BA.

Société Nigérienne des Télécommunications (SONITEL): ave du Général de Gaulle, BP 208, Niamey; tel. 20-72-29-98; fax 20-72-

24-78; e-mail info@sonitel.ne; internet www.sonitel.ne; f. 1998; 51% jtly owned by ZTE Corpn (People's Republic of China) and Laaico (Libya), 46% state-owned; Dir-Gen. MOUSSA BOUBACAR.

Sahel Com: BP 208, Niamey; internet www.sahelcom.ne; f. 2002; mobile cellular telecommunications in Niamey.

Regulatory Authorities

Autorité de Régulation Multisectorielle: 64 rue des bâtisseurs, BP 13179, Niamey; tel. 20-73-90-08; fax 20-73-85-91; e-mail arm@ armniger.org; internet www.armniger.org; f. 1999; Pres. AMINATA GARBA.

Conseil National de Régulation: Niamey; Pres. ALMOUSTAPHA BOUBACAR.

Haut Commissariat à l'Informatique et aux Nouvelles Technologies de l'Information et de la Communication: Niamey; High Commissioner SOUMANA HAMMA BEIDI.

BROADCASTING

Regulatory Authority

Observatoire National de la Communication (ONC): rue Presidence, BP 9999, Niamey; internet www.csc-niger.ne; f. 2010 to replace Conseil Supérieur de la Communication (CSC); Pres. ABDOURAHAMANE OUSMANE; 13 mems.

Radio

Independent radio stations have been permitted to operate since 1994, although the majority are concentrated in the capital, Niamey. In 2000 the first of a network of rural stations, RURANET, which were to broadcast mainly programmes concerned with development issues, mostly in national languages, was established.

Anfani FM: blvd Nali-Béro, BP 2096, Wadata, Niamey; tel. 20-74-08-80; fax 20-74-00-52; e-mail anfani@intnet.ne; private radio station, broadcasting to Niamey, Zinder, Maradi and Diffa; Dir ISMAËL MOUTARI.

Office de Radiodiffusion-Télévision du Niger (ORTN): BP 309, Niamey; tel. 20-72-31-63; fax 20-72-35-48; internet www.ortn.ne; f. 1967; state broadcasting authority; Dir-Gen. LOÏC CRESPIN.

Ténéré FM: BP 13600, Niamey; tel. 20-73-65-76; fax 20-73-46-94; e-mail tenerefm@intnet.ne; f. 1998; Dir ABIBOU GARBA; Editor-in-Chief SOULEYMANE ISSA MAÏGA.

La Voix du Sahel: BP 361, Niamey; tel. 20-72-22-02; fax 20-72-35-48; e-mail ortny@intnet.ne; internet www.ortn.ne; f. 1958; govt-controlled radio service; programmes in French, Hausa, Djerma, Kanuri, Fulfuldé, Tamajak, Toubou, Gourmantché, Boudouma and Arabic; Dir IBRO NA-ALLAH AMADOU.

RURANET: Niamey; internet membres.lycos.fr/nigeradio; f. 2000; network of rural radio stations, broadcasting 80% in national languages, with 80% of programmes concerned with devt issues; 31 stations operative in April 2002.

La Voix de l'Hémicycle: BP 12234, Niamey; f. 2002 as the radio station of the Assemblée nationale; broadcasts parliamentary debates and analysis for 15 hours daily in French and national languages to Niamey and environs.

Sudan FM: Dosso; auth. 2000; private radio station; Dir HIMA ADAMOU.

RFI, BBC, la Voix de l'Amérique, Deutsch Welle and Radio Chine Internationala are also broadcast to Niger.

Television

Office de Radiodiffusion-Télévision du Niger (ORTN): see Radio

Tal TV: BP 309, Niamey; f. 2001; broadcasts 72 hours of programmes each week.

Télé-Sahel: BP 309, Niamey; tel. 20-72-31-55; fax 20-72-35-48; govt-controlled television service; broadcasts daily from 13 transmission posts and six retransmission posts, covering most of Niger; Dir-Gen. ABDOU SOULEY.

Radio Télévision Bonferey: rue du Collège Mariama, BP 2260, Niamey; tel. 20 74 1717; e-mail bonferey@yahoo.fr; internet www.bonferey.net; f. 2007; Dir-Gen. MAHAMANE CHAIBOU.

Télévision Ténéré (TTV): BP 13600, Niamey; tel. 20-73-65-76; fax 20-73-77-75; e-mail tenerefm@intnet.ne; f. 2000; independent broadcaster in Niamey; Dir ABIBOU GARBA.

Other television channels include Dounia, Canal 3 and Bonferey. The independent operator, Télé Star, broadcasts several international or foreign channels in Niamey and environs, including TV5 Monde, Canal Horizon, CFI, RTL9, CNN and Euro News. Canal+Media Overseas, another independent operator, broadcasts over 50 television channels, both international and African, as well as a number of radio channels.

Finance

(cap. = capital; res = reserves; dep. = deposits; m. = million; brs = branches; amounts in francs CFA)

BANKING

In 2009 there were 10 commercial banks and one financial institution in Niger.

Central Bank

Banque Centrale des Etats de l'Afrique de l'Ouest (BCEAO): rue de l'Uranium, BP 487, Niamey; tel. 20-72-24-91; fax 20-73-47-43; HQ in Dakar, Senegal; f. 1962; bank of issue for the mem. states of the Union Economique et Monétaire Ouest-Africaine (UEMOA, comprising Benin, Burkina Faso, Côte d'Ivoire, Guinea-Bissau, Mali, Niger, Senegal and Togo); cap. 134,120m., res 1,474,195m., dep. 2,124,051m. (Dec. 2009); Gov. KONÉ TIÉMOKO MEYLIET; Dir in Niger ABDOULAYE SOUMANA; brs at Maradi and Zinder.

Commercial Banks

Bank of Africa—Niger (BOA—Niger): Immeuble BOA, rue du Gawèye, BP 10973, Niamey; tel. 20-73-36-20; fax 20-73-38-18; e-mail information@boaniger.com; internet www.boaniger.com; f. 1994 to acquire assets of Nigeria International Bank Niamey; 42.6% owned by African Financial Holding; cap. 3,500m., res 4,072m., dep. 92,026m. (Dec. 2009); Pres. PAUL DERREUMAUX; Dir-Gen. MAMADOU SÉNÉ; 8 brs.

Banque Atlantique Niger: BP 375, Rond Point Liberté, Niamey; tel. 20-73-98-88; fax 20-73-98-91; e-mail ban@banqueatlantique.net; internet www.banqueatlantique.net; f. 2005; 73% owned by Atlantic Financial Group, Lomé; total assets US $19.5m. (Dec. 2006); Chair. KONE DOSSONGUI; Man. Dir AMADOU MOUSTAPHA DIOUF.

Banque Commerciale du Niger (BCN): rue du Combattant, BP 11363, Niamey; tel. 20-73-39-15; fax 20-73-21-63; e-mail info@bcn .ne; internet www.bcn-niger.com; f. 1978; 83.15% owned by Libyan Arab Foreign Bank, 16.85% state-owned; cap. and res 1,477m., total assets 14,618m. (Dec. 2003); Administrator BASHIR M. SAMALOUS.

Banque Internationale pour l'Afrique au Niger (BIA—Niger): ave de la Mairie, BP 10350, Niamey; tel. 20-73-31-01; fax 20-73-35-95; e-mail bia@intnet.ne; internet www.bianiger.com; f. 1980; 35% owned by Groupe Belgolaise (Belgium); cap. 2,800m., res –25m., dep. 78,367m. (Dec. 2008); Pres. AMADOU HIMA SOULEY; Dir-Gen. OUHOUMOUDOU MAHAMADOU; 11 brs.

Banque Islamique du Niger pour le Commerce et l'Investissement (BINCI): Immeuble El Nasr, BP 12754, Niamey; tel. 20-73-27-30; fax 20-73-47-35; e-mail binci@intnet.ne; f. 1983; fmrly Banque Masraf Faisal Islami; 33% owned by Dar al-Maal al-Islami (Switzerland), 33% by Islamic Development Bank (Saudi Arabia); cap. 1,810m., total assets 7,453m. (Dec. 2003); Pres. ABDERRAOUF BENESSAÏAH; Dir-Gen. AISSANI OMAR.

Ecobank Niger: blvd de la Liberté, angle rue des Bâtisseurs, BP 13804, Niamey; tel. 20-73-71-81; fax 20-73-72-04; e-mail ecobankni@ ecobank.com; internet www.ecobank.com; f. 1999; 99.85% owned by Ecobank Transnational Inc, Lomé; total assets 100,385m. (Dec. 2009); Chair. IBRAHIM IDDI ANGO; Dir-Gen. MOUKARAMOU CHANOU.

Société Nigérienne de Banque (SONIBANK): ave de la Mairie, BP 891, Niamey; tel. 20-73-47-40; fax 20-73-46-93; e-mail sonibank@ intnet.ne; internet www.sonibank.net; f. 1990; 25% owned by Société Tunisienne de Banque; cap. 5,000m., res 7,355m., dep. 92,222m. (Dec. 2010); Pres. ILLA KANÉ; Dir-Gen. MOUSSA HAITOU; 6 brs.

Development Banks

Caisse de Prêts aux Collectivités Territoriales (CPCT): route Torodi, BP 730, Niamey; tel. 20-72-34-12; fax 20-72-30-80; f. 1970; 100% state-owned (94% by organs of local govt); cap. and res 744m., total assets 2,541m. (Dec. 2003); Administrator ABDOU DJIBO (acting).

Crédit du Niger (CDN): 11 blvd de la République, BP 213, Niger; tel. 20-72-27-01; fax 20-72-23-90; e-mail cdb-nig@intnet.ne; f. 1958; 54% state-owned, 20% owned by Caisse Nationale de Sécurité Sociale; transfer to full private ownership pending; cap. and res 1,058m., total assets 3,602m. (Dec. 2003); Administrator ABDOU DJIBO (acting).

Fonds d'Intervention en Faveur des Petites et Moyennes Entreprises Nigériennes (FIPMEN): Immeuble Sonara II, BP 252, Niamey; tel. 20-73-20-98; f. 1990; state-owned; cap. and res 124m. (Dec. 1991); Chair. AMADOU SALLA HASSANE; Man. Dir IBRAHIM BEIDARI.

Savings Bank

FINAPOSTE: BP 11778, Niamey; tel. 20-73-24-98; fax 20-73-35-69; fmrly Caisse Nationale d'Epargne; Chair. Mme PALFI; Man. Dir HASSOUME MATA.

STOCK EXCHANGE

Bourse Régionale des Valeurs Mobilières (BRVM): c/o Chambre de Commerce et d'Industrie du Niger, pl. de la Concertation, BP 13299, Niamey; tel. 20-73-66-92; fax 20-73-69-47; e-mail imagagi@brvm.org; internet www.brvm.org; f. 1998; national branch of BRVM (regional stock exchange based in Abidjan, Côte d'Ivoire, serving the member states of UEMOA); Man. IDRISSA S. MAGAGI.

INSURANCE

Agence Nigérienne d'Assurances (ANA): pl. de la Mairie, BP 423, Niamey; tel. 20-72-20-71; f. 1959; cap. 1.5m.; owned by L'Union des Assurances de Paris; Dir JEAN LASCAUD.

Caren Assurance: BP 733, Niamey; tel. 20-73-34-70; fax 20-73-24-93; e-mail carenas@intnet.ne; insurance and reinsurance; Dir-Gen. IBRAHIM IDI ANGO.

Leyma—Société Nigérienne d'Assurances et de Réassurances (SNAR—Leyma): BP 426, Niamey; tel. 20-73-57-72; fax 20-73-40-44; f. 1973; restructured 2001; Pres. AMADOU HIMA SOULEY; Dir-Gen. GARBA ABDOURAHAMANE.

La Nigérienne d'Assurance et de Réassurance: BP 13300, Niamey; tel. 20-73-63-36; fax 20-73-73-37; Dir-Gen. OUMAROU ALMA.

Union Générale des Assurances du Niger (UGAN): rue de Kalley, BP 11935, Niamey; tel. 20-73-54-06; fax 20-73-41-85; f. 1985; cap. 500m.; Pres. PATHÉ DIONE; Dir-Gen. MAMADOU TALATA; 7 brs.

Trade and Industry

GOVERNMENT AGENCIES

Centre National d'Energie Solaire (ONERSOL): BP 621, Niamey; tel. 20-72-39-23; e-mail cnes@intnet.ne; frmly Office National de l'Energie Solaire (ONERSOL), present name adopted 1998; govt agency for research and devt, commercial production and exploitation of solar devices; Dir ABDOUSSALAM BA.

Office des Eaux du Sous-Sol (OFEDES): BP 734, Niamey; tel. 20-74-01-19; fax 20-74-16-68; govt agency for the maintenance and devt of wells and boreholes; Pres. DJIBO HAMANI.

Office du Lait du Niger (OLANI): BP 404, Niamey; tel. 20-73-23-69; fax 20-73-36-74; f. 1971; devt and marketing of milk products; transferred to majority private ownership in 1998; Dir-Gen. M. DIENG.

Office National des Ressources Minières du Niger (ONAREM): Rond-Point Kennedy, BP 12716, Niamey; tel. 20-73-59-28; fax 20-73-28-12; f. 1976; govt agency for exploration, exploitation and marketing of all minerals; Pres. MOUDY MOHAMED; Dir-Gen. A. A. ASKIA.

Office des Produits Vivriers du Niger (OPVN): pl. du Petit Marché, BP 474, Niamey; tel. 20-73-44-43; fax 20-73-24-68; e-mail opvn@opvn.net; internet www.opvn.net; govt agency for developing agricultural and food production; Dir-Gen. SEYDOU SADOU.

Riz du Niger (RINI): BP 476, Niamey; tel. 20-71-13-29; fax 20-73-42-04; f. 1967; cap. 825m. francs CFA; 30% state-owned; transfer to 100% private ownership proposed; production and marketing of rice; Pres. YOUSSOUF MOHAMED ELMOCTAR; Dir-Gen. M. HAROUNA.

DEVELOPMENT ORGANIZATIONS

Agence Française de Développement (AFD): 203 ave du Gountou-Yéna, BP 212, Niamey; tel. 20-72-33-93; fax 20-72-26-05; e-mail afdniamey@groupe-afd.org; internet www.afd.fr; Country Dir EMMANUEL DEBROISE.

Stichting Nederlandse Vrijwilligers Niger (SNV): ave des Zarmakoye, BP 10110, Niamey; tel. 20-75-36-33; fax 20-75-35-06; e-mail snvniger@snv.ne; internet www.snvniger.org; present in Niger since 1978; projects concerning food security, agriculture, the environment, savings and credit, marketing, water and communications; operations in Tillabéri, Zinder and Tahoua provinces; Dir-Gen. NIKO PATER.

CHAMBER OF COMMERCE

Chambre de Commerce d'Agriculture, d'Industrie et d'Artisanat du Niger: BP 209, Niamey; tel. 20-73-22-10; fax 20-73-46-68; e-mail cham209n@intnet.ne; internet www.ccaian.org; f. 1954; comprises 80 full mems and 40 dep. mems; Pres. IBRAHIM IDI ANGO; Sec.-Gen. SADOU AISSATA.

INDUSTRIAL AND TRADE ORGANIZATIONS

Centre Nigérien du Commerce Extérieur (CNCE): pl. de la Concertation, BP 12480, Niamey; tel. 20-73-22-88; fax 20-73-46-68;

f. 1984; promotes and co-ordinates all aspects of foreign trade; Dir AÏSSA DIALLO.

Société Nationale de Commerce et de Production du Niger (COPRO-Niger): Niamey; tel. 20-73-28-41; fax 20-73-57-71; f. 1962; monopoly importer of foodstuffs; cap. 1,000m. francs CFA; 47% state-owned; Man. Dir DJIBRILLA HIMA.

EMPLOYERS' ORGANIZATIONS

Syndicat des Commerçants Importateurs et Exportateurs du Niger (SCIMPEXNI): Chambre de Commerce, d'Agriculture, d'Industrie et d'Artisanat du Niger, Niamey; tel. 20-73-33-17; Pres. M. SILVA; Sec.-Gen. INOUSSA MAÏGA.

Syndicat National des Petites et Moyennes Entreprises et Industries Nigériennes (SYNAPEMEIN): Chambre de Commerce, d'Agriculture, d'Industrie et d'Artisanat du Niger, Niamey; tel. 20-73-50-97; Pres. ALZOUMA SALEY; Sec.-Gen. HASSANE LAWAL KADER.

Syndicat Patronal des Entreprises et Industries du Niger (SPEIN): BP 415, Niamey; tel. 20-73-24-01; fax 20-73-47-07; f. 1994; Pres. AMADOU OUSMANE; Sec.-Gen. NOUHOU TARI.

UTILITIES
Electricity

Société Nigérienne d'Electricité (NIGELEC): 46 ave du Gen. de Gaulle, BP 11202, Niamey; tel. 20-72-26-92; fax 20-72-32-88; e-mail nigelec@intnet.ne; f. 1968; 95% state-owned; 51% transfer to private ownership proposed; production and distribution of electricity; Dir-Gen. ALHASSANE HALID.

Water

Société d'Exploitation des Eaux du Niger (SEEN): blvd Zarmaganda, BP 12209, Niamey; tel. 20-72-25-00; fax 20-73-46-40; fmrly Société Nationale des Eaux; 51% owned by Veolia Environnement (France); production and distribution of drinking water; Pres. ABARY DAN BOUZOUA SOULEYMENE; Dir-Gen. SEYNI SALOU.

Société de Patrimoine des Eaux du Niger: Immeuble Sonara II, 6ème étage, BP 10738, Niamey; tel. 20-73-43-40; fax 20-73-46-40; e-mail infos@spen.ne; internet www.spen.ne; f. 2000; Dir-Gen. ISSAKA HASSANE DJÉGOULÉ.

TRADE UNION FEDERATIONS

Confédération Démocratique des Travailleurs du Niger (CDTN): 1046 ave de l'Islam, BP 10766, Niamey; tel. 20-74-38-34; fax 20-74-28-55; e-mail c_cdtn@yahoo.fr; f. 2000; Sec.-Gen. ISSOUFOU SIDIBE.

Confédération des Travailleurs du Niger (CTN): Niamey; Sec.-Gen. MAMADOU SAKO.

Entente des Travailleurs du Niger (ETN): Bourse du Travail, BP 388, Niamey; tel. and fax 20-73-52-56; f. 2005 by merger of Confédération Nigérienne du Travail, Union Generale des Travailleurs du Niger and Union des Syndicats des Travailleurs du Niger.

Transport
ROADS

Niger is crossed by highways running from east to west and from north to south, giving access to neighbouring countries. A road is under construction to Lomé, Togo, via Burkina Faso, and the 428-km Zinder–Agadez road, scheduled to form part of the Trans-Sahara Highway, has been upgraded. In 2010 there were 19,267 km of classified roads, including 10,667 km of main roads and 2,096 km of secondary roads.

Société Nationale des Transports Nigériens (SNTN): BP 135, Niamey; tel. 20-72-24-55; fax 20-74-47-07; e-mail stratech@intnet.ne; f. 1963; operates passenger and freight road-transport services; 49% state-owned; Chair. MOHAMED ABDOULAHI; Man. Dir BARKE M. MOUSTAPHA.

RAILWAYS

There are as yet no railways in Niger, although the country uses the Benin and Togo railway lines, which transport goods from seaports to the Niger border.

Organisation Commune Bénin-Niger des Chemins de Fer et des Transports (OCBN): BP 38, Niamey; tel. 20-73-27-90; f. 1959; 50% owned by Govt of Niger, 50% by Govt of Benin; manages the Benin-Niger railway project (begun in 1978); also operates more than 500 km within Benin (q.v.); extension to Niger proposed; transfer to private ownership proposed; Dir-Gen. RIGOBERT AZON.

INLAND WATERWAYS

The River Niger is navigable for 300 km within the country. Access to the sea is available by a river route from Gaya, in south-western Niger, to the coast at Port Harcourt, Nigeria, between September and March. Port facilities at Lomé, Togo, are used as a commercial outlet for land-locked Niger.

Société Nigérienne de Transit (NITRA): Zone Industrielle, BP 560, Niamey; tel. 20-73-22-53; fax 20-73-26-38; f. 1974; 48% owned by SNTN; customs agent, freight-handling, warehousing, etc.; manages Nigerien port facilities at Lomé, Togo; Pres. Mounkaila Seydou; Man. Dir Sade Fatimata.

Société Nigérienne des Transports Fluviaux et Maritimes (SNTFM): Niamey; tel. 20-73-39-69; river and sea transport; cap. 64.6m. francs CFA; 99% state-owned; Man. Dir Bertrand Dejean.

CIVIL AVIATION

There are international airports at Niamey (Hamani Diori), Agadez (Mano Dayak) and Zinder, and major domestic airports at Diffa, Maradi and Tahoua.

Agence Nationale de l'Aviation Civile (ANAC-NIGER): BP 1096, Niamey; fax 20-73-58-95; f. 2010; Dir-Gen. Amadou Seydou Yaye.

Air Inter Afrique: Niamey; tel. 20-73-85-85; fax 20-73-69-73; f. 2001; operates services within West Africa; CEO Cheikh Ousmane Diallo.

Nigeravia: BP 10454, Niamey; tel. 20-73-30-64; fax 20-74-18-42; e-mail nigavia@intnet.ne; internet www.nigeravia.com; f. 1991; operates domestic, regional and international services; Pres. and Dir-Gen. Jean Sylvestre.

Sahel Airlines: rue de Rivoli, BP 10154, Niamey; tel. 20-73-65-71; fax 20-73-65-33; e-mail sahelair@intnet.ne; Dir-Gen. Abdoul Aziz Larabou.

Société Nigérienne des Transports Aériens (SONITA): Niamey; f. 1991; owned by private Nigerien (81%) and Cypriot (19%) interests; operates domestic and regional services; Man. Dir Abdoulaye Maiga Goudoubaba.

Tourism

The Aïr and Ténéré Nature Reserve, covering an area of 77,000 sq km, was established in 1988. In 2010 74,278 tourists entered Niger, while receipts from tourism totalled US $79m.

Centre Nigerien de Promotion Touristique (CNPT): ave de Président H. Luebke, BP 612, Niamey; tel. 20-73-24-47; fax 20-73-28-07; e-mail CNPT2@yahoo.fr; internet www.maisontourism-niger.com; Dirs Boulou Akano, Ibrahim Halidou, Kiepiw Toyé Fanta.

Defence

As assessed at November 2012, Niger's armed forces totalled 5,300 men (army 5,200; air force 100). Paramilitary forces numbered 5,400 men, comprising the gendarmerie (1,400 men), the republican guard (2,500) and the national police force (1,500). Conscription is selective and lasts for two years.

Defence Expenditure: Estimated at 23,400m. francs CFA in 2011.

Chief of General Staff of the Armed Forces: Brig.-Gen. Souleymane Salou.

Chief of General Staff of the Land Army: Col Salifou Mody.

Chief of General Staff of the Air Force: Col Hassane Mossi.

Education

Education is available free of charge, and is officially compulsory for eight years between the ages of seven and 15 years. Primary education begins at the age of six or seven and lasts for six years. Secondary education begins at the age of 13 years, and comprises a four-year cycle followed by a three-year cycle. According to UNESCO estimates, primary enrolment in 2010/11 included 62% of children in the appropriate age-group (boys 68%; girls 57%). Secondary enrolment in 2007/08 included only 10% of the relevant age-group (boys 13%; girls 8%). The Abdou Moumouni University (formerly the University of Niamey) was inaugurated in 1973, and the Islamic University of Niger, at Say (to the south of the capital), was opened in 1987. Some 11,292 students were enrolled at those institutions in 2009/10. In December 2001 the Assemblée nationale approved legislation providing for the introduction of teaching in all local languages, with the aim of improving the country's literacy rate—one of the lowest in the world. Public expenditure on education in 2010 represented 16.9% of total spending.

NIGERIA

Introductory Survey

LOCATION, CLIMATE, LANGUAGE, RELIGION, FLAG, CAPITAL

The Federal Republic of Nigeria is a West African coastal state on the shores of the Gulf of Guinea, with Benin to the west, Niger to the north, Chad to the north-east, and Cameroon to the east and south-east. The climate is tropical in the southern coastal areas, with an average annual temperature of 32°C (90°F) and high humidity. It is drier and semi-tropical in the north. Average annual rainfall is more than 2,500 mm (98 ins) in parts of the south-east, but in certain areas of the north is as low as 600 mm (24 ins). English is the country's official language. In 2003 the principal religious groups were Muslims (50.5%) and Christians (48.2%). The national flag (proportions 1 by 2) has three equal vertical stripes, of green, white and green. The capital is Abuja, to which the Federal Government was formally transferred in December 1991; however, many non-government institutions remained in the former capital, Lagos.

CONTEMPORARY POLITICAL HISTORY

Historical Context

The territory of present-day Nigeria, except for the section of former German-controlled Cameroon, was conquered by the United Kingdom, in several stages, during the second half of the 19th century and the first decade of the 20th century. The British dependencies of Northern and Southern Nigeria were merged into a single territory in 1914, administered largely by traditional native rulers, under the supervision of the colonial authorities. In 1947 the United Kingdom introduced a new Nigerian Constitution, establishing a federal system of government, based on three regions: Northern, Western and Eastern. The federal arrangement was an attempt to reconcile religious and regional tensions, and to accommodate Nigeria's diverse ethnic groups, notably the Ibo (in the east), the Yoruba (in the west) and the Hausa and Fulani (in the north). The Northern Region, which was predominantly Muslim, contained about one-half of Nigeria's total population.

In 1954 the federation became self-governing, and the first federal Prime Minister, Alhaji Abubakar Tafawa Balewa (a Muslim northerner), was appointed in August 1957. A constitutional conference, convened in 1958, agreed that Nigeria should become independent in 1960, and elections to an enlarged federal legislature took place in December 1959. The Northern People's Congress (NPC), which was politically dominant in the north, became the single largest party in the new legislature, although lacking an overall majority. Tafawa Balewa (a prominent member of the NPC) continued to head a coalition government of the NPC and the National Council for Nigeria and the Cameroons (NCNC), which attracted most support in the Eastern Region.

On 1 October 1960, as scheduled, the Federation of Nigeria achieved independence, initially as a constitutional monarchy. In June 1961 the northern part of the UN Trust Territory of British Cameroons was incorporated into Nigeria's Northern Region as the province of Sardauna, and in August 1963 a fourth region, the Mid-Western Region, was created by dividing the existing Western Region. On 1 October a revised Constitution was adopted, and the country was renamed the Federal Republic of Nigeria, although it remained a member of the Commonwealth. Dr Nnamdi Azikiwe of the NCNC took office as Nigeria's first President (then a non-executive post).

Domestic Political Affairs

In January 1966 Balewa's civilian Government was overthrown by junior army officers (mainly Ibos from the Eastern Region). The Commander-in-Chief of the Armed Forces, Maj.-Gen. Johnson Aguiyi-Aronsi (an Ibo), formed a Supreme Military Council, suspended the Constitution and imposed emergency rule. In July Aguiyi-Aronsi was killed in a further coup, staged by northern troops, and power was transferred to the Chief of Army Staff, Lt-Col (later Gen.) Yakubu Gowon, a Christian northerner. Gowon subsequently reintroduced the federal system, which had been suppressed after the January coup, and in April 1968 the four existing regions were replaced by 12 states.

Increasing opposition to Gowon's regime culminated in his overthrow in July 1975. Gowon was replaced as Head of State by Brig. (later Gen.) Murtala Ramat Muhammed, hitherto Federal Commissioner for Communications, who, in October, announced a detailed timetable for a transition to civilian rule. In February 1976, however, Muhammed was assassinated during an unsuccessful coup attempt. Power was immediately assumed by Lt-Gen. (later Gen.) Olusegun Obasanjo, the Chief of Army Staff, who promised to fulfil his predecessor's programme for the restoration of civilian rule.

In March 1976 the number of states was increased from 12 to 19, and it was announced that a new federal capital was to be constructed near Abuja, in central Nigeria. In September 1978 a new Constitution was promulgated, and the state of emergency, in force since 1966, was ended. At the same time the 12-year ban on political activity was revoked. Elections took place in July 1979 to a new bicameral National Assembly (comprising a Senate and a House of Representatives), and for State Assemblies and State Governors. The National Party of Nigeria (NPN), which included many prominent members of the former NPC, was the most successful in all the elections. The NPN's presidential candidate, Alhaji Shehu Shagari (who had served as an NPC federal minister prior to 1966 and as a federal commissioner in 1970–75), was elected to the new post of executive President in August 1979. He took office on 1 October, whereupon the military regime transferred power to the newly elected civilian authorities and the new Constitution came into effect.

In December 1983 the civilian Government was deposed in a bloodless military coup, led by Maj.-Gen. Muhammadu Buhari, who had been Federal Commissioner for Petroleum in 1976–78. The Government was replaced by a Supreme Military Council (SMC), headed by Buhari; the National Assembly was dissolved, and all political parties were banned. However, in August 1985 Buhari's administration was deposed in a bloodless coup, led by Maj.-Gen. (later Gen.) Ibrahim Babangida, the Chief of Army Staff and a member of the SMC. A new military administration, the Armed Forces Ruling Council (AFRC), was established, with Babangida as President.

Babangida's announcement in February 1986 that Nigeria had been accepted as a full member of the Organization of Islamic Cooperation (OIC, see p. 413) prompted concern in the non-Muslim sector of the population at increasing 'Islamization' in Nigeria. In July 1987 Babangida announced details of a programme to transfer power to a civilian government on 1 October 1992. In September 1987 the number of states was increased to 21. In May 1988 a Constituent Assembly, comprising 450 members elected by local government and 117 members nominated by the AFRC, commenced preparation of a draft constitution. The progress of the Constituent Assembly was impeded, however, by controversy over the proposed inclusion of Islamic (Shari'a) courts in the new document.

In May 1989 Babangida announced the end of the prohibition on political parties, and the new Constitution (which was scheduled to take effect on 1 October 1992) was promulgated. Only 13 of the existing parties managed to fulfil the requirements for registration by the stipulated date in July 1989. In September the National Electoral Commission (NEC) submitted six political associations to the AFRC for consideration; in October, however, it was decided to dissolve all the newly formed political parties, on the grounds that they were too closely associated with discredited former parties. In their place, the AFRC created two new organizations, the Social Democratic Party (SDP) and the National Republican Convention (NRC), provoking widespread criticism.

Following the completion of registration for membership of the SDP and the NRC, party executives were elected for each state in July 1990, taking the place of government-appointed administrators. In August Babangida replaced nine government ministers, and the position of Chief of General Staff, held by Vice-Adm. (later Adm.) Augustus Aikhomu, was replaced by the office of Vice-President (to which Aikhomu was immediately appointed).

In October 1990 the Movement for the Survival of the Ogoni People (MOSOP) was formed to co-ordinate opposition to the exploitation of petroleum reserves in territory of the Ogoni ethnic group (Ogoniland), in the south-central Rivers State, by the Shell Petroleum Development Co of Nigeria. Following a demonstration, organized by MOSOP in protest at environmental damage resulting from petroleum production, it was reported that security forces had killed some 80 Ogonis.

In September 1991, in an apparent attempt to relieve ethnic tensions, nine new states were created, increasing the size of the federation to 30 states. On 12 December the Federal Government was formally transferred from Lagos to Abuja, the new federal capital. In January 1992 Babangida formed a new Council of Ministers. In the same month the Government announced that elections to a bicameral National Assembly, comprising a 593-member House of Representatives and a 91-member Senate, would take place on 7 November, and would be followed by a presidential election on 5 December. The formal installation of a civilian government was consequently rescheduled for 2 January 1993, rather than 1 October 1992.

The 1992 elections

Elections to the National Assembly were brought forward to 4 July 1992. The SDP secured a majority in both chambers, with 52 seats in the Senate and 314 seats in the House of Representatives, while the NRC won 37 seats in the Senate and 275 seats in the House of Representatives. The formal inauguration of the National Assembly, due to take place on 27 July, was, however, postponed until 5 December, the stipulated date for the presidential election, prompting concern at the AFRC's apparent reluctance to relinquish legislative power.

Voting in primary elections for presidential candidates took place in September 1992. In October, however, shortly before a final round of voting was due to take place, Babangida suspended the primary elections, pending the outcome of an investigation by the NEC into alleged incidents of electoral malpractice. In November Babangida postponed the presidential election until 12 June 1993.

On 5 December 1992 Babangida inaugurated the National Assembly. On 2 January 1993 the AFRC and the Council of Ministers were dissolved, and a civilian Transitional Council and the National Defence and Security Council (NDSC—which comprised the President, Vice-President, the heads of the armed forces and senior members of the Transitional Council) were formally installed. The Chairman of the Transitional Council, Chief Ernest Adegunle Shonekan, was officially designated Head of Government (although supreme power was vested in the NDSC and the President), while Aikhomu retained the post of Vice-President. In accordance with the new programme for the transition to civilian rule, party congresses to select presidential candidates were conducted in February–March; the NRC elected Alhaji Bashir Othman Tofa and the SDP Chief Moshood Kastumawo Olawale Abiola to contest the presidential election.

Following a series of court rulings provoking widespread confusion, the results of the presidential election, which took place on 12 June 1993, were declared invalid by the Abuja High Court. It had been reported that Abiola had secured the majority of votes in 19 states, and Tofa in 11. On 23 June, in what it claimed was an effort to uphold the judicial system, the NDSC annulled the results of the presidential election, suspended the NEC and halted all proceedings pertaining to the election. Babangida subsequently announced that the poll had been marred by widespread irregularities (despite reports by international observers that voting had been conducted fairly), but insisted that he remained committed to the transition to civilian rule on 27 August. The SDP and the NRC were to select two new presidential candidates, under the supervision of a reconstituted NEC. The annulment of the election attracted international criticism, particularly from the USA and the United Kingdom, which announced the imposition of military sanctions against Nigeria. In July the NDSC announced that a new presidential election was to take place on 14 August. Legal proceedings initiated by Abiola in the Lagos Supreme Court, in an attempt to uphold his claim to the presidency, were abandoned after Babangida introduced legislation that prohibited any legal challenges to the annulment of the election.

At the end of July 1993 Babangida announced that an Interim National Government (ING) was to be established, on the grounds that there was insufficient time to permit the scheduled transition to civilian rule on 27 August. On 26 August Babangida resigned; on the following day a 32-member interim Federal Executive Council (FEC), headed by Shonekan as the new President, was installed, while the transitional period for the return to civilian rule was extended to 31 March 1994.

Supporters of democracy criticized the inclusion in the ING of several members of the now-dissolved NDSC, including Gen. Sani Abacha, who was appointed to the new post of Vice-President. Shonekan pledged his commitment to the democratic process, initiated negotiations with the Nigerian Labour Congress (NLC), which had announced industrial action in protest at the continuation of military rule, and effected the release of several journalists and opposition figures. In September 1993 a series of military appointments, which included the nomination of Lt-Gen. Oladipo Diya to the office of Chief of Defence Staff, effectively removed supporters of Babangida from significant posts within the armed forces. Later in September the NRC and SDP agreed to a new timetable whereby local government elections and a presidential election would take place concurrently in February 1994.

On 17 November 1993, following a meeting with senior military officials, Shonekan resigned as Head of State and immediately transferred power to Abacha (confirming widespread speculation that the latter had effectively assumed control of the Government following Babangida's resignation). On the following day Abacha dissolved all state institutions that had been established under the transitional process, replaced the State Governors with military administrators, prohibited political activity (thereby proscribing the NRC and the SDP), and announced the formation of a Provisional Ruling Council (PRC), which was to comprise senior military officials and principal members of a new FEC. He insisted, however, that he intended to relinquish power to a civilian government, and pledged to convene a conference with a mandate to determine the constitutional future of the country. Restrictions on the media were revoked. On 21 November Abacha introduced legislation that formally restored the 1979 Constitution and provided for the establishment of the new government organs. In an apparent attempt to counter domestic and international criticism, several prominent supporters of Abiola, including Baba Gana Kingibe, and four former members of the ING were appointed to the PRC and FEC, which were installed on 24 November. Abacha subsequently removed 17 senior military officers who were believed to be loyal to Babangida. Also in November the NLC agreed to abandon strike action after the Government acted to limit the increase in the price of petroleum products.

In December 1993 the United Kingdom announced that member nations of the European Union (EU, see p. 281) were to impose further sanctions against Nigeria, including restrictions on the export of armaments. In April 1994 the Government announced the establishment of a National Constitutional Conference (NCC), which was to submit recommendations, including proposals for a new draft constitution, to the PRC in October. The ban on political activity was to end in January 1995. In May 1994 a new pro-democracy organization, comprising former politicians, retired military officers and human rights activists, the National Democratic Coalition (NADECO), demanded that Abacha relinquish power by the end of that month and urged a boycott of the NCC. In the same month the leader of MOSOP, Ken Saro-Wiwa, was arrested in connection with the deaths, during political violence, of four Ogoni traditional leaders. Saro-Wiwa was alleged to have incited his supporters to commit the murders. (The trial of Saro-Wiwa, together with a further 14 Ogoni campaigners, by a Special Military Tribunal in Port Harcourt began in January 1995.) Following a public gathering, at which he declared himself Head of State and President of a parallel government, Abiola was arrested by security forces. He was arraigned before a special High Court in Abuja in July 1994 and charged with treason. In February 1995 the Federal Court of Appeal dismissed legal action by Abiola challenging the jurisdiction of the High Court in Abuja.

In February 1995 Abacha dissolved the FEC, after a number of ministers announced their intention of engaging in political activity in the forthcoming transitional period. In March some 150 military officials were arrested, and the authorities subsequently confirmed reports of a conspiracy to overthrow the Government. The arrest of the former Head of State, Olusegun Obasanjo, and his former deputy, Maj.-Gen. (retd) Shehu Musa Yar'Adua, together with other prominent critics of the Government, prompted international protests. In mid-March Abacha appointed a new, 36-member FEC. In May more than 40 people, including Obasanjo and Yar'Adua, were arraigned before a Special Military Tribunal in Lagos, in connection with the alleged coup attempt in March.

Transition to civilian rule

In June 1995 the NCC (having initially been scheduled to complete its preparations in October 1994) submitted a draft Constitution to Abacha, who rescinded the ban on political activity; a programme for transition to civilian rule was to be announced on 1 October. (A number of political organizations subsequently emerged, in response to the removal of the ban.) At the end of June it was reported that Yar'Adua and a further 13 military officers had been sentenced to death for conspiring to overthrow the Government, while several other defendants, including Obasanjo, received custodial terms. The Government subsequently confirmed that a total of 43 had been convicted in connection with the coup attempt, prompting protests and appeals for clemency from the international community. On 1 October, however, Abacha officially commuted the death sentences to terms of imprisonment and reduced the custodial sentences (although he did not withdraw the capital charges against Abiola). At the same time he announced the approval of the new Constitution (which was due to be formally endorsed in 1998) and the adoption of a three-year programme for transition to civilian rule, whereby a new President was to be inaugurated on 1 October 1998, following elections at local, state and national level.

At the end of October 1995 Saro-Wiwa and a further eight Ogoni activists were sentenced to death by the Special Military Tribunal in Port Harcourt, having been convicted of involvement in the murder of the four Ogoni leaders in May 1994; six defendants were acquitted. Although the defendants were not implicated directly in the incident, the nine convictions were based on the premise that the MOSOP activists had effectively incited the killings. An international campaign against the convictions and numerous appeals for clemency ensued. However, on 10 November the nine convicted Ogonis were executed, prompting immediate condemnation by the international community. Nigeria was suspended from the Commonwealth, and threatened with expulsion if the Government failed to restore democracy within a period of two years. Later that month the EU reaffirmed its commitment to existing sanctions that had been imposed in 1993 (notably an embargo on the export of armaments and military equipment to Nigeria), and extended visa restrictions to civilian members of the administration. The Governments of the USA, South Africa and the EU member nations recalled their diplomatic representatives from Nigeria in protest at the executions. The Nigerian Government condemned the imposition of sanctions and, in turn, withdrew its diplomatic representatives from the USA, South Africa and the EU member countries.

In June 1996 Nigerian officials met the Commonwealth Ministerial Action Group (CMAG) in an attempt to avert the Commonwealth's threatened imposition of sanctions against Nigeria. It was finally agreed that the Commonwealth would suspend the adoption of sanctions, but that the situation would subsequently be reviewed. In September CMAG agreed that the Commonwealth delegation would visit Nigeria, despite conditions imposed by the military authorities, which insisted that it would not be permitted access to opposition activists or political prisoners.

In June 1996 legislation governing the formation of political parties was promulgated. Five of 15 political organizations that applied for registration were granted legal status in September. NADECO condemned the disqualification of the remaining 10 parties, which were subsequently dissolved by decree; it was widely believed that the associations that had been granted registration were largely sympathetic towards the military administration. In October Abacha announced the creation of a further six states, increasing the total size of the federation to 36 states.

In early 1997 escalating tension between the Ijaw and Itsekiri ethnic groups in the town of Warri, in south-western Nigeria, severely disrupted operations in the region of the Niger Delta by the Shell Petroleum Development Co of Nigeria. In March Ijaw protesters seized Shell installations and took about 100 employees hostage, in an attempt to force the Government to accede to their demands. In May the authorities established a commission of inquiry to investigate the cause of the unrest and submit recommendations for restoring order in the region. Persistent attacks by Ijaw activists against petroleum installations resulted in the imposition of a state of emergency at the end of December 1998.

Meanwhile, at a summit meeting of the Commonwealth Heads of Government, which took place in Edinburgh, United Kingdom, in October 1997, Nigeria's suspension from the organization was extended for an additional year; it was further indicated that the country would be expelled from the Commonwealth if Abacha reneged on his pledge to restore democratic rule by 1 October 1998. The Government had announced a new electoral timetable and it was maintained that the new elected organs of government would be installed by 1 October 1998. Elections to the state legislatures, which were contested by the five registered parties, took place on 6 December 1997; the United Nigeria Congress Party (UNCP) won 637 of the 970 contested seats, securing a majority in 29 of the 36 State Assemblies. The other four parties subsequently attributed the success of the UNCP to malpractice, and threatened to withdraw from the remainder of the electoral process. In mid-December Abacha appointed a predominantly new FEC.

On 8 June 1998 Abacha died unexpectedly from heart failure. The PRC designated the Chief of Defence Staff, Maj.-Gen. Abdulsalami Abubakar, as Abacha's successor, and on 9 June he was inaugurated as Head of State (having been promoted to the rank of General). Abubakar pledged to continue the Abacha Government's scheduled transition to civilian rule. In mid-June Abubakar ordered the release of about 26 political prisoners, including Obasanjo (ostensibly on grounds of ill health). In July, following discussions with UN officials, the authorities agreed to release Abiola from detention. Shortly after his release, however, Abiola collapsed and subsequently died. Violent rioting ensued, amid widespread speculation that the authorities were responsible for Abiola's death. Although an autopsy confirmed that he had died of heart failure, it was indicated that his period in detention had contributed to his poor health. Later in July Abubakar announced that the transition to civilian rule would be completed on 29 May 1999 (rather than 1 October 1998). The Government annulled the results of the elections that had previously been conducted, and dissolved the five authorized political parties. In August a new, 31-member FEC, which included a number of civilians, was appointed to remain in office pending the formal transition to civilian rule; an Independent National Electoral Commission (INEC) was also established. Later that month the INEC announced that local government elections would take place on 5 December 1998 and state legislative elections on 9 January 1999, followed by elections to a bicameral national legislature on 20 February and a presidential election on 27 February. On 7 September 1998 the Government published the draft Constitution that had been submitted by the NCC in June 1995.

Some 25 new political organizations submitted applications for registration to the INEC. The commission provisionally approved nine political associations, notably the People's Democratic Party (PDP), which principally comprised former opponents of the Abacha administration. In October 1998 CMAG recommended that Commonwealth member states end sanctions against Nigeria, in preparation for the country's readmission to the Commonwealth. At the end of that month, in response to the democratization measures undertaken by the Government, the EU ended a number of sanctions against Nigeria (while maintaining the embargo on the export of armaments).

In January 1999 several prominent members of former administrations announced that they intended to seek nomination to contest the forthcoming presidential election. In early February the All Nigeria People's Party (ANPP) and the Alliance for Democracy (AD), which, despite the stated opposition of the INEC, had established an electoral alliance, nominated a joint candidate, Samuel Oluyemisi Falae (a former Minister of Finance in the Babangida administration). Later that month Obasanjo (who had joined the PDP in October 1998) was elected as the presidential candidate of that party. At the elections to the bicameral legislature, which took place on 20 February, the PDP secured 215 seats in the 360-member House of Representatives and 66 seats in the 109-member Senate. (Voting in the Niger Delta region was postponed, owing to continued unrest, and a further by-election for the vacant seat to the National Assembly took place in March.)

Obasanjo becomes President

On 27 February 1999 Obasanjo was elected to the presidency with 62.8% of votes cast. The Constitution was promulgated on 5 May and Obasanjo was formally inaugurated as President on 29 May; on the same day Nigeria was readmitted as a full member of the Commonwealth. On 3 June the inaugural session of the National Assembly took place. Obasanjo nominated a new Cabinet, principally comprising members of the PDP, which was approved by the Senate later that month. He also undertook a reorganization of the armed forces, removing more than 150 military officers who had served under the Abacha Government.

The Christian Association of Nigeria threatened to initiate a legal challenge to the introduction of Islamic *Shari'a* law, announced in Kano and Zamfara States in December 1999 and January 2000, respectively, on the grounds that it contravened the principle of secularity enshrined in the Constitution. In February 2000 a demonstration by Christians in the northern town of Kaduna in protest at the proposed imposition of *Shari'a* in Kaduna State precipitated violent hostilities between Muslims and Christians, in which more than 300 people were killed; government troops eventually suppressed the unrest. However, more than 50 people were killed in further clashes between Christians and Muslims in the south-eastern towns of Aba and Umuahia, which ensued in reprisal for the violence in the north. At an emergency meeting at the end of February, chaired by Obasanjo, the Governors of the 18 northern states agreed, in the interests of peace, to withdraw the new legislation introducing *Shari'a* law, and to revert to the provisions for *Shari'a* in the existing penal code, in accordance with the federal Constitution. However, the Governors of a number of the states subsequently announced that they would not comply with the federal government order, but would proceed with the implementation of *Shari'a* law. In March religious rioting in Niger State (where the adoption of the *Shari'a* law had been declared) was reported. In May some 150 people were killed in further clashes between Christians and Muslims in Kaduna; government troops were again deployed in the town to restore order.

In August 2000 *Shari'a* law was formally adopted in the northern states of Katsina, Jigawa and Yobe (to enter into effect later that year). In September the Governor of Borno State also announced the adoption of *Shari'a*. Although the Governors of most of these states had declared that Christians would be exempt from the provisions of *Shari'a*, social segregation of men and women and the application of punishments stipulated under Islamic law had been widely implemented in Zamfara and Kano States. In view of the violence in Kaduna State, the Governor announced that the form of *Shari'a* to be introduced in the state was to be modified to allow Islamic courts to exist in conjunction with special courts upholding secular laws.

In June 2001 religious and ethnic unrest in northern and central Nigeria intensified; some 1,000 people were killed in fighting between Christians and Muslims in Bauchi (which had become the 10th northern state to adopt *Shari'a* law). In early 2002 the death sentence imposed on a woman in northern Sokoto State, who had been convicted in October 2001 under *Shari'a* law on charges of adultery, attracted increasing international attention. Following pressure from the international community, in March the Minister of Justice urged the 12 State Governors who had adopted *Shari'a* law to discontinue its strict enforcement, on the grounds that it contravened the Constitution for reasons of discrimination (applying only to Muslims). A Court of Appeal subsequently overturned the sentence against the convicted woman, ruling that there was insufficient evidence to justify the death penalty. However, the Governors of several northern states insisted that they would continue to implement *Shari'a*.

In June 2002 the INEC announced that, of 24 political parties that had applied for official registration, only three had been recognized (increasing the total number of legal associations to six). Following a long-standing dispute between Obasanjo and the Senate over control of public finances, in August the House of Representatives adopted a resolution demanding that Obasanjo resign from office or face impeachment, on charges of mismanagement and abuse of power. Obasanjo refused to comply with the resolution, and at the end of that month the PDP voted in favour of drafting a list of charges against the President. In December the INEC granted registration to a further 24 political associations, after the Supreme Court upheld an appeal by five opposition parties against their exclusion, and ordered less restrictive regulations for legalization. Later that month the Commission announced that legislative elections were to be conducted on 12 April 2003, followed by a presidential election on 19 April and elections to regional Houses of Assembly on 3 May. In January Obasanjo was formally elected as the presidential candidate of the PDP.

Obasanjo's second term
Incidences of violence and malpractice were reported during the federal legislative elections on 12 April 2003. The PDP secured an overwhelming majority in both legislative chambers (213 seats in the House of Representatives and 73 in the Senate), while the ANPP was the only other party to win significant

representation (95 seats in the House of Representatives and 28 in the Senate). At the presidential election on 19 April, Obasanjo was elected for a second term by 61.9% of the valid votes cast, while Maj.-Gen. Muhammadu Buhari received 32.2% of votes. Opposition leaders, notably Buhari, contested the results, claiming that widespread electoral malpractice had been perpetrated, and indicated that violent protests might ensue. International monitors, although generally satisfied with the organization of the elections, declared that irregularities had taken place, particularly in the region of the Niger Delta. At gubernatorial elections, which also took place on 19 April, the PDP gained eight state governorships from the ANPP and AD, losing only one (that of Kano). Later that month Obasanjo criticized a statement by EU monitors, who claimed that they had obtained evidence of electoral malpractice perpetrated in 13 states. Meanwhile, at the end of April four offshore petroleum rigs, operated by a US enterprise, Transocean, in the Niger Delta were seized by protesting Nigerian employees, who took hostage 97 foreign national workers. Military naval forces were dispatched to the region and all hostages were airlifted from the rigs.

Obasanjo officially dissolved the Federal Government on 21 May 2003. He was sworn in on 29 May (after a legal challenge against his inauguration by Buhari was rejected by the federal Court of Appeal), and in early June began to nominate ministers to his new administration. In mid-July Obasanjo finally inaugurated the new, 40-member Federal Government, which included the hitherto Vice-President of the World Bank, Dr Ngozi Okonjo-Iweala, as the Minister of Finance and the Economy.

In early April 2004 the Government announced that some 20 army officials had been arrested, following the discovery of a conspiracy to seize power, believed to have been instigated by a former head of security in the Abacha administration, Maj. Hama al-Mustapha. (In October three senior military officers, including al-Mustapha, were charged with planning to overthrow the Government with an attack on the presidential helicopter.) Later in April reports emerged of severe clashes between Christian and Muslim tribes in farming villages on the border of Plateau State, reportedly as a result of land ownership disputes; by early May some 650 people, mainly Muslims, had been killed in the fighting. Muslims subsequently rioted in Kano in reprisal, resulting in the deaths of an estimated 600 Christians. Later in May Obasanjo dispatched security forces to restore order and imposed a state of emergency in Plateau State (which was ended in November).

In September 2004 renewed hostilities between the Ijaw and Itsekiri in the Niger Delta prompted further concern, particularly after an Ijaw militia, the Niger Delta People's Volunteer Force (NDPVF), threatened a campaign to disrupt petroleum supplies by attacking installations. Following a peace accord between the Government and the activists, reached in October, fighting in the Niger Delta region declined significantly; however, Ijaw militia failed to disarm by the scheduled date at the end of December. In September 2005 tension again increased in the region, following the arrest of the leader of the NDPVF, Mujahid Dokubo-Asari, who had threatened to continue hostilities unless his demands that the Ijaw people of the region be granted self-determination were met. In October Dokubo-Asari was officially charged with treason before the Abuja Federal High Court. Later that month the leader of the Movement for the Actualization of the Sovereign State of Biafra (MASSOB), Chief Ralph Uwazurike, was arrested and subsequently charged with treason (on the grounds that he had attempted to overthrow the Federal Government). Protests by members of MASSOB against the arrest of their leader culminated in clashes, in which some 20 people were killed.

In January 2006 four foreign nationals employed by companies subcontracted by the Shell Petroleum Development Co were seized by militants in Bayelsa State; a hitherto unknown organization, the Movement for the Emancipation of the Niger Delta (MEND), claimed responsibility for the kidnappings. At the end of January MEND announced the release of the hostages on humanitarian grounds, but maintained that it would continue attacks in the Niger Delta region and seized a further nine foreign nationals employed by a subcontracted US enterprise, Willbros. Six of the hostages were released one week later, while the remaining three (two US and one British national) were released in late March. Also in February a High Court in Port Harcourt ruled that the Shell Petroleum Development Co pay US $1,500m. in compensation to the Ijaw population in the Niger Delta for environmental damage, in compliance with a decision by the National Assembly in 2000. The situation worsened during mid-2006 and in June five Nigerian soldiers were killed in a raid by MEND on a petroleum installation. In August Obasanjo ordered the establishment of a joint operation between the armed forces and the police to patrol the Niger Delta region.

The 2007 elections

In early 2006 the Nigerian Constitutional Committee conducted a series of public debates on proposed amendments to the Constitution, which would allow Obasanjo to seek a third term in office. In May, however, the National Assembly rejected the proposals, thus preventing Obasanjo from contesting the 2007 presidential election. In the months prior to the presidential and legislative elections, scheduled to be held on 14 and 21 April 2007, respectively, several government reorganizations were effected. In June 2006 Obasanjo reassigned Okonjo-Iweala to the foreign affairs portfolio, amid concerns over the durability of the Government's financial management and economic reforms. However, Okonjo-Iweala resigned from the new position in August, having been dismissed from her role as head of the economic reform team; Prof. Joy Ogwu replaced her at the Ministry of Foreign Affairs. Further changes to the Government were carried out in mid-January 2007, when almost one-third of the ministries were dissolved or merged to simplify the administration's structure.

With Obasanjo prohibited from contesting the presidential election, Abubakar emerged as the primary presidential candidate. However, his relationship with the President had become increasingly strained and Obasanjo strongly opposed Abubakar's candidacy. In September 2006 Obasanjo submitted a report to the Senate containing allegations of fraudulent activity involving Abubakar, who was subsequently charged by the Economic and Financial Crimes Commission (EFCC). As Vice-President, Abubakar held immunity against prosecution unless impeached. Later in September he was suspended from the PDP for three months; although he retained his position as Vice-President, the suspension prevented him from seeking nomination from the PDP to stand as its presidential candidate. Abubakar continually denied the allegations against him, and it subsequently emerged that he would represent the Action Congress of Nigeria (ACN), a new party formed by the merger of several minor political parties, in the presidential election. Abubakar was disqualified from contesting the election by the INEC in mid-March 2007, owing to his indictment for corruption, but following a number of legal challenges, his candidature was confirmed by a Supreme Court ruling on 16 April.

Gubernatorial and state assembly elections took place on 14 April 2007: the PDP secured control of 28 states and the ANPP of five. Ensuing outbreaks of violence marred the conduct of the presidential election, which was held concurrently with the elections to the National Assembly, as scheduled, on 21 April. According to official results, the PDP candidate, Alhaji Umaru Musa Yar'Adua (the younger brother of the late Maj.-Gen. (retd) Shehu Musa Yar'Adua, former Vice-President in Obasanjo's military Government during the 1960s), secured a decisive victory, receiving about 70.0% of the votes cast. Buhari, who contested the election as the candidate of the ANPP, was second placed with 18.7% of the ballots, while Abubakar secured 7.3%. In the legislative elections, the PDP increased its majority in both the House of Representatives and the Senate, winning 263 seats and 87 seats, respectively, while the ANPP secured 63 seats in the lower house and 14 seats in the upper chamber. Despite claims by the INEC that the elections had been conducted successfully, international observers cast doubt on the credibility of the polls as reports emerged that no voting took place in some states due to delays in the distribution of ballot papers. Opposition parties rejected the outcome of the presidential election, and Buhari and Abubakar instigated legal proceedings to have the results of the ballot annulled. Yar'Adua was sworn in as President on 29 May. In June the House of Representatives for the first time elected a woman, Patricia Etteh, as Speaker. (However, following allegations regarding the misappropriation of funds, Etteh resigned in November, and was replaced by Dimeji Bankole.) President Yar'Adua named a new Cabinet in Augus; four more ministers were appointed in October. Yar'Adua assumed responsibility for the petroleum resources portfolio, as Obasanjo had before him, and pledged to continue with reforms to the energy sector that had been commenced under the previous administration.

At a final hearing in Abuja in February 2008 five judges dismissed the case brought by Buhari and Abubakar, citing insufficient grounds for overruling the result of the presidential election. The two defeated candidates announced their intention to appeal against the decision in the Supreme Court. By this time the election of eight State Governors had been nullified by the Court of Appeal, following challenges by opposition candidates, and in April the election of a further two Governors was also ruled invalid; polls were subsequently repeated in those states.

The Yar'Adua presidency

In August 2008 Yar'Adua announced a revision of the command structure of the armed forces, replacing the Chief of Defence Staff and heads of services. In September Yar'Adua approved the restructuring of several government departments, including the creation of a new Ministry of Niger Delta Affairs and the division of the Ministry of Energy into two separate ministries, the Ministry of Power and the Ministry of Petroleum Resources. He also dismissed the Secretary to the Government of the Federation, Baba Gana Kingibe, following suggestions in the media that he planned to challenge for the presidency. A total of eight ministers and 12 ministers of state were removed from the Cabinet in November. In the following month Yar'Adua named his new Government, in which only three members of the outgoing administration retained their positions. The new Cabinet featured 19 new appointees, most notably, Dr Rilwanu Lukman (a former Secretary-General of the Organization of the Petroleum Exporting Countries, see p. 418), who was appointed Minister of Petroleum Resources. Meanwhile, in late November there was significant unrest in the Plateau State town of Jos, where clashes between Christian and Muslim groups resulted in the deaths of some 400 people. The rioting followed a dispute over local elections in mid-November, at which the PDP had defeated the largely Muslim-supported ANPP.

Meanwhile, as part of President Yar'Adua's pledge that his administration would give special priority to the continued unrest in the Niger Delta, militia leader Dokubo-Asari, who had been in detention since October 2005, was released on bail in June 2007. However, in August a cease-fire negotiated by the Nigerian Government and MEND in May broke down and further abductions of petroleum workers and disruptions to petroleum production were reported during late 2007. In February 2008 MEND leader Henry Okah and another senior member of the movement, Edward Atatah, were extradited from Angola, where they had been arrested in September 2007 on weapons charges; in March 2008 treason charges were filed against both men. MEND claimed responsibility for a number of attacks on oil installations and pipelines owned by Royal Dutch Shell in April and May, which was forced to halt production. In September the Nigerian military carried out a large-scale bombardment of a MEND position in Rivers State, prompting the declaration of an 'oil war' by the rebels: after a week of intensified attacks on oil installations, MEND declared a cease-fire. However, there was a resumption of hostilities in early 2009, after rebels affiliated to MEND launched an assault on an oil platform and kidnapped six crew members. On 31 January MEND officially ended its cease-fire in response to a military offensive against one of its bases; attacks on oil and gas installations continued, and there was an increase in the number of foreign nationals and oil workers being kidnapped in the region, leading to a two-day strike by workers at the French company Total. In early June settlement was reached on a protracted legal case brought against Royal Dutch Shell in the USA by relatives of Ken Saro-Wiwa and other Ogoni leaders executed in 1995, who accused the corporation of complicity in human rights atrocities committed against the Ogoni people of the Niger Delta in the 1990s, including the executions; Royal Dutch Shell admitted no accountability but agreed to pay US $15.5m. to establish a trust fund for the Ogoni people shortly before the trial was due to start. Later in June 2009 Yar'Adua proposed a 60-day period of amnesty for all members of MEND, including its leaders, to allow a process of disarmament, which would begin in early August. In July Okah was released from prison, after accepting the presidential offer of amnesty.

In July 2009 police in Bauchi State arrested several suspected members of a militant Islamist group opposed to Western education and culture, known as Boko Haram, prompting retaliatory attacks against police stations by its followers in Bauchi and other northern states. Government forces were deployed in the capital of Borno State, Maiduguri, believed to be the base of Boko Haram, and launched an offensive against the compound of the movement's leader, Ustaz Mohammed Yusuf, and a nearby mosque. It was reported that Yusuf and some 300 militants had escaped. However, at the end of July he was captured by security forces and killed in custody; according to the police statement

Yusuf's death occurred while he was trying to escape. The authorities estimated that a total of 700 people had been killed during the clashes.

After the period of amnesty for insurgents entered into effect in early August 2009, it was reported that other prominent leaders of MEND had accepted a government pardon by early October and that large numbers of rebels had surrendered their armaments. Later that month Yar'Adua approved a plan to allocate 10% of revenue from Nigeria's oil and gas ventures to the population of the Niger Delta, in an effort to satisfy the long-standing demands of the insurgents. Although it was reported that MEND had initially responded favourably to the proposal, at the end of January 2010 the movement announced an end to its cease-fire, on the grounds that the Government had failed to fulfil pledges made in exchange for disarmament.

Goodluck Jonathan becomes President

The emergency hospitalization of President Yar'Adua in Saudi Arabia in late November 2009 prompted increasing demands for his resignation. In early December 56 politicians, including prominent PDP members, issued a statement urging Yar'Adua to transfer power to Vice-President Dr Goodluck Ebele Jonathan. However, the Government agreed unanimously that there were no grounds upon which to seek the resignation of Yar'Adua, who resisted pressure to cede power. In January 2010 the Federal High Court, rejecting an appeal by the Nigerian Bar Association, ruled that Yar'Adua was not obliged under the Constitution to transfer power or to inform the legislature of his absence; the Government issued a statement that he remained capable of governing. However, Yar'Adua's continued medical treatment for a heart condition in Saudi Arabia created an impasse regarding the adoption of the 2010 budget and attracted widespread criticism, including from within factions of the PDP, with opposition rallies and demands for the President's impeach-ment. In early February Yar'Adua announced his decision to transfer power to Jonathan. On 10 February Jonathan became Acting President and Commander-in-Chief of the Armed Forces, after both legislative chambers adopted motions allowing him to assume interim executive powers while Yar'Adua was unfit for office. Jonathan immediately reorganized the Government, and pledged to continue the amnesty process for insurgents in the Niger Delta. Yar'Adua unexpectedly returned to Nigeria in late February, but failed to appear in public.

Meanwhile, in January 2010 it was reported that some 400 people had been killed in further clashes between Muslim and Christian groups in Jos; in early March it was reported that about 500 members of the Christian Berom community had been killed by Muslim Hausa-Fulani herders near Jos, apparently in reprisal for the violence in January. The recurrent hostilities were widely attributed to long-standing divisions between mainly Christian indigenous ethnic groups and predominantly Muslim ethnic groups, who were classified as settlers, over land and resources in the region. In mid-March MEND claimed responsibility for two bomb explosions, in which four people were killed, at a government building on the occasion of an amnesty conference at Warri; the movement claimed that these had been intended as an attack against the Governor of Delta State in retaliation for his declaration in the press that the movement was a 'media creation'.

In early March 2010 Jonathan removed the National Security Adviser, a close associate of Yar'Adua, replacing him with Aliyu Gusau. On 17 March Jonathan dissolved the Cabinet. A new Government (which included 13 members of the previous administration) was installed on 6 April. Olusegun Olutoyin Aganga, hitherto a senior executive at an investment bank in the United Kingdom, became the new Minister of Finance and was also appointed Chairman of a new National Economic Team, which was entasked with effecting economic recovery. On 5 May the death of Yar'Adua was announced; on the following day Jonathan was sworn in as Head of State. Jonathan's nomination of the Governor of Kaduna State, Namadi Sambo, as his Vice-President was confirmed by the House of Representatives and the Senate on 18 May.

On 1 October 2010 12 people were killed and 17 others injured, when two car bombs exploded in Abuja during a celebration marking the 50th anniversary of Nigeria's independence; MEND declared responsibility for the bomb attacks. Okah was again detained in Johannesburg, South Africa, and charged with engaging in terrorist activity; several other suspects, including Okah's son and brother, were also arrested. (In March 2013 Okah was sentenced to 27 years' imprisonment by a South African court on 13 charges in connection with the bomb attacks.) Later

in October 2010 the Government deployed some 400 armed police officers and troops in the north-eastern town of Maiduguri, following a series of violent incidents that were attributed to Boko Haram, including the killings of five police officers and six civilians. In early November seven foreign nationals (including two US citizens) were seized by MEND militia from the Okoro oilfield, in the Niger Delta. After the Nigerian military launched a major offensive against MEND bases in the region, the seven foreign nationals, together with 12 Nigerian hostages, were released by the rebels later that month; however, MEND issued a statement declaring its intention to continue its insurgent campaign. In May 2011 Royal Dutch Shell lost a legal appeal against a court ruling that the corporation pay rent to the local community of the Niger Delta for the use of land where its major oil terminal was located.

The 2011 presidential and legislative elections

In November 2010 the INEC announced that the presidential election, which had been scheduled for January 2011, had been postponed until 9 April to allow more time for preparation; it was confirmed that the legislative elections would be conducted on 2 April, and the gubernatorial and state legislative elections on 16 April. Reports of violent incidents increased during December 2010; these included further clashes at the end of the month between Muslims and Christians in Jos, in which some 80 people were killed. On 14 January 2011 Jonathan was elected as the PDP candidate for the forthcoming presidential election, secur-ing 2,736 votes, while his closest contender, Abubakar, received 805 votes. The nomination of Jonathan (a southern Christian) prompted a number of protests against senior PDP officials in northern cities (the PDP having previously agreed to adopt election candidates alternately from the north and the south of the country). In the same month Buhari was selected as the presidential candidate of the Congress for Progressive Change (CPC), which had been established by former members of the ANPP in 2009 and which he had joined in March 2010. In February 2011 at least 11 people were killed in a stampede at an election campaign rally for Jonathan at a sports stadium in Port Harcourt, when a police officer fired a gun to disperse supporters. On 22 February the House of Representatives approved legislation increasing the powers of the authorities with regard to counter-terrorism; notably, judges were hence-forth permitted to order the detention of suspects for up to 30 days without charge. In March three people were killed in a bomb attack staged against a PDP election rally in Abuja, while numerous other incidents included an explosion at INEC offices in the town of Suleja, near the capital, in which eight people were killed.

In early April 2011 the INEC rescheduled all the forthcoming elections for several days later, owing to organizational difficul-ties, including the delivery of ballot papers. The legislative elections were finally conducted on 9 April: partial results indi-cated a significant loss in the parliamentary strength of the PDP, which obtained 123 of the 234 seats declared in the House of Representatives, while the ACN took 47 seats, the CPC 30 seats and the ANPP 25 seats; the PDP received 45 and the ACN 13 of the 74 seats declared in the elections to the Senate. (The INEC had announced that polls in 15 senatorial districts and 48 federal constituencies were to be postponed further, until 26 April.) The presidential election, which was contested by 19 candidates, took place on 16 April: according to provisional results, Jonathan secured a decisive majority of 58.9% of votes cast, while Buhari of the CPC was second placed, with about 32% of the votes (mainly receiving support in northern regions). Voter turn-out of 58.7% was recorded. International election observers, including an EU mission, generally declared that the conduct of the polls dem-onstrated a significant improvement compared with those of 2007. On 18 April 2011 the INEC announced that Jonathan had won the presidential election; the outcome prompted rioting in the northern regions, particularly in the towns of Kano and Kaduna, where protesters attacked the residences of Jonathan's supporters. Buhari, claiming that widespread electoral irregu-larities, particularly in the south of the country, had been observed, declared that the CPC would submit a legal challenge to the results and appealed for an end to the disturbances. (Meanwhile, Jonathan replaced the Minister of the Interior.) However, increasing violence directed against Christians in the north, which had prompted reprisal attacks against Muslims, had by late April resulted in the deaths of more than 500 people. On 25 April three people were killed in four bomb attacks in Maiduguri, which were attributed to Boko Haram. Together with the remaining federal legislative polls, the gubernatorial and state assembly elections proceeded in 24 of the 26 contested states on 26 April (owing to previously repeated polls in 10 states, after challenges to the April 2007 election results, the mandate of 10 Governors had not expired); despite the explosion of further bombs in Maiduguri, the elections were considered to have taken place relatively peacefully. On 28 April 2011 the final gubernatorial and state assembly elections took place in Kano and Bauchi States, where voting had been delayed for two days as a result of the unrest. According to official results, PDP candidates were elected Governors in 18 states, the ACN in three and the ANPP in three; consequently the PDP controlled 23 of the 36 states overall, compared with 27 previously. On 8 May the CPC submitted an appeal to a special tribunal against the election of Jonathan, accusing INEC and PDP officials of perpetrating electoral malpractice in a number of regions. Nevertheless, Jonathan was inaugurated as President on 29 May, when a series of bomb explosions in Abuja and four northern cities were also staged. Boko Haram claimed responsibility for three bomb attacks in the following month, including Nigeria's first suicide bombing at the national police headquarters in Abuja on 16 June. A new Government was formed in July; notably, Ngozi Okonjo-Iweala, hitherto Managing Director of the World Bank, and who had served in the Obasanjo administration, was appointed Minister of Finance. At the beginning of November the tribunal dismissed the CPC challenge to Jonathan's election, and ruled that the conduct of the election had been in accordance with democratic standards.

Escalation in Boko Haram operations

On 26 August 2011 24 people were killed and some 80 injured in a suicide bomb attack against the UN headquarters in Abuja. Boko Haram claimed responsibility for the attack (in addition to others against a police station and two banks in the north-eastern town of Gombi on the previous day), and demanded the release of all members of the movement in detention as a precondition to negotiations with the authorities. (It was reported that two prominent members of Boko Haram had been arrested earlier in August.) In October a cameraman working for the state-controlled television network and a parliamentary deputy were shot dead in Maiduguri, in separate incidents that were attributed to Boko Haram. In the same month three former State Governors were arrested, followed an investigation into allegations that they had abused their office in the award of public contracts and embezzlement of funds. Meanwhile, Boko Haram operations increased, particularly in Yobe State: in November some 65 people were reported to have been killed in a number of attacks against churches and mosques, as well as at the Yobe state police headquarters, in the town of Damaturu by Boko Haram members, who subsequently clashed with security forces; attacks were also staged in the nearby town of Potiskum. The US Administration expressed concern at the international threat presented by Boko Haram, which was believed to have links with the al-Qa'ida network.

In late December 2011 further violence erupted in Damaturu, after attacks by Boko Haram were followed by sustained fighting between its members and security forces, killing at least 24 and prompting the displacement of several thousand civilians. On 25 December Boko Haram staged numerous attacks at churches during Christmas Day services in several towns, notably including a suicide bomb attack against a church in Madalla, Niger State, in which 36 people were killed. The attacks attracted particular international condemnation and were denounced by Nigerian Muslim leaders. On 31 December Jonathan declared a state of emergency in Borno, Yobe, Niger and Plateau States, closed the country's borders with Chad and Niger, and also ordered the establishment of a special counter-terrorism unit within the armed forces. In January 2012 a number of co-ordinated bomb and armed attacks were staged against security service headquarters and police stations in the town of Kano, killing more than 185 people. In the same month government troops were deployed in Abuja and Lagos to suppress popular protests against the removal of a fuel subsidy; some 15 people were reported to have been killed. The protests and national strike action ended after Jonathan agreed partially to reinstate the subsidy. On 27 January the Supreme Court ordered the resignation of five PDP State Governors who had won repeated polls in 2008, ruling that their tenures had expired. (Three of the incumbent Governors were subsequently returned to office, while new PDP candidates were elected in the two other states.) In March two foreign hostages (one British and one Italian), who had been kidnapped in May 2011 by an Islamist militant group, were killed during a failed rescue attempt by Nigerian and British security forces in Sokoto; Boko Haram was widely believed to be responsible for the incident.

In a video released on the internet in early April 2012, the spiritual leader of Boko Haram, Imam Muhammad Abubakar Shekau (who had succeeded Yusuf), declared his intention to bring about the downfall of Jonathan's Government. Numerous attacks attributed to Boko Haram during that month included co-ordinated suicide bombings at the offices of *This Day* newspaper in Abuja and Kaduna, in which five people were killed, gun attacks against churches in Maiduguri and Kano, in which a total of 19 people died, and an attack at Bayero University (where Christians were holding a service) in Kano, which resulted in some 15 deaths. A further video released by Boko Haram indicated that the bombings of the offices of *This Day* were in retaliation for the newspaper's publication, in 2002, of an article concerning the Prophet Muhammad that many Muslims had considered blasphemous. In early May the suspected leader of the attack at Bayero University was killed in an operation by security forces in Kano. Later that month some 56 people were killed in an attack at a cattle market in Potiskum.

Meanwhile, a parliamentary report that was issued in April 2012 following the January fuel subsidy protests stated that senior officials of the state-owned Nigeria National Petroleum Corporation and Petroleum Products Pricing and Regulatory Agency were responsible for the mismanagement and embezzlement of some US $6,800m. during 2009–11, and urged the initiation of criminal proceedings against them. (In February 2013 a parliamentary deputy was charged with receiving a bribe in connection with the investigation.) Boko Haram staged further assaults against Christian targets in June 2012, amongst them three co-ordinated attacks on churches in the town of Zaira, in Kaduna State, in which some 19 people died; more than 50 Muslims in the city of Kaduna were reported to have been killed in reprisals by Christian youths. Later in June President Jonathan removed the Minister of Defence, Bello Mohammed, and the national security adviser. (Jonathan subsequently assumed control of the defence portfolio.) In September Abubakar Shekau confirmed that Boko Haram's public spokesman, Anwal Kontagora (also known as Abu Qaqa), had been captured by security forces, but denied governments claims that the militant group had sought dialogue with the authorities. Meanwhile, small numbers of Boko Haram militants were killed in further clashes with security forces. In October at least eight people died and more than 100 others were injured in a suicide bomb attack against a church in Kaduna city, which prompted further reprisal killings by Christians. (According to a report by international pressure group Human Rights Watch, some 815 people were killed in a total of 275 militant attacks between January and October.)

In December 2012 the mother of the Minister of Finance was abducted in Delta State (she was released several days later), while four nationals of the Republic of Korea and a Nigerian citizen were briefly held hostage in Bayelsa State. In the same month a newly emerged Islamist militant group affiliated to al-Qa'ida, known as Ansaru, announced that it had kidnapped a French employee of an energy company in Katsina State, in protest at a ban on the Islamic veil in France and at French military action against Islamist insurgents in Mali. Despite Boko Haram's public declaration of a cease-fire on 28 January 2013, further militant attacks were staged against police stations and banks in Kaduna and Kano States at the end of that month. In February members of the Ansaru group seized seven foreign employees (one British, one Italian, one Greek and four Lebanese nationals) in an attack on Lebanese construction company Setraco in Bauchi State; Ansaru announced in early March that the seven hostages had been killed. A French family of seven, kidnapped in Cameroon in late February, was reported to be being held in Nigeria by a Boko Haram group, which demanded the release of Boko Haram members detained by the Nigerian authorities.

Recent developments: proposed amnesty for Boko Haram

In early February 2013 Jonathan (who retained the defence portfolio) nominated Chinedu Osita Nebo as Minister of Power and Kabiru Tanimu Turaki as Minister of Special Duties; the appointments were subsequently confirmed by the Senate. In the same month it was announced that the ACN, the ANPP, the All Progressives Grand Alliance and the CPC had merged to form a new opposition association, the All Progressive Congress, in an effort to oust the PDP from government in the next elections. In

March some 25 people were killed in five bomb attacks attributed to Boko Haram at a bus station in a predominantly Christian area of Kano. Following consultations with political and religious leaders in the north, in early April President Jonathan, who had previously expressed reluctance, agreed to the proposal that Boko Haram militants be granted a government amnesty. It was reported shortly afterwards that Abubakar Shekau had rejected the suggested amnesty, on the grounds that the group's members had committed no wrongdoing. Later in April, however, Jonathan established a high-level committee, which was to develop a framework for granting an amnesty to Boko Haram members and for disarmament of the movement. In early May at least 55 people were killed in a series of co-ordinated attacks on a police station, military barracks and government buildings in Bama in Borno State. Later that month Jonathan declared a state of emergency in Borno State, as well as in Adamawa and Yobe States, and approved increased troop deployments to those areas.

Foreign Affairs

Nigeria has adopted a leading role in African affairs and is a prominent member of the Economic Community of West African States (ECOWAS, see p. 268) and other regional organizations. The Nigerian Government has contributed a significant number of troops to the ECOWAS Monitoring Group (ECOMOG), which was deployed in Liberia from August 1990 in response to the conflict between government forces and rebels in that country. In 1993 Nigerian troops were dispatched to Sierra Leone, in response to a formal request by the Sierra Leonean Government for military assistance to repulse attacks by rebels in Liberia. Following the completion of the transition to civilian rule in Nigeria in May 1999, a phased withdrawal of Nigerian troops from Sierra Leone commenced. By the end of April 2000 all Nigerian troops belonging to ECOMOG had left Sierra Leone; however, Nigeria continued to contribute troops to the UN Mission in Sierra Leone (UNAMSIL). In September an official visit to Nigeria by the US President, Bill Clinton, the first by a US Head of State since 1978, provided for a number of new trade and development initiatives. After further full-scale conflict in Liberia in mid-2003, the Liberian President, Charles Taylor, finally accepted an offer of asylum from Obasanjo, following pressure from the international community, and took up residence in Calabar, in south-eastern Nigeria, in early August. Some 1,500 Nigerian troops, which were deployed in the country, under an ECOWAS mandate, at the end of August, were incorporated into the replacement contingent, the UN Mission in Liberia (UNMIL, see p. 90), on 1 October. In October the Nigerian Government strongly protested at the US authorities' approval of the offer of a reward of some US $2m. for the arrest of Taylor (who had been indicted by the Special Court established in Sierra Leone to try war crime suspects). In March 2006 Nigeria announced that it had received a formal request from the new Liberian Government to extradite Taylor to the Special Court. Obasanjo agreed to return him to the Liberian authorities, but failed to comply with demands by the Chief Prosecutor of the Special Court and the USA to take him into custody. Taylor fled from his residence in Calabar, but was apprehended two days later in Borno State, near the border with Cameroon, and dispatched to Liberia, from where he was immediately extradited by UNMIL peace-keepers to the Special Court.

In 1991 the Nigerian Government claimed that Cameroonian security forces had annexed several Nigerian fishing settlements in Cross River State (in south-eastern Nigeria), following a long-standing border dispute, based on a 1913 agreement between Germany and the United Kingdom that ceded the Bakassi peninsula in the Gulf of Guinea (a region with significant petroleum reserves) to Cameroon. Subsequent negotiations between Nigerian and Cameroonian officials in an effort to resolve the dispute achieved little progress, and in February 1994 the Cameroonian Government announced that it was to submit the dispute for adjudication by the UN, the Organization of African Unity (OAU, now the African Union, see p. 191) and the International Court of Justice (ICJ). Subsequent reports of clashes between Cameroonian and Nigerian forces in the region prompted fears of a full-scale conflict between the two nations. In March 1996 the ICJ ruled that Cameroon had failed to provide sufficient evidence to support its contention that Nigeria had instigated the border dispute, and ordered both nations to cease military operations in this respect, to withdraw troops to former positions, and to co-operate with a UN investigative mission. In April, however, clashes continued, with each Government accusing the other of initiating the attacks. The UN investigative mission visited the Bakassi region in September. Further clashes between Nigerian and Cameroonian forces were reported in December 1997 and February 1998. In March 1998 the Nigerian Government contested the jurisdiction of the ICJ to rule on the Bakassi issue, on the grounds that the two countries had agreed to settle the dispute through bilateral negotiations. In June, however, the Court pronounced that it held the necessary jurisdiction.

In October 2002 the ICJ finally ruled that the disputed Bakassi region was part of Cameroon, under the terms of the 1913 agreement. Obasanjo criticized the decision, in support of strong opposition expressed by the Nigerian majority inhabitants of the peninsula, although he subsequently pledged to abide by the ruling. In August 2003, following UN mediation, Nigeria and Cameroon finally adopted a framework agreement for the implementation of the ICJ's judgment; all military and administrative personnel were to be withdrawn from the Bakassi region, and a commission, comprising Nigerian, Cameroonian and UN officials, was to resolve outstanding issues for the redemarcation of boundaries between the two countries, in a process that was expected to continue for up to three years. However, the Nigerian Government subsequently announced that the transfer of authority in the peninsula, scheduled for September 2004, had been postponed, citing technical difficulties in the final redemarcation of the joint border. Following a meeting in May 2005 between Obasanjo and the Head of State of Cameroon, conducted in Geneva, Switzerland, under the aegis of the UN Secretary-General, it was announced that the two sides had agreed to draft a new programme for Nigeria's withdrawal from the Bakassi peninsula. On 12 June 2006 an accord was signed, according to which Nigeria agreed to withdraw troops from the region within 60 days, and on 14 August Nigerian troops left the peninsula. Although the territory would remain under Nigerian control during the interim period, a full transfer of the Bakassi peninsula was scheduled to be completed by June 2008.

An agreement was reached in March 2008 which finalized the position of the two countries' long-disputed maritime boundary in the Gulf of Guinea, and the transfer of the Bakassi peninsula to Cameroon was scheduled for August that year. There was further violence in the peninsula in June, when five Cameroonian troops and a local government official, Felix Morfan, were abducted and later killed. In the following month members of the self-styled Niger Delta Defence and Security Council (NDDSC), a rebel group seeking to prevent the agreed transfer of the Bakassi peninsula, attacked a Cameroonian security patrol in Bakassi. The NDDSC also claimed responsibility for a further attack on a Cameroon military post in the same month. None the less, on 14 August the transfer was finally completed with an official flag-exchange ceremony which, for security reasons, took place in the city of Calabar, more than 100 miles from the peninsula. Formal delineation of the boundary began in December 2009. At a UN-mediated meeting of the border commission, held in Abuja in December 2012, Nigerian and Cameroonian representatives pledged commitment to expediting the boundary demarcation process.

CONSTITUTION AND GOVERNMENT

Under the terms of the Constitution of the Federal Republic of Nigeria, which entered into effect on 31 May 1999, executive power is vested in the President, who is the Head of State. The President, who is elected for a term of four years (and is restricted to two mandates), nominates a Vice-President and a Cabinet, subject to confirmation by the Senate. Legislative power is vested in the bicameral National Assembly, which comprises a 360-member House of Representatives and a 109-member Senate, and is elected by universal suffrage for a four-year term. Nigeria is a federation of 36 states, composed of 774 local government areas. The executive power of a state is vested in the Governor of that state, who is elected for a four-year term, and the legislative power in the House of Assembly of that state.

REGIONAL AND INTERNATIONAL CO-OPERATION

Nigeria is a member of the African Union (see p. 191) and of the Economic Community of West African States (see p. 268), which aims to promote trade and co-operation in West Africa.

Nigeria became a member of the UN in 1960 and was admitted to the World Trade Organization (WTO, see p. 444) in 1995. Nigeria participates in the Group of 15 (G15, see p. 461) and the Group of 77 (G77, see p. 461) developing countries, and is a member of the Organization of the Petroleum Exporting Countries (OPEC, see p. 418). In October 2009 Nigeria was elected as a non-permanent member of the UN Security Council for 2010 and 2011.

ECONOMIC AFFAIRS

In 2011, according to estimates by the World Bank, Nigeria's gross national income (GNI), measured at average 2009–11 prices, was US $195,333m., equivalent to $1,200 per head (or $2,300 per head on an international purchasing-power parity basis). During 2002–11, it was estimated, the population increased, in real terms, at an average annual rate of 2.5%, while gross domestic product (GDP) per head rose by an average of 4.7% per year. Overall GDP increased, in real terms, at an average annual rate of 7.4% in 2002–11; growth was 6.7% in 2011.

Agriculture (including hunting, forestry and fishing) contributed an estimated 33.1% of GDP in 2012. According to FAO estimates, agriculture engaged 22.7% of the total labour force in mid-2013. The principal cash crops are cocoa (which accounted for only 0.3% of total merchandise exports in 2006), rubber and oil palm. Staple food crops include cassava, yams, maize, millet, taro, rice and sorghum. Timber production, the raising of livestock (principally goats, sheep, cattle and poultry), and artisanal fisheries are also important. According to the African Development Bank (AfDB), agricultural GDP increased at an average annual rate of 4.8% in 2000–07. Growth in agricultural GDP was 4.0% in 2012, according to official figures.

Industry (including mining, manufacturing, construction and power) engaged an estimated 3.4% of the employed labour force in 2006, and contributed an estimated 39.3% of GDP in 2012. According to the AfDB, industrial GDP increased at an average annual rate of 3.7% in 2000–07. Sectoral growth was 2.4% in 2012, according to official figures.

Mining contributed an estimated 37.4% of GDP in 2012, although the sector engaged just 0.1% of the employed labour force in 2007. The principal mineral is petroleum, of which Nigeria is Africa's leading producer (providing an estimated 92.0% of total export earnings in 2008 and 34.5% of GDP in 2009). As a member of OPEC, Nigeria is subject to production quotas agreed by the Organization's Conference. Nigeria also possesses substantial deposits of natural gas and coal. In late 1999 the Nigerian Government commenced exports of liquefied natural gas, and by 2004 natural gas accounted for 8.8% of earnings. A 678-km pipeline, which would transport natural gas from the Escravos field, in Delta State, to Benin, Togo and Ghana, commenced operations in April 2007. In June 2009 it was announced that Russian state-controlled natural gas company Gazprom had signed an agreement investing some US $2,500m. in a joint venture with the Nigerian National Petroleum Corporation to explore and develop the country's gas reserves. Tin and iron ore are also mined, while there are plans to exploit recently discovered deposits of uranium. The GDP of the mining sector was estimated by the IMF to have declined by an average of 0.1% per year in 1997–2001; mining GDP increased by 0.6% in 2001. According to official figures, mining GDP declined by 0.5% in 2012.

Manufacturing contributed an estimated 1.7% of GDP in 2012, and engaged about 1.5% of the employed labour force in 2007. The principal sectors are food-processing, brewing, petroleum-refining, iron and steel, motor vehicles (using imported components), textiles, cigarettes, footwear, pharmaceuticals, pulp and paper, and cement. According to the AfDB, manufacturing GDP increased at an average annual rate of 7.3% in 2000–07. Manufacturing GDP increased by 7.6% in 2012, according to official figures.

The construction sector contributed an estimated 1.3% of GDP in 2012, and engaged 0.6% of the employed labour force in 2007. According to official figures, construction GDP increased by 12.6% in 2012.

Energy is derived principally from natural gas, which provided some 64.3% of electricity in 2009, and hydroelectric power (22.9%); petroleum provided 12.8%. Mineral fuels comprised 1.4% of the value of merchandise imports in 2010.

The services sector contributed an estimated 26.3% of GDP in 2012, and engaged 39.1% of the employed labour force in 2007. According to the AfDB, the GDP of the services sector increased at an average annual rate of 9.6% in 2000–07. The GDP of the services sector increased by 12.4% in 2012, according to official figures.

In 2011 Nigeria recorded a merchandise trade surplus of US $30,851m. and there was a surplus of $8,689m. on the current account of the balance of payments. In 2011 the principal source of imports (providing 18.0% of the total) was the USA; other major suppliers were the People's Republic of China and Brazil. The USA was also the principal market for exports (accounting for 22.5% of the total) in that year; other significant purchasers were Brazil, the United Kingdom, Spain, France (incl. Monaco) and Italy. The principal exports in 2011 were mineral products, followed by plastics and rubber articles. The principal imports in 2011 were machinery and mechanical appliances, prepared foodstuffs and beverages, vehicles and aircraft equipment, vegetable products, mineral products, plastic and rubber articles, base metals and articles, food and live animals, and chemical products.

Nigeria's overall budget deficit for 2011 was an estimated ₦1,433,000m. Nigeria's general government gross debt was ₦6,519,938m. in 2011, equivalent to 17.3% of GDP. The country's external debt totalled US $7,883m. at the end of 2010, of which $4,686m. was public and publicly guaranteed debt. In that year, the cost of servicing long-term public and publicly guaranteed debt and repayments to the IMF was equivalent to 0.4% of the value of exports of goods, services and income (excluding workers' remittances). The annual rate of inflation averaged 12.0% in 2008–12; consumer prices increased by 12.3% in 2012. An estimated 4.5% of the labour force were unemployed at the end of 1997.

Nigeria is one of Africa's most powerful economies, but, despite considerable agricultural and mineral resources, political instability has severely impeded economic reform. Following the accumulation of unsustainably high levels of external debt in the early 2000s, Nigeria settled its entire debt to the 'Paris Club' of creditor countries in 2006, under an agreement that was part of an IMF-approved government reform programme. From 2006 increased violence in the Niger Delta region, including a series of attacks against petroleum pipelines, resulted in frequent disruptions and partial suspensions in oil production. Goodluck Jonathan, who became Head of State in May 2010, undertook further stabilization measures, including the establishment of a new National Economic Team tasked with effecting economic recovery. Also in May, it was announced that the Government had secured a concessionary loan from the World Bank of US $915m., which was to finance infrastructural development over a five-year period. In August the Government announced plans to privatize the successor companies of the Power Holding Company of Nigeria, as part of reforms to address long-standing energy shortages (although subsequent progress in the programme was slow). The Government also proposed to adopt a Petroleum Industry Bill, which would replace the existing 16 oil sector laws with one legal framework, in an effort to improve transparency. In November 2011 the Central Bank implemented a 3.2% devaluation of the naira, following the depletion of foreign reserves. In January 2012, however, President Jonathan's removal of a fuel subsidy, resulting in sharp increases in petrol prices and transport fares, prompted national strike action and popular protests (obliging Jonathan partially to reinstate the subsidy). A parliamentary report released in April concluded that the fuel subsidies scheme had been marred by corruption and mismanagement, including major embezzlement by senior officials, and urged reform of the system. GDP growth of nearly 7% in 2011 was sustained at about the same level in 2012 (supported by high international oil prices), while by January 2013 consumer prices had been reduced to 9% year on year (according to official figures). The level of foreign investment remained robust in 2012, reflecting the fiscal stabilization efforts of Jonathan's Government; however, Nigeria was ranked 143rd lowest of 183 countries listed on Transparency International's 2011 index of public sector corruption. Furthermore, a critical increase in attacks perpetrated by the militant Islamist Boko Haram in northern regions (see Domestic Political Affairs), in addition to continued unrest in the Niger Delta, presented a major deterrent to foreign investment. An escalation in kidnappings of foreign national workers by Boko Haram and another militant Islamist group in early 2013 was a further source of concern for the Nigerian authorities.

PUBLIC HOLIDAYS

2014: 1 January (New Year's Day), 13 January* (Mouloud, Birth of the Prophet), 18–21 April (Easter), 28 July* (Id al-Fitr, end of Ramadan), 1 October (National Day), 4 October* (Id al-Kabir, Feast of the Sacrifice), 25–26 December (Christmas).

* These holidays are dependent on the Islamic lunar calendar, and may vary by one or two days from the dates given.

Statistical Survey

Sources (unless otherwise stated): National Bureau of Statistics, Plot 762, Independence Avenue, Central Business District, PMB 127, Garki, Abuja; tel. (9) 2731085; fax (9) 2731084; internet www.nigerianstat.gov.ng; Central Bank of Nigeria, Central Business District, PMB 187, Garki, Abuja; tel. (9) 61639701; fax (9) 61636012; e-mail info@cenbank.org; internet www.cenbank.org.

Area and Population

AREA, POPULATION AND DENSITY

Area (sq km)	909,890*
Population (census results)	
28–30 November 1991†	88,992,220
21–27 March 2006	
Males	71,345,488
Females	69,086,302
Total	140,431,790
Population (UN estimates at mid-year)‡	
2011	162,470,733
2012	166,629,385
2013	170,901,150
Density (per sq km) at mid-2013	187.8

* 351,310 sq miles.
† Revised 15 September 2001.
‡ Source: UN, *World Population Prospects: The 2010 Revision*.

POPULATION BY AGE AND SEX
(UN estimates at mid-2013)

	Males	Females	Total
0–14	37,348,909	35,702,491	73,051,400
15–64	46,506,618	45,491,992	91,998,610
65 and over	2,726,978	3,124,162	5,851,140
Total	86,582,505	84,318,645	170,901,150

Source: UN, *World Population Prospects: The 2010 Revision*.

STATES
(population at 2006 census)

	Area (sq km)	Population	Density (per sq km)	Capital
Abia	4,900	2,845,380	581	Umuahia
Adamawa . . .	38,700	3,178,950	82	Yola
Akwa Ibom . . .	6,900	3,902,051	556	Uyo
Anambra	4,865	4,177,828	859	Awka
Bauchi	49,119	4,653,066	95	Bauchi
Bayelsa	9,059	1,704,515	188	Yenogoa
Benue	30,800	4,253,641	138	Makurdi
Borno	72,609	4,171,104	57	Maiduguri
Cross River . . .	21,787	2,892,988	133	Calabar
Delta	17,108	4,112,445	240	Asaba
Ebonyi	6,400	2,176,947	340	Abakaliki
Edo	19,187	3,233,366	169	Benin City
Ekiti	5,435	2,398,957	441	Ado-Ekiti
Enugu	7,534	3,267,837	434	Enugu
Gombe	17,100	2,365,040	138	Gombe
Imo	5,288	3,927,563	743	Owerri
Jigawa	23,287	4,361,002	187	Dutse
Kaduna	42,481	6,113,503	144	Kaduna
Kano	20,280	9,401,288	464	Kano
Katsina	23,561	5,801,584	246	Katsina
Kebbi	36,985	3,256,541	88	Birnin Kebbi
Kogi	27,747	3,314,043	119	Lokoja
Kwara	35,705	2,365,353	66	Ilorin
Lagos	3,671	9,113,605	2,483	Ikeja
Nassarawa . . .	28,735	1,869,377	65	Lafia
Niger	68,925	3,954,772	57	Minna
Ogun	16,400	3,751,140	229	Abeokuta
Ondo	15,820	3,460,877	219	Akure

—continued	Area (sq km)	Population	Density (per sq km)	Capital
Osun	9,026	3,416,959	379	Oshogbo
Oyo	26,500	5,580,894	211	Ibadan
Plateau	27,147	3,206,531	118	Jos
Rivers	10,575	5,198,716	492	Port Harcourt
Sokoto	27,825	3,702,676	133	Sokoto
Taraba	56,282	2,294,800	41	Jalingo
Yobe	46,609	2,321,339	50	Damaturu
Zamfara	37,931	3,278,873	86	Gusau
Federal Capital Territory (Abuja) .	7,607	1,406,239	185	Abuja
Total	909,890	140,431,790	154	—

PRINCIPAL TOWNS
(unrevised census of November 1991)

Lagos (federal capital)* . . .	5,195,247	Enugu	407,756
Kano . . .	2,166,554	Oyo	369,894
Ibadan . . .	1,835,300	Warri	363,382
Kaduna . . .	933,642	Abeokuta . . .	352,735
Benin City . .	762,719	Onitsha . . .	350,280
Port Harcourt .	703,421	Sokoto . . .	329,639
Maiduguri . .	618,278	Okene . . .	312,775
Zaria . . .	612,257	Calabar . . .	310,839
Ilorin . . .	532,089	Katsina . . .	259,315
Jos	510,300	Oshogbo . . .	250,951
Aba	500,183	Akure . . .	239,124
Ogbomosho . .	433,030	Bauchi . . .	206,537

* Federal capital moved to Abuja (population 107,069) in December 1991.

Mid-2011 ('000 incl. suburbs, UN estimate): Abuja 2,153 (Source: UN, *World Urbanization Prospects: The 2011 Revision*).

BIRTHS AND DEATHS
(annual averages, UN estimates)

	1995–2000	2000–05	2005–10
Birth rate (per 1,000)	42.2	41.5	40.4
Death rate (per 1,000)	18.7	16.7	15.1

Source: UN, *World Population Prospects: The 2010 Revision*.

Life expectancy (years at birth): 51.9 (males 51.1; females 52.7) in 2011 (Source: World Bank, World Development Indicators database).

EMPLOYMENT
('000 persons aged 14 years and over)

	2005	2006	2007
Agriculture, hunting, forestry and fishing	29,017	30,682	31,278
Mining and quarrying	69	73	81
Manufacturing	908	960	821
Electricity, gas and water	427	451	n.a.
Construction	273	289	n.a.
Wholesale and retail trade; repairs of motor vehicles and motorcycles and personal and household articles	104	110	140
Hotels and restaurants	96	102	130
Transport, storage and communications	416	440	1,108
Financial intermediation	281	297	303
Real estate, renting and business activities	60	64	81
Public administration, defence and compulsory social security	5,067	5,358	5,338
Education	9,473	10,017	10,444
Health and social welfare	296	313	308
Other community, social and personal service activities	2,999	3,171	3,280
Total employed	49,486	52,327	54,030

Mid-2013 (estimates in '000): Agriculture, etc. 12,314; Total labour force 54,306 (Source: FAO).

Health and Welfare

KEY INDICATORS

Total fertility rate (children per woman, 2010)	5.5
Under-5 mortality rate (per 1,000 live births, 2010)	143
HIV/AIDS (% of persons aged 15–49, 2009)	3.6
Physicians (per 1,000 head, 2008)	0.4
Hospital beds (per 1,000 head, 2004)	0.5
Health expenditure (2009): US $ per head (PPP)	136
Health expenditure (2009): % of GDP	6.1
Health expenditure (2009): public (% of total)	35.1
Access to water (% of persons, 2010)	58
Access to sanitation (% of persons, 2010)	31
Total carbon dioxide emissions ('000 metric tons, 2008)	95,756.4
Carbon dioxide emissions per head (metric tons, 2008)	0.6
Human Development Index (2011): ranking	156
Human Development Index (2011): value	0.459

For sources and definitions, see explanatory note on p. vi.

Agriculture

PRINCIPAL CROPS
('000 metric tons)

	2009	2010	2011
Wheat*	50	51	52
Rice, paddy	3,546	4,473	4,567
Maize	7,358	7,677	9,180
Millet	4,930	5,170	1,271
Sorghum	5,279	7,141	6,897
Potatoes*	915	900	950
Sweet potatoes*	2,747	2,704	2,725
Cassava	36,822	42,533	52,404
Taro (Coco yam)	3,033	2,957	3,266
Yams	29,092	34,162	37,116
Sugar cane	1,402	1,402	1,450*
Cow peas, dry	2,372	3,368	1,861
Cashew nuts*	650	683	813
Kolanuts	162	170	138†
Soybeans (Soya beans)	427	285	564
Groundnuts, with shell	2,978	3,799	2,963
Coconuts	194†	211†	215*
Oil palm fruit*	8,500	8,500	8,500
Sesame seed	120	149	229
Melonseed	403	507	510*

—continued	2009	2010	2011
Tomatoes	1,750*	1,800	1,505
Chillies and peppers, green*	845	500	450
Onions and shallots, green*	180	236	236
Onions, dry	1,300*	1,346	1,238
Carrots and turnips*	199	213	210
Okra	1,050*	1,084	1,061
Maize, green*	538	706	740
Plantains	2,700*	2,676	2,700*
Citrus fruits*	3,769	3,488	3,500
Guavas, mangoes and mangosteens*	831	790	795
Pineapples*	875	910	920
Papayas*	764	704	705
Cocoa beans	364	399	400*
Ginger	169	162	160*
Tobacco, unmanufactured*	14	17	17
Natural rubber*	145	144	144

* FAO estimate(s).
† Unofficial figure.

Aggregate production ('000 metric tons, may include official, semi-official or estimated data): Total cereals 21,229 in 2009, 24,590 in 2010, 22,048 in 2011; Total roots and tubers 72,609 in 2009, 83,256 in 2010, 96,460 in 2011; Total vegetables (incl. melons) 10,399 in 2009, 11,830 in 2010, 11,440 in 2011; Total fruits (excl. melons) 10,022 in 2009, 9,780 in 2010, 9,870 in 2011.

Source: FAO.

LIVESTOCK
('000 head, year ending September)

	2009	2010	2011
Horses*	209	211	212
Asses*	1,065	1,200	1,220
Cattle	16,435	16,013	18,871
Camels*	19	19	20
Pigs	7,184	7,472	7,700
Sheep	34,687	37,423	38,000*
Goats	55,145	56,524	57,300*
Chickens	183,156	192,313	192,313*

* FAO estimate(s).

Source: FAO.

LIVESTOCK PRODUCTS
('000 metric tons, FAO estimates)

	2009	2010	2011
Cattle meat	298.4	301.6	338.0
Sheep meat	148.8	170.5	171.6
Goat meat	284.3	287.7	292.1
Pig meat	226.3	234.0	239.4
Chicken meat	256.5	268.0	268.0
Game meat	144.9	155.0	163.0
Cows' milk	472	496	563
Hen eggs	613	623	636

Source: FAO.

Forestry

ROUNDWOOD REMOVALS
('000 cubic metres, excluding bark, FAO estimates)

	2009	2010	2011
Sawlogs, veneer logs and logs for sleepers	7,100	7,100	7,100
Pulpwood	39	39	39
Other industrial wood	2,279	2,279	2,279
Fuel wood	62,793	63,215	63,600
Total	72,211	72,633	73,018

Source: FAO.

SAWNWOOD PRODUCTION
('000 cubic metres, including railway sleepers)

	1995	1996	1997
Broadleaved (hardwood) . . .	2,356	2,178	2,000

1998–2011: Broadleaved (hardwood) production as in 1997.

Source: FAO.

Fishing

('000 metric tons, live weight)

	2008	2009	2010
Capture	601.4	598.2	617.0
Tilapias	47.6	54.2	56.6
Elephant snout fishes . .	22.4	22.6	23.0
Torpedo-shaped catfishes . .	32.8	35.2	37.8
Sea catfishes . . .	20.8	18.4	17.2
West African croakers . .	11.3	9.2	7.5
Sardinellas	63.5	67.5	67.6
Bonga shad . . .	22.1	23.4	24.8
Southern pink shrimp . . .	11.4	9.4	7.7
Other shrimps and prawns .	1.9	11.5	13.5
Aquaculture	143.2	152.8	200.5
Total catch	744.6	751.0	817.5

Source: FAO.

Mining

(metric tons unless otherwise indicated)

	2009	2010	2011
Coal, bituminous	40,612	45,713	39,213
Kaolin	154,000	139,000	155,000
Gypsum	300,000	320,000	320,000
Crude petroleum ('000 barrels) .	780,348	896,043	866,245
Tin concentrates	510	680	740

Source: US Geological Survey.

Natural gas (million cu m, excl. gas flared or recycled): 24,796 in 2009; 36,588 in 2010; 39,864 in 2011 (Source: BP, *Statistical Review of World Energy*).

Industry

SELECTED PRODUCTS
('000 metric tons unless otherwise indicated)

	2009	2010	2011
Palm oil*†	1,380	1,350	1,350
Beer of barley*‡	1,600	1,760	1,960
Plywood ('000 cubic metres)†* .	56	56	56
Wood pulp*†	23	23	23
Paper and paperboard*† . .	19	19	19
Liquefied petroleum gas ('000 barrels)	1,200	1,900	1,200
Motor spirit—petrol ('000 barrels)	3,102	6,400	10,900
Kerosene ('000 barrels) . .	2,530	5,000	5,800
Gas-diesel (distillate fuel) oil ('000 barrels)	4,168	7,000	8,200
Residual fuel oils ('000 barrels) .	4,060	6,600	9,300
Cement	10,000	11,000	11,600
Electric energy (million kWh)§ .	19,777	n.a.	n.a.

* Source: FAO.
† Estimates.
‡ Unofficial figures.
§ Source: UN Industrial Commodity Statistics Database.

Raw sugar: 21,000 metric tons in 2008 (Source: UN Industrial Commodity Statistics Database).

Source (unless otherwise indicated): US Geological Survey.

Finance

CURRENCY AND EXCHANGE RATES

Monetary Units
100 kobo = 1 naira (₦).

Sterling, Dollar and Euro Equivalents (31 December 2012)
£1 sterling = 245.016 naira;
US $1 = 155.270 naira;
€1 = 204.863 naira;
1,000 naira = £4.081 = $6.440 = €4.881.

Average Exchange Rate (naira per US $)
2010   150.298
2011   154.740
2012   156.810

FEDERAL BUDGET
(₦ '000 million)

Revenue	2010	2011*	2012†
Petroleum revenue	1,555	1,924	2,180
Non-petroleum revenue . . .	675	788	1,003
Import and excise duties . .	139	153	178
Companies' income tax . . .	306	367	453
Value-added tax	76	91	112
Total	2,229	2,712	3,183

Expenditure	2010	2011*	2012†
Recurrent expenditure . . .	3,080	3,342	3,460
Goods and services . . .	2,480	2,388	2,391
Personnel and pension . .	1,564	1,661	1,835
Overhead cost	916	727	556
Interest payments	352	500	623
Transfers	248	455	446
Capital expenditure	900	803	1,062
Total	3,980	4,145	4,522

* Estimates.
† Projections.

Source: IMF, *Nigeria: Staff Report for the 2011 Article IV Consultation* (July 2012).

INTERNATIONAL RESERVES
(US $ million at 31 December)

	2009	2010	2011
Gold (national valuation) . . .	0	0	0
IMF special drawing rights . .	2,380	2,580	2,572
Foreign exchange	42,382	32,339	32,640
Total	44,763	34,919	35,212

Source: IMF, *International Financial Statistics*.

MONEY SUPPLY
(₦ '000 million at 31 December)

	2009	2010	2011
Currency outside depository corporations	927.2	1,082.4	1,245.1
Transferable deposits . . .	3,575.5	4,137.6	4,906.0
Other deposits	5,708.0	5,941.4	6,526.2
Broad money	10,210.7	11,161.4	12,677.2

Source: IMF, *International Financial Statistics*.

COST OF LIVING
(Consumer Price Index at November; base: November 2009 = 100)

	2010	2011	2012
Food (excl. beverages)	114.4	125.4	139.8
Alcoholic beverages, tobacco and kola	112.2	118.9	125.3
Clothing (incl. footwear) . . .	112.0	121.9	138.2
Rent, fuel and light	112.6	128.1	152.3
Household goods and maintenance	113.1	120.2	134.1
Medical care and health . . .	111.1	122.7	133.5
Transport	111.7	123.3	138.9
Education	107.7	114.2	128.8
All items (incl. others) . . .	112.8	124.7	140.0

NATIONAL ACCOUNTS
(₦ '000 million at current basic prices)

Expenditure on the Gross Domestic Product

	2009	2010*	2011*
Government final consumption expenditure	3,213.2	4,963.9	5,356.6
Private final consumption expenditure	18,859.6	20,408.9	19,908.8
Increase in stocks	1.8	2.2	2.1
Gross fixed capital formation .	3,048.0	4,663.6	5,991.4
Total domestic expenditure .	25,122.6	30,038.7	31,259.0
Exports of goods and non-factor services	7,766.2	15,640.7	18,650.9
Less Imports of goods and non-petroleum services	7,663.6	11,354.6	12,081.7
GDP in basic prices . . .	25,225.1	34,324.8	37,828.1
GDP in constant basic 1990 prices	594.2	609.9	608.2

2011 (revised figures): Government final consumption expenditure 4,979.9; Private final consumption expenditure 22,840.8; Increase in stocks 2.3; Gross fixed capital formation 3,908.3; *Total domestic expenditure* 31,731.3; Exports of goods and non-factor services 19,961.2; Imports of goods and non-petroleum services –13,675.6; *GDP in basic prices* 38,017.0.

Gross Domestic Product by Economic Activity

	2009	2010*	2011*
Agriculture, hunting, forestry and fishing	9,186.3	10,310.7	11,590.1
Mining and quarrying . . .	7,458.8	14,551.5	15,328.1
Crude petroleum	7,418.1	14,505.8	15,275.7
Manufacturing	612.3	643.1	694.7
Electricity, gas and water . .	62.1	70.3	80.7
Construction	347.7	394.7	456.0
Wholesale and retail trade . .	4,082.4	4,648.7	5,388.0
Hotels and restaurants . . .	99.0	113.8	130.8
Transport and communications .	762.7	791.6	858.7
Finance, insurance	444.2	507.8	574.3
Real estate and business services .	1,213.0	1,348.2	1,515.3
Government services	255.4	292.7	333.1
Other community, social and personal services	270.3	311.8	353.6
GDP at factor cost . . .	24,794.2	33,984.8	37,303.4
Indirect taxes (net)†	430.9	340.0	524.7
GDP in basic prices . . .	25,225.1	34,324.8	37,828.1

* Provisional.
† Figures obtained as residuals.

2011(revised figures): Agriculture, hunting, forestry and fishing 11,593.4; Mining and quarrying 15,408.2 (Crude petroleum and natural gas 15,285.0); Manufacturing 624.1; Electricity, gas and water 80.7; Construction 456.3; Wholesale and retail trade 5,385.8; Hotels and restaurants 130.8; Transport and communications 860.3; Finance and insurance 668.2; Real estate and business services 1,515.3; Government services 333.1; Other community, social and personal services 353.6; *GDP at factor cost* 37,409.9; Indirect taxes (net) 607.1; *GDP in basic prices* 38,017.0.

2012: Agriculture, hunting, forestry and fishing 13,413.8; Mining and quarrying 15,144.1 (Crude petroleum and natural gas 15,004.6); Manufacturing 681.3; Electricity, gas and water 91.3; Construction 539.7; Wholesale and retail trade 6,284.9; Hotels and restaurants 151.8; Transport and communications 997.5; Finance and insurance 636.0; Real estate and business services 1,813.3; Government services 381.1; Other community, social and personal services 409.1; *GDP at factor cost* 40,544.1; Indirect taxes (net) 637.5; *GDP in basic prices* 41,181.6.

BALANCE OF PAYMENTS
(US $ million)

	2009	2010	2011
Exports of goods	56,121	76,733	92,504
Imports of goods	–30,779	–46,374	–61,653
Balance on goods	25,342	30,359	30,851
Exports of services	2,218	3,092	3,387
Imports of services	–18,697	–21,412	–24,573
Balance on goods and services	8,863	12,040	9,665
Primary income received . . .	935	1,001	898
Primary income paid	–15,339	–20,513	–23,682
Balance on goods, services and primary income	–5,541	–7,472	–13,120
Secondary income received . .	19,826	21,262	22,281
Secondary income paid . . .	–464	–480	–472
Current balance	13,821	13,310	8,689
Direct investment assets . . .	–1,525	–915	–817
Direct investment liabilities . .	8,555	6,049	8,842
Portfolio investment assets . .	–822	–1,121	–1,610
Portfolio investment liabilities .	476	3,717	5,150
Other investment assets . . .	–6,488	–13,499	–17,394
Other investment liabilities . .	1,799	–2,150	730
Net errors and omissions . . .	–26,331	–15,119	–3,285
Reserves and related items .	–10,515	–9,730	306

Source: IMF, *International Financial Statistics*.

External Trade

PRINCIPAL COMMODITIES
(distribution by HS, ₦ '000 million)

Imports c.i.f.	2009	2010	2011
Live animals and animal products	157.0	190.0	567.4
Vegetable products	268.6	270.8	1,169.7
Prepared foodstuffs; beverages, spirits and vinegar and tobacco .	176.9	207.7	1,430.2
Mineral products	118.1	176.6	1,059.1
Chemicals and related products .	434.7	476.3	510.1
Plastics, rubber and articles thereof	392.3	490.1	659.8
Base metals and articles thereof .	531.4	598.2	604.7
Machinery and mechanical appliances	1,449.0	1,931.0	1,924.3
Vehicles, aircraft, vessels and associated transport equipment .	1,003.8	1,404.5	1,199.9
Total (incl. others)	5,047.9	6,648.5	9,892.6

Exports f.o.b.	2009	2010	2011
Prepared foodstuffs; beverages, spirits and vinegar and tobacco .	240.0	240.1	224.4
Mineral products	6,720.2	11,415.9	17,335.6
Plastics, rubber and articles thereof	49.1	147.5	1,177.5
Raw hides and skins, leather, furskins and articles thereof .	76.6	461.1	121.1
Total (incl. others)	7,434.5	13,009.9	19,440.4

PRINCIPAL TRADING PARTNERS
(₦ '000 million)*

Imports c.i.f.	2009	2010	2011
Brazil	168.0	216.9	549.0
China, People's Republic . . .	893.2	1,100.8	1,461.0
France (incl. Monaco) . . .	292.1	388.7	444.3
Germany	45.4	30.8	466.0
Italy	99.0	300.2	278.4
Japan	144.1	171.8	447.1
Netherlands	31.3	52.8	233.9
Spain	10.8	48.8	149.7
United Kingdom	229.5	185.6	262.8
USA	303.7	1,192.8	1,781.0
Total (incl. others)	5,047.9	6,648.5	9,892.6

Exports f.o.b.		2009	2010	2011
Brazil	. . . .	593.5	908.0	1,632.8
Canada	. . . . . .	261.4	382.5	225.2
China, People's Republic	. . .	78.1	216.5	392.6
France (incl. Monaco)	. . . .	407.4	526.9	1,140.1
Germany	. . . . . .	67.7	84.3	197.2
Italy	. . . .	309.7	458.0	991.0
Netherlands	. . . . .	199.4	591.6	414.5
Spain	. . . .	324.3	425.3	1,146.0
United Kingdom	. . . .	156.6	190.5	1,210.6
USA	. . . .	2,026.6	4,471.4	4,381.3
Total (incl. others)	. . . . .	7,434.5	13,009.9	19,440.4

* Imports by country of consignment; exports by country of destination.

Transport

RAILWAYS
(traffic)

		2006	2007	2008
Passenger journeys ('000)	. . .	708.8	1,478.7	1,996.3
Passenger-km (million)	. . .	256.6	535.3	722.7
Freight ('000 metric tons)	. .	41,219	31,405	47,409
Net freight ton-km (million)	. .	34.3	26.0	41.1

ROAD TRAFFIC
(motor vehicles in use, estimates)

		1995	1996
Passenger cars	. . . .	820,069	885,080
Buses and coaches	. . . . . .	1,284,251	903,449
Lorries and vans	. . . . . .	673,425	912,579
Motorcycles and mopeds	. . . . .	481,345	441,651

2007 ('000 motor vehicles in use): Passenger cars 4,560; Motorcycles and mopeds 3,040.

Source: IRF, *World Road Statistics*.

SHIPPING
Flag Registered Fleet
(at 31 December)

		2010	2011	2012
Number of vessels	. . . . .	382	417	462
Total displacement ('000 grt)	. .	2,041.1	2,035.9	2,094.0

Source: Lloyd's List Intelligence (www.lloydslistintelligence.com).

International Sea-borne Freight Traffic
(estimates, '000 metric tons)

		1991	1992	1993
Goods loaded	. . . . .	82,768	84,797	86,993
Goods unloaded	. . . . .	10,960	11,143	11,346

Source: UN Economic Commission for Africa, *African Statistical Yearbook*.

CIVIL AVIATION
(traffic on scheduled services)

		2007	2008	2009
Kilometres flown (million)	. . .	18	24	23
Passengers carried ('000)	. . .	1,365	1,461	1,365
Passenger-km (million)	. . .	1,528	1,978	1,873
Total ton-km (million)	. . . .	143	179	169

Source: UN, *Statistical Yearbook*.

Passengers carried ('000): 1,555 in 2010 (Source: World Bank, World Development Indicators database).

Tourism

ARRIVALS BY NATIONALITY*

Country		2008	2009	2010
Benin	. . . .	822,695	855,605	855,712
Cameroon	. . . .	223,984	233,274	233,370
Chad	. . . .	178,100	185,527	185,633
France	. . . .	129,668	134,609	134,718
Germany	. . . .	126,488	131,309	131,418
Ghana	. . . .	43,420	45,157	45,406
Italy	. . . .	137,473	142,712	142,813
Liberia	. . . .	225,153	234,160	234,254
Niger	. . . .	1,224,399	1,273,378	1,273,550
Sudan	. . . .	132,130	137,128	137,288
Total (incl. others)	. . . . .	5,820,497	6,053,318	6,113,384

* Figures refer to arrival at frontiers of visitors from abroad, including same-day visitors (excursionists).

Tourism receipts (US \$ million, excl. passenger transport): 602 in 2009; 571 in 2010; 601 in 2011 (provisional).

Source: World Tourism Organization.

Communications Media

	2009	2010	2011
Telephones ('000 main lines in use)	1,482.0	1,050.2	719.4
Mobile cellular telephones ('000 in use)	74,518.3	87,297.8	95,167.3
Internet subscribers ('000) . .	188.0	222.2	n.a.
Broadband subscribers ('000) . .	82.0	99.1	215.7

Source: International Telecommunication Union.

Education

(2008 unless otherwise specified)

	Institutions	Teachers	Students Males	Females	Total
Primary* . .	54,434	586,930	11,483,943	9,810,575	21,294,518
Secondary* . .	18,238	270,650	3,682,141	2,943,802	6,625,943
Poly/Monotechnic†	178	16,499	n.a.	n.a.	237,708
University . .	95	23,535†	n.a.	n.a.	724,856†

* Provisional.
† 2005 figure.

Pupil-teacher ratio (primary education, UNESCO estimate): 36.0 in 2009/10 (Source: UNESCO Institute for Statistics).

Adult literacy rate (UNESCO estimates): 61.3% (males 72.1%; females 50.4%) in 2010 (Source: UNESCO Institute for Statistics).

Directory

Federal Government

HEAD OF STATE

President and Commander-in-Chief of the Armed Forces: Dr GOODLUCK EBELE JONATHAN (sworn in 6 May 2010; re-elected 16 April 2011).

Vice-President: NAMADI SAMBO.

CABINET
(May 2013)

Minister of Labour and Productivity: CHUKWUEMEKA NGOZI WOGU.

Minister of Women's Affairs: Hajiya ZAINAB MAINA.

Minister of Science and Technology: Prof. ITA OKON BASSEY EWA.

Minister of Aviation: STELLA ODUAH-OGIEMWONYI.

Minister of the Federal Capital Territory: BALA MOHAMMED.

Minister of Petroleum Resources: DEZIANI ALISON-MADUEKE.

Minister of the Interior: ABBA MORO.

Minister of Niger Delta Affairs: PETER GODSDAY ORUBEBE.

Minister of Health: Prof. CHRISTIAN OTU ONYEBUCHI.

Minister of Works: MIKE ONOLEMEMEN.

Minister of Police Affairs: Capt. CALEB OLUBOLADE.

Minister of Power: CHINEDU OSITA NEBO.

Minister of Education: Prof. RUQAYYATU RUFAI.

Minister, Chairman of the National Planning Commission: Dr SHAMSUDEEN USMAN.

Minister of Mines and Steel Development: MUSA MOHAMMED SADA.

Minister of Special Duties: KABIRU TANIMU TURAKI.

Attorney-General and Minister of Justice: MOHAMMED BELLO ADOKE.

Minister of Sports: Mallam BOLAJI ABDULLAHI.

Minister of Trade and Investment: OLUSEGUN OLUTOYIN AGANGA.

Minister of Information and Communication: LABARAN MAKU.

Minister of Foreign Affairs: OLUGBENGA ASHIRU.

Minister of Transport: IDRIS A. UMAR.

Minister of Agriculture and Natural Resources: Dr AKINWUNMI AYO ADESINA.

Minister of Culture and Tourism: EDEM DUKE.

Minister of the Environment: HADIZA IBRAHIM MAILAFA.

Minister of Finance: NGOZI OKONJO-IWEALA.

Minister of Communication Technology: OMOBOLA JOHNSON OLUBUSOLA.

Minister of Lands and Housing: AMA PEPPLE.

Minister of Water Resources: SARAH RENG OCHEPKE.

There were, in addition, 11 Ministers of State.

MINISTRIES

Office of the Head of State: New Federal Secretariat Complex, Shehu Shagari Way, Central Area District, Abuja; internet www .statehouse.gov.ng; tel. (9) 5233536.

Ministry of Agriculture and Natural Resources: Area 11, Secretariat Complex, Garki, PMB 135, Abuja; tel. (9) 3141931; e-mail aruma@nigeria.gov.ng.

Ministry of Aviation: New Federal Secretariat Complex, Shehu Shagari Way, Central Area District, PMB 146, Abuja; tel. (9) 5237487.

Ministry of Communication Technology: Federal Secretariat Complex, Phase I, Annex III, Shehu Shagari Way, Abuja; e-mail roundtable@commtech.gov.ng; internet commtech.gov.ng.

Ministry of Culture and Tourism: Phase II Federal Secretariat, Block A, 1st Floor, Shehu Shagari Way, Abuja; tel. (9) 2348311; fax (9) 23408297; e-mail akayode@nigeria.gov.ng; internet www .visit-nigeria.gov.ng.

Ministry of Defence: Ship House, Central Area, Abuja; tel. (9) 2340534; fax (9) 2340714; e-mail mamed@nigeria.gov.ng.

Ministry of Education: New Federal Secretariat Complex, Shehu Shagari Way, Central Area District, PMB 146, Abuja; tel. (9) 5237838; e-mail enquires@fme.gov.ng; internet www.fmegovng.org.

Ministry of the Environment: 340 Indepence Way, Central Area, PMB 468, Garki, Abuja; tel. and fax (9) 5233611; e-mail info@ environment.gov.ng; internet environment.gov.ng.

Ministry of the Federal Capital Territory: 2 Kapital St, off Obafemi Awolowo St, Garki Area 11, PMB 24, Garki, Abuja; tel. (9) 4603600; e-mail info@fct.gov.ng; internet www.fct.gov.ng.

Ministry of Finance: Ahmadu Bello Way, Central Area, PMB 14, Garki, Abuja; tel. (9) 2346290; e-mail enquiries@fmf.gov.ng; internet www.fmf.gov.ng.

Ministry of Foreign Affairs: Sir Tafawa Balewa House, Federal Secretariat, PMB 130, Abuja; tel. (9) 5230570; e-mail omaduekwe@ nigeria.gov.ng.

Ministry of Health: New Federal Secretariat Complex, Ahmadu Bello Way, Central Business District, Phase III, Ahmadu Bello Way, PMB 083, Garki, Abuja; tel. (9) 5238362; fax (9) 5234590; e-mail info@ fmh.gov.ng; internet www.fmh.gov.ng.

Ministry of Information and Communication: New Federal Secretariat Complex, Shehu Shagari Way, Central Area District, PMB 1278, Abuja; tel. (9) 5237183; e-mail jodey@nigeria.gov.ng.

Ministry of the Interior: Block F, Old Federal Secretariat, Area 1, PMB 7007, Garki, Abuja; tel. and fax (9) 6713526; e-mail gabbe@ nigeria.gov.ng; internet interior.gov.ng.

Ministry of Justice: New Federal Secretariat Complex, Shehu Shagari Way, Central Area, PMB 192, Garki, Abuja; tel. (9) 5235208; fax (9) 5235194; internet www.fmj.gov.ng.

Ministry of Labour and Productivity: New Federal Secretariat Complex, Shehu Shagari Way, Central Area, PMB 04, Garki, Abuja; tel. (9) 5235980; e-mail hlawal@nigeria.gov.ng.

Ministry of Lands and Housing: Mabushi District, Garki, Abuja; tel. (9) 2346550; fax (9) 2340174.

Ministry of Mines and Steel Development: New Federal Secretariat Complex, Shehu Shagari Way, Central Area, PMB 107, Garki, Abuja; tel. (9) 5235830; fax (9) 5235831; e-mail info@mmsd.gov.ng; internet www.mmsd.gov.ng.

Ministry of Niger Delta Affairs: New Federal Secretariat Complex, 11th Floor, Abuja; e-mail director@mnda.gov.ng; internet mnda .gov.ng.

Ministry of Petroleum Resources: 1st and 2nd Floors, New Federal Secretariat Complex, Shehu Shagari Way, Garki, Abuja; tel. (9) 5230763.

Ministry of Police Affairs: 8th Floor, New Federal Secretariat Complex, Shehu Shagari Way, Garki, Abuja; tel. (9) 2340422; internet www.policeaffairs.gov.ng.

Ministry of Power: Annex 3, Federal Secretariat Complex, Shehu Shagari Way, Central Area, PMB 278, Garki, Abuja; tel. (9) 5239462; fax (9) 5236652; e-mail info@mpr.gov.ng; internet www.power.gov .ng.

Ministry of Science and Technology: New Federal Secretariat Complex, Shehu Shagari Way, Central Area, PMB 331, Garki, Abuja; tel. (9) 5233397; fax (9) 5235204.

Ministry of Special Duties: Block 3, 3rd Floor, Phase II New Federal Secretariat Complex, Shehu Shagari Way, Garki, Abuja.

Ministry of Sports: Abuja.

Ministry of Trade and Investment: Area 1, Secretariat Complex, Garki, PMB 88, Abuja; e-mail info@fmti.gov.ng; internet www.fmti .gov.ng; tel. (9) 2341662.

Ministry of Transport: Dipcharima House, Central Business District, off 3rd Ave, PMB 0336, Garki, Abuja; tel. (9) 2347451; fax (9) 2347453; e-mail info@fmt.gov.ng; internet www.fmt.gov.ng.

Ministry of Water Resources: Area 11, Secretariat Complex, Garki, PMB 135, Abuja; tel. (9) 3141931; e-mail aruma@nigeria .gov.ng.

Ministry of Women's Affairs: Ahmadu Bello Way, Central Business District, PMB 229, Garki, Abuja; tel. (9) 5237112; fax (9) 5233644; e-mail enquiries@womenaffairs.gov.ng; internet www .womenaffairs.gov.ng.

Ministry of Works: Mabushi District, Garki, Abuja; tel. (9) 2346550; fax (9) 2340174; e-mail info@works.gov.ng; internet www .works.gov.ng.

National Planning Commission: 421 Constitution Ave, Central Business District, PMB 234, Abuja; tel. 98709063 (mobile); e-mail info@npc.gov.ng; internet www.npc.gov.ng.

National Sports Commission: ICT Unit, Room 4A 158, 1st Floor, Federal Secretariat Complex, Phase I, Shehu Shagari Way, Central Business District, Abuja; tel. 8031552606 (mobile); e-mail info@ sportscommission.gov.ng; internet www.sportscommission.gov.ng.

President and Legislature

PRESIDENT

Presidential Election, 16 April 2011, provisional results

Candidate	Votes	% of votes
Goodluck Ebele Jonathan (People's Democratic Party)	22,495,187	58.87
Muhammadu Buhari (Congress for Progressive Change)	12,214,853	31.97
Malam Nuhu Ahmed Ribadu (Action Congress of Nigeria)	2,079,151	5.44
Ibrahim Shekarau (All Nigeria People's Party)	917,012	2.40
Mahmud Mudi Waziri (People For Democratic Change)	82,243	0.22
Others*	421,532	1.10
Total	**38,209,978**	**100.00**

* There were 15 other candidates.

NATIONAL ASSEMBLY

House of Representatives

Speaker of the House of Representatives: AMINU WAZIRI TAMBUWAL.

Election, 9 April 2011

Party	Seats
People's Democratic Party	152
Action Congress of Nigeria	53
Congress for Progressive Change	31
All Nigeria People's Party	23
Others	20
Total	**279***

* There are 360 seats; however, results in 81 constituencies were not immediately made available.

Senate

Speaker of the Senate: DAVID MARK.

Election, 9 April 2011

Party	Seats
People's Democratic Party	53
Action Congress of Nigeria	18
Congress for Progressive Change	6
All Nigeria People's Party	4
Others	4
Total	**85***

* There are 109 seats; however, full results of the senatorial elections were not immediately made available.

Election Commission

Independent National Electoral Commission (INEC): Plot 436 Zambezi Cres., Maitama District, PMB 0184, Garki, Abuja; tel. (9) 2224632; e-mail contact@inecnigeria.org; internet www.inecnigeria .org; f. 1998; Chair. Prof. ATTAHIRU JEGA.

Political Organizations

Prior to legislative and presidential elections in April 2003, three political associations were granted registration by the Independent National Electoral Commission (INEC) in June 2002, as were a further 24 in December. According to the INEC, by 2011 63 parties had been officially registered. However, in December 2012 28 of these were deregistered. A further two political parties were deregistered in February 2013.

Action Congress of Nigeria (ACN): PMB 141, Garki, Abuja; tel. (9) 2730102; internet www.acnigeria.com; f. 2006 by a merger of the Alliance for Democracy, the Justice Party, the Advanced Congress of Democrats and several minor parties; Chair. Chief BISI AKANDE; Nat. Sec. LAWAL SHUAIBU.

Advanced Congress of Democrats (ACD): Suite 35/36, Mazafala Complex, Kuru, Abuja; tel. 8044107989 (mobile); Chair. YUSUF BABA; Nat. Sec. Dr KENNETH KALU.

Alliance for Democracy (AD): Plot 2096, Bumbona Close, Zone 1, Wuse, Abuja; tel. (9) 5239357; e-mail info@allliancefordemocracy .org; f. 1998; Chair. MOJISOLUWA AKINFEWA.

All Nigeria People's Party (ANPP): Bassan Plaza, Plot 759, Central Business Area, Abuja; tel. (9) 2347556; f. 1998; Chair. Dr OGBONNAYA ONU; Nat. Sec. Alhaji TIJANI TUMSHA.

All Progressives Grand Alliance (APGA): House 4, Rd 116, Gwarimpa Housing Estate, Abuja; e-mail feedback@apganigeria .com; internet apganigeria.com; regd June 2002; Chair. VICTOR C. UMEH; Nat. Sec. Alhaji SHIKAFI .

Congress for Progressive Change (CPC): Suite 212, Banex Plaza, Plot 750, Aminu Kano Cres., Zone A7, Wuse II, Abuja; Nat. Chair. Prince TONY MOMOH; Nat. Sec. BUBA GALADIMA.

Democratic People's Party (DPP): 20 Oro Ago St, opp. Holy Trinity Hospital, off Muhammadu Buhari Way, old CBN, Garki II, Abuja; Chair. BIODUN OGUNBIYI; Nat. Sec. Dr ADEMOLA ADEBO.

Fresh Democratic Party: 4 Park Close, Aguyi Ironsi St, Maitma, Abuja; Chair. Rev. CHRIS OKOTIE; Nat. Sec. SOLA SALAKO.

Movement for the Actualization of the Sovereign State of Biafra (MASSOB): Okwe, Imo; tel. 7039015000 (mobile); e-mail massob_1999@yahoo.com; f. 1999; Leader Chief RALPH UWAZURIKE.

Movement for the Emancipation of the Niger Delta (MEND): f. 2005; main Ijaw militant group operating in the Niger Delta; Leader Maj.-Gen. GODSWILL TAMUNO.

Movement for the Survival of the Ogoni People (MOSOP): 17 Kenule St, Bori, Khana Local Govt Area, Ogoni; tel. (84) 233907; e-mail info@mosop.org; internet www.mosop.org; f. 1990 to organize opposition to petroleum production in Ogoni territory; Pres. LEDUM MITEE; Sec.-Gen. MOSES DAMGBOR.

National Conscience Party (NCP): 18 Phase 1 Low Cost Housing Estate, Lake City Ave, Gwagwalada, Abuja; tel. (9) 4937279; Chair. Dr TANKO YUNUSA.

National Democratic Party (NDP): Plot 39, Durban St, off Ademola Adetokunbo Cres., Wuse II, Abuja; tel. (9) 6704070; regd June 2002; Chair. Alhaji ALIYU HABU FARI; Nat. Sec. ADEMOLA AYOADE.

Niger Delta People's Volunteer Force (NDPVF): prominent Ijaw militant group operating in the Niger Delta; Leader Alhaji MUJAHID DOKUBO-ASARI.

People For Democratic Change (PDC): Kalabari St, Karu Site, Karu, Abuja; Nat. Chair. MAHMUD MUDI WAZIRI; Nat. Sec. BENJAMIN EMEKA IGWE.

People's Democratic Party (PDP): Wadata Plaza, Michael Okpara Way, Zone 5, Wuse, Abuja; tel. (9) 5232589; e-mail info@ peopledemocraticparty.org; internet www.peoplesdemocraticparty .com.ng; f. 1998; supports greater federalism; ruling party; Chair. Alhaji BAMANGA TUKUR; Nat. Sec. Chief OLISA METUH.

Progressive People's Alliance (PPA): 36 Moses A. Majekodunmi Cres., Utako District, Abuja; tel. 7038263544 (mobile); internet ppanigeria.com; Chair. SAM NKIRE; Nat. Sec. DAHIRU MUSA MOHAMMED.

Diplomatic Representation

EMBASSIES AND HIGH COMMISSIONS IN NIGERIA

Algeria: Plot 203, Etim Inyang Cres., POB 55238, Falomo, Lagos; tel. (1) 612092; fax (1) 2624017; Ambassador HAFRAD ALI.

Angola: 5 Kasumu Ekomode St, Victoria Island, POB 50437, Falomo Ikoyi, Lagos; tel. (1) 611702; fax (1) 618675; Ambassador EVARISTO DOMINGOS KIMBA.

Argentina: 1611 Yusuf Maitama Sule St, Asokoro District, Abuja; tel. (9) 7800651; fax (9) 3148683; e-mail enige@mrecic.gov.ar; internet www.nigeria.embajada-argentina.gov.ar; Ambassador MARIA SUSANA PATARO.

Australia: 5th Floor, Oakland Centre, 48 Aguiyi Ironsi St, Maitama, Abuja; PMB 5152, Abuja; tel. (9) 4612780; fax (9) 4612782; e-mail ahc .abuja@dfat.gov.au; internet www.nigeria.embassy.gov.au; High Commissioner DAVID JONATHAN RICHARDSON.

Austria: Plot 9, Usuma St, Maitama, Abuja; tel. 7064183226 (mobile); fax (9) 4612715; e-mail abuja-ob@bmeia.gv.at; Ambassador Dr STEFAN SCHOLZ.

Belarus: Sheraton Abuja Hotel, RM 317, Ladi Kwali Street, Maitama, Abuja; tel. 8092349803 (mobile); e-mail nigeria@mfa.gov.by; Ambassador VYACHESLAV BESKOSTY.

Belgium: 9 Usuma St, Maitama, Abuja; tel. (9) 4131859; fax (9) 4132015; e-mail abuja@diplobel.fed.be; internet www.diplomatie.be/ abuja; Ambassador DIRK VERHEYEN.

Benin: 4 Abudu Smith St, Victoria Island, POB 5705, Lagos; tel. (1) 2614411; fax (1) 2612385; Ambassador PATRICE HOUNGAVOU.

Brazil: Plot 173, Mississippi St, Maitama, Abuja; tel. (9) 4134067; fax (9) 4134066; Ambassador João André Pinto Dias Lima.

Bulgaria: 10 Euphrates St, off Aminu Kano Cres., Maitama, Abuja; tel. (9) 4130034; fax (9) 4132741; e-mail bulembassy@yahoo.com; internet www.mfa.bg/abuja; Ambassador Miroslav Nikolaev Komarov.

Burkina Faso: No. 4, Freetown St, off Ademola Adetokunbo Cres., Wuse II, Abuja; tel. (9) 4130491; fax (9) 4130492; e-mail ebfn@nova .net.ng; Ambassador Dramane Yaméogo.

Cameroon: 469, Lobito Cres., Wuse II, Abuja; tel. (1) 4611355; e-mail haucocamabuja@yahoo.fr; High Commissioner Abbas Ibrahima Salaheddine.

Canada: 15 Bobo St, Maitama, POB 5144, Abuja; tel. (9) 4612900; fax (9) 4612901; e-mail abuja@international.gc.ca; internet www .canadainternational.gc.ca/nigeria; High Commissioner Christopher Cooter.

Chad: 10 Mississippi St, PMB 488, Abuja; tel. (9) 4130751; fax (9) 4130752; Ambassador Mahamat Habib Doutoum.

China, People's Republic: Plot 302–303, Central Area, Abuja; tel. (9) 4618661; fax (9) 4618660; e-mail chinaemb_ng@mfa.gov.cn; internet ng.china-embassy.org; Ambassador Deng Boqing.

Congo, Republic: 447 Lobito Cres., Abuja; tel. (9) 4137407; fax (9) 4130157; Ambassador Peter Ngui.

Côte d'Ivoire: 2630 Gourara St, Abuja; tel. (9) 4133087; fax (9) 4133137; e-mail cotedivoire@micro.com.ng; Ambassador Maman Touré.

Cuba: Plot 339, Diplomatic Zone, Area 10, Garki, Abuja; tel. (9) 4614821; fax (9) 4614820; e-mail embajada@ng.embacuba.cu; internet emba.cubaminrex.cu/nigeriaing; Ambassador Elio Savón Oliva.

Czech Republic: Plot 1223, 5 Gnassingbé Eyadéma St, Asokoro District, POB 4628, Abuja; tel. 7037571096 (mobile); e-mail abuja@ embassy.mzv.cz; internet www.mzv.cz/abuja; Ambassador Jaroslav Siro.

Egypt: 8 Buzi Close, off Amazon St, Maitama, Abuja; PMB 5069, Wuse, Abuja; tel. (9) 4136091; fax (9) 4132602; Ambassador Youssef Hassan Shawki.

Equatorial Guinea: 20 Dakala St, off Parakou Cres., off Aminu Kano Cres., Wuse II, Abuja; tel. and fax (9) 7816867; e-mail egembassyabj@hotmail.com; Ambassador Job Obiang Esono Mbengono.

Eritrea: Plot 1510, Yedseram St, off IBB Way, Maitama, Abuja; tel. 8139856889 (mobile); fax (9) 4136085; e-mail eriemba_nigeria@ yahoo.com; Ambassador Mohammed Ali Omaro.

Ethiopia: 19 Ona Cres., Maitama, POB 2488, Abuja; tel. (1) 4131691; fax (1) 4131692; e-mail etabuja@primair.net; Ambassador Yohaness Genda.

Finland: 9 Iro Dan Musa St, Asokoro, Abuja; tel. 8037851150 (mobile); e-mail sanomat.aba@formin.fi; internet www .finlandnigeria.org; Ambassador Riitta Korpivaara.

France: 37 Udi Hills St, off Aso Dr., Abuja; tel. (9) 5235510; fax (9) 5235482; e-mail sec-amb.abuja-amba@diplomatie.gouv.fr; internet www.ambafrance-ng.org; Ambassador Jean-Michel Dumond.

Gabon: 8 Norman Williams St, SW Ikoyi, POB 5989, Lagos; tel. (1) 684566; fax (1) 2690692; Ambassador Corentin Hervo-Akendengue.

The Gambia: 7 Misratah St, off Parakou Cres., Wuse II, PMB 5058, Abuja; tel. (9) 5241224; fax (9) 5241228; e-mail ghcabuja@yahoo.com; High Commissioner Angela Colley.

Germany: 9 Lake Maracaibo Close, off Amazon St, Maitama, Abuja; tel. (9) 4130962; fax (9) 4130949; e-mail info@abuja.diplo.de; internet www.abuja.diplo.de; Ambassador Dorothee Janetzke-Wenzel.

Ghana: 21–25 King George V Rd, POB 889, Lagos; tel. (1) 2630015; fax (1) 2630338; High Commissioner Alhaji Baba Kamara.

Greece: 6 Seguela St, Wuse II, POB 11525, Abuja; tel. (9) 4612775; fax (9) 4612778; e-mail gremb.abj@mfa.gr; internet www.mfa.gr/ abuja; Ambassador Haralambos Dafaranos.

Guinea: No. 349, Central Business District, opp. United Nations Premises, POB 591, Abuja; tel. (9) 4618612; fax (9) 4618611; e-mail ambaguinig@yahoo.com; Ambassador Dr Cheick Abdoul Camara.

Holy See: Pope John Paul II Cres., Maitama, PMB 541, Garki, Abuja; tel. (9) 4138381; fax (9) 4136653; e-mail nuntiusabj@hotmail .com; Apostolic Nuncio Augustine Kasujja (Titular Archbishop of Caesarea in Numidia).

Hungary: 61 Jose Marti Cres., Asokoro, POB 5299, Abuja; tel. 7064786188 (mobile); e-mail mission.abv@kum.hu; internet www .mfa.gov.hu/emb/abuja; Ambassador Zsolt Maris.

India: 15 Rio Negro Close, off Yedseram St, Maitama, Abuja; tel. (9) 4602800; fax (9) 4602805; e-mail hoc.abuja@mea.gov.in; internet www.indianhcabuja.com; High Commissioner Mahesh Sachdev.

Indonesia: 5B Anifowoshe St, Victoria Island, POB 3473, Marina, Lagos; tel. (1) 2614601; fax (1) 2613301; e-mail unitkomigs@hyperia .com; Ambassador Sudirman Haseng.

Iran: 1 Udi Hills St, off Aso Dr., Maitama, Abuja; tel. (1) 5238048; fax (1) 5237785; e-mail iranabuja@gmail.com; Ambassador Saeed Koozechi.

Ireland: 11 Negro Cres., Maitama District, Abuja; tel. (9) 4620611; fax (9) 4620613; e-mail abujaembassy@dfa.ie; internet www .embassyofireland.org.ng; Ambassador Kyle O'Sullivan.

Israel: Plot 12, Mary Slessor St, Asokoro, POB 10924, Abuja; tel. (9) 4605500; e-mail info@abuja.mfa.gov.il; internet abuja.mfa.gov.il; Ambassador Moshe Ram.

Italy: 21st Cres., off Constitution Ave, Central Business District, Abuja; tel. (9) 4614722; fax (9) 4614709; e-mail ambasciata.abuja@ esteri.it; internet www.ambabuja.esteri.it; Ambassador Roberto Colaminè.

Jamaica: Plot 247, Muhammadu Buhari Way, Central Area District, Abuja; tel. and fax (9) 2345107; e-mail jamaicanembassy@ yahoo.com; High Commissioner Ann Scott.

Japan: 9 Bobo St, off Gana St, Maitama, PMB 5070, Abuja; tel. (9) 4138898; fax (870) 600-315-545 (satellite); Ambassador Ryuichi Shoji.

Kenya: 18 Yedseram St, Maitama, PMB 5160, Abuja; tel. (9) 4139155; fax (9) 4139157; e-mail abuja@mfa.go.ke; High Commissioner Daniel Mepukori Koikai.

Korea, Democratic People's Republic: Plot 350, Central Area, Cadastral Zone, AO, POB 407, Garki, Abuja; tel. (9) 2347200; fax (9) 2347199; Ambassador Jong Hak Se.

Korea, Republic: 9 Ovia Cres., off Pope John Paul St, Maitama, POB 6870, Abuja; tel. (9) 4612701; fax (9) 4612702; e-mail emb-ng@ mofat.go.kr; internet nga-abuja.mofat.go.kr; Ambassador Choi Jong-Hyun.

Liberia: 3 Idejo St, Plot 162, off Adeola Odeku St, Victoria Island, POB 70841, Lagos; tel. (1) 2618899; Ambassador Prof. Al-Hassan Conteh.

Libya: Plot 1591, Mike Okoye Cl., off George Sowemimo St, Asokoro Ext., POB 435, Garki, Abuja; tel. (9) 3148356; fax (9) 3148354; Ambassador Eng. Mansour O. Osman.

Malaysia: 4A, Plot 2232B, Rio Negro Close, off Yedseram St, Maitama, PMB 5217, Wuse, Abuja; tel. (9) 7809379; internet www .kln.gov.my/abuja; e-mail malabuja@kln.gov.my; High Commissioner Nik Mustafa Kamal Nik Ahmad.

Mauritania: Plot 31, Gaffar Animashaun St, Victoria Island Annex, POB 53569, Lagos; tel. (1) 2618966; Ambassador Bâ Abderrahmane.

Mexico: 39 Usuma St, off Ghana St, Maitama District, PMB 718, Garki, Abuja; tel. (9) 4620630; e-mail embnigeria@sre.gob.mx; Ambassador Marco Antonio Garcia Blanco.

Morocco: 5 Mary Slessor St, off Udo Udoma Cres., Asokoro, Abuja; tel. (9) 8746697; fax (9) 3141959; e-mail mcherkaoui45@yahoo.fr; Ambassador Mustapha Bouh.

Namibia: Plot 1738, T. Y. Danjuma St, Cadasdral Zone, A4 Asokoro, Abuja; tel. (9) 7809441; e-mail namibiahighcomabuja@yahoo.com; internet www.namibiahc.com.ng; High Commissioner Selma Ashipala-Musavyi.

Netherlands: 21st Cres., off Constitution Ave, Central Business District, Abuja; tel. (9) 4611200; fax (9) 4611240; e-mail abj@minbuza .nl; internet nigeria.nlembassy.org; Ambassador Bert Ronhaar.

Niger: 15 Adeola Odeku St, Victoria Island, PMB 2736, Lagos; tel. (1) 4136206; fax (1) 4136205; Ambassador Moussa Elhadji Ibrahim.

Norway: 54 T.Y. Danjuma St, Asokoro, Abuja; tel. (9) 8746989; fax (9) 3149309; e-mail emb.abuja@mfa.no; internet www.emb-norway .com.ng; Ambassador Rolf Kristian Ree.

Pakistan: 4 Samora Machel Street, Asokoro, Abuja; tel. (9) 3141650; fax (9) 3141652; e-mail pahicabuja@yahoo.com; High Commissioner Mohamad Ashraf Saleem.

Philippines: 2 Kainji St, cnr Lake Chad Cres., Maitama, Abuja; tel. (9) 4137981; fax (9) 4137650; e-mail pe.abuja@dfa.gov.ph; Ambassador Nestor Nabayra Padalhin.

Poland: 10 Ona Cres., off Lake Chad Cres., Maitama, 900271, Abuja; tel. 8052000204 (mobile); e-mail contact@abuja-polemb.net; internet www.abuja.polemb.net; Ambassador Przemysław Niesiołowski.

Portugal: Usama St 53, Maitama, Abuja; tel. (9) 4611443; fax (9) 4602629; e-mail portemb@rosecom.net; Ambassador Simeão Archer Pinto de Mesquita.

Romania: Nelson Mandela St, No. 76, Plot 498, Asokoro, Abuja; tel. (9) 3142304; fax (9) 3142306; e-mail romembabujaconsularsection@ gmail.com; internet www.romnig.com; Chargé d'affaires a.i. Barbu Nicolae Moldoveanu.

Russia: 5 Walter Carrington Cres., Victoria Island, POB 2723, Lagos; tel. (1) 2613359; fax (1) 4619994; Ambassador ALEXANDER DIMITRIEVICH POLYAKOV.

Rwanda: Abuja; High Commissioner JOSEPH HABINEZA.

Saudi Arabia: Plot 347H, off Adetokunbo Ademola Cres., Wuse II, Abuja; tel. (9) 4131880; fax (9) 4134906; Ambassador (vacant).

Senegal: 14 Kofo Abayomi Rd, Victoria Island, PMB 2197, Lagos; tel. (1) 2611722; Ambassador SAOUDATOU NDIAYE SECK.

Serbia: 11, Rio Negro Close, off Yedseram St, Cadastral Zone A6, Maitama District, Abuja; tel. 8059738141 (mobile); fax (9) 4130078; e-mail mail@ambnig.com; Ambassador RIFAT RONDIC.

Sierra Leone: Plot 308 Mission Rd, opp Ministry of Defence (Ship House), Diplomatic Zone, Central Business District, Abuja; tel. (9) 8766435; fax (9) 8725413; e-mail slhcnig@yahoo.com; High Commissioner HENRY O. MACAULEY.

Slovakia: POB 1290, Lagos; tel. (1) 2621585; fax (1) 2612103; e-mail obeo.sk@micro.com.ng; Ambassador MIROSLAV HACEK.

Somalia: Plot 1270, off Adeola Odeka St, POB 6355, Lagos; tel. (1) 2611283; Ambassador M. S. HASSAN.

South Africa: 71 Usuma St, off Gana St, Maitama, Abuja; tel. (9) 4133776; fax (9) 4133829; e-mail sahcabuja@yahoo.co.uk; High Commissioner J. N. K. MAMABOLO.

Spain: 8 Bobo Close, Maitama, PMB 5120, Wuse, Abuja; tel. (9) 4613258; fax (9) 4613259; e-mail emb.abuja@maec.es; internet www.maec.es/embajadas/abuja; Ambassador ALVARO CASTILLO AGUILAR.

Sudan: Plot 337, Misson Rd Zone, Central Area District, Abuja; tel. (9) 6700668; fax (9) 2346265; e-mail sudaniabj@hotmail.com; Ambassador AHMED ALTIGANI SALEH.

Sweden: PMB 569, Garki, Abuja; tel. (9) 8746913; fax (870) 782-248-789 (satellite); e-mail ambassaden.abuja@foreign.ministry.se; internet www.swedenabroad.com/abuja; Ambassador SVANTE KILANDER.

Switzerland: 157 Adetokumbo Ademola Cres., Wuse II, Abuja; tel. (9) 4610540; fax (9) 4610548; e-mail abu.vertretung@eda.admin.ch; internet www.eda.admin.ch/abuja; Ambassador Dr ANDREAS BAUM.

Syria: 25 Kofo Abayomi St, Victoria Island, Lagos; tel. (1) 2615860; Chargé d'affaires a.i. MUSTAFA HAJ-ALI.

Tanzania: 8 Agoro Odiyan St, Victoria Island, POB 6417, Lagos; tel. (1) 613604; fax (1) 610016; e-mail tanabuja@lytos.com; High Commissioner (vacant).

Thailand: 24 Tennesse Cres., off Panama St, Maitama, Abuja; tel. (9) 8723746; fax (9) 4135193; e-mail thaiabj@mfa.go.th; Ambassador N. SATHAPORN.

Togo: Plot 976, Oju Olobun Close, Victoria Island, POB 1435, Lagos; tel. (1) 2617449; fax (1) 617478; Ambassador FOLI-AGBENOZAN TET-TEKPOE.

Trinidad and Tobago: 7 Casablanca St, off Nairobi St, off Amino Kano Cres., Wuse II, Abuja; tel. (9) 6411118; fax (9) 4611117; e-mail trinitobagoabj@yahoo.co.uk; internet www.ttmissionsnigeria.com; High Commissioner NYAHUMA MENTHUHOTEP OBIKA.

Turkey: 5 Amazon St, Minister's Hill, Maitama, Abuja; tel. (9) 4139787; fax (9) 4139457; e-mail embassy.abuja@mfa.gov.tr; internet www.abuja.emb.mfa.gov.tr; Ambassador ALI RIFAT KÖKSAL.

Ukraine: Plot 15, Moundou St, Wuse II, Abuja; tel. (9) 5239577; fax (9) 5239578; e-mail emb_ng@mfa.gov.ua; internet www.mfa.gov.ua/nigeria; Ambassador VALERII VASYLIEV.

United Kingdom: Dangote House, Aguiyi Ironsi St, Wuse, Abuja; tel. (9) 4132010; fax (9) 4623223; e-mail information.abuja@fco.gov.uk; internet www.ukinnigeria.fco.gov.uk; High Commissioner Dr ANDREW JOHN POCOCK.

USA: Plot 1075, Diplomatic Dr., Central District Area, Abuja; tel. (9) 4614000; fax (9) 4614171; e-mail consularabuja@state.gov; internet abuja.usembassy.gov; Ambassador TERENCE PATRICK MCCULLEY.

Venezuela: Plot 1361 Hon, Justice Sowemino St, Asokoro District, Abuja; tel. (9) 3140900; fax (9) 3140903; e-mail evenigeria@yahoo.com; Ambassador BORIS ENRÍQUEZ MARTÍNEZ.

Zambia: 351 Mission Rd, Central Area District, Garki, Abuja; tel. (9) 4618605; fax (9) 4618602; e-mail zambiahc@yahoo.com; High Commissioner GEORGE MPOMBO.

Zimbabwe: 19 Tiamiyu Savage St, POB 50247, Victoria Island, Lagos; tel. (1) 2619328; e-mail zimabuja@yahoo.co.uk; High Commissioner Dr JOHN SHUMBA MVUNDURA.

Judicial System

The Constitution provides for both federal and state courts, in addition to election tribunals. The Supreme Court is the highest court of Nigeria. There are also Magistrate, Area and Customary Courts with limited jurisdiction, which are established by the National Assembly in respect of the Federal Capital Territory, Abuja, and the State House of Assembly in respect of a state.

Supreme Court: Three Arms Complex, Central District, PMB 308, Abuja; tel. 8152576253 (mobile); internet supremecourt.gov.ng; consists of a Chief Justice and up to 15 Justices, appointed by the President, on the recommendation of the National Judicial Council (subject to the approval of the Senate); has original jurisdiction in any dispute between the Federation and a state, or between states, and hears appeals from the Federal Court of Appeal; Chief Justice ALOMA MARIAM MUKHTAR.

Court of Appeal: consists of a President and at least 35 Justices, of whom three must be experts in Islamic (*Shari'a*) law and three experts in Customary law; has 12 divisions in various states.

Federal High Court: 24 Oyinkan Abayomi Dr., Ikoyi, PMB 40012, Falomo, Lagos; internet www.fhc-ng.com; Chief Judge IBRAHIM NDAH AUTA.

Each state has a **High Court**, consisting of a Chief Judge and a number of judges, appointed by the Governor of the state on the recommendation of the National Judicial Council (subject to the approval of the House of Assembly of the state). If required, a state may have a **Shari'a Court of Appeal** (dealing with Islamic civil law) and a **Customary Court of Appeal**. **Special Military Tribunals** have been established to try offenders accused of crimes such as corruption, drugs-trafficking and armed robbery; appeals against rulings of the Special Military Tribunals are referred to a **Special Appeals Tribunal**, which comprises retired judges.

Religion

ISLAM

According to the 2003 Nigeria Demographic and Health Survey, Muslims comprised 50.5% of the total population.

Spiritual Head: Col MUHAMMADU SA'AD ABUBAKAR (the Sultan of Sokoto).

CHRISTIANITY

According to the 2003 Nigeria Demographic and Health Survey, 48.2% of the population were Christians.

Christian Council of Nigeria: 139 Ogunlana Dr., Surulere, POB 2838, Lagos; tel. (1) 7923495; f. 1929; 15 full mems and six assoc. mems; Pres. Most Rev. EMMANUEL UDOFIA; Gen. Sec. Rev. IKECNUKWU OKORIE.

The Anglican Communion

Anglicans are adherents of the Church of the Province of Nigeria, comprising 139 dioceses. Nigeria, formerly part of the Province of West Africa, became a separate Province in 1979; in 1997 it was divided into three separate provinces and a 10-province structure for the Church of Nigeria (Anglican Communion) was proclaimed in January 2003.

Primate, Archbishop of the Province of Abuja: Most Rev. NICHOLAS DIKERIEHI OROGODO OKOH, Bishopscourt, Cable Point, POB 216, Asaba; tel. (56) 280682; e-mail primate@anglican-nig.org; internet www.anglican-nig.org.

Archbishop of the Province of Bendel and Bishop of Esan: Most Rev. FRIDAY JOHN IMAEKHAI, 24 Douala St, Wuse Zone 5, POB 212, Abuja; tel. (9) 5236950; fax (9) 5230986.

Archbishop of the Province of Ibadan and Bishop of Ibadan: Most Rev. JOSEPH AKINFENWA, POB 3075, Mapo; tel. (2) 8101400; fax (2) 8101413; e-mail ibadan@anglican.skannet.com.ng.

Archbishop of the Province of Jos and Bishop of Maiduguri: Most Rev. EMMANUEL KANA MANI, Bishopscourt, off Lagos St, GRA POB 1693, Maiduguri; tel. (76) 234010; e-mail maiduguri@anglican-nig.org.

Archbishop of the Province of Kaduna and Bishop of Kaduna: Most Rev. JOSIAH IDOWU-FEARON, POB 72, Kaduna; tel. (62) 240085; fax (62) 244408; e-mail manasoko@infoweb.abs.net.

Archbishop of the Province of Lagos and Bishop of Lagos: Most Rev. EPHRAIM ADEBOLA ADEMOWO, 29 Marina, POB 13, Lagos; tel. (1) 2636026; fax (1) 2636536; e-mail lagos@anglican.skannet.com.ng.

Archbishop of the Province of the Niger and Bishop of Awka: Most Rev. MAXWELL SAMUEL CHIKE ANIKWENWA, Bishopscourt, Ifite Rd, POB 130, Awka; tel. (48) 550058; fax (48) 550052; e-mail angawka@infoweb.abs.net.

Archbishop of the Niger Delta and Bishop of Aba: Most Rev. UGOCHUCKWU UWAOMA EZUOKE, Bishopscourt, 70/72 St Michael's Rd, POB 212, Aba; tel. (82) 227666; e-mail aba@anglican-nig.org.

Archbishop of the Province of Ondo and Bishop of Ekiti: Most Rev. SAMUEL ADEDAYE ABE, Bishopscourt, POB 12, Okesa St, Ado-Ekiti, Ekiti; tel. (30) 250305; e-mail ekiti@anglican.skannet.com.ng.

Archbishop of the Province of Owerri and Bishop of Orlu: Most Rev. BENNETT C. I. OKORO, Bishopscourt, POB 260, Nkwerre; tel. (82) 440538.

General Secretary: Ven. EMMANUEL ADEKUNLE, 24 Douala St, Wuse Zone 5, POB 212, Abuja; tel. (9) 5236950; fax (9) 5230987; e-mail general_secretary@anglican-nig.org.

The Roman Catholic Church

Nigeria comprises nine archdioceses, 43 dioceses and two Apostolic Vicariates. An estimated 15% of the population are Roman Catholics.

Catholic Bishops' Conference of Nigeria

Plot 459, Cadastral Zone B2, Southern Park, Durumi 1, Garki, POB 6523, Abuja; tel. (9) 5239413; fax (9) 5230881; e-mail cathsec1@infoweb.abs.net; internet www.cbcn-ng.org.

f. 1976; Pres. Most Rev. FELIX ALABA ADEOSIN JOB (Archbishop of Ibadan); Sec.-Gen. of Secretariat Rev. Fr MATTHEW HASSAN KUKAH.

Archbishop of Abuja: Cardinal JOHN OLORUNFEMI ONAIYEKAN, Archdiocesan Secretariat, POB 286, Garki, Abuja; tel. (9) 2340661; fax (9) 2340662; e-mail onaiyekan7@hotmail.com.

Archbishop of Benin City: AUGUSTINE OBIORA AKUBEZE, Archdiocesan Secretariat, POB 35, Benin City, Edo; tel. (52) 253787; fax (52) 255763; e-mail cadobc@infoweb.abs.net.

Archbishop of Calabar: Most Rev. JOSEPH EFFIONG EKUWEM, Catholic Secretariat, PMB 1044, 1 Bishop Moynagh Ave, Calabar, Cross River; tel. (87) 231666; fax (87) 239177; e-mail archdical@yahoo.com.

Archbishop of Ibadan: Most Rev. FELIX ALABA JOB, Archbishop's House, PMB 5057, 8 Bale Latosa Rd, Onireke, Ibadan, Oyo; tel. (22) 2413544; fax (22) 2414855; e-mail archdiocese.ibadan@skannet.com.

Archbishop of Jos: Most Rev. IGNATIUS AYAU KAIGAMA, Archdiocesan Secretariat, 20 Joseph Gomwalk Rd, POB 494, Jos, Plateau; tel. (73) 452878; fax (73) 451547; e-mail josarch@hisen.com.

Archbishop of Kaduna: Most Rev. MATTHEW MAN-OSO NDAGOSO, Archbishop's House, 71 Tafawa Balewa Way, POB 248, Kaduna; tel. (62) 246076; fax (62) 240026; e-mail catholickaduna@yahoo.com.

Archbishop of Lagos: Most Rev. ALFRED ADEWALE MARTINS, Archdiocesan Secretariat, 19 Catholic Mission St, POB 8, Lagos; tel. (1) 2635729; fax (1) 2633841; e-mail arclagos@yahoo.com.

Archbishop of Onitsha: Most Rev. VALERIAN OKEKE, Archdiocesan Secretariat, POB 411, Onitsha, Anambra; tel. (46) 413298; fax (46) 413913; e-mail secretariat@onitsha-archdiocese.org.

Archbishop of Owerri: Most Rev. ANTHONY JOHN VALENTINE OBINNA, Villa Assumpta, POB 85, Owerri, Imo; tel. (83) 250115; fax (83) 230760; e-mail owcatsec@owerriarchdiocese.org.

Other Christian Churches

Brethren Church of Nigeria: c/o Kulp Bible School, POB 1, Mubi, Adamawa; f. 1923; Gen. Sec. Rev. JINATU WAMDEO; 100,000 mems.

Church of the Lord (Aladura) Worldwide: 10/12 Primate Oshitelu St, Ogere-Remo, POB 71 Shagamu, Ogun; tel. (803) 3307288; fax (805) 3257190; e-mail cla_primate@yahoo.com; internet www.tclaw.org; f. 1925; Primate Most Rev. Dr RUFUS OKIKIOLA OSITELU; 3.8m. mems.

Lutheran Church of Christ in Nigeria: POB 21, Hospital Rd, Numan, Adamawa; tel. (75) 772330; fax (75) 625093; e-mail nemuelbabba@hotmail.com; Pres. Archbishop CHRISTIAN EKONG; 1.9m. mems (2010).

Lutheran Church of Nigeria: POB 49, Obot Idim Ibesikpo, Uyo, Akwa Ibom; tel. (85) 200505; fax (85) 200451; e-mail chrisekonglcn@yahoo.com; internet www.lutheranchurchnigeria.org; f. 1936; Pres. Most Rev. CHRISTIAN EKONG; 142,000 mems (2010).

Methodist Church Nigeria: Wesley House, 21–22 Marina, POB 2011, Lagos; tel. (1) 2702563; fax (1) 2702710; 483,500 mems; Patriarch Rev. Dr SUNDAY OLA KAKINDE.

Nigerian Baptist Convention: Baptist Bldg, PMB 5113, Ibadan; tel. (2) 2412267; fax (2) 2413561; e-mail baptconv@nigerianbaptist.org; internet nigerianbaptist.org; Pres. Rev. Dr REUBEN I. CHUGA; Gen. Sec. Dr SAMSON OLASUPO AYOKUNLE; 3.5m. mems.

The Presbyterian Church of Nigeria: 26–29 Ehere Rd, Ogbor Hill, POB 2635, Aba, Imo; tel. (82) 222551; f. 1846; Moderator Rt Rev. Dr UBON B. USUNG; Synod Clerk Rev. NDUKWE NWACHUKWU EME; 1m. mems.

The Redeemed Church of Christ, the Church of the Foursquare Gospel, the Qua Iboe Church and the Salvation Army are prominent among numerous other Christian churches active in Nigeria.

AFRICAN RELIGIONS

The beliefs, rites and practices of the people of Nigeria are very diverse, varying between ethnic groups and between families in the same group.

The Press

DAILIES

Al-Mizan: internet almizan.faithweb.com; Hausa; Editor IBRAHIM MUSA.

Aminiya: 20 POW Mafemi Cres., off Solomon Lar Way, Utako, Abuja; tel. (9) 6726241; internet aminiya.dailytrust.com; Hausa; Editor-in-Chief MANNIR DAN ALI.

BusinessDay: 72 Festac Link Rd, Amuwo Odofin, Lagos; tel. 8034694482 (mobile); internet www.businessdayonline.com; Editor PHILLIP ISAKPA.

Daily Champion: Isolo Industrial Estate, Oshodi-Apapa, Lagos; fax (1) 4526011; e-mail letters@champion-newspapers.com; internet www.champion-newspapers.com; Man. Editor UGO ONUOHA.

Daily Independent: Independent Newspapers Ltd, Block 5, Plot 7D, Wempco Rd, Ogba, PMB 21777, Ikeja, Lagos; tel. (1) 4962136; e-mail newseditor@idailyindependentnig.com; internet www.dailyindependentnig.com; f. 2001; Editor IKECHUKWU AMAECHI.

Daily Triumph: Triumph Publishing Co Ltd, Gidan Sa'adu Zungur, PMB 3155, Kano; tel. (64) 633875; fax (64) 630273; internet www.triumphnewsng.com; Editor Dr MUKHTARI MAGAJI.

Daily Trust: 20 POW Mafemi Cres., off Solomon Lar Way, Utako, Abuja; tel. (9) 6726241; e-mail dailytrust@yahoo.co.uk; internet www.dailytrust.com; f. 2001; Editor HABEEB PINDIGA.

The Guardian: Guardian Newspapers Ltd, Rutam House, Isolo Expressway, Isolo, PMB 1217, Oshodi, Lagos; tel. (1) 4524111; fax (1) 4524080; e-mail editday@ngrguardiannews.com; internet www.ngrguardiannews.com; f. 1983; independent; Editor-in-Chief EMEKA IZEZE; Editor DEBO ADESINA; circ. 80,000.

Leadership: 8A Umuozu Close, off Samuel Ladoke Akintola Blvd, POB 9514, Garki, Abuja; tel. (9) 2345055; fax (9) 2345360; e-mail leadershipnigeria@yahoo.com; internet leadershipnigeria.com.

The Nation: Vintage Press Ltd, 27B Fatai Atere Way, Matori, Mushin, Lagos; tel. (1) 8168361; e-mail info@thenationonlineng.com; internet www.thenationonlineng.net; f. 2006; Editor GBENGA OMOTOSO.

National Daily: e-mail editor@nationaldailyngr.com; internet www.nationaldailyngr.com; f. 2006; Exec. Editor SYLVESTER EBHODAGHE; circ. 50,000.

New Age: Lagos; e-mail ebiz@newage-online.com; internet www.newage-online.com; Editor STEVE OSUJI.

New Nigerian: New Nigerian Newspapers Ltd, 4/5 Ahmadu Bello Way, POB 254, Kaduna; tel. (62) 245220; fax (62) 245221; internet www.newnigerians.com; f. 1965; govt-owned; Editor-in-Chief NDANUSA ALAO; circ. 80,000.

Nigerian Compass: 10 Western Industrial Ave, Compass Media Village, Isheri, Ogun; tel. (1) 7400001; internet www.compassnews.net; Editor GABRIEL AKINADEWO.

Nigerian Observer: Bendel Newspaper Co Ltd, 24 Airport Rd, PMB 1334, Benin City; tel. (52) 240050; e-mail info@nigerianobservernews.com; internet nigerianobservernews.com; f. 1968; Editor TONY IKEAKANAM; circ. 150,000.

Nigerian Tribune: African Newspapers of Nigeria Ltd, Imalefalafi St, Oke-Ado, POB 78, Ibadan; tel. (2) 2312844; e-mail editornigeriantribune@yahoo.com; internet www.tribune.com.ng; f. 1949; Editor EDWARD DICKSON; circ. 109,000.

Peoples Daily: 35 Ajose Adeogun St, Peace Park Plaza, 1st Floor, Utako, Abuja; tel. (9) 9702136; e-mail editor@peoplesdaily-online.com; internet www.peoplesdaily-online.com; Editor AHMED SHEKARAU.

The Port Harcourt Telegraph: NUJ Bldg, Ernest Ikoli Press Centre, Moscow Rd, Port Harcourt; tel. 8036002239 (mobile); e-mail phtelegraph@yahoo.com; internet www.phctelegraphnews.com; 3 a week; Editor-in-Chief OGBONNA NWUKE.

The Punch: 1 Olu Aboderin St, Onipetesi, PMB 21204, Ikeja, Lagos; tel. (1) 7748081; e-mail editor@punchontheweb.com; internet www.punchng.com; f. 1976; Editor-in-Chief ADEMOLA OSINUBI; circ. 150,000.

The Sun: The Sun Publishing Ltd, 2 Coscharis St, Kirikiri Industrial Layout, Apapa, PMB 21776 Ikeja, Lagos; tel. (1) 5875560; fax (1) 5875561; e-mail thesun@sunnewsonline.com; internet www.sunnewsonline.com; f. 2003; Editor STEVE NWOSU.

This Day: 35 Creek Rd, Apapa, Lagos; tel. 8022924721 (mobile); fax (1) 4600276; e-mail info@thisdayonline.com; internet www.thisdaylive.com; f. 1995; Editor IJEOMA NWOGWUGWU.

The Tide: Rivers State Newspaper Corpn, 1 Ikwerre Rd, POB 5072, Port Harcourt; tel. 8034780061 (mobile); e-mail webmaster@thetidenewsonline.com; internet www.thetidenewsonline.com; f. 1971; Editor SOYE WILSON JAMABO; circ. 30,000.

Vanguard: Kirikiri Canal, PMB 1007, Apapa; e-mail vanguard@linkserve.com.ng; internet www.vanguardngr.com; f. 1984; Editor MIDENO BAYAGBON; circ. 130,000.

SUNDAY NEWSPAPERS

New Nigerian on Sunday: 4/5 Ahmadu Bello Way, POB 254, Kaduna; tel. (62) 245220; fax (62) 245221; e-mail auduson@newnigerian.com; internet www.newnigeriannews.com/sunday; f. 1981; weekly; Editor MALAM TUKUR ABDULRAHMAN; circ. 120,000.

Next on Sunday: Timbuktu Media, 235 Igbosere Rd, Lapal Plaza, 2nd Floor, Lagos; tel. (1) 8977685; e-mail MediaRelations@TimbuktuMedia.com; internet 234next.com; Editor MUFU OGUNBUNMI.

Sunday Compass: 10 Western Industrial Ave, Compass Media Village, Isheri, Ogun; tel. (1) 7400001; internet www.compassnews.net; Editor DOTUN OLADIPO.

Sunday Observer: Bendel Newspapers Co Ltd, 24 Airport Rd, PMB 1334, Benin City; e-mail info@nigerianobservernews.com; internet www.nigerianobservernews.com; f. 1968; Editor T. O. BORHA; circ. 60,000.

Sunday Sun: The Sun Publishing Ltd, 2 Coscharis St, Kirikiri Industrial Layout, Apapa, PMB 21776 Ikeja, Lagos; tel. (1) 5875560; fax (1) 5875561; e-mail thesun@sunnewsonline.com; internet www.sunnewsonline.com; Editor FUNKE EGBEMODE.

Sunday Tide: Rivers State Newspaper Corpn, 4 Ikwerre Rd, POB 5072, Port Harcourt; f. 1971; Editor AUGUSTINE NJOAGWUANI.

Sunday Tribune: Imalefalafi St, POB 78, Oke-Ado, Ibadan; tel. (2) 2310886; e-mail editornigeriantribune@yahoo.com; internet www.tribune.com.ng; Editor DEBO ABDULLAHI.

Sunday Triumph: Triumph Publishing Co Ltd, Gidan Sa'adu Zungur, PMB 3155, Kano; tel. (64) 633875; fax (64) 630273; internet www.triumphnewspapers.com; Editor MUSA AHMAD TIJJANI.

WEEKLIES

Business Hallmark: 109B Adeniyi Jones Ave, Ikeja, Lagos; tel. (1) 8034026226 (mobile); fax (1) 7397008; e-mail info@bizhallmark.com; internet bizhallmark.com; Editor-in-Chief PRINCE EMEKA OBASI.

Business World: 7B Regina Omolara St, off Opebi Rd, Opebi, Lagos; tel. (1) 8742199; e-mail info@businessworldng.com; internet businessworldng.com/web; Editor NIK OGBULI.

The News: 27 Acme Rd, Agidingbi, PMB 21531, Ikeja, Lagos; tel. (1) 7939286; e-mail info@thenewsng.com; internet thenewsng.com; independent; Editor-in-Chief JENKINS ALUMONA.

Newswatch: 3 Billingsway Rd, Oregun, Ikeja, Lagos; tel. (1) 7619660; e-mail newswatch@newswatchngr.com; internet www.newswatchngr.com; f. 1985; English; CEO RAY EKPU; Editor-in-Chief DAN AGBESE.

Nigerian Newsworld: A1 AMAC Plaza, Zone 3, Wuse, Abuja; tel. (9) 7816987; internet nigeriannewsworld.com; f. 2010; Editor-in-Chief DENNIS O. SAMI.

Technology Times: 9 Olufunlola Okikiolu St, off Toyin St, Ikeja, Lagos; tel. (1) 8968161; e-mail info@technologytimes.com.ng; internet www.technologytimes.com.ng; 2004; Man. Editor SHINA BADARU.

Tell Magazine: PMB 21749, Ikeja, Lagos; tel. (1) 7747910; e-mail newsroom@tellng.com; internet www.tellng.com; f. 1991; Editor AYO AKINKUOTU.

Truth (The Muslim Weekly): 45 Idumagbo Ave, POB 418, Lagos; tel. (1) 2668455; f. 1951; Editor S. O. LAWAL.

Weekly Insight: 33 Oron Road, Uyo; contemporary issues; Editor AUGUSTINE DAVID; circ. 5,000.

Weekly Trust: 20 POW Mafemi Cres., off Solomon Lar Way, Utako, Abuja; tel. (9) 6726241; internet www.weeklytrust.com.ng; Editor ABDULKAREEM BABA AMINU.

ENGLISH-LANGUAGE PERIODICALS

The Catholic Ambassador: PMB 2011, Iperu-Remo, Ogun; tel. 802350348; e-mail ambassadorpublications@yahoo.com; internet www.mspfathers.org; f. 1980; quarterly; Roman Catholic; Editor-in-Chief Rev. Fr PATRICK EBITO AKEKPE; circ. 20,000.

Economic Confidential: Abuja; e-mail info@economicconfidential.com; internet www.economicconfidential.net; f. 2007; monthly; Editor SANYA ADEJOKUN.

Financial Standard: 2 IPM Ave, CBD, Alausa-Ikeja, Lagos; tel. (1) 4934894; fax (1) 4934891; e-mail info@financialstandardnews.com; internet www.financialstandardnews.com; f. 1999; Mon.–Fri.; Editor-in-Chief SUNDAY SAMUEL ADEBOLA ONANUGA; circ. 60,000.

The Leader: 19A Assumpta Press Ave, Industrial Layout, PMB 1017, Owerri, Imo; tel. 8088227344 (mobile); e-mail leaderpress@yahoo.com; internet www.leadernewspaperowerri.com; f. 1956; weekly; Roman Catholic; Editor-in-Chief Rev. CHIMARAOKE SAMUEL OFFURUM.

Nigerian Journal of Economic and Social Studies: Nigerian Economic Society, c/o Dept of Economics, University of Ibadan, PMB 22004, Ibadan, Oyo; tel. (2) 8700395; e-mail journaleditor@nigerianeconomicsociety.org; internet www.nigerianeconomicsociety.org; f. 1957; 3 a year; Editor Prof. ABDUL GANIYU GARBA.

Nigerian Journal of Science: Science Asscn of Nigeria, c/o Dept of Computer Science, University of Ibadan, POB 4039, Ibadan, Oyo; tel. 8023382550 (mobile); e-mail editor@sciencenigeria.org; internet www.sciencenigeria.org; publ. of the Science Asscn of Nigeria; f. 1966; 2 a year; Editor Prof. I. FAWOLE; circ. 1,000.

Nigerian Medical Journal: Office of the Nigerian Medical Journal, Paediatric Surgery Unit, Department of Surgery, Jos University Teaching Hospital, PMB 2076, Jos, Plateau; e-mail nmj@nigeriannma.org; internet nigeriamedj.com; quarterly; Editor Prof. FRANCIS A. UBA.

VERNACULAR PERIODICAL

Gaskiya ta fi Kwabo: New Nigerian Newspapers Ltd, 4/5 Ahmadu Bello Way, POB 254, Kaduna; tel. (62) 245220; fax (62) 245221; internet www.newnigeriannews.com; f. 1939; 3 a week; Hausa; Editor ALHAJI NASIRU GARBA TOFA (acting).

NEWS AGENCY

News Agency of Nigeria (NAN): Independence Avenue, Central Business District, PMB 7006, Garki, Abuja; tel. (9) 6732189; e-mail nanhq@nanngr.com; internet www.nannewsngr.com; f. 1976; state-owned; Man. Dir OLUREMI OYO; Editor-in-Chief DIPO OGBEDE.

Publishers

Africana First Publishers Ltd: Book House Trust, 1 Africana-First Dr., PMB 1639, Onitsha; tel. (46) 485031; f. 1973; study guides, general science, textbooks; Chair. RALPH O. EKPEH; Man. Dir J. C. ODIKE.

Ahmadu Bello University Press: PMB 1094, Zaria; tel. (69) 550054; f. 1972; history, Africana, social sciences, education, literature and arts; Man. Dir SA'IDU HASSAN ADAMU.

Albah International Publishers: 100 Kurawa, Bompai-Kano, POB 6177, Kano City; f. 1978; Africana, Islamic, educational and general, in Hausa; Chair. BASHARI F. ROUKBAH.

Cassava Republic: Abuja; e-mail info@cassavarepublic.biz; internet www.cassavarepublic.biz; f. 2006; Publishers BIBI BAKARE-YUSUF, JEREMY WEATE.

Daar Communications PLC: Daar Communications Centre, Kpaduma Hills, off Gen. T. Y. Danjuma St, Asokoro, Abuja; tel. (9) 3144802; fax (9) 3300512; broadcasting and information services; Man. Dir LADI LAWAL.

Evans Brothers (Nigeria Publishers) Ltd: Jericho Rd, PMB 5164, Ibadan; tel. (2) 2414394; fax (2) 2410757; f. 1966; general and educational; Chair. Dr ADEKUNLE OJORA; Man. Dir GBENRO ADEGBOLE.

Fourth Dimension Publishing Co Ltd: 16 Fifth Ave, City Layout, PMB 01164, Enugu; tel. (42) 459969; fax (42) 456904; e-mail nwankwov@infoweb.abs.net; internet www.fdpbooks.com; f. 1977; periodicals, fiction, verse, educational and children's; Chair. ARTHUR NWANKWO; Man. Dir V. U. NWANKWO.

HEBN Publishers PLC: 1 Ighodaro Rd, Jericho, PMB 5205, Ibadan; tel. (2) 2412268; fax (2) 2411089; e-mail info@hebnpublishers.com; internet www.hebnpublishers.com; f. 1962; educational, law, medical and general; Chair. AYO OJENIYI; Man. Dir OLAWEPO SOGO.

Heritage Books: The Poet's Cottage, Artistes Village, Ilogbo-Eremi, Badagry Expressway, POB 610, Apapa, Lagos; tel. (1) 5871333; f. 1971; general; Chair. NAIWU OSAHON.

Ibadan University Press: Publishing House, University of Ibadan, PMB 16, IU Post Office, Ibadan; tel. (2) 400550; e-mail iup-unibadan@yahoo.com; f. 1951; scholarly, science, law, general and educational; Dir F. A. ADESANOYE.

Literamed Publications Ltd (Lantern Books): Plot 45, Alausa Bus-stop, Oregun Industrial Estate, Ikeja, PMB 21068, Lagos; tel. (1) 7901129; fax (1) 7936521; e-mail information@lantern-books.com; internet www.lantern-books.com; f. 1969; children's, medical and scientific; Chair. O. M. LAWAL-SOLARIN.

Longman Nigeria Ltd: 52 Oba Akran Ave, PMB 21036, Ikeja, Lagos; tel. (1) 4978925; fax (1) 4964370; e-mail longman@linkserve .com; f. 1961; general and educational; Man. Dir J. A. OLOWONIYI.

Macmillan Nigeria Publishers Ltd: Ilupeju Industrial Estate, 4 Industrial Ave, POB 264, Yaba, Lagos; tel. (1) 4962185; e-mail macmillan@hotmail.com; internet www.macmillan.nigeria.com; f. 1965; educational and general; Exec. Chair. J. O. EMANUEL; Man. Dir Dr A. I. ADELEKAN.

Northern Nigerian Publishing Co Ltd: Gaskiya Bldg, POB 412, Zaria; tel. (69) 332087; fax (69) 331348; internet www.nnpchausa .com; f. 1966; general, educational and vernacular texts; Gen. Man. MAHMUD BARAU BAMBALE.

Obobo Books: The Poet's Cottage, Artistes Village, Ilogbo-Eremi, Badagry Expressway, POB 610, Apapa, Lagos; tel. and fax (1) 5871333; e-mail theendofknowledge@yahoo.com; internet www .theendofknowledge.com; f. 1981; children's books; Editorial Dir BAKIN KUNAMA.

Ogunsanya Press Publishers and Bookstores Ltd: SW9/1133 Orita Challenge, Idiroko, POB 95, Ibadan; tel. (2) 310924; f. 1970; educational; Man. Dir Chief LUCAS JUSTUS POPO-OLA OGUNSANYA.

Spectrum Books Ltd: Spectrum House, Ring Rd, PMB 5612, Ibadan; tel. (2) 2310058; fax (2) 2318502; e-mail admin1@ spectrumbooksonline.com; internet www.spectrumbooksonline .com; f. 1978; educational and fiction; Chair. JOOP BERKHOUT; Man. Dir SINA OKEOWO.

University of Lagos Press: University of Lagos, POB 132, Akoka, Yaba, Lagos; tel. (1) 825048; e-mail library@rcl.nig.com; university textbooks, monographs, lectures and journals; Man. Dir S. BODUNDE BANKOLE.

University Publishing Co: 11 Central School Rd, POB 386, Onitsha; tel. (46) 210013; f. 1959; primary, secondary and university textbooks; Chair. E. O. UGWUEGBULEM.

West African Book Publishers Ltd: Ilupeju Industrial Estate, 28–32 Industrial Ave, POB 3445, Lagos; tel. (1) 7754518; fax (1) 2799127; e-mail w_bookafricapubl@hotmail.com; internet www.wabp.com; f. 1963; textbooks, children's, periodicals and general; Chair. B. A. IDRIS-ANIMASHAUN; Man. Dir FOLASHADE B. OMO-EBOH.

PUBLISHERS' ASSOCIATION

Nigerian Publishers' Association: Book House, NPA Permanent Secretariat, Jericho G.R.A., POB 2541, Ibadan; tel. (2) 2413396; f. 1965; Pres. S. B. BANKOLE.

Broadcasting and Communications

TELECOMMUNICATIONS

In early 2012 there were five mobile cellular telephone operators and 16 fixed-line or fixed wireless operators. At December 2011 there were 719,406 subscribers to fixed-line and fixed wireless telephone services, and 90,566,238 subscribers to mobile telephone services. In addition, there were 4.6m. subscribers to CDMA telephone services, provided by four operators.

Airtel Nigeria: Plot L2, Banana Island, Foreshore Estate, Ikoyi, Lagos; tel. 8021900000 (mobile); fax (1) 3200477; e-mail customercare.ng@airtel.com; internet www.ng.airtel.com; f. 2000; fmrly Celtel Nigeria, subsequently Zain Nigeria, present name adopted in 2010; Chair. Dr OBA OTUDEKO; CEO SEGUN OGUNSANYA; 18m. subscribers (Dec. 2011).

EMTS Ltd (Etisalat): tel. 8090000200 (mobile); fax 8090000201 (mobile); e-mail care@etisalat.com.ng; internet www.etisalat.com .ng; f. 2007; 10m. subscribers (Dec. 2011).

Globacom Nigeria Ltd: Mike Adenuga Towers, 1 Mike Adenuga Cl., off Adeola Odeku, Victoria Island, Lagos; tel. 8050020121 (mobile); e-mail customercare@gloworld.com; internet www .gloworld.com; f. 2003; Chair. Dr MIKE ADENUGA, Jr; 19m. subscribers (Dec. 2011).

MTN Nigeria Communications Ltd: Golden Plaza Bldg, Awolowo Rd, Falomo, Ikoyi, PMB 80147, Lagos; tel. 8032005638 (mobile); fax 8039029636 (mobile); e-mail info@mtnnigeria.net; internet www .mtnonline.com; f. 2001; CEO BRETT GOSCHEN; 41m. subscribers (Dec. 2011).

Multi-Links Telecommunication Ltd: 231 Adeola Odeku St, Victoria Island, POB 3453, Marina, Lagos; tel. (1) 7740000; fax (1)

7912345; internet www.multilinks.com; f. 1994; owned by Telkom SA; Chair. MARTINS DIRKS; 70,795 subscribers (Dec. 2011).

Nigerian Mobile Telecommunications Ltd (M-TEL): 2 Bissau St, off Herbert Macaulay Way, Wuse Zone 6, Abuja; tel. (9) 5233031; internet www.mtelnigeria.com; f. 1996; Chair. OLULADE ADEG-BOYEGA; 258,520 subscribers (Dec. 2011).

Nigerian Telecommunications Ltd (NITEL): 2 Bissau St, off Herbert Macaulay Way, Wuse Zone 6, Abuja; tel. (9) 5233021; f. 1984; 51% owned by Transnational Corporation of Nigeria PLC, 49% govt-owned; Chair. Dr MARTINS IGBOKWE; 58,750 subscribers (Dec. 2011).

Reliance Telecoms (Zoom): Zoom Mobile House 8A, Adeola Odeku St, Victoria Island, Lagos; tel. 07074800211; fax 07074800241; e-mail corporatecomm@zoomnigeria.com; f. 1998; fixed wireless and CDMA; CEO EDWIN MOMIFE; 43,784 fixed and 315,619 subscribers (Dec. 2011).

Starcomms: Starcomms House, Plot 1261 Bishop Kale Close, off Saka Tinubu St, Victoria Island, Lagos; tel. (1) 8041234; fax (1) 8110301; e-mail customerservice@starcomms.com; internet www .starcomms.com; f. 1999; fixed wireless and CDMA; Chair. Chief MANN LABABIDI; CEO LOGAN PATHER; 367,367 fixed wireless and 980,109 CDMA subscribers (Dec. 2011).

Telnet (Nigeria) Ltd: Plot 242, Kofo Abayomi St, Victoria Island, POB 53656, Falomi Ikoyi, Lagos; tel. (1) 4611747; e-mail contact@ iteco.com; internet www.telnetng.com; f. 1985; telecommunications engineering and consultancy services; Group Exec. Dir BENJAMIN ISHAKU.

21st Century Technologies: 249A, Muri Okunola St, Victoria Island, Lagos; tel. (1) 2710083; e-mail commercial@21ctl.com; internet www.21ctl.com; fixed-line services; Chair. TUNDE AJISOMO; CEO WALE AJISEBUTU; 70,087 subscribers (Dec. 2011).

Regulatory Authority

Nigerian Communications Commission (NCC): Plot 423, Aguiyi Ironsi St, Maitama, Abuja; tel. (9) 4617000; fax (9) 4617514; e-mail ncc@ncc.gov.ng; internet www.ncc.gov.ng; f. 1932; Chair. PETER EGBE IGOH; Exec. Chair. and CEO Dr EUGENE JUWAH.

BROADCASTING

According to the National Broadcasting Commission, there are 100 radio stations and 147 television stations in the country.

Regulatory Authority

National Broadcasting Commission: Plot 20, Ibrahim Taiwo St, Asokoro District, POB 5747, Garki, Abuja; tel. (9) 7805730; fax (9) 3147522; e-mail infonbc@nbc.gov.ng; internet www.nbc.gov.ng; Dir-Gen. Eng. YOMI BOLARINWA.

Radio

Federal Radio Corpn of Nigeria (FRCN): Radio House, Herbert Macaulay Way, Area 10, PMB 452, Garki, Abuja; tel. (9) 2345230; fax (9) 2346486; e-mail info@radionigeria.net; internet www .radionigeria.net; f. 1976; controlled by the Fed. Govt and divided into five zones: Lagos (English); Enugu (English, Igbo, Izon, Efik and Tiv); Ibadan (English, Yoruba, Edo, Urhobo and Igala); Kaduna (English, Hausa, Kanuri, Fulfulde and Nupe); Abuja (English, Hausa, Igbo and Yoruba); Dir-Gen. YUSUF NUHU.

Imo Broadcasting Corpn: Egbu Rd, PMB 1129, Owerri, Imo; tel. (42) 250327; operates one radio station in Imo State; CEO SAMFO NWANKWO.

Ray Power Radio 100.5 FM: Abeokuta Express Way, Ilapo, Alagbado, Lagos; tel. (1) 2644814; fax (1) 2644817; 100% owned by DAAR Communications Ltd; commenced broadcasting Sept. 1994; commercial; Chair. Chief ALEOGHO RAYMOND DOKPESI.

Voice of Nigeria (VON): 6th and 7th Floor, Radio House, Herbert Macaulay Way, Area 10, Garki, Abuja; tel. (9) 2344017; fax (9) 2346970; e-mail info@voiceofnigeria.org; internet www .voiceofnigeria.org; f. 1990; controlled by the Fed. Govt; external services in English, French, Arabic, Ki-Swahili, Hausa and Fulfulde; Dir-Gen. Alhaji ABUBAKAR BOBBOYI JIJIWA.

Television

Nigerian Television Authority (NTA): Television House, Area 11, Garki, PMB 13, Abuja; tel. (9) 2345907; fax (9) 2345914; f. 1976; controlled by the Fed. Govt; operates a network of 31 terrestrial broadcasters, which share national programming but also broadcast local programmes; also operates c. 70 regional channels; Chair. BENSON ABOUNU; Dir-Gen. Dr MAGAWATA MOHAMMED USMAN.

Africa Independent Television (AIT): Kpaduma Hill, off T. Y. Danjuma, Asokoro Extension, Abuja; e-mail info@daargroup.com; internet www.daargroup.com; f. 1994; 100% owned by DAAR Communications Ltd; Exec. Chair. Dr ALEOGHO RAYMOND DOKPESI.

Minaj Broadcast International (MBI): Minaj Media Group, 130/132, Ladipo St, Matori, Mushin, POB 70811, Victoria Island, Lagos; tel. (1) 4529203; fax (1) 4528500; e-mail info@minajmedia.com; internet www.minajmedia.com; provides free-to-air services; Chair. Chief MIKE AJEGBO.

Murhi International Television (MITV): MITV Plaza, Ikeja Central Business District, Obafemi Awolowo Way, Alausa, Lagos; tel. (1) 4931271; fax (1) 4931272; e-mail mitv@murhi-international.com; Chair. MURI GBADEYANKA BUSARI.

Finance

(cap. = capital; res = reserves; dep. = deposits; m. = million; brs = branches; amounts in naira)

BANKING

In early 2011 there were 24 commercial banks and five development finance institutions in Nigeria. In June Stanbic IBTC Bank PLC received a preliminary licence to provide Islamic banking services. Jaiz International PLC was also granted approval, in principle, to open the country's first Islamic bank.

Central Bank

Central Bank of Nigeria: Plot 33, Abubakar Tafawa Balewa Way, Central Business District, Cadestral Zone, PMB 0187, Garki, Abuja; tel. (9) 46239701; fax (9) 46236012; e-mail info@cenbank.org; internet www.cenbank.org; f. 1958; bank of issue; cap. 5,000m., res 320,165m., dep. 4,971,643m. (Dec. 2006); Gov. SANUSI LAMIDO AMINU SANUSI; 28 brs.

Commercial Banks

Access Bank: Plot 1665, Oyin Jolayemi St, Victoria Island, Lagos; tel. (1) 2805628; e-mail contactcenter@accessbankplc.com; internet www.accessbankplc.com; Chair. GBENGA OYEBODE; CEO AIGBOJE AIG-IMOUKHUEDE.

Citibank Nigeria Ltd: 27 Kofo Abayomi St, Victoria Island, POB 6391, Lagos; tel. (1) 2798400; fax (1) 2618916; internet www.citibanknigeria.com; f. 1984; cap. 2,793.7m., res 34,900.5m., dep. 97,969.5m. (Dec. 2008); Chair. OLAYEMI CARDOSO; Country Officer EMEKA EMUWA; 4 brs.

Diamond Bank PLC: Plot 1261, Adeola Hopewell St, Victoria Island, POB 70381, Lagos; tel. (1) 2701500; fax (1) 2619728; e-mail info@diamondbank.com; internet www.diamondbank.com; f. 2005 by merger with Lion Bank of Nigeria PLC; cap. 6,579.6m., res. 100,941.0m., dep. 410,094.0m. (April 2008); Chair. IGWE NNAEMEKA ALFRED ACHEBE; Man. Dir and CEO ALEX OTTI.

Enterprise Bank Ltd: 143 Ahmadu Bello Way, Victoria Island, Lagos; tel. (1) 2623780; internet www.springbankplc.com; f. 2004 by merger of ACB International Bank PLC, Citizens International Bank PLC, Fountain Trust Bank PLC, Guardian Express Bank PLC, Omegabank (Nigeria) PLC and Trans International Bank PLC; acquired by Platinum Habib Bank Group in 2008; name changed as above following nationalization in August 2011; Chair. EMEKA ONWUKA; Man. Dir AHMED KURU.

First Bank of Nigeria PLC: Samuel Asabia House, 35 Marina, POB 5216, Lagos; tel. (1) 2665900; fax (1) 2669073; e-mail firstcontact@firstbanknigeria.com; internet www.firstbanknigeria.com; f. 1894 as Bank of British West Africa; cap. 12,432m., res 338,622m., dep. 1,150,816m. (March 2009); Chair. Dr OBA OTUDEKO; CEO and Man. Dir STEPHEN OLABISI ONASANYA; 302 brs.

Guaranty Trust Bank PLC: Plot 635, Akin Adesola St, PMB 75455, Victoria Island, Lagos; tel. (1) 2715227; e-mail corpaff@gtbank.com; internet www.gtbank.com; f. 1990; cap. 9,326.9m., res 160,507.5m., dep. 728,859.7m. (Dec. 2009); Chair. OLUWOLE S. ODUYEMI; 161 brs.

Keystone Bank Ltd: 1 Bank PHB Cres., Victoria Island, Lagos; tel. (1) 4485742; e-mail phblink@bankphb.com; internet www.bankphb.com; frmly Bank PHB, name changed following nationalization in August 2011; Chair. JACOB AJEKIGBE; Man. Dir OTI IKOMI.

Mainstreet Bank Ltd: 51–55 Broad St, PMB 12021, Lagos; tel. (1) 2641566; fax (1) 2669763; e-mail info@afribank.com; internet www.afribank.com; f. 1969 as International Bank for West Africa Ltd; fmrly Afribank Nigeria Ltd, name changed as above following nationalization in August 2011; cap. 3,065.0m., res 31,822.0m., dep. 280,290.1m. (March 2008); Chair. FALALU BELLO; Man. Dir and CEO FAITH TUEDOR-MATTHEWS; 137 brs.

Skye Bank PLC: 3 Akin Adesola St, Victoria Island, Lagos; tel. (1) 2701600; e-mail info@skyebankng.com; internet www.skyebankng.com; Chair. MORONKEJI ONASANYA; Group Man. Dir KEHINDE DUROSINMI-ETTI.

Stanbic IBTC Bank PLC: I.B.T.C. Place, Walter Carrington Cres., POB 71707, Victoria Island, Lagos; tel. (1) 2712400; fax (1) 2806998;

e-mail customercarenigeria@stanbic.com; internet www.ibtc.com/portal/site/nigeria; f. 1989 as Investment Banking & Trust Co Ltd; name changed as above 2008 following merger with Stanbic Bank (Nigeria) Ltd; cap. 9,375.0m., res 67,241.7m., dep. 181,093.1m. (Dec. 2008); Chair. ATEDO N.A. PETERSIDE; CEO SOLA DAVID-BORHA; 57 brs.

Sterling Bank: Sterling Towers, 20 Marina, POB 12735, Lagos; tel. (1) 2600420; fax (1) 2633294; e-mail tradeservices@sterlingbankng.com; internet www.sterlingbankng.com; f. 2005 following merger of Indo-Nigerian Bank Ltd, Magnum Trust Bank, NAL Bank PLC, NBM Bank and Trust Bank of Africa Ltd; cap. 6,281.5m., res. 23,957.3m., dep. 184,730.2m. (Sept. 2008); Chair. Alhaji SULEIMAN ADEBOLA ADEGUNWA; Man. Dir RAZACK ADEYEMI ADEOLA.

Union Bank of Nigeria Ltd: 36 Marina, PMB 2027, Lagos; tel. (1) 2716800; fax (1) 2805798; e-mail info@unionbankng.com; internet www.unionbankng.com; f. 1917 as Colonial Bank, Barclays Bank acquired Colonial Bank in 1925; cap. 101,049m., res 1,493m., dep. 482,382m. (March 2007); Chair. RICHARD KRAMER; Man. Dir and CEO OLUNFUNKE IYABO OSIBODU; 379 brs.

United Bank for Africa (Nigeria) Ltd: UBA House, 57 Marina, POB 2406, Lagos; tel. (1) 2808822; fax (1) 2808448; e-mail cic@ubagroup.com; internet www.ubagroup.com; f. 1961; cap. 8,622m., res 179,533m., dep. 1,258,035m. (Sept. 2008); Chair. FERDINAND NGOGO ALABRABA; Man. Dir TONY O. ELUMELU; 428 brs.

Unity Bank PLC: Plot 785, Herbert Macaulay Way, Central Business District, POB 52463, Abuja; tel. (9) 4616700; fax (9) 4616730; e-mail we_care@unitybankng.com; internet www.unitybankng.com; f. 2005; cap. 21,752.9m., res. 9,015.0m., dep. 79,683.5m. (June 2006); Chair. Prof. AKIN L. MABOGUNJE; Man. Dir and CEO Alhaji FALALU BELLO.

Wema Bank Ltd: Wema Towers, PMB 12862, 54 Marina, Lagos; tel. (1) 2668043; fax (1) 2669236; e-mail info@wemabank.com; internet www.wemabank.com; f. 1945; cap. 5,035.0m., res 19,781.7m., dep. 125,476.0m. (March 2007); Chair. Chief SAMUEL BOLARINDE; Man. Dir SEGUN OLOKETUYI; 146 brs.

Zenith Bank PLC: Plot 84, Ajose Adeogun St, Victoria Island, POB 75315, Lagos; tel. (1) 2788000; fax (1) 2618212; e-mail enquiry@zenithbank.com; internet www.zenithbank.com; f. 1990; name changed as above in 2004; cap. 8,372.4m., res. 330,111.7m., dep. 1,167,335.2m. (Sept. 2008); Man. Dir JIM OVIA.

Merchant Banks

FBN Capital Ltd: 16 Keffi St, off Awolowo Rd, Ikoyi, Lagos; tel. (1) 2798300; fax (1) 2633600; e-mail info@fbncapital.com; internet www.fbncapital.com; Chair. OYEKANMI HASSAN-ODUKALE; Man. Dir and CEO KAYODE AKINKUGBE.

Fidelity Bank PLC: 2 Kofo Abayomi St, Victoria Island, Lagos; tel. (1) 2713487; fax (1) 2610414; e-mail info@fidelitybankplc.com; internet www.fidelitybankplc.com; f. 1988; cap. 14,481.3m., res 114,892.5m., dep. 356,137.3m. (June 2009); Chair. Chief CHRISTOPHER EZEH; CEO REGINALD IHEJIAHI; 20 brs.

First City Monument Bank Ltd: Primrose Tower, 17A Tinubu St, POB 9117, Lagos; tel. (1) 2665944; fax (1) 2665126; e-mail fcmb@fcmb-ltd.com; internet www.firstcitygroup.com; f. 1983; cap. 8,136.0m., res 119,322.0m., dep. 349,441.8m. (April 2009); Chair. Dr JONATHAN A.D. LONG; Man. Dir and CEO LADI BALOGUN; 12 brs.

Development Finance Institutions

Bank of Industry (BOI) Ltd: 23 Marina, POB 2357, Lagos; tel. (1) 2665528; fax (1) 2665286; e-mail info@boi-ng.com; internet www.boinigeria.com; f. 1964 as the Nigerian Industrial Development Bank Ltd to provide medium and long-term finance to industry, manufacturing, non-petroleum mining and tourism; name changed as above Oct. 2001; cap. 6,585.1m., dep. 3,500m. (Dec. 2005); Chair. Alhaji ABDULSAMAD RABIU; Man. Dir Dr EVELN N. OPUTU; 8 brs.

The Federal Mortgage Bank of Nigeria (FMBN): Mortgage House, Plot 266, Cadastral AO, Central Business District, PMB 2273, Garki, Abuja; tel. (9) 4602102; e-mail info@fmbnigeria.org; internet www.fmbnigeria.org; f. 1956 as Nigerian Building Society (NBS); Chair. Alhaji ADEDAMOLA ATTA; Man. Dir GIMBA YA'U KUMO.

Nigerian Agricultural, Co-operative and Rural Development Bank Ltd (NACRDB): Yakubu Gowoh, PMB 2155, Kaduna; tel. (62) 244417; fax (62) 244612; e-mail nacb@infoweb.abs.net; internet www.nacrdb.com; f. 1973 for funds to farmers and co-operatives to improve production techniques; name changed as above Oct. 2000, following merger with People's Bank of Nigeria; cap. 1,000m. (2002); Chair. Chief GORDON BOZIMO; Man. Dir Dr MOHAMMED SANTURAKI; 200 brs.

The Nigerian Export-Import Bank (NEXIM): NEXIM House, Plot 975, Cadastral Zone AO, Central Business District, PMB 276, Garki, Abuja; tel. (9) 6281630; fax (9) 6281640; e-mail neximabj@neximbank.com.ng; internet www.neximbank.com.ng; f. 1991; CEO ROBERTS U. ORYA.

The Urban Development Bank of Nigeria PLC (UDBN): Plot 977, Central Business Area, PMB 272, Garki, Abuja; tel. (9) 6710863; e-mail enquiries@udbng.com; internet www.udbng.com; f. 1992; Chair. HAKEEM O. SANUSI.

Bankers' Association

Chartered Institute of Bankers of Nigeria: PC 19 Adeola Hopewell St, POB 72273, Victoria Island, Lagos; tel. (1) 2703494; fax (1) 4618930; e-mail cibn@cibng.org; internet www.cibng.org; Chair. JOSEPH LAOYE JAIYEOLA; CEO Dr UJU M. OGUBUNKA.

STOCK EXCHANGE

Securities and Exchange Commission (SEC): SEC Towers, Plot 272, Samuel Adesujo Ademulegun St, Central Business District, PMB 315, Garki, Abuja; tel. (9) 6330000; fax (9) 2346276; internet www.sec.gov.ng; f. 1979 as govt agency to regulate and develop capital market and to supervise stock exchange operations; Chair. UDOMA UDO UDOMA; Dir-Gen. DAISY EKINEH.

Nigerian Stock Exchange: Stock Exchange House, 2–4 Customs St, POB 2457, Lagos; tel. (1) 2660287; fax (1) 2668724; e-mail info@nigerianstockexchange.biz; internet www.nigerianstockexchange.com; f. 1960; Pres. ALIKO DANGOTE; CEO OSCAR ONYEMA; 6 brs.

INSURANCE

In 2011 the insurance sector comprised 51 registered companies, seven life insurance companies, 23 non-life insurance companies, 19 composite companies and two reinsurance companies. Since 1978 they have been required to reinsure 20% of the sum insured with the Nigeria Reinsurance Corpn.

Regulatory Authority

National Insurance Commission (NAICOM): Shippers Plaza, Micheal Okpara St, Wuse Zone 5, PMB 457, Garki, Abuja; tel. (9) 6733520; fax (9) 6735649; e-mail info@naicom.gov.org; internet www.naicom.gov.ng; f. 1992 as National Insurance Supervisory Board; present name adopted 1997; Chair. Hajia INNA MARYAM CIROMA; Commr for Insurance FOLA DANIEL.

Insurance Companies

African Alliance Insurance Co Ltd: 112 Broad St, POB 2276, Lagos; tel. (1) 7227666; fax (1) 2660943; e-mail info@africanallianceinsurance.com; internet www.africanallianceinsurance.com; f. 1960; life assurance and pensions; Man. Dir ALPHONSUS OKPOR; 30 brs.

Aiico International Insurance (AIICO): AIICO Plaza, Plot PC 12, Afribank St, Victoria Island, POB 2577, Lagos; tel. (1) 2610651; fax (1) 2799800; e-mail info@aiicoplc.com; internet www.aiicoplc.com; CEO S. D. A SOBANJO.

Ark Insurance Group: Glass House, 11A Karimu Kotun St, Victoria Island, POB 3771, Marina, Lagos; tel. (1) 2615826; fax (1) 2615850; e-mail info@arkinsurancegroup.com; internet www.arkinsurancegroup.com; Chair. FRANCIS OLUWOLE AWOGBORO.

Continental Reinsurance Co Ltd: St. Nicholas House, 8th Floor, 6 Catholic Mission St, POB 2401, Lagos; tel. (1) 2665350; fax (1) 2665370; e-mail info@continental-re.com; internet www.continental-re.com; Chair. S. A. LAGUDA; CEO Dr FEMI OYETUNJI.

Cornerstone Insurance Co PLC: POB 75370, Victoria Island, Lagos; tel. (1) 2631832; fax (1) 2633079; e-mail marketing@cornerstone.com.ng; internet www.cornerstone.com.ng; f. 1991; Chair. ADEDOTUN SULAIMAN; Man. Dir and CEO LIVINGSTONE MAGORIMBO.

CrystaLife: 12th and 13th Floor, Eleganza House, 15B Joseph St, POB 1514, Lagos; tel. (1) 2636800; fax (1) 2637095; e-mail equilifekn@equity-lifeinsurance.com; internet www.crystalifeassurance.com; Chair. AKINSOLA AKINFEMIWA; Man. Dir and CEO OLUSEYI IFATUROTI.

Equity Assurance PLC: 19 Circular Road, Presidential Estate, POB 2709, Port Harcourt; tel. (84) 236114; fax (84) 236115; e-mail portharcourt@equityassuranceplc.com; f. 1991; Chair. OLUFEMI SOMOLU; COO OLUMIDE FALOHUN.

Great Nigeria Insurance Co PLC: 8 Omo-Osaghie St, off Obafemi Awolono Rd, Ikoyi S/W, Ikoyi, POB 2314, Lagos; tel. (1) 2695805; fax (1) 2693483; e-mail info@gniplc.com; internet www.gniplc.com; f. 1960; all classes; Chair. SEGUN OLOKETUYI; Man. Dir CECILIA O. SIPITAN.

Guinea Insurance PLC: Reinsurance Bldg, 10th Floor, 46 Marine, POB 1136, Lagos; tel. (1) 2665201; e-mail info@guineainsurance.com; internet www.guineainsurance.com; f. 1958; all classes; Man. Dir and CEO SOJI EMIOLA.

Industrial and General Insurance Co Ltd: Plot 741, Adeola Hopewell St, PMB 80181, Victoria Island, Lagos; tel. (1) 6215010; fax

(1) 2621146; e-mail info@iginigeria.com; internet www.iginigeria.com; Chair. YAKUBU GOWON.

Law Union and Rock Insurance PLC: 14 Hughes Ave, Alagomeji, Yaba, POB 944, Lagos; e-mail enquiry@lur-ng.com; tel. (1) 8995010; fax (1) 3425077; internet www.lawunioninsurance.com; fire, accident and marine; Chair. AKINSOLA AKINFEMIWA; Man. Dir and CEO YINKA BOLARINWA; 6 brs.

Leadway Assurance Co Ltd: 121/123 Funsho Williams Ave, Iponri, Lagos; tel. (1) 2700700; fax (1) 2700800; e-mail insure@leadway.com; internet www.leadway.com; f. 1970; all classes; Man. Dir OYEKANMI ABIODUN HASSAN-ODUKALE.

Lion of Africa Insurance Co Ltd: St Peter's House, 3 Ajele St, POB 2055, Lagos; tel. (1) 2600950; fax (1) 2636111; internet thelionofafrica.org; f. 1952; all classes; Man. Dir and CEO PETER MONYE.

National Insurance Corpn of Nigeria (NICON): 5 Customs St, POB 1100, Lagos; tel. (1) 2640230; fax (1) 2666556; f. 1969; all classes; cap. 200m.; Chair. JIMOH IBRAHIM; 28 brs.

N.E.M. Insurance Co (Nigeria) Ltd: 138/146 Broad St, POB 654, Lagos; tel. (1) 5861920; internet www.nem-insurance.com; all classes; Chair. Chief ADEWALE TELUWO; Man. Dir TOPE SMART.

Niger Insurance PLC: 48/50 Odunlami St, POB 2718, Marina, Lagos; tel. (1) 2631329; fax (1) 2662196; e-mail info@nigerinsurance.com; internet www.nigerinsurance.com; f. 1962; all classes; Chair. BALA ZAKARIYA'U; Man. Dir Dr JUSTUS URANTA; 6 brs.

Nigeria Reinsurance Corpn: 46 Marina, PMB 12766, Lagos; tel. (1) 2667049; fax (1) 2668041; e-mail info@nigeriare.com; internet www.nigeriareinsurance.com; all classes of reinsurance; Man. Dir T. T. MIRILLA.

Royal Exchange PLC: New Africa House, 31 Marina, POB 112, Lagos; tel. (1) 7404158; e-mail info@royalexchangeplc.com; internet portal.royalexchangeplc.com; 1921; all classes; Chair. KENNETH EZENWANI ODOGWU; Man. Dir CHIKE MOKWUNYE; 25 brs.

UnityKapital Assurance PLC: 497 Abogo Largema St, off Constitution Ave, Central Business District, POB 2044, Abuja; tel. (9) 4619900; fax (9) 4619901; e-mail info@unitykapital.com; internet www.unitykapital.com; f. 1973; Chair. Alhaji FALALU BELLO; CEO MOHAMMED KARI.

Unity Life and Fire Insurance Co Ltd: 25 Nnamdi Azikiwe St, POB 3681, Lagos; tel. (1) 2662517; fax (1) 2662599; all classes; Man. Dir R. A. ODINIGWE.

West African Provincial Insurance Co: WAPIC House, 119 Awolowo Rd, POB 55508, Falomo-Ikoyi, Lagos; tel. (1) 2672770; fax (1) 2693838; e-mail wapic@alpha.linkserve.com; Man. Dir D. O. AMUSAN.

Insurance Association

Nigerian Insurers' Association (NIA): 42 Saka Tinubu St, Victoria Island, POB 9551, Lagos; tel. (1) 7743813; fax (1) 2621298; e-mail info@nigeriainsurers.org; internet www.nigeriainsurers.org; f. 1971; Chair. REMI OLOWUDE; Dir-Gen. SUNDAY THOMAS.

Trade and Industry

GOVERNMENT AGENCIES

Bureau of Public Enterprises: The Presidency, Bureau of Public Enterprises, 11 Osun Cres., off IBB Way, Maitama District, PMB 442, Garki, Abuja; tel. (9) 4604400; fax (9) 4604411; e-mail bpe@bpeng.org; internet www.bpeng.org; Dir-Gen. BOLANLE ONAGORUWA.

Corporate Affairs Commission: Plot 420, Tigris Cres., off Aguiyi Ironsi St, Maitama, PMB 198, Garki, Abuja; tel. (9) 4618594; fax (9) 2342669; e-mail info@cac.gov.ng; internet www.cac.gov.ng; Chair. Chief Dr JIMOH IBRAHIM; Registrar-Gen./CEO BELLO MAHMUD.

National Council on Privatisation: Bureau of Public Enterprises, NDIC Bldg, Constitution Ave, Central Business District, PMB 442, Garki, Abuja; tel. (9) 5237405; fax (9) 5237396; e-mail bpegen@micro.com.ng; internet www.bpe.gov.ng; Chair. NAMADI SAMBO.

Nigeria Export Processing Zones Authority (NEPZA): 2 Zambezi Cres., Cadastral Zone A6, off Aguiyi Ironsi St, Maitama, PMB 037, Garki, Abuja; tel. (9) 4131598; fax (9) 4131550; e-mail info@nepza.gov.ng; internet www.nepza.gov.ng; Man. Dir SINA A. AGBOLUAJE.

Nigeria Sovereign Investment Authority: Abuja; f. 2011; Chair. Alhaji MAHEY RASHEED; Man. Dir UCHE ORJI.

DEVELOPMENT ORGANIZATIONS

Chad Basin Development Authority (CBDA): Dikwa Rd, PMB 1130, Maiduguri; tel. (76) 232015; f. 1973; irrigation and agriculture-

allied industries; Man. Dir Dr ABUBAKAR GARBA ILLIYA; Gen. Man.
Alhaji BUNU S. MUSA.

Cross River Basin Development Authority (CRBDA): 32 Target Rd, PMB 1249, Calabar; tel. (87) 223163; f. 1976; Gen. Man. SIXTUS ABETIANBE.

Federal Institute of Industrial Research, Oshodi (FIIRO): FIIRO Rd, by Cappa Bus Stop, off Agege Motor Rd, Oshodi, Ikeja, PMB 21023, Lagos; tel. (1) 4701846; fax (1) 4525880; e-mail info@fiiro.gov.ng; internet www.fiiro-ng.org; f. 1956; plans and directs scientific research for industrial and technological development; provides tech. assistance and information to industry; specializes in foods, minerals, textiles, natural products and industrial intermediates; Dir-Gen. Dr GLORIA NWAKAEGHO ELEMO.

Industrial Training Fund: 1, Kufang Village, Miango Rd, PMB 2199, Jos, Plateau; tel. and fax (73) 462395; e-mail dp@itf-nigeria.com; internet www.itf-nigeria.com; f. 1971 to promote and encourage skilled workers in trade and industry; Dir-Gen. Prof. OLU E. AKEREJOLA.

Kaduna Industrial and Finance Co Ltd: Investment House, 27 Ali Akilu Rd, PMB 2230, Kaduna; tel. 8037035577 (mobile); fax (62) 290781; e-mail info@kadunainvest.com; internet www.kadunainvest.com; f. 1989; provides devt finance; Man. Dir and CEO ALHAJI SHEHU MUHAMMAD SHITU.

Kwara State Investment Corpn: Charlets, 109–112 Fate Rd, PMB 1344, Ilorin, Kwara; tel. (31) 220510.

Lagos State Development and Property Corpn: 2/4 Town Planning Way, Ilupeju Industrial Estate, PMB 21050, Lagos; tel. (1) 7621424; e-mail info@lsdpc.gov.ng; internet www.lsdpc.gov.ng; f. 1972; planning and devt of Lagos; Man. Dir BIODUN OKI.

New Nigerian Development Co Ltd: 18/19 Ahmadu Bello Way, Ahmed Talib House, PMB 2120, Kaduna; tel. (62) 249355; fax (62) 245482; e-mail nndc@skannet.com.ng; f. 1949; owned by the govts of 19 northern states; investment finance; 8 subsidiaries, 83 assoc. cos; Chair. Prof. HALIDU IBRAHIM ABUBAKAR.

Niger Delta Development Commission (NDDC): 167 Aba Rd, Port Harcourt; e-mail info@nddc.gov.ng; internet www.nddc.gov.ng; f. 2000; Chair. Dr TARILAH TEBEPAH; Man. Dir Dr CHRISTIAN OBOH.

Odu'a Investment Co Ltd: Cocoa House Complex, Oba Adebimpe Rd, PMB 5435, Ibadan; tel. (2) 2001037; fax (2) 413000; e-mail odua@oduainvestmentcompany.com; internet www.oduainvestmentcompany.com; f. 1976; jtly owned by Ogun, Ondo and Oyo States; Man. Dir A. K. JIMOH.

Projects Development Institute (PRODA): Emene Industrial Layout, Proda Rd, POB 01609, Enugu; tel. 7098811745 (mobile); fax (42) 457691; e-mail info@proda-ng.org; internet proda-ng.org; f. 1970; promotes the establishment of new industries and develops industrial projects utilizing local raw materials; Dir BASIL K. C. UGWA.

Raw Materials Research and Development Council (RMRDC): Plot 427, Aguiyi, Ironsi St, Maitama District, PMB 232, Garki, Abuja; tel. (9) 4134716; fax (9) 4136034; e-mail icsd_liaison@rmrdc.gov.ng; internet www.rmrdc.gov.ng; f. 1988; Dir.-Gen. Prof. AZIKIWE PETER ONWUALU.

Rubber Research Institute of Nigeria (RRIN): PMB 1049, Benin City; tel. 8033197241; e-mail rubberresearchnig@yahoo.com; internet www.rrin.org; f. 1961; conducts research into the production of rubber, gum arabic and other latex bearing plants of economic importance; Exec. Dir OSAYANMO I. EGUAVOEN; Chair Air Cdre JOHN A. EHIWERE.

CHAMBERS OF COMMERCE

Nigerian Association of Chambers of Commerce, Industry, Mines and Agriculture (NACCIMA): 8A Oba Akinjobi Way, PMB 12816, Lagos; tel. (1) 4964727; fax (1) 4964737; e-mail contact@naccima.com; internet www.naccima.com; f. 1960; Pres. Dr HERBERT ADEMOLA AJAYI; Dir-Gen. JOHN ISEMEDE.

Aba Chamber of Commerce and Industry: UBA Bldg, Ikot Expene Rd/Georges St, POB 1596, Aba; tel. (82) 352084; fax (82) 352067; f. 1971; Pres. Chief KALU OMOJI KALU.

Abeokuta Chamber of Commerce and Industry: Commerce House, Nr Govt House, Oke Igbehin, Ibaha, POB 937, Abeokuta; tel. (39) 241230; Pres. Chief S. O. AKINREMI.

Abuja Chamber of Commerce, Industry, Mines & Agriculture: International Trade Fair Complex, KM8, Airport Rd, PMB 86, Garki, Abuja; tel. 8033139347 (mobile); e-mail abuccima@hotmail.com; f. 1986; Pres. DELE KELVIN OYE.

Adamawa Chamber of Commerce and Industry: c/o Palace Hotel, POB 8, Jimeta, Yola; tel. (75) 255136; Pres. Alhaji ISA HAMMANYERO.

Akure Chamber of Commerce and Industry: 57 Oyemekun Rd, POB 866, Akure; tel. (34) 242540; f. 1984; Pres. OMOLADE OWOSENI.

Awka Chamber of Commerce and Industry: 220 Zik Ave, POB 780, Awka; tel. (45) 550105; Pres. Lt-Col (retd) D. ORUGBU.

Bauchi Chamber of Commerce and Industry: 96 Maiduguri Rd, POB 911, Bauchi; tel. (77) 43727; f. 1976; Pres. Alhaji MAGAJI MU'AZU.

Benin Chamber of Commerce, Industry, Mines and Agriculture: 10 Murtala Muhammed Way, POB 2087, Benin City; tel. (52) 255761; Pres. Chief SIMON UDUIGHO EKWENUKE.

Benue Chamber of Commerce, Industry, Mines and Agriculture: Suite 7, IBB Sq, High Level, PMB 102344, Makurdi; tel. (44) 32573; Chair. Col (retd) R. V. I. ASAM.

Borno Chamber of Commerce and Industry: Grand Stand, Ramat Sq., off Central Bank, PMB 1636, Maiduguri; tel. 8076974846 (mobile); e-mail bsumar@hotmail.com; f. 1973; Pres. Alhaji MOHAMMED RIJYA; Sec.-Gen. BABA SHEHU BUKAR.

Calabar Chamber of Commerce and Industry: Desan House Bldg, 38 Ndidem Iso Rd, POB 76, Calabar, Cross River; tel. (87) 221558; 92 mems; Pres. Chief TAM OFORIOKUMA.

Enugu Chamber of Commerce, Industry, Mines and Agriculture (ECCIMA): Secretariat Complex, Old International Trade Fair Complex, Abakaliki Rd, POB 734, Enugu; tel. (42) 290481; e-mail enuguchamber@yahoo.com; internet www.enuguchamber.org; f. 1963; Pres. Dr THEO OKONKWO; Dir-Gen. EMEKA OKEREKE.

Franco-Nigerian Chamber of Commerce: 5th Floor, Big Leaf House, 7 Oyin Jolayemi St, POB 70001, Victoria Island, Lagos; tel. (1) 4611201; fax (1) 4613501; e-mail fncci@ccife.org; internet franco-nigerian.com; f. 1985; Pres. MARCEL HOCHET; Gen. Man. AKIN AKINBOLA.

Gongola Chamber of Commerce and Industry: Palace Hotel, POB 8, Jimeta-Yola; tel. (75) 255136; Pres. Alhaji ALIYU IBRAHIM.

Ibadan Chamber of Commerce and Industry: Commerce House, Ring Rd, Challenge, PMB 5168, Ibadan; tel. 7056778489 (mobile); e-mail ibdcci@yahoo.com; internet ibadanchamberofcommerce.net; Pres. ELDER DIIMEJI MIKE-FOWOWE.

Ijebu Chamber of Commerce and Industry: 51 Ibadan Rd, POB 604, Ijebu Ode; tel. (37) 432880; Pres. DOYIN DEGUN.

Ikot Ekpene Chamber of Commerce and Industry: 47 Aba Rd, POB 50, Ikot Ekpene; tel. (85) 400153; Pres. G. U. EKANEM.

Kaduna Chamber of Commerce, Industry, Mines and Agriculture: POB 728, Rigachikun, Kaduna; tel. 7023228854 (mobile); fax 7023228908 (mobile); e-mail kadunachamberofcommerce@yahoo.com; internet www.kadccima.org.ng; f. 1973; Pres. UMAR YAHAYA.

Kano Chamber of Commerce, Industry, Mines and Agriculture: Trade Fair Complex, Zoo Rd, POB 10, Kano City, Kano; tel. (64) 666936; fax (64) 667138; Pres. Alhaji AHMAD RABIU.

Katsina Chamber of Commerce and Industry: IBB Way, POB 789, Katsina; tel. (65) 31974; Pres. ABBA ALI.

Kwara Chamber of Commerce, Industry, Mines and Agriculture: 9A Kwara Hotel Premises, Ahmadu Bello Ave, POB 1634, Ilorin; tel. 8035888047 (mobile); fax (31) 224131; e-mail kwaccima@yahoo.com; internet www.kwaccima.com; f. 1965; Pres. Dr HEZEKIAH ADEDIJI.

Lagos Chamber of Commerce and Industry: Commerce House, 1 Idowu Taylor St, Victoria Island, POB 109, Lagos; tel. (1) 7746617; fax (1) 2701009; e-mail inform@micro.com.ng; internet www.lagoschamber.com; f. 1888; 1,500 mems; Pres. Chief OLUSOLA FALEYE.

Niger Chamber of Commerce and Industry: Trade Fair Site, Paiko Rd, POB 370, Minna; tel. (66) 223153; Pres. Alhaji U. S. NDANUSA.

Nnewi Chamber of Commerce, Industry, Mines and Agriculture: 31A Nnobi Rd, POB 1471, Nnewi, Anambra State; tel. (70) 35187662; f. 1987; Pres. PRINCE EMEKA A. AYABAZU.

Osogbo Chamber of Commerce and Industry: Obafemi Awolowo Way, Ajegunle, POB 870, Osogbo, Osun; tel. (35) 231098; Pres. Prince VICTOR ADEMLE.

Owerri Chamber of Commerce and Industry: OCCIMA Secretariat, 123 Okigwe Rd, POB 1439, Owerri; tel. (83) 234849.

Oyo Chamber of Commerce and Industry: Ogbomosho Rd, opp. Apaara Methodist Church, POB 588, Oyo; tel. (38) 240691; Pres. B. A. LASEBIKAN.

Plateau State Chambers of Commerce, Industry, Mines and Agriculture: POB 74, 21A Nassarawa Rd, Jos; tel. (73) 453918; f. 1976; Pres. SILAS JANGA.

Port Harcourt Chamber of Commerce, Industry, Mines and Agriculture: Alesa Eleme, POB 585, Port Harcourt; tel. (84) 239536; f. 1952; Pres. VINCENT FURO.

Remo Chamber of Commerce and Industry: 7 Sho Manager Way, POB 1172, Shagamu; tel. (37) 640962; Pres. Chief ADENIYI OGUNSANYA.

Sapele Chamber of Commerce and Industry: 144 New Ogorode Rd, POB 154, Sapele; tel. and fax (54) 42323; Pres. Chief DAVID IWETA.

Sokoto Chamber of Commerce and Industry: 12 Racecourse Rd, POB 2234, Sokoto; tel. (60) 231805; Pres. Alhaji ALIYU WAZIRI BODINGA.

Umahia Chamber of Commerce: 44 Azikiwe Rd, Umahia; tel. (88) 223373; fax (88) 222299; Pres. GEORGE AKOMAS.

Uyo Chamber of Commerce and Industry: 141 Abak Rd, POB 2960, Uyo, Akwa Ibom; Pres. Chief DANIEL ITA-EKPOTT.

Warri Chamber of Commerce, Industry, Mines and Agriculture: Block 1, Edewor Shopping Centre, PMB 302, Warri; tel. (53) 253709; internet www.waccima.com; f. 1963; Pres. AUSTIN E. EGBEGBADIA.

INDUSTRIAL AND TRADE ASSOCIATIONS

Federation of Agriculture Commodity Associations of Nigeria (FACAN): Lagos; f. 2011; Pres. Dr VICTOR IYAMA; AKIN GBADAMOSI.

National Cashew Association of Nigeria (NCAN): 32/35 Calcutta Cres., Apapa-Lagos; tel. (1) 5870966; Pres. OLATUNJI OWOEYE.

National Coffee and Tea Association of Nigeria: Old NRC Bldg, Gembu, Taraba; tel. (75) 624486.

National Cotton Association of Nigeria (NACOTAN): 48/50 Namagwatse House, Ahmadu Bello Way, Kaduna; Pres. Alhaji ALIYU ISAH DANMARAYA.

Nigerian Export Promotion Council (NEPC): Plot 40, Blantyre St, Wuse 2, Abuja; tel. (9) 5230932; fax (9) 5230931; e-mail info@nepc.gov.ng; internet www.nepc.gov.ng; f. 1977; Chair. Alhaji ISIAKA ADELEKE; CEO DAVID ADULUGBA.

Nigerian Investment Promotion Commission (NIPC): Plot 1181, Aguiyi Ironsi St, Maitama District, PMB 381, Garki, Abuja; tel. (9) 4134380; e-mail infodesk@nipc.gov.ng; internet www.nipc.gov.ng; Chair. FELIX OMOIKHOJE AIZOBEOJE OHIWEREI; Exec. Sec. Alhaji MUSTAFA BELLO.

Potato Growers, Processors and Marketers Association of Nigeria (POGPMAN): Lagos; Pres. BAYO AJIBADE.

EMPLOYERS' ORGANIZATIONS

Association of Advertising Agencies of Nigeria (AAAN): Plot 8, Otunba Jobi Fele-Way, Central Business District, Alausa, Ikeja, Lagos; tel. and fax (1) 4970842; e-mail lekan@aaanigeria.com; internet www.aaanigeria.com; Pres. FUNMI ONABOLU; CEO LEKAN FADOLAPO.

Chartered Institute of Bankers of Nigeria: PC 19 Adeola Hopewell St, POB 72273, Victoria Island, Lagos; tel. (1) 2703494; fax (1) 4618930; e-mail cibn@cibng.org; internet www.cibng.org; Chair. JOSEPH LAOYE JAIYEOLA; CEO Dr UJU M. OGUBUNKA.

Institute of Chartered Accountants of Nigeria: Plot 16, Professional Layout Centre, Idowu Taylor St, Victoria Island, POB 1580, Lagos; tel. (1) 7642294; fax (1) 7642295; e-mail info.ican@ican.org.ng; internet www.ican-ngr.org; f. 1965; CEO and Registrar ADEDOYIN OWOLABI; Pres. SEBASTIAN ACHULIKE OWUAMA.

Nigeria Employers' Consultative Association: NECA House, Plot A2, Hakeem Balogun St, Central Business District, Alausa, Ikeja, POB 2231, Marina, Lagos; tel. (1) 7746352; fax (1) 7912941; e-mail neca@neca.org.ng; internet www.neca.org.ng; f. 1957; Pres. R. U. UCHE; Dir-Gen. O. A. OSHINOWO.

Nigerian Institute of Architects (NIA): 2 Kukawa Close, off Gimbiya St, Area 11, Garki, Abuja; tel. (9) 4802518; e-mail info@niarchitects.org; internet niarchitects.org; f. 1960; Pres. OLATUNJI OLUMIDE BOLU.

Nigerian Institute of Building (NIOB): House No 24, Road 37, Gwarinpa Housing Estate, Abuja; tel. and fax (9) 7831243; e-mail niob@niobuilding.org; internet www.niobuilding.org; f. 1967; Pres. DACHOLLOM DALYOP JAMBOL.

Nigerian Institution of Estate Surveyors and Valuers: Plot 759, BASSAN Plaza, Wing C, Last Floor, Central Business District, Independence Ave, PMB 5147 Abuja; tel. 8078193014 (mobile); e-mail admin@niesv.org.ng; internet www.niesv.org.ng; f. 1969; Pres. EMEKA D. ELEH; Nat. Sec. ADEKUNLE G. AWOLAJA.

Nigerian Society of Engineers (NSE): National Engineering Centre, Plot 1035 Cadastral, off National Mosque-Labour House Rd, Central Business Area, PMB 13866, Abuja; tel. (9) 6735096; e-mail info@nseng.org; internet www.nse.org.ng; f. 1958; Pres. MUSTAPHA BALARABE SHEHU.

UTILITIES

Electricity

Following the liberalization of the electricity sector in 2005, the Power Holding Company of Nigeria (PHCN), the national producer and distributor of electricity, was dissolved in early 2012, and its assets and responsibilities were transferred to 17 successor companies. The privatization process was scheduled to be completed by mid-2013.

Nigerian Electricity Regulatory Commission (NERC): Adamawa Plaza, Plot 1099, First Ave, off Shehu Shagari Way, Central Business District, PMB 136, Garki, Abuja; tel. (9) 6700991; e-mail info@nercng.org; internet www.nercng.org; f. 2005; Chair. and CEO Dr SAM AMADI.

Gas

Nigeria Liquefied Natural Gas Co Ltd (NLNG): C. & C. Towers, Plot 1684, Sanusi Fafunwa St, Victoria Island, PMB 12774, Marina, Lagos; tel. (1) 2624190; fax (1) 2616976; internet www.nigerialng.com; f. 1989; Man. Dir CHIMA IBENECHE.

TRADE UNIONS

Federations

Nigerian Labour Congress (NLC): Labour House, Plot 820/821, Central Business District, Abuja; tel. (9) 6276042; fax (9) 6274342; e-mail gsec@nlcng.org; internet www.nlcng.org; f. 1978; comprised 36 affiliated industrial unions in 2009; Pres. ABDULWAHED IBRAHIM OMAR; Gen. Sec. OWEI LAKEMFA.

Trade Union Congress of Nigeria (TUC): Express House, 338 Ikorodu Rd, Maryland, Lagos; tel. (1) 4701699; e-mail info@tucnigeria.org; internet www.tucnigeria.org; Pres.-Gen. PETER ESELE; Gen. Sec. JOHN KOLAWOLE; 24 mem. orgs.

Transport

RAILWAYS

In 2005 there were about 3,528 km of mainly narrow-gauge railways. The two principal lines connect Lagos with Nguru and Port Harcourt with Maiduguri. In 2010 there were plans for the construction of a 21-km monorail in Enugu. Construction of a 35–km light rail system was under way in Lagos in early 2013.

Nigerian Railway Corpn: PMB 1037, Ebute-Metta, Lagos; tel. (1) 7747320; fax (1) 5831367; e-mail info.nrc@nrc-ng.org; internet www.nrc-ng.org; f. 1955; restructured in 1993 into three separate units: Nigerian Railway Track Authority; Nigerian Railways; and Nigerian Railway Engineering Ltd; Chair. Dr BELLO HALIRU MOHAMMED; Man. Dir ADESEYI SIJUWADE.

ROADS

In 2011 the Nigerian road network totalled 198,000 km, including 15,688 km of highways and 18,719 km of secondary roads; some 9,660 km were paved.

Federal Roads Maintenance Agency (FERMA): Plot 163, Aminu Kano Cres., Wuse II, Abuja; e-mail information@ferma.ng.gov; internet www.ferma.gov.ng; f. 2002; Chair. Eng. ABDULKHADIR A. KURE; Man. Dir and CEO Eng. SANI HALIRU.

Nigerian Road Federation: Ministry of Transport, National Maritime Agency Bldg, Central Area, Abuja; tel. (9) 5237053.

Road Transport Employers' Association of Nigeria (RTEAN): Plot 2082, Harper Cres., Beside Police Officers Mess, Wuse Zone 7, FCT, Abuja; internet rtean.com; Pres. JOSIAH OLUFEMI OLUFEMI AJEWOLE; Sec.-Gen. Alhaji DANLAMI GARBA NAVOM.

INLAND WATERWAYS

National Inland Waterways Authority (NIWA): PMB 1004, Adankolo, Lokoja, Kogi State; tel. (58) 2220965; internet niwagovng.com; f. 1997; responsible for all navigable waterways; Man. Dir AHMED AMINU YAR'ADUA.

SHIPPING

The principal ports are the Delta Port complex (including Warri, Koko, Burutu and Sapele ports), Port Harcourt and Calabar; other significant ports are situated at Apapa and Tin Can Island, near Lagos. The main petroleum ports are Bonny and Burutu. At 31 December 2012 Nigeria's flag registered fleet comprised 462 vessels, with a total displacement of 2,094,038 grt. Some 101 shipping companies were registered in 2010.

Nigerian Maritime Administration and Safety Agency (NIMASA): 4 Burma Rd, Apapa; tel. 5452843; e-mail info@nimasa.gov.ng; internet nimasa.gov.ng; f. 2007 following merger of National Maritime Authority and Joint Maritime Labour Industrial Council; Chair. ALHAJI AHMADU ADAMU MU'AZU; Dir-Gen. ZAIKEDE PATRICK AKPOBOLOKEMI.

Nigerian Ports Authority: 26/28 Marina, PMB 12588, Lagos; tel. (1) 2600620; fax (1) 2636719; e-mail telnpo@infoweb.abs.net; internet www.nigerianports.org; f. 1955; Man. Dir OMAR SULEIMAN.

Nigerian Green Lines Ltd: Yinka Folawiyo Plaza, 38 Yinka Folawiyo Ave (fmrly Warehouse Rd), Apapa; tel. (1) 5450436; fax (1) 5450204; f. 1972; Yinka Folawiyo Group; 2 vessels totalling 30,751 grt; Chair. Alhaji W. I. FOLAWIYO.

Association

Nigerian Shippers' Council: Shippers' Tower, 4 Park Lane, Apapa, Lagos; tel. (1) 5452307; fax (1) 5452906; e-mail info@shipperscouncil.com; internet www.shipperscouncil.com; Chair. Chief Dr MARIAN ALI; CEO Capt. ADAMU A. BIU.

CIVIL AVIATION

The principal international airports are at Lagos (Murtala Mohammed Airport), Kano, Port Harcourt and Abuja. There are also 18 airports servicing domestic flights. In 2012 Nigerian airports handled a total of some 13.4m. passengers.

Federal Airports Authority of Nigeria (FAAN): Murtala Mohammed Airport, PMB 21607, Ikeja, Lagos; tel. (1) 4970335; fax (1) 4970342; e-mail contact@faannigeria.org; internet www.faannigeria.org; Chair. EBITIMI BANIGO; CEO GEORGE ESEZOBOR URIESI.

Nigerian Civil Aviation Authority (NCAA): Nnandi Azikwe International Airport, Abuja; e-mail info@ncaa.gov.ng; internet www.ncaa.gov.ng; Dir-Gen. Capt. FOLA AKINKUOTU.

Principal Airlines

Aero Nigeria: Private Terminal, Domestic Wing, Murtala Mohammed Airport, Ikeja, Lagos; tel. (1) 6284140; e-mail customercare@acn.aero; internet www1.flyaero.com; f. 1959; Man. Dir OBARO IBRU (acting).

Air Nigeria: 3rd Floor, Ark Towers, Plot 17, Ligali Ayorinde St, Victoria Island Extension, Ikeja, Lagos; tel. (1) 4600505; internet www.flyairnigeria.com; f. Sept. 2004, name changed as above in 2010; private flag carrier; owned by Air Nigeria Development Ltd; scheduled domestic regional and international services; operations suspended owing to financial difficulties in September 2012; Chair. JIMOH IBRAHIM; CEO KINFE KAHASSAYE.

Arik Air: Murtala Mohammed Airport, POB 10468, Ikeja, Lagos; tel. (1) 2799900; fax (1) 4975940; e-mail info@arikair.com; internet www.arikair.com; f. 2002; Chair. JOSEPH ARUMEMI-IKHIDE; Group CEO Dr MICHAEL ARUMEMI-IKHIDE.

Chanchangi Airlines Nigeria Ltd: Kaduna; f. 1994; domestic scheduled services; Chair. Alhaji AHMADU CHANCHANGI; Man. Dir TREVOR WORTHINGTON.

Dana Air: 51 Allen Ave, Ikeja, Lagos; tel. (1) 2809888; e-mail contact@flydanaair.com; internet www.flydanaair.com; CEO JACKY HATHIRAMANI.

IRS Airlines Ltd: 62 Micheal Otedola Cres., off Joel Ogunnaike GRA, Ikeja, Lagos; tel. (1) 2704486; fax (1) 2704486; e-mail rirabiu@flyirsairlines.com; internet www.flyirsairlines.com; f. 2001; domestic services; Chair. Alhaji ISYAKU RABIU.

Tourism

Potential attractions for tourists include fine coastal scenery, dense forests and the rich diversity of Nigeria's arts. A total of 6.1m. tourists visited Nigeria in 2010. Receipts from tourism in 2011 amounted to an estimated US $601m.

Nigerian Tourism Development Corpn: Old Federal Secretariat, Area 1, Garki, PMB 167, Abuja; tel. (9) 2342764; fax (9) 2342775; e-mail ntdc@metrong.com; internet www.nigeria.tourism.com; Chair. Prince ADESUYI HAASTRUP; CEO OMOTAYO OMOTOSHO.

Defence

As assessed at November 2012, the total strength of the armed forces was 80,000: the army totalled 62,000 men, the navy 8,000 and the air force 10,000. There was also a paramilitary force of 82,000. Military service is voluntary. In 2012 a total of 5,183 Nigeria troops were stationed abroad, of which 75 were observers.

Defence Expenditure: Budgeted at ₦326,000m. in 2012.

Commander-in-Chief of the Armed Forces: Dr GOODLUCK EBELE JONATHAN.

Chief of Defence Staff: Vice-Adm. OLA SA'AD IBRAHIM.

Chief of Army Staff: Maj.-Gen. ONYEABO AZUBIKE IHEJIRIKA.

Chief of Naval Staff: Rear-Adm. DELE EZEOBA.

Chief of Air Staff: Air Vice-Marshal ALEX BADEH.

Education

Education is partly the responsibility of the state governments, although the Federal Government has played an increasingly important role since 1970. Primary education begins at six years of age and lasts for six years. Secondary education begins at 12 years of age and lasts for a further six years, comprising two three-year cycles. Education to junior secondary level (from six to 15 years of age) is free and compulsory. According to UNESCO estimates, in 2009/10 primary enrolment was equivalent to 83% of children in the relevant age-group (males 87%; females 79%), while the comparable ratio for secondary enrolment in that year was equivalent to 44% (males 47%; females 41%). In 2005 724,856 students were enrolled at Nigerian universities. Expenditure on education by the Federal Government in 2005 was ₦82,797m., equivalent to 5.0% of total spending in the federal budget.

NORWAY

Introductory Survey

LOCATION, CLIMATE, LANGUAGE, RELIGION, FLAG, CAPITAL

The Kingdom of Norway forms the western part of Scandinavia, in northern Europe. It is bordered to the east by Sweden and, within the Arctic Circle, by Finland and Russia. A long, indented coast faces the Atlantic Ocean. Norway exercises sovereignty over the Svalbard archipelago, Jan Mayen island and the uninhabited dependencies of Bouvetøya and Peter I Øy. Dronning Maud Land, in Antarctica, is also a Norwegian dependency. Norway's climate is temperate on the west coast, but colder inland. Annual average temperatures range from −2°C (28°F) to 8°C (46°F). There are two forms of the Norwegian language, which are officially recognized as equal. About 80% of children in schools use the older form, *Bokmål*, as their principal language, whereas only 20% use the newer form, *Nynorsk* (Neo-Norwegian). Lappish is also spoken by the Sámi population, in northern Norway. Almost all of the inhabitants profess Christianity: the Evangelical Lutheran Church is the established religion, with about 77% of the population professing adherence in 2011. The civil flag (proportions 8 by 11) has a dark blue cross, bordered with white, on a red background, the upright of the cross being to the left of centre; the state flag (16 by 27) displays the same cross, but forms a triple swallow-tail at the fly. The capital is Oslo.

CONTEMPORARY POLITICAL HISTORY

Historical Context

Norway, formerly linked to the Swedish crown, declared its independence in 1905. The union with Sweden was peacefully dissolved and the Norwegians elected their own monarch, Prince Karl of Denmark, who took the title of King Håkon VII. He reigned until his death in 1957, and was succeeded by his son, Olav V. Olav's son, Crown Prince Harald (who had acted as regent since May 1990, when his father suffered a stroke), became King Harald V upon Olav's death in January 1991.

During the Second World War Norway was occupied by German forces between 1940 and 1945. Norway abandoned its traditional policy of neutrality after the war, joining the North Atlantic Treaty Organization (NATO, see p. 380) in 1949. Norway was also a founder member of the Nordic Council (see p. 477) in 1952 and of the European Free Trade Association (EFTA, see p. 461) in 1960.

Domestic Political Affairs

Det norske Arbeiderparti (DnA—Norwegian Labour Party) governed from 1935 to 1965, except for the period of German occupation, when a pro-Nazi 'puppet' regime was administered by Vidkun Quisling, and an interlude of one month in 1963. Norway applied for membership of the European Community (EC, now European Union—EU, see p. 281) in 1962, and again in 1967. A general election to the Storting (parliament) in September 1965 resulted in a defeat for the DnA Government of Einar Gerhardsen, who had been Prime Minister almost continuously since 1955. His administration was replaced in October 1965 by a non-socialist coalition under Per Borten, leader of the Senterpartiet (Sp—Centre Party). Borten resigned in March 1971, following revelations that he had deliberately disclosed confidential details of Norway's negotiations with the EC. He was succeeded by a minority DnA Government, led by Trygve Bratteli. The terms of Norway's entry into the EC were agreed in December 1971, and a preliminary Treaty of Accession was signed in January 1972. In September, however, a consultative referendum on the agreed terms produced a 53.3% majority against entering the EC. The application was withdrawn, and Bratteli resigned in October. A coalition of Venstre (Liberal), the Sp and the Kristelig Folkeparti (KrF—Christian Democratic Party) subsequently formed a minority Government, with Lars Korvald of the KrF as Prime Minister.

Following the general election of September 1973, Bratteli formed another minority DnA Government, dependent on the support of a socialist alliance known from 1975 as the Sosialistisk Venstreparti (SV—Socialist Left Party). In January 1976 Odvar Nordli replaced Bratteli as Prime Minister. Nordli resigned in

February 1981, citing ill health, and was succeeded by Gro Harlem Brundtland. At the general election in September DnA lost support to centre-right groups. In October a minority administration, led by Kåre Willoch, became Norway's first Høyre (Conservative) Government since 1928. In June 1983 a coalition of Høyre with the Sp and the KrF was formed, with 79 of the 165 parliamentary seats. Willoch's Government was returned to power, although lacking an overall majority in the Storting, following the general election in September 1985. In May 1986 Willoch resigned when the Storting narrowly rejected a proposal to increase taxation on petrol. The Norwegian Constitution did not permit a general election before the expiry of the Storting's term (due in 1989). Brundtland accepted an invitation by the King to form a minority DnA administration.

At the general election in September 1989 both DnA and Høyre lost support to more radical parties. The SV gained nine seats, to achieve a total of 17 seats. The Fremskrittspartiet (FrP—Progress Party) increased its representation from two to 22 seats, despite attracting allegations of racism during the election campaign. Brundtland's Government resigned in October, following an agreement made by Høyre, the Sp and the KrF to form a coalition. The new Government, led by Jan Syse of Høyre, controlled only 62 seats in the Storting and was dependent upon the support of the FrP. Also in September 1989 the Sámi (Lapps) of northern Norway elected 39 representatives for a new Sameting (Consultative Assembly), to be based in Karasjok. This followed an amendment to the Constitution the previous year, which recognized the Sámi as an indigenous people and an ethnic minority. There was considerable support among the Sámi for a degree of autonomy, in order to protect their traditional way of life. The Sámi had officially ceased to exist by 1900, with their culture and language being declared illegal, but by 2000 they had formed a joint council representing Sámi populations in Norway, Sweden, Finland and Russia, and received a parliament building, opened in November by King Harald V. The issue of land rights, however, remained unresolved. This was aggravated by the discovery, in 2001, of substantial platinum deposits in Finnmark, an area to which the Sámi laid claim.

While Høyre had supported EC membership since 1988, the Sp remained strongly opposed to it. In October 1990 the Government announced that the Norwegian krone was to be linked to the European Currency Unit (ECU). Later that month the coalition collapsed, following disagreement between Høyre and the Sp regarding Norwegian demands in the negotiations between EFTA and the EC on the creation of a joint European Economic Area (EEA). In November DnA formed another minority Government, led by Brundtland.

In October 1991 agreement was finally reached on the terms of the EEA treaty, including arrangements whereby EC countries were to be allowed to take extra quotas of fish from Norwegian waters, while Norwegian fish products were to have increased access to EC markets. Many Norwegians remained opposed to membership of the EC, fearing, in particular, that government subsidies to remote rural and coastal communities would no longer be permitted. The EEA treaty was ratified by the Storting in October 1992 and entered into effect on 1 January 1994. A proposal by Brundtland to apply for EC membership was endorsed by the Storting in November 1992, and an application was duly submitted.

At the September 1993 general election DnA increased its representation in the Storting, from 63 to 67 seats. The Sp increased its total from 11 to 32 seats, thereby becoming the second largest party in the Storting, while Høyre won only 28 seats, compared with 37 at the previous election.

Negotiations on Norway's entry to the EU, as the EC had been restyled, were concluded in March 1994. However, at a national referendum held on 27–28 November (shortly after Sweden and Finland had voted to join the Union), 52.4% of voters rejected EU membership. The success of the campaign opposing Norway's entry to the EU was attributed to several factors: in particular, farmers feared the impact of an influx of cheaper agricultural goods from the EU, and fisheries workers feared that fish stocks would be severely depleted if EU boats were granted increased access to Norwegian waters. There was also widespread concern that national sovereignty would be compromised by the transfer to the EU of certain executive responsibilities.

The general elections of 1997 and 2001

In October 1996 Brundtland resigned as Prime Minister and was succeeded by Thorbjørn Jagland, who had replaced Brundtland as DnA leader in November 1992. By the end of the year, however, the Government's credibility had been seriously undermined, after Terje Röd-Larsen, the newly appointed Minister of National Planning, and Grete Faremo, the Minister of Petroleum and Energy, were forced to resign, following, respectively, allegations of financial irregularities and abuse of power.

At the general election in September 1997 DnA attracted the largest level of support, winning 65 seats, ahead of the FrP and the KrF with 25 seats each and Høyre with 23 seats. In October Jagland resigned, honouring a pre-election pledge to stand down should DnA fail to attain the level of popular support that it attracted at the 1993 poll. Kjell Magne Bondevik, the parliamentary leader of the KrF, had organized an alliance of the KrF, the Sp and Venstre (with representation totalling 42 seats), and was invited to form a coalition government on that basis. The new Council of State was dominated by the KrF. There was some uncertainty regarding the durability of the Government after the Prime Minister took more than three weeks' leave from his post from the end of August 1998, owing to depression. Bondevik was reported to have been under intense pressure as a result of recent economic instability, largely attributable to the sharp decline in international prices for petroleum, necessitating the postponement of a child-care scheme promoted by the Prime Minister. In November, furthermore, the Government was obliged to abandon proposed tax increases in order to secure the support of the FrP (and thus parliamentary approval) for the 1999 budget.

In March 2000 Bondevik resigned following his defeat in a confidence motion in the Storting. The vote was called to resolve a dispute over government plans to postpone the construction of gas-fired power plants. Jens Stoltenberg, who had replaced Jagland as leader of DnA in February, subsequently formed a single-party minority Government. The new Council of State included Jagland as Minister of Foreign Affairs. The new Government pledged to reform the public sector, resume the country's privatization programme, forge stronger links with Europe and continue Norway's role as a mediator in international peace negotiations.

At a general election conducted on 10 September 2001, DnA received only 24.3% of the valid votes cast (its poorest electoral performance since 1909), attaining 43 seats. Høyre secured 38 seats, the FrP 26, the SV 23 and the KrF 22. DnA formed a minority Government, but was unable to attract enough political support to control a majority in the Storting. Stoltenberg consequently resigned on 17 October, and DnA was replaced in government by a minority centre-right coalition comprising Høyre, the KrF and Venstre, with Bondevik as Prime Minister. The coalition gained a majority in the Storting with the informal support of the FrP.

In February 2003 the Government announced its decision to expel Mullah Krekar, the Iraqi-born alleged founder of the Kurdish guerrilla organization Ansar al-Islam, who was suspected by both the USA and the UN of having links to terrorism, and possibly to the radical Islamist al-Qa'ida organization. However, Krekar, who had stated that he would not leave Norway voluntarily, was not taken into custody or otherwise compelled to leave the country. The following month the Government announced that the case merited further investigation, and that the launch of the US-led military action in Iraq that month posed difficulties for his repatriation. Krekar was eventually detained and subsequently released, following an appearance on Dutch television during which he stated that Ansar al-Islam had suicide bombers ready to attack US citizens. He was arrested again in December and charged with plotting the murder of his political rivals in Iraq in 2000–01, and was imprisoned in January 2004 while prosecutors investigated the charges against him. Despite the prosecutors' efforts to keep Krekar in custody, he was freed by the Lagmannsrett (Court of Appeal) in February. The charges against Krekar were withdrawn in June owing to insufficient evidence. In 2005 Krekar's expulsion was further delayed pending a guarantee from the Iraqi authorities that he would not face the death penalty. (Norwegian law forbids extradition to countries with the death penalty.) In November 2007 the Høyesterett (Supreme Court) upheld the decision to expel Krekar, judging him to be a 'danger to national security'. However, in April 2008 it was reported that the Government had failed to reach an agreement with the Iraqi authorities over his extradition and that Krekar was to be allowed to remain in Norway indefinitely. In January 2010 Krekar survived a suspected assassination attempt at his home in Oslo. In March 2012 Krekar was sentenced to five years' imprisonment following repeated death threats made by him against a number of individuals, including several Norwegian politicians.

In 2004 Norway introduced transitional rules aimed at limiting (for an initial period of two years) the entry of migrant workers from the eight Central and Eastern European countries that joined the EU on 1 May. While Norway was not itself a member of the EU, it nevertheless had commitments arising from its membership of the EEA and the EU's Schengen agreement on border controls. In 2008, partly in response to domestic labour shortages, the Norwegian Government eased the restrictions on migrant workers from the new EU member states (now including Romania and Bulgaria, which joined the Union in 2007).

Stoltenberg regains the premiership

At the general election of 12 September 2005, DnA received 32.7% of the votes cast and won 61 of the 169 seats in the enlarged Storting, thus retaining its position as the largest parliamentary party. DnA contested the election at the head of a centre-left alliance also comprising the SV (which secured 15 seats) and the Sp (11 seats). The FrP won 38 seats, while Høyre received 23, the KrF 11 and Venstre 10. DnA, the SV and the Sp subsequently formed the first majority Government since 1985, led by Jens Stoltenberg. The new coalition Government's programme included proposals to increase welfare spending, raise taxes and eradicate social inequality.

In September 2006 Dag Terje Andersen, of DnA, succeeded party colleague Odd Eriksen as Minister of Trade and Industry. In September 2007 Odd Roger Enoksen resigned as Minister of Petroleum and Energy. The appointment of his successor, the leader of the Sp, Aslaug Haga, created Norway's first government composed of a majority of women, who occupied 10 of the 19 ministerial positions. A minor government reorganization took place in October and included new appointments by the SV, following significant losses for the party in nation-wide local elections in September, which were widely attributed to popular disenchantment with the SV members of the Council of State. Helen Bjørnøy and Øystein Djupedal, responsible for the environment and education portfolios, respectively, were removed from the Government, while DnA's Manuela Ramin-Osmundsen was appointed Minister of Children and Equality. In February 2008, however, Ramin-Osmundsen resigned from the Council of State, following media allegations of favouritism in her appointment of a government lawyer and close friend, Ida Hjort Kraby, as children's ombudsman. Ramin-Osmundsen was succeeded later that month by Anniken Huitfeldt. Hjort Kraby subsequently resigned from the post of children's ombudsman.

In June 2008 Haga resigned both as Minister of Petroleum and Energy and as leader of the Sp, citing ill health, following media accusations of tax irregularities in connection with the letting of a holiday home. Stoltenberg subsequently effected a reorganization of the Council of State. The Sp's Terje Riis-Johansen, hitherto Minister of Agriculture and Food, was assigned the post of Minister of Petroleum and Energy, while Lars Peder Brekk, who had been appointed as interim leader of the Sp, assumed the agriculture and food portfolio. In September the Minister of Transport and Communications, Liv Signe Navarsete, was elected as the new leader of the Sp.

On 19 June 2009 the Lagting and the Odelsting, the upper and lower houses of the Storting, met for the final time as separate bodies in their 195-year history, in accordance with a bill approved in February 2007 providing for their abolition. Previously members of the Storting had elected one-quarter of their own body to form the Lagting, while the other three-quarters had constituted the Odelsting. In practice, debates in the Lagting had become an unnecessary formality, since the composition of parties in both chambers was so similar that decisions made in the upper house were virtually identical to those in the lower house.

The 2009 general election

At the general election of 14 September 2009 DnA, led by Stoltenberg, remained the largest party in the Storting after securing 35.4% of the votes cast, increasing its parliamentary representation by three seats, to 64. The other two members of the DnA-led, centre-left coalition—the SV and the Sp—obtained 11 seats each in the 169-seat legislature, with both parties attracting 6.2% of the votes cast, thereby giving the three incumbent parties a total of 86 seats and a very slim majority (of two seats). The two main right-wing parties, the FrP and Høyre, increased their representation in the Storting, winning 41 seats (22.9% of the vote) and 30 seats (17.2%), respectively, while the KrF secured 10 seats (5.5%) and Venstre two (3.9%). The rate of participation by the electorate was 76.4%. Environmental issues, immigration and asylum, and education were subsequently announced as the main priorities of the new administration.

Stoltenberg reorganized the Council of State in October 2009, assigning one-half of the cabinet positions to women. Notably, the finance portfolio was allocated to Sigbjørn Johnsen, Minister of Finance during 1990–96, while the erstwhile incumbent, SV leader Kristin Halvorsen, became Minister of Education, and former Minister of Defence, Anne-Grete Strøm-Erichsen, was reassigned to the health ministry after being replaced by Grete Faremo. In November the Government was accused of reneging on earlier promises to tackle climate change, when a tax on biodiesel, previously exempt, received legislative approval, attracting widespread criticism and causing division within the ruling coalition.

Terje Riis-Johansen resigned as Minister of Petroleum and Energy in March 2011, having sustained repeated criticism regarding his ministerial competence: in particular, he had been widely blamed for allowing a pioneering plan to install a carbon capture and storage facility at the Mongstad gas-fired power station to fall well behind its original schedule. Riis-Johansen was also responsible for a highly controversial decision to erect overhead power lines through the scenic Hardanger district in western Norway, which had been finalized earlier in March. He was replaced by his Sp colleague Ola Borten Moe.

Recent developments: the Oslo bombing and the Utøya massacre

On 22 July 2011 the relative peace and stability traditionally enjoyed by Norway were seriously undermined by a bomb attack and mass shooting which left 77 people dead and 242 injured. In mid-afternoon on that day eight people were killed in a bomb explosion outside government buildings in Oslo and less than two hours later a lone gunman opened fire on participants at a summer youth camp organized by the Arbeiderpartiet (as the DnA had renamed itself earlier in the year) on the small island of Utøya, around 32 km north-west of the capital, killing a further 69 people. The perpetrator of both attacks was a 32-year-old, right-wing extremist Norwegian named Anders Behring Breivik, who willingly surrendered to the police and openly admitted responsibility for the murders. At his first court appearance, on 25 July, Breivik claimed to have carried out the two-pronged attack in an attempt to save Europe from 'Muslim domination' and to prevent further recruitment to the Arbeiderpartiet, which he accused of permitting excessive levels of Muslim immigration. He further asserted that Europe's Christian heritage and culture were being destroyed by the left-wing's advocacy of multiculturalism. It was subsequently revealed that Breivik had been a member of the right-wing FrP from 1999 until 2006, but had left the party claiming that its policies were not radical enough. Despite his assertions of links with other right-wing extremist organizations in Europe, it was generally believed that Breivik was a sociopath who had acted alone. Prime Minister Stoltenberg expressed his Government's resolve to uphold the country's staunch defence of diversity and tolerance and, amid criticism of the police response to the attacks, an independent commission was established in August to investigate the events surrounding the outrage. In an apparent backlash against right-wing extremism, support for the FrP in local elections held in September fell to 11.4% of the total votes, compared with the 22.9% achieved in the 2009 general election.

Following the resignation of the Minister of Justice and Public Security, Knut Storberget, on 11 November 2011, the Prime Minister carried out a reorganization of the Council of State. Storberget was replaced by the erstwhile Minister of Defence, Grete Faremo, and the defence portfolio was assumed by Espen Barth Eide. Although Storberget claimed that he had resigned for personal reasons, his political standing had been damaged by allegations that in August he had attempted to persuade a lawyer acting on behalf of victims of the Utøya massacre to moderate her criticism of the police response to Breivik's attacks.

The issue of religious extremism came to the fore again in mid-November 2011 when the trial commenced in Oslo of three Norwegian residents (all of whom were Muslim) who were charged with conspiring to carry out an attack on the office of a Danish newspaper that had provoked widespread condemnation from Muslims around the world by printing cartoons of the Prophet Muhammad in 2005. In January 2012, in the first convictions under Norway's anti-terrorism legislation, two of the defendants were given jail sentences (of seven years and three-and-a-half years), while the third was cleared of terrorism charges but convicted of helping to acquire explosives and sentenced to four months' imprisonment.

In January 2012 the head of Norway's Police Security Service (Politiets sikkerhetstjeneste—PST), Janne Kristiansen, was forced to resign following remarks made by her during a parliamentary hearing that Norway had secret intelligence agents operating in Pakistan; the Minister of Justice and Public Security claimed that such comments constituted a 'potential breach of confidentiality'. Kristiansen had also been much criticized during the preceding months for the PST's perceived mishandling of events surrounding Breivik's attacks. Following the publication in August of the government-commissioned report on the massacre, which claimed that the bombing could have been prevented if existing security proposals had been implemented and which criticized the length of time that it took for the police to respond to the shootings as 'unacceptable', Norway's police chief, Øystein Mæland, resigned. In turn, Prime Minister Stoltenberg, expressing deep regret at the mistakes that had been made, accepted responsibility for the events and announced a package of new security measures.

In early March 2012 Breivik was formally charged with having perpetrated acts of terrorism; his trial commenced in Oslo on 16 April. On 24 August Breivik was declared sane (despite assertions by the prosecution that he was criminally insane and should therefore be committed to psychiatric care) and found guilty; he was sentenced to at least 21 years in prison.

Meanwhile, on 24 May 2012 more than 30,000 public sector workers participated in a nation-wide strike, following the collapse of negotiations over pay increases and improved working conditions; this constituted the first such industrial action by state employees since 1984. In July 2012 the Government used emergency powers (to protect the country's interests) to force offshore workers at Norway's key oil and gas fields to abandon a 16-day strike launched in June following the breakdown of negotiations on wages and pensions.

A number of government and party changes took place during 2012: in early March Audun Lysbakken was forced to resign as Minister of Children, Equality and Social Inclusion on the grounds of conflicts of interest and improper use of government funds, and was replaced by Inga Marte Thorkildsen; and, later in the month, the Minister of the Environment and of International Development, Erik Solheim, was replaced by Bård Vegar Solhjell in the environment ministry and by Heikki Holmås in the international development ministry. Also in March, Minister of Education and Research Kristin Halvorsen resigned as leader of the SV; she was replaced as party head by Lysbakken (following the latter's resignation from the Council of State several days earlier). In mid-June Lars Peder Brekk was replaced by Trygve Slagsvold Vedum as Minister of Agriculture and Food, while Marit Arnstad was appointed Minister of Transport and Communications. A major cabinet reorganization in September—effected by Stoltenberg in an apparent attempt to boost the waning popularity of the Arbeiderpartiet in advance of the general election in September 2013—included the appointment of Strøm-Erichsen as Minister of Defence, and that of Eide as Minister of Foreign Affairs. Also of note was the installation of Norway's first Muslim cabinet minister, Hadia Tajik, who was given responsibility for the culture portfolio.

Foreign Affairs

Regional relations

Norway was a founder member of the Nordic Council (see p. 477) in 1952 and of the European Free Trade Association (EFTA, see p. 461) in 1960. In 1977 Norway declared an exclusive economic zone extending to 200 nautical miles (370 km) from its coastline, and also unilaterally established a fisheries protection zone around its territory of Svalbard. Following negotiations with Iceland in 1980, Norway declared a corresponding economic zone around Jan Mayen island, and in 1981 reached further agreement with Iceland regarding contested fishing and mineral rights. However, a similar dispute with Denmark, acting for Greenland, was not resolved, and in 1988 Denmark requested arbitration by the International Court of Justice, in The Hague, Netherlands, which gave its judgment on the delimitation of the disputed zones in June 1993 (see Jan Mayen). During 1994 incidents were reported between vessels of the Norwegian coast-guard and Icelandic fishing boats, within the economic zone surrounding the Norwegian island of Spitsbergen (see Svalbard). In October 2005 Norway detained two Russian vessels that were illegally transferring fish within the same zone.

In April 2009 the UN Commission on the Limits of the Continental Shelf finalized its recommendations on the extension of the Norwegian continental shelf, assigning responsibility for an additional 235,000 sq km of seabed in the Arctic Ocean to Norway, including the right to exploit any mineral resources present. However, the delimitation of Norwegian and Russian waters in the Barents Sea, a point of contention since 1974, remained in dispute until April 2010, when agreement was finally reached on the maritime border; the Sea was to be divided into two areas of approximately equal size. The accord was signed in September and was formally ratified by the respective legislatures of Norway and Russia in June 2011. The Norwegian state petroleum company, Statoil, announced two discoveries, in April 2011 and in January 2012, of large reserves of petroleum and natural gas in the Norwegian sector of the Barents Sea.

In May 2011 Norway and the other members of the Arctic Council (see p. 459) (Canada, Denmark, Finland, Iceland, Russia, Sweden and the USA) signed an agreement which included the establishment of a permanent secretariat to be located in Tromsø.

Other external relations

Norway was a founder member of the North Atlantic Treaty Organization (NATO, see p. 380) in 1949. From 1999 Norway contributed 520 troops to the NATO-led Kosovo Force (KFOR) peace-keeping mission in Kosovo. In 2004 Norway increased its contribution to KFOR, dispatching four helicopters and support personnel. At January 2013 Norway's contribution stood at just three troops.

During 1993 the Norwegian Government was instrumental in conducting secret negotiations between the Israeli Government and the Palestine Liberation Organization (PLO), which led to agreement on Palestinian self-rule in certain areas occupied by Israel. Norway won international acclaim for its role in furthering peace in the Middle East through these negotiations, and continues to be involved in the advancement of the peace process.

In February 2000 Norway extended its role as an international mediator, agreeing to broker negotiations between the Sri Lankan Government and Tamil separatists in an attempt to end the 17-year conflict. A cease-fire agreement was signed by the two parties in February 2002, supervised by the Norwegian-led Sri Lanka Monitoring Mission (SLMM). However, the SLMM's activities were terminated in January 2008, following an escalation of violence in the country and the Government's withdrawal from the cease-fire agreement.

In April 2001 Norway agreed to host peace negotiations between the Philippine Government and the Philippine dissident communist alliance, the National Democratic Front. These formal negotiations stalled in 2004 and again in 2005, although Norway continued to act as a mediator between the two parties. Representatives of both parties held informal discussions in Oslo in November 2008. However, the talks collapsed without agreement owing to the Philippine Government's insistence upon a cease-fire as a precondition for the resumption of formal negotiations. Formal talks resumed in Oslo in February 2011, at the end of which the two parties agreed to work towards ending the conflict by June 2012. In March 2012 Norway sent a civilian contingent to the southern Philippine island of Mindanao to participate in the international monitoring team tasked with overseeing the implementation of a cease-fire agreement between the Philippine Government and the rebels; the agreement was signed in October.

Following a moratorium on commercial whaling, adopted by the International Whaling Commission (IWC, see p. 453) in 1982 with effect from 1986, Norway continued to hunt small numbers of whales ostensibly for the purpose of scientific research. Norway registered an objection to the moratorium on hunting minke whales, claiming that (according to the findings of the IWC's scientific commission) this species was plentiful enough to allow whaling on a sustainable basis and that many Norwegian coastal communities depended on whaling for their existence. In 1992 the Norwegian Government declared that it would permit the resumption of commercial hunting of minke whales in 1993, as it was not bound by the moratorium, having reserved its position when the ban was introduced. In December 2005 the Norwegian Government announced an increase in its quota for minke

whales from 797 in 2005 to 1,052 in 2006, the highest quota since 1993. The narrow approval, at an IWC meeting in June 2006, of a Norwegian-backed resolution for an eventual resumption of commercial whaling provoked strong protests from countries opposed to whaling. Although the vote was not binding, it was considered to represent a further step towards a return for the IWC to a role of setting limits for the capture of whales, rather than one of protection. Norway prompted further controversy following its decision to raise its quota for minke whales from 885 in 2009 to 1,286 in 2010 (the highest level for 25 years). Conservationists claimed that this increase was politically motivated and that demand for whale meat had in fact fallen in recent years. The annual quota level was retained at 1,286 whales in 2011–13, despite the fact that actual catches were around one-half (or less) of this number.

In January 2002, following the US-led military campaign against the Taliban and al-Qa'ida militants in Afghanistan in 2001, Norway contributed 180 troops to the International Security Assistance Force (ISAF), deployed in the Afghan capital, Kabul, and at Bagram airbase to help maintain security in the region. Norway also contributed special forces troops to the US-led operation 'Enduring Freedom', the main aim of which was to combat al-Qa'ida's terrorist network in Afghanistan. In August 2004 the mandate of Norway's ISAF troops in northern Afghanistan was extended indefinitely. In January 2006 Norway withdrew almost all its remaining troops from 'Enduring Freedom' and increased its commitment to ISAF. The number of Norwegian troops stationed in Afghanistan was reduced from 433 in early 2012 to 98 in February 2013, as responsibility for the country's security was gradually transferred to Afghan personnel.

In July 2003 Norway sent 150 soldiers to Iraq to help repair roads and bridges and to clear land mines, following the success of the US-led military action in removing the regime of Saddam Hussein earlier in the year. Norway had not supported the war, and insisted that its troops were in Iraq as part of a humanitarian 'stabilizing force' mandated by UN Security Council Resolution 1483, and that they would remain separate from peace-keeping forces dispatched by the USA, the United Kingdom, Denmark and Poland. Norway withdrew its troops from Iraq in mid-2004. However, a small number of staff officers remained until December 2005.

Relations with Iran were strained in December 2009, when Norway (and Sweden) condemned the Iranian authorities' confiscation of the Nobel Peace Prize medal from the Iranian human rights campaigner Shirin Ebadi—an act that was denied by the Iranian Government. Further tension arose in early 2010 following the defection of an Iranian diplomat at the embassy in Oslo, Mohammed Reza Heydari, in protest against the suppression of anti-Government demonstrations in Iran; Heydari was subsequently granted asylum in Norway, despite Iran's disapproval of the decision. In February 2013 it was reported that another high-ranking diplomat at the Iranian embassy in Oslo had defected and applied for asylum.

The award by the Norwegian Nobel Committee of the 2010 Nobel Peace Prize to the Chinese political rights activist Liu Xiaobo seriously damaged relations between Norway and the People's Republic of China, which responded to the announcement of the award in October of that year by refusing to attend negotiations on a proposed free trade agreement between the two countries. In November it was reported that China had suspended the trade negotiations indefinitely. China withheld its ambassador from Liu's award ceremony in Oslo in December (which Liu himself was prevented from attending by the Chinese authorities) and urged other nations to do likewise. However, in early 2013 it was reported that, despite China's continuing campaign of political/diplomatic snubs, the Norwegian Government had reversed its earlier plans to block China's application to be a permanent observer on the Arctic Council.

Nearly 21 years after being awarded the 1991 Nobel Peace Prize, Aung San Suu Kyi, the leader of the Myanma opposition party, the National League for Democracy (see Myanmar), arrived in Oslo in June 2012 to deliver her long-delayed acceptance speech.

CONSTITUTION AND GOVERNMENT

Norway is a constitutional monarchy. Legislative power is held by the Storting (parliament), with 169 members elected for four years by universal adult suffrage, on the basis of proportional representation. Under a constitutional amendment which took effect from October 2009, the internal division of the Storting into two chambers, the Lagting (upper house) and the Odelsting (lower house), was abolished. Executive power is nominally held by the monarch, but is, in effect, exercised by the Statsråd (Council of State), led by the Prime Minister. The Council is appointed by the monarch in accordance with the will of the Storting, to which the Council is responsible. Norway comprises 19 counties (*fylker*) and 430 municipalities (*kommuner*).

REGIONAL AND INTERNATIONAL CO-OPERATION

Norway is a founding member of the Nordic Council (see p. 477) and the Nordic Council of Ministers (see p. 477). In addition to its membership of EFTA, Norway is a member of the European Economic Area (EEA), which incorporates Norway (together with Iceland and Liechtenstein) into the internal market of the European Union (EU, see p. 281). Although Norway is not a member of the EU, it joined the EU's Schengen agreement on the abolition of border controls in May 1999 (Denmark, Finland and Sweden—all EU members—had already joined in 1996) by virtue of its membership in the Nordic passport union. Norway is a member of the Arctic Council (see p. 459), which is based in Norway, and was a founder member of both the Council of Europe (see p. 260) and the Council of the Baltic Sea States (see p. 258). It participates in the Organization for Security and Co-operation in Europe (OSCE, see p. 397).

Norway was a founder member of the UN in 1945. As a contracting party to the General Agreement on Tariffs and Trade, Norway joined the World Trade Organization (WTO, see p. 444) on its establishment in 1995. It is a founder member of the North Atlantic Treaty Organization (NATO, see p. 380), and participates in the Organisation for Economic Co-operation and Development (OECD, see p. 388).

ECONOMIC AFFAIRS

In 2011, according to estimates by the World Bank, Norway's gross national income (GNI), measured at average 2009–11 prices, was US $440,185m., equivalent to $88,890 per head (or $62,970 per head on an international purchasing-power parity basis). During 2002–11, it was estimated, the population increased by an average of 1.0% per year, while gross domestic product (GDP) per head increased, in real terms, by an average of 0.5% per year. Norway's overall GDP increased, in real terms, at an average annual rate of 1.4% in 2002–11; real GDP grew by 1.2% in 2011.

The contribution of agriculture (including hunting, forestry and fishing) to GDP in 2011 was estimated at 1.4%. In 2012 the agricultural sector engaged 2.2% of the employed labour force. Around 3.4% of the land surface is cultivated, and the most important branch of the sector is livestock-rearing. Fish farming has been intensively developed by the Government since the early 1970s. The fishing industry provided an estimated 5.5% of total export revenue in 2012. In 2010 Norway produced some 939,600 metric tons of farmed salmon. According to official figures, agricultural GDP increased at an average annual rate of 3.1% during 2002–11. Agricultural GDP grew by 8.0% in 2010, but decreased by 0.7% in 2011.

Industry (including mining, manufacturing, construction, power and public utilities) contributed an estimated 42.0% of GDP in 2011, and engaged 20.1% of the employed labour force in 2012. During 2002–11 industrial GDP decreased, in real terms, at an average annual rate of 1.0%, according to official figures. Industrial GDP (including service activities incidental to the oil and gas sector) decreased by 2.8% in 2010 and by 0.8% in 2011.

Mining (including gas and petroleum extraction) provided an estimated 25.8% of GDP in 2011, and engaged 2.3% of the employed labour force in 2012. Extraction of petroleum and natural gas dominates the sector, accounting for 25.6% of GDP in 2011 and 1.0% of employment in 2012. Norway possesses substantial reserves of petroleum and natural gas (exports of petroleum and petroleum products accounted for 39.9% of total export earnings in 2012). Most of the reserves are located off shore. During 1995–2005 the production of crude petroleum from fields on the Norwegian continental shelf decreased at an average annual rate of 0.6%, while output of natural gas grew at an average rate of 11.8% per year, according to the Norwegian Petroleum Directorate. Norway's other mineral reserves include iron ore, iron pyrites, copper, lead and zinc. A large terminal to pump natural gas via a 1,200-km pipeline to the United Kingdom was completed in Aukra, on the island of Gossa, in 2007.

Manufacturing contributed 7.7% of GDP in 2011, and employed 9.2% of the working population in 2012. In 2006 the most important branches of manufacturing were food products,

transport equipment (including ships and oil platforms), metals and metal products, electrical and optical equipment, chemicals and chemical products, and pulp and paper products. During 2002–11, according to official figures, manufacturing GDP increased, in real terms, by an average of 2.0% per year. Manufacturing GDP increased by 2.0% in 2011.

In 2011 hydroelectric power accounted for 95.3% of Norway's electricity production, thermal power for 3.7% and wind power for 1.0%. Domestic energy demands are comfortably met, and Norway has exported hydroelectricity since 1993. Norway's extensive reserves of petroleum and natural gas are mainly exploited for sale to foreign markets, since the domestic market is limited.

Construction contributed 5.5% of GDP in 2011, and the sector engaged some 7.5% of the employed labour force in 2012.

The services sector contributed 56.6% of GDP in 2011, and engaged 77.7% of the employed labour force in 2012. The GDP of the services sector increased, in real terms, by an average of 2.7% per year during 2002–11, according to official figures. Services GDP grew by 2.6% in 2011.

Although shipbuilding has declined since the early 1970s, Norway remains a leading shipping nation. The establishment of the Norwegian International Ship Register in 1987 allowed an expansion of the merchant fleet by more than 300%, in terms of gross tonnage. At 31 December 2012 the total displacement of Norway's flag registered fleet amounted to 17.9m. grt, of which the Norwegian International Ship Register accounted for 13.9m. grt.

In 2011, according to IMF figures, Norway recorded a visible merchandise trade surplus of US $70,108m. and there was a surplus of $70,319m. on the current account of the balance of payments. In 2012 the EU (excluding the Nordic countries) provided 64.3% of imports and took 80.6% of exports; fellow members of the European Free Trade Association (EFTA, see p. 461) accounted for 1.7% of Norway's imports and 1.1% of exports in the same year. The principal source of imports in 2012 was Sweden (providing 13.6% of the total), followed by Germany, the People's Republic of China, Denmark, the United Kingdom and the USA; the principal market for exports was the United Kingdom (taking 25.6%), followed by Germany, the Netherlands, France and Sweden. In 2012 the principal exports were petroleum and petroleum products, natural gas, machinery and transport equipment, basic manufactures (most notably aluminium), and food and live animals; the principal imports were machinery and transport equipment, basic manufactures, miscellaneous manufactured articles, chemicals and related products, petroleum, petroleum products, metalliferous ores and metal scrap, and food and live animals.

In 2011 Norway recorded an overall surplus of 368,280m. kroner in the general budget (equivalent to some 13.4% of GDP in purchasers' values). Norway's general government gross debt was 1,349,586m. kroner in 2011, equivalent to 49.6% of GDP. During 2002–12 the average annual rate of inflation was 1.8%; consumer prices increased by 0.8% in 2012. The annual average rate of unemployment was 3.2% in 2012, according to official figures.

The Norwegian economy is highly dependent on its hydrocarbons sector. It has traditionally maintained a stable exchange rate and a prudent fiscal position, reinvesting a substantial proportion of petroleum revenues abroad through the Government Pension Fund—Global (formerly the Government Petroleum Fund), partly in preparation for future increased demands on pensions and also to offer a degree of protection to the economy against fluctuations in the petroleum sector. Budgetary guidelines introduced in 2001 state that government spending of hydrocarbons revenues should equate to the expected annual return on the Pension Fund (assumed to be 4%) in the long term, while allowing for a more expansionary fiscal policy during an economic downturn (as occurred during 2009–11 when government expenditure exceeded the 4% ceiling). In 2012 the Pension Fund was considerably boosted by large rises in equity indexes around the world. By the end of that year the Fund was worth some 3,800,000m. kroner, compared with 3,300,000m. kroner in 2011, and the annual return on its fixed-income investments was 6.7%. In the early years of the 21st century a sturdy policy framework underpinned enviable prosperity and a high degree of social equity in Norway. The strong tradition of social cohesiveness and solidarity ensured that the use of the country's petroleum wealth benefited people at all levels of society, and would continue to profit future generations well after the petroleum itself was depleted. Following a period of healthy economic expansion during the mid-2000s, however, the rate of growth slowed in 2008, before contracting by an estimated 1.7% in 2009, as the economy suffered the adverse effects of the global financial crisis. In January 2009 the Government announced fiscal measures designed to stimulate economic recovery, which included a significant increase in public spending, principally on infrastructure projects, as well as reductions in the level of taxation for businesses. Such measures helped to lessen the effects of the global downturn, and the fiscal stimulus was gradually withdrawn from 2011 as the economy recovered. Low production levels in the petroleum sector contributed to an overall GDP growth rate of just 0.7% in 2010, although 'mainland' GDP (which excludes the 'off-shore' industries) grew by 2.2%, an expansion that was driven mainly by a rise in household consumption fuelled by increased export revenue from the petroleum sector owing to higher commodity prices. Overall GDP increased by 1.2% in 2011 and by 3.2% ('mainland' 3.5%) in 2012. The surge in the rate of growth in the latter year was largely as a result of strong performances in the petroleum and ocean transport sectors. The prospects for Norway's sustained economic recuperation were boosted by reports in the latter half of 2011 that recent discoveries of petroleum reserves in the North Sea by the state oil company, Statoil, were the largest in more than 20 years. Furthermore, there were also reports of substantial reserves of petroleum and natural gas being discovered by Statoil in the Norwegian sector of the Barents Sea in 2011 and early 2012. According to official projections overall GDP was forecast to increase by 2.8% in 2013 and 'mainland' GDP by 2.9%.

PUBLIC HOLIDAYS

2014: 1 January (New Year's Day), 17 April (Maundy Thursday), 18 April (Good Friday), 21 April (Easter Monday), 1 May (Labour Day), 17 May (Constitution Day), 29 May (Ascension Day), 9 June (Whit Monday), 25–26 December (Christmas).

Statistical Survey

Sources (unless otherwise stated): Statistics Norway, Kongensgt. 6, Oslo; tel. 21-09-00-00; fax 21-09-49-73; e-mail biblioteket@ssb.no; internet www.ssb.no; Nordic Statistical Secretariat (Copenhagen), *Yearbook of Nordic Statistics*.

Area and Population

AREA, POPULATION AND DENSITY

Area (sq km)	
Land	304,248
Inland water	19,539
Total	323,787*
Population (census results)	
3 November 2001 . . .	4,520,947
19 November 2011	
Males	2,495,777
Females	2,484,178
Total	4,979,955
Density (per sq km) at 2011 census†	16.4

* 125,015 sq miles.
† Excluding inland water.

POPULATION BY AGE AND SEX
(population at 2011 census)

	Males	Females	Total
0–14	473,302	450,464	923,766
15–64	1,683,043	1,606,707	3,289,750
65 and over	339,432	427,007	766,439
Total	2,495,777	2,484,178	4,979,955

COUNTIES
(population at 2011 census)

	Land area (sq km)*	Population	Density (per sq km)
Østfold	3,888	278,014	71.5
Akershus	4,579	554,881	121.2
Oslo	426	612,314	1,437.4
Hedmark	26,084	192,722	7.4
Oppland	23,784	187,019	7.9
Buskerud	13,796	264,742	19.2
Vestfold	2,147	236,120	110.0
Telemark	13,854	169,930	12.3
Aust-Agder	8,314	111,370	13.4
Vest-Agder	6,677	174,184	26.1

—continued	Land area (sq km)*	Population	Density (per sq km)
Rogaland	8,589	442,265	51.5
Hordaland	14,525	489,786	33.7
Sogn og Fjordane . . .	17,676	108,124	6.1
Møre og Romsdal . . .	14,583	256,381	17.6
Sør-Trøndelag . . .	17,840	297,584	16.7
Nord-Trøndelag . . .	20,778	133,104	6.4
Nordland	36,079	237,856	6.6
Troms	24,866	158,147	6.4
Finnmark	45,762	73,694	1.6
Total	304,248	4,979,955	16.4

* Excluding inland waters, totalling 19,539 sq km.

PRINCIPAL TOWNS
(estimated population of urban settlements at 1 January 2011)

Oslo (capital) . .	906,681		Tønsberg . . .	48,350
Bergen	235,046		Ålesund . . .	47,772
Stavanger/Sandnes .	197,852		Haugesund . .	43,913
Trondheim . .	164,953		Moss	42,781
Fredrikstad/				
Sarpsborg . .	104,382		Sandefjord . .	41,811
Drammen . .	100,303		Bodø . . .	37,834
Porsgrunn/Skien .	88,335		Arendal . . .	33,303
Kristiansand .	69,380		Hamar . . .	30,565
Tromsø . .	56,466		Larvik . . .	24,252

BIRTHS, MARRIAGES AND DEATHS

	Registered live births		Registered marriages*		Registered deaths†	
	Number	Rate (per 1,000)	Number	Rate (per 1,000)	Number	Rate (per 1,000)
2004 . .	56,951	12.4	22,354	4.9	41,200	9.0
2005 . .	56,756	12.3	22,392	4.9	41,232	8.9
2006 . .	58,545	12.6	21,721	4.7	41,253	8.9
2007 . .	58,459	12.5	23,471	5.0	41,954	9.0
2008 . .	60,497	12.8	25,125	5.3	41,712	8.8
2009 . .	61,807	12.7	24,582‡	5.1‡	41,449	8.5
2010 . .	61,442	12.6	23,577‡	4.9‡	41,499	8.5
2011 . .	60,220	12.1	23,135‡	4.6‡	41,393	8.3

* Where bridegroom or older spouse (for same-sex marriages) is resident in Norway.
† Including deaths of residents temporarily abroad.
‡ Including same-sex marriages.

Life expectancy (years at birth): 81.0 (males 78.9; females 83.2) in 2010 (Source: World Bank, World Development Indicators database).

IMMIGRATION AND EMIGRATION

	2009	2010	2011
Immigrants	65,186	73,852	79,498
Emigrants	26,549	31,506	32,466

ECONOMICALLY ACTIVE POPULATION
('000 persons aged 16 to 74 years)*

	2010	2011	2012
Agriculture, fishing and forestry	63	59	57
Mining and quarrying (incl. petroleum and gas)	46	53	59
Manufacturing	236	236	237
Electricity, gas and water	31	32	29
Construction	179	190	194
Trade, restaurants and hotels	414	415	426
Transport and communications	230	239	247
Financing, insurance, real estate and business services	311	302	315
Public administration and defence	157	153	163
Education	208	211	214
Health and social work	529	547	545
Other services	102	102	100
Sub-total	2,506	2,539	2,586
Activities not adequately described	2	4	5
Total employed	2,508	2,543	2,591
Unemployed	94	86	86
Total labour force	2,602	2,629	2,677
Males	1,378	1,387	1,419
Females	1,224	1,243	1,259

* Figures are annual averages, based on quarterly sample surveys; totals may not be equal to the sum of components, owing to rounding.

Health and Welfare

KEY INDICATORS

Total fertility rate (children per woman, 2010)	1.9
Under-5 mortality rate (per 1,000 live births, 2010)	3
HIV/AIDS (% of persons aged 15–49, 2009)	0.1
Physicians (per 1,000 head, 2009)	4.2
Hospital beds (per 1,000 head, 2009)	3.3
Health expenditure (2009): US $ per head (PPP)	5,353
Health expenditure (2009): % of GDP	9.7
Health expenditure (2009): public (% of total)	84.1
Total carbon dioxide emissions ('000 metric tons, 2008)	49,992.2
Carbon dioxide emissions per head (metric tons, 2008)	10.5
Human Development Index (2011): ranking	1
Human Development Index (2011): value	0.943

For sources and definitions, see explanatory note on p. vi.

Agriculture

PRINCIPAL CROPS
('000 metric tons)*

	2009	2010	2011
Wheat	278.0	331.4	265.0
Barley	473.0	541.2	460.0
Rye	27.4	34.2	16.0
Oats	276.5	299.0	220.0
Potatoes	332.5	341.9	297.6
Rapeseed	6.9	11.0	10.0
Cabbages and other brassicas	47.1	30.9	41.2†
Tomatoes	12.7	12.9	13.1†
Cucumbers and gherkins	17.8	18.7	19.9†
Onions and shallots, green	20.6	15.5	16.0†
Carrots and turnips	44.7	40.2	40.1†
Apples	13.9	12.2	12.8†

* Figures refer to holdings with at least 0.5 ha of agricultural area in use.
† FAO estimate.

Aggregate production ('000 metric tons, may include official, semi-official or estimated data): Total cereals 1,055 in 2009, 1,206 in 2010, 961 in 2011; Total roots and tubers 333 in 2009, 342 in 2010, 298 in 2011; Total vegetables (incl. melons) 190 in 2009, 150 in 2010, 162 in 2011; Total fruits (excl. melons) 31 in 2009, 24 in 2010, 26 in 2011.

Source: FAO.

LIVESTOCK
('000 head)*

	2009	2010	2011
Horses	35.5	36.4	36.2
Cattle	876.4	874.2	862.5
Sheep	2,289.9	2,308.3	2,300.0†
Goats	68.3	67.5	68.0†
Pigs	845.0	850.4	845.0†
Chickens	3,879	3,891	3,900†

* Figures refer to holdings with at least 0.5 ha of agricultural area in use.
† FAO estimate.

Source: FAO.

LIVESTOCK PRODUCTS
('000 metric tons)

	2009	2010	2011
Cattle meat	84.8	83.5	73.5*
Sheep meat	23.9	24.4	24.0†
Pig meat	123.6	128.8	126.0†
Chicken meat	71.2	75.9	76.0†
Cows' milk	1,558.1	1,562.4	1,515.0†
Goats' milk	21.6	21.7	20.0†
Hen eggs	58.9	59.9	57.8†
Honey	1.1	1.3	1.3†
Wool, greasy	4.6	4.6	4.5†

* Unofficial figure.
† FAO estimate.

Source: FAO.

Forestry

ROUNDWOOD REMOVALS
('000 cubic metres, excl. bark)

	2009	2010	2011
Sawlogs, veneer logs and logs for sleepers	3,060	4,375	4,335
Pulpwood	3,549	3,921	4,149
Other industrial wood	22	27	22
Fuel wood	2,253	2,121	1,785
Total	8,884	10,444	10,291

Source: FAO.

SAWNWOOD PRODUCTION
('000 cubic metres, incl. railway sleepers)

	2009	2010	2011
Coniferous (softwood)	1,850	2,115	2,271
Broadleaved (hardwood) . . .	0	3	0
Total	1,850	2,118	2,271

Source: FAO.

Fishing

('000 metric tons, live weight)

	2008	2009	2010
Capture	2,431.4	2,524.4	2,675.3
Atlantic cod	215.4	242.8	283.3
Saithe (Pollock)	227.3	202.4	227.9
Blue whiting (Poutassou) . .	418.3	226.0	194.3
Sandeels (Sandlances) . . .	81.6	27.4	78.0
Capelin	40.9	232.6	272.4
Atlantic herring	1,027.9	1,070.4	921.3
Atlantic mackerel	121.5	121.2	234.0
Aquaculture	848.4	961.8	1,008.0
Atlantic salmon	737.7	862.9	927.9
Total catch	3,279.7	3,486.3	3,683.3

Note: Figures exclude aquatic plants ('000 metric tons, wet weight, capture): n.a. in 2008–10. Also excluded are aquatic mammals, recorded by number rather than by weight. The number of minke whales caught was: 535 in 2008; 484 in 2009; 468 in 2010. The number of harp seals caught was: 1,263 in 2008; 8,035 in 2009; 4,793 in 2010. The number of hooded seals caught was: nil in 2008; 402 in 2009; 178 in 2010.

Source: FAO.

Mining

('000 metric tons unless otherwise indicated)

	2009	2010	2011
Coal (all grades)	2,437	1,685	1,800*
Crude petroleum (million metric tons) .	108.8	98.6	93.4
Natural gas ('000 million cu m) . .	103.7	106.4	101.4
Iron ore†	896	3,105	3,200*

* Estimate.
† Metal content of ore.

Sources: US Geological Survey; BP, *Statistical Review of World Energy*.

Industry

SELECTED PRODUCTS
('000 metric tons unless otherwise indicated)

	2009	2010	2011
Mechanical wood pulp (dry weight)*	1,072	1,179	1,067
Chemical wood pulp (dry weight)*	600	704	702
Particle board ('000 cu m)* . .	293	348	316
Paper and paperboard* . . .	1,577	1,695	1,492
Kerosene ('000 barrels) . . .	5,800	5,800	5,800†
Naphthas ('000 barrels) . . .	10,000	10,000	10,000†
Gas-diesel (distillate fuel) oil ('000 barrels) . .	50,000	50,000	50,000†
Residual fuel oil ('000 barrels) .	12,000	12,000	12,000†
Cement†	1,700	1,700	1,800
Ferro-silicon (75% basis) . . .	233	230	230†
Other ferro-alloys	150	150	150†
Crude steel	579	514	620
Nickel (refined): primary . .	88.6	88.0	88.0†
Copper (refined): primary and secondary	34	32†	32†
Aluminium (refined): primary .	1,090.0	1,060.0	1,070.0
Aluminium (refined): secondary† .	350.0	300.0	300
Zinc (refined): primary . . .	137.6	147.8	150.0†
Electric energy (million kWh) .	132,778	n.a.	n.a.

* Source: FAO.
† Estimated or unofficial figure(s).

Sources (unless otherwise indicated): UN Industrial Commodity Statistics Database; US Geological Survey.

Finance

CURRENCY AND EXCHANGE RATES

Monetary Units
100 øre = 1 Norwegian krone (plural: kroner).

Sterling, Dollar and Euro Equivalents (31 December 2012)
£1 sterling = 8.789 kroner;
US $1 = 5.570 kroner;
€1 = 7.349 kroner;
100 Norwegian kroner = £11.38 = $17.95 = €13.61.

Average Exchange Rate (kroner per US $)
2010   6.0442
2011   5.6045
2012   5.8175

GENERAL BUDGET
(accrued values, million kroner)

Revenue	2009	2010	2011
Taxation	1,000,694	1,085,240	1,169,278
Taxes on income, profits and wealth	478,476	532,391	588,226
Taxes on goods and services .	284,923	306,142	318,221
Capital taxes	2,431	2,377	1,754
Social security contributions .	234,864	244,330	261,077
Property income	273,679	263,494	318,979
Interest	91,435	86,190	88,349
Dividends	74,790	70,198	94,807
Withdrawals from income of quasi-corporations . . .	100,119	100,461	128,956
Land rent, road rent, etc. . .	7,335	6,644	6,867
Administrative fees and charges .	63,124	67,532	70,785
Current transfers	7,903	8,491	10,044
Total	1,345,401	1,424,757	1,569,085

Expenditure		2009	2010	2011
General public services	. . .	115,186	115,613	115,041
Defence	. . . . .	40,291	38,275	42,732
Public order and safety	. . .	23,465	24,764	26,376
Economic affairs	. . . .	103,377	110,061	114,686
Environmental protection	. .	15,449	17,134	18,181
Housing and community amenities		16,548	17,635	18,379
Health	. . . . .	179,034	187,638	198,195
Recreation, culture and religion	.	31,988	32,831	35,125
Education	. . . . .	142,677	148,344	151,694
Social protection	. . . .	426,490	449,934	480,395
Statistical discrepancy		−1	−2	1
Total		**1,094,504**	**1,142,227**	**1,200,805**

INTERNATIONAL RESERVES
(excluding gold, US $ million at 31 December)

		2009	2010	2011
IMF special drawing rights	. .	2,508.7	2,455.5	2,338.9
Reserve position in IMF	. . .	632.1	602.2	1,445.7
Foreign exchange	. . . .	45,718.6	49,740.2	45,612.4
Total		**48,859.3**	**52,797.9**	**49,397.1**

Source: IMF, *International Financial Statistics*.

MONEY SUPPLY
('000 million kroner at 31 December)

		2004	2005	2006
Currency outside banks	. . .	43.34	46.57	48.25
Demand deposits at commercial and savings banks	. . .	700.07	791.12	923.21
Total money (incl. others)	. .	**743.44**	**839.01**	**971.48**

Source: IMF, *International Financial Statistics*.

COST OF LIVING
(Consumer Price Index; base: 1998 = 100)

	2010	2011	2012
Food and non-alcoholic beverages	122.4	122.3	123.8
Alcoholic beverages and tobacco .	147.8	157.2	162.3
Housing and utilities	159.0	160.5	157.6
Clothing and footwear . . .	57.6	55.9	55.2
All items (incl. others) . . .	**128.8**	**130.4**	**131.4**

NATIONAL ACCOUNTS
(million kroner at current prices)

Expenditure on the Gross Domestic Product

	2009	2010	2011
Government final consumption expenditure	530,682	558,469	590,783
Private final consumption expenditure	1,027,714	1,089,953	1,131,731
Increase in stocks*	14,892	110,207	125,872
Gross fixed capital formation . .	515,580	481,985	536,754
Total domestic expenditure	**2,088,868**	**2,240,614**	**2,385,140**
Exports of goods and services . .	953,870	1,029,969	1,140,919
Less Imports of goods and services	660,408	726,317	776,098
GDP in purchasers' values	**2,382,330**	**2,544,266**	**2,749,963**
GDP at constant 2005 prices .	**2,024,839**	**2,034,520**	**2,059,297**

* Including statistical discrepancy.

Gross Domestic Product by Economic Activity

		2009	2010	2011
Agriculture, hunting and forestry .		14,692	15,837	14,423
Fishing and fish farming	. . .	14,391	22,028	20,293
Petroleum and gas extraction	.	463,032	510,466	628,866
Other mining and quarrying	. .	4,089	4,436	5,347
Manufacturing		170,973	179,091	189,854
Electricity, gas and water . . .		62,831	72,067	72,508
Construction		121,389	122,932	135,144
Wholesale and retail trade; repair of motor vehicles		171,069	181,634	187,653
Hotels and restaurants	. . .	28,789	29,252	30,906
Transport, storage and communications*		198,839	208,667	194,344
Financing, insurance, real estate and business services . . .		346,214	364,036	382,508
Administration and support service activities		56,782	57,702	66,131
Public administration and defence		119,083	124,786	133,870
Education		98,090	104,211	108,467
Health and social work . . .		209,623	220,781	239,599
Arts, entertainment and other service activities		41,161	42,694	45,006
Sub-total		**2,121,047**	**2,260,620**	**2,454,919**
Taxes, less subsidies		261,283	283,646	295,045
GDP in purchasers' values		**2,382,330**	**2,544,266**	**2,749,963**

* Including transportation of petroleum and gas by pipeline.

BALANCE OF PAYMENTS
(US $ million)

		2009	2010	2011
Exports of goods	. . . .	112,885	129,122	159,209
Imports of goods	. . . .	−68,126	−73,836	−89,101
Balance on goods	. . . .	**44,759**	**55,285**	**70,108**
Exports of services	. . . .	35,405	41,860	44,244
Imports of services	. . . .	−37,073	−45,131	−47,428
Balance on goods and services		**43,091**	**52,014**	**66,924**
Primary income received	. . .	27,324	33,754	40,700
Primary income paid	. . . .	−24,550	−28,871	−32,152
Balance on goods, services and primary income		**45,865**	**56,897**	**75,471**
Secondary income received	. .	3,229	3,337	3,606
Secondary income paid	. . .	−7,813	−8,202	−8,759
Current balance		**41,281**	**52,032**	**70,319**
Capital account (net)	. . . .	−173	−213	−263
Direct investment assets	. . .	−25,517	−25,667	−13,306
Direct investment liabilities	. .	7,482	20,990	−796
Portfolio investment assets	. .	−4,172	−51,376	−60,669
Portfolio investment liabilities	. .	7,069	33,113	14,711
Other investment assets	. .	43,903	−22,403	−20,741
Other investment liabilities	. .	−95,067	8,472	−9,908
Net errors and omissions	. . .	16,277	−11,406	17,800
Reserves and related items	.	**−8,918**	**3,543**	**−2,853**

Source: IMF, *International Financial Statistics*.

OFFICIAL ASSISTANCE TO DEVELOPING COUNTRIES
(million kroner)

		2008	2009	2010
Bilateral assistance	. . . .	10,230	12,004	13,461
Multilateral-bilateral assistance	.	5,910	6,485	6,986
Multilateral assistance	. . .	5,500	5,748	5,782
Administration		1,222	1,387	1,452
Total official development assistance		**22,862**	**25,624**	**27,681**

External Trade

PRINCIPAL COMMODITIES
(distribution by SITC, million kroner)

Imports c.i.f.*	2010	2011	2012
Food and live animals . . .	27,703	31,070	32,800
Crude materials (inedible) except fuels	32,786	38,905	33,039
Metalliferous ores and metal scrap	22,291	27,725	21,930
Mineral fuels, lubricants, etc. (incl. electric current) . . .	32,190	34,028	33,058
Petroleum, petroleum products, etc.	23,151	26,121	28,973
Chemicals and related products	47,673	49,962	49,220
Basic manufactures . . .	68,517	75,198	77,533
Metal manufactures . . .	18,259	19,744	23,544
Machinery and transport equipment	180,189	195,097	192,859
Machinery specialized for particular industries . .	15,856	19,338	20,743
General industrial machinery, equipment and parts . .	21,921	23,558	27,104
Office machines and automatic data-processing equipment .	15,155	15,839	16,200
Telecommunications and sound equipment	18,601	18,380	19,147
Other electrical machinery, apparatus, etc. . . .	22,782	23,731	24,934
Road vehicles and parts† . .	43,770	49,328	51,387
Other transport equipment† . .	33,249	35,020	22,936
Miscellaneous manufactured articles	69,239	73,554	75,316
Clothing and accessories (excl. footwear)	15,131	16,212	15,528
Total (incl. others)	467,284	508,996	506,641

Exports f.o.b.	2010	2011	2012
Food and live animals . . .	55,556	55,234	54,220
Fish and fish preparations‡ . .	52,490	52,123	50,862
Mineral fuels, lubricants, etc. (incl. electric current) . . .	503,129	606,404	647,346
Petroleum, petroleum products, etc.	320,132	380,358	370,486
Gas (natural and manufactured) .	178,886	220,608	271,051
Chemicals and related products	44,887	45,769	40,706
Basic manufactures . . .	74,461	76,476	69,153
Non-ferrous metals	44,096	46,418	39,868
Machinery and transport equipment	74,851	70,023	74,336
Miscellaneous manufactured articles	20,533	20,920	23,491
Total (incl. others)	788,119	892,715	929,475

* Equipment imported directly to the Norwegian sector of the continental shelf is excluded.
† Excluding tyres, engines and electrical parts.
‡ Including crustaceans and molluscs.

PRINCIPAL TRADING PARTNERS
(million kroner)

Imports c.i.f.	2010	2011	2012
Belgium	8,567.8	9,309.0	10,219.0
Brazil	6,348.0	7,643.0	8,457.0
Canada	14,953.0	20,635.0	14,578.0
China, People's Repub. . . .	39,673.0	46,197.0	46,941.0
Denmark	29,011.0	32,165.0	31,666.0
Finland	11,919.5	12,908.0	14,073.0
France	16,694.0	16,541.0	16,466.0
Germany	57,447.0	60,984.0	62,914.0
Ireland	4,822.0	4,599.0	3,846.0
Italy	12,662.8	13,176.0	14,162.0
Japan	10,235.8	11,063.0	11,907.0

Imports c.i.f.—*continued*	2010	2011	2012
Korea, Republic	14,158.3	13,492.7	6,574.6
Netherlands	17,451.0	21,283.0	19,962.0
Poland	11,727.0	13,338.0	15,121.0
Russia	12,157.0	10,557.0	10,311.0
Spain	6,130.2	9,913.8	6,943.0
Sweden	65,303.0	68,255.0	68,724.0
Switzerland	4,786.6	5,851.0	7,065.0
United Kingdom	27,677.0	28,518.0	31,139.0
USA	25,655.0	27,242.0	27,467.0
Total (incl. others)	467,284.0	508,996.0	506,641.0

Exports f.o.b.	2010	2011	2012
Belgium	20,313.0	24,702.0	26,502.0
Canada	13,175.3	14,467.0	4,353.0
China, People's Repub. . .	13,520.0	16,230.0	13,906.0
Denmark	25,384.0	32,373.0	34,480.0
Finland	9,880.2	14,127.0	13,761.0
France	49,495.0	58,429.0	59,281.0
Germany	87,186.0	95,005.0	117,280.0
Ireland	8,433.8	9,785.0	9,575.0
Italy	19,275.0	20,644.0	20,699.0
Japan	9,524.2	10,334.0	8,794.0
Korea, Republic	12,404.0	8,735.0	25,519.0
Netherlands	93,721.0	103,334.0	111,423.0
Poland	12,884.0	15,695.0	14,065.0
Spain	14,426.0	13,241.0	15,733.0
Sweden	55,307.0	58,150.0	58,937.0
United Kingdom	216,355.0	249,792.0	238,159.0
USA	39,000.0	49,859.0	45,458.0
Total (incl. others)	788,119.0	892,715.0	929,475.0

Transport

STATE RAILWAYS
(traffic)

	2009	2010	2011
Passengers carried (million) . .	57.9	58.4	59.4
Goods carried ('000 metric tons) .	22,961	27,237	28,305
Passenger-km (million) . . .	3,080	3,134	3,013
Freight ton-km (million) . . .	3,506	3,498	3,574

ROAD TRAFFIC
(motor vehicles registered at 31 December)

	2009	2010	2011
Passenger cars (incl. station wagons and ambulances) . .	2,244,039	2,308,548	2,376,426
Buses	21,474	20,348	19,240
Vans	387,546	397,279	410,730
Combined vehicles	53,911	48,432	43,371
Goods vehicles, etc.	82,694	81,330	80,160
Tractors and special purpose vehicles	250,995	254,674	257,521
Motorcycles	141,235	146,592	151,650
Snow scooters	66,426	68,766	70,961
Mopeds	165,557	168,904	171,846

SHIPPING

Flag Registered Fleet
(all registers at 31 December)

	2010	2011	2012
Number of vessels	2,392	2,383	2,365
Total displacement ('000 grt) . .	17,873.6	17,778.9	17,865.3

Source: Lloyd's List Intelligence (www.lloydslistintelligence.com).

International Sea-borne Freight Traffic*
('000 metric tons)

	2009	2010	2011
Goods loaded	122,664	120,288	119,676
Goods unloaded	20,712	24,420	24,384

* Figures exclude transit traffic (other than Swedish iron ore), packing and re-export.

Source: UN, *Monthly Bulletin of Statistics*.

CIVIL AVIATION
(traffic on scheduled services)*

	2007	2008	2009
Kilometres flown (million) . .	40	126	102
Passengers carried ('000) . .	2,583	12,735	10,927
Passenger-km (million) . . .	3,449	10,723	8,818
Total ton-km (million)	490	1,214	960

* Including an apportionment (2/7) of the international services of Scandinavian Airlines System (SAS), operated jointly with Denmark and Sweden.

Source: UN, *Statistical Yearbook*.

Passengers carried ('000): 399 in 2010 (Source: World Bank, World Development Indicators database).

Tourism

VISITOR ARRIVALS BY COUNTRY OF ORIGIN*

	2008	2009	2010
Denmark	540,630	512,279	519,076
Finland	67,649	66,825	75,487
France	201,231	209,560	219,043
Germany	729,381	664,459	708,652
Italy	139,001	157,245	168,845
Japan	103,796	95,316	100,836
Netherlands	309,379	291,484	285,860
Spain	213,336	181,531	197,336
Sweden	579,329	568,062	601,797
United Kingdom	562,212	445,286	439,444
USA	289,944	250,686	302,146
Total (incl. others)	4,893,806	4,426,610	4,798,028

* Non-residents staying in all types of accommodation establishments.

Total tourist arrivals ('000): 2,973 in 2011 (provisional).

Tourism receipts (US $ million, excl. passenger transport): 4,154 in 2009; 4,707 in 2010; 5,301 in 2011 (provisional).

Source: World Tourism Organization.

Communications Media

	2009	2010	2011
Telephones ('000 main lines in use)	1,771	1,650	1,529
Mobile cellular telephones ('000 subscribers)	5,359.6	5,648.7	5,694.0
Internet subscribers ('000) . .	1,684	1,734	1,786
Broadband subscribers ('000) . .	1,678.8	1,723.7	1,745.6

Source: International Telecommunication Union.

Education

(2011 unless otherwise indicated)

	Institutions	Teachers	Students
Pre-primary	6,469	71,588	282,737
Primary and lower secondary	3,000	65,376*	614,413
Upper secondary . . .	434	21,215†‡	195,418
Folk high schools . . .	n.a.	n.a.	7,164
Other upper secondary programmes	n.a.	n.a.	10,809†§

* 2003.
† 2010.
‡ Full-time equivalent 'man years'.
§ Private educational programmes between lower secondary and higher education, but not consistent with upper secondary education (e.g. bible schools).

Higher and further education (2011 unless otherwise indicated): *Institutions* (2003): 59 colleges of higher education and 11 universities (or equivalent). *Teachers* (full-time equivalent 'man years'): 18,984. *Students:* Higher vocational 11,744; other higher education (incl. university) 250,456. Note: In addition 470,673 students were engaged in adult education in 2011, and 17,162 students were enrolled in distance learning programmes in 2010.

Pupil-teacher ratio (primary education, UNESCO estimate): 10.5 in 2003/04 (Source: UNESCO Institute for Statistics).

Directory

The Government

HEAD OF STATE

Sovereign: HM King HARALD V (succeeded to the throne 17 January 1991; sworn in 21 January 1991).

COUNCIL OF STATE
(Statsråd)
(May 2013)

A coalition of Arbeiderpartiet (AP—fmrly DnA), the Sosialistisk Venstreparti (SV) and the Senterpartiet (Sp).

Prime Minister: JENS STOLTENBERG (AP).

Minister of the Environment: BÅRD VEGAR SOLHJELL (SV).

Minister of Local Government and Regional Development: LIV SIGNE NAVARSETE (Sp).

Minister of Foreign Affairs: ESPEN BARTH EIDE (AP).

Minister of Justice and Public Security: GRETE FAREMO (AP).

Minister of Finance: SIGBJØRN JOHNSEN (AP).

Minister of Trade and Industry: TROND GISKE (AP).

Minister of Defence: ANNE-GRETE STRØM-ERICHSEN (AP).

Minister of Health and Care Services: JONAS GAHR STØRE (AP).

Minister of Education and Research: KRISTIN HALVORSEN (SV).

Minister and Chief of Staff in the Office of the Prime Minister: KARL EIRIK SCHJØTT-PEDERSEN (AP).

Minister of Labour: ANNIKEN HUITFELDT (AP).

Minister of Government Administration, Reform and Church Affairs, and of Nordic Co-operation: RIGMOR AASRUD (AP).

Minister of Fisheries and Coastal Affairs: LISBETH BERG-HANSEN (AP).

Minister of Transport and Communications: MARIT ARNSTAD (Sp).

Minister of Petroleum and Energy: OLA BORTEN MOE (Sp).

Minister of International Development: HEIKKI HOLMÅS (SV).

Minister of Children, Equality and Social Inclusion: INGA MARTE THORKILDSEN (SV).

Minister of Agriculture and Food: TRYGVE SLAGSVOLD VEDUM (Sp).

Minister of Culture: HADIA TAJIK (AP).

MINISTRIES

Office of the Prime Minister: Glacisgt. 1, POB 8001 Dep., 0030 Oslo; tel. 22-24-90-90; fax 22-24-95-00; e-mail postmottak@smk.dep .no; internet www.regjeringen.no/smk.

Ministry of Agriculture and Food: Teatergt. 9 (R6), POB 8007 Dep., 0030 Oslo; tel. 22-24-90-90; fax 22-24-95-55; e-mail postmottak@lmd.dep.no; internet www.regjeringen.no/lmd.

Ministry of Children, Equality and Social Inclusion: Akersgt. 59, POB 8036 Dep., 0030 Oslo; tel. 22-24-90-90; fax 22-24-95-15; e-mail postmottak@bld.dep.no; internet www.regjeringen.no/bld.

Ministry of Culture: Akersgt. 59 (R5), POB 8030 Dep., 0030 Oslo; tel. 22-24-90-90; fax 22-24-95-50; e-mail postmottak@kud.dep.no; internet www.regjeringen.no/kud.

Ministry of Defence: Glacisgt. 1, POB 8126 Dep., 0032 Oslo; tel. 23-09-80-00; fax 23-09-60-51; e-mail postmottak@fd.dep.no; internet www.regjeringen.no/fd.

Ministry of Education and Research: Kirkegt. 18, POB 8119 Dep., 0032 Oslo; tel. 22-24-90-90; fax 22-24-95-40; e-mail postmottak@kd.dep.no; internet www.regjeringen.no/kd.

Ministry of the Environment: Myntgt. 2, POB 8013 Dep., 0030 Oslo; tel. 22-24-90-90; fax 22-24-95-60; e-mail postmottak@md.dep .no; internet www.regjeringen.no/md.

Ministry of Finance: Akersgt. 40, POB 8008 Dep., 0030 Oslo; tel. 22-24-90-90; fax 22-24-95-14; e-mail postmottak@fin.dep.no; internet www.regjeringen.no/fin.

Ministry of Fisheries and Coastal Affairs: Grubbegt. 1, POB 8118 Dep., 0032 Oslo; tel. 22-24-90-90; fax 22-24-95-85; e-mail postmottak@fkd.dep.no; internet www.regjeringen.no/fkd.

Ministry of Foreign Affairs: 7 juni pl./Victoria Terrasse, POB 8114 Dep., 0032 Oslo; tel. 23-95-00-00; fax 23-95-00-99; e-mail post@ mfa.no; internet www.regjeringen.no/ud; also incl. Ministry of International Development.

Ministry of Government Administration, Reform and Church Affairs: Akersgt. 59, POB 8004 Dep., 0030 Oslo; tel. 22-24-90-90; fax 22-24-95-16; e-mail postmottak@fad.dep.no; internet www .regjeringen.no/fad.

Ministry of Health and Care Services: Teatergt. 9, POB 8011 Dep., 0030 Oslo; tel. 22-24-90-90; e-mail postmottak@hod.dep.no; internet www.regjeringen.no/hod.

Ministry of Justice and Public Security: Gullhaug Torg 4A, POB 8005 Dep., 0030 Oslo; tel. 22-24-90-90; e-mail postmottak@jd.dep.no; internet www.regjeringen.no/jd.

Ministry of Labour: Akersgt. 64, POB 8019 Dep., 0030 Oslo; tel. 22-24-90-90; fax 22-24-87-11; e-mail postmottak@ad.dep.no; internet www.regjeringen.no/ad.

Ministry of Local Government and Regional Development: Akersgt. 59, POB 8112 Dep., 0032 Oslo; tel. 22-24-90-90; e-mail postmottak@krd.dep.no; internet www.regjeringen.no/krd.

Ministry of Petroleum and Energy: Akersgt. 59, POB 8148 Dep., 0033 Oslo; tel. 22-24-90-90; fax 22-24-95-65; e-mail postmottak@oed .dep.no; internet www.regjeringen.no/oed.

Ministry of Trade and Industry: Kongens gt. 8, POB 8014 Dep., 0030 Oslo; tel. 22-24-90-90; fax 22-24-01-30; e-mail postmottak@nhd .dep.no; internet www.regjeringen.no/nhd.

Ministry of Transport and Communications: Akersgt. 59 (R5), POB 8010 Dep., 0030 Oslo; tel. 22-24-90-90; fax 22-24-95-71; e-mail postmottak@sd.dep.no; internet www.regjeringen.no/sd.

Legislature

Storting

Karl Johansgt. 22, 0026 Oslo; tel. 23-31-30-50; fax 23-31-38-17; e-mail info@stortinget.no; internet www.stortinget.no.

President: DAG TERJE ANDERSEN (AP).

First Vice-President: ØYVIND KORSBERG (FrP).

General Election, 14 September 2009

Party	Votes	% of votes	Seats
Arbeiderpartiet (AP)* . . .	949,060	35.37	64
Fremskrittspartiet (FrP) . .	614,724	22.91	41
Høyre (H)	462,465	17.24	30
Sosialistisk Venstreparti (SV) .	166,366	6.20	11
Senterpartiet (Sp) . . .	165,014	6.15	11
Kristelig Folkeparti (KrF) .	148,750	5.54	10
Venstre (V)	104,148	3.88	2
Rødt (R)	36,220	1.35	—
Others	36,201	1.35	—
Total	2,682,948	100.00	169

* Changed its name from Det norske Arbeiderparti (DnA) to Arbeiderpartiet in 2011.

Political Organizations

Arbeiderpartiet (AP) (Norwegian Labour Party): Youngstorget 2A, 5th floor, POB 8743, 0028 Oslo; tel. 24-14-40-00; fax 24-14-40-01; e-mail post@arbeiderpartiet.no; internet www.arbeiderpartiet.no; f. 1887; social democratic; changed its name from Det norske Arbeiderparti (DnA) in 2011; 50,269 mems (Dec. 2009); Leader JENS STOLTENBERG; Gen. Sec. RAYMOND JOHANSEN.

Fremskrittspartiet (FrP) (Progress Party): Karl Johans gt. 25, 0159 Oslo; tel. 23-13-54-00; fax 23-13-54-01; e-mail frp@frp.no; internet www.frp.no; f. 1973 as Anders Langes Parti; present name adopted 1977; anti-tax; favours privatization, the diminution of the welfare state and less immigration; Chair. SIV JENSEN; Sec.-Gen. FINN EGIL HOLM.

Høyre (H) (Conservative): Stortingsgt. 20, POB 1536 Vika, 0117 Oslo; tel. 22-82-90-00; fax 22-82-90-80; e-mail politikk@hoyre.no; internet www.hoyre.no; f. 1884; aims to promote economic growth and sound state finances, to achieve a property-owning democracy, and to uphold democratic govt, social security, private property, private initiative and personal liberty; 67,000 mems; Leader ERNA SOLBERG; Sec.-Gen. LARS ARNE RYSSDAL.

Kristelig Folkeparti (KrF) (Christian Democratic Party): Øvre Slottsgt. 18–20, POB 478 Sentrum, 0105 Oslo; tel. 23-10-28-00; fax 23-10-28-10; e-mail krf@krf.no; internet www.krf.no; f. 1933; aims to promote a democratic policy based on Christian values; Chair. KNUT ARILD HAREIDE; Sec.-Gen. KNUT H. JAHR.

Kystpartiet (Coastal Party): Grennsen 8B, 0159 Oslo; tel. 22-33-68-10; e-mail post@kystpartiet.no; internet www.kystpartiet.no; nationalist; Leader BENGT S. JOHANSEN; Sec. KRISTIN BRENNHAUG.

Miljøpartiet De Grønne (Green Party of Norway): Skippergt. 33, 0154 Oslo; tel. 23-69-94-11; e-mail mdg@mdg.no; internet www.mdg .no; f. 1988; Principal Speakers HARALD NISSEN, HANNA ELISE MARCUSSEN.

Norges Kommunistiske Parti (NKP) (Communist Party of Norway): Helgesensgt. 21, POB 9288 Grønland, 0134 Oslo; tel. 22-71-60-44; fax 22-71-79-07; e-mail nkp@nkp.no; internet www.nkp.no; f. 1923; Chair. SVEND HAAKON JACOBSEN.

Pensjonistpartiet (Pensioners' Party): Prinsensgt. 3A, 0152 Oslo; tel. 21-42-05-15; e-mail post@pensjonistpartiet.no; internet www .pensjonistpartiet.no; Leader EINAR LONSTAD.

Rødt (R): Osterhausgt. 27, 0183 Oslo; tel. 22-98-90-50; fax 22-98-90-55; e-mail raudt@raudt.no; internet roedt.no; f. 2007 by merger of Rød Valgallianse (Red Electoral Alliance) and Arbeidernes Kommunistparti (Workers' Communist Party); left-wing group; Leader BJØRNAR MOXNES; Sec. MARI EIFRING.

Senterpartiet (Sp) (Centre Party): Akersgt. 35, POB 1191 Sentrum, 0107 Oslo; tel. 23-69-01-00; fax 23-69-01-01; e-mail epost@ senterpartiet.no; internet www.senterpartiet.no; f. 1920 as the Bondepartiet (Farmers' Party), name changed 1959; advocates a decentralized society that will secure employment and diversified settlements in all parts of the country; opposes Norwegian membership of the EU; encourages the devt of an ecologically balanced society; Leader LIV SIGNE NAVARSETE; Sec.-Gen. KNUT M. OLSEN.

Sosialistisk Venstreparti (SV) (Socialist Left Party): Akersgt. 35, 0158 Oslo; tel. 21-93-33-00; fax 21-93-33-01; e-mail post@sv.no; internet www.sv.no; f. 1975 by merger of the Socialist People's Party, the Democratic Socialists and other socialist forces united previously in the Socialist Electoral League; advocates non-alignment and socialism independent of international centres, based on workers' control, decentralized powers, gender equality and ecological principles; Chair. AUDUN LYSBAKKEN; Sec. SILJE SCHEI TVEITDAL.

Venstre (V) (Liberal): Møllergt. 16, 0179 Oslo; tel. 22-40-43-50; fax 22-40-43-51; e-mail venstre@venstre.no; internet www.venstre.no; f. 1884; in 1988 reunited with Det Liberale Folkepartiet (Liberal

Democratic Party, f. 1972); advocates the promotion of national and democratic progress on the basis of the present system by gradual economic, social and cultural reforms; Leader Trine Skei Grande; Sec.-Gen. Trond Enger.

Diplomatic Representation

EMBASSIES IN NORWAY

Afghanistan: Gange–Rolvs gt. 5, 0244 Oslo; tel. 22-12-35-70; fax 22-12-35-71; e-mail info@afghanistanembassy.no; internet www.afghanistanembassy.no; Ambassador Manizha Bakhtari.

Algeria: Inkognitogt. 7, 0256 Oslo; tel. 22-55-75-31; fax 25-55-75-30; e-mail ambalgoslo@live.fr; Ambassador Boubakeur Ogab.

Argentina: Drammensvn 39, 0244 Oslo; tel. 22-55-24-49; fax 22-44-16-41; e-mail enoru@mrecic.gov.ar; internet www.enoru.mrecic.gov.ar; Ambassador Juan Manuel Ortiz de Rosas.

Austria: Thomas Heftyes gt. 19–21, 0244 Oslo; tel. 22-54-02-00; fax 22-55-43-61; e-mail oslo-ob@bmeia.gv.at; internet www.bmeia.gv.at/botschaft/oslo; Ambassador Dr Thomas Wunderbaldinger.

Belgium: Drammensvn 103D, 0244 Oslo; tel. 23-13-32-20; fax 23-13-32-32; e-mail oslo@diplobel.fed.be; internet www.diplomatie.be/oslo; Ambassador Michel Godfrind.

Bosnia and Herzegovina: Drammensvn 105, 0244 Oslo; tel. 22-54-09-60; fax 22-54-09-63; e-mail info@bhembassy.no; internet www.bhembassy.no; Ambassador Emir Poljo.

Brazil: Sigurd Syrs gt. 4, 0244 Oslo; tel. 22-54-07-30; fax 22-44-39-64; e-mail brasil@brasil.no; internet oslo.itamaraty.gov.br/pt-br; Ambassador Flávio Helmold Macieira.

Bulgaria: Tidemands gt. 11, 0244 Oslo; tel. 22-55-40-40; fax 22-55-40-24; e-mail bulgemb@online.no; internet www.mfa.bg/oslo; Chargé d'affaires a.i. Kiril Dimitrov.

Burundi: Inkognitogt. 33A, 1st Floor, 0256 Oslo; tel. 21-38-57-82; e-mail info@burundi-embassy-oslo.org; Chargé d'affaires a.i. Nadine Muhimpundu.

Canada: Wergelandsvn 7, 4th Floor, 0244 Oslo; tel. 22-99-53-00; fax 22-99-53-01; e-mail oslo@international.gc.ca; internet www.canadainternational.gc.ca/norway-norvege; Ambassador David Sproule.

Chile: Meltzersgt. 5, 0244 Oslo; tel. 22-44-89-55; fax 22-44-24-21; e-mail echile.noruega@minrel.gov.cl; Ambassador Juan Aníbal Barría García.

China, People's Republic: Tuengen allé 2B, 0244 Oslo; tel. 22-49-20-52; fax 22-92-19-78; e-mail webmaster@chinese-embassy.no; internet www.chinese-embassy.no; Ambassador Zhao Jun.

Colombia: Oscarsgt. 34, 0258 Oslo; tel. 23-12-01-50; fax 23-12-01-51; e-mail enoruega@cancilleria.gov.co; internet embajadadecolombiaoslo.axesnet.com; Ambassador Victoriana Mejía-Marulanda.

Costa Rica: Skippergt. 33, 8th Floor, 0154 Oslo; tel. 22-42-58-23; fax 22-33-04-08; e-mail embassy@costarica.no; Ambassador Manuel Rodríguez.

Croatia: Drammensvn 82, 0244 Oslo; tel. 23-01-40-50; fax 23-01-40-60; e-mail croemb.oslo@mvep.hr; Ambassador Mario Horvatić.

Cuba: Oscarsgt. 78B, 0244 Oslo; tel. 23-08-32-60; fax 23-08-32-61; e-mail enoruega@online.no; internet www.embacuba.no; Ambassador María Esther Fiffe Cabreja.

Czech Republic: Fritzners gt. 14, 0244 Oslo; tel. 22-12-10-31; fax 22-55-33-95; e-mail oslo@embassy.mzv.cz; internet www.mzv.cz/oslo; Ambassador Dr Milan Dufek.

Denmark: Olav Kyrres gt. 7, 0244 Oslo; tel. 22-54-08-00; fax 22-55-46-34; e-mail oslamb@um.dk; internet www.amboslo.um.dk; Ambassador Hugo Østergaard-Andersen.

Egypt: Drammensvn 90A, 0244 Oslo; tel. 23-08-42-00; fax 22-56-22-68; e-mail information@egypt-embassy.no; internet www.mfa.gov.eg/oslo_emb; Ambassador Ashraf M. Elmoafi.

Estonia: Parkvn 51A, 0244 Oslo; tel. 22-54-00-70; fax 22-54-00-71; e-mail embassy.oslo@mfa.ee; internet www.estemb.no; Ambassador Simmu Tiik.

Finland: Thomas Heftyes gt. 1, 0244 Oslo; tel. 22-12-49-00; fax 22-12-49-49; e-mail sanomat.osl@formin.fi; internet www.finland.no; Ambassador Maimo Susanne Henriksson.

France: Drammensvn 69, 0244 Oslo; tel. 23-28-46-00; fax 23-28-46-70; e-mail ambafrance.oslo@diplomatie.gouv.fr; internet www.ambafrance-no.org; Ambassador Jean-Marc Rives.

Georgia: Neuberggt. 19, 0367 Oslo; tel. 95-92-79-93; e-mail oslo.emb@mfa.gov.ge; internet www.norway.mfa.gov.ge; Ambassador Mamuka Tsikhelashvili.

Germany: Oscars gt. 45, 0244 Oslo; tel. 23-27-54-00; fax 22-44-76-72; e-mail info@oslo.diplo.de; internet www.oslo.diplo.de; Ambassador Dr Axel Berg.

Greece: Nobels gt. 45, 0244 Oslo; tel. 22-44-27-28; fax 22-56-00-72; e-mail gremb.osl@mfa.gr; Ambassador Antonios Vlavianos.

Guatemala: Drammensvn 126B, 0277 Oslo; tel. 22-55-60-04; fax 22-55-60-47; e-mail guatemala@guate.no; Ambassador Marta Eulalia Estrada Xicara de Leiva.

Hungary: Sophus Lies gt. 3, 0244 Oslo; tel. 22-55-24-18; fax 22-44-76-93; e-mail mission.osl@mfa.gov.hu; internet www.mfa.gov.hu/kulkepviselet/no; Ambassador Géza Jeszenszky.

Iceland: Stortingsgt. 30, 0244 Oslo; tel. 23-23-75-30; fax 22-83-07-04; e-mail emb.oslo@mfa.is; internet www.island.no; Ambassador Dr Gunnar Pálsson.

India: Niels Juels gt. 30, 0244 Oslo; tel. 24-11-59-24; fax 24-11-59-12; e-mail amb.oslo@mea.gov.in; internet www.indemb.no; Ambassador Rajendra Kumar Tyagi.

Indonesia: Fritznersgt. 12, 0244 Oslo; tel. 22-12-51-30; fax 22-12-51-31; e-mail kbrioslo@online.no; internet www.indonesia-oslo.no; Ambassador Esti Andayani.

Iran: Drammensvn 88E, 0244 Oslo; tel. 23-27-29-60; fax 22-55-49-19; e-mail info@iranembassy.no; internet www.iran-embassy-oslo.no; Ambassador Sayed Hussain Rezvani.

Iraq: Tidemands gt. 9, 0244 Oslo; tel. 22-00-60-00; fax 22-00-60-01; e-mail oslemb@mofaml.gov.iq; Ambassador Sundus Omar Albayr-aqdar.

Ireland: Haakon VIIs gt. 1, 0244 Oslo; tel. 22-01-72-00; fax 22-01-72-01; e-mail osloembassy@dfa.ie; internet www.embassyofireland.no; Ambassador Angela O'Farrell.

Israel: Parkvn 35, POB 534 Skøyen, 0214 Oslo; tel. 21-01-95-00; fax 21-01-95-30; e-mail israel@oslo.mfa.gov.il; internet oslo.mfa.gov.il; Ambassador Naim Araidi.

Italy: Inkognitogt. 7, 0244 Oslo; tel. 23-08-49-00; fax 22-44-34-36; e-mail ambasciata.oslo@esteri.it; internet www.amboslo.esteri.it; Ambassador Antonio Bandini.

Japan: Wergelandsvn 15, 0244 Oslo; tel. 22-99-16-00; fax 22-44-25-05; e-mail info@os.mofa.go.jp; internet www.no.emb-japan.go.jp; Ambassador Akio Shirota.

Kazakhstan: Nedre Vollgt. 3, 2nd Floor, 0158 Oslo; tel. 22-42-06-40; fax 22-42-06-42; e-mail oslo@mfa.kz; internet www.kazembassy.no; Chargé d'affaires a.i. Nurzhan Bazylbekov.

Korea, Republic: Inkognitogt. 3, 0244 Oslo; tel. 22-54-70-90; fax 22-56-14-11; e-mail kornor@mofat.go.kr; internet nor.mofat.go.kr; Ambassador Lee Byong-Hyun.

Latvia: Bygdøy allé 76, POB 3163 Elisenberg, 0208 Oslo; tel. 22-54-22-80; fax 22-54-64-26; e-mail embassy.norway@mfa.gov.lv; internet www.am.gov.lv/lv/norway; Ambassador Indulis Ābelis.

Lithuania: Dronningens gt. 3, 0244 Oslo; tel. 22-12-92-00; fax 22-12-92-01; e-mail amb.no@urm.lt; internet no.mfa.lt; Ambassador Andrius Namavičius.

Macedonia, former Yugoslav republic: Erling Skjalgssons gt. 19B, 0267 Oslo; tel. 22-55-15-44; fax 22-55-06-22; e-mail oslo@mfa.gov.mk; Ambassador Enver Abdulahi.

Morocco: Holtegt. 28, 0355 Oslo; tel. 23-19-71-50; fax 23-19-71-51; e-mail oslosifam@yahoo.com; Ambassador Saadia Alaoui.

Netherlands: Oscarsgt. 29, 0244 Oslo; tel. 23-33-36-00; fax 23-33-36-01; e-mail osl@minbuza.nl; internet www.netherlands-embassy.no; Ambassador Richard van Rijssen.

Pakistan: Eckersbergs gt. 20, 0244 Oslo; tel. 23-13-60-80; fax 22-55-50-97; e-mail info@pakistanembassy.no; internet www.pakistanembassy.no; Ambassador Ishtiaq Hussain Andrabi.

Philippines: Nedre Vollgt. 4, 4th Floor, 0158 Oslo; tel. 22-40-09-00; fax 22-41-74-01; e-mail ambassador@philembassy.no; internet www.philembassy.no; Ambassador Bayani Mercado.

Poland: Olav Kyrres pl. 1, 0244 Oslo; tel. 24-11-08-50; fax 22-44-48-39; e-mail oslo.info@msz.gov.pl; internet oslo.msz.gov.pl; Ambassador Stefan Czmur.

Portugal: Josefines gt. 37, 0244 Oslo; tel. 23-33-28-55; fax 22-56-43-55; e-mail embassyportugal.oslo@mne.pt; Ambassador Maria Clara dos Santos.

Romania: Oscars gt. 51, 0244 Oslo; tel. 22-44-15-12; fax 22-43-16-74; e-mail oslo@mae.ro; internet oslo.mae.ro; Ambassador Daniel Ioniță.

Russia: Drammensvn 74, 0244 Oslo; tel. 22-55-32-78; fax 22-55-00-70; e-mail rembassy@online.no; internet www.norway.mid.ru; Ambassador Vyacheslav Pavlovsky.

Saudi Arabia: Drammensvn 102H, 0244 Oslo; tel. 22-04-90-10; fax 22-04-90-14; e-mail osemb@mofa.gov.sa; Ambassador Khalid Alnafisee.

Serbia: Munkedamsvn 59B, 0244 Oslo; tel. 23-11-52-20; fax 22-83-83-14; e-mail ambasada@serbianembassy.no; internet www.serbianembassy.no; Ambassador MILAN SIMURDIĆ.

Slovakia: Thomas Heftyes gt. 24, 0244 Oslo; tel. 22-04-94-70; fax 22-04-94-74; e-mail emb.oslo@mzv.sk; internet www.oslo.mfa.sk; Ambassador FRANTIŠEK KAŠICKÝ.

South Africa: Drammensvn 88C, 0204 Oslo; tel. 23-27-32-20; fax 22-44-39-75; e-mail oslo.reception@foreign.gov.za; internet www.saemboslo.no; Ambassador QUEEN ANNE ZONDO.

South Sudan: Prinsessealléen 2, 0276 Oslo; tel. 22-44-99-39; fax 22-55-88-93; Ambassador BOL WEK AGOTH.

Spain: Halvdan Svartes gt. 13, 0268 Oslo; tel. 22-92-66-90; fax 22-92-66-66; e-mail emb.oslo@maec.es; internet www.maec.es/embajadas/oslo; Ambassador ANTONIO LÓPEZ MARTÍNEZ.

Sri Lanka: Sjølyst pl. 4, 5th Floor, 0158 Oslo; tel. 23-13-69-50; fax 23-31-70-90; e-mail embassy@srilanka.no; internet www.srilanka.no; Ambassador MUSTHAFA MOHAMED JAFFEER.

Sudan: Holtegt. 28, 0355 Oslo; tel. 22-60-33-55; fax 22-69-83-44; e-mail sudanembassy@sudanoslo.com; Ambassador NADIA MOHAMED E. GOFOUN.

Sweden: Nobels gt. 16, 0244 Oslo; tel. 24-11-42-00; fax 22-55-15-96; e-mail ambassaden.oslo@foreign.ministry.se; internet www.swedenabroad.com/oslo; Ambassador INGRID HJELT AF TROLLE.

Switzerland: Bygdøynesvn 13, 0244 Oslo; tel. 22-43-05-90; e-mail osl.vertretung@eda.admin.ch; internet www.eda.admin.ch/oslo; Ambassador JEAN-PHILIPPE TISSIÈRES.

Thailand: Eilert Sundtsgt. 4, 0244 Oslo; tel. 22-12-86-75; fax 22-04-99-69; e-mail thaioslo@online.no; internet www.thaiembassy.no; Ambassador THEERAKUN NIYOM.

Tunisia: Drammensvn 82C, 0271 Oslo; tel. 22-41-72-01; fax 22-41-72-04; e-mail at.oslo@online.no; Chargé d'affaires a.i. SIHEM SELTENE.

Turkey: Halvdan Svartesgt. 5, 0244 Oslo; tel. 22-12-87-50; fax 22-55-62-63; e-mail embassy.oslo@mfa.gov.tr; internet www.oslo.be.mfa.gov.tr; Ambassador K. ŞANIVAR OLGUN.

Ukraine: Arbins gt. 4, 0253 Oslo; tel. 22-83-55-60; fax 22-83-55-57; e-mail embassy@ukremb.no; internet www.mfa.gov.ua/norway; Ambassador YURII ONISCHENKO.

United Kingdom: Thomas Heftyesgt. 8, 0264 Oslo; tel. 23-13-27-00; fax 23-13-27-41; e-mail britemb@online.no; internet ukinnorway.fco.gov.uk; Ambassador JANE OWEN.

USA: Henrik Ibsens gt. 48, 0244 Oslo; tel. 21-30-85-40; fax 22-44-83-77; e-mail osloirc@state.gov; internet norway.usembassy.gov; Ambassador BARRY B. WHITE.

Venezuela: Drammensvn 82, POB 2820 Solli, 0204 Oslo; tel. 22-43-06-60; fax 22-43-14-70; e-mail embajada@venezuela.no; Ambassador JOSÉ DE JESÚS SOJO REYES.

Viet Nam: St Olavsgt. 21C, 0165 Oslo; tel. 22-20-33-00; fax 22-20-33-01; e-mail vietnamnorway@gmail.com; Ambassador TA VAN THONG.

Judicial System

The judicial system in Norway is organized on three levels. The courts of first instance are the District (Herredsrett) and City (Byrett) Courts. The country is divided into 93 judicial areas, most of which are served by one professional judge and one or two deputies (in the major cities the number of judges ranges from three to 52). The Court of Appeal (Lagmannsrett) consists of six jurisdictions, each with between 10 and 52 judges, and two divisions (Appeals and Criminal Divisions). The Supreme Court (Høyesterett) sits in Oslo and decides cases in the last instance. The Court, which is served by 19 judges appointed by the Crown and presided over by a Chief Justice, is competent to try all factual and legal aspects of cases in civil and criminal cause. However, in criminal cases, the competence of the Court is limited to questions concerning the application of the law, the nature of the penalty, and procedural errors of the lower courts. Appeals to the Supreme Court may not be based on errors in the assessment of evidence in connection with the question of guilt.

SUPREME COURT

Høyesterett: Høyesteretts pl. 1, POB 8016 Dep., 0030 Oslo; tel. 22-03-59-00; fax 22-33-23-55; e-mail post@hoyesterett.no; internet www.domstol.no/hoyesterett; f. 1814; pronounces judgment in the final instance; hears both civil and criminal cases, and has jurisdiction in all areas of law; composed of 18 ordinary justices of the Supreme Court and one Chief Justice; individual cases are heard by five justices—in some instances cases are heard by all of the justices sitting in plenary session; works in two parallel and equal divisions; Supreme Court justices also sit on the Appeals Selection Committee of the Supreme Court, which is classed as a separate court; cases brought before the Appeals Selection Committee are heard by three justices; any matter brought before the Supreme Court must initially be considered by the Appeals Selection Committee; justices sit in both divisions of the Supreme Court and on the Appeals Selection Committee in accordance with a rota system; Chief Justice of the Supreme Court TORE SCHEI.

COURTS OF APPEAL

Agder Lagmannsrett (Court of Appeal in Skien): Gjerpensgt. 16, POB 2644, 3702 Skien; tel. 35-54-05-00; fax 35-52-10-09; e-mail agder.lagmannsrett@domstol.no; internet www.domstol.no/agder; f. 1936; Presiding Judge DAG BUGGE NORDÉN.

Borgarting Lagmannsrett (Court of Appeal in Oslo): Keysersgt. 13, POB 8017 Dep., 0030 Oslo; tel. 21-55-80-00; fax 21-55-80-38; e-mail borgadm@domstol.no; internet www.domstol.no/borg; Presiding Judge OLA DAHL.

Eidsivating Lagmannsrett (Court of Appeal in Hamar): Østregt. 41, POB 4450, 2326 Hamar; tel. 62-55-06-00; fax 62-55-06-20; e-mail eidsivating.lagmannsrett@domstol.no; internet www.domstol.no/eidsivating; Presiding Judge SVERRE NYHUS.

Frostating Lagmannsrett (Court of Appeal in Trondheim): Trondheim tinghus, Munkegt. 20, POB 2315, 7004 Trondheim; tel. 73-54-24-60; fax 73-54-24-84; e-mail frostating.lagmannsrett@domstol.no; internet www.frostating.no; Presiding Judge AAGE RUNDBERGET.

Gulating Lagmannsrett (Court of Appeal in Bergen): Gulatings pl. 1, POB 7414, 5020 Bergen; tel. 55-69-39-00; fax 55-69-39-01; e-mail gulating@domstol.no; internet www.domstol.no/gulating; Presiding Judge BJØRN SOLBAKKEN.

Hålogaland Lagmannsrett (Court of Appeal in Tromsø): Fridtjof Nansens pl. 17, POB 2511, 9271 Tromsø; tel. 77-66-00-35; fax 77-66-00-60; e-mail halogaland.lagmannsrett@domstol.no; internet www.domstol.no/halogaland; Presiding Judge ARILD O. EIDESEN.

CIVIL COURTS

In each municipality there is a Conciliation Board (Forliksråd) consisting of three lay members elected by the municipal council for four years. With a few exceptions, no case may be taken to a court of justice without a prior attempt at mediation by a Conciliation Board. In addition to mediation, the Conciliation Board has a judicial capacity and is intended to settle minor cases in a simple manner without great expense to the parties involved.

The ordinary lower courts are the District and City Courts, which decide all cases not adjudicated upon by the Conciliation Board, and they also act as courts of appeal from judgments given in the Conciliation Board. During the main hearing, the court is generally convened with only one professional judge, but each of the parties may request that the court be convened with two lay judges, in addition to the professional judge. When the court finds it advisable, it may also summon lay judges on its own initiative.

Judgments delivered in the District and City Courts may be taken, on appeal, to the Court of Appeal or to the Supreme Court. In the Court of Appeal cases are judged by three professional judges, but, if requested by one of the parties, lay judges may be summoned.

CRIMINAL COURTS

The criminal courts are: the Court of Examination and Summary Jurisdiction (Forhørsretten), the District and City Courts, the Court of Appeal and the Supreme Court. In the Court of Examination and Summary Jurisdiction the professional judge presides alone, but in the District and City Courts two lay judges also sit. Following the implementation of a major reform in 1995, all criminal cases now begin in a District or City Court. The gravest offences were previously tried directly before a jury in the Court of Appeal and the possibilities for appeal were thus limited. Now, however, the issue of guilt can be appealed to the Court of Appeal in all cases. (Such cases are tried either by three professional judges, and four lay judges with equal votes, or by three professional judges and a jury of 10 members. For a guilty verdict to be upheld in the latter case, at least seven members of the jury must support the original decision of the lower court. In other cases appeal is directly to the Supreme Court.) The maximum penalty permissible under Norwegian law is 21 years of imprisonment.

OMBUDSMAN

The office of Parliamentary Ombudsman was established in 1962. An Ombudsman is elected by the Storting after every general election for a four-year term (with the possibility of re-election). The Ombudsman is accessible to all citizens, and attempts to ensure against the public administration committing any injustice to the individual citizen. The Ombudsman does not cover private legal affairs, and does not have the right to reverse an official decision, but his pronouncements are normally complied with.

Sivilombudsmannen—Stortingets ombudsmann for forvaltningen (Parliamentary Ombudsman for Public Administration): Akersgt. 8, 6th Floor, POB 3 Sentrum, 0101 Oslo; tel. 22-82-85-00; fax 22-82-85-11; e-mail postmottak@sivilombudsmannen.no; internet www.sivilombudsmannen.no; Ombudsman ARNE FLIFLET.

Religion

CHRISTIANITY

Citizens are considered to be members of the National Church unless they explicitly associate themselves with another denomination; around 77% of the population nominally belonged to the Church in 2011, although actual church attendance is low. Other Protestant Christian denominations accounted for some 5.4% of the population. There is a very small number of Orthodox Christians in Norway.

The National Church

Church of Norway

The Church Synod, Rådhusgt. 1-3, POB 799 Sentrum, 0106 Oslo; tel. 23-08-12-00; fax 23-08-12-01; e-mail post.kirkeradet@kirken.no; internet www.kirken.no.

The Evangelical Lutheran Church is the established religion; there are 11 dioceses, 105 archdeaconries and 1,260 parishes. The highest representative body of the Church is the Synod, summoned for the first time in 1984. In 2011 3,851,145 persons belonged to the Church of Norway.

Bishop of Oslo: OLE CHRISTIAN MÆLEN KVARME.

Bishop of Borg: ATLE SOMMERFELDT.

Bishop of Hamar: SOLVEIG FISKE.

Bishop of Tunsberg: LAILA RIKSAASEN DAHL.

Bishop of Agder and Telemark: STEIN REINERTSENL.

Bishop of Stavanger: ERLING J. PETTERSEN.

Bishop of Bjørgvin: HALVOR NORDHAUG.

Bishop of Møre: INGEBORG SYNØVE MIDTTØMME.

Bishop of Nidaros: TOR SINGSAAS.

Bishop of Sør-Hålogaland: TOR BERGER JØRGENSEN.

Bishop of Nord-Hålogaland: PER OSKAR KJØLAAS.

The Roman Catholic Church

For ecclesiastical purposes, Norway comprises the diocese of Oslo and the territorial prelatures of Tromsø and Trondheim. The diocese and the prelatures are directly responsible to the Holy See. In 2011 there were an estimated 83,000 adherents in Norway. The Bishop of Oslo participates in the Scandinavian Episcopal Conference (based in Västra Frölunda, Sweden).

Bishop of Oslo: Rt Rev. BERNT IVAR (MARKUS) EIDSVIG, Oslo Katolske Bispedømme, Akersvn 5, POB 8270, 0177 Oslo; tel. 23-21-95-00; fax 23-21-95-01; e-mail okb@katolsk.no; internet www.katolsk.no.

Other Churches

Church of England (Anglican Chaplaincy in Norway): St Edmund's Anglican Church, Møllergt. 30, Oslo; tel. 22-69-22-14; e-mail j-heil@online.no; internet www.osloanglicans.net; 1,800 mems (2010); also in Stavanger, Bergen and Trondheim; part of the Diocese of Gibraltar in Europe; Chaplain Rev. Canon JANET HEIL.

Evangelical Lutheran Free Church of Norway: Linstow gt. 3, POB 6702, St Olavs pl., 0129 Oslo; tel. 22-74-86-00; fax 22-74-86-01; e-mail post@frikirken.no; internet www.frikirken.no; f. 1877; c. 21,600 mems (2012); Chair. of Synod ARNFINN LØYNING.

Norwegian Baptist Union: Micheletsvei 62C, 1368 Stabekk; tel. 67-10-35-60; fax 67-10-35-69; e-mail post@baptist.no; internet www.baptist.no; f. 1860; 10,200 mems (2011); Gen. Sec. TERJE AADNE.

Pinsebevegelsen i Norge (Pentecostal Movement): POB 7007, St Olavs pl. 0130 Oslo; tel. 40-41-30-43; e-mail post@pinsebevegelsen.no; internet www.pinsebevegelsen.no; f. 1907; Admin. Leader JAN EILERT AAKRE; 39,700 mems (2013).

United Methodist Church: POB 2744 St Hanshaugen, 0131 Oslo; tel. 23-33-27-00; e-mail post@metodistkirken.no; internet www.metodistkirken.no; f. 1856; 12,000 mems (2011); Council Dir GUNNAR BRADLEY.

In 2011 there were 11,739 Jehovah's Witnesses in Norway and 5,066 Seventh-day Adventists.

OTHER RELIGIONS

In 2011 there were 106,735 Muslims, 14,580 Buddhists, 5,858 Hindus, 2,975 Sikhs and 819 Jews in Norway.

The Press

The principle of press freedom is safeguarded in the Norwegian Constitution. There is no law specifically dealing with the press. Editors bear wide responsibility in law for the content of their papers, especially regarding such matters as libel. Although a journalist is legally entitled to conceal his source he may be required to disclose this information under penalty of imprisonment, but such instances are rare. A three-member Council of Conduct gives judgments in cases of complaint against a paper or of disputes between papers. It has no powers of enforcement but its judgments are highly respected. The Press Association has a code of ethics aimed at maintaining the standards and reputation of the profession.

The eastern region dominates press activity. Oslo dailies are especially influential throughout this area, and four of these—*Aftenposten*, *Dagsavisen*, *Dagbladet* and *Verdens Gang*—have a national readership. Nevertheless, in Norway's other major cities the large local dailies easily lead in their own districts. In 2012 the most popular newspapers were *Verdens Gang* (Oslo), *Aftenposten* (Oslo), *Dagbladet* (Oslo), *Dagens Næringsliv* (Oslo), *Bergens Tidende* (Bergen) and *Adresseavisen* (Trondheim).

PRINCIPAL NEWSPAPERS

(circulation figures refer to the year 2011, unless otherwise indicated)

Ålesund

Sunnmørsposten: Røysegt. 10, POB 123, 6001 Ålesund; tel. 70-12-00-00; fax 70-12-46-42; e-mail redaksjon@smp.no; internet www.smp.no; f. 1882; Liberal; Editor HANNA RELLING BERG; circ. 29,974.

Arendal

Agderposten: POB 8, 4801 Arendal; tel. 37-00-37-00; fax 37-00-38-38; e-mail redaksjonen@agderposten.no; internet www.agderposten.no; f. 1874; independent; Editor MORTEN RØD; circ. 21,262.

Bergen

Bergens Tidende: Krinkelkroken 1, POB 7240, 5020 Bergen; tel. 55-21-45-02; fax 55-21-48-48; e-mail webmaster@bt.no; internet www.bergens-tidende.no; f. 1868; Editor TRINE EILERTSEN; circ. 79,467.

Bergensavisen: Chr. Michelsensgt. 4, POB 824 Sentrum, 5807 Bergen; tel. 55-23-50-00; fax 55-31-00-30; e-mail nyhet@ba.no; internet www.ba.no; f. 1927; independent, social democratic; Editor-in-Chief ANDERS NYLAND; circ. 19,773.

Dagen: Fjøsangervn 45, POB 2394, 5054 Bergen; tel. 47-77-37-75; fax 55-55-97-20; e-mail redaksjonen@dagen.no; internet www.dagen.no; f. 1919; religious daily; Editor VEBJØRN SELBEKK; circ. 10,060.

Billingstad

Budstikka: Billingstadsletta 17, POB 133, 1376 Billingstad; tel. 66-77-00-00; fax 66-77-00-60; e-mail redaksjonen@budstikka.no; internet www.budstikka.no; f. 1898; 6 a week; fmrly *Asker og Baerums Budstikke*; Conservative; Editor ANDREAS GJØLME; circ. 24,761.

Bodø

Avisa Nordland: Storgt. 38, 8002 Bodø; tel. 75-50-50-00; fax 75-50-50-60; e-mail kundeservice@an.no; internet www.an.no; f. 1910; Labour; Editor JAN-ELRIK HANSSEN; circ. 21,312.

Drammen

Drammens Tidende: Bragernes Torg 2A, POB 7033, 3007 Drammen; tel. 32-20-40-00; fax 32-20-40-61; e-mail redaksjonen@dt.no; internet www.dt.no; f. 1832 and 1883; Conservative daily; Dir METTE THRONDSEN; Editor GEIR ARNE BORE; circ. 6,109.

Fredrikstad

Fredrikstad Blad: Stortorvet 3, POB 143, 1606 Fredrikstad; tel. 46-80-77-77; e-mail tips@f-b.no; internet www.f-b.no; f. 1889; Conservative; Editor ERLING OMVIK; circ. 23,442 (2007).

Gjøvik

Oppland Arbeiderblad: Sommerrovn 1, POB 24, 2801 Gjøvik; tel. 61-18-93-00; fax 61-17-98-56; e-mail redaksjonen@oa.no; internet www.oa.no; f. 1924; daily; Labour; Editor-in-Chief JENS OLAI JENSSEN; circ. 24,528.

Hamar

Hamar Arbeiderblad: Grønnegt. 64, POB 264, 2317 Hamar; tel. 62-51-96-99; fax 62-51-96-18; e-mail red@h-a.no; internet www.h-a.no; f. 1925; daily; Labour; Editor CARSTEN BLENESS; circ. 24,915.

Harstad

Harstad Tidende: Storgt. 11, POB 85, 9481 Harstad; tel. 77-01-80-00; fax 77-01-80-05; e-mail redaksjonen@ht.no; internet www.ht.no; f. 1887; Conservative; Editor BÅRD MICHALSEN; circ. 11,587.

Haugesund

Haugesunds Avis: Karmsundgt. 74, POB 2024, 5504 Haugesund; tel. 52-72-00-00; fax 52-72-04-44; e-mail redaksjonen@haugesunds-avis.no; internet www.h-avis.no; f. 1895; independent; Editor BÅRD BORCH MICHALSEN; circ. 27,834.

Hønefoss

Ringerikes Blad: POB 68, 3502 Hønefoss; tel. 32-17-95-00; fax 32-17-95-01; e-mail redaksjonen@ringblad.no; internet www.ringblad.no; f. 1845; independent; Editor ØYVIND LIEN; circ. 12,030.

Kongsvinger

Glåmdalen: POB 757, 2204 Kongsvinger; tel. 62-88-25-00; fax 62-88-25-01; e-mail redaksjon@glomdalen.no; internet www.glomdalen.no; f. 1926; daily; Labour; Editor EIVIND LID; circ. 18,002.

Kristiansand

Fædrelandsvennen: Svanedamsvn 10, POB 369, 4664 Kristiansand; tel. 38-11-30-00; fax 38-11-30-01; e-mail 03811@fvn.no; internet www.fvn.no; f. 1875; daily; Liberal independent; Editor EIVIND LJØSTAD; circ. 36,604.

Lillehammer

Gudbrandsdølen Dagningen: Jernbanegt. 13, POB 954, 2604 Lillehammer; tel. 61-22-10-00; fax 61-26-09-60; e-mail redaksjonen@gd.no; internet www.gd.no; f. 1841 and 1894; independent; Editor-in-Chief KRISTIAN SKULLERUD; circ. 24,577.

Lillestrøm

Romerikes Blad: POB 235, 2001 Lillestrøm; tel. 63-80-50-50; fax 63-80-48-70; e-mail redaksjonen@rb.no; internet www.rb.no; f. 1913; Labour; Editor THOR WOJE; circ. 31,897.

Molde

Romsdals Budstikke: POB 2100, 6402 Molde; tel. 71-25-00-00; fax 71-25-00-11; e-mail redaksjon@r-b.no; internet www.rbnett.no; f. 1843; Conservative independent; Editor OLE BJØRNER LOE WELDE; circ. 17,220.

Moss

Moss Avis: POB 248/250, 1530 Moss; tel. 69-20-50-00; fax 69-20-50-02; e-mail jan.tollefsen@moss-avis.no; internet www.moss-avis.no; f. 1876; Liberal/Conservative independent; Editor PÅL ENGHAUG; circ. 14,335.

Oslo

Aftenposten: Biskop Gunnerus gt. 14A, 0185 Oslo; tel. 22-86-30-00; fax 22-42-63-25; e-mail aftenposten@aftenposten.no; internet www.aftenposten.no; f. 1860; Conservative independent; Editor HILDE HAUGSGJERD; circ. morning 235,795, evening 101,754.

Akers Avis/Groruddalen Budstikke: Trondheimsvn 459, POB 100 Grorud, 0905 Oslo; tel. 22-91-88-20; fax 22-16-01-05; e-mail redaksjonen@groruddalen.no; internet www.groruddalen.no; f. 1928; 2 a week; non-political; Editor HJALMAR KIELLAND; circ. 13,122.

Dagbladet: Langkaia 1, POB 1184 Sentrum, 0107 Oslo; tel. 24-00-10-00; fax 22-31-05-10; e-mail 2400@db.no; internet www.dagbladet.no; f. 1869; daily; Editor-in-Chief JOHN ARNE MARKUSSEN; circ. 98,989.

Dagens Næringsliv: Christian Krohgs gt. 16, POB 1182 Sentrum, 0107 Oslo; tel. 22-00-10-00; fax 22-00-10-70; e-mail redaksjonen@dn.no; internet www.dn.no; Editor SVEIN-THORE GRAN; circ. 82,595.

Dagsavisen: Grubbegt. 6, POB 1183 Sentrum, 0107 Oslo; tel. 22-99-80-00; fax 22-64-92-82; e-mail abonnement@dagsavisen.no; internet www.dagsavisen.no; f. 1884; Labour; Editors ARNE STRAND, KAIA STORVIK; circ. 24,524.

Nationen: Schweigaardsgt. 34E, POB 9390 Grønland, 0135 Oslo; tel. 21-31-00-00; fax 21-31-00-90; e-mail hans.eldegard@nationen.no; internet www.nationen.no; f. 1918; daily; Centre; Editor MARI VELSAND; circ. 12,824.

Vårt Land: Grubbegt. 6, POB 1180 Sentrum, 0107 Oslo; tel. 22-31-03-10; fax 22-31-03-05; e-mail sentral@vl.no; internet www.vl.no; f. 1945; independent, religious daily; Editor HELGE SIMONNES; circ. 24,448.

Verdens Gang (VG): Akersgt. 55, POB 1185 Sentrum, 0107 Oslo; tel. 22-00-00-00; fax 22-42-67-80; e-mail redaksjonen@vg.no; internet www.vg.no; f. 1945; independent; Editor-in-Chief TORRY PEDERSEN; circ. 233,295 (2010).

Sandefjord

Sandefjords Blad: POB 143, 3201 Sandefjord; tel. 33-42-00-00; fax 33-46-29-91; e-mail redaksjonen@sb.no; internet www.sb.no; f. 1861; Conservative; Editor JAN ROALDSET; circ. 13,191.

Sarpsborg

Sarpsborg Arbeiderblad: Sandesundsvn 2, POB 83, 1701 Sarpsborg; tel. 69-11-11-11; fax 69-11-11-00; e-mail redaksjonen@sa.no; internet www.sa.no; f. 1929; independent; Editor BERNT LYNGSTAD; circ. 13,364.

Skien

Telemarksavisa AS: POB 2833, Kjørbekk, 3702 Skien; tel. 35-58-55-00; fax 35-52-82-09; e-mail redaksjonen@ta.no; internet www.ta.no; f. 1921; independent; Editor OVE MELLINGEN; circ. 20,778.

Varden: POB 2873 Kjørbekk, 3702 Skien; tel. 35-54-30-00; fax 35-52-83-23; e-mail redaksjonen@varden.no; internet www.varden.no; f. 1874; Conservative; Editor LARS KISE; circ. 23,723.

Stavanger

Stavanger Aftenblad: Nykirkebakken 2, POB 229, 4001 Stavanger; tel. 05150; fax 51-89-30-05; e-mail redaksjonen@aftenbladet.no; internet www.aftenbladet.no; f. 1893; independent; Editor LARS HELLE; circ. 63,283.

Steinkjer

Trønder-Avisa: Hamnegt. 20, POB 2590, 7738 Steinkjer; tel. 74-12-12-00; fax 74-12-13-13; e-mail redaksjonen@t-a.no; internet www.t-a.no; Centre/Liberal; Editor ARVE LØBERG; circ. 21,975.

Tønsberg

Tønsbergs Blad: POB 33, 3101 Tønsberg; tel. 33-37-00-00; fax 33-37-30-10; e-mail redaksjonen@tb.no; internet www.tb.no; f. 1870; Conservative; Editor-in-Chief HÅKON BORUD; circ. 26,789.

Tromsø

Nordlys: Rådhusgt. 3, POB 2515, 9272 Tromsø; tel. 77-62-35-00; fax 77-62-35-01; e-mail firmapost@nordlys.no; internet www.nordlys.no; f. 1902; Labour; Editor ANDERS OPDAHL; circ. 23,627.

Trondheim

Adresseavisen: Industrivn 13, POB 3200, 7003 Trondheim; tel. 07200; fax 72-50-15-00; e-mail redaksjon@adresseavisen.no; internet www.adressa.no; f. 1767; Editor ARNE BLIX; circ. 71,657.

POPULAR PERIODICALS

Allers: Stenersgt. 2, POB 1169, 0107 Oslo; tel. 21-30-10-00; fax 21-30-12-04; e-mail elisabeth@allers.no; internet www.allers.no; family weekly; Editor-in-Chief ELISABETH LUND-ANDERSEN; circ. 123,578.

Bedre Helse: Gullhaugvn 1, 0441 Oslo; tel. 22-58-50-00; fax 22-58-58-79; e-mail bedre-helse@hm-media.no; internet www.bedrehelse.com; health; Editor INGVILD HAGEN; circ. 35,000 (2007).

Bonytt: Gullhaugvn 1, 0441 Oslo; tel. 22-58-50-00; fax 22-58-05-85; e-mail bonytt@hm-media.no; internet www.klikk.no/bonytt; home and furnishing; 14 a year; Editor JAN THORESEN; circ. 68,000 (2003).

Byavisa: Munkegt. 66E, 7011 Trondheim; tel. 73-95-49-00; fax 73-99-05-60; e-mail redaksjon@byavisa.no; internet www.byavisa.no; f. 1996; weekly; Editor-in-Chief PAUL JOSTEIN AUNE; circ. 82,000.

Familien: Gullhaugvn 1, 0441 Oslo; tel. 22-58-57-00; fax 22-58-07-64; e-mail abo-familien@hm-media.no; internet www.familien.no; family fortnightly; Editor-in-Chief IVAR MOE; circ. 111,448 (2009).

Foreldre & Barn: 0441 Oslo; tel. 22-58-50-00; fax 22-58-05-80; e-mail foreldreogbarn@hm-media.no; internet www.foreldreogbarn.no; 11 a year; for parents of young children; Editor TJODUNN ELTVIK DYRNES; circ. 59,210.

Foreldremagasinet: Gullhaugvn 1, 0483 Oslo; tel. 22-58-55-39; e-mail vibeke.ostelie@hm-media.no; monthly; for parents; circ. 20,470.

Henne: Stenersgt 2–8, POB 1169 Sentrum, 0107 Oslo; tel. 21-30-10-00; e-mail redaksjonen@henne.no; internet www.henne.no; women's interest; Editor-in-Chief ELLEN ARNSTAD; circ. 45,586.

Hjemmepc: Gullhaugvn 1, 0441 Oslo; tel. 22-58-50-00; e-mail hjemmepc@hm-media.no; internet www.hjemmepc.no; home computers; Editor-in-Chief HALLVARD LUNDE; circ. 28,963 (2003).

Hjemmet: Nydalsvn 12, 0441 Oslo; tel. 22-77-20-00; e-mail hjemmet@egmonthm.no; internet www.egmonthm.no; family weekly; Editor-in-Chief LISE HANSEN; circ. 169,258 (2013).

Hytteliv: Gullhaugvn 1, 0441 Oslo; tel. 22-58-50-00; fax 22-58-58-59; e-mail hytteliv@hm-media.no; internet www.klikk.no/ produkthjemmesider/hytteliv; f. 1972; 9 a year; for second-home owners; Editor TURID RØSTE; circ. 55,000.

I form: Trim.no AS, 6789 Loen; tel. 22-37-30-50; fax 91-38-59-26; e-mail redaksjonen@trim.no; internet www.iform.no; monthly; health and fitness; Editor-in-Chief GEIR TVERDAL; circ. 46,551.

Jærbladet: POB 23, 4349 Bryne; tel. 51-77-99-00; fax 51-48-37-40; internet redaksjon@jbl.no; internet www.jbl.no; 3 days a week; independent; Editor IVAR RUSDAL; circ. 12,477.

KK (Kvinner og Klær): Stenersgt. 2–8, POB 1169 Sentrum, 0107 Oslo; tel. 21-30-10-00; fax 22-63-61-02; e-mail leserservice@kk.no; internet www.kk.no; women's weekly; Editor-in-Chief PETTER DANBOLT; circ. 88,158.

Mann: Gullhaugvn 1, 0441 Oslo; tel. 22-58-50-00; fax 22-58-05-69; e-mail post@mann.no; internet www.mann.no; men's magazine; Editor-in-Chief KNUT CHRISTIAN MOENG; circ. 20,000.

Mat & Drikke: POB 40, 0411 Oslo; tel. 90-04-64-40; e-mail olav@ matogdrikke.no; internet www.matogdrikke.no; 7 a year; food and wine; Editor-in-Chief LINDAN SANNUM; circ. 23,032.

Norsk Ukeblad: Gullhaugvn 1, 0441 Oslo; tel. 22-58-58-00; fax 22-58-05-69; e-mail nu-tips@hm-media.no; internet www.norskukeblad .no; family weekly; Editor-in-Chief KJERSTI MOEN; circ. 102,347 (2009).

Det Nye: Gullhaugvn 1, 0441 Oslo; tel. 22-58-50-00; fax 22-58-58-09; e-mail detnye@hm-media.no; internet www.detnye.com; for young women; 14 a year; Editor-in-Chief MARI MIDTSTIGEN; circ. 72,000.

Programbladet: POB 1151 Sentrum, 0107 Oslo; tel. 22-31-03-10; fax 22-31-04-55; e-mail elins@programbladet.no; internet www .programbladet.no; f. 1946; radio and television weekly; Editor TRUDE HUSJORD; circ. 65,000.

Se og Hør: POB 1169 Sentrum, 0107 Oslo; tel. 22-41-51-80; fax 22-41-51-70; f. 1978; news weekly (radio and TV); Editors-in-Chief KNUT HÅVIK, ODD J. NELVIK; circ. 174,552 (2009).

TOPP: POB 169 Sentrum, 0107 Oslo; tel. 21-30-12-28; e-mail vilvite@topp.no; internet www.topp.no; monthly; for young people aged between 10 and 17 years; Editor PETTER DANBOLT; circ. 48,011.

Vi Menn: Gullhaugvn 1, 0441 Oslo; tel. 22-58-50-00; fax 22-58-05-71; e-mail vimenn@egmonthm.no; internet www.vimenn.no; f. 1951; men's weekly; publ. by Egmont Hjemmet Mortensen; Man. Editor ALEXANDER OEYSTAA; circ. 75,000.

SPECIALIST PERIODICALS

Alt om Fiske: Gullhaugvn 1, 0441 Oslo; tel. 22-58-50-00; fax 22-58-59-59; e-mail fiske@hm-media.no; internet www.klikk.no/ altomfiske; angling; circ. 22,906 (2005); Chief Editor JON LENÆS.

Barnemagasinet BAM: Gullhaugvn 1, 0484 Oslo; tel. 23-00-81-80; fax 23-00-81-89; e-mail postmaster@bam.no; internet www.bam.no; for expectant and new parents; 3 additional titles, *BAM Gravid*, *BAM Nyfødt* and *BAM Spedbarn*; circ. 80,000 (2000).

Batmagasinet: Stenersgt. 2A, POB 1169 Sentrum, 0107 Oslo; tel. 21-30-10-00; fax 21-30-12-59; e-mail hans.due@aller.no; internet www.batmagasinet.no; f. 1985; owned by Aller Media AS; 12 a year; boating, powerboats; Editor-in-Chief HANS DUE; circ. 22,500.

Bilforlaget AS: Hovfaret 17B, POB 63 Skoyen, 0212 Oslo; tel. 23-03-66-00; fax 23-03-66-40; e-mail info@bilforlaget.no; internet www .bladetbil.no; f. 1975; 10 a year; motoring; Editor STEIN PETTERSEN; circ. 43,312.

Bondebladet: POB 9303 Grønland, 0135 Oslo; tel. 21-31-44-00; fax 21-31-44-01; e-mail redaksjon@bondebladet.no; internet www .bondebladet.no; f. 1974; weekly; farming; Editor LARS OLAV HAUG; circ. 85,593.

Fjell og Vidde: Den Norske Turistforening, Youngstorget 1, 0181 Oslo; tel. 40-00-18-68; fax 22-42-64-27; e-mail redaksjonen@ turistforeningen.no; internet www.turistforeningen.no; f. 1967; 6 a year; organ of The Norwegian Mountain Touring Asscn; Editor HELLE ANDRESEN; circ. 160,000.

Hagen for alle: POB 433, Sentrum, 0103 Oslo; tel. 22-40-12-00; e-mail post@hagenforalle.no; internet www.hagenforalle.no; monthly; gardening; Editor ARILD SANDGREN; circ. 30,000.

Hundesport: POB 163 Bryn, 0611 Oslo; tel. 21-60-09-00; fax 21-60-09-01; e-mail hundesport@nkk.no; internet www.nkk.no; monthly; for dog-owners; circ. 60,000.

IngeniørNytt AS: POB 164, 1332 Østerås; Nils Lassons vei 5, 1359 Eiksmarka; tel. 67-16-34-99; fax 67-16-34-55; e-mail post@ ingeniornytt.no; internet www.ingeniornytt.no; every 2 weeks; engineering, architecture; Editor KARI LARSSEN-AAS; circ. 65,000.

Jakt & Fiske: POB 94, 1378 Nesbru; tel. 66-79-22-00; fax 66-90-15-87; e-mail jaktogfiske@njff.no; internet www.jaktogfiske.info; monthly; hunting and angling; Editor VIGGO KRISTIANSEN; circ. 76,710.

Kampanje: Prinsengracht 22, 0157 Oslo; tel. 22-33-50-00; fax 22-15-40-86; e-mail kampanje@kampanje.com; internet www.kampanje .com; marketing and media; Editor-in-Chief KNUT KRISTIAN HAUGER; circ. 11,340 (2000).

Kapital: POB 724 Skøyen, 0214 Oslo; tel. 23-29-63-00; fax 23-29-63-01; e-mail wenchew@kapital.no; internet www.hegnar.no; fortnightly; business, management; Editor-in-Chief FINN ØYSTEIN BERGH; circ. 40,000.

Motor: POB 494 Sentrum, 0105 Oslo; tel. 22-58-50-00; fax 22-58-59-59; e-mail svein.ola@motor.no; internet www.naf.no; 8 a year; motoring, travel and leisure; publ. by Norwegian Automobile Federation (NAF); Editor SVEIN OLA HOPE; circ. 400,000.

Norsk Hagetidend: POB 53 Manglerud, 0612 Oslo; tel. 23-03-16-00; fax 23-03-16-01; e-mail postkasse@hageselskapet.no; internet www.hageselskapet.no; f. 1885; monthly; gardening; Editor BERGLJOT GUNDERSEN; circ. 41,878.

Norsk Landbruk: POB 9309 Grønland, 0135 Oslo; tel. 21-31-44-09; fax 21-31-44-92; e-mail norsk.landbruk@tunmedia.no; internet www .norsklandbruk.no; f. 1882; 22 a year; agriculture, horticulture and forestry; Editor-in-Chief MARIANNE RØHME; circ. 16,172.

Okonomisk Rapport: POB 1180 Skøyen, 0213 Oslo; tel. 22-31-02-10; fax 22-40-41-01; e-mail rapport@orapp.no; internet www.orapp .no; business; Editor TERJE AURDAL; circ. 24,946 (2000).

PCPro: Gullhaugvn 1, 0441 Oslo; POB 5001 Majorstua, 0301 Oslo; tel. 22-58-50-00; e-mail pcpro@hm-media.no; internet www.pcpro .no; f. 2000; 8 a year; computing; circ. 25,000; Editor-in-Chief KJETIL ENSTAD.

Seilmagasinet: Gartnervn 1, 1394 Nesbru; tel. 21-37-77-90; fax 66-77-40-61; e-mail morten.jensen@seilmagasinet.no; internet www .seilmagasinet.no; f. 1975; publ. by MediaNavigering A/S; 10 a year; sailing; Editor MORTEN JENSEN; circ. 14,000.

SKOGeieren: POB 1438 Vika, 0115 Oslo; tel. 22-01-05-50; fax 22-42-16-90; e-mail anders.hals@skog.no; f. 1914; 12 a year; forestry; Editor ANDERS HALS; circ. 46,100.

Snø og Ski: Kongevn 5, 0787 Oslo; tel. 22-92-32-00; fax 22-92-32-50; quarterly; winter and summer sports; Editor KRISTIN MOE KROHN; circ. 42,000.

Ta del: POB 9202, 0134 Oslo; tel. 21-03-36-50; fax 85-02-85-03-9; e-mail tadel@delta.no; internet www.tadel.no; f. 1936; 9 a year; organ of Norwegian Confederation of Municipal Employees; Editor AUDUN HOPLAND; circ. 54,000.

Teknisk Ukeblad (Technology Review Weekly): POB 5844 Majorstua, 0308 Oslo; tel. 23-19-93-00; fax 23-19-93-01; e-mail redaksjonen@tu.no; internet www.tu.no; f. 1854; technology, industry, management, marketing and economics journal; Editor-in-Chief TORMOD HAUGSTAD; circ. 93,542.

Tidsskriftet Sykepleien: POB 456 Sentrum, 0104 Oslo; tel. 22-04-32-00; fax 22-04-33-756; internet www.sykepleien.no; f. 1912; 21 a year; health personnel, nursing; Editor-in-Chief BARTH THOLENS; circ. 69,000.

Utdanning: POB 9191 Grønland, 0134 Oslo; tel. 24-14-20-00; fax 24-14-21-55; e-mail redaksjonen@utdanning.ws; internet www .utdanning.ws; f. 1934; fmrly *Norsk Skoleblad*; weekly; teaching; Editor KNUT HOVLAND; circ. 129,423.

Utsyn: Sinsenvn 25, 0572 Oslo; tel. 22-00-72-00; fax 22-00-72-02; e-mail utsyn@nlm.no; internet www.utsyn.no; 25 a year; organ of Norsk Luthersk Misjonssamband (Norwegian Lutheran Mission); circ. 17,000.

Vi Menn Båt: Gullhaugvn 1, 0441 Oslo; tel. 22-58-50-00; fax 22-58-05-66; e-mail inger.storodegord@hm-media.no; internet www .vimenn.no; f. 1992; 7 a year; boats; Editor ALEXANDER ØYSTÅ; circ. 77,000 (2004).

Vi Menn Bil: Gullhaugvn 1, 0441 Oslo; tel. 90-02-69-96; e-mail post@frontpress.no; internet www.frontpress.no; f. 1996; 8 a year; cars; Editor ALEXANDER ØYSTÅ.

Vi Menn Fotball: Gullhaugvn 1, 0441 Oslo; tel. 22-58-50-00; e-mail erika-o.asker@hm-media.no; internet www.vimenn.no; football; circ. 30,000 (2000).

Villmarksliv: Gullhaugvn 1, 0441 Oslo; tel. 22-58-50-00; fax 22-58-59-59; e-mail knut.brevik@hm-media.no; internet www.villmarksliv .no; f. 1972; monthly; angling, hunting, photography; Editor-in-Chief KNUT BREVIK; circ. 45,600 (2006).

NEWS AGENCIES

Bulls Pressetjeneste A/S: Ebbellsgt. 3, 0179 Oslo; tel. 22-98-26-60; fax 22-20-49-78; e-mail info@bulls.no; internet www.bulls.no; Man. PAUL E. VATNE.

A/S Norsk Telegrambyrå (NTB) (Norwegian News Agency): Akersgt. 55, POB 6817 St Olavs pl., 0130 Oslo; tel. 22-03-44-00; fax 22-20-12-29; e-mail ntb@ntb.no; internet www.ntb.no; f. 1867; Editor-in-Chief PÅL BJERKETVEDT.

PRESS ASSOCIATIONS

Mediebedriftenes Landsforening (Norwegian Media Businesses' Asscn): Tollbugt. 27, 0157 Oslo; tel. 22-86-12-00; fax 22-42-26-11; e-mail info@mediebedriftene.no; internet www.mediebedriftene.no; Man. Dir ARVID SAND.

Den Norske Fagpresses Forening (Specialized Press Asscn): Akersgt. 41, 0158 Oslo; tel. 24-14-61-00; fax 24-14-61-10.

Norsk Journalistlag (Norwegian Union of Journalists): Torggt. 5, 5th Floor, POB 8793 Youngstorget, 0028 Oslo; tel. 22-05-39-50; fax 22-41-33-70; e-mail nj@nj.no; internet www.nj.no; f. 1946; Sec.-Gen. JAHN-ARNE OLSEN; 8,770 mems (2004).

Norsk Presseforbund (Norwegian Press Asscn): Rådhusgt. 17, POB 46 Sentrum, 0101 Oslo; tel. 22-40-50-40; fax 22-40-50-55; e-mail np@presse.no; internet www.presse.no; f. 1910; asscn of newspapermen, editors and journalists; Pres. KJETIL HAANES; Sec.-Gen. PER EDGAR KOKKVOLD.

Publishers

Antropos Forlag: Josefinesgt. 12, 0351 Oslo; tel. 22-46-03-74; fax 22-69-64-50; e-mail bokhandel@antropos.no; internet www.antropos.no.

H. Aschehoug & Co (W. Nygaard): Sehestedsgt. 3, POB 363 Sentrum, 0102 Oslo; tel. 22-40-04-00; fax 22-20-63-95; e-mail epost@aschehoug.no; internet www.aschehoug.no; f. 1872; general non-fiction, fiction, reference, children's, educational, textbooks; Man. Dir MADS NYGAARD.

Boksenteret Erik Pettersen & Co A/S: Krusesgt. 11, POB 3125 Elisenberg, 0207 Oslo; tel. 22-54-07-00; fax 22-54-07-07; e-mail bs@boksenteret.no; internet www.boksenteret.no; f. 1999; illustrated, non-fiction, craft, DIY; Man. Dir ERIK PETTERSEN.

Bokvennen Forlag: POB 6794, 0133 Oslo; tel. 22-19-14-25; fax 22-19-14-26; e-mail post@bokvennen.no; internet www.vidarforlaget.no; f. 1989; fiction, essays, biographies; Mans MORTEN CLAUSSEN, JAN M. CLAUSSEN.

Cappelen Akademisk Forlag: POB 350 Sentrum, 0055 Oslo; tel. 21-61-65-00; fax 21-61-65-01; e-mail cafinfo@cappelen.no; internet www.cappelendamm.no; f. 1946; textbooks for universities and colleges, social sciences, law, economics, medicine, health and nursing, educational science, psychology; Publr ESTER MOEN.

Cappelen Damm AS: Akersgt. 47, 0180 Oslo; tel. 21-61-65-00; fax 21-61-65-01; e-mail web@cappelen.no; internet www.cappelendamm.no; f. 1829; general, educational, popular science, fiction, maps, children's, encyclopedias; Man. Dir PIP HALLÉN.

Dreyers Forlag: POB 2336 Solli, 0201 Oslo; tel. 23-13-69-38; fax 23-13-69-39; e-mail post@dreyersforlag.no; internet www.dreyersforlag.no; fmrly Andresen & Butenschøn A/S.

Egmont Hjemmet Mortensen A/S: Gullhaugvn 1, Nydalen, 0441 Oslo; tel. 22-58-50-00; fax 22-58-50-68; e-mail firmapost@hm-media.no; internet www.hm-media.no; f. 1941; fiction, non-fiction, children's; Man. Dir ANNE BRITT BERENSTEN.

Eide Forlag A/S: POB 6050 Postterminalen, 5892 Bergen; tel. 55-38-88-00; fax 55-38-88-01; e-mail post@eideforlag.no; internet www.eideforlag.no; f. 1880; general, children's, textbooks, fiction, non-fiction; Publrs ARNO VIGMOSTAD, ARNSTEIN BJORKE.

Fagbokforlaget: POB 6050, Postterminalen, 5892 Bergen; tel. 55-38-88-00; fax 55-38-88-01; e-mail fagbokforlaget@fagbokforlaget.no; internet www.fagbokforlaget.no; f. 1992; general and scientific; also owns Forlaget Fag og Kultur A/S; Publrs ARNO VIGMOSTAD, ARNSTEIN BJØRKE.

Falken Forlag: Helgesens gt. 21, 0553 Oslo; tel. 22-35-54-00; e-mail falkenforlag@falkenforlag.no; internet www.falkenforlag.no; f. 1946; fiction, non-fiction; Publr KIRSTI KRISTIANSEN.

Fonna Forlag: Underhaugsveien 9A, 0354 Oslo; tel. 22-69-10-10; fax 22-20-12-01; e-mail fonna@fonna.no; internet www.fonna.no; f. 1934; limited co; general, fiction; Man. Dir ARNT ÅRNES.

Frifant Forlag A/S: Leinvn 10, 1453 Bjørnemyr; tel. 66-91-29-40; fax 66-91-29-41; e-mail frifor@online.no; internet www.frifant.no; f. 1997.

Genesis Forlag: Fetveien 1D, POB 83, 2027 Kjeller; tel. 63-80-30-99; fax 63-81-69-22; e-mail genesis@genesis.no; internet www.genesis.no; f. 1996; Dir SVEIN ANDERSEN.

John Grieg Forlag A/S: Spelhaugen 20, 5147 Bergen; tel. 55-16-13-44; fax 66-16-13-44; e-mail post@grieg1721.no; internet www.grieg1721.no; f. 1721; children's, art, education, aquaculture; Publr SVEIN SKOTHEIM.

Gyldendal Akademisk: Sehestedsgt. 4, POB 6860, St Olavs pl., 0130 Oslo; tel. 22-03-41-00; fax 22-03-43-05; e-mail akademisk@gyldendal.no; internet www.gyldendal.no/akademisk; f. 1992; university textbooks; Man. Dir FREDRIK NISSEN.

Gyldendal Norsk Forlag A/S: Sehestedsgt. 4, POB 6860 St Olavs pl., 0130 Oslo; tel. 22-03-41-00; fax 22-03-41-05; internet www.gyldendal.no; f. 1925; general, non-fiction, fiction, biography, religion, cookery, school and university textbooks, children's, manuals; Man. Dir BJØRGUN HYSING.

Imprintforlaget A/S: Huitfeldtsgt. 15, POB 2336 Solli, 0201 Oslo; tel. 23-13-69-30; fax 23-13-69-39; e-mail imprint@imprint.no; internet www.imprint.no; imprints: Omnipax, Pegasus, Unipax; Publr BJØRN SMITH-SIMONSEN.

Kolibri Forlag A/S: POB 44 Øvre Ullern, 0311 Oslo; tel. 92-45-25-29; e-mail post@kolibriforlag.no; internet www.kolibriforlag.no; f. 1982; fantasy, non-fiction, cookery, children's, humour, leisure; Publr ELSE LILL BJØNNES.

Kolon Forlag: Sehestedsgt. 4, POB 6860 St Olavs pl., 0130 Oslo; tel. 22-03-42-02; fax 22-03-41-05; e-mail kolon@gyldendal.no; internet www.kolonforlag.no; f. 1995; modern Norwegian poetry and fiction; Publr BJØRN AAGENÆS.

Kunnskapsforlaget: Gullhaug Torg 1, POB 4432 Nydalen, 0403 Oslo; tel. 22-02-22-00; fax 22-02-22-99; e-mail resepsjonen@kunnskapsforlaget.no; internet www.kunnskapsforlaget.no; f. 1975; reference books, encyclopedias, dictionaries, atlases, electronic reference titles; Man. Dir MARIANNE BRATTLAND.

Libretto Forlag: Øvre Vollgt. 15, 0158 Oslo; tel. 22-41-03-85; e-mail post@librettoforlag.no; internet www.librettoforlag.no; f. 1990; children's, gift books and handbooks; Publr TOM THORSTEINSEN.

Lunde Forlag A/S: Sinsenvn 25, 0572 Oslo; tel. 22-00-73-50; fax 22-00-73-73; e-mail post@lundeforlag.no; internet www.lundeforlag.no; f. 1905; religious, general, fiction, children's; Dir TORLEIF BELT.

Luther Forlag: Grensen 3, 0159 Oslo; tel. 22-00-87-80; fax 22-00-87-81; e-mail post@lutherforlag.no; internet www.lutherforlag.no; religious, fiction, general; Dir MORTEN DAHLE STÆRK.

Lydbokforlaget A/S: Søreggen 2, POB 64, 7224 Melhus; tel. 72-85-60-70; fax 72-85-60-90; e-mail info@lydbokforlaget.no; internet www.lydbokforlaget.no; f. 1987; owned by H. Aschehoug & Co (33%), Gyldendal Norsk Forlag (33%) and Stiftergruppen (34%); Publr HERBORG HONGSET.

Messel Forlag: Øvre Vollgt. 15, 0158 Oslo; tel. 22-42-14-20; e-mail info@messelforlag.no; internet www.messelforlag.no; f. 1992; Pub. Dir ANNE-GRETHE MESSEL.

NKI Forlaget: Hans Burumsvn 30, POB 111, 1319 Bekkestua; tel. 67-58-89-00; fax 67-58-19-02; e-mail faordre@nki.no; internet www.nkiforlaget.no; f. 1972; textbooks for secondary and technical schools and colleges; Publr MARIANNE LØVDAHL.

Norsk Bokreidingslag: POB 6045, 5892 Bergen; tel. 55-30-18-99; fax 55-32-03-56; e-mail post@bodonihus.no; internet www.bokreidingslaget.no; f. 1939; fiction, folklore, linguistics, cultural history; Man. FROYDIS LEHMANN.

Det Norske Samlaget: Jens Bjelkesgt. 12, POB 4672 Sofienberg, 0506 Oslo; tel. 22-70-78-00; fax 22-68-75-02; e-mail kontakt@samlaget.no; internet www.samlaget.no; f. 1868; fiction, non-fiction, poetry, children's, textbooks; Man. Dir TOVE LIE.

Forlaget Oktober A/S: Kr. Augustsgt. 11, POB 6848 St Olavs pl., 0130 Oslo; tel. 23-35-46-20; fax 23-35-46-21; e-mail oktober@oktober.no; internet www.oktober.no; f. 1970; fiction, politics, social and cultural books; Publr GEIR BERDAHL.

Pantagruel Forlag A/S: Inkognitogt. 33, POB 2370 Solli, 0201 Oslo; tel. 23-27-28-10; fax 23-27-28-15; e-mail alle@pantagruel.no; internet www.pantagruel.no; Pub. Dir ALEXANDER ELGURÉN.

Pax Forlag A/S: Huitfeldtgt. 15, POB 2336 Solli, 0201 Oslo; tel. 23-13-69-00; fax 23-13-69-19; e-mail pax@pax.no; internet www.pax.no; f. 1964; fiction, non-fiction, feminism, social sciences; Man. Dir BJØRN SMITH-SIMONSEN.

Schibsted Forlagene AS: Apotekergt. 12, POB 6974 St Olavs pl., 0130 Oslo; tel. 24-14-68-00; fax 24-14-68-01; e-mail post@schibstedforlag.no; internet www.schibstedforlag.no; f. 2004 by merger of Chr. Schibsteds Forlagene A/S (f. 1839) and other units within Schibsted Group; reference, biographies, handbooks, children's, food and drink, sports, foreign language, guides, fiction, comics; Group Dir ROLV ERIK RYSSDAL.

Snøfugl Forlag: POB 95, 7221 Melhus; tel. 72-87-24-11; fax 72-87-10-13; e-mail snoefugl@online.no; internet www.snøfuglforlag.no; f. 1972; fiction, general; Man. ÅSMUND SNØFUGL.

Solum Forlag A/S: Hoffsvn 18, POB 140 Skøyen, 0212 Oslo; tel. 22-50-04-00; fax 22-50-14-53; e-mail info@solumforlag.no; internet www.solumforlag.no; f. 1974; fiction, human sciences, general; Man. Dir KNUT ENDRE SOLUM.

Spartacus Forlag A/S: POB 6673 St Olavs pl. 0129 Oslo; tel. 22-44-56-70; fax 22-44-46-50; e-mail post@spartacus.no; internet www.spartacus.no; f. 1989; Publr PER NORDANGER.

Spektrum Forlag AS: Rosencrantzgt. 22, 0160 Oslo; tel. 22-00-82-60; fax 85-03-64-78; e-mail post@spektrum-forlag.no; internet www.spektrum-forlag.no; f. 1992; Pub. Dir CYRUS BRANTENBERG.

Stabenfeldt A/S: Sothammargeilen 3, 4029 Stavanger; tel. 51-84-54-00; fax 51-84-54-90; f. 1913; general fiction, adventure, reference; Man. Dir JENS OTTO HANSEN.

Tell Forlag A/S: Slemmestadveien 416, 1390 Vollen; tel. 66-78-09-18; fax 66-90-05-72; e-mail post@tell.no; internet www.tell.no; f. 1987; textbooks and educational books; Man. TELL-CHR. WAGLE.

Tiden Norsk Forlag: Sehestedsgt. 4, POB 6704 St Olavs pl., 0130 Oslo; tel. 23-32-76-60; fax 23-32-76-97; e-mail tiden@tiden.no; internet www.tiden.no; f. 1933; literary fiction, crime, thrillers, fantasy, non-fiction; Pub. Dir RICHARD AARØ.

Tun Forlag A/S: Schweigaardsgt. 34A POB 9303 Grønland, 0135 Oslo; tel. 21-31-44-00; e-mail post@tunforlag.no; internet www.boktunet.no; f. 2005; agriculture, hunting, fishing, outdoor, handicrafts, culture, horses, dogs; Man. HEIDI JANNICKE ANDERSEN.

Universitetsforlaget AS: Sehestedsgt. 3, POB 508 Sentrum, 0105 Oslo; tel. 24-14-75-00; fax 24-14-75-01; e-mail post@universitetsforlaget.no; internet www.universitetsforlaget.no; f. 1950; publishers to the Universities of Oslo, Bergen, Trondheim and Tromsø and various learned societies; school books, university textbooks, specialized journals; Man. Dir SVEIN SKARHEIM.

Verbum Forlag: Bernhard Getzgt. 3, POB 6624 St Olavs pl., 0129 Oslo; tel. 22-93-27-00; fax 22-93-27-27; e-mail verbumforlag@verbumforlag.no; internet www.verbumforlag.no; f. 1820; Christian literature; Man. TURID BARTH PETTERSEN.

Forlaget Vett & Viten AS: Ramstadsletta 15, 1363 Høvik; tel. 66-84-90-40; fax 66-53-11-52; e-mail vv@vettviten.no; internet www.vettviten.no; f. 1987; medical, technical and engineering textbooks; Publr JAN WIBE LIEN.

Wigestrand Forlag A/S: POB 621, 4003 Stavanger; tel. 51-51-76-10; fax 51-51-76-40; e-mail forlag@wigestrand.no; internet www.wigestrand.no; f. 1998; Publr ØYVIND WIGESTRAND.

PUBLISHERS' ASSOCIATION

Den norske Forleggerforening (Norwegian Publishers' Asscn): Øvre Vollgt. 15, 0158 Oslo; tel. 22-00-75-80; fax 22-33-38-30; e-mail dnf@forleggerforeningen.no; internet www.forleggerforeningen.no; f. 1895; Chair. GEIR BERDAHL; Sec. KRISTENN EINARSSON; 88 mem. firms.

Broadcasting and Communications

TELECOMMUNICATIONS

NetCom AS: Sandakervn 140, 0484 Oslo; tel. 92-40-50-50; internet www.netcom.no; f. 1990; mobile cellular telecommunications; owned by TeliaSonera AB (Sweden); Man. Dir AUGUST BAUMANN.

Network Norway AS: Innspurten 15, 0663 Oslo; tel. 51-84-64-00; fax 51-84-64-01; e-mail 09060@networknorway.no; internet www.networknorway.no; f. 2005; mobile cellular telecommunications and broadband internet services; owned by Tele2 Norge AS; Man. Dir ARILD E. HUSTAD.

Norkring AS: Telenor Broadcast, 1331 Fornebu; tel. 67-89-20-00; fax 67-89-36-11; e-mail norkring@telenor.com; internet www.norkring.no; f. 1996; provides fixed and mobile telephone services; owned by Telenor Broadcast Holding A/S; CEO TORBJOERN TEIGEN.

Telenor ASA: Snarøyvn 30, 1331 Fornebu; tel. 67-89-40-00; e-mail infomaster@telenor.no; internet www.telenor.no; offers fixed-line telecommunications, broadband internet and digital television services; 53.97% stake owned by the Government of Norway; Man. Dir BERIT SVENDSEN.

djuice: Snarøyvn 30, 1331 Fornebu; tel. 81-07-70-00; fax 67-89-00-00; e-mail infomaster@telenor.com; internet www.djuice.no; mobile cellular telecommunications; subsidiary of Telenor ASA.

Tele2 Norge AS: Innspurten 15, 0663 Oslo; tel. 21-31-90-00; fax 21-31-91-00; internet www.tele2.no; f. 1995; fixed-line and mobile cellular telecommunications services, also broadband internet access; subsidiary of Tele2 AB (Sweden); Man. Dir ARILD HUSTAD.

REGULATORY AUTHORITY

Post- og Teletilsynet (NPT) (Norwegian Post and Telecommunications Authority): Nygård 1, POB 93, 4791 Lillesand; tel. 22-82-46-00; fax 22-82-46-40; e-mail firmapost@npt.no; internet www.npt.no; f. 1987; issues and supervises regulations, concessions and licences; expanded to incorporate postal matters in 1997; Dir-Gen. TORSTEIN OLSEN.

BROADCASTING

Radio

Norsk Rikskringkasting (NRK) (Norwegian Broadcasting Corpn): Bj. Bjørnsons pl. 1, 0340 Oslo; tel. 23-04-25-20; fax 23-04-27-20; e-mail info@nrk.no; internet www.nrk.no; autonomous public corpn; operates 3 national services (including a youth programme), 18 regional services (including 1 in the language of the Sámi—Lappish) and an international service, Radio Norway International; Chair. WILLIAM NYGAARD; CEO (Broadcasting) THOR GJERMUND ERIKSEN.

P4—Radio Hele Norge ASA: Serviceboks, 2626 Lillehammer; tel. 61-24-88-44; fax 61-24-84-45; e-mail p4@p4.no; internet www.p4.no; f. 1993; private commercial station; Man. Dir KALLE LISBERG.

Radio Norge: Kråkerøyvn 2 POB 144, 1601 Fredrikstad; tel. 69-70-76-00; fax 69-70-76-01; e-mail redaksjon@radionorge.com; internet www.radionorge.com; f. 2004 as Kanal24; present name adopted 2008; 77% stake owned by SBS Radio Norge AS; Man. Dir BENTE KLEMETSDAL.

Television

Digital terrestrial broadcasting began in 2007. Analogue signals were discontinued in December 2009.

Canal Digital AS: Snarøyvn 30, 1331 Fornebu; tel. 67-89-00-00; fax 67-89-11-93; e-mail corporate@canaldigital.com; internet www.canaldigital.no; digital satellite and cable television services; also broadband internet access; owned by Telenor ASA; Man. Dir PATRIK HOFBAUER.

Norsk Rikskringkasting (NRK) (Norwegian Broadcasting Corpn): CEO THOR GJERMUND ERIKSEN.

RiksTV AS: Økernvn 145, POB 393, Økern, 0513 Oslo; tel. 22-88-37-90; fax 22-88-37-91; e-mail post@rikstv.no; internet www.rikstv.no; f. 2005; a digital terrestrial, cable and satellite television service, offering up to 26 channels; co-owned by NRK, Telenor Broadcast Holding and TV 2 Gruppen; Man. Dir CHRISTIAN BIRKELAND.

TV 2: Nøstegaten 72, POB 7222, 5020 Bergen; tel. 02255; fax 21-00-60-03; e-mail 02255@tv2.no; internet www.tv2.no; f. 1992; private commercial station; Man. Dir ALF HILDRUM; Dir of Programmes PIL GUNDELACH BRANDSTRUP.

TV Norge AS: Nydalen Allé 37, POB 4800, 0484 Oslo; tel. 21-02-20-00; fax 22-05-10-00; e-mail tvnorge@tvnorge.no; internet www.tvnorge.no; private commercial television channel; owned by ProSiebenSat1 (Germany); Man. Dir HARALD STRØMME; Dir of Programmes JARLE NAKKEN.

Finance

At April 2013 there were 17 commercial banks (comprising the major banks, some large regional banks and a number of smaller regional and local banks) and 109 savings banks.

Finanstilsynet (Financial Supervisory Authority of Norway): Revierstredet 3, POB 1187, Sentrum, 0107 Oslo; tel. 22-93-98-00; fax 22-63-02-26; e-mail post@finanstilsynet.no; internet www.finanstilsynet.no; f. 1986; finance inspectorate; Dir-Gen. MORTEN BALTZERSEN.

BANKING

(cap. = capital; res = reserves; dep. = deposits; m. = million; brs = branches; amounts in kroner, unless otherwise specified)

Central Bank

Norges Bank: Bankplassen 2, POB 1179 Sentrum, 0107 Oslo; tel. 22-31-60-00; fax 22-41-31-05; e-mail central.bank@norges-bank.no; internet www.norges-bank.no; f. 1816; holds the exclusive right of note issue; cap. and res 59,887m., dep. 2,690,419m. (Dec. 2008); Chair., Supervisory Bd REIDAR SANDAL; Gov. SVEIN GJEDREM; 12 brs.

Principal Commercial Banks

Bank 1 Oslo Akershus AS: Hammersborggt. 2, POB 778 Sentrum, 0106 Oslo; tel. 07040; fax 21-02-50-51; e-mail bank1@sparebank1.no; internet www.oslo.sparebank1.no; f. 1898; present name adopted 2011; cap. 341m., res 200m., dep. 20,600m. (Dec. 2011); CEO TORBJØRN VIK; Chair. ELDAR MATHISEN; 17 brs.

DNB Bank A/S: Aker Brygge, Stranden 21, 0021 Oslo; tel. 91-50-30-00; fax 24-02-53-00; e-mail 04800@dnbnor.no; internet www.dnb.no; f. 2004 by merger of Den norske Bank ASA and Union Bank of Norway; fmr name DnB NOR Bank ASA; name changed to present 2011; cap. 18,314m., res 20,612m., dep. 1,258,085m. (Dec. 2011); Chair. ANNE CARINE TANUM; Pres. and CEO RUNE BJERKE; 185 brs.

Nordea Bank Norge ASA: Middelthunsgt. 17, POB 1166 Sentrum, 0107 Oslo; tel. 22-48-50-00; fax 22-48-47-49; internet www.nordea.no; fmrly Christiania Bank og Kreditkasse ASA; present name adopted 2001; part of Nordea Bank Group (Sweden); cap. 4,411m., res 3,478m., dep. 447,749m. (Dec. 2012); Group Pres. and CEO CHRISTIAN CLAUSEN; Senior Exec., Norway GUNN WÆRSTED; 130 brs.

Principal Savings Banks

Sparebank 1 Nord-Norge: Storgt. 65, POB 6800, 9298 Tromsø; tel. 91-50-22-44; fax 77-62-22-91; e-mail 02244@snn.no; internet www.snn.no; f. 1989 as Sparebanken Nord-Norge, following merger of Sparebanken Nord and Tromsø Sparebank; present name adopted 2008; cap. 1,655m., res 4,753m., dep. 51,205m. (Dec. 2011); Chair. KJELL OLAV PETTERSEN; CEO HANS OLAV KARDE; 81 brs.

Sparebank 1 SMN: Sondregt. 4, 7467 Trondheim; tel. 73-58-51-11; fax 73-58-64-50; e-mail smn@smn.no; internet www.smn.no; f. 1823 as Trondhjems Sparebank; fmrly Sparebanken Midt-Norge; present name adopted 2008; cap. 2,373m., res 4,566m., dep. 61,875m. (Dec. 2011); Chair. PER AXEL KOCHE; Man. Dir FINN HAUGAN; 53 brs.

SpareBank 1 SR-Bank ASA: Bjergsted Terrasse 1, POB 250, 4066 Stavanger; tel. 91-50-20-02; fax 51-53-54-67; e-mail kundesenter@sr-bank.no; internet www.sr-bank.no; f. 1839 as Egersund Sparebank; merged with 22 savings banks in 1976; name changed from SpareBank 1 SR-Bank to SpareBank 1 SR-Bank ASA in Dec. 2011; cap. 3,180m., res 3,946m., dep. 74,717m. (Dec. 2011); CEO TERJE VAREBERG; 52 brs.

Sparebanken Hedmark: Strandgt. 15, POB 203, 2302 Hamar; tel. 62-51-20-00; fax 62-53-29-75; e-mail kundesenter@sparebanken-hedmark.no; internet www.sparebanken-hedmark.no; f. 1845; dep. 26,803m. total assets 43,241m. (Dec. 2011); Chair. RICHARD H. HEIBERG; Man. Dir HARRY KONTERUD; 29 brs.

Sparebanken Møre: Keiser Wilhelmsgt. 29–33, POB 121, 6002 Ålesund; tel. 70-11-30-00; fax 70-12-26-70; e-mail kundeservice@sbm.no; internet www.sbm.no; f. 1985; cap. 784m., res 935m., dep. 28,347m. (Dec. 2011); CEO OLAV-ARNE FISKERSTRAND; 31 brs.

Sparebanken Pluss: Rådhusgt. 7–9, POB 200, 4662 Kristiansand; tel. 38-17-35-00; fax 38-17-35-04; e-mail firmapost@sparebankenpluss.no; internet www.sparebankenpluss.no; f. 1824; merged with 4 savings banks in 1987; cap. 125m., res 35m., dep. 27,964m. (Dec. 2011); Chair. ARVID GRUNDEKJØN; Man. Dir STEIN HANNEVIK.

Sparebanken Sør: Vestervn. 1, POB 782, 4800 Arendal; tel. 37-02-50-00; fax 37-02-19-36; e-mail international@sor.no; internet www.sor.no; f. 1825; cap. 2,895m., res 14m., dep. 27,490m. (Dec. 2011); Chair. ALICE JERVELL; Man. Dir MORTEN KRAFT; 27 brs.

Sparebanken Vest: Kaigt. 4, POB 7999, 5016 Bergen; tel. 91-50-55-55; fax 55-21-73-50; e-mail sparebanken.vest@spv.no; internet www.spv.no; f. 1823 as Bergens Sparebank; merger 1982 of 25 savings banks; cap. 765m., res 847m., dep. 69,741m. (Dec. 2011); Man. Dir STEIN KLAKEGG; 63 brs.

Bankers' Associations

Finansnæringens Fellesorganisasjon (FNO) (Finance Norway): Hansteensgt. 2, POB 2473 Solli, 0202 Oslo; tel. 23-28-42-00; fax 23-28-42-01; e-mail firmapost@fno.no; internet www.fno.no; f. 2010; trade organization for banks, insurance companies and other financial institutions; 180 mems; Chair. RUNE BJERKE; Man. Dir ARNE HYTTNES.

Sparebankforeningen i Norge (Savings Banks Asscn): Universitetsgt. 8, St Olavs pl., POB 6772, 0130 Oslo; tel. 22-11-00-75; fax 22-36-25-33; e-mail firmapost@sparebankforeningen.no; internet www.sparebankforeningen.no; f. 1914; Pres. TERJE VAREBERG (Sparebank 1 SR-Bank); Man. Dir ARNE HYTTNES; 121 mems.

STOCK EXCHANGE

Oslo Børs (Oslo Stock Exchange): Tollbugt. 2, POB 460 Sentrum, 0105 Oslo; tel. 22-34-17-00; e-mail communications@oslobors.no; internet www.oslobors.no; f. 1819; owned by Oslo Børs VPS Holding ASA; Pres. and CEO BENTE A. LANDSNES.

INSURANCE

Assuranceforeningen Skuld: Ruseløkkvn. 26, POB 1376 Vika, 0114 Oslo; tel. 22-00-22-00; fax 22-42-42-22; e-mail osl@skuld.com; internet www.skuld.com; f. 1897; mutual, shipowners' protection and indemnity; Chair. KLAUS KJÆRULFF; Pres. and CEO DOUGLAS JACOBSOHN.

Gjensidige Forsikring ASA: Drammensvn 228, POB 276, 1326 Lysaker; tel. 91-50-31-00; fax 22-96-92-00; e-mail epost@gjensidigenor.no; internet www.gjensidige.com; f. 1847; merged with Forenede Norge Forsikring and Forenede Skadeforsikring in 1993; Chair. INGE K. HANSEN; Group CEO HELGE LEIRO BAASTAD.

Kommunal Landspensjonskasse (KLP): Trelastgt. 3, 0191 Oslo; tel. 22-03-35-00; fax 22-03-36-00; internet www.klp.no; f. 1949; Group CEO SVERRE THORNES.

Nordea Liv AS: POB 7078, 5020 Bergen; tel. 22-48-50-00; fax 55-17-33-80; internet www.nordealiv.no; f. by merger of Norske Liv AS and Vesta Liv AS; life insurance; Dir JØRUND VANDVIK.

TrygVesta: Folke Bernadottesvei 50, 5020 Bergen; tel. 55-17-10-00; e-mail kundeservice@trygvesta.no; internet www.tryg.com; f. 1884 as Vesta; bought by Tryg-Baltica in 1999; current name adopted 2002; includes Skadeforsikringsselskapet Vesta A/S (general insurance), Vesta Liv A/S (life insurance), Vesta Finans A/S (financial services); Chair. MIKAEL OLUFSEN; CEO MORTEN HÜBBE.

Uni Storebrand: Prof. Kohtsvei 9, POB 500, 1327 Lysaker; tel. 22-31-50-50; e-mail international@storebrand.no; internet www.storebrand.no; f. 1991 by merger of Storebrand (f. 1947) and Uni Forsikring (f. 1984); group includes life, non-life and international reinsurance operations; taken over by govt administrators in 1992 and new holding co (Uni Storebrand New) formed, following suspension of payments to creditors; CEO ODD ARILD GREFSTAD.

Insurance Association

Finansnæringens Fellesorganisasjon (FNO) (Finance Norway): (see Bankers' Associations).

Trade and Industry

GOVERNMENT AGENCIES

Enova SF: Prof. Brochsgt. 2, POB 5700 Sluppen, 7437 Trondheim; tel. 73-19-04-30; e-mail post@enova.no; internet www.enova.no; f. 2001; owned by the Ministry of Petroleum and Energy; advises the Ministry on matters related to energy efficiency and new renewable energy; Man. Dir NILS KRISTIAN NAKSTAD.

Innovasjon Norge (Innovation Norway): Akersgt. 13, POB 448 Sentrum, 0104 Oslo; tel. 22-00-25-00; fax 22-00-25-01; e-mail post@innovasjonnorge.no; internet www.innovasjonnorge.no; f. 2004 to replace Norges Turistråd (Norwegian Tourist Board), Norges Eksportråd (Norwegian Trade Council), Statens nærings- og distriktsutviklingsfond (SND—Industrial and Regional Development Fund) and Statens Veiledningskontor for Oppfinnere (SVO—Government Consultative Office for Inventors); state-owned; operates in all Norwegian counties and more than 30 countries worldwide; Chair. REIDAR SANDAL; Pres. and CEO GUNN OVESEN.

CHAMBERS OF COMMERCE

Bergen Næringsråd (Bergen Chamber of Commerce and Industry): POB 843, Sentrum, 5807 Bergen; tel. 55-55-39-00; fax 55-55-39-01; e-mail firmapost@bergen-chamber.no; internet www.bergen-chamber.no; f. 1915; Chair. JOHANNES D. NETELAND; Man. Dir MARIT WARNCKE.

Oslo Handelskammer (Oslo Chamber of Commerce): Henrik Ibsensgt. 100, POB 2874 Solli, 0230 Oslo; tel. 22-12-94-00; fax 22-12-94-01; e-mail mail@chamber.no; internet www.chamber.no; Man. Dir LARS-KÅRE LEGERNES.

INDUSTRIAL AND TRADE ASSOCIATION

Norges Skogeierforbund (Norwegian Forest Owners' Fed.): Roald Amundsensgt. 6, POB 1438 Vika, 0115 Oslo; tel. 23-00-07-50; fax 22-42-16-90; e-mail post@skog.no; internet www.skog.no; f. 1913; aims to promote the economic and technical interests of forest owners, a general forest policy in the interests of private ownership and cooperation between the affiliated asscns; Man. Dir GUDBRAND KVAAL; 40,000 mems.

EMPLOYERS' ASSOCIATIONS

Næringslivets Hovedorganisasjon (NHO) (Confederation of Norwegian Business and Industry): Middelthunsgt. 27, POB 5250 Majorstua, 0303 Oslo; tel. 23-08-80-00; fax 23-08-80-01; e-mail firmapost@nho.no; internet www.nho.no; f. 1989; rep. org. for industry, crafts and service industries; Pres. KRISTIN SKOGEN LUND; Dir-Gen. JOHN G. BERNANDER; c. 21,500 mems who must also belong to one of the 20 affiliated national asscns, chief among which are the following:

Bensinforhandlernes Bransjeforening (BBF) (Petrol Retailers' Organization): POB 5488, Majorstua, 0305 Oslo; tel. 23-08-87-50; fax 23-08-87-51; e-mail kbs@nho.no; internet www.bensinforhandlerne.no; Man. Dir JAN CARHO; approx. 600 mems.

Energi Norge (Energy Norway): Middelthunsgt. 27, POB 7184 Majorstua, 0307 Oslo; tel. 23-08-89-00; fax 23-08-89-01; e-mail post@energinorge.no; internet www.energinorge.no; fmrly Energibedriftenes Landsforening; present name adopted in 2009; Chair. TORE OLAF RIMMEREID.

Fiskeri- og Havbruksnæringens Landsforening (FHL) (Fish and Aquaculture Industries): Middelthunsgt. 27, POB 5471 Majorstua, 0305 Oslo; tel. 99-11-00-00; fax 23-08-87-31; e-mail firmapost@fhl.no; internet www.fhl.no; Dir-Gen. GEIR ANDREASSEN.

NHO Grafisk (Fed. of Graphic Arts Enterprises): Middelthunsgt. 27, 0369, POB 5495, Majorstua, 0305 Oslo; tel. 23-08-78-70; fax 23-08-78-71; e-mail post@nhografisk.no; internet www.nhografisk .no; f. 1906; fmrly Visuell Kommunikasjon Norge; Dir-Gen. BJØRN MOEN; 240 mems.

NHO Håndverk (Norwegian Fed. of Craft Industries): Middelthunsgt. 27, POB 5250, Majorstua, 0303 Oslo; tel. 23-08-80-00; fax 23-08-87-61; e-mail handverk@nho.no; internet www .nhohandverk.no; f. 1993; Chair. MERETHE SUNDE; 2,000 mems.

NHO Luftfart (Fed. of Norwegian Aviation Industries): POB 5474 Majorstua, 0305 Oslo; tel. 23-08-85-70; fax 23-08-85-71; e-mail nholuftfart@nho.no; internet www.nholuftfart.no; Dir TORBJØRN LOTHE.

NHO Mat og Drikke (Fed. of Norwegian Food and Drink Industry): Middelthunsgt. 27, POB 5472 Majorstua, 0305 Oslo; tel. 23-08-87-00; e-mail firmapost@nhomd.no; internet www .nhomatogdrikke.no; Admin. Dir KNUT MARONI.

NHO Reiseliv (Norwegian Hospitality Asscn): Middelthunsgt. 27, POB 5465 Majorstua 0305 Oslo; tel. 23-08-86-20; fax 23-08-86-21; e-mail post@nhoreiseliv.no; internet www.nhoreiseliv.no; f. 1997 as Reiselivsbedriftenes Landsforening; present name adopted 2006; Pres. OLE WARBERG; 2,400 mems.

NHO Service (Nat. Fed. of Service Industries): Middelthunsgt. 27, POB 5473, Majorstua, 0305 Oslo; tel. 23-08-86-50; fax 23-08-86-59; e-mail baard.fiksdal@nhoservice.no; internet www.nhoservice .no; f. 1989; Admin. Dir PETTER FURULUND; 1,187 mems.

NHO Transport (TL) (Fed. of Norwegian Transport Cos): Middelthunsgt. 27, POB 5477 Majorstua, 0305 Oslo; tel. 23-08-86-00; fax 23-08-86-01; e-mail post@transport.no; internet www .transport.no; f. 1929 as Norges Rutebileieres Forbund; present name adopted 2011; Dir-Gen. JON H. STORDRANGE.

Norges Bilbransjeforbund (NBF) (Asscn of Norwegian Motor Car Dealers and Services): Majorstua, POB 5486, 0305 Oslo; tel. 22-54-21-00; fax 23-08-79-80; e-mail firmapost@nbf.no; internet www.nbf.no; f. 1928; Admin. Dir STIG MORTEN NILSEN; 1,200 mems.

Norsk Industri (Fed. of Norwegian Industries): Middelthunsgt. 27, POB 7072 Majorstua, 0306 Oslo; tel. 23-08-88-00; e-mail post@ norskindustri.no; internet www.norskindustri.no; f. 2005 by merger of Teknologibedriftenes Landsforening (Fed. of Norwegian Manufacturing Industries) and Prosessindustriens Landsforening (Fed. of Norwegian Process Industries); Chair. PER A. SØRLIE; Admin. Dir STEIN LIER-HANSEN; c. 2,200 mems.

Skogbrukets Landsforening (SL) (Forestry Asscn): Middelthunsgt. 27, POB 5496, Majorstua 0305 Oslo; tel. 23-08-86-80; fax 23-08-86-75; e-mail firmapost@skogbruk.no; internet www .skogbruk.no; f. 1928 as Skogbrukets Arbeidsgiverforening; present name adopted 1994; Admin. Dir GAUTE LENVIK; 120 mems.

Treforedlingsindustriens Bransjeforening (TFB) (Norwegian Pulp and Paper Association): Middelthunsgt. 27, POB 7072, Majorstua, 0306 Oslo; tel. 23-08-88-08; fax 23-08-78-99; e-mail mhf@norskindustri.no; internet www.norskindustri.no/ treforedling; f. 1891; Man. Dir MARIT HOLTERMANN FOSS; 18 mems.

Bryggeri- og Drikkevareforeningen (Norwegian Breweries and Soft Drink Producers): POB 7087 Majorstua, 0306 Oslo; tel. 23-08-86-96; fax 23-08-87-01; e-mail info@drikkeglede.no; internet www .drikkeglede.no; f. 1901; Man. Dir PETTER NOME; 40 mems.

Entreprenørforeningen—Bygg og Anlegg (General Contractors): Middelthunsgt. 27, POB 5485 Majorstua, 0305 Oslo; tel. 23-08-75-00; fax 23-08-75-30; e-mail firmapost@eba.no; internet www .ebanett.no; Chair. SVEN CHRISTIAN ULVATNE; 220 mems.

Hovedorganisasjonen Virke (Federation of Commercial and Service Enterprises): Henrik Ibsensgt. 90, POB 2900 Solli, 0230 Oslo; tel. 22-54-17-00; fax 22-56-17-00; e-mail info@virke.no; internet www .virke.no; f. 1990 by merger; 15,000 mem. cos; Pres. SVERRE LEIRO.

Norsk olje og gass (Oil and Gas Industry): Vassbotnen 1, POB 8065, 4068 Stavanger; tel. 51-84-65-00; e-mail firmapost@norog.no; internet www.norskoljeoggass.no; Admin. Dir GRO BRÆKKEN.

UTILITIES
Electricity

Bergenshalvøens Kommunale Kraftselskap AS (BKK): Kokstadvegen 37, POB 7050, 5020 Bergen; tel. 55-12-70-00; fax 55-12-70-01; e-mail firmapost@bkk.no; internet www.bkk.no; f. 1920; production, distribution and supply of electricity; supplies customers throughout western Norway; 49.9% stake owned by Statkraft AS, 37.75% owned by Bergen city council, 12.35% owned by 16 other municipalities; Chair. MARTIN SMITH-SIVERTSEN; CEO ATLE NETELAND.

Fjordkraft AS: Folke Bernadottes Vei 38, POB 3507, Fyllingsdalen, 5845 Bergen; tel. 06-11-0; fax 33-46-63-73; e-mail kundeservice@ fjordkraft.no; internet www.fjordkraft.no; electricity supplier; owned by BKK, Skagerak Energi and Statkraft; Man. Dir SVERRE GJESSING; c. 325,000 customers.

Hafslund ASA: Drammensvn 144, 0247 Oslo; tel. 22-43-50-00; internet www.hafslund.no; f. 1898; electrical generation (9 hydroelectric plants), sales, distribution, safety, installation, security and network infrastructure; Chair. BIRGER MAGNUS; CEO FINN BJØRN RUYTER.

Lyse Energi AS: Breiflåtvn 18, POB 8124, 4017 Stavanger; tel. 51-90-80-00; internet www.lyse.no; f. 1998; production, distribution and supply of electricity; also supplier of natural gas and telecommunications services; owned by 16 municipalities in south Rogaland (incl. Stavanger city council); Chair. IVAR RUSDAL; Man. Dir EIMUND NYGAARD.

Nordkraft AS: Teknologivn 2A, POB 55, 8517 Narvik; tel. 02-27-5; e-mail post@nordkraft.no; internet www.nordkraft.no; f. 2006 by merger of Nordkraft AS and Narvik Energi AS; production of electricity (hydroelectric power plants and wind power farms); 50.01% owned by Narvik municipal council, 33.33% owned by DONG Energy A/S (Denmark), 16.66% owned by Hålogaland Kraft AS; Chair. SIGVE NILS STOKLAND; Admin. Dir JEAN-OTTO KARLSEN.

Salten Kraftsamband AS (SKS): Eliasbakken 7, POB 606, 8205 Fauske; tel. 75-40-22-00; e-mail firmapost@sks.no; internet www.sks .no; production, distribution and supply of electricity nation-wide; 40% owned by Bodø municipal council, 23.7% by DONG Energy A/S (Denmark); Man. Dir LEIF FINSVEEN.

Statkraft Varme AS: Sluppenv. 6, POB 2400, 7005 Trondheim; tel. 73-96-10-11; fax 73-96-11-90; e-mail firmapost@statkraftvarme.no; internet www.statkraftvarme.no; f. 1901 as Trondheim Energiverk; present name adopted 2011; production and supply of electricity in Sør-Trøndelag; owned by Statkraft AS; Chair. JON BRANDSAR.

Statnett SF: Husebybakken 28B, POB 5192 Majorstua, 0302 Oslo; tel. 23-90-30-00; fax 23-90-30-01; e-mail firmapost@statnett.no; internet www.statnett.no; f. 1992; national power grid co; supervises and co-ordinates the operation of the entire Norwegian power system, also operates own transmission lines and submarine cables, as well as sub-stations and switching stations; state-owned co under the jurisdiction of the Ministry of Petroleum and Energy; Pres. and CEO AUKE LONT.

Ustekveikja Energi AS: Geilovegen 68, 3580 Geilo; tel. 32-08-70-00; fax 32-08-70-10; e-mail post@ustekveikja.no; internet www .ustekveikja.no; f. 1992; producer and retailer of electricity; supplies customers throughout Norway; Man. Dir BJØRN SKARET.

Other major production and distribution companies include Agder Energi AS, Åkershus Energi AS, Bodø Energi AS, Fredrikstad Energi AS, Haugaland Kraft AS, HelgelandsKraft AS, Istad AS, Oppland Energi AS, Østfold Energi AS, Skagerak Energi AS, Sira-Kvina Kraftselskap, Troms Kraft AS, TrønderEnergi AS and Agder Energiverk.

Water
Responsibility for water supply in Norway lies with the municipalities.

TRADE UNIONS

National Confederations

Landsorganisasjonen i Norge (LO) (Norwegian Confederation of Trade Unions): Folkets Hus, Youngstorget 11, 0181 Oslo; tel. 23-06-10-00; fax 23-06-11-00; e-mail inter@lo.no; internet www.lo.no; f. 1899; Pres. GERD KRISTIANSEN; 880,000 mems in 22 affiliated unions (2013).

Unio (Confederation of Unions for Professionals): Stortingsgt 2, 0158 Oslo; tel. 22-70-88-50; fax 22-70-88-60; e-mail post@unio.no; internet www.unio.no; f. 2001; Pres. ANDERS FOLKESTAD; 300,000 mems in 10 affiliated unions (Jan. 2012).

Yrkesorganisasjonenes Sentralforbund (YS) (Confederation of Vocational Unions): Brugt. 19, 0186 POB 9232, Grønland, Oslo; tel. 21-01-36-00; fax 21-01-37-20; e-mail post@ys.no; internet www.ys .no; f. 1977; Pres. TORE EUGEN KVALHEIM; 215,000 mems in 21 affiliated unions.

Transport

RAILWAYS

In 2011 there were 4,191 km of railways, of which 2,516 km were electrified. There is a 60 km high-speed railway line in Gardermoen, between the Oslo Central station and Eidsvoll via Oslo airport. In June 2010 the first phase of the Bergen Light Rail, a 9.8-km line with 15 stations connecting Bergen Valley to Nesttun, was opened. Fur-

www.europaworld.com

ther construction from Nesttun to Rådal started in January 2011 and was expected to open in mid-2013.

Jernbaneverket (JBV) (Norwegian National Rail Administration): POB 4350, 2308 Hamar; Stortorvet 7, Oslo; tel. 22-45-50-00; fax 22-45-54-99; e-mail dsft@jbv.no; internet www.jernbaneverket .no; f. 1996; manages railway infrastructure; Dir-Gen. ELISABETH ENGER.

Norges Statsbaner AS (NSB) (Norwegian State Railways): Prinsensgt. 7–9, 0048 Oslo; tel. 23-62-00-00; fax 23-15-33-00; internet www.nsb.no; f. 1854 as private line; govt-owned; Chair. INGEBORG MOEN BORGERUD; CEO GEIR ISAKSEN.

ROADS

In 2010 there were 93,509 km of public roads in Norway, of which 417 km were motorways and 10,496 km were national main roads.

Statens vegvesen Vegdirektoratet: Brynsengfaret 6A, POB 8142 Dep., 0033 Oslo; tel. 91-50-20-30; fax 22-07-37-68; e-mail firmapost@ vegvesen.no; internet www.vegvesen.no; f. 1864; Dir TERJE MOE GUSTAVSEN.

SHIPPING

At 31 December 2012 the Norwegian flag registered fleet numbered 2,365 vessels, with a combined displacement of 17.9m. grt. of which 59 were bulk vessels, 619 were fishing vessels and 237 were general cargo ships. The total includes vessels on the Norwegian International Ship Register (established in 1987), which numbered 569 vessels at 31 December 2012, with a combined displacement of 13.9m. grt.

Port Authorities

Port of Ålesund: Skansekaia, 6002 Ålesund; tel. 70-16-34-00; fax 70-16-34-01; e-mail post@alesund.havn.no; internet www.alesund .havn.no; Harbour Master BIRGER FLEM.

Port of Bergen: POB 6040, 5892 Bergen; Bergen & Omland Havnevesen, Nøstegt. 30, 5010 Bergen; tel. 55-56-89-50; fax 55-56-89-86; e-mail bergen.havn@bergen.kommune.no; internet www .bergenhavn.no; Port Dir INGE TANGERÅS.

Port of Bodø: POB 138, 8001 Bodø; Bodøterminalen, 4th Floor, Rønvikleira; tel. 75-55-10-80; fax 75-55-10-90; e-mail firmapost@ bodohavn.no; internet www.bodohavn.no; Port Dir INGVAR M. MATHISEN.

Borg Harbour: Borg Havnevesen, Øravn 27, 1630 Gamle Fredrikstad; tel. 69-35-89-00; fax 69-35-89-20; e-mail firmapost@borg-havn .no; internet www.borg-havn.no; Harbour Dir TORE LUNDESTAD.

Flekkefjord Port: Flekkefjord Havnevesen, Kirkegt 50, 4400 Flekkefjord; tel. 38-32-80-00; fax 38-32-80-09; e-mail post@ flekkefjord.kommune.no; internet flekkefjord.kommune.no; Harbour Master PETTER TAGHOLDT.

Flora Hamn KF: POB 17, 6901 Florø; tel. 57-75-67-40; fax 57-74-09-16; e-mail audun.korneliussen@flora.kommune.no; internet florahamn.no; Harbour Master AUDUN KORNELIUSSEN.

Grenland Harbour: Grenland Havnevesen, POB 20, 3991 Brevik; tel. 35-93-10-00; fax 35-93-10-11; e-mail ghv@grenland-havn.no; internet www.grenland-havn.no; Port Dir FINN FLOGSTAD.

Halden Port: Halden Havnevesen, Langbrygga 3 Halden 1750 Halden; tel. 69-18-32-00; fax 69-18-06-80; e-mail post@haldenhavn .no; internet www.haldenhavn.no; Harbour Master ØYVIND JOHANNESSEN.

Port of Hammerfest: Hammerfest Havnevesen KF, POB 123, 9615 Hammerfest; tel. 78-40-74-00; fax 78-40-74-01; e-mail post@ hammerfest.havn.no; internet www.hammerfesthavn.no; f. 1828; Harbour Master ROLL HARTO STIANSEN.

Haugesund Port Authority: Karmsund Interkommunale Havnevesen, Killingøy, POB 186, 55001 Haugesund; tel. 52-70-37-50; e-mail postmottak@karmsund-havn.no; internet www .karmsund-havn.no; Port Dir SIGURD EIKJE.

Horten Port: Horten Havnevesen, Tollbugt. 2, POB 167, 3192 Horten; tel. 33-08-64-00; fax 33-08-63-91; e-mail postmottak@ hortenhavn.no; internet www.hortenhavn.no; Harbour Master ERIK ANDERSEN.

Karmsund Port: Karmsund Havnevesen, Skillebekkgt 1, POB 186, 5501 Haugesund; tel. 52-70-37-50; fax 52-70-37-65; e-mail post@ karmsund-havn.no; internet www.karmsund-havn.no; Harbour Master FRODE JØRGENSEN.

Kirkenes Port: Municipality of Sør-Varanger, Storgt. 5, POB 406, 9915 Kirkenes; tel. 78-97-74-44; fax 78-97-75-89; e-mail havnevesenet@svk.no; internet www.kirkenes-havn.no; Port Capt. MAUNG SAN LWIN; Port Dir EIVIND GADE-LUNDLIE.

Kristiansund and Nordmøre Port: Kristiansand Havn KF, Gravane 4, POB 114, 4662 Kristiansand; tel. 38-00-60-00; fax 38-02-70-99; e-mail post@kristiansand-havn.no; internet www .kristiansand-havn.no; Port Dir JAN ODDVAR SKISLAND.

Kristiansund Port: Kristiansund og Nordmøre Havn IKS, Astrupsgt. 9, 6509 Kristiansund; tel. 40-00-65-04; fax 71-67-14-83; e-mail info@knhavn.no; internet www.knhavn.no; Port Capt. ERLEND FURU.

Port of Larvik: Larvik Havn KF, POB 246 Sentrum, Havnegt. 5, 3251 Larvik; tel. 33-18-07-72; fax 33-16-57-59; e-mail post@larvik .havn.no; internet www.larvik.havn.no; Port Dir JAN FREDRIK JONAS.

Port of Mandal: Mandal Havnevesen KF, POB 905, 4509 Mandal; tel. 40-00-51-52; fax 38-27-34-76; e-mail mandalhavn@mandal .kommune.no; internet www.mandal-kommune.no/mandalhavn; Dir KIRSTEN HUSER LESCHBRANDT.

Port of Mongstad: Statoil Mongstad, 5954 Mongstad; tel. 56-34-40-00; fax 56-34-47-29; e-mail jja@statoilhydro.com; Port Capt. JON M. JAKOBSEN.

Port of Moss: Moss Havnevesen, Moss Maritime Centre, Strandgt. 10, POB 118, 1501 Moss; tel. 69-20-87-00; e-mail firmapost@ moss-havn.no; internet www.moss-havn.no; Harbour Master REIDAR MAGNUS HANSEN.

Port of Narvik: Narvik Havn KF, POB 627, 8508 Narvik; tel. 76-95-03-70; fax 76-95-03-84; e-mail post@narvikhavn.no; internet www .portofnarvik.com; Port Dir. RUNE J. ARNØY.

Port of Orkanger: Orkanger Havnevesen, POB 83, 7300 Orkanger; tel. 72-48-00-09; fax 72-48-10-03; e-mail tom.hamborg@orkdal .kommune.no; Port Man. TOM HAMBORG.

Port of Oslo: POB 230 Sentrum, 0103 Oslo; tel. 81-50-06-06; fax 22-41-54-02; e-mail postmottak@hav.oslo.kommune.no; internet www .oslohavn.no; Port Dir ANNE SIGRID HAMRAN.

Sandefjord Port: Sandefjord Havnevesen, Tollbugt. 1, 3210 Sandefjord; tel. 33-41-64-38; fax 33-46-26-13; e-mail havnefogd@ sandefjord.kommune.no; internet www.cruisesandefjord.com; Harbour Master BJØRNAR CHRISTIANSEN.

Port of Sauda: Sauda Havnekontor, 4200 Sauda; tel. 52-78-62-21; fax 52-78-39-68; Harbour Master HARALD HALVORSEN LOELAND.

Port of Stavanger: Stavangerregionen Havnedrift, Strandkaien 46, 4005 Stavanger; tel. 51-50-12-00; fax 51-50-12-21; e-mail post@ stavanger.havn.no; internet www.stavanger.havn.no; Port Dir FINN P. OLSEN.

Tønsberg Port: Tønsberg Havnevesen, Nedre Langgate 36, 3126 Tønsberg; tel. 33-35-45-00; fax 33-33-26-75; e-mail tonsberg.havn@ tonsberg.kommune.no; internet www.tonsberghavn.no; Harbour Master PER SVENNAR.

Port of Tromsø: Tromsø Havnevesen, Kirkegt. 1, POB 392, 9254 Tromsø; tel. 77-66-18-50; fax 77-66-18-51; e-mail adm@tromso.havn .no; internet www.tromso.havn.no; f. 1827; Port Dir HALVAR PETTERSEN.

Trondheim Port: Trondheim Havn, POB 1234 Sluppen, 7462 Trondheim; tel. 73-99-17-00; fax 73-99-17-17; e-mail firmapost@ trondheim.havn.no; internet www.trondheim.havn.no; Port Dir WOLLERT KROHN-HANSEN.

Vardø Port: Vardø Havn KF, Kaigt. 26A, POB 50, 9951 Vardø; tel. 78-98-72-76; fax 78-98-78-28; e-mail vardhavn@online.no; internet www.vardoport.no; f. 2003; Harbour Master INGOLF ERIKSEN.

Shipping Organizations

NHO Sjøfart (Federation of Norwegian Coastal Shipping): Middelthunsgt. 27, POB 5201 Majorstua, 0302 Oslo; tel. 23-08-85-60; fax 23-08-85-61; e-mail post@nhosjofart.no; internet www.nhosjofart .no; Man. Dir HARALD THOMASSEN.

Nordisk Skibsrederforening (Nordisk Defence Club): Kristinelundvn 22, POB 3033 Elisenberg, 0207 Oslo; tel. 22-13-56-00; fax 22-43-00-35; e-mail post@nordisk.no; internet www.nordisk.no; f. 1889; Chair. NILS P. DYVIK.

Norges Rederiforbund (Norwegian Shipowners' Asscn): Rådhusgaten 25, POB 1452 Vika, 0116 Oslo; tel. 22-40-15-00; fax 22-40-15-15; e-mail post@rederi.no; internet www.rederi.no; f. 1909; Pres. TROND KLEIVDAL; Dir-Gen. STURLA HENRIKSEN.

Norsk Skipsmeglerforbund (Norwegian Shipbrokers' Asscn): Rådhusgt. 25, POB 1895 Vika, 0158 Oslo; tel. 22-33-02-00; e-mail mail@shipbroker.no; internet www.shipbroker.no; f. 1919; Pres. THOMAS MACODY LUND; Gen. Man. KNUT FRODE ERIKSEN; 138 mems.

Det Norske Veritas (DNV): Veritasvn 1, POB 300, 1322 Høvik; tel. 67-57-99-00; e-mail dnv.corporate@dnv.com; internet www.dnv.no; f. 1864; global provider of services for managing risk; acts on behalf of 130 national maritime authorities; CEO HENRIK O. MADSEN.

Principal Companies

Bergshav Management AS: POB 8, 4891 Grimstad; tel. 37-25-63-00; fax 37-25-63-01; e-mail mgmt@bergshav.com; internet www .bergshav.com; Chair. ATLE BERGSHAVEN.

BW Gas ASA: Prof. Kohtsvei 5, POB 443, 1327 Lysaker; tel. 67-21-16-00; fax 67-21-16-01; e-mail bwgas@bwgas.com; internet www

.bwgas.com; f. 1935; fmrly Bergesen d.y. ASA; Chair. MORTEN SIG. BERGESEN; Group CEO ANDREAS SOHMEN-PAO.

Grieg Shipping AS: Sundtsgt. 17–19, POB 234 Sentrum, 5804 Bergen; tel. 55-57-66-00; fax 55-57-68-55; internet www.grieg.no; Chair. ELISABETH GRIEG.

Leif Høegh & Co ASA: Wergelandsvn 7, POB 2596 Solli, 0203 Oslo; tel. 22-86-97-00; fax 22-20-14-08; e-mail ihc@hoegh.no; internet www.hoegh.no; f. 1927; vessels for the transport of liquefied gas, ores and other bulk materials, car and ro-ro ships and reefers; world-wide services; Chief Exec. THOR J. GUTTORMSEN; Chair. WESTYE HØEGH.

Hurtigruten ASA: Havnegata 2, POB 8514, Narvik; tel. 81-00-30-30; fax 76-96-76-01; e-mail firmapost@hurtigruten.com; internet www.hurtigruten.com; f. 1893; coastal ferries and cruise ships; CEO DANIEL SKJELDAM.

Jahre-Wallem AS: Strandpromenaden 9, POB 271, 3201 Sandefjord; tel. 33-48-44-44; e-mail jawa@jawa.no; subsidiary of the Wallem Group; Man. Dir HENRIK LIAN.

Jebsens Management AS: Gullskogarden, Bryggen 47, 5003 Bergen; tel. 53-05-00-00; fax 53-05-00-51; e-mail jema@jebsens.no; internet www.jebsens.com; f. 1929; services in Scandinavia, and to Europe, Far East, Australia and the Americas; Chair. BJØRN JEBSEN.

Torvald Klaveness & Co AS: Drammensvn 260, POB 182 Skøyen, 0212 Oslo; tel. 22-52-60-00; fax 22-52-67-40; e-mail management@klaveness.com; internet www.klaveness.com; Chair. TROND HARALD KLAVENESS; CEO LASSE KRISTOFFERSEN.

Knutsen OAS Shipping AS: Smedasundet 40, POB 2017, 5504 Haugesund; tel. 52-70-40-00; fax 52-70-40-40; e-mail firmapost@knutsenoas.com; internet www.knutsenoas.com; Man. Dir TRYGVE SEGLEM.

AS J. Ludwig Mowinckels Rederi: Bradbenken 1, POB 4130 Dreggen, 5835 Bergen; tel. 55-21-64-00; fax 55-21-63-10; e-mail msm@mshipm.com; internet www.jlmr.no; f. 1898; tankers and cargo services; CEO GEIR BELSNES.

Norbroker Shipping & Trading AS: Elvegt. 2, POB 34, 4401 Flekkefjord; tel. 38-32-61-00; fax 38-32-61-01; e-mail drycargo@norbroker.no; internet www.norbroker.no; f. 1993; Man. Dir ARNT IVAR BJOERNELI.

Odfjell ASA: Conrad Mohrsveg 29, POB 6101 Postterminalen, 5892 Bergen; tel. 55-27-00-00; fax 55-28-47-41; e-mail presscontact@odfjell.com; internet www.odfjell.no; f. 1916; transportation and storage of liquid chemicals; Chair. LAURENCE WARD ODFJELL.

Fred.Olsen Marine Services AS: Prinsensgt. 2B, POB 374 Sentrum, 0101 Oslo; tel. 22-34-11-00; e-mail foms@foms.no; internet www.fredolsen-marine.com; Man. Dir LEIF LAURITZEN.

OSM Ship Management AS: Rådhusgt. 3, POB 69, 4661 Kristiansand; tel. 41-49-20-00; fax 40-47-98-00; e-mail osm.krs@osm.no; internet www.osm.no; part of OSM Group; fmrly Rasmussen Maritime Services AS; Man. Dir DAGFINN ANDERSEN.

Det Stavangerske Dampskibsselskab: POB 848, 4004 Stavanger; tel. 51-84-56-00; fax 51-84-56-01; e-mail mail@dsd-shipping.no; internet www.dsd-shipping.no; f. 1855; Man. Dir ODDVAR HAUSKEN.

Teekay Shipping Norway AS: Vervn. 4, POB 8035, 4068 Stavanger; tel. 51-44-27-00; fax 51-44-28-00; fmrly called Bona Shipping; Dir and Chair. C. SEAN DAY.

Uglands Rederi AS: POB 128, 4891 Grimstad; tel. 37-29-26-00; fax 37-04-47-22; e-mail jjuc@jjuc.no; internet www.jjuc.no; f. 1930; part of J. J. Ugland Cos.

A. Wilhelmsen Gruppen AS: Beddingen 8, Aker Brygge, POB 1583 Vika, 0118 Oslo; tel. 22-01-42-00; fax 22-01-43-74; e-mail thagen@awilco.no; internet awilhelmsen.no; Chair. ARNE ALEXANDER WILHELMSEN; Group CEO SIGURD E. THORVILDSEN.

Wilh. Wilhelmsen ASA: Strandvn 20, POB 33, 1324 Lysaker; tel. 67-58-40-00; fax 67-58-40-80; e-mail ww@wilhelmsen.com; internet www.wilhelmsen.com; f. 1861; regular fast freight services world-wide; Chair. DIDERIK SCHNITLER; CEO JAN EYVIN WANG.

CIVIL AVIATION

In 2010 there were 98 airports in Norway, the principal international airport being Gardermoen Airport, 47 km north of Oslo.

Avinor AS: POB 150, 2061 Gardermoen; Oslo Atrium, Dronning Eufemias gt. 6, 0191 Oslo; tel. 81-53-05-50; fax 64-81-20-01; e-mail post@avinor.no; internet www.avinor.no; f. 2003; state-owned; owns and operates 46 airports in Norway and responsible for air traffic control services; Chair. OLA MØRKVED RINNAN; CEO FALK PETERSEN.

Luftfartstilsynet (Civil Aviation Authority): POB 243, 8001 Bodø; tel. 75-58-50-00; fax 75-58-50-05; e-mail postmottak@caa.no; internet luftfartstilsynet.no; f. 2000; independent administrative body under the Ministry of Transport and Communications; Aviation Dir STEIN ERIK NODELAND.

Principal Airlines

Norwegian Air Shuttle ASA: Oksenøyvn 3, POB 115, 1330 Fornebu; tel. 67-59-30-00; fax 67-59-30-01; e-mail post@norwegian.no; internet www.norwegian.no; f. 1966; present name since 1993; low-cost carrier, offering flights to domestic and European destinations; established Norwegian Cargo SA in 2013; CEO BJØRN KJOS.

SAS Norge ASA: 0800 Oslo; tel. 64-81-77-00; fax 67-58-78-77; internet www.sas.no; f. 2004 as SAS Braathens; present name adopted 2007; wholly owned subsidiary of the Scandinavian Airlines System (SAS) Group; Gen. Man. OLA H. STRAND.

Scandinavian Airlines System (SAS): Head Office: Snarøyvn 57, 0080 Oslo; tel. 64-81-60-50; e-mail cr@sas.no; internet www.sas.no; f. 1946; the national carrier of Denmark, Norway and Sweden; consortium owned two-sevenths by SAS Danmark A/S, two-sevenths by SAS Norge ASA and three-sevenths by SAS Sverige AB; parent org. 50% owned by the Govt and 50% by private shareholders; SAS group includes the consortium and the subsidiaries in which the consortium has a majority or otherwise controlling interest; the Board consists of 2 members from each of the parent cos and the chairmanship rotates among the 3 national chairmen on an annual basis; strategic alliance with Lufthansa (Germany) formed in 1995; Chair. FRITZ H. SCHUR; Pres. and CEO RICKARD GUSTAFSON.

Widerøes Flyveselskap AS: Langstranda 6, POB 247, 8001 Bodø; tel. 75-51-35-00; fax 75-51-35-81; e-mail kundservice@wideroe.no; internet www.wideroe.no; f. 1934; subsidiary of Scandinavian Airlines System (SAS) Group; scheduled domestic service and flights to destinations in Denmark, Russia, Sweden and the United Kingdom; Pres. and CEO LARS KOBBERSTAD.

Tourism

Norway is a popular resort for tourists who prefer holidays in rugged, peaceful surroundings. It is also a centre for winter sports. In 2011 visitor arrivals totalled some 3m.; receipts from tourism amounted to an estimated US $5,301m. that year.

Innovasjon Norge (Innovation Norway): Akersgt 13, POB 448 Sentrum, 0104 Oslo; tel. 22-00-25-00; fax 22-00-25-01; e-mail post@innovasjonnorge.no; internet www.innovasjonnorge.no; f. 2004 to replace Norges Turistråd (Norwegian Tourist Board), Norges Eksportråd (Norwegian Trade Council), Statens nærings- og distriktsutviklingsfond (SND-Industrial and Regional Development Fund) and Statens Veiledningskontor for Oppfinnere (SVO-Government Consultative Office for Inventors); state-owned; operates in all Norwegian counties and more than 30 countries worldwide; Chair. REIDAR SANDAL; Pres. and CEO GUNN OVESEN.

Defence

Norway is a member of the North Atlantic Treaty Organization (NATO). Every male is liable for 12 months' national service at the age of 19. Periodical refresher programmes are also compulsory until the age of 44. The total strength of the armed forces, as assessed at November 2012, was 24,450 (including 7,700 conscripts): army 8,900 (4,400 conscripts); navy 3,900 (1,450 conscripts); air force 3,650 (including 850 conscripts); home guard 500; and central support, administration and command 7,750 (conscripts 1,000). There is also a mobilization reserve of 45,190 (army 270, navy 320, home guard 44,250 and central support 350). In November 2004 the European Union (EU) ministers responsible for defence agreed to create 13 'battlegroups' (each numbering about 1,500 men), which could be deployed at short notice to crisis areas around the world. The EU battlegroups, two of which were to be ready for deployment at any one time, following a rotational schedule, reached full operational capacity from 1 January 2007. In December 2004 the Storting gave qualified approval for Norway's participation, with Finland and Sweden, in a joint Nordic Battlegroup, which was subsequently joined by Estonia and Ireland. Norway provides 150 of the group's 2,850 soldiers (most of whom are provided by Sweden). In November 2012 Denmark, Finland, Iceland, Norway and Sweden agreed to operate military transport aircraft jointly.

Defence Expenditure: Budget estimated at 40,500m. kroner for 2012.

Chief of Defence: Gen. HARALD SUNDE.

Chief of Defence Staff: Vice-Adm. JAN EIRIK FINSETH.

Chief of the Army Staff: Maj.-Gen. PER SVERRET OPEDAL.

Chief of the Naval Staff: Rear Adm. BERNT GRIMSTVEDT.

Chief of the Air Force Staff: Maj.-Gen. FINN KRISTIAN HANNESTAD.

Chief of the Home Guard Staff: Maj.-Gen. KRISTIN LUND.

Education

The Ministry of Education and Research has overall responsibility for education and manages tertiary education directly. Compulsory education is supervised by the municipal authorities, while upper secondary education is managed by the county authorities. Non-compulsory pre-primary education is offered to children less than six years of age. Compulsory education begins at six years of age and lasts for 10 years. Elementary education is divided into two phases. The primary phase (*Barnetrinnet*) is meant for children between the ages of six and 12 years, and the lower secondary phase (*Ungdomstrinnet*) for children between 13 and 16 years of age. Completion of lower secondary entitles pupils to transfer to an upper secondary school (*Videregående skole*) for a course lasting three years. Primary enrolment in 2010/11 included 99% of children in the relevant age-group, while the comparable rate for secondary enrolment was 94%.

Adults who did not complete compulsory education, or who wish to refresh their competence, have a statutory right to lower secondary education. This also applies to special education. Upon completion of a three-year course at an upper secondary school, pupils may seek admission to one of Norway's seven universities or other colleges. In 2008/09 there were 77 institutes of higher education (including universities) in Norway. From the age of 25 years adults have the right to be assessed for admittance to higher education based on non-formal learning. A broader system of higher professional education has been organized on a regional basis, including colleges of education and technology. In 2011 some 250,456 students were enrolled in higher education establishments, including universities. General government expenditure on education in 2011 was estimated at 151,694m. kroner (equivalent to 12.6% of total government expenditure).

NORWEGIAN EXTERNAL TERRITORIES
SVALBARD

Introductory Survey

LOCATION AND CLIMATE

The Svalbard archipelago is the northernmost part of the Kingdom of Norway. It lies in the Arctic Sea, 657 km north of mainland Norway, between latitudes 74°N and 81°N and longitudes 10°E and 35°E, comprising a total area of 61,022 sq km (23,561 sq miles). The group consists of nine principal islands—the main island, Spitsbergen (formerly Vestspitsbergen), Kvitøya, Edgeøya, Barentsøya, Nordaustlandet, Prins Karls Forland, Kong Karls Land, Hopen and Bjørnøya (Bear Island), some 204 km to the south of the main island—together with numerous small islands. Mild Atlantic winds lessen the severity of the Arctic climate, but almost 60% of the land area is covered with glaciers. Average temperatures range from −16°C (3°F) to 6°C (43°F), and precipitation in the lowlands averages some 200 mm per year. The main settlement is Longyearbyen.

CONTEMPORARY POLITICAL HISTORY

The existence of Svalbard has probably been known since Viking exploration in the 12th century. There were conflicting claims to sovereignty by England and Scotland, the Netherlands and the joint entity of Denmark and Norway in the 17th century, when the area was an important centre for whale hunting, but interest subsequently lapsed until the early years of the 20th century, when coal deposits were discovered. On 9 February 1920 14 nations signed a treaty recognizing Norwegian sovereignty over Svalbard (another 27 nations subsequently signed the treaty). International rights of access and economic exploitation were agreed, but the use of the islands for military purposes and the construction of fortifications were expressly forbidden. Svalbard was formally incorporated as part of the Kingdom of Norway in 1925.

In 1941 the population was evacuated by Allied forces for the duration of the Second World War; three years later the USSR, to which Svalbard was of considerable strategic interest, unsuccessfully sought Norway's agreement to a revision of the 1920 treaty whereby part of the archipelago would become a Soviet-Norwegian condominium. Russia currently maintains a helicopter station, a mobile radar station and a consulate adjoining its coal-mining settlement at Barentsburg on Spitsbergen. Russia (as the USSR before it) continues to refuse to recognize Norway's unilateral declaration (made in 1977) of a 370-km fisheries protection zone around Svalbard. The Norwegian coastguard regularly detains Russian fishing vessels operating within this zone. In September 2010 Russia and Norway signed a treaty establishing the maritime border between the Svalbard archipelago and the Novaya Zemlya archipelago.

Owing to its international rights of access, Svalbard, unlike mainland Norway, is not covered by the terms of the Schengen agreement of the European Union (EU), which abolishes border controls between signatories. In order to aid compliance with the Schengen agreement, in February 2011 the Norwegian authorities introduced identity controls for all arrivals in Svalbard, including Norwegian nationals.

Particularly since the promulgation of a Royal Decree in 1971, the Norwegian administration has endeavoured to protect the flora, fauna and environment of Svalbard. The protected areas, which total 39,815 sq km of land, or 64% of the land area, and 76,293 km of sea, include seven national parks, the most recently created (September 2005) being at Indre Wijdefjorden in northern Spitsbergen. From April 2007 visitors to Svalbard were required to pay an 'environment fee', the income from which was to be added to the territory's environmental protection fund.

Apart from a small permanent research station established by Poland, only Norway and Russia maintain permanent settlements on Svalbard. In order to continue Norwegian occupation of Svalbard, thus ensuring its future as a Norwegian territory and protecting it from potential, rival claims for sovereignty, notably from Russia, in 2000 the Svalbard administration proposed the establishment of a new coal mine on Spitsbergen to exploit newly discovered reserves; the new mine, at Svea Nord, about 60 km south of Longyearbyen, was opened in the following year and is operated by Store Norske Spitsbergen Grubekompani AS (SNSG)—a wholly-owned subsidiary of the Norwegian state-owned coal company Store Norske Spitsbergen Kulkompani (SNSK). SNSK has two other susidiaries—Store Norske Boliger, which owns and lets the group's residential accommodation to tenants, and Store Norske Gull, which conducts gold-prospecting operations. There is another, smaller SNSG-run coal mine, the Gruve 7 mine (which has been in production since 1975),

lying some 15 km from Longyearbyen, and the company planned to open a third mine, at Lunkefjell, about 2 km from Svea Nord, in September 2013. Following the outbreak in October 2006 of an underground fire at the coal mine operated by Russian state-owned coal company Arktikugol in the Russian/Ukrainian settlement of Barentsburg, no mining took place until the recommencement of operations at the end of 2010. Svalbard has also been promoted as a centre for scientific research; at the end of 2000 there were more than 20 scientific stations from foreign countries on the islands. The University Centre in Svalbard, which was established in Longyearbyen in 1993, offers courses in arctic sciences to around 350 students. In June 2005 the Arctic Marine Laboratory was opened at Ny-Ålesund on Spitsbergen. In February 2008 the Svalbard Global Seed Vault was officially opened by the Norwegian Prime Minister, Jens Stoltenberg. Established at a depth of 130 m in the permafrost of a mountain at Longyearbyen, the vault was designed to store up to 4.5m. seed samples from around the world, in order to preserve biological diversity for future generations.

In November 2001 Norwegians resident on Spitsbergen conducted, for the first time, elections for a local council. The new Longyearbyen Council (Longyearbyen Lokalstyre) replaced the incumbent Svalbard Council, which had been partly appointed by the SNSK. The new 15-seat Council was to exercise only limited power in issues relating to health, education and the Church, which would all continue ultimately to be controlled by the State. The rate of participation in the local elections was only 51.5% of the electorate; a multi-party grouping won eight seats on the Council, while Det norske Arbeiderparti (DnA—Norwegian Labour Party) secured six seats; Høyre (Conservative) took the remaining seat. At the elections held in October 2003, DnA won six seats on the Council, while the multi-party grouping secured five seats; the Fremskrittspartiet (FrP—Progress Party) and Høyre each took two seats. The Council's mandate was increased from two to four years. DnA again emerged as the largest party following the elections of October 2007, winning seven seats on the Council; the multi-party grouping secured four seats, while Høyre received three seats and the FrP lost its representation. The rate of voter participation was recorded at just 40.3% of the electorate. At elections to the Council on 10–11 October 2011 the Arbeiderpartiet (as the DnA had renamed itself earlier in the year) won seven seats, two multi-party groupings took a combined total of five seats and Høyre secured three seats.

CONSTITUTION AND GOVERNMENT

Svalbard has been part of the Kingdom of Norway since it was formally incorporated in 1925. The territory is administered by a Sysselmann (Governor), resident at Longyearbyen, on Spitsbergen, which is the administrative centre of the archipelago. The Sysselmann is responsible to the Polar Affairs Department of the Ministry of Justice and Public Security. The Norwegian Polar Institute acts in an advisory capacity to the administration. Svalbard lies within the same judicial jurisdiction as the city of Tromsø on the mainland.

In accordance with the Svalbard Treaty of 1920, the Norwegian Government prescribed a mining code in 1925, regulating all mineral prospecting and exploitation in the islands and their territorial waters extending to 4 nautical miles (7.4 km). The Mining Code is administered by the Directorate for Mineral Management of Mines at Svalbard (Direktoratet for mineralforvaltning med Bergmesteren for Svalbard).

ECONOMIC AFFAIRS

The total population of Svalbard at 1 July 2012 was 2,642, of whom 2,195 were resident in Norwegian settlements (including 407 foreign nationals), 439 were in the Russian/Ukrainian settlement of Barentsburg and 8 in the Polish research station. There are limited recreational, transport, financial and educational facilities on Svalbard. There are hospitals in the capital, Longyearbyen (which had a population of 2,090 at 31 December 2012, according to official figures), and in Barentsburg.

Mining and quarrying is the dominant industry, with coal the islands' main product. In 2011 some 1,639,618 metric tons were shipped from mines on Svalbard (all from Norwegian mines). The Norwegian state-owned company Store Norske Spitsbergen Kulkompani (SNSK) directly employs some 390 people. SNSK produced some 1.4m. tons of coal in 2011, a decline of 28.4% compared to the previous year. SNSK's most productive mine, at Svea Nord, about 60 km from Longyearbyen, was opened in 2001 to exploit significant newly discovered reserves of coal. The coal is of high calorific value and therefore burns more cleanly than normal coal. Svea is extremely well-placed for exporting coal to Europe, as it is located only 10 km from the port at Kapp Amsterdam; the mine is linked to the port by road, and in 2004 a conveyor belt was constructed to transport the coal out of the mountain directly to the trucks. Another Norwegian coal-mining camp, Gruve 7, some 15 km from Longyearbyen, is used largely to supply a coal-burning power station, which provides electricity for Longyearbyen. In April 2011 SNSK received permission from the Svalbard Sysselmann (Governor) to open a new mine at Lunkefjell, some 2 km from Svea Nord. Following approval by the Norwegian Ministry of the Environment in December 2011, the Lunkefjell mine was scheduled to begin production in September 2013; main production was due to commence in 2015, in which year stocks at Svea Nord were expected to be exhausted.

Russia had only one settlement on Svalbard in early 2013, at Barentsburg (which had a population of 471 at 31 December 2012, according to official figures). In 2006 some 88,140 tons of coal were produced at the coal mine operated by Russian state-owned coal company Arktikugol at Barentsburg and shipped to Russia. The outbreak of an underground fire in October of that year meant that no mining took place at Barentsburg until the recommencement of operations at the end of 2010. Barentsburg, located about 55 km south-west of Longyearbyen, has its own coal-fired power station.

Deep onshore drillings for petroleum have been carried out by Norwegian and other companies, but no commercially-viable deposits were discovered. Offshore exploration for petroleum or natural gas is not permitted by the Norwegian authorities for environmental reasons. In 2003 Store Norske Gull, a subsidiary of SNSK, was founded in order to explore the potential for gold mining in Svalbard. In January 2011 the company reported that gold deposits had been discovered, although it was not yet clear if they were significant enough to be commercially exploited. Svalbard's other mineral resources include reserves of phosphate, asbestos, iron ore, anhydrite, limestone and various sulphides.

Total turnover in Svalbard in 2011 was 3,498m. kroner. The construction sector comprised 16 companies in 2011, which had a turnover of 390.0m. kroner in that year, accounting for 11.1% of the total.

Tourism has been encouraged on Svalbard; cruise ships make stops at the islands and there is also a small industry in skiing and trekking across the wilderness. In recent years, however, the authorities have become increasingly concerned about the adverse effects of the encroachment of hundreds of tourists on Svalbard's small settlements and fragile environment. Consequently, legislation has been passed, due to come into effect from the beginning of 2014, imposing strict restrictions on the size of visiting cruise ships. In 2011 visitors spent a total of 84,744 nights in Svalbard, of which 46,871 were spent by those visiting for recreational purposes. The services sector has grown substantially in recent years, particularly in the areas of education and research. Many jobs are connected to Norwegian government organizations, such as Statsbygg, the state-owned building agency, and Longyearbyen Elementary and High School.

For 2005 the Svalbard budget was 195.2m. kroner, of which 135.9m. kroner was a direct subsidy from the Norwegian state budget. In addition to the major revenue sources of coal mining, tourism and international scientific research, Svalbard also raises some revenue from the sale of hunting and fishing licences. There is no value-added tax in Svalbard.

Statistical Survey

Source: Statistics Norway, Kongensgt. 6, Oslo; tel. 21-09-00-00; fax 21-09-49-73; e-mail biblioteket@ssb.no; internet www.ssb.no.

AREA AND POPULATION

Area: 61,022 sq km (23,561 sq miles).

Population: 1,718 Norwegian nationals (1,037 males, 681 females) at census of 19 November 2011. *1 July 2012* (official estimates): 2,642 (Norwegian settlements 2,195—including 407 foreign nationals, Russian/Ukrainian settlements 439, Polish settlement 8). Note: Figure for Russian/Ukrainian settlements at 1 September 2012.

Density (at 1 July 2012): 0.04 per sq km.

Population by Age and Sex (Norwegian nationals at 2011 census): *0–14:* 337 (males 191, females 146); *15–64:* 1,341 (males 820, females 521); *65 and over:* 40 (males 26, females 14); *Total* 1,718 (males 1,037, females 681).

Economically Active Population (2003): Mining and quarrying 233; Manufacturing 8; Construction 194; Wholesale and retail trade 107; Hotels and restaurants 100; Transport and storage 177; Supporting and auxiliary transport activities 120; Public administration 147; Education, health and social work 133; Other community, social and personal service activities 15; *Total* 1,234.

MINING

Coal Shipments (Norwegian mines, '000 metric tons): 2,436.8 in 2009; 1,684.5 in 2010; 1,639.6 in 2011.

FINANCE

(Norwegian currency is used)

Budget (million kroner, 2005): Estimated revenue 195.2 (incl. direct grant of 135.9 from central Govt); Budgeted expenditure 195.2.

TRANSPORT

Road Traffic (vehicles registered at 31 December 2008): Passenger cars 1,257; Buses 39; Goods vehicles 462; Mopeds and motorcycles 187; Snow scooters 1,904.

Civil Aviation (2004, metric tons unless otherwise specified): Passengers (number) 92,958; Goods received 541; Goods sent 42; Mail received 341; Mail sent 42.

TOURISM

Overnight Stays: 79,038 in 2010; 84,744 in 2011.

Foreign Visitors by Country of Nationality (2011): Denmark 1,601; Germany 2,499; Netherlands 1,037; Norway 65,866; Sweden 2,974; United Kingdom 2,975; Total (incl. others) 84,744.

EDUCATION

(2006 unless otherwise indicated)

Pre-primary: Schools 2; Teachers 29; Pupils 137 (2011).

Primary and Lower Secondary: Schools 1; Pupils 228 (2011/12).

Upper Secondary (2004): Schools 1; Pupils 55.

Directory

The Government

(May 2013)

ADMINISTRATION

Governor (Sysselmann): ODD OLSEN INGERØ.

OFFICES

Office of the Governor: Sysselmannen på Svalbard, POB 633, 9171 Longyearbyen, Svalbard; tel. 79-02-43-00; fax 79-02-11-66; e-mail firmapost@sysselmannen.no; internet www.sysselmannen.no.

Ministry of Justice and the Public Security (Polar Affairs Department): Gullhaug Torg 4A, POB 8005 Dep., 0030 Oslo; tel. 22-24-56-01; fax 22-24-95-30; e-mail postmottak@jd.dep.no; responsible for the administration of Svalbard and Jan Mayen, and for the Norwegian Antarctic dependencies.

Norsk Polarinstitutt på Svalbard (Norwegian Polar Institute in Svalbard): Forskningsparken, POB 505, 9171 Longyearbyen, Svalbard; tel. 79-02-26-00; fax 79-02-26-04; e-mail post@npolar.no; internet www.npolar.no; f. 1928 as Norges Svalbard- og Ishavs-undersøkelser; adopted present name and expanded functions in 1948; branch of Norwegian Polar Institute, Tromsø; mapping and research institute; responsible for advising Govt on matters concerning Svalbard, Jan Mayen and the Antarctic dependencies; monitors and investigates environment of the territories; organizes regular Antarctic research expeditions; establishes and maintains aids to navigation in Svalbard waters; Dir JAN-GUNNAR WINTHER.

Norsk Polarinstitutts Forskningsstasjon (Norwegian Polar Institute Research Station): Sverdrupstasjonen, 9173 Ny-Ålesund, Svalbard; tel. 79-02-74-00; fax 79-02-70-02; permanent research base in Svalbard.

LONGYEARBYEN COUNCIL

Longyearbyen Lokalstyre: POB 350, 9171 Longyearbyen, Svalbard; tel. 79-02-21-50; fax 79-02-21-51; e-mail postmottak@lokalstyre.no; internet www.lokalstyre.no; f. 2002; first locally elected body in Svalbard; replaced Svalbard Council; 15 mems; Leader CHRISTIN KRISTOFFERSEN.

Svalbard, as an integral part of the Kingdom of Norway, has provision for its Norwegian inhabitants to participate in the national elections. For judicial matters Svalbard lies in the jurisdiction of the Nord-Troms District Court (based in Tromsø). The state Evangelical Lutheran Church provides religious services.

Press

There is only one newspaper published in the Svalbard archipelago.

Svalbardposten: POB 503, 9171 Longyearbyen, Svalbard; tel. 79-02-47-00; fax 79-02-47-01; e-mail post@svalbardposten.no; internet www.svalbardposten.no; f. 1948; weekly; Editor-in-Chief BIRGER AMUNDSEN; circ. 3,380 (2004).

Finance

Norwegian currency is used. Most banking facilities are available.

Sparebank 1 Nord-Norge: POB 518, 9171 Longyearbyen, Svalbard; tel. 79-02-29-10; fax 79-02-29-11; e-mail kundesenter@snn.no; internet www.snn.no; savings bank; Man. Dir HANS OLAV KARDE.

Trade and Industry

Bydrift Longyearbyen A/S: POB 350, 9171 Longyearbyen, Svalbard; tel. 79-02-21-50; fax 79-02-23-01; e-mail bydrift@lokalstyre.no; internet www.lokalstyre.no; state-owned; operates most local services, incl. utilities, and undertakes infrastructure devt; Admin. Dir IVAR UNDHEIM.

Direktoratet for mineralforvaltning med Bergmesteren for Svalbard (Directorate for Mineral Management of Mines at Svalbard): POB 520,9171 Longyearbyen; tel. 79-02-12-92; fax 79-02-14-24; e-mail per.brekke@dirmin.no; from 2003 the Commissioner of Mines at Svalbard was merged into the Norwegian Directorate of Mining; name changed from the Directorate of Mines at Svalbard in Jan. 2010; Dir PER ZAKKEN BREKKE.

Store Norske Spitsbergen Kulkompani A/S (SNSK): POB 613, 9171 Longyearbyen, Svalbard; tel. 79-02-52-00; fax 79-02-18-41; e-mail firmapost@snsk.no; internet www.snsk.no; state-owned; develops the Store Norske group's proprietary and coal mining rights on Svalbard, with the exception of the Svea area; Chair. BÅRD MIKKELSEN; CEO BJØRN ARNESTAD.

Store Norske Spitsbergen Grubekompani A/S (SNSG): f. 2002; manages all assets, rights, contractual obligations and liabilities in connection with the Svea Nord mine, responsible for coal production and sales in Longyearbyen and Svea, and for exploration at both its own and SNSK's claims; 350 employees.

Store Norske Boliger A/S: f. 2002; manages the group's accommodation in Longyearbyen and some of the accommodation in Svea.

Transport

The airport near Longyearbyen was opened in 1975. SAS operates services to Oslo, via Tromsø, up to six times per week. There are air strips at Ny-Ålesund and Svea, and a Russian helicopter facility at Barentsburg. Apart from helicopters, and a fixed-wing service between Longyearbyen and Ny-Ålesund, internal traffic is little developed.

AIRPORT

Svalbard Airport: POB 550, 9170 Longyearbyen, Svalbard; tel. 67-03-54-00; fax 67-03-54-01; e-mail morten.ulsnes@avinor.no; internet www.avinor.no/lufthavn/svalbard; f. 1975; owned by Avinor; Man. MORTEN ULSNES.

Tourism

Svalbard Reiseliv AS: POB 232, 9171 Longyearbyen, Svalbard; tel. 79-02-55-50; fax 79-02-55-51; e-mail info@svalbard.net; internet www.svalbard.net; f. 2001; represents and promotes tourism-related enterprises in Svalbard; produces brochures for tourists and collates statistics.

JAN MAYEN

The lofty volcanic island of Jan Mayen is located in the Arctic Ocean, some 910 km west-north-west of Bodø on the Norwegian mainland, 610 km north-north-east of Iceland and 480 km east of Greenland (Denmark). The island is 53 km in length and has a total area of 377 sq km (145 sq miles). The highest point is the summit of Mt Beerenberg, which is an active volcano (2,277 m above sea level). The climate is severe, cold and usually misty.

The sea north and west of Jan Mayen (which was frequented by various whalers and hunters for around 23 years in the 17th century) has been an important area for seal hunting by Norwegians since the mid-19th century. Partly to assist their navigation, the Norwegian Meteorological Institute instigated activities on the island in the early 20th century. In 1922 Jan Mayen was declared annexed by the Institute, and on 8 May 1929 Norwegian sovereignty was proclaimed by Royal Decree. The island was made an integral part of the Kingdom of Norway by the Jan Mayen Act of 1930. Jan Mayen is not included in the Svalbard Treaty.

The island's sole exploitable mineral resource is gravel (from a site at Trongskaret), and the island is largely barren. However, geologists believe that the Jan Mayen Ridge, which lies beneath the surrounding waters, may contain reserves of petroleum and natural gas. Fishing in the surrounding waters is intermittently productive. In 1970 there was a violent volcanic eruption on the island, the first since the early 19th century. In the course of the first few days of the eruption a huge glacier melted and millions of cubic metres of ice disappeared as steam. Lava poured into the sea and formed about 3.5 sq km of new land. The last volcanic eruption on the island occurred in 1985. The island's main use remains as a meteorological, navigational and radio station.

During the Second World War Jan Mayen remained the only part of Norway under Norwegian rule, following the German invasion of the mainland. Despite some conflict, the Norwegian Government and its allies maintained the strategic meteorological station and established a radio-locating station on the island during the war.

In 1946 a new base was established at Nordlaguna, both as a meteorological and a coastal radio station. As a result of a North Atlantic defence co-operation exercise in 1959–60, a long-range navigation (LORAN) network was established, with one base on Jan Mayen. At the same time, it was decided to build an airstrip near the new LORAN-C base, and in 1962 the personnel of the weather and coastal radio services also moved to the same area. In recent years the use of LORAN has declined significantly, being replaced primarily by the satellite-based Global Positioning System (GPS). In 2010 the coastguards of both the USA and Canada ceased transmitting LORAN signals.

Following negotiations with Iceland in 1980, the Norwegian Government declared an economic zone extending for 200 nautical miles (370 km) around the coast of Jan Mayen. In 1981 a further agreement was made with Iceland, regarding mineral and fishing rights. A dispute with Denmark, acting on behalf of Greenland, concerning the delimitation of maritime economic zones between Greenland and Jan Mayen was referred by Denmark to the International Court of Justice (based in The Hague, Netherlands) in 1988. The Court delivered its judgment in June 1993, deciding that 57% of the disputed area belonged to Norway. A subsequent accord on maritime delimitation, agreed between the Governments of Norway, Greenland and Iceland in November 1997, established the boundaries of a 1,934-sq km area of Arctic sea that had been excluded from the terms of the 1993 settlement.

In September 2009, following a visit to the island by the Minister of Petroleum and Energy, Terje Riis-Johansen, the Norwegian Government initiated the process of opening the territorial waters surrounding Jan Mayen to possible future petroleum exploration. Earlier in 2009 the Icelandic Government had offered petroleum exploration licences for the portion of the undersea Jan Mayen Ridge that lay within Iceland's territorial waters; in December 2012 provisional licences to explore this area were granted to a multinational joint venture, comprising Iceland Petroleum, the Norwegian state-owned company Petoro and the United Kingdom–based independent company Faroe Petroleum.In October 2010 the Norwegian Government allocated 10m. kroner towards an environmental impact assessment in connection with the proposed opening of the Jan Mayen waters to petroleum exploration. In March 2011 the Government announced that it was to commit 180m. kroner to the seismic mapping of the Jan Mayen Ridge by the Norwegian Petroleum Directorate (Oljedirektoratet) and the University of Bergen during 2012–14.

According to a Royal Decree drawn up in November 2010 Jan Mayen and its adjacent territorial waters became a protected nature reserve under Norwegian jurisdiction.

Since 1995 Jan Mayen has chiefly been administered by the County Governor (Fylkesmann) of the northern Norwegian county of Nordland, which it is closest to. However, the commanding officer in charge of the LORAN-C base also exerts some authority over the island. The officer is directly responsible for the 18–35 inhabitants (who usually remain on the island for only one year at a time), and is accountable to the Chief of Police for Salten district (headquartered in Bodø), and the Ministry of Justice and Public Security (as in Svalbard). The commander may grant permission for visits of not more than 24 hours. For longer visits, the Chief of Police or the Ministry must approve the application. Visits are normally allowed only for scientific purposes and only if private provision has been made for transport. There is no public transport or accommodation on Jan Mayen.

Station Commander: HALLVARD JACOBSEN, LORAN-C Base, 8099 Jan Mayen; tel. 32-17-79-00; fax 32-17-79-01; e-mail post@www .jan-mayen.no; internet www.jan-mayen.no.

Chief of Police (Salten district): GEIR OVE HEIR, Kongensgt. 81, POB 1023, 8001 Bodø; tel. 75-54-58-00; e-mail post.salten@politiet .no; internet www.politi.no/salten.

For the Ministry of Justice and Public Security, and the Norsk Polarinstitutt (Norwegian Polar Institute), see under Svalbard.

NORWEGIAN DEPENDENCIES

Norway's so-called 'Antarctic' dependencies are all uninhabited and were acquired as a result of Norwegian whaling interests in the region since the 1890s. The three territories are dependencies of the Kingdom of Norway, and are administered by the Polar Affairs Department of the Ministry of Justice and Public Security, with the advice of the Norsk Polarinstitutt (Norwegian Polar Institute: for details, see under Svalbard) and the assistance of the Ministry of the Environment.

Bouvetøya

Bouvetøya (Bouvet Island) is a volcanic island in the South Atlantic Ocean, some 2,400 km south-west of the Cape of Good Hope (South Africa) and 1,600 km north of Antarctica. The island lies north of the Antarctic Circle (it is not, therefore, encompassed by the terms of the Antarctic Treaty). Bouvetøya has an area of 49 sq km, but about 93% of the surface is covered by ice. The climate is maritime antarctic, with a mean annual temperature of −1°C and a persistent heavy fog.

Regular landings on the island occurred only as part of Norwegian Antarctic expeditions in the 1920s and 1930s. Bouvetøya was claimed for Norway in 1927, placed under its sovereignty in 1928, and declared a Norwegian dependency in 1930. A Royal Decree of 1971 declared the entire island and its adjoining territorial waters to be a nature reserve. An automated weather station was established in 1977, and the island is regularly visited by Norwegian scientific expeditions.

Dronning Maud Land

Dronning Maud Land (Queen Maud Land) is that sector of the Antarctic continent lying between the longitudes of 20°W (adjoining the British Antarctic Territory to the west) and 45°E (neighbouring the Australian Antarctic Territory). The territory is, in area, several times the size of Norway, and 98% of its surface is covered by ice. The climate is severe, the usual temperature always being below 0°C and, in the winter months of mid-year, falling to −60°C on the coast and −88°C inland. The territory's coast is divided into five named sectors (the exact delimitations of which, and of the territory as a whole, have varied at different periods): Kronprinsesse Märtha Kyst (Crown Princess Märtha Coast), Prinsesse Astrid Kyst, Prinsesse Ragnhild Kyst, Prins Harald Kyst and Kronprins Olav Kyst.

The first Norwegian territorial claims in Antarctica were made in 1929, following many years of Norwegian involvement in the exploration and survey of the continent. Further claims were made in 1931 and 1936–37. These claims were formalized by the Norwegian authorities, and the land placed under their sovereignty, only in 1939. The extent of Dronning Maud Land then received its current limits, between the British and Australian claims. Norway now follows a policy that upholds its claim to sovereignty but supports the pattern of international co-operation, particularly that established under the terms of the Antarctic Treaty (signed in 1959), to which the Kingdom of Norway is an original signatory. In 2005 the Troll research station, previously suitable only for summer use, reopened as an all-year station; an airstrip to serve the facility was also opened. A further, summer-only research station is also in operation. In addition to these two Norwegian stations, there are a further 10 active research stations (five summer-only and five all-year) operated by a number of other countries.

Peter I Øy

Peter I Øy (Peter I Island) is located in the Bellingshausen Sea, some 450 km north of Antarctica and more than 1,800 km south-west of Chile, the nearest inhabited territory. It covers an area of some 156 sq km, 95% of which is covered by ice. The island lies within the Antarctic Circle and the area covered by the terms of the Antarctic Treaty. The first recorded landing on the island was not made until 1929, by a Norwegian expedition, which then claimed the island. A Royal Proclamation placed Peter I Øy under Norwegian sovereignty in 1931, and the island was declared a dependency in 1933. The island became subject to the Antarctic Treaty in 1961. Few landings have been made since 1929, but in 1987 the Norsk Polarinstitutt (Norwegian Polar Institute) conducted a relatively long survey and established an automated weather station on the island.

OMAN

Introductory Survey

LOCATION, CLIMATE, LANGUAGE, RELIGION, FLAG, CAPITAL

The Sultanate of Oman occupies the extreme east and south-east of the Arabian peninsula. It is bordered to the west by the United Arab Emirates (UAE), Saudi Arabia and Yemen. A detached portion of Oman, separated from the rest of the country by UAE territory, lies at the tip of the Musandam peninsula, on the southern shore of the Strait of Hormuz. Oman has a coastline of more than 1,600 km (1,000 miles) on the Indian Ocean, and is separated from Iran by the Gulf of Oman. In Muscat average annual rainfall is 100 mm and the average temperature varies between 21°C (70°F) and 35°C (95°F). Rainfall is heavier on the hills of the interior, and the south-western province of Dhofar is the only part of Arabia to benefit from the summer monsoon. The official language is Arabic. Islam is the official religion. The majority of the population are Ibadi Muslims; there are also Sunni Muslim, Hindu and Christian minorities. The national flag (proportions 1 by 2) has three equal horizontal stripes, of white, red and green, with a vertical red stripe at the hoist. In the upper hoist is a representation, in white, of the state emblem, two crossed swords and a dagger (khanjar), surmounted by a belt. The capital is Muscat.

CONTEMPORARY POLITICAL HISTORY

Historical Context

Officially known as Muscat and Oman until 1970, the Sultanate has had a special relationship with the United Kingdom since the 19th century. Full independence was confirmed by a treaty of friendship with the United Kingdom on 20 December 1951, although the armed forces and police retain some British officers on loan service. Sultan Said bin Taimur succeeded his father in 1932 and maintained a strictly conservative and isolationist rule until July 1970, when he was overthrown by his son in a bloodless palace coup. The new Sultan, Qaboos bin Said al-Said, then began a liberalization of the regime, and spending on development was increased.

Domestic Political Affairs

A Consultative Assembly (comprising representatives of the Government, the private sector and the regions, appointed by the Sultan) was created in 1981, in order to advise Sultan Qaboos on economic and social development. In November 1990 it was announced that the Assembly was to be replaced by a Consultative Council (Majlis al-Shura), comprising regional representatives, which was intended to extend participation by Omani citizens in national affairs. A selection process was duly announced whereby representatives of each of the country's 59 districts (wilayat—increased to 61 in 2006) would nominate three candidates; the nominations would then be submitted to the Deputy Prime Minister for Legal Affairs, who, with the Sultan's approval, would choose one representative for each district to join the new Majlis. No government official or civil servant would be eligible for election to the new body. The President of the Majlis al-Shura would be appointed by royal decree; other executive officers and committee members would be designated by, and from among, the local delegates. Although the role of the Majlis was strictly advisory, government ministers were to be obliged to submit reports to the assembly and to answer any questions addressed to them. The Majlis was formally established by royal decree in November 1991 and was convened in January 1992, when its members were sworn in for a three-year term. In 1994 membership of the Majlis was increased from 59 to 80, to include an additional member for any district with 30,000 or more inhabitants. For the first time, women were nominated as candidates in six regions in and around the capital; two women were subsequently appointed to the enlarged Majlis.

The Basic Statute of the State and the formation of the Majlis Oman

In November 1996 Sultan Qaboos issued a decree promulgating a Basic Statute of the State, a constitutional document defining for the first time the organs and guiding principles of the state. The Statute provided for a Council of Oman (Majlis Oman), to be composed of the Majlis al-Shura and a new State Council (Majlis al-Dawlah). The latter was to be appointed from among prominent Omanis, and would liaise between the Government and the people of Oman. In December a Defence Council was established by royal decree, comprising the Minister of the Royal Court, the heads of the armed and police forces, and the chief of internal security. The Basic Statute defined a process of succession to the Sultan, requiring that the ruling family determine a successor within three days of the throne's falling vacant, failing which the Defence Council would confirm the appointment of a successor predetermined by the Sultan.

Voting was organized in October 1997 to select candidates for appointment to the Majlis al-Shura. Women from all regions were permitted to seek nomination. Of a total of 736 candidates, 164 were chosen, from whom the Sultan selected the 82 members of the newly expanded Majlis in November. The two female members of the outgoing Majlis were returned to office. In December Sultan Qaboos issued a decree appointing the 41 members of the Majlis al-Dawlah, which was reportedly dominated by former politicians, business leaders and academics. A further decree established the Majlis Oman, which was formally inaugurated by the Sultan on 27 December.

The elections to the Majlis al-Shura held on 14 September 2000 were the first in which members were directly elected rather than appointed by the Sultan. However, voting rights were restricted to prominent business leaders, intellectuals, professionals and tribal chiefs. Of a total of 541 candidates, 21 of whom were women, 83 (including two women) were elected to the (further expanded) Majlis. The number of eligible voters had tripled, to some 150,000, since the previous election; according to official figures, an estimated 90% of the electorate participated in the poll. A new Majlis al-Dawlah was appointed in October, and the Majlis Oman convened for its second term on 4 November.

In March 2003 Sultan Qaboos issued a decree establishing a Public Authority for Craft Industries. The President of the Authority, Sheikha Aisha bint Khalfan bin Jumiel al-Siyabiah, was given the rank of Minister, and thus became the first female to be appointed to that level of government. Elections to the Majlis al-Shura were held on 4 October, for which voting rights were granted to all Omani citizens over 21 years of age—some 820,000 people. A total of 506 candidates, 15 of them women, stood for election to the 83-seat assembly. Critics of the polls claimed that tribal loyalties had guided the decision-making of most voters, resulting in a predictable set of results—a situation that was exacerbated by the lack of legislative power wielded by council members. Moreover, turn-out was recorded at just 32%. A royal decree issued later in October extended the term of office for members of both the Majlis al-Shura and the Majlis al-Dawlah from three to four years. In November a new Majlis al-Dawlah was appointed, with an expanded membership of 57 (including eight women); membership of the Majlis was subsequently increased to 59 (nine of whom were women) and then again, to 70.

A royal decree signed in March 2004 appointed Dr Rawya bint Saud bin Ahmad al-Busaidiyah as Minister of Higher Education (the first female member of the Council of Ministers) and Sheikh Yahya bin Mahfoudh al-Mantheri as President of the Majlis al-Dawlah. In June the Sultan created a Ministry of Tourism; another woman, Rajha bint Abd al-Amir bin Ali, was appointed as the new minister. Dr Sharifah bint Khalfan bin Nasser al-Yahyaia became the third woman to be appointed to the Council of Ministers when she was awarded the role of Minister of Social Development in October.

In September 2007 Sultan Qaboos carried out a reorganization of the Council of Ministers, which included the creation of new Ministries of Fisheries and of Environment and Climate Affairs, as well as a Public Authority for Electricity and Water. Sheikh Ahmad bin Muhammad al-Issai was appointed as President of the Majlis al-Shura, elections to which were held on 27 October. Membership of the Majlis was increased from 83 to 84. The polls were contested by 632 candidates, 21 of them women; however, none of the contested seats were secured by women. The majority of elected members of the new Majlis al-Shura were tribal leaders or businessmen. Turn-out of some 62.7% was recorded. A new Majlis al-Dawlah, comprising 70 members (including 14 women), was appointed on 5 November.

The Government had, in 1998, introduced measures aimed at reducing the number of expatriates in the labour force and replacing them with trained Omani personnel, a process termed 'Omanization'. By 2000 the proportion of Omanis employed in the state services sector exceeded the set target of 72%. Several amendments to Oman's Labour Law were introduced in November 2009, imposing stringent regulations on the utilization of foreign labour, including the provision of prison sentences and fines for employers or sponsors of illegal workers, and stipulating increased financial penalties for employers failing to meet Omanization targets. According to unofficial estimates, there were up to 125,000 unregistered or illegal expatriate workers in Oman in 2009. In January 2010 the Government announced a two-month amnesty programme to enable foreign nationals employed illegally in the country either to acquire correct documentation or to leave the Sultanate without prosecution. The amnesty was subsequently extended until 31 May and then again, to 31 July. However, it was reported in August that only 20,000 people had responded to the initiative.

Recent developments: the protests of early 2011 and tentative signs of democratic reform

Amid a series of popular uprisings that took place in the Middle East and North Africa during 2011, on 17 January a demonstration was held in Muscat by protesters who demanded lower food prices and the removal of government ministers perceived to be corrupt. A second rally was held in the capital on 18 February, at which the demands further included political reform and job creation. On 25 February the protests intensified, and two days later violence erupted in the northern industrial port of Sohar, with many official buildings reportedly being vandalized and shops set on fire. As protesters in Sohar began a sit-in, blocking access roads to the port, and some reportedly tried to break into a police station, two demonstrators were said to have died in clashes with security forces. The unrest spread to other cities, including Muscat and Salalah, despite a pledge by Sultan Qaboos to create 50,000 public sector jobs and to introduce unemployment benefits. Nevertheless, unlike the instigators of pro-democracy protests in other parts of the Gulf and wider region, Omanis did not directly challenge the rule of their leader, who in July 2010 had celebrated the 40th anniversary of his accession to power.

On 26 February 2011 Sultan Qaboos replaced six cabinet ministers and promised improved benefits to students. On 5 March the Sultan effected a further limited reshuffle of the Council of Ministers, which included the replacement of the Minister of the Royal Palace Office, Gen. Ali bin Majid al-Ma'amari. Two days later Qaboos announced a more substantial reorganization of the 29-member Government: 12 ministers were removed from office and several other portfolios changed hands. It was announced that the Ministry of National Economy—the minister of which, Ahmad bin Abd al-Nabi Macki, had been a target of the protesters' anger—was to be dissolved, while the former Minister of Commerce and Industry, Maqbool bin Ali Sultan (who had on 26 February been awarded the transport and communications portfolio), was also removed from his post. Saad bin Muhammad bin Said al-Mardhouf al-Saadi became the new Minister of Commerce and Industry, while Darwish bin Ismail bin Ali al-Balushi was named as the new Minister Responsible for Financial Affairs. The Minister of the Interior, Saud bin Ibrahim al-Busaidi, and the Minister of the Diwan of the Royal Court, Sayed Ali bin Hamoud al-Busaidi, also lost their posts; the former was replaced by Hamoud bin Faisal bin Said al-Busaidi and the latter by Khalid bin Hilal bin Saud al-Busaidi. Six of the newly appointed ministers were reported to be elected members of the Majlis al-Shura.

On 13 March 2011 Sultan Qaboos issued a decree in which he pledged to grant legislative and audit powers to both chambers of the Majlis Oman. The decree provided for the establishment of a technical committee of experts, which would formulate a draft amendment to the Basic Statute of the State and submit a report to the Sultan. The Sultan also announced the creation of 50,000 employment opportunities, an increase to the national minimum wage and the introduction of unemployment benefits. However, the protests continued, and a reported 7,000 Omanis signed a petition later in March urging the Government to bring corruption charges against three of the ministers recently removed from office—Macki, Sultan and Gen. Ali al-Ma'amari. (There were subsequent demands by the protesters for other serving

cabinet ministers to leave office in order to face allegations of corruption.) However, the Public Prosecutor ruled at the end of the month that it would not investigate the claims against the three former ministers owing to a lack of evidence, prompting demands for the Attorney-General to stand down.

Meanwhile, the security forces were reported to have arrested more than 100 people on 29 March 2011 during efforts to bring to an end the sit-in that protesters had staged in Sohar for the past month. The authorities described those detained as 'law-breaking vandals', who were charged with a range of violations including damage to property, obstructing free movement and damaging the country's reputation. On 31 March the human rights organization Amnesty International published a report in which it condemned the arrests, expressing concern that the protesters may have been apprehended 'solely for peacefully exercising their right to freedom of expression'. One protester was shot dead during violent clashes between demonstrators and the authorities in Sohar on 1 April, prompting the staging of a sit-in outside the Majlis al-Shura building in Muscat on the following day by protesters demanding that the police officer responsible for the fatality be prosecuted. The authorities insisted that only rubber bullets had been used to break up the protests, but there were numerous reports of live gunfire in the area. The sit-ins outside the Majlis building and in Sohar continued throughout April, together with protest marches in various locations across Oman.

Responding to the ongoing protests, on 7 May 2011 the Government proposed a series of amendments to the country's labour legislation. The proposed reforms included the introduction of a standard five-day working week in both the public and private sectors, and an increase in the holiday entitlement of private sector workers to match that of their public sector counterparts. Nevertheless, around a dozen people were arrested on 13–14 May, after protesters continued a sit-in outside the Majlis al-Shura building. Violent clashes were also reported between protesters and the authorities in the southern towns of Salalah and Sur, with police again using tear gas, water cannons and rubber bullets in their attempts to disperse the demonstrators.

On 28 June 2011 16 people were convicted on charges related to the protests: nine were sentenced to five-year prison terms, having been found to have forced the closure of the Ministry of Manpower's local office in Sohar during protests in late March, while the remaining seven received gaol terms of between three and six months for having blocked roads and 'humiliated' civil servants; a further 21 people were acquitted of disturbing public order. On 7 July seven people were convicted of possessing explosive materials and plotting terrorist activities in Sohar and were sentenced to two-and-a-half years' imprisonment, while five others who were convicted of aiding and abetting the seven were given three-month prison terms. Largely peaceful protests continued to be staged in Sohar and other towns, with participants urging the Government to release the imprisoned protesters.

Elections to the 84-member Majlis al-Shura were held on 15 October 2011 and were contested by 1,133 candidates, of whom 77 were women. Turn-out was recorded at 76% of the registered electorate. As in the 2003 and 2007 polls, tribal loyalties were believed to have guided the decision-making of most voters; however, one woman and three members of the pro-democracy movement were also elected. The Sultan appointed a new, expanded 83-member Majlis al-Dawlah, which included 15 women, on 18 October 2011.

On 19 October 2011 Sultan Qaboos issued a decree announcing amendments to the Basic Statute of the State. Adhering to his pledge in March, the Sultan confirmed that both chambers of the Majlis Oman were henceforth to be empowered with legislative and audit powers. Among the most significant changes, draft laws prepared by the Council of Ministers would now be referred to the Majlis Oman for approval or amendment before being submitted to the Sultan. National development plans and the annual state budget were also to be referred to the Majlis Oman for review. The President of the Majlis al-Shura, hitherto appointed by royal decree, was henceforth to be elected by the members of the Majlis, via secret ballot. On 29 October Sheikh Khalid bin Hilal bin Nasser al-Ma'awali became the chamber's first elected President. The popular response to the amendments was mixed; while some welcomed them as cause for optimism about Oman's prospects of genuine democratic reform, others expressed disappointment that proposals made by the Majlis Oman remained unbinding, with the Sultan retaining the authority to reject its views in favour of those expressed by the Council of Ministers.

In a bid to address the growing issue of illegal immigration, particularly by nationals of South Asian countries, from the latter half of 2011 the Omani authorities intensified efforts to apprehend illegal immigrants across the Sultanate. The Minister of Manpower warned in September that companies found to be employing illegal workers would be heavily fined or even closed down. Later that month more than 1,300 illegal immigrants, the majority of whom were reported to originate from Bangladesh, India and Pakistan, were arrested during raids in Muscat governorate; many of those apprehended were employed within the construction industry. In mid-October 41 people, mostly Pakistani nationals, were arrested by the Omani authorities near Sohar on suspicion of seeking to enter Oman without a visa and/or a residence permit. Many hundreds more illegal immigrants were arrested during late 2011 and into 2012, including 1,104 immigrants detained in a series of raids across Muscat governorate in December 2011, a further 269 immigrants detained in Ruwi in March 2012 and 835 immigrants arrested in various coastal districts in June. Some 600 illegal South Asian immigrants were deported in February 2012, and in June the authorities were preparing to deport another 116 illegal immigrants, some of whom originated from the Horn of Africa.

A government reorganization effected in late February 2012 comprised six new appointments, including those of Sheikh Abd al-Malik bin Abdullah bin Ali al-Khalili as Minister of Justice, Dr Abd al-Munem bin Mansour bin Said al-Hasni as Minister of Information and Ali bin Massoud bin Ali al-Sunaidi as Minister of Commerce and Industry. In an apparent concession to the pro-democracy movement by the Government, on 22 December municipal elections were held for the first time in Oman's history; more than 1,400 candidates (among them 46 women) contested a total of 192 council seats, which were to have an advisory role.

Nevertheless, during mid-2012 further protests concerning the perceived delay on the part of the Government in implementing political and economic reforms were held in various parts of the country. In late May at least 1,000 employees of the state-owned Petroleum Development Oman took strike action in demand of higher salaries and improved working conditions. A reported 400 of the employees who lost their jobs as a result of their decision to go on strike were subsequently allowed to return to work following the intervention of members of the Majlis al-Shura. Also in May the Omani authorities declared that those activists who were openly critical of Sultan Qaboos or the Government would henceforth faces charges of sedition. This firmer stance by the authorities regarding the ongoing protest movement, particularly towards those who protested using social networking websites, led in that month to the detention of further pro-democracy campaigners, some of whom had criticized the Sultan personally. Among a number of convictions on similar charges during the second half of 2012, in early July nine such campaigners were found guilty of sedition and given prison sentences of between six and 18 months, while in early September six activists were sentenced to gaol terms of between 12 and 18 months for their alleged 'abusive and provocative' criticism of the Government in articles that had been published on the internet.

Foreign Affairs

Regional relations

An agreement on the demarcation of Oman's border with Yemen, which had been the subject of a lengthy dispute with the former People's Democratic Republic of Yemen, was signed in October 1992 and ratified in December; demarcation was completed in June 1995. In July 1996 Oman withdrew an estimated 15,000 troops from the last of the disputed territories on the Yemeni border, in accordance with the 1992 agreement, and in May 1997 the border demarcation maps were signed in Muscat. Several bilateral economic co-operation accords were announced in September 1998, and a free trade zone was subsequently established near the border at al-Mazyona. From March 2011 the Omani authorities were reported to have increased security along the country's border with Yemen, where a series of demonstrations by protesters demanding the resignation of President Ali Abdullah Saleh were in some cases violently suppressed by security forces. The Omani Government feared that, unless border security was improved, a possible influx of Yemeni refugees fleeing the escalating violence—which ultimately led to President Saleh's resignation in November—might use the free trade zone at al-Mazyona to enter Oman illegally.

Having signed a preliminary border accord in June 2002, Oman and the UAE reached agreement on the final delineation of their mutual land borders in July 2008. Although the two countries have traditionally enjoyed good relations, in January 2011 the Omani authorities revealed that they were investigating the existence of an espionage network originating in the UAE, which was allegedly engaged in spying on the Omani Government and security forces. Several Omani nationals were arrested in connection with the investigation. The UAE Government denied any knowledge of such a network, and, although it pledged to co-operate fully with the Omani investigation into the matter, the issue provoked considerable tension. However, following an intervention by the Amir of Kuwait and the staging of remedial talks between senior Omani and UAE government officials, the two countries were reported to have reconciled their differences over the issue in March and Sultan Qaboos pledged his commitment further to enhance bilateral relations. This process continued during 2012, with further meetings taking place between senior officials of both countries.

Agreement was reached between Oman and Saudi Arabia in July 1995 providing for the formal demarcation of the common border. However, relations were compromised by the conclusion, in October 2005, of a free trade agreement between Oman and the USA. The Saudi Government had previously argued that the Cooperation Council for the Arab States of the Gulf (the Gulf Cooperation Council—GCC, see p. 255) should negotiate a trade deal as a single body and had claimed that a similar trade pact concluded between the USA and Bahrain in September 2004 contravened the GCC's external tariff agreement. In a bid to strengthen bilateral relations, Oman and Saudi agreed in 2006 to construct a road link between the two countries. Construction of the 1,400-km road, which would connect the Saudi capital, Riyadh, with Oman's al-Dhahira region, commenced in 2007 and was expected to be completed by the end of 2013.

Despite Oman's strong relations with the USA and other Western powers, the Sultanate also maintains close ties with Iran, supporting the right of the Iranian regime to pursue the peaceful development of nuclear energy and opposing any use of military force against Iran. Since June 2007 Oman and Iran have been engaged in negotiations concerning a joint venture to develop Iran's Kish gasfield, at an estimated cost of more than US $9,000m. The proposed deal would involve Oman providing finance for the project in exchange for a guaranteed gas supply of at least 1,000m. cu ft per day. Bilateral relations were further extended during 2008–09; in August 2009 Sultan Qaboos undertook his first visit to the Iranian capital, Tehran, since the 1979 Islamic Revolution. During the visit several co-operation agreements were signed in the fields of security and education, and the establishment of a $800m. petrochemicals joint venture was confirmed. However, no agreement was reached concerning the ongoing gas supply negotiations. In January 2010 the establishment of an Iranian trade centre in Oman was announced—the first such initiative in a GCC member state. In August the Omani and Iranian ministers of defence signed a military co-operation accord in Muscat. In February 2011 the two countries staged a joint naval exercise in the Gulf of Oman and affirmed their mutual commitment to developing closer military ties.

In April 1994 the Israeli Deputy Minister of Foreign Affairs, Yossi Beilin, participated in talks in Oman. This constituted the first official visit by an Israeli government member to an Arab Gulf state since Israel's declaration of independence in 1948. In September 1994, moreover, Oman and the other GCC member states announced the partial ending of their economic boycott of Israel. In December the Israeli Prime Minister, Itzhak Rabin, made an official visit to Oman to discuss the Middle East peace process, and in February 1995 it was announced that low-level diplomatic relations were to be established between Oman and Israel. An Omani trade office was opened in Tel-Aviv, Israel, in August 1996, despite concerns that bilateral relations would be undermined by the uncompromising stance adopted by the new Israeli Government of Binyamin Netanyahu. In March 1997 ministers responsible for foreign affairs of the countries of the League of Arab States (the Arab League, see p. 372) recommended, in condemnation of Israeli settlement policy, the suspension of involvement in multilateral negotiations with Israel, a reassertion of the primary economic boycott and the ending of efforts to normalize bilateral relations. In October 2000, in view of the deepening crisis in Israeli–Palestinian relations, Oman closed both its trade office in Tel-Aviv and the Israeli trade office in Muscat. Oman hosted the annual summit meeting of GCC heads of state in December 2001, at the close of which a statement was issued blaming Israel for the collapse of the peace process and expressing support for the Palestinian leadership.

Demonstrations subsequently took place in Muscat to demand an end to Israeli military incursions into Palestinian territory. Nevertheless, according to reports in the Israeli daily newspaper *Ha'aretz*, senior officials from Israel's Ministry of Foreign Affairs visited Muscat in November 2009, ostensibly to attend a conference on water desalination, and held discussions on the Middle East peace process with their Omani counterparts.

Other external relations

Negotiations between Oman and the USA concerning a bilateral free trade agreement took place in March–October 2005, and the deal was signed following their conclusion. The accord was ratified by both countries' institutions in 2006 and entered into force on 1 January 2009. The US-Omani agreement followed similar accords between the USA and Bahrain, Israel, Jordan and Morocco, with a view to establishing a wider free trade area across the Middle East, and was a source of considerable displeasure to the Saudi Government (see Regional relations).

Dr Manmohan Singh, the Prime Minister of India, visited Oman in November 2008 for a two-day state visit—the first by an Indian premier for more than a decade. Since the establishment of an India-Oman Joint Commission in 1995 bilateral relations progressed considerably, with the signing of several agreements on trade and defence co-operation. During Prime Minister Singh's visit the two countries agreed to upgrade bilateral relations to a strategic partnership, and two significant memorandums of understanding were signed: one concerning labour co-operation and another on the establishment of an India-Oman Joint Investment Fund. In December 2010 Omani and Indian government representatives signed an agreement identifying nine fields in which bilateral co-operation was to be enhanced—namely, agriculture, chemicals and fertilizers, education, health care, infrastructural development, mining, oil and gas, power, and tourism.

CONSTITUTION AND GOVERNMENT

The Basic Statute of the State, which was promulgated by Royal Decree on 6 November 1996, and amended by Royal Decree on 19 October 2011, defines Oman's organs of government. The Sultan, who is head of state, is empowered to promulgate and ratify legislation. He is assisted in formulating and implementing the general policy of the state by a Council of Ministers. Members of the Council of Ministers are appointed by the Sultan, who presides, or may appoint a Prime Minister to preside, over the Council. There is no legislature. However, a Majlis al-Shura (Consultative Council) is elected for four years at national polls. With effect from elections held in October 2003, voting rights have been granted to all Omani citizens over 21 years of age. The Majlis is composed of one representative from each *wilaya* (district) with fewer than 30,000 inhabitants, and two from each *wilaya* with 30,000 or more inhabitants. The Majlis al-Shura elected in October 2011 comprised 84 members. A Majlis al-Dawlah (State Council) is appointed by the Sultan from among prominent Omanis; members also serve a four-year term of office. The Majlis al-Dawlah appointed in October 2011 comprised 83 members. The two Councils together comprise the Majlis Oman (Council of Oman). Under the terms of the amendment to the Basic Statute of the State issued on 19 October 2011, legislative and audit powers were granted to both chambers of the Majlis Oman (see Contemporary Political History).

Following the creation of seven new governorates as a result of a decree issued by Sultan Qaboos in October 2011, Oman comprised a total of 11 governorates and five regions, which are subdivided into 61 *wilayat*; each *wilaya* has its own governor (*wali*).

REGIONAL AND INTERNATIONAL CO-OPERATION

Oman was a founder member of the Cooperation Council for the Arab States of the Gulf (the Gulf Cooperation Council—GCC, see p. 255). The GCC's six members established a unified regional customs tariff in 2003. The economic convergence criteria for a common market and monetary union were agreed at a GCC summit in Abu Dhabi, the UAE, in 2005. However, it was announced in February 2007 that the Omani authorities had decided to withdraw their participation from the proposed monetary union, owing to concerns regarding the convergence criteria. The common market was officially launched in January 2008. Oman is also a member of the League of Arab States (the Arab League, see p. 372).

Oman became a member of the UN in October 1971 and was admitted to the World Trade Organization (WTO, see p. 444) in November 2000. The country also participates in the

Organization of Islamic Cooperation (OIC, see p. 413) and the Group of 77 (G77, see p. 461) developing countries.

ECONOMIC AFFAIRS

In 2010, according to estimates by the World Bank, Oman's gross national income (GNI), measured at average 2008–10 prices, was US $53,598m., equivalent to $19,260 per head (or $25,770 per head on an international purchasing-power parity basis). During 2002–11, it was estimated, the population increased at an average annual rate of 2.4%, while real gross domestic product (GDP) per head increased, in real terms, by an average of 2.3% per year. Overall GDP increased, in real terms, at an average annual rate of 5.3% in 2002–10; the rate of GDP growth was 4.5% in 2011, according to provisional official figures.

Agriculture (including fishing) contributed 1.1% of GDP in 2011, according to provisional figures, while 26.9% of the labour force was estimated to be engaged in the sector in mid-2013, according to FAO data. The major crops are dates, tomatoes, watermelons, bananas and other fruits. The production of frankincense, formerly an important export commodity, has been revived. Livestock and fishing are also important. The real GDP of the agricultural sector increased by an average of 2.5% annually in 2002–10. Real agricultural GDP expanded by 2.3% in 2011, according to provisional official figures.

Industry (including mining and quarrying, manufacturing, construction, and power) provided 66.7% of GDP in 2011, according to provisional figures, and employed 27.9% of the working population in 2003. Real industrial GDP increased by an average of 3.8% annually in 2002–10. The sector's real GDP increased by 1.6% in 2011, according to provisional official figures.

The mining sector contributed 50.2% of the country's GDP in 2011 according to provisional figures, and engaged 2.8% of the employed labour force in 2003. The principal mineral reserves are petroleum and natural gas, which together provided around 49.8% of GDP in 2011. There were proven petroleum reserves of 5,500m. barrels at the end of 2011—sufficient to maintain output at that year's levels, which averaged an estimated 891,000 barrels per day (b/d), for more than 17 years. Exports of Omani crude petroleum provided 58.9% of total export earnings in 2011. Natural gas is also an important mineral resource; there were proven reserves of some 900,000m. cu m at the end of 2011, sustainable for more than 36 years at that year's production levels (output in 2011 totalled 26,500m. cu m). Budgetary revenue from petroleum and natural gas contributed some 85.8% of the total in 2012, according to provisional figures. Chromite, gold, silver, salt, marble, gypsum and limestone are also mined, and the exploitation of coal deposits is planned. The GDP of the mining sector (including petroleum activities) declined at an average annual rate of 0.1% in 2002–11; however, according to provisional official figures, mining GDP (including petroleum activities) recorded an increase of 2.3% in 2011.

Manufacturing contributed 10.5% of GDP in 2011, according to provisional figures, and engaged 8.2% of the employed labour force in 2003. The most important branches of the sector are petroleum-refining, construction materials, cement production and copper-smelting. Assembly industries, light engineering and food-processing are being encouraged at Oman's industrial estates, which include those at Nizwa, Sohar, al-Buraymi and Sur. The Government is also promoting light industry in free trade zones at Sohar and Salalah Ports. The GDP of the manufacturing sector increased, in real terms, at an average rate of 8.6% annually in 2002–10. The sector's real GDP contracted by 3.1% in 2011, according to provisional official figures.

Construction contributed 4.9% of GDP in 2011, according to provisional figures, and engaged 16.1% of the labour force in 2003. The real GDP of the construction sector increased at an average annual rate of 19.6% in 2002–10. Real construction GDP expanded by 1.6% in 2011, according to provisional official figures.

Energy is derived almost exclusively from domestic supplies of natural gas (which accounted for 82.0% of electricity produced in 2009) and petroleum. Imports of fuel products comprised just 10.8% of total imports in 2011. A regional electricity grid, linking countries of the Cooperation Council for the Arab States of the Gulf (the Gulf Cooperation Council—GCC, see p. 255), became fully operational in November 2012, when Oman was connected to the grid; it was eventually to achieve regional self-sufficiency up to 2058.

Services provided 32.2% of GDP in 2011, according to provisional figures, and engaged 64.0% of the employed population in 2003. With the Government seeking to diversify Oman's petroleum-dependent economy, the construction of several large-scale tourism projects has been initiated in recent years. Pre-eminent among these was Al-Madina al-Zarqa (Blue City) resort, the plans for which were announced in June 2005, and which was expected to take some 15 years to complete. However, in April 2011 the Government assumed control of the US $20,000m. project, after it had been beset by a series of problems, including a legal dispute over ownership, funding difficulties and a disappointing level of interest in the properties for sale. The Government intended to increase the number of tourist arrivals from an estimated 2m. in 2012 (in which year Muscat was the nominated Arab Tourism Capital) to 12m. by 2020. The GDP of the services sector increased, in real terms, at an average rate of 7.5% per year during 2002–10. Real services GDP expanded by 7.8% in 2011, according to provisional official figures.

In 2011 Oman recorded a visible merchandise trade surplus of US $25,594m., while there was a surplus of $10,263m. on the current account of the balance of payments. In 2011 the principal source of imports was the United Arab Emirates (UAE—which supplied 27.4% of total imports). Japan, the USA and Saudi Arabia were also important suppliers. The most important market for non-petroleum exports in 2011 was the UAE (taking 25.3%). The People's Republic of China, India and Saudi Arabia were also important markets for non-petroleum exports. Petroleum and natural gas was, by far, the principal export category in 2011. Chemical products made the most notable contribution to export revenue of all non-oil exports of Omani origin in the same year. The principal imports in that year were: machinery and transport equipment; basic manufactures; minerals, fuels and lubricants; food and live animals; chemicals and related products; and miscellaneous manufactured articles.

Oman recorded an estimated overall budgetary surplus of RO 1,753.3m. in 2011 (equivalent to some 6.5% of GDP in that year). Oman's general government gross debt was RO 1,267m. in 2010, equivalent to 5.7% of GDP. Annual inflation increased by an average of 3.5% in 2002–11, and consumer prices grew by an average of 2.9% in 2012. Although Oman has traditionally relied on a high level of immigrant labour (non-Omanis accounted for 57.6% of the employed labour force in 2003), employment opportunities for young Omanis declined in the early 1990s and, according to census results, unemployment among Omanis stood at 11.9% in 1993; the figure was estimated at 12%–15% in 2006, although unemployment in rural areas was assumed to be far greater.

Oman's limited petroleum reserves and fluctuations in the price of petroleum have necessitated a series of five-year development plans to diversify the country's economic base, in particular through the expansion of the private sector since 1994. Under the eighth Development Plan (2011–15), emphasis was to be placed on improvements to the health, education and transport systems. However, despite ongoing efforts to develop the non-petroleum sector (with gas-based industry and tourism being notable targets), an estimated RO 6,000m. of the allocated RO 30,000m. was to be spent on the oil industry. Following sustained government investment in enhanced petroleum recovery techniques, a steady decline in petroleum production during 2001–07 has subsequently been reversed; production increased by 3.8%, to reach some 918,500 b/d, in 2012, according to official figures, while gas output also increased, by 3.3%, to reach 98.2m. cu m/d. By 2012 more than 20 foreign oil companies were engaged in exploration and production projects in Oman, and a number of potentially significant oil and gas discoveries were announced by the state-owned Petroleum Development Oman in February of that year and in March 2013. In addition to a major programme of investment in Oman's hydrocarbons sector (with spending forecast to exceed US $100,000m. during 2013–22), the Government was also committed to developing the tourism sector's infrastructure, with plans announced later for, *inter alia*, the construction of six airports and the expansion, by 2014, of Muscat International and Salalah airports. Having benefited from foreign investment, tourism's contribution to GDP reportedly increased from an estimated 0.9% in 2008 to 3.0% in 2011, and was expected to increase further, to 3.5%, by 2015. The completion of new commercial facilities at Duqm Port in March 2013 and the planned construction of a regional railway network linking Oman with other GCC member states were also expected to attract investment into the country, as well as improving trading opportunities for Omani businesses. The budget for 2013 anticipated government expenditure of RO 12,900m. (a 29% increase on the amount forecast in the 2012 budget) and revenue of RO 11,200m. Following the protests of 2011, there was a focus on social and educational infrastructure investment, including on health care and housing provision, and further measures were announced to address persistently high levels of unemployment.

PUBLIC HOLIDAYS

2014: 13 January* (Mouloud, Birth of the Prophet), 26 May* (Leilat al-Meiraj, Ascension of the Prophet), 28 June* (Ramadan begins), 23 July (Renaissance Day), 28 July* (Id al-Fitr, end of Ramadan), 4 October* (Id al-Adha, Feast of the Sacrifice), 24 October* (Muharram, Islamic New Year), 18 November (National Day), 19 November (Birthday of Sultan Qaboos).

* These holidays are dependent on the Islamic lunar calendar and may vary by one or two days from the dates given.

Statistical Survey

Sources (unless otherwise stated): National Center for Statistics and Information, Supreme Council for Planning, POB 881, Muscat 100; tel. 24698900; fax 24698467; internet www.ncsi.gov.om; Central Bank of Oman, POB 1161, 44 Mutrah Commercial Centre, Ruwi 112; tel. 24777777; fax 24788995; e-mail cboccr@omantel.net.om; internet www.cbo-oman.org.

Area and Population

AREA, POPULATION AND DENSITY

Area (sq km)	309,500*
Population (census results)	
1 December 2003	2,340,815†
12 December 2010	
Males	1,612,411
Females	1,161,068
Total	2,773,479‡
Population (official estimate at mid year)	
2011§	3,295,298
Density (per sq km) at mid-2011	10.6

* 119,500 sq miles.

† Comprising 1,781,558 Omani nationals and 559,257 non-Omanis.

‡ Comprising approximately 1,957,336 Omani nationals and 816,143 non-Omanis. Note: The number of non-Omanis was believed to have been reduced significantly by the proximity of the census to the Christmas holiday season.

§ Estimate not adjusted to take account of the 2010 census.

POPULATION BY AGE AND SEX
(population estimates at mid-2011)

	Males	Females	Total
0–14	378,538	361,487	740,025
15–64	1,661,667	799,818	2,461,485
65 and over	50,678	43,110	93,788
Total	2,090,883	1,204,415	3,295,298

Estimates not adjusted to take account of results of the 2010 census.

ADMINISTRATIVE DIVISIONS
(population estimates at mid-2011)

	Area (sq km)*	Population†	Density (per sq km)
Muscat Governorate . . .	3,900	1,003,742	257.4
Al-Batinah Region . . .	12,500	818,381	65.5
Musandam Governorate . .	1,800	31,025	17.2
Al-Dhahira Region . . .	44,000	157,006	3.6
Al-Dakhliya Region . . .	31,900	342,017	10.7
Al-Sharqiya Region . . .	36,400	415,656	11.4
Al-Wosta Region . . .	79,700	30,624	0.4
Dhofar Governorate . . .	99,300	315,324	3.2
Al-Buraymi Governorate . .	n.a.	78,535	n.a.
Total (incl. others)	309,500	3,295,298	10.6

* Figures for area are rounded, and totals may not be equal to the sum of components as a result; area data predate the creation, from al-Dhahira Region, of al-Buraymi Governorate in October 2006.
† Estimates not adjusted to take account of results of the 2010 census; total also includes 102,988 persons of unspecified location.

PRINCIPAL TOWNS
(population at 2010 census)

Al-Seeb	302,992	Ibri	116,416
Bawshar	192,235	Nizwa	84,528
Salalah	172,570	Al-Rustaq	79,720
Mutrah	150,124	Sur	64,988
Sohar	140,006	Al-Buraymi (Buraimi) .	63,159

Muscat (capital): 27,216.

BIRTHS AND DEATHS
(Omani nationals only, official estimates)

	2009	2010	2011
Live births	59,461	59,903	67,922
Birth rate (per 1,000) . . .	29.5	31.0	31.2
Deaths	6,092	6,444	7,667
Death rate (per 1,000) . . .	3.0	3.3	3.3

Registered marriages: 26,544 (marriage rate 8.1 per 1,000) in 2011.

Life expectancy (years at birth, official figures): 73.3 (males 71.0, females 75.8) in 2011.

EMPLOYMENT
(persons aged 15 years and over, 2003 census)

	Omanis	Non-Omanis	Total
Agriculture and fishing . . .	14,210	43,904	58,114
Mining and quarrying	11,998	8,117	20,115
Manufacturing	13,831	45,661	59,492
Electricity, gas and water . . .	1,826	2,219	4,045
Construction	10,128	108,129	118,257
Trade, hotels and restaurants .	24,999	84,158	109,157
Transport, storage and communications	17,202	10,472	27,674
Finance, insurance and real estate	12,657	12,543	25,200
Public administration and defence	144,699	18,043	162,742
Other community, social and personal services	54,923	83,299	138,222
Sub-total	306,473	416,545	723,018
Activities not adequately defined .	5,973	7,633	13,606
Total employed	312,446	424,178	736,624
Males	258,655	364,337	622,992
Females	53,791	59,841	113,632

Mid-2013 (estimates in '000): Agriculture, etc. 321; Total labour force 1,193 (Source: FAO).

Health and Welfare

KEY INDICATORS

Total fertility rate (children per woman, 2010)	2.3
Under-5 mortality rate (per 1,000 live births, 2010) . . .	9
HIV/AIDS (% of persons aged 15–49, 2009)	0.1
Physicians (per 1,000 head, 2008)	1.9
Hospital beds (per 1,000 head, 2009)	1.8
Health expenditure (2009): US $ per head (PPP) . . .	826
Health expenditure (2009): % of GDP	3.0
Health expenditure (2009): public (% of total) . . .	78.8
Access to water (% of persons, 2010)	89
Access to sanitation (% of persons, 2010)	99
Total carbon dioxide emissions ('000 metric tons, 2008) . .	45,749.5
Carbon dioxide emissions per head (metric tons, 2008) . .	17.3
Human Development Index (2011): ranking	89
Human Development Index (2011): value	0.705

For sources and definitions, see explanatory note on p. vi.

Agriculture

PRINCIPAL CROPS
('000 metric tons)

	2009	2010	2011
Sorghum	42.0	26.1	36.2
Potatoes	10.0	7.2	8.1
Tomatoes	74.0	82.2	53.7
Onions, dry	5.2	4.4	7.8
Watermelons	15.4	19.1	18.6
Bananas	29.0	56.7	61.6
Lemons and limes	6.4	6.4	6.5
Mangoes, mangosteens and guavas	10.2	10.2	8.9
Dates	259.0	276.4	268.0
Papayas	1.9	1.9	1.7

Aggregate production ('000 metric tons, may include official, semi-official or estimated data): Total cereals 47.0 in 2009, 31.7 in 2010, 42.5 in 2011; Total roots and tubers 10.0 in 2009, 7.2 in 2010; 8.1 in 2011; Total vegetables (incl. melons) 234.4 in 2009, 340.7 in 2010, 284.8 in 2011; Total fruits (excl. melons) 305.9 in 2009, 351.6 in 2010, 346.8 in 2011.

Source: FAO.

LIVESTOCK
('000 head, year ending September)

	2009	2010	2011
Asses*	28.5	28.5	28.5
Cattle	326	333	340
Camels	127	130	132
Sheep	381	389	396
Goats	1,685	1,719	1,754
Chickens*	4,300	4,390	4,450

* FAO estimates.

Source: FAO.

LIVESTOCK PRODUCTS
('000 metric tons)

	2009	2010	2011
Cattle meat*	5.2	5.3	5.6
Camel meat*	6.7	7.4	7.7
Sheep meat*	19.5	19.7	20.1
Goat meat*	14.5	15.0	15.7
Chicken meat*	5.9	5.9	6.0
Cows' milk	49.6	69.6	71.0
Sheep's milk*	4.1	4.2	4.3
Goats' milk*	71.9	100.6	100.8
Hen eggs	9.3	9.3	10.7

* FAO estimates.

Source: FAO.

Fishing

('000 metric tons, live weight)

	2008	2009	2010
Capture	151.9	158.6	163.9
Groupers	5.5	6.0	5.2
Emperors (Scavengers)	9.0	11.3	10.8
Porgies and seabreams	7.4	10.3	9.9
Hairtails and scabbardfishes	3.8	5.7	6.7
Demersal percomorphs	4.3	7.6	6.3
Indian oil sardine	33.5	36.6	32.1
Longtail tuna	7.8	8.1	8.6
Yellowfin tuna	7.0	7.0	3.2
Indian mackerel	9.0	11.0	10.1
Sharks, rays, skates, etc.	5.2	4.8	5.3
Cuttlefish and bobtail squids	9.2	6.6	9.8
Aquaculture	0.1	0.1	0.1
Total catch	152.0	158.7	164.1

Source: FAO.

Mining

('000 metric tons unless otherwise indicated)

	2008	2009	2010
Crude petroleum	35,947	38,700	41,000
Natural gas (million cu m)	24,056	24,760	27,100
Chromium	859.7	798.5	801.9
Gold (kg)	49	28	—
Marble	501.4	630.8	507.7
Salt	11.4	30.6	12.3
Gypsum	348.8	254.2	395.5

2011: Crude petroleum 42,100; Natural gas (million cu m) 26,500.

Sources: BP, *Statistical Review of World Energy*; US Geological Survey.

Industry

SELECTED PRODUCTS
('000 barrels, unless otherwise indicated, estimates)

	2008	2009	2010
Jet fuel and kerosene	3,037	3,225	2,720
Motor spirit (petrol)	6,514	6,604	6,426
Gas-diesel (distillate fuel) oils	8,132	6,662	6,639
Residual fuel oils	18,561	19,697	15,685
Electric energy (million kWh)	16,048	17,823	19,159

Electric energy (million kWh): 21,354 in 2011; 25,018 in 2012.

Source: mainly US Geological Survey.

Finance

CURRENCY AND EXCHANGE RATES

Monetary Units
1,000 baiza = 1 rial Omani (RO).

Sterling, Dollar and Euro Equivalents (31 December 2012)
£1 sterling = 606.7 baiza;
US $1 = 384.5 baiza;
€1 = 507.3 baiza;
10 rials Omani = £16.48 = $26.01 = €19.71.

Exchange Rate: Since January 1986 the official exchange rate has been fixed at US $1 = 384.5 baiza (1 rial Omani = $2.6008).

BUDGET
(RO million)

Revenue	2009	2010	2011
Petroleum revenue (net)	4,490.5	5,470.1	9,664.9
Gas revenues	731.3	929.9	1,172.9
Other current revenue	1,492.6	1,464.2	1,596.5
Taxes and fees	761.8	707.6	728.5
Income tax on enterprises	370.1	272.6	282.0
Customs duties	158.1	179.6	161.2
Non-tax revenue	730.8	756.6	868.0
Surplus from public authorities	24.8	9.2	10.3
Income from government investments	378.9	379.9	512.0
Capital revenue	24.0	29.9	17.6
Capital repayments	10.0	22.4	39.3
Total	6,748.4	7,916.5	12,491.2

Expenditure	2009	2010	2011
Current expenditure	4,218.5	4,791.3	6,103.8
Defence and national security	1,726.4	1,888.2	2,563.7
Civil ministries	2,216.7	2,613.5	3,186.9
Investment expenditure	2,690.9	2,596.8	2,959.5
Share of PDO expenditure*	696.1	613.5	624.3
Participation and subsidies	519.3	577.2	1,674.6
Total	7,428.7	7,965.3	10,737.9

* Referring to the Government's share of current and capital expenditure by Petroleum Development Oman.

2012 (RO million, provisional): *Revenue:* Petroleum revenue (net) 10,436.7; Gas revenues 1,562.9; Customs duties 220.8; Income tax on enterprises 351.9; Capital revenue 11.8; Other revenues 1,397.4; Total 13,981.5. *Expenditure* Current expenditure 6,266.6; Investment expenditure 2,663.8; Participation and subsidies 1,828.3; Total 10,758.7.

INTERNATIONAL RESERVES
(US $ million at 31 December)

	2009	2010	2011
Gold (national valuation)	0.7	0.9	1.0
IMF special drawing rights	290.8	285.8	268.8
Reserve position in IMF	55.9	67.2	113.3
Foreign exchange	11,856.3	12,671.3	13,983.2
Total	12,203.7	13,025.2	14,366.3

Source: IMF, *International Financial Statistics*.

MONEY SUPPLY
(RO million at 31 December)

	2009	2010	2011
Currency outside depository corporations	624.2	702.0	843.1
Transferable deposits	2,073.1	2,596.1	2,600.2
Other deposits	5,192.6	5,369.5	6,342.2
Securities other than shares	—	117.2	69.4
Broad money	7,889.9	8,784.8	9,854.9

Source: IMF, *International Financial Statistics*.

COST OF LIVING
(Consumer Price Index; base: 2000 = 100)

	2010	2011	2012
Food, beverages and tobacco	154.4	161.4	164.9
Textiles, clothing and footwear	104.5	105.2	108.0
Rent, electricity, water and fuel	134.3	138.0	141.0
All items (incl. others)	133.7	139.1	143.2

NATIONAL ACCOUNTS
(RO million in current prices)

Expenditure on the Gross Domestic Product

	2008	2009	2010*
Final consumption expenditure .	10,507.8	10,876.4	11,775.3
General government . . .	3,316.4	3,601.1	4,065.2
Households	7,179.2	7,254.7	7,697.2
Non-profit institutions serving households	12.2	20.6	12.9
Gross capital formation . .	7,863.7	4,707.8	5,630.7
Gross fixed capital formation .	7,028.0	6,421.3	6,261.4
Changes in inventories . .	835.7	−1,713.5	−630.7
Total domestic expenditure	18,371.5	15,584.2	17,406.0
Balance on goods and services .	4,980.0	2,975.0	5,367.0
GDP in purchasers' values .	23,351.5	18,559.1	22,773.0
GDP at constant 2000 prices .	11,079.5	11,513.0	12,083.5

* Provisional figures.

Gross Domestic Product by Economic Activity

	2009	2010*	2011*
Agriculture and fishing . .	261.5	283.0	316.0
Mining and quarrying . . .	7,500.6	10,508.9	14,239.9
Crude petroleum . . .	6,743.4	9,558.6	13,117.9
Natural gas	674.6	869.8	1,022.7
Non-petroleum	82.6	80.7	99.3
Manufacturing	2,160.1	2,459.7	2,965.2
Electricity and water . . .	231.6	271.0	322.2
Construction	1,237.6	1,263.4	1,390.1
Wholesale and retail trade . .	1,618.0	1,816.4	1,945.3
Hotels and restaurants . .	168.5	174.4	175.0
Transport, storage and communications	1,138.3	1,280.0	1,346.1
Financial intermediation . .	910.7	956.3	1,053.5
Real estate	915.1	996.8	1,043.9
Public administration and defence	1,376.8	1,588.5	1,861.6
Other community, social and personal services . . .	1,446.7	1,645.2	1,708.8
Sub-total	18,965.5	23,243.6	28,367.6
Less Financial intermediation services indirectly measured .	424.9	465.0	513.8
Gross value added in basic prices	18,540.6	22,778.6	27,853.8
Taxes on imports	18.5	−5.6	−949.6
GDP in purchasers' values .	18,559.1	22,773.0	26,904.2

* Provisional figures.

Note: Totals may not be equal to the sum of components, owing to rounding.

BALANCE OF PAYMENTS
(US $ million)

	2009	2010	2011
Exports of goods	27,651	36,601	47,092
Imports of goods	−16,052	−17,874	−21,498
Balance on goods . . .	11,600	18,726	25,594
Exports of services . . .	1,620	1,899	2,148
Imports of services . . .	−5,482	−6,291	−7,066
Balance on goods and services	7,738	14,334	20,676
Primary income received . .	653	869	697
Primary income paid . . .	−3,671	−3,628	−3,896
Balance on goods, services and primary income . . .	4,720	11,574	17,477
Secondary income paid . .	−5,316	−5,704	−7,215
Current account . . .	−596	5,871	10,263
Capital account (net) . . .	55	−65	−146
Direct investment assets . .	−109	−1,012	−572
Direct investment liabilities .	1,509	1,142	788
Portfolio investment assets . .	−156	−284	−310
Portfolio investment liabilities	246	571	−447
Other investment assets . .	2,165	−3,026	−7,376
Other investment liabilities .	−1,015	−1,764	299
Net errors and omissions . .	−1,024	65	−1,037
Reserves and related items .	1,076	1,499	1,462

Source: IMF, *International Financial Statistics.*

External Trade

PRINCIPAL COMMODITIES
(RO million)

Imports c.i.f. (distribution by SITC)*	2009	2010	2011
Food and live animals	639.6	778.9	806.1
Beverages and tobacco	60.9	82.1	99.9
Crude materials (inedible) except fuels	167.0	204.3	415.8
Minerals, fuels, lubricants, etc. .	387.5	559.1	978.2
Chemicals and related products .	578.5	670.9	772.6
Basic manufactures	1,202.9	1,263.0	1,560.7
Machinery and transport equipment	3,368.4	3,510.6	3,821.9
Miscellaneous manufactured articles	385.6	451.2	496.2
Commodities not elsewhere classified	24.9	23.9	30.6
Total (incl. others)	6,864.6	7,603.3	9,081.8

Exports f.o.b.	2009	2010	2011
Petroleum and natural gas .	6,947.9	9,703.3	12,826.0
Crude petroleum	5,359.5	8,007.7	10,659.6
Refined petroleum	618.9	519.4	697.1
Natural gas	969.5	1,176.2	1,469.3
Non-oil and -gas exports . .	1,849.5	2,448.2	3,033.2
Live animals and animal products	126.2	160.3	173.4
Mineral products	400.9	612.7	422.1
Chemicals and related products .	311.6	709.0	1,181.4
Total†	10,632.2	14,073.2	18,106.8

* Excluding unrecorded imports (RO million): 31.4 in 2009; 76.2 in 2010; 153.4 in 2011.
† Including re-exports (RO million): 1,834.8 in 2009; 1,921.7 in 2010; 2,247.6 in 2011.

PRINCIPAL TRADING PARTNERS
(RO million)

Imports c.i.f.	2009	2010	2011
Australia	138.2	158.9	155.4
Bahrain	42.4	91.1	147.1
Belgium	76.8	77.7	61.1
China, People's Republic . .	330.1	368.0	420.8
France	103.0	172.3	148.6
Germany	295.8	279.6	315.4
India	404.6	344.0	437.6
Italy	158.5	124.0	169.9
Japan	1,030.7	1,271.6	1,148.0
Korea, Republic	242.2	256.2	350.2
Kuwait	83.2	103.3	76.7
Malaysia	177.1	89.2	110.6
Netherlands	113.2	78.5	105.6
Pakistan	72.1	50.0	66.5
Saudi Arabia	242.0	240.8	454.4
Singapore	68.8	107.1	63.3
Thailand	163.1	188.3	217.4
United Arab Emirates . . .	1,631.8	2,156.0	2,490.3
United Kingdom	157.0	171.4	177.8
USA	442.6	374.6	535.7
Total (incl. others)	6,864.6	7,603.3	9,081.8

Exports f.o.b.*	2009	2010	2011
China, People's Republic . .	184.4	276.8	566.0
Egypt	52.4	26.7	42.0
Hong Kong	51.3	65.6	91.4
India	241.3	371.6	468.0
Indonesia	37.3	59.6	173.0
Iran	246.4	185.1	154.0
Iraq	69.1	63.2	64.0
Jordan	14.2	22.5	14.8
Korea, Republic	73.1	88.5	85.0
Kuwait	19.1	26.6	128.3
Libya	32.7	28.2	2.0
Netherlands	37.5	28.9	88.1

Exports f.o.b.*—continued	2009	2010	2011
Pakistan	84.1	72.0	152.1
Qatar	129.5	66.9	50.7
Saudi Arabia	216.34	265.5	388.6
Singapore	171.6	97.9	65.6
Somalia	40.9	26.9	47.6
United Arab Emirates	1,309.8	1,626.4	1,338.6
United Kingdom	42.4	40.4	76.2
USA	75.6	118.5	129.1
Yemen	55.6	38.9	44.7
Total (incl. others)	3,684.3	4,369.9	5,280.7

* Excluding petroleum exports.

Transport

ROAD TRAFFIC
(registered vehicles at 31 December)

	2001	2002	2003
Private cars	309,217	335,771	284,902
Taxis	20,901	23,639	23,761
Commercial	132,920	140,270	109,118
Government	27,788	29,175	14,861
Motorcycles	5,195	5,436	3,977
Diplomatic	1,274	1,386	561
Other	23,631	24,625	7,320
Total	520,926	560,302	444,500

2007 (registered vehicles at 31 December): Passenger cars 453,362; Buses 26,387; Vans and Lorries 113,341; Motorcycles and mopeds 6,297 (Source: IRF, *World Road Statistics*).

SHIPPING

Flag Registered Fleet
(at 31 December)

	2010	2011	2012
Number of vessels	43	46	47
Total displacement (grt)	48,545	51,284	52,164

Source: Lloyd's List Intelligence (www.lloydslistintelligence.com).

International Sea-borne Freight Traffic
('000 metric tons, unless otherwise indicated)

	2009	2010	2011
Port Sultan Qaboos:			
Vessels entered (number)	1,737	1,858	4,647
Goods loaded	838	911	803
Goods unloaded	4,366	4,082	4,018
Salalah Port:			
Vessels entered (number)	1,591	1,639	1,103
Goods loaded	2,970	5,345	5,556
Goods unloaded	752	935	963
Mina al-Fahal Coastal Area			
Vessels entered (number)	447	456	382
Petroleum loaded	33,328	37,250	37,331
Petroleum products unloaded	1,677	1,518	1,515

2012: *Port Sultan Qaboos:* Goods loaded 829; Goods unloaded 4,229. *Salalah Port:* Goods loaded 6,058; Goods unloaded 1,193.

CIVIL AVIATION
(aircraft movements, passengers and cargo handled at Muscat International Airport)

	2010	2011	2012
International flights:			
flights (number)	60,467	61,441	65,859
passengers ('000)	5,196	5,865	6,836
goods handled (metric tons)	95,411	92,521	n.a.
Domestic flights:			
flights (number)	6,269	6,943	7,987
passengers ('000)	555	613	700
goods handled (metric tons)	1,284	1,400	n.a.

Tourism

FOREIGN TOURIST ARRIVALS*

Country of nationality	2008	2009	2010
Bahrain	13,363	15,759	9,567
Egypt	22,648	26,853	26,807
France	39,704	35,828	38,217
Germany	101,737	85,768	81,372
India	156,723	162,832	158,739
Italy	23,544	21,849	20,909
Kuwait	16,102	20,728	13,487
Netherlands	20,615	22,327	18,638
Pakistan	21,867	18,149	20,878
Saudi Arabia	24,177	25,312	17,550
Switzerland	24,423	25,366	23,898
United Arab Emirates	112,785	130,487	93,585
United Kingdom	122,723	100,671	81,677
USA	38,630	111,304	66,761
Total (incl. others)	1,378,078	1,279,678	1,048,052

* Figures refer to international arrivals at hotels and similar establishments.

Tourism receipts (US $ million, incl. passenger transport, unless otherwise indicated): 1,113 in 2008; 1,108 in 2009; 775 in 2010 (excl. passenger transport).

Source: World Tourism Organization.

Communications Media

	2009	2010	2011
Telephones ('000 main lines in use)	296.4	281.8	287.3
Mobile cellular telephones ('000 subscribers)	3,970.6	4,606.1	4,809.2
Internet subscribers ('000)	78.1	73.9	89.1
Broadband subscribers ('000)	41.1	45.4	52.6

Source: International Telecommunication Union.

Education

(state schools; 2011/12, unless otherwise indicated)

			Pupils/Students		
	Institutions	Teachers	Males	Females	Total
Pre-primary*	5	529	4,973	4,456	9,429
Basic†	855	38,650	184,137	182,136	366,273
General†:					
Grades 1–6	238	1,098	8,066	7,787	15,853
Grades 7–9		2,911	12,723	12,535	25,258
Grades 10–12		9,684	55,557	54,112	109,669
Higher‡§	34	1,608	12,282	11,004	23,286
University‖	1	1,181	8,371	8,123	16,494

* 2005/06.
† The Basic education system began to replace the General education system from 1998/99.
‡ Comprising six teacher-training colleges, the College of *Shari'a* and Law, five technical colleges, the Academy of Tourism and Catering, the College of Banking and Financial Studies, 16 institutes of health, and four vocational-training centres.
§ 2004/05.
‖ 2010/11.

Pupil-teacher ratio (primary education, UNESCO estimate): 11.8 in 2008/09 (Source: UNESCO Institute for Statistics).

Adult literacy rate (UNESCO estimates): 86.6% (males 90.0%; females 80.9%) in 2008 (Source: UNESCO Institute for Statistics).

Directory

The Government

HEAD OF STATE

Sultan: QABOOS BIN SAID AL-SAID (assumed power on 23 July 1970, after deposing his father).

COUNCIL OF MINISTERS
(May 2013)

Prime Minister and Minister of Foreign Affairs, Defence and Finance: Sultan QABOOS BIN SAID AL-SAID.

Deputy Prime Minister for the Council of Ministers: Sayyid FAHD BIN MAHMOUD AL-SAID.

Minister Responsible for Defence Affairs: Sayyid BADR BIN SAUD BIN HAREB AL-BUSAIDI.

Minister of Legal Affairs: Dr ABDULLAH BIN MUHAMMAD BIN SAID AL-SAEEDI.

Minister of Oil and Gas: Dr MUHAMMAD BIN HAMAD BIN SAIF AL-RUMHI.

Minister of Justice: Sheikh ABD AL-MALIK BIN ABDULLAH BIN ALI AL-KHALILI.

Minister Responsible for Financial Affairs: DARWISH BIN ISMAIL BIN ALI AL-BALUSHI.

Minister of Awqaf (Religious Endowments) and Religious Affairs: Sheikh ABDULLAH BIN MUHAMMAD BIN ABDULLAH AL-SALIMI.

Minister Responsible for Foreign Affairs: YOUSUF BIN AL-ALAWI BIN ABDULLAH.

Minister of Information: Dr ABD AL-MUNEM BIN MANSOUR BIN SAID AL-HASNI.

Minister of Housing: Sheikh SAIF BIN MUHAMMAD AL-SHABIBI.

Minister of Education: MADEEHA BINT AHMAD BIN NASIR AL-SHIBANIYAH.

Minister of Higher Education: Dr RAWYA BINT SAUD BIN AHMAD AL-BUSAIDIYAH.

Minister of Heritage and Culture: Sayyid HAITHAM BIN TARIQ AL-SAID.

Minister of Tourism: AHMAD BIN NASSER BIN HAMAD AL-MEHRZI.

Minister of Social Development: Sheikh MUHAMMAD BIN SAID BIN SAIF AL-KALBANI.

Minister of Manpower: ABDULLAH BIN NASSER AL-BAKRI.

Minister of Sports Affairs: SAAD BIN MUHAMMAD BIN SAID AL-MARDHOUF AL-SAADI.

Minister of Transport and Communications: AHMAD BIN MUHAMMAD BIN SALIM AL-FUTAISI.

Minister of the Interior: Sayyid HAMOUD BIN FAISAL BIN SAID AL-BUSAIDI.

Minister of Commerce and Industry: Eng. ALI BIN MASSOUD BIN ALI AL-SUNAIDI.

Minister of Agriculture and Fisheries: Dr FUAD BIN JAAFAR BIN MUHAMMAD AL-SAJWANI.

Minister of Environment and Climate Affairs: MUHAMMAD BIN SALIM BIN SAID AL-TOOBI.

Minister of Health: Dr AHMAD BIN MUHAMMAD BIN OBAID AL-SAEEDI.

Minister of Regional Municipalities and Water Resources: AHMAD BIN ABDULLAH BIN MUHAMMAD AL-SHUHI.

Minister of the Civil Service: Sheikh KHALID BIN OMAR BIN SAID AL-MARHOON.

Minister of State and Governor of Muscat: Sayyid SAUD BIN HILAL BIN HAMAD AL-BUSAIDI.

Minister of State and Governor of Dhofar: Sayyid MUHAMMAD BIN SULTAN BIN HAMOUD AL-BUSAIDI.

Minister of the Diwan of the Royal Court: Sayyid KHALID BIN HILAL BIN SAUD AL-BUSAIDI.

Minister of the Royal Office: Lt-Gen. SULTAN BIN MUHAMMAD AL-NUMANI.

MINISTRIES

Diwan of the Royal Court: POB 632, Muscat 113; tel. 24738711; fax 24739427.

Ministry of Agriculture and Fisheries: POB 3738, Ruwi 112; tel. 24700896; fax 24707939; e-mail info@maf.gov.om; internet www.maf.gov.om.

Ministry of Awqaf (Religious Endowments) and Religious Affairs: POB 3232, Ruwi 112; tel. 24696870; e-mail info@mara.gov.om; internet www.maraoman.net.

Ministry of the Civil Service: POB 3994, Ruwi 112; tel. 24696000; fax 24601365; internet www.mocs.gov.om.

Ministry of Commerce and Industry: POB 550, Muscat 113; tel. 24813500; fax 24817238; e-mail info@mocioman.gov.om; internet www.mocioman.gov.om.

Ministry of Defence: POB 113, Muscat 113; tel. 24312605; fax 24702521.

Ministry of Education: POB 3, Muscat 113; tel. 24775209; e-mail moe@moe.gov.om; internet www.moe.gov.om.

Ministry of Environment and Climate Affairs: POB 323, Muscat 100; tel. 24404805; fax 24603993.

Ministry of Finance: POB 506, Muscat 100; tel. 24738201; fax 24737028; e-mail info@mof.gov.om; internet www.mof.gov.om.

Ministry of Foreign Affairs: POB 252, Muscat 112; tel. 24699500; fax 24696141; e-mail info@mofa.gov.om; internet www.mofa.gov.om.

Ministry of Health: POB 393, Muscat 113; tel. 24602177; fax 24602647; e-mail webmaster@moh.gov.om; internet www.moh.gov.om.

Ministry of Heritage and Culture: POB 668, Muscat 113; tel. 24641300; fax 24641331; e-mail info@mhc.gov.om; internet www.mhc.gov.om.

Ministry of Higher Education: POB 82, Ruwi 112; tel. 24340999; fax 24340172; e-mail info_dept@mohe.gov.om; internet www.mohe.gov.om.

Ministry of Housing: POB 173, Ruwi 100; tel. 24601276; e-mail dept.infopr@housing.gov.om; internet eservices.housing.gov.om.

Ministry of Information: POB 600, Muscat 113; tel. 24603222; fax 24693770; e-mail omanet@omantel.net.om; internet www.omanet.om.

Ministry of the Interior: POB 127, Ruwi 112; tel. 24602244; fax 24696660; internet www.moi.gov.om.

Ministry of Justice: POB 354, Ruwi 112; tel. 24697699; fax 24607716; e-mail webmaster@moj.gov.om; internet www.moj.gov.om.

Ministry of Legal Affairs: POB 578, Ruwi 112; tel. 24605802; fax 24482309; e-mail inquiry@mola.gov.om; internet www.mola.gov.om.

Ministry of Manpower: POB 413, Muscat 113; tel. 24816739; fax 24816234; e-mail webmaster@manpower.gov.om; internet www.manpower.gov.om.

Ministry of Oil and Gas: POB 551, Muscat 100; tel. 24640555; fax 24691046; internet www.mog.gov.om.

Ministry of Regional Municipalities and Water Resources: POB 461, Muscat 112; tel. 24692550; fax 24694015; e-mail admin@mrmwr.gov.om; internet www.mrmwr.gov.om.

Ministry of the Royal Office: POB 2227, Ruwi 112; tel. 24600841.

Ministry of Social Development: Muscat; internet mosd.gov.om.

Ministry of Sports Affairs: POB 211, Muscat 113; tel. 24755240; fax 24704558; e-mail feedback@sportsoman.com; internet www.sportsoman.com.

Ministry of Tourism: Madinat al-Sultan Qaboos, POB 200, Muscat 115; tel. 24588700; fax 24588880; e-mail info@omantourism.gov.om; internet www.mot.gov.om.

Ministry of Transport and Communications: POB 684, Ruwi 112; tel. 24685000; fax 24685757; e-mail info@motc.gov.om; internet www.motc.gov.om.

MAJLIS OMAN
(Council of Oman)

Majlis al-Shura
(Consultative Council)

POB 981, 111 Muscat; tel. 24510444; fax 24510560; e-mail info@shura.om; internet www.shura.om.

President: Sheikh KHALID BIN HILAL BIN NASSER AL-MA'AWALI.

The Majlis al-Shura was established by royal decree in November 1991. Initially, members of the Majlis were appointed by the Sultan from among nominees selected at national polls, but from the September 2000 elections members were directly elected. Two representatives are elected in each *wilaya* (district) of more than 30,000 inhabitants, and one in each *wilaya* of fewer than 30,000 inhabitants. Members of the Majlis are appointed for a single four-year term of office. The Majlis elected in October 2011 comprised 84 members. The duties of the Majlis include the approval and amendment of all social and economic draft laws prior to their enactment by the Sultan;

public service ministries are required to submit reports and answer questions regarding their performance, plans and achievements. A decree issued by Sultan Qaboos bin Said al-Said on 19 October 2011 granted members of both chambers of the Majlis Oman the right to propose draft legislation, while members of the Majlis al-Shura may issue a request to question government ministers. The President of the Majlis is elected by an absolute majority of its members.

Majlis al-Dawlah
(State Council)

POB 59, Muscat; tel. 24699677; fax 24698719; e-mail statecouncil@statecouncil.om.

President: Sheikh YAHYA BIN MAHFOUDH AL-MANTHERI.

The Majlis al-Dawlah was established in December 1997, in accordance with the terms of the Basic Statute of the State. Like the Majlis al-Shura, it is an advisory body, the function of which is to serve as a liaison between the Government and the people of Oman. Its members are appointed by the Sultan for a four-year term. A new Majlis al-Dawlah, comprising 70 members, was appointed on 1 November 2011.

Political Organizations

There are no political organizations in Oman.

Diplomatic Representation

EMBASSIES IN OMAN

Algeria: POB 216, Muscat 115; tel. 24694945; fax 24694419; e-mail afcongem@omantel.net.om; Ambassador MUHAMMAD YOUSFI.

Bahrain: al-Khuwair, POB 66, Madinat Qaboos; tel. 24605133; fax 24605072; e-mail muscat.mission@mofa.gov.bh; Ambassador MUHAMMAD BIN SALEH AL-SHEIKH ALI.

Bangladesh: St 664, Bldg 5903, POB 3959, Ruwi 112; tel. 24698660; fax 24698789; e-mail bangla@omantel.net.om; Ambassador NURUL ALAM CHOWDHURY.

Brazil: al-Khuwair, Villa 1424, Way 1521, POB 1149, Muscat; Ambassador MITZI GURGEL VALENTE DA COSTA.

Brunei: Shatti al-Qurum, St 3050, Villa 4062, POB 91, Ruwi 112; tel. 24603533; fax 24605910; e-mail kbopuni@omantel.net.om; Ambassador Dato' Seri Setia Dr Haji BESAR BIN Haji BAKAR.

China, People's Republic: House No. 1368, Shatti al-Qurum, POB 315, Muscat 112; tel. 24696698; fax 24602322; e-mail chinaemb_om@mfa.gov.cn; internet om.chineseembassy.org; Ambassador WU JIU-HONG.

Egypt: Jamiat al-Dowal al-Arabiya St, Diplomatic City, al-Khuwair, POB 2252, Ruwi 112; tel. 24600411; fax 24603626; e-mail eg.emb_muscat@mfa.gov.eg; Ambassador AMR AHMAD ABD AL-MAJEED AL-ZAYAT.

France: Diplomatic City, al-Khuwair, POB 208, Madinat Qaboos 115; tel. 24681800; fax 24681843; e-mail diplofr1@omantel.net.om; internet www.ambafrance-om.org; Ambassador YVES OUDIN.

Germany: POB 128, Ruwi 112; tel. 24832482; fax 24835690; e-mail info@maskat.diplo.de; internet www.maskat.diplo.de; Ambassador HANS-CHRISTIAN FREIHERR VON REIBNITZ.

India: New Chancery Complex, Jamiat al-Dowal al-Arabiya St, al-Khuwair, POB 1727, Ruwi 112; tel. 24684500; fax 24698291; e-mail indiamct@omantel.net.om; internet www.indemb-oman.org; Ambassador J. S. MUKUL.

Iran: Diplomatic Area, Jamiat al-Dowal al-Arabiya St, POB 3155, Ruwi 112; tel. 24696944; fax 24696888; e-mail iranembassy@hotmail.com; internet www.iranembassy.gov.om; Ambassador ALI AKBAR SEBAWYEH.

Iraq: Shatti al-Qurum, Way 3015, House No. 1073, POB 262, Muscat 115; tel. 24603642; fax 24602026; e-mail musemb@iraqmofamail.net; Ambassador MUIZ KADIM SALMAN AL-NOAH.

Italy: Shatti al-Qurum, Way No. 3034, House No. 2697, POB 520, Ruwi 115; tel. 24693727; fax 24695161; e-mail ambasciata.mascate@esteri.it; internet www.ambmascate.esteri.it; Ambassador PAULA AMADI.

Japan: Shatti al-Qurum, Villa No. 760, Way No. 3011, Jamiat al-Dowal al-Arabiya St, POB 3511, Ruwi 112; tel. 24601028; fax 24698720; e-mail embjapan@omantel.net.om; internet www.oman.emb-japan.go.jp; Ambassador GEORGE HISAEDA.

Jordan: Diplomatic City, Arab League St, POB 70, al-Adhaiba 130; tel. 24692760; fax 24692762; e-mail embhkjom@omantel.net.om; Ambassador MITEB ZAIN.

Kenya: Muscat; Chargé d'affaires a.i. YABESH MONARI.

Korea, Republic: POB 377, Madinat Qaboos 115; tel. 24691490; fax 24691495; e-mail emboman@mofat.go.kr; internet omn.mofat.go.kr; Ambassador CHOE JONG-HYUN.

Kuwait: Diplomatic Area, al-Khuwair, Arab League St, Blk 13, Bldg 58, POB 1798, Ruwi 112; tel. 24699626; fax 24604732; e-mail muscat@mofa.gov.kw; Ambassador SALIM GHASAB AL-ZIMNAN.

Lebanon: Shatti al-Qurum, Way No. 3019, Villa No. 1613, al-Harthy Complex, POB 67, Muscat 118; tel. 24695844; fax 24695633; e-mail lebanon1@omantel.net.om; Ambassador AFIF AYYUB.

Malaysia: Shatti al-Qurum, Villa No. 1611, Way No. 3019, POB 3939, Ruwi 112; tel. 24698329; fax 24605031; e-mail mwmuscat@omantel.net.om; internet www.kln.gov.my/web/omn_muscat; Ambassador Dato' RUSTUM BIN YAHAYA.

Morocco: Shatti al-Qurum, Villa No. 2443, Way No. 3030, POB 3125, Ruwi 112; tel. 24696152; fax 24601114; e-mail sifamamu@omantel.net.om; Ambassador NOURDINE BEN OMAR.

Netherlands: Shatti al-Qurum, Way No. 3017, Villa No. 1366, POB 3302, Ruwi 112; tel. 24603706; fax 24603778; e-mail mus@minbuza.nl; internet www.mfa.nl/mus; Ambassador STEFAN VAN WERSCH.

Pakistan: Way No. 2133, POB 1302, Madinat Qaboos, Ruwi 112; tel. 24603439; fax 24697462; e-mail parepmuscat@hotmail.com; internet www.mofa.gov.pk/oman; Ambassador (vacant).

Philippines: POB 420, Madinat Qaboos 115; tel. 24605140; fax 24605176; e-mail muscatpe@omantel.net.om; internet www.muscatpe.org; Ambassador JOSELITO A. JIMENO.

Qatar: Diplomatic City, Jamiat al-Dowal al-Arabiya St, al-Khuwair, POB 802, Muscat 113; tel. 24691152; fax 24691156; e-mail sad707@omantel.net.om; Ambassador ABDULLAH BIN MUHAMMAD BIN KHALID AL-KHATIR.

Russia: Shatti al-Qurum, Way No. 3032, Surfait Compound, POB 745, Ruwi 115; tel. 24602894; fax 24604189; e-mail rusoman@omantel.net.om; internet www.oman.mid.ru; Ambassador SERGEI N. PESKOV.

Saudi Arabia: Diplomatic City, Jamiat al-Dowal al-Arabiya St, POB 1411, Ruwi 112; tel. 24698780; fax 24607418; e-mail omemb@mofa.gov.sa; Ambassador ABD AL-AZIZ BIN SULAIMAN AL-TURKI.

Senegal: Muscat; tel. 24694139; fax 24694151; Ambassador AL-SHAIKH AL-TIJANI.

Somalia: Mumtaz St, Villa Hassan Jumaa Baker, POB 1767, Ruwi 112; tel. and fax 24697977; e-mail danjsiad@omantel.net.om; Ambassador HASSAN MOHAMED SYAAD BERI.

South Africa: al-Harthy Complex, POB 231, Muscat 118; tel. 24694791; fax 24694792; e-mail southae@omantel.net.om; Ambassador YOUSEF SALOJI.

Spain: Shatti al-Qurum, Way No. 2834, House No. 2573, POB 3492, Ruwi 112; tel. 24691101; fax 24698969; e-mail emb.mascate@mae.es; Ambassador JOSÉ LUIS ROSELLÓ SERRA.

Sri Lanka: POB 95, Madinat Qaboos 115; tel. 24697841; fax 24697336; e-mail lankaemb@omantel.net.om; Ambassador MADU-KANDE ASOKA KUMARA GIRIHAGAMA.

Sudan: Diplomatic City, al-Khuwair, POB 3971, Ruwi 112; tel. 24697875; fax 24699065; e-mail suanimt@gto.net.om; Ambassador AWADH MUHAMMAD AHMED.

Syria: al-Ensharah St, Villa No. 2826, POB 85, Madinat Qaboos, Muscat 115; tel. 24697904; fax 24603895; e-mail syria@omantel.net.om; internet www.syrianembassy.gov.om; Ambassador FAROUK MAHMOUD QADDOUR.

Thailand: Shatti al-Qurum, Villa No. 1339, Way No. 3017, POB 60, Ruwi 115; tel. 24602684; fax 24605714; e-mail thaimct@omantel.net.om; Ambassador Dr PORNCHAI DANVIVATHANA.

Tunisia: al-Ensharah St, Way No. 1507, POB 220, Muscat 115; tel. and fax 24603486; Ambassador TARIQ EL-ADAB.

Turkey: Shatti al-Qurum, Bldg No. 3270, St No. 3042, POB 47, Mutrah 115; tel. 24697050; fax 24697053; e-mail embassy.muscat@mfa.gov.tr; internet muscat.emb.mfa.gov.tr; Ambassador KEREM AHMET KIRATLI.

United Arab Emirates: Diplomatic City, al-Khuwair, POB 551, Muscat 111; tel. 24400000; fax 24602584; e-mail muscat@mofa.gov.ae; Ambassador ABD AL-REDHA ABDULLAH KHOURI.

United Kingdom: POB 185, Mina al-Fahal 116; tel. 24609000; fax 24609010; e-mail enquiries.muscat@fco.gov.uk; internet ukinoman.fco.gov.uk; Ambassador JAMES BOWDEN.

USA: Jamiat al-Dowal al-Arabiya St, POB 202, Madinat Qaboos, Muscat 115; tel. 24643400; fax 24643740; e-mail answersom@state.gov; internet oman.usembassy.gov; Ambassador GRETA HOLTZ.

Yemen: Shatti al-Qurum, Area 258, Way No. 2840, Bldg No. 2981, POB 105, Madinat Qaboos 115; tel. 24600815; fax 24605008; e-mail yemenom@hotmail.com; Ambassador ABD AL-RAHMAN KHAMIS UBAID.

Judicial System

Oman's Basic Statute guarantees the independence of the judiciary. The foundation for the legal system is *Shari'a* (Islamic law), which is the basis for family law, dealing with matters such as inheritance and divorce. Separate courts have been established to deal with commercial disputes and other matters to which *Shari'a* does not apply.

Courts of the First Instance are competent to try cases of criminal misdemeanour; serious crimes are tried by the Criminal Courts; the Court of Appeal is in Muscat. There are district courts throughout the country. Special courts deal with military crimes committed by members of the armed and security forces.

The Basic Statute provides for a Supreme Council to supervise the proper functioning of the courts.

An Administrative Court, to review the decisions of government bodies, was instituted in April 2001.

The office of Public Prosecutor was established in 1999, and the first such appointment was made in June 2001.

Religion

ISLAM

The majority of the population (estimated at 89.2% in 2001) are Muslims, of whom approximately three-quarters are of the Ibadi sect and about one-quarter are Sunni Muslims.

Grand Mufti of Oman: Sheikh AHMAD BIN HAMAD AL-KHALILI.

HINDUISM

According to 2001 estimates, 6.0% of the population are Hindus.

CHRISTIANITY

According to 2001 estimates, 2.9% of the population are Christians.

Protestantism

The Protestant Church in Oman: POB 1982, Ruwi 112; tel. 24702372; fax 24789943; e-mail pcomct@omantel.net.om; internet 76.12.38.165/occ2003/skur/history.htm; joint chaplaincy of the Anglican Church and the Reformed Church of America; four interdenominational churches in Oman, at Ruwi and Ghala in Muscat, at Sohar, and at Salalah; Senior Pastor Rev. MICHAEL PEPPIN.

The Roman Catholic Church

A small number of adherents, mainly expatriates, form part of the Apostolic Vicariate of Southern Arabia. The Vicar Apostolic is resident in the United Arab Emirates.

The Press

Article 31 of Oman's Basic Statute guarantees the freedom of the press, printing and publishing, according to the terms and conditions specified by the law. Published matter 'leading to discord, harming the State's security or abusing human dignity or rights' is prohibited.

NEWSPAPERS

Oman: POB 3002, Ruwi 112; tel. 24699689; fax 24697443; e-mail editor@omandaily.com; internet www.omandaily.com; daily; Arabic; publ. by Oman Establishment for Press, Publication and Advertising; Editor-in-Chief ABDULLAH BIN NASSER AL-RAHBI; circ. 26,000.

Al-Shabiba (Youth): POB 2998, Ruwi 112; tel. 24814373; fax 24811722; e-mail editor@shabiba.com; internet www.shabiba.com; f. 1993; daily; Arabic; culture, leisure and sports; publ. by Muscat Press and Publishing House SAOC; Editor-in-Chief AHMAD BIN ESSA AL-ZEDJALI; circ. 15,000.

Al-Watan (The Nation): POB 463, Muscat 113; tel. 24491919; fax 24491280; e-mail alwatan@omantel.net.om; internet www.alwatan.com; f. 1971; daily; Arabic; Editor-in-Chief MUHAMMAD BIN SULAYMAN AL-TAI; circ. 40,000.

English Language

Oman Daily Observer: POB 3002, Ruwi 112; tel. 24699647; fax 24600362; e-mail editor@omanobserver.com; internet www.omanobserver.com; f. 1981; daily; publ. by Oman Establishment for Press, News, Publication and Advertising; Chair. ABDULLAH BIN NASSER AL-RAHBI; Editor IBRAHIM BIN SAIF AL-HAMDANI; circ. 22,000.

Oman Tribune: POB 463, Muscat 113; tel. 24491919; fax 24498444; e-mail eomantribune@omantribune.com; internet www.omantribune.com; f. 2004; Chair. MUHAMMAD BIN SULAYMAN AL-TAI; Editor-in-Chief ABD AL-HAMID BIN SULAYMAN AL-TAI.

Times of Oman: POB 770, Ruwi 112; tel. 24811953; fax 24813153; e-mail online@timesofoman.com; internet www.timesofoman.com; f. 1975; daily; publ. by Muscat Press and Publishing House SAOC; Founder, Chair. and Editor-in-Chief ESSA BIN MUHAMMAD AL-ZEDJALI; Man. Dir ANIS BIN ESSA AL-ZEDJALI; circ. 34,000.

TheWeek: POB 2616, Ruwi 112, Muscat; tel. 24799388; fax 24793316; e-mail theweek@apexstuff.com; internet www.theweek.co.om; f. 2003; weekly; free; publ. by Apex Press and Publishing; CEO and Man. Editor MOHANA PRABHAKAR; circ. 50,743 (copies per week).

PERIODICALS

Al-Ain al-Sahira (The Vigilant Eye): Royal Oman Police, POB 302, Mina' al-Fahl 116; tel. 24569270; fax 24567161; internet www.rop.gov.om; quarterly magazine of Royal Oman Police; Editor-in-Chief Col ABDULLAH BIN ALI AL-HARTHI.

Alam Aliktisaad Wala'mal (AIWA) (World of Economy and Business): POB 3305, Ruwi 112; tel. 24700896; fax 24707939; e-mail avi@umsoman.com; f. 2007; monthly; Arabic; business magazine; publ. by United Press and Publishing LLC; Business Head AVI TITUS.

Al-'Aqida (The Faith): POB 1001, Ruwi 112; tel. 24701000; fax 24709917; weekly illustrated magazine; Arabic; political; Editor SAID AL-SAMHAN AL-KATHIRI; circ. 10,000.

Business Today: POB 2616, Ruwi 112; tel. 24799388; fax 24793316; e-mail editorial@apexstuff.com; internet www.businesstoday.co.om; monthly; publ. by Apex Press and Publishing; Man. Editor MOHANA PRABHAKAR.

The Commercial: POB 2002, Ruwi 112; tel. 24704022; fax 24795885; e-mail omanad@omantel.net.om; f. 1978; monthly; Arabic and English; business news; Man. MUHAMMAD AYOOB; Chief Editor ALI BIN ABDULLAH AL-KASBI; circ. 10,000.

Al-Ghorfa (The Chamber): POB 1400, Ruwi 112; tel. 24703082; fax 24708497; e-mail alghorfa@chamberoman.com; internet www.chamberoman.com; f. 1978; bi-monthly; English and Arabic; business; publ. by Oman Chamber of Commerce and Industry; Editor HAMOOD HAMAD AL-MAHROUQ; circ. 10,500.

Al-Jarida al-Rasmiya (Official Gazette): POB 578, Ruwi 112; tel. 24605802; fax 24605697; f. 1972; fortnightly; publ. by Ministry of Legal Affairs.

Jund Oman (Soldiers of Oman): Ministry of Defence, POB 113, Muscat 113; tel. 24613615; fax 24613369; f. 1974; monthly; Arabic; illustrated magazine of the Ministry of Defence; Supervisor Chief of Staff of the Sultan's Armed Forces.

Al-Mar'a (Woman): United Media Services, POB 3305, Ruwi 112; tel. 24700896; fax 24707939; e-mail almara@umsoman.com; internet www.almaraonline.com; monthly; Arabic and English; women's interest; publ. by United Press and Publishing LLC.

Al-Markazi (The Central): POB 1161, Ruwi 112; tel. 24702222; fax 24707913; e-mail cboccr@omantel.net.om; internet www.cbo-oman.org; f. 1975; bi-monthly economic magazine; Arabic and English; publ. by Cen. Bank of Oman; Editor-in-Chief HAIDER BIN ABD AL-REDHA AL-LAWATI.

Al-Nahda (The Renaissance): POB 979, Muscat 113; tel. 24563104; fax 24563106; weekly illustrated magazine; Arabic; political and social; Editor TALEB SAID AL-MEAWALY; circ. 10,000.

Nizwa: POB 855, 117 Wadi Kabir; tel. 24601608; fax 24694254; e-mail nizwa99@nizwa.com; internet www.nizwa.com; f. 1994; quarterly; Arabic; literary and cultural; publ. by Oman Establishment for Press, News, Publication and Advertising; Editor-in-Chief SAIF AL-RAHBI.

Oman Economic Review: POB 3305, Ruwi 112; tel. 24700896; fax 24707939; e-mail editor@oeronline.com; internet www.oeronline.com; f. 1998; monthly; English; business news; publ. by United Press and Publishing LLC; Editor-in-Chief Sayyid TARIK BIN SHABIB; circ. 25,000.

Oman Today: POB 2616, Ruwi 112; tel. 24799388; fax 24793316; e-mail editorial@apexstuff.com; internet www.omantoday.co.om; f. 1981; monthly; English; leisure and sports; publ. by Apex Press and Publishing; Man. Editor MOHANA PRABHAKAR; circ. 20,000.

Al-Omaniya (Omani Woman): POB 3303, Ruwi 112; tel. 24792700; fax 24707765; f. 1982; monthly; Arabic; Editor AIDA BINT SALIM AL-HUJRI; circ. 10,500.

Risalat al-Masjid (The Mosque Message): POB 6066, Muscat; tel. 24561178; fax 24560607; issued by Diwan of the Royal Court Protocol Dept (Schools and Mosques Section); Editor JOUMA BIN MUHAMMAD BIN SALEM AL-WAHAIBI.

Al-Usra (The Family): POB 440, Mutrah 114; tel. 24794922; fax 24795348; e-mail admeds@omantel.net.om; f. 1974; fortnightly; Arabic; socio-economic illustrated magazine; Chief Editor SADEK ABDOWANI; circ. 15,000.

NEWS AGENCY

Oman News Agency: Ministry of Information, POB 3659, Ruwi 112; tel. 24698891; fax 24699657; e-mail onaoman@omantel.net.om; internet www.omannews.gov.om; f. 1986; Dir-Gen. and Editor-in-Chief MAJID BIN MUHAMMAD BIN FARAJ AL-ROWAS.

Publishers

Apex Press and Publishing: POB 2616, Ruwi 112, Muscat; tel. 24799388; fax 24793316; e-mail editorial@apexstuff.com; internet www.apexstuff.com; f. 1980; art, history, trade directories, maps, leisure and business magazines, and guidebooks; publs incl. *TheWeek* (English weekly), *Business Today* (business monthly), *Oman Today* (leisure monthly); Pres. SALEH M. TALIB AL-ZAKWANI; Man. Editor MOHANA PRABHAKAR.

Muscat Press and Publishing House SAOC: POB 770, Ruwi 112; tel. 24811953; fax 24813153; publs incl. *Times of Oman* (English daily) and *Al-Shabiba* (Arabic daily); Chair. ESSA BIN MUHAMMAD AL-ZEDJALI; CEO AHMAD BIN ESSA AL-ZEDJALI.

National Publishing and Advertising LLC: POB 3112, Ruwi 112; tel. 24793098; fax 24708445; e-mail advertising@npaoman.com; internet www.npaoman.com; f. 1987; Man. ASHOK SUVARNA.

Oman Establishment for Press, News, Publication and Advertising (OEPNPA): POB 974, al-Qurum, Muscat 113; tel. 24649458; fax 24649469; f. 1996 as Oman Newspaper House; publs include *Oman* (Arabic daily), *Oman Daily Observer* (English language) and *Nizwa* (Arabic quarterly); three regional offices in Dhofar, Nizwa and Sohar; CEO ABDULLAH BIN NASSER AL-RAHBI; Editor-in-Chief FAHMI BIN KHALID AL-HARTHI.

United Press and Publishing LLC (UPP): POB 3305, Ruwi 112; tel. 24700896; fax 24707939; internet www.renaissanceoman.com; f. 1995; part of Renaissance Services SAOG; publishes *Alam Aliktisaad Wala'mal* (Arabic monthly) and *Oman Economic Review* (English monthly); Chief Exec. SANDEEP SEHGAL.

Broadcasting and Communications

TELECOMMUNICATIONS

Oman Telecommunications Company SAOC (Omantel): POB 789, Ruwi 112; tel. 24631417; fax 24697066; e-mail info@omantel.net .om; internet www.omantel.om; f. 1999 as successor to Gen. Telecommunications Org.; provider of fixed-line, mobile and internet services; held a monopoly on fixed-line services until 2008; 70% stake owned by the Government of Oman; Chair. Eng. SULTAN BIN HAMDOUN AL-HARTHI; CEO Dr AMER BIN AWADH AL-RAWAS.

Oman Mobile Telecommunications Company LLC (Oman Mobile): POB 694, al-Azaiba 130; tel. 24474000; e-mail enquiry@ omanmobile.om; internet www.omanmobile.om; f. 2004; Chair. Eng. SULTAN BIN HAMDOUN AL-HARTHI.

Omani Qatari Telecommunications Co SAOC (Nawras): POB 874, Muscat 111; tel. 95011500 (mobile); fax 95011555; e-mail customerservice@nawras.om; internet www.nawras.om; f. 2004; awarded Oman's second mobile cellular telecommunications licence 2004; awarded Oman's second fixed-line licence 2008; jt venture between Qatar Telecommunications Corpn (Q-Tel), TDC A/S (Denmark) and several Omani investors; Chair. Sheikh SALIM BIN MUSTAHIL AL-MA'ASHANI; CEO ROSS CORMACK.

Regulatory Authority

Telecommunications Regulatory Authority: POB 579, Ruwi 112; tel. 24574300; fax 24565464; e-mail traoman@tra.gov.om; internet www.tra.gov.om; f. 2002 to oversee the privatization of Omantel and to set tariffs and regulate the sale of operating licences; Chair. MUHAMMAD BIN NASSER AL-KHUSAIBI.

BROADCASTING

The Law on Private Radio and Television Stations, enacted in 2004, provided for the establishment of private broadcasters for the first time.

Radio

Sultanate of Oman Radio: Ministry of Information, POB 600, Muscat 113; tel. 24602058; fax 24601393; e-mail omanet@omantel .net.om; internet www.oman-radio.gov.om; f. 1970; operates four services: General Arabic Channel, Al-Shabab Channel (youth service), English-language FM service, Holy Koran Channel; Dir-Gen. NASSER SULAYMAN AL-SAIBANI.

The first private radio licences were issued in 2005, and broadcasts began in 2007 with the launch of Hala FM (Arabic, entertainment and music) and Hi FM (English, entertainment and music). A third private station, Al-Wisal FM, began broadcasting in Arabic in 2008.

Television

Sultanate of Oman Television: Ministry of Information, POB 600, Muscat 113; tel. 24603222; fax 24605032; e-mail feedback_tv@ oman-tv.gov.om; internet www.oman-tv.gov.om; began broadcasting in 1974; programmes broadcast via Arabsat and Nilesat satellite networks.

Finance

(cap. = capital; res = reserves; dep. = deposits; m. = million; brs = branches; amounts in rials Omani)

BANKING

At the end of March 2010 there were 17 commercial banks (seven local and 10 foreign) and two specialized banks, with a total network of 451 domestic branch offices operating throughout Oman.

Central Bank

Central Bank of Oman: POB 1161, 44 Mutrah Commercial Centre, Ruwi 112; tel. 24777777; fax 24788995; e-mail cboccr@omantel.net .om; internet www.cbo-oman.org; f. 1974; cap. 400m., res 774m., dep. 2,851m. (Dec. 2009); 100% state-owned; Dep. Chair. Dr ALI BIN MUHAMMAD BIN MOUSA; 2 brs.

Commercial Banks

Ahli Bank SAOG: POB 545, Mina al-Fahal 116; tel. 24577000; fax 24568001; e-mail info@ahlibank-oman.com; internet www .ahlibank-oman.com; f. 1997 as Alliance Housing Bank; renamed as above 2008; privately owned; cap. 80m., res 24m., dep. 696m. (Dec. 2011); Chair. HAMDAN ALI NASSER AL-HINAI; CEO ABD AL-AZIZ AL-BALUSHI; 12 brs.

Bank Dhofar SAOG: POB 1507, Ruwi 112; tel. 24790466; fax 24797246; e-mail info@bankdhofar.com; internet www.bankdhofar .com; f. 1990 as Bank Dhofar al-Omani al-Fransi SAOG; renamed as above in 2004 after merger with Majan Int. Bank SAOC; cap. 91m., res 115m., dep. 1,519m. (Dec. 2011); Chair. Eng. ABD AL-HAFIDH SALIM RAJAB AL-AUJAILI; CEO ANTHONY MAHONEY; 54 brs.

BankMuscat SAOG: POB 134, Ruwi 112; tel. 24768888; fax 24785572; e-mail banking@bkmuscat.com; internet www .bankmuscat.com; f. 1993 by merger as Bank Muscat Al-Ahli Al-Omani; renamed Bank Muscat Int. in 1998, and as above in 1999; merged with Commercial Bank of Oman Ltd SAOG in 2000 and with Industrial Bank of Oman in 2002; 88.8% owned by Omani shareholders; cap. 154m., res 562m., dep. 5,587m. (Dec. 2011); Chair. Sheikh KHALID BIN MUSTAHAIL AL-MASHANI; Chief Exec. ABD AL-RAZAK ALI ISSA; 129 brs in Oman, 2 brs abroad.

Bank Sohar SAOG: POB 44, Hay al-Mina, Muttrah 114; tel. 24730000; fax 24793972; e-mail info@banksohar.net; internet www.banksohar.net; f. 2007; 32.5% owned by Oman Govt, 12% by Al Ghadir Al Arabia LLC, 55.5% by various Omani shareholders; cap. 100m., res 4m., dep. 1,171m. (Dec. 2011); Chair. Sheikh Dr SALIM SAID AL-FANNAH AL-ARAIMI; CEO Dr MUHAMMAD ABD AL-AZIZ KALMOOR; 11 brs.

HSBC Bank Oman SAOG: POB 240, Ruwi 112; tel. 80074722; internet www.hsbc.co.om; merged with Oman International Bank SAOG in June 2012; Chair. SIMON COOPER.

National Bank of Oman SAOG (NBO): POB 751, Ruwi 112; tel. 24778000; fax 24778585; e-mail ask@nbo.co.om; internet www.nbo .co.om; f. 1973; 100% Omani-owned; cap. 108m., res 117m., dep. 1,611m. (Dec. 2011); Chair. OMAR HUSSAIN AL-FARDAN; CEO SALAAM BIN SAEED AL-SHAKSY; 64 brs in Oman, 6 brs abroad.

Oman Arab Bank SAOC: POB 2010, Ruwi 112; tel. 24706265; fax 24797736; e-mail mktoab@omantel.net.om; internet www .oman-arabbank.com; f. 1984; purchased Omani European Bank SAOG in 1994; 51% Omani-owned, 49% by Arab Bank PLC (Jordan); cap. 85m., res 54m., dep. 772m. (Dec. 2010); Chair. RASHAD MUHAMMAD AL-ZUBAIR; CEO ABD AL-QADER ASKALAN; 46 brs.

Development Banks

Oman Development Bank SAOC: POB 3077, Ruwi 112; tel. 24812507; fax 24813100; e-mail customer.care@odboman.net; internet www.odb.com.om; f. 1977; absorbed Oman Bank for Agriculture and Fisheries in 1997; provides finance for devt projects in industry, agriculture and fishing; state-owned; cap. 70m., res 8m., dep. 2m. (Dec. 2010); Chair. Sheikh YAQOOB BIN HAMAD AL-HARTHY; Gen. Man. SAMIR BIN BECHIR AL-SAID; 9 brs.

Oman Housing Bank SAOC: POB 2555, Ruwi 112; tel. 24704444; fax 24704071; e-mail ohb@ohb.co.om; internet www.ohb.co.om; f. 1977; long-term finance for housing devt; 100% state-owned;

cap. 30m., res 55m., dep. 14m. (Dec. 2010); Gen. Man. ADNAN HAIDAR DARWISH AL-ZA'ABI; 9 brs.

STOCK EXCHANGE

Muscat Securities Market (MSM): POB 3265, Muscat 112; tel. 24823600; fax 24823706; e-mail info@msm.gov.om; internet www .msm.gov.om; 221 cos listed (Jan. 2009); f. 1989; Chair. HASSAN BIN ALI JAWAD AL-LAWATI; Dir-Gen. AHMAD SALEH AL-MARHOON.

Supervisory Body

Capital Market Authority (CMA): POB 3359, Ruwi 112; tel. 24823224; fax 24817471; e-mail info@cma.gov.om; internet www .cma.gov.om; f. 1998 to regulate capital market and insurance sector; Chair. Eng. ALI BIN MASSOUD BIN ALI AL-SUNAIDI (Minister of Commerce and Industry); Exec. Pres. YAHYA BIN SAID ABDULLAH AL-JABRI.

INSURANCE

In 2008 there were 23 licensed insurance companies operating in Oman. Of these, 11 were local firms and the remainder were branches of non-resident companies.

Al-Ahlia Insurance Co SAOG: POB 1463, Ruwi 112; tel. 24766800; fax 24797151; e-mail aaic@alahliaoman.com; internet www .alahliaoman.com; f. 1985; part of Royal and Sun Alliance Group (United Kingdom); cap. 6.0m., total assets 63.1m. (June 2008); Man. Dir LLOYD EAST; 23 brs.

Dhofar Insurance Co SAOG: POB 1002, Ruwi 112; tel. 24705305; fax 24793641; e-mail dhofar@dhofarinsurance.com; internet www .dhofarinsurance.com; f. 1989; cap. 20.0m. (Dec. 2007); Chair. Sheikh SALIM BIN MUBARAK AL-SHANFARI; Man. Dir and CEO TAHER T. AL-HERAKI.

Falcon Insurance Co SAOC: POB 2279, Ruwi 112; tel. 24660900; fax 24566476; e-mail info@falconinsurancesaoc.com; internet www .falconinsurancesaoc.com; f. 1977 as Al-Ittihad al-Watani; assoc. co of Al Anwar Holdings SAOG; cap. 5.4m.; Gen. Man. MICHAEL JAN WRIGHT.

Al Madina Insurance Co SAOC: POB 1805, Athaiba 130; tel. 24771888; fax 24771899; e-mail contact@amicoman.com; internet www.amicoman.com; f. 2006; cap. 10m. (Dec. 2006); CEO GAUTAM DATTA.

Muscat Insurance Co SAOC: POB 72, Ruwi 112; tel. 24478897; fax 24481847; e-mail info@muscatlife.com; internet www.omzest.com/mic.htm; f. 1995 as Muscat Insurance Co SAOG; restructured in 1999 as Muscat Nat. Holding Co SAOG (parent co), Muscat Insurance Co SAOC and Muscat Life Assurance Co SAOC; subsidiary of Omar Zawawi Establishment (OMZEST); Gen. Man. ANDREW M. WOODWARD.

National Life and General Insurance Co SAOC: POB 798, Wadi Kabir 117; tel. 24730999; fax 24795222; e-mail natlife@nlicgulf.com; internet www.nlicgulf.com; f. 1983; subsidiary of Oman Nat. Investment Corpn Holding SAOG; Gen. Man. S. VENKATACHALAM.

Oman Qatar Insurance Co SAOC: POB 3660, Ruwi 112; tel. 24700798; fax 24700815; e-mail contact@oqic.com; internet www .qatarinsurance.com/net_oman.htm; subsidiary of Qatar Insurance Co; CEO GEOFFREY BLOFELD.

Oman United Insurance Co SAOG: POB 1522, Ruwi 112; tel. 24477300; fax 24477334; e-mail info@omanutd.com; internet www .omanutd.com; f. 1985; cap. 10.0m., total assets 65.4m. (Dec. 2007); Chair. and CEO SAID SALIM BIN NASSIR AL-BUSAIDI.

Trade and Industry

GOVERNMENT AGENCY

The Public Authority for Investment Promotion and Export Development (PAIPED): POB 25, al-Wadi Kabir 117, Muscat; tel. 24623300; fax 24623331; e-mail info@paiped.com; internet www .paiped.com; f. 1996; promotes investment to Oman and the devt of non-oil Omani exports; Chair. Dr SALEM NASSER AL-ISMAILI.

CHAMBER OF COMMERCE

Oman Chamber of Commerce and Industry: POB 1400, Ruwi 112; tel. 24707674; fax 24708497; e-mail occi@chamberoman.com; internet www.chamberoman.com; f. 1973; Chair. KHALIL BIN ABDULLAH BIN MUHAMMAD AL-KHONJI; 142,881 mems (Sept. 2008).

STATE HYDROCARBONS COMPANIES

National Gas Co SAOG: POB 95, Rusayl 124; tel. 24446073; fax 24446307; e-mail info@nationalgasco.net; internet www .nationalgasco.net; f. 1979; bottling of LPG; Chair. Sheikh KHALID AHMAD SULTAN AL-HOSNI; CEO GOUTAM SEN; 158 employees.

Oman Gas Co SAOC (OGC): POB 799, al-Khuwair 133; tel. 24681600; fax 24681678; e-mail info@oman-gas.com.om; internet www.oman-gas.com.om; f. 2000; govt-owned (80% Ministry of Oil and Gas; 20% Oman Oil Co SAOC); operates gas network and builds pipelines to supply power plants and other industries in Oman; Chair. Dr MUHAMMAD BIN HAMAD BIN SAIF AL-RUMHI (Minister of Oil and Gas); CEO YOUSUF BIN MUHAMMAD AL-OJAILI.

Oman LNG LLC: POB 560, Mina al-Fahal 116; tel. 24609999; fax 24609900; e-mail info@omanlng.co.om; internet www.omanlng.com; f. 1994; 51% state-owned; Royal Dutch Shell 30%; manages 6.6m.-metric-tons-per-year LNG plant at Qalhat; manufacturing, shipping and marketing; Chair. NASSER BIN KHAMIS AL-JASHMI; CEO and Gen. Man. Dr BRIAN BUCKLEY; 225 employees.

Oman Oil Co SAOC (OOC): POB 261, Ruwi 118; tel. 24573100; fax 24573101; e-mail info@oman-oil.com; internet www.oman-oil.com; f. late 1980s to invest in foreign commercial enterprises and oil-trading operations; incorporated 1996; 100% state-owned; Chair. NASSIR BIN KHAMIS AL-JASHMI; CEO AHMAD AL-WAHAIBI.

Oman Refineries and Petroleum Industries Co SAOC (ORPIC): POB 3568, Ruwi 112; tel. 24561200; fax 24561384; internet orpic.om; f. 2010 after merger of Oman Refineries and Petrochemicals Co, Aromatics Oman and Oman Polypropylene; production of light petroleum products; 75% owned by Oman Govt, 25% by Oman Oil Co SAOC; Chair. Dr MUHAMMAD BIN HAMAD BIN SAIF AL-RUMHI (Minister of Oil and Gas); CEO Dr MUSAB AL-MAHRUQI; 1,600 employees.

Petroleum Development Oman LLC (PDO): POB 81, Muscat 113; tel. 24678111; fax 24677106; e-mail external-affairs@pdo.co.om; internet www.pdo.co.om; incorporated in Sultanate of Oman by royal decree as an LLC since 1980; 60% owned by Oman Govt, 34% by Royal Dutch Shell; exploration and production of crude petroleum and gas; crude petroleum production (2007) averaged 561,000 b/d from over 100 fields, linked by a pipeline system to terminal at Mina al-Fahal, near Muscat; gas production (2007) totalled 63.3m. cu m/d; Chair. Dr MUHAMMAD BIN HAMAD BIN SAIF AL-RUMHI (Minister of Oil and Gas); Man. Dir JOHN MALCOLM; 5,000 employees.

Qalhat LNG SAOC: POB 514, al-Khuwair 133; tel. 24574004; fax 24574090; e-mail info@qalhatlng.co.om; internet www.qalhatlng .com; f. 2003; production of LNG; 46.84% owned by Oman Govt, 36.80% by Oman LNG LLC, 16.36% by foreign investors; Chair. Sheikh AL-FADHIL BIN MUHAMMAD AL-HARTHY; CEO HARIB AL-KITANI.

UTILITIES

As part of its privatization programme, the Omani Government is divesting the utilities on a project-by-project basis. Private investors have already been found for several municipal wastewater projects, desalination plants and regional electricity providers.

Supervisory Body

Public Authority for Electricity and Water (PAEW): POB 1889, al-Azaiba 130; tel. 24611100; fax 24611133; e-mail dg-project@paew .gov.om; internet www.paew.gov.om; f. 2007 following restructuring of fmr Ministry of Housing, Electricity and Water; Chair. MUHAMMAD BIN ABDULLAH BIN MUHAMMAD AL-MAHROUQI.

Electricity

Authority for Electricity Regulation (AER): POB 954, al-Khuwair 133; tel. 24609700; fax 24609701; e-mail enquiries@ aer-oman.org; internet www.aer-oman.org; f. 2004 to regulate and facilitate the privatization of the electricity and related water sector; Chair. Dr SALEH MUHAMMAD AL-ALAWI; Exec. Dir JOHN CUNEEN.

Electricity Holding Co SAOC (EHC): POB 850, Mina al-Fahal 116; tel. 24559200; fax 24559288; e-mail ehcoman@omantel.net.om; internet www.ehcoman.com; f. 2005; state-owned; established to hold Govt's ownership in 9 utility cos and to facilitate the commercial restructuring of the sector; Al-Rusail Power Co was privatized in 2007; of the remaining 8 successor cos, 6 are currently scheduled for privatization; Chair. MUHAMMAD BIN ABDULLAH BIN MUHAMMAD AL-MAHROUQI; CEO KARL MATACZ.

Principal subsidiaries of the EHC include:

Muscat Electricity Distribution Co SAOC (MEDC): POB 3732, al-Ghubrah 112; tel. 24588600; fax 24588666; e-mail medc@medcoman.com; internet www.medcoman.com; f. 2005; responsible for all distribution in the Governorate of Muscat; Chair. Eng. SALEH AL-FARSI; Gen. Man. Eng. ZAHIR AL-ABRI.

Oman Electricity Transmission Co SAOC (OETC): POB 1224, al-Hamriya 131; tel. 24573221; fax 24573222; e-mail info@ omangrid.com; internet www.omangrid.com; f. 2003; owns and operates the Main Interconnected System, which covers the north of Oman and accounts for 90% of the Sultanate's electricity transmission; scheduled for privatization; Chair. Eng. SAIF ABDULLAH RASHID AL-SUMRY; Gen. Man. ALI AL-HADABI.

Oman Power and Water Procurement Co SAOC: POB 1388, Ruwi 112; e-mail vacancies@omanpwp.com; internet www .omanpwp.co.om; f. 2003; responsible for forecasting and managing the supply and demand of electricity and water; Chair. SAUD NASSIR AL-SHUKAILY; CEO BOB WHITELAW.

Other subsidiaries of the EHC are: Al-Ghubrah Power and Desalination Co, Majan Electricity Co, Mazoon Electricity Co, Rural Areas Electricity Co and Wadi Jizzi Power Co.

Water

Ministry of Regional Municipalities and Water Resources: (see The Government); assesses, manages, develops and conserves water resources.

Oman Power and Water Procurement Co SAOC: see Electricity.

Oman Wastewater Services Co SAOC (Haya Water): POB 1047, al-Khuwair 133; tel. 24590544; fax 24693418; e-mail customerservice@omanwsc.com; internet www.owsc.com.om; f. 2002; devt and operation of a wastewater system in the Governorate of Muscat; govt-owned; CEO OMAR KHALFAN AL-WAHAIBI.

Transport

RAILWAYS

There are no railways in Oman, although plans for a regional rail network, connecting Oman with member countries of the Cooperation Council for the Arab States of the Gulf (or Gulf Cooperation Council—GCC), were finalized in late 2009. A feasibility study into the proposed first phase of the Omani section of the GCC network, a 230-km line linking Sohar and Muscat, was carried out by a French contractor in 2009. Tenders for contracts to design and manage the Omani rail project were issued in April 2010.

ROADS

A network of adequate graded roads links all the main centres of population, and only a few mountain villages are inaccessible by off-road vehicles. In 2010 there were an estimated 59,363 km of roads, of which 1,791 km were dual carriageways and a further 28,903 km were asphalted roads. The eighth Development Plan (2011–15) provided for several large-scale road-building projects, including the third phase of a new 240-km al-Batinah coastal road linking Barka and Sohar with Khatmat Malaha on the border with the United Arab Emirates. A new 81-km dual carriageway linking Sohar with Buraimi, in north-eastern Oman, was inaugurated in January 2010.

Directorate-General of Roads: Ministry of Transport and Communications, POB 338, Ruwi 112; tel. 24697870; fax 24696817; e-mail dgroads@omantel.net.om; internet www.motc.gov.om/en/edgr/edgr.html; Dir-Gen. of Roads Sheikh MUHAMMAD BIN HILAL AL-KHALILI.

Oman National Transport Co SAOG (ONTC): POB 620, Muscat 113; tel. 24490046; fax 24490152; e-mail info@ontcoman.com; internet www.ontcoman.com; f. 1972; re-established in 1984; operates local, regional and long-distance bus services from Muscat; Chair. MAJID SAID SALIM AL-RUWAHI; Gen. Man. MAJID AL-MANDHRY.

SHIPPING

Port Sultan Qaboos (Mina Sultan Qaboos), at the entrance to the Persian (Arabian) Gulf, was built in 1974 to provide nine deep-water berths varying in length from 250 ft to 750 ft (76 m to 228 m), with draughts of up to 43 ft (13 m), and three berths for shallow-draught vessels drawing 12 ft to 16 ft (3.7 m to 4.9 m) of water. A total of 12 new berths have been opened, and two of the existing berths have been upgraded to a container terminal capable of handling 60 containers per hour. The port also has a 3,000-metric-ton-capacity cold store, which belongs to the Oman Fisheries Co. In the 1990s Port Sultan Qaboos underwent a further upgrade and expansion. A new terminal for passenger cruise ships was inaugurated in February 2010.

The oil terminal at Mina al-Fahal can also accommodate the largest super-tankers on offshore loading buoys. Similar facilities for the import of refined petroleum products exist at Mina al-Fahal. Salalah Port, formerly known as Mina Raysut, is Oman's largest transshipment terminal and serves as a major transshipment centre for the region. Salalah has been developed into an all-weather port, and, in addition to container facilities, has six deep-water berths with an annual capacity of 4.5m. 20-ft equivalent units; plans for the construction of three additional deep-water berths were announced in 2008. A major redevelopment of the port at Duqm, on the Gulf of Masirah, was announced in 2007. In 2008 the authorities announced that the project would be significantly expanded to provide: deep-water berths of 18 m; a deepened approach channel; breakwaters expanded to 7.7 km; a new dry dock for ships of up to 400,000 tons; and a new ship repair yard. The project was allocated an initial

RO 700m. in government investment and was completed in March 2013.

At 31 December 2012 Oman's flag registered fleet totalled 47 vessels, with an aggregate displacement of 52,164 grt.

Port Authorities and Regulatory Body

Directorate-General of Ports and Maritime Affairs: POB 684, Ruwi 113; tel. 24685994; fax 24685992; e-mail dgpma@omantel.net .om; Dir-Gen. Eng. QASSIM AHMAD ABD AL-MOHSEN AL-SHIZAWI.

Port Services Corpn SAOG (PSC): POB 133, Muscat 113; tel. 24714000; fax 24714007; e-mail mktg@pscoman.com; internet www .pscoman.com; f. 1976; jointly owned by the Govt of Oman and private shareholders; responsible for management and operation of Port Sultan Qaboos; cap. RO 7.9m. (2007); CEO SAUD BIN AHMAD AL-NAHARI.

Salalah Port Services Co SAOG (SPS): POB 105, Muscat 118; tel. 24601003; fax 24600736; e-mail info@salalahport.com; internet www .portofsalalah.com; f. 1997; holds a 30-year concession to manage and develop Salalah Port; CEO PETER FORD.

Principal Shipping Companies

National Ferries Co SAOC: Jibroo, Blk 1, nr DHL, Muscat; tel. 24715252; fax 24711333; e-mail reservation@nfcoman.com; internet www.nfcoman.com; f. 2006; govt-owned; operates a high-speed, passenger and vehicle ferry service between Muscat and Khasab, on the Strait of Hormuz; Chair. MEHDI MUHAMMAD AL-ABDUWANI.

Oman Shipping Co SAOC (OSC): al-Harthy Complex, POB 104, Madinat Sultan Qaboos St, Muscat 118; tel. 24400900; fax 24400922; e-mail info@omanship.co.om; internet www.omanship.co.om; f. 2003; govt-owned (Ministry of Finance 80%, Oman Oil Co SAOC 20%); owns and operates a fleet of over 30 vessels; transportation of LNG, crude petroleum and petrochemical products; subsidiaries include: Oman Charter Co, Duqm Maritime Transportation Co, Liwa Maritime Transportation Co, Energy Spring LNG Carrier SA, Oasis LNG Carrier SA; Dep. Chair. AHMAD BIN MUHAMMAD BIN SALIM AL-FUTAISI (Minister of Transport and Communications); CEO NICHOLAS FISHER.

CIVIL AVIATION

Domestic and international flights operate from Muscat International Airport (known as Seeb International Airport prior to February 2008). In 2010 5.8m. passengers passed through the airport; a project designed to increase annual passenger capacity to 12m. was expected to be completed by 2014. Oman's second international airport, at Salalah, was completed in 1978; in 2010 455,000 passengers passed through the airport. Both Seeb and Salalah were effectively privatized in October 2001. Responsibility for the management and refurbishment of the airports passed to Oman Airports Management Co (OAMC), 75% of which was owned by foreign investors and 25% by the Omani Government; however, following the failure of the Government successfully to agree financial terms for the privatization and ongoing development of the airports with OAMC, the 25-year contract was cancelled in October 2004 and Seeb and Salalah airports were returned to state control. OAMC continues to manage and operate Oman's airports, but it is now a wholly government-owned entity. Plans for substantial development and expansion of both international airports to provide additional terminals and increase passenger-handling capacity were announced as part of the Government's seventh Development Plan in 2006. There are also airports at Sur, Masirah, Khasab and Diba, with six further airports planned for Sohar, Duqm, Ras Al Hadd, Adam, Haima and Shaleem. Three new private airfields, owned and operated by Petroleum Development Oman, were opened in 2008 at Marmul, Qarn Alam and Fahud.

Directorate-General of Civil Aviation Affairs: POB 1, CPO Muscat International Airport, Muscat 111; tel. 24519356; fax 24519880; e-mail hakeem@dgcam.gov.om; internet www.met.gov .om; Dir of Airports ABD AL-HAKEEM AMUR AL-KIYUMI.

Oman Air SAOC: POB 58, Muscat International Airport, Muscat 111; tel. 24531111; fax 24765121; e-mail wycallcenter@omanair .aero; internet www.omanair.aero/wy; f. 1993 as a subsidiary of Oman Aviation Services Co (f. 1981); whole corpn renamed Oman Air 2008; state-owned; cap. US $1,300m.; air-charter, maintenance, handling and catering; operators of Oman's domestic and international commercial airline; operates a fleet of 21 aircraft; carried over 2.3m. passengers in 2009; Chair. DARWISH BIN ISMAIL BIN ALI AL-BALUSHI (Minister Responsible for Financial Affairs); CEO WAYNE PEARCE.

Oman Airports Management Co SOAC: POB 1707, Muscat 111; tel. 24518030; fax 24518088; e-mail oamcinfo@omanairports.com; f. 2002; originally 75% owned by private investors; 100% owned by Oman Govt since 2004; operates Muscat International and Salalah airports; Chair. AHMAD BIN MUHAMMAD BIN SALIM AL-FUTAISI (Minister of Transport and Communications); CEO GEORGE BELLEW.

Tourism

Tourism, introduced in 1985, is strictly controlled. Oman's attractions, apart from the capital itself, include Nizwa, ancient capital of the interior, Dhofar, and the forts of Nakhl, Rustaq and al-Hazm. The country also possesses an attractive and clean environment, including around 1,700 km of sandy beaches. The tourism sector has been undergoing a period of intensive investment and development in recent years, overseen by the Oman Tourism Development Co (Omran). The emphasis has been on the development of extensive luxury resorts in areas of outstanding natural beauty. By 2011 there were 11,779 hotel rooms, with plans to increase this to 18,000 by 2015. In 2010 there were 1,048,052 visitor arrivals in Oman, and tourism receipts totalled US $775m. (excluding passenger transport).

Directorate-General of Tourism: Madinat al-Sultan Qaboos, POB 200, Muscat 115; tel. 24588700; fax 24588880; e-mail info@omantourism.gov.om; internet www.omantourism.gov.om; Dir-Gen. MUHAMMAD ALI SAID.

Oman Tourism Development Co (Omran): POB 479, Muttrah 114; tel. 24773700; fax 24793929; e-mail enquiries@omran.om; internet www.omran.om; f. 2005; CEO WAEL BIN AHMAD AL-LAWATI.

Defence

Chief of Staff of the Sultan's Armed Forces: Lt-Gen. AHMED BIN HARITH AL-NABHANI.

Commander of the Royal Army of Oman: Maj.-Gen. MATAR BIN SALIM AL-BALUSHI.

Commander of the Royal Air Force of Oman: Air Vice-Marshal MATAR BIN ALI AL-OBAIDANI.

Commander of the Royal Navy of Oman: Rear Adm. ABDULLAH KHAMIS AL-RAISI.

Commander of the Royal Guard of Oman: Maj.-Gen. KHALIFA BIN ABDULLAH AL-JUNAIBI.

Defence Budget (2012): RO 2,590m.

Total armed forces (as assessed at November 2012): 42,600: army 25,000; navy 4,200; air force 5,000; plus 2,000 expatriate personnel. There is a 6,400-strong Royal Guard.

Paramilitary forces: 4,400: tribal Home Guard (*Firqat*) 4,000; police coastguard 400.

Education

Great advances have been made in education since 1970, when Sultan Qaboos came to power. Although education is still not compulsory, it is provided free to Omani citizens from primary to tertiary level, and attendance has increased greatly. Primary education begins at six years of age and lasts for six years. The next level of education, divided into two equal stages (preparatory and secondary), lasts for a further six years. In 1998/99 a new system, comprising 10 years of basic education and two years of secondary education, was introduced in 17 schools; it was to be implemented gradually throughout the country. In 2011/12 there were 1,040 schools in the state sector, as well as 406 private kindergartens and schools regulated by the Ministry of Education. In total, 517,606 students were in state education and 71,274 in private education in 2011/12. As a proportion of the school-age population, the total enrolment at primary, preparatory and secondary schools increased from 25% (boys 36%; girls 14%) in 1975 to 76% (boys 78%; girls 74%) in 1997/98. Primary enrolment in 2008/09 included 94% of children in the relevant age-group, while secondary enrolment included 90% of children in the relevant age-group. In 2010 there were six teacher-training colleges, five vocational institutes, seven technical colleges and 16 institutes of health, together with the College of Shari'a and Law, the Academy of Tourism and Catering, and the College of Banking and Financial Studies. There are 26 private universities and technical colleges. Oman's first national university, named after Sultan Qaboos, was opened in late 1986, and had 16,494 students in 2010/11. In the 2012 budget, a total of RO 1,300m. was allocated to education, equivalent to 13% of total government expenditure.

PAKISTAN

Introductory Survey

LOCATION, CLIMATE, LANGUAGE, RELIGION, FLAG, CAPITAL

The Islamic Republic of Pakistan lies in southern Asia, bordered by India to the east and by Afghanistan and Iran to the west. It has a short frontier with the People's Republic of China in the far north-east. The climate is dry and generally hot, with an annual average temperature of 27°C (80°F), except in the mountainous areas, which have very cold winters. Temperatures in Karachi are generally between 13°C (55°F) and 34°C (93°F), with negligible rainfall. The principal languages are Punjabi (the language usually spoken in 44.2% of households in 1998), Pushto/Pashtu (15.4%), Sindhi (14.1%) and Saraiki (10.5%). Urdu (7.6%) is the national language, and English is extensively used. The state religion is Islam, embracing more than 96% of the population in 1998, the remainder being mainly Hindus or Christians. The national flag (proportions 2 by 3) has a vertical white stripe at the hoist, while the remainder is dark green, with a white crescent moon and a five-pointed star in the centre. The capital is Islamabad.

CONTEMPORARY POLITICAL HISTORY

Historical Context

Pakistan was created in August 1947 by the partition of the United Kingdom's former Indian Empire into the independent states of India and Pakistan, in response to demands by elements of the Muslim population in the subcontinent for the establishment of a specifically Islamic state. Pakistan originally comprised two distinct regions: East Pakistan and West Pakistan, separated by some 1,600 km (1,000 miles) of Indian territory, and united only by a common religion. Although the majority of the population lived in the smaller East Pakistan, political and military power was concentrated in the west, where the Muslim League was the dominant political movement. The leader of the Muslim League, Muhammad Ali Jinnah, popularly known as Quaid-i-Azam ('Great Leader'), became the first Governor-General of Pakistan but died in 1948. The country, formerly a dominion with the British monarch as Head of State, became a republic on 23 March 1956, when Pakistan's first Constitution was promulgated. At the same time Maj.-Gen. Iskander Mirza was appointed as Pakistan's first President.

Pakistan came under military rule in early October 1958, when President Mirza abrogated the Constitution, declared martial law, dismissed the national and provincial governments, and dissolved all political parties. In late October, however, Gen. (later Field Marshal) Muhammad Ayub Khan, the Martial Law Administrator appointed by Mirza, removed Mirza from office and became President himself. Ayub Khan's autocratic but modernizing regime lasted until March 1969, when he was forced to resign following widespread unrest. Gen. Agha Muhammad Yahya Khan, the Commander-in-Chief of the Army, replaced him, and martial law was reimposed.

In December 1970 the country's first general election was held for a national assembly. Sheikh Mujibur Rahman's Awami League, which advocated autonomy for East Pakistan, won almost all the seats in the east (thus gaining an absolute majority in the National Assembly), while the Pakistan Peoples Party (PPP), led by Zulfikar Ali Bhutto, won a majority of seats in the west. Following the failure of negotiations to achieve a coalition government of the two parties, on 23 March 1971 East Pakistan declared its independence as the People's Republic of Bangladesh. Civil war immediately broke out, as Pakistani troops clashed with Bengali irregular forces. In December the Indian army intervened in the conflict to support the Bengalis, and the Pakistani army was forced to withdraw, thus permitting Bangladesh firmly to establish its independence. In the truncated Pakistan that remained in the west Yahya Khan resigned, military rule was ended, and Bhutto became the new President.

Domestic Political Affairs

Premiership of Zulfikar Ali Bhutto (1973–77)

A new Constitution, which came into effect in August 1973, provided for a parliamentary system of government. Bhutto was appointed executive Prime Minister, while Fazal Elahi Chaudry, hitherto Speaker of the National Assembly, became constitutional President. The PPP won an overwhelming majority of seats in elections to the National Assembly in March 1977. However, the opposition Pakistan National Alliance (PNA) accused the PPP of widespread electoral malpractice and launched a nation-wide campaign of civil disobedience. An estimated 1,000 people died in subsequent clashes between troops and demonstrators, and some 40,000 people were arrested. In July the armed forces intervened in the crisis: Bhutto was deposed in a bloodless military coup and a martial law regime was instituted, with Gen. Mohammad Zia ul-Haq, the Army Chief of Staff, as Chief Martial Law Administrator. President Chaudry remained in office as Head of State. Bhutto was subsequently charged with instigating the murder of a PPP dissident and a member of the dissident's family in 1974. He was sentenced to death in March 1978 and executed in April 1979.

Pakistan under Gen. Mohammad Zia ul-Haq (1977–88)

In September 1978 President Chaudry resigned and Gen. Zia became President. General elections were postponed several times by the military administration, and in October 1979 Gen. Zia announced an indefinite postponement of the polls. Opposition to the military regime was rigorously suppressed. In March 1981 nine political parties formed an opposition alliance, the Movement for the Restoration of Democracy (MRD), which advocated an end to military rule. Several opposition politicians were subsequently interned or placed under house arrest. In August 1983 the MRD, led by the PPP, launched a civil disobedience campaign to press for the restoration of parliamentary democracy on the basis of the 1973 Constitution. The campaign enjoyed considerable support in Sindh province, where anti-Government protests resulted in numerous deaths. However, there was limited popular support elsewhere in the country, and the campaign ended in December 1983. Many political leaders and activists, including Benazir Bhutto (daughter of the former President and herself a leading PPP activist), were subsequently imprisoned or went into exile.

Gen. Zia's regime zealously pursued a policy of 'Islamization' of the country's institutions, including the enforcement of Islamic penal codes, and the introduction of Islamic economic principles, such as interest-free banking. In December 1984 a referendum was held, which sought affirmation of the Islamization process and, indirectly, endorsement of a further five-year term for Gen. Zia. The referendum was boycotted by the MRD, but, according to official figures, 98% of those participating supported the proposal. However, there were widespread allegations of electoral malpractice.

In February 1985 a general election was held for a national assembly, followed shortly afterwards by elections to four provincial assemblies. The elections were held on a non-party basis, but widespread dissatisfaction with the regime was indicated by the defeat of several of Zia's cabinet ministers and close supporters. The largest two groupings in the new National Assembly were composed of a faction of the Pakistan Muslim League (PML, the successor to the Muslim League) known as the Pagara Group and former members of the PPP. In late March Gen. Zia appointed Muhammad Khan Junejo, a member of the PML (Pagara Group), as Prime Minister, and an almost entirely civilian Cabinet was formed.

In October 1985 the National Assembly approved changes to the Constitution (the 'Eighth Amendment') proposed by Gen. Zia, which introduced a powerful executive presidency and indemnified all actions of the military regime during the previous eight years. On 30 December Gen. Zia announced the repeal of martial law and the restoration of the Constitution (as amended in October). The military courts were dissolved, and military personnel were removed from civilian posts, with the exception of Gen. Zia, who remained as President and head of the armed forces. Junejo retained the post of Prime Minister in a new Cabinet. However, the MRD continued to demand the restoration of the unamended 1973 Constitution. In April 1986 the opposition's cause was strengthened by the return from exile of

Benazir Bhutto, who travelled throughout the country holding political rallies that attracted thousands of supporters. She demanded the resignation of President Zia and the holding of a free general election, open to all political parties. In May Benazir Bhutto and her mother, Nusrat Bhutto, were elected as Co-Chairwomen of the PPP. In August the Government adopted a less tolerant approach towards the MRD by banning all rallies scheduled for Independence Day and by detaining hundreds of opposition members, including Benazir Bhutto. The arrests provoked violent anti-Government demonstrations in a number of cities.

The rise of ethnic communalism in Pakistan was reflected in the results of local elections held throughout the country in November 1987. The party of the Urdu-speaking Mohajirs (who migrated from India when the subcontinent was partitioned in 1947), the Mohajir Qaumi Movement (MQM), won the majority of seats in Karachi and was also successful in other urban areas of Sindh province.

In May 1988, in accordance with the authority vested in him through the Eighth Amendment, President Zia dismissed the Prime Minister and his Cabinet, and dissolved the National Assembly and the four provincial assemblies. Zia became head of an interim administration, which was to govern until a general election was held. In July Zia announced that the elections would be held in November. However, on 17 August President Zia was killed in an air crash in eastern Pakistan. Subsequent speculation that the cause of the crash was sabotage was not officially confirmed. The Chairman of the Senate, Ghulam Ishaq Khan, was appointed acting President, and an emergency National Council (composed of senior military officers, the four provincial governors and four federal ministers) was appointed to take charge of government.

Benazir Bhutto and the Pakistan Peoples Party assume power (1988–90)

Despite the imposition of a state of emergency after the death of Zia, the general election took place, as scheduled, in November 1988. The PPP won 93 of the 207 directly elected seats in the National Assembly, and was the only party to secure seats in each of Pakistan's four provinces. The Islamic Democratic Alliance (IDA), a grouping of nine Islamic and right-wing parties (including the PML), gained 54 seats. However, the PPP did not achieve such a high level of support in the elections to the provincial assemblies, held three days later. The PPP was able to form coalition governments in Sindh and the NWFP, but the IDA took power in Punjab, the most populous province. At the federal level, a coalition Government was formed by the PPP and the MQM, which together had a working majority in the National Assembly (the MQM held 14 seats). Benazir Bhutto was appointed Prime Minister on 1 December, thus becoming the first female leader of a Muslim country. The state of emergency was repealed on the same day. A new Cabinet was formed, and later in December an electoral college (comprising the Senate, the National Assembly and the four provincial assemblies) elected Ghulam Ishaq Khan as President.

Benazir Bhutto's attempts, in early 1989, to repeal the Eighth Amendment to the Constitution, which severely constrained her powers as Prime Minister, proved unsuccessful. Moreover, the fragile coalitions that the PPP had formed in the provincial assemblies soon collapsed. In the same month the opposition was strengthened by the formation of an informal parliamentary grouping, the Combined Opposition Party (COP), comprising the IDA, the ANP, Jamiat-e-Ulema-e-Islam (JUI) and the Pakistan Awami Ittehad. In October the Government suffered a serious reversal when the MQM transferred its parliamentary support from the PPP to the opposition, claiming that the former had failed to honour any of the promises made in their original co-operation agreement. In November a parliamentary motion of no confidence, proposed by the COP against the Government, was narrowly defeated. In January 1990 the COP organized a campaign to undermine the Government, accusing it of corruption, political bribery and mismanagement. Rallies and demonstrations in Sindh province culminated in violence between supporters of the PPP and the MQM and the deaths of about 100 people in clashes with police.

By mid-1990 the popularity of the PPP Government had declined considerably: the maintenance of law and order had worsened; no significant new legislation had been introduced; the economic situation was deteriorating; and there were widespread allegations of corruption against high-ranking officials. On 6 August the President, in accordance with his constitutional

powers, dissolved the National Assembly, dismissed the Prime Minister and her Cabinet, and declared a state of emergency. He also announced that a general election would take place in October. The President alleged that the ousted Government had violated the Constitution, accusing it of corruption, nepotism and incompetence. Ghulam Mustafa Jatoi, the leader of the COP in the National Assembly, was appointed acting Prime Minister in an interim Government. The four provincial assemblies were also dissolved, and 'caretaker' Chief Ministers appointed. Benazir Bhutto claimed that the dissolution of her administration was illegal and strongly denied the various charges made against her Government. At the end of August several of Benazir Bhutto's former ministers were arrested, and in the following month she herself was indicted on more than 10 charges of corruption and abuse of power. In early October Benazir Bhutto's husband, Asif Ali Zardari, was arrested on charges of extortion, kidnapping and financial irregularities (he was later acquitted on all counts).

Mohammad Nawaz Sharif and the Islamic Democratic Alliance head the Government (1990–93)

At the general election, which took place on 24 October 1990, the IDA doubled its representation in the National Assembly, leaving it only four seats short of an absolute majority, while the People's Democratic Alliance (PDA, an electoral alliance comprising the PPP and three smaller parties) suffered a heavy defeat. The PPP unexpectedly lost control of Sindh in provincial elections, while the MQM and ANP continued to expand their influence in Sindh and the NWFP, respectively. On 6 November Mohammad Nawaz Sharif, the leader of the IDA and the former Chief Minister of Punjab, was elected as the new Prime Minister. He officially ended the three-month state of emergency, and appointed a new Cabinet, which included several ministers who had served under President Zia. Nawaz Sharif promised that one of the Government's major priorities was to establish lasting peace in Sindh, where ethnic conflict and general lawlessness continued to prevail. However, it was alleged that the Government's subsequent campaign of suppression in the province, in response to numerous local murders and kidnappings, was aimed primarily at supporters of the PPP, hundreds of whom were arrested.

In May 1991 the National Assembly adopted legislation incorporating *Shari'a*, the Islamic legal code, in Pakistan's legal system. The Assembly also approved legislation providing for the Islamization of the educational, economic and judicial systems. Benazir Bhutto criticized these measures as being extreme and fundamentalist, while the right-wing JUI claimed that the new laws' provisions were not stringent enough. The fundamentalist Jamaat-e-Islami Pakistan (JIP) left the IDA in May 1992, in protest against the Government's decision to support the new moderate *mujahidin* Government in Kabul, Afghanistan, and at its failure to effect the full Islamization of Pakistan. Meanwhile, violent clashes between two factions of MQM provoked a military crackdown and mass arrests in Karachi, in the aftermath of which most of the MQM members of the National Assembly and Sindh Assembly resigned in protest.

In November 1992 the PDA intensified its campaign of political agitation and was now supported by the majority of the components of the newly formed opposition National Democratic Alliance (NDA), including the National People's Party (NPP—which had been expelled from the IDA in March). The large-scale demonstrations and marches organized by Benazir Bhutto were ruthlessly suppressed by the Government. However, by mid-December tensions between the Government and opposition had eased considerably, and in January 1993, in an apparently conciliatory move on the part of Nawaz Sharif's administration, Benazir Bhutto was elected Chairperson of the National Assembly's Standing Committee on Foreign Affairs. Shortly after Benazir Bhutto had accepted the nomination, her husband, Asif Ali Zardari, was released on bail.

In March 1993 a growing rift between the Prime Minister and the President became evident when the Government initiated discussions regarding proposed modifications to the provisions of the Eighth Constitutional Amendment. By mid-April a total of eight ministers had resigned from the Cabinet in protest against Nawaz Sharif's continued tenure of the premiership. On 18 April the President dissolved the National Assembly and dismissed the Prime Minister and his Cabinet, accusing Nawaz Sharif of 'maladministration, nepotism and corruption'. However, the provincial assemblies and governments remained in power, despite demands by the PDA and the NDA for their dissolution. A member of the dissolved National Assembly, Mir Balakh Sher

Mazari, was subsequently appointed acting Prime Minister and a broadly based interim Cabinet, including Asif Ali Zardari, was sworn in at the end of April. In May the PML (Junejo Group) split into two factions: one led by Nawaz Sharif, the other by Hamid Nasir Chattha (with the support of the President).

On 26 May 1993, in an historic and unexpected judgment, the Supreme Court ordered that the National Assembly, the Prime Minister and the Cabinet (dismissed in April) should be restored to power immediately, stating that President Khan's order had been unconstitutional. The President agreed to honour the Court's ruling, and the National Assembly and Nawaz Sharif's Government were reinstated with immediate effect. However, renewed political turmoil ensued following the dissolution, through the machinations of supporters of the President, of the provincial assemblies in Punjab and the NWFP. Lacking effective authority in each of the four provinces, in June Nawaz Sharif resorted to the imposition of federal government's rule on Punjab. However, the Punjab provincial government refused to obey the federal Government's orders, prompting the Government to threaten the imposition of a military administration. In early July the Chief of Army Staff assumed the role of inter-mediary in talks between the President and Prime Minister in an attempt to resolve the growing political crisis. On 18 July, in accordance with an agreement reached under the auspices of the army, both Khan and Nawaz Sharif resigned from their posts, the federal legislature and the provincial assemblies were dissolved, the holding of a general election in October was announced, and neutral administrations were established at both federal and provincial level. As specified in the Constitution, Khan was succeeded by the Chairman of the Senate, Wasim Sajjad Jan. A small, apolitical Cabinet was sworn in, headed by Moeenuddin Ahmad Qureshi, a former Executive Vice-President of the World Bank.

Benazir Bhutto's second term as Prime Minister (1993–96)

The general election, held in early October 1993 under military supervision, was widely considered to have been fair, although the turn-out, which some officials estimated to be less than 50%, was disappointing. The polling was closely contested between the PML faction led by Nawaz Sharif—PML (N)—and the PPP (the MQM boycotted the elections to the National Assembly, claiming systematic intimidation by the army, but took part in the provincial assembly elections a few days later). Neither of the two leading parties won an outright majority in the federal elections, and in the provincial elections an outright majority was only achieved by the PPP in Sindh. Following intensive negotiations with smaller parties and independents in the National Assembly, on 19 October Benazir Bhutto was elected to head a coalition Government. On the following day a PPP-led coalition assumed control of the provincial administration in Punjab (traditionally a PML stronghold). However, the provincial governments in the NWFP and in Balochistan were headed by alliances led by the PML (N).

In November 1993 the PPP's candidate, Sardar Farooq Ahmad Khan Leghari, was elected President, comfortably defeating the incumbent acting President, Wasim Sajjad Jan, who stood as the candidate of the PML (N). On assuming office, Leghari stated that he intended to end his political ties with the PPP and that he hoped for the early repeal or modification of the controversial Eighth Constitutional Amendment.

In February 1994 the President imposed governor's rule in the NWFP, following the thwarted introduction of a vote of no confidence against the PML (N)-led coalition by the PPP. In April a PPP member was elected as Chief Minister of the newly revived provincial government in the NWFP; the opposition alliance boycotted the proceedings.

Meanwhile, uprisings in the northern regions of Malakand and Swat in late 1994 prompted military action, while ethnic and criminal violence Karachi escalated to dangerous levels. The rise of Islamist extremism was also apparent, with the bombing of the Egyptian embassy in Islamabad in November (see Sectarian, Ethnic and Political Violence in Pakistan).

In March 1996 the Supreme Court in Karachi ruled that the Government's appointments of judges to the higher courts would require the consent of the Chief Justices of the High Courts and the Chief Justice of Pakistan. This ruling provoked considerable controversy since it deprived the executive of substantial authority within the national judicial system.

The Government's popularity was undermined by the necessary introduction of an austere budget in June 1996, in an attempt to reduce the budget deficit. The volatile political situation was intensified by a bomb explosion at Lahore airport in July, a series of debilitating public sector strikes and by a resurgence of violence in Karachi. In addition, the appointment of the Prime Minister's unpopular husband, Asif Ali Zardari, as Minister of Investment in July aroused much controversy and criticism. At the end of that month about 16 opposition parties, including the PML (N), the MQM and the JIP, established an informal alliance with a one-point agenda: to oust Prime Minister Bhutto and her Government. Pakistan was thrown into further political turmoil in September following the fatal shooting of Benazir Bhutto's estranged brother, Mir Murtaza Bhutto, in a gun battle with police in Karachi. A number of opposition politicians accused the Prime Minister and her husband of complicity in the killing, while Benazir Bhutto implied in a number of public statements that she believed that the President and the army were to blame. In 1995 Mir Murtaza Bhutto had established a rival faction of the PPP, known as the PPP (Shaheed Bhutto Group), charging his sister's Government with corruption and misrule; however, the breakaway faction attracted no substantial support.

Amid mounting public discontent, President Leghari dismissed Prime Minister Benazir Bhutto and her Government and dissolved the National Assembly on 5 November 1996 (the state assemblies were dissolved over the following week), citing as justification the deteriorating law and order situation, severe economic problems, widespread corruption, disregard for judicial authority and the violation of various constitutional provisions. A former Speaker of the National Assembly, Malik Meraj Khaled, who claimed no affiliation to any political party, was named as acting Prime Minister and an interim Cabinet was appointed. Following the dismissal of her Government, it was reported that several leading members of Benazir Bhutto's PPP, including her husband, had been arrested. In mid-November the President promulgated a decree providing for a five-year disqualification from public office of politicians (with the exception of the President and members of the judiciary and armed forces) involved in corruption and abuses of power.

Meanwhile, in January 1997, with sectarian violence escalating in several parts of the country, the President instituted an official advisory role for the military, with the formation of a 10-member Council of Defence and National Security (CDNS) to advise the Government on a broad range of issues from national security to the economy. The President chaired the new body, which comprised the Prime Minister, senior cabinet ministers and senior military officials.

Mohammad Nawaz Sharif's second term as Prime Minister (1997–99)

The general election, which was held on 3 February 1997, was marred by an extremely low turn-out (an estimated 30%–40%). The PML (N) won a decisive victory, obtaining 134 seats in the National Assembly, while the PPP was routed, winning only 18 seats. The MQM emerged as the country's third political force (obtaining 12 seats), while the Pakistan Tehreek-e-Insaf (PTI—Pakistan Movement for Justice), a political party founded in 1996 by former international cricketer Imran Khan, failed to win a single seat. Nawaz Sharif was sworn in as Prime Minister on 17 February; a small Cabinet was appointed the following week.

Nawaz Sharif's political authority was strengthened considerably in April 1997, when both the National Assembly and the Senate voted unanimously to repeal the major components of the 1985 Eighth Constitutional Amendment, thereby divesting the President of the power to appoint and dismiss the Prime Minister and Cabinet, to dissolve the legislature, to order a national referendum on any national issue, and to appoint provincial Governors, the Chairman of the Joint Chiefs of Staff and the three armed forces chiefs (these functions and appointments were, in future, to be carried out subject to mandatory advice from the Prime Minister). The President thus became a largely ceremonial figure whose main executive role was the appointment of judges. President Leghari was reported to have 'willingly agreed' to the constitutional changes.

In July 1997 Asif Ali Zardari was formally charged with ordering the killing of Mir Murtaza Bhutto. In September the Swiss police ordered four banks in Geneva to freeze the accounts of Benazir Bhutto and her family after Pakistan's Accountability Commission alleged that up to US $80m. had been illegally transferred to them. In March 1998 the Sindh High Court issued an arrest warrant for the leader of the PPP on a charge of misuse of power during her second term in office as Prime Minister. In

April the High Court in Lahore ordered that all assets belonging to Benazir Bhutto, her husband and her mother be frozen as the government investigation into allegations of corruption continued.

Meanwhile, in the latter half of 1997 a serious rift developed between Nawaz Sharif and the Chief Justice of the Supreme Court, Sajjad Ali Shah, over the appointment of new judges to the Court. In early November a compromise was reached between the Supreme Court and the Government, allowing the former to appoint five new judges while confirming the right of the legislature to determine the total number of judges. Nevertheless, the Supreme Court subsequently charged Nawaz Sharif with contempt for slandering the Court and for defying its orders. The Prime Minister, who, if found guilty, was liable to be disqualified from office, denied the charges. However, the Chief Justice was forced to adjourn Nawaz Sharif's trial in late November, when thousands of the Prime Minister's supporters stormed the Supreme Court in Islamabad. The constitutional crisis came to a dramatic end on 2 December when the Chief Justice was suspended from office by rebel members of the Supreme Court; on the same day President Leghari also stood down from office. The Chairman of the Senate, Wasim Sajjad Jan, assumed the position of acting President. It was widely speculated that the army, in tacitly supporting the Prime Minister, had exerted considerable influence in resolving the constitutional impasse. Nawaz Sharif strengthened his hold on power on 31 December when his nominee and fellow Punjabi, Mohammad Rafiq Tarar, won the presidential election by a record margin.

Despite the temporary public euphoria and heightened popularity of the Prime Minister arising from the conduct of controversial nuclear tests in May 1998 (see Foreign Affairs), the repercussions (particularly the international sanctions) left Pakistan in dire financial straits. In August the Prime Minister introduced the Fifteenth Constitutional Amendment Bill to the National Assembly, seeking to replace Pakistan's legal code with *Shari'a*. Nawaz Sharif attempted to allay fears of a move towards Islamist extremism by promising to uphold women's rights and to safeguard minorities, but the Bill was denounced by human rights activists as 'regressive'. It was passed in the National Assembly in October, but was never ratified by the Senate.

The Government suffered a severe reverse in October 1998 when the Muttahida Qaumi Movement—MQM—(formerly known as the Mohajir Qaumi Movement) withdrew its support for the PML (N)-led provincial administration in Sindh. On 30 October the provincial legislature was suspended and the province was placed under governor's rule in an effort to curb the violence. In November the Prime Minister announced the establishment of anti-terrorist military courts in Karachi, and the suspension of civil rights in Sindh.

In April 1999 the Lahore High Court found Benazir Bhutto (now in self-imposed exile abroad) and her husband guilty of corruption; they were each sentenced to five years' imprisonment, their property was confiscated and they were jointly fined US $8.6m. The verdict automatically removed the former Prime Minister and Asif Ali Zardari (who was already in prison serving a separate sentence) from their seats in the National Assembly and Senate, respectively.

Meanwhile, in January 1999 the Prime Minister escaped an apparent assassination attempt when a bomb exploded near his country residence in Punjab, killing four people; it was followed by an upsurge in sectarian violence in the province. In February the Supreme Court ruled that military trials could not be used for cases against civilians, thus sparing 14 people from death sentences imposed in the military tribunals in Sindh and effectively barring the establishment of military courts throughout the country (as the Government had proposed). The Supreme Court ordered the transfer of the cases to civilian anti-terrorist courts.

A dangerous escalation in the Kashmir crisis between Pakistan and India in mid-1999 (see Foreign Affairs) elicited considerable international condemnation and represented a major turning-point in the fortunes of the PML (N) Government. Many of Nawaz Sharif's opponents in Pakistan declared that the Prime Minister's seeming haste to agree to a Pakistani withdrawal in the face of US pressure constituted a national 'betrayal'. In September Nawaz Sharif's position looked increasingly precarious following the formation of a Grand Democratic Alliance by 19 opposition parties, including the PPP, the MQM and the ANP, which demanded the Prime Minister's immediate resignation. The various Islamist parties, including the JIP, also stepped up their anti-Government protests and rallies throughout the country. However, the opposition was weakened to some extent by the fact that Benazir Bhutto was unwilling to return to Pakistan for fear of being arrested.

Pakistan under Gen. Pervez Musharraf (1999–2008)

Events took a dramatic turn on 12 October 1999, when, shortly after Nawaz Sharif's announcement of a decision to dismiss Chief of Army Staff and Chairman of the Joint Chiefs of Staff Committee Gen. Pervez Musharraf, the army chief flew back from an official tour in Sri Lanka and promptly mounted a bloodless military coup in Islamabad. Nawaz Sharif and his Government were overthrown, and the deposed Prime Minister was placed under house arrest. On 15 October Gen. Musharraf assumed the position of Chief Executive, declared a nation-wide state of emergency, and suspended the Constitution, the National Assembly, the Senate, the four provincial legislatures and all political officials, with the exception of the President and judiciary. He also ensured, by means of a Provisional Constitution Order (PCO), that his actions could not be challenged by any court of law, thus imposing virtual martial law. On 18 October Pakistan was suspended from participation in meetings of the Commonwealth with immediate effect (it was not readmitted to full membership until May 2004). On 22 October 1999 Musharraf appointed four new provincial governors, and on 26 October he installed a three-member Cabinet (which was later expanded) and named the members of a National Security Council (NSC), which was expected to be the supreme executive body of the country.

Following his seizure of power, Musharraf attempted to win over international opinion by portraying himself as a moderate, liberal leader. He was aided in this respect by the fact that the majority of the Pakistani people appeared to support the army's coup (it was a widely held opinion that the military had no provincial bias and represented all levels of society—rather than purely the landed élite). Musharraf promised an eventual return to civilian rule and announced wide-ranging measures to tackle corruption, regional instability and religious extremism. The new regime's stated major priority was the revival of the almost bankrupt economy.

In November 1999 the National Accountability Bureau was formed to investigate cases of corruption. In April 2000 Nawaz Sharif was sentenced to life imprisonment on charges of terrorism (a charge subsequently lifted following appeal) and hijacking (in relation to the alleged refusal of landing rights to the aircraft carrying Musharraf from Sri Lanka to Karachi in October 1999); in addition, all of the former Prime Minister's property in Pakistan was to be confiscated by the State. Six other defendants—including Muhammad Shahbaz Sharif, Nawaz Sharif's brother and former Chief Minister of Punjab—were acquitted. In July Nawaz Sharif was convicted of corruption and sentenced to 14 years' imprisonment, and barred from holding public office for 21 years. In August Musharraf issued a decree disqualifying all those convicted of criminal offences and of terrorist acts from holding public office. The decision was viewed by many as an effective ban on convicted political leaders, notably former Prime Ministers Benazir Bhutto and Nawaz Sharif.

Meanwhile, in January 2000 Musharraf was accused of undemocratic conduct and of attempting to erode the independence of the judiciary when he dismissed the country's Chief Justice, Saeeduzzaman Siddiqui, together with five other judges of the Supreme Court, following their refusal to swear allegiance to the military regime under a new oath. In May Musharraf's regime was strengthened by a unanimous decision by the now pro-military Supreme Court to validate the October 1999 coup as having been necessary to spare the country from chaos and bankruptcy. At the same time, the Court announced that the Chief Executive should name a date not later than 90 days before the expiry of the three-year period from 12 October 1999 for the holding of elections to the National Assembly, the provincial assemblies and the Senate; Musharraf stated that he would comply with this ruling.

In July 2000 Musharraf issued a decree to revive the Islamic provisions of the suspended Constitution and to incorporate them in the PCO, thereby preventing the passage of any law that conflicted with Islamic principles. In August the NSC was reconstituted and redefined as the supreme executive body, comprising the three chiefs of staff and the Ministers of Foreign Affairs, of the Interior, of Finance and of Commerce.

In late 2000 Nawaz Sharif and Benazir Bhutto, together with the heads of 16 other smaller political parties, formed the Alliance for the Restoration of Democracy (ARD), with the aim of ending military rule and accelerating a return to democracy. The new alliance superseded the PPP-led Grand Democratic Alliance. On 10 December Nawaz Sharif was unexpectedly released from prison and sent into exile in Saudi Arabia. The Government announced that the deposed Prime Minister had been granted a 'presidential pardon' and had been permitted to leave the country to seek medical treatment. In return, Nawaz Sharif relinquished his personal and business assets, promised not to return to Pakistan for 10 years, and agreed not to take part in Pakistani politics for 21 years. In May 2001 a warrant was issued for Benazir Bhutto's arrest on her return to Pakistan. However, owing to her continued exile in Dubai, United Arab Emirates, in June she was sentenced, *in absentia*, to three years' imprisonment for failing to appear in court to answer these latest corruption allegations; this criminal conviction effectively disqualified Bhutto from holding further public office in Pakistan.

Musharraf insisted that a ban on party political activity in public would be maintained until after the forthcoming parliamentary elections, and opposition attempts at organizing pro-democracy rallies in March and May 2001 were suppressed by the authorities, who detained thousands of ARD supporters. On 20 June Musharraf unexpectedly assumed the presidency, having dismissed Mohammad Rafiq Tarar. Musharraf immediately issued a formal dissolution of both houses of the federal legislature (which had been suspended since October 1999) in preparation for the elections. In August Musharraf confirmed that elections to the four provincial legislatures and to the bicameral federal parliament would be conducted between 1 and 11 October 2002, thereby providing for the full restoration of democratic institutions by 12 October (the deadline established by the Supreme Court).

As one of only three states to have recognized the legitimacy of the Taliban administration in Afghanistan, and as the most significant trading partner and political associate of the Afghan regime, Pakistan's support was crucial to the efforts of the US-led anti-terrorism coalition in the aftermath of the 11 September 2001 terrorist attacks on the US mainland, and Musharraf was left in little doubt that his refusal to co-operate with the campaign to apprehend those members of the al-Qa'ida organization held responsible for the attacks would result in Pakistan's increased economic and political isolation. Therefore, Musharraf's political opponents in the PML and PPP appeared to accept his declaration of co-operation with US requests for shared intelligence and use of airspace with resignation. However, large-scale popular opposition to the President's decision was inevitable, particularly in the NWFP bordering Afghanistan, which was home to large numbers of Pakhtoon (Pashtun) Pakistanis who were fiercely opposed to any assault on the Pashtun-dominated Taliban. Despite Musharraf's insistence that the US-led activities in the region did not represent an attack on Islam, protests against the action spread throughout the country. Of particular note was the widely alleged opposition from within the armed forces and the Inter-Services Intelligence (ISI) agency to Pakistan's official support for the intervention in Afghanistan; both of these bodies were believed to have nurtured particularly close links with the Taliban. In October, having extended indefinitely his term of office as Chief of Army Staff, Musharraf implemented a radical reorganization of the military high command and the intelligence service, replacing a number of senior personnel with known sympathies for the country's militant Islamist cause, including Lt-Gen. Mahmood Ahmed, head of the ISI. Popular protests against co-operation with the US-led coalition continued, but Musharraf's resolve remained firm (strengthened, in part, by the promise of financial recognition of his political support from the USA and the European Union—EU), and despite the uncompromising response of the security forces to sporadic rioting there were surprisingly few casualties. In early November the leaders of the JUI and the JIP were detained following allegations that they were continuing to promote anti-Government activities and demonstrations. In the border regions of the NWFP and Balochistan reports began to emerge of large numbers of armed local tribesmen crossing the border as willing recruits for the Taliban, and it was alleged that supply lines for the Taliban were being maintained into north-western Pakistan. However, by mid-November the anti-Taliban forces of the United National Islamic Front for the Salvation of Afghanistan (commonly known as the United Front or Northern Alliance), with the support of the US-led coalition, had taken Kabul (the Afghan capital). As the rout of Taliban forces in Afghanistan continued in December and the USA intensified its bombardment of suspected al-Qa'ida positions in southern Afghanistan, Pakistan substantially reinforced security personnel along its north-western border in order to intercept fleeing combatants.

On 30 April 2002, despite a boycott by the opposition, a national referendum was held to seek endorsement for Musharraf's term of office as President to be extended by five years and approval of the Government's political and economic programme. According to official figures, turn-out was 70%, with 98% of those participating supporting the proposal; however, there were widespread allegations of gross irregularities and fraud, and opposition parties and independent monitors estimated that turn-out was only about 5%. In late June Musharraf dismissed the head of the political wing of the ISI and chief organizer of the presidential referendum, Maj.-Gen. Ehtesam Zamir, after being forced to admit that his referendum victory had been fraudulent.

On 21 August 2002 President Musharraf unilaterally enacted the Legal Framework Order (LFO), which validated all the military decrees approved since the coup in 1999, and introduced 29 amendments to the Constitution, including: a reduction in the parliamentary term from five years to four; a lowering of the voting age from 21 years to 18 years; a restriction in the number of terms premiers or provincial chief ministers could hold in office to two; and disqualification of those members of the legislature who had criminal convictions, had defaulted on loans or had absconded (the last two amendments were widely considered to be aimed at preventing former Prime Ministers Benazir Bhutto and Nawaz Sharif from returning to office). Musharraf's powers were enlarged considerably: the President was restored the right to dissolve the National Assembly and to dismiss the Prime Minister and Cabinet; furthermore, he was given the authority to override parliamentary majorities and provincial assemblies in order to appoint a Prime Minister and provincial governors himself if necessary. The amendments allowed the President to appoint Supreme Court judges and to extend his term in office. One of the most significant amendments, the permanent establishment of an NSC, which would include Musharraf in his capacity as President and Chief of Army Staff, as well as the three other armed forces chiefs, the Prime Minister, the provincial chief ministers, the leader of the parliamentary opposition, the Chairman of the Senate and the Speaker of the National Assembly, was also authorized. The NSC would provide consultation to the elected government on strategic issues. Inevitably, the changes were heavily criticized by the PML (N) and PPP. However, Musharraf insisted that a formal role for the military in governing the country was necessary to ensure a stable transition to democracy and to forestall a potential military coup. According to the LFO, the size of the National Assembly would be increased to 342 members, with 60 seats reserved for women and 10 seats reserved for non-Muslims. The Senate would consist of 100 members.

Meanwhile, in July 2002 Benazir Bhutto was re-elected as leader of the PPP. However, the newly introduced decree barring parties from contesting an election if any of its office-holders had a criminal conviction prompted the PPP in early August to create the Pakistan Peoples Party Parliamentarians (PPPP) under new leadership to contest the forthcoming general election. At the same time Shahbaz Sharif was elected leader of the PML (N). Bhutto's plans to return to the political arena were thwarted in late August when election officials in Sindh rejected her candidacy in the National Assembly elections, owing to her criminal conviction. In response, Nawaz Sharif withdrew his nomination papers (although they had been accepted by the Election Commission), reportedly in solidarity with Bhutto. In September Shahbaz Sharif was disqualified from contesting the general election for defaulting on a bank loan. Meanwhile, a pro-Musharraf faction of the PML, the Quaid-i-Azam group, was reportedly receiving covert support from the Government.

On 9 October 2002 Musharraf declared that he was relinquishing the title of Chief Executive. The following day elections for the National Assembly and provincial assemblies took place. In elections to the National Assembly the PML (Quaid-i-Azam—Q) won 77 of the 272 directly elective seats (25.7% of the votes cast). The PPPP secured 25.8% of the vote, but only 63 seats. A surprising outcome was the success of the Muttahida Majlis-e-Amal (MMA), an alliance of six Islamist parties, in obtaining 45 seats (11.3% of the vote). The PML (N) won only 14 seats (9.4% of the vote). According to the Election Commission, the turn-out at the elections was 41.8%. Opposition parties, independent analysts and the Human Rights Commission of Pakistan claimed that the army had provided financial and other support to the PML (Q), while hampering other parties' campaign efforts, while

EU election monitors reported that the poll was 'seriously flawed'. The emergence of the MMA as a political force suggested that a significant proportion of the population objected to Musharraf's support for the US-led military action against the Taliban and al-Qa'ida in Afghanistan. The PML (Q) and PPPP each attempted to gain the support of the MMA in order to form a governing coalition. By mid-November the parties had yet to reach a compromise; nevertheless, the National Assembly convened and elected a Speaker and Deputy Speaker. Shortly beforehand, the President revived the 1973 Constitution, which had been in abeyance since he assumed power in 1999—it was believed that the Constitution incorporated the controversial LFO—and took an oath to begin his new five-year term as President. On 21 November the PML (Q) candidate, Zafarullah Khan Jamali, was elected Prime Minister by the National Assembly. Jamali's victory ensured a PML (Q)-led, pro-army Government with a slim majority. Musharraf agreed to transfer power to the elected Government, but emphasized that he would continue to carry out his 'important role'.

In the provincial elections held concurrently in October 2002 the MMA won a majority in the NWFP and formed a coalition government in Balochistan with the PML (Q). The PML (Q) assumed power in Punjab, and a coalition government comprising the PML (Q), the MMA and several smaller parties was appointed in Sindh in December (following the failure of the PPPP—which had won the largest number of seats—to form a provincial administration). At the delayed Senate elections in February 2003, in which the majority of seats were elected by the provincial assemblies, the PML (Q) became the largest single party in the Senate; the PML (Q) candidate, Mohammad Mian Soomro, was elected unopposed as Chairman of the Senate after opposition parties boycotted the vote in protest against alleged military interference in the Senate elections. The opposition instigated a campaign of disruption of proceedings in the National Assembly, repeatedly demanding that the President submit the LFO for parliamentary approval. In June 2003 the MMA-led legislative assembly in the NWFP unanimously voted in favour of legislation to implement *Shari'a* throughout the province (giving Islamic law precedence over secular provincial law).

In September 2003, following negotiations between the Government and opposition, the Cabinet endorsed a modified version of the LFO. In December Musharraf announced seven further concessionary amendments to the LFO, including his commitment to resign as Chief of Army Staff by December 2004. On 29 December 2003 the National Assembly approved the Constitution (Seventeenth Amendment) Bill, which comprised the seven modifications. The opposition ARD boycotted the parliamentary proceedings, dismissing the concessions as 'cosmetic'. According to the Bill, which became law on 31 December following the Senate's approval, a new NSC (the existing body having been inactive since its creation) was to be established by an act of parliament, rather than be incorporated into the Constitution by the LFO. Furthermore, while the President would have the right to dismiss the National Assembly, he would be obliged to refer the matter to the Supreme Court within 15 days. Despite the concessions, Musharraf retained most of the special powers that he had awarded himself in 2002. In January 2004 the federal and provincial legislatures passed votes of confidence in Musharraf, allowing him to complete his five-year term as President (which was due to expire in 2007). In April 2004, amid strong protest by opposition members, the National Assembly passed legislation on the establishment of the NSC, which gave the armed forces a formal, albeit supervisory, role in civilian politics for the first time in Pakistan's history.

In August 2003 Asif Ali Zardari was acquitted of all charges relating to the 1998 murder of Sajjad Hussain, the former Chairman of Pakistan Steel Mills. In November 2003 opposition parties held widespread protests on the seventh anniversary of Zardari's arrest to demand his release from prison. Zardari, now largely considered a political prisoner, was implicated in 14 pending criminal cases, but had been convicted on only one corruption charge. In November 2004 the Supreme Court ordered that Zardari be released on bail. Meanwhile, his wife, Benazir Bhutto, faced further corruption cases in Pakistan, Switzerland, the United Kingdom and the USA. In November 2005 Bhutto claimed that President Musharraf had offered to abandon all remaining charges against her, on the condition that she declined to contest elections scheduled for 2007; she asserted that she was unable to accept the condition.

In 2003 sectarian violence between Sunni and Shi'a Muslims escalated; in addition, attacks by militant Islamists on Western targets continued to take place. Despite a ban on several militant Islamist groups, imposed in November, in December the President narrowly escaped two assassination attempts by suspected Islamist militants near his residence in Rawalpindi (see Sectarian, Ethnic and Political Violence in Pakistan).

In December 2003 the Government admitted that it was investigating allegations that Pakistan had transferred nuclear technology to other countries, and that Dr Abdul Qadeer Khan, the founder of Pakistan's nuclear weapons programme, was being questioned. However, the authorities were quick to deny any official involvement. Khan was reportedly placed under house arrest and in January 2004 was removed from his post as scientific adviser to the Prime Minister. In February Khan confessed on television that during the past 15 years he had provided Iran, the Democratic People's Republic of Korea (North Korea) and Libya with designs and technology to develop nuclear weapons. Taking full responsibility for his actions, he denied any government involvement and absolved the military and his fellow scientists. Dr Khan's plea for clemency was promptly granted by Musharraf, who stated, nevertheless, that the scientist would remain under strict surveillance. It was widely acknowledged that prosecuting Dr Khan would have led to unrest throughout the country (he had been long revered as the 'father' of Pakistan's nuclear bomb and had the status of a national hero) and to political problems (there were fears that if put on trial the scientist would provide evidence that incriminated Pakistani leaders and generals). Analysts declared that it was unlikely that the transfer of nuclear materials could have been conducted without the knowledge and involvement of at least parts of the military.

In June 2004 Prime Minister Jamali tendered his resignation, having been placed under considerable pressure to do so by Musharraf. The President was reportedly frustrated at the weakness of Jamali's Government and, in particular, its apparent inability to curb sectarian violence in Pakistan. Later in the same month Musharraf's nominee, Chaudhry Shujaat Hussain, President of the newly formed PML (which had been created following the merger of several factions of the PML and the Sindh Democratic Alliance), was elected to serve as interim Prime Minister. It was reported that Minister of Finance Shaukat Aziz was Musharraf's choice to serve in the post permanently, but, as Aziz was a Senator, he would first need to be elected to the House of Representatives. In August, following victories in two constituency by-elections, Aziz was elected as Prime Minister and leader of the house by the National Assembly. In the following month a new Cabinet was appointed, which included the 20 members of Chaudhry Shujaat Hussain's interim Government and incorporated an additional 13 members.

In October 2004 the National Assembly approved legislation enabling Musharraf to retain his dual role as President and Chief of Army Staff, contrary to his December 2003 pledge that he would resign from his military position by the end of 2004. To counter opposition protests that the bill was unconstitutional, the Government claimed that the ongoing terrorist threat necessitated Musharraf's retention of both roles. In November, having been approved by the Senate, the bill was signed into law. In the following month Musharraf formally confirmed that he intended to retain his military position until the end of his presidential term in 2007. In April 2005 the Supreme Court dismissed all petitions challenging Musharraf's dual role as unconstitutional.

In October 2005 a huge earthquake devastated Azad Kashmir and much of the NWFP, resulting in the deaths of more than 81,000 people and leaving many thousands homeless. The response of the Government and armed forces to the disaster attracted criticism for its tardiness and lack of co-ordination, although the logistical challenge of delivering relief to many of the remote areas affected was considerable. At a meeting of donors held in November in Islamabad, a total of US $5,800m. was pledged by the international community for the relief and reconstruction effort.

In November 2006 the federal legislature approved the Women's Protection Bill, giving civil courts jurisdiction in rape cases and revoking the death penalty for extra-marital sexual intercourse. Religious groups voiced their opposition to the bill, arguing that it was 'un-Islamic', while others complained that it did not go far enough. In March 2007 Musharraf suspended the Chief Justice of the Supreme Court, Iftikhar Mohammad Chaudhry—who was widely recognized for his independent stance on controversial issues and for his investigations into human rights violations—on charges of abuse of office. This controversial action provoked the holding of large-scale, violent demonstrations by the legal community and the resignation of several senior judicial officials. In May Chaudhry arrived in Karachi to address a political rally organized by his supporters, but was unable to leave the airport because the roads into the city were blocked. Demonstrations in Karachi subsequently escalated into violent clashes between supporters of the Government and the opposition, resulting in some 41 fatalities. The campaign to reinstate Chaudhry appeared to have succeeded when the Supreme Court voted to restore him to the position of Chief Justice in July.

Sectarian violence and terrorist attacks continued to pose a threat to internal security and stability throughout the country in 2006 and 2007. Matters came to a head in July 2007 with violent clashes between paramilitary forces and occupants of the Lal Masjid compound in central Islamabad (see Sectarian, Ethnic and Political Violence in Pakistan).

Meanwhile, conjecture about the possible return to Pakistan of Benazir Bhutto and Nawaz Sharif intensified. In August 2007 the Supreme Court decided that, regardless of the terms of his exile agreement, Nawaz Sharif was entitled to return to the country; however, upon his arrival in Islamabad in the following month, Nawaz Sharif was sent back to Saudi Arabia, prompting a legal challenge to the deportation. In early October Musharraf passed a National Reconciliation Ordinance, giving Bhutto and other politicians immunity from prosecution under charges brought during 1986–99. Despite the absence of a conclusive agreement, Bhutto entered Pakistan later that month. She was greeted by hundreds of thousands of supporters in Karachi, but fears for her safety were confirmed when a bomb attack on her procession resulted in approximately 139 fatalities. Bhutto herself was unharmed.

On 6 October 2007 Musharraf was re-elected as President by the incumbent national and provincial legislatures, securing 671 votes against the eight received by former Supreme Court judge Wajihuddin Ahmed. Members of the MMA, the PML (N) and other opposition parties had resigned from the National Assembly in protest prior to the ballot, while the PPP abstained from the vote. Just before the vote, the Supreme Court had ruled that the victor could not be declared until the legality of the election had been confirmed pending legal challenges from the opposition. The Supreme Court was also expected to rule on the legality of the National Reconciliation Ordinance. On 3 November Musharraf declared a state of emergency and suspended the Constitution, citing, among other contributing factors, the deteriorating law and order situation and the judiciary's interference in government affairs. Immediate measures included the dismissal of Chief Justice Chaudhry and the swearing in of Abdul Hameed Dogar as his replacement. Members of the judiciary were reportedly among those detained, together with lawyers, opposition figures and human rights activists who had taken part in demonstrations to protest against the imposition of emergency measures. The National Assembly was dissolved on 15 November, and the Chairman of the Senate, Mohammad Mian Soomro, was sworn in to lead an interim Government the following day. The Punjab, Balochistan and Sindh provincial legislatures were subsequently dissolved, the provincial assembly of NWFP having been dissolved in October. On 20 November the Chief Election Commissioner confirmed that parliamentary and provincial assembly elections would be held on 8 January 2008. Musharraf resigned as Chief of Army Staff on 28 November 2007, following the Supreme Court's dismissal, on 22 November, of the final legal challenge to Musharraf's re-election as President, thus facilitating Musharraf's inauguration as civilian head of state (which duly took place on 29 November). Musharraf revoked the state of emergency on 15 December.

Meanwhile, the possibility of a power-sharing agreement between Musharraf and Bhutto appeared increasingly unlikely as PPP supporters joined the ranks of opposition members detained under the emergency measures, and Bhutto herself was placed under temporary house arrest to prevent her participation in political rallies. In mid-November 2007 Bhutto announced an end to negotiations with Musharraf and indicated a willingness to consider the formation of a coalition government with other opposition parties. Nawaz Sharif was permitted to return to Pakistan at the end of November, following the reported intervention of the King of Saudi Arabia. However, in late December, as the country prepared for elections, there was a dramatic turn of events when Benazir Bhutto was killed in a suicide bomb attack on a PPP rally in Rawalpindi. The Gov-

ernment was criticized for not arranging adequate security measures, and some voiced suspicion about the perpetrators' possible links to sections of the Government or the intelligence establishment, a claim that Musharraf vehemently denied. According to officials, Baitullah Mehsud, an extremist from the FATA, and al-Qa'ida were involved in the attack. News of the assassination provoked rioting in several cities, resulting in more than 45 deaths. On 30 December 19-year-old Bilawal Bhutto Zardari was named to succeed his mother as leader of the PPP upon the completion of his university studies, with Asif Ali Zardari assuming the role in an interim capacity.

At the legislative elections, which were held later than scheduled, on 18 February 2008, the PPPP secured a total of 121 seats in the National Assembly (including seats reserved for women and non-Muslims). The PML (N) won 91 seats, while the PML, which supported Musharraf, took just 54 seats. Turn-out was estimated at some 45% of the electorate. The PML was also defeated in all of the provincial assemblies except Balochistan. A coalition Government, mainly composed of PPP and PML (N) members, was sworn in at the end of March, under the premiership of Yousaf Raza Gilani of the PPP. Shortly after assuming office, Gilani ordered the release of several judges arrested in November 2007.

Musharraf steps down and Asif Ali Zardari assumes the presidency

The fragility of the new coalition Government was demonstrated almost immediately, when a disagreement over the reinstatement of the judges who had been dismissed in November 2007 necessitated prolonged negotiations between the PPP and the PML (N) in April–May 2008. The PML (N) wanted to return Chaudhry and the other judges to their positions, while the PPP was hesitant, perhaps fearing the consequences of their reinstatement (i.e. the rescinding of the National Reconciliation Ordinance). In the absence of a resolution, in mid-May the PML (N) announced the withdrawal of its ministers from the Cabinet, although Nawaz Sharif gave an assurance of his party's continuing support for the coalition in the legislature. In the following month a campaign instigated by lawyers to reinstate the judges gained momentum and increasingly targeted the President, with thousands of people participating in a march from Lahore to Islamabad. In August Musharraf announced his resignation from the presidency, prompted by the prospect of impending impeachment proceedings (on charges of violating the Constitution and gross misconduct) initiated by the PPP and the PML (N). The Chairman of the Senate, Mohammad Mian Soomro, was appointed President in an acting capacity, pending the parliamentary election of a successor.

At the presidential election held on 6 September 2008, Zardari defeated the PML (N) candidate, former Chief Justice of the Supreme Court Saeeduzzaman Siddiqui, by 481 votes to 153; a third candidate, Mushahid Hussain Syed, supported by the PML (Q), received only 44 votes. The rift between the PPP and the PML (N) appeared to widen in February 2009, when the Supreme Court upheld a verdict barring Nawaz Sharif and his brother, Shahbaz Sharif, from elected office on account of their previous criminal convictions. The latter was dismissed from his position as Chief Minister of Punjab, and governor's rule was imposed in the province. Nawaz Sharif protested against the ruling, claiming that Zardari was behind the decision and reiterating his demand for the reinstatement of the judges. In mid-March, in an apparent attempt to defuse the political crisis and to end the agitation by the lawyers and PML (N) activists that threatened to destabilize the country, the Government agreed to reinstate Chaudhry as Chief Justice. At the end of the month, in a further conciliatory move, President Zardari lifted central rule in Punjab and Shahbaz Sharif was restored as Chief Minister of the province.

In December 2009 the Supreme Court ruled that the National Reconciliation Ordinance of October 2007 (which had allowed for the return of Benazir Bhutto and her husband, Zardari, to take an active role in Pakistani politics, as well as acting as a political amnesty for thousands of other politicians and officials) was unconstitutional and ordered that it be abolished with immediate effect. Although Zardari was immune from criminal prosecution while he held the presidency, Nawaz Sharif demanded his resignation on moral grounds. As well as the President's political future looking increasingly unstable, a number of his government colleagues, including the Minister of the Interior, Rehman Malik, were also confronted by the prospect of renewed charges of corruption.

These political developments took place against a background of increasing instability and violence in Pakistan. As fighting and bombings continued in the NWFP and FATA, there were concerns about the expanding power base of the militants. Numerous terrorist attacks (many of which were perpetrated by Islamist extremists) took place in major cities throughout Pakistan in 2008 and 2009. The emergence in the latter half of the 2000s of the Tehrik-e-Taliban Pakistan (TTP), or the so-called Pakistani Taliban, a coalition of more than 10 militant factions operating in north-west Pakistan and reportedly led by Baitullah Mehsud, represented a disturbing development. Prime Minister Gilani vowed to tackle terrorism, but he also declared a willingness to negotiate with militants on the condition of their cessation of violence. Receiving particular media attention was the situation in the Swat Valley (see Sectarian, Ethnic and Political Violence in Pakistan).

The abolition of the Seventeenth Amendment; increasing unrest and instability

In April 2010 a number of far-reaching constitutional reforms (the Eighteenth Amendment Bill), ceding key presidential powers to the Prime Minister and legislature, were signed into law, following unanimous approval by the National Assembly and Senate earlier that month. The main components of the amendments, which effectively terminated the Seventeenth Amendment enacted by President Musharraf in December 2003 (including the LFO) and transformed the President into a largely titular head of state, were: the divestment of the presidential mandate to dismiss elected governments and to appoint military chiefs and the Chief Election Commissioner, and the devolution of these powers to the Prime Minister; the transfer of responsibility for the appointment of judges from the President to a judicial commission headed by the Chief Justice (with nominations to be approved by a parliamentary committee); the termination of the election of the Prime Minister and of provincial chief ministers by secret ballot; the divestment of the presidential power unilaterally to impose emergency rule in a province; the lifting of the two-term limit on the holding of the premiership (thus allowing for Nawaz Sharif potentially to stand for another term as Prime Minister); and the renaming of the NWFP as Khyber Pakhtoonkhwa (a long-standing demand of the ethnic Pashtuns who dominate that region).

Political events in Pakistan were overshadowed by devastating floods that began in late July 2010 following unusually heavy monsoon rains. The floods, which were described as the country's worst in more than 80 years, affected around 100,000 sq km of land throughout the Indus river basin, killing at least 1,600 people, damaging or destroying around 1.6m. homes, ravaging vast areas of agricultural land and adversely affecting 20m. people. With up to 8m. people in urgent need of emergency relief, the UN appealed for US $460m. in international aid. Widespread public anger at the perceived ineffectiveness of the authorities' relief operation was reported in numerous areas, and consequently the profile of various Islamic charities that provided relief to flood victims was raised considerably, prompting concerns that a number of these charities had links to militant groups. In addition, the Government's civilian authority was undermined by the dominant role played by the army in the relief effort. President Zardari came under particular criticism for completing a European tour during the height of the flooding.

Meanwhile, Karachi, the capital of Sindh province and Pakistan's largest city, which had enjoyed a period of relative stability over the previous decade, suffered an intensification of political and sectarian violence from 2010. At the same time minority religious groups (including Shi'a Muslims, Christians and members of the Sufi branch of Islam) in other parts of the country were increasingly targeted by extremists. Conflict arose over the controversial blasphemy law, with the assassination of two prominent reformists, PPP Governor of Punjab Salman Taseer and Minister of Minorities Shahbaz Bhatti in January and March 2011, respectively (see Sectarian, Ethnic and Political Violence in Pakistan).

As agreed in the Eighteenth Amendment Bill, in December 2010 the Cabinet approved the devolution of five federal ministries to the provinces as part of a programme to increase the latter's administrative and financial autonomy (another 12 ministries were devolved in 2011). In December 2010 the Government suffered a setback when the JUI (Fazl—F) left the coalition following the dismissal of one its members from the Cabinet. On 2 January 2011 the Government appeared even more fragile when the MQM also withdrew from the coalition, in protest against economic reforms, including the introduction of a sales tax and the imposition of a fuel price increase (instigated under pressure from the IMF). To prevent the collapse of the Government, Prime Minister Gilani cancelled the controversial reforms; on 7 January the MQM pledged to reinstate its support for the coalition (but not to rejoin the Cabinet). The following month, as part of the Government's plans to reduce public expenditure in response to the deteriorating economic situation, the number of cabinet ministers was reduced from 42 to 22.

In February 2011 an anti-terrorism court in Rawalpindi issued a warrant for the arrest of Musharraf with regard to the 2007 assassination of Benazir Bhutto, claiming that the former President had failed to provide adequate security protection for the PPP leader. Musharraf, from his self-imposed exile in the United Kingdom, refuted all the allegations.

In April 2011, in an effort to address the Government's narrowing parliamentary majority, a new coalition agreement between the PPP and the PML—still widely known in Pakistan as the PML (Q)—was concluded. On 2 May Prime Minister Gilani incorporated 14 new PML ministers and ministers of state into the Cabinet. Chaudhry Pervaiz Elahi, a senior PML official and leader of the party's Punjab wing, was appointed Senior Minister, a post that was regarded as the de facto deputy premiership, and allocated additional responsibility for defence production and for industries. The Government was further strengthened by the decision of the MQM to rejoin the Cabinet; three MQM members were inducted into the Cabinet on 11 May. However, the new coalition arrangement appeared to intensify internal divisions within the PML; in mid-May the newly appointed PML Minister of Production, Amir Muqam, resigned in protest against the terms of the coalition deal, and several members of the PML announced their intention to support the opposition in the National Assembly. Also in mid-May the Lahore High Court ruled that President Zardari's dual role as head of state and Co-Chairman of the ruling PPP was unconstitutional, as the President was required to function with impartiality. The ruling prompted opposition demands for Zardari's resignation from the presidency.

Meanwhile, the Government came under intense domestic and international pressure following the killing of Osama bin Laden, the founder of al-Qa'ida, by US special forces during a covert raid on a fortified compound in Abbottabad, Khyber Pakhtoonkhwa, on 2 May 2011. Four other inhabitants of the compound, including one of bin Laden's sons, were reportedly killed during the operation, which was apparently carried out without prior consultation with the Pakistani authorities. The discovery of the al-Qa'ida leader in a town containing a prominent Pakistani military academy and located less than 120 km from Islamabad prompted widespread assertions that senior Pakistani officials, most likely from the ISI or the army, must have sanctioned bin Laden's presence in the country. While the Pakistani Government publicly welcomed bin Laden's demise, Prime Minister Gilani described the clandestine operation as a violation of national sovereignty, and rejected all allegations of official involvement in harbouring the militant leader. However, the Government's professed ignorance of the presence of the notorious fugitive and its inability to prevent the USA from conducting a unilateral military operation within Pakistani territory exposed it to persistent accusations of weakness and incompetence. The incident also reinforced existing doubts about the Government's capacity for exerting control over the security apparatus in Pakistan. Gilani initiated an internal investigation into the circumstances of bin Laden's presence in Pakistan (the so-called Abbottabad Commission report was presented to Gilani's successor as Prime Minister, Raja Pervaiz Ashraf, in January 2013, but its findings were not immediately released to the public).

At the end of June 2011 the three MQM ministers resigned from the Cabinet again (as did the MQM members of the provincial government in Sindh), in protest against the postponement of elections to two seats in the legislature of Azad Kashmir and citing their inability to continue working with an 'undemocratic and dictatorial' administration. However, Prime Minister Gilani refused to accept the resignations and asserted that the MQM politicians' status as ministers remained intact (they resumed their ministerial responsibilities in October). In July, at the request of President Zardari, who wished to restore a degree of stability to Karachi (where there had been a recent upsurge in ethnic and sectarian violence), the MQM's Ishratul Ibad Khan resumed office as Governor of Sindh. In the same month 34-year-old Hina Rabbani Khar of the PPP was sworn in as the country's first female—as well as youngest ever—Minister of Foreign Affairs. In October the MQM ministers in the federal Government and in the provincial cabinet of Sindh announced that, in the national interest, they were resuming their ministerial responsibilities.

Recent developments: state institutions in conflict; the 2013 general election

In October 2011 relations between the Government and the military came under strain following the publication of allegations that the Pakistani ambassador to the USA, Husain Haqqani (a close ally of Zardari), had issued a memorandum seeking US help for the Pakistani civilian authorities to avert a military coup by the country's powerful generals in the wake of the killing of bin Laden in May. Haqqani denied having committed any such action, but resigned from his post the following month. However, the repercussions of the affair persisted; Zardari denied having authorized the dispatch of the alleged memorandum, while the military dismissed continuing rumours of an imminent coup. The US authorities, for their part, claimed that they had indeed received the memorandum (which was reportedly unsigned) but had not acted on it. The Supreme Court instigated an official inquiry into the allegations at the end of the month. In January 2012 Prime Minister Gilani claimed that the Chief of Army Staff, Gen. Ashfaq Pervez Kayani, and the head of the ISI, Lt-Gen. Ahmad Shuja Pasha, had acted unconstitutionally by submitting evidence to the inquiry. A few days later, in an apparent show of defiance against the military, Gilani dismissed the Defence Secretary, Naeem Khalid Lodhi, on the grounds of alleged 'gross misconduct'.

In January 2012 relations between the Government and the judiciary deteriorated when the Supreme Court launched contempt of court proceedings against Prime Minister Gilani for his refusal to obey a 2009 court order formally to request that the Swiss authorities reopen a corruption investigation against the President (dating back to the 1990s). Gilani asserted that, as Head of State, Zardari was immune from prosecution. The President, in turn, continued to reject the corruption charges as politically motivated. On 12 April 2012, as part of what the media described as preparations for the court proceedings, Moula Baksh Chandio was replaced as Minister of Law and Justice, and of Parliamentary Affairs by Farooq H. Naek, the former Chairman of the Senate. A more extensive cabinet reorganization was effected a week later, increasing the total of government ministers to 53. On 26 April the Supreme Court found Prime Minister Gilani guilty of contempt of court; however, he was given only a symbolic sentence (of several minutes' detention in the courtroom) and was not required to serve a term in prison. Despite demands by the opposition that Gilani be automatically disqualified from holding office for the next five years, the Court issued no such order and the Prime Minister remained in power.

In the mean time, the beleaguered PPP was given a considerable boost in March 2012 when it made gains in elections to the Senate, becoming the party with the largest representation (41 seats) in the upper house for the first time in almost 15 years and, together with is allies, holding a comfortable majority.

With opposition leaders continuing to agitate for Gilani's removal from the premiership, in June the Supreme Court ruled that, in the absence of an appeal from the Prime Minister against his contempt of court conviction, he was disqualified from holding office. The initial candidate to replace him, PPP Minister of the Textile Industry Makhdoom Shahabuddin, was withdrawn after an arrest warrant was issued in relation to his previous position as Minister of Health. The second candidate, former Minister of Water and Power Raja Pervaiz Ashraf (also of the PPP), was elected as Prime Minister by a significant margin of votes in the National Assembly on 22 June. A new Cabinet was sworn in, retaining most members of the previous Government. Chaudhry Pervaiz Elahi of the PML was appointed as Deputy Prime Minister and Minister responsible for Industries, while Syed Naveed Qamar remained as Minister of Defence, having recently been transferred from the position of Minister of Water and Power for a reportedly poor performance. The erstwhile Minister of Defence, Chaudhry Ahmed Mukhtar, was allocated the crucial water and power portfolio. Meanwhile, the former Minister of the Interior, Rehman Malik, was reappointed as a prime ministerial adviser on the interior, having been disqualified from membership of the Senate due to his dual nationality.

Ashraf promised to hold free and fair elections and to concentrate on addressing the country's power crisis. However, his appointment was not without controversy—the new Prime Minister faced corruption charges from his tenure as Minister of Water and Power. In addition, he was under renewed pressure from the Supreme Court to reopen the corruption case against President Zardari. Legislation granting government officials immunity from contempt of court charges was passed in July 2012, but the Supreme Court dismissed this as unconstitutional in August. In September Ashraf finally conceded, informing the Supreme Court that he had begun the process of contacting the Swiss authorities to withdraw the request for corruption charges against Zardari to be annulled. After much discussion, the proposed letter from Farooq H. Naek, the Minister of Law and Justice, and of Parliamentary Affairs, to the Swiss authorities was agreed upon by the Supreme Court in October. Nevertheless, in January 2013 the Supreme Court ordered Ashraf's arrest on corruption charges, following claims he accepted bribes while serving as Minister of Water and Power. At the same time, the cleric Tahirul Qadri and thousands of his supporters protested in Islamabad to demand the ousting of the Government in advance of the forthcoming elections, scheduled for May. Concerns about a potential political crisis were allayed when the Government agreed to dissolve Parliament in March in order to halt the protests. Ashraf's arrest also appeared unlikely in light of the National Accountability Bureau's reluctance to follow through on the case without further evidence.

Meanwhile, discussions took place between the Government and the opposition over the election process. According to recent legislation, the crucial post of Chief Election Commissioner (CEC) would be appointed by consensus, with equal input from the Government and the opposition. In July 2012 a former Supreme Court judge, Fakhruddin G. Ebrahim, was named CEC through this process. In February 2013 Saleem Mandvi Walla replaced Abdul Hafeez Sheikh as Minister of Finance, Revenue, Planning and Development, Economic Affairs and Statistics, as speculation mounted over the composition of the new caretaker cabinet. In the following month the National Assembly was dissolved and the PPP-led Government duly stood down, becoming the first democratically elected administration to complete a full term in the country's history. President Zardari announced the date of 11 May for the elections, and negotiations to determine appointments to the caretaker government began. When these talks failed to reach a consensus, in late March the Election Commission of Pakistan chose Mir Hazar Khan Khoso, a retired judge, to act as caretaker Prime Minister; a 15-member interim Cabinet was sworn in on 2 April.

Extensive media attention was focused on the return of Pervez Musharraf from exile in late March 2013. Musharraf, who declared his intention to stand in the May elections, had been granted a protective bail order, but several court cases against him were pending in Pakistan. With a mixed reaction among the public to his arrival, and the rejection of his nomination papers in four districts, his decision to return was judged by analysts as a miscalculation. In mid-April Musharraf was arrested on charges of having illegally detained judges while he was in power in 2007. Meanwhile, there was an upsurge in violence in the weeks leading up to the May elections, as mainly Islamist militants launched attacks on political rallies in various parts of the country; in early May it was reported that more than 100 people had been killed in such attacks since the beginning of April. Although the violence initially targeted the main secular parties, by early May Islamist political parties were also subject to militant attacks, with the TTP declaring its complete opposition to the 'un-Islamic' democratic process.

The general election took place, as scheduled, on 11 May 2013. Despite rising levels of violence as polling day approached, turnout was an estimated 60%, a considerable increase on the 45% recorded in 2008. According to provisional results, the PML (N) performed strongly and the party was expected to gain sufficient seats to form a government, albeit with the support of independent deputies; Mohammad Nawaz Sharif was poised to return as Prime Minister for the third time. The PPP appeared to have suffered heavy losses, as expected, while the arrival as a political force of the PTI was confirmed, as Imran Khan's party was expected to rival the PPP for the status of main opposition party. (By 16 May, with provisional results declared in 261 out of 272 elective seats, the PML (N) had secured 124 seats, the PPP had 31 seats, the PTI had won 27 seats and the MQM had 18 seats.) In concurrent provincial elections, according to provisional results, the PML (N) won an overwhelming majority in Punjab Province, while the PPP retained control of the Sindh Assembly (although the MQM dominated in the urban centres of Karachi and

Hyderabad). In Khyber Pakhtoonkhwa, the PTI performed strongly and was expected to lead a coalition administration in the province; in Balochistan, seats were divided between Balochi nationalist parties, the PML (N) and independents. While the elections were widely viewed as a significant advance for democracy in Pakistan, not least because they represented the first democratic transfer of power between two civilian governments in the country's history, numerous allegations of vote-rigging (notably in Karachi) were under investigation by the ECP in the immediate aftermath of the polling. Nawaz Sharif indicated that if appointed Prime Minister his priorities would include the introduction of extensive economic reforms, the reinvigoration of relations with India and a renegotiation of Pakistan's relationship with the USA.

Sectarian, Ethnic and Political Violence in Pakistan

Since the 1970s Pakistan has encountered a steady rise in violence resulting from sectarian and ethnic conflicts. Among the prominent sources of unrest have been conflicts between rival ethnic groups (notably Mojahirs, Pathans and Punjabis), clashes between rival Sunni and Shi'a (mainly Hazara) groups, and the resurgence of militant separatism in Balochistan. Meanwhile, Karachi, in particular, has increasingly been riven by a combination of sectarian violence between Sunni and Shi'a Muslims, clashes between rival factions of the Mohajir Qaumi Movement (MQM—later renamed the Muttahida Qaumi Movement), and fighting between rival criminal gangs. Another problematic and interlinked development has been the growing activity and influence of Islamist militant groups, particularly in the FATA and in Khyber Pakhtoonkhwa. Boosted by widespread opposition to Pakistan's official support for US-led military campaigns in Afghanistan and Iraq, and simmering Pakistani–Indian tensions, such groups have proliferated since 2002. Analysts have asserted that some militant groups have benefited from clandestine support from elements within the Pakistani military, who have sought to use the militants as proxy forces in conflicts with domestic and regional rivals—notably along Pakistan's borders with India and Afghanistan. Relationships between the aforementioned groups are complex and volatile: while in some situations the interests of militant groups may converge, in other cases conflict between rival groups exacerbates the adverse security situation.

The rise of ethnic communalism was highlighted in late 1986, when violent clashes occurred in Karachi, Quetta and Hyderabad as a result of disputes between rival ethnic groups—primarily between the Pathans, originally from the North-West Frontier Province (NWFP, renamed Khyber Pakhtoonkhwa in 2010) and Afghanistan, and the Urdu-speaking Mohajirs, who migrated from India when the subcontinent was partitioned in 1947. The violence was most severe in Karachi, where some 170 people were killed in December 1986. The MQM subsequently gained much ground at local elections in Sindh.

In response to continuing violence in Sindh, the Government launched 'Operation Clean-up' in May 1992, whereby the army was to apprehend criminals and terrorists, and seize unauthorized weapons. A violent clash between two factions of the MQM (the majority Altaf faction and the small breakaway Haqiqi faction) in Karachi in June provided the armed forces with the opportunity to suppress extremist elements within the MQM; the resultant military operation prompted criticism from the leader of the MQM, Altaf Hussain, and precipitated the resignations of most of the MQM members of the National Assembly and the Sindh assembly. By late 1994 the police and paramilitary forces appeared to be losing control of Karachi, which was riven by rapidly escalating ethnic and criminal violence; nearly 170 people were killed in the city in December alone, following 'Operation Clean-up' and the withdrawal of the army in the previous month. Much of the violence stemmed from the bloody rivalry between the opposing factions of the MQM, while other killings were linked to drugs mafias and to sectarian disputes between Sunni and Shi'a Muslims. By June 1995 the security forces had lost control of large areas of Karachi to MQM activists. It was estimated that during that year almost 2,000 people (including about 250 members of the security forces) were killed as a result of the political and ethnic violence in Karachi.

Meanwhile, in November 1994 the Government was confronted with a series of uprisings staged by heavily armed tribesmen in the mountainous regions of Malakand and Swat demanding the enforcement of *Shari'a* law. The fundamentalist revolt was suppressed by paramilitary forces (but only after the deaths of several hundred people), and *Shari'a* measures were implemented in the tribal areas.

In November 1995 18 people were killed when a car bomb exploded at the Egyptian embassy in Islamabad; within hours of the attack three militant Islamist groups in Egypt had claimed responsibility for the bombing. During the previous year the Pakistani Government had been co-operating with Egypt in attempts to apprehend and extradite members of illegal Islamist militant organizations operating in the NWFP or across the border in Afghanistan. (In 1993–95 the Pakistani authorities, concerned at the country's growing reputation as a refuge for Islamist extremists, expelled more than 2,000 Arabs, the majority of whom were reported to have been involved in the civil war in Afghanistan.)

Sectarian violence between Sunni and Shi'a Muslims escalated in January 1997, culminating in a bomb blast outside a district court in Lahore, which killed 25 people, including the leader of the Sunni extremist group Sipah-e-Sahaba Pakistan. In January 1998 at least 24 Shi'a Muslims were massacred in Lahore by a clandestine Sunni group. In response, the Government approved measures to control illicit weapons in an attempt to curb terrorism. (A controversial anti-terrorist law had been passed in August 1997, giving the security forces extensive powers of arrest and enabling the Government to ban any group or association without parliamentary approval.)

In response to the rise in sectarian and ethnically motivated violence, in June 2001 the Government approved new legislation to tackle terrorist activity. Earlier in the month Pakistan's military ruler, Gen. Pervez Musharraf, had complained that Pakistan's growing reputation as a centre for militant religious intolerance and fundamentalism was having a detrimental effect on the country's international standing and on its economic prospects. In August Musharraf announced an immediate ban on the activities of two militant Islamist groups: the Sunni Lashkar-e-Jhangvi and the Shi'a Sipah-e-Mohammad. Following the 11 September terrorist attacks on the US mainland, Musharraf's support for the US-led invasion of Afghanistan attracted large-scale popular opposition in Pakistan (see Domestic Political Affairs).

Meanwhile, relations with India had become openly hostile as a result of the deteriorating security situation in Kashmir and the increasingly violent activities of Pakistan's militant Islamist groups in India (see Foreign Affairs—Relations with India). Following intense international pressure (particularly from the USA) to address the continuing security risk presented by these groups, in December 2001 the security forces began to detain some of their most prominent members, financial assets were frozen and offices closed down. Moreover, in January 2002 Musharraf announced an indefinite ban on the activities of five predominantly separatist groups (Tehrik-e-Nifaz-e-Shariat-e-Mohammadi, Sipah-e-Sahaba Pakistan, Jaish-e-Mohammed, Tehrik-e-Jafria and Lashkar-e-Taiba) and plans to reform and regulate the country's system of *madrassa* religious schools, many of which were accused of promoting extremism.

In early 2002 a US journalist, Daniel Pearl, was abducted in Karachi and murdered by a militant Islamist group. Confounding speculation that suspects in the case would be extradited for trial in the USA, in July Ahmed Omar Saeed Sheikh and three alleged accomplices were convicted on charges of kidnapping, murder and terrorism at a specially instituted anti-terrorism court in Karachi; Saeed Sheikh was sentenced to death and his co-defendants were each sentenced to life imprisonment. Following an anti-US grenade attack on the Protestant International Church in Islamabad in March, in which five people (including the wife and daughter of a US diplomat) were killed, Musharraf dismissed five senior police officers for what he considered a serious lapse in security. It was widely believed that intelligence proceeding from Pakistani investigations to discover the identities of the assailants was a crucial factor in the arrest of Abu Zubaydah, one of al-Qa'ida's most senior commanders, by officers of the US Federal Bureau of Investigation (FBI) in Faisalabad at the end of March. However, another attack occurred in June outside the US consulate in Karachi, killing 12 people. One month later two Pakistani members of the al-Alami faction of the banned Harakat ul-Mujahideen claimed responsibility for the attack on the US consulate as well as other attacks on Western targets. In September Pakistani security forces arrested 12 alleged members of al-Qa'ida in Karachi, including the Yemeni-born Ramzi Binalshibh, a principal suspect in the attacks on the USA on 11 September 2001. The USA took custody of Binalshibh and four other al-Qa'ida suspects.

In an apparent breakthrough in the campaign against religious extremism, the alleged operations chief of the al-Qa'ida

network, Khalid Sheikh Mohammed, who was suspected of
having planned the attacks on the USA in September 2001,
was arrested in Rawalpindi in March 2003. It was hoped that the
suspect, who was promptly taken into US custody, would provide
information on the identity and whereabouts of al-Qa'ida cells in
Pakistan and elsewhere in the world. The ISI's involvement in
the arrest suggested that the intelligence agency was genuinely
attempting to curb militant activity. Furthermore, in early
March the ISI declared that since 11 September 2001 Pakistan
had arrested 442 suspected foreign militants, of whom 346 had
been handed over to US custody. However, the discovery of
Mohammed in a house owned by an army officer's brother raised
further questions about links between al-Qa'ida and the Pakistani military. In addition, the proprietor's prominent role in
Jamaat-e-Islami Pakistan generated speculation about that
political party's connections with al-Qa'ida.

In October 2003, following reports of increased militant activity in South Waziristan, Pakistani forces mounted several operations targeting militants and tribal elders who were suspected
of providing Taliban members with shelter. However, there were
claims that Pakistani troops continued to allow Taliban movement across the Afghan–Pakistani border and that senior Taliban members were openly living in Quetta in Balochistan. In the
first half of 2004 the search for suspected militants remained
focused on South Waziristan, where the USA believed Osama bin
Laden and other al-Qa'ida leaders were receiving shelter. Several thousand Pakistani troops were deployed to force al-Qa'ida
fugitives across the border into Afghanistan, where US soldiers
were active (US troops were not permitted to operate from
Pakistani soil). Fighting between Pakistani troops and militants
in March resulted in the deaths of more than 100 people,
although many militants were believed to have evaded capture
and escaped.

Meanwhile, the legislator and leader of Millat-e-Islamia Pakistan, Maulana Azam Tariq, was assassinated in Islamabad in
October 2003 as sectarian violence between Sunnis and Shi'as
increased. In addition, attacks by militant Islamists on Western
targets continued. In November Musharraf proscribed six militant Islamist groups under the 1997 Anti-Terrorist Act. Three of
the organizations—Islami Tehrik-e-Pakistan (formerly Tehrik-
e-Jafria-e-Pakistan), Millat-e-Islamia Pakistan (formerly Sipah-
e-Sahaba Pakistan) and Khudam ul-Islam (formerly Jaish-e-
Mohammed)—had disregarded an earlier ban by changing their
names. Some commentators doubted the effectiveness of
Musharraf's approach to militant Islamism, claiming that the
groups would continue to receive covert support from the army
and judiciary. Indeed, in December 2003 the President narrowly
escaped two assassination attempts by suspected Islamist militants. It was suggested that al-Qa'ida was responsible for organizing the attacks.

The issue of religious extremism continued to resonate in
Pakistani society, with rising levels of sectarian violence continuing to disrupt and unsettle the country's major cities. Meanwhile, in May 2005 it was announced that Abu Faraj al-Libbi,
reported to be the operational head of al-Qa'ida in Pakistan, had
been captured in the city of Mardan in the NWFP. Al-Libbi was
subsequently transferred into US custody for interrogation. In
July 2005, following the discovery that at least two of the four
British Muslim suicide bombers who had attacked the transport
network in London, United Kingdom, in that month had previously visited Pakistan and had allegedly received instruction at
one of the country's many *madrassas*, President Musharraf
announced the implementation of a more stringent policy to
prevent the spread of Islamist extremism. Hundreds of suspected Islamist militants were arrested and several *madrassas*
suspected of being involved in extremism were raided. Legislation regulating the activities of *madrassas* was passed in August.

Despite the signing of peace accords between the Government
and tribal leaders—in North Waziristan in September 2006 and
in the Bajaur region of the FATA in March 2007—the conflict
between the army and the militants did not cease and the death
toll on both sides continued to rise. In July Baitullah Mehsud (a
militant later accused of involvement in Benazir Bhutto's assassination in December), along with a group of tribal leaders,
declared an end to the cease-fire in North Waziristan.

In 2007 members of the Lal Masjid and its two *madrassas* were
involved in increasingly overt challenges to authority, issuing a
fatwa (Islamic edict) against a government minister and even
abducting security officers and alleged prostitutes. Following the
collapse of negotiations between the two sides, the security forces
invaded the compound in July. It was later estimated that some

100 people, many of them Lal Masjid followers, had been killed,
but some estimates were much higher. The siege aggravated
anti-Government sentiment in certain quarters, and resulted in
a spate of retaliatory attacks.

In the Swat Valley the provincial government was reported to
have signed a peace agreement with pro-Taliban radicals in May
2008. However, sporadic fighting continued, as did attacks on
girls' schools. In February 2009 a further cease-fire agreement
was announced, under the terms of which large parts of the
NWFP's Malakand Division (which includes the Swat Valley)
would be brought under *Shari'a* law. However, in April, following pressure from the USA, government forces launched a fresh
offensive against the Taliban militants who—in violation of the
peace agreement—were attempting to expand their power base
southwards towards Islamabad. In early May the peace agreement appeared to have collapsed, with increasingly frequent
violent clashes and rising casualties on both sides, and large-
scale internal displacement of civilians. There was huge political, public and media support for the army's intervention. In
July the Pakistani Government, having taken control of the key
town of Mingora, declared that its offensive in the Swat Valley
had been a success; however, despite the return of tens of
thousands of refugees the cycle of violence continued. In August
the army's struggle against the militants was given a major boost
when the leader of the Tehrik-e-Taliban Pakistan (TTP), Baitullah Mehsud (who was alleged to have been responsible for the
assassination of Benazir Bhutto, as well as for recent bomb blasts
in various Pakistani cities), was reported to have been killed by a
US missile strike; he was replaced as leader of the TTP by
Hakimullah Mehsud.

In September 2009 there was a notable upsurge in militant
attacks (particularly suicide bombings) against civilian and
army targets in the NWFP. The army itself was also accused
of carrying out human rights violations (including extrajudicial
killings) against the Taliban fighters. In mid-October the army
launched a fresh offensive against Taliban militants in South
Waziristan, one of the agencies of the FATA. The fierce fighting
that ensued led to another exodus of refugees from the area of
conflict and also prompted an escalation in retaliatory suicide
bombings and armed attacks against government, military and
civilian targets throughout Pakistan. One of the worst such
incidents took place in Peshawar in late October when a car bomb
killed at least 118 people in a crowded market. In December the
army claimed to have achieved a victory against the militants in
South Waziristan, but subsequent reports of terrorist activity
appeared to verify that the Taliban remained active in the
region. Unsubstantiated claims that Hakimullah Mehsud had
been mortally wounded in January 2010 were strongly denied by
the militants. (Similar allegations of the TTP leader's death were
made by the Pakistan military in January 2012, but no firm
evidence either way was forthcoming.) In February 2010 US-
Pakistani co-operation in the fight against Islamist terrorism
appeared to be working effectively when US officials reported the
capture in Karachi of the high-ranking Afghan Taliban military
commander Mullah Abdul Ghani Baradar, who was widely
believed to be second-in-command to the supreme leader of the
Taliban, Mullah Mohammad Omar. Meanwhile, in June 2010 it
was reported that a founding member of al-Qa'ida, Mustafa Abu
al-Yazid, who was alleged to have aided the financing of the
September 2001 attacks in the USA, had been killed in an
unmanned US military aircraft ('drone') attack in north-west
Pakistan.

Karachi also experienced an increase in violence from 2010. In
August, following the assassination of a leading local MQM
politician, Raza Haider, at least 100 people were reported to
have been killed in clashes. Further unrest erupted in September
following the murder in London, United Kingdom, of a founding
member of the MQM, Dr Imran Farooq. More than 50 people
were killed during several days of intense violence following a by-
election for Haider's former parliamentary seat in October,
fuelling a growing sense of crisis in the city. According to the
Government, about 500 people died as a result of targeted
attacks in Karachi during 2010; human rights organizations
estimated the death toll to be considerably higher, at around 775
people. In the first half of 2011 alone it was estimated that a
further 500 people had been killed during the unrest.

From 2010 minority religious groups increasingly came under
attack. In April Taliban militants were suspected of having
carried out attacks on two mosques (belonging to the minority
Ahmadi sect) in Lahore that left around 90 people dead. In
November a Christian woman, Asia Bibi, was sentenced to death

for blasphemy. The conviction prompted a public debate about reforming the controversial blasphemy law, which sanctioned the death penalty as a punishment for insulting Islam. Critics of the law claimed that accusations of blasphemy were often based on hearsay or imprecise evidence and that the legislation was frequently used to persecute Christians and other religious minorities or in pursuit of a personal vendetta. However, opponents of reform mounted large demonstrations throughout the country from late December, demanding the retention of the existing legislation, and public support for change was gradually stifled by increasingly menacing threats of violent retaliation issued by extremist groups against would-be supporters of liberalization. Events took a grave turn in January 2011 when the PPP Governor of Punjab, Salman Taseer, who had demanded the reform of the blasphemy law and had described Asia Bibi's sentence as 'disgraceful', was murdered by one of his own bodyguards in Islamabad. The liberal sectors of Pakistan's population expressed their disapproval when the assassination was openly welcomed by Islamist extremists throughout Pakistan and the murderer (who was sentenced to death in October) was hailed as a hero of Islam. However, the Government itself failed directly to condemn Taseer's murder (despite the Governor having been a close associate of President Zardari), and the Minister of the Interior, Rehman Malik, pledged to prevent any attempt to amend the blasphemy law. Pakistan's faltering image as a moderate Islamic state was further undermined in March when Minister of Minorities Shahbaz Bhatti, the only Christian member of the Cabinet, was killed by suspected Islamist activists in Islamabad. Bhatti was apparently targeted because of his support for the rights of religious minorities and his opposition to the blasphemy legislation. Responsibility for the attack was reportedly claimed by the TTP. The debate over the blasphemy legislation again came to the fore with the case of a Christian girl who was alleged to have desecrated the Koran in August 2012. The girl, whose age was disputed, was arrested, but it later emerged that she had learning disabilities. The case against her was condemned by several religious leaders and was widely reported internationally. A local cleric was arrested for planting evidence in the case in September, and all charges against her were dropped in November.

On 13 May 2011 at least 82 people were killed and more than 100 injured in a double suicide bomb attack on a training base of the paramilitary Frontier Constabulary in Charsadda District, Khyber Pakhtoonkhwa. The TTP issued a statement claiming that it had carried out the attack in reprisal for the killing of bin Laden (see Domestic Political Affairs) and vowed to launch further retaliatory attacks. Later that month a small group of TTP militants launched an audacious attack on the heavily guarded Mehran naval airbase in central Karachi, during which 10 security personnel were killed in a 17-hour gun battle and several aircraft were destroyed. This attack appeared to give further credence to allegations that members of the Pakistani armed forces were colluding with extremist elements, and a former Pakistani navy commando was subsequently detained in connection with the incident. In June an army brigadier was arrested on suspicion of working with the banned Islamist group Hizb-ut-Tahrir. Meanwhile, earlier that month it was reported that the alleged mastermind behind the attack on the Mehran base, Ilyas Kashmiri (a senior al-Qa'ida operative and leader of the outlawed Harkat-ul-Jihad al-Islami), had been killed in a US drone attack in South Waziristan.

The levels of violence in Karachi rose dramatically in August 2011—in that month alone it was estimated that some 300 people died as a result of targeted attacks by gangs associated with different political parties and ethnicities. In response, the federal Government deployed paramilitary troops in the worst-affected areas of the city. In the same month the Supreme Court published its findings from an official inquiry into the epidemic of violence in Karachi, asserting that political parties (notably the MQM) were directly involved in the violence and that a major cause of the breakdown in law and order was the politicization of the security forces in the city. The situation in Karachi did not improve in 2012: that year's death toll from violent crimes was reportedly 2,500, a significant increase on the previous year.

Sectarian attacks on Shi'as intensified in several regions of Pakistan in 2012 and early 2013. It was estimated that more than 400 Shi'as had lost their lives in sectarian violence in 2012, with the death toll particularly high in Balochistan. In January 2013, after a brutal attack in which more than 90 Shi'as were killed in Quetta, the Balochistan provincial government was dismissed and the province was brought under federal rule. However,

another bomb attack in a Shi'a area in Quetta in February resulted in some 90 further fatalities. An upsurge in sectarian violence was also reported in the Azad Kashmir region of Gilgit-Baltistan, where Shi'as were increasingly targeted. An estimated 93 people were reported to have died in such violence in the area in 2012.

Meanwhile, in October 2012 the TTP's targeting of a school bus carrying Malala Yusufzai, a 15-year-old activist for girls' education, provoked an international outcry. Yusufzai, who was from the Swat area of Khyber Pakhtoonkhwa province, was shot in the head by TTP gunmen, but survived the attack and became the focus of a surge of anti-Taliban sentiment. In February 2013 it was reported that the TTP had offered to enter peace talks with the Government, subject to certain conditions.

Foreign Affairs
Relations with India

Relations with India have dominated Pakistan's foreign policy since the creation of the two states in 1947. Relations deteriorated during the late 1970s and early 1980s, owing to Pakistan's nuclear weapons programme, and as a result of major US weapons deliveries to Pakistan. The other major contentious issue between the two states was the disputed region of Kashmir, where, since 1949, a cease-fire line, known as the Line of Control (LoC), has separated Indian-controlled Kashmir (the state of Jammu and Kashmir) and Pakistani Kashmir, which comprises Azad (Free) Kashmir and the Northern Areas. While Pakistan demanded that the sovereignty of the region be decided in accordance with earlier UN resolutions (which advocated a plebiscite in both parts of the region), India argued that a solution should be reached through bilateral negotiations.

Relations between Pakistan and India reached a crisis in late 1989, when the outlawed Jammu and Kashmir Liberation Front (JKLF) and several other Muslim groups in Indian-controlled Kashmir intensified their campaigns of terrorism, strikes and civil unrest, in support of demands for an independent Kashmir or unification with Pakistan. In response, the Indian Government dispatched troops to Jammu and Kashmir; numerous civilians were killed in resulting clashes between troops and protesters. The opposition parties in Pakistan organized nationwide strikes, to express their sympathy for the Muslims in Jammu and Kashmir, and urged the Government to adopt more active measures regarding the crisis.

In December 1990 discussions were held between the Ministers of External Affairs of Pakistan and India, at which an agreement not to attack each other's nuclear facilities was finalized, but no solution was found to the Kashmiri problem. Further high-level talks held between the two countries during the first half of the 1990s made no progress in resolving the crisis, and skirmishes between Pakistani and Indian troops along the border in Kashmir continued. In January 1996 relations between the two countries deteriorated when the Pakistani Government accused the Indian forces of having launched a rocket attack on a mosque in Azad Kashmir, which killed 20 people. The Indian authorities claimed that the deaths had been caused by misfired Pakistani rockets. Tensions between Pakistan and India were also exacerbated in early 1996 by allegations that each side was on the verge of conducting nuclear tests. Later that year, India's holding of state assembly elections in Jammu and Kashmir (described as 'farcical' by Benazir Bhutto) and its refusal to sign the Comprehensive Test Ban Treaty (CTBT) did nothing to encourage an improvement in bilateral relations. Despite the resumption in March 1997 of bilateral talks (which had been suspended since 1994), little progress was made during the course of the year to ease the tension.

In April 1998 the arms race between Pakistan and India escalated dramatically after the former successfully test-fired a new intermediate-range missile (capable of reaching deep into Indian territory); in the following month India conducted five underground nuclear test explosions. The test programme was condemned world-wide, and the USA imposed economic sanctions against India. The US President, Bill Clinton, and the UN Security Council urged Pakistan to show restraint in not conducting its own retaliatory test explosions. However, at the end of May Pakistan carried out six underground atomic test explosions. In early June the Pakistani Government ordered a 50% reduction in public expenditure in an attempt to mitigate the effects of the resultant economic sanctions imposed by various foreign countries, including the USA. Immediately after the nuclear tests, India and Pakistan announced self-imposed moratoriums on further testing and engaged in intense diplomatic activity. In September, however, the Pakistani Minister of Foreign Affairs categorically stated that Pakistan would not sign the CTBT until all of the sanctions were lifted and other legitimate concerns addressed.

Indo-Pakistani talks at foreign secretary level regarding Kashmir and other issues were resumed in Islamabad in October 1998. In February 1999 the Indian Prime Minister, Atal Bihari Vajpayee, made an historic journey (inaugurating the first passenger bus service between India and Pakistan) over the border to Lahore. Following his welcome by the Pakistani Prime Minister, the two leaders signed the Lahore Declaration, which, with its pledges regarding peace and nuclear security, seemed designed to allay world-wide fears of a nuclear 'flashpoint' in South Asia. However, the contentious subject of Jammu and Kashmir was largely avoided.

In May 1999 the Kashmir conflict intensified to reach what was termed a 'near-war situation' following the reported infiltration of 600–900 well-armed Islamist militants, reinforced by regular Pakistani troops, across the LoC into the area around Kargil in the Indian-held sector of Kashmir. The Pakistani Government claimed that it had no direct involvement whatsoever with the Islamist insurgents. In response, the Indian troops launched a series of air-strikes against the militants at the end of the month, the first peacetime use of air power in Kashmir. Artillery exchanges increased along the LoC (with both sides suffering heavy casualties), and reports of the massing of troops and evacuation of villages along the international border aroused considerable concern. In early July, however, Indian military dominance combined with US diplomatic pressure prompted Nawaz Sharif to agree to the withdrawal of all 'intruders' from Indian-controlled Kashmir.

In November 2000 the Indian Government declared the suspension of combat operations against Kashmiri militants during the Muslim holy month of Ramadan. The unilateral cease-fire began at the end of November (and was subsequently extended, at intervals, until the end of May); however, Indian security forces were authorized to retaliate if fired upon. The Pakistani authorities described the cease-fire as 'meaningless' without simultaneous constructive dialogue. The moderate All-Party Hurriyat Conference in Indian-administered Kashmir welcomed the development and offered to enter negotiations with Pakistan in order to prepare for tripartite discussions. However, the Hizbul Mujahideen and other militant groups in Pakistan-administered Kashmir rejected the offer of talks and continued their campaign of violence, extending their activities as far as the Red Fort in Old Delhi, India, where three people were shot dead in December. In January 2001 the Indian High Commissioner to Pakistan held talks with Gen. Musharraf, the first high-level contact since the military coup in Pakistan in 1999. The two officials urged an early resumption of negotiations on the Kashmir question.

Relations with India appeared to improve following the earthquake in Gujarat in January 2001, when Pakistan offered humanitarian relief to India. In July Prime Minister Vajpayee and Gen. Musharraf held negotiations in Agra, India. However, there was no breakthrough on the issue of Kashmir, with the divergent views of the two sides on the priority issue in the dispute (cross-border terrorism according to India, and Kashmiri self-determination in the opinion of Pakistan) appearing to be more firmly entrenched than ever. Tension with India was heightened considerably following a guerrilla-style attack on the state assembly building in Srinagar, Jammu and Kashmir, in October, which caused an estimated 38 deaths. The Indian Government attributed responsibility for the attack to the Pakistan-based Jaish-e-Mohammed and Lashkar-e-Taiba (LeT) groups; although Gen. Musharraf publicly condemned the attack, he rejected official Indian requests to ban the activities of the organizations in Pakistan.

On 13 December 2001 five armed assailants attempted to launch an apparent suicide attack on the Indian union parliament building in New Delhi. Although no parliamentary deputies were hurt in the attack, nine people were killed in the botched assault (as were the five assailants). Tensions between India and Pakistan were exacerbated when Mohammed Afzal, a member of Jaish-e-Mohammed arrested in Kashmir on suspicion of complicity in the incident, admitted his involvement and alleged publicly that Pakistani security and intelligence agencies had provided support to those directly responsible for the attack. India recalled its High Commissioner from Islamabad and announced that overground transport services between the two countries would be suspended from 1 January 2002. As

positions were reinforced with troops and weapons on both sides of the LoC, there was considerable international concern that such brinkmanship might propel the two countries into renewed armed conflict. Mindful of the potential detriment to security at Pakistan's border with Afghanistan that could result from escalated conflict in Kashmir, the USA applied increased pressure on the beleaguered Pakistani Government (already facing vociferous domestic opposition to its accommodation of US activities in Afghanistan) to adopt a more conciliatory attitude towards India's security concerns, and in December the Pakistani authorities followed the US Government's lead in freezing the assets of the two groups held responsible for the attack by India. Although the leaders of the two groups were later detained by the Pakistani authorities, the Indian Government dismissed much of the Pakistani response as superficial and demanded that the two men be extradited to stand trial in India.

In January 2002 Musharraf yielded to relentless international pressure by publicly condemning the activities of militant extremists based in Pakistan and announcing the introduction of a broad range of measures to combat terrorist activity and religious zealotry, including the proscription of five extremist organizations (among them Jaish-e-Mohammed and LeT). However, in mid-May suspected Islamist militants attacked an Indian army camp in Jammu and Kashmir, killing more than 30 people. In response, India expelled Pakistan's High Commissioner from New Delhi. Indo-Pakistani relations deteriorated further following the assassination by suspected Islamist militants of Abdul Ghani Lone, the leader of the moderate All-Party Hurriyat Conference, on 21 May. India accused the Pakistani Government of supporting the extremists. Despite US attempts to calm tensions, artillery fire was exchanged along the LoC. More than 1m. soldiers were mobilized on both sides of the border as the two countries appeared once more to be on the verge of war. In June, following intense diplomatic efforts by British and US officials, the threat of conflict appeared to diminish. However, the killing of 27 Hindu civilians by suspected Islamist militants in Jammu in July disrupted attempts to improve diplomatic relations between India and Pakistan, and the Indian Government decided to delay the appointment of a new High Commissioner to Pakistan. President Musharraf dismissed elections in Jammu and Kashmir in September–October as a 'sham'.

In early 2003 tensions were exacerbated by India conducting its latest set of 'routine' ballistic-missile tests without advance warning (thus ignoring the procedures specified in the 1999 Lahore Declaration—Pakistan responded in kind), the continuing violence in Kashmir and India's new military agreement with Russia. In October a series of confidence-building measures (including more transport links) announced by the Indian Government was met with a cautious welcome on the part of Pakistan, and in November Pakistani Prime Minister Zafarullah Khan Jamali announced a unilateral cease-fire along the LoC. India reciprocated the gesture, but reserved the right to fire at so-called 'infiltrators'. In December Indian and Pakistani officials signed a three-year agreement on the restoration from January 2004 of a passenger and freight train service between New Delhi and Lahore. Meanwhile, in November 2003 President Musharraf banned six Islamist militant groups (three of which had been banned in 2002 but had re-emerged under different names), closed down their offices and froze their bank accounts.

At a ground-breaking summit meeting of the South Asian Association for Regional Cooperation (SAARC, see p. 430) in Islamabad in January 2004, Musharraf assured Vajpayee that he would not permit any territory under Pakistan's control to be used to support terrorism; in return, Vajpayee agreed to begin negotiations on all bilateral issues, including Kashmir. In June several rounds of discussions took place between Indian and Pakistani officials in New Delhi, following which both sides stressed their renewed commitment to reaching a negotiated final settlement on the Kashmir issue and agreed to restore their diplomatic missions to full strength. In September Pakistan and India held their first, official, ministerial-level talks in more than three years, in New Delhi. In November Pakistan welcomed a move by India to reduce the number of troops deployed in Jammu and Kashmir, and in February 2005 the two countries agreed to open a bus service across the LoC, linking Srinagar with Muzaffarabad. Despite militant threats of disruption the service commenced in April. In March India had expressed disapproval of the US decision to supply Pakistan with F-16 fighter aircraft, stating its concerns that the deal would exacerbate security tensions in the region. However, in April Musharraf travelled to India for the first time since 2001 and met with Prime Minister

Manmohan Singh in Delhi for further peace talks; the two leaders subsequently issued a statement referring to the peace process as 'irreversible' and agreeing to improve trade and transport links over the LoC.

In October 2005 the devastating consequences of the massive earthquake centred in Azad Kashmir had significant implications for the ongoing peace process. In the aftermath of the disaster, Pakistan accepted an Indian offer of aid. Following a series of negotiations, the two countries agreed to open a number of crossing points on the LoC, in order to facilitate the reunification of divided families. However, fears on the part of both countries that the other would take advantage of the situation to conduct military surveillance hampered prospects for more extensive co-operation.

In March 2006, after the opening of a rail link between Sindh and Rajasthan, Pakistan and India agreed that trade links would be further developed, as part of efforts to restore normal relations through the improvement of economic and commercial ties. Relations became temporarily strained in the aftermath of the Mumbai train bombings in July (see the chapter on India), when Singh suggested the perpetrators had links to Pakistan. In November the two countries agreed to form an intelligence-sharing panel to combat terrorism; the panel's first meeting took place in Islamabad in March 2007.

The explosions on the Delhi–Lahore Samjhauta Express train in February 2007, which claimed 68 lives, were widely believed to have been a deliberate attempt to sabotage forthcoming negotiations between Pakistan and India. Fighting across the LoC in July 2008 threatened to destabilize relations between the two countries, with India accusing Pakistan of the most 'serious violation' of the cease-fire yet. In the same month a suicide bombing at the Indian embassy in Kabul, Afghanistan, resulted in more than 40 fatalities; the Indian Government intimated that the plot had originated in Pakistan. In the aftermath of the November Mumbai attacks, when more than 170 people were killed in co-ordinated offensives against public targets, the Indian Government suggested that the perpetrators were all from Pakistan. The Pakistani authorities initially issued a denial, but subsequently conceded that the sole gunman captured alive, Mohammed Ajmal Amir Qasab, was indeed a Pakistani citizen. Moreover, in February 2009, in an unexpected turnaround, a senior official of the Pakistani Government publicly admitted that the Mumbai attacks had been partly planned in Pakistan and stated that six suspects belonging to LeT had been arrested. The Indian Government described this ground-breaking admission as a 'positive development' and demanded that the suspects be extradited to India; however, Pakistan insisted that any prosecutions be carried out internally. (Qasab was sentenced to death in May 2010, and was executed in Maharashtra in November 2012.)

The first high-level direct talks between India and Pakistan since the 2008 Mumbai attacks, which were held in New Delhi in February 2010, proved fruitless, with both sides accusing each other of supporting terrorism and of tolerating human rights abuses. In May tension was further exacerbated by the Pakistan Supreme Court's decision to release from custody the alleged founder of LeT and the leader of its political wing, Jamaat-ud-Dawa, Hafiz Mohammad Saeed, who the Indian authorities believed to have been one of the masterminds behind the Mumbai attacks. In July the Indian Minister of External Affairs met his Pakistani counterpart in Islamabad in an attempt to relaunch formal peace negotiations. However, the Pakistani minister accused the Indian delegation of being ill-prepared for the talks and refusing to discuss the Kashmir issue; the summit culminated in mutual recriminations. A controversial accusation made just prior to the negotiations, by Indian Home Secretary G. K. Pillai, in which he claimed that the ISI had co-ordinated the 2008 Mumbai attacks (the first time that an Indian official had publicly accused the Pakistani authorities of a direct role in the attacks), had done little to alleviate mutual tensions.

In February 2011 it was announced that Pakistan and India had agreed to a formal resumption of comprehensive bilateral discussions at foreign secretary level, to be held in July in New Delhi. In March relations appeared to thaw further when Prime Minister Gilani made his first official visit to India, having accepted an invitation from Indian Prime Minister Singh to attend an international cricket match in Punjab; the two leaders reportedly discussed 'all outstanding issues' concerning bilateral relations. Meanwhile, following a meeting between senior Indian and Pakistani officials, held in New Delhi in advance of the prime-ministerial summit, agreement was reportedly reached on a number of measures to improve co-operation in counter-terrorism efforts; in addition, security officials from Pakistan and India were to be permitted access to each other's country to facilitate investigations into the 2008 Mumbai attacks. Although no major breakthroughs were achieved as a result of the talks held between the two countries' foreign secretaries in New Delhi in late July 2011, relations were reported to have been 'on the right track'. In September, during an official visit by a Pakistani trade delegation to the Indian capital, Pakistan and India agreed to double bilateral trade over the next three years through a programme of liberalization measures. In November the Pakistani Government approved the award of 'most favoured nation' trading status to India (which had granted Pakistan this status in 1996), thus allowing the lifting of stringent barriers to the sale of Indian goods. The improvement in relations was furthered later that month by the holding of amicable talks between Prime Minister Gilani and Prime Minister Manmohan Singh during a SAARC summit in the Maldives. In March 2012 a Pakistani team of officials arrived in Mumbai to investigate the 2008 attacks. In the following month, during a private visit to India, President Zardari held talks with the Indian Prime Minister in New Delhi—the first visit to India by a Pakistani Head of State for seven years. Less than a week later India agreed to permit foreign direct investment from Pakistan. In April 2012 an avalanche on the Siachen glacier resulted in the deaths of 129 Pakistani soldiers and 11 civilians. As a result, Gen. Ashfaq Pervez Kayani, the Chief of Army Staff, called for a withdrawal of Indian and Pakistani troops from the glacier to avoid future casualties. In June secretaries of defence from both countries met to discuss the disputed territory. Relations between Pakistan and India were tense in early 2013 over alleged ceasefire violations in Kashmir. In January India accused the Pakistani army of beheading one of its soldiers; a total of two Indian soldiers and three Pakistani soldiers were killed in that month.

Other regional relations

Relations with Afghanistan were strained during the 1980s and early 1990s, as rebel Afghan tribesmen (*mujahidin*) used areas inside Pakistan (notably the city of Peshawar) as bases for their activities. Soviet and Afghan government troops launched frequent cross-border attacks against these bases. In early 1988 there were an estimated 3.2m. Afghan refugees in Pakistan, most of them in the NWFP. In 1988 Pakistan signed the Geneva Accords on the withdrawal of Soviet troops from Afghanistan, which included agreements on the voluntary repatriation of Afghan refugees from Pakistan. Following the withdrawal of Soviet troops from Afghanistan in 1989, Pakistan maintained its support for the guerrillas' cause, while denying accusations by the Afghan Government that it was taking an active military part in the conflict, or that it was acting as a conduit for arms supplies to the *mujahidin*. The Pakistani Government welcomed the overthrow of the Afghan regime by the guerrillas in April 1992 and supported the interim coalition Government that was formed to administer Afghanistan pending the holding of free elections. However, relations between Pakistan and Afghanistan deteriorated in 1994. The turbulence and increasing anti-Pakistan feeling in Afghanistan not only threatened to result in an extension of the violence into the Pakhtoon (Pashtun) areas of the NWFP, but also obstructed the trade route from the Central Asian republics of the former USSR to the Arabian Sea at Karachi. The situation worsened in September 1995 when the Pakistani embassy in Kabul was burned down by a mob of about 5,000 Afghans protesting against Pakistan's alleged active support for the Islamist Taliban militia, which opposed the more moderate *mujahidin* Government. In the following month the Afghan ambassador to Pakistan was expelled from the country. Following the capture of Kabul by Taliban militia in September 1996 and their assumption of power, the Pakistani Government formally recognized the Taliban leaders as the new Afghan Government.

In December 1999, following the imposition of UN-mandated sanctions on Afghanistan the previous month for refusing to surrender the Saudi-born terrorist suspect Osama bin Laden, Pakistan closed down a number of Afghan banking operations in Pakistan. The Pakistani Government continued to offer financial and diplomatic support to the Taliban, although Gen. Musharraf repeatedly and strongly denied giving military assistance. However, allegations regarding the involvement of Pakistan's special forces in the Taliban campaign against the forces of the opposition *mujahidin* grew following the Taliban's successful offensive in August–September 2000. The Pakistani Government agreed to implement the UN sanctions imposed on Afghanistan in

January 2001, but announced that it would attempt to mitigate the effect of the restrictions, warning of a steep increase in refugee numbers and a worsening of the civil war. Following the September 2001 terrorist attacks on the US mainland, the failure of (somewhat unconvincing) attempts by senior Pakistani military officers to persuade the Taliban administration to comply with US demands that bin Laden and members of his al-Qa'ida terrorist organization, thought to be in hiding in Afghanistan, be handed over to the US authorities ultimately resulted in a US-led military campaign to remove the Taliban from power. Despite considerable opposition from ethnic Pashtuns in north-western Pakistan and from elements of the armed forces who had spent years consolidating relations with the Taliban regime (the majority of which was composed of Pashtuns), Musharraf was forced to co-operate with the US-led coalition to avoid potentially devastating economic and political isolation. Long-standing enmity between the Pakistani Government and the Afghan forces of the United Front, arising from Pakistani sponsorship of the Taliban regime, was exacerbated by the participation of Pakistani nationals in the armed resistance to the United Front's renewed military campaign (supported by the international coalition) to recapture Afghanistan. As the United Front continued to make impressive territorial gains in Afghanistan, culminating in the capture of the capital, Kabul, and the collapse of the Taliban regime in mid-November, the Pakistani Government announced the closure of all Taliban consular offices in Pakistan, including the embassy in Islamabad. It was hoped that the broad-based ethnicity of the Afghan Interim Authority (which included Pashtun representatives) installed in December would help to foster improved relations between the Pakistani authorities and the United Front.

Publicly, Musharraf supported Hamid Karzai, President of the new Afghan Transitional Authority. However, Afghan officials remained convinced that the Pakistani ISI was giving sanctuary to senior Taliban members and other Afghan military commanders, such as Gulbuddin Hekmatyar, who were opposed to the new Government in Kabul. In April 2003, during an official visit to Pakistan, President Karzai urged the Pakistani Government to assist in curbing cross-border attacks by militant Islamists. In July the Pakistani embassy in Afghanistan was stormed and raided by hundreds of Afghans in protest against alleged incursions by Pakistani border troops into Afghan territory. In January 2004 the Pakistani Prime Minister paid his first ever official visit to Afghanistan; the two countries agreed to work together to combat cross-border infiltration. In 2005–06, however, despite a number of meetings between Afghan and Pakistani officials, relations remained strained, with mutual public recriminations being made over cross-border activities and the fight against the Taliban.

In late 2006 Pakistan's plans to lay land-mines and construct a series of fences along sections of the Afghan–Pakistani border to prevent insurgents based in Pakistan from launching cross-border raids, while also reducing drugs-smuggling from Afghanistan, were criticized as divisive by Karzai. Construction continued in 2007 despite disagreement over the border demarcation. Nevertheless, relations between the two countries appeared to improve with the holding of a joint 'peace *jirga* (council)' in Kabul in August, attended by some 650 tribal leaders from both countries, along with Karzai, President Musharraf and other senior government officials, in order to address shared issues such as security and terrorism. In February 2008 the Pakistani ambassador to Afghanistan was abducted by suspected Taliban militants in the Khyber Agency in Pakistan; he was released unharmed in May. In February 2009 the new US Secretary of State, Hillary Clinton, hosted a meeting with the foreign ministers of Pakistan and Afghanistan in Washington, DC, and announced that these trilateral negotiations would be held on a regular basis to discuss mutually strategic issues. In August President Karzai and the Pakistani Prime Minister, Yousaf Raza Gilani, agreed to co-operate in combating terrorism and militancy. In early 2010 the Pakistani authorities appeared to be adhering to their pledge to co-operate in the fight against the insurgents when a number of high-ranking Afghan Taliban figures were arrested in Pakistan.

Relations between Pakistan and Afghanistan were given a boost in October 2010 when the two sides signed a US-sponsored Afghan-Pakistan Transit Trade Agreement (APTTA), which was to replace a 1965 bilateral trade agreement and would facilitate the transport of Afghan exports through Pakistan to markets in India, as well as providing access to Central Asian markets for Pakistani exports; the APTTA was officially implemented in June 2011. The positive trend in relations continued in December 2010 following Prime Minister Gilani's first official visit to Afghanistan, during which he held wide-ranging discussions with President Karzai. In January 2011 members of the Afghan High Peace Council, which had been established by Karzai in September 2010 and which was led by former Afghan President Burhanuddin Rabbani, held talks with the Pakistani President and Prime Minister in Islamabad regarding Pakistan's future role in peace negotiations with the Afghan Taliban. The first meeting of an Afghan-Pakistani peace and reconciliation commission, chaired by Karzai and Gilani and involving senior Afghan and Pakistani military and intelligence officials, was held in Islamabad in June 2011. However, relations between the two countries were again placed under strain when Afghan officials accused the Pakistani ISI of collusion in the murder of Burhanuddin Rabbani in September by a suspected Islamist suicide bomber in Kabul. In December Pakistan boycotted an international conference, held in Bonn, Germany, on the future of Afghanistan following the killing in November of 24 Pakistani soldiers by a North Atlantic Treaty Organization (NATO) airstrike at two crossing points on the Afghan border. However, Karzai participated in negotiations with the presidents of Pakistan and Iran in Islamabad in mid-February 2012, which were reported to have focused on the incorporation of members of the Taliban into the peace process and on the extension of the APTTA to cover the countries of Central Asia. In the following week Prime Minister Gilani publicly urged the Taliban to enter into direct peace negotiations with the Afghan Government, the first time that the Pakistani authorities had made such an appeal. Pakistan subsequently appeared to play a more dynamic role in promoting peace negotiations between the Taliban and the Afghan Government, taking part in a series of trilateral talks with Afghanistan and the United Kingdom and releasing numerous Taliban prisoners to facilitate peace talks. However, tension mounted over shelling in the border province of Kunar in September 2012, which Pakistan blamed on the TTP, members of which it believed to be hiding in Afghanistan. In spite of this, in November Pakistan and Afghanistan began talks on a strategic partnership agreement.

Meanwhile, as the UN High Commissioner for Refugees (UNHCR) pointed out, Pakistan continued to host 'one of the largest and most protracted refugee situations in the world'. According to reports, between early 2002 and early 2012 more than 3.7m. refugees returned to Afghanistan from Pakistan, but, as at January 2012, some 1.7m. Afghan refugees remained in Pakistan.

Relations between Pakistan and Bangladesh improved in 1976: ambassadors were exchanged, and trade, postal and telecommunication links were resumed. In September 1991 Pakistan finally agreed to initiate a process of phased repatriation and rehabilitation of some 250,000 Urdu-speaking Bihari Muslims (who openly supported Pakistan in Bangladesh's war of liberation in 1971) still remaining in refugee camps in Bangladesh. The first group of Bihari refugees returned to Pakistan from Bangladesh in January 1993, but the repatriation process proved very slow. (In May 2008 the Dhaka High Court concluded that approximately 150,000 Biharis—those who had been minors in 1971 or who had been born in the intervening years—could become citizens of Bangladesh.) A diplomatic row arose in September 2000 over who was responsible for the events during Bangladesh's war of liberation, culminating in the withdrawal of the Pakistani Deputy High Commissioner to Bangladesh. In July 2002 Pakistani President Pervez Musharraf paid a visit to Bangladesh, during which he expressed regret for the atrocities committed by Pakistani troops during the 1971 war. In February 2006 Bangladeshi Prime Minister Khaleda Zia visited Islamabad to hold talks with her Pakistani counterpart, Shaukat Aziz; the latter hailed the visit, during which the two sides signed four memorandums of understanding on trade, agriculture, tourism, and standardization and quality control, as a turning point in bilateral relations. A fifth round of Pakistan-Bangladesh bilateral consultations (primarily covering trade and investment) was held, after a three-year hiatus, in Islamabad in November 2010, during which the Bangladeshi delegation requested a formal apology from Pakistan for the war of liberation; other issues discussed reportedly included the proposed repatriation of more Bihari refugees and the division of state assets pertaining to the period before Bangladesh's independence. In addition, the Bangladeshi delegation formally raised the issue of war reparations for the first time. During her visit to the Bangladeshi capital Dhaka in November 2012 the Pakistani

Minister of Foreign Affairs, Hina Rabbani Khar, refused to provide a formal apology for the war of liberation.

Other external relations

In foreign relations Pakistan has traditionally pursued a policy of maintaining close links with Islamic states in the Middle East and Africa and with the People's Republic of China, while continuing to seek aid and assistance from the USA. Pakistan's controversial nuclear programme prompted the USA to terminate development aid in April 1979, but, as a result of the Soviet invasion of Afghanistan in December of that year, military and economic assistance was renewed in 1981. However, increased concern about Pakistan's ability to develop nuclear weapons and its refusal to sign the Nuclear Non-Proliferation Treaty (NPT) led to the suspension of military and economic aid by the US Government again in 1990. In February 1992 the Pakistani Government admitted for the first time that Pakistan had nuclear-weapons capability, but added that it had frozen its nuclear programme at the level of October 1989, when its capabilities were insufficient to produce a nuclear device. In January 1996 the US Government agreed to resume economic aid to Pakistan, and in August the first consignment of military equipment released by the US Government after a six-year delay arrived in Pakistan. In December 1998 Prime Minister Nawaz Sharif held talks with President Clinton in the US capital in an attempt to gain support for Pakistan's ailing economy and to persuade the US leader further to ease sanctions imposed on Pakistan following nuclear tests carried out by the latter in May. During 1998–99 the USA lifted some of the sanctions imposed on Pakistan and India, while reiterating requests that the two countries sign the CTBT and exercise restraint in their respective missile development programmes. During 2000 US foreign policy appeared to favour closer co-operation with India at the expense of improved relations with Pakistan. However, Pakistan's strategic importance to US efforts to dismantle the Taliban regime in Afghanistan and thus apprehend members of the al-Qa'ida terrorist organization held responsible for the devastating attacks on New York and Washington, DC, of September 2001 resulted in attempts by the USA to promote Pakistan's political rehabilitation in the Western international community. In September the US Government withdrew sanctions imposed on Pakistan in May 1998.

Despite the international acclaim that greeted Musharraf's public declaration of his commitment to the eradication of militant religious extremism in January 2002, US concerns persisted about the proliferation of armed fundamentalist groups in Pakistan's border regions, and the possibility of their assisting scattered al-Qa'ida units to regroup in these areas (see Sectarian, Ethnic and Political Violence in Pakistan).

In March 2003 Pakistan, influenced by widespread protest marches against US-led military action to remove the regime of Saddam Hussein in Iraq, stated that it would not support the USA in this action. In the same month the USA removed all remaining sanctions imposed on Pakistan after the 1999 military coup and in early April 2003 agreed to waive a total of US $1,000m. in debt, in recognition of Pakistan's efforts in the 'war on terror'. During Musharraf's visit to the USA in June, the US President, George W. Bush, offered an aid package of $3,000m. in financial and military assistance to cover the following five years. However, the Bush Administration declined to cancel a further $1,800m. debt, owing to reservations over whether the Pakistani authorities were acting sufficiently to curb militant activity and to prevent the infiltration of separatist militants into Indian-controlled Kashmir. During a visit to Pakistan in March 2004, the US Secretary of State announced that, in recognition of the close military relations between the two countries, the USA had decided to designate Pakistan a 'major non-NATO ally'. Shortly afterwards President Bush announced that all remaining US sanctions against Pakistan would be lifted.

In February 2005, in a move indicative of the improved relations between the two countries, the USA revived the deal that it had suspended in 1990 to supply Pakistan with F-16 fighter aircraft. Following the devastating earthquake of October 2005, however, the purchase of the aircraft was postponed, in order that the funds could be allocated instead to the reconstruction effort.

Accounts of attacks by US drones in the FATA and cross-border incursions served to strain relations between Pakistan and the USA in 2007 and 2008, with the former demanding the latter respect its sovereignty and the latter refusing publicly to acknowledge the existence of its drones programme. The report-

edly high civilian death toll was also perceived to have an extremely counter-productive effect on public sentiment. Furthermore, it was argued by human rights organizations that the drone strikes represented extrajudicial killings. The new US President, Barack Obama, who took office in January 2009, emphasized his 'commitment to a strong partnership' with Pakistan in February, including an increase in the provision of non-military aid. However, there was a marked rise in the frequency of the controversial US drone attacks in north-west Pakistan (particularly in North Waziristan) in 2009–10, as the USA intensified its struggle against the Islamist militants who were based in that area.

In October 2009 the US Administration pledged US $7,500m. in non-military aid to Pakistan over a five-year period, on the condition that the country remained committed to fighting terrorism; that it did not permit its territory to be used as a base for attacks against other countries; that it committed itself to nuclear non-proliferation; and that the army did not interfere in Pakistan's political or judicial processes. The conditions attached to the so-called Kerry-Lugar-Berman Bill, which were to be strictly monitored and certified by US officials within Pakistan itself, prompted serious Pakistani criticism on the grounds that they undermined the country's sovereignty. In May 2010 the US authorities arrested a Pakistani-born US citizen and two Pakistani nationals for their alleged involvement in a failed bomb attack in the centre of New York that was foiled earlier that month. In October a plot by another Pakistani-born US national to carry out a bomb attack on the Metrorail system in Washington, DC, was uncovered by the US authorities; the suspect, Farooque Ahmed, was sentenced to 23 years in prison in April 2011.

During the latter half of 2010 Pakistan's military leadership resisted US demands that Pakistan launch a major offensive against militants in North Waziristan, claiming that their troops were already overstretched. In November it was reported that the USA was seeking to expand its drone operations in Pakistan; Pakistan responded that it would never allow this. (However, it was widely understood, although not officially admitted, that Pakistani intelligence provided the US military with information for these strikes, of which there was a record total of some 118 in 2010.) Furthermore, in the following month Pakistan warned the USA that their counter-terrorism partnership would be terminated if there was any encroachment by US ground forces across the Afghan border into Pakistani territory (as the US military was reported to have recently requested).

In January 2011 Pakistani-US relations were severely strained following the fatal shooting in Lahore of two Pakistani civilians by a US consulate official, Raymond Davis, who, it later transpired, was employed by the US Central Intelligence Agency—CIA—to monitor militant Islamist groups in Pakistan (without the knowledge of the Pakistani authorities). Davis, who claimed to have been acting in self-defence, was charged with murder but was acquitted by a Pakistani court in March when relatives of the victims accepted so-called 'blood money' in exchange for his release. However, the incident provoked a marked increase in anti-US sentiment throughout Pakistan. In April it was reported that Pakistan had requested that the USA substantially reduce the number of CIA agents in the country, provide detailed information regarding the assignments of the agency's remaining personnel, and limit the number of drone attacks in the north-west tribal areas (such attacks were estimated to have killed hundreds of civilians in addition to the numerous targeted Taliban and al-Qa'ida militants).

In May 2011 bilateral relations were brought to a crisis point following the covert US raid in Abbottabad at the beginning of May 2011 during which Osama bin Laden, the founder of al-Qa'ida and the USA's 'most-wanted' terrorist target, was killed (see Domestic Political Affairs). The US decision apparently to conduct the operation without consulting the Pakistani authorities appeared to illustrate the low level of trust that existed between the two countries, especially with regard to counter-terrorism and security issues. The Pakistani Government angrily rejected US suggestions that the al-Qa'ida leader could not have taken refuge in Abbottabad without the co-operation of senior Pakistani officials. The incident provoked intense political debate in both the USA and Pakistan concerning the viability of the strategic alliance between the two countries. Members of the US Senate urged the Obama Administration to halt military aid to Pakistan until the Pakistani authorities demonstrated greater commitment to supporting US counter-terrorism objectives in the region; Pakistan had received some US $20,000m. in military and non-military aid since 2001. In mid-May 2011 John Kerry, Chairman of the US Senate Foreign Affairs Committee, travelled to Islamabad for talks with Pakistan's civilian and military leaders concerning the bin Laden incident and the crisis confronting bilateral relations. Pointedly, in an official visit to China during the same week, Prime Minister Gilani thanked China for its unwavering support and solidarity and described the host nation as Pakistan's 'best and most trusted friend'. At the end of May US Secretary of State Hillary Clinton and the Chairman of the US Joint Chiefs of Staff, Adm. Michael Mullen, held talks in Islamabad with President Zardari, Prime Minister Gilani and high-ranking Pakistani army officials on the subject of reinforcing the two countries' joint campaign against militancy. However, at the end of June a further deterioration in relations between Pakistan and the USA was made evident by the Pakistani Government's demand that US drone operations from the Shamsi airbase in Balochistan be terminated. Earlier in the month the director of the CIA, during an unannounced visit to Pakistan, had directly accused elements of the ISI of colluding with Islamist militants. Furthermore, in early July Adm. Mullen asserted that the Pakistani military had 'sanctioned' the kidnap and murder of an investigative journalist, Saleem Shahzad, in May (shortly before his death, Shahzad had written an article in which he claimed that the Pakistani navy had been infiltrated by al-Qa'ida). In mid-July, following Pakistan's expulsion of US military-training personnel in the previous month, it was reported that the US authorities were suspending $800m. of military aid for Pakistan. Moreover, in September Adm. Mullen accused the ISI of providing safe havens in North Waziristan for the notorious Haqqani militant Islamist network.

In November 2011 US-Pakistani relations suffered further damage following reports that 24 Pakistani soldiers had been killed during NATO air-strikes at two checkpoints on the Pakistan–Afghanistan border; Afghan officials claimed that the NATO forces had been responding to gunfire from the Pakistani side of the border, an allegation strenuously denied by the Pakistani military, which countered that the attack had been completely unprovoked. The Pakistani authorities described the incident as a serious violation of national sovereignty and announced the immediate suspension of NATO logistical supply routes through Pakistan (by land and air), while ordering US personnel to vacate the Shamsi airbase within two weeks. In November the US Administration announced that it was suspending a further US $700m. in military aid to Pakistan owing to the latter's failure adequately to prevent the cross-border operations of militant groups in the FATA. In February 2012 the Pakistani Government gave permission for the temporary recommencement of food supplies to NATO personnel in Afghanistan via Pakistani airspace. In the same month, however, the Pakistani authorities strongly condemned the presentation of a resolution in the US Congress in support of independence for Balochistan. In April 2012 the US authorities announced the offer of a bounty of $10m. for information leading to the arrest of Hafiz Mohammad Saeed, the leader of Jamaat-ud-Dawa, with alleged links to LeT. (Saeed had recently launched the Pakistan Defence Council, a coalition of right-wing, mainly Islamist, organizations that was vehemently opposed to Pakistan's alliance with the USA). India welcomed this announcement, while Pakistan continued to claim that it lacked sufficient evidence to prosecute Saeed. The impasse between Pakistan and the USA was finally resolved in July, when Clinton issued an apology for the deaths of the Pakistani soldiers in 2011; the Pakistani Government promptly agreed to reopen NATO supply routes. However, tensions remained over the USA's continuing use of drones to attack militants within Pakistan's borders. In September 2012 a report by Stanford University and New York University stated that a significant number of the fatalities caused by drone attacks between June 2004 and mid-September 2012 were that of civilians, including children. There was widespread public opposition to the attacks among the Pakistani public.

In 1995 Pakistan, China, Kazakhstan and Kyrgyzstan signed a transit trade agreement, restoring Pakistan's overland trade route with Central Asia, through China. During a commemorative visit to Pakistan by the Chinese Premier, organized in May 2001 to celebrate 50 years of bilateral relations, the two countries concluded a number of agreements on technical and economic co-operation. In January 2002 it was reported that China had supplied several dozen fighter aircraft and air defence missiles to Pakistan. In May 2004 the two countries signed an agreement to construct a second nuclear power plant at Chashma in Punjab province, with substantial assistance from the Chinese National Nuclear Corporation (a first plant having opened in 2001); the second Chashma facility was inaugurated in May 2011. Relations between Pakistan and China were further strengthened by the signing of a Treaty of Friendship, Co-operation and Good-Neighbourly Relations in April 2005 and of a landmark free trade agreement in November 2006. It was hoped that the latter accord would lead to the tripling of bilateral trade within five years. In April 2008 the Pakistani navy took delivery of the first of four advanced Chinese-constructed frigates that had been ordered in 2005. The new Pakistani President, Asif Ali Zardari, made China the destination of his first official state visit in October 2008, during which it was reported that the two countries agreed to expand their nuclear co-operation. In April 2009 Pakistan and China signed an agreement to construct a further two nuclear power plants at Chashma. In mid-2010 the USA and India expressed their concern at the proposed expansion of Pakistan's nuclear sector, but China insisted that its civilian nuclear co-operation with Pakistan was for purely peaceful purposes. According to the guidelines of the Nuclear Suppliers' Group (NSG, which China had joined in 2004), member states should not export civil nuclear technology to countries that had not signed the NPT (Pakistan being one of these). China argued, however, that its nuclear co-operation programme with Pakistan pre-dated its joining the NSG. China's role as a counterweight to US influence in Pakistan was underlined in May 2011 when Chinese Premier Wen Jiabao, in the midst of a US–Pakistani diplomatic crisis following the killing of Osama bin Laden (see above), extended to Prime Minister Gilani China's unqualified support, during a bilateral summit in Beijing to mark the 60th anniversary of the establishment of Sino-Pakistani relations. During the summit China finalized arrangements for the supply of 50 JF-17 fighter aircraft to Pakistan; details of a joint venture agreement to produce additional fighter aircraft in Pakistan were also announced.

In early 1992 the Economic Cooperation Organization (see p. 274), comprising Pakistan, Iran and Turkey, was reactivated, and by the end of the year had been expanded to include Afghanistan, Azerbaijan and the five Central Asian, mainly Muslim, republics of the former USSR. Trade delegations from Turkey and the new republics visited Pakistan, and an agreement for the restoration and construction of highways in Afghanistan, to link Pakistan with these republics, was signed. In October 2010 the Pakistani Government formally approved the framework agreement for the construction of the 1,680-km Turkmenistan-Afghanistan-Pakistan-India (TAPI) gas pipeline. The pipeline, which was to be funded by the Asian Development Bank (see p. 214) at an estimated cost of US $7,600m. and was projected to be operational by 2016, was to extend from the Dauletabad gas field in Turkmenistan to the town of Fazilka in the Indian state of Punjab (via Afghanistan and Pakistan). Furthermore, despite international pressure (notably from the USA) to abandon the project, Pakistan signed an agreement with Iran in March 2010 to construct a 2,775-km gas pipeline at an estimated cost of $7,500m. from Asalouyeh in the South Pars gas field in southern Iran to Multan (via Karachi) in Pakistan. In July 2011 Iran announced the completion of its section of the pipeline; Pakistan was contracted to finish the construction of its section by the end of 2014.

Pakistan withdrew from the Commonwealth in January 1972, in protest against the United Kingdom's role in the East Pakistan crisis. Pakistan recognized Bangladesh in February 1974, but attempts to rejoin the organization in the late 1970s and early 1980s were thwarted by India. In 1989, following a decision by India to discontinue its opposition to Pakistan's application to rejoin, Pakistan's Commonwealth membership was resumed. However, in October 1999, following the military coup, Pakistan was suspended from participation in meetings of the Commonwealth. In May 2004 the Commonwealth Ministerial Action Group (CMAG) agreed to restore fully Pakistan's Commonwealth membership, stating that it had decided that the country had consolidated the progress made towards democracy following the October 2002 general election, owing to President Musharraf's statement that he would step down as Chief of Army Staff by the end of 2004 and the subsequent legislative vote of confidence in his leadership. In February 2005 the CMAG criticized Musharraf for reneging on his pledge to become a civilian president and insisted that he must relinquish his military role by 2007. Following Musharraf's imposition of a state of emergency and suspension of the Constitution in November 2007, the CMAG once again suspended Pakistan from participation in meetings. However, full membership was restored in May 2008 as a result of the reinstatement of democratic government in February.

CONSTITUTION AND GOVERNMENT

The Constitution was promulgated on 10 April 1973, and amended on a number of subsequent occasions. Several provisions were suspended following the imposition of martial law in 1977. The (amended) Constitution was restored on 30 December 1985. The Constitution was placed in abeyance on 15 October 1999 following the overthrow of the Government in a military coup. The Constitution, incorporating a Legal Framework Order (LFO), which greatly increased the powers held by the President, was revived on 15 November 2002. The LFO, however, was effectively repealed by the Eighteenth Amendment Bill, which was passed in April 2010 and which transformed the President into a largely titular Head of State.

The President is a constitutional Head of State, who is normally elected for five years by an electoral college, comprising the Federal Legislature and the four provincial assemblies. The former consists of a lower and upper house—the National Assembly and Senate. There are 342 seats in the National Assembly, with 272 members directly elected (on the basis of adult suffrage), 60 seats reserved for women and 10 for non-Muslims. The term of the National Assembly is five years. The Senate comprises 104 seats; the provincial assemblies directly elect 92 members—of whom four have to be non-Muslims, 16 have to be women and a further 16 technocrats (including *ulema*, Muslim legal scholars)—and of the remaining 12 members, the Federally Administered Tribal Areas (FATA) return eight members and the remaining four are elected from the Federal Capital Territory by members of the Provincial Assemblies. The term of the Senate is six years, with one-half of the membership being renewed every three years. The Prime Minister is elected by the National Assembly and he/she and the other ministers in the Cabinet are responsible to it.

Pakistan comprises four provinces (each with an appointed Governor and provincial government), the federal capital of Islamabad, and the FATA.

REGIONAL AND INTERNATIONAL CO-OPERATION

Pakistan is a member of the South Asian Association for Regional Cooperation (SAARC, see p. 430), of the Asian Development Bank (ADB, see p. 214) and of the Colombo Plan (see p. 460). Pakistan is also a founder member of the Islamic Financial Services Board.

Having joined the UN in 1947, Pakistan is a member of the Economic and Social Commission for Asia and the Pacific (ESCAP, see p. 31). As a contracting party to the General Agreement on Tariffs and Trade (GATT), Pakistan joined the World Trade Organization (WTO, see p. 444) on its establishment in 1995.

ECONOMIC AFFAIRS

In 2011, according to estimates by the World Bank, Pakistan's gross national income (GNI), measured at average 2009–11 prices, was US $197,604m., equivalent to $1,120 per head (or $2,880 per head on an international purchasing-power parity basis). During 2002–11, it was estimated, the population grew at an average annual rate of 1.8%, while gross domestic product (GDP) per head increased, in real terms, by an average of 2.9% per year. Overall GDP rose, in real terms, at an average annual rate of 4.8% in 2002–11. According to official provisional figures, growth reached 3.7% in 2011/12.

Agriculture (including forestry and fishing) contributed an estimated 21.1% of GDP in 2011/12. Some 44.7% of the employed labour force was engaged in the sector at 30 June 2008. The principal cash crops are cotton and rice; sugar cane, wheat and maize are also major crops. Fishing and leather production provide significant export revenues. According to the Asian Development Bank (ADB), during 2002–11 agricultural GDP increased at an average annual rate of 3.5%. According to official provisional figures, the sector grew by 3.1% in 2011/12.

Industry (including mining, manufacturing, power and construction) engaged an estimated 20.1% of the employed labour force at 30 June 2008, and provided an estimated 25.5% of GDP in 2011/12. During 2002–11, according to the ADB, industrial GDP increased by an average of 5.8% per year. According to official provisional figures, industrial GDP grew by 3.4% in 2011/12.

Mining and quarrying contributed an estimated 2.3% of GDP in 2011/12, and, according to the International Labour Organization (ILO), engaged only 0.1% of the employed labour force at 30 June 2008. Petroleum and petroleum products are the major mineral exports. Limestone, rock salt, gypsum, silica sand, natural gas and coal are also mined. In addition, Pakistan has reserves of graphite, copper and manganese. The GDP of the mining sector increased at an average annual rate of 4.9% during 2002–11 according to the ADB. According to official provisional figures, mining GDP decreased by 1.3% in 2010/11, but increased by 4.4% in 2011/12.

Manufacturing contributed an estimated 19.0% of GDP in 2011/12, and engaged about 13.0% of the employed labour force at 30 June 2008. The most important sectors include the manufacture of textiles, food products, automobiles and electrical goods, and also petroleum-refining. During 2002–11 manufacturing GDP increased at an average annual rate of 6.9% according to the ADB. According to official provisional figures, manufacturing GDP rose by 3.6% in 2011/12.

Construction contributed an estimated 2.1% of GDP in 2011/12, while the sector engaged some 6.3% of the employed labour force at 30 June 2008. According to the ADB, construction GDP increased at an average annual rate of 3.5% during 2002–11. According to official figures, sectoral GDP declined by 7.1% in 2010/11; however, according to provisional figures, the sector grew by 6.5% in 2011/12.

Energy is derived principally from natural gas (providing 29.4% of the total electrical energy supply in 2009), hydroelectric power (29.4%) and petroleum (38.0%). Imports of mineral fuels, lubricants, etc. comprised about 35.4% of the cost of total imports in 2011/12.

Services engaged 35.2% of the employed labour force at 30 June 2008, and provided an estimated 53.4% of GDP in 2011/12. The combined GDP of the service sectors increased at an average rate of 5.3% per year in 2002–11 according to the ADB. According to official provisional figures, the GDP of services expanded by 4.0% in 2011/12.

According to the IMF, Pakistan recorded a visible merchandise trade deficit of US $12,545m. in 2011 and there was a deficit of $2,234m. on the current account of the balance of payments. The flow of remittances from Pakistanis working abroad showed strong and steady growth during the 2000s, increasing from $4,600m. in 2005/06 to a record $13,187m. in 2011/12. The principal source of imports in 2011/12 was the United Arab Emirates (UAE—which provided 17.1% of the total); other major suppliers were the People's Republic of China, Saudi Arabia, Kuwait and Malaysia. The principal market for exports was the USA (which accounted for 15.0% of the total); other major purchasers were the UAE, Afghanistan, China and the United Kingdom. The principal exports in 2011/12 were cotton fabrics, yarn and thread, garments and hosiery, and rice. The principal imports were mineral fuels and lubricants, machinery and transport equipment, chemicals and related products, basic manufactures, and animal and vegetable oil and fats.

For the financial year ending 30 June 2012, there was an estimated budgetary deficit of Rs 369,459m. Pakistan's general government gross debt was Rs 10,860,123m. in 2011, equivalent to 60.2% of GDP. According to the ADB, Pakistan's total external debt was US $55,626m. at the end of 2010. The cost of debt-servicing in that year was equivalent to 18.0% of earnings from exports of goods and services. During 2002–12, according to the ILO, the average annual rate of inflation was 9.8%. According to official figures, consumer prices rose by 13.7% in 2010/11 and by 11.0% in 2011/12. About 5.9% of the labour force was estimated to be unemployed at 30 June 2011.

Following a period of steady growth in the first half of the 2000s, in 2007/08 the Pakistani economy reached crisis point, with massive rises in levels of external debt, the trade deficit and the current account deficit. Increases in food prices, worsening political strife, energy shortages and poor export figures combined to have a negative impact on GDP growth. The threat to Pakistan's economic stability was somewhat alleviated by the implementation of an IMF-supported stabilization programme (worth US $7,600m.) in November 2008. In August 2009 the total amount of projected IMF financial support was increased to $11,300m. In July 2010 the World Bank approved a four-year lending programme for Pakistan worth a total of $6,200m. However, devastating floods from late July led to a reduction in agricultural output and severely damaged the country's transport and communications networks. Flood damage was estimated to total some $9,500m. GDP growth was measured at a weak 2.4% in 2010/11. In January 2011 the Pakistani Government was criticized by the IMF for succumbing to political pressure and cancelling the planned introduction of power tariffs and a new general sales tax. The IMF continued to refuse to revive its suspended standby arrangement programme (with remaining disbursements of up to $3,600m. withheld since May 2010) until Pakistan made further progress with economic reform. High rates of inflation have persisted in recent years, with inflation reaching a peak of 21.0% in 2008/09; however, the rate was projected to moderate to 9.5% in 2012/13. Levels of foreign direct investment fell from a high of $5,409.8m. in 2007/08 to just $812.6m. in 2011/12 in response to widespread concerns over security and inadequate infrastructure. Large-scale losses incurred by state-owned enterprises and increases in the wages of government employees have contributed to rising budget deficits, from 5.3% of GDP in 2008/09 to an estimated 8.5% in 2011/12. The economy remained sluggish in 2011/12 and 2012/13, as acute energy shortages and political instability continued to hamper growth. The rate of GDP growth was put at 3.7% in 2011/12; GDP was projected to rise at a similar rate in 2012/13.

PUBLIC HOLIDAYS

2014: 13 January* (Eid-i-Milad-un-Nabi, Birth of the Prophet), 23 March (Pakistan Day, proclamation of republic in 1956), 1 May (Labour Day), 28 June* (Ramadan begins), 28 July* (Id al-Fitr, end of Ramadan), 14 August (Independence Day), 6 September (Defence of Pakistan Day), 11 September (Anniversary of Death of Quaid-i-Azam), 4 October* (Id al-Adha, Feast of the Sacrifice), 24 October* (Muharram, Islamic New Year), 9 November (Allama Iqbal Day), 2 November* (Ashoura), 25 December (Birthday of Quaid-i-Azam).

* These holidays are dependent on the Islamic lunar calendar and may vary by one or two days from the dates given.

Statistical Survey

Sources (unless otherwise stated): Pakistan Bureau of Statistics, 5-SLIC Building, F-6/4, Blue Area, Islamabad; fax (51) 99203233; e-mail pbs@pbs.gov.pk; internet www.pbs.gov.pk; State Bank of Pakistan, Karachi; internet www.sbp.org.pk.

Area and Population

AREA, POPULATION AND DENSITY*

Area (sq km)	796,095†
Population (census results)	
2 March 1998	
Males	68,873,686
Females	63,478,593
Total	132,352,279
12 September 2011 (preliminary)‡	192,288,944
Density (per sq km) at 2011 census	241.5

* Excluding data for the disputed territory of Jammu and Kashmir. The Pakistani-held parts of this region are known as Azad ('Free') Kashmir, with an area of 11,639 sq km (4,494 sq miles) and a population of 1,980,000 in 1981, and Gilgit-Baltistan (the former Northern Areas), with an area of 72,971 sq km (28,174 sq miles) and a population of 870,347 in 1998. Also excluded are Junagardh and Manavadar. The population figures exclude refugees from Afghanistan (estimated to number 1,702,000 in late 2011).
† 307,374 sq miles.
‡ Excluding data for Khuzdar, Kech and Panjgur districts of Balochistan.

POPULATION BY AGE AND SEX
(population at 1998 census)

	Males	Females	Total
0–14	29,241,025	26,823,722	56,064,747
15–64	35,504,033	33,082,093	68,586,126
65 and over	2,476,581	2,048,494	4,525,075
Total	67,221,639	61,954,309	129,175,948

Note: Figures exclude population of Federally Administered Tribal Areas (FATA), numbering 3,176,331.

ADMINISTRATIVE DIVISIONS
(population at 2011 census, preliminary)

	Area (sq km)	Population*	Density (per sq km)
Provinces:			
Balochistan	347,190	13,162,222	37.9
North-West Frontier Province† .	74,521	26,896,829	360.9
Punjab	205,344	91,379,615	445.0
Sindh	140,914	55,245,497	392.1
Federally Administered Tribal			
Areas	27,220	4,452,913	163.6
Federal Capital Territory:			
Islamabad	906	1,151,868	1,271.4
Total	796,095	192,288,944	241.5

* Excluding data for Khuzdar, Kech and Panjgur districts of Balochistan.
† Renamed Khyber Pakhtoonkhwa in April 2010.

PRINCIPAL TOWNS
(population at 1998 census)

Karachi . . .	9,269,265	Bahawalpur . .	408,395
Lahore . . .	5,143,495	Sukkur . . .	335,551
Faisalabad		Jhang Maghiana	
(Lyallpur) . .	2,008,861	(Jhang Sadar) .	293,366
Rawalpindi . . .	1,409,768	Shekhupura . .	280,263
Multan . . .	1,197,384	Larkana . . .	270,283
Hyderabad . .	1,166,894	Gujrat . . .	251,792
Gujranwala . .	1,042,509	Mardan . . .	244,511
Peshawar . .	988,005	Kasur . . .	241,649
Quetta . . .	565,137	Rahimyar Khan .	233,537
Islamabad (capital) .	529,180	Sahiwal . . .	207,388
Sargodha . .	455,360	Okara . . .	201,815
Sialkot . . .	421,502		

2010 (official estimates): Karachi 13,386,730; Lahore 7,214,954; Faisalabad (Lyallpur) 2,912,269; Rawalpindi 2,013,876; Gujranwala 1,676,357; Multan 1,610,180; Hyderabad 1,521,231; Peshawar 1,386,529; Islamabad 972,669; Quetta 871,643.

BIRTHS AND DEATHS
(annual averages, UN estimates)

	1995–2000	2000–05	2005–10
Birth rate (per 1,000)	34.4	28.9	28.1
Death rate (per 1,000)	8.8	8.0	7.7

Source: UN, *World Population Prospects: The 2010 Revision*.

Crude rates (per 1,000): *Births:* 28.0 in 2010; 27.5 in 2011; 27.2 in 2012. *Deaths:* 7.4 in 2010; 7.3 in 2011; 7.2 in 2012 (Source: Ministry of Finance, *Economic Survey, 2011/12*).

Life expectancy (years at birth): 65.2 (males 64.3; females 66.1) in 2010 (Source: World Bank, World Development Indicators database).

ECONOMICALLY ACTIVE POPULATION
('000 persons aged 10 years and over, excl. armed forces, at 30 June)

	2006	2007	2008
Agriculture, hunting, forestry and fishing	20,364	20,780	21,919
Mining and quarrying	43	52	57
Manufacturing	6,499	6,454	6,377
Electricity, gas and water . . .	308	360	343
Construction	2,880	3,127	3,088
Wholesale and retail trade, and restaurants and hotels . . .	6,886	6,872	7,178
Transport, storage and communication	2,697	2,569	2,681
Financing, insurance, real estate and business services . . .	518	544	692
Community, social and personal services	6,739	6,868	6,706
Sub-total	46,934	47,626	49,041
Activities not adequately defined .	18	25	49
Total employed	46,952	47,651	49,090
Unemployed	3,103	2,680	2,694
Total labour force	50,055	50,331	51,784
Males	39,974	39,925	40,825
Females	10,081	10,406	10,959

Source: ILO.

2011 ('000 persons aged 10 years and over, excl. armed forces, at 30 June): Total employed 53,840; Unemployed 3,400; Total labour force 57,240 (Source: Ministry of Finance, *Economic Survey, 2011/12*).

Health and Welfare

KEY INDICATORS

Total fertility rate (children per woman, 2010)	3.4
Under-5 mortality rate (per 1,000 live births, 2010) . .	87
HIV/AIDS (% of persons aged 15–49, 2009)	0.1
Physicians (per 1,000 head, 2009)	0.8
Hospital beds (per 1,000 head, 2010)	0.6
Health expenditure (2008): US $ per head (PPP) . . .	62
Health expenditure (2008): % of GDP	2.6
Health expenditure (2008): public (% of total)	32.3
Access to water (% of persons, 2010)	92
Access to sanitation (% of persons, 2010)	48
Total carbon dioxide emissions ('000 metric tons, 2008) . .	163,177.8
Carbon dioxide emissions per head (metric tons, 2008) . .	1.0
Human Development Index (2011): ranking	145
Human Development Index (2011): value	0.504

For sources and definitions, see explanatory note on p. vi.

Agriculture

PRINCIPAL CROPS
('000 metric tons)

	2009	2010	2011
Wheat	24,033	23,311	25,214
Rice, paddy	10,325	7,235	6,160
Barley	82	71	71
Maize	3,262	3,707	4,271
Millet	293	346	304
Sorghum	154	141	137
Potatoes	2,941	3,142	3,492
Sugar cane	50,045	49,373	55,309
Sugar beet	93*	53	21
Beans, dry	129	88	104
Chick peas	741	562	496
Groundnuts, with shell . . .	53	68	88
Sunflower seed	420	325	404
Rapeseed	199	162	195
Tomatoes	562	477	530
Cauliflower and broccoli . . .	235	213	228
Pumpkins, squash and gourds .	265	252	252
Onions, dry	1,704	1,701	1,940
Carrots and turnips	246	219	242
Okra	116	107	103
Watermelons	416*	420†	463†
Cantaloupes and other melons† .	300	290	333
Bananas	155	1471†	130†
Oranges*	1,492	1,505	1,388
Tangerines, mandarins, clementines and satsumas* .	554	559	515
Lemons and limes	85*	86*	79
Apples	366	526	599
Apricots	194	190	189
Peaches and nectarines . . .	54	53	54
Plums and sloes	57	56	54†
Guavas, mangoes and mangosteens	1,728	1,846	1,888
Dates	735	524	557
Pimento and allspice	187	172	203†
Tobacco, unmanufactured . .	105	119	103

* Unofficial figure(s).
† FAO estimate(s).

Aggregate production ('000 metric tons, may include official, semi-official or estimated data): Total cereals 38,157 in 2009, 34,811 in 2010, 36,157 in 2011; Total roots and tubers 3,383 in 2009, 3,570 in 2010, 3,986 in 2011; Total vegetables (incl. melons) 5,269 in 2009, 5,064 in 2010, 5,457 in 2011; Total fruits (excl. melons) 6,091 in 2009, 6,370 in 2010, 6,340 in 2011.

Source: FAO.

LIVESTOCK
('000 head, year ending September)

	2009	2010	2011
Cattle	33,029	34,285	35,568
Buffaloes	29,883	29,413	31,726
Sheep	27,432	27,757	28,086
Goats	58,279	59,858	61,480
Horses	350	352	354
Asses	4,509	4,600	4,700
Mules	165	167	170
Camels	958	970	983
Chickens*	295,000	321,000	349,000
Ducks*	3,500	3,700	3,700

* FAO estimates.

Source: FAO.

LIVESTOCK PRODUCTS
('000 metric tons)

	2009	2010	2011
Cattle meat	707	733	761
Buffalo meat	730	752	775
Sheep meat	155	156	158
Goat meat	271	278	285
Chicken meat	651	707	767
Cows' milk	11,985	12,437	12,906
Buffaloes' milk	21,622	22,279	22,955
Sheep's milk	36	36	36
Goats' milk	719	739	759
Hen eggs*	529.1	556.4	604.3
Other poultry eggs†	7.2	8.0	8.0
Wool, greasy	41.5	42.0	42.5

* Unofficial figures.
† FAO estimates.

Source: FAO.

Forestry

ROUNDWOOD REMOVALS
('000 cubic metres, excl. bark)

	2007	2008	2009*
Sawlogs, veneer logs and logs for sleepers	2,008	2,023	2,023
Pulpwood	56	59	59
Other industrial wood	897	908	908
Fuel wood	29,520	29,660	29,660
Total	32,481	32,650	32,483

* FAO estimates.

2010–11: Production assumed to be unchanged from 2009 (FAO estimates).
Source: FAO.

SAWNWOOD PRODUCTION
('000 cubic metres, incl. railway sleepers)

	2006	2007	2008
Coniferous (softwood)	432	453	462
Broadleaved (hardwood)	881	910	919
Total	1,313	1,363	1,381

2009–11: Production assumed to be unchanged from 2008 (FAO estimates).
Source: FAO.

Fishing

('000 metric tons, live weight)

	2008	2009	2010
Capture	451.4	446.4	453.3
Freshwater fishes	108.0	112.4	115.3
Sea catfishes	28.3	23.9	32.3
Croakers and drums	14.7	13.6	20.0
Largehead hairtail	22.7	20.4	20.9
Indian oil sardine	31.5	26.9	20.1
Other clupeoids	16.3	14.8	17.3
Jacks and crevalles	5.0	9.1	7.6
Requiem sharks	8.5	5.9	4.8
Skates, rays and mantas	7.3	6.6	6.2
Aquaculture*	135.1	138.1	140.1
Total catch*	586.5	584.5	593.4

* FAO estimates.

Source: FAO.

Mining
('000 metric tons unless otherwise indicated)

	2008/09	2009/10	2010/11
Barite	63	57	32
Chromite	90	257	148
Limestone	33,186	37,1137	32,021
Gypsum	800	854	885
Rock salt	1,917	1,944	1,954
Coal	3,679	3,536	3,292
Crude petroleum (million barrels)	24	24	24
Natural gas ('000 million cu m)	41	42	42

Source: Ministry of Finance, *Economic Survey, 2011/12.*

Natural gas (million cu m, excluding flared or recycled gas): 38,400 in 2009; 39,600 in 2010; 39,200 in 2011 (Source: BP, *Statistical Review of World Energy*).

Industry

SELECTED PRODUCTS
('000 metric tons unless otherwise indicated, year ending 30 June)

	2008/09	2009/10	2010/11
Cotton cloth (million sq m)	1,020	1,010	1,030
Cotton yarn	2,862	2,881	2,939
Refined sugar	3,190	3,132	4,169
Vegetable ghee	1,062	1,076	1,081
Cement	28,380	31,160	28,723
Urea	4,918	5,057	4,552
Superphosphate	187	149	173
Sulphuric acid	98	85	128
Soda ash	365	410	378
Caustic soda	245	182	172
Chlorine gas	17	16	15
Cigarettes ('000 million)	76	65	65
Ammonium nitrate	344	346	275
Nitrophosphate	306	304	252
Pig-iron	791	483	433
Paper and paperboard	421	427	435
Tractors (number)	60,107	71,730	n.a.
Bicycles ('000)	420	447	342
Motor tyres and tubes ('000)	21,604	28,825	28,448
Bicycle tyres and tubes ('000)	10,089	10,678	9,408
Electric energy (million kWh)	92,430	94,222	n.a.

Source: Ministry of Finance, *Economic Survey, 2011/12.*

Finance

CURRENCY AND EXCHANGE RATES

Monetary Units
100 paisa = 1 Pakistani rupee.

Sterling, Dollar and Euro Equivalents (31 December 2012)
£1 sterling = 153.28 rupees;
US $1 = 97.14 rupees;
€1 = 128.16 rupees;
1,000 Pakistani rupees = £6.52 = $10.29 = €7.80.

Average Exchange Rate (Pakistani rupees per US $)
2010	85.194
2011	86.343
2012	93.395

CENTRAL GOVERNMENT BUDGET
(million rupees, year ending 30 June)

Revenue	2010/11	2011/12	2012/13*
Tax revenue	1,679,400	1,945,698	2,503,575
Income and corporate taxes†	602,500	731,579	914,000
Other direct taxes	24,400	363	18,000
Excise duty	132,900	122,014	125,000
Sales tax†	654,600	809,310	1,076,500
Taxes on international trade	173,300	218,215	247,500
Other taxes revenue	91,700	64,217	122,575
Non-tax revenue (incl. surcharges)	556,500	478,475	730,332
Total	2,235,900	2,424,173	3,233,907

Expenditure	2010/11	2011/12	2012/13*
Current expenditure	2,295,921	2,209,324	2,611,941
General public service	1,655,566	1,526,979	1,876,839
Defence†	444,640	507,159	545,386
Economic affairs	79,960	40,966	53,642
Development expenditure	202,661	380,422	360,282
Capital expenditure	179,549	203,886	294,085
Total	2,678,131	2,793,632	3,266,308

* Budget estimates.
† Exclusively federal.

INTERNATIONAL RESERVES
(US $ million, last Thursday of the year)

	2010	2011	2012
Gold*	2,864	3,566	3,555
IMF special drawing rights	1,230	1,054	921
Foreign exchange	13,115	13,474	9,320
Total	17,209	18,094	13,796

* Revalued annually, in June, on the basis of London market prices.

Source: IMF, *International Financial Statistics*.

MONEY SUPPLY
(million rupees, last Thursday of the year)

	2010	2011	2012
Currency outside depository corporations	1,508,986	1,585,720	1,826,742
Transferable deposits	3,040,414	3,482,924	4,223,926
Other deposits	1,566,688	1,783,699	1,968,534
Securities other than shares	111	59	83
Broad money	6,116,199	6,852,402	8,019,285

Source: IMF, *International Financial Statistics*.

COST OF LIVING
(Consumer Price Index; base: 2007/08 = 100; year ending 30 June)

	2009/10	2010/11	2011/12
Food and non-alcoholic beverages	139.1	164.6	182.8
Alcoholic beverages and tobacco	136.7	151.6	165.0
Clothing and footwear	119.2	133.3	153.5
Housing and utilities	122.1	135.3	146.2
Health	114.3	123.8	138.0
Transport	132.8	149.0	171.4
Education	119.4	128.2	143.8
All items (incl. others)	128.9	146.5	162.6

NATIONAL ACCOUNTS
(million rupees at current prices, year ending 30 June)

Expenditure on the Gross Domestic Product

	2009/10	2010/11	2011/12*
Government final consumption expenditure	1,178,732	1,430,122	1,720,759
Private final consumption expenditure	12,188,896	15,159,996	18,031,743
Gross fixed capital formation	2,066,945	2,069,243	2,255,864
Increase in stocks	236,858	288,526	330,462
Total domestic expenditure	15,671,431	18,947,887	22,338,828
Exports of goods and services	2,009,463	2,552,620	2,575,359
Less Imports of goods and services	2,877,243	3,467,636	4,260,319
Gross domestic product (GDP) in market prices	14,803,651	18,032,871	20,653,868
GDP at constant 1999/2000 prices	5,317,244	5,483,634	5,653,474

* Provisional figures.

Gross Domestic Product by Economic Activity

	2009/10	2010/11	2011/12*
Agriculture, forestry and fishing	2,972,660	3,697,068	3,899,313
Mining and quarrying	437,899	391,267	446,526
Manufacturing	2,484,699	3,181,980	3,694,464
Electricity and gas distribution	327,305	354,055	413,861
Construction	319,315	336,993	410,863
Wholesale and retail trade	2,463,640	3112,125	3,574,101
Transport, storage and communications	1,832,760	2,143,403	2,476,789
Finance and insurance	609,944	685,110	807,807
Ownership of dwellings	345,760	401,354	459,829
Public administration and defence	757,061	983,924	1,119,328
Community, social and personal services	1,482,586	1,805,624	2,133,944
GDP at factor cost	14,033,629	17,092,903	19,436,825
Indirect taxes	842,899	1,014,853	1,274,467
Less Subsidies	72,877	74,885	57,424
GDP in market prices	14,803,651	18,032,871	20,653,868

* Provisional figures.

BALANCE OF PAYMENTS
(US $ million)

	2009	2010	2011
Exports of goods	18,357	21,482	26,308
Imports of goods	−28,536	−32,842	−38,852
Balance on goods	−10,179	−11,360	−12,545
Exports of services	3,957	6,575	5,021
Imports of services	−6,616	−7,175	−8,044
Balance on goods and services	−12,838	−11,960	−15,567
Primary income received	607	681	844
Primary income paid	−4,221	−3,868	−3,942
Balance on goods, services and primary income	−16,452	−15,147	−18,665
Secondary income received	12,552	13,930	16,603
Secondary income paid	−93	−137	−172
Current balance	−3,993	−1,354	−2,234
Capital account (net)	484	109	221
Direct investment assets	−71	−47	−62
Direct investment liabilities	2,338	2,018	1,309
Portfolio investment assets	−26	6	−1
Portfolio investment liabilities	−582	−114	−39
Other investment assets	−3	−283	−574
Other investment liabilities	2,813	1,359	988
Net errors and omissions	703	−1,000	116
Reserve and related items	1,662	694	−276

Source: IMF, *International Financial Statistics*.

External Trade

Note: Data exclude trade in military goods.

PRINCIPAL COMMODITIES
(million rupees, year ending 30 June)

Imports c.i.f. (excl. re-imports)	2009/10	2010/11	2011/12
Food and live animals . . .	141,005.7	214,132.4	179,555.6
Mineral fuels, lubricants, etc.	883,653.4	1,084,764.7	1,420,173.6
Animal and vegetable oils, fats and waxes	120,975.4	190,133.7	228,731.4
Chemicals and related products .	492,227.1	528,988.9	637,823.7
Basic manufactures	294,972.2	369,322.2	482,498.6
Machinery and transport equipment	616,893.3	639,389.0	699,993.9
Total (incl. others)	2,910,975.3	3,455,285.6	4,009,093.0

Exports f.o.b. (excl. re-exports)	2009/10	2010/11	2011/12
Rice	183,370.3	184,674.6	184,405.0
Fish and fish preparations . .	19,049.8	25,313.9	28,597.6
Raw cotton	16,365.5	31,168.4	41,392.6
Leather, leather manufactures and dressed furskins	28,698.3	39,744.3	39,841.2
Carpets and rugs	11,119.1	11,034.4	10,113.5
Cotton fabrics, cotton yarn and thread	271,703.4	412,528.6	381,563.3
Garments and hosiery . . .	294,059.9	375,740.5	331,790.7
Sports goods	25,020.8	28,208.4	30,241.0
Total (incl. others)	1,617,457.6	2,120,846.7	2,110,605.5

PRINCIPAL TRADING PARTNERS
(million rupees, year ending 30 June)

Imports c.i.f. (excl. re-imports)	2007/08	2008/09	2009/10
Australia	32,589	39,039	47,440
Belgium	14,946	20,828	20,786
Canada	31,927	37,419	33,729
China, People's Republic . . .	294,684	319,640	370,231
France	30,776	30,422	35,747
Germany	79,950	102,534	98,663
Hong Kong	11,797	9,469	8,238
India	106,872	93,471	102,872
Indonesia	73,998	65,742	53,774
Iran	34,654	72,111	80,634
Italy	34,639	66,338	47,637
Japan	114,510	98,549	128,832
Korea, Republic	42,567	50,449	57,989
Kuwait	188,502	180,947	201,803
Malaysia	96,935	125,582	146,345
Netherlands	22,282	27,682	25,193
Saudi Arabia	336,590	334,132	283,555
Singapore	48,764	43,140	68,235
Switzerland	23,475	24,894	31,406
Thailand	37,259	46,102	60,128
Turkey	9,742	10,093	13,271
United Arab Emirates . . .	214,561	n.a.	n.a.
United Kingdom	48,373	71,652	50,022
USA	153,278	146,205	134,999
Total (incl. others)	2,512,072	2,723,570	2,910,975

Exports f.o.b. (excl. re-exports)	2007/08	2008/09	2009/10
Afghanistan	71,974	109,330	n.a.
Australia	8,689	7,494	n.a.
Bangladesh	21,501	30,073	n.a.
Belgium	25,743	30,803	36,082
Canada	12,347	13,595	16,710
China, People's Republic . . .	43,164	54,888	n.a.
France	22,905	24,601	26,739
Germany	51,255	57,731	66,514
Hong Kong	32,595	29,602	n.a.
Italy	45,391	45,321	50,822

Exports f.o.b. (excl. re-exports)— *continued*	2007/08	2008/09	2009/10
Japan	8,585	8,668	n.a.
Korea, Republic	12,523	11,625	n.a.
Netherlands	32,303	36,343	31,237
Saudi Arabia	23,981	35,699	32,959
Spain	33,992	31,674	36,413
Turkey	27,244	31,547	42,284
United Arab Emirates	130,549	114,752	144,233
United Kingdom	64,597	68,470	86,115
USA	232,758	261,362	281,683
Total (incl. others)	1,196,638	1,383,718	1,617,458

2010/11: Total imports 3,455,285.6; Total exports 2,120,846.7.

2011/12: Total imports 4,009,093.0; Total exports 2,110,605.5.

Transport

RAILWAYS
(year ending 30 June)

	2008/09	2009/10	2010/11
Passenger journeys ('000) . . .	82,542	74,903	64,900
Passenger-km (million) . . .	25,702	23,522	20,619
Freight ('000 metric tons) . . .	6,937	5,836	2,610
Net freight ton-km (million) . .	5,896	4,847	1,757

ROAD TRAFFIC
('000 vehicles in use, year ending 30 June)

	2009/10	2010/11	2011/12*
Motorcycles and scooters . . .	5,412.1	5,468.8	5,503.5
Passenger cars	2,387.2	2,822.2	3,205.0
Jeeps	78.3	78.5	78.6
Station wagons	171.4	175.2	178.3
Road tractors	940.8	970.9	1,008.7
Buses	123.3	125.6	129.2
Taxicabs	146.4	154.6	158.7
Rickshaws	89.1	89.8	102.4
Delivery vans and pick-ups . .	300.7	308.9	317.9
Trucks and tankers	211.6	220.9	224.2

* Provisional figures.

Source: Ministry of Finance, *Economic Survey, 2011/12.*

SHIPPING

Flag Registered Fleet
(at 31 December)

	2010	2011	2012
Number of vessels	47	46	48
Total displacement ('000 grt) . .	433,299	387,163	391,106

Source: Lloyd's List Intelligence (www.lloydslistintelligence.com).

International Sea-borne Shipping
(port of Karachi, year ending 30 June)

	2008/09	2009/10	2010/11
Goods ('000 long tons):			
loaded	13,364	13,528	12,846
unloaded	25,367	27,892	28,589

Source: Ministry of Finance, *Economic Survey, 2011/12.*

CIVIL AVIATION
(PIA only, domestic and international flights, '000, financial year based on calendar year)

	2009	2010	2011
Kilometres flown	80,108	81,588	84,898
Passengers carried	5,535	5,538	5,953
Passenger-km ('000) . . .	13,891	15,657	15,664

Source: Ministry of Finance, *Economic Survey, 2011/12.*

Tourism

FOREIGN TOURIST ARRIVALS
('000)

Country of nationality	2007	2008	2009
Afghanistan	80.5	66.4	96.6
Canada	36.5	39.9	43.0
China, People's Republic	30.4	30.1	30.1
Germany	23.9	22.4	21.4
India	48.2	54.1	42.7
Japan	11.0	8.3	6.7
United Kingdom	275.5	285.7	275.4
USA	121.9	114.1	117.5
Total (incl. others)	839.5	822.8	854.9

Total arrivals ('000): 907 in 2010.

Receipts from tourism (US $ million, excl. passenger transport): 305 in 2010; 358 in 2011 (provisional).

Source: partly World Tourism Organization.

Communications Media

	2008	2009	2010
Television receivers ('000 in use)*	9,940.1	10,556.5	9,940.1
Telephones ('000 main lines in use)	4,416.7	6,144.2	6,079.1
Mobile cellular telephones ('000 subscribers)	88,019.7	94,342.0	99,185.8
Internet subscribers ('000)	3,500	3,700	3,236
Broadband subscribers ('000)	148.5	302.8	531.8
Daily newspapers: number	324	252	360
average circulation ('000)	6,068.0	n.a.	n.a.
Other newspapers and periodicals: number	875	454	592
average circulation ('000)	1,137.3	n.a.	n.a.

*Estimates as at 30 June; includes Azad Kashmir and Gilgit-Baltistan (former Northern Areas).

2011: Telephones ('000 main lines in use) 5,721.7; Mobile cellular telephones ('000 subscribers) 108,894.5; Fixed internet subscribers ('000) 2,881.7; Broadband subscribers ('000) 737.8.

Source: partly International Telecommunication Union.

Education

(estimates in '000, 2011/12)

	Institutions	Teachers	Students
Primary*	154.6	435.5	19,571
Middle	42.6	342.6	5,718
Secondary	25.8	463.9	2,725
Higher: arts and science colleges	3.6	85.0	1,291
professional	1.7	45.4	1,015
universities/degree-awarding institutes	0.135†	72.6	1,414

* Including mosque schools.
† 2010/11.

Source: Ministry of Finance, *Economic Survey, 2011/12*.

Pupil-teacher ratio (primary education, UNESCO estimate): 40.5 in 2009/10 (Source: UNESCO Institute for Statistics).

Adult literacy rate (UNESCO estimates): 54.9% (males 68.6%; females 40.3%) in 2009 (Source: UNESCO Institute for Statistics).

Directory

The Government

HEAD OF STATE

President: ASIF ALI ZARDARI (sworn in 9 September 2008).

CABINET
(May 2013)

In mid-March 2013 the Government of Prime Minister Raja Pervaiz Ashraf, led by the Pakistan Peoples Party, completed its term of office. The Election Commission of Pakistan subsequently selected Mir Hazar Khan Khoso, a retired judge, to serve as caretaker Prime Minister. Khan Khoso appointed an interim administration to oversee preparations for a general election. At the election, which took place on 11 May, the Pakistan Muslim League (Nawaz) secured the largest number of seats and was expected to form a government under the leadership of Mohammad Nawaz Sharif.

Prime Minister: MIR HAZAR KHAN KHOSO (acting).

Minister of Commerce and of the Textile Industry: MAQBOOL H. H. RAHIMTOOLA (acting).

Minister of Communications, and of Ports and Shipping: ASADULLAH KHAN MANDOKHEL (acting).

Minister of Housing and Works: Dr YOUNIS SOOMRO (acting).

Minister of Information and Broadcasting, and of Postal Services: ARIF NIZAMI (acting).

Minister of the Interior and of Narcotics Control: MALIK MOHAMMAD HABIB KHAN (acting).

Minister of Inter-Provincial Co-ordination, and of National Food Security and Research: MIR HASSAN DOMKI (acting).

Minister of Human Rights, of Law and Justice, and of Parliamentary Affairs: AHMER BILAL SOOFI (acting).

Minister of National Heritage and Integration, of National Harmony, of National Regulations and Services, and of Religious Affairs: SHAHZADA JAMAL NAZIR (acting).

Minister for Overseas Pakistanis: FEROZE JAMAL SHAH KAKAKHEL (acting).

Minister of Petroleum and Natural Resources: Dr SOHAIL WAJAHAT H. SIDDIQUI (acting).

Minister of Industries and of Production: SHAHZADA ASHAN ASHRAF SHEIKH (acting).

Minister of Railways: Dr ABDUL MALIK KASI (acting).

Minister of Education and Training, of Science and Technology, and of Information Technology: Dr SANIA NISHTAR (acting).

Minister of Water and Power: Dr MUSADIK MALIK (acting).

MINISTRIES

Office of the President: Aiwan-e-Sadr, Islamabad; tel. (51) 9206060; fax (51) 9208046; internet www.presidentofpakistan.gov.pk.

Office of the Prime Minister's Secretariat: Cabinet Secretariat, Cabinet Div., Islamabad; tel. (51) 925190512; e-mail contact@cabinet.gov.pk; internet www.cabinet.gov.pk.

Ministry of Climate Change: G-5/2, Islamabad; tel. (51) 9224174; fax (51) 9224890; e-mail minister@moenv.gov.pk.

Ministry of Commerce: Blk A, Pakistan Secretariat, Islamabad; tel. (51) 9205708; fax (51) 9205241; e-mail mincom@commerce.gov.pk; internet www.commerce.gov.pk.

Ministry of Communications: Islamabad; tel. (51) 9204918; fax (51) 9204917; internet www.communication.gov.pk.

Ministry of Defence: Pakistan Secretariat, No. II, Rawalpindi 46000; tel. (51) 9271107; fax (51) 9271113; e-mail tahir@mod.gov.pk; internet www.mod.gov.pk.

Ministry of Defence Production: Islamabad; internet www.modp.gov.pk.

Ministry of Economic Affairs and Statistics: Islamabad; tel. (51) 9213204; e-mail minister@finance.gov.pk; internet www.ead.gov.pk.

Ministry of Education and Training: Blk C, Pakistan Secretariat, Islamabad; tel. (51) 9213933; fax (51) 9203742; internet moptt.gov.pk.

Ministry of Finance, Revenue and Planning and Development: Blk Q, Pakistan Secretariat, Islamabad; tel. (51) 9202576; fax (51) 9206354; e-mail webmaster@finance.gov.pk; internet www.finance.gov.pk.

Ministry of National Food Security and Research: Islamabad.

Ministry of Foreign Affairs: Constitution Ave, Islamabad; tel. (51) 9210335; fax (51) 9207600; internet www.mofa.gov.pk.

Ministry of Housing and Works: Blk B, Pakistan Secretariat, Islamabad; tel. (51) 9214121; fax (51) 9209125; e-mail minister@housing.gov.pk; internet www.pha.gov.pk.

Ministry of Human Resource Development: 5th & 6th Floors, Blk B, Pakistan Secretariat, Islamabad; tel. (51) 9210077; fax (51) 9201088; internet www.hrd.gov.pk.

Ministry of Human Rights: 3rd Floor, Old USAID Bldg, Attaturk Ave, G-5/1, Islamabad; tel. (51) 9206022; fax (51) 9201631; internet www.mohr.gov.pk.

Ministry of Industries: Blk A, Pakistan Secretariat, Islamabad; tel. (51) 9212164; fax (51) 9205130; e-mail moip@moip.gov.pk; internet www.moip.gov.pk.

Ministry of Information and Broadcasting: Cyber Wing, 4th Floor, Cabinet Blk, Pakistan Secretariat, Islamabad; tel. (51) 9206176; fax (51) 9207629; e-mail webmaster@infopak.gov.pk; internet www.infopak.gov.pk.

Ministry of Information Technology: 4th Floor, Evacuee Trust Bldg, Aga Khan Rd, F-5/1, Islamabad; tel. (51) 9201990; fax (51) 9205233; e-mail minister@moitt.gov.pk; internet www.moitt.gov.pk.

Ministry of the Interior: Blk R, Room 404, Pakistan Secretariat, Islamabad; tel. (51) 9212026; fax (51) 9202624; e-mail ministry.interior@gmail.com; internet www.interior.gov.pk.

Ministry of Inter-Provincial Co-ordination: Cabinet Secretariat, Cabinet Div., Islamabad; tel. (51) 9203248; fax (51) 9207760; internet www.ipc.gov.pk.

Ministry of Kashmir Affairs and Gilgit-Baltistan: Blk R, Pakistan Secretariat, Islamabad; tel. (51) 9208442; fax (51) 9207084; e-mail minister@moka.gov.pk; internet www.kana.gov.pk.

Ministry of Law and Justice: Blk R, Pakistan Secretariat, Islamabad; tel. (51) 9211278; fax (51) 9201722; e-mail contact@molaw.gov.pk; internet www.molaw.gov.pk.

Ministry of Narcotics Control: 30 St 48, F-8/4, Islamabad; tel. (51) 9260207; fax (51) 9260208; e-mail info@narcon.gov.pk; internet www.narcon.gov.pk.

Ministry of National Harmony: Islamabad.

Ministry of National Heritage and Integration: Islamabad.

Ministry of National Regulations and Services: Islamabad.

Ministry of Overseas Pakistanis: Shahrah-e-Jamhuriat, Sector G-5/2, POB 1470, Islamabad; tel. (51) 9203267; fax (51) 9224335; internet www.opf.org.pk.

Ministry of Parliamentary Affairs: Islamabad.

Ministry of Petroleum and Natural Resources: 3rd Floor, Blk A, Pakistan Secretariat, Islamabad; tel. (51) 9210220; fax (51) 9213180; e-mail minister@mpnr.gov.pk; internet www.mpnr.gov.pk.

Ministry of Ports and Shipping: 3rd Floor, Block D, Pakistan Secretariat, Islamabad; tel. (51) 9210322; fax (51) 9215740; e-mail minister@mops.gov.pk; internet www.mops.gov.pk.

Ministry of Postal Services: Islamabad; tel. (51) 9260179; fax (51) 9261570; internet www.pakpost.gov.pk.

Ministry of Privatisation: 5-A, EAC Bldg, Constitution Ave, Islamabad 44000; tel. (51) 9205146; fax (51) 9203076; e-mail info@privatisation.gov.pk; internet www.privatisation.gov.pk.

Ministry of Production: Islamabad; tel. (51) 9103891; fax (51) 9103893; internet www.mop.gov.pk.

Ministry of Professional and Technical Training: Islamabad; internet moptt.gov.pk.

Ministry of Railways: Blk D, Pakistan Secretariat, Islamabad; tel. (51) 9218515; fax (51) 9210247; e-mail minister@railways.gov.pk; internet www.railways.gov.pk.

Ministry of Religious Affairs: 20 Civic Centre, G-6 Markaz, Islamabad; tel. (51) 9214856; fax (51) 9205833; e-mail minister@mora.gov.pk; internet www.mora.gov.pk.

Ministry of Science and Technology: 4th Floor, Evacuee Trust Complex, Aga Khan Rd, F-5/1, Islamabad; tel. (51) 9208026; fax (51) 9204541; e-mail minister@most.gov.pk; internet www.most.gov.pk.

Ministry of States and Frontier Regions: Islamabad; tel. (51) 9211405; fax (51) 9218772; e-mail minister@safron.gov.pk; internet www.safron.gov.pk.

Ministry of Textile Industry: 2nd Floor, FBC Bldg, Attaturk Ave, G-5/2, Islamabad; tel. (51) 9212799; fax (51) 9214015; e-mail minister@textile.gov.pk; internet www.textile.gov.pk.

Ministry of Water and Power: Blk A, 15th Floor, Shaheed-e-Millat, Pakistan Secretariat, Islamabad; tel. (51) 9212442; fax (51) 9224825; e-mail fminister@mowp.gov.pk; internet www.mowp.gov.pk.

Federal Legislature

SENATE

The Eighteenth Amendment Bill, promulgated in April 2010, increased the number of seats in the Senate from 100 to 104. The provincial assemblies were directly to elect 92 members—of whom four were to be non-Muslims, 16 were to be women and a further 16 technocrats (including *ulema*, Muslim legal scholars)—and of the remaining 12 members the Federally Administered Tribal Areas were to return eight members and four were to be elected from the Federal Capital Territory by members of the Provincial Assemblies. The term of office of the Senate is six years, but one-half of its membership is renewed after three years. The most recent election was held on 2 March 2012.

Chairman: NAYYAR ALI BUKHARI.

Deputy Chairman: SABIR BALOCH.

Distribution of Seats, March 2012

	Seats
Pakistan Peoples Party Parliamentarians	41
Pakistan Muslim League (Nawaz)	14
Awami National Party	12
Jamiat-e-Ulema-e-Islam (F)	7
Muttahida Qaumi Movement	7
Pakistan Muslim League	5
Balochistan National Party (Awami)	4
Pakistan Muslim League (Functional)	1
National Party	1
Independents	12
Total	**104**

NATIONAL ASSEMBLY

General Election, 11 May 2013, preliminary results

	Seats
Pakistan Muslim League (Nawaz)	124
Pakistan Peoples Party Parliamentarians	31
Pakistan Tehreek-e-Insaf	27
Muttahida Qaumi Movement	18
Jamiat-e-Ulema-e-Islam (Fazlur)	10
Pakistan Muslim League (Functional)	5
Jamaat-e-Islami Pakistan	3
Pukhtoonkhwa Milli Awami Party	3
Others	12
Independents	28
Undecided	11
Reserved	70
Total	**342**

Provincial Governments
(April 2013)

Pakistan comprises the four provinces of Sindh, Balochistan, Punjab and Khyber Pakhtoonkhwa (the former North-West Frontier Province), plus the federal capital and Federally Administered Tribal Areas.

BALOCHISTAN
(Capital—Quetta)

Governor: Nawab ZULFIQAR ALI MAGSI.

Chief Minister: Nawab GHOUS BAKHSH BAROZAI (acting).

Legislative Assembly: 65 seats (Pakistan Peoples Party Parliamentarians 15, Like Minded Group 13, Jamiat-e-Ulema-e-Islam 10, Balochistan National Party—Awami 7, Pakistan Muslim League—Quaid-e-Azam 6 Awami National Party 3, Jamiat-e-Ulema-e-Islam—Ideological 1, National Party 1, Pakistan Muslim League—Nawaz 1, independents 8.

KHYBER PAKHTOONKHWA
(Capital—Peshawar)

Governor: SHAUKATULLAH KHAN.

Chief Minister: TARIQ PERVAIZ (acting).

Legislative Assembly: 124 seats (Awami National Party 48, Pakistan Peoples Party Parliamentarians 30, Muttahida Majlis-e-Amal 15, Pakistan Muslim League—Nawaz 9, Pakistan Peoples Party—Sherpao 6, Pakistan Muslim League—Quaid-e-Azam 7, independents 9).

PUNJAB
(Capital—Lahore)

Governor: SARDAR MUHAMMAD LATIF KHAN KHOSA.

Chief Minister: NAJAM SETHI (acting).

Legislative Assembly: 371 seats (Pakistan Muslim League—Nawaz 171, Pakistan Peoples Party Parliamentarians 106, Pakistan Muslim League—Quaid-e-Azam 81, Pakistan Muslim League—Functional 3, Muttahida Majlis-e-Amal 2, Pakistan Muslim League—Zia 1, independents 6, vacant or withheld 1).

SINDH
(Capital—Karachi)

Governor: ISHRATUL IBAD KHAN.

Chief Minister: ZAHID KURBAN ALAVI (acting).

Legislative Assembly: 168 seats (Pakistan Peoples Party Parliamentarians 93, Muttahida Qaumi Movement 51, Pakistan Muslim League—Quaid-e-Azam 11, Pakistan Muslim League—Functional 8, National People's Party 3, Awami National Party 2).

Election Commission

Election Commission of Pakistan: Secretariat, Election House, Constitution Ave, G-5/2, Islamabad; tel. (51) 9206939; fax (51) 9205402; e-mail info@ecp.gov.pk; internet www.ecp.gov.pk; independent; Chief Election Commr Justice FAKHRUDDIN G. IBRAHIM.

Political Organizations

In April 2013 there were more than 160 political parties registered with the Election Commission of Pakistan, including the following:

All Jammu and Kashmir Muslim Conference: f. 1948; advocates the holding of a free plebiscite in the whole of Kashmir; Leader Sardar ATTIQ AHMED KHAN.

Awami Muslim League (AML): Lal Haveli, Rawalpindi; tel. (51) 5554242; fax (51) 5772708; e-mail info@aml.org.pk; internet www.aml.org.pk; f. 2008; Pres. SHEIKH RASHID AHMED.

Awami National Party (ANP) (People's National Party): Bacha Khan Markaz, Pajagai Rd, POB 306, Peshawar; tel. (91) 2246851; fax (91) 2252406; e-mail info@anp.org.pk; internet www.anp.org.pk; f. 1986 by the merger of the National Democratic Party, the Awami Tehrik (People's Movement) and the Mazdoor Kissan (Labourers' and Peasants' Party); federalist and nationalist; the Pakhtoonkhawa Qaumi Party merged with the ANP in February 2006, followed by the National Awami Party Pakistan in June of the same year; Pres. ASFANDYAR WALI KHAN.

Awami Qiyadat Party (People's Leadership Party): 1 Nat. Park Rd, Rawalpindi Cantt; f. 1995; Chair. Gen. (retd) MIRZA ASLAM BEG.

Balochistan National Party—Awami (BNP—A): Istaqlal Bldg, Quarry Rd, Quetta; Leader SYED EHSAN SHAH; Pres. Sardar AKHTER JAN MANGAL.

Balochistan National Party—Maingal (BNP—M): Quetta; e-mail bnpwebadmin@balochistan.net; Leader Sardar MOHAMMAD AKHTAR MAINGAL.

Jamaat-e-Islami Pakistan (JIP): Mansoorah, Multan Rd, Lahore 54570; tel. (42) 37844605; fax (42) 37832194; e-mail info@jamaat.org; internet www.jamaat.org; f. 1941; seeks the establishment of Islamic order through adherence to teaching of Maulana MAUDUDI, founder of the party; revivalist; right-wing; Chair. Amir S. MUNAWAR HASSAN; c. 5m. mems (2005).

Jamhoori Watan Party (Bugti) Balochistan: Bugti House, Dera Bugti, Quetta; tel. (81) 32827743; fax (81) 32845559; Pres. Nawab TALAL AKBAR KHAN BUGTI.

Jamiat-e-Ulema-e-Islam (JUI): Jamia al-Maarf, al-Sharia, Dera Ismail Khan; f. 1950; mem. Muttahida Majlis-e-Amal alliance; advocates adoption of a constitution in accordance with (Sunni) Islamic teachings; split into factions led by Maulana Fazlur Rehman (JUI—F; Sec.-Gen. Maulana Abdul Ghafoor Haideri) and Sami ul-Haq (JUI—S).

Jamiat-e-Ulema-e-Pakistan (JUP): Burns Rd, Karachi; f. 1948; mem. Muttahida Majlis-e-Amal alliance; advocates progressive (Sunni) Islamic principles and enforcement of Islamic laws in Pakistan; Pres. Dr ABUL KHAIR MOHAMMAD ZUBAIR (acting); Gen. Sec. QARI ZAWWAR BAHADUR.

Muttahida Qaumi Movement (MQM): 494/8 Azizabad, Federal Area B, Karachi; tel. (21) 36313690; fax (21) 36329955; e-mail mqm@mqm.org; internet www.mqm.org; f. 1984 as Mohajir Qaumi Movement; name changed as above in 1997; associated with the All Pakistan Muttahida Students' Organization (f. 1978 as the All Pakistan Mohajir Students' Organization; name changed July 2006); represents the interests of Muslim, Urdu-speaking immigrants (from India) in Pakistan; seeks the designation of Mohajir as fifth nationality (after Sindhi, Punjabi, Pathan and Balochi); aims to abolish the prevailing feudal political system and to establish democracy; Founder and Leader ALTAF HUSSAIN; Pres. AFTAB SHEIKH.

National Party: Firdosi Bldg, 4th Floor, Rustam G Line, Jinnah Rd, Quetta; f. 2003 following merger of Balochistan National Movement and Balochistan National Democratic Party; Chair. Dr ABDUL HAYEE BALOCH.

National People's Party (NPP): 18 Khayaban-e-Shamsheer, Defence Housing Authority, Phase V, Karachi; tel. (21) 35854522; fax (21) 35853500; f. 1986; centre left-wing party advocating a just, democratic welfare state for Pakistan; breakaway faction from PPP; Chair. GHULAM MUSTAFA JATOI; Parl. Leader ARIF MUSTAFA JATOI.

Pakhtoonkhwa Milli Awami Party: Central Secretariat, Jinnah Rd, Quetta; Leader MEHMOOD KHAN ACHAKZAI.

Pakistan Awami Tehreek (PAT): 365M Model Town, Lahore; fax (42) 35169114; e-mail info@pat.com.pk; internet www.pat.com.pk; Pres. MUHAMMAD TAHIR UL-QADRI; Sec.-Gen. Dr ANWAAR AKHTAR.

Pakistan Muslim League (PML): PML House, F-7/3, Islamabad; tel. (51) 9102669; fax (51) 2611061; e-mail mushahid.hussain@gmail.com; internet www.pml.org.pk; f. 2002 following merger of PML Quaid-i-Azam Group, PML (Junejo), PML (Functional), PML (Zia-ul-Haq Shaheed), PML (Jinnah) and the Sindh Democratic Alliance; PML (Functional) subsequently split from party; commonly known as PML (Q) within Pakistan; Pres. CHAUDHRY SHUJAAT HUSSAIN; Sec.-Gen. Sen. MUSHAHID HUSSAIN SYED.

Pakistan Muslim League—Functional (PML—F): Islamabad; merged with PML Quaid-e-Azam Group, PML (Junejo), PML (Zia-ul-Haq Shaheed), PML (Jinnah) and the Sindh Democratic Alliance in 2004 but subsequently split from party; Leader PIR PAGARA.

Pakistan Muslim League—Nawaz (PML—N): 20-H, St 10, F-8/3, Islamabad; tel. and fax (51) 2852662; e-mail pmlisb@hotmail.com; internet www.pmln.org.pk; f. 1993 as faction of Pakistan Muslim League (Junejo); Pres. MIAN NAWAZ SHARIF; Chair. RAJA ZAFARUL HAQ; Gen. Sec. IQBAL ZAFAR JHAGRA.

Pakistan Peoples Party (PPP): 8, St 19, F-8/2, Islamabad; tel. (51) 2255264; fax (51) 2282741; e-mail ppp@comsats.net.pk; internet www.ppp.org.pk; formed Pakistan Peoples Party Parliamentarians (PPPP) 2002 in order to meet electoral requirements; advocates Islamic socialism, democracy and a non-aligned foreign policy; Leaders BILAWAL BHUTTO ZARDARI, ASIF ALI ZARDARI.

Pakistan Peoples Party (Shaheed Bhutto Group): 70 Clifton, Karachi; tel. (21) 35865370; fax (21) 35861224; e-mail pppsb@pppsb.net; internet www.pppsb.net; f. 1995 as a breakaway faction of the PPP; Chair. GHINWA BHUTTO; Sec.-Gen. Dr GHULAM HUSSAIN.

Pakistan Tehreek-e-Insaf (PTI) (Pakistan Movement for Justice): 2, St 84, Sector G-6/4, Islamabad; tel. (51) 2270744; fax (51) 2873893; e-mail info@insaf.org.pk; internet www.insaf.org.pk; f. 1996; Pakistan Democratic Party merged into Tehreek-e-Insaf in March 2012; Chair. IMRAN KHAN; Pres. JAVED HASHMI; Sec.-Gen. ARIF ALVI.

Punjabi Pakhtoon Ittehad (PPI): f. 1987 to represent the interests of Punjabis and Pakhtoons in Karachi; Pres. MALIK MIR HAZAR KHAN.

Sindh National Front (SNF): Pres. MUMTAZ BHUTTO.

Sindh Taraqi Passand Party (STPP): Leader Dr QADIR MAGSI.

Diplomatic Representation

EMBASSIES AND HIGH COMMISSIONS IN PAKISTAN

Afghanistan: 8, St 90, G-6/3, Islamabad 44000; tel. (51) 2824505; fax (51) 2824504; e-mail contact@islamabad.mfa.gov.af; internet islamabad.mfa.gov.af; Ambassador MUHAMMAD DAUDZAI.

Algeria: 107, St 9, E-7, POB 1038, Islamabad; tel. (51) 2653773; fax (51) 2653795; internet algerianembpk.com; Ambassador Dr AHMED BENFLIS.

Argentina: 60, St 1, F-6/3, POB 1015, Islamabad; tel. (51) 8438120; fax (51) 2825564; e-mail epaki@mrecic.gov.ar; internet www.pakistan.embajada-argentina.gov.ar; Ambassador RODOLFO MARTIN-SARAVIA.

Australia: Diplomatic Enclave 1, Constitution Ave and Isphani Rd, G-5/4, POB 1046, Islamabad; tel. (51) 8355500; fax (51) 2820112; e-mail consular.islm@dfat.gov.au; internet www.pakistan.embassy.gov.au; High Commissioner PETER HEYWARD.

Austria: 13, St 1, F-6/3, POB 1018, Islamabad 44000; tel. (51) 2209710; fax (51) 2828366; e-mail islamabad-ob@bmeia.gv.at; Ambassador AXEL WECH.

Azerbaijan: Plot 1D and 1E, Diplomatic Enclave II, Islamabad; tel. (51) 2600704; fax (51) 2600720; internet azembassy-pakistan.com; Ambassador DASHGIN SHIKAROV.

Bahrain: 5, St 83, G-6/4, Islamabad; tel. (51) 2831115; fax (51) 2831060; internet www.mofa.gov.bh/islamabad; Ambassador MUHAMMAD EBRAHIM MUHAMMAD ABD AL-QADIR.

Bangladesh: 1, St 5, F-6/3, Islamabad; tel. (51) 2279267; fax (51) 2279266; e-mail bdhcisb@yahoo.com; internet www.bdhcpk.org; High Commissioner SUHRAB HOSSAIN.

Belgium: 24, St 4, F-6/3, Islamabad; tel. (51) 2822293; fax (51) 2820972; e-mail islamabad@diplobel.fed.be; internet www.diplomatie.be/islamabad; Ambassador PETER CLAES.

Bosnia and Herzegovina: 195A, St 10, E-7, Islamabad 44000; tel. (51) 2654018; fax (51) 2654017; e-mail info@bembassy.org; internet www.bembassy.org; Ambassador ARMIN LIMO.

Brazil: 1, St 72, Sector F-8/3, Islamabad; tel. (51) 2287189; fax (51) 2287199; e-mail brasemb@isb.compol.com; internet islamabade.itamaraty.gov.br; Ambassador ALFREDO CESAR MARTINHO LEONI.

Brunei: 5, St 6, F-6/3, Islamabad; tel. (51) 2879636; fax (51) 2823688; e-mail islamabad.pakistan@mfa.gov.bn; High Commissioner Pehin Dato' Haji Panglima Col (retd) Haji ABDUL JALIL BIN Haji AHMAD.

Bulgaria: Plot 6/11, Diplomatic Enclave, Ramna 5, POB 1483, Islamabad; tel. (51) 2279196; fax (51) 2279195; e-mail embassy.islamabad@mfa.bg; internet www.mfa.bg/embassies/pakistan; Ambassador ROUMEN PIRONCTHEV.

Canada: Diplomatic Enclave, Sector G-5, POB 1042, Islamabad; tel. (51) 2086000; fax (51) 2086900; e-mail isbad@international.gc.ca; internet www.international.gc.ca/missions/pakistan; High Commissioner GREG GIOKAS.

China, People's Republic: Diplomatic Enclave, Ramna 4, Islamabad; tel. (51) 8355059; fax (51) 2872660; e-mail chinaemb_pk@mfa.gov.cn; internet pk.china-embassy.org; Ambassador LIU JIAN.

Cuba: 37 School Rd, Sector F-6/2, Islamabad; tel. (51) 2824078; fax (51) 8357339; e-mail eocuba2@nayatel.pk; internet www.cubadiplomatica.cu/pakistan; Ambassador JESÚS ZENÉN BUERGO CONCEPCIÓN.

Czech Republic: 49, St 27, Sector F-6/2, POB 1335, Islamabad; tel. (51) 2274304; fax (51) 2825327; e-mail islamabad@embassy.mzv.cz; internet www.mzv.cz/islamabad; Ambassador MIROSLAV KRENEK.

Denmark: 16, St 21, F-6/2, POB 1118, Islamabad; tel. (51) 2099800; fax (51) 2823483; e-mail isbamb@um.dk; internet pakistan.um.dk; Ambassador OLE MOESBY.

Egypt: Plot 38–51, UN Blvd, Diplomatic Enclave, Ramna 5/4, POB 2088, Islamabad; tel. (51) 2209072; fax (51) 2279552; internet www.mfa.gov.eg/Islamabad_Emb; Ambassador MOHAMED EL-SAID HINDAM.

Eritrea: 28, St 33, F-8/1, Islamabad; tel. (51) 2816131; fax (51) 2816133; e-mail eritrea@comsats.net.pk; Ambassador (vacant).

France: G-5, Diplomatic Enclave, POB 1068, Islamabad; tel. (51) 2011414; fax (51) 2011400; e-mail ambafrance.islamabad@diplomatie.gouv.fr; internet www.ambafra-pk.org; Ambassador PHILIPPE THIEBAUD.

Germany: Diplomatic Enclave, Ramna 5, POB 1027, Islamabad 44000; tel. (51) 2279430; fax (51) 2279436; internet www.islamabad.diplo.de; Ambassador Dr CYRIL NUNN.

Greece: 33A School Rd, Sector F-6/2, Islamabad; tel. (51) 2825186; fax (51) 8358985; e-mail gremb.isl@mfa.gr; internet www.mfa.gr/islamabad; Ambassador PETROS MAVROIDIS.

Holy See: Apostolic Nunciature, St 5, G-5, Diplomatic Enclave 1, POB 1106, Islamabad 44000; tel. (51) 2278218; fax (51) 2820847; e-mail vatipak@isb.comsatas.net.pk; Apostolic Nuncio Most Rev. EDGAR PEÑA PARRA.

Hungary: 12 Margalla Rd, F-6/3, POB 1103, Islamabad; tel. (51) 2823352; fax (51) 2825256; e-mail mission.isl@kum.hu; internet www.mfa.gov.hu/emb/islamabad; Ambassador ISTVAN SZABÓ.

India: G-5, Diplomatic Enclave, Islamabad; tel. (51) 2206950; fax (51) 2823102; e-mail info2.islamabad@mea.gov.in; internet www.india.org.pk; High Commissioner SHARAT SABHARWAL.

Indonesia: St 5, G-5/4, Diplomatic Enclave, POB 1019, Islamabad; tel. (51) 2832017; fax (51) 2832013; e-mail unitkom@kbri-islamabad.go.id; internet www.indonesianembassy-isb.pk; Ambassador BURHAN MUHAMMAD.

Iran: Plot No. 222–238, St 2, F-5/1, Islamabad; tel. (51) 8318901; fax (51) 8318906; e-mail info@iranembassy.pk; internet www.iranembassy.pk; Ambassador ALIREZA HAGHIGHIAN.

Iraq: 57, St 48, F-8/4, Islamabad; tel. (51) 2253734; fax (51) 2253688; e-mail iraqembpk@yahoo.com; Ambassador Dr RUSHDI MAHMOOD AL-ANI.

Italy: St 17, Diplomatic Enclave, G–5, POB 1008, Islamabad; tel. (51) 2833183; fax (51) 2833179; e-mail segreteria.ambislamabad@esteri.it; internet www.ambislamabad.esteri.it; Ambassador ADRIANO CHIODI CIANFARANI.

Japan: Plot 53–70, Diplomatic Enclave 1, Ramna 5/4, POB 1119, Islamabad 44000; tel. (51) 9072500; fax (51) 9072352; e-mail japanemb@comsats.net.pk; internet www.pk.emb-japan.go.jp; Ambassador HIROSHI OE.

Jordan: 99 Main Double Rd, F-10/1, Islamabad; tel. (51) 2279124; fax (51) 2279130; e-mail islamabad@fm.gov.jo; Ambassador NAWAF SARAIREH.

Kazakhstan: 11, St 45, F-8/1, Islamabad 44000; tel. (51) 2262926; fax (51) 2262806; e-mail islamabad@mfa.kz; internet www.kazembpakistan.com; Ambassador BAKHITBEK SHABARBAYEV.

Kenya: Plot 1–3, St 27, Ramna 5, Diplomatic Enclave, Islamabad; tel. (51)2601504; fax (51) 2601507; e-mail info@kenyahighcommission.com.pk; High Commissioner MISHI MASIKA MWATSAHU.

Korea, Democratic People's Republic: 9, St 18, F-8/2, Islamabad; tel. (51) 2252756; fax (51) 2252754; Ambassador RO KYONG CHOL.

Korea, Republic: Blk 13, St 29, G-5/4, Diplomatic Enclave 2, POB 1087, Islamabad; tel. (51) 2279380; fax (51) 2279391; e-mail pakistan@mofat.go.kr; internet koreanembassy-pakistan.org; Ambassador CHOI CHOONG-JOO.

Kuwait: Plot 1, 2 and 24, Diplomatic Enclave 2, Islamabad; tel. (51) 2279413; fax (51) 2279411; Ambassador NAWAF AL-ENEZI.

Kyrgyzstan: 163, St 36, F-10/1, Islamabad; tel. (51) 2212196; fax (51) 2212169; e-mail kyrgyzembassy@dsl.net.pk; internet www.kyrgyzembassy.com.pk; Ambassador ALIK K. OROZOV.

Lebanon: 6, St 27, F-6/2, Islamabad; tel. (51) 2278338; fax (51) 2826410; e-mail lebemb@comsats.net.pk; Ambassador WAFIC MUHAMMAD REHAIME.

Libya: 736 Margalla Rd, F-10/2, Islamabad; tel. (51) 2214348; fax (51) 2290093; Ambassador IBRAHIM AL-ABID MUKHTAR.

Malaysia: 34, St 56, F-7/4, Islamabad; tel. (51) 2656092; fax (51) 2656012; e-mail malislamb@kln.gov.my; internet www.kln.gov.my/perwakilan/islamabad; High Commissioner Dr HASRUL SANI BIN MUJTABAR.

Maldives: 27A, St 2, F-8/3, Islamabad; tel. (51) 2286903; fax (51) 2286904; e-mail admin@maldiveshighcom.pk; internet www.maldiveshighcom.pk; High Commissioner Dr AISHATH SHEHENAZ ADAM.

Mauritius: 13, St 26, F-6/2, POB 1084, Islamabad; tel. (51) 2824658; fax (51) 2824656; e-mail mauripak@dsl.net.pk; High Commissioner MOHAMMAD RASHAD DAUREEAWO.

Morocco: 6 Gomal Rd, E-7, POB 1179, Islamabad; tel. (51) 2654744; fax (51) 2654741; e-mail sifamapak@morocco-embassy.com.pk; Ambassador MUSTAPHA SALAHDDINNE.

Myanmar: 273, St 6, F-10/3, Islamabad; tel. (51) 2114148; fax (51) 2114149; e-mail embassy_myanmar@yahoo.com; Ambassador SAN MYINT OO.

Nepal: 11A, St 13, F-7/2, Islamabad; tel. (51) 2655182; fax (51) 2655184; e-mail info@nepalembassy.pk; internet www.nepalembassy.pk; Ambassador BHARAT RAJ PAUDYAL.

Netherlands: Plot 167, St 15, Sector G-5, Diplomatic Enclave, POB 1065, Islamabad; tel. (51) 2004444; fax (51) 2004333; e-mail isl@minbuza.nl; internet pakistan.nlembassy.org; Ambassador HUGO GAJUS SCHELTEMA.

Nigeria: 132–135 Isphani Rd, G-5/4, Diplomatic Enclave 1, POB 1075, Islamabad; tel. (51) 2823542; fax (51) 2824104; e-mail nigeria@isb.comsats.net.pk; High Commissioner DAUDA DANLADI.

Norway: 25, St 19, Sector F-6/2, POB 1336, Islamabad; tel. (51) 2077700; fax (51) 2279726; e-mail emb.islamabad@mfa.no; internet www.norway.org.pk; Ambassador CECILIE LANDSVERK.

Oman: 53, St 48, F-8/4, POB 1194, Islamabad; tel. (51) 2254955; fax (51) 2255074; Ambassador RIYADH BIN YOUSUF AL-RA'EESI.

Philippines: 7A Koshar Rd, F-7/2, Islamabad; tel. (51) 2653661; fax (51) 2653665; e-mail isdpe@isb.comsats.net.pk; internet www.isdpe.com.pk; Ambassador DOMINGO LUCENARIO.

Poland: St 24, G-5/4, Diplomatic Enclave 2, POB 1032, Islamabad; tel. (51) 2600844; fax (51) 2600852; e-mail islamabad.amb.sekretariat@msz.gov.pl; internet islamabad.msz.gov.pl; Ambassador Dr ANDRZEJ ANANICZ.

Portugal: 66, Main Margalla Rd, F-7/2, Islamabad; tel. (51) 2652491; fax (51) 2652492; e-mail portugal@dsl.net.pk; Ambassador Dr ANTONIO JOSÉ M. SANTOS BRAGA.

Qatar: 20 University Rd, Diplomatic Enclave, G-5/4, Islamabad; tel. (51) 2270768; fax (51) 2600957; e-mail islamabad@mofa.gov.qa; Ambassador SAYYAR BIN ABDUL REHMAN AL-MAWADA.

Romania: 13, St 88, Ramna G-6/3, Islamabad; tel. (51) 2826514; fax (51) 2826515; e-mail amb.rom.isb@gmail.com; internet www.islamabad.mae.ro; Ambassador EMILIAN ION.

Russia: Khayaban-e-Suhrawardy, Diplomatic Enclave, Ramna 4, Islamabad; tel. (51) 2600812; fax (51) 2600814; e-mail rusemb.pak@gmail.com; internet www.pakistan.mid.ru; Ambassador BUDNIK ANDREY.

Saudi Arabia: 14 North Service Rd, Diplomatic Enclave, G-4, Islamabad; tel. (51) 2600900; fax (51) 2278816; e-mail pkemb@mofa.gov.sa; internet embassies.mofa.gov.sa/sites/pakistan/AR/Pages/default.aspx; Ambassador ABDUL AZIZ AL-GHADEER.

Somalia: 17, St 60, F-8/4, Islamabad; tel. and fax (51) 2854733; tel. (51) 2826117; e-mail webmaster@somaligov.net; internet www.pakistan.somaligov.net; Ambassador ABDISALAM Haji AHMED LIBAN.

South Africa: 48 Main Margalla Rd, Khayaban-e-Iqbal, F-8/2, Islamabad; tel. (51) 2262354; fax (51) 2250114; e-mail xhosa@isb.comsats.net.pk; High Commissioner MPENDULO KUMALO.

Spain: St 6, G-5, Diplomatic Enclave 1, POB 1144, Islamabad; tel. (51) 2088777; fax (51) 2088774; e-mail embspain@dsl.net.pk; Ambassador JAVIER M. CARBAJOSA SANCHEZ.

Sri Lanka: 2C,St 55, F-6/4, POB 1497, Islamabad; tel. (51) 2828723; fax (51) 2828751; e-mail srilanka@dsl.net.pk; internet www.slhcpakistan.org; High Commissioner Air Chief Marshal (retd) JAYALATH WEERAKKODY.

Sudan: 1A, St 32, F-8/1, Islamabad; tel. (51) 2263926; fax (51) 2264404; e-mail sudanipk@isb.compol.com; Ambassador AL-SHAFIA AHAMMAD MOHAMMAD.

Sweden: 4, St 5, Sector F-6/3, POB 1100, Islamabad; tel. (51) 2072600; fax (51) 2825284; e-mail ambassaden.islamabad@gov.se; internet www.swedenabroad.com/en-GB/Embassies/Islamabad/; Ambassador LARS HJALMAR WIDE.

Switzerland: St 6, G-5/4, Diplomatic Enclave, POB 1073, Islamabad 44000; tel. (51) 2279291; fax (51) 2279286; e-mail isl.vertretung@eda.admin.ch; internet www.eda.admin.ch/islamabad; Ambassador CHRISTOPH BUBB.

Syria: 30 Hill Rd, F-6/3, Islamabad; tel. (51) 2279470; fax (51) 2279472; e-mail syremb@comsats.net.pk; Ambassador ALI AL-MOHRA.

Tajikistan: 295, St 35, F-11/3, Islamabad 44000; tel. (51) 2293462; fax (51) 2299710; e-mail tajemb_islamabad@mail.ru; internet www.tajikembassy.pk; Ambassador SHERALI JONONOV.

Thailand: Plot 1–20, Diplomatic Enclave 1, Sector G-5/4, Islamabad; tel. (51) 8431270; fax (51) 8431288; e-mail royalthaiembassyislamabad@gmail.com; internet www.thaiembassy.org/islamabad; Ambassador MARWIN TAN-ATTANAWIN.

Tunisia: 221, St 21, E-7, Islamabad; tel. (51) 2652387; fax (51) 2653564; e-mail atisl@comsats.net.pk; internet /www.atunisia-pk.org; Ambassador MOURAD BOUREHLA.

Turkey: St 1, Diplomatic Enclave, Islamabad; tel. (51) 8319810; fax (51) 2278752; e-mail consulate.islamabad@mfa.gov.tr; internet islamabad.emb.mfa.gov.tr; Ambassador MUSTAFA BABUR HEZLAN.

Turkmenistan: 22A Nazim-Ud-Din Rd, F-7/1, Islamabad; tel. (51) 2611817; fax (51) 2611816; e-mail turkmen@trkmn.org; internet www.trkmn.org; Ambassador ATADJAN MOVLAMOV.

Ukraine: 4, St 5, Sector F-7/3, Islamabad; tel. (51) 2608966; fax (51) 2608967; e-mail emb_pk@mfa.gov.ua; internet www.mfa.gov.ua/pakistan; Ambassador VOLODYMYR LAKOMOV.

United Arab Emirates: Plot No. 1-22, Quaid-e-Azam University Rd, G-5, Diplomatic Enclave, POB 1111, Islamabad; tel. (51) 2099999; fax (51) 2279063; e-mail islamabad@mofa.gov.ae; internet uae-embassy.ae/Embassies/pk; Ambassador ESSA ABDULLAH AL-NOAIMI.

United Kingdom: Diplomatic Enclave, Ramna 5, POB 1122, Islamabad; tel. (51) 2012000; fax (51) 2012043; e-mail Islamabad-general.enquiries@fco.gov.uk; internet ukinpakistan.fco.gov.uk; High Commissioner ADAM THOMSON.

USA: Diplomatic Enclave, Ramna 5, POB 1048, Islamabad; tel. (51) 2080000; fax (51) 2276427; e-mail infoisb@state.gov; internet islamabad.usembassy.gov; Ambassador RICHARD OLSON.

Uzbekistan: 2, St 2, F-8/3, Islamabad; tel. (51) 2264746; fax (51) 2261739; e-mail Pakistan@tiv.uz; internet www.uzbekembassypakistan.org; Ambassador PARVIZ M. ALIEV.

Viet Nam: 117, St 11, Sector E-7, Islamabad; tel. (51) 2655785; fax (51) 2655783; e-mail vnemb.pakistan@yahoo.com; internet www.vietnamembassy-pakistan.org; Ambassador NGUYEN VIET HUNG.

Yemen: 90 Main Double Rd, F-10/2, Islamabad; tel. (51) 2102448; fax (51) 2102417; e-mail yemen22@isb.apollo.net.pk; Ambassador ABDO ALI ABDUL RAHMAN.

Judicial System

SUPREME COURT

The Supreme Court, consisting of the Chief Justice and 16 other judges, exercises original jurisdiction in case of inter-governmental disputes and, along with the High Courts, has original jurisdiction in matters associated with the enforcement of fundamental rights. The Supreme Court has appellate jurisdiction in civil and criminal matters, and has advisory jurisdiction with regard to assisting the Government on legal issues.

Supreme Court: Constitution Ave, Islamabad; tel. (51) 9220581; fax (51) 9213452; e-mail mail@supremecourt.gov.pk; internet www.supremecourt.gov.pk.

Chief Justice: IFTIKHAR MUHAMMAD CHAUDHRY.

Attorney-General: IRFAN QADIR.

FEDERAL SHARIAT COURT

The Federal Shariat Court consists of eight Muslim judges including the Chief Justice, all of whom are appointed through a Judicial Commission headed by the Chief Justice of Pakistan. The Court examines and determines whether the provisions of law are in accordance with the injunctions of Islam.

Federal Shariat Court: G-5/2, Constitution Ave, Islamabad; tel. (51) 9208679; e-mail registrar@federalshariatcourt.gov.pk; internet www.federalshariatcourt.gov.pk.

Chief Justice: AGHA RAFIQ AHMED KHAN.

HIGH COURTS

There is a High Court in each of the four provinces and one in the federal capital, Islamabad. The Courts exercise original jurisdiction in the enforcement of fundamental rights and appellate jurisdiction on judgments of the subordinate courts in civil and criminal matters.

Balochistan High Court: Hali Rd, Quetta, Balochistan; tel. (81) 9203277; fax (81) 9202784; e-mail bhc@bhc.gov.pk; internet bhc.gov.pk; Chief Justice FAEZ ISA.

Islamabad High Court: internet www.ihc.gov.pk; Chief Justice MUHAMMAD ANWAR KHAN KASI.

Lahore High Court: Shahra-e-Quaid-e-Azam, Lahore; tel. (42) 99212951; internet www.lhc.gov.pk; Chief Justice UMAR ATA BANDIAL.

Peshawar High Court: Khyber Rd, Peshawar; tel. (91) 9210149; fax (91) 9210170; e-mail info@peshawarhighcourt.gov.pk; internet www.peshawarhighcourt.gov.pk; Chief Justice DOST MUHAMMAD KHAN.

Sindh High Court: Nr Passport Office, Saddar and Sindh Secretariat, Karachi; tel. (21) 99203151; fax (21) 99203221; e-mail info@sindhhighcourt.gov.pk; internet www.sindhhighcourt.gov.pk; Chief Justice MUSHIR ALAM.

Religion

ISLAM

Islam is the state religion. The majority of the population are Sunni Muslims, while estimates of the Shi'a sect vary between 5% and 20% of the population. Only about 0.001% are of the Ahmadi sect.

CHRISTIANITY

About 3% of the population are Christians.

National Council of Churches in Pakistan: 32-B, Shahrah-e-Fatima Jinnah, POB 357, Lahore 54000; tel. (42) 37592167; fax (42) 37569782; e-mail nccp@lhr.comsats.net.pk; internet nccpakistan .org.pk; f. 1949; four mem. bodies, 14 assoc. mems; Gen. Sec. VICTOR AZARIAH.

The Roman Catholic Church

For ecclesiastical purposes, Pakistan comprises two archdioceses, four dioceses and one apostolic prefecture. At 31 December 2007 there were an estimated 1,139,333 adherents in the country.

Bishops' Conference: Pakistan Catholic Bishops' Conference, St 55, F-8/4, Kaghan Rd, Islamabad 44000; e-mail cbcp2000@isb .comsats.net.pk; internet www.pcbcsite.org; f. 1976; Pres. Most Rev. LAWRENCE J. SALDANHA (Archbishop of Lahore, retd); Sec.-Gen. Rt Rev. ANTHONY LOBO (Bishop of Islamabad-Rawalpindi).

Archbishop of Karachi: Most Rev. EVARIST PINTO, St Patrick's Cathedral, Shahrah-e-Iraq, Karachi 74400; tel. (21) 37781533; fax (21) 37781532.

Archbishop of Lahore: (vacant), Sacred Heart Cathedral, 1 Mian Mohammad Shafi Rd, POB 909, Lahore 54000; tel. (42) 6366137; fax (42) 6368336; e-mail info@archdioceselahore.org; internet www .archdioceselahore.org.

Protestant Churches

Church of Pakistan: Moderator Rt Rev. Dr ALEXANDER JOHN MALIK (Bishop of Lahore), Bishopsbourne, Cathedral Close, The Mall, Lahore 54000; tel. (42) 7233560; fax (42) 7221270; e-mail bishop_lahore@hotmail.com; f. 1970 by union of the fmr Anglican Church in Pakistan, the United Methodist Church in Pakistan, the United Church in Pakistan (Scots Presbyterians) and the Pakistani Lutheran Church; eight dioceses; c. 700,000 mems (1993); Gen. Sec. HUMPHREY PETERS.

Presbyterian Church of Pakistan: Gujranwala Theological Seminary, Civil Lines, POB 13, Gujranwala; tel. (431) 259512; fax (431) 258314; e-mail kamil65@gjr.paknet.com.pk; f. 1961; c. 340,000 mems (1989); Moderator Rev. Dr ARTHUR JAMES; Sec. Rev. Dr MAGSOOD KAMIL.

Other denominations active in the country include the Associated Reformed Presbyterian Church and the Pakistan Salvation Army.

HINDUISM

Hindus comprise about 1.8% of the population.

BAHÁ'Í FAITH

National Spiritual Assembly: 56, H-8/4, Islamabad; tel. (51) 4444699; fax (51) 4444691; e-mail nsapakistan@cyber.net.pk; internet www.bahai.org; f. 1956; Gen. Sec. Prof. MEHRDAD YOSUF.

The Press

The Urdu press comprises almost 800 newspapers, with the *Daily Jang, Daily Khabrain, Nawa-i-Waqt, Daily Express* and *Jasarat* among the most influential. The daily newspaper with the largest circulation is the *Daily Jang*. Although the English-language press reaches only a small percentage of the population, it is influential in political, academic and professional circles. The four main press groups in Pakistan are Jang Publications (the *Daily Jang, The News*, the *Daily News* and the weekly *Akhbar-e-Jehan*), the Dawn or Herald Group (the *Dawn*, and the monthly *Herald* and *Spider*), the Khabrain Group (the *Daily Khabrain*) and the Nawa-i-Waqt Group (the *Nawa-i-Waqt, The Nation*, the *Daily Express* and the weekly *Family*).

PRINCIPAL DAILIES

Islamabad

Al-Akhbar: 25, Shameem Akbar Tower-i, Lilly Market, Blk G, Srialimar Rd, Swan Garden, Islamabad; tel. (51) 5738551; fax (51) 5738554; e-mail alakabar@dsl.net.pk; internet www.alakhbar.com .pk; f. 1994; Urdu; also publ. in Peshawar and Lahore; Chief Editor GHULAM AKBAR; Editor MANZOOR SADIQ.

Daily Awam: Flat No. 2, Blk 15, PHA Apartments, G-7/1 Zero Point, Islamabad 44000; tel. (51) 2890427; fax (51) 2890437; e-mail awam@ awam.com.pk; internet www.dailyawam.net; evening; Urdu; also publ. in Quetta and Hub; Editor-in-Chief WASEEM AHMED.

The Nation: Nawa-i-Waqt House, Zero Point, Islamabad; tel. (51) 2202641; fax (51) 2202645; e-mail editor@nation.com.pk; internet www.nation.com.pk; English; Man. Dir and Editor-in-Chief MAJID NIZAMI; circ. 15,000.

National Herald Tribune: Islamabad; internet www.dailynht .com; f. 2005; English; Editor-in-Chief GHULAM AKBAR.

Pakistan Observer: Al-Akbar House, Markaz G-8, Islamabad 44870; tel. (51) 2852027; fax (51) 2262258; e-mail observer@ pakobserver.net; internet www.pakobserver.net; f. 1988; English; independent; Editor-in-Chief ZAHID MALIK.

Karachi

Aghaz: 11 Japan Mansion, Preedy St, Sadar, Karachi 74400; tel. (21) 32720228; fax (21) 32722125; e-mail ex101@hotmail.com; f. 1962; evening; Urdu; Chief Editor MOHAMMAD ANWAR FAROOQI.

Amn: Deen Muhammad Wafai Rd, opposite NED City Campus, Karachi; tel. (21) 32634451; fax (21) 32634454; e-mail info@dailyamn .net; internet dailyamn.net; f. 1972; Urdu; Editor AJMAL DEHLVI.

Anjam Daily: 2nd Floor, New Blk No. II, Hockey Stadium, off Shahrah-e-Faisal, Karachi; tel. (21) 35672941; fax (21) 35672942; e-mail chiefeditordailyanjam@gmail.com; f. 1996; Urdu; Editor Dr ABDUL JABBAR KHATTAK.

Awami Awaz: 2nd Floor, New Blk No. II, Hockey Stadium, off Shahrah-e-Faisal, Karachi; tel. (21) 35672949; fax (21) 35672946; e-mail awamiawaz@hotmail.com; internet www.awamiawaz.com; f. 1989; Sindhi; Publr and Editor Dr ABDUL JABBAR KHATTAK; Editor Dr KHAIR MUHAMMAD JUNO; circ. 70,000.

Barsat: 246/D-6, PECHS, Karachi; tel. (21) 34535228; fax (21) 34535227; f. 1993; Urdu; Publr FAROOQUE AHMED DAUDPUTA.

Beopar: 205 Alfalah Court, I. I. Chundrigar Rd, Karachi; tel. (21) 32636442; fax (21) 32630784; e-mail beopar@yahoo.com; internet www.dailybeopaar.com; f. 1990; Urdu; Editor YOUNUS RIAZ.

Business Daily: Suite 209, 2nd Floor, Prime Office Lobby, Pak Towers, Clifton, Karachi; tel. (21) 35820100; fax (21) 35821655; Editor QAISAR MAHMOOD.

Business Recorder: Recorder House, 531 Business Recorder Rd, Karachi 74550; tel. (21) 32250071; fax (21) 32228644; e-mail ed.khi@ br-mail.com; internet www.brecorder.com; f. 1965; English; Editor-in-Chief WAMIQ A. ZUBERI.

Daily Express: Plot 5, Expressway, off Korangi Rd, Karachi; tel. (21) 35800051; fax (21) 35800050; f. 1998; Urdu; also publ. in Islamabad and Peshawar; Publr and Editor SULTAN ALI LAKHANI.

Daily Islam: Nazimabad 4, Karachi; tel. (21) 36682380; fax (21) 36622240; e-mail editor@dailyislam.pk; internet www.dailyislam .pk; Editor MUFTI ABDUL RASHEED.

Daily Jang: HQ Printing House, I. I. Chundrigar Rd, POB 52, Karachi; tel. (21) 32637111; fax (21) 32636066; e-mail jangkarachi@ janggroup.com.pk; internet www.jang.com.pk; f. 1940; morning; Urdu; also publ. in Quetta, Rawalpindi, Lahore and London; Editor-in-Chief Mir SHAKIL-UR-RAHMAN; combined circ. 750,000.

Daily Naya Akhbar: 1301, Mehmoodabad No. 6, Masjid-e-Awais Qarni Rd, Blk 7, Karachi Administration Society, Karachi; tel. (21) 111-558-855; fax (21) 5805207; internet naya-akhbar.epaper.pk; Urdu; Publr ZIA SHAHID; Editor AMTNAN SHAHID.

Daily News: Al-Rahman Bldg, I. I. Chundrigar Rd, Karachi; tel. (21) 32637111; fax (21) 32634395; e-mail dailynews@janggroup.com.pk; f. 1962; evening; English; Editor S. M. FAZAL; circ. 25,000.

Daily Sindh Sujag: Suite 414, 6th Floor, Amber Medical Centre, M. A. Jinnah Rd, Karachi; tel. (21) 32700252; fax (21) 32700249; Sindhi; political; Publr NASIR DAD BALOCH.

Daily Times: Plot No. SR 5/12/1, 2nd Floor, Nelson Chamber, I. I. Chundrigar Rd, Karachi; tel. (21) 32213822; fax (21) 32213874; e-mail yousaf@dailytimes.com.pk; internet www.dailytimes.com .pk; Editor YOUSAF RAFIQ.

Daily Ummat: Room No. 1, Blk IV, Hockey Club of Pakistan Stadium, Liaquat Barracks, Karachi; tel. (21) 35655270; fax (21) 35655275; e-mail info@ummatpublication.com; Editor NASEER HASHMI.

Dawn: Haroon House, Dr Ziauddin Ahmed Rd, POB 3740, Karachi 74200; tel. (21) 35670001; fax (21) 35683801; e-mail editor@dawn .com; internet www.dawn.com; f. 1947; English; also publ. from Islamabad, Rawalpindi and Lahore; CEO HAMEED HAROON; Editor ZAFFAR ABBAS; circ. 110,000 (weekdays), 125,000 (Sundays).

Deyanet: 4th Floor, Al Warid Centre, off I. I. Chundrigar Rd, nr APP, Karachi; tel. (21) 32631555; fax (21) 32631999; Urdu; also publ. in Sukkur; Editor NAJMUDDIN SHAIKH.

The Finance: 9th Floor, Uni Towers, I. I. Chundrigar Rd, Karachi; tel. (21) 32411665; fax (21) 32422560; e-mail tfinance@super.net.pk; English; Publr SYED SAJJAD HUSSAIN SHAH.

Financial Daily: 11-C, Jami Commercial St No. 11, Phase VII, DHA, Karachi; tel. (21) 35311893; e-mail info@thefinancialdaily .com; internet thefinancialdaily.com; publ. by Data Research & Communications.

Financial Post: 3rd Floor, Bldg No. 2/C, Highland Apartments, 6th Sunset Lane, Phase II, Extension, Defence Housing Authority, Karachi; tel. (21) 35381626; fax (21) 35390493; e-mail editor@ dailyfpost.com; internet www.dailyfpost.com; f. 1994; English; Editor-in-Chief and Chief Exec. QUDSIA K. KHAN; Publr WAJID JAWAD; circ. 26,000.

Hilal-e-Pakistan: Court View Bldg, 2nd Floor, M. A. Jinnah Rd, POB 3737, Karachi 74200; tel. (21) 32624997; fax (21) 32212096; internet www.dailyhilal.com; Sindhi; Editor MOHAMMAD IQBAL DAL.

Janbaz: 9th Floor, Uni Tower, I. I. Chundrigar Rd, Karachi; tel. (21) 32411665; fax (21) 32422560; Urdu; Publr SYED SAJJAD HUSSAIN SHAH.

Jasarat: 3rd Floor, Syed House, I. I. Chundrigar Rd, Karachi 74200; tel. (21) 32630391; fax (21) 32629344; e-mail jasarat@cyber.net.pk; internet www.jasarat.com; f. 1970; Urdu; Publr IFTIKHAR AHMED; circ. 50,000.

Jurat: Jurat House, off I. I. Chundrigar Rd, Dr Bilmoria House, Karachi; tel. (21) 32637641; fax (21) 32637640; Urdu; Publr MUKHTAR AAQIL.

The Leader: 1st Floor, Haji Bldg, Khushhal Daas St, off I. I. Chandrigar Rd, Burns Garden, Karachi; tel. (21) 35863801; fax (21) 35872206; f. 1958; English; independent; Publr MUNIR M. LADHA; circ. 7,000.

The Nation: Blk I, Hockey Stadium, off Khayaban-e-Shamsher, Phase V, Defence Housing Authority, Karachi; tel. (21) 5843720; fax (21) 5854932; e-mail editor@nation.com.pk; internet www.nation .com.pk; English; Editor MAJEED NIZAMI.

The News International: Printing House, I. I. Chundrigar Rd, POB 52, Karachi 74200; tel. (21) 32630611; fax (21) 32418343; e-mail thenewskarachi@thenews.com.pk; internet www.thenews.com.pk; f. 1990; English; also publ. from Lahore and Rawalpindi/Islamabad; Editor-in-Chief Mir SHAKIL-UR-RAHMAN.

Qaumi Akhbar: 14 Ramzan Mansion, Arif Jeeja St, I. I. Chundrigar Rd, Karachi; tel. (21) 32633381; fax (21) 2636688; e-mail news@ qaumiakhbar.com; internet www.qaumiakhbar.com; f. 1988; Urdu; offices in Islamabad; Publr ILYAS SHAKIR.

The Regional Times of Sindh: 6/1-E, Mohammad Ali Society, Karachi; tel. (21) 34398762; fax (21) 34398763; e-mail editor@ regionaltimes.com; internet regionaltimes.com; also publ. from Hyderabad; Editor-in-Chief KAZI SAJJAD ABBASI.

Lahore

Daily Khabrain: 12 Lawrence Rd, Lahore; tel. (42) 36309155; fax (42) 36314658; e-mail khabrain@khabrain.com; internet www .khabrain.com; Urdu; also publ. in Karachi, Islamabad and Multan; Editor and Proprietor ZIA SHAHID.

Daily Pakistan: 41 Jail Rd, Lahore; tel. (42) 37576301; fax (42) 37586251; e-mail marketing@dailypak.com; internet www.dailypak .com; f. 1990; Urdu; Chief Editor MUJIBUR RAHMAN SHAMI.

Daily Times: Media Times (Pvt) Ltd, 41-N, Industrial Area, Gulberg II, Lahore; tel. (42) 35878614; fax (42) 35878620; e-mail editorial@ dailytimes.com.pk; internet www.dailytimes.com.pk; Editor RASHED RAHMAN.

Daily Wifaq: 6A Warris Rd, Lahore; tel. (42) 36367467; fax (42) 38405989; e-mail wifaqtimes@yahoo.com; internet dailywifaq.com; Urdu; also publ. in Sargodha; Editor MUSTAFA SADIQ; circ. 50,000.

Millat: 310 B, Pak Arab Society, Ferozepore Rd, Lahore; tel. (33) 28452580; fax (42) 45924421; e-mail info@millat.com; internet www .millat.com; f. 1998; Urdu and English; independent; Chief Editor ASADULLAH GHALIB; circ. 22,550.

The Nation: NIPCO House, 4 Sharah-e-Fatima Jinnah, POB 1815, Lahore 54000; tel. (42) 36367580; fax (42) 36367005; e-mail editor@ nation.com; internet www.nation.com.pk; f. 1986; English; also publ. in Karachi, Islamabad and Multan; Man. Dir MAJEED NIZAMI; circ. 52,000.

Nawa-i-Waqt (Voice of the Time): 4 Sharah-e-Fatima Jinnah, Lahore 54000; tel. (42) 36367580; fax (42) 36367005; internet www .nawaiwaqt.com.pk; f. 1940; English, Urdu; also publ. edns in Karachi, Islamabad and Multan; Editor MAJID NIZAMI; combined circ. 560,000.

News Time Pakistan: Lahore; e-mail editor@newstimepakistan .com; internet www.newstimepakistan.com; f. 2011; English; Founder and Chief Editor AHMED FARAZ RAO.

Pakistan Today: 4 Shara-i-Fatima Jinnah, Lahore; tel. (42) 36298305; fax (42) 36298302; e-mail editorial@pakistantoday.com .pk; internet www.pakistantoday.com.pk; f. 2010; English; Founder and Editor ARIF NIZAMI.

Tijarat: Tijarat House, 14 Abbot Rd, opp. Nishat Cinema, Lahore; tel. (42) 36312462; fax (42) 36362767; Urdu; Publr JAMIL ATHAR.

Rawalpindi

Daily Asas: Asas Plaza, B-27, Murree Rd, Rawalpindi; tel. (51) 111272711; fax (51) 4428315; e-mail info@dailyasas.com.pk; internet www.dailyasas.com.pk; f. 1993; also printed from Islamabad, Lahore, Karachi and Faisalabad; Editor DANISH IFTIKHAR.

Daily Jang: Murree Rd, Rawalpindi; tel. (51) 5962444; fax (51) 5962277; internet www.jang.com.pk; f. 1940; also publ. in Quetta, Karachi, Lahore and London; Urdu; independent; Editor Mir JAVED REHMAN; circ. (Rawalpindi) 65,000.

Daily Mahasib: M-40E, Bank Rd, Saddar, Rawalpindi; tel. (51) 5567341; fax (51) 5700464; e-mail ce@mahasib.com.pk; internet www.mahasib.com.pk; Urdu; also publ. from Abbotabad, Muzaffar-abad, Mirpur and Gilgit; Chief Editor ZAFAR HIJAZI.

Daily Wifaq: Mohallah Waris Khan 604, Murree Rd, Rawalpindi; tel. (51) 553979; e-mail dailywifaq@hotmail.com; internet dailywifaq .com; f. 1959; also publ. in Lahore, Sargodha and Rahimyar Khan; daily publ. in Urdu, monthly magazine in English *The Times*; Editor MUSTAFA SADIQ.

The News: Al-Rehman Bldg, Murree Rd, Rawalpindi; tel. (51) 5962444; fax (51) 5962277; e-mail thenews@isb.comsats.net.pk; internet www.jang-group.com; f. 1991; also publ. in Lahore and Karachi; English; independent; Chief Editor Mir SHAKIL-UR-RAHMAN.

Other Towns

Aftab: Opposite WASA Office, Bagh Langay Khan Rd, Multan; tel. (61) 4546080; fax (61) 4786083; f. 1975; Urdu; also publ. from Lahore, Quetta and Karachi; Publr MUMTAZ A. TAHIR; Editor ASAD MUMTAZ SEYAL.

Al Falah: Al Falah House, Al Falah Bazar, nr State Life Bldg, Mall Rd, Peshawar; tel. (91) 5853694; fax (91) 5854454; f. 1938; Urdu; Editor SYED BADRUDDIN SHAH.

Al-Jamiat-e-Sarhad: Kocha Gilania Chakagali, Karimpura Bazar, Peshawar; tel. (91) 2212093; e-mail sagha@brain.net.pk; f. 1941; Urdu and Pashtu; Propr and Chief Editor S. M. HASSAN GILANI.

Balochistan Times: Aiwan-e-Shafhat, Zamana St, Industrial State, Sirkee Rd, Quetta; tel. (81) 2451401; fax (81) 2453170; e-mail dailyz@yahoo.com; f. 1976; English; Publr and Editor SYED FASIH IQBAL.

Daily Business Report: Railway Rd, Faisalabad; tel. (41) 2629668; fax (41) 2621207; f. 1948; Urdu; Publr FARKHANDA JABEEN; Editor ABDUL RASHID GHAZI; circ. 26,000.

Daily Ibrat Hyderabad: Ibrat Building, Gadi Khata, Hyderabad; tel. (22) 2728571; fax (22) 2784300; e-mail ibrat@hyd.paknet.com.pk; internet www.dailyibrat.com; Sindhi; Man. Editor Qazi ASAD ABID.

Frontier Post: 27 Abdara Rd, University Town, POB 1161, Pesha-war; tel. (91) 5844317; fax (91) 5703687; e-mail tfpost@brain.net.pk; internet www.thefrontierpost.com; f. 1984; English; left-wing; also publ. in Lahore, Karachi, Islamabad and Quetta; closed down temporarily in January 2001, reopened in June; Chief Editor REHMAT SHAH AFRIDI; Man. Editor MAHMOOD AFRIDI; Man. Editor JALIL AFRIDI.

Jihad: 15A Islamia Club Bldg, Khyber Bazar, Peshawar; tel. (91) 2210522; fax (91) 2553890; e-mail jehad@pes.comsats.net.pk; Urdu; Publr SHARIF FAROOQ.

Kaleem: Madina Complex, opp. Makki Masjid, Minara Rd, POB 88, Sukkur; tel. (71) 5627833; fax (71) 5622087; e-mail kaleemsukkur@ yahoo.com; Urdu; Editor SHAHID MEHR SHAMSI.

Kawish: B/2 Civil Lines, Hyderabad; tel. (22) 2780026; fax (22) 2780772; e-mail kawish12@gmail.com; internet www.thekawish .com; f. 1991; Sindhi; Editor MUHAMMAD ALI QAZI.

Pasban: Pasban Press, Gari Khata, Hyderabad; tel. (22) 2783693; fax (22) 2780556; Urdu; Publr NOMAN JAFFERI.

Sindhu: Popular Printers, Ibrat Bldg, Gadi Khata, Thandi Sarak, Hyderabad; tel. (22) 2728272; fax (22) 2728971; Sindhi; political; Publr KAZI ASAD ABID.

The Statesman: Bilal Town, GT Rd, POB 1107, Peshawar; tel. (91) 2651151; fax (91) 2584471; internet www.statesman.com.pk; f. 2002; English; also publ. from Islamabad, Lahore and Karachi; Editor-in-Chief SYED AYAZ BADSHAH.

Watan: St 7, Gulbahar Colony 2, Peshawar; tel. (91) 2651332; fax (91) 2264635; Urdu; Publr BARI MALIK.

Zamana: Aiwan-e-Shafhat, Zamana St, Industrial State, Sirkee Rd, Quetta; tel. (81) 2453170; fax (81) 2442606; Urdu; Publr SYED FASIH IQBAL; circ. 5,000.

SELECTED WEEKLIES

Akhbar-e-Jehan: Printing House, off I. I. Chundrigar Rd, POB 32, Karachi; tel. (21) 32271313; fax (21) 32635701; e-mail editor-in-chief@akhbar-e-jehan.com; internet www.akhbar-e-jehan.com; f. 1967; Urdu; independent; illustrated family magazine; Publr and Editor Mir JAVED RAHMAN; circ. 285,000.

Amal: Shah Qabool Colony, POB 185, Peshawar; tel. (91) 5704673; e-mail maab_kaifi@hotmail.com; f. 1958; Urdu, Pashtu and English; Chief Editor F. M. ZAFAR KAIFI; Publr MUNAZIMA MAAB KAIFI.

Family Magazine: Nipco House 4, Shara-i-Fatima Jinnah, Lahore 54000; tel. (42) 36367551; fax (42) 36367583; internet family.nawaiwaqt.com.pk; f. 1989; Urdu; Editor MAJID NIZAMI; circ. 100,000.

The Friday Times: 72-F. C. C. Gulberg IV, Lahore 54000; tel. (42) 35673510; fax (42) 35751025; e-mail tft@thefridaytimes.com; internet www.thefridaytimes.com; f. 1989; English; independent; Editor-in-Chief NAJAM SETHI; Man. Editor and Publr JUGNU MOHSIN.

Insaf: P/929, Banni, Rawalpindi 46000; tel. and fax (51) 5550903; e-mail insafrwp@isb.paknet.com.pk; f. 1955; Editor Mir WAQAR AZIZ.

Nida-i-Millat: NIPCO House, 4 Sharah-e-Fatima Jinnah, Lahore 54000; tel. (42) 6367551; fax (42) 6367583; Urdu; Publr MAJID NIZAMI.

Pak Kashmir: Pak Kashmir Office, Soikarno Chowk, Liaquat Rd, Rawalpindi; tel. (51) 74845; f. 1951; Urdu; Editor M. MUSADDIQ ABBASI.

Pakistan and Gulf Economist (PAGE): Economist Publications, C-158/B-2, Blk 2, KDA Scheme 5, Clifton, Karachi; tel. (21) 35838572; fax (21) 35838517; e-mail info@pgeconomist.com; internet www.pakistaneconomist.com; f. 1960; English; financial; also publ. from Islamabad; Editor ALI HAIDER GOKAL; circ. 30,000.

Parsi Sansar and Loke Sevak: 8 Mehrabad, 5 McNeil Rd, Karachi 75530; tel. and fax (21) 35656217; e-mail organ@cyber.net.pk; f. 1909; English and Gujarati; Editor NUSSERWANJI OGRA.

Qalandar: Peshawar; f. 1950; Urdu; Editor M. A. K. SHERWANI.

Takbeer: Rm 1–3, VIP Enclosure, Hockey Club of Pakistan, Liaquat Barracks, Karachi; tel. (21) 35655270; fax (21) 35655275; f. 1984; Urdu; Publr ABDUL RAFIQ AFGHAN; circ. 70,000.

Times of Kashmir: P/929, Banni, Rawalpindi 46000; tel. (51) 5550903; fax (51) 4411348; e-mail insafrwp@isb.paknet.com.pk; f. 1982; English; Editor Mir IQBAL AZIZ.

SELECTED PERIODICALS

Aadab Arz: 190 N. Ghazali Rd, Saman Abad, Lahore 54500; tel. (42) 37582449; monthly; Editor KHALID BIN HAMID.

Air World: G51, Defence View, Phase II, Karachi; e-mail airworld_fmajeed@hotmail.com; internet www.airworldonline.com; monthly; aviation, defence and travel trade; Chief Editor FARRUKH MAJEED.

Akhbar-e-Watan: 35-C, 12th Commercial St, Rm No. 4, Phase-II, Extension DHA, Karachi; tel. (21) 35394747; fax (21) 34252012; e-mail akhbarewatan@hotmail.com; f. 1977; monthly; Urdu; cricket; Publr and Editor MUNIR HUSSAIN; circ. 63,000.

Albalagh: Korangi Industrial Area, Karachi 75180; tel. (21) 35123222; monthly; publ. by Jamia Darul-Uloom Karachi; Editor-in-Chief MUHAMMED TAQI USMANI; Exec. Editor MUHAMMAD WALI RAAZI.

Al-Ma'arif: Institute of Islamic Culture, Club Rd, Lahore 54000; tel. (42) 6363127; f. 1950; quarterly; Urdu; Dir and Editor-in-Chief Dr RASHID AHMAD JALLANDHRI.

Anchal: Rm 7, Farid Chambers, Abdullah Haroon Rd, Karachi 74400; tel. (21) 35620771; fax (21) 35620773; e-mail info@aanchal.com.pk; internet www.aanchal.com.pk; monthly; Chief Editor MUSHTAQ AHMED QURESHI; Exec. Editor TAHIR AHMED QURESHI.

Archi Times: B-34, Blk 15, Gulshan-e-Iqbal, Karachi; tel. (21) 34977652; fax (21) 34967656; e-mail architimes@cyber.net.pk; internet www.archpresspk.com; f. 1986; monthly; English; architecture; Editor MURTAZA SHIKOH.

Architecture and Interiors: B-34, Blk 15, Gulshan-e-Iqbal, Karachi 75300; tel. (21) 34977652; fax (21) 34967656; e-mail aplusi@cyber.net.pk; internet www.archpresspk.com; f. 2001; quarterly; English; Editor MUTJUBA HUSSAIN; Man. Editor MURTUZA SHIKOH.

Automark: 68-D, Block 9, Clifton, Karachi; tel. (21) 32218526; e-mail magazine@automark.pk; internet www.automark.pk; monthly; English; Editor MUHAMMAD HANIF MEMON.

Bachoon Ka Risala: 108–110 Adam Arcade, Shaheed-e-Millat Rd, Karachi; tel. (21) 3419616; monthly; Urdu; children's; Editor RUKHSANA SEHAM MIRZA.

Beauty: Plot No. 4-C, 14th Commercial St, Defence Housing Authority, Phase II Extension, Karachi; tel. (21) 35805391; fax (21) 35896269; e-mail riazmansuri@hotmail.com; f. 2000; bi-monthly; English; Chief Editor RIAZ AHMED MANSURI.

Beemakar (Insurer): R-3, Row 5, Blk A, NCES Gulshan-e-Iqbal, 10A Karachi; tel. (31) 22220939; fax (31) 34990243; e-mail beemakar@gmail.com; internet www.beemakar.com; f. 1990; monthly; Urdu; Man. Editor KHAN MUHAMMED AYAZ; Editor AYAZ KHAN.

Chand: 190 N. Ghazali Rd, Saman Abad, Lahore 54500; tel. (42) 7582449; e-mail chaand.news@gmail.com; monthly; Editor MASOOD HAMID.

The Cricketer: Plot No. 4-C, 14th Commercial St, Defence Housing Authority, Phase II Extension, Karachi; tel. (21) 35805391; fax (21) 35896269; e-mail riazmansuri@hotmail.com; f. 1972; monthly; English/Urdu; Chief Editor RIAZ AHMED MANSURI.

Dastarkhuan: Plot No. 4-C, 14th Commercial St, Defence Housing Authority, Phase II Extension, Karachi; tel. (21) 35805391; fax (21) 35896269; e-mail riazmansuri@hotmail.com; f. 1998; monthly; Urdu; Chief Editor RIAZ AHMED MANSURI.

Defence Journal: SMS Block, Defence Hockey Stadium, Phase-V, Karachi; tel. (21) 35843502; fax (21) 35843416; e-mail defjrnl@pathfinder9.com; internet www.defencejournal.com; f. 1975; monthly; English; Editor-in-Chief IKRAM SEHGAL.

Dosheeza: 110 Adam Arcade Shaheed-e-Millat Rd, Karachi; tel. (21) 34934369; fax (21) 34939823; e-mail pearlpublications@hotmail.com; monthly; Urdu; Publr MUNAZZA SEHAM MIRZA.

Duniya-e-Tibb: Eveready Chambers, 2nd Floor, Mohd Bin Qasim Rd, off I. I. Chundrigar Rd, POB 1385, Karachi 1; tel. (21) 32630985; fax (21) 32637624; e-mail mcm@digicom.net.pk; f. 1986; monthly; Urdu; modern and Asian medicine; Editor QUTUBUDDIN; circ. 12,000.

Economic Review: Al-Masiha, 3rd Floor, 47 Abdullah Haroon Rd, POB 7843, Karachi 74400; tel. (21) 37728963; fax (21) 37728957; f. 1969; monthly; economic, industrial and investment research; Editor AHMAD MUHAMMAD KHAN.

Engineering Horizons: 13-J, Markaz F-7, Islamabad 44000; tel. (51) 2650174; fax (51) 2650943; e-mail islamabad@engghorizons.com; internet www.engghorizons.com; f. 1988; monthly; English; Chief Editor IMTIAZ SHEIKH.

Engineering Review: 305 Spotlit Chambers, Dr Billimoria St, off I. I. Chundrigar Rd, POB 807, Karachi 74200; tel. (21) 32632567; fax (21) 32639378; e-mail engineer@engineeringreview.com.pk; internet www.engineeringreview.com.pk; f. 1975; fortnightly; English; Editor RIAZUL HASAN; circ. 5,000.

Global Science: 139 Sunny Plaza, Hasrat Mohani Rd, Karachi 74200; tel. (21) 32625545; e-mail globalscience@yahoo.com; internet www.globalscience.com.pk; f. 1998; monthly; Urdu; Editor ALEEM AHMED.

Good Food: Plot No. 4-C, 14th Commercial St, Defence Housing Authority, Phase II Extension, Karachi; tel. (21) 35805391; fax (21) 35896269; e-mail riazmansuri@hotmail.com; f. 1997; bi-monthly; English; Chief Editor RIAZ AHMED MANSURI.

Hamdard-i-Sehat: Hamdard Foundation Pakistan, Nazimabad 3, Karachi 74600; tel. (21) 36620945; fax (21) 36611755; e-mail hfp@hamdardfoundation.org; internet hamdardfoundation.org; f. 1933; monthly; Urdu; Editor-in-Chief SADIA RASHID; circ. 9,400.

Hamdard Islamicus: Hamdard Foundation Pakistan, Hamdard Centre, Nazimabad 3, Karachi 74600; tel. (21) 36620949; fax (21) 36611755; e-mail hfp@hamdardfoundation.org; internet hamdardfoundation.org; f. 1978; quarterly; English; Editor-in-Chief SADIA RASHID; circ. 750.

Hamdard Medicus: Hamdard Foundation Pakistan, Nazimabad 3, Karachi 74600; tel. (21) 36620949; fax (21) 36611755; e-mail hfp@hamdardfoundation.org; internet hamdardfoundation.org; f. 1957; quarterly; English; Editor-in-Chief SADIA RASHID; circ. 1,000.

Hamdard Naunehal: Hamdard Foundation Pakistan, Nazimabad 3, Karachi 74600; tel. (21) 36620949; fax (21) 36611755; e-mail hfp@hamdardfoundation.org; internet hamdardfoundation.org; f. 1952; monthly; Urdu; Editor MASOOD AHMAD BARAKATI; circ. 32,000.

The Herald: Haroon House, Dr Ziauddin Ahmed Rd, Karachi 74200; tel. (21) 35670001; fax (21) 35683188; e-mail letters.herald@dawn.com; internet www.dawn.com/herald; f. 1970; monthly; English; Editor ARIFA NOOR; circ. 38,000.

Hikayat: 26 Patiala Ground, Link McLeod Rd, Lahore; monthly; Editor SHAHID JAMIL; circ. 25,000.

Hilal: Hilal Rd, Rawalpindi 46000; tel. (51) 9271617; fax (51) 56134605; e-mail hilalenglish@gmail.com; internet www.pakistanarmy.gov.pk/hilal; f. 1948; monthly; Urdu and English; illustrated armed forces; Chief Editor SHAHID ZAHUR; circ. 90,000.

Islamic Studies: Islamic Research Institute, Faisal Masjid Campus, POB 1035, Islamabad 44000; tel. (51) 2281289; fax (51) 2254879; e-mail islamicstudies.iri@gmail.com; internet iri.iiu.edu.pk; f. 1962; quarterly; English, Urdu (Fikro-Nazar) and Arabic (Al Dirasat al-Islamiyyah) edns; Islamic literature, religion, history, geography, language and the arts; Editor Dr KHALID MASUD; circ. 3,000.

Journal of the Pakistan Historical Society (Historicus): Bait al-Hikmah, Madinatt al-Hikmah, Karachi 74700; tel. (21) 36620945;

fax (21) 36611755; e-mail hfp@hamdardfoundation.org; internet hamdardfoundation.org; f. 1953; quarterly; English; Editor Dr ANSAR ZAHID KHAN; circ. 475.

Khwateen Digest: 51–52, Aurangzeb Market, M. A. Jinnah Rd, Karachi; tel. (21) 32721777; fax (21) 32766872; monthly; Urdu; Publr AZAR RIAZ.

Kiran Digest: 35, Aurangzeb Market, M. A. Jinnah Rd, Karachi; tel. (21) 32721777; fax (21) 32766872; Urdu; monthly; Publr AZAR RIAZ.

The Leather News: Iftikhar Chambers, opp. UNI Plaza, Altaf Hussain Rd, POB 4323, Karachi 74000; tel. (21) 32630861; fax (21) 32631545; e-mail arsintl@yahoo.com; f. 1989; Editor ABDUL RAFAY SIDDIQI.

Ma'arif Feature: D-35, Blk 5, Federal 'B' Area, Karachi 75950; tel. (21) 36349840; fax (21) 36361040; e-mail info@irak.pk; internet www .irak.pk; f. 1999; journal of the Islamic Research Acad; fortnightly; Urdu; Editor SYED SHAHID HASHMI.

Naey-Ufaq: 7 Farid Chambers, Abdullah Haroon Rd, Karachi; tel. (21) 35620771; fax (21) 35620773; Urdu; monthly; Publr MUSHTAQ AHMED QURESHI.

NGM Communication: NGM House, 319/1A, Makkah Colony, Gulberg-3 Lahore 54660; tel. (42) 35879524; e-mail anjeeam@ yahoo.com; f. 1980; owned by Nizam Nizami; English; lists newly released Pakistani publications on the internet; updated weekly; Editor GHUFRAN NIZAMI.

Pakistan Journal of Applied Economics: Applied Economics Research Centre, University of Karachi, POB 8403, Karachi 75270; tel. (21) 99261541; fax (21) 99261545; e-mail pjae@aerc.edu.pk; internet www.aerc.edu.pk; twice a year; Editor MUHAMMAD SABI-HUDDIN BUTT.

Pakistan Journal of Scientific and Industrial Research: Pakistan Council of Scientific and Industrial Research, Scientific Information Centre, PCSIR Laboratories Campus, Shahrah-e-Dr Salimuzzaman Siddiqui, Karachi 75280; tel. (21) 34651739; fax (21) 34651738; e-mail info@pjsir.org; internet www.pjsir.org; f. 1958; bi-monthly; English; Editor-in-Chief Dr SHOUKAT PARVEZ; Exec. Editor Dr GHULAM QADIR SHAIKH; circ. 1,000.

Pakistan Management Review: Pakistan Institute of Management, Management House, Shahrah Iran, Clifton, Karachi 75600; tel. (21) 99251711; fax (21) 99251715; e-mail pimkhi@pim.com.pk; internet www.pim.com.pk; f. 1960; quarterly; English; Editor IQBAL A. QAZI.

Pakistan Textile Journal: B-4, 2nd Floor, 64/21 Miran Mohd Shah Rd, M. A. H. S., Karachi; tel. (21) 34533616; fax (21) 35206188; e-mail ptj@cyber.net.pk; internet www.ptj.com.pk; f. 1951; Editor-in-Chief AMINA BAQAI; Publr NADEEM MAZHAR.

Phool: 23 Queen's Rd, Lahore 54000; tel. (42) 36314099; fax (42) 36309661; e-mail editor@phool.com.pk; internet www.phool.com.pk; f. 1989; monthly; children's; Chief Editor MAJID NIZAMI; Editor MUHAMMAD SHOAIB MIRZA; circ. 50,000.

Progress: 4th Floor, PIDC House, Dr Ziauddin Ahmed Rd, Karachi 75530; tel. (21) 111-568-568; fax (21) 35680005; e-mail h_saquib@ppl .com.pk; internet www.ppl.com.pk/content/ monthly-progress-magazine; f. 1956; monthly; publ. by Pakistan Petroleum Ltd; Editor and Publr SAQUIB HANIF; Chief Exec./Man. Dir ASIM MURTAZA KHAN.

Qaumi Digest: 50 Lower Mall Rd, Lahore; tel. and fax (42) 37241713; monthly; Urdu; Publr MUJIBUR REHMAN SHAMI.

Sabrang Digest: 47–48 Press Chambers, I. I. Chundrigar Rd, Karachi 1; f. 1970; monthly; Urdu; Editor SHAKEEL ADIL ZADAH; circ. 150,000.

Sach-Chee Kahaniyan: 110 Adam Arcade, Shaheed-e-Millat Rd, Karachi; tel. (21) 34934369; fax (21) 34930470; monthly; Urdu; Publr MUNAZZA JAMIL AHMED.

Sayyarah Digest: 240 Main Market Riwaz Garden, Lahore 54000; tel. (42) 37245412; fax (42) 37325080; e-mail sayyaradigest@gmail .com; f. 1963; monthly; Urdu; Chief Editor AMJAD RAUF KHAN; Editor KAMRAN AMJAD KHAN; circ. 40,000.

Seep: Alam Market, Block No. 16, Federal B Area, Karachi; quarterly; literary; Editor NASIM DURRANI.

Sindh Quarterly: 36D Karachi Administrative Co-operative Housing Society, off Shaheed-e-Millat Rd, Karachi 75350; tel. (21) 34531988; f. 1973; Editor SAYID GHULAM MUSTAFA SHAH.

Smash: Plot No. 4-C, 14th Commercial St, Defence Housing Authority, Phase II Extension, Karachi; tel. (21) 35805391; fax (21) 35896269; e-mail riazmansuri@hotmail.com; f. 2000; monthly; English; Chief Editor RIAZ AHMED MANSURI.

Spider: Haroon House, Dr Ziauddin Ahmed Rd, Karachi 74200; tel. (21) 111-444-777; fax (21) 35681544; e-mail reba@spider.tm; internet www.spider.tm; f. 1998; internet monthly; Editor REBA SHAHID; CEO HAMEED HAROON.

Talimo Tarbiat: Ferozsons (Pvt) Ltd, 60 Shahrah-e-Quaid-e-Azam, Lahore 54000; tel. (42) 36301196; fax (42) 36369204; e-mail support@ ferozsons.com.pk; f. 1941; children's monthly; Urdu; Publr and Editor ZAHEER SALAM; circ. 50,000.

Textile Times: 1183 House, St 1, Sector G-9/2, Islamabad 44000; tel. (51) 2855125; e-mail info@textiletimes.com; internet www.aiousoft .com/textile/; monthly; English; Chief Editor KANWAR ABDUL MAJEED; Exec. Editor RAHEEL MAJEED KHAN.

Trade Chronicle: Iftikhar Chambers, Altaf Hussain Rd, POB 5257, Karachi 74000; tel. (21) 32631587; fax (21) 32635007; e-mail arsidiqi@ptcl.net; f. 1953; monthly; English; trade, politics, finance and economics; Editor ABDUL RAB SIDDIQI; circ. 6,000.

Urdu Digest: 21-Acre Scheme, Samanabad, Lahore 54500; tel. (42) 37589957; fax (42) 37563646; e-mail urdudigest42@hotmail.com; monthly; Urdu; Editor ALTAF HASAN QURESHEE.

Women's Own: Plot No. 4-C, 14th Commercial St, Defence Housing Authority, Phase II Extension, Karachi; tel. (21) 35805391; fax (21) 35896269; e-mail riazmansuri@hotmail.com; f. 1987; monthly; English; Chief Editor RIAZ AHMED MANSURI.

Yaqeen International: Darut Tasnif (Pvt) Ltd, Main Hub River Rd, Mujahidabad, Karachi 75760; tel. (21) 32814432; fax (21) 32811304; e-mail daruttasnif@yaqeendtl.com; f. 1952; English and Arabic; Islamic organ; Editor Dr HAFIZ MUHAMMAD ADIL.

Yaran-e-Watan: Overseas Pakistanis Foundation, Shahrah-e-Jamhuriate, G-5/2, POB 1470, Islamabad 44000; tel. (51) 9224518; fax (51) 9211613; e-mail yw@opf.org.pk; f. 1982; monthly; Urdu; publ. by the Overseas Pakistanis Foundation; Editor TANVIR HUSSAIN.

NEWS AGENCIES

Associated Press of Pakistan (APP): 18 Mauve Area, Zero Point, G-7/1, POB 1258, Islamabad; tel. (51) 2203064; fax (51) 2203074; e-mail news@app.com.pk; internet app.com.pk; f. 1948; Dir-Gen. MANSOOR SOHAIL.

National News Agency (NNA): 491-C, Margalla Town, Islamabad 45510; tel. (51) 2840896; fax (51) 2841746; e-mail nnaisb@yahoo.com; f. 1990; Chief Editor SUHAIL ILYAS.

News Network International: 2nd Floor, Blk 19, PHA Apts, G-7/1, Islamabad 44000; tel. (51) 2204760; fax (51) 2204757; e-mail news@ nni-news.com.pk; internet www.nni-news.com.pk; f. 1992; independent international news agency; news in Arabic, Urdu and English; provides services to 435 newspapers and radio and television channels in South Asia, Europe, the Middle East, the Far East and the USA; Editor-in-Chief QAISAR JAVED; Editor MUHAMMAD TAHIR KHAN.

Online International News Network (OINN): 69 Bhattai Rd, F-7/4, Islamabad; tel. (51) 111888666; fax (51) 2611472; e-mail online@ dsl.net.pk; internet www.onlinenews.com.pk; 11 national offices; provides services to 132 local and 30 int. media orgs; Chief Editor MOHSIN JAMIL BAIG.

Pakistan—International Press Agency (PPA): 6, St 39, G-6/2, Islamabad 44000; tel. (51) 2279830; fax (51) 2272405; e-mail khalidathar@gmail.com; f. 1991; Urdu and English; Chief Editor KHALID ATHAR.

Pakistan Press International (PPI): Press Centre, Shahrah Kamal Atatürk, POB 541, Karachi; tel. (21) 32633215; fax (21) 32217069; e-mail ppi@ppinewsagency.com; internet www .ppinewsagency.com; f. 1956; pvt ltd co; Chair. OWAIS ASLAM ALI.

Sharp Eye: 111 Lytton Rd, Qurtaba Chowk (Mozang Chungi), Lahore; tel. (42) 37313401; fax (42) 37313405; e-mail editor@ sharpeye.com.pk; internet www.sharpeye.com.pk; f. 2000; Chief Editor MIAN MUHAMMAD AZHAR AMIN.

United Press of Pakistan (Pvt) Ltd (UPP): 1 Victoria Chambers, Haji Abdullah Haroon Rd, Karachi 74400; tel. (21) 35683235; fax (21) 35682694; e-mail pnrupp2000@yahoo.com; f. 1949; Chair. MAHMUD UL-AZIZ; 5 brs.

PRESS ASSOCIATIONS

All Pakistan Newspaper Employees Confederation: Karachi Press Club, M. R. Kayani Rd, Karachi; f. 1976; confed. of all press industry trade unions; Chair. SHAFIUDDIN ASHRAF; Sec.-Gen. PERVAIZ SHAUKAT.

All Pakistan Newspapers Society: ST-1/E, Blk 16, KDA Scheme-36, Gulistan-e-Jauhar, Karachi; tel. (21) 34012491; fax (21) 34012495; e-mail apns@apns.com.pk; internet www.apns.com.pk; f. 1949; Pres. SARMAD ALI; Sec.-Gen. MASOOD HAMID.

Council of Pakistan Newspaper Editors: c/o United Press of Pakistan, 1 Victoria Chambers, Haji Abdullah Haroon Rd, Karachi 74400; tel. and fax (21) 35682694; f. 1957; Pres. JAMAL AKHTAR KAZI; Sec.-Gen. ILYAS SHAKIR.

Pakistan Federal Union of Journalists (PFUJ): Suite 210, 2nd Floor, Avaque Trust Complex, Aga Khan Rd, F-5/1, Islamabad; tel.

(51) 2870220; fax (51) 2870223; e-mail info@pfuj.pk; internet pfuj.pk; Pres. PERVAIZ SHAUKAT; Sec.-Gen. AMIN YOUSUF.

Pakistan Press Foundation: Press Centre, Shahrah Kamal Ataturk, Karachi 74200; tel. (21) 32633215; fax (21) 32217069; e-mail ppf@pakistanpressfoundation.org; internet www.pakistanpress foundation.org; f. 1967; independent media research and training centre for promotion of press freedom; Sec.-Gen. OWAIS ASLAM ALI.

Publishers

Alhamra Publishing: Shop 3–4, Chauburji Qtrs Mosque, Arya Nagar Scheme, Poonch Rd, Lahore; tel. and fax (51) 924237582414 (mobile); e-mail contact@alhamra.com; internet www.alhamra.com; f. 2000; publs broad range of subjects incl. fiction, literary criticism, languages, history, education and religion in Urdu and English translations; Man. Dir SHAFIQ NAZ.

Al-Noor Publishers: 15x DHA, Ghazi Rd, Lahore; tel. (42) 35733700; e-mail alnoorcentraloffice@yahoo.com; CEO NIGHAT YASMIN HASHMI.

Anjuman Taraqqi-e-Urdu Pakistan: D-159, Block 7, Gulshan-e-Iqbal, Karachi 75300; tel. (21) 34811406; fax (21) 34973296; e-mail quami.zaban@yahoo.com; f. 1903; literature, religion, textbooks, Urdu dictionaries, literary and critical texts; promotion and preservation of Urdu language; Pres. AFTAB AHMED KHAN; Hon. Sec. JAMIL UDDIN AALI.

Book Group: 187/2–C, Blk 2, PECHS, Karachi; tel. (21) 34310641; fax (21) 34395264; e-mail info@bookgroup.org.pk; internet www .bookgroup.org.pk; Chair. SYED SAMI MUSTAFA.

Chronicle Publications: Iftikhar Chambers, Altaf Hussain Rd, POB 5257, Karachi 74000; tel. (21) 32631587; fax (21) 32635007; e-mail arsidiqi@ptcl.net; f. 1953; reference, directories, religious books; Dir ABDUL RAUF SIDDIQI.

Darussalam Publishers and Distributors: D. C. H. S., Main Tariq Rd, Karachi; tel. (21) 4393936; fax 4393937; e-mail info@ darussalampk.com; internet www.darussalampk.com; Man. Dir MUHAMMAD AYUB SIPRA.

Dawah Academy International Islamic University: Faisal Masjid, Islamabad; tel. (51) 2262031; fax (51) 9263442; e-mail hairankhatak@yahoo.com; internet www.dawahacademy.com; Dir Dr SAJID UR-RAHMAN.

Educational Resource Development Centre (ERDC): A 735, Blk H, North Nazimabad, Karachi; tel. (21) 36723454; fax (21) 36678748; e-mail info@erdconline.org; internet www.erdconline .org; Dir SALMAN ASIF SIDDIQUI.

Elite Publishers Ltd: D-118, SITE, Karachi 75700; tel. (21) 32573435; fax (21) 32564720; e-mail elite@elite.com.pk; internet www.elite.com.pk; f. 1951; general commercial printing and packaging; Chair. AHMED MIRZA JAMIL; Chief Exec. KHALID JAMIL.

Fazlee's Book Super Market: 507/3, Temple Rd, Urdu Bazar, Nr Radio Pakistan, Karachi; tel. (21) 32629724; fax (21) 32633887; e-mail fazleebook@hotmail.com; internet www.fazleebooks.com; f. 1997; publishing and bookselling; fiction, poetry, literary criticism, research, history, education, religion and children's books; Propr SAJID REHMAN.

Ferozsons (Pvt) Ltd: 60 Shahrah-e-Quaid-e-Azam, Lahore; tel. (42) 111-626-262; fax (42) 36369204; e-mail support@ferozsons .com.pk; internet www.ferozsons.com.pk; f. 1894; general books, school books, periodicals, maps, atlases, stationery products; Man. Dir ZAHEER SALAM; Dir (Business Development) MUQEET SALAM.

Fiction House: 18, Mozang House, Lahore; printing and publishing; publs quarterly social science journal *Tareekh*.

Frontline Publishing Co: 22, Urdu Bazar, Lahore; tel. (42) 37247310; fax (42) 37247323; e-mail azam.fpc@gmail.com; f. 1951; academic and general; Dirs AZAM MUHAMMAD, AMIR MUHAMMAD.

Gaba Educational Books: Urdu Bazar, 1/2 Urdu Manzil, Karachi; tel. (21) 32628266; fax (21) 32630606; e-mail gebpak@cyber.net.pk; internet www.gabaedu.com; Man. Dir MUHAMMAD HAROON GABA.

Sh. Ghulam Ali and Sons (Pvt) Ltd: 14 Lawrence Rd, Lahore 54000; tel. (42) 37352908; fax (42) 36315478; e-mail info@ghulamali .com.pk; internet www.ghulamali.com.pk; f. 1887; general, religion, technical, textbooks; Dirs NIAZ AHMAD, ASAD NIAZ.

Gohar Publishers: 1 and 2 Quran Mahal, Urdu Bazar, M. A. Jinnah Rd, Karachi; tel. (21) 32639320; fax (21) 32623884; e-mail gohar .publishers@live.com; internet goharpublishers.com; academic; Dir ABU ZAR GHAFFARI.

Ilmi Kitab Khana: Kabeer St, Urdu Bazar, Lahore; tel. (42) 37353510; e-mail contactus@ilmikitabkhana.com; internet www .ilmikitabkhana.com; f. 1948; technical, professional, historical and law; Propr JAVED IQBAL.

INAYAT Sons: YMCA Bldg, 16 The Mall, Lahore 54000; tel. (42) 38401335; fax (42) 37231896; e-mail general@inayatsons.com; internet www.inayatsons.com; f. 1971; Propr S. PERVEZ.

Indus Publications: 25 Fared Chambers, Abdullah Haroon Rd, Karachi; tel. (21) 35660242; e-mail muzaffar_indus@hotmail.com; f. 1959; printers, publishers and importers of books; Dir AATIF SAFDAR.

Iqbal Sons Educational Publishers: Urdu Bazar, M. A. Jinnah Rd, Karachi; tel. (21) 32218838; fax (21) 34387943; e-mail info@ al-iqbaledu.com; internet www.al-iqbaledu.com; Propr MUHAMMAD SOHAIL IQBAL GABA.

Islamic Book Centre: 25B Masson Rd, POB 1625, Lahore 54000; tel. (42) 36361803; fax (42) 36360955; e-mail lsaeed@paknetl.ptc.pk; religion in Arabic, Urdu and English; Islamic history, textbooks, dictionaries and reprints; Propr and Man. Dir SUMBLEYNA SAJID SAEED.

Islamic Publications (Pvt) Ltd: 3 Court St, Lower Mall, Lahore 54000; tel. (42) 37248676; fax (42) 37214974; e-mail islamicpak@ hotmail.com; internet www.islamicpak.com.pk; f. 1959; Islamic literature in Urdu and English; Man. Dir Prof. MUHAMMAD AMIN JAVED; Gen. Man. AMANAT ALI.

Kazi Publications: 121 Zulqarnain Chambers, Ganpat Rd, POB 1845, Lahore; tel. (42) 37311359; fax (42) 37350805; e-mail kazip@ brain.net.pk; internet www.brain.net.pk/~kazip; f. 1978; Islamic literature, religion, law, biographies; Propr MUHAMMAD IKRAM SIDDIQI.

Liberty Books (Pvt) Ltd: 3 Rafiq Plaza, M. R. Kayani Rd, opposite Navy Fleet Club, Saddar, Karachi; tel. (21) 35656567; fax (21) 35684319; e-mail info@libertybooks.com; internet www .libertybooks.com; f. 1980; Man. Dir SALEEM ABDUL HUSSAIN.

Lion Art Press (Pvt) Ltd: 112 The Mall, Lahore 54000; tel. (42) 36304444; fax (42) 36367728; e-mail lionart786@hotmail.com; f. 1919; general publs in English and Urdu; Chief Exec. KHALID A. SHEIKH; Dir ASMA KHALID.

Maktaba Darut Tasnif: Main Hub River Rd, Mujahidabad, Karachi 75760; tel. (21) 32814432; fax (21) 32811307; e-mail daruttasnif@yaqeendtl.com; f. 1951; Koran Majeed and Islamic literature; Dir ABDUL BAQI FAROOQI.

Malik Sirajuddin & Sons: 48-C, Lower Mall, Lahore 54000; tel. (42) 37225809; fax (42) 37224586; e-mail sirajco@brain.net.pk; f. 1905; general, religion, law, textbooks; Man. MALIK ABDUL ROUF.

Medina Publishing Co: M. A. Jinnah Rd, Karachi 1; f. 1960; general literature, textbooks; Propr HAKIM MOHAMMAD TAQI.

Sh. Muhammad Ashraf: 7 Aibak Rd, New Anarkali, Lahore 7; tel. (42) 37353171; fax (42) 37353489; e-mail shashraf@brain.net.pk; f. 1923; books in English on all aspects of Islam; Man. Dir SHAHZAD RIAZ SHEIKH.

Nafees Academy: Qasr-e-Maryam, Govali Lane No. 3, Ratan Talab, Urdu Bazar, Karachi; tel. (21) 32722080; fax (21) 32751247; e-mail nafeesacademy@cyber.net.pk; Propr KHAWAR IFTIKHAR.

National Book Foundation: G 8/4, 6 Mauve Area, Taleemi Chowk, POB 1169, Islamabad; tel. (51) 9261036; fax (51) 9261534; e-mail books@nbf.org.pk; internet www.nbf.org.pk; f. 1972; Man. Dir MAZHAR-UL-ISLAM.

National Book Service: 22 Urdu Bazar, Lahore; tel. (42) 37247310; fax (42) 37247323; e-mail fpc_pak@hotmail.com; internet www.fpcpk .com; f. 1950; academic and primary, secondary and ELT school books; Execs MUHAMMAD ARIF, MUHAMMAD AMIR, MUHAMMAD ASIM.

Noorsons Publishers: 16-Urdu Bazar, Lahore; tel. (42) 37124664; fax (42) 37231377; e-mail info@noorsons.com.pk; internet www .noorsons.com.pk.

Oxford University Press: Plot No. 38, Sector 15, Korangi Industrial Area, POB 8214, Karachi 74900; tel. (21) 35050835; fax (21) 35055071; e-mail oup.pk@oup.com; internet www.oup.com.pk; f. 1952; academic, educational and general; Man. Dir AMEENA SAIYID.

Pak Book Corpn: Aziz Chambers, 21 Queen's Rd, Lahore 54000; tel. (42) 36363222; fax (42) 36362328; e-mail info@pakbook.com; internet www.pakbook.com; f. 1975; Chief Exec. M. IQBAL CHEEMA.

Pakistan Law House: Pakistan Chowk, POB 90, Karachi 1; tel. (21) 32212455; fax (21) 32627549; e-mail pak_law_house@hotmail.com; internet www.pakistanlawhouse.com; f. 1950; importers and exporters of legal books and reference books; Man. K. NOORANI.

Pakistan Publishing House: 2 Victoria Chambers, A. Haroon Rd, Karachi 75400; tel. (21) 35681457; fax (21) 32627549; e-mail danyalbooks@hotmail.com; f. 1959; Propr HOORI NOORANI; Gen. Man. AAMIR HUSSAIN.

Paramount Publishing Enterprise: 152/0, Blk 2, PECHS, Karachi 75400; tel. (21) 34310030; fax (21) 34553772; e-mail info@ paramountbooks.com.pk; internet www.paramountbooks.com.pk; f. 1948; business management, children, computer science, medical, science, social science, etc.; Man. Dir IQBAL SALEH MUHAMMAD.

Pioneer Book House: 1-Sami Chambers, opp. D. M. C., M. A. Jinnah Rd, Karachi 74400; tel. (21) 32628739; fax (21) 32620971; agent for state and federal govt publications; periodicals, gazettes, maps and reference works in English, Urdu and other regional languages.

Publishers United (Pvt) Ltd: c/o Gulam Ali Medicine Market, Chowk Lohari Gate, POB 1689, Lahore 54000; tel. (42) 36361306; fax (42) 36316015; e-mail smalipub2@hotmail.com; f. 1950; Islamic studies, history, art, archaeology, literature, Oriental studies, genealogy, scientific, medical, humanities and social sciences; Man. Dir ASAD NIAZ.

Punjab Religious Books Society: Anarkali, Lahore 2; educational, religious, law and general; Gen. Man. A. R. IRSHAD; Sec. NAEEM SHAKIR.

Royal Book Co: BG-5, Rex Centre, Basement, Fatima Jinnah Rd, Karachi 75530; tel. (21) 35653418; fax (21) 37015472; e-mail royalbook@hotmail.com; Dir YOUSUF MIRZA.

Sang-e-Meel Publications: 25 Lower Mall, Lahore 54000; tel. (42) 37220100; fax (42) 37245101; e-mail smp@sang-e-meel.com; internet www.sang-e-meel.com; f. 1962; CEO AFZAAL AHMAD.

Say Publishing (Pvt) Ltd: SA 1-3, Shahnawaz Arcade, Shahid-e-Millat Rd, Karachi; tel. (21) 34945541; fax (21) 35834777; e-mail saybooks@gerrys.net; f. 1982; Man. Dir AHSON JAFFRI.

Sindh Education Foundation (SEF): Plot No. 9, Blk 7, Clifton 5, Karachi 75600; tel. (21) 111-424-111; fax (21) 99251652; e-mail info@sef.org.pk; internet www.sef.org.pk; f. 1992; Man. Dir Prof. ANITA GHULAM ALI.

Sindhi Adabi Board (Sindhi Literary and Publishing Organization): Hyderabad; tel. (221) 771276; e-mail bookinfo@sindhiadabiboard.org; internet www.sindhiadabiboard.org; f. 1951; history, literature, culture of Sindh; in Sindhi, Urdu, English, Persian and Arabic; translations into Sindhi, especially of literature and history; chaired by Minister of Education and Literacy, Sindh; Sec. AIJAZ AHMED MANGI.

Taj Co Ltd: Basement Aewan-e-ilm Plaza, Urdu bazar, Lahore; tel. (42) 37310638; fax (42) 37310641; internet www.tajcom.com; f. 1929; religious books; Man. Dir A. H. KHOKHAR.

The Times Press (Pvt) Ltd: C-18, Al-Hilal Society, off University Rd, Karachi 74800; tel. (21) 34932931; fax (21) 34935602; e-mail timekhi@cyber.net.pk; internet www.timespresspk.com; f. 1948; printers, publishers and stationery manufacturers, incl. security printing (postal stationery and stamps); registered publishers of Koran, school textbooks, etc.; Dir S. M. MINHAJUDDIN.

Urdu Academy Sind: Main Urdu Bazar, M. A. Jinnah Rd, Karachi; tel. (21) 32628655; fax (21) 32625992; e-mail urduacademy@cyber.net.pk; f. 1947; brs in Hyderabad and Lahore; academic, reference, general and textbooks; Man. Dir AZIZ KHALID.

Vanguard Books (Pvt) Ltd: 72-FCC, Gulberg IV, Lahore; tel. (42) 35763510; fax (42) 35751025; e-mail vbl@brain.net.pk; Chief Exec. NAJAM SETHI.

West-Pak Publishing Co (Pvt) Ltd: 17 Urdu Bazar, Lahore; tel. (42) 37230555; fax (42) 37120077; e-mail pakcompany@hotmail.com; f. 1932; textbooks and religious books; Chief Exec. SYED AHSAN MAHMUD.

GOVERNMENT PUBLISHING HOUSE

Government Publications: Office of the Deputy Controller, Stationery and Forms, nr Old Sabzi Mandi, University Rd, Karachi 74800; tel. (21) 99231989; publ. *Gazette of Pakistan*; Dep. Controller MUHAMMAD AMIN BUTT.

PUBLISHERS' ASSOCIATION

Pakistan Publishers' and Booksellers' Association: 6 Gunpat Rd, Lahore; tel. (42) 37722043; Chair. NAJAM SETHI; Gen. Sec. ZUBAIR SAEED.

Broadcasting and Communications

TELECOMMUNICATIONS

Regulatory Authority

Pakistan Telecommunication Authority (PTA): F-5/1, Islamabad 44000; tel. (51) 2878143; fax (51) 2878155; e-mail administration@pta.gov.pk; internet www.pta.gov.pk; f. 1997; regulatory authority; Chair. Dr MOHAMMAD YASEEN; Dir-Gen. CH. MOHAMMAD DIN.

Service Providers

Burraq Telecom (Pvt) Ltd: Plot 94A, St 7, Sector I-10/3, Islamabad; tel. (51) 111-287-727; fax (51) 2112380; e-mail info@burraqtel.com.pk; internet www.burraqtel.com.pk; f. 2004; CEO SADIQ YOUSAF YALMAZ.

China Mobile Pakistan Ltd: 7 Mauve Area, Islamabad; tel. (51) 111222111; fax (51) 111031031; internet www.zong.com.pk; f. 2008; Chair. WANG JIANZHOU.

Mobilink: Mobilink House 1A, Kohistan Rd, F-8 Markaz, Islamabad; tel. (21) 32273984; fax (21) 32826999; e-mail customercare@mobilink.net; internet www.mobilinkgsm.com; subsidiary of Orascom Telecom, Egypt; Pres. and CEO RASHID KHAN.

National Telecommunication Corporation: NTC Bldg, F-5/1, Islamabad; tel. (51) 9206450; e-mail infolhr@ntc.net.pk; internet www.ntc.net.pk; f. 1996; govt-owned; Chair. MUHAMMAD YOUNAS.

Pakistan Telecommunications (Pvt) Ltd (PTCL): Blk E, G-8/4, Islamabad 44000; tel. (51) 4844463; fax (51) 4843991; e-mail shahzad.khalil@ptcl.net.pk; internet www.ptcl.com.pk; f. 1990; 74% state-owned; 26% owned by Etisalat (United Arab Emirates); Chair. SAEED AHMAD KHAN; Pres. and CEO WALID IRSHAID.

   Ufone: 13-B, F-7 Markaz, Jinnah Super Market, Islamabad; fax (51) 111-333-100; e-mail customercare@ufonegsm.net; internet www.ufone.com; f. 2001; subsidiary of Pakistan Telecommunications (Pvt) Ltd; private mobile telephone co; Pres. and Chief Exec. ABDUL AZIZ.

TeleCard Ltd: 7th Floor, World Trade Centre, 10 Khayaban-e-Roomi, Blk 5, Clifton, Karachi 75600; tel. (21) 111-222-124; fax (21) 35867850; e-mail customerservices@telecard.com.pk; internet www.telecard.com.pk; Chair. SULTAN UL-ARFEEN; CEO SYED AAMIR HUSSAIN.

Telenor: 13-K, Moaiz Centre, F-7 Markaz, Islamabad; tel. (51) 111-345-700; fax (51) 2651923; internet www.telenor.com.pk; f. 2004; private mobile telephone co; CEO SIGVE BREKKE.

Warid Telecom (Pvt) Ltd: 9th Floor, EFU Bldg, Jail Rd, Lahore; e-mail customerservice@waridtel.com; internet www.waridtel.com; owned by Abu Dhabi Group; CEO MUNEER FAROOQUI.

Wateen Telecom (Pvt) Ltd: 4th Floor, New Auriga Complex, Main Blvd, POB 3527, Lahore; fax (21) 34324096; e-mail info@wateen.com; internet www.wateen.com; subsidiary of the Abu Dhabi Group, UAE; mobile and fixed line telephone services; internet, television and multimedia provider; CEO NAEEM ZAMINDAR.

Other Companies

Megatech Communications (Pvt) Ltd: 47 Banglore Town, off Tipu Sultan Rd, Karachi 75350; tel. (21) 34528954; fax (21) 34533768; e-mail info@megatech.com.pk; internet www.megatech.com.pk; f. 1992; supplier of new digital telephone systems integrated with ISDN/BRI; Sales Dir FARHAT ABBAS.

Telephone Industries of Pakistan (TIP): Khanpur Rd, Haripur 22630; tel. (995) 611469; fax (995) 610490; e-mail mdtip@tip.org.pk; internet www.tip.org.pk; f. 1952; Man. Dir NADEEM AHMAD KHAN; mfrs of telecommunications equipment.

BROADCASTING

Regulatory Authority

Pakistan Electronic Media Regulatory Authority (PEMRA): 6th Floor, Green Trust Tower, Blue Area, Islamabad; tel. (51) 9107105; fax (51) 9107107; e-mail exec_member@pemra.gov.pk; internet www.pemra.gov.pk; regulates the establishment and operation of broadcast media and distribution services; Chair. MUSHTAQ MALIK.

Radio

Pakistan Broadcasting Corporation: G-5 Constitution Ave, Islamabad; tel. (51) 9208306; fax (51) 9223827; e-mail cac.pbc@gmail.com; internet www.radio.gov.pk; f. 1947 as Radio Pakistan; national broadcasting network of 42 stations; Dir-Gen. MURTAZA SOLANGI.

CityFM89: 11 Dockyard Rd, West Wharf Industrial Area, Karachi; tel. (21) 32331095; fax (21) 32331099; e-mail info@cityFM89.com; internet cityfm89.com; f. 2004; owned by Kohinoor Airwaves (Pvt) Ltd; broadcasts in Karachi, Lahore, Islamabad and Faisalabad; Chief Operating Officer NERMEEN CHINOY.

FM-100: Plot 43-5, E/3, Blk 6, Karachi; tel. (21) 32630611; fax (21) 32629311; e-mail info@fm100pakistan.com; internet www.fm100pakistan.com; f. 1995; music station; broadcasts in Karachi, Lahore and Islamabad.

Radio1 FM91: 11F, Main Karsaz Rd, KDA Scheme 1, Karachi; tel. (21) 34525190; fax (21) 34522253; e-mail info@91radio1.fm; internet www.fm91.com.pk; broadcasts in Karachi, Lahore, Islamabad and Gawadar; entertainment programmes.

Television

Aaj TV: 531 Recorder House, Business Recorder Rd, Karachi 74550; fax (21) 32237067; e-mail aajcomments@aaj.tv; internet www.aaj.tv; privately owned by Business Recorder Group; digital satellite channel broadcasting news, current affairs and entertainment programmes; also operates from Islamabad and Lahore; Dir MASOOM USMANI.

ARY News: 6th Floor, Madina City Mall, Abdullah Haroon Rd, Saddar, Karachi; tel. (21) 35657315; fax (21) 35657314; e-mail info@arydigital.tv; internet www.thearynews.com.

ATV Shalimar Television Network Channel (Shalimar Recording and Broadcasting Co Ltd): 36, H-9, POB 1246, Islamabad; tel. (51) 9257396; fax (51) 4434830; e-mail contact@srbc.com.pk; internet www.srbc.com.pk; f. 1976 as Shalimar Recording Co; 92.81% state-owned, 7.19% privately owned; 20 terrestrial stations throughout Pakistan; Chief Exec. and Dir FAZALUR REHMAN MALIK.

CNBC Pakistan: Techno City Corporate Tower, 13/F Hasrat Mohani Rd, Karachi; tel. (21) 111-262-275; fax (21) 32270852; e-mail info@cnbcpakistan.com; internet www.cnbcpakistan.com.

Geo TV: I. I. Chundrigar Rd, Jang Building, Karachi; tel. (21) 32637111; fax (21) 32271403; e-mail feedback@geo.tv; internet www.geo.tv; f. 2003; Pakistan's first private broadcasting network; broadcasts in Urdu; operates four channels; Pres. IMRAN ASLAM.

HUM TV: Plot 10/11, Hassan Ali St, Karachi; tel. (21) 35374258; fax (21) 32628840; e-mail feedback@hum.tv; internet www.hum.tv; transmits 24 hrs daily; entertainment channel.

Indus TV Network: 2nd Floor, Shafi Court, Civil Lines, Mereweather Rd, Karachi; tel. (21) 35693801; fax (21) 35693813; e-mail info@indus.tv; internet www.indus.tv; f. 2000; Pakistan's first independent satellite channel; CEO GHAZANFAR ALI.

Pakistan Television Corpn Ltd: Federal TV Complex, Constitution Ave, POB 1221, Islamabad; tel. (51) 9212222; fax (51) 99202202; e-mail md@ptv.com.pk; internet ptv.com.pk; f. 1964; transmits 24 hrs daily; 6 channels; Man. Dir YOUSAF BAIG MIRZA.

SAMAA TV: 16th Floor, Techno City Corporate Tower, Karachi; tel. (21); fax (21) 32270856; e-mail interactive@samaa.tv; internet www.samaa.tv; broadcasts in Karachi, Lahore, Islamabad, Quetta and Peshawar.

WAQT Television: 23 Queens Rd, Lahore; tel. (42) 36367580; fax (42) 36367005; internet www.waqtnews.tv; f. 2007; Dir TARIQ MAHMOOD.

Finance

(cap. = capital; auth. = authorized; p.u. = paid up; res = reserves; dep. = deposits; m. = million; brs = branches; amounts in rupees unless otherwise stated)

BANKING

Central Bank

State Bank of Pakistan: Central Directorate, I. I. Chundrigar Rd, POB 4456, Karachi 2; tel. (21) 99212400; fax (21) 99217234; e-mail info@sbp.org.pk; internet www.sbp.org.pk; f. 1948; bank of issue; controls and regulates currency and foreign exchange; cap. 1.0m., res 349.7m., dep. 512.7m. (June 2009); Gov. YASIN ANWAR; 16 brs.

Commercial Banks

Allied Bank Ltd: Central Office, Main Clifton Rd, Bath Island, Karachi; tel. (21) 35370499; fax (21) 35370500; e-mail info@abl.com.pk; internet www.abl.com.pk; f. 1942 as Australasia Bank Ltd; name changed as above 2005; cap. 8,603m., res 14,480m., dep. 399,560.8m. (Dec. 2011); 49% state-owned; CEO KHALID A. SHERWANI; Chair. MOHAMMAD NAEEM MUKHTAR; 741 brs in Pakistan.

Askari Bank Ltd: AWT Plaza, The Mall, POB 1084, Rawalpindi; tel. (51) 99063000; fax (51) 99272455; e-mail president@askaribank.com.pk; internet www.askaribank.com.pk; f. 1992; cap. 8,130.7m., res 10,552.3m., dep. 306,930m. (Dec. 2012); Chair. Lt-Gen. JAVED IQBAL; Pres. and Chief Exec. MUHAMMAD RAFIQUDDIN MEHKARI; 121 brs.

Bank Al Habib Ltd: Mackinnons Bldg, I. I. Chundrigar Rd, Karachi; tel. (21) 32412421; fax (21) 32419752; e-mail info@bankalhabib.com; internet www.bankalhabib.com; f. 1991; cap. 10,103.8m., res 9,252.5m., dep. 340,286.5m. (Dec. 2012); Chair. ALI RAZA D. HABIB; Chief Exec. and Man. Dir ABBAS D. HABIB; 263 brs in Pakistan and abroad.

Bank Alfalah Ltd: BA Bldg, I. I. Chundrigar Rd, POB 6773, Karachi; tel. (21) 32416811; fax (21) 32424901; e-mail figroup@bankalfalah.com; internet www.bankalfalah.com; f. 1992 as Habib Credit and Exchange Ltd; name changed as above 1998; cap. 13,491m., res 6,888m., dep. 401,245.7m. (Dec. 2011); 60.7% owned by Abu Dhabi Consortium, 15.6% non-residents, 23.2% general public, employees and cos, 0.5% others; Chair. SHEIKH HAMDAN BIN MUBARAK AL NAHAYAN; 231 brs.

The Bank of Khyber: 24 The Mall, Peshawar; tel. (521) 111-959-595; fax (915) 278146; e-mail bokforex@psh.paknet.com.pk; internet www.bok.com.pk; f. 1991; cap. 8,228m., res 1,387.6m., dep. 45,548m. (Dec. 2011); 51% state-owned; 49% public shareholders; the main branch in Peshawar began Islamic banking operations in June 2003; Man. Dir BILAL MUSTAFA; Chair. ATTAULLAH KHAN; 34 brs.

The Bank of Punjab: BOP Tower, 10-B, Blk-E-II, Main Blvd, Gulberg-III, POB 2254, Lahore; tel. (42) 35783700; e-mail sajjad.hussain@bop.com.pk; internet www.bop.com.pk; f. 1989; cap. 5,287.9m., res 6,113.8m., dep. 165,292.3m. (Dec. 2008); 51% owned by provincial govt; Chair. GHAFOOR MIRZA; Pres. and CEO NAEEMUDDIN KHAN; 280 brs.

Faysal Bank Ltd: ST-02, Faysal House, 4th Floor, FIG, Main Shahrah-e-Faisal, Karachi; tel. (21) 32795306; fax (21) 32793131; e-mail fbl@faysalbank.com; internet www.faysalbank.com; f. 1995; merged with Al-Faysal Investment Bank Ltd 2002; took over Royal Bank of Scotland (RBS) Pakistan in Jan. 2011; cap. 9,273.5m., res 8,558.1m., dep. 240,712.8m. (Dec. 2012); Pres. and CEO NAVED A. KHAN; 107 brs.

Habib Bank Ltd: 22 Habib Bank Plaza, I. I. Chundrigar Rd, Karachi 75650; tel. (21) 32411530; fax (21) 32411556; e-mail zmahmood@hblpk.com; internet www.habibbankltd.com; f. 1941; cap. 12,122.7m., res 52,164.6m., dep. 1,227.2m. (Dec. 2012); transferred to private sector Feb. 2004; 51% owned by Agha Khan Fund for Economic Development (United Kingdom), 41% by State Bank of Pakistan and 8% by Government and National Bank of Pakistan; Pres. and CEO ZAKIR MAHMOOD; 1,437 brs in Pakistan; 39 foreign brs.

Habib Metropolitan Bank Ltd: Mezzanine Floor, Spencer's Bldg, I. I. Chundrigar Rd, POB 1289, Karachi; tel. (21) 32638080; fax (21) 32630404; e-mail info@hmb.com.pk; internet www.hmb.com.pk; f. 1992; fmrly Metropolitan Bank; merged with Habib Bank AG Zurich in 2006; cap. 10,478m., res 11,674.5m., dep. 217,670.8m. (Dec. 2012); Chair. KASSIM PAREKH; Pres. and CEO SIRAJUDDIN AZIZ; 110 brs (incl. 4 Islamic banking brs).

JS Bank Ltd: 1st Floor, Shaheen Commercial Complex, Dr Ziauddin Ahmed Rd, Karachi 74200; tel. (21) 111-572-265; fax (21) 32631803; e-mail info@jsbl.com; internet www.jsbl.com; f. 2006; cap. 10,724.6m., res −1,590.7m., dep. 61,934.7m. (Dec. 2011); Pres. and CEO KALIM UR RAHMAN; Chair. JAHANGIR SIDDIQUI; 39 brs.

KASB Bank Ltd: Business and Finance Centre, I. I. Chundrigar Rd, Karachi 74000; tel. (21) 32446005; fax (21) 32446781; e-mail international@kasb.com; internet www.kasbbank.com; f. 1995 as Platinum Commercial Bank Ltd; name changed as above 2003; cap. 19,508m., res −6,357.8m., dep. 61,993m. (Dec. 2011); Pres. and CEO AAMER H. ZAIDI; 73 brs.

MCB Bank Ltd: MCB Tower, I. I. Chundrigar Rd, POB 4976, Karachi 74000; tel. (21) 32270075; fax (21) 32270076; e-mail atif.bajwa@mcb.com.pk; internet www.mcb.com.pk; f. 1947; cap. 8,362m., res 52,539.9m., dep. 491,146.9m. (Dec. 2011); Chair. Mian MUHAMMAD MANSHA; Pres. and CEO M. U. A. USMANI; 1,057 brs in Pakistan, 4 brs abroad.

National Bank of Pakistan (NBP): NBP Bldg, I. I. Chundrigar Rd, POB 4937, Karachi 2; tel. (21) 99212100; fax (21) 99212774; e-mail nbp@nbp.com.pk; internet www.nbp.com.pk; f. 1949; cap. 18,500m., res 66,257.5m., dep. 1,038,094.9m. (Dec. 2012); 100% state-owned; Pres. QAMAR HUSSAIN; 1,491 brs in Pakistan and 22 brs abroad.

NIB Bank Ltd: Muhammadi House, I. I. Chundrigar Rd, Karachi; tel. (21) 32420333; fax (21) 32472258; e-mail info@nibpk.com; internet www.nibpk.com; f. 2003; PICIC Commercial Bank Ltd and Prime Commercial Bank Ltd merged into NIB in December 2007; cap. 103,028.5m., res −45,563.5m., dep. 91,094.4m. (Dec. 2012); Pres. and CEO BADAR KAZMI; 179 brs (2012).

Samba Bank Ltd: 5th & 6th Floor, Sidco Avenue Centre, Maulana Deen Mohammad Wafai Rd, Karachi 74000; tel. (21) 111-999-333; internet www.cresbank.com; f. 2002 as Crescent Commercial Bank Ltd; cap. 14,334.7m., res 192.7m., dep. 22,753.6m. (Dec. 2012); Pres. and CEO TAWFIQ A. HUSAIN; Chair. SYED SAJJAD RAZVI; 18 brs.

Silkbank: Saudi Pak Bldg, I. I. Chundrigar Rd, Karachi; tel. (21) 32460466; fax (21) 32460464; fmrly Saudi Pak Commercial Bank Ltd, rebranded as above in 2009; cap. 26,716m., res −12,961.9m., dep. 69,050.4m. (Dec. 2012); Chair. MUNNAWAR HAMID; Pres. and CEO AZMAT TARIN; 38 brs.

Soneri Bank Ltd: 87 Shahrah-e-Quaid-e-Azam, POB 49, Lahore; tel. (42) 36368142; fax (42) 36368138; e-mail main.lahore@soneribank.com; internet www.soneribank.com; f. 1991; cap. 10,022.3m., res 362.6m., dep. 120,830.5m. (Dec. 2012); Chair. ALAUDDIN FEERASTA; Pres. and CEO MOHAMMAD AFTAB MANZOOR; 216 brs.

Standard Chartered Bank (Pakistan) Ltd: 3rd Floor, Main Br., POB 5556, I. I. Chundrigar Rd, Karachi; tel. (21) 32450288; fax (21)

32414914; e-mail badar.kazmi@pk.standardchartered.com; internet www.standardchartered.com/pk; f. 2006; cap. 38,715.8m., res 9,035.4m., dep. 266,598.5m. (Dec. 2011); Pres. and CEO MOHSIN ALI NATHANI; 144 brs.

Summit Bank Ltd: 6B, F–6, Supermarket, Islamabad; tel. (21) 111-124-725; fax (21) 2463566; e-mail syedadnanali@arifhabibbank.com; internet www.summitbank.com.pk; f. 2006 as Arif Habib Bank Ltd; name changed as above in Aug. 2010; cap. 10,779.8m., res –1,645.9m., dep. 96,815.3m. (Dec. 2012); Pres. and Chief Exec. HUSAIN LAWAI; Chair. NASSER ABDULLAH HUSSAIN LOOTAH; 80 brs and sub brs.

United Bank Ltd: State Life Bldg, No. 1, I. I. Chundrigar Rd, POB 4306, Karachi 74000; tel. (21) 32417021; fax (21) 32413492; e-mail president@ubl.com.pk; internet www.ubl.com.pk; f. 1959; cap. 12,241.8m., res 47,553.7m., dep. 755,264.2m. (Dec. 2012); privatized in 2002; Pres. and CEO ATIF BOKHARI; 1,172 brs in Pakistan and 16 brs abroad.

Leasing Banks (*Modarabas*)

The number of leasing banks (*modarabas*), which conform to the strictures placed upon the banking system by *Shari'a* (the Islamic legal code), rose from four in 1988 to about 45 in 2002. The following are among the most important *modarabas* in Pakistan.

Asian Leasing Corporation Ltd: 85-B Jail Rd, Gulberg, POB 3176, Lahore; tel. (42) 484417; fax (42) 484418.

Atlas Lease Ltd: Ground Floor, Federation House, Shahrah-e-Firdousi, Main Clifton, Karachi 75600; tel. (21) 35866817; fax (21) 35870543; e-mail all@atlasgrouppk.com; Chair. YUSUF H. SHIRAZI.

B. R. R. International Modaraba: 1500A Saima Trade Towers, I. I. Chundrigar Rd, Karachi 74000; tel. (21) 32271874; fax (21) 32271912; e-mail brr@firstdawood.com; internet www.firstdawood.com/brr.

Dadabhoy Leasing Co Ltd: 5th Floor, Maqbool Commercial Complex, JCHS Block, Main Shahrah-e-Faisal, Karachi; tel. (21) 34548171; fax (21) 34547301; Man. (Finance) MOHAMMAD AYUB.

English Leasing Ltd: D-16, Block 3, Clifton, Scheme 5, Karachi; tel. (21) 35810453; fax (21) 35375770; e-mail info@engl.com.pk; Chair. ASIM MAHBOOB SHEIKH.

First Habib Bank Modaraba: 18 Habib Bank Plaza, I. I. Chundrigar Rd, Karachi 75650; tel. (21) 32635949; fax (21) 32627373; e-mail fhm@habibmodaraba.com; internet www.habibmodaraba.com; f. 1991; wholly owned subsidiary of Habib Bank Ltd; Chair. WAZIR MUMTAZ AHMED; CEO MUHAMMAD SHOAIB.

Orix Leasing Pakistan Ltd: Overseas Investors Chamber of Commerce Bldg, Talpur Rd, Karachi 74000; tel. (21) 32425896; fax (21) 32425897; e-mail olp@orixpakistan.com; internet www.orixpakistan.com; f. 1986; cap. US $10m. (June 2004); Chief Exec. TAIZA KISET.

Pakistan Industrial and Commercial Leasing Ltd: 504 Park Ave, 24-A, Blk 6, PECHS, Shahrah-e-Faisal, Karachi 75210; tel. (21) 324551045; fax (21) 32452065; e-mail picl@super.net.pk; internet www.piclltd.com; f. 1987; Exec. Chair. ZAHEERUL HAQUE.

Standard Chartered Modaraba: Standard Services of Pakistan (Pvt) Ltd, Standard Bank Bldg, I. I. Chundrigar Rd, POB 5556, Karachi 74000; tel. (21) 32450378; fax (21) 38140801; e-mail contact@scmodaraba.com; internet www.scmodaraba.com; fmrly First Grindlays Modaraba; Man. Dir SYED ZAHIR MEHDI.

Islamic Banks

BankIslami Pakistan Ltd: 11th Floor, Executive Tower One, Dolmen City, Marine Dr., Blk 4, Clifton, Karachi; tel. (21) 35839906; fax (21) 35378373; e-mail info@bankislami.com.pk; internet www.bankislami.com.pk; cap. 5,279.7m., res 192.8m., dep. 64,110.6m. (Dec. 2012); CEO MAHBOOB AHMED.

Burj Bank Ltd: Trade Centre, I. I. Chundrigar Rd, Karachi 74000; tel. (21) 32637174; fax (21) 32272466; e-mail info@burjbankltd.com; internet www.burjbankltd.com; cap. 7,410m., res 43.8m., dep. 20,341m. (Dec. 2011); fmrly Dawood Islamic Bank Ltd, name changed as above July 2011; Pres. and CEO KHALID MOHAMMAD AL-ABOODI.

Dubai Islamic Bank Pakistan Ltd: Hassan Chambers, Plot DC-7, Blk 7, Clifton, Karachi; tel. (21) 35368786; fax (21) 35308921; e-mail saad.zaman@dib.ae; internet www.dibpak.com; f. 2006; cap. 6,776m., res 80.3m., dep. 38,841.6m. (Dec. 2011); CEO JUNAID AHMED.

Meezan Bank Ltd: 2nd and 3rd Floors, PNSC Bldg, Moulvi Tamizuddin Khan Rd, Karachi 74000; tel. (21) 35610582; fax (21) 35610375; e-mail info@meezanbank.com; internet www.meezanbank.com; f. 1997 as Al-Meezan Investment Bank; became commercial bank 2002 and name changed as above; cap. 8,029.9m., res 2,540.3m., dep. 170,022.4m. (Dec. 2011); Pres. and CEO IRFAN SIDDIQUI; Gen. Man. ARIFUL ISLAM; 37 brs.

Investment Banks

Asset Investment Bank Ltd: Rm 1-B, 1st Floor, Ali Plaza, Khaya-ban-e-Quaid-e-Azam, Blue Area, Islamabad; tel. (51) 2270625; fax (51) 2272506; Chief Exec. SYED NAVEED ZAIDI.

Atlas Investment Bank Ltd: 3rd Floor, Federation House, Abdullah Shah Ghazi Rd, Main Clifton, Karachi; tel. (21) 111-333-225; fax (21) 35870543; e-mail info@atlasbank.com.pk; internet www.atlasbank.com.pk; 15% owned by Bank of Tokyo-Mitsubishi UFJ Ltd; Chair. YUSUF H. SHIRAZI; CEO AZIZ RAJKOTWALA.

Escorts Investment Bank Ltd: Escorts House, 26 Davis Rd, Lahore; tel. (42) 36371931; fax (42) 36375950; e-mail mailmanager@escortsbank.net; internet escortsbank.net; Pres. and CEO RASHID MANSUR.

IGI Investment Bank Ltd: 7th Floor, The Forum, Suite 701–703, 4-20, Blk 9, Khayaban-e-Jami, Clifton, Karachi; tel. (21) 111-234-234; fax (21) 111-567-567; e-mail contact.center@igi.com.pk; internet www.igiinvestmentbank.com.pk; Man. Dir and CEO SYED BABAR ALI.

Orix Investment Bank Pakistan Ltd: 2nd Floor, Islamic Chamber of Commerce Bldg, St 2/A, Block 9, Clifton, Karachi 75600; tel. (21) 35861266; fax (21) 35868862; e-mail oibpl@orixbank.com; internet www.orixbank.com; f. 1995; Man. Dir and CEO NAIM FAROOQUI.

Development Finance Organizations

First MicroFinanceBank Ltd: President's Secretariat, 62-C, 25th Commercial St, Tauheed Commercial Area, DHA Phase V, Karachi; tel. (21) 35822432; fax (21) 35822434; e-mail information@mfb.com.pk; internet www.mfb.com.pk; Pres. and CEO HUSSAIN TEJANY.

First Women Bank Ltd: S.T.S.M. Foundation Bldg, CL-10/20/2 Beaumont Rd, Civil Lines, Karachi 75530; tel. (21) 111-676-767; fax (21) 35657756; e-mail info@fwbl.com.pk; internet www.fwbl.com.pk; f. 1989; cap. 1,080m., res 359m., dep. 13,814.8m. (Dec. 2011); Pres. SHAFQAT SULTANA; 38 brs.

House Building Finance Corpn: Finance and Trade Centre, 3rd Floor, Shahrah-e-Faisal, Karachi 74400; tel. (21) 99202301; fax (21) 99202360; e-mail info@hbfc.com.pk; internet www.hbfc.com.pk; provides loans for the construction and purchase of housing units; Man. Dir and CEO AZHAR A. JAFFRI.

Industrial Development Bank of Pakistan: State Life Bldg No. 2, Wallace Rd, off I. I. Chundrigar Rd, POB 5082, Karachi 74000; tel. (21) 99213601; fax (21) 99213644; e-mail idbp@idbp.com.pk; internet www.idbp.com.pk; f. 1961; provides credit facilities for small and medium-sized industrial enterprises in the private sector; 100% state-owned; Chair. and Man. Dir JAMAL NASIM; 14 brs.

Khushhali Bank: 94W, 4th Floor, Jinnah Ave, Blue Area, Islamabad 44000; tel. (51) 111-092-092; fax (51) 9245120; internet www.khushhalibank.com.pk; f. 2000 by the Govt under the Asian Development Bank's micro-finance sector development programme; provides micro-loans to the poor and finances reforms in the micro-finance sector; cap. 1,705m. (Aug. 2000); Pres. GHALIB NISHTAR.

National Investment Trust Ltd: NBP Bldg, 6th Floor, I. I. Chundrigar Rd, POB 5671, Karachi; tel. (21) 32419061; fax (21) 32430623; e-mail info@nit.com.pk; internet www.nit.com.pk; f. 1962; an open-ended mutual fund, mobilizes domestic savings to meet the requirements of growing economic development and enables investors to share in the industrial and economic prosperity of the country; 67,000 unit holders (1999/2000); Man. Dir TARIQ IQBAL KHAN.

Network Microfinance Bank Ltd: 202 Azayam Plaza, opp. FTC Bldg, SMCHS, Shahrah-e-Faisal, Karachi; fax (21) 34311722; e-mail info@networkmicrobank.com; internet www.networkmicrobank.com; Pres. and CEO ZAINUL AABEDIN MEMON.

Pak Oman Microfinance Bank Ltd: 2nd Floor, Tower C, Finance and Trade Centre, Shahrah-e-Faisal, Karachi; tel. (21) 35630941; fax (21) 35630999; e-mail info@pomicro.com; internet www.pomicro.com; f. 2005; Pres. and CEO MUNAWAR SULEMAN.

Pakistan Industrial Credit and Investment Corpn Ltd (PICIC): State Life Bldg No. 1, I. I. Chundrigar Rd, POB 5080, Karachi 74000; tel. (21) 32414220; fax (21) 32419100; f. 1957 as an industrial development bank to provide financial assistance in both local and foreign currencies, for the establishment of new industries in the private sector and balancing modernization, replacement and expansion of existing industries; merchant banking and foreign exchange activities; total assets 33,949m., cap. 2,736m., res 4,188m. (June 2005); held 97.9% and 2.1% by local and foreign investors, respectively; Man. Dir MOHAMMAD ALI KHOJA; Chair. ALTAF M. SALEEM; 19 brs.

Pakistan Kuwait Investment Co (Pvt) Ltd: Tower 'C', 4th Floor, Finance and Trade Centre, Shahrah-e-Faisal, POB 901, Karachi 74400; tel. (21) 35630901; fax (21) 35630939; e-mail info@pkic.com; internet www.pkic.com; jt venture between the Govt and Kuwait to promote investment in industrial and agro-based enterprises; Man. Dir SHAMSUL HASAN.

Pak-Libya Holding Co (Pvt) Ltd: Finance and Trade Centre, 5th Floor, Tower 'C', Shahrah-e-Faisal, POB 10425, Karachi 74400; tel. (21) 111-111-115; fax (21) 35630665; e-mail info@paklibya.com.pk; internet www.paklibya.com.pk; jt venture between the Govts of Pakistan and Libya to promote industrial investment in Pakistan; Chair. RAMADAN A. HAGGIAGI; Man. Dir KAMAL UDDIN KHAN.

Saudi Pak Industrial and Agricultural Investment Co (Pvt) Ltd: Saudi Pak Tower, 61-A Jinnah Ave, Islamabad; tel. (51) 111-222-003; fax (51) 111-222-004; e-mail saudipak@saudipak.com; internet www.saudipak.com; f. 1981 jtly by Saudi Arabia and Pakistan to finance industrial and agro-based projects and undertake investment-related activities in Pakistan; cap. 2,000m., res 732m., dep. 5,900m. (March 2001); CEO MUHAMMAD RASHID ZAHIR; Chair. ABDULLAH T. AL-THENAYAN; 1 br.

SME Bank Ltd: Jang Plaza, 2nd Floor, 40 Fazal-ul-Haq Rd, Blue Area, POB 1587, Islamabad; tel. (51) 9217000; fax (51) 9217001; e-mail info@smebank.org; internet www.smebank.org; formed through merger of Regional Development Finance Corpn (RDFC) and Small Business Finance Corpn (SBFC); provides loans for small businesses; Pres. and CEO R. A. CHUGHTAI.

Zarai Taraqiati Bank Ltd (ZTBL): 1 Faisal Ave, POB 1400, Islamabad; tel. (51) 9252805; fax (51) 9252737; e-mail contactus@ztbl.com.pk; internet www.ztbl.com.pk; f. 1961; provides credit facilities to agriculturists (particularly small-scale farmers) and cottage industrialists in the rural areas and for allied projects; 100% state-owned; Pres. MUHAMMAD ZAKA ASHRAF; 24 zonal offices and 342 brs.

Banking Associations

Investment Banks Association of Pakistan: 7th Floor, Shaheen Commercial Complex, Dr Ziauddin Ahmed Rd, POB 1345, Karachi; tel. (21) 32631396; fax (21) 32630678; internet www.ibap.biz; Chair. RASHID MANSUR.

NBFI & Modaraba Association of Pakistan: 6th Floor, Progressive Centre, 30A, Blk 6, PECHS, Shahrah-e-Faisal, Karachi; tel. (21) 34322440; fax (21) 34389775; e-mail association@nbfi-modaraba.com.pk; internet www.nbfi-modaraba.com.pk; f. 2010; Chair. RAHEEL Q. AHMAD.

Pakistan Banks' Association: D-126, Blk 4, Clifton, Karachi 2; tel. (21) 35822986; fax (21) 35823418; e-mail pba@pakistanbanks.org; internet www.pakistanbanks.org; Chair. M. YOUNAS KHAN; Sec. A. GHAFFAR K. HAFIZ.

Banking Organizations

Banking Mohtasib Pakistan: Secretariat, 5th Floor, Shaheen Complex, POB 604, M. R. Kiyani Rd, Karachi; tel. (21) 99217334; fax (21) 99217375; e-mail info@bankingmohtasib.gov.pk; internet www.bankingmohtasib.gov.pk; resolves public grievances against banks and disputes between banking institutions; offices in Quetta, Lahore, Rawalpindi and Peshawar; Banking Ombudsman AZHAR HAMID.

Pakistan Banking Council: Habib Bank Plaza, I. I. Chundrigar Rd, Karachi; f. 1973; acts as a co-ordinating body between the nationalized banks and the Ministry of Finance; Chair. MUHAMMAD ZAKI; Sec. Mir WASIF ALI.

Pakistan Development Banking Institute: 4th Floor, Sidco Ave Centre, Stratchen Rd, Karachi; tel. (21) 35688049; fax (21) 35688460.

STOCK EXCHANGES

Securities and Exchange Commission of Pakistan: NIC Bldg, 63 Jinnah Ave, Blue Area, Islamabad 44000; tel. (51) 9207091; fax (51) 9204915; e-mail enquiries@secp.gov.pk; internet www.secp.gov.pk; oversees and co-ordinates operations of exchanges and registration of companies; registration offices in: Faisalabad (356-A, 1st Floor, Al-Jamil Plaza, People's Colony, Small D Ground, Faisalabad; tel. (41) 713841); Karachi (No. 2, 4th Floor, State Life Building, North Wing, Karachi; tel. (21) 2415855); Lahore (3rd and 4th Floors, Associated House, 7 Egerton Rd, Lahore; tel. (42) 9202044); Multan (61 Abdali Rd, Multan; tel. (61) 542609); Peshawar (Hussain Commercial Bldg, 3 Arbab Rd, Peshawar); Quetta (382/3, IDBP House, Shahrah-e-Hall, Quetta; tel. (81) 844138); and Sukkur (B-30, Sindhi Muslim Housing Society, Airport Rd, Sukkur; tel. (71) 30517); Chair. MUHAMMAD ALI.

Islamabad Stock Exchange (Guarantee) Ltd: ISE Towers, 55B, Jinnah Ave, Islamabad; tel. (51) 2275045; fax (51) 2275044; e-mail info@ise.com.pk; internet www.ise.com.pk; f. 1991; 121 mems; Chair. MUHAMMAD RASHID ZAHIR; Sec. Mian AYYAZ AFZAL.

Karachi Stock Exchange (Guarantee) Ltd: Stock Exchange Bldg, Stock Exchange Rd, Karachi 74000; tel. (21) 111-001-122; fax (21) 32410825; e-mail info@kse.com.pk; internet www.kse.com

.pk; f. 1947; 200 mems, 654 listed cos (Jan. 2007); Chair. MUNEER KAMAL; Man. Dir NADEEM NAQVI.

Lahore Stock Exchange (Guarantee) Ltd: Lahore Stock Exchange Bldg, 19 Khayaban-e-Aiwan-e-Iqbal, POB 1315, Lahore 54000; tel. (42) 36368000; fax (42) 36368484; e-mail info@LSE.com.pk; internet www.lse.com.pk; f. 1970; 511 listed cos, 151 mems; Chair. AFTAB AHMAD KHAN; Man. Dir/CEO AFTAB AHMAD CH.

Pakistan Mercantile Exchange Ltd: 9th Floor, PIC Towers, 32-A Lalazar Drive, M. T. Khan Rd, Karachi; tel. (21) 111-623-623; fax (21) 35611263; e-mail support@pmex.com.pk; internet www.pmex.com.pk; f. 2002; online commodity futures exchange; regulated by Securities and Exchange Commission of Pakistan; fmrly National Commodity Exchange Ltd; name changed as above 2011; Man. Dir SAMIR AHMED.

INSURANCE

Insurance Division: Securities and Exchange Commission, 4th Floor, NIC Bldg, Jinnah Ave, Islamabad; tel. (51) 9207091; fax (51) 9204915; e-mail enquiries@secp.gov.pk; internet www.secp.gov.pk; under the Ministry of Finance; Commissioner of Insurance MOHAMMED ASIF ARIF; Exec. Dir S. GULREZ YAZDANI.

Life Insurance

American Life Insurance Co (Pakistan) Ltd: Dolmen City Mall, 13th Floor (Level 16), Blk 4, Scheme 5, Clifton, Karachi 75600; tel. (21) 111-111-711; fax (21) 35290042; e-mail alico@cyber.net.pk; internet www.alico.com.pk; Chair. and Chief Exec. ARIF SULTAN MUFTI.

Asia Care Health and Life Insurance Co Ltd: 15C and 17C, 2nd Floor, Zamzama 5th Commercial Lane, Karachi; tel. (21) 35302072; fax (21) 35302076; e-mail info@asiacare.net; Man. Dir MEHDI KAZMI.

EFU Life Assurance Ltd: 37-K, Blk 6, PECHS, Karachi; tel. (21) 111-338-111; fax (21) 34535079; e-mail info@efulife.com; internet www.efulife.com; f. 1932; Chair. RAFIQUE R. BHIMJEE; Man. Dir and CEO TAHER G. SACHAK.

Postal Life Insurance Organization: 2nd and 3rd Floors, Karachi GPO Bldg, I. I. Chundrigar Rd, Karachi; tel. (21) 99211102; e-mail dg@pakpost.gov.pk; f. 1884; life and group insurance; Dir-Gen. ABDUL HAMEED.

State Life Insurance Corpn of Pakistan: State Life Bldg No. 9, Dr Ziauddin Ahmed Rd, POB 5725, Karachi 75530; tel. (21) 111-111-888; fax (21) 99202868; e-mail dhasp@statelife.com.pk; internet www.statelife.com.pk; f. 1972; life and group insurance and pension schemes; Chair. SHAHID AZIZ SIDDIQI.

General Insurance

ACE Insurance Ltd: 6th Floor, NIC Bldg, Abbasi Shaheed Rd, off Shahrah-e-Faisal, Karachi; tel. (21) 35681320; fax (21) 35683935; e-mail zehra.naqvi@acegroup.com; internet www.ace-ina.com; f. 1948; Chief Exec. ZEHRA NAQVI.

Adamjee Insurance Co Ltd: Adamjee House, 6th Floor, I. I. Chundrigar Rd, POB 4850, Karachi 74000; tel. (21) 2412623; fax (21) 2412627; e-mail info@adamjeeinsurance.com; internet www.adamjeeinsurance.com; f. 1960; Man. Dir MANZAR MUSHTAQ.

Agro General Insurance Co Ltd: 612 Qamar House, M. A. Jinnah Rd, Karachi 74000; tel. (21) 2313181; fax (21) 2313182; e-mail agiho@cyber.net.pk; f. 1987; Man. Dir and CEO M. JALILULLAH.

Alfalah Insurance Co Ltd: 5 Saint Mary Park, Gulberg, Lahore; tel. (42) 111-786-234; fax (42) 35774329; e-mail afi@alfalahinsurance.com; internet www.alfalahinsurance.com; Chair. Sheikh HAMDAN BIN MUBARAK AL-NAHAYAN; Man. Dir and CEO NASAR US-SAMAD QURESHI.

Alpha Insurance Co Ltd: State Life Bldg No. 1B–1C, 2nd Floor, off I. I. Chundrigar Rd, POB 4359, Karachi 74000; tel. (21) 32416041; fax (21) 32419968; e-mail info@alphainsurance.com.pk; internet www.alphainsurance.com.pk; f. 1952; Man. Dir UMAIR KHAN; 9 brs.

Asia Insurance Co Ltd: 456K Blk, Model Town, Lahore; tel. (42) 35916801; fax (42) 35865579; e-mail info@asiainsurance.com.pk; f. 1979; Chair. IHTESHAM-UL-HAQ QURESHI.

Askari General Insurance Co Ltd: 4th Floor, AWT Plaza, The Mall, POB 843, Rawalpindi; tel. (51) 9272425; fax (51) 9272424; e-mail info@agico.com.pk; internet www.agico.com.pk; f. 1995; Chair. TAHIR MAHMOOD.

Atlas Insurance Ltd: 3 Bank Sq., Shahrah-e-Quaid-e-Azam, Lahore; tel. (42) 37320542; fax (42) 37234742; e-mail info@atlasinsurance.com; internet www.atlasinsurance.com.pk; f. 1935; Chair. YUSUF H. SHIRAZI; Chief Exec. ARSHAD P. RANA.

Capital Insurance Co Ltd: Muradia Rd, Nr Lone House Model Town, Sialkot; tel. (52) 3563771; fax (52) 3552958; e-mail info@capital-insurance.net; internet www.capital-insurance.net; f. 1998; Chief Exec. EHTESHAM UL-HAQ MALIK.

Central Insurance Co Ltd: Dawood Centre, 5th Floor, M. T. Khan Rd, POB 3988, Karachi 75530; tel. (21) 35686001; fax (21) 35680218; e-mail info.cic@dawoodgroup.com; internet www.ceninsure.com; f. 1960; owned by the Dawood Group; Chair. A. SAMAD DAWOOD; Chief Exec. VIQUAR SIDDIQUE.

Century Insurance Co Ltd: 11th Floor, Lakson Square Bldg No. 3, Sarwar Sheheed Rd, POB 4895, Karachi 74200; tel. (21) 35698000; fax (21) 35671665; e-mail info@cicl.com.pk; internet www.cicl.com.pk; f. 1988; Chair. and Chief Exec. IQBALALI LAKHANI; Man. Dir and CEO MUHAMMAD HUSSAIN HIRJI.

CGU Inter Insurance PLC: 74/1-A, Lalazar, M. T. Khan Rd, POB 4895, Karachi 74000; tel. (21) 35611802; fax (21) 35611456; f. 1861; general and life insurance; Country Chief MOIN M. FUDDA; 3 brs.

Co-operative Insurance Society of Pakistan Ltd: Co-operative Insurance Bldg, Shahrah-e-Quaid-e-Azam, POB 147, Lahore; tel. (42) 37352306; fax (42) 37352794; f. 1949; Chief Exec. and Gen. Man. MUZAFFAR SHAH.

Credit Insurance Co Ltd: Asmat Chambers, 68 Mazang Rd, Lahore; tel. (42) 36316774; fax (42) 36368868; f. 1995; Chief Exec. MUHAMMAD IKHLAQ BUTT.

Crescent Star Insurance Co Ltd: Nadir House, I. I. Chundrigar Rd, POB 4616, Karachi 74000; tel. (21) 32415471; fax (21) 32415474; e-mail info@cstar.com.pk; internet www.cstar.com.pk; f. 1957; Man. Dir MUNIR I. MILLWALA.

East West Insurance Co Ltd: 310, EFU House, M. A. Jinnah Rd, POB 6693, Karachi 74000; tel. (21) 32311662; fax (21) 32311667; e-mail info@eastwestlifeco.com; internet www.eastwestlifeco.com; f. 1983; Chair. MIAN MAHBOOB AHMAD.

EFU General Insurance Ltd: EFU House, M. A. Jinnah Rd, Karachi 74000; tel. (21) 32313471; fax (21) 32310450; e-mail info@efuinsurance.com; internet www.efuinsurance.com; f. 1932; Man. Dir and Chief Exec. SAIFUDDIN N. ZOOMKAWALA.

Excel Insurance Co Ltd: 38/C-1, Blk 6, PECH Society, Shahrah-e-Faisal, Karachi 75400; tel. (21) 111-777-666; fax (21) 34548076; e-mail eicl@cyber.net.pk; f. 1991; Man. Dir GHULAM H. ALI MOHAMMAD.

Habib Insurance Co Ltd: Insurance House, 6 Habib Sq., M. A. Jinnah Rd, POB 5217, Karachi 74000; tel. (21) 32424038; fax (21) 32421600; e-mail info@habibinsurance.net; internet www.habibinsurance.net; f. 1942; Chair. RAFIQ A. HABIB; Man. Dir and Chief Exec. ALI RAZA D. HABIB.

IGI Insurance Ltd: 7th Floor, The Forum, Suite 701–713m G-20, Blk 9, Khayaban-e-Jami, Clifton, Karachi 75600; tel. (21) 35301726; fax (21) 35301729; e-mail skhalid@igi.com.pk; internet www.igiinsurance.com.pk; Chair. SYED BABAR ALI.

Ittefaq General Insurance Co Ltd: H-16 Murree Rd, Rawalpindi; tel. (51) 5771333; f. 1982; Chief Exec. and Man. Dir Dr SYED ISHTIAQ HUSSAIN SHAH.

National General Insurance Co Ltd: 401-B, Satellite Town, nr Commercial Market, Rawalpindi; tel. (51) 4411792; fax (51) 4427361; f. 1969; Gen. Man. F. A. JAFFERY.

National Insurance Corpn: NIC Bldg, Abbasi Shaheed Rd, Karachi 74400; tel. (21) 99202741; fax (21) 99202779; e-mail info@nicl.com.pk; internet www.nicl.com.pk; govt-owned; sole govt insurance co; Chair. and CEO MUHAMMAD AYYAZ NIAZI.

New Jubilee Insurance Co Ltd: 2nd Floor, Jubilee Insurance House, I. I. Chundrigar Rd, POB 4795, Karachi 74000; tel. (21) 32416022; fax (21) 32416728; e-mail nji@cyber.net.pk; internet www.nji.com.pk; f. 1953; Chair. TOWFIQ H. CHINOY.

New Hampshire Insurance Co (Pakistan): 1st Floor, Dadex House, 34-A/1, Blk 6, PECHS, Shahrah-e-Faisal, Karachi 75400; tel. (21) 35205443; fax (21) 34169013; e-mail info-pakistan@chartisinsurance.com; internet www.chartisinsurance.com/about-us_840_204502.html; f. 1949; forms part of the Chartis insurance group.

North Star Insurance Co Ltd: 37–38 Basement, Sadiq Plaza, 69 The Mall, Lahore 54000; tel. (42) 36314308; fax (42) 36375366; e-mail northstarins@hotmail.com; f. 1995; Chief Exec./Man. Dir M. RAFIQ CHAUDHRY.

Pak Equity Insurance Co Ltd: M. K. Arcade, 32 Davis Rd, Lahore; tel. (42) 36361536; fax (42) 36365959; f. 1984; Chief Exec. CH. ATHAR ZAHOOR.

Pakistan General Insurance Co Ltd: 3 Bank Sq., Shahrah-e-Quaid-e-Azam, POB 1364, Lahore; tel. (42) 37323569; fax (42) 37230634; f. 1948; Chair. CH. MANZOOR AHMAD; Pres. and CEO CH. ZAHOOR AHMAD.

Pakistan Reinsurance Co Ltd: PRC Towers, 32 A Lalazar Dr., M. T. Khan Rd, POB 4777, Karachi 74000; tel. (21) 99202908; fax (21) 99202921; e-mail prcl@pakre.org.pk; internet www.pakre.org.pk; Chair. RUKHSANA SALEEM.

PICIC Insurance Ltd: 8th Floor, Shaheen Complex, M. R. Kiyani Rd, Karachi; tel. (21) 32219550; fax (21) 32219561; e-mail info@picicinsurance.com; internet www.picicinsurance.com; Man. Dir and CEO AHMED SALAHUDDIN.

Premier Insurance Ltd: 2-A State Life Bldg, 5th Floor, Wallace Rd, off I. I. Chundrigar Rd, POB 4140, Karachi 74000; tel. (21) 32416331; fax (21) 32416572; e-mail prinscop@super.net.pk; internet www.pil.com.pk; f. 1952; Chair. ZAHID BASHIR; CEO FAKHIR A. RAHMAN.

Prime Insurance Co Ltd: 505–507, Japan Plaza, M. A. Jinnah Rd, POB 1390, Karachi; tel. (21) 37770801; fax (21) 37725427; f. 1989; Chief Exec. ABDUL MAJEED.

Raja Insurance Co Ltd: Panorama Centre, 5th Floor, 256 Fatimah Jinnah Rd, POB 10422, Karachi 4; tel. (21) 35670619; fax (21) 35681501; f. 1981; Chair. RAJA ABDUL RAHMAN; Man. Dir Sheikh HUMAYUN SAYEED.

Reliance Insurance Co Ltd: Reliance Insurance House, 181-A, Sindhi Muslim Co-operative Housing Society, POB 13356, Karachi 74400; tel. (21) 34539415; fax (21) 34539412; e-mail reli-ins@cyber.net.pk; internet www.relianceins.com; Chair. ISMAIL H. ZAKARIA.

Royal Exchange Assurance: P&O Plaza, I. I. Chundrigar Rd, POB 315, Karachi 74000; tel. (21) 32635141; fax (21) 32631369; Man. (Pakistan) Dr MUMTAZ A. HASHMI.

Saudi Pak Insurance Co Ltd: 2nd Floor, State Life Bldg, No. 2A, Wallace Rd, Karachi; tel. (21) 32418430; fax (21) 32417885; e-mail info@saudipakinsurance.com.pk; internet www.saudipakinsurance.com.pk; Man. Dir and CEO Capt. AZHAR EHTESHAM AHMED.

Seafield Insurance Co Ltd: 86-Q, Blk 2, Allama Iqbal Rd, PECHS, Karachi; tel. (21) 34527592; fax (21) 34527593; e-mail sifcpk89@hotmail.com; f. 1989; Man. Dir ADNAN HAFEEZ.

Security General Insurance Co Ltd: 18-C/E–1, SGI House, Gulberg III, Lahore; tel. (42) 35775024; fax (42) 35775030; e-mail sgi@sgicl.com; f. 1996; CEO NABIHA SAMAD.

Shaheen Insurance Co Ltd: 10th Floor, Shaheen Complex, M. R. Kayani Rd, Karachi 74200; tel. (21) 2630370; fax (21) 2626674; e-mail sihifc@cyber.net.pk; internet www.shaheeninsurance.com; f. 1996; Chief Exec. ASIF SULEMAN.

Silver Star Insurance Co Ltd: Silver Star House, 2nd Floor, 5 Bank Sq., POB 2533, Lahore 54000; tel. (42) 37324488; fax (42) 37229966; e-mail info@silverstarinsurance.com; internet www.silverstarinsurance.com; f. 1984; Man. Dir and Chief Exec. ZAHIR MUHAMMAD SADIQ; Chair. CHAUDHRY MUHAMMAD SADIQ.

TPL Direct Insurance Ltd: 172-B, 2nd Floor, Najeeb Centre, Blk 2, PECHS, Karachi; tel. (21) 34322555; fax (21) 34322515; e-mail insurance@trakkerdirect.com; internet tplinsurance.com; CEO SAAD NISSAR.

UBL Insurers Ltd: 8th Floor, State Life Bldg, No. 2, Wallace Rd, off I. I. Chundrigar Rd, Karachi; tel. (21) 111-845-111; fax (21) 2463117; e-mail khalid.hamid@ublinsurers.com; internet www.ublinsurers.com; CEO and Man. Dir KHALID HAMID.

Union Insurance Co of Pakistan Ltd: Adamjee House, 9th Floor, I. I. Chundrigar Rd, Karachi; tel. (21) 32416171; fax (21) 32420174; e-mail unionins@cyber.net.pk; Pres. NISHAT RAFFIQ.

United Insurance Co of Pakistan Ltd: Nizam Chambers, 5th Floor, Shahrah-e-Fatima Jinnah, POB 532, Lahore; tel. (42) 36361471; fax (42) 36375036; e-mail uicp@xcess.net.pk; internet www.theunitedinsurance.com; f. 1959; Chair. and CEO M.A. SHAHID.

Universal Insurance Co Ltd: Universal Insurance House, 63 Shahrah-e-Quaid-e-Azam, POB 539, Lahore; tel. (42) 37353458; fax (42) 37230326; e-mail tuic@nexlinx.net.pk; internet www.uic.com.pk; f. 1958; Chief Exec. Begum ZEB GAUHAR AYUB KHAN; Man. Dir SARDAR KHAN.

Insurance Associations

Insurance Association of Pakistan: 1713–1715, 17th Floor, Saima Trade Tower A, I. I. Chundrigar Rd, POB 4932, Karachi 74000; tel. (21) 32277165; fax (21) 32277170; e-mail iapho@cyber.net.pk; internet www.iap.net.pk; f. 1948; mems comprise 39 non-life insurance cos and 4 life insurance cos; establishes rules for insurance in the country; regional office in Lahore; Chair. HASANALI ABDULLAH; Sec. N. A. USMANI.

Pakistan Insurance Institute: 30B Lalazar Drive, M. T. Khan Rd, Karachi; tel. (21) 35611063; fax (21) 35610020; e-mail customer.service@pii.com.pk; internet www.pii.com.pk; f. 1951 to encourage insurance education; Chair. FARZANA SIDDIQUE.

Trade and Industry

GOVERNMENT AGENCIES

Alternative Energy Development Board (AEDB): F-8/3, Islamabad; tel. (51) 9262947; fax (51) 9261426; e-mail support@aedb.org; internet www.aedb.org; f. 2003; mandate incl. development of national plans and policies, undertaking promotion and dissemination of activities in field of renewable energy technologies, facilitation of power generation projects using alternative or renewable energy resources; CEO ARIF ALAUDDIN.

Board of Investment (BOI): Government of Pakistan, Ataturk Ave, Sector G-5/1, Islamabad; tel. (51) 9224103; fax (51) 9215554; e-mail secretary@pakboi.gov.pk; internet www.pakboi.gov.pk; promotes domestic and foreign investment in all sectors of the economy; operates under the presidency of the Prime Minister of Pakistan; Chair. SALEEM H. MANDVI WALLA; Sec. MUNIR QURESHI (acting).

Competition Commission of Pakistan: 7th Floor, South ISE Towers, 55B, Jinnah Ave, Islamabad; tel. (51) 9100260; fax (51) 9100251; e-mail rhassan@cc.gov.pk; internet www.cc.gov.pk; Chair. RAHAT KAUNAIN HASSAN.

Engineering Development Board: 5-A, Constitution Ave, SEDC Bldg (STP), Sector F-5/1, Islamabad 44000; tel. (51) 9205595; fax (51) 9203584; e-mail ceo@edb.gov.pk; internet www .engineeringpakistan.com; CEO AITAZAZ A. NIAZI.

Export Processing Zones Authority (EPZA): Landhi Industrial Area Extension, Mehran Highway, Landhi, Karachi 75150; tel. (21) 111-777-222; fax (21) 35082009; e-mail info@epza.gov.pk; internet www.epza.gov.pk; Chair. MUHAMMAD TARIQ HASSAN.

Federal Board of Revenue: Constitution Ave, G-5, Islamabad; tel. (51) 9207545; fax (51) 9207540; e-mail helpline@cbr.gov.pk; internet www.cbr.gov.pk; tax authority; Chair. MUMTAZ HAIDER RIZVI.

Geological Survey of Pakistan: Sariab Rd, POB 15, Quetta; tel. (81) 9211032; fax (81) 9211018; e-mail qta@gsp.gov.pk; internet www .gsp.gov.pk; Dir-Gen. IMRAN KHAN.

Intellectual Property Organization of Pakistan (IPO-PAKISTAN): House 23, St 87, Ataturk Ave (West), G-6/3, Islamabad; tel. (51) 9208581; fax (51) 9208157; e-mail info@ipo.gov.pk; internet www.ipo.gov.pk; f. 2005; Chair. HAMEED ULLAH JAN AFRIDI.

National Economic Council: supreme economic body; the governors and chief ministers of the four provinces and fed. ministers in charge of economic ministries are its mems; sr fed. and provincial officials in the economic field are also associated; Chair. Prime Minister.

National Energy Conservation Centre (ENERCON): ENERCON Bldg, G-5/2, Islamabad; tel. (51) 9206005; fax (51) 9202657; e-mail ferts@enercon.gov.pk; internet www.enercon.gov.pk; f. 1987; Man. Dir HAMID ALI KHAN.

National Fertilizer Corpn of Pakistan (Pvt) Ltd (NFC): Al-Falah Bldg, 1st Floor, Shahrah-e-Quaid-e-Azam, POB 1730, Lahore; tel. (42) 36284983; fax (42) 36284989; e-mail info@nfc.gov.pk; internet www.nfc.gov.pk; under the supervision of the Ministry of Industries; mfg and distribution of fertilizers and devt of the associated sector; Chair. Maj.-Gen. (retd) ZAFAR ABBAS; Gen. Man. (Technical) T. I. CHUGHTAI.

National Tariff Commission: State Life Bldg, No. 5, Blue Area, Jinnah Ave, POB 1689, Islamabad 44000; tel. (51) 9202839; fax (51) 9221205; e-mail ntc@ntc.gov.pk; internet www.ntc.gov.pk; f. 1990; Chair. ABBAS KHAN.

Oil and Gas Regulatory Authority: Tariq Chambers, Civic Centre, G-6, Islamabad; tel. (51) 9204524; fax (51) 9204762; e-mail secretary@ogra.org.pk; internet www.ogra.org.pk; regulates oil and gas sector.

Pakistan National Accreditation Council (PNAC): Ministry of Science and Technology, 4th Floor, Evacuee Trust Complex, Aga Khan Rd, F-5/1, Islamabad; tel. (51) 9222310; fax (51) 9209510; e-mail info@pnac.org.pk; internet www.pnac.org.pk; f. 1998; Dir-Gen. KHALID MEHMOOD.

Pakistan Software Export Board (Guarantee) Ltd: 2nd Floor, Evacuee Trust Complex, F-5/1, Aga Khan Rd, Islamabad; tel. (51) 9204074; fax (51) 9204075; e-mail info@pseb.org.pk; internet www .pseb.org.pk; Man. Dir AZHER ALI CHOUDHRY.

Pakistan Standards and Quality Control Authority (PSQCA): Pakistan Secretariat, Block 77, Karachi 74400; tel. and fax (21) 99206290; fax (21) 99206263; e-mail psqcadg@super.net.pk; internet www.psqca.com.pk; f. 1996; regulates standards in industry; Dir-Gen. PIR BAKHSH KHAN JAMALI.

Pakistan Stone Development Co: I. C. C. I. Bldg, 2nd Floor, Mauve Area, G-8/1, Islamabad; tel. (51) 9263465; fax (51) 9263664; e-mail info@pasdec.com.pk; internet www.pasdec.org; f. 2006; promotes devt of marble and granite sector; Chair. IHSANULLAH KHAN.

Pakistan Tobacco Board: 46-B Office Enclave, Phase-V, Hayatabad, POB 188, Peshawar; tel. (91) 9217156; fax (91) 9217149; f. 1968; regulates, controls and promotes the export of tobacco and related products, and fixes grading standards; Chair. Maj. SAHIBZADA MUHAMMAD KHALID; Research and Devt Dir MOHAMMAD TARIQ.

Privatisation Commission: Experts Advisory Cell Bldg, 5A Constitution Ave, Islamabad 44000; tel. (51) 9205146; fax (51) 9203076; e-mail info@privatisation.gov.pk; internet www.privatisation.gov .pk; supervised by Ministry of Privatisation.

Sindh Board of Investment: 1st Floor, Tower B, Finance and Trade Centre, Shahra-e-Faisal, Karachi; tel. (21) 99207512; fax (21) 99207515; e-mail info@sbi.gos.pk; internet www.sbi.gos.pk; Chair. MUHAMMAD ZUBAIR MOTIWALA.

Sindh Privatisation Commission: Sindh Secretariat, 4-A, Block 15, Court Rd, Karachi; tel. (21) 99202077; fax (21) 99202071; e-mail spcsecretary@yahoo.com; Sec. SYED ZULFIQAR ALI SHAH.

Trade Development Authority of Pakistan (TDAP): Finance and Trade Centre, Block A, 3rd Floor, POB 1293, Shahrah-e-Faisal, Karachi 75200; tel. (21) 99206487; fax (21) 99206461; e-mail tdap@ tdap.gov.pk; internet www.tdap.gov.pk; f. 1963 as Export Promotion Bureau (EPB) affiliated to the Ministry of Commerce; est. in 2006 to assume all functions fmrly dispatched by the EPB; Chief Exec. TARIQ PURI; Sec. JAVED ANWAR KHAN.

Trading Corporation of Pakistan: 4th and 5th Floors, Finance and Trade Centre, Main Shahrah-e-Faisal, Karachi 75530; tel. (21) 99202947; fax (21) 99202722; e-mail tcp@tcp.gov.pk; internet www .tcp.gov.pk; f. 1967; public sector trading house handling bulk import requirements, such as edible oil and other essential food items; deals in exports of Pakistani products, such as textiles, wheat, leather, rice, etc.; Chair. TAHIR RAZA NAQVI.

Utility Stores Corporation of Pakistan: Plot No. 2039, G-7/F-7, POB 1339, Jinnah Ave, Blue Area, Islamabad; tel. (51) 9245030; fax (51) 9210982; e-mail usc_ho@yahoo.com; internet www.usc.com.pk; f. 1971; Chair. AZIZ AHMAD BILOUR; Sec. SULTAN MAHMOOD.

DEVELOPMENT ORGANIZATIONS

Balochistan Development Authority: Civil Secretariat, Block 7, Quetta; tel. (81) 9202491; created for economic devt of Balochistan; exploration and exploitation of mineral resources; development of infrastructure, water resources, etc.

Capital Development Authority: G-7/4, Islamabad; tel. (51) 9253003; fax (51) 9253009; e-mail info@cda.gov.pk; internet www .cda.gov.pk; f. 1960; Chair. FARKHAND IQBAL.

Center for International Private Enterprise (Pakistan) (CIPE): Glass Tower, Suite 214–15, 2 Ft 3, adjacent to PSO House, Main Clifton Rd, Karachi 75530; tel. (21) 35656993; e-mail pakistan@ cipe.org; internet www.cipe.org; international org.; affiliate of US Chamber of Commerce and key member of National Endowment for Democracy; US Agency for International Development supports programs of CIPE; Country Dir M. MOIN FUDDA.

Council for Works and Housing Research (CWHR): F-40, SITE Area Hub River Rd, Karachi 75730; tel. (23) 32577236; fax (23) 32577235; e-mail cwhr@khi.comsats.net.pk; f. 1964; Chair. NAJMUL HASAN TAQVI.

Faisalabad Industrial Estate Development & Management Co (FIEDMC): 1st Floor, FCCI Complex, East Canal Rd, Canal Park, Faisalabad; tel. (41) 9230231; fax (41) 9230235; e-mail fiedmc@ fiedmc.com.pk; internet www.fiedmc.com.pk; established by the Punjab state government under the Public Private Partnership system to promote devt of industrial estates; Chair. KH. ASEM KHURSHID; CEO MUSADAQ ZULQARNAIN.

Gwadar Development Authority: Governor House Rd, Gwadar; tel. and fax (86) 9201010; fax (86) 9201020; e-mail info@gda.gov.pk; internet www.gda.gov.pk; f. 2003; Dir-Gen. Dr SHOAIB AHMED GOLA.

Infrastructure Project Development Facility (IPDF): House No. 2, St 59, F-7/4, Islamabad; tel. (51) 9100168; fax (51) 9100169; e-mail adil.anwar@ipdf.gov.pk; internet ipdf.gov.pk; f. 2006; devt of public infrastructure projects; CEO ADIL ANWAR.

Lahore Development Authority (LDA): LDA Plaza, 9th Floor, Egerton Rd, Lahore; tel. (42) 99201510; internet www.lda.gop.pk; f. 1975; Dir of Admin. ABDUL HAMEED CHAUDHRY.

Lasbela Industrial Estate Development Authority (LIEDA): Hub Industrial Trading Estate, Lasbella, Balochistan; tel. (853) 303361; fax (853) 302470; e-mail lieda@lieda.gov.pk; internet www .lieda.gov.pk; est. under section 3 of Government of Balochistan Ordinance IX (1989); promotes devt of industrial concerns over 1,000-acre Coastal Highway region; Man. Dir MUHAMMAD ASLAM SHAKIR.

Malir Development Authority: Main National Highway, Opp. Chowkandi Tombs, Shah Latif Town, Karachi; tel. (21) 4100451; fax (21) 4100452; e-mail dg@mda.com.pk; internet mda.com.pk; f. 1994.

Pakistan Agricultural Research Council: 20, Ataturk Ave, G-5/1, Islamabad; tel. (51) 8442280; fax (51) 9202968; e-mail webmaster@ parc.gov.pk; internet www.parc.gov.pk; f. 1981; agricultural research; Chair. NAVEED SALIMI.

Pakistan Gems & Jewellery Development Co (PGJDC): Regent Plaza Hotel and Convention Centre, M-3 Mezzanine Floor, Shahra-e-Faisal, Karachi; tel. (21) 35631395; fax (21) 35631398; e-mail info@pgjdc.org; internet www.pgjdc.org; f. 2006; supervised by the Ministry of Industries and Production; subsidiary of Pakistan

Industrial Devt Corpn; promotes devt of Pakistan's gem and jewellery industry; CEO Bakhtiar Khan.

Pakistan Industrial Development Corpn (PIDC): PIDC House, 2nd Floor, Dr Ziauddin Ahmad Rd, Karachi; tel. (21) 39205754; fax (21) 99204376; internet pidc.com.pk; f. 1962; parastatal body; devt of the industrial sector and establishment of industrial units; est. 94 industrial units during 1952–88; current subsidiaries active in engineering, furniture, gems and jewellery, technical training; Chair. Ch. Anwar Ali Cheema; CEO Gul Muhammad Rind.

Pakistan Industrial Technical Assistance Centre (PITAC): 234 Maulana Jalaluddin Roomi Rd (old Ferozepur Rd), Lahore 54600; tel. (42) 99230699; fax (42) 99230589; e-mail info@pitac.gov.pk; internet www.pitac.gov.pk; f. 1962 by the Govt to provide prototype tooling facilities and spare parts to manufacturing industries and advanced training to industrial personnel in the fields of metal trades and tool engineering design and related fields; provides human resource devt programmes and technical training; Gen. Man. Tariq Ahmad Chaudhary.

Pakistan Poverty Alleviation Fund: House No. 1, Hill View Rd, Banigala, Islamabad; tel. (51) 111-000-102; fax (51) 2613931; e-mail info@ppaf.org.pk; internet www.ppaf.org.pk; f. 1997 by the Government; funded by the World Bank; works with non-governmental organizations and private sector institutions to alleviate poverty; 68 partner orgs nation-wide; Chief Exec. and Man. Dir Kamal Hayat.

Provincial Disaster Management Authority (Sindh): C-52, Blk 2, Clifton, Karachi; tel. (21) 99925158; fax (21) 35830087; e-mail info@pdma.gos.pk; internet www.pdma.pk/dn; crisis management, resource mobilization, planning; headed by the Chief Minister of Sindh; Dir-Gen. Danish Saeed.

Quetta Development Authority: Sarai Rd, Quetta; tel. (81) 9211069; f. 1978.

Sarhad Development Authority (SDA): PIA Bldg, Arbab Rd, POB 172, Peshawar; tel. (91) 9211608; fax (91) 9211605; e-mail sda.psh@ntc.net.pk; internet www.sda.org.pk; f. 1972; promotes industrial and commercial devt in Khyber Pakhtoonkhwa; Chair. Dr Hammad Awais Agha.

Sindh Katchi Abadis Authority (SKAA): Maulana Din Muhammad Wafai Rd, Karachi 74200; tel. (21) 99211278; fax (21) 99211272; e-mail skaa@khi.compol.com; f. 1987; govt agency established to regulate and improve slums in Pakistan's southern province; Dir-Gen. Mir Nasir Abbas.

Small and Medium Enterprises Development Authority (SMEDA): 6th Floor, LDA Plaza, Egerton Rd, Lahore; tel. (42) 111-111-456; fax (42) 36304926; e-mail helpdesk@smeda.org.pk; internet www.smeda.org.pk; f. 1998; four brs; 18 regional business centres; CEO Yousaf Naseem Khokhar.

CHAMBERS OF COMMERCE

The Federation of Pakistan Chambers of Commerce and Industry: Federation House, Main Clifton, Sharea Firdousi, Karachi 75600; tel. (21) 35873691; fax (21) 35874332; e-mail info@fpcci.com.pk; internet www.fpcci.com.pk; f. 1950; 144 mem. bodies; Pres. Haji Fazal Kadir Khan Sherani; Sec.-Gen. Syed Masood Alam Rizvi.

Islamic Chamber of Commerce and Industry: St 2/A, Block 9, KDA Scheme 5, Clifton, Karachi 75600; tel. (21) 35874756; fax (21) 35870765; e-mail icci@icci-oic.org; internet www.iccionline.net; f. 1979; Pres. Sheikh Saleh bin Abdullah Kamel; Sec.-Gen. Dr Bassem Awadallah.

Overseas Investors' Chamber of Commerce and Industry: Chamber of Commerce Bldg, Talpur Rd, POB 4833, Karachi 74000; tel. (21) 32410814; fax (21) 32427315; e-mail info@oicci.org; internet www.oicci.org; f. 1860 as the Karachi Chamber of Commerce, name changed to above in 1968; 175 mem. bodies; Pres. Humayun Bashir; Sec.-Gen. Md Abdul Aleem.

Principal Affiliated Chambers

Bahawalpur Chamber of Commerce and Industry: 43-A/1, Tipu Shaheed Rd, Model Town A, Bahawalpur; tel. (62) 2883192; fax (62) 2889283; e-mail info@bahawalpurchamber.com; internet www.bahawalpurchamber.com; Pres. Muzammil-ur-Rasheed Abbasi.

Dera Ghazi Khan Chamber of Commerce and Industry: Block 34, Khakwani House, Dera Ghazi Khan, Punjab; tel. (64) 9260503; fax (64) 9260507; Pres. Dr Muhammad Haris.

Faisalabad Chamber of Commerce and Industry: East Canal Rd, Canal Park, Faisalabad; tel. (41) 9230265; fax (41) 9230270; e-mail info@fcci.com.pk; internet www.fcci.com.pk; Pres. Muzammil Sultan; Vice-Pres. Rehan Naseem Bharara.

Gujranwala Chamber of Commerce and Industry: Aiwan-e-Tijarat Rd, Gujranwala; tel. (55) 3256701; fax (55) 3254440; e-mail info@gcci.org.pk; internet www.gcci.org.pk; f. 1978; Pres. Chadda Khalid Mehmood; Sec. Syed Ali Asim.

Gujrat Chamber of Commerce and Industry: G. T. Rd, Gujrat; tel. (53) 3523012; fax (53) 3523011; e-mail gujrat.chamber@yahoo.com; internet www.gtcci.org; f. 1994; Pres. Mirza Mohammad Mushtaq.

Haripur Chamber of Commerce and Industry: Chamber House, GPO Rd, Haripur; tel. (995) 613364; fax (995) 614664; e-mail haripur-chamber@yahoo.com; Pres. Haji Fakhar-e-Alam; Sec.-Gen. Faqir Muhammad Khan.

Hyderabad Chamber of Commerce and Industry: Aiwan-e-Tijarat Rd, Saddar, POB 99, Hyderabad 71000; tel. (22) 2784972; fax (22) 2784977; e-mail hcci@muchomail.com; internet www.hcci.com.pk; f. 1961; Pres. Goharullah; Sec.-Gen. Dr Mohamad Ali Mian.

Islamabad Chamber of Commerce and Industry: Aiwan-e-Sana't-o-Tijarat Rd, Mauve Area, Sector G-8/1, Islamabad; tel. (51) 2250526; fax (51) 2252950; e-mail icci@brain.net.pk; internet www.icci.com.pk; f. 1984; Pres. Mian Shaukat Masud; Sec.-Gen. Majid Shabbir.

Jhang Chamber of Commerce and Industry: Aamir Colony, Yousaf Shah Rd, Jhang; tel. (47) 7611780; fax (47) 7612371; e-mail jcci@paknet4.ptc.pk; Pres. Haji Abad Hussain Khokhar.

Karachi Chamber of Commerce and Industry: Aiwan-e-Tijarat Rd, off Shahrah-e-Liaquat, POB 4158, Karachi 74000; tel. (21) 99218001; fax (21) 99218010; e-mail info@kcci.com.pk; internet www.kcci.com.pk; f. 1959; 18,333 mems; Pres. Muhammad Haroon Agar; Sec.-Gen. Syed Mazahir Hussain Rizvi.

Lahore Chamber of Commerce and Industry: 11 Shahrah-e-Aiwan-e-Tijarat, POB 597, Lahore; tel. (42) 36305538; fax (42) 36368854; e-mail sect@lcci.org.pk; internet www.lcci.org.pk; f. 1923; 18,000 mems; Pres. Farooq Iftikhar; Sec.-Gen. Syed Muhammad Saqlain.

Larkana Chamber of Commerce and Industry: 21–23 Kenedy Market, POB 78, Larkana, Sindh; tel. (741) 457136; fax (741) 440709; e-mail president@larkanachamber.com; Pres. Masood Ahmed Shaikh.

Lasbela Chamber of Commerce and Industry: LIEDA Office Bldg, Ground Floor, Hub District, Lasbela, Balochistan; tel. (853) 303410; fax (853) 302431; e-mail info@lasbelachamber.com; internet www.lasbelachamber.com; f. 1995; Pres. Muhammad Aslam.

Multan Chamber of Commerce and Industry: Shahrah-e-Aiwan-e-Tijarat-o-Sanat, Multan; tel. (61) 4517087; fax (61) 4570463; e-mail mccimultan@hotmail.com; internet www.mcci.org.pk; Pres. Shahid Naseem Khokhar; Sec. Khurram Javed.

Quetta Chamber of Commerce and Industry: Zarghoon Rd, POB 117, Quetta 87300; tel. (81) 2821943; fax (81) 2821948; e-mail qcci@hotmail.com; Pres. Ghulam Farooq; Sec. Muhammad Ahmed.

Rawalpindi Chamber of Commerce and Industry: 39 Mayo Rd, Civil Lines, Rawalpindi; tel. (51) 5110514; fax (51) 5111055; e-mail rcci@rcci.org.pk; internet www.rcci.org.pk; f. 1952; Pres. Javed Akhtar Bhatti; Sec. Irfan Manan Khan (acting).

SAARC Chamber of Commerce and Industry: House No. 397, St No. 64, I-8/3, Islamabad; tel. (51) 4860611; fax (51) 8316024; e-mail info@saarcchamber.com; internet www.saarcchamber.com; f. 1993; Pres. Annisul Huq.

Sargodha Chamber of Commerce and Industry: 80/2-A, Satellite Town, Sargodha 40100; tel. (48) 9230883; fax (48) 9230835; e-mail info@scci.pk; internet www.scci.pk; f. 1986; Pres. Tariq Yaqoob Mian; Sec.-Gen. Khalique Ahmad Khan.

Sarhad Chamber of Commerce and Industry: Sarhad Chamber House, Family Park, G. T. Rd, Peshawar; tel. (91) 9213314; fax (91) 9213316; e-mail scci.psh@gmail.com; internet kpcci.org.pk; f. 1958; 3,159 mems; Pres. Afan Aziz.

Sheikhupura Chamber of Commerce and Industry: Chamber House, km 23 Lahore–Sheikhupura Rd, Qila Sattar Shah, Sheikhupura; tel. (42) 37971367; fax (42) 37970667; e-mail info@scci.net.pk; internet www.scci.net.pk; Jt Sec. Muzaffar Hameed Rana.

Sialkot Chamber of Commerce and Industry: Shahrah-e-Aiwan-e-Sanat-o-Tijarat, POB 1870, Sialkot 51310; tel. (52) 4261881; fax (52) 4268835; e-mail directorrnd@scci.com.pk; internet www.scci.com.pk; f. 1982; 7,500 mems; Pres. Hassan Ali Bhatti; Sec. Nawaz Ahmed Toor.

South Punjab Women's Chamber of Commerce and Industry: 116, Metro Plaza, Qasim Rd, Multan; tel. (61) 4002389; fax (61) 4027621; e-mail spwcci@hotmail.com; Pres. Aneela Iftikhar.

Sukkur Chamber of Commerce and Industry: Sukkur Chamber House, 1st Floor, opp. Mehran View Plaza, Bunder Rd, Sukkur; tel. (71) 5623938; fax (71) 5623059; e-mail info@sukkurcci.org.pk; internet www.sukkurcci.org.pk; Pres. Shakeel Ahmed Mukhtar; Sec. Mirza Iqbal Beg.

INDUSTRIAL AND TRADE ASSOCIATIONS

Advertising Association of Pakistan: 30-C, Mezzanine Floor, Wheel House, 1st Badar Commercial St, Phase V, DHA, Karachi; tel.

(21) 8750352; e-mail info@aap-pakistan.com; internet www .aap-pakistan.com; Chair. SHAHNOOR AHMED; Sec. QAZI MASOOD.

Air Cargo Agents' Association of Pakistan: Suite 305, 3rd Floor, Fortune Centre, 45-A, Block 6, PECHS, Shahrah-e-Faisal, Karachi 75400; tel. (21) 34383501; fax (21) 34383502; e-mail acaap@pk .netsolir.com; internet www.acaap.org; Chair. TAHIR MALIK.

All Pakistan Cement Manufacturers' Association: House 27-28/3A FCC, Gulberg-IV, Lahore; tel. (42) 5871632; fax (42) 5874442; e-mail apcma@apcma.com; internet apcma.com; Chair. AIZAZ MAN-SOOR SHEIKH.

All Pakistan Cloth Merchants' Association: 4th Floor, Hasan Ali Centre, Hussaini Cloth Market, nr Mereweather Tower, M. A. Jinnah Rd, Karachi; tel. (21) 32444274; fax (21) 32401423; e-mail pcma@cyber.net.pk; f. 1947; Chair. SALMAN YOUSUF; Sec.-Gen. RAFIQ KHAN.

All Pakistan Cotton Powerlooms' Association: P-79/3, Montgomery Bazaar, Faisalabad; tel. (41) 2612929; fax (41) 2613636; Chair. KHALID MAHMOOD CHEEMA.

All Pakistan Textile Mills' Association (APTMA): APTMA House, 44A Lalazar, off Moulvi Tamizuddin Khan Rd, POB 5446, Karachi 74000; tel. (21) 35611710; fax (21) 35610193; e-mail aptma@ cyber.net.pk; internet www.aptma.org.pk; f. 1959; Chair. MOHSIN AZIZ.

Association of Builders and Developers of Pakistan: ABAD House, St 1/D, Blk 16, Gulistan-e-Jauhar, Karachi 75290; tel. (21) 34613645; fax (21) 34613648; e-mail info@abad.com.pk; internet www.abad.com.pk; f. 1972; Sec-Gen. S. JAVED JAFRI.

Cigarette Manufacturers' Association of Pakistan: Caesars Towers (opp. Aisha Bawany Academy), Rm 102, 1st Floor, Main Shahrah-e-Faisal, Karachi 75400; tel. and fax (21) 32789555; e-mail cmaofpak@cyber.net.pk; Sec. TARIQ FAROOQ.

Cotton Board: Dr Abbasi Clinic Bldg, 76 Strachan Rd, Karachi 74200; fax (21) 35680422; f. 1950; Dep. Sec. Dr MUHAMMAD USMAN.

Federal 'B' Area Association of Trade and Industry: ST-7, Block 22, Federal 'B' Area, Karachi 75950; tel. (21) 36340362; fax (21) 36360203; e-mail info@fbati.com; internet www.fbati.com; Chair. MASROOR AHMAD ALVI.

Karachi Cotton Association: The Cotton Exchange, I. I. Chundrigar Rd, Karachi; tel. (21) 32425007; fax (21) 32413035; e-mail kcapak@cyber.net.pk; internet www.kcapk.org; Chair. MUHAMMAD ATIF DADA; Sec. YUNUS HUSSAIN KHAN.

Korangi Association of Trade and Industry: ST-4/2, 1st Floor, Aiwan-e-Sanat, Sector 23, Korangi Industrial Area, Karachi 74900; tel. (21) 35061211; fax (21) 35061215; e-mail kati@kati.pk; internet www.kati.pk; Chair. MUHAMMAD ZUBAIR CHHAYA; Sec.-Gen. NIHAL AKHTAR.

Management Association of Pakistan: 36-A/4, Lalazar, opp. Beach Luxury Hotel, Karachi 74000; tel. (21) 35610903; fax (21) 35611683; e-mail info@mappk.org; internet www.mappk.org; f. 1964; Pres. KAMAL A. CHINOY.

Pakistan Agricultural Machinery and Implements Manufacturers' Association: Samundari Rd, Faisalabad; tel. (41) 8719471; fax (41) 8729072; e-mail info@pamima.pk; internet www.pamima .pk; Chair. AMJAD ALI AMJAD.

Pakistan Arms and Ammunition Merchants' and Manufacturers' Association: Metropole Cinema Bldg, Rm 7, Abbot Rd, Lahore; tel. (42) 37239973; fax (42) 37230170; e-mail ssalimali@ hotmail.com.

Pakistan Art Silk Fabrics and Garments Exporters' Association: 60, The Mall, Lahore; tel. (42) 36360919; fax (42) 36361291; e-mail pasfgea@hotmail.com; internet www.pasfgea.org; Chair. JAMIL MEHBOOB MAGOON; Sec.-Gen. IFTIKHAR AHMED KHAN.

Pakistan Association of Automotive Parts and Accessories Manufacturers: 16-B, Westwood Colony, Thokar Niaz Baig, Lahore; tel. (42) 37498474; fax (42) 37498476; e-mail chairman@ paapam.com; internet www.paapam.com; Chair. MUNIR BANA.

Pakistan Association of Printing and Graphic Arts Industry: CC-25, Central Plaza, 3 Civic Centre, Barkat Mkt, Grden Town, Lahore; tel. (42) 35889229; fax (42) 35889228; e-mail papgaipk@ yahoo.com; internet www.papgai.org; f. 1959; affiliated with the Fed. of Pakistan Chambers of Commerce and Industry; promotion and devt of the printing and graphic arts industry; Chair. FARAZ AHMAD.

Pakistan Automotive Manufacturers' Association: 1st Floor, Block-C, Finance & Trade Centre, Shahrah-e-Faisal, Karachi; tel. (21) 35630992; fax (21) 35630995; e-mail info@pama.org.pk; internet www.pama.org.pk; Chair. KEIICHIRO UTSUMI.

Pakistan Bedwear Exporters' Association: 245-1-V, Block 6, PECHS, Karachi 75400; tel. (21) 34541149; fax (21) 34541192; e-mail bedwear@max.com.pk; internet www.pakbedwear.com; Chair. SHABIR AHMED; Sec. S. IFTIKHAR HUSSAIN.

Pakistan Beverage Manufacturers' Association: C, 1st Floor, Kiran Centre, M-28, Model Town Extension, Lahore; tel. (42) 35167306; fax (42) 35167316.

Pakistan Broadcasters Association (PBA): 177/2, 1st Floor, I. E. P Bldg, Liaquat Barracks, Shahrah-e-Faisal, Karachi; tel. (21) 32793075; fax (21) 32793045; e-mail info@pba.org.pk; internet www.pba.org.pk; Exec. Dir MUHAMMAD ALI BUTT.

Pakistan Canvas and Tents Manufacturers' and Exporters' Association: 15/63, Shadman Commercial Market, Afridi Mansion, Lahore 3; tel. (42) 37578836; fax (42) 37577572; e-mail pctmea@wol .net.pk; internet www.pctmea.org; f. 1984; Chair. SHABAB AHMAD; Sec.-Gen. IJAZ HUSSAIN.

Pakistan Carpet Manufacturers' and Exporters' Association: 23–D, Block 6, PECHS, Shahrah-e-Faisal, Karachi; tel. (21) 34382728; fax (21) 34382739; e-mail pcmeaho@gerrys.net; Chair. ABDUL GHAFOOR SAJID.

Pakistan Chemicals and Dyes Merchants' Association: Chemicals and Dyes House, Rambharti St, Jodia Bazar, Karachi; tel. (21) 32432752; fax (21) 32430117; e-mail pcdma@super.net.pk; internet www.pcdma.com.pk; Chair. NASIRUDDIN FATEH KUKDA.

Pakistan Cotton Fashion Apparel Manufacturers' and Exporters' Association: 5, Amber Court, 2nd Floor, Shahrah-e-Faisal, Shaheed-e-Millat Rd, Karachi 75350; tel. (21) 34522936; fax (21) 34546711; e-mail pcfa@cyber.net.pk; internet www.pcfa .pk; f. 1982; 650 mems; Chair. SHAHZAD ARSAD.

Pakistan Cotton Ginners' Association: PCGA House, M.D.A. Rd, Multan; tel. (61) 4549815; fax (61) 4549817; e-mail pcga@pgca.org; internet www.pcga.org; Chair. AMANULLAH QURESHI; Sec. AIJAZUDDIN GHAURI.

Pakistan Dairy Association: 7-B/2, Aziz Ave, Gulberg 5, Lahore; tel. (42) 35779423; fax (42) 35779424; e-mail info@pda.com.pk; internet www.pda.com.pk; Chair. IMRAN AMJAD.

Pakistan Electronics Manufacturers' Association: Rm Nos 901-902, 9th Floor, Q. M. House, Ellender Rd, Karachi; tel. (21) 35658872; fax (21) 35620877; Chair. HAROON NIAZI.

Pakistan Engineering Council: Atatürk Ave (East), Sector G-5/2, Islamabad; tel. (51) 2829348; fax (51) 2276224; e-mail info@pec.org .pk; internet www.pec.org.pk; f. 1976; Chair. SYED ABDUL QADIR SHAH.

Pakistan Film Producers' Association: Regal Cinema Bldg, Shahrah-e-Quaid-e-Azam, Lahore; tel. (42) 37322904; fax (42) 37241264; Chair. Mian AMJAD FARZEND; Sec. SAMI DEHLVI.

Pakistan Flour Mills' Association: 676, Shadman Colony-1, Lahore; tel. (42) 37596330; fax (42) 37573967; e-mail info@ thepfma.com; internet www.thepfma.com; f. 1961; Chair. MUHAMMAD NAEEM BUTT.

Pakistan Footwear Manufacturers' Association: 6-F, Rehman Business Centre, 32-B-III, Gulberg III, Lahore 54660; tel. (42) 35750051; fax (42) 35780276; e-mail pfma@pakfootwear.com; internet www.pakfootwear.org; f. 1984; Chair. MUHAMMAD YOUNAS; Sec.-Gen. Col (retd) ARSHAD AYYAZ.

Pakistan Glass Manufacturers' Association: 33A, St 13, F-7/2, Islamabad; tel. (51) 2825045; fax (51) 5857692.

Pakistan Gloves Manufacturers' and Exporters' Association: PGMEA Bldg, Kashmir Rd, POB 1330, Sialkot; tel. (52) 4272959; fax (52) 4274860; e-mail pgmea@brain.net.pk; internet www.pgmea.org .pk; f. 1978; Chair. KHURRAM AZIM KHAN; Sec.-Gen. MUHAMMAD ATIF (acting).

Pakistan Hardware Merchants' Association: 47 Nishtar Rd, Lahore 54000; tel. (42) 37631182; e-mail phmasbcircle@hotmail.com; internet www.phma.info; f. 1961; more than 1,500 mems; Chair. SARDAR USMAN GHANI.

Pakistan Hosiery Manufacturers' Association: PHMA House, 37-H, Block 6, PECHS, Karachi; tel. (21) 34544765; fax (21) 34543774; e-mail info@phmaonline.com; internet www .phmaonline.com; f. 1960; Chair. SALAMAT ALI.

Pakistan Iron and Steel Merchants' Association: Mustafa Cloth Market, M. A. Jinnah Rd, Karachi; tel. (21) 32464567; fax (21) 32464568; Chair. AKBAR ABDULLAH.

Pakistan Jute Mills' Association: PJMA House, 18 D-E, 2 Gulberg III, Lahore 546600; tel. (42) 35774400; fax (42) 35774402; e-mail secretary@pjma.com.pk; internet www.pjma.com.pk; Chair. IRFAN ASLAM.

Pakistan Knitwear and Sweaters Exporters' Association: Rm Nos 1014–1016, 10th Floor, Park Ave, Block 6, PECHS, Shahrah-e-Faisal, Karachi 95350; tel. (21) 34544035; fax (21) 34544039; e-mail info@paksea.com; internet www.paksea.com; Chair. M. KAMRAN CHANDNA.

Pakistan Leather Garments Manufacturers' and Exporters' Association: 60-C, Mezzanine Floor, 11th Commercial St, DHA Phase II (Extension), Karachi; tel. (21) 35387365; fax (21) 35388799;

e-mail plgmea@plgmea.pk; internet www.plgmea.pk; f. 2001; Chair. CH. AHMED ZULFIQAR HAYAT.

Pakistan Paint Manufacturers' Association: St 6/A, Block 14, Federal 'B' Area, Karachi 38; tel. (21) 36321103; fax (21) 32560468; f. 1953; Chair. WASSIM A. KHAN; Sec. SYED AZHAR ALI.

Pakistan Petroleum Exploration and Production Companies' Association: 1 St 49, Sector F-6/4, Islamabad; tel. (51) 2823928; fax (51) 2276084; e-mail mail@ppepca.com; internet www.ppepca.com; f. 1995; Chair. JANOS FEHRER; Sec.-Gen. MAZHAR FAROOQ.

Pakistan Pharmaceutical Manufacturers' Association: 430–431, Hotel Metropole, Karachi; tel. (21) 35211773; fax (21) 35675608; e-mail ppma@cyber.net.pk; internet www.ppma.org.pk; Chair. MUHAMMAD ASAD.

Pakistan Plastic Manufacturers' Association: Suite 8, 2nd Floor, B-9/B-2, Estate Ave, Metro Chowrangi, S.I.T.E, Karachi; tel. (21) 36040111; fax (21) 32585050; e-mail ppma@pakplas.com.pk; internet www.pakplas.com.pk; Chair. SHAKEEL AHMED.

Pakistan Poultry Association: 219 Mashriq Centre, Block 14, Sir Shah Muhammad Suleman Rd, Gulshan-e-Iqbal, Karachi; tel. (21) 34940362; fax (21) 34940364; e-mail ppasee@cyber.net.pk; Chair. HASSAN SAROSH AKRAM.

Pakistan Pulp, Paper and Board Mills' Association: 402 Burhani Chambers, Abdullah Haroon Rd, Karachi 74400; tel. (21) 37726150; Chair. KAMRAN KHAN.

Pakistan Readymade Garments Manufacturers' and Exporters' Association (PRGMEA): Shaheen View Bldg, Mezzanine Floor, Plot No. 18A, Block 6, PECH Society, Shahrah-e-Faisal, Karachi 75400; tel. (21) 34382602; fax (21) 34539669; e-mail info@prgmea.org; internet www.prgmea.org; f. 1981; Chair. SAJID MINHAS.

Pakistan Seafood Industries' Association: A-2, Fish Harbour, West Wharf, Karachi; tel. (21) 32311117; fax (21) 32310939; e-mail psiapk@hotmail.com.

Pakistan Ship Breakers' Association: 608, S. S. Chamber, Siemens Chowrangi, S.I.T.E., Karachi; tel. (21) 3293958; fax (21) 3256533.

Pakistan Silk and Rayon Mills' Association: Rms Nos 44, 48 and 49, Textile Plaza, 5th Floor, M. A. Jinnah Rd, Karachi 2; tel. (21) 32410288; fax (21) 32415261; e-mail ctech@edu.pk; f. 1974.

Pakistan Small Units Powerlooms' Association: 2nd Floor, Waqas Plaza, Aminpura Bazar, POB 8647, Faisalabad; tel. (411) 627992; fax (411) 633567.

Pakistan Soap Manufacturers' Association: 148 Sunny Plaza, Hasrat Mohani Rd, Karachi 74200; tel. (21) 32218937; fax (21) 32634648; e-mail psma@com.com.pk; internet www.psma.com.pk; f. 1969; Gen. Sec. SYED AIJAZ AHMED.

Pakistan Software Houses Association (PASHA): Rm 310, 3rd Floor, Business Center, Blk 6, PECHS, Karachi; tel. (21) 35418121; fax (21) 34547759; e-mail secretariat@pasha.org.pk; internet www.pasha.org.pk; f. 1992; Pres. JEHAN ARA.

Pakistan Sports Goods Manufacturers' and Exporters' Association: 298–99 Shah Faisal Rd, Model Town, Sialkot 51310; tel. (52) 3256930; fax (52)3256920; e-mail psga@brain.net.pk; Asst Sec. USMAN ZAHOOR.

Pakistan Steel Melters' Association: 30-S, Gulberg Centre, 84-D/1, Main Boulevard, Gulberg-III, Lahore; tel. (42) 35759284; fax (42) 35712028; e-mail steelmelters@angelfire.com; Chair. ILYAS AZIZ MALIK.

Pakistan Steel Re-rolling Mills' Association: Rashid Chambers, 6-Link McLeod Rd, Lahore 54000; tel. (42) 37227136; fax (42) 37231154; e-mail steel_re_rollers@hotmail.com; Chair. Mian TARIQ WAHEED.

Pakistan Sugar Mills' Association: 24D Rashid Plaza Mezzanine Floor, Jinnah Ave, Islamabad; tel. (51) 2270525; fax (51) 2274153; e-mail center@psmaonline.com; internet www.psmaonline.com; Chair. JAVED A. KAYANI; Sec.-Gen. K. INAYATULLAH KHAN.

Pakistan Tanners' Association: Plot No. 46-C, 21st Commercial St, Phase II Extension, Defence Housing Authority, Karachi 75500; tel. (21) 35880180; fax (21) 35880093; e-mail info@pakistantanners.org; internet www.pakistantanners.org; Chair. S. M. NASEEM.

Pakistan Tea Association: Suite 307, Business Plaza, Mumtaz Hassan Rd, off I. I. Chundrigar Rd, Karachi; tel. (21) 32422161; fax (21) 32422209; e-mail pta@cyber.net.pk; Chair. MOHAMMED HANIF JANOO.

Pakistan Textile Exporters Association: 30/7, Civil Lines, Faisalabad; tel. (41) 644750; fax (41) 617985; e-mail info@ptea.org; internet www.ptea.org; Chair. WASEEM LATIF.

Pakistan Vanaspati Manufacturers' Association: 386, St No. 11, Sector I-8/2, Islamabad; tel. (51) 2502004; fax (51) 4440773; e-mail info@pvma.com.pk; Chair. ABDUL WAHEED.

Pakistan Woollen Mills' Association: 25A, Davis Rd, Lahore 54000; tel. (42) 36307691; fax (42) 36306881; e-mail pwma@brain.net.pk; Chair. Mian MUZAFFAR ALI; Sec. MUHAMMAD RAHEEL CHOHAN.

Pakistan Yarn Merchants' Association: Rms Nos 802–803, Business Centre, 8th Floor, Dunolly Rd, Karachi 74000; tel. (21) 32410320; fax (21) 32424896; e-mail pyma@cyber.net.pk; internet www.pyma.com.pk; Chair. Mohammad USMAN.

Rice Exports Association of Pakistan: 4th Floor, Sadiq Plaza, The Mall, Lahore; tel. and fax (42) 36280146; fax (42) 36280196; e-mail reap@cyber.net.pk; internet www.reap.com.pk; Chair. JAVED ISLAM AGHA.

Towel Manufacturers' Association of Pakistan: 77-A, Block A, Sindhi Muslim Co-operative Housing Society, Karachi 74400; tel. (21) 4382801; fax (21) 34551628; e-mail tma@towelassociation.com; internet www.towelassociation.com; Chair. FEROZE ALAM LARI.

EMPLOYERS' ORGANIZATION

Employers' Federation of Pakistan: 2nd Floor, State Life Bldg No. 2, Wallace Rd, off I. I. Chundrigar Rd, POB 4338, Karachi 74000; tel. (21) 32411551; fax (21) 32439347; e-mail info@efp.org.pk; internet www.efp.org.pk; f. 1950; Pres. KHAWAJA MUHAMMAD NAUMAN; Sec. S. SAUD AALAM.

UTILITIES

Water and Power Development Authority (WAPDA): WAPDA House, Shahrah-e-Quaid-e-Azam, Lahore; tel. (42) 99202222; fax (42) 99202505; e-mail chairman@wapda.gov.pk; internet www.wapda.gov.pk; f. 1958 for devt of irrigation, water supply and drainage, building of replacement works under the World Bank-sponsored Indo-Pakistan Indus Basin Treaty; flood-control and watershed management; reclamation of waterlogged and saline lands; inland navigation; generation, transmission and distribution of hydroelectric and thermal power; partial transfer to private ownership carried out in 1996; Chair. SYED RAGHIB ABBAS SHAH.

Electricity

National Electric Power Regulatory Authority (NEPRA): OPF Bldg, 2nd Floor, Shahrah-e-Jamhuriat, G-5/2, Islamabad 44000; tel. (51) 9207200; fax (51) 9210215; e-mail info@nepra.org.pk; internet www.nepra.org.pk; f. 1997; fixes the power tariff; Chair. (vacant).

Hub Power Co Ltd (Hubco): Islamic Chamber Bldg, 3rd Floor, St 2/A, Block No. 9, Clifton, POB 13841, Karachi 75600; tel. (21) 35874677; fax (21) 35870397; e-mail info@hubpower.com; internet www.hubpower.com; f. 1991; supplies electricity; Chair. MOHAMMAD AHMED ZAINAL ALIREZA; Chief Exec. ZAFAR IQBAL SOBANI.

Karachi Electric Supply Corpn Ltd (KESC): Aimai House, Abdullah Haroon Rd, POB 7197, Karachi; tel. (21) 35685492; fax (21) 35682408; internet www.kesc.com.pk; f. 1913; Chair. ABDUL AZIZ HAMEED AL-JOMAIH; CEO TABISH GAUHAR.

Kohinoor Energy Ltd: Near Tablighi Ijtima, PO Kohinoor Energy, Raiwind Bypass, Lahore; tel. (42) 35392317; fax (42) 35393415; e-mail info@kel.com.pk; internet www.kel.com.pk; f. 1994; jt venture of Saigols Group of Cos and Toyota Tsusho Corpn; Chair. M. NASEEM SAIGOL; CEO MUNEKI UDAKA.

Kot Addu Power Co (KAPCO): 404 Siddiq Trade Centre, 72-Main Blvd, Gulberg, Lahore; tel. (42) 35781631; fax (42) 35781636; e-mail info@kapco.com.pk; internet www.kapco.com.pk; f. 1996; 46% owned by Pakistan Water and Power Development Authority; Chair. SHAKIL DURRANI.

National Power Construction Corpn (Pvt) Ltd: 9 Shadman II, Lahore 54000; tel. (42)37566019; fax (42)37566022; e-mail npcc@wol.net.pk; internet www.npcc.com.pk; f. 1974; execution of power projects on turnkey basis, e.g. extra high voltage transmission lines, distribution networks, substations, power generation plants, industrial electrification, external lighting of housing complexes, etc.; Chair. MUHAMMAD ISMAIL QURESHI; Man. Dir MUHAMMAD AJAZ MALIK; project office in Jeddah (Saudi Arabia).

Pakistan Atomic Energy Commission (PAEC): POB 1114, Islamabad; tel. (51) 9206384; fax (51) 9204908; e-mail feedback@paec.gov.pk; internet www.paec.gov.pk; operates Karachi Nuclear Power Plant—KANUPP (POB 3183, Karachi 75400; tel. (21) 9202222; fax (21) 9202240; e-mail knpc@khi.comsats.net.pk) and Chashma Nuclear Power Plant (CHASNUPP) at Chashma District, Mianwali (tel. (459) 241481; fax (459) 241505; email chasnupp1@ntc.net.pk); a second nuclear power station at Chashma opened in 2011; responsible for harnessing nuclear energy and for devt of nuclear technology as part of the nuclear power programme; establishing research centres, incl. Pakistan Institute of Nuclear Science and Technology (PINSTECH); promoting peaceful use of atomic energy in agriculture, medicine, industry and hydrology; Chair. ANSAR PARVEZ; Dir-Gen. (KANUPP) JAWED IQBAL; Dir-Gen. (CHASNUPP) SAFDER HABIB.

Pakistan Electric Power Co: WAPDA House, Lahore; tel. (42) 99203846; fax (42) 99202402; e-mail info@pepco.gov.pk; internet www.pepco.gov.pk; f. 1998; Man. Dir FAZL AHMED KHAN.

Pakistan Nuclear Regulatory Authority (PNRA): POB 1912, Islamabad 44000; tel. (51) 9263017; fax (51) 9263007; e-mail officialmail@pnra.org; internet www.pnra.org; f. 2001 by presidential ordinance; Chair. JAMSHED AZIM HASHMI.

Private Power and Infrastructure Board (PPIB): 50 Nazimuddin Rd, F-7/4, Islamabad; tel. (51) 9205421; fax (51) 9217735; e-mail ppib@ppib.gov.pk; internet www.ppib.gov.pk; f. 1994; facilitates participation of private sector in national power generation; Man. Dir MOHAMMAD YOUSUF MEMON.

Quetta Electric Supply Co Ltd (QESCO): Zarghoon Rd, Quetta Cantt, Balochistan; tel. (81) 9202211; fax (81) 836554; e-mail qesco@qta.infolink.net.pk; internet www.qesco.com.pk; f. 1998; CEO MUHAMMAD KHATTAK.

Gas

Hydrocarbon Development Institute of Pakistan: Plot 18, Street 6, H-9/1, POB 1308, Islamabad; tel. (51) 9258301; fax (51) 9258310; e-mail info@hdip.com.pk; internet www.hdip.com.pk; f. 1975; re-established Jan. 2006 under Ministry of Petroleum and Natural Resources; national petroleum research and devt org.; provides consultancy and laboratory services to petroleum industry; Chair. ASIM HUSSAIN; Dir-Gen. and Chief Exec. HILAL A. RAZA.

Mari Gas Co Ltd (MGCL): 21 Mauve Area, 3rd Rd, Sector G-10/4, POB 1614, Islamabad; tel. (51) 111-410-410; fax (51) 2297686; e-mail info@marigas.com.pk; internet www.marigas.com.pk; 20% govt-owned; Chair. Lt-Gen. (retd) SYED ARIF HASSAN; Resident Gen. Man. Col (retd) AMJAD JAVED.

Oil and Gas Development Co Ltd (OGDCL): OGDC House, Blue Area, Islamabad; tel. (51) 9209882; fax (51) 9209859; f. 1961; became a publicly limited co in 1997; 85% govt-owned; plans, promotes, organizes and implements programmes for the exploration and devt of petroleum and gas resources, and the production, refining and sale of petroleum and gas; transfer to private ownership pending; Man. Dir and CEO BASHARAT A. MIRZA (acting); 11,624 employees (Aug. 2005).

Oil and Gas Regulatory Authority: Tariq Chambers, Main Civic Centre, Islamabad; tel. (51) 9204524; fax (51) 9204762; e-mail registrar@ogra.org.pk; internet www.ogra.org.pk; f. 2002; Chair. TAUQIR SADIQ; Vice-Chair. RASHID FAROOQ.

Pakistan Petroleum Ltd (PPL): PIDC House, 4th Floor, Dr Ziauddin Ahmed Rd, POB 3942, Karachi 75530, Sindh; tel. (21) 111-568-568; fax (21) 35680005; e-mail info@ppl.com.pk; internet www.ppl.com.pk; 78.4% govt-owned, 15.5% owned by private Pakistani shareholders and 6.1% owned by International Finance Corpn; Pakistan's largest producer of natural gas; cap. and res Rs 18,393m., sales Rs 10,732m. (July–Dec. 2004); Chief Exec./Man. Dir KHALID RAHMAN; 2,520 employees (2006).

Petroleum Institute of Pakistan (PIP): Federation House, 1st Floor, St 28, Block V, Kehkashan, Clifton, Karachi 75600; tel. (21) 35378701; fax (21) 35378704; e-mail info@pip.org.pk; internet www.pip.org.pk; f. 1963; represents all sectors of the petroleum industry (incl. exploration, production, refining, marketing and natural gas); promotes and co-ordinates industry activities; mem. of the International Gas Union and World Petroleum Council; 25 Industrial Collective mems, over 860 individual industry mems; Chair. TARIQ KHAMISANI.

Sui Northern Gas Pipelines Ltd: Gas House, 21 Kashmir Rd, Lahore; tel. (42) 99201451; fax (42) 99201302; e-mail info@sngpl.com.pk; internet www.sngpl.com.pk; f. 1964; 36% state-owned; transmission and distribution of natural gas in northern Pakistan; sales Rs 107,897.3m. (2005/06); Chair. MIAN MISBAH UR-RAHMAN; Man. Dir ABDUL RASHID LONE.

Sui Southern Gas Co Ltd: 4B Sir Shah Suleman Rd, Block 14, Gulshan-e-Iqbal, Karachi 75000; tel. (21) 99231602; fax (21) 99231604; e-mail info@ssgc.com.pk; internet www.ssgc.com.pk; f. 1988; 70% state-owned; Chair. SALIM ABBAS JILANI; Man. Dir Dr FAIZULLAH ABBASI.

Water

Faisalabad Development Authority (Water and Sanitation Agency) (FDA): Jail Rd, POB 229, Faisalabad; tel. (41) 9210053; fax (41) 9210054; e-mail wasa_fsd@yahoo.com; internet www.wasafaisalabad.gop.pk; f. 1978; Man. Dir SYED ZAHID AZIZ.

Karachi Water and Sewerage Board: 9th Mile, Karsaz, Shahrah-e-Faisal, Karachi; tel. (21) 99231882; fax (21) 99231814; e-mail mdkwsb@yahoo.co.uk; internet www.kwsb.gos.pk; f. 1983; Man. Dir FAZAL-UR-REHMAN.

Lahore Development Authority (Water and Sanitation Agency): 4-A Gulberg V, Jail Rd, Lahore; tel. (42) 35752483; fax (42) 35752960; internet www.lda.gop.pk; f. 1967; Dir-Gen. RAJA MUHAMMAD ABBAS.

TRADE UNIONS

National Trade Unions Federation Pakistan: 628 Mashriq Centre, Gulshan-e-Iqbal, Blk 14, National Stadium Rd, Karachi; tel. (21) 7075324; fax (21) 34853685; e-mail info@ntufpak.org; internet www.ntufpak.org; f. 1999; 50 affiliated unions; covers following fields: steel, agriculture, textiles, garments, leather, automobiles, pharmaceuticals, chemicals, transport, printing, food, shipbuilding, engineering and power; Pres. MUHAMMAD RAFIQUE; Gen. Sec. SALEEM RAZA.

Pakistan Workers Federation (PWF): Bakhtiar Labour Hall, 28 Nisbet Rd, Lahore; tel. (42) 37229192; fax (42) 37239529; e-mail cpr@pwf.org.pk; internet www.pwf.org.pk; f. 2005 following the merger of the All Pakistan Federation of Trade Unions, Pakistan National Federation of Trade Unions and All Pakistan Federation of Labour; affiliated with the International Confederation of Free Trade Unions; 10 regional offices; 419 workers' unions; Pres. CH. TALIB NAWAZ; Chair. MUHAMMAD AHMED; Gen. Sec. KHURSHID AHMED.

The principal affiliated federations are:

Muttahida Labour Federation: 24, Circular Bldg, Risala Rd, Hyderabad; c. 120,000 mems; Pres. GUL REHMAN KHAN; Sec.-Gen. KHAMASH GUL KHATTAK.

National Labour Federation (NLF): 28, Circular Rd, Hyderabad; Pres. MERAJ-UD-DIN KHAN.

Pakistan Central Federation of Trade Unions: 220 Al-Noor Chambers, M. A. Jinnah Rd, Karachi; tel. (21) 728891.

Pakistan Railway Employees' Union (PREM): City Railway Station, Karachi; tel. (21) 32415721; Divisional Sec. ISHTIAQ AHMED ASSI.

Pakistan Trade Union Federation: Khamosh Colony, Karachi; Pres. KANIZ FATIMA; Gen. Sec. SALEEM RAZA.

Pakistan Transport Workers' Federation: 110 McLeod Rd, Lahore; 17 unions; 92,512 mems; Pres. ATIA SALEEM.

Other affiliated federations include: Pakistan Bank Employees' Federation, Pakistan Insurance Employees' Federation, Automobile, Engineering and Metal Workers' Federation, Pakistan Teachers Organizations' Council, Sarhad WAPDA Employees' Federation, and Balochistan Ittehad Trade Union Federation.

Transport

RAILWAYS

In 2011/12 the total length of Pakistan's railway network was 7,791 route-km, of which 293 route-km were electrified. The network carried 41.1m. passengers and 1.3m. metric tons of freight traffic in that year. By mid-2011 preliminary studies had been completed for the first part of an Asian Development Bank-sponsored railways modernization programme, involving the rehabilitation of 132 km of track between Lahore and Lalamusa in Punjab province.

Pakistan Railways: Empress Rd, Lahore; tel. (42) 99201700; fax (42) 99201669; e-mail gmopr@pr.gov.pk; internet pakrail.com; state-owned; seven divisions (Karachi, Lahore, Multan, Quetta, Rawalpindi, Peshawar and Sukkur); Chair. JAVED IQBAL; Gen. Man. ASHFAQ KHATAK.

ROADS

The total length of roads in June 2006 was 260,420 km, 65.36% of which were paved, including 11,488 km of highways and motorways. In 2010 the World Bank approved additional financing of US $130m. for the ongoing Pakistan Highways Rehabilitation Project covering nearly 1,000 km of highways. In June 2011 the Government approved nine roads projects proposed by the National Highway Authority, costing Rs 56,900m. The projects involved roads development works in all provinces, including post-floods reconstruction.

National Highway Authority (NHA): 27 Mauve Area, G-9/1, Islamabad; e-mail info@nha.gov.pk; internet www.nha.gov.pk; f. 1991; responsible for planning, maintenance and devt of nat. highways and strategic roads; Chair. ALTAF AHMED CHOWDHRY; Dir-Gen. ATHAR HUSSAIN KHAN.

SHIPPING

The chief port is Karachi. A second port, Port Qasim, started partial operation in 1980 and another port, Port Pasni, which is situated on the Balochistan coast, was completed in 1988. A fourth port, Port Gwadar, has been developed as a deep-water seaport; the port opened in 2007. The US $115.8m. Karachi Port Improvement Project was endorsed by the World Bank in 2010. The scope of the project included channel- and harbour-deepening as well as reconstruction of old berths. At December 2012 Pakistan's flag registered fleet had a total of 48 vessels, with a total displacement of 391,106 grt.

Regulatory and Port Authorities

Ports and Shipping Division: Ministry of Ports and Shipping, Pakistan Secretariat, Islamabad; tel. (51) 9215354; fax (51) 9215349; see Ministries; Sec. MUHAMMAD SALEEM KHAN.

Gwadar Port Authority: GPA Complex, Fish Harbour Rd, Gwadar 92100; tel. (864) 210073; fax (864) 210075; e-mail mail@gwadarport .gov.pk; internet www.gwadarport.gov.pk.

Karachi Port Trust (KPT): Eduljee Dinshaw Rd, Karachi 74000; tel. (21) 99214530; fax (21) 99214329; e-mail chairman@kpt.gov.pk; internet www.kpt.gov.pk; Chair. NASREEN HAQUE; Gen. Operations Man. Rear-Adm. AGHA DANISH; Sec. KHALID MOBIN ARSHAD.

Mercantile Marine Dept: 70/4, Timber Pond, N. M. Reclamation, Keamari, Karachi 74000; tel. (21) 99263014; fax (21) 99263018; e-mail info@mercantilemarine.gov.pk; internet www .mercantilemarine.gov.pk; f. 1930; ensures safety of life and property at sea and prevention of marine pollution through implementation of nat. legislation and international conventions; Prin. Officer Capt. MUHAMMAD ASLAM SHAHEEN.

Port Qasim Authority (PQA): Bin Qasim, Karachi 75020; tel. (21) 99272111; fax (21) 34730108; e-mail webmaster@portqasim.org.pk; internet www.portqasim.org.pk; f. 1973; Chair. Vice-Adm. MUHAMMAD SHAFI; Sec. ANWAR MEHTAB ZAIDI.

Shipping Companies and Terminal Operators

Engro Vopak Terminal Ltd: 1st Floor, Bahrai Complex 1, 24 M. T. Khan Rd, POB 5736, Karachi 74000; tel. (21) 35610388; fax (21) 35611394; e-mail info@engrovopak.com; internet www.engrovopak .com; jt venture between Engro Chemicals Pakistan Ltd and Royal Vopak of Netherlands; engaged in handling and storage of chemicals and LPG; Man. IMRAN UL-HAQUE.

Al-Hamd International Container Terminal (Pvt) Ltd: Plot No. 28, O & L Trans Lyari Quarters, Hawkesbay Rd, New Truck Stand, Karachi; tel. (21) 32352660; fax (21) 32351556; e-mail sshipping@ cyber.net.pk; internet www.aictpakistan.com; CEO HUSSAIN ISLAM; Gen. Man. Col (retd) SHAHZADA FARRUKH ZAMAN.

Karachi International Container Terminal (KICT): Administration Bldg, Berths 28–30, Dockyard Rd, West Wharf, Karachi 74000; tel. (21) 35273599; fax (21) 32313816; e-mail info@kictl.com; internet www.kictl.com; f. 1996; Chief Exec. ANJUM SAJID.

Karachi Shipyard and Engineering Works Ltd: POB 4419, West Wharf, Dockyard Rd, Karachi 74000; tel. (21) 99214045; fax (21) 99214020; e-mail contact@karachishipyard.com.pk; internet www.karachishipyard.com.pk; f. 1953; building and repairing ships; general engineering; Man. Dir SYED HASAN NASIR SHAH.

Pakistan International Container Terminal Ltd: 2nd Floor, Business Plaza, Mumtaz Hussain Rd, Karachi 74000; tel. (21) 32855701; fax (21) 32855715; e-mail sh_pervez@pict.com.pk; internet www.pict.com.pk; Dir AASIM A. SIDDIQI; CEO Capt. ZAFAR IQBAL AWAN.

Pakistan National Shipping Corpn: PNSC Bldg, M. T. Khan Rd, POB 5350, Karachi 74000; tel. (21) 99203980; fax (21) 99203974; e-mail communication@pnsc.com.pk; internet www.pnsc.com.pk; f. 1979 by merger; state-owned; national flag carrier; undertakes global shipping operations; Chair. Vice-Adm. AHMED SALEEM MENAI; Sec. ZAINAB SULEMAN.

Qasim International Container Terminal: Berths 5–7, Marginal Wharfs, POB 6425, Port Mohammad Bin Qasim, Karachi 75020; tel. (21) 34739100; fax (21) 34730021; e-mail info@qict.net; internet www .dpworldkarachi.com; f. 1994; CEO CHANGEZ NIAZI.

Associations

All Pakistan Shipping Association: 01-E, 1st Floor, Sattar Chambers, West Wharf Rd, Karachi; tel. (21) 32200742; fax (21) 32200743; e-mail apsa-pak@cyber.net.pk; Chair. MUHAMMAD F. QAISER.

Pakistan Ship's Agents Association (PSAA): GSA House, Suite 1, 1st Floor, 19 Timber Pound, Keamari, Karachi 75620; tel. (21) 32850837; fax (21) 32850836; e-mail psaa@cyber.net.pk; internet www.psaa.org.pk; f. 1976; Chair. AVA A. COWASJEE.

Terminal Association of Pakistan: 8th Floor, Adamjee House, I. I. Chundrigar Rd, Karachi 74000; tel. (21) 32417131; fax (21) 32416477; e-mail terasspak@cyber.net.pk; Chair. MOHAMMED KASIM HASHIM; Sec. AKHTAR SULTAN.

CIVIL AVIATION

Islamabad, Karachi, Lahore, Rawalpindi, Peshawar, Quetta, Faisalabad and Gwadar have international airports. Construction of a new international airport at Islamabad commenced in 2007, following a series of postponements; the project was to cost an estimated Rs 35,000m. and would handle 6.5m. passengers annually upon completion, scheduled for 2014.

Civil Aviation Authority: Terminal 1 Bldg, Karachi Airport, Karachi; tel. (21) 99242070; fax (21) 99242071; e-mail chief.hr@ caapakistan.com.pk; internet www.caapakistan.com.pk; controls all the civil airports; Chair. Lt-Gen. (retd) SYED ATHAR ALI; Sec. ASHRAF M. HAYAT.

Air Blue Ltd: 55B, Jinnah Ave, Islamabad; e-mail wearelistening@ airblue.com; internet www.airblue.com; f. 2004; CEO and Chair. TARIQ CHAUDHARY.

Pakistan International Airlines Corpn (PIA): Jinnah International Airport, Karachi 75200; tel. (21) 111-786-786; fax (21) 34570419; e-mail info@piac.com.pk; internet www.piac.com.pk; f. 1955; merged with Orient Airways in 1955; 57.7% govt-owned; operates domestic services to 35 destinations and international services to 40 destinations in 31 countries; Chair. CHAUDHRY AHMED MUKHTAR; Man. Dir NADEEM KHAN YOUSUFZAI.

Shaheen Air International: Jinnah International Airport, Karachi 75200; tel. (21) 99242951; fax (21) 99242965; e-mail info@ shaheenair.com; internet www.shaheenair.com; f. 1993; operates scheduled domestic services and international services to the Gulf region; Chair. and CEO EHSAN KHALID SEHBAI.

Tourism

The Himalayan hill stations of Pakistan provide magnificent scenery, a fine climate and excellent opportunities for field sports, mountaineering, trekking and winter sports. The archaeological remains and historical buildings are also impressive.

In 2010 Pakistan received some 907,000 foreign visitors and receipts from tourism (excluding passenger transport) amounted to an estimated US $305m.

Pakistan Tourism Development Corpn (PTDC): Flashman's Hotel, The Mall, Rawalpindi; tel. (51) 9211510; fax (51) 9211509; e-mail info@tourism.gov.pk; internet www.tourism.gov.pk; f. 1970; Man. Dir Mir SHAHJAHAN KHETRAN.

Travel Agents' Association of Pakistan (TAAP): 115, Central Hotel Bldg, 1st Floor, Mereweather Rd, Karachi 75530; tel. (21) 35656022; fax (21) 35684469; e-mail taap.khi@gmail.com; internet www.taap.org.pk; f. 1974; Chair. YAYHA POLANI; Sec.-Gen. MOHAMMAD SALEEM.

Defence

As assessed at November 2012, the total strength of the armed forces was 642,000: army 550,000, navy 22,000, air force 70,000. There was also a paramilitary force of as many as 304,000 (including a National Guard of 185,000). Military service is voluntary.

Defence Expenditure: Estimated at Rs 518,000m. in 2012.

Chairman of Joint Chiefs of Staff Cttee: Gen. KHALID SHAMIM WYNE.

Chief of Army Staff: Gen. ASHFAQ PERVEZ KAYANI.

Chief of Air Staff: Air Marshal TAHIR RAFIQUE BUTT.

Chief of Naval Staff: Adm. MUHAMMAD ASIF SANDILA.

Education

Universal and free primary education is a constitutional right, but education is not compulsory. Primary education begins at five years of age and lasts for five years. Secondary education, beginning at the age of 10, is divided into two stages, of three and four years respectively. In 2011/12 there were an estimated 154,600 primary schools (including mosque schools), and total enrolment at those institutions amounted to some 19.5m. With the assistance of the World Bank, a Primary Education Project has been launched to increase educational facilities and improve the quality of instruction.

There were an estimated 42,600 middle schools and 25,800 secondary schools in 2011/12. Enrolment in that year was estimated at about 5.7m. in middle schools and 2.7m. in secondary schools. The secondary education sector includes secondary vocational institutes (an estimated 3,121 schools and 263,000 enrolled pupils in 2007/08).

In 2008/09 enrolment at secondary schools was equivalent to 85% of students in the relevant age-group (92% of males; 77% of females), while enrolment at secondary level in the same year was equivalent to 33% of students in the relevant age-group (37% of males; 29% of females).

In 2009/10, according to estimates, there were 3,399 arts and science colleges and 1,275 professional colleges (including educational colleges); enrolment totalled 1,147,800 and 458,835, respectively. There were 135 universities (including degree-awarding institutes) and 1.1m. enrolments in 2010/11. The Open University has been established with the technical support of the British Open University.

With the assistance of the Asian Development Bank, 11 polytechnic institutes and a national teacher-training college have been established by the federal Government. Training is provided for teachers at polytechnic, commercial and vocational institutes.

In 2010/11, according to UNESCO, the adult literacy rate in Pakistan was an estimated 55% (males 67%; females 42%).

RELATED TERRITORIES

The status of Jammu and Kashmir has remained unresolved since the 1949 cease-fire agreement, whereby the area was divided into sectors administered by India and Pakistan separately. Pakistan administers Azad (Free) Kashmir and Gilgit-Baltistan (the former Northern Areas) as *de facto* dependencies, being responsible for foreign affairs, defence, coinage, currency and the implementation of UN resolutions concerning Kashmir.

AZAD KASHMIR

Area: 11,639 sq km (4,494 sq miles).

Population: 1,980,000 (1981 census).

Administration: Government is based on the Azad Jammu and Kashmir Interim Constitution Act of 1974. There are seven administrative districts: Bagh, Bhimber, Kotli, Mirpur, Muzaffarabad, Poonch and Sudhnuti.

Legislative Assembly: consists of 49 members: 41 directly elected and eight indirectly elected, including five women.

Azad Jammu and Kashmir Council: consists of the President of Pakistan as Chairman, the President of Azad Kashmir as Vice-Chairman, five members nominated by the President of Pakistan, six members by the Legislative Assembly, and, *ex officio*, the Pakistan Minister of Kashmir Affairs and Gilgit-Baltistan.

President of Azad Kashmir: SARDAR MUHAMMAD YAQOOB KHAN.

Prime Minister of Azad Kashmir: CHAUDHRY ABDUL MAJID (PPP).

GILGIT-BALTISTAN

Area: 72,971 sq km (28,174 sq miles).

Population: 870,347 (1998 census).

Administration: There are two divisions, Gilgit and Baltistan, which are, in turn, divided into seven districts: the Baltistan districts of Skardu and Ghanche, and the Gilgit districts of Gilgit, Ghizer, Diamer, Astore and Hunza-Nagar.

Legislative Assembly: consists of 33 members: 24 directly elected and nine indirectly elected (six women and three technocrats), headed by a Chief Minister.

Gilgit-Baltistan Council: consists of the Prime Minister of Pakistan as Chairman and the Governor of Gilgit-Baltistan as Vice-Chairman.

Governor of Gilgit-Baltistan: PIR KARAM ALI SHAH.

Chief Minister of Gilgit-Baltistan: SYED MEHDI SHAH.

PALAU

Introductory Survey

LOCATION, CLIMATE, LANGUAGE, RELIGION, FLAG, CAPITAL

The Republic of Palau (also known as Belau) consists of more than 200 islands, in a chain about 650 km (400 miles) long, lying about 7,150 km (4,450 miles) south-west of Hawaii and about 1,160 km (720 miles) south-west of Guam. With the Federated States of Micronesia (q.v.), Palau forms the archipelago of the Caroline Islands. Palau is subject to heavy rainfall, and seasonal variations in precipitation and temperature are generally small. Palauan and English are the official languages. The principal religion is Christianity, much of the population being Roman Catholic. The flag (proportions 3 by 5) features a large golden disc (representing the moon), placed off-centre, towards the hoist, on a light blue background. The capital is Ngerulmud, in the state of Melekeok, which is located on the island of Babeldaob.

CONTEMPORARY POLITICAL HISTORY

Historical Context

From 1965 there were increasing demands for local autonomy within the Trust Territory of the Pacific Islands. In that year the Congress of Micronesia was formed, and in 1967 a commission was established to examine the future political status of the islands. In 1970 the commission declared Micronesians' rights to sovereignty over their own lands, self-determination, the right to their own constitution and to revoke any form of free association with the USA. In May 1977, after eight years of negotiations, US President Jimmy Carter announced that his Administration intended to adopt measures to terminate the trusteeship agreement by 1981. In the Palau District a referendum in July 1979 approved a proposed local Constitution, which came into effect on 1 January 1981, when the district became the Republic of Palau. The USA signed a Compact of Free Association with the Republic of Palau in August 1982, and reached agreement with the Marshall Islands and the Federated States of Micronesia in October. The trusteeship of the Pacific territory was due to end after the principle and terms of Compacts of Free Association had been approved by the respective peoples and legislatures of the new countries, by the US Congress and by the UN Security Council. Under the Compacts, the four countries (including the Northern Mariana Islands) would be independent of each other and would manage both their internal and foreign affairs separately, while the USA would be responsible for defence and security. In addition, the USA was to allocate some US $3,000m. in aid to the islands. (For history prior to 1965, see the Marshall Islands.)

Domestic Political Affairs

More than 60% of Palauans voted in February 1983 to support their Compact, but fewer than the required 75% approved changing the Constitution to allow the transit and storage of nuclear materials. A revised Compact, which contained no reference to nuclear issues, was approved by 66% of votes cast in a referendum in September 1984. However, the US Government had hoped for a favourable majority of 75% of the votes cast, which would have allowed the terms of the Compact to override the provisions of the Palau Constitution in the event of a conflict between the two.

In June 1985 President Haruo Remeliik of Palau was assassinated. Relatives of a rival candidate in the 1984 presidential election, Roman Tmetuchl, were convicted of the murder, but an appeal against their conviction was upheld, on the grounds of unreliable evidence, by Palau's Supreme Court in August 1987. In March 1993 Palau's Minister of State, John Ngiraked, and his wife, Emerita Kerradel, were found guilty of aiding and abetting Remeliik's murder. Meanwhile, Lazarus Salii was elected President in September 1985.

In January 1986 representatives of the Palau and US administrations reached a preliminary agreement on a new Compact, whereby the USA consented to provide US $421m. in economic assistance to the islands. However, the proportion of votes in favour of the new Compact at a referendum in the following month was still less than that required for the constitutional ban on nuclear material to be waived. Both Salii and US President Ronald Reagan supported the terms of the Compact, arguing that a simple majority would suffice for its approval, as the USA had guaranteed that it would observe the constitutional ban on nuclear material.

In May 1986 the UN Trusteeship Council endorsed the US Administration's request for the termination of the existing trusteeship agreement with the islands. However, a writ was subsequently submitted to the Palau High Court, in which it was claimed that approval of the Compact with the USA was unconstitutional because it had failed to obtain the requisite 75% of votes. The High Court ruled in favour of the writ, but the Palau Government appealed against the ruling and in October the Compact was approved by the US Congress. At a new plebiscite in December, however, only 66% of Palauans voted in favour of the Compact; ratification of the Compact thus remained impossible. A fifth plebiscite on the proposed Compact, in June 1987, again failed to secure the 75% endorsement required by the Constitution. Under alleged physical intimidation by pro-nuclear supporters of the Compact, the House of Delegates (the lower house of the Palau National Congress) agreed to a further referendum in August. In this referendum an amendment to the Constitution was approved, ensuring that a simple majority would henceforth be sufficient to approve the Compact. This was duly achieved in a further referendum in the same month. When a writ was entered with the Supreme Court challenging the legality of the decision to allow approval of the Compact by a simple majority, a campaign of arson and bombing followed, and one person was murdered.

In February 1988 a team from the US General Accounting Office travelled to Palau to investigate allegations of government bribery and intimidation. Approval of the Compact by the US Congress was to be delayed until the investigators had published their findings. However, in April a ruling by Palau's Supreme Court invalidated the procedure by which the Compact had finally been approved by a simple majority in the previous August. Salii, the principal subject of the bribery allegations, apparently committed suicide in August, and, following an election in November, was replaced as President by Ngiratkel Etpison, who advocated the proposed Compact. Only 60% of voters approved the proposed Compact at a seventh referendum in February 1990. In July the US Department of the Interior declared its intention to impose stricter controls on the administration of Palau, particularly in financial matters.

Legislative and presidential elections were held in November 1992. (The electoral system had been modified earlier in the year to include primary elections for the selection of two presidential candidates.) At the presidential election the incumbent Vice-President, Kuniwo Nakamura, narrowly defeated Johnson Toribiong. A concurrent referendum endorsed a proposal that, in future polls, a simple majority be sufficient to approve the adoption of the Compact of Free Association. Around 62% of voters were in favour of the proposal, which was approved in 14 of Palau's 16 states. Some 68.3% of participating voters approved the proposed Compact in a further referendum in November 1993, giving the Government a mandate to proceed with its adoption. Despite continued opposition to the changes in the polling system, two legal challenges to the amendments, which claimed that the Compact's approval had been procured by coercion, were dismissed, and on 1 October 1994 Palau achieved independence under the Compact of Free Association, thereby marking the end of the Trust Territory of the Pacific Islands, of which Palau had been the final component. Palau was admitted to the UN in December.

A preliminary round of voting in the presidential election took place in September 1996; the incumbent Kuniwo Nakamura secured 52.4% of total votes, Johnson Toribiong received 33.5%, and Yutaka Gibbons 14.2%. Nakamura and Toribiong were, therefore, expected to proceed to a second electoral round due to take place in November. However, Toribiong withdrew his candidacy, following the revelation that his vice-presidential running-mate had been involved in repair work alleged to have been responsible for the collapse in late September of the bridge linking the islands of Koror and Babeldaob; the collapse of the bridge had killed two people and had disastrous economic repercussions for Palau, which was reliant on the route for all communications. Gibbons thus re-entered the contest by default; none the less, at the second round of the presidential poll, held concurrently with legislative elections on 5 November, Nakamura was re-elected with 62.0% of total votes.

At the presidential election conducted on 7 November 2000, Thomas E. (Tommy) Remengesau, Jr, the incumbent Vice-President, received 52% of the votes cast, thus defeating Senator Peter Sugiyama. Sandra Pierantozzi was elected as Vice-President. Despite Remengesau's pledges to improve transparency in public office, there were several instances of fraudulent use of official funds in the early 2000s. In December 2002 the Speaker of the House of Delegates, Mario Gulibert, was arrested on charges relating to the alleged misuse of travel expenses (he was dismissed on unrelated charges in March 2004). In February 2003 the former Governor of Ngardmau state, Albert Ngirmekur, was fined and sentenced to six months' imprisonment following his impeachment for theft. In late 2003 Remengesau was obliged to veto an attempt by legislators to eliminate the Office of the Special Prosecutor, which had conducted a number of investigations into alleged misuse of public funds. In February 2004, however, members of the National Congress under investigation for alleged misuse of expenses agreed to pay some US $250,000 on condition that the cases against them be withdrawn. In November the Senate (the upper house of the National Congress) overturned Remengesau's veto of a bill to ease bank-licensing restrictions, although this decision was reversed in December, following the threat of international financial sanctions.

At the presidential election of 2 November 2004, President Remengesau was re-elected with 6,494 of the votes cast; his opponent, Polycarp Basilius, received 3,268 votes. Elias Camsek Chin was elected Vice-President. Concurrent to the presidential election, voters also approved various amendments to the Constitution: to restrict members of the National Congress to three terms of four years, to permit dual US-Palauan citizenship, to provide for the joint election of the country's President and Vice-President as a team, and to adjust congressional members' salaries. A plan to hold a constitutional convention was approved by some 53% of the votes cast. In April 2005 16 state delegates and nine delegates-at-large were elected to the Constitutional Convention, which ended its deliberations in June, following consultations with the general public and special-interest groups. The Convention concluded with 251 proposals, of which 22 were to be submitted for the electorate's consideration at a referendum to be held concurrently with the elections scheduled for 2008.

Financial issues and the elections of 2008

The issue of misuse of public funds gained further prominence in 2006–08. In March 2006 the legislature of Peleliu state approved a resolution to impeach Governor Jackson Ngiraingas on charges of treason, unlawful spending of state finances and the lodging of accusations, against President Remengesau and others, purporting to be on the state's behalf. Ngiraingas was removed from office in April and subsequently filed a civil suit, claiming that the allegations against him were false and not necessarily grounds for impeachment, and that his removal from office was unconstitutional. The Supreme Court invalidated the legislature's resolution in the following month, deciding that Ngiraingas had been denied due process. Ngiraingas remained Governor of Peleliu until his appointment as Minister of Public Infrastructure, Industry and Commerce in February 2009. Meanwhile, in March 2006 the Ngardmau state legislature adopted a resolution to impeach Governor J. Schwartz Tudong. Tudong was accused of illegally spending state funds and making payments to himself without legal authority; in May Akiko C. Sugiyama was elected to succeed him. In August Augustine Mesebeluu, the Speaker of the House of Delegates, was charged on numerous counts related to personal use of public finances. (Mesebeluu later agreed to repay costs that he had incurred during trips abroad.)

The closure of the Pacific Savings Bank, which went into receivership in late 2006, was followed by charges against the bank's President, Timothy Taunton, and other employees in 2007. However, Taunton fled from Palau shortly after the failure of the bank and could not subsequently be traced. In December 2010 the Palau Government announced that it was to reimburse some depositors of the bank, following the provision of a US $900,000 grant from Taiwan, which was to be released in instalments; as a result, only those depositors with an unpaid claim not in excess of $4,000 would initially be eligible for a refund. In December 2011 three former employees of the bank were sentenced to suspended prison terms of between 25 and 30 years, having been found guilty of numerous counts of grand larceny and money-laundering, and ordered to pay restitution and fines. They were granted presidential pardons in January 2013, but the Office of the Attorney-General filed a petition against the pardons in the following month.

Meanwhile, in October 2006 Palau's seat of government was relocated from Koror to the new capital, Melekeok, on the island of Babeldaob. Following the death of the President of the Senate, Johnny Reklai, in March 2007, Joshua Koshiba was subsequently elected as his successor; however, a successful legal appeal by some members of the Senate resulted in Koshiba's replacement by Surangel Whipps.

In June 2008 the US General Accountability Office published an audit report examining Palau's financial accountability and the provisions of the Compact with the USA, which was due to expire in 2009. The report judged that Palau had made progress in providing financial accountability and that the country had complied with most of the Compact's conditions; however, problems of internal control persisted. Meanwhile, the Palau Compact Review Commission was established earlier in 2008.

Elections took place on 4 November 2008 for the 16 seats in the House of Delegates and the 13 seats in the newly expanded Senate, concurrently with polling for the country's presidency. In the presidential contest (for which primary elections to determine the candidates had been held in September), Johnson Toribiong defeated Vice-President Elias Camsek Chin by a narrow margin, having obtained 5,040 of the votes cast, compared with the 4,828 received by Chin; Toribiong's running-mate, Kerai Mariur, thus became the new Vice-President. The level of voter participation was 74%. President Toribiong took office in January 2009; Vice-President Mariur also assumed the role of Minister of Administration and of Finance. In the legislative elections several incumbents were re-elected to the House of Delegates and to the Senate, but other members of the National Congress, including a number of long-serving senators, were unable to stand for re-election owing to the implementation of the limit of a maximum of three terms of office. Outgoing President Remengesau was elected to a seat in the Senate, as were two women, who thus became the country's first female senators. In a concurrent referendum held on 4 November 2008, 22 proposed constitutional amendments were submitted to the electorate; voters endorsed a proposal henceforth to elect the President and Vice-President separately.

In January 2009 the Speaker of the Koror state legislature, Timothy Uehara, was convicted of perjury and of misconduct in public office. Uehara was found to have sub-leased government properties and embezzled tenants' rental payments from the Koror State Public Lands Authority. In March he received a six-year prison sentence and a fine of US $10,000; however, he was to serve only one year of the prison sentence, with the remainder being suspended. In April the Governor of Melekeok state, Lazarus Kodep, was formally charged with misconduct. It was alleged that between 2003 and 2007 Kodep had used public funds to repay a personal bank loan. Kodep subsequently pleaded guilty to misconduct and misuse of public funds, and resigned as Governor in March 2010; in April he was sentenced to five years' imprisonment, four-and-a-half of which were suspended, and was fined $10,000. Meanwhile, in December 2009 Senator Remengesau was fined $156,000, following his conviction in the previous month on 12 counts of failure to disclose assets during his term as President.

Recent developments: renewal of the Compact of Free Association and the 2012 elections

In March 2009 the Compact with the USA was extended for one year from the end of September, following a meeting in Washington, DC, between President Toribiong and US Secretary of State Hillary Clinton. Negotiations to reach a new long-term agreement were held during the latter half of the year. In October an offer extended by the USA of direct economic assistance of US $156m. for the period 2010–24 was summarily rejected by Palau, which dismissed the stipulated amount as 'inadequate' and stated that it expected the level of assistance to remain at current levels. Palau finally accepted a $250m. aid programme for the next 15 years at the beginning of 2010, although the signing of the agreement was delayed for a number of months, owing to several unresolved points of contention, including a US demand that the $250m. aid programme incorporate a $21m.

subsidy pledged for postal services. Of this subsidy, $16.8m. was intended for US postal services to the Marshall Islands and the Federated States of Micronesia and was therefore of no benefit to Palau—a provision that was strongly contested by the Palau Government.

In early September 2010 a Palau delegation headed by President Toribiong travelled to Hawaii to meet with US officials to discuss the outstanding issues. In the following week Palau and the USA finally signed the agreement, formally renewing the Compact for a further 15 years. The contentious inclusion of the US $21m. postal subsidy remained within the final agreed terms, but the US delegation made concessions on certain other demands, including the stipulation that charitable donations no longer be tax deductible, a measure that the Palau Government had denounced as 'highly intrusive'. The terms of the agreement provided for the creation of an economic and financial reforms body, the composition of which was to be approved by the US Government. Throughout 2011 and 2012 President Toribiong urged the US Congress to approve the Compact, warning that failure to do so threatened to erode the confidence of Palauans in their relations with the USA. However, at early 2013 the final agreement on the Compact had yet to be approved by the US Congress.

In November 2010 Toribiong introduced to the Senate draft legislation proposing to increase incrementally the government-mandated minimum hourly wage from US $2.50 (at which level it had remained since its implementation in 1997) to $3.50 from October 2011. Having stalled within the Senate's Ways and Means Committee, the legislation was finally approved by the upper house in February 2013 and was passed to the House of Delegates for consideration.

A state of emergency was declared by President Toribiong in early November 2011, following a fire at Palau's largest power plant, in Aimeliik, which severely affected the supply of electricity in the country and led to power rationing (which remained in place until early January 2012). On the same day as declaring the state of emergency, Toribiong unilaterally enacted a law authorizing and appropriating US $1.5m. in emergency funds, and on the following day he enacted a further law increasing this sum to $3.0m., prompting claims that he had acted beyond his constitutional remit. In mid-February 2012 Senator Alan Seid filed a civil lawsuit against Toribiong, arguing that the declaration of a state of emergency had been invalid since the Constitution authorized such action only in instances where 'war, external aggression, civil rebellion or natural catastrophe threatens the lives or property of a significant number of people in Palau'. Seid stressed both his resolve not to politicize the issue and his respect for Toribiong as President, stating that he was motivated purely by the urge to protect the Constitution and the rule of law. However, the President dismissed the lawsuit as 'frivolous'. In late February a resolution proposing the filing of a separate lawsuit against Toribiong—on the grounds of misuse of funds provided by the US Government in 2009 for the resettlement of a number of Chinese Uygur (Uighur) Muslims formerly held at the USA's detention centre in Guantánamo Bay, Cuba, and of unauthorized government expenditure allegedly committed between 2009 and 2011—failed to elicit the support of the majority of the Senate; none the less, a group of five senators opted to proceed with filing lawsuits related to the two issues in early March 2012. In August the Supreme Court issued a decision denying a motion by President Toribiong's lawyers seeking the dismissal of the lawsuit concerning the state of emergency. Similarly, in October the Court further denied a motion to dismiss the lawsuits regarding the Uygur Muslims and alleged unauthorized expenditure. The three cases were thus permitted to proceed. Toribiong defended his actions, claiming that the lawsuits were politically motivated. Meanwhile, despite the ongoing controversy surrounding the President, in mid-January 2012 all 16 state governors endorsed a declaration of support for the candidacy of Toribiong in the forthcoming presidential election, due to be held, concurrently with legislative elections, in November.

Primary elections to determine the candidates for the presidency and vice-presidency were held in late September 2012; as stipulated by the recently introduced constitutional amendment, elections to the two positions were now conducted separately. The legislative polls were held on 6 November, concurrently with the presidential and vice-presidential elections. In the presidential contest, former President Tommy Remengesau defeated the incumbent Toribiong by 6,140 votes to 4,287 (including absentee votes), while Antonio Bells was victorious over the incumbent

Kerai Mariur in the polling for the vice-presidency, securing 5,303 of the votes cast, compared with Mariur's tally of 4,847 votes. President Remengesau took office on 17 January 2013 and nominated his new cabinet members in the following week; Vice-President Bells was given the additional responsibility of the justice portfolio. By 6 March three of the President's ministerial nominees had been confirmed in their posts by the Senate, but on 20 March the Senate rejected, for the third time, the appointments of Secilil Eldebechel as Minister of Finance and Andrew Tabelual as Minister of Education. In early April the Council of Chiefs reiterated President Remengesau's earlier pleas by appealing to the Senate to endorse the two appointments as soon as possible, claiming that its failure to do so to date was proving detrimental to the good of the country by preventing the proper functioning of government. Later that month, following a fourth rejection of Eldebechel and Tabelual by the Senate, Remengesau designated Elbuchel Sadang as Minister of Finance and Charles Obichang as Minister of Public Infrastructure, Industries and Commerce. At early May their nominations, together with that of Tabelual, remained subject to confirmation, while a new Minister of State had yet to be named.

Regional Affairs

In mid-1999 a delegation from Solomon Islands visited Palau to discuss the possibility of allowing Solomon Islanders to work in Palau, in an attempt to resolve the latter's severe labour shortage. In August 2001, however, the Government imposed a ban on the hiring of Indian and Sri Lankan workers, citing rising tensions and disputes with local employers which the Government claimed were largely due to religious differences. In July 2002 the Senate approved a bill that would amend the islands' immigration law in order to give greater authority over immigration affairs to the President of Palau. (Non-Palauan nationals were estimated to represent about 73% of the islands' population in 2003.) In March 2003 the Government introduced a measure to extend employment permits for foreign workers which allowed a new maximum extension of two years. In April some 200 Chinese migrant employees of a failed clothing business were stranded in Palau and placed under house arrest. However, the migrants were subsequently repatriated, following diplomatic intervention from the People's Republic of China. In January 2006 legislation banning the employment of Bangladeshi nationals in Palau for a period of one year was implemented, making an exception for those Bangladeshis already contracted to work in the country, who would be allowed to complete their terms; in December the House of Delegates voted to extend the ban indefinitely, subject to ongoing review. The ban was subsequently extended on several occasions, latterly in October 2009, and remained in place at early 2013. In October 2009 President Johnson Toribiong banned the employment of Myanma nationals, citing a lack of diplomatic relations and cultural differences, and issued an executive order introducing a quota for the number of foreign workers in Palau. At that time there were reported to be some 5,432 foreign nationals employed in the country; as a result of the executive order, this number would not be permitted to increase beyond 6,000. In July 2010 President Toribiong was forced to defend a newly introduced law requiring foreign nationals to register with, and pay an administrative fee to, the Government. Critics of the legislation argued that it constituted a tax on foreigners, but the President insisted that the new measure was intended merely to give a clear indication of the number of foreigners resident on the island. However, the Supreme Court repealed the legislation in February 2011. In January 2013 the Senate was considering the introduction of a foreign labour tax in an attempt to encourage employers to hire Palauans rather than foreign workers.

Diplomatic relations were established, at ambassadorial level, with Taiwan in late 1999. The first Taiwanese ambassador to Palau was formally appointed in April 2000. Reports in December of that year that the Palau Government was considering establishing diplomatic relations with the People's Republic of China were denied, and President-elect Thomas Remengesau reaffirmed Palau's diplomatic relations with Taiwan. In early 2000, meanwhile, Palau and Taiwan signed an agreement undertaking to develop bilateral projects in a number of areas, including agriculture, fisheries and tourism. In January 2005 President Chen Shui-bian of Taiwan visited Palau to discuss economic co-operation and to strengthen bilateral political relations. President Remengesau travelled to Taiwan in May 2008 to attend the inauguration of President Ma Ying-jeou. In March 2010 President Ma paid a reciprocal visit to Palau, on the last stage of a tour of Taiwan's six Pacific allies; during his visit, which focused on cultural exchanges, he met with President Toribiong and various members of the Cabinet. A bilateral memorandum of understanding, which was intended to foster greater co-operation in the fields of aquaculture, food-processing and tourism, was signed in October. Palau and Taiwan also agreed to convene regularly to discuss the economic development of the Pacific nation. Following the implementation in 2009 of a ban on commercial shark-fishing in Palauan waters, thereby creating the world's first shark sanctuary, in December 2011 a Taiwanese vessel was boarded and its crew detained after being caught fishing for, and removing the fins of, sharks within the sanctuary during a joint patrol organized by the Palau Government and the international environmental activist organization Greenpeace. The vessel and captain were both banned from Palauan waters for one year and the operators of the vessel were fined US $65,000. In August 2011 a summit of regional leaders agreed to implement a shark sanctuary throughout Micronesian waters by the end of 2012; although the sanctuary was not fully established by this date, considerable progress had been made by individual states with regard to the protection of sharks.

Palau maintains strong diplomatic links with Japan, which has been a leading source of tourism revenue since the 1980s. The Japanese Government provided US $25m. for the reconstruction of the Koror bridge (see Domestic Political Affairs) and contributed to the construction of a new terminal building at Palau International Airport, which opened in May 2003. Palauan support for Japan's position on international whaling was withdrawn in June 2010; announcing the change in strategy, President Toribiong stated that Palau would henceforth be advocating a quota system by which it was envisaged that the hunting of whales would be reduced by one-half.

Palau and Australia signed a 'partnership for development' agreement in August 2010 that was welcomed by both sides as the beginning of a 'new era' of bilateral co-operation. It was hoped that the accord would facilitate an improvement in living standards and national development in Palau. Australia's official development assistance to Palau for 2012/13 was budgeted at $A2.3m. As part of its aid provision, Australia committed $A1.4m. over 2011–13 to support the clearance of unexploded ordnance left over from the Second World War, including land mines and cluster munitions.

Diplomatic relations with Indonesia were established in July 2007. In July 2009 former Malaysian Prime Minister Abdullah Badawi headed a delegation to Palau, dispatched to discuss the possibility of establishing diplomatic and trade links. Meanwhile, in March 2009 Palau and the Philippines held discussions regarding the delineation of their maritime border. In March 2010 President Toribiong created a task force to negotiate Palau's maritime boundaries with the Philippines and Indonesia. In January 2012 the Philippine Government announced that it was to close its embassy in Koror by the end of July owing to budgetary constraints. Later in January President Toribiong submitted a formal request to the Philippine Government urging it to keep the embassy open, arguing that it was an essential source of support for the 5,000-strong Filipino community in Palau. A petition against the planned closure was reported to have attracted the signatures of several hundred Filipinos resident in Palau by March 2012. Despite the level of opposition, however, the embassy was closed down as planned. Filipino workers were estimated to account for some 60% of total foreign workers, and 20% of the total population, in Palau in 2011.

Palau's consulates on Saipan (Northern Mariana Islands) and Guam were closed owing to a lack of funding in December 2009 and March 2010, respectively. However, the 2010/11 budget allocated funding to enable the reopening of the Guam consulate, prompting an angry response from Palauans resident on Saipan, who appealed to the Government similarly to reopen the Saipan consulate. Meanwhile, Palau has appeared keen to increase its diplomatic representation in recent years, most latterly establishing diplomatic relations with Georgia in October 2011, Brunei in December 2011 and Luxembourg and Poland in February 2012.

CONSTITUTION AND GOVERNMENT

In October 1994 Palau, the last remaining component of the Trust Territory of the Pacific Islands (a United Nations Trusteeship administered by the USA), achieved independence under the Compact of Free Association. Administrative authority was transferred to the Government of Palau (with the USA retaining responsibility for the islands' defence). The Compact of Free Association was renewed for a 15-year period in 2010, pending approval by the US Congress.

A locally drafted Constitution of the Republic of Palau entered into effect on 1 January 1981. Under the Constitution, executive authority is vested in the President, elected by direct suffrage for a four-year term. Legislative power is exercised by the Olbiil era Kelulau ('House of Whispered Decisions', or Palau National Congress), composed of the directly elected House of Delegates (comprising one delegate from each of the 16 states of Palau) and the Senate (comprising 13 senators). Members of the National Congress are elected for a four-year term.

Local governmental units are the municipalities and villages. Elected Magistrates and Councils govern the municipalities. Village government is largely traditional.

REGIONAL AND INTERNATIONAL CO-OPERATION

Palau is a member of the Pacific Community (see p. 422), the Pacific Islands Forum (see p. 426) and the Asian Development Bank (ADB, see p. 214). It is also an associate member of the UN's Economic and Social Commission for Asia and the Pacific (ESCAP, see p. 31), having been admitted to the UN in 1994, and acceded to the UN's International Maritime Organization (see p. 145) in 2011.

ECONOMIC AFFAIRS

In 2011, according to estimates by the World Bank, Palau's gross national income (GNI), measured at average 2009–11 prices, totalled US $149m., equivalent to $7,250 per head (or $12,330 per head on an international purchasing-power parity basis). During 2002–11, it was estimated, the population increased at an average annual rate of 0.6%, while gross domestic product (GDP) per head rose, in real terms, by an average of 1.0% per year. In 2002–11, according to the Asian Development Bank (ADB), overall GDP expanded, in real terms, at an average annual rate of 0.4%. The ADB estimated that real GDP expanded by 5.8% in the year ending 30 September 2011 and by 4.0% in 2011/12.

The agricultural sector (including forestry and fishing) engaged 7.8% of the employed labour force in 2005, and, according to the ADB, provided 5.6% of GDP in 2011. Agriculture is mainly on a subsistence level, the principal crops being coconuts, root crops and bananas. Pigs and chickens are kept for domestic consumption. Eggs are produced commercially, and the introduction of cattle-ranching on Babeldaob was under consideration in the early 2000s. Fishing licences have been sold to foreign fleets, including those of Taiwan, the USA, Japan and the Philippines. Fish has traditionally been a leading export, earning US $6.3m. in 2011. According to the ADB, agricultural GDP increased, in real terms, by an average of 8.8% per year in 2002–11; the sector's GDP contracted by 0.8% in 2010, but expanded by 0.2% in 2011.

The industrial sector (including mining and quarrying, manufacturing, construction and utilities) engaged 18.7% of the employed labour force in 2005. According to the ADB, the sector provided 8.1% of GDP in 2011. The only manufacturing activity of any significance is the production of garments; the sector employs mainly foreign workers. Manufacturing accounted for only 1.2% of GDP in 2011, according to the ADB, and provided 2.3% of employment in 2005. Construction is the most important industrial activity; the sector contributed 3.9% of GDP in 2011, according to the ADB, and engaged 14.0% of the employed labour force in 2005. Electrical energy, output of which totalled an estimated 152m. kWh in 2009, is produced by two power plants, at Aimeliik and Malakal. In July 2008 it was announced that the World Bank was to provide financial and technical assistance in the exploration for reserves of petroleum and gas in an area north-east of Babeldaob. According to the ADB, the real GDP of the industrial sector contracted by an average of 12.2% per year in 2002–11; sectoral GDP declined by 15.0% in 2010 and by 4.8% in 2011.

Service industries dominate Palau's economy, providing 86.3% of GDP in 2011, according to the ADB, and engaging 73.5% of the employed labour force in 2005. The Government is a significant employer within the sector, public administration engaging 17.7% of the total employed labour force in 2005. The tourism sector has expanded rapidly since the 1980s, to become an important source of foreign exchange. Receipts from tourism (including passenger transport) totalled US $124m. in 2010. The trade, hotels and restaurants sector engaged 17.1% of the employed labour force in 2005, and trade provided 18.9% of GDP in 2011, according to the ADB. Visitor arrivals (mostly from

Japan, Taiwan and the Republic of Korea—South Korea) increased by 8.9% in 2012, to 118,754. The Micronesian Games were held in Palau in August 2010. The GDP of the services sector increased, in real terms, by an average of 1.3% per year in 2002–11, according to the ADB; sectoral GDP increased by 1.6% in 2010 and by 6.6% in 2011.

In the year ending September 2011 the visible merchandise trade deficit was estimated at US \$117.5m., while there was a surplus on the current account of the balance of payments of \$9.0m. The principal sources of imports in 2004 were the USA (including Guam), which supplied 45.0% of the total, and Singapore (27.9%). Other significant suppliers were Japan, South Korea and Taiwan. The principal imports in 2011 were mineral fuels, metals and mineral products (accounting for 39.6% of total imports), machinery and transport equipment, food and live animals, chemicals, manufactured goods, and beverages and tobacco. The principal export in 2011 was fish, accounting for 92.4% of total exports.

The islands record a persistent budget deficit, which reached US \$7.8m. in the year ending 30 September 2011, equivalent to 3.5% of GDP, according to the ADB. The fiscal deficit narrowed slightly in 2011/12, to 3.2% of GDP, mainly owing to an increase in tourism revenue. Financial assistance from the USA contributes a large part of the islands' external revenue. Upon implementation of the Compact of Free Association with the USA in 1994, Palau became eligible for an initial grant of \$142m. and for annual aid of \$23m. over the period until 2009. Following a renegotiation of the Compact in 2010, the USA was to provide \$250m. over a 15-year period (see Contemporary Political History). Palau's external debt was estimated by the ADB at \$80m. in 2012. The cost of debt-servicing was equivalent to 52.5% of the value of exports of goods and services in that year. The annual rate of inflation averaged 4.1% in 2002–11. Consumer prices rose by 4.7% in 2011. At the 2005 census 4.2% of the total labour force were unemployed.

The economy of Palau has benefited greatly from the substantial aid payments from the US Government that followed the implementation in 1994 of the Compact of Free Association, which was renegotiated in 2010, pending approval by the US Congress. Grants accounted for some 49.2% of government revenue in 2010/11. The decline in real GDP that prevailed during 2006–09 was attributed mainly to a contraction in tourist arrivals, which decreased by some 10% in both 2008 and 2009. However, the tourism sector registered a substantial improvement in 2010–12, in tandem with economic recovery in Asia, while overseas marketing campaigns were intensified and new flight routes from Asian countries were established. The opening in Ngardmau in mid-2011 of the Palau Eco Theme Park, a US \$2.2m. facility comprising a 'zipline' adventure cable course and a monorail system, was expected further to boost tourism. Visitor arrivals rose by an impressive 27.4% in 2011 and by a further 8.9% in 2012, according to the Palau Visitors' Authority. Fiscal spending was reduced by nearly 7% in 2009/10 and by 4% in 2010/11. However, observers noted that significant investment in public infrastructure programmes was required. In 2011/12 the Government of Taiwan provided 'stimulus' funding of \$10m. (as in the previous year) for Palau's economic development: much of the aid was disbursed on the rehabilitation of the road network. In October 2011 the ADB approved a \$16m. loan to improve Palau's water and sanitation services; this was the first loan agreement between the ADB and Palau. In a report published in December, the ADB identified the implementation of broader tax reforms (including the introduction of a value-added tax), as well as the reduction of the public sector wage bill (which typically accounts for about one-third of total government expenditure), as being imperative if medium- to long-term fiscal sustainability were to be achieved. These proposals were reiterated in an IMF report published in March 2013, which also advocated the promotion of private sector development in order to sustain economic growth. The rate of growth of real GDP was forecast to moderate to 3.0% in 2012/13.

PUBLIC HOLIDAYS

2014: 1 January (New Year's Day), 14 March (for Youth Day), 5 May (Senior Citizens' Day), 2 June (for Presidents' Day), 9 July (Constitution Day), 1 September (Labor Day), 1 October (Independence Day), 24 October (United Nations Day), 27 November (Thanksgiving), 25 December (Christmas Day).

Statistical Survey

Source (unless otherwise indicated): Office of Planning and Statistics, Ministry of Finance, POB 6011, Koror; tel. 767-1269; fax 767-5642; e-mail ops@palaugov.net; internet www.palaugov.net/stats/index.htm.

AREA AND POPULATION

Area: 508 sq km (196 sq miles); Babeldaob (Babeldaop, Babelthuap) island 409 sq km (158 sq miles).

Population: 19,129 at census of 15 April 2000; 19,907 (males 10,699, females 9,208) at census of 1 April 2005. *Mid-2013* (Secretariat of the Pacific Community estimate): 20,901. Source: Pacific Regional Information System.

Density (at mid-2013): 41.1 per sq km.

Population by Age and Sex (Secretariat of the Pacific Community estimates at mid-2013): *0–14:* 4,082 (males 2,084, females 1,998); *15–64:* 15,523 (males 8,502, females 7,021); *65 and over:* 1,296 (males 587, females 709); *Total* 20,901 (males 11,172, females 9,729). Source: Pacific Regional Information System.

Principal Towns (population at 2005 census): Koror (capital) 10,743; Meyuns 1,153. Source: Thomas Brinkhoff, *City Population* (internet www.citypopulation.de).

Births and Deaths (Secretariat of the Pacific Community estimates, 2010): Registered live births 279 (birth rate 13.6 per 1,000); Registered deaths 158 (death rate 7.7 per 1,000). Source: Pacific Regional Information System.

Life Expectancy (years at birth, WHO estimates): 72 (males 68; females 77) in 2009. Source: WHO, *World Health Statistics*.

Economically Active Population (persons aged 16 years and over, 2005 census): Agriculture 451; Forestry and fishing 310; Mining 34; Manufacturing 225; Utilities and sanitary services 208; Construction 1,365; Transport and communications 561; Trade, restaurants, etc. 1,670; Finance, insurance and real estate 132; Public administration 1,734; Professional and related services 1,466; Private households 915; Other personal services 387; Other services 319; *Total employed* 9,777 (males 5,982, females 3,795); Unemployed 426 (males 232, females 194); *Total labour force* 10,203 (males 6,214, females 3,989).

HEALTH AND WELFARE

Key Indicators

Total Fertility Rate (children per woman, 2010): 1.7.

Under-5 Mortality Rate (per 1,000 live births, 2010): 19.

Physicians (per 1,000 head, 2010): 1.4.

Hospital Beds (per 1,000 head, 2010): 4.8.

Health Expenditure (2009): US \$ per head (PPP): 1,431.

Health Expenditure (2009): % of GDP: 10.6.

Health Expenditure (2009): public (% of total): 78.0.

Total Carbon Dioxide Emissions ('000 metric tons, 2008): 212.7.

Carbon Dioxide Emissions Per Head (metric tons, 2008): 10.5.

For sources and definitions, see explanatory note on p. vi.

AGRICULTURE, ETC.

Fishing (metric tons, live weight, 2010, FAO estimates): Marine fishes 920; Total catch (incl. others) 1,012. Source: FAO.

INDUSTRY

Production (2009): Electric energy 152 million kWh (estimate). Source: UN Industrial Commodity Statistics Database.

FINANCE

Currency and Exchange Rates: United States currency is used: 100 cents = 1 United States dollar (US \$). *Sterling and Euro*

Equivalents (31 December 2012): £1 sterling = US $1.5780; €1 = US $1.3194; US $100 = £63.37 = €75.79.

Budget (US $ million, year ending 30 September 2011): *Revenue:* Current revenue 41.6 (Taxes 32.0, Non-tax revenue 9.6); Grants 40.3; Total 81.9. *Expenditure:* Current expenditure 72.2; Capital expenditure 17.5; Total 89.7. Source: Asian Development Bank.

Cost of Living (Consumer Price Index, base: June 2008 = 100): All items 102.3 in 2009; 103.7 in 2010; 108.6 in 2011.

Gross Domestic Product (US $ '000 at current prices): 204,319 in 2009; 208,162 in 2010; 220,706 in 2011. Source: Asian Development Bank.

Expenditure on the Gross Domestic Product (US $ '000 at current prices, 2011): Government final consumption expenditure 69,864; Private final consumption expenditure 110,844; Increase in stocks 2,638; Gross fixed capital formation 52,810; *Total domestic expenditure* 236,156; Exports of goods and services 162,688; *Less* Imports of goods and services 154,257; Statistical discrepancy –23,881; *GDP in purchasers' values* 220,706. Source: Asian Development Bank.

Gross Domestic Product by Economic Activity (US $ '000 at current prices, 2011): Agriculture and fishing 11,641; Mining (incl. electricity, gas and water) 6,185; Manufacturing 2,572; Construction 8,190; Trade (including hotels and restaurants) 39,554; Transport and communications 18,962; Financial intermediation 8,665; Public administration 50,818; Other services 62,531; *Sub-total* 209,118; Taxes on imports, less imputed bank service charges 11,588; *GDP in purchasers' values* 220,706. Source: Asian Development Bank.

Balance of Payments (US $ million, year ending September 2011): Exports of goods f.o.b. 6.8; Imports of goods f.o.b. –124.3; *Trade balance* –117.5; *Services and income (net)* 100.9; *Balance on goods, services and income* –16.6; Current transfers (net) 25.5; *Current balance* 9.0; Capital and financial account (net) 24.3; Net errors and omissions 33.2; *Overall balance* 66.5. Source: Asian Development Bank.

EXTERNAL TRADE

Principal Commodities (US $ '000, 2011): *Imports f.o.b.:* Food and live animals 20,952; Beverages and tobacco 6,820; Mineral fuels, metals and mineral products 49,287; Chemicals 8,709; Manufactured goods 8,168; Machinery and transport equipment 22,700; Miscellaneous manufactured articles 2,818; Total (incl. others) 124,323. *Exports:* Fish 6,316; Total (incl. others) 6,837 (Source: Pacific Regional Information System).

Principal Trading Partners (US $ '000, year ending September 2004): *Imports:* Japan 8,531; Korea, Republic 5,411; Philippines 6,934; Singapore 29,885; Taiwan 5,343; USA (incl. Guam) 48,225; Total (incl. others) 107,280. *Exports:* Total 5,882. *2011* (US $ '000): Total imports 124,323; Total exports 6,837 (Source: Pacific Regional Information System).

TRANSPORT

International Shipping (freight traffic, metric tons, 2006): Goods loaded 8,767; Goods unloaded 94,693. *Flag Registered Fleet* (at 31 December 2012): Vessels 3; Displacement 28,522 grt (Source: Lloyd's List Intelligence—www.lloydslistintelligence.com).

Civil Aviation (2006): Aircraft movements 1,054; Passengers enplaned 98,808; Cargo loaded 2,170,648 lbs.

TOURISM

Tourist Arrivals: 85,593 in 2010; 109,057 in 2011; 118,754 in 2012 (Source: Palau Visitors' Authority).

Tourist Arrivals by Country of Residence (2012): China, People's Republic 4,471; Guam 1,233; Japan 39,353; Korea, Republic 19,465; Taiwan 38,649; USA (mainland) 6,530; Total (incl. others) 118,754 (Source: Palau Visitors' Authority).

Tourism Receipts (US $ million, excl. passenger transport): 113 in 2009; 124 in 2010 (Source: World Tourism Organization).

COMMUNICATIONS MEDIA

Telephones (2011): 6,900 main lines in use.

Mobile Cellular Telephones (2011): 15,400 subscribers.

Internet Subscribers (2011): 1,300.

Broadband Subscribers (2011): 500.

Source: International Telecommunication Union.

EDUCATION

Pre-primary (public institutions only, 2006/07): 13 schools; 30 teachers; 509 pupils.

Enrolment (2006/07): *Elementary:* Total 2,683 (Public 2,135, Private 548). *Secondary:* Total 1,309 (Public 810, Private 499).

Teachers (1999/2000, estimates): *Elementary:* 124. *Secondary:* 126.

Institutions (2006/07): *Elementary:* Total 21 (Public 19, Private 2). *Secondary:* Total 6 (Public 1, Private 5).

Tertiary (Palau Community College): 54 teachers (full-time and part-time, 2005/06); 545 students (at 2005 census).

Pupil-teacher Ratio (primary education, UNESCO estimate): 12.5 in 2004/05 (Source: UNESCO Institute for Statistics).

Directory

The Government

HEAD OF STATE

President: THOMAS (TOMMY) E. REMENGESAU, Jr (took office 17 January 2013).

Vice-President and Minister of Justice: ANTONIO BELLS.

CABINET
(May 2013)

Tommy Remengesau was sworn in as President on 17 January 2013. By early May four of his ministerial nominees had been confirmed in their posts, while three still awaited approval by the Senate. A Minister of State had yet to be named.

Minister of Health: GREG NGIRMANG.

Minister of Finance: ELBUCHEL SADANG (nominated).

Minister of Public Infrastructure, Industries and Commerce: CHARLES OBICHANG (nominated).

Minister of Natural Resources, Environment and Tourism: UMIICH SENGEBAU.

Minister of Education: ANDREW TABELUAL (nominated).

Minister of Justice: ANTONIO BELLS.

Minister of Community and Cultural Affairs: BAKLAI TEMENGIL.

Minister of State: (vacant).

COUNCIL CHIEFS

The Constitution provides for an advisory body for the President, comprising the 16 highest traditional chiefs from the 16 states. The chiefs advise on all traditional laws and customs, and on any other public matter in which their participation is required.

Chairman: Ibedul YUTAKA GIBBONS (Koror).

GOVERNMENT OFFICES AND MINISTRIES

Office of the President: POB 6051, Koror, PW 96940; tel. 488-2403; fax 488-1662; e-mail pres@palaunet.com.

Department of the Interior, Office of Insular Affairs (OIA): OIA Field Office, POB 6031, Koror, PW 96946; tel. 488-2601; fax 488-2649; internet www.doi.gov/oia/islands/palau.cfm.

Ministry of Community and Cultural Affairs: POB 100, Koror, PW 96940; tel. 767-1126; fax 767-3354; e-mail mcca@palaunet.com.

Ministry of Education: POB 819, Koror, PW 96940; tel. 767-1464; fax 767-1465; e-mail moe@palaumoe.net; internet www.palaumoe.net.

Ministry of Finance: Exec. Bldg, 3rd Floor, Ngerulmud, PW 96939; tel. 767-2501; fax 767-2168; e-mail bpss@palaugov.net.

Ministry of Health: One Hospital Rd, POB 6027, Koror, PW 96940; tel. 767-5552; fax 767-0722; e-mail moh@palau-health.net; internet www.palau-health.net.

Ministry of Justice: POB 3022, Koror, PW 96940; tel. 488-3198; fax 488-4567; e-mail justice@palaunet.com.

PALAU

Directory

Ministry of Natural Resources, Environment and Tourism: Exec. Bldg, 1st Floor, Ngerulmud, PW 96939; tel. 767-5435; fax 767-3380; e-mail mnret@palaugov.net.

Ministry of Public Infrastructure, Industries and Commerce: POB 1471, Ngerulmud, PW 96940; tel. 767-2111; fax 767-3207; e-mail mincat@palaunet.com.

Ministry of State: Ngerulmud, Melekeok; tel. 767-2509; fax 767-2443; e-mail state@palaugov.net.

The new capital Ngerulmud, in the state of Melekeok, was opened in October 2006. All national government offices were to be transferred from Koror to Ngerulmud. Each state has its own administrative headquarters.

President and Legislature

PRESIDENT

At the presidential election held on 6 November 2012, Thomas E. (Tommy) Remengesau, Jr, the President in 2001–09, defeated the incumbent Johnson Toribiong by 6,140 votes to 4,287 (including absentee votes).

OLBIIL ERA KELULAU
(Palau National Congress)

The Palau National Congress comprises two chambers, the Senate and the House of Delegates. The Senate has 13 elected members, and the House of Delegates consists of 16 elected members. The most recent election was held on 6 November 2012.

President of the Senate: CAMSEK E. CHIN.

Vice-President of the Senate: HOKKONS BAULES.

Speaker of the House of Delegates: SABINO ANASTACIO.

Vice-Speaker of the House of Delegates: ALEXANDER MEREP.

National Congress: National Capitol Bldg, Ngerulmud, Melekeok; tel. 767-2455; fax 767-2633; e-mail senate@palaunet.com; internet www.palauoek.net.

Election Commission

Palau Election Commission: POB 826, Koror, PW 96940; tel. 488-1554; fax 488-3327; Chair. SANTOS BORJA.

Political Organizations

(There are currently no active political parties in Palau)

Palau Nationalist Party: c/o Olbiil era Kelulau, Koror, PW 96940; inactive; Leader JOHNSON TORIBIONG.

Ta Belau Party: c/o Olbiil era Kelulau, Koror, PW 96940; inactive; Leader KUNIWO NAKAMURA.

Diplomatic Representation

EMBASSIES IN PALAU

Japan: POB 6050, Palau Pacific Resort, Arakebesang, Koror, PW 96940; tel. 488-6455; fax 488-6458; internet www.palau.emb-japan.go.jp; Ambassador YOSHIYUKI SADAOKA.

Taiwan (Republic of China): WCTC Bldg, Of. 3F, POB 9087, Koror, PW 96940; tel. 488-8150; fax 488-8151; e-mail roc@palautelecoms.com; Ambassador MAGGIE TIEN.

USA: POB 6028, Koror, PW 96940; tel. 587-2920; fax 587-2911; e-mail usembassykoror@palaunet.com; internet palau.usembassy.gov; Ambassador HELEN REED-ROWE.

Judicial System

The judicial system of the Republic of Palau consists of the Supreme Court (including Trial and Appellate Divisions), presided over by the Chief Justice, the National Court (inactive), the Court of Common Pleas and the Land Court.

Supreme Court of the Republic of Palau: POB 248, Koror, PW 96940; tel. 488-4979; fax 488-1597; e-mail cjngiraklsong@palaunet.com; internet www.palausupremecourt.net; Chief Justice ARTHUR NGIRAKLSONG.

Office of the Attorney-General: 1365 Koror, PW 96940; tel. 488-2481; fax 488-3329; e-mail agoffice@palaunet.com; Attorney-Gen. ERNESTINE RENGIIL.

Religion

The population is predominantly Christian, mainly Roman Catholic. The Assembly of God, Baptists, Seventh-day Adventists, the Church of Jesus Christ of Latter-day Saints (Mormons) and the Bahá'í and Modignai (or Modeknai) faiths are also represented.

CHRISTIANITY
The Roman Catholic Church

Palau forms part of the diocese of the Caroline Islands, suffragan to the archdiocese of Agaña (Guam). The Bishop, who is resident in Chuuk, Eastern Caroline Islands (see the Federated States of Micronesia), participates in the Catholic Bishops' Conference of the Pacific, based in Suva, Fiji.

MODIGNAI FAITH

Modignai Church: Koror, PW 96940; an indigenous, non-Christian religion; also operates a high school.

The Press

Moonshadow Publications: POB 9006, Koror, PW 96940; tel. 488-8655; fax 779-3440; e-mail jerome@palaunet.com; internet jerometemengil.synthasite.com; Publr JEROME TEMENGIL.

Palau Gazette: POB 100, Koror, PW 96940; tel. 488-3257; fax 488-1662; e-mail roppresoffice@palaunet.com; newsletter publ. by Govt; monthly; Publr ROMAN YANO.

Roureur Belau: POB 477, Koror, PW 96940; tel. 488-6365; fax 488-4810; e-mail myu@palaunet.com; weekly; Publr CLIFFORD 'SPADE' EBAS.

Tia Belau (This is Palau): POB 477, Koror, PW 96940; tel. 488-6365; fax 488-4810; e-mail tiabelau@palaunet.com; f. 1992; weekly; English and Palauan; Editor RAOUL G. BRIONES; Publr MOSES ULUDONG; circ. 1,500.

Broadcasting and Communications

TELECOMMUNICATIONS

Palau National Communications Corpn (PNCC): POB 99, Koror, PW 96940; tel. 587-9000; fax 587-1888; e-mail pncc@palaunet.com; internet www.palaunet.com; f. 1982; mem. of the Pacific Islands Broadcasting Asscn; telephone, internet and digital television operator; 24 hrs daily; Chair. JENNIFER L. ANSON; Gen. Man. RICHARD L. MISECH.

Palau Mobile Corpn (PMC): POB 8084, Koror, PW 96940; tel. 488-4088; fax 488-2111; e-mail marklin@palaumobile.com; internet www.palaumobile.com; mobile telephone operator.

BROADCASTING
Radio

High Adventure Ministries: POB 66, Koror, PW 96940; tel. 488-2162; fax 488-2163; e-mail hamadmin@palaunet.com; f. 1992; broadcasts religious material; Engineering Man. BENTLEY CHAN.

KRFM: Sure Save Store, Koror, PW 96940; tel. 488-1359; e-mail rudimch@palaunet.com.

T8AA (Eco Paradise): POB 279, Koror, PW 96940; tel. 488-2417; fax 488-1932; broadcasts news, entertainment and music; govt-owned.

WSZB Broadcasting Station: POB 279, Koror, PW 96940; tel. 488-2417; fax 488-1932; Station Man. ALBERT SALUSTIANO.

WWFM: POB 1327, Koror, PW 96940; tel. 488-4848; fax 488-4420; e-mail wwfm@palaunet.com; internet www.brouhaha.net/palau/wwfm.html; Man. ALFONSO DIAZ.

Television

Oceania Television Network (OTV): 1724 Media Lane, Koror, PW 96940; tel. 488-6884; e-mail sales@oceaniatv.net; internet www.oceaniatv.net; f. 2007; broadcasts 24 hrs daily across Polynesian and Micronesian islands; Pres. JEFF BARABE.

PNCC Digital Television: POB 39, Koror, PW 96940; tel. 587-3515; fax 587-1888; e-mail pncc@palaunet.com; internet www.palaunet.com; owned by the Palau Nat. Communications Corpn; fmrly Island Cable Television.

3544

Finance

(cap. = capital; res = reserves; amounts in US dollars)

BANKING

Regulatory Authority

Financial Institutions Commission: POB 10243, Koror, PW 96940; tel. 488-3560; fax 488-3564; e-mail info@ropfic.org; internet www.ropfic.org; f. 2001; regulates and supervises banks and credit institutions; Chair. Okada Techitong; Exec. Commr G. Semdiu Decherong.

Banks

Bank of Guam: POB 338, Koror, PW 96940; tel. 488-2696; fax 488-1384; internet www.bankofguam.com; Man. Matthew Cruz.

Bank of Hawaii (USA): Medalaii Hamlet, Koror, PW 96940; tel. 488-2602; fax 488-2427; internet www.boh.com.

Bank Pacific: Lebuu St, Tngerongel Hamlet, Koror; tel. 488-5635; fax 488-4752; internet www.bankpacific.com; Sr Country Officer Joseph Koshiba.

National Development Bank of Palau: POB 816, Koror, PW 96940; tel. 587-2578; fax 587-2579; e-mail ndbp@palaunet.com; internet www.ndbp.com; f. 1982; total assets 15.6m. (Sept. 2009); 100% govt-owned; Pres. Sandra Mincer; Chair. Joshua Koshiba.

INSURANCE

Century Insurance Co: POB 318, Koror, PW 96940; tel. 488-8580; fax 488-8632; e-mail knakamura@palaunet.com.

Moylan's Insurance Underwriters Palau: POB 156, Koror, PW 96940; tel. 488-2765; fax 488-2744; e-mail palau@moylans.net; internet www.moylansinsurance.com; Branch Man. Kenji Dengokl.

NECO Insurance Underwriters Ltd: POB 129, Koror, PW 96940; tel. 488-2325; fax 488-2880; e-mail necogroup@palaunet.com.

Poltalia National Insurance: POB 12, Koror, PW 96940; tel. 488-2254; fax 488-2834; e-mail psata@palaunet.com; f. 1974; Pres. and CEO Ephram Polycarp.

Trade and Industry

CHAMBER OF COMMERCE

Palau Chamber of Commerce: POB 6021, Koror, PW 96940; tel. 488-4581; fax 488-2732; e-mail reklai@reklai.com; f. 1984; Pres. Surangel Whipps, Jr.

CO-OPERATIVES

These include the Palau Fishermen's Co-operative, the Palau Boatbuilders' Assen and the Palau Handicraft and Woodworkers' Guild. In 1990, of the 13 registered co-operatives, eight were fishermen's co-operatives, three consumers' co-operatives (only two in normal operation) and two farmers' co-operatives (one in normal operation).

DEVELOPMENT ORGANIZATION

Palau Conservation Society: POB 1811, Koror, PW 96940; tel. 488-3993; fax 488-3990; e-mail pcs@palaunet.com; internet www.palauconservation.org; f. 1994; sustainable devt, environmental protection; Chair. Maura Gordon; Exec. Dir Elbuchel Sadang.

Transport

ROADS

Tarmac and concrete roads are found in the more important islands. Other islands have stone- and coral-surfaced roads and tracks. The Government is responsible for 36 km (22 miles) of paved roads and 25 km (15 miles) of coral- and gravel-surfaced roads. Most paved roads are located on Koror. A major project to construct a new 85-km (53-mile) road around Babeldaob was completed in 2007, funded with US $150m. from the Compact of Free Association.

SHIPPING

Most shipping in Palau is government-organized. However, the Micronesia Transport Line operates a service from Sydney, Australia, to Palau. A twice-weekly inter-island service operates between Koror and Peleliu. There is one commercial port at Malakal Harbor, which is operated by the privately owned Belau Transfer and Terminal Company.

CIVIL AVIATION

There is an international airport on Babeldaob. Domestic airfields (former Japanese military airstrips) are located on Angaur and Peleliu. Continental Micronesia (Northern Mariana Islands and Guam) provides daily flights to Koror from Guam, and twice-weekly flights from Manila (Philippines). Cebu Pacific operates direct flights from Davao (Philippines) to Koror. In May 2008 China Airlines began operating charter flights between Taiwan and Palau. Palau Trans Pacific also operates from Taiwan. In July 2008 two South Korean carriers, Korean Air and Asiana Airlines, reached an agreement with the Palau Government, allowing for up to seven passenger flights and four cargo flights per week. Following the suspension by Japan Airlines of its charter flights from Tokyo, US carrier Delta Airlines inaugurated a regular service between the Japanese capital and Palau in December 2010.

Palau Airways: RTMRI Bldg, Koror, PW 96940; tel. 488-2468; fax 448-2228; e-mail service@palauairways.com; internet www.palauairways.com; CEO Teo Yong-Hwee.

Rock Island Airlines: managed by Aloha Airlines (Hawaii).

Tourism

Tourism is becoming increasingly important in Palau. The islands are particularly rich in their marine environment, and the Government has implemented measures to conserve and protect these natural resources. The myriad Rock Islands, now known as the Floating Garden Islands, are a noted reserve in the lagoon to the west of the main group of islands. There were 959 hotel rooms in 2004. In 2012 visitor arrivals increased by 8.9%, to reach 118,754. Most visitors come from Japan, Taiwan and the Republic of Korea. Tourism revenue reached US $124m. in 2010. The Seventh Micronesian Games were held in Palau in August 2010.

Belau Tourism Association: POB 9032, Koror, PW 96940; tel. 488-4377; fax 488-1725; e-mail bta@palaunet.com; Pres. Mari Kishigawa.

Palau Visitors' Authority: POB 256, Koror, PW 96940; tel. 488-2793; fax 488-1453; e-mail pva@visit-palau.com; internet www.visit-palau.com; f. 1982; Chair. Eyos Rudimch; Man. Dir Darin De Leon.

Defence

The USA is responsible for the defence of Palau, according to the Compact of Free Association implemented in October 1994, and has exclusive military access to Palau's waters, as well as the right to operate two military bases on the islands. The US Pacific Command is based in Hawaii.

Education

The educational system is similar to that of the USA. The Government of Palau is now responsible for the state school system, which most children attend. Education is free and compulsory between the ages of six and 14, and secondary education may be obtained at the public High School or one of the five private ones.

In 2006/07 there were 509 pupils enrolled in pre-primary public schools, 2,683 in primary schools, and 1,309 in secondary schools. According to the results of the 2005 census, there were 545 students in tertiary education in that year. In 2006/07 government schools totalled 20, one of which was a secondary school. The Micronesian Occupational College, based in Koror, provides two-year training programmes. Government expenditure on education totalled US $9.1m. in 1999/2000, equivalent to 10.7% of total budgetary expenditure.

PALESTINIAN TERRITORIES

Introductory Survey

LOCATION, CLIMATE, LANGUAGE, RELIGION, FLAG, CAPITAL

The Palestinian Territories are located in the West Bank and the Gaza Strip. (For a more detailed description of the location, see Constitution and Government.) The West Bank lies in western Asia, to the west of the Jordan river and the Dead Sea, with the State of Israel to the north, west and south. The Gaza Strip lies on the easternmost coast of the Mediterranean, with Israel to the north and east, and Egypt to the south. The Interim Agreement of September 1995 (see Contemporary Political History) provides for the creation of a corridor, or safe passage, linking the Gaza Strip with the West Bank. A 'southern' safe passage between Hebron and Gaza was opened in October 1999 (although it has been closed since October 2000). Including East Jerusalem, the West Bank covers an area of 5,655 sq km. Precipitation ranges between 600 mm and 800 mm on the Mount Hebron massif and 200 mm in the Jordan valley. Apart from the urban centres of Beit Lahm (Bethlehem) and Al-Khalil (Hebron) to the south, the majority of the Palestinian population is concentrated in the northern localities around Ram Allah (Ramallah), Nabulus (Nablus), Janin (Jenin) and Tulkarm. The Gaza Strip covers an area of 365 sq km. Annual average rainfall is 300 mm. The language of Palestinians in the West Bank and Gaza is Arabic. The majority of the Palestinian population are Muslims, with a Christian minority representing about 2% of the Palestinian population of the territories. This minority, in turn, represents about 45% of all Palestinian Christians. The national flag (proportion 1 by 2) comprises three equal horizontal stripes of black, white and green, with a red triangle with its base corresponding to the hoist. Ramallah is the centre of administration for the Palestinian (National) Authority. In November 1988 the Palestine National Council (PNC) proclaimed Jerusalem as the capital of the newly declared independent State of Palestine. Israel (q.v.) declares Jerusalem as its capital. In 1967 East Jerusalem was formally annexed by the Israeli authorities, although the annexation has never been recognized by the UN. The permanent status of Jerusalem remains subject to negotiation on so-called 'final status' issues under the Oslo accords.

CONTEMPORARY POLITICAL HISTORY

Historical Context

Until the end of the 1948 Arab–Israeli War, the West Bank formed part of the British Mandate of Palestine, before becoming part of the Hashemite Kingdom of Jordan under the Armistice Agreement of 1949. It remained under Jordanian sovereignty, despite Israeli occupation in 1967, until King Hussein of Jordan formally relinquished legal and administrative control on 31 July 1988. Under Israeli military occupation, the West Bank was administered by a military government, which divided the territory into seven sub-districts. The Civil Administration, as it was later termed, did not extend its jurisdiction to the many Israeli settlements that were established under the Israeli occupation; settlements remained subject to the Israeli legal and administrative system. By October 2000 approximately 17.2% of the West Bank was under exclusive Palestinian jurisdiction and security control, although Israel retained authority over access to and from the zone; about 23.8% was under Israeli military control, with responsibility for civil administration and public order transferred to the Palestinian (National) Authority (PA); the remaining 59% was under Israeli occupation.

An administrative province under the British Mandate of Palestine, Gaza was transferred to Egypt after the 1949 armistice and remained under Egyptian administration until June 1967, when it was invaded by Israel. Following Israeli occupation, the Gaza Strip, like the West Bank, became an 'administered territory'. Until the provisions of the Declaration of Principles on Palestinian Self-Rule (see The Palestinian–Israeli Conflict) began to take effect, the management of day-to-day affairs was the responsibility of the area's Israeli military commander. Neither Israeli laws nor governmental and public bodies—including the Supreme Court—could review or alter the orders of the military command to any great extent. In 2001 an estimated 42% of the Gaza Strip was under Israeli control, including settlements, military bases, bypass roads and a 'buffer zone' along the border with Israel. Israel withdrew its settlers and military personnel from Gaza in August–September 2005.

The Palestinian–Israeli Conflict

The Oslo accords

In accordance with the Declaration of Principles on Palestinian Self-Rule of 13 September 1993, and the Cairo Agreement on the Gaza Strip and Jericho of 4 May 1994, the Palestine Liberation Organization (PLO) assumed control of the Jericho area of the West Bank, and of the Gaza Strip, on 17 May 1994. In November–December 1995, under the terms of the Israeli-Palestinian Interim Agreement on the West Bank and the Gaza Strip, concluded on 28 September 1995, Israeli armed forces withdrew from the West Bank towns of Nablus, Ramallah, Jenin, Tulkarm, Qalqilya and Bethlehem. (These three agreements and associated accords are referred to collectively as the 'Oslo accords'.) In late December the PLO assumed responsibility in some 17 areas of civil administration in the town of Hebron, with a view to assuming eventual full responsibility for civil affairs in the 400 surrounding villages. However, despite a partial withdrawal from Hebron in January 1997, Israeli armed forces were to retain freedom of movement to act against potential hostilities there, and to provide security for some 400 settlers. Responsibility for security in the rest of Hebron (excluding access roads) passed to the Palestinian police force. Following the first phase of the redeployment, and the holding of elections to a Palestinian Legislative Council and for a Palestinian Executive President, Israel was to have completed a second redeployment from rural areas by July 1997. The Israeli occupation was to be maintained in military installations, East Jerusalem and the settlements in Gaza and the West Bank, as well as those around Jerusalem, until the conclusion of 'final status' negotiations between Israel and the Palestinians, scheduled for May 1999.

Diplomatic developments within the context of the Oslo peace process led to a new timetable for Israeli redeployment, which envisaged two phases, subsequent to the Hebron withdrawal, to be completed by October 1997 and August 1998. Discussions on 'final status' issues—borders, Jerusalem, Jewish settlements and Palestinian refugees—were to commence within two months of the signing of the agreement on Hebron. As guarantor of the Oslo accords, the USA undertook to obtain the release from Israeli custody of Palestinian prisoners, and to ensure that Israel continued to engage in negotiations for the establishment of a Palestinian airport in the Gaza Strip and for safe passage for Palestinians between the West Bank and Gaza. The USA also endeavoured to ensure that the Palestinians would continue to combat terrorism, complete the revision of the Palestinian National Charter (or PLO Covenant—adopted in 1964 and amended in 1968), and consider Israeli requests to extradite Palestinians suspected of involvement in attacks in Israel.

In February 1997 the Israeli Government of Binyamin Netanyahu announced the construction of a new settlement at Jabal Abu Ghunaim (Har Homa in Hebrew), near Beit Sahur, which would prejudice 'final status' negotiations concerning Jerusalem because it would effectively separate East Jerusalem from the West Bank. In response, the PA withdrew from 'final status' talks scheduled to commence in March. The start of construction work at Jabal Abu Ghunaim provoked rioting among Palestinians and a resumption of attacks by the military wing of the Islamic Resistance Movement (Hamas) on Israeli civilian targets. Israel responded by ordering a general closure of the West Bank and Gaza. Both the Jabal Abu Ghunaim construction and Israel's unilateral decision to redeploy its armed forces from only 9% of West Bank territory (announced in March) were regarded by many observers as a vitiation of both the Oslo and the subsequent post-Hebron agreements.

In June 1997 the US House of Representatives voted in favour of recognizing Jerusalem as the undivided capital of Israel and of transferring the US embassy to the city from Tel-Aviv. The vote (which was opposed by US President Bill Clinton) coincided with violent clashes between Palestinian civilians and Israeli troops in Gaza and Hebron. In July, on the eve of a scheduled visit by Dennis Ross, the US Special Co-ordinator to the Middle East, to reactivate negotiations between Israel and the PA, Hamas carried out a suicide bomb attack at a Jewish market in Jerusalem, in which 14 civilians were killed. Ross cancelled his visit, and the Israeli Government immediately halted payment of tax revenues to the PA and closed the Gaza Strip and the West Bank. The PA undertook a campaign to detain members of Hamas and another militant organization, Islamic Jihad. As a result of US diplomacy, Israeli and Palestinian officials agreed to resume negotiations focusing on the outstanding issues of the Oslo accords in October.

It was reported in December 1997 that, under further US pressure, the Israeli Cabinet had agreed in principle to withdraw troops from an unspecified area of the West Bank. However, the Israeli Government subsequently reiterated that it would not redeploy until the Palestinian leadership had adopted effective measures to counter terrorism, had reduced the strength of its security forces from 40,000 to 24,000, and had revised the Palestinian National Charter to recognize explicitly Israel's right to exist. In January 1998 the Israeli Cabinet issued a communiqué detailing 'vital and national interests' in the West Bank, amounting to some 60% of the entire territory that it was not prepared to relinquish, including the territory surrounding Jerusalem. (Within the framework of the Oslo accords, it was planned for Israel to relinquish 90% of the West Bank.) Direct contacts between Palestinian representatives and the Israeli Prime Minister subsequently collapsed.

On 7 July 1998 the UN General Assembly overwhelmingly approved a resolution to upgrade the status of the PLO at the UN. The new provision, which the USA and Israel had opposed, allowed the PLO to participate in debates, co-sponsor resolutions and raise points of order during discussions of Middle East affairs. In June, meanwhile, the adoption by the Israeli Cabinet of a plan to extend the boundaries of Jerusalem and construct homes there for a further 1m. people was denounced by the PA as amounting to a de facto annexation of territories that were officially subject to 'final status' negotiations.

The Wye River Memorandum and subsequent US-sponsored peace negotiations

On 19–22 July 1998 Israeli and Palestinian delegations held direct negotiations in order to discuss a new US initiative to expedite the commencement of 'final status' talks. In September Netanyahu and Arafat met in Washington, DC, and agreed to participate in a peace conference in the USA. This summit meeting, also attended by President Clinton, commenced at the Wye Plantation, Maryland, USA, on 15 October and culminated in the signing, on 23 October, of an agreement intended to facilitate the implementation of the Oslo accords. Under the terms of the Wye River Memorandum, to be implemented within three months of its signing, Israel was to transfer a further 13.1% of West Bank territory from exclusive Israeli control to joint Israeli-Palestinian control. An additional 14% of the West Bank was to be transferred from joint Israeli-Palestinian control to exclusive Palestinian control. The Wye Memorandum also stipulated that: negotiations with regard to a third Israeli redeployment (under the terms of the Oslo accords) should proceed concurrently with 'final status' discussions; the PA should reinforce anti-terrorism measures and arrest 30 suspected terrorists; the strength of the Palestinian police force should be reduced by 25%; Israel should carry out the phased release of 750 Palestinian prisoners (including political detainees); the Palestine National Council (PNC) should annul those clauses of the PLO Covenant deemed to be anti-Israeli; Gaza International Airport was to become operational with an Israeli security presence; and an access corridor between the West Bank and the Gaza Strip should be opened. On 20 November Israel redeployed its armed forces from about 500 sq km of the West Bank (with the PA assuming responsibility for all civil affairs and for security affairs in some 400 sq km); released some 250 (mainly non-political) Palestinian prisoners; and signed a protocol for the opening of Gaza International Airport. Israel retained the right to decide which airlines could use the airport, which was officially inaugurated by Arafat on 24 November.

Prior to a planned visit by Bill Clinton to Israel and the Gaza Strip in December 1998, violent clashes erupted in the West Bank between Palestinians and Israeli security forces. One cause of the unrest was a decision by Israel to suspend further releases of Palestinian prisoners under the terms of the Wye Memorandum, and its insistence that no Palestinians convicted of killing Israelis, nor members of Hamas or Islamic Jihad, would be released. On 14 December, in the presence of President Clinton, the PNC voted to annul articles of the Palestinian National Charter deemed to be anti-Israeli. However, at a summit meeting the following day between Clinton, Netanyahu and Arafat at the Erez crossing between Israel and the Gaza Strip, the Israeli Prime Minister further demanded that the Palestinians should cease incitement to violence and formally relinquish plans for a unilateral declaration of Palestinian statehood on 4 May 1999 (the original deadline as established by the Oslo accords). Netanyahu announced that Israel would not proceed with the second scheduled redeployment of its armed forces on 18 December 1998, and on 20 December the Israeli Cabinet voted to suspend implementation of the Wye Memorandum.

Following a meeting of the Palestinian Central Council (PCC), together with Hamas representatives, in Gaza in late April 1999, it was announced that a declaration on Palestinian statehood would be postponed until after the Israeli elections scheduled for May. The decision was applauded internationally, but provoked violent demonstrations among many Palestinians.

Meeting at Sharm el-Sheikh, Egypt, on 4 September 1999, during a visit to the region by the US Secretary of State, Madeleine Albright, Arafat and the new Israeli Prime Minister, Ehud Barak, signed the Sharm el-Sheikh Memorandum (or Wye Two accords), outlining a revised timetable for implementation of the outstanding provisions of the original Wye agreement. Under the terms of the Memorandum, on 9 September Israel released some 200 Palestinian 'security' prisoners, and the following day Israel transferred a further 7% of the West Bank to PA control. A ceremonial opening of 'final status' negotiations between Israel and the PA took place at the Erez checkpoint on 13 September. In early October, however, the Palestinians' chief negotiator, Yasser Abd al-Rabbuh, warned that the PA would boycott 'final status' talks unless Israel ended its settlement expansion programme. Barak, also under pressure from left-wing groups in Israel, responded by ordering the dismantling of 12 illegal 'settlement outposts' in the West Bank. Meanwhile, Israel released a further 151 Palestinian prisoners under the terms of Wye Two. The first 'safe passage' between the West Bank and Gaza was inaugurated on 25 October. Israel asserted that it would maintain almost complete control over this 'southern route', which linked Hebron to the Erez checkpoint.

'Final status' negotiations between Israel and the PA commenced in Ramallah on 8 November 1999, following a summit meeting held earlier in the month in Oslo, Norway, between Arafat, Barak and Clinton. A further redeployment of Israeli armed forces from 5% of the West Bank, scheduled for 15 November, was postponed, owing to disagreement over the areas to be transferred. In early December Palestinian negotiators withdrew from the talks, following reports that settlement activity had intensified under Barak. Apparently in response to US pressure, the Israeli Prime Minister subsequently announced a halt to settlement construction until the close of negotiations regarding a framework agreement on 'final status'. In late December Arafat conducted talks in Ramallah with Barak, who became the first Israeli premier to hold peace discussions on Palestinian territory. At the end of the month Israel released some 26 Palestinian 'security' prisoners as a gesture of 'goodwill'. Israeli armed forces withdrew from a further 5% of the West Bank on 6–7 January 2000. Israel subsequently announced that a scheduled third redeployment from 6.1% of the territory would be postponed until Barak had returned from the USA (where revived talks on the Israeli-Syrian track of the peace process ended in failure). During a subsequent meeting with Arafat, Barak was reported to have proposed that the deadline for reaching a framework agreement be postponed for two months. The approval by the Israeli Cabinet of a withdrawal of its troops from a sparsely populated area of the West Bank led the PA to break off negotiations in February. The resumption of 'final status' talks was announced on 21 March, shortly after Israel released 15 Palestinian 'security' prisoners. Israeli armed forces withdrew from a further 6.1% of the West Bank the following day.

In mid-April 2000, following talks between Barak and Clinton in Washington, DC, Israel was said to have agreed to Palestinian demands for greater US involvement in future discussions. Moreover, the Israeli premier reportedly indicated that a Palestinian entity could be established in what was now PA-controlled territory—covering 60%–70% of the West Bank—although he refused to speak of a Palestinian 'state'. At the third round of 'final status' talks between Israel and the PA, which opened at the Israeli port of Eilat on 30 April, Palestinian negotiators denounced a recent decision by the Israeli Government to construct 174 new homes in the West Bank. At crisis talks between Arafat and Barak in Ramallah in early May, mediated by Dennis Ross, Barak reportedly proposed the transfer to full PA control of three Palestinian villages close to Jerusalem, on condition that the third West Bank redeployment (scheduled to be implemented in June) be postponed. After PA negotiators admitted that the 13 May deadline for reaching a framework agreement would not be met, 'final status' talks were suspended. On 21 May Israel suspended 'secret' talks being conducted between Israeli and Palestinian representatives in Stockholm, Sweden, after an Israeli child was seriously wounded in continuing violence in the West Bank. (The latest unrest came after Palestinians declared 15 May—the anniversary of the declaration of the State of Israel in 1948—to be a 'day of rage', and amid growing anger over the apparent unaccountability of the PA leadership.) The Israeli Government also reversed its decision to transfer the three Arab villages to PA control, demanding that Arafat take action to curb Palestinian unrest. On 21 June, two days prior to the scheduled date, the PA reportedly agreed to a postponement of the third redeployment of Israeli forces from the West Bank.

The PCC convened on 2 July 2000, and after two days of discussions stated that the PLO would declare a State of Palestine on or before 13 September. A peace summit in mid-July between Arafat and Barak at the US presidential retreat at Camp David, Maryland, mediated by Clinton with the aim of achieving a framework agreement on 'final status', ended without agreement. Nevertheless, Israel and the PA pledged to continue peace negotiations and to avoid 'unilateral actions'—interpreted as Arafat's intention unilaterally to declare an independent Palestinian state on 13 September. Amid intense international pressure, the PCC reconvened in Gaza on 9–10 September and agreed to postpone the declaration of statehood for an indefinite period. Negotiations between Israeli and PA officials subsequently resumed in the USA, and on 20 September an agreement was signed allowing for construction of the Gaza seaport to begin (although the work failed to progress thereafter).

The al-Aqsa intifada

From late September 2000 the West Bank and Gaza Strip was engulfed in what became known as the al-Aqsa *intifada* (uprising—the first *intifada* lasted from 1987 to 1993), as Palestinians demonstrated their frustration at the lack of progress in the Oslo peace process and at their failure to achieve statehood. The catalyst for the violence was a visit by Ariel Sharon, leader of Israel's right-wing Likud party, to Temple Mount/Haram al-Sharif in Jerusalem—the site of the al-Aqsa Mosque and the Dome of the Rock—on 28 September. Sharon's visit to the Islamic holy sites provoked violent protests and stone-throwing by Palestinians, to which Israeli security forces responded forcefully. Clashes spread rapidly: by the end of October at least 140 people had died—all but eight of them Palestinians—and thousands had been wounded. In early October Arafat and Barak travelled to Paris, France, for negotiations led by the US Secretary of State, Madeleine Albright. The Israeli authorities subsequently sealed off the borders of the West Bank and Gaza, and on 7 October the UN Security Council issued a resolution condemning the 'provocation carried out' at Temple Mount/Haram al-Sharif and the 'excessive use of force' employed by the Israeli security forces against Palestinians. Israel accused Arafat of failing to intervene to halt the violence, as members of Arafat's own Fatah movement joined Hamas and other militant groups in the quickly escalating *intifada*. In an attempt to prevent the crisis from developing into a major regional conflict, a US-sponsored summit meeting between Barak and Arafat was convened on 16–17 October at Sharm el-Sheikh. At the close of the meeting US President Clinton announced that the Israeli and Palestinian leaders had agreed the terms of a truce to halt the spiralling violence, and to the formation of a US-appointed committee to investigate the clashes. Clinton subsequently named the five-member commission, chaired by former US Senator George Mitchell, in early November. Barak, meanwhile, demanded that Arafat rearrest some 60 militant Islamists whom the PA had freed in early October.

At the end of October 2000 Islamic Jihad claimed responsibility for a suicide bombing on an Israeli army post in Gaza, signalling a new campaign against Israeli forces by militant Palestinian organizations opposed to the Oslo process. Israel responded with air-strikes on Fatah military bases, and declared a new strategy of targeting leading officials of militant Islamist

groups suspected of terrorist activities (subsequently termed 'targeted killings'). On 1 November Arafat held a crisis meeting in Gaza with the Israeli Minister for Regional Co-operation, Shimon Peres; the two sides were reported to have agreed a cease-fire, based on the truce brokered in Egypt in October. The following day, however, a car bomb exploded in Jerusalem, for which Islamic Jihad claimed responsibility. Meeting with Clinton in the USA in early November 2000, Arafat demanded that the USA support Palestinian requests for the establishment of a UN peace-keeping force in the self-rule areas, despite Barak's opposition to such a force. Israel imposed an economic blockade on the West Bank and Gaza in mid-November, and launched air-strikes against PA offices in Gaza later that month, in reprisal for the deaths of two people in the bombing of a school bus for Israeli settlers. A further round of peace talks opened in December, at which Clinton was reported to have proposed a peace deal that included plans for a future Palestinian state covering the Gaza Strip and some 95% of the West Bank, as well as granting the Palestinians sovereignty over the Islamic holy sites in the Old City of Jerusalem. However, the US plan also required that Palestinians renounce the right of return for 3.7m. refugees, which the PA deemed unacceptable. The negotiations broke down in late December after two Israelis died in bombings by Palestinian militants in Tel-Aviv and the Gaza Strip.

The election of Ariel Sharon as Israeli Prime Minister in February 2001 provoked violent demonstrations by Palestinians, who held Sharon responsible—as Israel's Minister of Defence at that time—for the Phalangist massacre of Palestinian refugees in Lebanese camps in 1982. Immediately after Sharon's election Palestinian militants carried out a car bombing in Jerusalem, and in mid-February a Palestinian bus driver launched an attack on Israeli soldiers and civilians in Tel-Aviv, killing nine people. Israel again responded by sealing off the Palestinian territories.

In June 2001 21 Israelis were killed in a suicide bomb attack, apparently perpetrated by Hamas, at a Tel-Aviv nightclub. The PA agreed the following day to implement the recommendations listed in the final report of the international commission of inquiry under George Mitchell (the Sharm el-Sheikh Fact-Finding Committee, or 'Mitchell Committee'), published in May. The Mitchell Report recommended a freeze on Israeli settlement expansion; a clear statement by the PA demanding an end to Palestinian violence; an 'immediate and unconditional' end to the conflict and the disengagement of forces by both sides; and the resumption of security co-operation. The PA also agreed to an extended cease-fire brokered by the US Central Intelligence Agency (CIA) Director, George Tenet, although in July both Hamas and Islamic Jihad formally announced that the cease-fire was ended.

Following a Hamas suicide bombing in August 2001 that killed at least 15 Israelis at a restaurant in central Jerusalem, Israel ordered its armed forces to occupy PA offices including Orient House, the PA's de facto headquarters in East Jerusalem. Israeli troops subsequently entered the West Bank town of Jenin—the first Israeli reoccupation of territory transferred to full PA control under the terms of the Oslo accords. Palestinian officials called the action a 'declaration of war'. Later in the month Abu Ali Moustafa, the leader of the Popular Front for the Liberation of Palestine (PFLP), was assassinated by Israeli forces in the West Bank.

The unprecedented scale of the suicide attacks on the USA on 11 September 2001 precipitated efforts by the US Administration of George W. Bush to encourage Israel and the PA to end the violence in the Palestinian territories. Yasser Arafat, who had condemned the attacks in the strongest terms, declared that he had ordered militant Palestinian groups to halt their actions against Israelis, while Israel agreed to withdraw from PA-controlled areas of the West Bank. However, Sharon stated that his Government required 48 hours without violence prior to any resumption of peace talks. Arafat and Peres met in the Gaza Strip in late September, in an attempt to consolidate the cease-fire arrangements outlined in the Mitchell Report. However, on the first anniversary of the al-Aqsa *intifada* five Palestinians were shot dead by Israeli forces in Gaza, and retaliatory attacks between the two sides resumed.

President Bush disclosed for the first time in October 2001 that the USA would accept the creation of a Palestinian state, on condition that Israel's existence was not threatened. In late October Israel order its armed forces into six major West Bank towns following the assassination in Jerusalem of its ultra-nationalist Minister of Tourism, Rechavam Ze'evi, by three members of the PFLP—apparently in revenge for the murder of the PFLP leader in August. Arafat subsequently banned all military factions of Palestinian political groups, and his security forces arrested several PFLP militants; however, the PA refused Israeli demands for their extradition. At least five Palestinians reportedly died in a raid by Israeli forces searching for Ze'evi's assassins. Towards the end of October Israel stated that it would carry out a phased withdrawal from the six West Bank towns; however, its 'anti-terrorist' operation continued in Jenin and Tulkarm, and Israeli tanks continued to surround Ramallah.

The Israeli blockade of Arafat's West Bank headquarters

Hamas claimed responsibility for a series of attacks in Jerusalem and Haifa over a 24-hour period in December 2001, in which at least 25 Israelis were killed. Palestinian security forces subsequently stated that they had arrested more than 150 militants, mostly in Jenin, and were also reported to have placed the spiritual leader of Hamas, Sheikh Ahmad Yassin, under house arrest. Meanwhile, Israel conducted a missile strike on Arafat's official residence in Gaza, and Israeli tanks advanced to the edge of the presidential compound in Ramallah. The Israeli Prime Minister increasingly began to draw parallels between Israel's efforts to suppress the *intifada* and the US 'war on terror', describing the PA as a 'terror-supporting entity'. In mid-December Israel responded to an assault on a settlers' bus in the West Bank (in which some 10 Israelis died) by declaring Arafat to be 'irrelevant', owing to his failure to prevent such attacks, and announced that it was severing all contacts with the PA leader. The Israeli military launched air raids across the West Bank and Gaza, reoccupied large areas of Ramallah, and reinforced its military blockade of Arafat's headquarters; several Palestinian police officers and civilians were killed during the Israeli operations.

In January 2002 Arafat ordered an investigation into Israeli and US claims that the PA was complicit in a massive shipment of largely Iranian-produced weaponry intercepted by Israeli forces in the Red Sea; the freighter, the *Karine A*, was apparently en route for the Gaza Strip. In February Arafat, on behalf of his administration, accepted responsibility for the shipment. Following a gun attack by members of the militant Al-Aqsa Martyrs Brigades, in which six guests at a bar mitzvah ceremony in northern Israel were killed, Sharon ordered tanks and armoured vehicles to tighten the blockade of Arafat's Ramallah headquarters. Israeli forces also briefly reoccupied Tulkarm, in order to arrest Palestinian militants, in what was reported to be the largest military incursion since the start of the al-Aqsa *intifada*. In February Israel carried out the 'targeted killing' of at least four members of the radical Democratic Front for the Liberation of Palestine (DFLP) in the Gaza Strip.

There were renewed efforts to restart peace negotiations in February 2002. Ariel Sharon met leading PA representatives, while Shimon Peres held discussions with the Palestinian Legislative Council (PLC) Speaker, Ahmad Quray. However, Israeli officials were angered when a large number of Palestinian militants were freed during Israeli air-strikes on the PA's security headquarters in Nablus. Requests for calm by the UN, and attempts by the European Union (EU, see p. 281) to launch a new peace initiative, failed to prevent an escalation of violence in the Palestinian territories. Israel subsequently agreed to withdraw its tanks from Arafat's compound, but refused to allow the Palestinian leader freedom of movement beyond Ramallah. This travel ban remained in place despite the arrest by Palestinian security forces of three militants believed to have been responsible for Ze'evi's murder, prompting PA security officials again to suspend bilateral talks.

As violence continued in the West Bank, Crown Prince Abdullah of Saudi Arabia made proposals for a Middle East peace settlement, prior to a summit meeting of the League of Arab States (the Arab League, see p. 372) Council, due to be held in Beirut, Lebanon, in March 2002. Abdullah's proposals centred on Arab recognition of the State of Israel and the normalization of diplomatic relations, in exchange for agreement by Israel to withdraw from all Arab land occupied since 1967 and on the establishment of a Palestinian state with East Jerusalem as its capital. Arafat stated that he would not attend the Beirut conference, because of threats by Sharon to prevent his return to the West Bank and Gaza. Meanwhile, in response to a suicide bombing by a Palestinian woman at an Israeli army checkpoint, Israel for the first time sent ground troops into two refugee camps in the West Bank, which it claimed were centres of Islamist

militancy. Fierce fighting ensued, and the PA announced subsequently that it was suspending all contacts with the Israeli Government. The USA urged Israel to show restraint, and UN and EU officials demanded an immediate Israeli withdrawal from the camps. Several Palestinians were killed as Israeli forces entered Ramallah, Bethlehem and Tulkarm in an attempt to find the perpetrators of two attacks, in which 20 Israelis had died, for which the Al-Aqsa Martyrs Brigades were held responsible. The US Secretary of State, Gen. Colin Powell, publicly criticized Sharon's declared aim of forcing the PA to return to peace talks by defeating them militarily. An estimated 40 Palestinians died during the fierce fighting that followed the killing of five settler students by Hamas gunmen in Gaza. Meanwhile, Sharon declared that Arafat had met the conditions for the restoration of free movement after a fifth suspect in Ze'evi's murder was arrested by Palestinian security forces in early March 2002. However, after a suicide bombing in Jerusalem, in which 11 Israelis were killed, and a shooting in Netanya in which two died, Israel's 'inner' Security Cabinet voted to intensify the military offensive. Tanks entered Qalqilya and the Jabalia refugee camp in Gaza (where 18 Palestinians, including four Hamas members, were reported to have been killed), and Arafat's headquarters in Gaza was destroyed by Israeli helicopters and gunboats.

In mid-March 2002 Israel announced that it was lifting its travel ban on Arafat, although the Palestinian leader would still not be permitted to travel abroad. Some 20,000 Israeli troops then began a massive ground offensive in the Palestinian territories. Hundreds of Palestinian men were detained for questioning, and several civilians died, in what was reported to be the largest Israeli operation against Palestinian militants since the 1982 invasion of Lebanon. Israeli forces again took control of most of Ramallah, with tanks coming to within a short distance of Arafat's presidential compound. The UN Security Council adopted Resolution 1397, demanding an immediate end to all acts of violence by both sides, and urging Israel and the Palestinians to co-operate in implementation of the Mitchell Report and Tenet recommendations. Apparently under US pressure, Israeli forces withdrew from Ramallah, Tulkarm and Qalqilya, although they continued to surround the towns, and subsequently also agreed to redeploy its troops from Bethlehem and Beit Jala. However, after talks between Israeli and Palestinian security officials ended without agreement, the Israeli Government again ordered troops into much of the West Bank and detained several alleged militants. After a further suicide attack by the Al-Aqsa Martyrs Brigades, which killed three Israelis in central Jerusalem, the USA added the group to its list of proscribed terrorist organizations.

The Arab League summit proceeded in Beirut on 27–28 March 2002, although both President Mubarak of Egypt and King Abdullah of Jordan did not attend. Palestinian officials were angered that Arafat was refused permission to address the session via satellite link from Ramallah: the Lebanese authorities stated that they feared an Israeli disruption of such a broadcast. At the close of the conference, the participating Arab states unanimously endorsed the Saudi peace initiative, which included a clause calling for a 'just solution' to the question of Palestinian refugees.

'Operation Defensive Shield'

The Israeli–Palestinian crisis deepened at the end of March 2002, following the deaths of 30 people in an attack by a Hamas suicide bomber at a hotel in the Israeli town of Netanya, during the Jewish festival of Passover. Although Arafat personally condemned the bombing, and reportedly ordered the immediate arrest of four prominent West Bank militants, Sharon blamed the PA for its failure to prevent such attacks. In response to what was swiftly called the 'Passover massacre', and with Arafat effectively isolated at his compound in Ramallah, Israeli armed forces began a huge campaign of incursions into West Bank towns—code-named 'Operation Defensive Shield'—on 29 March, with the declared aim of dismantling the Palestinian 'terrorist infrastructure'. The UN Security Council met in emergency session and demanded, in Resolution 1402, an immediate Israeli withdrawal from all towns that had been transferred to the PA under the Oslo accords. After a Hamas suicide bomber killed 15 Israelis at a café in Haifa, Sharon declared that Israel was 'at war', and his 'inner' Security Cabinet gave the army permission to broaden its offensive in the West Bank. By early April Israel had effectively reoccupied most major towns in the West Bank and detained more than 1,000 Palestinians; Ramallah and Bethlehem were declared 'closed military areas'. The UN Security Council unanimously adopted a further resolution (No. 1403), demanding the implementation of Resolution 1402 (i.e. an Israeli withdrawal from Palestinian territories) 'without delay'. However, Israel ruled out the prospect of further withdrawals from the West Bank following the deaths of several of its reservists in ambushes in the Jenin refugee camp, and those of at least eight people in a Hamas suicide bombing of a bus near Haifa. In mid-April Marwan Barghouthi, a PLC member and the Fatah leader in the West Bank (whom Israel claimed to be the commander of the Al-Aqsa Martyrs Brigades), was arrested by Israeli forces in Ramallah; on charges of leading Palestinian 'terrorist' groups in the West Bank and orchestrating suicide bombings against Israeli citizens. Sharon announced on 21 April that the first stage of Operation Defensive Shield had been completed; however, Israeli forces were to remain in Ramallah and Bethlehem. According to Palestinian sources, at least 100 Palestinians died during the Israeli invasion; 23 Israelis were believed to have been killed. Some reports stated that more than 4,000 Palestinians were detained during the offensive, although many were subsequently released. (In May 2004 Barghouthi was convicted by a court in Tel-Aviv on five counts of murder and of leading a 'terrorist organization' that had launched assaults on Israeli forces and settlers, although he was acquitted on 33 counts of resistance attacks because of lack of evidence. He was subsequently sentenced to five terms of life imprisonment, with two additional 20-year terms.)

Yasser Arafat was freed by the Israeli authorities at the beginning of May 2002, under a US-brokered arrangement whereby Israel agreed to end its siege of Ramallah on condition that the PA leader handed over six prisoners, who were sheltering in the presidential compound, wanted by Israel in connection with 'terrorist' activities. In late April four of the prisoners had been convicted by an ad hoc Palestinian court, inside the compound, of direct involvement in the assassination of Rechavam Ze'evi, and were sentenced to between one and 18 years' imprisonment. The other two detainees were the PFLP leader, Ahmad Saadat, and a militant implicated in the *Karine A* affair. The six prisoners were subsequently transferred to Jericho, where they were to remain in 'international custody' under US and British guard. In response to a series of fatal suicide attacks against Israeli citizens by Palestinian militants in late June and July, Israel again ordered its armed forces into several towns in the West Bank and Gaza.

Israel responded to a suicide bombing in Tel-Aviv in September 2002 by announcing that it would seek to isolate Arafat: Israeli forces began the systematic destruction of Arafat's compound in Ramallah, while the PA leader reportedly remained inside one of the office buildings. Israel also launched a series of incursions into the Gaza Strip, which increasingly became the focus of its military operations. The siege of Arafat's headquarters was brought to an end in late September, after the UN Security Council issued a resolution (No. 1435), demanding the immediate cessation of Israeli military actions in and around Ramallah.

The 'roadmap' peace plan and the construction of Israel's 'security fence'

The peace process was temporarily revived by the publication of the 'roadmap' peace plan (sponsored by the Quartet group, comprising the USA, Russia, the UN and the EU) at the end of April 2003. The release of the roadmap, which had originally been agreed in December 2002, and which envisaged an end to the Israeli–Palestinian conflict and the establishment of a sovereign Palestinian state by 2005–06, was conditional on the announcement of a new Palestinian Cabinet under Prime Minister Mahmud Abbas (see Domestic Political Affairs). Palestinian responsibilities under the terms of the roadmap were broadly restricted to a commitment to ending militant actions against Israeli targets and the establishment of a civilian and government infrastructure; critical issues concerning the Palestinian population, such as the borders of a future state, the status of refugees and Jerusalem, were to be decided during Israel's negotiations with Lebanon, Syria and other Arab states. Initially, Sharon objected to the issue of the right to return of Palestinian refugees and refused to consider the dismantling of settlements, but in late May 2003 the Israeli Cabinet accepted the terms of the roadmap. At the end of the month Sharon made the unprecedented acknowledgement that Israel was in occupation of the Palestinian areas. In early June Sharon, Abbas and President Bush met in Aqaba, Jordan, to discuss the implementation of the roadmap, and Israeli troops had begun dismantling settlements in the West Bank

Violence resumed by mid-June 2003, with an Israeli assassination attempt on the prominent Hamas leader, Abd al-Aziz al-Rantisi, and a retaliatory suicide attack against a bus in Jerusalem, in which 16 people died. Israeli helicopter gunships attacked targets in Gaza, and 26 people were killed in the renewed violence. Nevertheless, Israel continued to dismantle some settlements, to withdraw troops from certain areas of the West Bank and Gaza, and to release Palestinian prisoners. This last was not a condition of the roadmap, but was viewed as a 'goodwill' gesture to Mahmud Abbas, who was now apparently engaged in a power struggle with Arafat. Some 400 prisoners were released in August, but excluded those members of Hamas and Islamic Jihad who had been involved in planning or executing attacks against Israeli targets. Along with Fatah, the two militant groups had declared a three-month cease-fire at the end of June. Following the cease-fire declaration, Israeli troops withdrew from key parts of northern and central Gaza and removed roadblocks from the arterial north–south highway. In July Bethlehem was handed over to Palestinian control.

The successful implementation of the roadmap was threatened, however, by Israel's ongoing construction, despite international criticism, of a 'security fence' in the West Bank, as a barrier against infiltration by Palestinian militants. In October the Israeli Cabinet approved the next phase of the security fence; although the new sections were not contiguous to those already built, they would completely enclose Israeli settlements in the West Bank. Meanwhile, a senior commander of Islamic Jihad in Hebron was killed by Israeli forces in mid-August, as part of the continuing policy of raids against and 'targeted killings' of Palestinian militant leaders. A suicide bomber subsequently killed 20 Israelis on a bus in Jerusalem, an attack for which both Hamas and Islamic Jihad claimed responsibility.

In December 2003 Israel declared that, unless the PA started disarming and disbanding Palestinian militant groups, it was prepared to initiate a 'disengagement plan', involving the accelerated construction of the 'security fence' in the West Bank and the physical separation of Israel from the Palestinian territories. In an interview published in the *Ha'aretz* newspaper in February 2004, Ariel Sharon stated that a plan had been drawn up for the evacuation of all Israeli settlements in the Gaza Strip. This was welcomed by the recently appointed Palestinian Prime Minister, Ahmad Quray.

In March 2004 10 Israelis were killed in a double suicide bombing—for which both Hamas and the Al-Aqsa Martyrs Brigades claimed responsibility—at the southern Israeli port of Ashdod. In response, the founder and spiritual leader of Hamas, Sheikh Ahmad Yassin, and several of his entourage were killed by Israeli helicopter gunships as they left a mosque. A UN Security Council resolution condemning the killing was vetoed by the USA, since the text did not refer to Hamas as a terrorist organization. Abd al-Aziz al-Rantisi was appointed to lead Hamas in Gaza, but was himself killed in a targeted air-strike by Israeli forces in Gaza City in April. Hamas did not disclose the identity of al-Rantisi's successor, reportedly adopting a policy of 'collective leadership' in order to prevent future individual leaders of the organization from being targeted by Israel. Khalid Meshaal remained the head of the group's political bureau, based in Damascus, Syria.

In July 2004 the International Court of Justice (ICJ) in The Hague, Netherlands, issued a non-binding ruling that the Israeli 'security fence' breached international law and effectively constituted the annexation of Palestinian land. The ICJ urged Israel to remove sections of the fence and to pay compensation to affected Palestinians. Sharon rejected the court's findings. In August Sharon approved the construction of 1,000 new settlement homes in the West Bank. In September, following the deaths of 16 people in a double suicide bombing by Hamas in Beersheba, Israel, Israeli tanks and aircraft attacked a Hamas training camp in the Gaza Strip. The UN reported in October that 135 Palestinians had been killed and an estimated 95 homes destroyed following a 16-day Israeli military assault on Gaza, prompted by a Hamas rocket that killed two Israeli children in Sderot.

Meanwhile, further details of Sharon's 'disengagement plan' were published in Israeli newspapers: it combined a complete Israeli withdrawal from the Gaza Strip, and evacuation of all settlements there, with the consolidation of six settlement blocs in the West Bank. In October 2004 the Israeli Knesset voted in favour of Sharon's proposal to dismantle all 21 settlements in Gaza, and four in the northern West Bank, entailing the eviction of about 9,000 settlers. The removal of settlements in Gaza was scheduled to commence in July 2005, but was later postponed until August.

Following the death of Yasser Arafat in November 2004, Sharon expressed hope that the new Palestinian leadership would understand the need to end 'terrorist' attacks before relations between the two sides could be improved and outstanding issues resolved. Israel and Egypt agreed in December that 750 Egyptian troops would be deployed along the country's border with Gaza in advance of the planned Israeli withdrawal; however, settlers in Gaza vowed to resist eviction. Also in December Mahmud Abbas issued an appeal (rejected by Hamas) for an end to the continuing use of violence in resistance to Israeli occupation. Israel announced that it would withdraw troops from Palestinian areas prior to the Palestinian presidential election, and that its military would remain outside towns in the West Bank and Gaza Strip for 72 hours. Towards the end of December Israel released 159 Palestinian prisoners as a gesture of 'goodwill'.

In January 2005, following the deaths of six Israelis in a Palestinian militant attack at the Karni crossing, Sharon severed ties with the Palestinian leadership, and ordered raids on several areas of Gaza. Following a demand by the PLO leadership that Palestinians should cease all military action against Israel, Sharon called off the offensive and announced that Israel would co-operate on security issues, although he instructed troops to prepare for a full-scale assault on an area in the northern Gaza Strip from where rockets were being fired on Israeli targets.

Negotiations with Israel and Israeli withdrawal from Gaza

At security talks between Palestinian and Israeli officials in January 2005, agreement was reached on the deployment of Palestinian security forces in the southern Gaza Strip in order to reduce attacks on Israeli targets. Some 2,500 Palestinian security forces were already patrolling northern Gaza, on the orders of the new PA President, Mahmud Abbas.) The former Palestinian Minister of Security, Muhammad Dahlan, and the Israeli Minister of Defence, Shaul Mofaz, subsequently agreed to the withdrawal of Israeli troops and the deployment of PA security forces in the five West Bank towns of Ramallah, Qalqilya, Tulkarm, Jericho and Bethlehem.

Abbas and Sharon met in February 2005 at a summit meeting held in Sharm el-Sheikh, with Egypt's President Mubarak and King Abdullah of Jordan also in attendance. Abbas announced a cease-fire, and Sharon declared that Israeli military operations would end if Palestinian militant attacks stopped; Sharon also agreed to release 500 Palestinian prisoners as a 'goodwill' gesture. Some Palestinian militant groups agreed to observe the cease-fire, but Hamas demanded that Israel cease all acts of aggression against Palestinians and release all Palestinian prisoners before it would agree to a formal cease-fire, although it apparently agreed to an informal truce. Israel suspended plans to withdraw from the five West Bank towns after four Israelis were killed in a suicide bombing by Islamic Jihad outside a nightclub in Tel-Aviv in late February. In March, however, Israel officially surrendered Jericho to Palestinian security control, and also announced plans to remove all 24 settlement outposts constructed since Sharon became Prime Minister in February 2001, after a ministerial report condemned the illegal use of budget funds to develop the outposts. Although this fulfilled a condition of the roadmap, not all of the 105 outposts would be dismantled. Israeli forces withdrew from the West Bank town of Tulkarm at the end of March 2005.

Meanwhile, in February 2005 Israel announced plans to alter the route of the 'security fence' so that it would cut out 7% of the territory of the West Bank instead of the 16% outlined in the original route. In March, to Palestinian protest, the Israeli Government announced that the completed barrier would divide the town of Bethlehem and also separate East Jerusalem and the settlement of Ma'aleh Edomin from the rest of the West Bank.

Abbas travelled to Washington, DC, in May 2005 for his first meeting with President Bush since becoming President of the PA. Bush reportedly offered US $50m. in direct aid to the PA to develop the Gaza Strip after the Israeli withdrawal. The US President also urged Israel to dismantle illegal settlement outposts in the West Bank, to end the expansion of settlements and to ensure that the 'security fence' did not become a 'political border'. Abbas spoke in favour of starting 'final status' negotiations with Israel after its disengagement from the Gaza Strip. Israel released some 398 Palestinian prisoners in June.

However, following a series of Palestinian militant attacks claimed to be in retaliation for Israeli violations of the cease-fire, in June Israel carried out raids across the West Bank and detained around 50 members of Islamic Jihad. Israeli forces also launched a missile strike on Gaza, in a failed attempt to kill an Islamic Jihad activist. The Palestinian Minister of the Interior and National Security, Maj.-Gen. Nasser Yousuf, declared a state of emergency in the Gaza Strip, and authorized his forces to prevent militants launching rocket and mortar attacks against targets in Israel. As clashes broke out between members of the Palestinian security services and Hamas militants, Israel carried out further air attacks on Hamas targets, killing seven. Israeli troops re-entered Tulkarm in July, after it was reported that a suicide bomber who had killed four Israelis in Netanya had come from a nearby village. Meanwhile, a series of rocket attacks by Hamas, in which an Israeli woman was killed, prompted Israel to launch air-strikes on targets in Gaza

Israel completed its withdrawal from the Gaza Strip (according to the terms of its unilateral Disengagement Plan) on 12 September 2005. In November, following intervention by the US Secretary of State, Condoleezza Rice, Israel reached an agreement with Palestinian officials to reopen Gaza's southern crossing into Egypt at Rafah later that month. The PA was to manage the crossing, with additional remote monitoring by Israeli and EU observers.

In September 2005 21 people were killed when a Palestinian truck carrying rockets exploded during a Hamas parade in the Jabalia refugee camp in the Gaza Strip. Hamas accused Israel of having fired a missile at the truck from a remote-controlled drone aircraft; both Israel and the PA denied the accusation. However, Hamas responded by launching mortars into Sderot. The Israeli Government decided at an emergency meeting to permit the army to use any means necessary to suppress militants. Accordingly, the Israeli army stationed tanks and artillery batteries on Gaza's eastern and northern borders, began seizing Hamas and Islamic Jihad activists in the West Bank, and used air-strikes to kill militants in Gaza and to destroy a weapons store and weapons-production facilities, despite a pledge from Hamas to end attacks and return to the cease-fire. In October Israeli security forces also killed two senior Islamic Jihad militants in Tulkarm and arrested five other members of the Tulkarm cell, which it believed to be responsible for the suicide attacks in Tel-Aviv in February and in Netanya in July. Islamic Jihad avenged the 'targeted killings' by launching a suicide bomb attack on a market in Hadera, resulting in the deaths of five Israelis. Israeli Prime Minister Ariel Sharon declared a 'broad and continuous' offensive against militant Islamist groups, and hours later the Israeli army launched an air-strike on a car carrying two senior Islamic Jihad militants in Gaza: eight Palestinians, mostly civilians, died. In December Islamic Jihad launched a further suicide attack in Netanya, killing five Israelis.

Developments following Hamas's 2006 electoral victory

Israel reacted to Hamas's victory in the legislative elections held in January 2006 (see Domestic Political Affairs) by declaring that it would not negotiate with a Palestinian authority that included 'an armed terrorist organization' that advocated Israel's destruction. US President Bush announced that his country would also refuse to deal with Hamas until it renounced its call to destroy Israel, and stated that the USA would consider halting aid to the Palestinians. At the end of the month the Quartet group announced that financial assistance to a future Palestinian administration would depend on the extent to which Hamas fulfilled the following conditions: that it renounce violence, respect agreements approved under the Fatah regime and recognize Israel's right to exist. Egypt and Jordan also demanded that the militant organization reject violence and accept Israel's existence. The head of Hamas's political bureau, Khalid Meshaal, announced that his organization could enter into a long-term truce with Israel under certain conditions, including the return of Israel to its pre-1967 borders. However, Meshaal asserted that violent resistance to the occupation was legal.

Israel announced in February 2006 that, in order to punish the new Palestinian regime until it renounced violence and recognized Israel's right to exist, it would stop collecting customs and tax revenues on Palestinians' behalf, and would ask foreign donors to cease all payments to the PA; however, it would permit the transfer of humanitarian aid to Palestinians. President Abbas announced that the PA faced a financial crisis, while Hamas asserted that Arab and Islamic countries would compensate for a reduction in aid from Israel and the West. Later in the month the EU, which—like Israel and the USA—considered

Hamas to be a terrorist organization, announced that it was to give the PA US $140m. worth of aid to save the interim administration from financial collapse. However, following the installation of the new Hamas-led Cabinet on 28 March, both the USA and the EU announced that they were withdrawing direct aid to the PA until Hamas fulfilled the three conditions placed on it by the Quartet group.

Meanwhile, as Israel continued to kill militants in the Palestinian territories following further missile strikes, it declared that, should Hamas resume attacks on Israel, all members of the organization would be deemed to be legitimate targets for assassinations, including Prime Minister-designate Ismail Haniya and future ministers. In March 2006 Israeli forces stormed the gaol in Jericho in which the Secretary-General of the PFLP, Ahmad Saadat, was being held prisoner, detaining him and other inmates suspected of involvement in attacks against Israel. US and British monitors had left the gaol immediately prior to the raid, ostensibly to protest against poor security arrangements there. A Palestinian high court had announced in 2002 that there was no evidence that Saadat had been involved in Rechavam Ze'evi's murder, and both President Abbas and Hamas had recently announced plans to release him, as he had been elected to the PLC at the elections in January 2006. Israel, however, still wished to interrogate Saadat in connection with the murder, and therefore resolved to detain him before the Palestinian authorities released him. The raid, in which two Palestinians were killed, provoked unrest throughout the territories. Palestinians set fire to the British Council building in Jericho in protest at perceived British collusion with the Israeli authorities, and gunmen briefly kidnapped 11 foreign workers. The PFLP vowed to avenge Saadat's capture, which President Abbas condemned as a crime and a humiliation for Palestinians. In April the Israeli Ministry of Justice announced that a pre-trial inquiry had not produced enough evidence to try Saadat for Ze'evi's murder, but that he would be tried for other security offences. However, four other militant PFLP members detained with him were charged with the murder, among them the man accused of firing the fatal shot.

Israel's new Government under Prime Minister Ehud Olmert, which was appointed in May 2006, was at this time pursuing plans to establish Israel's permanent borders, if necessary unilaterally, by 2010. Olmert's so-called Convergence Plan entailed the annexation of West Bank settlement blocs to Israel and the transfer of other, majority-Palestinian, sections of the West Bank to full PA control. (Israel would retain the whole of Jerusalem under the plans.) The Israeli premier affirmed that Israel was, however, seeking to secure an internationally supported peace plan with Hamas, but that such a solution required the group to reject violence and adhere to peace agreements signed by Israel and the previous Fatah administration. Khalid Meshaal dismissed the Convergence Plan as allowing Israel to: illegally retain its possession of the largest section of the West Bank and its 'security fence'; reject concessions on the status of Jerusalem; and thwart the 'right of return' of Palestinian refugees.

In June 2006 Palestinians claimed that the shelling of a beach in the northern Gaza Strip, in which seven members of one family were killed, had been carried out by Israeli forces firing from gunboats. (The Israeli Prime Minister later declared that a technical failure had been to blame for the deaths, and issued an apology to the Palestinian authorities.) On 25 June Hamas militants from Gaza launched a cross-border raid, which resulted in the kidnapping of an Israeli soldier, Corporal Gilad Shalit; two other Israeli soldiers were killed during the raid, as were two of the militants. The following day Palestinian militant groups issued a statement demanding that Israel release all female Palestinian prisoners and detainees under 18 years of age in exchange for Shalit. Israel responded by launching air-strikes on Gaza and entering the southern part of the Strip. Israel's military actions (code-named 'Operation Summer Rains') to seek to secure the release of Corporal Shalit in the Gaza Strip continued despite the conflict that began between Israel and Hezbollah in July. Several bridges and official buildings were bombed by the Israeli military, while the territory's only power plant was also destroyed, leaving thousands of Gazans without electricity or water.

On 29 June 2006 Israeli security forces arrested 64 senior Palestinian officials, including eight Hamas ministers from the Cabinet and 20 other parliamentarians, for questioning in relation to their alleged involvement in attacks against Israeli targets. On the following day an Israeli missile destroyed the

offices of the Ministry of the Interior and Civil Affairs in Gaza City. On 2 July an Israeli air-strike destroyed the office of the Palestinian Prime Minister, Ismail Haniya. The crisis continued to escalate during July, and many Palestinians died in the ensuing violence: it was estimated that Israeli troops killed more than 160 Palestinians in the period between late June and 23 July. Israel arrested the Speaker of the PLC, Dr Aziz Duweik, in August, while some of the cabinet ministers arrested in June were released during subsequent weeks. Duweik was subsequently imprisoned for three years for being a member of Hamas, and was released, two months early, in June 2009.

In November 2006 Israeli armed forces began a new military offensive in the town of Beit Hanoun, in northern Gaza. 'Operation Autumn Clouds' was aimed at destroying the infrastructure and weapons supplies used by Palestinian militants across the border in order to prevent the firing of rockets into Israel by the armed groups. It was reported that more than 50 Palestinians, including many civilians, were killed in the operation. However, a cease-fire between the sides was secured by President Abbas towards the end of the month, and Israel withdrew its troops from Gaza. The number of Palestinians killed by Israeli security forces in the West Bank and Gaza was reported by the Israeli human rights organization B'Tselem to have tripled, to 657, in 2006, of whom 322 were believed to have been civilians. Most of these fatalities had occurred in the Gaza Strip, following the intensification of Israeli bombardments of the territory from mid-2006. Relations between Israel and the PA deteriorated once again in early 2007, after the truce was broken by militant Palestinian groups, who continued to launch large numbers of rockets against Israeli targets such as the town of Sderot. In mid-April Abbas and Olmert held discussions concerning a future Palestinian state and a possible prisoner exchange, in what was intended to be the first of a series of regular fortnightly meetings between the two leaders. However, in late April Hamas militants, announcing that they were ending the truce brokered in November 2006, resumed the firing of rockets into Israel from Gaza. Israel responded in May 2007 by conducting a series of air-strikes against alleged militant targets in Gaza; a number of Hamas legislators, ministers and local government officials were also detained by Israeli security forces.

Following the takeover of the Gaza Strip by militants of Hamas on 14 June 2007 and the subsequent naming of an Emergency Cabinet—consisting principally of independents and technocrats—by President Abbas in the West Bank on 17 June (see Domestic Political Affairs), on 24 June the Israeli Government agreed to transfer tax revenues to the PA that it had withdrawn following Hamas's election victory of January 2006. On 25 June 2007 a summit meeting was held in Sharm el-Sheikh between Abbas, Olmert, Egypt's President Mubarak and King Abdullah of Jordan, aimed at expressing solidarity with Abbas's newly appointed Emergency Cabinet in the West Bank. Olmert declared that Israel was to free 250 Palestinian security prisoners as a gesture of 'goodwill' to the Palestinian President; a final total of 255 (mainly Fatah-affiliated) prisoners were duly released on 20 July. In that month Israel also granted an amnesty for some 180 Fatah militants who were sought by the Israeli security forces in the West Bank, provided that the men renounced violence against Israel and handed themselves over to the PA.

Abbas held discussions with Olmert in Jericho on 6 August 2007—the first meeting between Israeli and Palestinian leaders on Palestinian territory since May 2000—in preparation for the US-sponsored Middle East peace meeting scheduled for November. The two leaders held further talks on 'fundamental issues' in late August and early September 2007. On 5 September Israel's Supreme Court issued a ruling that the route of a further section of the 'security fence' along Israel's boundary with the West Bank should be altered in order to improve the living conditions of Palestinians residing at the affected village of Bil'in whose homes had been separated from the land they were cultivating. During late September the Israeli military took action against the continued launching by Palestinian militants of rockets against northern Israel by carrying out air raids and sending tanks into the northern Gaza Strip; at least 12 Palestinians were reported to have died during the military campaign. Nevertheless, Israel released another 57 (mainly Fatah) Palestinian prisoners to the West Bank and 29 to the Gaza Strip in early October.

In October 2007 President Abbas for the first time outlined his specific demands with regard to the territory on which a future

Palestinian state should be established: Abbas demanded that the state should cover 6,205 sq km (2,400 sq miles) of the West Bank and Gaza Strip—the exact amount of territory occupied by Israel in 1967. Towards the end of October 2007 the Israeli Government responded to the launching of missiles from Gaza into northern Israel by confirming a policy of reducing fuel and electricity supplies to Gaza, which it now classified as a 'hostile entity'.

The Annapolis conference on peace in the Middle East

An international peace meeting intended officially to relaunch the Middle East peace process was held in Annapolis, Maryland, USA, on 27 November 2007, with members of the Quartet group and the Arab League in attendance. At the close of the summit, US President George W. Bush read a statement of joint understanding between Ehud Olmert and Mahmud Abbas, who expressed their commitment to achieving a final settlement of the outstanding issues of contention between Israelis and Palestinians by the end of 2008. It was announced that: an Israeli-Palestinian steering committee would oversee 'vigorous, ongoing and continuous' negotiations between the two sides; the Israeli and Palestinian leaders would continue to meet on a fortnightly basis; and both Israel and the PA would comply with their obligations as agreed under the terms of the roadmap signed in 2003. However, on 4 December 2007 Palestinians complained that Israel had again contravened its obligations by issuing tenders for 307 new homes to be built at the Jabal Abu Ghunaim settlement in East Jerusalem. Moreover, Olmert appeared to indicate that Israel would not be required to conclude a peace treaty with the PA by the end of 2008 if it considered that the Palestinians had not met their security obligations; the Israeli leader was reported to have told his Cabinet that there was 'no commitment to a specific timetable' made at Annapolis. A Hamas spokesman reportedly responded to the Annapolis meeting by pledging that Palestinian 'resistance' to Israeli occupation would continue. Nevertheless, the Israeli authorities released a further 429 Palestinian prisoners (408 to the West Bank and 21 to Gaza—none of whom had been involved in attacks against Israelis) on 3 December 2007 as a further 'goodwill' gesture to President Abbas; most of those freed were Fatah members from the West Bank, with no Hamas or Islamic Jihad detainees on the list.

Meanwhile, on 2 December 2007 Hamdi Koran, one of the PFLP militants who had been seized when Israeli forces stormed the gaol in Jericho in March 2006, was sentenced in a court in Jerusalem to a term of life imprisonment (and an additional 100 years in prison), after he was convicted of having assassinated the Israeli Minister of Tourism, Rechavam Ze'evi, in October 2001, as well as involvement in other attacks against Israeli citizens.

The first session of the Israeli-Palestinian steering committee established at the Annapolis peace meeting was held on 12 December 2007 but failed to achieve significant progress. Israeli air-strikes against alleged militant targets in the Gaza Strip continued, with several members of Islamic Jihad believed to have fired rockets into Sderot being targeted. According to B'Tselem at the end of December, 344 Palestinians had been killed as a result of inter-factional violence in 2007—the highest number since the start of the second *intifada* in 2000. However, the number of Palestinians killed by Israeli troops during 2007 was reported by B'Tselem to have declined to 373, of whom 131 were estimated to be civilians and 53 minors; 290 of the deaths occurred in the Gaza Strip. During a visit to Israel and the West Bank in the second week of January 2008, and amid an intensification of Israel's military campaign in Gaza since the beginning of the month, US President Bush asserted that a future Palestinian state should be contiguous territory and not a 'Swiss cheese' of separate cantons; he also urged Israel to withdraw from Arab territory that its forces had occupied in 1967. Bush reiterated his demand that the PA dismantle the territories' militias.

On 17 January 2008 Israel imposed virtually a complete blockade on the Gaza Strip, which prompted vehement international criticism: the Israeli response to Palestinian violence targeted at its citizens was widely viewed as 'collective punishment' of the people of Gaza for the actions of a minority of militants. The blockade resulted in severe disruption to Gaza's electricity supplies, although Olmert did subsequently agree to allow some essential supplies into the Strip. None the less, on 23 January hundreds of thousands of Palestinians entered Egypt from Gaza in search of food, fuel and medical supplies, after Hamas militants had breached the Rafah crossing separating

the two territories. (The crossing had been almost permanently closed since Hamas's takeover of the Strip in June 2007 because the Egyptian Government, as did Israel, refused to recognize Hamas as the legitimate administration there.) Egyptian officials responded by offering their backing to a plan proposed by President Abbas that would allow for the PA, rather than Hamas, to assume control of the Egypt–Gaza border. Although the breaches in the border were repaired by 3 February 2008, there were reports of exchanges of gunfire between Egyptian security forces and Palestinian gunmen as tensions continued. The UN estimated that 700,000 Gazans (about 50% of the territory's population) had crossed the border into Egypt. On 4 February the Al-Aqsa Martyrs Brigades reportedly claimed responsibility for the first suicide bombing in Israel for more than a year, in the southern town of Dimona (in which an Israeli woman died), although a Hamas representative apparently alleged that militants from its Hebron branch had in fact carried out the attack. The Israeli Government implied that the perpetrator of the bombing, whom it believed to be Gazan, must have entered Israel via Egypt as a direct result of the border having been breached. As Israeli officials threatened a full-scale invasion of the Gaza Strip and also pledged to restart the policy of 'targeted killings' of Hamas and other militants, Olmert declared that he considered the status of Jerusalem to be the final 'core issue' to be negotiated by the two parties—a proposal that was rejected strongly by many Palestinians.

In March 2008 a militant Palestinian, believed to be a resident of East Jerusalem, entered a Jewish religious college in West Jerusalem and shot dead eight students. As with the Dimona bombing, the issue of whether ultimate responsibility for the shooting could be attributed to Hamas remained unclear. Shortly after the Jerusalem shooting, Olmert approved a plan to construct a further 330 homes for settlers in the West Bank. In April 12 Palestinian militant factions (excluding Fatah and Hamas), meeting in Cairo, reportedly agreed to new proposals for a cease-fire to be reached with Israel: a cessation of violence was to be implemented gradually, beginning in the Gaza Strip and then being undertaken in the West Bank, provided Israel also ended its economic blockade of Gaza. Talks between Abbas and Olmert, under the terms agreed at Annapolis, had resumed earlier that month. However, with regard to a proposed cease-fire deal between Israel and Hamas, Olmert emphasized during discussions in Jerusalem with the Egyptian intelligence chief, Lt-Gen. Omar Suleiman, that Israel demanded an end to the weapons-smuggling by Palestinian militants into Gaza and the release of Corporal Gilad Shalit in order for any sustainable truce to be realized.

Following several violent incidents in previous weeks, in mid-June 2008 a formal cease-fire was finally agreed between Israel and Hamas representatives in the Gaza Strip, after lengthy negotiations led by Egyptian mediators. Israel was to end its economic blockade of the Strip and cease military action in the territory, on condition that Hamas militants and those of other Palestinian groups refrained from conducting any cross-border attacks on Israeli targets. The truce was to remain in place for at least six months, but to take effect in stages. Towards the end of June Israeli officials complained of a 'grave violation' of the cease-fire by Palestinian militants who had launched a rocket attack against the town of Sderot, and responded by closing Israel's border crossings into Gaza. The rocket attack was alleged to have been carried out by Islamic Jihad in retaliation for an Israeli military raid in the West Bank, which caused two Palestinian deaths. Hamas asserted in July that, since Israel was not abiding by the terms of the recent truce, it had suspended bilateral negotiations concerning a proposed prisoner exchange involving the release of Corporal Shalit. Meanwhile, three Israelis were killed by a Palestinian militant in Jerusalem. In August the Israeli Government released 198 Palestinian prisoners as a gesture of 'goodwill' to President Abbas. The list included two of the longest-serving Palestinian detainees, who—contrary to Israel's usual policy of not freeing those with 'blood on their hands'—had been responsible for the deaths of two Israeli citizens in the 1970s.

In November 2008 the first direct clashes between Israeli armed forces and Hamas militants since the cease-fire agreement of June took place in the Gaza Strip. Israel launched a renewed military campaign in the territory and reimposed its blockade, while Hamas and Islamic Jihad fighters responded by firing rockets into northern Israel. Officials from the US Administration conceded that it was no longer possible to achieve an Israeli-Palestinian peace agreement by the end of the year, as envisaged by the November 2007 Annapolis meeting. Nevertheless, at the first meeting held between Abbas and Olmert for two months, Olmert promised to free a further 250 Palestinian prisoners as a 'confidence-building measure' towards the Palestinian President. After a government committee agreed to the release of only 230 Palestinians, on 15 December 2008 a total of 227 prisoners (none of whom were from Hamas or Islamic Jihad) were freed. On 16 December the UN Security Council approved Resolution 1850, which reiterated its endorsement of a two-state solution to the Israeli–Palestinian conflict and affirmed that the peace process was 'irreversible'. The resolution urged all parties involved in the negotiations to intensify their efforts to achieve a comprehensive and lasting peace in the Middle East.

'Operation Cast Lead'

On 19 December 2008, following discussions with other Palestinian factions in the Gaza Strip, Hamas formally declared an end to its six-month truce with Israel, asserting that Israel had not adhered to its requirements under the terms of the agreement. Rocket and mortar attacks by Palestinian militants against towns in northern Israel followed, and Israel launched air-strikes against Gaza. On 27 December Olmert ordered a campaign of intensive air-strikes against targets in the Strip, as the first phase of its offensive code-named 'Operation Cast Lead', undertaken in response to the increased cross-border attacks. The principal targets initially appeared to be security headquarters and police stations, as well as the tunnels used by militants to smuggle weapons used to launch attacks against Israelis. At least 225 Palestinians were reported to have been killed on the first day of the Israeli military operation. In late December the UN Security Council expressed 'serious concern at the escalation of the situation in Gaza' and urged an immediate halt to all violence.

Having declared an 'all-out war against Hamas' on 29 December 2008, the Israeli Government sanctioned a wider campaign of air-strikes, which now targeted government offices, presidential buildings and the Islamic University in Gaza. The UN Relief and Works Agency for Palestine Refugees in the Near East (UNRWA) stated that the ongoing Israeli bombardment had inflicted considerable damage on the Gaza Strip's already fragile public infrastructure, and that it had erased the territory's public service capacity. On 3 January 2009 Israel launched a major ground assault into the Strip. The declared aim of the operation, which effectively divided the enclave into two, was to guarantee the long-term security of Israel's citizens by preventing the continued firing of rockets and mortars by Hamas militants against towns in southern Israel; the Israeli military sought to destroy Hamas's infrastructure, weapons factories and supplies. Heavy fighting ensued in densely populated districts of Gaza City and other urban centres. There was condemnation from the international community on 6 January, when an Israeli mortar attack close to an UNRWA-administered school in the Jabalia refugee camp resulted in the deaths of 43 Palestinians; at that time around 25 UNRWA-run schools were serving as temporary shelters to Palestinians who had been displaced by the ongoing violence, and a further two of these had also come under attack. Soon afterwards UNRWA temporarily suspended its movements through Gaza (including food distribution activities) owing to Israeli air-strikes on humanitarian convoys that had caused several fatalities. On 8 January the UN Security Council adopted Resolution 1860, which demanded: an immediate and durable cease-fire in Gaza, culminating in the full withdrawal of Israeli forces; the unimpeded provision throughout Gaza of food, fuel and medical treatment; improved international arrangements to prevent arms- and ammunition-smuggling; intra-Palestinian reconciliation; and renewed efforts to achieve a comprehensive long-term peace between Israel and the Palestinians. The USA abstained from the vote. Hostilities continued, however, and on 15 January UNRWA's Gaza field headquarters was struck and set alight by Israeli shells that reportedly contained incendiary white phosphorus; the UN Secretary-General, Ban Ki-Moon, protested strongly against the attack. On the same day Said Siyam, the Minister of the Interior and Civil Affairs in the Hamas administration, was killed, along with two members of his family, in an Israeli air attack on the Jabalia camp. On 17 January 2009 the Israeli Government declared a unilateral cease-fire in its conflict with Hamas, with Prime Minister Olmert asserting that the objectives of Operation Cast Lead had been achieved. Hours after the cease-fire entered into effect, on 18 January, Hamas also announced a week-long cessation of hostilities against Israeli targets, in order to permit Israel to withdraw its armed forces from the Gaza Strip; the Israeli

withdrawal was completed on 21 January. UNRWA reported that by the time of the cease-fire 1,340 Palestinians had been killed (including 460 children and 106 women), and some 5,320 wounded (including 1,855 children and 795 women), during the 22-day Israeli offensive. In addition, thousands of Palestinian homes, as well as commercial and industrial buildings, had been destroyed by Israeli forces. Some 13 Israelis (including 10 soldiers) were reported to have died, and at least 680 to have been injured. A report published by B'Tselem on 9 September claimed that 1,387 Palestinians had been killed during Operation Cast Lead, of whom 773 were civilians (including 320 children and 109 women), 330 were combatants and 248 were Hamas police officers who died in an Israeli bombing raid at the start of the offensive; the status of the remaining 36 was unknown. These figures differed markedly from those of the Israeli Defence Forces (IDF), which reportedly assessed that 1,166 Palestinians had been killed during the campaign, of whom 295 were civilians and 709 were Hamas fighters; the IDF claimed that 162 of the fatalities had an unclear status.

In early 2009 international diplomatic efforts were conducted in the region with the aim of securing a more formal, permanent truce between Israel and Hamas, thereby ensuring that international arrangements would be put in place to prevent the smuggling of weapons into Gaza, and to allow for the unimpeded provision of humanitarian aid within Gaza and the subsequent reconstruction of the territory's infrastructure. An international summit was held in Sharm el-Sheikh in January, hosted by Mubarak and attended by Abbas). Delegates—mainly from the EU and Arab League—agreed to intensify efforts to provide much-needed humanitarian aid to Gaza's population, to support Egypt in its ongoing mediation between Hamas and Israel, and to maintain a dialogue with the Israeli Government. In February the Israeli Government stated that border crossings into Gaza would not be reopened, and an official long-term cease-fire would not be concluded, until Gilad Shalit was released by Hamas.

A new Israeli Government led by Binyamin Netanyahu

The inauguration of Barack Obama as US President on 20 January 2009 resulted in renewed US engagement in efforts to resolve the Israeli–Palestinian situation. In March the new US Secretary of State, Hillary Clinton, declared her support for the creation of a Palestinian state in the West Bank and Gaza. However, at the end of the month a new Israeli Government took office under the premiership of Binyamin Netanyahu, who, shortly after his appointment, stated that he would not endorse a two-state solution to the Israeli–Palestinian conflict. Moreover, the new Israeli Minister of Foreign Affairs, Avigdor Lieberman, declared that decisions reached at the November 2007 Annapolis meeting had 'no validity'. In April 2009 President Obama restated the US Administration's strong support for the commitments made at Annapolis. In May, during a meeting with Netanyahu in Washington, DC, Obama declared his commitment to a two-state solution, and identified the expansion of Israeli settlements as the chief obstacle to the resumption of peace negotiations.

In June 2009 Prime Minister Netanyahu indicated, for the first time during his premiership, his acceptance of the idea of a sovereign Palestinian state. However, he insisted that the formation of such a state would be conditional on the complete demilitarization of the Palestinian territories and Arab recognition of Israel as a Jewish state, with an undivided Jerusalem as its capital. Netanyahu also rejected the 'right of return' of Palestinian refugees. The proposal was rejected by the Palestinian leadership, on the grounds that it placed unacceptable limitations on the sovereignty of a future Palestinian state. An invitation to resume direct negotiations, issued by President Abbas in July, was turned down, with the Palestinians refusing to resume peace talks, frozen since the launch of the Israeli offensive in the Gaza Strip in December 2008, until a complete cessation of Israeli settlement activity had been implemented.

Between June and September 2009 George Mitchell, the US Special Envoy to the Middle East, and other senior-level US diplomats were engaged in intensive efforts aimed at reviving the peace process. However, the prospects for a revival of peace talks were undermined in September when the Israeli Ministry of Defence granted approval for the construction of 455 new housing units in settlements in the West Bank. A temporary moratorium on new housing units in the West Bank, proposed by Netanyahu, was deemed inadequate by the Palestinian negotiators, who continued to demand a complete cessation of all settlement construction in the West Bank and East Jerusalem. No significant breakthrough was achieved when President

Obama hosted a meeting between Netanyahu and Abbas at the UN General Assembly in New York in September. Abbas met with US Secretary of State Hillary Clinton in Abu Dhabi, United Arab Emirates (UAE), at the end of October, where he again rejected a resumption of talks based on a partial suspension of settlement activity.

Meanwhile, the UN Fact Finding Mission on the Gaza Conflict—appointed in April 2009 to investigate violations of human rights and humanitarian law committed during Operation Cast Lead, and headed by South African judge Richard Goldstone—issued its final report in September. The report concluded that both the Israeli armed forces and Hamas militants had committed war crimes during the conflict, and outlined evidence of possible crimes against humanity committed by both sides. The most serious allegations were levelled against Israel's armed forces, who were accused of: launching a disproportionate operation, which aimed to 'punish, humiliate and terrorize' the civilian population of Gaza; targeting civilian and commercial infrastructure; and using inappropriate armaments, including white phosphorous. On the Palestinian side, the report highlighted: indiscriminate rocket attacks against Israel; the possible use of 'human shields' by militants in Gaza; and arbitrary arrests and extra-judicial executions carried out by the authorities in both Gaza and the West Bank. Hamas denied the report's claims regarding its own conduct, but supported its referral to the UN Security Council. At the beginning of October, shortly before a scheduled vote at UN Human Rights Council concerning referral of the report to the Security Council, PA representatives unexpectedly requested that the vote be deferred for six months. The request provoked protests against Abbas in the Gaza Strip and the West Bank, and drew strong criticism from the leaders of several Arab states; a planned visit by Abbas to Damascus was cancelled by the Syrian authorities. Abbas reversed his earlier decision, announcing that the PA would resubmit the report to the Human Rights Council. The council duly endorsed the Goldstone report, and in November the UN General Assembly adopted a resolution demanding that Israel conduct an investigation into allegations that its forces had committed war crimes. In January 2010 the de facto Hamas administration in Gaza submitted to the Human Rights Council a report of an internal investigation into the findings of the UN Fact Finding Mission. According to the internal report, Hamas militants had been instructed to attack military targets only, and any civilian casualties resulting from Hamas operations were accidental. The report apparently contained an unprecedented apology for Israeli civilian casualties caused by Hamas rockets. However, the apology was subsequently retracted and denounced by Hamas officials.

Following pressure from the US Administration, in late November 2009 Netanyahu formally announced the imposition of a 10-month moratorium on the construction of new housing units in settlements in the West Bank, excluding some 3,000 units that were already under construction or for which permission had already been granted. Crucially, the moratorium did not apply to settlements within East Jerusalem, which Netanyahu described as part of Israel's 'sovereign capital'. In February 2010 it was confirmed by the Israeli Ministry of Defence that construction work had continued in some 29 settlements in the West Bank, despite the moratorium on settlement-building activity. In March the start of the so-called 'proximity talks' was delayed after the Israeli authorities approved plans for a further 1,600 new homes to be built in the settlement of Ramat Shlomo, in East Jerusalem.

Following the assassination of Mahmoud al-Mabhouh, a senior member of Hamas, in Dubai, UAE, on 19 January 2010, Hamas accused the Israeli external intelligence service, Mossad, of involvement in the killing. The Israeli Government insisted that there was no evidence to support such a claim. In February the authorities in Dubai issued details of 11 individuals suspected of involvement in the assassination, all of whom had travelled to the emirate using false or stolen British, Australian, Irish, French and German passports, and announced that they were '99% certain' of Mossad's involvement in the operation. Meanwhile, reports from Gaza emphasized the alleged involvement of two former members of Fatah's security service, who had been arrested in Jordan in connection with the investigation into al-Mabhouh's death. In June the Polish authorities were reported to have arrested, at Germany's request, a suspected Mossad agent on charges relating to the killing; however, the Israeli Government continued to maintain that there was no proof that its intelligence service had been involved in the killing.

Meanwhile, Hamas announced in February 2010 that it had suspended its role in talks over the release of Corporal Gilad Shalit, in part owing to the allegations of Israel's involvement in the killing of al-Mabhouh. In May Israel denied that the release of Muhammad Abu Tir—a senior Hamas member of the PLC who had been among scores of Palestinian officials to be arrested after Shalit's abduction—was connected to a prisoner exchange deal involving Shalit's release. (Abu Tir was the 10th Hamas parliamentarian to be freed by the Israeli authorities in recent months, although he was rearrested in July and threatened with deportation, together with three other Hamas-backed politicians.)

A short-lived resumption of peace negotiations and partial easing of the Gaza blockade

It was reported in January 2010 that a US proposal to revive the peace process through indirect negotiations, to be mediated by George Mitchell and other US diplomats, was under consideration by Palestinian and Israeli officials. Abbas resolved to consult with other Arab leaders before accepting the proposal. In March the Arab League granted approval to the plan, although with the provision of a four-month time limit; the PLO subsequently voted in favour of indirect talks. In May, reportedly after Netanyahu had assured President Obama that Israel would temporarily delay the expansion of Ramat Shlomo and would not approve the construction of any large new settlements in Jerusalem while the talks were under way, the indirect negotiations began when George Mitchell visited Ramallah for talks with Abbas; Mitchell returned to the region later that month to continue the dialogue. However, both the Israeli and Palestinian electorates were highly sceptical about the prospects for a successful outcome, while Hamas declared its opposition to the decision of the PA in the West Bank to enter into indirect negotiations with Israel.

Plans announced by the Israeli Government in February 2010 to incorporate into a Jewish heritage project two holy sites in the West Bank, Rachel's Tomb in Bethlehem and the Tomb of the Patriarchs in Hebron (both of which are venerated by Jews, Muslims and Christians), provoked violent protests by Palestinians in Hebron. The reopening of the Hurva synagogue in East Jerusalem in mid-March was also deemed a provocative measure by many Palestinians, who believed that it reflected a programme to promote the Jewish character of the Old City. Hamas called for a 'day of rage' in response. Widespread rioting occurred in the city on 16 March. Israeli riot police were deployed in Jerusalem at the end of March when Palestinian protesters attacked visitors to the al-Aqsa mosque, in the belief that they were Jewish extremists intending to pray at the site. In June Israeli municipal authorities in East Jerusalem endorsed a plan to demolish 22 Palestinian homes in the Silwan district of the city as part of a significant redevelopment involving the construction of an archaeological park. The UN Secretary-General, US Department of State officials and even senior Israeli cabinet ministers such as the Deputy Prime Minister and Minister of Defence, Ehud Barak, criticized the decision as being detrimental to attempts to further the Palestinian-Israeli peace negotiations.

On 31 May 2010 nine pro-Palestinian Turkish activists were killed, and many more injured, during a raid by Israeli naval forces on a ship that was part of a flotilla attempting to breach the Israeli blockade of Gaza in order to deliver humanitarian aid and materials to the population there. Although the Israeli military, seven of whose naval commandos were also wounded, insisted that its forces had acted in self-defence, their actions were widely condemned by foreign governments and international organizations. On 1 June Egypt temporarily opened the Rafah crossing on its border with Gaza to permit the free movement of both people and humanitarian supplies. On 5 June the Israeli Government rejected a recommendation by the UN Secretary-General that a multinational inquiry be launched into what exactly occurred on the Turkish ship. Instead, the Israeli leadership declared on 8 June that two internal committees—one military and one government—would be formed to investigate the incident; the latter would include two foreign observers. Activists announced that a second flotilla would, in June–July 2011, attempt to breach the blockade of Gaza to deliver aid and other materials. However, the attempt was aborted by the majority of participants amid claims of Israeli sabotage of a number of the vessels involved. Only one vessel managed to approach Gaza, and on 19 July this was boarded, without violent incident, by Israeli naval commandos and escorted to the Israeli port of Ashdod. A further two vessels attempting to reach Gaza in November were intercepted, again without violence, by the Israeli navy.

Meanwhile, following a meeting with President Obama in Washington, DC, on 9 June 2010, President Abbas received an assurance from the US President that his Administration would provide a further US $400m. to the PA, and that it was seeking to persuade Israel to reconsider its blockade of the Gaza Strip. On 14 June the International Committee of the Red Cross described the Israeli blockade as 'a collective punishment' of the people of Gaza, which was 'in clear violation of Israel's obligations under international humanitarian law'. The Israeli Government did announce an easing of the blockade on 17 June, following discussions between Netanyahu and the former British Prime Minister, Tony Blair, in his capacity as the international Quartet group's special envoy to the Middle East. Henceforth, only weapons and other items that could be used by Hamas militants to target Israelis were to be banned from entry into Gaza, thus allowing into the territory humanitarian aid, food and so-called 'dual-use' materials intended to be used in internationally supervised civilian reconstruction projects; Israel also pledged to improve the efficiency of its procedures for checking both goods and people at the border crossings. Nevertheless, a report issued by 21 international charities and human rights organizations in November demanded that Israel bring an immediate end to the blockade, assessing that, five months after the partial easing, there was little evidence that it had improved the lives of the Gazan population since many vital supplies were still being prevented from reaching their intended destination.

Direct negotiations between Prime Minister Netanyahu and President Abbas commenced in Washington, DC, on 2 September 2010, chaired by Hillary Clinton and attended by George Mitchell. These negotiations—the first direct Israeli-Palestinian talks since December 2008—followed meetings held on the previous day between President Obama and both leaders, as well as with King Abdullah of Jordan and President Mubarak of Egypt. However, the talks were preceded by further violence in the West Bank, where four settlers were killed by militants belonging to Hamas, which did not recognize the legitimacy of the talks. During September Obama urged the Israeli premier to extend the 10-month moratorium on settlement-building in the West Bank, which came to an end on 26 September; however, Netanyahu was unwilling to implement a complete freeze on construction. A second round of direct negotiations took place in Sharm el-Sheikh on 14 September and in Jerusalem on the following day. However, while it appeared that some progress was being made in the talks (for example, the Israeli and Palestinian leaders reportedly agreed to hold further fortnightly meetings), following the expiry of Israel's temporary settlement ban—a prerequisite for the PA and the Arab League as far as continuing the discussions was concerned—the PA suspended its involvement in the peace process, stating that it would resume talks only when Israel had agreed to end settlement construction and its blockade of Gaza. In November Clinton announced that the US Administration was offering the PA another US $150m. to ameliorate its financial situation and to assist with the further development of Palestinian institutions and security forces. In December US diplomats acknowledged that their attempts to persuade the Israeli Government to impose a new partial suspension of settlement-building in the West Bank had failed, although they insisted that the Obama Administration remained committed to pursuing a comprehensive peace in the Middle East.

The prospect of a resumption of peace talks was further diminished by a series of violent incidents during 2011. In early March five members of a settler family, including three children, were killed in their home at the Itamar settlement in the West Bank; in the following month, following an extensive Israeli investigation, two Palestinian men were arrested on suspicion of carrying out the killings, which were condemned by Abbas as 'immoral and inhuman'. In mid-March one person was killed and up to 50 injured in a bomb explosion near the central bus station in Jerusalem; Palestinian militants were widely suspected of carrying out the attack, although no group officially acknowledged responsibility. Later that month militants in the Gaza Strip launched a series of rocket attacks against towns in southern Israel, prompting Israeli air-strikes against Hamas and Islamic Jihad targets, in which at least eight people were reported to have been killed. Following further Israeli air-strikes in Gaza that claimed the lives of at least three militants in early April, Hamas warned of 'consequences'. The conclusion of a so-called 'unity' agreement between Hamas and Fatah in early May

(see Domestic Political Affairs) was strongly condemned by the Israeli Government, which announced that it was temporarily to suspend the transfer of tax revenues to the PA, citing concerns that the funds could be used to finance operations against Israeli interests by Hamas militants. In mid-May George Mitchell resigned as the US Special Envoy to the Middle East; he was replaced by his deputy, David Hale.

A report issued by B'Tselem in mid-June 2011 claimed that Israel had accelerated its policy of demolishing Palestinian homes in the Jordan valley, in the eastern part of the West Bank. As a result, the report claimed, more than 700 Palestinians had been rendered homeless there since the start of 2011. Israel continued to defend its demolitions policy, arguing that it targeted only homes that had been erected without building permits or that were within military firing zones. However, critics alleged that the demolitions formed part of a deliberate policy to displace Palestinians from the area. There was an upsurge in violence from mid-August after eight Israelis (including six civilians) were killed, and 25 others were injured, when a group of suspected Palestinian militants who had crossed into southern Israel over the Egyptian border carried out a series of attacks on buses and cars near Eilat; five of the assailants were reported to have been killed by Israeli soldiers. Israeli officials claimed to possess intelligence indicating that the militants had originated from the Gaza Strip, and more than a dozen Palestinians were reported to have been killed in retaliatory Israeli air-strikes in the territory by the end of the month. Palestinian militants responded by launching a number of rocket attacks into Israeli territory, as a result of which one Israeli was reported to have been killed in Beersheba and six others were injured in Ashdod.

Palestinian application for statehood at the UN

Following an announcement by the PA that it intended unilaterally to seek, through the UN, formal recognition of an independent Palestinian state, on the basis of its pre-1967 borders, and with East Jerusalem as its capital, the Israeli Government was reported to have threatened, in July 2011, to renounce all previous agreements with the Palestinians, including the Oslo accords. The Arab League offered its formal endorsement of the Palestinian bid, pledging to urge the UN Security Council and UN General Assembly to support 'full membership of a Palestinian state'. Admission to UN membership would require a two-thirds' majority in the General Assembly, following a recommendation from the Security Council. Despite intense US diplomatic activity aimed at persuading Abbas to abandon the unilateral pursuit of statehood, in mid-September Abbas reaffirmed his resolve to proceed with the application, noting that UN recognition of a Palestinian state would not preclude the possibility of a resumption of direct Israeli-Palestinian negotiations.

The PA formally submitted its application for full membership of the UN as an independent state to UN Secretary-General Ban Ki-Moon on 23 September 2011, although the Obama Administration made clear its intention to veto the application should it proceed to a Security Council vote. The Security Council announced in November that it was unable unanimously to recommend the Palestinian application for full membership, since only eight of the 15 Security Council members were prepared to support the application—one short of the majority required to force the USA to use its veto to prevent the application being approved. Meanwhile, following UNESCO's vote, at the end of October, to admit 'Palestine', the Israeli and US Governments both announced that they were to freeze their funding for the agency. Furthermore, Israel announced that it was to accelerate the construction of 2,000 new homes in settlements in East Jerusalem and the West Bank. In mid-November King Abdullah visited the West Bank (his first visit to the territory since April 2000) for talks with Abbas.

In October 2011, after more than five years spent in Palestinian detention, Gilad Shalit was finally released by Hamas and allowed to return to Israel, via Cairo. Shalit (now a sergeant-major, following a promotion on the eve of his release) was freed as part of a prisoner exchange agreement concluded, with Egyptian mediation, between Hamas and Israel, which provided for the release by the latter of 477 predominantly Palestinian prisoners immediately following the release of Shalit, and of a further 550 prisoners (including 300 members of Fatah) in December. Of the 1,027 prisoners in total, around 280 were reported to have been serving life sentences for planning or perpetrating terrorist attacks against Israeli targets. Abbas welcomed the exchange, but stressed that the Palestinian authorities would continue to press for the release of all remaining Palestinian prisoners detained within Israel.

In early January 2012 the first meetings between Palestinian and Israeli peace negotiators in more than a year were held in Amman; however, the exploratory talks were reported to have ended without any significant progress. Nevertheless, at a press conference held shortly afterwards, Ban Ki-Moon commended both sides for their participation in the talks, while urging them to cease all provocative acts and to pursue confidence-building measures. The PA continued to insist that it would not resume formal peace talks until Israel had suspended all settlement-building activity, while the Israeli Government maintained that it would not participate in such talks until the PA had removed all preconditions to the resumption of formal negotiations.

Tensions were exacerbated by the re-arrest, in mid-January 2012, of Aziz Duweik, the Speaker of the PLC; Duweik was apprehended by Israeli soldiers at a checkpoint near Ramallah, on suspicion of 'involvement in terrorist attacks'. Hamas officials insisted that Abbas should, in protest, suspend Palestinian involvement in the exploratory peace talks. An Israeli judge subsequently ordered that Duweik be placed under 'administrative detention', allowing custody for up to six months without charge or trial.

A Palestinian man was shot dead during a violent confrontation with Israeli soldiers at a checkpoint near Ramallah in February 2012, and in early March a Palestinian youth was fatally shot by Israeli soldiers near Hebron. The Secretary-General of the Hamas-aligned Popular Resistance Committees was among several militants killed in what were stated to be preventive Israeli air-strikes on Gaza in early March. In the ensuing exchange of retaliatory rocket attacks on Israel and further strikes on Gaza, some 25 Palestinians were killed; one Israeli was reported to have been seriously injured. A cease-fire was agreed between Israel and Hamas, with Egyptian mediation, in mid-March.

In late March 2012 the Israeli Government announced the suspension of co-operation with the UN Human Rights Council, after the body voted in favour of dispatching a mission to investigate the impact of Israeli settlements on Palestinians' civil, political, economic, social and cultural rights.

At the beginning of April 2012 a female Palestinian detainee from Jenin was released from Israeli custody and exiled to Gaza, under an arrangement whereby she ended a hunger strike begun following her detention without trial (i.e. under administrative detention) in mid-February. The detainee, a supporter of Islamic Jihad, had previously been among prisoners released under the terms of the October 2011 agreement, but had been rearrested for alleged involvement in planned attacks by Islamic Jihad. Her forced exile was condemned by the PA, as well as by Israeli human rights activists, while the International Committee of the Red Cross, which facilitated a meeting of the released woman with her family at the Erez crossing-point, urged Israel to comply with international humanitarian law, which prohibits such forcible transfer. The protest against administrative detention (under which some 300 Palestinians were held in custody) escalated during April 2012, with a mass hunger strike extending by the end of the month to some 1,500 Palestinians in Israeli detention. In early May the Israeli Supreme Court rejected an appeal against the terms of their imprisonment by two Palestinians, held in administrative detention on security grounds, who had maintained a hunger strike for more than 70 days. In mid-May, following a direct request by President Abbas and mediation assistance by Egypt and Jordan, an agreement was reached to end the mass protest. Among its terms, Israel undertook not to renew detentions without charge in the absence of further evidence, while the prisoners would be required to sign a commitment to refrain while in custody from activities liable to contravene security. At the end of May, also under terms of the agreement ending the hunger strike, Israel transferred to the PA the remains of 91 Palestinians killed in suicide bombings and other attacks on Israel over a period of more than 35 years.

Direct confrontation was renewed in the second half of June 2012, as a series of Israeli air-strikes on targets in Gaza provoked retaliatory rocket attacks for which Hamas's military wing—which had effectively refrained from such operations over a prolonged period—claimed responsibility. At least seven Palestinians were killed in the engagements; although the Israeli strikes were targeting militants preparing to launch rocket attacks, a six-year-old boy was among the dead. In late June Hamas stated that a senior member of the organization, Kamal Ghanaja, who had reportedly been a close associate of Mahmoud al-Mabhouh (killed in Dubai in 2010), had been assassinated in Damascus. In early August it was reported that an air-strike on the Gaza Strip had targeted a militant held responsible for an exchange in June on Israel's border with Egypt, in which an Israeli civilian was killed in an attack from Sinai.

Operation 'Pillar of Defence'

There was a major escalation in the situation from mid-November 2012, when, in response to protracted rocket fire from the Gaza Strip into southern Israel, Israeli forces began an intensive series of strikes from the air and sea against Hamas, Islamic Jihad and other militant groups, and their missile capabilities and weapons storage facilities. Among the targets of 'Operation Pillar of Defence' was the head of Hamas's military wing, Ahmad Said Khalil al-Jabari, who, together with another Hamas official, was killed in an air-strike on their vehicle in Gaza City on 14 November. As the confrontation deepened, Egypt led efforts to bring about a cease-fire. Hillary Clinton travelled to Israel for talks with Netanyahu and other government officials, and subsequently to Ramallah for discussions with Abbas, before proceeding to Cairo to meet with President Muhammad Mursi. It was reported that Israel had come under intense international pressure not to begin a ground offensive in Gaza. The diplomatic initiative was also joined by the UN Secretary-General, who held talks with regional leaders. After eight days of offensives and counter-strikes (during which Israeli missiles caused considerable damage to the complex of the Hamas-led administration in Gaza City, including the offices of its head, Ismail Haniya, and rockets fired from Gaza reached as far as outer Tel-Aviv), a cease-fire took effect on 21 November. Under its terms, Israel was to cease hostilities and targeted killings, enter discussions on the reopening of border crossings with Gaza, and ease restrictions on the movement of goods and people, while the Palestinian militant organizations were required to halt rocket attacks and border assaults. At the conclusion of hostilities, according to initial reporting by the UN Office for the Co-ordination of Humanitarian Affairs, there had been 158 deaths in Gaza, including 103 civilian deaths; at least 30 children were killed. Six Israelis were killed, four of them civilians. In April 2013 an interim report by the Israeli Military Advocate General into allegations of misconduct on the part of the Israeli military during Operation Pillar of Defence found that considerable emphasis had been put on minimizing 'collateral damage to uninvolved civilians and civilian property'; and, although 'certain professional flaws' were detected in a limited number of incidents, these did not constitute a criminal offence. The deaths of 10 members of one family and two of their neighbours in an attack on a house in Gaza were notably found to be 'regrettable', but were the result of an attack aimed at an alleged senior terrorist operative (who had escaped unharmed) and other militants. The investigation also found, *inter alia*, that damage caused to a hospital and other medical facilities in Gaza had been the unintentional result of attacks against terrorist targets or weapons held in close proximity to such facilities.

UN General Assembly Resolution 67/19, and a new coalition government in Israel

On 29 November 2012 the UN General Assembly adopted a resolution (67/19) according (by 138 votes to nine, with 41 abstentions) Palestine the status of Non-Member Observer State. Netanyahu denounced the decision effectively to upgrade the Palestinian territories' status as meaningless, and reiterated that there could be no establishment of a Palestinian state in the absence of a settlement guaranteeing Israel's security. The USA voted against the resolution. In early December the Israeli Ministry of Finance announced its intention to appropriate some NIS 460m. in tax and customs revenues due to the PA, in partial payment for debts owed for power supply. Also in early December Israel confirmed that it would proceed with its project to construct 3,000 settlement homes on land effectively separating East Jerusalem from the West Bank; plans were also advanced later in the month with regard to 1,500 housing units announced in 2010; and planning approval was given for more than 2,600 homes on land between southern Jerusalem and Bethlehem.

The outcome of the January 2013 Knesset election in Israel (q.v), in which Binyamin Netanyahu's Likud, in alliance with Israel Beytenu, lost support, suggested a shift in voter sentiment in areas including Israeli-Palestinian relations. This, in conjunction with the inauguration for a second term of US President Obama, allowed for initial, guarded optimism among some commentators regarding the prospect of a renewed impetus in the peace process. The outgoing US Secretary of State, Hillary Clinton, signalled that she considered the election result as likely to be conducive to such an initiative, and her successor, John Kerry, was generally considered to favour a new US-led effort to restart negotiations. The agreement of Tzipi Livni to join Israel's new coalition Government with a mandate to lead negotiations with the Palestinians was also recognized as a development likely to expedite renewed contacts. However, the inclusion in the coalition of the nationalist Jewish Home suggested that pressure to proceed with settlement-building would remain within the administration.

At the end of January 2013 a report of the UN Human Rights Council stated that the incumbent Israeli administration had contributed to the consolidation and expansion of settlements, and emphasized that the transfer of Israeli citizens to occupied territory was in violation of both international humanitarian and international criminal law. Israel, which had boycotted a mandatory review of the Council that month, responded that the report further indicated the Council's bias against it. Meanwhile, the PA indicated that, should the new Israeli Government proceed with plans to construct settlements east of Jerusalem, it might seek recourse to the International Criminal Court (which it had become eligible to join upon adoption as a Non-Member Observer State at the UN).

In March 2013, shortly after the inauguration of the new Israeli coalition Government, President Obama made his first visit to Palestinian territory—travelling to the West Bank from Israel. While in Israel, Obama (similarly also on his first official visit) notably spoke of the need for a viable, independent Palestinian state, and stated that continued settlement expansion on occupied land did not advance the cause of peace; however, he emphasized the strength of US-Israeli ties, not least in military and intelligence co-operation. Following talks with President Abbas in Ramallah, Obama reiterated his commitment to a two-state solution, and stated that settlement activity represented an obstacle to advancing the cause of peace. However, he appealed to the Palestinians to abandon their demand for a freeze in settlement-building as a precondition for the resumption of peace talks, urging both sides to 'push through' areas of disagreement. The US President offered no new proposals for reviving peace talks during his visit, but stated that Secretary of State Kerry—who accompanied him on his visit, and then subsequently held separate talks with both Abbas and Netanyahu—would take up the task of narrowing differences between the Palestinians and Israel with the aim of renewing negotiations. At the end of a further, three-day visit to Israel and the West Bank in early April, Kerry stated that the USA was preparing a programme of incentives to stimulate economic activity in the West Bank, with the aim of facilitating renewed political negotiations. (In late March, meanwhile, the US Administration had agreed to release almost US $500m. in budgetary assistance to the PA which had been blocked by Congress since late 2012; Israel had also agreed to resume the transfer of tax revenues to the PA.) However, prospects for a revival of the peace process were put into further doubt with the announcement of the resignation of the PA Prime Minister in mid-April (see Domestic Political Affairs). Furthermore, there was an escalation in tensions at the end of April, when the Israeli military conducted its first targeted killing in Gaza since the November 2012 conflict. The target of the attack was alleged to be a weapons expert within a militant group held responsible for recent rocket attacks, including an attack from Sinai by Gaza-based militants on the southern Israeli city of Eilat. Also in late April an Israeli settler in the West Bank was stabbed to death by a Palestinian (who was wounded and apprehended by Israeli security personnel), reportedly provoking retaliatory attacks by settler groups on Palestinian villages.

Visiting Washington, DC, at the end of April 2013, an Arab League delegation led by the Qatari Prime Minister apparently offered concessions on the terms of peace adopted at its summit meeting in Beirut in 2002. The acknowledgement that land swaps could form part of an eventual settlement between Israel and the Palestinians was welcomed by the PA, the US Administration and the Israeli Government, but was rejected by the Hamas-led administration in Gaza. Kerry was expected to make a further visit to the Middle East to meet Abbas and Netanyahu later in May 2013. Meanwhile, Abbas and Netanyahu made separate, near-simultaneous visits to the People's Republic of China in early May. Abbas, during his visit, met with the new Chinese President, Xi Jinping, and Premier, Li Keqiang, and

signed agreements regarding economic, technical and cultural co-operation.

The issue of conditions of detention of Palestinians again came under scrutiny in February 2013, as violent clashes broke out between Palestinian protesters and Israeli armed forces in West Bank towns; in one confrontation near Ramallah, more than 60 demonstrators were injured. The protesters were demanding the release of four Palestinians, in administrative detention, who were on hunger strike; one of the detainees had been refusing food at intervals for more than 200 days. Tensions escalated in late February, following the sudden death in custody of a Palestinian from the West Bank who had been arrested on suspicion of stone-throwing. The Israeli authorities stated that the detainee had suffered a heart attack, but Palestinians claimed that there was evidence that he had died as a result of torture. In protest, most Palestinian detainees observed a one-day hunger strike; and clashes persisted between demonstrators and Israeli forces in the West Bank. A Palestinian demonstrator who was shot in the head in one such confrontation later died in hospital in Tel-Aviv. There were further protests by Palestinians in Israeli custody in early April, following the death of a prisoner who had been suffering from cancer. President Abbas was understood to have intervened personally to influence the release of the inmate on compassionate grounds, but the request for parole had not been processed by the time of his death. Later in April the Israeli authorities stated that an agreement had been reached to end a hunger strike by a detainee who had been released in 2011, under the terms of the agreement whereby Gilad Shalit had been freed, but later rearrested; by the new arrangement, the detainee, who had begun a hunger strike in August 2012, was to be released by the end of 2013.

At December 2012, according to figures published by the Israeli Prison Service, there were 4,517 Palestinians in Israeli detention, of whom 1,031 were awaiting the conclusion of legal proceedings and 178 were in administrative detention; 170 were under 18 years of age. The UN Children's Fund (UNICEF), in a paper published in March 2013, stated that there appeared to be a pattern of ill treatment during the arrest, transfer and interrogation of Palestinian minors within the Israeli military detention system, and made recommendations to improve protection for children in conformity with international standards, such as the prohibition of blindfolding and solitary confinement. UNICEF none the less reported some recent improvements in the treatment of Palestinian children in the Israeli military system, including the raising the age of majority from 16 to 18 years.

Domestic Political Affairs

Legislative elections took place on 20 January 1996, with the participation of some 79% of the estimated 1m. eligible Palestinian voters, selecting 88 deputies to the 89-seat PLC. (One seat was reserved for the President of the Council's executive body—the Palestinian President.) At the concurrent election for a Palestinian Executive President, Yasser Arafat defeated his only rival, Samiha Khalil, winning 88.1% of the votes cast, and took office as President on 12 February. Deputies returned to the PLC automatically became members of the PNC, the existing 483 members of which were subsequently permitted to return from exile by the Israeli authorities. The PLC held its first session in Gaza City on 7 March, electing Ahmad Quray as its Speaker. At the 21st session of the PNC, held in Gaza City on 22–24 April, the PNC voted to amend the Palestinian National Charter (or PLO Covenant) by annulling those clauses that sought the destruction of the State of Israel and those that were inconsistent with the agreement of mutual recognition concluded by Israel and the PLO in September 1993. At the close of its session, the PNC elected a new PLO Executive Committee, and in May 1996 President Arafat appointed a Palestinian Cabinet. The appointments were approved by the PLC in July.

In April 1997 Arafat's audit office disclosed evidence of the misappropriation by PA ministers of some US $326m. of public funds. In August the findings of a parliamentary committee appointed by Arafat to investigate the affair led to the resignation of the Cabinet. New appointments were made in early 1998, but the Cabinet resigned again in June, apparently in order to obstruct a second vote of no confidence in Arafat's leadership, in protest partly at alleged corruption within the PA. A new Cabinet was appointed by Arafat in August, but soon attracted criticism from officials of the principal international organizations granting funds to the PA. In November donors pledged aid worth more than $3,000m., to be disbursed over the next five years. In October 1998 the PA was again accused of financial mismanagement, after customs revenues amounting to some $70m. allegedly failed to be deposited at the PA treasury.

US officials reportedly confirmed in March 1998 that the CIA was assisting the Palestinian security forces in the spheres of espionage, information-gathering and interrogation, in an attempt to reassure the Israeli Government of the PA's ability to take effective action against groups involved in attacks on Israeli targets. (Under the terms of the Wye Memorandum—see The Palestinian–Israeli Conflict—the CIA was to monitor the PA's compliance with the security provisions of the accord.) In October the PA detained 11 journalists who had attempted to obtain an interview with the spiritual leader of Hamas, Sheikh Ahmad Yassin (who was subsequently placed under house arrest). In subsequent weeks several radio and television stations, as well as press offices, were closed down by the PA, and numerous journalists were imprisoned. There was also a marked increase in self-censorship in the state-controlled and pro-administration media.

In January 1999 the PLC approved a motion urging an end to political detentions and the release of all those imprisoned on exclusively political charges; the motion further demanded the formation of a special committee to assess the case of every political prisoner in the Palestinian territories and to recommend prisoner releases. The committee was duly appointed in February, under the chairmanship of the Minister of Justice. However, despite the release of 37 political prisoners by the PA, in late January Hamas and Islamic Jihad activists began a hunger strike in Jericho and Nablus, in protest against their continued detention without trial. In February some 3,000 protesters marched to the headquarters of the PA, which they accused of 'subservience to Israel and the CIA'. In March a security agent and former member of Hamas's military wing was sentenced to death for the killing of a Palestinian intelligence officer in Rafah. The verdict provoked serious clashes between Palestinian police and protesters in the Gaza Strip, and Arafat was forced to curtail an official visit to Jordan to address the domestic security crisis. In November 20 leading Palestinian intellectuals (including members of the PLC) issued a joint statement in which they criticized alleged corruption, mismanagement and abuse of power within the PA, and accused Palestinian officials of ineffectiveness in the peace talks with Israel. An official crackdown on Arafat's critics was subsequently instigated, during which several of the document's signatories were detained or placed under house arrest (they were later released on bail). The establishment, announced in January 2000, of a Higher Council for Development under Arafat's chairmanship was welcomed by foreign donors as a major step towards ending corruption and mismanagement within the Palestinian administration.

In August 1999 a Palestinian national dialogue conference was held in Cairo, Egypt, between representatives of Fatah and the PFLP. Later in August Arafat and the Secretary-General of the DFLP, Nayef Hawatmeh, met, also in Cairo, for the first time since 1993. At the end of the month representatives of nine Palestinian political factions, meeting in Ramallah, agreed on an agenda for a comprehensive national dialogue; Hamas and Islamic Jihad, however, refused to participate. In September 1999 the PFLP's deputy leader, Abu Ali Moustafa, was permitted by the Israeli Government to return to the West Bank from exile in Jordan, in order to participate in reconciliation talks with Arafat. George Habash stepped down as leader of the PFLP in April 2000, and Abu Ali Moustafa was elected to lead the organization in July. (Following Moustafa's assassination in August 2001, Ahmad Saadat assumed the party leadership.)

In June 2002, following Arafat's release from Israeli house arrest in the previous month, the President implemented major government changes: membership of the Cabinet was reduced from 31 ministers to 21, with several ministries being either merged or abolished. Maj.-Gen. Abd al-Razzaq al-Yahya was appointed Minister of the Interior—a position previously held by Arafat. Dr Salam Fayyad was named as the new Minister of Finance. The new Cabinet was described as an interim administration, its main task to be the preparation and supervision of far-reaching reforms, including the organization of municipal elections towards the end of 2002 and of presidential and legislative elections by early 2003. The planned reforms would also include the streamlining of the Palestinian security services. Perhaps most importantly, draft legislation was prepared in order to create a new post of Prime Minister, to be responsible for the day-to-day administration of the PA. In September 2002 the entire Palestinian Cabinet resigned in order to prevent a vote of

no confidence being brought in the legislature; a new administration was announced in the following month. Meanwhile, the PA President set 20 January 2003 as the day on which legislative and presidential elections were to be held. However, in December 2002 Arafat announced a postponement of the polls, claiming that it would be untenable to hold elections while Israel continued to occupy PA-controlled population centres in the West Bank and Gaza.

In March 2003 the PLC endorsed a bill defining the role to be played by a future Palestinian Prime Minister, after having rejected amendments to the legislation proposed by Arafat according to which the President would retain authority over the appointment of cabinet ministers. In the proposed power-sharing arrangement, the President was reportedly to control security and foreign affairs and would also have the authority to appoint and dismiss a premier, while the Prime Minister would nominate ministers and retain responsibility for domestic affairs. Mahmud Abbas, the Secretary-General of the PLO Executive Committee, formally accepted the post of Prime Minister on 19 March; on 29 April the Palestinian legislature endorsed his appointment. A newly expanded Palestinian Cabinet was announced on that day, comprising 25 ministers under the premiership of Mahmud Abbas (who also became Minister of the Interior). Muhammad Dahlan was confirmed as the Minister of State for Security Affairs, while Dr Nabil Shaath was named as the Minister of External Affairs and Saeb Erakat as the Minister of Negotiation Affairs. The announcement of the new PA Cabinet prompted the publication of the Quartet-sponsored 'roadmap' peace plan.

In May 2003 Erakat, regarded as an Arafat ally, resigned as Minister of Negotiation Affairs apparently in protest against his omission from the Palestinian delegation, which included Abbas, Muhammad Dahlan and the Speaker of the PLC, Ahmad Quray, due to hold talks with Ariel Sharon and leading Israeli officials. Immediately following the summit with Sharon, Abbas engaged in a round of discussions with Hamas and Islamic Jihad, which in June resulted in the implementation of a cease-fire in attacks by those groups against Israeli targets, with the support of Fatah. However, in September Abbas resigned as Prime Minister, seemingly representing the culmination of his power struggle with Arafat over control of the Palestinian security apparatus. Arafat nominated Quray to replace him. Meanwhile, Erakat was reinstated as the Minister of Negotiation Affairs, and it appeared that Arafat had effectively regained control of the PA. In October the Palestinian President declared a state of emergency in the West Bank and Gaza, following Israel's continuing construction of the 'security fence' (see The Palestinian–Israeli Conflict) and the arrest of a key member of Islamic Jihad; he also announced the establishment of an eight-member Emergency Cabinet. In early November the PLC approved Ahmad Quray's first full Cabinet. Ministers who retained their portfolios from the previous administration under Mahmud Abbas included Shaath as Minister of Foreign Affairs and Fayyad as Minister of Finance. Rafiq al-Natsheh was elected Speaker of the PLC (but was replaced by Rawhi Fattouh in March 2004).

An audit of the PA's finances carried out by the IMF in 2003 estimated that during 1995–2000 nearly US $900m. had been diverted into accounts controlled by Yasser Arafat. Moreover, documents seized by Israeli forces during the reoccupation of Palestinian areas in 2001 reportedly revealed that some EU funds intended for the PA had in fact been used by the Al-Aqsa Martyrs Brigades. In February 2004 Israeli soldiers raided banks in Ramallah in an operation to seize funds reputedly belonging to Palestinian militant groups.

Arafat's authority was further threatened in July 2004 by mass disorder in the Gaza Strip, in protest against PA corruption and incompetence, as well as a threat by Prime Minister Quray to bring about the collapse of the administration if his powers were not increased. In mid-July Arafat took measures against the growing anarchy in Gaza, discharging two senior security commanders, declaring a state of emergency and sending loyal troops to protect official buildings in Gaza. He also replaced the national police chief and the commander of general security forces in Gaza (the latter with his cousin, Musa Arafat), and amalgamated eight rival security forces into three. However, Fatah members demanding reforms rejected those introduced by the President as 'superficial and unconvincing', and pressure on Arafat (especially from the Al-Aqsa Martyrs Brigades) apparently forced him to reverse his decision to appoint his cousin as head of security. In late July Quray reportedly announced his resignation (which was rejected by Arafat) after chaos erupted in Gaza following the kidnapping of the Palestinian police commander, a colonel in the PA security forces and four French aid workers. However, Quray later announced his intention to stay in office as caretaker Prime Minister, having, according to one of his ministers, urged Arafat to forgo some of his powers to prevent the PA from collapsing further. In August Nahid al-Rayyis resigned as Minister of Justice, citing the ongoing disorder in Gaza.

Developments following the death of Yasser Arafat

It was announced on 11 November 2004 that Yasser Arafat, who had been undergoing treatment at a military hospital in France, had died. In accordance with Palestinian law, the Speaker of the PLC, Rawhi Fattouh, was sworn in as acting President, pending an election due to take place in the territories within 60 days. Mahmud Abbas assumed the chairmanship of the PLO, and Quray was chosen to head the Palestinian National Security Council (PNSC) in addition to taking charge of the administration of the PA. Farouk Kaddoumi was appointed leader of Fatah. In late November Abbas was nominated as Fatah's only candidate in the forthcoming election, which in early December both Hamas and Islamic Jihad announced they would boycott. Palestinian election officials declared that a total of 10 candidates had qualified for registration, including a human rights activist, Mustafa Barghouthi, who was to stand as an independent. Having initially registered his candidacy, Marwan Barghouthi later withdrew from the campaign, following pressure on him to give Abbas the best chance of securing the presidency; it had been feared that, had Marwan Barghouthi won the ballot, Israel would have refused to negotiate with him owing to his imprisonment.

The first municipal elections to be held in the West Bank since 1976 began on 23 December 2004, at which Hamas, participating in an election in the Palestinian territories for the first time, won 16 councils and Fatah secured nine, with the two movements to share control of one municipality. At the local elections held in the Gaza Strip in late January 2005, Hamas secured control of seven of the 10 councils. The lack of support for Fatah was attributed to its association with corruption, while voters were encouraged by Hamas's provision of welfare and educational services and by its opposition to Israel.

The election to appoint a successor to Yasser Arafat was held in the West Bank, Gaza Strip and East Jerusalem on 9 January 2005. The Palestinian Central Elections Commission (CEC) asserted that the presence of Israeli forces in Jerusalem interfered with the voting process, forcing international observers to intervene. Nevertheless, these observers considered the overall conduct of the election to have been free and fair. Final results showed that, from the seven candidates, Abbas had received 62.5% of votes cast and Mustafa Barghouthi 19.5%. The other candidates had all secured less than 4% of the votes. Abbas was sworn in as Executive President of the PA on 15 January.

In February 2005 the PLC voted to approve a new Cabinet under Prime Minister Ahmad Quray. Dr Nabil Shaath, hitherto Minister of Foreign Affairs, was appointed Deputy Prime Minister and Minister of Information. Quray pledged the new administration's determination to heighten security and combat poverty. In March, after militants from the Fatah-affiliated Al-Aqsa Martyrs Brigades reportedly shot at the presidential compound in Ramallah, President Abbas removed the military chief in the West Bank and the Ramallah district commander, explaining that the security apparatus had failed and needed to be reorganized. In an effort to consolidate various (often rival) factions into a unified command, in the following month Abbas nominated four new heads of security forces in the West Bank and Gaza Strip, and ordered 10 senior officers to resign.

A reported 82% of eligible voters took part in a second round of municipal elections in the West Bank and Gaza Strip on 5 May 2005. According to official results, 45 of the 84 municipal districts contested were to be governed by councils with a majority of Fatah representatives (which took 56% of votes). Hamas, which had not participated in the presidential election, took 23 councils (33% of votes), and left-wing and independent lists secured 16 councils. Later in the month the CEC declared that elections to the PLC, scheduled for July, would be delayed while the PLC ratified a new elections law, intended to replace the system of simple majority by which the 1996 general election had been held, with a 'mixed' electoral system. The PLC ratified the new law in June 2005. In August Abbas issued a decree setting 25 January 2006 as the date for the legislative elections. A third round of municipal elections was held in 82 towns and villages in the West Bank on 29 September 2005. Fatah won a reported 54% of the votes, and Hamas took 26%. At local elections in some of the

largest cities in the West Bank conducted on 15 December, Fatah secured 35% of the 414 contested seats, while Hamas won 26%. However, although Fatah retained control of Ramallah, Hamas notably gained control of Nablus and Jenin.

Factional conflict following Hamas's victory in the 2006 legislative elections

At legislative elections held on 25 January 2006, Hamas, competing as the Change and Reform list in order to avoid a ban on its direct participation, secured 74 of the 132 seats, and Fatah only 45. A large part of Change and Reform's election campaign had focused on the movement's social welfare programme and its strong stance against official corruption. Other groups, including the PFLP (contesting the poll as Martyr Abu Ali Moustafa) and independents, also achieved representation. Quray announced the resignation of his administration on 26 January.

The new PLC was inaugurated on 18 February 2006. Dr Aziz Duweik was appointed to replace Rawhi Fattouh as Speaker, and President Abbas called on Hamas to establish a new administration. Hamas subsequently held discussions with Abbas and other factions, including Fatah, concerning the possibility of forming a coalition administration of national unity, and nominated Ismail Haniya, who had held senior positions within Hamas and survived an Israeli assassination attempt in 2003, as Prime Minister. Hamas began to assert its authority at a PLC session in early March 2006 when it reversed legislation that the Fatah-led parliament had approved immediately prior to its dissolution. Fatah deputies walked out of the session, asserting that Hamas had no right to reverse their decisions. The new laws had given President Abbas further powers, apparently in an attempt to increase his authority and curb that of parliament, in anticipation of Hamas's domination of the legislature. One of the rulings had provided for the establishment of a constitutional court and granted Abbas the right to elect its members.

After weeks of discussions between the two factions, Fatah rejected Hamas's offer of entering into an administration of national unity, and the Islamist organization decided to form a cabinet alone. One of the most important matters of dispute had been Hamas's rejection of bilateral Israeli-Palestinian agreements approved by the former legislature: Hamas considered that by recognizing these accords it would be accepting Israeli occupation of Palestinian territory. The PLC approved Hamas's proposed Cabinet on 28 March, and on the following day President Abbas inaugurated the new administration, which included Nasser al-Shaer as Deputy Prime Minister and Minister of Education and Higher Education.

In the weeks following the elections to the PLC, there were sporadic violent clashes between rival militias and security forces of Hamas and Fatah. The increased tensions in the Palestinian territories were aggravated by the decision of the USA and the EU to withdraw all direct aid to the PA until Hamas fulfilled the three conditions that the Quartet group had placed on it (see The Palestinian–Israeli Conflict). Nevertheless, in June 2006 Hamas and Fatah reportedly agreed to a joint political platform which contained implicit recognition of Israel's existence. The representatives approved a document drawn up in May by a group of Palestinian political prisoners in Israeli gaols, led by Marwan Barghouthi and Sheikh Abd al-Khaliq al-Natsheh of Hamas, which detailed 18 points for a return to negotiations with Israel. The so-called 'prisoners' document' urged the formation of an administration of national unity in which all political parties that accepted the terms of the document would be represented, as well as the establishment of a 'unified resistance front' against Israeli occupation. Shortly afterwards Hamas endorsed the prisoners' document and agreed in principle to share power with Fatah in an administration committed to a two-state settlement and negotiations with Israel on the basis of an independent Palestinian state on territories occupied in 1967. (The group had been under intense pressure from President Abbas to accept the proposals or face a referendum.) However, the agreement was rejected by Hamas's military wing and the organization's political leaders-in-exile. Moreover, it failed to achieve the immediate resumption of foreign aid to the PA, which was urgently required in order to allow the authorities to begin paying workers' salaries.

In September 2006 a general strike was organized by public sector workers in protest against unpaid wages. In early November Arab ministers responsible for foreign relations, meeting in Cairo, pledged to increase levels of financial assistance given to the PA; Iran also gave funds to the Hamas-led administration in the following month. In mid-November it was announced that

Fatah and Hamas had agreed to nominate Muhammad Shbeir, a former head of the Islamic University in Gaza, as Prime Minister in a coalition administration. However, despite lengthy discussions, it proved impossible for Shbeir to form a cabinet. On 8 February 2007 Fatah and Hamas—represented by President Abbas and Khalid Meshaal, respectively—signed an agreement to form a national unity administration; the accord followed two days of discussions in Mecca, Saudi Arabia, held at the invitation of King Abdullah. Although Hamas continued to reject an acceptance of Israel's right to exist, it was reported that the organization had agreed, for the first time, to 'respect and work to implement' the 'land-for-peace' proposal adopted at the Beirut summit in 2002.

Finally, on 17 March 2007 the PLC approved the composition of a new Cabinet, which replaced the former Hamas-dominated administration with a coalition of ministers from Hamas and Fatah, together with independents and representatives from the DFLP and the Palestinian People's Party. Hamas's Ismail Haniya retained the post of Prime Minister, while Azzam al-Ahmad, of Fatah, became Deputy Prime Minister. Three prominent ministries were allocated to independents: Hani Talab al-Qawasmeh was appointed Minister of the Interior, Dr Ziad Abu Amr Minister of Foreign Affairs and Dr Salam Fayyad was again named as Minister of Finance. At the end of March EU ministers responsible for foreign affairs, meeting in Germany, declared their support for the peace initiative revived in Saudi Arabia a few days previously, and announced that they would be willing to have contacts with non-Hamas members of the new Palestinian Cabinet. Israel declared that it would continue its boycott of the PA, however, until the new administration met the conditions demanded by the Quartet group. The resignation from the Cabinet of al-Qawasmeh in May appeared to demonstrate the divisions within the administration with regard to the difficult security issues facing the West Bank and Gaza; Prime Minister Haniya assumed the interior portfolio in an acting capacity.

Abbas announced in March 2007 that he had appointed Muhammad Dahlan as Secretary of the newly re-established PNSC, which in theory meant that he became general commander of the Palestinian security forces; Dahlan, however, was profoundly disliked by Hamas. Following several unsuccessful attempts to achieve a lasting cease-fire between the rival militias in the Palestinian territories, a new security plan to restore order in Gaza was announced by the Cabinet in May. Yet the factional fighting between gunmen from Hamas and Fatah continued, leading Abbas, speaking in June on the 40th anniversary of Israeli occupation, to warn of the threat of a Palestinian civil war. In mid-2007 scores of Palestinians were killed in the violence, some of which even occurred within hospital buildings. On 12 June gun battles between Hamas and Fatah fighters intensified across the Gaza Strip. As Hamas began to demonstrate its military superiority, it seized control of the headquarters of security forces in the north and south of the Strip, before taking over Gaza City itself. At the same time Fatah militias in the West Bank stormed Hamas-controlled institutions, seeking revenge for the Islamist movement's takeover of the Strip. On 14 June Abbas dissolved the national unity Cabinet under Haniya's premiership, declared a state of emergency and appointed Salam Fayyad as Prime Minister. As a respected economist and former employee of the World Bank and the IMF, Fayyad had wide support in Israel, the USA and the EU. Meanwhile, Haniya sought to consolidate authority at the head of the Hamas-led administration in the Gaza Strip by naming a new chief of security in the territory, Maj.-Gen. Said Fanouna.

An Emergency Cabinet, consisting principally of independents and technocrats, as well as one Fatah representative, was sworn in by President Abbas in Ramallah on 17 June 2007. Besides assuming the premiership, Fayyad also held charge of the finance portfolio and, briefly, that of foreign affairs. (Riyad al-Maliki assumed responsibility for the latter from September.) Fatah's Abd al-Razzaq al-Yahya became Minister of the Interior and of Civil Affairs. The hope was that this administration would restore law and order throughout the Palestinian territories, but it became apparent that divisions between the Fatah-controlled West Bank and Hamas-administered Gaza Strip were widening. Abbas refused to enter into a dialogue with Hamas until it withdrew its militias from former Fatah positions in Gaza. Moreover, the President granted himself the power to take decisions without the endorsement of the PLC, where Hamas held a majority of the seats. Abbas also declared that he was outlawing Hamas's paramilitary wing and other militias associated with the Islamist group. On 18 June the USA and the EU,

in a demonstration of support for President Abbas and his formation of an administration that excluded Hamas ministers, lifted their 15-month economic and political boycott of the PA. The Bush Administration additionally pledged assistance valued at some US $190m. to the Ramallah-based Cabinet.

Upon the expiry of the 30-day state of emergency, on 13 July 2007 President Abbas accepted the resignation of the Emergency Cabinet and appointed three new ministers to a reorganized Cabinet, which was to function as a caretaker administration until either the PLC convened or new legislative elections were called. (Hamas was unwilling for a vote to be held in the PLC as, with so many of its legislators in Israeli detention, it would lose its parliamentary majority.) Hamas leaders again refused to recognize the legitimacy of this interim administration. On 4 July, three days after Israel began transferring US $117m. of withheld Palestinian taxes to the Fayyad administration, thousands of Palestinian civil servants began receiving their first full salaries since March 2006. However, the West Bank administration continued to withhold the salaries of thousands of civil servants in the Gaza Strip. On 19 July 2007, at the first meeting of the international Quartet group since the appointment of former British Prime Minister Tony Blair as its special envoy to the Middle East, members of the Quartet affirmed their joint refusal to deal with Hamas. Muhammad Dahlan resigned as National Security Adviser on 26 July, citing ill health; however, some reports alleged that Dahlan had been asked to resign after his security forces in Gaza had allowed Hamas militants to oust Fatah from power in Gaza (when Dahlan was undergoing medical treatment abroad). Nevertheless, the resignation was essentially a formality since President Abbas had dissolved the PNSC following Hamas's takeover of Gaza. In August Fayyad issued a statement outlining the conditions required for inter-Palestinian dialogue to begin: Hamas should renounce any claims to be the legal authority governing Gaza (although Fayyad did not insist on an annulment of the 2006 election results) and disband all armed militias. This demand apparently included the Hamas Executive Force, which was responsible for maintaining law and order in Gaza. The third anniversary of the death of Yasser Arafat in November 2007 provoked a further outbreak of factional violence; eight Palestinians were reported to have died in clashes between rival Fatah and Hamas supporters in Gaza City.

International aid organizations stated in early March 2008 that the humanitarian crisis afflicting the Gazan population was the worst in the territory since 1967; in that month both the USA and the EU released to the PA the first instalments of funds pledged at the December 2007 donors' conference. In late March 2008 Hamas and Fatah signed a reconciliation agreement brokered by the Yemeni President, Ali Abdullah Saleh, and thus termed the San'a Declaration, which included a pledge to resume direct discussions between the feuding parties and affirmed the 'unity of the Palestinian people, territory and authority'. However, doubts were immediately expressed as to exactly what preconditions had been agreed, and productive dialogue was not pursued. In July a bomb exploded near the beach at Gaza City, killing five suspected Hamas members and a child. The Hamas-controlled security forces subsequently arrested up to 160 people associated with Fatah, which Hamas publicly blamed for the crime. Fatah, meanwhile, denied involvement and claimed that the atrocity had resulted from infighting within Hamas; an increase in numbers of Hamas members detained by Fatah-controlled PA security forces in the West Bank ensued. In August the two factions agreed to participate in a national committee aimed at calming the spate of politically motivated arrests and facilitating the release of detainees.

In September 2008 Abbas declared that he would remain President beyond the formal expiry, on 8 January 2009, of his term of office, pending the organization of national elections. In early October 2008 it was reported that the Fatah and Hamas leaderships, as well as representatives of other Palestinian factions, had agreed to meet to discuss national reconciliation under mediation by Egyptian government officials. Later in October the Egyptian Government, following a series of consultations with relevant parties, released a draft proposal for achieving Palestinian national unity, urging the immediate formation of a united government that would have responsibility for rebuilding the Palestinian security forces and for organizing legislative and presidential elections, for which a date was to be scheduled without delay. Under the Egyptian proposal, the currently Fatah- and Hamas-controlled security forces were to be managed at the national level and thereby removed from involvement in factional politics. In addition, any future peace deal reached by President Abbas with the Israeli Government was to be submitted to a national referendum or else presented to a restructured PLO that was to encompass Hamas and other factions opposed to the peace process. On 8 November, however, Hamas, alleging that politically motivated arrests of its members were continuing to be ordered by the PA in the West Bank, announced its withdrawal from a conference that had been planned for the following day to discuss the Egyptian proposal.

Hamas-Fatah reconciliation negotiations

The reconciliation process received new impetus in early 2009 in the aftermath of Operation Cast Lead. As reports emerged that intra-Palestinian tensions were causing delays in transfers of aid to Gaza, and that many international donors considered it preferable to pledge assistance to a united government, it appeared that continuing political divisions might undermine urgently required reconstruction activities in the Strip. In February representatives of Fatah, Hamas and 11 other Palestinian factions met in Cairo to begin a newly arranged series of Egyptian-mediated negotiations, with the principal aims of pursuing reconciliation, and reaching agreement on the staging of elections and the formation of a national unity coalition. Five negotiating committees were established to discuss: reconciliation; elections; the proposed interim government; security; and PLO-Hamas integration. The participants also decided to draft a new agreement to govern use of the Rafah crossing between Gaza and Egypt. In mid-March the parties to the negotiations jointly determined that concurrent presidential and legislative elections should be held by 25 January 2010. Progress on the formation of the planned national unity administration, however, remained deadlocked over several contentious issues, including conflicting perspectives on Israel's right to exist, on the use of state violence and on the legitimacy of existing Israeli-Palestinian agreements.

In an effort to facilitate the reconciliation negotiations, Prime Minister Fayyad submitted his resignation, and that of his Cabinet, on 7 March 2009. At the beginning of April Fayyad announced that, at the request of President Abbas, he would remain in office until the conclusion of the ongoing Egyptian-mediated negotiations. Further reconciliation talks at the end of April and in mid-May ended without agreement, and on 19 May Abbas appointed a new transitional government led by Prime Minister Fayyad, which excluded representatives of Hamas. The new, enlarged Cabinet consisted principally of Fatah members, independents and representatives of smaller Palestinian factions including the DFLP, the Palestinian Popular Struggle Front (PPSF) and the Palestinian Democratic Union—FIDA. Several ministers, including Minister of Foreign Affairs Riyad al-Maliki, retained positions that they had held in the previous administration; newly appointed cabinet members included Saeed Abu Ali, a Fatah official, who was appointed Minister of the Interior. President Abbas stated that he did not intend to abandon the reconciliation negotiations with Hamas, and promised that the transitional government would be disbanded upon the conclusion of any Fatah-Hamas reconciliation agreement. However, Hamas refused to recognize the legitimacy of the administration and warned that its appointment would deepen intra-Palestinian divisions and imperil the prospects for the reconciliation negotiations. At the end of June the PA's Minister of Jerusalem Affairs, Hatem Abd al-Qader, tendered his resignation, having reportedly been angered by the inadequate level of funding allocated to his department and the insufficient support offered by the PA to those Palestinian residents of East Jerusalem who were subject to house demolitions by Israeli forces. In mid-July it was reported that Fayyad would assume responsibility for the relevant ministry, and al-Qader subsequently became an adviser to the President on Jerusalem affairs.

Factional tensions increased at the end of May 2009, when an attempt by PA security forces to arrest a senior Hamas militant in the West Bank town of Qalqilya escalated into a gun battle; three police officers, two Hamas militants and a civilian were killed in the fighting. The PA security forces mounted a series of raids on suspected militants around Qalqilya in the following days; another police officer and two Hamas fighters were killed in an operation on 4 June. In reprisal, Hamas security forces reportedly arrested numerous Fatah supporters in the Gaza Strip. Nevertheless, representatives of the two factions reconvened in Cairo on 28 June for a new round of negotiations, subject to a deadline of 7 July for conclusion of an agreement. However, despite reports that progress had been made concerning electoral reform and a joint security force, on 1 July the negotiations

were suspended, with new talks scheduled for 25 July and the deadline for reaching an agreement extended until 28 July. Preliminary discussions in mid-July were hampered by discord over security operations and political prisoners, and the new round of negotiations was postponed until 25 August. Meanwhile, representatives of smaller Palestinian factions, including the PFLP, the DFLP, the PPSF and FIDA, continued to protest against their exclusion from the Egyptian-brokered reconciliation talks.

The long-awaited sixth Fatah convention opened in Bethlehem, in the West Bank, on 4 August 2009 (the last party conference having been held in Tunisia in 1989). The week-long convention, which was attended by more than 2,000 delegates, many of whom were making a rare return from exile in Syria, Lebanon and Jordan, marked the emergence of a new generation to the party leadership. Some 13 new members secured representation in the first elections in more than 20 years to the 23-member Fatah Central Committee. Newly elected representatives to the faction's ruling body included Marwan Barghouthi, who was serving five sentences of life imprisonment in Israel, and Muhammad Dahlan, Fatah's leading official in the Gaza Strip and the erstwhile PA security chief. Prominent members of the old guard who lost their seats on the Committee included former Prime Minister Ahmad Quray and Farouk Kaddoumi, hitherto Secretary-General of the Central Committee. Abbas, who was reappointed Chairman of the Central Committee, reaffirmed Fatah's commitment to the pursuit of a negotiated peace settlement with Israel, but also reiterated the organization's entitlement to engage in 'resistance' against Israel if necessary. More than 400 Gaza-based delegates were reportedly prevented from attending the convention after Hamas barred them from travelling to the West Bank; Hamas had demanded the release of hundreds of its prisoners in the West Bank in exchange for granting exit permits to Fatah members. On 26–27 August a special session of the PNC was convened in Ramallah to replace members of the 18-member PLO Executive Committee who had died since the last such meeting in 1996 (including former President Yasser Arafat). Among the six new members were Quray, Saeb Erakat, and parliamentary deputy and former cabinet minister Hanan Ashrawi, who became the first woman to join the Executive Committee. Also in August 2009 Prime Minister Fayyad launched a plan intended to achieve unilateral Palestinian statehood by 2011; Palestinian officials began actively to secure international backing for the proposal.

In early October 2009 representatives of Fatah reportedly signed a new Egyptian-brokered reconciliation agreement, which included the proposal to hold presidential and legislative elections on 28 June 2010; however, Hamas demanded further amendments, including an increase in the proposed 25% of parliamentary seats to be elected by district, rather than proportional, representation to at least 40%. Hamas subsequently withdrew from the negotiations, partly in protest against Abbas's decision to delay Palestinian endorsement of the report of the UN Fact Finding Mission on the Gaza conflict, headed by South African judge Richard Goldstone. Furthermore, on 16 October Fayyad accepted the resignation of the PA Minister of National Economy, Bassem Khoury, who disagreed with the administration's decision not to discuss the Goldstone report; he was succeeded on 25 October by Dr Hasan Abu-Libdeh, founder of the Palestinian Central Bureau of Statistics and a former Chairman of the Palestine Securities Exchange. Other members of the PA Cabinet, of Fatah and of the PLO were also strongly critical of the President's stance with regard to the UN report, and the PLO announced the holding of a domestic inquiry into the PA's decision-making processes. Meanwhile, following the suspension of the reconciliation talks, on 23 October Abbas declared that legislative and presidential elections would be held on 24 January 2010, upon the expiry of the PLC's term. Hamas leaders rejected the declaration and announced that they would prevent the holding of elections in the Gaza Strip; furthermore, the Islamist faction warned that such elections would serve to exacerbate the internal Palestinian divisions. Earlier in October 2009 Meshaal had described Abbas as 'an illegal president' whose term of office had ended on 9 January, exactly four years after his election victory. In early November Abbas announced that he would not stand for re-election in the forthcoming presidential election, citing his frustration at the failure of PA efforts to restart peace talks with Israel and, in particular, at the policy of the new US Administration under President Obama with regard to Israeli settlement expansion in the West

Bank. However, on 19 November, in response to recommendations from the CEC, the President announced the postponement of the planned elections. In mid-December the Central Council of the PLO approved a decision to extend indefinitely the terms of President Abbas and the PLC, pending a resolution of the Hamas–Fatah schism, and the holding of fresh elections.

Hamas-Fatah negotiations resumed in early 2010; however, progress was hampered by a dispute concerning the status of both the interim Cabinet in the West Bank and the de facto Hamas administration in Gaza, following the expiry of the PLC's scheduled term on 24 January. A further dispute arose in early February when the interim Cabinet in Ramallah scheduled municipal elections in the West Bank and Gaza for 17 July. Following Hamas's decision to boycott the forthcoming municipal elections, in late April 2010 it was announced that, while voting would be postponed in the Gaza Strip, it would proceed as scheduled in the West Bank. In mid-February, meanwhile, President Abbas suspended from office his chief of staff, Rafiq al-Husseini, following allegations of impropriety regarding the allocation of jobs to female applicants, details of which were broadcast on an Israeli television channel, along with further allegations of widespread financial corruption among PA officials. Although cleared of corruption charges by an internal PA inquiry, al-Husseini was dismissed from his post in mid-April for 'tarnishing the office of the President'. In early June the Cabinet announced that it had decided to postpone the municipal elections due to be held in the West Bank on 17 July for an indefinite period. Officials from the Ministry of Local Government explained that the elections were being delayed in the interests of maintaining unity between the West Bank and Gaza.

Seemingly inspired by the anti-government uprisings across the Middle East and North Africa, a series of rallies by protesters demanding an end to the ongoing tensions between the main political factions took place Ramallah, Gaza City and elsewhere in the West Bank and Gaza in mid-March 2011. In mid-February Prime Minister Fayyad had tendered the resignation of his administration to President Abbas, in order to facilitate a long-awaited cabinet reorganization; Fayyad was immediately requested by Abbas to lead the new administration. The CEC had earlier that month announced that municipal elections would be held in July, and PA officials indicated that presidential and legislative elections would finally take place in September, despite warnings by Hamas that it would prevent the polls from taking place in Gaza. Unexpectedly, it was reported in late April that the new Egyptian Government had initiated reconciliation talks between Hamas and Fatah. At a meeting in Cairo on 3 May, representatives of 13 Palestinian groups, including Hamas and Fatah, signed a so-called 'unity' agreement; this was intended to lead to the formation of a joint administration for both the West Bank and Gaza, principally comprising figures independent of both main factions, with elections to the PLC and the presidency to follow within 12 months. Abbas and Meshaal travelled to the Egyptian capital the following day for a formal ceremony to mark the agreement. However, implementation stalled in June, as Hamas and Fatah failed to agree on the appointment of a Prime Minister—with Hamas having rejected Abbas's proposal that Fayyad be reappointed to the post.

The Rafah crossing between Gaza and Egypt was reopened in late May 2011 by the Egyptian authorities, despite Israeli protests that this development would inevitably facilitate the smuggling of arms into Gaza. The opening of the crossing had been one of the incentives offered by Egypt in exchange for Palestinian reconciliation. Disputes over operational procedures prompted the temporary reclosure of the crossing in early June, but it was reopened again later that month, nominally allowing the visa-free, two-way transfer of all women and children and of men above the age of 40 years, as well as medical supplies. However, reports in late June indicated that, in practice, no more than 300–400 people per day were being permitted to leave Gaza via the crossing. The route remained closed to commercial traffic.

In November 2011 Abbas and Meshaal met in Cairo, for the first time since the signing of the unity agreement in May. The discussions were stated by both leaders to have been constructive, and both factions reaffirmed their commitment to the holding of legislative and presidential elections. Abbas and Meshaal met again in Qatar in February 2012, following which it was announced that the two had agreed to form a unity government with Abbas as Prime Minister. This prompted a rift over the decision within Hamas's senior leadership, and in mid-February Hamas officials outlined new conditions for the formation of the unity government, reportedly including demands that, in

exchange for agreeing to the appointment of Abbas as interim Prime Minister, Hamas representatives be allowed to retain the key ministerial portfolios of finance, interior and justice, and maintain control of security arrangements in the Gaza Strip, and that Fayyad be excluded from the transitional administration. Hamas was also reported to have demanded that the composition of the administration, including the designation of Abbas as interim premier, be subject to a vote of confidence by the PLC.

Following further talks in Cairo in late February 2012, Hamas and Fatah agreed to allow themselves more time to form the interim unity government; and in early March it was announced that presidential and legislative elections were to be postponed, from May, until such time as the outstanding differences between the two factions had been resolved. No further progress was achieved, and in mid-May a new PA Cabinet took office. Fayyad was reappointed as Prime Minister, although he ceded the finance portfolio to an independent, Nabil Qassis (a former President of Birzeit University). Other notable appointees to the Government included Ali Muhanna as Minister of Justice, and Adnan Husseini as Minister of Jerusalem Affairs. Hamas denounced the appointment of the new administration as over-riding both the February Doha accord and the Cairo agreement of November 2011; and stated the Government was not the choice of the Palestinian people, and did not have the support of the PLC.

In mid-July 2012 Abbas travelled to Cairo to meet with the new Egyptian President, Muhammad Mursi, who stated that Egypt would continue to assist in efforts to bring about a reconciliation between Fatah and Hamas, and that it would not show preferential treatment to either side. Mursi received Meshaal the following day. During talks in Cairo at the end of the month, Mursi and the head of the Hamas-led administration in Gaza, Ismail Haniya, discussed possible measures to alleviate the impact on the Gaza Strip of the continued economic blockade of the territory; these were understood to include provision to increase the rate of transit of Qatari-supplied fuel to Gaza, in order to ease chronic shortages of electricity. Prior to Haniya's visit, the Egyptian authorities were reported to have eased some restrictions on the allocation of visas to Palestinians of less than 40 years of age. However, no indication was given at this time that Egypt would move fully to open the frontier with the Gaza Strip.

The first stage of municipal council elections, originally scheduled for 2010, took place in the West Bank on 20 October 2012. Hamas boycotted the elections, having refused to recognize their legitimacy; and more than one-half of all councils stood uncontested because of a lack of candidates. Overall turn-out was some 55% of eligible voters. Official results assigned 440 of just over 1,000 seats contested, in around 90 municipalities, to Fatah candidates. However, independent lists of 'breakaway' former Fatah members won control in four key municipalities, including Ramallah and Jenin, while a list of independent and leftist candidates narrowly defeated Fatah in Bethlehem.

The vote of the UN General Assembly, on 29 November 2012, to accord Palestine the status of Non-Member Observer State was regarded within the Palestinian territories as a success for the diplomacy of President Abbas, and was welcomed by all factions in the West Bank and Gaza, including Hamas.

Khalid Meshaal made his first visit to the Gaza Strip in early December 2012, having been permitted to enter from Egypt via the Rafah crossing-point. (Meshaal had left Damascus earlier in the year, and had since been based in Egypt and Qatar.) During his visit to Gaza, Meshaal visited the home of Ahmed Said Khalil al-Jabari, the head of Hamas's military wing who had been killed by Israeli forces as the start of the November conflict, and met relatives of a family that had lost 10 of its members in an Israeli air-strike during the offensive. He also travelled to the home of Sheikh Ahmad Yassin, the organization's spiritual leader who had been assassinated in 2004. Addressing a mass rally in Gaza City at the start of celebrations of the 25th anniversary of Hamas's foundation, Meshaal spoke of reconciliation with Fatah (members of which attended the rally) and of the need for a united political platform with a single authority, president and legislature. He also reiterated his organization's commitment to armed struggle, and emphasized that there could be no recognition of Israel's right to exist. In the following week the PA authorized a rally by Hamas in Nablus, which was attended by some 5,000 supporters; this was the first time such a gathering had been permitted in the West Bank since 2007. A further, 3,000-strong group marched near an Israeli security point in Hebron. A reciprocal mass rally by Fatah took place in Gaza City in early January 2013, in the presence of senior Fatah officials; Fatah stated that about 500,000 supporters attended the rally, while Hamas put the number at 200,000. Meeting in Cairo in shortly afterwards, with mediation by President Mursi, Abbas and Meshaal agreed to renew efforts to implement the 2011 unity agreement. This was achieved despite an apparent reverse caused, shortly before talks began, by the sentencing of a member of the Fatah-affiliated Al-Aqsa Martyrs Brigades to 15 years' imprisonment by a Hamas-administered court in the Gaza Strip, following his conviction on charges of terrorism and illegal possession of weapons and explosives. In late March, at the annual summit meeting of Arab League heads of state, held in Doha, Qatar, the Qatari Amir, Sheikh Hamad bin Khalifa Al Thani, proposed the convening of a summit meeting, to be held in Egypt, to further the reconciliation process. The summit meeting also approved Sheikh Hamad's proposal for the establishment of an assistance fund for East Jerusalem, intended to support the preservation of the city's Arab and Islamic character. The US $1,000m. fund (one-quarter of which was pledged by Qatar) was to be administered by the Islamic Development Bank. At the beginning of April Meshaal was re-elected for a further four-year term as head of Hamas's political bureau by the organization's governing council.

In mid-April 2013, following several weeks of speculation regarding the tenability of his position, Salam Fayyad resigned as Prime Minister. In accepting his resignation, President Abbas asked Fayyad to remain in office pending the formation of a new government. Relations between Fayyad and Abbas had been strained for some time on issues of economic policy, and had deteriorated markedly in early March when Fayyad accepted the resignation of Nabil Qassis—a close associate of the President—as Minister of Finance. The US Secretary of State, John Kerry, was understood to have intervened personally in an effort to influence an accommodation between the PA President and Prime Minister that would have allowed Fayyad, who commanded considerable respect internationally, to remain in office.

CONSTITUTION AND GOVERNMENT

In accordance with the Declaration of Principles on Palestinian Self-Rule and the Cairo Agreement on the Gaza Strip and Jericho, the PLO assumed control of the Jericho area of the West Bank and of the Gaza Strip on 17 May 1994. In November and December 1995, under the terms of the Israeli-Palestinian Interim Agreement on the West Bank and the Gaza Strip concluded in September 1995, Israeli armed forces withdrew from the West Bank towns of Nablus, Ramallah, Jenin, Tulkarm, Qalqilya and Bethlehem. In late December the PLO assumed responsibility in some 17 areas of civil administration in the town of Hebron. The Interim Agreement divided the West Bank into three zones: Areas A, B and C. As of July 1998, the PA had sole jurisdiction and security control in Area A (2% of the West Bank), but Israel retained authority over movement into and out of the area. In Area B (26% of the West Bank) the PA had some limited authority while Israel remained in control of security. Area C, the remaining 72% of the West Bank, was under Israeli military occupation. In accordance with the Wye Memorandum of October 1998, Israel effected a further redeployment of its armed forces from approximately 500 sq km of West Bank territory in November. Of this, about 400 sq km became Area A territory and the remainder Area B territory. The Sharm el-Sheikh Memorandum of September 1999 was intended to facilitate completion of outstanding commitments under agreements previously signed, as well as to enable the resumption of 'final status' negotiations with Israel. By October 2000 approximately 17.2% of the West Bank (Area A) was under sole Palestinian jurisdiction and security control, although Israel retained authority over access to and from the zone; about 23.8% (Area B) was under Israeli military control, with the PA responsible for civil administration and public order; the remaining 59% (Area C) remained under Israeli military occupation. Israel implemented its unilateral Disengagement Plan, according to which it dismantled Israeli military installations and settlements in the Gaza Strip, and withdrew from four settlements in the West Bank, in August–September 2005. The total area of the territory over which the PA will eventually assume control, and the extent of its jurisdiction there, remain subject to 'final status' talks. (For further details, see Contemporary Political History.)

REGIONAL AND INTERNATIONAL CO-OPERATION

'Palestine' was granted non-member observer state status at the UN General Assembly on 29 November 2012. An application for full membership in the UN submitted by the Palestinian (National) Authority (PA) in September 2011 officially remained under review in early 2013, although it was considered unlikely to succeed owing to opposition from the USA (which had indicated its intention to veto the application in a vote of the UN Security Council). 'Palestine' was admitted to membership in UNESCO in October 2011. The PA is also represented at the League of Arab States (the Arab League, see p. 372) and the Organization of Islamic Cooperation (see p. 413).

ECONOMIC AFFAIRS

In 2005, according to estimates by the World Bank, the gross national income (GNI) of the West Bank and the Gaza Strip, measured at average 2003–05 prices, was US $4,452m., equivalent to $1,230 per head. During 2002–11, it was estimated, the population increased at an average annual rate of 2.5%, while in 2000–07 gross domestic product (GDP) per head decreased, in real terms, by an average of 5.1% per year. According to official figures, overall GDP increased, in real terms, at an average annual rate of 7.7% in 2002–11; real GDP grew by 9.3% in 2010 and by 12.2% in 2011.

Agriculture and fishing contributed 6.7% of the GDP of the West Bank and Gaza Strip in 2011, according to official figures. In 2008 agriculture (including hunting, forestry and fishing) engaged 15.6% of the classified employed Palestinian labour force. Citrus fruits are the principal export crop, and horticulture also makes a significant contribution to trade. Other important crops are tomatoes, cucumbers, olives and grapes. The livestock sector is also significant. Agricultural GDP increased at an average annual rate of 6.9% during 2002–11. The GDP of the sector declined by 1.8% in 2010, but recorded growth of 32.2% in 2011.

Industry (including mining, manufacturing, electricity and water supply, and construction) contributed 23.2% of GDP in the West Bank and Gaza Strip in 2011. In 2008 the industrial sector engaged 13.5% of the classified employed labour force of the West Bank and Gaza. During 2002–11 industrial GDP increased at an average rate of 10.8% annually. The sector's GDP increased by 13.4% in 2010, and by 36.7% in 2011.

Mining and quarrying contributed 0.8% of GDP in the West Bank and Gaza Strip in 2011, and engaged 0.3% of the classified employed labour force in 2008. Two significant gasfields were discovered off the Gazan coast in 1999; however, the exploration and supply of this offshore gas is dependent upon agreement being reached with Israel, which was expected to be the principal purchaser before its own discovery of significant offshore gas reserves in 2009. During 2002–11 mining GDP increased at an average annual rate of 10.9%. The sector's GDP increased by 7.5% in 2010, and by some 102.1% 2011.

Manufacturing contributed 12.3% of the GDP of the West Bank and Gaza Strip in 2011. In 2007 12.3% of the classified employed labour force were engaged in the sector. Palestinian manufacturing is characterized by small-scale enterprises, which typically engage in food-processing and the production of textiles and footwear. The frequent closure of the West Bank and Gaza by the Israeli authorities has prompted the development of free trade industrial zones on the Palestinian side of the boundaries separating Israel from the territories: Israeli and Palestinian enterprises can continue to take advantage of low-cost Palestinian labour at times of closure, and the zones also benefit from tax exemptions and export incentives. Manufacturing GDP increased at an average annual rate of 4.8% during 2002–11. The GDP of the sector increased by 0.7% in 2010, and by a further 14.8% in 2011.

Construction accounted for 8.3% of GDP in 2011, while it employed 12.7% of the classified employed labour force in 2008. During 2002–11 construction GDP contracted at an average annual rate of 28.4%. The sector's GDP increased by 38.4% in 2010, and by some 67.2% in 2011.

The energy sector (comprising electricity and water supply) accounted for an estimated 1.8% of GDP in the West Bank and Gaza Strip in 2011. Electricity, gas and water utilities together employed 0.5% of the employed labour force of the West Bank and Gaza in 2008. In the West Bank, the Jerusalem District Electric Company supplies electric power to Jerusalem, Bethlehem, Jericho, Ramallah and Al-Birah, while the National Electric Company operates in the northern West Bank. The Israel Electric Corporation (IEC) was the only source of electricity to municipalities in the Gaza Strip prior to the establishment of the Palestine Electric Company in 1999, and Palestinian utility firms remain principally reliant on the purchase of electricity from the IEC.

In 2011 the services sector contributed 70.2% of GDP in the West Bank and Gaza Strip. Services engaged 71.0% of the classified employed labour force in 2008. Although in recent years the Palestinian tourism industry was all but halted by the ongoing violence in the territories, tourism officials reported a record number of almost 5m. visitors in 2010, when the sector's contribution to GDP was close to 15%. The GDP of the services sector increased at an average rate of 5.8% per year during 2002–11. The sector's GDP grew by 6.9% in 2011.

In 2011 according to preliminary estimates, the West Bank and Gaza Strip recorded a visible trade deficit of US $4,625.9m. while there was a deficit of $2,192.6m. on the current account of the balance of payments. In the absence of seaport facilities and of an airport (Gaza International Airport was opened in 1998 but closed by the Israeli authorities in 2001), foreign trade (in terms of value) has been conducted almost exclusively with Israel since occupation. In 2009 Israel was the source of 73.6% of all imports and took 87.5% of all exports; Jordan was the second most significant trading partner, taking 5.6% of all exports in that year. Most Palestinian exports are of basic manufactures followed by agricultural or horticultural products. One notable feature of this trade is that Palestinian goods have often been exported to Israel, and subsequently re-exported as originating in Israel.

In 2012, according to Ministry of Finance, the PA recorded an overall budget deficit of US $834.0m. The annual rate of inflation in the West Bank and Gaza averaged 4.0% in 2002–11; consumer prices increased by an average of 2.9% in 2011. According to official figures, some 20.9% of the labour force in the Palestinian territories (17.3% in the West Bank; 28.7% in Gaza) were unemployed in 2011. Unemployment rose to 23.0% in 2012, according to preliminary official figures.

The prospects for an improvement in economic conditions in the Palestinian territories, which remain highly dependent on Israel, are inextricably linked to the full implementation of the Oslo accords—which provide for the development of seaport facilities, the opening of Gaza International Airport, and the creation of a safe passage linking the Gaza Strip with the West Bank—and the outcome of (currently stalled) 'final status' negotiations between the PA and Israel.

In a report published in March 2013, the IMF stated that urgent action was needed on the part of the PA, the Government of Israel and external donors in order to stabilize the fiscal position and stimulate growth in the Palestinian territories. The report found that economic activity had slowed from the final quarter of 2012, highlighting persistent restrictions on movement and access, and increasing political uncertainty. Large increases in arrears and domestic debt were notably affecting government operations, with a likely adverse impact on institution-building and social stability. Concern was expressed regarding the sustainability of public finances, which continued to be eroded by a combination of diminishing domestic bank and non-bank finance, delays in the transfer of tax and customs clearance revenues by Israel, and a shortfall in donor funding to offset the fiscal deficit. Delays in the payment of wages by the PA (jobs in the public sector account for more than one-fifth of total employment) had led to unrest in the West Bank in late 2012, and arrears persisted into 2013. IMF projections suggested a financing gap of US $400m. in the draft budget for 2013 (on a commitment basis), assuming donor budget support of $1,000m. and the payment of salary arrears from 2012. The conflict between Hamas and Israel in November 2012 and continued Israeli settlement-building, as well as wider regional uncertainty, had further undermined prospects for the economy. Preliminary official estimates for 2012 put real GDP growth at 5.9% in 2012, and growth in GDP per head at 2.7%. The IMF study projected real overall GDP growth of 5% for 2013 and growth averaging 4% in 2013–16, with a declining trend in both the West Bank and Gaza, noting that there was a large gap between the territories' potential and actual growth rates. Youth unemployment was particularly high—reported by the IMF to be 28% in the West Bank and 49% in Gaza in the final quarter of 2012. In March 2013 the US Administration released some $500m. in assistance to the PA, as efforts were stepped up to revive the stalled peace process, and Israel agreed to release previously blocked tax transfers. However, the likelihood of immediate measures by the PA to address its precarious public finances was put into doubt by the resignation of Prime Minister Salam Fayyad—who was known to command the respect of the international donor community—as Prime Minister in April 2013.

PUBLIC HOLIDAYS

2014: 13 January* (Mouloud/Yum al-Nabi, Birth of Muhammad), 26 May* (Leilat al-Meiraj, Ascension of Muhammad), 28 July* (Id al-Fitr, end of Ramadan), 4 October* (Id al-Adha, Feast of the Sacrifice), 15 November (Independence Day), 25 December (Christmas).

*These holidays are dependent on the Islamic lunar calendar and may vary by one or two days from the dates given.

Christian holidays are observed by the Christian Arab community.

Statistical Survey

Source (unless otherwise indicated): Palestinian Central Bureau of Statistics (PCBS), POB 1647, Ramallah; tel. (2) 2406340; fax (2) 2406343; e-mail diwan@pcbs.gov.ps; internet www.pcbs.gov.ps.

Note: Unless otherwise indicated, data include East Jerusalem, annexed by Israel in 1967.

Area and Population

AREA, POPULATION AND DENSITY

Area (sq km)	6,020*
Population (census of 9 December 1997)†	2,895,683
Population (census of December 2007)‡	
Males	1,877,028
Females	1,821,229
Total	3,698,257
Population (official projected estimates at mid-year)	
2011	4,168,860
2012	4,293,313
2013	4,420,549
Density (per sq km) at mid-2013	734.3

* 2,324 sq miles. The total comprises: West Bank 5,655 sq km (2,183 sq miles); Gaza Strip 365 sq km (141 sq miles).

† Figures include an estimate of 210,209 for East Jerusalem and an adjustment of 83,805 for estimated underenumeration. The total comprises 1,873,476 (males 951,693, females 921,783) in the West Bank (including East Jerusalem) and 1,022,207 (males 518,813, females 503,394) in the Gaza Strip. The data exclude Jewish settlers. According to official Israeli estimates, the population of Israelis residing in Jewish localities in the West Bank (excluding East Jerusalem) and Gaza Strip was 243,900 at 31 December 2004 (West Bank 235,700, Gaza Strip 8,200). The withdrawal of Israeli settlers residing in Jewish localities in the Gaza Strip was completed in September 2005.

‡ Includes population counted between 25 December 2007 and 8 January 2008, and estimates for underenumeration.

Note: Official projected estimates of a total world-wide Palestinian population of 10,094,565 at 31 December 2006 included 1,134,293 Palestinians resident in Israel and 2,799,440 resident in Jordan.

POPULATION BY AGE AND SEX
(official projected estimates at mid-2013)

	Males	Females	Total
0–14	904,352	866,778	1,771,130
15–64	1,286,172	1,234,801	2,520,973
65 and over	54,876	73,570	128,446
Total	2,245,400	2,175,149	4,420,549

GOVERNORATES
(census of December 2007)

	Area (sq km)	Population*	Density (per sq km)
West Bank			
Janin (Jenin)	583	251,807	431.9
Tubas	402	48,164	119.8
Tulkarm	246	156,792	637.4
Qalqilya	166	88,574	533.6
Salfeet	204	58,800	288.2
Nabulus (Nablus)	605	315,956	522.2
Ram Allah (Ramallah) and Al-Birah	855	262,941	307.5
Al-Quds (Jerusalem)† . . .	345	350,051	1,014.6
Ariha (Jericho) and Al-Aghwar	593	40,403	68.1
Beit Lahm (Bethlehem) . .	659	169,966	257.9
Al-Khalil (Hebron)	997	538,260	539.9
Gaza Strip			
North Gaza	61	270,246	4,430.3
Gaza	74	496,411	6,708.3
Deir al-Balah	58	205,535	3,543.7
Khan Yunus (Khan Yunis) .	108	270,979	2,509.1
Rafah	64	173,372	2,708.9
Total	6,020	3,698,257	614.3

* Figures exclude Jewish settlers.

† Figures refer only to the eastern sector of the city.

PRINCIPAL LOCALITIES
(estimated population at mid-2002, excluding Jewish settlers)

West Bank			
Al-Quds (Jerusalem)	242,081*	Al-Dhahiriya . .	25,348
Al-Khalil (Hebron) .	147,291	Al-Ram and Dahiyat	
Nabulus (Nablus) .	121,344	al-Bareed . . .	23,038
		Ram Allah	
Tulkarm . .	41,109	(Ramallah) . .	22,493
Qalqilya . . .	39,580	Halhul	19,345
Yattah (Yatta) . .	38,023	Dura	19,124
Al-Birah . . .	34,920	Ariha (Jericho) . .	18,239
Janin (Jenin) . .	32,300	Qabatiya . . .	17,788
Beit Lahm			
(Bethlehem) . .	26,847		
Gaza Strip			
Ghazzah (Gaza) .	361,651	Beit Lahya . . .	50,576
Khan Yunus (Khan		Deir al-Balah . .	43,593
Yunis)	110,677	Bani Suhaylah . .	28,761
Jabalyah (Jabalia) .	104,620	Beit Hanoun . .	27,341
Rafah	62,452	Tel al-Sultan Camp .	21,477
Al-Nuseirat . . .	56,449	Al-Maghazi Camp .	21,278

* The figure refers only to the eastern sector of the city.

Mid-2011 (incl. suburbs, UN estimate): Ramallah 74,792 (Source: UN, *World Urbanization Prospects: The 2011 Revision*).

BIRTHS AND DEATHS
(West Bank only, official estimates)*

	2009	2010	2011
Live births	68,579	69,809	64,519
Deaths	6,241	6,209	6,398

* Excluding Jewish settlers.

Gaza Strip (2007): Live births 50,075; Deaths 4,483.

Birth rate (official estimates per 1,000): 32.7 in 2009; 32.8 in 2010–11.

Death rate (official estimates per 1,000): 4.3 in 2009; 4.1 in 2010; 4.0 in 2011.

MARRIAGES
(number registered)

	2009	2010	2011
West Bank	19,839	20,185	20,165
Gaza Strip	18,477	17,043	16,199

Marriage rate (rates per 1,000, official estimates): West Bank: 8.1 in 2009; 8.0 in 2010; 7.8 in 2011. Gaza Strip: 12.4 in 2009; 11.1 in 2010; 10.1 in 2011.

ECONOMICALLY ACTIVE POPULATION
(persons aged 15 years and over)

	2006	2007	2008
Agriculture, hunting, forestry and fishing	107,024	103,721	86,447
Mining and quarrying . . .	2,237	1,542	1,462
Manufacturing	80,543	81,964	n.a.
Electricity and gas	2,500	2,230	2,780
Construction	73,905	72,722	70,688
Wholesale and retail trade . .	114,662	116,408	111,537
Hotels and restaurants . . .	13,492	13,407	19,599
Transport, storage and communications	38,242	37,404	32,046
Financial intermediation . . .	4,503	4,214	4,916
Real estate, renting and business activities	11,217	11,380	n.a.
Public administration and defence	98,922	99,584	101,723
Education	67,704	68,034	71,114
Health and social work . . .	24,400	24,525	27,265

—continued	2006	2007	2008
Services	19,426	20,594	19,189
Extra-territorial organizations and bodies	7,221	7,411	6,449
Households with employed persons	348	182	483
Sub-total	666,345	665,322	555,698
Unclassified	30	298	91,324
Total employed . . .	666,375	665,620	647,022
Unemployed	206,150	183,689	227,990
Total labour force	872,525	849,309	875,012
Males	721,153	691,695	715,822
Females	151,372	157,615	159,192

Source: ILO.

Health and Welfare

KEY INDICATORS

Total fertility rate (children per woman, 2010)	4.2
Under-5 mortality rate (per 1,000 live births, 2005–06) . .	28.2
Physicians (per 1,000 head, 2009, official estimate) . .	1.9
Hospital beds (per 1,000 head, 2011, official estimate) . .	1.3
Access to water (% of persons, 2008)	91
Access to sanitation (% of persons, 2008)	89
Total carbon dioxide emissions ('000 metric tons, 2008) . .	2,053.5
Carbon dioxide emissions per head (metric tons, 2008) . .	0.5
Human Development Index (2011): ranking	114
Human Development Index (2011): value	0.641

For other sources and definitions, see explanatory note on p. vi.

Agriculture

PRINCIPAL CROPS
('000 metric tons, FAO estimates)

	2009	2010	2011
Wheat	30.0	17.0	17.8
Barley	9.8	6.0	5.8
Potatoes	69.5	40.0	48.6
Sweet potatoes	2.5	0.2	0.0
Olives	85.4	103.6	115.6
Cabbages and other brassicas .	25.1	24.5	22.3
Tomatoes	222.4	204.8	198.2
Cauliflowers and broccoli . .	25.7	26.2	34.6
Cucumbers and gherkins . .	208.2	233.8	255.2
Aubergines (Eggplants) . .	57.4	48.0	47.9
Onions, dry	44.6	49.8	52.7
Watermelons	20.0	5.0	5.0
Grapes	55.4	55.2	55.3
Plums and sloes	9.5	8.9	10.3
Oranges	40.8	42.5	44.3
Tangerines, mandarins, clementines and satsumas . .	7.7	8.4	8.7
Lemons and limes	16.5	16.3	16.8
Grapefruit and pomelos . .	1.9	1.8	1.6
Bananas	5.5	5.5	5.6
Strawberries	3.4	3.3	3.4

Aggregate production ('000 metric tons, may include official, semi-official or estimated data): Total cereals 40.0 in 2009, 23.3 in 2010, 23.9 in 2011; Total roots and tubers 74.2 in 2009, 40.8 in 2010, 49.4 in 2011; Total vegetables (incl. melons) 735.1 in 2009, 695.4 in 2010, 728.5 in 2011; Total fruits (excl. melons) 171.1 in 2009, 171.7 in 2010, 178.0 in 2011.

Source: FAO.

LIVESTOCK
('000 head)

	2009	2010	2011
Cattle	28.3*	27.4*	30.0†
Sheep†	650.0	613.0	640.0
Goats	300.0*	219.4	200.0†
Chickens†	7,500	7,500	7,600

* Unofficial figure.
† FAO estimate(s).

Source: FAO.

LIVESTOCK PRODUCTS
('000 metric tons)

	2009	2010	2011
Cattle meat	4.3*	5.8*	6.0†
Chicken meat†	47.1	49.0	52.0
Goat meat†	4.9	4.3	4.3
Sheep meat†	11.3	10.7	10.7
Cows' milk†	95.0	98.3	98.3
Hen eggs†	39.7	40.5	40.5

* Unofficial figure.
† FAO estimate(s).

Source: FAO.

Fishing

GAZA STRIP
(metric tons, live weight)

	2008	2009	2010
Capture	2,843	1,525	1,699
Bogue	27	10	25
Jack and horse mackerels . .	44	57	82
Sardinellas	1,983	337	702
Chub mackerel	109	15	39
Cuttlefish and bobtail squids . .	18	17	8
Aquaculture	65	115	280
Total catch	2,908	1,640	1,979

Source: FAO.

Finance

CURRENCY AND EXCHANGE RATES

Monetary Units:
At present, there is no domestic Palestinian currency in use. The Israeli shekel, the Jordanian dinar and the US dollar all circulate within the West Bank and the Gaza Strip.

BUDGET OF THE PALESTINIAN AUTHORITY
(US $ million, estimates)

Revenue	2002	2003*	2004†
Domestic revenue	185	259	298
Revenue clearances‡	150	442	508
Total	335	701	806

Expenditure	2002	2003*	2004†
Central administration . . .	141.8	128.0	109.2
Public security and order . . .	310.4	392.1	433.9
Financial affairs	292.5	352.2	410.7
Foreign affairs	13.8	17.2	25.6
Economic development . . .	35.8	39.8	43.1
Social services	340.5	432.9	526.6
Cultural and information services	25.4	29.2	32.8
Transport and communication services	10.4	12.1	14.2
Total	1,170.6	1,403.5	1,596.1

* Revised estimates.
† Provisional figures.
‡ Figures refer to an apportionment of an agreed pool of selected tax revenues arising as a result of the de facto customs union between Israel and the Palestinian territories. Israel is the collecting agent for these receipts and periodically makes transfers to the Palestinian Authority.

Source: Ministry of Finance, Ramallah.

2010 (US $ million): *Revenue:* Local taxes 707; Clearing 1,320; Total 2,027. *Expenditure and net lending:* Wages and salaries 1,550; Other current expenditure 1,370; Net lending 250; Total 3,170.

2011 (US $ million): *Revenue:* Local taxes 812; Clearing 1,442; Total 2,254. *Expenditure and net lending:* Wages and salaries 1,710; Other current expenditure 1,363; Net lending 160; Total 3,232.

2012 (US $ million): *Revenue:* Local taxes 812; Clearing 1,542; Total 2,354. *Expenditure and net lending:* Wages and salaries 1,793; Other current expenditure 1,290; Net lending 105; Total 3,188.

Source: Ministry of Finance, Palestinian National Authority.

COST OF LIVING
(Consumer Price Index; base: 2000 = 100)

	2006	2007	2008
Food	118.8	124.3	147.4
Electricity, gas and other fuels .	135.8	140.3	160.8
Clothing	103.5	102.7	102.4
Rent	109.0	100.8	119.5
All items (incl. others) . . .	123.5	126.9	139.2

2009: Food 152.7; All items (incl. others) 143.1.

2010: Food 157.8; All items (incl. others) 148.4.

2011: Food 161.6; All items (incl. others) 152.7.

Source: ILO.

NATIONAL ACCOUNTS*
(US $ million at current prices)

Expenditure on the Gross Domestic Product

	2009	2010	2011
Final consumption expenditure .	8,966.2	10,263.8	12,352.1
Households	6,869.5	7,868.5	9,094.3
Non-profit institutions serving households	340.9	356.2	337.4
General government . . .	1,755.8	2,039.1	2,920.4
Gross capital formation . . .	1,232.9	1,541.1	1,688.9
Gross fixed capital formation .	1,209.2	1,445.3	2,020.6
Changes in inventories . . .	23.7	95.8	−331.7
Total domestic expenditure .	10,199.1	11,804.9	14,041.0
Exports of goods and services .	905.3	1,151.6	1,509.7
Less Imports of goods and services	4,384.8	4,625.9	5,775.4
GDP in purchasers' values .	6,719.6	8,330.6	9,775.3

Gross Domestic Product by Economic Activity

	2009	2010	2011
Agriculture and fishing . . .	373.8	430.3	575.1
Mining and quarrying	48.8	33.2	68.2
Manufacturing	670.2	849.0	1,061.6
Electricity and water supply . .	157.8	168.0	153.8
Construction	265.6	365.2	710.9
Wholesale and retail trade . .	1,013.5	1,326.7	1,507.7
Transport, storage and communications	616.4	681.8	790.9
Financial intermediation . . .	270.8	307.4	341.2
Real estate, renting and business services	417.4	526.2	506.1
Community, social and personal services	28.3	34.9	42.3
Hotels and restaurants . . .	98.7	126.7	72.2
Education	523.2	605.7	786.5
Health and social work . . .	223.8	267.0	361.5
Public administration and defence	969.5	1,236.0	1,440.9
Households with employed persons	3.7	5.7	6.0
Other services	140.7	182.5	187.7
Sub-total	5,822.2	7,146.3	8,612.6
Less Financial intermediation services indirectly measured .	202.7	236.2	236.2
Gross value added	5,619.5	6,910.1	8,376.4
Taxes on imports	1,100.1	1,420.5	1,398.9
GDP in purchasers' values .	6,719.6	8,330.6	9,775.3

* Referring to the West Bank and Gaza Strip, but excluding that part of Jerusalem annexed in 1967.

BALANCE OF PAYMENTS
(US $ million, preliminary estimates)

	2009	2010	2011
Exports of goods f.o.b.	631.3	666.1	848.0
Imports of goods f.o.b.	−4,135.7	−4,318.9	−5,473.9
Trade balance	−3,504.4	−3,652.8	−4,625.9
Exports of services	579.3	830.7	954.6
Imports of services	−931.1	−1,142.8	−1,058.2
Balance on goods and services	−3,856.2	−3,964.9	−4,729.5
Other income received (net) . .	876.2	1,098.1	1,217.2
Balance on goods, services and income	−2,980.0	−2,866.8	−3,512.3
Current transfers (net) . . .	2,267.5	2,175.9	1,319.8
Current balance	−712.5	−690.9	−2,192.6
Capital account (net)	719.0	846.1	536.2
Direct investment abroad (net) .	315.9	103.0	605.2
Portfolio investment (net) . . .	−367.0	−453.4	−69.5
Other investment (net) . . .	191.5	341.0	1,050.2
Net errors and omissions . . .	−158.1	−109.6	36.9
Overall balance	−11.1	36.4	−33.7

External Trade

PRINCIPAL COMMODITIES
(US $ million)

Imports c.i.f.	2009	2010	2011
Food and live animals	628.4	703.7	714.7
Beverages and tobacco . . .	137.1	166.1	161.0
Crude materials (inedible) except fuels	36.8	39.3	78.1
Mineral fuels, lubricants, etc. .	1,141.4	1,247.5	1,380.8
Animal and vegetable oils and fats	17.6	21.1	22.6
Chemicals and related products .	294.3	353.2	352.3
Basic manufactures	553.5	651.0	699.7
Machinery and transport equipment	571.2	536.6	596.6
Miscellaneous manufactured articles	220.4	239.9	215.3
Total	3,600.8	3,958.5	4,221.1

Exports f.o.b.	2009	2010	2011
Food and live animals	61.3	79.4	105.2
Beverages and tobacco . . .	22.0	24.0	30.1
Crude materials (inedible) except fuels	7.2	11.6	94.3
Mineral fuels, lubricants, etc. .	2.7	1.5	1.6
Animal and vegetable oils and fats	14.6	15.8	19.9
Chemicals and related products .	67.7	74.0	51.9
Basic manufactures	210.5	244.9	240.5
Machinery and transport equipment	30.0	33.0	30.8
Miscellaneous manufactured articles	102.2	91.2	145.3
Total	518.4	575.5	719.6

PRINCIPAL TRADING PARTNERS
(US $ million)

Imports c.i.f.	2007	2008	2009
China, People's Republic . . .	143.8	126.0	161.8
Egypt	27.5	23.5	35.3
France (incl. Monaco) . . .	23.5	27.6	38.8
Germany	57.3	82.9	97.3
Israel	2,307.9	2,767.7	2,651.1
Italy	30.9	69.9	40.4
Japan	103.1	17.0	18.7
Jordan	44.8	52.2	48.1
Korea, Republic	12.9	27.7	50.5
Spain	27.5	23.4	33.5
Sweden	21.2	13.9	31.3
Switzerland	35.3	52.8	—
Thailand	25.5	8.3	14.3
Turkey	82.0	68.5	113.8
United Kingdom	20.7	16.7	21.2
USA	24.3	37.7	40.4
Total (incl. others)	3,141.3	3,568.7	3,600.8

Exports f.o.b.	2007	2008	2009
Algeria	1.0	0.8	8.9
Israel	455.2	499.4	453.5
Jordan	27.8	34.1	28.9
Netherlands	8.8	0.3	0.8
Saudi Arabia	1.8	3.6	4.2
United Arab Emirates . . .	2.4	3.7	—
USA	3.4	3.6	6.1
Total (incl. others)	513.0	558.4	518.4

Source: UN, *International Trade Statistics Yearbook*.

Transport

ROAD TRAFFIC
(registered motor vehicles holding Palestinian licence, 2011 unless otherwise indicated)

	West Bank	Gaza Strip*
Private cars	100,406	30,830
Taxis	8,706	2,841
Buses	1,533	615
Trucks and commercial cars	24,999	11,172
Motorcycles and mopeds	373	14,083
Tractors	1,246	738

* 2010 figures.

Tourism

ARRIVALS OF VISITORS AT HOTELS*

	2009	2010	2011
Total	452,625	577,383	510,435

* Including Palestinians.

2009: Total guest nights in hotels 1,042,290 (Palestinians 115,978; European Union members 402,316; Israelis 80,312; Asians 85,562).

2010: Total guest nights in hotels 1,285,661 (Palestinians 120,142; European Union members 512,637; Israelis 77,191; Asians 142,271).

2011: Total guest nights in hotels 1,254,496 (Palestinians 141,973; European Union members 469,135; Israelis 73,538; Asians 129,728).

Communications Media

	2007	2008	2009
Telephones ('000 main lines in use)	348.8	354.8	368.2
Mobile cellular telephones ('000 subscribers)	1,021.5	1,314.4	1,800.0
Internet subscribers ('000) . .	102.3	102.9	114.7
Broadband subscribers ('000) .	55.6	n.a.	n.a.

Personal computers: 195,000 (54.6 per 1,000 persons) in 2005.

Source: International Telecommunication Union.

Education

(2011/12 unless otherwise indicated)

	Institutions	Teachers	Students
Pre-primary	862*	3,285†	63,007*
Primary	1,792 }	43,560† {	980,213
Secondary	915		149,325
Higher:			
universities, etc. . . .	11‡ }	6,861§ {	213,973§
other	23‡		

* West Bank only.
† 2007/08.
‡ 2006/07.
§ 2010/11.

Pupil-teacher ratio (primary education, UNESCO estimate): 27.8 in 2009/10 (Source: UNESCO Institute for Statistics).

Adult literacy rate (persons aged 15 and over, UNESCO estimates): 94.9% (males 97.6%; females 92.2%) in 2010 (Source: UNESCO Institute for Statistics).

Directory

Administration

PALESTINIAN NATIONAL AUTHORITY

Appointed in May 1994, the Palestinian National Authority, generally known internationally as the Palestinian Authority (PA), has assumed some of the civil responsibilities formerly exercised by the Israeli Civil Administration in the Gaza Strip and parts of the West Bank.

Executive President: MAHMUD ABBAS (assumed office 15 January 2005).

CABINET
(May 2013)

On 13 April 2013 the Prime Minister, Dr Salam Khaled Abdullah Fayyad, submitted his resignation to the Executive President of the Palestinian (National) Authority, Mahmud Abbas. President Abbas accepted Fayyad's submission, while requesting that he remain in post until a new Cabinet could be formed. Fayyad's decision followed a deterioration in relations with Abbas, after the resignation in early March of Minister of Finance Nabil Qassis, which had been accepted by Fayyad despite Abbas's opposition.

The executive is formed by Fatah, the Democratic Front for the Liberation of Palestine, the Palestinian Democratic Union and independents.

Prime Minister: Dr SALAM KHALED ABDULLAH FAYYAD.

Minister of Finance: (vacant).

Minister of the Interior: SAID ABU ALI.

Minister of Foreign Affairs: Dr RIYAD NAJIB AL-MALIKI.

Minister of the Environment: YOUSEF ABU SAFIEH.

Minister of Local Government: KHALED AL-QAWASMI.

Minister of Tourism: ROLA MA'AIYA.

Minister of National Economy: JAWAD NAJI.

Minister of Education: LAMIS AL-ALAMI.

Minister of Higher Education: Dr ALI AL-JARBAWI.

Minister of Health: HANI ABDEEN.

Minister of Awqaf (Religious Endowments): MAHMUD SIDQI AL-HABBASH.

Minister of Transport: ALI ABU ZUHRI.

Minister of Telecommunications and Information Technology: SAFA NASSER EL-DIN.

Minister of Detainees' Affairs: ISSA QARAQE'.

Minister of Women's Affairs: RABIHA THIAB.

Minister of Social Affairs: MAJIDA AL-MASRI.

Minister of Justice: ALI MUHANNA.

Minister of Labour: Dr AHMAD AL-MAJDALANI.

Minister of Agriculture: WALID ASSAF.

Minister of Culture: SIHAM AL-BARGHOUTHI.

Minister of Public Works and Housing: MAHER GHANIM.

Minister of Jerusalem Affairs: ADNAN HUSSEINI.

Minister of State for Planning: MAHMOUD ABU RAMADAN.

MINISTRIES

Office of the President: Ramallah.

Ministry of Agriculture: POB 197, Ramallah; tel. (2) 2961080; fax (2) 2961212; e-mail moa@planet.edu.

Ministry of Awqaf (Religious Endowments): POB 17412, Jerusalem; tel. (2) 6282085; fax (2) 2986401.

Ministry of Culture: POB 147, Ramallah; tel. (2) 2986205; fax (2) 2986204; e-mail moc@moc.pna.ps.

Ministry of Detainees' Affairs: Ramallah; tel. (2) 2961713; internet www.mod.gov.ps.

Ministry of Education: POB 576, al-Masioun, Ramallah; POB 5285, al-Wihda St, Gaza; tel. (2) 2983200; fax (2) 2983222; e-mail moehe.p@gmail.com; internet www.moehe.gov.ps.

Ministry of Environment: Ramallah.

Ministry of Finance: POB 795, Sateh Marhaba, al-Birah/Ramallah; POB 4007, Gaza; tel. (2) 2825255; fax (2) 2848900; e-mail mof@mof.ps; internet www.mof.gov.ps.

Ministry of Foreign Affairs: POB 1336, Ramallah; tel. (2) 2405040; fax (2) 2403772; e-mail info@mofa-gov.ps; internet www.mofa.gov.ps.

Ministry of Health: POB 14, al-Mukhtar St, Nablus; POB 1035, Abu Khadra Center, Gaza; tel. (9) 2384772; fax (9) 2384777; e-mail moh@gov.ps; tel. (8) 2829173; fax (8) 2826295; internet www.moh.gov.ps.

Ministry of Higher Education: Ramallah.

Ministry of the Interior: Ramallah; tel. (2) 2429873; fax (2) 2429872.

Ministry of Jerusalem Affairs: POB 20479, Jerusalem; tel. (2) 6273330; fax (2) 6286820.

Ministry of Justice: POB 267, Ramallah; POB 1012, Gaza; tel. (2) 2987661; fax (2) 2974491; e-mail info@moj.gov.ps; internet www.moj.gov.ps.

Ministry of Labour: POB 350, al-Irsal St, Ramallah; tel. (2) 2982800; fax (2) 2982801; e-mail info@mol.gv.ps; internet www.mol.gov.ps.

Ministry of Local Government: POB 731, Albaloo, al-Birah/Ramallah; Gaza; tel. (2) 2401092; fax (2) 2401091; tel. (8) 2820272; fax (8) 2828474; e-mail info@molg.gov.ps; internet www.molg.pna.ps.

Ministry of National Economy: POB 1629, Umm al-Sharayet, Ramallah; POB 4023, Maqqusi Bldg, al-Nasser St, Gaza; tel. (2) 2981218; fax (2) 2981207; tel. (8) 2874146; fax (8) 2874145; e-mail info@met.gov.ps; internet www.met.gov.ps.

Ministry of State for Planning: POB 4557, al-Birah/Ramallah; POB 4017, Gaza; tel. (2) 2973010; fax (2) 2973012; tel. (8) 2828825; fax (8) 2830509; e-mail mop@gov.ps; internet www.mop-gov.ps.

Ministry of Public Works and Housing: Gaza; tel. (8) 2829232; fax (8) 2823653; e-mail mopgaza@palnet.com.

Ministry of Social Affairs: POB 3525, Ramallah; tel. (2) 2986181; fax (2) 2985239; e-mail msa@hally.net; internet www.mosa.gov.ps.

Ministry of Telecommunications and Information Technology: Ramallah; Gaza; tel. (2) 2829720; fax (2) 2829740; e-mail smadoukh@gov.ps; internet www.mtit.gov.ps.

Ministry of Tourism: POB 534, Manger St, Bethlehem; Gaza; tel. (2) 2741581; fax (2) 2743753; tel. (7) 2824866; fax (7) 2824856; e-mail mota@visit-palestine.com; internet www.dach.pna.ps.

Ministry of Transport: POB 399, Ramallah; tel. (2) 2986945; fax (2) 2986943.

Ministry of Women's Affairs: al-Birah/Ramallah; tel. (2) 2403315; e-mail contactus@mowa.ps; internet www.mowa.gov.ps.

President and Legislature

Presidential and legislative elections had been due to take place by 25 January 2010; however, the polls were postponed indefinitely owing to the ongoing dispute between the Palestinian (National) Authority Cabinet and the de facto Hamas administration in the Gaza Strip. Following the signature of a unity agreement by the main Palestinian factions in early May 2011, it had been expected that elections would take place later that year. However, by early 2013 no further progress had been made, and elections had yet to be scheduled.

PRESIDENT

Election, 9 January 2005

Candidates							Votes	%
Mahmud Abbas (Fatah)	.	.	.	.	.	.	501,448	62.52
Mustafa Barghouthi (Ind.)		.	.	.	.	.	156,227	19.48
Tayseer Khalid (DFLP)	.	.	.	.	.		26,848	3.35
Abd al-Halim al-Ashqar (Ind.)		.	.	.	.		22,171	2.76
Bassam el-Salhi (PPP)	.	.	.	.	.		21,429	2.67
Al-Said Baraka (Ind.)	.	.	.	.	.		10,406	1.30
Abd al-Karim Shbeir (Ind.)		.	.	.	.		5,717	0.71
Invalid votes	.	.	.	.	.		57,831	7.21
Total	.	.	.	.	.	.	802,077	100.00

Palestinian Legislative Council
e-mail info@plc.gov.ps; internet www.plc.gov.ps.

Speaker: Dr AZIZ DUWAIK.

General Election, 25 January 2006

Parties, Lists and Coalitions	Seats		
	Majority system	Proportional system	Total
Change and Reform* .	29	45	74
Fatah	28	17	45
Martyr Abu Ali			
Moustafa† . . .	3	0	3
The Third Way . .	2	0	2
The Alternative‡ . .	2	0	2
Independent			
Palestine§ . . .	2	0	2
Independents . . .	0	4	4
Total	**66**	**66**	**132**

* The Islamic Resistance Movement (Hamas) contested the elections as Change and Reform.

† The Popular Front for the Liberation of Palestine contested the elections as Martyr Abu Ali Moustafa.

‡ Electoral list comprising the Palestinian Democratic Union, the Coalition of the Democratic Front (representing the Democratic Front for the Liberation of Palestine) and the Palestinian People's Party.

§ Coalition comprising independents and representatives of the Palestinian National Initiative.

Election Commission

Central Elections Commission (CEC): POB 2319, Qasr al-Murjan Bldg, Al-Balou, nr Jawwal Circle, Ramallah; tel. (2) 2969700; fax (2) 2969712; e-mail info@elections.ps; internet www.elections.ps; f. 2002; independent; comprises 9 mems, appointed by the Exec. Pres. of the PA; Chair. Dr HANNA NASIR; Sec.-Gen. Dr RAMI HAMDALLAH.

Political Organizations

Alliance of Palestinian Forces: f. 1994; comprises representatives of the PLF, the PPSF, the PRCP and the PFLP—GC; opposes the Declaration of Principles on Palestinian Self-Rule signed by Israel and the PLO in September 1993, and subsequent agreements concluded within its framework (the 'Oslo Accords'). The PFLP and DFLP left the Alliance in 1996. The **Fatah Revolutionary Council,** headed by Sabri Khalil al-Banna, alias 'Abu Nidal', split from Fatah in 1973. Its headquarters were formerly in Baghdad, Iraq, but the office was closed down and its staff expelled from the country by the Iraqi authorities in November 1983; a new base was established in Damascus, Syria, in December. Al-Banna was readmitted to Iraq in 1984, having fled Syria. With 'Abu Musa' (whose rebel Fatah group is called **Al-Intifada** or 'Uprising'), Abu Nidal formed a joint rebel Fatah command in February 1985, and both had offices in Damascus until June 1987, when those of Abu Nidal were closed by the Syrian Government. Forces loyal to Abu Nidal surrendered to Fatah forces at the Rashidiyeh Palestinian refugee camp near Tyre, northern Lebanon, in 1990. Abu Nidal was reportedly found dead in Baghdad in August 2002.

Arab Liberation Front (ALF): Ramallah; internet alfpalestine.org; f. 1969; fmrly supported by Iraq's Arab Baath Socialist Party under the leadership of former President Saddam Hussain; member of the PLO; opposes Oslo Accords; Sec.-Gen. RAKAD SALIM (imprisoned in 2002).

Democratic Front for the Liberation of Palestine (DFLP) (Al-Jabha al-Dimuqratiyya li-Tahrir Filastin): Damascus, Syria; tel. (11) 4448993; fax (11) 4442380; Ramallah; tel. (2) 2954438; fax (2) 2980401; e-mail dflp-palestine@dflp-palestine.org; internet www.dflp-palestine.net; f. 1969 following split with PFLP; Marxist-Leninist; contested Jan. 2006 legislative elections on The Alternative electoral list as the Coalition of the Democratic Front; Sec.-Gen. NAIF HAWATMEH (Damascus).

Fatah (Harakat al-Tahrir al-Watani al-Filastin—Palestine National Liberation Movement): POB 1965, Ramallah; tel. (2) 2986892; fax (2) 2987947; e-mail fact@palnet.com; internet www.fateh.ps; f. 1957; militant group that became the single largest Palestinian org. and strongest faction in both the administration and Palestinian Legislative Council until the legislative elections of Jan. 2006; leadership is nominally shared by the members of the Cen. Cttee, who were elected at Fatah's Sixth Gen. Conference on 10 Aug. 2009; Chair. of Cen. Cttee MAHMUD ABBAS.

Islamic Jihad (Al-Jihad al-Islami): Damascus, Syria; f. 1979–80 by Palestinian students in Egypt; militant Islamist; opposed to the Oslo Accords; Sec.-Gen. RAMADAN ABDULLAH SHALLAH.

Islamic Resistance Movement (Hamas—Harakat al-Muqawama al-Islamiyya): Gaza; Damascus, Syria; f. 1987; originally welfare organization Mujama (f. 1973) led by the late Sheikh AHMAD YASSIN (killed by Israeli forces in March 2004); militant Islamist; opposes the Oslo Accords; following the killing by Israeli forces of Hamas's leader in the Gaza Strip, Abd al-Aziz al-Rantisi, in April 2004, the group announced that it was adopting a policy of 'collective leadership'; contested Jan. 2006 legislative elections as Change and Reform; Head of Political Bureau KHALID MESHAAL (Doha, Qatar); Gen. Commdr of military wing, Izz al-Din al-Qassam Brigades, MUHAMMAD DEIF (in hiding from the Israeli authorities since 1992, though presumed to be in Gaza).

Palestine Liberation Front (PLF): f. 1977 following split with PFLP—GC; the PLF split into three factions in the early 1980s, all of which retained the name PLF; one faction (Leader MUHAMMAD 'ABU' ABBAS) was based in Tunis, Tunisia, and Baghdad, Iraq, and remained nominally loyal to Yasser Arafat; the second faction (Leader TALAAT YAQOUB) belonged to the anti-Arafat National Salvation Front and opened offices in Damascus, Syria, and Libya; a third group derived from the PLF was reportedly formed by its Central Cttee Secretary, ABD AL-FATTAH GHANIM, in June 1986; the factions of Yaqoub and Ghanim were reconciled in early 1985; at the 18th session of the PNC a programme for the unification of the PLF was announced, with Yaqoub (died November 1988) named as Secretary-General and Abu Abbas appointed to the PLO Executive Committee, while unification talks were held. The merging of the two factions was announced in June 1987, with Abu Abbas becoming Deputy Secretary-General. Abu Abbas was apprehended by US-led coalition forces in Iraq in April 2003, and reportedly died of natural causes in March 2004 while still in US custody; Sec.-Gen. WASSEL ABU YUSUF.

Palestine Liberation Organization (PLO) (Munazzimat al-Tahrir al-Filastiniyya): Negotiations Affairs Dept, POB 4120, Ramallah; tel. (2) 2963741; fax (2) 2963740; internet www.nad-plo.org; f. 1964; the supreme organ of the PLO is the Palestine Nat. Council (PNC; Pres. SALIM AL-ZA'NUN), while the PLO Exec. Cttee (Chair. MAHMUD ABBAS; Sec.-Gen. FAROUK KADDOUMI) deals with day-to-day business. Fatah (the Palestine Nat. Liberation Movement) joined the PNC in 1968, and all the guerrilla orgs joined the Council in 1969. In 1973 the Palestinian Cen. Council (PCC; Chair. SALIM AL-ZA'NUN) was established to act as an intermediary between the PNC and the Exec. Cttee. The Council meets when the PNC is not in session and approves major policy decisions on its behalf; Chair. MAHMUD ABBAS.

Palestine Revolutionary Communist Party (PRCP) (Al-Hizb al-Shuyu'i al-Thawri al-Filastini): principally based in Lebanon; promotes armed struggle in order to achieve its aims; Sec.-Gen. ARABI AWAD.

Palestinian Democratic Union (FIDA): POB 247, Ramallah; tel. 2954072; fax (2) 2954071; e-mail info@fida.ps; internet www.fida.ps; f. 1990 following split from the DFLP; contested Jan. 2006 legislative elections on The Alternative electoral list; Leader YASSER ABD AL-RABBUH; Sec.-Gen. ZAHIRA KAMAL.

Palestinian National Initiative (Al-Mubadara): Ramallah; tel. (5) 9293006; e-mail almubadara@almubadara.org; internet www.almubadara.org; f. 2002; seeks peaceful resolution of conflict with Israel through establishment of an independent, unified, viable and democratic Palestinian state, with East Jerusalem as its capital; advocates reform of internal political structures, and aims to fight corruption and injustice, and to uphold citizens' rights; contested Jan. 2006 legislative elections as part of the Independent Palestine coalition; Sec.-Gen. Dr MUSTAFA BARGHOUTHI.

Palestinian People's Party (PPP) (Hezb al-Sha'ab): Ramallah; tel. (2) 2963593; fax (2) 2963592; e-mail info@ppp.ps; internet www.palpeople.org; f. 1921 as Palestine Communist Party; adopted current name in 1991; admitted to the PNC at its 18th session in 1987; contested Jan. 2006 legislative elections on The Alternative electoral list; Sec.-Gen. BASSAM EL-SALHI.

Palestinian Popular Struggle Front (PPSF) (Jabhat al-Nidal al-Sha'biyya al-Filastiniyya): f. 1967; has reportedly split into two factions which either support or oppose the PA; the pro-PA faction (Leader AHMAD AL-MAJDALANI) is based in the West Bank; the anti-PA faction (Leader KHALID ABD AL-MAJID) is based in Damascus, Syria.

Popular Front for the Liberation of Palestine (PFLP) (Al-Jabha al-Sha'biyya li-Tahrir Filastin): Damascus, Syria; internet www.pflp.ps; f. 1967; Marxist-Leninist; publr of *Democratic Palestine* (English; monthly); contested Jan. 2006 legislative elections as Martyr Abu Ali Moustafa; Sec.-Gen. AHMAD SAADAT (imprisoned in 2002).

Popular Front for the Liberation of Palestine—General Command (PFLP—GC): Damascus, Syria; internet www.palestinesons

.com; f. 1968 following split from the PFLP; pro-Syrian; Leader AHMAD JIBRIL.

Popular Front for the Liberation of Palestine—National General Command: Amman, Jordan; split from the PFLP—GC in 1999; aims to co-operate with the PA; Leader ATIF YUNUS.

Al-Saiqa (Thunderbolt, or Vanguard of the Popular Liberation War): f. 1968; Syrian-backed; pan-Arab; opposed to the Oslo Accords; Sec.-Gen. ISSAM AL-QADI.

The formation of the **Right Movement for Championing the Palestinian People's Sons** by former members of Hamas was announced in April 1995. The movement, based in Gaza City, was reported to support the PA. The **Al-Aqsa Martyrs Brigades**, consisting of a number of Fatah-affiliated activists, emerged soon after the start of the al-Aqsa *intifada* in September 2000, and have carried out attacks against Israeli targets in Israel, the West Bank and Gaza Strip.

Diplomatic Representation

On 29 November 2012 an application to the UN General Assembly by the PLO (as Palestine) for non-member observer status was approved. Of the 193 member states, 138 voted in favour of the application, while nine voted against. A further 46 countries abstained from the vote or were absent. An earlier application for full membership in the UN officially remained under consideration in early 2013, although it appeared unlikely that it would gain the necessary approval from the UN Security Council.

Countries with which the PLO maintains diplomatic relations include:

Afghanistan, Albania, Algeria, Angola, Argentina, Austria, Azerbaijan, Bahrain, Bangladesh, Belarus, Benin, Bolivia, Bosnia and Herzegovina, Brazil, Brunei, Bulgaria, Burkina Faso, Cambodia, Cameroon, Chad, Chile, China (People's Rep.), Comoros, Congo (Rep.), Costa Rica, Côte d'Ivoire, Cuba, Cyprus, Djibouti, Dominican Republic, Ecuador, Egypt, El Salvador, Ethiopia, Gabon, The Gambia, Georgia, Ghana, Guinea, Guinea-Bissau, Guyana, the Holy See, Honduras, Hungary, India, Indonesia, Iran, Iraq, Jordan, Kazakhstan, Kenya, Korea (Dem. People's Rep.), Kuwait, Laos, Lebanon, Libya, Malawi, Malaysia, Maldives, Mali, Malta, Mauritania, Mauritius, Mongolia, Montenegro, Morocco, Mozambique, Namibia, Nicaragua, Niger, Nigeria, Norway, Oman, Pakistan, Paraguay, Peru, Philippines, Poland, Qatar, Romania, Russia, Saudi Arabia, Senegal, Serbia, Seychelles, Slovakia, Somalia, South Africa, Sri Lanka, Sudan, Syria, Swaziland, Sweden, Tajikistan, Tanzania, Tunisia, Turkey, Uganda, Uruguay, the United Arab Emirates, Uzbekistan, Vanuatu, Venezuela, Viet Nam, Yemen, Zambia and Zimbabwe.

The following states, while they do not recognize Palestine, allow the PLO to maintain a regional office: Australia, Belgium, Canada, Colombia, Denmark, Estonia, Finland, France, Germany, Greece, Iceland, Ireland, Korea (Rep.), Italy, Japan, Latvia, Lithuania, Luxembourg, Mexico, the Netherlands, New Zealand, Portugal, Slovenia, Spain, Switzerland, Syria and the United Kingdom.

Judicial System

In the Gaza Strip, the West Bank towns of Jericho, Nablus, Ramallah, Jenin, Tulkarm, Qalqilya, Bethlehem and Hebron, and in other, smaller population centres in the West Bank, the PA has assumed limited jurisdiction with regard to civil affairs. However, the situation is confused owing to the various and sometimes conflicting legal systems which have operated in the territories occupied by Israel in 1967: Israeli military and civilian law; Jordanian law; and acts, orders-in-council and ordinances that remain from the period of the British Mandate in Palestine. Religious and military courts have been established under the auspices of the PA.

Higher State Security Court: Gaza; f. 1995; decides on security crimes both inside and outside the PA's area of jurisdiction; and to implement all valid Palestinian laws, regulations, rules and orders in accordance with Article 69 of the Constitutional Law of the Gaza Strip of 5 March 1962.

General Prosecutor of the PA: AHMAD AL-MOGHANI.

Religion

The vast majority of Palestinians in the West Bank and Gaza are Muslims, while a small (and declining) minority are Christians of the Greek Orthodox and Roman Catholic rites.

ISLAM

The PA-appointed Grand Mufti of Jerusalem and the Palestinian Lands is the most senior Muslim cleric in the Palestinian territories.

Mufti of Jerusalem: Sheikh MUHAMMAD AHMAD HUSSEIN.

CHRISTIANITY

The Roman Catholic Church

Latin Rite

The Patriarchate of Jerusalem covers Israel and the Occupied Territories, the Palestinian territories, Jordan, and Cyprus.

Patriarchate of Jerusalem: Patriarcat Latin, POB 14152, Jerusalem 91141; tel. (2) 6282323; fax (2) 6271652; e-mail latinvic@latinpat.org; internet www.lpj.org; Patriarch His Beatitude Archbishop FOUAD TWAL; Vicar-General Emeritus for Jerusalem KAMAL HANNA BATHISH (Titular Bishop of Jericho); Vicar-General for Israel GIACINTO-BOULOS MARCUZZO (Titular Bishop of Emmaus Nicopolis).

Melkite Rite

The Greek-Melkite Patriarch of Antioch and all the East, of Alexandria, and of Jerusalem (GRÉGOIRE III LAHAM) is resident in Damascus, Syria.

Patriarchal Vicariate of Jerusalem: Patriarcat Grec-Melkite Catholique, POB 14130, Porte de Jaffa, Jerusalem 91141; tel. (2) 6282023; fax (2) 6289606; e-mail gcpjer@p-ol.com; about 3,300 adherents (31 December 2007); Protosyncellus Archim. Archbishop JOSEPH JULES ZEREY (Titular Archbishop of Damietta).

The Greek Orthodox Church

The Patriarchate of Jerusalem covers Israel and the Occupied Territories, the Palestinian territories, Jordan, Kuwait, the UAE, and Saudi Arabia.

Patriarchate of Jerusalem: POB 14518, Jerusalem 91145; tel. (2) 6274941; fax (2) 6282048; e-mail secretariat@jerusalem-patriarchate.info; internet www.jerusalem-patriarchate.info; Patriarch THEOPHILOS III.

The Press

NEWSPAPERS

Al-Ayyam: POB 1987, al-Ayyam St, Commercial Area, Ramallah; tel. (2) 2987341; fax (2) 2987342; e-mail info@al-ayyam.com; internet www.al-ayyam.ps; f. 1995; weekly; Arabic; publ. by Al-Ayyam Press, Printing, Publishing and Distribution Co; Editor-in-Chief AKRAM HANIYA.

Al-Ayyam al-Arabi: POB 1987, al-Ayyam St, Commercial Area, Ramallah; tel. 2-2987341; fax 2-2987342; e-mail info@al-ayyam.com; internet www.al-ayyam.com; f. 1995; daily; Arabic; publ. by Al-Ayyam Press, Printing, Publishing and Distribution Co; Editor-in-Chief AKRAM HANIYA.

Filastin al-Thawra (Palestine of the Revolution): fmrly publ. in Beirut, Lebanon, but resumed publication from Cyprus in November 1982; weekly newspaper of the PLO; Arabic.

Al-Hadaf (The Target): e-mail alhadaf@alhadafmagazine.com; internet www.alhadafmagazine.com; f. 1969 in Beirut, Lebanon; weekly; Arabic; organ of the Popular Front for the Liberation of Palestine.

Al-Hayat al-Jadidah: POB 1822, Ramallah; tel. (2) 2407251; fax (2) 2407250; e-mail info1@alhayat-j.com; internet www.alhayat-j.com; f. 1994; weekly; Arabic; Editor NADIL AMR.

Al-Hourriah (Liberation): POB 11488, Damascus, Syria; tel. (1) 6319455; fax (1) 6319125; e-mail hourriah@hotmail.com; internet www.alhourriah.org; Arabic; organ of the Democratic Front for the Liberation of Palestine; publ. in Beirut (Lebanon) and Damascus; Editor-in-Chief HAMADEH MU'TASIM.

Al-Istiqlal (Independence): al-Thawra St, Gaza City; e-mail alesteqlal@p-i-s.com; weekly; Arabic; organ of Islamic Jihad; Sec. TAWFIQ AL-SAYYID SALIM.

Palestine Times: POB 10355, London, NW2 3WH, United Kingdom; e-mail palestimes@ptimes.org; internet www.ptimes.org; f. 2006; monthly; English; privately owned; independent; Editor-in-Chief AHMAD KARMAWI; circ. 5,000.

Al-Quds (Jerusalem): POB 19788, Jerusalem; tel. (2) 5833501; fax (2) 5856937; e-mail info@alquds.com; internet www.alquds.com; Arabic; independent; pro-PA; supports peace negotiations; reportedly has largest circulation of all Palestinian newspapers; daily; Editor MAHER AL-ALAMI.

Al-Risala (Letter): Gaza City; weekly; Arabic; affiliated with the Islamic Resistance Movement (Hamas); Editor-in-Chief GHAZI HAMAD.

Directory

Al-Watan: Gaza City; weekly; Arabic; supports Hamas.

PERIODICALS

Filastin (Palestine): Gaza City; e-mail adel@falasteen.com; internet www.falasteen.com; f. 1994; weekly; Arabic; pro-Hamas, banned from publication and distribution in the West Bank; Editor-in-Chief MUSTAFA AL-SAWWAF.

The Jerusalem Times: POB 20185, 19 Nablus Rd, Jerusalem; tel. (2) 2961078; fax (2) 2961079; e-mail tjt@yahoo.com; internet www .jerusalemtimes.info; f. 1994; weekly; English; independent; Publr HANNA SINIORA; Man. Editor HALIMA ABU HANEYA.

Al-Karmel Magazine: POB 1887, Ramallah; tel. (2) 2965934; fax (2) 2987374; e-mail editor@alkarmel.org; internet www.alkarmel.org; f. 1981 in Beirut, Lebanon; literature; Editor-in-Chief HASAN KHADER.

Madar: Madar—al-Markaz al-Filastini lil-Dirasat al-Israiliyah, Ramallah; publ. by Madar—The Palestinian Centre for Israeli Studies; political; Editor SALMAN NATOUR.

Palestine Report: Jerusalem Media and Communications Centre, POB 25047, 7 Nablus Rd, Jerusalem 97300; tel. (2) 5838266; fax (2) 5836837; e-mail jmcc@jmcc.org; internet www.jmcc.org; f. 1990; weekly; English; current affairs; publ. by the Jerusalem Media and Communications Centre; Editor-in-Chief JOHARAH BAKER; Man. Dir OMAR KARMI.

The Youth Times: Orabi Bldg, 2 Ramallah St, Jerusalem; tel. (2) 2426280; fax (2) 2426281; e-mail pyalara@pyalara.org; internet www .pyalara.org; f. 1998; monthly; Arabic and English; publ. by the Palestinian Youth Association for Leadership and Rights Activation; Editor-in-Chief HANIA BITAR.

NEWS AGENCY

Wikalat Anbaa' Filastiniya (WAFA, Palestine News Agency): POB 5300, Gaza City; tel. (8) 2824036; fax (8) 2824046; e-mail edit@wafa.ps; internet www.wafa.ps; official PLO news agency; Editor ZIAD ABD AL-FATTAH.

Publishers

Al-Ayyam Press, Printing, Publishing and Distribution Co: POB 1987, Ramallah; tel. (2) 2987341; fax (2) 2987342; e-mail info@ al-ayyam.com; internet www.al-ayyam.com; f. 1995; publishes *Al-Ayyam al-Arabi* daily newspaper, *Al-Ayyam* weekly newspaper, books and magazines.

Beit Al-Maqdes for Publishing and Distribution: Ramallah; history, politics, fiction, children's.

Centre for Palestine Research and Studies (CPRS): POB 132, Nablus; tel. (9) 2380383; fax (9) 2380384; f. 1993; history, politics, strategic studies and economics; Dir SAID KANAAN.

Ogarit Centre for Publishing and Distribution: Ramallah; non-fiction, children's.

Broadcasting and Communications

TELECOMMUNICATIONS

A monopoly on fixed-line services is held by the Palestine Telecommunications Co PLC (PalTel). However, a second mobile telephone licence was awarded to Wataniya Mobile in 2006.

Palestine Telecommunications Co PLC (PalTel): POB 1570, Nablus; tel. (9) 2390108; fax (9) 2350140; e-mail paltel@palnet.net; internet www.paltel.ps; f. 1995; following acquisition of 56% stake by Zain Kuwait in May 2009, PalTel was merged with Zain Jordan; provider of fixed-line, mobile (cellular) and internet services; Chair. SABIH T. MASRI; CEO AMMAR AKER.

Palestine Cellular Co (Jawwal): POB 3999, al-Birah/Ramallah; tel. (2) 2402440; fax (2) 2968636; e-mail atyourservice@jawwal.ps; internet www.jawwal.ps/index.php; f. 1999; wholly owned subsidiary of PalTel; 700,000 subscribers (May 2006), representing some 55% of the Palestinian mobile (cellular) telecommunications market; CEO AMMAR AKER.

Wataniya Mobile: POB 4236, al-Birah/Ramallah; tel. (2) 2415000; fax (2) 2423044; e-mail hanin.khoury@wataniya.ps; internet www .wataniya-palestine.com; awarded the second mobile telephone licence 2006; commenced services in the West Bank Nov. 2009; 57% owned by Wataniya Telecom (Kuwait), 43% owned by Palestine Investment Fund; Chair. MUHAMMAD MUSTAFA; CEO FAYEZ HUSSEINI.

BROADCASTING

Palestinian Broadcasting Co (PBC): POB 984, al-Birah/Ramallah; tel. (2) 2959894; fax (2) 2959893; e-mail pbcinfo@pbc.gov.ps; internet www.pbc.gov.ps/English/about_us.htm; f. 1994; state-controlled; Chair. BASEM ABU SUMAYA.

Sawt Filastin (Voice of Palestine): c/o Police HQ, Jericho; tel. (2) 921220; f. 1994; official radio station of the PA; broadcasts in Arabic from Jericho and Ramallah; Dir RADWAN ABU AYYASH.

Palestine Television: f. 1994; broadcasts from Ramallah and Gaza City; broadcasts online on JumpTV; Dir RADWAN ABU AYYASH.

Finance

(cap. = capital; p.u. = paid up; res = reserves; dep. = deposits; brs = branches; m. = million)

BANKING

The Palestine Monetary Authority (PMA) is the financial regulatory body in the Palestinian territories, and is expected to evolve into the Central Bank of Palestine. Three currencies circulate in the Palestinian economy—the Jordanian dinar, the Israeli shekel and the US dollar—and the PMA currently has no right of issue. According to the PMA, there were 17 banks operating in the West Bank and Gaza in early 2013.

Palestine Monetary Authority (PMA): POB 452, Nablus Rd, Ramallah; POB 4026, Nasrah St, Gaza; tel. (2) 2415250; fax (2) 2409922; tel. (8) 2407779; fax (8) 2409646; e-mail info@pma.ps; internet www.pma.ps; f. 1994; began licensing, inspection and supervision of the Palestinian and foreign commercial banks operating in the Gaza Strip and the Jericho enclave in the West Bank in July 1995; assumed responsibility for 13 banks in the Palestinian territories over which the Central Bank of Israel had hitherto exercised control in Dec. 1995; Gov. Dr JIHAD AL-WAZIR.

National Banks

Bank of Palestine PLC (BOP): POB 471, Court St, Ain Misbah, Ramallah; tel. (2) 2965010; fax (2) 2964703; e-mail info@ bankofpalestine.com; internet www.bankofpalestine.com; f. 1960; cap. US $100m., res $42m., dep. $1,313m. (Dec. 2010); Gen. Man. Dr HANI HASHEM SHAWA; 31 brs and sub-brs in West Bank and Gaza.

Palestine Commercial Bank: POB 1799, Michael Tanous Bldg, Alawda St, Ramallah; tel. (2) 2979999; fax (2) 2979977; internet www .pcb.ps; f. 1992; as Commercial Bank of Palestine; name changed as above 2009; cap. US $35m. (May 2008); Pres. MAHMOUD ZUHDI MALHAS; 5 brs.

Palestine International Bank: al-Birah/Ramallah; tel. (2) 2983300; fax (2) 2983344; e-mail issam@ias.intranets.com; internet www.pibank.net; f. 1997; cap. US $20m.; Chair. OSAMA MUHAMMAD KHADIR; 4 brs.

Investment Banks

Arab Palestinian Investment Bank: POB 1260, al-Harji Bldg, Ramallah; tel. (2) 2987126; fax (2) 2987125; e-mail apibank@palnet .com; internet www.apibank.ps; f. 1996; Arab Bank of Jordan has a 51% share; cap. US $15m.; Dir ABD AL-MAJID SHOMAN; Gen. Man. BESHARA DABBAH.

Palestine Investment Bank PLC: POB 3675, al-Helal St, al-Birah/Ramallah; tel. (2) 2407880; fax (2) 2407887; e-mail info@ pinvbank.com; internet www.pinvbank.com; f. 1995 by the PA; some shareholders based in Jordan and the Gulf states; cap. US $60m.; provides full commercial and investment banking services throughout the West Bank and Gaza; Chair. ABD AL-AZIZ ABU DAYYEH; 7 brs.

Al-Quds Bank for Development and Investment (Quds Bank): POB 2471, Ramallah; tel. (2) 2961750; fax (2) 2961754; e-mail quds@ qudsbank.ps; internet www.alqudsbank.ps; f. 1995; merchant bank; cap. p.u. US $50m.; Gen. Man. AZZAM A. SHAWWA; 8 brs and 12 offices.

Islamic Banks

Arab Islamic Bank: POB 631, Nablus St, al-Birah/Ramallah; tel. (2) 2407060; fax (2) 2407065; e-mail aib@arabislamicbank.com; internet www.aibnk.com; f. 1995; cap. US $40m., res $9m., dep. $231m. (Dec. 2010); Chair. WALID T. FAKHOURI; Gen. Man. SAMI SAIDI; 8 brs.

Palestine Islamic Bank: POB 1244, Omar al-Mukhtar St, Gaza City; tel. (8) 2827360; fax (8) 2825269; e-mail info@islamicbank.ps; internet www.islamicbank.ps; f. 1996; Chair. MUHAMMED FAYEZ JABER ZAKARNEH.

STOCK EXCHANGE

Palestine Exchange (PEX): POB 128, 4th Floor, Amman St, Nablus; tel. (9) 2390999; fax (9) 2390998; e-mail pex@pex.ps; internet www.pex.ps; f. 1995; CEO AHMAD AWEIDAH.

INSURANCE

A very small insurance industry exists in the West Bank and Gaza.

Ahleia Insurance Group Ltd (AIG): POB 1214, al-Jalaa Tower, Remal, Gaza; tel. (8) 2824035; fax (8) 2824015; e-mail info@aig.ps; internet www.aig.ps; f. 1994; Chair. and CEO Dr MUHAMMAD AL-SABAWI; 11 brs.

Arab Insurance Establishment Co Ltd (AIE): POB 166, al-Qasr St, Nablus; tel. (9) 2341040; fax (9) 2341033; e-mail info@aie.com.ps; f. 1975; Chair. WALID ALOUL.

National Insurance Co: POB 1819, 34 Municipality St, al-Birah/Ramallah; tel. (2) 2983800; fax (2) 2407460; e-mail nic@nic-pal.com; internet www.nic-pal.com; f. 1992; Chair. MUHAMMAD MAHMOUD MASROUJI; Gen. Man. AZIZ MAHMOUD ABD AL-JAWAD; 8 brs.

DEVELOPMENT FINANCE ORGANIZATIONS

Arab Palestinian Investment Co Ltd: POB 2396, Kharaz Center, Yafa St, Industrial Zone, Ramallah; tel. (2) 2981060; fax (2) 2981065; e-mail apic@apic.com.jo; internet www.apic.ps; f. 1995; headquarters in Amman, Jordan; Chair. and CEO TAREK OMAR AGGAD.

Jerusalem Real Estate Investment Co: POB 1876, Ramallah; tel. (2) 2965215; fax (2) 2965217; e-mail jrei@palnet.com; f. 1996; Chair. AWNI ALSAKET.

Palestine Development & Investment Co (PADICO): POB 316, Nablus; tel. (9) 2384480; fax (9) 2384355; e-mail padico@padico.com; internet www.padico.com; f. 1993; 12 subsidiary and affiliate cos; Chair. MUNIB R. AL-MASRI; CEO Dr SAMIR HULILEH.

Palestine Real Estate Investment Co (Aqaria): POB 4049, Gaza; tel. (8) 2824815; fax (8) 2824845; e-mail aqaria@rannet.com; internet www.aqaria.com; f. 1994; Chair. NABIL SARAF; Vice-Chair. OMAR AL-ALAMI.

Palestinian Economic Council for Development and Reconstruction (PECDAR): POB 54910, Dahiyat al-Barid, Jerusalem; tel. (2) 2974300; fax (2) 2974331; e-mail info@pecdar.pna.net; internet www.pecdar.org; privately owned; Pres. Dr MUHAMMAD SHTAYYEH.

Trade and Industry

CHAMBERS OF COMMERCE

Federation of Chambers of Commerce, Industry and Agriculture: tel. (2) 2344923; fax (2) 2344924; e-mail fpccia@palnet.com; internet www.pal-chambers.org; f. 1989; 14 chambers, 32,000 mems.

Bethlehem Chamber of Commerce and Industry: POB 59, Bethlehem; tel. (2) 2742742; fax (2) 2764402; e-mail bcham@palnet.com; internet www.bethlehem-chamber.org; f. 1952; 2,800 mems; Chair. of Bd SAMIR HAZBOUN.

Gaza Chamber of Commerce, Industry and Agriculture: POB 33, Sabra Quarter, Gaza; tel. and fax (8) 2864588; e-mail gazacham@palnet.com; internet www.gazacham.ps; f. 1954; Chair. MUHAMMAD QUDWAH; Man. Dir BASSAM MORTAJA; 14,000 mems.

Hebron Chamber of Commerce and Industry: POB 272, Hebron; tel. (2) 2228218; fax (2) 2227490; e-mail ceo@hebroncci.org; internet www.hebroncci.org; f. 1953; Chair. M. GHAZI HERBAWI; 7,350 mems.

Jenin Chamber of Commerce, Industry and Agriculture: Jenin; tel. (4) 2501107; fax (4) 2503388; e-mail jencham@hally.net; internet www.pal-chambers.org/chambers/jenin.html; f. 1953; 3,800 mems.

Jericho Chamber of Commerce, Industry and Agriculture: POB 91, Jericho 00970; tel. (2) 2323313; fax (2) 2322394; e-mail jericho@pal-chambers.org; internet www.pal-chambers.org/chambers/jericho.html; f. 1953; 400 mems; Chair. HAJ MANSOUR SALAYMEH; Sec.-Gen. SELMI HAMAD.

Jerusalem Arab Chamber of Commerce and Industry: POB 19151, Jerusalem 91191; tel. (2) 2344923; fax (2) 2344914; e-mail chamber@jerusalemchamber.org; internet www.jerusalemchamber.org; f. 1936; 2,050 mems; Chair. AHMAD HASHEM ZUGHAYAR; Dir AZZAM ABU SAUD.

Nablus Chamber of Commerce and Industry: POB 35, Nablus; tel. (9) 2380335; fax (9) 2377605; e-mail nabluschamber@gmail.com; internet www.pal-chambers.org/chambers/nablus.html; f. 1943; Pres. MA'AZ NABULSI; Dir TAJ EL-DIN BITAR; 7,000 mems.

Palestinian-European Chamber of Commerce: Jerusalem; tel. (2) 894883; Chair. HANNA SINIORA.

Qalqilya Chamber of Commerce, Industry and Agriculture: POB 13, Qalqilya; tel. (9) 2941473; fax (9) 2940164; e-mail chamberq@hally.net; internet www.pal-chambers.org/chambers/qalqilya.html; f. 1972; 1,068 mems.

Ramallah Chamber of Commerce and Industry: POB 256, al-Birah/Ramallah; tel. (2) 2955052; fax (2) 2984691; e-mail ramallahcci@gmail.com; internet www.ramallahcci.org; f. 1950; Chair. KHALIL RIZEQ; Vice-Chair. MUHAMMAD ZEID; 3,566 mems.

Salfeet Chamber of Commerce, Industry and Agriculture: Salfeet; tel. and fax (9) 2515970; e-mail salfeetchamber@hotmail.com; internet www.pal-chambers.org/chambers/salfeet1.html; f. 1997; Chair. FOUAD AWAD.

Tulkarm Chamber of Commerce, Industry and Agriculture: POB 51, Tulkarm; tel. (9) 2671010; fax (9) 2675623; e-mail tulkarm@palnet.com; internet www.tulkarmchamber.org; f. 1945; 2,000 mems; Chair. SHUKRI AHMAD JALLAD.

TRADE AND INDUSTRIAL ORGANIZATIONS

Palestinian General Federation of Trade Unions (PGFTU): POB 1216, Nablus; tel. (9) 2385136; fax (9) 2384374; e-mail pgftu@pgftu.org; internet www.pgftu.org; f. 1965; Sec.-Gen. SHAHER SAED.

Union of Industrialists: POB 1296, Gaza; tel. (8) 2866222; fax (8) 2862013; Chair. MUHAMMAD YAZIJI.

UTILITIES

Electricity

Palestinian Energy Authority (PEA): POB 3591, Nablus St, al-Birah/Ramallah; POB 3041, Gaza; tel. (2) 2986190; fax (2) 2986191; tel. (8) 2821702; fax (8) 2824849; e-mail pea@palnet.com; internet pea-pal.tripod.com; f. 1994; Chair. Dr ABD AL-RAHMAN T. HAMAD.

Jerusalem District Electricity Co (JDECO): POB 19118, 15 Salah el-Din St, Jerusalem; tel. (2) 6269333; fax (2) 6282441; e-mail info@jdeco.net; internet www.jdeco.net; Gen. Man. HISHAM OMARI.

National Electric Co (NEC): West Bank; f. 2000.

Palestine Electric Co (PEC): POB 1336, Gaza; tel. (8) 2823800; fax (8) 2823297; e-mail info@pec-gpgc.com; internet www.pec-gpgc.com; f. 1999; 33% state-owned; Chair. SAID KHOURY; CEO WALID SALMAN.

Water

Palestinian Water Authority (PWA): POB 2174, Baghdad St, Ramallah; tel. (2) 2429022; fax (2) 2429341; e-mail pwa@pwa.ps; internet www.pwa.ps; f. 1995; Dir Dr SHADDAD AL-ATTILI.

Transport

ROADS

In 2006, according to estimates by the International Road Federation, the Palestinian territories had 5,147 km of paved roads, of which 535 km were highways or main roads, 438 km were secondary roads and 4,175 km were other roads.

CIVIL AVIATION

Palestinian Civil Aviation Authority (PCAA): Yasser Arafat International Airport, POB 4043, Rafah, Gaza; tel. and fax (8) 2827844; e-mail abuhalib@gaza-airport.org; internet www.gaza-airport.org; f. 1994; Gaza International Airport (renamed as above after Arafat's death in Nov. 2004) was formally inaugurated in November 1998 to operate services by Palestinian Airlines (its subsidiary), EgyptAir and Royal Jordanian Airline; Royal Air Maroc began to operate services to Amman (Jordan), Abu Dhabi and Dubai (both UAE), Cairo (Egypt), Doha (Qatar), Jeddah (Saudi Arabia), Istanbul (Turkey) and Larnaca (Cyprus), and intends to expand its network to Europe; the airport was closed by the Israeli authorities in February 2001 and the runway seriously damaged by Israeli airstrikes in late 2001 and early 2002; Dir-Gen. SALMAN ABU HALIB; Admin. Man. JAMAL AL-MASHHARAWI.

Palestinian Airlines: POB 4043, Gaza; tel. and fax (8) 2827844; e-mail commercial@palairlines.com; internet www.palairlines.com; f. 1994; state-owned; operates flights from el-Arish, Egypt, and Amman, Jordan; Dir-Gen. Capt. ZEYAD ALBADDA; Commercial. Dir YASSER IRQAYEQ.

Tourism

Although the tourism industry in the West Bank was virtually destroyed as a result of the 1967 Arab–Israeli War, by the late 1990s the sector was expanding significantly, with a number of hotels being opened or under construction. Much of the tourism in the West Bank centres around the historical and biblical sites of Jerusalem and Bethlehem. However, the renewed outbreak of Israeli–Palestinian conflict in the West Bank and Gaza Strip from late 2000, as well as the recent increase in inter-Palestinian violence, has generally prevented the recovery of the tourism industry.

Ministry of Tourism and Antiquities: See Administration.

NET—Near East Tourist Agency: POB 19015, 30 Mount of Olives Rd, Jerusalem 91190; tel. (2) 5328720; fax (2) 5328701; internet new.netours.com; f. 1964; CEO Sami Abu Dayyeh; Man. Steve Ustin.

Defence

Commander of the Palestinian National Security Forces: Maj.-Gen. Nidal Abu Dukhan.

Commander of the Interior Forces and the Civil Police: Maj.-Gen. Hazem Atallah.

Commander of General Intelligence: Maj.-Gen. Majid Faraj.

Estimated Public Security and Order Budget (2004): US $433.9m.

Paramilitary Forces (as assessed at November 2012): Paramilitary forces in the Gaza Strip and in the areas of the West Bank where the PA has assumed responsibility for security totalled an estimated 56,000; however, figures for personnel strength in the various forces were impossible to confirm, owing to the uncertain situation in the Palestinian territories at that time. There is, *inter alia*, a Presidential Security Force, a Preventative Security Force, a Civil Defence Force and a Police Force. Units of the Palestine National Liberation Army (PNLA) have been garrisoned in various countries in the Middle East and North Africa; however, much of the PNLA's personnel strength has now been incorporated into the PA's various security forces.

Education

According to the World Bank, Palestinians are among the most highly educated of any Arab group. However, basic and secondary education facilities in the West Bank and Gaza Strip are described as poor. In the West Bank, the Jordanian education system is in operation. Services are provided by the Israeli Civil Administration, the UN Relief and Works Agency for Palestine Refugees in the Near East (UNRWA) and private, mainly charitable, organizations. Vocational education is offered by the Civil Administration and UNRWA. All university and most community college education is provided by private, voluntary organizations. There are 20 community and teacher training colleges in the West Bank, and six universities (including an open university). The Egyptian system of education operates in the Gaza Strip, where there are three universities and one teacher training college. Palestinian education has been severely disrupted since the first *intifada* (uprising) of 1987, and more recently as a result of the al-Aqsa *intifada*, which began in late 2000. Universities have played a major role in the political activities of the West Bank and Gaza, and were closed by the Israeli Civil Administration during 1987–1992.

Since May 1994 the PA has assumed responsibility for education in Gaza and parts of the West Bank. Some 980,213 pupils attended 1,792 primary institutions across the Palestinian territories in 2011/12, while 149,325 students were enrolled at 915 secondary institutions. In 2010/11 213,973 students attended universities or equivalent third-level institutions, while teachers numbered 6,861. In 2011/12 UNRWA operated 99 schools in the West Bank and 245 in the Gaza Strip, providing education to 51,695 pupils in the West Bank and to 225,098 pupils in Gaza. Education personnel in that year numbered 3,134 in the West Bank and 9,444 in Gaza. In addition, UNRWA operated four vocational training centres (two in the West Bank and two in Gaza). In 2009/10 UNRWA budgeted some US $187.1m. for expenditure on education in the Palestinian territories.

PANAMA

Introductory Survey

LOCATION, CLIMATE, LANGUAGE, RELIGION, FLAG, CAPITAL

The Republic of Panama is a narrow country situated at the southern end of the isthmus separating North and South America. It is bounded to the west by Costa Rica and to the east by Colombia in South America. The Caribbean Sea is to the north, and the Pacific Ocean to the south. Panama has a tropical maritime climate (warm, humid days and cool nights). There is little seasonal variation in temperatures, which average 23°C–27°C (73°F–81°F) in coastal areas. The rainy season is from April until December. Spanish is the official language. Almost all of the inhabitants profess Christianity, and some 83% are Roman Catholics. The national flag (proportions 2 by 3) is composed of four equal rectangles: on the top row the quarter at the hoist is white, with a five-pointed blue star in the centre, while the quarter in the fly is red; on the bottom row the quarter at the hoist is blue, and the quarter in the fly is white, with a five-pointed red star in the centre. The capital is Panamá (Panama City).

CONTEMPORARY POLITICAL HISTORY

Historical Context

Panama was subject to Spanish rule from the 16th century until 1821, when it became independent as part of Gran Colombia. Panama remained part of Colombia until 1903, when it declared its separate independence with the support of the USA. In that year the USA purchased the concession for construction of the Panama Canal, which was opened in 1914. The 82-km Canal links the Atlantic and Pacific Oceans, and is a major international sea route. Under the terms of the 1903 treaty between Panama and the USA concerning the construction and administration of the Canal, the USA was granted ('in perpetuity') control of a strip of Panamanian territory, called the Canal Zone, extending for 8 km on either side of the Canal route. The treaty also established Panama as a protectorate of the USA. In exchange for transferring the Canal Zone, Panama was to receive an annuity from the USA.

In 1939 a revised treaty with the USA ended Panama's protectorate status. A new Constitution for Panama was adopted in 1946. Following a period of rapidly changing governments, the 1952 presidential election was won by Col José Antonio Remón. President Remón negotiated a more favourable treaty with the USA, whereby the annuity payable to Panama was increased. In January 1955, however, before the treaty came into force, Remón was assassinated. He was succeeded by José Ramón Guizado, hitherto the First Vice-President, but, less than two weeks after assuming power, the new President was implicated in the plot to assassinate Remón. Guizado was removed from office and later imprisoned. Remón's Second Vice-President, Ricardo Arias Espinosa, completed the presidential term, which expired in 1956, when Ernesto de la Guardia was elected President. The next presidential election was won by Roberto Chiari, who held office in 1960–64, and his successor was Marco Aurelio Robles (1964–68). During this period there were frequent public demands for the transfer to Panama of sovereignty over the Canal Zone.

The presidential election of 1968 was won by Dr Arnulfo Arias Madrid, the candidate supported by the coalition Unión Nacional (which included his own Partido Panameñista). Dr Arias had been President in 1940–41 and 1949–51, but both terms had ended in his forcible removal from power. He took office for a third term in October 1968 but, after only 11 days, he was deposed by the National Guard, led by Col (later Brig.-Gen.) Omar Torrijos Herrera, who accused him of planning to establish a dictatorship. The Asamblea Nacional (National Assembly) was dissolved, and political activity suspended. Political parties were banned in 1969.

Domestic Political Affairs

In 1972 elections were held to a new legislative body, the 505-member Asamblea Nacional de Corregidores (National Assembly of Community Representatives). The Asamblea conferred extraordinary powers on Gen. Torrijos as Chief of Government for six years.

In 1974 representatives of Panama and the USA concluded an agreement on principles for a new treaty whereby the USA would surrender its jurisdiction over the Canal Zone. Intensified talks in 1977 resulted in two new Canal treaties, which were approved by referendum and became effective from October 1979. Panama assumed control of the former Canal Zone, which was abolished. Administration of the Canal was placed under the control of a joint Panama Canal Commission until the end of 1999. US military forces in Panama were to remain until 2000, and the USA was to be entitled to defend the Canal's neutrality thereafter.

In 1978 elections were held to the Asamblea Nacional de Corregidores; the new representatives elected Dr Arístides Royo Sánchez to be President for a six-year term. Gen. Torrijos resigned as Chief of Government, but continued in the post of Commander of the National Guard, and effectively retained power until his death in 1981. President Royo failed to gain the support of the National Guard, and in July 1982 he was forced to resign by Col Rubén Darío Paredes, who had ousted Col Florencio Flores as Commander-in-Chief in March. The Vice-President, Ricardo de la Espriella, was installed as President, and, under the direction of Col Paredes, promoted business interests and pursued a foreign policy more favourable to the USA.

In April 1983 a series of amendments to the Constitution were approved by referendum. However, de facto power remained with the armed forces, whose position was strengthened by a decision in September to unite all security forces within one organization (subsequently known as the National Defence Forces). In June Paredes was succeeded as Commander-in-Chief by Brig. (later Gen.) Manuel Antonio Noriega Morena. In February 1984 Dr Jorge Illueca, hitherto the Vice-President, became Head of State after the sudden resignation of President de la Espriella, who was believed to have been ousted from power by the National Defence Forces.

Elections to the presidency and the legislature (the new 67-member Asamblea Legislativa—Legislative Assembly) took place in 1984. Dr Nicolás Ardito Barletta, the candidate of the Partido Revolucionario Democrático (PRD), narrowly defeated Arias Madrid, representing the Partido Panameñista Auténtico (PPA). However, Ardito was unable to secure a political base to support his administration, and in September 1985 he resigned. There was considerable speculation that Ardito had been forced to resign by Gen. Noriega, to prevent a public scandal over the alleged involvement of the National Defence Forces in the murder of Dr Hugo Spadafora, a leading critic of Noriega. Ardito was succeeded as President in September by Eric Arturo Delvalle, formerly First Vice-President.

In 1986 US sources alleged that Noriega was involved in the trafficking of illegal drugs and weapons and in the transfer of proceeds from these activities through Panamanian banks. In addition, Noriega was implicated in the sale of US national security information and restricted technology to Cuba. There were also renewed allegations of his involvement in the murder of Dr Spadafora and in electoral fraud. Demonstrations in support of demands for Noriega's dismissal resulted in violent clashes with the National Defence Forces. The US Senate approved a resolution urging the establishment of democracy in Panama, the suspension of Noriega and the holding of an independent investigation into the allegations against him. The Government responded by accusing the USA of interfering in Panamanian affairs, and a wave of anti-US sentiment was unleashed, including an attack on the US embassy building. The USA subsequently suspended economic and military aid to Panama and downgraded its official links with the country.

In February 1988 Noriega was indicted in the USA on charges of drugs-smuggling and racketeering. President Delvalle subsequently dismissed Noriega from his post. However, leading members of the ruling coalition and the National Defence Forces united in support of their Commander-in-Chief, and on the following day the Asamblea Legislativa voted to remove President Delvalle from office. The Minister of Education, Manuel Solís Palma, was appointed acting President. Delvalle refused to accept his dismissal, and the US Administration declined to recognize the new leadership. At the end of the month, following Delvalle's demand that the US Government impose an economic boycott on Panama, US courts authorized a 'freeze' on Panamanian assets held in US banks. This move, coupled with a general strike, brought economic chaos to Panama.

Presidential and legislative elections were held in May 1989. The presidential candidate of the pro-Government electoral alliance, the Coalición de Liberación Nacional (COLINA), was Carlos Duque Jaén, the leader of the PRD and a close associate of Noriega. Guillermo Endara Galimany of the PPA was the candidate of the opposition Alianza Democrática de Oposición Civilista (ADOC). The election campaign was dominated by accusations of electoral malpractice, and, following the voting, both ADOC and COLINA claimed victory, despite indications from exit polls and unofficial sources that ADOC had received between 50% and 75% of votes cast. A group of international observers declared that the election had been conducted fraudulently. Endara declared himself President-elect. On 10 May the election results were annulled by the Electoral Tribunal, which cited US interference.

On 31 August 1989, following intervention by the Organization of American States (OAS, see p. 404), Panama's General State Council announced the appointment of a provisional Government and a 41-member Legislative Commission to preserve 'institutional order'. The holding of elections was to be considered within six months, but this was to be largely dependent upon the cessation of US 'hostilities' and the withdrawal of US economic sanctions. On 1 September Francisco Rodríguez, a known associate of Noriega, was inaugurated as President. The USA immediately severed diplomatic relations with Panama. In October an attempted coup was suppressed by forces loyal to Noriega.

US invasion and removal of Noriega

In November 1989 the Asamblea Nacional de Corregidores was provisionally restored. This body, now numbering 510 members, was intended to fulfil a consultative and (limited) legislative function. Noriega was elected as its 'national co-ordinator'. In December the Asamblea adopted a resolution declaring Noriega to be Head of Government, and announced that a state of war existed with the USA. On 20 December a US military offensive (Operation Just Cause), involving some 24,000 troops, was launched against Noriega and the headquarters of the National Defence Forces from US bases within Panama. The objects of the assault were swiftly brought under US control, although Noriega eluded capture long enough to take refuge in the residence of the Papal Nuncio in Panama. On 21 December Endara was officially inaugurated as President. He declared that the Panamanian judicial system was inadequate to try Noriega. Following his surrender to US forces in January 1990, Noriega was immediately transported to the USA and arraigned on several charges of involvement in drugs-trafficking and money-laundering operations. In 1992 Noriega was sentenced to 40 years' imprisonment (reduced to 30 years in 1999).

Following the appointment of a new Cabinet in December 1989, the Endara administration declared itself to be a 'democratic Government of reconstruction and national reconciliation'. Shortly afterwards the Electoral Tribunal revoked its annulment of the May elections and announced that ADOC had obtained 62% of the votes cast in the presidential election. In February 1990 the composition of the Asamblea Legislativa was announced. The National Defence Forces were officially disbanded, and a new, 'non-political' Public Force was created. In April the USA revoked the economic restrictions that had been imposed two years previously, and in May Congress approved financial assistance to Panama totalling $420m.

Long-standing political differences within the Government reached a crisis in March 1991 when one of the parties in the ruling coalition, the Partido Demócrata Cristiano (PDC), initiated proceedings to impeach Endara for involving the US armed forces in suppressing an uprising in December 1990. Although the proposal was rejected by the Asamblea Legislativa, Endara dismissed the five PDC members of his Cabinet. Two further alleged coup attempts were suppressed in October 1991 and February 1992. In November the President suffered a serious reverse, when proposals for more than 50 reforms (including the constitutional abolition of the armed forces) were rejected by 64% of voters in a referendum.

Noriega was, following a trial in 1993, found guilty of ordering the assassination of Dr Spadafora and sentenced to 20 years' imprisonment *in absentia*. Further convictions followed in 1994 and 2001. Noriega completed his prison sentence in the USA in 2007, having served 17 years, but remained in detention pending the outcome of an extradition request from France. In April 2010 he was extradited to France, and following a retrial, in July a French court sentenced Noriega to seven years' imprisonment and ordered the seizure of €2.3m. of his assets. In November 2011, however, a French appeals court approved the extradition of Noriega to Panama, in response to a request from the Panamanian Government. (The consent of the US authorities had also been required under the terms of the agreement allowing Noriega's extradition to France, as he had not yet served his full sentence there.) On his return to Panama in December, Noriega was immediately imprisoned to serve three concurrent 20-year terms, for the murder of Spadafora and other political opponents. Despite the penal code allowing convicts aged over 70 to serve sentences under house arrest, the 78-year-old Noriega remained in prison in March 2013.

Presidents Pérez Balladares and Moscoso, 1994–2004

At a presidential election held in May 1994, Ernesto Pérez Balladares, the candidate of the Pueblo Unido alliance (that included the PRD), won a narrow victory over Mireya Moscoso de Gruber (the widow of former President Arias Madrid). Moscoso was the nominee of the Alianza Democrática, comprising the Partido Arnulfista (PA, formerly a faction of the PPA), the Partido Liberal (PL), the Partido Liberal Auténtico (PLA), the Unión Democrática Independiente and the Partido Nacionalista Popular (PNP). Post-electoral political manoeuvring resulted in the creation of the Alianza Pueblo Unido y Solidaridad, Pérez Balladares' electoral alliance having secured the additional support of the Partido Solidaridad in the Asamblea. Pérez Balladares assumed the presidency on 1 September 1994. A new Cabinet included former members of the PA and the PDC who had resigned their party membership in order to take up their posts.

At a presidential election conducted in May 1999, Mireya Moscoso de Gruber, this time the candidate of the Unión por Panamá alliance (comprising the PA, Movimiento Liberal Republicano Nacionalista—MOLIRENA, Movimiento de Renovación Nacional and Cambio Democrático), was elected, ahead of Martín Torrijos Espino, son of former dictator Omar Torrijos, the candidate of the Nueva Nación alliance (comprising the PRD, the Partido Solidaridad, the Partido Liberal Nacional—PLN—and the Movimiento Papa Egoró—MPE). However, the Unión por Panamá failed to secure a majority in the concurrent legislative election. Moscoso assumed the presidency on 1 September. The new administration included members of the Partido Solidaridad, the PLN, the PDC and the Partido Renovación Civilista (PRC), each of which had abandoned their respective electoral alliances in order to form a 'Government of national unity', thereby giving Moscoso a narrow majority in the legislature. However, in August of the following year the governing coalition lost its majority after the PRD and the PDC formed an alliance.

On 31 December 1999 the USA officially relinquished ownership of the Canal to Panama.

Following the discovery of human remains in a former military barracks in Tocumen, in 2000 President Moscoso announced the establishment of a Truth Commission to investigate 'disappearances' during the military dictatorships of 1968–89. In March 2004 the Asamblea approved the establishment of a Special Prosecutor's Office to investigate crimes committed during the military dictatorships.

Presidential and legislative elections took place in May 2004. Martín Torrijos Espino, the candidate of the PRD (which contested the elections as part of the Patria Nueva electoral alliance with the Partido Popular), won the presidential ballot, with 47% of the votes cast. Former President Endara, representing the Partido Solidaridad, came second with 31% of the ballot. The Patria Nueva also performed well in the concurrently held elections to the enlarged, 78-seat Asamblea Legislativa, securing a total of 43 seats, 42 of which were won by the PRD.

The presidency of Martín Torrijos, 2004–09

Even before he assumed the presidency on 1 September 2004, Torrijos was successful in bringing about several constitutional amendments. In July his proposed reform of the Asamblea Legislativa received legislative approval. The number of seats in the legislature—which was to be renamed the Asamblea Nacional (National Assembly)—was to be reduced to 71 (from 78) from 2009. Furthermore, parliamentary immunity from prosecution was abolished and the authority to ratify constitutional amendments transferred from the legislature to a constituent assembly.

In October 2004 some 5,000 people participated in a protest march organized by the Frente Nacional por la Defensa de la Seguridad Social (FRENADESSO), the social organization established to resist privatization of the social security fund, the Caja de Seguro Social (CSS). The new Government denied intentions fully to privatize the CSS, but emphasized the need for reform in light of the institution's estimated deficit of between US $2,500m. and $3,000m. Proposed social security reforms included an increase in the retirement age, a reduction in retirement benefits and the transfer of some pensions into private funds. Despite further protests, the pension reforms received legislative approval in June 2005, although they included a number of concessions. None the less, industrial unrest continued. A revised series of measures was voted into law in December.

In April 2006 the Autoridad del Canal de Panamá (ACP) announced plans to expand the Canal's capacity to allow the passage of larger commercial container vessels, by constructing a third set of locks at either end of the waterway. The projected cost of US $5,250m. of the project was to be funded by toll revenues and loans totalling an estimated $2,270m. While widely considered to be vital to the future of the Canal, concerns were raised relating to the environmental consequences of the expansion and the possible relocation of farmers in communities bordering the Canal. The ACP's plan was none the less overwhelmingly approved by the Asamblea Nacional in July and by 78% of voters in a referendum conducted in October (although participation was just 43% of the electorate). It was anticipated that the expansion, which would not disrupt normal operations, would be completed in October 2014.

The Asamblea Nacional approved legislation aimed at improving internal security in May 2008. The Government claimed the new law introduced a more uncompromising stance against crime, increasing maximum prison sentences, and recognizing 37 new offences. In the following month the legislature granted Torrijos temporary powers to introduce security reforms by decree. The reforms included the creation of a single national intelligence and security service, a proposal that met with widespread opposition owing to fears that the agency would wield excessive power. FRENADESO (Frente Nacional por la Defensa de los Derechos Económicos y Sociales, as FRENADESSO had been restyled) mobilized over 15,000 people in marches in the capital and other cities in August to protest against both the decree and rising living costs, and a national strike followed on 5 September.

Martinelli in power

The presidential election, which was held on 3 May 2009, was won decisively by Ricardo Martinelli Berrocal, the owner of a large chain of supermarkets, on behalf of the Alianza por el Cambio, comprising his own Cambio Democrático party, the Partido Panameñista (PP, as the PA had been renamed in 2005), MOLIRENA and the Unión Patriótica (UP), which had been formed by the merger of the PLN and the Partido Solidaridad. Martinelli, whose campaign had concentrated on crime and poverty reduction, secured 60.0% of the valid votes cast, while Balbina del Carmen Herrera Araúz, representing the PRD-led Un País para Todos alliance, obtained 37.7%; former President Endara, of the Vanguardia Moral de la Patria, took just 2.3%. A turn-out of 74.0% was recorded. The Alianza por el Cambio also won an overall majority in the Asamblea Nacional. Martinelli appointed his Vice-President-elect, Juan Carlos Varela Rodríguez, as Minister of Foreign Affairs and Alberto Vallarino Clement, also of the PP, as Minister of the Economy and Finance. The President of the UP, José Raúl Mulino, was allocated the interior and justice portfolio.

The new President acted swiftly to initiate the implementation of several of the pledges he made during his electoral campaign: a salary increase of US $100 per month for police officers; monthly payments, also of $100, for those aged over 70 without pensions; and the creation of a government agency to supervise the construction of a metro system in Panama City. Martinelli's administration also sought to demonstrate its commitment to addressing government corruption. A judicial investigation into bribery allegations by the Moscoso Government was reopened in July 2009, and two former PRD Ministers of Education in the Torrijos Government, Belgis Castro and Salvador Rodríguez, were arrested on charges of embezzlement in September and December. In January 2010, moreover, former President Pérez Balladares was placed under house arrest after being charged with money-laundering. (He was acquitted of this charge in April 2011 in a ruling that was upheld on appeal in January 2012.) However, Martinelli's appointment of two close allies to fill vacant positions in the Supreme Court of Justice in December 2009 provoked criticism, as did his suspected involvement in the following month in the Court's decision to suspend the PRD-appointed Ana Matilde Gómez from the post of Procurator-General pending an investigation into her alleged abuse of office (on the grounds that she had failed to seek the Court's approval before authorizing the interception of conversations involving a prosecutor being investigated for corruption). Gómez was dismissed in August, after being convicted of abuse of office by the Supreme Court, but claimed that the verdict was politically motivated. Her replacement, Guiseppe Bonissi, resigned in December, amid allegations that his office had been infiltrated by organized criminals, following the release from custody in November of four suspected drugs-traffickers.

Considerable controversy was provoked in June 2010 by the approval of legislation that reformed regulations affecting a wide range of areas, including civil aviation, the environment, the police and the labour code. Most contentious were the amendments to the labour code—which notably permitted the suspension of the contracts of striking workers—and the abolishment of the requirement for environmental impact studies to be conducted into projects declared to be 'in the social interest'. The labour reforms were suspended for 90 days in July, after three people were killed and more than 100 injured in violent clashes between protesters and the police in the province of Bocas del Toro. Following discussions with trade unions, President Martinelli agreed to repeal the law entirely in October, although the Government intended to propose separate bills addressing each of the various areas individually. New legislation covering labour rights and environmental protection adopted later that month omitted the controversial elements of the previous law. In March 2011 President Martinelli was forced to revoke another controversial law, adopted the previous month, which would have allowed investment by foreign governments in the mining sector, following widespread protests by environmentalists and civil society groups, as well as by indigenous communities fearing the development of mineral reserves within their territories.

In January 2011 the constitutional committee of the Asamblea Nacional rejected a bill proposed to amend the Constitution to permit the President to seek a second consecutive term in office. President Martinelli none the less announced his intention to seek the approval of other constitutional reforms, including a reduction in the number of years that a former President was required to wait before contesting the presidency again from 10 to five, and in April a committee of legal experts was formally established to consider possible constitutional changes. Italo Antinori, who had initially been appointed to head the committee, had notably stood down from this position the previous month, after being accused of leading a group of senior officials who had allegedly orchestrated Gómez's removal as Procurator-General in 2010. In April 2011 José Abel Almengor, one of the two judges appointed by Martinelli to the Supreme Court of Justice in December 2009, also resigned his post in connection with the alleged plot against Gómez. Civil society groups criticized the President's nomination of Harry Díaz González as Almengor's replacement, claiming that, as Díaz had acted as deputy finance minister in Martinelli's administration, it violated a constitutional provision prohibiting those who had held executive positions during the current constitutional period from being appointed as magistrates in the Supreme Court.

Relations between Cambio Democrático and its principal coalition partner, the PP, which had become strained over the abandoned proposal to allow consecutive presidential re-election, deteriorated further in May 2011, owing to disagreement regarding Cambio Democrático's desire to introduce a second round in presidential elections if no candidate managed to secure a majority in the first round. Cambio Democrático's position in the legislature had been strengthened since the May 2009 elections by defections from other parties (mainly the PRD) and the absorption of the UP in March 2011, increasing its representation from 14 seats to 29 seats, compared with the PP's 20 seats. Further signs of the disintegration of the alliance between the two parties were apparent in June and July: first, José Muñoz Molina, the President of the Asamblea Nacional, stated that his party, Cambio Democrático, had commenced the process of selecting a candidate for the 2014 presidential election (despite an expectation that the PP would provide the ruling coalition's candidate, having supported Martinelli's candidacy in the 2009 election), while the election of Héctor Aparicio, also of Cambio Democrático, to succeed Muñoz as President of the

Asamblea in July contravened an agreement between the two parties to alternate the office. However, Cambio Democrático suffered a minor set-back in August, when the Electoral Tribunal rejected the integration of MOLIRENA into the party, on the grounds that the vote that MOLIRENA had held on the merger in July had not been conducted, as required, by secret ballot.

The rupture of Cambio Democrático's coalition with the PP was confirmed at the end of August 2011, when Martinelli dismissed Vice-President Varela as Minister of Foreign Affairs, accusing him of neglecting his ministerial duties in favouring of pursuing his aspiration to secure election to the presidency in 2014. Despite remaining Vice-President, Varela announced that he intended to fulfil the role of leader of the opposition henceforth, and his dismissal prompted the resignations of the other PP ministers from the Government. As part of the ensuing cabinet reorganization, Varela was replaced at the Ministry of Foreign Affairs by Roberto Henríquez, the Vice-President of Cambio Democrático and hitherto Minister of Commerce and Industry, who was himself succeeded by Ricardo Quijano, while José Domingo Arias was appointed as Minister of Housing, in place of the PP's Carlos Dubois. Martinelli initially refused to accept the resignation of the Minister of the Economy and Finance, Vallarino, under whose tenure Panama had recorded high rates of economic growth, but in October Frank de Lima, Vallarino's erstwhile deputy, was promoted to the post. Meanwhile, the Cambio Democrático secured a working majority of 36 of the legislature's 71 seats, when several PP deputies transferred their allegiance to the party.

The return of Noriega to Panama in December 2011, to serve prison terms for the murder of political opponents (see US invasion and removal of Noriega), prompted renewed interest in human rights violations committed during the military dictatorships of 1968–89, and in January 2012 the Government announced that the Truth Commission that had been established under the Moscoso administration would be reactivated to identify victims of abuses perpetrated during that period.

Roxana Méndez, the Minister of the Interior, became Mayor of Panama City in January 2012, following the resignation of Bosco Ricardo Vallarino of the PP, officially on health grounds, although members of the PP and the PRD claimed that he had been pressured to resign by the President. Méndez, who had been Deputy Mayor of the capital prior to her appointment to the Government (see above), was replaced as Minister of the Interior by Jorge Ricardo Fábrega Sosa, hitherto Director-General of the Autoridad de Tránsito y Transporte Terrestre.

Recent developments: reform agenda frustrated

In January 2012 the committee established some nine months earlier to consider changes to the Constitution submitted its conclusions to the President. Proposed reforms included the creation of a constitutional court, the prohibition of consecutive re-election for deputies, and the expansion of the Supreme Court of Justice from nine members to 12. Notably omitted from the draft legislation were the controversial revisions previously mooted by either the Cambio Democrático or President Martinelli regarding consecutive presidential re-election, a reduction in the number of years that a former President was required to wait before contesting the presidency again and the introduction of a second round in the presidential ballot.

Indigenous groups from the Ngöbe-Buglé *comarca* (a region under the administrative control of the indigenous population) commenced a blockade of part of the Pan-American Highway, linking Panama to the rest of Central America, in late January 2012 in protest against draft mining legislation that omitted previous provisions on the protection of natural resources in Ngöbe-Buglé. As unrest spread to other areas of the country, two people were killed and more than 40 injured in clashes with the police. The protests were halted in early February when the Government agreed to the reconsideration of the mining bill by the Asamblea Nacional. Following further negotiations between the indigenous groups and the Government, an agreement concluded in March provided for the cancellation of all mining concessions in the Ngöbe-Buglé *comarca* and the establishment of a special framework for the protection of natural resources in the region. Moreover, construction of the Barro Blanco hydroelectric project in the *comarca* was temporarily suspended until an environmental impact assessment could be carried out, and any future applications for hydroelectric dams in the area would require the approval of the Ngöbe-Buglé authorities.

President Martinelli's popularity fell further in April 2012 following the arrest in Italy of Valter Lavitola, a close ally of former Italian Prime Minister Silvio Berlusconi on fraud charges. Allegations emerged that Martinelli had accepted bribes from Lavitola in exchange for the awarding of contracts to Italian construction companies to build prisons in Panama. Vice-President Varela revealed that, during his tenure as Minister of Foreign Affairs, Martinelli had asked him on three separate occasions to appoint Lavitola honorary consul in Rome. The President denied the accusations, and countered that Varela was using his position as Vice-President to further his presidential ambitions. In early May the rupture between the head of state and his deputy deepened after Martinelli brought a civil suit against Varela, claiming damages of US $30m. for slander.

In June 2012 the PP, the Partido Revolucionario Democrático (PRD) and the Partido Popular formed an opposition alliance, the Frente por la Democracia, to contest the 2014 elections. The announcement by the three parties, traditionally rival groupings, came in response to President Martinelli's appointment of three judges to the proposed new constitutional court. The Frente accused the President of behaving undemocratically, as the creation of the court had not yet been ratified by the legislature. In addition, it opposed the Government's proposal to sell one-half of its 49% share in the telecommunications company Cable & Wireless Panama, claiming it was a ruse by the CD administration to raise money before the 2014 elections. Opposition protests in the capital against the plans descended into violence and led to 47 arrests, and a congressional session on 19 June was suspended after fighting broke out between deputies. Martinelli bowed to pressure on the following day and withdrew both proposals.

Nevertheless, in September 2012 the CD and MOLIRENA succeeded in gaining legislative approval for a series of electoral reforms in advance of the 2014 elections. Included in the changes were the ending of the proportional representation system under which 45 deputies were elected to the 71-seat Asamblea, the permitting of independent candidates to run for office, limiting the official electoral campaign to six months, and a stipulation that women comprise at least 50% of candidates in internal party ballots. The opposition claimed the reforms did nothing to strengthen the democratic process, citing the absence of a tightening of rules on electoral financing. The Tribunal Electoral also criticized the measures, asserting, *inter alia*, that a reform allowing candidates to contest more than one post at the same time threatened the separation of powers.

The Government's privatization agenda suffered a further setback in late October 2012 after President Martinelli was forced to repeal a law, approved nine days earlier, allowing the sale of land within the Colón Free Zone. Passage of the bill in the CD-controlled legislature had prompted widespread popular protests in Colón that resulted in the deaths of three people, including a nine-year-old boy. The Government claimed that sale of the land would fund regeneration of the region and that 35% of any profits would be reinvested in the Colón area; however opposition groupings countered that it was another attempt to improve government finances in advance of the 2014 elections. Trade unions announced a 24-hour general strike and indigenous groups in Ngöbe-Buglé recommenced a blockade of the Pan-American Highway in protest at the proposed sell-off.

Juan Carlos Navarro, a former Mayor of Panama City and the PRD Secretary-General, was chosen to be that party's presidential candidate in the May 2014 elections following a primary election in early March 2013. Later the same month Vice-President Varela was confirmed as the PP's nominee. The CD was scheduled to hold its primary election in May: President Martinelli was constitutionally barred from standing for re-election. In late February the Minister of Foreign Affairs, Rómulo Roux, had resigned his post in order to seek the party's nomination; he was replaced by Fernando Núñez Fábrega. Meanwhile, FRENADESO was seeking to secure the adherence of the 63,500 members required to achieve registration as a political party, the Frente Amplio por la Democracia, in order to contest the 2014 polls.

Foreign Affairs

In 1997, in the light of the increasing number of incursions by Colombian guerrillas and paramilitary groups into Panamanian territory, the Government deployed security forces to Darién Province to secure the border with Colombia. Following bilateral discussions, an agreement on improved co-operation concerning border security was reached. In 1999, following further incursions by Colombian guerrillas into Darién Province, Panama and Colombia agreed further to strengthen military patrols on both sides of the countries' joint border. Negotiations towards a bilateral free trade agreement commenced in March 2010, although they were suspended in October, reportedly by the Panamanian Government. In 2012, none the less, following a meeting with his Colombian counterpart, Panama's Minister of Commerce and Industry, Ricardo Quijano, announced the resumption of negotiations on the proposed free trade accord; a sixth round of talks was under way in March 2013.

In 1993 President Endara signed a protocol to establish Panama's membership of the Central American Parliament (Parlacen), a regional political forum with its headquarters in Guatemala. Endara, together with the five Presidents of the member nations of the Central American Common Market (CACM, see p. 237), also signed a protocol to the 1960 General Treaty on Central American Integration, committing Panama to fuller economic integration in the region. However, in 1994 Pérez Balladares stated that his administration considered further regional economic integration to be disadvantageous to Panama, owing to the differences between Panama's services-based economy and the reliance on the agricultural sector of the other Central American states. A free trade agreement with El Salvador entered into force in 2003, and similar accords with Costa Rica, Honduras, Guatemala and Nicaragua took effect in 2008 and 2009. In late 2009 Panama unilaterally withdrew from Parlacen, fulfilling a pre-election pledge made by President Martinelli. In October 2010 the Central American Court of Justice ruled that Panama's departure from Parlacen required the approval of the remaining Parlacen members, but the Government rejected the Court's verdict. However, in January 2013 the legislature voted to rejoin the regional grouping in acknowledgement of a supreme court ruling in the previous year that Panama's departure from Parlacen had been unconstitutional.

Although Panama was excluded from the negotiations towards a Dominican Republic-Central American Free Trade Agreement with the USA, a bilateral free trade agreement with the USA was signed and ratified by the Asamblea Nacional in 2007. However, the accord was not ratified by the US legislature until October 2011, owing to US concerns over Panama's tax regime; the agreement entered into force on 31 October 2012. In 2009 the Organisation for Economic Co-operation and Development (OECD) included Panama on its so-called 'grey list' of territories that had committed to improving financial transparency, but had yet substantially to implement reform. The Martinelli administration finally secured the 12 bilateral tax information agreements necessary to secure its removal from the 'grey list' in 2011, including one with the USA. This milestone, confirmed by OECD in July, was crucial in gaining US congressional approval for the trade promotion agreement in October. Panama's ambassador to the USA, Jaime Alemán, resigned in December 2010, after the publication of a US diplomatic cable by WikiLeaks, an organization publishing leaked private and classified content, that questioned the propriety of the awarding, in July 2009, of the contract for the construction of new locks for the Panama Canal to a Spanish-led consortium, to which Alemán had apparently provided legal representation. Meanwhile, in May 2010 negotiations were concluded on an association agreement between Central American countries, including Panama, and the European Union (see p. 281), while the Panamanian Government also signed a free trade agreement with Canada.

CONSTITUTION AND GOVERNMENT

Under the terms of the 1972 Constitution, legislative power is vested in the unicameral Asamblea Nacional (National Assembly), with a total of 71 members elected for five years by universal adult suffrage. Executive power is held by the President, also directly elected for a term of five years, assisted by two elected Vice-Presidents and an appointed Cabinet. Panama is divided into nine provinces and three autonomous Indian Reservations. Each province has a governor, appointed by the President.

REGIONAL AND INTERNATIONAL CO-OPERATION

Panama is a member of the Central American Integration System (see p. 237), the Inter-American Development Bank (see p. 341) and the Organization of American States (see p. 404), and of the Community of Latin American and Caribbean States (see p. 475), which was formally inaugurated in December 2011. The country has observer status within the Andean Community of Nations (see p. 199). Panama was a founder member of the UN in 1945 and was admitted to the World Trade Organization (see p. 444) in 1997. Panama was party to a Central American association agreement concluded with the European Union (see p. 281) in 2010. Panama became the 13th member of Latin

American Integration Association (see p. 370) in February 2012 and also joined the Central American Integration System (see p. 237) in July of that year.

ECONOMIC AFFAIRS

In 2011, according to estimates by the World Bank, Panama's gross national income (GNI), measured at average 2009–11 prices, was US $28,258m., equivalent to $7,910 per head (or $14,740 on an international purchasing-power parity basis). During 2002–11, it was estimated, the population increased at an average annual rate of 1.7%, while gross domestic product (GDP) per head increased, in real terms, by an average of 6.1% per year. Overall GDP increased, in real terms, at an average annual rate of 7.9% in 2002–11; according to official estimates, growth was 10.8% in 2011.

Agriculture (including hunting, forestry and fishing) contributed an estimated 4.0% of GDP (measured at constant prices) in 2011. The sector engaged some 16.7% of the employed labour force in 2012. Rice, maize and beans are cultivated as subsistence crops, while the principal cash crops are bananas (which accounted for an estimated 9.0% of total export earnings in 2010), sugar cane, melons and pineapples. Cattle-raising, tropical timber and fisheries (particularly shrimps and yellowfin tuna for export) are also important. Fish exports were increasingly important. In 2010 exports of yellowfin tuna and fish fillet accounted for an estimated 19.1% of export revenue. According to official figures, agricultural GDP increased by an average of 0.2% annually during 2002–11; the sector decreased by an estimated 14.2% in 2010 and by an estimated 0.6% in 2011.

Industry (including mining, manufacturing, construction and power) contributed an estimated 16.6% of GDP (measured at constant prices) in 2011. The sector engaged 18.2% of the employed labour force in 2012. According to official figures, industrial GDP increased at an average annual rate of 7.8% during 2002–11; the sector's GDP increased by an estimated 11.3% in 2011.

Mining contributed an estimated 1.6% of GDP (measured at constant prices) in 2011 and engaged 0.2% of the employed labour force in 2012. Panama has significant deposits of copper and coal. The GDP of the mining sector increased by an estimated average of 16.5% per year in 2002–11; the sector expanded by an estimated 7.3% in 2010 and by a further 21.6% in 2011.

Manufacturing contributed an estimated 5.5% of GDP (measured at constant prices) in 2011. The sector engaged an estimated 6.9% of the employed labour force in 2012. The most important sectors were refined petroleum products, food-processing, beverages, and cement, lime and plaster. Manufacturing GDP increased by an average of 2.2% annually during 2002–11; the sector increased by an estimated 3.2% in 2011.

The construction sector contributed an estimated 6.7% of GDP (measured at constant prices) in 2011 and engaged some 10.3% of the employed labour force in 2012. The GDP of the mining sector increased by an average annual rate of 16.1% in 2002–11; the sector increased by an estimated 7.0% in 2010 and by a further 18.9% in 2011.

The country's topography and climate make it ideal for hydro-electric power, and in 2009 approximately 56.1% of Panama's total output of electricity was water-generated. A hydroelectric project, under construction from 2011, on the Tabasará river in the Ngäbe-Buglé *comarca* (see Domestic Political Affairs) was expected to provide 28.8 MW of energy upon completion. Petroleum accounted for most of the remainder (43.6%) of the country's generating capacity. In 2010 imports of mineral products accounted for 19.3% of the value of merchandise imports.

Panama's economy is dependent upon the services sector, which contributed an estimated 79.4% of GDP (measured at constant prices) in 2011. The sector engaged 65.1% of the employed labour force in 2012. Panama is an important 'offshore' financial centre, and important contributions to the economy are also made by trade in the Colón Free Zone (CFZ—in which some 2,500 companies were situated in 2012), and by the registration of merchant ships under a 'flag of convenience' in Panama. The tourism sector was also an increasingly significant economic contributor: in 2011 tourism receipts totalled a provisional US $1,926m., compared with $1,676m. in the previous year. According to official figures, the GDP of the services sector increased by an average of 8.4% per year in 2002–11; the sector grew by an estimated 10.7% in 2011.

In 2011 Panama recorded a visible merchandise trade deficit of US $6,015.8m., and there was a deficit of $3,873.6m. on the current account of the balance of payments. According to preliminary figures, in 2011 the principal source of imports (24.9%) was the USA, which was also the principal market for exports (20.8%). Other major trading partners are Canada, Sweden, Costa Rica and the People's Republic of China. The principal exports in 2010 were fresh and frozen fish and fillets, bananas and melons. The principal imports in that year were machinery and apparatus, mineral products, food and live animals, transport material, chemicals, and metals and metal manufactures.

In 2011 there was an estimated overall budgetary surplus of 688.6m. balboas, equivalent to 2.2% of GDP. Panama's general government gross debt was 11,563m. balboas in 2011, equivalent to 37.8% of GDP. Panama's external debt at the end of 2010 was US $11,412m., of which $10,421m. was public and publicly guaranteed debt. In that year, the cost of debt-servicing long-term public and publicly guaranteed debt and repayments to the IMF was equivalent to 5.7% of the value of exports of goods, services and income (excluding workers' remittances). Annual inflation averaged 3.8% in 2003–11; consumer prices increased by 5.9% in 2011. Some 4.0% of the labour force were unemployed in August 2012.

The Panama Canal provided the Government with a considerable source of funds. Expansion of the Canal at a cost of US $5,250m. was scheduled for completion in late 2014. The project was expected to increase GDP growth by 1%–2% per year until 2025 and in May 2012 the Government created a sovereign wealth fund to save the additional revenue generated by the expanded Canal. Meanwhile, in 2011 the Government announced the discovery of some 900m. barrels of crude petroleum reserves in Panamanian territory, estimating that this could provide $15,000m. of revenue in royalties and taxes over a 20-year period, while the enactment of a free trade agreement

with the USA in October 2012 was also expected to boost growth and investment in the medium and long term. Strong growth since the Government of President Ricardo Martinelli took office in 2009 was driven by a large rise in investment, linked to the expansion of the Canal, as well as infrastructure projects, including the construction of a metro system in Panama City and the development of the main international airport. Panama enjoyed the largest growth rate (10.8%) in Latin America in 2012, and the economy was forecast to expand by a further 8.5% in 2012. However, at the same time there were concerns about the rise in public debt levels, which reached 13,800m. balboas in June 2012, compared with 10,421m. balboas in 2010. Critics also highlighted the high levels of government spending in advance of the 2014 elections. The IMF envisaged GDP growth of 7.5% in 2013.

PUBLIC HOLIDAYS

2014: 1 January (New Year's Day), 6 January (for National Martyrs' Day), 3–4 March (Carnival), 5 March (Ash Wednesday), 17 April (Maundy Thursday), 18 April (Good Friday), 1 May (Labour Day), 15 August (Foundation of Panama City, Panama City only)*, 11 October (Revolution Day), 1 November (National Anthem Day)*, 2 November (Day of the Dead), 3 November (Independence from Colombia), 4 November (Flag Day)*, 5 November (Independence Day, Colón only), 10 November (First Call for Independence), 1 December (for Independence from Spain), 8 December (Immaculate Conception, Mothers' Day), 25 December (Christmas).

* Official holiday: banks and government offices closed.

Statistical Survey

Sources (unless otherwise stated): Instituto Nacional de Estadística y Censo, Contraloría General de la República, Avda Balboa y Federico Boyd, Apdo 5213, Panamá 5; tel. 210-4800; fax 210-4801; e-mail cgrdec@contraloria.gob.pa; internet www.contraloria.gob.pa/inec; Ministry of the Economy and Finance, Edif. Ogawa, Vía España, Apdo 5245, Panamá 5; e-mail webmaster@mef.gob.pa; internet www.mef.gob.pa.

Area and Population

AREA, POPULATION AND DENSITY

Area (sq km)	75,517*
Population (census results)	
14 May 2000	2,839,177
16 May 2010	
Males	1,712,584
Females	1,693,229
Total	3,405,813
Population (official estimates at mid-year)	
2011	3,723,821
2012	3,787,511
2013	3,850,735
Density (per sq km) at mid-2013	51.0

* 29,157 sq miles.

POPULATION BY AGE AND SEX
(official population estimates at mid-2013)

	Males	Females	Total
0–14	552,863	530,110	1,082,973
15–64	1,250,586	1,238,004	2,488,590
65 and over	130,815	148,357	279,172
Total	1,934,264	1,916,471	3,850,735

ADMINISTRATIVE DIVISIONS
(population at 2010 census)

Province	Population	Capital (and population)*
Bocas del Toro	125,461	Bocas del Toro (16,135)
Chiriquí	416,873	David (144,858)
Coclé	233,708	Penonomé (85,737)
Colón	241,928	Colón (206,553)
Comarca Emberá . . .	10,001	—
Comarca Kuna Yala . .	33,109	—
Comarca Ngöbe-Buglé .	156,747	—
Darién	48,378	Chepigana (30,110)
Herrera	109,955	Chitré (50,684)
Los Santos	89,592	Las Tablas (27,146)
Panamá	1,713,070	Panamá (880,691)
Veraguas	226,991	Santiago (88,997)
Total	3,405,813	—

* Population of district in which capital is located.

PRINCIPAL TOWNS
(population at 2010 census)

Panamá (Panama City, capital) . .	430,299	Puerto Armuelles .	55,775
San Miguelito . .	315,019	Pacora	52,494
Santiago . .	88,997	Pedregal . . .	51,641
David . . .	82,907	Nuevo Arraiján .	41,041
Tocumen . .	74,952	Colón	34,655
La Chorrera . .	62,803	Changuinola .	31,223

Mid-2011 (incl. suburbs, UN estimate): Panama City 1,426,110 (Source: UN, *World Urbanization Prospects: The 2011 Revision*).

BIRTHS, MARRIAGES AND DEATHS

	Registered live births		Registered marriages*		Registered deaths	
	Number	Rate (per 1,000)†	Number	Rate (per 1,000)†	Number	Rate (per 1,000)†
2004 . .	62,743	19.8	10,290	3.2	13,475	4.2
2005 . .	63,645	19.7	10,512	3.3	14,180	4.4
2006 . .	65,764	20.0	10,747	3.3	14,358	4.4
2007 . .	67,364	20.2	11,516	3.4	14,775	4.4
2008 . .	68,759	20.3	11,508	3.4	15,115	4.5
2009 . .	68,364	19.8	12,273	3.6	15,498	4.5
2010 . .	67,955	19.4	12,981	3.7	16,542	4.7
2011 . .	73,292	19.7	15,135	4.1	16,367	4.4

* Excludes tribal Indian population.
† Based on official mid-year population estimates.

Life expectancy (years at birth): 76.1 (males 73.6, females 78.8) in 2011 (Source: World Bank, World Development Indicators database).

ECONOMICALLY ACTIVE POPULATION

(labour force survey at August, '000 persons aged 15 years and over)

	2010	2011	2012
Agriculture, hunting, forestry and fishing	253.6	254.5	270.6
Mining and quarrying	2.8	3.1	3.8
Manufacturing	120.5	107.2	111.6
Electricity, gas and water supply .	7.6	15.9	12.6
Construction	141.3	162.0	166.3
Wholesale and retail trade; repair of motor vehicles, motorcycles and personal and household goods	253.5	276.5	295.7
Hotels and restaurants . .	74.7	77.3	80.3
Transport, storage and communications . .	113.4	124.9	135.8
Financial intermediation . .	27.6	38.4	39.9
Real estate, renting and business activities	82.8	101.6	107.6
Public administration and defence; compulsory social service . .	86.6	105.1	105.8
Education	82.5	83.8	87.7
Health and social work . .	65.5	57.8	60.2
Other community, social and personal service activities . .	73.1	56.7	66.8
Private households with employed persons	68.8	71.5	74.3
Extra-territorial organizations and bodies	1.3	1.6	1.9
Total employed	1,455.6	1,538.1	1,621.1
Unemployed	101.5	72.2	68.4
Total labour force	1,557.1	1,610.4	1,689.5
Males	959.6	992.1	1,022.7
Females	597.5	618.1	666.8

Health and Welfare

KEY INDICATORS

Total fertility rate (children per woman, 2010) . . .	2.5
Under-5 mortality rate (per 1,000 live births, 2010) . .	20
HIV/AIDS (% of persons aged 15–49, 2009)	0.9
Physicians (per 1,000 head, 2000)	1.5
Hospital beds (per 1,000 head, 2009)	2.2
Health expenditure (2009): US $ per head (PPP) . . .	1,054
Health expenditure (2009): % of GDP	8.1
Health expenditure (2009): public (% of total) . . .	74.8
Access to water (% of persons, 2008)	93
Access to sanitation (% of persons, 2008)	69
Total carbon dioxide emissions ('000 metric tons, 2008) . .	6,912.3
Carbon dioxide emissions per head (metric tons, 2008) . .	2.0
Human Development Index (2011): ranking	58
Human Development Index (2011): value	0.768

For sources and definitions, see explanatory note on p. vi.

Agriculture

PRINCIPAL CROPS
('000 metric tons)

	2009	2010	2011*
Rice, paddy	241.5	274.0	311.9
Maize	85.5	87.6	84.7
Sugar cane	1,913.9	2,095.0	2,095.0
Watermelons	79.7	54.9	55.8
Cantaloupes and other melons .	43.9	13.6	13.6
Bananas	320.5	338.3	340.3
Plantains	99.3	95.2	97.4
Oranges	49.1	50.7	53.4
Coffee, green	13.0	12.5	12.0
Tobacco, unmanufactured* . .	2.6	2.4	3.0

* FAO estimates.

Aggregate production ('000 metric tons, may include official, semi-official or estimated data): Total cereals 331.4 in 2009, 366.3 in 2010, 401.5 in 2011; Total roots and tubers 80.1 in 2009, 77.0 in 2010–11; Total vegetables (incl. melons) 212.0 in 2009, 178.7 in 2010, 187.5 in 2011; Total fruits (excl. melons) 592.6 in 2009, 618.1 in 2010, 636.5 in 2011.

Source: FAO.

LIVESTOCK
('000 head, year ending September)

	2009	2010	2011
Horses*	191	195	197
Mules*	4	4	4
Cattle	1,621	1,641	1,661*
Pigs	273	276	278*
Goats*	6	6	6
Chickens	16,483	17,263	18,719
Ducks*	235	235	235
Turkeys*	40	40	40

* FAO estimate(s).

Source: FAO.

LIVESTOCK PRODUCTS
('000 metric tons)

	2009	2010	2011
Cattle meat	74.5	79.4	80.3*
Pig meat	31.3	29.5	30.9†
Chicken meat	118.7	125.8	136.8*
Cows' milk	193.1	198.0	198.0†
Hen eggs	23.9	24.6	24.6†

* Unofficial figure.
† FAO estimate.

Source: FAO.

Forestry

ROUNDWOOD REMOVALS
('000 cubic metres, excluding bark)

	2009	2010	2011
Sawlogs, veneer logs and logs for sleepers	79	86	97
Other industrial wood* . . .	1	—	1
Fuel wood*	1,143	1,128	1,112
Pulp wood*	90	90	90
Total*	1,313	1,304	1,300

* FAO estimates.

Source: FAO.

SAWNWOOD PRODUCTION
('000 cubic metres, incl. railway sleepers, unofficial figures)

	2009	2010	2011
Total (all broadleaved) . . .	15	40	45

Source: FAO.

Fishing

('000 metric tons, live weight)

	2008	2009	2010
Capture	223.4	222.5	163.5
Snappers and jobfishes . . .	6.5	6.9	6.3
Pacific thread herring . . .	36.8	28.9	35.4
Pacific anchoveta	47.4	62.5	19.4
Skipjack tuna	50.8	36.7	30.6
Yellowfin tuna	34.3	38.8	34.9
Bigeye tuna	11.0	11.5	10.8
Marine fishes	10.3	11.1	10.0
Aquaculture	8.2	6.4	6.2
Whiteleg shrimp	7.8	5.9	5.5
Total catch	231.6	228.9	169.7

Note: Figures exclude crocodiles. The number of spectacled caimans caught was: 2,205 in 2008; 995 in 2009; 9,902 in 2010.

Source: FAO.

Industry

SELECTED PRODUCTS
('000 metric tons, unless otherwise indicated)

	2009	2010	2011*
Salt	20	28	17
Sugar	144	146	170
Beer (million litres)	230	235	247
Wines and spirits (million litres) .	13	13	16
Evaporated, condensed and powdered milk	23	19	19
Fish oil	10	3	4
Footwear ('000 pairs)	9	—	—
Electricity (million kWh, net) .	6,638	7,121	7,530

* Preliminary.

Finance

CURRENCY AND EXCHANGE RATES

Monetary Units
100 centésimos = 1 balboa (B).

Sterling, Dollar and Euro Equivalents (31 December 2012)
£1 sterling = 1.578 balboas;
US $1 = 1.000 balboas;
€1 = 1.319 balboas;
100 balboas = £63.37 = $100.00 = €75.79.

Exchange Rate: The balboa's value is fixed at par with that of the US dollar.

BUDGET
(consolidated general government budget, '000 balboas)

Revenue	2009	2010	2011*
Central government revenue . .	6,474,147	6,323,571	7,305,161
Current revenue	4,333,890	5,212,028	5,579,941
Tax revenue	2,739,413	3,101,841	3,536,601
Direct taxes	1,511,981	1,588,067	1,644,367
Income tax	1,310,105	1,346,839	1,385,987
Taxes on property and inheritance	150,914	182,384	193,204
Educational insurance .	50,962	58,844	65,177
Indirect taxes	1,227,432	1,513,773	1,892,234
Non-tax revenue	1,477,376	1,602,106	1,833,643
Panama Canal	n.a.	n.a.	n.a.
Transfers from balance of public sector . . .	5,084	5,010	5,539
Other current revenue . .	117,101	169,874	80,717
Surplus on cash account . .	12,167	286,626	84,323
Capital revenue	2,128,090	1,111,544	1,725,220
Decentralized institutional revenue	3,577,000	3,798,000	4,221,700
State enterprises	2,341,000	2,936,300	3,121,100
Non-financial	778,500	953,700	997,300
Financial	1,562,500	1,982,600	2,123,800
Municipalities	140,200	161,500	150,800
Total revenue	12,532,347	13,219,400	14,798,800

Expenditure	2009	2010	2011*
Central government expenditure .	6,468,305	6,323,373	7,302,093
Current expenditure . . .	4,928,625	3,975,156	4,564,107
National Assembly . . .	69,561	62,634	60,327
State treasury	47,620	61,310	70,400
Ministry of the Presidency .	63,563	74,732	75,194
Ministry of the Interior and Justice	329,565	380,620	n.a.
Ministry of Foreign Affairs .	44,877	41,453	41,332
Ministry of Social Development	56,521	23,919	25,841
Ministry of the Economy and Finance	160,233	223,383	380,758
Ministry of Education . .	760,699	797,006	867,444
Ministry of Commerce and Industry	28,431	31,540	42,595
Ministry of Public Works .	27,751	65,751	29,962
Ministry of Agricultural Development	48,744	59,078	52,533
Ministry of Public Health .	725,451	795,132	829,900
Ministry of Labour and Social Welfare	15,918	15,853	16,922
Ministry of Housing . . .	15,520	16,925	40,003
Judiciary	55,388	57,602	64,154
Ombudsman	—	—	

Expenditure—*continued*	2009	2010	2011*
Electoral tribunal	51,311	29,018	50,049
Other institutions . . .	49,696	—	—
Other expenditures of administration . . .	12,059	12,652	13,374
Debt-servicing	2,288,623	1,113,174	1,322,975
Education fund	77,094	54,917	60,943
Ministerial development expenditure	1,539,680	2,348,217	2,737,986
Decentralized institutional expenditure	2,722,400	3,325,000	3,610,600
State enterprises	2,204,400	2,845,200	3,049,200
Municipalities	128,400	151,100	148,300
Total	11,523,500	12,644,700	14,110,200

* Preliminary figures.

Note: Totals may not be equal to the sum of components, as some figures have been rounded.

INTERNATIONAL RESERVES
(excl. gold, US $ million at 31 December)

	2009	2010	2011
IMF special drawing rights . .	268.2	263.3	262.4
Reserve position in IMF . . .	18.6	18.3	18.2
Foreign exchange	2,741.5	2,432.9	2,023.1
Total	3,028.3	2,714.5	2,303.7

Note: US treasury notes and coins form the bulk of the currency in circulation in Panama.

Source: IMF, *International Financial Statistics*.

MONEY SUPPLY
(million balboas at 31 December)

	2009	2010	2011
Transferable deposits	4,403.5	5,230.4	6,229.3
Other deposits	17,378.7	18,963.7	20,020.2
Securities other than shares . .	29.9	40.1	27.0
Broad money	21,812.1	24,234.2	26,276.5

Source: IMF, *International Financial Statistics*.

COST OF LIVING
(Consumer Price Index, base: 2003 = 100)

	2009	2010	2011
Food (incl. beverages)	138.8	142.8	151.2
Rent, fuel and light	112.4	115.3	n.a.
Clothing (incl. footwear) . . .	98.3	100.8	n.a.
All items (incl. others) . . .	122.8	127.1	134.6

Source: ILO.

NATIONAL ACCOUNTS

National Income and Product
(million balboas at current prices)

	2009	2010	2011*
Compensation of employees . .	7,829.6	8,260.4	9,317.5
Operating surplus	9,852.7	11,432.8	13,264.6
Net mixed income	3,200.9	3,560.6	4,193.2
Domestic factor incomes . .	20,883.2	23,253.8	26,775.3
Consumption of fixed capital . .	1,350.3	1,518.0	1,766.4
Gross domestic product (GDP) at factor cost	22,233.5	24,771.8	28,541.7
Indirect taxes	2,111.7	2,592.4	3,078.4
Less Subsidies	182.4	311.2	304.3
GDP in purchasers' values .	24,162.9	27,053.0	31,315.8
Less Net factor income paid to the rest of the world	1,821.6	2,226.6	2,343.6
Gross national product . .	22,341.3	24,826.4	28,972.2
Less Consumption of fixed capital	1,350.3	1,518.0	1,766.4
National income in market prices	20,991.0	23,308.4	27,205.8
Other current transfers from abroad (net)	−1.9	33.3	81.3
National disposable income .	20,989.1	23,341.7	27,287.1

* Preliminary figures.

Expenditure on the Gross Domestic Product
(million balboas at current prices)

	2009	2010	2011*
Government final consumption expenditure	3,078.1	3,545.9	3,860.0
Private final consumption expenditure	11,702.7	16,176.0	18,859.8
Increase in stocks	253.6	267.5	339.5
Gross fixed capital formation .	5,932.0	6,639.3	8,179.5
Total domestic expenditure .	20,966.4	26,628.7	31,238.8
Exports of goods and services .	19,581.7	20,337.0	26,379.9
Less Imports of goods and services	16,385.2	19,912.7	26,302.9
GDP in purchasers' values .	24,162.9	27,053.0	31,315.8

* Preliminary figures.

Gross Domestic Product by Economic Activity
(million balboas at constant 1996 prices)

	2009	2010	2011*
Agriculture, hunting, forestry and fishing	1,043.5	895.6	889.9
Mining and quarrying	270.8	290.7	353.5
Manufacturing	1,163.9	1,176.7	1,214.7
Electricity, gas and water . .	540.5	575.2	610.7
Construction	1,170.4	1,252.3	1,489.1
Wholesale and retail trade, repair of vehicles, motorcycles and other household goods . . .	2,737.5	3,009.5	3,443.7
Hotels and restaurants . . .	549.7	607.0	664.0
Transport, storage and communications	4,269.0	4,890.1	5,578.8
Financial intermediation . . .	1,661.4	1,754.6	1,886.5
Renting, real estate and business services	2,947.7	3,150.9	3,395.2
General government services .	1,353.5	1,393.4	1,468.1
Social services and private education and health . . .	307.5	332.1	346.9
Other community, social and personal services	575.5	609.1	663.1
Private households with employed persons	113.8	115.5	119.5
Sub-total	18,704.7	20,052.7	22,123.7
Less Financial intermediation services indirectly measured .	430.5	446.7	470.3
Gross value added in basic prices	18,274.2	19,606.0	21,653.4
Import duties and other taxes, less subsidies	1,264.2	1,388.4	1,618.7
GDP in market prices . . .	19,538.4	20,994.4	23,272.1

* Preliminary figures.

BALANCE OF PAYMENTS
(US $ million)*

	2009	2010	2011
Exports of goods	12,071.0	12,691.8	16,925.7
Imports of goods	−14,214.3	−17,230.4	−22,941.5
Balance on goods	−2,143.3	−4,538.6	−6,015.8
Exports of services	5,477.4	6,042.9	7,130.8
Imports of services	−2,189.4	−2,637.0	−3,317.9
Balance on goods and services	1,144.7	−1,132.7	−2,202.9
Primary income received . . .	1,458.0	1,519.2	1,950.4
Primary income paid	−2,906.8	−3,377.7	−3,749.8
Balance on goods, services and primary income	−304.1	−2,991.2	−4,002.3
Secondary income received . .	749.0	782.9	761.4
Secondary income paid . . .	−622.7	−653.5	−632.7
Current balance	−177.8	−2,861.8	−3,873.6
Capital account (net)	30.0	42.5	8.9
Direct investment assets . .	173.8	167.9	−468.1
Direct investment liabilities . .	1,085.5	2,182.2	3,257.9
Portfolio investment assets . .	−1,021.0	−1,169.9	−645.5
Portfolio investment liabilities .	1,323.0	2.7	169.9
Financial derivatives and employee stock options (net)	—	2.7	1.5
Other investment assets . . .	−1,568.2	−3,625.8	−3,840.6
Other investment liabilities . .	307.8	5,358.9	5,750.4
Net errors and omissions . . .	451.2	357.4	−707.0
Reserves and related items .	604.3	456.8	−346.2

* Including the transactions of enterprises operating in the Colón Free Zone.

Source: IMF, *International Financial Statistics*.

External Trade

PRINCIPAL COMMODITIES
('000 balboas)

Imports c.i.f.	2008	2009	2010*
Food and live animals	990,839	925,817	1,079,823
Mineral products	2,003,609	1,411,224	1,763,150
Chemicals and chemical products .	780,094	791,707	856,870
Plastics, rubber and articles thereof	343,952	319,476	399,110
Textiles and articles thereof . .	276,245	344,974	418,048
Metals and manufactures of metal	826,700	600,600	712,198
Machinery and apparatus . .	1,768,606	1,537,853	1,805,318
Transport materials	932,841	794,304	901,680
Total (incl. others)	9,009,934	7,788,849	9,145,308

Exports f.o.b.†	2008	2009	2010*
Sugar	15,149	13,349	19,193
Bananas	98,748	62,146	65,198
Melons	213,994	81,856	50,324
Pineapples	36,503	33,063	32,064
Coffee	16,049	9,618	13,874
Shellfish	40,683	43,925	35,384
Fresh and frozen fish and fillets (incl. yellowfin tuna) . . .	275,133	165,022	138,472
Meat from cattle	14,512	14,047	14,846
Total (incl. others)	1,144,046	821,918	725,155

* Preliminary.
† Including re-exports.

2011: Total imports 11,341,514; total exports 785,249.

PRINCIPAL TRADING PARTNERS*
('000 balboas)

Imports c.i.f.†	2009	2010‡	2011‡
Argentina	45,056	47,886	124,814
Brazil	144,406	244,917	217,392
China, People's Republic . .	327,450	489,560	689,721
Colombia	258,368	300,066	469,560
Costa Rica	408,631	444,470	509,791
El Salvador	83,760	82,605	103,805
Germany	103,358	141,007	166,082
Guatemala	161,507	173,498	196,544
Japan	284,161	289,095	292,071
Korea, Republic	202,517	292,789	303,798
Mexico	355,042	394,606	445,296
Spain	113,839	163,002	294,443
USA	2,258,105	2,518,507	2,826,654
Total (incl. others)	7,788,849	9,145,308	11,341,514

Exports f.o.b.	2009	2010‡	2011‡
Canada	9,446	75,872	121,049
Chile	2,911	6,086	9,182
China, People's Republic . . .	20,218	36,086	38,809
Colombia	15,731	9,712	9,265
Costa Rica	60,895	49,517	52,388
Dominican Republic	19,442	8,273	n.a.
El Salvador	5,375	8,610	7,614
Honduras	11,387	16,905	16,327
India	4,565	7,272	19,063
Italy	16,965	14,421	20,028
Korea, Republic	3,766	5,032	18,613
Netherlands	53,938	50,563	34,484
Nicaragua	10,628	14,781	18,991
Portugal	4,828	4,376	9,103
Spain	50,802	19,920	16,173
Sweden	49,735	49,974	55,010
Taiwan	24,027	36,495	34,722
United Kingdom	11,996	8,419	10,010
USA	349,675	211,482	163,338
Viet Nam	4,499	5,763	8,675
Total (incl. others)	821,918	725,155	785,249

* Including trade with the Colón Free Zone (CFZ) ('000 balboas): *Imports:* 919,322 in 2009; 1,030,035 in 2010 (preliminary); 1,176,037 in 2011 (preliminary). *Exports:* 18,166 in 2009; 15,523 in 2010 (preliminary); 28,926 in 2011 (preliminary).
† Including imports to the Petroleum Free Zone ('000 balboas): 1,089,977 in 2009; 1,486,609 in 2010 (preliminary); 2,258,607 in 2011 (preliminary).
‡ Preliminary.

Transport

RAILWAYS
(traffic)

	2002*	2003	2004
Passenger-km (million) . . .	35,693	52,324	53,377
Freight ton-km (million) . . .	20,665	41,863	52,946

* Panama Railway only.

Source: UN, *Statistical Yearbook*.

ROAD TRAFFIC
(motor vehicles in use)

	2000	2001	2002
Cars	223,433	219,372	224,504
Buses and coaches	16,865	15,558	16,371
Lorries and vans	75,454	73,139	74,247

2007: Motorcycles and mopeds 20,133.

2010: Cars 359,266; Buses and coaches 19,661; Lorries and vans 104,774.

Source: IRF, *World Road Statistics*.

SHIPPING

Flag Registered Fleet
(at 31 December)

	2010	2011	2012
Number of vessels	9,192	9,369	9,326
Total displacement (grt) . . .	211,363.4	222,739.6	228,548.2

Source: Lloyd's List Intelligence (www.lloydslistintelligence.com).

International Sea-borne Freight Traffic
(national ports authority, '000 metric tons)

	2009	2010	2011*
Goods handled	56,461	57,002	64,831
Container goods	28,778	37,683	45,883

*Preliminary.

Panama Canal Traffic

	2009/10	2010/11	2011/12
Transits	14,230	14,684	14,544
Cargo ('000 long tons)	204,854.5	222,357.1	218,059.2

Source: Panama Canal Authority.

CIVIL AVIATION
(traffic on scheduled services)

	2007	2008	2009
Kilometres flown (million) . .	81	98	94
Passengers carried ('000) . .	2,519	6,900	6,348
Passenger-km (million) . . .	7,942	8,970	8,414
Total ton-km (million)	841	951	894

Source: UN, *Statistical Yearbook*.

Passengers carried ('000): 7,365.6 in 2010 (Source: World Bank, World Development Indicators database).

Tourism

VISITOR ARRIVALS BY COUNTRY OF ORIGIN
(arrivals at Tocumen International Airport)

	2008	2009	2010
Argentina	23,598	41,989	47,216
Brazil	18,603	24,338	31,520
Canada	44,171	37,849	48,029
Colombia	213,776	177,224	219,250
Costa Rica	65,438	37,759	39,524
Ecuador	50,129	22,172	30,861
Guatemala	27,629	26,064	32,780
Mexico	51,533	44,904	48,132
Peru	23,251	11,853	15,431
Spain	22,242	25,200	30,845
USA	272,386	234,190	252,837
Venezuela	34,403	162,581	131,608
Total (incl. others)	1,136,079	1,054,663	1,162,713

Total tourist arrivals ('000): 1,473 in 2011 (provisional).

Tourism receipts (US $ million, excl. passenger transport): 1,483 in 2009; 1,676 in 2010; 1,926 in 2011 (provisional).

Source: World Tourism Organization.

Communications Media

	2009	2010	2011*
Telephones ('000 main lines in use)	536.4	539.3	542.5
Mobile cellular telephones ('000 subscribers)	6,066.7	6,646.3	7,281.1
Internet subscribers ('000) . .	244.4	285.1	n.a.
Broadband subscribers ('000) .	233.9	255.5	282.8

*Preliminary.

Personal computers: 96,823 (28.5 per 1,000 persons) in 2008.

Source: International Telecommunication Union.

Education

(2009/10 unless otherwise indicated, provisional)

	Institutions*	Teachers	Students		
			Males	Females	Total
Pre-primary .	1,662	5,348	47,195	45,472	92,667
Primary . .	3,116	18,746	228,177	211,569	439,746
Secondary .	442	18,501	140,061	143,686	283,747
General .	n.a.	14,769	117,043	121,812	238,855
Vocational .	n.a.	3,732	23,032	21,891	44,932
Tertiary† .	24	13,512	54,604	80,605	135,209

*2001/02 figures.
†2008/09.

Sources: Ministry of Education; UNESCO, *Statistical Yearbook*; UNESCO Institute for Statistics.

Pupil-teacher ratio (primary education, UNESCO estimate): 23.5 in 2009/10 (Source: UNESCO Institute for Statistics).

Adult literacy rate (UNESCO estimates): 94.1% (males 94.7%; females 93.5%) in 2010 (Source: UNESCO Institute for Statistics).

Directory

The Government

HEAD OF STATE

President: RICARDO A. MARTINELLI BERROCAL (took office 1 July 2009).

Vice-President: JUAN CARLOS VARELA RODRÍGUEZ.

THE CABINET
(May 2013)

The Government is formed by representatives of Cambio Democrático (CD), several Independents (Ind.) and a dissident member of the Partido Revolucionario Democrático (PRD).

Minister of Foreign Affairs: FERNANDO NÚÑEZ FÁBREGA (CD).

Minister of Public Security: JOSÉ RAÚL MULINO (CD).

Minister of the Interior: JORGE RICARDO FÁBREGA SOSA (CD).

Minister of Public Works: JAIME FORD CASTRO (CD).

Minister of the Economy and Finance: FRANK GEORGE DE LIMA GERCICH (CD).

Minister of Agricultural Development: OSCAR ARMADO OSORIO CASAL (Ind.).

Minister of Commerce and Industry: RICARDO QUIJANO (CD).

Minister of Health: JAVIER DÍAZ VERÓN (CD).

Minister of Labour and Social Welfare: ALMA LORENA CORTÉS AGUILAR (CD).

Minister of Education: LUCINDA MOLINAR (Ind.).

Minister of Housing and Land Management: YASMINA PIMETEL (CD).

Minister of the Presidency: ROBERTO HENRÍQUEZ (CD).

Minister of Social Development: GUILLERMO ANTONIO FERRUFINO BENÍTEZ (CD).

Minister of Canal Affairs: ROBERTO ROY (CD).

Minister of Tourism: SALOMÓN SHAMAH ZUCHIN (Ind.).

Minister of Micro-, Small and Medium-sized Enterprises: GISELLE BURILLO SÁIZ (PRD dissident).

MINISTRIES

Office of the President: Palacio de Las Garzas, Corregimiento de San Felipe, Panamá 1; tel. 527-9600; fax 527-9034; e-mail prensa@presidencia.gob.pa; internet www.presidencia.gob.pa.

Ministry of Agricultural Development: Edif. 576, Calle Manuel E. Melo, Altos de Curundú, Apdo 0816-01611, Panamá 5; tel. 507-0600; e-mail infomida@mida.gob.pa; internet www.mida.gob.pa.

Ministry of Commerce and Industry: Plaza Edison, Sector El Paical, 2° y 3°, Apdo 0815-0111, Panamá 4; tel. 560-0600; fax 261-1942; e-mail contactenos@mici.gob.pa; internet www.mici.gob.pa.

Ministry of the Economy and Finance: (Economy) Edif. Ogawa, Vía España y Calle 52 Este, Calle del Santuario Nacional, Apdo 5245, Panamá 5; (Finance) Antiguo Edif. de Hacienda y Tesoro, Calle 34 y 35, Avda Perú, Calidonia, Panamá; tel. (Economy) 507-7000; tel. (Finance) 507-7600; e-mail prensa@mef.gob.pa; internet www.mef.gob.pa.

Ministry of Education: Villa Cárdenas, Ancón, Apdo 0816-04049, Panamá 3; tel. 511-4400; fax 511-4440; e-mail meduca@meduca.gob.pa; internet www.meduca.gob.pa.

Ministry of Foreign Affairs: Edif. 26, Palacio Bolívar, Calle 3, San Felipe, Panamá 4; tel. 511-4100; fax 511-4022; e-mail prensa@mire.gob.pa; internet www.mire.gob.pa.

Ministry of Health: Apdo 2048, Panamá 1; tel. and fax 512-9202; e-mail saludaldia@minsa.gob.pa; internet www.minsa.gob.pa.

Ministry of Housing and Land Management: Edif. Plaza Edison, 4°, Avda Ricardo J. Alfaro y Calle El Paical, Corregimiento de Bethania, Apdo 5228, Panamá 5; tel. 579-9200; fax 579-9651; e-mail info@miviot.gob.pa; internet www.miviot.gob.pa.

Ministry of the Interior: Avda 7 y Calle 3, Central San Felipe, Apdo 1628, Panamá 1; tel. 512-7600; fax 512-2126; e-mail despachosuperior@mingob.gob.pa; internet www.mingob.gob.pa.

Ministry of Labour and Social Welfare: Plaza Edison, 5°, Avda Ricardo J. Alfaro (Tumba Muerto) Betania, Apdo 2441, Panamá 3; tel. 560-1100; fax 560-1117; e-mail mitradel@mitradel.gob.pa; internet www.mitradel.gob.pa.

Ministry of the Presidency: Palacio de Las Garzas, Corregimiento de San Felipe, Apdo 2189, Panamá 1; tel. 527-9600; e-mail ofasin@presidencia.gob.pa; internet www.presidencia.gob.pa.

Ministry of Public Security: Avda 7 y Calle 3, Central San Felipe, Apdo 1628, Panamá 1; tel. 512-2000; fax 512-2174; e-mail prensa@minseg.gob.pa; internet www.minseg.gob.pa.

Ministry of Public Works: Edif. Principal 1019, Curundú, Zona 1, Apdo 1632, Panamá 1; tel. 507-9400; fax 507-9561; e-mail info@mop.gob.pa; internet www.mop.gob.pa.

Ministry of Social Development: Plaza Edison, 4°, Avda Ricardo J. Alfaro, Apdo 680-50, El Dorado, Panamá; tel. 500-6001; fax 500-6020; e-mail mides@mides.gob.pa; internet www.mides.gob.pa.

President and Legislature

PRESIDENT

Election, 3 May 2009

Candidate	Votes	% of valid votes
Ricardo A. Martinelli Berrocal (Alianza por el Cambio*)	952,333	60.03
Balbina del Carmen Herrera Araúz (Un País para Todos†)	597,227	37.65
Guillermo Endara Galimany (Vanguardia Moral de la Patria)	36,867	2.32
Total valid votes‡	1,586,427	100.00

* Electoral alliance comprising Cambio Democrático, the Partido Panameñista, the Movimiento Liberal Republicano Nacionalista and the Unión Patriótica.

† Electoral alliance comprising the Partido Revolucionario Democrático, the Partido Popular and the Partido Liberal.

‡ In addition, there were 19,105 blank and 30,976 invalid ballots.

ASAMBLEA NACIONAL
(National Assembly)

President: SERGIO R. GÁLVEZ EVERS.

The unicameral Asamblea Nacional comprises 71 members, elected for five years by universal adult suffrage. The last election was held on 3 May 2009.

Distribution of Seats, July 2012

Party	Seats
Cambio Democrático	36
Partido Revolucionario Democrático	17
Partido Panameñista	12
Movimiento Liberal Republicano Nacionalista (MOLIRENA)	4
Partido Popular	1
Independent	1
Total	71

Election Commission

Tribunal Electoral: Edif. del Tribunal Electoral-Dirección Superior, Avda Ecuador y Calle 33, Apdo 5281, Panamá 5; tel. 507-8000; e-mail secretaria-general@tribunal-electoral.gob.pa; internet www.tribunal-electoral.gob.pa; f. 1956; independent, comprised of three magistrates, one each appointed by the legislature, the executive and the judiciary; Pres. ERASMO PINILLA CASTILLERO; Exec. Dir YARA IVETTE CAMPO B.

Political Organizations

Cambio Democrático (CD): Parque Lefevre, Plaza Carolina, arriba de la Juguetería del Super 99, Panamá; tel. 217-2643; fax 217-2645; e-mail cambio.democratico@hotmail.com; internet www.cambiodemocratico.org.pa; formally registered 1998; contested the 2009 elections as part of the Alianza por el Cambio; merged with the Unión Patriótica in March 2011; Pres. RICARDO A. MARTINELLI BERROCAL; Sec.-Gen. GIACOMO TAMBURELLI.

Frente Amplio por la Democracia (FAD): Panamá; tel. 396-6679; e-mail frenadeso@frenadesonoticias.com; internet www.frenadesonoticias.org; f. 2011 by Frente Nacional por la Defensa de los Derechos Económicos y Sociales (FRENADESO); Pres. FERNANDO CEBAMANOS.

Movimiento Liberal Republicano Nacionalista (MOLIRENA): Calle 66 (Calle Belén), Casa Duplex 46-A, Corregimiento de San Francisco, Panamá; tel. 399-5280; fax 399-5288; formally registered 1982; conservative; contested the 2009 elections as part of the Alianza por el Cambio; Pres. SERGIO GONZÁLEZ RUIZ; Sec.-Gen. ARTURO GONZÁLEZ BASO.

Partido Liberal: Edif. Torre Universal, 11°, Avda Federico Boyd, Panamá; tel. 209-2574; fax 209-2575; e-mail partidoliberal@elveloz .com; f. 2005; contested the 2009 elections as part of the Un País para Todos alliance; Pres. JOAQUÍN F. FRANCO, III.

Partido Panameñista (PP): Avda Perú y Calle 37, No 37–41, al lado de Casa la Esperanza, Apdo 9610, Panamá 4; tel. 227-0028; fax 227-0951; e-mail partidopanamenista@hotmail.com; internet partidopanamenista.com; f. 1990 by Arnulfista faction of the Partido Panameñista Auténtico as Partido Arnulfista (PA); name changed as above in Jan. 2005; contested the 2009 elections as part of the Alianza por el Cambio; mem. of Frente por la Democracia alliance from June 2012; Pres. JUAN CARLOS VARELA RODRÍGUEZ; Sec.-Gen. ALCIBÍADES VÁSQUEZ.

Partido Popular: Avda Perú, frente al Parque Porras, Apdo 6322, Panamá 5; tel. 225-2381; fax 227-3944; e-mail comunicacion@ partidopopular.org.pa; internet www.panamaprimermundo.org; f. 1960 as Partido Demócrata Cristiano; name changed as above in 2001; contested the 2009 elections as part of the Un País para Todos alliance; mem. of Frente por la Democracia alliance from June 2012; Pres. MILTON COHEN-HENRÍQUEZ; Sec.-Gen. JOSÉ RAMOS REYES.

Partido Revolucionario Democrático (PRD): Edif. Policentro, Avda México, entre Calle 26 y 27, Panamá 3; tel. 225-8462; fax 225-8476; e-mail info@prd.org.pa; internet www.prd.org.pa; f. 1979; supports policies of late Gen. Omar Torrijos Herrera; combination of Marxists, Christian Democrats and some business interests; mem. of Frente por la Democracia alliance from June 2012; Pres. BENICIO ROBINSON; Sec.-Gen. JUAN CARLOS NAVARRO.

Diplomatic Representation

EMBASSIES IN PANAMA

Argentina: PH Torre Global, 24°, Calle 50, Apdo 832-0458, Panamá 1; tel. 302-0003; fax 302-0004; e-mail epnma@mrecic.gov.ar; internet www.epnma.mrecic.gov.ar; Ambassador ANA CRISTINA BERTA DE ALBERTO.

Belize: Villa de la Fuente 1, F-32, Calle 22, POB 0819-12255, Panamá; tel. 236-3762; fax 236-4132; e-mail nmusag@cwpanama .net; Ambassador ALFREDO MARTÍNEZ.

Bolivia: Calle G, Casa 3, El Cangrejo, Apdo 0823-05603, Panamá; tel. 269-0274; fax 264-3868; e-mail emb_bol_pan@cwpanama.net; internet embolivia-panama.com.pa; Chargé d'affaires a.i. BORIS FROILAN CALDERON ARANDIA.

Brazil: Edif. El Dorado 24, 1°, Calle Elvira Méndez y Avda Ricardo Arango, Urb. Campo Alegre, Apdo 4287, Panamá 5; tel. 263-5322; fax 269-6316; e-mail brasemb.panama@itamaraty.gov.br; internet www .embrasil.org.pa; Ambassador ADALNIO SENNA GANEM.

Canada: Edif. World Trade Center, Torres de las Américas, Torre A, 11°, Punta Pacífica, Apdo 0832-2446, Panamá; tel. 294-2500; fax 294-2514; e-mail panam@international.gc.ca; internet www .canadainternational.gc.ca/panama; Ambassador SYLVIA CESARATTO.

Chile: Torres de las Américas, 7°, Punta Pacífica, Apdo 7341, Panamá 5; tel. 294-8901; fax 294-8904; e-mail echilepa@tdla.com.pa; internet chileabroad.gov.cl/panama; Ambassador ALBERTO LABBÉ GALILEA.

Colombia: Edif. World Trade Center, Of. 1801, 18°, Calle 53, Urb. Marbella, Panamá; tel. 264-9513; fax 223-1134; e-mail epanama@ cancilleria.gov.co; internet www.embajadaenpanama.gov.co; Ambassador ANGELA MARÍA BENEDETTI VILLANEDA.

Costa Rica: Edif. Plaza Omega, 3°, Calle Samuel Lewis, Apdo 0816-02038, Panamá; tel. 264-2980; fax 264-4057; e-mail embajadacr@ cwpanama.net; Chargé d'affaires a.i. DEYANIRA RAMIREZ.

Cuba: Avda Cuba y Ecuador 33, Apdo 6-2291, Bellavista, Panamá; tel. 227-5277; fax 225-6681; e-mail segundojefemision@pa.embacuba .cu; internet www.cubadiplomatica.cu/panama; Ambassador REINALDO CARLOS CALVIAC LAFERTÉ.

Dominican Republic: Torre Delta, 16°, Calle Elvira Méndez, Área Bancaria, Apdo 6250, Panamá 5; tel. 263-6324; fax 263-7725; e-mail embajadompa.zlg@cableonda.net; Ambassador OCTAVIO ALFREDO LEÓN LISTER HENRÍQUEZ.

Ecuador: Edif. Torre 2000, 6°, Calle 50, Marbella, Bellavista, Panamá; tel. 264-2654; fax 223-0159; e-mail ecuador@ibw.com.ni; Chargé d'affaires a.i. EDWIN MARTINEZ BEDON.

Egypt: Calle 55, No 15, El Cangrejo, Apdo 7080, Panamá 5; tel. 263-5020; fax 264-8406; e-mail egempma@hotmail.com; internet www .mfa.gov.eg/PanamaCity_Emb; Ambassador AHMED MOHAMED TAHA DAWOUD.

El Salvador: Edif. ADR, 8°, Avda Samuel Lewis y Calle 58, Apdo 0823-05432, Panamá; tel. 223-3020; fax 264-6148; e-mail embasalva@cwpanama.net; Ambassador EFRÉN ARNOLDO BERNAL CHÉVEZ.

France: Plaza de Francia 1, Las Bovedas, San Felipe, Apdo 0816-07945, Panamá 1; tel. 211-6200; fax 211-6201; e-mail cad .panama-amba@diplomatie.gouv.fr; internet www.ambafrance-pa .org; Ambassador HUGUES GOISBAULT.

Germany: Edif. World Trade Center, 20°, Calle 53E, Marbella, Apdo 0832-0536, Panamá 5; tel. 263-7733; fax 223-6664; e-mail germpanama@cwp.net.pa; internet www.panama.diplo.de; Ambassador HERMANN-JOSEF SAUSEN.

Guatemala: Edif. World Trade Center, 2°, Of. 203, Calle 53, Urb. Marbella, Panamá 9; tel. 269-3475; fax 223-1922; e-mail embpanama@minex.gob.gt; Ambassador STELLA RIEGER WEISS.

Haiti: Edif. Dora Luz, 2°, Calle 1, El Cangrejo, Apdo 442, Panamá 9; tel. 269-3443; fax 223-1767; e-mail embhaitipan@cableonda.net; Chargé d'affaires a.i. HERBERT DANIER.

Holy See: Punta Paitilla, Avda Balboa y Vía Italia, Apdo 0816-00457, Panamá 5 (Apostolic Nunciature); tel. 269-2102; fax 264-2116; e-mail secretarionunciatura@cableonda.net; Apostolic Nuncio Most Rev. ANDRÉS CARRASCOSA COSO (Titular Archbishop of Elo).

Honduras: Edif. Bay Mall, 1°, Avda Balboa 112, Apdo 0816-03427, Panamá 5; tel. 264-5513; fax 264-4628; e-mail info@ embajadadehonduras.com.pa; internet www.embajadadehonduras .com.pa; Ambassador NERY M. FÚNES PADILLA.

India: Avda Federico Boyd y Calle 51, Bella Vista, Apdo 0823-05815, Panamá 7; tel. 264-3043; fax 209-6779; e-mail ambassador@ indempan.org; internet www.indempan.org; Ambassador YOGESHWAR VARMA.

Indonesia: Torres de Alba Hotel & Suites, Rm 1123, Avda Eusebio A. Morales, El Cangrejo, Panamá; tel. 300-7130; fax 300-7153; e-mail embajaindonesiapanama@gmail.com; Ambassador DWI AYU ARIMAMI.

Israel: Edif. Torre Banco General, 17°, Calle Aquilino de la Guardia, Urb. Marbella, Panamá; tel. 208-4700; fax 208-4755; e-mail info@ panama.mfa.gov.il; internet panama.mfa.gov.il; Ambassador ALEXANDER GALILEE.

Italy: Torre Banco Exterior, 25°, Avda Balboa, Apdo 0816-04453, Panamá 9; tel. 225-8950; fax 227-4906; e-mail ambpana.mail@esteri .it; internet www.ambpanama.esteri.it; Ambassador GIANCARLO MARIA CURCIO.

Japan: Calle 50 y 60E, Urb. Obarrio, Apdo 0816-06807, Panamá 1; tel. 263-6155; fax 263-6019; e-mail taiship2@cwpanama.net; internet www.panama.emb-japan.go.jp; Ambassador IKUO MIZUKI.

Korea, Republic: Edif. Victoria Plaza, 4°, Calle 53, Urb. Obarrio, Apdo 8096, Panamá 7; tel. 264-8203; fax 264-8825; e-mail panama@ mofat.go.kr; internet pan.mofat.go.kr; Ambassador DOO JUNG-SOO.

Libya: Avda Balboa y Calle 32 (frente al Edif. Atalaya), Apdo 6-894, El Dorado, Panamá; tel. 227-3342; fax 227-3886; Chargé d'affaires a.i. NAGI A. S. KSUDA.

Mexico: Edif. Torre ADR, 10°, Avda Samuel Lewis y Calle 58, Urb. Obarrio, Corregimiento de Bella Vista, Apdo 0823-05788, Panamá; tel. 263-4900; fax 263-5446; e-mail embamexpan@cwpanama.net; internet www.sre.gob.mx/panama; Ambassador ALEJANDRA MARÍA GABRIELA BOLOGNA ZUBIKARAI.

Netherlands: Edif. World Trade Center, 9°, Of. 904, Calle 53, Marbella, Panamá; tel. 264-7275; fax 264-7257; e-mail pan@ minbuza.nl; internet panama.nlambassade.org; Ambassador WIEGE DE BOER.

Nicaragua: Edif. De Lessep's, 3°, Calle Manuel Maria Icaza, Urb. Obarrio, Panamá; tel. 264-3080; fax 264-5425; e-mail embapana@ sinfo.net; Ambassador ANTENOR ALBERTO FERREY PERNUDI.

Paraguay: Edif. Galerías Balboa, 3°, Of. 45, Avda Balboa y Aquilino de la Guardia, Bella Vista, Panamá; tel. 263-4782; fax 269-4247; e-mail panamaembaparsc@mre.gov.py; Chargé d'affaires a.i. MARÍA ADORACIÓN AMARILLA ACOSTA.

Peru: Edif. World Trade Center, 12°, Calle 53, Urb. Marbella, Apdo 4516, Panamá 5; tel. 223-1112; fax 269-6809; e-mail embaperu@ cableonda.net; Ambassador GUILLERMO JOSÉ MIGUEL RUSSO CHECA.

Russia: Torre IBC, 10°, Avda Manuel Espinosa Batista, Apdo 6-4697, El Dorado, Panamá; tel. 264-1408; fax 264-1588; e-mail emruspan@sinfo.net; internet www.panama.mid.ru; Ambassador ALEXEI A. ERMAKOV.

Spain: Plaza de Belisario Porras, entre Avda Perú y Calle 33A, Apdo 0816-06600, Panamá 1; tel. 227-5122; fax 227-6284; e-mail emb

.panama@maec.es; internet www.maec.es/subwebs/Embajadas/Panama; Ambassador JESÚS SILVA FERNÁNDEZ.

Taiwan (Republic of China): Edif. Torre Hong Kong Bank, 10°, Avda Samuel Lewis, Apdo 7492, Panamá 5; tel. 269-1347; fax 264-9118; e-mail panama@mail.gio.gov.tw; internet www .taiwanembassy.org/pa; Ambassador DIEGO-LIN CHOW.

United Kingdom: MMG Tower, 4°, Calle 53, Urb. Marbella, Apdo 0816-07946, Panamá 1; tel. 269-0866; fax 263-5138; e-mail britemb@cwpanama.net; internet ukinpanama.fco.gov.uk; Ambassador MICHAEL JOHN HOLLOWAY.

USA: Edif. 783, Avda Demetrio Basilio Lakas, Apdo 0816-02561, Clayton, Panamá 5; tel. 207-7000; fax 317-5568; e-mail panamaweb@state.gov; internet panama.usembassy.gov; Ambassador JONATHAN DON FARRAR.

Uruguay: Edif. Los Delfines, Of. 8, Avda Balboa, Calle 50E Este, Apdo 0816-03616, Panamá 5; tel. 264-2838; fax 264-8908; e-mail urupanam@cwpanama.net; internet www.urupana.org; Ambassador FRANCISCO HEBER PURIFICATTI GAMARRA.

Venezuela: Torre HSBC, 5°, Avda Samuel Lewis, Apdo 661, Panamá 1; tel. 269-1244; fax 269-1916; e-mail info@venezuela.org.pa; internet www.venezuela.org.pa; Ambassador HELENA SALCEDO.

Viet Nam: 52 José Gabriel Duque, La Cresta, Apdo 12434-6A, El Dorado, Panamá; tel. 264-2551; fax 265-6056; e-mail convietnam@cwpanama.net; Ambassador NGUYEN DUY AN.

Judicial System

The judiciary in Panama comprises the following courts and judges: Corte Suprema de Justicia (Supreme Court of Justice), with nine judges appointed for a 10-year term; 10 Tribunales Superiores de Distrito Judicial (High Courts) with 36 magistrates; 54 Jueces de Circuito (Circuit Judges), and 89 Jueces Municipales (Municipal Judges).

Panama is divided into four judicial districts and has seven High Courts of Appeal. There are two additional special High Courts of Appeal: the first hears maritime, labour, family and infancy cases and the second deals with anti-trust cases and consumer affairs.

Corte Suprema de Justicia: Edif. 236, Calle Culebra, Ancón, Apdo 1770, Panamá 1; tel. 262-9833; e-mail informatica@organojudicial .gob.pa; internet www.organojudicial.gob.pa; Pres. ALEJANDRO MONCADA LUNA.

Procurator-General: ANA ISABEL BELFÓN VEJAS.

Religion

The Constitution recognizes freedom of worship and the Roman Catholic Church as the religion of the majority of the population.

CHRISTIANITY

The Roman Catholic Church

For ecclesiastical purposes, Panama comprises one archdiocese, five dioceses, the territorial prelature of Bocas del Toro and the Apostolic Vicariate of Darién. Some 83% of the population are Roman Catholics.

Bishops' Conference

Conferencia Episcopal de Panamá, Secretariado General, Apdo 870933, Panamá 7; tel. 223-0075; fax 223-0042; internet www .iglesia.org.pa.

f. 1958statutes approved 1986; Pres. Rt Rev. JOSÉ LUIS LACUNZA MAESTROJUAN (Bishop of David).

Archbishop of Panamá: Most Rev. JOSÉ DIMAS CEDEÑO DELGADO, Arzobispado Metropolitano, Calle 1a Sur Carrasquilla, Apdo 6386, Panamá 5; tel. 261-0002; fax 261-0820; e-mail asccn4@keops.utp.ac .pa.

The Baptist Church

Baptist Convention of Panama (Convención Bautista de Panamá): Apdo 0816-01761, Panamá 5; tel. and fax 259-5485; e-mail convencionbautistadepanama@hotmail.com; f. 1959; Pres. FRANCISCO MEDINA; Sec. ESMERALDA DE TUY; 7,573 mems.

The Anglican Communion

Panama comprises one of the five dioceses of the Iglesia Anglicana de la Región Central de América.

Bishop of Panama: Rt Rev. JULIO MURRAY, Edif. 331A, Calle Culebra, Apdo R, Balboa; tel. 212-0062; fax 262-2097.

BAHÁ'Í FAITH

National Spiritual Assembly of the Bahá'ís: Apdo 850-625, Las Cumbres, Panamá 15; tel. 231-1191; fax 231-6909; e-mail panbahai@cwpanama.net; internet panamabahai.net; mems resident in 529 localities; Nat. Sec. YOLANDA RODRÍGUEZ VILLAREAL.

The Press

DAILIES

Crítica Libre: Vía Fernández de Córdoba, Apdo B-4, Panamá 9A; tel. 261-0575; fax 230-0132; e-mail esotop@epasa.com; internet www .critica.com.pa; f. 1925; morning; Pres. RICARDO CHANIS; Dir JUAN PRITSIOLAS; circ. 40,000.

DIA a DIA: Vía Ricardo J. Alfaro, al lado de la USMA, Apdo B-4, Panamá 9A; tel. 230-7777; fax 230-2279; e-mail editor.diaadia@epasa .com; internet www.diaadia.com.pa; Pres. FRANCISCO ARIAS V.; Gen. Man. ELIZABETH M. DE LAO.

La Estrella de Panamá: Calle Alejandro Duque, Vía Transístmica y Frangipani, Panamá; tel. 227-0555; fax 227-1026; e-mail laestre@estrelladepanama.com; internet www.estrelladepanama.com; f. 1853; morning; Dir GERARDO BERROA; circ. 10,000.

El Panamá América: Vía Ricardo J. Alfaro, al lado de la USMA, Apdo 0834-02787, Panamá 9A; tel. 230-7777; fax 230-7773; e-mail director@epasa.com; internet pa-digital.com.pa; f. 1925; morning; independent; affiliated to Interamerican Press Asscn; Dir DUSTIN GUERRA; Editor JULIO RUILOBA; circ. 25,000.

La Prensa: Avda 12 de Octubre y Calle C, Hato Pintado, Pueblo Nuevo, Apdo 0819-05620, Panamá; tel. 222-1222; fax 221-7328; e-mail editor@prensa.com; internet www.prensa.com; f. 1980; morning; independent; Dir LOURDES DE OBALDÍA; Editor FERNÁN MOLINOS DELASWSKY; circ. 38,000.

El Siglo: Calle Alejandro Duque y Avda Frangipani, Apdo 0515-00662, Panamá; tel. 204-0982; fax 204-0974; e-mail digital@elsiglo .com; internet www.elsiglo.com; f. 1985; morning; Pres. EDUARDO ANTONIO QUIRÓS; Editor OCTAVIO COGLEY; circ. 30,000.

PERIODICALS

FOB Colón Free Zone: Apdo 0819-06908, El Dorado, Panamá; tel. 225-6638; fax 225-0466; e-mail info@colonfreezone.com; internet www.colonfreezone.com; f. 1971; annual; bilingual trade directory; publ. by Focus Publications (Int.), SA; Editor ISRAEL ARGUEDAS; circ. 60,000.

Focus Panama: 742 Calle 2A, Perejil, Panamá; tel. 225-6638; fax 225-0466; e-mail focusint@cableonda.net; internet www .focuspublicationsint.com; f. 1970; 2 a year; publ. by Focus Publications; visitors' guide; separate English and Spanish edns; Dir KENNETH J. JONES; circ. 100,000.

Instituto Nacional de Estadística y Censo: Avda Balboa y Federico Boyd, Apdo 0816-01521, Panamá 5; tel. 510-4800; fax 510-4801; e-mail cie_dec@contraloria.gob.pa; internet www .contraloria.gob.pa/inec; f. 1941; publ. by the Contraloría General de la República; statistical survey in series according to subjects; Controller-Gen. GIOCONDA TORRES DE BIANCHINI; Dir of Statistics and Census DANIS P. CEDEÑO H.

Mi Diario, La Voz de Panamá: Avda 12 de Octubre y Calle C, Hato Pintado, Pueblo Nuevo, Apdo 0819-05620, Panamá; tel. 222-9000; fax 222-9090; e-mail midiario@midiario.com; internet www.midiario .com; f. 2003 by La Prensa (q.v.); Dir LORENZO ABREGO.

Revista SIETE: Vía Ricardo J. Alfaro, al lado de la USMA, Apdo B-4, Panamá 9A; tel. 230-7777; fax 230-1033; e-mail revista.siete@epasa .com; internet siete.panamaamerica.com.pa; weekly; Editor NAYLA G. MONTENEGRO.

El Visitante/The Visitor: Calle 2, Perejil 742, Apdo 0819-06908, El Dorado, Panama; tel. 225-6638; fax 225-0466; e-mail focusint@cableonda.net; internet www.thevisitorpanama.com; bilingual; weekly; Editor JACOB EHRLER.

PRESS ASSOCIATION

Sindicato de Periodistas de Panamá (SPP): Edif. 287, Avda Gorgas, Panamá; tel. 214-0163; fax 214-0164; e-mail sindiperpana@yahoo.com; f. 1949; Sec.-Gen. FILEMÓN MEDINA RAMOS.

Publishers

Editora Géminis, SA: Edif. Don Tomás, Planta Baja, Calle 7, Vista Hermosa, Apdo 0819-04188, El Dorado, Panamá; tel. 229-2972; fax 229-1010; e-mail info@editorageminis.com; internet www .editorageminis.com; f. 1985; dictionaries, general fiction, school texts; Dir-Gen. RAÚL ESQUIVEL.

Editora Panamá América, SA (EPASA): Avda Ricardo J. Alfaro, al lado de la USMA, Apdo 0834-02787, Panamá R; tel. 230-7777; fax 230-7773; e-mail gerente.general@epasa.com; internet www.epasa .com; Pres. RICARDO CHANIS CORREA; Gen. Man. LUIS STANZIOLA S.

Exedra Books: esq. de Vía España y Vía Brasil, diagonal a Galerias Obarrio, Apdo 0831-00125, Paitilla, Panamá; tel. 264-4252; fax 264-4266; e-mail info@exedrabooks.com; internet www.exedrabooks .com; general fiction and non-fiction; Dir-Gen. SHEILA DE TERÁN.

Focus Publications: Calle 2A 742, Perejil, Apdo 0819-06908, El Dorado, Panamá; tel. 225-6638; fax 225-0466; e-mail focusint@sinfo .net; internet www.focuspublicationsint.com; f. 1970; guides, trade directories, yearbooks and maps; Pres. KENNETH J. JONES.

Piggy Press, SA: Apdo 0413-00110, Boquete, Chiriquí; tel. 720-1072; e-mail info@piggypress.com; internet www.piggypress.com; f. 2001; multilingual children's literature; Pres. PAT ALVARADO.

Ruth Casa Editorial: Edif. Los Cristales, Of. 6, Calle 38 y Avda Cuba, Apdo 2235, Zona 9A, Panamá; e-mail ruthcasaeditorial@yahoo .com; internet www.ruthcasaeditorial.org; Pres. FRANÇOIS HOUTART.

Serapis Bey Editores, SA: Parque Lefevre, Calle W-2, Casa 46-B-21, Apdo 0834-01726, Panamá; tel. 302-0213; fax 302-0214; e-mail jorgecarrizo@serapisbey.com; internet www.serapisbey.com; f. 1989; spiritual literature; Gen. Man. JORGE A. CARRIZO.

SIJUSA (Sistemas Juridicos, SA): Edif. Bank Boston, 2°, Vía España y Calle Elvira Méndez, Panamá; tel. 223-2764; fax 223-2766; e-mail servicioalcliente@sijusa.com; internet www.sijusa.com; f. 1989; law and politics; Dir-Gen. JOSÉ ALEJANDRO ESPINO.

Susaeta Ediciones Panamá, SA: Apdo. 0819-08750, Panamá; tel. 220-0833; fax 220-4561; e-mail susaeta@susaetapanama.com; internet www.susaetapanama.net; f. 1982; children's literature; includes the imprints Ediesco, Nacho and Susaeta; Dir-Gen. MIRNA DE DÍAZ.

GOVERNMENT PUBLISHING HOUSE

Editorial Mariano Arosemena: Instituto Nacional de Cultura, Apdo 662, Panamá 1; tel. 501-4000; fax 211-4016; e-mail secretariageneral@inac.gob.pa; internet www.inac.gob.pa; f. 1974; division of National Institute of Culture; literature, history, social sciences, archaeology; Dir-Gen. MARIA EUGENIA HERRERA DE VICTORIA.

ASSOCIATION

Cámara Panameña del Libro: Edif. Tula, Of. 6C, Vía España, entrada de Vía Argentina, arriba del Blockbuster, Apdo 0823-04289, Panamá; tel. 390-4738; fax 390-4739; e-mail info@capali.com.pa; internet www.capali.com.pa; f. 1997; organizes international book fairs; 28 active mems, 3 honorary mems, 2 associate mems; Pres. RENÉE AVILA; Sec. MIRNA DE DÍAZ.

Broadcasting and Communications

REGULATORY AUTHORITY

Autoridad Nacional de los Servicios Públicos: Edif. Office Park, Vía España, Apdo 0816-01235, Panamá 5; tel. 508-4500; fax 508-4600; e-mail adminweb@asep.gob.pa; internet www.asep.gob.pa; f. 1996 as Ente Regulador de los Servicios Públicos; name changed as above in 2006; state regulator with responsibility for television, radio, telecommunications, water and electricity; Administrator-Gen. ZELMAR RODRÍGUEZ CRESPO; Exec. Dir ANTONIO TERCERO GONZÁLEZ.

TELECOMMUNICATIONS

Cable & Wireless Panama: Apdo 0834-00659, Panamá; e-mail cwp@cwpanama.com; internet www.cwpanama.com.pa; 49% govt-owned, 49% owned by Cable & Wireless; major telecommunications provider; Pres. JORGE NICOLAU.

Digicel: Edif. Digicel, Vía Transístimica, Panamá; tel. 306-0600; fax 300-0469; e-mail servicioalcliente.pa@digicelgroup.com; internet www.digicelpanama.com; f. 2001; Gen. Man. COLM DELVES; 11m. subscribers.

Galaxy Communications Corpn (ClaroCOM): Edif. Alegre, 4°, Calle 49B Oeste El Cangrejo, Bella Vista, Apdo 0832-2657, Panamá; tel. 200-5555; fax 263-3403; e-mail info@clarocom.com; internet www .clarocom.com; f. 2001; Chair. SETH REDLICH; CEO PEDRO CORDOVEZ.

Movistar: Edif. Magna, Area Bancaria, Calle 51 Este y Manuel M. Icaza, Panamá; tel. 265-0955; internet www.movistar.com; f. 1996 as BellSouth Panamá, SA; acquired by Telefónica Móviles, SA (Spain) in 2004; name changed as above in 2005; mobile telephone services; Gen. Man. CLAUDIO HIDALGO.

BROADCASTING

Radio

La Mega 98.3 FM: Casa 35, Calle 50 y 77 San Francisco, Panamá; tel. 270-3242; fax 226-1021; e-mail ventas@lamegapanama.com; internet www.lamegapanama.com; f. 2000.

Omega Stereo: Calle G, El Cangrejo 3, Panamá; e-mail omegaste@ omegastereo.com; internet www.omegastereo.com; f. 1981; Pres. GUILLERMO ANTONIO ADAMES.

RPC Radio: Avda 12 de Octubre, Apdo 0827-00116, Panamá; tel. 390-6700; e-mail mtalessandria@medcom.com.pa; internet www .rpcradio.com; f. 1949; broadcasts news, sports and commentary; Man. MARÍA TERESA ALESSANDRÍA.

SuperQ: Edif. Dominó, 1°, Of. 9, Vía España, Apdo 0816-03034, Panamá; tel. 263-5298; fax 263-0362; e-mail info@superqpanama .com; internet www.superqpanama.net; f. 1984; Pres. G. ARIS DE ICAZA.

WAO 97.5: Edif. Plaza 50, 2°, Calle 50 y Vía Brasil, Panamá; tel. 223-8348; fax 223-8351; e-mail info@wao975.fm; internet www.wao975 .fm; Gen. Man. ROGELIO CAMPOS.

Television

Fundación para la Educación en la Televisión—FETV (Canal 5): Vía Ricardo J. Alfaro, Apdo 6-7295, El Dorado, Panamá; tel. 230-8000; fax 230-1955; e-mail comentarios@fetv.org; internet www.fetv .org; f. 1992; Pres. FÁTIMA CUPAS DE MORENO; Gen. Man. FERNANDO TOVAR.

Medcom Panamá, SA (RPC): Avda 12 de Octubre, Hato Pintado, Apdo 0827-00116, Panamá 8; tel. 390-6700; fax 390-6895; e-mail murrutia@medcom.com.pa; internet www.rpctv.com; f. 1998 by merger of RPC Televisión (Canal 4) and Telemetro (Canal 13); commercial; also owns Cable Onda 90 and RPC Radio; CEO NICOLÁS GONZÁLEZ-REVILLA.

Sistema Estatal de Radio y Televisión (Canal 11): Curundu, diagonal al Ministerio de Obras Públicas, Apdo 0843-0256, Panamá; tel. 507-1500; e-mail aportal@sertv.gob.pa; internet www.sertv.gob .pa; f. 1978 as Radio y Televisión Educativa; restructured and assumed present name in 2005; educational and cultural; Dir-Gen. MARISÍN LUZCANDO.

Televisora Nacional—TVN (Canal 2): Edif. TVN-TV-MAX, Avda Ricardo J. Alfaro, Apdo 0819-07129, Panamá; tel. 294-6400; fax 236-2987; e-mail tvn@tvn-2.com; internet www.tvn-2.com; f. 1962; Dir JAIME ALBERTO ARIAS.

Broadcasting Association

Asociación Panameña de Radiodifusión: Apdo 7387, Estafeta de Paitilla, Panamá; tel. 263-5252; fax 226-4396; Pres. PEDRO SOLIS.

Finance

(cap. = capital; res = reserves; dep. = deposits; m. = million; br.(s) = branch(es); amounts in balboas, unless otherwise stated)

BANKING

Superintendencia de Bancos (Banking Superintendency): Torre HSBC, 18°, Avda Samuel Lewis, Apdo 0832-2397, Panamá 1; tel. 506-7800; fax 506-7706; e-mail superbancos@superbancos.gob.pa; internet www.superbancos.gob.pa; f. 1970 as Comisión Bancaria Nacional (National Banking Commission); licenses and controls banking activities within and from Panamanian territory; Comisión Bancaria Nacional superseded by Superintendencia de Bancos in June 1998 with enhanced powers to supervise banking activity; Supt ALBERTO DIAMOND.

National Bank

Banco Nacional de Panamá: Vía España y Calle 55, Apdo 5220, Panamá 5; tel. 505-2000; fax 505-0211; e-mail atencionclientes@ banconal.com.pa; internet www.banconal.com.pa; f. 1904; govt-owned; cap. 500m., res 11.8m., dep. 5,461.3m. (Dec. 2009); Pres. CARLOS RICARDO HENRÍQUEZ LÓPEZ; Gen. Man. DARIO ERNESTO BERBEY DE LA ROSA; 66 brs.

Savings Bank

Caja de Ahorros: Vía España y Calle Thays de Pons, Apdo 1740, Panamá 1; tel. 205-1000; fax 269-3674; e-mail atencionalcliente@ cajadeahorros.com.pa; internet www.cajadeahorros.com.pa; f. 1934; govt-owned; cap. 150.7m., res 47.9m., dep. 170.9m. (Dec. 2006); Pres. RICCARDO FRANCOLINI AROSEMENA; Gen. Man. JAYSON E. PASTOR; 42 brs.

Domestic Private Banks

Banco General, SA: Calle Aquilino de la Guardia, Apdo 0816-00843, Panamá 5; tel. 227-3200; fax 265-0210; e-mail info@bgeneral .com; internet www.bgeneral.com; f. 1955; purchased Banco Comercial de Panamá (BANCOMER) in 2000; cap. 550m., res 44.7m., dep. 7,227m. (Dec. 2011); Chair. and CEO FEDERICO HUMBERT; Exec. Vice-Pres. and Gen. Man. RAÚL ALEMÁN Z.; 59 brs.

Banco Panameño de la Vivienda (BANVIVIENDA): Edif. Grupo Mundial, Avda La Rotonda y Blvd Costa del Este, Bella Vista, Apdo 0816-03366, Panamá 5; tel. 300-4700; fax 300-1133; e-mail bpvger@ pty.com; internet www.banvivienda.com; f. 1981; cap. 60.3m., res 53.2m., dep. 764.5m. (Dec. 2011); Pres. FERNANDO LEWIS NAVARRO; Gen. Man. JUAN RICARDO DE DIANOUS; 3 brs.

Banco Pichincha Panamá: Edif. Parque Urraca, entre Avda Federico Boyd y Avda Balboa, Apdo 0832-01382Panamá; tel. 297-4500; fax 264-6129; e-mail banco@pichinchapanama.com; internet www.pichinchapanama.com; f. 2006; Pres. FIDEL DARIO EGAS GRIJALVA; Gen. Man. ALBERTO ANTONIO BARRIOS ICAZA.

Banco Universal: Torre Banco Universal, Calle B Norte y Avda 1, Apdo 0426-00564, David, Chiriquí; tel. 777-9400; fax 777-9432; e-mail cosorio@bancouniversal.com; internet www.bancouniversal .com; f. 1970; present name adopted 1994; cap. 10m., res −1.9m., dep. 290.1m. (Dec. 2011); Pres. JOSÉ ISAAC VIRZI LÓPEZ; Gen. Man. CARLOS RAÚL BARRIOS ICAZA; 10 brs.

Global Bank Corporation: Torre Global Bank, Calle 50, Apdo 0831-01843, Paitilla, Panamá; tel. 206-2000; fax 206-2072; e-mail global@pan.gbm.net; internet www.globalbank.com.pa; f. 1994; cap. 78.2m., res 22.5m., dep 2,380.7m. (Jun. 2012); Pres. LAWRENCE MADURO; Gen. Man. JORGE VALLARINO STRUNZ.

Multibank: Edif. Prosperidad, planta baja, Vía España 127, Apdo 8210, Panamá 7; tel. 294-3500; fax 264-4014; e-mail banco@ grupomulticredit.com; internet www.multibank.com.pa; f. 1990 as Multi Credit Bank; current name adopted 2008; cap. 182.6m., res −11.4m., dep. 1,465.5m. (Dec. 2011); Pres. ALBERTO S. BTESH; Gen. Man. RAFAEL SÁNCHEZ GARRÓS.

Towerbank International Inc: Edif. Tower Plaza, Calle 50 y Beatriz M. de Cabal, Apdo 0819-06769, Panamá; tel. 269-6900; fax 269-6800; e-mail towerbank@towerbank.com; internet www .towerbank.com; f. 1971; cap. 71.8m., res −1.7m., dep. 582m. (Dec. 2011); Pres. FRED KARDONSKI; Gen. Man. JOSÉ CAMPA.

Foreign Banks

Principal Foreign Banks with General Licence

BAC Panamá (USA): Edif. BAC Credomatic, Calle Aquilino de la Guardia, Apdo 6-3654, Panamá; tel. 213-0822; fax 269-3879; e-mail infobac@pa.bac.net; internet www.bac.net/panama; f. 1995; bought by Grupo Aval de Colombia in Dec. 2010; Gen. Man. JAIME MORENO RUBIO.

Balboa Bank & Trust Corpn: Torre Generali, 19°, Avda Samuel Lewis y Calle 54, Urb. Obarrio, Panamá; tel. 208-7300; fax 263-4165; e-mail customerservice@balboabanktrust.com; internet www .balboabanktrust.com; f. 2003 as Stanford Bank (Panamá), SA; taken over by the Superintendencia de Bancos de Panamá in 2009; renamed in April 2010; Pres. RAMÓN FERNÁNDEZ QUIJANO.

Banco Aliado, SA: Calle 50 y 56, Urb. Obarrio, 0831-02109 Paitilla, Panamá; tel. 302-1555; fax 302-1556; e-mail bkaliado@bancoaliado .com; internet www.bancoaliado.com; f. 1992; cap. 100m., res −0.9m., dep. 1,183.4m. (June 2011); Pres. MOISÉS CHREIM; Gen. Man. ALEXIS A. ARJONA.

Banco Bilbao Vizcaya Argentaria (Panama), SA (Spain): Torre BBVA, Avda Balboa, Calles 42 y 43, Apdo 8673, Panamá 5; tel. 227-0973; fax 227-3663; e-mail fperezp@bbvapanama.com; internet www .bbvapanama.com; f. 1982; cap. 28.7m., res 88.5m., dep. 1,633.3m. (Dec. 2012); Chair. FRANCISCO GONZÁLEZ; Gen. Man. ANTONIO ALONSO; 19 brs.

Banco Davivienda (Panamá), SA (Colombia): Avda Manuel María Icaza y Calle 52E, No 18, Campo Alegre, Apdo 0834-00384, Panamá 9A; tel. 366-6500; fax 263-6115; e-mail info@davivienda.com .pa; internet www.davivienda.com.pa; f. 1966 as Banco Cafetero; name changed as Bancafe in 1995; present name adopted in 2012; cap. 29.1m., res 5.5m., dep. 433m. (Dec. 2010); Pres. EFRAÍN FORERO FONSECO; Gen. Man. FRANCISCO GÓNZALEZ RODRÍGUEZ; 2 brs.

Banco Delta, SA (BMF): Edif. Torre Delta, planta baja, Vía España 122 y Calle Elvira Méndez, Apdo 0816-07831, Panamá; tel. 340-0000; fax 340-0019; e-mail mguerra@bandelta.com; internet www .bandelta.com; f. 2006; Pres. ARTURO MÜLLER; Gen. Man. GINA DE SÁENZ.

Banco Internacional de Costa Rica, SA: Casa Matriz, Calle Manuel M. Icaza 25, Apdo 0816-07810, Panamá 1; tel. 208-9500; fax 208-9581; e-mail informacion@bicaspan.net; internet www .bicsapan.com; f. 1976; cap. 100.3m., res 0.2m., dep. 804m. (Dec. 2011); Gen. Man. FEDERICO CARRILLO ZURCHER.

Banco Latinoamericano de Comercio Exterior SA (BLADEX) (Multinational): Torre V, Business Park, Avda La Rotonda, Urb. Costa del Este, Panamá; tel. 210-8500; fax 269-6333; e-mail webmaster@bladex.com; internet www.blx.com; f. 1979 as Banco Latinoamericano de Exportaciones; name changed as above in 2009; groups together 254 Latin American commercial and central banks, 22 international banks and some 3,000 New York Stock Exchange shareholders; cap. US $280m., res $124.4m., dep. $2,317.3m. (Dec. 2012); CEO RUBENS V. AMARAL, Jr.

Citibank Panamá (USA): Edif. Banco Cuscatlán, Calle Aquilino de la Guardia, Apdo 555, Panamá 9A; tel. 210-5900; fax 210-5901; internet www.citibank.com.pa; f. 1904; cap. 124.7m., res 3.8m., dep. 699.5m. (Dec. 2011); Gen. Man. MARCELO GORRINI; 14 brs.

Credicorp Bank, SA: Edif. Plaza Credicorp Bank, Nicanor de Obarrio, Calle 50, Apdo 833-0125, Panamá; tel. 210-1111; fax 210-0100; internet www.credicorpbank.com; f. 1992; cap. 60.3m., res 0.9m., dep. 837.1m. (Jun. 2010); Pres. RAYMOND HARARI; Gen. Man. MAX J. HARARI; 25 brs.

Helm Bank (Panama), SA: Edif. World Trade Center, 19°, Calle 53, Urb. Marbella, Apdo 0819-07070, Panamá; tel. 265-2820; fax 214-9715; e-mail servicioalcliente@helmpanama.com; internet www .helmpanama.com; f. as Banco de Crédito (Panama) SA, renamed in 2002 as Banco de Crédito Helm Financial Sevices (Panama), and as above in 2009; owned by Helm Bank SA (Colombia); cap. US $38.6m., res US $−0.5m., dep. US $499.9m. (Dec. 2010); Gen. Man. CARLOS HUMBERTO ROJAS M.

HSBC Bank (Panama), SA: Plaza HSBC, Calle Aquilino de la Guardia, Urb. Marbella, Panamá; tel. 263-5855; fax 263-6009; e-mail panama_investrel@hsbc.com.pa; internet www.hsbc.com.pa; cap. US $1,293.7m., dep. $11,137.7m. (Dec. 2009); acquired the Panama operations of Chase Manhattan Bank in 2000 and Primer Banco del Istmo (Banistmo) in 2006; bought by Bancolombia in 2013; CEO ANTONIO MIGUEL LOSADA; 62 brs.

Principal Foreign Banks with International Licence

Austrobank Overseas (Panamá), SA: Edif. MMG, planta baja, Calle 53, Este Marbella, Apdo 0819-07030, El Dorado, Panamá 6; tel. 223-5105; fax 264-6918; e-mail gerencia@austrobank.com; internet www.austrobank.com; f. 1995; Gen. Man. JOSÉ ENRIQUE CÓRDOVA.

Banco Agrícola (Panamá), SA: Edif. Global Bank, 17°, Local E y F, Calle 50, Apdo 6-2637, Panamá; tel. 263-5762; fax 263-5626; e-mail info@bancoagricola.com; internet www.bancoagricolapanama.com; f. 2002; Exec. Pres. RAFAEL BARRAZA DOMÍNGUEZ.

Banco de la Nación Argentina: Edif. World Trade Center 501, Calle 53, Urb. Marbella, Panamá; tel. 269-4666; fax 269-6719; e-mail bnapanama@bna.com.pa; internet www.bna.com.ar; f. 1977; Pres. JUAN CARLOS FABREGA; Gen. Man. RUBÉN DARÍO NOCERA.

Banco de Occidente (Panama), SA: Edif. American International, Calle 50 y Aquilino de la Guardia, Apdo 6-7430, El Dorado, Panamá; tel. 263-8144; fax 269-3261; internet www.bancoccidente .com.pa; f. 1982; cap. US $9.6m., res $7.8m., dep. $575.4m. (Dec. 2010); Pres. EFRAÍN OTERO ALVAREZ; Gen. Man. OSCAR LUNA GORDILLO.

Banco del Pacífico (Panama), SA: Calle Aquilino de la Guardia y Calle 52, esq. Edif. Banco del Pacifico, Apdo 0819-07070, El Dorado, Panamá; tel. 263-5833; fax 263-7481; e-mail bpacificopanama@ pacifico.fin.ec; internet www.bancodelpacifico.com.pa; f. 1980; cap. 11.3m., res −0.2m., dep. 150.4m. (Dec. 2010); Pres. and Gen. Man. ANA ESCOBAR.

Bancolombia (Panamá), SA: Edif. Bancolombia, Plaza Marbella, Calle Aquilino de la Guardia y Calle 47, Apdo 0816-03320, Panamá; tel. 263-6955; fax 269-1138; e-mail bancolombiapanama@allus.com .co; internet www.bancolombiapanama.com; f. 1973; current name adopted in 1999; cap. 14m., res 20.8m., dep. 6,434m. (Dec. 2011); Pres. CARLOS RAUL YEPES JIMÉNEZ; Gen. Man. PABLO EMILIO DÍAZ GÓMEZ.

FPB Bank Inc: Torre de las Américas, Torre C, 26°, Of. 2601, Punta Pacífica, Panamá; tel. 210-6600; fax 210-6649; internet www .fpbbank.com; f. 2005; Pres. EDUARDO ROSA PINHEIRO; Gen. Man. JOSÉ APARECIDO PAULUCCI.

Popular Bank Ltd Inc: Edif. Torre Banco General, Calle 47E y Avda Aquilini de la Guardia, Marbella, Apdo 0816-00265, Panamá; tel. 269-4166; fax 269-1309; e-mail contactenos@popularbank.com .pa; internet www.popularbank.com.pa; f. 1983 as Banco Popular Dominicano (Panama), SA; current name adopted in 2003; cap. 50.4m., res 0.1m., dep. 521.8m. (Dec. 2010); Pres. ALEJANDRO E. SANTELISES; Gen. Man. GIANNI VERSARI.

Banking Association

Asociación Bancaria de Panamá (ABP): Torre Hong Kong Bank, 15°, Avda Samuel Lewis, Apdo 4554, Panamá 5; tel. 263-7044; fax 223-5800; e-mail abp@orbi.net; internet www.asociacionbancaria

.com; f. 1962; 79 mems; Pres. CARLOS E. TROETSCH SAVAL; Exec. Vice-Pres. MARIO DE DIEGO, Jr.

STOCK EXCHANGE

Bolsa de Valores de Panamá: Edif. Bolsa de Valores de Panamá, Avda Federico Boyd y Calle 49, Apdo 823-00963, Panamá; tel. 269-1966; fax 269-2457; e-mail bvp@panabolsa.com; internet www.panabolsa.com; f. 1960; Pres. FELIPE E. CHAPMAN; Gen. Man. ROBERTO BRENES PÉREZ.

INSURANCE

Acerta, Cía de Seguros: Avda Ricardo Arango y Calle Santa Ana, Urb. Obarrio, Apdo 0823-04175, Panamá; tel. 307-3000; fax 307-3001; e-mail info@acertaseguros.com; internet www.acertaseguros.com; Pres. JUAN CARLOS FÁBREGA.

Arca Internacional de Reaseguros, SA: Edif. Bolsa de Valores, 1°, Avda Federico Boyd, Frente al Restaurante Rinos, Panamá; tel. 300-2858; fax 300-2859; f. 1996; Gen. Man. CARLOS G. DE LA LASTRA.

Aseguradora Ancón, SA: Avda Samuel Lewis y Calle 54, Urb. Obarrio, Panamá; tel. 210-8700; fax 210-8790; e-mail info@asegurancon.com; internet www.asegurancon.com; f. 1992; Pres. TOBIAS CARRERO NACAR; Sec. CARLOS G. CHAMORRO.

ASSA Cía de Seguros, SA: Edif. ASSA, Avda Nicanor de Obarrio (Calle 50), Apdo 0816-01622, Panamá 5; tel. 300-2772; fax 300-2729; e-mail servicioalcliente@assanet.com; internet www.assanet.com; f. 1973; Pres. STANLEY MOTTA.

Assicurazioni Generali, Spa: Torre Generali, Avda Samuel Lewis y Calle 54, Urb. Obarrio, Apdo 0816-02206, 507 Panamá; tel. 206-9100; fax 206-9105; e-mail mercadeo@generali.com.pa; internet www.generali.com.pa; f. 1977; Gen. Man. GABRIEL R. DE OBARRIO, III.

Cía Interoceánica de Seguros, SA: Plaza Marbella, Frente Banco HSBC, Calle Alquilino de la Guardia, Panamá; tel. 205-0700; fax 264-7668; e-mail info@interoceanica.com; internet www.interoceanica.com; f. 1978; Gen. Man. SALVADOR MORALES BACA.

Empresa General de Seguros, SA: Edif. Plaza 2000, Calles 50 y 53, 1° y 2°, Panamá; tel. 303-2222; fax 264-1107; e-mail scliente-gseguros@egs.com.pa; internet www.asecomer.com; f. 1987; Gen. Man. LUIS E. BANDERA.

HSBC Seguros (Panamá), SA (CONASE): Edif. HSBC, No 62, Calle 50, Apdo 5303, Panamá 5; tel. 205-0300; fax 223-4865; e-mail hsbcseguros@hsbc.com.pa; f. 1957 as Cía Nacional de Seguros, SA; current name adopted July 2007; Pres. ERNESTO FERNÁNDEZ.

Internacional de Seguros, SA: Edif. Plaza Credicorp Bank, 17°, Avda Nicanor de Obarrio, Calle 50, Panamá; tel. 227-4000; e-mail conase@conase.net; internet www.iseguros.com; f. 1910; Pres. RICHARD A. FORD.

Mitsui Sumitomo Insurance Co Ltd: Of. 701, 7°, Plaza Credicorp Bank Panamá, Panamá; tel. 210-0133; fax 210-0122; internet www.msilm.com; f. 1979; Gen. Man. TA KASHI MORIMOTO.

Panama Mapfré: Edif. MAPFRE, 1°, Costa del Este, Panamá; tel. 378-5900; fax 378-5916; e-mail info@mapfre.com.pa; internet www.mapfre.com.pa; f. 1937; general; Gen. Man. DINO MON.

Provincial Re Panamá, SA: Edif. Alexandra, Of. 3A, Avda Octavio de Icaza, Panamá; tel. 836-5660; fax 260-5055; internet www.provincialre.com; f. 1984; Gen. Man. JOSÉ FRANCISCO LÓPEZ ANTÓN.

QBE del Istmo Cía de Reaseguros, Inc: Costa del Este, Avda Paseo del Mar y Calle Vista del Pacífico, Apdo 51, Panamá; tel. 306-2200; fax 306-2270; internet www.istmore.com; f. 1979; Pres. and CEO RAMÓN E. FERNÁNDEZ.

La Seguridad de Panamá, Cía de Seguros, SA: Edif. American International, Calle 50, esq. Aquilino de la Guardia, Apdo 5306, Panamá 5; tel. 263-6700; f. 1986; Gen. Man. MARIELA OSORIO.

Seguros Sura: Calle Aquilino De La Guardia, entre calle 47 y 48, Plaza Marbella, Apdo 0831-0784, Paitilla, Panamá; tel. 2050700; e-mail atencionalasegurado@sura.com.pa; internet www.sura.com.pa; Gen. Man. SALVADOR MORALES BACA.

Trade and Industry

Colón Free Zone (CFZ): Avda Roosevelt, Apdo 1118, Colón; tel. 445-1033; fax 445-2165; e-mail zonalibre@zolicol.org; internet www.zonalibredecolon.com.pa; f. 1948 to manufacture, import, handle and re-export all types of merchandise; some 2,500 companies active in 2012, employing 27,347 people; the total area of the CFZ was 450 ha; Gen. Man. LEOPOLDO BENEDETTI.

GOVERNMENT AGENCIES

Autoridad de la Micro, Pequeña y Mediana Empresa: Calle Maritza Alabarca, Edif. 1005 y 1010, Clayton, Panamá; tel. 500-5602; e-mail atencionalcliente@ampyme.gob.pa; internet www.ampyme.gob.pa; f. 2000; promotes the devt of micro-, small and medium enterprises; Dir-Gen. GISELLE BURILLO SÁIZ.

CHAMBERS OF COMMERCE

American Chamber of Commerce and Industry of Panama: POB 0843-00152, Panamá; tel. 301-3881; fax 301-3882; e-mail amcham@panamcham.com; internet www.panamcham.com; Pres. JUAN CARLOS ARIAS; Exec. Dir MAURICE BELANGER.

Cámara de Comercio, Industrias y Agricultura de Panamá: Avda Cuba y Ecuador 33A, Apdo 74, Panamá 1; tel. 207-3440; fax 207-3422; e-mail infocciap@cciap.com; internet www.panacamara.com; f. 1915; Pres. FEDERICO HUMBERT ARIAS; Exec. Dir RAFAEL ZUÑIGA BRID; 1,300 mems.

Cámara Oficial Española de Comercio: Avda Balboa, Edif. Banco BBVA, Torre Menor, 7°, Apdo 1857, Panamá 1; tel. 225-1487; fax 225-6608; e-mail caespan@cwpanama.net; internet www.caespan.com.pa; Pres. MARCO ANTONIO SAAVEDRA CATALÁ; Exec. Dir MARÍA JESÚS ALONSO ROS.

INDUSTRIAL AND TRADE ASSOCIATIONS

Asociación Panameña de Exportadores (APEX): Edif. Ricardo Galindo Quelquejeu, Avda Ricardo J. Alfaro, Urb. Sara Sotillo, Panamá; tel. 230-0169; e-mail apex@cableonda.net; internet www.apexpanama.org; f. 1971; export asscn; Pres. JUAN PLANELLS; Sec. JAIME ORTIZ.

Cámara Panameña de la Construcción: Calle Aquilino de la Guardia y Calle 52, Área Bancaria, diagonal al Hotel Ejecutivo, Apdo 0816-02350, Panamá 5; tel. 265-2500; fax 265-2571; e-mail informacion@capac.org; internet www.capac.org; represents interests of construction sector; Pres. GASTÓN E. REGIS R.; Dir-Gen. EDUARDO RODRÍGUEZ.

Sindicato de Industriales de Panamá: Vía Ricardo J. Alfaro, Entrada Urb. Sara Sotillo, Apdo 6-4798, Estafeta El Dorado, Panamá; tel. 230-0169; fax 230-0805; e-mail sip@cableonda.net; internet www.industriales.org; f. 1945; represents and promotes activities of industrial sector; Pres. JUAN F. KIENER; Sec.-Gen. MÁXIMO GALLARDO.

EMPLOYERS' ORGANIZATIONS

Asociación Panameña de Ejecutivos de Empresas (APEDE): Avda Justo Arosemena, Calle 31, frente a la Piscina Adán Gordón, Apdo 0816-06785, Panamá; tel. 204-1500; fax 204-1510; e-mail apede@apede.org; internet www.apede.org; Pres. FÉLIX H. CUEVAS S.; Exec. Dir YARA GONZÁLEZ.

Consejo Nacional de la Empresa Privada (CONEP): Avda Morgan, Balboa, Ancón, Casa 302A-B, Zona 1, Apdo 0816-07197, Panamá 1; tel. 211-2672; fax 211-2694; e-mail conep1@cwpanama.net; internet www.conep.org.pa; Pres. GABRIEL DIEZ; Exec. Dir ALFREDO BURGOS.

UTILITIES

Regulatory Authority

Autoridad Nacional de los Servicios Públicos: see Broadcasting and Communications—Regulatory Authority.

Electricity

AES Panama: Torre Banco Continental, 25°, Calle 50 y Aquilino de la Guardia, CP 0816-01990, Panamá; tel. 206-2600; fax 206-2645; e-mail aespanama@aes.com; internet www.aespanama.com; f. 1998 upon acquisition by AES Corpn of 49% interest in Empresa de Generación Electrica Bayano and Empresa de Generación Electrica Chiriquí; operates three hydroelectric facilities in Bayano (248 MW), Estí (120 MW) and Chiriquí (90 MW) and one 43-MW thermal facility; Pres. JAIME TUPPER; Gen. Man. JAIME COOPER.

Empresa de Transmisión Eléctrica, SA (ETESA): Plaza Sun Tower, 3°, Avda Ricardo J. Alfaro, El Dorado, Panamá; tel. 501-3800; fax 501-3506; e-mail gerinfo@etesa.com.pa; internet www.etesa.com.pa; f. 1998; state-owned transmission co; Pres. FRANK DE LIMA; Gen. Man. FERNANDO A. MARCISCANO R.

ENSA, SA: Costa del Este, Business Park-Torre Oeste, 3°, Panamá; tel. 340-4600; internet www.ensa.com.pa; f. 1998; fmrly known as Elektra Noreste, SA; electricity distribution; Gen. Man. JAVIER PARIENTE.

Natural Gas Fenosa: Albrook, Edif. 812, Avda Diógenes de la Rosa, Balboa, Ancón, Panamá; tel. 315-7600; e-mail edemet-edechi@ufpanama.com; internet www.ufpanama.com; f. 1998 by acquisition of Empresa de Distribución Eléctrica Metro Oeste (EDEMET) and Empresa de Distribución Eléctrica Chiriquí (EDECHI) by Unión FENOSA, Spain; electricity distributor; includes 2 subsidiaries: Ufinet and ESEPSA; Pres. RICARDO BARRANCO.

Water

Instituto de Acueductos y Alcantarillados Nacionales (IDAAN) (National Waterworks and Sewage Systems Institute): Apdo 5234, Panamá; tel. 523-8567; e-mail relaciones.publicas@idaan .gob.pa; internet www.idaan.gob.pa; state-run; Pres. JOSÉ ANTONIO DÍAZ.

TRADE UNIONS

Central General Autónoma de Trabajadores de Panamá (CGTP): Edif. CGTP, Calle 3a Perejil, detrás del Colegio Javier, Panamá; tel. 269-9741; fax 223-5287; e-mail cgtpan@cwpanama.net; internet www.cgtp.org.pa; fmrly Central Istmeña de Trabajadores; Sec.-Gen. MARIANO E. MENA.

Confederación Nacional de Unidad Sindical Independiente (CONUSI): 0421B Calle Venado, Ancón, Apdo 830344, Zona 3, Panamá; tel. 212-3865; fax 212-2565; e-mail conusipanama@ hotmail.com; Sec.-Gen. GENARO LÓPEZ.

Confederación de Trabajadores de la República de Panamá (CTRP) (Confederation of Workers of the Republic of Panama): Calle 31, entre Avdas México y Justo Arosemena 3-50, Apdo 0816-03647, Panamá 5; tel. 225-0293; fax 225-0259; e-mail ctrp@hotmail.es; f. 1956; admitted to ITUC/ORIT; Sec.-Gen. GUILLERMO PUGA; 62,000 mems from 13 affiliated groups.

Transport

RAILWAYS

In 1998 there was an estimated 485 km of track in Panama. In 2001 the 83-km Trans-Isthmian railway, originally founded in 1855, reopened. The construction of a metro system in Panama City began in 2011. The first phase of the project, funded by the Corporación Andina de Fomento (CAF) with $400m., was construction of Consorcio Línea 1. Operations were expected to begin in 2014 and the Government was expected to launch a tender for the second subway line in the same year. Four such lines were planned, one of which was to run above the canal.

Panama Canal Railway Company: Edif. T-376, Corozal Oeste, Apdo 2669, Balboa Ancón, Panamá; tel. 317-6070; fax 317-6061; e-mail info@panarail.com; internet www.panarail.com; private investment under 50-year govt concession; 83 km linking Panama City and Colón, running parallel to Panama Canal; operation on concession by Kansas City Southern (KS, USA) and Mi-Jack Products (IL, USA); modernization programme completed in 2001; operates daily passenger and cargo service; Dir-Gen. THOMAS KENNA.

ROADS

In 2010, according to preliminary figures, there were 15,137 km of roads, of which some 42% were paved. The Pan-American Highway to Mexico City runs for 545 km in Panama and is expected to be extended towards Colombia. The Trans-Isthmian Highway runs from Panama City to Colón. There is also a highway to San José, Costa Rica. The Coastal Beltway, or Cinta Costera, road development project aimed to reduce congestion in Panama City. The first phase of the project was completed in 2009 at a cost of US $189.1m. In the same year, the Government approved $52m. for the second phase, and in 2010 the final phase, expected to cost $776.9m., was approved.

Autoridad del Tránsito y Transporte Terrestre (ATTT): ; tel. 502-0547; internet www.transito.gob.pa; f. 1999; regulatory authority; Dir-Gen. ROBERTO MORENO.

MiBus: Panamá; internet www.mibus.com.pa; f. 2009; operates the Metro bus system in Panamá; Man. IVÁN POSADA.

SHIPPING

Some 5% of all the world's sea-borne trade passes through the Panama Canal. It is 82 km long, and ships take an average of nine hours to complete a transit. In 2011/12 some 14,544 transits were recorded. The widening of the narrowest section of the Canal, the Culebra Cut, was completed in 2005. Plans were also announced to construct a 203-ha international cargo-handling platform at the Atlantic end of the Canal, including terminals, a railway and an international airport. Terminal ports are Balboa, on the Pacific Ocean, and Cristóbal, on the Caribbean Sea. Further expansion of the Canal's capacity to allow the passage of larger commercial container vessels, by constructing a third set of locks at either end of the waterway, was initially scheduled to be completed in October 2014, although this was likely to be delayed.

The Panamanian flag registered fleet was the second largest in the world in December 2012, comprising 9,326 vessels, totalling 228.5m. gross registered tons.

Autoridad del Canal de Panamá (ACP): Administration Bldg, Balboa, Ancón, Panamá; tel. 272-7602; fax 272-7693; e-mail info@ pancanal.com; internet www.pancanal.com; f. 1997; manages, operates and maintains the Panama Canal; succeeded the Panama Canal Commission, a US govt agency, on 31 December 1999, when the waterway was ceded to the Govt of Panama; the ACP is the autonomous agency of the Govt of Panama; there is a Board of 11 mems; Chair. ROBERTO ROY; Administrator JORGE LUIS QUIJANO.

Autoridad Marítima de Panamá: Edif. PanCanal Albrook, Diablo Heights, Balboa, Ancón, Apdo 0843-0533, Panamá 7; tel. 501-5196; fax 501-5406; e-mail ampadmin@amp.gob.pa; internet www.amp .gob.pa; f. 1998 to unite and optimize the function of all state institutions with involvement in the maritime sector; Administrator ROBERTO LINARES TRIBALDOS.

Panama City Port Authority and Foreign Trade Zone 65: Apdo 15095, Panamá; FL 32406, USA; tel. 767-3220; e-mail wstubbs@ portpanamacityusa.com; internet www.portpanamacityusa.com; Chair. GEORGE NORRIS; Exec. Dir WAYNE STUBBS.

CIVIL AVIATION

Tocumen (formerly Omar Torrijos) International Airport, situated 19 km (12 miles) outside Panamá (Panama City), is the country's principal airport and is served by many international airlines. The France Airport in Colón and the Rio Hato Airport in Coclé province have both been declared international airports. There are also 11 smaller airports in the country.

Air Panama: Marcos A. Gelabert Airport, Albrook, Panamá; tel. 316-9000; e-mail info@flyairpanama.com; internet www .flyairpanama.com; operates flights throughout Panama and to Costa Rica; Gen. Man. EDUARDO STAGG.

Compañía Panameña de Aviación, SA (COPA): Avda Justo Arosemena 230 y Calle 39, Apdo 1572, Panamá 1; tel. 227-2522; fax 227-1952; e-mail proquebert@mail.copa.com.pa; internet www .copaair.com; f. 1947; scheduled passenger and cargo services from Panamá (Panama City) to Central America, South America, the Caribbean and the USA; Chair. STANLEY MOTTA; CEO PEDRO O. HEILBRON.

Tourism

Panama's attractions include Panamá (Panama City), the ruins of Portobelo and 800 sandy tropical islands, including the resort of Contadora, one of the Pearl Islands in the Gulf of Panama, and the San Blas Islands, lying off the Atlantic coast. In 2011 the number of visitor arrivals stood at 1,473,000 and income from tourism was US $1,926m.

Asociación Panameña de Agencias de Viajes y Turismo (APAVIT): Edif. Balmoral, Vía Argentina, diagonal a la Universidad de Panamá, Panamá; tel. 263-9104; fax 263-8937; e-mail info@apavit .org; internet www.apavit.org; f. 1957; Pres. ERNESTO REINA.

Autoridad de Turismo Panamá (IPAT): Edif. Central, 1°, Avda Samuel Lewis y calle Gerardo Ortega, Panamá 5; tel. 526-7000; fax 526-7100; e-mail gerencia@atp.gob.pa; internet www.atp.gob.pa; f. 1960; Dir-Gen. SALOMON SHAMAH.

Defence

In 1990, following the overthrow of Gen. Manuel Antonio Noriega Morena, the National Defence Forces were disbanded and a new Public Force was created. The new force was representative of the size of the population and affiliated to no political party. As assessed at November 2012, the Public Force numbered an estimated 12,000, comprising the National Police (11,000) and the National Aeronaval Service (1000).

Security Expenditure: budgeted at an estimated US $548m. in 2012.

Director of National Civil Protection System: ARTURO ALVARADO DE ICAZA.

Director of National Police: JULIO MOLTÓ.

Director of National Aero-Naval Service: BELSIO GIOLIS GONZALEZ SÁNCHEZ.

Education

The education system in Panama is divided into elementary, secondary and university schooling, each of six years' duration. Education is free up to university level and is officially compulsory between six and 15 years of age. Primary education begins at the age of six and secondary education, which comprises two three-year cycles, at the age of 12. In 2007/08 enrolment at primary schools included 98% of children in the relevant age-group, while secondary enrolment included 66% of children in the relevant age-group. There are four public universities and 11 private ones, including one that specializes in distance learning. In 2011 a plan to improve educational standards in indigenous schools was announced. The project was to be financed by a US $30m. loan from the Inter-American Development Bank. Budgetary expenditure on education by the central Government in 2010 amounted to a preliminary 749.9m. balboas.

PAPUA NEW GUINEA

Introductory Survey

LOCATION, CLIMATE, LANGUAGE, RELIGION, FLAG, CAPITAL

The Independent State of Papua New Guinea lies east of Indonesia and north of the north-eastern extremity of Australia. It comprises the eastern section of the island of New Guinea (the western section being Papua (West Papua), formerly Irian Jaya, which forms part of Indonesia) and about 600 smaller islands, including the Bismarck Archipelago (mainly New Britain, New Ireland and Manus) and the northern part of the Solomon Islands (mainly Bougainville and Buka). The climate is hot and humid throughout the year, with an average maximum temperature of 33°C (91°F) and an average minimum of 22°C (72°F). Rainfall is high on the coast but lower inland: the annual average varies from about 1,000 mm (40 ins) to 6,350 mm (250 ins). There are more than 850 native languages, but Pidgin and, to a lesser extent, standard English are also spoken, and, together with Motu, are the official languages in Parliament. More than 90% of the population profess Christianity. The national flag (proportions 3 by 4) is divided diagonally from the upper hoist to the lower fly: the upper portion displays a golden bird of paradise in silhouette on a red ground, while the lower portion has five white five-pointed stars, in the form of the Southern Cross constellation, on a black ground. The capital is Port Moresby.

CONTEMPORARY POLITICAL HISTORY

Historical Context

Papua New Guinea was formed by the merger of the Territory of Papua, under Australian rule from 1906, with the Trust Territory of New Guinea, a former German possession which Australia administered from 1914, first under a military Government, then under a League of Nations mandate, established in 1921, and later under a trusteeship agreement with the UN. During the Second World War, parts of both territories were occupied by Japanese forces from 1942 to 1945.

A joint administration for the two territories was established by Australia in July 1949. The union was named the Territory of Papua and New Guinea. A Legislative Council was established in November 1951 and was replaced by a House of Assembly, with an elected indigenous majority, in June 1964. The territory was renamed Papua New Guinea in July 1971. It achieved internal self-government in December 1973 and full independence on 16 September 1975, when the House of Assembly became the National Parliament.

Domestic Political Affairs

Michael Somare, who from 1972 served as Chief Minister in an interim coalition Government, became Prime Minister on independence. He remained in office until 1980, despite widespread allegations of inefficiency in government ministries and of discrimination against the Highland provinces. The first general election since independence was held in mid-1977, following which Somare's Pangu (Papua New Guinea Unity) Pati formed a governing coalition, first with the People's Progress Party (PPP) and later with the United Party (UP).

In March 1980 the Government lost a vote of confidence, the fourth in 15 months, and Sir Julius Chan, the leader of the PPP and a former Deputy Prime Minister, succeeded to the premiership. Somare became Prime Minister again following a general election in June 1982. In 1983 the Somare Government effected a constitutional change to provide the central authorities with greater control of the provincial governments as a means of preventing abuse of their powers. As a result, between 1983 and 1991 a total of nine provincial governments were suspended by the central Government for alleged maladministration.

In March 1985 a motion expressing no confidence in Somare's Government was introduced in Parliament by Chan, who nominated Paias Wingti (hitherto Deputy Prime Minister and a member of the Pangu Pati) as alternative Prime Minister. Somare quickly formed a coalition, comprising the ruling Pangu Pati, the National Party (NP) and the Melanesian Alliance (MA), and the motion was defeated. Fourteen Members of Parliament

(MPs) who had supported the motion were expelled from the Pangu Pati, and subsequently formed a new political party, the People's Democratic Movement (PDM), under the leadership of Wingti.

In August 1985 the NP withdrew from Somare's coalition Government, and in November Chan presented another motion of no confidence, criticizing Somare's handling of the economy. Somare was defeated and Wingti took office as Prime Minister, heading a new five-party coalition Government (comprising the PDM, the PPP, the NP, the UP and the MA), with Chan as Deputy Prime Minister.

At the mid-1987 election to the National Parliament Somare's Pangu Pati won 26 of the 109 elective seats, while Wingti's PDM obtained 18. However, by forming a coalition with minor parties, Wingti succeeded in securing a parliamentary majority and was re-elected Prime Minister. In July 1988 Wingti was defeated in a no confidence motion, proposed by Rabbie Namaliu, who had replaced Somare as leader of the Pangu Pati. As a result, Namaliu took office as Prime Minister and announced a new coalition Government, comprising members of the Pangu Pati and five minor parties: the People's Action Party (PAP), the MA, the NP, the League for National Advancement (LNA) and the Papua Party. In August Ted Diro, the leader of the PAP, was acquitted on a charge of perjury by the Supreme Court (having been accused of illegally appropriating funds for his party). An amendment to the Constitution, whereby a motion expressing no confidence in the Prime Minister could not be proposed until the premier had completed 18 months in office, was approved by Parliament in August 1990 and incorporated into the Constitution in July 1991.

In September 1991 a leadership tribunal found Ted Diro, the leader of the PAP, guilty of 81 charges of misconduct in government office. However, the Governor-General, Sir Serei Eri, refused to ratify the tribunal's decision and reinstated Diro as Deputy Prime Minister, despite recommendations that he be dismissed. A constitutional crisis subsequently arose, during which a government envoy was sent to the United Kingdom to request that the Queen (as head of state of Papua New Guinea) dismiss Eri. However, the Governor-General and Diro both resigned in October. A new Governor-General, Wiwa Korowi, was elected by the National Parliament in November.

In 1992 the Government continued to be troubled by allegations of corruption and misconduct (notably bribery and misuse of public funds). Campaigning for the general election began amid serious fighting among the various political factions, which led to rioting, in April, by some 10,000 supporters of rival candidates. At the election in June a total of 59 members of the legislature (including 15 ministers) lost their seats. The final result gave the Pangu Pati 22 of the 109 elective seats, while the PDM secured 15. Independent candidates won a total of 31 seats. Paias Wingti of the PDM was subsequently elected Prime Minister by the National Parliament, defeating Rabbie Namaliu of the Pangu Pati by a single vote. Wingti formed a coalition Government, comprising PDM, PPP and LNA members, as well as several independents. As part of the new administration's anti-corruption policy, Wingti suspended six provincial governments for financial mismanagement in October, and threatened to abolish the entire local government system.

In early 1993 a resurgence of tribal violence, mainly in the Enga Province, resulted in the deaths of more than 100 people. This development, together with a continued increase in violent crime throughout the country (despite the implementation in 1991 of severe measures to combat crime, including the introduction of the death penalty) prompted the National Parliament to approve a new internal security act in May 1993. The measures, which included an amendment of the legal system that required defendants accused of serious crimes to prove their innocence, rather than be proven guilty, were criticized by the opposition as oppressive. In May 1994 the Supreme Court nullified six of the 26 sections of the act (most of which concerned the extension of police powers), denouncing them as unconstitutional.

In September 1993 Prime Minister Wingti announced his resignation. The Speaker immediately requested nominations for the premiership, and Wingti was re-elected unopposed with 59 of the 109 votes. According to the Constitution, a motion of no confidence in the Prime Minister could not be presented for at least 18 months, and Wingti claimed that his action had been necessary in order to secure a period of political stability for the country. However, opposition members described the events as an abuse of the democratic process, and several thousand demonstrators gathered in the capital to demand Wingti's resignation. In December the National Court rejected a constitutional challenge from the opposition to Wingti's re-election, but in August 1994 the Supreme Court declared Wingti's re-election invalid. Wingti did not contest the ensuing parliamentary vote for a new Prime Minister, in which Sir Julius Chan of the PPP defeated the Speaker, Bill Skate, by 66 votes to 32; Chris Haiveta, the leader of the Pangu Pati, was appointed Deputy Prime Minister.

The abolition of the directly elected provincial government system, as proposed by Wingti, was rejected by Chan's Government, although a series of reforms were presented to Parliament in early 1995. The controversial legislation was approved in June, and the new regional authorities, comprising national politicians and selected local councillors and led by appointed governors, were appointed in that month. Wingti resigned as parliamentary Leader of the Opposition in order to assume the post of Governor in the Western Highlands Province, and was replaced by another PDM member, Roy Yaki.

The involvement of mercenaries to counter the secessionist movement on the island of Bougainville in early 1997 led to a period of extreme instability throughout the country, culminating in Chan's temporary resignation and the appointment of John Giheno as acting Prime Minister for about two months. The atmosphere of political uncertainty was exacerbated by serious outbreaks of violence in the weeks preceding the general election in mid-June. The Government imposed a dusk-to-dawn curfew and a nation-wide ban on the sale of alcohol. Many senior politicians, including Giheno and Wingti, failed to secure re-election at the polls. Following a period of intense political manoeuvring, former Speaker Bill Skate of the People's National Congress (PNC), who was currently the Governor of the National Capital District (NCD), was elected Prime Minister in July, defeating Sir Michael Somare (who had established a new party—the National Alliance—in 1996) by 71 votes to 35. Skate was supported by a coalition of the PNC, PDM, PPP, Pangu Pati and independent members. A new Government was appointed in late July 1997, and extensive changes in the functional responsibilities of ministries were announced.

In September 1997 the Government declared a national disaster following a prolonged period of drought, which, by the end of the year, had resulted in the deaths of more than 1,000 people. Several countries and organizations that had provided relief funds during the disaster were highly critical of the Government's management of the aid it received. The Minister for Finance, Roy Yaki, was dismissed, in part for his role in the affair. It was subsequently revealed that less than one-half of the relief aid received had been deployed to help the victims of the disaster.

In November 1997 Silas (later Sir Silas) Atopare was appointed Governor-General, defeating Sir Getake Gam, head of the Evangelical Lutheran Church, by 54 votes to 44 in the legislature. A serious political scandal erupted later that month, following allegations of corruption against the Prime Minister. The accusations centred on a videotape broadcast on Australian television, which appeared to show Skate arranging bribes and boasting of his strong connections with criminal elements in Port Moresby. The Prime Minister dismissed his recorded comments (and the resultant allegations), stating that he had been drunk at the time of filming. Several senior politicians, including Somare, demanded his resignation over the affair. Meanwhile, Skate dismissed the leaders of the Pangu Pati and the PPP (Chris Haiveta and Andrew Baing, respectively), his coalition partners, accusing them of conspiring against him. The situation intensified in December with the announcement that the Pangu Pati and the PPP would join the opposition. However, the PPP rejoined the Government shortly afterwards, having voted to replace Baing as leader of the party with Michael Nali. Similarly, four Pangu Pati ministers rejoined the Government, thereby restoring Skate's majority in the National Parliament.

In April 1998 the Prime Minister announced the formation of a new political grouping, the Papua New Guinea First Party,

which absorbed the PNC, the Christian Country Party and several other minor parties. The Government's majority was undermined in mid-1998 when the Court of Disputed Returns declared the election in 1997 of seven government MPs to be null and void. Furthermore, in June 1998 the Pangu Pati officially joined the opposition, thereby reducing the Government's representation in the National Parliament to 61 members. Rumours of a forthcoming motion of no confidence in the Prime Minister prompted the establishment of a new pro-Skate coalition in the National Parliament in July. The PPP left the governing coalition in October.

In May 1999 the Speaker, John Pundari, established a new political party, the PNG Liberal Party (relaunched in June as the Advance PNG Party—APP). In a government reorganization in early June, Skate dismissed the PDM leader, Sir Mekere Morauta (a former Governor of the central bank), and three other PDM ministers; both the PDM and the United Resource Party (URP) withdrew completely from the coalition Government later that month, following the resignation of nine government ministers. Both parties were expected to support the APP, in an attempt to subject the Prime Minister to a vote of no confidence. In July, however, Skate unexpectedly resigned. At the opening session of the National Parliament Iairo Lasaro defeated the opposition candidate, Bernard Narokobi of the PDM, to become Speaker. However, on the next day Morauta was elected Prime Minister by an overwhelming majority, following his nomination by Pundari, who had transferred his allegiance from Skate, having refused to accept the latter's nomination of himself as candidate for the premiership. Lasaro immediately resigned as Speaker, and Narokobi was elected unopposed to the position. Morauta subsequently appointed a new coalition Government, with Pundari as Deputy Prime Minister.

The Morauta administration

In August 1999 Sir Mekere Morauta presented a 'mini-budget', in an attempt to combat various economic problems which, he claimed, were a consequence of the previous Government's mismanagement. In December the Prime Minister expelled the APP from the coalition Government and dismissed Pundari as Deputy Prime Minister, claiming that this constituted a further move towards the restoration of political stability. (Pundari was rumoured to have conspired with the opposition leader, Skate, to oust the Prime Minister.) Following Pundari's sudden dismissal, four small political parties within the governing coalition—the National Alliance, the People's National Party, the Melanesian Alliance and the Movement for Greater Autonomy—joined together to form the People's National Alliance (subsequently known as the National Alliance—NA). Also in that month, Skate (who had been charged with attempted fraud during his term in office as Governor of the NCD) announced that his party, the PNC, which had 10 MPs, was to join the coalition Government.

The parliamentary strength of the ruling coalition was increased to 76 MPs in April 2000, following the readmission of the APP to government, including the appointment of Pundari to the post of Minister of Lands and Physical Planning. In an attempt to increase government stability, Morauta proposed legislation in August that would restrict the ability of MPs to change their party allegiance within a parliamentary session, and announced the adjournment of Parliament between January and July 2001, the only period during which votes of no confidence could be tabled. (The Constitution forbade such votes in the 18 months following the election of a Prime Minister, and in the 12 months prior to a general election.) In November 2000, however, a revolt by 25 MPs (including six government ministers) prevented a vote on the so-called Political Parties Integrity Bill. The rebellion prompted a major government reorganization, in which all of the ministers involved in the revolt were dismissed. Morauta secured the parliamentary approval of the bill in December.

Allegations of corruption and mismanagement resulted in the suspension of four provincial governments (Western Province, Southern Highlands, Enga and the NCD) in late 2000 and early 2001. Moreover, in January 2001 the Minister for Provincial and Local Government, Iairo Lasaro, was arrested for the alleged misappropriation of public funds, and in March Bill Skate was charged with the same crime, having been acquitted earlier in the month of conspiring to defraud an insurance company.

A Commonwealth report into the Papua New Guinea Defence Force, published in January 2001, recommended reducing the number of army personnel by one-third. Subsequent plans by the Government to make more than 2,000 soldiers redundant (equivalent to some 50% of the entire Defence Force) resulted in a revolt at the Port Moresby barracks in March. It was believed that senior officers had helped to distribute weapons to the rebels, who demanded the resignation of the Prime Minister and the transfer of power to an interim administration. The rebellion ended two weeks later with an amnesty for the soldiers involved, during which hundreds of looted weapons were surrendered.

In April 2001 the APP was dissolved and merged with the PDM, led by the Prime Minister. In May Morauta expelled the NA from the ruling coalition and dismissed the party's ministers from the National Executive Council, accusing Somare, the party's leader, of attempting to destabilize the Government. In October, following a further reallocation of ministerial portfolios, the Minister for Foreign Affairs, John Pundari, was dismissed. His removal from office followed his criticism of the Government's participation in Australia's 'Pacific Solution', whereby 216 refugees, who had attempted to enter Australia by boat, were being housed in a former military prison on Manus Island. In January 2002 the Government decided to accept 784 additional asylum seekers. It was understood that they were to remain only until their asylum claims had been processed. The agreement with Australia to accommodate the asylum seekers on Manus Island was extended for a further 12 months in October 2002 and was to provide for the reception of an additional 1,000 people. In August 2003 the Australian Government announced that it intended to close the facility. However, the facility was reopened in November 2012.

At a general election in June 2002 many polling stations failed to open as scheduled, amid reports of the theft of ballot papers and strike action by electoral staff. Some 25 people were killed in election-related violence, much of which occurred in the High-lands provinces as a result of disputes between clan-based candidates. A Commonwealth inquiry was subsequently planned to investigate the events surrounding the election, which was described as the worst in the country's history. In the final results, announced in August, six seats in the Highlands provinces remained vacant where voting had been unable to proceed (elections for these seats were held in April and May 2003). Of the 103 seats determined, Somare's NA won 19 and Morauta's PDM secured 12. Independent candidates won 17 seats, with the remainder divided among a large number of minor parties, many of which had been formed specifically to contest the election.

Somare's third term as Prime Minister

On 5 August 2002 Sir Michael Somare was elected unopposed as Prime Minister, receiving 88 parliamentary votes. Bill Skate, who had played an important part in Somare's campaign, was elected Speaker. After appointing a 28-member National Executive Council (which included 19 newly elected MPs), Somare began his third term as Prime Minister, pledging to restore stability, halt the privatization programme initiated by his predecessor and reduce state expenditure.

In June 2003 the Government submitted proposals for a number of changes to the political system, including a mandatory general election following the approval of a no confidence motion and stricter rules governing the switching of party allegiances among members of the National Parliament. In addition, the Government proposed legislation that would extend the period during which a new government should be exempt from votes of no confidence, from 18 months to three years. Both attempts to introduce these constitutional changes were unsuccessful, despite government inducements of some US $25,000 for MPs to support the proposals.

In September 2003 Sir Albert Kipalan was elected Governor-General, defeating former Minister for Foreign Affairs Sir Paulias Matane by a single vote. However, questions were raised concerning possible irregularities in the polling procedure and the Supreme Court subsequently declared the election to be invalid. The parliamentary Speaker, Bill Skate, was appointed acting Governor-General pending a fresh election in December, at which Sir Pato Kakaraya was the successful candidate. However, Kipalan, who had also contested the election, challenged the result and was granted a legal injunction against Kakaraya's inauguration, which had been due to take place in January 2004. In March the Supreme Court declared the election of Sir Pato Kakaraya to be null and void. Following four rounds of voting, Sir Paulias Matane was narrowly elected Governor-General in late May; he took office in the following month.

In May 2004 Somare dismissed the Deputy Prime Minister, Moses Maladina, together with all the PNC members of the National Executive Council who had refused to support proposed

government legislation and who were believed to be planning a vote of no confidence in the Government. In August the National Parliament was adjourned for a period of three months after both the Government and the opposition expressed concern over the number of legislators who were reported to be bringing firearms into the parliament building. In January 2005 Somare announced a reorganization of ministerial portfolios, which included the appointment of his son, Arthur, to the role of Minister for National Planning and Monitoring. In February 2006, however, Arthur Somare resigned from his government position following allegations of misappropriation of public funds; he was referred to the Public Prosecutor for failing to submit annual statements on time and to account for the application of local grants. A major reorganization of the National Executive Council was carried out in July, in which Arthur Somare, whose case with the Public Prosecutor was still pending, was reappointed to the Government as Minister for State Enterprise, Communication and Information.

In April 2006 it was reported that the Public Prosecutor had found enough evidence to justify the establishment of a leadership tribunal to investigate alleged misconduct on the part of Puka Temu, the Minister for Lands and Physical Planning, and Andrew Baing, the Deputy Leader of the Opposition. In February 2007 a tribunal was formed to examine allegations of misconduct against Melchior Pep, who had previously served as Minister for Correctional and Administrative Services. In May a leadership tribunal recommended the dismissal of Sir Moi Avei, the former Deputy Prime Minister who had subsequently held the government portfolio of petroleum and energy, over charges of financial misconduct.

The election of 2007

Polling took place, under a new 'limited preferential voting' system, in relatively peaceful circumstances between 30 June and 15 July 2007, although there were some fatalities. The NA won 27 of the 109 parliamentary seats, with its nearest rival, the Papua New Guinea Party, taking only eight. The PAP won six seats, while the Pangu Pati, the PDM and the URP each took five seats. Following coalition negotiations with several smaller parties, Sir Michael Somare was re-elected as Prime Minister in August. Sir Mekere Morauta became Leader of the Opposition. In the new National Executive Council the NA, which provided a total of 13 ministers, was allocated a number of important portfolios: Puka Temu was appointed Deputy Prime Minister and Minister for Lands, Physical Planning and Mining, while Patrick Pruaitch assumed responsibility for the finance and treasury portfolio, and a new government appointee, Samuel Abal, became Minister for Foreign Affairs and Trade. Bob Dadae of the UP was appointed Minister for Defence, and Allan Marat of the Melanesian Liberal Party (MLP) received the justice portfolio. Other parties represented included the PAP and the PNC.

In July 2009 the National Parliament approved the formation of two new provinces, to take effect in 2012: Hela (hitherto part of Southern Highlands Province) and Jiwaka (hitherto part of Western Highlands), bringing the total number of provinces to 22. A total of 14 members of the governing coalition joined the opposition in that month, claiming that the Government was corrupt and that they had been warned that funds would not be allocated to their local districts if they did not support the administration. In February 2010 the Chief Justice announced an investigation into allegations of financial misconduct by the Minister for Finance and Treasury, Patrick Pruaitch; in June the Supreme Court ordered his suspension, pending an appeal against his referral to the tribunal.

In March 2010 the Governor of the NCD, Powes Parkop, founded a new political party, with the aim of combating corruption and ensuring the fair distribution of resources, in particular those derived from the imminent exploitation of the country's reserves of natural gas. (Initially known as the United Democratic Front, the party subsequently assumed the name of Social Democratic Party.) Also in March, a commission of inquiry, established three years previously, reported that the Department of Finance had paid large sums, amounting to hundreds of millions of kina, in response to fraudulent claims against the state. In the same month the Ombudsman Commission, which had been examining the conduct of the Government in the Moti affair (see Regional Affairs), concluded that both Somare and Polye had acted wrongly, and recommended a criminal investigation; however, the National Parliament voted to reject the Commission's report. In May Parliament approved amendments to the Defence Force Act to allow the legal participation of troops from Papua New Guinea in international combat or civil operations. As part of the same bill, Parliament agreed to establish an International Relations Committee, which was to advise the National Executive Council on international issues.

The election to choose a replacement for Governor-General Sir Paulias Matane descended into uproar in June 2010 when the National Parliament appeared unwittingly to approve a second term uncontested for Matane, despite three other candidates having been nominated. The Speaker had initially requested the MPs to conduct an open ballot on the elegibility of Matane to seek a second term in office and, this vote having been carried by an absolute majority, the Prime Minister subsequently presented a motion for Parliament to resolve that Matane be supported in his second term as Governor-General. The Government claimed that the MPs' earlier approval of Matane's eligibility circumvented any need for the holding of a secret multi-candidate ballot, since the MPs had, in effect, already voted in favour of returning the Governor-General to office. The Leader of the Opposition, Sir Mekere Morauta, claimed that this action by the Government constituted an abuse of parliamentary democracy and pledged to challenge the decision in court.

In July 2010 the Supreme Court ruled that a law governing the conduct of MPs and political parties was unconstitutional: since the Organic Law on the Integrity of Political Parties and Candidates (OLIPAC, which had been introduced in 2001) prohibited MPs from voting against a party resolution or switching allegiance, it was deemed to contravene their rights and freedom of choice. The annulment of the OLIPAC meant that Parliament was now constitutionally free to introduce a vote of no confidence against the Prime Minister. As the opposition made plans and garnered support for such a vote, Attorney-General Ano Pala and three government ministers (Deputy Prime Minister Puka Temu, Minister for Forestry Belden Namah and Minister for Culture and Tourism Charles Abel) announced their defection to the opposition. Following an unsuccessful attempt to present a parliamentary motion of no confidence against the Prime Minister in late July (the Government avoided the vote by adjourning Parliament until November), the opposition stated its intention to force an early recall of Parliament through the judiciary (claiming that the legislature had not convened for the minimum number of 63 days, as specified in the Constitution). In early August Somare attracted further criticism when he abrogated the constitution of the NA and cancelled a party conference in an apparent attempt to allow his son, Arthur, to assume the party leadership unchallenged. In October Morauta announced his resignation as leader of the Papua New Guinea Party (being replaced by Belden Namah), while remaining as parliamentary Leader of the Opposition.

Political instability

Prime Minister Somare's political future appeared increasingly uncertain in early December 2010 when the acting Public Prosecutor announced plans to refer the premier to a leadership tribunal to answer charges of alleged misconduct in office (with some of the charges dating back nearly 20 years). Somare's referral to the tribunal was expected to force him to resign from the premiership and be replaced by the Deputy Prime Minister. In a seeming attempt to bolster his support within government prior to his departure, Somare unexpectedly carried out a ministerial reorganization, which included the replacement of Deputy Prime Minister Don Polye by Samuel Abal. In addition, former Chief Justice Sir Arnold Amet was appointed as the new Attorney-General. The Government came under greater pressure when the Supreme Court ruled that the parliamentary Speaker, Jeffrey Nape, had acted unconstitutionally by reappointing Matane to a second term as Governor-General in June. Matane's reappointment was consequently ruled invalid and Nape became acting Governor-General pending the election of a permanent replacement.

In an unexpected development, Prime Minister Somare announced in mid-December 2010 that he was temporarily relinquishing the premiership pending the investigation by the leadership tribunal into the allegations of financial misconduct that had been made against him; he was replaced, in an acting capacity, by newly appointed Deputy Prime Minister Abal. In response, the opposition claimed that Abal's appointment as Deputy Prime Minister (together with the other ministerial reallocations effected by Somare earlier that month) had been unconstitutional and that, therefore, Polye was still the official Deputy Prime Minister. In the mean time, Polye refused to take up his new cabinet portfolio of foreign affairs and immigration. On 14 January 2011 Michael Ogio, the Minister for Higher Education, Research, Science and Technology and the

candidate favoured by the NA, was elected as the new Governor-General, defeating Sir Pato Kakaraya by 65 votes to 23. Following the election, Parliament adjourned until May.

In mid-January 2011 it was reported that Somare had resumed the premiership. In mid-March the leadership tribunal (comprising three judges from the United Kingdom, Australia and New Zealand) ruled that Somare could continue as Prime Minister during the misconduct hearing; however, later that month it found Somare guilty on 13 counts of official misconduct for failing properly to lodge financial returns. Although the Public Prosecution Office demanded that the tribunal impose the maximum penalty of dismissal from office, Somare was merely suspended from the premiership, without pay, for two weeks, commencing on 4 April. The opposition reacted by claiming that this lenient sentence made a mockery of the rule of law. Somare subsequently underwent major heart surgery in Singapore, and remained on medical leave for several months. In June of that year members of Somare's family announced his retirement from public office on the grounds of ill health. As Abal continued in the role of acting Prime Minister, conflict between rival factions within the NA became increasingly apparent. In June Abal dismissed Don Polye, the Minister for Foreign Affairs and Immigration, claiming that he was acting to restore discipline to the Government. The NA announced its decision in the following month to suspend Abal from the organization for acting in a way that was described as against the party's interests.

Meanwhile, investigations into allegations of misconduct against members of the Government continued during 2011, with finance minister Patrick Pruaitch and Arthur Somare, the Minister for Public Enterprise, suspended from office in July. Another cabinet member, Mark Maipakai, the Minister for Intergovernmental Relations and District Development, was under investigation by the Public Prosecution Office in October for alleged financial misconduct.

Increasing divisions within the Government led some 49 of its members to defect to the opposition and to support a parliamentary vote in early August 2011 to have the Prime Minister's office declared vacant. The lack of clarity regarding the long-term absence of Prime Minister Somare and the ability of Abal to continue in the role in an acting capacity, given the unpopularity of his leadership, had contributed to a climate of political instability. Minister for Transport and Works Peter O'Neill was subsequently elected to the premiership with 70 parliamentary votes to Abal's 24. He appointed a National Executive Council that included many relatively unknown members, as well as former Leader of the Opposition and leader of the Papua New Guinea Party Belden Namah as Deputy Prime Minister. Don Polye, the former Minister for Foreign Affairs and newly elected leader of the NA, and William Duma, the former Minister for Energy and Petroleum, who had both been dismissed by Abal in June, returned to the Government. However, the constitutional legitimacy of the new Government was disputed by many observers. Meanwhile, in early September, following his return from Singapore, the National Parliament voted to remove Somare from his parliamentary seat for non-attendance of three consecutive sessions without permission.

One of the most significant acts of the new Government was the decision to present a supplementary budget in September 2011, detailing planned expenditure for the projected budgetary surplus of K600m., around one-half of which was to be used to provide free elementary education and heavily subsidized higher education. O'Neill announced a similar plan for health care in January 2012.

On 13 December 2011 the Supreme Court ordered the reinstatement of Sir Michael Somare as Prime Minister, ruling that the election of O'Neill to the premiership in August had been unlawful, and on 14 December Somare and his cabinet were sworn in to office by Governor-General Ogio. However, O'Neill refused to accept the ruling and used his parliamentary majority to effect a vote suspending the Governor-General. A parliamentary vote held immediately afterwards resulted in the appointment of Speaker Jeffrey Nape as acting Governor-General; Nape then reinstated O'Neill and his cabinet. In chaotic scenes Somare was ejected from the parliament building by police officers. The apparent loyalty of the security forces to O'Neill was again illustrated when police secured the state-owned print works in order that newspapers declaring O'Neill to be the country's Prime Minister could be printed. On 19 December Ogio's suspension as Governor-General was lifted, after he affirmed his recognition of O'Neill's premiership. In mid-January 2012 Somare reappeared in Parliament, bearing legal documents that supported his reinstatement, but was again ejected from the building. Later in the month a retired colonel, Yaura Sasa, attempted to stage a coup, taking control of the country's military headquarters and briefly holding the armed forces' Commander-in-Chief, Brig.-Gen. Francis Agwi, hostage, and demanded Somare's restoration as Prime Minister. Sasa was subsequently arrested and charged with mutiny.

Meanwhile, following continued divisions with the NA, Don Polye announced the deregistration of the party in January 2012 (despite the continued existence of a rival faction) and the formation of a new political organization, the Triumph Heritage Empowerment Party (THE). In March Chief Justice Sir Salamo Injia was charged with obstructing a police investigation into his management of the Supreme Court, and in early April the National Parliament voted to suspend the Chief Justice and another Supreme Court judge, Nicholas Kirriwon, from office, after the former refused to disqualify himself from overseeing hearings into the O'Neill Government's legitimacy. However, the Court subsequently placed a stay order on the controversial judicial conduct law that had been invoked by Parliament to suspend the judges, effectively restoring them to their posts. In an escalation of the dispute between the legislative and judicial branches of government, in mid-April the National Parliament adopted legislation restricting the powers of the Supreme Court. Amid claims that the Government and Parliament were acting unconstitutionally, Deputy Prime Minister Namah levelled the same accusation at the judiciary, asserting that the Supreme Court did not have the right to impede the implementation of legislation. Meanwhile, in early April Parliament voted in favour of ordering the Electoral Commissioner, Andrew Trawen, to request that Governor-General Ogio suspend the organization of a general election, scheduled to be held in June and July, for six months. However, Trawen opposed any delay, insisting that the Constitution provided for a strict five-year parliamentary term. In May Somare's spokesperson, his daughter Betha, announced that he would not stand for office in the election.

Recent developments: the 2012 general election

A total of 3,443 candidates from some 46 political groups contested the general election held between 23 June and 17 July 2012. O'Neill's PNC secured the strongest representation in the National Parliament, with 27 of the 111 seats, followed by Polye's THE, with 12 seats. The Papua New Guinea Party won eight parliamentary seats, while the NA and URP each secured seven, and the PPP and the People's Party garnered six each; 16 independent candidates were elected. A turn-out of 76.9% was recorded. The National Parliament convened in early August, when O'Neill was elected to the premiership with 94 out of 108 votes and Theo Zurenuoc of the PPP was elected Speaker. Following the formation of a broad governing coalition, which included the PNC, the THE, the NA, the URP, the PPP and the People's Party, as well as several more minor parties, the composition of a 33-member cabinet was announced. Somare made a public statement expressing the importance of supporting the new Government in the interests of national stability. However, the stability of the new administration was threatened by the record number of challenges filed against the results of the election. By September it was reported that more than 80 of the 111 seats had been officially challenged. In addition to allegations of electoral malpractice, some observers reported witnessing intimidation and coercion in certain areas, including an incident in the newly established province of Jiwaka, where armed men overpowered electoral staff to burn some 100,000 counted ballot papers. In December warrants were issued for the arrest of five police officers accused of carrying out the incident. In March 2013 the Minister for Higher Education, Research, Science and Technology, David Arore of the THE, was charged with bribery and corruption in relation to the election. He was subsequently suspended from office pending the outcome of the case against him, being replaced in an acting capacity by Polye, the Minister for Treasury.

In an attempt to increase political stability, in November 2012 O'Neill proposed an extension of the post-election period during which the submission of motions of no confidence in the Prime Minister was not permitted, from 18 months to 30 months. The requisite constitutional amendment was approved in February 2013 by 90 votes to 14. Also in February, the National Parliament voted to repeal legislation adopted during the 2012 political impasse that had accorded the Government the power to remove judges and had restricted the powers of the Supreme Court. In the previous month the PNC, which had already attracted a number of independents and defectors from other parties since

the 2012 election, increased its parliamentary representation further, to 40 seats, following the decision of the People's Party's to merge into the ruling party.

In early May 2013 O'Neill proposed an increase in maximum sentences for violent crimes, including the application in some cases of the death penalty, which had not been implemented since being reintroduced in 1991.

Bougainville and the Issue of Secession

From the late 1980s the status of Bougainville (the island which, with the smaller neighbouring islands, forms the easternmost part of Papua New Guinea, and is geographically and ethnically distinct from the rest of the country) became a matter of dispute that developed into civil unrest and a long-term national crisis. In April 1988 landowners on the island of Bougainville submitted claims for financial compensation for land that had been mined by the Australian-owned Bougainville Copper Ltd since 1972. When no payment was forthcoming, acts of sabotage were perpetrated in late 1988 by the Bougainville Revolutionary Army (BRA), led by Francis Ona, a former mine surveyor and land-owner, and the copper mine was obliged to suspend operations. Members of the national security forces were deployed in the area and production at the mine recommenced in December, but a curfew was imposed after further violence in January 1989.

The BRA increasingly favoured secession from Papua New Guinea for Bougainville (and for North Solomons Province as a whole), together with the closure of the mine, until their demands for compensation and secession had been met. In May 1989, as the violent campaign on the island intensified, the mine was forced once more to suspend production, and, in June, the Papua New Guinea Government declared a state of emergency on Bougainville, sending 2,000 security personnel to the island. In September a minister in the Bougainville provincial government, who had been negotiating an agreement with Bougainville landowners to increase their share of mining royalties from 5% to 20%, was shot dead. The signing of the accord, due to take place the following day, was postponed indefinitely. In early 1990 the owners of Bougainville Copper Ltd completed a full withdrawal and Australian nationals were evacuated by their Government.

In March 1990 the Government negotiated a cease-fire with the BRA and withdrew its security forces; later in that month it imposed an economic blockade on Bougainville, now under the control of the BRA. The blockade was intensified in May, when banking, telecommunications and public services on the island were suspended. In that month Ona proclaimed Bougainville's independence and declared himself interim President. The unilateral declaration of independence was immediately dismissed by the central Government as unconstitutional and invalid. Negotiations between the BRA and the Government in July resulted in the BRA representatives agreeing to defer implementation of the May declaration of independence and to hold further discussions on the political status of the island. The Government agreed to end the blockade, and to restore essential services to the island. However, there was a resurgence in violence between the BRA and armed forces in September, leading to many reported deaths, after the Government sent troops to take control of the island of Buka, claiming that Buka islanders had petitioned for help.

In January 1991 further negotiations between representatives of the Papua New Guinea Government and of Bougainville in Honiara, the capital of Solomon Islands, resulted in the 'Honiara Accord'. The Papua New Guinea Government agreed not to station its security forces on Bougainville if the BRA disbanded and surrendered all prisoners and weapons to a multinational peace-keeping force. The Bougainville secessionists were guaranteed immunity from prosecution. However, the agreement made no provision for any change in the political status of Bougainville, and by early March it appeared to have failed. Government troops launched a further attack on Bougainville in April. In June Col Leo Nuia was dismissed from his post as Commander of the Papua New Guinea Defence Force, after admitting that his troops had committed atrocities during fighting on Bougainville in early 1990. Further allegations of human rights abuses and summary executions of BRA members and sympathizers by government troops prompted the Prime Minister, Rabbie Namaliu, to announce plans for an independent inquiry into the claims. (The report, published in late 1996, identified numerous problems contributing to a lack of discipline among the troops, and recommended a thorough reorganization of the country's armed forces.)

Fighting continued throughout 1991, and in early 1992, in an attempt to force the Government to end its economic blockade of the island, the BRA intercepted and set fire to a supply ship, and held its crew hostage. As a result, all shipping and air services to Bougainville were suspended, and in October government troops began a major offensive against rebel-held areas of Bougainville. Violence on the island intensified in early 1993, and allegations of atrocities and violations of human rights by both sides were widely reported.

Talks between government representatives and Bougainville secessionists in Honiara during 1994 led to the signing of a cease-fire agreement in September. Under the terms of the agreement, a regional peace-keeping force, composed of troops from Fiji, Vanuatu and Tonga, was deployed in October (with the Governments of Australia and New Zealand in a supervisory role) and the economic blockade of Bougainville was ended. In the following month Prime Minister Chan and a group of non-BRA Bougainville leaders signed the Charter of Mirigini, which provided for the establishment of a transitional Bougainville government. The BRA declared its opposition to the proposed authority, reiterating its goal of outright secession.

In April 1995, following the suspension of the Bougainville provincial government, Theodore Miriong, a former legal adviser to Ona, was sworn in as Premier of a 32-member transitional administration. Three seats reserved for the BRA leaders, Ona, Gen. Sam Kauona and Joseph Kabui (a former Premier of North Solomons Province), remained vacant, as the rebels urged their supporters to reject the new administration. The murder of several more members of the security forces in March 1996 led the Government to abandon all talks with the secessionists and to reimpose a military blockade on Bougainville. An escalation of violence in mid-1996 culminated in a major military offensive against rebel-held areas in June. By August it was estimated that some 67,000 Bougainvilleans were taking refuge in 59 government 'care centres'. In the same month defence forces arrested Miriong, accusing him of incitement regarding the killing of 13 government soldiers at an army camp. In October Miriong was assassinated by unidentified gunmen, later found by an official inquiry to be a group of government soldiers, assisted by pro-Government civilians (known as 'resistance fighters'). Meanwhile, Gerard Sinato was elected as the new Premier of the Bougainville Transitional Government.

In February 1997, in response to unofficial reports, Prime Minister Chan confirmed that a company based in the United Kingdom, Sandline International (a subsidiary of Executive Outcomes, a supplier of private armed forces in Africa), had been commissioned to provide military advice and training for soldiers on Bougainville. Subsequent reports of mercenary activity on the island and of the large-scale purchase of military equipment and of weapons provoked condemnation from numerous international sources. The situation developed into a major crisis in mid-March when the Commander of the Defence Force, Brig.-Gen. (later Maj.-Gen.) Jerry Singirok, announced that the mercenaries (most of whom were from South Africa) had been captured by the armed forces and were being detained while arrangements were made for their deportation. Singirok demanded the immediate resignation of Chan, but denied that his actions constituted a coup attempt. On the following day the Prime Minister dismissed Singirok, replacing him with Col Alfred Aikung. However, the armed forces rejected the new leadership, remaining loyal to Singirok. Popular support for the army's stance became increasingly vocal, as several thousand demonstrators rampaged through the streets of the capital, looting and clashing with security forces. The contract with Sandline International was suspended and the remaining mercenaries left the country. Aikung was replaced as Commander of the Defence Force by Col Jack Tuat. However, demands for the Prime Minister's resignation intensified, and following large-scale demonstrations and appeals by military, political and religious leaders, as well as the Governor-General, Chan resigned from office, along with the Deputy Prime Minister and the Minister for Defence. John Giheno, the erstwhile Minister for Mining and Petroleum, was subsequently elected acting Prime Minister.

In June 1997 an inquiry into the mercenary affair concluded that Chan had not been guilty of misconduct and, as a result, Chan announced his immediate resumption of his former position. Shortly after resuming office, Chan again provoked controversy by reappointing Col Leo Nuia to the position of Commander of the Defence Force. A second inquiry into the mercenary affair, begun following the election of a new Govern-

ment, concluded in September 1998 that former Deputy Prime Minister Chris Haiveta had been the beneficiary of corrupt payments from Sandline, but upheld the first inquiry's finding that Chan had not been guilty of any wrongdoing. Meanwhile, in March government soldiers reacted angrily to the prosecution of military leaders involved in the operation to oust Sandline mercenaries from Bougainville. Nuia was imprisoned in his barracks by members of the Defence Force, while Maj. Walter Enuma, who was being held while awaiting trial on charges of 'raising an illegal force', was freed by rebel soldiers.

Throughout 1997 talks were held at the Burnham army base in New Zealand between secessionists and representatives of the Bougainville Transitional Government, which concluded in October with the signing of the 'Burnham Truce'. Both sides agreed to a series of interim measures, which included refraining from acts of armed confrontation pending a formal meeting of government and secessionist leaders in early 1998. The Prime Ministers of both Papua New Guinea and Solomon Islands made an extended visit to Bougainville in December 1997 to demonstrate their united support for the truce; however, Ona, who appeared to be becoming increasingly marginalized within the BRA, refused to give his support. Further talks held at Lincoln University in Christchurch, New Zealand, in January 1998 resulted in the 'Lincoln Agreement', providing for an extension to the truce, the initiation of a disarmament process and the phased withdrawal of government troops from the island. The Prime Minister also issued a public apology for the mistakes of successive administrations during the conflict, which was estimated to have resulted in the deaths of some 20,000 people.

A permanent cease-fire agreement was signed in Arawa, the main town on Bougainville, on 30 April 1998. Ona declined to take part in the ceremony, reiterating his opposition to the peace agreement. In June government troops were withdrawn from Arawa, and reconstruction projects on Bougainville were initiated.

Bougainville's progression to autonomy

In August 1998 more than 2,000 representatives from different groups in Bougainville met in Buin (in the south of the island) to discuss their response to the 'Burnham Truce'. In the resultant 'Buin Declaration' the islanders stated their united aspiration for independence through peaceful negotiation. In October the National Parliament voted to amend the Constitution to allow the Bougainville Reconciliation Government to replace the Bougainville Transitional Government. The new authority came into existence on 1 January 1999, following the renewed suspension of the Bougainville provincial government, and at its first sitting elected Sinato and Kabui as its co-leaders. In April an agreement signed by Bougainville and Papua New Guinea government representatives (although not acknowledged by the BRA), known as the Matakana and Okataina Understanding, reaffirmed both sides' commitment to the cease-fire, while undertaking to discuss options for the political future of the island.

Elections to the Bougainville People's Congress (BPC, formerly the Bougainville Reconciliation Government) were held in early May 1999. At the first session of the BPC, Kabui was elected President by an overwhelming majority, securing 77 of the 87 votes, defeating his former co-leader, Sinato. Ona refused Kabui's invitation to join the BPC, despite the latter's stated intention to campaign for independence for Bougainville. Prime Minister Bill Skate responded that, although there was no possibility of independence (as this was not provided for in the Constitution), Parliament would consider terms for greater autonomy for the island. In August the suspension of the Bougainville provincial government was extended for a further six months in an attempt to find a peaceful resolution to the autonomy issue. The Minister for Bougainville Affairs and for Foreign Affairs, Sir Michael Somare (as he had become), stated that the Government was willing to allow Bougainville to be self-governing in all matters except foreign affairs, defence and policing, all of which would remain the responsibility of the central Government. The proposal was welcomed by members of the BPC, although they also announced their intention not to surrender their weapons until the Government had agreed to hold a referendum on independence.

In October 1999 a Supreme Court ruling declared the suspension of the Bougainville provincial government illegal on technical grounds. On 9 December the provincial government was formally recognized, in theory: however, the provincial government comprised only four members—the Bougainville Regional Member of Parliament, John Momis, who thus became Governor-elect (although he agreed not to exercise his powers for the time being) and the three other Bougainville parliamentarians. Further talks regarding the future status of Bougainville between Somare and members of the BPC, the BRA and elders of the island took place in late 1999 and early 2000, and led to an agreement known as the Loloata Understanding. This allowed for the eventual holding of a referendum on independence, once full autonomy had been implemented, and the formal establishment of the Bougainville Interim Provincial Government (BIPG), composed of an Executive Council and a 25-member Provincial Assembly (including the four original members).

At the end of March 2000 the Provincial Assembly and the Executive Council were sworn in by the Governor-General. Six seats were left vacant in the Provincial Assembly for other Bougainville officials such as Kabui and Ona; however, Kabui stated that, rather than joining the BIPG, he would await the establishment of a fully autonomous government (which he hoped would be in place by early 2001). In May 2000 the Office of Bougainville Affairs was renamed the Office of Peace and Reconstruction. Following a further round of peace talks in November, Kabui confirmed that he had secured an agreement from Somare that a future referendum would include a legally binding option of independence, although disagreement over how soon the vote should be held persisted.

In February 2001 agreement on the terms of the referendum was finally reached, following the intervention of the Australian Minister for Foreign Affairs. The agreement stated that the referendum would be held in 10–15 years' time and would contain the option of independence. In the interim the provincial government was to be granted increased autonomy and the BRA would be expected to disarm. In May commanders of the BRA and the Bougainville Resistance Force (BRF, a militia that was allied to the Government during the civil conflict on Bougainville) signed an agreement to surrender their weapons. In the following month an agreement was reached on autonomy for the island, with the Government ceding to demands that Bougainville be accorded its own system of criminal law and an autonomous police force. On 30 August the Government and island leaders signed the Bougainville Peace Agreement in Arawa. Although he signed the accord, which was still to be approved by the National Parliament, Ishmael Toroama, the BRA's Chief of Defence, stated that the BRA would campaign for the referendum to be held in three to five years' time and would continue to seek full independence. (Francis Ona did not attend the signing ceremony; he died in July 2005.)

Weapons disposal by the BRA and BRF began in December 2001, and the UN Observer Mission on Bougainville (UNOMB) formally acknowledged the Bougainville Peace Agreement later in that month. In March 2002 the Papua New Guinea Defence Force began its withdrawal from Bougainville. The withdrawal of troops was completed in late December.

In August 2003 the Government of Papua New Guinea formally announced its plan for autonomy in Bougainville, allowing the provincial authorities to proceed with the establishment of a constitution and the eventual organization of elections for an autonomous government leader and local assembly. In March 2004 the BIPG approved legislation providing for its merger with the BPC to establish the Bougainville Constituent Assembly (BCA), which was finally convened later that month to consider the third and final draft of the proposed constitution. In December the Government of Papua New Guinea finally approved Bougainville's Constitution, and the UN agreed to extend its Observer Mission by a further six months to cover the period of the forthcoming election. Elections for the President of the new Autonomous Bougainville Government (ABG) and for 39 members of the first local assembly began on 20 May 2005 and continued for two weeks to allow islanders, some of whom had to travel for several days on foot or by canoe, sufficient time to reach the polling stations. Despite attempts by armed rebels to disrupt the election process, it was deemed to have been largely successful. Joseph Kabui was declared to be Bougainville's first President, with 37,928 votes, defeating several other candidates (the closest of whom, former Governor John Momis, received 23,861 votes). The inauguration of the autonomous assembly, the Bougainville House of Representatives, took place on 14 June, with the President occupying the 40th seat. Kabui appointed a 10-member Bougainville Executive Council several days later.

In September 2000 a group of landowners from Bougainville had initiated legal action in a US court against Rio Tinto, the operator of the Panguna copper mine between 1972 and 1988. The group was reported to be suing the company for the envir-

onmental and social damage caused by its activities, including health problems experienced by workers and islanders living near the mine. Moreover, their case alleged that the company had effectively transformed the Papua New Guinea Defence Force into its own private army and was therefore responsible for the deaths of some 15,000 civilians in military action and a further 10,000 as a result of the economic blockade on the island. In 2007 the US Ninth Court of Appeals upheld the Bougainville residents' right to sue. A committee was established by the provincial Government in late 2005 to work on reopening the mine following an overwhelming vote in favour of the proposal.

In June 2008 Joseph Kabui, the President of Bougainville, died of a heart attack. John Tabinaman was appointed as his temporary replacement, and at a by-election in December, James Tanis, a former BRA commander and an unsuccessful opponent of Kabui in the first presidential election in 2005, secured victory. Tanis undertook to remove roadblocks in the remaining 'no go zones', and in March 2009 it was reported that the ABG had concluded an agreement with the principal rebel group in the Me'ekamui area. The possible reopening of the Panguna copper mine was a major topic of debate during the 2010 election campaign.

Polling commenced on 7 May 2010 and lasted for a fortnight; the election process was monitored by a team from the Pacific Islands Forum. In an indication of the efficacy of the peace process, for the first time since the signing of the 2001 peace agreement polling was to be permitted by rebel leaders in the areas surrounding the Panguna mine. Having secured 43,047 votes (more than 52% of the total cast), John Momis, the leader of the New Bougainville Party, was elected President. James Tanis, his nearest rival, received 17,205 votes (21%). More than three-quarters of incumbent legislators lost their seats in the House of Representatives in a vote that was widely held to reflect the public's disenchantment with the ABG's perceived lack of progress in recent years. Independent candidates were reported to have won 23 seats and the New Bougainville Party 14 seats. Momis pledged to work towards fully implementing autonomy in preparation for the holding of the referendum on independence between 2015 and 2020, to complete the weapons-disposal programme, to combat corruption, to improve the general welfare of the population through economic development and to investigate means of generating revenue for the completion of much-needed infrastructure projects. During an official visit to the People's Republic of China by President Momis in November 2010 various agreements were signed regarding future joint business ventures, including the proposed establishment of an airline company in Bougainville.

Ongoing violence in the Konnou region in the south of Bougainville (one of the few areas of rebel resistance that remained on the island), which had led to the killing of more than 50 people since 2006, persisted during 2011. Damien Koike, a militant leader who was based in that region, had apparently launched a violent campaign called 'Operation Leader Out', which aimed to overthrow the ABG. President Momis announced in May that he was prepared to seek the return of UN peace-keeping troops if negotiations did not succeed in ending the violence, which threatened to jeopardize the conditions under which a referendum could be held, according to the peace agreement. In November, however, the rebels signed a cease-fire agreement.

At a series of public meetings throughout Bougainville in late 2012, strong support was expressed for the reopening of the Panguna copper mine by Bougainville Copper Ltd. Momis stated that any decision to reopen the mine must be taken by the ABG with local residents and landowners, rather than by the central Government of Papua New Guinea.

Exploitation of Natural Resources and Tribal Conflict

Papua New Guinea's wealth of mineral deposits and forestry resources are important for the country's economy and have attracted considerable foreign investment. However, the operations of foreign business interests have sometimes caused serious environmental damage, with the interests of local inhabitants frequently being ignored, and legislative controls proving difficult to enforce.

In 1989 the Government gave Ok Tedi Mining Ltd (OTML), the owners of a gold and copper mine in Western Province, permission to discharge 150,000 metric tons of toxic waste per day into the Fly River. In 1994 some 6,000 people living in the region began a compensation claim against the Australian company operating the mine for damage caused by the resultant pollution. A settlement worth some $A110m. was reached in an Australian court in 1995 (and a further settlement worth $A400m. for the establishment of a containment system was concluded in mid-1996), despite opposition from the Papua New Guinea Government, which feared that such action might adversely affect the country's prospects of attracting foreign investment in the future. Similar claims were initiated by people living near the Australian-controlled Porgera gold-mine in Enga Province in early 1996 for pollution of the Strickland River system, as well as by landowners near the Kutubu oilfield, while the Panguna copper mine on Bougainville was believed to have caused severe environmental problems. The results of an independent review, carried out by the World Bank and published in March 2000, recommended the closure of the Ok Tedi mine on environmental grounds, but also emphasized the potentially damaging impact of the mine's early closure on both the local economy and world copper markets. In October 2001 BHP Billiton, the Australian operator, announced its withdrawal from the OTML venture and in early 2002 it transferred its 52% stake in the company to a development fund called the PNG Sustainable Development Programme Ltd. In early 2006 the managing director of OTML acknowledged that mining operations had caused major damage to the Ok Tedi and Fly River systems, resulting in flooding and forest dieback. Furthermore, the toxic effects of this waste were believed to be threatening supplies of ground and drinking water. In 2009 OTML achieved record sales, amounting to US $1,500m., and was reportedly the single largest business contributor to the Papua New Guinea economy. In December 2012 landowners reached an agreement with the mine operators to extend commercial operations at Ok Tedi (which had been expected to cease in 2013) until 2025.

Activity in the forestry sector increased dramatically in the early 1990s, and an official report published in 1994 indicated that the current rate of logging was three times the sustainable yield of the country's forests. However, attempts to introduce new regulations to govern the industry were strongly opposed by several Malaysian logging companies with operations in the country. In early 2000, however, environmentalists welcomed a commitment by the Papua New Guinea Government to impose a moratorium on all new forestry licences and to review all existing licences. Concern continued among conservation organizations as the Government failed to enforce laws promoting sustainable forestry activity, which, if upheld, were deemed sufficient to ensure the long-term survival of the forestry sector. In March 2011 the UN expressed its concern to the Government of Papua New Guinea that it was involved in the allocation of large areas of forestry land for 'logging by stealth' through Special Agricultural Business Leases.

Controversy surrounding the role of foreign interests in the exploitation of the country's natural resources re-emerged in early 2005 when a group representing tribal landowners near the Porgera gold mine protested at the mysterious deaths of villagers while panning for alluvial gold near the mine. The group claimed that a number of local people (totalling 29 by early May) had been shot dead by Porgera security personnel and that others had been seriously assaulted. Mine officials denied the allegations, stating that most of the deaths had been accidental, and that any shootings by their security guards had been carried out in self-defence. Violent incidents between miners and villagers living near the Porgera mine continued sporadically. In May 2009 villagers reportedly claimed that their homes had been destroyed by security personnel who had been sent to the mine in the previous month to quell alleged tribal warfare and halt illegal mining activities. Also in May, violence between local workers and foreign employees over the issue of labour conditions broke out at the Chinese-owned Ramu nickel/cobalt mine, in Madang Province, forcing it to close temporarily; protests against delays in the previously agreed relocation of residents led to a further closure in early 2010.

Tribal conflicts, principally between the Ujimap and Wagia tribes, broke out near Mendi, the capital of Southern Highlands Province, in December 2001, apparently in a dispute over the governorship of the province. A brief cease-fire was brokered in January 2002, by which time more than 120 people had been killed since the onset of the fighting.

Ethnic and tribal violence continued in several regions of the country during 2003. Eight people were killed in fighting near Port Moresby in May, and 17 died during inter-clan violence involving more than 1,000 people in Enga Province in July. By mid-2004 further ethnic violence in Enga, Morobe, Chimbu and East Highlands Provinces had resulted in many more deaths. Concerns regarding the conduct of the national police force in tackling such conflicts intensified following an incident in

August when a confrontation between security personnel and a group of youths in Enga Province resulted in police setting fire to an entire village, shooting dead a villager and injuring several others, and killing domestic animals. Ethnic violence continued in 2005. Some 5,000 villagers were left homeless following fighting in Chimbu Province in April. Further violence during the year, particularly in the Highlands provinces, resulted in many more deaths. In one outbreak of fighting in July, resulting from a land dispute, an estimated 7,000 guns were believed to have been used and police officers declined to intervene as they were considerably less well-armed. In another incident fuel shortages prevented police from attending a serious tribal conflict in which many people were killed. A report published in July claimed that the majority of illegal firearms in circulation in the country originated from the Papua New Guinea Defence Force or from police stocks.

A reported increase in murders involving allegations of sorcery was a cause of concern for officials in 2008. In January 2009 the police estimated that as many as one-half of all the murders in the country in the previous year were linked to accusations of 'black magic', which, according to human rights organizations, frequently led to the persecution of innocent individuals. The issue gained prominence again in mid-2012, when 29 residents of Madang Province were arrested for the sorcery-related killings of seven people, which included acts of cannibalism. The murder in Mount Hagen, Western Highlands Province, in February 2013 of a young woman who was burnt alive in front of a large crowd of onlookers following accusations of sorcery attracted international condemnation. Human rights organizations urged the Government to introduce specific legislation to address sorcery-related murders, which appeared to be increasing. Following the beheading on Bougainville of a further woman accused of sorcery, in April the Prime Minister proposed repealing the current controversial law on the practice, which had been cited as a defence by those alleged to have committed sorcery-related murders.

During 2009 it became evident that plans for the exploitation of natural gas deposits in Southern Highlands and Gulf Provinces, although expected to result in an enormous increase in the national income, were also a cause of conflict among rival groups claiming to be the traditional landowners at the construction sites. The signing of a benefit-sharing agreement by the Government and representatives of some 60,000 landowners was postponed from March until May, in order to identify legitimate claimants, and during 2010 demands for recognition continued to be made by other groups.

In May 2010, according to official reports, more than 10,000 mainly Sepik settlers had been displaced and two killed as a result of the violent unrest between the settlers and the local Watut and Patep people in the Bulolo mining township in Morobe Province.

Tribal conflict, reportedly prompted by different groups making accusations about who had been responsible for an increase in crime, led to the killing of 15 people and the burning of the settlement of Kaianantu in Eastern Highlands Province in October 2011. Meanwhile, in the following month similar disagreements between people in Lae, Morobe Province, and those from the Highlands provinces led to fighting in which nine people were killed and some 1,000 were left homeless.

Other Environmental Concerns and Health Issues

Fears that rising sea levels caused by global warming might have very serious consequences for Pacific islanders intensified in May 2003 when an emergency operation was undertaken to save the inhabitants of Carteret and Mortlock Islands, near Bougainville. Food supplies were sent to the islands, the 2,000 inhabitants of which were reported to be suffering from starvation and health problems related to poor diet, since the failure of their crops, which had been flooded by sea water. Some islanders were reluctant to accept a government proposal to relocate them to the main island of Bougainville, fearing the loss of their distinct Polynesian culture and way of life. None the less, in 2009 the relocation of the world's first so-called climate change refugees, from the Carteret Islands, commenced.

A series of severe floods in late 2003 and early 2004 affected 5,000 people in Morobe Province and more than 10,000 in West Highlands Province. In November 2007 Cyclone Guba struck Papua New Guinea, causing major floods that resulted in the deaths of at least 163 people and the displacement of thousands more. A state of emergency was declared in Oro Province, the worst-affected region. In December of the following year the northern coast was hit by tsunamis, which affected an estimated 75,000 people.

In late 2009 and 2010 outbreaks of cholera and dysentery were reported in several provinces, and the representative of the World Health Organization (WHO) in Papua New Guinea warned that outbreaks would continue if the country's sanitation and water supply systems were not improved. In April 2010, meanwhile, WHO described the occurrence of HIV and AIDS in Papua New Guinea as an epidemic, while communicable diseases, such as malaria and tuberculosis, were still the principal cause of death.

Regional Affairs

Papua New Guinea's most influential relationships have been with its immediate neighbours, Australia (the former ruling power), Indonesia and Solomon Islands. The country's large mineral resources have also attracted considerable investment from China and Japan. Papua New Guinea is a member of the Commonwealth and of numerous other international and regional organizations (see Regional and International Co-operation).

Relations with Australia and the Pacific islands

Relations with Australia, the former administrative power and a major source of investment and aid, have remained close, although affected by various developments. In December 2003 Australia announced the deployment of some 250 of its security personnel to different regions of Papua New Guinea, as part of plans for a five-year operation costing US $325m., aimed at restoring order to troubled areas of the country. Moreover, the Australian Government was to send up to 70 officials to Papua New Guinea to assume senior public roles in the spheres of finance, justice, public sector management, immigration, border security and transport safety. The agreement, known as the Enhanced Co-operation Program (ECP), incorporated a substantial aid programme. Prime Minister Somare had initially been reluctant to accept Australia's expanded role in the country, fearing that it would erode national sovereignty, but had been obliged to reconsider when the Australian Prime Minister, John Howard, implied that aid payments to Papua New Guinea were dependent on the country's co-operation. A report by the Australian Strategic Policy Institute, published in 2004, claimed that Papua New Guinea risked economic and social collapse, and that government and state institutions had become too weak to prevent drugs- and weapons-smuggling, human-trafficking and money-laundering activities by international criminal groups that had relocated to Papua New Guinea from South-East Asia in recent years. Furthermore, Australian journalists alleged in early 2005 that Chinese mafia groups had infiltrated the highest levels of Papua New Guinea's police force. It was also believed that the criminals had been recruiting Port Moresby's notorious 'raskol' gangs (groups of heavily armed, disaffected young men responsible for much of the violent crime in the capital) to commit armed robberies, assaults and other crimes in support of their activities. The ECP suffered a serious reversal in mid-2005 when Australian security personnel began to return to Australia following Papua New Guinea's Supreme Court ruling that their deployment was unconstitutional (principally because they had been given immunity from prosecution). In February 2006 an internal police investigation that had begun in 2003 revealed that as many as 66 Papua New Guinea police officers had been implicated in corrupt activities, such as receiving funds from Asian crime syndicates.

Relations with Australia became increasingly strained towards the end of 2006 over the extradition of the newly appointed Solomon Islands Attorney-General, Julian Moti, who was wanted by the authorities in Australia on a child molestation charge. Moti had been arrested in Port Moresby in September, but escaped to Solomon Islands in October, reportedly on an aircraft of the Papua New Guinea Defence Force. Prime Minister Somare denied any knowledge of the operation. Australia subsequently imposed a ban on ministerial exchanges with Papua New Guinea and ministerial-level travel to Australia. In November it was reported that the Papua New Guinea Chief Secretary, the Commander of the Defence Force and the acting Police Commissioner had been suspended, ostensibly owing to the Moti affair. In February 2007 a Papua New Guinea Defence Force inquiry issued a summons to Somare, following a testimony that he had given instructions to fly Moti out to Solomon Islands. Somare's dismissal of the Minister for Defence, Martin Aini, who had established the board of inquiry and admitted that the Prime Minister had exerted pressure on

him to disband it, prompted further speculation over Somare's involvement. In September 2007 the National Court overruled Somare's attempt to dismiss the inquiry's conclusions. The new Australian Prime Minister, Kevin Rudd, paid a three-day visit to Papua New Guinea in March 2008, and announced an increase in aid to Papua New Guinea. In April 2009, during a return visit to Australia by Somare, Rudd criticized the distribution of Australia's aid in Papua New Guinea, stating that too much aid was being spent on the engagement of consultants.

In March 2010 Papua New Guinea's Ombudsman Commission concluded that Somare had been responsible for the order to transport Moti to Solomon Islands, and recommended a criminal investigation; however, the Commission's findings were rejected by the legislature. (In December 2011 the Australian High Court granted Moti a permanent stay of prosecution, ruling that correct procedures had not been followed in his extradition from Solomon Islands to Australia.)

In March 2011 the Australian authorities stated that they would adopt a 'zero tolerance' approach towards fraud in their annual aid programme to Papua New Guinea. At a meeting between the Australian Prime Minister, Julia Gillard, and Papua New Guinea's new Prime Minister, Peter O'Neill, in October 2011, a number of new aid projects were announced. These included the establishment of a sovereign wealth fund to enable Papua New Guinea to manage its revenue from major resource projects more effectively and the creation of secondment opportunities for officials from Papua New Guinea in Australian government departments. Amid ongoing concerns about corruption, O'Neill announced the establishment of an independent commission to combat institutional corruption, for which Australia was to provide technical and advisory support. In September 2012 the Governments of Australia and Papua New Guinea signed a memorandum of understanding on the resumption of the processing of asylum seekers who had sought entry to Australia on Manus Island, in Papua New Guinea, with the first group of asylum seekers arriving from Australia in November. In February 2013, however, the office of the UN High Commissioner for Refugees expressed concern regarding conditions at the processing centre on Manus Island. Gillard made her first official visit to Papua New Guinea in May, signing a joint declaration with O'Neill aimed at broadening the bilateral relationship, as well as an agreement on enhanced defence co-operation. During their discussions O'Neill expressed dissatisfaction with Australian arrangements for processing the visas of Papua New Guineans visiting Australia.

From 1990 relations with Solomon Islands were overshadowed by the conflict on Bougainville. Solomon Islands (the inhabitants of which are culturally and ethnically very similar to Bougainville islanders) protested against repeated incursions by Papua New Guinea defence forces into Solomon Islands' territorial waters, while the Papua New Guinea Government consistently accused Solomon Islands of harbouring members of the BRA and providing them with supplies. Despite several attempts during the 1990s to improve the situation between the two countries (including an agreement by Solomon Islands in 1993 to close the BRA office in the capital, Honiara), relations remained tense. In June 1997 Papua New Guinea and Solomon Islands concluded a maritime border agreement (which took effect in January 1998) that delineated the sea boundary between the two countries and provided a framework for co-operation in matters of security, natural disaster, customs, quarantine, immigration and conservation.

In May 2010 the importance attached to relations between Papua New Guinea and Solomon Islands was underlined by the official opening of a new chancery building in Port Moresby; this building constituted the first permanent location for the High Commission of Solomon Islands in any country with which it maintained diplomatic relations. At a meeting with his Solomon Islands counterpart in October 2011, Papua New Guinea's Prime Minister, Peter O'Neill, announced a commitment to provide Solomon Islands with financial assistance totalling K100m. over the next five years.

In March 1988, meanwhile, Papua New Guinea signed an agreement with Vanuatu and Solomon Islands to form the Melanesian Spearhead Group, which was subsequently joined by Fiji. The grouping was dedicated to the preservation of Melanesian cultural traditions and to achieving independence for the French Overseas Territory of New Caledonia. In March 2007 the members of the Melanesian Spearhead Group signed a constitution.

Relations with Asia

In 1989 Papua New Guinea increased its links with South-East Asia, signing a Treaty of Amity and Co-operation with the Association of Southeast Asian Nations (ASEAN, see p. 218). During an official visit to the Philippines in April 2009, and a visit by the Indonesian President to Papua New Guinea in March 2010, Somare appealed for the support of both countries for Papua New Guinea's ambition to attain full membership of ASEAN.

In 1984 more than 9,000 refugees crossed into Papua New Guinea from the western section of the island of New Guinea, the Indonesian province of Irian Jaya (officially known as Papua from January 2002), as a consequence of operations by the Indonesian army against Melanesian rebels of the pro-independence Organisasi Papua Merdeka (Free Papua Movement—OPM). For many years relations between Papua New Guinea and Indonesia had been strained by the conflict in Irian Jaya, not least because the independence movement drew sympathy from many among the largely Melanesian population of Papua New Guinea. A new border treaty was signed in October 1984, and attempts were made to repatriate the refugees, based on assurances by the Indonesian Government that there would be no reprisals against those who returned. In 1988 the Government condemned incursions by Indonesian soldiers into Papua New Guinea, in search of OPM members, and the resultant violence and killings, as a breach of bilateral accords, and affirmed that Papua New Guinea would not support Indonesia in its attempt to suppress the OPM. In late 1995 violent confrontations resulted in the killing of several rebels and security personnel and the kidnapping by OPM activists of some 200 villagers. Australia urged the Papua New Guinea Government to accept several thousand refugees living in camps along the border, and in May 1996 the Government announced that 3,500 Irian Jayans would be allowed to remain in Papua New Guinea on condition that they were not involved in OPM activities. During 2000 hundreds of refugees were voluntarily repatriated to Indonesia (including more than 600 in a major operation in early September), although approximately 7,000 were believed to remain in Papua New Guinea in September. In late 2000 it was reported that Indonesian security forces had made some 400 incursions into Papua New Guinea in the previous two months while pursuing separatists. In December the border with Irian Jaya was officially closed.

The number of Indonesian troops along the border increased from about 150 in late 2002 to a reported 1,500 in early 2003. In late January the Government of Papua New Guinea ordered its security forces to arrest OPM rebels believed to be staying in refugee camps along the border, following complaints from the Indonesian authorities that rebels based there were carrying out operations in the province of Papua. In January 2009 it was reported that 700 West Papuans would voluntarily return to Indonesia, although observers were sceptical about their reasons for departing. In March 2010 the President of Indonesia, Susilo Bambang Yudhoyono, paid an official visit to Papua New Guinea during which agreements on co-operation in defence, agricultural development and commerce were concluded.

In January 2011 the Government of Papua New Guinea launched a joint forces security operation, reportedly at the request of the people of West Sepik Province, in an alleged attempt to curb illegal weapons- and drugs-trafficking, poaching activities and people-smuggling. By early February more than 170 people (many of whom were reported to be suspected OPM activists) had been arrested and detained for their purported illegal movement across the border from Indonesia.

Diplomatic relations with the People's Republic of China were established in 1976. In February 2004 Prime Minister Sir Michael Somare led a delegation of 80 officials (the largest such group Papua New Guinea had ever sent on a state visit) to China. Almost one-half of the delegates were representatives from the mining sector, who were hoping to secure agreements with Chinese interests relating to petroleum, gas and other mineral developments in Papua New Guinea. Major Chinese investments in Papua New Guinea include the Ramu mine in Madang Province, extracting nickel and cobalt, and China was expected to be one of the principal customers for Papua New Guinea's liquefied natural gas (LNG) after the planned commencement of exports in 2014/15. Bilateral relations were further strengthened in August 2010 when two Chinese warships docked at Port Moresby during a three-day intensive exchange programme between technical naval staff of the two countries. Chinese financial assistance worth some US $2,300m.,

announced in late 2012, was to be used to fund the Highlands highway project, as well as the development of ports and telecommunications services.

Relations with Taiwan came under international scrutiny in May 2008, when two senior members of the Taiwanese Government were forced to resign over a major funding controversy involving the use of intermediaries to secure diplomatic recognition for Taiwan by Papua New Guinea. The affair, which highlighted the practice of so-called 'chequebook diplomacy', prompted Somare to issue a denial of any involvement. In March 2010 a contract was signed for the supply of Papua New Guinea's LNG to Taiwan over a period of 20 years from the expected commencement of production in 2014/15.

Meanwhile, it was announced in 2009 that two Japanese companies had won the contract for providing the production and processing facilities for Papua New Guinea's LNG project, and during an official visit to Japan in March 2010 Somare announced that Japan was to buy more than 50% of Papua New Guinea's LNG output.

CONSTITUTION AND GOVERNMENT

Executive power is vested in the British monarch (the head of state), represented locally by the Governor-General, who is appointed on the proposal of the National Executive Council (cabinet) in accordance with the decision of the National Parliament by simple majority vote. The Governor-General acts on the advice of the National Executive Council, which is led by the Prime Minister. The Prime Minister is appointed and dismissed by the head of state on the proposal of the National Parliament. Legislative power is vested in the unicameral National Parliament, with 111 members elected by universal adult suffrage for a term of five years. The National Executive Council is responsible to the National Parliament. The local government system underwent extensive reform in 1995, when the directly elected provincial governments were replaced by new regional authorities, composed of members of the National Parliament and local councillors, and led by an appointed Governor. The National Capital District (NCD) has its own governing body. Papua New Guinea comprises 22 provinces.

In January 2005 the National Government approved the final draft of the proposed Constitution for the province of Bougainville, and elections for the President of the new autonomous Government and for the 39 members of the House of Representatives commenced in May. In June the new President of the Autonomous Bougainville Government was sworn in and the House of Representatives was inaugurated. The second Bougainville elections took place in mid-2010.

REGIONAL AND INTERNATIONAL CO-OPERATION

Papua New Guinea is a member of Asia-Pacific Economic Co-operation (APEC, see p. 208), the Asian Development Bank (ADB, see p. 214), the Colombo Plan (see p. 460), the Pacific Community (see p. 422), the Pacific Islands Forum (see p. 426) and the UN's Economic and Social Commission for Asia and the Pacific (ESCAP, see p. 31). Papua New Guinea is also a member of the Melanesian Spearhead Group, which, besides other benefits, provides for free trade among member countries (the others being Fiji, Solomon Islands and Vanuatu).

The country was admitted to the World Trade Organization (WTO, see p. 444) in 1996. Papua New Guinea is also a member of the International Cocoa Organization (see p. 456) and of the International Coffee Organization (see p. 456).

ECONOMIC AFFAIRS

In 2011, according to estimates by the World Bank, Papua New Guinea's gross national income (GNI), measured at average 2009–11 prices, was US $10,387m., equivalent to $1,480 per head (or $2,590 per head on an international purchasing-power parity basis). During 2002–11, it was estimated, the population increased at an average annual rate of 2.4%, while gross domestic product (GDP) per head increased, in real terms, by an average of 2.8% per year. Overall GDP grew, in real terms, at an average annual rate of 5.2% in 2002–11. According to the Asian Development Bank (ADB), real GDP increased by 9.2% in 2012.

Agriculture (including hunting, forestry and fishing) contributed an estimated 31.1% of GDP in 2011. In mid-2013, according to FAO, the sector was expected to engage an estimated 67.4% of the labour force. The principal cash crops are oil palm and coffee. Other significant crops are cocoa and coconuts (for the production of copra and coconut oil), rubber, tea and vanilla. Roots and tubers, vegetables, bananas and melons are grown as food crops. Forestry is an important activity, and Papua New Guinea is one of the world's largest exporters of unprocessed tropical timber. However, serious concerns have been raised with regard to the environmental damage caused by extensive logging activity in the country (see Contemporary Political History). Exports of forest products accounted for 4.7% of total export earnings in 2011, when revenue reached K768.3m. The sale of fishing licences to foreign fleets has provided a substantial source of revenue. During 2002–11, according to figures from the World Bank, agricultural GDP expanded at an average annual rate of 3.5%. According to the ADB, the GDP of the agricultural sector increased by 0.2% in 2012.

Industry (including mining, manufacturing, construction and power) contributed an estimated 43.9% of GDP in 2011. During 2002–11 industrial GDP increased by an average of 4.9% per year, according to figures from the World Bank. According to the ADB, industrial GDP rose by 15.9% in 2012.

Mining and quarrying provided an estimated 18.5% of GDP in 2011. Gold, which accounted for 36.5% of the country's total export revenue in 2011, copper (18.6%) and crude petroleum (14.9%) are the sector's major exports. Other mineral deposits include cobalt, nickel, silver, chromite and quartz. The country's largest petroleum refinery, at Napa Napa, began production in 2004. Papua New Guinea also has substantial reserves of natural gas. Construction of a 700-km pipeline from Southern Highlands Province to the capital of Port Moresby commenced in 2010, part of a liquefied natural gas project (LNG), which was scheduled for completion in 2013/14 (see below). The GDP of the mining sector declined at an average annual rate of 1.7% during 2002–11, according to ADB data; sectoral GDP increased by 0.3% in 2012.

Manufacturing contributed an estimated 6.8% of GDP in 2011. The sector is limited, employing only 1.1% of the working population in 2000. The principal branches of manufacturing are food products, beverages, tobacco, wood products, metal products, machinery and transport equipment. Several fish canneries have been established since the 1990s. In addition to a large tuna-loining plant in Wewak, it was announced in May 2009 that a major tuna cannery was to be built with Chinese assistance in Morobe Province; the project was expected to create 3,000 jobs. According to the World Bank, during 2002–11 manufacturing GDP increased by an average of 4.5% per year. The sector's GDP expanded by 3.0% in 2011.

Construction contributed an estimated 16.5% of GDP in 2011. According to ADB data, during 2002–11 the GDP of the construction sector increased by an average of 12.6% per year; the sector's GDP rose by 4.5% in 2012.

Energy is derived principally from hydroelectric power, which in 2000 accounted for more than 50% of electricity supplies. Output of electric energy reached 3,131m. kWh in 2009. However, more than 90% of the population are estimated to have no access to electricity, and in 2009, with assistance from the ADB, the Government formulated a new development plan for the country's power sector. In 2011 fuel imports accounted for 18.4% of the value of total merchandise imports.

The services sector contributed an estimated 25.0% of GDP in 2011. Tourism is an expanding industry, although political instability and reports of widespread violent crime have had a detrimental effect on the sector. Total foreign visitor arrivals increased from 146,350 in 2010 to 165,059 in 2011. Tourism receipts were worth an estimated US $2.0m. in 2011. The GDP of the services sector increased at an average annual rate of 3.5% in 2002–11, according to figures from the World Bank. According to the ADB, the sector's GDP expanded by 10.1% in 2012.

In 2011 Papua New Guinea recorded a visible merchandise trade surplus of K6,343m., while there was a deficit of K407m. on the current account of the balance of payments. In 2011 the principal source of imports (40.0%) was Australia; other major suppliers were the USA and Singapore. In that year Australia

was also the principal market for exports (42.0%), followed by Japan, the Philippines, the People's Republic of China, Germany and the Netherlands. The principal exports in 2011 were mineral products (specifically gold, copper and crude petroleum) and agricultural products, while the principal imports in that year were machinery and transport equipment, mineral fuels, miscellaneous manufactured articles, food and live animals and basic manufactures.

An overall budget deficit of K63.7m. was recorded in 2011, according to the ADB, equivalent to 0.2% of GDP. Of total projected expenditure of K10,560.3m. in the budget for 2012, K4,437.1m. was allocated to the development budget. Papua New Guinea receives grants for budgetary aid from Australia. In 2012/13 official development assistance from Australia was projected at $A493.2m. New Zealand's allocation of aid totalled $NZ27.0m. in 2011/12. According to the ADB, Papua New Guinea's external debt totalled US $1,260m. at the end of 2012. In that year the cost of debt-servicing was equivalent to 0.3% of the value of exports of goods and services. A large informal sector supports the majority of the population. At the census of 2000, 2.8% of the registered labour force were reported to be unemployed. In urban areas, however, the unemployment rate was estimated at some 70%. In the rural areas underemployment remained a serious problem. The annual rate of inflation averaged 5.9% in 2002–11. Consumer prices increased by 4.1% in 2012.

The Government's Medium-Term Development Plan for 2011–15 focused on the effective utilization of the substantial revenue inflows expected from the US $16,000m. LNG project; among the proposed measures was the establishment of a sovereign wealth fund with the aim of managing such revenue in a transparent manner. Legislation to create the sovereign wealth fund was formally approved in February 2012. The plan also encouraged the introduction of private sector competition to a number of state-owned enterprises, and aimed to improve general living standards by upgrading basic services and infrastructure. Despite the continuing economic growth of the resource-rich country, poverty was still believed to be affect 50% of the population. Papua New Guinea remained vulnerable to extreme climatic conditions and to variations in world commodity prices. Meanwhile, plans to revitalize the coffee industry, encompassing the period 2008–18, were implemented; a particularly good crop and high global prices led to an 88% increase in coffee export earnings in 2011. Fish-processing was expected to increase in importance from 2012 and to be a significant source of employment, following the announcement that several canning operations were to be expanded, with additional investment announced for new plants. The 2013 budget contained an K80m. stimulus package for small businesses, which aimed to create 500,000 new enterprises and 2m. new jobs by 2050. Construction work on the LNG project, which was being developed in collaboration with an international consortium, led to accelerated economic growth in 2010–12. The scheme was forecast to have an annual output of 6.6m. metric tons of LNG by 2014/15, but was not expected to generate significant revenue until 2023 owing to the high cost of development. Meanwhile, plans were under way for the establishment of a second LNG project, in Gulf Province. Having expanded for the 11th consecutive year in 2012 (when growth of 9.2% was recorded), GDP was forecast by the ADB to increase by a more modest 5.5% in 2013.

PUBLIC HOLIDAYS

2014: 1 January (New Year's Day), 18 April (Good Friday), 21 April (Easter Monday), 9 June (Queen's Official Birthday), 23 July (Remembrance Day), 16 September (Independence Day and Constitution Day), 25–26 December (Christmas).

Statistical Survey

Source (unless otherwise stated): Papua New Guinea National Statistical Office, POB 337, Waigani, NCD; tel. 3011200; fax 3251869; e-mail pmaime@nso.gov .pg; internet www.nso.gov.pg.

Area and Population

AREA, POPULATION AND DENSITY

Area (sq km)	462,840*
Population (census results)	
9 July 2000	5,190,786
10 July 2011†	
Males	3,663,249
Females	3,396,404
Total	7,059,653
Population (UN estimates at mid-year)‡	
2012	7,170,115
2013	7,327,276
Density (per sq km) at mid-2013	15.8

* 178,704 sq miles.
† Preliminary figures.
‡ Source: UN, *World Population Prospects: The 2010 Revision*; estimates not adjusted to take account of 2011 census results.

POPULATION BY AGE AND SEX
(UN estimates at mid-2013)

	Males	Females	Total
0–14	1,442,270	1,339,788	2,782,058
15–64	2,204,599	2,127,144	4,331,743
65 and over	91,147	122,328	213,475
Total	3,738,016	3,589,260	7,327,276

Source: UN, *World Population Prospects: The 2010 Revision*.

PRINCIPAL TOWNS
(census of 9 July 2000, provisional)

Port Moresby (capital)	254,158	Mount Hagen	27,782
Lae	78,038	Madang	27,394
Arawa	36,443	Kokopo/Vunamami	20,262

Source: Thomas Brinkhoff, *City Population* (internet www.citypopulation.de).

Mid-2011 (incl. suburbs, UN estimate): Port Moresby 342,904 (Source: UN, *World Urbanization Prospects: The 2011 Revision*).

BIRTHS AND DEATHS
(annual averages, UN estimates)

	1995–2000	2000–05	2005–10
Birth rate (per 1,000)	35.8	33.7	31.5
Death rate (per 1,000)	9.5	8.7	7.9

Source: UN, *World Population Prospects: The 2010 Revision*.

2003 (incomplete registration): Registered live births 192,817; Registered deaths 7,054 (Source: UN, *Population and Vital Statistics Report*).

Life expectancy (years at birth): 62.8 (males 60.7; females 65.0) in 2011 (Source: World Bank, World Development Indicators database).

ECONOMICALLY ACTIVE POPULATION
(census of 9 July 2000, persons aged 10 years and over)

Agriculture, hunting and forestry	1,666,247
Fishing	30,024
Mining and quarrying	9,282
Manufacturing	25,557
Electricity, gas and water	2,208
Construction	48,312
Wholesale and retail trade; repair of motor vehicles, motorcycles and personal and household goods	353,186
Hotels and restaurants	4,395
Transport, storage and communications	24,513
Financial intermediation	3,670
Real estate, renting and business activities	27,459
Public administration and defence; compulsory social security	32,043
Education	27,118
Health and social work	12,341
Other community, social and personal service activities	31,409
Private households with employed persons	15,523
Extra-territorial organizations and bodies	163
Activities not adequately defined	31,284
Total employed	2,344,734
Unemployed	68,623
Total labour force	2,413,357
Males	1,256,887
Females	1,156,470

Source: ILO.

Mid-2013 (estimates in '000): Agriculture, etc. 2,249; Total labour force 3,335 (Source: FAO).

Health and Welfare

KEY INDICATORS

Total fertility rate (children per woman, 2010)	4.0
Under-5 mortality rate (per 1,000 live births, 2010)	61
HIV/AIDS (% of persons aged 15–49, 2009)	0.9
Physicians (per 1,000 head, 2008)	0.05
Hospital beds (per 1,000 head, 1990)	4.0
Health expenditure (2009): US $ per head (PPP)	85
Health expenditure (2009): % of GDP	3.7
Health expenditure (2009): public (% of total)	70.6
Access to water (% of persons, 2010)	40
Access to sanitation (% of persons, 2010)	45
Total carbon dioxide emissions ('000 metric tons, 2008)	2,108.5
Carbon dioxide emissions per head (metric tons, 2008)	0.3
Human Development Index (2011): ranking	153
Human Development Index (2011): value	0.466

For sources and definitions, see explanatory note on p. vi.

Agriculture

PRINCIPAL CROPS
('000 metric tons)

	2009	2010	2011
Cassava (Manioc)*	111	135	120
Sweet potatoes*	595	642	567
Yams*	322	448	396
Taro (Cocoyam)*	292	252	223
Sugar cane*	330	335	335
Coconuts	1,196†	1,196†	1,238*
Oil palm fruit*	1,730	1,730	1,730
Pineapples*	23.5	20.0	19.3
Bananas*	980	1,050	1,000
Coffee, green	60.2†	40.0*	40.0*
Cocoa beans	59.4†	39.4†	39.4*
Tea*	7.6	5.0	5.0
Natural rubber	7.5†	7.5*	7.5*

* FAO estimate(s).
† Unofficial figure.

Aggregate production ('000 metric tons, may include official, semi-official or estimated data): Total cereals 15.3 in 2009, 13.1 in 2010, 14.8 in 2011; Total oil crops 684 in 2009, 712 in 2010, 738 in 2011; Total vegetables (incl. melons) 532 in 2009, 537 in 2010, 468 in 2011; Total fruits (excl. melons) 2,076 in 2009, 2,111 in 2010, 2,023 in 2011.

Source: FAO.

LIVESTOCK
('000 head, year ending September, FAO estimates)

	2009	2010	2011
Horses	2	2	2
Cattle	94	94	94
Pigs	1,900	1,800	1,785
Sheep	7	7	7
Goats	3	3	3
Chickens	4,200	4,000	3,800

Source: FAO.

LIVESTOCK PRODUCTS
('000 metric tons, FAO estimates)

	2009	2010	2011
Cattle meat	3.2	3.2	3.2
Pig meat	72	68	68
Chicken meat	5.9	5.9	5.8
Game meat	380	355	355
Hen eggs	4.8	4.5	4.5

Source: FAO.

Forestry

ROUNDWOOD REMOVALS
('000 cubic metres, excluding bark)

	2008	2009	2010
Sawlogs, veneer logs and logs for sleepers	2,958*	2,863	4,435
Pulpwood	82*	41	41
Fuel wood*	5,533	5,533	5,533
Total*	8,573	8,437	10,009

* FAO estimate(s).

2011: Production assumed to be unchanged from 2010 (FAO estimates).

Source: FAO.

SAWNWOOD PRODUCTION
('000 cubic metres, including railway sleepers, unofficial figures)

	2007	2008	2009
Coniferous (softwood) . . .	10	10	10
Broadleaved (hardwood) . . .	51	51	71
Total	61	61	81

2010–11: Production assumed to be unchanged from 2009 (unofficial figures).

Source: FAO.

Fishing

('000 metric tons, live weight)

	2008	2009	2010
Capture	222.4	229.6	224.5
Mozambique tilapia* . . .	2.3	2.3	2.3
Other freshwater fishes* . .	6.7	6.7	6.7
Sea catfishes*	1.9	1.9	1.9
Skipjack tuna	147.0	160.8	160.5*
Yellowfin tuna	53.3	44.7	41.5*
Aquaculture	1.1	1.4	1.6
Total catch*	223.6	231.0	226.1

* FAO estimate(s).

Note: Figures exclude crocodiles, recorded by number rather than weight. The number of estuarine crocodiles caught was: 14,074 in 2008, 11,910 in 2009; 5,519 in 2010. The number of New Guinea crocodiles caught was: 16,955 in 2008, 18,840 in 2009; 10,821 in 2010. Figures also exclude shells ('000 metric tons): 0.4 in 2008, 0.3 in 2009; 0.3 in 2010.

Source: FAO.

Mining

	2009	2010	2011*
Petroleum, crude ('000 barrels) .	12,806	12,500*	12,500
Copper ('000 metric tons)† .	166.7	159.8	130.0
Silver (metric tons)†	50.0	46.0	45.0
Gold (metric tons)†	63.6	62.9	62.2

* Estimate(s).
† Figures refer to metal content of ore.

Source: US Geological Survey.

Industry

SELECTED PRODUCTS
('000 metric tons unless otherwise indicated)

	2007	2008	2009
Beer of barley*	60	65	60
Palm oil*	382	465	478
Raw sugar	35	35	35
Electric energy (million kWh) .	3,112	3,131	3,131†

* Unofficial figures.
† Estimated production.

Wood products ('000 cu m, excl. furniture): 1,611 in 2003.

2010 ('000 metric tons, unofficial figures): Beer of barley 60; Palm oil 500.

2011 ('000 metric tons, unofficial figures): Beer of barley 70; Palm oil 520.

Sources: FAO; UN Industrial Commodity Statistics Database.

Finance

CURRENCY AND EXCHANGE RATES

Monetary Units
100 toea = 1 kina (K).

Sterling, Dollar and Euro Equivalents (30 November 2012)
£1 sterling = 3.370 kina;
US $1 = 2.099 kina;
€1 = 2.725 kina;
100 kina = £29.68 = $47.65 = €36.69.

Average Exchange Rate (kina per US $)
2009   2.7551
2010   2.7193
2011   2.3710

Note: The foregoing information refers to the mid-point exchange rate of the central bank. In October 1994 it was announced that the kina would be allowed to 'float' on foreign exchange markets.

BUDGET
(million kina)

Revenue*	2010	2011†	2012‡
Taxation	6,434.7	7,904.2	8,519.7
Personal tax	1,494.0	2,158.8	2,417.4
Company tax	2,668.4	3,446.4	3,564.1
Other direct tax	505.7	538.8	561.4
Import duties	188.6	281.4	223.3
Excise duties	610.5	737.0	985.7
Export tax	173.6	210.6	215.6
Goods and services tax	778.1	525.5	545.3
Other indirect tax	15.8	5.7	6.8
Non-tax revenue	435.1	350.3	520.1
Dividends	339.2	239.7	258.0
Interest revenue/fees	1.3	12.8	4.0
Other internal revenue	94.6	97.8	130.1
Injection from trust accounts	—	—	128.0
Total	6,869.8	8,254.5	9,039.8

Expenditure§	2010	2011†	2012‡
Recurrent expenditure	4,160.5	5412.6	6,123.2
National departmental	2,474.3	3,396.9	3,998.3
Provincial governments	1,046.2	1,290.6	1,304.4
Interest payments	353.1	416.3	459.8
Foreign	47.8	63.8	50.7
Domestic	305.3	352.5	409.1
Other grants and expenditure	288.1	315.9	360.7
Development expenditure	3,278.9	3,194.2	4,437.1
National projects	2,623.1	2,555.4	3,549.7
Provincial projects	655.8	638.8	887.4
Additional priority expenditure	653.3	781.8	—
Total	8,092.7	9,388.6	10,560.3

* Excluding grants received from abroad, tax credits and trust accounts (million kina): 1,409.1 in 2010; 1,070.4 in 2011 (preliminary figure); 1,520.5 in 2012 (budget figure).
† Preliminary figures.
‡ Budget figures.
§ Excluding net lending (million kina): –1.2 in 2010; –7.1 in 2011 (preliminary figure); 0 in 2012 (Budget figure).

Source: Bank of Papua New Guinea, Port Moresby.

INTERNATIONAL RESERVES
(US $ million at 31 December)

	2009	2010	2011
Gold (national valuation)	46.40	58.40	66.24
IMF special drawing rights	182.19	15.50	14.68
Reserve position in IMF	0.69	0.67	0.67
Foreign exchange	2,377.73	3,017.56	4,241.04
Total	2,607.01	3,092.13	4,322.63

Source: IMF, *International Financial Statistics*.

MONEY SUPPLY
(million kina at 31 December)

	2009	2010	2011
Currency outside depository corporations	788.95	954.91	1,188.33
Transferable deposits	5,443.73	6,688.71	8,431.35
Other deposits	5,537.23	5,323.39	5,611.73
Securities other than shares	52.66	66.91	61.98
Broad money	11,822.57	13,033.92	15,293.39

Source: IMF, *International Financial Statistics*.

COST OF LIVING
(Consumer Price Index; base: 1977 = 100)

	2009	2010	2011
Food	1,039.1	1,094.9	1,178.3
Clothing and footwear	531.2	544.2	601.4
Rent, fuel and power	384.8	406.8	443.7
All items (incl. others)	973.6	1,032.2	1,119.3

NATIONAL ACCOUNTS
(million kina at current prices)

National Income and Product

	2004	2005	2006
Compensation of employees	2,450.5	2,491.1	2,550.9
Operating surplus	9,163.8	10,505.1	11,994.5
Domestic factor incomes	11,614.3	12,996.2	14,545.4
Consumption of fixed capital	828.9	876.7	985.0
Gross domestic product (GDP) at factor cost	12,443.2	13,872.9	15,530.4
Indirect taxes, less subsidies	1,016.3	1,221.8	1,366.2
GDP in purchasers' values	13,459.3	15,094.7	16,896.5
Net factor income from abroad	–1,408.8	–1,670.0	–2,462.0
Gross national product	12,050.7	13,424.7	14,434.6
Less Consumption of fixed capital	828.9	876.7	985.0
National income in market prices	11,221.8	12,548.0	13,449.6

Source: Bank of Papua New Guinea, Port Moresby.

Expenditure on the Gross Domestic Product

	2004	2005	2006
Government final consumption expenditure	2,237.6	2,437.6	2,837.6
Private final consumption expenditure	7,047.5	7,239.2	7,959.0
Increase in stocks	580.2	150.0	350.0
Gross fixed capital formation	2,294.3	2,489.3	2,302.6
Total domestic expenditure	12,159.6	12,316.1	13,449.2
Exports of goods and services	9,143.4	11,245.7	13,986.2
Less Imports of goods and services	7,843.7	8,467.1	10,538.9
GDP in purchasers' values	13,459.3	15,094.7	16,896.5
GDP at constant 1998 prices	8,299.1	8,625.2	8,823.1

Source: Bank of Papua New Guinea, Port Moresby.

Gross Domestic Product by Economic Activity
(million kina, provisional)

	2009	2010	2011
Agriculture, hunting, forestry and fishing	7,207.9	8,106.9	9,102.3
Mining and quarrying	4,714.9	5,916.8	5,402.3
Manufacturing	1,328.8	1,500.1	1,980.8
Electricity, gas and water . . .	461.7	538.0	640.1
Construction	2,912.3	3,632.0	4,814.3
Wholesale and retail trade . .	1,621.8	1,944.8	2,493.4
Transport, storage and communications	603.7	772.2	973.2
Finance, insurance, real estate and business services*	933.1	1,084.2	1,314.6
Community, social and personal services (incl. defence) . . .	2,010.1	2,211.4	2,522.8
Sub-total	21,794.3	25,706.4	29,243.8
Import duties, less subsidies . .	536.7	688.9	597.7
GDP in purchasers' values .	22,331.0	26,395.3	29,841.5

* Including services of owner-occupied dwellings.

Source: Asian Development Bank.

BALANCE OF PAYMENTS
(million kina)

	2009	2010	2011
Exports of goods f.o.b.	12,101	15,623	16,396
Imports of goods f.o.b.	−7,909	−9,597	−10,053
Trade balance	4,192	6,026	6,343
Exports of services	511	844	1,006
Imports of services	−5,070	−7,497	−7,030
Balance on goods and services	−367	−627	319
Other income received . . .	128	114	95
Other income paid	−1,849	−1,724	−1,400
Balance on goods, services and income	−2,088	−2,237	−986
Current transfers received . .	1,046	1,192	1,368
Current transfers paid	−569	−676	−789
Current balance	−1,611	−1,721	−407
Capital account (net)	74	101	73
Direct investment abroad . .	−12	−1	−2
Direct investment from abroad .	1,166	79	−734
Portfolio investment assets . .	414	−284	1,019
Portfolio investment liabilities .	−1	0	0
Financial derivatives assets . .	58	−21	−79
Other investment assets . .	1,232	3,216	1,348
Other investment liabilities . .	363	−55	−26
Net errors and omissions . . .	42	−249	−96
Overall balance	1,725	1,065	1,096

Source: Bank of Papua New Guinea, Port Moresby.

External Trade

PRINCIPAL COMMODITIES
(million kina)

Imports f.o.b.	2010	2011
Food and live animals	1,111.3	1,119.1
Mineral fuels, lubricants and related materials.	1,750.3	1,845.7
Chemicals and related products	337.0	313.2
Basic manufactures	685.8	647.8
Machinery and transport equipment . . .	3,619.1	3,546.9
Miscellaneous manufactured articles . . .	1,432.7	1,759.2
Total (incl. others)	9,576.2	10,033.5

Exports f.o.b.	2009	2010	2011
Agricultural products	2,223.5	2,961.3	3,789.8
Forestry products	409.9	743.7	768.3
Logs	383.1	705.9	732.0
Mineral products	9,057.0	11,782.8	11,558.2
Crude petroleum	1,610.4	2,224.8	2,434.0
Copper	2,025.9	3,089.3	3,047.1
Gold	5,366.7	6,380.3	5,974.2
Total (incl. others)	11,902.8	15,601.8	16,376.1

Source: Bank of Papua New Guinea, Port Moresby.

PRINCIPAL TRADING PARTNERS
(million kina)

Imports c.i.f.	2009	2010	2011
Australia	3,346.6	3,919.3	4,016.6
China, People's Republic . . .	405.8	355.4	442.3
Hong Kong	99.2	120.0	138.1
Indonesia	91.7	95.5	80.2
Japan	271.7	440.5	348.5
Malaysia	145.9	229.6	181.1
New Zealand	223.0	253.3	261.9
Singapore	901.6	1,440.3	1,235.4
USA	1,741.7	1,938.0	2,655.9
Total (incl. others)	7,890.0	9,576.2	10,033.5

Exports f.o.b.	2009	2010	2011
Australia	5,691.6	7,277.8	6,872.6
China, People's Republic . . .	415.8	1,036.0	985.3
Germany	587.4	615.3	940.9
Italy	112.1	90.8	267.8
Japan	1,751.6	2,319.6	2,273.4
Korea, Republic	463.9	579.8	401.4
Malaysia	129.4	178.1	236.2
Netherlands	157.5	398.2	836.9
Philippines	867.6	1,140.9	1,188.3
Singapore	348.5	307.3	146.9
Spain	314.6	317.8	253.1
United Kingdom	164.6	295.5	322.3
USA	164.9	122.0	275.5
Total (incl. others)	12,079.8	15,601.8	16,376.1

Source: Bank of Papua New Guinea, Port Moresby.

Transport

ROAD TRAFFIC
('000 vehicles in use)

	1999	2000	2001
Passenger cars	18.8	24.9	24.9
Commercial vehicles	87.0	87.8	87.8

Source: UN, *Statistical Yearbook*.

2007 ('000 vehicles in use at 31 December): Passenger cars 38,173; Coaches and buses 6,561; Vans and lorries 11,333; Motorcycles and mopeds 1,193 (Source: IRF, *World Road Statistics*).

SHIPPING

Flag Registered Fleet
(at 31 December)

	2010	2011	2012
Number of vessels	98	104	112
Total displacement ('000 grt) . .	97.6	106.5	117.5

Source: Lloyd's List Intelligence (www.lloydslistintelligence.com).

International Sea-borne Freight Traffic

	1997	1998	1999
Cargo unloaded ('000 metric tons).	2,208.6	2,209.0	2,062.8
Cargo loaded ('000 metric tons) .	735.9	823.3	788.1

Source: Papua New Guinea Harbours Board, *Monthly Shipping Register Form*.

CIVIL AVIATION
(traffic on scheduled services)

	2007	2008	2009
Kilometres flown (million) . .	14	14	14
Passengers carried ('000) . .	919	905	847
Passenger-km (million) . .	791	780	728
Total ton-km (million) . . .	104	102	94

Source: UN, *Statistical Yearbook*.

Passengers carried ('000): 1,158 in 2010 (Source: World Bank, World Development Indicators database).

Tourism

FOREIGN TOURIST ARRIVALS

Country of origin	2008	2009	2010
Australia	58,724	66,842	75,355
Canada	1,745	1,937	1,927
Germany	1,408	1,219	1,680
Japan	3,865	2,767	3,804
Malaysia	4,772	5,017	5,915
New Zealand	5,399	5,685	7,043
Philippines . . .	7,661	7,333	9,551
United Kingdom . . .	3,800	3,669	5,102
USA	6,109	6,630	8,435
Total (incl. others)	114,207	125,891	146,350

Total tourist arrivals: 165,059 in 2011.

Receipts from tourism (US $ million, excl. passenger transport): 1.0 in 2009; 2.0 in 2010; 2.0 in 2011 (provisional).

Source: World Tourism Organization.

Communications Media

	2009	2010	2011
Telephones ('000 main lines in use)	91.1	121.2	130.0
Mobile cellular telephones ('000 subscribers)	1,417.5	1,909.1	2,400.0
Internet users ('000)	125	n.a.	n.a.
Broadband subscribers ('000) . .	4.5	6.1	7.5

Source: International Telecommunication Union.

Education

(2007/08)

	Institutions	Teachers	Students
Pre-primary	5,908	12,140	422,592
Primary	3,549	20,942	715,764
Secondary	208	3,476	94,192
Vocational	99	947	19,661
Tertiary*	13	557	10,520

*Includes national high schools, technical colleges and teacher training colleges.

Sources: National Department of Education, *Statistical Bulletin* (2008).

Pupil-teacher Ratio (primary education, UNESCO estimate): 35.8 in 2005/06 (Source: UNESCO Institute for Statistics).

Adult Literacy Rate (UNESCO estimates): 60.6% (males 63.9%; females 57.3%) in 2010 (Source: UNESCO Institute for Statistics).

Directory

The Government

HEAD OF STATE

Queen: HM Queen ELIZABETH II.
Governor-General: MICHAEL OGIO (sworn in 25 February 2011).

NATIONAL EXECUTIVE COUNCIL
(May 2013)

The cabinet includes members of the People's National Congress (PNC), Triumph Heritage Empowerment Rural Party (THE), the United Resources Party (URP), National Alliance (NA), People's Party, People's Progress Party (PPP), Indigenous People's Party (IPP), Our Development Party, People's Democratic Movement (PDM), Social Democratic Party (SDP), United Party and Independents.

Prime Minister: PETER O'NEILL (PNC).
Deputy Prime Minister and Minister for Inter-Government Relations: LEO DION (THE).
Minister for Foreign Affairs and Immigration: RIMBINK PATO (United Party).
Minister for Trade, Commerce and Industry: RICHARD MARU (United Party).
Minister for Defence: FABIAN POK (URP).
Minister for Police: NIXON DUBAN (PNC).
Minister for Justice and Attorney-General: KERENGA KUA (Ind.).
Minister for Treasury: DON POLYE (THE).

Minister of Finance: JAMES MARAPE (PNC).
Minister for Agriculture and Livestock: TOMMY TOMSCOLL (PDM).
Minister for Communication and Information Technology: JIM MIRINGTORO (PNC).
Minister for Tourism, Arts and Culture: BOKA KONDRA (PNC).
Minister for Environment and Conservation: JOHN PUNDARI (People's Party).
Minister for Mining: BYRON CHAN (PPP).
Minister for Fisheries and Marine Resources: MAO ZEMING (PNC).
Minister for Public Service: Sir PUKA TEMU (Our Development Party).
Minister for Health and HIV/AIDS: MICHAEL MALABAG (PNC).
Minister for Education: PARU AIHI (PNC).
Minister for Higher Education, Research, Science and Technology: DON POLYE (THE) (acting).
Minister for Housing and Urban Development: PAUL ISIKELI (PNC).
Minister for Forests and Climate Change: PATRICK PRUAITCH (NA).
Minister for Labour and Industrial Relations: MARK MAIPAKAI (THE).
Minister for National Planning: CHARLES ABEL (PNC).
Minister for Petroleum and Energy: WILLIAM DUMA (URP).

Minister for Public Enterprise and State Investment: BEN MICAH (PPP).

Minister for Lands and Physical Planning: BENNY ALLAN (PNC).

Minister for Civil Aviation: DAVIS STEVEN (People's Party).

Minister for Autonomous Regions: STEVEN KAMA PIRIKA (URP).

Minister for Community Development, Religion and Youth: LOUJAYA TONI (IPP).

Minister for Sports and Pacific Games: JUSTIN TKATCHENKO (SDP).

Minister for Correctional Services: JIM SIMITAB (NA).

Minister for Transport: ANO PALA (PNC).

Minister for Works and Implementation: FRANCIS AWESA (PNC).

GOVERNMENT DEPARTMENTS AND OFFICES

Office of the Prime Minister: POB 639, Waigani, NCD; tel. 3276525; fax 3277328; e-mail chiefsectogov@pmnec.gov.pg; internet www.pm.gov.pg.

Department of Agriculture and Livestock: POB 417, Konedobu 125; tel. 3231848; fax 3230563; e-mail dalit@daltron.com.pg; internet www.agriculture.gov.pg.

Department of the Attorney-General and of Justice: POB 591, Waigani, NCD; tel. 3230138; fax 3233661.

Department of Autonomous Regions: Boroko, NCD.

Department of Communications and Information: POB 1122, Waigani, NCD; tel. 3250148; fax 3250412; e-mail hiduhu@gopng.gov .pg.

Department of Community Development, Religion and Youth: Sambra Investment House, Waigani, NCD; tel. 3250120; fax 3250118.

Department of Defence: CDC House, MacGregor St, Port Moresby; tel. 3200633; fax 3200611; internet www.defence.gov.pg.

Department of Education: Fincorp Haus, POB 446, Waigani, NCD; tel. 3013555; fax 3254648; internet www.education.gov.pg.

Department of Environment and Conservation: POB 6601, Boroko 111, NCD; tel. 3014500; fax 3250180; e-mail wamini@dec.gov .pg; internet www.dec.gov.pg.

Department of Finance: POB 710, Waigani, Vulupindi Haus, NCD; tel. 3128449; fax 3128431; e-mail inquires@finance.gov.pg; internet www.finance.gov.pg.

Department of Fisheries and Marine Resources: POB 2016, Port Moresby; tel. 3271799; fax 3202074.

Department of Foreign Affairs and Immigration: POB 422, Waigani 131, NCD; tel. 3014158; fax 3277480.

Department of Health: POB 807, Waigani, NCD; tel. 3013827; fax 3013742; e-mail andrew_solien@health.gov.pg; internet www.health .gov.pg.

Department of Higher Education, Research, Science and Technology: Mutual Rumana Bldg, Boroko, NCD; tel. 3277528; fax 3277480.

Department of Housing and Urban Development: POB 1550, Boroko, NCD; tel. 3259344; fax 3259918.

Department of Inter-Government Relations: Somare Foundation Bldg, Waigani, NCD; tel. 3250251; fax 3217462.

Department of Labour and Industrial Relations: POB 5644, Boroko, NCD; tel. 3235758; fax 3256655; e-mail enquiries@ workpermits.gov.pg; internet www.workpermits.gov.pg.

Department of Lands and Physical Planning: Aopi Centre, Tower 2, Levels 2, 3 and 4, Waigani Drive, Boroko, NCD; tel. 3013206; fax 3013205; e-mail onnoj@lands.gov.pg; internet www .lands.gov.pg.

Department of Mining: PMB, Port Moresby Post Office, Port Moresby 121; tel. 3214011; fax 3217958; internet www.mineral .gov.pg.

Department of National Planning: POB 631, Waigani, NCD; tel. 3288302; fax 3288384; e-mail dnpm_enquiries@planning.gov.pg; internet www.planning.gov.pg.

Department of Petroleum and Energy: POB 1993, Port Moresby, NCD; tel. 3224261; fax 3224222; e-mail enquiry@petroleum.gov.pg; internet www.petroleum.gov.pg.

Department of Police: Police Headquarters, POB 85, Konedobu, NCD; tel. 3226100; fax 3226113.

Department of Public Enterprise and State Investment: Pacific Place Bldg, Level 11, POB 320, Port Moresby NCD; tel. 3212977; fax 3210192.

Department of Public Service: Waigani, NCD; tel. 3276418; fax 3250835.

Department of Sport and Pacific Games: Boroko, NCD.

Department of Tourism, Arts and Culture: Port Moresby, NCD.

Department of Trade, Commerce and Industry: Waigani, NCD; tel. 3277346; fax 3013205.

Department of Transport and Civil Aviation: POB 1489, Port Moresby; tel. 3236460; fax 3200236.

Department of Treasury: POB 542, Waigani 131, NCD; tel. 3128817; fax 3128844; e-mail enquiries@treasury.gov.pg; internet www.treasury.gov.pg.

Department of Works and Implementation: POB 1108, Boroko 111, NCD; tel. 3222500; fax 3200236; e-mail webmaster@works.gov .pg; internet www.works.gov.pg.

Correctional Service: POB 6889, Boroko, NCD III; tel. 3232496; fax 3232707; e-mail rsikani@hq.cs.gov.pg.

Papua New Guinea Forest Authority: POB 5055, Boroko, NCD; tel. 3277841; fax 3254433; e-mail info_general@pngfa.gov.pg; internet www.forestry.gov.pg.

Legislature

NATIONAL PARLIAMENT

The unicameral legislature has 111 elective seats: 89 representing open constituencies and 22 representing provincial constituencies. There is constitutional provision for up to three nominated members.

Speaker: THEO ZURENUOC.

General Election, 23 June–17 July 2012

Party	Seats
People's National Congress	27
Triumph Heritage Empowerment Party	12
Papua New Guinea Party	8
National Alliance	7
United Resources Party	7
People's Party*	6
People's Progress Party	6
People's United Assembly Party	3
Social Democratic Party	3
Coalition for Reform Party	2
Melanesian Liberal Party	2
People's Democratic Movement	2
People's Movement for Change Party	2
PNG Country Party	2
Indigenous People's Party	1
New Generation Party	1
Our Development Party	1
Pangu Pati	1
PNG Constitutional Democratic Party	1
Stars Alliance Party	1
United Party	1
Independents and others	14
Total	111

* The People's Party merged into the People's National Congress in January 2013.

Autonomous Region

BOUGAINVILLE ASSEMBLY

Elections for 39 of the 40 seats in Bougainville's second autonomous assembly and for the President of the Autonomous Bougainville Government took place over a period of two weeks commencing on 7 May 2010. John Momis of the New Bougainville Party was elected President of the Autonomous Bougainville Government, winning 52.3% of the total votes cast, thus defeating the incumbent James Tanis (20.9%) and five other candidates. More than three-quarters of incumbent legislators lost their seats in the House of Representatives. Independent candidates were reported to have won 23 seats and the New Bougainville Party 14 seats. Three of the 39 seats are reserved for women and three for former combatants. The President occupies the 40th seat in the assembly. The incoming President and the House of Representatives were inaugurated on 15 June 2010.

President: JOHN MOMIS.

Vice-President: PATRICK NISIRA.

Speaker: ANDREW MIRIKI.

Election Commission

Election Commission of Papua New Guinea: POB 5348, Boroko, NCD; tel. 3258187; fax 3258650; e-mail info@pngec.gov.pg; internet www.pngec.gov.pg; Electoral Commr ANDREW TRAWEN.

Political Organizations

In May 2012 46 political parties were registered.

Christian Democratic Party: POB 41, Waigani, NCD; tel. 3443301; e-mail kpokeya@hotmail.com; internet www.cdppng.org; Pres. JACOB POPUNA; Leader Dr BANARE BUN.

Coalition for Reform Party: POB 903, Port Moresby; tel. 3424836; fax 3216233; e-mail coalition4reform@gmail.com; Pres. EDWARD DIRO; Gen. Sec. PHILEMON WASS.

Customary Land Rights-holders Party: f. 2011; promotes wealth creation, co-operation and equal devt among all customary land rights-holders and citizens; Pres. PETER DONIGI; Sec.-Gen. EMMANUEL MUNGU.

Melanesian Alliance (MA): POB 484, Waigani, NCD; tel. 71783787; f. 1978; socialist; Pres. SIMON EYORK; Gen. Sec. NICK KLAPAT.

Melanesian Liberal Party: POB 250, University, NCD; tel. 3112798; fax 3251093; Pres. LUI POE; Gen. Sec. GABRIEL BUAKIA.

National Alliance (NA): POB 424, Boroko, NCD; tel. 3232899; fax 3230250; e-mail nappng@daltron.com.pg; f. 1996; est. to combat corruption in public life; split into two factions in 2011, one of which, comprising many of the NA's members of Parliament, est. a new party, Triumph Heritage Empowerment Rural Party, in early 2012; Pres. SIMON KAIWI; Leader PATRICK PRUAITCH.

New Generation Party: POB 1853, Waigani, NCD; tel. 3260462; Pres. GEORGE LEAHY; Leader Dr WILLIAM TONGAMP.

Pangu Pati (PANGU) (Papua New Guinea Unity): POB 446, Gordons, NCD; tel. 73291927; f. 1968; urban- and rural-based; Pres. MILO TIMINI; Leader ANDREW KUMBAKOR.

Papua New Guinea Country Party (Kantri Pati): POB 7134, Boroko, NCD; tel. 71135856; fax 3270480; e-mail png.cp@hotmail.com; Pres. KILROY GENIA; Gen. Sec. WILSON T. ORLEGGE.

Papua New Guinea Greens Party: POB 511, Port Moresby, NCD; tel. 72657588; f. 2001; Pres. DOROTHY TEKWIE; Gen. Sec. ANDREW KUTAPAE.

Papua New Guinea Party: POB 6902, Boroko, NCD; tel. 3212163; fax 3217986; e-mail admin@pngparty.com; internet www.pngparty.com; f. 2007; Pres. PHILIP ELEDUME; Leader BELDEN NAMAH.

People's Action Party (PAP): POB 525, Waigani, NCD; tel. 71895394; e-mail bolesimon@yahoo.com; f. 1985; Acting Pres. and Gen. Sec. SIMON BOLE.

People's Democratic Movement (PDM): POB 635, Gordons, NCD; tel. 72175054; f. 1985; merged with Advance PNG Party in 2001; Pres. GEOFFREY BULL; Leader PAIAS WINGTI.

People's Movement for Change Party: POB 4458, Boroko, NCD; tel. 3254291; fax 4728289; e-mail tjsipa@daltron.com.pg; Pres. SIMON MERTON; Gen. Sec. PAUL POPLE.

People's National Congress (PNC): POB 4172, Boroko, NCD; tel. 71665849; internet www.pncpng.com; absorbed the People's Party in Jan. 2013; Pres. SIMON KORAWA; Leader PETER O'NEILL.

People's Progress Party (PPP): POB 785, Boroko, NCD; tel. 72735931; f. 1970; Parliamentary Leader JULIUS CHAN; Pres. BROWN SINAMOI; Gen. Sec. PHILIP KUWIMB.

People's United Assembly Party: POB 228, Port Moresby, NCD; tel. 3214847; fax 3214849; Pres. RAYMOND KAUI; Gen. Sec. BENJAMIN AGAWI.

Rural Development Party: POB 1012, Boroko, NCD; tel. 9829123; Pres. JOHN ROBIN.

Social Democratic Party (SDP): POB 5076, Boroko, NCD; tel. 3422701; fax 3233259; f. 2010; est. as United Democratic Front; aims to eliminate corruption and 'power politics, power-play and politics of convenience'; Leader POWES PARKOP; Pres. WESLEY SANARUP.

Triumph Heritage Empowerment Party (THE): POB 2975, Boroko, NCD; tel. 3416168; f. 2012; est. by fmr mems of National Alliance; Pres. DOUGLAS TOMURIESA; Leader DON POLYE.

United Party: POB 2266, Boroko, NCD; tel. 3202973; fax 3277380; Pres. CHRIS KOPYOTO; Leader BOB DADAE.

United Resources Party (URP): POB 155, Gordons, NCD; tel. 3430421; f. 1997; aims to secure greater representation in govt for resource owners; Pres. KEN YAPANE; Leader WILLIAM DUMA.

Other parties that contested the 2012 election included the Stars Alliance Party, PNG Constitutional Democratic Party, Our Development Party and Indigenous People's Party (IPP).

Diplomatic Representation

EMBASSIES AND HIGH COMMISSIONS IN PAPUA NEW GUINEA

Australia: Godwit Rd, Waigani, NCD; tel. 3259333; fax 3256647; internet www.png.embassy.gov.au; High Commissioner DEBORAH STOKES.

China, People's Republic: POB 1351, Boroko, NCD; tel. 3259903; fax 3254191; e-mail chinaemb_pg@mfa.gov.cn; internet pg.china-embassy.org; Ambassador QIU BOHUA.

Fiji: Defens Haus, 4th Floor, Champion Parade, POB 6117, Boroko, NCD; tel. 3211914; fax 3217220; High Commissioner ROMANU TIKOTIKOCA.

France: Defens Haus, 6th Floor, Champion Parade, POB 1155, Port Moresby, NCD 121; tel. 3215550; fax 3215549; e-mail cad.port-moresby-amba@diplomatie.gouv.fr; internet www.ambafrance-pg.org; Ambassador ALAIN WAQUET.

Holy See: POB 98, Port Moresby; tel. 3256021; fax 3252844; e-mail nunciaturepng@datec.net.pg; Apostolic Nuncio Most Rev. SANTO ROCCO GANGEMI (Titular Archbishop of Umbriatico).

India: Lot 20, Section 8, Unit 2, Tanatana St, Boroko, NCD; tel. 3254757; fax 3253138; e-mail hcipom@datec.net.pg; High Commissioner A. M. GONDANE.

Indonesia: POB 7165, Boroko, NCD; tel. 3253116; fax 3250535; e-mail kbripom@daltron.com.pg; internet www.deplu.go.id/portmoresby; Ambassador ANDREAS SITEPU.

Japan: POB 1040, Port Moresby; tel. 3211800; fax 3214868; e-mail sceoj@online.net.pg; Ambassador HIROHARU IWASAKI.

Korea, Republic: POB 381, Port Moresby; tel. 3215822; fax 3215828; e-mail embpng@mofat.go.kr; internet png.mofat.go.kr; Ambassador LEE WHIE-JIN.

Malaysia: POB 1400, Port Moresby; tel. 3252076; fax 3252784; e-mail malpmresby@kln.gov.my; internet www.kln.gov.my/web/png_port-moresby; Ambassador Datin BLANCHE OLBERY.

New Zealand: POB 1051, Waigani, NCD; tel. 3259444; fax 3250565; e-mail nzhcpom@dg.com.pg; High Commissioner MARION CRAWSHAW.

Philippines: POB 5916, Boroko, NCD; tel. 3256414; fax 3231803; e-mail pompe@datec.net.pg; Ambassador BIENVENIDO V. TEJANO.

Solomon Islands: Waigani, Port Moresby; e-mail sihicomm@daltron.com.pg; High Commissioner WILLIAM HAOMAE.

United Kingdom: Kiroki St, Waigani 131, NCD; tel. 3251677; fax 3253547; e-mail ukinpng@datec.net.pg; internet www.ukinpng.fco.gov.uk; High Commissioner JACQUELINE BARSON.

USA: POB 1492, Port Moresby; tel. 3211455; fax 3211593; e-mail png@state.gov; internet portmoresby.usembassy.gov; Ambassador WALTER NORTH.

Judicial System

The Supreme Court is the highest judicial authority in the country, and deals with all matters involving the interpretation of the Constitution, and with appeals from the National Court. The National Court has unlimited jurisdiction in both civil and criminal matters. All National Court Judges (except acting Judges) are Judges of the Supreme Court. District Courts are responsible for civil cases involving compensation, for some indictable offences and for the more serious summary offences, while Local Courts deal with minor offences and with such matters as custody of children under the provision of Custom. There are also Children's Courts, which judge cases involving minors. Appeal from the District, Local and Children's Courts lies to the National Court. District and Local Land Courts deal with disputes relating to Customary land, and Warden's Courts with civil cases relating to mining. In addition, there are other courts with responsibility for determining ownership of government land and for assessing the right of Customary landowners to compensation. Village Courts, which are presided over by Magistrates with no formal legal qualification, are responsible for all Customary matters not dealt with by other courts.

Supreme Court: POB 7018, Boroko, NCD; tel. 3245700; fax 3234492; internet www.pngjudiciary.gov.pg; Chief Justice Sir SALAMO INJIA.

Office of the Attorney-General: POB 591, Waigani, NCD; tel. 3230138; fax 3233661; e-mail fred_tomo@justice.gov.pg; internet www.lawandjustice.gov.pg; Attorney-General KERENGA KUA.

PAPUA NEW GUINEA

Directory

Religion

The belief in magic or sorcery is widespread, even among the significant proportion of the population that has adopted Christianity (nominally 97% in 1990). Pantheism also survives. There are many missionary societies.

CHRISTIANITY

Papua New Guinea Council of Churches: POB 1015, Boroko, NCD; tel. 3259961; fax 3251206; f. 1965; 7 mem. churches; Chair. EDEA KIDU; Gen. Sec. SOPHIA W. R. GEGEYO.

The Anglican Communion

Formerly part of the Province of Queensland within the Church of England in Australia (now the Anglican Church of Australia), Papua New Guinea became an independent Province in 1977. The Anglican Church of Papua New Guinea comprises five dioceses and had 246,000 members in 2000.

Archbishop of Papua New Guinea and Bishop of Popondota: Most Rev. JOSEPH KIFAU KOPAPA, POB 26, Popondetta, Oro Province; tel. 3297194; fax 7297476; e-mail acpngpop@online.net.pg.

General Secretary: RICHARD RABIAFI, POB 673, Lae, Morobe Province; tel. 4724111; fax 4721852; e-mail acpnggensec@global.net.pg.

The Roman Catholic Church

For ecclesiastical purposes, Papua New Guinea comprises four archdioceses and 15 dioceses. At 31 December 2007 there were 1,826,012 adherents.

Catholic Bishops' Conference of Papua New Guinea and Solomon Islands

POB 398, Waigani, NCD; tel. 3259577; fax 3232551; e-mail cbcgensec@catholic.org.pg; internet www.catholicpng.org.pg. f. 1959; Pres. Most Rev. JOHN RIBAT (Bishop of Bereina); Gen. Sec. LAWRENCE STEPHENS.

Archbishop of Madang: Most Rev. STEPHEN JOSEPH REICHERT, Archbishop's Residence, POB 750, Madang 511; tel. 8522599; fax 8522596; e-mail Kurtz_caom@global.net.pg.

Archbishop of Mount Hagen: Most Rev. DOUGLAS YOUNG, Archbishop's Office, POB 54, Mount Hagen, Western Highlands Province 281; tel. 5421285; fax 5422128; e-mail dwyoung@global.net.pg.

Archbishop of Port Moresby: Most Rev. JOHN RIBAT, Archbishop's House, POB 1032, Boroko, NCD 111; tel. 3251192; fax 3256731; e-mail archpom@daltron.com.pg.

Archbishop of Rabaul: Most Rev. FRANCESCO PANFILO, Archbishop's House, POB 357, Kokopo 613, East New Britain Province; tel. 9828369; fax 9828858; e-mail abkhesse@online.net.pg.

Other Christian Churches

Baptist Union of Papua New Guinea Inc: POB 705, Mount Hagen, Western Highlands Province; tel. 5422805; fax 5320100; e-mail bupng@global.net.pg; f. 1976; Gen. Dir JOHN KISANYI KAEWA; 80,000 mems.

Evangelical Lutheran Church of Papua New Guinea: POB 80, Lae, Morobe Province; tel. 4723711; fax 4721056; e-mail bishop.admin@global.net.pg; internet www.elcpng.org; f. 1956; Head Bishop Rt Rev. GIEGERE WENGE; 1.2m. mems.

Gutnius Lutheran Church of Papua New Guinea: Bishop Rev. DAVID P. PISO, POB 111, 291 Wabag, Enga Province; tel. 5471280; fax 5471235; e-mail dpisoglc@online.net.pg; f. 1948; Gen. Sec. RICHARD R. MOSES; 149,455 mems.

Papua New Guinea Union Mission of the Seventh-day Adventist Church: POB 86, Lae, Morobe Province 411; tel. 4721488; fax 4721873; internet pngum.adventist.org.pg; Sec. LEIGH RICE; 200,000 adherents.

The United Church in Papua New Guinea: POB 1401, Port Moresby; tel. 3211744; fax 3214930; e-mail ucpng@daltron.com.pg; internet www.ucpng.com; f. 1968; formed by union of the Methodist Church in Melanesia, the Papua Ekalesia and United Church, Port Moresby; Moderator Sir SAMSON LOWA; 700,000 mems; Gen. Sec. Rev. SIULANGI KAVORA.

BAHÁ'Í FAITH

National Spiritual Assembly: PMB 9, Boroko, NCD; tel. 3250286; fax 3236474; e-mail nsasecretary@bahai.org.pg; internet www.bahai.org.pg.

ISLAM

In 2000 the Muslim community in Papua New Guinea numbered about 1,500, of whom approximately two-thirds were believed to be expatriates. The religion was introduced to the island in the 1970s.

The country's first mosque was opened in 2000 at Poreporena Highway, Hohola, Port Moresby; Imam MIKHAIL KORAH (acting).

The Press

There are numerous newspapers and magazines published by government departments, statutory organizations, missions, sporting organizations, local government councils and regional authorities. They are variously in English, Tok Pisin (Pidgin), Motu and vernacular languages.

Ailans Nius: POB 1239, Rabaul, East New Britain Province; weekly.

Foreign Affairs Review: Dept of Foreign Affairs, Central Government Offices, Kumul Ave, Post Office, Wards Strip, Waigani, NCD; tel. 3271401; fax 3254886.

Hailans Nius: Mount Hagen, Western Highlands Province; weekly.

Lae Nius: POB 759, Lae, Morobe Province; 2 a week.

The National: POB 6817, Boroko, NCD; tel. 3246888; fax 3246868; e-mail national@thenational.com.pg; internet www.thenational.com.pg; f. 1993; daily; Editor DANIEL KORIMBAU; circ. 30,000.

Papua and New Guinea Education Gazette: Dept of Education, Fincorp Haus, POB 446, Waigani, NCD; tel. 3272413; fax 3254648; monthly; Editor J. OBERLENTER; circ. 8,000.

Papua New Guinea Post-Courier: POB 85, Port Moresby; tel. 3091000; fax 3212721; e-mail postcourier@ssp.com.pg; internet www.postcourier.com.pg; f. 1969; daily; English; published by News Corpn; Editor YEHIURA HRIEHWAZI; circ. 25,044.

Sunkamap Times: POB 322, Buka, Bougainville, North Solomons Province; e-mail stephen@viscom.co.nz; internet www.viscom.co.nz/SunkamapTimes; monthly; f. 2004; community newsletter.

Wantok (Friend) Niuspepa: POB 1982, Boroko, NCD; tel. 3252500; fax 3252579; e-mail word@global.net.pg; f. 1970; weekly in New Guinea Pidgin; mainly rural readership; Publr ANNA SOLOMON; Editor NEVILLE CHOI; circ. 10,000.

Publishers

Gordon and Gotch (PNG) Pty Ltd: POB 107, Boroko, NCD; tel. 3254855; fax 3250950; e-mail ggpng@online.net.pg; f. 1970; books, magazines and stationery; Gen. Man. PETER G. PORTER.

Scripture Union of Papua New Guinea: POB 280, University, Boroko, NCD; tel. and fax 3253987; f. 1966; religious; Chair. RAVA TAVIRI.

Word Publishing Co Pty Ltd: POB 1982, Boroko, NCD; tel. 3252500; fax 3252579; e-mail word@global.net.pg; f. 1982; 60% owned by the Roman Catholic Church, 20% by Evangelical Lutheran, 10% by Anglican and 10% by United Churches; Gen. Man. JEREMY BURGESS.

Broadcasting and Communications

REGULATORY AUTHORITY

National Information and Communications Technology Authority (NICTA): POB 8444, Boroko, NCD; tel. 3033223; fax 3004829; e-mail licensing@nicta.gov.pg; internet www.nicta.gov.pg; f. 2009; CEO CHARLES PUNAHA.

TELECOMMUNICATIONS

Datec: Poreporena Freeway, POB 504, Port Moresby; tel. 3031333; fax 3259066; e-mail concierge@datec.net.pg; internet www.datec.net.pg; internet service provider.

Bemobile: POB 1055, Port Moresby, NCD; tel. 3259400; e-mail support@bemobile.com.pg; internet www.bemobile.com.pg; f. 2009; CEO STUART KELLY.

Digicel (PNG) Ltd: POB 1618, Port Moresby, NCD; tel. 72222222 (mobile); fax 3253652; e-mail customercarepng@digicelgroup.com; internet www.digicelpng.com; GSM services; CEO JOHN MANGOS.

Telikom PNG Pty Ltd: POB 736, Waigan, Port Moresby, NCD; tel. 3004688; fax 3004689; e-mail webadmin@telikompng.com.pg; internet www.telikompng.com.pg; fixed-line, satellite and broadband services; Chair. GEREA AOPI; CEO PETER LOKO.

BROADCASTING
Radio

National Broadcasting Corporation of Papua New Guinea: POB 1359, Boroko, NCD; tel. 3255233; fax 3256296; e-mail info@nbc.com.pg; internet www.nbc.com.pg; f. 1973; commercial and free govt

www.europaworld.com

radio programmes services; broadcasting in English, Melanesian, Pidgin, Motu and 30 vernacular languages; Chair. CHRIS RANGATIN; Man. Dir Dr MEMAFU KAPERA.

Kalang Service (FM): POB 1359, Boroko, NCD; tel. 3255233; commercial radio co established by National Broadcasting Commission; Chair. CAROLUS KETSIMUR.

Nau FM/Yumi FM: POB 774, Port Moresby; tel. 3201996; fax 3201995; e-mail reception@naufm.com.pg; internet www .pngvillage.net; f. 1994; holding co PNG FM, owned by Communications Fiji Ltd; Gen. Mans MARK ROGERS, JUSTIN KILI.

Television

EM TV: POB 443, Boroko, NCD; tel. 3257322; fax 3254450; internet www.emtvpng.com; f. 1988; operated by Media Niugini Pty Ltd; CEO BHANU SUD.

Kundu 2 (National Television Service): f. 2008; state-owned.

Finance

(cap. = capital; res = reserves; dep. = deposits; m. = million; brs = branches; amounts in kina unless otherwise stated)

BANKING

Central Bank

Bank of Papua New Guinea: POB 121, Port Moresby 121; tel. 3227200; fax 3211617; e-mail info@bankpng.gov.pg; internet www .bankpng.gov.pg; f. 1973; bank of issue since 1975; cap. 145.5m., res 205.3m., dep. 3,452m. (Dec. 2011); Gov. LOI MARTIN BAKANI; Deputy Gov. BENNY POPOITAI.

Commercial Banks

Australia and New Zealand Banking Group (PNG) Ltd: POB 1152, Port Moresby 121; tel. 3211079; fax 3223302; e-mail cshdpg@ anz.com; internet www.anz.com/Png; f. 1976; cap. 5.0m., res 2.2m., dep. 3,055.3m. (Sept. 2008); Chair. JOHN MORSCHEL; Man. Dir VISHNU MOHAN; 12 brs.

Bank of South Pacific Ltd: POB 78, Cnr Douglas and Musgrave Sts, Port Moresby; tel. 3201212; fax 3211954; e-mail servicebsp@bsp .com.pg; internet www.bsp.com.pg; f. 1974; acquired from National Australia Bank Ltd by Papua New Guinea consortium (National Investment Holdings, now BSP Holdings Ltd) in 1993; merged with Papua New Guinea Banking Corpn in 2002; 10% stake acquired by International Finance Corporation in mid-2010; cap. 426.4m., res 196.3m., dep. 9,444.1m. (Dec. 2011); Chair. KOSTAS CONSTANTINOU; CEO IAN B. CLYNE; 35 brs.

Maybank (PNG) Ltd: Cnr Waigani Rd and Islander Dr., POB 882, Waigani, NCD; tel. 3258028; fax 3256128; e-mail maybankpom@ datec.net.pg; internet maybank.com.my/maybank-worldwide/ papua-new-guinea; f. 1995; Chair. ALISTER MAITLAND.

Westpac Bank—PNG—Ltd: POB 706, Port Moresby; tel. 3220511; fax 3220636; e-mail westpacpng@westpac.com.au; internet www .westpac.com.pg; f. 1910; est. as Bank of New South Wales, present name adopted 1982; 93.5% owned by Westpac Banking Corpn (Australia); cap. 5.8m., res 78.5m., dep. 2,206m. (Sept. 2010); Man. Dir ASHLEIGH MATHESON; 16 brs.

Development Bank

National Development Bank (NDB): POB 686, Waigani, NCD; tel. 3247500; fax 3259817; e-mail rbank@devbank.com.pg; internet www.ndb.com.pg; f. 1967; est. as Agriculture Bank of Papua New Guinea; later known as Rural Development Bank of Papua New Guinea; name changed as above in 2007; statutory govt agency; Chair. WILLIAM LAMUR; Man. Dir MOSES LIU (acting); 18 brs.

Savings and Loan Societies

Registry of Savings and Loan Societies: Bank of Papua New Guinea, Banking Supervision Dept, POB 121, Port Moresby; tel. 3227200; fax 3214548; e-mail gawap@bankpng.gov.pg; internet www .bankpng.gov.pg; 22 savings and loan societies; 243,003 mems (2010); total funds 756.8m., loans outstanding 219.4m., investments 341.1m. (Dec. 2010); Man. GEORGE AWAP.

STOCK EXCHANGE

Port Moresby Stock Exchange (POMSoX) Ltd: POB 1531, Level 4, Defence Haus, Port Moresby; tel. 3201980; fax 3201981; e-mail pomsox@pomsox.com.pg; internet www.pomsox.com.pg; f. 1999; Chair. FRANK DUNPHY; Gen. Man. GEOFF MASON.

INSURANCE

Capital Life Insurance Co: Tisa Haus, 2nd Floor, Wardship, Waigani, Port Moresby; tel. 3234036; fax 3232533; e-mail marketing@tsl.org.pg; f. 1993; fmrly Pan Asia Pacific Assurance (PNG); 100% owned by Teachers' Savings & Loan Society Ltd (TISA).

Kwila Insurance Corpn: POB 1457, Boroko, NCD; tel. 3258811; fax 3112867; e-mail jmcllvena@kwilainsurance.com.pg; internet www.kwilainsurance.com.pg; f. 1977; Gen. Man. JASON R. MCILVENA.

Pacific MMI Insurance Ltd: POB 331, Port Moresby; tel. 3214077; fax 3218437; e-mail enquiries@pacificmmi.com; internet www .pacificmmi.com; f. 1998; fmrly Niugini Insurance Corpn Ltd; jt venture; general and life insurance; financial services; Chair. WAYNE DORGAN; Gen. Man. LAURENS VAN DER GAAG.

There are branches of several insurance companies from Australia and the United Kingdom in Port Moresby, Rabaul, Lae and Kieta.

Trade and Industry

GOVERNMENT AGENCIES

Independent Public Business Corpn (IPBC): POB 320, Port Moresby, NCD; tel. 3212977; fax 3212916; e-mail ipbc@ipbc.com.pg; internet www.ipbc.com.pg; f. 2002; assets manager of all govt enterprises of Papua New Guinea; Chair. GEREA AOPI; Man. Dir GLENN BLAKE.

Investment Promotion Authority (IPA): POB 5053, Boroko, NCD 111; tel. 3213900; fax 3213049; e-mail ipa@ipa.gov.pg; internet www.ipa.gov.pg; f. 1992; est. following reorganization of National Investment and Development Authority; statutory body responsible for the promotion of foreign investment; recommends priority areas for investment to the Govt; also co-ordinates investment proposals; Man. Dir IVAN POMALEU.

Mineral Resources Authority (MRA): POB 1906, Port Moresby; tel. 3213511; fax 3215711; e-mail info@mra.gov.pg; internet www .mra.gov.pg; f. 2006; Man. Dir KEPAS WALI.

DEVELOPMENT ORGANIZATION

Industrial Centres Development Corporation (ICDC): POB 1571, Boroko, NCD; tel. 3112211; fax 3112212; e-mail henlytaka@ hotmail.com; internet www.icdc.gov.pg; f. 1990; owned by govt of Papua New Guinea under the Ministry of Commerce and Industry; promotes foreign investment in non-mining sectors through establishment of industrial estates; Sr Marketing Officer HENLY TAKA.

CHAMBERS OF COMMERCE

Lae Chamber of Commerce Inc: POB 265, Lae, Morobe Province; tel. 4722340; fax 4726038; e-mail lcci@global.net.pg; internet www .lcci.org.pg; Pres. ALAN MCLAY.

Papua New Guinea Chamber of Commerce and Industry: POB 1621, Port Moresby; tel. 3213057; fax 3210566; e-mail pngcci@global .net.pg; internet www.pngcci.org.pg; Pres. JOHN LEAHY; Vice-Pres. MICHAEL MAYBERRY.

Port Moresby Chamber of Commerce and Industry: POB 75, Port Moresby; tel. 3213077; fax 3214203; e-mail bizcentre@pomcci .org.pg; internet www.pomcci.com; Pres. RON SEDDON; Chief Exec. DAVID CONN.

INDUSTRIAL AND TRADE ASSOCIATIONS

Cocoa Board of Papua New Guinea: POB 532, Rabaul, East New Britain Province; tel. 9829083; fax 9828712; e-mail l.tautea@global .net.pg; f. 1974; Chair. JIMMY SIMITAB; CEO LAVATAU TAUTEA.

Coffee Industry Corpn Ltd: POB 137, Goroka, Eastern Highlands Province; tel. 7321266; fax 7321214; e-mail cicgka@daltron.com.pg; internet www.coffeecorp.org.pg; CEO NAVI ANIS.

Fishing Industry Association (PNG) Inc: POB 5860, Boroko, NCD; tel. 3258222; fax 3258994; e-mail netshop1@daltron.com.pg; Pres. PETE CELSO.

Forest Industries Association: POB 229, Waigani, NCD; internet www.fiapng.com; Pres. ANTHONY HONEY; CEO ROBERT TATE.

Growers Association Inc: POB 14, Kokopo, East New Britain Province 613; tel. 9829123; fax 9829264; e-mail growers@global.net .pg; Pres. ROBIN MERIBA; Exec. Dir PAUL ARNOLD.

Kokonas Indastri Korporesen (KIK): POB 81, Port Moresby; tel. 3211133; fax 3214257; e-mail infor@kik.com.pg; f. 2002; regulates the marketing of all coconut products in Papua New Guinea; represents producers, processors and exporters of coconut products; fmrly Copra Marketing Board of Papua New Guinea (f. 1950s); govt-owned; Chair. MAKENA GENO; Man. Dir TORE OVASURU.

Manufacturers' Council of Papua New Guinea: POB 598, Port Moresby; tel. 3259512; fax 3230199; e-mail pngmade@global.com.pg; Chair. WAYNE GOLDING; CEO BRUCE REVILLE.

Mineral Resources Development Corporation: POB 1076, Port Moresby, NCD 121; tel. 3255822; fax 3252633; e-mail enquiry@mrdc.com.pg; internet www.mrdc.com.pg; f. 1975; manages landowner and provincial govt interests in major mineral resources projects; subsidiaries incl. Mineral Resources Star Mountains Ltd, Mineral Resources Ok Tedi No 2 Ltd, Mineral Resources Enga Ltd, Petroleum Resources Kutubu Ltd, Petroleum Resources Gobe Ltd and Petroleum Resources Moran Ltd; Chair. SIMON TOSALI; Man. Dir AUGUSTINE SANGA MANO.

National Fisheries Authority: POB 2016, Port Moresby; tel. 3212643; fax 3202061; e-mail nfa@fisheries.gov.pg; internet www.fisheries.gov.pg; Man. Dir SYLVESTER POKAJAM.

National Housing Corpn (NHC): POB 1550, Boroko, NCD; tel. 3252124; fax 3259918; e-mail managingdirector@nhc.gov.pg; f. 1990; man. and promotion of nat. housing projects; Man. Dir TARCISSIUS MUGANAUA (acting).

Palm Oil Producers Association: Port Moresby; Chair. BROWN BAI.

Papua New Guinea Chamber of Mines and Petroleum: POB 1032, Port Moresby; tel. 3212988; fax 3217107; e-mail conf@pngchamberminpet.com.pg; internet www.pngchamberminpet.com.pg; Exec. Dir GREG ANDERSON; Pres. Dr ILA TEMU.

Papua New Guinea Forest Authority: POB 5055, Boroko, NCD; tel. 3277800; fax 3254433; e-mail info_general@pngfa.gov.pg; internet www.forestry.gov.pg; Man. Dir KANAWI POURU; Chair. JOSEPH LELANG.

Petromin PNG Holdings Ltd: POB 2032, Port Moresby 121, NCD; tel. 3256333; fax 3257019; e-mail contact@petrominpng.com.pg; internet www.petrominpng.com.pg; f. 2007; Chair. BROWN BAI; CEO JOSHUA KALINOE.

Rural Industries Council: POB 1530, Port Moresby; tel. 3215773; fax 3217223; e-mail ric@daltron.com.pg; Chair. BROWN BAI.

UTILITIES

Electricity

PNG Power Ltd (PPL): POB 1105, Boroko, NCD; tel. 3243200; fax 3250072; e-mail marketing@pngpower.com.pg; internet www.pngpower.com.pg; prev. PNG Electricity Commission (Elcom); Commission privatized and name changed to above in 2002; undertakes regulatory role on behalf of Consumer and Competition Commission; Chair. ISAAC WAIGAVARA (acting); Chief Exec. TONY KOIRI.

Water

Eda Ranu (Our Water): PMB, Waigani, NCD; tel. 3122133; fax 3122196; e-mail info@edaranu.com.pg; internet www.edaranu.com.pg; fmrly Port Moresby Water Supply Company; CEO BILLY IMAR.

Water PNG: POB 2779, Boroko, NCD; tel. 3235700; fax 3256298; e-mail pamini@pngwater.com.pg; internet www.waterpng.com.pg; f. 1986 as PNG Waterboard; govt-owned; operates 17 water supply systems throughout the country; Man. Dir PATRICK AMINI.

TRADE UNIONS

Papua New Guinea Trade Unions Congress (PNGTUC): POB 4279, Boroko, NCD; tel. 3257642; fax 3257890; e-mail tucl@daltron.com.pg; Pres. MICHAEL MALABAG; Gen. Sec. JOHN PASKA; 52 affiliates, 76,000 mems.

Transport

There are no railways in Papua New Guinea. The capital city, Port Moresby, is not connected by road to other major population centres. Therefore, air and sea travel are of particular importance.

ROADS

In 2000 there were an estimated 19,600 km of roads in Papua New Guinea, of which 3.5% were paved.

National Roads Authority: POB 2578, Boroko, NCD; tel. 3259576; fax 3113502; e-mail nraadmin@nra.gov.pg; internet www.nra.gov.pg; f. 2004; statutory authority; maintains the road network, particularly the Highlands Highway; CEO ROY MUMU.

SHIPPING

Papua New Guinea has 16 major ports. At 31 December 2012 the flag registered fleet comprised 112 vessels, with a total displacement of 117,455 grt, of which 30 were general cargo ships.

PNG Ports Corporation Ltd: POB 671, Port Moresby, NCD; tel. 3084200; fax 3211546; e-mail business@pngports.com.pg; internet www.pngports.com.pg; CEO STANLEY ALPHONSE.

Port Authority of Kieta: POB 149, Kieta, North Solomons Province; tel. 9956066; fax 9956255; Port Man. CHARLES TARURAVA.

Port Authority of Lae: POB 563, Lae, Morobe Province; tel. 4723464; fax 4723543; Port Man. SAKEUS GEM.

Port Authority of Port Moresby: POB 671, Port Moresby; tel. 211400; fax 3211546; Gen. Man. BEN PUKAI.

Port Authority of Rabaul: POB 592, Rabaul, East New Britain Province; tel. 9821533; fax 9821535; Port Man. JOHN TUNGAPIK.

Shipping Companies

Coastal Shipping Co Ltd: Sulphur Creek Rd, POB 423, Rabaul, East New Britain Province; tel. 9821746; fax 9821734; e-mail coastco@global.net.pg; f. 1967; Man. Dir HENRY CHOW.

Lutheran Shipping: POB 789, Madang; tel. 8522577; fax 8522180; e-mail finance.luship@global.net.pg; CEO TONESSI EWEBI (acting).

Morehead Shipping Pty Ltd: POB 1908, Lae, Morobe Province; tel. 4423602.

New Guinea Australia Line Pty Ltd: POB 145, Stanley Esplanade, Port Moresby, NCD 121; tel. 3212377; fax 3201825; f. 1952; est. by The China Navigation Co, a fully owned shipping wing of John Swire & Sons (PNG) Ltd; operates regular container services between Australia, Papua New Guinea, Singapore, Indonesia, Vanuatu, Tuvalu and Solomon Islands; Chair. CHRIS PRATT.

P&O Maritime Services (PNG) Ltd: MMI House, 3rd Floor, Champion Parade, POB 1403, Port Moresby; tel. 3229200; fax 3229251; e-mail cgcpom@popng.com.pg; internet www.pomaritime.com; owned by P&O (Australia); Country Man. JOHN HULSE.

Papua New Guinea Shipping Corporation Pty Ltd: POB 634, Port Moresby; tel. 3220290; fax 3212815; e-mail shipping@steamships.com.pg; f. 1977; owned by Steamships Trading Co Ltd; provides a container/break-bulk service to Australia and the Pacific islands; Chair. CHRISTOPHER PRATT; Man. Dir JOHN DUNLOP.

South Sea Lines Proprietary Ltd: POB 5, Lae, Morobe Province; tel. 4423455; fax 4424884; Man. Dir R. CUNNINGHAM.

Steamships Trading Co Ltd: Champion Parade, POB 1, Port Moresby; tel. 3220222; fax 3213595; internet www.steamships.com.pg; f. 1924; Chair. W. L. ROTHERY; Man. Dir D. H. COX.

Western Tug & Barge Co P/L: POB 1403, Port Moresby; tel. 3229290; fax 3229251; division of P & O PNG; operates 24 vessels.

CIVIL AVIATION

There is an international airport, Jackson's Airport, at Port Moresby. International services also operate from Lae and Mount Hagen airports. There are more than 400 other airports and airstrips throughout the country. In mid-2011 it was announced that the Asian Development Bank was to invest US $480m. over eight years to upgrade the country's airports.

Air Niugini: POB 7186, Boroko, NCD; tel. 3259000; fax 3273482; e-mail airniugini@airniugini.com.pg; internet www.airniugini.com.pg; f. 1973; govt-owned national airline; operates scheduled domestic cargo and passenger services within Papua New Guinea and international services to Australia, Fiji, Solomon Islands, Philippines, Hong Kong, Singapore and Japan; fleet comprises 20 aircraft (2010); Chair. GARTH MCLLWAIN; CEO SIMON FOO.

Airlines PNG: POB 170, Boroko, NCD; tel. 3252011; fax 3252219; e-mail apng@apng.com; internet www.apng.com; f. 1984; est. as Milne Bay Air (MBA); operates domestic scheduled and charter services; Chair. SIMON WILD; CEO MURALEE SIVA.

National Aviation Services: Boroko, NCD; f. 2005; provides services between all small airstrips in Central, Oro, Gulf and Western Provinces, primarily for the transport of agricultural products to markets; Operations Man. GILBERT YENBARI; Propr and CEO TED DIRO.

Tourism

Papua New Guinea's attractions include the tribal customs, spectacular scenery and abundant wildlife. Foreign visitor arrivals rose from 146,350 in 2010 to 165,059 in 2011. Tourism receipts amounted to an estimated US $2m. in the same year.

PNG Tourism Promotion Authority: POB 1291, Port Moresby; tel. 3200211; fax 3200223; e-mail info@pngtourism.org.pg; internet www.pngtourism.org.pg; CEO PETER VINCENT.

Tour Operators Association of Papua New Guinea (TOAPNG): POB 101, Boroko; tel. 3417130; fax 3234518; e-mail seepapuanewguinea@gmail.com; internet www.toa.org.pg; f. 2005; Pres. MICHAEL BULEAU.

Defence

As assessed at November 2012, the Papua New Guinea Defence Force had a total strength of some 3,100 (army 2,500, navy 400 and air force 200). Military service is voluntary. Australian training forces stationed in the country totalled 38. Government expenditure on defence in 2012 was budgeted at K229m.

Commander-in-Chief of Papua New Guinea Defence Force: Brig.-Gen. FRANCIS WANGI AGWI.

Education

Most education facilities have remained inadequate and unevenly distributed. In August 2011, however, it was announced that from the beginning of 2012 elementary education was to be provided free of charge and that 75% of the cost of higher education was to be subsidized by the Government. In 2007/08 there were 3,549 primary schools, with 715,764 pupils and 20,942 teachers. In that year there were 208 secondary schools (with 94,192 pupils and 3,476 teachers)

and 99 vocational schools (with 19,661 pupils and 947 teachers). There are two universities. Preparatory work to establish a new university was under way in 2013.

Children attend school from seven years of age. At the age of 13 they move from community schools to provincial high schools for a further three years and are then eligible to spend another two years at the national high schools, where they are prepared for entrance to tertiary education.

In 2008 the total enrolment at primary schools was equivalent to 60% (males 63%; females 57%) of children in the relevant age-group. In 1998 secondary enrolment was equivalent to only 19% (males 23%; females 16%) of children in the relevant age-group. In some areas, such as East New Britain and Port Moresby, almost all eligible children attend primary schools, whereas in others, such as the Highlands provinces, attendance is as low as 34%. Access to secondary education ranges from 7% in the Eastern Highlands to almost 50% in East New Britain. In 2010, according to UNESCO estimates, adult literacy averaged 60.6% (males 63.9%; females 57.3%).

Central government expenditure on education was projected at K1,400m. for 2012.

PARAGUAY

Introductory Survey

LOCATION, CLIMATE, LANGUAGE, RELIGION, FLAG, CAPITAL

The Republic of Paraguay is a land-locked country in central South America. It is bordered by Bolivia to the north, by Brazil to the east, and by Argentina to the south and west. The climate is sub-tropical. Temperatures range from an average maximum of 34.3°C (93.7°F) in January to an average minimum of 14°C (51°F) in June. The official languages are Spanish and Guaraní, the latter, an indigenous Indian language, being spoken by the majority of the population. Almost all of the inhabitants profess Christianity, and some 92% adhere to the Roman Catholic Church, the country's established religion. There is a small Protestant minority. The national flag (proportions 3 by 5) has three equal horizontal stripes, of red, white and blue. It is the only national flag with a different design on each side, having a varying emblem in the centre of the white stripe: the obverse side bears the state emblem (a white disc with a red ring bearing the words 'República del Paraguay', in yellow capitals, framing a blue disc with the five-pointed 'May Star', in yellow, surrounded by a wreath, in green), while the reverse side carries the seal of the Treasury (a white disc with a red ribbon bearing the words 'Paz y Justicia' in yellow capitals above a lion supporting a staff, surmounted by the red 'Cap of Liberty'). The capital is Asunción.

CONTEMPORARY POLITICAL HISTORY

Historical Context

Paraguay, ruled by Spain from the 16th century, achieved independence in 1811. In 1865 Paraguay was involved in a disastrous war against Brazil, Argentina and Uruguay (the Triple Alliance), resulting in the loss of more than one-half of its population. Paraguay also suffered heavy losses in the Chaco Wars of 1928–30 and 1932–35 against Bolivia, but won a large part of the disputed territory when the boundary was fixed in 1938. Gen. Higinio Morínigo established an authoritarian regime in 1940, but the return of a number of political exiles in 1947 precipitated a civil war in which supporters of the right-wing Asociación Nacional Republicana (commonly known as the Partido Colorado) defeated the Liberals and the Partido Revolucionario Febrerista, leading to the overthrow of Gen. Morínigo in June 1948. A period of great instability ensued. In 1954 Gen. Alfredo Stroessner Mattiauda, the Army Commander-in-Chief, assumed power in a military coup. He nominated himself for the presidency, as the Colorado candidate, and was elected unopposed in July to complete the term of office of his predecessor, Federico Chávez. In 1955 Stroessner assumed extensive powers, and established a state of siege. Regular purges of the Partido Colorado membership, together with the mutual co-operation of the ruling party, the armed forces and the business community, enabled Stroessner to become the longest-serving dictator in South America: he was re-elected President, by large majorities, at five-yearly elections in 1958–88.

Domestic Political Affairs

In February 1978 President Stroessner revoked the state of siege in all areas except Asunción. The assassination of the former Nicaraguan dictator, Gen. Anastasio Somoza Debayle, in Asunción in September 1980, however, prompted Stroessner to reimpose the state of siege throughout the country; harassment of leaders of the political opposition and of peasant and labour groups continued. The leader of the Partido Demócrata Cristiano, Luis Alfonso Resck, was expelled from the country in 1981, and Domingo Laíno, leader of the Partido Liberal Radical Auténtico (PLRA), was deported in 1982. After Ronald Reagan took office as President of the USA in 1981, Paraguay encountered less pressure from the US Administration to curb abuses of human rights, and the use of torture against detainees reportedly became widespread once more. It was estimated at this time that more than 60% of all Paraguayans resided outside the country.

The majority of opposition parties boycotted the presidential and legislative elections of February 1983, enabling Stroessner to obtain more than 90% of the votes cast in the presidential poll.

In May the Government instigated a campaign of repression against students and trade unionists. In February 1984 opposition parties organized demonstrations in Asunción for the first time in 30 years.

Divisions over Stroessner's continuance in office led to factionalism within the Partido Colorado in the mid-1980s. In 1987 Stroessner announced that the state of siege was to be ended. However, the suppression of civil liberties and of political activity continued under the new penal code that replaced the state of siege. Stroessner received 89% of the votes cast in the 1988 presidential election. However, opposition leaders (who had urged voters to boycott the elections) complained of electoral malpractice, and denounced Stroessner's re-election as fraudulent.

On 3 February 1989 Gen. Stroessner was overthrown in a coup led by Gen. Andrés Rodríguez, the second-in-command of the armed forces. Stroessner was allowed to leave for exile in Brazil, as Gen. Rodríguez assumed the presidency and appointed a new Council of Ministers. The interim President pledged to respect human rights and to strengthen links with neighbouring countries. At the presidential election in May Rodríguez, the candidate of the Partido Colorado, was confirmed as President. The Partido Colorado also won the largest number of seats in both the Cámara de Diputados (Chamber of Deputies) and the Senado (Senate). Despite widespread allegations of electoral fraud, all parties agreed to respect the results.

In July 1989 the Cámara ratified the San José Pact on Human Rights, adopted by the Organization of American States (OAS, see p. 404) in 1978. In August 1989 the Congreso Nacional (National Congress—comprising the Cámara de Diputados and the Senado) initiated judicial proceedings against former government officials for violations of human rights. Following the repeal of laws that had provided a basis for political repression under the Stroessner regime, the Partido Comunista Paraguayo (PCP) was formally legalized. In November 1990, however, Rodríguez vetoed congressional proposals for the establishment of a legislative commission to investigate alleged violations of human rights.

In August 1991 the Congreso Nacional approved proposals for a complete revision of the 1967 Constitution. In anticipation of the elections to a National Constituent Assembly, President Rodríguez and military leaders made concerted efforts to forge unity within the Partido Colorado, with the result that the party's three main factions were persuaded to present a single list of candidates. In the December elections the Partido Colorado secured an overwhelming majority of the Assembly's 198 seats.

In November 1991 new legislation, drafted by President Rodríguez in co-operation with military leaders, was approved by the Congreso Nacional. The law appeared to guarantee the autonomy of the armed forces, and the definition of the role of the military was expanded to include responsibility, at the request of the head of state, for civil defence and internal order. Apparently in contradiction of the 1990 electoral code, no restrictions were placed on political activities by serving members of the armed forces. Provision was made for the President to delegate the functions of Commander-in-Chief of the Armed Forces to a senior military officer. Opposition parties protested that, should the new legislation be entrenched in the new Constitution, the armed forces would remain a 'parallel' political force, following the transition to civilian rule.

On 22 June 1992 the new Constitution was promulgated. The Constituent Assembly had ostensibly disregarded the November 1991 military legislation by confirming the President as Commander-in-Chief of the Armed Forces and excluding officers on active duty from participating directly in politics. The President and Vice-President (a new post) were to be elected by a simple majority of votes.

Wasmosy's presidency, 1993–98

At the general election of May 1993 the Colorado candidate, Juan Carlos Wasmosy, was elected President with 40% of the votes cast. However, the Partido Colorado failed to gain a majority in either the Cámara or the Senado. Moreover, the far-right faction of the Partido Colorado led by Luis María Argaña, the Movimiento de Reconciliación Colorada, negotiated with the PLRA and the Partido Encuentro Nacional (PEN) to exclude supporters of the President-elect from appointment to important posts in the Congreso Nacional. The opposition expressed some concern over the composition of Wasmosy's first Council of Ministers, many of whom had served in the administrations of Rodríguez and Stroessner. Despite Wasmosy's apparent desire to restrict the influence of the military, the designation of Gen. Lino César Oviedo Silva as Commander of the Army provoked further criticism, since, prior to the elections, Oviedo had publicly stated that the army would not accept an opposition victory.

A preliminary agreement on a 'governability pact' between the Government and the opposition, initiated in an attempt to facilitate the implementation of a coherent economic and legislative programme, was signed in October 1993, and this, in turn, facilitated an agreement between the Government and the legislature towards resolving the controversial question of judicial reform. Under the latter agreement, the two were to appoint members of the Supreme Court and the Supreme Electoral Tribunal by consensus.

In May 1995 an investigation into corruption at the Central Bank revealed the existence of an illegal 'parallel' financial system involving a network of institutions, including the Central Bank. The investigation precipitated the collapse of the system and a severe liquidity crisis. In December the Government issued an emergency decree extending the powers of intervention of the Central Bank, with the aim of restoring confidence in the banking sector. By the end of the year the Central Bank had disbursed almost US $400m. of reserves in order to contain the liquidity crisis, which had resulted in the closure of several financial institutions.

In April 1996 a serious confrontation arose between President Wasmosy and Gen. Oviedo, with the result that a military coup was only narrowly averted. Following an attempt by Oviedo to postpone the internal elections of the Partido Colorado, Wasmosy accused Oviedo of contravening the ban on political activity by serving members of the military, and demanded his resignation as Commander of the Army. When Oviedo refused to comply, Wasmosy dismissed him. Oviedo rejected the decision, and installed himself at the army headquarters in Asunción, from where he issued demands for Wasmosy's resignation and threatened, with the support of the army, violently to overthrow the Government. Wasmosy took refuge in the US embassy building. On the following day, in a demonstration of popular support for Wasmosy, thousands rallied outside the presidential palace. Declarations of support were also issued by the Commanders of the Navy and the Air Force, and by the Congreso Nacional. External pressure for Wasmosy to resist the overthrow of democratic rule came from the USA, which immediately suspended military aid, and from neighbouring South American countries, and was sufficient to prompt Wasmosy to seek a compromise: in return for his retirement from military service, Oviedo was given the position of Minister of Defence. However, the measure was condemned by the legislature, and was also strongly opposed by the public, and, following Oviedo's retirement from military service, Wasmosy withdrew the offer of the defence portfolio. Despite fears of an outright coup, Oviedo accepted the final outcome of the dispute.

In May 1996 Oviedo announced the creation of a new faction of the Partido Colorado, the Unión Nacional de Colorados Eticos (UNACE). In that month, in an effort to purge the armed forces of officers sympathetic to Oviedo, Wasmosy announced the retirement of some 20 high-ranking officers. In June Oviedo was placed under house arrest on charges of insurrection and insubordination with respect to the events of April. In the following month his detention was revised from house arrest to imprisonment. Wasmosy continued to reorganize the military hierarchy, replacing several senior officers. In August an appeal court acquitted Oviedo of the charge of insurrection on the grounds of insufficient evidence and in December he was acquitted of the lesser charge of insubordination.

Amid continuing divisions within the ruling party, in 1997 Oviedo succeeded in securing the Partido Colorado's presidential nomination. However, Argaña's faction, which effectively controlled the party's executive board, refused to accept the outcome of the ballot, claiming that it had been fraudulent.

In October 1997 Wasmosy issued an executive order for the 'disciplinary arrest', for a period of 30 days, of Oviedo; the grounds for the detention were contempt of the President and

Commander-in-Chief of the Armed Forces, after Oviedo had publicly accused Wasmosy of corruption. In December, following endorsement of the arrest order by the Supreme Court, Oviedo surrendered to the military authorities. Furthermore, a special military tribunal, established by Wasmosy to investigate the events of the April 1996 coup attempt, ordered that he be detained indefinitely pending the results of the inquiry. In March 1998 the tribunal found Oviedo guilty of crimes committed against the order and security of the armed forces, and also of sedition, and sentenced him to 10 years' imprisonment. The Supreme Court ratified the military tribunal's decision, and the Supreme Electoral Tribunal consequently annulled Oviedo's presidential candidacy.

Election and impeachment of Cubas Grau, 1998–99

The presidential election of 10 May 1998 resulted in victory for the Colorado replacement candidate, Raúl Cubas Grau. Colorado candidates were also most successful at legislative elections and at elections for provincial administrators held concurrently. Cubas Grau's election campaign had emphasized his support for his long-time political ally, Oviedo. Prior to the inauguration of the new administration, in July Vice-President-elect Argaña (a staunch opponent of Oviedo) concluded an informal political pact involving his faction of the Partido Colorado and the opposition PLRA and PEN, effectively depriving Cubas Grau of a congressional majority, while in August President Wasmosy implemented a comprehensive reorganization of the military high command, which promoted the interests of many of Oviedo's military opponents.

Cubas Grau duly took office on 15 August 1998, and a new Council of Ministers, largely composed of supporters of Oviedo, was sworn in on the same day. One of Cubas Grau's first acts as President was to issue a decree commuting Oviedo's prison sentence to time already served, a deliberate circumvention of a new law restricting presidential pardons. On the following day the Congreso Nacional voted to condemn the decree and to initiate proceedings to impeach the President for unconstitutional procedure. In December the Argaña faction-controlled central apparatus of the Partido Colorado expelled Oviedo from the party. While the Congreso Nacional was unable to muster the two-thirds' majority support necessary to impeach President Cubas Grau, the country remained in effective political deadlock.

In March 1999, however, the political impasse ended dramatically. On 23 March Vice-President Argaña was assassinated, prompting nation-wide speculation that Oviedo was behind the attack, and galvanizing the Congreso Nacional sufficiently to secure the support of the two-thirds' majority needed to initiate Cubas Grau's impeachment. Increasing tensions were exacerbated three days later by the killing of seven protesters who were demonstrating in Asunción in support of demands for the resignation of the President. On 28 March Cubas Grau resigned the presidency and sought refuge in Brazil, while Oviedo crossed the border to Argentina. (Cubas Grau surrendered to the Paraguayan authorities in February 2002 and was placed under house arrest until June 2003, when the charges against him were dismissed.) In April 1999, the judicial authorities ordered the arrest of Oviedo for involvement in the death of Argaña, after three of his close collaborators were identified as the assassins. (In 2000 Maj.-Gen. Reinaldo Servin, Constantino Rodas and Pablo Vera Esteche were sentenced to long prison terms for their roles in the assassination.)

Presidency of González Macchi, 1999–2003

Meanwhile, in accordance with the terms of the Constitution, in the absence of the elected President and Vice-President, the President of the Congreso Nacional—the pro-Argaña Colorado senator Luis González Macchi—was swiftly installed as head of state. He announced the composition of a multi-party Government of National Unity at the end of March 1999. In April the Supreme Court ruled that González Macchi should serve the remainder of Cubas Grau's presidential term. The Court also ruled that an election to select a new Vice-President should be conducted. Hoping to consolidate the new Government, González Macchi announced that his own party would not present a vice-presidential candidate. Prominent figures within the Partido Colorado decided to contest the election none the less, precipitating tension with the PLRA, which had effectively been promised the post. Meanwhile, factionalism within the PLRA placed increasing strains on the Government of National Unity. Events culminated in February 2000 when PLRA members voted to withdraw from the ruling coalition, depriving the Government of a legislative majority.

In 1999 González Macchi forcibly retired more than 145 army officers, including several high-ranking supporters of Oviedo. However, the reorganization did not prevent a coup attempt, in May 2000, by rebellious soldiers thought to be sympathetic to Oviedo. It was swiftly defeated by the Government, which declared a 30-day state of emergency, assuming extraordinary powers that resulted in the arrest of more than 70 people, mostly members of the security forces. Oviedo denied any involvement with the coup, but in June he was arrested in Brazil. In March 2001 the Brazilian Chief Prosecutor ruled that Oviedo could be extradited, but in December the Supreme Court rejected the ruling, stating that Oviedo was a victim of political persecution, and released him from imprisonment.

The initial popularity of the Government of National Unity collapsed as thousands of peasants, assembled by rural organizations, mobilized on several occasions during 1999 to protest against the Government's lack of action on rural issues. In response, in November the Government offered a US $168m. rescue package for the agricultural sector and in March 2000 announced a scheme to assist 250,000 small farmers. However, by the end of the month there were an estimated 10,000 smallholders camped outside the Congreso building. (The protest continued until March 2001, when government concessions were eventually secured.) Strikes were also undertaken by workers in the power, telecommunications and public sectors during 2000. However, the Government insisted that it would continue with its 'state restructuring' programme. In November the Congreso Nacional approved legislation allowing for the sale of the state railway, water and telecommunications companies.

At the vice-presidential election, finally held on 13 August 2000, the 53-year Colorado monopoly on power was ended when Félix Argaña, son of the late Vice-President, was narrowly defeated by the PLRA candidate, Julio César Franco. The election of Franco, whose candidacy was endorsed by Oviedo, increased the divisions within the Partido Colorado and resulted in the resignation of the Minister of National Defence, Nelson Argaña, another son of the late Vice-President.

A corruption scandal in May 2001 forced the President of the Central Bank, Washington Ashwell, to resign over his alleged involvement in the fraudulent transfer of US $16m. to a US bank account. An opposition attempt to impeach the President over his alleged involvement in the fraud was defeated by the Cámara de Diputados in August. In September several thousand protesters marched in Asunción to demand the resignation of González Macchi. In April 2002 González Macchi was formally charged with involvement in the corruption scandal.

Throughout 2002 an alliance of farmers, trade unions and left-wing organizations staged mass protests throughout the country to call for an end to the Government's free market policies and to protest at widely perceived government corruption. In response to the mounting opposition, in June the Government suspended its planned privatization of the state telecommunications company. Nevertheless, the protests continued as the economic situation worsened, prompting González Macchi to declare a state of emergency in July, which was lifted two days later after clashes between anti-Government protesters and security forces resulted in two fatalities.

In December 2002 the Cámara de Diputados voted in favour of the impeachment of President González Macchi on five charges of corruption. In an attempt to avoid the charges, González Macchi offered to resign early from office, immediately following the presidential election due in April 2003 (his term of office officially ended in August). However, in February the Senado voted narrowly against impeachment. Proceedings began against González Macchi in 2004 on charges relating to the May 2001 embezzlement scandal; in 2005 further charges were brought against him for misuse of public funds and irregularities connected to the sale of two state-owned banks. He was found guilty on charges of embezzlement and false testimony and was sentenced to eight years' imprisonment in December 2006.

Duarte's presidency, 2003–08

The presidential election of April 2003 was won by the Colorado candidate, Nicanor Duarte Frutos. However, the Partido Colorado lost its majority in the Cámara de Diputados in the concurrently held legislative ballot. Duarte announced his intention to effect wide-ranging judicial reform; to this effect, in October the Congreso reached consensus on impeachment proceedings against six Supreme Court judges suspected of corruption. Four of the judges resigned during the impeachment process, which finally resulted in the indictment of the remaining two judges in December. However, despite hopes that political influ-

ence in the selection of new judges might be avoided, two of the six new Supreme Court judges appointed in March 2004 were Colorado supporters.

In June 2004 Oviedo returned voluntarily from Brazil and was immediately taken to a military prison to serve the remainder of his 10-year sentence for organizing the 1996 attempted coup. In October, however, he was provisionally acquitted of having organized the failed coup attempt of 2000, and in 2005 charges against him relating to a discovered arms cache were dismissed. In March the Supreme Court ruled that Oviedo would nevertheless have to serve out his prison sentence.

In October 2004 the kidnap and murder of Cecilia Cubas, the daughter of former President Cubas Grau, provoked a vociferous public outcry against the perceived deterioration of security in Paraguay. In response, President Duarte dismissed the Minister of the Interior, Orlando Fiorotto Sánchez (who was replaced by Nelson Mora), and the head of the national police. In February 2005 Mora was himself dismissed—in addition to some 50 senior members of the police force—following the discovery of the girl's body. Twelve of the 15 people charged with involvement in the kidnap and murder, all of whom were members or sympathizers of the left-wing Partido Patria Libre (PPL), were found guilty in November 2006.

Throughout 2003 and 2004 strikes, roadblocks, marches and illegal land occupations were organized by farmers and indigenous groups in protest at a range of government policies, including agrarian reform and privatization. In response to the continuing civil unrest, in September 2004 the Government signed an agreement to distribute some 13,000 ha of land to landless peasants; however, the main peasant grouping, the Federación Nacional Campesina, maintained its demand for the redistribution of some 100,000 ha of land. Illegal land occupations and other protests continued in 2004 and 2005, resulting in the arrest of hundreds of protesters and several fatalities.

In November 2005 President Duarte announced plans to reform the Constitution in order to allow for presidential re-election. At that time, Duarte was also seeking re-election to the leadership of the Partido Colorado. However, opposition groups argued that it was unconstitutional for the President to hold any additional public office, although a motion to impeach Duarte, proposed by the opposition Patria Querida, was defeated. In January 2006 the Supreme Electoral Tribunal also rejected criminal charges against Duarte, brought by the Frente Colorado faction, for attempting to hold two public offices, although the Court ruled that it would be unconstitutional for Duarte to hold another office concurrently with the presidency of the Republic. Duarte won a convincing victory in the Partido Colorado leadership election, in March 2006, and in the same month the Supreme Court overturned the Supreme Electoral Tribunal's earlier ruling forbidding the President from holding an additional office. On assuming leadership of the party, the President proposed a referendum on allowing presidential re-election. In response to the Supreme Court ruling, opposition groups again initiated impeachment proceedings against Duarte, as well as against the five judges of the Court's Constitutional Panel. Faced with such resistance, the following day Duarte resigned from the party presidency.

In February 2007 a group of more than 30 social and labour organizations joined the principal opposition parties in signing an accord to form the Concertación Nacional (CN). The new coalition announced its intention to present a single candidate in the presidential election in 2008 in the hope of providing an effective challenge to the Partido Colorado. In July six of the eight political parties in the CN, including the PLRA and the PEN, announced their support for Fernando Lugo Méndez, a popular former Roman Catholic bishop known for his frequent pronouncements on social justice. However, Patria Querida and UNACE rejected Lugo's nomination and subsequently withdrew from the CN. As a result, Lugo founded the Alianza Patriótica para el Cambio (APC) to support his candidacy. In September 2007 Oviedo was granted conditional release from gaol by a military tribunal. In the following month the Supreme Court acquitted him of involvement in the 1996 coup attempt, thereby making him eligible to stand for the presidency, and he was declared the UNACE candidate in January 2008.

The Lugo Méndez presidency, 2008–12

At the presidential election, held on 20 April 2008, Lugo won a comfortable victory, securing 40.9% of votes cast, against 30.6% for the Colorado candidate, Blanca Ovelar, and 21.9% for Oviedo. In the concurrent legislative elections the Partido Colorado narrowly retained its status as the largest party in both chambers of the Congreso Nacional, securing 30 of the 80 seats in the Cámara de Diputados and 15 out of 45 seats in the Senado. The PLRA (the largest party in Lugo's APC) obtained 27 seats in the lower house and 14 in the upper, while UNACE won 15 and nine seats, respectively. In order to achieve a working majority in the Congreso, Lugo secured the support of UNACE and the 'Nicanorista' faction of the Partido Colorado, the latter comprising supporters of President Duarte. However, the stability of the new legislature was threatened by a dispute regarding the fact that Duarte had been elected to a seat in the Senado, in apparent contravention of the Constitution (which granted former Presidents a non-voting seat for life in the chamber, but prohibited a serving President from exercising any additional public office).

President Lugo was inaugurated on 15 August 2008. His cabinet included four representatives of different factions of the PLRA (in addition to the Vice-President, Federico Franco Gómez) and a number of non-affiliated ministers. In the first month of Lugo's presidency the dispute over Duarte's senatorial seat continued to disrupt relations between the new Government and the Congreso Nacional. On 26 August an inquorate session of the Senado chaired by the chamber's pro-Duarte President, Enrique González Quintana of UNACE, swore Duarte into office as an elected senator, but later the same day the PLRA Vice-President of the Senado, in defiance of González Quintana, chaired a session dominated by anti-Duarte senators that swore the former President's nominated alternate, Jorge Céspedes, into the same seat. The impasse, which appeared to indicate an inability of Lugo's allies to co-operate, was ended in early September after Lugo publicly accused Duarte and Oviedo, along with González Quintana and other senior political figures, of plotting a coup to overthrow the new Government. Although Duarte and Oviedo both strongly denied the allegations, UNACE subsequently relinquished its support for Duarte; on 4 September Céspedes was legitimately sworn in as a senator and Duarte was afforded the honorary position of senator for life. However, in a controversial judgment, the Supreme Court in September 2010 authorized Duarte to assume his elective seat in the Senado, raising concerns that the dispute would be reignited.

One of Lugo's main campaign pledges was to initiate a process of land reform. In 2008 peasants organized by the Mesa Coordinadora Nacional de Organizaciones Campesinas staged a series of land invasions, demanding the implementation of a comprehensive land redistribution programme. In October the government body responsible for rural development, the Instituto Nacional del Desarrollo Rural y de la Tierra, declared that it would no longer allow foreigners to acquire land in Paraguay; the large proportion of land in foreign (especially Brazilian) ownership was a major source of tension between landowners and landless peasants. In October the Government announced the purchase of some 22,000 ha from 11 Brazilian farmers in the department of San Pedro for redistribution to landless families; none the less, protests by peasants continued, and were countered in December with demonstrations by landowners. In January 2009 the Government announced the first stage of its land reform programme, which concentrated on rural development and did not include any redistributive measures.

The APC's weak position in the Congreso Nacional, exacerbated by divisions within the alliance, impeded the passage of the Government's legislative proposals throughout 2009. In August representatives of the main parties in the Congreso signed a 'democratic accord', reaffirming their commitment to a political system based on representative democracy; the agreement, which Lugo refused to sign, was interpreted by observers as being a response to the President's proposal to hold a referendum on the performance of the Congreso.

Lugo replaced the Commanders of the Armed Forces, the Army, Air Force and Navy in November 2009, following rumours of a coup. Meanwhile, tensions between the Congreso and the President continued to intensify, as a number of senators threatened to initiate impeachment proceedings against Lugo on various grounds: an alleged failure to address security concerns, following the abduction in October of a rancher by the Ejército del Pueblo Paraguayo (EPP, a small guerrilla group linked to the PPL); comments by Lugo that they claimed were an incitement to 'class warfare'; and alleged corruption related to the purchase of 22,000 ha of land in San Pedro for redistribution to landless families.

In January 2010 Lugo ordered a military and police offensive against the EPP in San Pedro, but little progress was made in suppressing the movement. A deadly attack by EPP guerrillas near the San Pedro–Concepción border in April prompted Lugo to declare a 30-day state of emergency in five northern departments and to mobilize security forces to bolster the operation against the rebels. The Congreso also temporarily granted extensive powers of arrest to the police in the affected departments and restricted the freedom of assembly. New anti-terrorism legislation came into effect in June, although there were fears that the new laws could be inappropriately used against legitimate demonstrators. Between July and September a number of suspected EPP leaders were arrested or killed by the security forces. Nevertheless, the Minister of National Defence, Gen. (retd) Luis Bareiro Spaini, was forced to resign in August after a dispute involving the theft of military weapons by alleged EPP members led to the initiation of impeachment proceedings against him; Spaini was replaced by Gen. (retd) Cecilio Pérez Bordón. In a further change to the leadership of the armed forces, in September Lugo replaced the commanders of each branch of the military (the fourth time that he had done so since taking office). In October 2011 Lugo authorized a further state of emergency in two northern departments, following multiple EPP attacks during the previous month. Troops were mobilized for 60 days, but, once again, little progress was made in subduing the rebel group. EPP raids, predominantly directed against wealthy landowners, continued to be reported throughout 2012. The police complained of a lack of co-operation from peasant communities, an apparent consequence of the EPP's popularity in rural areas.

Meanwhile, the creation of a new organization in support of the President, the Movimiento 20 de Abril, was announced in February 2010. In the following month Frente Guasú (FG), a coalition of political organizations and social movements supportive of Lugo, was also established. Municipal elections were conducted on 7 November and resulted in victory for the opposition Partido Colorado, which secured a majority of the contested municipalities, including the key municipality of Asunción. Infighting within the APC—primarily resulting from ongoing tensions between Lugo's supporters and anti-Lugo elements in the PLRA centred around Vice-President Franco (who had organized a protest rally against the President, attended by 5,000 people, in April)—had undermined the ruling coalition's efforts to present a coherent challenge to the Partido Colorado.

Minister of Foreign Affairs Héctor Lacognata resigned in March 2011 following press reports that he was working illegally as a consultant. (According to the Constitution, public officials are not permitted to receive more than one salary.) Jorge Lara Castro, hitherto Lacognata's deputy, was appointed as his replacement. Ostensibly owing to FG pressure, in June Lugo dismissed Minister of Public Works and Communications Efraín Alegrem and Minister of the Interior Rafael Filizzola, prominent members of the PLRA and Partido Democrático Progresista, respectively. In the subsequent cabinet reorganization, Cecilio Pérez Bordón received the public works portfolio and was replaced as Minister of National Defence by Brig.-Gen. (retd) Catalino Luis Roy Ortíz, while Federico Acuña became the new Minister of the Interior (although he was succeeded by Carlos Filizzola in August after resigning on grounds of ill health). Lugo claimed that Alegrem and Filizzola had demonstrated insufficient commitment to their ministerial responsibilities. However, both men were known critics of an FG campaign to modify the Constitution to enable the re-election of the President, and analysts suggested that this may have been a factor in their dismissal. Although the Senado voted against the contentious constitutional reform proposals in July, the episode sharply exacerbated the existing tensions within the APC, resulting in the de facto dissolution of the coalition. Meanwhile, in a referendum held in October, 78.4% of participants endorsed a constitutional amendment conferring voting rights upon Paraguayan citizens resident outside the country (many of whom had fled during the repressive Stroessner era), thereby expanding the electoral register by approximately 25%. Turnout was recorded at just 12.5%, however.

The Franco presidency

Confronted by continued opposition in the Congreso and the effective collapse of his coalition, by mid-2012 Lugo had only made limited progress with his reform agenda, particularly with respect to land reform, which had precipitated a renewed campaign of protests and land invasions by landless peasants from mid-2011. Carlos Filizzola was stripped of the interior portfolio on 16 June 2012 after 17 people lost their lives during a police raid on a peasant-occupied estate in Canindeyú. The Congreso, however, held Lugo ultimately responsible for the tragedy and moved swiftly to initiate impeachment proceedings against the President, citing his failure to address the broader rural conflict (as well as other alleged transgressions). Deputies voted in favour of the impeachment motion on 21–22 June, and Lugo was immediately succeeded as head of state by Vice-President Franco, who formed a new Government. Lugo claimed that the legislature's actions constituted a 'coup', but the Supreme Court rejected this interpretation, declaring that the Congreso had acted in accordance with the Constitution. Nevertheless, the removal from office of an elected President caused widespread alarm within the region, and the prevailing view among regional leaders was that the impeachment process had violated democratic norms. Consequently, on 29 June Paraguay was suspended from the Mercado Común del Sur (Mercosur, see p. 439) and the Union of South American Nations (UNASUR, see p. 479), although it was indicated that the country would be readmitted to both organizations after the 21 April 2013 presidential and legislative elections. UNASUR member states also withdrew their ambassadors from Paraguay.

Recent developments: the election of Horacio Cartes

Following primary elections in December 2012, it was determined that Horacio Cartes would represent the Partido Colorado in the upcoming presidential poll, while Efraín Alegre was selected as the PLRA's candidate. Further primaries were conducted in January 2013, with Aníbal Carrillo Iramain endorsed as FG's nominee and Mario Ferreiro due to stand for the Avanza País coalition, which had been formed by FG dissidents in November 2012. Oviedo, who had been named as UNACE's presidential candidate, died in a helicopter accident in February 2013; he was succeeded by his nephew, Lino César Oviedo Sánchez. The PLRA and UNACE formed an electoral alliance in early April.

In the election held on 21 April 2013 Cartes won the presidency convincingly, with 45.80% of the votes cast, according to the Tribunal Superior de Justicia Electoral. Alegre, his nearest rival, attracted 36.94% of the total ballot, while Ferreiro of the Avanza País garnered 5.88% of the ballot and the FG's Carrillo Iramain won only 3.32% of the vote. Cartes was scheduled to take office on 15 August. The Partido Colorado won a majority of seats in concurrent elections to the Cámara de Diputados, as well as 19 seats in the 45-seat Senado.

Foreign Affairs

In 1991 the Presidents and Ministers of Foreign Affairs of Argentina, Brazil, Uruguay and Paraguay signed a formal agreement in Asunción creating a common market of the 'Southern Cone' countries, the Mercado Común del Sur (Mercosur). The agreement allowed for the dismantling of trade barriers between the four countries, and entered into full operation in 1995.

Following Fernando Lugo's accession to the presidency in 2008, relations with Brazil were dominated by the new President's stated commitment to renegotiate the treaty governing the Itaipú hydroelectric project on the border between Brazil and Paraguay. The Treaty of Itaipú, signed in 1973 and due to expire in 2023, apportioned to each country one-half of the electricity produced by the project, and bound each country to sell to the other any surplus (in the case of Paraguay, some 95% of its share) at the cost of production. In 2009 President Lugo and his Brazilian counterpart, Lula da Silva, signed an agreement tripling the amount paid by Brazil to Paraguay for surplus electricity from Itaipú and permitting Paraguay to sell energy direct to Brazilian utility companies, rather than solely through the state-controlled Centrais Elétricas Brasileiras, SA (Eletrobrás). Brazil also agreed to provide financing for various infrastructure projects in Paraguay, including the construction of an electrical transmission line from Itaipú to central Paraguay. However, the Brazilian Government refused to allow Paraguay to sell its surplus production to third parties. The agreement was ratified by the Brazilian Senado Federal in May 2011.

Paraguay's relations with the USA were strained in 2006 when the Government announced that US military personnel operating in that country would no longer enjoy immunity from prosecution. Unlike other Mercosur countries, Paraguay had signed an agreement with the USA in 2005 protecting US soldiers from extradition to the International Criminal Court. The decision by Paraguay not to renew this agreement prompted the USA to announce the withdrawal of humanitarian and medical services that it had been providing to people living in remote rural areas of Paraguay.

CONSTITUTION AND GOVERNMENT

Under the 1992 Constitution, legislative power is held by the bicameral Congreso Nacional (National Congress), whose members serve for five years. The Senado (Senate) has 45 members, and the Cámara de Diputados (Chamber of Deputies) 80 members. Elections to the legislature are by universal adult suffrage. Executive power is held by the President, directly elected for a single term of five years at the same time as the legislature. The President of the Republic governs with the assistance of a Vice-President and an appointed Council of Ministers. Judicial power is exercised by the Supreme Court of Justice and by the tribunals. Paraguay is divided into 17 departments, each administered by an elected governor.

REGIONAL AND INTERNATIONAL CO-OPERATION

Paraguay is a member of the Inter-American Development Bank (see p. 341), of the Latin American Integration Association (see p. 370), of the Latin American Economic System (see p. 462), of the Organization of American States (see p. 404) and of the Mercado Común del Sur (Mercosur, see p. 439), although the country was suspended from Mercosur in June 2012. In December 2004 Paraguay was one of 12 countries that were signatories to the agreement creating the South American Community of Nations, intended to promote greater regional economic integration. A constitutive treaty for the community—renamed the Union of South American Nations (UNASUR, see p. 479) in 2007—was ratified in September 2011, with full functionality of economic union tentatively scheduled for 2019, although following the impeachment of President Lugo in June 2012 (see above), Paraguay was suspended from the community. The country is a member of the Community of Latin American and Caribbean States (see p. 475), which was formally inaugurated in December 2011.

Paraguay was a founder member of the UN in 1945. As a contracting party to the General Agreement on Tariffs and Trade, Paraguay joined the World Trade Organization (see p. 444) on its establishment in 1995.

ECONOMIC AFFAIRS

In 2011, according to estimates by the World Bank, Paraguay's gross national income (GNI), measured at average 2009–11 prices, was US $19,511m., equivalent to $2,970 per head (or $5,310 per head on an international purchasing-power parity basis). During 2002–11, it was estimated, the population increased at an average annual rate of 1.9%, while gross domestic product (GDP) per head increased, in real terms, by an average of 2.8% per year. Overall GDP increased, in real terms, at an average annual rate of 4.4% in 2002–11; GDP increased, according to preliminary figures, by 13.1% in 2010 and by 4.3% in 2011.

Agriculture (including forestry, hunting and fishing) contributed 21.4% of GDP in 2011, according to preliminary figures. In October–December 2011 some 26.5% of the economically active population were employed in the sector. The principal cash crop is soybeans, which accounted for an estimated 31.3% of total export revenue in 2012. Other significant crops are sugar cane, cassava, sunflowers, cotton, wheat and maize. Timber and wood manufactures provided an estimated 1.8% of export revenues in 2012. The raising of livestock (particularly cattle and pigs) is also important. Meat accounted for an estimated 15.7% of export earnings in 2012. According to official preliminary figures, agricultural GDP increased at an average annual rate of 5.7% in 2002–11; real agricultural GDP increased by 32.0% in 2010 and by 2.8% in 2011.

Industry (including mining, manufacturing, construction and power) contributed 27.5% of GDP in 2011, according to preliminary figures, and employed 17.6% of the working population in October–December 2011. According to official preliminary figures, industrial GDP increased by an average of 2.5% per year in 2002–11; the sector increased by 1.2% in 2011.

Paraguay has almost no commercially exploited mineral resources, and the mining sector, which employed only 0.3% of the labour force in 2007, contributed just 0.1% of GDP in 2011, according to preliminary figures. Production is confined to gypsum, kaolin and limestone. According to official preliminary figures, mining GDP increased by an average of 4.8% per year in 2002–11; the sector increased by 5.3% in 2011.

Manufacturing contributed 11.7% of GDP in 2011, according to preliminary figures, and the sector (including mining) employed 10.5% of the working population in October–December 2011. The main branch of manufacturing was production of food and beverages. The other principal sectors were wood and wood products, handicrafts, paper, printing and publishing, hides and furs, and non-metallic mineral products. According to official preliminary figures, manufacturing GDP increased at an average annual rate of 2.1% in 2002–11; real GDP of the sector increased by 6.1% in 2010, but declined by 1.1% in 2011.

The construction sector contributed 7.2% of GDP in 2011, according to preliminary figures, and engaged 6.6% of the working population in October–December 2011. According to official preliminary figures, construction GDP increased by an average of 5.6% per year in 2002–11; the sector increased by 13.0% in 2010 and only by 1.5% in 2011.

Energy is derived almost completely from hydroelectric power. Imports of mineral fuels comprised 15.8% of the value of total merchandise imports in 2012, according to preliminary figures. Ethyl alcohol (ethanol), derived from sugar cane, is widely used as a component of vehicle fuel. In 2013 the Government announced a significant discovery of natural gas in Alto Paraná.

The services sector contributed 51.0% of GDP in 2011, according to preliminary figures, and engaged 56.0% of the working population in October–December 2011. Paraguay traditionally serves as an entrepôt for regional trade. According to official preliminary figures, the GDP of the services sector increased by an average of 4.8% per year in 2002–11; the sector increased by 8.9% in 2010 and by 5.5% in 2011.

In 2011 Paraguay recorded a visible merchandise trade deficit of US $1,393.3m., and there was a deficit of $270.2m. on the current account of the balance of payments. According to preliminary figures, in 2012 the principal source of registered imports was the People's Republic of China (27.7%); other major suppliers in that year were Brazil, Argentina and the USA. Brazil was the principal market for registered exports in that year (an estimated 21.1% of total exports); other notable purchasers were Uruguay, Argentina and Russia. The principal exports in 2012 were soybeans, cereals, and meat. The principal imports were motors, general industrial machinery equipment and parts, mineral fuels, chemical products, and transport equipment.

In 2011 there was a central government budget deficit of 787,000m. guaraníes (equivalent to 0.7% of GDP). Paraguay's general government gross debt was 13,103,575m. guaraníes in 2011, equivalent to 12.0% of GDP. Paraguay's total external debt was US $4,938m. at the end of 2010, of which $2,369m. was public and publicly guaranteed debt. In that year, the cost of servicing long-term public and publicly guaranteed debt and repayments to the IMF was equivalent to 4.6% of the value of exports of goods, services and income (excluding workers' remittances). Annual inflation averaged 7.6% in 2002–11; consumer prices increased by an average of 8.2% in 2011. An estimated 5.6% of the labour force were unemployed in October–December 2011.

The economy contracted in 2009 as the increasingly severe global economic crisis stifled demand for Paraguayan exports. Nevertheless, a bumper harvest, combined with a resurgence in demand and prices for the country's key exports (soybeans and beef), resulted in a strong economic recovery throughout 2010. The flourishing agricultural sector supported renewed growth in other parts of the economy, including services and construction, and real GDP increased by an impressive 13.1% in that year. Economic growth moderated to 4.3% in 2011, again supported by the agricultural sector. However, in September foot and mouth disease was detected in cattle in the department of San Pedro, with a further outbreak reported in January 2012. Paraguayan meat exports were suspended while the authorities undertook measures to contain the disease, resulting in estimated losses to the industry of some US $300m. This set-back for the agricultural sector was compounded in late 2011 by the onset of a severe drought, which caused extensive crop damage and also affected the navigability of the commercially important Paraguay river. The Government provided funding to support small-scale farmers affected by the crisis. The Government also implemented a countercyclical spending strategy during 2012 in an attempt to offset the damage inflicted by these economic shocks. Nevertheless, the IMF estimated that real GDP contracted by 1.5% in 2012, although growth of around 11% was expected in 2013 as the agricultural sector recovered.

PUBLIC HOLIDAYS

2014: 1 January (New Year's Day), 3 March (for Heroes' Day), 17 April (Maundy Thursday), 18 April (Good Friday), 1 May (Labour Day), 15 May (Independence Day), 12 June (Peace of Chaco), 15 August (Founding of Asunción), 29 September (Battle of Boquerón), 8 December (Immaculate Conception), 25 December (Christmas Day).

Statistical Survey

Sources (unless otherwise stated): Dirección General de Estadística, Encuestas y Censos, Naciones Unidas, esq. Saavedra, Fernando de la Mora, Zona Norte; tel. (21) 51-1016; fax (21) 50-8493; internet www.dgeec.gov.py; Banco Central del Paraguay, Avda Federación Rusa y Marecos, Casilla 861, Barrio Santo Domingo, Asunción; tel. (21) 61-0088; fax (21) 60-8149; e-mail ccs@bcp.gov.py; internet www.bcp.gov.py; Secretaría Técnica de Planificación, Presidencia de la República, Iturbe y Eligio Ayala, Asunción.

Area and Population

AREA, POPULATION AND DENSITY

Area (sq km)	406,752*
Population (census results)	
26 August 1992	4,152,588
28 August 2002	
Males	2,627,831
Females	2,555,249
Total	5,183,080
Population (official estimates at mid-year)	
2011	6,561,785
2012	6,672,631
2013	6,783,374
Density (per sq km) at mid-2013	16.7

* 157,048 sq miles.

POPULATION BY AGE AND SEX
('000, official estimates at mid-2013)

	Males	Females	Total
0–14	1,114.2	1,073.7	2,187.8
15–64	2,137.5	2,091.6	4,229.1
65 and over	174.9	191.6	366.5
Total	3,426.5	3,356.9	6,783.4

Note: Totals may not be equal to the sum of components, owing to rounding.

DEPARTMENTS

(official population estimates at mid-2011)

	Area (sq km)	Population	Density (per sq km)	Capital
Alto Paraguay (incl. Chaco) .	82,349	11,245	0.1	Fuerte Olimpo
Alto Paraná .	14,895	769,692	51.7	Ciudad del Este
Amambay .	12,933	125,474	9.7	Pedro Juan Caballero
Asunción .	117	516,897	4,417.9	—
Boquerón (incl. Nueva Asunción) .	91,669	59,429	0.6	Doctor Pedro P. Peña
Caaguazú . .	11,474	481,911	42.0	Coronel Oviedo
Caazapá . . .	9,496	151,349	15.9	Caazapá
Canindeyú . .	14,667	187,555	12.8	Salto del Guairá
Central . .	2,465	2,144,591	870.0	Asunción
Concepción . .	18,051	190,194	10.5	Concepción
Cordillera . .	4,948	279,959	56.6	Caacupé
Guairá . .	3,846	197,528	51.4	Villarrica
Itapúa . .	16,525	540,711	32.7	Encarnación
Misiones . .	9,556	117,874	12.3	San Juan Bautista
Ñeembucú . .	12,147	83,977	6.9	Pilar
Paraguarí . .	8,705	239,601	27.5	Paraguarí
Presidente Hayes	72,907	105,130	1.4	Pozo Colorado
San Pedro . .	20,002	358,668	17.9	San Pedro
Total . . .	406,752	6,561,785	16.1	—

PRINCIPAL TOWNS

(population at 2002 census, incl. rural environs)

Asunción (capital) .	510,910	Lambaré . . .	119,830
Ciudad del Este* .	222,109	Fernando de la Mora	113,990
San Lorenzo . .	203,150	Caaguazú . . .	100,132
Luque	185,670	Encarnación . .	97,000
Capiatá	154,520	Pedro Juan Caballero . . .	88,530

* Formerly Puerto Presidente Stroessner.

Mid-2011 ('000, incl. suburbs, UN estimate): Asunción 2,139 (Source: UN, *World Urbanization Prospects: The 2011 Revision*).

BIRTHS, MARRIAGES AND DEATHS

	Live births Number	Rate (per 1,000)	Marriages Number	Rate (per 1,000)	Deaths Number	Rate (per 1,000)
2003 . .	45,669	8.0	17,717	3.1	19,593	3.4
2004 . .	49,857	8.6	17,763	3.1	20,283	3.5
2005 . .	51,444	8.7	19,826	3.4	17,360	2.9
2006 . .	49,473	8.2	19,476	3.2	19,298	3.2
2007 . .	49,879	8.2	19,726	3.2	21,049	3.4
2008 . .	51,423	8.3	18,832	3.0	20,053	3.2
2009 . .	52,540	8.3	17,965	2.8	18,753	3.0
2010 . .	53,441	8.3	18,099	2.8	21,257	3.3

Note: Rates were derived from estimates of mid-year population.

Life expectancy (years at birth): 72.5 (males 70.25; females 74.6) in 2011 (Source: World Bank, World Development Indicators database).

ECONOMICALLY ACTIVE POPULATION

(household survey, '000 persons aged 10 years and over, October–December unless otherwise indicated)

	2009	2010	2011
Agriculture, hunting, forestry and fishing	872,905	782,639	801,914
Manufacturing, mining and quarrying	325,486	322,732	318,996
Electricity, gas and water . . .	12,152	16,371	14,065
Construction	171,751	210,388	198,979
Trade, restaurants and hotels .	728,949	711,376	768,920
Transport, storage and communications	128,548	111,766	126,420
Financing, insurance, real estate and business services . . .	115,284	131,183	137,763
Community, social and personal services	600,500	630,467	662,788
Sub-total	2,955,575	2,916,922	3,029,845
Activities not adequately described	5,268	1,814	4,926
Total employed	2,960,843	2,918,736	3,034,771
Unemployed	202,398	175,571	180,739
Total labour force	3,163,241	3,094,307	3,215,510

Health and Welfare

KEY INDICATORS

Total fertility rate (children per woman, 2010)	3.0
Under-5 mortality rate (per 1,000 live births, 2010) . . .	25
HIV/AIDS (% of persons aged 15–49, 2009)	0.3
Physicians (per 1,000 head, 2002)	1.1
Hospital beds (per 1,000 head, 2006)	1.3
Health expenditure (2009): US $ per head (PPP) . . .	295
Health expenditure (2009): % of GDP	6.6
Health expenditure (2009): public (% of total)	39.0
Access to water (% of persons, 2010)	86
Access to sanitation (% of persons, 2010)	71
Total carbon dioxide emissions ('000 metric tons, 2008) . .	4,118.0
Carbon dioxide emissions per head (metric tons, 2008) . .	0.7
Human Development Index (2011): ranking	107
Human Development Index (2011): value	0.665

For sources and definitions, see explanatory note on p. vi.

Agriculture

PRINCIPAL CROPS

('000 metric tons)

	2009	2010	2011
Wheat	1,067	1,402	1,461
Rice, paddy	215	315	408
Maize	1,858	3,109	3,346
Sorghum	26	150	150
Sweet potatoes	45	43	45
Cassava (Manioc)	2,610	2,624	2,454
Sugar cane	4,800	5,131	5,339
Beans, dry	43	49	53
Soybeans (Soya beans) . . .	3,855	7,460	8,310
Oil palm fruit*	152	152	152
Sunflower seed	194	262	109
Tomatoes	44	58	45
Onions, dry*	32	35	28

—continued	2009	2010	2011
Carrots and turnips	11	12	12
Watermelons*	125	130	103
Cantaloupes and other melons* .	30	38	30
Bananas	59	80	60
Oranges	226	230	230
Tangerines, mandarins, clementines and satsumas . .	45	44	44
Grapefruit and pomelos . . .	41	42	42
Guavas, mangoes and mangosteens*	30	32	30
Pineapples	55	59	59
Maté	77	85	85

* FAO estimate(s).

Aggregate production ('000 metric tons, may include official, semi-official or estimated data): Total cereals 3,166 in 2009, 4,976 in 2010, 5,365 in 2011; Total roots and tubers 2,655 in 2009, 2,668 in 2010, 2,503 in 2011; Total vegetables (incl. melons) 282 in 2009, 323 in 2010, 257 in 2011; Total fruits (excl. melons) 531 in 2009, 568 in 2010, 542 in 2011.

Source: FAO.

LIVESTOCK
('000 head, year ending September)

	2009	2010	2011
Cattle	11,643	12,305	12,437
Horses*	285	290	295
Pigs	1,100*	1,182	1,241
Sheep*	380	400	410
Goats*	130	135	137
Chickens*	18,000	20,000	20,000
Ducks*	1,050	1,100	1,200
Geese and guinea fowls* . . .	115	115	115
Turkeys*	185	190	195

* FAO estimate(s).

Source: FAO.

LIVESTOCK PRODUCTS
('000 metric tons, FAO estimates)

	2009	2010	2011
Cattle meat	315	385	411
Pig meat	144	160	164
Chicken meat	36	37	38
Cows' milk	467	396	396
Hen eggs	128	128	128

Source: FAO.

Forestry

ROUNDWOOD REMOVALS
('000 cubic metres, excluding bark, FAO estimates)

	2009	2010	2011
Sawlogs, veneer logs and logs for sleepers	3,515	3,515	3,515
Other industrial wood	529	529	529
Fuel wood	6,466	6,576	6,684
Total	10,510	10,620	10,728

Source: FAO.

SAWNWOOD PRODUCTION
('000 cubic metres, including railway sleepers)

	1995	1996	1997
Total (all broadleaved) . . .	400	500	550

1998–2011: Annual production as in 1997 (FAO estimates).

Source: FAO.

Fishing
('000 metric tons, live weight, FAO estimates)

	2008	2009	2010
Capture	1.7	1.7	1.7
Characins	0.6	0.6	0.6
Freshwater siluroids . . .	0.8	0.8	0.8
Other freshwater fishes . . .	0.3	0.3	0.3
Aquaculture	2.5	2.6	3.0
Total catch	4.2	4.3	4.7

Source: FAO.

Industry

SELECTED PRODUCTS
('000 metric tons)

	2008	2009	2010
Soya bean oil*†	267	301	336
Hydraulic cement‡§	620	620	620

* Unofficial figures.
† Data from FAO.
‡ Data from US Geological Survey.
§ Estimates.

2011: Soya bean oil 374 (unofficial figure).

Finance

CURRENCY AND EXCHANGE RATES

Monetary Units
    100 céntimos = 1 guaraní (G).

Sterling, Dollar and Euro Equivalents (31 October 2012)
    £1 sterling = 7,179.7 guaraníes;
    US $1 = 4,455.0 guaraníes;
    €1 = 5,788.4 guaraníes;
    100,000 guaraníes = £13.93 = $22.45 = €17.28.

Average Exchange Rate (guaraníes per US dollar)
    2009   4,965.4
    2010   4,735.5
    2011   4,191.4

BUDGET
(central government operations, '000 million guaraníes)

Revenue	2009	2010	2011
Taxation	9,207	11,406	13,211
Corporate taxes	2,193	2,096	2,611
Value-added tax	4,450	5,908	6,786
Import duties	977	1,526	1,704
Non-tax revenue and grants . .	4,422	4,517	5,115
Capital revenues	278	347	675
Total	13,907	16,270	19,001

Expenditure	2009	2010	2011
Current expenditure . . .	10,606	11,869	13,973
Personal	6,079	6,951	8,047
Other	4,527	4,919	5,926
Capital expenditure . . .	3,256	3,227	4,241
Total	13,862	15,096	18,214

INTERNATIONAL RESERVES
(excl. gold, US $ million at 31 December)

	2009	2010	2011
IMF special drawing rights . .	173.00	170.08	169.76
Reserve position in IMF . . .	33.67	33.07	32.97
Foreign exchange	3,631.97	3,933.66	4,747.33
Total	3,838.64	4,136.81	4,950.06

Source: IMF, *International Financial Statistics.*

MONEY SUPPLY
('000 million guaraníes at 31 December)

	2009	2010	2011
Currency outside depository corporations	4,344.60	5,195.27	5,761.73
Transferable deposits . . .	12,102.11	14,249.69	15,364.78
Other deposits	9,145.53	10,535.67	11,908.53
Securities other than shares . .	6,888.16	8,676.49	11,843.76
Broad money	32,480.39	38,657.12	44,878.79

Source: IMF, *International Financial Statistics.*

COST OF LIVING
(Consumer Price Index for Asunción; base: 2000 = 100)

	2008	2009	2010
Food (incl. beverages) . . .	246.1	247.5	268.6
Housing (incl. fuel and light) . .	172.0	175.2	184.5
Clothing (incl. footwear) . . .	146.0	150.6	153.2
All items (incl. others) . . .	196.9	202.1	211.5

2011: Food (incl. beverages) 304.4; All items (incl. others) 228.9.

Source: ILO.

NATIONAL ACCOUNTS
('000 million guaraníes at current prices)

Expenditure on the Gross Domestic Product

	2009	2010*	2011*
Final consumption expenditure .	63,234.6	76,578.5	90,870.5
Households†	54,592.8	66,661.8	79,714.3
General government . .	8,641.8	9,916.6	11,156.2
Gross capital formation . . .	10,911.5	15,404.4	17,632.7
Gross fixed capital formation .	10,684.8	15,049.5	17,231.6
Changes in inventories‡ . .	226.7	355.0	401.1
Total domestic expenditure .	74,146.1	91,982.9	108,503.3
Exports of goods and services .	40,479.9	51,863.0	53,148.4
Less Imports of goods and services	35,508.9	48,911.6	52,857.0
GDP in purchasers' values .	79,117.2	94,934.3	108,794.6
GDP at constant 1994 prices .	20,282.3	22,937.8	23,933.5

* Preliminary figures.
† Including non-profit institutions serving households.
‡ Including acquisitions, less disposals, of valuables.

Gross Domestic Product by Economic Activity

	2009	2010*	2011*
Agriculture, hunting, forestry and fishing	13,657.7	19,339.4	21,143.9
Mining and quarrying	105.7	114.7	136.0
Manufacturing	9,186.7	10,614.5	11,535.7
Construction	4,625.1	5,844.9	7,096.0
Electricity and water	9,221.3	9,272.3	8,430.6
Trade	12,734.6	14,963.2	21,064.4
Transport and communications .	5,164.4	5,470.4	5,737.0
Financial intermediation . .	2,505.7	3,393.4	4,345.9
Government services	7,480.8	8,523.9	9,703.0
Real estate, renting and business activities	2,607.6	2,890.2	3,257.0
Hotels and restaurants . . .	789.4	924.5	1,050.5
Other services	4,118.9	4,497.6	5,230.7
Gross value added in basic prices	72,197.9	85,848.8	98,730.7
Net taxes on products	6,919.2	9,085.4	10,063.9
GDP in market prices . . .	79,117.2	94,934.3	108,794.6

* Preliminary figures.

BALANCE OF PAYMENTS
(US $ million)

	2009	2010	2011
Exports of goods	6,013.5	8,604.4	10,620.8
Imports of goods	−6,880.4	−9,868.2	−12,014.2
Balance on goods	−866.9	−1,263.8	−1,393.3
Exports of services	1,257.1	1,341.5	1,632.9
Imports of services	−539.1	−755.3	−903.7
Balance on goods and services	−148.9	−677.7	−664.1
Primary income received . . .	349.8	328.2	443.9
Primary income paid	−652.1	−861.6	−750.9
Balance on goods, services and primary income	−451.2	−1,211.1	−971.1
Secondary income received . .	520.3	558.9	702.3
Secondary income paid . .	−1.4	−1.4	−1.4
Current balance	67.7	−653.6	−270.2
Capital account (net)	47.0	40.0	40.0
Direct investment assets . . .	38.4	−135.4	71.4
Direct investment liabilities . .	186.1	475.1	412.0
Other investment assets . . .	184.0	1.7	212.8
Other investment liabilities . .	125.2	326.7	15.3
Net errors and omissions . . .	278.9	264.8	302.9
Reserves and related items .	927.3	319.4	784.2

Source: IMF, *International Financial Statistics.*

External Trade

PRINCIPAL COMMODITIES
(US $ million)

Imports f.o.b.	2010	2011*	2012*
Food and live animals	361.9	454.1	459.6
Beverages and tobacco . . .	309.7	350.1	351.5
Mineral fuels	1,072.8	1,506.5	1,693.4
Chemical products	682.1	939.1	892.1
Road vehicles	314.7	448.5	429.0
Transport equipment and accessories	677.2	905.6	779.4
Electrical appliances . . .	344.4	366.0	323.6
Motors, general industrial machinery equipment and parts	2,851.7	3,094.5	2,651.5
Total (incl. others)	9,399.8	11,502.2	10,689.6

Exports f.o.b.	2010	2011*	2012*
Meat	919.8	753.0	796.0
Cereals	549.2	607.6	1,044.9
Soya seeds	1,590.8	2,294.6	1,582.9
Vegetable oil	275.6	339.7	184.2
Flour	349.2	416.7	228.0
Wood and wooden products . .	101.6	96.6	89.1
Cotton fibres	39.2	32.6	n.a.
Total (incl. others)	4,533.8	5,517.4	5,058.1

* Preliminary figures.

PRINCIPAL TRADING PARTNERS
(US $ million)

Imports f.o.b.	2010	2011*	2012*
Argentina	1,460.2	1,620.5	1,712.8
Brazil	2,280.0	3,049.0	2,516.0
Chile	116.5	143.8	137.6
China, People's Republic . . .	3,255.2	3,428.5	2,964.7
Germany	147.1	205.8	188.6
Japan	320.9	359.4	287.0
Korea, Republic	139.0	198.5	253.2
Mexico	87.8	178.6	156.6
Switzerland-Liechtenstein . .	90.7	87.6	60.6
USA	404.9	603.6	854.6
Uruguay	140.2	159.5	142.9
Venezuela	208.6	361.6	122.5
Total (incl. others)	9,399.8	11,502.2	10,689.6

Exports f.o.b.	2010	2011*	2012*
Argentina	538.1	972.6	776.7
Bolivia	34.9	55.8	89.3
Brazil	660.5	782.9	1,067.4
Cayman Islands	24.3	26.0	n.a.
Chile	547.4	488.5	103.0
France	60.5	78.6	10.8
India	71.9	28.5	14.9
Israel	62.8	104.7	112.7
Italy	77.7	99.3	81.2
Japan	39.0	52.2	31.0
Netherlands	126.5	87.3	32.0
Peru	127.5	114.2	65.1
Russia	238.7	224.9	551.2
Spain	89.9	100.0	23.7
Switzerland-Liechtenstein . .	99.7	290.3	233.4
Turkey	67.7	17.2	1.5
USA	63.7	146.5	137.7
Uruguay	995.7	1,061.6	919.7
Venezuela	110.2	91.5	60.5
Total (incl. others)	4,533.8	5,517.4	5,058.1

* Preliminary figures.

Transport

RAILWAYS
(traffic)

	1988	1989	1990
Passengers carried	178,159	196,019	125,685
Freight (metric tons)	200,213	164,980	289,099

Source: UN, *Statistical Yearbook*.

Passenger-km: 3.0 million per year in 1994–96.

Freight ton-km: 5.5 million in 1994.

Source: UN Economic Commission for Latin America and the Caribbean.

ROAD TRAFFIC
(vehicles in use)

	1999	2000
Cars	267,587	274,186
Buses	8,991	9,467
Lorries	41,329	42,992
Vans and jeeps	134,144	138,656
Motorcycles	6,872	8,825

Source: Organización Paraguaya de Cooperación Intermunicipal.

2009: (vehicles in use): Passenger cars 177,166; Buses and coaches 5,408; Vans and lorries 157,302; Motorcycles and mopeds 167,273.

SHIPPING
Flag Registered Fleet
(at 31 December)

	2010	2011	2012
Number of vessels	140	151	155
Total displacement ('000 grt) . .	134.0	148.7	157.1

Source: Lloyd's List Intelligence (www.lloydslistintelligence.com).

CIVIL AVIATION
(traffic)

	2009	2010	2011
Passengers carried ('000) . . .	569.6	699.3	792.5
Freight carried ('000 metric tons) .	15.0	19.0	23.1

Tourism

ARRIVALS BY NATIONALITY

	2008	2009	2010
Argentina	195,948	196,149	218,418
Brazil	134,985	131,429	159,280
Chile	9,517	11,115	9,829
Germany	10,467	10,289	7,173
USA	13,241	14,012	10,142
Uruguay	9,327	11,130	11,216
Total (incl. others)	428,215	439,246	465,264

Total arrivals ('000): 524 in 2011 (provisional).

Tourism receipts (US $ million, incl. passenger transport, unless otherwise indicated): 247 in 2009; 217 in 2010 (excl. passenger transport); 241 in 2011 (excl. passenger transport, provisional).

Source: World Tourism Organization.

Communications Media

	2009	2010	2011
Telephones ('000 main lines in use)	387.3	361.8	372.4
Mobile cellular telephones ('000 subscribers)	5,618.6	5,920.9	6,529.1
Internet subscribers ('000) . .	156.9	105.7	n.a.
Broadband subscribers ('000) . .	15.8	28.1	60.5

Source: International Telecommunication Union.

Education

(2008/09 unless otherwise indicated)

	Institutions*	Teachers	Students
Pre-primary schools . .	4,071	6,304.5†	154,866
Primary	7,456	32,998.2†	852,168
Secondary	2,149	34,340.7†	549,482
Tertiary: university level .	111	1,844‡	236,194

* 1999.
† 2007/08.
‡ 1999/2000.

Source: partly UNESCO Institute for Statistics.

Pupil-teacher ratio (primary education, UNESCO estimate): 26.5 in 2007/08 (Source: UNESCO Institute for Statistics).

Adult literacy rate (UNESCO estimates): 93.9% (males 94.8%; females 92.9%) in 2010 (Source: UNESCO Institute for Statistics).

Directory

The Government

HEAD OF STATE

President: LUIS FEDERICO FRANCO GÓMEZ (took office 22 June 2012 following the impeachment of Fernando Lugo Méndez).

President-elect: HORACIO MANUEL CARTES JARA (scheduled to take office 15 August 2013).

Vice-President: OSCAR DENIS.

COUNCIL OF MINISTERS
(May 2013)

The Government comprises members of the Partido Liberal Radical Auténtico, Asociación Nacional Republicana (Partido Colorado) and Unión Nacional de Ciudadanos Eticos. A new administration was scheduled to be formed by the Asociación Nacional Repúblicana (Partido Colorado) in August 2013.

Minister of the Interior: CARMELO CABALLERO.

Minister of Foreign Affairs: JOSÉ FÉLIX FERNÁNDEZ ESTIGARRIBIA.

Minister of Finance: MANUEL ADOLFO FERREIRA BRUSQUETTI.

Minister of Industry and Commerce: DIEGO ZAVALA.

Minister of Public Works and Communications: ENRIQUE SALYN BUZARQUIS.

Minister of National Defence: MARÍA LIZ ARNOLD GARCÍA.

Minister of Public Health and Social Welfare: ANTONIO ARBO.

Minister of Justice and Labour: MARÍA LORENA SEGOVIA AZUCAS.

Minister of Agriculture and Livestock: RODY GODOY.

Minister of Education and Culture: HORACIO GALEANO PERRONE.

Secretary-General to the Presidency: MARTÍN BURT.

Minister for Women: GLORIA RUBIN.

MINISTRIES

Office of the President: Palacio de los López, Asunción; tel. (21) 414-0200; internet www.presidencia.gov.py.

Ministry of Agriculture and Livestock: Edif. San Rafael, Yegros, entre 25 de Mayo y Cerro Corá 437, Apdo 825, Asunción; tel. (21) 45-0937; fax (21) 49-7965; e-mail prensa@mag.gov.py; internet www .mag.gov.py.

Ministry of Education and Culture: Edif. La Consolidada, Chile 719, Casi Eduardo V. Haedo, Asunción; tel. (21) 45-0014; fax (21) 45-0015; e-mail comunicacion@mec.gov.py; internet www.mec.gov.py.

Ministry of Finance: Chile 252, entre Palma y Presidente Franco, Asunción; tel. (21) 44-0010; fax (21) 44-8283; e-mail info@hacienda .gov.py; internet www.hacienda.gov.py.

Ministry of Foreign Affairs: Edif. Benigno López, Palma y 14 de Mayo, Asunción; tel. (21) 49-3928; fax (21) 49-3910; e-mail sistemas@ mre.gov.py; internet www.mre.gov.py.

Ministry of Industry and Commerce: Avda Mariscal López 3333, esq. Dr Wiss, Villa Morra, Casilla 2151, Asunción; tel. (21) 616-3012; fax (21) 616-3118; e-mail sprivada@mic.gov.py; internet www.mic .gov.py.

Ministry of the Interior: Chile 1002, esq. Manduvira, Asunción; tel. (21) 415-2000; fax (21) 44-6448; e-mail ministro@mdi.gov.py; internet www.mdi.gov.py.

Ministry of Justice and Labour: Avda Dr José Gaspar Rodríguez de Francia, esq. Estados Unidos, Asunción; tel. (21) 49-3209; fax (21) 20-8469; e-mail info@mjt.gov.py; internet www.mjt.gov.py.

Ministry of National Defence: Avda Mariscal López, esq. Vice-presidente Sánchez y 22 de Septiembre, Asunción; tel. (21) 21-0052; fax (21) 21-1815; e-mail ministro@mdn.gov.py; internet www.mdn .gov.py.

Ministry of Public Health and Social Welfare: Avda Pettirossi, esq. Brasil, Asunción; tel. (21) 20-4601; fax (21) 20-6700; internet www.mspbs.gov.py.

Ministry of Public Works and Communications: Oliva y Alberdi 411, Casilla 1221, Asunción; tel. (21) 414-9000; fax (21) 44-4421; e-mail comunicaciones@mopc.gov.py; internet www.mopc.gov.py.

Ministry for Women: Edif. Ayfra, 13°, entre Bloque B y Planta Baja, Avda Presidente Franco, esq. Ayolas, Asunción; tel. (21) 45-0036; fax (21) 45-0041; e-mail info@mujer.gov.py; internet www .mujer.gov.py.

President and Legislature

PRESIDENT

Election, 21 April 2013

Candidate	Votes	% of votes
Horacio Manuel Cartes Jara (ANR) . .	1,095,469	45.80
Pedro Efraín Alegre Sasiain (PLRA) . .	883,630	36.94
Mario Aníbal Ferreiro Sanabría (Avanza País)	140,622	5.88
Aníbal Enrique Carrillo Iramain (FG) .	79,327	3.32
Miguel Carrizosa Galiano (PPQ) .	27,036	1.13
Lino César Oviedo Sánchez (UNACE) .	19,124	0.80
Others	15,777	0.66
Total votes	2,391,790*	100.00

* Including 71,388 blank and 59,417 invalid ballots.

CONGRESO NACIONAL

President of the Senado and the Congreso Nacional: ALFREDO LUIS JAEGGLI (PLRA) (acting).

Senado

Senate: Calle 14 de Mayo, esq. Avda. de la República, 1°, Asuncíon; tel. (21) 414-5198; e-mail informes@senado.gov.py; internet www .senado.gov.py.

General Election, 21 April 2013, preliminary results

Party	Seats
Asociación Nacional Republicana (Partido Colorado)	19
Partido Liberal Radical Auténtico	12
Frente Guasú	5
Partido Democrático Progresista	3
Avanza País	2
Unión Nacional de Ciudadanos Eticos	2
Partido Encuentro Nacional	1
Partido Patria Querida	1
Total	**45**

Cámara de Diputados

Chamber of Deputies: Avda República y 15 de Agosto, Asunción; tel. (21) 414-4000; e-mail dircom@diputados.gov.py; internet www.diputados.gov.py.

President of the Cámara de Diputados: VÍCTOR ALCIDES BOGADO GONZÁLEZ (ANR).

General Election, 21 April 2013, preliminary results

Party	Seats
Asociación Nacional Republicana (Partido Colorado)	44
Partido Liberal Radical Auténtico	27
Unión Nacional de Ciudadanos Eticos	2
Avanza País	2
Partido Encuentro Nacional	2
Others	3
Total	**80**

Election Commission

Tribunal Superior de Justicia Electoral (TSJE): Avda Eusebio Ayala 2759 y Santa Cruz de la Sierra, Casilla 1209, Asunción; tel. and fax (21) 618-0111; e-mail protocolo@tsje.gov.py; internet www.tsje.gov.py; f. 1995; Pres. ALBERTO RAMÍREZ ZAMBONINI.

Political Organizations

Asociación Nacional Republicana (ANR) (Partido Colorado): Casa de los Colorados, 25 de Mayo 842, Asunción; tel. (21) 45-2543; fax (21) 45-4136; e-mail contacto@anr.gov.py; internet www.anr.org.py; f. 19th century; Pres. LILIAN SAMANIEGO.

Avanza País: Eligio Ayala 1728, casi República Francesa, Asunción; tel. (21) 20-4392; e-mail info@avanzapais.com; internet avanzapais.com; f. 2012 by breakaway mems of the Frente Guasú; Leader MARIO FERREIRO.

Convergencia Popular Socialista (CPS): Caballero 766, Asunción; tel. (21) 44-3705; e-mail prensapcps@gmail.com; internet partidoconvergencia.wordpress.com; f. 2002; Sec.-Gen. RAMÓN MEDINA VELAZCO.

Frente Guasú: Teniente Bauza 4121, con Cerro Corá, Asunción; tel. (21) 20-1494; e-mail frenteguasu@frenteguasu.org.py; internet frenteguasu.org.py; f. 2010; a coalition of political orgs and social movts supportive of Fernando Lugo Méndez, incl. the constituent parties of the APC; Sec.-Gen. RICARDO CANESE.

Movimiento 20 de Abril: Colón 262, entre Avda Presidente Franco y Avda Palma, Asunción; tel. (21) 49-0991; e-mail movimiento20deabril2012@gmail.com; internet movimiento20deabril.blogspot.com; f. 2010 by supporters of Fernando Lugo Méndez; Leader MIGUEL ANGEL LÓPEZ PERITO; Sec.-Gen. LIZ TORRES.

Partido Comunista Paraguayo (PCP): Brasil 228, Asunción; internet www.pcparaguay.org; f. 1928; banned 1928–46, 1947–89; Leader ANANÍAS MAIDANA; Sec.-Gen. NAJEEB AMADO.

Partido Demócrata Cristiano (PDC): Dupuis 962, entre Montevideo y Colón, Asunción; tel. (21) 42-0434; e-mail info@pdc.org.py; internet www.pdc.org.py; f. 1960; 20,500 mems; Pres. ALBA ESPINOLA DE CRISTALDO; Sec.-Gen. ANÍBAL RODAS.

Partido Democrático Progresista (PDP): Avda 25 de Mayo, entre Constitución y Brasil, Asunción; tel. (21) 22-5354; e-mail info@pdp.org.py; internet www.pdp.org.py; f. 2007; democratic socialist; Pres. DESIRÉE MASI.

Partido Encuentro Nacional (PEN): Avda Mariscal López, con General Aquino 834, Asunción; tel. (21) 21-0229; fax (21) 21-4716;

e-mail prensa.pen@gmail.com; internet www.encuentronacional.org.py; f. 1991 as Movimiento Encuentro Nacional; Pres. FERNANDO CAMACHO PAREDES.

Partido Frente Amplio: Antequera 764, esq. Fulgencio R. Moreno, Asunción; tel. (21) 44-1389; e-mail arevalovicente@hotmail.com; Gen. Sec. VÍCTOR BAREIRO ROA.

Partido Humanista Paraguayo: San Francisco 1318, San Antonio, Barrio Jara, Asunción; tel. (21) 23-3085; e-mail phfernandodelamora@hotmail.com; f. 1985; legally recognized 1989; campaigns for the protection of human rights and environmental issues; Pres. ROBERTO CARLOS FERREIRA FRANCO.

Partido Liberal Radical Auténtico (PLRA): Iturbe 936, entre Manuel Domínguez y Teniente Fariña, Asunción; tel. (21) 49-8442; fax (21) 49-8443; e-mail prensa@plra.org.py; internet www.plra.org.py; f. 1978; centre; 806,000 mems; Pres. BLAS ANTONIO LLANO RAMOS; Sec.-Gen. AMANDA ROSALIA NUÑEZ DE FIGUEREDO.

Partido del Movimiento al Socialismo (PMAS): Jejui y 15 de agosto 582, Asunción; tel. (21) 45-5977; e-mail prensa@pmas.org.py; internet p-mas.org.py; f. 2006; Pres. CAMILO SOARES; Sec.-Gen. RODRIGO BUONGERMINI.

Partido País Solidario: Avda 5, esq. Méjico, Asunción; tel. (21) 39-1271; e-mail presidencia@paissolidario.org.py; internet www.paissolidario.org.py; f. 2000; mem. of Socialist International; Pres. Dr CARLOS FILIZZOLA PALLARÉS; Exec. Sec. MARÍA TERESA FERREIRA.

Partido Patria Querida (PPQ): Padre Cardozo 469, Asunción; tel. 21-3300; e-mail comunicaciones@patriaquerida.org; internet www.patriaquerida.org; f. 2002; legally recognized 2004; Pres. SEBASTIÁN ACHA; Sec.-Gen. ARSENIO OCAMPOS VELÁZQUEZ.

Partido Popular Tekojojá: Carios, esq. Médicos del Chaco, Asunción; tel. and fax (21) 55-4104; e-mail tekojoja@tekojoa.org.py; internet www.tekojoja.org; f. 2006; left-wing, mainly comprising social and indigenous groups; Pres. STILBER VALDES; Sec. SANDRA GALLARDO.

Partido Revolucionario Febrerista (PRF): Casa del Pueblo, Manduvira 522, entre 14 de Mayo y 15 de Agosto, Asunción; tel. (21) 49-4041; e-mail partyce@mixmail.com; internet www.prf.org.py; f. 1951; social democratic; mem. of Socialist International; Pres. HILDA JOSEFINA DUARTE BENÍTEZ; Sec.-Gen. OSVALDO SEGOVIA.

Partido Social Demócrata (PSD): 25 de Mayo, esq. Tacuarí, Asunción; tel. (21) 45-3293; e-mail partidosocialdemocrata.paraguay@gmail.com; f. 2007; Pres. MANUEL DOLDÁN DEL PUERTO.

Partido de los Trabajadores (PT): Hernandarias y Piribebuy 890, Asunción; tel. (21) 44-5009; e-mail info@ptparaguay.org; internet www.ptparaguay.org; f. 1989; Socialist; Pres. JULIO LÓPEZ.

Partido de la Unidad Popular (PUP): Palma 571, entre 14 de Mayo y 15 de Agosto, Planta Alta, Asunción; tel. (21) 21-5059; fax (21) 49-8018; e-mail p.unidadpopular@gmail.com; legally recognized 2004; Pres. JUAN DE DIOS ACOSTA MENA.

Unión Nacional de Ciudadanos Eticos (UNACE): Avda Mariscal López, Saturio Ríos, Asunción; tel. (21) 59-1900; e-mail loviedo@unace.org.py; internet www.unace.org.py; f. 1996 as Unión Nacional de Colorados Eticos, a faction of the Partido Colorado, current name adopted 2002; left-wing; Exec. Sec. HERMINIO CHENA VALDEZ.

Diplomatic Representation

EMBASSIES IN PARAGUAY

Argentina: Avda España, esq. Avda Perú, Casilla 757, Asunción; tel. (21) 21-2320; fax (21) 21-1029; e-mail contacto_epara@cancilleria.gov.ar; internet www.embajada-argentina.org.py; Chargé d'affaires a.i. LUIS PABLO NISCOVOLOS.

Bolivia: Campos Cervera 6421, Barrio Villa Aurelia, Asunción; tel. (21) 61-4984; fax (21) 60-1999; e-mail emboliviapy@tigo.com.py; Chargé d'affaires a.i. ZANDRA ELIZABETH RODRÍGUEZ CAMPOY.

Brazil: Coronel Irrazábal, esq. Eligio Ayala, Casilla 22, Asunción; tel. (21) 248-4000; fax (21) 21-2693; e-mail parbrem@embajadabrasil.org.py; internet assuncao.itamaraty.gov.br; Chargé d'affaires a.i. RAFAEL DE MELLO VIDAL.

Chile: Capital Emilio Nudelman 351, esq. Campos Cervera, Asunción; tel. (21) 61-3855; fax (21) 66-2755; e-mail echilepy@tigo.com.py; Ambassador CRISTIÁN MAQUEIRA ASTABURUAGA.

Colombia: Coronel Francisco Brizuela 3089, esq. Ciudad del Vaticano, Asunción; tel. (21) 22-9888; fax (21) 22-9703; e-mail easuncio@cancilleria.gov.co; internet www.embajadaenparaguay.gov.co; Ambassador JUAN ALBERTO BARRANTE ULLOA.

Cuba: Luis Morales 757, esq. Luis de León y Luis de Granada, Barrio Jara, Asunción; tel. (21) 22-2108; fax (21) 21-3879; e-mail embajada@embacuba.org.py; internet www.cubadiplomatica.cu/paraguay; Ambassador BERNARDO GUANCHE.

Dominican Republic: Edif. Asturias, 9°, Suite C, Avda Mariscal López, esq. Dr Pane 127, Asunción; tel. (21) 21-3143; e-mail embajadadominicanapy@hotmail.com; Ambassador MARINO BERIGÜETE.

Ecuador: Dr Bestard 861, esq. Juan XXIII, Barrio Manorá, Casilla 13162, Asunción; tel. (21) 61-4814; fax (21) 61-4813; e-mail eecuparaguay@mmree.gov.ec; internet www.ecuador.com.py; Chargé d'affaires a.i. PABLO SEBASTIÁN MARTÍNEZ MENDUIÑO.

France: Avda España 893, esq. Padre Pucheu, Casilla 97, Asunción; tel. (21) 21-2449; fax (21) 21-1690; e-mail chancellerie@ambafran.gov .py; internet www.ambafrance-py.org; Ambassador OLIVIER POUPARD.

Germany: Avda Venezuela 241, Casilla 471, Asunción; tel. (21) 21-4009; fax (21) 21-2863; e-mail info@asuncion.diplo.de; internet www .asuncion.diplo.de; Ambassador Dr CLAUDE ROBERT ELLNER.

Holy See: Ciudad del Vaticano 350, casi con 25 de Mayo, Casilla 83, Asunción (Apostolic Nunciature); tel. (21) 21-5139; fax (21) 21-2590; e-mail nunciatura@tigo.com.py; Apostolic Nuncio Most Rev. ELISEO ANTONIO ARIOTTI (Titular Archbishop of Vibiana).

Italy: Quesada 5871 con Bélgica, Asunción; tel. (21) 61-5620; fax (21) 61-5622; e-mail amb.assunzione@cert.esteri.it; internet www .ambassunzione.esteri.it; Ambassador ANTONELLA CAVALLARI.

Japan: Avda Mariscal López 2364, Casilla 1957, Asunción; tel. (21) 60-4616; fax (21) 60-6901; e-mail embajaponpy@rieder.net.py; internet www.py.emb-japan.go.jp; Ambassador TAKESHI KAMITANI.

Korea, Republic: Avda Rep. Argentina Norte 678, esq. Pacheco, Casilla 1303, Asunción; tel. (21) 60-5606; fax (21) 60-1376; e-mail paraguay@mofat.go.kr; internet pry.mofat.go.kr; Ambassador PARK DONG-WON.

Lebanon: San Francisco 629, esq. República Siria y Juan de Salazar, Asunción; tel. (21) 22-9375; fax (21) 23-2012; e-mail embajadadelibano@tigo.com.py; Ambassador ZEIN EL MOUSSAWI (designate).

Mexico: Avda España 1428, casi San Rafael, Casilla 1184, Asunción; tel. (21) 618-2000; fax (21) 618-2500; e-mail embamex@embamex .com.py; internet embamex.sre.gob.mx/paraguay; Ambassador FERNANDO ESTRADA SÁMANO.

Panama: Carmen Soler 3912, esq. Radio Operadores del Chaco, Barrio Seminario, Asunción; tel. and fax (21) 21-1091; e-mail embapana@gmail.com.py; Ambassador SABRINA DEL CARMEN GARCÍA BARRERA.

Peru: Edif. Santa Teresa, Dept 8B, Avda Santa Teresa 2415, Aviadores del Chaco, Casilla 433, Asunción; tel. (21) 60-0226; fax (21) 60-0901; e-mail embperu@embperu.com.py; internet www .embperu.org.py; Chargé d'affaires a.i. AUGUSTO ERNESTO SALAMANCA CASTRO.

Russia: Edif. Las Palmas, Molas López, esq. Dr C. Caceres y Julio Correa, Barrio Las Lomas, Asunción; tel. (21) 62-3733; fax (21) 62-3735; e-mail embruspar@ya.ru; internet www.paraguay.mid.ru; Ambassador GRIGÓRY MASHKÓV.

Spain: Edif. S. Rafael, 5° y 6°, Yegros 437, Asunción; tel. (21) 49-0686; fax (21) 44-5394; e-mail emb.asuncion@maec.es; internet www .maec.es/embajadas/asuncion; Ambassador DIEGO BERMEJO ROMERO DE TERREROS.

Switzerland: Edif. Parapití, 4°, Ofs 419–423, Juan E. O'Leary 409, esq. Estrella, Casilla 552, Asunción; tel. (21) 44-8022; fax (21) 44-5853; e-mail asu.vertretung@eda.admin.ch; internet www.eda .admin.ch/asuncion; Ambassador ALAIN-DENIS HENCHOZ.

Taiwan (Republic of China): Avda Mariscal López 1133 y Vicepresidente Sánchez, Casilla 503, Asunción; tel. (21) 21-3362; fax (21) 21-2373; e-mail embroc01@rieder.net.py; internet www .taiwanembassy.org/py; Ambassador JOSÉ MARÍA LIU.

USA: Avda Mariscal López 1776, Casilla 402, Asunción; tel. (21) 21-3715; fax (21) 21-3728; e-mail paraguayusembassy@state.gov; internet paraguay.usembassy.gov; Ambassador JAMES H. THESSIN.

Uruguay: Edif. Maria Luisa, 3°, Avda Boggiani 5832, esq. Alas Paraguayas, Asunción; tel. (21) 66-4244; fax (21) 60-1335; e-mail uruasun@embajadauruguay.com.py; internet www.embajada uruguay.com.py; Ambassador JUAN ENRIQUE FISCHER (recalled in June 2012).

Venezuela: Soldado Desconocido 348, Avda España, Barrio Manorá, Asunción; tel. (21) 66-4682; fax (21) 66-4683; e-mail despacho2@ embaven.org.py; internet paraguay.embajada.gob.ve; Ambassador JOSÉ FRANCISCO JAVIER ARRÚE DE PABLO.

Judicial System

The Corte Suprema de Justicia (Supreme Court of Justice) is composed of nine judges appointed on the recommendation of the Consejo de la Magistratura (Council of the Magistracy).

Corte Suprema de Justicia: Palacio de Justicia, 10°, Torre Norte, entre Avdas Alonso y Testanova, Asunción; tel. (21) 439-4000; internet www.pj.gov.py; Pres. Dr ANTONIO FRETES.

Attorney-General: JAVIER DÍAZ VERÓN.

Religion

The Roman Catholic Church is the established religion, although all sects are tolerated.

CHRISTIANITY

The Roman Catholic Church

For ecclesiastical purposes, Paraguay comprises one archdiocese, 11 dioceses and two Apostolic Vicariates. Some 91% of the population are Roman Catholics.

Bishops' Conference

Conferencia Episcopal Paraguaya, Calle Alberdi 782, Casilla 1436, 1209 Asunción; tel. (21) 49-0920; fax (21) 49-5115; e-mail cep@infonet .com.py; internet www.episcopal.org.py.

f. 1977, statutes approved 2000; Pres. Most Rev. EUSTAQUIO PASTOR CUQUEJO VERGA (Archbishop of Asunción).

Archbishop of Asunción: Most Rev. EUSTAQUIO PASTOR CUQUEJO VERGA, Arzobispado, Avda Mariscal López 130 esq. Independencia Nacional, Casilla 654, Asunción; tel. (21) 44-5551; fax (21) 44-4150; e-mail asa@pla.net.py.

The Anglican Communion

Paraguay constitutes a single diocese of the Iglesia Anglicana del Cono Sur de América (Anglican Church of the Southern Cone of America). The Presiding Bishop of the Church is the Bishop of Northern Argentina.

Bishop of Paraguay: Rt Rev. JOHN ELLISON, Iglesia Anglicana, Avda España casi Santos, Casilla 1124, Asunción; tel. (21) 20-0933; fax (21) 21-4328; e-mail iapar@sce.cnc.una.py.

The Baptist Church

Baptist Evangelical Convention of Paraguay: Casilla 1194, Asunción; tel. (21) 22-7110; fax (21) 21-0588; e-mail cebp@sce.cnc .una.py; internet www.ublaonline.org/paises/paraguay.htm; Exec. Sec. AUGUSTO VEGA.

THE LUTHERAN CHURCH

Evangelical Lutheran Church of Paraguay: Hohenau II, Itapua; e-mail ielpar@gmail.com; internet www.iglesialuterana.org.py; f. 1937; 4,009 mems (2011); Pres. Rev. NORBERTO GERKE.

BAHÁ'Í FAITH

National Spiritual Assembly of the Bahá'ís of Paraguay: Eligio Ayala 1456, Apdo 742, Asunción; tel. (21) 22-5747; e-mail bahai@ highway.com.py; internet www.bahai.org.py; Sec. MIRNA LLAMOSAS DE RIQUELME.

The Press

DAILIES

ABC Color: Yegros 745, Apdo 1421, Asunción; tel. (21) 49-1160; fax (21) 415-1310; e-mail azeta@abc.com.py; internet www.abc.com.py; f. 1967; independent; Dir ELENO MARTÍNEZ; Editor MABEL REHNFELDT; circ. 45,000.

La Nación: Avda Zavala Cué entre 2da y 3ra, Fernando de la Mora, Asunción; tel. (21) 51-2520; fax (21) 51-2535; e-mail redaccion@ lanacion.com.py; internet www.lanacion.com.py; f. 1995; Dir ALEJANDRO DOMÍNGUEZ WILSON-SMITH; Editor NÉSTOR INSAURRALDE; circ. 10,000.

Popular: Avda Mariscal López 2948, Calle McArthur, Asunción; tel. and fax (21) 60-3400; e-mail popular@mm.com.py; internet www .diariopopular.com.py; owned by Grupo Multimedia; circ. 28,000.

Ultima Hora: Benjamín Constant 658, Asunción; tel. (21) 49-6261; fax (21) 44-7071; e-mail ultimahora@uhora.com.py; internet www .ultimahora.com; f. 1973; independent; Dir OSCAR AYALA BOGARÍN; Editor ESTELA RUIZ; circ. 30,000.

PERIODICALS

Acción: CEPAG, Vicepresidente Sánchez 612, casi Azara, Asunción; tel. (21) 23-3541; e-mail revistaaccion@cepag.org.py; internet www .cepag.org.py/revistas_accion.php; f. 1923; monthly; published by the

Centro de Estudios Paraguayos Antonio Guasch (CEPAG—Jesuit org.); Sec. NURIDIA MOLINAS.

Revista Zeta: Eligio Ayala 2002, esq. Gral Bruguez, Asunción; tel. (21) 61-3392; fax (21) 61-3393; e-mail zeta@revistazeta.com.py; f. 2000; monthly; general interest; Dir ZUNI CASTIÑEIRA.

TVO: Santa Margarita de Youville 250, Santa María, Asunción; tel. (21) 67-2079; fax (21) 21-1236; e-mail sugerencias@teveo.com.py; internet www.teveo.com.py; f. 1992; fmrly *TeVeo*; weekly; news and society; Commercial Dir MARTINA LECLERCQ.

NEWS AGENCY

Información Pública Paraguay (IP Paraguay): Palacio de los López, Asunción; e-mail ipparaguay@gmail.com; internet www .ipparaguay.com.py; f. 2009; attached to the Office of the President.

Publishers

Arandurã Editorial: Tte Fariña, Asunción; fax (21) 21-4295; e-mail arandura@tigo.com.py; internet www.arandura.pyglobal.com; f. 1991; poetry, literature, social history.

La Colmena, SA: Asunción; tel. (21) 20-0428; Dir DAUMAS LADOUCE.

Dervish SA, Editorial: Avda Mariscal López 1735, CP 1584, Asunción; tel. (21) 21-2062; fax (21) 22-2580; e-mail dervish@ dervish.com.py; f. 1989; Co-ordinator JORGELINA MIGLIORISI; Vice-Pres. and Dir JANINE GIANI PATTERSON.

Ediciones Diálogo: Brasil 1391, Asunción; tel. (21) 20-0428; f. 1957; fine arts, literature, poetry, criticism; Man. MIGUEL ANGEL FERNÁNDEZ.

Ediciones Nizza: Eligio Ayala 1073, Casilla 2596, Asunción; tel. (21) 44-7160; medicine; Pres. Dr JOSÉ FERREIRA MARTÍNEZ.

Editorial Comuneros: Cerro Corá 289, Casilla 930, Asunción; tel. (21) 44-6176; fax (21) 44-4667; e-mail rolon@conexion.com.py; f. 1963; social history, poetry, literature, law; Man. OSCAR R. ROLÓN.

Editorial Servilibro: 25 de Mayo y México, Plaza Uruguaya, Asunción; fax (21) 44-4770; e-mail servilibro@gmail.com; internet www.servilibro.com.py; Dir-Gen. ELIZABETH BÁEZ.

Librería Intercontinental: Caballero 270, Calle Mariscal, Estigarribia, Asunción; tel. (21) 49-6991; fax (21) 44-8721; e-mail agatti@ libreriaintercontinental.com.py; internet www.libreriainter continental.com.py; political science, law, literature, poetry; Dir ALEJANDRO GATTI VAN HUMBEECK.

R. P. Ediciones: Eduardo Víctor Haedo 427, Asunción; tel. (21) 49-8040; Man. (vacant).

Santillana: Avda Venezuela 276, Asunción; fax (21) 20-2942; e-mail cls@santillana.com.py; internet www.santillana.com.py; educational books; Dir-Gen. JAVIER BARRETO.

ASSOCIATION

Cámara Paraguaya del Libro (CAPEL): Ayolas 129, esq. Benjamin Constant, Asunción; tel. (21) 49-7352; fax (21) 44-7053; internet www.capel.org.py; Pres. EDGAR RUIZ DÍAZ.

Broadcasting and Communications

REGULATORY AUTHORITY

Comisión Nacional de Telecomunicaciones (CONATEL): Presidente Franco 780, esq. Ayolas, Asunción; tel. (21) 44-0020; fax (21) 49-8982; e-mail info@conatel.gov.py; internet www.conatel.gov.py; Pres. CARLOS LEOPOLDO GÓMEZ ZELADA.

TELECOMMUNICATIONS

Claro (AMX Paraguay, SA): Avda Mariscal López 1730, Asunción; tel. (21) 249-9000; fax (21) 249-9099; e-mail empresaspy@claro.com .py; internet www.claro.com.py; subsidiary of América Móvil, SA de CV (Mexico); fmrly CTI Móvil; mobile cellular telephone services; Gen. Man. LUCIANO MAURONI.

Corporación Paraguaya de Comunicaciones, SA (COPACO): Edif. Morotí, 1°–2°, esq. Gen. Bruguez y Teodoro S. Mongelos, Casilla 2042, Asunción; tel. (21) 20-3800; fax (21) 20-3888; e-mail infoweb@ copaco.com.py; internet www.copaco.com.py; fmrly Administración Nacional de Telecomunicaciones (ANTELCO); adopted current name in 2001; state-owned; Pres. FRANCISCO JAVIER GALIANO.

VOX (Hola Paraguay, SA): Avda Mariscal López 3958, Calle República Argentina, Asunción; tel. (21) 619-9000; e-mail unidaddecompras@vox.net.py; internet www.vox.com.py; f. 1999; cellular service provider; Dir SANTE VALLESE.

Personal Paraguay (Núcleo, SA): Avda España 224, casi Máximo Lira, Asunción; tel. (21) 217-7000; internet www.personal.com.py;

f. 1998; subsidiary of Telecom Argentina; Gen. Man. JUAN CARLOS PEPE.

Tigo Paraguay: Edif. Casa Central Tigo, Avda Mariscal López 4050, esq. Avda República Argentina, Asunción; tel. (21) 618-9000; internet www.tigo.com.py; fmrly Telefónica Celular del Paraguay; relaunched in 2004 as Tigo; largest mobile operator with 2.8m. subscribers; subsidiary of Grupo Millicom International Cellular, Luxembourg; Gen. Man. TOM GUTJAHR.

BROADCASTING

Radio

FM Popular 103.1: Avda Mariscal López 2948, casi McArthur, Asunción; tel. (21) 60-3400; e-mail redaccion@mm.com.py; internet www.fmpopular.com; owned by Grupo Multimedia; Man. DAHIANA BRESANOVICH.

Radio Arapysandú: Avda Mariscal López y Capitán del Puerto San Ignacio, Misiones; tel. (82) 2374; fax (82) 2206; e-mail arapysanduam@gmail.com; internet arapysanduam.blogspot.com; f. 1982; AM; Dir HECTOR BOTTINO.

Radio Asunción: Avda Artígas y Capitán Lombardo 174, Asunción; tel. and fax (21) 28-2662; fax (21) 28-2661; e-mail radioasuncion@ cmm.com.py; internet www.radioasuncion.comyr.com; AM; Propr MIGUEL GERÓNIMO FERNÁNDEZ; Dir-Gen. BIBIANA LANDO MEYER.

Radio Cardinal: Comendador Nicolás Bó 1334 y Guaraníes, Casilla 2532, Lambaré, Asunción; tel. (21) 31-0555; fax (21) 30-3089; e-mail info@cardinal.com.py; internet www.cardinal.com.py; f. 1991; AM and FM; Pres. ALFREDO CHENA; Man. Dir ANDREA BITTAR.

Radio Cáritas: Avda Kubitschek 661 y Azara, Asunción; tel. (21) 21-3570; fax (21) 20-4161; e-mail caritas@caritas.com.py; internet www .caritas.com.py; f. 1936; station of the Archdiocese of Asunción and the Universidad Católica Nuestra Señora de la Asunción; AM; Dir-Gen. JORGE BAZÁN.

Radio Guairá: Presidente Franco 788 y Alejo García, Villarica; tel. (541) 42130; fax (541) 42385; e-mail fmguaira@gmail.com; internet www.fmguaira.com; f. 1950; AM and FM; Dir ENRIQUE TRAVERSI.

Radio Itapiru SRL: Avda San Blás, esq. Coronel Julián Sánchez, Ciudad del Este; tel. (61) 57-2207; fax (61) 57-2210; internet www .radioitapiru.com; f. 1969; AM and FM; Dir-Gen. RICHARD ARANDA.

Radio Nacional del Paraguay: Blas Garay 241, esq. Iturbe y Yegros, Asunción; tel. (21) 39-0374; fax (21) 39-0375; e-mail direccion@radionacionaldelparaguay.com.py; internet www .radionacionaldelparaguay.com.py; f. 1957; AM and FM; Dir JUDITH MARIA VERA DE BIRBAUMER.

Radio Ñandutí: Choferes del Chaco y Carmen Soler, Asunción; tel. (21) 60-4308; fax (21) 60-6074; e-mail prensaam@holdingderadio .com.py; internet www.nanduti.com.py; f. 1962; FM; Dir HUMBERTO LEÓN RUBÍN.

Radio Primero de Marzo: Avda Gen. Perón y Concepción Prieto Yegros, Casilla 1456, Asunción; tel. (21) 30-0380; fax (21) 33-3427; e-mail prensa@780am.com.py; internet www.780am.com.py; AM and FM; Dir-Gen. ANGEL R. GUERREÑOS.

Radio Uno: Avda Mariscal López 2948, Asunción; tel. (21) 61-2151; fax prensa650@mm.com.py; internet www.radiouno.com.py; f. 1968 as Radio Chaco Boreal; AM; Dir JAVIER MARÍA PIROVANO SILVA.

Radio Venus: Avda República Argentina y Souza, Asunción; tel. (21) 61-0151; fax (21) 60-6484; e-mail info@venus.com.py; internet www.venus.com.py; f. 1987; FM; Dir ANGEL AGUILERA.

Radio Ysapy: Independencia Nacional 1260, 1°, Asunción; tel. (21) 44-4037; e-mail info@radioysapy.com.py; internet www.radioysapy .com.py; FM; Dir JOSÉ TOMÁS CABRIZA SALVIONI.

Television

Paravision: Bélgica 4498, casi Mariscal López, Asunción; tel. (21) 66-4380; e-mail francisco.gomez@paravision.com.py; internet www .paravision.com.py; Exec. Dir MARIAN ALONSO; Gen. Man. FRANCISCO GÓMEZ.

Red Guaraní (Canal 2): Complejo Textilia, Gen. Santos 1024, casi Concordia, Asunción; tel. (21) 20-5444; e-mail oescobar@redguarani .com.py; internet www.redguarani.com.py; Exec. Dir FLAVIO FLORENTÍN; Gen. Man. OSCAR ESCOBAR.

Sistema Nacional de Televisión Cerro Corá—Canal 9 (SNT): Avda Carlos Antonio López 572, entre Colón y Santiago Leguizamón, Asunción; tel. (21) 42-4222; e-mail info@snt.com.py; internet www .snt.com.py; f. 1965; commercial; Dir MARCELO FLEITAS.

La Tele-Canal 11 (Hispanoamérica TV del Paraguay): Avda Eusebio Ayala 2995, esq. Pasaje Tembetary, Asunción; tel. (21) 415-7400; e-mail prensa@latele.com.py; internet www.latele.com.py; Dir LEONARDO SALOMÓN.

Teledifusora Paraguaya—Canal 13: Comendador Nicolás Bó y Guaraníes, Lambaré, Asunción; tel. (21) 33-2823; fax (21) 33-2826;

e-mail info@canal13.com.py; internet www.rpc.com.py; f. 1981; Pres. ANDREA VITTAR DE BENÍTEZ; Dir-Gen. GUSTAVO CUBILLA.

Telefuturo-Canal 4 (TV Acción, SA): Andrade 1499 y O'Higgins, Asunción; tel. (21) 618-4000; fax (21) 618-4166; e-mail telefuturo@telefuturo.com.py; internet www.telefuturo.com.py; Gen. Man. MARCOS GALANTI.

TV Pública Paraguay-Canal 14: Avda Alberdi 633, casi Gen. Díaz, Asunción; tel. (21) 49-4000; fax (21) 49-4050; e-mail info@tvpublica.com.py; internet www.tvpublica.com.py; Dir CRISTIAN TURRINI.

Finance

(cap. = capital; res = reserves; dep. = deposits; m. = million; brs = branches; amounts in guaraníes, unless otherwise indicated)

BANKING

Superintendencia de Bancos: Edif. Banco Central del Paraguay, Avda Federación Rusa y Avda Marecos, Barrio Santo Domingo, Asunción; tel. (21) 60-8148; fax (21) 419-2403; e-mail informaciones@bcp.gov.py; Supt NELSON DANIEL VALIENTE SAUCEDO.

Central Bank

Banco Central del Paraguay: Avda Federación Rusa y Cabo 1° Marecos, Casilla 861, Barrio Santo Domingo, Asunción; tel. (21) 60-8011; fax (21) 619-2328; e-mail informaciones@bcp.gov.py; internet www.bcp.gov.py; f. 1952; cap. 683,092.0m., res –1,577,631.0m., dep. 11,942,860.0m. (Dec. 2009); Pres. JORGE RAÚL CORVALÁN MENDOZA; Gen. Man. JORGE AURELIO VILLALBA LEGUIZAMON.

Development Banks

Banco Nacional de Fomento: Independencia Nacional, entre Cerro Cora y 25 de Mayo, Asunción; tel. (21) 44-4440; fax (21) 44-6056; e-mail correo@bnf.gov.py; internet www.bnf.gov.py; f. 1961 to take over the deposit and private banking activities of the Banco del Paraguay; cap. 294,108.5m., res 131,108m., dep. 2,305,433.3m. (Dec. 2011); Pres. CARLOS ALBERTO PEREIRA OLMEDO; Sec.-Gen. CÉSAR LEONARDO FURIASSE ROLÓN; 52 brs.

Crédito Agrícola de Habilitación (CAH): Caríos 362 y Willam Richardson, Asunción; tel. (21) 569-0100; fax (21) 55-4956; e-mail info@cah.gov.py; internet www.cah.gov.py; f. 1943; Pres. CARLOS JAVIER GONZÁLEZ DEL PUERTO.

Fondo Ganadero: Avda Mariscal López 1669 esq. República Dominicana, Asunción; tel. (21) 22-7288; fax (21) 22-7378; e-mail info@fondogan.gov.py; internet www.fondogan.gov.py; f. 1969; govt-owned; Pres. JUAN FERNANDO PERONI CAZAL RIBEIRO.

Commercial Banks

Banco Amambay, SA: Avda Aviadores del Chaco, entre San Martín y Pablo Alborno, Asunción; tel. (21) 60-8831; fax (21) 60-8813; e-mail bcoama@bancoamambay.com.py; internet www.bancoamambay.com.py; f. 1992; cap. 138,870m., res 56,597.6m., dep. 1,144,845.1m. (Dec. 2011); Pres. and Gen. Man. HUGO JAVIER PORTILLO SOSA; 6 brs.

Banco Atlas, SA: Avda Eligio Ayala 1049, entre Avdas Estados Unidos y Brasil, Asunción; tel. (21) 217-5000; fax (21) 217-5142; e-mail consultas@atlas.com.py; internet www.bancoatlas.com.py; f. 1989 as Cristal Financiera, SA; changed name as above in 2010; cap. 16,200m., res 27,690.6m., dep. 337,957m. (Dec. 2010); Pres. MIGUEL A. ZALDÍVAR SILVERA; Gen. Man. JUAN CARLOS MARTÍN.

Banco Bilbao Vizcaya Argentaria Paraguaya, SA: Yegros 435, esq. 25 de Mayo, Casilla 824, Asunción; tel. (21) 417-6000; fax (21) 44-8103; e-mail info@bbva.com.py; internet www.bbva.com.py; f. 1961 as Banco Exterior de España, SA; present name adopted in 2000; cap. 325,000m., res 89,390.1m., dep. 5,920,062.4m. (Dec. 2011); Pres. VICENTE LUIS BOGLIOLO DEL RÍO; 5 brs.

Banco Continental, SAECA: Estrella 621, Calle 15 de Agosto, Asunción; tel. (21) 44-2002; fax (21) 44-2001; e-mail contil@connexion.com.py; internet www.bancontinental.com.py; f. 1980; cap. 299,027.0m. (Dec. 2010), res 520,557m., dep. 18,260m. (Dec. 2011); Pres. CARLOS ESPÍNOLA; 28 brs.

Banco Itaú Paraguay: Oliva 349, esq. Chile y Alberdi, Asunción; tel. (21) 617-1000; fax (21) 417-1372; e-mail sac@itau.com.py; internet www.itau.com.py; f. 1978; known as Interbanco until 2009; cap. 500,000m., res 264,151.9m., dep. 6,750,901m. (Dec. 2011); Pres. VIVIANA VARAS; 17 brs.

Sudameris Bank, SAECA: Independencia Nacional y Cerro Corá, Casilla 1433, Asunción; tel. (21) 44-8670; fax (21) 44-4024; e-mail gerencia@sudameris.com.py; internet www.sudamerisbank.com.py; f. 1961; savings and commercial bank; cap. 160,194.6m., res 102,411.7m., dep. 2,394,456.2m. (Dec. 2011); Chair. CONOR McENROY; Vice-Chair. GERMÁN ROJAS; 8 brs.

Banking Association

Asociación de Bancos del Paraguay: Aca Caraya 397, esq. Leandro Prieto, Asunción; tel. (21) 22-3571; fax (21) 21-0440; e-mail asoban@asoban.org.py; internet asoban.org.py; mems: Paraguayan banks and foreign banks with brs in Asunción; Pres. PEDRO JERÓNIMO NASSER.

STOCK EXCHANGE

Bolsa de Valores y Productos de Asunción, SA: 15 de Agosto 640, esq. General Díaz y Víctor Haedo, Asunción; tel. (21) 44-2445; fax (21) 44-2446; e-mail rodrigo.callizo@bvpasa.com.py; internet www.bvpasa.com.py; f. 1977; Pres. RODRIGO CALLIZO LÓPEZ MOREIRA.

INSURANCE

Supervisory Authority

Superintendencia de Seguros: Edif. Banco Central del Paraguay, 1°, Federación Rusa y Sargento Marecos, Asunción; tel. (21) 619-2380; fax (21) 619-2637; e-mail dmarti@bcp.gov.py; internet www.bcp.gov.py; Supt DIEGO ARTURO MARTÍNEZ SÁNCHEZ.

Principal Companies

La Agrícola SA de Seguros Generales: Mariscal López 5377 y Concejal Vargas, Asunción; tel. (21) 60-9509; fax (21) 60-9606; e-mail sagricola@tigo.com.py; internet www.seguroslaagricola.com.py; f. 1982; general; Pres. CARLOS ALBERTO LEVI SOSA.

ALFA SA de Seguros y Reaseguros: Yegros 944 esq. Tte Fariña, Asunción; tel. (21) 44-9992; fax (21) 44-9991; e-mail alfa.seg@conexion.com.py; Pres. NICOLÁS SARUBBI ZAYAS.

Aseguradora del Este SA de Seguros: Avda República Argentina 778, entre Pacheco y Souza, Asunción; tel. (21) 60-5015; e-mail ngoiris@aesaseguros.com.py; internet www.aesaseguros.com.py; Pres. VÍCTOR ANDRÉS RIBEIRO ESPÍNOLA.

Aseguradora Paraguaya, SA (ASEPASA): Avda Guido Boggiani 5848, Asunción; tel. (21) 61-2870; fax (21) 22-2217; e-mail asepasa@asepasa.com.py; internet www.asepasa.com.py; f. 1976; Pres. and Gen. Man. GERARDO TORCIDA CONEJERO.

Aseguradora Yacyretá SA de Seguros y Reaseguros: Oliva 685, esq. Juan E. O'Leary y 15 de Agosto, Asunción; tel. (21) 45-2374; fax (21) 44-6478; e-mail spalomar@yacyreta.com.py; internet yacyretaseguros.com; f. 1980; Pres. OSCAR HARRISON JACQUET; Vice-Pres. NORMAN HARRISON PALEARI; Gen. Man. EDUARDO BARRIOS PERINI; 5 brs.

Atalaya SA de Seguros Generales: Independencia Nacional 565, 1°, esq. Azara y Cerro Corá, Asunción; tel. (21) 49-2811; fax (21) 49-6966; e-mail ataseg@telesurf.com.py; internet www.atalayaseguros.com; f. 1964; general; Pres. KARIN M. DOLL.

Cenit, SA: Ayolas 1082, Calle Jejui, Asunción; tel. (21) 49-4972; fax (21) 44-9502; e-mail cenit@cenit.com.py; internet www.cenit.com.py; Pres. Dr FELIPE OSCAR ARMELE BONZI.

Central SA de Seguros: Edif. Betón I, 1° y 2°, Eduardo Víctor Haedo 179, Independencia Nacional, Casilla 1802, Asunción; tel. (21) 49-4654; fax (21) 49-4655; e-mail centralseguros@centralseguros.com.py; internet www.centralseguros.com.py; f. 1977; Pres. MIGUEL JACOBO VILLASANTI; Gen. Man. ALBERTO AYALA.

El Comercio Paraguayo SA Cía de Seguros Generales: Alberdi 453 y Oliva, Asunción; tel. (21) 49-2324; fax (21) 49-3562; e-mail elcomercioparaguayo@elcomercioparaguayo.com.py; internet www.elcomercioparaguayo.com.py; f. 1947; Dir VICTORIA MARTÍNEZ DE ELIZECHE.

La Consolidada SA de Seguros y Reaseguros: Chile 719 y Eduardo Víctor Haedo, Casilla 1182, Asunción; tel. (21) 49-5174; fax (21) 44-5795; e-mail info@consolidada.com.py; internet www.consolidada.com.py; f. 1961; Pres. JUAN CARLOS DELGADILLO ECHAGÜE.

Fénix SA de Seguros y Reaseguros: Iturbe 823 y Fulgencio R. Moreno, Asunción; tel. (21) 49-4909; fax (21) 44-5643; e-mail fenixsa@fenixseguros.com.py; internet www.fenixseguros.com.py; Pres. JAIME LAUFER.

Garantía SA de Seguros y Reaseguros: 25 de Mayo 640, Asunción; tel. (21) 44-5452; fax (21) 49-0678; e-mail administracion@migarantia.com.py; internet www.migarantia.com.py; Pres. ESTEBAN PARDO.

Grupo General de Seguros: Avda España 2210, Asunción; tel. (21) 23-4000; fax (21) 23-4200; e-mail general_de_seguros@ggeneral.com.py; internet www.ggeneral.com.py; Pres. HUGO FERNANDO CAMPERCHIOLI.

La Independencia de Seguros y Reaseguros, SA: Edif. Parapatí, 1°, Juan E. O'Leary 409, esq. Estrella, Casilla 980, Asunción; tel. (21) 44-7021; fax (21) 44-8996; e-mail liseguros@laindependencia.com.py;

internet www.laindependencia.com.py; f. 1965; Pres. EDMUNDO EMILIO RICHER BÉCKER.

Intercontinental SA de Seguros y Reaseguros: Iturbe 1047 con Teniente Fariña, Altos, Asunción; tel. (21) 49-2348; fax (21) 49-1227; e-mail info@intercontinentaldeseguros.com.py; internet www .intercontinentaldeseguros.com.py; f. 1978; Pres. Dr JUAN MÓDICA LUCENTE; Gen. Man. MARIO VICENTE MÓDICA LUCENTE.

Mapfre Paraguay, SA: Avda Mariscal López 910 y General Aquino, Asunción; tel. (21) 217-6000; fax (21) 217-6107; e-mail sac@mapfre .com.py; internet www.mapfre.com.py; Pres. ZAIDA GABAS DE REQUENA.

La Meridional Paraguaya SA de Seguros: Iturbe 1046, Teniente Fariña, Asunción; tel. (21) 49-4756; fax (21) 49-8826; e-mail f .mujica@meridional.com.py; internet www.meridional.com.py; Pres. TITO LIVIO MUJICA VARELA.

La Paraguaya SA de Seguros: Estrella 675, 7°, Asunción; tel. (21) 49-1367; fax (21) 44-8235; e-mail lps@laparaguaya.com.py; internet www.laparaguaya.com.py; f. 1905; Pres. JUAN BOSCH BEYNEN.

Patria SA de Seguros y Reaseguros: General Santos 715 esq. Siria, Asunción; tel. (21) 22-5250; fax (21) 21-4001; e-mail segurospatria@segurospatria.com.py; f. 1967; general; Pres. Dr PABLO PARRA GARCÍA.

El Productor SA de Seguros y Reaseguros: Ind. Nacional 811 esq. Fulgencio R. Moreno, 8°, Asunción; tel. (21) 44-8620; fax (21) 49-1599; e-mail info@elproductor.com.py; internet www.elproductor .com.py; Pres. REINALDO PAVÍA MALDONADO.

Regional SA de Seguros y Reaseguros: Avda Irrazábal y Ruta VI, Encarnación; tel. (71) 20-3700; fax (21) 20-6640; e-mail regisesa@ itacom.com.py; Pres. JUAN A. DIAZ DE VIVAR PRIETO.

Rumbos SA de Seguros: Estrella 851, Ayolas, Casilla 1017, Asunción; tel. (21) 44-9488; fax (21) 44-9492; e-mail rumbos@rumbos.com .py; internet www.rumbos.com.py; f. 1960; general; Pres. MIGUEL A. LARREINEGABE LESME; Man. Dir MIGUEL LARREINEGABE BENZA.

La Rural SA de Seguros: Avda Mariscal López 1082, esq. Mayor Bullo, Casilla 21, Asunción; tel. (21) 22-8805; fax (21) 44-1592; e-mail larural@larural.com.py; internet www.larural.com.py; f. 1920; Pres. MARIA CRISTINA MATSUMIYA DE TANAKA; Gen. Man. JUAN FRANCISCO PEREZ SALDÍVAR.

Seguros Chaco SA de Seguros y Reaseguros: Mariscal Estigarribia 982, Casilla 3248, Asunción; tel. (21) 44-7118; fax (21) 44-9551; e-mail seguroschaco@pla.net.py; f. 1977; general; Pres. EMILIO VELILLA LACONICH.

Seguros Generales, SA (SEGESA): Edif. SEGESA, 1°, Oliva 393 esq. Alberdi, Casilla 802, Asunción; tel. (21) 49-1362; fax (21) 49-1360; e-mail segesa@segesa.com.py; internet segesa.com.py; f. 1956; Pres. CÉSAR AVALOS.

El Sol del Paraguay, Cía de Seguros y Reaseguros, SA: Cerro Corá 1031, Asunción; tel. (21) 49-1110; fax (21) 21-0604; e-mail elsol@ elsol.com.py; internet www.elsol.com.py; f. 1978; Pres. MIGUEL ANGEL BERNI CENTURIÓN; Vice-Pres. CAROLINA VEGA DE ONETTO.

Insurance Association

Asociación Paraguaya de Cías de Seguros: 15 de Agosto, esq. Lugano, Casilla 1435, Asunción; tel. (21) 44-6474; fax (21) 44-4343; e-mail apcs@consultronic.com.py; internet www.apcs.org.py; f. 1963; Pres. ANTONIO VACCARO PAVIA; Sec. GERARDO RUBÉN RAPPENECKER COSCIA.

Trade and Industry

GOVERNMENT AGENCIES

Instituto Nacional de Desarrollo Rural y de la Tierra (INDERT): Tacuary 276, esq. Mariscal Estigarribia, Asunción; tel. and fax (21) 44-3161; e-mail presidencia@indert.gov.py; internet www.indert.gov.py; f. 2003; land reform institute; Pres. JUAN CARLOS RAMÍREZ MONTALBETTI; Gen. Man. JORGE GALEANO.

Instituto Nacional de Tecnología, Normalización y Metrología (INTN): Avda General Artigas 3973 y General Roa, Casilla 967, Asunción; tel. (21) 29-0160; fax (21) 29-0873; e-mail intn@intn.gov .py; internet www.intn.gov.py; national standards institute; Dir-Gen. MARIO GUSTAVO LEIVA ENRIQUE.

Instituto de Previsión Social: Edif. de la Caja Central, Constitución y Luis Alberto de Herrera, Casilla 437, Asunción; tel. (21) 22-3141; fax (21) 22-3654; e-mail secretaria_general@ips.gov.py; internet www.ips.gov.py; f. 1943; responsible for employees' welfare and health insurance scheme; Pres. LUIS ALBERTO LÓPEZ GONZÁLEZ.

DEVELOPMENT ORGANIZATIONS

Alter Vida (Centro de Estudios y Formación para el Ecodesarrollo): Itapúa 1372, esq. Primer Presidente y Río Monday, Barrio Trinidad,

Asunción; tel. (21) 29-8842; fax (21) 29-8845; e-mail info@altervida .org.py; internet www.altervida.org.py; f. 1985; ecological devt; Exec. Dir VÍCTOR BENÍTEZ INSFRÁN.

Centro de Cooperación Empresarial y Desarrollo Industrial (CEDIAL): Edif. UIP, 2°, Cerro Corá 1038, esq. Estados Unidos y Brasil, Asunción; tel. and fax (21) 23-0047; e-mail cedial@cedial.org .py; internet www.cedial.org.py; f. 1991; promotes commerce and industrial devt; Gen. Man. HERNÁN RAMÍREZ.

Centro de Información y Recursos para el Desarrollo (CIRD): Avda Mariscal López 2029, esq. Acá Carayá, Casilla 1580, Asunción; tel. (21) 22-6071; fax (21) 21-2540; e-mail cird@cird.org.py; internet www.cird.org.py; f. 1988; information and resources for devt orgs; Exec. Pres. AGUSTÍN CARRIZOSA.

Instituto de Biotecnología Agrícola (INBIO): Avda Brasilia 939, Calle Ciancio, Asunción; tel. (21) 23-3892; e-mail info@inbio.org.py; internet www.inbio.org.py; bio-technological research for agricultural devt; Pres. RICARDO WOLLMEISTER; Sec. LUIS MARÍA CORVALÁN.

Instituto Paraguayo de Artesanía (IPA): Teófilo del Puerto, entre Capt. Pedro Villamayor y Dr Prieto, Barrio Villa Aurelia, Asunción; tel. (21) 52-6533; fax (21) 60-0035; e-mail ipa@artesania .gov.py; internet www.artesania.gov.py; f. 2004; promotes handicraft industries; Pres. CLAUDIA ALDANA DÍAZ CORTAZAR.

Instituto Paraguayo del Indígena (INDI): Don Bosco 745, entre Haedo y Humaita, Asunción; tel. (21) 49-7317; fax (21) 44-0046; e-mail informes@indi.gov.py; internet www.indi.gov.py; f. 1981; responsible for welfare of Indian population; Pres. RUBÉN QUESNEL.

Red de Inversiones y Exportaciones (REDIEX): Avda Mariscal López 3333, CP 1892, Asunción; tel. (21) 616-3028; fax (21) 616-3034; e-mail info@rediex.gov.py; internet www.rediex.gov.py; replaced ProParaguay in 2007; responsible for promoting investment in Paraguay and the export of national products; Dir OSCAR STARK ROBLEDO.

Red Rural de Organizaciones Privadas de Desarrollo (Red Rural): Paraguari 1162, Calle Gaspar Rodríguez de Francia, Asunción; tel. (21) 44-3022; e-mail redrural@redrural.org.py; internet www.redrural.org.py; f. 1989; co-ordinating body for rural devt orgs; Gen. Co-ordinator HERMES GARCÍA; Sec. JOSÉ LARROZA.

Secretaría Técnica de Planificación: Estrella 505, esq. 14 de Mayo, Asunción; tel. (21) 45-0422; fax (21) 49-6510; e-mail comunicacion@stp.gov.py; internet www.stp.gov.py; govt body responsible for overall economic and social planning; Minister RICHARD WILLIAM KENT FERREIRA.

CHAMBERS OF COMMERCE

Cámara Nacional de Comercio y Servicios de Paraguay: Estrella 540, esq. 14 de Mayo y 15 de Agosto, Asunción; tel. (21) 49-3321; fax (21) 44-0817; e-mail info@ccparaguay.com.py; internet www.ccparaguay.com.py; f. 1898; fmrly Cámara y Bolsa de Comercio; adopted current name 2002; Pres. BELTRÁN MACCHI SALIN; Gen. Man. MIGUEL RIQUELME OLAZAR.

Cámara de Comercio Paraguayo-Americana: 25 de Mayo 2090, esq. Mayor Bullo, Asunción; tel. (21) 22-2160; fax (21) 22-1926; e-mail kcoronel@pamcham.com.py; internet www.pamcham.com.py; f. 1981; Pres. ALEJANDRO CONTI; Exec. Dir KAREN CORONEL; c. 300 mem. cos.

Cámara de Comercio Paraguayo-Argentina: Banco de la Nación Argentina, entre Palma y Alberdi (al lado del Consulado Argentino), Asunción; tel. (21) 49-7804; fax (21) 49-7805; e-mail administracion@ campyarg.org.py; internet www.campyarg.org.py; f. 1991; Pres. ERNESTO GÓMEZ ESPECHE; Man. MARCELA ESCOBAR.

Cámara de Comercio Paraguayo-Británica: Edif. Internacional Faro, 2°, Avda Gen. Díaz 521, Asunción; tel. (21) 49-8274; e-mail britcham@conexion.com.py; internet www.britchampy.com; Pres. GUILLERMO ALONSO.

Cámara de Comercio Paraguayo-Francesa (CCPF): Yegros 837, 1°, Of. 12, CP 3009, Asunción; tel. (21) 49-7852; fax (21) 44-6324; e-mail info@ccpf.com.py; internet www.ccpf.com.py; Pres. ANTONIO LUIS PECCI MILTOS; Man. IRIS FELIU DE FLEITAS.

Cámara de Industria y Comercio Paraguayo-Alemana: Avda República Argentina 1616, Calle Alfredo Seiferheld, Casilla 1887, Asunción; tel. (21) 61-5848; fax (21) 61-5844; e-mail rrpp@ahkasu .com.py; internet www.ahkasu.com.py; f. 1956; Pres. WILFRIDO FERNÁNDEZ; Gen. Man. HELMUT L. ZAGEL.

AGRICULTURAL, INDUSTRIAL AND EMPLOYERS' ORGANIZATIONS

Asociación de Empresas Financieras del Paraguay (ADEFI): Edif. Ahorros Paraguayos, Torre II, 6°, Of. 05, General Díaz 471, Asunción; tel. (21) 44-8298; fax (21) 49-8071; e-mail adefi@adefi.org .py; internet www.adefi.org.py; f. 1975; grouping of financial cos; Pres. JULIO ALBERTO SQUEF; Sec. FELIPE BURRÓ GUSTALE.

Asociación Paraguaya de la Calidad: Eduardo Victor Haedo 680, O'Leary, Asunción; tel. (21) 44-7348; fax (21) 45-0705; e-mail apc@apc.org.py; internet www.apc.org.py; f. 1988; grouping of cos to promote quality of goods and services; Pres. JORGE MIGUEL BRUNOTTE; Sec. SANTIAGO LLANO CAVINA.

Asociación de Productores de Soja, Oleaginosas y Cereales del Paraguay (APS): Edif. Maynumby, 1°, Of. 11, Avda Mariscal López, Ciudad del Este, Alto Paraná; tel. (61) 570-115; e-mail aps_central@aps.org.py; internet www.aps.org.py; soya and grain producers' asscn; Pres. FRANCISCO REGIS MERELES; Sec. FABIAN PEREIRA.

Asociación Rural del Paraguay (ARP): Ruta Transchaco, Km 14, Mariano Roque Alonso; tel. (21) 75-4412; e-mail ania@arp.org.py; internet www.arp.org.py; grouping of agricultural cos and farmers; Pres. GERMÁN RUIZ; Exec. Dir VÍCTOR PERSANO.

Cámara Paraguaya de Exportadores de Cereales y Oleaginosas (CAPECO): Avda Brasilia 840, Asunción; tel. (21) 20-8855; fax (21) 21-3971; e-mail capeco@capeco.org.py; internet www.capeco.org.py; f. 1980; grain exporters' asscn; Pres. ULRICH BAUER; Gen. Man. IGNACIO SANTIVIAGO.

Centro de Importadores del Paraguay (CIP): Avda Brasilia 1947, casi Artigas, Casillas 2609, Asunción; tel. (21) 29-9800; e-mail cip@cip.org.py; internet www.cip.org.py; f. 1939; importers' asscn; Pres. MAX HABER NEUMANN; Man. JULIO SÁNCHEZ LASPINA.

Federación de Cooperativas de Producción Ltda (FECOPROD): Sacramento 2279, Calle Teniente Silverio Molinas, Asunción; tel. (21) 29-7050; fax (21) 29-4277; e-mail info@fecoprod.com.py; internet www.fecoprod.com.py; f. 1975; agricultural producers' org.; Pres. GUSTAV SAWATZKY; Sec. ANDREAS ENS.

Federación de la Producción, Industria y Comercio (FEPRINCO): Edif. Union Club, Palma 751, 3°, esq. O'Leary y Ayolas, Asunción; tel. (21) 44-4963; fax (21) 44-6638; e-mail feprinco@quanta.com.py; internet www.feprinco.org.py; org. of private sector business execs; Pres. MAX HABER.

Unión de Gremios de la Producción (UGP): Avda Brasilia 939 y Calle Ciancio, Asunción; tel. (21) 22-4232; internet www.ugp.org.py; f. 2005; agricultural producers' org.; Pres. RAMÓN SÁNCHEZ VEGA.

Unión Industrial Paraguaya (UIP): Avda Sacramento 945, Calle Profesor Chávez, Asunción; tel. (21) 60-6988; fax (21) 21-3360; e-mail uip@uip.org.py; internet www.uip.org.py; f. 1936; org. of business entrepreneurs; Pres. EDUARDO FELIPPO; Sec. RAÚL HOECKLE.

UTILITIES

Electricity

Administración Nacional de Electricidad (ANDE): Avda España 1268, casi Padre Cardozo, Asunción; tel. (21) 21-1001; fax (21) 21-2371; e-mail luis_rojas@ande.gov.py; internet www.ande.gov.py; f. 1949; national electricity board; Pres. CARLOS DIONISIO HEISELE SOSA; Sec.-Gen. LUIS RAMÓN ROJAS IBARRA.

Entidad Binacional Yacyretá: General Díaz 831 esq. Ayolas y Montevideo, Edif. Héroes de Marzo, Asunción; tel. and fax (21) 44-5611; internet www.eby.gov.py; owned jtly by Paraguay and Argentina; operates the hydroelectric dam at Yacyretá on the Paraná river, completed in 1998; installed capacity of 3,200 MW; 14,673 GWh of electricity produced in 2007; Dir (Paraguay) ENRIQUE CÁCERES.

Itaipú Binacional: Centro Administrativo, Ruta Internacional Km 3.5, Avda Monseñor Rodríguez 150, Ciudad del Este, Depto Alto Paraná; tel. (61) 599-8989; e-mail itaipu@itaipu.gov.br; internet www.itaipu.gov.py; f. 1974; jtly owned by Paraguay and Brazil; hydroelectric power station on Brazilian–Paraguayan border; 98,287 GWh of electricity produced in 2012; Dir-Gen. (Paraguay) FRANKLIN RAFAEL BOCCIA ROMAÑACH.

Water

Empresa de Servicios Sanitarios del Paraguay, SA (ESSAP): José Berges 516, entre Brasil y San José, Asunción; tel. (21) 21-0330; fax (21) 21-2624; e-mail secretaria@essap.com.py; internet www.essap.com.py; f. 1954 as Corporación de Obras Sanitarias (CORPOSANA); responsible for public water supply, sewage disposal and drainage; Pres. ANDRÉS RIVAROLA CASACCIA.

TRADE UNIONS

Central Nacional de Trabajadores (CNT): Piribebuy 1078, Asunción; tel. (21) 44-4084; fax (21) 49-2154; e-mail cnt@cnt.org.py; internet www.cnt.org.py; Sec.-Gen. MIGUEL ZAYAS; 120,840 mems (2007).

Central Unitaria de Trabajadores Autentica (CUT-A): R. Moreno 566, esq. Paraguari y México, Asunción; tel. (21) 45-1212; e-mail cutautentica@hotmail.com; internet cutautentica.org.py; Pres. BERNARDO ROJAS DACOSTA; Sec.-Gen. VICTOR PEDRO FERREIRA.

Confederación Paraguaya de Trabajadores (CPT): Yegros 1333, esq. Simón Bolívar, Asunción; tel. 981878479 (mobile); e-mail conpartra@gmail.com; f. 1951; Sec.-Gen. FRANCISCO BRITEZ RUIZ; 43,500 mems from 189 affiliated groups.

Coordinadora Agrícola del Paraguay (CAP): Juan B. Flores y Tacuary, Hernandarias; tel. (983) 52-7003; e-mail bhjca@tigo.com.py; farmers' org.; Pres. HÉCTOR CRISTALDO; Sec.-Gen. ALBERTO ESTECHE.

Federación Nacional Campesina (FNC): Nangariry 1196, esq. Cacique Cará Cará, Asunción; tel. (21) 51-2384; internet fncmarandu.blogspot.com; grouping of peasants' orgs; Sec. ADRIÁN VÁZQUEZ.

Transport

RAILWAYS

Ferrocarriles del Paraguay, SA (FEPASA): México 145, Casilla 453, Asunción; tel. (21) 44-6789; fax (21) 44-3273; e-mail informaciones@ferrocarriles.com.py; internet www.ferrocarriles.com.py; f. 1854; state-owned since 1961; scheduled for privatization; 376 km of track; Pres. MARCELO WAGNER.

ROADS

In 2010 there were an estimated 32,059 km of roads, of which 15.2% were paved. The Pan-American Highway runs for over 700 km in Paraguay and the Trans-Chaco Highway extends from Asunción to Bolivia. In 2011 the Government announced a US $170m. plan to improve some 5,150 km of roads and 189 bridges in the country's eastern region, under its national rural roads programme.

SHIPPING

The rivers Paraguay and Paraná constitute the principal waterways for cargo transportation in the country. There are 3,100 km of navigable waterways. The country has six ports of which the port of Asunción is the most important. At December 2012 the flag registered fleet comprised 155 vessels, totalling 157,086 grt.

Administración Nacional de Navegación y Puertos (ANNP) (National Shipping and Ports Administration): Colón y El Paraguayo Independiente, Asunción; tel. (21) 49-2883; fax (21) 49-7485; e-mail gciacomercial@annp.gov.py; internet www.annp.gov.py; f. 1965; responsible for ports services and maintaining navigable channels in rivers and for improving navigation on the Paraguay and Paraná rivers; Pres. VIDAL FRANCIA ZARACHO.

Compañía Paraguaya de Navegación de Ultramar, SA (Copanu): Avda. General Artigas 4145, Calle General Delgado, Asunción; tel. (21) 28-3665; fax (21) 28-1224; e-mail info@copanu.com.py; internet www.copanu.com.py; f. 1963; 10 vessels; Exec. Pres. IAN BOSCH.

Navemar, SA: Avda República Argentina 1412, Casilla 273, Asunción; tel. (21) 61-2527; fax (21) 61-2526; e-mail navemar@navemar.com.py; internet www.navemar.com.py; f. 1969; shipping agency, stowage, fleet operations and management; 5 vessels; Dir RICARDO DOS SANTOS.

Transporte Fluvial Paraguayo SACI: Edif. de la Encarnación, 13°, 14 de Mayo 563, Asunción; tel. (21) 49-3411; fax (21) 49-8218; e-mail tfpsaci@tm.com.py; Pres. MARCELO TOYOTOSHI; Man. EINAR DOMÍNGUEZ; 1 vessel.

CIVIL AVIATION

There are two major international airports: Aeropuerto Internacional Silvio Pettirossi, situated 15 km from Asunción; and Aeropuerto Internacional Guaraní, 30 km from Ciudad del Este.

Transportes Aéreos del Mercosur (TAM Mercosur): Aeropuerto Internacional Silvio Pettirossi, Hangar TAM/ARPA, Luque, Asunción; tel. (21) 49-1039; fax (21) 64-5146; e-mail tammercosur@uninet.com.py; internet www.tam.com.py; f. 1963 as Líneas Aéreas Paraguayas (LAP); name changed as above in 1997; services to destinations within South America; 80% owned by TAM Linhas Aéreas (Brazil); Pres. LÍBANO MIRANDA BARROSO.

Tourism

Tourism is undeveloped, but, with recent improvements in infrastructure, efforts were being made to promote the sector. Tourist arrivals in Paraguay in 2011 totalled 524,000, according to provisional data. In the same year tourism receipts were estimated at US $241m. (excluding passenger transport).

Secretaría Nacional de Turismo: Palma 468, Calle 14 de Mayo, Asunción; tel. (21) 49-4110; fax (21) 49-1230; e-mail infosenatur@senatur.gov.py; internet www.senatur.gov.py; f. 1998; Exec. Sec. LIZ ROSANNA CRÁMER CAMPOS.

Defence

As assessed at November 2012, Paraguay's armed forces numbered 10,650, of which 2,550 were conscripts. There was an army of 7,600 and an air force of 1,100. The navy, which is largely river-based, had 1,950 members, including 900 marines and a naval air force of 100. There is also a 14,800-strong paramilitary police force, including 4,000 conscripts. Military service, which is compulsory, lasts for 12 months in the army and for two years in the navy.

Defence Budget: 1,054,000m. guaraníes in 2011.

Commander-in-Chief of the Armed Forces: President of the Republic.

Commander of the Armed Forces: Gen. MIGUEL CHRIST JACOBS.

Commander of the Army: Gen. JORGE FRANCISCO RAMÍREZ GÓMEZ.

Commander of the Air Force: Gen. LUIS NOCEDA.

Commander of the Navy: Adm. PABLO RICARDO OSORIO FLEITAS.

Education

Education is, where possible, compulsory for six years, to be undertaken between six and 12 years of age. Primary education begins at the age of six and lasts for six years. Secondary education, beginning at 12 years of age, lasts for a further six years. In 2009 enrolment at primary schools included 85% of children in the relevant age-group, while enrolment at secondary schools included 60% of those in the relevant age-group. There are 12 universities in Paraguay. The 2013 budget allocated an estimated 111,000m. guaraníes to the Ministry of Education and Culture.

PERU

Introductory Survey

LOCATION, CLIMATE, LANGUAGE, RELIGION, FLAG, CAPITAL

The Republic of Peru lies in western South America, bordered by Ecuador and Colombia to the north, by Brazil and Bolivia to the east, and by Chile to the south. Peru has a coastline of more than 2,300 km (1,400 miles) on the Pacific Ocean. The climate varies with altitude, average temperatures being about 11°C (50°F) lower in the Andes mountains than in the coastal plain. The rainy season is between October and April, with heavy rainfall in the tropical forests. Temperatures in Lima are usually between 13°C (55°F) and 28°C (82°F). The three official languages are Spanish, Quechua and Aymará. Almost all of the inhabitants profess Christianity, and the great majority are adherents of the Roman Catholic Church. The civil flag (proportions 2 by 3) has three equal vertical stripes, of red, white and red. The state flag additionally has the national coat of arms (a shield divided into three unequal segments: red, with a golden cornucopia spilling coins of yellow and white at the base, blue, with a yellow vicuña in the dexter chief, and white, with a green tree in the sinister chief; all surmounted by a green wreath, and framed by branches of palm and laurel, tied at the bottom with a red and white ribbon) in the centre of the white stripe. The capital is Lima.

CONTEMPORARY POLITICAL HISTORY

Historical Context

Following independence from Spain, declared in 1821 and finally achieved in 1824, Peruvian politics were characterized by alternating periods of civilian administration and military dictatorship. In the early 1920s opposition to the dictatorial regime of President Augusto Bernardino Leguía resulted in the creation of the Alianza Popular Revolucionaria Americana (APRA), Peru's oldest political party to command mass support. The party, founded as a nationalist revolutionary movement, was formally established in Peru as the Partido Aprista Peruano (PAP) in 1930, when Leguía was deposed and the party's founder (and its leader for more than 50 years), Dr Víctor Raúl Haya de la Torre, returned from enforced exile in Mexico. A long-standing tradition of hostility developed between the Apristas and the armed forces, and the party was banned in 1931–45, and again in 1948–56.

During 1945–63 political power shifted regularly between the armed forces and elected government. In 1948 Dr José Luis Bustamente y Rivera was deposed by Gen. Manuel Odría, following a right-wing military rebellion. Odría established a military junta which governed until 1950, when the General was elected unopposed to the presidency, and subsequently appointed a cabinet composed of military officers and civilians. In 1956 Odría was succeeded by Dr Manuel Prado y Ugartache (who had been President in 1939–45). An inconclusive presidential election in 1962 precipitated military intervention, and power was assumed by Gen. Ricardo Pérez Godoy, at the head of a military junta. In March 1963, however, Pérez was supplanted by his second-in-command, Gen. Nicolás Lindley López.

Fernando Belaúnde Terry, the joint candidate of his own Acción Popular (AP) party and the Partido Demócrata Cristiano, was elected President in 1963. An increase in internal disturbances in predominantly Indian areas resulted in the temporary suspension of constitutional guarantees in 1965–66 and an intensive military campaign of counter-insurgency. Lack of congressional support for the Government contributed to a succession of ministerial crises which, together with continuing internal unrest, prompted renewed military intervention in 1968, when Gen. Juan Velasco Alvarado assumed the presidency, dissolved Congress and appointed a military cabinet.

Despite the re-emergence of internal disturbances and dissension within the armed forces, Velasco retained power until August 1975, when he was overthrown and replaced by Gen. Francisco Morales Bermúdez. In 1977 President Morales announced plans for the restoration of civilian rule. Accordingly, a national election was conducted in June 1978 to select the members of a constituent assembly, which was to draft a new constitution in preparation for elections. PAP emerged as the largest party, and in July the assembly elected the 83-year-old Dr Haya de la Torre to be its President. The new Constitution, adopted in July 1979, provided for elections by universal adult suffrage, and extended the franchise to the sizeable illiterate population.

Domestic Political Affairs

The presidential contest of May 1980 was won decisively by Belaúnde. At the same time, the AP won an outright majority in the Cámara de Diputados (Chamber of Deputies) and also secured the greatest representation in the Senado (Senate). While Belaúnde sought to liberalize the economy, much of his term of office was dominated by the threat to stability posed by the emergence of the Maoist rebel group Sendero Luminoso (SL—Shining Path). The situation deteriorated following the uncompromising response of the armed forces to terrorist activity in a designated emergency zone, which extended to 13 provinces (primarily in the departments of Ayacucho, Huancavelica and Apurímac) by mid-1984, and a dramatic increase in violent deaths and violations of human rights was reported.

At elections in 1985 Alan García Pérez (the candidate for PAP) received 46% of the votes in the presidential poll, while PAP secured a majority in both houses of the Congreso (legislature). García's victory was ensured in May, prior to a second round of voting, when his closest opponent, Dr Alfonso Barrantes Lingán (of the left-wing Izquierda Unida coalition), withdrew his candidature.

Widespread opposition to the Government's economic programme was manifested in a succession of well-supported general strikes in 1987–88. Government plans for the nationalization of Peru's financial sector encountered considerable opposition, and prompted the creation of Libertad, a 'freedom movement' expressing opposition to the plans (which were subsequently modified), established under the leadership of a well-known writer, Mario Vargas Llosa. The authority of the García administration was further undermined by persistent rumours of military unrest, by allegations of links between members of the Government and a right-wing paramilitary 'death squad', and by the continuing terrorist activities of the SL and a resurgence of activity by the Movimiento Revolucionario Túpac Amaru (MRTA) guerrilla group, in north-east Peru. In addition, the Government was criticized by international human rights organizations for its methods of combating political violence.

The Fujimori era

General elections took place in April 1990, despite the attempts of the SL to disrupt them. In the presidential poll Vargas Llosa, the candidate of the centre-right Frente Democrático (FREDEMO) alliance (established in 1988 by the AP, Libertad and the Partido Popular Cristiano), obtained the largest percentage of the votes cast, followed by a hitherto little-known agronomist, Alberto Fujimori, the candidate of the Cambio 90 group of independents. In a second round of voting, conducted in June, Fujimori was victorious, having attracted late support from left-wing parties and from PAP.

Subsidies for consumers were abolished in August 1990, thereby increasing prices by more than 3,000% for petrol and by as much as 600% for basic foods. Although these reforms secured Peru's rehabilitation within the international financial community, they provoked industrial unrest. In November 1991, despite public and congressional dissent, Fujimori took advantage of a 150-day period of emergency legislative powers to issue a series of decrees. These represented a continuation of policies concerning the elimination of state monopolies of telecommunications, postal networks and railways, the opening to private investment of the power sector, the privatization of schools and a reform of the health and social security services.

On 5 April 1992 Fujimori suspended the 1979 Constitution and dissolved the Congreso, pending a restructuring of the legislature. The President maintained that the reform of the Congreso was essential in order to eradicate 'corruption and inefficiency', to enable him to implement a programme of 'pacification' of the nation by combating terrorism and drugs-trafficking, and also fully to implement free market economic policies. In the interim an Emergency and National Reconstruction Government would govern the country, and legislative power would be exercised by the President, with the approval of the Council of Ministers. Fujimori also announced a reform of the judiciary. The constitutional coup (or 'autogolpe') was implemented with the full co-operation and support of the armed forces. On the following day the President of the Council of Ministers, Alfonso de los Heros Pérez Albela, resigned in protest, and was replaced by Oscar de la Puente. Fujimori's actions prompted outrage from politicians, the judiciary and the media; however, popular reaction to the 'autogolpe' was less hostile. Bolstered by demonstrations of public support for his actions, Fujimori dismissed 13 of Peru's 28 Supreme Court judges, whom he accused of corruption, and detained several prominent opposition party figures. The President of the Central Bank was also removed from office, as were 134 judges. The Organization of American States (OAS, see p. 404) deplored Fujimori's actions, and dispatched a mission to attempt to effect a reconciliation between the legislature and the executive.

The threat posed to Fujimori's programme of radical reform by economic constraints resulting from the suspension of international financial aid to Peru prompted the revision of the timetable for a return to democracy, and in June 1992 Fujimori confirmed that national elections would be conducted in October to a unicameral constituent congress, which would then draft a new constitution. The President also announced that, pending approval of a new document, the 1979 Constitution would be reinstated without certain articles that might 'impede the progress of the Government'.

A 'National Dialogue for Peace and Development', comprising a series of discussions with representatives of the political opposition and with the public, sought to identify important issues for future consideration by the new Congreso Constituyente Democrático (CCD). Elections to the CCD, conducted on 22 November 1992 and attended by OAS observers, were a qualified success for pro-Government parties. An electoral coalition of Cambio 90 and the Nueva Mayoría (a new independent party supported by many former cabinet ministers), headed by Fujimori's former Minister of Energy and Mines, Jaime Yoshiyama Tanaka, secured a majority of seats. TThe CCD's immediate aims were the restoration of the autonomy of the judiciary, the eradication of terrorism, the generation of employment and of favourable conditions for foreign investment, and the projection of an enhanced national image abroad. In January 1993, having formally reinstated the 1979 Constitution, the CCD confirmed Fujimori as constitutional Head of State. Following the resignation of de la Puente's Government in July, Alfonso Bustamente y Bustamante was appointed prime minister in August.

The final text of the draft Constitution, which enhanced presidential powers and provided for the establishment of a unicameral legislature, was approved by the CCD in September 1993. Among the text's most controversial articles were the introduction of the death penalty for convicted terrorists and a provision permitting a President of the Republic to be re-elected for a successive five-year term of office. The Constitution was narrowly approved at a national referendum in October and promulgated on 29 December.

In a presidential election in April 1995, Fujimori secured an unexpected outright victory over his closest opponent, Javier Pérez de Cuéllar de la Guerra (the former UN Secretary-General and the candidate of the Unión por el Perú—UPP). In concurrent legislative elections, Fujimori's coalition movement, Cambio 90-Nueva Mayoría, also secured an absolute majority in the unicameral Congreso.

On 17 December 1996 MRTA activists launched an assault on the residence of the Japanese ambassador in Lima, and detained more than 500 people attending an evening reception. Among those taken hostage were the Ministers of Foreign Affairs and of Agriculture, at least nine foreign ambassadors and other diplomatic personnel, leading police and security officials and representatives of the business community. The MRTA activists' demands included the release of all 458 MRTA prisoners, safe passage to Peru's central highlands, greater economic assistance to the country's poorest people and payment of a 'war tax'. The siege lasted until 22 April 1997 when Peruvian troops launched an unexpected assault on the ambassador's residence. Two soldiers and all 14 of the MRTA activists were killed in the operation, and one of the 72 remaining hostages died of heart failure; it was later alleged that some of the MRTA members might have been killed after having surrendered to army officers.

Ongoing concerns regarding the President's circumvention of the traditional role of the judiciary intensified in May 1998 when Fujimori introduced draconian anti-crime legislation by decree (subsequently approved by the Congreso) seeking to extend the extreme powers and penalties employed in recent successful anti-terrorism initiatives to other areas of criminal activity. Among the provisions of the new law were plans to increase the powers of military tribunals to try civilians. Despite appeals by international observers and opposition groups for greater judicial independence and respect for human rights, in December the Congreso voted to extend the period of judicial reorganization initiated by Fujimori's administration for a further two-year period.

Fujimori's continuing efforts to secure support for a third presidential term were encouraged by the defeat in the Congreso, in September 1998, of an opposition proposal to decide the question of Fujimori's eligibility by a national referendum. A broad range of labour unions and political parties held a one-day general strike in April 1999 expressing opposition to Fujimori's potential re-election. However, in December Fujimori announced his candidature on behalf of the newly created Perú 2000 alliance. On 1 January 2000 the Jurado Nacional Electoral (JNE—National Electoral Board), which was dominated by Fujimori's supporters, ratified his candidacy, precipitating street protests.

The general election proceeded on 9 April 2000. Opposition candidates and international observers alleged that the ballot was marred by fraud. US officials issued increasingly strong statements stressing the need for a second round of voting as the only credible proof of legitimacy. Fujimori officially received 49.9% of the votes cast and Alejandro Toledo (the first presidential candidate of Amerindian descent) 40.2%. The JNE resisted pressure for a postponement of the second round, in order to correct irregularities noted in the first round. In response, Toledo withdrew his candidature and urged his supporters to spoil their votes. Violent incidents, including the fire-bombing of the presidential palace, followed. Amid further mass demonstrations, Fujimori contested the election on 28 May effectively unopposed (although the JNE refused to remove Toledo's name from the ballot papers), taking 51% of the total votes; Toledo received 18%. Excluding spoiled (30%) and blank (1%) papers, the incumbent was thus returned to office with 74% of the valid votes cast. The result was denounced as invalid by the opposition and by the US Government (though it later moderated its position, describing the outcome as imperfect). Fujimori's inauguration on 28 July was accompanied by violent protests in Lima.

In September 2000 a major political scandal erupted after the disclosure of a video that allegedly showed Vladimiro Montesinos, the head of the national intelligence service and a close ally of the President, bribing an opposition member of the Congreso. In response, Fujimori declared that new elections would be held, in which he would not participate. He also announced that the national intelligence service would be disbanded. At the same time, 10 Perú 2000 deputies defected to the opposition, thus depriving Fujimori of his majority in the legislature. Demonstrations, led by Toledo, demanded the immediate resignation of Fujimori and the arrest of Montesinos, who fled to Panama. In October the Congreso approved OAS-mediated proposals paving the way for power to be transferred from Fujimori to his successor in mid-2001, as well as the disbandment of the Congreso to make way for a newly elected legislature.

The political crisis deepened in late October 2000 when Montesinos returned from Panama. His apparent impunity supported the widely held view that the armed forces were protecting him. At the same time, the first Vice-President, Francisco Tudela, resigned in protest against government attempts to make new elections conditional upon an amnesty for those in the armed forces accused of human rights violations. Further OAS-sponsored negotiations led to the announcement that new elections would be held on 8 April 2001, without any conditions attached. In mid-November 2000 the Congreso voted to replace its pro-Fujimori President, Martha Hildebrandt Pérez Treviño, with Valentín Paniagua Corazao, effectively giving the opposition control of the legislature. The following day Fujimori travelled to Japan, from where, on 20 November, he resigned the presidency. However, the Congreso refused to accept the resignation, and instead voted to dismiss Fujimori.

On 22 November 2000 Paniagua was appointed interim President. A new cabinet was sworn in three days later, which included Javier Pérez de Cuéllar as prime minister and Minister of Foreign Affairs. Several days later the new Minister of Defence, Walter Ledesma Rebaza, announced the decision to retire 13 generals who were associates of Montesinos. A congressional commission, established to investigate the activities of Montesinos, uncovered hundreds of secret videotapes that seemed to compromise the integrity of judges, politicians, military officers, businessmen and bishops. In early December the commission's investigations were extended to Fujimori. In mid-December it was announced that Fujimori had taken up Japanese citizenship and was thus, in effect, protected from the threat of extradition from Japan. Nevertheless, in February 2001 corruption charges were formally filed against him. Furthermore, in August the Congreso voted unanimously to lift Fujimori's constitutional immunity and issued an international warrant for his arrest on the charge of dereliction of duty. Further charges of embezzlement and illicit enrichment were subsequently filed against the former President. However, the Japanese Government stated that it had no intention of allowing Fujimori's extradition.

In June 2001 Montesinos was arrested in Venezuela. He was sent back to Peru and, in July 2002, sentenced to nine years' imprisonment. A further 80 indictments against him, including murder, bribery and the illegal sale of weapons and narcotics, were subsequently brought against him. In 2003 Montesinos was convicted on corruption charges and sentenced to a further five years' imprisonment. In 2004 Montesinos was found guilty of bribing newspaper editors to support Fujimori's re-election attempt in 2000, and was sentenced to a further 15 years' imprisonment. (In 2005 eight newspaper chiefs were sentenced to five years in gaol after being convicted of receiving payments from Montesinos.) In 2006 Montesinos received another gaol term of 20 years after being convicted of arms-trafficking.

The election of Toledo

In January 2001, only a few days after corruption charges against him were ruled to have expired under the statute of limitations, former President Alan García Pérez returned to Peru to launch his campaign for the forthcoming presidential election. Toledo won 37% of the votes cast at the first round of the election on 8 April, while García attracted 26% of the ballot and Lourdes Flores Nano of the Unidad Nacional alliance 24%. In the second round, held on 3 June, Toledo won, with 53% of the vote. Toledo was inaugurated on 28 July. A broad-based, 15-member cabinet was appointed, headed by lawyer Roberto Dañino. The new Government promised to create more jobs, to reduce poverty and to put an end to the corruption of the Fujimori regime. In the previous month a congressional commission implicated 180 people in corruption scandals that took place during Fujimori's presidencies, including Gen. Walter Chacón Málaga, the recently appointed head of the armed forces.

However, the popularity of the Toledo Government declined sharply after only a few months in power, as high public expectations were not matched by an increase in economic prospects. In September and October 2001 popular protests erupted throughout Peru as workers demanded more jobs and improvements to transport infrastructure and health care. The protests proliferated, and in June 2002, following a week of violent demonstrations in protest against government plans to privatize two regional electricity companies in Arequipa, the Minister of the Interior, Fernando Rospigliosi Capurro, resigned and the privatization process was suspended indefinitely. An extensive cabinet reorganization was carried out in July, in which the Secretary-General of Perú Posible (PP), Luis Solari, replaced Dañino as prime minister.

In January 2003 the Constitutional Tribunal ruled that anti-terrorism legislation adopted by the Fujimori administration had violated the Constitution. In order to alleviate the potential pressure on the judiciary, and to prevent the release of large numbers of alleged terrorists, the Congreso granted President Toledo exceptional temporary powers to legislate by decree on security issues. In February the Government announced that all military sentences passed during Fujimori's presidency were to be annulled. The courts would have 60 days to decide whether to release convicted individuals or commit them for retrial. In March anti-terrorism legislation received congressional approval.

In February 2003 coca growers staged demonstrations to demand the suspension of the Government's coca eradication policy. The demonstrations escalated after a coca growers' federation leader, Nelson Palomino La Serna, was imprisoned on terrorism charges. Following negotiations, the Government

agreed to give US $11m. in direct aid to farmers affected by the eradication efforts. In April thousands of coca growers began a protest march towards Lima to demand subsidies for alternative crops and an increase in the amount of coca that could legally be grown. Later that month President Toledo signed into law a decree pledging that the eradication programme would be gradual and that the Government would discuss policy with the growers.

President Toledo, his family and his advisers were implicated in several major scandals during 2003–04. In September 2003 Adm. (retd) Alfonso Panizzo, director of the national intelligence service, resigned, after it emerged that the intelligence agency had been spying on journalists investigating corrupt practices in public office. Panizzo's successor, Gen. (retd) Daniel Mora, held the post until March 2004, when the revelation that the agency had been compiling a dossier on the Minister of the Interior, Fernando Rospigliosi Capurro, forced his resignation. In late March Toledo announced that the national intelligence agency was to be abolished. A government committee was formed to oversee the establishment of a successor body, the Agencia de Inteligencia Estratégica. In May Rospigliosi Capurro himself was forced to resign from the Government, having been held responsible for the authorities' inability to quell violent disturbances in the southern region of Puno, which had culminated in April in the lynching of a local mayor. Javier Reátegui was named as the new Minister of the Interior.

In July 2004 the President's sister, Margarita Toledo, was ordered by a judge not to leave the country pending investigations into an alleged large-scale forging of signatures in 1999 in order to register PP for the 2000 legislative elections. Toledo and her husband were placed under house arrest in January 2005. A special congressional commission was established to investigate the case. Meanwhile, in July 2004 President Toledo granted investigators the authority to probe bank accounts held in Peru and abroad by himself and his wife, following media accusations that they had accepted bribes. In mid-July a general strike was held in protest against, *inter alia*, the perceived corruption of the Toledo administration and its failure to fulfil electoral promises, as well as at the proposed free trade agreement with the USA and the Government's failure to act upon the findings of the Truth Commission (see below). In May 2005 a congressional committee concluded that Toledo and his associates had violated electoral law by forging signatures to register PP for the 2000 elections. However, on 20 May the Congreso voted not to impeach President Toledo.

Reátegui resigned as Minister of the Interior in January 2005, in response to public dissatisfaction with the authorities' handling of the forcible occupation of a police station in the southern province of Andahuaylas by an ultra-nationalist grouping, the Movimiento Etnocacerista (allied to the Movimiento Nacionalista Peruana). The uprising resulted in the deaths of seven people, including four police officers, before the insurgents surrendered. In August, following the resignation of the Minister of Foreign Affairs, Manuel Rodrígues Cuadros, President Toledo appointed the outspoken leader of the Frente Independiente Moralizador, Fernando Olivera, to succeed him. However, Olivera's appointment caused dissent within the Council of Ministers (ostensibly over his approval of the legalization of coca cultivation for traditional use in the province of Cusco), and prompted the resignation of the prime minister, Ferrero Costa. Three days after his appointment, Olivera resigned.

The criminal conviction of Fujimori

In November 2005 Fujimori was arrested on his arrival in Chile, where he had arrived unannounced. It was believed that the former President, who had declared his intention to contest the presidential election scheduled for April 2006, had planned to conduct his election campaign from Chile. In September 2007 Fujimori was extradited to Peru on seven charges and in December the former President went on trial before the Supreme Court on four of those charges: namely, responsibility for the killing of 15 civilians in Barrios Altos in 1991, and of nine students and a professor at Lima's La Canuta university in 1992, by an assassination squad known as the Colina group (see below); and the abductions of a journalist and a businessman, also in 1992. In April 2009 Fujimori was convicted of all four charges and sentenced to 25 years' imprisonment (upheld by the Supreme Court in January 2010). The trial, which was praised by international human rights organizations for its rigour and fairness, was the first of a Latin American President in his own country on charges of human rights violations. Fujimori received further sentences (of seven years and six years' imprisonment, respectively) for embezzlement and corruption later in 2009.

The return of García

Presidential and legislative elections were held on 9 April 2006. A left-wing nationalist candidate, Lt-Col (retd) Ollanta Humala Tasso, who was the nominee of a coalition of his own party, the Partido Nacionalista Peruano (PNP), and the UPP, won the first round of the presidential ballot with 31% of the valid votes cast, while former President García, representing PAP, secured 24%. A high turn-out, of 89%, was recorded. In the legislative elections the UPP emerged as the largest party in the new Congreso, although it failed to secure an outright majority. At a second round of presidential voting, on 4 June, García defeated Humala, securing 53% of the votes cast.

García took office on 28 July 2006. At his inauguration the new President focused on the need to reduce poverty, announcing plans to lower administrative expenses and to invest some US $1,600m. in rural areas to improve public infrastructure and the provision of education and health care. Nine independents were appointed to the 16-member Council of Ministers, including Luis Carranza Ugarte, a former director of the Central Bank, as Minister of Economy and Finance, while Jorge del Castillo Gálvez, a Secretary-General of PAP and a close ally of García, was designated President of the Council.

Although the UPP-PNP coalition had secured the largest number of seats in the legislature, divisions within the alliance soon became apparent, with the UPP favouring the adoption of a less confrontational approach towards García's administration. In August 2006 the UPP announced that it had severed ties with Humala and the PNP, leaving PAP as the largest bloc in the Congreso. Humala suffered a further setback in late August, when he was formally charged with human rights abuses based on allegations of murder and torture by counter-insurgency troops under his command at a military base in the department of San Martín in 1992; the former army officer claimed that the charges were a form of political persecution. In December Humala was also charged with rebellion in relation to his alleged involvement in the uprising at a police station in Andahuaylas in January 2005 (led by his imprisoned brother, Antauro).

Environmental issues and indigenous unrest

Civil unrest and violence continued in various parts of the country during 2008. In August a state of emergency was declared in several provinces after members of 65 indigenous groups erected roadblocks and picketed energy installations in protest against two decrees relating to the sale of native land. The protesters claimed that the new laws, which allowed indigenous communities to sell their land if more than 50% of the community voted in favour of the sale (rather than a two-thirds' majority, as was previously the case), would have put large areas of the Amazon rainforest at risk of development by energy companies. The controversial decrees were revoked by the Congreso in late August.

In October 2008 a series of tape recordings emerged that appeared to indicate that a senior official of Perupetro, the government agency responsible for the development of the petroleum industry, had accepted bribes in exchange for the awarding of exploration contracts to a small Norwegian company, Discover Petroleum. The Minister of Energy and Mines, Juan Valdivia Romero, resigned in response to the allegations, as did the head of the state oil company, Petroperú. Three days later, on 10 October, the entire Council of Ministers tendered its resignation, following allegations that the prime minister, del Castillo, had been involved in the affair. Yehude Simon Munaro was appointed as prime minister. It was thought that the appointment of Simon, a left-winger who had been imprisoned under the Fujimori Government for supposed links to the MRTA (for which he was subsequently pardoned), would help to diminish tension between the Government and the regions in the wake of further strikes and protests in early October.

In June 2009 indigenous protests against the industrial development of the Amazon rainforest led to serious violent clashes in which many people were killed. Groups of indigenous people in the Amazonas region in Bagua province had gathered to protest against controversial legislation relating to the rainforest that had been agreed during negotiations on a free trade agreement with the USA. According to official reports, a total of 33 people were killed (including 24 police officers); however, indigenous groups claimed that at least 40 of their people had been massacred and their bodies dumped in an attempt to conceal the killings. The prime minister and Minister of the Interior nar-

rowly avoided official censure in a motion to the Congreso immediately after the incident, amid calls for their resignations. One member of the cabinet, the Minister of Women and Social Development, Carmen Vildoso, resigned her post in protest against the Government's handling of the affair. In late June the Congreso repealed the two most controversial pieces of legislation, which allocated 45m. ha of the Amazonian rainforest (some 50% of the Peruvian Amazon) for development by international companies with mining, logging or mineral exploration interests and which allowed these operators to do so without the consent of local communities.

A series of strikes and demonstrations organized across the country in July 2009, in support of the indigenous communities involved in the previous month's violence and in protest against the Government's economic and social policies, prompted Simon's resignation as prime minister. He was replaced by Javier Velásquez Quesquén, and a major cabinet reorganization was effected, which included the appointment of former national police chief Octavio Salazar as Minister of the Interior, replacing Cabanillas, who had faced intense criticism over the Government's handling of the crisis.

The Minister of Justice, Aurelio Pastor Valdivieso, was dismissed in March 2010, following controversy over his involvement in the decision in December 2009 to pardon José Enrique Crousillat, the former owner of América Televisión, who had been sentenced to eight years' imprisonment in 2006 after being convicted of accepting bribes from Montesinos to provide favourable coverage of former President Fujimori. PAP was damaged in April 2010 by corruption scandals involving the party's joint Secretaries-General, former prime minister del Castillo and Omar Quesada Martínez, both of whom had been considered potential candidates for the presidential election scheduled for April 2011. Tape recordings emerged that appeared to indicate that del Castillo had lobbied in favour of Petrolera Monterrico, an oil company owned by an associate, during his premiership, while Quesada was accused of involvement in corrupt land sales made by a state agency he headed, the Organismo de Formalización de la Propiedad Informal (Cofopri). Quesada stood down as executive director of Cofopri and both men temporarily resigned from their party positions, although they denied the allegations against them. Several Cofopri officials were subsequently arrested.

Further demonstrations against government plans related to the mining and energy sectors took place during 2010. Five people were reportedly killed in Arequipa in April during clashes between police and protesters opposed to a recently approved decree that prohibited unregulated gold-panning and dredging of rivers. In response to the unrest, prime minister Velásquez agreed to create a commission, including representatives of the informal mining sector, to discuss the decree. In May the Congreso adopted legislation requiring the state to consult indigenous communities on projects affecting their territories, but in June President García refused to promulgate the law in its current form on the grounds that it would impede national economic development. Velásquez declared a state of emergency in the Echarate district of Cusco at the beginning of August, following several days of violent protests against the exportation of natural gas, in which one person had died, with many more injured. The protests ended later that month, when the prime minister addressed concerns regarding domestic shortages of gas by guaranteeing that gas from one of the Camisea field's two blocs would be exclusively for domestic use; a new processing plant and pipeline would supply regional demand. In December a company exploring for gold in the Catac district of the northern region of Ancash had its licence revoked, following major demonstrations by indigenous groups in the regional capital, Huaraz.

Regional elections held in October 2010 were marked by the success of local movements and the poor performance of the traditional, national parties; PAP secured just one of the 25 regional presidencies (compared with three in the 2006 polls). In concurrent municipal elections, Susana Villarán, of the centre-left Partido Decentralista Fuerza Social, was notably elected mayor of Lima, narrowly defeating the conservative Lourdes Flores Nano, who had unsuccessfully contested the presidential elections of 2001 and 2006.

Chang resigned as President of the Council of Ministers and as Minister of Education in March 2011. The Minister of Justice, Rosario Fernández, assumed the premiership for the remaining four months of President García's term in office. Protests against mining projects continued during that period, leading to the cancellation, in April, of a contract for the development of a copper mine near Arequipa, following the deaths of three protestors in clashes with police, and to the withdrawal, in June, of a silver mining concession in the Puno region from a Canadian-based company, after a series of demonstrations in which five protesters died.

The election of Humala

The first round of the presidential and legislative elections was held on 10 April 2011. PAP notably did not contest the presidency, its representative, former Minister of Economy and Finance Mercedes Aráoz Fernández, having withdrawn her candidacy in protest against the inclusion on the party's list for the congressional elections of del Castillo, who remained under investigation in relation to the scandal that led to his resignation as prime minister in 2008. Ollanta Humala, the candidate of Gana Perú (a PNP-led alliance of left-wing parties), won 31.7% of the valid votes cast in the presidential ballot, while his closest rival, Keiko Fujimori, daughter of imprisoned former President Fujimori, who stood for the right-wing Fuerza 2011, took 23.6%. Pedro Pablo Kuczynski, President of the Council of Ministers in 2005–06, who was representing the Alianza por el Gran Cambio (a grouping of four centre-right parties, including the Partido Popular Cristiano), was placed third, with 18.5%, followed by former President Toledo, of PP, with 15.6%. In the legislative elections, Gana Perú became the largest grouping in the new 130-seat Congreso, securing 47 seats, followed by Fuerza 2011, with 37, while PP won 21 seats and the Alianza por el Gran Cambio 12. A turn-out of 83.7% was recorded. At a second round of presidential voting on 5 June the nationalist Humala, who had conducted a far more moderate campaign than he had done in the 2006 vote, narrowly defeated Fujimori, securing 51.5% of the valid votes cast.

President Humala was inaugurated on 28 July 2011. Controversially taking the oath of office in accordance with the 1979 Constitution, rather than the current charter enacted by Alberto Fujimori in 1993, Humala pledged to promote social inclusion, while pursuing continued economic growth through existing free market policies. Specific measures promised included increases in the minimum wage and in pensions for those over 65, while the imposition of a 'windfall' tax on mining companies was also proposed. The composition of the new administration was generally well received by the financial markets and the business community, which, despite assurances to the contrary, had feared that Humala's election would herald a radical shift to the left. Luis Castilla Rubio, who had served as Deputy Minister of Finance in the outgoing administration, became Minister of the Economy and Finance, and Julio Velarde Flores was retained as President of the Central Bank, while Salomón Lerner Ghitis, a wealthy businessman who had managed Humala's election campaign, was appointed President of the Council of Ministers. Having endorsed Humala's candidacy in the second round of the presidential poll, PP received two ministerial portfolios (defence and labour and employment) in return for its support in the Congreso, thus providing Gana Perú with a working majority.

In August 2011 the Congreso approved a new law enshrining the rights of local (mainly indigenous) communities to be consulted about proposed development projects in their territories; the Government hoped that greater consultation would avert the social unrest that had increasingly occurred under the García administration. In a second success for Humala that month, agreement was reached with mining companies on the introduction of a new regulatory framework for the sector, including a royalty tax on operating profits, which, it was estimated, could generate an additional US $1,100m. in public revenue per year. The creation of a Ministry of Development and Social Inclusion was approved by the Congreso in September, in a significant move towards the implementation of the President's primary election pledge.

Humala announced a major purge of the police force in October 2011, as part of efforts to combat corruption, retiring 30 of the country's 45 police generals (not all owing to alleged wrongdoing) and replacing the commander of the police force. However, corruption allegations affected the Government later that month, when the Second Vice-President, Omar Chehade, was accused of attempting to secure the eviction of protesting workers from a sugar plantation, in order to facilitate its return to its owners. Chehade stood down temporarily from his post in November, while denying any wrongdoing, pending an investigation into the allegations against him, but he resigned permanently in January 2012, one day before the Congreso narrowly rejected a report accused him of 'illegal sponsorship'.

Recent developments: mining protests and social unrest

Protests against mining projects in northern Peru escalated in late 2011, representing a reverse for the Government's efforts to reduce social unrest. Construction work at the proposed Conga expansion of Peru's largest gold mine, Yanacocha, in the region of Cajamarca, was suspended by operator Newmont Mining Corporation of the USA in late November, after at least 10 people were injured during protests. However, protests continued over the potential environmental affects, particularly on water supplies, of the US $4,800m. project (which had been approved by the García administration). The Deputy Minister of the Environment, Jose de Echave, notably resigned from the Goverment over the issue, asserting that environmental impact studies into the project were 'weak, outdated and lacking in credibility'. Talks between government officials and the protesters, who were supported by Cajamarca's regional President, collapsed in December.

Lerner unexpectedly resigned as President of the Council of Ministers on 10 December 2011, precipitating a major reorganization of the Government, in which 11 ministers were replaced, less than five months after Humala's inauguration. Observers noted that Lerner had failed to unite the Council of Ministers, which had appeared disorganized and undisciplined. The appointment of Oscar Valdés Dancuart, hitherto Minister of the Interior and a former lieutenant-colonel in the army, as Lerner's successor, was considered to be an indication that Humala intended to respond more firmly to any further social unrest, while the replacement of a number of leftist ministers with more technocratic appointees was welcomed by the business community, but not by Humala's traditional supporters. Moreover, Toledo described the appointment of Valdés as the 'militarization' of the Government, from which he withdrew PP's two ministers and the party's congressional support.

Soon after taking office, Valdés announced that the environmental impact assessment of the Conga project would be reviewed by independent experts. None the less, a national march in defence of the right to clean water supplies, which had commenced in Cajamarca, arrived in Lima in mid-February 2012, comprising around 1,000 participants, who protested against the establishment of mines at the head of water sources and demanded the prohibition of the use of cyanide and mercury in mining projects in order to avoid water pollution. In April the three international experts tasked with evaluating the environmental assessment of the Conga project presented their report to the Government. The Minister of the Environment, Manuel Pulgar-Vidal, noted that the report recommended improvements to the project, but that further analysis would be required before the Government made a final decision on the project's future. Further protests in Cajamarca took place in mid-2012 and resulted in the deaths of five people when demonstrators clashed with police in July. Meanwhile, in the southern region of Madre de Dios, informal miners, estimated to number some 30,000 in that area (and 100,000 in the entire country), declared an indefinite strike in March in protest against three government decrees that aimed to formalize artisanal mining and to criminalize illegal mining. The Government maintained that restrictions were required to ensure that small-scale mining was pursued legally and without damaging the environment. Illegal mining was believed to account for almost one-quarter of total gold exports and to be worth an estimated US $1,800m. After clashes between the protesters and the police resulted in three deaths, the Government held talks with the local miners' federation, which ended the strike two weeks after it began, having accepted government assistance in formalizing its members' mining activities. However, demonstrations by informal miners continued in other areas of the country throughout 2012.

In May 2012 Daniel Lozada and Alberto Otárola, the interior and defence ministers, respectively, resigned in order to avoid a motion of censure in the Congreso relating to their management of a recent hostage crisis (see below). They were replaced by José Urquizo in the defence portfolio and by retired army general Wilver Calle Girón as interior minister. However, in July Humala carried out his third cabinet reorganization, in which Urquizo and Calle Girón were both replaced (by security consultant Pedro Cateriano Bellido and former director of the prison service Wilfredo Pedraza, respectively), in addition to four other ministers. Although the rapid turnover of personnel in certain ministerial roles led to accusations of instability within Humala's Government, the President countered that continuity in the crucial areas of finance, and energy and mines, would ensure that investor confidence would not be harmed. The reorganization was also notable for increasing the representation of women, with a record number of six ministerial portfolios being held by female members of the Government. Furthermore, Valdés, who had been subject to increasing criticism over his management of the Conga mine conflict and other ongoing social disputes throughout the country (estimated to total 243 in mid-2012), was replaced as prime minister by Juan Jiménez Mayor. Upon his appointment, the new prime minister attempted to set a different tone for the Government by renaming the Office for the Management of Social Conflicts as the Office of National Dialogue. He also announced a 'water before gold' policy in negotiations between local representatives and mine operators in the Conga project. Following an announcement confirming the indefinite suspension of the project by the US firm Newmont Mining Corporation in August, Jiménez Mayor stated that development of the mine was no longer a priority for the Government, which would focus on resolving the social issues in the area.

A period of instability and violence in early 2013 led opponents of Humala to accuse his Government of neglecting public security. The head of the national police, Gen. Raúl Salazar, resigned in March following criticism of his force. Later that month Minister of the Interior Pedraza announced the creation of a specialized police unit to investigate criminal gangs. However, the measures did not satisfy the opposition, who summoned Humala to appear before the Congreso in April to answer criticisms of his security policies.

The Resurgence of Sendero Luminoso

In the early 1990s the SL intensified its attacks against government and military targets, strategic power installations, commercial enterprises and rural defence groups. Following Fujimori's 'autogolpe' of 1992 (effected partly in response to continuing congressional opposition to his efforts to expand the role of the armed forces), considerable concern was expressed by human rights organizations that the security forces would be permitted an increasing degree of autonomy. In September of that year government forces captured the SL's founder and leader, Abimael Guzmán Reynoso, together with 20 prominent SL members. Guzmán was tried by a military court, where he was found guilty of treason and sentenced to life imprisonment. However, the SL remained highly active, and in 1993 was held responsible for the assassination of 20 candidates campaigning in local elections. The Government actively pursued its offensive against terrorist organizations in the mid-1990s, and publicized the detention of leading members of the SL, the MRTA and the dissident SL 'Sendero Rojo' faction (which advocated a continuation of the armed struggle). In 1999 Oscar Ramírez Durand, the leader of Sendero Rojo, was captured and sentenced to life imprisonment.

The SL emerged again in 2001, with at least 31 deaths attributed to the terrorist organization in that year. In 2002 a car bomb killed 10 people and injured at least 40 more near the US embassy in Lima. The attack was attributed to a radical wing of the SL. In 2003 the Government attributed the abduction of 60 pipeline construction workers in the Ayacucho region to the remnants of the SL; the hostages were subsequently released unharmed. In 2004 a retrial of Guzmán and 16 other SL militants began in a civilian court after the Constitutional Tribunal ruled that their convictions by military court in 1992 were invalid. However, President Toledo's announcement in advance of the verdict that none of the defendants would go free contributed to the collapse of the retrial. In 2005, however, the retrial of Guzmán began anew. Guzmán and his former second-in-command, Elena Iparraguirre, were both sentenced to life imprisonment in October 2006, while the 10 other defendants being retried received lengthy prison sentences.

Meanwhile, it was believed that the SL was increasingly turning away from its ideological struggle in favour of protecting the illegal drugs trade, from which it allegedly derived a substantial part of its funding. In December 2005 some 13 police officers were killed by SL guerrillas in rural provinces known to be centres of coca cultivation and cocaine production. In January 2006 President Toledo announced the establishment of a new police unit to combat the resurgence of the SL. Eight people, including five police officers, were killed in December in an ambush mounted against a coca eradication operation near the town of Machente in Ayacucho. The Government dispatched some 500 commandos to the area, following the deployment of 1,500 special troops to combat terrorism and drugs-trafficking in the regions of Ayacucho and Huancayo. An attack on a police station in Ocobamba, Apurímac, by some 50–80 armed men in November 2007, was blamed on SL members. In mid-2008 the army launched an offensive in the area of the Apurímac-Ene valley aimed at defeating the larger of the two remaining SL contingents; none the less, attacks by the guerrilla group in the area intensified. In October the SL inflicted its most deadly attack on the army in 11 years when it ambushed a military convoy in a coca-producing area in Huancavelica: 13 soldiers from an anti-terrorist unit and at least three civilians were killed. In April 2009 two co-ordinated ambushes by the SL in the Huanta province of Ayacucho resulted in the deaths of another 13 soldiers.

A series of small-scale attacks against military targets by the SL in late 2009 and early 2010 reinforced the belief that the organization was becoming more active. Moreover, leaked documents revealed in January 2010 appeared to provide evidence of growing links with the Colombian guerrilla organization Fuerzas Armadas Revolucionarias de Colombia (FARC). The murders of two coca eradication workers and a police officer in the Huallaga province of San Martín in April were attributed to the SL. In October the arrest was reported of Edgar Mejía, a senior SL commander. Following the deaths of 10 military personnel in attacks by the SL in 2011, the Minister of Defence announced that the armed forces would assume full control of security, including policing, in the Apurímac-Ene valley. Following the capture of Florindo Eleuterio Flores Hala (alias 'Comrade Artemio'), the leader of the SL faction operating in the group's other main stronghold, the Upper Huallaga valley, and those of his suspected successors, Walter Díaz Vega and Jaime Arenas Caviedes, in early 2012, President Humala declared that the SL had been defeated in the Upper Huallaga valley and that the Government's objective was to intensify efforts to eradicate the SL contingent based in the Apurímac-Ene valley. The trial of Flores on terrorism and drugs-trafficking charges began in January 2013. Cuarto 'Jaime' Chujandama Pinedo, believed to be Flores' security chief, was arrested in March. In mid-April 2012 the Government declared a 60-day state of emergency in the district of Echarate, Cusco, where a group of workers employed by a Swedish company constructing a natural gas plant had been abducted by presumed members of the SL faction in the Apurímac-Ene valley, dispatching some 1,500 troops to the area. All 36 hostages were released after six days in captivity, when hundreds of troops surrounded their kidnappers, forcing them to flee, according to the Ministry of Defence; at least four members of the security forces were killed in the operation.

During 2012 the SL appeared to be renewing efforts to extend its political influence in the country by means of the Movimiento por Amnistía y Derechos Fundamentales (Movadef) organization. The group, which maintains that the SL is a political rather than a terrorist organization and supports an amnesty for all imprisoned SL activists, had applied unsuccessfully to register as a political party in 2011. In an attempt to limit the influence of the group, Humala proposed legislation in August 2012 that would impose legal sanction (in the form of a prison sentence of between four and eight years) on individuals who publicly deny or justify terrorist acts committed in Peru. Moreover, in September he rejected the suggestion that the Government might hold peace talks with the SL. According to some reports, Movadef was attempting to gain influence within other large organizations in Peru, particularly some trade unions, and hoping to exploit some of the country's existing social disputes to further its own interests.

Human Rights Issues and the Illegal Drugs Trade

The Peruvian Government attracted criticism from human rights organizations for its methods in achieving the apparent subjugation of the terrorist movements in the 1990s. In 1999 Peru withdrew from the jurisdiction of the Inter-American Court of Human Rights (IACHR, see p. 405), a branch of the OAS, after the court ruled that new trials should be held for four Chilean activists who were serving life sentences. However, in 2001, the Congreso approved Peru's return to the jurisdiction of the IACHR. In September 2001 the Attorney-General charged Fujimori with responsibility for two mass killings by the right-wing Colina death squad in the early 1990s; he was subsequently convicted of these crimes (see above). In 2006 the IACHR ruled that the Peruvian state was responsible for the killings of 41 suspected members of the SL during an assault by the security forces on a prison in 1992, ordering the Government to pay compensation totalling some US $20m. to relatives of the deceased and to injured survivors. In a separate case, the court also held the state responsible for the abduction and subsequent summary execution by Colina of 10 civilians at La Canuta university (which constituted one of the charges against Fujimori); compensation of $1.8m. was to be paid to the victims' relatives.

In 2001 a Truth Commission, composed of church leaders and civil and military representatives, was established to investigate the impact of the campaign against the guerrilla groups in the 1980s and 1990s. The Commission conducted some 17,000 interviews, and initially secured the support of the Peruvian army (although the navy refused to co-operate). In 2003 the group presented its findings, which estimated the number of deaths during the conflict at some 69,000, twice the previous official total, with some 6,000 individuals reported as 'disappeared'. Nevertheless, despite the report's conclusion that the SL was responsible for the greater part of the killings, its conclusions were criticized by elements of the Roman Catholic Church, the military and PAP. In November President Toledo publicly apologized for the state's actions during the period and announced a US $817m. plan to improve social conditions in the regions most affected by the violence.

In 1990 the Presidents of Peru, Colombia, Bolivia and the USA signed the Cartagena Declaration, pledging the intensification of efforts to combat the consumption, production and trafficking of illegal drugs. However, commitments to fund subsequent anti-drugs schemes in Peru were suspended by the US Administration as a result of international criticism of the Peruvian Government's record on human and democratic rights. In 1996 responsibility for combating the drugs trade was transferred from the military to the national police force, following a series of allegations that army officers had themselves been involved in trafficking. The Andean Trade Promotion and Drug Eradication Act was approved by the US Congress in that year. In 2003 a new US $3,000m. development strategy for the regions of Peru affected by coca cultivation was announced; the plans envisaged the reforestation of 1m. ha of arable land judged to be capable of producing coca, and the replanting of some 500,000 ha with alternative crops. The Government also envisaged that the new initiatives would lead to the creation of some 2.5m. jobs by 2020, with the complete elimination of coca in the area under illegal cultivation (which totalled approximately 24,600 ha). However, in 2005 it was reported that US funding to the Andean region for drugs eradication would prioritize Colombia over Bolivia and Peru. There was speculation that the reduction in funding reflected the US Administration's disappointment with the lack of progress made by the Toledo Government in coca eradication. In 2007 the Minister of Agriculture in García's new Government, Juan José Salazar, proposed a shift in Peru's counter-narcotics policy, to focus more on combating the production and smuggling of cocaine rather than the eradication of coca. Salazar provoked controversy in May by signing an agreement with coca producers in the Cusco region that committed the Government to re-evaluating its membership of the Vienna Convention on Narcotic Drugs (which required that the authorities implement measures to control coca production). Salazar resigned over the issue and his replacement stated that henceforth coca eradication was the sole responsibility of the state anti-narcotic agency. The US Drug Enforcement Administration (DEA) projected that potential cocaine production in Peru exceeded that of Colombia in 2010, reaching 325 tons, a 44% increase from 2009 and the highest level since 1995. The DEA also warned that Mexican drugs-trafficking organizations were expanding their activities into Peru and Bolivia. The Humala Government that took office in July 2011 asserted that coca eradication alone would not prevent illicit drugs production, identifying additional priorities for its counter-narcotics policy, including an increased focus on combating organized crime and money-laundering, on controlling processing materials and on providing alternative livelihoods for rural communities. However, the appointment of Ricardo Soberón as the new head of the anti-drugs body was criticized, owing to his alleged close links with coca-growing associations. Soberón resigned in January 2012 amid disagreements within the administration regarding forced coca eradication, the effectiveness of which Soberón doubted; his replacement, Carmen Masías Claux, notably stated that coca eradication fell within the remit of the Ministry of the Interior. A report published by the UN in late 2012 stated that coca production in Peru rose by 5.2% in 2011, with the area under cultivation increasing to 64,400 ha in that year, compared with 61,200 ha in 2010.

Foreign Affairs

Meeting in Caracas, Venezuela, in May 1991, the Presidents of the five South American nations comprising the Andean Group (now the Andean Community of Nations, see p. 199) formalized their commitment to the full implementation of an Andean free trade area by the end of 1995, to be achieved by a gradual reduction in tariffs and other trade barriers. An agreement to restructure the Group into the Andean Community, thus strengthening regional integration, was signed in 1996 in Trujillo. In 1997 the Peruvian Government announced plans to abolish tariffs on some 2,500 goods entering Peru from within the Community (with immediate effect), and its intention to remove tariffs on a further 3,500 goods (including more than 600 deemed 'sensitive') by 2005. Peru was admitted as an associate member of the Southern Common Market (Mercosur—Mercado Común del Sur, see p. 439) in 2003. The US Andean Trade Promotion and Drug Eradication Act (ATPDEA), which awarded Peru significant new tariff reductions on exports to the USA, including clothing and manufactures, came into operation in 2002, but expired at the end of 2010. Meanwhile, a free trade agreement between Peru and the USA was enacted in 2009, in spite of vociferous opposition from left-wing and indigenous groups. Peru signed a number of further free trade accords in recent years: an agreement with the People's Republic of China, a major trading partner, came into effect in 2010, as did one with the Republic of Korea in the same year. An accord was reached with the European Union in 2012, although this awaited ratification by the Peruvian legislature. President Humala made official visits to Japan and the Republic of Korea in mid-2012 with the aim of strengthening bilateral trading relations.

A long-standing border dispute with Ecuador over the Cordillera del Cóndor descended into armed conflict in January 1981. A cease-fire was declared a few days later, under the auspices of the guarantors (Argentina, Brazil, Chile and the USA) of the Rio de Janeiro Protocol of 1942, which had awarded the area, affording access to the Amazon river basin, to Peru. However, the Protocol had never been recognized by Ecuador, and, despite mutual efforts to achieve a constructive dialogue, the matter continued to be a source of tension and recurrent skirmishes between the two countries. In January 1995 serious fighting broke out. Representatives of both countries, meeting in Brazil under the auspices of the Rio de Janeiro Protocol guarantors, approved a provisional cease-fire. Following further negotiations, both countries signed the Itamaraty Peace Declaration. The withdrawal of forces from the disputed border area was achieved by mid-May. None the less, reports of further armed clashes prompted requests from both countries for an extension of the observer mission. Agreement on the delimitation of a demilitarized zone in the disputed Cenepa river region came into effect in August. In September Fujimori agreed to reopen the border with Ecuador for commercial purposes, and in November both countries agreed to pursue further confidence-building measures. In 1996 the Ministers of Foreign Affairs of both countries, meeting in Chile under the auspices of the guarantor countries, signed the Santiago Agreement, which was to provide a framework for a settlement of the border issue.

Following further negotiations, in 1998 a number of commissions were established to examine specific aspects of a potential agreement between Peru and Ecuador, including a trade and navigation treaty and the fixing of frontier markers on the ground in the Cordillera del Cóndor. Talks culminated in the signing of an accord in Brasília, Brazil, in October by the Ministers of Foreign Affairs of Peru and Ecuador. The accord confirmed Peru's claim regarding the delineation of the border, but granted Ecuador navigation and trading rights on the Amazon and its tributaries and the opportunity to establish two trading centres in Peru (although this was not to constitute sovereign access). Moreover, Ecuador was given 1 sq km of territory, as private property, at Tiwintza in Peru, where many Ecuadorean soldiers, killed during the conflict in 1995, were buried. Although considerable opposition to the accord was expressed in Peru, international reaction was very favourable and resulted in several offers of finance from multilateral agencies for cross-border development projects.

In 1992 the Presidents of Peru and Bolivia concluded an agreement whereby Bolivia would be granted access to the Pacific Ocean via the Peruvian port of Ilo (which would be jointly developed as a free zone). In return, Bolivia agreed to help facilitate Peruvian access to the Atlantic Ocean (through Brazil) by way of the Bolivian town of Puerto Suárez. In 2004, following negotiations on economic integration, the Presidents of Peru and

Bolivia signed a declaration of intent to create a special zone in Ilo for the exportation of Bolivian gas. In 2010 the Peruvian and Bolivian Presidents signed an agreement expanding the 1992 accord, by allowing Bolivia to construct docks, storage facilities and a naval academy in Ilo.

The support of President Chávez for Humala in the presidential election of 2006 severely strained Peru's relations with Venezuela. President Toledo criticized Chávez for interfering in Peru's domestic affairs and withdrew Peru's ambassador from Venezuela, prompting Chávez to recall the Venezuelan ambassador from Peru a few days later. Full diplomatic relations were restored in 2007. The establishment in March 2008 of a congressional committee to investigate the Casas del Alba—ostensibly humanitarian organizations founded in previous months by Peruvian supporters of Chávez—once again strained relations between the two countries. Venezuela strongly denied allegations by the Peruvian Government that the offices, named after Chávez's regional integration project, the Bolivarian Alliance for the Peoples of our America (Alianza Bolivariana para los Pueblos de Nuestra América—ALBA), were funded by the Venezuelan Government as a means of promoting 'Bolivarian' ideology in Peru. Nevertheless, in March 2009 a report published by the congressional committee concluded that both Venezuela and Bolivia, another ALBA member country, had interfered in Peru's internal affairs; the report recommended that the Congreso close all 146 Casas del Alba and submit formal protests to the Governments of Venezuela and Bolivia. Relations with Venezuela were further impaired in April by the Peruvian Government's decision to grant asylum to the Venezuelan opposition leader and former presidential candidate, Manuel Rosales, who had taken refuge in Peru after being charged with corruption offences in his home country. Venezuela recalled its ambassador in response to the incident.

Peru's relations with Chile, which had been strained during Toledo's presidency, improved significantly after García took office in 2006. In August the two countries agreed to expand the scope of a bilateral economic agreement reached in 1998 by including provisions related to cross-border investment and trade in services. It was hoped that this would eventually lead to the conclusion of a free trade agreement. García also urged the Chilean Government to rejoin the Andean Community as an associate member (which it did in November 2006), and an agreement on military co-operation was reached in October. Notwithstanding these advances, an ongoing dispute over maritime boundaries was rekindled in August 2007 by the Peruvian Government's publication of an official map that restated the country's long-standing claim to some 37,900 sq km of the Pacific Ocean controlled by Chile. The move prompted the Chilean Government, which maintained that the issue had already been resolved by previous bilateral treaties, to recall its ambassador for consultations. In January 2008 Peru presented an application to the International Court of Justice (see p. 26) for adjudication on the disputed border. Public hearings on the case began in December 2012.

CONSTITUTION AND GOVERNMENT

A new Constitution, drafted by the Congreso Constituyente Democrático, was approved by a national referendum on 31 October 1993, and was promulgated on 29 December. Under the terms of the Constitution, executive power is vested in the President, who is elected for a five-year term by universal adult suffrage and is eligible for re-election for a successive term of office. Two Vice-Presidents are also elected. The President governs with the assistance of an appointed Council of Ministers. Legislative power is vested in a single chamber Congreso (removing the distinction in the 1979 Constitution of an upper and lower house) consisting of 130 members (increased from 120 following the 2011 elections, in accordance with a constitutional amendment adopted in September 2009). The members of the Congreso are elected for a five-year term by universal adult suffrage. For administrative purposes, Peru comprises 25 regions, which are subdivided into 195 provinces; the provinces are further subdivided into districts.

REGIONAL AND INTERNATIONAL CO-OPERATION

Peru is a member of the Andean Community of Nations (see p. 199), the Inter-American Development Bank (IDB, see p. 341), the Southern Common Market (Mercosur—Mercado Común del Sur, see p. 439) and the Latin American Integration Association (ALADI, see p. 370), all of which encourage regional economic development, and of the Rio Group (formerly the Group of Eight Countries, see p. 478), which attempts to reduce regional indebtedness. Peru became a member of the Asia-Pacific Economic Co-operation group (APEC, see p. 208) in 1998. In December 2004 Peru was one of 12 countries that were signatories to the agreement, signed in Cusco, creating the South American Community of Nations (which was inaugurated, as the Unión Suramericana de Naciones—UNASUR—in May 2008), intended to promote greater regional economic integration. The country is a member of the Organization of American States (OAS, see p. 404), and of the Community of Latin American and Caribbean States (see p. 475), which was formally inaugurated in December 2011. In June 2012 the Presidents of Peru, Chile, Colombia and Mexico signed a framework agreement in Antofagasta, Chile, creating a new regional economic bloc, the Pacific Alliance (see p. 463).

Peru became a member of the UN in 1945. The country has been a member of the World Trade Organization (WTO, see p. 444) since January 1995. Peru is a member of the Group of 15 (G15, see p. 461) and the Group of 77 (G77, see p. 461) organization of developing states.

ECONOMIC AFFAIRS

In 2011, according to estimates by the World Bank, Peru's gross national income (GNI), measured at average 2009–11 prices, was US $161,701m., equivalent to $5,500 per head (or $10,160 per head on an international purchasing-power parity basis). During 2002–11, it was estimated, the population increased by an average of 1.1% per year, while gross domestic product (GDP) per head increased, in real terms, at an average annual rate of 5.3%. According to official figures, overall GDP increased, in real terms, at an average annual rate of 6.5% in 2002–11; growth was 6.9% in 2011.

Agriculture (including forestry and fishing) contributed 6.9% of GDP in 2011, and the sector engaged 8.1% of the economically active population residing in urban areas in 2008. Rice, maize and potatoes are the principal food crops. The principal cash crop is coffee. Peru is the world's leading producer of coca, and the cultivation of this shrub, for the production of the illicit drug cocaine, reportedly generates revenue of US $1,500m.–$2,500m. per year. Fishing, particularly for the South American pilchard and the anchoveta, provides another important source of revenue, and the fishing sector contributed an estimated 0.8% of GDP in 2011. Fishing accounted for 1.8% of the total value of exports in 2010. During 2002–11 agricultural GDP increased at an average annual rate of 4.2%; the sector's GDP increased by 5.7% in 2011.

Industry (including mining, manufacturing, construction and power) provided 36.5% of GDP in 2011 and employed 20.8% of the working population in 2008. During 2002–11 industrial GDP increased by an average of 6.5% per year; industrial GDP increased by 4.3% in 2011.

Mining (including hydrocarbon extraction) contributed 12.3% of GDP in 2011 and employed 1.0% of the urban working population in 2008. Production of natural gas rose sharply following the opening of the Camisea natural gas export pipeline in 2004, and stood at 418,795m. cu ft in 2012. Peru's first natural gas liquefaction plant was inaugurated in 2010. Copper accounted for 17.5% of total export earnings in 2010. Zinc, gold, petroleum and its derivatives, lead and silver are also major mineral exports. During 2002–11 the GDP of the mining and petroleum sector increased at an average annual rate of 3.5%; real GDP grew by 0.1% in 2011.

Manufacturing contributed 14.7% of GDP and employed 10.1% of the employed population in 2011. The principal branches of manufacturing were food products, petroleum refineries, non-ferrous metals, beverages, and textiles and clothing. During 2002–11 manufacturing GDP increased by an average of 6.4% per year. The sector's GDP increased by 6.0% in 2011.

Construction contributed 7.6% of GDP and employed 5.7% of the employed population in 2011. During 2002–11 the GDP of the construction sector increased at an average annual rate of 10.1%; real GDP grew by 3.0% in 2011

Energy is derived principally from domestic supplies of hydro-electric power (57.6% of total electricity production in 2009) and natural gas (34.3%). Imports of mineral fuels and lubricants comprised 14.2% of the value of merchandise imports in 2010.

The services sector contributed 56.6% of GDP and employed 57.2% of the total working population in 2011. Tourism is gradually emerging as an important source of foreign revenue (US $2,360m. in 2011, according to provisional figures). In 2002–

11 the GDP of the services sector increased at an average annual rate of 6.8%; the sector's GDP grew by 8.3% in 2011.

In 2011 Peru recorded a visible merchandise trade surplus of US $10,005m., while there was a deficit of $3,341m. on the current account of the balance of payments. In 2010 the principal source of imports (19.5%) was the USA, which was also the principal market for exports (16.4%). Other major trading partners were the People's Republic of China and Brazil for imports, and China, Switzerland-Liechtenstein, Canada and Japan for exports. The principal exports in 2010 were crude materials (particularly copper and zinc), food and live animals, basic manufactures, mineral fuels and lubricants, and miscellaneous manufactured articles. The principal imports in the same year were machinery and transport equipment, basic manufactures, chemicals and related products, mineral fuels and lubricants, and food and live animals.

In 2011 there was a preliminary general budgetary surplus of 8,944m. new soles, equivalent to 1.8% of GDP. In 2011 Peru's general government gross debt was 101,790m. new soles, equivalent to 20.9% of GDP. Peru's external debt at the end of 2010 was US $36,271m., of which $20,027m. was long-term public and publicly guaranteed debt. In that year, the cost of servicing long-term public and publicly guaranteed debt and repayments to the IMF was equivalent to 16.7% of the value of exports of goods, services and income (excluding workers' remittances). The annual rate of inflation averaged 2.8% in 2002–11. Consumer prices increased by an average of 3.4% in 2011. According to official figures, 4.0% of the labour force were unemployed in 2011.

The election of the nationalist Ollanta Humala to the presidency in 2011 initially prompted fears among investors of a radical shift to the left in economic policy; however, the new President insisted that he would adhere to free market policies while promoting social inclusion, and the composition of his Government, which included a number of technocrats and orthodox economists, was welcomed by the business community. His administration set several economic targets for its five-year term of office, including annual real GDP growth of at least 6% and public debt equivalent to no more than 15% of GDP. Upon completion of his first year in office Humala pledged to increase social spending and to reduce the percentage of people living in poverty from some 30% to 15% by the end of his term. Humala's Government also reached early agreement with mining companies on a new royalty tax on operating profits, although mining-related social unrest caused difficulties for the sector and for the Government later in 2011 and throughout 2012. The economy is vulnerable to fluctuations in international commodity prices and a steep decline in mineral prices caused by the global financial crisis led to a sharp deceleration in GDP growth, to 0.9%, in 2009, reducing the value of exports and levels of foreign investment. GDP growth recovered to 8.8% in 2010, as private investment, domestic demand and export revenue rose strongly, and remained relatively robust at 6.9% in 2011. GDP growth of 6.3% was recorded in 2012, although slower rates of 5.1% and 4.8% were forecast for 2013 and 2014, respectively, owing to an expected contraction in the construction sector and to reduced demand for Peru's mineral exports from the Chinese market.

PUBLIC HOLIDAYS

2014: 1 January (New Year's Day), 17 April (Maundy Thursday), 18 April (Good Friday), 1 May (Labour Day), 24 June (Day of the Peasant, half-day only), 30 June (for St Peter and St Paul), 28–29 July (Independence), 30 August (St Rose of Lima), 8 October (Battle of Angamos), 1 November (All Saints' Day), 8 December (Immaculate Conception), 25 December (Christmas Day).

Statistical Survey

Sources (unless otherwise stated): Banco Central de Reserva del Perú, Jirón Antonio Miró Quesada 441–445, Lima 1; tel. (1) 4267041; fax (1) 4275880; e-mail webmaster@bcrp.gob.pe; internet www.bcrp.gob.pe; Instituto Nacional de Estadística e Informática, Avda General Garzón 658, Jesús María, Lima; tel. (1) 2218990; fax (1) 4417760; e-mail infoinei@inei.gob.pe; internet www.inei.gob.pe.

Area and Population

AREA, POPULATION AND DENSITY
(excluding Indian jungle population)

Area (sq km)	
Land	1,280,086
Inland water	5,130
Total	1,285,216*
Population (census results)†‡	
11 July 1993	22,048,356
21 October 2007	
Males	13,622,640
Females	13,789,517
Total	27,412,157
Population (official estimates at mid-year)	
2011	29,797,694
2012	30,135,875
2013	30,475,144
Density (per sq km) at mid-2013	23.8

* 496,225 sq miles.
† Excluding adjustment for underenumeration, estimated at 2.35% in 1993.
‡ An additional census was compiled, according to different methodology, during 18 July–20 August 2005. The total population was recorded at 27,219,264 in that year, including adjustment for an estimated 3.92% underenumeration (when the enumerated total was 26,152,265).

POPULATION BY AGE AND SEX
(official estimates at mid-2013)

	Males	Females	Total
0–14	4,460,007	4,294,456	8,754,463
15–64	9,936,642	9,876,185	19,812,827
65 and over	874,413	1,033,441	1,907,854
Total	15,271,062	15,204,082	30,475,144

REGIONS
(official estimates at mid-2013)

	Area (sq km)	Population	Density (per sq km)	Capital
Amazonas . .	39,249	419,404	10.7	Chachapoyas
Ancash . .	35,915	1,135,962	31.6	Huaraz
Apurímac . .	20,896	454,324	21.7	Abancay
Arequipa . .	63,345	1,259,162	19.9	Arequipa
Ayacucho . .	43,815	673,609	15.4	Ayacucho
Cajamarca . .	33,318	1,519,764	45.6	Cajamarca
Callao* . . .	147	982,800	6,685.7	Callao
Cusco . .	71,987	1,300,609	18.1	Cusco (Cuzco)
Huancavelica .	22,131	487,472	22.0	Huancavelica
Huánuco . .	36,849	847,714	23.0	Huánuco
Ica . . .	21,328	771,507	36.2	Ica
Junín . . .	44,197	1,331,253	30.1	Huancayo
La Libertad .	25,500	1,814,276	71.1	Trujillo
Lambayeque .	14,231	1,239,882	87.1	Chiclayo
Lima . . .	34,802	9,540,996	274.2	Lima
Loreto . .	368,852	1,018,160	2.8	Iquitos

—continued	Area (sq km)	Population	Density (per sq km)	Capital
Madre de Dios .	85,301	130,876	1.5	Puerto Maldonado
Moquegua . .	15,734	176,736	11.2	Moquegua
Pasco . . .	25,320	299,807	11.8	Cerro de Pasco
Piura . . .	35,892	1,814,622	50.6	Piura
Puno . . .	71,999	1,389,684	19.3	Puno
San Martín .	51,253	818,061	16.0	Moyabamba
Tacna . . .	16,076	333,276	20.7	Tacna
Tumbes . .	4,669	231,480	49.6	Tumbes
Ucayali . .	102,411	483,708	4.7	Pucallpa
Total . .	.1,285,216	30,475,144	23.7	—

* Province.

PRINCIPAL TOWNS
(population of towns and urban environs at 21 October 2007)

Lima (capital) . .	8,472,935*	Iquitos	370,962
Arequipa . .	749,291	Cusco (Cuzco) . .	348,935
Trujillo . . .	682,834	Chimbote . . .	334,568
Chiclayo . . .	524,442	Huancayo . . .	323,054
Callao . . .	515,200†	Tacna	242,451
Piura . . .	377,496	Ica	219,856

* Metropolitan area (Gran Lima) only.
† Estimated population of town, excluding urban environs, at mid-1985.
Mid-2013 (incl. suburbs, official estimates): Lima (capital) 9,585,636.

BIRTHS, MARRIAGES AND DEATHS

	Registered live births		Registered marriages		Registered deaths	
	Number	Rate (per 1,000)	Number	Rate (per 1,000)	Number	Rate (per 1,000)
2005 . .	611,459	22.0	82,277	3.0	103,207	3.7
2006 . .	637,974	22.7	89,162	3.2	105,074	3.7
2007 . .	663,056	23.3	90,883	3.2	107,249	3.8
2008 . .	679,122	23.6	94,971	3.3	108,100	3.8
2009 . .	660,716	22.7	87,561	3.0	110,811	3.8
2010 . .	637,902	21.7	82,043	2.8	108,178	3.7

Life expectancy (years at birth): 74.0 (males 71.4; females 76.6) in 2011 (Source: World Bank, World Development Indicators database).

EMPLOYMENT
('000 persons aged 14 years and over, urban areas)

	2006	2007	2008
Agriculture, hunting and forestry .	857.3	698.5	710.7
Fishing	42.0	58.7	59.0
Mining and quarrying	94.2	97.2	98.8
Manufacturing	1,135.7	1,292.2	1,316.6
Electricity, gas and water . . .	26.3	21.1	35.8
Construction	431.6	469.8	512.0
Wholesale and retail trade; repair of motor vehicles, motorcycles and personal and household goods	2,035.2	2,087.6	2,101.4
Hotels and restaurants . . .	631.1	680.5	730.2
Transport, storage and communications	750.7	840.5	907.0
Financial intermediation . . .	74.5	69.5	92.3
Real estate, renting and business activities	426.8	483.0	486.4

—continued	2006	2007	2008
Public administration and defence; compulsory social security . .	396.5	437.6	423.2
Education	545.7	650.3	641.5
Health and social work . . .	201.1	248.4	270.5
Other services	568.7	587.1	634.5
Private households	476.0	474.3	423.4
Extra-territorial organizations .	0.7	1.5	2.2
Total employed	8,694.0	9,197.8	9,445.5

Source: ILO.

2007 (persons aged 14 years and over, census figures): Total employed 10,166,179 (males 6,563,384, females 3,602,795); Unemployed 474,464 (males 316,021, females 158,443); *Total labour force* 10,640,643 (males 6,879,405, females 3,761,238).

2011 ('000 persons, national household survey): Agriculture, fishing and mining 4,142; Manufacturing 1,548; Construction 866; Commerce 2,789; Transport and communications 1,226; Other services 4,734; *Total employed* 15,307 (males 8,554, females 6,753); Unemployed 642 (males 331, females 311; *Total labour force* 15,949 (males 8,885, females 7,064).

Health and Welfare

KEY INDICATORS

Total fertility rate (children per woman, 2010)	2.5
Under-5 mortality rate (per 1,000 live births, 2010) . . .	19
HIV/AIDS (% of persons aged 15–49, 2009)	0.4
Physicians (per 1,000 head, 1999)	1.2
Hospital beds (per 1,000 head, 2004)	0.9
Health expenditure (2009): US $ per head (PPP)	466
Health expenditure (2009): % of GDP	5.3
Health expenditure (2009): public (% of total)	57.7
Access to water (% of persons, 2010)	85
Access to sanitation (% of persons, 2010)	71
Total carbon dioxide emissions ('000 metric tons, 2008) . .	40,535.0
Carbon dioxide emissions per head (metric tons, 2008) . .	1.4
Human Development Index (2011): ranking	80
Human Development Index (2011): value	0.725

For sources and definitions, see explanatory note on p. vi.

Agriculture

PRINCIPAL CROPS
('000 metric tons)

	2009	2010	2011
Wheat	226.3	219.5	214.1
Rice, paddy	2,991.2	2,831.4	2,624.5
Barley	213.2	216.2	201.2
Maize	1,559.8	1,541.2	1,514.4
Potatoes	3,765.3	3,814.4	4,073.6
Sweet potatoes	262.7	263.5	299.1
Cassava (Manioc)	1,166.0	1,240.1	1,116.7
Sugar cane	9,937.0	9,660.9	9,884.9
Beans, dry	98.6	92.8	87.8
Oil palm fruit	268.3	291.8	361.7
Cabbages	39.8	37.0	37.1
Asparagus	313.9	335.2	392.3
Tomatoes	221.6	224.9	186.0
Pumpkins, squash and gourds .	190.5	179.5	199.0
Chillies and peppers, green* . .	10.7	11.4	11.5
Onions, dry	606.1	724.0	726.9
Garlic	58.0	63.0	88.5
Peas, green	105.2	102.3	100.8
Broad beans, dry	69.6	67.1	64.7
Carrots and turnips	162.4	182.4	183.9
Maize, green	394.2	408.2	368.6
Plantains	1,866.6	2,007.3	1,967.9
Oranges	377.6	394.6	418.6

—continued	2009	2010	2011
Tangerines, mandarins, clementines and satsumas . .	166.1	221.3	236.3
Lemons and limes	208.0	233.0	224.7
Apples	137.2	143.9	149.5
Grapes	264.4	280.5	296.4
Watermelons	106.9	91.7	87.0
Guavas, mangoes and mangosteens	170.6	457.8	355.4
Avocados	157.4	184.4	212.9
Pineapples	274.4	310.6	400.4
Papayas	173.9	186.8	125.8
Coffee, green	243.5	264.6	313.6

* FAO estimates.

Aggregate production ('000 metric tons, may include official, semi-official or estimated data): Total cereals 5,049.9 in 2009, 4,868.1 in 2010, 4,614.5 in 2011; Total roots and tubers 5,490.1 in 2009, 5,621.1 in 2010, 5,802.3 in 2011; Total vegetables (incl. melons) 2,678.8 in 2009, 2,846.6 in 2010, 2,884.0 in 2011; Total fruits (excl. melons) 4,199.2 in 2009, 4,821.2 in 2010, 4,811.6 in 2011.

Source: FAO.

LIVESTOCK
('000 head, year ending September)

	2009	2010	2011
Horses*	732	735	740
Asses*	635	635	635
Mules*	300	300	300
Cattle	5,459	5,520	5,689
Pigs	3,257	3,254	3,263
Sheep	14,138	14,160	14,050
Goats	1,929	1,968	1,946
Chickens	137,838	130,779	128,943

* FAO estimates.
Source: FAO.

LIVESTOCK PRODUCTS
('000 metric tons)

	2009	2010	2011
Cattle meat	164.7	171.9	178.6
Sheep meat	33.5	33.7	35.3
Pig meat	114.7	115.7	117.4
Chicken meat	964.4	1,020.0	1,084.8
Cows' milk	1,652.1	1,678.4	1,745.5
Hen eggs	268.7	285.1	317.7
Wool, greasy	10.3	8.7*	8.7*

* FAO estimate.
Source: FAO.

Forestry

ROUNDWOOD REMOVALS
('000 cubic metres, excluding bark)

	2009	2010	2011
Sawlogs, veneer logs and logs for sleepers	1,192	1,212	1,373
Other industrial wood	155	140	123
Fuel wood	7,343	7,338	7,425
Total	**8,690**	**8,690**	**8,921**

Source: FAO.

SAWNWOOD PRODUCTION
('000 cubic metres, including railway sleepers)

	2009	2010	2011
Coniferous (softwood)	7	2	9
Broadleaved (hardwood) . . .	619	626	702
Total	**626**	**628**	**711**

Source: FAO.

Fishing
('000 metric tons, live weight)

	2008	2009	2010
Capture	7,394.5	6,914.5	4,216.1
Chilean jack mackerel . . .	169.5	74.7	17.6
Anchoveta (Peruvian anchovy) .	6,258.0	5,935.2	3,450.6
Jumbo flying squid	533.4	411.8	369.8
Aquaculture	43.1	44.3	89.0
Total catch	**7,437.7**	**6,958.8**	**4,305.1**

Note: Figures exclude aquatic plants ('000 metric tons, all capture): 13.8 in 2008; 5.7 in 2009; 4.4 in 2010.

Source: FAO.

Mining
('000 metric tons unless otherwise indicated)*

	2010	2011	2012
Crude petroleum ('000 barrels) .	57,363.0	55,741.2	55,991.3
Natural gas (million cu ft) . .	255,609.2	401,169.4	418,794.8
Copper	1,024.0	1,024.8	1,120.7
Lead	241.2	211.9	228.9
Molybdenum	16.3	18.4	16.1
Tin	29.4	25.1	22.7
Zinc	1,258.4	1,075.2	1,096.3
Iron ore	6,139.3	7,123.1	6,791.5
Gold ('000 kg)	159.4	161.4	156.7
Silver ('000 kg)	3,422.6	3,214.3	3,270.9

* Figures for metallic minerals refer to metal content only.

Industry

SELECTED PRODUCTS
('000 metric tons, unless otherwise indicated)

	2010	2011	2012
Canned fish	77.8	118.7	64.0
Wheat flour	1,214	1,249	1,255
Raw sugar	1,039.2	1,076.2	1,097.8
Beer ('000 hl)	12,303	13,054	13,643
Motor spirit (petrol, '000 barrels)* .	15,185†	n.a.	n.a.
Kerosene ('000 barrels)* . . .	80†	n.a.	n.a.
Distillate fuel oils ('000 barrels)* .	24,606†	n.a.	n.a.
Residual fuel oils ('000 barrels)* .	10,124†	n.a.	n.a.
Portland cement	6,941	7,026	8,038
Crude steel*	750‡	n.a.	n.a.
Copper (refined)	111.5	110.6	86.0
Electric energy (million kWh) .	35,500.3	38,701.4	40,985.2

* Source: US Geological Survey.
† Preliminary figure.
‡ Estimate.

Finance

CURRENCY AND EXCHANGE RATES

Monetary Units
100 céntimos = 1 nuevo sol (new sol).

Sterling, Dollar and Euro Equivalents (31 October 2012)
£1 sterling = 4.176 new soles;
US $1 = 2.592 new soles;
€1 = 3.367 new soles;
100 new soles = £23.94= $38.59 = €29.70.

Average Exchange Rate (new soles per US $)
2009   3.0115
2010   2.8251
2011   2.7541

Note: On 1 February 1985 Peru replaced its former currency, the sol, with the inti, valued at 1,000 soles. A new currency, the nuevo sol (equivalent to 1m. intis), was introduced in July 1991.

CENTRAL GOVERNMENT BUDGET
(million new soles, preliminary figures)

Revenue	2009	2010	2011
Taxation	52,566	64,429	75,482
Taxes on income, profits, etc.	20,346	25,802	33,627
Taxes on imports (excl. VAT) .	1,493	1,803	1,380
Value-added tax	29,519	35,536	40,424
Domestic	17,322	19,629	22,029
Imports	12,197	15,907	18,395
Excises	4,146	4,670	4,720
Fuel duty	2,255	2,410	2,231
Other taxes	4,400	4,566	5,043
Less Refunds	7,339	7,948	9,712
Other current revenue	8,265	10,283	12,668
Capital revenue*	444	747	288
Total	61,275	75,459	88,438

Expenditure	2009	2010	2011
Current non-interest expenditure .	47,577	51,441	58,379
Compensation of employees .	15,160	15,823	17,644
Goods and non-labour services .	13,341	15,537	17,051
Transfers	19,077	20,081	23,685
Interest payments	4,867	4,766	5,219
Internal	1,801	1,875	2,430
External	3,066	2,891	2,789
Capital expenditure	14,537	19,048	20,499
Gross capital formation . . .	9,878	13,452	13,918
Total	66,982	75,256	84,097

* Net of payments to the American International Group and the Perú-Alemania Agreement.

General Budget (million new soles, preliminary figures): *2009:* Total revenue 72,649 (current 72,201, capital 448); Total expenditure 78,336 (current non-interest 51,938, capital 21,496, interest payments 4,902). *2010:* Total revenue 87,692 (current 86,948, capital 744); Total expenditure 88,363 (current non-interest 57,141, capital 26,231, interest payments 4,992). *2011:* Total revenue 102,380 (current 102,089, capital 290); Total expenditure 93,436 (current non-interest 63,322, capital 24,503, interest payments 5,610).

INTERNATIONAL RESERVES
(US $ million at 31 December)

	2009	2010	2011
Gold	1,217.7	1,564.9	1,722.3
IMF special drawing rights . .	821.6	807.2	805.0
Foreign exchange	30,999.8	41,652.8	46,096.5
Total	33,039.1	44,024.9	48,623.8

Source: IMF, *International Financial Statistics*.

MONEY SUPPLY
(million new soles at 31 December)

	2009	2010	2011
Currency outside banks . .	19,497	24,449	27,643
Demand deposits at commercial and development banks . . .	30,194	33,472	38,079
Total money (incl. others) . .	50,511	60,909	68,349

Source: IMF, *International Financial Statistics*.

COST OF LIVING
(Consumer Price Index, Lima metropolitan area; base: 2000 = 100)

	2005	2006	2007
Food (incl. beverages)	107.6	110.2	113.0
Rent	120.3	123.3	124.5
Electricity, gas and other fuels .	129.7	132.5	132.9
Clothing (incl. footwear) . . .	107.5	109.1	111.9
All items (incl. others) . . .	110.1	112.3	114.3

2008: Food (incl. beverages) 123.3; All items (incl. others) 120.9.
2009: Food (incl. beverages) 128.5; All items (incl. others) 124.4.
2010: Food (incl. beverages) 131.8; All items (incl. others) 126.3.
2011: Food (incl. beverages) 138.2; All items (incl. others) 130.6.
Source: ILO.

NATIONAL ACCOUNTS
(million new soles at current prices)

Expenditure on the Gross Domestic Product

	2009	2010	2011
Government final consumption expenditure	39,452	42,271	45,842
Private final consumption expenditure	248,970	269,045	296,004
Gross capital formation . . .	87,402	118,266	134,582
Total domestic expenditure .	375,824	429,582	476,428
Exports of goods and services . .	93,707	114,095	141,468
Less Imports of goods and services	77,602	98,897	120,066
GDP in purchasers' values .	391,929	444,781	497,831
GDP at constant 1994 prices .	193,108	210,063	224,624

Gross Domestic Product by Economic Activity

	2009	2010	2011
Agriculture, hunting and forestry .	23,834	24,996	28,077
Fishing	2,555	2,559	3,512
Mining and quarrying	37,377	46,535	56,220
Manufacturing	51,667	59,808	67,149
Electricity and water	7,440	7,758	8,619
Construction	27,082	32,690	34,802
Wholesale and retail trade . .	52,025	59,545	66,790
Restaurants and hotels . . .	14,631	16,478	18,982
Transport and communications .	34,114	37,701	42,718
Government services	27,108	28,051	30,294
Other services	83,593	91,251	100,165
Gross value added at basic prices	361,425	407,372	457,329
Import duties	29,012	35,606	39,122
Taxes on products	1,493	1,803	1,380
GDP in purchasers' values .	391,929	444,781	497,831

BALANCE OF PAYMENTS
(US $ million)

	2009	2010	2011
Exports of goods	26,962	35,565	46,269
Imports of goods	−20,808	−28,390	−36,264
Balance on goods	**6,153**	**7,175**	**10,005**
Exports of services	3,439	3,273	3,666
Imports of services	−4,818	−6,044	−6,501
Balance on goods and services	**4,775**	**4,404**	**7,169**
Primary income received . . .	1,400	1,149	1,111
Primary income paid	−9,785	−12,361	−14,821
Balance on goods, services and primary income	**−3,610**	**−6,808**	**−6,540**
Secondary income received . .	2,894	3,033	3,210
Secondary income paid . . .	−7	−7	−11
Current balance	**−723**	**−3,782**	**−3,341**
Capital account (net)	−78	−115	−109
Direct investment assets . .	−411	−266	−113
Direct investment liabilities . .	6,431	8,455	8,233
Portfolio investment assets . .	−3,058	−1,145	−1,472
Portfolio investment liabilities .	758	6,358	921
Other investment assets . . .	116	−1,949	−1,343
Other investment liabilities . .	278	1,938	2,919
Net errors and omissions . .	−1,411	1,476	−1,011
Reserves and related items .	**1,902**	**10,970**	**4,684**

Source: IMF, *International Financial Statistics*.

External Trade

PRINCIPAL COMMODITIES
(distribution by SITC, US $ million)

Imports c.i.f.	2008	2009	2010
Food and live animals . . .	2,348.9	1,943.0	2,498.2
Cereals and cereal preparations .	1,240.5	877.7	1,044.2
Vegetables and fruits	133.9	133.1	171.8
Mineral fuels, lubricants and related materials	5,467.5	3,085.6	4,248.4
Petroleum, petroleum products and related materials	5,125.5	2,974.5	4,147.0
Chemicals and related products	4,078.1	3,289.3	4,386.0
Medicinal and pharmaceutical products	458.3	520.8	587.4
Plastics in primary forms . . .	1,136.3	745.9	1,179.5
Basic manufactures	4,915.6	3,470.1	4,969.1
Iron and steel	2,056.3	1,155.1	1,741.0
Machinery and transport equipment	10,095.0	7,617.8	10,449.9
Machinery specialized for particular industries	1,421.9	1,118.9	1,528.7
General industrial machinery, equipment, etc.	1,724.5	1,340.1	1,594.2
Office machines and automatic data-processing machines . .	780.7	711.3	901.1
Telecommunications, sound-recording and -reproducing equipment	1,574.4	1,011.8	1,350.2
Road vehicles	2,767.4	1,901.5	3,108.9
Miscellaneous manufactured articles	1,724.2	1,533.5	1,971.9
Professional, scientific and controlling instruments . .	333.3	310.4	357.9
Total (incl. others)	**29,952.8**	**21,869.7**	**29,879.5**

Exports f.o.b.	2008	2009	2010
Food and live animals . . .	4,497.3	4,278.4	5,239.1
Fish, crustaceans, molluscs and preparations thereof	609.5	510.6	635.5
Coffee	645.1	585.4	889.1
Crude materials	9,032.0	7,132.5	10,789.1
Iron ore and concentrates . . .	385.1	297.7	523.3
Copper ores and concentrates . .	4,897.5	3,920.9	6,153.9
Lead ores and concentrates . .	801.3	895.1	1,277.3
Zinc ores and concentrates . .	1,294.0	1,123.1	1,473.3
Molybdenum ores and concentrates (excl. roasted)	1,079.4	275.9	492.4
Mineral fuels and lubricants .	2,860.5	2,068.3	3,345.3
Petroleum, petroleum products and related materials	2,850.6	1,923.5	2,810.9
Basic manufactures	5,760.7	3,723.6	4,765.7
Non-ferrous metals	4,813.0	2,952.1	3,852.3
Copper	3,127.1	2,192.2	3,068.4
Miscellaneous manufactured articles	2,071.2	1,512.6	1,573.6
Total (incl. others)	**31,288.2**	**26,738.3**	**35,073.2**

Source: UN, *International Trade Statistics Yearbook*.

PRINCIPAL TRADING PARTNERS
(US $ million)

Imports c.i.f.	2008	2009	2010
Argentina	1,582.0	875.1	1,107.0
Brazil	2,417.8	1,682.9	2,178.7
Canada	436.1	410.4	541.8
Chile	1,183.4	997.3	1,047.9
China, People's Republic . .	4,069.5	3,268.8	5,115.3
Colombia	1,283.0	950.0	1,325.2
Ecuador	1,776.0	1,022.1	1,422.0
France (incl. Monaco) . . .	266.8	205.9	246.0
Germany	857.4	715.4	888.2
India	504.1	311.0	498.1
Italy	731.1	392.8	410.1
Japan	1,277.0	930.2	1,367.0
Korea, Republic	780.0	667.9	1,044.3
Mexico	1,163.5	735.3	1,119.3
Nigeria	73.3	435.8	647.6
Spain	422.0	313.5	403.3
United Kingdom	174.8	143.8	n.a.
USA	5,647.5	4,339.3	5,815.4
Venezuela	333.0	256.8	96.8
Total (incl. others)	**29,952.8**	**21,869.7**	**29,879.5**

Exports f.o.b.	2008	2009	2010
Belgium	411.8	381.9	581.0
Bolivia	350.9	321.8	382.7
Brazil	895.4	508.1	947.5
Canada	1,949.9	2,310.9	3,319.7
Chile	1,840.8	752.2	1,371.8
China, People's Republic . . .	3,735.0	4,078.0	5,425.9
Colombia	708.7	643.8	795.0
Ecuador	504.1	576.5	814.2
Germany	1,028.0	1,042.4	1,514.5
Italy	927.2	607.5	938.4
Japan	1,860.0	1,376.5	1,790.4
Korea, Republic	552.0	749.6	894.9
Mexico	298.7	242.5	285.7
Netherlands	788.3	466.0	621.9
Panama	296.1	91.4	254.0
Spain	1,023.9	736.5	1,163.1
Switzerland-Liechtenstein . .	3,410.3	3,954.3	3,844.4
United Kingdom	377.5	229.0	230.6
USA	5,835.3	4,603.8	5,767.0
Venezuela	1,079.5	614.2	512.9
Total (incl. others)	**31,288.2**	**26,738.3**	**35,073.2**

Source: UN, *International Trade Statistics Yearbook*.

Transport

RAILWAYS
(traffic)*

	2003	2004	2005
Passenger-km (million) . . .	103	119	126
Freight ton-km (million) . . .	1,117	1,147	1,115

* Including service traffic.

Source: UN, *Statistical Yearbook*.

ROAD TRAFFIC
(motor vehicles in use, excl. motorcycles)

	2008	2009	2010
Passenger cars	996,755	1,203,135	1,275,821
Buses and coaches	49,882	64,018	68,096
Lorries and vans	534,061	718,242	790,518

Source: IRF, *World Road Statistics*.

SHIPPING

Flag Registered Fleet
(at 31 December)

	2010	2011	2012
Number of vessels	189	200	206
Total displacement ('000 grt) . .	310.3	443.6	448.1

Source: Lloyd's List Intelligence (www.lloydslistintelligence.com).

International Sea-borne Freight Traffic
('000 metric tons)

	2008	2009	2010
Goods loaded	10,620	9,816	10,152
Goods unloaded	14,280	12,204	16,428

2012 ('000 metric tons): Goods loaded 13,056; Goods unloaded 21,876.

Source: UN, *Monthly Bulletin of Statistics*.

CIVIL AVIATION
(traffic on scheduled services)

	2007	2008	2009
Kilometres flown (million) . .	60	83	88
Passenger-km (million) . .	6,472	8,720	8,765
Total ton-km (million) . . .	236	222	107

Source: UN Economic Commission for Latin America and the Caribbean, *Statistical Yearbook*.

Tourism

ARRIVALS BY NATIONALITY

	2008	2009	2010
Argentina	90,914	114,176	119,771
Bolivia	85,245	91,789	84,315
Brazil	62,902	80,940	85,662
Canada	50,306	52,899	51,236
Chile	445,590	456,896	587,866
Colombia	75,538	86,055	97,319
Ecuador	126,852	134,666	150,915
France	62,901	64,960	65,774
Germany	50,737	50,228	51,357
Japan	42,745	36,394	26,769
Spain	74,196	79,386	84,637
United Kingdom	65,800	57,949	53,403
USA	370,945	374,659	362,906
Total (incl. others)	2,057,620	2,139,961	2,299,187

Total arrivals ('000): 2,598 in 2011 (provisional).

Tourism receipts (US $ million, excl. passenger transport): 2,014 in 2009; 2,008 in 2010; 2,360 in 2011 (provisional).

Source: World Tourism Organization.

Communications Media

	2009	2010	2011
Telephones ('000 main lines in use)	3,158.8	3,159.9	3,688.4
Mobile cellular telephones ('000 subscribers)	24,700.4	29,115.1	32,461.4
Internet subscribers ('000) . .	823.8	924.5	1,197.2
Broadband subscribers ('000) . .	809.6	911.6	1,190.3

Personal computers: 2.8m. (100.6 per 1,000 persons) in 2005.

Source: International Telecommunication Union.

Education

(2012 unless otherwise indicated)

	Institutions	Teachers	Pupils
Nursery	42,173	67,285	1,387,134
Primary	35,917	191,537	3,436,170
Secondary	12,527	170,219	2,390,708
Higher: universities* . . .	78	33,177	435,637
Higher: other tertiary . . .	943	21,586	376,782
Special	441	3,564	17,446
Vocational	1,644	9,576	230,421

* Figures for 2000.

Source: Ministerio de Educación del Perú.

Pupil-teacher ratio (primary education, UNESCO estimate): 19.7 in 2009/10 (Source: UNESCO Institute for Statistics).

Adult literacy rate (UNESCO estimates): 89.6% (males 94.9%; females 84.6%) in 2007 (Source: UNESCO Institute for Statistics).

Directory

The Government

HEAD OF STATE

President: Lt-Col (retd) OLLANTA MOISÉS HUMALA TASSO (took office 28 July 2011).

First Vice-President: MARISOL ESPINOZA CRUZ.

COUNCIL OF MINISTERS
(May 2013)

The Government was formed by a coalition led by the Partido Nacionalista Peruano, and independents.

President of the Council of Ministers: JUAN FEDERICO JIMÉNEZ MAYOR.

Minister of Foreign Affairs: EDA ADRIANA RIVAS FRANCHINI.

Minister of Defence: PEDRO ALVARO CATERIANO BELLIDO.

Minister of Economy and Finance: LUIS MIGUEL CASTILLA RUBIO.

Minister of the Interior: GERÓNIMO WILFREDO PEDRAZA SIERRA.

Minister of Justice and Human Rights: DANIEL FIGALLO.

Minister of Education: PATRICIA SALAS O'BRIEN.

Minister of Health: MIDORI MUSME DE HABICH ROSPIGLIOSI.

Minister of Agriculture: MILTON MARTÍN VON HESSE LA SERNA.

Minister of Labour and Employment: NANCY TERESA LAOS CÁCERES.

Minister of International Trade and Tourism: JOSÉ LUIS SILVA MARTINOT.

Minister of Transport and Communications: CARLOS EDUARDO PAREDES RODRÍGUEZ.

Minister of Housing, Construction and Sanitation: RENÉ CORNEJO DÍAZ.

Minister of Energy and Mines: JORGE HUMBERTO MERINO TAFUR.

Minister of Production: GLADYS MÓNICA TREVIÑO CHANG.

Minister of Culture: LUIS ALBERTO PEIRANO FALCONÍ.

Minister of Women and Vulnerable Populations: ANA JARA VELÁSQUEZ.

Minister of the Environment: MANUEL PULGAR-VIDAL.

Minister of Development and Social Inclusion: CAROLINA TRIVELLI AVILA.

MINISTRIES

Office of the President of the Council of Ministers: Jirón Carabaya, cuadra 1 s/n, Anexo 1105-1107, Lima; tel. (1) 2197000; fax (1) 4449168; e-mail atencionciudadana@pcm.gob.pe; internet www.pcm.gob.pe.

Ministry of Agriculture: Avda La Universidad 200, La Molina, Lima; tel. (1) 2098625; e-mail portal@minag.gob.pe; internet www.minag.gob.pe.

Ministry of Culture: Avda Javier Prado Este 2465, San Borja, Lima 41; tel. (1) 6189393; e-mail comunicaciones@mcultura.gob.pe; internet www.mcultura.gob.pe.

Ministry of Defence: Edif. Quiñones, Avda de la Peruanidad s/n, Jesús María, Lima 1; tel. (1) 2098530; e-mail despacho@mindef.gob.pe; internet www.mindef.gob.pe.

Ministry of Development and Social Inclusion: Avda Paseo de la República 3101, San Isidro, Lima; tel. (1) 2098000; e-mail fosorio@midis.gob.pe; internet www.midis.gob.pe.

Ministry of Economy and Finance: Jirón Junín 319, 4°, Circado de Lima, Lima 1; tel. (1) 3115930; e-mail postmaster@mef.gob.pe; internet www.mef.gob.pe.

Ministry of Education: Biblioteca Nacional del Perú, Avda de la Poesía 160, San Borja, Lima 41; tel. (1) 6155800; fax (1) 4370471; e-mail webmaster@minedu.gob.pe; internet www.minedu.gob.pe.

Ministry of Energy and Mines: Avda Las Artes Sur 260, San Borja, Lima 41; tel. (1) 4111100; e-mail webmaster@minem.gob.pe; internet www.minem.gob.pe.

Ministry of the Environment: Avda Javier Prado Oeste 1440, San Isidro, Lima; tel. (1) 6116000; fax (1) 2255369; e-mail minam@minam.gob.pe; internet www.minam.gob.pe.

Ministry of Foreign Affairs: Jirón Lampa 535, Lima 1; tel. (1) 2042400; e-mail informes@rree.gob.pe; internet www.rree.gob.pe.

Ministry of Health: Avda Salaverry 801, Jesús María, Lima 11; tel. (1) 3156600; fax (1) 6271600; e-mail webmaster@minsa.gob.pe; internet www.minsa.gob.pe.

Ministry of Housing, Construction and Sanitation: Edif. de Petroperú, Avda Paseo de la República 3361, San Isidro, Lima; tel. (1) 2117930; e-mail webmaster@vivienda.gob.pe; internet www.vivienda.gob.pe.

Ministry of the Interior: Plaza 30 de Agosto s/n, Urb. Córpac, San Isidro, Lima 27; tel. (1) 5180000; fax (1) 2242405; e-mail dm@mininter.gob.pe; internet www.mininter.gob.pe.

Ministry of International Trade and Tourism: Calle Uno Oeste 50, Urb. Córpac, San Isidro, Lima 27; tel. (1) 5136100; fax (1) 2243362; e-mail webmaster@mincetur.gob.pe; internet www.mincetur.gob.pe.

Ministry of Justice and Human Rights: Scipión Llona 350, Miraflores, Lima 18; tel. (1) 2048020; fax (1) 4223577; e-mail webmaster@minjus.gob.pe; internet www.minjus.gob.pe.

Ministry of Labour and Employment: Avda Salaverry 655, cuadra 8, Jesús María, Lima 11; tel. (1) 6306000; fax (1) 6306060; e-mail informes@trabajo.gob.pe; internet www.mintra.gob.pe.

Ministry of the Presidency: Jirón de la Unión s/n, Cuadra 1, Lima 1; tel. (1) 3113900; fax (1) 3114300; internet www.presidencia.gob.pe.

Ministry of Production: Calle Uno Oeste 60, Urb. Córpac, San Isidro, Lima 27; tel. (1) 6162222; e-mail portal@produce.gob.pe; internet www.produce.gob.pe.

Ministry of Transport and Communications: Jirón Zorritos 1203, Lima 1; tel. (1) 6157800; e-mail atencionalciudadano@mtc.gob.pe; internet www.mtc.gob.pe.

Ministry of Women and Vulnerable Populations: Jirón Camaná 616, Lima 1; tel. (1) 4165200; fax (1) 4261665; e-mail postmaster@mimp.gob.pe; internet www.mimp.gob.pe.

President and Legislature

PRESIDENT

Election, first round, 10 April 2011

Candidate	Valid votes cast	% of votes
Lt-Col (retd) Ollanta Moisés Humala Tasso (Gana Perú*)	4,643,064	31.70
Keiko Sofía Fujimori Higuchi (Fuerza 2011) .	3,449,562	23.56
Pedro Pablo Kuczynski Godard (Alianza por el Gran Cambio)	2,711,332	18.51
Alejandro Toledo Manrique (Perú Posible) .	2,289,540	15.63
Luis Castañeda Lossio (Solidaridad Nacional)	1,440,242	9.83
Others	113,423	0.78
Total valid votes†	14,647,163	100.00

* An alliance led by the Partido Nacionalista Peruano.
† In addition, there were 1,477,696 blank votes and 574,875 invalid votes cast.

Election, second round, 5 June 2011

Candidate	Valid votes cast	% of votes
Lt-Col (retd) Ollanta Moisés Humala Tasso (Gana Perú)	7,937,704	51.45
Keiko Sofía Fujimori Higuchi (Fuerza 2011) .	7,490,647	48.55
Total*	15,428,351	100.00

* In addition, there were 116,335 blank votes and 921,711 invalid votes cast.

CONGRESO

President: VÍCTOR ISLA ROJAS.

General Election, 10 April 2011

Parties	% of valid votes	Seats
Gana Perú*	25.43	47
Fuerza 2011	22.91	37
Perú Posible	14.82	21
Alianza por el Gran Cambio	14.35	12
Solidaridad Nacional	10.19	9
Partido Aprista Peruano	6.46	4
Cambio Radical	2.68	—
Asociación Nacional de Fonavistas de los Pueblos del Perú	1.33	—
Others	1.83	—
Total†	100.00	130

* An alliance led by the Partido Nacionalista Peruano.
† Excluding blank votes and spoiled votes.

Election Commissions

Jurado Nacional de Elecciones (JNE): Avda Nicolás de Piérola 1070, Lima 1; tel. (11) 3111700; e-mail consultas@jne.gob.pe; internet www.jne.gob.pe; f. 1931; autonomous electoral body; 5-mem. council; Pres. FRANCISCO ARTEMIO TÁVARA CÓRDOVA.

Oficina Nacional de Procesos Electorales (ONPE): Jirón Washington 1894, Lima 1; tel. (1) 4170630; e-mail informes@onpe.gob.pe; internet www.onpe.gob.pe; f. 1995; independent; Nat. Dir MARIANO CUCHO ESPINOZA.

Regional Presidents
(May 2013)

Amazonas: José Arista Arbildo.

Ancash: César Joaquín Alvarez Aguilar.

Apurímac: Elías Segovia Ruiz.

Arequipa: Juan Manuel Guillén Benavides.

Ayacucho: Wilfredo Oscorima Núñez.

Cajamarca: Gregorio Santos Guerrero.

Callao: Félix Moreno Caballero.

Cusco: Jorge Acurio Tito.

Huancavelica: Maciste Díaz.

Huánuco: Luis Raúl Picón Quedo.

Ica: Alonso Alberto Navarro Cabanillas.

Junín: Vladimir Cerrón Rojas.

La Libertad: José Humberto Murgia Zannier.

Lambayeque: Humberto Acuña Peralta.

Lima (Provincias): Jesús Alvarado Gonzáles del Valle.

Loreto: Yván Enrique Vásquez Valera.

Madre de Dios: José Luis Aguirre Pastor.

Moquegua: Martín Vizcarra Cornejo.

Pasco: Klever Meléndez.

Piura: Javier Atkins.

Puno: Mauricio Rodríguez Rodríguez.

San Martín: César Villanueva Arévalo.

Tacna: Tito Chocano.

Tumbes: Gerardo Fidel Viñas Dioses.

Ucayali: Jorge Velásquez Portocarrero.

Political Organizations

The following parties were active at a national level in 2013:

Acción Popular (AP): Paseo Colón 218, Lima 1; tel. and fax (1) 3321965; e-mail webmaster@accionpopular.pe; internet accionpopular.com.pe; f. 1956; 1.2m. mems; liberal; contested the 2011 elections as part of the Perú Posible alliance; Pres. Javier Alva Orlandini; Sec.-Gen. Mesias Antonio Guevara Amasifuen.

Alianza para la Alternativa de la Humanidad (APHU): f. 2010; indigenous grouping; not yet officially registered by the Oficina Nacional de Procesos Electorales; Leader Alberto Pizango.

Alianza por el Gran Cambio: Avda Salaverry 2007, Lima; tel. (1) 4710985; e-mail contacto@ppk.pe; internet www.ppk.pe; f. 2010; right-wing coalition formed to contest the 2011 elections; Presidential candidate Pedro Pablo Kuczynski; comprises the following parties:

Alianza para el Progreso: Avda de la Policía 643, entre Cuadra 8 y 9 de Gregorio Escobedo, Jesús María, Lima; tel. (1) 4613197; e-mail informes@app-peru.org.pe; internet www.app-peru.org.pe; f. 2001; Founder and Pres. César Acuña Peralta; Nat. Exec. Sec. Luis Carlos Antonio Iberico Nuñez.

Partido Humanista Peruano (PHP): Canaval y Moreyra 680, San Isidro, Lima; tel. (1) 2241243; e-mail contactenos@partidohumanista.org.pe; internet www.partidohumanista.org.pe; Pres. Yehudé Simón Munaro; Sec.-Gen. Marco Cardoso Montoya.

Partido Popular Cristiano (PPC): Avda Alfonso Ugarte 1484, Breña, Lima; tel. (1) 4238722; fax (1) 4238721; e-mail estflores@terra.com.pe; internet www.ppc.pe; f. 1967; 250,000 mems; Pres. Raúl Castro Stagnaro; Sec.-Gen. Rafael Yamashiro Oré.

Restauración Nacional: Avda Arequipa 3750, San Isidro, Lima; tel. (1) 3117546; f. 2005; evangelical Christian party; Pres. Humberto Lay Sun; Sec.-Gen. Rubén Gavino Sánchez.

APRA: see entry for PAP.

Asociación Nacional de Fonavistas de los Pueblos del Perú (ANFPP): Jirón Caylloma 824, Of. 102, Lima; tel. (1) 4242913; e-mail informes@fonavistas.com; internet www.fonavistas.com; Pres. Andrés Avelino Alcantara Paredes; Vice-Pres. Luis Luzuriaga Garibotto.

Despertar Nacional: Avda Benavides 2470, Miraflores, Lima 18; tel. (1) 3583657; e-mail comunicaciones@despertarnacional.com; internet www.despertarnacional.com; f. 1999; Leader Ricardo Noriega Salaverry.

Fuerza Popular: Paseo Colón 422, Cercado de Lima, Lima; tel. 999383300 (mobile); e-mail contacto@fuerza2011.com; internet www.fuerzapopular.pe; contested the 2011 elections as Fuerza 2011; Pres.

Keiko Sofía Fujimori Higuchi; Sec.-Gen. Clemente Jaime Yoshiyama Tanaka.

Partido Aprista Peruano (PAP): Avda Alfonso Ugarte 1012, Breña, Lima 5; tel. (1) 4250218; e-mail ofisistemapap@apra.pe; internet www.apra.pe; f. in Mexico 1924, in Peru 1930; legalized 1945; democratic left-wing party; although legally known as PAP, the party is commonly known as APRA; Pres. Alan Gabriel Ludwig García Pérez; Secs-Gen. Carlos Arana Vivar, Omar Quezada Martínez; 700,000 mems.

Partido Descentralista Fuerza Social: Jíron Cápac Yupanqui 1076, Jesús María, Lima; tel. (1) 4717895; e-mail central@fuerzasocial.pe; internet fuerzasocial.pe; f. 2007; Pres. Gustavo Guerra-García; Nat. Co-ordinator Rocío Peñafiel.

Partido Nacionalista Peruano (PNP): Avda Arequipa 3410, Lima 27; tel. (1) 4223592; internet www.partido nacionalistaperuano.net; f. 2005; contested the 2011 elections as part of the Gana Perú alliance; Pres. Lt-Col (retd) Ollanta Moisés Humala Tasso.

Partido Político Adelante: Jirón Ricardo Palma 120, San Isidro, Lima; tel. (1) 2212563; e-mail 2004adelante@gmail.com; internet www.adelante.org.pe; f. 2004; Sec.-Gen. Rafael Belaunde Aubry.

Perú Posible (PP): Avda Faustino Sánchez Carrión 601, Jesús María, Lima 11; tel. (1) 4602493; fax (1) 2612418; e-mail sgpp@mixmail.com; internet www.peruposible.org.pe; f. 1994; contested the 2011 elections in alliance with Acción Popular and Somos Perú; Leader Alejandro Toledo Manrique; Sec.-Gen. Luis Alberto Thais Díaz.

Renovación Nacional: Avda Camino Real 1206, 2°, San Isidro, Lima; tel. (1) 5673798; f. 1992; contested the 2011 elections in alliance with Fuerza 2011 (now Fuerza Popular); Pres. Rafael Rey; Sec.-Gen. Wilder Ruíz Silva.

Solidaridad Nacional (SN): Amador Merino Reyna 140, San Isidro, Lima 27; tel. (1) 4213348; e-mail fsandoval@psn.org.pe; internet www.psn.org.pe; f. 1999; centre-left; Pres. Luis Castañeda Lossio; Sec.-Gen. José León Luna Glavez.

Somos Perú (Partido Democrático Somos Perú): Mariscal Las Heras 393, Lince, Lima 14; tel. (1) 4714484; e-mail postmaster@somosperu .org.pe; internet www.somosperu.org.pe; f. 1998; contested the 2011 elections as part of the Perú Posible alliance; Pres. Fernando Andrade Carmona; Sec.-Gen. Víctor Yuri Vilela Seminario.

Unión por el Perú (UPP): Avda Cuba 543, Jesús María, Lima; tel. (1) 4271941; e-mail ivega@partidoupp.org; internet www .partidopoliticoupp.org; f. 1994; ind. movt; Pres. Eduardo Espinoza Ramos; Sec.-Gen. José Vega Antonio.

ILLEGAL GROUPS

Movimiento Nacionalista Peruano (MNP) (Movimiento Etnocacerista): Pasaje Velarde 188, Of. 204, Lima; tel. (1) 4338781; e-mail eletnocacerista@yahoo.com; internet eletnocacerista.galeon.com; ultra-nationalist paramilitary group; Pres. Dr Isaac Humala Núñez; Leader of paramilitary wing Maj. (retd) Antauro Igor Humala Tasso (arrested Jan. 2005 following an armed uprising in Andahuaylas).

Movimiento Por Amnistía y Derechos Fundamentales (Movadef): Jirón Pasco 3679, San Martín de Porres; e-mail movadefperu@hotmail.com; internet movamnsitiayderfundamentales.blogspot.co .uk; f. 1990; political wing of Sendero Luminoso (Shining Path) f. 1970; began armed struggle 1980; splinter group of Partido Comunista Peruano; active in the Apurímac-Ene and Upper Huallaga valleys; advocated the policies of Mao Zedong in the People's Republic of China; from the mid-2000s it became increasingly involved in the illegal drugs trade; founder Dr Abimael Guzmán Reynoso (alias 'Chairman Gonzalo'—arrested Sept. 1992); leaders Víctor Quispe Palomino (alias 'Comrade José'—commander of the Apurímac-Ene contingent), 'Comrade Artemio' (identified as Florindo Eleuterio Flores Hala—commander of the Upper Huallaga contingent).

Diplomatic Representation
EMBASSIES IN PERU

Algeria: Avda El Rosario 380, San Isidro, Lima; tel. (1) 4217582; fax (1) 4217580; e-mail embarg@embajadadeargelia.com; internet www .argelia-pe.org; Ambassador Muhammad Bensabri.

Argentina: Avda Las Flores 326, San Isidro, Lima 1; tel. (1) 4414444; fax (1) 4224304; e-mail contacto_eperu@mrecic.gov.ar; internet eperu.mrecic.gov.ar; Ambassador Darío Pedro Alessandro.

Australia: Avda La Paz 1049, 10°, Miraflores, Lima 18; tel. (1) 6300500; fax (1) 6300520; e-mail consular.lima@dfat.gov.au; internet www.embassy.gov.au/peru; Ambassador John M. L. Woods.

Austria: Edif. de las Naciones, Avda República de Colombia 643, 5°, San Isidro, Lima 27; tel. (1) 4420503; fax (1) 4428851; e-mail lima-ob@

bmeia.gv.at; internet www.aussenministerium.at/lima; Ambassador ANDREAS LIEBMANN MEIÁN.

Belgium: Avda Angamos Oeste 380, Miraflores, Lima 18; tel. (1) 2417566; fax (1) 2416379; e-mail lima@diplobel.fed.be; internet www .diplomatie.be/lima; Ambassador BEATRIX VAN HEMELDONCK.

Bolivia: Los Castaños 235, San Isidro, Lima 27; tel. (1) 4402095; fax (1) 4402298; e-mail embajada@boliviaenperu.com; Ambassador JORGE LEDEZMA CORNEJO.

Brazil: Avda José Pardo 850, Miraflores, Lima; tel. (1) 5120830; fax (1) 4452421; e-mail embajada@embajadabrasil.org.pe; internet lima .itamaraty.gov.br; Ambassador CARLOS LAZARY TEIXEIRA.

Canada: Calle Bolognesi 228, Miraflores, Casilla 18-1126, Lima; tel. (1) 3193200; fax (1) 4464912; e-mail lima@international.gc.ca; internet www.canadainternational.gc.ca/peru-perou; Ambassador PATRICIA FORTIER.

Chile: Avda Javier Prado Oeste 790, San Isidro, Lima; tel. (1) 7102211; fax (1) 7102223; e-mail contacto@chileabroad.gov.cl; internet chileabroad.gov.cl/peru; Ambassador FAVIO VIO UGARTE.

China, People's Republic: Jirón José Granda 150, San Isidro, Apdo 375, Lima 27; tel. (1) 2220841; fax (1) 4429467; e-mail chinaemb_pe@mfa.gov.cn; internet www.embajadachina.org.pe; Ambassador HUANG MINHUI.

Colombia: Avda J. Basadre 1580, San Isidro, Lima 27; tel. (1) 4410954; fax (1) 4419806; e-mail elima@cancilleria.gov.co; internet www.embajadaenperu.gov.co; Ambassador LUÍS ELADIO PÉREZ BONILLA.

Costa Rica: Baltazar La Torre 828, San Isidro, Lima; tel. (1) 2642999; fax (1) 2642799; e-mail embcr.peru@gmail.com; Ambassador MELVIN ALFREDO SÁENZ BIOLLEY.

Cuba: Coronel Portillo 110, San Isidro, Lima; tel. (1) 5123400; fax (1) 2644525; e-mail embacuba@pe.embacuba.cu; internet www .cubadiplomatica.cu/peru; Ambassador JUANA MARTÍNEZ GONZÁLEZ.

Czech Republic: Baltazar La Torre 398, San Isidro, Lima 27; tel. (1) 2643374; fax (1) 2641708; e-mail lima@embassy.mzv.cz; internet www.mfa.cz/lima; Ambassador VLADIMIR EISENBRUK.

Dominican Republic: Calle Tudela y Varela 360, San Isidro, Lima 27; tel. (1) 4219765; fax (1) 4219763; e-mail embdomperu@speedy .com.pe; internet www.embajadadominicanaperu.org; Ambassador RAFAEL JULIÁN CEDANO.

Ecuador: Las Palmeras 356 y Javier Prado Oeste, San Isidro, Lima 27; tel. (1) 2124171; fax (1) 4220711; e-mail embajada@ mecuadorperu.org.pe; internet www.mecuadorperu.org.pe; Chargé d'affaires a.i. IVÁN MALDONADO VACA.

Egypt: Avda Jorge Basadre 1470, San Isidro, Lima 27; tel. (1) 4222531; fax (1) 4402369; e-mail egipto@sspeedy.com.pe; internet embajadadeegipto.webs.com; Ambassador AHMAD SALAMA.

El Salvador: Avda Javier Prado 2108, San Isidro, Lima 27; tel. (1) 4403500; fax (1) 2212561; e-mail embajadasv@terra.com.pe; Ambassador IDALIA GERTRUDIZ MENJIVAR CAMPOS.

Finland: Edif. Real Tres, Of. 502, 5°, Avda Víctor Andrés Belaúnde 147, San Isidro, Lima; tel. (1) 2224466; fax (1) 2224463; e-mail sanomat.lim@formin.fi; internet www.finlandia.org.pe; Ambassador JUHA VIRTANEN.

France: Avda Arequipa 3415, Lima 27; tel. (1) 2158400; fax (1) 2158410; e-mail france.chancellerie@ambafrance-pe.org; internet www.ambafrance-pe.org; Ambassador JEAN-JACQUES BEAUSSOU.

Germany: Avda Arequipa 4202–4210, Miraflores, Lima 18; tel. (1) 2125016; fax (1) 4226475; e-mail info@lima.diplo.de; internet .lima.diplo.de; Ambassador JOACHIM CHRISTOPH SCHMILLEN.

Greece: Avda Principal 190, Urb. Santa Catalina, La Victoria, Lima 13; tel. (1) 4761548; fax (1) 2232486; e-mail gremb.lim@mfa.gr; internet www.mfa.gr/lima; Ambassador DIMITRIS HATZOPOULOS.

Guatemala: Inca Ripac 309, Jesús María, Lima 11; tel. (1) 4602078; fax (1) 4635885; e-mail embperu@minex.gob.gt; internet www .embajadadeguatemalaenperu.org; Ambassador GABRIEL AGUILERA PERALTA.

Holy See: Avda Salaverry, 6a cuadra, Lima 11 (Apostolic Nunciature); tel. (1) 7174897; fax (1) 7174896; e-mail nunciaturaperu@inbox .com; Apostolic Nuncio Most Rev. JAMES PATRICK GREEN (Titular Archbishop of Altinum).

Honduras: Calle Juan Dellepiani 231, 2°, San Isidro, Lima 27; tel. (1) 2644600; fax (1) 2640008; e-mail info@embhonpe.org; internet www .embhonpe.org; Ambassador HUMBERTO LÓPEZ VILLAMIL OCHOA.

India: Avda Salaverry 3006, San Isidro, Lima 27; tel. (1) 4602289; fax (1) 4610374; e-mail hoc@indembassy.org.pe; internet www .indembassy.org.pe; Ambassador MANPREET VOHRA.

Indonesia: Avda Las Flores 334-336, San Isidro, Lima; tel. (1) 2220308; fax (1) 2222684; e-mail kbrilima@indonesia-peru.org.pe; internet www.indonesia-peru.org.pe; Ambassador YOSEF BERTY FERNANDEZ.

Israel: Edif. El Pacifico, 6°, Plaza Washington, Natalio Sánchez 125, Santa Beatriz, Lima; tel. (1) 4180500; fax (1) 4180555; e-mail info@ lima.mfa.gov.il; internet lima.mfa.gov.il; Ambassador MODI EPHRAIM.

Italy: Avda Giuseppe Garibaldi 298, Apdo 0490, Lima 11; tel. (1) 4632727; fax (1) 4635317; e-mail ambasciata.lima@esteri.it; internet www.amblima.esteri.it; Ambassador GUGLIELMO ARDIZZONE.

Japan: Avda San Felipe 356, Apdo 3708, Jesús María, Lima 11; tel. (1) 2181130; fax (1) 4630302; e-mail cultjapon@embajadajapon.org .pe; internet www.pe.emb-japan.go.jp; Ambassador MASAJIRO FUJUKAWA.

Korea, Democratic People's Republic: Los Nogales 227, San Isidro, Lima; tel. (1) 4411120; fax (1) 4409877; e-mail embcorea@ hotmail.com; Ambassador RI MUN GYU.

Korea, Republic: Avda Principal 190, 7°, Urb. Santa Catalina, La Victoria, Lima; tel. (1) 4760815; fax (1) 4760950; e-mail peru@mofat .go.kr; internet per.mofat.go.kr; Ambassador PARK HEE-KWON.

Malaysia: Avda Daniel Hernández 350, San Isidro, Lima 27; tel. (1) 4220297; fax (1) 2210786; e-mail mallima@kln.gov.my; internet www .kln.gov.my/perwakilan/lima; Ambassador AYAUF BACHI.

Mexico: Avda Jorge Basadre 710, esq. Los Ficus, San Isidro, Lima; tel. (1) 6121600; fax (1) 6121627; e-mail info@mexico.org.pe; internet embamex.sre.gob.mx/peru; Ambassador MANUEL RODRÍGUEZ ARRIAGA.

Morocco: Calle Tomás Edison 205, San Isidro, Lima; tel. (1) 4403117; fax (1) 4404391; e-mail sifa@embajadamarruecoslima .com; internet www.embajadamarruecoslima.com; Ambassador OUMAMA AOUAD LAHRECH.

Netherlands: Torre Parque Mar, 13°, Avda José Larco 1301, Miraflores, Lima; tel. (1) 2139800; fax (1) 2139805; e-mail info@ nlgovlim.com; internet www.nlgovlim.com; Ambassador ARJAN HAMBURGER.

Nicaragua: Avda Alvarez Calderón 738, San Isidro, Lima 27; tel. (1) 4223892; fax (1) 4223895; e-mail embanic@telefonica.net.pe; Ambassador MARCELA MARTHA PERÉZ SILVA.

Panama: Avda Trinidad Morán 1426, Lince, Lima; tel. (1) 4228084; fax (1) 4227871; e-mail secretaria@panaembaperu.com.pe; internet www.panaembaperu.com.pe; Ambassador CARLOS LUIS LINARES BRIN.

Paraguay: Alcanfores 1286, Miraflores, Lima; tel. (1) 4474762; fax (1) 4442391; e-mail embaparpe@infonegocio.net.pe; Chargé d'affaires a.i. FELIPE SANTIAGO JARA AGUERO.

Poland: Avda Salaverry 1978, Jesús María, Lima 11; tel. (1) 4713920; fax (1) 4714813; e-mail lima.amb.sekretariat@msz.gov.pl; internet www.lima.polemb.net; Ambassador IZABELA MATUSZ.

Portugal: Calle Antequera 777, 3°, San Isidro, POB 3692, Lima 100; tel. (1) 4409905; fax (1) 4215979; e-mail limaportugal@hotmail.com; Ambassador HELENA MARGARIDA REZENDE DE ALMEIDA COUTINHO.

Qatar: Avda Santa Cruz 1136, Miraflores, Lima; tel. (1) 6373500; fax (1) 6384574; e-mail lima@mofa.gov.ga; Ambassador JAMAL NASSER AL-BADER.

Romania: Avda Jorge Basadre 690, San Isidro, Lima; tel. (1) 4224587; fax (1) 4210609; e-mail ambrom@terra.com.pe; Chargé d'affaires a.i. ŞTEFAN NICOLAE.

Russia: Avda Salaverry 3424, San Isidro, Lima 27; tel. (1) 2640036; fax (1) 2640130; e-mail embrusa@infonegocio.net.pe; internet www .embajada-rusa.org; Ambassador NIKOLAY V. SOFINSKIY.

South Africa: Edif. Real Tres, Avda Víctor Andrés Belaúnde 147, Of. 801, Lima 27; tel. (1) 6124848; fax (1) 4223881; e-mail general .peru@dirco.gov.za; Ambassador ELSA DRY.

Spain: Jorge Basadre 498, San Isidro, Lima 27; tel. (1) 2125155; fax (1) 4402020; e-mail emb.lima@maec.es; internet www.maec.es/ embajadas/lima; Ambassador JUAN CARLOS SÁNCHEZ ALONSO.

Switzerland: Avda Salaverry 3240, San Isidro, Lima 27; tel. (1) 2640305; fax (1) 2641319; e-mail lim.vertretung@eda.admin.ch; internet www.eda.admin.ch/lima; Ambassador ANNE-PASCALE KRAUER MÜLLER.

Thailand: Avda Coronel Portillo 678, San Isidro, Lima 27; tel. (1) 6375620; fax (1) 6384073; e-mail thailim@mfa.go.th; internet www .thaiembassyperu.org; Ambassador RUENGDEJ MAHASARANOND.

Turkey: Calle Miguel de Cervantes 504-510, San Isidro, Lima 27; tel. (1) 2047000; fax (1) 4216304; e-mail embajada.lima@mfa.gov.tr; Ambassador NAMIK GÜNER ERPUL.

Ukraine: José Dellepiani 470, San Isidro, Lima 27; tel. (1) 2642884; fax (1) 2642892; e-mail emb_pe@mfa.gov.ua; internet www.mfa.gov.ua/ peru; Ambassador OLEKSANDR MYKHALCHUK.

United Kingdom: Torre Parque Mar, 22°, Avda José Larco 1301, Miraflores, Lima; tel. (1) 6173000; fax (1) 6173100; e-mail belima@fco .gov.uk; internet www.ukinperu.fco.gov.uk; Ambassador JAMES DAURIS.

USA: Avda La Encalada 17, Surco, Lima 33; tel. (1) 6182000; fax (1) 6182397; internet lima.usembassy.gov; Ambassador ROSE M. LIKINS.

Uruguay: José D. Anchorena 84, San Isidro, Lima 27; tel. (1) 7192550; fax (1) 7192865; e-mail uruinca@americatelnet.com.pe; Ambassador JUAN JOSÉ ARTEAGA SÁENZ DE ZUMARÁN.

Venezuela: Avda Arequipa 298, Lima; tel. (1) 4334511; fax (1) 4331191; e-mail consulve@millicom.com.pe; Ambassador ALEXANDER YAÑEZ DELEUZE.

Judicial System

The Supreme Court consists of a President and 17 members. There are also Higher Courts and Courts of First Instance in provincial capitals.

SUPREME COURT

Corte Suprema de Justicia: Palacio de Justicia, 2°, Avda Paseo de la República, Cercado, Lima 1; tel. (1) 4284457; fax (1) 4269437; internet www.pj.gob.pe; f. 1971; Pres. Dr ENRIQUE JAVIER MENDOZA RAMÍREZ.

Attorney-General: JOSÉ ANTONIO PELÁEZ BARDALES.

Religion

CHRISTIANITY

The Roman Catholic Church

For ecclesiastical purposes, Peru comprises seven archdioceses, 19 dioceses, 10 territorial prelatures and eight Apostolic Vicariates. According to the latest census (2007), some 81% of the population are Roman Catholics.

Bishops' Conference

Conferencia Episcopal Peruana, Jirón Estados Unidos 838, Apdo 310, Lima 100; tel. (1) 4631010; fax (1) 4636125; e-mail sgc@iglesiacatolica.org.pe; internet www.iglesia.org.pe.

f. 1981; Pres. HÉCTOR MIGUEL CABREJOS VIDARTE (Archbishop of Trujillo).

Archbishop of Arequipa: JAVIER AUGUSTO DEL RIO ALBA, Arzobispado, Moral San Francisco 118, Apdo 149, Arequipa; tel. (54) 234094; fax (54) 242721; e-mail arzobispadoaqp@planet.com.pe.

Archbishop of Ayacucho or Huamanga: SALVADOR PIÑEIRO GARCÍA-CALDERÓN, Arzobispado, Jirón 28 de Julio 148, Apdo 30, Ayacucho; tel. and fax (64) 812367; e-mail arzaya@mail.udep.edu.pe.

Archbishop of Cusco: JUAN ANTONIO UGARTE PÉREZ, Arzobispado, Herrajes, Hatun Rumiyoc s/n, Apdo 148, Cusco; tel. (84) 225211; fax (84) 222781; e-mail arzobisp@terra.com.pe.

Archbishop of Huancayo: PEDRO RICARDO BARRETO JIMENO, Arzobispado, Jirón Puno 430, Apdo 245, Huancayo; tel. (64) 234952; fax (64) 239189; e-mail arzohyo@hotmail.com.

Archbishop of Lima: Cardinal JUAN LUIS CIPRIANI THORNE, Arzobispado, Jirón Carabaya, Plaza Mayor, Apdo 1512, Lima 100; tel. (1) 4275980; fax (1) 4271967; e-mail arzolim@terra.com.pe; internet www.arzobispadodelima.org.

Archbishop of Piura: JOSÉ ANTONIO EGUREN ANSELMI, Arzobispado, Libertad 1105, Apdo 197, Piura; tel. and fax (74) 327561; e-mail ocordova@upiura.edu.pe.

Archbishop of Trujillo: HÉCTOR MIGUEL CABREJOS VIDARTE, Arzobispado, Jirón Mariscal de Orbegozo 451, Apdo 42, Trujillo; tel. (44) 256812; fax (44) 231473; e-mail arztrujillo@terra.com.pe.

The Anglican Communion

The Iglesia Anglicana del Cono Sur de América (Anglican Church of the Southern Cone of America), formally inaugurated in April 1983, comprises seven dioceses, including Peru. The Presiding Bishop of the Church is the Bishop of Northern Argentina.

Bishop of Peru: Rt Rev. HAROLD WILLIAM GODFREY, Apdo 18-1032, Miraflores, Lima 18; tel. and fax (1) 4229160; e-mail diocesisperu@anglicanperu.org; internet www.peru.anglican.org.

The Methodist Church

There are an estimated 4,200 adherents of the Iglesia Metodista del Perú.

President: Rev. JORGE BRAZO CABALLERO, Baylones 186, Lima 5; Apdo 1386, Lima 100; tel. (1) 4245970; fax (1) 4318995; e-mail iglesiamp@computextos.com.pe; internet www.iglesiametodista.org.pe.

Other Protestant Churches

Among the most popular are the Iglesia Evangélica del Perú (accounting for some 12% of the population at the 2007 census), the Asamblea de Dios, the Iglesia del Nazareno, the Alianza Cristiana y Misionera and the Iglesia de Dios del Perú.

BAHÁ'Í FAITH

National Spiritual Assembly of the Bahá'ís of Peru: Horacio Urteaga 827, Jesús María, Apdo 11-0209, Lima 11; tel. (1) 4316077; fax (1) 4333005; e-mail bahai@pol.com.pe; mems resident in 220 localities.

The Press

DAILIES

Lima

El Bocón: Jirón Jorge Salazar Araoz 171, Urb. Santa Catalina, Apdo 152, Lima 1; tel. (1) 6908090; fax (1) 6908127; e-mail web@grupoepensa.pe; internet www.elbocon.com.pe; f. 1994; football; Editorial Dir JORGE ESTÉVES ALFARO; circ. 90,000.

El Comercio: Empresa Editora 'El Comercio', SA, Jirón Antonio Miró Quesada 300, Lima; tel. (1) 3116310; fax (1) 4260810; e-mail editorweb@comercio.com.pe; internet www.elcomercioperu.com.pe; f. 1839; morning; Editor JUAN CARLOS LUJÁN; Dir-Gen. FRANCISCO MIRÓ QUESADA; circ. 150,000 weekdays, 220,000 Sundays.

Expreso: Jirón Antonio Elizalde 753, Lima; tel. (1) 6124000; fax (1) 6124024; e-mail sugerencias@expreso.com.pe; internet www.expreso.com.pe; f. 1961; morning; conservative; Dir LUIS GARCÍA MIRÓ; circ. 100,000.

Extra: Jirón Libertad 117, Miraflores, Lima; tel. (1) 4447088; fax (1) 4447117; e-mail extra@expreso.com.pe; f. 1964; evening edition of Expreso; Dir CARLOS SÁNCHEZ; circ. 80,000.

Gestión: Miró Quesada 247, 8°, Lima 1; tel. (1) 3116370; fax (1) 3116500; e-mail gestion2@diariogestion.com.pe; internet www.gestion.pe; f. 1990; Dir JULIO LIRA SEGURA; Editor DAVID REYES; circ. 131,200.

Ojo: Jirón Jorge Salazar Araoz 171, Urb. Santa Catalina, Apdo 152, Lima; tel. (1) 4709696; fax (1) 4761605; internet www.ojo.com.pe; f. 1968; morning; Dir VÍCTOR RAMÍREZ; circ. 100,000.

Perú 21: Jirón Miró Quesada 247, 6°, Lima; tel. (1) 3116500; fax (1) 3116391; e-mail lectores@peru21.com; internet www.peru21.com; independent; Dir FRITZ DU BOIS; Editor MANUEL TUMI.

El Peruano (Diario Oficial): Avda Alfonso Ugarte 873, Lima 1; tel. (1) 3150400; fax (1) 4245023; e-mail gbarraza@editoraperu.com.pe; internet www.elperuano.com.pe; f. 1825; morning; official State Gazette; Dir JOSÉ LUIS BRAVO RUSSO; circ. 27,000.

La República: Jirón Camaná 320, Lima 1; tel. (1) 7116000; fax (1) 2511029; e-mail otxoa@larepublica.com.pe; internet www.larepublica.pe; f. 1982; left-wing; Dir GUSTAVO MOHME SEMINARIO; circ. 50,000.

Arequipa

Noticias: Calle Consuelo 404, Arequipa; tel. (54) 281026; fax (54) 280784; e-mail diarionoticiasarequipa@yahoo.es; internet www.diarionoticias.com.pe; morning; Dir RONALD IBÁÑEZ BARREDA; Editor JAVIER ARISTA VALDIVIA.

El Pueblo: Sucre 213, Arequipa; tel. and fax (54) 205086; internet www.elpueblo.com.pe; f. 1905; morning; independent; Pres. DANIEL MACEDO GUTIÉRREZ; Dir CARLOS MENESES CORNEJO; circ. 70,000.

Chiclayo

La Industria: Jiron Tacna 610, Chiclayo; tel. (74) 237952; fax (74) 227678; f. 1952; Dir JULIO ALBERTO ORTIZ CERRO; circ. 20,000.

Cusco

El Diario del Cusco: Centro Comercial Ollanta, Avda El Sol 346, Cusco; tel. (84) 229898; fax (84) 229822; e-mail buzon@diariodelcusco.com; internet www.diariodelcusco.com; morning; independent; Exec. Pres. WASHINTON ALOSILLA PORTILLO; Gen. Man. JOSÉ FERNANDEZ NÚÑEZ.

Huacho

El Imparcial: Avda Grau 203, Huacho; tel. (34) 2392187; fax (34) 2327942; e-mail elimparcial1891@hotmail.com; f. 1891; evening; Dir ADÁN MANRIQUE ROMERO; circ. 5,000.

Huancayo

Primicia: Calle Real 455, Interior 1, Huancayo; tel. (64) 201309; fax (64) 216594; e-mail criverab@diarioprimicia.pe; internet www .diarioprimicia.pe; f. 1997; Dir ABEL EGOÁVIL SORIANO.

Ica

La Opinión: Avda Los Maestros 801, Apdo 186, Ica; tel. (56) 235571; f. 1922; evening; independent; Dir GONZALO TUEROS RAMÍREZ.

La Voz de Ica: Castrovirreyna 193, Ica; tel. and fax (56) 232112; e-mail lavozdeica1918@yahoo.es; internet www.lavozdeica.com; f. 1918; Dir ATILIO NIERI BOGGIANO; Man. MARIELLA NIERI DE MACEDO; circ. 4,500.

Pacasmayo

Diario Ultimas Noticias: Jiron 2 de Mayo 33, Pacasmayo, La Libertad; tel. (44) 528319; fax (44) 523022; e-mail escribanos@ ultimasnoticiasdiario.com; internet www.ultimasnoticiasdiario .com; f. 1973; morning; independent; Editor MARÍA DEL CARMEN BALLENA RAZURI; circ. 3,000.

Piura

El Tiempo: Jíron Ayacucho 751, Piura; tel. (74) 325141; fax (74) 327478; e-mail rlaban@eltiempo.com.pe; internet www.eltiempo .com.pe; f. 1916; morning; independent; Dir ROSARIO ARÁMBULO; Editor ROSA LABÁN; circ. 18,000.

Trujillo

La Industria: Jirón Gamarra 443, Trujillo; tel. (44) 295757; fax (44) 290901; e-mail redaccion@laindustria.com; internet laindustria.pe; f. 1895; morning; independent; Dir JOSÉ BRINGAS; circ. 8,000.

PERIODICALS

Business: Avda La Molina 1110, Of. 203, La Molina, Lima 12; tel. (1) 2500596; fax (1) 2500597; e-mail info@businessperu.com.pe; internet www.businessperu.com.pe; f. 1994; monthly; Dir DANIEL VALERA LOZA.

Caretas: Jirón Huallaya 122, Portal de Botoneros, Plaza de Armas, Lima 1; Apdo 737, Lima 100; tel. (1) 4289490; fax (1) 4262524; e-mail info@caretas.com.pe; internet www.caretas.com.pe; weekly; current affairs; Dir MARCO ZILERI DOUGALL; Editor JAIME BEDOYA; circ. 90,000.

Cosas: Calle Alcanfores 1262, Miraflores, Lima 18; tel. (1) 2023000; fax (1) 4473776; e-mail suscripcionesperu@cosas.com; internet www .cosas.pe; f. 1992; weekly; society; Editor ELIZABETH DULANTO DE MIRÓ QUESADA; Editor ISABEL DE MIRÓ QUESADA.

Debate Agrario: Avda Salaverry 818, Lima 11; tel. (1) 4336610; fax (1) 4331744; e-mail fegurenl@cepes.org.pe; internet www.cepes.org .pe/debate/debate.htm; f. 1987 by Centro Peruano de Estudios Sociales; annual; rural issues; Dir FERNANDO EGUREN L.

Gente Peru: Calle Durero 320, San Borja, Lima 14; tel. (1) 4340957; fax (1) 4413646; e-mail correo@revista-gente.com; internet www .revista-gente.com; f. 1958; monthly; circ. 25,000; Dir ENRIQUE ESCARDÓ.

Industria Peruana: Los Laureles 365, San Isidro, Apdo 632, Lima 27; tel. (1) 6164444; fax (1) 6164440; e-mail industriaperuana@sni .org.pe; internet www.sni.org.pe/servicios/publicaciones; f. 1932; monthly publication of the Sociedad Nacional de Industrias; Editor-Gen. ENZO CHAPARRO.

Orbita: Parque Rochdale 129, Lima; tel. (1) 4610676; e-mail redaccion@orbitamagazine.com; internet www.orbitamagazine .com; monthly; music; f. 1970; Dir ALBERTO SÁNCHEZ; Editor FERNANDO FUENTES.

Perú Económico: Apdo 671, Lima 100; tel. (1) 2425656; fax (1) 4455946; internet perueconomico.com; f. 1978; monthly.

The Peruvian Times: Paseo de la República 291, Of. 702, Lima 1; tel. (1) 4676609; e-mail egriffis@peruviantimes.com; internet www .peruviantimes.com; f. 1940, successor to West Coast Leader (f. 1912); refounded 2007 as an online publ; general news, analysis and features; English; daily; Publr ELEANOR GRIFFIS; Editor RICK VECCHIO.

QueHacer: León de la Fuente 110, Lima 17; tel. (1) 6138300; fax (1) 6138308; e-mail monica@desco.org.pe; internet www.desco.org.pe/ quehacer; f. 1979; 6 a year; supported by Desco research and devt agency; Editor-in-Chief MARTÍN PAREDES; Dir ABELARDO SÁNCHEZ-LEÓN; circ. 5,000.

Revista Agraria: Avda Salaverry 818, Lima 11; tel. (1) 4336610; fax (1) 4331744; e-mail agraria@cepes.org.pe; internet www .larevistaagraria.org; f. 1987 by Centro Peruano de Estudios Sociales; monthly review of rural problems; Dir FERNANDO EGUREN; circ. 100,000.

Semana Económica: Avda 28 de Julio 1370, Miraflores, Lima 18; tel. (1) 2130600; fax (1) 4445240; e-mail redaccion@se.pe; internet semanaeconomica.com; f. 1985; weekly; Exec. Dir GONZALO ZEGARRA MULANOVICH; Editor ANDREA STIGLICH WATSON.

NEWS AGENCY

Andina—Agencia de Noticias Peruana: Avda Alfonso Ugarte 873, Lima 1; tel. (1) 3150400; fax (1) 4312849; e-mail andina@ editoraperu.com.pe; internet www.andina.com.pe; f. 1981; state-owned; Pres. HUGO COYA HONORES; Dir JOSÉ LUIS BRAVO RUSSO.

PRESS ASSOCIATIONS

Asociación Nacional de Periodistas del Perú: Jirón Huanca-vélica 320, Of. 501, Apdo 2079, Lima 1; tel. (1) 4270687; fax (1) 4278493; internet www.anp.org.pe; f. 1928; 8,800 mems; Pres. ROBERTO MARCOS MEJÍA ALARCÓN; Sec.-Gen. ZULIANA LAINEZ OTERO.

Federación de Periodistas del Perú (FPP): Avda Abancay 173, 3°, Lima; tel. (1) 4261806; e-mail fpp@omco.org; internet www.omco .org/fpp; f. 1950; Pres. JESÚS GERMÁN LLANOS CASTILLO; Sec.-Gen. OLGGER SEVERO PODESTÁ.

Publishers

Asociación Editorial Bruño: Avda Arica 751, Breña, Lima 5; tel. (1) 4237890; fax (1) 4240424; e-mail federico@brunoeditorial.com.pe; internet www.brunoeditorial.com.pe; f. 1950; educational; Man. FEDERICO DÍAZ TINEO.

Biblioteca Nacional del Perú: Avda de la Poesia 160, San Borja, Lima 41; tel. (1) 5136900; fax (1) 5137060; e-mail contactobnp@bnp .gob.pe; internet www.bnp.gob.pe; f. 1821; general non-fiction, directories; Dir RAMÓN ELÍAS MUJICA PINILLA.

Borrador Editores: Avda Fray Luis de León 39, San Borja; tel. (1) 2710192; e-mail borradoreditores@gmail.com; internet www .borradoreditores.blogspot.com; Man. PEDRO VILLA GAMARRA.

Ediciones del Hipocampo: Avda Alfredo Franco 195, Urb. Chama, Lima 33; tel. (1) 3586783; fax (1) 3586783; e-mail editor@hipocampo .com.pe; internet www.hipocampo.com.pe; f. 2000; travel literature; Gen. Man. JOSÉ MIGUEL HELFER ARGUEDAS.

Ediciones PEISA: Avda 2 de Mayo 1285, San Isidro, Lima; tel. and fax (1) 2215988; e-mail peisa@terra.com.pe; internet www.peisa.com .pe; f. 1968; fiction and scholarly; Dir GERMÁN CORONADO.

Ediciones SM: Calle Micaela Bastidas 125, San Isidro, Lima; tel. (1) 6148900; fax (1) 6148914; e-mail contacto@ediciones-sm.com.pe; internet www.ediciones-sm.com.pe; textbooks, education, children's literature; Gen. Man. SIMÓN BERNILLA CARRILLO.

Edigraber Editora Gráfica: Avda Tacna 685, 5°, Of. 54, Lima; tel. and fax (1) 4287073; e-mail info@edigraberperu.com; internet www .edigraberperu.com; Gen. Man. SIMÓN BERNILLA CARRILLO.

Editora Normas Legales, SA: Angamos Oeste 526, Miraflores, Lima; tel. and fax (1) 4861410; e-mail ventas@normaslegales.com; internet www.normaslegales.com; law textbooks; Man. JAVIER SANTA MARÍA SILVE.

Editorial Arkabas: Jirón Miraflores 291, Barranco, Lima; tel. (1) 6525350; internet www.arkabas.com; Gen. Man. DANIEL ZÚÑIGA-RIVERA.

Editorial Casatomada: Avda Mariátegui 1600, Of. 803, Jesús María, Lima; tel. (1) 6245992; e-mail ecasatomada@gmail.com; internet www.editorialcasatomada.com; f. 2005; fiction, folklore; Dir GABRIEL RIMACHI SIALER.

Editorial Cuzco, SA: Calle 5 Marzo, Jirón Lote 3, Urb. Las Magnolias, Surco, Lima; tel. (1) 4453261; e-mail ccuzco@camaralima.org .pe; law; Man. SERGIO BAZÁN CHACÓN.

Editorial Horizonte: Avda Nicolás de Piérola 995, Lima 1; tel. (1) 4279364; fax (1) 4274341; e-mail damonte@terra.com.pe; f. 1968; social sciences, literature, politics; Man. HUMBERTO DAMONTE.

Editorial Milla Batres, SA: Lima; f. 1963; history, literature, art, archaeology, linguistics and encyclopaedias on Peru; Dir-Gen. CARLOS MILLA BATRES.

Editorial Océano Peruana, SA: Ricardo Angulo 795, 5°, Urb. Corpac, San Isidro, Lima; tel. (1) 2230800; fax (1) 4219773; e-mail ocelibros@oceano.com.pe; general interest and reference; Gen. Man. JORGE A. DAVELOUIS SARTORI.

Editorial Salesiana: Avda Brasil 218, Apdo 0071, Lima 5; tel. (1) 4235225; internet www.libreriasalesiana.com; f. 1918; religious and general textbooks; Man. Dir Dr FRANCESCO VACARELLO.

Editorial San Marcos: Jirón Dávalos Lissón 135, Lima; tel. (1) 3311535; fax (1) 3302405; e-mail informes@editorialsanmarcos.com; internet www.editorialsanmarcos.com; educational, academic, legal; Gen. Man. ANÍBAL JESÚS PAREDES GALVÁN.

Editorial Santillana: Avda Primavera 2160, Santiago de Surco, Lima; tel. (1) 3134000; fax (1) 3134001; e-mail santillana@santillana .com.pe; internet www.gruposantillana.com.pe; literature, scholarly and reference; Man. ANA CECILIA HALLO.

Grijley: Jirón Lampa 1221, Lima; tel. (1) 4273147; e-mail info@ grijley.com; internet www.grijley.com; law.

Grupo Editorial Mesa Redonda: Pasaje José Payán 141, Miraflores, Lima; tel. (1) 2212957; e-mail editoramesaredonda@gmail .com; internet www.editorialmesaredonda.com; f. 2003; literature, humanities; imprints incl. Mesa Redonda and Calcomanía; Dir JUAN MIGUEL MARTHANS.

Palestra Editores: Jirón Ica 435, Of. 201, Lima 1; tel. (1) 4261363; fax (1) 4271025; e-mail palestra@palestraeditores.com; internet www.palestraeditores.com; law; Gen. Man. PEDRO GRANDEZ CASTRO.

Pontificia Universidad Católica del Perú, Fondo Editorial: Avda Universitaria 1801, San Miguel, Lima 32; tel. (1) 6262650; fax (1) 6262913; e-mail feditor@pucp.edu.pe; internet www.pucp.edu.pe; Dir-Gen. ANA PATRICIA ARÉVALO MAJLUF.

Sociedad Bíblica Peruana, AC: Avda Petit Thouars 991, Apdo 14-0295, Lima 100; tel. (1) 4336608; fax (1) 4336389; internet www .casadelabiblia.org; f. 1821; Christian literature and bibles; Gen. Sec. PEDRO ARANA-QUIROZ.

Universidad Nacional Mayor de San Marcos: Of. General de Editorial, Avda República de Chile 295, 5°, Of. 508, Lima; tel. (1) 4319689; internet www.unmsm.edu.pe; f. 1850; textbooks, education; Man. Dir JORGE CAMPOS REY DE CASTRO.

PUBLISHING ASSOCIATIONS

Alianza Peruana de Editores (ALPE): Lima; tel. (1) 2759081; e-mail alianzaeditores@gmail.com; internet alpe.wordpress.com; f. 2007; independent publrs' asscn; Pres. GERMÁN CORONADO.

Cámara Peruana del Libro: Avda Cuba 427, esq. Jesús María, Apdo 10253, Lima 11; tel. (1) 4729516; fax (1) 2650735; e-mail cp-libro@amauta.rep.net.pe; internet www.cpl.org.pe; f. 1946; 102 mems; Pres. CARLOS A. BENVIDES AGUIJE; Exec. Dir LOYDA MORÁN BUSTAMANTE.

Vida y Espiritualidad: Avda Pedro de Osma 434, Barranco, Lima; tel. (1) 4672548; fax (1) 4617153; e-mail consultas@ vidayespiritualidad.com; internet vidayespiritualidad.com; f. 1984; Dir KLAUS BERCKHOLTZ BENAVIDES.

Broadcasting and Communications

TELECOMMUNICATIONS

Claro Perú: Avda Nicolás Arriola 480, Urb. Santa Catalina, Lima; tel. (1) 6131000; e-mail prensa@claro.com.pe; internet www.claro .com.pe; f. 2005; owned by América Móvil, SA de SV (Mexico); mobile cellular telecommunications services; Exec. Dir JUAN JOSÉ RIVADE-NEYRA SÁNCHEZ.

Nextel del Perú: Avda República de Colombia 791, 14°, esq. Cuadra 34, Paseo D, San Isidro, Lima; tel. (1) 6117777; fax (1) 6111111; internet www.nextel.com.pe; f. 1998; subsidiary of NII Holdings, USA; Gen. Man. MIGUEL EDUARDO RIVERA AGUIRRE.

Telefónica del Perú, SA: Avda Arequipa 1155, Santa Beatriz, Lima 1; tel. (1) 2101013; internet www.telefonica.com.pe; tv and internet services operated under the Movistar brand; Pres. JAVIER MANZA-NARES GUTIÉRREZ.

Regulatory Authorities

Dirección General de Regulación y Asuntos Internacionales de Telecomunicaciones: Avda Jirón Zorritos 1203, Lima 1; tel. (1) 6157800; Dir-Gen. PATRICIA CARREÑO FERRÉ.

Instituto Nacional de Investigación y Capacitación de Tele-comunicaciones (INICTEL): Avda San Luis 1771, esq. Bailetti, San Borja, Lima 41; tel. (1) 6261400; fax (1) 6261402; e-mail informes@inictel-uni.edu.pe; internet www.inictel-uni.edu.pe; Pres. MANUEL ADRIANZEN.

Organismo Supervisor de Inversión Privada en Telecomuni-caciones (OSIPTEL): Calle de la Prosa 136, San Borja, Lima 41; tel. (1) 2251313; fax (1) 4751816; e-mail jgutierrez@osiptel.gob.pe; internet www.osiptel.gob.pe; f. 1993; established by the Peruvian Telecommunications Act to oversee competition and tariffs, to monitor the quality of services and to settle disputes in the sector; Pres. GONZALO MARTÍN RUIZ DÍAZ.

BROADCASTING

Instituto Nacional de Radio y Televisión Peruana (IRTP): Avda José Galvez 1040, Lima 1; tel. (1) 6190707; fax (1) 6190723; e-mail comercial@irtp.com.pe; internet www.irtp.com.pe; f. 1996; state-run, part of the Ministry of Culture from 2010; Exec. Pres.

MARÍA LUISA MÁLAGA SILVA; Gen. Man. Dr LUIGINO PILOTTO CARREÑO; runs the following stations:

Radio Nacional del Perú: Avda Petit Thouars 447, Lima 1; tel. (1) 6190660; e-mail lllontop@irtp.com.pe; internet www.radionacional .com.pe; f. 1925; state broadcaster; Gen. Man. LUIS ENRIQUE LLONTOP SAMILLAN.

Televisión Nacional del Perú (TV Perú): Avda José Gálvez 1040, Santa Beatriz, Lima; tel. (1) 6190704; e-mail adelgado@irtp.com.pe; internet www.tvperu.gob.pe; f. 1958 as Radio y Televisión Peruana; state broadcaster; 22 stations; Gen. Man. ANGELA DELGADO POPOLIZIO.

Radio

Radio Agricultura del Perú, SA—La Peruanísima: Casilla 625, Lima 11; tel. (1) 4246677; e-mail radioagriculturadelperu@yahoo .com; internet www.laperuanisima.com; f. 1963; Gen. Man. LUZ ISABEL DEXTRE NÚÑEZ.

Radio América: Montero Rosas 1099, Santa Beatriz, Lima 1; tel. (1) 2653841; fax (1) 2653844; f. 1943; Dir-Gen. KAREN CROUSILLAT.

Radio Cutivalú, La Voz del Desierto: Jirón Ignacio de Loyola 300, Urb. Miraflores, Castilla, Piura; tel. (73) 343370; e-mail cutivalu630am@hotmail.com; internet www.radiocutivalu.org; f. 1986; Pres. FRANCISCO MUGUIRO IBARRA; Dir RODOLFO AQUINO RUIZ.

Emisoras Cruz del Perú: Jirón Victorino Laynes 1402, Urb. Elio, Lima 1; tel. (1) 3190240; fax (1) 3190244; e-mail info@emisorascruz .com.pe; internet www.emisorascruz.com.pe; Pres. FERNANDO CRUZ MENDOZA; Gen. Man. MARCO CRUZ MENDOZA.

Radio Panamericana: Paseo Parodi 340, San Isidro, Lima 27; tel. (1) 4226787; fax (1) 4221182; internet www.radiopanamericana.com; f. 1953.

Radio Programas del Perú (GRUPORPP): Avda Paseo de la República 3866, San Isidro, Lima; tel. (1) 2150200; fax (1) 2150269; internet www.rpp.com.pe; Pres. HUGO DELGADO NACHTI-GAL; Gen. Man. MANUEL DELGADO PARKER.

Television

América Televisión, Canal 4: Jirón Montero Rosas 1099, Santa Beatriz, Lima; tel. (1) 4194000; fax (1) 2656979; e-mail web@ americatv.com.pe; internet www.americatv.com.pe; CEO and Gen. Man. ERIC JURGENSEN.

ATV, Canal 9: Avda Arequipa 3570, San Isidro, Lima 27; tel. (1) 2118800; fax (1) 4427636; e-mail webmaster@atv.com.pe; internet www.tuteve.tv; f. 1983; Gen. Man. MARCELLO CÚNEO LOBIANO.

Frecuencia Latina, Canal 2: Avda San Felipe 968, Jesús María, Lima; tel. (1) 2191000; fax (1) 2656660; internet www .frecuencialatina.com.pe; Pres. BARUCH IVCHER.

Panamericana Televisión SA: Avda Arequipa 1110, Santa Bea-triz, Lima 1; tel. (1) 4113200; internet www.24horas.com.pe.

RBC Televisión, Canal 11: Avda Manco Cápac 333, La Victoria, Lima; tel. (1) 6132929; fax (1) 4331237; internet www.rbctelevision .com; f. 1966; Pres. FERNANDO GONZÁLEZ DEL CAMPO; Gen. Man. JUAN SÁENZ MARÓN.

Uranio, Canal 15: Avda Arequipa 3570, 6°, San Isidro, Lima; e-mail agamarra@atv.com.pe; Gen. Man. ADELA GAMARRA VÁSQUEZ.

Regulatory Authority

Coordinadora Nacional de Radio: Avda Javier Prado Oeste 109, Magdalena del Mar; tel. (1) 2616257; fax (1) 4715808; e-mail prensa@ cnr.org.pe; internet www.cnr.org.pe; f. 1978; Pres. CARLOS SÁNCHEZ; Exec. Dir RODOLFO AQUINO RUIZ.

Association

Asociación Peruana de Radio y Televisión (APERTV): Avda Manco Capac 333, La Victoria, Lima 13; tel. (1) 3321656; internet www.apertv.org; Pres. RICARDO BELMONT CASSINELLI.

Finance

BANKING

(cap. = capital; res = reserves; dep. = deposits; m. = million; brs = branches; amounts in new soles)

Superintendencia de Banca y Seguros: Los Laureles 214, San Isidro, Lima 27; tel. (1) 6309000; fax (1) 6309236; e-mail mostos@sbs .gob.pe; internet www.sbs.gob.pe; f. 1931; Supt DANIEL SCHYDLOWSKY ROSENBERG; Sec.-Gen. MARCO OJEDA PACHECO.

Central Bank

Banco Central de Reserva del Perú: Jirón Antonio Miró Quesada 441-445, Lima 1; tel. (1) 6132000; fax (1) 4273091; e-mail webmaster@bcrp.gob.pe; internet www.bcrp.gob.pe; f. 1922; refounded 1931; cap. 591.3m., res 1,385m., dep. 54,458.4m. (Dec. 2009); Chair. JULIO VELARDE FLORES; Gen. Man. RENZO ROSSINI MIÑÁN; 7 brs.

Other Government Banks

Banco de la Nación: Avda República de Panamá 3664, San Isidro, Lima 1; tel. (1) 5192164; fax (1) 5192217; e-mail dep_ccorporativa@bn.com.pe; internet www.bn.com.pe; f. 1966; cap. 1,000m., res 355.1m., dep. 20,401.6m. (Dec. 2011); conducts all commercial banking operations of official govt agencies; Exec. Pres. CARLOS MANUEL DÍAZ MARIÑOS; Gen. Man. JUAN GALFRÉ GARCÍA; 444 brs.

Corporación Financiera de Desarrollo (COFIDE): Augusto Tamayo 160, San Isidro, Lima 27; tel. (1) 6154000; fax (1) 4423374; e-mail postmaster@cofide.com.pe; internet www.cofide.com.pe; f. 1971; also owners of Banco Latino; Pres. ALFONSO ZÁRATE; 11 brs.

Commercial Banks

Banco de Comercio: Avda Paseo de la República 3705, San Isidro, Lima; tel. (1) 5136000; fax (1) 4405458; e-mail postmaster@bancomercio.com.pe; internet www.bancomercio.com; f. 1967; fmrly Banco Peruano de Comercio y Construcción; cap. 133.2m., res 9.6m., dep. 1,345.8m. (Dec. 2012); Pres. JOSÉ RICARDO STOK CAPELLA; Gen. Man. CARLOS ALBERTO MUJICA CASTRO; 23 brs.

Banco de Crédito del Perú: Calle Centenario 156, Urb. Las Laderas de Melgarejo, Apdo 12-067, Lima 12; tel. (1) 3132000; internet www.viabcp.com; f. 1889; cap. 2,557.7m., res 2,299m., dep. 47,820.2m. (Dec. 2011); Pres. and Chair. DIONISIO ROMERO PAOLETTI; Gen. Man. WALTER BAYLY; 326 brs.

Banco Interamericano de Finanzas, SA: Avda Rivera Navarrete 600, San Isidro, Lima 27; tel. (1) 6133000; fax (1) 2212489; e-mail gchang@bif.com.pe; internet www.bif.com.pe; f. 1991; cap. 291.5m., res 28.6m., dep. 3,943m. (Dec. 2011); Pres. FRANCISCO ROCHE; Gen. Man. and CEO JUAN IGNACIO DE LA VEGA; 37 brs.

BBVA Banco Continental: Avda República de Panamá 3055, San Isidro, Lima 27; tel. (1) 2111000; fax (1) 2111788; internet www.bbvabancocontinental.com; f. 1951; merged with BBVA of Spain in 1995; 92.01% owned by Holding Continental, SA; cap. 1,944.2m., res 609.4m., dep. 30,492.5m. (Dec. 2011); Pres. and Chair. PEDRO BESCIA CAFFERATA; Gen. Man. EDUARDO TORRES-LLOSA VILLACORTA; 250 brs.

INTERBANK (Banco Internacional del Perú): Carlos Villarán 140, Urb. Santa Catalina, Lima 13; tel. (1) 2192347; fax (1) 2192336; e-mail krubin@intercorp.com.pe; internet www.interbank.com.pe; f. 1897; commercial bank; cap. 1,172.6m., res 247m., dep. 13,188.3m. (Dec. 2011); Chair. and Pres. CARLOS RODRÍGUEZ-PASTOR; Gen. Man. LUIS FELIPE CASTELLANOS LÓPEZ-TORRES; 232 brs.

Scotiabank Perú, SAA: Avda Dionisio Derteano 102, San Isidro, Apdo 1235, Lima; tel. (1) 2116060; fax (1) 4407945; e-mail scotiaenlinea@scotiabank.com.pe; internet www.scotiabank.com.pe; f. 2006 by merger of Banco Sudamericano (owned by Scotiabank, Canada) and Banco Wiese Sudameris; cap. 2,299.3m., res 804.2m., dep. 20,117.6m. (Dec. 2011); Chair. PETER CARDINAL; Vice-Pres. and CEO CARLOS GONZÁLEZ-TABOADA.

Banking Association

Asociación de Bancos del Perú: Calle 41, No 975, Urb. Córpac, San Isidro, Lima 27; tel. (1) 6123333; fax (1) 6123316; e-mail estudioseconomicos@asbanc.com.pe; internet www.asbanc.com.pe; f. 1929; refounded 1967; Pres. OSCAR JOSÉ RIVERA; Gen. Man. ADRIÁN REVILLA.

STOCK EXCHANGE

Bolsa de Valores de Lima: Pasaje Acuña 106, Lima 1; tel. (1) 6193333; fax (1) 6193354; internet www.bvl.com.pe; f. 1860; Pres. CHRISTIAN LAUB BENAVIDES; Gen. Man. FRANCIS STENNING DE LAVALLE.

Regulatory Authority

Superintendencia del Mercado de Valores: Santa Cruz 315, Miraflores, Lima; tel. (1) 6106300; fax (1) 6106325; e-mail webmaster@smv.gob.pe; internet www.smv.gob.pe; f. 1968; regulates the securities and commodities markets; responsible to Ministry of Economy and Finance; Supt. LILIAN ROCCA CARBAJAL.

INSURANCE

ACE Seguros, SA: Calle Amador Merino Reyna 267, Of. 402, San Isidro, Lima; tel. (1) 4175000; fax (1) 2212943; internet www.acelatinamerica.com; Pres. JUAN CARLOS PUYÓ.

CARDIF del Perú Cía de Seguros y Reaseguros: Avda Canaval y Moreyra 380, 1101°, San Isidro, Lima; tel. (1) 6151700; fax (1) 6151721; e-mail servicioalcliente@cardif.com.pe; internet www.cardif.com.pe; Pres. FRANCISCO VALENZUELA CORNEJO; Gen. Man. DANIEL WEIS CILLERO.

Interseguro Cía de Seguros, SA: Avda Pardo y Aliaga 640, 2°, San Isidro, Lima; tel. (1) 6114700; fax (1) 6114725; e-mail gonzalo.basadre@interseguro.com.pe; internet www.interseguro.com.pe; f. 1998; life and non-life, annuities; owned by Intergroup Financial Services; Chair. FELIPE MORRIS GUERINONI; CEO GONZALO BASADRE BRAZZINI.

Invita Seguros de Vida, SA: Torre Wiese, Canaval y Moreyra 532, San Isidro, Lima; tel. (1) 2222222; fax (1) 2211683; e-mail servicioalcliente@invita.com.pe; internet www.invita.com.pe; f. 2000; life; fmrly Wiese Aetna, SA; Pres. CARIDAD DE LA PUENTE WIESE; Gen. Man. JAVIER FREYRE TRIVELLI.

Mapfre Perú Cía de Seguros: Avda 28 de Julio 873, Miraflores, Apdo 323, Lima 100; tel. (1) 2137373; fax (1) 2433131; e-mail fmarco@mapfreperu.com; internet www.mapfreperu.com; f. 1994; general; fmrly Seguros El Sol, SA; Pres. RENZO CALDA GIURATO.

Pacífico, Cía de Seguros y Reaseguros: Avda Juan de Arona 830, San Isidro, Lima 27; tel. (1) 5184000; fax (1) 5184295; e-mail arodrigo@pps.com.pe; internet www.pacificoseguros.com; f. 1943; general; Pres. DIONISIO ROMERO SEMINARIO; Gen. Man. DAVID SAETTONE WATMOUGH.

La Positiva Cía de Seguros y Reaseguros, SA: Esq. Javier Prado Este y Francisco Masías 370, San Isidro, Lima; tel. (511) 2110000; fax (511) 2110011; e-mail lineapositiva@lapositiva.com.pe; internet www.lapositiva.com.pe; f. 1947; Pres. JUAN MANUEL PEÑA ROCA; Gen. Man. GUSTAVO CERDEÑA RODRÍGUEZ.

Rimac Seguros: Las Begonias 475, 3°, San Isidro, Lima; tel. (1) 4111111; fax (1) 4210570; e-mail jortecho@rimac.com.pe; internet www.rimac.com.pe; f. 1896; acquired Seguros Fénix in 2004; Gen. Man. RAFAEL VENEGAS.

SECREX: Avda Angamos Oeste 1234, Apdo 0511, Miraflores, Lima; tel. (1) 4424033; fax (1) 4423890; e-mail ciaseg@secrex.com.pe; internet www.secrex.com.pe; f. 1980; mem. of Grupo CESCE.

Insurance Association

Asociación Peruana de Empresas de Seguros (APESEG): Arias Araguez 146, Miraflores, Lima 18; tel. (1) 4442294; fax (1) 4468538; e-mail seguros@apeseg.org.pe; internet www.apeseg.org.pe; f. 1904; Pres. ALFREDO JOCHAMOWITZ STAFFORD; Gen. Man. RAÚL DE ANDREA DE LAS CARRERAS.

Trade and Industry

GOVERNMENT AGENCIES

Agencia de Promoción de la Inversión Privada (ProInversión): Avda Enrique Canaval Moreyra 150, 9°, San Isidro, Lima 27; tel. (1) 2001200; fax (1) 2212941; e-mail contact@proinversion.gob.pe; internet www.proinversion.gob.pe; f. 2002 to promote economic investment; Exec. Dir JAVIER ILLESCAS; Sec.-Gen. GUSTAVO VILLEGAS DEL SOLAR.

Empresa Nacional de la Coca, SA (ENACO): Avda Arequipa 4528, Miraflores, Lima; tel. (1) 4442292; fax (1) 4471667; e-mail jjara@enaco.com.pe; internet www.enaco.com.pe; f. 1949; agency with exclusive responsibility for the purchase and resale of legally produced coca and the promotion of its derivatives; Pres. JULIO BALTAZAR JARA LADRÓN DE GUEVARA; Gen. Man. JUAN CARLOS GALDOS TEJADA.

Fondo Nacional de Cooperación para el Desarrollo Social (FONCODES): Avda Paseo de la República 3101, San Isidro, Lima; tel. (1) 4212102; fax (1) 4214128; e-mail cacurio@foncodes.mimdes.gob.pe; internet www.foncodes.gob.pe; f. 1991; responsible for social devt and eradicating poverty; Exec. Dir CÉSAR AURELIO ACURIO ZAVALA.

Instituto de Investigaciones de la Amazonía Peruana (IIAP): Avda Abelardo Quiñones Km 2.5, Apdo 784, Loreto; tel. (65) 265516; fax (65) 2265527; e-mail info@iiap.org.pe; internet www.iiap.org.pe; promotes sustainable devt of Amazon region; Pres. LUIS CAMPOS BACA.

Perúpetro, SA: Luis Aldana 320, San Borja, Lima; tel. (1) 6171800; fax (1) 6171801; e-mail asistemas@perupetro.com.pe; internet www.perupetro.com.pe; f. 1993; responsible for promoting investment in hydrocarbon exploration and exploitation; Chair. AURELIO ERNESTO OCHOA ALENCASTRE; CEO ISABEL TAFUR MARÍN.

DEVELOPMENT ORGANIZATIONS

Asociación de Exportadores (ADEX): Avda Javier Prado Este 2875, San Borja, Lima 41; Apdo 1806, Lima 1; tel. (1) 6183333; fax (1) 6183355; e-mail prensa@adexperu.org.pe; internet www.adexperu.org.pe; f. 1973; exporters' asscn; Pres. JUAN MANUEL VARILLAS VELÁSQUEZ; Gen. Man. JUAN C. LEÓN SILES; 600 mems.

Asociación Kallpa para la Promoción Integral de la Salud y el Desarrollo: Pasaje Capri 140, Urb. Palomar Norte, La Victoria, Lima 13; tel. (1) 2243344; fax (1) 2429693; e-mail peru@kallpa.org.pe; internet www.kallpa.org.pe; health devt for youths; Pres. AUREA BOLAÑOS HIDALGO; Sec. MARIE SPRUAGLI.

Asociación Nacional de Centros de Investigación, Promoción Social y Desarrollo: Belisario Flores, Lince, Lima 14; tel. (1) 4728888; fax (1) 4728962; e-mail anc@anc.org.pe; internet www.anc.org.pe; umbrella grouping of devt orgs; Pres. FRANCISCO SOBERÓN GARRIDO; Exec. Sec. JOSEFINA HUAMÁN.

Asociación para la Naturaleza y Desarrollo Sostenible (ANDES): Calle Ruinas 451, Casilla 567, Cusco; tel. (8) 4245021; fax (8) 4232603; e-mail tammy@andes.org.pe; internet www.andes.org.pe; f. 2007; poverty alleviation, biodiversity management, recognition and strengthening of traditional community rights; Exec. Dir CÉSAR ARGUMEDO.

Grupo ACP: Avda Domingo Orue 165, 5°, Surquillo, Lima 34; tel. (1) 4181930; fax (1) 2224166; e-mail grupoacp@grupoacp.com.pe; internet www.grupoacp.com.pe; f. 1969; fmrly Acción Comunitaria del Perú; promotes economic, social and cultural devt; Chair. LUIS FELIPE DERTEANO MARIE.

Sociedad Nacional de Industrias (SNI) (National Industrial Association): Los Laureles 365, San Isidro, Apdo 632, Lima 27; tel. (1) 6164444; fax (1) 6164433; e-mail sni@sni.org.pe; internet www.sni.org.pe; f. 1896; comprises permanent commissions covering various aspects of industry including labour, integration, fairs and exhibitions, industrial promotion; its Small Industry Cttee groups over 2,000 small enterprises; Pres. LUIS SALAZAR; Gen. Man. ROSA ASCA; 90 dirs (reps of firms); 2,500 mems; 60 sectorial cttees.

Centro de Desarrollo Industrial (CDI): Los Laureles 365, San Isidro, Lima; tel. (1) 2158888; fax (1) 2158877; e-mail cdi@sni.org.pe; internet www.cdi.org.pe; f. 1986; Exec. Dir LUIS TENORIO PUENTES.

CHAMBERS OF COMMERCE

Cámara de Comercio de Lima (Lima Chamber of Commerce): Avda Giuseppe Garibaldi 396, Jesús María, Lima 11; tel. (1) 4633434; fax (1) 2191674; e-mail secreceex@camaralima.org.pe; internet www.camaralima.org.pe; f. 1888; Pres. CARLOS DURAND CHAHUD; Gen. Man. JOSÉ ROSAS BERNEDO; 5,500 mems.

Cámara Nacional de Comercio, Producción y Servicios (PER-UCAMARAS): Giuseppe Garibaldi 396, 6°, Jesús María, Lima 11; tel. (1) 2191580; fax (1) 2191586; e-mail cnadministracion@perucam.com; internet www.perucam.com; Pres. SAMUEL GLEISER KATZ; Gen. Man. RUBÉN RONDINELLI ZAGA.

EMPLOYERS' ORGANIZATIONS

Asociación Automotriz del Perú: Avda Javier Prado Oeste 278, Apdo 1248, San Isidro, Lima 27; tel. (1) 6403636; fax (1) 4428865; e-mail aap@aap.org.pe; internet www.aap.org.pe; f. 1926; asscn of importers of motor cars and accessories; 360 mems; Pres. EDWIN DERTEANO DYER; Gen. Man. ENRIQUE PRADO REY.

Asociación de Ganaderos Lecheros del Perú (Agalep) (Association of Stock Farmers of Peru): Pumacahua 877, 3°, Jesús María, Lima; f. 1915; Gen. Man. JAVIER VALERA.

Confederación Nacional de Instituciones Empresariales Privadas (CONFIEP): Edif. Real Tres, Of. 401, Avda Víctor Andrés Belaúnde 147, San Isidro, Lima; tel. (1) 4223311; e-mail postmaster@confiep.org.pe; internet www.confiep.org.pe; f. 1984; federation of 20 employers' orgs; Pres. HUMBERTO SPEZIANI; Gen. Man. GABRIEL AMARO ALZAMORA.

Junta Nacional del Café (JNC): Jr Ramón Dagnino 369, Jesús María, Lima; tel. (1) 4331477; fax (1) 3327914; e-mail jnc@juntadelcafe.org.pe; internet www.juntadelcafe.org.pe; reps of govt and industrial coffee growers; Pres. CÉSAR RIVAS PEÑA; Gen. Man. LORENZO CASTILLO.

Sociedad Nacional de Minería y Petróleo: Francisco Graña 671, Magdalena del Mar, Lima 17; tel. (1) 2159250; fax (1) 4601616; e-mail postmaster@snmpe.org.pe; internet www.snmpe.org.pe; f. 1940; asscn of cos involved in mining, petroleum and energy; Pres. PEDRO MARTÍNEZ CARLEVARINO; Gen. Man. CATERINA PODESTÁ MEVIUS.

Sociedad Nacional de Pesquería (SNP): Avda Javier Prado Oeste 2442, San Isidro, Lima 27; tel. (1) 2612970; fax (1) 2617912; e-mail snpnet@snp.org.pe; internet www.snp.org.pe; f. 1952; private sector fishing interests; Pres. RICHARD INURRITEGUI BAZÁN; Gen. Man. VIVECA AMORÓS.

STATE HYDROCARBONS COMPANY

Petroperú (Petróleos del Perú, SA): Avda Enrique Canaval Moreyra 150, Lima 27; tel. (1) 2117800; fax (1) 6145000; internet www.petroperu.com; f. 1969; state-owned petroleum-refining co; Pres. HÉCTOR REYES CRUZ; Gen. Man. PEDRO MÉNDEZ MILLA.

UTILITIES

Electricity

Distriluz: Edif. Torre el Pilar, 13°, Avda Camino Real 348, San Isidro, Lima 27; tel. (1) 2115500; e-mail central@distriluz.com.pe; internet www.distriluz.com.pe; generation and distribution of electricity; operates 4 energy distribution cos: Electronoroeste, Electronorte, Hidrandina and Electrocentro; Pres. GENARO VÉLEZ CASTRO.

Edegel (Empresa de Generación Eléctrica de Lima): Lima; e-mail comunicacion@edegel.com; internet www.edegel.com; privatized in 1995; generates electricity; Pres. BLANCO FERNÁNDEZ; Gen. Man. CARLOS ALBERTO LUNA CABRERA.

Electroperú: Prolongación Pedro Miotta 421, San Juan de Miraflores, Lima 29; tel. (1) 2170600; fax (1) 2170621; internet www.electroperu.com.pe; state-owned; Pres. DAVID ABRAHAM GRÁNDEZ GÓMEZ; Gen. Man. CÉSAR RAÚL TENGAN MATSUTAHARA.

EnerSur: Avda República de Panamá 3490, San Isidro, Lima 27; tel. (1) 6167979; fax (1) 6167878; e-mail contacto@enersur.com.pe; internet www.enersur.com.pe; f. 1996; part of Grupo GDF SUEZ; electricity generation and transmission; Gen. Man. PATRICK EECKELERS.

Water

Autoridad Nacional del Agua: Calle Diecisiete 355, Urb. El Palomar, San Isidro, Lima; tel. and fax (1) 2243298; e-mail comunicaciones@ana.gob.pe; internet www.ana.gob.pe; f. 2008; Dir HUGO EDUARDO JARA FACUNDO.

TRADE UNIONS

Central Unitaria de Trabajadores del Perú (CUT-PERU): Alejandro Tirado 780, Santa Beatriz, Lima 1; tel. (1) 4723691; e-mail juliocesarbazan@gmail.com; internet www.cutperu.org.pe; f. 1993; Pres. JULIO CÉSAR BAZÁN FIGUEROA; includes:

Confederación General de Trabajadores del Perú (CGTP): Plaza 2 de Mayo 4, Lima 1; tel. (1) 4242357; e-mail cgtp@cgtp.org.pe; internet www.cgtp.org.pe; f. 1968; Pres. CARMELA SIFUENTES INOSTROZA; Sec.-Gen. MARIO HUAMÁN RIVERA.

Confederación Nacional de Trabajadores (CNT): Avda Iquitos 1198, Lima; tel. (1) 4711385; e-mail david.quintana@cnt.pe; affiliated to the PPC; c. 12,000 mems; Sec.-Gen. DAVID QUINTANA.

Confederación de Trabajadores del Perú (CTP): Jirón Ayacucho 173, CP 3616, Lima 1; tel. (1) 4261310; e-mail ctp7319@hotmail.com; affiliated to PAP; Sec.-Gen. ELÍAS GRIJALVA.

Transport

RAILWAYS

In 2010 there were some 2,020 km of track.

Consorcio Ferrocarriles del Perú: in 1999, following the privatization of the state railway company, Empresa Nacional de Ferrocarriles (ENAFER), the above consortium won a 30-year concession to operate the following lines:

Ferrocarril Tacna–Arica: Avda Aldarracín 484, Tacna; 62 km open; Administrator ORLANDO ANGULO BLANCO.

Ferrocarril Transandino, SA (Southern Railway): Avenida Tacna y Arica 200, Arequipa; tel. (54) 215350; fax (54) 231603; internet www.ferrocarriltransandino.com; 915 km open; operates Ferrocarril del Sur y Oriente; also operates steamship service on Lake Titicaca; Gen. Man. ALBERTO VALDEZ GALDÓS.

Ferrovías Central Andina, SA: Avda José Galvez Barrenechea 566, 5°, San Isidro, Lima; tel. (1) 2266363; e-mail reservas@fcca.com.pe; internet www.ferroviasperu.com.pe; f. 1999; operates Ferrocarril del Centro del Perú; Gen. Man. JAIME FERNANDO BLANCO RAVINA.

ROADS

There are 125,045 km of roads in Peru as estimated in 2010, of which approximately 23,596 km are highways and national roads. The most important highways are: the Pan-American Highway (3,008 km), which runs from the Ecuadorean border along the coast to Lima; Camino del Inca Highway (3,193 km) from Piura to Puno; Marginal de la Selva (1,688 km) from Cajamarca to Madre de Dios; and the Trans-Andean Highway (834 km), which runs from Lima to Pucallpa on the River Ucayali via Oroya, Cerro de Pasco and Tingo María. In 2010 plans were announced for the Línea Amarilla toll road in Lima, funded by the Inter-American Development Bank. The estimated total cost of the project was US $600m.

SHIPPING

Most trade is through the port of Callao, but there are 13 deep-water ports. There are river ports at Iquitos, Pucallpa and Yurimaguas, aimed at improving communications between Lima and Iquitos, and a further port is under construction at Puerto Maldonado. At December 2012 the flag registered fleet comprised 206 vessels, totalling 448,060 grt.

Agencia Naviera Maynas, SA: Avda San Borja Norte 761, San Borja, Lima 41; tel. (1) 4752033; fax (1) 4759680; e-mail lima@navieramaynas.com.pe; internet www.peruvianamazonline.com.pe; f. 1970; owned by the Naviera Yacu Puma, SA; liner services to and from Amazon river ports and Gulf of Mexico; Pres. LUIS VARGAS V.; Gen. Man. ROBERTO MELGAR BARABINO.

Asociación Marítima del Perú: Avda Camino Real 479, Of. 701, San Isidro, Apdo 3520, Lima 27; tel. and fax (1) 4214939; fax (1) 2215856; internet www.asmarpe.org.pe; f. 1957; asscn of 14 int. and Peruvian shipping cos; Pres. GUILLERMO ACOSTA RODRÍGUEZ.

Consorcio Naviero Peruano, SA: Avda República de Colombia 643, 7° y 8°, San Isidro, Lima 27; tel. (1) 4116500; fax (1) 4116599; e-mail cnp@cnpsa.com; internet www.cnpsa.com; f. 1959; Gen. Man. ALEJANDRO JOSÉ PEDRAZA MACLEAN.

Empresa Nacional de Puertos, SA (Enapu): Avda Manco Capac 255, Callao; tel. (1) 6517828; fax (1) 4691010; e-mail enapu@inconet.net.pe; internet www.enapu.com.pe; f. 1970; govt agency administering all coastal and river ports; Pres. JAIME THORNE; Gen. Man. JUAN ARRISUEÑO GÓMEZ DE LA TORRE.

Naviera Humboldt, SA: Edif. Pacífico–Washington, 9°, Natalio Sánchez 125, Apdo 3639, Lima 1; tel. (1) 4334005; fax (1) 4330503; e-mail info@humboldt.com.pe; internet www.humboldt.com.pe; f. 1970; cargo services; Pres. AUGUSTO BEDOYA CAMERE; Gen. Man. ERNESTO FERRARO AMICO.

Naviera Transoceánica, SA (PETRANSO): Edif. Macros, 12°, Manuel Olguín 501, Lima 33; tel. (1) 5139300; fax (1) 5139321; e-mail comercial@navitranso.com; internet www.navitranso.com; f. 1956 as Petrolera Transoceánica; privatized in 1993; CEO LUIS RAFAEL MEDINA ZAMBRANO; Gen. Man. ALVARO VALDEZ.

CIVIL AVIATION

Of Peru's 294 airports and airfields, the major international airport is Jorge Chávez Airport near Lima. Other important international airports are Coronel Francisco Secada Vignetta Airport, near Iquitos, Velasco Astete Airport, near Cusco, and Rodríguez Ballón Airport, near Arequipa.

Corporación Peruana de Aeropuertos y Aviación Comercial: Aeropuerto Internacional Jorge Chávez, Avda Elmer Faucett, Callao; tel. (1) 6301000; fax (1) 5745578; e-mail sugerencias@corpac.gob.pe; internet www.corpac.gob.pe; f. 1943; Pres. WALTER HUGO TELLO CASTILLO; Gen. Man. JUAN CARLOS CROVETTO LUNA.

Domestic Airlines

Aero Cóndor: Juan de Arona 781, San Isidro, Lima; tel. (1) 4425215; fax (1) 2215783; domestic services; Pres. CARLOS PALACÍN FERNÁNDEZ; Exec. Dir LUIS EDUARDO PALACÍN.

LAN Perú, SA: Centro Comercial Real Plaza, Avda Garcilazo de la Vega 1337, Tienda 1001, Lima; tel. (1) 2138200; internet www.lan.com; f. 1999; CEO JORGE VILCHEZ; Gen. Man. NICOLAS GOLDSTEIN.

StarPerú: Avda Comandante Espinar 331, Miraflores, Lima 18; tel. (1) 7059000; fax (1) 3324789; e-mail atencionalcliente@starperu.com; internet www.starperu.com; f. 1997; operates services to 8 domestic destinations; Gen. Man. ROMÁN KASIANOV.

Tourism

Tourism is centred on Lima, with its Spanish colonial architecture, and Cusco, with its pre-Inca and Inca civilization, notably the 'lost city' of Machu Picchu. Lake Titicaca, lying at an altitude of 3,850 m above sea level, and the Amazon jungle region to the north-east are also popular destinations. In 2011 Peru received an estimated 2,598,000 visitors. Receipts from tourism generated a provisional US $2,360m. (excluding passenger transport) in that year.

Cámara Nacional de Turismo del Perú (CANATUR): Avda Paseo de la República No 6348, Miraflores, Lima; tel. (1) 2057500; fax (1) 2427555; e-mail secretaria@canaturperu.org; internet www.canaturperu.org; f. 1971; Pres. CARLOS CANALES ANCHORENA; Exec. Dir CESAR ALCORTA SUERO.

Comisión de Promoción del Perú (PromPerú): Edif. Mitinci, Calle Uno Oeste, 13°, Urb. Corpac, San Isidro, Lima 27; tel. (1) 2243279; fax (1) 2243323; e-mail postmaster@promperu.gob.pe; internet www.peru.info; f. 1993; Dir of Tourism MARÍA DEL CARMEN DE REAPARAZ.

Defence

As assessed at November 2012, Peru's armed forces numbered 115,000: army 74,000, navy 24,000, air force 17,000. Paramilitary police forces numbered 77,000. There were 188,000 army reserves. Compulsory military service was reintroduced in 2013.

Defence Budget: an estimated 6,420m. new soles for defence and domestic security in 2012.

President of the Joint Command of the Armed Forces: Adm. JOSÉ CUETO ASERVI.

Commander-General of the Army: Gen. RICARDO MONCADA NOVOA.

Commander-General of the Air Force: Gen. JAIME MARIN FIGUEROA OLIVOS.

Commander-General of the Navy: Adm. CARLOS ROBERTO TEJADA MERA.

Education

The educational system in Peru is divided into three levels: the first level is for children up to six years of age in either nurseries or kindergartens. Basic education is provided at the second level. It is free and, where possible, compulsory between six and 15 years of age. Primary education lasts for six years. Secondary education, beginning at the age of 12, is divided into two stages, of two and three years, respectively. In 2009/10 enrolment at primary schools included 95% of pupils in the relevant age-group, while secondary enrolment included 78% of students in the relevant age-group. Higher education includes the pre-university and university levels. There were 78 universities in 2000. There is also provision for adult literacy programmes and bilingual education. Budget proposals for 2012 allocated some 95,535m. new soles to education.

THE PHILIPPINES

Introductory Survey

LOCATION, CLIMATE, LANGUAGE, RELIGION, FLAG, CAPITAL

The Republic of the Philippines lies in the western Pacific Ocean, east of mainland South-East Asia. The island of Borneo is to the south-west, and New Guinea to the south-east. The principal islands of the Philippine archipelago are Luzon, in the north, and Mindanao, in the south. Between these two (which together account for 66% of the country's area) lie the 7,000 islands of the Visayas. The climate is maritime and tropical. It is generally hot and humid, except in the mountains. There is abundant rainfall, and the islands are frequently in the path of typhoons. At the 1995 census there were 102 languages; the most frequently used were Tagalog (by 29.3% of the population), Cebuano (21.2%), Ilocano (9.3%), Hiligaynon (Ilongo—9.1%) and Bicol (5.7%). Filipino, based on Tagalog, is the native national language. English is widely spoken, and Spanish is used in some communities. At the 2000 census 92.7% of the population were Christians (81.1% Roman Catholics) and 5.0% were Muslims. The national flag (proportions 1 by 2) has two equal horizontal stripes, of blue and red, with a white triangle, enclosing a yellow 'Sun of Liberty' (with eight large and 16 small rays) and three five-pointed yellow stars (one in each corner), at the hoist. The capital is Manila, on the island of Luzon.

CONTEMPORARY POLITICAL HISTORY

Historical Context

The Philippines became a Spanish colony in the 16th century. During the Spanish–American War, the independence of the Philippines was declared on 12 June 1898 by Gen. Emilio Aguinaldo, leader of the revolutionary movement, with the support of the USA. Under the Treaty of Paris, signed in December 1898, Spain ceded the islands to the USA. A new Constitution, ratified by plebiscite in May 1935, gave the Philippines internal self-government and provided for independence after 10 years. During the Second World War the islands were occupied by Japanese forces from 1942, but, after Japan's surrender in 1945, US rule was restored. The Philippines became an independent republic on 4 July 1946, with Manuel Roxas as its first President. A succession of Presidents, effectively constrained by US economic interests and the Filipino land-owning class, did little to help the peasant majority or to curb disorder and political violence.

Domestic Political Affairs

At elections in November 1965 the incumbent President, Diosdado Macapagal of the Liberal Party (LP), was defeated by Ferdinand Marcos of the Nacionalista Party (NP). Rapid development of the economy and infrastructure followed. President Marcos was re-elected in 1969. His second term was characterized by civil unrest, economic difficulties and an increase in guerrilla activity (see Separatist Tensions and Militancy).

In September 1972, before completing the (then) maximum of two four-year terms of office, President Marcos declared martial law in order to address subversive activity and to introduce drastic reforms. The bicameral Congress was suspended, opposition leaders were arrested, the private armies of the landed oligarchs were disbanded, stringent press censorship was introduced, and Marcos began to rule by decree. In November a new Constitution was approved by a constitutional convention, and in January 1973 it was ratified by Marcos. It provided for a unicameral National Assembly and a Constitutional President, with executive power held by a Prime Minister, to be elected by the legislature. Transitional provisions gave the incumbent President the combined authority of the presidency (under the 1935 Constitution) and the premiership, without any fixed term of office. Under martial law, the definitive provisions of the new Constitution remained in abeyance.

A referendum in July 1973 approved Marcos's continuation in office beyond his elected term. Referendums in February 1975 and October 1976 approved the maintenance of martial law and the adoption of constitutional amendments, including a provision for the formation of an interim assembly. In December 1977 a fourth referendum approved the extension of Marcos's presidential term.

Criticism of President Marcos became more widespread after November 1977, when a sentence of death was imposed by a military tribunal on the principal opposition leader, Benigno Aquino, Jr—a former senator and Secretary-General of the LP, who had been detained since 1972—for alleged murder, subversion and the possession of firearms. Marcos allowed a stay of execution, and conceded some relaxation of martial law in 1977. Elections to the interim National Assembly took place in April 1978. Opposition parties were permitted to participate, but the pro-Government Kilusang Bagong Lipunan (KBL—New Society Movement), founded in 1978 by Marcos and former members of the NP, won 151 of the Assembly's 165 elective seats. The Assembly was inaugurated in June, when Marcos was also confirmed as Prime Minister. Martial law remained in force, and Marcos retained the power to legislate by decree. In May Aquino was released from prison to undergo medical treatment in the USA.

In January 1981 martial law was ended, although Marcos retained most of his former powers. A referendum in April approved constitutional amendments that permitted Marcos to renew his presidential mandate by direct popular vote and to nominate a separate Prime Minister. In June, amid allegations of electoral malpractice, Marcos was re-elected President for a six-year term. In April 1982 the United Nationalist Democratic Organization (UNIDO), an alliance of opposition groups, formed an official coalition: it included Lakas ng Bayan (the People's Power Movement, founded by Benigno Aquino in 1978) and the Pilipino Democratic Party (PDP), which merged to form PDP-Laban in 1983.

In August 1983 Benigno Aquino, returning from exile in the USA, was shot dead on arrival at Manila airport. Rolando Galman, the alleged communist assassin, was killed immediately by military guards. A commission of inquiry, nominated by the Government, concluded that Aquino's murder had been a military conspiracy. However, the Supreme Court announced in December 1985 that the evidence submitted to the commission was inadmissible, acquitted the 26 military personnel who had been accused of conspiring to murder Aquino and upheld the Government's assertion that the assassin was Galman. At elections to the National Assembly in May 1984, public participation was high, and, after numerous accusations by the opposition of electoral fraud and corruption by Marcos, the opposition won 59 of the 183 elective seats.

In November 1985, in response to US pressure, Marcos announced that a presidential election would be held in February 1986, 18 months earlier than scheduled. Corazon Aquino, the widow of Benigno Aquino, was chosen as the UNIDO presidential candidate, in spite of her lack of political experience. More than 100 people were killed in violence during the election campaign. Vote-counting was conducted by the government-controlled National Commission on Elections (Comelec) and by the independent National Citizens' Movement for Free Elections (Namfrel). Allegations of electoral fraud and irregularities, apparently perpetrated by supporters of Marcos, were substantiated by international observers. The National Assembly declared Marcos the winner of the presidential election, with 10.8m. votes, compared with 9.3m. for Corazon Aquino, according to figures from Comelec. According to Namfrel figures (based on 69% of the total votes), Aquino was in the lead. Marcos immediately announced the resignation of the Cabinet, and declared his intention to establish a council of presidential advisers.

Later in February 1986 Lt-Gen. (later Gen.) Fidel Ramos, the acting Chief of Staff of the Armed Forces, and Juan Ponce Enrile, the Minister of National Defense, along with about 300 troops, established a rebel headquarters in the Ministry of National Defense (later moving to the police headquarters), stating that they no longer accepted Marcos's authority and asserting that Corazon Aquino was the rightful President. Attempts by forces loyal to Marcos to attack the rebels were foiled by large unarmed crowds, which gathered to protect them at the instigation of the

Catholic Archbishop of Manila, Cardinal Jaime Sin. Troops supporting Ramos subsequently secured control of the government broadcasting station. Rival ceremonies were held, at which both Marcos and Aquino were sworn in as President. However, later the same day, under pressure from the USA, Marcos agreed to withdraw, and left the Philippines for the US state of Hawaii.

President Aquino appointed her Vice-President, Salvador Laurel (the President of UNIDO), to be Prime Minister and Minister of Foreign Affairs, while Enrile retained the post of Minister of National Defense. Ramos was appointed Chief of Staff of the Armed Forces. At the end of February 1986 Aquino ordered the controversial release of all political prisoners, including communist leaders. In March the Government announced the restoration of habeas corpus, the abolition of press censorship and the suspension of local government elections (scheduled for May). The Government also secured the resignation of all Justices of the Supreme Court, as well as the resignation of Comelec members. Aquino announced that the 1973 Constitution was to be replaced by an interim document, providing for the immediate abolition of the National Assembly and for the inauguration of a provisional government, with the President being granted emergency powers. The post of Prime Minister was temporarily abolished, and in May a commission was appointed to draft a new constitution.

In March 1986 military leaders pledged their loyalty to President Aquino. The Government then began to implement a programme of military reform, in accordance with the demands of officers of the Rebolusyonaryong Alyansang Makabayan (RAM—Nationalist Revolutionary Alliance—also known as the Reform the Armed Forces Movement), who had supported the February revolution. In September the Supreme Court ordered the retrial of the members of the military who had earlier been acquitted of the murder of Benigno Aquino. In September 1990 a special court convicted 16 members of the armed forces of the murder of both Aquino and Galman.

In July 1986 an abortive coup took place in Manila, led by Arturo Tolentino, a former Minister of Foreign Affairs and Marcos's vice-presidential candidate, and a group of 300 pro-Marcos troops. One of the principal reasons for military dissatisfaction was the new Government's conciliatory attitude towards communist insurgents. In November a group of army officers attempted to gain control of several military camps and to replace Aquino with Nicanor Yniguez, a former Speaker of the National Assembly. The rebellion was quelled by Ramos and troops loyal to Aquino; Enrile was dismissed from the Cabinet. In January 1987 a further coup attempt by 500 disaffected soldiers was suppressed by forces loyal to the President, and an attempt by Marcos to return to the Philippines was thwarted by US officials.

In February 1987 a new Constitution was approved by 76% of voters in a national plebiscite. The new Constitution gave President Aquino a mandate to rule until 30 June 1992, and established an executive presidency. An order followed disbanding all 'fraternal organizations' (such as the RAM) within the armed forces, because they 'encouraged divisiveness'. Elections to the bicameral Congress of the Philippines took place in May 1987, at which more than 83% of the electorate participated. Aquino's UNIDO coalition (under the name Lakas ng Bayan) secured 180 of the 200 elective seats in the House of Representatives and 22 of the 24 seats in the Senate.

In August 1987 Ramos and troops loyal to Aquino averted a serious coup attempt, when rebel officers (led by Col Gregorio Honasan, an officer closely associated with Enrile) occupied the army headquarters, and captured a radio and television station. In the intense fighting that ensued in Manila and Cebu, 53 people were killed. Honasan and his supporters fled, successfully evading capture until December. (However, Honasan escaped from detention in April 1988.) In December 1990 a military court sentenced 81 members of the armed forces to prison terms of up to 32 years for their part in the rebellion.

In October 1988 former President Marcos and his wife, Imelda, were indicted in the USA and charged with the illegal transfer into the country of some US $100m. that had allegedly been obtained by embezzlement and racketeering. In February 1989 Laurel (who had formally dissociated himself from Aquino) began to campaign for Marcos to be permitted to return to the Philippines. In May Marcos's NP was revived, with Laurel as President and Enrile as Secretary-General. The Philippine Government launched the first of 35 planned civil suits against Marcos *in absentia* on charges of corruption in September. However, the former President died in Hawaii later that month.

In July 1990, in New York, USA, Imelda Marcos was acquitted of charges of fraud and of the illegal transfer of stolen funds to the USA.

In December 1989 an abortive coup was staged by members of two élite military units, in collusion with the now illicit RAM and officers loyal to Marcos. President Aquino subsequently addressed a rally of 100,000 supporters, accusing Laurel and Enrile (who were both included in an eight-member provisional junta named by the rebels) of involvement in the coup attempt. Dissident members of the armed forces continued their campaign to destabilize the Government in 1990, carrying out a series of bombings of allegedly corrupt businesses associated with the Government or owned by US interests.

In July 1991 Ramos resigned as Secretary of National Defense in order to contest the presidential election (scheduled for 1992). Having failed to secure the nomination of the ruling party, Laban ng Demokratikong Pilipino (LDP—formed in 1988 by members of pro-Government parties), Ramos, with Aquino's endorsement, resigned from the LDP and registered a new party, EDSA-LDP, with the support of 25 former LDP members of Congress. (EDSA was the popular acronym for the Epifanio de los Santos Avenue, the main site of the February 1986 uprising.) The party, which subsequently altered its title to Lakas ng EDSA, formed an alliance with the National Union of Christian Democrats to become Lakas-NUCD.

Presidential, legislative and local elections took place on 11 May 1992. Fidel Ramos was elected to the presidency, winning 23.6% of the votes cast; his closest rivals were Miriam Defensor Santiago, a former Secretary of Agrarian Reform (with 19.7%), and Eduardo Cojuangco, Aquino's estranged cousin, whose wing of the NP had been renamed the Nationalist People's Coalition (NPC—with 18.2%). However, in the legislative elections the LDP (the only party that had local bases in every province) won 16 of the 24 seats in the Senate and 89 of the 200 elective seats in the House of Representatives. Despite his party's poor representation in Congress, Ramos, who was inaugurated on 30 June, managed to gain the support of the NPC, the LP and 55 defectors (now known as Laban) from the LDP, to form a 'rainbow coalition', comprising 145 of the 200 elected members of the House of Representatives. The Senate remained under the control of the LDP. On assuming power, Ramos gave priority to persuading mutinous right-wing soldiers, communist insurgents and Muslim separatists to abandon their armed struggle (see Separatist Tensions and Militancy).

In September 1993 Imelda Marcos (who had returned to the Philippines in 1991) was convicted of corruption and sentenced to 18 years' imprisonment; she remained at liberty pending an appeal against the conviction. In February 1994 a court in Hawaii awarded US $2,000m. in punitive damages to 10,000 Filipinos tortured under President Marcos's administration, following a court ruling in October 1992 that victims of abuses of human rights under the Marcos regime could sue his estate for compensation. Imelda Marcos announced that she would appeal against the decision. Further charges of embezzlement were filed against her in April and June 1994 and in September 1995. Meanwhile, in February 1993 Congress adopted legislation (which was signed into law in December) to reinstate the death penalty, which had been banned under the 1987 Constitution.

Prior to legislative and local elections held on 8 May 1995, in which an estimated 80% of all eligible voters participated, more than 80 people were killed in campaign violence. The ruling coalition won the vast majority (about 70%) of seats in the House of Representatives, and an electoral alliance between Lakas-NUCD and the LDP—known as Lakas-Laban—won nine of the 12 contested seats in the Senate. One of the three opposition seats was secured by Honasan, despite a campaign by Aquino against his candidacy. Imelda Marcos obtained a seat in the House of Representatives, having been allowed to contest the elections pending the outcome of her appeal, although she was not permitted to take her seat until November, when the Supreme Court ruled in her favour.

The presidency of Joseph Estrada

The formation of an opposition grouping, the Laban ng Makabayang Masang Pilipino (LaMMP—Struggle of Nationalist Filipino Masses), to contest the elections scheduled for May 1998 was announced in June 1997. The LaMMP was composed of the Partido ng Masang Pilipino, led by Joseph 'Erap' Estrada, the LDP (which had withdrawn from its alliance with Lakas-NUCD in February 1996), led by Edgardo Angara, and the NPC, led by Ernesto Maceda. Estrada was a famous former action-film star who for many years had held the position of mayor of the Metro

Manila municipality of San Juan before being elected to the Senate in 1987. In December 1997 Estrada and Angara were formally endorsed as the LaMMP's presidential and vice-presidential candidates, respectively.

Presidential, legislative and local elections took place on 11 May 1998; an estimated 80% of the electorate participated in the polls. Some 51 people were killed in pre-election violence (mostly in the southern province of Mindanao). Estrada was elected to the presidency with 39.9% of the votes cast. His closest rival was the Lakas-NUCD candidate, Jose de Venecia (who was responsible for negotiations with both the Islamist separatists and the left-wing National Democratic Front—NDF—see Separatist Tensions and Militancy), who secured 15.9% of the votes. The vice-presidency was won by Gloria Macapagal Arroyo (the daughter of former President Diosdado Macapagal), who had supported de Venecia's candidacy. Seven of the victorious senators were members of the LaMMP, while the other five were Lakas-NUCD candidates. However, Lakas-NUCD dominated the House of Representatives, winning 106 seats, compared with only 66 for the LaMMP. In a development indicative of the weakness of the party system, many congressional members subsequently defected to Estrada's party, which was renamed Laban ng Masang Pilipino (Fight of the Filipino Masses).

In Estrada's inaugural address, in June 1998, the new President reiterated campaign pledges to eradicate poverty and corruption, but also assured the business sector that he would continue Ramos's programme of economic reform. His new Cabinet comprised members from a wide political and social spectrum, including wealthy ethnic Chinese business executives, former associates of Marcos, and allies from Estrada's career as mayor and senator, as well as former activists from the communist movement and left-wing non-governmental organizations. Five members of Lakas-NUCD were allocated portfolios and Ramos accepted a post as Senior Adviser. However, Estrada was criticized for appointing friends and relatives to lucrative and influential positions. Additional concerns about a reversion to the Marcos era of 'cronyism' were raised by the return to prominence of former Marcos associates, some of whom had made substantial financial contributions to Estrada's presidential campaign fund. The Marcoses' daughter, Imee, and their son, Ferdinand, Jr, were elected to Congress and the governorship of Ilocos Norte, respectively.

In spite of widespread apprehension regarding his leadership abilities, Estrada was credited with several successes during his first year in office, including a dramatic reduction in kidnappings for ransom, facilitated by the creation in July 1998 of the Presidential Anti-Organized Crime Task Force. Estrada also effectively abolished 'pork barrel' funds (state funds from which congress members financed projects in their constituencies), which had led to corruption and the reinforcement of patronage politics.

In October 1998 Imelda Marcos was acquitted of charges of corruption, although numerous civil suits remained pending against her. Estrada favoured a negotiated settlement with the Marcos family to resolve the dispute over funds misappropriated by the former President and also gave his support to the burial of Ferdinand Marcos in the National Heroes' Cemetery. However, popular outrage prompted Imelda Marcos to postpone the burial indefinitely. Meanwhile, the Swiss Supreme Court ruled in January 1998 that all funds held by Marcos in Swiss bank accounts be released (to be disbursed by the Philippine courts), rejecting an appeal by the Marcos family in April. In February 1999 the Marcos family agreed to pay a total of US $150m. in damages to 9,539 victims of human rights abuses. (In July 2003 the Philippines Supreme Court ruled that the sum of approximately $658m. that had been held by Ferdinand Marcos in several Swiss bank accounts should be released to the Philippine Government.)

In late 1999 President Estrada's hitherto excellent popularity ratings began to decline owing to his perceived failure to alleviate poverty and amid increasing concern about 'cronyism' and corruption in his administration. In August Aquino and Cardinal Sin mobilized 100,000 demonstrators in a democracy rally to protest particularly against government plans to amend the 1987 Constitution. Critics feared the potential removal from the Constitution of the stipulation limiting the President to a single term of office. Later in August 1999 Estrada relaunched the ruling coalition, restyling it the Lapian ng Masang Pilipino (LAMP—Party of the Filipino Masses).

Following a report by the World Bank in November 1999 claiming that 20% of the Philippine budget was lost to corrup-

tion, President Estrada pledged to intensify investigations of officials suspected of dishonesty. In the same month, in a further attempt to dispel criticism, Estrada established the EDSA People Power Commission to promote the ideals of the 1986 uprising; its 15 members included Aquino, Ramos and Estrada. However, these measures proved inadequate to reverse a trend that was compounded by the unexpected resignation of the respected Secretary of Finance, Edgardo Espiritu, in January 2000 and by Espiritu's subsequent accusations of undue influence being exerted by unelected associates of Estrada. Estrada responded to growing public dissatisfaction by announcing the reform of his administration. He dismissed his informal advisers, replacing them with a six-member Economic Co-ordinating Council to promote coherence in economic affairs, and recruited five eminent business leaders to act as an economic advisory council. The proposed constitutional reforms were suspended and replaced by plans to achieve economic liberalization through legislation. Estrada's attempts to improve his popularity were swiftly undermined by the testimony in January of the Chairman of the Securities and Exchange Commission, Perfecto Yasay, to a Senate Committee investigating allegations of illegal share trading; Yasay alleged that Estrada had pressed him to exonerate one of Estrada's close associates who was suspected of illegally manipulating share prices. Estrada denied the intervention, although he admitted telephoning Yasay four times in relation to the investigation.

Despite the President's denial in October 2000 of allegations that he had accepted large sums of money in bribes from illegal gambling businesses, in November the House of Representatives endorsed the impeachment of Estrada after more than one-third of its members signed a petition favouring this action. Supporters of Estrada condemned the impeachment proceedings as unconstitutional since they had not been submitted to a formal vote in the House of Representatives. At an impeachment trial held in the Senate in December Estrada pleaded not guilty to charges of bribery, corruption, betrayal of public trust and violation of the Constitution. However, the trial was adjourned indefinitely in January 2001 after prosecutors failed to obtain the disclosure of bank records as evidence against him. This effective acquittal of the President provoked mass demonstrations against him. Estrada had lost the support of many members of his Cabinet, the police and the armed forces, and, in response to a request by Vice-President Arroyo, who had resigned as Secretary of Social Welfare and Development in October 2000 and proceeded to establish an alliance of opposition parties, the Supreme Court declared the presidency to be vacant.

President Arroyo's first term

Gloria Arroyo was sworn in as President on 20 January 2001, and the Supreme Court affirmed the legitimacy of her office in March. In April Estrada was formally indicted for a number of alleged offences, including one of economic plunder, which was punishable by the death penalty. Estrada was arrested for the first time in mid-April and charged with corruption and perjury. At the beginning of May supporters of Estrada attempted to storm the presidential palace in Manila. Three senators were arrested for having allegedly conspired to bring down the Government, and President Arroyo declared a state of rebellion, which permitted her to deploy the armed forces to quell the unrest. Estrada, who had subsequently been rearrested, was removed to a detention centre outside Manila, having had his application for bail denied.

Legislative and local elections were held on 14 May 2001. Lakas-NUCD secured 87 seats in the House of Representatives, followed by the NPC with 62. The People Power Coalition (PPC—a coalition of Lakas-NUCD, the LP and several smaller parties, which had been formed by President Arroyo to contest the elections) won eight seats in the Senate, while allies of the Laban ng Demokratikong Pilipino-Pwersa ng Masa (LDP-PnM—the opposition coalition formed to support Estrada) secured four. The remaining seat went to an independent candidate. President Arroyo thus succeeded in securing a majority in both chambers. As a result of violence throughout the election period, 83 people died. The elections were further marred by reports of widespread corruption.

In October 2001 Jose Miguel Arroyo, the husband of the President, was investigated by the Senate over allegations that he had diverted funds from a state lottery in order to finance electoral campaigns for prospective senators. In the same month Estrada's trial on charges of perjury and plunder commenced. In November the Supreme Court rejected a legal challenge brought by Estrada against his trial and affirmed the constitutionality of the anti-plunder law under which he was being tried. After the suspension of two senior judges involved in the trial, the trial was adjourned and was resumed in January 2002 in a special anti-graft court. In July 2004 the court ruled that Estrada had not been guilty of money-laundering when he opened a bank account under a different name in 2000. A few days later the court approved Estrada's transfer from military detention to house arrest. In September 2007 Estrada was convicted of plunder, having been found to have misappropriated some US \$80m. during his tenure of office, and was sentenced to life imprisonment; he was acquitted of the charge of perjury. However, after apparently agreeing not to seek political office, Estrada was pardoned by President Arroyo in October. The pardon, and in particular the swiftness with which it had been granted, provoked considerable controversy.

Meanwhile, in June 2002 the defection of a senator to the opposition deprived the PPC of its narrow majority in the upper chamber. In November President Arroyo announced that she did not intend to contest the presidential election scheduled to take place in 2004, claiming that she wished to spare the country further political division. The Absentee Voting Bill, which rendered Filipino citizens living and working abroad eligible to vote in future legislative and presidential elections, was enacted in February 2003.

In July 2003 approximately 350 disaffected members of the armed forces staged a mutiny, taking control of a shopping centre in the Manila commercial district of Makati. The rebels, who demanded the resignation of President Arroyo and Secretary of National Defense Angelo Reyes, finally surrendered peacefully. While the Government claimed that the mutiny constituted an attempted coup, those who had participated claimed that they were merely seeking a chance to air their grievances, which included allegations that senior military personnel were guilty of systematic collusion with Muslim rebels in the south of the country. Later in July the head of military intelligence, Brig.-Gen. Victor Corpus, who had been accused of misconduct by the rebels, resigned. In the aftermath of the mutiny Arroyo declared a nation-wide state of rebellion, which was removed in August. In that month charges were filed against more than 1,000 people, including Senator Gregorio Honasan, in connection with the mutiny. Meanwhile, Secretary of National Defense Reyes resigned, while denying the allegations of corruption; Eduardo Ermita was appointed as his successor in September. In November the criminal charges that had been filed against 290 of those who had taken part in the July mutiny were abandoned; however, it was announced that the officers believed to have led the mutiny would be tried by a civilian court. In addition, all 321 soldiers were to appear at a court martial on separate charges related to their involvement in the mutiny. As a result of the court martial, which was conducted during 2005–08, the defendants received various sentences, including demotion, dishonourable discharge and terms of imprisonment. Meanwhile, the civilian trial of 20 of the 29 officers on separate charges of mounting a coup continued; in April 2008, having changed their plea to guilty, two of the officers were sentenced to life imprisonment, while seven received prison terms ranging from six to 12 years, although all nine were granted presidential pardons in May. (In November 2007 several of the defendants had briefly attempted to stage a further coup, but swiftly surrendered—see The elections of 2007.)

Meanwhile, in October 2003, in a reversal of her statement of December 2002, President Arroyo announced that she did now intend to contest the next presidential election, scheduled to take place in May 2004. Vice-President Teofisto Guingona, Jr, resigned from Lakas-NUCD (which restyled itself as Lakas-Christian Muslim Democrats—Lakas-CMD—in 2003), in advance of the announcement, citing differences of principle, but he retained his cabinet position. In November 2003 Secretary of Finance Jose Isidro Camacho tendered his resignation; he was replaced by Under-Secretary Juanita Amatong. In the same month two armed men occupied the air traffic control tower at the Ninoy Aquino International Airport in Manila, protesting against government corruption and prompting speculation concerning another coup attempt. Both men were shot dead by the police.

The elections of 2004

In advance of the May 2004 legislative and presidential elections, Senator Edgardo Angara, President of the opposition LDP, announced that his party had merged with the PDP-Laban group and Estrada's Pwersa ng Masang Pilipino (PMP—Force of the Filipino Masses, as the Partido ng Masang Pilipino had been renamed) to form the Koalisyon ng Nagkakaisang Pilipino

(KNP—Coalition of the United Filipino). The KNP subsequently announced that it had nominated the film actor Fernando Poe, Jr, as its presidential candidate. However, former chief of police Brig.-Gen. Panfilo Lacson stated his intention to stand as the official presidential candidate of the LDP, while former Secretary of Education, Culture and Sports Raul Roco, who had resigned in August 2002, secured the presidential nomination of Aksyon Demokratiko. The fifth presidential candidate to emerge was Eduardo Villanueva, the leader of the 'Jesus is Lord' Church, who was to represent the newly established Bangon Pilipinas (Rise Philippines). President Arroyo formed a new coalition in support of her candidacy—the Koalisyon ng Katapatan at Karanasan sa Kinabukasan (K-4)—which consisted of Lakas-CMD, the LP, Reporma and Probinsya Muna Development Intiatives. The coalition replaced the PPC, which had effectively been disbanded following the withdrawal of its most important members.

Presidential, legislative and local elections were held as planned on 10 May 2004. Almost 100 people were killed as a result of violence during the campaign period, despite the deployment of some 230,000 police officers and troops at polling stations throughout the country. Arroyo won a narrow victory in the presidential election, receiving 40.0% of the votes cast, compared with Poe's 36.5%. Poe refused to accept the result, alleging widespread fraud. Noli de Castro, representing Lakas-CMD, was elected to the vice-presidency. Lakas-CMD also performed well in the legislative elections, securing 93 of the 212 elective seats in the House of Representatives, while the NPC won 54 seats and the LP 34. Seven candidates of the K-4 coalition, dominated by Lakas-CMD, were elected to the Senate, with the remaining five contested seats taken by the KNP.

On being sworn in for a second term of office in June 2004, President Arroyo pledged to curb corruption, to improve basic services and to reform the economy, notably promising to create 6m. new jobs during her six-year term. In July Angelo Reyes, a close ally of the President, returned to the Government as Secretary of the Interior and Local Government, following the resignation of Jose Lina from that position. Later in that month Poe and his defeated vice-presidential candidate, Loren Legarda, lodged separate complaints with the Supreme Court, demanding a recount of votes on the grounds of electoral fraud. Poe died in December after suffering a stroke.

In August 2004 Arroyo announced a cabinet reorganization, in which former Executive Secretary Alberto Romulo succeeded Delia Domingo-Albert as Secretary of Foreign Affairs; Eduardo Ermita, hitherto Secretary of National Defense, replaced Romulo, and was in turn replaced by Avelino Cruz, the President's former chief legal adviser. In January 2005 the Secretary of Finance, Juanita Amatong, and the Secretary of Energy, Vicente Perez, resigned from office. The finance portfolio was allocated to Cesar Purisima, hitherto Secretary of Trade and Industry, who was replaced by Juan Santos. Perez agreed to remain in his post until the end of March, when he was succeeded by Raphael Lotilla.

In June 2005 a major political scandal arose over a recording of a telephone conversation held between President Arroyo and an election official while votes in the 2004 presidential poll were still in the process of being counted. Arroyo acknowledged that she had made an 'error of judgement' by speaking with an election official at that time, but strenuously denied having tried to influence the outcome of the poll. A number of cabinet members, including Secretary of Finance Purisima, resigned in July 2005, in protest against what they perceived to be the illegality of Arroyo's presidency. Margarito Teves assumed responsibility for the finance portfolio later in July. In September Congress formally rejected three separate impeachment cases against Arroyo, deeming the complaints too weak to stand up to legislative scrutiny.

In January 2006 the influential Catholic Bishops' Conference urged that investigations into the allegations of malpractice against Arroyo be continued since previous efforts were perceived to have been undermined by 'acts of evasion and obstruction of truth'. In February the National Bureau of Investigation announced that, since the recording of the conversation had been adjudged to have been tampered with, there was no longer any sound basis for continuing with its own investigation into the incident. In the same month an estimated 20,000 people marched through the capital to demand Arroyo's resignation as they marked the 20th anniversary of the ousting of former President Marcos. In March it was reported that members of the opposition were compiling evidence with which to file another impeachment complaint against Arroyo, regarding not only the vote manipulation allegations but also accusations concerning the mismanagement of state funds for a fertilizer scheme, which, it was claimed, had been misappropriated by Arroyo and her allies to help finance her presidential election campaign in 2004. A fresh impeachment motion against Arroyo was defeated in the House of Representatives in August 2006. A Senate inquiry into the vote-manipulation allegations commenced in September 2007; however, in December 2008 the Supreme Court barred the Senate from continuing its investigations on the grounds of incorrect procedure. In February 2009 a Senate committee recommended the prosecution of former Under-Secretary of Agriculture Jocelyn Bolante and nine others in connection with the fertilizer scandal, but found no direct evidence to link Arroyo to the controversy.

Meanwhile, in February 2006 a minor explosion within the presidential palace compound at Malacañang led to rumours of a potential military coup. A statement purporting to be from a rebel military faction, the Young Officers' Union-new generation (YOUng), claimed responsibility for the explosion; however, the YOUng leadership distanced itself from the statement, and, furthermore, forensic tests revealed the blast to have been the result of an accidental chemical reaction, rather than of terrorist activity. In late February it was reported that an attempted military coup had been averted after 14 junior army officers had confessed to their involvement in the plot. A few days later Arroyo declared a state of emergency, in response to the 'clear threat' to the nation, a decision that attracted considerable censure from the opposition, the media and civil liberties groups, which criticized the President for infringing upon public freedoms. One week after the military's announcement that the threat had been successfully countered, Arroyo removed the state of emergency. In the same month a special task force, comprising élite army units, was created in order to counter any further threats to the Government. In April 49 people, including members of the legislature and the military, were charged with rebellion for their alleged involvement in the February coup plot. In May the Supreme Court ruled that Arroyo's declaration of a state of emergency had been legal, but that several actions that had followed the declaration, including certain arrests, were unlawful. In June 2007 the Supreme Court dismissed charges of rebellion against six members of the legislature.

In June 2006 President Arroyo ratified a law that abolished the death penalty. In February 2007 Congress approved the Human Security Act, anti-terrorism legislation giving security officials powers of detention for a period of up to three days in the absence of a warrant or charge, and allowing access to suspicious financial accounts. Critics, including human rights organizations, opposition politicians and the Roman Catholic Church, expressed concern that the Act could be used to suppress legitimate political dissent.

The increasing occurrence of extra-judicial killings and human rights violations was highlighted in 2006 and 2007 by several independent reports. In February 2007 the UN Special Rapporteur on extra-judicial, summary or arbitrary executions, Philip Alston, contended that, although the highest level of Government recognized the gravity of the situation, the army was 'in a state of almost total denial of its need to respond effectively and authentically to the significant number of killings which have been convincingly attributed to them'. Also in February, an inquiry supported by the Government and led by Jose Melo, a retired judge, found links between sections of the military and politically motivated murders. As part of efforts to address the issue, the armed forces and the national police established their own human rights offices, and in March the Chief Justice designated special tribunals to try cases of political killings. In November Arroyo ordered the creation of a task force against political violence. On the following day Alston's final report was released, in which he concluded that claims by the armed forces that extra-judicial killings of leftist activists were a result of internal purges within communist groups were 'strikingly unconvincing' and observed that no one had been convicted of these killings. Other victims identified by Alston included civil society leaders, human rights activists, trade unionists and advocates of land reform. While welcoming measures initiated by the Government to combat the problem, Alston noted that they had yet to succeed.

The elections of 2007

Legislative and local elections held on 14 May 2007 were marred by numerous reports of fraud, voter intimidation and violence; some 120 people had been killed in election-related violence since the beginning of the year. Polling in 13 towns in the province of Lanao del Sur on Mindanao was postponed owing to the threat of violence, finally taking place on 26 May, amid heightened security. Moreover, six days before the elections at least eight people were killed in a bomb attack in the city of Tacurong, on Mindanao, which the security forces attributed to the regional militant organization Jemaah Islamiah (JI).

In the elections for 12 of the 24 seats in the Senate, the pro-Arroyo TEAM (Together Everyone Achieves More) Unity coalition—including Lakas-CMD, Kabalikat ng Malayang Pilipino (Kampi, founded in 1997 to support Arroyo) and the LDP—won three seats, while the Genuine Opposition (GO) coalition—including the LP, the PDP-Laban and the NP—won seven, giving a majority to opponents of President Arroyo. Notably elected for the GO was Antonio Trillanes IV, who remained in detention for his alleged role in the 2003 mutiny. The remaining two seats in the Senate were secured by independent candidates, one of whom was Gregorio Honasan, who was on bail accused of involvement in the same mutiny (the charges were dismissed in July 2007). None the less, supporters of Arroyo retained control of the House of Representatives, with parties belonging to TEAM Unity reportedly securing 168 elective seats compared with the GO's 44. Voter turn-out was estimated at 68% for the upper chamber and 70% for the lower chamber.

In September 2007 President Arroyo suspended a US $329m. contract signed by the Government and the Chinese ZTE Corporation in April for the provision of a national broadband telecommunications network, amid claims that Philippine officials brokering the agreement had both solicited and offered bribes. Among those implicated in the scandal were the President's husband, Jose Miguel Arroyo, and the Chairman of Comelec, Benjamin Abalos. The contract with ZTE Corporation, the bid of which had been substantially higher than those of rival companies, was cancelled in October. In November a new impeachment complaint against President Arroyo based on her alleged failure to act on the bribery accusations concerning Abalos, who had resigned in October, was dismissed owing to 'lack of substance'.

A bomb exploded outside the House of Representatives in November 2007, killing four people, including Wahab Akbar, the suspected target, who represented the island of Basilan in the lower chamber. The attack was attributed to the Islamist secessionist group Abu Sayyaf (see Separatist Tensions and Militancy), of which Akbar was allegedly a former member. Later in that month several military officers walked out of a court in Manila where they were being tried on charges of staging a coup in July 2003 (see President Arroyo's first term) and occupied a nearby hotel, from where, joined by other dissident soldiers, former Vice-President Teofisto Guingona, Jr, and a number of Catholic priests, among others, they appealed to the armed forces to withdraw support for President Arroyo. More than 1,000 heavily armed troops were deployed to quash the rebellion. Having failed to inspire a mass uprising, the leaders of the mutiny, Senator Antonio Trillanes IV and Brig.-Gen. Danilo Lim, surrendered to the authorities after several hours. Most of the rebels were detained, and an overnight curfew was imposed in Manila. In December 2007 Trillanes, Lim, Guingona and 33 others were charged with rebellion and incitement to rebellion; the charges against 18 civilians, including Guingona, were dismissed later in that month.

The controversy over the broadband contract with ZTE Corporation persisted in early 2008, as the Senate hearings into the affair continued, with further witnesses corroborating the bribery allegations. Jose de Venecia, formerly a close ally of President Arroyo, was removed as Speaker of the House of Representatives in a vote in February, after accusing Arroyo and the Government of corruption, and resigned as President of Lakas-CMD in March; he was succeeded in both posts by Prospero Nograles. (A company owned by de Venecia's son had unsuccessfully bid for the broadband contract.) Meanwhile, in February an estimated 10,000 people participated in a demonstration in Manila to demand the resignation of Arroyo over the corruption scandal, while more than 50 former government officials issued a joint statement also urging the President to leave office. At the end of the month former Presidents Corazon Aquino and Joseph Estrada addressed an anti-Government rally attended by some 15,000 people in the capital, while smaller demonstrations were held in other towns. Yielding to considerable pressure, notably from the Catholic Bishops' Conference, in March Arroyo revoked a controversial executive order issued in September 2005 that prevented public officials from attending congressional hearings on alleged government corruption unless permitted by the President. Meanwhile, it was announced that three suspected militants, believed to have links to Abu Sayyaf or JI, had been arrested on suspicion of plotting to bomb foreign embassies in Manila and to assassinate Arroyo. In July 2008 it was announced that a human rights lawyer and four former military officers had been arrested in connection with a new plot to oust President Arroyo; however, all five were acquitted of the charges against them in early 2009.

Juan Ponce Enrile, considered to be an ally of Arroyo, was elected President of the Senate in November 2008, following the resignation of the incumbent, NP President Manuel Villar, who had recently been embroiled in controversy over the funding of a road project and had lost the support of the majority of senators. In December the House of Representatives rejected a fourth impeachment complaint against Arroyo, which detailed various accusations of corruption and human rights abuses under her administration. Further corruption allegations against the President's husband emerged in early 2009, when he was linked to claims of collusion between government officials and contractors in bids for road development contracts.

Constitutional reform was considered in 2008–09. In April 2008 12 senators proposed a resolution on the formation of a constituent assembly to amend the Constitution by introducing a federal system of government, comprising 11 states and one administrative region centred on Manila, while retaining the presidency and a bicameral legislature. However, later in that month the House of Representatives' committee on constitutional amendments deferred a planned vote on the need for constitutional change, instead approving a motion to conduct nation-wide public consultations on the issue. Opposition politicians alleged that the President's supporters in the legislature intended to attempt to extend her tenure or to introduce a parliamentary system of government (under which she could assume the premiership); Arroyo's administration rejected these claims. In December several thousand opponents of constitutional reform, supported by former Presidents Aquino and Estrada, attended a rally in Manila. In February 2009 the House of Representatives' committee on constitutional amendments approved a resolution seeking to remove constitutional restrictions on foreign ownership of companies and land. Opponents of the proposal argued that, once the process of reforming the Constitution's economic provisions began, more controversial amendments might follow. In April Luis Villafuerte, the President of Kampi, filed a congressional resolution to form a constituent assembly. However, the death in August of former President Aquino, which provoked a period of national mourning during which tens of thousands of Filipinos took to the streets to pay their last respects to their erstwhile leader, appeared to diminish hopes of achieving charter change in the foreseeable future. Aquino had been vociferous in her objections to reform of the Constitution, which her administration had introduced in 1987, and several prominent politicians urged members of the House of Representatives to refrain from demanding constitutional reform out of deference to the late Aquino.

Meanwhile, Lakas-CMD and Kampi were merged in May 2009, thereby forming Lakas-Kampi-CMD, in a move that was deeply unpopular among significant factions within both Lakas-CMD and Kampi. De Venecia filed a petition with the Supreme Court in November, seeking the cancellation, by Comelec, of Lakas-Kampi-CMD's registration and for Lakas-CMD to be reinstated as the ruling party. However, the Supreme Court upheld the legality of the merger in December. Meanwhile, in the President's State of the Nation address in July 2009, Arroyo publicly refuted ongoing claims that she was seeking to change the Constitution in order to secure a second six-year term of office.

The Maguindanao massacre

In mid-November 2009 some 57 people were killed when a convoy of supporters of local politician Ismael Mangudadatu was ambushed by a group of armed men on the island of Mindanao; the convoy had been on its way to file nomination papers for Mangudadatu, who had previously announced his intention to stand against local mayor Andal Ampatuan, Jr (son of the incumbent Governor of Maguindanao, Andal Ampatuan, Sr, and a prominent member of the powerful provincial Ampatuan clan) in municipal polls due to be held, concurrently with legislative and presidential elections, in May 2010. Witnesses described seeing the group of armed men, estimated to number some 100, shoot the victims at close range before burying their bodies in shallow graves; Mangudadatu's wife and two sisters,

along with 30 journalists, were among the dead. Arroyo declared a state of emergency in the region in order to assist the authorities in their search for the perpetrators of the violence. Witnesses were reported to have identified Ampatuan, Jr, as the main assailant; shortly thereafter, he was expelled from the ruling Lakas-Kampi-CMD party, together with his brother, Zaldy Ampatuan, who was also suspended as Governor of the Autonomous Region of Muslim Mindanao (see Separatist Tensions and Militancy), and his father, who was dismissed as Governor of Maguindanao. Ampatuan, Jr, surrendered to the authorities at the end of November 2009 but denied any involvement in the attack. In early December martial law was imposed in Maguindanao, coinciding with the launch, by the police and armed forces, of a large-scale operation against militants in the region. It was also announced that the entire provincial police force was to be replaced by personnel from other regions in order to ensure an impartial investigation of the murders, without fear of relatives and supporters of the Ampatuan clan within the Maguindanao police force sabotaging the investigation.

Martial law was removed in mid-December 2009, following widespread criticism by the opposition that its implementation had been a disproportionate response. Ampatuan, Jr, formally pleaded not guilty to 41 charges of murder in January 2010. In February 196 people were charged with involvement in the attack, among them Andal Ampatuan, Sr, Zaldy Ampatuan and other prominent members of the clan. In April the acting Secretary of Justice, Alberto Agra, directed prosecutors to dismiss multiple murder charges against Zaldy Ampatuan and his cousin, Akmad Ampatuan, the mayor of Mamasapano, owing to an apparent lack of evidence. In the following week the families of 43 of the victims filed a joint motion for reconsideration of Agra's directive, contending that it was a reflection of Arroyo's indebtedness to the Ampatuan clan, which had supported her throughout her presidency; the Government repudiated such claims. However, Agra reversed his decision in May, citing the emergence of new evidence that appeared to incriminate both Zaldy and Akmad Ampatuan. In June the two men lodged separate petitions with the Court of Appeals seeking to nullify Agra's revocation of his initial directive on the grounds that their constitutionally guaranteed right to due process had been violated. Akmad Ampatuan's petition was rejected by the Court of Appeals in August 2011, and that of Zaldy Ampatuan was dismissed in November; an appeal lodged by Akmad Ampatuan was dismissed by the Court of Appeals in January 2012.

Meanwhile, the trial of 19 of the 196 people charged in connection with the massacre, including principal suspects Andal Ampatuan, Jr, and his father, commenced in September 2010. Given the naming of 200 witnesses by the prosecution and of a further 300 by the defence, the trial was not expected to be concluded rapidly. With less than one-half of the 196 charged persons in custody by the time the trial opened, there were widespread reports of attempts to intimidate investigators and witnesses by supporters of the Ampatuan clan. At least five people reported to have provided, or agreed to provide, incriminatory testimony against the Ampatuans were killed prior to the commencement of the trial. A report published by Human Rights Watch in November claimed that during the previous 20 years the Ampatuan clan had been responsible for at least 56 killings in addition to those of the Maguindanao massacre.

In June 2011 the Court of Appeals ordered that some US $23m. of assets belonging to the Ampatuan family be frozen, pending an investigation into how the family's wealth had been accumulated. Complaints about the slow progress of the trial increased in late 2011, with relatives of the victims and human rights groups voicing anger in November that, some two years after the massacre, the trial was still engaged in bail proceedings and only 93 of the 196 people suspected of involvement in the incident had been arrested. The trial remained ongoing at May 2013.

In August 2011 Ismael Mangudadatu narrowly avoided serious injury when a car bomb was detonated near the vehicle in which he was travelling in Tacurong, in the southern province of Sultan Kudarat. One person was killed in the attack.

The election of Benigno Aquino

In January 2010 it was announced that about 100,000 additional police officers and soldiers were to be deployed across the Philippines in advance of the forthcoming elections, in order to help enforce a ban on all unlicensed weapons and to encourage private militias to disband. Presidential, legislative and local elections, held on 10 May, were, as on previous occasions, marred by numerous reports of fraud and 'vote-buying'. At least 10 people were reported to have died in election-related violence, although polling in the majority of areas was generally conducted in a peaceful manner. However, the first national computerized elections in the history of the Philippines were reported to have presented significant problems in both the casting and the counting of ballots. According to some sources, as many as 8m. people had been unable to cast their vote owing to the failure of numerous automated counting machines. Amid allegations of serious electoral fraud, the Chairman of Comelec, Jose Melo, insisted that the fully computerized system made it impossible to counterfeit results without detectable irregularities appearing in the data.

In the presidential election, according to the official results released by Comelec on 8 June 2010, Benigno 'NoyNoy' Aquino, the son of the late former President Corazon Aquino, received 41.9% of the total votes cast. Joseph Estrada secured 26.1% of the ballot, NP President Manuel Villar 15.4% and the former Lakas-Kampi-CMD Chairman and Secretary of National Defense, Gilberto Teodoro, 11.3%. Despite the considerable margin of victory secured by Aquino, whose popularity had been boosted following the death in August 2009 of his mother, Estrada's second placing represented a far better performance than had been expected of the former President. The election for the vice-presidency was narrowly won by Jejomar 'Jojo' Binay, leader of the PDP-Laban group and Estrada's running mate, who defeated Aquino's running mate, Manuel 'Mar' Roxas II of the LP (the grandson of former President Roxas). Meanwhile, Arroyo secured a congressional seat. (Her decision to contest the elections had been criticized by the opposition, which contended that it represented a calculated bid by the outgoing President to retain immunity from potential corruption charges.)

Lakas-Kampi-CMD secured 107 of the 286 seats in the House of Representatives, the LP 45 and the NP 26. In the elections for 12 of the 24 seats in the Senate, the LP and an alliance of the NP and the NPC won three seats each, Lakas-Kampi-CMD and the PMP secured two each, and the People's Reform Party (PRP) took one seat. The remaining seat was secured by an independent candidate.

Benigno Aquino was sworn in as President on 30 June 2010. In his inauguration speech, the new President identified a number of priorities for his administration, including combating corruption, addressing the persistent budget deficit, reducing bureaucracy in order to render the country more attractive to potential investors, enhancing national infrastructure and improving the education system. On the previous day Aquino had announced the composition of his new Cabinet, which was dominated by members of the LP, technocrats and representatives of the business sector. Alberto Romulo retained the foreign affairs portfolio, while Voltaire Gazmin was appointed Secretary of National Defense; both men had been close allies of former President Corazon Aquino. Cesar Purisima, who had resigned from the post of Secretary of Finance in 2005 in protest against the perceived illegality of Arroyo's presidency, resumed responsibility for the finance portfolio. Other notable members of the incoming Cabinet included Leila de Lima, hitherto Chairperson of the Commission on Human Rights of the Philippines, who became Secretary of Justice, an appointment that was well received by human rights and anti-corruption groups.

On 1 July 2010 Arroyo filed a congressional resolution appealing for a constitutional convention to propose changes to the Constitution, furthering concerns among her critics that she was seeking the introduction of a parliamentary system of government with a view to returning to power in a prime-ministerial position. Aquino stated that he would not endorse proposals to reform the Constitution unless there was proof that such action was urgently required. At the end of July Aquino revoked by executive order some 977 'midnight appointments' authorized by the Arroyo administration during its final weeks, and established the Philippines Truth Commission of 2010, which was to investigate alleged anomalies from the Arroyo presidency.

Nicanor Faeldon voluntarily surrendered to the authorities in July 2010 'in recognition of the legitimacy' of Aquino's presidency; Faeldon was one of several military officers who in November 2007 had walked out of court during their trial on charges of staging a coup in July 2003 and occupied a hotel in protest against the perceived illegitimacy of Arroyo's presidency. In October 2010 Aquino announced a presidential proclamation granting amnesty to rebel soldiers involved in the military uprisings of 2003 and 2006. Senator Antonio Trillanes IV was among those released from prison in December 2010, and was able to take up his seat in the Senate for the first time in January 2011.

Recent developments: controversies and efforts to combat corruption

The first crisis of the Aquino administration arose when eight Hong Kong tourists were killed following the hijacking of a bus in Manila in August 2010 by a former Filipino police officer, Rolando Mendoza, who had recently been dismissed on suspicion of extortion and brutality. An 11-hour siege was finally concluded when armed police officers approached the bus and fatally shot Mendoza. The Aquino administration attracted criticism for its handling of the incident, with local police officers and government officials apparently having been left to tackle the situation without direct federal assistance. Aquino issued a public apology for the outcome of the affair and pledged to reprimand those found to be responsible. Witnesses stated that negotiation efforts appeared to have been leading to a peaceful resolution to the impasse when the authorities decided to approach the bus and that it was the advance of the police officers that had provoked Mendoza into opening fire on his hostages. Of further embarrassment to the Philippine authorities was the revelation by Secretary of Justice de Lima in September that the Government was investigating the theory that some of the tourists killed might have been shot by the police officers trying to rescue them.

In October 2010 the Supreme Court upheld the constitutionality of the Human Security Act, which was known to have been invoked just twice since its implementation in July 2007. Several human rights groups and legislators had lodged separate petitions seeking to revoke the legislation, arguing that its definition of 'terrorism' was too broad-based and that it posed a significant threat to civil liberties. In December 2010 the Supreme Court ruled that the Truth Commission established in July was unlawful since it 'singled out' an individual, Arroyo, which contravened the terms of the Constitution. Aquino expressed concern at the ruling, which he denounced as a setback for anti-graft reform, but vowed to continue his efforts undeterred. The Secretary of Justice dismissed the ruling as being politically motivated, an apparent reference to the fact that 14 of the 15 Supreme Court justices had been appointed by Arroyo, including the Chief Justice, Renato Corona, whose 'midnight appointment' in April had not been challenged by the incoming Aquino administration. In October a petition filed by Bai Omera Dianalan-Lucman appealing against the revocation of his 'midnight appointment' as Secretary of the National Commission on Muslim Filipinos was upheld by the Supreme Court, prompting an angry response from Aquino, who argued that the ruling had the potential to derail the Government's efforts to streamline the bureaucracy and restore good governance. Further petitions were subsequently filed by other officials dismissed as a result of Aquino's revocation of Arroyo's 'midnight appointments'; the petitioners alleged that Aquino had summarily dismissed them without just cause and due process. The Supreme Court remanded six such petitions to the Court of Appeals in February 2012; one petition was dismissed in April and the other five in September.

In January 2011 the US district court of Hawaii approved the disbursement of US $1,000 to each of 7,526 victims of human rights abuses perpetrated during the regime of former President Ferdinand Marcos. The US court also held Imelda Marcos and Ferdinand Marcos, Jr, in contempt for violating a court order requesting information on assets belonging to the Marcos estate, and fined them $353.6m., which was to fulfil in part the $2,000m. ruling against the Marcos estate in 1994.

In February 2011 Albert del Rosario was appointed acting Secretary of Foreign Affairs, in place of Romulo (being confirmed in this post in May). On the same day Edcel Lagman was elected to succeed Gloria Arroyo as National Chairman of Lakas-Kampi-CMD, while Ramon Bong Revilla, Jr, was chosen as the party's National President.

The issue of corruption continued to attract much attention throughout the first two years of Aquino's administration, which appeared keen to use public scandals dating from Arroyo's presidency to its political advantage. In February 2011 former cabinet minister Angelo Reyes, a close ally of Arroyo who had served as army Chief of Staff in 2000–01, died in an apparent suicide shortly prior to a scheduled appearance before a congressional committee investigating allegations of corruption (involving diverted state funds) within the military. Aquino pledged to punish those officers found to have embezzled state funds and charged his newly appointed military Chief of Staff, Lt-Gen. Eduardo Oban, with effecting radical reform of the military so as to eradicate large-scale vice, insisting that corruption would no longer be tolerated as, Aquino claimed, it had been by his predecessor. In March the House of Representatives voted to impeach the Ombudsman, Merceditas Gutierrez, another close ally of Arroyo, on the charge of betraying public trust. The motion accused Gutierrez of failing properly to address corruption allegations against Arroyo and other senior officials during her presidency, including the recent military graft scandal as well as that emanating from the tape recording during which Arroyo was apparently heard trying to influence the vote-counting process during the 2004 presidential election (see The elections of 2004). Citing the likelihood of protracted impeachment proceedings against her distracting attention from important legislative considerations, Gutierrez announced her resignation in April 2011.

Amid mounting speculation that Gloria and Jose Miguel Arroyo were to be charged in connection with electoral fraud pertaining to the 2004 and 2007 elections, in October 2011 the Department of Justice placed the former President and her husband on a travel 'watch list', forcing them to seek permission from the authorities before leaving the country. The Government denied a request by Gloria Arroyo to travel abroad for medical treatment in early November, citing concern that her itinerary included a number of destinations with which the Philippines did not have an extradition treaty. Supporters of the former President argued that the application of the travel ban was unconstitutional and that both she and Jose Miguel Arroyo remained innocent until proven guilty, further noting that no formal charges had yet been filed against either of them. The Supreme Court, still heavily dominated by justices appointed by former President Arroyo, ruled on 15 November that the travel ban was unlawful. Nevertheless, shortly afterwards Arroyo was prevented from boarding a flight to Singapore; Secretary of Justice de Lima subsequently stated that her department had not yet received the Supreme Court order rescinding the travel ban. On 18 November Arroyo was arrested on electoral sabotage charges pertaining to the 2007 Senate polls and was detained under hospital arrest. Arroyo, who denied any wrongdoing, alleging that the charges against her were politically motivated, was transferred from her private hospital to a court-approved military hospital in December 2011, pending a decision on whether she would be permitted to be detained under house arrest, as requested by her lawyers. In February 2012 the Government accepted a court decision to allow Arroyo to remain under hospital arrest; prosecutors had argued that the former President should be detained in gaol. Later that month Arroyo pleaded not guilty to the charges against her, which carried a potential sentence of life imprisonment.

Meanwhile, two civil lawsuits were filed against Gloria Arroyo during 2011. In June the United Church of Christ, a Protestant church grouping, filed a lawsuit claiming that during Arroyo's administration security forces had detained and tortured many of its members and had killed at least six. (A report published by the international human rights organization Amnesty International in the previous month had claimed that more than 200 disappearances and at least 305 extra-judicial killings that took place during the Arroyo presidency remained unresolved.) In November relatives of 15 of the victims of the Maguindanao massacre also filed a civil lawsuit against Arroyo, alleging that the former President, in her capacity as Commander-in-Chief at the time of the killings, was liable for their deaths owing to her connections with the Ampatuans and to the 'sense of impunity' that her administration had bestowed upon the clan.

In December 2011 the House of Representatives voted to impeach Chief Justice Renato Corona. The motion accused Corona, *inter alia*, of a betrayal of public trust 'marked by partiality and subservience in cases involving the Arroyo administration'; of affording Arroyo 'an opportunity to escape prosecution and to frustrate the ends of justice', a reference to the Supreme Court order rescinding the travel ban against Arroyo and her husband; and of failure to disclose his statement of assets, liabilities and net worth as required by the Constitution, leading to suspicion that he had accumulated 'ill-gotten wealth'. The impeachment complaint was referred to the Senate, which initiated trial proceedings against Corona, who denied any wrongdoing, in January 2012. In late May Chief Justice Corona was convicted by the Senate on charges of failing to declare all but a small percentage of his sizeable assets, in contravention of the Constitution, and immediately resigned from his post.

Meanwhile, in January 2012 Lakas-Kampi-CMD National Chairman Edcel Lagman resigned from the party and as the minority leader of the House of Representatives, citing disagreements with minority legislators 'beholden' to former President Arroyo. Lagman, who declared himself an independent hence-

forth, subsequently accused Arroyo of having orchestrated a plot to oust him as minority leader in favour of Danilo Suarez, who duly assumed the post later in January. In May Lakas-Kampi-CMD reverted to its former name of Lakas-CMD in an overhaul of the party aimed at improving its electoral prospects in 2013. Many former members of Kampi had previously left the party to form the National Unity Party.

Arrest warrants were issued for Gloria and Jose Miguel Arroyo, and for former Secretary of Transportation and Communications Leandro Mendoza and former Comelec Chairman Benjamin Abalos, in March 2012 in connection with corruption allegations pertaining to the ZTE Corporation scandal (see The elections of 2007). The Arroyos and Abalos pleaded not guilty to the charges against them at the special anti-graft court in April, while Mendoza's arraignment, at which he also entered a not guilty plea, was deferred until May owing to ill health. In late July Gloria Arroyo left the military hospital where she was receiving treatment, having been released on bail following a judicial ruling that the evidence against her regarding charges of electoral sabotage was too weak to justify her continuing detention. In early October, one day after applying for re-election to Congress, Arroyo was arrested in a military hospital on plunder charges (a non-bailable offence in the Philippines) for allegedly diverting some US $8.8m. from the state lottery charity fund for her personal advantage.

Meanwhile, in late August 2012 six days of national mourning were called and a state funeral conducted following the death of the popular Secretary of the Interior and Local Government, Jesse Robredo, in an aeroplane crash. Robredo had been greatly admired by the public on account of his perceived lack of corruption and his apparently genuine wish to better the lives of all Filipinos.

The implementation in early October 2012 of a controversial new law aimed at preventing 'cybercrime' (including online child pornography, identity theft and, most notably, libel) prompted protests by those who were concerned that the legislation would be used by the authorities to curb free speech and target government opponents. Under the Cybercrime Prevention Act, anyone found guilty of making libellous comments online, including on social networking sites and blogs, could be fined or imprisoned for up to 12 years. In response to the vehement opposition, the act was suspended a few days later by the Supreme Court for a period of 120 days. Another contentious piece of legislation, allowing for free access to state-funded contraception and family planning, was approved by Congress in December, despite the staunch opposition of the powerful Roman Catholic Church. The Church claimed that the Responsible Parenthood Act, which had been debated for around 14 years, would corrupt moral values, while the legislation's supporters asserted that its introduction was vital in an impoverished country that had the highest birth rate and one of the highest maternal mortality rates in the region. However, in March 2013 the Supreme Court delayed the implementation of the act pending the hearing of arguments disputing its legality in June. The adoption in December 2012 of another new law, providing for the potential imposition of a life sentence on state officials convicted of the abduction of individuals ('enforced disappearances'), was welcomed by human rights groups.

In late February 2013 President Aquino enacted a law ensuring the provision of compensation (including monetary compensation as well as social and psychological assistance where required) to the thousands of victims of human rights abuses under the regime of Ferdinand Marcos. The Government had set aside around US $224m. to fund this programme, having recovered large amounts of money from the secret Swiss bank accounts of the former President.

Local and legislative elections were scheduled to be held on 13 May 2013.

Separatist Tensions and Militancy

During the early 1970s there was an increase in guerrilla activity, by the New People's Army (NPA), the armed wing of the outlawed (Maoist) Communist Party of the Philippines (CPP), part of the left-wing National Democratic Front (NDF) alliance, in the north of the country, and by the Moro National Liberation Front (MNLF), a mainly Muslim separatist movement, in the south. The Philippines continued to be affected by regional instability during the years that followed, owing to the activities of these and other insurgent groups.

Upon his inauguration in June 1992, President Fidel Ramos gave priority to persuading the various factions to abandon their armed struggle. In July two communist leaders were conditionally released, and Ramos submitted to Congress an amnesty proclamation for about 4,500 members of the NPA, the MNLF and renegade former members of the armed forces who had already applied for amnesty. In August, following the formation of the National Unification Commission (NUC), which was charged with consulting rebel groups and formulating a viable amnesty programme, Ramos ordered the temporary release from prison of more communist leaders, including the Commander of the NPA, Romulo Kintanar, and NDF Spokesperson Saturnino Ocampo, and also of 16 rebel soldiers. In December seven military renegades, including Gregorio Honasan (see Domestic Political Affairs), emerged from hiding to sign a preliminary agreement to take part in talks with the Government. Discussions between the NUC and representatives of the RAM and the Young Officers' Union (YOU—a progressive offshoot of the RAM, which was alleged to have played an important role in the December 1989 coup attempt) began in January 1993, but were subsequently suspended.

In March 1994 Ramos proclaimed a general amnesty for all rebels and for members of the security forces charged with offences committed during counter-insurgency operations, as recommended by the NUC; however, the amnesty did not include persons convicted of torture, arson, massacre, rape and robbery. The RAM rejected the amnesty on the grounds that it failed to address the causes of the rebellion, while Saturnino Ocampo dismissed the proclamation as being biased against the communist rebels. Following agreement between the RAM and the Government during 1994 on certain government programmes and the issue of electoral reform, in 1995 formal negotiations resumed. In October the RAM and the YOU signed a peace agreement with the Government, which provided for the return of the rebels' military weapons within 90 days and the reintegration of members of the two organizations into the armed forces.

The NDF, the CPP and the NPA

In August 1992 the Government began discussions with exiled representatives of the NDF in the Netherlands. In September President Ramos repealed anti-subversion legislation, in place since 1957, that proscribed the CPP. Nevertheless, the exiled leadership of the NDF pledged that the CPP would continue its armed struggle, although there were widening divisions within the CPP over co-operation with the NUC.

In July 1993 the CPP's influential Metro Manila-Rizal regional committee publicly broke away from the CPP Central Committee led by Jose Maria Sison, a founder member of the CPP who had been based in the Netherlands since his release from prison in 1986, and who had assumed the party chairmanship in April 1992. This followed the attempted dissolution by Sison of the region's leading committee and its armed unit, the Alex Boncayao Brigade (ABB), accused of factionalism and military excesses. The Metro Manila-Rizal organization, which comprised about 40% of CPP members, was subsequently joined by the CPP regional committee of the Visayas. In October four communist leaders, including Kintanar, were expelled from the CPP and the NPA for refusing to recognize the authority of Sison.

In March 1998 the Government and the NDF signed a Comprehensive Agreement on Respect for Human Rights and International Law, the first of four agreements that would complete the peace process. Despite Joseph Estrada's inclusion of former communist activists in the Government upon his inauguration as President in June, the leadership of the NDF-CPP-NPA condemned his administration. In July Estrada approved the human rights agreement that had been reached by the NDF and the Ramos administration, and invited the exiled leadership of the NDF to the Philippines to resume peace negotiations. In February 1999, however, Estrada suspended peace talks with the communists following the NPA's abduction of three hostages. The Government also suspended the Joint Agreement on Safety and Immunity Guarantees, exposing NDF-CPP-NPA members to the risk of arrest. Five hostages were released by the NPA in April, although the communists continued to reject other conditions for negotiations.

In May 1999 the NDF withdrew from peace negotiations in response to the Senate's ratification of a defence treaty with the USA (see Foreign Affairs). Estrada subsequently adopted a position of outright hostility towards the movement. In an attempt to divide the communist movement, Estrada entered into negotiations with several breakaway factions, but failed to make substantial progress. In January 2000 the Government suspended military operations against the communists to facilitate the release of two NPA hostages. In December Estrada

announced that a peace agreement had been concluded with the Revolutionary Proletarian Army-ABB. The agreement, which applied only to the central Philippines, was accompanied by a presidential amnesty for some political prisoners whose death sentences had been upheld by the Supreme Court, and by the release of an additional 235 political detainees. In the same month the NPA rejected an offer by the Government of a truce.

In April 2001 the Government of President Gloria Arroyo held peace talks with the NDF in Oslo, Norway. The talks were reported to have made some progress, with both sides agreeing to undertake confidence-building measures, including the release of political prisoners. Further discussions were held in May, but were suspended in June when the NDF was implicated in the assassination of Congressman Rodolfo Aguinaldo. In November 28 people were killed on the island of Mindanao when fighting broke out between the NPA and government soldiers. However, despite the renewal of violence, exiled NDF members announced shortly afterwards that they had agreed to resume peace talks with the Government in Oslo in December. In the same month Arroyo announced a temporary cease-fire with the NDF, following its offer to suspend hostilities for one month if the Government made a reciprocal gesture. However, the arrival of US troops in the Philippines in 2002 (see Foreign Affairs) threatened further peace negotiations, as the NDF continued to oppose any US involvement in the country. In May Arroyo called off further peace negotiations following a number of political assassinations.

In August 2002 the USA added the CPP and the NPA to its list of international terrorist organizations. The Philippine Government formally designated the NDF a terrorist organization in October, while emphasizing that it remained willing to continue peace negotiations. However, Sison continued to oppose any negotiations between the CPP and the Government while Arroyo remained President. In June 2003 fighting broke out between government troops and NPA rebels on the island of Samar, and sporadic clashes continued throughout the latter half of the year. In January 2004 NPA rebels attacked a power station near Manila, causing eight deaths.

Peace negotiations between the Government and the NDF finally recommenced in Oslo in February 2004, despite ongoing clashes between the two sides. A third round of talks took place in Oslo in June. Negotiations were scheduled to resume in August, but were suspended after the NDF claimed that the Government was failing to meet its demands, including the implementation of measures to secure the removal of the CPP and the NPA from the USA's list of international terrorist organizations. Sporadic violence continued, and at the end of 2004 the armed forces announced that a total of 182 NPA members had been killed in clashes with government troops in that year and a further 910 had surrendered or been captured. In February 2005 14 NPA rebels and two government soldiers were killed in skirmishes in the town of Compostela, some 930 km south-east of Manila. Negotiations between the NDF and the Government resumed during the first half of 2005, but were abandoned by the former in August in response to the political scandal surrounding President Arroyo (see Domestic Political Affairs). Discussions between the two sides resumed in September. However, hopes for a peaceable resolution to the ongoing conflict suffered a setback in November, when at least nine soldiers were killed in an ambush near Calinog, in the province of Iloilo, which was alleged to have been carried out by NPA members. Furthermore, in January 2006 a group of suspected NPA members conducted a raid on a prison in Barangay Cuta, Iloilo, during which they released 14 detainees. Later in that month it was reported that Philippine troops had killed at least 18 NPA rebels during fierce clashes in Santa Ignacia, north of Manila.

In May 2007 five police officers were killed on the island of Mindoro by a landmine believed to have been planted by the NPA. In August Sison was arrested in the Netherlands, where he remained in exile, on suspicion of ordering the assassinations of former associates Romulo Kintanar and Arturo Tabara in 2003 and 2004, respectively; he was released in September owing to lack of evidence. In an effort to restart the stalled peace negotiations, in September 2007 Arroyo signed a proclamation offering amnesty to communist rebels who relinquished their weapons. However, the NPA continued its activities, and persistent sporadic violence resulted in further fatalities on both sides in late 2007 and early 2008. Little progress appeared to have been made at two rounds of informal talks between the Government and the NDF held in Oslo in May and November, with the NDF reportedly rejecting the Government's demand for an indefinite cease-fire as a condition for the resumption of formal peace negotiations. In December the military announced that five soldiers had been killed in an NPA attack on an army vehicle in the province of Surigao del Norte. Philippine troops captured an NPA base on Mindanao in February 2009, following fighting in which at least 11 rebels and five soldiers died. At least nine further rebels and one soldier were killed in December during a raid by Philippine troops on an NPA camp near the town of Valencia.

Meanwhile, the Government and the CPP agreed in August 2009 to renew peace talks following the release by the Government of two senior CPP leaders. However, hopes of a resumption of formal talks were threatened by the arrest in February 2010 of 43 people attending a health convention on suspicion of belonging to the NPA. The detainees denied any connection to the NPA and accused the authorities of fabricating incriminating evidence against them.

Upon assuming power in June 2010, the administration of President Benigno Aquino emphasized its commitment to concluding a peace settlement with the NDF, the NPA and the CPP. In July Aquino announced the formation of two government 'peace panels', one to facilitate negotiations with the NDF, the NPA and the CPP, and the other to focus on the peace process with the Moro Islamic Liberation Front (MILF—see The activities of the MILF). The NDF continued to appeal for the release of all political prisoners and meaningful land reform, while sporadic violent clashes were reported throughout 2010. In August NPA members killed a local official and eight police officers on Samar island. In December 2010 Aquino ordered the release of the 43 people arrested at the health convention in February, declaring that their 'right to due process' had been denied during the full term of their detention. In the same month 10 government soldiers were killed in an ambush by NPA rebels, just two days before the scheduled commencement of an 18-day cease-fire between government troops and the NPA, the longest cease-fire agreed in some 10 years. Nevertheless, the cease-fire appeared to be observed by both sides. Following its conclusion in January 2011, senior NPA leader Tiro Alcantara (alias Ka or Comrade Bart) was arrested and charged with more than 20 counts of murder. Formal peace talks between the Government and the NDF were reconvened in February, and were reported to have been constructive, with both sides expressing their resolve to conclude a comprehensive settlement by June 2012. Further talks were due to have been held in June 2011; however, in a letter sent early in the month to Alex Padilla, the Government's chief negotiator, Luis Jalandoni, Padilla's NDF counterpart, warned that the continued detention of 17 NDF members 'seriously prejudiced' the peace talks and urged that the process be suspended pending their release. Formal negotiations were subsequently rescheduled for late October, but earlier in the month Padilla announced the indefinite suspension of the talks owing to the NDF's 'unreasonable demands'. In April 2012 at least 10 Philippine soldiers and one civilian were reportedly killed in an ambush by the NPA on an army convoy in a village in Ifugao province. At April 2013 no further peace talks had taken place between the NDF and the Government, despite the former's stated willingness to resume the negotiation process.

The activities of the MNLF

The Government of Corazon Aquino established a cease-fire with the MNLF in September 1986, following an announcement by the Government that it would grant legal and judicial autonomy to four predominantly Muslim provinces in Mindanao. Further talks ensued—under the auspices of the Organization of the Islamic Conference (OIC), which was renamed the Organization of Islamic Cooperation (see p. 413) in 2011—and on 5 January 1987 the MNLF signed an agreement to relinquish demands for complete independence in Mindanao, and to accept autonomy. The new Constitution, which was approved by plebiscite in the following month, granted eventual autonomy to Muslim provinces in Mindanao, which had been promised by President Ferdinand Marcos in 1976. In February 1988, however, the MNLF resumed its offensive against the Government, which had attempted to prevent the MNLF from gaining membership of the OIC (which would imply that the MNLF was regarded as representing an independent state). In November 1989 a referendum was held, in the country's 13 southern provinces and nine cities in Mindanao, on proposed legislation that envisaged the autonomy of these provinces and cities, with direct elections to a unicameral legislature in each province; this contrasted with the MNLF's demand for autonomy in 23 provinces, to be granted without a referendum. Four provinces (Lanao del Sur, Maguin-

danao, Tawi-Tawi and Sulu) voted in favour of the government proposal, and formed the Autonomous Region of Muslim Mindanao (ARMM).

In February 1990 the candidate favoured by Aquino, Zacaria Candao (formerly the legal representative of the MNLF), was elected to the governorship of Muslim Mindanao. In October the autonomous regional government was granted limited executive powers. Under Ramos's programme of reconciliation, the MNLF participated in discussions with the NUC. In October 1992 the leader of the MNLF, Nur Misuari, agreed to return to the Philippines from exile in Libya to facilitate negotiations. In January 1993 talks were suspended, and violence in Mindanao escalated prior to the impending elections for the region's Governor and Assembly. At the elections, which took place on 25 March, a former ambassador, Lininding Pangandaman, was elected Governor, with the unofficial support of Ramos.

In April 1993 exploratory discussions in Jakarta, Indonesia, between Nur Misuari and representatives of the Philippine Government led to an agreement on the resumption of formal peace talks under the auspices of the OIC. Further exploratory talks took place in Saudi Arabia in June, prior to the first formal negotiations in October in Jakarta, where the MNLF demanded the creation of an autonomous Islamic state in the south, as agreed in 1976. In November 1993 the two sides signed a memorandum of understanding (MOU) and an interim cease-fire was agreed. The cease-fire was implemented in January 1994.

The second round of formal peace negotiations between the Government and the MNLF took place in Jakarta in April 1994. Agreement was subsequently reached on government administration in the proposed autonomous region, Islamic law, education and revenue-sharing between Manila and the autonomous zones. In August 1995 Misuari agreed for the first time to a referendum (which was required under the Constitution) prior to the establishment of an autonomous zone, but demanded the immediate establishment of a provisional MNLF government to ensure that the referendum was conducted fairly.

In June 1996 it was announced that the MNLF and the Government had finally reached agreement on a proposal by Ramos for the establishment of a transitional administrative council, to be known as the Southern Philippines Council for Peace and Development (SPCPD), which was to derive powers from the Office of the President. The five-member SPCPD, which was to be headed by Misuari, was to co-ordinate peace-keeping and development efforts in 14 provinces and 10 cities in Mindanao, with the assistance of an 81-member Consultative Assembly and a religious advisory council. After a period of three years a referendum was to be conducted in each province and city to determine whether it would join the existing ARMM (the MNLF had abandoned its demands for autonomy in 23 provinces in Mindanao). In July government officials announced that, under the peace agreement, Muslims were to be allocated one cabinet post, and were to be granted representation in state-owned companies and constitutional commissions. In addition, Ramos offered to support the candidacy of Misuari in the forthcoming gubernatorial election in the ARMM. In September the Government and the MNLF signed a final draft of the peace agreement in Jakarta. In the same month elections took place peacefully in the ARMM for the region's Governor and Assembly; Misuari, who, as agreed, contested the gubernatorial election with the support of Lakas-NUCD, was elected unopposed. In October it was announced that Misuari had been officially appointed Chairman of the SPCPD. In March 1997 more than 1,000 former MNLF members were integrated into the armed forces under the terms of the peace accord.

In August 2001, after some delay, the referendum was finally held: the city of Marawi and the province of Basilan elected to join the ARMM; however, 10 provinces and 13 cities rejected the offer of membership, and the electoral turn-out was low. In November around 600 supporters of Governor Misuari (who had been dismissed from the leadership of the MNLF in April owing to his widespread unpopularity) led an armed uprising against military and police outposts on the island of Jolo, resulting in the deaths of more than 100 people. The violence was reportedly intended to prevent an election to the governorship of the ARMM, scheduled for late November, from taking place. By instigating the rebellion, Misuari had violated the terms of his five-year peace accord with the Government, although he claimed that by holding an election the Government was itself breaking the terms of the agreement. Shortly afterwards President Arroyo suspended Misuari from his post. Later in

November Misuari and six of his supporters were arrested by the Malaysian authorities for attempting to gain illegal entry into the country. On 26 November polls to elect a new governor, vice-governor and 44 regional legislators for the province were conducted. The turn-out was low, a fact partly attributed to the escalating military presence in the region. The next day government forces launched air-strikes on MNLF insurgents who remained in Zamboanga City, killing 25 rebels and one civilian. As they attempted to flee, the rebels took several local residents hostage. The next day the hostages were released in return for the rebels' safe passage out of the city, thus bringing an end to the confrontation. In December the President's favoured candidate, former MNLF member Farouk Hussein, was declared Governor. He immediately urged the establishment of peace in the troubled region and stated that he would seek to open a dialogue with the remaining followers of Misuari and other radical groups in the area, including Abu Sayyaf. In January 2002 Misuari was finally deported from Malaysia to stand trial in Manila on charges of inciting a rebellion; he subsequently refused to enter a plea to the charges against him. In January 2003 the four factions comprising the MNLF signed a declaration of unity in advance of the election of a new leadership; significantly, Misuari's name was excluded from the statement, preventing him from regaining the chairmanship of the group.

In February 2005 more than 500 MNLF rebels loyal to Misuari, led by Habier Malik, attacked government troops in several towns on the island of Jolo, in retaliation for a recent army assault, which military leaders insisted had been targeted at Abu Sayyaf, rather than the MNLF; an estimated 30 soldiers and 70 MNLF fighters were killed in the ensuing clashes. Elections to the governorship and Regional Legislative Assembly of the ARMM took place in August; Zaldy Ampatuan, the candidate of Lakas-CMD, was elected Governor. At least nine MNLF rebels were killed in April 2007 during an offensive by government troops on a base commanded by Malik, who was believed to be responsible for a recent attack on an army outpost in which two soldiers and a child had died; some 8,000 people reportedly fled the violence. The OIC appealed for both sides to cease fighting and to abide by the 1996 peace agreement, but, as in 2005, the military maintained that the operation was not targeted at the MNLF, but rather at Malik and his followers, who had allegedly aligned themselves with Abu Sayyaf. Misuari, who remained under house arrest near Manila but was yet to be convicted, contested the Sulu gubernatorial election in May 2007, but was overwhelmingly defeated. In August President Arroyo insisted that efforts would be made to maintain the cease-fire with the MNLF, despite the apparent involvement of members of the group in clashes between the armed forces and Abu Sayyaf (see The activities of Abu Sayyaf).

Tripartite talks involving the OIC, the Philippine Government and the MNLF were held in Jeddah, Saudi Arabia, in November 2007 with the aim of addressing complaints by the MNLF that the Government had failed fully to implement the 1996 agreement; a second round of discussions was held in Istanbul, Turkey, in February 2008. Meanwhile, there was disquiet among MNLF members over the accord being negotiated between the Government and the MILF (see The activities of the MILF), amid fears that it would violate the group's own peace agreement. The appointment by the MNLF Central Committee of Muslimin Sema, hitherto Secretary-General of the group, as its Chairman was rejected by Misuari loyalists in April, prompting the OIC to express concern at the internal divisions within the group. Misuari was released from house arrest on bail later in that month. In May leaders of various factions of the MNLF, meeting in Tripoli, Libya, agreed to form a 'transitional leadership and unification committee', comprising six members, including Misuari and Sema, with the aim of resolving their differences. However, it later appeared that Misuari, who had sent two representatives to the meeting rather than attending himself, was unwilling to accept this arrangement. A third round of tripartite discussions, which was scheduled to be held in Manila in late May, was postponed indefinitely, reportedly as a result of the uncertainty over the leadership of the MNLF. Gubernatorial and regional legislative elections were held in the ARMM on 11 August; Ampatuan was re-elected Governor of the region. Later in that month, following a meeting with Sema, the Secretary of the Interior and Local Government, Ronaldo Puno, announced that a total of 5,000 former MNLF fighters had been integrated into the armed forces, and a further 1,600 into the police force. The third round of tripartite talks finally took place in Manila in March 2009, at which the Government and the

MNLF agreed to form a joint legal panel to propose amendments to the 1996 agreement; the MNLF delegation was reportedly headed by Misuari and also included Sema. Further talks were held in Damascus, Syria, in May 2009. In the same month skirmishes between MNLF and MILF rebels caused an estimated 2,000 families to flee from Maguindanao and Sultan Kudarat. Following allegations of his involvement in the killing of 57 people on Mindanao in November 2009, Governor Ampatuan was suspended from office and replaced by his deputy, Ansaruddin Adiong, in an acting capacity.

Sporadic clashes between MNLF and government troops were reported to have resulted in the deaths of about 20 MNLF members and several government soldiers during the latter half of 2009. In April 2010 an MOU emphasizing the intention of both the MNLF and the Government to work towards 'just, meaningful and lasting peace and development in Mindanao' was signed in Libya, and in the following month arrangements for the Bangsamoro Development Assistance Fund were concluded in Surabaya, Indonesia. In December consensus points for proposed amendments to the 1996 ARMM peace accord were initialled by government and MNLF representatives meeting at the Indonesian embassy in Manila. A number of issues of contention remained, but both sides welcomed the initialling of consensus points as a sign of meaningful progress having been made.

Clashes between hundreds of rival MNLF and MILF members in January–February 2011 were reported to have killed at least 13 rebels; some 3,000 local villagers were displaced by the violence. The fourth round of tripartite talks was held in Jeddah in February; the formation of three panels of experts, which were to report to the OIC, was approved. In June the panels of experts reported to the OIC, after which an agreement was signed by the Government, the MNLF and the OIC. The agreement recognized the MNLF as a 'principal partner' of the Government in ensuring 'sound and meaningful autonomy' for Muslims in the southern regions and acknowledged the ARMM as the 'complementary mechanism' for the full implementation of the 1996 peace accord. In December 2011 Mujib Hataman was appointed as caretaker Governor of the ARMM, pending elections scheduled to be held in mid-May 2013 (concurrently with national local and legislative elections). Following further tripartite talks in Bandung in March 2012, Sema reaffirmed the MNLF's willingness to co-operate with the Government in order to improve governance in the ARMM. Meanwhile, Sema, who had been elected Vice-Mayor of Cotabato City in June 2010, was seriously injured in an ambush by armed assailants in January 2012.

The activities of the MILF

The MILF, an Islamist fundamentalist grouping demanding secession for Mindanao, which was formed as a breakaway movement from the MNLF in 1978, was covered by the government cease-fire implemented in January 1994 but was not a party to the peace talks. The grouping was widely suspected of having taken advantage of negotiations between the MNLF and the Government to strengthen its position, both by an accumulation of weapons and the recruitment of young militants disaffected with the compliance of the MNLF. In April 1996 the Government and the MILF agreed to a cease-fire in North Cotabato.

In August 1996, for the first time, MILF and government officials met in Davao City for preliminary peace discussions. The MILF had rejected the peace agreement with the MNLF and continued to demand separatism for 23 provinces in Mindanao. Alternating hostilities and short-term cease-fires, together with a high incidence of abductions by the rebels, characterized relations between the Government and the MILF between late 1996 and late 1997. Despite further clashes between the MILF and the Government in January 1998, with mutual accusations of violations of a cease-fire agreement signed in November 1997, peace negotiations continued in February 1998, when the MILF demanded recognition of 13 MILF camps in Mindanao as 'legitimate territories'. In March the two sides agreed to create a 'quick response team' to resolve conflicts and confrontations before they escalated into serious clashes. In October the MILF and the Government agreed to disclose the location of their forces to prevent accidental encounters. However, in January 1999, following a statement by the MILF advocating independence for Mindanao, Estrada conducted successive offensives against the MILF, causing the collapse of the 1997 cease-fire agreement. Up to 60 people were estimated to have died in the ensuing fighting and 90,000 residents were displaced. A new cease-fire was implemented at the end of January 1999, and in February the Presidential Adviser, Robert Aventajado, was sent to Mindanao to meet the leader of the MILF, Hashim Salamat, inside a MILF camp. They agreed to the resumption of peace negotiations and to a meeting between Salamat and Estrada to re-establish goodwill between the two sides. However, Estrada cancelled the meeting, as a result of a dispute over its location and security considerations. In March Salamat and Nur Misuari met for the first time in 20 years in an attempt to promote the peace process.

Negotiations between the Government and the MILF took place in October 1999, despite MILF protests against continued government attacks on MILF camps in Mindanao. Formal peace negotiations commenced in January 2000 but failed to achieve substantial progress. In that month Estrada announced a new anti-insurgency programme, the National Peace and Development Plan, which aimed to remove the causes of insurgency in Mindanao, including poverty, injustice and disease. Peace talks resumed in March after negotiations scheduled for February were suspended owing to escalating violence, during which the Government claimed to have captured an important MILF base, Camp Omar. Several incendiary devices planted on buses in Mindanao in February, which resulted in nearly 50 civilian deaths, were attributed by government sources to the MILF; however, the MILF claimed that the bombings were perpetrated by government agents in an attempt to justify the intensification of the military campaign against the separatists. At further talks in March a protocol was signed with enhanced cease-fire provisions, whereby the Government agreed to recognize 39 MILF camps as 'safe areas' while the MILF representatives agreed to carry a government identity card during talks (which they had formerly claimed would represent a surrender of sovereignty). Intense fighting between the MILF and government forces in Lanao del Norte and Maguindanao provinces prompted Estrada to convene a meeting of the National Security Council in March.

In May 2000 the MILF was reported to have withdrawn from a section of the Narciso Ramos highway, a strategically significant route, which it had controlled for more than five years. The withdrawal appeared to augur well for the resumption of peace negotiations, although the Government held Islamist separatist movements responsible for bomb attacks in Manila and Mindanao in the same month. Peace negotiations between the Government and the MILF resumed later in May, and in June the MILF was reported to be assessing an improved offer of autonomy by the Government. However, the MILF subsequently rejected the extension of the deadline for its acceptance of this offer from 1 July to 15 December, owing to a stipulation that it should meanwhile abandon its pursuit of independence. In late June, following a major offensive, government forces captured the MILF's military headquarters at Abubakar. In December the MILF appeared to have resumed its armed struggle after an attack on government forces on Jolo island was attributed to the movement. Bomb explosions in Manila at the end of the month, in which 22 people died, were also blamed on the group. (In January 2009 three Muslim militants with alleged links to both the MILF and JI were sentenced to life imprisonment in connection with the bombings.)

The new Cabinet appointed by President Arroyo in January 2001 included two members who originated from Mindanao. The incoming President stated that she would seek to resume peace negotiations with the MILF, and in February the Government's military campaign against the MILF ceased. The MILF welcomed the Government's offer to resume talks, although sporadic clashes between its forces and those of the Government continued throughout February. In late March the Government announced that it had reached an agreement with the MILF to resume peace negotiations, and appeared prepared to accept the MILF's condition that renewed talks should be held in an OIC member state. In April the MILF announced a unilateral cease-fire, declaring its intention to observe this until the conclusion of a peace agreement. In June government representatives initiated talks with the MILF in Libya, leading to the conclusion of a preliminary cease-fire agreement in July. Following a new round of peace talks, a further cease-fire agreement was signed in August. In the same month the MILF also reached an accord with the MNLF. In September sporadic fighting between the MILF and army troops on Mindanao, which led to the deaths of 15 rebels, threatened to undermine the peace process. However, in October the MILF signed a pact with the Government to safeguard the recent cease-fire agreement. In November the Pentagon Gang, formed in 2000 and mainly comprising renegade members of the MILF, kidnapped an Italian priest, Father

Giuseppe Pierantoni, in northern Manila. The leader of the faction, Akiddin Abdusalem, was shot dead as he attempted to escape from custody after being captured by government troops. In January 2002 39 MILF guerrillas surrendered to government forces and relinquished a large cache of weapons. In February the MILF announced that it was to hold a new series of discussions with the Government as the situation had been complicated by the arrival of US troops on the island of Basilan. In April government troops finally secured the release of Father Pierantoni after conducting intensive operations against the Pentagon Gang.

In May 2002 the Government signed several new peace agreements with the MILF in Putrajaya, Malaysia. In December the MILF denied responsibility for an ambush on Mindanao that resulted in the deaths of 12 employees of a Canadian mining company, as well as for a bomb attack that killed 17 people in the same week; the group claimed that it continued to observe the cease-fire agreed upon in 2001. Meanwhile, President Arroyo succeeded in deterring the US Government from classifying the MILF as an international terrorist organization, citing concerns that the ongoing negotiation process might be undermined by such an action. In February 2003 peace negotiations broke down when government troops assumed control of the important MILF base of Pikit, on Mindanao, in violation of the cease-fire arrangement. The Government claimed that it had ordered the military action in an attempt to capture members of the Pentagon Gang, who it believed were being sheltered by the MILF. Although President Arroyo called a halt to the operation several days later and proposed a peace agreement, many rebels were believed to have been killed in the fighting that had resulted. Insurgency in the area continued to intensify, as the MILF refused to negotiate unless government troops withdrew from Pikit. A number of attacks occurred, the most serious of which took place in March when a bomb exploded near Davao Airport, resulting in the deaths of 23 people. Although the MILF denied responsibility for the attack, the police subsequently filed charges against 150 of its members; four of the group's leaders were charged with murder and warrants issued for their arrest. (Five alleged members of the MILF were arrested in late 2004 in connection with the bomb attack. One of those detained reportedly claimed to have been trained by a leader of JI.) In late March 2003 the MILF sent representatives for preliminary discussions with government officials in Malaysia, and in April the Government declared that formal peace negotiations would restart, although with the exclusion of those indicted in connection with the March attack on Davao Airport, including MILF leader Hashim Salamat. However, shortly afterwards the MILF was responsible for several further outbreaks of violence in the area and, in May, the Government abandoned peace talks and renewed its military offensive against the organization. Later in that month the MILF declared a 10-day unilateral cease-fire in order, it claimed, to prepare the way for the renewal of negotiations, but the Government rejected the offer following the perpetration of further attacks by the MILF during the cease-fire period. Nevertheless, at the request of the Malaysian Government, the MILF extended the cease-fire by a further 10 days in June and, later in that month, Salamat announced that the group had renounced terrorism, an important precondition for any peace agreement. Despite this, the Government continued to take military action against the organization. However, in July it was announced that the two sides had finally concluded a peace agreement. In August it was reported that Hashim Salamat had died as a result of a heart attack in the previous month; he was replaced as MILF Chairman by Murad Ebrahim.

Following exploratory talks in February 2004, formal peace negotiations were to take place in April, but were postponed owing to the May elections (see Domestic Political Affairs). In April the MILF protested against the arrest of four of its members on suspicion of collaborating with JI, claiming it contravened the cease-fire agreement. In July it was announced that the MILF had agreed to co-operate with the armed forces in operations against kidnapping gangs and JI elements based in Mindanao. A 60-member International Monitoring Team (IMT), led by Malaysia, was deployed in Mindanao in October to oversee the ongoing cease-fire between the government forces and the MILF. Further exploratory talks aimed at restarting the stalled formal peace negotiations were held in December; the two sides reportedly made progress on the contentious issue of ancestral domain. In January 2005 at least six government soldiers were killed in an attack on an army outpost by MILF rebels. The Government stated that it regarded the attack, which had not been sanctioned by the MILF leadership, as an isolated incident. Exploratory talks between the two sides were conducted between February and December.

In March 2005 the Government and the MILF finally agreed to resume formal peace negotiations in Malaysia, which commenced in February 2006 at Port Dickson, near Kuala Lumpur. ARMM Governor Zaldy Ampatuan urged the holding of a plebiscite to assist the efforts to resolve the contentious issue of ancestral domain. In March rumours circulated of a failed attempt to oust Murad Ebrahim from the MILF leadership, but senior MILF members denied such reports. In June a bomb explosion in Mindanao resulted in several fatalities and precipitated clashes between local paramilitaries and MILF rebels after the latter was accused of responsibility for the attack. The MILF denied perpetrating further bomb attacks in Mindanao in October, but suspicions were raised about the group's links to JI and Abu Sayyaf. Several MILF members were reported to be among at least 47 prisoners who escaped during an attack on a prison in Mindanao by a group of around 25 armed men in February 2007; the MILF denied any involvement in the incident. An Italian priest, Father Giancarlo Bossi, was kidnapped in June in his parish on Mindanao by suspected renegade members of the MILF. In July clashes between some 300 rebels and a group of marines who were searching for the priest on Basilan resulted in the deaths of 14 marines, 10 of whom were beheaded. Father Bossi was released later in that month on Mindanao. There was speculation that Abu Sayyaf members might have been involved in the kidnapping or the ensuing fighting.

In November 2007 the Government announced that the latest round of peace negotiations with the MILF in Malaysia had resulted in agreement on the demarcation of the land and maritime boundaries of a proposed new autonomous area on Mindanao, to be known as the Bangsamoro Juridical Entity (BJE). Although no details of the borders were disclosed, it was reported that the BJE would cover a larger area than the ARMM. However, talks faltered in December over continued disagreement on ancestral domain, with the MILF opposed to the Government's position that any agreement should be implemented through the 'constitutional process', i.e. by conducting a plebiscite in the villages to be added to the ARMM to create the proposed BJE. Apparently frustrated at the lack of progress in the negotiations, Malaysia withdrew 28 of its cease-fire monitors from the IMT in May 2008. Finally, in July it was announced that the Government and the MILF had concluded a Memorandum of Agreement on Ancestral Domain (MOA-AD), which would be signed in a formal ceremony in Kuala Lumpur on 5 August. The accord envisaged the creation of the BJE by extending the ARMM to include a further 712 villages, subject to the approval of their residents in a plebiscite to be conducted within 12 months, and outlined the expanded political and economic powers to be devolved to the new entity. However, the MOA-AD provoked considerable controversy, particularly within predominantly Christian communities intended for inclusion in the BJE, and a protest against the accord held in Zamboanga City in early August was attended by an estimated 15,000 people. On 4 August, in response to a number of petitions challenging the constitutionality of the MOA-AD, the Supreme Court issued a temporary restraining order, preventing the signing ceremony from taking place on the following day.

Tensions in the south subsequently escalated, as MILF rebels reportedly occupied some 15 villages in North Cotabato, prompting renewed fighting with government troops, which led to the displacement of an estimated 160,000 people in the province and the deaths of at least two soldiers and more than 20 militants. By mid-August 2008 the armed forces had secured control of the occupied villages, and people began to return home. However, on 18 August raids by MILF forces on several towns and villages in the provinces of Lanao del Norte and Sarangani left more than 30 civilians dead and forced thousands to flee, while seven soldiers died in a MILF ambush in Lanao del Sur. The MILF leadership claimed that the three commanders held responsible for the attacks were 'renegades', but refused to surrender them to the armed forces. The Government declared the MOA-AD defunct a few days later, and in early September the President ordered the dissolution of the peace panel responsible for negotiating with the MILF and announced a new policy of promoting direct dialogue with local communities, stating that future negotiations with armed groups would focus on disarmament, demobilization and reintegration. The National Disaster Coordinating Council (NDCC) estimated that a total of some 500,000 people had been displaced by the violence by the end of September. In October the Supreme Court ruled the MOA-AD to be unconstitutional (by a narrow margin of eight votes to seven), noting that its implementation would require constitutional amendments that the President did not have the authority to guarantee would be adopted. Malaysia withdrew altogether from the IMT in November, although monitors from Brunei, Libya and Japan were to continue their participation.

Despite the re-establishment of the government peace panel in December 2008, talks with the MILF remained in abeyance and sporadic fighting between MILF rebels and government troops continued during late 2008 and early 2009. The two sides agreed to a cease-fire in July 2009, by which month more than 1,000 people were reported to have been killed and nearly 750,000 people displaced by the conflict since the failure of peace talks in August 2008. In February 2009, meanwhile, more than 112,000 of those displaced in August–September 2008 remained in camps, according to the NDCC, while a further 200,000 were believed to be residing with friends or relatives.

In December 2009 the Government and the MILF reconvened for formal peace negotiations, held in Kuala Lumpur; the two sides agreed to revive an international monitoring team of cease-fire observers and announced that they hoped to reach a peace deal by April 2010. A second round of talks was held in January of that year, at which the Philippine Government submitted a draft power-sharing proposal; however, this was rejected by the MILF, which argued that the draft contained provisions that had not been discussed previously and did not offer sufficient autonomy. However, in what was welcomed by government negotiators as a positive development in the quest for peace, the MILF officially abandoned its demands for full independence and a separate Islamic state, instead envisaging, in the words of a prominent MILF negotiator, 'a real state and sub-state relationship where we can have real governance and control over our lives'.

While the objective of securing an agreement by April 2010 was not met, it was hoped that the election of Benigno Aquino as President in May would provide a boost to the peace process. One of Aquino's principal election pledges had been to intensify efforts to negotiate peace with the various separatist groups, and upon assuming office the new President reiterated his Government's commitment to resuming talks with the MILF by October. In September Aquino announced the formation of an advisory body to assist the Government's negotiating team and to facilitate 'greater transparency and accountability' during the forthcoming peace negotiations with the MILF. An attack by MILF rebels later that month on a military outpost on Mindanao was interpreted by some observers as an attempt by certain elements within the MILF to disrupt the peace process. Tensions as a result of the incident, together with a disagreement over the Malaysian facilitator, led to a delay in the resumption of the talks. The Philippine Government claimed that Othman Razak, who had been facilitating the peace talks between the Government and the MILF since 2003, was biased towards the latter, and demanded his replacement with an impartial intermediary; the MILF denied that Razak had demonstrated any such bias and insisted that he be allowed to continue as facilitator in order to ensure continuity in the talks. The arrest of a senior MILF leader, Abraham Yap Alonto, in October 2010 was condemned by the MILF leadership as 'a direct blow to the early resumption of the negotiations'. In the same month a bomb explosion on a bus in North Cotabato province in the southern Philippines, which claimed the lives of eight people, was believed by the authorities to have been carried out by a splinter group of JI in an attempt further to delay the resumption of peace talks between the Government and the MILF. A bomb attack on a bus terminal in North Cotabato in November, which killed one person, was similarly attributed to Islamist militants seeking to disrupt the peace process. In January 2011 a further bomb explosion on a bus, in Manila, killed five people; no claim of responsibility was immediately issued, but the authorities stated that the device used in the bombing was similar to those used in recent attacks on Mindanao.

Despite the apparent efforts to impede the peace process, formal negotiations between the MILF and the Philippine Government were reconvened in Kuala Lumpur in February 2011, with both sides expressing confidence that a peace agreement could be concluded within 12 months. The MILF presented its 'comprehensive compact' for peace, which the Government subsequently confirmed did not include the demand for independence. A second round of negotiations was held in April, brokered by a new facilitator, Tengku Dato' Ab Ghafar Tengku Mohamed, former secretary of Malaysia's National Security Council; both sides expressed support for the appointment. During the discussions the MILF submitted a draft proposal for the creation of Bangsamoro sub-state in Mindanao. A third round of talks was held in June, but was cut short after the Government announced that it was to defer the presentation of its counter-proposal until the next round of talks, which was scheduled to be held later in the year. Meanwhile, shortly before the resumption of talks in February it was revealed that a splinter group of the MILF had been formed. Headed by Ustadz Ameril Umbra Kato, the so-called Bangsamoro Islamic Freedom Fighters (BIFF) was identified as a threat to the peace process by both the MILF and the Government. In April the MILF leadership announced that Kato had been expelled from the MILF after refusing to disband his armed grouping. In July the MILF issued a statement urging those engaged in 'anti-MILF seminars'—widely believed to be a reference to Kato and other BIFF commanders—to cease all efforts to obstruct the peace process, and accusing such individuals and groups of undermining 'the legitimate aspirations of the Bangsamoro people'.

Aquino met with Murad Ebrahim in the Japanese capital, Tokyo, in early August 2011—the first time that a Philippine President had met with a MILF Chairman during the protracted negotiations; both sides pledged to accelerate the peace process. Despite an outbreak of violence between the MILF and a splinter group in mid-August, owing to a land dispute as well as disagreements over peace negotiations with the Government, the fourth round of formal talks were convened between government and MILF representatives in Kuala Lumpur later that month. During the three-day session the Government presented its counter-proposal for peace, which included the offer of 'a more empowered, more workable and thus more genuine autonomy' in exchange for the surrender by the MILF of its weapons; the proposal also included plans for 'a system of co-operation' through which the Government and the MILF could share revenues generated by the exploitation of natural resources in the region. The MILF rejected the proposal as 'inadequate', arguing that it did not address the central political issues behind the long-running conflict, but reaffirmed its continued commitment to the peace talks. A revised proposal was submitted to the Government by the MILF in October; however, the outbreak of fierce fighting between government and MILF forces later that month in Zamboanga and on Basilan threatened to undermine the ongoing peace process. Nevertheless, following further talks held in Kuala Lumpur in April 2012, the Government and the MILF concluded a set of principles to guide subsequent negotiations: the two sides notably agreed to create a new autonomous political entity, with a ministerial form of government, to replace the ARMM, while reference was also made to 'wealth-sharing' and 'power-sharing', although the national Government would retain power over certain areas, including defence and external security, foreign policy, trade, monetary policy and citizenship. Following an extensive consultation process (involving members of both the Muslim and Christian communities), a major breakthrough was achieved on 15 October when, with President Aquino and Murad Ebrahim among the witnesses, the government and MILF negotiators formally signed a framework peace agreement at the presidential palace in Manila providing for the establishment of a new autonomous region to be known as Bangsamoro; the two sides committed themselves to reaching a 'comprehensive deal' by the end of the year. It was planned to establish a joint transition commission, to finalize outstanding issues and ultimately to put the whole proposal to a referendum before the expiry of Aquino's term of office in 2016. Among the stipulations incorporated in the draft agreement was the gradual decommissioning of the MILF forces (numbering an estimated 12,000) and the phased transfer of the region's law enforcement from the army to the Bangsamoro police. At April 2013 no comprehensive peace agreement had yet been achieved—although a 15-member Transition Commission (TransCom), chaired by MILF chief negotiator Mohaqher Iqbal, had been appointed in February—and the MILF and the Government agreed to postpone further negotiations until after the elections in mid-May.

The activities of Abu Sayyaf

In early June 1994 the Government undertook a major offensive against Abu Sayyaf, which was held responsible for numerous attacks, principally on the islands of Jolo and Basilan, to the south of Mindanao. In retaliation for the capture by the armed forces of its base on Jolo, the group took a number of Christians hostage on Basilan, killing 15 of them. All but one of the remaining 21 hostages were released in mid-June, following the apparent payment of a ransom and the intercession of the MNLF. Later in June government troops captured the Abu Sayyaf's main headquarters in Basilan. In August the group's remaining hostage was released, and the authorities announced that Abu Sayyaf had been 'eliminated'. In April 1995, however, the group was believed to be responsible for an attack on the town of Ipil, in Mindanao, in which as many as 100 people were killed. Some of the assailants were also believed to belong to a splinter group of the MNLF, the Islamic Command Council. Some 14 hostages were reportedly killed as the army pursued the rebels in their retreat from Ipil. Despite intense counter-insurgency measures by government troops, Abu Sayyaf perpetrated a further assault in Tungawan, south of Ipil, in which six civilians were killed. In April 1996 two bomb explosions in Zamboanga City were widely attributed to Abu Sayyaf or to other groups opposed to the peace negotiations between the Government and the MNLF. Abu Sayyaf subsequently denounced the MNLF's peace agreement with the Government. In December 1998 the leader of Abu Sayyaf, Abdurajat Abubakar Janjalani, was killed by government security forces; he was subsequently replaced by his younger brother, Khadafi Janjalani.

Under the leadership of Khadafi Janjalani, Abu Sayyaf began to employ a new tactic of kidnapping hostages to use them as both a means of political bargaining and a source of financing, often demanding high ransoms from the families of those abducted. In April 2000 armed Abu Sayyaf troops abducted 21 people, including 10 foreign tourists, from the island resort of Sipadan in Malaysia, and held them hostage on Jolo. One month earlier members of a separate Abu Sayyaf group had seized a number of Filipino hostages on the island of Basilan where, demanding the release of convicted Islamist terrorists held in US prisons, they had at the end of April managed to evade capture by government forces by which they had been besieged. The Government's military response to the hostage crisis remained largely ineffective, and a stalemate lasting several months ensued, punctuated by both formal and informal negotiations and a partially successful intervention, involving the payment of ransoms, by Libyan mediators. Although sporadic releases were secured, some hostages were also killed by their captors. In April 2001 President Arroyo declared 'all-out war' against Abu Sayyaf.

In May 2001 Abu Sayyaf rebels abducted 20 people, including three US tourists, from a holiday resort off the western island of Palawan. President Arroyo immediately ordered a military response, although the group threatened to kill the hostages if it was attacked. In June the rebels succeeded in fleeing from a military siege; nine Filipino captives escaped as a result. Later in the same month the Government was forced to bring in a Malaysian mediator in order to avert the threatened execution of the three US hostages still being held. It was reported that one had already been beheaded, although his body had not been found. In July two Filipino hostages were released, but Abu Sayyaf stated that it intended to continue attacking US and European citizens until government forces had been withdrawn from the southern Philippines. Nadzmie Sabtulah, the rebel leader alleged to have planned the May abductions, was arrested, together with three other members of the group. However, Abu Sayyaf activities continued, and in August a group of Abu Sayyaf guerrillas raided the town of Lamitan on the island of Basilan, taking at least 36 hostages and beheading 10. The next day 11 hostages were released and soon afterwards 13 more were freed, following an armed raid by government troops. However, the military failed to capture any members of the Abu Sayyaf leadership and 21 hostages remained in captivity, leading to allegations of collusion between Abu Sayyaf and the Philippine military. Soon afterwards three Chinese nationals were abducted as they tried to negotiate the release of a Chinese engineer who had been held by the group since June 2001. Two of the Chinese hostages were later killed following a clash between the kidnappers and government forces in Sultan Kudurat province.

In October 2001 Abu Sayyaf was responsible for two explosions in Zamboanga City. Meanwhile, government soldiers were reported to have cornered the kidnappers and their hostages following two days of fighting, which had resulted in the deaths of 21 guerrillas. Shortly afterwards the group threatened to behead its two remaining US hostages—Martin and Gracia Burnham—prior to President Arroyo's scheduled November visit to the USA, unless the military halted its offensive. In late October an explosion in Zamboanga, which killed six people, was attributed to the group. In the following month a Canadian national was abducted by men claiming to be Abu Sayyaf separatists. The group then released one hostage, followed a week later by a further seven. In December government troops succeeded in rescuing the Canadian man. Three hostages remained—the Burnhams and Ediborah Yap, a Filipino nurse. The military offensive against Abu Sayyaf was intensified by the arrival of US troops on Basilan in 2002. In April a series of bombs exploded in the southern city of General Santos, killing 15 people and prompting President Arroyo to declare a state of emergency in the area. The police later arrested five men in connection with the attacks. While the suspects were initially thought to be connected to the MILF, Abu Sayyaf claimed responsibility for the bombings. Shortly afterwards four men reported to be members of Abu Sayyaf were killed during a gun battle with police in the area. In June Gracia Burnham was rescued in a military operation, but her husband and Ediborah Yap were killed. Later in the same month it was reported that Aldam Tilao (alias Abu Sabaya), a senior member of the organization, had died during a gunfight at sea.

In July 2002 the joint US-Philippine military exercises that had been conducted on Basilan were formally concluded; President Arroyo subsequently ordered the redeployment of government forces to combat insurgency elsewhere in the country. Although it was thought that the exercises had achieved some success in defeating Abu Sayyaf, in August the group was responsible for the kidnapping of eight members of a Christian sect on Jolo; although two of the hostages were released, a further two were beheaded. Following the group's threat to perpetrate attacks in retaliation for the military offensive being conducted against it, in early October a bomb exploded in Zamboanga City, resulting in the deaths of three people, including a US soldier. Responsibility for the attack was attributed to Abu Sayyaf. Later in the same month two further explosions in Zamboanga, which led to the deaths of seven people, were also suspected to have been carried out by members of Abu Sayyaf, although there was speculation that JI members might also have been involved. The bombings followed the terrorist attack on the island of Bali, Indonesia, several days previously. Meanwhile, a bomb exploded on a bus in Manila, killing at least three people.

In January 2003 three government soldiers were killed during a battle with Abu Sayyaf rebels on the island of Jolo. In the following month further fighting broke out in advance of the resumption of counter-terrorism exercises between US and Philippine troops in the area. In May the final two members of the Christian sect captured in August 2002 were freed from captivity, and in June 2003 the last hostage to have been taken from Sipadan in April 2000 escaped. Meanwhile, the Government announced the establishment of a commission to investigate claims by former hostage Gracia Burnham that collusion had taken place between Abu Sayyaf and Philippine military forces during her time in captivity. In December 2003 it was announced that government forces had captured Galib Andang, a senior Abu Sayyaf figure, following a gun battle in Sulu.

Abu Sayyaf claimed responsibility for a bomb explosion in February 2004 that caused a fire on a passenger ferry in Manila Bay in which 116 were presumed to have died. In March the Government announced that it had apprehended six members of Abu Sayyaf, thought to have connections to JI, who were believed to have been planning a bomb attack on Manila; one of those detained also allegedly confessed to planting the bomb on the ferry. In April the armed forces claimed to have killed Hamsiraji Sali, a leading member of Abu Sayyaf for whose capture the USA had offered a reward of US $1m., following a gun battle on the island of Basilan. Also in April at least eight members of Abu Sayyaf were among 53 prisoners who escaped from a prison on Basilan, using smuggled firearms; within four days 34 of the prisoners had been killed or recaptured by the security forces. In August 17 members of Abu Sayyaf were sentenced to death, having been convicted of kidnapping Ediborah Yap and three other hospital workers in 2001; four of the defendants were among those who had escaped in April 2004 and were sentenced *in absentia*. In October President Arroyo announced that six members of Abu Sayyaf had been charged with murder and attempted murder in connection with the ferry bombing in February; two of the accused had been arrested in March, but the other four remained at large. A bomb exploded in a market in General Santos in December, killing 16 people. The police arrested five men in connection with the attack, for which Abu Sayyaf was suspected of being responsible.

In January 2005 the armed forces commenced a major offensive against Abu Sayyaf. Some 30,000 people fled the heavy fighting that ensued in the following month on the island of Jolo

between government troops and Abu Sayyaf members, joined by followers of former MNLF leader Nur Misuari. Meanwhile, in February Abu Sayyaf claimed responsibility for three co-ordinated bomb explosions, in Manila, General Santos and Davao City, in which 12 people were killed. Amid fears of further attacks, the Government increased security at airports, seaports, bus terminals and shopping centres. In March the security forces quashed an uprising at a prison near Manila, killing at least 22 detainees, including three Abu Sayyaf leaders. Abu Sayyaf subsequently threatened to retaliate for the deaths of its members.

In the southern Philippines in August 2005 three explosive devices were detonated in Zamboanga City, injuring 26 people. In the same month a bomb exploded on a ferry, injuring at least 30 people. The Philippine authorities attributed the attacks to Abu Sayyaf. In October two alleged Abu Sayyaf members were sentenced to death, together with a suspected member of JI, for their part in a bomb attack on a bus in Manila's financial district, which had killed four people in February. In November at least 23 alleged Abu Sayyaf members were killed in violent clashes with government troops on the island of Jolo. In February 2006, in another suspected Abu Sayyaf attack, an explosion near an army base that was being used by US troops killed one person. In January 2007 the campaign against Abu Sayyaf seemed to have made significant progress when it was reported that Jainal Antel Sali, or Abu Sulaiman, a senior Abu Sayyaf leader wanted for his alleged involvement in the kidnapping of several tourists in 2001 (see above) and the bombing of a ferry in 2004, had been killed by government forces on Jolo island. In the same month DNA tests confirmed earlier reports that the leader of Abu Sayyaf, Khadafi Janjalani, had been killed in September 2006. Four Filipinos later received a US $10m. reward from the US authorities for providing information that led to the two killings. None the less, Abu Sayyaf militants remained active, decapitating seven Christians whom they had taken hostage on Jolo in April 2007, and sending the severed heads to military camps on the island.

In August 2007 President Arroyo ordered the temporary transfer of the headquarters of the armed forces to Zamboanga City and announced that a major offensive had been launched against Abu Sayyaf on Jolo and Basilan, following clashes on Jolo in which 26 soldiers and an estimated 31 militants died. Rogue elements of the MNLF were also reported to be involved in the fighting, which prompted some 24,000 people to flee their homes. Later in that month the armed forces claimed to have killed 42 members of Abu Sayyaf in an attack on a camp on Basilan. Clashes continued in the following months, with further casualties reported on both sides. Abu Sayyaf was also held responsible for a bomb explosion outside the House of Representatives in Manila in November, in which four people died. In December 14 members of Abu Sayyaf were sentenced to life imprisonment for the May 2001 abduction of 20 people from a holiday resort off Palawan (see above). Later in that month government troops killed Mobin Abdurajak, a senior leader of Abu Sayyaf and brother-in-law of Khadafi Janjalani, who was wanted for the April 2000 abduction of 21 people from a Malaysian resort (see above). A Catholic priest who had reportedly been receiving death threats from Abu Sayyaf was abducted and killed on the island of Tawi-Tawi in January 2008. Two minor bomb explosions in Zamboanga City in April were attributed to Abu Sayyaf. A further bomb attack outside an air force base in Zamboanga City in late May killed two people; the MILF rejected suggestions that its members had perpetrated the bombing jointly with Abu Sayyaf. It was announced in August that a member of Abu Sayyaf who was wanted for his alleged involvement in the ferry bombing in 2004, as well as several other bomb attacks, had been arrested in Bahrain and deported to the Philippines. Moreover, in November 2008 an Abu Sayyaf commander suspected of involvement in the April 2000 abduction was captured on Jolo, while another senior member of the movement wanted for kidnapping was killed during a gunfight with troops in Sulu.

Three aid workers from the International Committee of the Red Cross (ICRC) were abducted by members of Abu Sayyaf on Jolo in January 2009. In March 10 people were killed in fighting between troops and militants holding the three ICRC workers captive. Later in that month Abu Sayyaf threatened to behead one of the ICRC hostages if all troops had not been withdrawn from several villages on Jolo by 31 March. At least 800 of 1,000 soldiers subsequently retreated, although the Government insisted that a complete withdrawal would compromise the security of residents. At the end of that month, as the deadline imposed by the rebels approached, the Governor of Sulu imposed a state of emergency in the province. At the beginning of April one of the hostages was released; another hostage escaped from captivity later in that month, and the remaining hostage was released in July. Clashes between Abu Sayyaf members and government troops on Basilan in August reportedly resulted in the deaths of more than 20 government soldiers and of at least 30 militants. The group was believed to be responsible for the kidnapping in October of a teacher on Jolo; in the following month the teacher was beheaded after his family refused to pay the ransom demanded by his kidnappers.

In December 2009 the authorities announced the capture of a founding member of Abu Sayyaf, Abdul Basir Latip, who was alleged to have been involved in the kidnapping of foreigners and Christians. The killing by the security forces of Albader Parad, a senior Abu Sayyaf commander held responsible for the abduction of the three ICRC workers, during an operation on Jolo in February 2010 was thought to represent another significant loss for the group. Later that month at least 11 people were reported to have been killed when a group of about 70 Abu Sayyaf members attacked a village on Basilan, in an apparent act of revenge for the killing of Parad. In the following month it emerged that Khair Mundus, who was on the US Federal Bureau of Investigation (FBI)'s list of 'most wanted' terrorists, with a US $500,000 reward offered for information leading to his capture, had become Abu Sayyaf's leader on Basilan; it was feared that the prominent involvement of Mundus, who was reported to have links to Malaysian and Saudi financial sources, would result in a significant increase in the levels of the group's foreign funding. Mundus and another senior Abu Sayyaf leader, Puruji Indama, were the intended targets of a security operation on Sakol island in March 2011; Indama, who was thought to have co-ordinated a number of kidnappings, was alleged to have links to Malaysian bomber Zulkifli bin Hir (alias Marwan), a prominent member of JI, for information leading to whose capture the FBI was offering a $5m. reward. However, both men escaped unharmed and were believed to have fled to Basilan.

Meanwhile, in early August 2010 an apparent suicide bombing at Zamboanga airport claimed the lives of two people, including the perpetrator, and injured 24 others, among them the Governor of Sulu, Sakur Tan. The attack was believed to have been an attempt to assassinate Sakur Tan, who had spearheaded campaigns targeting members of the Abu Sayyaf grouping. At the end of August the Philippine Government filed a petition with a court on Basilan seeking to outlaw Abu Sayyaf as a terrorist organization under the terms of the controversial Human Security Act of 2007 (see Domestic Political Affairs); if approved, the petition would allow the Government to arrest members of Abu Sayyaf without them having committed any crime other than belonging to the group, and would enable the Government to seek assistance from foreign law enforcement agencies in order to freeze Abu Sayyaf's funding from external sources.

Sporadic violent clashes between Abu Sayyaf rebels and government forces continued to be reported during 2011 and into 2012. In July 2011 seven government troops were killed during a gun battle with Abu Sayyaf militants in Sulu. A further two soldiers and 13 militants were killed in clashes on Jolo in September. Meanwhile, in July a Filipino-American woman was kidnapped, together with her son and her Filipino nephew, by suspected Abu Sayyaf militants in Zamboanga. The kidnappers were reported subsequently to have demanded payment of a large ransom in exchange for the hostages' release. The woman was released unharmed in October, prompting speculation that the Philippine Government, wishing to safeguard relations with the USA, had agreed to pay the ransom; however, both the Philippine and US authorities denied that any money had been paid. The nephew and son both managed to escape later in the year. An Australian national was abducted by suspected Abu Sayyaf militants in December. Again, a sizeable ransom was demanded for his safe release. However, the Australian Government ruled out paying any ransom, and the man was released in March 2013. Meanwhile, in early February 2012 a regional Abu Sayyaf commander was reported to have been killed in an air-strike in Sulu, along with 15 other suspected militants, including Marwan and another senior JI leader (who was a Singaporean national). The resumption in February 2013 of fighting between forces of the MNLF and Abu Sayyaf in Sulu reportedly resulted in the deaths of at least 30 militants.

Foreign Affairs
Regional relations
The Philippines' engagement with the Association of Southeast Asian Nations (ASEAN, see p. 218) deepened during the administrations of Presidents Fidel Ramos and Joseph Estrada. At the ASEAN ministerial meeting in Manila in July 1998, Secretary of Foreign Affairs Domingo Siazon, Jr, joined his Thai counterpart in expressing support for 'constructive intervention' in member countries' internal affairs, in marked contrast to ASEAN's policy of non-interference hitherto. In January 2007 the Philippines hosted the 12th annual ASEAN summit meeting, as well as the second East Asia summit (comprising the member states of ASEAN together with the People's Republic of China, Japan and the Republic of Korea), in Cebu. In October 2008 the Philippines ratified the new ASEAN Charter, which codified the principles and purposes of the Association and came into effect in December of that year; President Gloria Arroyo had previously suggested that the Philippines would not ratify the new Charter while Myanma opposition leader Aung San Suu Kyi remained under house arrest. During 2009 and early 2010 the Philippines was outspoken in its appeals for Myanmar's first legislative elections since 1990, due to be held before the end of 2010, to be genuinely inclusive, with the opposition able fully to participate in a free and fair contest. At an ASEAN summit meeting held in Hanoi, Viet Nam, in October 2010, the Philippine delegation communicated the view of President Benigno Aquino's administration that the forthcoming elections, which were held on 7 November, were 'a farce to democratic values', following recent developments that indicated that the polls would be neither free nor fair (see Myanmar). The Philippine Secretary of Foreign Affairs, Albert del Rosario, made an official visit to the Myanma administrative capital, Nay Pyi Taw, in February 2012, during which he commended the new (nominally civilian) administration of Myanma President Thein Sein for its implementation of a series of significant political, economic and social reforms, including the release of a number of political prisoners and the participation of opposition political parties, including Suu Kyi's National League for Democracy, within the political process. Thein Sein expressed gratitude to the Philippine Government for its support for proposals to ease international economic sanctions against Myanmar, and invited Philippine businesses to invest in the Myanma economy. In June the Myanma Minister of Foreign Affairs, Wunna Maung Lwin, paid a reciprocal visit to the Philippines, during which the two countries concluded a bilateral mechanism that would allow them to co-operate in a wide field of mutual interests, including politics, trade and culture.

Relations with Malaysia were somewhat strained, owing to the Philippines' claim to the Malaysian state of Sabah, dating from 1962, before Sabah joined the Federation of Malaysia; attempts by both Presidents Ferdinand Marcos and Corazon Aquino to abandon the claim were thwarted by the Senate. In August 1993 the Philippine and Malaysian ministers responsible for foreign affairs signed a memorandum creating a commission to address bilateral issues, including the Philippines' claim to Sabah. In the latter half of 1998 bilateral relations were strained by Estrada's public condemnation of the arrest and mistreatment of the former Malaysian Deputy Prime Minister, Dato' Seri Anwar Ibrahim (see Malaysia). Estrada's decision to hold a private meeting with Anwar's wife during her visit to the Philippines in May 1999 further displeased the Malaysian Government. In November 2001 relations were jeopardized again when the Malaysian authorities detained rebel leader Nur Misuari for attempting to enter the country illegally. After some vacillation, Misuari was finally deported in January 2002 and relations remained cordial. However, in August the bilateral relationship deteriorated following the implementation of stringent new laws in Malaysia whereby all illegal immigrants remaining in the country risked harsh penalties and deportation. Many of those affected were Filipino workers. The Arroyo administration filed a formal complaint against Malaysia over its treatment of the immigrants and sent an official delegation to investigate allegations of maltreatment. Malaysia subsequently suspended implementation of the legislation. In March 2009 Arroyo met with Malaysian Prime Minister Abdullah Badawi to request assistance in peace talks with the MILF (see Separatist Tensions and Militancy). Bilateral relations were threatened by the abduction of two Malaysian labourers in Sabah by a group of unidentified Philippine assailants in February 2010. However, the safe return of the pair was secured in December, and was welcomed by the Malaysian embassy in Manila as a 'reflection of the close co-operation' between the two countries' police forces.

In early February 2013 it was reported that a group of around 200 men (some of whom were armed) from the Philippine island province of Sulu had landed in Lahad Datu, a remote area of Sabah, and had raised the Philippine flag in the coastal village of Tanduo. The Government of the Philippines denied having sanctioned the actions of the group, which described itself as the 'Royal Security Forces (RSF)' of the Sultanate of Sulu and North Borneo' and which was led by Agbimuddin Kiram, the brother of self-proclaimed Sultan of Sulu Jamalul Kiram III, and urged the men to withdraw at once. The group asserted that Sabah, which had been given to the Sultan of Sulu by the Sultan of Brunei in the 17th century, was still part of Sulu (and, by extension, part of the Philippines). The Malaysian authorities, in turn, claimed that Sabah had, in effect, been sold (rather than simply leased) to the British North Borneo Company by the Sultan of Sulu through a contract drawn up between the two parties in 1878. Following a stand-off between the RSF and the Malaysian security forces, the situation turned violent at the end of February 2013; two police officers and 12 Philippine rebels were reportedly killed in the ensuing shoot-outs. In early March, as tensions escalated and the death toll rose, the Malaysian authorities dispatched additional troops (including fighter jets) to Sabah, while the Philippine Secretary of Foreign Affairs, Albert del Rosario, was sent to Malaysia to attempt to arrange peace talks between the RSF and the Malaysian Government. The Malaysian Government rejected the subsequent offer of a cease-fire made by the rebel group, demanding instead its unconditional surrender. By mid-March more than 70 people had been killed in the conflict and around 5,000 civilians displaced. In April there were reports that about 1,000 members of the Philippine Muslim group the MNLF had broken through the Malaysian-Philippine naval blockades to land on Sabah, where they offered their assistance to the RSF.

In August 2001 Indonesian President Megawati Sukarnoputri visited the Philippines on her first overseas trip since assuming power. During her brief stay she met with President Arroyo, and the two leaders promised to assist each other in overcoming the separatist violence endemic in both their countries. In March 2002 bilateral relations threatened to become strained when the Philippine police filed charges against three Indonesian men who had been arrested at Manila Airport for illegal possession of explosives. One of those arrested was believed to be a member of the Majelis Mujahidin Indonesia (MMI—Indonesian Mujahidin Council), an extremist Islamist organization, and to have links to JI. The Indonesian Government was reported to have been angered by the arrests and stated that the detentions should not be used as a pretext to portray Indonesia as a haven for Islamist extremists. However, in early 2003 it was reported that Philippine rebels were engaged in smuggling weapons to militant groups in Indonesia, despite increased anti-terrorism co-operation between the two countries as a result of a trilateral security treaty signed by the Philippines, Indonesia and Malaysia in May 2002. In October 2003 Fathur Rohman al-Ghozi, believed to be a senior Indonesian member of JI, was shot dead by Philippine government forces on Mindanao three months after his escape from a prison in Manila, where he had been detained following his conviction for illegal possession of explosives. In November 2006 an additional security pact between the Philippines and Indonesia was signed, which was intended further to improve co-operation in combating transnational crime and terrorism.

Diplomatic relations were established with the People's Republic of China in 1975, at which time the Philippine Government recognized Taiwan as an 'inalienable' part of the People's Republic. However, conflicting claims to the Spratly Islands, in the South China Sea, were a source of tension between the Philippines and China. (Viet Nam, Brunei, Malaysia and Taiwan also claimed sovereignty over some or all of the islands.) Bilateral animosity was exacerbated by intermittent incidents during the early 1990s, including the occupation by the Chinese armed forces of Mischief Reef, which lay within the Philippines' 200-mile exclusive economic zone (EEZ) established by the UN Convention on the Law of the Sea (UNCLOS). Following two days of consultations in August 1995, however, the Chinese Government agreed for the first time to settle disputes in the South China Sea according to international law, rather than insisting that historical claims should take precedence. The Chinese and Philippine Governments issued a joint statement agreeing on a code of conduct to reduce the possibility of a military confrontation in the area. A similar agreement was signed with Viet Nam in November 1995. In March 1996 the Philippines and China agreed to co-operate in combating piracy, which was also a source of tension between the two countries as pirate vessels in the area often sailed under Chinese flags. Despite these agreements, sporadic tension continued during 1996–99.

In April 1999 the Philippines and Viet Nam agreed to joint military operations and leisure activities to reduce the risk of confrontation over the Spratly Islands. In October, however, the Philippines lodged a protest at the Vietnamese embassy, following an incident in which Vietnamese forces had fired on a Philippine aircraft patrolling in the South China Sea. In November ASEAN officials agreed on a regional code of conduct drafted by the Philippines to prevent conflicts in the Spratlys. In the same month the Chinese Premier, Zhu Rongji, visited the Philippines, and he and Estrada agreed to strengthen co-operation between the two countries. However, China rejected the proposed regional code of conduct. In early 2000 China proposed a new draft code omitting previous references to a ban on construction on islands or atolls and excluding the Paracel Islands, which China had seized from Viet Nam in 1974. However, China did meet with all the ASEAN representatives to discuss the draft, a departure from its previously exclusively bilateral approach. In May 2000 Estrada made a visit to China, where he met President Jiang Zemin and signed a joint statement on the framework for co-operation between China and the Philippines.

In mid-2002 relations with China were jeopardized when the Philippine Secretary of Justice, Hernando Perez, demanded that the Chinese ambassador be expelled from the country. His request marked the culmination of a dispute regarding the fate of more than 100 Chinese fishermen, who had been arrested over the preceding months and accused of fishing illegally in Philippine waters. Perez accused the ambassador of reneging on an agreement whereby the fishermen would be freed on condition that they entered guilty pleas and paid fines, claiming that the ambassador had attempted to coerce the Philippine Government into releasing the fishermen without penalty. However, Perez subsequently withdrew his expulsion demand and, shortly afterwards, the Chinese Minister of Defence paid a goodwill visit to the country. In November the improvement in bilateral relations was demonstrated when a senior delegation from the Chinese Communist Party arrived in the Philippines. Also in that month a 'declaration on the conduct of parties in the South China Sea' was signed by the ministers responsible for foreign affairs of China and the ASEAN member states. In September 2004, during a three-day state visit by President Arroyo to China, her first foreign trip since her election, the two countries signed five bilateral agreements, including one to conduct joint marine research in the South China Sea. It was also agreed to explore the possibility of defence co-operation. In March 2005 the national oil companies of the Philippines, China and Viet Nam signed a three-year agreement on undertaking joint research into petroleum resources in the South China Sea.

In March 2006 the Chinese Government granted the Philippine administration US $3m. with which to establish a Chinese-language military training programme, in return for the Philippines' continued adherence to the 'one China' policy, which recognized Taiwan as an integral part of the People's Republic of China. The Chinese Government also donated engineering equipment and invited the Philippines to participate in joint naval exercises. In January 2007 the Chinese Premier, Wen Jiabao, spent two days in Manila, after attending the 10th ASEAN-China summit and other ASEAN-related meetings in Cebu. During his visit several bilateral accords were signed, most notably a framework agreement on expanding economic and trade co-operation. President Arroyo visited China in October, shortly after suspending a telecommunications contract with China's ZTE Corporation, following allegations of bribery in the bidding process (see Domestic Political Affairs). In talks with the Chinese President, Hu Jintao, Arroyo sought to ensure that the cancellation of the contract did not adversely affect bilateral relations. However, Arroyo's administration was subsequently forced to defend the propriety of other economic agreements with China, amid criticism from Philippine opposition parties. Tension over sovereignty in the South China Sea re-emerged in February 2009, when the Philippines adopted legislation seeking to define the country's maritime boundaries: this referred to the disputed Kalayaan group of islands (more commonly known as the Spratly Islands and referred to as the

Nansha Islands by China) and the Scarborough Shoal (or Huangyan) as being part of a 'regime of islands under the Republic of the Philippines'. The Chinese Government denounced the territorial claims as illegal and invalid. However, in October the two countries signed the Philippines-China Joint Action Plan for Strategic Co-operation, which set out the direction of bilateral co-operation in the fields of, *inter alia*, politics, the economy, trade and investment, and tourism during 2010–15, and the Philippines-China Consular Agreement, which was the first consular accord that the Philippines had signed since the multilateral Vienna Convention on Consular Relations in 1963.

However, relations with China were compromised by the killing of eight Hong Kong tourists in Manila in a bus hijacking in August 2010 (see Domestic Political Affairs). The affair also had a negative impact on relations with the Government of Hong Kong: Chief Executive Donald Tsang described the management of the incident by the Philippine authorities as 'disappointing', and his administration issued a warning against all travel to the Philippines. The Chinese Government demanded a thorough investigation into the handling of the incident. President Benigno Aquino conceded that the authorities' response to the hijacking had been unsatisfactory and pledged to improve standards within the police force.

Proposals to formulate a binding code of conduct for the Spratly Islands were espoused in October 2010, but discussions to this end were not reported to have yielded any tangible results as of early 2013. Tensions between the Philippines and China (and, to a lesser extent, Viet Nam) over sovereignty of the islands intensified from early 2011, with the Philippine Government alleging numerous incursions into its territorial waters by Chinese vessels. In April the Philippines announced that it had lodged a formal protest with the UN against China's claims, formally submitted to the organization in 2009, to the Spratly Islands and surrounding waters. Tensions were further heightened in June 2011 by the holding of Chinese navy exercises, including live fire drills, in the disputed waters. To the consternation of the Chinese Government, joint US-Philippines naval exercises were held close to the Spratly Islands at the end of the month. In July the Philippine Secretary of Foreign Affairs, Albert del Rosario, met with his Chinese counterpart during a visit to the Chinese capital, Beijing, but no significant developments on the territorial dispute were reported. A visit to Pagasa Island in mid-July by a five-member Philippine delegation prompted an angry response from Chinese government officials. Relations were ameliorated by a five-day state visit to Beijing by President Aquino in late August–early September, during which he met with President Hu Jintao and Premier Wen Jiabao; both countries pledged to seek a peaceful, diplomatic resolution to the ongoing territorial dispute, and an agreement seeking to increase annual bilateral trade to US \$60,000m. within five years was signed.

Renewed tensions arose in April 2012, however, when the Philippine navy claimed to have found illegally caught fish and coral on eight Chinese fishing vessels while patrolling the area of the Scarborough Shoal; two Chinese surveillance ships subsequently arrived in the area, placing themselves between the warship and the fishing vessels, and thus preventing the navy from making arrests. The Philippine Government lodged a protest with the Chinese ambassador over the incident, but China reasserted its sovereignty over the area. A second protest was lodged later that month, after the Philippines alleged that Chinese ships and aircraft were 'harassing' a research ship in the area. Del Rosario proposed jointly referring the issue of sovereignty over the waters surrounding the Scarborough Shoal to the International Tribunal for the Law of the Sea (see p. 363). The stand-off between Chinese and Philippine vessels continued into May, with dozens more Chinese fishing and utility boats arriving in the area during the month, according to Philippine officials. Tensions were eased in June following the withdrawal of the two Philippine naval vessels, citing stormy weather. Meanwhile, further joint US-Philippines military exercises took place in the area in the latter half of April. In July the Philippine Government announced plans to auction off three areas in the South China Sea for oil and gas exploration; the blocks were located off the coast of Palawan province, near Reed Bank, in an area that was also claimed by China. However, the Philippine Government asserted that the blocks were located well within the country's EEZ. President Aquino risked exacerbating tensions when he signed an order in September renaming areas of the South China Sea, including the Spratly Islands and Scarborough Shoal, the

West Philippine Sea. Following repeated refusals by China to discuss the maritime dispute through the diplomatic avenues offered by ASEAN, the Philippines announced in January 2013 that it intended to challenge China's territorial claims through an arbitration tribunal under UNCLOS (which both countries had signed).

In September 2006 Arroyo and the Japanese Prime Minister, Junichiro Koizumi, signed an economic partnership agreement, which would eliminate tariffs on almost 95% of trade and provide for the entry of more Filipino workers to Japan. The agreement was approved by the Japanese legislature in December 2006, but did not enter into force until December 2008, following considerable controversy over, *inter alia*, provisions apparently granting Japanese investors rights almost equal to those of Filipinos. Bilateral co-operation was expected to be bolstered following the announcement by the Japanese Government in November 2010 that it was to invest some US \$5,500m. in the Philippines. Relations were further consolidated by a four-day state visit to Japan in September 2011 by President Aquino, during which a number of business agreements were concluded and Japan pledged to promote private investment and support infrastructural development projects in the Philippines.

Australia, along with the USA and Japan, was one of the Philippines' leading bilateral aid donors in the early 21st century; total assistance for 2012/13 was budgeted at \$A128.7m., which was primarily to be disbursed on improving education, local government capacity to deliver basic services (notably through road infrastructure development), disaster risk reduction and climate change adaptation, and conditions for peace and security. Meanwhile, in May 2007 President Arroyo and the Australian Prime Minister, John Howard, signed a new security pact designed to assist the Philippines in its efforts to combat insurgents in the south of the country. Under the agreement, Australian special forces would train Philippine troops and joint counter-terrorism exercises would be organized.

The Philippines contributed 1,000 troops to a UN multinational force to restore peace and security in East Timor (which became Timor-Leste upon its accession to independence in May 2002), following the violence that erupted after the East Timorese voted in a referendum for independence from Indonesia. The Philippines also participated in subsequent UN missions in Timor-Leste, most recently the UN Integrated Mission in Timor-Leste (UNMIT), which was established in August 2006. A number of bilateral agreements were signed in August 2008, during José Ramos Horta's first state visit to the Philippines since taking office as President of Timor-Leste in May 2007. During another visit to the Philippines, in July 2010, Ramos Horta met with President Benigno Aquino, expressing his belief that bilateral relations would be enhanced under the new presidency. The Timorese President voiced gratitude for the Philippine contribution to UNMIT, as a result of which, he declared, peace and stability had returned to Timor-Leste. Ramos Horta also appealed for greater Philippine investment in Timorese infrastructure development projects.

Other external relations

The Philippines and the USA enjoy long-standing cordial relations and close military co-operation. In November 1991 the US military formally transferred management of the Clark Air Base to the Philippines, in accordance with the Philippine Constitution's stipulation that foreign military bases should not be allowed in the country from the end of that year. US personnel withdrew from Subic Naval Bay in September 1992, and from the Cubi Point Naval Air Station in November.

Following the occupation, by the People's Republic of China, of a reef in the Spratly Islands claimed by the Philippines (see Regional relations), in July 1995 Philippine and US forces staged a joint naval exercise about 100 km from the Spratly Islands. Owing to the intensification of the dispute with China over the Islands, the Philippines signed an agreement with the USA in October 1998 to allow for the formal resumption of joint military exercises. The first phase of such exercises, which took place in January 2000, provoked popular protests outside the US embassy in Manila against the return to the Philippines of US troops. Meanwhile, in February 1998 the Philippine and US Governments signed a Visiting Forces Agreement (VFA), which, *inter alia*, authorized the unrestricted movement of US military aircraft and vessels within the Philippines, and allowed the US Government to retain jurisdiction over US military personnel accused of committing crimes in the Philippines, unless the crimes were of particular significance to the latter country.

Despite significant opposition to the VFA, it was ratified by the Philippine Senate in May 1999.

Following the terrorist attacks on the USA, attributed to the al-Qa'ida Islamist network, in September 2001, President Gloria Arroyo offered US President George W. Bush the Philippine Government's unqualified support for the US campaign against terrorism, volunteering logistical and intelligence assistance, the use of Philippine airspace, and the former US military bases at Clark and Subic Bay to the US Government. An offer of combat troops was also made, pending congressional approval. In November Arroyo paid a state visit to the USA, where she addressed the UN General Assembly and held talks with Bush. In return for the ongoing support of the Philippines in the US anti-terrorist campaign, Bush promised the country US $100m. in military assistance and further development aid for Mindanao. The funds included $39m. to aid the Government in its continuing war against Abu Sayyaf, which had proven links to al-Qa'ida. However, President Arroyo declined an offer of direct US military involvement, limiting the role of the USA to the provision of technical and financial assistance for the offensive.

In January 2002 it was reported that the US Government had sent 660 soldiers to the southern Philippines to participate in joint training exercises with Philippine troops; however, they were not to engage in any direct combat as this would contravene the Constitution. The deployment marked the first significant extension of the US-led 'war on terror' beyond Afghanistan, and prompted widespread criticism of Arroyo within the Philippines, with several members of Congress claiming that the exercises were intended to conceal a US offensive against Abu Sayyaf. Her most outspoken critic was the Vice-President and Secretary of Foreign Affairs, Teofisto Guingona, Jr, whose stance was a decisive factor in his resignation from the foreign affairs portfolio in July. Meanwhile, in February more than 20 people died following clashes in the city of Jolo between police and soldiers; a later bomb blast in the city killed a further five people. A second explosion in Zamboanga, which was serving as a temporary base for US service personnel, occurred on the same day. The incidents were attributed to opponents of the ongoing military exercises. In April Arroyo sanctioned the deployment of hundreds more US troops to the region and extended the deadline for their departure, owing to the apparent success of the exercises in containing terrorist activities in the Philippines. The exercises were formally concluded at the end of July and the US troops left the Philippines in September; however, about 600 troops remained, forming the counter-insurgency Joint Special Operations Task Force-Philippines (JSOTF-P). In August 2009 US Secretary of Defense Robert Gates announced that JSOTF-P was to remain in the Philippines for the foreseeable future.

Meanwhile, in late 2002 the US Government signed a five-year military agreement with the Philippines, pledging to extend co-operation between the armed forces of the two countries and to facilitate the movement of heavy equipment and logistical supplies. In January 2003 an advance deployment of US Special Forces troops arrived in Zamboanga to commence anti-terrorism training exercises. In February the USA announced that it intended to send a new deployment of soldiers to the island of Jolo, a stronghold of Abu Sayyaf; it specified, controversially, that the troops would assume a combat role for the first time. However, the Philippine Government stressed later that US forces would play an entirely non-combative role in any counter-terrorism exercises. In March Arroyo stated that, owing to local opposition, military exercises would not be conducted on Jolo; in April it was announced that they were to take place in various alternative locations across the Philippines.

During a visit to the USA by President Arroyo in May 2003, US President Bush designated the Philippines as a Major Non-North Atlantic Treaty Organization (NATO) Ally (MNA), entitling it to increased US military co-operation and supplies of armaments. Later in that month the Government stated that it expected to receive a total of US $356m. in military assistance from the USA. In October Bush visited the Philippines during a tour of the region and thanked the country for its continued co-operation in the US-led 'war on terror'. Relations with the USA were strained in July 2004 by Arroyo's decision to withdraw the small Philippine contingent from the US-led coalition forces in Iraq a month ahead of schedule, in order to comply with the demands of militants who had taken a Filipino civilian hostage in the country. Nevertheless, joint US-Philippine military exercises continued during 2004–06. In December 2006 the USA threatened to cancel the joint exercises scheduled for the follow-

ing year owing to a bilateral dispute that had arisen over the conviction, by a Philippine court, of a US soldier on the charge of having raped a Filipino woman, which, the USA argued, was counter to the terms of the VFA signed in 1998; however, in January 2007 the USA announced that the exercises were to go ahead as planned.

Arroyo met with Bush's successor as President, Barack Obama, during a visit to the USA in July 2009; in a joint press conference, Obama affirmed the significance of US-Philippine relations and emphasized the Philippines' importance as a vital link between the USA and Asia. In November US Secretary of State Hillary Clinton, who had met with Arroyo during a visit by the latter to Washington, DC, in February, visited Manila to show solidarity with the Philippine people in the aftermath of a series of destructive typhoons that had struck the country in previous weeks, killing several hundred people and causing extensive damage.

President Benigno Aquino visited New York in September 2010, his first overseas visit since assuming the presidency in June. During his week-long stay in the USA he attended the second summit meeting of US and ASEAN leaders, at which the South China Sea dispute was among a number of issues discussed. In the course of his visit Aquino also secured a number of agreements collectively worth an estimated US $2,800m.

During a visit to Washington, DC, in late June 2011, Secretary of Foreign Affairs Albert del Rosario held discussions with US Secretary of State Clinton. In a joint press conference, Clinton urged all involved parties to seek a swift and peaceful resolution to the ongoing dispute over the Spratly Islands. However, she also stressed the continued relevance of the US-Philippine Mutual Defense Treaty and the US Administration's 'commitment to the defence of the Philippines', appearing to indicate tacit US support for the Philippines; Clinton also noted that the USA had assisted the Philippines to establish a coastal radar system to enable it to monitor its waters more closely. The staging of joint US-Philippines naval exercises close to the disputed Spratly Islands at the end of June provoked an angry response from China. During a visit to the Philippines in November, Clinton reaffirmed the US Government's commitment to strong military ties between the two countries; Clinton and del Rosario signed a declaration appealing for multilateral talks to resolve maritime disputes. President Benigno held talks with Obama during a visit to the USA in June 2012; among the topics discussed were the peace negotiations with the MILF, the recent stand-offs with China in the South China Sea, the development of good governance and political transparency in the Philippines, and the proposed expansion of bilateral trade. Amid rising tension in the Asia-Pacific region, in December the USA announced that it planned significantly to increase its rotational military presence in the Philippines—in April 2013 12 US F/A-18 fighter aircraft (the largest number to date) were deployed in the annual military exercises conducted by the two countries in Tarlac province.

In the course of a visit to St Petersburg, Russia, in June 2009, President Arroyo met with Russian President Dmitrii Medvedev and the two leaders signed a number of formal and informal agreements, including one that provided for the supply of Russian liquefied natural gas to the Philippines for the first time. Arroyo and Medvedev also agreed further to consolidate military co-operation. An air services agreement was signed between the two countries in December (replacing an existing agreement signed in 1992), which provided for the opening of direct scheduled flights between the Russian capital of Moscow and several locations within the Philippines, including Manila and Cebu; the new accord was expected to facilitate increased bilateral tourism, trade and investment. It was hoped that the establishment of the Philippine-Russian Business Council in November 2011 would further contribute to the strengthening of bilateral ties. In April 2013 the two countries signed a Customs Mutual Administrative Assistance Agreement, aimed at preventing smuggling and strengthening co-operation in the fight against transnational crimes and commercial fraud.

CONSTITUTION AND GOVERNMENT

The Constitution, which was approved by a national referendum on 2 February 1987, provided for a bicameral Congress, comprising a Senate, with 24 members directly elected by universal suffrage (for a six-year term, with one-half of the membership being elected every three years), and a House of Representatives (with a three-year mandate), with a maximum of 286 members (with effect from the 2010 elections), one being directly elected from each legislative district. In addition, one-fifth of the total number of representatives was to be elected under a party list system from lists of nominees proposed by minority groups.

The President is Head of State, Chief Executive of the Republic and Commander-in-Chief of the Armed Forces. The President is elected by the people for a six-year term, and is not eligible for re-election. The President cannot prevent the enactment of legislative proposals if they are approved by a two-thirds' majority vote in Congress. The President may declare martial law in times of national emergency, but Congress is empowered to revoke such actions at any time by a majority vote of its members. The President appoints a Cabinet and other officials, with the approval of the Commission on Appointments (drawn from members of both chambers of Congress).

Local government is by Barangays (citizens' assemblies), and autonomy is granted to any region where its introduction is endorsed in a referendum. The Autonomous Region of Muslim Mindanao (ARMM), granted autonomy in November 1989, has its own 24-seat Regional Legislative Assembly (RLA). As part of a draft peace agreement signed between the Government and the Moro Islamic Liberation Front (MILF) in October 2012, however, the ARMM was to be replaced by a new autonomous region, Bangsamoro, in the near future.

REGIONAL AND INTERNATIONAL CO-OPERATION

The Philippines is a member of the Association of Southeast Asian Nations (ASEAN, see p. 218), the Asia-Pacific Economic Cooperation (APEC, see p. 208) forum, the Asian Development Bank (ADB, see p. 214), the UN's Economic and Social Commission for Asia and the Pacific (ESCAP, see p. 31) and the Colombo Plan (see p. 460).

The Philippines became a member of the UN in 1945. As a contracting party to the General Agreement on Tariffs and Trade, the Philippines joined the World Trade Organization (WTO, see p. 444) on its establishment in 1995. The Philippines is also a member of the International Labour Organization (ILO, see p. 142) and the Non-aligned Movement (see p. 477).

ECONOMIC AFFAIRS

In 2011, according to estimates by the World Bank, the Philippines' gross national income (GNI), measured at average 2009–11 prices, was US $209,450m., equivalent to $2,210 per head (or $4,160 per head on an international purchasing-power parity basis). During 2002–12, it was estimated, the population increased at an average annual rate of 1.8%, while gross domestic product (GDP) per head increased, in real terms, by an average of 3.1% per year. According to official figures, overall GDP increased, in real terms, at an average annual rate of 5.0% in 2004–12; GDP increased by 3.9% in 2011 and by 6.6% in 2012.

Agriculture (including hunting, forestry and fishing) contributed 11.9% of GDP in 2012 and engaged 32.3% of the employed labour force at October 2012. Rice, maize and cassava are the main subsistence crops. None the less, the Philippines has traditionally relied on substantial imports of rice to meet domestic demand. In April 2008, however, the Government announced a 43,700m. pesos programme of investment in the agricultural sector, aimed at improving general food security and achieving self-sufficiency in rice by 2013. In April 2013 the Secretary of Agriculture, Proceso Alcala, stated that the Philippines was close to reaching this objective, with imports of only 187,000 metric tons of rice being required that year. The principal crops cultivated for export are sugar cane, coconuts, bananas and pineapples. Livestock (mainly pigs, buffaloes, goats and poultry) and fisheries are important. Agricultural GDP increased at an average annual rate of 2.3% during 2004–12; the sector's GDP grew by 2.7% in 2012.

Industry (including mining, manufacturing, construction and power) contributed 31.1% of GDP in 2012 and engaged 15.2% of the employed labour force at October 2012. Industrial GDP increased at an average annual rate of 4.7% in 2004–12; sectoral GDP increased by 6.5% in 2012.

Mining contributed 1.1% of GDP in 2012 and engaged 0.7% of the employed labour force at October 2012. Copper is the Philippines' leading mineral product; coal, nickel, silver, gold and chromium are also extracted. Commercial production of crude petroleum began in 1979. Production from a substantial natural gas field and petroleum reservoir, off the island of Palawan, commenced in 2001. Mining GDP increased at an average annual rate of 7.7% in 2004–12; the GDP of the mining sector expanded by 7.0% in 2011, but declined by 3.7% in 2012.

Manufacturing contributed 20.5% of GDP in 2012 and engaged 8.3% of the employed labour force at October 2012. The most important branches of manufacturing include food products and beverages, electronic products and components (mainly telecommunications equipment), petroleum products and chemicals. The GDP of the manufacturing sector increased at an average annual rate of 4.1% in 2004–12, expanding by 5.4% in 2012.

Construction contributed 5.9% of GDP in 2012 and engaged 5.8% of the employed labour force at October 2012. The GDP of the construction sector increased at an average annual rate of 7.2% in 2004–12; the sector's GDP declined by 7.3% in 2011, but rose by 14.4% in 2012.

The energy sector's reliance on imported petroleum has decreased, as new sources of power have become available. In 2009 natural gas accounted for 32.1% of the total amount of electrical energy produced, coal for 26.6%, hydroelectric power for 15.8% and petroleum for 8.7%. A Renewable Energy Act was adopted in 2008, as part of the Government's long-term programme to increase the contribution of renewable sources (including biomass plants and solar power) to the electricity supply. In 2012 mineral fuels accounted for 22.2% of the value of total merchandise imports.

The services sector contributed 57.1% of GDP in 2012 and engaged 52.6% of the employed labour force at October 2012. Although periodically affected by political unrest, tourism remains a significant sector of the economy, with receipts (excluding passenger transport) estimated at US $3,152m. in 2011. Foreign visitor arrivals rose from 1.9m. in 2003 to more than 3.9m. (including Filipinos resident overseas) in 2011. The provision of business process outsourcing facilities and attendant call-centre services has expanded rapidly, to become a significant sector of the economy. Revenue from these activities increased by an estimated 19% in 2009, and in 2012 more than 600,000 workers were employed in these services. The GDP of the services sector increased at an average annual rate of 5.8% in 2004–12, expanding by 7.4% in 2012.

In 2011 the Philippines recorded a visible merchandise trade deficit of US $16,522m., while there was a surplus of $6,988m. on the current account of the balance of payments. Remittances from Filipino workers abroad make a vital contribution to the economy, rising steadily from $10,689m. in 2005 to $21,391m. in 2012. In 2012 the principal source of imports was the USA (accounting for 11.5% of the total); other significant suppliers were the People's Republic of China, Japan, Taiwan, the Republic of Korea, Singapore and Thailand. The principal market for exports in that year was Japan (19.0%); other major purchasers were the USA, China, Singapore, Hong Kong and the Republic of Korea. The principal imports in 2012 were mineral fuels, telecommunications equipment and electric machinery, materials acquired for the manufacture of electronic equipment, chemical products, manufactured goods, power-generating and special machines, and food and live animals. The principal exports in that year were electronic products (notably semiconductors and electronic data-processing devices), machinery and transport equipment, woodcraft and furniture, and metal components.

A budget deficit of 242,827m. pesos was recorded in 2012, equivalent to 2.3% of GDP. The general government gross debt was 4,079,200m. pesos in 2011, equivalent to 41.9% of GDP. According to the Asian Development Bank (ADB), the Philippines' external debt totalled US $60,337m. at the end of 2012; in that year the cost of servicing the debt was equivalent to 7.4% of the value of exports of goods and services. According to official figures, the annual rate of inflation averaged 4.6% in 2002–12; consumer prices increased by 3.2% in 2012. According to the labour force survey of October 2012, 6.8% of the labour force were unemployed at that date (compared with 11.8% in 2004).

A major issue confronting President Benigno Aquino, who took office in June 2010, was the persistently high rate of unemployment. Although unemployment declined from 7.4% in 2010 to 6.8% in 2012, the rate of underemployment increased from 18.8% to 20.0%, while youth unemployment remained high, at just under 19%. A national development plan for 2011–16, approved in March 2011, envisaged the generation of 1m. new employment opportunities annually, as well as a reduction in the incidence of poverty from 26.5% in 2009 to 16.6% by 2015. Other priorities under the plan, which targeted annual GDP growth of 7%–8%, included infrastructural development, anti-corruption measures, increasing investment levels and improving access to social services. Meanwhile, the new Government also undertook to decrease government debt and to restrict the budget deficit to 2.0% of GDP by 2013 (the latter aim being achieved in 2011, but not in 2012, when the deficit rose to 2.3% of GDP). Remittances from overseas workers increased from US $20,117m. in 2011 to a record $21,391m. in 2012, in turn sustaining domestic demand. Following weak investment inflows in 2011 in the aftermath of the tsunami disaster in Japan (a major provider of investment financing and also of development assistance to the Philippines), foreign direct investment was estimated to have risen by 9.8% in 2012, to reach some $2,000m.—a level that was none the less still lower than in other South-East Asian countries. A 7.6% increase in export revenues in 2012 resulted in a smaller trade deficit and, with the help of substantial remittance inflows, a narrowing of the current account surplus. After rising to 4.7% in 2011, owing to higher food and petroleum prices, the inflation rate moderated to 3.2% in 2012 (its lowest level for five years), aided by better harvests and generally stable global commodity prices. Inflation was expected to increase to about 3.6% in 2013 as a result of strong domestic demand and higher taxes on alcohol and tobacco. Following robust GDP growth in 2010, growth slowed to 3.9% in 2011, primarily as a result of the contraction in export earnings and weak government spending; strong consumer spending, an increase in net exports and an acceleration in public and private investment drove growth of 6.6% in 2012. According to the ADB,

the rate of GDP growth was forecast to decelerate slightly to 6.0% in 2013. Overall, the short-term prospects for the Philippine economy appeared positive as a result of improvements to fiscal management, increasing levels of remittances, strong growth in the tourism sector and high levels of consumption and investment.

PUBLIC HOLIDAYS

2014: 1 January (New Year's Day), 9 April (Bataan Day—Araw ng Kagitingan), 17 April (Maundy Thursday), 18 April (Good Friday), 1 May (Labour Day), 12 June (Independence Day, anniversary of 1898 declaration), 24 June (Araw ng Maynila)*, 28 July (Id al-Fitr)†, 19 August (Quezon Day)‡, 21 August (Ninoy Aquino Day), 25 August (National Heroes' Day), 4 October (Id al-Adha)†, 1 November (All Saints' Day), 1 December (Bonifacio Day), 25 December (Christmas Day), 29 December (for Rizal Day), 31 December (Last Day of the Year).

* Observed only in Metro Manila.

† These holidays are dependent on the Islamic lunar calendar and may vary by one or two days from the dates given.

‡ Observed only in Quezon City.

Statistical Survey

Source (unless otherwise stated): National Statistics Office, Solicarel 1, R. Magsaysay Blvd, Santa Mesa, 1008 Metro Manila; tel. (2) 7160807; fax (2) 7137073; internet www.census.gov.ph.

Area and Population

AREA, POPULATION AND DENSITY

Area (sq km)	300,000*
Population (census results)	
1 August 2007	
Males	44,757,788
Females	43,788,299
Total	88,546,087
1 May 2010†	92,337,852
Population (UN estimates at mid-year)‡	
2011	94,852,031
2012	96,471,460
2013	98,112,778
Density (per sq km) at mid-2013	327.0

* 115,831 sq miles.

† Includes 2,739 Filipinos in Philippine embassies, consulates and missions abroad.

‡ Source: UN, *World Population Prospects: The 2010 Revision*; estimates not adjusted to take account of 2010 census.

POPULATION BY AGE AND SEX
(UN estimates at mid-2013)

	Males	Females	Total
0–14	17,237,973	16,435,681	33,673,654
15–64	30,353,791	30,323,725	60,677,516
65 and over	1,588,401	2,173,207	3,761,608
Total	49,180,165	48,932,613	98,112,778

Source: UN, *World Population Prospects: The 2010 Revision*.

REGIONS
(population at 2010 census)

	Population
National Capital Region	11,855,975
Ilocos (Region I)	4,748,372
Cagayan Valley (Region II)	3,229,163
Central Luzon (Region III)	10,137,737
CALABARZON (Region IV-A)*	12,609,803
MIMAROPA (Region IV-B)*	2,744,671
Bicol (Region V)	5,420,411
Western Visayas (Region VI)	7,102,438
Central Visayas (Region VII)	6,800,180
Eastern Visayas (Region VIII)	4,101,322
Zamboanga Peninsula (Region IX)†	3,407,353
Northern Mindanao (Region X)	4,297,323
Davao (Region XI)‡	4,468,563
SOCCSKSARGEN (Region XII)§	4,109,571
Cordillera Administrative Region	1,616,867
Autonomous Region of Muslim Mindanao	3,256,140
Caraga	2,429,224
Total	92,337,852‖

* Southern Tagalog region prior to September 2001.

† Western Mindanao region prior to September 2001.

‡ Southern Mindanao region prior to September 2001.

§ Including area designated Central Mindanao region prior to September 2001.

‖ Total includes Filipinos in Philippine embassies, consulates and missions abroad (2,739 persons).

PRINCIPAL TOWNS
(population at 2010 census)

Quezon City*	2,761,720		Bacolod City	511,820
Manila (capital)*	1,652,171		Muntinlupa City*	459,941
Caloocan City*	1,489,040		Iloilo City	424,619
Davao City	1,449,296		Marikina City	424,150
Cebu City	866,171		Pasay City*	392,869
Zamboanga City	807,129		Mandaue City	331,320
Pasig City*	669,773		Mandaluyong City*	328,699
Cagayan de Oro City	602,088		Angeles City	326,336
Parañaque City	588,126		Iligan City	322,821
Valenzuela City	575,356		Baguio City	318,676
Las Piñas City	552,573		Butuan City	309,709
Gen. Santos City	538,086		Cotabato City	271,786
Makati City*	529,039		Olongapo City	221,178

* Part of Metropolitan Manila.

BIRTHS, MARRIAGES AND DEATHS*

	Registered live births		Registered marriages		Registered deaths	
	Number	Rate (per 1,000)	Number	Rate (per 1,000)	Number	Rate (per 1,000)
1997	1,653,236	23.1	562,808	7.9	339,400	4.7
1998	1,632,859	22.3	549,265	7.5	352,992	4.8
1999	1,613,335	21.6	551,445	7.4	347,989	4.7
2000	1,766,440	23.1	577,387	7.5	366,931	4.8
2001	1,714,093	22.0	559,162	7.2	381,834	4.9
2002	1,666,773	21.0	583,167	7.3	396,297	5.0
2003	1,669,442	20.6	593,553	7.3	396,331	4.9
2004	1,710,994	20.7	582,281	7.0	403,191	4.9

* Registration is incomplete. According to UN estimates, the average annual rates per 1,000 were: births 30.2 in 1995–2000, 29.0 in 2000–05, 25.9 in 2005–10; deaths 6.1 in 1995–2000, 6.0 in 2000–05, 5.9 in 2005–10 (Source: UN, *World Population Prospects: The 2010 Revision*).

2008: Registered live births 1,784,316; Registered marriages 486,514.

2009: Registered live births 1,745,585 (18.9 per 1,000); Registered marriages 492,254 (5.3 per 1,000); Registered deaths 480,820 (5.2 per 1,000).

2010: Registered marriages 482,480 (5.1 per 1,000).

Life expectancy (years at birth): 68.8 (males 65.5; females 72.2) in 2011 (Source: World Bank, World Development Indicators database).

ECONOMICALLY ACTIVE POPULATION
('000 persons aged 15 years and over)

	2006	2007	2008
Agriculture, hunting and forestry	10,254	10,342	10,604
Fishing	1,428	1,444	1,426
Mining and quarrying	139	149	158
Manufacturing	3,053	3,059	2,926
Electricity, gas and water	128	135	130
Construction	1,677	1,778	1,834
Wholesale and retail trade; repair of motor vehicles, motorcycles and personal and household goods	6,202	6,354	6,446
Hotels and restaurants	887	907	953
Transport, storage and communications	2,483	2,599	2,590
Financial intermediation	344	359	368
Real estate, renting and business activities	783	885	953
Public administration and defence; compulsory social security	1,485	1,551	1,676
Education	999	1,035	1,071
Health and social work	359	373	391
Other community, social and personal services	801	849	833
Private households with employed persons	1,612	1,740	1,729
Extra-territorial organizations and bodies	2	2	2
Total employed	32,636	33,560	34,089
Unemployed	2,829	2,653	2,716
Total labour force	35,465	36,213	36,805
Males	21,811	22,217	22,673
Females	13,653	13,996	14,131

Source: ILO.

2012 ('000 persons aged 15 years and over, labour force survey at July): Total employed 37,584; Unemployed 2,842; Total labour force 40,426.

Health and Welfare

KEY INDICATORS

Total fertility rate (children per woman, 2010)	3.1
Under-5 mortality rate (per 1,000 live births, 2010)	29
HIV/AIDS (% of persons aged 15–49, 2009)	<0.1
Physicians (per 1,000 head, 2004)	0.58
Hospital beds (per 1,000 head, 2006)	1.3
Health expenditure (2009): US $ per head (PPP)	133
Health expenditure (2009): % of GDP	3.6
Health expenditure (2009): public (% of total)	35.1
Access to water (% of persons, 2010)	92
Access to sanitation (% of persons, 2010)	74
Total carbon dioxide emissions ('000 metric tons, 2008)	83,156.6
Carbon dioxide emissions per head (metric tons, 2008)	0.9
Human Development Index (2011): ranking	112
Human Development Index (2011): value	0.644

For sources and definitions, see explanatory note on p. vi.

Agriculture

PRINCIPAL CROPS
('000 metric tons)

	2009	2010	2011
Rice, paddy	16,266	15,772	16,684
Maize	7,034	6,377	6,971
Potatoes	119	125	121
Sweet potatoes	561	542	516
Cassava (Manioc)	2,044	2,101	2,210
Taro	115	111	111
Yams	23	22	18
Sugar cane*	32,500	34,000	34,000
Beans, dry	28	27	33
Groundnuts, with shell	31	30	30
Coconuts	15,668	15,510	15,245
Oil palm fruit	516	565	541
Cabbages and other brassicas	125	129	125
Tomatoes	199	204	204
Pumpkins, squash and gourds	351	342	318
Aubergines (Eggplants)	201	208	208
Onions, dry	127	135	128
Watermelons	97	110	102
Bananas	9,013	9,101	9,165
Grapefruit and pomelos	34	33	31
Guavas, mangoes and mangosteens	786	844	801
Avocados	23	22	21
Pineapples	2,199	2,169	2,247
Papayas	177	166	158
Coffee, green	96	95	89
Ginger	27	27	28
Tobacco, unmanufactured	36	41	45
Natural rubber†	129	130	141

* FAO estimates.
† Unofficial figures.

Aggregate production ('000 metric tons, may include official, semi-official or estimated data): Total cereals 23,301 in 2009, 22,149 in 2010, 23,656 in 2011; Total roots and tubers 2,878 in 2009, 2,916 in 2010, 2,990 in 2011; Total vegetables (incl. melons) 5,814 in 2009, 6,299 in 2010, 6,205 in 2011; Total fruits (excl. melons) 15,980 in 2009, 16,182 in 2010, 16,139 in 2011.

Source: FAO.

LIVESTOCK
('000 head, year ending 30 June)

	2009	2010	2011
Cattle	2,586	2,571	2,518
Pigs	13,596	13,398	12,303
Buffaloes	3,321	3,270	3,075
Horses*	240	240	240
Goats	4,222	4,178	3,882
Sheep*	30	30	30
Chickens	158,663	158,984	162,813
Ducks	10,577	10,268	10,126

* FAO estimates.

Source: FAO.

LIVESTOCK PRODUCTS
('000 metric tons)

	2009	2010	2011
Cattle meat*	189.5	193.5	197.3
Buffalo meat†	98.9	105.6	105.6
Pig meat*	1,595.7	1,613.5	1,649.3
Chicken meat*	715.0	744.0	777.9
Cows' milk	14.4	15.6	16.2
Hen eggs	368.5	387.3	403.4
Other poultry eggs†	74.0	77.8	77.8

* Unofficial figures.
† FAO estimates.

Source: FAO.

Forestry

ROUNDWOOD REMOVALS
('000 cubic metres, excl. bark)

	2009	2010	2011
Sawlogs, veneer logs and logs for sleepers	689	518	780
Pulpwood	109	35	87
Other industrial wood*	3,000	3,000	3,000
Fuel wood*	12,469	12,362	12,250
Total*	16,267	15,915	16,117

* FAO estimates.

Source: FAO.

SAWNWOOD PRODUCTION
('000 cubic metres, incl. railway sleepers)

	2009	2010	2011
Total (all broadleaved)	304	377	372

Source: FAO.

Fishing

('000 metric tons, live weight)

	2008	2009	2010
Capture	2,561.2	2,602.5	2,611.7
Scads (Decapterus)	414.0	379.0	415.4
Sardinellas	369.2	467.9	448.6
Frigate and bullet tunas	156.3	152.3	149.6
Skipjack tuna	222.0	251.5	228.2
Yellowfin tuna	169.4	152.9	147.7
Indian mackerel	91.3	87.4	93.4
Aquaculture	741.1	737.4	744.7
Nile tilapia	188.1	189.4	168.4
Milkfish	350.8	347.6	349.4
Total catch	3,302.3	3,339.9	3,356.4

Note: Figures exclude aquatic plants ('000 metric tons): 1,667.0 (capture 0.4, aquaculture 1,666.6) in 2008; 1,740.4 (capture 0.4, aquaculture 1,740.0) in 2009; 1,801.8 (capture 0.5, aquaculture 1,801.3) in 2010.

Source: FAO.

Mining

('000 metric tons unless otherwise indicated)

	2008	2009	2010
Coal	3,610	4,687	6,650
Crude petroleum ('000 barrels)	965	2,920	3,059
Chromium ore (gross weight)	15.3	14.3	14.8
Copper ore*	21.2	49.1	58.4
Salt (unrefined)	510	516	558
Nickel ore*	75	144	204
Gold (metric tons)*	35.7	37.0	40.8
Silver (metric tons)*	14.2	33.8	41.0
Dolomite	1,150.0	1,177.0	1,259.2
Limestone†	31,528	33,090	35,540

* Figures refer to the metal content of ores and concentrates.
† Excludes limestone for road construction.

Source: US Geological Survey.

Industry

SELECTED PRODUCTS
('000 metric tons unless otherwise indicated)

	2007	2008	2009
Plywood ('000 cubic metres)	281	235	295
Mechanical wood pulp*	38	38	38
Chemical wood pulp	147	147	147
Paper and paperboard*	1,097	5,000	5,000
Jet fuels	771	716	675
Motor spirit—petrol	1,470	1,410	1,077
Kerosene	166	133	129
Distillate fuel oils	3,659	3,302	2,426
Residual fuel oils	3,206	2,413	1,628
Liquefied petroleum gas	253	305	282
Cement	13,048	13,369	14,865
Smelter (unrefined) copper	220	240	230
Electric energy (million kWh)	59,612	60,821	61,934

* Estimates.

2010: Electric energy (million kWh) 67,743; Cement 15,900; Smelter (unrefined) copper 216; Plywood ('000 cubic metres) 318; Mechanical wood pulp 38 (FAO estimate); Chemical wood pulp 147; Paper and paperboard 5,000 (FAO estimate).

2011: Plywood ('000 cubic metres) 300; Mechanical wood pulp 38 (FAO estimate); Chemical wood pulp 147; Paper and paperboard 5,000 (FAO estimate).

Sources: FAO; UN Industrial Commodity Statistics Database; Asian Development Bank; US Geological Survey.

Finance

CURRENCY AND EXCHANGE RATES

Monetary Units
  100 centavos = 1 Philippine peso.

Sterling, Dollar and Euro Equivalents (31 December 2012)
  £1 sterling = 65.00 pesos;
  US $1 = 41.19 pesos;
  €1 = 54.35 pesos;
  1,000 Philippine pesos = £15.38 = $24.28 = €18.40.

Average Exchange Rate (pesos per US $)
  2010   45.110
  2011   43.313
  2012   42.229

GENERAL BUDGET
(million pesos)

Revenue*	2003	2004	2005†
Tax revenue	537,684	596,408	677,707
Taxes on net income and profits	243,735	278,848	319,102
Taxes on property	712	798	914
Taxes on domestic goods and services	186,784	203,779	225,041
General sales tax	82,444	93,727	109,094
Excises on goods	56,865	51,433	50,699
Taxes on international trade	106,453	112,983	132,650
Non-tax revenue	87,748	79,491	80,239
Bureau of the Treasury income	56,657	40,735	45,369
Fees and charges	29,375	22,993	24,643
Privatization	1,716	1,000	500
Other non-tax revenue	—	14,763	9,726
Total	**625,432**	**675,898**	**757,945**

Expenditure‡	2003	2004	2005†
Economic services	169,881	155,585	159,158
Agriculture	32,932	25,262	25,941
Natural resources and the environment	6,752	6,776	6,803
Trade and industry	2,722	2,833	3,020
Tourism	1,182	1,200	1,412
Power and energy	1,099	1,999	1,512
Water resources, development and flood control	7,007	6,180	6,471
Transport and communications	67,149	54,908	54,949
Other economic services	1,688	7,077	5,982
Allotment to local government units	49,350	49,350	53,068
Social services	237,532	247,888	254,297
Education, culture and training	128,995	133,321	135,470
Health	12,400	12,880	12,927
Social security, welfare and employment	39,096	38,381	40,080
Housing and community development	3,019	2,577	1,739
Land distribution	907	4,284	4,422
Other social services	945	4,275	3,558
Allotment to local government units	52,170	52,170	56,101
Defence	44,439	43,847	44,193
General public services	141,233	137,278	140,650
General administration	43,442	42,254	40,143
Public order and safety	52,565	53,213	54,290
Other general public services	5,746	2,331	3,763
Allotment to local government units	39,480	39,480	42,454
Interest payments	226,408	271,531	301,692
Total	**819,493**	**856,129**	**899,990**

* Excluding grants received (million pesos): 1,198 in 2003; 511 in 2004; 527 in 2005 (forecast).

† Forecasts.

‡ Excluding net lending (million pesos): 5,620 in 2003; 5,500 in 2004; 7,600 in 2005 (forecast).

2010: *Revenue:* Tax revenue 1,093,643; Non-tax revenue 113,877; Total revenue 1,207,520 (excl. grants 406). *Expenditure:* Allotment to local government units 279,552; Interest payments 294,244; Subsidy 21,005; Equity 2,149; Tax expenditures 39,693; Others 876,483; Total expenditure 1,513,126 (excl. net lending 9,258).

2011: *Revenue:* Tax revenue 1,202,066; Non-tax revenue 157,621; Total revenue 1,359,687 (excl. grants 255). *Expenditure:* Allotment to local government units 315,114; Interest payments 278,996; Subsidy 53,705; Equity 12,889; Tax expenditures 25,831; Others 853,106; Total expenditure 1,539,641 (excl. net lending 18,055).

2012: *Revenue:* Tax revenue 1,247,001; Non-tax revenue 161,483; Total revenue 1,408,484 (excl. grants 91). *Expenditure:* Allotment to local government units 273,546; Interest payments 282,337; Subsidy 25,627; Equity 1,170; Others 924,219; Total expenditure 1,506,899 (excl. net lending 28,976).

INTERNATIONAL RESERVES
(US $ million at 31 December)

	2009	2010	2011
Gold*	5,460	7,010	8,013
IMF special drawing rights	1,141	1,121	1,118
Reserve position in IMF	138	251	472
Foreign exchange	37,504	53,991	65,700
Total	**44,243**	**62,373**	**75,303**

* Valued at market-related prices.

Source: IMF, *International Financial Statistics*.

MONEY SUPPLY
('000 million pesos at 31 December)

	2009	2010	2011
Currency outside depository corporations	461.49	478.43	514.93
Transferable deposits	773.88	899.32	1,010.44
Other deposits	3,635.63	3,948.54	4,076.06
Securities other than shares	113.87	201.78	220.02
Broad money	**4,984.88**	**5,528.07**	**5,821.45**

Source: IMF, *International Financial Statistics*.

COST OF LIVING
(Consumer Price Index; base: 2006 = 100)

	2010	2011	2012
Food and non-alcoholic beverages	129.5	136.6	139.8
Alcoholic beverages and tobacco	116.4	122.6	128.7
Clothing (incl. footwear)	114.2	118.4	123.9
Housing, fuel, light and water	114.5	120.3	125.8
Health	120.4	124.3	128.1
Transport	115.6	122.9	125.7
Communication	92.6	92.4	92.5
Recreation and culture	105.2	106.7	109.5
Education	124.3	130.3	136.3
All items (incl. others)	120.4	126.1	130.1

NATIONAL ACCOUNTS
('000 million pesos at current prices)

Expenditure on the Gross Domestic Product

	2010	2011	2012
Government final consumption expenditure	875.3	931.7	1,096.8
Private final consumption expenditure	6,442.0	7,177.0	7,836.2
Gross fixed capital formation	1,847.7	1,857.3	2,076.7
Change in inventories*	1.6	256.7	−23.5
Total domestic expenditure	**9,166.7**	**10,222.7**	**10,986.2**
Exports of goods and services	3,133.5	3,019.7	3,196.2
Less Imports of goods and services	3,296.7	3,506.9	3,587.3
Statistical discrepancy	—	—	−26.7
GDP in purchasers' values	**9,003.5**	**9,735.5**	**10,568.4**
GDP at constant 2000 prices	**5,701.5**	**5,924.4**	**6,314.9**

* Including intellectual property products.

Gross Domestic Product by Economic Activity

	2010	2011	2012
Agriculture, hunting, forestry and fishing	1,108.7	1,245.2	1,256.7
Mining and quarrying	128.7	143.0	114.7
Manufacturing	1,930.8	2,047.7	2,164.1
Electricity, gas and water	321.5	330.3	374.3
Construction	551.2	535.4	628.7
Wholesale and retail trade, restaurants and hotels	1,563.8	1,695.9	1,869.7
Transport, storage and communications	586.2	627.3	689.1
Real estate, renting and business services	979.1	1,115.6	1,252.4
Financial intermediation	622.4	684.1	760.6
Public administration	372.3	392.6	433.6
Other services	838.7	918.3	1,024.5
GDP in purchasers' values	9,003.5	9,735.5	10,568.4

Source: Central Bank of the Philippines, Manila.

BALANCE OF PAYMENTS
(US $ million)

	2009	2010	2011
Exports of goods	29,781	37,555	38,890
Imports of goods	−39,433	−49,883	−55,412
Balance on goods	−9,652	−12,328	−16,522
Exports of services	11,824	15,457	16,451
Imports of services	−8,900	−11,360	−11,876
Balance on goods and services	−6,728	−8,231	−11,947
Primary income received	5,712	6,093	6,987
Primary income paid	−5,905	−5,588	−5,694
Balance on goods, services and primary income	−6,921	−7,726	−10,654
Secondary income received	16,910	17,478	18,503
Secondary income paid	−631	−830	−861
Current balance	9,358	8,922	6,988
Capital account (net)	104	98	171
Direct investment assets	−1,108	−953	−616
Direct investment from liabilities	2,712	1,635	1,869
Portfolio investment assets	−2,715	−2,872	395
Portfolio investment liabilities	2,090	9,522	5,129
Financial derivatives and employee stock options assets	403	429	1,541
Financial derivatives and employee stock options liabilities	−371	−620	−539
Other investment assets	−1,967	−2,773	−3,252
Other investment liabilities	−2,784	5,192	529
Net errors and omissions	398	−1,987	−2,042
Reserves and related items	6,119	16,593	10,173

Source: IMF, *International Financial Statistics*.

External Trade

PRINCIPAL COMMODITIES
(distribution by SITC, US $ million)

Imports c.i.f.	2008	2009	2010
Food and live animals	5,866.2	4,806.9	5,911.8
Mineral fuels, lubricants, etc.	12,803.6	7,654.2	9,840.9
Petroleum, petroleum products, etc.	11,582.0	6,635.5	8,757.0
Crude petroleum oils, etc.	7,683.6	3,354.6	5,504.6
Chemicals and related products	5,166.6	4,482.7	5,554.1
Basic manufactures	4,893.9	3,639.5	4,670.0
Textile yarn, fabrics, etc.	872.5	604.2	648.0
Machinery and transport equipment	27,396.9	21,540.8	27,436.6
Office machines and automatic data-processing equipment	4,757.6	3,989.4	4,424.8
Parts and accessories for office machines, etc.	4,435.4	3,663.6	4,094.3

Imports c.i.f.—*continued*	2008	2009	2010
Telecommunications and sound equipment	1,297.8	1,200.8	1,189.4
Other electrical machinery, apparatus, etc.	16,118.5	11,638.7	14,996.3
Thermionic valves, tubes, etc.	14,126.8	9,897.7	12,703.2
Electronic microcircuits	5,123.8	4,243.8	5,411.8
Parts for electronic microcircuits	8,693.4	5,434.7	6,910.0
Road vehicles and parts (excl. tyres, engines and electrical parts)	2,093.8	2,044.4	2,863.6
Miscellaneous manufactured articles	1,730.9	1,603.5	1,927.1
Total (incl. others)	60,419.7	45,877.7	58,228.6

Exports f.o.b.	2008	2009	2010
Food and live animals	2,340.6	2,079.5	2,157.8
Basic manufactures	3,958.3	2,678.1	3,354.3
Machinery and transport equipment	33,030.8	26,623.7	36,090.2
Office machines and automatic data-processing equipment	9,016.4	8,210.1	10,297.3
Automatic data-processing machines and units	6,852.0	5,753.1	8,207.0
Digital automatic data-processing machines and units thereof	1,447.1	1,397.2	1,756.3
Digital central storage units, separately consigned	1,651.4	1,106.0	1,765.9
Parts and accessories for data-processing machines	2,013.4	2,346.9	1,981.7
Telecommunications and sound equipment	1,061.9	841.5	1,122.3
Other electrical machinery, apparatus, etc.	19,741.5	14,710.8	21,480.0
Thermionic valves, tubes, etc.	15,572.7	11,066.7	16,546.2
Diodes, transistors, etc.	1,789.3	1,458.0	2,591.1
Electronic microcircuits	13,165.2	8,815.8	13,003.3
Road vehicles and parts (excl. tyres, engines and electrical parts)	2,213.6	1,567.3	1,860.8
Miscellaneous manufactured articles	4,090.5	3,381.0	3,855.0
Clothing and accessories (excl. footwear)	1,979.0	1,534.1	1,764.4
Total (incl. others)	49,077.5	38,435.8	51,431.7

Source: UN, *International Trade Statistics Yearbook*.

2011 (US $ million): *Imports:* Capital goods 15,280.1; Raw materials and intermediate goods 24,834.6; Mineral fuels, lubricants and related materials 12,552.0; Consumer goods 6,985.9; Special transactions 843.1; Total 60,495.8. *Exports:* Electronic products 23,795.4 (Semiconductor devices 17,782.0; Electronic data-processing devices 4,242.0); Articles of apparel and clothing accessories 1,895.7; Wiring sets for vehicles, aircraft and ships 1,109.8; Coconut oil 1,425.4; Woodcraft and furniture 1,848.0; Metal components 785.1; Machinery and transport equpment 2,806.2; Total (incl. others) 48,304.9.

2012 (US $ million): *Imports:* Capital goods 17,391.7; Raw materials and intermediate goods 22,283.6; Mineral fuels, lubricants and related materials 13,665.3; Consumer goods 7,690.1; Special transactions 629.1; Total 61,659.8. *Exports:* Electronic products 22,557.0 (Semiconductor devices 17,469.7; Electronic data-processing devices 3,037.0); Articles of apparel and clothing accessories 1,572.8; Wiring sets for vehicles, aircraft and ships 1,446.5; Coconut oil 1,016.1; Woodcraft and furniture 2,339.5; Metal components 1,963.6; Machinery and transport equpment 5,310.1; Total (incl. others) 51,994.0.

PRINCIPAL TRADING PARTNERS
(US $ million)

Imports c.i.f.	2008	2009	2010
Australia	956.8	784.7	902.1
China, People's Republic	4,561.1	4,060.4	4,933.9
France (incl. Monaco)	821.3	546.4	692.4
Germany	1,148.4	1,008.0	1,182.3
Hong Kong	2,101.6	1,547.6	1,563.8
India	654.3	532.3	565.8
Indonesia	1,602.3	1,915.1	2,399.7
Iran	292.7	106.0	115.8
Ireland	644.2	185.4	321.7
Japan	7,121.9	5,764.9	7,304.7
Korea, Republic	3,128.5	3,160.9	4,034.4
Malaysia	2,583.2	1,787.1	2,562.5
Saudi Arabia	5,154.4	1,558.5	2,451.3
Singapore	6,217.9	3,931.1	5,439.5
Thailand	2,997.6	2,595.7	4,098.4
Viet Nam	1,800.7	1,401.7	1,750.8
United Arab Emirates	1,377.9	807.6	1,413.8
USA	7,738.1	5,488.2	6,292.5
Total (incl. others)	60,419.7	45,877.7	58,228.6

Exports f.o.b.	2008	2009	2010
Australia	470.8	296.3	348.8
Belgium	639.8	492.5	347.0
China, People's Republic	5,469.2	2,933.9	5,701.5
Germany	2,440.1	2,505.6	2,657.3
Hong Kong	4,987.5	3,213.3	4,334.0
Indonesia	602.7	382.7	449.2
Japan	7,707.1	6,208.4	7,827.5
Korea, Republic	2,522.5	1,828.2	2,228.2
Malaysia	1,957.6	1,359.9	1,396.5
Netherlands	3,708.4	3,743.5	2,428.9
Singapore	2,606.7	2,477.3	7,331.2
Thailand	1,509.0	1,236.1	1,784.2
United Kingdom	482.8	296.7	395.0
USA	8,216.4	6,797.1	7,568.2
Total (incl. others)	49,077.5	38,435.8	51,431.7

Source: UN, *International Trade Statistics Yearbook*.

2011 (US $ million): *Imports:* China, People's Republic 6,085.1; Indonesia 2,459.2; Japan 6,516.4; Korea, Republic 4,419.5; Malaysia 2,597.6; Singapore 4,899.5; Taiwan 4,209.1; Thailand 3,463.0; United Arab Emirates 1,729.6; USA 6,535.5; Total (incl. others) 60,495.8. *Exports:* China, People's Republic 6,237.3; Germany 1,729.8; Hong Kong 3,701.5; Japan 8,886.1; Korea, Republic 2,237.2; Malaysia 1,099.1; Singapore 4,278.6; Taiwan 1,993.2; Thailand 1,906.0; USA 7,101.9; Total (incl. others) 48,304.9.

2012 (US $ million): *Imports:* China, People's Republic 6,663.7; Indonesia 2,732.3; Japan 6,446.0; Korea, Republic 4,504.1; Malaysia 2,407.4; Singapore 4,402.5; Taiwan 4,832.7; Thailand 3,446.6; United Arab Emirates 1,944.5; USA 7,118.2; Total (incl. others) 61,659.8. *Exports:* China, People's Republic 6,159.8; Germany 1,956.6; Hong Kong 4,776.1; Japan 9,881.3; Korea, Republic 2,862.0; Malaysia 1,016.9; Singapore 4,863.9; Taiwan 1,915.3; Thailand 2,446.0; USA 7,395.4; Total (incl. others) 51,994.0.

Transport

RAILWAYS
(traffic)

	2002	2003	2004
Passenger-km (million)	93	83	84
Freight ton-km ('000)	63	69	76

Source: UN, *Statistical Yearbook*.

ROAD TRAFFIC
(registered motor vehicles)

	2008	2009	2010
Passenger cars	761,919	780,252	808,583
Utility vehicles	1,595,162	1,643,878	1,700,795
Sports utility vehicles (SUVs)	198,497	221,980	261,213
Buses	29,745	33,033	34,933
Trucks	296,276	311,582	317,903
Motorcycles and mopeds*	2,982,511	3,200,968	3,482,149
Trailers	27,162	28,740	29,279

* Including tricycles.

Source: Land Transportation Office, Manila.

SHIPPING

Flag Registered Fleet
(at 31 December)

	2010	2011	2012
Number of vessels	985	988	986
Total displacement ('000 grt)	4,964.4	4,816.3	4,320.8

Source: Lloyd's List Intelligence (www.lloydslistintelligence.com).

International Sea-borne Shipping
(freight traffic)

	1994	1995	1996
Vessels ('000 net registered tons):			
entered	53,453	61,298	n.a.
cleared	53,841	61,313	n.a.
Goods ('000 metric tons):			
loaded	14,581	16,658	15,687
unloaded	38,222	42,418	51,830

CIVIL AVIATION
(traffic on scheduled services)

	2007	2008	2009
Kilometres flown (million)	92	101	108
Passengers carried ('000)	8,818	9,508	10,481
Passenger-km (million)	18,084	18,698	18,254
Total ton-km (million)	2,142	2,167	2,005

Source: UN, *Statistical Yearbook*.

2010 ('000): Passengers carried 18,933 (Source: World Bank, World Development Indicators database).

Tourism

FOREIGN VISITOR ARRIVALS

Country of residence	2009	2010	2011
Australia	132,330	147,469	170,736
Canada	99,012	106,345	117,423
China, People's Republic	155,019	187,446	243,137
Germany	55,912	58,725	61,193
Hong Kong	122,786	133,746	112,106
Japan	324,980	358,744	375,496
Korea, Republic	497,936	740,622	925,204
Malaysia	68,679	79,694	91,752
Singapore	98,305	121,083	137,802
Taiwan	102,274	142,455	181,738
United Kingdom	91,009	96,925	104,466
USA	582,537	600,165	624,527
Total (incl. others)*	3,017,099	3,520,471	3,917,400

* Including Philippine nationals permanently resident abroad.

Source: Department of Tourism, Manila.

Tourism receipts (US $ million, excl. passenger transport): 2,330 in 2009; 2,630 in 2010; 3,152 in 2011 (provisional) (Source: World Tourism Organization).

Communications Media

	2009	2010	2011
Telephones ('000 main lines in use)	4,100.0	3,335.4	3,556.0
Mobile cellular telephones ('000 subscribers)	75,586.6	83,150.1	94,189.8
Internet subscribers ('000) . .	3,600.0	4,320.0	5,184.0
Broadband subscribers ('000) . .	1,722.4	1,722.4	1,791.0

Personal computers: 6,300,000 (72.3 per 1,000 persons) in 2006.

Source: International Telecommunication Union.

Education

(2010/11 unless otherwise stated, estimates)

	Institutions	Teachers	Pupils
Pre-primary . . . . . }	45,964	413,872	{ 1,650,232
Primary schools . }			14,166,066
Secondary schools . .	12,950	201,435	6,954,946
University and other tertiary education* . .	1,619	111,225	2,402,315

* 2004/05 figures.

Sources: Department of Education; Commission on Higher Education.

Pupil-teacher ratio (primary education, UNESCO estimate): 31.4 in 2008/09 (Source: UNESCO Institute for Statistics).

Adult literacy rate (UNESCO estimates): 95.4% (males 95.0%; females 95.8%) in 2008 (Source: UNESCO Institute for Statistics).

Directory

The Government

HEAD OF STATE

President: BENIGNO AQUINO, III (assumed office 30 June 2010).
Vice-President: JEJOMAR BINAY.

CABINET
(May 2013)

The Cabinet comprises members of the Liberal Party and numerous unaffiliated representatives of the public and private sectors.

Executive Secretary: PAQUITO OCHOA, Jr.
Secretary of the Interior and Local Government: MAR ROXAS.
Secretary of Foreign Affairs: ALBERT DEL ROSARIO.
Secretary of Finance: CESAR PURISIMA.
Secretary of Justice: LEILA L. DE LIMA.
Secretary of National Defense: VOLTAIRE GAZMIN.
Secretary of Education: Brother ARMIN A. LUISTRO.
Secretary of the Budget and Management: FLORENCIO ABAD.
Secretary of Agriculture: PROCESO V. ALCALA.
Secretary of Energy: CARLOS JERICHO PETILLA.
Secretary of the Environment and Natural Resources: RAMON PAJE.
Secretary of Health: Dr ENRIQUE T. ONA.
Secretary of Labor and Employment: ROSALINDA BALDOZ.
Secretary of Public Works and Highways: ROGELIO SINGSON.
Secretary of Science and Technology: Dr MARIO G. MONTEJO.
Secretary of Social Welfare and Development: CORAZON SOLIMAN.
Secretary of Tourism: RAMON JIMENEZ, Jr.
Secretary of Trade and Industry: GREGORY L. DOMINGO.
Secretary of Transportation and Communications: MANUEL ROXAS, II.
Secretary of Agrarian Reform: VIRGILIO DE LOS REYES.
Secretary of Presidential Communications Development and Strategic Planning: RAMON CARANDANG.
Secretary of the Presidential Communications Operations Office: HERMINIO COLOMA, Jr.
Director-General of the National Economic and Development Authority: ARSENIO M. BALISACAN.

There are a further 11 officials of cabinet rank.

MINISTRIES

Office of the President: New Exec. Bldg, Malacañang Palace Compound, J. P. Laurel St, San Miguel, Metro Manila; tel. (2) 7356201; fax (2) 9293968; e-mail op@president.gov.ph; internet www.president.gov.ph.

Office of the Vice-President: PNB Financial Center, 7th Floor, President Diosdado Macapagal Blvd, Pasay City, 1300 Metro Manila; tel. (2) 8333311; fax (2) 8316676; e-mail vp@ovp.gov.ph; internet www.ovp.gov.ph.

Department of Agrarian Reform: DAR Bldg, Elliptical Rd, Diliman, Quezon City, Metro Manila; tel. (2) 9287031; fax (2) 9293088; e-mail dar.gov.ph@gmail.com; internet www.dar.gov.ph.

Department of Agriculture: DA Bldg, 4th Floor, Elliptical Rd, Diliman, Quezon City, Metro Manila; tel. (2) 9288756; fax (2) 9203987; e-mail web@da.gov.ph; internet www.da.gov.ph.

Department of the Budget and Management: DBM Bldg, Gen. Solano St, Malacañang, San Miguel, Metro Manila; tel. (2) 7332993; fax (2) 7354809; e-mail fbabad@dbm.gov.ph; internet www.dbm.gov.ph.

Department of Education: DepED Complex, Meralco Ave, Pasig City, 1600 Metro Manila; tel. (2) 6361663; fax (2) 6388634; e-mail action@deped.gov.ph; internet www.deped.gov.ph.

Department of Energy: Energy Center, Merritt Rd, Fort Bonifacio, Taguig, 1201 Metro Manila; tel. and fax (2) 8402278; e-mail info@doe.gov.ph; internet www.doe.gov.ph.

Department of the Environment and Natural Resources: DENR Bldg, Visayas Ave, Diliman, Quezon City, 1100 Metro Manila; tel. (2) 9296626; fax (2) 9204352; e-mail osec@denr.gov.ph; internet www.denr.gov.ph.

Department of Finance: DOF Bldg, BSP Complex, Roxas Blvd, 1004 Metro Manila; tel. (2) 5236051; fax (2) 5268474; e-mail helpdesk@dof.gov.ph; internet www.dof.gov.ph.

Department of Foreign Affairs: DFA Bldg, 2330 Roxas Blvd, Pasay City, 1330 Metro Manila; tel. (2) 8344000; fax (2) 8321597; e-mail webmaster@dfa.gov.ph; internet www.dfa.gov.ph.

Department of Health: San Lazaro Compound, Rizal Ave, Santa Cruz, 1003 Metro Manila; tel. (2) 7438301; fax (2) 7431823; e-mail ftduque@co.doh.gov.ph; internet www.doh.gov.ph.

Department of the Interior and Local Government: A. Francisco Gold Condominium II, Epifanio de los Santos Ave, cnr Mapagmahal St, Diliman, Quezon City, 1100 Metro Manila; tel. (2) 9250330; fax (2) 9250332; e-mail marroxas@dilg.gov.ph; internet www.dilg.gov.ph.

Department of Justice: Padre Faura St, Ermita, 1000 Metro Manila; tel. (2) 5238481; fax (2) 5267643; e-mail communications@doj.gov.ph; internet www.doj.gov.ph.

Department of Labor and Employment: DOLE Exec. Bldg, 7th Floor, Muralla Wing, Muralla St, Intramuros, 1002 Metro Manila; tel. (2) 5278000; fax (2) 5273494; e-mail osec@dole.gov.ph; internet www.dole.gov.ph.

Department of National Defense: DND Bldg, 3rd Floor, Camp Aguinaldo, Quezon City, 1110 Metro Manila; tel. (2) 9116402; fax (2) 9111651; e-mail webmaster@dnd.gov.ph; internet www.dnd.gov.ph.

Department of Public Works and Highways: DPWH Bldg, Bonifacio Dr., Port Area, Metro Manila; tel. (2) 3043000; fax (2) 5275635; e-mail bonoan.manuel@dpwh.gov.ph; internet www.dpwh.gov.ph.

Department of Science and Technology: DOST Compound, Gen. Santos Ave, Bicutan, Taguig, 1631 Metro Manila; tel. (2) 8372071; fax (2) 8378937; e-mail efa@dost.gov.ph; internet www.dost.gov.ph.

Department of Social Welfare and Development: Batasang Pambansa, Constitution Hills, Quezon City, Metro Manila; tel. (2) 9318101; fax (2) 9318191; e-mail lfp@dswd.gov.ph; internet www.dswd.gov.ph.

Department of Tourism: T. F. Valencia Circle, T. M. Kalaw St, Rizal Park, Metro Manila; tel. (2) 5238411; fax (2) 5238411; e-mail webmaster@tourism.gov.ph; internet www.wowphilippines.com.ph.

Department of Trade and Industry: Industry and Investments Bldg, 385 Sen. Gil J. Puyat Ave, Buendia, Makati City, 1200 Metro Manila; tel. (2) 7513330; fax (2) 8956487; e-mail mis@dti.dti.gov.ph; internet www.dti.gov.ph.

Department of Transportation and Communications: Columbia Tower, 17th Floor, Ortigas Ave, Mandaluyong City, 1555 Metro Manila; tel. (2) 7277960; fax (2) 7234925; e-mail webmaster@dotc.gov .ph; internet www.dotc.gov.ph.

National Economic and Development Authority (NEDA—Department of Socio-Economic Planning): NEDA-sa-Pasig Bldg, 12 St Josemaria Escriva Dr., Ortigas Center, Pasig City, 1605 Metro Manila; tel. (2) 6310945; fax (2) 6313282; e-mail info@ neda.gov.ph; internet www.neda.gov.ph.

Philippine Information Agency (Office of the Press Secretary): Media Center Bldg, Visayas Ave, Diliman, Quezon City, 1101 Metro Manila; tel. (2) 9204345; fax (2) 9204390; e-mail angie .villapando@gmail.com; internet www.pia.gov.ph.

President and Legislature

PRESIDENT

Election, 10 May 2010

Candidate	Votes	% of votes
Benigno Aquino III (Liberal Party—LP) .	15,208,678	41.87
Joseph Estrada (Pwersa ng Masang Pilipino—PMP)	9,487,837	26.12
Manuel Villar (Nacionalista Party—NP) .	5,573,835	15.35
Gilberto Teodoro (Lakas-Kampi-CMD)* .	4,095,839	11.28
Eduardo Villanueva (Bangon Pilipinas) .	1,125,878	3.10
Richard Gordon (Bagumbayan-VNP) . .	501,727	1.38
Vetellano Acosta (Kilusang Bagong Lipunan—KBL)	181,985†	0.50
Nicanor Perlas (Independent) . . .	54,575	0.15
Jamby Madrigal (Independent) . . .	46,489	0.13
John Carlos de los Reyes (Ang Kapatiran).	44,244	0.12
Total	36,321,087	100.00

* Lakas-Kampi-CMD was renamed Lakas-CMD in May 2012.
† Candidate was disqualified after ballot papers had been printed; all votes for Vetellano Acosta were therefore deemed invalid.

THE CONGRESS OF THE PHILIPPINES

Senate

President of the Senate: JUAN PONCE ENRILE.

Elections for 12 of the 24 seats were held on 10 May 2010. The LP and the NP-Nationalist People's Coalition (NPC) alliance both won three seats, while Lakas-Kampi-CMD and the PMP secured two seats each, and the People's Reform Party took one. The remaining seat was secured by an independent candidate. Elections for 12 of the 24 seats were due to take place on 13 May 2014.

House of Representatives

Speaker of the House: FELICIANO BELMONTE.

A general election was due to take place on 13 May 2013.

General Election, 10 May 2010

	Seats
Lakas-Kampi-CMD*	107
Liberal Party (LP)	45
Nacionalista Party (NP)	26
Independents	7
Pwersa ng Masang Pilipino (PMP)	6
Others	38
Party lists†	57‡
Total	286

* Lakas-Kampi-CMD was renamed Lakas-CMD in May 2012.
† Reserved for members of minority and cause-orientated groups allocated under the concurrent party list elections.
‡ Including one unoccupied seat owing to a disqualification process.

Autonomous Region

MUSLIM MINDANAO

The Autonomous Region of Muslim Mindanao (ARMM) originally comprised the provinces of Lanao del Sur, Maguindanao, Tawi-Tawi and Sulu. The Region was granted autonomy in November 1989. Elections took place in February 1990, and the formal transfer of limited executive powers took place in October of that year. In August 2001 a plebiscite was conducted in 11 provinces and 14 cities in Mindanao to determine whether or not they would become members of the ARMM. The city of Marawi and the province of Basilan subsequently joined the Region. The Regional Legislative Assembly was expanded to 24 seats, from 21 previously, at elections held on 8 August 2005. A total of six candidates contested the concurrent gubernatorial election; Zaldy Ampatuan, the candidate of Lakas ng EDSA-Christian Muslim Democrats (Lakas-CMD), won an estimated 63.7% of the votes cast, defeating Mahid Mutilan of the Ompia Party, a Muslim grouping, and Ibrahim Paglas of the Liberal Party, who received 24.3% and 11.8% of the votes respectively. Ampatuan was re-elected Governor on 11 August 2008. However, owing to his alleged involvement in the killing of 57 people on Mindanao in November 2009, Ampatuan was subsequently suspended from office and replaced by his deputy, Ansaruddin Adiong, in an acting capacity. In December 2011 Mujib Hataman was appointed as a caretaker Governor, pending elections scheduled to be held in May 2013.

In October 2012 the Government and the rebel Moro Islamic Liberation Front (MILF—which had abandoned its demand for the establishment of an independent Islamic state in Mindanao) concluded a framework peace agreement, providing for the replacement of the ARMM with a new autonomous political entity with enhanced political and economic powers, to be named Bangsamoro. The territory of Bangsamoro would comprise the existing geographical area of the ARMM, several municipalities and barangays (districts) that had voted in favour of inclusion in the ARMM in the 2001 plebiscite and the cities of Cotabato and Isabela. A comprehensive accord had yet to be reached at early May 2013, with the MILF and the Government having agreed to postpone further negotiations until after that month's elections, although a 15-member Transition Commission had been appointed in February.

Governor: MUJIB HATAMAN (acting).

Vice-Governor: BAINON KARON (acting).

Election Commission

Commission on Elections (COMELEC): Postigo St, Intramuros, 1002 Metro Manila; tel. (2) 5275581; e-mail asd@comelec.gov.ph; internet www.comelec.gov.ph; f. 1940; Chair. SIXTO BRILLANTES, Jr.

Political Organizations

Akbayan (Citizens' Action Party): 36B Madasalin St, Teacher's Village West, Diliman, Quezon City, 1101 Metro Manila; tel. (2) 4336933; fax (2) 9252936; e-mail secretariat@akbayan.org; internet www.akbayan.org.ph; f. 1998; left-wing party list; Chair. RONALD LLAMAS; Pres. CONRAD CASTILLO; Sec.-Gen. DANNY EDRALIN.

Aksyon Demokratiko (Democratic Action Party): 16th Floor, Strata 2000 Bldg, F. Ortigas Jr Rd, Ortigas Center, Pasig City, 1600 Metro Manila; tel. (2) 6385381; fax (2) 6343072; e-mail senator@ raulroco.com; f. 1997; est. to support presidential candidacy of RAUL ROCO; joined Alyansa ng Pag-asa in 2003 to contest 2004 elections; Chair. and Pres. HERMINIO S. AQUINO; Sec.-Gen. ERNESTO M. RAMEL, Jr.

Bagumbayan-Volunteers for a New Philippines (Bagumbayan-VNP): Unit 3C, Classica Condominium I, H. V. Dela Costa St, Makati City, Metro Manila; tel. (2) 8131257; e-mail join@ bagumbayan-vnp.com; f. 2009; Chair. RICHARD GORDON; Pres. LEON B. HERRERA.

Bangon Pilipinas (Rise Philippines): 8th Floor, Dominion Bldg, 833 Arnaiz Ave, Legaspi Village, Makati City, 1200 Metro Manila; tel. (2) 8113355; fax (2) 8111110; e-mail feedback@bangonpilipinas .org; internet bangonpilipinas.com; Pres. and Chair. EDUARDO VILLANUEVA.

Bayan Muna (People First): 153 Scout Rallos St, Kamuning, Quezon City, 1103 Metro Manila; tel. (2) 4251045; fax (2) 9213473; e-mail information@bayanmuna.net; internet www.bayanmuna .net; f. 1999; Pres. SATUR C. OCAMPO; Chair. Dr REYNALDO LESACA, Jr.

Centrist Democratic Party of the Philippines (Ang Partido ng Tunay na Demokrasya—CDP): Mille Bldg, 2nd Floor, 335-337 Gil Puyat Ave, Pasay City, Metro Manila; tel. (2) 3852669; e-mail info@ cdp.ph; internet www.cdp.ph; f. 2012; Chair. LITO MONICA

LORENZANA; Pres. RUFUS RODRIGUEZ; Sec.-Gen. LORELYN GALARRITA TURTOSA-DUMAUG.

Kilusang Bagong Lipunan (KBL) (New Society Movement): Metro Manila; f. 1978 by Pres. MARCOS and fmr mems of the Nacionalista Party; Chair. IMELDA MARCOS.

Laban ng Demokratikong Pilipino (LDP) (Fight of Democratic Filipinos): 3-B, Osmena Bldg, 1991 A. Mabini St, Malate, Metro Manila; internet www.edangara.com; f. 1987; reorg. 1988 as an alliance of Lakas ng Bansa and a conservative faction of the PDP-Laban Party; mem. of Lapian ng Masang Pilipino (LAMP) until Jan. 2001; split into two factions, led by EDGARDO ANGARA and AGAPITO AQUINO, to contest 2004 elections; Angara faction joined Koalisyon ng Nagkakaisang Pilipino (KNP) in Dec. 2003 to support presidential candidacy of FERNANDO POE, Jr; Aquino faction supported presidential candidacy of PANFILO LACSON; Pres. EDGARDO ANGARA.

Lakas-CMD: Unit AB, Lower Penthouse, One Burgundy Plaza Condominium, 307 Katipunan Ave, Loyola Heights, Quezon City; tel. (2) 4330115; internet www.lakaskampicmd.org.ph; f. 2009; est. by merger of Lakas ng EDSA-Christian Muslim Democrats and Kabalikat ng Malayang Pilipino (Kampi); name reverted to Lakas-CMD in 2012; Nat. Chair. RAMON BONG REVILLA, Jr; Nat. Pres. FERDINAND MARTIN ROMUALDEZ.

Liberal Party (LP): Expo Centro, EDSA cnr McArthur Ave, Araneta Centre, Cubao City, Metro Manila; tel. (2) 7093817; fax (2) 7093829; e-mail liberalpartyphils@gmail.com; f. 1946; represents centre-liberal opinion of the fmr Nacionalista Party, which split in 1946; joined Koalisyon ng Katapatan at Karanasan sa Kinabukasan (K-4) in Jan. 2004 to contest 2004 elections; Chair. BENIGNO S. AQUINO III; Pres. MANUEL ROXAS, II.

Nacionalista Party (NP): 2nd Floor, Starmall EDSA, cnr Shaw Blvd, Mandaluyong City, 1552 Metro Manila; tel. (2) 7224727; fax (2) 7274223; e-mail secretariat@nacionalistaparty.com; internet www.nacionalistaparty.com; formed alliance with NPC in April 2010 to contest election in May; Pres. MANUEL VILLAR; Sec.-Gen. ALAN PETER CAYETANO.

Nationalist People's Coalition (NPC): 8 Bouganvilla St, cnr Balete Dr., Mariana, Quezon City, 1112 Metro Manila; tel. (2) 5847518; fax (2) 5847568; e-mail npcparty@gmail.com; internet npcparty.org; f. 1991; breakaway faction of the NP, with which it formed an alliance in April 2010, in advance of the legislative election in May; mem. of Lapian ng Masang Pilipino (LAMP) from 1997 until Jan. 2001; Chair. FAUSTINO DY, Jr; Pres. FRISCO SAN JUAN.

Partido Demokratiko Pilipino-Lakas Ng Bayan (PDP-Laban): 721 J. P. Rizal St, Makati City, Metro Manila; internet www.pdplaban.org; tel. (2) 8901792; fax (2) 8900858; f. 1983; est. following merger of Pilipino Democratic Party (f. 1982 by fmr mems of the Mindanao Alliance) and Laban (Lakas ng Bayan—People's Power Movement, f. 1978 and led by BENIGNO S. AQUINO, Jr, until his assassination in 1983); centrist; formally dissolved in Sept. 1988, following formation of the LDP, but a faction continued to function as a political movement; formed United Nationalist Alliance (UNA) alliance with the PMP in advance of the May 2013 elections; Chair. JEJOMAR BINAY; Pres. AQUILINO PIMENTEL, III; Sec.-Gen. JOSE DE VENECIA, III.

Partido Demokratiko Sosyalista ng Pilipinas (PDSP) (Philippine Democratic Socialist Party): 45 Melchor St, Varsity Hills, Quezon City, Metro Manila; tel. and fax (2) 4161325; fax 9286678; e-mail secretariat@pdsp.net; internet pdsp.net; f. 1981; formed by mems of the Batasang Pambansa allied to the Nacionalista (Roy faction), Pusyon Visaya and Mindanao Alliance parties; joined People Power Coalition (PPC) in Feb. 2001; Chair. NORBERTO GONZALES.

Partido ng Manggagawang Pilipino (Filipino Workers' Party): e-mail pinoy_bolshevik@yahoo.com; internet manggagawang pilipino.tripod.com; f. 2002; est. by fmr supporters of the CPP.

Partido para sa Demokratikong Reporma: Chateau Bldg, Pasig City, Metro Manila; joined People Power Coalition (PPC) in Feb. 2001; Chair. RENATO DE VILLA; Sec.-Gen. RAFAEL COLET.

People's Reform Party (PRP): Narsan Bldg, 4th Floor, 3 West Fourth St, West Triangle Quezon Ave, Quezon City, Metro Manila; e-mail miriam@miriam.com.ph; f. 1991; formed by MIRIAM DEFENSOR SANTIAGO to support her candidacy in the 1992 presidential election; Santiago re-elected to Senate for a third term in 2010; Pres. MIRIAM DEFENSOR SANTIAGO.

Probinsya Muna Development Initiatives (PROMDI): 7 Pasteur St, Lahug, Cebu City; tel. (32) 2326692; fax (32) 2313609; f. 1997; Leader EMILIO ('LITO') OSMEÑA.

Pwersa ng Masang Pilipino (PMP): 409 Shaw Bld, Mandaluyong City, Metro Manila; e-mail pmp_power@yahoo.com; formed United Nationalist Alliance (UNA) alliance with PDP-Laban in advance of the May 2013 elections; Pres. JOSEPH EJERCITO ESTRADA; Chair. JUAN PONCE ENRILE; Sec.-Gen. JINGGOY ESTRADA.

United Negros Alliance (UNA): Negros Occidental; formed alliance with the NPC in advance of the May 2010 elections; Chair. ALFREDO MARAÑON, Jr.

The following organizations are, or have been, in conflict with the Government:

Abu Sayyaf (Bearer of the Sword): Mindanao; radical Islamist group seeking the establishment of an Islamic state in Mindanao; breakaway grouping of the MILF; est. strength 1,500 (2000); Leader RADULAN SAHIRON.

Alex Boncayao Brigade (ABB): communist urban guerrilla group, fmrly linked to CPP; formed alliance with Revolutionary Proletarian Party in 1997; est. strength 500 (April 2001); Leader NILO DE LA CRUZ.

Islamic Command Council (ICC): Mindanao; splinter group of MNLF; Leader MELHAM ALAM.

Maranao Islamic Statehood Movement: Mindanao; f. 1998; armed grouping seeking the establishment of an Islamic state in Mindanao.

Mindanao Independence Movement (MIM): Mindanao; claims a membership of 1m; Leader REUBEN CANOY.

Moro Islamic Liberation Front (MILF): Camp Abubakar, Lanao del Sur, Mindanao; comprises a faction that broke away from the MNLF in 1978; its armed wing, the Bangsa Moro Islamic Armed Forces, has c. 12,500 armed regulars; having abandoned its demand for the establishment of an Islamic state in Mindanao, the MILF concluded a framework peace agreement with the Govt in Oct. 2012, providing for the creation of a new autonomous political entity with enhanced political and economic powers to replace the ARMM; Chair. Al-Haj MURAD EBRAHIM.

Moro Islamic Reform Group: Mindanao; breakaway faction from MNLF; est. strength of 200 in 2000.

Moro National Liberation Front (MNLF): internet mnlf.net; seeks autonomy for Muslim communities in Mindanao; signed a peace agreement with the Govt in Sept. 1996; its armed wing, the Bangsa Moro Army, comprised an est. 10,000 mems in 2000; Chair. and Pres. of Cen. Cttee Dr NUR MISUARI.

Moro National Liberation Front—Islamic Command Council (MNLF—ICC): Basak, Lanao del Sur; f. 2000; Islamist separatist movement committed to urban guerrilla warfare; breakaway faction from MNLF.

National Democratic Front (NDF): a left-wing alliance of 14 mem. groups; Chair. MARIANA OROSA; Spokesman FIDEL V. AGCAOILI.

The NDF includes:

Communist Party of the Philippines (CPP): f. 1968; breakaway faction of the Partido Komunista ng Pilipinas (PKP, f. 1930); legalized Sept. 1992; in July 1993 the Metro Manila-Rizal and Visayas regional committees, controlling 40% of total CPP membership (est. 15,000 in 1994), split from the Central Committee; Chair. JOSE MARIA SISON; Gen. Sec. BENITO TIAMZON.

New People's Army (NPA): f. 1969; est. as the military wing of the CPP; based in central Luzon, but operates throughout the Philippines; est. strength 9,500; Leader JOVENCIO BALWEG; Spokesman GREGORIO ROSAL.

Revolutionary Proletarian Party: Metro Manila; f. 1996; comprises mems of the Metro Manila-Rizal and Visayas regional committees, which broke away from the CPP in 1993; has a front organization called the Bukluran ng Manggagawang Pilipino (Association of Filipino Workers); Leader ARTURO TABARA.

National Unity Party (NUP): Metro Manila; e-mail feedback@nup.ph; internet www.nup.ph; f. 2011; est. by fmr members of Lakas-Kampi-CMD (mostly fmr members of Kampi); Chair. PABLO P. GARCIA; Nat. Pres. RODOLFO ANTONINO; Sec.-Gen. ROGER G. MERCADO.

Rajah Solaiman Movement (RSM): Mindanao; f. 2002; radical Islamist group seeking to establish an Islamic state in the Philippines; predominantly composed of converts to Islam.

Workers and Peasants Party (WPP): Unit 113, Legaspi Suites, 11th Floor, 178 Salcedo St, Legaspi Village, Makati City, Metro Manila; fmrly known as Lapiang Mangagawa; Pres. JOSE MALVAR VILLEGAS, Jr; Sec.-Gen. FRANK PASION.

Diplomatic Representation

EMBASSIES IN THE PHILIPPINES

Argentina: 8th Floor, Liberty Center, 104 H. V. de la Costa St, Salcedo Village, Makati City, 1227 Metro Manila; tel. (2) 8453218; fax (2) 8453220; e-mail efili@mrecic.gov.ar; Ambassador JOAQUÍN DANIEL OTERO.

Australia: 23rd Floor, Tower II, RCBC Plaza, 6819 Ayala Ave, Makati City, 1200 Metro Manila; tel. (2) 7578100; fax (2) 7578268; e-mail public-affairs-MNLA@dfat.gov.au; internet www.australia.com.ph; Ambassador WILLIAM TWEDDEL.

Austria: Prince Bldg, 4th Floor, 117 Rada St, Legaspi Village, POB 2411, Makati City, 1200 Metro Manila; tel. (2) 8179191; fax (2) 8134238; e-mail manila-ob@bmeia.gv.at; internet www.aussenministerium.at/manila; Ambassador WILHELM DONKO.

Bangladesh: Universal-Re Bldg, 2nd Floor, 106 Paseo de Roxas, Legaspi Village, Makati City, 1226 Metro Manila; tel. (2) 8175001; fax (2) 8164941; e-mail info@bangladeshembassymanila.org; internet bangladeshembassymanila.org; Ambassador Maj.-Gen. (retd) JOHN GOMES.

Belgium: Multinational Bancorporation Center, 9th Floor, 6805 Ayala Ave, Makati City, Metro Manila; tel. (2) 8451869; fax (2) 8452076; e-mail manila@diplobel.fed.be; internet www.diplomatie.be/manila; Ambassador CHRISTIAN MEERSCHMAN.

Brazil: 16th Floor, Liberty Center, 104 H. V. de la Costa St, Salcedo Village, Makati City, 1227 Metro Manila; tel. (2) 8453651; fax (2) 8453676; e-mail brascom@info.com.ph; internet www.brasemb.org.ph; Ambassador GEORGE NEY DE SOUZA FERNANDES.

Brunei: Bank of the Philippine Islands Bldg, 11th Floor, Ayala Ave, cnr Paseo de Roxas, Makati City, 1227 Metro Manila; tel. (2) 8162836; fax (2) 8916646; e-mail manila.philippines@mfa.gov.bn; Ambassador MALAI Hajah HALIMAH MALAI YUSSOF.

Cambodia: Unit 7A, 7th Floor, Country Space One Bldg, Sen. Gil J. Puyat Ave, Makati City, Metro Manila; tel. (2) 8189981; fax (2) 8189983; e-mail camemb.phl@mfa.gov.kh; Ambassador TUOT PANHA.

Canada: 6th–8th Floors, Tower 2, RCBC Plaza, 6819 Ayala Ave, POB 2098, Makati City, 1200 Metro Manila; tel. (2) 8579000; fax (2) 8431082; e-mail manil@international.gc.ca; internet www.canadainternational.gc.ca/philippines; Ambassador CHRISTOPHER THORNLEY.

Chile: 17th Floor, Liberty Center, 104 H. V. de la Costa St, cnr Leviste St, Salcedo Village, Makati City, 1227 Metro Manila; tel. (2) 8433461; fax (2) 8431976; e-mail echileph@eastern.com.ph; internet www.embachileph.com; Ambassador ROBERTO MAYORGA LORCA.

China, People's Republic: 4896 Pasay Rd, Dasmariñas Village, Makati City, Metro Manila; tel. (2) 8443148; fax (2) 8452465; e-mail chinaemb_ph@mfa.gov.cn; internet ph.chineseembassy.org; Ambassador MA KEQING.

Cuba: 101 Aguirre St, cnr Trasierra St, Cacho-Gonzales Bldg Penthouse, Legaspi Village, Makati City, Metro Manila; tel. (2) 8171192; fax (2) 8164094; e-mail embacuba@pldtdsl.net; Ambassador JUAN CARLOS ARENCIBIA CORRALES.

Czech Republic: 30th Floor, Rufino Pacific Tower, 6784 Ayala Ave, 1200 Makati City, Metro Manila; tel. (2) 8111155; fax (2) 8111020; e-mail manila@embassy.mzv.cz; internet www.mzv.cz/manila; Ambassador JOSEF RYCHTAR.

Egypt: 2229 Paraiso St, cnr Banyan St, Dasmariñas Village, Makati City, Metro Manila; tel. (2) 8439232; fax (2) 8439239; Ambassador (vacant).

France: Pacific Star Bldg, 16th Floor, Makati Ave, cnr Sen. Gil J. Puyat Ave, 1200 Makati City, Metro Manila; tel. (2) 8576900; fax (2) 8576951; e-mail consulat@ambafrance-ph.org; internet www.ambafrance-ph.org; Ambassador M. GILLES GARACHON.

Germany: 25th Floor, Tower 2, RCBC Plaza, 6819 Ayala Ave, Makati City, Metro Manila; tel. (2) 7023000; fax (2) 7023015; e-mail deboma@pldtdsl.net; internet www.manila.diplo.de; Ambassador JOACHIM HEIDORN.

Greece: 7th Floor, SEDCCO Bldg, Legaspi Village, Makati City, 1229 Metro Manila; tel. (2) 8174444; fax (2) 8120202; e-mail gremb.man@mfa.gr; Ambassador CONSTANTINA KOLIOU.

Holy See: 2140 Taft Ave, POB 3364, 1099 Metro Manila (Apostolic Nunciature); tel. (2) 5210306; fax (2) 5211235; e-mail nuntiusp@info.com.ph; Apostolic Nuncio Most Rev. GIUSEPPE PINTO.

India: 2190 Paraiso St, Dasmariñas Village, POB 2123, Makati City, MCPO, Metro Manila; tel. (2) 8430101; fax (2) 8158151; e-mail info@embindia.org.ph; internet www.embindia.org.ph; Ambassador AMIT DASGUPTA.

Indonesia: 185 Salcedo St, Legaspi Village, POB 1671, MCPO, Makati City, Metro Manila; tel. (2) 8925061; fax (2) 8925878; e-mail fungsipensosbud@yahoo.com.ph; internet www.kbrimanila.org.ph; Ambassador YOHANNES KRISTIARTO SOERYO LEGOWO.

Iran: 2224 Paraiso St, cnr Pasay Rd, Dasmariñas Village, Makati City, Metro Manila; tel. (2) 8884757; fax (2) 8884777; e-mail mrouzbehani@gmail.com; Ambassador ALI ASGHAR MOHAMMADI.

Israel: Trafalgar Plaza, 23rd Floor, 105 H. V. de la Costa St, Salcedo Village, Makati City, 1227 Metro Manila; tel. (2) 8839500; fax (2) 8839555; e-mail info@manila.mfa.gov.il; internet embassies.gov.il/manila; Ambassador MENASHE BAR-ON.

Italy: Zeta II Bldg, 6th Floor, 191 Salcedo St, Legaspi Village, Makati City, Metro Manila; tel. (2) 8924531; fax (2) 8171436; e-mail informazioni.manila@esteri.it; internet www.ambmanila.esteri.it; Ambassador MASSIMO ROSCIGNO.

Japan: 2627 Roxas Blvd, Pasay City, 1300 Metro Manila; tel. (2) 5515710; fax (2) 5515780; e-mail jicc-mnl@japanembassy.ph; internet www.ph.emb-japan.go.jp; Ambassador TOSHINAO URABE.

Korea, Republic: 122 Upper Mckinley Rd, Mckinley Town Center, Fort Bonifacio, Taguig City, 1634 Metro Manila; tel. (2) 8569210; fax (2) 8569019; e-mail philippines@mofat.go.kr; internet embassy_philippines.mofat.go.kr; Ambassador LEE HYUK.

Kuwait: 1230 Acacia Rd, Dasmariñas Village, POB 2033, Makati City, Metro Manila; tel. (2) 8876880; fax (2) 8876887; Ambassador WALEED AHMAD AL-KANDARI.

Laos: 34 Lapu-Lapu St, Magallanes Village, Makati City, Metro Manila; tel. and fax (2) 8525759; Ambassador LUMEN B. ISLETA.

Libya: 1644 Dasmariñas St, cnr Mabolo St, Dasmariñas Village, Makati City, Metro Manila; tel. (2) 8177331; fax (2) 8177337; e-mail lpbmanila@skynet.net; Chargé d'affaires a.i. BASHIR A. M. ELAKKARI.

Malaysia: 107 Tordesillas St, Salcedo Village, Makati City, 1200 Metro Manila; tel. (2) 8640761; fax (2) 8640727; e-mail mwmanila@indanet.com; internet www.kln.com.my/perwakilan/manila; Ambassador MOHD ZAMRI BIN MOHD KASSIM.

Mexico: 150 Legaspi St, G. C. Corporate Plaza, Legaspi Village, Makati City, Metro Manila; tel. (2) 8122211; fax (2) 8927635; e-mail embmxfil@info.com.ph; internet portal.sre.gob.mx/filipinaseng; Ambassador TOMAS JAVIER CALVILLO UNNA.

Myanmar: Gervasia Corporate Center, 8th Floor, 152 Amorsolo St, Legaspi Village, Makati City, Metro Manila; tel. (2) 8931944; fax (2) 8928866; e-mail myanila@mydestiny.net; Ambassador AUNG KHIN SOE.

Netherlands: Equitable PCI Bank Tower, 26th Floor, 8751 Paseo de Roxas, Makati City, Metro Manila; tel. (2) 7866666; fax (2) 7866600; e-mail man@minbuza.nl; internet www.netherlandsembassy.ph; Ambassador ROBERT BRINKS.

New Zealand: BPI Buendia Center, 23rd Floor, Sen. Gil J. Puyat Ave, POB 3228, MCPO, Makati City, Metro Manila; tel. (2) 8915358; fax (2) 8915357; e-mail nzmanila@nxdsl.com.ph; internet www.nzembassy.com/philippines; Ambassador REUBEN LEVERMORE.

Nigeria: 2211 Paraiso St, Dasmariñas Village, POB 3174, Makati City, 1271 Metro Manila; tel. (2) 8439866; fax (2) 8439867; e-mail embassy@nigeriamanila.org; internet www.nigeriamanila.org; Ambassador Dr YEMI FAROUNBI.

Norway: Petron Mega Plaza Bldg, 21st Floor, 358 Sen. Gil J. Puyat Ave, Makati City, 1209 Metro Manila; tel. (2) 8863245; fax (2) 8863384; e-mail emb.manila@mfa.no; internet www.norway.ph; Ambassador KNUT SOLEM.

Pakistan: Alexander House, 6th Floor, 132 Amorsolo St, Legaspi Village, Makati City, Metro Manila; tel. (2) 8172776; fax (2) 8400229; e-mail pakrepmanila@yahoo.com; internet www.cpsctech.org/~pkembphil; Ambassador MOHSIN RAZI.

Palau: Marbella Condominium II, Unit 101, Ground Floor, 2071 Roxas Blvd, Malate, Manila; tel. (2) 5221982; fax (2) 5210402; e-mail ropembassy-pi@pldtdsl.net; Chargé d'affaires a.i. NGERIKL BAULES.

Panama: 11th Floor, National Life and Insurance Bldg, 6762 Ayala Ave, 1200 Makati City; tel. (2) 3283810; fax (2) 3388841; e-mail panamaph@pldtdsl.net; Ambassador ROBERTO C. VALLARINO.

Papua New Guinea: 3rd Floor, Corinthian Plaza Condominium Bldg, cnr Paseo de Roxas and Gamboa St, Makati City, Metro Manila; tel. (2) 8113465; fax (2) 8113466; e-mail kundumnl@pngembmnl.com.ph; Ambassador CHRISTOPHER VIHRURI.

Qatar: 1398 Cabellero St, cnr Lumbang St, Dasmariñas Village, Makati City, Metro Manila; tel. (2) 8874944; fax (2) 8876406; e-mail gemanila2000@yahoo.com; Ambassador ABDULLAH AHMED YOUSIF AL-MUTAWA.

Romania: 1216 Acacia Rd, Dasmariñas Village, Makati City, Metro Manila; tel. (2) 8439014; fax (2) 8439063; e-mail amarom@zpdee.net; Ambassador VALERIU GHEORGHE.

Russia: 1245 Acacia Rd, Dasmariñas Village, Makati City, Metro Manila; tel. (2) 8930190; fax (2) 8109614; e-mail RusEmb@i-manila.com.ph; internet www.philippines.mid.ru; Ambassador NIKOLAI R. KUDASHEV.

Saudi Arabia: Saudi Embassy Bldg, 389 Sen. Gil J. Puyat Ave Ext., Makati City, Metro Manila; tel. (2) 8564444; fax (2) 8953493; e-mail phemb@mofa.gov.sa; internet www.saudiembassy.com.ph; Ambassador ABDULLAH AL-HASSAN.

Singapore: 505 Rizal Drive, Bonifacio, 1634 Taguig City, Metro Manila; tel. (2) 8569922; fax (2) 8569932; e-mail singemb_mnl@sgmfa.gov.sg; internet www.mfa.gov.sg/manila; Ambassador V. P. HIRUBALAN.

South Africa: 29th Floor, Yuchengco Tower, RCBC Plaza, 6819 Ayala Ave, Makati City, 1227 Metro Manila; tel. (2) 8899383; fax (2) 8899337; e-mail manila@foreign.gov.za; Ambassador AGNES NYAMANDE-PITSO.

Spain: 27th Floor, Equitable Bank Tower, 8751 Paseo de Roxas, 1226 Metro Manila; tel. (2) 8176676; fax (2) 8174892; e-mail emb .manila@maec.es; Ambassador JORGE DOMECQ.

Sri Lanka: 7th Floor, G. C. Corporate Plaza, 150 Legaspi St, Legaspi Village, Makati City, Metro Manila; tel. (2) 8120124; fax (2) 8120126; e-mail slembmanila@pldtdsl.net; internet www .slembmanila.ph; Ambassador NAWALAGE B. COORAY.

Switzerland: Equitable Bank Tower, 24th Floor, 8751 Paseo de Roxas, Makati City, 1226 Metro Manila; tel. (2) 8454545; fax (2) 8454538; e-mail man.vertretung@eda.admin.ch; internet www.eda .admin.ch/manila; Ambassador IVO SIEBER.

Thailand: 107 Rada St, Legaspi Village, Makati City, 1229 Metro Manila; tel. (2) 8154220; fax (2) 8154221; e-mail infomnl@pldtdsl.net; internet www.thaiembassymnl.ph; Ambassador PRASAS PRASASVI- NITCHAI.

Timor-Leste: 17th Floor, Centerpoint Condominium, Rm 1703, cnr Julia Vargas Ave, Ortigas Center, Pasig City, 1605 Metro Manila; tel. (2) 6379405; fax (2) 6379408; e-mail timorlesteembassyinmanila@ yahoo.com; Ambassador JUVÊNCIO DE JESUS MARTINS.

Turkey: 2268 Paraiso St, Dasmariñas Village, Makati City, Metro Manila; tel. (2) 8439705; fax (2) 8439702; e-mail turkembm@info.com .ph; Ambassador HATICE P. IŞIK.

United Arab Emirates: Renaissance Bldg, 2nd Floor, 215 Sakedo St, Legaspi Village, Makati City, Metro Manila; tel. (2) 8173906; fax (2) 8183577; Ambassador MUSA ABDUL WAHED ABDUL GHAFAR AL- KHAJA.

United Kingdom: Locsin Bldg, 15th–17th Floors, 6752 Ayala Ave, cnr Makati Ave, Makati City, 1226 Metro Manila; tel. (2) 5808700; fax (2) 8197206; e-mail uk@info.com.ph; internet www .ukinthephilippines.fco.gov.uk; Ambassador STEPHEN LILLIE.

USA: 1201 Roxas Blvd, Ermita, 1000 Metro Manila; tel. (2) 3012000; fax (2) 3012399; internet manila.usembassy.gov; Ambassador HARRY THOMAS, Jr.

Venezuela: Unit 17A, Multinational Bancorporation Center, 6805 Ayala Ave, Makati City, Metro Manila 1226; tel. (2) 8452841; fax (2) 8452866; e-mail venezemb@info.com.ph; Chargé d'affaires a.i. YELITZA VENTURA POLANCO.

Viet Nam: 670 Pablo Ocampo St, Malate, Metro Manila; tel. (2) 5216843; fax (2) 5260472; e-mail vnembph@yahoo.com; internet www.vietnamembassy-philippines.org; Ambassador NGUYEN VU TU.

Judicial System

The Philippine judicial system comprises the Supreme Court, the Court of Appeals, Regional Trial Courts, Metropolitan Trial Courts, Municipal Courts in Cities, Municipal Courts and Municipal Circuit Trial Courts. There is also a special court for trying cases of corruption (the Sandiganbayan). The Office of the Ombudsman (Tanodbayan) investigates complaints concerning the actions of public officials. Islamic *Shari'a* courts were established in the southern Philippines in July 1985 under a presidential decree of February 1977. They are presided over by three district magistrates and six circuit judges.

Supreme Court: New Supreme Court Bldg Annex, 3rd Floor, Padre Faura St, Ermita, 1000 Metro Manila; tel. (2) 5225090; fax (2) 5268129; e-mail pio@sc.judiciary.gov.ph; internet sc.judiciary.gov .ph; comprises a Chief Justice and 14 Associate Justices; the Court may sit *en banc* or in divisions of three, five or seven members; Justices of the Supreme Court are appointed by the President from a list of a minimum of three nominees prepared by a Judicial and Bar Council; Chief Justice MARIA LOURDES SERENO.

Court of Appeals: Maria y Orosa St, Ermita, 1000 Metro Manila; tel. (2) 5241241; e-mail ca_manila@yahoo.com; internet ca.judiciary .gov.ph; consists of a Presiding Justice and 68 Associate Justices; Presiding Justice ANDRES B. REYES, Jr.

Religion

According to the results of the 2000 census, 81.1% of the population were Roman Catholics and 11.6% belonged to other Christian denominations. The Islamic community constituted 5% of the population, Buddhists accounted for 0.1%, while indigenous and other religious traditions comprised a further 1.7%. Atheists and persons who did not state a religious preference accounted for 0.5%.

CHRISTIANITY

Sangguniang Pambansa ng mga Simbahan sa Pilipinas (National Council of Churches in the Philippines): 879 Epifanio de los Santos Ave, West Triangle, Quezon City 1104, Metro Manila; tel. (2) 9293745; fax (2) 9267076; e-mail library@nccphilippines.org;

internet www.nccphilippines.org; f. 1963; 10 mem. churches, 9 assoc. mems; Gen. Sec. Rev. REX R. B. REYES, Jr.

The Roman Catholic Church

For ecclesiastical purposes, the Philippines comprises 16 archdioceses, 55 dioceses, six territorial prelatures, one military ordinate and seven apostolic vicariates. At 31 December 2007 approximately 81.2% of the population were adherents.

Catholic Bishops' Conference of the Philippines (CBCP) 470 General Luna St, Intramuros, 1076 Metro Manila; tel. (2) 9414471; fax (2) 5279634; e-mail cbcpmonitor@cbcpworld.net; internet cbcponline.net.

f. 1945; statutes approved 1952; Pres. Most Rev. JOSÉ SEROFIA PALMA, III

Archbishop of Caceres: Most Rev. LEONARDO Z. LEGASPI, Archbishop's House, Elias Angeles St, POB 6085, 4400 Naga City; tel. (54) 4738483; fax (54) 4738383; e-mail chancerynaga@yahoo.com.

Archbishop of Cagayan de Oro: Most Rev. ANTONIO J. LEDESMA, Archbishop's Residence, POB 113, 9000 Misamis Oriental, Cagayan de Oro City; tel. (8822) 722375; fax (8822) 726304; e-mail acdo_chancery@yahoo.com.

Archbishop of Capiz: Most Rev. JOSE F. ADVINCULA, Chancery Office, POB 44, 5800 Roxas City; tel. (36) 6215595; fax (36) 6211053.

Archbishop of Cebu: Most Rev. JOSÉ SEROFIA PALMA, Archbishop's Residence, cnr P. Gomez St and P. Burgos St, POB 52, 6000 Cebu City; tel. (32) 2541861; fax (32) 2530123; e-mail adelito@skynet.net.

Archbishop of Cotabato: Most Rev. ORLANDO B. QUEVEDO, Archbishop's Residence, 158 Sinsuat Ave, POB 186, 9600 Cotabato City; tel. (64) 4212918; fax (64) 4211446.

Archbishop of Davao: Most Rev. ROMULO G. VALLES, Archbishop's Residence, 247 Florentino Torres St, POB 80418, 8000 Davao City; tel. (82) 2275992; fax (82) 2279771; e-mail bishopdavao@yahoo.com.

Archbishop of Jaro: Most Rev. ANGEL N. LAGDAMEO, Archbishop's Residence, Jaro, 5000 Iloilo City; tel. (33) 3294442; fax (33) 3293197; e-mail abpjaro@yahoo.com.

Archbishop of Lingayen-Dagupan: Most Rev. SOCRATES B. VILLEGAS, Archbishop's House, Jovellanos St, 2400 Pangasinan, Dagupan City; tel. (75) 5235357; fax (75) 5221878; e-mail maximo82158@ gmail.com; internet www.lingayen-dagupan.org.

Archbishop of Lipa: Most Rev. RAMON C. ARGÜELLES, Archbishop's House, St Lorenzo Ruiz Rd, Lipa City, 4217 Batangas; tel. (43) 7562572; fax (43) 7560005; e-mail chancery@batangas.net.ph; internet www.archlipa.org.

Archbishop of Manila: Cardinal LUIS ANTONIO TAGLE, Arzobispado, 121 Arzobispo St, Intramuros, POB 132, 1099 Metro Manila; tel. (2) 5277631; fax (2) 5273956; e-mail rcamaoc@yahoo.com; internet www.rcam.org.

Archbishop of Nueva Segovia: Most Rev. ERNESTO A. SALGADO, Archbishop's House, Vigan, 2700 Ilocos Sur; tel. (77) 7222018; fax (77) 7221591; e-mail nschancery@yahoo.com.ph.

Archbishop of Ozamis: Most Rev. JESUS A. DOSADO, Archbishop's House, POB 2760, Rizal Ave, Banadero, 7200 Ozamis City; tel. (65) 5212820; fax (65) 5211574.

Archbishop of Palo: Most Rev. JOHN FORROSUELO DU, Archdiocesan Chancery, Palo, 6501 Leyte; POB 173, Tacloban City, 6500 Leyte; tel. (53) 3232213; fax (53) 3235607; e-mail rcap@mozcom.com.

Archbishop of San Fernando (Pampanga): Most Rev. PACIANO B. ANICETO, Chancery Office, San José, San Fernando, 2000 Pampanga; tel. (45) 9612819; fax (45) 9616772; e-mail rca@pamp.pworld.net.ph; internet www.rcasf.com.

Archbishop of Tuguegarao: Most Rev. SERGIO LASAM UTLEG, Archbishop's House, Rizal St, Tuguegarao, 3500 Cagayan; tel. (78) 8441663; fax (78) 8462822; e-mail chancerycat@lycos.com.

Archbishop of Zamboanga: Most Rev. ROMULO G. VALLES, Sacred Heart Centre, POB 1, Justice R. T. Lim Blvd, 7000 Zamboanga City; tel. (62) 9911329; fax (62) 9932608; e-mail zambochancery-10@yahoo .com.

Other Christian Churches

Convention of Philippine Baptist Churches: POB 263, 5000 Iloilo City; tel. (33) 3290621; fax (33) 3290618; e-mail gensec@iloilo .net; f. 1935; Gen. Sec. HUDSON HERVILLA; Pres. DAN L. PEDROSA.

Episcopal Church in the Philippines: POB 10321, Broadway Centrum, Quezon City, 1112 Metro Manila; tel. (2) 7228481; fax (2) 7211923; e-mail ecpnational@yahoo.com.ph; internet www .episcopalchurchphilippines.org; f. 1901; seven dioceses; Prime Bishop Most Rev. EDWARD MALECDAN.

Iglesia Evangélica Metodista en las Islas Filipinas (Evangelical Methodist Church in the Philippines): Beulah Land, Iemelif Center, Greenfields 1, Subdivision, Marytown Circle, Novaliches,

Quezon City, 1123 Metro Manila; tel. (2) 9356519; fax (2) 4185017; f. 1909; 40,000 mems (2003); Gen. Supt Bishop NATHANAEL P. LAZARO.

Iglesia Filipina Independiente (Philippine Independent Church): POB 2484, 1000 Metro Manila; tel. (2) 5237242; fax (2) 5213932; e-mail gensec@ifi.ph; internet www.ifi.ph; f. 1902; 34 dioceses; 6m. mems; Obispo Maximo (Supreme Bishop) Most Rev. EPHRAIM S. FAJUTAGANA.

Iglesia ni Cristo: 1 Central Ave, New Era, Quezon City, 1107 Metro Manila; tel. (2) 9814311; fax (2) 9814333; f. 1914; 6m. mems; Exec. Minister Brother EDUARDO V. MANALO.

Lutheran Church in the Philippines: 4461 Old Santa Mesa, 1008 Metro Manila; POB 507, 1099 Metro Manila; tel. (2) 7157084; fax (2) 7142395; internet www.lutheranphilippines.org; f. 1946; Pres. Rev. JAMES CERDEÑOLA.

Union Church of Manila: cnr Legaspi St and Rada St, Legaspi Village, Makati City, Metro Manila; tel. (2) 8126062; fax (2) 8172386; e-mail ucmweb@unionchurch.ph; internet www.unionchurch.ph; Senior Pastor Rev. STEVE RUESTCHLE.

United Church of Christ in the Philippines: 1667 A. Vasquez St, Malate, Metro Manila; tel. (2) 9240215; fax (2) 9240207; e-mail uccpnaof@manila-online.net; internet uccp.org.ph; f. 1948; 900,000 mems (1996); Gen. Sec. Rev. ELIEZER PASCUA (Bishop).

Among other denominations active in the Philippines are the Iglesia Evangélica Unida de Cristo and the United Methodist Church.

ISLAM

Some 14 different ethnic groups profess the Islamic faith in the Philippines. Mindanao and the Sulu and Tawi-Tawi archipelago, in the southern Philippines, are predominantly Muslim provinces, but there are 10 other such provinces, each with its own Imam, or Muslim religious leader. More than 500,000 Muslims live in the north of the country (mostly in, or near to, Manila).

Islamic Da'wah Council of the Philippines (IDCP): Suite 400, FUBC Bldg, Escolta, Metro Manila; tel. (2) 2458456; fax (2) 2415142; e-mail info@halalislamicdawah-ph.com; internet www .halalislamicdawah-ph.com; f. 1982; federation of 95 mem. orgs; Pres. ABDUL RAHAM R. T. LINZAG.

BAHÁ'Í FAITH

National Spiritual Assembly: 1070 A. Roxas St, cnr Bautista St, Singalong Subdiv., Malate, 1004 Metro Manila; POB 4323, 1099 Metro Manila; tel. (2) 5240404; fax (2) 5232449; e-mail nsa.bahai.ph@ gmail.com; internet bahai.ph; mems resident in 129,949 localities; Chair. ALFREDO RAMIREZ; Sec.-Gen. MA ADORACION NEWMAN.

The Press

The Office of the President implements government policies on information and the media. Freedom of the press and freedom of speech are guaranteed under the Constitution.

METRO MANILA

Dailies

Abante: 167 Liberty Bldg, Roberto S. Oca St, Port Area, Metro Manila; tel. (2) 5276722; fax (2) 5280147; e-mail abante@ abante-tonite.com; internet www.abante.com.ph; morning; Filipino and English; Man. Editor NICOLAS V. QUIJANO, Jr; circ. 417,000.

Abante Tonite: 167 Liberty Bldg, Roberto S. Oca St, Port Area, Metro Manila; tel. (2) 5276722; fax (2) 5279838; e-mail tonite@ abante-tonite.com; internet www.abante-tonite.com; afternoon; Filipino and English; Man. Editor NICOLAS V. QUIJANO, Jr; circ. 277,000.

Balita: Liwayway Publishing Inc, 2249 Pasong Tamo, Makati City, Metro Manila; tel. (2) 5278121; fax (2) 4000095; e-mail balitamb@ yahoo.com; f. 1972; morning; Filipino; Publr HERMOGENES P. POBRE; circ. 151,000.

BusinessMirror: Dominga Bldg (Annex), 2nd Floor, 2113 Chino Roces Ave, cnr De La Rosa St, Makati City, Metro Manila; tel. (2) 8179467; fax (2) 8137025; e-mail news@businessmirror.com.ph; internet www.businessmirror.com.ph; f. 2005; Editor-in-Chief LOURDES M. FERNANDEZ; Man. Editor VLADIMIR S. BUNOAN.

BusinessWorld: Raul L. Locsin Bldg I, 95 Balete Dr. Ext., New Manila, Quezon City, 1112 Metro Manila; tel. (2) 5359901; fax (2) 5359926; internet www.bworldonline.com; f. 1987; Exec. Editor ARNOLD E. BELLEZA; Man. Editor WILFREDO G. REYES; circ. 54,000.

Daily Tribune: Penthouse Suites, GLC Bldg, T. M. Kalaw St, cnr A. Mabini St, Ermita, Metro Manila; tel. (2) 5215584; fax (2) 5215522; e-mail nco@tribune.net.ph; internet www.tribune.net.ph; f. 2000; English; Publr and Editor-in-Chief NINEZ CACHO-OLIVARES.

Malaya Business Insight: Leyland Bldg, 20th St, cnr Railroad St, Port Area, Metro Manila; tel. (2) 3393324; fax (2) 5271839; e-mail malayanews@yahoo.com; internet www.malaya.com.ph; f. 1981; originally Filipino; English since 1983; Exec. Editor ENRIQUE P. ROMUALDEZ; Editor-in-Chief JOY DE LOS REYES; circ. 175,000.

Manila Bulletin: Bulletin Publishing Corpn, Muralla St, cnr Recoletos St, Intramuros, POB 769, 1002 Metro Manila; tel. (2) 5278121; fax (2) 5277510; e-mail bulletin@mb.com.ph; internet www .mb.com.ph; f. 1900; English; Pres. and Publr HERMOGENES P. POBRE; Editor-in-Chief Dr CHRIS J. ICBAN, Jr; circ. 443,110.

Manila Standard Today: Leyland Bldg, 21st St, cnr Railroad St, Port Area, Metro Manila; tel. (2) 5278351; fax (2) 5246649; e-mail mst@manilastandardtoday.com; internet www .manilastandardtoday.com; f. 1987 as Manila Standard; name changed as above in 2005, following merger with rival newspaper *Today*; morning; English; Editor-in-Chief JOJO ROBLES; circ. 96,000.

Manila Times: 371A Bonifacio Dr., Port Area, Metro Manila; tel. (2) 5245664; fax (2) 3019552; e-mail newsboy1@manilatimes.net; internet www.manilatimes.net; f. 1945; morning; English; Publr and Editor-in-Chief FRED DELA ROSA.

People's Journal: Universal-Re Bldg, 6th Floor, 106 Paseo de Roxas, cnr Perea and Gallardo Sts, Legaspi Village, Makati City, Metro Manila; tel. (2) 5278421; fax (2) 5274627; internet www .journal.com.ph; English and Filipino; Editor AUGUST B. VILLANUEVA; circ. 219,000.

People's Taliba: 6th Floor, Universal-Re Bldg, 106 Paseo de Roxas, cnr Perea and Gallardo Sts, Legaspi Village, Makati City, Metro Manila; fax (2) 5274627; Filipino; Editor BENJAMIN DEFENSOR; circ. 229,000.

People's Tonight: 6th Floor, Universal-Re Bldg, 106 Paseo de Roxas, cnr Perea and Gallardo Sts, Legaspi Village, Makati City, Metro Manila; tel. (2) 5278421; fax (2) 5274627; f. 1978; English and Filipino; Editor FERDIE RAMOS; circ. 500,000.

Philippine Daily Inquirer: Philippine Daily Inquirer Bldg, Chino Roces Ave, cnr Mascardo and Yague Sts, Pasong Tamo, POB 2353, Makati City, 1263 Metro Manila; tel. (2) 8978808; fax (2) 8974793; e-mail feedback@inquirer.com.ph; internet www.inquirer.com.ph; f. 1985; English; Editor-in-Chief LETTY JIMENEZ-MAGSANOC; circ. 250,000.

Philippine Star: 202 Railroad St, cnr 13th St, Port Area, 1016 Metro Manila; tel. (2) 5276856; fax (2) 5276851; e-mail editor@ philstar.com; internet www.philstar.com; f. 1986; Editor-in-chief ANA MARIE PAMINTUAN; circ. 275,000.

Pilipino Star Ngayon: 202 Railroad St, cnr 13th St, Port Area, 1016 Metro Manila; tel. (2) 5272389; fax (2) 5272403; e-mail psngayon@ philstar.net.ph; internet www.philstar.com/ngayon; f. 1986; Filipino tabloid; Chief Editor ALFONSO G. PEDROCHE; circ. 286,452.

Tempo: Bulletin Publishing Corpn, Muralla St, cnr Recoletos St, Intramuros, POB 769, 1002 Metro Manila; tel. (2) 5278121; fax (2) 5277510; internet www.tempo.com.ph; f. 1982; English and Filipino; Editor-in-Chief BAMBANG HARYMURTI; circ. 230,000.

United Daily News: 812–818 Benavides St, Binondo, 1006 Metro Manila; tel. (2) 2447171; e-mail united_dailynews@yahoo.com; f. 1973; Chinese; Editor-in-Chief CHUA KEE; circ. 85,000.

Selected Periodicals

Weeklies

Bannawag: c/o Manila Bulletin Publishing Corpn, Muralla St, cnr Recoletos St, Intramuros, Metro Manila; tel. (2) 5278121; fax (2) 5277510; e-mail bannawagmagazine.mb@gmail.com; f. 1934; Ilocano; Editor CLES B. RAMBAUD; circ. 55,500.

Bisaya: c/o Manila Bulletin Publishing Corpn, Muralla St, cnr Recoletos St, Intramuros, Metro Manila; tel. (2) 5278121; fax (2) 5277510; f. 1934; Cebu-Visayan; Editor EDGAR S. GODIN; circ. 90,000.

Liwayway: c/o Manila Bulletin Publishing Corpn, Muralla St, cnr Recoletos St, Intramuros, Metro Manila; tel. (2) 5278121; fax (2) 5277510; f. 1922; Tagalog; circ. 102,400.

Panorama: Manila Bulletin Publishing Corpn, Muralla St, cnr Recoletos St, Intramuros, POB 769, Metro Manila; tel. and fax (2) 5277509; e-mail panorama@mb.com.ph; internet www.panorama .com.ph; f. 1968; English; Editor RANDY V. URLANDA; circ. 239,600.

Philippine Starweek: 13th St, cnr Railroad St, Port Area, Metro Manila; tel. (2) 5277901; fax (2) 5275819; e-mail feedback@philstar .net.ph; internet www.philstar.com; English; Editor JOSEPH NACINO; circ. 268,000.

SELECTED PROVINCIAL PUBLICATIONS

The Aklan Reporter: 1227 Rizal St, Kalibo, Panay, 5600 Aklan; tel. (36) 2684158; f. 1971; weekly; English and Aklanon; Editor SUNRA ROJO; circ. 1,000.

Baguio Midland Courier: 16 Kisad Rd, POB 50, Baguio City; tel. (74) 4422444; fax (74) 4439485; e-mail baguiomidlandcourier@yahoo.com; internet www.baguiomidlandcourier.com.ph; f. 1947; weekly; English; Publr CHARLES M. HAMADA; circ. 24,500.

Bayanihan Weekly News: Bayanihan Publishing Co, P. Guevarra Ave, Santa Cruz, Laguna; f. 1966; Mon.; Filipino and English; Editor ARTHUR A. VALENOVA; circ. 1,000.

Bohol Chronicle: 56 B. Inting St, Tagbilaran City, 6300 Bohol; tel. and fax (38) 5010077; fax (38) 4113100; e-mail editor@boholchronicle.com; internet www.boholchronicle.com; f. 1954; 2 a week; English and Cebuano; Editor and Publr ZOILO DEJARESCO; circ. 5,500.

The Bohol Times: 100 Gallares St, Tagbilaran City, 6300 Bohol; tel. (38) 4112961; fax (38) 4112656; e-mail boholtimes@yahoo.com; Publr Dr LILIA A. BALITE; Editor-in-Chief SALVADOR D. DIPUTADO.

The Ilocos Times: Barangay 23, M. H. del Pilar St, 2900 Laoag City; tel. (77) 7720976; fax (77) 7711378; e-mail publisher@ilocostimes.net; internet www.ilocostimes.net; f. 1920; weekly; publ. by Ilocos Publishing Corpn; English and Iluko; Publr and Editor EFREN S. RAMOS, Jr; circ. 5,000.

The Kapawa News: L. V. Moles and Jose Abad Santos Sts, Tangub, POB 365, 6100 Bacolod City; tel. and fax (34) 4441941; e-mail LM-Kapawa@eudoramail.com; f. 1966; weekly; Sat.; Hiligaynon and English; Publr HENRY G. DOBLE; circ. 2,000.

Mindanao Post: Blk 16, Lot 3, SIR New Matina, Davao City, Mindanao; f. 1999; Editor-in-Chief DOMING ROSAL.

Mindanao Times: UMBN Bldg, Ponciano Reyes St, Davao City, Mindanao; tel. 2273252; e-mail editorial.mtimes@gmail.com; internet www.mindanaotimes.com.ph; daily; Editor-in-Chief AMALIA B. CABUSAO; circ. 5,000.

Pagadian Times: 0519 Alano St, 7016 Pagadian City; tel. (62) 2141721; fax (62) 2151504; e-mail pagtimes@mozcom.com; f. 1969; weekly; English; Publr PEDE G. LU; Editor REMAI ALEJADS; circ. 7,000.

Panay News: Panay News Complex, Q. Abeto St, Mandurriao, Iloilo City; tel. (33) 3212749; fax (33) 5094159; e-mail pnnews@panaynewsphilippines.com; internet www.panaynewsphilippines.com; Editor-in-Chief DANNY FAJARDO.

Sorsogon Today: 2903 Burgos St, East District, 4700 Sorsogon; tel. and fax (56) 4215306; fax (56) 2111340; e-mail sortoday@yahoo.com; f. 1977; weekly; Publr and CEO MARCOS E. PARAS, Jr; circ. 2,250.

Sun Star Cebu: Sun Star Bldg, 3rd Floor, cnr of P. del Rosario St and P. Cui St, Cebu City; tel. (32) 2546100; fax (32) 2537256; e-mail centralnewsroom@sunstar.com.ph; internet www.sunstar.com.ph/cebu; f. 1982; daily; English; Editor-in-Chief PACHICO A. SEARES; Gen. Man. JULIUS NERI.

Superbalita Davao: 5–6 Granland Business and Warehouse Center, R. Castillo St, Agdao, Davao City; tel. (82) 2351004; fax (82) 2351006; e-mail ssdavao@gmail.com; internet www.sunstar.com.ph/superbalitadavao; daily; Editor-in-Chief STELLA ESTREMERA.

The Tribune: Jarlego & Sons Bldg, Maharlika Highway, 2301 Cabanatuan City, Luzon; f. 1960; weekly; English and Filipino; Editor and Publr ORLANDO M. JARLEGO; circ. 8,000.

The Valley Times: Daang Maharlika, San Felipe, Ilagan, Isabela; f. 1962; weekly; English; Editor AUREA A. DE LA CRUZ; circ. 4,500.

The Visayan Tribune: 1973 Mezzanine Floor, Masonic Temple Bldg, Plaza Libertad 5000, Iloilo City; f. 1959; weekly; English; Editor HERBERT L. VEGO; circ. 5,000.

The Voice of Islam: Davao City; f. 1973; monthly; English and Arabic; official Islamic news journal; Editor and Publr NASHIR MUHAMMAD AL'RASHID AL HAJJ.

NEWS AGENCY

Philippines News Agency: Media Center Bldg, 2nd Floor, Visayas Ave, Diliman, Quezon City, Metro Manila; tel. (2) 9206551; fax (2) 9206566; e-mail bert.panganiban@gmail.com; internet www.pna.gov.ph; f. 1973; Gen. Man. VITTORIO V. VITUG; Exec. Editor DANILO C. TAGUIBAO (acting).

PRESS ASSOCIATION

National Press Club of the Philippines: National Press Club Bldg, Magallanes Drive, Intramuros, 1002 Metro Manila; tel. (2) 3010521; fax (2) 5219300; e-mail ad-nationalpressclub@yahoo.com; f. 1952; Pres. BENNY ANTIPORDA; Vice-Pres. ROLLY GONZALO; 1,405 mems.

Publishers

Abiva Publishing House Inc: Abiva Bldg, 851 Gregorio Araneta Ave, Quezon City, 1113 Metro Manila; tel. (2) 7120245; fax (2) 7120486; e-mail mmrabiva@i-manila.com.ph; internet www.abiva.com.ph; f. 1937; reference and textbooks; Pres. JORGE GARCIA.

Ateneo de Manila University Press: Bellarmine Hall, Ateneo de Manila University, Katipunan Ave, Loyola Heights, Quezon City, Metro Manila; tel. (2) 4265984; fax (2) 4265909; e-mail unipress@admu.edu.ph; internet www.ateneopress.org; f. 1972; literary, textbooks, humanities, social sciences, reference books on the Philippines; Dir MARICOR E. BAYTION.

Bookman, Inc: 373 Quezon Ave, Quezon City, 1114 Metro Manila; tel. (2) 7123587; fax (2) 7408108; e-mail sales@bookmanphilippines.com; internet bookmanphilippines.com; f. 1945; textbooks, reference, educational; Pres. LINA PICACHE-ENRIQUEZ.

Capitol Publishing House, Inc: 13 Team Pacific Bldg, Jose C. Cruz St, cnr F. Legaspi St, Barrio Ugong, Pasig City, Metro Manila; tel. (2) 6712662; fax (2) 6712664; e-mail cacho@mozcom.com; f. 1947; Gen. Man. MANUEL L. ATIENZA.

Heritage Publishing House: 33 4th Ave, cnr Main Ave, Cubao, Quezon City, POB 3667, Metro Manila; tel. (2) 7216218; fax (2) 7220468; e-mail heritage@skydsl.com.ph; art, anthropology, history, political science; Pres. MARIO R. ALCANTARA; Man. Dir GEORGE B. ALCANTARA.

The Lawyers' Co-operative Publishing Co Inc: 1071 Del Pan St, Makati City, 1206 Metro Manila; tel. (2) 5634073; fax (2) 5642021; e-mail lawbooks@info.com.ph; f. 1908; law, educational; Pres. ELSA K. ELMA.

Manila Bulletin Publishing Corpn: Muralla cnr Recoletos, Intramuros, 1002 Metro Manila; tel. (2) 5278121; fax (2) 5277510; e-mail bulletin@mb.com.ph; internet www.mb.com.ph; f. 1900; Chair. Dr EMILIO T. YAP; Pres. HERMOGENES P. POBRE.

Mutual Books Inc: Rm 208, Jovan Condominium, 600 Shaw Blvd, Mandaluyong City, Metro Manila; tel. (2) 5329656; fax (2) 5342665; internet mutualbooks.com; f. 1959; textbooks on accounting, management and economics, computers and mathematics; Pres. ALFREDO S. NICDAO, Jr.

Reyes Publishing Inc: Mariwasa Bldg, 4th Floor, 717 Aurora Blvd, Quezon City, 1112 Metro Manila; tel. (2) 7221827; fax (2) 7218782; e-mail reyespub@skyinet.net; f. 1964; art, history and culture; Pres. LOUIE REYES.

SIBS Publishing House Inc: Phoenix Bldg, 927 Quezon Ave, Quezon City, Metro Manila; tel. (2) 3764041; fax (2) 3764034; e-mail sibsbook@sibs.com.ph; internet www.sibs.com.ph; f. 1996; science, language, religion, literature and history textbooks; Pres. MA. ERLINDA SIBAL.

Sinag-Tala Publishers Inc: GMA Lou-Bel Plaza, 6th Floor, Chino Roces Ave, cnr Bagtikan St, San Antonio Village, Makati City, 1203 Metro Manila; tel. (2) 8971162; fax (2) 8969626; e-mail stpi@info.com.ph; internet www.sinagtala.com; f. 1972; educational textbooks; business, professional and religious books; Man. Dir LUIS A. USON.

University of the Philippines Press: Epifanio de los Santos St, U. P. Campus, Diliman, Quezon City, 1101 Metro Manila; tel. (2) 9266642; fax (2) 9282558; e-mail press@up.edu.ph; internet uppress.com.ph; f. 1965; literature, history, political science, sociology, cultural studies, economics, anthropology, mathematics; Dir MARIA LUISA T. CAMAGAY.

Vibal Publishing House, Inc: 1253 G. Araneta Ave, cnr Maria Clara St, Talayan, Quezon City, Metro Manila; tel. (2) 7122722; fax (2) 7118852; e-mail inquire@vibalpublishing.com; internet www.vibalpublishing.com; f. 1953; linguistics, social sciences, mathematics, religion; Pres. and Gen. Man. ESTHER A. VIBAL.

PUBLISHERS' ASSOCIATIONS

Philippine Educational Publishers' Asscn: 84 P. Florentino St, Santa Mesa Heights, Quezon City, 1113 Metro Manila; tel. (2) 7402698; fax (2) 7115702; e-mail info@pepa.org.ph; internet www.pepa.org.ph; Pres. DOMINADOR D. BUHAIN.

Publishers' Association of the Philippines Inc: Unit 206 Cityland 8, 98 Sen. Gil Puyat Ave, Makati City 1200, Metro Manila; tel. (2) 8929278; fax (2) 8944687; e-mail papi@gawab.com; internet papiphilippines.org; f. 1974; more than 1,000 mems; Pres. JUAN P. DAYANG.

Broadcasting and Communications

TELECOMMUNICATIONS

BayanTel: Diliman Corporate Center, Bayan Bldg, Maginhawa St, cnr Malingap St, Teacher's Village East, Quezon City, 1101 Metro Manila; tel. (2) 4121212; fax (2) 4492174; e-mail bayanserve@bayantel.com.ph; internet www.bayantel.com.ph; fixed lines and internet services provider; 359,000 fixed lines (1999); Chair. OSCAR M. LOPEZ; Pres. and CEO EUGENIO L. LOPEZ III.

Bell Telecommunications Philippines (BellTel): Pacific Star Bldg, 3rd Floor, Sen. Gil J. Puyat Ave, cnr Makati Ave, Makati City,

Metro Manila; tel. (2) 68002355; fax (2) 8915618; e-mail info@belltel .ph; internet www.belltel.ph; f. 1997; Pres. EDGARDO REYES.

Capitol Wireless Inc: Spirit of Communications Centre, 4th Floor, 106 Carlos Palanca St, Makati City, Metro Manila; tel. (2) 8159961; fax (2) 8184482; f. 1962; Pres. EPITACIO R. MARQUEZ.

Digital Telecommunications Philippines Inc (DIGITEL): 110 Eulogio Rodriguez Jr Ave, Bagumbayan, Quezon City, 1110 Metro Manila; tel. and fax (2) 3978888; e-mail customerservice@digitel.ph; internet digitel.webready.ph; f. 2003; Philippine Long Distance Telephone Co acquired 51.55% stake in Digitel in 2011; provision of fixed line telecommunications services; over 400,000 fixed lines; Pres. and CEO ORLANDO VEA.

Digital Mobile Philippines Inc: 110 Eulogio Rodriguez Jr Ave, Bagumbayan, Quezon City, 1110 Metro Manila; tel. (2) 3958000; e-mail customerservice@digitel.ph; internet www.suncellular.com .ph; f. 2003; wireless services under the brand name Sun Cellular; CEO CHARLES LIM.

Domestic Satellite Philippines Inc (DOMSAT): Solid House Bldg, 4th Floor, 2285 Pasong Tamo Ext., Makati City, 1231 Metro Manila; tel. (2) 8105917; fax (2) 8671677; Pres. SIEGFRED MISON.

Globe Telecom (GMCR) Inc: Globe Telecom Plaza 1, 5th Floor, Pioneer St, cnr Madison St, 1552 Mandaluyong City, Metro Manila; tel. (2) 7301000; fax (2) 7390072; e-mail ir@globetel.com.ph; internet www.globe.com.ph; fixed line, mobile telecommunication and internet services; 23.2m. mobile telephone subscribers (2009); Chair. JAIME AUGUSTO ZOBEL DE AYALA; Pres. and CEO ERNEST CU.

Philippine Communications Satellite Corpn (PhilcomSat): 12th Floor, Telecoms Plaza, 316 Sen. Gil J. Puyat Ave, Makati City, Metro Manila; tel. (2) 8158406; fax (2) 8179430; e-mail inquiry@ philcomsat.com.ph; internet philcomsat.com.ph; Pres. ERLINDA BILDNER.

Philippine Global Communications, Inc (PhilCom): 8755 Paseo de Roxas, Makati City, 1259 Metro Manila; tel. (2) 8451101; fax (2) 8189720; e-mail helpdesk@philcom.com; internet www .philcom.com; Chair. WILLY N. OCIER; CEO SALVADOR M. CASTILLO.

Philippine Long Distance Telephone Co (PLDT): Ramon Cojuangco Bldg, Makati Ave, POB 2148, Makati City, Metro Manila; tel. (2) 6882700; fax (2) 8446654; e-mail customercare@pldt.com; internet www.pldt.com.ph; f. 1928; monopoly on overseas telephone service until 1989; transferred to private sector in 2007; major fixed line and internet services provider; 44.7m. subscribers (2010); Chair. MANUEL V. PANGILINAN; Pres. and CEO NAPOLEON L. NAZARENO.

Smart Communications, Inc (SCI): SMART Tower, 6799 Ayala Ave, Makati City, 1226 Metro Manila; tel. (2) 8881111; fax (2) 8488830; e-mail cbg@smart.com.ph; internet www.smart.com.ph; f. 1993; mobile and internet services provider; 43.2m. subscribers (2010); Pres. and CEO NAPOLEON L. NAZARENO.

REGULATORY AUTHORITY

National Telecommunications Commission (NTC): NTC Bldg, BIR Rd, East Triangle, Diliman, Quezon City, 1104 Metro Manila; tel. (2) 9244042; fax (2) 9244048; e-mail bsd@ntc.gov.ph; internet www.ntc.gov.ph; f. 1979; supervises and controls all private and public telecommunications services; Commr GAMALIEL A. CORDOBA.

BROADCASTING

The Philippines was scheduled to switch from analogue to digital television by the end of 2015. In 2012 radio stations were still largely dependent on analogue broadcasting.

Radio

Bureau of Broadcast Services (BBS) (Philippine Broadcasting Service): Media Centre Bldg, 4th Floor, Visayas Ave, Diliman, Quezon City, 1100 Metro Manila; tel. (2) 9203968; fax (2) 9203961; e-mail pbs.inquiry@gmail.com; internet www.pbs.gov.ph; f. 1952; est. as Philippine Broadcasting Service; govt-operated; 32 radio stations; Dir JOHN S. MANALILI.

Cebu Broadcasting Co: Star City Complex, Vicente Sotto St, Roxal Blvd, Pasay City; tel. (2) 8326134; fax (2) 8326133; e-mail ed_montilla@hotmail.com; Chair. HADRIAN ARROYO.

Far East Broadcasting Co Inc: 62 Karuhatan Rd, Karuhatan, Valenzuela City, 1441 Metro Manila; tel. (2) 2921152; fax (2) 2925790; e-mail info@febc.org.ph; internet www.febc.org.ph; f. 1948; 18 stations; operates a classical music station, eight domestic stations and an overseas service in 64 languages throughout Asia; Pres. DAN ANDREW CURA.

Filipinas Broadcasting Network: Legaspi Towers 200, Room 306, Paseo de Roxas, Makati City, Metro Manila; tel. (2) 8176133; fax (2) 8177135; six stations; Gen. Man. DIANA C. GOZUM.

GMA Network Inc: GMA Network Center, EDSA cnr Timog Ave, Diliman, Quezon City, 1103 Metro Manila; tel. (2) 9827777; e-mail corporateaffairs@gmanetwork.com; internet www.gmanetwork

.com; f. 1950; fmrly Republic Broadcasting System Inc; 21 stations; Chair. and CEO FELIPE L. GOZON; Pres. GILBERTO R. DUAVIT, Jr.

Manila Broadcasting Co: Star City Complex, Vicente Sotto St, Roxas Blvd, Pasay City; tel. (2) 8326142; fax (2) 8326143; e-mail junic@mbcradio.net; internet www.mbcsales.com.ph; f. 1946; affiliate of Philippine Broadcasting Service; 16 stations; Chair. FRED J. ELIZALDE; Pres. RUPERTO NICDAO, Jr.

Nation Broadcasting Corpn: 8th–9th Floors, Jacinta Bldg 2, Edsa Guadalupe, Makati City; tel. (2) 8821622; fax (2) 8821400; e-mail radio@philexport.com; f. 1963; 13 stations; Pres. MANUEL PANGILINAN.

Newsounds Broadcasting Network Inc: 2406 Nobel, cnr Edison St, Makati City, 3117 Metro Manila; tel. (2) 8430116; fax (2) 8430122; 10 stations; Gen. Man. E. BILLONES; Office Man. HERMAN BASBANO.

Pacific Broadcasting System: c/o Manila Broadcasting Co, Star City Complex, Vicente Sotto St, Roxas Blvd, Metro Manila; tel. (2) 8326142; fax (2) 8326143; three stations; Pres. RUPERTO NICDAO, Jr; Dir RUDOLPH JULARBAL.

PBN Broadcasting Network Inc: Ersan Bldg, 3rd Floor, 32 Quezon Ave, Quezon City, Metro Manila; tel. (2) 7120190; fax (2) 7438162; e-mail pbnbroadcasting@yahoo.com; internet www .pbnbicol.com; f. 1958; five radio stations, two TV stations; Chair. JORGE D. BAYONA.

Philippine Federation of Catholic Broadcasters: 201 Sunrise Condominium, 226 Ortigas Ave, North Greenhills, San Juan, Metro Manila 1503; tel. (2) 7249850; fax (2) 7249962; e-mail cmnftd@ cmn-ftd.org; internet www.catholicmedianetwork.org; f. 1965; operates under the brand name Catholic Media Network (CMN); all 51 radio stations are broadcast via the Dream Satellite; Chair. Bishop BERNARDINO CORTEZ; Pres. Fr FRANCIS LUCAS.

Radio Philippines Network, Inc: Broadcast City, Capitol Hills, Diliman, Quezon City, Metro Manila; tel. (2) 9318618; fax (2) 4357403; e-mail dody_lacuna@yahoo.com; internet www.rpn9.com; f. 1969; 14 radio stations; Pres. ANTONIO ALBANO; Gen. Man. JESS A. YU.

Radio Veritas Asia: Buick St, Fairview Park, POB 2642, Quezon City, Metro Manila; tel. (2) 9390011; fax (2) 9381940; e-mail rveritas-asia@rveritas-asia.org; internet www.rveritas-asia.org; f. 1969; Catholic short-wave station; broadcasts in 14 languages; owned by Philippine Radio Educational and Information Center, Inc; Pres. and Chair. Cardinal LUIS ANTONIO TAGLE; Gen. Man. Fr ROBERTO M. EBISA (SVD).

UM Broadcasting Network: cnr P. Reyes and Palma Gil Sts, Davao City; tel. (82) 2279535; fax (82) 2217824; e-mail umbndvo@ mozcom.com; internet www.umbn.com.ph; f. 1949; 13 stations; Exec. Vice-Pres. WILLY TORRES.

Vanguard Radio Network: Cityland Pasong Tamo Tower, Rm 520, Chino Roces Ave, Makati City; tel. (2) 8929565; fax (2) 7160899; Pres. MANUEL GALVEZ.

Television

ABC Development Corpn (TV5): 762 Quirino Highway, Barangay San Bartolome, Novaliches, Quezon City; tel. (2) 9385837; fax (2) 8128840; internet www.tv5.com.ph; Pres. and CEO RAY ESPINOSA.

ABS-CBN Corpn: ABS-CBN Broadcasting Center, Sgt E. Esguerra Ave, cnr Mother Ignacia St, Quezon City, 1103 Metro Manila; tel. (2) 9244101; fax (2) 4163567; e-mail feedback_web@abs-cbn.com; internet www.abs-cbn.com; Pres. and CEO ROSARIO SANTOS-CONCIO.

AMCARA Broadcasting Network: ABS-CBN Broadcasting Centre, Mother Ignacia St, cnr Sgt Esguerra Ave, Quezon City, 1103 Metro Manila; tel. (2) 4152272; fax (2) 4121259; e-mail studio23@abs-cbn.com; internet www.studio23.tv; Man. Dir ANTONIO VENTOSA.

Channel V Philippines: 89 Timog Ave, South Triangle, Quezon City; tel. (2) 9292151; e-mail feedback@channelv.ph; internet www .channelv.ph; Head ROMEL V. SINGSON.

GMA Network, Inc: (see Radio) transmits nation-wide through 47 VHF and 1 affiliate station and in Asia, Australia and Hawaii through Measat-2 satellite.

Intercontinental Broadcasting Corpn: Broadcast City Complex, Capitol Hills, Diliman, Quezon City, Metro Manila; tel. (2) 9318781; fax (2) 9524002; e-mail ibcpres@ibc.com.ph; 5 stations; Pres. ROBERTO DEL ROSARIO.

National Broadcasting Network (NBN): Broadcast Complex, Visayas Ave, Quezon City, Metro Manila; tel. (2) 4075143; fax (2) 9204342; internet www.nbn.ph; f. 1974; public television network; fmrly People's Television Network (PTV4); Gen. Man JOSE S. ISABELO.

Radio Mindanao Network: State Condominium, 4th Floor, 1 Salcedo St, Legaspi Village, Makati City, Metro Manila; tel. (2) 8158304; fax (2) 8163680; e-mail sales@rmn.com.ph; internet rmn .ph; f. 1952; 2 stations; Pres. ERIC S. CANOY.

Directory

Radio Philippines Network, Inc: (see Radio) operates 7 TV stations.

Rajah Broadcasting Network, Inc (RJ TV 29): 5F, Ventures I Bldg, 7849 Gen. Luna St, cnr Makati Ave, Makati City, Metro Manila; tel. (2) 8962962; fax (2) 8933404; e-mail rjofc@compass .com; f. 1993; Chair. RAMON JACINTO.

Southern Broadcasting Network, Inc: Suite 2902, Jollibee Plaza, 29th Floor, Ortigas Jr Rd, Ortigas Center, Pasig City, Metro Manila; tel. (2) 6363286; fax (2) 6363288; e-mail gemceo@ sbnphilippines.net; 8 stations; Pres. and CEO TEOFILO A. HENSON; Vice-Pres. GERMELINA DINOPOL.

United Broadcasting Network: FEMS Tower 1, 11th Floor, 1289 Zobel Roxas, cnr South Superhighway, Malate; tel. (2) 5216138; fax (2) 5221226; Pres. and CEO JOSEPH HODREAL.

Broadcasting Association

Kapisanan ng mga Brodkaster ng Pilipinas (KBP) (Association of Broadcasters in the Philippines): LTA Bldg, 6th Floor, 118 Perea St, Legaspi Village, Makati City, 1226 Metro Manila; tel. (2) 8151990; fax (2) 8151993; e-mail info@kbp.org.ph; internet www.kbp.org.ph; f. 1973; est. in order to regulate the broadcasting industry, elevate standards, disseminate govt information and strengthen relations with advertising industry; Chair. BASBAÑO HERMAN; Pres. RUPERTO NICDAO, Jr.

Finance

(cap. = capital; res = reserves; dep. = deposits; m. = million; brs = branches; amounts in pesos, unless otherwise stated)

BANKING

In 1994 legislation providing for the establishment in the Philippines of additional foreign bank branches was enacted. By the end of 2011 there were 18 commercial banks and 16 foreign bank branches and subsidiaries in Philippines.

Central Bank

Bangko Sentral ng Pilipinas (Central Bank of the Philippines): A. Mabini St, cnr Pablo Ocampo St, Malate, 1004 Metro Manila; tel. (2) 7087701; fax (2) 7087416; e-mail bspmail@bsp.gov.ph; internet www .bsp.gov.ph; f. 1993; cap. 20,000m., surplus and res 117,738.2m., dep. 2,581,692.3m. (Dec. 2011); Gov. AMANDO M. TETANGCO, Jr; 18 brs.

Principal Commercial Banks

Allied Banking Corpn: 6754 Allied Bank Centre, Ayala Ave, cnr Legaspi St, Makati City, 1200 Metro Manila; tel. (2) 8163311; fax (2) 8160921; e-mail info@alliedbank.com.ph; internet www.alliedbank .com.ph; f. 1977; cap. 3,302.4m., res 2,664.5m., dep. 148,205m. (Dec. 2011); Chair. DOMINGO T. CHUA; Pres. ANTHONY Q. CHUA; 285 brs.

Bank of Commerce: San Miguel Properties Centre, 7 Saint Francis St, Mandaluyong City 1550; tel. (2) 6335501; fax (2) 6332430; e-mail mscallangan@bankcom.com.ph; internet www.bankcom.com.ph; f. 1983; fmrly Boston Bank of the Philippines; merged with Traders Royal Bank 2001; cap. 8,620.4m., res 6,583.1m., dep. 87,188.2m. (Dec. 2010); Chair. JOSE T. PARDO; Pres. and CEO SERGIO G. EDEZA; 117 brs.

Bank of the Philippine Islands: BPI Bldg, 6768 Ayala Ave, Makati City, 1226 Metro Manila; tel. (2) 8185541; fax (2) 8910170; e-mail expressonline@bpi.com.ph; internet www.bpiexpressonline .com; f. 1851; merged with Far East Bank and Trust Co in April 2000; merged with DBS Bank Philippines, Inc, 2001; cap. 35,562m., res 11,947m., dep. 682,818m. (Dec. 2011); Pres. and Dir AURELIO R. MONTINOLA, III; Chair. JAIME ZOBEL DE AYALA, II; 819 local brs; 4 overseas br.

BDO Unibank Inc: 7899 Makati Ave, Makati City, 0726 Metro Manila; tel. (2) 8407000; e-mail irandcorplan@bdo.com.ph; internet www.bdo.com.ph; f. 1996; fmrly known as Banco de Oro Unibank; cap. 96,000m., dep. 857,000m. (Dec. 2011); Chair. TERESITA T. SY; Pres. NESTOR V. TAN; 743 brs.

China Banking Corpn: CBC Bldg, 8745 Paseo de Roxas, cnr Villar St, Makati City, 1226 Metro Manila; tel. (2) 8855555; fax (2) 8920220; e-mail online@chinabank.com.ph; internet www.chinabank.ph; f. 1920; cap. 11,798m., res 3,260m., dep. 216,133m. (Dec. 2011); Chair. HANS T. SY; Pres. and CEO PETER S. DEE; 206 brs.

ChinaBank Savings Inc (CBS): VGP Centre, 6772 Ayala Ave, Makati City, 1226 Metro Manila; tel. (2) 9645011; fax (2) 8109226; internet www.cbs.com.ph; f. 1999; est. as Manila Banking Corpn; present name adopted following acquisition by China Banking Corpn in 2007; Pres. SAMUEL L. CHIONG; Chair. RICARDO R. CHUA; 26 brs.

Development Bank of the Philippines: DBP Bldg, Makati Ave, cnr Sen. Gil J. Puyat Ave, Makati City, 1200 Metro Manila; tel. (2) 8189511; fax (2) 8934311; e-mail info@dbp.ph; internet www.dbp.ph;

f. 1947; est. as the Rehabilitation Finance Corpn; govt-owned; provides medium- and long-term loans for strategic devt projects; cap. 19,025m., res –1,242.2m., dep. 131,221.3m. (Dec. 2010); Chair. JOSÉ A. NUÑEZ, Jr; Pres. and CEO GIL A. BUENAVENTURA; 86 brs.

East West Banking Corpn: Beaufort, 5th Ave cnr 23rd St, Fort Bonifacio Global City, Taguig City; tel. (2) 8150233; fax (2) 3250412; e-mail service@eastwestbanker.com; internet www.eastwestbanker .com; f. 1994; cap. 6,873.5m., res 28.7m., dep. 76,669m. (Dec. 2011); Chair. JONATHAN T. GOTIANUN; Pres. and CEO ANTONIO C. MONCUPA, Jr; 89 brs.

Land Bank of the Philippines: POB 2284, Manila Central Post Office, Metro Manila; tel. (2) 5220000; fax (2) 5288502; e-mail landbank@mail.landbank.com; internet www.landbank.com; f. 1963; specialized govt bank with universal banking licence; cap. 11,971m., res 17,787.6m., dep. 428,715.1m. (Dec. 2009); Chair. CESAR V. PURISIMA; Pres. and CEO GILDA E. PICO; 324 brs.

Maybank Philippines Inc: Legaspi Towers 300, Pablo Ocampo St, cnr Roxas Blvd, Malate, 1004 Metro Manila; tel. (2) 5237777; fax (2) 5218514; e-mail customerservice@maybank.com.ph; internet www .maybank2u.com.ph; f. 1961; cap. 4,280m., res 300.5m., dep. 22,164.1m. (June 2010); Chair. Dato' MOHD SALEH Haji HARUN; Pres. and CEO ONG SEET JOON; 53 brs.

Metropolitan Bank and Trust Co (Metrobank): Metrobank Plaza, Sen. Gil J. Puyat Ave, Makati City, 1200 Metro Manila; tel. (2) 8700700; fax (2) 8176248; e-mail customercare@metrobank.com .ph; internet www.metrobank.com.ph; f. 1962; acquired Global Business Bank (Globalbank) 2002; cap. 42,228m., res 25,233m., dep. 680,993m. (Dec. 2011); Chair. ARTHUR TY; Pres. FABIAN S. DEE, Jr; 700 local brs, 35 overseas brs.

Philippine Bank of Communications: PBCOM Tower, 6795 Ayala Ave, cnr V. A. Rufino St, Makati City, 1226 Metro Manila; tel. (2) 8307000; fax (2) 8182598; e-mail info@pbcom.com.ph; internet www.pbcom.com.ph; f. 1939; merged with AsianBank Corpn in 1999; cap. 8,260m., res 4,828.5m., dep. 27,817m. (Dec. 2011); Chair. ERIC O. RECTO; Pres. and CEO NINA D. AGUAS; 66 brs.

Philippine National Bank (PNB): PNB Financial Center, President Diosdado Macapagal Blvd, Pasay City, 1300 Metro Manila; tel. (2) 5738888; fax (2) 5734580; e-mail customercare@pnb.com.ph; internet www.pnb.com.ph; f. 1916; partially transferred to the private sector in 1996 and 2000; 10.93% govt-owned; cap. 26,490m., res 5,737.6m., dep. 237,534m. (Dec. 2011); Chair. FLORENCIA G. TARRIELA; Pres. and CEO CARLOS A. PEDROSA; 324 local brs, 5 overseas brs.

Philippine Veterans Bank: PVB Bldg, 101 V. A. Rufino St, cnr de la Rosa St, Legaspi Village, Makati City, Metro Manila; tel. (2) 9021600; fax (2) 9021700; e-mail corpcomm@veteransbank.com.ph; internet www.veteransbank.com.ph; cap. 2,758.5m., res 1,192m., dep. 47,590.2m. (Dec. 2011); Chair. EMMANUEL V. DE OCAMPO; Pres. and CEO RICARDO A. BALBIDO, Jr; 45 brs.

Philtrust Bank (Philippine Trust Co): Philtrust Bank Bldg, United Nations Ave, cnr San Marcelino St, Ermita, 1045 Metro Manila; tel. (2) 5249061; fax (2) 5217309; e-mail ptc@philtrustbank .com; internet www.philtrustbank.com; f. 1916; cap. 10,000m., res 378.3m., dep. 87,594.5m. (Dec. 2011); Pres. ANTONIO H. OZAETA; Chair. JAIME C. LAYA; 46 brs.

Rizal Commercial Banking Corpn: Yuchengco Tower, RCBC Plaza, 6819 Alaya Ave, Makati City, 0727 Metro Manila; tel. (2) 8949000; fax (2) 8949958; e-mail customercontact@rcbc.com; internet www.rcbc.com; f. 1960; cap. 11,427m., res 11,808m., dep. 255,460m. (Dec. 2011); Chair. HELEN Y. DEE; Pres. and CEO LORENZO V. TAN, Jr; 287 brs.

Security Bank Corpn: 6776 Ayala Ave, Makati City, 0719 Metro Manila; tel. (2) 8676788; fax (2) 8932563; e-mail ccad@securitybank .com.ph; internet www.securitybank.com; f. 1951; fmrly Security Bank and Trust Co; cap. 5,023.5m., res 3,592m., dep. 119,365.6m. (Dec. 2011); Pres. and CEO ALBERTO S. VILLAROSA; Chair. FREDERICK Y. DY; 125 brs.

Union Bank of the Philippines: Union Bank Plaza, Meralco Ave, cnr Onyx and Sapphire Sts, Ortigas Center, Pasig City, 1605 Metro Manila; tel. (2) 6676388; fax (2) 6366289; e-mail online@ unionbankph.com; internet www.unionbankph.com; f. 1982; cap. 6,414.3m., res 8,413.5m., dep. 204,210.2m. (Dec. 2011); Chair. and CEO JUSTO A. ORTIZ; Pres. VICTOR B. VALDEPEÑAS; 111 brs.

United Coconut Planters Bank (UCPB): UCPB Bldg, 7907 Makati Ave, Makati City, 0728 Metro Manila; tel. (2) 8119000; fax (2) 8119706; e-mail crc@ucpb.com; internet www.ucpb.com; f. 1963; cap. 1,484.8m., res 12,973m., dep. 153,836m. (Dec. 2010); Chair. MENARDO R. JIMENEZ; Pres. and CEO JERONIMO U. KILAYKO; 178 brs.

Rural Banks

Small private banks have been established with the assistance of the Government in order to promote the rural economy. Their principal objectives are to provide credit facilities on reasonable terms and, in co-operation with other agencies of the Government, to give advice on management.

Thrift Banks

Thrift banks mobilize small savings and provide loans to lower-income groups. The thrift banking system comprises savings and mortgage banks, stock savings and loan associations, and private development banks.

Islamic Bank

Al-Amanah Islamic Investment Bank of the Philippines: 4th Floor, DBP Bldg, Makati Ave, Makati City, Metro Manila; tel. (2) 8934350; fax (2) 8195249; e-mail info@al-amanahbank.com; internet www.al-amanahbank.com.ph; f. 1989; Chair. and CEO JOSE LUIS L. VERA.

Banking Associations

Bankers Association of the Philippines: Sagittarius Cond. Bldg, 11th Floor, H. V. de la Costa St, Salcedo Village, Makati City, Metro Manila; tel. (2) 8103858; fax (2) 8103860; e-mail secretariat@bap.org .ph; 23 mems; Pres. ALBERTO VILLAROSA; Exec. Dir CESAR O. VIRTUSIO.

Bankers Institute of the Philippines, Inc (BAIPhil): Kanlaon Tower, 6th Floor, Unit 66, Paseo de Roxas, Pasay City, Metro Manila; tel. (2) 8534457; fax (2) 8530889; e-mail secretariat@baiphil.org; internet www.baiphil.org; f. 1941; est. as Nat. Asscn of Auditors and Comptrollers; name changed to Bank Administration Institute in 1968, and as above in 2001; Pres. AGNES C. BRILLANTE SANTOS.

Chamber of Thrift Banks: Cityland 10 Condominium Tower 1, Unit 614, H. V. de la Costa St, Salcedo Village, Makati City, Metro Manila; tel. (2) 8126974; fax (2) 8127203; internet www.ctb.com.ph; 52 mems; Pres. PATRICK D. CHENG.

Offshore Bankers' Association of the Philippines, Inc: MCPO 3088, Makati City, 1229 Metro Manila; tel. (2) 8103554; Chair. TERESITA MALABANAN.

Rural Bankers' Association of the Philippines: RBAP Bldg, 2nd Floor, A. Soriano Jr Ave, cnr Arzobispo St, Intramuros, Metro Manila; tel. (2) 5272968; fax (2) 5272980; e-mail info@rbap.org; internet www.rbap.org; Pres. EDWARD LEANDRO Z. GARCIA, Jr.

STOCK EXCHANGES

Securities and Exchange Commission: SEC Bldg, Epifanio de los Santos Ave, Greenhills, Mandaluyong City, Metro Manila; tel. (2) 5840923; fax (2) 5845293; e-mail mis@sec.gov.ph; internet www.sec .gov.ph; f. 1936; Chair. TERESITA J. HERBOSA.

Philippine Stock Exchange: Ayala Triangle, Ayala Ave, Makati City, 1226 Metro Manila; tel. (2) 819-4100; fax (2) 891-9004; e-mail pirs@pse.com.ph; internet www.pse.com.ph; f. 1994; est. following the merger of the Manila and Makati Stock Exchanges; 362 listed cos (2012); Chair. JOSE T. PARDO; Pres. HANS B. SICAT.

INSURANCE

At March 2012 a total of 116 insurance companies were authorized by the Insurance Commission to transact in the Philippines. Of these 30 were life insurance companies, 83 for non-life insurance and three composite insurance companies. Foreign companies were also permitted to operate in the country.

Principal Domestic Companies

Ayala Life Assurance Inc: Ayala Life-FGU Center, 14th–15th Floors, 6811 Ayala Ave, Makati City, Metro Manila; tel. (2) 8885433; fax (2) 8180171; e-mail customer.service@ayalalife.com.ph; internet www.ayalalife.com.ph; Chair. XAVIER LOINAZ.

BPI/MS Insurance Corpn: Ayala Life-FGU Center, 11th Floor, 6811 Ayala Ave, Makati City, 1226 Metro Manila; tel. (2) 8409000; fax (2) 8409099; e-mail insure@bpims.com; internet www.bpims .com; f. 2002; est. by merger of FGU Insurance Corpn and FEB Mitsui Marine Insurance Corpn; jt venture of Bank of the Philippine Islands and Sumitomo Insurance Co (Japan); cap. 731m. (2006), sales 2,140m.; Chair. AURELIO R. MONTINOLA, III; Pres. TAKAAKI UEDA.

Central Surety & Insurance Co: 2nd Floor, Universal-Re Bldg, 106 Paseo de Roxas, Legaspi Village, Makati City, 1200 Metro Manila; tel. (2) 8174931; fax (2) 8170006; f. 1945; bonds, fire, marine, casualty, motor car; Pres. FERMIN T. CASTAÑEDA.

Commonwealth Insurance Co: BDO Plaza, 10th Floor, 8737 Paseo de Roxas, Makati City, Metro Manila; tel. (2) 8187626; fax (2) 8138575; e-mail info@cic.com.ph; internet www.cic.com.ph; f. 1935; Pres. MARIO NOCHE.

Co-operative Insurance System of the Philippines: CISP Bldg, 80 Malakas St, Diliman, Quezon City, Metro Manila; tel. (2) 4359100; fax (2) 4333211; e-mail cisplife@cisplife.com; internet www.cisplife .com; Chair. LEONIDA V. CHAVEZ; Pres. AMBROSIO M. RODRIGUEZ.

Empire Insurance Co: Prudential Life Bldg, 2nd Floor, 843 Arnaiz Ave, Legaspi Village, Makati City, 1229 Metro Manila; tel. (2) 8159561; fax (2) 8152599; e-mail empire_ins_co@yahoo.com; f. 1949; fire, bonds, marine, accident, motor car, extraneous perils; Pres. and CEO JOSE MA G. SANTOS.

Equitable Insurance Corpn: Equitable Bank Bldg, 4th Floor, 262 Juan Luna St, Binondo, POB 1103, Metro Manila; tel. (2) 2430291; fax (2) 2415768; e-mail info@equitableinsurance.com.ph; internet www.equitableinsurance.com.ph; f. 1950; fire, marine, casualty, motor car, bonds; Pres. NORA T. GO; Exec. Vice-Pres. ANTONIO C. OCAMPO.

Great Domestic Insurance Co of the Philippines: 5th Floor, Champ Bldg, Anda Circle, Bonifacio Drive, Port Area, Manila; tel. (2) 5273044; fax (2) 5273052; e-mail grdomic@intertasia.com.ph; internet www.greatdomesticph.com; f. 1946; cap. 10m.; Pres. and Chair. MAR S. LOPEZ.

Insular Life Assurance Co Ltd: Insular Life Corporate Center, Insular Life Drive, Filinvest Corporate City, Alabang, 1781 Muntinlupa City; tel. (2) 5821818; fax (2) 7711717; e-mail corplan@ insular.com.ph; internet www.insularlife.com.ph; f. 1910; members' equity 14,000m. (Dec. 2009); Chair. and CEO VICENTE R. AYLLÓN.

Makati Insurance Co Inc: BPI Buendia Center, 19th Floor, Sen. Gil J. Puyat Ave, Makati City, 1200 Metro Manila; tel. (2) 8459576; fax (2) 8915229; f. 1965; non-life; Pres. and Gen. Man. JAIME L. DARANTINAO; Chair. OCTAVIO V. ESPIRITU.

Malayan Insurance Co Inc: Yuchengco Tower I, 4th Floor, 484 Quintin Paredes St, Binondo, 1099 Metro Manila; tel. (2) 2428888; fax (2) 2412188; e-mail malayan@malayan.com; internet www .malayan.com; f. 1949; cap. 100m.; insurance and bonds; Pres. YVONNE S. YUCHENGCO; Chair. ADELITA VERGEL DE DIOS.

Manila Surety & Fidelity Co Inc: 66 P. Florentino St, Quezon City, Metro Manila; tel. (2) 7122251; fax (2) 7124129; f. 1945; cap. p.u. 50m., members' equity 85m. (Dec. 2003); Pres. MARIA LOURDES V. PEÑA; Vice-Pres. MARIA EDITHA PEÑA-LIM; 4 brs.

Metropolitan Insurance Co: Ateneum Bldg, 3rd Floor, 160 L. P. Leviste St, Salcedo Village, Makati City, Metro Manila; tel. (2) 8672888; fax (2) 8162294; f. 1933; non-life; Pres. JOSE M. PERIQUET, Jr; Exec. Vice-Pres. ROBERTO ABAD.

National Life Insurance Co of the Philippines: National Life Insurance Bldg, 6762 Ayala Ave, Makati City, Metro Manila; tel. (2) 8100251; fax (2) 8178718; f. 1933; Pres. BENJAMIN L. DE LEON; Sr Vice-Pres. DOUGLAS MCLAREN.

National Reinsurance Corpn of the Philippines: AXA Life Center, 18th Floor, Sen. Gil J. Puyat Ave, cnr Tindalo St, Makati City, 1200 Metro Manila; tel. (2) 7595801; fax (2) 7595886; e-mail nrcp@nrcp.com.ph; internet www.nrcp.com.ph; f. 1978; Chair. HELEN Y. DEE; Pres. and CEO ROBERTO B. CRISOL.

Paramount Life and General Insurance Corpn: Sage House, 14th and 15th Floors, 110 V. A. Rufino St, Legaspi Village, Makati City, 1229 Metro Manila; tel. (2) 8127956; fax (2) 8131140; e-mail insure@paramount.com.ph; internet www.paramount.com.ph; f. 1950; fmrly Paramount General Insurance Corpn; name changed to Paramount Union Insurance Corpn in 2001; name changed as above in 2002; fire, marine, casualty, motor car; Chair. PATRICK L. GO; Pres. GEORGE T. TIU.

Philippine American Life and General Insurance Co (Philamlife): Philamlife Bldg, United Nations Ave, Metro Manila; POB 2167, 0990 Metro Manila; tel. (2) 5269404; fax (2) 5222863; e-mail philamwebmaster@aig.com; internet www.philamlife.com; Pres. TREVOR BULL.

Philippine AXA Life Insurance Corpn: Philippine AXA Life Centre, Sen. Gil J. Puyat Ave, cnr Tindalo St, Makati City, Metro Manila; tel. (2) 5815292; fax (2) 8192631; e-mail customer.service@ axa.com.ph; internet www.axa.com.ph; Pres. and CEO SEVERINUS HERMANS.

Philippine Charter Insurance Coprn: Skyland Plaza, Sen. Gil J. Puyat Ave, cnr Tindalo St, Makati City 1203; tel. (2) 5806800; fax (2) 8154797; e-mail customerservice@philcharter.com.ph; internet www.philcharter.com.ph; f. 1960; Chair. BIENVENIDO E. LAGUESMA; Pres. MELECIO MALLILLIN.

Pioneer Insurance and Surety Corpn: Pioneer House Makati, 108 Paseo de Roxas, Legaspi Village, Makati City, 1229 Metro Manila; tel. (2) 8127777; fax (2) 8171461; e-mail info@pioneer.com .ph; internet www.pioneer.com.ph; f. 1954; cap. 5,441m. (2009); Pres. and CEO DAVID C. COYUKIAT.

Rizal Surety and Insurance Co: Prudential Life Bldg, 3rd Floor, 843 Arnaiz Ave, Legaspi Village, Makati City, Metro Manila; tel. (2) 8159561; fax (2) 8152599; e-mail rizalsic@mkt.weblinq.com; f. 1939; fire, bond, marine, motor car, accident, extraneous perils; Chair. and Pres. S. CORPUS.

Standard Insurance Co Inc: Petron Mega Plaza Bldg, 28th Floor, Sen. Gil J. Puyat Ave, Makati City, Metro Manila; tel. (2) 9886388; f. 1958; Chair. LOURDES T. ECHAUZ; Pres. PATRICIA CHILIP.

Sterling Insurance Co: Zeta II Annex Bldg, 6th Floor, 191 Salcedo St, Legaspi Village, Makati City, Metro Manila; tel. and fax (2) 8923794; f. 1960; fmrly Dominion Insurance Corpn; renamed as above Nov. 2001; fire, marine, motor car, accident, engineering, bonds; Pres. RAFAEL GALLAGA.

Tico Insurance Co Inc: Trafalgar Plaza, 7th Floor, 105 H. V. de la Costa St, Salcedo Village, Makati City, 1227 Metro Manila; tel. (2) 8140143; fax (2) 8140150; f. 1937; fmrly Tabacalera Insurance Co Inc; Chair. and Pres. CARLOS CATHOLICO.

UCPB General Insurance Co Inc: UCPB Bldg, 5th Floor, 7907 Makati Ave, Makati City; tel. (2) 8111788; fax (2) 2773333; e-mail ucpbgen@ucpbgen.com; internet www.ucpbgen.com; f. 1963; non-life; Pres. ISABELO P. AFRICA; Chair. JUAN ANDRES D. BAUTISTA.

Universal Reinsurance Corpn: Ayala Life Bldg, 9th Floor, 6786 Ayala Ave, Makati City, Metro Manila; tel. (2) 7514977; fax (2) 8173745; f. 1949; life and non-life; Chair. JAIME AUGUSTO ZOBEL DE AYALA II; Pres. HERMINIA S. JACINTO.

Regulatory Body

Insurance Commission: 1071 United Nations Ave, Metro Manila; tel. and fax (2) 5238461; e-mail pubassist_ic@yahoo.com.ph; internet www.insurance.gov.ph; regulates the private insurance industry by, among other things, issuing certificates of authority to insurance companies and intermediaries and monitoring their financial solvency; Commr EMMANUEL F. DOOC.

Trade and Industry

GOVERNMENT AGENCIES

Board of Investments: Industry and Investments Bldg, 385 Sen. Gil J. Puyat Ave, Makati City, 1200 Metro Manila; tel. (2) 8976682; fax (2) 8958233; e-mail nerbac@boi.gov.ph; internet www.boi.gov.ph; Chair. GREGORY L. DOMINGO.

Bureau of Domestic Trade (BDT): Trade and Industry Bldg, Ground Floor, 361 Sen. Gil J. Puyat Ave, Makati City, Metro Manila; tel. (2) 7513223; fax (2) 7513324; e-mail bdt@dti.gov.ph; Dir MEYNARD R. ORBETA.

Cagayan Economic Zone Authority: Westar Bldg, 7th Floor, 611 Shaw Blvd, Pasig City, 1603 Metro Manila; tel. (2) 6365774; fax (2) 6313997; e-mail info@ceza.gov.ph; internet ceza.gov.ph; Administrator and CEO JOSÉ MARI B. PONCE.

Clark Development Corpn: Bldg 2122, C. P. Garcia St, Clark Freeport Zone, Pampanga; tel. (45) 5999000; fax (45) 5992507; e-mail info@clark.com.ph; internet www.clark.com.ph; Chair. EDUARDO OBAN; Pres. and CEO BENIGNO N. RICAFORT.

Industrial Technology Development Institute: DOST Compound, Gen. Santos Ave, Bicutan, Taguig, 1631 Metro Manila; tel. (2) 8372071; fax (2) 8373167; e-mail adiv@dost.gov.ph; internet itdibiz.com; Dir Dr NUNA E. ALMANZOR.

Maritime Industry Authority (MARINA): Parkview Plaza, 984 Taft Ave, cnr T. M. Kalaw St, Ermita, Manila; tel. (2) 5239078; fax (2) 5242746; e-mail oadm@marina.gov.ph; internet www.marina.gov .ph; f. 1974; development of inter-island shipping, overseas shipping, shipbuilding and repair, and maritime power; Administrator MARIA ELENA H. BAUTISTA, Jr.

National Tobacco Administration: NTA Bldg, Scout Reyes St, cnr Panay Ave, Quezon City, Metro Manila; tel. (2) 3743987; fax (2) 3742505; e-mail mis@nta.gov.ph; internet www.nta.da.gov.ph; f. 1987; Administrator CARLITOS S. ENCARNACION.

Philippine Coconut Authority (PCA): PCA Compound, Elliptical Rd, Diliman, Quezon City, 1100 Metro Manila; tel. (2) 9284501; fax (2) 9216173; e-mail pca_cpo@yahoo.com.ph; internet www.pca.da .gov.ph; f. 1973; Chair. ARTHUR C. YAP; Administrator OSCAR G. GARIN.

Philippine Council for Advanced Science and Technology Research and Development (PCASTRD): DOST Main Bldg, Gen. Santos Ave, Bicutan, Taguig, 1631 Metro Manila; tel. (2) 8377522; fax (2) 8373168; e-mail pcastrd@dost.gov.ph; internet www.pcastrd.dost.gov.ph; f. 1987; Exec. Dir Dr REYNALDO V. EBORA.

Philippine Economic Zone Authority: Roxas Blvd, cnr San Luis St, Pasay City, Metro Manila; tel. (2) 5513454; fax (2) 8916380; e-mail info@peza.gov.ph; internet www.peza.gov.ph; f. 1995; Dir-Gen. Dr LILIA B. DE LIMA.

Privatization and Management Office: Department of Finance, 104 Gamboa St, Legaspi Village, Makati City, 1229 Metro Manila; tel. (2) 8932383; fax (2) 8933453; e-mail pmo@eastern.com.ph; internet www.pmo.gov.ph; f. 2002; formed to handle the privatization of govt assets; succeeded Asset Privatization Trust; Chief Privatization Officer GUILLERMO N. HERNANDEZ.

Subic Bay Metropolitan Authority: Administration Bldg, 229 Waterfront Rd, Subic Bay Freeport Zone, 2222 Zambales; tel. (47) 2524000; fax (47) 2524216; e-mail webteam@sbma.com; internet www.sbma.com; Chair. FELICIANO G. SALONGA; CEO and Administrator ARMAND C. ARREZA.

DEVELOPMENT ORGANIZATIONS

Bases Conversion and Development Authority: Bonifacio Technology Center, 2nd Floor, 31st St, Cres. Park West, Bonifacio Global City, POB 42, Taguig, 1634 Metro Manila; tel. (2) 8166666; fax (2) 8160996; e-mail bcda@bcda.gov.ph; internet www.bcda.gov.ph; f. 1992; est. to facilitate the conversion, privatization and development of fmr military bases; Chair. ALOYSIUS R. SANTOS; Pres. and CEO NARCISO L. ABAYA.

Bureau of Land Development: DAR Bldg, Elliptical Rd, Diliman, Quezon City, Metro Manila; tel. (2) 9287031; fax (2) 9260971; Dir EUGENIO B. BERNARDO.

Capital Market Development Council (CMDC): Unit 1901, 19th Floor, 139 Corporate Center, Valero St, Salcedo Village, Makati City, Metro Manila; tel. (2) 8114052; fax (2) 8114185; e-mail cmdcphil@yahoo.com.ph; internet www.cmdc-phil.net; f. 1991; Chair. ABELARDO V. CORTEZ; Exec. Dir RESCINA BHAGWANI.

Cooperative Development Authority: CDA Bldg, Ground Floor, 827 Aurora Blvd, Immaculate Conception Village, Quezon City, Metro Manila; tel. (2) 3736894; fax (2) 3712077; e-mail cda.oed@gmail.com; internet www.cda.gov.ph; Chair. LECIRA V. JUAREZ; Exec. Dir NIEL A. SANTILLAN.

Micro, Small and Medium Enterprise Development Council: Oppen Bldg, 3rd Floor, 349 Sen. Gil J. Puyat Ave, Makati City, Metro Manila; tel. and fax (2) 8967916; e-mail bsmbd@mnl.sequel.net; f. 2008; est. to replace Small and Medium Enterprise Devt Council; initiates and implements programmes and projects addressing the specific needs of micro, small and medium enterprises in areas concerning entrepreneurship, institutional development, productivity improvement, organization, financing and marketing; chaired by Sec. of Trade and Industry; Vice-Chair. JOSE CONCEPCION, III

> **Bureau of Micro, Small and Medium Enterprise Development (BMSMED):** Trade and Industry Bldg, 5th Floor, 361 Sen. Gil J. Puyat Ave, Makati City, Metro Manila; tel. (02) 8971693; fax (02) 8967916; e-mail bmsmed@dti.gov.ph; f. 2008, to replace Bureau of Small and Medium Business Development; Secr. of the MSMED Council.

National Development Co (NDC): NDC Bldg, 8th Floor, 116 Tordesillas St, Salcedo Village, Makati City, 1227 Metro Manila; tel. (2) 8404838; fax (2) 8404862; e-mail info@ndc.gov.ph; internet www.ndc.gov.ph; f. 1919; govt-owned corpn engaged in the organization, financing and management of subsidiaries and corpns, incl. commercial, industrial, mining, agricultural and other enterprises assisting national economic devt; also jt industrial ventures with other ASEAN countries; Chair. PETER B. FAVILA; Gen. Man. LOURDES F. RUBUENO.

Philippine National Oil Co (PNOC): PNOC Bldg 6, Energy Center, Merritt Rd, Fort Bonifacio, Taguig City, Metro Manila; tel. (2) 7897662; internet www.pnoc.com.ph; f. 1973; state-owned energy devt agency mandated to ensure stable and sufficient supply of oil products and to develop domestic energy resources; Chair. ANGELO T. REYES; Pres. and CEO ANTONIO M. CAILAO.

Southern Philippines Development Authority: Basic Petroleum Bldg, 104 Carlos Palanca, Jr, St, Legaspi Village, Makati City, Metro Manila; fax (2) 8183907; Chair. ROBERTO AVENTAJADO; Manila Rep. GERUDIO 'KHALIQ' MADUENO.

CHAMBERS OF COMMERCE AND INDUSTRY

Cebu Chamber of Commerce and Industry (CCCI): CCCI Center, cnr Commerce and Industry Sts, North Reclamation Area, Cebu City; tel. (32) 2323938; fax (32) 4129461; internet www.cebuchamber.org; f. 1903; Pres. PRUDENCIO GESTA.

Chamber of Mines of the Philippines: Rm 809, Ortigas Bldg, Ortigas Ave, Pasig City, 1605 Metro Manila; tel. (2) 6354123; fax (2) 6354160; e-mail info@chamberofmines.com.ph; internet www.chamberofmines.com.ph; f. 1975; Chair. ARTEMIO F. DISINI; Pres. BENJAMIN PHILIP G. ROMUALDEZ.

Federation of Filipino-Chinese Chambers of Commerce and Industry Inc: Federation Center, 6th Floor, Muelle de Binondo St, Binondo, POB 23, Metro Manila; tel. (2) 2419201; fax (2) 2422361; internet www.ffcccii.com.ph/main.html; f. 1954; Pres. TAN CHING.

Philippine Chamber of Coal Mines (Philcoal): Rm 1007, Princeville Condominium, S. Laurel St, cnr Shaw Blvd, 1552 Mandaluyong City, Metro Manila; tel. (2) 5330518; fax (2) 5315513; f. 1980; Exec. Dir BERTRAND GONZALES.

Philippine Chamber of Commerce and Industry (PCCI): 3rd Floor, Commerce and Industry Plaza, cnr 1030 Campus Ave, Park Avenue McKinley Town Center, Fort Bonifacio, Taguig City; tel. (2)

8468196; fax (2) 8468619; e-mail pcci@philippinechamber.com; internet www.philippinechamber.com; f. 1978; Pres. MIGUEL B. VARELA; Chair. ALFREDO M. YAO.

FOREIGN TRADE ORGANIZATIONS

Bureau of Export Trade Promotion (BETP): New Solid Bldg, 6th Floor, 357 Sen. Gil J. Puyat Ave, Makati City, 1200 Metro Manila; tel. (2) 8904707; fax (2) 8904693; e-mail infobetp@dti.gov.ph; internet www.tradelinephil.dti.gov.ph; Dir FERNANDO P. CALA, II.

Bureau of Import Services (BIS): Tara Bldg, 3rd Floor, 389 Sen. Gil J. Puyat Ave, Makati City, Metro Manila; tel. (2) 8964431; fax (2) 8964430; e-mail bis@dti.gov.ph; Dir LUIS M. CATIBAYAN.

Garments and Textile Export Board (GTEB): New Solid Bldg, 2nd and 3rd Floors, 357 Sen. Gil J. Puyat Ave, Makati City, Metro Manila; tel. (2) 8978723; fax (2) 4904653; e-mail gtebebs@dti.gov.ph; manages and supervises the garment textile quota system; Exec. Dir FELICITAS R. AGONCILLO REYES.

Philippine International Trading Corpn (PITC): NDC Bldg, 5th Floor, 116 Tordesillas St, Salcedo Village, 1227 Metro Manila; tel. (2) 8189801; fax (2) 8920782; e-mail pitc@pitc.com.ph; internet www.pitc.gov.ph; f. 1973; state trading company to conduct international marketing of general merchandise, industrial and construction goods, raw materials, semi-finished and finished goods, and bulk trade of agri-based products; also provides financing, bonded warehousing, shipping, cargo and customs services; Chair. PETER B. FAVILA; Pres. and CEO JORGE MENDOZA JUDAN.

INDUSTRIAL AND TRADE ASSOCIATIONS

Beverage Industry Association of the Philippines: SMPC Bldg, 23rd Floor, St Francis St, Mandaluyong City, Metro Manila; tel. (2) 6346840; fax (2) 6318672; e-mail rbkmlo@mnl.sequel.net; f. 1988; Pres. HECTOR GUBALLA.

Chamber of Automotive Manufacturers of the Philippines (CAMPI): Suite 1206, 12th Floor, Jollibee Center, San Miguel Ave, Ortigas Center, Pasig City, 1600 Metro Manila; tel. (2) 6329733; fax (2) 6339941; e-mail campi@globelines.com.ph; internet www.campiauto.org; f. 1995; 11 mems; Pres. ROMMEL R. GUTIERREZ.

Construction Industry Authority of the Philippines (CIAP): Jupiter I Bldg, 4th Floor, Jupiter St, Makati City, Metro Manila; tel. (2) 8979336; e-mail pocb@skynet.net; Officer-in-Charge KATHERINE T. DELA CRUZ.

Cotton Development Administration (CODA): ATI Bldg, 1st Floor, Elliptical Rd, Diliman, Quezon City, 1100 Metro Manila; tel. (2) 9208878; fax (2) 9209238; e-mail coda@da.gov.ph; internet www.coda.da.gov.ph; f. 1998; Administrator Dr EUGENIO D. ORPIA, Jr.

Federation of Philippine Industries (FPI): Unit 701, Atlanta Center, 31 Annapolis St, Greenhills, San Juan City, Metro Manila; tel. (2) 7223409; fax (2) 7229737; e-mail fpi@fpi.ph; internet www.fpi.ph; f. 1991; 129 mems; Chair. MENELEO J. CARLOS, Jr; Pres. JESUS L. ARRANZA.

Fiber Industry Development Authority: Asiatrust Bank Annex Bldg, 1424 Quezon Ave, Quezon City, Metro Manila; tel. (2) 3737494; fax (2) 4944126; e-mail fida@pldtdsl.net; internet www.fida.da.gov.ph/home.html.html; f. 1977; Administrator CECILIA GLORIA J. SORIANO.

Philippine Association of Electrical Industries: Banks of the Philippines Bldg, Suite 702, Plaza Cervantes, Binondo, Metro Manila; tel. and fax (2) 2421144; Pres. RICARDO SY.

Philippine Fisheries Development Authority: PCA Annex Bldg, 2nd Floor, Elliptical Rd, Diliman, Quezon City, 1101 Metro Manila; tel. (2) 9256141; fax (2) 9256138; e-mail cvmaranan@yahoo.com; internet www.pfda.da.gov.ph; f. 1976; Gen. Man. CLARO V. MARANAN.

Philippine Liquefied Petroleum Gas Association: 218 San Vicente St, Binondo, Metro Manila; tel. (2) 2412668; fax (2) 6337781; f. 1966; Pres. JOSELITO ASENTERO.

Semiconductor and Electronic Industries in the Philippines (SEIPI): Unit 902, RCBC Plaza, Tower 2, Ayala Ave, cnr Sen. Gil J. Puyat Ave, Makati City, 1200 Metro Manila; tel. (2) 8449028; fax (2) 8449037; e-mail philippine.electronics@seipi.org.ph; internet www.seipi.org.ph; f. 1984; 240 mems; Pres. DAN C. LACHICA.

EMPLOYERS' ORGANIZATIONS

Cement Manufacturers' Association of the Philippines (CeMAP): Corporal Cruz St, cnr E. Rodriguez Jr Ave, Bagong Ilog, Pasig City, Metro Manila; tel. and fax (2) 6717585; e-mail cementinfo@cemap.org.ph; internet www.cemap.org.ph; f. 1957; est. as Cement Institute of the Philippines; renamed in 1965 as Cement Asscn of the Philippines, in 1973 as Philippine Cement Corpn, and in 1980 as Philippine Cement Mfrs' Corpn; present name adopted in 2003; 14 mems; Chair. RENATO SUNICO; Pres. ERNESTO M. ORDOÑEZ.

Employers' Confederation of the Philippines (ECOP): ECC Bldg, 2nd Floor, 355 Sen. Gil J. Puyat Ave, Makati City, Metro Manila; tel. (2) 8904845; fax (2) 8958623; e-mail ecop@webquest.com; internet www.ecop.org.ph; f. 1975; Chair. MIGUEL B. VARELA; Pres. SERGIO ORTIZ-LUIS, Jr.

Filipino Shipowners' Association: Victoria Bldg, Rm 503, 429 United Nations Ave, Ermita, 1000 Metro Manila; tel. (2) 5227318; fax (2) 5243164; e-mail filiship@info.com.ph; internet www.filipinoshipowners.com.ph; f. 1950; 24 mems, incl. 6 assoc. mems; Chair. CARLOS C. SALINAS; Exec. Sec. AUGUSTO Y. ARREZA, Jr.

Philippine Coconut Producers' Federation, Inc: Wardley Bldg, 2nd Floor, 1991 Taft Ave, cnr San Juan St, Pasay City, 1300 Metro Manila; tel. (2) 5230918; fax (2) 5211333; e-mail cocofed@pworld.net.ph; Pres. MARIA CLARA L. LOBREGAT.

Philippine Retailers' Association (PRA): Unit 2610, Jollibee Plaza, F. Ortigas Jr Rd, Ortigas Center, Pasig City, Metro Manila; tel. (2) 6874180; fax (2) 6360825; e-mail philretailers@gmail.com; internet www.philretailers.com; f. 1976; est. as Chamber of Philippine Dept Stores and Retailers, Inc; present name adopted 1991; Pres. JORGE MENDIOLA.

Philippine Sugar Millers' Association Inc: 1402 Security Bank Centre, 6776 Ayala Ave, Makati City, 1226 Metro Manila; tel. (2) 8911138; fax (2) 8911144; e-mail psma@psma.com.ph; internet www.psma.com.ph; f. 1922; Chair. JULIO O. SY; Pres. PEDRO E. ROXAS.

Textile Mills Association of the Philippines (TMAP): Ground Floor, Alexander House, 132 Amorsolo St, Legaspi Village, Makati City, 1229 Metro Manila; tel. (2) 8186601; fax (2) 8183107; e-mail tmap@pacific.net.ph; f. 1956; 11 mems; Pres. HERMENEGILDO C. ZAYCO; Chair. JAMES L. GO.

Textile Producers' Association of the Philippines, Inc: Downtown Center Bldg, Rm 513, 516 Quintin Paredes St, Binondo, Metro Manila; tel. (2) 2411144; fax (2) 2411162; Pres. GO CUN UY; Exec. Sec. ROBERT L. TAN.

UTILITIES

Energy Regulatory Commission: Pacific Center Bldg, San Miguel Ave, Ortigas Center, Pasig City, 1600 Metro Manila; tel. (2) 9145000; fax (2) 6315818; e-mail info@erc.gov.ph; internet www.erc.gov.ph; f. 2001; Chair. and CEO ZENAIDA CRUZ-DUCUT; Exec. Dir FRANCIS SATURNINO C. JUAN.

Electricity

Davao Light and Power Co: 163–165 C. Bangoy Sr St, 8000 Davao City; tel. (82) 2293572; internet www.davaolight.com; f. 1929.

Manila Electric Co (Meralco): Lopez Bldg, 2nd Floor, Meralco Center, Ortigas Ave, Pasig City, 0300 Metro Manila; tel. (2) 6312222; fax (2) 6315591; e-mail finplan.inv.relations@meralco.com.ph; internet www.meralco.com.ph; f. 1903; partially privatized in 1991; 34% govt-owned; supplies electric power to Manila and seven provinces in Luzon; largest electricity distributor, supplying 54% of total consumption in 2000; Chair. MANUEL V. PANGILINAN; Pres. and CEO OSCAR S. REYES.

National Power Corpn (NAPOCOR): Quezon Ave, cnr BIR Rd, Quezon City, Metro Manila; tel. (2) 9213541; fax (2) 9212468; e-mail webmaster@napocor.gov.ph; internet www.napocor.gov.ph; f. 1936; state-owned corpn supplying electric and hydroelectric power throughout the country; partially privatized in 2007; Pres. and CEO FROILAN TAMPINCO.

Gas

First Gen Corpn: Benpres Bldg, 3rd Floor, Exchange Rd, cnr Meralco Ave, Pasig City, Metro Manila; tel. and fax (2) 4496400; fax (2) 6378366; e-mail info@firstgen.com.ph; internet www.firstgen.com.ph; f. 1998; major interests in power generation and distribution; Chair. OSCAR M. LOPEZ; Pres. FEDERICO R. LOPEZ.

Water

Regulatory Authority

Metropolitan Waterworks and Sewerage System: 4th Floor, Administration Bldg, MWSS Complex, 489 Katipunan Rd, Balara, Quezon City, 1105 Metro Manila; tel. (2) 9223757; fax (2) 9212887; e-mail info@mwss.gov.ph; internet www.mwss.gov.ph; govt regulator for water supply, treatment and distribution within Metro Manila; Chair. RAMON B. ALIKPALA; Administrator GERARDO ESQUIVEL (acting).

Distribution Companies

Davao City Water District: Km 5, Jose P. Laurel Ave, Bajada, 8000 Davao City; tel. (82) 2219400; fax (82) 2264885; e-mail davaowater@davao-water.gov.ph; internet www.davao-water.gov.ph; f. 1973; public utility responsible for the water supply of Davao City; Chair. EDUARDO A. BANGAYAN; Gen. Man. EDWIN V. REGALADO (acting).

Manila Water: MWSS Administration Bldg, 489 Katipunan Rd, Balara, Quezon City, 1105 Metro Manila; tel. (2) 9267999; fax (2) 9818164; e-mail info@manilawater.com; internet www.manilawater.com; f. 1997 following the privatization of Metro Manila's water and wastewater services; responsible for water supply and wastewater services to Manila East until 2037; Chair. FERNANDO ZOBEL DE ALAYA; Pres. and CEO GERARDO C. ABLAZA, Jr.

Maynilad Water: MWSS Compound, 489 Katipunan Rd, Balara, Quezon City, 1105 Metro Manila; tel. (2) 9813333; fax (2) 9223759; e-mail customer.helpdesk@mayniladwater.com.ph; internet www.mayniladwater.com.ph; f. 1998; est. following the privatization of Metro Manila's water services; responsible for water supply, sewage and sanitation services for Manila West until 2021; Pres. ROGELIO SINGSON.

Metropolitan Cebu Water District: Magallanes St, cnr Lapulapu St, 6000 Cebu City; tel. (32) 2548434; fax (32) 2545391; e-mail mcwd@cvis.net.ph; internet www.mcwd.gov.ph; f. 1974; public utility responsible for water supply and sewerage of Cebu City and surrounding towns and cities; Chair. JUAN SAUL F. MONTECILLO; Gen. Man. ARMANDO H. PAREDES.

TRADE UNION FEDERATIONS

Katipunang Manggagawang Pilipino (KMP-TUCP) (Trade Union Congress of the Philippines): TUCP Training Center Bldg, TUCP-PGEA Compound, Masaya St, cnr Maharlika St, Diliman, Quezon City, 1101 Metro Manila; tel. and fax (2) 5253522; e-mail secrtucp@tucp.org.ph; internet www.tucp.org.ph; f. 1975; 39 affiliates; 1.0m. mems; Pres. ERNESTO F. HERRERA; Gen. Sec. JOSE P. UMALI.

INDEPENDENT LABOUR FEDERATIONS

The following organizations are not affiliated to the KMP-TUCP:

Associated Marine Officers and Seamen's Union of the Philippines (AMOSUP): Seaman's Centre, cnr Cabildo and Sta Potenciana Sts, Intramuros, Metro Manila; tel. (2) 5278491; fax (2) 5273534; e-mail s_center@amosup.org; internet www.amosup.org.ph; f. 1960; 23 affiliated unions with 55,000 mems; Pres. GREGORIO S. OCA.

Federation of Free Workers (FFW): FFW Bldg, 1943 Taft Ave, Malate, Metro Manila; tel. (2) 5219435; fax (2) 4006656; internet www.ffw.org.ph; f. 1950; affiliated to Int. Trade Union Confed. (ITUC); 300 affiliated local unions and 400,000 mems; Pres. ANTONIO ASPER.

Kilusang Mayo Uno (KMU): 63 Narra St, Barangay Claro, Quezon City, 1102 Metro Manila; tel. (2) 4210986; fax (2) 4210768; e-mail obrero@kilusangmayouno.org; internet www.kilusangmayouno.org; f. 1980; Chair. ELMER LABOG; Sec.-Gen. WILSON BALDONAZA.

Lakas ng Manggagawa Labor Center: Metro Manila; tel. and fax (2) 5280482; a grouping of 'independent' local unions; Chair. OSCAR M. ACERSON.

Manggagawa ng Komunikasyon sa Pilipinas (MKP): 22 Libertad St, Mandaluyong City, Metro Manila; tel. (2) 5313701; fax (2) 5312109; f. 1951; Pres. PETE PINLAC.

National Confederation of Labor: Suite 402, Carmen Bldg, Ronquillo St, cnr Evangelista St, Quiapo, Metro Manila; tel. and fax (2) 7334474; f. 1994 by fmr mems of Kilusang Mayo Uno; Pres. ANTONIO DIAZ.

Philippine Social Security Labor Union (PSSLU): Carmen Bldg, Suite 309, Ronquillo St, Quiapo, Metro Manila; f. 1954; Nat. Pres. ANTONIO B. DIAZ; Nat. Sec. OFELIA C. ALAVERA.

Samahang Manggagawang Pilipino (SMP-NATOW) (National Alliance of Teachers and Office Workers): 236 J. Romualdez St, Mandaluyong City, Metro Manila; tel. and fax 9176242569 (mobile); e-mail smpnatow@smpnatow.org; internet smpnatow.org; Pres. JOSEPH JOVELLANOS; Sec.-Gen. MILAGROS C. OGALINDA.

Solidarity Trade Conference for Progress: Rizal Ave, Dipolog City; tel. and fax (65) 2124303; Pres. NICOLAS E. SABANDAL.

Trade Unions of the Philippines and Allied Services (TUPAS): Med-dis Bldg, Suites 203–204, Solana St, cnr Real St, Intramuros, Metro Manila; tel. (2) 493449; affiliated to the World Fed. of Trade Unions; 280 affiliated unions and 75,000 mems; Nat. Pres. DIOSCORO O. NUÑEZ; Pres. VLADIMIR R. TUPAZ.

Transport

RAILWAYS

The railway network is confined mainly to the island of Luzon. Following a dispute over costs and other issues, work on a major programme of network improvements and expansion, which was to include an extension to the Clark Special Economic Zone and a branch line to Subic, was suspended in May 2011.

Light Rail Transit Authority (Metrorail): Adm. Bldg, LRTA Compound, Aurora Blvd, Pasay City, Metro Manila; tel. (2) 8530041; fax (2) 8316449; e-mail lrtamain@lrta.gov.ph; internet www.lrta.gov.ph; managed and operated by Light Rail Transit Authority (LRTA); electrically driven mass transit system; Line 1 (15 km, Baclaran to Monumento) began commercial operations in Dec. 1984; Line 2 (13.8 km, Santolan to Recto) became fully operational in Oct. 2004; Line 1 South Extension (12 km, Baclaran to Bacoot) planned; Chair. JOSEPH EMILIO M. ABAYA.

Philippine National Railways: PNR Exec. Bldg, Mayhaligue St, Tondo, Metro Manila; tel. (2) 3190041; fax (2) 3190169; e-mail info@pnr.gov.ph; internet www.pnr.gov.ph; f. 1887; govt-owned; northern line services run from Manila to Caloocan, 6 km (although the track extends to San Fernando, La Union); southern line services run from Manila to Legaspi, Albay, 479 km; Chair. GERARD L. RABONZA; Gen. Man. JUNIO M. RAGRAGIO.

ROADS

In 2009 there were 213,151 km of roads in the Philippines, of which 29,898 km were national roads and 183,253 km were covered by provincial, city, municipal and barangay roads; an estimated 53,596 km of the total network were paved. Bus services provided the most widely used form of inland transport.

Department of Public Works and Highways: Bonifacio Dr., Port Area, Metro Manila; tel. (2) 3043300; e-mail singson.rogelio@dpwh.gov.ph; internet www.dpwh.gov.ph; responsible for the construction and maintenance of roads and bridges; Sec. ROGELIO L. SINGSON.

Land Transportation Franchising and Regulatory Board: East Ave, Diliman, Quezon City, Metro Manila; tel. (2) 9257191; fax (2) 4262515; e-mail officeofthechairman@ltfrb.gov.ph; internet www.ltfrb.gov.ph; f. 1987; Chair. JAIME D. JACOB.

Land Transportation Office (LTO): East Ave, Quezon City, 1100 Metro Manila; tel. (2) 9219072; fax (2) 9219071; e-mail ltombox@lto.gov.ph; internet www.lto.gov.ph; f. 1987; plans, formulates and implements land transport rules, regulations and safety measures; registration of motor vehicles; issues licences; Asst Sec. VIRGINIA TORRES; Exec. Dir ALFONSO V. TAN, Jr.

SHIPPING

The eight major ports are Manila, Cebu, Iloilo, Cagayan de Oro, Zamboanga, General Santos, Polloc and Davao. In December 2012 the flag registered fleet comprised 986 vessels, with a total displacement of 4,320,810 grt, of which 340 were general cargo ships.

Pangasiwaan ng Daungan ng Pilipinas (Philippine Ports Authority): Bonifacio Dr., South Harbour, Port Area, 1018 Metro Manila; tel. (2) 5274856; fax (2) 5274853; e-mail info@ppa.com.ph; internet www.ppa.com.ph; f. 1977; supervises all ports within the Philippine Ports Authority port system; Gen. Man. JUAN C. SANTA ANA.

Philippine Shippers' Bureau (PSB): Trade and Industry Bldg, 2nd Floor, 361 Sen. Gil J. Puyat Ave, Makati City, Metro Manila; tel. and fax (2) 7513304; fax (2) 7513305; e-mail psb@dti.gov.ph; shipping facilitator for international and domestic trade; promotes and protects the interests of shippers, exporters, importers and domestic traders; Dir PEDRO VICENTE C. MENDOZA.

Domestic Lines

2GO Travel: Times Plaza Bldg, 15th Floor, United Nations Ave, cnr Taft Ave, Ermita, 1000 Metro Manila; tel. and fax (2) 5287000; e-mail info@2go.com.ph; internet travel.2go.com.ph; fmrly Negros Navigation; changed name as above in 2012; Chair. FRANCIS C. CHUA; Pres. and CEO SULFICIO O. TAGUD, Jr.

Albar Shipping and Trading Corpn: 2649 Molave St, cnr East Service Rd, United Hills Village, Parañaque, 1713 Metro Manila; tel. (2) 8232391; fax (2) 8233046; e-mail info@albargroup.com.ph; internet www.albargroup.com.ph; f. 1974; manning agency (maritime), trading, ship husbanding; Chair. AKIRA S. KATO; Pres. JOSE ALBAR G. KATO.

Candano Shipping Lines, Inc: Victoria Bldg, 6th Floor, 429 United Nations Ave, Ermita, 2802 Metro Manila; tel. (2) 5238051; fax (2) 5211309; e-mail candano888@yahoo.com; f. 1953; inter-island and Far East chartering, cargo shipping; Pres. and Gen. Man. TRINIDAD CANDANO.

Delsan Transport Lines Inc: Magsaysay Center Bldg, 520 T. M. Kalaw St, Ermita, Metro Manila; tel. (2) 5219172; fax (2) 2889331; Pres. VICENTE A. SANDOVAL; Gen. Man. CARLOS A. BUENAFE.

Eastern Shipping Lines, Inc: ESL Bldg, 54 Anda Circle, Port Area, POB 4253, 2803 Metro Manila; tel. (2) 5277841; fax (2) 5273006; e-mail eastship@skyinet.net; f. 1957; services to Japan; Pres. ERWIN L. CHIONGBIAN; Exec. Vice-Pres. ROY L. CHIONGBIAN.

Loadstar Shipping Co Inc: Loadstar Bldg, 1294 Romualdez St, Paco, 1007 Metro Manila; tel. (2) 5238381; fax (2) 5218061; Pres. and Gen. Man. TEODORO G. BERNARDINO.

Lorenzo Shipping Corpn: 20th Floor, Times Plaza Bldg, United Nations Ave, cnr Taft Ave, Ermita, Metro Manila; tel. (2) 5672180; fax (2) 5672030; internet www.lorenzoshipping.com; Chair. DORIS MAGSAYSAY HO.

Luzteveco (Luzon Stevedoring Corpn): Magsaysay Bldg, 520 T. M. Kalaw St, Ermita, Metro Manila; f. 1909; two brs; freight-forwarding, air cargo, world-wide shipping, broking, stevedoring, salvage, chartering and oil-drilling support services; Pres. JOVINO G. LORENZO; Vice-Pres. RODOLFO B. SANTIAGO.

National Shipping Corpn of the Philippines: Metro Manila; tel. (2) 473631; fax (2) 5300169; services to Hong Kong, Taiwan, Korea, USA; Pres. TONY CHOW.

Philippine Pacific Ocean Lines Inc: Delgado Bldg, Bonifacio Drive, Port Area, POB 184, Metro Manila; tel. (2) 478541; Vice-Pres. C. P. CARANDANG.

Philippine President Lines, Inc: PPL Bldg, 1000–1046 United Nations Ave, POB 4248, Metro Manila; tel. (2) 5249011; fax (2) 5251308; trading world-wide; Chair. EMILIO T. YAP.

Sulpicio Lines, Inc: Don Sulpicio Go Bldg, Sulpicio Go St, Reclamation Area, POB 137, 6000 Cebu City; tel. (32) 2325361; fax (32) 2321216; internet www.sulpiciolines.com; Chair. ENRIQUE S. GO; Man. Dir CARLOS S. GO.

Transocean Transport Corpn: Magsaysay Bldg, 8th Floor, 520 T. M. Kalaw St, Ermita, POB 21, Metro Manila; tel. (2) 506611; Pres. and Gen. Man. MIGUEL A. MAGSAYSAY; Vice-Pres. EDUARDO U. MANESE.

United Philippine Lines, Inc: Plaza Santiago Bldg, Santa Clara St, Intramuros, POB 127, Metro Manila; tel. (2) 5277491; fax (2) 3380087; e-mail mailadmin@uplines.net; internet www.uplines.net; services world-wide; Pres. FERNANDO V. LISING.

CIVIL AVIATION

In addition to the international airports in Metro Manila (Ninoy Aquino International Airport), Cebu (Mactan International Airport), Angeles City (Clark International Airport) and Olongapo City (Subic Bay International Airport), there are alternative international airports at Laoag City, Ilocos Norte; Davao City; Zamboanga City; Gen. Santos (Tambler) City; Silay City (Bacolod-Silay International Airport); Iloilo City; and Puerto Princesa City, Palawan. There are also numerous domestic and private airports.

Civil Aviation Authority: MIA Rd, Pasay City, Metro Manila; tel. (2) 8799104; fax (2) 8340143; e-mail information@mis.caap.gov.ph; internet www.caap.gov.ph; implements govt policies for the development and operation of a safe and efficient aviation network; Dir-Gen. Lt-Gen. (retd) WILLIAM K. HOTCHKISS, III.

Civil Aeronautics Board: CAB Bldg, Old MIA Rd, Pasay City, Metro Manila; tel. (2) 8537259; fax (2) 8516911; e-mail tmanalac@cab .gov.ph; internet cab.gov.ph; exercises general supervision and regulation of, and jurisdiction and control over, air carriers, their equipment facilities and franchise; Chair. JOSEPH EMILIO AGUINALDO ABAYA; Exec. Dir CARMELO L. ARCILLA.

Manila International Airport Authority (MIAA): Metro Manila; tel. (2) 8322938; fax (2) 8331180; e-mail gm@miaa.gov.ph; internet www.miaa.gov.ph; Gen. Man. Maj.-Gen. (retd) JOSE ANGEL HONRADO.

Cebu Pacific Air: Airlines Operations Center Bldg, Manila Domestic Airport Complex, Pasay City, Metro Manila; tel. (2) 2308888; fax (2) 8512871; e-mail customerservice@cebupacificair.com; internet www.cebupacificair.com; f. 1995; domestic and international services; Chair. RICARDO J. ROMULO; Pres. and CEO LANCE Y. GOKONGWEI.

PAL Express: PNB Financial Centre, CCP Complex, Pasay City, Metro Manila; tel. (2) 3208300; e-mail reservations@airphilexpress .com; internet www.flypalexpress.com; f. 1995; domestic and regional services; Chair. DOMINGO T. CHUA; Pres. and CEO IÑIGO ZOBEL.

Philippine Airlines Inc (PAL): PNB Financial Center, Pres. Diosdado Macapagal Ave, CCP Complex, Pasay City, Metro Manila; tel. (2) 5562220; fax (2) 5562221; e-mail webmgr@pal.com.ph; internet www.philippineairlines.com; f. 1941; in Jan. 1992 67% of PAL was transferred to the private sector; operates domestic, regional and international services to destinations in the Far East, Australasia, the Middle East, the USA and Canada; Chair. and CEO LUCIO C. TAN; Pres. and COO RAMON S. ANG.

Spirit of Manila Airlines: Roxas Sea Front Garden, Roxas Blvd, cnr Ortigas St, Pasay City; tel. (2) 5444188; fax (2) 5567377; e-mail sales@spiritofmanilaairlines.com; internet www .spiritofmanilaairlines.com; regional and international passenger services from Manila to destinations in Asia and the Middle East; Pres. and CEO BASILIO P. REYES.

Zest Airways Inc: General Aviation Area, Pasay City; e-mail customerrelations@zestair.com.ph; internet www.zestair.com.ph; f. 1995; est. as Asian Spirit; following takeover by AMY Holdings, renamed as above 2008; operates services to about 20 domestic destinations, and international services to the Republic of Korea (South Korea); three aircraft; Chair. DONALD DEE; Pres. and CEO ALFREDO YAO.

Tourism

Although intermittently affected by political unrest, tourism remains an important sector of the economy. In 2011 visitor arrivals totalled 3,917,400 (including Filipinos permanently resident overseas), compared with 3,520,471 in the previous year. According to provisional figures, tourism receipts, excluding passenger transport, totalled US $3,152m. in 2011.

Philippine Tourism Promotions Board: Legaspi Towers, 4th Floor, 300 Roxas Blvd, 1004 Metro Manila; tel. (2) 5259318; fax (2) 5253314; e-mail pcvcnet@dotpcvc.gov.ph; internet www.dotpcvc.gov .ph; COO DOMINGO RAMON ENERIO, III.

Tourism Infrastructure and Enterprise Zone Authority: Department of Tourism Bldg, T. M. Kalaw St, Teodoro F. Valencia Circle, Ermita, 1000 Metro Manila; tel. (2) 5247141; fax (2) 5218113; e-mail info@philtourism.gov.ph; internet www.tieza.com.ph; CEO MARK T. LAPID.

Defence

As assessed at November 2012, the total strength of the armed forces was estimated at 125,000: army 86,000, navy an estimated 24,000 (including 8,300 Marines), air force an estimated 15,000. Active paramilitary forces, comprising the Philippine National Police (under the Department of Interior and Local Government), numbered 40,500. The Citizen Armed Forces Geographical Units (CAFGU), which replaced the civil home defence force, numbered about 50,000. Military service is voluntary.

Defence Expenditure: Budgeted at an estimated 113,000m. pesos for 2012.

Chief of Staff of the Armed Forces: Gen. EMMANUEL T. BAUTISTA.

Chief of Staff (Army): Lt-Gen. NOEL COBALLES.

Chief of Staff (Navy): Vice-Adm. JOSE LUIS M. ALANO.

Chief of Staff (Air Force): Maj.-Gen. LAURO DE LA CRUZ.

Education

The 1987 Constitution commits the Government to provide free elementary and high school education; elementary education is compulsory. The organization of education is the responsibility of the Department of Education.

There were 45,964 pre-primary and primary schools in 2010/11. In that year there were 1,650,232 pupils enrolled at pre-primary schools and 14,166,066 pupils enrolled at primary schools. Total enrolment at pre-primary level in 2008/09 included 39% (males 38%; females 39%) of children in the relevant age-group. In the same year 88% (males 88%; females 89%) of all children in the relevant age-group were enrolled at primary schools. In 2010/11 there were a total of 12,950 secondary schools, at which 6,954,946 pupils were enrolled. In 2008/09 enrolment at secondary level included 62% of children in the relevant age group (males 56%; females 67%). In 2004/05 there were a total of 1,619 tertiary level institutions, at which 2,402,315 pupils were enrolled. In 2005/06 total enrolment at tertiary level was equivalent to 28% (males 25%; females 32%) of the relevant age-group. Instruction is in both English and Filipino at elementary level, and English is the usual medium at the secondary and tertiary levels. The 2012 budget allocated 238,800m. pesos to education.

POLAND

Introductory Survey

LOCATION, CLIMATE, LANGUAGE, RELIGION, FLAG, CAPITAL

The Republic of Poland is situated in eastern Europe, bounded to the north by the Baltic Sea and an exclave of the Russian Federation (Kaliningrad Oblast), to the north-east by Lithuania, to the east by Belarus, to the south-east by Ukraine, to the west by Germany, and to the south by the Czech Republic and Slovakia. The climate is temperate in the west but continental in the east. Poland has short summers and cold, snowy winters. Temperatures in Warsaw are generally between −6°C (21°F) and 24°C (75°F). The official language is Polish, spoken by almost all of the population, and there is a small German-speaking community. Most of the inhabitants profess Christianity: more than 95% are adherents of the Latin-rite Catholic Church, but there are numerous other denominations. The national flag (proportions 5 by 8) has two equal horizontal stripes of white and red. The capital is Warsaw (Warszawa).

CONTEMPORARY POLITICAL HISTORY

Historical Context

Poland, partitioned since the 18th century, was declared an independent republic on 11 November 1918, at the end of the First World War. The country was ruled by a military regime from 1926 until 1939, when Poland was invaded by and partitioned between Germany and the USSR. After Germany declared war on the USSR in June 1941, its forces occupied the whole of Poland until they were expelled by Soviet troops in March 1945.

At the end of the Second World War a pro-communist 'Polish Committee of National Liberation', established under Soviet auspices in July 1944, was transformed into a Provisional Government. Under the Potsdam Agreement, signed by the major Allied powers in 1945, the former German territories lying east of the rivers Oder and Neisse (which now comprise one-third of Poland's total area) came under Polish sovereignty, while Poland's frontier with the USSR was shifted westward. These border changes were accompanied by a major resettlement of the population in the affected areas.

The communist-led 'democratic bloc' claimed victory in national elections, held in January 1947. In February a People's Republic, dominated by the Polish Workers' Party (PPR) of Władysław Gomułka was established. Gomułka's reluctance to implement the collectivization of agriculture demanded by the Soviet authorities led to his dismissal as First Secretary of the PPR in 1948. In December the PPR merged with the Polish Socialist Party to form the Polish United Workers' Party (PZPR). Two other parties, the United Peasants' Party (ZSL) and the Democratic Party (SD), were permitted to remain in existence, but were closely controlled by the PZPR, and Poland effectively became a one-party state.

In 1956 mass demonstrations, provoked by food shortages, were suppressed by security forces. In the ensuing political crisis, Gomułka was returned to office, despite Soviet opposition. In December 1970 a sharp rise in food prices led to strikes and demonstrations in the Baltic port of Gdańsk and in other cities. Many demonstrators were killed or injured in clashes with the police and army, and Gomułka was forced to resign as First Secretary of the PZPR; he was succeeded by Edward Gierek.

In July 1980 an increase in meat prices again prompted widespread labour unrest, and shipyard employees in the Baltic ports, notably at Gdańsk, demanded the right to form free trade unions. The Government finally granted permission for several self-governing trade unions to be established, under the guidance of Solidarity, the organization involved in the Gdańsk strike, which was led by a local worker, Lech Wałęsa. As labour unrest continued, Gierek was replaced as First Secretary of the PZPR by Stanisław Kania. Under the growing influence of Solidarity (which claimed an estimated 10m. members by 1981), strikes continued throughout the country, and in February Józef Pińkowski resigned as Chairman of the Council of Ministers. He was succeeded by Gen. Wojciech Jaruzelski, Minister of Defence (a post he retained) since 1968. Despite further concessions to Solidarity, the crisis forced Kania's resignation in October; he was succeeded by Jaruzelski, who thus held the leading posts in both the PZPR and the Government.

On 13 December 1981 martial law was imposed throughout Poland. A governing Military Council of National Salvation, led by Jaruzelski, was established; all trade union activity was suspended, and Wałęsa and other Solidarity leaders were detained. Violent clashes between workers and security forces ensued, and thousands of protesters were arrested. Sporadic disturbances continued in 1982, particularly in response to legislation abolishing all trade unions. Wałęsa was released in November, and in December martial law was suspended and some prisoners were freed. (During 1982 about 10,000 people were detained, and at least 15 demonstrators killed.) In July 1983 martial law was formally ended; the Military Council of National Salvation was dissolved, and an amnesty was declared for most political prisoners and activists. In October Wałęsa was awarded the Nobel Peace Prize.

In July 1984, to mark the 40th anniversary of the establishment of the communist regime in Poland, some 35,000 detainees were granted amnesty. In August US sanctions (imposed following the declaration of martial law) were relaxed. However, the murder, in October, of Fr Jerzy Popiełuszko, a well-known pro-Solidarity Catholic priest, provoked renewed unrest. In February 1985 four officers from the Ministry of Internal Affairs were found guilty of the murder.

Legislative elections took place in October 1985. New regulations gave voters a choice of two candidates for 410 of the 460 seats in the Sejm (Assembly), the remaining 50 deputies being elected unopposed on a national list. Solidarity appealed for a boycott of the poll and disputed the Government's claim that 79% of the electorate had participated. In November Jaruzelski resigned as Chairman of the Council of Ministers, in order to become President of the Council of State (Head of State). He was succeeded by Prof. Zbigniew Messner.

In December 1986, in an effort to broaden the regime's support, Jaruzelski established a 56-member Consultative Council, comprising mainly non-PZPR members. Nevertheless, Solidarity activists attempted to disrupt the official May Day celebrations in several cities in 1987, and in June there were violent clashes between police and protesters during a visit by Pope John Paul II to his native country. Significant price rises were imposed in 1988, prompting widespread protests and strike action.

The Messner Government resigned in September 1988. Dr Mieczysław Rakowski, Deputy Chairman in 1981–85, was appointed Chairman of a new Council of Ministers, which included several non-PZPR and reformist politicians. However, the Government's announcement that the Lenin Shipyard in Gdańsk was to be closed provoked further strike action. By April 1989 agreement had been reached on the restoration of legal status to Solidarity, as well as on the holding of elections to a new, bicameral legislature, the Zgromadzenie Narodowe (National Assembly). Solidarity and other non-communist groups were to be permitted to contest all the seats in a new upper chamber, the Senat (Senate), which would have a limited right of veto over the lower chamber, the Sejm. Just 35% of the seats in the Sejm were to be subject to free elections, with the remainder open only to candidates of the PZPR and its associate organizations. A new post of executive President was also to be introduced. The necessary amendments to the Constitution were duly approved by the Sejm. In May the Catholic Church, which enjoyed widespread support and adherence among the population, was accorded legal status.

Elections to the new legislature took place on 4 and 18 June 1989. In the elections to the Senate, the electoral wing of Solidarity, the Solidarity Citizens' Committee, secured all but one of the 100 seats. In the elections to the 460-member Sejm, Solidarity secured all the 161 seats that it was permitted to contest, and the other 299 seats were divided between the PZPR (173 seats), its allied parties—the ZSL (76) and the SD (27)—and members of Catholic organizations (23), including the communist-aligned PAX Association (10). The new legislature narrowly elected Jaruzelski, unopposed, as executive President. He was replaced as First Secretary of the PZPR by Rakowski. Jaruzelski accepted Wałęsa's proposal of a coalition of Solidarity, the SD and the ZSL. The appointment of Tadeusz Mazowiecki, a newspaper editor and member of Solidarity, as Chairman of the Council of Ministers, was approved by the Sejm on 24 August 1989, thereby bringing an end to exclusively communist rule. A Solidarity-dominated administration was formed in September.

The new Government's programme of radical political and economic reforms emphasized the creation of democratic institutions and the introduction of a market economy. In December 1989 the legislature voted to rename the country the Republic of Poland, and the pre-communist national symbols were reintroduced. In January 1990 the PZPR was dissolved to allow the establishment of a new party, Social Democracy of the Republic of Poland (SdRP). Local elections held in May were the first entirely free elections in Poland for more than 50 years. Candidates of the Solidarity Citizens' Committee won more than 41% of the seats, while nominally independent candidates secured 38%. By mid-1990 tension had developed between Wałęsa, who advocated accelerated economic reform, and the more cautious Mazowiecki.

Domestic Political Affairs

In September 1990 Jaruzelski agreed to resign, to permit a direct presidential election to take place. In the first round, held on 25 November, Mazowiecki was placed third, behind Wałęsa and an émigré business executive, Stanisław Tymiński. At the second round of voting on 9 December, Wałęsa won 74.3% of the votes cast. Wałęsa resigned the chairmanship of Solidarity (he was replaced in February 1991 by Marian Krzaklewski), and in December 1990 was inaugurated as President for a five-year term. Jan Krzysztof Bielecki, a reformist economist, became Prime Minister. The new regime rapidly encountered challenges to its reform programme, including, in May 1991, a nation-wide day of strikes and demonstrations organized by Solidarity.

Democratic consolidation

Legislative elections took place on 27 October 1991, with the participation of 43.2% of the electorate. Some 29 parties won representation in the Sejm. The party with the largest number of deputies (62) was Mazowiecki's Democratic Union (UD). The Democratic Left Alliance (SLD), an electoral coalition of the SdRP and the All Poland Trade Unions' Alliance, won 60 seats. The UD was also the largest single party in the Senat, with 21 seats, compared with Solidarity's 11. After Bronisław Geremek of the UD failed to form a government, Wałęsa nominated Jan Olszewski of the Centre Alliance (PC) as Prime Minister. An attempt by Olszewski to submit his resignation was rejected by the Sejm, which proceeded, in December, to approve a new centre-right Council of Ministers, incorporating members of the PC, the Peasant Alliance and the Christian-National Union (ZChN).

In June 1992, following controversy regarding government attempts to expose alleged communist conspirators, the Sejm approved a motion of no confidence in the Olszewski Government. After the failure of Waldemar Pawlak of the Polish People's Party (PSL) to form a government, the Sejm approved the appointment of Hanna Suchocka of the UD as Prime Minister of a seven-party coalition administration dominated by the UD and the ZChN. In December an interim 'Small Constitution' entered into effect, pending a comprehensive revision of the 1952 Constitution. A motion of no confidence in the Suchocka administration, proposed by the Solidarity group after the failure of negotiations between the Government and striking teachers and health workers, was narrowly approved by the Sejm in May 1993. However, Wałęsa refused to accept Suchocka's resignation; instead, he dissolved the Sejm, scheduling new elections to both houses of parliament for September. The electoral code was amended, with a new stipulation that a party (with the exception of organizations representing national minorities) must secure at least 5% of the total votes cast (8% in the case of an electoral alliance) in order to achieve parliamentary representation.

The general election held on 19 September 1993 resulted in victory for parties of the left, as voters demonstrated their dissatisfaction with the immediate consequences of recent reforms. The SLD and the PSL, both dominated by former communists and their allies, won, respectively, 171 and 132 seats in the Sejm (with 20.4% and 15.4% of the votes cast), and 37 and 36 seats in the Senat. The UD took 74 seats in the Sejm (with 10.6% of the votes cast) and four in the Senat, while Solidarity won 10 seats in the Senat. Wałęsa's Non-Party Bloc for Reform, established in June, won 16 seats in the Sejm and two seats in the

Senat. Almost 35% of the votes cast in elections to the Sejm were for parties that received fewer than 5% of the total votes, notably the PC and the ZChN, and therefore secured no representation; the rate of participation by voters was 52.1%. In October Pawlak formed a coalition Government, dominated by members of his PSL and the SLD. In early 1994 the Deputy Prime Minister and Minister of Finance, Marek Borowski (of the SLD), resigned.

In January 1995 Wałęsa refused to endorse legislation to increase rates of personal income tax; however, after his actions were ruled to be unconstitutional, he was obliged to approve the legislation. Relations between the Government and the President deteriorated sharply in February, when Wałęsa demanded the Prime Minister's resignation and threatened to dissolve parliament if he failed to comply. Further conflict was averted by Pawlak's departure, and in March Józef Oleksy, a member of the SLD and hitherto Marshal (Speaker) of the Sejm, took office as Prime Minister.

The first round of the 1995 presidential election took place on 5 November. The two leading candidates, Aleksander Kwaśniewski, the Chairman of the SdRP (and formerly a leading member of the PZPR), and Wałęsa proceeded to a second round on 19 November, when Kwaśniewski achieved a narrow victory, with 51.7% of the votes cast. Kwaśniewski took office on 23 December. Following Kwaśniewski's election, the ministers responsible for foreign affairs, internal affairs and national defence submitted their resignations. The outgoing Minister of Internal Affairs, Andrzej Milczanowski, claimed that Oleksy had acted on behalf of Soviet (and subsequently Russian) espionage agents since the 1980s; despite denying the charges, Oleksy resigned as Prime Minister in January 1996 (an official report, published in October, exonerated him of all charges). Oleksy was subsequently elected Chairman of the SdRP, replacing Kwaśniewski, who had resigned his party membership following his election as President. Włodzimierz Cimoszewicz of the SLD was appointed as Prime Minister in February.

In June 1996 some 25 centre-right political parties, including Solidarity, the PC and the ZChN, established a new electoral bloc, Solidarity Electoral Action (AWS). In September Cimoszewicz dismissed Jacek Buchacz as Minister of Foreign Economic Relations, prompting his party, the PSL, to withdraw for several weeks from government negotiations on proposed administrative reforms. Agreement was subsequently reached on the distribution of ministerial portfolios.

The 1997 Constitution

On 2 April 1997 the legislature voted to adopt a new Constitution, which slightly reduced presidential powers and provided for the maintenance of a social market economy, pending its approval by national referendum. In the referendum, held on 25 May, some 52.7% of the votes cast were in support of the new text (42.9% of the electorate participated). Among the prominent opponents of the document were AWS and the conservative Movement for the Reconstruction of Poland (ROP). The new Constitution came into force on 17 October.

In the general election of 21 September 1997, AWS secured 201 seats in the Sejm (with 33.8% of the valid votes cast) and 51 in the Senat, while the SLD won 164 seats in the Sejm (with 27.1% of the votes) and 28 in the Senat. The PSL retained only 27 seats in the Sejm and three in the Senat. The rate of voter participation was 48%. Krzaklewski, the leader of AWS, subsequently initiated coalition talks with the economically liberal Freedom Union (UW) and the ROP, which had won, respectively, 60 and six seats in the Sejm, and eight and five in the Senat. Jerzy Buzek of Solidarity was nominated as Prime Minister in mid-October. Following lengthy negotiations, AWS and the UW signed a coalition agreement later that month, despite some opposition from two members of the AWS alliance, the ZChN and the PC. A new Council of Ministers included Leszek Balcerowicz, leader of the UW, as Deputy Prime Minister, Minister of Finance and Chairman of the Economic Committee. In November the Sejm approved the new Government's programme, which prioritized rapid integration with the North Atlantic Treaty Organization (NATO, see p. 380) and the European Union (EU, see p. 281), and accelerated privatization and government reform. Shortly afterwards, the Social Movement of Solidarity Electoral Action, which was to replace Solidarity within AWS, applied for registration as a new political party.

In July 1998 a new structure of local and regional government was approved, reducing the number of voivodships (provinces) from 48 to 16. At local elections in October, the opposition SLD was returned as the largest party in nine voivodships, although the governing AWS-UW coalition won the largest number of seats overall, and secured control of the seven remaining voivodships. Meanwhile, the approval of the divestment of the Gdańsk shipyard (which was completed in September) prompted six AWS deputies to withdraw their support for the Government. (In preceding weeks nine other deputies had also left the ruling coalition.)

In June 1998 the Sejm adopted a resolution (which was opposed by the SLD) condemning the communist regime imposed on post-war Poland by the USSR. In September the Sejm approved legislation granting access for Polish citizens to files compiled on them by the security services during the communist era. In February 1999 it was announced that the leader of the Self-Defence Trade Union (which had organized a series of protests by farmers in the previous year), Andrzej Lepper, was to stand trial for having organized illegal road blocks. During March the Prime Minister undertook a major government reorganization. The Secretary-General of the UW resigned in protest at two of the ministerial appointments.

In May 1999 farmers resumed protests against agricultural policy. An estimated 80 people were injured in August, when violence erupted between police and farmers demonstrating against the low price of grain in northern Poland. Protests against the economic slowdown and government reforms in education, health and pensions provision culminated, in September, in a march through Warsaw by agricultural and industrial workers (as well as opposition SLD and PSL members). In the same month the Deputy Prime Minister and Minister of Internal Affairs and Administration, Janusz Tomaszewski, announced his resignation. Following a minor government reorganization in October, AWS and the UW renewed their coalition agreement for a further two years. In late October the Government reached a compromise with miners' representatives from Solidarity regarding the restructuring of the industry. It was announced in December that Solidarity was to withdraw from political activities and become an 'organization of employees'. In January 2000 Lepper announced the formation of the Self-Defence Party of the Republic of Poland (SRP), a populist party opposed to Polish membership of the EU that incorporated elements of several farmers' organizations and trade unions, under his leadership.

At the end of May 2000 the UW announced its withdrawal from the governing coalition, in protest at the blocking of Balcerowicz's proposals for economic reform by AWS parliamentary deputies. Negotiations on re-establishing the coalition collapsed in June, and Buzek subsequently formed a minority AWS Government.

In the presidential election, held on 8 October 2000, Kwaśniewski was re-elected with 53.9% of the valid votes cast, ahead of Andrzej Olechowski, an independent former foreign minister, who secured 17.3% of the votes; Krzaklewski obtained 15.6%, Lepper 3.1% and Wałęsa just 1.0%. The rate of participation by the electorate was 61.1%. Krzaklewski resigned as leader of AWS in January 2001, and was succeeded by Prime Minister Buzek. Meanwhile, Balcerowicz resigned the leadership of the UW in November 2000, and became President of the National Bank in December.

In January 2001 Olechowski, together with the Marshal of the Sejm, Maciej Plazyński of AWS, and a Vice-Marshal of the Senat, Donald Tusk of the UW, founded a new centre-right, economically liberal political movement, the Civic Platform (PO). In April Kwaśniewski signed a new electoral law introducing a system of proportional representation. Significant political realignment took place in advance of legislative elections scheduled for September, and in May AWS was restructured as Solidarity Electoral Action of the Right (AWSP), in alliance with the ROP. At the end of May the conservative Catholic, nationalist League of Polish Families (LPR), which opposed Polish membership of the EU, was registered as a party. Also in May Lepper was sentenced to 16 months' imprisonment, after being found guilty of charges relating to the farmers' blockades of 1998–99. Lepper commenced an appeal against the sentence.

Left-wing coalition government

Legislative elections took place on 23 September 2001, with a rate of voter participation of 46.3%. Neither AWSP nor the UW received the requisite 8% of the votes cast to obtain seats in the Sejm, although both parties contested the elections to the Senat as part of the Blok Senat 2001 (also comprising the PO, the ROP, and Law and Justice—PiS—a conservative party founded earlier in the year by former members of AWS), which won 15 of the 100 seats in the upper chamber. Support for conservative parties was divided between PiS, which obtained 44 seats in the Sejm, and

the LPR, which secured 38 seats in the Sejm and two in the Senat. Another party elected to the Sejm for the first time was the SRP, which obtained 53 seats in the Sejm and two in the Senat. An electoral coalition of the SLD and the Union of Labour (UP) won 216 seats in the Sejm and 75 seats in the Senat, falling short of an overall majority. The PO, which received 65 seats in the Sejm, rejected an initial proposal to form a coalition with the SLD-UP. Instead, on 9 October the SLD and the UP signed a coalition agreement with the PSL, which had obtained 42 seats in the elections to the Sejm and four seats in the Senat. The leader of the SLD, Leszek Miller, was sworn in as Prime Minister and Chairman of the European Integration Committee on 19 October; the PSL's leader, Jarosław Kalinowski, and the leader of the UP, Marek Pol, were appointed as Deputy Prime Ministers. Miller announced that a referendum on entry to the EU would be held in mid-2003.

In November 2001 Lepper was dismissed as a Vice-Marshal of the Sejm. In March 2002, on appeal, Lepper's prison sentence was reduced to a suspended one-year term. Government changes in July included the resignation of Marek Belka as Minister of Finance; Grzegorz Kołodko subsequently assumed the post, being appointed additionally as a Deputy Prime Minister.

In January 2003 the Prime Minister reorganized the Government, consolidating the Ministries of the Economy and of Labour into a new Ministry of the Economy, Labour and Social Policy, under Jerzy Hausner. On 1 March Miller expelled the PSL from the Government, after it voted with opposition deputies against new tax legislation in the Sejm. In mid-March the Sejm rejected a motion, proposed by the LPR, to dissolve parliament. The following day the SLD-UD coalition formed a parliamentary alliance with the Peasant Democratic Party (PLD), although it remained 13 seats short of a majority. In June Miller transferred responsibility for economic policy from the Ministry of Finance to Hausner's Ministry of the Economy, Labour and Social Policy, prompting the resignation of Kołodko from the Government. Hausner assumed Kołodko's former responsibilities as a Deputy Prime Minister (while retaining his previous portfolio), while Andrzej Raczko became Minister of Finance.

In January 2004 Miller appointed Deputy Chairman of the SLD and former premier Oleksy as Deputy Prime Minister and Minister of Internal Affairs and Administration. In late January the PLD withdrew its support for the ruling coalition, thereby reducing the Government's majority in parliament. In February Miller announced that he was to resign as Chairman of the SLD, but retain the premiership, to enable him to focus on Poland's planned accession to the EU on 1 May. On 6 March Krzysztof Janik was elected as the new party Chairman, although later in the month more than 20 deputies, led by Borowski, announced that they were to defect from the SLD in order to establish a new party, Polish Social Democracy (SDPL); Borowski subsequently resigned as Marshal of the Sejm. On 26 March Miller acknowledged the loss of support for his leadership and announced that he would resign as Prime Minister on 2 May. Three days later President Kwaśniewski nominated former Minister of Finance Belka (latterly Director of Economic Policy in the US-led Coalition Provisional Authority in Iraq) to head a new government; Belka announced that he intended to retain key ministers, including Hausner, who had devised a controversial economic austerity programme for 2004–07. In late April Oleksy was elected as the new Marshal of the Sejm.

Poland acceded to full membership of the EU, as planned, on 1 May 2004. Miller resigned one day later, as announced, and Belka's Government, principally composed of SLD members and independents, took office, pending approval by the Sejm. In mid-May, however, the Sejm rejected the nomination to the premiership of Belka, forcing the resignation of the new Government. The Sejm failed to propose a new candidate within the requisite two weeks, and Kwaśniewski duly renominated Belka. In late June the Sejm approved Belka's appointment by 236 votes to 215. In order to secure the support of the SDPL, Belka agreed to hold a further confidence vote in October to confirm his mandate to govern.

In October 2004 Belka won the scheduled vote of confidence in the Sejm, by 234 votes to 218. Ahead of the vote Belka had announced to the lower chamber that Poland would begin reducing its 2,500-strong military contingent in Iraq from early 2005. Krzysztof Pater resigned as Minister of Social Policy in November, after the Sejm rejected austerity measures on corporate social insurance and pensions. In December Oleksy was elected Chairman of the SLD, defeating Krzysztof Janik. A few days later, following extensive investigations, the Vetting Court ruled that Oleksy had concealed his collaboration with the communist-era military intelligence services; Oleksy, who strongly denied the charges against him, announced that he would appeal against the verdict. In response to mounting pressure, Oleksy resigned as Marshal of the Sejm, and in January 2005 Włodzimierz Cimoszewicz, hitherto Minister of Foreign Affairs, was elected as his replacement. Adam Rotfeld assumed the foreign affairs portfolio.

In February 2005 Hausner resigned from the SLD, after the party's national council voted against holding early legislative elections in June. In March he also resigned as Deputy Prime Minister and Minister of the Economy and Labour, to which position Jacek Piechota was subsequently appointed. In late February Hausner and the leader of the UW, Władysław Frasyniuk, announced plans to create a new centrist political organization, the Democratic Party (PD), the founding congress of which was held in May. In March Belka urged the Sejm to dissolve itself to allow early elections to take place, as the minority Government lacked sufficient legislative support for proposed budget reforms. However, the Sejm voted to reject three motions submitted by opposition parties for its dissolution, and President Kwaśniewski rejected Belka's resignation, tendered on 6 May, stating that the Government should remain in office until the forthcoming legislative elections. In late May Wojciech Olejniczak was elected as Chairman of the SLD, succeeding Oleksy. In June Belka made public his police file, in response to allegations that he had collaborated with the communist security services.

The Law and Justice Government

In the legislative elections, held on 25 September 2005, in which 40.5% of the electorate participated, PiS obtained the largest number of seats in both the Sejm (taking 155 of the 460 seats, with 27.0% of the votes) and the Senat (with 49 of the 100 seats). PO won 133 seats in the Sejm (with 24.1% of the votes) and 34 seats in the Senat, whereas the incumbent SLD received just 55 seats in the Sejm (with 11.3% of the votes cast). Two days later, the leader of PiS, Jarosław Kaczyński, proposed Kazimierz Marcinkiewicz for the premiership; Kaczyński's twin brother, Lech, the Mayor of Warsaw, was to contest the forthcoming presidential election as the candidate of the PiS.

After a first round of voting in the presidential election, conducted on 9 October 2005, PO leader Donald Tusk (who obtained 36.3% of the votes) and Lech Kaczyński (33.1%) progressed to a second round on 23 October. Kaczyński emerged as the winner in the run-off poll, with 54.0% of the votes. The rate of participation by the electorate was 49.7% in the first round and 51.0% in the second. Kaczyński was inaugurated as President on 23 December.

Meanwhile, although PiS and the more economically liberal PO, as the two principal parties of the centre-right, had been widely expected to negotiate a coalition government, the parties were unable to agree on the distribution of senior positions, and on 31 October 2005 Marcinkiewicz was appointed as Prime Minister of a minority Government, comprising nine members of PiS and eight independents. Bogdan Borusewicz, an independent, was appointed Marshal of the Senat, and Marek Jurek of PiS became Marshal of the Sejm. On 10 November the Government won a motion of confidence in the Sejm, by 272 to 187 votes, with the support of several smaller, mostly right-wing, parties (the SRP, the LPR and the PSL).

In January 2006 the Minister of the Treasury, Andrzej Mikosz, resigned, following media allegations that his wife had been involved in financial misdemeanours; he was succeeded by Wojciech Jasiński in the following month. Also in January Teresa Lubinska was dismissed as Minister of Finance; she was succeeded by Zyta Gilowska, who also became Deputy Prime Minister. In late April PiS signed a coalition agreement with the SRP and the LPR, giving the Government a majority in the Sejm for the first time. The Minister of Foreign Affairs, Stefan Meller, subsequently resigned in protest at the Government's decision to co-operate with the SRP. Several new ministers were appointed to the Government on 5 May. The leaders of both the SRP and the LPR were awarded with deputy prime ministerial positions, with Lepper additionally gaining responsibility for agriculture and rural development, while the leader of the LPR, Roman Giertych, also became the Minister of National Education.

In June 2006 Gilowska resigned from the Council of Ministers, following the opening of an investigation into claims that she had lied about collaborating with the secret services during the communist era. (Former members of the Soviet-backed secret services were eligible to hold public office, but falsely denying

such links was considered a serious offence.) She was succeeded as Minister of Finance by Paweł Wojciechowski. In early July Marcinkiewicz tendered his resignation, reportedly owing to disagreements with the leader of his party, Jarosław Kaczyński, over economic policy, as a result of which the entire Government was constitutionally obliged to resign. Shortly afterwards President Kaczyński nominated his twin brother as Marcinkiewicz's replacement; after the Sejm approved this appointment Jarosław Kaczyński was sworn into office on 14 July, together with his new Council of Ministers, to which only one change had been made—the replacement of Wojciechowski by Stanisław Kluza, hitherto Deputy Minister of Finance. However, in September, after she had been cleared of the accusations levied against her, Gilowska was reappointed as Deputy Prime Minister and Minister of Finance, and Kluza left the Government. Also in September, following several policy disagreements, President Kaczyński dismissed Lepper. In response, the SRP withdrew from the ruling coalition, which thereby lost its parliamentary majority. However, in October, a few days prior to a planned parliamentary vote on an opposition-initiated motion for the legislature to dissolve itself, Lepper's dismissal was retracted and the alliance between PiS and the SRP revived.

Also in October 2006 both pro- and anti-Government rallies were held in Warsaw, following the broadcast in late September of a video purporting to show an aide of Prime Minister Kaczyński attempting to buy the support of a member of the opposition. The Prime Minister rejected demands that he resign and insisted that his aide had been engaged in legitimate political bargaining. In local elections held in November, PiS performed robustly overall, but crucially lost the mayoralty of Warsaw, which was secured by Hanna Gronkiewicz-Waltz of PO, a former Governor of the Central Bank.

In February 2007 the Minister of National Defence, Radosław Sikorski, resigned; he was succeeded by a former head of the presidential chancellery, Aleksander Szczygło. In the same month Ludwik Dorn resigned the internal affairs portfolio (while initially retaining the post of Deputy Prime Minister). A former Prosecutor-General, Janusz Kaczmarek, became the new Minister of Internal Affairs and Administration. In April 2007 Dorn was elected Marshal of the Sejm, after Jurek resigned from that position in response to the chamber's failure to adopt a constitutional amendment that would have enforced stricter legislation on abortion. Jurek also resigned from PiS to form a new party, the Right of the Republic, which was to emphasize pro-life and other traditional Catholic policies. In July Prime Minister Kaczyński again removed Lepper from his government post, on the grounds that he was under investigation for corrupt practice in the designation of agricultural land. Lepper announced that the SRP would provisionally remain in the Government. However, on 13 August President Kaczyński dismissed the remaining SRP representatives and the LPR members from the Government, thereby ending the ruling coalition; they were replaced by PiS representatives on an interim basis, and it was announced that early legislative elections were to be organized.

Civic Platform elected to power

On 7 September 2007 the Sejm voted to dissolve itself. Elections to both parliamentary chambers were scheduled for 21 October. Prime Minister Kaczyński dismissed all 15 government ministers to prevent a motion of no confidence planned by the PO; they were subsequently reappointed on an interim basis. At the elections to the Sejm, conducted on 21 October, the PO obtained 209 seats, receiving 41.5% of the votes cast, with PiS receiving 166 seats (32.1% of the votes); an SLD-led coalition, known as Left and Democrats (LiD), secured 53 seats (13.2%), and the PSL 31 seats (8.9%). The rate of participation was 53.8% of the electorate. Neither the LPR nor the SRP obtained legislative representation. Later in October Giertych resigned from the leadership of the LPR. On 5 November Prime Minister Kaczyński submitted the resignation of his minority Government. On 9 November President Kaczyński nominated Tusk as Prime Minister. Tusk, as leader of PO, reached a coalition agreement with the PSL; together, the two parties held 240 seats in the 460-member Sejm.

In early September 2008 the trial began of Gen. (retd) Wojciech Jaruzelski and seven other former communist officials, on charges relating to the imposition of martial law in 1981. In the same month the Government announced a financial plan to prevent the bankruptcy of three major shipyards, situated at Gdynia, Gdańsk and Szczecin, following an investigation by the European Commission into use of state aid by the Polish authorities to support the shipyards, seemingly in a manner that contravened EU regulations. However, in November 2008 the European Commission issued a decision ordering the Government to sell the assets of the Gdynia and Szczecin shipyards by May 2009 (this deadline was subsequently extended) in order to enable the Government to reimburse some €2,300m. in aid.

At elections to the European Parliament, held on 7 June 2009, the PO secured 44.4% of the votes cast and 25 of the 50 contested seats, while PiS won 27.4% of the votes and 15 seats, the SLD (in alliance with the UP) 12.3% of the votes and seven seats, and the PSL 7.0% of the votes and three seats; the rate of participation by voters was recorded at 24.5% of the electorate.

In October 2009 the parliamentary leader of the PO, Zbigniew Chlebowski, resigned from his post, after media allegations of his involvement in a corruption scandal. The parliamentarian was accused of offering assistance to the gambling industry by refusing to support proposed tax rises as part of a new gambling law. The Deputy Prime Minister and Minister of Internal Affairs and Administration, Grzegorz Schetyna, and two other ministers were replaced in mid-October.

The death of President Kaczyński and election of Bronisław Komorowski

On 10 April 2010 Kaczyński was killed, with 96 others, principally senior political, military and cultural figures, in an air crash near Smolensk, Russia, while travelling to mark the 70th anniversary of the massacre of Poles by Soviet troops at Katyń. There were no survivors, and among those killed were the President of the National Bank of Poland, Sławomir Skrzypek, and the Chief of Staff of the Defence Forces, Gen. Franciszek Gągor, as well as the President's wife. In accordance with the Constitution, Bronisław Komorowski, as the Marshal of the Sejm, was appointed acting President; he immediately declared a week of national mourning. A presidential election was scheduled for 20 June. Komorowski was to stand as the PO candidate in the election, which was also to be contested by the deceased President's twin brother, Jarosław Kaczyński, as the candidate of PiS. On 10 May some 2,500 people demonstrated outside the presidential palace in Warsaw to demand an independent international inquiry into the crash, expressing dissatisfaction with the ongoing, joint Russian-Polish inquiry (see Regional relations).

In the first round of voting in the early presidential election, which was duly held on 20 June 2010, Komorowski was placed first, with 41.5% of the votes cast. He and Jarosław Kaczyński (who received 36.5%) proceeded to a second round. In the run-off ballot, contested on 4 July, Komorowski was elected President, receiving 53.0% of the votes cast. Some 54.9% of citizens voted in the first round of polling, and 52.0% participated in the run-off vote. On 8 July Schetyna was elected to replace Komorowski as Marshal of the Sejm, serving as acting President until Komorowski's inauguration on 6 August.

The 2011 legislative elections

Tusk became the first Prime Minister of Poland to secure two successive terms of office since the end of the communist regime in 1989, after the PO won 39.2% of the votes and 207 seats in the Sejm, while securing 63 of 100 seats in the Senat, at legislative elections held on 9 October 2011. (However, voter participation was comparatively low, at around 50% of the electorate.) The PO's nearest rival was the PiS, which took 29.9% of the vote in the Sejm and 157 seats, and 31 seats in the Senat. A newly formed, socially liberal, anti-clerical party, Palikot's Movement (RP), was placed third in the elections to the Sejm, receiving 10.0% of the votes cast and obtaining 40 seats. The PSL obtained 8.4% of the votes cast and 28 seats, while the SLD obtained 8.2% and 27 seats. The cabinet was inaugurated on 18 November, and was largely unaltered from the previous administration. The only ministerial change was the appointment of Jacek Cichocki as Minister of the Interior. In March 2012 several members of PO left the party to join RP, and in the same month several prominent members of PiS, including 20 deputies, two senators and four members of the European Parliament, announced their defection from the party and their affiliation to a newly formed group, Polish Solidarity (SP). Former Minister of Justice Zbigniew Ziobro, was elected as the leader of SP later in the month.

In July 2012 the long-standing Minister of Agriculture and Rural Development, Marek Sawicki of the PSL, resigned, after a business newspaper published transcripts of a video recording in which two senior agricultural officials discussed corrupt practices within the ministry involving PSL officials. Sawicki was replaced by Stanisław Kalemba. Amid a further slowdown in

economic growth (see Economic Affairs) and a concomitant decline in popular support for Tusk, at the end of September PiS organized a mass anti-Government protest in Warsaw. On 12 October Tusk won (by 233 to 219 votes) a parliamentary motion of confidence, which he had requested in an attempt to counter the increasing criticism of his economic management. Following the organization of rival demonstrations to commemorate Independence Day celebrations on 11 November, the police forcibly suppressed protests by nationalist groups that had degenerated into violent rioting. Later that month the authorities announced that they had thwarted a plan by a radical nationalist to stage a bomb attack outside the parliamentary building.

Recent developments: government changes

On 17 November 2012 Pawlak tendered his resignation as Deputy Prime Minister and Minister of the Economy after he lost an election for the chairmanship of the PSL to Janusz Piechociński, stating that the government post should be held by the most senior member of the party. Consequently, in early December Piechociński also succeeded Pawlak as Deputy Prime Minister and Minister of the Economy. Meanwhile, in November PO, with the support of the SLD and RP, initiated a parliamentary motion that would allow former Prime Minister Jarosław Kaczyński to be tried by the country's Tribunal of State for abusing his constitutional powers to harass political opponents while in office; a similar motion against Ziobro, who had served in Kaczyński's administration, for constitutional violations was also planned. In late February 2013 Tusk announced a government reorganization, in which the Minister of Finance, Jacek Vincent-Rostowski, also became a deputy premier, while Bartłomiej Sienkiewicz, a prominent, non-party, journalist, replaced Cichocki as Minister of the Interior. In early March a vote of no confidence in the Government, submitted by the PiS in response to the recent downturn in economic growth, was defeated in the Sejm. In early April a vote of no confidence in the Minister of Transport, Sławomir Nowak was also defeated.

In mid-April Tusk dismissed the non-partisan Mikołaj Budzanowski as Minister of the State Treasury, after it emerged that a memorandum on co-operation with the Russian state-owned corporation, Gazprom, had been signed by the deputy chairman of the state gas company, Polish Oil and Gas Co (PGNiG), without the ministry's knowledge. Budzanowski was replaced by Włodzimierz Karpiński of PO. Later in the month Jarosław Gowin was dismissed as Minister of Justice after he made a series of controversial comments and disputes with his government colleagues; he was succeeded in early May by Marek Biernacki.

Foreign Affairs

Regional relations

After 1991, close relations were retained with the Czech Republic, Hungary and Slovakia through the structures of the Visegrad Group and the Central European Free Trade Agreement. In 1991–92 Poland established diplomatic relations with the former republics of the USSR, developing particularly strong links with Ukraine. In May 1997 the Polish and Ukrainian Presidents signed a declaration of reconciliation, which included the condemnation of the killing of tens of thousands of Poles by Ukrainian nationalists in 1942–43, and of the 'Wisła Operation' of 1947, in which more than 100,000 Ukrainians were forcibly deported from their homes in south-east Poland.

All former Soviet combat troops were withdrawn from Poland by November 1992, and the last remaining Russian military presence was withdrawn in September 1994. Although relations between Poland and Russia deteriorated after Poland acceded to NATO in 1999, in July 2000 President Kwaśniewski became the first Polish head of state to pay an official visit to Moscow, the Russian capital, since the collapse of communist rule, and Russian President Vladimir Putin made an official visit to Poland in January 2002. In 2005 Poland expressed concern at plans to construct a North European Natural Gas Pipeline between Russia and Germany, under the Baltic Sea, effectively bypassing Poland.

In April 2010 President Lech Kaczyński and 96 others died in an air crash near Smolensk, Russia, while travelling to attend a 70th anniversary ceremony of a massacre of Poles by Soviet troops at Katyń (see Domestic Political Affairs). Days before the Smolensk crash, the Russian premier Putin had met Polish Prime Minister Tusk at the site of the massacre. Having previously been accused of concealing evidence, in May Russia provided acting Polish President Bronisław Komorowski with historical documents relating to the 1940 massacre. In November 2010 Russia's Federal Assembly issued an historic declaration accepting that former Soviet leader Iosif Dzhugashvili (Stalin) had given the order for the massacre in 1940; it was only in 1990 that Russia ceased blaming Germany's Nazi regime for the Katyń atrocities.

A report by Russian aviation investigators into the Smolensk air crash, released in January 2011, concluded that pilot error had caused the crash, confirming that the pilot had failed to heed repeated warnings by Russian air traffic control staff to divert to an alternative airport owing to poor weather conditions in Smolensk. The Minister of Internal Affairs and Administration, Jerzy Miller, accepted the findings but stated that Russian officials had also been at fault. The late President's brother, however, rejected the conclusions of the report, while there were public demands for an independent investigation into the incident. In August the body of one of the victims of the Smolensk crash, a PiS deputy, was exhumed at the request of a relative, following the discovery of serious inconsistencies between existing Polish medical records and the findings of a Russian autopsy carried out after the disaster. After two further exhumations in March 2012, the Polish authorities acknowledged that at least four of the victims of the air crash had been wrongly identified. In November a leading newspaper, *Rzeczpospolita*, was obliged to retract a report (which was strenuously denied by government officials and resulted in the dismissal of the publication's senior editors) that traces of explosives had been discovered in the airplane wreckage.

In April 2013 Russian state-controlled monopoly Gazprom announced that it had reached a preliminary agreement with EuRoPol GAZ (its joint venture with the state-owned Polish Oil and Gas Co—PGNiG) for the construction of a new gas pipeline across Poland to Slovakia, and that a feasibility study was to be undertaken on the project. However, Prime Minister Tusk and other government officials subsequently denied any knowledge of the accord.

In July 2005 Poland recalled its ambassador to Belarus, and appealed to the EU for assistance in protecting the Polish minority there, after the main Polish-language newspaper in the country was closed by the authorities, and the leadership of a principal Polish non-governmental organization in the country—the Union of Poles in Belarus (UPB)— was replaced and its offices sequestrated. The Polish ambassador returned to Belarus in October. In March 2006 Belarus briefly recalled its ambassador to Poland, after a number of Polish journalists and parliamentarians were refused entry to Belarus in advance of the presidential election there, and a former Polish ambassador to Belarus was imprisoned for 15 days after participating in an unauthorized protest. In February 2010 several members of the UPB were imprisoned, accused of organizing an unauthorized demonstration, prompting condemnation from Poland. Relations remained strained in 2011, following the re-election of Belarusian President Alyaksandr Lukashenka in December 2010 and the arrest, shortly after the election, of several opposition candidates. Poland appealed to other EU states collectively to impose or reimpose travel restrictions on Lukashenka's associates while facilitating travel abroad for Belarusian citizens. In reprisal for the subsequent expansion of EU sanctions, in February 2012 the Belarusian authorities announced the expulsion of the Polish ambassador and EU representatives, which was followed by the withdrawal of all EU ambassadors. Following the release of a prominent Belarusian opposition leader, the ambassadors of EU member states returned to Belarus in April.

In November 1990 Poland and Germany signed a border treaty confirming their post-1945 borders, and in June 1991 the two countries signed a treaty of 'good neighbourliness and friendly co-operation'. Poland welcomed the establishment, announced in February 1999, of a compensation fund for over 2m. Poles who were employed as forced labour in German companies during the Second World War. In December it was agreed that German companies would pay a total of DM 10,000m. into a compensation fund. The German Chancellor, Gerhard Schröder, attended a ceremony in Warsaw in August 2004 to mark the 60th anniversary of the city's failed uprising against the Nazi occupation, the first German leader to participate in such an event. In January 2005 the German President, Horst Köhler, attended a ceremony in Poland to commemorate the 60th anniversary of the liberation of the Nazi concentration camp at Oświęcim (Auschwitz). In March 2007 German Federal Chancellor Angela Merkel met President Kaczyński during an official visit to Poland. Subse-

quently, Prime Minister Tusk sought to forge closer relations with Germany.

A national referendum on EU membership took place in June 2003, at which some 77% of the votes cast by 58.9% of the electorate were in favour of accession. In October, in preparation for its accession to the EU, Poland introduced visa requirements for Belarusian, Moldovan, Russian and Ukrainian citizens, in accordance with EU requirements, although special arrangements were instituted for residents of the Russian exclave of Kaliningrad. Poland became a full member of the EU on 1 May 2004. In December 2007 Poland implemented the EU's Schengen Agreement on freedom of travel, effectively removing border controls between those states subject to the Agreement. On 9 April 2008 President Kaczyński approved a law allowing him to ratify the EU's Lisbon Treaty (signed in December 2007), after it had been endorsed by both legislative chambers earlier in the month, although he did not do so until October 2009. Poland assumed the presidency of the Council of the EU for a period of six months from July 2011, during which the successful completion of accession treaty negotiations with Croatia was achieved.

In February 2013 the Sejm approved ratification of the EU's Treaty on Stability, Co-ordination and Governance in the Economic and Monetary Union (the 'fiscal compact'), which was supported by the government parties; however, PiS strenuously opposed the Treaty, and demanded that Poland's prospective entry to the euro area (which was, however, required by the terms under which Poland had entered the EU in 2004) be referred to a national referendum. In March Prime Minister Tusk indicated that he would agree to the organization of a referendum on adoption of the euro (despite lack of popular support for the measure, according to opinion surveys), in order to secure PiS support for the necessary constitutional amendments.

Other external relations

The Polish Government strongly supported the US-led military campaign to remove from power the Iraqi President, Saddam Hussain, in 2003; Poland was subsequently offered the opportunity to manage one of three reconstruction zones in Iraq, under overall US command. In September the USA transferred responsibility for security in an area of central Iraq to a 9,500-strong multinational force led by Poland, which contributed some 2,500 troops. In early 2005 Poland reduced its military contingent in Iraq to 1,700 troops. The final Polish contingent left Iraq in October 2008. In March 2009 Prime Minister Donald Tusk announced that the 1,600-member Polish force supporting the US-led coalition in Afghanistan would be reinforced by 400 troops, and by mid-2011 Polish troops numbered 2,600. Following agreement on the staged withdrawal of the US-led mission in Afghanistan by the end of 2014, in September 2012 the Polish Government announced that its contingent in the country would be reduced to 1,800 in 2013 and to 1,000 in 2014.

At a NATO summit meeting, which took place in Bucharest, Romania, in April 2008, member states endorsed US plans to position missile defence bases (forming part of its proposed National Missile Defence programme) in Poland and the Czech Republic. In August a treaty was signed in Warsaw between Polish Minister of Foreign Affairs Radosław Sikorski and US Secretary of State Condoleezza Rice, providing for the installation of 10 US anti-missile interceptors and guaranteeing the permanent stationing of US missiles in Poland. The announcement prompted immediate protests by Russia: in September the Russian Minister of Foreign Affairs, Sergei Lavrov, during a visit to Warsaw, reiterated that the missile installation presented a threat to Russian security. However, following the election of US President Barack Obama in November, the new US Administration indicated in early 2009 that it would review security policy, including the planned missile defence system. On 17 September President Obama informed Tusk that the US Administration had cancelled plans for the permanent missile defence installation in Poland. In October Poland reached agreement on the deployment of a much smaller-scale installation of US anti-missile interceptors. In March 2013 the US Administration announced that the planned establishment of long-range anti-missile interceptors in Poland (and Romania) had been abandoned, although the Polish Government was subsequently issued assurances by US officials that shorter-range interceptors would be installed in Poland.

CONSTITUTION AND GOVERNMENT

Under the Constitution, which came into force in October 1997, legislative power is vested in the bicameral Zgromadzenie Narodowe (National Assembly), which is elected for a four-year term and comprises the 100-member Senat (Senate, upper chamber) and the 460-member Sejm (Assembly, lower chamber). The Senat reviews the laws adopted by the Sejm and may propose their rejection. Senators and deputies are elected by universal, direct suffrage. In the Sejm, deputies are elected under a system of proportional representation. Executive power is vested in the President of the Republic, who is directly elected (a second ballot being held if necessary) for a five-year term and may be re-elected only once, and in the appointed Council of Ministers, led by the Prime Minister. The Council of Ministers is responsible to the Sejm for its activities. The judiciary is independent. Poland is divided into 16 voivodships (provinces) and 308 powiats (districts).

REGIONAL AND INTERNATIONAL CO-OPERATION

Poland is a member of the European Bank for Reconstruction and Development (EBRD, see p. 276) and the Council of Europe (see p. 260). In May 2004 Poland became a full member of the European Union (EU, see p. 281).

Poland became a member of the UN in 1955. As a contracting party to the General Agreement on Tariffs and Trade, Poland joined the World Trade Organization (WTO, see p. 444) in 1995. Poland is also a member of the Organisation for Economic Co-operation and Development (OECD, see p. 388) and the North Atlantic Treaty Organization (NATO, see p. 380).

ECONOMIC AFFAIRS

In 2011, according to the World Bank, Poland's gross national income (GNI), measured at average 2009–11 prices, was US $477,009m., equivalent to $12,480 per head (or $20,480 per head on an international purchasing-power parity basis). During 2002–11 the population remained constant, while gross domestic product (GDP) per head increased, in real terms, at an average annual rate of 4.5%. Overall GDP increased, in real terms, at an average annual rate of 4.5% in 2002–11; GDP grew by 4.3% in 2011.

Agriculture contributed 4.0% of GDP in 2012 and engaged 12.7% of the employed labour force in 2011. The principal crops are sugar beet, potatoes, wheat, barley and rye. Livestock production is important to the domestic food supply. According to World Bank estimates, during 2002–10 the GDP of the agricultural sector increased, in real terms, by an average annual rate of 1.1%; real agricultural GDP increased by 9.5% in 2009, but decreased by 1.5% in 2010.

Industry (including mining, manufacturing, power and construction) accounted for 32.3% of GDP in 2012 and engaged 30.6% of the employed labour force in 2011. According to World Bank estimates, during 2002–10 industrial GDP increased, in real terms, by an average of 6.8% per year; real industrial GDP increased by 8.2% in 2010.

Mining and quarrying contributed 2.5% of GDP in 2012 and engaged 1.6% of the employed labour force in 2011. Poland is a significant producer of copper, silver and sulphur, and there are also considerable reserves of natural gas and coal. At the end of 2011 Poland's proven coal reserves stood at 5,709m. metric tons.

The manufacturing sector contributed 17.8% of GDP in 2012 and engaged 18.8% of the employed labour force in 2011. According to World Bank estimates, in 2002–10 manufacturing GDP increased, in real terms, at an average annual rate of 9.4%. Manufacturing GDP increased by 5.2% in 2010.

The construction sector contributed 7.3% of GDP in 2012 and engaged 8.2% of the employed labour force in 2011.

Energy is derived principally from coal, which satisfied 88.1% of the country's total energy requirements in 2010. Mineral fuels and lubricants accounted for 12.6% of the value of merchandise imports in 2011.

The services sector contributed 63.7% of GDP in 2012 and engaged 56.7% of the employed labour force in 2011. According to World Bank estimates, the GDP of the services sector increased, in real terms, by an average of 3.5% per year in 2002–10. Real services GDP increased by 1.9% in 2010.

In 2011 Poland recorded a visible merchandise trade deficit of US $14,036m., and there was a deficit of $25,023m. on the current account of the balance of payments. In 2011 the principal source of imports was Germany (accounting for 22.3% of the total); other major suppliers were Russia, the People's Republic of China and Italy. Germany was also the principal market for exports (26.1% of the total); other significant purchasers were the United Kingdom, the Czech Republic, France and Italy. The principal imports in 2011 were machinery and transport equipment, basic manufactures, chemicals and related products, mineral fuels and lubricants, miscellaneous manufactured articles, and food and live animals. The principal exports in that year were machinery and transport equipment, basic manufactures, miscellaneous manufactured articles, food and live animals, and chemicals and related products.

Poland's budgetary deficit was some 56,393m. złotys in 2010, equivalent to 4.0% of GDP. Poland's general government gross debt was 858,931m. złotys in 2011, equivalent to 56.3% of GDP. Poland's external debt totalled US $218,022m. at the end of 2008, of which $43,426m. was public and publicly guaranteed debt. In 2008 the cost of debt-servicing was equivalent to 25.0% of the value of exports of goods, services and income. According to ILO estimates, the average annual rate of inflation was 2.8% in 2002–12. Consumer prices increased by 3.7% in 2012. In 2011 9.7% of the labour force were unemployed.

Despite the economic downturn, Poland was the only EU country to avoid recession in 2009, partially as a result of its lack of reliance on export trade. However, the general government deficit increased from less than 2% of GDP in 2007 to 7.9% in 2010. In late 2009 the Government announced plans for a large-scale privatization programme, and that it intended to delay the country's adoption of the euro until at least 2015. The election of Bronisław Komorowski as President in July 2010 brought about a consolidation of power, with both the President and the Prime Minister, Donald Tusk, being members of the reformist Civic Platform party. As part of its fiscal consolidation measures, Tusk's Government (which was returned to office in legislative elections in October 2011) introduced legislation in May 2012 that would increase the statutory retirement age to 67 (by 2020 for men and by 2040 for women). In September the Government acknowledged that its budget deficit for 2012 would reach 3.5% of GDP (failing to meet EU fiscal requirements for reduction of the deficit to below 3%). After a further fall in economic growth, to just over 2% in 2012, was projected, in October the Government announced an ambitious investment programme, under which state assets would be transferred to the state-owned Bank Gospodarstwa Krajowego (National Economy Bank), and would be used to provide some 40,000m. złotys for infrastructural projects. The authorities were also to continue the planned construction of the country's first nuclear power station, at a projected cost of 50,000m. złotys, with the aim of reducing the energy sector's dependence on coal. In January 2013 the IMF approved a new, two-year flexible credit arrangement of $33,800m., which was again intended to be precautionary. Komorowski announced, meanwhile, that a date for the country's adoption of the euro should not be decided until after elections in 2015, while the insistence of the Law and Justice party that a referendum be conducted on the issue, in view of lack of public support, constituted a prospective obstacle.

PUBLIC HOLIDAYS

2014: 1 January (New Year's Day), 21 April (Easter Monday), 1 May (State Holiday), 3 May (Polish National Day, Proclamation of 1791 Constitution), 30 May (Corpus Christi), 15 August (Assumption), 1 November (All Saints' Day), 11 November (Independence Day), 25–26 December (Christmas).

Statistical Survey

Source (unless otherwise indicated): Główny Urząd Statystyczny (Central Statistical Office), 00-925 Warsaw, Al. Niepodległości 208; tel. (22) 6083161; fax (22) 6083869; internet www.stat.gov.pl.

Area and Population

AREA, POPULATION AND DENSITY

Area (sq km)	
Land	311,888
Inland water	791
Total	312,679*
Population (census results)†	
20 May 2002	38,230,080
31 March 2011‡	
Males	18,643,900
Females	19,867,900
Total	38,511,800
Population (official estimate at mid-year)	
2012	38,533,789
Density (per sq km) at mid-2012	123.2

* 120,726 sq miles.
† Figures exclude civilian foreign nationals within the country and include civilian nationals temporarily outside the country.
‡ Figures rounded to nearest 100 persons.

POPULATION BY AGE AND SEX
('000 at 2011 census)

	Males	Females	Total
0–14	2,991.6	2,840.6	5,832.2
15–64	13,673.7	13,775.8	27,449.5
65 and over	1,978.6	3,251.5	5,230.1
Total	18,643.9	19,867.9	38,511.8

VOIVODSHIPS
(population at 2011 census, rounded figures)

	Area (sq km)	Population ('000)	Density*	Principal city
Dolnośląskie . .	19,947	2,915.2	146.1	Wrocław
Kujawsko-Pomorskie . .	17,972	2,097.6	116.7	Bydgoszcz
Lubelskie . .	25,122	2,175.7	86.6	Lublin
Lubuskie . .	13,988	1,022.8	73.1	Gorzów Wlkp†
Łódzkie . .	18,219	2,538.7	139.3	Łódź
Małopolskie . .	15,183	3,337.5	219.8	Kraków
Mazowieckie . .	35,558	5,268.7	148.2	Warsaw
Opolskie . .	9,412	1,016.2	108.0	Opole
Podkarpackie . .	17,845	2,127.3	119.2	Rzeszów
Podlaskie . .	20,187	1,202.4	59.6	Białystok
Pomorskie . .	18,310	2,276.2	124.3	Gdańsk
Śląskie . .	12,333	4,630.4	375.4	Katowice
Świętokrzyskie . .	11,711	1,280.7	109.4	Kielce
Warmińsko-Mazurskie . .	24,174	1,452.1	60.1	Olsztyn
Wielkopolskie . .	29,826	3,447.4	115.6	Poznań
Zachodniopomorskie . .	22,892	1,722.9	75.3	Szczecin
Total	312,679	38,511.8	123.2	—

* Per sq km.
† Gorzów Wielkopolski.

PRINCIPAL TOWNS
(official estimates at 1 January 2012)

Warszawa (Warsaw, the capital) . .	1,708,491	Bytom	176,106
Kraków	759,137	Olsztyn	175,420
Łódź	725,055	Bielsko-Biała . .	174,503
Wrocław . . .	631,235	Ruda Śląska . .	143,024
Poznań	553,564	Rybnik	140,944
Gdańsk	460,517	Tychy	129,322
Szczecin . . .	409,596	Dąbrowa Górnicza .	125,475
Bydgoszcz . . .	363,020	Gorzów Wielkopolski . .	124,554
Lublin	348,567	Płock	124,318
Katowice . . .	309,304	Elbląg	124,257
Białystok . . .	294,298	Opole	122,439
Gdynia	248,939	Wałbrzych . . .	119,955
Częstochowa . .	235,798	Zielona Góra . .	119,197
Radom	220,602	Włocławek . . .	116,345
Sosnowiec . . .	215,262	Tarnów	113,593
Toruń	204,921	Chorzów	111,536
Kielce	201,815	Koszalin	109,233
Gliwice	186,868	Kalisz	105,122
Zabrze	180,332	Legnica	102,979
Rzeszów	180,031		

BIRTHS, MARRIAGES AND DEATHS

	Registered live births		Registered marriages		Registered deaths	
	Number	Rate (per 1,000)	Number	Rate (per 1,000)	Number	Rate (per 1,000)
2005 . .	364,383	9.6	206,916	5.4	368,285	9.7
2006 . .	376,035	9.8	226,181	5.9	369,686	9.7
2007 . .	387,873	10.2	248,702	6.5	377,226	9.9
2008 . .	414,499	10.9	257,744	6.8	379,399	9.9
2009 . .	417,589	11.0	250,794	6.6	384,940	10.1
2010 . .	413,300	10.8	228,337	6.0	378,478	9.9
2011 . .	388,400	10.2	206,500	5.4	375,500	9.7
2012 . .	389,700	10.1	203,800	5.3	380,100	9.9

Life expectancy (official figures, years at birth): 76.5 (males 72.4; females 80.9) in 2011.

IMMIGRATION AND EMIGRATION
('000)*

	2010	2011	2012
Immigrants	15.2	15.5	15.0
Emigrants	17.4	19.9	20.7

* Figures refer to immigrants arriving for permanent residence in Poland and emigrants leaving for permanent residence abroad.

ECONOMICALLY ACTIVE POPULATION*
('000 persons aged 15 years and over, annual averages)

	2009	2010	2011
Agriculture, hunting, forestry and fishing	2,107	2,050	2,045
Mining and quarrying	221	230	255
Manufacturing	3,059	2,961	3,025
Electricity, gas and water supply	346	336	335
Construction	1,308	1,285	1,318
Wholesale and retail trade; repair of motor vehicles, motorcycles, and personal and household goods	2,332	2,376	2,377
Hotels and restaurants	329	350	355
Transport, storage and communications	1,207	1,202	1,215
Financial intermediation	372	371	389
Real estate, renting and business activities	1,001	1,077	1,128
Public administration and defence; compulsory social security	1,021	1,049	1,064
Education	1,227	1,254	1,228
Health and social work	881	935	924
Other community, social and personal service activities	428	448	439
Sub-total	15,839	15,924	16,097
Activities not adequately defined and unallocated	29	37	34
Total employed	15,868	15,961	16,131
Unemployed	1,411	1,699	1,723
Total labour force	17,279	17,660	17,853
Males	9,455	9,643	9,771
Females	7,824	8,017	8,082

* Excluding regular military personnel living in barracks, and conscripts.

Note: Totals may not be equal to the sum of component parts, owing to rounding.

Health and Welfare

KEY INDICATORS

Total fertility rate (children per woman, 2010)	1.4
Under-5 mortality rate (per 1,000 live births, 2010)	6
HIV/AIDS (% of persons aged 15–49, 2009)	0.1
Physicians (per 1,000 head, 2005)	2.0
Hospital beds (per 1,000 head, 2005)	5.2
Health expenditure (2009): US $ per head (PPP)	1,391
Health expenditure (2009): % of GDP	7.4
Health expenditure (2009): public (% of total)	72.3
Access to sanitation (% of total population, 2008)	90
Total carbon dioxide emissions ('000 metric tons, 2008)	316,066.1
Carbon dioxide emissions per head (metric tons, 2008)	8.3
Human Development Index (2011): ranking	39
Human Development Index (2011): value	0.813

For sources and definitions, see explanatory note on p. vi.

Agriculture

PRINCIPAL CROPS
('000 metric tons)

	2009	2010	2011
Wheat	9,789.6	9,487.8	9,339.2
Barley	3,983.9	3,533.0	3,325.9
Maize	1,706.6	1,716.2	1,659.7*
Rye	3,712.9	2,851.7	2,600.7
Oats	1,415.4	1,334.4	1,381.6
Triticale (wheat-rye hybrid)	5,234.0	4,575.8	4,235.3
Mixed grain	3,628.8	3,008.0	3,113.0
Potatoes	9,702.8	8,766.0	8,196.7
Sugar beet	10,849.2	9,972.6	11,674.2
Rapeseed	2,496.8	2,228.7	1,861.8
Cabbages and other brassicas	1,337.4	1,047.0	1,288.7
Tomatoes	709.2	558.1	712.3

—continued	2009	2010	2011
Cauliflowers and broccoli	291.1	273.0	297.6
Cucumbers and gherkins	480.6	442.2	510.9
Onions, dry	707.8	578.0	677.0
Carrots and turnips	913.3	764.6	887.4
Mushrooms and truffles*	199.1	173.4	198.2
Apples	2,626.3	1,877.9	2,493.1
Pears	83.0	46.5	62.8
Sour (Morello) cherries	189.2	147.2	175.0
Plums and sloes	120.7	83.8	91.8
Strawberries	198.9	153.4	166.2
Currants	196.5	196.7	169.6

* FAO estimate(s).

Aggregate production ('000 metric tons, may include official, semi-official or estimated data): Total cereals 29,571 in 2009, 26,653 in 2010, 25,775 in 2011; Total roots and tubers 9,703 in 2009, 8,766 in 2010, 8,197 in 2011; Total vegetables (incl. melons) 5,805 in 2009, 5,056 in 2010, 5,778 in 2011; Total fruits (excl. melons) 3,685 in 2009, 2,781 in 2010, 3,462 in 2011.

Source: FAO.

LIVESTOCK
('000 head, year ending September)

	2009	2010	2011
Horses	298	291	254
Cattle	5,700	5,724	5,717
Pigs	14,279	14,865	13,509
Sheep	286	258	251
Chickens	124,129	117,845	127,542
Geese and guinea fowls	4,039	2,976	3,720
Turkeys	8,065	7,398	8,458
Ducks	4,327	3,647	3,583

Source: FAO.

LIVESTOCK PRODUCTS
('000 metric tons)

	2009	2010	2011
Cattle meat	396.9	400.9	394.9
Pig meat	1,735.7	1,894.8	1,935.3
Horse meat	14.1	14.4	13.3
Game meat*	14.0	10.9	10.9
Chicken meat	1,059.8	1,123.0†	1,150.0*
Duck meat*	17.0	17.2	16.8
Turkey meat*	100.0	100.0	100.0
Cows' milk	12,447.2	12,278.7	12,413.8
Hen eggs	605.0	618.5	576.7
Honey	14.0	12.5	13.4

* FAO estimate(s).
† Unofficial figure.

Source: FAO.

Forestry

ROUNDWOOD REMOVALS
('000 cubic metres, excl. bark)

	2009	2010	2011
Sawlogs, veneer logs and logs for sleepers	13,604	14,320	14,722
Pulpwood	15,385	15,600	16,015
Other industrial wood	1,486	1,423	1,464
Fuel wood	4,154	4,124	4,980
Total	34,629	35,467	37,180

Source: FAO.

SAWNWOOD PRODUCTION
('000 cubic metres, incl. railway sleepers)

	2009	2010	2011
Coniferous (softwood) . . .	3,383	3,765	3,946
Broadleaved (hardwood) . . .	468	455	476
Total	**3,850**	**4,220**	**4,422**

Source: FAO.

Fishing

('000 metric tons, live weight)

	2008	2009	2010
Capture	142.5	223.9	189.7
Freshwater fishes	16.0	16.0	16.0
European flounder	9.1	9.7	11.2
Atlantic cod	11.3	12.4	14.8
Atlantic herring	16.8	22.2	24.9
European sprat	55.6	83.4	59.3
Antarctic krill	8.0	8.1	7.0
Aquaculture*	36.8	36.5	30.8
Common carp	17.2	18.1	15.4
Rainbow trout	16.5	14.9	12.9
Total catch*	**179.3**	**260.4**	**220.5**

* FAO estimates.

Source: FAO.

Mining

('000 metric tons unless otherwise indicated)

	2009	2010	2011
Hard coal	78,064	76,728	76,454
Brown coal (incl. lignite) . . .	57,108	56,510	62,841
Crude petroleum	687	686	617
Salt (unrefined)	3,831	4,097	4,282
Native sulphur	263	517	657
Copper ore (metric tons)* . . .	498,960	480,600	479,300
Lead ore (metric tons)* . . .	80,400	63,800†	59,000†
Magnesite ore—crude . . .	47,000	63,000	60,000†
Silver (metric tons)* . . .	1,221	1,175	1,280†
Zinc ore (metric tons)* . . .	116,000	95,000†	65,000
Natural gas (million cu metres) .	5,537	5,667	5,825

* Figures refer to the metal content of ores.
† Estimate.

Source: US Geological Survey.

Industry

SELECTED PRODUCTS
('000 metric tons unless otherwise indicated)

	2009	2010	2011
Refined sugar	1,683	1,754	2,159
Margarine	363	390	397
Beer ('000 hl)	36,236	36,800	38,067
Wine, mead and other fermented beverages ('000 hl) . . .	1,881	1,816	1,667
Cigarettes (million) . . .	125,204	144,651	150,490
Leather footwear ('000 pairs) . .	11,433	11,784	12,049
Mechanical wood pulp* . . .	20,290	18,800	20,000
Chemical wood pulp* . . .	826,266	881,001	894,322
Newsprint*	166	149	149
Rubber tyres ('000)[1] . . .	51,945	60,875	64,796
Sulphuric acid—100% . . .	1,243	1,686	1,889
Caustic soda—96% . . .	75	53	59
Nitrogenous fertilizers (a)[2] . .	4,472	4,709	4,987
Phosphate fertilizers (b)[2] . .	146	310	392
Motor spirit—Petrol[3] . . .	4,283	4,222	3,925

—continued	2009	2010	2011
Diesel oils	9,016	9,893	10,739
Coke-oven coke	5,305	7,200	6,417
Cement	15,422	15,812	18,993
Pig-iron[4]	2,984	3,638	3,975
Crude steel	7,128	7,993	8,776
Rolled steel products . . .	6,232	6,658	7,504
Aluminium—unwrought[5] . .	10.3	10.1	6.1
Refined copper—unwrought . .	458	470	482
Refined lead—unwrought . .	50.6	35.8	31.0
Zinc—unwrought[5] . . .	110	98	109
Radio receivers ('000) . . .	18	17	10
Television receivers ('000)[6] . .	21,559	26,349	20,674
Merchant ships launched (gross reg. tons) . . .	338	27	64
Passenger motor cars ('000) . .	819	785	741
Lorries and tractors (number) . .	52,213	76,131	86,245
Domestic washing machines ('000) .	3,221	4,048	4,054
Domestic refrigerators and freezers ('000) . . .	1,886	1,867	2,066
Electric energy (million kWh) .	151,720	157,658	162,923

* Source: FAO.
[1] Tyres for passenger motor cars and commercial vehicles, including inner tubes and tyres for animal-drawn road vehicles, and tyres for non-agricultural machines and equipment.
[2] Fertilizer production is measured in terms of (a) nitrogen or (b) phosphoric acid. Phosphate fertilizers include ground rock phosphate.
[3] Including synthetic products.
[4] Including blast furnace ferro-alloys.
[5] Figures refer to both primary and secondary metal. Zinc production includes zinc dust and remelted zinc.
[6] Including monitors.

Finance

CURRENCY AND EXCHANGE RATES

Monetary Units
100 groszy (singular: grosz) = 1 złoty.

Sterling, Dollar and Euro Equivalents (31 December 2012)
£1 sterling = 4.891 złotys;
US $1 = 3.100 złotys;
€1 = 4.090 złotys;
100 złotys = £20.45 = $32.26 = €24.45.

Average Exchange Rate (złotys per US dollar)
2010   3.015
2011   2.963
2012   3.257

GOVERNMENT FINANCE
(general government transactions, non-cash basis, million złotys)

Summary of Balances

	2008	2009	2010
Revenue	496,968	497,099	532,242
Less Expense	512,023	550,623	588,635
Net operating balance . .	**−15,055**	**−53,524**	**−56,393**
Less Net acquisition of non-financial assets . . .	32,867	42,456	54,975
Net lending/borrowing . .	**−47,922**	**−95,980**	**−111,368**

Revenue

	2008	2009	2010
Taxes	291,832	274,128	292,154
Taxes on income, profits and capital gains . . .	102,529	93,083	91,306
Taxes on goods and services .	165,851	158,124	176,099
Social contributions . . .	144,337	152,085	156,981
Grants	7,826	12,743	23,896
Other revenue	52,973	58,143	59,211
Total	**496,968**	**497,099**	**532,242**

Expense/Outlays

Expense by economic type	2008	2009	2010
Compensation of employees . .	126,714	137,447	143,021
Use of goods and services . .	76,027	71,601	86,075
Consumption of fixed capital . .	22,513	24,252	25,241
Interest	30,491	34,863	36,673
Subsidies	7,306	7,541	7,611
Grants	13,529	14,291	15,274
Social benefits	206,659	228,715	241,366
Other expense	28,784	31,913	33,374
Total	512,023	550,623	588,635

Outlays by functions of government*	2008	2009	2010
General public services . . .	69,530	77,841	83,672
Defence	20,560	12,468	19,142
Public order and safety . . .	25,670	25,722	26,967
Economic affairs	62,008	70,916	82,311
Environmental protection . .	7,799	9,973	9,579
Housing and community amenities	10,785	12,299	13,834
Health	60,071	67,910	69,911
Recreation, culture and religion .	15,596	17,653	19,883
Education	66,886	71,267	76,713
Social protection	205,985	227,030	241,598
Total	544,890	593,079	643,610

* Including net acquisition of non-financial assets.

Source: IMF, *Government Finance Statistics Yearbook*.

INTERNATIONAL RESERVES
(US $ million at 31 December)

	2009	2010	2011
Gold (national valuation) . .	3,652.9	4,666.4	5,209.9
IMF special drawing rights . .	2,099.5	2,006.5	1,797.5
Reserve position in IMF . . .	430.3	497.9	1,160.8
Foreign exchange	73,393.6	86,317.4	89,688.1
Total	79,576.3	93,488.2	97,856.4

Source: IMF, *International Financial Statistics*.

MONEY SUPPLY
(million złotys at 31 December)

	2009	2010	2011
Currency outside depository corporations	89,778	92,707	101,848
Transferable deposits . . .	298,567	356,485	366,205
Other deposits	329,507	331,904	405,268
Securities other than shares . .	4,332	4,100	11,156
Broad money	722,184	785,196	884,477

Source: IMF, *International Financial Statistics*.

COST OF LIVING
(Consumer Price Index; base: 2000 = 100)

	2010	2011	2012
Food (incl. alcoholic beverages) .	131.1	137.4	142.8
All items (incl. others) . . .	131.2	136.9	142.0

Source: ILO.

NATIONAL ACCOUNTS
(million złotys at current prices)

Expenditure on the Gross Domestic Product

	2010	2011	2012
Final consumption expenditure .	1,136,237	1,207,585	1,256,700
Gross capital formation . . .	297,449	333,187	334,045
Total domestic expenditure .	1,433,686	1,540,772	1,590,745
Exports of goods and services . .	598,369	688,739	734,578
Less Imports of goods and services	615,470	706,266	729,440
GDP in market prices . .	1,416,585	1,523,245	1,595,883

Gross Domestic Product by Economic Activity
(preliminary)

	2010	2011	2012
Agriculture, hunting, forestry and fishing	46,637	54,093	56,657
Mining and quarrying . . .	30,587	36,949	35,560
Manufacturing	209,714	235,169	250,537
Electricity, gas and water supply .	59,995	62,625	66,861
Construction	101,026	107,534	102,521
Wholesale and retail trade; repair of motor vehicles, motorcycles and personal and household goods	242,150	251,415	264,980
Transport, storage and communication	116,255	124,766	136,927
Hotels and restaurants . . .	14,630	16,444	17,170
Financial intermediation . . .	55,110	59,106	65,218
Real estate, renting and business activities	156,038	165,556	179,812
Public administration and defence; compulsory social security . .	66,517	67,345	71,308
Education	60,717	64,134	68,074
Health and social work . . .	48,694	51,374	52,854
Other community, social and personal service activities . .	10,379	11,156	11,393
Private households with employed persons	6,486	7,040	7,288
Other services	22,716	22,798	23,500
Gross value added in basic prices	1,247,651	1,337,504	1,410,661
Taxes, *less* subsidies, on products .	168,934	185,741	185,222
GDP in market prices . . .	1,416,585	1,523,245	1,595,883

BALANCE OF PAYMENTS
(US $ million)

	2009	2010	2011
Exports of goods	142,081	165,721	195,209
Imports of goods	−149,702	−177,519	−209,245
Balance on goods	−7,621	−11,798	−14,036
Exports of services	28,990	32,706	37,556
Imports of services	−24,191	−29,620	−31,894
Balance on goods and services	−2,822	−8,712	−8,374
Primary income received . . .	6,625	8,029	8,534
Primary income paid	−23,176	−27,109	−31,414
Balance on goods, services and primary income	−19,373	−27,792	−31,254
Secondary income received . .	10,349	9,936	12,520
Secondary income paid . . .	−8,131	−6,174	−6,289
Current balance	−17,155	−24,030	−25,023
Capital account (net)	7,040	8,620	10,017
Direct investment assets . . .	−5,928	−10,213	−3,744
Direct investment liabilities . .	14,388	17,074	15,296
Portfolio investment assets . .	−1,448	−1,111	726
Portfolio investment liabilities .	16,202	26,649	16,109
Financial derivatives and employee stock options liabilities . . .	−1,692	−787	−562
Other investment assets . . .	5,275	−3,901	−3,457
Other investment liabilities . .	8,129	13,293	6,065
Net errors and omissions . . .	−10,050	−10,488	−9,314
Reserves and related items .	14,761	15,106	6,113

Source: IMF, *International Financial Statistics*.

External Trade

PRINCIPAL COMMODITIES
(distribution by SITC, US $ million)

Imports c.i.f.	2009	2010	2011
Food and live animals	10,301	11,641	13,810
Crude materials (inedible) except fuels	4,086	5,414	7,351
Mineral fuels, lubricants, etc. .	14,105	19,020	26,779
Chemicals and related products .	20,960	25,386	30,139
Basic manufactures	26,043	31,722	38,667
Machinery and transport equipment	53,170	61,103	67,389
Miscellaneous manufactured articles	15,917	18,253	20,824
Total (incl. others)	149,570	178,063	212,331

Exports f.o.b.	2009	2010	2011
Food and live animals	13,065	14,744	17,652
Crude materials (inedible) except fuels	2,577	3,706	4,488
Mineral fuels, lubricants, etc. .	4,214	6,536	9,232
Chemicals and related products .	10,706	13,634	17,005
Basic manufactures	26,674	32,362	40,566
Machinery and transport equipment	59,034	65,687	73,966
Miscellaneous manufactured articles	18,037	20,558	24,262
Total (incl. others)	136,641	159,758	190,247

PRINCIPAL TRADING PARTNERS
(US $ million)*

Imports c.i.f.	2009	2010	2011
Austria	2,601.0	2,995.8	3,912.9
Belgium	3,467.0	4,254.2	4,708.3
China, People's Republic . . .	13,914.4	16,703.3	18,386.4
Czech Republic	5,399.6	6,746.7	7,919.3
Denmark	2,053.7	2,181.1	2,770.8
Finland	1,933.5	1,791.6	2,133.5
France (incl. Monaco) . . .	6,892.8	7,713.6	8,874.9
Germany	33,418.5	39,015.7	47,442.5
Hungary	2,804.7	3,104.2	3,736.1
Italy	10,165.7	10,166.5	11,477.6
Japan	2,957.1	3,613.1	3,711.0
Korea, Republic	4,481.2	4,866.8	4,647.3
Netherlands	5,434.9	6,618.1	7,968.9
Norway	1,891.1	2,676.3	3,340.1
Russia	12,834.4	18,206.0	25,534.5
Slovakia	3,054.2	3,683.5	4,392.4
Spain	3,344.8	3,615.5	4,165.8
Sweden	2,767.1	3,350.8	4,291.5
Turkey	1,925.8	2,131.9	2,328.4
United Kingdom	4,417.6	4,874.5	5,575.8
USA	3,441.2	4,480.3	4,791.1
Total (incl. others)	149,569.8	178,062.9	212,330.9

Exports f.o.b.	2009	2010	2011
Austria	2,591.4	3,059.4	3,651.7
Belgium	3,291.5	3,798.4	4,421.0
Czech Republic	8,005.7	9,574.2	11,884.5
Denmark	2,533.1	2,984.0	3,501.2
France (incl. Monaco) . . .	9,498.9	10,857.9	11,645.3
Germany	35,679.6	41,786.3	49,687.8
Hungary	3,699.0	4,504.7	4,882.2
Italy	9,314.4	9,510.4	10,156.8
Lithuania	1,662.1	1,854.6	2,688.6
Netherlands	5,751.6	7,028.1	8,310.5
Norway	2,556.8	2,340.2	3,819.0

Exports f.o.b.—*continued*	2009	2010	2011
Romania	1,833.2	2,188.8	2,936.6
Russia	5,015.2	6,617.9	8,531.5
Slovakia	3,131.9	4,332.8	4,671.6
Spain	3,584.6	4,261.5	4,556.6
Sweden	3,667.1	4,738.6	5,437.4
Turkey	1,755.1	2,483.1	2,328.4
Ukraine	3,433.2	3,917.3	4,688.0
United Kingdom	8,771.6	10,076.7	12,265.9
USA	2,482.4	2,873.3	3,693.1
Total (incl. others)	136,641.3	159,757.6	190,247.4

* Imports by country of purchase; exports by country of sale.

Transport

POLISH STATE RAILWAYS
(traffic)

	2009	2010	2011
Paying passengers ('000 journeys)	282,729	261,314	263,509
Passenger-km (million) . . .	18,671	17,921	18,161
Freight carried ('000 metric tons) .	201,226	216,899	248,606
Freight ton-km (million) . . .	43,455	48,707	53,746

ROAD TRAFFIC
('000 motor vehicles registered at 31 December)

	2009	2010	2011
Passenger cars	16,495	17,240	18,125
Lorries and vans (incl. road tractors)	2,797	2,982	3,131
Buses and coaches	95	97	100
Motorcycles	975	1,013	1,069

INLAND WATERWAYS
(traffic, including coastal transport)

	2009	2010	2011
Passengers carried ('000) . .	1,671	1,397	1,519
Passenger-km (million) . . .	30	23	24
Freight carried ('000 metric tons) .	5,655	5,141	5,093
Freight ton-km (million) . . .	1,020	1,030	909

SHIPPING

Flag Registered Fleet
(at 31 December)

	2010	2011	2012
Number of vessels	259	260	260
Total displacement ('000 grt) . .	162.5	160.1	157.3

Source: Lloyd's List Intelligence (www.lloydslistintelligence.com).

Sea Transport
(by owned or leased ships)

	2009	2010	2011
Passengers carried ('000) . . .	658	672	637
Passenger-miles (million) . . .	89	168	156
Freight carried ('000 metric tons) .	9,378	8,362	7,737
Freight ton-miles (million) . . .	12,883	19,773	21,341

International Sea-borne Shipping at Polish Ports

	2009	2010	2011
Vessels entered ('000 net reg. tons)	62,457	69,857	71,905
Vessels entered (number) . . .	20,094	19,710	18,864
Passengers ('000): arrivals . .	713	759	792
Passengers ('000): departures .	724	781	836
Cargo ('000 metric tons): loaded* .	22,095	30,932	24,165
Cargo ('000 metric tons): unloaded*	22,984	28,575	33,574

* Including ships' bunkers and transshipments.

Source: Centre of Maritime Statistics.

CIVIL AVIATION
(traffic on all services)

	2009	2010	2011
Passengers carried ('000) . . .	4,350	4,990	6,491
Passenger-km (million) . . .	7,428	8,273	11,065
Freight carried ('000 metric tons) .	37	41	47
Total ton-km (million) . . .	85	114	129

Kilometres flown (million): 92 in 2007; 97 in 2008; 89 in 2009 (Source: UN, *Statistical Yearbook*).

Tourism

FOREIGN TOURIST ARRIVALS
('000, including visitors in transit)

Country of residence	2010	2011	2012
Belarus	3,090	3,450	3,920
Czech Republic	9,240	10,840	12,380
Germany	25,860	25,740	26,720
Lithuania	2,690	2,420	3,010
Russia	1,530	1,850	2,670
Slovakia	6,010	5,620	6,630
Ukraine	5,030	5,830	6,740
Total (incl. others)	58,340	60,745	67,390

Source: Institute of Tourism.

Receipts from tourism (US $ million, excluding passenger transport): 9,011 in 2009; 9,526 in 2010; 10,687 in 2011 (provisional) (Source: World Tourism Organization).

Communications Media

	2009	2010	2011
Radio subscribers ('000)* . . .	7,027	6,939	6,888
Television subscribers ('000)* . .	6,797	6,707	6,652
Telephones ('000 main lines in use)†	8,493.5	7,667.1	6,852.6
Mobile cellular telephones ('000 subscribers)†	44,806.6	46,952.1	50,160.2
Internet subscribers ('000)† . .	5,036.3	4,963.0	n.a.
Broadband subscribers ('000)† .	4,798.1	4,960.5	5,622.4
Book production: titles‡ . . .	28,128	29,539	31,511
Book production: copies (million)‡ .	69.5	83.4	95.7
Daily and non-daily newspapers: number	56	51	44
average circulation ('000 copies)	4,299	3,722	3,671
Other periodicals: number . .	7,367	7,604	7,520
Other periodicals: average circulation ('000 copies) . . .	83,055	87,075	85,747

* At 31 December.
† Source: International Telecommunication Union.
‡ Including pamphlets.

Personal computers: 6,456,000 (169.3 per 1,000 persons) in 2006 (Source: International Telecommunication Union).

Education

(2008/09 unless otherwise indicated)

			Students ('000)		
	Institutions	Teachers	Males	Females	Total
Pre-primary .	17,337*	54,318	469.8	449.3	919.1
Primary . .	15,344†	238,741	1,182.2	1,112.2	2,294.4
Secondary . .	17,825†	276,969	1,519.0	1,439.2	2,958.2
Tertiary . .	400†	101,390	905.4	1,244.6	2,150.0

* 2001/02 figure.
† 2004/05 figure.

Source: partly UNESCO Institute for Statistics.

Pupil-teacher ratio (primary education, UNESCO estimate): 9.6 in 2008/09 (Source: UNESCO Institute for Statistics).

Adult literacy rate (UNESCO estimates): 99.5% (males 99.7%; females 99.4%) in 2010 (Source: UNESCO Institute for Statistics).

Directory

The Government
HEAD OF STATE

President: Bronisław Komorowski (elected 4 July 2010, assumed office 6 August).

COUNCIL OF MINISTERS
(May 2013)

A coalition comprising Civic Platform (PO), the Polish People's Party (PSL) and Independents.

Prime Minister: Donald Tusk (PO).

Deputy Prime Minister and Minister of the Economy: Janusz Piechociński (PSL).

Deputy Prime Minister and Minister of Finance: Jan (Jacek) Vincent-Rostowski (PO).

Minister of Administration and Digitization: Michał Boni (PO).

Minister of Agriculture and Rural Development: Stanisław Kalemba (PSL).

Minister of Culture and National Heritage: Bogdan Zdrojewski (PO).

Minister of the Economy: Piotr Grzegorz Woźniak (PO).

Minister of the Environment: Marcin Korolec (Independent).

Minister of Foreign Affairs: Radosław Sikorski (PO).

Minister of Health: Bartosz Arłukowicz (PO).

Minister of the Interior: Bartłomiej Sienkiewicz (Independent).

Minister of Justice: Marek Biernacki (PO).

Minister of Labour and Social Policy: Władysław Kosiniak-Kamysz (PSL).

Minister of National Defence: Tomasz Siemoniak (PO).

Minister of National Education: Krystyna Szumilas (PO).

Minister of Regional Development: Elżbieta Bieńkowska (PO).

Minister of Science and Higher Education: Barbara Kudrycka (PO).

Minister of Sport and Tourism: Joanna Mucha (PO).

Minister of the State Treasury: Włodzimierz Karpiński (PO).

Minister of Transport, Construction and Maritime Economy: Sławomir Nowak (PO).

Minister, responsible for the Standing Committee of the Council of Ministers, Head of the Chancellery of the Prime Minister: Jacek Cichocki (Independent).

MINISTRIES

Chancellery of the President: 00-902 Warsaw, ul. Wiejska 10; tel. (22) 6952900; fax (22) 6952238; e-mail listy@prezydent.pl; internet www.prezydent.pl.

Chancellery of the Prime Minister: 00-583 Warsaw, Al. Ujaz-dowskie 1/3; tel. (22) 6946000; fax (22) 6252637; e-mail kontakt@kprm.gov.pl; internet www.premier.gov.pl.

Ministry of Administration and Digitization: ul. Stefana Bator-ego 5, 02-591 Warsaw; tel. (22) 6947815; e-mail smb@mac.gov.pl; internet www.mac.gov.pl.

Ministry of Agriculture and Rural Development: 00-930 War-saw, ul. Wspólna 30; tel. (22) 6231000; fax (22) 6232750; e-mail kanceleria@minrol.gov.pl; internet www.minrol.gov.pl.

Ministry of Culture and National Heritage: 00-071 Warsaw, ul. Krakowskie Przedmieście 15/17; tel. (22) 4210100; fax (22) 4210131; e-mail minister@mkidn.gov.pl; internet www.mkidn.gov.pl.

Ministry of the Economy: 00-507 Warsaw, pl. Trzech Krzyży 3/5; tel. (22) 6935000; fax (22) 6934048; e-mail mg@mg.gov.pl; internet www.mg.gov.pl.

Ministry of the Environment: 00-922 Warsaw, ul. Wawelska 52/54; tel. (22) 5792900; fax (22) 5792511; e-mail info@mos.gov.pl; internet www.mos.gov.pl.

Ministry of Finance: 00-916 Warsaw, ul. Świętokrzyska 12; tel. (22) 6945555; fax (22) 6944177; e-mail kancelaria@mofnet.gov.pl; internet www.mf.gov.pl.

Ministry of Foreign Affairs: 00-580 Warsaw, Al. Szucha 23; tel. (22) 5239000; fax (22) 6287819; e-mail dabw.sekretariat@msz.gov.pl; internet www.msz.gov.pl.

Ministry of Health: 00-952 Warsaw, ul. Miodowa 15; tel. (22) 6349600; fax (22) 6349213; e-mail kancelaria@mz.gov.pl; internet www.mz.gov.pl.

Ministry of the Interior: 02-591 Warsaw, ul. Stefana Batorego 5; tel. (22) 6212020; fax (22) 6013988; e-mail kancelaria.glowna@mswia.gov.pl; internet www.msw.gov.pl.

Ministry of Justice: 00-950 Warsaw, Al. Ujazdowskie 11; tel. (22) 5212888; fax (22) 6286552; e-mail kontakt@ms.gov.pl; internet ms.gov.pl.

Ministry of Labour and Social Policy: 00-513 Warsaw, ul. Nowogrodzka 1/3/5; tel. (22) 6610100; fax (22) 6611336; e-mail info@mpips.gov.pl; internet www.mpips.gov.pl.

Ministry of National Defence: 00-909, ul. Klonowa 1; tel. and fax (22) 6840213; e-mail newsroom.dpimon@mon.gov.pl; internet www.mon.gov.pl.

Ministry of National Education: 00-918 Warsaw, Al. Szucha 25; tel. (22) 3474100; e-mail informacja@men.gov.pl; internet www.men.gov.pl.

Ministry of Regional Development: 00-926 Warsaw, ul. Wspólna 2/4; tel. (22) 2737000; e-mail media@mrr.gov.pl; internet www.mrr.gov.pl.

Ministry of Science and Higher Education: 00-529 Warsaw, ul. Wspólna 1/3; tel. (22) 5292718; fax (22) 6280922; e-mail ssekretariat.bm@nauka.gov.pl; internet www.nauka.gov.pl.

Ministry of Sport and Tourism: 00-082 Warsaw, ul. Senatorska 14; tel. (22) 2443142; fax (22) 2443255; e-mail kontakt@msport.gov.pl; internet www.msport.gov.pl.

Ministry of the State Treasury: 00-522 Warsaw, ul. Krucza 36; tel. (22) 6958000; fax (22) 6280872; e-mail minister@msp.gov.pl; internet www.msp.gov.pl.

Ministry of Transport, Construction and Maritime Economy: 00-928 Warsaw, ul. Chałubińskiego 4/6; tel. (22) 6301000; fax (22) 6301116; e-mail info@transport.gov.pl; internet www.transport.gov.pl.

President

Presidential Election, First Ballot, 20 June 2010

Candidates				Votes	%
Bronisław Komorowski	.	.	.	6,981,319	41.54
Jarosław Kaczyński	.	.	.	6,128,255	36.46
Grzegorz Napieralski	.	.	.	2,299,870	13.68
Others .	.	.	.	1,396,726	8.31
Total	.	.	.	**16,806,170**	**100.00**

Second Ballot, 4 July 2010

Candidates				Votes	%
Bronisław Komorowski	.	.	.	8,933,887	53.01
Jarosław Kaczyński	.	.	.	7,919,134	46.99
Total	.	.	.	**16,853,021**	**100.00**

Legislature

The Zgromadzenie Narodowe (National Assembly) is bicameral, comprising: the Sejm (Assembly), the lower chamber; and the Senat (Senate), the upper chamber.

Sejm
(Assembly)

00-902 Warsaw, ul. Wiejska 2/6; tel. (22) 6942500; fax (22) 6941446; e-mail zjablon@sejm.gov.pl; internet www.sejm.gov.pl.

Marshal: GRZEGORZ SCHETYNA.

Election, 9 October 2011

Parties	Votes	% of votes	Seats
Civic Platform (PO)	5,629,773	39.18	207
Law and Justice (PiS) . . .	4,295,016	29.89	157
Palikot's Movement (RP) . . .	1,439,490	10.02	40
Polish People's Party (PSL) . .	1,201,628	8.36	28
Democratic Left Alliance (SLD) . .	1,184,303	8.24	27
German Minority (MN) . . .	28,014	0.19	1
Others	591,279	4.12	—
Total	**14,369,503**	**100.00**	**460**

Senat
(Senate)

00-902 Warsaw, ul. Wiejska 6; tel. (22) 6949284; fax (22) 6949570; internet www.senat.gov.pl.

Marshal: BOGDAN BORUSEWICZ.

Election, 9 October 2011

Parties and alliances	Seats
Civic Platform (PO)	63
Law and Justice (PiS)	31
Polish People's Party (PSL)	2
Independent	4
Total	**100**

Election Commission

Państwowa Komisja Wyborcza (PKW) (State Election Commission): 00-902 Warsaw, ul. Wiejska 10; tel. (22) 6250617; fax (22) 6293959; internet www.pkw.gov.pl; Pres. STEFAN JAN JAWORSKI.

Political Organizations

Civic Platform (PO) (Platforma Obywatelska): 00-159 Warsaw, ul. Andersa 21; tel. (22) 6357879; fax (22) 6357641; e-mail donald.tusk@sejm.pl; internet www.platforma.org; f. 2001; liberal-conservative; Pres. DONALD TUSK.

Democratic Left Alliance (SLD) (Sojusz Lewicy Demokratycz-nej): 00-419 Warsaw, ul. Rozbrat 44 A; tel. (22) 6210341; fax (22) 6216069; e-mail rk@sld.org.pl; internet www.sld.org.pl; f. 1999; contested 2007 legislative elections as mem. of Left and Democrats coalition; Chair. LESZEK MILLER.

Democratic Party (PD) (Partia Demokratyczna): 00-581 Warsaw, ul. Marszałkowska 2/4; tel. (22) 3355800; fax (22) 4651284; e-mail sekretariat@demokraci.pl; internet www.demokraci.pl; f. 2005 to replace Freedom Union (UW); contested 2007 legislative elections as mem. of Left and Democrats coalition; Leader BRYGIDA KUŹNIAK.

German Minority (MN) (Mniejszość Niemiecka): 45-004 Opole, ul. M. Konopnickiej 6; tel. (77) 4021070; concerned with cultural and educational issues to help combat social problems; Chair. RASCH NORBERT.

Law and Justice (PiS) (Prawo i Sprawiedliwość): 02-018 Warsaw, ul. Nowogrodzka 84/86; tel. (22) 6215035; fax (22) 6216767; e-mail biuro@pis.org.pl; internet www.pis.org.pl; f. 2001; conservative; Pres. JAROSŁAW KACZYŃSKI.

League of Polish Families (LPR) (Liga Polskich Rodzin): 00-528 Warsaw, ul. Hoża 9; tel. (22) 6223648; fax (22) 6223138; e-mail info@lpr.pl; internet www.lpr.pl; f. 2001 as alliance comprising the National Party, All-Poland Youth, the Polish Accord Party, the Catholic National movement and the Peasant National Bloc; Roman Catholic, nationalist, anti-EU; Pres. WITOLD BAŁAŻAK.

Palikot's Movement (RP) (Ruch Palikota): 00-446 Warsaw, ul. Fabryczna 16/22, lok. 24; tel. (22) 4010247; e-mail biuro@

ruchpalikota.org.pl; internet www.ruchpalikota.org.pl; f. 2011 on basis of Movement of Support; anti-clerical; Chair. JANUSZ PALIKOT.

Polish Labour Party (PPP) (Polska Partia Pracy): 00-570 Warsaw, ul. Wyzwolenia 18; tel. (22) 3929180; e-mail bzietek@wzz.org.pl; internet www.partiapracy.pl; f. 2001; Chair. BOGUSŁAW ZIĘTEK.

Polish People's Party (PSL) (Polskie Stronnictwo Ludowe): 00-924 Warsaw, ul. Kopernika 36/40; tel. (22) 6206020; fax (22) 6543583; e-mail biuronkw@psl.org.pl; internet www.psl.pl; f. 1990 on basis of United Peasant Party (f. 1949) and Polish Peasant Party—Rebirth (f. 1989); centrist, advocates devt of agriculture and social market economy; Chair. JANUSZ PIECHOCIŃSKI.

Polish Social Democracy (SDPL) (Socjaldemokracja Polski): 00-560 Warsaw, ul. Mokotowska 29A; tel. (22) 6213640; fax (22) 6215342; e-mail sdpl@sdpl.pl; internet www.sdpl.pl; f. 2004; contested 2007 legislative elections as mem. of Left and Democrats coalition; Chair. WOJCIECH FILEMONOWICZ.

Polish Solidarity (SP) (Solidarna Polska): 00-902 Warsaw, ul. Wieska 4/6/8/134; internet www.klubsp.pl; f. 2012 by fmr members of Law and Justice (q.v.); Pres. ZBIGNIEW ZIOBRO; 1,700 mems (Mar. 2012).

Right of the Republic (PR) (Prawica Rzeczypospolitej): 00-687 Warsaw, ul. Wspólna 61/105; tel. (22) 3920554; e-mail lech .luczynski@prawicarzeczypospolitej.org; internet www.prawica rzeczypospolitej.org; f. 2007; opposed to abortion, euthanasia, and supportive of traditional Roman Catholic values; Leader MAREK JUREK.

Self-Defence Party of the Republic of Poland (SRP) (Partia Samoobrona Rzeczypospolitej Polskiej): 00-024 Warsaw, Al. Jerozolimskie 30; tel. (22) 6250472; fax (22) 6250477; e-mail partia@ samoobrona.org.pl; internet www.samoobrona.pl; agrarian, populist, anti-EU; Leader ANDRZEJ LEPPER.

Union of Labour (UP) (Unia Pracy): 00-513 Warsaw, ul. Nowogrodzka 4; tel. (22) 6256776; e-mail biuro@uniapracy.pl; internet www.uniapracy.org.pl; f. 1992; contested 2007 legislative elections as mem. of Left and Democrats coalition; Chair. WALDEMAR WITKOWSKI.

Women's Party (PK) (Partia Kobiet): 00-278 Warsaw, ul. Kanonia 24/26; tel. (22) 644434; e-mail przewodniczaca@partiakobiet.org.pl; internet www.polskajestkobieta.org; f. 2007; socially liberal; Chair. IWONA PIĄTEK.

Diplomatic Representation

EMBASSIES IN POLAND

Afghanistan: 02-954 Warsaw, ul. Goplańska 1; tel. (22) 8855410; fax (22) 8856500; e-mail warsaw@afghanembassy.com.pl; internet www .afghanembassy.com.pl; Chargé d'affaires SAYED GHAZANFAR HUSSAINY.

Albania: 02-386 Warsaw, ul. Altowa 1; tel. (22) 8241427; fax (22) 8241426; e-mail embassy.warsaw@mfa.gov.al; Ambassador FLORENT ÇELIKU.

Algeria: 03-932 Warsaw, ul. Dąbrowiecka 21; tel. (22) 6175855; fax (22) 6160081; e-mail ambalggovdz@zigzag.pl; Ambassador ABDELKADER KHEMRI.

Angola: 02-616 Warsaw, ul. Goszczyńskiego 12; tel. (22) 8440994; fax (22) 8447452; e-mail embaixada@emb-angola.pl; Ambassador DOMINGOS CULOLO.

Argentina: 03-973 Warsaw, ul. Brukselska 9; tel. (22) 6176028; fax (22) 6177162; e-mail epolo@home.pl; Ambassador PATRICIA BEATRIZ SALAS.

Armenia: 02-803 Warsaw, ul. Bekasów 50; tel. (22) 8990940; fax (22) 8990935; e-mail secretariat@armenia.internetdsl.pl; Ambassador ASHOT GOLOIAN.

Australia: 00-513 Warsaw, ul. Nowogrodzka 11, 3rd Floor, Nautilus Bldg; tel. (22) 5213444; fax (22) 6273500; e-mail ambasada .australia@dfat.gov.au; internet www.poland.embassy.gov.au/ wsaw/home.html; Ambassador JEAN DUNN.

Austria: 00-748 Warsaw, ul. Gagarina 34; tel. (22) 8410081; fax (22) 8410085; e-mail warschau-ob@bmaa.gv.at; internet www .ambasadaaustrii.pl; Ambassador HERBERT KRAUSS.

Azerbaijan: 03-941 Warsaw, ul. Zwycięców 12; tel. (22) 6162188; fax (22) 6161949; e-mail warsaw@mission.mfa.gov.az; internet www .azembassy.pl; Ambassador HASAN AZIZ HASANOV.

Belarus: 02-952 Warsaw, ul. Wiertnicza 58; tel. (22) 7420990; fax (22) 7420980; e-mail poland@mfa.gov.by; internet poland.mfa.gov .by; Ambassador VIKTAR GAISENAK.

Belgium: 00-095 Warsaw, ul. Senatorska 34; tel. (22) 5512800; fax (22) 8285711; e-mail warsaw@diplobel.fed.be; internet www .diplomatie.be/warsawfr; Ambassador RAOUL ROGER DELCORDE.

Bosnia and Herzegovina: 00-789 Warsaw, ul. Humańska 10; tel. (22) 8569935; fax (22) 8481521; e-mail amb-bih.pl@poczta .internetdsl.pl; Ambassador KOVILJKA ŠPIRIĆ.

Brazil: 03-963 Warsaw, ul. Bajońska 15; tel. (22) 6174800; fax (22) 6178689; e-mail brasil@brasil.org.pl; internet www.brasil.org.pl; Ambassador JORGE GERALDO KADRI.

Bulgaria: 00-540 Warsaw, Al. Ujazdowskie 33/35; tel. (22) 6294071; fax (22) 6282271; e-mail Embassy.Warsaw@mfa.bg; internet www .mfa.bg/embassies/poland; Ambassador VASILIY TAKEV.

Canada: 00-481 Warsaw, ul. Matejki 1/5; tel. (22) 5843100; fax (22) 5843192; e-mail wsaw@international.gc.ca; internet www.canada .pl; Ambassador ALEXANDRA BUGAILISKIS.

Chile: 02-925 Warsaw, ul. Okrężna 62; tel. (22) 8582330; fax (22) 8582329; e-mail echile.polonia@minrel.gov.cl; internet www .chileabroad.gov.cl; Ambassador JOSÉ MANUEL SILVA VIDAURRE.

China, People's Republic: 00-203 Warsaw, ul. Bonifraterska 1; tel. (22) 8313836; fax (22) 6354211; e-mail ambchina@pol.pl; internet www.chinaembassy.org.pl; Ambassador XU JIAN.

Colombia: 03-936 Warsaw, ul. Zwycięzców 29; tel. (22) 6170973; fax (22) 6176684; e-mail embcol@medianet.pl; Ambassador VICTORIA GONZÁLEZ ARIZA.

Croatia: 02-611 Warsaw, ul. Ignacego Krasickiego 25; tel. (22) 8442393; fax (22) 8444808; e-mail croemb.warszawa@mvep.hr; internet pl.mvp.hr; Ambassador IVAN DEL VECHIO.

Cuba: 02-516 Warsaw, ul. Rejtana 15/8; tel. (22) 8481715; fax (22) 8482231; e-mail embacuba@medianet.pl; internet emba.cubaminrex .cu/polonia; Ambassador JUAN DAGOBERTO CASTRO MARTINEZ.

Cyprus: 02-629 Warsaw, ul. Pilicka 4; tel. (22) 8444577; fax (22) 8442558; e-mail ambasada@ambcypr.pl; Ambassador ANDREAS ZENONOS.

Czech Republic: 00-555 Warsaw, ul. Koszykowa 18; tel. (22) 5251850; fax (22) 5251898; e-mail warsaw@embassy.mzv.cz; internet www.mfa.cz/warsaw; Ambassador JAKUB KARFIK.

Denmark: 00-061 Warsaw, ul. Marszałkowska 142; tel. (22) 5652900; fax (22) 5652970; e-mail wawamb@um.dk; internet www .ambwarszawa.um.dk; Ambassador STEEN HOMMEL.

Ecuador: 02-516 Warsaw, ul. Rejtana 15/15; tel. (22) 8487230; fax (22) 8488196; e-mail eccupolonia@mmrree.gov.ec; Ambassador FABIÁN VALDIVIESO EGUIGUREN.

Egypt: 03-972 Warsaw, ul. Alzacka 18; tel. (22) 6176973; fax (22) 6179058; e-mail embassyofegypt@neostrada.pl; Ambassador FAHMY AHMED FAYED SALAMA.

Estonia: 02-639 Warsaw, ul. Karwińska 1; tel. (22) 8811810; fax (22) 8811812; e-mail embassy@estemb.pl; internet www.estemb.pl; Ambassador TAAVI TOOM.

Finland: 00-559 Warsaw, ul. Chopina 4/8; tel. (22) 5989500; fax (22) 6213442; e-mail sanomat.var@formin.fi; internet www.finland.pl; Ambassador JARI VILÉN.

France: 00-477 Warsaw, ul. Piękna 1; tel. (22) 5293000; fax (22) 5293001; e-mail presse@ambafrance-pl.org; internet www .ambafrance-pl.org; Ambassador PIERRE BUHLER.

Georgia: 03-976 Warsaw, ul. Berneńska 6; tel. (22) 6166221; fax (22) 6166226; e-mail warsaw.emb@mfa.gov.ge; internet www.poland .mfa.gov.ge; Ambassador NIKOLOZ NIKOLOZISHVILI.

Germany: 00-467 Warsaw, ul. Jazdów 12; tel. (22) 5841700; fax (22) 5841739; e-mail warszawa@wars.diplo.de; internet www.warschau .diplo.de; Ambassador RÜDIGER FREIHERR VON FRITSCH.

Greece: 00-432 Warsaw, ul. Górnośląska 35; tel. (22) 6229460; fax (22) 6229464; e-mail gremb.war@mfa.gr; internet www.greece.pl; Ambassador TASSIA ATHANASSIOU.

Holy See: 00-582 Warsaw, Al. J. Ch. Szucha 12, POB 163; tel. (22) 6288488; fax (22) 6284556; e-mail nuncjatura@episkopat.pl; Apostolic Nuncio Most Rev. CELESTINO MIGLIORE (Titular Archbishop of Canosa).

Hungary: 00-559 Warsaw, ul. Chopina 2; tel. (22) 6284451; fax (22) 6218561; e-mail mission.vao@mfa.gov.hu; internet www.mfa.gov .hu/kulkepviselet/PL/HU; Ambassador IVAN GYURCSIK.

India: 02-516 Warsaw, ul. Rejtana 15/2–7; tel. (22) 8495800; fax (22) 8496705; e-mail ambassador.office@indianembassy.pl; internet indembwarsaw.in; Ambassador MONIKA MOHTA.

Indonesia: 03-903 Warsaw, ul. Estońska 3–5; tel. (22) 6175108; fax (22) 6174455; e-mail comwar@indonesianembassy.pl; internet www .indonesianembassy.pl; Ambassador DARMANSJAH DJUMALA.

Iran: 03-928 Warsaw, ul. Królowej Aldony 22; tel. (22) 6171585; fax (22) 6178452; e-mail iranemb@iranemb.warsaw.pl; internet iranemb.pl; Ambassador SAMAD ALI LAKIZADEH.

Iraq: 03-932 Warsaw, ul. Dąbrowiecka 9A; tel. (22) 6175773; fax (22) 6177065; e-mail ambasada.irak@neostrada.pl; Ambassador Dr SAAD JAWAD QINDEEL.

Ireland: 00-496 Warsaw, ul. Mysia 5; tel. (22) 8496633; fax (22) 8498431; e-mail warsawembassy@dfa.ie; internet www .embassyofireland.pl; Ambassador EUGENE HUTCHINSON.

Israel: 02-078 Warsaw, ul. Krzywickiego 24; tel. (22) 5970500; fax (22) 8251607; e-mail ambass-sec@warsaw.mfa.gov.il; internet www .israel.pl; Ambassador ZVI RAV-NER.

Italy: 00-055 Warsaw, pl. Dąbrowskiego 6; tel. (22) 8263471; fax (22) 8278507; e-mail ambasciata.varsavia@esteri.it; internet www .ambvarsavia.esteri.it; Ambassador RICCARDO GUARIGLIA.

Japan: 00-464 Warsaw, ul. Szwoleżerów 8; tel. (22) 6965000; fax (22) 6965001; e-mail info-cul@wr.mofa.go.jp; internet www.pl.emb-japan .go.jp; Ambassador MAKOTO YAMANAKA.

Kazakhstan: 02-954 Warsaw, ul. Królowej Marysieńki 14; tel. (22) 6425388; fax (22) 6423427; e-mail kazdipmis@hot.pl; internet www .kazakhstan.pl; Ambassador ERIK UTEMBAYEV.

Korea, Democratic People's Republic: 00-728 Warsaw, ul. Bobrowiecka 1A; tel. (22) 8405813; fax (22) 8405710; e-mail korembpl@yahoo.com; Ambassador KIM PYONG IL.

Korea, Republic: 00-464 Warsaw, ul. Szwoleżerów 6; tel. (22) 5592900; fax (22) 5592905; e-mail koremb_waw@mofat.go.kr; Ambassador YOUNG-SUN PAEK.

Kuwait: 00-486 Warsaw, ul. Franciszka Nullo 13; tel. (22) 6222860; fax (22) 6274314; e-mail embassy@kuwait-embassy.pl; Ambassador ADEL MUHAMMAD A. H. HAYAT.

Latvia: 03-928 Warsaw, ul. Królowej Aldony 19; tel. (22) 6171105; fax (22) 6171106; e-mail embassy@mfa.gov.lv; internet www .latvia.pl; Ambassador EINARS SEMANIS.

Lebanon: 02-516 Warsaw, ul. Starościńska 1B/10–11; tel. (22) 8445065; fax (22) 6460030; e-mail embassy@lebanon.com.pl; internet en.lebanon.pl; Chargé d'affaires a.i. SONIA ABOU AZAR.

Lithuania: 00-478 Warsaw, Al. Ujazdowskie 14; tel. (22) 6253368; fax (22) 6253440; e-mail amb.pl@urm.lt; internet pl.mfa.lt; Ambassador LORETTA ZAKAREVIČIENĖ.

Luxembourg: 00-789 Warsaw, ul. Słoneczna 15; tel. (22) 5078650; fax (22) 5078661; e-mail varsovie.amb@mae.etat.lu; Ambassador CONRAD BRUCH.

Macedonia, former Yugoslav republic: 02-954 Warsaw, ul. Królowej Marysieńki 40; tel. (22) 6517291; fax (22) 6517292; e-mail ambrmwar@zigzag.pl; Ambassador FATMIR XHELADINI.

Malaysia: 03-902 Warsaw, ul. Gruzińska 3; tel. (22) 6174413; fax (22) 6176256; e-mail mwwarsaw@poczta.neostrada.pl; Ambassador JAMALUDDIN BIN SABEH.

Malta: 02-520 Warsaw, ul. Wiśniowa 40/4; tel. (22) 6464639; fax (22) 6464685; e-mail maltaembassy.warsaw@gov.mt; Ambassador VINCENZO ANTONIO MANNO.

Mexico: 02-017 Warsaw, Al. Jerozolimskie 123, 20th Floor; tel. (22) 3112900; fax (22) 3112901; e-mail info@emexico.pl; internet www.sre .gob.mx/polonia; Ambassador RICARDO VILLANUEVA HALLAL.

Moldova: 02-710 Warsaw, ul. Imielińska 1; tel. and fax (22) 6462099; e-mail varsovia@mfa.md; internet www.polonia.mfa.md; Ambassador LURIE BODRUG.

Mongolia: 02-516 Warsaw, ul. Rejtana 15/16; tel. (22) 8499391; fax (22) 8482063; e-mail mongemb@ambasadamongolii.pl; internet www.ambasadamongolii.pl; Ambassador AMGALANBAATARYN GANBAATAR.

Montenegro: Warsaw, Al. Ujazdowskie 41; tel. 531208600; e-mail dragica.ponorac@mfa.gov.me; Ambassador RAMIZ BAŠIĆ.

Morocco: 02-516 Warsaw, ul. Starościńska 1/11–12; tel. (22) 8496341; fax (22) 8481840; e-mail info@moroccoembassy.org.pl; Ambassador MOHA OUALI TAGMA.

Netherlands: 00-468 Warsaw, ul. Kawalerii 10; tel. (22) 5591200; fax (22) 8402638; e-mail war@minbuza.nl; internet www.nlembassy .pl; Ambassador MARCEL KURPERSHOEK.

New Zealand: 00-536 Warsaw, Al. Ujazdowskie 51; tel. (22) 5210500; fax (22) 5210510; e-mail nzwsw@nzembassy.pl; internet www.nzembassy.com/poland; Chargé d'affaires a.i. WENDY HINTON.

Nigeria: 02-953 Warsaw, ul. Kosiarzy 22B; tel. (22) 6515305; fax (22) 6515378; e-mail nigeria.warsaw@mfa.gov.ng; internet www .embassyofnigeria.pl; Ambassador SAMUEL WODI JIMBA.

Norway: 00-559 Warsaw, ul. Chopina 2A; tel. (22) 6964030; fax (22) 6280938; e-mail emb.warsaw@mfa.no; internet www.amb-norwegia .pl; Ambassador KARSTEN KLEPSVIK.

Pakistan: 02-516 Warsaw, ul. Starościńska 1/1–2; tel. (22) 8494808; fax (22) 8491160; e-mail parepwarsaw@gmail.com; Ambassador MURAD ALI.

Panama: 02-946 Warsaw, ul. Biedronki 13A; tel. (22) 6422143; fax (22) 6517616; e-mail panamaembassy@neostrada.pl; Ambassador LUIS ALBERTO MADRID CABALLERO.

Peru: 02-516 Warsaw, ul. Starościńska 1/3; tel. (22) 6468806; fax (22) 6468617; e-mail embperpl@perupol.pl; internet www.perupol.pl; Ambassador MARTHA CHAVARRI DUPUY.

Philippines: 00-956 Warsaw, ul. Lentz 11; tel. (22) 4902025; fax (60) 2541012; e-mail pe.warsaw@gmail.com; Ambassador PATRICIA ANN PAEZ.

Portugal: 03-905 Warsaw, ul. Francuska 37; tel. (22) 5111010; fax (22) 5111013; e-mail embaixada@embport.internetdsl.pl; Ambassador JOSÉ DUARTE SEQUEIRA E SERPA.

Qatar: 00-493 Warsaw, ul. Prusa 2/271; tel. (22) 6222288; fax (22) 6225566; e-mail qtrembassypl@yahoo.com; Ambassador HADI NASER MANSOUR AL-HAJRI.

Romania: 00-559 Warsaw, ul. Chopina 10; tel. (22) 6215983; fax (22) 6285264; e-mail office@roembassypl.org; internet varsovia.mae.ro; Chargé d'affaires a.i. IOANA GABRIELA COSTACHE.

Russia: 00-761 Warsaw, ul. Belwederska 49; tel. (22) 6213453; fax (22) 6253016; e-mail embassy@rusemb.pl; internet www.rusemb.pl; Ambassador ALEKSANDR ALEKSEYEV.

Saudi Arabia: 00-739 Warsaw, ul. Stępińska 55; tel. (22) 8400000; fax (22) 8405636; e-mail info@saudiembassy.pl; internet www .saudiembassy.pl; Ambassador WALEED TAHER RADWAN.

Serbia: 00-556 Warsaw, Al. Róż 5; tel. (22) 6285161; fax (22) 6297173; e-mail embassy.warsaw@mfa.rs; internet warsaw.mfa.rs; Ambassador RADOJKO BOGOJEVIĆ.

Slovakia: 00-581 Warsaw, ul. Litewska 6; tel. (22) 5258110; fax (22) 5258122; e-mail emb.warsaw@mzv.sk; internet www.mzv.sk/ varsava; Ambassador VASIL GRIVNA.

Slovenia: 02-516 Warsaw, ul. Starościńska 1/23–24; tel. (22) 8498282; fax (22) 8484090; e-mail vvr@gov.si; Ambassador MARJAN ŠETINC.

South Africa: 00-675 Warsaw, ul. Koszykowa 54, 6th Floor; tel. (22) 6256228; fax (22) 6256270; e-mail warsaw.political@foreign.gov.za; internet www.southafrica.pl; Ambassador L. S. TED PEKANE.

Spain: 00-459 Warsaw, ul. Myśliwiecka 4; tel. (22) 5834000; fax (22) 6225408; e-mail embesppl@mail.mae.es; Ambassador AGUSTÍN NÚÑEZ MARTÍNEZ.

Sri Lanka: 02-737 Warsaw, Niedźwiedzia 2C; tel. (22) 8538896; fax (22) 8538897; e-mail mission@srilankaembassy.com.pl; internet www.srilankaembassy.com.pl; Ambassador PAMELA J. DEEN.

Sweden: 00-585 Warsaw, ul. Bagatela 3; tel. (22) 6408900; fax (22) 6408983; e-mail ambassaden.warszawa@gov.se; internet www .swedenabroad.com/warsaw; Ambassador STAFFAN HERRSTRÖM.

Switzerland: 00-540 Warsaw, Al. Ujazdowskie 27; tel. (22) 6280481; fax (22) 6210548; e-mail var.vertretung@eda.admin.ch; internet www.eda.admin.ch/warsaw; Ambassador LUKAS BEGLINGER.

Syria: 02-610 Warsaw, ul. Goszczyńskiego 30; tel. (22) 8484809; fax (22) 8489178; e-mail embsyria@palmyra.neostrada.pl; internet www .syrian-embassy.com; Chargé d'affaires a.i. Dr WISSAL ISSA.

Thailand: 00-790 Warsaw, ul. Willowa 7; tel. (22) 8496414; fax (22) 8492630; e-mail thaiemb@thaiemb.internetdsl.pl; internet www .thaiembassy.pl; Ambassador BANSARN BUNNAG.

Tunisia: 00-459 Warsaw, ul. Myśliwiecka 14; tel. (22) 6286330; fax (22) 6216295; e-mail at.varsovie@ambtun.pl; Ambassador SLIM BEN JAÂFAR.

Turkey: 02-622 Warsaw, ul. Malczewskiego 32; tel. (22) 8546111; fax (22) 6464325; e-mail embassy.warsaw@mfa.gov.tr; internet warsaw .emb.mfa.gov.tr; Ambassador YUSUF ZIYA ÖZCAN.

Ukraine: 00-580 Warsaw, Al. J. Ch. Szucha 7; tel. (22) 6293446; fax (22) 6298103; e-mail emb.pl@mfa.gov.ua; internet poland.mfa.gov .ua; Ambassador MARKIYAN Z. MALSKY.

United Kingdom: 00-468 Warsaw, ul. Kawalerii 12; tel. (22) 3110000; fax (22) 3110313; e-mail info@britishembassy.pl; internet ukinpoland.fco.gov.uk; Ambassador ROBIN BARNETT.

USA: 00-540 Warsaw, Al. Ujazdowskie 29/31; tel. (22) 5042000; fax (22) 5042688; e-mail publicwrw@state.gov; internet poland .usembassy.gov; Ambassador STEPHEN MULL.

Uruguay: 02-516 Warsaw, ul. Rejtana 15/12; tel. (22) 8495040; fax (22) 6466887; e-mail urupol@urupol.ikp.pl; Ambassador CARLOS BRUGNINI GARCÍA LAGOS.

Uzbekistan: 02-804 Warsaw, ul. Kraski 21; tel. (22) 8946230; fax (22) 8946231; e-mail uzembassy@gmail.com; internet www .uzbekistan.pl; Chargé d'affaires a.i. IKROM NAZAROV.

Venezuela: 02-516 Warsaw, ul. Rejtana 15/20–21; tel. (22) 6468760; fax (22) 6468761; e-mail embajada@embavenez.pl; Chargé d'affaires a.i. JESÚS MIGUEL CRUZ GUEVARA.

Viet Nam: 02-956 Warsaw, ul. Resorowa 36; tel. (22) 6516098; fax (22) 6516095; e-mail vnemb.pl@mofa.gov.vn; internet www .vietnamembassy-poland.org; Ambassador NGUYEN VAN XUONG.

Yemen: 02-956 Warsaw, ul. Królewicza Jakuba 54; tel. (22) 6176025; fax (22) 6176022; e-mail office@embassy-of-yemen.pl; internet www .embassy-of-yemen.pl; Ambassador ALI ALI ABD AL-AZIZ AQLAN.

Judicial System

Supreme Court (Sąd Najwyższy Rzeczpospolitej Polskiej): 00-951 Warsaw, pl. Krasińskich 2/4/6; tel. (22) 5308000; fax (22) 5309100; e-mail ppsek@sn.pl; internet www.sn.pl; the highest judicial organ; exercises supervision over the decision-making of all other courts; justices are appointed by the President of the Republic on motions of the National Council of Judiciary and serve until the age of retirement. The First President of the Supreme Court is appointed from among the Supreme Court Justices by the President of the Republic, and serves a six-year term. The First President is also the Chairman of the Tribunal of State (Trybunał Stanu), before which certain, constitutionally determined, high state positions are accountable for violations of the Constitution or statutes; First Pres. STANISŁAW DĄBROWSKI.

Supreme Administrative Court (Naczelny Sąd Administracyjny): 00-011 Warsaw, ul. Gabriela Piotra Boduena 3/5; tel. (22) 5516000; fax (22) 8267506; e-mail informacje@nsa.gov.pl; internet www.nsa.gov.pl; f. 1980; examines complaints concerning the legality of administrative decisions; 11 regional brs; Pres. ROMAN HAUSER.

Constitutional Tribunal (Trybunał Konstytucyjny): 00-918 Warsaw, Al. J. Ch. Szucha 12A; tel. (22) 6574586; fax (22) 6574503; e-mail prasainfo@trybunal.gov.pl; internet www.trybunal.gov.pl; comprises 15 judges, each appointed by the Sejm for a nine-year term; supervises compliance of legislation with the Constitution; Pres. ANDRZEJ RZEPLIŃSKI.

Religion

CHRISTIANITY

The Roman Catholic Church

The Roman Catholic Church was granted full legal status in May 1989, when legislation guaranteeing freedom of worship was approved. The Church was also permitted to administer its own affairs, and to operate schools, hospitals and other charitable organizations. A Concordat, agreed by the Polish Government and the Holy See in 1993, was ratified in January 1998.

For ecclesiastical purposes, Poland comprises 15 archdioceses (including one for the Catholics of the Byzantine-Ukrainian rite) and 28 dioceses (including one for the Catholics of the Byzantine-Ukrainian rite), an Ordinariate for the faithful of the Oriental rite, and a Military Ordinariate. There were some 34.3m. adherents in Poland (96.1% of the population) at 31 December 2008.

Bishops' Conference: 01-015 Warsaw, Skwer Kardynała Stefana Wyszyńskiego 6; tel. (22) 5304800; fax (22) 8380967; Pres. Most Rev. JÓZEF MICHALIK (Latin Rite Archbishop of Przemyśl).

Latin Rite

Archbishop of Białystok: Most Rev. EDWARD OZOROWSKI, 15-087 Białystok, Pl. Jana Pawła II 1; tel. (85) 7416473; fax (85) 7322213; e-mail sekretariat@bialystok.opoka.org.pl.

Archbishop of Częstochowa: Most Rev. STANISŁAW NOWAK, 42-200 Częstochowa, Al. Najśw. Maryi Panny 54; tel. (34) 3241044; fax (34) 3651182; e-mail kuria@czestochowa.opoka.org.pl.

Archbishop of Gdańsk: Most Rev. SŁAWOJ LESZEK GŁÓDŹ, 80-330 Gdańsk-Oliwa, ul. Biskupa Edmunda Nowickiego 1; tel. (58) 5520051; fax (58) 5522775; e-mail kuria@diecezja.gda.pl.

Archbishop of Gniezno, Primate of Poland: Most Rev. JÓZEF KOWALCZYK, 62-200 Gniezno, ul. Kanclerza Jana Łaskiego 7; tel. (61) 4262102; fax (61) 4262105; e-mail kuriagni@gniezno.opoka.org.pl.

Archbishop of Katowice: Most Rev. WIKTOR SKWORC, 40-043 Katowice, ul. Jordana 39; tel. (32) 2512160; fax (32) 2514830; e-mail kancelaria@kuria.katowice.pl.

Archbishop of Kraków: Cardinal STANISŁAW DZIWISZ, 31-004 Kraków, ul. Franciszkańska 3; tel. (12) 6288100; fax (12) 4294617; e-mail kuria@diecezja.krakow.pl.

Archbishop of Łódź: Most Rev. WŁADYSŁAW ZIÓŁEK, 90-458 Łódź, ul. Ks Ignacego Skorupki 1; tel. (42) 6648700; fax (42) 6648796; e-mail kuria@archidiecezja.lodz.pl.

Archbishop of Lublin: Most Rev. STANISŁAW BUDZIK, 20-950 Lublin, ul. Ks Prymasa Stefana Wyszyńskiego 2; tel. (81) 5321058; fax (81) 5346141; e-mail kanclerz@kuria.lublin.pl; internet www .diecezja.lublin.pl.

Archbishop of Poznań: Most Rev. STANISŁAW GĄDECKI, 61-109 Poznań, ul. Ostrów Tumski 2; tel. (61) 8512800; fax (61) 8512814; e-mail kuria@archpoznan.org.pl.

Archbishop of Przemyśl (Latin Rite): Most Rev. JÓZEF MICHALIK, 37-700 Przemyśl, pl. Katedralny 4A; tel. (16) 6786694; fax (16) 6782674; e-mail kuria@przemysl.opoka.org.pl.

Archbishop of Szczecin-Kamień: Most Rev. ANDRZEJ DZIĘGA, 71-459 Szczecin, ul. Papieża Pawła VI 4; tel. (91) 4542292; fax (91) 4536908; e-mail kuria@szczecin.opoka.org.pl.

Archbishop of Warmia: Most Rev. WOJCIECH ZIEMBA, 10-006 Olsztyn, ul. Pieniężnego 22; tel. (89) 5272280; fax (89) 5355172; e-mail kuria@olsztyn.opoka.org.pl.

Archbishop of Warsaw: Cardinal KAZIMIERZ NYCZ, 00-246 Warsaw, ul. Miodowa 17/19; tel. (22) 5317200; fax (22) 6354324; e-mail kanclerz@mkw.pl; internet www.spp.episkopat.pl.

Archbishop of Wrocław: Most Rev. MARIAN GOŁĘBIEWSKI, 50-328 Wrocław, ul. Katedralna 13; tel. (71) 3271111; fax (71) 3228269; e-mail kuria@archidiecezja.wroc.pl.

Byzantine-Ukrainian Rite

Archbishop of Przemyśl-Warsaw: Most Rev. IVAN MARTYNIAK, 37-700 Przemyśl, ul. Basztowa 13; tel. and fax (16) 6787868; e-mail kuria@przemyslgr.opoka.pl.

The Orthodox Church

Polish Autocephalous Orthodox Church (Polski Autokefaliczny Kościół Prawosławny): 03-402 Warsaw, Al. Solidarności 52; tel. (22) 6190886; fax (22) 6192996; e-mail kancelaria@orthodox.pl; internet www.orthodox.pl; comprises six dioceses, six archbishoprics and three bishoprics; 515,000 mems (2001); Archbishop of Warsaw and Metropolitan of All Poland Sawa MICHAŁ HRYCUNIAK.

Protestant Churches

In 1999 there were an estimated 148,738 Protestants in Poland.

Evangelical Augsburg (Lutheran) Church in Poland (Kościół Ewangelicko-Augsburski czyli Luterański w Polsce): 00-246 Warsaw, ul. Miodowa 21; tel. (22) 8870200; fax (22) 8870218; e-mail biskup@luteranie.pl; internet www.luteranie.pl; 75,000 mems, 134 parishes (2007); Bishop and Pres. of Consistory JERZY SAMIEC.

Pentecostal Church in Poland (Kościół Zielonoświątkowy w Polsce): 00-825 Warsaw, ul. Sienna 68/70; tel. and fax (22) 5951820; e-mail sekretariat@kz.pl; internet www.kz.pl; f. 1910; 20,000 mems (2000); Chief Presbyter Bishop MIECZYSŁAW CZAJKO.

There are also several other small Protestant churches, including the Church of Christ, the Church of Evangelical Christians, the Evangelical Christian Church, the Jehovah's Witnesses, the Pentecostal Church, the Seventh-day Adventist Church and the United Methodist Church.

ISLAM

In 1999 there were about 5,125 Muslims, principally of Tatar origin, in Białystok Voivodship (Prefecture), in eastern Poland, and smaller communities in Warsaw, Gdańsk and elsewhere.

Religious Union of Muslims in Poland (Muzułmański Związek Religijny): 15-426 Białystok, Rynek Kosciuszki 26/2; tel. (85) 414970; Chair. STEFAN MUCHARSKI.

JUDAISM

The overwhelming majority of the Jewish population of Poland were killed during the occupation by Nazi Germany in the Second World War (1939–45). In the mid-2000s there were believed to be between 10,000 and 20,000 Jews in Poland.

Union of Jewish Communities in Poland (Związek Gmin Wyznaniowych Żydowskich w Rzeczypospolitej Polskiej): 00-950 Warsaw, ul. Twarda 6; tel. (22) 6204324; fax (22) 6201037; e-mail union@ jewish.org.pl; 14 synagogues and about 2,500 registered mems; Pres. PIOTR KADLČIK.

The Press

In 2010 there were 46 newspapers in Poland, with an average circulation of 3.9m. In that year there were 7,419 periodicals, with an average circulation of 85.0m. copies.

Axel Springer Polska Sp. z o.o.: 02-672 Warsaw, ul. Domaniewska 52; tel. (22) 2320000; fax (22) 2325534; e-mail asp@axelspringer.pl; internet axelspringer.pl; subsidiary of Axel Springer AG (Germany); publishes two major dailies, *Dziennik* and *Fakt*, and is the country's second largest magazine publisher, printing women's, fiction, computer, food, economics, news and motoring magazines; CEO ANDREAS TILK.

WARSAW DAILIES

Dziennik (Daily): 02-672 Warsaw, ul. Domaniewska 52; tel. (22) 2320519; fax (22) 2325550; e-mail dziennik@dziennik.pl; internet www.dziennik.pl; f. 2006; Mon.–Sat; publ. by Axel Springer Polska; Editor-in-Chief ROBERT KRASOWSKI; circ. 77,750 (Nov. 2008).

Fakt (Fact): 02-672 Warsaw, ul. Domaniewska 52; tel. (22) 6085554; fax (22) 6085508; e-mail redakcja@efakt.pl; internet www.efakt.pl; f. 2003; owned by Axel Springer Polska; Editor KATARZYNA SIELICKA; circ. 410,756 (Nov. 2010).

Gazeta Wyborcza: 00-732 Warsaw, ul. Czerska 8/10; tel. (22) 5556000; fax (22) 5557990; e-mail redakcja_portalu@agora.pl; internet www.wyborcza.pl; f. 1989; non-party; national edn and 20 local edns; weekend edn: *Gazeta Swiateczna*; special supplements; Editor-in-Chief ANDRZEJ OLEJNICZAK; circ. 411,192 (2008).

Nasz Dziennik (Our Daily): 04-476 Warsaw, ul. Żeligowskiego 16/20; tel. (22) 5157777; fax (22) 5157778; e-mail redakcja@naszdziennik.pl; internet www.naszdziennik.pl; national; Editor-in-Chief EWA NOWINA KONOPKA; circ. 250,000.

Polska Zbrojna (Military Poland): 00-909 Warsaw, Al. Jerozolimskie 97; tel. (22) 6845365; fax (22) 6845503; e-mail sekretariat@zbrojni.pl; internet www.polska-zbrojna.pl; f. 1943; Editor KATARZYNA PIETRASZEK; circ. 50,000.

Przegląd Sportowy (Sports Review): 02-672 Warsaw, Al. Domaniewska 52; tel. (22) 2320503; fax (22) 2325523; e-mail redakcja@przeglad.com.pl; internet www.sports.pl; f. 1921; Editor MARCIN KALITA; circ. 64,332 (2008).

Rzeczpospolita (The Republic): 00-838 Warsaw, ul. Prosta 51; tel. (22) 6283401; fax (22) 6280588; e-mail p.aleksandrowicz@rzeczpospolita.pl; internet www.rp.pl; f. 1982; 51% owned by Orkla (Norway); Editor-in-Chief PAWEŁ LISICKI; circ. 157,136 (2008).

Super Express: 00-939 Warsaw, ul. Jubilerska 10; tel. (22) 5159100; fax (22) 5159010; e-mail internet@se.com.pl; internet www.se.pl; f. 1991; popular; Editor-in-Chief SŁAWOMIR JASTRZĘBOWSKI; circ. 183,976 (Nov. 2010).

Życie Warszawy (Warsaw Life): 00-838 Warsaw, Prosta 51; tel. (22) 6530433; fax (22) 4630011; e-mail sekretariat@zw.com.pl; internet www.zw.com.pl; f. 1944; independent; Editor-in-Chief TOMASZ SOBIECKI; circ. 3,753 (2009).

REGIONAL DAILIES

Dziennik Bałtycki (Baltic Newspaper): 80-894 Gdańsk, Targ Drzewny 9/11; tel. (58) 3003300; fax (58) 3003303; e-mail internet@prasa.gda.pl; internet www.dziennikbaltycki.pl; f. 1945; non-party; Editor-in-Chief GRZEGORZ POPŁAWSKI; circ. 41,330 (Nov. 2010).

Dziennik Łódzki (Łódź Daily): 90-532 Łódź, ul. Ks. Skorupki 17/19; tel. (42) 6659100; fax (42) 6659101; e-mail dziennik@dziennik.lodz.pl; internet www.dziennik.lodz.pl; f. 1945; non-party; Editor ROBERT SAKOWSKI; circ. 38,376 (Nov. 2010).

Dziennik Polski (Polish Daily): 31-072 Kraków, ul. Wielopole 1; tel. (12) 6199200; fax (12) 6199275; e-mail redakcja@dziennik.krakow.pl; internet www.dziennik.krakow.pl; f. 1945; Mon.–Sat; Editor PIOTR LEGUTKO; circ. 39,145 (Nov. 2010).

Dziennik Wschodni (Eastern Daily): 20-081 Lublin, ul. Staszica 20; tel. (81) 4626800; fax (81) 4626801; e-mail redakcja@dziennikwschodni.pl; internet www.dziennikwschodni.pl; Chief Editor KRZYSZTOF WIEJAK; circ. 13,084 (Nov. 2010).

Dziennik Zachodni (Western Daily): 41-203 Sosnowiec, ul. Baczyńskiego 25A; tel. (32) 6342200; fax (32) 1538196; e-mail redakcja@dz.com.pl; internet www.dz.com.pl; f. 1945; absorbed Trybuna Śląska in 2004; non-party; Editor-in-Chief MAREK TWARÓG; circ. 69,600 (Nov. 2010).

Echo Dnia (Echo of the Day): 25-520 Kielce, ul. Targowa 18; tel. (41) 3495353; fax (41) 3682218; e-mail redakcja@echodnia.eu; internet www.echodnia.eu; f. 1971; Chief Editor STANISŁAW WRÓBEL; circ. 37,573 (Nov. 2010).

Gazeta Krakowska (Kraków Gazette): 31-548 Kraków, Al. Pokoju 3; tel. (12) 6888000; fax (12) 6888109; e-mail sekretariat@gk.pl; internet www.gk.pl; f. 1949; Editor-in-Chief TOMASZ LACHOWICZ; circ. 26,652 (Nov. 2010).

Gazeta Lubuska: 65-042 Zielona Góra, Al. Niepodległości 25, POB 120; tel. (68) 3248800; fax (68) 3248875; e-mail ar@gazetalubuska.pl; internet www.gazetalubuska.pl; f. 1952; independent; Chief Editor IWONA ZIELIŃSKA; circ. 40,193 (Nov. 2010).

Gazeta Olsztyńska (Olsztyn Gazette): 10-364 Olsztyn, ul. Tracka 5; tel. (89) 5397700; e-mail internet@gazetaolsztynska.pl; internet gazetaolsztynska.wm.pl; f. 1886; Editor-in-Chief EWA BARTNIKOWSKA; circ. 24,293 (Nov. 2010).

Gazeta Pomorska: 85-063 Bydgoszcz, ul. Zamoyskiego 2; tel. (52) 3263100; fax (52) 3221542; e-mail gp.redakcja@pomorska.pl;

internet www.pomorska.pl; f. 1948; independent; Editor-in-Chief WOJCIECH POTOCKI; circ. 66,512 (Nov. 2010).

Gazeta Wrocławska (Wrocław Gazette): 53-611 Wrocław, ul. Strzegomska 42A; tel. (71) 3748151; fax (71) 3748175; e-mail redakcja@gazeta.wroc.pl; internet www.gazetawroclawska.pl; Editor-in-Chief ARKADIUSZ FRANAS; circ. 26,945 (Nov. 2010).

Gazeta Współczesna: 15-419 Białystok, POB 193, ul. Św. Mikołaja 1; tel. (85) 7487400; fax (85) 7487401; e-mail gazeta@wspolczesna.pl; internet www.wspolczesna.pl; f. 1951; Editor KONRAD KRUSZEWSKI; circ. 14,033 (Nov. 2010).

Głos Pomorza (Voice of Pomerania): 76-200 Słupsk, ul. Pobożnego 19; tel. (59) 8488100; fax (59) 8488104; e-mail akcja@gp24.pl; internet www.gp24.pl; f. 1952; Chief Editor KRZYSZTOF NAŁĘCZ; circ. 43,952 (Nov. 2010).

Głos Szczeciński (Szczecin Voice): 71-875 Szczecin, ul. Nowy Rynek 3; tel. (91) 4813300; fax (91) 4334864; e-mail akcja@gs24.pl; internet www.gs24.pl; f. 1947; Chief Editor KRZYSZTOF NAŁĘCZ; circ. 30,000 (weekdays), 100,000 (weekends).

Głos Wielkopolski (Voice of Wielkopolska): 60-782 Poznań, ul. Grunwaldzka 19; tel. (61) 8694100; fax (61) 8606115; e-mail redakcja@glos.com; internet www.glos.com; f. 1945; independent; Editor-in-Chief ADAM PAWŁOWSKI; circ. 45,534 (Nov. 2010).

Kurier Lubelski (Lublin Courier): 20-002 Lublin, Krakowskie Przedmieście 10/1; tel. (81) 4462800; fax (81) 4462830; e-mail redakcja@kurierlubelski.pl; internet www.kurierlubelski.pl; f. 1830; independent; evening; Editor-in-Chief DARIUSZ KOTLARZ; circ. 7,322 (Nov. 2010).

Kurier Szczeciński (Szczecin Courier): 70-550 Szczecin, pl. Hołdu Pruskiego 8; tel. (91) 4429101; fax (91) 4429105; e-mail t.kowalczyk@kurier.szczecin.pl; internet www.24kurier.pl; Editor-in-Chief TOMASZ KOWALCZYK; circ. 20,054 (Nov. 2010).

NoWiny 24 (News): 35-016 Rzeszów, ul. Kraszewskiego 2; tel. (17) 8672210; fax (17) 8672201; e-mail online@nowiny24.pl; internet www.nowiny24.pl; f. 1949; evening; Editor-in-Chief STANISŁAW SOWA; circ. 100,000.

Nowa Trybuna Opolska (New Opole Tribune): 45-086 Opole, ul. Powstańców Śląskich 9; tel. (77) 4432500; fax (77) 4432515; e-mail nto@nto.pl; internet www.nto.pl; f. 1952; independent; Editor KRZYSZTOF ZYZIK; circ. 27,112 (Nov. 2010).

PERIODICALS

Computerworld Polska: 04-204 Warsaw, ul. Jordanowska 12, POB 73; tel. (22) 3217800; fax (22) 3217888; e-mail cw@idg.com.pl; internet www.computerworld.pl; weekly; Editor-in-Chief ANDRZEJ GONTARZ; circ. 3,695 (2009).

Dobre Rady (Good Advice): 00-034 Wrocław, ul. Warecka 11A; tel. (71) 3517758; fax (71) 3737288; e-mail dobrerady@burdamedia.pl; internet www.dobrerady.pl; f. 2002; publ. by Burda Polska; Editor-in-Chief ANNA MANDES-TARASSOV; circ. 508,844 (2009).

Dom i Wnętrze (Home and Interior): 00-480 Warsaw, ul. Wiejska 19; tel. (22) 5842200; fax (22) 5842591; e-mail info@domiwnetrze.pl; internet www.domiwnetrze.pl; f. 1991; illustrated monthly; Editor-in-Chief EWA MIERZEJEWSKA; circ. 20,945 (2009).

Dziecko (Child): 00-732 Warsaw, ul. Czerska 8/10; tel. (22) 5556882; e-mail dziecko@agora.pl; internet www.edziecko.pl; f. 1995; monthly; women's magazine concerning children's affairs; Editor JOANNA SZULC; circ. 65,984 (Mar. 2010).

Dziewczyna (Girl): 02-672 Warsaw, ul. Domaniewska 52, Axel Springer Polska; tel. (22) 2320750; e-mail redakcja@dziewczyna.pl; internet www.dziewczyna.pl; f. 2000; monthly; lifestyle magazine for young women; Publr DONATA CIESLIK; Editor-in-Chief ANDRZEJ GUMULAK; circ. 94,211 (2009).

Les Echos de Pologne: 02-530 Warsaw, ul. Kielecka 42/14; tel. (22) 4030870; fax (22) 4030872; e-mail echos@echos.pl; internet www.echos.pl; f. 2003; fortnightly; in French; Editor-in-Chief KRYSTYNA KOCERBA.

Gazeta Bankowa (Banking Gazette): 00-140 Warsaw, Al. Solidarności 117; tel. (22) 6525914; fax (22) 6525910; e-mail redakcja@wtrendy.pl; internet www.gb.pl; f. 1988; weekly; business and finance; Editor-in-Chief ANDRZEJ S. NARTOWSKI.

Głos Nauczycielski (Teachers' Voice): 00-389 Warsaw, ul. J. Smulikowskiego 6/8; tel. (22) 3189260; fax (22) 8281355; e-mail glos@glos.pl; internet www.glos.pl; f. 1917; weekly; organ of the Polish Teachers' Union; Chief Editor JAKUB RZEKANOWKSI; circ. 40,000.

Lubie Gotować (I Love Cooking): 00-732 Warsaw, ul. Czerska 8/10; tel. (22) 5556606; fax (22) 5556668; e-mail lubiegotowac@agora.pl; internet www.lubiegotowac.pl; f. 1997; monthly; cookery; Editor-in-Chief JOANNA NOWICKA; circ. 31,314 (2009).

Nie (No): 00-789 Warsaw, ul. Słoneczna 25; tel. (22) 8488448; fax (22) 8497258; e-mail nie@redakija.nie.com.pl; internet www.nie.com.pl; f. 1990; satirical; weekly; Editor JERZY URBAN; circ. 500,000.

Nowa Fantastyka (New Fantasy): 02-651 Warsaw, ul. Garażowa 7; tel. (22) 6077790; fax (22) 8482266; e-mail nowafantastyka@ fantastyka.pl; internet www.fantastyka.pl; f. 1982; monthly; science fiction and fantasy; Editor-in-Chief JAKUB WINIARSKI; circ. 9,889 (2009).

Nowe Życie Gospodarcze (New Economic Life): 00-549 Warsaw, ul. Piękna 24/26; tel. (22) 6280628; fax (22) 6288392; e-mail nzg@nzg .pl; e-mail sekretariat@nzg.pl; internet www.nzg.pl; f. 1945 as *Życie Gospodarcze* (Economic Life); weekly; economic; Chair. and Editor-in-Chief JERZY DZIĘCIOŁOWSKI; circ. 35,700.

Państwo i Prawo (State and Law): 00-330 Warsaw, ul. Nowy Świat 72; tel. (22) 6288296; e-mail panstwoiprawo@wolterskluwer.pl; internet www.panstwoiprawo.pl; f. 1946; monthly organ of the Polish Academy of Sciences; publ. by Wolters Kluwer Polska; Chief Editor Dr LESZEK KUBICKI; circ. 3,000.

Polityka (Politics): 02-309 Warsaw, ul. Słupecka 6, POB 13; tel. (22) 4516133; fax (22) 4516135; e-mail polityka@polityka.com.pl; internet www.polityka.pl; f. 1957; weekly; political, economic, cultural; Editor JERZY BACZYŃSKI; circ. 144,894 (2009).

Poradnik Gospodarski (Farmers' Guide): 60-163 Poznań, ul. Sieradzka 29; tel. and fax (61) 8685492; e-mail poradnik .gospodarski@wodr.poznan.pl; internet www.poradnik.wodr.poznan .pl; f. 1889; monthly; agriculture; Editor-in-Chief TADEUSZ SZALCZYK; circ. 10,000.

Przekrój (Review): 00-695 Warsaw, ul. Nowogrodzka 47A; tel. (22) 2842533; fax (22) 5259988; e-mail redakcja@przekroj.pl; internet www.przekroj.pl; f. 1945; weekly; illustrated; cultural; Chief Editor KATARZYNA JANOWSKA; circ. 52,657 (2009).

Przyjaciółka (Girlfriend): 00-480 Warsaw, ul. Wiejska 19; tel. (22) 5842438; fax (22) 5842436; e-mail info@przyjaciolka.pl; internet www.przyjaciolka.pl; f. 1948; weekly; women's magazine; Editor-in-Chief URSZULA ZUBCZYŃSKA; circ. 476,571 (2009).

Res Publica Nowa (The New Republic): 00-362 Warsaw 1, ul. Gałczyńskiego 5; tel. (22) 8260566; fax (22) 3430833; e-mail redakcja@res.publica.pl; internet www.publica.pl; f. 1987; monthly; political and cultural; Editor WOJCIECH PRZYBYLSKI; circ. 5,000.

Sprawy Międzynarodowe (International Affairs): Polish Institute of International Affairs, 00-950, Warsaw, ul. Warecka 1A, POB 1010; tel. (22) 5568000; fax (22) 5568099; e-mail sprawy@ pism.pl; internet www.pism.pl/publikacje/czasopisma/Sprawy_ Miedzynarodowe; f. 1948; quarterly; publ. by Polish Institute of International Affairs; Editor-in-Chief HENRYK SZLAJFER; circ. 1,000.

Świat Nauki (World of Science): 02-651 Warsaw, ul. Garażowa 7; tel. (22) 6077811; fax (22) 8482266; e-mail swiatnauki@ proszynskimedia.pl; internet www.swiatnauki.pl; f. 1991; monthly; Polish edn of *Scientific American*; Editor-in-Chief ELŻBIETA WIE-TESKA; circ. 18,746 (2009).

Szpilki (Needles): Warsaw; tel. (22) 6280429; f. 1935; weekly; illustrated; satirical; Editor JACEK JANCZARSKI; circ. 100,000.

Tygodnik Solidarność (Solidarity Weekly): 02-390 Warsaw, ul. Grójecka 186, POB 613; tel. and fax (22) 8822796; e-mail redakcja@ tygodniksolidarnosc.com; internet www.tygodniksolidarnosc.com; f. 1981; reactivated 1989; weekly; Editor-in-Chief JERZY KŁOSIŃSKI; circ. 60,000.

The Warsaw Voice: 01-452 Warsaw, ul. Księcia Janusza 64; tel. (22) 3359700; fax (22) 3359710; e-mail voice@warsawvoice.pl; internet www.warsawvoice.pl; f. 1988; weekly; political, social, cultural and economic; in English; Editor ANDRZEJ JONAS; circ. 10,500.

Wiedza i Życie (Knowledge and Life): 02-651 Warsaw, ul. Garażowa 7; tel. (22) 6077753; fax (22) 8482266; e-mail wiedzaizycie@ proszynskimedia.pl; internet www.wiz.pl; f. 1926; monthly; popular science; Editor ELŻBIETA WIETESKA; circ. 35,677 (2009).

Wprost (To The Point): 02-672 Warsaw, ul. Domaniewska 39A, Horizon Plaza; tel. (22) 5291100; fax (22) 4299101; e-mail redakcja@wprost.pl; internet www.wprost.pl; f. 1982; weekly; news and comment; Publr TOMASZ PLATA; Editor-in-Chief TOMASZ LIS; circ. 98,549 (2009).

NEWS AGENCY

Polska Agencja Prasowa (PAP) (Polish Press Agency): 00-502 Warsaw, ul. Bracka 6/8; tel. (22) 5092222; fax (22) 5092234; e-mail newsroom@pap.pl; internet www.pap.com.pl; f. 1944; brs in 22 Polish towns and 13 foreign capitals; 240 journalist and photojournalist mems; Pres. KRZYSZTOF HOFMAN.

PRESS ASSOCIATION

Stowarzyszenie Dziennikarzy Polskich (SDP) (Polish Journalists' Association): 00-366 Warsaw, ul. Foksal 3/5; tel. and fax (22) 8278720; e-mail sdp@sdp.pl; internet www.sdp.pl; f. 1951; dissolved 1982, legal status restored 1989; Pres. KRZYSZTOF SKOWROŃSKI; Gen. Sec. STEFAN TRUSZCZYŃSKI; 2,700 mems.

Publishers

Bertelsmann Media Sp. z o.o.: 02-786 Warsaw, ul. Rosoła 10; tel. (22) 6458200; fax (22) 6484732; e-mail poczta@swiatksiazki.com.pl; internet www.swiatksiazki.com.pl; f. 1994 as Bertelsmann Publishing Świat Książki Sp. z o.o.; *belles lettres*, science fiction, popular science, albums, books for children and teenagers; Pres. ANDRZEJ KOSTARCZYK; Editor-in-Chief BOGUSŁAW DĄBROWSKI.

Dom Wydawniczy ABC Sp. z o.o.: 01-231 Warsaw, ul. Płocka 5A; tel. (22) 5358000; fax (22) 5358001; e-mail info@abc.com.pl; internet www.abc.com.pl; f. 1989; legal, business and financial books; part of Polskie Wydawnictwa Profesjonalne Sp. z o.o; owned by Wolters Kluwer (Netherlands); Owners WŁODZIMIERZ ALBIN, KRZYSZTOF BRZESKI.

Dom Wydawniczy Bellona: 00-844 Warsaw, ul. Grzybowska 77; tel. (22) 6204291; fax (22) 6522695; e-mail bellona@bellona.pl; internet www.bellona.pl; f. 1947; fiction, history and military; Pres. Col JÓZEF SKRZYPIEC; Dir ZBIGNIEW CZERWIŃSKI.

Dom Wydawniczy Rebis Sp. z o.o.: 60-171 Poznań, ul. Żmigrodzka 41/49; tel. (61) 8678140; fax (61) 8673774; e-mail rebis@rebis.com.pl; internet www.rebis.com.pl; f. 1990; historical fiction, history of art; Pres. and Man. Dir TOMASZ SZPONDER.

Drukarnia i Księgarnia św. Wojciecha (St Adalbert—Wojciech Printing and Publishing Co): 60-967 Poznań, pl. Wolności 1; tel. (61) 8529186; fax (61) 8523746; e-mail wydawnictwo@ksw.com.pl; internet www.ksw.com.pl; f. 1895; textbooks and Catholic publications; Dir Rev. BOGDAN REFORMAT; Editor-in-Chief BOŻYSŁAW WALCZAK.

Egmont Sp. z o.o.: 01-029 Warsaw, ul. Dzielna 60; tel. (22) 8384100; fax (22) 8384200; e-mail kluby@egmont.pl; internet www.egmont.pl; f. 1990; books and comics for children and teenagers; Man. Dir JACEK BEŁDOWSKI; Editor-in-Chief HANNA BALTYN.

Instytut Wydawniczy Pax (Pax Publishing Institute): 00-390 Warsaw, ul. Wybrzeże Kościuszkowskie 21A; tel. (22) 6253398; fax (22) 6251378; e-mail iwpax@iwpax.com.pl; internet sklep.iwpax.com .pl; f. 1949; theology, philosophy, religion, history, literature; Dir KRZYSZTOF PRZESTRZELSKI; Editor-in-Chief ZBIGNIEW BOROWIK.

Muza SA: 00-590 Warsaw, ul. Marszałkowska 8; tel. (22) 6211776; fax (22) 6292349; e-mail muza@muza.com.pl; internet www.muza .com.pl; f. 1991; albums, encyclopedias, lexicons, handbooks, dictionaries, *belles lettres*, books for children and youth; Man. Dir MARCIN GARLINSKI.

Oficyna Wydawnicza Volumen: 00-354 Warsaw, ul. Dynasy 2A/3; tel. and fax (60) 7678936; e-mail volumen@owvolumen.pl; internet owvolumen.pl; f. 1984 (working clandestinely as WERS), 1989 officially; science, popular history, anthropology and socio-political sciences; Dir MIROSŁAWA LATKOWSKA.

Pallottinum—Wydawnictwo Stowarzyszenia Apostolstwa Katolickiego: 60-959 Poznań, Al. Przybyszewskiego 30, POB 23; tel. (61) 8675233; fax (61) 8675238; e-mail pallottinum@pallottinum .pl; internet www.pallottinum.pl; f. 1947; religious and philosophical books; Dir STEFAN DUSZA.

Państwowe Wydawnictwo Rolnicze i Leśne (State Agricultural and Forestry Publishers): 02-272 Warsaw, ul. Malownicza 14; tel. and fax (22) 8684529; e-mail pwril@pwril.com; internet www.pwril .com; f. 1947; professional publications on agriculture, forestry, health and veterinary science; Dir and Editor-in-Chief JOLANTA KUCZYŃSKA.

Państwowy Instytut Wydawniczy (State Publishing Institute): 00-372 Warsaw, ul. Foksal 17; tel. (22) 8260201; fax (22) 8261536; e-mail piw@piw.pl; internet www.piw.pl; f. 1946; Polish and foreign classical and contemporary literature, fiction, literary criticism, biographies, performing arts, culture, history, popular science, and fine arts; Dir and Editor-in-Chief RAFAŁ SKĄPSKI.

Pierwszy Wybór Profesjonalisty: 01-231 Warsaw, ul. Płocka 5A; tel. (22) 5358000; fax (22) 5358001; e-mail obsluga.klienta@ wolterskluwer.pl; internet www.pwp.pl; country's largest legal publisher; Pres. ALBIN WŁODZIMIERZ.

Polskie Przedsiębiorstwo Wydawnictw Kartograficznych im. E. Romera (E. Romer Polish Cartographical Publishing House): 02-389 Warsaw, Al. Bohaterów Września 9; tel. (22) 5851800; fax (22) 5851801; e-mail ppwk@ppwk.com.pl; internet www.ppwk.com.pl; f. 1951; maps, atlases, travel guides, books on geodesy and cartography; Man. Dir JACEK BŁASCZYŃSKI.

Polskie Wydawnictwo Muzyczne (Polish Publishing House for Music): 31-111 Kraków, Al. Krasińskiego 11A; tel. (12) 4227044; fax (12) 4220174; e-mail pwm@pwm.com.pl; internet www.pwm.com.pl; f. 1945; music and books on music; Chair. and Man. Dir Dr SŁAWOMIR J. TABKOWSKI; Editor-in-Chief ANDRZEJ KOSOWSKI.

Prószyński i S-ka Publishing House: 02-651 Warsaw, ul. Garażowa 7; tel. (22) 6077700; fax (22) 6077704; e-mail wydawnictwo@ proszynski.pl; internet www.proszynski.pl; f. 1990; poetry, fiction, non-fiction, educational text and reference books, popular science, etc.; Pres. MIECZYSŁAW PRÓSZYŃSKI; 110 employees.

Spółdzielnia Wydawnicza Czytelnik ('Reader' Co-operative Publishing House): 00-490 Warsaw, ul. Wiejska 12A; tel. (22) 5831407; fax (22) 6283178; e-mail sekretariat@czytelnik.pl; internet www .czytelnik.pl; f. 1944; general, especially fiction, memoirs and contemporary Polish literature; Pres. MAREK ŻAKOWSKI; Editorial Dir ANNA RUCIŃSKA.

Spółdzielnia Wydawniczo-Handlowa 'Książka i Wiedza' ('Books and Knowledge' Trade Co-operative Publishing House): 00-375 Warsaw, ul. Smolna 13; tel. (22) 8275401; fax (22) 8279423; e-mail publisher@kiw.com.pl; internet www.kiw.com.pl; f. 1948; philosophy, religion, linguistics, literature and history; Chair. WŁODZIMIERZ GAŁĄSKA; Editor-in-Chief ELŻBIETA KONECKA.

Wydawnictwa Naukowo-Techniczne (Scientific-Technical Publishers): 00-048 Warsaw, ul. Mazowiecka 2/4, POB 359; tel. (22) 8267271; fax (22) 8268293; e-mail wnt@pol.pl; internet www.wnt .com.pl; f. 1949; scientific and technical; Man. Dir and Editor Dr ANIELA TOPULOS.

Wydawnictwa Szkolne i Pedagogiczne (WSiP) (School and Pedagogical Publishers): 00-965 Warsaw, Al. Jerozolimskie 136; tel. (22) 5762510; fax (22) 5762509; e-mail wsip@wsip.com.pl; internet www.wsip.pl; f. 1945; school textbooks and popular science books, scientific literature for teachers, visual teaching aids, periodicals for teachers and youth; Chair. of Bd JERZY GARLICKI.

Wydawnictwo Arkady: 00-344 Warsaw, ul. Dobra 28, POB 137; tel. (22) 4448650; fax (22) 8274194; e-mail info@arkady.eu; internet www .arkady.eu; f. 1957; publications on building, town-planning, architecture, fashion, photography, gardening, design, art and books for children; Dir and Pres. JANINA KRYSIAK.

Wydawnictwo C. H. Beck: 00-203 Warsaw, ul. Bonifraterska 17; tel. (22) 3377600; fax (22) 3377601; e-mail redakcja@beck.pl; internet www.beck.pl; f. 1993; law and economics; Man. Dir PAWEŁ ESSE.

Wydawnictwo Dolnośląskie Sp. z o.o.: 50-010 Wrocław, ul. Podwale 62; tel. (71) 7859040; fax (71) 7859066; e-mail sekretariat@wd .wroc.pl; internet www.wd.wroc.pl; f. 1986; *belles lettres*, essays, memoirs, translations, general non-fiction; Pres. of Bd ANDRZEJ ADAMUS.

Wydawnictwo Iskry (Sparks Publishing House Ltd): 00-375 Warsaw, ul. Smolna 11; tel. and fax (22) 8279415; e-mail iskry@iskry.com .pl; internet www.iskry.com.pl; f. 1952; travel, Polish and foreign fiction, science fiction, essays, popular science, history, memoirs; Chair. Dr WIESŁAW UCHAŃSKI; Editor-in-Chief MAGDALENA SŁYSZ.

Wydawnictwo Kurpisz: 01-341 Poznań, ul. Przemysława 46; tel. (61) 8331517; fax (61) 8351294; e-mail kurpisz@kurpisz.pl; internet www.kurpisz.pl; f. 1991; *belles lettres*, reprints, dictionaries, encyclopedias, periodicals; Dir KAZIMIERZ GRZESIAK.

Wydawnictwo Lekarskie PZWL (PZWL Medical Publishers): 02-019 Warsaw, ul. Grójecka 5; tel. and fax (22) 6954033; e-mail promocja@pzwl.pl; internet www.wydawnictwopzwl.pl; f. 1945; medical literature and manuals, lexicons, encyclopedias; Pres. MICHAŁ SKUBA.

Wydawnictwo Literackie (Literary Publishing House): 31-147 Kraków, ul. Długa 1; tel. (12) 4232254; fax (12) 4225423; e-mail redakcja@wl.net.pl; internet www.wl.net.pl; f. 1953; works of literature and *belles lettres*; Dir BARBARA DRWOTA; Editor-in-Chief MAŁGORZATA NYCZ.

Wydawnictwo Nasza Księgarnia (Our Booksellers' Publishing House): 02-868 Warsaw, ul. Sarabandy 24C; tel. (22) 6439389; fax (22) 6437028; e-mail naszaksiegarnia@nk.com.pl; internet www.nk.com .pl; f. 1921; books and periodicals for children and young readers; Pres. AGNIESZKA TOKARCZYK; Editor JOLANTA SZTUCZYŃSKA.

Wydawnictwo Naukowe PWN (PWN Scientific Publishers): 02-676 Warsaw, ul. Postepu 18; tel. (22) 6954180; fax (22) 6954288; e-mail international@pwn.com.pl; internet www.pwn.pl; f. 1951; reference, academic, incl. multimedia; Pres. BARBARA JOZWIAK.

Wydawnictwo Nowa Era: 02-305 Warsaw, Al. Jerozolimskie 146D; tel. (22) 5702580; fax (22) 5702581; e-mail nowaera@nowaera.com.pl; internet www.nowaera.com.pl; school textbooks; Chair. MARIUSZ KOPER.

Wydawnictwo Ossolineum (Ossolineum Publishing House): 50-062 Wrocław, pl. Solny 14A; tel. (71) 3436961; fax (71) 3448103; e-mail wydawnictwo@ossolineum.pl; internet www.ossolineum.pl; f. 1817; publishing house of the Polish Academy of Sciences; academic publications in humanities and sciences; Man. Dir WOJCIECH KARWACKI; Editor-in-Chief STANISŁAW ROŚCICKI.

Wydawnictwo Prawnicze LexisNexis—LexPolonia (LexPolonia—LexisNexis Legal Publishing House): Warsaw; tel. (22) 5729500; fax (22) 5729508; e-mail biuro@lexisnexis.pl; internet www.lexisnexis.pl; f. 1952; present name adopted 2003; Exec. Dir OLGA DYMKOWSKA-PULCHNY.

Wydawnictwo Publicat: 61-003 Poznań, ul. Chlebowa 24; tel. (61) 8679546; fax (61) 6529200; internet www.najlepszyprezent.pl; f. 1990 as Wydawnictwo Podsiedlik-Raniowski Sp. z o.o.; popular and children's literature, poetry, prose, classical works, educational books; Pres. MICHAŁ KAIK.

Wydawnictwo Śląsk Sp. z o.o. (Silesia Publishing House Ltd): 40-161 Katowice, Al. W. Korfantego 51; tel. (32) 580756; fax (32) 583229; e-mail biuro@slaskwn.com.pl; internet www.slaskwn.com.pl; f. 1952; social, popular science, technical, and regional literature; Chair. and Editor-in-Chief Dr TADEUSZ SIERNY.

Wydawnictwo W.A.B. (WAB Publishers): 02-502 Warsaw, ul. Łowicka 31; tel. (22) 6460510; fax (22) 6460511; e-mail wab@wab.com.pl; internet www.wab.com.pl; f. 1991; contemporary Polish fiction, historical and cultural essays, and literature for children.

Wydawnictwo Wam (For You Publishers): 31-501 Kraków, ul. Kopernika 26; tel. (12) 6293200; fax (12) 4295003; e-mail wam@ wydawnictwowam.pl; internet www.wydawnictwowam.pl; f. 1872; Roman Catholic textbooks, encyclopedias, non-fiction, fiction and children's books; Dir HENRYK PIETRAS.

Wydawnictwo Wiedza Powszechna (General Knowledge Publishers): 00-054 Warsaw, ul. Jasna 26; tel. and fax (22) 8270799; e-mail info@wiedza.pl; internet www.wiedza.pl; f. 1952; popular science books, Polish and foreign language dictionaries, foreign language textbooks, encyclopedias and lexicons; Dir TERESA KORSAK.

Wydawnictwo Zysk i S-ka (Zysk Publishers): 61-744 Poznań, ul. Wielka 10; tel. (61) 8532767; fax (61) 8526326; e-mail sekretariat@ zysk.com.pl; internet www.zysk.com.pl; f. 1994; *belles lettres*, popular, scientific and religious literature; Pres. TADEUSZ ZYSK.

Znak Społeczny Instytut Wydawniczy (Znak Social Publishing Institute): 30-105 Kraków, ul. Kościuszki 37; tel. (12) 6199500; fax (12) 6199502; internet www.znak.com.pl; f. 1959; religion, philosophy, *belles lettres*, essays, history; Chief Exec. HENRYK WOŹNIAKOWSKI; Editor-in-Chief JERZY ILLG.

Broadcasting and Communications

TELECOMMUNICATIONS

Orange Polska (TP—Telekomunikacja Polska): 00-105 Warsaw, ul. Twarda 18; tel. (22) 5270000; internet www.orange.pl; f. 1992; mem. of France Telecom group (France); provides mobile telecommunications and internet services; subsidiary company PTK Centertel provides certain mobile telecommunications services, also under the brand name Orange Polska; Chair. MACIEJ WITUCKI.

Polkomtel: 02-676 Warsaw, ul. Postępu 3; tel. (22) 4261000; fax (22) 4260103; e-mail pr@plus.pl; internet www.polkomtel.com.pl; f. 1996; provides mobile cellular telecommunications services under the brand names Plus GSM, SimplusTeam and mixPlus; internet service provider; 3G network commenced operations Sept. 2004; Pres. ZYGMUNT SOLORZ-ŻAK (acting).

Polska Telefonia Cyfrowa (PTC) (Polish Digital Telephone): 02-222 Al. Jerozolimskie 181, Warsaw; tel. (22) 4136000; fax (22) 4134949; e-mail biznes@era.pl; internet www.era.pl; f. 1996; provides mobile cellular telecommunications under the brand names Era, Heyah and Blue Connect; internet service provider; 70.5% owned by T-Mobile Deutschland GmbH; 22.5% owned by T-Mobile Poland Holding B.V.; CEO Dr MIROSLAV RAKOWSKI.

Regulatory Authority

Office of Electronic Communications (Urząd Komunikacji Elektronicznej—UKE): 01-211 Warsaw, ul. Kasprzaka 18/20; tel. (22) 5349190; fax (22) 5349162; e-mail uke@uke.gov.pl; internet www .uke.gov.pl; f. 2001; formerly the Office of Telecommunications and Post Regulation (URTIP); reorganized Jan. 2006; Pres. MAGDALENA GAJ.

BROADCASTING

Regulatory Authority

National Broadcasting Council (Krajowa Rada Radiofonii i Telewizji—KRRiTV): 01-015 Warsaw, Skwer Kardynała Stefana Wyszyńskiego, Prymasa Polski 9; tel. (22) 5973042; fax (22) 5973180; e-mail abonament@krrit.gov.pl; internet www.krrit.gov .pl; f. 1993; Chair. JAN DWORAK.

Radio

In 2006, in addition to the state-owned Polskie Radio, which operates four national channels, there were 22 other public radio stations: 17 regional; four city; and one local. There were also 179 independent radio broadcasters, of which three broadcast nation-wide, eight on a regional basis and 168 locally.

Polskie Radio (Polish Radio): 00-977 Warsaw, Al. Niepodległości 77/85; tel. (22) 6452445; fax (22) 6455924; e-mail sluchacze@ polskieradio.pl; internet www.polskieradio.pl; home service comprises four national channels, broadcasting 24 hours a day; foreign service broadcasts in Polish, English, German, Russian, Belarusian, Ukrainian and Hebrew; Chair. STANISŁAW JĘDRZEJEWSKI.

Radio Maryja: 87-100 Toruń, ul. Żwirki i Wigury 80; tel. (56) 6552361; fax (56) 6552362; e-mail radio@radiomaryja.pl; internet www.radiomaryja.pl; conservative Catholic; Dir TADEUSZ RYDZYK.

Radio Musyka Fakty (RMF FM): 30-204 Kraków, Al. Waszyngtona 1, Kopiec Kościuszki; tel. (12) 6622000; fax (12) 6622228; e-mail redakcja@rmf.fm; internet www.rmf.fm; Pres. and Dir THADDEUS SOLTYS.

Radio Zet: 00-503 Warsaw, ul. Żurawia 8; tel. (22) 5833300; fax (22) 6227900; e-mail radiozet@radiozet.pl; internet www.radiozet.com .pl; independent; 24 hours; wholly owned by the Eurozet media group; Pres. and Editor-in-Chief ROBERT KOZYRA.

Television

Telewizja Polska (Polish Television): 00-999 Warsaw, ul. J. P. Woronicza 17; tel. (22) 5474450; fax (22) 5477719; e-mail pr@tvp.pl; internet www.tvp.pl; f. 1952; Chair. JULIUSZ BRAUN.

PolSat: 04-175 Warsaw, ul. Ostrobramska 77; tel. (22) 5144000; fax (22) 5134295; internet www.polsat.pl; f. 1992; satellite broadcasts; Dir Gen. MIROSŁAW BŁASZCZYK.

TVN: 02-952 Warsaw, ul. Wiertnicza 166; tel. (22) 8566060; fax (22) 8566666; e-mail widzowie@tvn.pl; internet www.tvn.pl; f. 1997; Dir Gen. PIOTR WALTER.

Finance

(cap. = capital; res = reserves; dep. = deposits; m. = million; amounts in złotys; brs = branches)

BANKING

Foreign banks were permitted to operate freely in the country from 1997. In early 2010 there were 49 domestic commercial banks and 20 branches of credit institutions operating in Poland.

Supervisory Authority

Polish Financial Supervision Authority (PFSA) (Komisja Nadzoru Finansowego): 00-950 Warsaw, Plac Powstańców Warszawy 1; tel. (22) 3326600; fax (22) 3326602; e-mail knf@knf.gov.pl; internet www.knf.gov.pl; f. 2008 to succeed Financial Supervision Commission; Chair. STANISŁAW KLUZA.

National Bank

Narodowy Bank Polski—NBP (National Bank of Poland): 00-919 Warsaw, ul. Świętokrzyska 11/21, POB 1011; tel. (22) 6531000; fax (22) 6208518; e-mail listy@nbp.pl; internet www.nbp.pl; f. 1945; cap. 1,500.0m., res 969.3m., dep. 83,920.9m. (Dec. 2007); Pres. MAREK BELKA; 16 brs.

Other Banks

Bank BPH SA: 31-548 Kraków, Al. Pokoju 1; tel. (12) 5318095; fax (12) 5073152; e-mail bank@bphpbk.pl; internet www.bph.pl; f. 1989; fmrly Bank Przemysłowo-Handlowy PBK SA; present name adopted 2004; 52.1% owned by Bank Austria Creditanstalt AG (HVB Group, Austria); cap. 383.3m., res 3,842.4m., dep. 13,342.8m. (Dec. 2012); Pres. JÓZEF WANCER; 283 brs.

Bank Gospodarki Żywnościowej—BGZ (Bank of Food Economy): 01-211 Warsaw, ul. Kasprzaka 10/16; tel. (22) 8604000; fax (22) 8605000; e-mail info@bgz.pl; internet www.bgz.pl; f. 1919; present name adopted 1994; universal commercial bank; finances agriculture, forestry and food-processing; 37.3% state-owned; 44.5% owned by Rabobank (Netherlands); cap. 51.1m., res 3,281.1m., dep. 29,330.9m. (Dec. 2012); Exec. Pres. JACEK BARTKIEWICZ; 400 brs.

Bank Gospodarstwa Krajowego—BGK (National Economy Bank): 00-955 Warsaw, Al. Jerozolimskie 7, POB 41; tel. (22) 5229105; fax (22) 6270378; e-mail bgk@bgk.com.pl; internet www .bgk.com.pl; f. 1924; 100% state-owned; cap. 4,948.2m., res 374.9m., dep. 27,488.5m. (Dec. 2011); Pres. of Bd DOMINIK RADZIWIŁŁ; 23 brs.

Bank Millennium: 02-593 Warsaw, Stanisława Żaryna 2A; tel. (22) 5981565; fax (22) 5981563; e-mail wojciech.kaczorowski@ bankmillennium.pl; internet www.bankmillennium.pl; f. 1989 as Bank Inicjatyw Gospodarczych (BIG); present name adopted 2003; 65.0% owned by Banco Comercial Português SA (Portugal); cap. 1,213.1m., res 1,013.1m., dep. 42,656.1m. (Dec. 2012); Chair. of Bd BOGUSŁAW KOTT; 447 brs.

Bank Ochrony Środowiska—BOS (Environmental Protection Bank): 00-950 Warsaw 1, Al. Jana Pawła II 12, POB 150; tel. (22)

8508720; fax (22) 8508891; e-mail bos@bosbank.pl; internet www .bosbank.pl; f. 1991; 77.2% by Polish National Fund for the Protection of the Environment and Water; cap. 228.7m., res 579.5m., dep. 10,790.9m. (Dec. 2012); Pres. of Exec. Bd MARIUSZ KLIMCZAK; 48 brs.

Bank Polska Kasa Opieki—Bank Pekao: 00-950 Warsaw, ul. Grzybowska 53/57; tel. (22) 6560000; fax (22) 6560004; e-mail info@ pekao.com.pl; internet www.pekao.com.pl; f. 1929; universal bank; 52.9% owned by UniCredito Italiano SpA (Italy); cap. 262.5m., res 20,023.1m., dep. 109,401.9m. (Dec. 2012); CEO ALICJA KORNASIEWICZ; Chair. JERZY WOZNICKI; 720 brs and sub-brs.

Bank Zachodni WBK (Western Bank): 50-950 Wrocław, Dolnośląskie Rynek 9/11; tel. (71) 3701000; fax (71) 3702771; e-mail press .office@bzwbk.pl; internet www.bzwbk.pl; f. 1989; present name adopted 2001; 70.5% owned by AIB European Investments Ltd (Ireland); cap. 746.4m., res 6,577.1m., dep. 47,700.6m. (Dec. 2012); Pres. MATEUSZ MORAWIECKI; 526 brs.

BNP Paribas Bank Polska: 02-676 Warsaw, ul. Suwak 3; tel. (22) 5669300; fax (22) 5669079; internet www.bnpparibas.pl; f. 1990; fmrly Fortis Bank Polska; present name adopted 2011; 99.1% owned by BNP Paribas (France); cap. 1,434.6m., res 231.6m., dep. 10,447.3m. (Dec. 2012); CEO ALEXANDER PAKLONS; Chair. CAMILLE FOHL.

BRE Bank: 00-950 Warsaw, ul. Senatorska 18, POB 728; tel. (22) 8290000; fax (22) 8290033; e-mail info@brebank.pl; internet www .brebank.com.pl; f. 1987; present name adopted 1999; 70.3% owned by Commerzbank AG (Germany); specializes in corporate banking; cap. 168.6m., res 8,211.2m., dep. 56,735.7m. (Dec. 2012); Pres. and CEO MARIUSZ GRENDOWICZ; 172 brs.

Citibank Handlowy: 00-923 Warsaw, ul. Senatorska 16; tel. (22) 6577200; fax (22) 6925023; e-mail relacjeinwestorskie@citi.com; internet www.citibank.pl; f. 1870; trade and finance bank; specializes in corporate and investment banking; fmrly Bank Handlowy w Warszawie (Trade Bank in Warsaw); 75% owned by Citibank Overseas Investment Corpn (USA); cap. 522.6m., res 5,906.2m., dep. 25,109.5m. (Dec. 2012); Pres. SŁAWOMIR SIKORA; Chair. STANISŁAW SOŁTYSIŃSKI; 149 brs.

Deutsche Bank PBC: 00-609 Warsaw, Al. Armii Ludowej 26; tel. (22) 5799800; fax (22) 5799801; e-mail info@db-pbc.pl; internet www .deutsche-bank-pbc.pl; f. 1991; fmrly Bank Wspolpracy Regionalnej SA w Krakowie; present name adopted 2003; 99.7% owned by Deutsche Bank Privat- und Geschäftskunden Aktiengesellschaft (Germany); cap. 1,620.5m., res 192.4m., dep. 20,976.6m. (Dec. 2011); Chair. of Supervisory Bd GUIDO HEUVELDOP; Pres. LESZEK NIEMYCKI.

Getin Noble Bank SA: 02-675 Warsaw, ul. Domaniewska 39 B; tel. (32) 2008500; fax (32) 2008685; e-mail marketing@getinbank.pl; internet www.getinbank.pl; f. 1990; fmrly Górnośląski Bank Gospodarczy; renamed Getin Bank in 2004; present name adopted 2010 after merger with Noble Bank; cap. 2,650.1m., res 2,014.7m., dep. 51,181.6m. (Dec. 2012); Pres. MICHAŁ HANDZLIK; Chair. KRZYSZTOF ROSIŃSKI; 146 brs.

ING Bank Śląski: 40-086 Katowice, ul. Sokolska 34; tel. (32) 3570069; fax (32) 3577507; e-mail mampytanie@ingbank.pl; internet www.ing.pl; f. 1989; 75% owned by ING Bank NV (Netherlands); cap. 130.1m., res 1,997.3m., dep. 59,571.9m. (Dec. 2012); Chair. ANNA FORNALCZYK; Pres. MAŁGORZATA KOŁAKOWSKA; 439 brs.

Nordea Bank Polska: 81-303 Gdynia, ul. Kielecka 2, POB 11; tel. (58) 6691111; fax (58) 6691110; e-mail nordea@nordea.com; internet www.nordea.pl; f. 1991; 98.9% owned by Nordea Bank AB (Sweden); cap. 227.5m., res 1,870.7m., dep. 29,413.1m. (Dec. 2012); Pres. WLODZIMIERZ KICINSKI; Chair. WOJCIECH RYBOWSKI.

PKO Bank Polski—Powszechna Kasa Oszczędności Bank Państwowy—PKO (State Savings Bank): 00-975 Warsaw, ul. Pulawska 15, POB 183; tel. (22) 5218440; fax (22) 5218029; internet www.pkobp.pl; f. 1919; 51.5% state-owned; cap. 1,250m., res 19,812.7m., dep. 148,383.3m. (Dec. 2012); Pres. of Management Bd ZBIGNIEW JAGIEŁŁO; Chair. of Supervisory Bd CEZARY BANASIŃSKI; 1,153 brs and sub-brs.

Raiffeisen Bank Polska: 00-549 Warsaw, ul. Piekna 20, POB 53; tel. (22) 5852000; fax (22) 5852585; internet www.raiffeisen.pl; f. 1991; present name adopted 2000; 100% owned by Raiffeisen International Bank Holding AG (Austria); cap. 1,250.9m., res 1,448.8m., dep. 28,146.7m. (Dec. 2011); Pres. PIOTR CZARNECKI; Chair. HERBERT STEPIC; 37 brs.

STOCK EXCHANGE

The Warsaw Stock Exchange was re-established in April 1991. In January 1998 a derivatives market was launched. At the end of 2008 the Stock Exchange's shareholders included 35 entities, comprising banks, brokerage firms, an Exchange company and the State Treasury (which held a share of 98.8%).

Warsaw Stock Exchange: 00-498 Warsaw, ul. Książęca 4; tel. (22) 6283232; fax (22) 6281754; e-mail wse@wse.com.pl; internet www

.wse.com.pl; opened for trading in 1991; Pres. and Chief Exec. Dr LUDWIK SOBOLEWSKI.

INSURANCE

In late 2009 there were 30 insurance companies operating in Poland.

Allianz Życie Polska: 02-685 Warsaw, ul. Rodziny Hiszpańskich 1; tel. (22) 5294000; fax (22) 5294040; internet www.allianz.pl; f. 1997; life; Pres. PAWEŁ DANGEL.

Aviva Towarzystwo Ubezpieczeń na Życie: 00-838 Warsaw, ul. Prosta 70; tel. (22) 5574050; fax (22) 5574075; e-mail bok@aviva.pl; internet www.aviva.pl; f. 1991; Pres. MACIEJ JANKOWSKI.

Axa Życie Towarzystwo Ubezpieczeń: 00-867 Warsaw, ul. Budynek 51, Warsaw Trade Tower Bldg; tel. (22) 5550050; fax (22) 5550052; e-mail ubezpieczenia@axa-polska.pl; internet www .axa-polska.pl; f. 1993; Pres. MACIEJ SZWARC.

Grupa Powszechny Zakład Ubezpieczeń (PZU) (Polish National Insurance Group): 00-133 Warsaw, Al. Jana Pawła II 24; tel. (22) 3084940; fax (22) 3084942; internet www.pzu.pl; f. 1803; insurance group comprising two principal cos dealing in life and non-life insurance, and six support cos; Pres. ANDRZEJ KLESYK; 400 brs; 14,000 employees.

ING Towarzystwo Ubezpieczeń na Życie: 00-406 Warsaw, ul. Ludna 2; tel. (22) 5220000; fax (22) 5221111; e-mail info@ing.pl; internet www.ing.pl; f. 1994; Pres. JAROSŁAW JAMKA.

MetLife Amplico: 00-450 Warsaw, ul. Przemysłowa 26; tel. (22) 6271000; fax (22) 6271010; e-mail lifeinfo@amplico.pl; internet www .amplicolife.pl; f. 1990; Pres. ŁUKASZ KALINOWSKI.

Nordea Polska Towarzystwo Ubezpieczeń na Życie: 00-867 Warsaw, Al. Jana Pawła II/27; tel. (22) 5410100; fax (22) 5410101; e-mail zycie@nordeapolska.pl; internet www.nordeazycie.pl; f. 1994; Pres. MARIUSZ SOBIECH.

UNIQA Towarzystwo Ubezpieczeń na Życie: 90-520 Łódź, ul. Gdańska 132; tel. (42) 6344700; fax (42) 6377687; e-mail zycie@uniqa .pl; internet www.uniqa.pl; f. 1994; Pres. JAROSŁAW PARKOT.

Warta—Towarzystwo Ubezpieczeń i Reasekuracji Warta (Warta Insurance and Reinsurance Co): 00-805 Warsaw, ul. Chmielna 85/87; tel. (22) 5810100; fax (22) 5811375; e-mail info@ warta.pl; internet www.warta.pl; f. 1920; marine, air, motor, fire, luggage and credit; Chair. of Bd JOHN HOLLOWS; 25 brs.

Trade and Industry

GOVERNMENT AGENCIES

Agency for the Restructuring and Modernization of Agriculture (Agencja Restrukturyzacji i Modernizacji Rolnictwa): 00-175 Warsaw, Al. Jana Pawła II 70; fax (22) 3185330; e-mail info@arimr .gov.pl; internet www.arimr.gov.pl; f. 1994; Pres. Prof. GRZEGORZ SPYCHALSKI.

Agricultural Market Agency (Agencja Rynku Rolnego): 00-400 Warsaw, ul. Nowy Świat 6/12; tel. (22) 6617272; fax (22) 6289353; e-mail tpi@arr.gov.pl; internet www.eng.arr.gov.pl; f. 1991; implements selected schemes under the Common Agricultural Policy of the European Union; Pres. STANISŁAW GRZEGORZ KAMIŃSKI.

Polish Agency for Enterprise Development (PARP) (Polska Agencja Rozwoju Przedsiębiorczości): 00-834 Warsaw, ul. Pańska 81/83; tel. (22) 4328080; fax (22) 4328620; e-mail biuro@parp.gov.pl; internet www.parp.gov.pl; f. 2000; manages funds assigned from the state budget and the European Union for the support of entrepreneurship and devt of human resources, particularly concerning small and medium-sized enterprises; Chief Exec. DANUTA JABŁOŃSKA.

Polish Information and Foreign Investment Agency (Polska Agencja Informacji i Inwestycji Zagranicznych): 00-585 Warsaw, ul. Bagatela 12; tel. (22) 3349800; fax (22) 3349999; e-mail post@paiz.gov .pl; internet www.paiz.gov.pl; f. 2003; Pres. ANDRZEJ KANTHAK.

DEVELOPMENT AGENCY

Industrial Development Agency (Agencja Rozwoju Przemysłu): 02-675 Warsaw, ul. Wołoska 7, Budynek Mars, Klatka A; tel. (22) 4603636; fax (22) 4603637; e-mail lucyna.stepien@arp.com.pl; internet www.arp.com.pl; Pres. PAWEŁ BRZEZICKI.

CHAMBERS OF COMMERCE

Polish Chamber of Commerce (National Economic Chamber—Krajowa Izba Gospodarcza): 00-074 Warsaw, ul. Trębacka 4, POB 361; tel. (22) 6309600; fax (22) 8274673; e-mail kig@kig.pl; internet www.kig.pl; f. 1990; Pres. ANDRZEJ ARENDARSKI; Sec.-Gen. MAREK KŁOCZKO; 145 mems.

Foreign Investors' Chamber of Industry and Trade in Poland (Izba Przemysłowo-Handlowa Inwestorów Zagranicznych—IPHIZ): 00-834 Warsaw, ul. Pańska 73; tel. (22) 3147575; fax (22) 3147576;

e-mail biuro@iphiz.com.pl; internet www.iphiz.com.pl; f. 1989; Pres. ZDZISŁAW JAGODZIŃSKI.

UTILITIES

Energy Regulatory Authority (Urząd Regulacji Energetyki): 00-872 Warsaw, ul. Chłodna 64; tel. (22) 6616107; fax (22) 6616152; e-mail ure@ure.gov.pl; internet www.ure.gov.pl; Pres. Dr LESZEK JUCHNIEWICZ.

Electricity

The electricity sector has been reorganized into separate generation, transmission and distribution entities.

Koncern Energetyczny ENERGA: 80-557 Gdańsk, ul. Marynarki Polskiej 130; tel. (58) 3473013; fax (58) 3010152; internet www .energa.pl; f. 2004; renamed as above 2005; group of eight regional electricity distributors in central and northern Poland, known as G8; partial privatization suspended in 2004; Chief Exec. WALDEMAR BARTELIK; 7,500 employees.

PGE Polska Grupa Energetyczna: 00-496 Warsaw, ul. Mysia 2; tel. (22) 6931580; fax (22) 6285964; internet www.pgesa.pl; national transmission-system operator; fmrly Polskie Sieci Elektroenergetyczne (PSE); Chair. of Bd TOMASZ ZADROGA.

RWE Polska (RWE Poland): 02-384 Warsaw, ul. Włodarzewska 68; tel. (22) 8214646; fax (22) 8214647; e-mail info@rwe.pl; internet www .rwe.pl; f. 1993; fmrly STOEN SZE; transmits and distributes electric energy; privatized in 2002; 85% owned by RWE Energie AG (Germany); 15% state-owned; Chief Exec. HARRY SCHUR.

Gas

EuRoPol GAZ: 00-342 Warsaw, ul. Topiel 2; tel. (22) 5867000; fax (22) 5867070; e-mail info@europolgaz.com.pl; internet www .europolgaz.com.pl; f. 1993; jt venture between PGNiG and Gazprom (Russia); Pres. KAZIMIERZ ADAMCZYK.

Polish Oil and Gas Co (PGNiG) (Polskie Górnictwo Naftowe i Gazownictwo): 00-537 Warsaw, ul. Krucza 6/14; tel. (22) 5835000; fax (22) 5835856; e-mail pr@pgnig.pl; internet www.pgnig.pl; f. 1982; divided into six regional distribution subsidiaries in 2003; state-owned natural gas producer and supplier; scheduled for partial privatization; Pres. of Bd KRZYSZTOF GŁOGOWSKI; 47,300 employees.

TRADE UNIONS

All-Poland Alliance of Trade Unions (Ogólnopolskie Porozumienie Związków Zawodowych—OPZZ): 00-924 Warsaw, ul. Kopernika 36/40; tel. (22) 5515500; fax (22) 5515501; e-mail inter@opzz.org.pl; internet www.opzz.org.pl; f. 1984; Pres. JAN GUZ.

Transport

RAILWAYS

In 2011 there were 20,228 km of railway lines making up the state network in Poland, of which nearly 12,000 km were electrified.

Office for Railway Transport (Urząd Transportu Kolejowego): 00-928 Warsaw, ul. Chałubinskiego 4/6; tel. (22) 6301950; fax (22) 6301892; e-mail utk@utk.gov.pl; internet www.utk.gov.pl; fmrly General Railway Inspectorate; reorganized in July 2003; Pres. WIESŁAW JAROSIEWICZ; Dir-Gen. LIDIA OSTROWSKA.

Polish State Railways (Polskie Koleje Państwowe—PKP): 00-973 Warsaw, ul. Szczęśliwicka 62; tel. (22) 4749000; fax (22) 4749102; e-mail biuro.zarzadu@pkp.pl; internet www.pkp.pl; f. 1926; freight and passenger transport; PKP Group comprises 12 cos; from 2004 Regional Services (WKD), a principal subsidiary, has been operated by local govts; Polskie Koleje Państwowe Polskie Linie Kolejowe (PKP PLK) operates the railway network; Pres. ANDRZEJ WACH; Gen. Dir MACIEJ MECLĘWSKI; 125,000 employees.

ROADS

In 2010 there were 406,122 km of roads, of which 857 km were motorways; 69.9% of the road network was paved.

General Directorate of Public Roads and Motorways (Generalna Dyrekcja Dróg Krajowych i Autostrad): 00-848 Warsaw, ul. Żelazna 59; tel. (22) 3758888; fax (22) 3758763; e-mail kancelaria@ gddkia.gov.pl; internet www.gddkia.gov.pl; Dir ZBIGNIEW KOTLAREK.

INLAND WATERWAYS

Poland has 6,850 km of waterways, of which 3,660 km were navigable in 2009. The main rivers are the Wisła (Vistula), Odra (Oder), Bug, Warta and San. There are some 5,000 lakes. In addition, there is a network of canals.

SHIPPING

Poland has three large harbours on the Baltic Sea: Gdynia, Gdańsk and Szczecin. At 31 December 2012 the Polish flag registered fleet comprised 260 vessels, with a total displacement of 157,267 grt.

Authority of Szczecin and Świnoujście Authority Co: 70-603 Szczecin, ul. Bytomska 7; tel. (91) 4308240; fax (91) 4624842; e-mail info@port.szczecin.pl; internet www.port.szczecin.pl; f. 1950; Pres. and Man. Dir JANUSZ CATEWICZ.

Port of Gdańsk Authority Co: 80-955 Gdańsk, ul. Zamknięta 18; tel. (58) 7379100; fax (58) 7379485; e-mail info@portgdansk.pl; internet www.portgdansk.pl; f. 1997; management of land and port infrastructure; Pres. of Bd STANISŁAW CORA.

Port of Gdynia Authority Co: 81-337 Gdynia, ul. Rotterdamska 9; tel. (58) 6274002; fax (58) 6203191; e-mail marketing@port.gdynia .pl; internet www.port.gdynia.pl; f. 1922; Pres. JANUSZ JAROSIŃSKI.

Principal Shipping Companies

Polska Żegluga Bałtycka—Polferries (Polish Baltic Shipping Co—POLFERRIES): 78-100 Kołobrzeg, ul. Portowa 41; tel. (94) 3552102; fax (94) 3552208; internet www.polferries.pl; f. 1976; operates three ferries on four routes between Denmark and Sweden; also serves as travel agency and tour operator.

Polska Żegluga Morska (PZM) (Polish Steamship Co—Polsteam): 70-419 Szczecin, Pl. Rodła 8; tel. (91) 3594333; fax (91) 3594288; e-mail pzmmanagement@polsteam.com.pl; internet www.polsteam .com.pl; f. 1951; state-owned; world-wide tramping; operates 75 vessels totalling 2m. dwt, incl. four liquid-sulphur carriers; largest dry bulk carrier in Europe; operates ferry service between Poland and Sweden (Unity Line); Gen. Dir PAWEŁ SZYNKARUK; 2,800 employees.

Polskie Linie Oceaniczne (PLO) (Polish Ocean Lines): 81-364 Gdynia, ul. 10 Lutego 24; tel. (58) 6900670; fax (58) 6900672; e-mail pol@pol.com.pl; internet www.pol.com.pl; f. 1951; holding co for six shipping cos operating within PLO group; tonnage operated by the POL-Levant Shipping Lines; Pres. of Bd ANDRZEJ OSIECIMSKI.

CIVIL AVIATION

Fryderyk Chopin–Okęcie international airport is situated near Warsaw. In addition, international flights serve a number of other airports, including those at Bydgoszcz, Gdańsk, Katowice, Kraków, Łódź, Poznań, Rzeszów, Szczecin and Wrocław.

Civil Aviation Office (Urząd Lotnictwa Cywilnego): 00-848 Warsaw, ul. Żelazna 59; tel. (22) 5207200; fax (22) 5207300; e-mail kancelaria@ulc.gov.pl; internet www.ulc.gov.pl; Pres. GRZEGORZ KRUSZYŃSKI.

LOT—Polskie Linie Lotnicze (Polish Airlines): 00-906 Warsaw, ul. 17 Stycznia 39; tel. (22) 6066111; fax (22) 8460909; e-mail lot@lot .com; internet www.lot.com; f. 1929; 67.97% state-owned; domestic and international services; operates low-cost subsidiary Eurolot (f. 1996) providing domestic scheduled and international scheduled and charter services; Chair. of Bd SEBASTIAN MIKOSZ.

Tourism

Poland is rich in historic cities, such as Gdańsk, Wrocław, Kraków, Poznań and Warsaw. There are numerous health and climatic resorts, while the mountains, forests and rivers provide splendid scenery and excellent facilities for touring and sporting holidays. In 2012 Poland was visited by some 67.4m. foreign tourists. Receipts from tourism (excluding passenger transport) were provisionally estimated at US \$10,687m. in 2011.

Polish Tourist Organization (Polska Organizacja Turystyczna—POT): 00-613 Warsaw, ul. Chałubińskiego 8, XIX piętro; tel. (22) 5367070; fax (22) 5367004; e-mail pot@pot.gov.pl; internet www.pot .gov.pl; Pres. RAFAŁ SZMYTKE.

Defence

As assessed at November 2012, Poland's active armed forces numbered 96,000, comprising an army of 45,600, a navy of 7,600, air forces of 16,500, special forces of 2,200 and joint forces of 24,100. The 22,050 paramilitary forces comprised border guards (14,750) and interior ministry units (7,300, including 1,000 conscripts). Compulsory military service was abolished with effect from February 2009. Poland joined the 'Partnership for Peace' military co-operation programme of the North Atlantic Treaty Organization (NATO) in 1994 and became a full member of the alliance in 1999.

Defence Expenditure: Budgeted at 31,200m. złotys for 2013.

Chief of Staff of the Defence Forces: Gen. MIECZYSŁAW CIENIUCH.

Education

Education is free and compulsory for nine years. Before the age of seven, children may attend crèches and kindergartens. Compulsory basic schooling begins at seven years of age with primary school. Primary education lasts for six years, divided into two equal cycles. Lower secondary education (at the gimnazjum) is compulsory for three years. In 2008/09 net enrolment at primary schools included 96% of children in the relevant age-group. In the same year enrolment in secondary schools included 91% of children in the relevant age-group. Three years of education at general secondary schools commence at the age of 16 years, for pupils who successfully complete the entrance examination; there are general secondary schools, vocational technical schools and basic vocational schools. The latter provide courses consisting of three days' theoretical and three days' practical training per week, and in addition some general education is given. New post-secondary schools were introduced in 1999 to prepare students from technical and vocational schools for skilled jobs. Curriculums are standardized throughout Poland. In 2004/05 there were 400 higher education establishments, including 17 universities and 22 technical universities. In 2008/09 there were 2.2m. students of higher education. In 2010 state budgetary expenditure on education amounted to 76,713m. new złotys (11.9% of total spending).

PORTUGAL

Introductory Survey

LOCATION, CLIMATE, LANGUAGE, RELIGION, FLAG, CAPITAL

The mainland portion of the Portuguese Republic lies in Western Europe, on the Atlantic side of the Iberian peninsula, bordered by Spain to the north and east. The country also includes two archipelagos in the Atlantic Ocean, the Azores (Açores) and the Madeira Islands. The climate is mild and temperate, with an annual average temperature of 16°C (61°F). In the interior the weather is drier and hotter. Almost all of the inhabitants speak Portuguese and are adherents of the Roman Catholic Church. The national flag (proportions 2 by 3) has two vertical stripes, of green and red, the green occupying two-fifths of the total area; superimposed on the stripes (half on the green, half on the red) is the state coat of arms: a white shield, containing five small blue shields (each bearing five white roundels) in the form of an upright cross, with a red border containing seven yellow castles, all superimposed on a yellow armillary sphere. The capital is Lisbon (Lisboa).

CONTEMPORARY POLITICAL HISTORY

Historical Context

The monarchy that had ruled Portugal from the 11th century was overthrown in 1910, when the King was deposed in a bloodless revolution, and a republic was proclaimed. A period of great instability ensued until a military coup installed the regime of the Estado Novo (New State) in 1926. Dr António de Oliveira Salazar became Minister of Finance in 1928 and Prime Minister in 1932, establishing a right-wing dictatorial regime, influenced by Italian Fascism. A new Constitution, establishing a corporate state, was adopted in 1933. Only one political party was authorized, and suffrage was limited. Portugal remained neutral during the Second World War. The Government strove to achieve international acceptance, but Portugal was not admitted to the UN until 1955. Unlike the other European colonial powers, Portugal insisted on maintaining its overseas possessions, regarding them as 'inalienable'. In 1961 Portuguese enclaves in India were successfully invaded by Indian forces, and in the same year a rebellion against Portuguese rule began in Angola. Similar rebellions followed, in Portuguese Guinea (1963) and Mozambique (1964), and protracted guerrilla warfare ensued in the three African provinces. Salazar remained in power until illness forced his retirement in September 1968. He was succeeded by Dr Marcello Caetano, who had been Deputy Prime Minister in 1955–58. Caetano pursued slightly more liberal policies. Opposition parties were legalized for elections to the Assembléia Nacional in October 1969, but the União Nacional, the government party, won all 130 seats. Immediately after the elections, the opposition groups were outlawed again. The government party, renamed Acção Nacional Popular in February 1970, also won every seat at the next elections to the Assembléia, in October 1973, following the withdrawal of all opposition candidates.

The drain on Portugal's economy by the long wars against nationalist forces in the overseas provinces contributed to the overthrow of Caetano in a bloodless coup on 25 April 1974, initiated by the Movimento das Forças Armadas (MFA), a group of young army officers. Gen. António Ribeiro de Spínola, head of the Junta da Salvação Nacional (Junta of National Salvation) that assumed power, became President in May and promised liberal reforms. The new Government recognized the right of Portugal's overseas territories to self-determination. The independence of Guinea-Bissau (formerly Portuguese Guinea), proclaimed in September 1973, was recognized by Portugal in September 1974. The remaining African territories were all granted independence in 1975. Portugal also withdrew from Portuguese Timor (Timor-Leste) in that year.

Following a split between the Junta's right and left wings, President Spínola resigned in September 1974 and was replaced by Gen. Francisco da Costa Gomes. An abortive counter-coup by senior officers in March 1975 resulted in a move to the left. All existing organs of the MFA were dissolved, a Supreme Revolutionary Council (SRC) was created, and six of the country's political parties agreed that the SRC would stay in power for five years. On 25 April a general election was held for a Constituent Assembly. Of the 12 parties contesting the election, the Partido Socialista (PS) obtained the largest share of the votes cast and won 116 of the Assembly's 250 seats. However, disputes between Socialists and Communists provoked withdrawals from the new coalition Government, and the Prime Minister, Gen. Vasco Gonçalves, was dismissed. Adm. José Pinheiro de Azevedo became Prime Minister in August. In September a new Government of 'united action' was formed, including members of the armed forces, the PS, the Partido Popular Democrático (PPD) and the Partido Comunista Português (PCP). In November the Government suspended its activities, owing to a lack of support from the armed forces. An abortive leftist military coup resulted from the political turmoil. Changes took place within the SRC, and in December the armed forces announced a plan to reduce their political power.

Domestic Political Affairs

A new Constitution, committing Portugal to make a transition to socialism, took effect on 25 April 1976. The SRC was renamed the Council of the Revolution, becoming a consultative body, headed by the President, with powers to delay legislation and the right of veto in military matters. At the general election for the new Assembléia da República (Assembly of the Republic), the PS won 107 of the Assembléia's 263 seats. In June the Army Chief of Staff, Gen. António Ramalho Eanes, a non-party candidate supported by the PS, the PPD and the Centro Democrático Social (CDS), was elected President. He took office in July, when a minority Socialist Government was formed under Dr Mário Lopes Soares, who had been Minister of Foreign Affairs in 1974–75. The Government resigned in December 1977, but the President again invited Soares to take office as Prime Minister. A new PS-CDS coalition was established in January 1978, but it collapsed after only six months. A new Government was formed in November under Prof. Carlos Mota Pinto, but he resigned in July 1979. President Eanes appointed Dr Maria de Lourdes Pintasilgo to head a provisional Government.

The centre-right alliance, Aliança Democrática (AD), which included the Partido Social Democrata (PSD, formerly the PPD) and the CDS, won a majority in the Assembléia da República in an early general election held in December 1979. Dr Francisco Sá Carneiro, the leader of the PSD, was appointed Prime Minister. At the general election in October 1980 the AD increased its parliamentary majority. In December Sá Carneiro and his Minister of Defence, Adelino Amaro da Costa, were killed in an apparent air accident. (In 2004 tests revealed that a bomb had exploded on board the aircraft, and the eighth commission of inquiry into the crash cited Amaro da Costa's attempt to stop the illegal sale of arms to Iran as a possible motive for the bombing.) The presidential election took place as planned, however, and Eanes was re-elected. Dr Francisco Pinto Balsemão, co-founder of the PSD, was appointed Prime Minister. In March 1981 the offices of the President of the Republic and the Chief of Staff of the Armed Forces were formally separated.

In August 1982 the Assembléia da República approved the final draft of the new Constitution, which completed the transition to full civilian government. Following divisions within the PSD, and losses at local elections in December, Balsemão resigned as Prime Minister. In addition, the Deputy Prime Minister and leader of the CDS, Prof. Diogo Freitas do Amaral, resigned from all party and political posts. In February 1983 Mota Pinto became leader of the PSD. At an early general election, held in April, the PS won 101 of the 250 seats. Soares formed a coalition Government with the PSD (the AD having been dissolved).

In February 1985 Mota Pinto resigned as leader of the PSD, and subsequently as Deputy Prime Minister and Minister of Defence, and was replaced by Rui Machete, the Minister of Justice. In May Machete was replaced as party leader by Prof. Aníbal Cavaco Silva, a former Minister of Finance. In June, on the day after Portugal signed its treaty of accession to the European Community (EC, now European Union—EU, see

p. 281), the PS-PSD coalition disintegrated. Eanes called a general election for October, at which the PSD won 88 seats, while the PS won 57 seats and the Partido Renovador Democrático (PRD, a new party founded in early 1985 by supporters of President Eanes) secured 45 seats. Cavaco Silva was able to form a minority PSD-led Government.

During the mid-1980s a number of terrorist attacks were perpetrated by the radical left-wing group Forças Populares 25 de Abril (FP-25) and other groups. Targets included both Portuguese and foreign business interests, installations of the North Atlantic Treaty Organization (NATO, see p. 380) and the US embassy in Lisbon. In July 1985 the trial opened of more than 70 alleged members of FP-25—including Lt-Col Otelo Saraiva de Carvalho, the former revolutionary commander—but was adjourned owing to the fatal shooting of a key prosecution witness. The trial later resumed and, in May 1987, Saraiva de Carvalho was found guilty of subversion and sentenced to 15 years' imprisonment (subsequently increased to 18 years). In March 1996, following a personal initiative by President Soares, the Assembléia da República approved a pardon for Saraiva de Carvalho and other members of FP-25.

Four candidates contested the January 1986 presidential election. As no candidate achieved the requisite 50% majority, a second round of voting was held in February: Mário Soares narrowly defeated Freitas do Amaral, former leader of the CDS, to become Portugal's first civilian President for 60 years.

Cavaco Silva's minority Government encountered difficulties in securing the adoption of reformist legislation. In April 1987 the Prime Minister resigned, following his defeat in a motion of censure. At an early general election in July the PSD secured 148 seats in the Assembléia da República, becoming the first party since 1974 to win an absolute majority. The PS won 60 seats, and the Coligação Democrático Unitária (CDU, a new left-wing coalition comprising the PCP and the ecologist Partido Ecologista 'Os Verdes' and also known as the PCP-PEV) won 31 seats. Cavaco Silva was reappointed as Prime Minister and announced a programme of radical economic reform, which included the partial privatization of state-owned companies. A controversial bill to reform the restrictive labour laws was approved by the Assembléia da República in April, despite mass public protests; in the following month, however, the Constitutional Court ruled that the new legislation was unconstitutional. The legislation was also approved by the President in February 1989, although labour unrest persisted and amendments removing Marxist elements from the Constitution entered into force in August.

Soares was decisively re-elected President in January 1991. At legislative elections in October the PSD renewed its absolute majority, winning 135 of the 230 seats (reduced from 250) in the Assembléia da República. The PS secured 72 seats, the CDU won 17 and the CDS five. During 1992 tension between Soares and Cavaco Silva became more evident, owing to the President's increasingly frequent use of his power of veto in order to obstruct the passage of legislation.

The Government of António Guterres: 1995–2002

At legislative elections in October 1995 the PS won 112 of the 230 seats in the Assembléia da República. The PSD won 88 seats, the Centro Democrático Social-Partido Popular (CDS-PP—formerly the CDS) 15 and the CDU also 15. The Secretary-General of the PS, António Guterres, was appointed Prime Minister, leading a minority administration that incorporated several non-party ministers. At the presidential election in January 1996, Cavaco Silva was defeated by Jorge Sampaio, the former Mayor of Lisbon and erstwhile leader of the PS, who took office in March.

In August 1996 Guterres announced proposals for radical reform of the country's political system. The opening of electoral lists to independent citizens (thus ending the monopoly of the major parties) and provision for the holding of referendums on issues of national interest were among the changes envisaged. In early 1997 the ruling PS and the opposition PSD reached a broad consensus on these proposals, also agreeing upon the gradual establishment of a professional army and a reduction in compulsory military service. In September the Assembléia da República gave its approval to the reforms.

In February 1997, in a free vote, the Assembléia da República narrowly rejected proposals to liberalize the country's abortion law. The issue aroused bitter controversy, and created a deep division within the PS. However, in February of the following year the legislature voted by a narrow margin to relax the law. At a referendum in June some 51% of voters favoured the liberalization of the law, although the result was declared null and void, owing to the low rate of participation. Guterres suffered a setback in November when another referendum, on government proposals to divide mainland Portugal into eight administrative regions, each with a proposed elected local assembly and regional president, was rejected by 64% of participants. However, owing once again to a low participation rate, the result of this referendum was also declared invalid.

At the general election in October 1999 the PS secured 115 of the 230 seats in the Assembléia da República, while the PSD won 81 seats and the CDU 17 seats (including two seats allocated to the ecologist PEV). The recently established Bloco de Esquerda (BE), a militant left-wing grouping, unexpectedly obtained two seats. Thus, one seat short of an absolute majority, Guterres was returned to office. In November the incoming Government announced a programme of reforms aimed at narrowing the disparity between Portugal and the more developed member states of the EU. At a presidential election in January 2001 Sampaio was re-elected for a second term, obtaining 55.8% of the votes cast and defeating four other candidates.

Following municipal elections in December 2001, at which the PS suffered significant losses, Guterres resigned both as Prime Minister and as leader of the PS. The poor electoral results were widely attributed to a decline in the economy and to discontent with public services, which had been adversely affected by reductions in government expenditure. Guterres was replaced as Secretary-General of the PS by Eduardo Ferro Rodrigues. At an early general election in March 2002 the PSD, whose campaign had featured reductions in corporate taxation and public expenditure and the privatization of state services, won 105 seats in the Assembléia da República. The PS secured 96 seats, the CDS-PP 14 seats, the CDU alliance 12 and the BE three seats. The PSD leader, José Manuel Durão Barroso, was appointed Prime Minister and formed a centre-right coalition Government with the CDS-PP.

PSD-led Government: 2002–05

Durão Barroso's Government announced its intention to introduce austerity measures to counter the large public deficit, which contravened the country's obligations under the regulations for the European single currency. In mid-2002 the Government proposed a new labour code designed to increase the ease of recruitment and dismissal of staff and limit the power of the unions. In late 2002 two public sector one-day general strikes, involving up to 500,000 workers, were organized to protest against the measures.

In May 2003 Paolo Pedroso, the deputy leader and parliamentary spokesman of the PS, was arrested in connection with a child abuse scandal surrounding the Casa Pia children's homes. Several other establishment figures had been arrested earlier that year. Throughout his custody Pedroso maintained that the allegations against him were part of a PSD plot to discredit him. He was charged in December (with nine other prominent figures) on 23 counts of sexual abuse, although the charges against him were later dropped. (In September 2008 Pedroso was awarded damages of around €100,000, following a civil court case in which the judge ruled that his arrest and subsequent imprisonment constituted a 'grave error'.) Seven defendants in the Casa Pia case went on trial in late 2004; all were found guilty in September 2010. Meanwhile, the Government established a tribunal to consider compensation claims brought by victims of abuse at Casa Pia orphanages, which in March 2006 awarded a total of more than €50m. to 44 claimants.

In June 2004 Durão Barroso was unexpectedly invited to take over the role of President of the European Commission in October. In order to accept this appointment, Durão Barroso resigned as leader of the PSD, and as Prime Minister on 5 July; the populist Mayor of Lisbon and Secretary-General of the PSD, Pedro Santana Lopes, was elected as his successor.

In November 2004 directors and a prominent newscaster resigned from the state broadcasting company, Radiotelevisão Portuguesa (RTP), in protest at perceived pressure from the Government. The state media authority criticized the Government for attempting to limit RTP's freedom. Later that month President Sampaio informed Santana Lopes of his decision to dissolve parliament and call legislative elections. Prior to the dissolution, the President permitted time for the adoption of the 2005 budget. However, the expansionary budget, which was approved by the Assembléia da República in early December, proved controversial as it contained tax reductions and increases in the state pension that were likely to cause Portugal to breach the budget deficit limit (equivalent to 3% of gross domestic product—GDP) specified in the EU's Stability and Growth Pact.

At the elections in February 2005, the PS, which during the campaign had advocated institutional reform and policies to increase economic growth, won an outright majority, securing 121 seats in the Assembléia da República, with 45.0% of the votes cast; the CDU and the BE also performed well at the expense of the right. The PSD won 75 seats, while its junior partner in the previous Government, the CDS-PP, won 12 seats. Santana Lopes and Portas resigned as leader of the PSD and the CDS-PP, respectively. Luís Marques Mendes was subsequently elected leader of the PSD, while José Ribeiro e Castro became President of the CDS-PP.

The first Government of José Sócrates: 2005–09
A new 16-member Council of Ministers, headed by Sócrates, took office in March 2005. It included an equal number of PS members and independents, most notably former CDS leader Freitas do Amaral, who had been an outspoken critic of the US-led invasion of Iraq in 2003, as Minister of Foreign Affairs. Another independent, and former deputy governor of the Banco de Portugal, Luís Campos e Cunha, was allocated the finance portfolio.

On taking office the new Government adopted a policy of strict economic austerity in an effort to reduce the budget deficit, which was forecast to be considerably higher than the EU limit of 3% of GDP. Disagreements arose between Campos e Cunha and Sócrates, however, and the Minister of Finance resigned in July 2005; he was replaced by Fernando Teixeira dos Santos of the PS. Plans to increase value-added tax (VAT) and reduce government expenditure, notably on social security, led to a series of protests and strikes by public sector employees. A one-day general strike in July, observed by an estimated 500,000 workers, was followed, in September and October, by protests and industrial action staged by employees in various sectors. In November, and again in February 2006, public sector workers participated in large-scale protests against the reduction in social welfare benefits, a wage freeze and the raising of the retirement age.

Six candidates contested the presidential election on 22 January 2006, including former President Soares and former Prime Minister Cavaco Silva. (Sampaio was not eligible to stand for a third term.) Cavaco Silva narrowly won an overall majority (with 50.5% of the valid votes cast), and took office on 9 March, the first centre-right President since the coup of 1974.

In November 2006 the draft budget for 2007 was approved in the Assembléia da República with the sole support of the PS. All other parties opposed the budget, which included significant reductions in public expenditure, to be largely financed by a reform of public administration. The public sector trade unions organized a two-day strike to coincide with the passage of the legislation. A similar demonstration was organized by one of the principal trade union federations, the Confederação Geral dos Trabalhadores Portugueses-Intersindical Nacional (CGTP—General Confederation of Portuguese Workers) in October. In January 2007 the Government began negotiations with trade unions over the reform of labour legislation. The trade unions expressed vehement opposition to the proposals, which were likely to entail significant reductions in the number of civil servants. In June the Government approved a new system of remuneration and career progression for civil servants, despite ongoing opposition from the CGTP.

In a referendum held in February 2007, 59.2% of those voting approved plans to legalize abortion (hitherto permitted only in restricted circumstances) for all women up to the 10th week of pregnancy; however, only 43.6% of the electorate participated in the poll, below the 50% needed to make the result legally binding. None the less, Sócrates declared that the result represented a mandate for reform. Legislation providing for decriminalization was adopted by the Assembléia da República in March and, after receiving presidential approval in April, entered into force in July.

In September 2007 Luís Filipe Menezes was elected leader of the PSD, narrowly defeating the incumbent, Marques Mendes. However, Menezes resigned after only seven months in the post, citing ongoing disagreements within the PSD. Manuela Ferreira Leite, the former Minister of State and of Finance, was elected to succeed him as party leader in May 2008.

Relations between the two main parties deteriorated in 2009 as the PS and the PSD began preparations for the forthcoming general election. In January the Prime Minister accused his opponents of seeking to discredit him, following media reports linking him with an investigation into alleged financial improprieties related to the construction of a shopping centre on land in an environmental protection zone in Alcochete, near Lisbon;

Sócrates, who was Minister of the Environment and Territorial Planning at the time of the affair in 2002, denied any impropriety. The Government was further embarrassed in July when Manuel Pinho was forced to resign as Minister of the Economy and Innovation, after he had caused outrage by making an offensive gesture towards a PCP deputy during a debate in the Assembléia da República.

The re-election of Sócrates in 2009
At the general election on 27 September 2009 the PS remained the largest party in the Assembléia da República, but lost its majority, winning 97 of the 230 seats with 37.7% of the votes cast. The other parties all increased their representation: the PSD won 30.0% of the votes and took 81 seats, while the CDS-PP took 21 seats, the BE 16 and the CDU 15. Following unsuccessful negotiations with other parties on the formation of a coalition, Sócrates formed a minority administration, which, like the previous Government, contained an equal number of PS members and independents. Most of the senior ministers remained in their posts. In response to her party's poor performance in the general and local elections, Ferreira Leite resigned the PSD leadership; Pedro Passos Coelho was elected to succeed her.

On taking office for a second term, Sócrates declared that his administration would continue its policy of public investment in order to counteract the effects of the global economic crisis, confirming plans to invest some €60,000m. in infrastructure over the following decade. However, by early 2010 concerns in international financial markets over the size of Portugal's budget deficit (which was equivalent to 9.4% of GDP in 2009) had forced the Government to emphasize measures to reduce public spending. In February the Government was defeated in the Assembléia da República over amendments to a regional finance bill proposed by the opposition that would allow the autonomous regional governments of the Azores and Madeira to increase their levels of debt. Despite government concerns that the measures would undermine efforts to reduce the deficit and damage Portugal's international financial credibility, amendments were adopted later in February after storms and flooding caused severe damage on Madeira. In March public sector workers took part in a one-day strike in protest at austerity measures in the proposed budget, including a freeze on salaries. None the less, the budget received parliamentary approval later in the month after the PSD abstained.

Meanwhile, in February 2010 the Assembléia da República approved legislation to allow persons of the same sex to marry, while preventing married same-sex couples from adopting children. In January, at the bill's first reading, the legislature had rejected demands by the PSD that the question be decided by a referendum. In March President Cavaco Silva, who had made known his opposition to the bill, referred it to the Constitutional Court, which in April ruled that the legislation did not violate the Constitution. Despite speculation that the President might refuse to sign the bill, in May Cavaco Silva signed it into law, stating that he did not wish to distract the legislature's attention from the economic crisis.

Recent developments: the EU and IMF bail-out
In May 2010 the Government proposed new austerity measures including increases in VAT, income tax and corporate tax. Planned major infrastructure improvements, including a new Lisbon airport, were postponed. The PSD agreed to support the necessary legislation, and later in May a motion of censure proposed by the PCP, in protest at the plans, was defeated. Nevertheless, in the course of the year there was persistent speculation that Portugal would become the third member of the euro area (after Greece, in May, and Ireland, in November) to require emergency assistance from the EU and the IMF in order to avoid defaulting on its debts. This was repeatedly denied by the Government, which pointed out that its budgetary deficit and state debt were not as large as those of Greece and Ireland, and that, unlike in Ireland, there had been no crisis in the Portuguese banking sector, requiring massive government support. However, the international financial markets' lack of confidence in the Portuguese economy meant that the cost of borrowing reached record levels by the end of the year. In its budget for 2011, the Government proposed a third set of austerity measures, aiming to reduce the budget deficit to the equivalent of 4.5% of GDP in 2011, through tax increases (including raising VAT to 23%) and further reductions in public spending, notably on public sector pay, state pensions and family benefits. After some of its demands for less extensive tax increases had been met, the PSD agreed to abstain in the legislative vote on the

budget, which was duly adopted after a one-day general strike organized by the CGTP in protest at the proposals and at the resulting likelihood of an increase in the record levels of unemployment.

At the presidential election on 23 January 2011 the incumbent Cavaco Silva secured an easy victory, winning 53.0% of the valid votes cast, while his nearest rival, Manuel Alegre of the PS, secured 19.8%: only 46.5% of the electorate participated. The Bank of Portugal predicted that the economy would again fall into recession in 2011, and the cost to Portugal of borrowing on the international markets increased to levels that were widely regarded as unsustainable. Divisions within the legislature about the best way to respond to the economic crisis led to a climate of political instability, which contributed to the downgrading of Portugal's credit rating on the international markets, which, in turn, led to further increases in the country's borrowing costs. In March, in its fourth austerity programme in less than one year, the Government proposed yet more reductions in public spending. On this occasion, however, it did not first consult either the opposition parties or the President, and the proposals were defeated in the Assembléia da República. On 23 March Sócrates resigned, but remained as a caretaker Prime Minister, pending an early general election. On 7 April 2011 Portugal made a formal request for financial assistance from the EU and the IMF, which was approved on 16 May. Portugal was to receive emergency loans of €78,000m., of which about one-third was to be provided by the IMF. The country thus became the third nation in the euro area, after Greece and Ireland, to receive an EU-IMF bail-out in order to avert major economic catastrophe. The three-year agreement was conditional upon the imposition of yet further extensive austerity measures, intended to reduce the budget deficit from 9.8% of GDP in 2010 to 3% by 2013. These measures included significant reductions in expenditure on health and education, and in public sector pay and pensions, the reform of the country's public administration, and the implementation of an extensive privatization programme, that aimed to raise revenue totalling €5,500m.

At the general election on 5 June 2011 the centre-right PSD led by Passos Coelho won 40.3% of votes and 108 seats in the Assembléia da República. The PS secured 29.2% of the votes and 74 seats, representing a loss of 23 seats for the party. The CDS-PP increased its representation to 24 seats, the CDU secured 16 and the BE took just eight. The participation rate was the lowest on record at a legislative election in the country at 58.0% of eligible voters. In recognition of his party's defeat Sócrates immediately resigned as leader of the PS. President Cavaco Silva asked Passos Coelho to form a government with 'consistent majority support' in the legislature; the PSD subsequently formed a coalition with its traditional ally the conservative CDS-PP and four independent members. Passos Coelho and his 11-member Council of Ministers (only four of whom originated from his own party) were sworn in on 21 June.

The implementation of a wide range of austerity measures during 2011 resulted in a series of protests, including a one-day general strike in November and a rare protest rally by the armed forces. Despite the strict economic policies, some observers expressed concern at the apparent lack of progress in reducing the budget deficit or in reversing the contraction of GDP. The situation was compounded by the revelation in late 2011 that Madeira had underreported its debt since 2004 and a further €1,100m. was consequently added to the country's total debt for 2011. In November the Assembléia da República approved an austerity budget for 2012 that included severe reductions in the pay and pensions of public sector workers and substantial increases in taxes on energy. Popular protests against the measures continued during early 2012 with industrial action organized by the CGTP, demonstrations by some 400,000 people in Lisbon and Oporto, and defiance of the Government's cancellation of the country's famous Mardi Gras celebrations. In May the Government took the highly unusual decision to suspend four further public holidays from 2013 for at least five years, in an attempt to increase economic activity.

In September 2012 Passos Coelho agreed not to proceed with social security reforms, following intense opposition from the trade unions and the largest anti-austerity demonstrations of his tenure. Further protests and a general strike in November caused major disruption across the country and resulted in clashes with security forces in Lisbon, in which around 50 people were injured. The proposed budget for 2013 was opposed by every opposition party when it was debated in the Assembléia da República in November 2012. Several thousand demonstrators protested outside the parliament building against the proposals, which included substantial increases in income tax, further reductions in public spending and the sale of a wide range of state-owned companies. The Government maintained that without the measures the deficit would exceed its target of 5% of GDP as part of the terms of its EU-IMF bail-out agreement. The budget was approved by a narrow majority and signed into law by President Cavaco Silva on 31 December. However, on the following day, during his New Year address, the President announced that he was to take the highly unusual step of referring the budget to the constitutional court. Cavaco Silva, who claimed that the country was in a vicious cycle of austerity and recession, asked the court in particular to decide whether the tax increases were fairly distributed across all sectors of Portuguese society. Following the court's ruling in early April 2013 that certain measures could not be implemented, Passos Coelho announced that the Government would need to seek other ways to reduce the deficit.

One of the most notable effects of the economic situation was the increase in emigration, particularly among young people in search of employment. The rate of unemployment among those between the ages of 16 and 25 years was estimated at about 40% in early 2013, compared with some 16% for the population as a whole. Many of the estimated 240,000 people (equivalent to some 2% of the population) who left the country between 2011 and the beginning of 2013 were believed to have sought work opportunities in Portugal's former colonies in Africa and in Brazil.

Foreign Affairs

Regional relations

Portugal became a member of the European Community (EC, now European Union—EU, see p. 281) in January 1986, and participated in the introduction of the European single currency, the euro, on 1 January 1999. The EU Treaty establishing a Constitution for Europe was signed by the EU heads of state and of government in October 2004. In March 2005 the new PS administration announced its intention to hold a referendum on the EU constitutional treaty in October, after seeking the necessary constitutional amendment. However, following the rejection of the treaty in referendums in France and the Netherlands, in June 2005 the Portuguese Government postponed its own national referendum. The constitutional treaty was subsequently abandoned and, shortly after Portugal assumed the six-month rotating Presidency of the Council of the European Union, an Intergovernmental Conference was convened in Lisbon in July 2007 to draft a replacement. The resulting Treaty of Lisbon amending the Treaty on European Union and the Treaty establishing the European Community, which retained many of the provisions of the constitutional treaty (although it amended existing treaties rather than replacing them), was signed by EU leaders in December. In January 2008 Sócrates announced that the treaty was to be ratified by parliamentary vote in Portugal, rather than by a national referendum, as had been promised for the constitutional treaty. It was speculated that the Prime Minister had come under pressure from other European leaders who feared that a referendum in Portugal might jeopardize the ratification process in their own countries. The treaty was ratified by the Assembléia da República in April and received presidential approval in May; it entered into force in December 2009 following ratification by all 27 EU member states. In May 2011 Portugal became the third member of the euro area (after Greece and Ireland) to receive emergency assistance under the EU's financial stability mechanism, in order to avoid defaulting on its debts. In April 2012 Portugal became the first country to ratify the EU's 'fiscal compact', which it had signed in the previous month; this required members to adopt binding legislation on balancing their budgets. The deadline for meeting the agreed terms of the compact was extended for another year in early 2013.

Other external relations

Negotiations with the People's Republic of China on the question of the Portuguese overseas territory of Macao commenced in June 1986, and in April 1987 Portugal and China signed an agreement whereby Portugal would transfer the administration of Macao to China in December 1999. On 19 December 1999 the sovereignty of Macao was duly transferred (see Macao). In November 2010, during a state visit to Portugal by President Hu Jintao, China agreed to purchase Portuguese government bonds, and the two countries undertook to increase mutual trade and to conduct joint ventures, particularly in Portugal's former colonies of Angola and Mozambique.

The former Portuguese territory of Timor-Leste (East Timor) was unilaterally annexed by Indonesia in 1976. UN-sponsored negotiations between Portugal and Indonesia began in 1983, but proved inconclusive. Similarly, under UN auspices, talks on the Timor-Leste issue resumed in 1992, but again ended without agreement. In 1995 Portugal and Indonesia agreed to allow the UN to oversee talks between the factions of Timor-Leste. In August 1998, following a change of presidency in Indonesia and the country's subsequent troop withdrawals from the disputed region, the UN Secretary-General announced that Portugal and Indonesia would resume discussions on Timor-Leste. In March 1999 Portugal and Indonesia reached agreement on the holding of a referendum in the territory on the question of either autonomy or independence. The referendum in August resulted in an overwhelming endorsement of proposals for full independence for Timor-Leste. The result, however, prompted a rapid decline in the security situation, leading to the declaration of martial law in the territory and the deployment in mid-September of a multinational peace-keeping force, led by Australia. Following the restoration of order in Timor-Leste and the Indonesian Government's acceptance of the result of the referendum, in December 1999 Portugal and Indonesia resumed full diplomatic relations, which had been severed in 1975. Meanwhile, Portugal committed an initial 700 troops to the UN peace-keeping force that replaced the Australian-led force in early 2000 and pledged an annual sum of US $75m. towards the reconstruction of Timor-Leste. Official diplomatic relations with Timor-Leste were established with the creation of an embassy in Lisbon in 2002. Following a resurgence in violence in mid-June 2006 some 120 members of the National Republican Guard were dispatched to Timor-Leste. Portugal also contributed security personnel to the UN Integrated Mission in Timor-Leste, which was established in August.

Portugal played a significant role in the peace process in Angola, a former Portuguese overseas possession. Several meetings between representatives of the Angolan Government and the União Nacional para a Independência Total de Angola (UNITA) rebel group were held in Lisbon, culminating in the signing of a peace accord in 1991. However, in June 1993, following the resumption of hostilities, UNITA rejected Portugal's status as an observer in the new peace process. A new peace agreement was signed in November 1994. Following renewed hostilities in Angola, UNITA severed its links with Portugal and the other observers in the peace process in mid-1998, accusing them of bias towards the Angolan Government. Tensions between Angola and Portugal increased in 2000, following comments by the Angolan Minister of Social Communication, accusing the former Portuguese President, Mario Soares, and his son, João, of benefiting from UNITA's illegal trade in diamonds. The allegations were strongly denied by UNITA. Following the cessation of hostilities in Angola in April 2002, Portugal agreed to continue with military support, including overseeing the integration of UNITA soldiers into new armed forces.

Portugal was also involved in attempts to reach a peace settlement in Mozambique. Relations with Mozambique deteriorated in March 1989, however, when a Mozambican diplomat was expelled from Portugal, following his implication in the assassination, in April 1988, of a Mozambican resistance leader. Nevertheless, in January 1992 Portugal was invited to attend the peace talks as an observer, and in October a peace treaty was signed in Italy.

In July 1996 Portugal hosted the inaugural meeting of the Comunidade dos Países de Língua Portuguesa (CPLP, see p. 475), a grouping of lusophone countries (including Angola, Brazil, Mozambique and Guinea-Bissau), which aimed to promote closer political and economic co-operation. In late 1998, as part of a CPLP initiative, Portugal played a major role in the implementation of a peace agreement in Guinea-Bissau, ending several months of conflict between government and rebel forces in the former colony. In the aftermath of a coup in May 1999, the deposed President of Guinea-Bissau, João Vieira, was granted asylum in Portugal. Moreover, following a further coup in September 2003, the Portuguese Government provided US $1.5m. in aid to the new Government. New Portuguese legislation on immigration, effective from August 2007, aimed, *inter alia*, to integrate foreign workers by facilitating the granting of residence permits to undocumented migrants, the majority of whom came from Brazil and lusophone African countries.

Support for the proposed US-led military campaign to remove the regime of Saddam Hussain in Iraq by the Prime Minister, Durão Barroso, provoked strong opposition from rival politicians, including President Sampaio, and public disapproval in early 2003. In January the Government authorized the USA to use the Lajes airbase in the Azores in the event of war and affirmed its support for the proposed military action in Iraq, with or without a UN mandate. In March, Durão Barroso hosted an emergency summit between the leaders of the USA, the United Kingdom and Spain. However, following the rejection by the UN Security Council of a resolution endorsing military action against Iraq, a compromise on Portugal's stance was announced by Sampaio: Portuguese troops would not participate in the conflict, although transit facilities would be made available for use by coalition forces. The Government defeated motions of censure submitted to the Assembléia da República in March by the four left-wing opposition parties. In November some 120 members of the paramilitary National Republican Guard were sent to Iraq. The contingent returned to Portugal in February 2005, following democratic elections in Iraq.

In mid-2005 Portuguese troops were deployed in Afghanistan as part of the NATO-led International Security Assistance Force (ISAF). In March 2013 there were 141 Portuguese troops stationed in the country.

In November 2011 Prime Minister Passos Coelho made an official visit to Angola in response to Angola's programme of investment in Portugal. Angola, which had become Portugal's most important trading partner outside the EU, had invested a total of US $156m. in Portugal in 2009 (a dramatic increase compared with a figure of $2.1m. in 2002). However, some observers warned the Portuguese Government to exercise caution in accepting finance from that country because of its poor record on corruption. Portugal's programme of economic reforms, particularly its aim of privatizing state assets, prompted a similar visit to Mozambique in April 2012 when the Government ended a long-running dispute with the country by agreeing to sell its remaining stake in the Cahora Bassa hydroelectric dam plant. Ongoing economic difficulties in Portugal, particularly unemployment, resulted in an influx of migrants from that country to Angola. By late 2012 Portuguese nationals residing in Angola were believed to total more than 130,000, a dramatic increase compared with the estimated 20,000 residing in the country in 2003.

CONSTITUTION AND GOVERNMENT

A new Constitution, envisaging the construction of a socialist society in Portugal, was promulgated in 1976 and revised in 1982, when ideological elements were diminished. Subsequent revisions included the provision in 1997 for the holding of referendums on issues of national interest. The organs of sovereignty are the President, the Assembléia da República and the Government. The President, elected by popular vote for a five-year term, appoints the Prime Minister and, on the latter's proposal, other members of the Government, principally the Council of Ministers. The Council of State (Conselho de Estado) is a consultative body. The unicameral Assembléia has 230 members, including four representing Portuguese citizens abroad, elected by universal adult suffrage for four years (subject to dissolution). The mainland comprises 18 administrative districts. The Azores and Madeira (integral parts of the Portuguese Republic) were granted autonomy in 1976.

REGIONAL AND INTERNATIONAL CO-OPERATION

Portugal is a member of the European Union (EU, see p. 281), the Council of Europe (see p. 260) and the Organization for Security and Co-operation in Europe (OSCE, see p. 397).

Portugal joined the UN in 1955; it was elected as a non-permanent member of the Security Council for the period 2011–12. As a contracting party to the General Agreement on Tariffs and Trade, it joined the World Trade Organization (WTO, see p. 444) on its establishment in 1995. Portugal was a founding member of the North Atlantic Treaty Organization (NATO, see p. 380) and is a member of the Organisation for Economic Co-operation and Development (OECD, see p. 388) and the Comunidade dos Países de Língua Portuguesa (CPLP, see p. 475), which has its headquarters in Lisbon.

ECONOMIC AFFAIRS

In 2011, according to estimates by the World Bank, Portugal's overall gross national income (GNI), measured at average 2009–11 prices, was US $226,021m., equivalent to $21,250 per head (or

$24,480 on an international purchasing-power parity basis). During 2002–11, it was estimated, the population increased at an average rate of 0.3% per year, while gross domestic product (GDP) per head decreased, in real terms, by an average of 0.1% per year. According to the World Bank, overall GDP expanded, in real terms, at an average annual rate of 0.2% in 2002–11; in 2010 GDP increased by 1.4%, but decreased by 1.6%, measured at constant prices. According to chain-linked methodologies, GDP increased by 1.9% in 2010, but decreased by 1.6% in 2011.

Agriculture (including forestry and fishing) contributed an estimated 2.2% of GDP in 2011, and engaged 10.5% of the employed labour force in 2012. The principal crops are grapes, tomatoes, potatoes, maize, sugar beet, olives, wheat, pears, apples and oranges. The production of wine, particularly port, is significant. The fishing industry is important; the sardine catch, at 63,800 metric tons in 2010, being by far the largest. According to World Bank figures, agricultural GDP declined, in real terms, by an average of 0.4% during 2002–10. According to chain-linked methodologies, agricultural GDP increased by 0.6% in 2011.

Industry (comprising mining, manufacturing, construction and power) contributed an estimated 23.9% of GDP in 2011 and engaged 25.6% of the employed labour force in 2012. According to World Bank figures, the GDP of the industrial sector decreased, in real terms, by an average of 1.2% during 2002–10; industrial GDP decreased by 7.9% in 2009, but increased by 1.0% in 2010. The mining and quarrying industry makes a minimal contribution to GDP, engaging just 0.3% of the employed labour force in 2012. Limestone, granite, marble, copper pyrites, gold and uranium are the most significant products.

Manufacturing provided 14.5% of GDP in 2011, and engaged 16.6% of the employed labour force in 2012. According to the World Bank, manufacturing GDP decreased by 0.7% in 2002–10; manufacturing GDP decreased by 8.7% in 2009, and by 2.6% in 2010. The textile industry is the most important branch of manufacturing. Basic manufactures accounted for 22.3% of total export earnings in 2010. Other significant manufactured products include cork items, chemicals, electrical appliances, ceramics and paper pulp.

Construction provided 5.7% of GDP in 2011, and engaged 7.7% of the employed labour force in 2012. According to chain-linked methodologies, GDP of the construction sector declined by 9.7% in 2011.

In 2010 13.6% of electricity production was derived from coal, 28.1% from natural gas, 30.7% from hydroelectric power and 4.4% from petroleum. In 2010 imports of mineral fuels accounted for 14.3% of total import costs. Portugal's heavy dependence on petroleum was reduced in 1997 when a pipeline carrying natural gas from Algeria (via Morocco and Spain) was inaugurated. Investment in renewable energy sources has increased significantly during recent years, in accordance with the Government's aim to produce some 60% of Portugal's energy from renewable sources by 2020. In January 2007 the construction of an 11-MW solar power plant was completed in Serpa, some 200 km southeast of Lisbon; a photovoltaic plant at Moura, in the southern region of Alentejo, which was to be the largest in the world, was connected to the grid at the end of 2008. The use of wind power expanded the 2000s. In addition, a commercial wave-energy project was under way off the coast of northern Portugal. In February 2009 an agreement was signed between Energias de Portugal and the US-based Principle Power to generate electricity from wind turbines off the Portuguese coast.

Services provided 73.9% of GDP in 2011 and engaged 63.9% of the employed labour force in 2012. The tourism industry remained a significant source of foreign exchange earnings in 2011, when receipts (excluding passenger transport) totalled an estimated US $11,339m. In 2010 there were some 6.8m. tourist arrivals in Portugal. Emigrants' remittances are also important to the Portuguese economy. According to World Bank figures, the GDP of the services sector increased, in real terms, by an estimated average of 1.4% per year during 2002–10; services GDP decreased by 0.5% in 2009, but increased by 1.6% in 2010.

In 2011 Portugal recorded a visible merchandise trade deficit of US $18,461.8m., and there was a deficit of $15,539.4m. on the current account of the balance of payments. Most of Portugal's trade is with other members of the European Union (EU, see p. 281). In 2011 Spain (providing 32.3% of total imports) was the main source of imports; other major suppliers were Germany, France (including Monaco), Italy and the Netherlands. The principal export market was also Spain (which contributed 24.9% of the total exports) in that year; other major purchasers were Germany, France (including Monaco), the United Kingdom and Angola. The main exports in 2011 were machinery and electrical equipment, vehicles and transport equipment, textile goods, mineral products, base metals and articles of base metal, plastic goods, prepared foodstuffs, beverages, tobacco and manufactured substitutes, chemical products, and pulp wood and fibrous materials. The principal imports were mineral products, machinery and electrical equipment, vehicles and transport equipment, chemical products, base metals and articles of base metal, textile goods, plastic goods, and live animals and animal products.

The central government budget deficit for 2011 was estimated at €7,506.2m., equivalent to 4.4% of GDP. In 2011 Portugal's general gross government debt was estimated at €184,291m., equivalent to 107.8% of GDP. In 2002–11 the annual rate of inflation averaged 2.2%. Consumer prices rose by an average of 3.7% in 2011. The unemployment rate averaged 15.7% in 2012.

Following a period of slow economic growth during the 2000s, the Portuguese economy officially entered recession at the end of 2008, owing to the effects of the global economic crisis. GDP declined by 2.7% in 2009, and general government debt increased significantly in that year, reaching 93.3% of GDP in 2010. A series of austerity measures was introduced, including below-inflation increases in public sector salaries, the postponement of planned investment in transport infrastructure, increases in corporate tax, income tax and value-added tax (VAT). However, these unpopular measures failed to reduce the budget deficit sufficiently. Uncertainty on the international financial markets about Portugal's ability to pay its debts led to successive downgradings of its sovereign credit rating, and the cost of borrowing consequently increased such that by early 2011 government bond yields (i.e. the interest on debt) were in excess of 8%, regarded as an unsustainable level. In April, following the rejection by the legislature of further austerity measures, and the resignation of the Prime Minister, the caretaker Government was finally obliged to request emergency assistance from the EU and the IMF. A three-year programme of loans valued at €78,000m., approved by the EU and IMF in May, was conditional upon the adoption of new economic adjustment measures, including a major reorganization of the public sector and an extensive programme of privatization, with the aim of reducing the budget deficit to 3% of GDP by 2013. Portugal's GDP contracted by 1.6% in 2011 and by a further 3.2% in 2012. A decline of 1.9% was forecast for 2013. A similarly severe austerity budget was approved for 2013, but some of the controversial measures it contained, including substantial tax increases, were subsequently referred to the constitutional court by President Cavaco Silva as potentially unconstitutional (see Domestic Political Affairs). Meanwhile, the budget deficit and public debt remained alarmingly high at an estimated 6.6% and 119.1% of GDP, respectively in 2012. The rate of unemployment reached 16% in early 2013 and was forecast to increase to more than 18% during the year, with young people particularly badly affected by the lack of employment opportunities in the country. In early 2013 the Government negotiated with its EU and IMF creditors to extend the deadline for meeting its agreed fiscal targets by one more year.

PUBLIC HOLIDAYS

2014*: 1 January (New Year's Day), 4 March (Carnival Day)†, 18 April (Good Friday), 25 April (Liberty Day), 1 May (Labour Day), 10 June (Portugal Day), 13 June (St Anthony—Lisbon only)†, 24 June (St John the Baptist—Oporto only)†, 15 August (Assumption), 8 December (Immaculate Conception), 25 December (Christmas Day).

* In 2012 agreement was reached between the Government, the Vatican, employers and trade unions for four public holidays (two religious: Corpus Christi and All Saints' Day, and two secular: Proclamation of the Republic and Restoration of Independence) to be suspended until 2017.

† Optional.

Statistical Survey

Source (unless otherwise stated): Instituto Nacional de Estatística (INE), Av. António José de Almeida 2, 1000-043 Lisbon; tel. (21) 8426100; fax (21) 8426380; e-mail ine@ine.pt; internet www.ine.pt.

Area and Population

AREA, POPULATION AND DENSITY

Area (sq km)	
Land	91,906
Inland water	439
Total	92,345*
Population (census results)	
1 March 2001	10,356,117
21 March 2011	
Males	5,046,600
Females	5,515,578
Total	10,562,178
Density (per sq km) at 2011 census	114.9

* 35,655 sq miles.

POPULATION BY AGE AND SEX
(2011 census)

	Males	Females	Total
0–14	803,999	768,330	1,572,329
15–64	3,400,277	3,579,508	6,979,785
65 and over	842,324	1,167,740	2,010,064
Total	**5,046,600**	**5,515,578**	**10,562,178**

REGIONS
(population at 2011 census)

	Area (sq km)*	Population	Density (per sq km)
Continental Portugal	88,796	10,047,621	113.2
Norte	21,278	3,689,682	173.4
Centro	23,668	2,327,755	98.4
Lisboa e Vale do Tejo . . .	11,931	2,821,876	236.5
Alentejo	26,931	757,302	28.1
Algarve	4,988	451,006	90.4
Autonomous Regions	3,109	514,557	165.5
Os Açores (Azores)	2,330	246,772	105.9
Madeira	779	267,785	343.8
Total	**91,906**	**10,562,178**	**114.9**

* Excluding river estuaries (439 sq km).

PRINCIPAL TOWNS
(population at 2011 census)

Lisboa (Lisbon, the capital) . . .	547,733	Leiria	126,897
Vila Nova de Gaia .	302,295	Setúbal	121,185
Porto (Oporto) . .	237,591	Funchal	111,892
Braga . . .	181,494	Parede	86,854
		Algueirão-Mem	
Amadora . . .	175,136	Martins . . .	66,250
Guimarães . . .	158,124	Odivelas . . .	59,559
Coimbra	143,396	Amora	48,629

BIRTHS, MARRIAGES AND DEATHS

	Registered live births		Registered marriages		Registered deaths	
	Number	Rate (per 1,000)	Number	Rate (per 1,000)	Number	Rate (per 1,000)
2004 . .	109,356	10.4	49,178	4.7	102,371	9.7
2005 . .	109,399	10.4	48,671	4.6	107,462	10.2
2006 . .	105,449	10.0	47,857	4.5	101,990	9.6
2007 . .	102,492	9.7	46,329	4.4	103,512	9.8
2008 . .	104,594	9.8	43,228	4.1	104,280	9.8
2009 . .	99,491	9.4	40,391	3.8	104,434	9.8
2010 . .	101,381	9.5	39,993	3.8	105,954	10.0
2011 . .	96,856	9.2	36,035	3.4	102,848	9.7

Life expectancy (years at birth): 79.0 (males 76.1; females 82.1) in 2010 (Source: World Bank, World Development Indicators database).

ECONOMICALLY ACTIVE POPULATION
('000 persons aged 15 years and over)

	2010	2011	2012
Agriculture, hunting and forestry	524.1	460.6	469.9
Fishing	18.1	17.9	16.1
Mining and quarrying . . .	20.2	19.6	14.9
Electricity, gas and water supply.	48.2	49.5	46.7
Manufacturing	826.6	813.3	769.5
Construction	482.4	440.3	357.2
Wholesale and retail trade; repair of motor vehicles, motorcycles and personal and household goods	736.7	709.3	676.6
Hotels and restaurants . . .	291.5	290.4	280.8
Transport, storage and communications	282.5	255.8	256.7
Financial intermediation . . .	88.0	105.0	97.8
Real estate, renting and business activities	339.7	342.6	328.1
Public administration and defence; compulsory social security	313.3	311.9	293.7
Education	368.4	367.9	370.3
Health and social work . . .	349.5	367.2	374.9
Other community, social and personal service activities* .	140.9	148.3	146.5
Private households with employed persons	144.0	135.6	132.9
Extra-territorial organizations and bodies	4.2	1.9	2.0
Total employed*	**4,978.2**	**4,837.0**	**4,634.7**
Unemployed	602.5	706.2	860.1
Total labour force	**5 580.7**	**5,543.2**	**5,494.8**
Males	2,931.8	2,940.5	2,897.6
Females	2,648.9	2,602.6	2,597.2

* Including regular members of the armed forces, but excluding persons on compulsory military service.

Health and Welfare

KEY INDICATORS

Total fertility rate (children per woman, 2010)	1.3
Under-5 mortality rate (per 1,000 live births, 2010) . . .	4
HIV/AIDS (% of persons aged 15–49, 2009)	0.6
Physicians (per 1,000 head, 2010)	3.9
Hospital beds (per 1,000 head, 2009)	3.3
Health expenditure (2009): US $ per head (PPP) . . .	2,690
Health expenditure (2009): % of GDP	10.7
Health expenditure (2009): public (% of total) . . .	67.8
Total carbon dioxide emissions ('000 metric tons, 2008) . .	56,310.5
Carbon dioxide emissions per head (metric tons, 2008) . .	5.3
Human Development Index (2011): ranking	41
Human Development Index (2011): value	0.809

For sources and definitions, see explanatory note on p. vi.

Agriculture

PRINCIPAL CROPS
('000 metric tons)

	2009	2010	2011
Wheat	124	83	59
Rice, paddy	162	170	182
Barley	73	31	23
Maize	634	626	550
Rye	19	18	15
Oats	71	66	45
Triticale (wheat-rye hybrid) . .	35	30	20
Potatoes	435	384	390
Sweet potatoes*	21	18	19
Sugar beet	7	8	8
Olives	423	445	444
Sunflower seeds	12	8	13
Cabbages and other brassicas* .	163	170	151
Lettuce and chicory*	102	107	95
Tomatoes	1,347	1,406	1,245
Cauliflower and broccoli* . . .	42	44	39
Onions, dry*	124	129	114
Broad beans, horse beans, dry* .	19	21	17
Beans, green*	19	19	17
Carrots and turnips* . . .	156	163	144
Carobs*	22	22	31
Chestnuts	24	22	18
Bananas*	30	32	30
Oranges	183	194	228
Tangerines, mandarins, clementines and satsumas . .	34	34	34
Apples	263	213	247
Pears	200	177	230
Peaches and nectarines . . .	40	33	35
Grapes	785	947	745
Cantaloupes and other melons* .	22	23	21

* FAO estimates.

Aggregate production ('000 metric tons, may include official, semi-official or estimated data): Total cereals 1,118 in 2009, 1,019 in 2010, 895 in 2011; Total roots and tubers 458 in 2009, 404 in 2010, 410 in 2011; Total vegetables (incl. melons) 2,711 in 2009, 2,831 in 2010, 2,507 in 2011; Total fruits (excl. melons) 1,692 in 2009, 1,781 in 2010, 1,712 in 2011.

Source: FAO.

LIVESTOCK
('000 head, year ending September)

	2009	2010	2011
Horses*	19	16	18
Asses*	120	115	120
Cattle	1,495	1,447	1,503
Pigs	1,945	1,917	1,985
Sheep	2,368	2,226	2,170
Goats	425	419	413
Chickens*	39,000	40,000	40,000
Turkeys*	6,800	6,500	6,400

* FAO estimates.

Source: FAO.

LIVESTOCK PRODUCTS
('000 metric tons)

	2009	2010	2011
Cattle meat	103	93	96
Sheep meat	18	18	18
Pig meat	374	385	385
Chicken meat	246	249	246
Cows' milk	1,939	1,898	1,906
Sheep's milk	82	78	74
Goats' milk	27	27	27
Hen eggs	124	131	123

Source: FAO.

Forestry

ROUNDWOOD REMOVALS
('000 cubic metres, excluding bark)

	2009	2010*	2011*
Sawlogs, veneer logs and logs for sleepers	2,554	2,578	2,433
Pulpwood	6,230	6,288	5,935
Other industrial wood . . .	180	182	171
Fuel wood	600	600	600
Total	**9,564**	**9,648**	**9,140**

* Unofficial figures.

Source: FAO.

SAWNWOOD PRODUCTION
('000 cubic metres, including railway sleepers)

	2009	2010*	2011*
Coniferous (softwood)	958	929	922
Broadleaved (hardwood) . . .	135	116	122
Total	**1,093**	**1,045**	**1,044**

* Unofficial figures.

Source: FAO.

Fishing

('000 metric tons, live weight)

	2008	2009	2010
Capture	224.3	198.8	222.9
Atlantic redfishes	8.3	9.5	10.7
European pilchard (sardine) . .	71.2	60.9	63.8
Atlantic horse mackerel . . .	11.1	11.8	12.4
Chub mackerel	24.7	15.0	24.6
Blue shark	11.9	12.0	14.3
Octopuses	14.7	8.3	10.9
Aquaculture	7.4	6.7	3.2
Total catch	**231.6**	**205.5**	**226.1**

Note: Figures exclude aquatic plants ('000 metric tons): 0.2 in 2008; 0.4 in 2009; 0.5 in 2010. Also excluded are aquatic mammals, recorded by number rather than weight. The number of whales and porpoises caught was: 35 in 2008; nil in 2009; nil in 2010.
Source: FAO.

Mining

('000 metric tons)

	2009	2010	2011
Iron ore: gross weight* . . .	14.0	14.0	14.0†
Iron ore: metal content* . . .	10.0	10.0	10.0†
Copper ore‡	86.5	74.4	79.7
Tungsten ore (metric tons)‡ . .	1,038	1,007	1,032
Silver ore (metric tons)‡ . . .	22.5	23.7	28.4
Marble	572	94	n.a.
Kaolin	274.9	273.9	322.0
Salt (rock)	594.6	619.0	631.3
Gypsum and anhydrite . . .	335.2	336.8	337.3
Talc (metric tons)	11,567	11,981	15,462

* Estimates.
† Preliminary.
‡ Figures refer to the metal content of ores.

Source: US Geological Survey.

Industry

SELECTED PRODUCTS
('000 metric tons unless otherwise indicated)

	2007	2008	2009
Wheat flour	680	680	680
Soda ash (Sodium carbonate)* .	150	150	150
Jet fuels	745	748	782
Motor spirit (petrol)	2,591	2,091	2,056
Naphthas	1,071	1,151	992
Distillate fuel oils	4,634	4,484	3,810
Residual fuel oils	2,622	2,783	1,976
Liquefied petroleum gas . . .	366	369	326
Cement	12,631	6,650	6,900
Pig-iron*†	100	100	100
Crude steel (ingots)*	1,847	1,630	1,587
Electric energy (million kWh) .	49,041	45,969	50,207

* Source: US Geological Survey.
† Estimates.

2010 ('000 metric tons): Cement 7,200; Soda ash 150; Pig-iron 100; Crude steel (ingots) 1,351.

2011 ('000 metric tons): Cement 7,200; Soda ash 150 (preliminary); Pig-iron 100 (preliminary); Crude steel (ingots) 1,400 (preliminary).

Sources: mainly UN Industrial Commodity Statistics Database and US Geological Survey.

Finance

CURRENCY AND EXCHANGE RATES

Monetary Units
100 cent = 1 euro (€).

Sterling and Dollar Equivalents (31 December 2012)
£1 sterling = 1.196 euros;
US $1 = 0.757 euros;
€10 = £8.36 = $13.19.

Average Exchange Rate (euros per US dollar)
2010   0.7550
2011   0.7194
2012   0.7779

Note: The national currency was formerly the Portuguese escudo. From the introduction of the euro, with Portuguese participation, on 1 January 1999, a fixed exchange rate of €1 = 200.482 escudos was in operation. Euro notes and coins were introduced on 1 January 2002. The euro and local currency circulated alongside each other until 28 February, after which the euro became the sole legal tender.

BUDGET
(€ million)*

Revenue	2009	2010	2011†
Current revenue	65,460.8	67,058.4	69,275.3
Taxes on income and wealth .	15,146.3	15,222.3	16,962.6
Taxes on production and imports	21,486.7	23,039.5	23,389.8
Social contributions . . .	21,031.2	21,268.4	20,926.9
Other current revenue . . .	7,796.6	7,528.2	7,996.0
Capital revenue	1,246.2	4,911.9	7,641.0
Total	66,706.9	71,970.3	76,916.3

Expenditure	2009	2010	2011†
Current expenditure	77,155.6	79,087.8	77,588.9
Wages and salaries . . .	21,385.7	21,143.5	19,425.7
Social transfers	37,007.6	37,948.5	37,623.9
Intermediate consumption . .	8,389.9	8,923.2	8,019.1
Interest payments	4,807.5	4,891.2	6,911.2
Subsidies	1,270.6	1,294.3	1,198.9
Other current expenditure . .	4,294.4	4,887.0	4,410.2
Capital expenditure	6,686.8	9,899.3	6,833.6
Gross capital formation . .	5,244.3	6,572.3	4,402.5
Other	1,442.5	3,327.0	2,431.1
Total	83,842.4	88,987.0	84,422.5

* Figures refer to the consolidated accounts of the central Government, excluding assets and liabilities.
† Provisional.

INTERNATIONAL RESERVES
(US $ million at 31 December)

	2009	2010	2011
Gold (Eurosystem valuation) . .	13,577	17,343	19,362
IMF special drawing rights . .	1,306	1,283	1,217
Reserve position in IMF . . .	337	356	417
Foreign exchange	811	2,013	341
Total	16,031	20,995	21,337

Source: IMF, *International Financial Statistics*.

MONEY SUPPLY
(incl. shares, depository corporations, national residency criteria, € '000 million at 31 December)

	2009	2010	2011
Currency issued	19.13	19.91	21.00
Banco de Portugal . . .	1.19	0.87	−0.82
Demand deposits	53.29	51.71	48.11
Other deposits	144.62	166.90	180.27
Securities other than shares . .	79.73	83.15	97.18
Money market fund shares . .	0.01	0.05	0.07
Shares and other equity . . .	53.56	57.53	57.60
Other items (net)	−26.83	−36.67	−63.72
Total	323.51	342.57	340.50

Source: IMF, *International Financial Statistics*.

COST OF LIVING
(Consumer Price Index; base: 2000 = 100)

	2008	2009	2010
Food and beverages	121.1	116.9	116.5
Clothing	108.1	106.3	104.4
Electricity, gas and other fuels .	134.4	134.8	142.9
Rent	127.3	130.8	133.5
All items (incl. others)* . . .	126.4	125.2	126.8

* Excluding rent.

2011: Food and beverages 119.1; All items (incl. others) 131.6.

Source: ILO.

NATIONAL ACCOUNTS
(€ million at current prices)

Composition of the Gross National Income

	2009	2010	2011
Gross domestic product at market prices	168,503.6	172,834.8	171,039.9
Primary incomes received from abroad	10,541.1	14,034.1	12,126.0
Less Primary incomes paid abroad	17,405.5	19,959.1	18,603.3
Gross national income . . .	161,639.2	166,909.8	164,562.6
Less Consumption of fixed capital .	29,795.1	30,444.2	30,987.6
Net national income	131,844.1	136,465.6	133,575.0
Current transfers from abroad .	4,581.1	4,876.6	5,065.5
Less Current transfers paid abroad	3,420.5	3,514.0	3,527.2
Net national disposable income	133,004.6	137,828.2	135,113.3

Expenditure on the Gross Domestic Product

	2009	2010	2011
Final consumption expenditure .	146,934.1	151,289.8	148,048.6
Households and non-profit institutions serving households	109,773.8	113,978.7	113,777.4
General government	37,160.3	37,311.1	34,271.2
Gross capital formation . . .	34,050.9	34,874.7	30,442.3
Total domestic expenditure .	180,985.0	186,164.5	178,490.9
Exports of goods and services . .	47,235.8	54,109.4	61,168.1
Less Imports of goods and services	59,717.2	67,439.1	68,619.1
GDP in market prices . . .	168,503.6	172,834.8	171,039.9

Gross Domestic Product by Economic Activity

	2009	2010	2011
Agriculture, hunting, forestry and fishing	3,410.9	3,467.2	3,239.9
Electricity, gas and water . . .	5,325.1	5,832.8	5,510.7
Industry	19,375.7	20,915.9	21,625.8
Construction	9,964.2	9,465.5	8,526.4
Trade, restaurants and hotels . .	28,060.9	28,317.1	28,186.9
Transport, storage and communications	13,010.8	12,893.6	13,021.4
Finance, insurance and real estate	22,514.7	23,236.5	23,749.6
Other services	47,040.7	47,284.9	45,407.3
Gross value added in basic prices	148,703.2	151,413.5	149,268.0
Taxes on products (net) . . .	19,800.4	21,421.3	21,625.6
Statistical discrepancy	0.0	0.0	146.3
GDP in market prices . . .	168,503.6	172,834.8	171,039.9

BALANCE OF PAYMENTS
(US $ million)

	2009	2010	2011
Exports of goods	44,450.6	48,994.0	59,248.8
Imports of goods	−69,431.8	−72,966.8	−77,710.7
Balance on goods	−24,981.2	−23,972.8	−18,461.8
Exports of services	22,220.7	22,436.1	25,737.7
Imports of services	−13,647.0	−13741.1	−15,072.9
Balance on goods and services	−16,407.5	−15,277.8	−7,797.0
Primary income received . . .	11,531.3	15,402.5	13,411.0
Primary income paid . . .	−23,767.4	−25,826.8	−25,333.8
Balance on goods, services and primary income	−28,643.6	−25,702.0	−19,719.7
Secondary income received . .	8,930.5	8,850.1	10,467.0
Secondary income paid . . .	−5,939.1	−5,961.4	−6,286.7
Current balance	−25,652.2	−22,813.3	−15,539.4

—*continued*	2009	2010	2011
Capital account (net)	1,922.6	2,591.1	2,936.3
Direct investment assets . . .	−3,383.5	3,775.5	−15,206.1
Direct investment liabilities . .	5,319.2	6,187.1	13,074.2
Portfolio investment assets . .	−22,418.4	−3,866.2	33,489.4
Portfolio investment liabilities .	43,011.0	−8,423.2	−39,234.7
Financial derivatives and employee stock options (net)	210.0	504.5	577.9
Other investment assets . . .	−2,005.4	−9,570.8	1,004.9
Other investment liabilities . .	4,654.4	33,228.0	192.9
Net errors and omissions . . .	−562.9	−341.8	−1,185.8
Reserves and related items .	1,094.8	1,270.9	−19,890.4

Source: IMF, *International Financial Statistics*.

External Trade

PRINCIPAL COMMODITIES
(US $ million)

Imports c.i.f.	2008	2009	2010
Food and live animals . . .	8,860.7	7,653.3	8,392.4
Fish, crustaceans and molluscs .	1,875.4	1,582.2	1,780.0
Cereal and cereal preparations .	1,662.3	1,270.1	1,344.9
Mineral fuels, lubricants and related materials	15,139.2	9,033.6	11,025.7
Petroleum and petroleum products	11,371.8	6,631.5	8,714.6
Chemicals and related products	9,383.7	8,182.4	9,481.1
Medicinal and pharmaceutical products	2,931.9	3,011.6	2,972.3
Basic manufactures	13,501.0	9,235.2	11,293.9
Paper, paperboard and articles thereof	1,526.3	1,278.1	1,394.0
Textile yarn, fabrics and related products	1,921.9	1,441.6	1,892.7
Machinery and transport equipment	25,897.7	19,881.0	22,827.5
General industrial machinery and equipment	2,775.1	2,144.9	2,398.4
Office machines and data processing machines . . .	1,960.9	1,535.3	1,454.4
Telecommunications and sound recording equipment . . .	2,660.6	2,224.4	2,278.4
Miscellaneous manufactured articles	8,500.9	7,261.1	8,385.8
Articles of clothing and clothing accessories	2,244.4	2,029.0	2,405.7
Total (incl. others)	90,105.6	69,985.0	75,572.5

Exports f.o.b.	2008	2009	2010
Food and live animals . . .	3,188.6	2,916.4	3,411.1
Vegetables and fruit	855.3	832.9	959.5
Beverages and tobacco . . .	1,776.1	1,679.2	1,705.9
Wine	856.8	767.2	809.3
Crude materials (inedible), except fuels	2,148.5	1,760.9	2,473.2
Metalliferous ore and metal scrap .	930.9	604.5	935.1
Mineral fuels, lubricants and related materials	3,274.5	2,202.0	3,259.1
Petroleum and petroleum products	2,754.8	2,047.1	2,936.6
Chemicals and related products	3,820.9	3,094.2	4,029.7
Organic chemicals	794.0	382.6	669.4
Basic manufactures	11,639.3	9,469.9	10,871.1
Cork and wood manufactures .	1,599.9	1,236.9	1,307.9
Cork manufacture	1,033.5	852.4	916.7
Textile yarn, fabrics and related products	1,867.6	1,540.3	1,793.9

Exports f.o.b.—*continued*	2008	2009	2010
Non-metallic mineral manufactures	2,037.8	1,633.8	1,824.3
Iron and steel	1,481.2	897.1	1,168.8
Manufactures of metal	2,096.1	1,599.0	1,742.2
Machinery and transport equipment	16,810.0	11,632.5	13,225.3
General industrial machinery and equipment	2,229.5	1,644.0	1,721.5
Telecommunications and sound recording equipment . . .	1,548.1	1,331.7	1,660.8
Electrical machinery and appliances	4,371.3	2,227.0	2,587.4
Road vehicles	6,283.0	4,795.0	5,734.4
Miscellaneous manufactured articles	8,381.7	7,118.4	8,037.1
Total (incl. others)	55,940.7	43,396.5	48,743.6

Source: UN, *International Trade Statistics Yearbook*.

2011 (€ million, provisional): *Imports* Live animals and animal products 2,970.2; Vegetable products 2,587.6; Prepared foodstuffs, beverages, tobacco and manufactured substitutes 2,775.9; Mineral products 10,547.8; Textile articles 3,387.6; Chemical products 6,124.2; Plastic goods 3,295.7; Base metals and articles of base metal 4,841.7; Machinery and electrical equipment 9,076.8; Vehicles and transport equipment 6,303.9; Total (incl. others) 59,242.9. *Exports* Prepared foodstuffs, beverages, tobacco and manufactured substitutes 2,598.8; Pulp wood and fibrous materials 2,169.3; Mineral products 3,820.1; Textile articles 4,152.1; Chemical products 2,437.1; Plastic goods 2,905.6; Base metals and articles of base metal 3,435.1; Machinery and electrical equipment 6,262.6; Vehicles and transport equipment 5,555.9; Total (incl. others) 42,870.2.

PRINCIPAL TRADING PARTNERS
(US $ million)

Imports c.i.f.	2008	2009	2010
Algeria	1,040.9	384.3	356.8
Belgium	2,303.7	1,942.0	2,149.8
Brazil	1,986.1	1,217.4	1,384.0
China, People's Repub. . . .	1,956.5	1,545.4	2,079.3
France (incl. Monaco) . . .	7,164.1	5,982.9	5,466.1
Germany	10,401.4	8,668.3	10,459.6
Ireland	838.1	676.0	724.7
Italy	4,407.1	3,871.0	4,291.8
Japan	858.6	382.5	472.4
Libya	1,457.5	464.3	977.3
Netherlands	3,881.6	3,663.4	3,866.2
Nigeria	2,549.4	1,737.1	1,824.6
Norway	1,019.4	813.9	700.1
Russia	586.8	738.0	547.6
Saudi Arabia	987.4	562.7	693.6
Spain	26,033.2	22,066.8	23,557.4
Sweden	1,082.7	727.5	768.2
United Kingdom	2,738.3	2,243.9	2,847.3
USA	1,498.7	1,189.1	1,117.2
Total (incl. others)	90,105.6	69,985.0	75,572.5

Exports f.o.b.	2008	2009	2010
Angola	3,339.1	3,126.7	2,532.9
Belgium	1,310.9	1,045.3	1,382.2
Brazil	468.2	401.3	575.9
Denmark	366.2	315.8	335.9
Finland	340.0	183.1	308.3
France (incl. Monaco) . . .	6,098.2	5,236.8	5,728.6
Germany	6,878.6	5,643.9	6,262.3
Italy	1,930.0	1,614.4	1,827.7
Mexico	322.8	278.5	532.2
Netherlands	1,605.5	1,551.1	1,780.2
Poland	389.2	361.9	387.5
Singapore	1,271.5	114.7	69.4
Spain	14,116.8	11,390.0	12,917.4
Sweden	618.1	507.6	493.6
Switzerland (incl. Liechtenstein) .	420.1	378.2	436.3

Exports f.o.b.—*continued*	2008	2009	2010
Turkey	263.9	210.5	328.0
United Kingdom	2,902.3	2,401.0	2,655.8
USA	1,874.0	1,312.0	1,727.9
Total (incl. others)	55,940.7	43,396.5	48,743.6

Source: UN, *International Trade Statistics Yearbook*.

2011 (€ million, provisional): *Imports:* Algeria 776.2; Angola 1,177.5; Belgium 1,504.5; Brazil 1,461.9; China, People's Republic 1,499.8; France 4,008.5; Germany 7,332.4; Italy 3,235.0; Kazakhstan 854.0; Netherlands 2,829.5; Nigeria 1,528.7; Saudi Arabia 914.4; Spain 19,116.7; Sweden 623.7; United Kingdom 1,973.4; USA 1,134.3; Total (incl. others) 59,242.9. *Exports:* Angola 2,331.2; Belgium 1,350.3; Brazil 583.1; France 5,212.8; Germany 5,811.2; Italy 1,567.3; Mexico 461.6; Netherlands 1,675.4; Spain 10,679.7; Sweden 443.3; United Kingdom 2,234.1; USA 1,496.4; Total (incl. others) 42,870.2.

Transport

RAILWAYS
(traffic)

	2002	2003	2004
Passenger journeys (million) . .	161	151	153
Passenger-km (million) . . .	3,926	3,585	3,693
Freight ('000 metric tons) . . .	10,739	8,718	11,151
Freight ton-km (million) . . .	2,583	2,073	2,589

Passenger journeys (million): 151 in 2005; 155 in 2006; 157 in 2007; 158 in 2008; 166 in 2009.

ROAD TRAFFIC
(motor vehicles registered at 31 December)

	2001	2002	2003
Light and heavy vehicles . . .	7,361,572	7,690,019	7,910,572
Motorcycles	371,114	390,209	402,759
Tractors	309,775	322,283	329,761
Trailers and semi-trailers . . .	363,722	376,719	377,552

2006 (motor vehicles in use at 31 December): Passenger cars 5,234,477; Buses and coaches 29,741; Vans and lorries 118,965; Motorcycles and mopeds 558,720 (Source: IRF, *World Road Statistics*).

2009 (motor vehicles in use at 31 December): Vans and lorries 118,965; Motorcycles and mopeds 558,720 (Source: IRF, *World Road Statistics*).

SHIPPING

Flag Registered Fleet
(at 31 December)

	2010	2011	2012
Number of vessels	236	239	239
Total displacement (grt) . . .	278,812	301,649	305,242

Source: Lloyd's List Intelligence (www.lloydslistintelligence.com).

International Sea-borne Freight Traffic
(Figures exclude the Azores)

	2009	2010	2011
Vessels entered ('000 gross registered tons)	148,719	159,683	167,157
Goods loaded ('000 metric tons) .	19,802	23,103	24,482
Goods unloaded ('000 metric tons)	41,911	42,868	43,025

CIVIL AVIATION
(traffic on scheduled services, domestic and international)

	2007	2008	2009
Kilometres flown (million) . .	185	203	195
Passengers carried ('000) . . .	9,815	10,158	9,904
Passenger-km (million) . . .	20,900	23,182	22,820
Total ton-km (million)	2,245	2,462	2,385

Source: UN, *Statistical Yearbook*.

2010: Passengers carried ('000) 11,124 (Source: World Bank, World Development Indicators database).

Tourism

FOREIGN TOURIST ARRIVALS BY COUNTRY OF RESIDENCE*

Country of origin	2008	2009	2010
Belgium	169,913	154,990	152,851
Brazil	306,228	268,913	363,871
France	665,737	663,022	666,958
Germany	736,200	702,542	695,247
Ireland	168,705	149,809	151,786
Italy	380,226	330,105	364,908
Japan	63,486	57,641	61,690
Netherlands	363,215	337,349	356,749
Spain	1,365,372	1,419,354	1,438,984
Sweden	104,870	81,962	88,864
United Kingdom . . .	1,261,871	989,123	1,008,141
USA	227,068	228,776	256,151
Total (incl. others)	6,961,707	6,439,022	6,756,354

* Arrivals at all accommodation establishments.

Total tourist arrivals ('000): 7,432 in 2011.

Receipts from tourism (US $ million, excl. passenger transport): 9,635 in 2009; 10,077 in 2010; 11,339 in 2011 (provisional).

Source: World Tourism Organization.

Communications Media

	2009	2010	2011
Telephones ('000 main lines in use)	4,343.2	4,476.6	4,530.3
Mobile cellular telephones ('000 subscribers)	11,795.1	12,210.4	12,334.6
Internet subscribers ('000) . .	2,008.6	2,221.3	2,265.7
Broadband subscribers ('000) . .	1,911.8	2,126.7	2,239.7

Source: International Telecommunication Union.

Education

(public and private, 2010/11)

	Institutions	Teachers	Students
Pre-school	6,812	18,284	276,125
Basic: 1st cycle . . .	5,225	29,948	464,620
Basic: 2nd cycle . . .	1,179	34,086	278,263
Basic: 3rd cycle . . .	1,516	89,539	389,692
Secondary	937		440,895
Higher*	301	35,380	373,002

* 2008/09.

Pupil-teacher ratio (primary education, UNESCO estimate): 11.2 in 2008/09 (Source: UNESCO Institute for Statistics).

Adult literacy rate (UN estimates): 95.2% (males 96.9%; females 93.6%) in 2010 (Source: UNESCO Institute for Statistics).

Directory

The Government

HEAD OF STATE

President: ANÍBAL CAVACO SILVA (took office 9 March 2006; re-elected 23 January 2011).

COUNCIL OF MINISTERS
(May 2013)

A coalition of the Partido Social Democrata (PSD), the Centro Democrático Social-Partido Popular (CDS-PP) and independents (Ind.)

Prime Minister: PEDRO PASSOS COELHO (PSD).

Minister of State and of Finance: VÍTOR GASPAR (Ind.).

Minister of State and of Foreign Affairs: PAULO PORTAS (CDS-PP).

Minister of National Defence: JOSÉ PEDRO AGUIAR BRANCO (PSD).

Minister of Internal Administration: MIGUEL MACEDO (PSD).

Minister of Justice: PAULA TEIXEIRA DA CRUZ (PSD).

Minister of the Presidency and of Parliamentary Affairs: LUÍS MARQUES GUEDES (PSD).

Assistant Minister and Minister of Regional Development: MIGUEL POIARES MADURO (Ind.).

Minister of the Economy and Employment: ÁLVARO SANTOS PEREIRA (Ind.).

Minister of Agriculture, Sea, Environment and Spatial Planning: ASSUNÇÃO CRISTAS (CDS-PP).

Minister of Health: PAULO MACEDO (Ind.).

Minister of Education and Science: NUNO CRATO (Ind.).

Minister of Solidarity and Social Security: PEDRO MOTA SOARES (CDS-PP).

MINISTRIES

Office of the President: Presidência da República, Palácio de Belém, Calçada da Ajuda 11, 1349-022 Lisbon; tel. (21) 3614600; fax (21) 3636603; e-mail belem@presidencia.pt; internet www.presidencia.pt.

Office of the Prime Minister, Presidency of the Council of Ministers: Rua da Imprensa à Estrela 4, 1200-888 Lisbon; tel. (21) 3923500; fax (21) 3951616; e-mail pm@pm.gov.pt; internet www.portugal.gov.pt.

Ministry of Agriculture, Sea, Environment and Spatial Planning: Praça do Comércio, 1149-010 Lisbon; tel. (21) 3234652; fax (21) 3234604; e-mail gabministro@mamaot.gov.pt.

Ministry of the Economy and Employment: Rua da Horta Seca 15, 1200-221 Lisbon; tel. (21) 3245400; fax (21) 3245440; e-mail gabinete.ministro@mee.gov.pt.

Ministry of Education and Science: Av. 5 de Outubro 107, 1069-018 Lisbon; tel. (21) 7811800; fax (21) 7811835; e-mail gabinete.ministro@mec.gov.pt.

Ministry of Finance: Av. Infante D. Henrique 1, 1149-009 Lisbon; tel. (21) 8816800; fax (21) 8816862; e-mail gabinete.ministro@mf.gov.pt.

Ministry of Foreign Affairs: Palácio das Necessidades, Largo do Rilvas, 1399-030 Lisbon; tel. (21) 3946000; fax (21) 3946070; e-mail gabinete.ministro@mne.gov.pt.

Ministry of Health: Av. João Crisóstomo 9, 1000-179 Lisbon; tel. (21) 3305000; fax (21) 3305161; e-mail gabinete.ministro@ms.gov.pt.

Ministry of Internal Administration: Praça do Comércio, 1149-015 Lisbon; tel. (21) 3233000; fax (21) 3232035; e-mail gabinete.ministro@mai.gov.pt.

Ministry of Justice: Praça do Comércio, 1149-019 Lisbon; tel. (21) 3222300; fax (21) 3479208; e-mail gabinete.ministro@mj.gov.pt.

Ministry of National Defence: Av. Ilha da Madeira 1, 1400-204 Lisbon; tel. (21) 3034500; fax (21) 3034501; e-mail gabinete .ministro@mdn.gov.pt.

Ministry of Solidarity and Social Security: Praça de Londres 2, 16°, 1049-056 Lisbon; tel. (21) 8424100; fax (21) 8424108; e-mail gabinete.ministro@msss.gov.pt.

COUNCIL OF STATE

The Council of State (Conselho de Estado) is the political consultative organ of the President of the Republic. It is presided over by the President and comprises the President of the Assembleia da República (Assembly of the Republic), the Prime Minister, the President of the Constitutional Court, the Superintendent of Justice, the Presidents of the Regional Governments, certain former Presidents of the Republic, five citizens nominated by the President of the Republic and five citizens elected by the Assembly.

President

Election, 23 January 2011

Candidate	Votes	% of votes
Aníbal Cavaco Silva (PSD) (CDS-PP) .	2,231,603	52.95
Manuel Alegre (PS) (BE)	832,637	19.76
Fernando Nobre (Ind.)	594,068	14.10
Francisco Lopes (CDU—PCP-PEV) . .	300,921	7.14
José Coelho (PND)	189,091	4.49
Defensor Moura (Ind.)	66,112	1.57
Total	**4,214,432***	**100.00**

* Excluding 191,284 blank and 86,581 spoiled votes.

Legislature

Assembleia da República
(Assembly of the Republic)

Palácio de São Bento, 1249-068 Lisbon; tel. (21) 3919000; fax (21) 3917440; e-mail correio.geral@ar.parlamento.pt; internet www .parlamento.pt.

President: Assunção Esteves.

General Election, 5 June 2011

Party	Votes	% of votes	Seats
Partido Social Democrata (PSD)	2,159,181	40.30	108
Partido Socialista (PS) . . .	1,566,347	29.24	74
Centro Democrático Social-Partido Popular (CDS-PP) .	653,888	12.21	24
Coligação Democrática Unitária (PCP-PEV)	441,147	8.24	16
Bloco de Esquerda (BE) . . .	288,923	5.39	8
Others	247,126	4.61	—
Total	**5,356,612***	**100.00**	**230**

* Excluding 148,618 blank and 79,399 spoiled votes.

Autonomous Regions

Following the promulgation of a new Constitution in 1976, the mid-Atlantic archipelagos of the Azores and Madeira were officially designated as Autonomous Regions of the Portuguese Republic. Each region is afforded a degree of political and administrative autonomy, as well as the power to raise funds through taxation. Members of the Legislative Assemblies are elected by universal suffrage for a term of four years, according to a system of proportional representation. Executive functions are vested in a Regional Government. The state is represented in each region by a Minister of the Republic, who appoints both the President of the Regional Government and its members.

OS AÇORES
(The Azores)

President of the Regional Government: Vasco Ilídio Alves Cordeiro (PS).

Assembleia Legislativa da Região Autónoma dos Açores

Rua Marcelino Lima, 9901 858 Horta, Azores; tel. (292) 207600; fax (292) 293798; e-mail secgeral@alra.pt; internet www.alra.pt.

President of the Assembly: Francisco Coelho.

Election, 14 October 2012

Party	Seats
Partido Socialista (PS)	31
Partido Social Democrata (PSD)	20
Centro Democrático Social-Partido Popular (CDS-PP)	3
Bloco de Esquerda (BE)	1
Coligação Democrática Unitária (PCP-PEV) . . .	1
Partido Popular Monárquico (PPM)	1
Total	**57**

MADEIRA

President of the Regional Government: Dr Alberto João Jardim (PSD).

Assembleia Legislativa da Região Autónoma da Madeira

Av. do Mar e das Comunidades Madeirenses, 9004 506 Funchal, Madeira; tel. (291) 210500; fax (291) 232977; e-mail info@alram.pt; internet www.alram.pt.

President of the Assembly: José Miguel Jardim d'Olival de Mendonça.

Election, 9 October 2011

Party	Seats
Partido Social Democrata (PSD)	25
Centro Democrático Social-Partido Popular (CDS-PP)	9
Partido Socialista (PS)	6
Partido Trabalhista Português	3
Coligação Democrática Unitária (PCP-PEV) . . .	1
Nova Democrácia (PND)	1
Partido pelos Animais e pela Natureza (PAN) . .	1
Partido da Terra (MPT)	1
Total	**47**

Election Commission

Comissão Nacional de Eleições (CNE): Av. D. Carlos I 128, 7°, 1249-065 Lisbon; tel. (21) 3923800; fax (21) 3953543; e-mail cne@cne .pt; internet www.cne.pt; Pres. appointed by the judiciary, other mems by the Assembleia da República and the Govt; Pres. Dr Fernando Costa de Soares.

Political Organizations

Bloco de Esquerda (BE) (Left Bloc): Rua da Palma 268, 1100-394 Lisbon; tel. (21) 3510510; fax (21) 3510519; e-mail bloco.esquerda@ bloco.org; internet www.bloco.org; f. 1999 by several left-wing groups; Co-ordinators Catarina Martins, João Semedo; Parliamentary Leader Pedro Filipe Soares.

Centro Democrático Social-Partido Popular (CDS-PP) (Social Democratic Centre-Popular Party): Largo Adelino Amaro da Costa 5, 1149-063 Lisbon; tel. (21) 8814700; fax (21) 8860454; e-mail cds-pp@ cds.pt; internet www.cds.pt; f. 1974 as Centro Democrático Social; present name adopted 1993; centre-right; mem. of International Democrat Union; supports social market economy and reduction of public sector intervention in the economy; defended revision of 1976 Constitution; Pres. Paulo Sacadura Cabral Portas; Sec.-Gen. António Carlos Monteiro.

Coligação Democrática Unitária (CDU): coalition of left-wing parties, led by PCP:

Partido Comunista Português (PCP) (Portuguese Communist Party): Rua Soeiro Pereira Gomes 3, 1600-196 Lisbon; tel. (21) 7813800; fax (21) 7969126; e-mail pcp@pcp.pt; internet www.pcp .pt; f. 1921; legalized 1974; theoretical foundation is Marxism-Leninism; aims are the defence and consolidation of the democratic regime and the revolutionary achievements, and ultimately the building of a socialist society in Portugal; Sec.-Gen. Jerónimo de Sousa.

Partido Ecologista 'Os Verdes' (PEV) (The Greens): Rua Borges Carneiro 38, r/c esq., 1200–619 Lisbon; tel. (21) 3960291; fax (21) 3960424; e-mail pev@osverdes.pt; internet www.osverdes .pt; f. 1982; ecological party.

Nova Democracia (PND) (New Democracy Party): Rua da Trinidade 36, 1200-302 Lisbon; tel. (21) 3247020; fax (21) 3247029; e-mail partidonovademocracia@gmail.com; internet www.pnd.pt; f. 2003 by disaffected mems of the CDS-PP; right-wing, nationalist and Eurosceptic; Pres. Maria Augusta Montes; Sec.-Gen. Joel Viana.

Partido pelos Animais e pela Natureza (PAN) (Party for Animals and Nature): Rua Anchieta 5, 4° esq., 1200-023 Lisbon; tel. (21) 3426226; fax (21) 3430227; e-mail geral@pan.com.pt; internet www .pan.com.pt; f. 2011; Leader PAULO BORGES.

Partido Comunista dos Trabalhadores Portugueses/Movimento Revolucionário Português do Proletariado (PCTP/ MRPP) (Communist Workers' Party/Proletarian Portuguese Revolutionary Movement): Rua da Palma 159, 2° dto, 1100-391 Lisbon; tel. and fax (21) 8880780; e-mail pctp@pctpmrpp.org; internet www .pctpmrpp.org; f. 1970 as Movimento Reorganizativo do Partido do Proletariado; present name adopted 1976; Leader ANTÓNIO GARCIA PEREIRA.

Partido Nacional Renovador (PNR) (National Renewal Party): Apartado 8076, 1804-001 Lisbon; tel. 964378225; e-mail geral@pnr .pt; internet www.pnr.pt; extreme nationalist; f. 2000 by fmr mems of Movimento de Acção Nacional and Partido Renovador Democrático; Leader JOSÉ PINTO-COELHO.

Partido Popular Monárquico (PPM) (Popular Monarchist Party): Travessa da Pimenteira 2, r/c esq., 1300-460 Lisbon; tel. and fax (21) 3622153; e-mail ppm.geral@sapo.pt; f. 1974; advocates a system of constitutional monarchy; Pres. PAULO ESTÊVÃO.

Partido Social Democrata (PSD) (Social Democratic Party): Rua de São Caetano 9, 1249-087 Lisbon; tel. (21) 3918500; fax (21) 3976967; e-mail psd@psd.pt; internet www.psd.pt; f. 1974 as Partido Popular Democrático; present name adopted 1976; centre-right; aims to promote market economy, taking into account the welfare of the community; encourages European integration; Leader PEDRO PASSOS COELHO; Sec.-Gen. JOSÉ MATOS ROSA.

Partido Socialista (PS) (Socialist Party): Largo do Rato 2, 1269-143 Lisbon; tel. (21) 3822000; fax (21) 3822022; e-mail portal@ps.pt; internet www.ps.pt; f. 1973 from fmr Acção Socialista Portuguesa (Portuguese Socialist Action); affiliate of the Socialist International and Party of European Socialists; advocates a society of greater social justice and co-operation between public, private and co-operative sectors, while respecting public liberties and the will of the majority attained through free elections; Pres. MARIA DE BELÉM ROSEIRA; Sec.-Gen. ANTÓNIO JOSÉ SEGURO.

Partido da Terra (MPT) (The Earth Party): Rua da Beneficência 111, 1°, Apdo 43050, 1601-301 Lisbon; tel. (96) 9640021; fax (21) 8438029; e-mail mpt@mpt.pt; internet www.mpt.pt; f. 1993; contested 2005 election in coalition with PSD; Pres. JOHN ROSAS BAKER.

Partido Trabalhista Português (Portuguese Labour Party—PTP): Rua Portas de Santo Antão 117, 2°, 1150-265 Lisbon; tel. and fax (21) 3465222; e-mail ptp@trabalhista.pt; internet www .partidotrabalhista.org; advocates democracy and democratic socialism; Pres. AMÂNDIO CERDEIRA MADALENO; Sec. JOAQUIM DE JESUS MAGALHÃES FONSECA.

Diplomatic Representation

EMBASSIES IN PORTUGAL

Algeria: Rua Duarte Pacheco Pereira 58, 1400-140 Lisbon; tel. (21) 3041520; fax (21) 3010393; e-mail geral@emb-argelia.pt; internet www.emb-argelia.pt; Ambassador FATIHA SELMANE.

Andorra: Rua do Possolo 76, 2°, 1350-251 Lisbon; tel. (21) 3913740; fax (21) 3913749; e-mail ambaixada_portugal@govern.ad; Ambassador MARIA UBACH.

Angola: Av. da República 68, 1069-213 Lisbon; tel. (21) 7961830; fax (21) 7971238; internet www.embaixadadeangola.org; Ambassador JOSÉ MARCOS BARRICA.

Argentina: Av. João Crisóstomo 8, r/c esq., 1000-178 Lisbon; tel. (21) 7959223; fax (21) 7959225; e-mail eport@mrecic.gov.ar; Ambassador JORGE ARGÜELLO.

Australia: Av. da Liberdade 200, 2°, 1250-147 Lisbon; tel. (21) 33101500; fax (21) 3101555; e-mail austemb.lisbon@dfat.gov.au; internet www.portugal.embassy.gov.au; Ambassador ANNE PLUNKETT.

Austria: Av. Infante Santo 43, 4°, 1399-046 Lisbon; tel. (21) 3943900; fax (21) 3958224; e-mail lissabon-ob@bmeia.gv.at; internet www .embaixadadaaustria.pt; Ambassador BERNHARD WRABETZ.

Belgium: Praça Marquês de Pombal 14, 6°, 1269-024 Lisbon; tel. (21) 3170510; fax (21) 3561556; e-mail lisbon@diplobel.fed.be; internet www.diplomatie.be/lisbon; Ambassador BERNARD PIERRE.

Brazil: Quinta de Mil Flores, Estrada das Laranjeiras 144, 1649-021 Lisbon; tel. (21) 7248510; fax (21) 7267623; e-mail geral@ embaixadadobrasil.pt; internet lisboa.itamaraty.gov.br; Ambassador MÁRIO VILALVA.

Bulgaria: Rua do Sacramento à Lapa 31, 1200-792 Lisbon; tel. (21) 3976364; fax (21) 3979272; e-mail ebul@mail.telepac.pt; internet www.mfa.bg/embassies/portugal; Ambassador IVAN PETROV IVANOV.

Canada: Av. da Liberdade 198–200, 3°, 1269-121 Lisbon; tel. (21) 3164600; fax (21) 3164693; e-mail lsbon@international.gc.ca; internet www.canadainternational.gc.ca/portugal; Ambassador HEIDI KUTZ.

Cape Verde: Av. do Restelo 33, 1449-025 Lisbon; tel. (21) 3041440; fax (21) 3041466; e-mail info@embcv.pt; internet www.embcv.pt; Ambassador MARIA MADALENA BRITO NEVES.

Chile: Av. Miguel Bombarda 5, 1°, 1000-207 Lisbon; tel. (21) 3148054; fax (21) 3150909; e-mail embachile@net.novis.pt; internet www.emb-chile.pt; Ambassador LUIS PATRÍCIO EDUARDO DAMM.

China, People's Republic: Rua do Pau de Bandeira 11–13, 1200-756 Lisbon; tel. (21) 3928430; fax (21) 3928431; e-mail chinaemb_pt@ mfa.gov.cn; internet pt.china-embassy.org/pot; Ambassador HUANG SONGFU.

Colombia: Palácio Sottomayor, 6°, Av. Fontes Pereira de Melo 16, 1050-021 Lisbon; tel. (21) 3188480; fax (21) 3188499; e-mail embajada@embaixadadacolombia.pt; internet www .embaixadadacolombia.pt; Ambassador GERMÁN SANTAMARÍA BARRAGÁN.

Congo, Democratic Republic: Av. Fontes Pereira de Melo 31, 7°, 1050-117 Lisbon; e-mail ambalisbonne@minaffecirde.cd; Ambassador MULAMBA WATEMA SHABENDELO.

Croatia: Rua D. Lourenço de Almeida 24, 1400-126 Lisbon; tel. (21) 3021033; fax (21) 3021251; e-mail croemb.lisboa@mvpei.hr; Chargé d'affaires a.i. KATIJA MILIČIĆ.

Cuba: Rua Pero da Covilhã 14 (Restelo), 1400-297 Lisbon; tel. (21) 3041860; fax (21) 3011895; e-mail embaixada.cuba@netcabo.pt; Ambassador EDUARDO CARLOS GONZÁLEZ LERNER.

Cyprus: Av. da Liberdade 229, 1°, 1250-142 Lisbon; tel. (21) 3194180; fax (21) 3194189; e-mail chipre@netcabo.pt; internet www.mfa.gov.cy/embassylisbon; Ambassador THALIA PETRIDES.

Czech Republic: Rua Pêro de Alenquer 14, 1400-294 Lisbon; tel. (21) 3010487; fax (21) 3010629; e-mail czechembassylisbon@gmail .com; internet www.mfa.cz/lisbon; Ambassador Dr MARKÉTA SARBOCHOVÁ.

Denmark: Rua Castilho 14C, 3°, 1269-077 Lisbon; tel. (21) 3512960; fax (21) 3554615; e-mail lisamb@um.dk; internet www.portugal.um .dk; Ambassador HANS KOFOED-HANSEN.

Dominican Republic: Av. Campo Grande 35, 12° A, 1700-087 Lisbon; tel. (21) 7811120; fax (21) 7811129; e-mail embajadom@ mail.ptprime.pt; Ambassador JAIME DURAN HERNANDO.

Egypt: Av. D. Vasco da Gama 8, 1400-128 Lisbon; tel. (21) 3301018; fax (21) 3017909; e-mail egyptianembassyportugal@net.novis.pt; Ambassador HAMDI LOZA.

Estonia: Rua Filipe Folque 10°J, 2° esq., 1050-113 Lisbon; tel. (21) 3194150; fax (21) 3194155; e-mail embassy.lisbon@mfa.ee; internet www.embest.pt; Ambassador MARIN MÕTTUS.

Finland: Rua do Possolo 76, 1°, 1350-251 Lisbon; tel. (21) 3933040; fax (21) 3904758; e-mail sanomat.lis@formin.fi; internet www .finlandia.org.pt; Ambassador ASKO NUMMINEN.

France: Rua de Santos-o-Velho 5, 1249-079 Lisbon; tel. (21) 3939100; fax (21) 3939151; e-mail ambafrance@hotmail.com; internet www.ambafrance-pt.org; Ambassador PASCAL TEIXEIRA DA SILVA.

Germany: Campo dos Mártires da Pátria 38, 1169-043 Lisbon; tel. (21) 8810210; fax (21) 8853846; e-mail info@lissabon.diplo.de; internet www.lissabon.diplo.de; Ambassador HELMUT ELFENKÄMPER.

Greece: Rua do Alto do Duque 13, 1449-026 Lisbon; tel. (21) 3031260; fax (21) 3011205; e-mail gremb.lis@mfa.gr; Ambassador VASSILIOS COSTIS.

Guinea-Bissau: Rua de Alcolena 17A, 1400-004 Lisbon; tel. and fax (21) 3009081; Chargé d'affaires a.i. ALFREDO FERNANDES.

Holy See: Av. Luís Bivar 18, 1069-147 Lisbon; tel. (21) 3171130; fax (21) 3171149; e-mail nunciaturapt@netcabo.pt; Apostolic Nuncio Most Rev. RINO PASSIGATO (Titular Archbishop of Nova Caesaris).

Hungary: Calçada de Santo Amaro 85, 1349-042 Lisbon; tel. (21) 3630395; fax (21) 3632314; e-mail mission.lis@mfa.gov.hu; internet www.mfa.gov.hu/emb/lisbon; Ambassador NORBERT KONKOLY.

India: Rua Pêro da Covilhã 16, 1400-297 Lisbon; tel. (21) 3041090; fax (21) 3016576; e-mail hoc@indembassy-lisbon.org; internet www .indembassy-lisbon.org; Ambassador B. B. TYAGI.

Indonesia: Rua Miguel Lupi 12, 1°, 1249-080 Lisbon; tel. (21) 3932070; fax (21) 3932079; e-mail lisabon.kbri@kemlu.go.id; Ambassador ALBERT MATONDANG.

Iran: Rua do Alto do Duque 49, 1400-009 Lisbon; tel. (21) 3041850; fax (21) 3010777; e-mail info@iranembassy.com.pt; internet www .iranembassy.com.pt; Ambassador Dr HOSSEIN GHARIBI.

Iraq: Rua do Arriaga à Lapa 9, 1200-608 Lisbon; tel. (21) 3933310; fax (21) 3977052; e-mail iraqemblis@yahoo.com; internet www .mofamission.gov.iq/prt; Ambassador HUSSEIN SINJARI.

Ireland: Av. da Liberdade 200, 4°, 1250-147 Lisbon; tel. (21) 3308200; fax (21) 3977363; e-mail lisbonembassy@dfa.ie; internet www.embassyofireland.pt; Ambassador DECLAN O'DONOVAN.

Israel: Rua António Enes 16, 4°, 1050-025 Lisbon; tel. (21) 0455500; fax (21) 0455555; e-mail israelemb@lisbon.mfa.gov.il; internet lisbon .mfa.gov.il; Ambassador EHUD GOL.

Italy: Largo Conde de Pombeiro 6, 1150-100 Lisbon; tel. (21) 3515320; fax (21) 3154926; e-mail ambasciata.lisbona@esteri.it; internet www.amblisbona.esteri.it; Ambassador RENATO VARRIALE.

Japan: Av. da Liberdade 245, 6°, 1269-033 Lisbon; tel. (21) 3110560; fax (21) 3537600; e-mail cultural@embjapao.pt; internet www.pt .emb-japan.go.jp; Ambassador NOBUTAKA SHINOMIVA.

Korea, Republic: Edif. Presidente, Av. Miguel Bombarda 36, 7°, 1051-802 Lisbon; tel. (21) 7937200; fax (21) 7977176; e-mail embpt@ mofat.go.kr; internet prt.mofat.go.kr; Ambassador YOO JUNG-HEE.

Latvia: Rua Sacramento à Lapa 50–52, 1200-794 Lisbon; tel. (21) 3407170; fax (21) 3469045; e-mail embassy.portugal@mfa.gov.lv; internet www.am.gov.lv/portugal; Ambassador ALDA VANAGA.

Libya: Av. das Descobertas 24, 1400-092 Lisbon; tel. (21) 3016301; fax (21) 3012378; e-mail bureau.popular.libia@clix.pt; Sec. of the People's Bureau (vacant).

Lithuania: Av. 5 de Outubro 81, 1° esq., 1050-050 Lisbon; tel. (21) 7990110; fax (21) 7996363; e-mail amb.pt@urm.lt; internet pt.mfa.lt; Chargé d'affaires a.i. LAURA TUPE.

Luxembourg: Av. Engenheiro Duarte Pacheco Amoreiras Torre 1, 8°, 1070-101 Lisbon; tel. (21) 3931940; fax (21) 3901410; e-mail lisbonne.amb@mae.etat.lu; internet lisbonne.mae.lu; Ambassador PAUL SCHMIT.

Malta: Av. da Liberdade 49, 5° esq., 1250-139 Lisbon; tel. (21) 3405470; fax (21) 3405479; e-mail maltaembassy.lisbon@gov.mt; Ambassador JOSEPH A. FILLETTI.

Mexico: Estrada de Monsanto 78, 1500-462 Lisbon; tel. (21) 7621290; fax (21) 7620045; e-mail embamex@mail.telepac.pt; internet www.sre.gob.mx/portugal; Ambassador BENITO ANDIÓN SANCHO.

Moldova: Rua Gonçalo Velho Cabral 31A, 1400-188 Lisbon; tel. (21) 3009060; fax (21) 3009067; e-mail lisabona@mfa.md; internet www .portugalia.mfa.md/about-embassy-en; Ambassador VALERIU TUREA.

Morocco: Rua Alto do Duque 21, 1400-099 Lisbon; tel. (21) 3020842; fax (21) 3020935; e-mail sifmar@emb-marrocos.pt; internet www .emb-marrocos.pt; Ambassador KARIMA BENYAICH.

Mozambique: Av. de Berna 7, 1050-036 Lisbon; tel. (21) 7971994; fax (21) 7932720; e-mail embamoc.portugal@minec.gov.mz; Ambassador JACOB NYAMBIR.

Netherlands: Av. Infante Santo 43, 5°, 1399-011 Lisbon; tel. (21) 3914900; fax (21) 3914950; e-mail nlgovlis@netcabo.pt; internet www.emb-paisesbaixos.pt; Ambassador HENK J. W. SOETERS.

Nigeria: Av. D. Vasco da Gama 3, 1400-127 Lisbon; tel. (21) 3031290; fax (21) 3018152; e-mail nigerieemblisbon@portugal.pt; Ambassador IJEOMA BRISTOL.

Norway: Av. D. Vasco da Gama 1, 1400-127 Lisbon; tel. (21) 3009100; fax (21) 3009101; e-mail emb.lisbon@mfa.no; internet www.noruega.org.pt; Ambassador OVE THORSHEIM.

Pakistan: Rua António Saldanha 46, 1400-021 Lisbon; tel. (21) 3009070; fax (21) 3013514; e-mail parep.lisbon.1@mail.telepac.pt; Ambassador HUMAIRA HASAN.

Panama: Av. Helen Keller 15, Lote C, 4° esq., 1400-197 Lisbon; tel. (21) 3644576; fax (21) 3644589; e-mail panemblisboa@netcabo.pt; Ambassador FREDERICO HUMBERT.

Paraguay: Rua Alexandre Herculano 17, r/c esq., 1250-008 Lisbon; tel. (21) 7965907; fax (21) 7965905; e-mail embaparlisboa@net.novis .pt; Ambassador LUIS ANTONIO FRETES CARRERAS.

Peru: Rua Castilho 50, 4° dto, 1250-071 Lisbon; tel. (21) 3827470; fax (21) 3827479; e-mail info@embaixadaperu.pt; Ambassador NESTOR BARDALES.

Poland: Av. das Descobertas 2, 1400-092 Lisbon; tel. (21) 3041410; fax (21) 3041429; e-mail lizbona.amb.sekretariat@msz.gov.pl; internet lizbona.msz.gov.pl; Ambassador BRONISŁAW MISZTAL.

Romania: Rua de São Caetano à Lapa 5, 1200-828 Lisbon; tel. (21) 3968812; fax (21) 3960984; e-mail ambrom@mail.telepac.pt; internet lisabona.mae.ro; Ambassador VASILE POPOVICI.

Russia: Rua Visconde de Santarém 57, 1000-286 Lisbon; tel. (21) 8462423; fax (21) 8463008; e-mail mail@embrussia.ru; internet www .embrussia.ru; Chargé d'affaires a.i. ALEXEY V. DEMENTIEV.

São Tomé and Príncipe: Av. 5 de Outubro 35, 4°, 1050-047 Lisbon; tel. (21) 8461917; fax (21) 8461895; e-mail embaixada@ emb-saotomeprincipe.pt; Ambassador DAMIÃO ALMEIDA.

Saudi Arabia: Av. do Restelo 42, 1400-315 Lisbon; tel. (21) 3041750; fax (21) 3014209; e-mail saudiembassy@netcabo.pt; Chargé d'affaires a.i. OSAMAK KRENSHI.

Senegal: Av. da Liberdade 38, 4°, 1250-145 Lisbon; tel. (21) 3160180; fax (21) 3431067; e-mail ambassenelisbonne@mail.telepac.pt; Ambassador MAYMOUNA DIOP SY.

Serbia: Rua de Alcolena, 11, 1400-004 Lisbon; tel. (21) 3015311; fax (21) 3015313; e-mail serviaemba@netcabo.pt; internet www .embaixadaservia.pt; Ambassador MIRKO STEFANOVIĆ.

Slovakia: Av. da Liberdade 200, 5° esq., 1250-147 Lisbon; tel. (21) 3583300; fax (21) 3583309; e-mail emb.lisbon@mzv.sk; Chargé d'affaires a.i. ADAM MRIÁN.

South Africa: Av. Luís Bivar 10, 1069-024 Lisbon; tel. (21) 3192200; fax (21) 3535713; e-mail embsa@embaixada-africadosul.pt; internet www.embaixada-africadosul.pt; Ambassador KEITUMETSE MATT-HEWS.

Spain: Rua do Salitre 1, 1296-052 Lisbon; tel. (21) 3472381; fax (21) 3472384; e-mail emb.lisboa@maec.es; internet www.maec.es/ embajadas/lisboa; Ambassador EDUARDO JUNCO.

Sweden: Rua Miguel Lupi 12, 2° dto, 1249-077 Lisbon; tel. (21) 3942260; fax (21) 3942261; e-mail ambassaden.lissabon@foreign .ministry.se; internet www.swedenabroad.com/lissabon; Ambassador CAROLINE FLEETWOOD.

Switzerland: Travessa do Jardim 17, 1350-185 Lisbon; tel. (21) 3944090; fax (21) 3955945; e-mail lis.vertretung@eda.admin.ch; internet www.eda.admin.ch/lisbon; Ambassador LORENZO SCHNYDER VON WARTENSEE.

Thailand: Rua de Alcolena 12, 1400-005 Lisbon; tel. (21) 3014848; fax (21) 3018181; e-mail thai.lis@mail.telepac.pt; internet www .thaiembassy.org/lisbon; Ambassador CHAKORN SUCHIVA.

Timor-Leste: Largo dos Jerónimos 3, 1°, Santa Maria de Belém, 1400-209 Lisbon; tel. (21) 3933730; fax (21) 3933739; e-mail embaixada.rdtl@mail.telepac.pt; Ambassador NATÁLIA CARRASCA-LÃO.

Tunisia: Rua Rodrigo Rebelo 16, 1400-318 Lisbon; tel. (21) 3010330; fax (21) 3016817; e-mail at.lisbonne@netcabo.pt; Ambassador YOUSUF LOUZIR.

Turkey: Av. das Descobertas 22, 1400-092 Lisbon; tel. (21) 3003110; fax (21) 3017934; e-mail embassy.lisbon@mfa.gov.tr; internet lizbon .be.mfa.gov.tr; Ambassador EBRU BARUTÇU GÖKDENIZLER.

Ukraine: Av. das Descobertas 18, 1400-092 Lisbon; tel. (21) 3010043; fax (21) 3010059; e-mail emb_pt@mfa.gov.ua; internet www.mfa.gov.ua/portugal; Ambassador OLEKSANDR NYKONENKO.

United Kingdom: Rua de São Bernardo 33, 1249-082 Lisbon; tel. (21) 3924000; fax (21) 3924021; e-mail ppa.lisbon@fco.gov.uk; internet ukinportugal.fco.gov.uk; Ambassador JILL GALLARD.

USA: Av. das Forças Armadas (Sete Rios), 1600-081 Lisbon; Apdo 43033, 1601-301 Lisbon; tel. (21) 7273300; fax (21) 7269109; e-mail lisbonweb@state.gov; internet portugal.usembassy.gov; Ambassador ALLAN J. KATZ.

Uruguay: Rua Sampaio Pina 16, 2°, 1070-249 Lisbon; tel. (21) 3889265; fax (21) 3889245; e-mail urulusi@sapo.pt; Ambassador JÓSE IGNACIO KORZENIAK.

Venezuela: Av. Duque de Loulé 47, 4°, 1050-086 Lisbon; tel. (21) 3573803; fax (21) 3527421; e-mail embavenezlisboacentral@gmail .com; Ambassador LUCAS ENRIQUE RINCÓN ROMERO.

Judicial System

The judicial system of the Portuguese Republic comprises several categories of courts which, according to the Constitution, are sovereign bodies. The country is divided into four judicial districts, which are, in turn, divided into 37 judicial circuits. The principle of habeas corpus is recognized. Citizens who have been unjustly convicted are entitled to a review of their sentence and to compensation. The death penalty is prohibited by the Constitution. The jury system, reintroduced for certain types of crime in 1976, operates only at the request of the Public Prosecutor or defendant.

Judges are appointed for life and are irremovable. Practising judges may not hold any other office, whether public or private, except a non-remunerated position in teaching or research in the legal field. The Conselho Superior da Magistratura controls their appointment, transfer and promotion and the exercise of disciplinary action.

PUBLIC PROSECUTION

The state is represented in the courts by the Public Prosecution, whose highest organ is the Procuradoria-Geral da República (Attorney-General's Office).

Procuradoria-Geral da República: Rua da Escola Politécnica 140, 1269-269 Lisbon; tel. (21) 3921900; fax (21) 3975255; e-mail mailpgr@pgr.pt; internet www.pgr.pt; Attorney-General Dr FERNANDO JOSÉ MATOS PINTO MONTEIRO.

SUPREME COURT

Supremo Tribunal de Justiça: Praça do Comércio, 1149-012 Lisbon; tel. (21) 3218900; fax (21) 3474919; e-mail correio@lisboa .stj.pt; internet www.stj.pt; highest organ of the judicial system; consists of 60 judges, incl. the President; Pres. Luís António Noronha do Nascimento.

COURTS OF SECOND INSTANCE

There are five Courts of Second Instance (or Courts of Appeal):

Tribunal da Relação de Coímbra: Palácio da Justiça, Rua da Sofia, 3004-501 Coimbra; tel. (239) 852950; fax (239) 838985; e-mail coimbra.tr@tribunais.org.pt; internet www.trc.pt; 46 judges, incl. the President; Pres. António Joaquim Piçarra.

Tribunal da Relação de Évora: Palácio Barahona, Rua da República 141–143, 7004-501 Évora; tel. (266) 758800; fax (266) 701529; e-mail evora.tr@tribunais.org.pt; internet www.tre.pt; 39 judges, incl. the President; Pres. Dr Joaquim António Chambel Mourisco.

Tribunal da Relação de Guimarães: Largo João Franco 248, 4810-269 Guimarães; tel. (253) 439900; fax (253) 439999; e-mail guimaraes.tr@tibunais.org.pt; internet www.trg.mj.pt; 31 judges, incl. the President; Pres. Dr António Alberto Rodrigues Ribeiro.

Tribunal da Relação de Lisboa: Rua Arsenal, Letra G, 1100-038 Lisbon; tel. (21) 3222900; fax (21) 3222992; e-mail lisboa.tr@ tribunais.org.pt; internet www.trl.mj.pt; 108 judges, incl. the President; Pres. Dr Luís Maria Vaz das Neves.

Tribunal da Relação do Porto: Campo Mártires de Pátria, 4099-012 Porto; tel. (22) 2008531; fax (22) 2000715; e-mail porto.tr@ tribunais.org.pt; internet www.trp.pt; 91 judges, incl. the President; Pres. Dr José António de Sousa Lameira.

COURTS OF FIRST INSTANCE

There are 258 Courts of First Instance within Portuguese territory: 195 comarca courts hear cases of a general nature, while 46 labour courts hear specific matters. There are five family courts and two courts for the enforcement of sentences. Circuit Courts total 33.

CONSTITUTIONAL COURT

Tribunal Constitucional: Palácio Ratton, Rua de O Século 111, 1249-117 Lisbon; tel. (21) 3233600; fax (21) 3233649; e-mail tribunal@tribconstitucional.pt; internet www .tribunalconstitucional.pt; rules on matters of constitutionality according to the terms of the Constitution of the Portuguese Republic; exercises jurisdiction over all Portuguese territory; consists of 13 judges, incl. the President; Pres. Joaquim de Sousa Ribeiro.

SUPREME ADMINISTRATIVE COURT

Supremo Tribunal Administrativo: Rua de S. Pedro de Alcântara 75–79, 1269-137 Lisbon; tel. (21) 3216200; fax (21) 3466129; e-mail correio@lisboa.sta.mj.pt; internet www.stadministrativo.pt; highest organ of the administrative system; has jurisdiction over metropolitan Portugal, the Azores and Madeira; there is also a Supremo Tribunal Administrativo Norte and Sul; consists of 37 judges, incl. the President.; Pres. Lúcio Alberto de Assunção Barbosa.

Religion

There is freedom of religion in Portugal. The dominant Christian denomination is Roman Catholicism. In the 2011 census, of the 8,244,975 respondents to the question regarding religion, 7,281,887 of those over the age of 15 identified themselves as Catholic, 56,550 as Orthodox Christian, 75,571 as Protestant and 163,338 as other Christian. A further 3,061 were Jewish, 20,640 were Muslim and 28,596 followed another religion.

CHRISTIANITY

The Roman Catholic Church

For ecclesiastical purposes, Portugal comprises 17 dioceses, grouped into three metropolitan sees (the patriarchate of Lisbon and the archdioceses of Braga and Évora). At 31 December 2006 some 9,058,788 Portuguese were adherents of the Roman Catholic Church, representing 86.4% of the population.

Bishops' Conference

Conferência Episcopal Portuguesa, Quinta do Cabeço, Porta D, 1885-076 Moscavide, Lisbon; tel. (21) 8855460; fax (21) 8855461; e-mail cep .sgeral@ecclesia.pt; internet www.ecclesia.pt.

f. 1932; Pres. Most Rev. José da Cruz Policarpo (Patriarch of Lisbon); Sec. Fr Manuel Morujão.

Patriarch of Lisbon: Cardinal José da Cruz Policarpo, Casa Patriarcal, Quinta do Cabeço, 1800-076 Moscavide, Lisbon; tel.

(21) 9457310; fax (21) 9457329; e-mail gab.patriarca@ patriarcado-lisboa.pt; internet www.patriarcado-lisboa.pt.

Archbishop of Braga: Most Rev. Jorge Ferreira da Costa Ortiga, Paço Arquiepiscopal, Rua de Santa Margarida 181, 4710-306 Braga; tel. (253) 202820; fax (253) 203191; e-mail diocese@diocese-braga.pt; internet www.diocese-braga.pt.

Archbishop of Évora: Most Rev. José Francisco Sanches Alves, Cúria Arquidiocesana, Largo Marquês de Marialva, 7000-809 Évora; tel. (266) 748850; fax (266) 748851; e-mail informatica@diocese-evora .pt; internet www.diocese-evora.pt.

Other Christian Churches and Organizations

Associação de Igrejas Baptistas Portuguesas (Asscn of Portuguese Baptist Churches): Rua da Escola 18, Maceira, 2715 Pero Pinheiro; tel. (21) 9271150; f. 1955; Pres. Rev. João S. Regueiras.

Conselho Português de Igrejas Cristãs (COPIC) (Portuguese Council of Christian Churches): Praça do Coronel Pacheco 23, 4050-453 Porto; tel. (22) 2007410; e-mail bispo@igreja-methodista.pt; f. 1971; mems include the Igreja Lusitana Católica Apostólica Evangélica, the Igreja Evangélica Metodista Portuguesa and the Igreja Evangélica Presbiteriana de Portugal; Pres. Rt Rev. Fernando Luz Soares.

Convenção Baptista Portuguesa (Portuguese Baptist Convention): Rua Luís Simões 7, 1º, Apdo 3085, 2746-501 Queluz; tel. (21) 4365737; fax (21) 4343379; e-mail convencao.b.portuguesa@gmail .com; f. 1920; Pres. Pastor Abel Pego; Vice-Pres. João David Santos; 4,650 mems (2010).

Igreja Evangélica Metodista Portuguesa (Portuguese Evangelical Methodist Church): Praça Coronel Pacheco 23, 4050-453 Porto; tel. (22) 2007410; fax (22) 2086961; e-mail sede-geral@ igreja-metodista.pt; internet www.igreja-metodista.pt; Bishop Sifredo Teixeira.

Igreja Evangélica Presbiteriana de Portugal (Presbyterian Church of Portugal): Rua Eduardo Augusto Pedroso 12, 1°, 1495-047 Oeiras; tel. and fax (21) 4113048; e-mail office@iepp.org; internet www.iepp.org; f. 1952; Pres. Silvina Queiroz; Gen. Sec. Dulce Cabete.

Igreja Lusitana Católica Apostólica Evangélica—Comunhão Anglicana (Lusitanian Catholic Apostolic Evangelical Church—Anglican Communion): Rua de Afonso Albuquerque 86, Apdo 392, 4430-905 Vila Nova de Gaia; tel. (22) 3754018; fax (22) 3752016; e-mail centrodiocesano@igreja-lusitana.org; internet www .igreja-lusitana.org; f. 1880; extraprovincial diocese of the Anglican Communion under the metropolitan authority of the Archbishop of Canterbury (UK) since 1980; Bishop Rt Rev. Fernando Luz Soares.

ISLAM

Comunidade Islamica de Lisboa: Mesquita Central de Lisboa, Av. José Malhoa, 1000 Lisbon; tel. (21) 3874142; fax (21) 3872230; e-mail info@comunidadeislamica.pt; internet www .comunidadeislamica.pt; f. 1968; Pres. Abdul Majid Karim Vakil.

JUDAISM

There are Jewish communities in Lisbon, Oporto, Belmonte and Portimão.

Comunidade Israelita de Lisboa: Rua do Monte Olivete 16, r/c, 1200-280 Lisbon; tel. (21) 3931130; fax (21) 3931139; e-mail administrativo@cilisboa.org; internet www.cilisboa.org; Pres. Dr José Oulman Carp.

Comunidade Israelita do Porto: Rua Guerra Junqueiro 340, 4150–186 Oporto; tel. (22) 6092789; e-mail info@ comunidade-israelita-porto.org; internet comunidade -israelita-porto.org; f. 1923.

The Press

PRINCIPAL DAILIES

(circulation figures refer to 2011, unless otherwise indicated)

Aveiro

Diário de Aveiro: Av. Dr Lourenço Peixinho 15, 5°, 3800-801 Aveiro; tel. (234) 000030; fax (234) 000033; e-mail diarioaveiro@ diarioaveiro.pt; internet www.diarioaveiro.pt; f. 1985; morning; Dir Adriano Callé Lucas; circ. 3,334.

Braga

Diário do Minho: Rua de Santa Margarida 4A, 4710-306 Braga; tel. (253) 609460; fax (253) 609465; e-mail redaccao@diariodominho.pt; internet www.diariodominho.pt; f. 1919; morning; Dir Luís da Silva Pereira; circ. 4,706.

Coímbra

Diário as Beiras: Rua Abel Dias Urbano 4, 2°, 3000-001 Coímbra; tel. (239) 980280; fax (239) 983574; e-mail agostinho.franklin@ asbeiras.pt; internet www.asbeiras.pt; Dir AGOSTINHO FRANKLIN; circ. 7,899.

Diário de Coímbra: Rua Adriano Lucas, Apdo 542, 3020-264 Coímbra; tel. (239) 499900; fax (239) 499992; e-mail redac@ diariocoimbra.pt; internet www.diariocoimbra.pt; f. 1930; morning; *Domingo* publ. on Sun. (f. 1974; circ. 8,000); Dir ADRIANO CALLE LUCAS; circ. 7,816.

Évora

Diário do Sul: Estrada de Arraiolos, Évora; tel. (266) 730410; fax (266) 730411; internet www.diariodosul.com.pt; f. 1969; morning; Dir MANUEL MADEIRA PIÇARRA; circ. 5,418.

Leiria

Diário de Leiria: Edif. Maringá, Rua S. Franciso 7, 4° esq., 2400-232 Leiria; tel. (244) 000031; fax (244) 000032; e-mail diarioleiria@ diarioleiria.pt; internet www.diarioleiria.pt; f. 1987; morning; Dir ADRIANO CALLÉ LUCAS; circ. 1,737.

Lisboa
(Lisbon)

A Bola: Travessa da Queimada 23, 2°D r/c esq., 1294 Lisbon; tel. (21) 3463981; fax (21) 3432275; internet www.abola.pt; f. 1945; sport; Dir VICTOR SERPA.

Correio da Manhã: Av. João Crisóstomo 72, 1069-043 Lisbon; tel. (21) 3185200; fax (21) 3156146; e-mail geral@correiomanha.pt; internet www.correiomanha.pt; f. 1979; morning; independent; Dir OCTÁVIO RIBEIRO; circ. 120,994.

Diário Económico: Rua Vieira da Silva 45, 1350-342 Lisbon; tel. (21) 3236700; fax (21) 3236801; e-mail economico@economico.pt; internet diarioeconomico.sapo.pt; Dir ANTÓNIO COSTA; circ. 14,446.

Diário de Notícias: Av. Liberdade 266, 1250-149 Lisbon; tel. (21) 3187500; fax (21) 3187515; e-mail dn@dn.pt; internet dn.sapo.pt; f. 1864; morning; Dir JOÃO MARCELINO; circ. 34,987.

i (informação): Taguspark, Edif. Tecnologia I, Corpo 1, 2740-257 Oeiras; tel. (21) 0434000; fax (21) 0434011; e-mail info@ionline.pt; internet www.ionline.pt; f. 2009; morning; Dir EDUARDO OLIVEIRA E SILVA; circ. 7,405.

Público: Rua Viriato 13, 1069-315 Lisbon; tel. (21) 0111000; fax (21) 0111006; internet www.publico.pt; f. 1990; morning; Dir BÁRBARA REIS; circ. 32,032.

Record: Av. Conde Valbom 30, 4-5°, 1050-068 Lisbon; tel. (21) 0124900; fax (21) 3476279; e-mail record@record.pt; internet www .record.pt; f. 1949; sport; Dir ALEXANDRE PAIS; circ. 55,543.

Porto
(Oporto)

O Jogo: Rua de Gil Vicente 129, 1°, 4000-814 Porto; tel. (22) 5071900; fax (22) 5504550; e-mail ojogo@mail.telepac.pt; internet www.ojogo .pt; f. 1985; sporting news; Dir JOSÉ MANUEL RIBEIRO; circ. 23,273.

Jornal de Notícias: Rua de Gonçalo Cristóvão 195, 4049-011 Porto; tel. (22) 2096111; fax (22) 2096140; e-mail noticias@jn.pt; internet www.jn.pt; f. 1888; morning; Dir MANUEL TAVARES; circ. 82,401.

O Primeiro de Janeiro: Rua de Santa Catarina 489, 2°, 4000-452 Porto; tel. (22) 0967847; fax (22) 5103291; e-mail geral@ oprimeirodejaneiro.pt; internet www.oprimeirodejaneiro.pt; f. 1868; independent; morning; Dir RUI ALAS PEREIRA; circ. 20,200 (2007).

Setúbal

Correio de Setúbal: Rua Camilo Castelo Branco 163 F–H, Apdo 549, 2900-450 Setúbal; tel. (265) 538810; fax (265) 538813; e-mail correiodesetubal@sado2000.pt.

Viseu

Diário Regional de Viseu: Rua Alexandre Herculano 198, 2°, 3510-033 Viseu; tel. (232) 000031; fax (232) 000032; e-mail diarioviseu@ diarioregional.pt; internet www.diarioregional.pt; Dir ADRIANO CALLÉ LUCAS; circ. 2,386.

Notícias de Viseu: Av. do Convento 1, Apdo 3115, 3510-690 Viseu; tel. (232) 410410; fax (232) 410418; e-mail geral@noticiasdeviseu .com; internet www.noticiasdeviseu.com; f. 1974; Dir FERNANDO ABREU.

Os Açores
(The Azores)

Açoriano Oriental: Rua Dr Bruno Tavares Carreiro 36, 9500-055 Ponta Delgada; tel. (296) 202800; fax (296) 202825; e-mail pub.ao@ acorianooriental.pt; internet www.acorianooriental.pt; f. 1835; morning; Dir PAULO SIMÕES; circ. 4,167.

Correio dos Açores: Rua Dr João Francisco de Sousa 14, 9500 Ponta Delgada; tel. (296) 201060; fax (296) 286119; internet www .correiodosacores.net; f. 1920; morning; Dir AMÉRICO NATALINO VIVEIROS.

Diário dos Açores: Rua Dr João Francisco de Sousa 16, 9500-187 Ponta Delgada; tel. (296) 284355; fax (296) 284840; e-mail jornal@ diariodosacores.pt; internet www.diariodosacores.pt; f. 1870; morning; Dir PAULO HUGO VIVEIROS.

Diário Insular: Av. Infante D. Henrique 1, 9700-098 Angra do Heroísmo, Terceira; tel. (295) 401050; fax (295) 214246; e-mail diarioins@mail.telepac.pt; internet www.diarioinsular.com; f. 1946; morning; Dir JOSÉ LOURENÇO.

Madeira

Diário de Notícias: Rua Dr Fernão de Ornelas 56, 3°, 9054-514 Funchal; tel. (291) 202300; fax (291) 202306; e-mail dnmad@ dnoticias.pt; internet www.dnoticias.pt; f. 1876; morning; independent; Dir JOSÉ BETTENCOURT DA CÁMARA; circ. 11,797.

Jornal da Madeira: Rua Dr Fernão de Ornelas 35 r/c, 4°, 9001-905 Funchal; tel. (291) 210400; fax (291) 210401; e-mail secretariado@ jornaldamadeira.pt; internet www.jornaldamadeira.pt; f. 1927; morning; Catholic; Dir JOÃO AFONSO DE ALMEIDA.

PRINCIPAL PERIODICALS

Activa: Rua Calvet de Magalhães 242, Laveiras, 2770-022 Paço de Arcos; tel. (21) 4143078; fax (21) 4107050; internet activa.aeiou.pt; f. 1991; monthly; for women; Editor ROSÁRIA BARRETO; circ. 70,800 (2010).

Africa Hoje: Rua Joaquim António de Aguiar 45, 5° esq., 1070 Lisbon; tel. (21) 557175; fax (21) 3557667; e-mail geral@lucidus.pt; f. 1985; monthly; African affairs; Dir ALBÉRICO CARDOSO; circ. 30,000 (2007).

Anglo-Portuguese News: Apdo 113, 2766-902 Estoril, Lisbon; tel. (21) 4661471; fax (21) 4660358; e-mail apn@mail.telepac.pt; f. 1937; Thur.; English-language newspaper; Publr and Editor NIGEL BATLEY; circ. 30,000 (2007).

Autosport: Edif. São Francisco de Sales, Rua Calvet de Magalhães 242, 2770-022 Paço de Arcos; tel. (21) 4698197; fax (21) 4698552; e-mail autosport@autosport.pt; internet www.autosport.pt; weekly; motoring; Dir RUI FREIRE; circ. 15,523 (2010).

Avante: Av. Almirante Gago Coutinho 121, 1700-029 Lisbon; tel. (21) 7817190; fax (21) 7817193; e-mail avante.pcp@mail.telepac.pt; internet www.avante.pt; weekly; organ of the Portuguese Communist Party; Dir JOSÉ CASANOVA.

Brotéria—Revista de Cultura: Rua Maestro António Taborda 14, 1249-094 Lisbon; tel. (21) 3961660; fax (21) 3956629; e-mail geral@ broteria.pt; internet www.broteria.pt; f. 1902; monthly; review of culture; Dir ANTÓNIO VAZ PINTO; circ. 1,400 (2007).

Casa & Jardim: Rua da Misericórdia 137, s/loja, 1249-037 Lisbon; tel. (21) 3472127; fax (21) 3421490; e-mail direccao@casajardim.pt; f. 1978; monthly; home, interior and exterior design, fine arts, exhibitions and antique fairs; Dir EDUARDO FORTUNATO DE ALMEIDA; circ. 14,486 (2006).

Colóquio/Letras: Av. de Berna 45, 1067-001 Lisbon; tel. (21) 7823567; fax (21) 7823631; e-mail coloquioletras@gulbenkian.pt; internet www.coloquio.gulbenkian.pt; f. 1971; 3 a year; owned by Calouste Gulbenkian Foundation; literary; Dir Prof. NUNO JÚDICE; circ. 1,500.

Correio da Madeira: Rua do Carmo 19, 3° dto, 9000 Funchal; tel. (291) 20738; f. 1987; weekly newspaper; Dir JOSÉ CAMPOS; circ. 5,000.

Eles e Elas: Rua de São Bento 311, 3° esq., 1269-083 Lisbon; tel. (21) 3224660; fax (21) 3224679; e-mail gabinete1@gabinete1.pt; internet www.gabinete1.pt; f. 1983; monthly; fashion, culture, social events; Dir MARIA DA LUZ DE BRAGANÇA.

Elle: Rua Filipe Folque 40, 4°, 1050 Lisbon; tel. (21) 3156907; fax (21) 3164205; e-mail elle@hachette.pt; f. 1988; monthly; women's magazine; Dir FÁTIMA COTTA; circ. 44,533 (2010).

Expresso: Edif. S. Francisco de Sales, Rua Calvet de Magalhães 242, 2770-022 Paço de Arcos; tel. (21) 4544000; fax (21) 4435349; e-mail diretor@expresso.impresa.pt; internet www.expresso.sapo.pt; weekly newspaper; Dir RICARDO COSTA; circ. 104,131 (2010).

Gente e Viagens: Rua Joaquim António de Aguiar 45, 1099-058 Lisbon; tel. (21) 3839810; fax (21) 862746; e-mail lucidus@mail .telepac.pt; internet genteviagens.sapo.pt; f. 1980; monthly; tourism; circ. 30,000.

Guia—Revista Prática: Av. Almirante Gago Coutinho 113, 1749-087 Lisbon; tel. (21) 8474410; fax (21) 8474396; e-mail mpcorreia@ tvguia.pt; weekly; fashion and housekeeping; Dir MARGARIDA PINTO CORREIA; Editor-in-Chief PALMIRA SIMÕES; circ. 40,000.

JL (Jornal de Letras, Artes e Ideias): Rua Calvet de Magalhães 242, Laveiras, 2770-022 Paço de Arcos; tel. (21) 574520; e-mail jcvasconcelos@edimpresa.pt; internet aeiou.visao.pt/jornal -de-letras; f. 1981; fortnightly; Dir JOSÉ CARLOS DE VASCONCELOS; circ. 7,679 (2010).

Manchete: Rua de São Bernardo 27, 4°, 1200-823 Lisbon; tel. (21) 0999695; fax (21) 0999674; e-mail gabinete1@gabinete1.pt; internet www.gabinete1.pt; f. 1992; monthly; national and international events; Dir MARIA DA LUZ DE BRAGANÇA.

Maria: Av. Miguel Bombarda 33, 2745 Queluz; tel. 4364401; fax 4365001; internet www.impala.pt; f. 1977; weekly; women's magazine; Dir JACQUES RODRIGUES; Editor-in-Chief PAULA RODRIGUES; circ. 204,451 (2010).

Máxima: Arruamento D à Rua José Maria Nicolau, 1549-023 Lisbon; tel. (21) 3185200; e-mail lauratorres@maxima.cofina.pt; internet www.maxima.pt; f. 1989; women's magazine; Dir LAURA LUZES TORRES; circ. 68,459 (2006).

Moda & Moda: Rua Braamcamp 12, r/c esq., 1250-050 Lisbon; tel. (21) 3862426; fax (21) 3862426; e-mail modaemoda@netcabo.pt; f. 1984; 5 a year; fashion, beauty and art; Dir MARIONELA GUSMÃO; circ. 20,000 (2007).

Mulher Moderna: Rua da Impala 33A, 2710-070 Sintra; tel. (21) 9238218; fax (21) 9238463; internet www.impala.pt; f. 1988; weekly; women's magazine; Dir JACQUES RODRIGUES; Editor-in-Chief PAULA RODRIGUES; circ. 16,512 (2006).

Nova Gente: Rua da Impala 33A, 2710-070 Sintra; tel. (21) 9238130; fax (21) 9238197; internet www.impala.pt; f. 1979; weekly; popular; Dir JACQUES RODRIGUES; Editor-in-Chief ANTÓNIO SIMÕES; circ. 117,564 (2010).

Portugal Socialista: Largo do Rato 2, 1269-143 Lisbon; tel. (21) 3822000; f. 1967; quarterly; organ of the Socialist Party; Dir AUGUSTO SANTOS SILVA; circ. 5,000.

Povo Livre: Rua S. Caetano 9, 1249-087 Lisbon; tel. (21) 3918500; fax (21) 3976967; e-mail povolivre@psd.pt; weekly; organ of the Social Democratic Party; Dir JORGE MANUEL FERRAZ DE FREITAS NETO.

Revista ACP: Rua Rosa Araújo 24, 1250-195 Lisbon; tel. (21) 3180100; fax (21) 3180170; e-mail ricardo.barroso@acp.pt; internet www.acp.pt; f. 1908; monthly; motoring and tourism; Propr Automóvel Club de Portugal; Editor RICARDO BARROSO; circ. 180,000 (2013).

Revista Exame: Rua Calvet de Magalhães 242, Laveiras, 2770-022 Paço de Arcos; tel. (21) 4698000; fax (21) 4698500; e-mail icanha@edimpresa.pt; internet www.exame.pt; monthly; finance; Dir ISABEL CANHA; circ. 21,074 (2010).

Segredos de Cozinha: Edif. do Grupo Impala, Ranholas, 2710-460 Sintra; tel. (21) 92398033; fax (21) 9238044; e-mail gracamorais@impala.pt; internet www.impala.pt; f. 1985; weekly; cookery; Dir GRAÇA MORAIS; Editor-in-Chief PAULA RODRIGUES; circ. 12,271 (2010).

Selecções do Reader's Digest: Lagoas Park, Edif. 11-1°, 2740-270 Porto Salvo; tel. (21) 3810000; fax (21) 3859203; e-mail clientes .portugal@seleccoes.pt; internet www.seleccoes.pt; monthly magazine; Dir ISABEL BIVAR; circ. 103,690 (Oct.–Dec. 2007).

Semanário Económico: Rua da Oliveira ao Carmo 8, 5°, 1249-111 Lisbon; tel. (21) 3236774; fax (21) 3237603; e-mail seconomico@economicasgps.com; internet www.semanarioeconomico.com; weekly; economy, business and finance; Dir INÊS SERRA LOPES; circ. 10,616 (Oct.–Dec. 2007).

Sol: Rua de São Nicolau 120, 1100-550 Lisbon; tel. (21) 3246500; fax (21) 3246540; e-mail geral@sol.pt; internet sol.sapo.pt; f. 2006; weekly newspaper; Sat.; publ. by O Sol é Essencial; Dir JOSÉ ANTÓNIO SARAIVA; circ. 49,046 (Oct.–Dec. 2007).

TV Guia: Av. Almirante Gago Coutinho 113, 1749-087 Lisbon; tel. (21) 8474410; fax (21) 8474395; e-mail jgobern@tvguia.pt; weekly; TV programmes and general features; Dir JOÃO GOBERN; circ. 73,275 (2010).

TV 7 Dias: Av. Miguel Bombarda 33, 2745 Queluz; tel. 4364401; fax 4365001; internet www.tv7dias.pt; f. 1985; weekly; television magazine; Dir JOSÉ PAULO CANELAS; Editor-in-Chief FREDERICO VALARINHO; circ. 151,770 (2010).

Vida Económica: Rua Gonçalo Cristovão 111, 5°–7°, 4049-037 Porto; tel. (22) 3399400; fax (22) 2058098; e-mail ve@vidaeconomica.pt; internet www.vidaeconomica.pt; weekly; financial; Dir JOÃO PEIXOTO DE SOUSA; Editor-in-Chief JOÃO LUÍS DE SOUSA; circ. 12,202 (2010).

Visão: Rua Calvet de Magalhães 242, Laveiras, 2770-022 Paço de Arcos; tel. (22) 4698000; fax (22) 2698547; e-mail visao@impresa.pt; internet www.visaoonline.pt; f. 1993; weekly magazine; Dir-Gen. PEDRO CAMAHO; circ. 99,771 (2010).

NEWS AGENCY

Lusa (Agência de Notícias de Portugal, SA): Rua Dr João Couto, Lote C, 1500 Lisbon; tel. (21) 7116500; fax (21) 7116531; e-mail agencialusa@lusa.pt; internet www.lusa.pt; f. 1987; Pres. JOSÉ MANUEL DOS REIS BARROSO; News Editor LUÍS MIGUEL VIANA.

PRESS ASSOCIATIONS

Associação Portuguesa da Imprensa (APIMPRENSA) (Portuguese Press Association): Rua Gomes Freire 183, 4° esq., 1169-041 Lisbon; tel. (21) 3555092; fax (21) 3142191; e-mail geral@apimprensa .pt; internet www.apimprensa.pt; f. 1961; represents 600 publications, both local and national; Pres. JOÃO PALMEIRO; Sec.-Gen. JOANA RAMADA CURTO.

Associação da Imprensa Diária (Association of the Daily Press): Rua de Artilharia Um 69, 2°, 1250-138 Lisbon; tel. (21) 3857584; fax (21) 3873541; e-mail associacao.imprensa.diaria@gmail.com; f. 1938; 6 mems; Pres. FERNANDO ALVES MONTEIRO; Sec. ADRIANO CALLE LUCAS.

Associação da Imprensa Estrangeira em Portugal (AIEP): Sala da Imprensa, Palácio Foz, Praça dos Restauradores, 1250-187 Lisbon; fax (21) 3464145; e-mail belenchurg@yahoo.com; internet www.aiep.eu; f. 1976; Pres. BELÉN RODRIGO; Exec. Sec. ANNE GOVERNO.

Publishers

Âncora Editora: Av. Infante Santo 52, 3° esq., 1350-179 Lisbon; tel. (21) 3951223; fax (21) 3951222; e-mail ancora.editora@ancora-editora.pt; internet www.ancora-editora.pt; f. 1998; Portuguese literature and culture, factual and educational works.

Areal Editores: Rua da Torrinha 228H, 3°, 4050-610 Porto; tel. (22) 3393900; fax (22) 2005708; e-mail areal@arealeditores.pt; internet www.arealeditores.pt; educational.

Assírio & Alvim: Rua Passos Manuel 67B, 1150-258 Lisbon; tel. (21) 3583030; fax (21) 3583039; e-mail assirio@assirio.com; internet www .assirio.pt; f. 1972; poetry, fiction, essays, gastronomy, photography, art, children's literature, history, social sciences; Man. VASCO DAVID.

Bertrand Editora, SA: Rua Prof. Jorge da Silva Horta 1, 1500-499 Lisbon; tel. (21) 0305590; fax (21) 7607149; e-mail leitor@bertrand .pt; internet www.bertrand.pt; literature, arts, humanities, educational; Man. MARIO CORREIA.

Casa das Letras: Rua Cidade de Córdova 2, 2610-038 Alfragide; tel. (21) 0417410; fax (21) 4717737; e-mail servicocliente@leya.com; internet www.casadasletras.leya.com; fiction, politics, religion, history, economics, management, biographies, dictionaries, memoirs.

Circulo de Leitores: Rua Prof. Jorge da Silva Horta 1, 1500-499 Lisbon; tel. (21) 7626000; fax (21) 7607149; e-mail correio@circuloleitores.pt; internet www.circuloleitores.pt; f. 1971; fiction and non-fiction.

Coímbra Editora, Lda: Rua do Armado, Apdo 101, 3001-951 Coímbra; tel. (239) 8526540; fax (239) 852651; e-mail info@coimbraeditora.pt; internet www.coimbraeditora.pt; f. 1920; law, education, linguistics; Man. Dr JOÃO CARLOS A. OLIVEIRA SALGADO.

Edições Afrontamento, Lda: Rua de Costa Cabral 859, 4200-225 Porto; tel. (22) 5074220; fax (22) 5074229; e-mail editorial@edicoesafrontamento.pt; internet www.edicoesafrontamento.pt; f. 1963; fiction, poetry, cinema, children's books, history, sociology, philosophy, economics, politics, etc.; Dirs J. SOUSA RIBEIRO, A. SOUSA LUÍS.

Edições Almedina, SA: Rua Fernandes Tomás 76–80, 3000-167 Coimbra; tel. (239) 851903; fax (239) 851901; e-mail editora@grupoalmedina.net; internet www.grupoalmedina.net; f. 1955; law, education, economics, history, philosophy; CEO JOSÉ MIGUEL MARQUES MENDES.

Edições Asa: Rua Cidade de Córdova 2, 2610-038 Alfragide; tel. (22) 6166030; fax (22) 5322831; e-mail edicoes@asa.pt; internet www.asa .pt; f. 1951; literature, arts, schoolbooks, children's books, educational equipment; Gen. Man. AMÉRICO A. AREAL.

Edições Caixotim: Rua dos Clérigos 23, 4050-205 Porto; tel. (22) 3390831; fax (22) 3390833; e-mail edicoescaixotim@caixotim.pt; internet www.caixotim.pt; f. 2001; literature, history, criticism, essays, art, etc.; Publr and Editorial Dir PAULO SAMUEL.

Edições 70, Lda: Av. Fernão de Magalhães 584, 5°, 3000-174 Coimbra; tel. (21) 3190240; fax (21) 3190249; e-mail geral@edicoes70.pt; internet www.edicoes70.pt; f. 1970; history, linguistics, anthropology, philosophy, psychology, education, art, architecture, science, reference books; Dir CARLOS PINTO.

Editora Educação Nacional, Lda: Rua do Almada 125, 4018-001 Porto; tel. (22) 2005351; fax (22) 2080742; e-mail contacto@editoraeducnacional.pt; internet www.editoraeducnacional.pt; school textbooks and review, *Educação Nacional*.

Editora Livros do Brasil, SA: Estrada da Outurela 121, 2794-051 Carnaxide; tel. (21) 3462621; fax (21) 3428487; e-mail geral@livrosdobrasil.com; internet www.livrosdobrasil.com; f. 1944; literature, history, politics, science, management, health, children's books; Dir ANTÓNIO LUIS DE SOUZA PINTO.

Editora Pergaminho, Lda: Rua de Alegria 486A, Amoreira, 2645-167 Cascais; tel. (21) 4646110; fax (21) 4674008; e-mail info@ editorapergaminho.pt; internet www.editorapergaminho.pt; f. 1991; cinema, music, humour, fiction; Dir MÁRIO MENDES DE MOURA.

Editora Portugalmundo, Lda: Rua Gonçalves Crespo 47, r/c, 1150-184 Lisbon; tel. (21) 3304685; fax (21) 3590420; e-mail editoraportugalmundo@gmail.com; internet www .portugalmundoeditora.com; f. 1976; children's books, poetry, biographies, law, music, fiction, theatre; Dir MARIA ALEXANDRA SANTOS.

Editora Replicação, Lda: Rua Pedro Sintra 26A, 1400-277 Lisbon; tel. (21) 3021583; fax (21) 3021584; e-mail replic@mail.telepac.pt; f. 1982; textbooks, children's books, dictionaries, language materials; Dir JOSÉ CARLOS ANAIA CRISTO.

Editorial Bizancia, Lda: Largo Luis Chaves 11–11A, 1600-487 Lisbon; tel. (21) 7550228; fax (21) 7520072; e-mail bizancio@ editorial-bizancio.pt; internet www.editorial-bizancio.pt; f. 1998; general fiction and non-fiction.

Editorial Confluência: Calçada do Combro 99, 1200-112 Lisbon; tel. and fax (21) 3466917; e-mail livroshorizonte@mail.telepac.pt; f. 1945; dictionaries; Man. ROGÉRIO MENDES DE MOURA.

Editorial Estampa, Lda: Rua da Escola do Exército 9, r/c dto, 1169-090 Lisbon; tel. (21) 3555663; fax (21) 3141911; e-mail estampa@ estampa.pt; internet www.estampa.pt; f. 1960; sociology, economics, occult, fiction, sport, history, art, alternative medicine, children's; Dir ANTÓNIO CARLOS MANSO PINHEIRO.

Editorial Futura: Rua General Morais Sarmento 9, c/v esq., 1500-310 Lisbon; tel. and fax (21) 7155848; e-mail editorialfutura@netcabo .pt; literature, comics.

Editorial Minerva: Rua Luz Soriano 33, 1200-246 Lisbon; tel. (21) 3224950; fax (21) 3224952; e-mail minerva-beta@sapo.pt; internet www.editorialminerva.com; f. 1927; literature, politics, children's; Man. NARCISA FERNANDES.

Editorial Nova Ática, SA: Calçado Nova de S. Francisco, 10, 1° esq., 1200-300 Lisbon; tel. (21) 3420557; fax (21) 3420305; e-mail editorialnovaatica@sapo.pt; f. 1935; poetry, literature, essays, theatre, history, philosophy; Chief Execs VASCO SILVA, JOSÉ RODRIGUES.

Editorial Presença, SA: Estrada das Palmeiras 59, Queluz de Baixo, 2730-132 Barcarena; tel. (21) 4347000; fax (21) 4346502; e-mail info@presenca.pt; internet www.presenca.pt; f. 1960; social sciences, fiction, textbooks, computer books, business, leisure, health, children's books, etc.; Dir FRANCISCO ESPADINHA.

Editorial Verbo SA: Av. António Augusto de Aguiar 148, 6°, 1069-019 Lisbon; tel. (21) 3801100; fax (21) 3865396; e-mail babel@babel .pt; f. 1958; imprints include Editora Ulisseia; encyclopedias, dictionaries, reference, history, general science, textbooks, education and children's books; Dir FERNANDO GUEDES.

Europress—Editores e Distribuidores de Publicações, Lda: Rua João Saraiva 10A, 1700–249 Lisbon; tel. (21) 8444340; fax (21) 8492061; e-mail europress@mail.telepac.pt; internet www.europress .pt; f. 1982; academic, children's, law, poetry, health, novels, history, social sciences, medicine, etc.; Man. ANTÓNIO BENTO VINTÉM.

FCA (Editora de Informática, Lda): Rua D. Estefânia 183, r/c esq., 1000-154 Lisbon; tel. (21) 3532735; fax (21) 3577827; e-mail fca@fca .pt; internet www.fca.pt; f. 1991; computer science.

Gradiva—Publicações, Lda: Rua Almeida e Sousa 21, r/c esq., 1399-041 Lisbon; tel. (21) 3974067; fax (21) 3953471; e-mail geral@ gradiva.mail.pt; internet www.gradiva.pt; f. 1981; philosophy, education, history, fiction, science, social sciences, children's books, cartoons; Man. Dir GUILHERME VALENTE.

Guimarães Editores, Lda: Av. António Augusto de Aguiar, 148-6°, 1069-019 Lisbon; tel. (21) 3801100; fax (21) 3865396; e-mail babel@ babel.pt; internet www.babel.pt; f. 1899; literature, philosophy, history, etc.

Imprensa Nacional—Casa da Moeda, SA (INCM): Edif. Casa da Moeda, Av. António de José de Almeida, 1000-042 Lisbon; tel. (21) 7810700; fax (21) 7810754; e-mail incm@incm.pt; internet www.incm .pt; f. 1972 as Imprensa Nacional—Casa da Moeda, EP; changed status as above in 1999; Portuguese literature, arts, philosophy, history, geography, sociology, economics, encyclopedias, dictionaries, and the *Diário da República*; Dir Dr HELENA ESTEVES FELGAS.

Lello Editores, Lda: Rua Dom João de Castro 539, 4435-674 Baguim do Monte; tel. (22) 3326084; fax (22) 3326086; e-mail joselello@lelloeditores.com; internet www.lelloeditores.com; fiction, poetry, history, reference, biography, religion; Dir-Gen. JOSÉ MANUEL BERNARDES PEREIRA LELLO.

Lidel Edições Técnicas, Lda: Rua D. Estefânia 183, r/c dto, 1049-057 Lisbon; tel. (21) 3511440; fax (21) 3577827; e-mail lidel@lidel.pt; internet www.lidel.pt; f. 1963; Portuguese as a foreign language,

management, technology, computer science; Man. Dir FREDERICO CARLOS DA SILVA ANNES.

Lisboa Editora, Lda: Av. dos Estados Unidos da América 1B, 1700-163 Lisbon; tel. (21) 8430910; fax (21) 8430911; e-mail geral@ lisboaeditora.pt; internet www.lisboaeditora.pt; textbooks; Editorial Dirs MARIA DE LOURDES PAIXÃO, BRIGITTE THUDICHUM.

Livraria Civilização Editora: Rua Alberto Aires de Gouveia 27, 4050-023 Porto; tel. (22) 6050917; fax (22) 6050999; e-mail info@ civilizacao.pt; internet www.civilizacao.pt; f. 1920; social sciences, politics, economics, history, art, medicine, fiction, children's; Man. Dir MOURA BESSA.

Livraria Editora Figueirinhas, Lda: Rua do Freixo 643, 4300-217 Porto; tel. (22) 5309026; fax (22) 5309027; e-mail correio@ liv-figueirinhas.pt; f. 1898; literature, school textbooks; Dir FRANCISCO GOMES PIMENTA.

Livraria Multinova: Av. Santa Joana Princesa 12E, 1700-357 Lisbon; tel. (21) 8421820; fax (21) 8483436; e-mail geral@ multinova.pt; internet www.multinova.pt; f. 1970; school books, general, religion, Brazilian works; Dir CARLOS SANTOS.

Livraria Romano Torres: Rua Marcos Portugal 20A, 1200-258 Lisbon; tel. (21) 3880430; fax (21) 3040818; e-mail info@ estudodidactico.pt; f. 1885; fiction; Dir FRANCISCO NORONHA DE ANDRADE.

Livros Cotovia: Rua Nova da Trindade 24, 1200-303 Lisbon; tel. (21) 3471447; fax (21) 3470467; e-mail geral@livroscotovia.pt; internet www.livroscotovia.pt; f. 1988; literature, drama, poetry, etc.

Livros Horizonte, Lda: Rua das Chagas 17, 1° dto, 1200-106 Lisbon; tel. (21) 3466917; fax (21) 3159259; e-mail geral@ livroshorizonte.pt; internet www.livroshorizonte.pt; f. 1953; art, education, history, social sciences; Dir CLAUDIA MOURA.

Lusodidacta (Sociedade Portuguesa de Materia Didáctico, Lda): Rua Darío Cannas 5A, 2670-427 Loures; tel. (21) 9839840; fax (21) 9839847; e-mail loures1@lusodidacta.pt; internet www.lusodidacta .pt; f. 1976; textbooks, dictionaries, medicine.

PAULUS Editora: Rua Dom Pedro de Cristo 10, 1749-092 Lisbon; tel. (21) 8437620; fax (21) 8437629; e-mail editor@paulus.pt; internet www.paulus.pt; religion, theology, psychology, etc.; Dir DARLEI ZANON.

Plátano Editora, SARL: Av. de Berna 31, 2° esq., 1069-054 Lisbon; tel. (21) 7979278; fax (21) 7954019; e-mail geral@platanoeditora.pt; internet www.platanoeditora.pt; f. 1972; literature, educational, science, technical, dictionaries, etc.; Dir FRANCISCO PRATA GINJA.

Porto Editora, Lda: Rua da Restauração 365, 4099-023 Porto; tel. (22) 6088300; fax (22) 6088301; e-mail secretariado@portoeditora.pt; internet www.portoeditora.pt; f. 1944; general literature, school books, dictionaries, children's books, multimedia; Dirs VASCO TEIXEIRA, JOSÉ ANTÓNIO TEIXEIRA, ROSÁLIA TEIXEIRA.

Publicações Dom Quixote: Rua Cidade de Córdova 2, 2610-038 Alfragide; tel. (21) 4272200; fax (21) 4272201; e-mail info@dquixote .pt; internet www.dquixote.pt; f. 1965; general fiction, poetry, history, philosophy, psychology, politics, didactics and sociology; university textbooks; children's books.

Publicações Europa-América, Lda: Rua Francisco Lyon de Castro 2, Apdo 8, 2725-397 Mem Martins; tel. (21) 9267700; fax (21) 9267771; e-mail secretariado@europa-america.pt; internet www .europa-america.pt; f. 1945; imprints include Edições CETOP, Editorial Inquerito, Livros de Vida Editores, Lyon Edições and Publicações Alfa; fiction, current affairs, economics, reference, history, technical, children's; Dir TITO LYON DE CASTRO.

Quimera Editores, Lda: Rua do Vale Formoso 37, 1949-013 Lisbon; tel. (21) 8455950; fax (21) 8455951; e-mail quimera@ quimera-editores.com; internet www.quimera-editores.com; f. 1987; literature, art, history, photography, etc.; Dirs JOSÉ ALFARO, LUÍS VEIGA.

Rés—Editora, Lda: Praça Marquês de Pombal 78, 4000-390 Porto; tel. (22) 5024174; fax (22) 5026098; e-mail res-editora@res-editora .pt; internet www.res-editora.pt; f. 1975; economics, philosophy, law, sociology; Dir REINALDO DE CARVALHO.

Texto Editora, Lda: Rua Cidade de Córdova 2, 2610-038 Alfragide; tel. (21) 4272200; fax (21) 4272201; e-mail info@texto.pt; internet pt .textoeditores.com; f. 1977; school textbooks, management, pedagogy, health, beauty, cooking, children's books, multimedia; Man. Dir MANUEL JOSÉ DO ESPÍRITO SANTO FERRÃO.

PUBLISHERS' ASSOCIATION

Associação Portuguesa de Editores e Livreiros (Portuguese Association of Publishers and Booksellers): Av. dos Estados Unidos da América 97, 6° esq., 1700-167 Lisbon; tel. (21) 8435180; fax (21) 8489377; e-mail geral@apel.pt; internet www.apel.pt; f. 1927; Pres. PAULO TEIXEIRA PINTO; Sec.-Gen. MIGUEL FREITAS DA COSTA.

Broadcasting and Communications

REGULATORY AUTHORITY

Autoridade Nacional de Comunicações (ANACOM): Av. José Malhoa 12, 1009-017 Lisbon; tel. (21) 7211000; fax (21) 7211001; e-mail info@anacom.pt; internet www.anacom.pt; formerly Instituto das Comunicações de Portugal (ICP); Pres. JOSÉ MANUEL AMADO DA SILVA.

TELECOMMUNICATIONS

AR Telecom, SA: Edif. Diogo Cão, Doca de Alcântara Norte, 1350-352 Lisbon; tel. (21) 0301030; fax (21) 0301300; e-mail 16300@artelecom.pt; internet www.artelecom.pt; f. 2000 as Jazztel Portugal, SA; renamed as above in 2005; subsidiary of Grupo SGC; fixed-line operator.

Oni Communications, SA: Av. Fontes Pereira de Melo 27, 1069-447 Lisbon; tel. (21) 1154300; fax (21) 1154399; e-mail geral@oni.pt; internet www.oni.pt; f. 1998; fixed-line operator; CEO XAVIER RODRÍGUEZ-MARTÍN.

Optimus Telecomunicações, SA: Apartado 52121, 1721-501 Lisbon; tel. (21) 7233600; fax (21) 7546275; e-mail 1693@optimus.pt; internet www.optimus.pt; f. 1998; provides mobile telephone services; CEO MIGUEL ALMEIDA.

Portugal Telecom, SA (PT): Av. Fontes Pereira de Melo 40, 1069-300 Lisbon; tel. (21) 5002000; fax (21) 5000902; e-mail geral@telecom.pt; internet www.telecom.pt; f. 1994 by merger of 3 regional telecommunications operators; state holding reduced to 25% in 1997; relinquished monopoly on fixed-line operations in Jan. 2000; Chair. HENRIQUE GRANADEIRO; CEO ZEINAL BAVA.

Sonaecom-Serviços de Comunicações, SA: Rua Henrique Pousão 432, 7°, 4460-191 Senhora da Hora; tel. (93) 1002000; fax (22) 0111850; e-mail comunicacao@sonae.com; internet www.sonae.com; fixed-line operator; merged with Optimus Teleçomunicações, SA in 2007; Pres. PAULO TEIXEIRA DE AZEVEDO; CEO ÂNGELO GABRIEL DOS SANTOS PAUPÉRIO.

TMN (Telecomunicações Móveis Nacionais), SA: Av. Álvaro Pais 2, 1649-041 Lisbon; tel. (21) 7914400; fax (21) 7914440; e-mail tmn.comunica@tmn.pt; internet www.tmn.pt; f. 1991; part of Portugal Telecom; Pres. ZEINAL ABEDIN MAHOMED BAVA.

UZO: Av. Álvaro Pais 2, 1649-041 Lisbon; e-mail info@uzo.pt; internet www.uzo.pt; f. 2005; part of Portugal Telecom; mobile operator; Exec. Dir JOÃO MENDES.

Vodafone Portugal—Comunicações Pessoais, SA: Parque das Nações, Av. D. João II, Lote 1.04.01, 1998-017 Lisbon; tel. (21) 0915000; fax (21) 0915480; e-mail press.pt@vodafone.com; internet www.vodafone.pt; f. 1991; fmrly Telecel-Comunicações Pessoais; subsidiary of Vodafone Group PLC (UK); provides mobile and fixed-line telephone services; Chief Exec. MÁRIO VAZ.

Other fixed-line operators include Cabovisão, Coltel, Refer Telecom, Telemilénio, TV Cabo and TVTEL.

BROADCASTING

In 2006 there were around 350 radio stations in operation.

Radio

State-controlled Radio

Radio e Televisão de Portugal, SA (RTP): Av. Marechal Gomes da Costa 37, 1849-030 Lisbon; tel. (21) 7947000; fax (21) 7947570; internet www.rtp.pt; f. 1956; nationalized in 1975; became jt-stock co (with 100% public capital) in 1992; Pres. GUILHERME COSTA; Dir of Programmes RUI FERNANDES PÊGO.

Domestic Services:

Antena 1: tel. (21) 7947000; fax (21) 820199; e-mail antena1.programas@rtp.pt; internet www.rtp.pt/antena1; broadcasts 24 hours a day on medium-wave and FM; news, sport, music, etc.; Dir JOÃO COELHO.

Antena 2: tel. (21) 3820000; fax (21) 3820199; e-mail rdp.antena2@rtp.pt; internet tv1.rtp.pt/antena2; broadcasts classical music 24 hours a day on FM; Dir JOÃO ALMEIDA.

Antena 3: tel. (21) 3820000; fax (21) 3820017; e-mail antena3@programas.rdp.pt; internet tv1.rtp.pt/antena3; broadcasts 24 hours a day on FM; music and entertainment for young people; Dir JOSÉ MARINO CORREIA.

Commercial and Private Radio

Cidade FM: Rua Sampaio e Pina 24–26, 1099-044 Lisbon; tel. (21) 3821500; fax (21) 3821589; internet cidadefm.clix.pt; 1 FM transmitter; broadcasts 24 hours a day; Dir-Gen. JORDI JORDÀ; Dir of Programmes NUNO GONÇALVES.

Orbital FM: Travessa do Olival 6, 2685 Sacavém; tel. (21) 9401019; fax (21) 9427757; e-mail orbital@orbital.pt; internet www.orbital.pt; 1 FM transmitter; broadcasts 24 hours a day in Lisbon region.

Rádio Capital: Rua Viriato 25, 4° dto, 1050-234 Lisbon; tel. (21) 0105760; fax (21) 2740781; e-mail geral@radiocapital.fm; 1 FM transmitter; broadcasts 24 hours a day in Lisbon and Oporto.

Rádio Clube: Rua Sampaio e Pina 24, 1099-044 Lisbon; tel. (21) 3821500; fax (21) 3821589; e-mail internet@radiocomercial.pt; f. 1992; fmrly Radio Nostalgia; broadcasts music 24 hours a day on FM; Head LUÍS MONTEZ.

Rádio Comercial, SA: Rua Sampaio e Pina 24/26, 1000 Lisbon; tel. (21) 3821500; fax (21) 3821589; e-mail geral@radiocomercial.pt; internet www.radiocomercial.pt; f. 1979 as RDP-3; transferred to private ownership in 1993; broadcasts music, news and sport 24 hours a day on Rádio Comercial: (FM); since March 1998 on Rádio Nacional on MW to central and southern Portugal, also music, news and sport; Head PEDRO RIBEIRO; Dir of Programmes MIGUEL CRUZ.

Rádio Europa Lisboa: Rua Latino Coelho 50, 1°, 1050-137 Lisbon; tel. (21) 3510580; fax (21) 3510598; e-mail programas@radioeuropa.fm; internet www.radioeuropa.fm; fmrly Rádio Paris Lisboa; present name adopted 2006; one FM transmitter; broadcasts 24 hours a day; Dir ANTONIETA LOPES DA COSTA.

Rádio Juventude: Edif. Plátano, Loja A, Rua Prof. Hugo Correia Pardal, 6000-267 Castelo Branco; tel. (272) 341758; fax (272) 347660; e-mail radio.juventude@netvisao.pt; internet juventude.radios.pt; 1 FM transmitter; broadcasts 24 hours a day.

RR (Rádio Renascença): Rua Ivens 14, 1249-108 Lisbon; tel. (21) 3239200; fax (21) 3239299; e-mail mail@rr.pt; f. 1937; Roman Catholic station; broadcasts 24 hours a day on Rádio Renascença (FM, medium-wave and satellite; internet www.rr.pt), on RFM (FM and satellite; internet www.rfm.pt; Dir ANTÓNIO MENDES) and on MEGA FM (FM and satellite; internet www.mega.fm.pt; Dir NELSON CUNHA).

TSF—Rádio Jornal: Edif. Altejo, Sala 301, Rua 3 da Matinha, 1900-823 Lisbon; tel. (21) 8612500; fax (21) 8612510; e-mail tsf@tsf.pt; internet www.tsf.pt; broadcasts news and sport 24 hours a day on FM; Pres. JOAQUIM OLIVEIRA.

Television

State-controlled Television

Radio e Televisão de Portugal, SA (RTP): see Radio; 12 studios incl. Lisbon, Oporto, Ponta Delgada and Funchal; Pres. GUILHERME COSTA; Dir of Programmes JOSÉ MANUEL FRAGOSO.

Regional Centres:

RTP/Porto: Rua Conceição Fernandes 755, Apdo 174, 4402 Vila Nova de Gaia; tel. (22) 7156000; fax (22) 7110963; Dir DJALME NEVES.

RTP/Açores: Rua Castelo Branco, 9500-062 Ponta Delgada; tel. (296) 202100; fax (296) 201120; e-mail rtpa@rtp.pt; internet www.rtp.pt; Dir ANTÓNIO MAURÍCIO DE SOUSA.

RTP—Madeira: Rua Tenente Coronel Sarmento 15, 9000-020 Funchal; tel. (291) 202000; fax (291) 230753; e-mail rtp.madeira@rtp.pt; Dir Dr MARTIM FIGUEIROA GOMES SANTOS.

RTP/Internacional (RTPi): e-mail rtpi@rtp.pt; internet rtpi.rtp.pt; commenced satellite transmissions in June 1992; broadcasts in Portuguese 24 hours a day.

RTP/Africa: commenced transmissions to lusophone countries of Africa in 1997; broadcasts 24 hours a day; Dir JORGE GONÇALVES.

Cable, Commercial and Private Television

Cabovisão—Sociedade de Televisão por Cabo, SA: Lugar de Poços, Vale de Touros, 2950-425 Palmela; tel. (21) 0801080; fax (21) 0801000; e-mail info@cabovisao.pt; internet www.cabovisao.pt; authorized to operate in 156 municipalities (4.5m. homes).

Pluricanal Santarém: Edif. Ribatel, Estrada Nacional 3, S. Pedro, 2000 Santarém; tel. (244) 824925; fax (244) 824943.

SIC (Sociedade Independente de Comunicação, SA): Estrada da Outurela, Carnaxide, 2795 Linda-a-Velha; tel. 4173111; fax 4173118; e-mail atendimento@sic.pt; internet www.sic.pt; commenced transmissions in 1992; news and entertainment; Head FRANCISCO PINTO BALSEMÃO; Dir of Programmes NUNO SANTOS.

TVI (Televisão Independente, SA): Rua Mário Castelhano 40, 2734-502 Barcarena; tel. (21) 4347500; fax (21) 4347654; internet www.tvi.pt; commenced transmissions in 1993; Pres. MIGUEL DO AMARAL; Gen. Man. ROSA CULLELL.

TVTEL Comunicações, SA: Rua Delfim Ferreira 383, 4100-201 Porto; tel. (22) 0325800; fax (22) 6154949; internet www.zon.pt; 100% subsidiary of ZON TV Cabo.

Zon Multimédia—Serviços de Telecomunicações e Multimédia, SGPS, SA: Av. 5 de Outubro 208, 1069-203 Lisbon; tel. (21) 7824725; fax (21) 3564735; internet www.zon.pt; fmrly PT Multimédia; renamed as above in 2008; Chair. RODRIGO JORGE LUÍS DE ARAÚJO COSTA; 1.7m. customers.

ZON TV Cabo: Av. 5 de Outubro 208, 1069-203 Lisbon; tel. (21) 7824725; fax (21) 7824735; internet www.zon.pt; f. 1999; offers subscription-based television services, also broadband internet access and fixed-line telecommunications; Chair. RODRIGO JORGE LUÍS DE ARAÚJO COSTA.

ZON TV Cabo Açoreana, SA: Av. Antero de Quental 9C, 1°, 9500-160 Ponta Delgada; tel. (296) 302401; fax (296) 302405; e-mail cliente@zon-acores.pt; internet www.zon-acores.pt.

Zon TV Cabo Madeirense: Rua Estados Unidos da América, Nazaré, 9000-090 Funchal; tel. (291) 700800; fax (291) 766132; e-mail tvcabo@cabotvm.pt; internet www.zonmadeira.pt; f. 1992; 78% owned by ZON Multimedia; CEO NUNO AGUIAR.

Finance

(cap. = capital; res = reserves; dep. = deposits; m. = million; brs = branches; amounts in euros)

BANKING

Central Bank

Banco de Portugal: Rua do Ouro 27, 1100-150 Lisbon; tel. (21) 3213200; fax (21) 3464843; e-mail info@bportugal.pt; internet www.bportugal.pt; f. 1846; reorganized 1931 with the sole right to issue notes; nationalized in 1974; cap. 1m., res 6,017m., dep. 5,406m. (Dec. 2008); Gov. CARLOS DA SILVA COSTA; also maintains br. in Oporto; 10 brs.

Principal Banks

Banco Activobank SA (ActivoBank7): Rua Augusta 84, 1149-023 Lisbon; tel. (21) 4232673; fax (21) 0066883; e-mail ab7_dop@activobank7.pt; internet www.activobank7.pt; f. 1969 as Sociedade Financeira Portuguesa; nationalized 1975; privatized 1991 and name changed to Banco Mello, SA; name changed to above in 2010; owned by Banco Comercial Português, SA; cap. 23.5m., res 2.4m., dep. 211.4m. (Dec. 2009); Chair. PAULO TEIXEIRA PINTO.

Banco Bilbao Vizcaya Argentaria (Portugal), SA: Av. da Liberdade 222, 1250-148 Lisbon; tel. (21) 3117200; fax (21) 3117500; e-mail helpdesk@bbva.pt; internet www.bbva.pt; f. 1991 as Banco Bilbao Vizcaya; name changed 2000; cap. 280m., res 23.9m., dep. 7,444.9m. (Dec. 2010); Man. Dir ALBERTO CHARRO; 100 brs.

Banco BPI, SA: Rua Tenente Valadim 284, 4100-476 Porto; tel. (22) 2075000; fax (22) 6002954; e-mail dirint@bpi.pt; internet www.bancobpi.pt; f. 1998 following the absorption of Banco Fonseca e Burnay and Banco Borges e Irmão by Banco de Fomento e Exterior; cap. 990m., res −729.9m., dep. 28,183.7m. (Dec. 2011); Chair. FERNANDO ULRICH; 700 brs.

Banco Comercial Português (Millennium BCP): Praça D. João I 28, 4000-295 Porto; tel. (22) 7502424; fax (22) 2064139; internet www.millenniumbcp.pt; f. 1985; cap. 6,236.2m., res −329.2m., dep. 71,448m. (Dec. 2011); Chair., Exec. Bd NUNO MANUEL DA SILVA AMADO; 917 brs.

Banco Efisa, SA: Av. António Augusto de Aguiar 134, 4°, 1050-020 Lisbon; tel. (21) 3117800; fax (21) 3117915; e-mail dcb@bancoefisa.pt; f. 1994 by merger; nationalized in Nov. 2008; cap. 22m., res 4m., dep. 420m. (Dec. 2007); Man. Dir JOSÉ AUGUSTO OLIVEIRA COSTA.

Banco Espírito Santo, SA: Av. da Liberdade 195, 1250-142 Lisbon; tel. (21) 3501000; fax (21) 8557491; e-mail info@bes.pt; internet www.bes.pt; f. 1884; nationalized 1975; transfer to private sector completed 1992; 40% owned by BESPAR SGPS Lisbon, 10.8% owned by Crédit Agricole SA (France); cap. 4,242.1m., res 1,110.2m., dep. 53,409.3m. (Dec. 2011); Pres. and CEO RICARDO ESPÍRITO SANTO SILVA SALGADO; 457 brs.

Banco Finantia, SA: Rua General Firmino Miguel 5, 1600-100 Lisbon; tel. (21) 7202000; fax (21) 7202030; e-mail finantia@finantia.com; internet www.finantia.com; f. 1987; investment bank; 50% owned by Finantipar SGPS, SA; cap. 150m., res 4.8m., dep. 1,089m. (Dec. 2011); Pres. ANTÓNIO MANUEL AFONSO GUERREIRO; also br. in Oporto.

Banco Popular Portugal, SA: Rua Ramalho Ortigão 51, 1099-090 Lisbon; tel. (21) 0071000; fax (21) 0071996; e-mail s.mercados@bancopopular.pt; internet www.bancopopular.pt; f. 1991 as Banco Nacional de Crédito; present name adopted 2005; cap. 451m., res 83.7m., dep. 8,297.6m. (Dec. 2011); owned by Banco Popular Español (Spain); CEO RUI MANUEL MORGANHO SEMEDO; 174 brs.

Banco Santander Totta: Rua do Ouro 88, 1100-063 Lisbon; tel. (21) 3262000; fax (21) 3262271; e-mail santandertotta@santandertotta.pt; internet www.santandertotta.pt; f. 2004 by merger of Banco Totta & Açores, Banco Santander Portugal and Crédito Predial Português; owned by Banco Santander (Spain); cap. 656.7m., res 455.6m., dep. 20,866.8m. (Dec. 2011); CEO NUNO MANUEL DA SILVA AMADO; 763 brs.

Banif—Banco Internacional do Funchal SA: Rua de João Tavira 30, 9000-509 Funchal, Madeira; tel. (291) 207731; fax (291) 230221; e-mail info@banif.pt; internet www.banif.pt; f. 1988; cap. 764.5m., res 0.5m., dep. 10.7m. (Dec. 2011); absorbed Banco Banif e Comercial

dos Açores in 2008; Chair. HORÁCIO DA SILVA ROQUE; CEO Dr JOAQUIM FILIPE MARQUES DOS SANTOS; 290 brs.

BPN—Banco Português de Negócios, SA: Edif. Fronteira, Av. António Augusto de Aguiar 132, 1050-020 Lisbon; tel. (21) 3598000; fax (21) 3191622; e-mail marketing@banco.bpn.pt; internet www.bpn.pt; f. 1993; nationalized in Nov. 2008; cap. 380m., res 42.3m., dep. 1,890.1m. (Dec. 2011); Chair. FRANCISCO MANUEL MARQUES BANDEIRA; 213 brs.

Caixa-Banco de Investimento, SA (CaixaBI): Rua Barata Salgueiro 33, 1269-057 Lisbon; tel. (21) 3137300; fax (21) 3526327; e-mail caixabi@caixabi.pt; internet www.caixabi.pt; f. 1984 as Manufacturers Hanover Trust Co; present name adopted 2000; 99.7% owned by Caixa Geral de Depósitos, SA; cap. 81.3m., res 65.3m., dep. 1,109.6m. (Dec. 2011); Pres. and Chair. Dr JOSÉ LOURENÇO SOARES; CEO JORGE HUMBERTO CORREIA TOMÉ; 1 br.

Caixa Central de Crédito Agrícola Mútuo, CRL (Crédito Agrícola): Rua Castilho 233–233A, 1099-004 Lisbon; tel. (21) 3809900; fax (21) 3860996; e-mail dint.cccam@creditoagricola.pt; internet www.creditoagricola.com; f. 1984; 100% owned by 84 local co-operative banks; co-operative bank; cap. 867.6m., res 277.9m., dep. 11,448.8m. (Dec. 2011); Chair. and Pres. CARLOS COURELAS; CEO JOÃO ANTÓNIO MORAIS DA COSTA PINTO; 696 brs.

Caixa Económica Montepio Geral (Montepio Geral): Rua Áurea 219–241, POB 2882, 1100-062 Lisbon; tel. (21) 3248000; fax (21) 3248228; internet www.montepio.pt; f. 1844 as Caixa Económica de Lisboa; present name adopted 1991; cap. 1,245m., res −50.9m., dep. 16,449m. (Dec. 2011); Pres. ANTÓNIO TOMÁS CORREIA; 55 brs.

Caixa Geral de Depósitos, SA (CGD): Av. João XXI 63, 1000-300 Lisbon; tel. (21) 7953000; fax (21) 7905050; e-mail cgd@cgd.pt; internet www.cgd.pt; f. 1876; state-owned; grants credit for agriculture, industry, building, housing, energy, trade and tourism; cap. 5,150m., res −244.3m., dep. 75,198.3m. (Dec. 2011); Pres. and Chair. FERNANDO MANUEL BARBOSA FARIA DE OLIVEIRA; 830 brs.

Banking Association

Associação Portuguesa de Bancos (APB): Av. da República 35, 5°, 1050-186 Lisbon; tel. (21) 3510070; fax (21) 3579533; e-mail apbancos@apb.pt; internet www.apb.pt; f. 1984; Pres. Prof. ANTÓNIO DE SOUSA; Sec.-Gen. Dr JOÃO MENDES RODRIGUES; 28 mems.

STOCK EXCHANGE

Euronext Lisbon: Av. da Liberdade 196, 7°, 1250-147 Lisbon; tel. (21) 7900000; fax (21) 7952021; internet www.euronext.com; f. 1769 as Bolsa de Valores de Lisboa e Porto; merged with Euronext in 2002 and adopted current name; merged with New York Stock Exchange in 2007 to form NYSE Euronext; Chair. MIGUEL ATHAYDE MARQUES.

Regulatory Authority

Comissão do Mercado de Valores Mobiliários (CMVM): Av. da Liberdade 252, 1056-801 Lisbon; tel. (21) 3177000; fax (21) 3537077; e-mail cmvm@cmvm.pt; internet www.cmvm.pt; f. 1991; independent securities exchange commission; Pres. Dr CARLOS TAVARES.

INSURANCE

At the end of 2011 there were 43 insurance companies based in Portugal, of which 14 specialized in life insurance. In that year 35 foreign-owned companies were operating in Portugal.

Principal Companies

AXA-Portugal—Companhia de Seguros, SA: Rua Gonçalo Sampaio 39, 4002-001 Porto; tel. (22) 6081100; fax (22) 6081136; e-mail contacto@axa-seguros.pt; internet www.axa.pt; non-life; Pres. Dr JOÃO LEANDRO.

AXA-Portugal—Companhia de Seguros de Vida, SA: Praça Marquês de Pombal 14, Apdo 1953, 1990-156 Lisbon; tel. (21) 3506000; fax (21) 3506136; e-mail contacto@axa-seguros.pt; internet www.axa.pt; life and pension funds; Pres. Dr CARLOS PEDRO BRANDÃO DE MELO DE SOUSA E BRITO.

BPI Vida e Pensões—Companhia de Seguros, SA: Rua Braamcamp 11, 6°, 1250-049 Lisbon; tel. (21) 3111010; fax (21) 3111082; e-mail bpi.vida.reportes@bancobpi.pt; internet www.bpipensoes.pt; f. 1991; life and pension funds; owned by Banco BPI; Pres. Dr FERNANDO MARIA COSTA DUARTE ULRICH.

Companhia de Seguros Açoreana, SA: Largo da Matriz 45–52, 9501-908 Ponta Delgada; tel. (296) 201400; fax (296) 201483; e-mail info@csanet.pt; internet www.acornet.pt; f. 1892; life and non-life; Pres. DIOGO DA SILVEIRA.

Companhia de Seguros Allianz Portugal, SA: Rua Andrade Corvo 32, 1069-014 Lisbon; tel. (21) 3108300; fax (21) 3165570; e-mail info@allianz.pt; internet www.allianz.pt; f. 1907; fmrly Allianz Portugal; life, non-life and pension funds; CEO IVÁN JOSÉ DE LA SOTA DUÑABEITIA.

Companhia de Seguros Fidelidade–Mundial, SA: Largo do Calhariz 30, 1249-001 Lisbon; tel. (21) 3238000; fax (21) 3238001;

e-mail apoiocliente@fidelidademundial.pt; internet www
.fidelidademundial.pt; f. 1980 from merger of 4 cos; life, non-life and
pension funds; Pres. Dr JORGE MANUEL MAGALHÃES CORREIA.

Companhia de Seguros Tranquilidade, SA: Av. da Liberdade
242, 1250-149 Lisbon; tel. (21) 3503500; fax (21) 3503584; e-mail
lisboa@tranquilidade.pt; internet www.tranquilidade.pt; f. 1871;
non-life; privatized in 1990; Pres. LUÍS FREDERICO REDONDO LOPES.

Companhia de Seguros Tranquilidade Vida, SA (T-Vida): Av.
da Liberdade 230, 1250-149 Lisbon; tel. (21) 3167500; fax (21)
3153194; e-mail correio@tranquilidade-vida.pt; internet www
.tranquilidade.pt; life and pension funds; Pres. Dr LUÍS FREDERICO
REDONDO LOPES.

Cosec (Companhia de Seguro de Créditos, SA): Av. da República 58, 1069-057 Lisbon; tel. and fax (21) 7913700; fax (21) 7913720;
e-mail cosec@cosec.pt; internet www.cosec.pt; f. 1969; domestic and
export credit insurance; bond insurance; net profits 5.5m. (2007);
Chair. JOSÉ MIGUEL GOMES DA COSTA.

Crédito Agrícola Vida, SA: Rua Castilho 233A, 1050-185 Lisbon;
tel. (21) 3809900; fax (21) 3860996; e-mail linhadirecta@
creditoagricola.pt; internet www.credito-agricola.pt; life; Pres.
CARLOS COURELAS.

Eurovida, SA: Rua Ramalho Ortigão 51, 1099-090 Lisbon; tel. (21)
7924700; fax (21) 7924701; e-mail seguros@eurovida.pt; internet
www.eurovida.pt; Pres. Dr LUÍS EDUARDO DA SILVA BARBOSA.

Global—Companhia de Seguros, SA: Av. Duque de Avila 171,
1069-031 Lisbon; tel. (21) 3137500; fax (21) 3554021; e-mail
globalseguros@global-seguros.pt; internet www.global-seguros.pt;
non-life; Exec. Pres. ALBERTINO SILVA.

Groupama Seguros: Av. de Berna 24D, 1069-170 Lisbon; tel. (21)
7923100; fax (21) 7923232; e-mail group@ma.net; internet www
.groupama.pt; life and non-life; CEO JOÃO MARIA AZEVEDO DE
QUINTANILHA E MENDONÇA.

Império Bonança—Companhia de Seguros, SA: Largo do Calhariz 30, 1249-001 Lisbon; tel. (21) 3237201; fax (21) 3237839; e-mail
apoiocliente@imperiobonanca.pt; internet www.imperiobonanca.pt;
f. by merger of Companhia de Seguros Bonança, SA and Companhia
de Seguros Império, SA; Chair. Dr JORGE MANUEL BAPTISTA
MAGALHÃES CORREIA.

Liberty Seguros, SA: Av. Fontes Pereira de Melo 6–11, 1069-001
Lisbon; tel. (21) 3124300; fax (21) 3553300; e-mail geral@
libertyseguros.pt; internet www.libertyseguros.pt; f. 1922; life and
non-life; fmrly Companhia Europeia de Seguros, SA; CEO JOSÉ
ANTÓNIO DE SOUSA.

Lusitânia—Companhia de Seguros, SA: Rua São Domingos à
Lapa 35, 1249-130 Lisbon; tel. (21) 3926900; fax (21) 3973090; e-mail
sede@lusitania.pt; internet www.lusitania.pt; non-life; CEO JOSÉ
ANTÓNIO DE AREZ ROMÃO.

MAPFRE Seguros Gerais, SA: Rua Castilho 52, 1250-071 Lisbon;
tel. (21) 3819700; fax (21) 3819799; e-mail sim24@mapfre.pt; internet
www.mapfre.pt; f. 1998; non-life; net profits 5.5m., cap. 33.1m.
(2007); CEO ANTÓNIO MANUEL CARDOSO BELO.

Real Vida Seguros, SA: Edif. Capitólio, Av. de França 316, 2°, 4050-
276 Porto; tel. (22) 0410700; fax (22) 0410706; e-mail info.clientes@
realvidaseguros.pt; internet www.realvidaseguros.pt; f. 1988; non-
life; Pres. FRANCISCO DOMINGOS RIBEIRO NOGUEIRA LEITE.

**Santander Totta Seguros—Companhia de Seguros de Vida,
SA:** Rua da Mesquita 6, 1070-238 Lisbon; tel. (21) 3704000; fax (21)
3705978; e-mail ermelinda.martins@santander.pt; internet www
.santandertotta.pt; life; Pres. PEDRO AIRES CORUCHE DE CASTRO E
ALMEIDA.

Victoria—Seguros de Vida, SA/Victoria—Seguros, SA: Edif.
Victoria, Av. da Liberdade 200, 1250-147 Lisbon; tel. (21) 3134100;
fax (21) 3134700; e-mail victoria@victoria-seguros.pt; internet www
.victoria-seguros.pt; f. 1930/1981; transferred to private sector in
1993; life and pensions; non-life; Pres. JOSÉ ANTÓNIO PINTO RIBEIRO.

**Zurich—Companhia de Seguros, SA/Zurich—Companhia de
Seguros Vida, SA:** Rua Barata Salgueiro 41, 1269-058 Lisbon; tel.
(21) 3133100; fax (21) 3133111; e-mail zuritel.pt@zurich.com;
internet www.zurich.com/portugal; f. 1918; fmrly Companhia de
Seguros Metrópole; Pres. Dr NUNO MARIA SERRA SOARES DA FONSECA;
Chief Exec. JOSÉ M. COELHO.

Mutual Companies

Mútua dos Armadores da Pesca do Arrasto: Av. António
Augusto de Aguiar 7, 1°, 1069-117 Lisbon; tel. (21) 3515970; fax
(21) 3515999; e-mail info@mutuamar.com; f. 1942; marine and
workers' compensation, personal accident, sickness, fire, etc.; Pres.
Dr ANTÓNIO ALBERTO CARVALHO DA CUNHA.

Mútua dos Pescadores—Mútua dos Seguros, C.R.L.: Av. Santos
Dumont 57, 6°, 1050-202 Lisbon; tel. (21) 3936300; fax (21) 3936310;
e-mail geral@mutuapescadores.pt; internet www.mutuapescadores
.pt; f. 1942; co-operative; personal accident, marine, fire, workers'
compensation, etc.; net profits 0.5m. (2007); Dir-Gen. JERÓNIMO
TEIXEIRA.

Supervisory Authority

Instituto de Seguros de Portugal (ISP): Av. da República 76,
1600-205 Lisbon; tel. (21) 7903100; fax (21) 7938568; e-mail isp@isp
.pt; internet www.isp.pt; f. 1982; office in Oporto; Pres. FERNANDO
DIAS NOGUEIRA.

Insurance Association

Associação Portuguesa de Seguradores (APS): Rua Rodrigo da
Fonseca 41, 1250-190 Lisbon; tel. (21) 3848100; fax (21) 3831422;
e-mail aps@apseguradores.pt; internet www.apseguradores.pt;
f. 1982; Pres. PEDRO ROGÉRIO DE AZEVEDO SEIXAS VALE.

Trade and Industry
GOVERNMENT AGENCIES

AICEP Portugal Global: Av. 5 de Outubro 101, 1050-051 Lisbon;
tel. (21) 7909500; fax (21) 7935028; e-mail aicep@portugalglobal.pt;
internet www.portugalglobal.pt; f. 2007; fmrly Agência para o
Investimento e Comércio Externo de Portugal; promotes
internationalization of the Portuguese economy; Chair. and Chief
Exec. PEDRO REIS.

Autoridade de Segurança Alimentar e Económica (ASAE): Av.
Conde de Valbom 98, 1050-185 Lisbon; tel. (21) 7983600; fax (21)
7983654; e-mail correio.asae@asae.pt; internet www.asae.pt; f. 2005;
regulatory authority for food safety and economic activities (Ministry
of the Economy; Inspector-Gen. Dr ANTÓNIO NUNES.

Gabinete de Estratégia e Estudos (GEE): Rua da Prata 8, 1149-
057 Lisbon; tel. (21) 7921372; fax (21) 7921398; e-mail gee@gee
.min-economia.pt; internet www.gee.min-economia.pt; advises on
economic policy and strategy (Ministry of the Economy and
Employment); Dir JOÃO REIS LEÃO.

**Instituto de Apoio às Pequenas e Médias Empresas e a
Inovação (IAPMEI):** Edif. A, Estrada do Paço do Lumiar, 1649-
038 Lisbon; tel. (21) 3836000; fax (21) 3836283; internet www.iapmei
.pt; financial and technical support to small and medium-sized
enterprises (Ministry of the Economy and Employment); Pres. JAIME
SERRÃO ANDREZ.

Instituto de Financiamento da Agricultura e Pescas (IFAP):
Rua Castilho 45–51, 1269-163 Lisbon; tel. (21) 3846000; fax (21)
3846170; e-mail ifap@ifap.pt; internet www.ifap.min-agricultura.pt;
f. 2007; provides loans for agriculture and fisheries, acts as
intermediary with the European Agricultural Guarantee Fund
(EAGF), the European Agricultural Fund for Rural Development
(EAFRD) and the European Fisheries Fund (EFF); Pres. LUÍS
BARREIROS.

**Instituto Nacional de Engenharia Tecnologia e Inovação
(INETI):** Estrada do Paço do Lumiar, 1649-038 Lisbon; tel. (21)
0924600; fax (21) 7160901; e-mail atendimento@ineti.pt; internet
www.ineti.pt; f. 1977; industrial and technological research (Ministry of the Economy and Employment); Pres. Prof. MARIA TERESA
COSTA PEREIRA DA SILVA PONCE DE LEÃO.

Instituto Português de Apoio ao Desenvolvimento (IPAD): Av.
da Liberdade 192, 2°, 1250-147 Lisbon; tel. (21) 3176700; fax (21)
3147897; e-mail cooperacao.portuguesa@ipad.mne.gov.pt; internet
www.ipad.mne.gov.pt; f. 2003; part of Ministry of Foreign Affairs;
supports international devt; Pres. AUGUSTO MANUEL CORREIA.

Instituto Português da Qualidade (IPQ): Rua António Gião 2,
2829-513 Caparica; tel. (21) 2948100; fax (21) 2948101; e-mail ipq@
mail.ipq.pt; internet www.ipq.pt; manages and develops the
Portuguese Quality System (Ministry of the Economy and Employment); Pres. JOSÉ MANUEL DIOGO MARQUES DOS SANTOS.

DEVELOPMENT ORGANIZATIONS

**Centro para o Desenvolvimento e Inovação Tecnológicos
(CEDINTEC):** Rua de São Domingos à Lapa 117, 2° dto, 1200-834
Lisbon; tel. (21) 3955302; fax (21) 3961203; e-mail geral@cedintec.pt;
internet www.cedintec.pt; f. 1982; supports the creation of techno-
logical infrastructures; Pres. Dr PEDRO CASTELÃO DE ALMEIDA SOUSA
DIAS.

Cotec Portugal: Rua de Salazares 842, 4149-002 Porto; tel. (22)
6192910; fax (22) 6192919; e-mail secretariado@cotec.pt; internet
www.cotec.pt; f. 2003; Chair. Prof. JOÃO BENTO; CEO DANIEL BESSA.

Instituto do Vinho do Douro e do Porto (IVDP): Rua dos
Camilos 90, 5050–272 Peso da Régua; tel. (25) 4320130; fax (25)
4320149; e-mail ivdp@ivdp.pt; internet www.ivdp.pt; an official body
dealing with quality control and the promotion of port and Douro
wines; also gives technical advice to exporters; Pres. MANUEL DE
NOVAIS CABRAL.

Sociedade de Desenvolvimento da Madeira (SDM): Rua da
Mouraria 9, 1°, 9000-047 Funchal, Madeira; tel. (291) 201333; fax
(291) 201399; e-mail sdm@sdm.pt; internet www.sdm.pt; concessionaire of Madeira's International Business Centre; Chair. Dr
FRANCISCO COSTA.

Sociedade Nacional de Empreendimentos e Desenvolvimento Económico, SA (SNEDE): Av. Fontes Pereira de Melo 35, 19A, 1050-118 Lisbon; tel. and fax (21) 3139889; e-mail snede@snede.pt; internet www.snede.pt; f. 1976; private consultancy co in economy and management; Pres. Dr ALFREDO GONZALEZ ESTEVES BELO.

CHAMBERS OF COMMERCE AND TRADE ASSOCIATIONS

Associação Comercial e Industrial do Funchal/Câmara de Comércio e Indústria da Madeira (ACIF/CCIM): Rua dos Aranhas 24–26, 9000-044 Funchal; tel. (291) 206800; fax (291) 206868; e-mail geral@acif-ccim.pt; internet www.acif-ccim.pt; f. 1836; Pres. JOSÉ ALEXANDRE LEBRE THEOTÓNIO.

Associação Comercial de Lisboa/Câmara de Comércio e Indústria Portuguesa (ACL/CCIP): Palácio do Comércio, Rua das Portas de Santo Antão 89, 1169-022 Lisbon; tel. (21) 3224050; fax (21) 3224051; e-mail geral@acl.org.pt; internet www.acl.org.pt; f. 1834; Pres. BRUNO BOBONE; Sec.-Gen. Dr PEDRO MADEIRA RODRIGUES; 2,100 mems.

Associação Comercial do Porto/Câmara de Comércio e Indústria do Porto (ACP/CCIP): Palácio da Bolsa, Rua Ferreira Borges, 4050-253 Porto; tel. (22) 3399000; fax (22) 3399090; e-mail correio@cciporto.pt; internet www.cciporto.com; f. 1834; Chair. Dr RUI MOREIRA; 800 mems.

Associação Industrial Portuguesa—Câmara de Comércio e Indústria (AIP-CCI): Praça das Indústrias, Apdo 3200, EC Junqueira, 1301-918 Lisbon; tel. (21) 3601000; fax (21) 3641301; e-mail info@aip.pt; internet www.aip.pt; f. 1837; privately owned; Pres. JORGE ROCHA DE MATOS; 4,500 mems (2010).

Câmara de Comércio e Indústria de Ponta Delgada/Associação Empresarial das Ilhas de São Miguel e Santa Maria (CCIPD): Rua Ernesto do Canto 13–15, 9504-531 Ponta Delgada, Azores; tel. (296) 305000; fax (296) 305050; e-mail ccipd@ccipd.pt; internet www.ccipd.pt; f. 1979; Pres. MÁRIO FORTUNA; 800 mems.

OTHER INDUSTRIAL AND TRADE ASSOCIATIONS

Associação dos Comerciantes e Industriais de Bebidas Espirituosas e Vinhos (ACIBEV): Largo do Carmo 15, 1°, 1200-092 Lisbon; tel. (21) 3462318; fax (21) 3427517; e-mail acibevmail@acibev.pt; internet www.acibev.org; f. 1975; spirit and wine traders and manufacturers; Pres. Dr ANTÓNIO SOARES FRANCO.

Associação Empresarial de Portugal: Av. da Boavista 2671, 4100-135 Porto; tel. (22) 6158500; fax (22) 6158519; e-mail mjmagalhaes@aeportugal.com; internet www.aeportugal.pt; f. 1849; represents industry in northern Portugal in all sectors; organizes trade fairs, exhibitions, congresses, etc.; Pres. ANGELO LUDGERO MARQUES; 2,500 mems.

Associação Nacional de Comerciantes e Industriais de Produtos Alimentares (ANCIPA): Largo de São Sebastião da Pedreira 31, 1050-205 Lisbon; tel. (21) 3528803; fax (21) 3154665; e-mail geral@ancipa.pt; internet www.ancipa.pt; f. 1975; national asscn of food products manufacturers and traders; Pres. CARLOS GONÇALVES.

Associação Nacional das Indústrias de Vestuário e Confecção (ANIVEC/APIV): Av. da Boavista 3523, 7°, 4100-139 Porto; tel. (22) 6165470; fax (22) 6168714; e-mail geral@anivec.com; internet www.anivec.com; clothing manufacturers' asscn; Pres. ALEXANDRE MONTEIRO PINHEIRO.

Associação Portuguesa da Indústria de Cerâmica (APICER): Edif. C, Rua Col Veiga Simão, 3020-053 Coimbra; tel. (239) 497600; fax (239) 497601; e-mail info@apicer.pt; internet www.apicer.pt; ceramics asscn; Pres. DIAMANTINO NEVES LOPES.

Associação Portuguesa de Cortiça (APCOR) (Portuguese Cork Association): Av. Comendador Henrique Amorim 580, 4536-904 Sta Maria de Lamas; tel. (22) 7474040; fax (22) 7474049; e-mail info@apcor.pt; internet www.apcor.pt; f. 1956; asscn of cork manufacturers and exporters; Pres. JOÃO RUI FERREIRA.

Associação Portuguesa dos Industriais de Calçado, Componentes, e Artigos de Pele e seus Sucedâneos (APICCAPS): Rua Alves Redol 372, 4011-001 Porto; tel. (22) 5074150; fax (22) 5074179; e-mail apiccaps@mail.telepac.pt; internet www.apiccaps.pt; f. 1975; footwear and leather goods manufacturers' asscn; Pres. FORTUNATO FREDERICO.

Associação Têxtil e Vestuário de Portugal (ATP): Edif. do Citeve, Rua Fernando Mesquita 2785, 4760-034 Vila Nova de Famalicão; tel. (252) 303030; fax (252) 303039; e-mail atp@atp.pt; internet www.atp.pt; textile and ready-to-wear clothing industries; Pres. Dr JOÃO COSTA.

Confederação dos Agricultores de Portugal (CAP): Rua Mestre Lima de Freitas 1, 1549-012 Lisbon; tel. (21) 7100000; fax (21) 7166123; e-mail cap@cap.pt; internet www.cap.pt; f. 1975; farmers' confederation; Pres. JOÃO PEDRO GORJÃO CYRILLO MACHADO.

Confederação do Comércio e Serviços de Portugal (CCP): Av. D. Vasco da Gama 29, 1449-032 Lisbon; tel. (21) 3031380; fax (21) 3031401; e-mail ccp@ccp.pt; internet www.ccp.pt; f. 1976; Pres. Dr JOÃO MANUEL LANÇA VIEIRA LOPES; c. 100 mem. trade asscns.

Confederação Empresarial de Portugal (CIP): Praça das Indústrias, 1300-307 Lisbon; tel. (21) 3164700; fax (21) 3579986; e-mail geral@cip.org.pt; internet www.cip.org.pt; f. 1974; represents employers; Pres. ANTÓNIO SARAIVA; over 35,000 mems.

UTILITIES

In 2006 Spain and Portugal began operating an integrated electricity market, the Mercado Ibérico de Electricidade (MIBEL).

Regulatory Authority

Entidade Reguladora dos Serviços Energéticos (ERSE): Rua Dom Cristovão da Gama 1, 3°, 1400-113 Lisbon; tel. (21) 3033200; fax (21) 3033201; e-mail erse@erse.pt; internet www.erse.pt; regulator of electricity and natural gas in Portugal; Pres. Prof. VÍTOR MANUEL DA SILVA SANTOS.

Electricity

Rede Eléctrica Nacional, SA (REN): Av. Estados Unidos da América 55, 1749-061 Lisbon; tel. (21) 0013500; fax (21) 0013310; e-mail secretariaren@ren.pt; internet www.ren.pt; f. 1994; subsidiary of Redes Energéticas Nacionais, SGPS, SA; concessionaire of the Portuguese transmission grid and transmission system operator in mainland Portugal; Chair. and CEO RUI MANUEL JANES CARTAXO.

Energias de Portugal—EDP, SA: Praça Marquês de Pombal 12, 1250-162 Lisbon; tel. (21) 0012500; fax (21) 0021403; internet www.edp.pt; fmrly Electricidade de Portugal; production, purchase, transport, distribution and sale of electrical energy in Portugal and Spain (via Hidrocantábrico); partially privatized in 2004; Chair. EDUARDO CATROGA; CEO ANTÓNIO MEXIA.

EDP Comercial—Comercialização de Energia, SA: Rua Castilho 165, 4°, 1050-045 Lisbon; tel. (21) 0024321; fax (21) 0014330; Pres. Eng. JORGE CRUZ MORAIS.

EDP Distribuição—Energia, SA: Praça Marquês de Pombal 12, 1250-162 Lisbon; tel. (21) 0012500; fax (21) 0021403; internet www.edp.pt; electricity distribution.

EDP Produção—Gestão da Produção de Energia, SA: Praça Marquês de Pombal 12, 1250-162 Lisbon; tel. (21) 0012500; fax (21) 0021403; e-mail geral@edpproducao.edp.pt; internet www.edp.pt; production and sale of electrical energy; in 2005 the Govt reduced its stake from 30% to 10%; CEO ANTÓNIO LUÍS GUERRA NUNES MEXIA.

Gas

REN Gasodutos, SA: Av. Estados Unidos da América 55, 1749-061 Lisbon; tel. (21) 0013500; fax (21) 0013950; e-mail secretariaren@ren.pt; internet www.ren.pt; f. 2006; subsidiary of Redes Energéticas Nacionais, SGPS, SA; concessionaire of the national gas transmission network; Chair. RUI MANUEL JANES CARTAXO.

Galp Energia, SGPS, SA: Edif. Galp Energia, Rua Tomás de Fonseca, 1600-209 Lisbon; tel. (21) 7242500; fax (21) 7242965; e-mail galp@galpenergia.com; internet www.galpenergia.com; f. 1999; partially privatized in 2000; also comprises Petróleos de Portugal (Petrogal), SA, a petroleum refining co, and Gás de Portugal (GDP), SA, a gas distribution co; Chair. AMÉRICO FERREIRA DE AMORIM; CEO MANUEL FERREIRA DE OLIVEIRA.

Lisboagás GDL—Sociedade Distribuidora de Gás Natural de Lisboa, SA: Rua Tomás da Fonseca, Torre C, 4°, 1600-209 Lisbon; tel. (21) 7242500; fax (21) 8681161; e-mail lisboagas@galpenergia.com; f. 1995; regional natural gas distribution; there are 8 other regional distributors operating in Portugal: Beiragás, Dianagás, Duriensegás, Lusitaniagás, Medigás, Paxgás, Setgás and Tagusgás; Pres. Dr LUÍS FERNANDO MUÑOZ DE MOURA; Man. Dir Eng. CARLOS AUGUSTO.

Water

Águas de Portugal, SGPS, SA (AdP): Rua Visconde de Seabra 3, 1700-421 Lisbon; tel. (21) 2469400; fax (21) 2469401; e-mail info@adp.pt; internet www.adp.pt; f. 1993; Chair. AFONSO JOSÉ MARÇAL GRILO LOBATO DE FARIA.

TRADE UNIONS

National Confederations

Confederação Geral dos Trabalhadores Portugueses-Intersindical Nacional (CGTP-IN) (General Confederation of Portuguese Workers): Rua Victor Cordon 1, 2°, 1249-102 Lisbon; tel. (21) 3236500; fax (21) 3236695; e-mail cgtp@cgtp.pt; internet www.cgtp.pt; f. 1970; reorganized 1974; 83 affiliated unions; Sec.-Gen. ARMÉNIO CARLOS.

União Geral dos Trabalhadores de Portugal (UGT) (General Union of Portuguese Workers): Av. Almirante Gago Coutinho 132, 1700-033 Lisbon; tel. (21) 3931200; fax (21) 3974612; e-mail geral@

ugt.pt; internet www.ugt.pt; f. 1978; pro-socialist; comprises 58 unions and 2 feds; Pres. João de Deus Pires; Sec.-Gen. Carlos Silva.

Transport

RAILWAYS

In 2011 the total length of rail track stood at 2,793.9 km, of which 1,629.7 km was electrified. In 2005 the Government announced plans to develop high-speed rail links connecting Lisbon and Oporto with the Spanish capital, Madrid, and Vigo in north-west Spain. However, construction of the Lisbon–Madrid link was cancelled in 2012, and construction of the Lisbon–Oporto–Vigo line was delayed.

Comboios de Portugal (CP): Calçada do Duque 20, 1249-109 Lisbon; tel. (21) 1023000; fax (21) 3474468; e-mail webmaster@ mail.cp.pt; internet www.cp.pt; f. 1856; nationalized in 1975 as Caminhos de Ferro Portugueses; renamed as above in 2004; Pres. Manuel Queiró.

Metropolitano de Lisboa, EP (ML): Av. Fontes Pereira de Melo 28, 1069-095 Lisbon; tel. (21) 7980600; fax (21) 7980605; e-mail relacoes.publicas@metrolisboa.pt; internet www.metrolisboa.pt; f. 1948; new transport network opened 1959; operates the underground system, consisting of 52 stations and 4 lines covering 39.6 km (2010); Pres. José Manuel Silva Rodrigues.

Rede Ferroviária Nacional—REFER EPE: Estação de Santa Apolónia, 1100-105 Lisbon; tel. (21) 1022000; fax (21) 1021724; e-mail ci@refer.pt; internet www.refer.pt; f. 1997; assumed responsibility for rail infrastructure in 1999; Pres. Rui Lopes Loureiro.

ROADS

In 2010 there were 21,912 km of roads in continental Portugal of which 2,737 km were motorways.

Brisa (Auto-Estradas de Portugal, SA): Edif. Brisa, Quinta da Torre da Aguilha, 2785-599 São Domingos de Rana; tel. (21) 4448500; fax (21) 4448672; e-mail ir@brisa.pt; internet www.brisa.pt; f. 1972; responsible for construction, maintenance and operation of motorways; Pres. Vasco Maria Guimarães José de Mello.

Estradas de Portugal (EP): Praça da Portagem, 2809-013 Almada; tel. (21) 2879058; fax (21) 2879006; e-mail ep@estradasdeportugal .pt; internet www.estradasdeportugal.pt; f. 1999 as Instituto de Estradas de Portugal; merged with Instituto para a Conservação e Exploração da Rede Rodoviária (ICERR) and Instituto para a Construção Rodoviária (ICOR) in 2002; present name adopted 2004; road infrastructure policy, construction and maintenance of the road network; Pres. António Manuel Palma Ramalho.

SHIPPING

The principal Portuguese ports are Aveiro, Lisbon, Leixões (Oporto), Setúbal, Sines, and Funchal (Madeira). The ports of Portimão (Algarve) and the Azores regularly receive international cruise liners. At December 2012 Portugal's flag registered fleet comprised 239 vessels, totalling 0.3m. grt.

Principal Shipping Companies

Portline (Transportes Marítimos Internacionais, SA): Av. Infante D. Henrique 332, 3°, 1800-224 Lisbon; tel. (21) 8391800; fax (21) 8376680; e-mail mail@portline.pt; internet www.portline.pt; f. 1984; privatized 1991; marine transport; Gen. Man. Manuel Pinto de Magalhães.

Sacor Marítima, SA: Rua do Açúcar 86, 1950-010 Lisbon; tel. (21) 8625500; fax (21) 8687548; e-mail sacor.maritima@petrogal.pt; tanker transport; owned by Petrogal SA, subsidiary of Galp Energia; Chair. Luís Martins Carneiro.

CIVIL AVIATION

There are international airports at Lisbon, Oporto, Faro, Funchal (Madeira), Santa Maria and São Miguel (both Azores). Construction of a second international airport, serving Lisbon and replacing the existing Portela Airport, was expected to be completed by 2017. However, in 2010 the project was postponed owing to financial constraints.

SATA (Air Açores—Serviço Açoreano de Transportes Aéreos—EP): Av. Infante D. Henrique 55, 2°, 9505-528 Ponta Delgada, São Miguel, 9500 Azores; tel. (296) 209720; fax (296) 288631; e-mail contacts@sata.pt; internet www.sata.pt; f. 1941; owned by the regional govt of the Azores; inter-island services in the Azores archipelago; Pres. António Gomes de Menezes.

TAP Portugal: Aeroporto de Lisboa, Edif. 25, CP 50194, 1704-801 Lisbon; tel. (707) 205700; fax (21) 8416572; e-mail fale.connosco@tap .pt; internet www.flytap.com; f. 1945; state-owned; national airline serving destinations in Europe, Africa, North, Central and South America; scheduled, international and domestic, passenger and cargo services; joined Star Alliance in 2005; Chair., Supervisory Bd Manuel Pinto Barbosa; CEO Fernando Pinto.

Portugália Airlines (PGA): Aeroporto de Lisboa, Edif. 70, Rua C, 1749-078 Lisbon; tel. (21) 8425500; fax (21) 8425625; e-mail comunicacao@pga.pt; internet www.portugalia-airlines.pt; f. 1988; subsidiary of TAP Portugal; regional airline operating scheduled and charter, international and domestic flights from Lisbon; CEO Luiz Plácido Lapa.

Tourism

Portugal is popular with visitors because of its mild and clement weather. Apart from Lisbon and the Algarve on the mainland, Madeira and the Azores are much favoured as winter resorts. In 2011 the total number of tourist arrivals was 7.4m. In 2011 revenue from tourism (excluding passenger transport) was provisionally put at US $11.3m.

Turismo de Portugal: Rua Ivone Silva 6, 1050-124 Lisbon; tel. (21) 1140200; fax (21) 1140830; e-mail info@turismodeportugal.pt; internet www.turismodeportugal.pt; f. 2007 to replace the Direcção-Geral do Turismo, the Instituto de Formação Turística and the Instituto de Turismo de Portugal; an agency of the Ministry of the Economy and Employment; Pres. Luís Manuel dos Santos Silva Patrão.

Defence

Portugal is a member of the North Atlantic Treaty Organization (NATO, see p. 380). The total strength of the armed forces, as assessed at November 2012, was 42,600: army 25,700, navy 9,700 and air force 7,200. There were reserves of 211,950. The paramilitary National Republican Guard and the Public Security Police totalled 26,100 and 21,600, respectively. Compulsory military service was abolished in 2004. At November 2011 a total of 731 US troops were stationed in Portugal, mainly at the air force base at Lajes in the Azores. In November 2004 Portugal confirmed its participation in one of a number of European Union (EU, see p. 281) 'battlegroups' (with Italy, Spain and Greece). The battlegroups, two of which were to be ready for deployment to a crisis area at any one time, following a rotational schedule, reached full operational capacity from 1 January 2007. Portugal subsequently agreed to participate in a second EU battlegroup, led by Spain and also involving Germany and France.

Defence Budget: €2,090m. in 2013.

General Chief of Staff of the Armed Forces: Gen. Luís Evangelista Esteves de Araújo.

Army Chief of Staff: Gen. Artur Neves Pina Monteiro.

Navy Chief of Staff: Adm. José Carlos Torrado Saldanha Lopes.

Air Force Chief of Staff: Gen. José António de Magalhães Araújo Pinheiro.

Education

The Ministry of Education and Science is responsible for providing education in Portugal. Formal education at all levels is provided at both public and private institutions. Pre-school education, for children aged from three to five years, is not compulsory and is available free of charge. Education is compulsory between the ages of six and 18 years, and is provided free of charge in public schools. Primary education is divided into two cycles: the first lasts for four years, the second for two years. Lower secondary and upper secondary education each last for three years. Entry to the second cycle of primary education and to lower and upper secondary education is dependent on the successful completion of the previous cycle. In 2010/11 99% of children in the relevant age-group were enrolled in primary schools, while in 2008/09 some 88% of children in the relevant age-group were enrolled in secondary schools. At the non-tertiary level, above the age of 18 years, students can enrol for a Curso de Especialização Tecnológica (CET, specialized technological course). Higher education comprises university and polytechnic education. Fees are set by the institution depending on the course. Universities award the following academic degrees: the *licenciatura*, after four to six years of study; the *mestrado*, after one or two years of study and research work; and the *doutoramento*. Regional polytechnic institutes, grouping technical, management, educational and fine arts schools, offer three-year courses leading to the *bacharel* and specialized studies leading to a diploma after one to two years. In 2008/09 a total of 373,002 students were enrolled at some 301 institutions of higher education. Expenditure on education in 2010 was €11,150m (representing 6.5% of gross domestic product).

QATAR

Introductory Survey

LOCATION, CLIMATE, LANGUAGE, RELIGION, FLAG, CAPITAL

The State of Qatar occupies a peninsula, projecting northwards from the Arabian mainland, on the west coast of the Persian (Arabian) Gulf. It is bordered, to the south, by Saudi Arabia and the United Arab Emirates. The archipelago of Bahrain lies to the north-west. On the opposite side of the Gulf lies Iran. The climate is exceptionally hot in the summer, when temperatures may reach 49°C (120°F), with high humidity on the coast; conditions are relatively mild in the winter. Rainfall is negligible. The official language is Arabic. Almost all of the inhabitants are adherents of Islam, although an influx of guest workers in recent years has precipitated official recognition of Christian denominations. Native Qataris, who comprise less than one-quarter of the total population, belong mainly to the strictly orthodox Wahhabi sect of Sunni Muslims. The national flag (proportions 11 by 28) is maroon, with a broad vertical white stripe at the hoist, the two colours being separated by a serrated line. The capital is Doha.

CONTEMPORARY POLITICAL HISTORY

Historical Context

Qatar was formerly dominated by the Al Khalifa family of Bahrain. The peninsula became part of Turkey's Ottoman Empire in 1872, but Turkish forces evacuated Qatar at the beginning of the First World War (1914–18). The United Kingdom recognized Sheikh Abdullah Al Thani as Ruler of Qatar, and in 1916 made a treaty with him, providing British protection against aggression in return for supervision of Qatar's external affairs. A 1934 treaty extended fuller British protection to Qatar.

In October 1960 Sheikh Ali Al Thani, Ruler of Qatar since 1949, abdicated in favour of his son, Sheikh Ahmad. In 1968 the British Government announced its intention to withdraw British forces from the Persian (Arabian) Gulf area by 1971. In April 1970 Sheikh Ahmad announced a provisional Constitution, providing for a partially elected Consultative Assembly, although he retained effective power. In May the Deputy Ruler, Sheikh Khalifa Al Thani (a cousin of Sheikh Ahmad), was appointed Prime Minister. After the failure of attempts to agree terms for union with neighbouring Bahrain and Trucial Oman (now the United Arab Emirates—UAE), Qatar became fully independent on 1 September 1971, whereupon the Ruler took the title of Amir. The 1916 treaty was replaced by a new treaty of friendship with the United Kingdom.

In February 1972 Sheikh Ahmad was deposed in a bloodless coup by Sheikh Khalifa, who proclaimed himself Amir, while retaining the premiership. The new Amir adopted a policy of wide-ranging social and economic reform, and the previous extravagance and privileges of the ruling family were curbed. In accordance with the 1970 Constitution, the Amir appointed an Advisory Council in April 1972 to complement the ministerial Government. The Council was expanded from 20 to 30 members in 1975 and to 35 members in 1988. Its term has been extended at regular intervals since its establishment, most recently, for a period of three years, in 2010.

Domestic Political Affairs

Accession of Sheikh Hamad

On 27 June 1995 the Deputy Amir, Heir Apparent, Minister of Defence and Commander-in-Chief of the Armed Forces, Maj.-Gen. Sheikh Hamad bin Khalifa Al Thani, deposed his father in a bloodless coup. Sheikh Hamad proclaimed himself Amir, claiming the support of the ruling family and the Qatari people. Sheikh Khalifa, who was in Switzerland at the time of the coup, vowed to return to Qatar. Sheikh Hamad, however, reputedly enjoyed widespread support, and his domestic reforms were perceived as having contributed to Qatar's stability. The United Kingdom, the USA and Saudi Arabia swiftly recognized the new Amir. In July 1995 Sheikh Hamad reorganized the Council of Ministers and appointed himself Prime Minister, while retaining the posts of Minister of Defence and Commander-in-Chief of the Armed Forces.

In February 1996 security forces in Qatar were reported to have foiled an attempted coup. As many as 100 people were arrested, and a warrant was issued for the arrest of Sheikh Hamad bin Jasim bin Hamad Al Thani, a former government minister and a cousin of the Amir. Sheikh Khalifa denied any involvement, although he was quick to imply that the alleged plot indicated popular support for his return.

In October 1996 Sheikh Hamad named the third of his four sons, Sheikh Jasim bin Hamad bin Khalifa Al Thani, as Heir Apparent. The Amir subsequently appointed his younger brother, Sheikh Abdullah bin Khalifa Al Thani, as Prime Minister. In November 1996 Sheikh Hamad announced the creation of a new Defence Council, over which he would preside. The Council, to be comprised of senior ministers and armed forces and security personnel, was expected to function in an advisory and consultative capacity. It was also reported that the Amir had appointed the Gulf region's first female member of government (as Under-Secretary of State for Education and Culture). In March 1998 the Ministry of Information and Culture was dissolved, the post of Minister having been abolished two years earlier.

Elections to Qatar's new 29-member Central Municipal Council (CMC), held by universal suffrage on 8 March 1999, were the first in the country's history. Announced by Sheikh Hamad in November 1997 and provided for by law in July 1998, the CMC was to have a consultative role in the operations of the Ministry of Municipal Affairs and Agriculture. However, only about 22,000 voters of an eligible 40,000 actually participated in the elections.

The draft constitution

In July 1999 a 32-member constitutional committee was established to draft a permanent constitution; this was to include provision for the creation of a new National Assembly. The committee produced a draft constitution in July 2002, which provided for a separation of the executive, the judiciary and the legislature, but which would retain executive power in the hands of the Amir and the Council of Ministers. The draft constitution also guaranteed freedom of expression, religion and association, and provided for the establishment of an independent judiciary and of a new 45-member Consultative Council (to replace the Advisory Council), comprising 30 elected and 15 appointed members. Under the proposed constitution, the Amir would be obliged to provide reasons for rejecting draft laws adopted by the Council. The Amir would be required to approve such legislation sent to him a second time by the Council with two-thirds' majority support, although he would have a discretionary right to halt the implementation of laws in question on a temporary basis if he deemed this to be in the greater interests of the country. The parliament was to have a four-year mandate, and suffrage was to be extended to all citizens, including women, aged 18 years and above. In a referendum held on 29 April 2003, an overwhelming majority (96.6%) of the 71,406 voters approved the new Constitution, and the affirmative vote was expected to have led to legislative elections being conducted in 2004. However, the planned elections were repeatedly postponed.

Meanwhile, Sheikh Hamad bin Jasim bin Hamad Al Thani was arrested in July 1999 for his alleged role in the coup plot of 1996. The trial of those accused of involvement in the coup (which began in November 1997) ended in February 2000, with the former minister and 32 co-defendants sentenced to life imprisonment; 85 others were acquitted. Appeal proceedings were subsequently lodged by all 33 who had been convicted. In May 2001 the Court of Appeal overruled the previous sentences of life imprisonment, sentencing to death 19 of the defendants (including Sheikh Hamad bin Jasim bin Hamad); the court was also reported to have sentenced 26 defendants to terms of life imprisonment, and acquitted two others. However, Sheikh Hamad bin Jasim was subsequently granted an official pardon and released in September 2005.

In January 2002 it was reported that a group styling itself the General Congress of the Qatari Opposition had emerged to demand that the Amir stand down in favour of his son, Crown

Prince Jasim. The group, which claimed to include former members of the armed forces, tribal chiefs, businessmen, students and officials who had served under the previous regime, accused the Amir of pursuing 'reckless' policies, of corruption and of alienating Qatar's Gulf neighbours. This last charge was interpreted as possibly referring not only to Qatar's pursuit of an increasingly independent foreign policy but also to the activities of *Al Jazeera*, a satellite television broadcaster linked to the Al Thani family with a wide audience throughout the region. *Al Jazeera*'s reporting style and scope of coverage had caused several governments to threaten to restrict its freedom to operate in their countries.

The 2003 and 2007 elections to the Central Municipal Council

The second elections to the CMC were held on 7 April 2003. Turnout was estimated at about 35% of the registered electorate. A female candidate, Sheikha al-Jufairi, was elected unopposed after the competing candidates stood aside, and thus became the first woman in the Gulf region to hold elected office. In May Sheikha bint Ahmad al-Mahmoud became the first woman to join the Council of Ministers when she was appointed Minister of Education. Sheikh Jasim was replaced as Heir Apparent by Sheikh Tamim bin Hamad bin Khalifa Al Thani, the Amir's fourth eldest son, in August.

The Government approved an anti-terrorism law in February 2004. The legislation included the provision of the death penalty for anyone who killed 'through a terror act' and for anyone 'founding, organizing or managing a group or organization to commit a terror act'. In addition, the crime of assisting a terrorist group was to be punishable by a life sentence. In May a law permitting the formation of trade unions was approved. In addition, the legislation granted workers the right to strike, banned children aged under 16 years from employment and set a maximum eight-hour working day.

In April 2005 the Amir removed from their posts his Chief of Staff, Abdullah bin Muhammad bin Sa'ud Al Thani, and two recently appointed ministers—Muhammad bin Abd al-Latif bin Abd al-Rahman al-Mana, the Minister of Awqaf (Religious Endowments) and Islamic Affairs, and Muhammad bin Isa Hamad al-Mehannadi, the Minister of State for Council of Ministers' Affairs—amid allegations that three cabinet members and several businessmen had been questioned by officials with regard to alleged fraudulent activities relating to the sale of the state-owned Qatar Gas Transport Co (Nakilat) in early 2005. Faisal bin Abdullah al-Mahmud was awarded the religious affairs portfolio, Sultan bin Hassan al-Dhabit al-Dousary, the Minister of Municipal Affairs and Agriculture, received the position of Minister of State for Council of Ministers' Affairs in addition to his existing responsibilities, and Sheikh Abd al-Rahman bin Sa'ud Al Thani was appointed as the new Chief of Staff.

A bomb exploded outside a theatre frequented by Western expatriates in Doha in March 2005. A British citizen was killed in the suicide attack and 12 people were injured. A previously little-known militant grouping, Jund al-Sham (the Army of the Levant), claimed responsibility for the attack. Although the bombing was the first of its kind in Qatar, Western embassies had previously issued warnings to expatriates that the threat from terrorism in the emirate was high.

The third elections to the CMC, contested by 118 candidates, took place on 1 April 2007. Turn-out, although relatively low, exceeded expectations, at 51.1% of the electorate. Of the three female candidates standing for election, only Sheikha al-Jufairi was successful, securing re-election with 800 of the 879 votes cast in the Old Airport constituency—the highest proportion of votes achieved by any candidate. A few days later it was announced that the Prime Minister, Sheikh Abdullah, had resigned, but no explanation was offered for his decision. Sheikh Hamad bin Jasim bin Jaber Al Thani, hitherto First Deputy Prime Minister and Minister of Foreign Affairs, replaced him, while retaining the foreign affairs portfolio.

Administrative reorganizations, 2008–11

In July 2008 the Amir effected a major reorganization of the Council of Ministers. Seven new ministerial portfolios were created—including those of culture, arts and heritage, business and trade, environment, and international co-operation—bringing the number of members of the Council of Ministers to 20, in addition to the Amir himself. A new Minister of Public Health, Sheikha Ghalia bint Muhammad bin Hamad Al Thani, was appointed, increasing the number of female ministers to two.

However, both Sheika Ghalia and the Minister of Education and Higher Education, Sheikha bint Ahmad al-Mahmoud, were replaced in April 2009, following a minor reallocation of cabinet portfolios. Sheikha bint Ahmad al-Mahmoud rejoined the Government in June as Minister of State without Portfolio.

A major reorganization of Qatar's administrative structure was effected in August 2009. Several ministries were restructured and numerous, formerly autonomous state agencies were reintegrated into cabinet ministries. Notable developments included: the assignment of the Civil Aviation Authority and the Qatar Tourism Authority to the Ministry of Business and Trade; the reallocation of the Public Works Authority to the Ministry of Municipal Affairs and Urban Planning; and the division of the Ministry of Foreign Affairs into two separate departments, responsible for foreign affairs and for international co-operation, respectively. Furthermore, the Heir Apparent, Sheikh Tamim, was accorded direct responsibility for the General Secretariat for Development Planning (GSDP), the agency responsible for co-ordination of the National Development Strategy, which was intended to facilitate efforts to meet the objectives of the National Vision 2030—a long-term development programme launched under the supervision of the GSDP in October 2008, which aimed to promote and manage Qatar's ambitious economic and social development programme. The inaugural National Development Strategy (a five-year plan covering 2011–16) was launched in March 2011.

It had been hoped that a new electoral law approved by the Advisory Council in May 2008 would facilitate the organization of long-awaited elections to the Consultative Council provided for in the Constitution. However, the Advisory Council's term was subsequently extended (in June 2008) until June 2010, and (in June 2010) further to June 2013. In November 2010 the Amir announced that the Council of Ministers was reviewing the status of Qatar's foreign worker sponsorship system, by which employers sponsored foreign workers' residency; the Bahraini Government had abolished a similar system in 2009. The controversial system was widely regarded as an affront to workers' rights and as allowing employers excessive control over their workers: under its provisions, an employer had the authority, *inter alia*, to deny a worker's request to change jobs, and there were widespread reports of employers confiscating workers' passports. Human rights groups welcomed the Amir's announcement, urging the Government to take firm action on the issue. Despite an announcement in May 2012 that sponsorship would be replaced by a contractual system, by early 2013 the changes had yet to be implemented. On 11 June 2012 the Council of Ministers approved the formation of workers' committees in anticipation of Qatar's hosting of the 2022 International Federation of Association Football (Fédération internationale de football association—FIFA) World Cup. The following day the US-based organisation, Human Rights Watch, published a report recommending an overhaul of the country's labour laws.

In January 2011 the Amir announced the appointment of Abdullah bin Hamad al-Attiya, hitherto Deputy Prime Minister and Minister of Energy and Industry, to the position of Chairman of the Emiri Diwan. Al-Attiya, who had headed the energy portfolio since 1992, retained the deputy premiership and was replaced as Minister of Energy and Industry by Muhammad Saleh al-Sada. A government spokesperson stated that the changes were not indicative of any revision of the country's oil policy.

Meanwhile, in October 2008 the international Doha Centre for Media Freedom (DCMF) commenced operations, under the direction of Robert Ménard, founder of the Paris (France)-based advocacy group Reporters sans frontières (Reporters Without Borders). Heralded as the first body of its kind in the region, the DCMF had been established by the Amir, under the patronage of his wife, Sheikha Mozah bint Nasser al-Misnad, in December 2007. In addition to promoting media freedom, the centre was to provide refuge for journalists under threat of persecution. In February 2009 the DCMF published a report detailing government restrictions on the media in Qatar and the biased nature of *Al Jazeera*'s coverage of Qatari events. In June Ménard, who had attracted strong criticism from some Qatari newspapers, which accused him of promoting media content that they considered insulting to Muslims, resigned as Director-General, alleging that certain Qatari officials were obstructing the DCMF's operations and compromising its independent status. The resignation of Ménard, together with that of three other senior DCMF officials, led to a sustained suspension of the centre's activities. Meanwhile, Qatar's international reputation in the field of human rights received a boost in May 2009, with the opening in Doha of the UN Human Rights Training and Documentation Centre for South-West Asia and the Arab Region. The centre, which benefited from a US $1m. donation from the Qatari Government, was established to promote the development and documentation of human rights in the region.

Recent developments: the promise of democratic reform

Qatar remained largely unaffected by the anti-Government protests that spread across the Middle East and North Africa region from early 2011. However, observers were swift to note that, despite the Qatari Government's support for the revolts elsewhere, particularly in Libya, Qatar itself, with elections to the Consultative Council still pending, remained slow to embrace democracy. The Qatari authorities appeared to take heed of such criticism, and some progress towards reform became evident during the course of the year.

In late February 2011 Sheikh Hamad declared that elections to the Consultative Council would take place 'in the near future', in what was interpreted by some observers as a response to posts published on a social networking website appealing for the staging of a revolt in Doha on 16 March in order to overthrow the Amir. Although that date passed without incident, the posts had included demands that parliamentary elections finally be held, that greater welfare benefits be made available, that the US command post at Al-Udaid military base (see Foreign Affairs) be closed, and that Qatar sever all links with Iran and Israel. In November 2011 the Amir announced that elections to the Consultative Council were to take place in the latter half of 2013; however, by April no date had been confirmed. As stipulated by the Constitution approved in 2003, 30 members of the 45-seat legislature were to be elected, with the remaining 15 to be appointed by the Amir.

Meanwhile, the fourth elections to the CMC were held on 10 May 2011 and were contested by 117 candidates, including four women. Turn-out was just 43.3% of the registered electorate. As in the 2003 and 2007 polls, Sheikha al-Jufairi was the only successful female candidate, securing re-election to a third term.

The issue of media freedom gained increasing prominence in 2011. In March Sultan al-Khalaifi, a human rights activist who had recently criticized the censorship of books in Qatar, was arrested. Amid increasing appeals from international rights groups, al-Khalaifi was released without charge in April. Also in that month the DCMF announced that it had recommenced its activities. Draft legislation providing for greater media freedom was approved by the Council of Ministers in June. Upon ratification, the new law would allow journalists to write on all issues except those pertaining to 'national security and friendly countries', as well as prohibiting the detention of journalists for questioning by law enforcement agencies without a court order; journalists charged with defamation would, however, be liable to a fine of QR 50,000 or more. Although the legislation stated that there would be no censorship of the media, the Ministry of Culture, Arts and Heritage was to be granted the authority to 'license and monitor' the industry. In June 2012 the draft legislation was approved by the Advisory Council; however, in October Human Rights Watch urged the Amir not to approve the law, which, it argued, would compromise press freedom. Ratification of the legislation remained pending in early 2013.

Meanwhile, in May 2011 the Amir ratified legislation providing for the amendment of *Al Jazeera*'s legal status to 'a private organization devoted to public interest', which would allow the broadcaster greater freedom in its administrative and editorial functions. A secret US diplomatic cable published by the Wiki-Leaks organization in August indicated that the Director-General of *Al Jazeera*, Wadah Khanfar, had in 2005 agreed to a request by the US Defense Intelligence Agency to amend content on the broadcaster's website relating to the conflict in Iraq. Khanfar resigned in September 2011, and was replaced by a member of the Qatari ruling family, Sheikh Ahmad bin Jasim bin Muhammad Al Thani.

In November 2011 the poet Muhammad ibn al-Dheeb al-Ajami was arrested and detained, ostensibly for reciting a poem in which he insulted the Amir—an offence punishable by five years' imprisonment. However, al-Ajami was also thought to have angered the authorities by a poem he wrote in praise of the Arab uprisings of 2010–11. After several postponements of his trial and despite criticism of his detention by several human rights organisations al-Ajani was additionally charged with 'inciting to overthrow the ruling system', and sentenced to life imprisonment on 29 November 2012. The sentence was subsequently reduced to 15 years.

In early 2013 concerns were once again raised regarding the issue of workers' rights. In mid-January it was announced that some 6,000 complaints of labour rights violations had been made to the Ministry of Labour during 2012. Later in January 2013 the International Trade Union Confederation, jointly with an international trade union, filed a case with the International Labour Organization citing allegations of 'forced labour' in Qatar.

Qatar's Role as a Regional Mediator

In June 2007, and again in February 2008, Qatari negotiators played a leading role in brokering peace agreements between the Government of Yemen and rebels loyal to the late Shi'a cleric Hussain al-Houthi, who had been engaged in a sporadic civil war in Saada province since 2004. Although the Qatari-brokered accords ultimately failed to end the hostilities, they demonstrated Qatar's willingness and capability to act as an independent mediator in regional conflicts. In May 2008 Qatari diplomats brokered a deal in Doha to resolve an 18-month-long political stalemate between rival factions in Lebanon. The agreement, which provided for the formation of a power-sharing government, the election of a President and the drafting of a new electoral law, was widely believed to have averted the threat of civil war. Qatar's success in brokering the Lebanese accord was attributed to its independent foreign policy and lack of vested interests in the region, and significantly bolstered its reputation as a regional mediator. Following the collapse of the national unity coalition Government in January 2011, Sheikh Hamad and the Turkish Minister of Foreign Affairs, Prof. Dr Ahmet Davutoğlu, chaired negotiations between the rival Lebanese factions in an attempt to secure an end to the impasse; however, Qatar and Turkey announced a suspension of their mediation efforts on 19 January 'owing to certain reservations'.

Qatar played a key role in GCC efforts to bring an end to the ongoing impasse between the Yemeni Government and its opponents in 2011. In a statement released on 7 April, Sheikh Hamad bin Jasim bin Jaber Al Thani announced that the GCC hoped to finalize a deal that would provide for the transfer of power from President Ali Abdullah Saleh to Vice-President Maj.-Gen. Abd al-Rabbuh Mansur al-Hadi at the head of an interim government, while offering guarantees of safe protection for Saleh and his family. However, Saleh rejected the proposal, and withdrew Yemen's ambassador from Doha. The Yemeni President further alleged that Qatar was 'funding chaos' in the rest of the Arab world, and accused *Al Jazeera* of fuelling the popular protests in Yemen and elsewhere. A revised mediation plan announced by the GCC on 21 April was accepted by Saleh on 23 April. However, Qatar announced its withdrawal from the mediation process in May, citing 'indecision and delays in the signature of the proposed agreement' and the increasing intensity of clashes between government forces and protesters across Yemen.

Qatar was reported in January 2012 to have agreed in principle to the opening in Doha of a liaison office by the Afghan Taliban, in a development that was interpreted by some observers as a precursor to the staging of peace talks between the Taliban and the US Administration, in which Qatar would mediate. The office was eventually opened one year later. Qatari-mediated talks between rival Palestinian factions Hamas and Fatah in February led to them agreeing to form a unity government for the West Bank and the Gaza Strip.

Meanwhile, Qatari mediators were involved in efforts from 2008 to conclude a peace agreement between participants in the conflict in Darfur, Sudan. Talks between Darfur-based rebel group the Sudan Justice and Equality Movement (JEM) and the Government of Sudan, which were sponsored by the African Union (AU, see p. 191) and the League of Arab States (the Arab League), were held in Doha in February 2009 and resulted in the signing of a confidence-building agreement intended to lead to broader peace negotiations. Furthermore, negotiations between the Governments of Sudan and Chad, aimed at resolving a bilateral dispute arising from the conflict in the Darfur, commenced in Doha in April. The negotiations, which were sponsored by Qatar and Libya, resulted in the signing of a framework agreement on the normalization of bilateral relations in May. Meanwhile, talks between the JEM and Sudan's Government resumed in Doha in April and, following several rounds of negotiations during 2009, culminated in the signing of a provisional cease-fire and power-sharing agreement in February 2010. Qatar successfully mediated an end to the eight-year conflict between the JEM and the Sudanese Government in January 2011, and in July hosted a ceremony formally to mark the signing of the peace agreement (the Doha Document for Peace in Darfur–DDPD) by the Sudanese Government and the rebel Liberation and Justice Movement. Following intensive negotiations brokered by the Qatari Government and the AU, in early April 2013 in Doha the JEM also became a signatory to the DDPD.

Following Qatari-chaired negotiations intended to resolve a protracted border dispute between Djibouti and Eritrea in mid-2010, Prime Minister Sheikh Hamad announced in June that Eritrea had withdrawn its troops from contested border areas. A few days later an agreement was signed by Djibouti and Eritrea in Doha, under the terms of which the two countries agreed to entrust to Qatar the role of mediating in efforts to draft a 'final and binding resolution' to the bilateral dispute. Qatar's offer of mediation in the dispute was welcomed by many within the international community, including the UN Security Council, which pledged its 'full support' to Qatari efforts. Meanwhile, in April 2008 the Ethiopian authorities broke off diplomatic relations with Qatar, accusing the Middle Eastern country of promoting instability in the Horn of Africa and alleging that its relationship with Eritrea was a threat to Ethiopia's national security. In November 2012, however, diplomatic contacts between the two countries were restored.

Foreign Affairs

Regional relations

Qatar's relations with Bahrain have long been impeded by a protracted dispute over sovereignty of the Hawar islands (which had been awarded to Bahrain in 1939 by a British judgment) and the shoals of Fasht al-Dibal and Qit'at Jaradah (over which the British had recognized Bahrain's 'sovereign rights' in 1947). In December 1996 Bahrain boycotted the annual summit meeting of the Cooperation Council for the Arab States of the Gulf (Gulf Cooperation Council—GCC, see p. 255), which took place in Doha. The meeting, none the less, decided to establish a quad-ripartite committee, comprising those GCC countries not involved in the territorial dispute, to mediate between Qatar and Bahrain. The committee's efforts achieved a degree of success, and meetings between senior Qatari and Bahraini representatives in London, United Kingdom, and Manama, Bahrain, in early 1997 resulted in the announcement that diplomatic relations at ambassadorial level were to be established.

The Amir, Sheikh Hamad bin Khalifa Al Thani, made his first official visit to Manama in December 1999, during which it was agreed that a joint committee, headed by the heirs apparent of Bahrain and Qatar, would be established to encourage bilateral co-operation. A second senior-level meeting was held in January 2000, when the new Amir of Bahrain, Sheikh Hamad bin Isa Al Khalifa, made his first visit to Qatar. The two countries agreed to expedite the opening of embassies in Manama and Doha. In February, following the first meeting of the Bahrain-Qatar Supreme Joint Committee, it was announced that the possibility of constructing a causeway to link the two states was to be investigated. In May Bahrain announced its decision to suspend the activities of the Supreme Joint Committee pending a ruling on the dispute by the International Court of Justice (ICJ). The ICJ's final verdict, issued in March 2001, was virtually identical to the British judgment of 1939: Bahrain was found to have sovereignty over the Hawar islands and Qit'at Jaradah, while Qatar held sovereignty over Zubarah, Janan island and the low-tide elevation of Fasht al-Dibal; the Court drew a single maritime boundary between the two states. Both Qatar and Bahrain accepted the ICJ ruling, and declared that their territorial dispute was ended.

In August 2002 a Danish consortium completed a feasibility study for the construction of the planned causeway linking Qatar to Bahrain (the Friendship Bridge). Both Governments had approved the project by May 2004, and international companies were invited to present bids for the contract in late 2004. Following extensive negotiations, a US $3,000m. contract to design and build the causeway was signed in May 2008 by a consortium led by VINCI Construction, a French company, and the Qatar-Bahrain Causeway Foundation. However, substantial revisions to the design were required after a decision, in late 2008, to incorporate a railway line; the rail link was expected to add up to $1,000m. to the cost of the project. Construction had been expected to commence in 2010, with completion scheduled for 2015. Delays to the project were subsequently exacerbated by financial difficulties, and by early 2013 work on the causeway

had yet to commence. Relations had been damaged when a Bahraini fisherman was seriously injured by Qatari coastguards in a 'naval incident' in May 2010, which resulted in a renewal of hostilities over ownership of the Hawar islands. Tensions were further exacerbated later that month following the broadcasting by *Al Jazeera* of a television programme on poverty and the treatment of foreign labourers in Bahrain; the programme was widely interpreted as a public criticism of the Bahraini Government, which promptly announced a suspension of *Al Jazeera*'s operations in Bahrain, citing a 'breach of press and publishing regulations'. *Al Jazeera* was the cause of further bilateral tension in August 2011, owing to widespread coverage broadcast on its English-language service of popular protests in Bahrain, including claims that the Bahraini Government had committed human rights abuses in its attempts to suppress the demonstrations. Bahraini legislators accused *Al Jazeera* of heavy bias against the Bahraini authorities and of deliberately fomenting unrest in the country.

Qatar's relations with Saudi Arabia, subject to persistent border tensions from late 1992, appeared to improve in August 1995, when the Amir held talks with King Fahd in Saudi Arabia. In December, nevertheless, Qatar boycotted the closing session of the annual GCC summit, following the appointment of a Saudi national as the next GCC Secretary-General (in preference to a Qatari candidate). In March 1996 the dispute was reported to have been settled, after mediation by Oman, and in April Qatar and Saudi Arabia agreed to establish a joint committee to complete the demarcation of their mutual border. In March 2001, at a ceremony in Doha, Saudi and Qatari officials signed an apparently final agreement concerning the land and maritime demarcation of their joint border. Bilateral relations worsened in October 2002, however, when the Saudi ambassador to Qatar was recalled following the airing of a television programme via the *Al Jazeera* network that was deemed to be critical of the Saudi regime. Relations had already been strained by the expansion of US military facilities in Qatar and by the relocation, in April, of the main US air operations in the Gulf region from Saudi Arabia to Doha (see the chapter on Saudi Arabia). Furthermore, Saudi Arabia subsequently reopened the border dispute, despite the 2001 agreement, threatening in July 2007 to block a US $3,500m. gas pipeline between Qatar and the UAE on the grounds that undersea sections ran through what it claimed to be Saudi territory.

A visit to Jeddah, Saudi Arabia, undertaken by Sheikh Hamad in September 2007 engendered optimism for an improvement in Qatari-Saudi ties, with the announcement of a number of agreements arising from the Amir's dialogue with King Abdullah: Sheikh Hamad gave an assurance that *Al Jazeera* would not broadcast material that could be regarded as defamatory in respect of Saudi Arabia, in return for which *Al Jazeera* would be permitted to establish a presence in the kingdom. Saudi Arabia also confirmed the return of its diplomatic envoy to Qatar, and King Abdullah agreed to attend the forthcoming GCC summit in Doha (an invitation that he had refused in 2002, when Qatar had last hosted a meeting of the organization). Saudi objections to the Qatar–UAE gas pipeline were also resolved. The new Saudi ambassador to Qatar acceded to his position in March 2008, and relations were further bolstered in that month by an official visit to the emirate by Saudi Crown Prince Sultan ibn Abd al-Aziz Al Sa'ud for talks with the Amir on the countries' bilateral relations and other international issues.

In July 2008 the Qatari and Saudi Governments agreed to resolve the issue of border demarcation and to establish a Joint Co-ordination Council to encourage co-operation in military, industrial, agricultural and energy affairs. A Land and Maritime Border Delimitation Agreement was signed in December, together with various other agreements on bilateral co-operation, at the first meeting of the Saudi-Qatari Joint Co-ordination Council, and was registered with the UN in March 2009. Following the eighth meeting of the joint Qatari-Saudi technical committee for the demarcation of land and maritime borders in Doha in January 2010, a French company was awarded the contract for the completion of the land border demarcation, and the defining of the maritime border beyond Khor al-Udaid, in south-western Qatar. Relations were strengthened further in February when Sheikh Hamad visited the Saudi capital, Riyadh, for talks with King Abdullah on bilateral relations and regional affairs. Saudi Arabia recognized Qatari sovereignty over the southern shore of the disputed Khor al-Udaid inlet in early 2011 and granted Qatar Airways greater access to the Saudi market in July.

In September 1994 Qatar, along with the other GCC states, revoked aspects of the economic boycott of Israel, and Israel signed a memorandum of intent to purchase Qatari liquefied natural gas (LNG) in November 1995. Relations between the two countries were consolidated further in April 1996, when Shimon Peres made the first official visit to Qatar by an Israeli Prime Minister. However, later that year Israel declared that the memorandum of intent had expired, and Qatar stated that any deal would be dependent on progress in the Middle East peace process. Prior to the ninth conference of the Organization of the Islamic Conference (now Organization of Islamic Cooperation—OIC, see p. 413), held in Doha in November 2000, several Islamic states (notably Saudi Arabia and Iran) threatened to boycott the summit unless Qatar agreed to sever its low-level diplomatic relations with Israel. (Arab and Islamic states were keen to demonstrate support for the Palestinians in their renewed uprising against Israeli occupation from late September.) The Qatari leadership apparently bowed to regional pressure when, later in November, it announced that the Israeli trade office in Doha was to be closed, although the office continued to function until January 2009, exacerbating tensions with Saudi Arabia in particular.

Delegations from both Israel and Qatar attended the 62nd UN General Assembly in New York, USA, in September 2007. At a meeting with the Israeli Vice-Prime Minister and Minister of Foreign Affairs, Tzipi Livni, initiated by Sheikh Hamad, Livni reiterated the importance of the involvement of 'moderate' Arab states in regional discussions towards promoting political negotiations with the Palestinians, and appealed for greater solidarity with Israel against the emergence of extremist elements in the region. Despite Qatar's unprecedented, and isolated, invitation for Iran to attend the GCC's annual summit meeting, held in Doha in December, Livni maintained Israeli dialogue with Qatar and subsequently embarked on a series of diplomatic visits to the country in early 2008, including attendance at the Doha Forum on Democracy, Development and Free Trade in April. While Qatar, together with other GCC members, strongly condemned Israel's renewed military offensive in the Gaza Strip in January 2008, in February the country pledged its willingness to facilitate a cease-fire agreement between Israel and Hamas. However, Qatar's accommodation of the Israeli Minister of Foreign Affairs precipitated the withdrawal from the conference of several other participants, notably members of the Hezbollah-led opposition in Lebanon.

In response to the military offensive launched by Israel against Hamas targets in the Gaza Strip in late December 2008, Sheikh Hamad sought to convene an emergency summit of the League of Arab States (the Arab League, see p. 372) in Doha to formulate a unified Arab response to the crisis. During the summit, which was convened on 16 January 2009, the Qatari Government announced the closure of Israel's trade office in Doha and the suspension of diplomatic ties. The Doha summit, which was boycotted by several countries (notably Saudi Arabia and Egypt), together with a series of high-level meetings during the latter half of January, failed in its stated aim of developing a united Arab response to the Israeli aggression in Gaza. Instead, it highlighted regional divisions over the Palestinian issue, exemplified by the emergence of two opposing blocs: one broadly supportive of Hamas and open to Iranian influence, the other supportive of the Fatah-led Palestinian Authority (PA) and generally aligned with the USA. A Qatari offer to resume diplomatic and economic ties in return for an easing of the Israeli blockade of Gaza (see the chapter on the Palestinian Territories), so as to allow the import into Gaza of construction materials in order to facilitate rebuilding efforts within the territory, was rejected by Israel in May 2010. Further bilateral tensions emerged in August 2011 over Israeli objections to Qatar's perceived increasing support for Hamas, and to the support that Qatar as chair of the Arab League in that year had provided to the PA with regard to the latter's application (submitted in September) for full membership, as an independent state, of the UN. In October 2012, following a pledge of US $254m. (later increased to $400m.) for the reconstruction and modernization of Gaza, the Amir became the first Arab leader to visit the territory since its effective takeover by Hamas in 2007, in what was widely seen as an attempt to rehabilitate the movement's reputation in the international community. In early April 2013 Qatar and the PA signed a memorandum of understanding for co-operation on security issues.

Qatar invested heavily in Egypt's new, Islamist-led Government during the latter half of 2012, including in the form of a US $2,000m. deposit in the country's central bank in August and the announcement of a $18,000m. investment in tourism and industrial projects. Announcements of further aid in early 2013 prompted accusations that the Qatari Government was seeking to interfere in Egypt's domestic affairs, a claim denied by Prime Minister Sheikh Hamad. Sheikh Hamad further denied a bias on the part of Qatar towards the Muslim Brotherhood during a visit to Berlin, Germany, in April. Also that month Qatar pledged to increase its budgetary aid to Egypt to some $8,000m.

Despite maintaining significant military co-operation with the USA, Qatar has established outwardly strong relations with Iran, and has publicly supported Iran's right to pursue civil nuclear technology. The two states' shared ownership of the world's largest non-associated gasfield, Qatar's North Field and Iran's South Pars field, in the Persian (Arabian) Gulf, underlines the strategic importance of stable political and commercial relations. In December 2007 the Amir extended an unprecedented invitation to Iran's President, Mahmoud Ahmadinejad, to attend the 28th GCC summit in Doha. In October 2008 Qatar, Iran and Russia, the holders of the world's largest gas reserves, announced the formation of a strategic trilateral alliance to promote co-operation in the sector. Sheikh Hamad visited Iran in March 2009, and again in November, for discussions on bilateral relations and regional affairs with President Ahmadinejad. A bilateral memorandum of understanding on defence co-operation, encompassing joint training and counter-terrorism operations, was signed in February 2010. During a visit to Doha in November by Iran's First Vice-President, Muhammad Reza Rahimi, several bilateral agreements intended to bolster commerce, trade and customs co-operation were signed. However, despite the appearance of friendly co-operation, relations have in recent years seemed to be characterized by mutual mistrust. This view appeared to be confirmed by the publication in late 2010 of a series of leaked US diplomatic cables. In one such communiqué, the Amir was reported to have told US Senator John Kerry that Iran 'will give you 100 words; trust only one of the 100', while another cable indicated that the Qatari Government had secretly agreed in principle to allow the USA to launch an attack against Iran from Qatari territory if it were to receive security guarantees from the US Administration in return, and that Qatar had also demanded US assistance in retaining Qatari sovereignty over the North Field gasfield at the Qatari–Iranian border. (Iran's ambassador to Qatar had announced in January 2010 that a provisional agreement had been reached on demarcation of the two countries' maritime border; however, a final agreement had yet to be announced by early 2013.) A security agreement between Qatar and Iran, which provided for increased co-operation in the fields of border security, counter-terrorism and operations intended to address drugs- and human-trafficking, was reported to have been concluded in June 2011.

Qatar's international profile was further bolstered by its active involvement in the international coalition to enforce an air exclusion zone imposed on the Libyan regime of Col Muammar al-Qaddafi by the UN Security Council in March 2011. Qatar and the United Arab Emirates were the only Middle Eastern countries to contribute aircraft to the North Atlantic Treaty Organization (NATO) coalition force. Furthermore, Qatar was reported to have provided Libyan rebels with significant amounts of financial aid, military training and weapons, and in March 2011 became the first Arab state formally to recognize the rebel National Transitional Council as the sole legitimate representative of the Libyan people.

Qatar also played a leading role in regional and international efforts to halt the use of military force against anti-Government protesters in Syria from 2011. Qatar was instrumental in securing the suspension of Syria's membership of the Arab League in November, and the organization's subsequent imposition of sanctions against the Syrian Government. Meanwhile, in July 2011 Qatar closed its embassy in the Syrian capital, Damascus, and withdrew its diplomatic staff from the country. In a sign of its increasing confidence in its own international influence, in March 2012 Sheikh Hamad bin Jasim bin Jaber Al Thani accused the Syrian authorities of committing 'genocide' against its own people, and declared that Arab and other international troops should be deployed to Syria to protect the civilian population. Sheikh Hamad also urged all nations to recognize the opposition Syrian National Council as the legitimate representative of that country. Qatar further endorsed the Syrian National Council in March 2013 when, during the Arab League summit meeting at which it was invited to occupy the seat previously held by the Syrian Government, the movement was permitted to open an embassy in Doha.

Other external relations

There was reported to have been a significant increase in the amount of US military personnel and equipment positioned in Qatar following the suicide attacks against New York and Washington, DC, USA, in September 2001. Furthermore, the construction of a major air facility at the Al-Udaid military base enhanced its strategic importance within the US military network in the region; in December 2002 the US Department of Defense dispatched more than 600 personnel from the US military command centre to the base, which was to act as the main US command post in the Gulf. None the less, Qatar, concerned about the popular reaction to a US-led war in Iraq and the regional implications that such a conflict might have, continued to advocate a diplomatic solution to the crisis. By the time of the commencement of hostilities in March 2003, the USA had stationed some 3,000 air force personnel and 36 tactical jets at Al-Udaid. In March 2007 the Qatari Government announced that it would not allow from its soil the launch by the USA of any military action against Iran, and strongly advocated a peaceful resolution to the ongoing impasse between the US and Iranian Governments. However, a US diplomatic cable published by WikiLeaks in late 2010 appeared to indicate that the Qatari and US Governments had previously reached a covert agreement by which the USA would be able to launch a future attack against Iran from Qatari soil, in exchange for security assurances (see Regional relations). A separate diplomatic cable published by WikiLeaks, referred to Qatar as the 'worst in the region' vis-à-vis co-operation with the US Government in the field of counter-terrorism, accused the Qatari authorities of being hesitant to act against known terrorists for fear of appearing to be too closely aligned with the USA, and expressed concern about Qatar's perceived support of Hamas via charitable organizations.

During a state visit to the People's Republic of China by the Qatari Prime Minister and Minister of Foreign Affairs, Sheikh Hamad, in April 2008, economic relations were augmented through an agreement for Qatar, as the largest producer of LNG globally, to supply 2m. metric tons per year (t/y) of LNG to the China National Offshore Oil Corporation (CNOOC). A separate contract, incorporating the purchase of 3m. t/y of LNG from Qatar Liquefied Gas Co (Qatargas) by PetroChina over a period of 25 years, was also signed between the two companies and Royal Dutch Shell (Netherlands/United Kingdom) during Sheikh Hamad's discussions with Chinese President Hu Jintao as part of enhanced Qatari-Chinese investment and co-operative initiatives. Qatargas signed two further deals in November 2009, under the terms of which it was to provide CNOOC with a further 3m. t/y of LNG from 2013 and PetroChina with an additional 2m. t/y during 2010–15. In May 2010 Qatar Petroleum, Petro-China and Royal Dutch Shell signed a 30-year gas exploration and production-sharing agreement providing for the joint exploration in Qatar's Block D concession, which spans an area of more than 8,000 sq km on shore and off shore close to the north-eastern city of Ras Laffan. Qatari-Chinese relations were further boosted by a state visit to Doha by Chinese Premier Wen Jiabao in January 2012, during which he held discussions with both the Amir and the Prime Minister, and a series of bilateral co-operation agreements were signed, including an accord intended to facilitate investment co-operation.

Relations between Qatar and India have strengthened considerably in recent years. Sheikh Hamad visited India in 2005, followed by Prime Minister Sheikh Abdullah in 2006. Between 2004 and 2007 the volume of trade between the two countries increased three-fold; by 2008 Qatar was the largest supplier of LNG to India, exporting around 5m. metric tons annually, while there were an estimated 300,000 Indians living and working in Qatar. During an official visit to Doha by Indian Prime Minister Manmohan Singh in November 2008 two security co-operation agreements were signed, covering matters such as maritime security, intelligence-sharing and law enforcement. In April 2012 in New Delhi, India, the Amir signed several agreements with Prime Minister Singh including one on establishing a framework to enhance bilateral co-operation on oil and gas exploration.

The selection in December 2010 of Qatar as the host of the 2022 International Federation of Association Football (Fédération internationale de football association—FIFA) World Cup, the first time that the right to host the event had been awarded to a Middle Eastern country, was widely expected to boost Qatar's international profile. Subsequent allegations that Qatar had made illegal payments to FIFA officials to secure the right to host the tournament were denied by both FIFA and the Qatari authorities, although in January 2013 FIFA investigators confirmed that they intended to examine these claims further.

CONSTITUTION AND GOVERNMENT

According to the provisional Constitution that took effect in 1970, Qatar is an absolute monarchy, with full powers vested in the Amir as head of state. Executive power is exercised by the Council of Ministers, appointed by the head of state. An Advisory Council was formed in April 1972, with 20 nominated members (expanded to 30 in 1975 and to 35 in 1988). The Advisory Council's constitutional entitlements include the power to debate legislation drafted by the Council of Ministers before ratification and promulgation. It also has the power to request ministerial statements on matters of general and specific policy, including the draft budget. In March 1999 elections took place, by universal adult suffrage, for a 29-member Central Municipal Council, which was to have a consultative role in the operations of the Ministry of Municipal Affairs and Agriculture; further elections were held in April 2003 and April 2007. The Amir formally adopted a new Constitution following its approval at a referendum held on 29 April 2003. Under the Constitution, the Amir was to remain head of the executive, while a 45-member unicameral parliament, of which two-thirds were to be directly elected (the remainder being appointed by the Amir), was to have the power, *inter alia*, to legislate, review the state budget and monitor government policy. However, elections to the new legislature, after which the Advisory Council was to be abolished, were repeatedly postponed, most recently owing to the need to introduce an appropriate legal framework. A new electoral law was duly adopted by the Advisory Council in May 2008. In November 2011 the Amir announced that elections to the new legislature were finally to be held in the latter half of 2013. However, by early 2013 no date had been set.

REGIONAL AND INTERNATIONAL CO-OPERATION

Qatar is a member of the Cooperation Council for the Arab States of the Gulf (Gulf Cooperation Council—GCC, see p. 255). GCC member states created a unified regional customs tariff in January 2003. The economic convergence criteria for the proposed monetary union were agreed at a heads of state meeting in Abu Dhabi, United Arab Emirates, in December 2005, and in January 2008 the GCC launched its common market. The country is also a member of the League of Arab States (the Arab League, see p. 372) and the Organization of Arab Petroleum Exporting Countries (OAPEC, see p. 410).

Qatar joined the UN on 21 September 1971, having gained independence earlier that month. The country became a member of the World Trade Organization (WTO, see p. 444) in 1996. It also participates in the Organization of the Petroleum Exporting Countries (OPEC, see p. 418) and the Organization of Islamic Cooperation (OIC, see p. 413).

ECONOMIC AFFAIRS

In 1997, according to estimates by the World Bank, Qatar's gross national income (GNI), measured at average 1995–97 prices, was US $11,627m., equivalent to $22,147 per head. According to unofficial sources, GNI totalled $17,150m. in 2001 and $17,490m. in 2002 (equivalent to some $28,300 per head). According to the World Bank, during 2002–11, it was estimated, the population increased at an average annual rate of 13.0%, while gross domestic product (GDP) per head increased, in real terms, by an average of 1.5% per year during 2002–11. Non-Qataris accounted for some 80% of the total population by the beginning of the 21st century. Overall GDP was estimated to have increased, in real terms, at an average rate of 15.7% per year in 2004–11; according to preliminary official figures, real GDP growth was estimated at 13.0% in 2011.

Agriculture (including fishing) contributed 0.1% of GDP in 2011, according to provisional official figures. The sector engaged some 1.4% of the employed population in the same year. All agricultural land is owned by the Government, and most farm managers are immigrants employing a largely expatriate workforce. The main crops are cereals (principally barley), vegetables and dates. Qatar is self-sufficient in winter vegetables and nearly self-sufficient in summer vegetables. Some vegetables are exported to other Gulf countries. The Government has prioritized education in agricultural techniques and experimentation with unconventional methods of cultivation (including the use of sea water and solar energy to produce sand-based crops).

Livestock-rearing and fishing are also practised. The GDP of the agricultural sector was estimated to have increased by an average annual rate of 11.7% during 2004–11. Real agricultural GDP increased by 5.5% in 2011, according to preliminary official estimates.

Industry (including mining, manufacturing, construction and power) contributed 71.0% of GDP in 2011, according to provisional figures, and engaged 54.1% of the employed population in the same year. Industrial GDP was estimated to have increased by an average of 14.3% per year in 2004–11. According to preliminary figures, growth in the sector's real GDP was estimated at 14.0% in 2011.

The mining and quarrying sector (comprising principally the extraction and processing of petroleum and natural gas) provided 57.0% of GDP in 2011, according to provisional figures. The sector engaged just 6.4% of the employed population in the same year. Proven recoverable petroleum reserves at the end of 2011 were 24,683m. barrels, sufficient to maintain production for just over 39 years at 2011 levels—averaging some 1.72m. barrels per day (b/d). As a member of the Organization of the Petroleum Exporting Countries (OPEC, see p. 418), Qatar is subject to production quotas agreed by the Organization's Conference. Proven gas reserves were 25,047,000m. cu m at the end of 2011 (representing 12.0% of known world reserves at that date—behind only Russia and Iran), primarily located in the North Field, the world's largest gas reserve not associated with petroleum. The real GDP of the mining and quarrying sector was estimated to have increased at an average annual rate of 13.1% in 2004–11. According to preliminary figures, growth in the sector was an estimated 15.7% in 2011.

Manufacturing contributed 9.8% of GDP in 2011 (excluding activities related to petroleum and natural gas), according to provisional figures. The sector engaged 7.9% of the employed population in the same year. The principal manufacturing activities are linked to the country's oil and gas resources—petroleum-refining and the production of liquefied natural gas (LNG—developed as part of the North Field project), together with industrial chemicals (particularly fertilizers) and steel production. Manufacturing GDP (excluding hydrocarbons) was estimated to have increased by an average of 11.4% per year in 2004–11. According to preliminary figures, the sector's real GDP increased by an estimated 10.4% in 2011.

Construction contributed 3.7% of GDP in 2011, according to provisional figures, while the sector engaged 39.2% of the employed population in the same year. According to preliminary figures, the sector's GDP increased by an average of 27.1% per year in 2004–11. Construction GDP was estimated to have increased by 10.6% in 2011.

Electrical energy is derived almost exclusively from Qatar's natural gas resource. Solar energy is being developed in conjunction with desalination. The US $3,900m. Ras Laffan C independent water and power project was inaugurated at the end of May 2011; with a capacity of 2,730 MW of power and 63m. gallons of water a day, the project was the country's largest of its kind. The electricity and water generated by the project were to be sold through a 25-year power and water purchase agreement with the Qatar General Electricity and Water Corpn.

The services sector contributed 28.9% of GDP in 2011, according to provisional figures. The sector engaged 44.6% of the employed population in the same year. The establishment in March 2005 of the Qatar Financial Centre, which was to provide a hub for the emirate's financial services sector, had reportedly proved popular with investors by early 2006 and was expected to stimulate further activity in the sector. The GDP of the services sector was estimated to have increased by an average of 19.3% per year in 2004–11. According to preliminary figures, services GDP increased by an estimated 10.3% in 2011.

According to preliminary official figures for 2011, Qatar recorded a visible merchandise trade surplus of QR 318,037m., while there was a surplus of QR 189,200m. on the current account of the balance of payments. In 2011, according to preliminary official figures, the principal source of imports (11.5% of the total value) was the USA; other important suppliers in that year were the People's Republic of China, the United Arab Emirates (UAE), Germany, Italy, Japan and Saudi Arabia. In 2011, according to preliminary official figures, Japan took 26.1% of Qatar's exports by value (including re-exports); the Republic of Korea (South Korea), India, Singapore and the United Kingdom were also significant markets for exports. The principal exports were mineral products. The principal imports in 2011 were machinery and electrical equipment, vehicles, vessels, aircraft and other transport equipment, base metals and their articles, chemical products and mineral products.

In the financial year ending 31 March 2012 Qatar recorded a budget surplus of QR 54,342m., according to preliminary official figures. Qatar's gross government debt was QR 207,475m. in 2011, equivalent to 32.3% of GDP (compared with just 11.9% in 2008). According to ILO data, the annual rate of inflation averaged 5.5% in 2002–11; consumer prices declined by an average of 2.4%, in 2010, but increased by 0.4% in 2011. The Qatari economy is heavily dependent on immigrant workers, owing to a shortage of indigenous labour; according to the official figures, some 94.1% of the employed population were non-Qataris in 2011. The rate of unemployment among the total labour force was recorded at 0.5% in 2011, although 3.5% of the Qatari labour force was unemployed in that year.

Since 2006 Qatar has been the world's largest exporter of LNG. From 2008 the combined value of exports of LNG and other associated and non-associated gas products has exceeded that of crude petroleum, hitherto Qatar's principal export. Exports of LNG in 2011 reached some 75.5m. metric tons (31% of the global total), up from 55.7m. tons the previous year. Oil output, meanwhile, stood at 1.72m. b/d, compared to 1.57m. b/d and 1.35m. b/d in 2010 and 2009, respectively. Despite the dominance of its hydrocarbons sector and two decades of intensive expansion of its gas output, Qatar's long-term priority has been diversification of its economy: in 2005 a moratorium was imposed on the development of new projects in the country's North Field gas reservoir which was subsequently extended until at least 2015. Qatar's inaugural National Development Strategy, which was announced in March 2011 and covered the period 2011–16, was regarded as the first step in realizing the goals of the National Vision 2030 launched in 2008 (see Domestic Political Affairs), as well as in preparing to host the 2022 International Federation of Association Football (Fédération internationale de football association—FIFA) World Cup. The Strategy provided for expenditure of some $125,000m. during 2011–16 (equivalent to around 25% of projected GDP for the period). More than $65,000m. of this total was to be disbursed on upgrading infrastructure in advance of the FIFA World Cup. At early 2013 major infrastructure projects under development included the construction of a new international airport, a new port in Doha and a national rail network. Education, health, housing projects and transportation were also to benefit from the Strategy, while the respective roles of the private and non-hydrocarbons sectors were to be enhanced. In January 2013 the Ministry of Business and Trade completed the draft of a company law aimed at simplifying and facilitating the procedures of establishing new businesses. The National Development Strategy envisaged a narrowing of the fiscal surplus to (a still healthy) 5.7% of GDP by 2016 as a result of the stabilization of the hydrocarbons sector and increased government spending.

PUBLIC HOLIDAYS

2014: 11 February (National Sports Day), 26 May* (Leilat al-Meiraj, Ascension of the Prophet), 27 June (Anniversary of the Amir's Accession), 28 June* (Ramadan begins), 28 July* (Id al-Fitr, end of Ramadan), 4 October* (Id al-Adha, Feast of the Sacrifice), 24 October* (Muharram, Islamic New Year), 18 December* (National Day).

* These holidays are dependent on the Islamic lunar calendar and may differ by one or two days from the dates given.

Statistical Survey

Sources (unless otherwise stated): Dept of Economic Policies, Qatar Central Bank, POB 1234, Doha; tel. 4456456; fax 4413650; e-mail elzainys@qcb.gov.qa; internet www.qcb.gov.qa; Qatar Statistics Authority, POB 7283, Doha; tel. 4958888; fax 4839999; e-mail customer_services@planning.gov.qa; internet www.qsa .gov.qa.

Area and Population

AREA, POPULATION AND DENSITY

Area (sq km)	11,493*
Population (census results)†	
1 March 2004	744,029
20 April 2010	
Males	1,284,739
Females	414,696
Total	1,699,435
Population (official estimate at mid year)	
2011‡	1,732,717
Density (per sq km) at mid-2011	150.8

* 4,437 sq miles.
† Including resident workers from abroad.
‡ Estimate not adjusted to take account of the 2010 census.

POPULATION BY AGE AND SEX
(population at 2010 census*)

	Males	Females	Total
0–14	119,140	113,444	232,584
15–64	1,157,450	295,584	1,453,034
65 and over	8,149	5,668	13,817
Total	1,284,739	414,696	1,699,435

* Including resident workers from abroad.

PRINCIPAL TOWNS
(population of municipalities at 2010 census)

Al Dawhah (Doha) .	796,947	Umm Salal . . .	60,509
Al-Rayyan . . .	455,623	Al Daayen . . .	43,176
Al-Khawr (Al-Khor).	193,983	Al-Shamal . . .	7,975
Al-Wakrah . . .	141,222		

BIRTHS, MARRIAGES AND DEATHS

	Registered live births		Registered marriages		Registered deaths	
	Number	Rate (per 1,000)	Number	Rate (per 1,000)	Number	Rate (per 1,000)
2004 . .	13,190	17.5	2,649	3.5	1,341	1.8
2005 . .	13,401	16.8	2,734	3.4	1,545	1.9
2006 . .	14,120	16.8	3,019	3.6	1,750	2.1
2007 . .	15,681	12.8	3,206	2.6	1,776	1.5
2008 . .	17,210	11.9	3,235	2.2	1,942	1.3
2009 . .	18,351	11.2	3,153	1.9	2,008	1.2
2010 . .	19,504	11.2	2,977	1.7	1,970	1.1
2011 . .	20,623	11.9	3,293	1.9	1,949	1.1

Life expectancy (years at birth): 78.2 (males 78.5; females 77.9) in 2011 (Source: World Bank, World Development Indicators database).

ECONOMICALLY ACTIVE POPULATION
(population aged 15 years and over, 2011)

	Qatari	Non-Qatari	Total
Agriculture, hunting, forestry and fishing	78	17,209	17,287
Mining and quarrying	5,403	76,506	81,909
Manufacturing	798	100,206	101,004
Electricity, gas and water . . .	1,633	4,982	6,615
Construction	715	496,916	497,631
Wholesale and retail trade; repair of motor vehicles, motorcycles and personal and household goods	1,884	140,104	141,988
Hotels and restaurants . . .	33	30,336	30,369
Transport and storage	578	32,381	32,959
Information and communications .	2,388	7,536	9,924
Financial intermediation . . .	2,490	8,157	10,647
Real estate, renting and business activities	348	8,740	9,088
Public administration	43,974	32,534	76,508
Professional, scientific and technical activities	429	23,692	24,121
Administrative and support service activities	587	39,831	40,418
Education	8,407	18,840	27,247
Health and social work . . .	3,799	17,388	21,187
Arts, entertainment and recreation	962	3,695	4,657
Other community, social and personal service activities . .	158	4,176	4,334
Private households with employed persons	—	131,607	131,607
Extra-territorial organizations and bodies	16	1,558	1,574
Total employed	74,680	1,196,394	1,271,074
Unemployed	2,730	3,641	6,371
Total labour force	77,410	1,200,035	1,277,445
Males	50,093	1,069,164	1,119,257
Females	27,317	130,871	158,188

Health and Welfare

KEY INDICATORS

Total fertility rate (children per woman, 2010)	2.3
Under-5 mortality rate (per 1,000 live births, 2010) . . .	8
Physicians (per 1,000 head, 2006)	2.8
Hospital beds (per 1,000 head, 2009)	1.2
Health expenditure (2009): US $ per head (PPP)	1,965
Health expenditure (2009): % of GDP	2.6
Health expenditure (2009): public (% of total)	78.4
Total carbon dioxide emissions ('000 metric tons, 2008) . .	68,477.6
Carbon dioxide emissions per head (metric tons, 2008) . .	49.1
Human Development Index (2011): ranking	37
Human Development Index (2011): value	0.831

For sources and definitions, see explanatory note on p. vi.

Agriculture

PRINCIPAL CROPS
('000 metric tons)

	2009	2010	2011
Barley	0.7	0.7	0.5
Cauliflowers and broccoli	1.6	2.1	1.4
Pumpkins, squash and gourds	0.4	0.6	0.4
Aubergines (Eggplants)	4.5	4.7	3.6
Chillies and peppers, green	0.8	1.0	0.9
Onions, dry	2.4	2.8	2.6
Tomatoes	12.6	12.8	10.7
Cantaloupes and other melons	2.9	2.1	1.8*
Dates	20.8	21.5	20.7

*FAO estimate.

Aggregate production ('000 metric tons, may include official, semi-official or estimated data): Total cereals 2.2 in 2009, 2.7 in 2010, 1.7 in 2011; Total fruits (excl. melons) 21.6 in 2009, 22.3 in 2010, 21.6 in 2011; Total vegetables (incl. melons) 45.7 in 2009, 48.4 in 2010, 47.9 in 2011.

Source: FAO.

LIVESTOCK
('000 head, year ending September)

	2009	2010	2011
Horses	6.1	6.0	5.8*
Cattle	11.1	11.4	10.1
Camels	47.3	51.5	61.7
Sheep	199.8	213.8	241.4
Goats	165.6	171.6	190.0
Chickens	6,800.0	7,300.0	8,000.0

*FAO estimate.
Source: FAO.

LIVESTOCK PRODUCTS
('000 metric tons)

	2009	2010	2011
Camel meat*	1.2	1.3	1.4
Sheep meat*	9.5	8.6	8.7
Chicken meat*	7.3	8.1	9.2
Cows' milk*	6.8	7.0	6.9
Camels' milk*	4.6	4.9	4.9
Goats' milk*	5.9	6.0	6.0
Hen eggs	4.3	4.5	5.0

*FAO estimates.
Source: FAO.

Fishing

('000 metric tons, live weight)

	2008	2009	2010
Capture	17.7	14.1	13.8
Groupers	2.3	1.3	1.3
Grunts and sweetlips	1.0	0.7	0.8
Emperors (Scavengers)	5.0	4.7	4.1
Narrow-barred Spanish mackerel	2.6	1.8	2.1
Aquaculture	0.0	0.0	0.0
Total catch	17.7	14.1	13.8

Source: FAO.

Mining

	2009	2010	2011
Crude petroleum ('000 metric tons)	57,868	65,685	71,053
Natural gas (million cu m)*	89,300	116,700	146,850

*Excluding gas flared or recycled.

Source: BP, *Statistical Review of World Energy*.

Industry

SELECTED PRODUCTS
('000 metric tons unless otherwise indicated)

	2004	2005	2006
Ammonia (for fertilizer)	1,737.2	2,133.8	2,170.2
Urea (for fertilizer)	2,238.7	2,978.8	2,908.9
Organic fertilizers	24.0	42.0	57.0
Cement	1,202.0	1,182.0	2,169.0
'Super' petrol (motor spirit— gasoline)	801.0	754.6	889.4
'Premium' petrol (motor spirit— gasoline)	857.9	901.7	1,004.7
Jet fuel (incl. kerosene)	957.7	905.5	1,087.1
Gas diesel (distillate fuel) oils	995.1	925.6	997.9
Residual fuel oils	250.7	418.3	614.6
Liquefied petroleum gas	127.6	131.0	217.0
Natural gas condensate	1,545.1	1,556.1	1,667.9
Butane	963.0	1,075.4	1,151.8
Propane	1,242.6	1,403.1	1,576.2
Electric energy (million kWh)	12,992.6	14,395.9	14,983.2

Electric energy (million kWh): 19,462 in 2007; 21,616 in 2008; 24,796 in 2009 (Source: UN Industrial Commodity Statistics Database).

Finance

CURRENCY AND EXCHANGE RATES

Monetary Units
100 dirhams = 1 Qatar riyal (QR).

Sterling, Dollar and Euro Equivalents (31 December 2012)
£1 sterling = 5.744 riyals;
US $1 = 3.640 riyals;
€1 = 4.803 riyals;
100 Qatar riyals = £17.41 = $27.47 = €20.82.

Average Exchange Rate

Note: Since June 1980 the official mid-point rate has been fixed at US $1 = QR 3.64.

BUDGET
(QR million, year ending 31 March)

Revenue	2009/10	2010/11	2011/12*
Petroleum and natural gas	82,807	96,849	153,198
Investments	53,881	36,090	25,764
Other	32,454	22,968	41,132
Total	169,142	155,907	220,094

Expenditure	2009/10	2010/11	2011/12*
Current expenditure	75,788	98,127	115,661
Wages and salaries	21,594	23,065	29,613
Interest payments	3,998	5,577	9,613
Supplies and services	8,082	15,188	11,586
Other	42,114	54,297	64,849
Development expenditure	39,246	44,243	50,091
Total	115,034	142,370	165,752

*Preliminary figures.

INTERNATIONAL RESERVES
(US $ million at 31 December)

	2009	2010	2011
Gold (national valuation) . .	436.0	566.5	626.1
IMF special drawing rights . .	420.4	413.2	412.5
Reserve position in IMF . . .	80.4	96.0	144.6
Foreign exchange	17,868.9	30,111.6	15,641.3
Total	18,805.7	31,187.3	16,824.6

Source: IMF, *International Financial Statistics*.

MONEY SUPPLY
(QR million at 31 December)

	2009	2010	2011
Currency outside depository corporations	5,653	6,095	7,013
Transferable deposits	65,740	81,484	106,305
Other deposits	143,689	177,137	196,648
Broad money	215,082	264,716	309,966

Source: IMF, *International Financial Statistics*.

COST OF LIVING
(Consumer Price Index; base: 2007 = 100)

	2010	2011	2012
Food, beverages and tobacco . .	123.9	129.4	134.2
Clothing and footwear . . .	105.2	113.3	116.5
Rent, fuel and energy	91.9	87.4	84.6
Transport and communication .	107.2	114.1	116.7
All items (incl. others) . . .	106.9	108.9	111.0

NATIONAL ACCOUNTS
(QR million at current prices)

Expenditure on the Gross Domestic Product
(provisional)

	2008	2009	2010
Government final consumption expenditure	41,139	49,397	56,059
Private final consumption expenditure	64,223	68,621	68,758
Gross capital formation . .	174,534	159,204	163,612
Total domestic expenditure .	279,896	277,222	288,429
Exports of goods and services .	257,466	182,034	283,232
Less Imports of goods and services	117,779	103,269	108,171
GDP in purchasers' values .	419,583	355,986	463,489
GDP at constant 2004 prices .	217,486	243,492	284,226

Gross Domestic Product by Economic Activity

	2009	2010	2011*
Agriculture and fishing . . .	439	534	582
Mining and quarrying† . . .	159,467	239,745	364,458
Manufacturing	33,570	49,185	62,690
Electricity, gas and water . .	1,794	2,070	2,564
Construction	25,522	24,144	23,825
Trade, restaurants and hotels .	29,839	32,310	35,696
Transport and communications .	16,212	18,275	21,892
Finance, insurance, real estate and business services	58,099	62,119	73,727
Government services . . .	32,106	35,814	46,736
Social services	4,149	4,346	4,883
Other services	1,827	1,881	2,027
Sub-total	363,024	470,423	639,080
Import duties	3,114	4,019	3,546
Less Imputed bank service charge	10,152	10,953	11,743
GDP in purchasers' values .	355,986	463,489	630,883

* Provisional.
† Including services incidental to mining of petroleum and natural gas.

BALANCE OF PAYMENTS
(QR million)

	2009	2010	2011*
Exports of goods f.o.b.	174,745	272,309	416,047
Imports of goods f.o.b.	−81,726	−76,210	−98,010
Trade balance	93,019	196,099	318,037
Exports of services	7,288	10,961	26,913
Imports of services	−21,543	−31,961	−61,395
Balance on goods and services	78,764	175,099	283,555
Other income received . . .	3,594	8,698	22,445
Other income paid	−37,856	−55,813	−70,752
Balance on goods, services and income	44,502	127,984	235,248
Current transfers (net) . . .	−21,247	−41,362	−46,048
Expatriates' remittances . .	−25,827	−29,577	−37,543
Current balance	23,255	86,622	189,200
Capital account (net)	−6,538	−7,489	−13,121
Financial account (net) . . .	8,735	−31,379	−214,685
Net errors and omissions . .	4,806	−3,361	−13,605
Overall balance	30,258	44,393	−52,211

* Preliminary figures.

External Trade

PRINCIPAL COMMODITIES
(distribution by HS, QR million)

Imports	2009	2010	2011*
Live animals; animal products	2,285.3	2,718.2	3,181.3
Mineral products	2,646.1	3,237.8	5185.2
Chemical products, etc. . .	5,200.4	6,132.0	6,712.2
Base metals and articles of base metal	13,502.7	10,976.4	8,852.9
Articles of iron and steel . . .	9,877.2	6,180.4	5,069.3
Machinery and electrical equipment	38,669.3	27,744.4	22,423.1
Boilers, machinery and mechanical appliances and other apparatus (such as nuclear reactors)	23,297.3	16,087.2	12,333.6
Electrical machinery and equipment; sound and television recorders and reproducers . .	15,372.0	11,657.2	10,089.4
Vehicles, vessels, aircraft and other transport equipment .	10,220.8	13,278.9	13,065.8
Vehicles other than trains, vessels and air and spacecraft . . .	7,748.7	9,010.5	8,528.7
Total (incl. others)	90,715.9	84,593.0	81,275.1

Exports†	2009	2010	2011*
Mineral products	155,900.1	245,969.0	383,131.2
Mineral fuels and oils, and products thereof	155,708.5	245,271.0	381,728.6
Chemical products, etc. . .	7,788.3	8,329.6	11,062.5
Plastics, rubber and articles thereof	4,272.5	5,456.0	8,860.1
Plastics and articles thereof . .	4,265.3	5,438.7	8,846.8
Total (incl. others)	174,746.0	272,309.5	416,046.9

* Preliminary figures.
† Including re-exports (QR million): 4,248.4 in 2009; 7,317.8 in 2010; 5,590.8 in 2011 (preliminary).

PRINCIPAL TRADING PARTNERS
(QR million)

Imports	2009	2010	2011*
Australia	780.4	1,310.8	1,844.3
Bahrain	1,497.7	1,986.4	1,796.5
Belgium	987.5	980.4	703.1
Brazil	1,198.2	1,443.9	1,949.4
China, People's Republic	7,158.9	7,658.1	7,842.2
Egypt	1,067.7	1,044.5	967.6
France	4,483.9	4,026.2	2,723.7
Germany	6,829.2	6,130.0	5,644.8
India	3,313.5	2,553.2	2,672.1
Italy	6,790.7	5,497.9	4,644.2
Japan	6,602.8	6,373.3	4,557.3
Korea, Republic	3,234.9	2,642.2	2,048.5
Malaysia	1,267.0	1,252.9	1,030.6
Oman	1,012.0	852.6	603.3
Saudi Arabia	4,841.6	4,441.2	4,257.3
Spain	1,082.3	926.7	1,089.1
Sweden	790.1	819.6	1,398.1
Switzerland	2,032.8	1,387.9	1,927.4
Thailand	1,428.8	1,350.0	1,375.4
Turkey	1,428.7	980.1	876.4
United Arab Emirates	6,418.7	5,795.6	6,514.9
United Kingdom	4,125.1	4,307.3	4,023.4
USA	11,158.6	9,981.1	9,312.1
Total (incl. others)	90,715.9	84,593.0	81,275.1

Exports†	2009	2010	2011*
Belgium	4,818.3	4,855.6	7,188.8
China, People's Republic	3,360.4	8,098.5	16,361.6
France	177.9	4,282.1	6,301.8
India	14,691.2	23,285.6	39,375.4
Japan	56,323.4	78,032.0	108,394.0
Korea, Republic	25,086.4	43,788.7	73,294.5
New Zealand	2,036.0	1,520.8	2,757.5
Philippines	2,278.6	1,715.4	1,504.5
Saudi Arabia	1,310.1	3,859.3	3,136.2
Singapore	12,249.8	20,927.8	29,682.9
Spain	5,281.3	11,737.2	15,800.1
Taiwan	1,877.1	6,928.7	13,475.3
Thailand	4,936.2	7,912.9	8,784.9
Turkey	419.4	2,742.4	2,684.6
United Arab Emirates	9,592.1	15,571.4	15,861.6
United Kingdom	4,867.6	12,869.3	29,149.8
USA	1,376.5	2,848.3	3,803.7
Total (incl. others)	174,746.0	272,309.5	416,046.9

* Preliminary figures.

† Including re-exports (QR million): 4,248.4 in 2009; 7,317.8 in 2010; 5,590.8 in 2011 (preliminary).

Transport

ROAD TRAFFIC
(registered vehicles)

	2004	2005	2006
Private cars	265,609	293,355	337,056
Other private transport	114,115	126,541	148,436
Heavy equipment	11,162	13,262	17,438
Motorcycles and mopeds	4,420	4,698	5,048
Total (incl. others)	406,626	451,388	525,795

SHIPPING
Flag Registered Fleet
(at 31 December)

	2010	2011	2012
Number of vessels	146	152	152
Total displacement ('000 grt)	1,037.3	1,047.0	860.6

Source: Lloyd's List Intelligence (www.lloydslistintelligence.com).

INTERNATIONAL SEA-BORNE FREIGHT TRAFFIC
(2010)

	Traffic
Doha Port	
Vessels entered and cleared	1,144
Containers	472
Capacity ('000 grt)	19,079
Umm Said (Mesaieed) Port	
Vessels entered and cleared	2,159
Tankers	263
Containers	349
Capacity ('000 grt)	2,746,117
Halul Port	
Vessels entered and cleared	134
Tankers	134
Capacity ('000 grt)	19,946
Ras Laffan Port	
Vessels entered and cleared	1,719
Tankers	1,408
Capacity ('000 grt)	154,782
Total	
Vessels entered and cleared	5,156
Tankers	1,805
Containers	821
Capacity ('000 grt)	2,939,924

CIVIL AVIATION
(Doha International Airport)

	2004	2005	2006
Aircraft arrivals	49,614	60,828	67,472
Passenger arrivals ('000)*	2,790	3,654	4,424
Passengers in transit ('000)	1,589	2,185	4,573
Cargo and mail received (metric tons)	102,455	127,042	161,759
Cargo and mail dispatched (metric tons)	61,047	83,554	105,760

* Excluding private aircraft.

Aircraft arrivals: 50,603 in 2009; 59,088 in 2010; 68,734 in 2011.

Tourism

TOURIST ARRIVALS
(arrivals of non-resident tourists in hotels and similar establishments)

Region of residence	2008	2009	2010
Asia	216,742	264,550	298,395
Europe	329,059	406,725	730,034
Middle East	628,440	679,859	751,924
Total (incl. others)	1,404,850	1,658,569	1,866,471

Tourism receipts (US $ million, excl. passenger transport): 179 in 2009; 584 in 2010; 1,170 in 2011 (provisional).

Source: World Tourism Organization.

Communications Media

	2009	2010	2011
Telephones ('000 main lines in use)	287.9	292.2	306.0
Mobile cellular telephones ('000 in use)	1,948.8	2,186.4	2,302.3
Internet subscribers ('000) . .	145.8	150.4	167.4
Broadband subscribers ('000) . .	141.3	142.9	162.1

Source: International Telecommunication Union.

Education

(2010/11)

	Institutions	Teachers	Students Males	Females	Total
Private schools* . .	435	8,175	57,321	49,263	106,584
Pre-primary . .	185	1,448	12,636	11,296	23,932
Primary . . .	109	3,774	29,047	24,778	53,825
Preparatory . .	76	2,211	9,242	7,803	17,045
General secondary .	65	742	6,396	5,386	11,782
Independent schools† .	234	9,444	43,663	47,008	90,671
Pre-primary . .	36	566	2,411	3,173	5,584
Primary . . .	95	4,647	19,645	21,515	41,160
Preparatory . .	54	2,181	10,536	11,041	21,577
General secondary‡	49	2,050	11,071	11,279	22,350
Total	669	17,619	96,271	100,984	197,255
Pre-primary . .	221	2,014	15,047	14,469	29,516
Primary . . .	204	8,421	48,692	46,293	94,985
Preparatory . .	130	4,392	19,778	18,844	38,622
General secondary‡	114	2,792	17,467	16,665	34,132
University of Qatar§ .	—	721	2,339	7,454	9,793

* Including the Qatar Foundation for Education, Science and Community Development (including the Qatar Academy and the Qatar Leadership Academy and Learning Centre) and the Academy for Sports Excellence (Aspire).
† Including Government schools.
‡ Including specialized secondary schools.
§ Including Qatar Community College.

Pupil-teacher ratio (primary education, UNESCO estimate): 12.0 in 2009/10 (Source: UNESCO Institute for Statistics).

Adult literacy rate (UNESCO estimates): 96.3% (males 96.5%; females 95.4%) in 2010 (Source: UNESCO Institute for Statistics).

Directory

The Government

HEAD OF STATE

Amir and Commander-in-Chief of the Armed Forces: Maj.-Gen. Sheikh HAMAD BIN KHALIFA AL THANI (assumed power 27 June 1995).

Heir Apparent and Deputy Commander-in-Chief of the Armed Forces: Sheikh TAMIM BIN HAMAD BIN KHALIFA AL THANI.

COUNCIL OF MINISTERS
(May 2013)

Amir and Minister of Defence: Maj.-Gen. Sheikh HAMAD BIN KHALIFA AL THANI.

Prime Minister and Minister of Foreign Affairs: Sheikh HAMAD BIN JASIM BIN JABER AL THANI.

Deputy Prime Minister and Chairman of the Emiri Diwan: ABDULLAH BIN HAMAD AL-ATTIYA.

Deputy Prime Minister and Minister of State for Cabinet Affairs: AHMAD BIN ABDULLAH AL-MAHMOUD.

Minister of Energy and Industry: MUHAMMAD SALEH AL-SADA.

Minister of Economy and Finance: YOUSUF HUSSAIN KAMAL.

Minister of Business and Trade: Sheikh JASSIM BIN ABD AL-AZIZ BIN JASSIM BIN HAMAD AL THANI.

Minister of the Interior: Sheikh ABDULLAH BIN KHALID AL THANI.

Minister of Awqaf (Religious Endowments) and Islamic Affairs: Dr GHAITH BIN MUBARAK BIN IMRAN AL-KUWARI.

Minister of Municipal Affairs and Urban Planning: Sheikh ABD AL-RAHMAN BIN KHALIFA BIN ABD AL-AZIZ AL THANI.

Minister of the Environment: ABDULLAH BIN MUBARAK BIN ABOUD AL-MIDHADHI.

Minister of Justice: HASSAN BIN ABDULLAH AL-GHANEM.

Minister of Education and Higher Education: SAAD BIN IBRAHIM AL-MAHMOUD.

Minister of Social Affairs and Acting Minister of Labour: NASSER BIN ABDULLAH AL-HAMIDI.

Minister of Public Health: ABDULLAH BIN KHALID AL-QAHTANI.

Minister of Culture, Arts and Heritage: Dr HAMAD BIN ABD AL-AZIZ AL-KAWARI.

Minister of State for Foreign Affairs: Dr KHALID BIN MUHAMMAD AL-ATTIYA.

Minister of State for the Interior: Sheikh ABDULLAH BIN NASSER BIN KHALIFA AL THANI.

Ministers of State without Portfolio: Sheikh MUHAMMAD BIN KHALID AL THANI, Sheikha BINT AHMAD AL-MAHMOUD.

MINISTRIES

Ministry of Awqaf (Religious Endowments) and Islamic Affairs: POB 422, Doha; tel. 44470777; fax 44470700; e-mail awqaf@awqaf.gov.qa; internet www.islam.gov.qa.

Ministry of Business and Trade: POB 1968, Doha; tel. 44945555; fax 44945000; e-mail mbt@mbt.gov.qa; internet www.mbt.gov.qa.

Ministry of Culture, Arts and Heritage: POB 23700, Doha; tel. 44022222; fax 44022212; e-mail info@moc.gov.qa; internet www.moc .gov.qa.

Ministry of Defence: Qatar Armed Forces, POB 37, Doha; tel. 44614111.

Ministry of Economy and Finance: POB 83, Doha; tel. 44461608; fax 44413617; e-mail qatfin@mof.gov.qa; internet www.mof.gov.qa.

Ministry of Education and Higher Education: POB 80, al-Waqf Tower, al-Dafna, Doha; tel. 44941111; fax 44941445; e-mail e .alhorr@moe.edu.qa; internet www.moe.edu.qa.

Ministry of Energy and Industry: POB 2599, Doha; tel. 44846444; fax 44832024; e-mail did@mei.gov.qa; internet www .mei.gov.qa.

Ministry of the Environment: POB 7634, Doha; tel. 44207777; fax 44207000; e-mail responsibility@moe.gov.qa; internet www.moe.gov .qa.

Ministry of Foreign Affairs: POB 250, Doha; tel. 44334334; fax 44324131; e-mail webmaster@mofa.gov.qa; internet www.mofa.gov .qa.

Ministry of the Interior: POB 115, Doha; tel. 44330000; fax 44322927; e-mail info@moi.gov.qa; internet www.moi.gov.qa.

Ministry of Justice: POB 917, Doha; tel. 44842222; fax 44832875; e-mail info@moj.gov.qa; internet www.moj.gov.qa.

Ministry of Labour: POB 36, Doha; tel. 44841111; fax 44841441; e-mail customerservice@mol.gov.qa; internet www.mol.gov.qa.

Ministry of Municipal Affairs and Urban Planning: POB 22332, Main Bldg, Corniche St, Doha; tel. 44413331; fax 44430239; e-mail info@baladiya.gov.qa; internet www.baladiya.gov .qa.

Ministry of Public Health: POB 42, Doha; tel. 44070000; fax 44446294; e-mail info@nha.org.qa; internet www.nha.org.qa.

Ministry of Social Affairs: POB 36, Doha; tel. 44841137; fax 44841959; e-mail mosa@mosa.gov.qa; internet www.mosa.gov.qa.

Advisory Council

POB 2034, Doha; tel. 44416292; fax 44221222; e-mail fahad@shura .gov.qa.

The Advisory or *Shura* Council was established in 1972, with 20 nominated members. It was expanded to 30 members in 1975, and to 35 members in 1988. Under the terms of the new Constitution, promulgated in 2003, the Advisory Council was to be replaced by a 45-member unicameral parliament, of which two-thirds of the members were to be directly elected.

Speaker: MUHAMMAD BIN MUBARAK AL-KHOLAIFI.

Political Organizations

There are no political organizations in Qatar.

Diplomatic Representation

EMBASSIES IN QATAR

Afghanistan: POB 22104, Isteolal St, West Bay, Doha; tel. 44931511; fax 44932330; e-mail doha@afghanistan-mfa.net; Ambassador KHALID AHMAD ZEKRIYA.

Albania: POB 22659, Doha; tel. and fax 44953522; e-mail embassy .doha@mfa.gov.al; Ambassador RIDI KURTEZI.

Algeria: POB 2494, Doha; tel. 44838729; fax 44836072; Ambassador ABD AL-FATTAH ZAYYANI.

Azerbaijan: POB 23900, Doha; tel. 44932450; fax 44931755; e-mail azembassy@qatar.net.qa; Ambassador TOFIQ A. ABDULLAYEV.

Bahrain: al-Dafna St, Section 66, POB 24888, Doha; tel. 44839360; fax 44831018; e-mail doha.mission@mofa.gov.bh; Ambassador WAHEED MUBARAK ABDULLAH SAYYAR.

Bangladesh: POB 2080, 77 Mussab bin Omair St, Doha; tel. 44671927; fax 44671190; e-mail bdootqat@qatar.net.qa; internet www.bdembassydoha.com; Ambassador MUHAMMAD SHAHADAT HUSSAIN.

Belgium: POB 24418, al-Sanaa St, District 64, Doha; tel. 44931542; fax 44930151; e-mail doha@diplobel.fed.be; internet www .diplomatie.be/doha; Ambassador HERMAN MERCKX.

Benin: POB 24210, Doha; tel. 44930128; fax 44115713; e-mail ambabenin-doha@hotmail.com; Ambassador SAIDOU BAKU BUKHARI.

Bosnia and Herzegovina: POB 876, Doha; tel. 44113828; fax 44113234; e-mail ambasada@qatar.net.qa; internet www .bhembassyqatar.org; Ambassador NUDZEIM RECICA.

Brazil: POB 23122, Doha; tel. 44838227; fax 44838087; e-mail brasemb.doha@itamaraty.gov.br; internet doha.itamaraty.gov.br; Ambassador TADEU VALADARES.

Brunei: POB 22772, Doha; tel. 44831956; fax 44836798; e-mail bruemb@qatar.net.qa; Ambassador Haji NURUDDIN BIN Haji AHMAD.

China, People's Republic: POB 17200, Doha; tel. 44934203; fax 44934201; e-mail chinashi@qatar.net.qa; internet qa.china-embassy .org; Ambassador GAO YOUZHEN.

Cuba: POB 12017, Saha 76, New Dafna, West Bay Lagoon, Doha; tel. 44110713; fax 44110387; e-mail embacuba@qatar.net.qa; internet www.cubadiplomatica.cu/qatar; Ambassador ÉRNESTO D. PLASENCIA ESCALANTE.

Cyprus: POB 24482, 3 Saba Saha 12 St, District 63, West Bay, Doha; tel. 44934390; fax 44933087; e-mail kyprosdoha@qatar.net.qa; internet www.mfa.gov.cy/embassydoha; Ambassador CHARALAMBOS PANAYIDES.

Djibouti: POB 23796, Doha; tel. 44838461; fax 44839245; e-mail guarileh@gmail.com; Ambassador HASSAN MUMIN BARREH.

Dominican Republic: POB 23545, Doha; tel. 44113868; fax 44113267; e-mail info@domrepemb-qatar.com; internet www .domrepemb-qatar.com; Ambassador HUGO GUILIANI CURY.

Egypt: POB 2899, Doha; tel. 44832116; fax 44832196; e-mail eg .emb_doha@mfa.gov.eg; Ambassador MUHAMMAD MURSI AWAD.

El Salvador: POB 23031, Saha 72, Doha; tel. 44110195; fax 44110962; e-mail esvq@rree.gob.sv; Ambassador VICTOR MANUEL LAGOS PIZZATI.

Eritrea: POB 4309, D-Ring Rd 14, Doha; tel. 44667934; fax 44664139; Ambassador ALI IBRAHIM AHMED.

France: POB 2669, West Bay, Diplomatic Area, Doha; tel. 44021777; fax 44021701; e-mail ambadoha@qatar.net.qa; internet www .ambafrance-qa.org; Ambassador JEAN-CHRISTOPHE PEAUCELLE.

The Gambia: POB 12232, Doha; tel. 44657780; fax 44657391; Ambassador ANSUMANA JAMMEH.

Germany: POB 3064, 12 al-Jazeera al-Arabiya St, Doha; tel. 44082300; fax 44082333; e-mail germany@qatar.net.qa; internet www.doha.diplo.de; Ambassador ANGELIKA RENATE STORZ-CHAKARJI.

Hungary: POB 23525, Area 66, West Bay, Doha; tel. 44932531; fax 44932537; e-mail mission.doh@mfa.gov.hu; internet www.mfa.gov .hu/emb/doha; Ambassador Dr ISTVÁN ELTER.

India: POB 2788, Doha; tel. 44255777; fax 44670448; e-mail ambassadorindia@qatar.net.qa; internet www.indianembassy.gov .qa; Ambassador SANJIV ARORA.

Indonesia: POB 22375, al-Maheed St, Doha; tel. 44657945; fax 44657610; e-mail inemb@qatar.net.qa; internet www.kbridoha.com; Ambassador DEDDY SAIFUL AL-HADI.

Iran: POB 1633, Doha; tel. 44831950; fax 44831665; e-mail iranemb .doh@mfa.gov.ir; internet www.iranembassy.org.qa; Ambassador MUHAMMAD JAWAD.

Iraq: POB 1526, Doha; tel. 44216146; fax 44216152; e-mail dohemb@ iraqmofamail.net; Ambassador Dr JAWAD AL-HINDAWI.

Italy: POB 4188, St 913, Plot 83, Villa 31, Doha; tel. 44831828; fax 44831909; e-mail ambasciata.doha@esteri.it; internet www .ambdoha.esteri.it; Ambassador GUIDO DE SANCTIS.

Japan: POB 2208, Diplomatic Area, West Bay, Doha; tel. 44840888; fax 44832178; e-mail eojqatar@dh.mofa.go.jp; internet www.qa .emb-japan.go.jp/en; Ambassador KENJIRO MONJI.

Jordan: POB 2366, Doha; tel. 44832202; fax 44832173; e-mail jordand@qatar.net.qa; internet www.jordanembassy.com.qa; Ambassador ZAHI MUHAMMAD AL-SEMADI.

Kazakhstan: POB 23513, Doha; tel. 44128015; fax 44128014; e-mail embassykz@qatar.net.qa; Ambassador AZAMAT R. BERDYBAI.

Kenya: POB 23091, West Bay, Zone 66, St 840, Doha; tel. 44931870; fax 44831730; e-mail Information@kenyaembassydoha.com; Ambassador GALMA MUKHE BORU.

Korea, Republic: POB 3727, Diplomatic Area, West Bay, Doha; tel. 44832238; fax 44833264; e-mail koemb_qa@mofat.go.kr; internet qat .mofat.go.kr; Ambassador CHUNG KEE-JONG.

Kuwait: POB 1177, Doha; tel. 44832111; fax 44832042; e-mail kuwaitembassy@qatar.net.qa; Ambassador ALI SALMAN AL-HAIFI.

Lebanon: POB 2411, 63 United Nations St, al-Haditha Area, Doha; tel. 44933330; fax 44933331; e-mail embleb@qatar.net.qa; Ambassador HASSAN SAAD.

Libya: POB 574, Doha; tel. 44429546; fax 44429548; Ambassador ABD AL-MONSEF HAFIZ AL-BOURI.

Macedonia, former Yugoslav republic: POB 24262, Villa 54, al-Ithar St, Diplomatic Area, al-Dafna, Doha; tel. 44931374; fax 44831572; e-mail doha@mfa.gov.mk; Ambassador FUAD HASANOVIC.

Malaysia: POB 23760, Zone 66, Lusail St, West Bay, al-Dafna, Doha; tel. 44836463; fax 44836453; e-mail maldoha@kln.gov.my; internet www.kln.gov.my/perwakilan/doha; Ambassador AHMAD JAZRI BIN MUHAMMAD JOHAR.

Mauritania: POB 3132, Doha; tel. 44836003; fax 44836015; Ambassador SAYID AHMAD BAKAY OULD HAMADI.

Morocco: POB 3242, Doha; tel. 44831885; fax 44833416; e-mail moroccoe@qatar.net.qa; Ambassador EL MEKKI GAOUANE.

Nepal: POB 23002, St No. 810, Doha; tel. 44675681; fax 44675680; e-mail nembdoha@qatar.net.qa; internet www.nembdoha.org.qa; Ambassador Dr MAYA KUMARI SHARMA.

Netherlands: POB 23675, 6th Floor, al-Mirqab Tower, al-Dafna, Corniche, Doha; tel. 44954700; fax 44836340; e-mail doh@minbuza .nl; internet qatar.nlembassy.org; Ambassador J. C. M. GROFFEN.

Oman: POB 1525, 41 Ibn al-Qassim St, Villa 7, Doha; tel. 44931514; fax 44932278; e-mail doha@mofa.gov.om; Ambassador MUHAMMAD BIN NASSER HAMAD AL-WIHAIBI.

Pakistan: POB 334, Diplomatic Area, Plot 30, West Bay, Doha; tel. 44832525; fax 44832227; e-mail parepqat@qatar.net.qa; internet www.pakmissiondoha.com; Ambassador MUHAMMAD SARFRAZ AHMAD KHANZADA.

Philippines: POB 24900, Doha; tel. 44831585; fax 44831595; e-mail doha.pe@dfa.gov.ph; Ambassador CRESCENTE RELACION.

Poland: POB 23380, al-Qutaifiya 66, St 519, Saha 49, West Bay, Doha; tel. 44113230; fax 44110307; e-mail doha.amb.sekretariat@

msz.gov.pl; internet www.doha.polemb.net; Ambassador ROBERT ROSTEK.

Romania: POB 22511, Doha; tel. 44934848; fax 44934747; e-mail romamb@qatar.net.qa; internet doha.mae.ro; Ambassador ADRIAN MĂCELARU.

Russia: POB 15404, Doha; tel. 44836231; fax 44836243; e-mail rusemb@qatar.net.qa; internet www.qatar.mid.ru; Chargé d'affaires a.i. DMITRII TROFIMOV.

Saudi Arabia: POB 1255, Doha; tel. 44832030; fax 44832720; Ambassador AHMAD BIN ALI AL-QAHTANI.

Senegal: Ibn Almoutas St, House 65, al-Dafna, Doha; tel. 44837644; fax 44838872; Ambassador ADAMA SARR.

Singapore: POB 24497, New West Bay Area, Doha; tel. 44128082; fax 44128180; e-mail singemb_doh@sgmfa.gov.sg; internet www.mfa.gov.sg/doha; Ambassador WONG KWOK PUN.

Somalia: POB 1948, Doha; tel. and fax 44935751; Ambassador OMAR IDRIS.

South Africa: POB 24744, Doha; tel. 44857111; fax 44835961; e-mail doha.consular@foreign.gov.za; Ambassador SAAD CACHALIA.

Spain: POB 24616, Lusail St, West Bay, Doha; tel. 44835886; fax 44835887; e-mail emb.doha@maec.es; Ambassador MARÍA DEL CARMEN DE LA PEÑA CORCUERA.

Sri Lanka: 4 al-Kharja St, POB 19075, Doha; tel. 44677627; fax 44674788; e-mail lankaemb@qatar.net.qa; internet www.slembassy-qatar.com; Ambassador JAYANTHA PALIPANE.

Sudan: POB 2999, Doha; tel. 44831474; fax 44833031; e-mail suemdoha@yahoo.com; Ambassador YASSIR KHALAF ALLAH KHADIR.

Syria: POB 1257, Doha; tel. 44831844; fax 44832139; Ambassador Dr RIAD ISMAT.

Thailand: POB 22474, Doha; tel. 44934426; fax 44930514; e-mail thaidoh@qatar.net.qa; internet www.thaiembassy.org/doha; Ambassador PANYARAK POOLTHUP.

Tunisia: POB 21185, Doha; tel. 44128188; fax 44128938; e-mail at.doha@qatar.net.qa; Ambassador MUHAMMAD MONDHER DHERIF.

Turkey: POB 1977, al-Istiqlal St, Doha; tel. 44951300; fax 44951320; e-mail embassy.doha@mfa.gov.tr; internet www.doha.emb.mfa.gov.tr; Ambassador HAKKI EMRE YUNT.

United Arab Emirates: POB 3099, 22 al-Markhiyah St, Diplomatic Area, Khalifa Northern Town, Doha; tel. 44838880; fax 44836186; e-mail doha@mofa.gov.ae; internet www.uae-embassy.ae/embassies/qa; Ambassador JUMA RASHID SAIF AL-DHAHERI.

United Kingdom: POB 3, West Bay, Doha; tel. 44962000; fax 44962086; e-mail embassy.qatar@fco.gov.uk; internet ukinqatar.fco.gov.uk; Ambassador MICHAEL O'NEILL.

Uruguay: POB 23237, Doha; tel. 44113833; fax 44113540; e-mail uruqatar@uruguayembassy.org.qa; Ambassador Dr JOSÉ LUIS REMEDI.

USA: POB 2399, 22nd February St, al-Luqta District, Doha; tel. 44966000; fax 44884298; e-mail pasdoha@state.gov; internet qatar.usembassy.gov; Ambassador SUSAN L. ZIADEH.

Venezuela: POB 24470, Doha; tel. 44932730; fax 44932729; e-mail embavenqatar@gmail.com; internet www.embavenqatar.org; Ambassador JUAN ANTONIO HERNÁNDEZ.

Yemen: POB 3318, Doha; tel. 44432555; fax 44429400; Ambassador ABD AL-MALIK SAID.

Judicial System

The independence of the judiciary was guaranteed by the provisional Constitution and further augmented in the Constitution formally adopted by the Amir in April 2003. All aspects pertaining to the civil judiciary are supervised by the Ministry of Justice, which organizes courts of law through its affiliated departments. The *Shari'a* judiciary hears all cases of personal status relating to Muslims, other claim cases, doctrinal provision and crimes under its jurisdiction. Legislation adopted in 1999 unified all civil and *Shari'a* courts in one judicial body, and determined the jurisdictions of each type of court. The law also provided for the establishment of a court of cassation; this was to be competent to decide on appeals relating to issues of contravention, misapplication and misinterpretation of the law, and on disputes between courts regarding areas of jurisdiction. In addition, the law provided for the establishment of a supreme judiciary council, to be presided over by the head of the court of cassation and comprising, *inter alia*, the heads of the *Shari'a* and civil courts of appeal. The legislation came into effect in 2003. An Amiri decree published in June 2002 provided for the establishment of an independent public prosecution system. A Supreme Constitutional Court was established in 2008 to adjudicate on the constitutionality of laws and to arbitrate in disputes between different branches of the judiciary.

Presidency of Shari'a Courts: POB 232, Doha; tel. 44452222; Pres. Sheikh ABD AL-RAHMAN BIN ABDULLAH AL-MAHMOUD.

Public Prosecution Office: POB 705, Doha; tel. 4843333; fax 44843211; e-mail info@pp.gov.qa; internet www.pp.gov.qa; Attorney-Gen. Dr ALI BIN FITAISE AL-MERRI.

Supreme Judiciary Council: POB 9673, Doha; tel. 44859222; fax 44833939; e-mail sjc@sjc.gov.qa; internet www.sjc.gov.qa; f. 2003; Pres. MASOUD MUHAMMAD AL-AMRI.

Religion

The indigenous population are Muslims of the Sunni sect, most being of the strict Wahhabi persuasion. In March 2008 the first official Christian church (of the Roman Catholic branch) was consecrated in Doha; open worship among adherents of Christianity had previously been prohibited.

CHRISTIANITY

The Anglican Communion

Within the Episcopal Church in Jerusalem and the Middle East, Qatar forms part of the diocese of Cyprus and the Gulf. The Anglican congregation in Qatar is entirely expatriate. The Bishop in Cyprus and the Gulf is resident in Cyprus, while the Archdeacon in the Gulf is resident in Bahrain.

The Roman Catholic Church

An estimated 100,000 adherents in Qatar, mainly expatriates, form part of the Apostolic Vicariate of Northern Arabia. The Vicar Apostolic is resident in Bahrain.

The Press

NEWSPAPERS

Al-'Arab (The Arabs): POB 22612, Doha; tel. 44997333; fax 44997411; e-mail alarab@alarab.qa; internet www.alarab.qa; f. 1972; ceased publication in 1996, but recommenced following relaunch in Nov. 2007; daily; Arabic; publ. by Dar al-Ouroba Printing and Publishing; Editor-in-Chief Prof. AHMAD SAID AL-ROMAIHI.

Gulf Times: POB 2888, Doha; tel. 44350478; fax 44350474; e-mail edit@gulf-times.com; internet www.gulf-times.com; f. 1978; daily and weekly edns; English; political; publ. by Gulf Publishing and Printing Co; Man. Editor NEIL COOK; circ. 20,000 (daily).

The Peninsula: POB 3488, Doha; tel. 44557777; fax 44557746; e-mail editor@thepeninsulaqatar.com; internet www.thepeninsulaqatar.com; f. 1995; daily; English; political; publ. by Dar al-Sharq Printing, Publishing and Distribution; Chair. Sheikh THANI BIN ABDULLAH AL THANI; Man. Editor RACHEL MORRIS; circ. 8,000.

Qatar Tribune: POB 23493, Doha; tel. 44422077; fax 44416790; e-mail editor-in-chief@qatar-tribune.com; internet www.qatar-tribune.com; f. 2006; daily; English; Editor-in-Chief Dr HASSAN MUHAMMAD AL-ANSARI; circ. 10,000.

Al-Rayah (The Banner): POB 3464, Doha; tel. 44466636; fax 44320080; e-mail edit@raya.com; internet www.raya.com; f. 1979; daily and weekly edns; Arabic; political; publ. by Gulf Publishing and Printing Co; Editor NASSER AL-OTHMAN; circ. 25,000.

Al-Sharq (The Orient): POB 3488, Doha; tel. 44557702; fax 44557760; e-mail jaber.alharmi@gmail.com; internet www.al-sharq.com; f. 1985; daily; Arabic; political; publ. by Dar al-Sharq Printing, Publishing and Distribution; Editor-in-Chief JABER AL-HARAMI; Dep. Editor KHALED AL-JABER; circ. 45,018.

Al-Watan: POB 22345, Doha; tel. 44652244; fax 44654482; e-mail alwatan@qatar.net.qa; internet www.al-watan.com; f. 1995; daily; Arabic; political; publ. by Dar al-Watan Printing, Publishing and Distribution; Editor-in-Chief MUHAMMAD HAMAD AL-MERRI; circ. 25,000.

PERIODICALS

Glam: POB 3272, Doha; tel. 44672139; fax 44550982; e-mail contact@omsqatar.com; internet www.omsqatar.com/glam; monthly; English; fashion and lifestyle; publ. by Oryx Advertising Co; f. 2008; Editor-in-Chief YOUSUF JASSEM AL-DARWISH.

Al-Jawhara (The Jewel): POB 2531, Doha; tel. 44414575; fax 44671388; f. 1977; monthly; Arabic; magazine covering watches and jewellery; publ. by al-Ahd Establishment for Journalism, Printing and Publications Ltd; Editor-in-Chief ABDULLAH YOUSUF AL-HUSSAINI; circ. 8,000.

Al-Ouroba (Arabism): POB 663, Doha; tel. 44325874; fax 44429424; f. 1970; weekly; Arabic; political; publ. by Dar al-Ouroba Printing and Publishing; Editor-in-Chief YOUSUF NAAMA; circ. 12,000.

Qatar Al-Yom: POB 3272, Doha; tel. 44672139; fax 44550982; e-mail contact@omsqatar.com; internet www.omsqatar.com/qatar-al-yom; f. 2005; Arabic; news, business and lifestyle; publ. by Oryx Advertising Co; Editor-in-Chief YOUSUF JASSEM AL-DARWISH; circ. 22,000.

Qatar Today: POB 3272, Doha; tel. 44672139; fax 44550982; e-mail qtoday@omsqatar.com; internet www.omsqatar.com/qatar-today; f. 1978; monthly; English; news, business and lifestyle; publ. by Oryx Advertising Co; Editor-in-Chief YOUSUF JASSEM AL-DARWISH; circ. 27,000.

Al-Tarbiya (Education): POB 9865, Doha; tel. 44044596; fax 44044557; e-mail qnc@sec.gov.qa; f. 1971; quarterly; publ. by Qatar Nat. Comm. for Education, Culture and Science; Editor-in-Chief MUHAMMAD SIDDIQ; circ. 2,500.

Al-Tijara Wal A'amal: POB 272, Doha; tel. 44478042; fax 44478063; e-mail info@mashaheermedia.com; internet www.mashaheermedia.com; f. 2003; English; business and industry; publ. by Mashaheer Media Qatar.

Al-Ufuq: POB 3488, Doha; tel. 44602844; fax 44601294; e-mail alsharqpp@qatar.net.qa; f. 2002; monthly; Arabic; business; publ. by Dar al-Sharq Printing, Publishing and Distribution.

Al-Ummah: POB 893, Doha; tel. 44447300; fax 44447022; e-mail m_dirasat@islam.gov.qa; f. 1982; bi-monthly; Islamic thought and affairs, current cultural issues, book serializations.

Woman Today: POB 3272, Doha; tel. 44672139; fax 44550982; e-mail wtoday@omsqatar.com; internet www.omsqatar.com/woman-today; f. 2005; monthly; English; magazine aimed at working women; publ. by Oryx Advertising Co; Editor-in-Chief YOUSUF JASSEM AL-DARWISH; circ. 20,500.

NEWS AGENCY

Qatar News Agency (QNA): POB 3299, Doha; tel. 44450321; fax 44438316; e-mail info@qnaol.com; internet www.qnaol.net; f. 1975; affiliated to Ministry of Foreign Affairs; Dir and Editor-in-Chief AHMAD JASSIM AL-HUMAR.

Publishers

Ali bin Ali Media and Publishing: POB 75, Doha; tel. 44313245; fax 44411251; e-mail publishing@alibinali.com; internet www.abamediapublishing.com; part of Ali bin Ali Group; publrs of *Qatar Telephone Directory* and *Yellow Pages*; Chair. and Pres. ADEL ALI BIN ALI; Gen. Man. ANTOINE CHERFANE.

Bloomsbury Qatar Foundation Publishing: POB 5825, Villa 3, Qatar Education City, Doha; tel. 44542431; fax 44542438; e-mail bqfp@qf.org.qa; internet www.bqfp.com.qa; f. 2009; publr of fiction and non-fiction in English and Arabic, including educational, academic, reference and children's books; owned by the Qatar Foundation; Dir KATHY ROONEY.

Dar al-Sharq Printing, Publishing and Distribution: POB 3488, Doha; tel. 44557866; fax 44557871; e-mail alsharqpp@qatar.net.qa; internet www.al-sharq.com; publrs of *Al-Sharq* and *The Peninsula* newspapers, and *Al-Ufuq* magazine; distributor for various foreign newspapers; Gen. Man. ABD AL-LATIF AL-MAHMOUD.

Gulf Publishing and Printing Co: POB 533, Al Hilal Area, C Ring Rd, Doha; tel. 44350475; fax 44350474; e-mail gm@gulftimes.com; internet www.gulf-times.com; f. 1978; publrs of *Gulf Times* and *Al-Rayah*; Chair. ABDULLAH BIN KHALIFA AL-ATTIYA.

Oryx Advertising Co WLL: POB 3272, Doha; tel. 44672139; fax 44550982; e-mail info@omsqatar.com; internet www.omsqatar.com; f. 1973; publs include *Qatar Today*, *Qatar Al-Yom*, *Glam* and *Woman Today*; Publr and Editor-in-Chief YOUSUF JASSEM AL-DARWISH.

Qatar National Printing Press (QNPP): POB 355, Doha; tel. 44448452; fax 44449550; e-mail info@qnpp.net; internet www.qnpp.net; f. 1958; promotional printing, business forms, stationery, screenprinting, etc.; Gen. Man. JOSEPH DORLIAN.

Broadcasting and Communications

TELECOMMUNICATIONS

Supreme Council for Communications and Information Technology (ictQATAR): POB 23264, al-Mirqab Tower, al-Corniche St, Doha; tel. 44995333; fax 44935913; e-mail info@ict.gov.qa; internet www.ict.gov.qa; f. 2004 to oversee deregulation of telecommunications sector; Chair. Heir Apparent Sheikh TAMIM BIN HAMAD BIN KHALIFA AL THANI; Sec.-Gen. Dr HESSA SULTAN AL-JABER.

Qatar Telecommunications Corpn—Qatar Telecom (Q-Tel): POB 217, Doha; tel. 44830000; fax 44476231; e-mail customer.service@qtel.com.qa; internet www.qtel.com.qa; f. 1987; majority state-owned; provides telecommunications services within Qatar; Chair. Sheikh ABDULLAH BIN MUHAMMAD AL THANI; CEO Dr NASSER MARAFIH.

Vodafone Qatar QSC: POB 74057, Unit 207, Level 2, Tech 2, Qatar Science & Technology Park, Doha; tel. 44096666; internet www.vodafone.com.qa; f. 2008; majority shareholders Vodafone Group PLC (United Kingdom) and Qatar Foundation for Education, Science and Community Devt; initial public offering for Qatari nationals of 40% of shares conducted in April 2009; awarded Qatar's second mobile telephone operating licence in June 2008; Chair. Sheikh ABD AL-RAHMAN BIN SAUD AL THANI; CEO JOHN TOMBLESON (acting).

BROADCASTING

Regulatory Authority

Qatar Radio and Television Corpn (QRTC): POB 1414, Doha; tel. 44894444; fax 44882888; e-mail ksaid@rtc.gov.qa; f. 1997; autonomous authority reporting direct to the Council of Ministers; Dir-Gen. ABD AL-RAHMAN OBEIDAN.

Radio

Qatar Broadcasting Service (QBS): POB 3939, Doha; tel. 44894444; fax 44882888; f. 1968; govt service transmitting in Arabic, English, French and Urdu; programmes include Holy Quran Radio and Doha Music Radio; Dir ALI NASSER AL-KUBAISI.

Sout al-Khaleej: POB 1414, Doha; tel. 44888334; fax 44879999; e-mail info@soutalkhaleej.fm; internet www.soutalkhaleej.fm; f. 2002; Arabic arts broadcasting.

Television

Al Jazeera Satellite Network: POB 23123, Doha; tel. 44896044; fax 44873577; e-mail imr@aljazeera.net; internet www.aljazeera.net; f. 1996; 24-hr broadcasting of news and current affairs in Arabic; English-language service launched Nov. 2006; documentary channel launched Jan. 2007; Dir-Gen. Sheikh AHMAD BIN JASIM BIN MUHAMMAD AL THANI; Chief Editor AHMED SHEIKH.

Qatar Television Service (QTV): POB 1944, Doha; tel. 44894444; fax 44874170; f. 1970; operates 2 channels (of which 1 broadcasts in English); 24-hr broadcasting; Dir MUHAMMAD AL-KUWARI; Asst Dir ABD AL-WAHAB MUHAMMAD AL-MUTAWA'A.

Finance

(cap. = capital; res = reserves; dep. = deposits; m. = million; brs = branches; amounts in Qatar riyals)

STATE FINANCIAL AUTHORITIES

In March 2005 the Government established the Qatar Financial Centre (QFC), which was intended to attract international financial institutions and multinational corporations to Qatar, 'to establish business operations in a best-in-class international environment'. The QFC comprised the QFC Authority and the QFC Regulatory Authority (QFCRA—see below), as well as two legal bodies—the QFC Regulatory Tribunal and the QFC Civil and Commercial Court—which were charged with upholding the rule of law and ensuring the transparency of QFC transactions. In July 2007 plans were announced for the creation of a single, integrated, fully independent financial regulatory authority, which would merge the regulatory activities of the QFCRA, the Qatar Financial Markets Authority and the Qatar Central Bank, and oversee all banking, insurance, securities, asset management and other financial services.

Qatar Financial Centre Authority (QFCA): POB 23245, Doha; tel. 44967777; fax 44967676; e-mail info@qfc.com.qa; internet www.qfc.com.qa; f. 2005; charged with promoting Qatar as an attractive location for international banking, insurance and financial services; Chair. YOUSUF HUSSAIN KAMAL (Minister of Economy and Finance); CEO SHASHANK SRIVASTAVA (acting).

Qatar Financial Centre Regulatory Authority (QFCRA): POB 22989, Level 14, Qatar Financial Centre Tower, Doha; tel. 44956888; fax 44835031; e-mail info@qfcra.com; internet www.qfcra.com; f. 2005; charged with the regulation and supervision of a wide range of financial activities, incl. banking, insurance, asset management and financial advisory services; Chair. and CEO PHILLIP THORPE.

Qatar Financial Markets Authority: POB 25552, Doha; tel. 44289999; fax 44441221; e-mail info@qfma.org.qa; internet www.qfma.org.qa; f. 2007 to supervise the stock exchange and securities industry; Chair. YOUSUF HUSSAIN KAMAL (Minister of Economy and Finance); Chief Exec. NASSER AHMAD SHAIBI.

BANKING

Central Bank

Qatar Central Bank: POB 1234, Doha; tel. 44456456; fax 44414190; e-mail webmaster@qcb.gov.qa; internet www.qcb.gov .qa; f. 1966 as Qatar and Dubai Currency Bd; became Qatar Monetary Agency in 1973; renamed Qatar Cen. Bank in 1993; state-owned; cap. and res 9,982.5m., total assets 44,458.5m., currency in circulation 6,912.8m. (Dec. 2008); Gov. ABDULLAH BIN SAUD AL THANI.

Commercial Banks

Ahlibank QSC: POB 2309, Suhmin bin Hamad St, al-Sadd Area, Doha; tel. 44232222; fax 44232323; e-mail info@ahlibank.com.qa; internet www.ahlibank.com.qa; f. 1984 as Al-Ahli Bank of Qatar QSC; name changed as above in 2004; cap. 700m., res 1,689m., dep. 14,681m. (Dec. 2011); Chair. Sheikh FAISAL BIN ABD AL-AZIZ BIN JASIM AL THANI; CEO SALAH JASIM MURAD; 9 brs.

Commercial Bank of Qatar QSC (CBQ): POB 3232, Grand Hamad Ave, Doha; tel. 44900000; fax 44490070; e-mail info@cbq .com.qa; internet www.cbq.com.qa; f. 1975; cap. 2,474m., res 11,545m., dep. 46,374m. (Dec. 2011); Man. Dir HUSSAIN IBRAHIM AL-FARDAN; Group CEO ANDREW C. STEVENS; 23 brs.

Doha Bank: POB 3818, Grand Hamad Ave, Doha; tel. 44456600; fax 44410625; e-mail international@dohabank.com.qa; internet www .dohabank.com.qa; f. 1979; cap. 2,066m., res 4,807m., dep. 33,357m. (Dec. 2011); Chair. Sheikh FAHAD BIN MUHAMMAD BIN JABER AL THANI; Group CEO R. SEETHARAMAN; 35 brs in Qatar, 3 abroad.

International Bank of Qatar QSC (IBQ): POB 2001, Suhaim bin Hamad St, Doha; tel. 44473700; fax 44473745; e-mail qatarenq@ibq .com.qa; internet www.ibq.com.qa; f. 2000 as Grindlays Qatar Bank QSC; previously a branch of ANZ Grindlays Bank (f. 1956); name changed as above in 2004, after Nat. Bank of Kuwait SAK assumed management of the bank; announced plans to merge with Al-Khalij Commercial Bank in mid-2010; cap. 1,100m., res 2,791m., dep. 22,752m. (Dec. 2011); Chair. Sheikh HAMAD BIN JASIM BIN JABER AL THANI (Prime Minister and Minister of Foreign Affairs); Man. Dir GEORGE NASRA.

Al-Khalij Commercial Bank (QSC) (al-Khaliji): POB 28000, Doha; tel. 44996000; fax 44996020; e-mail info@alkhaliji.com; internet www.alkhaliji.com; f. 2007; announced plans to merge with Int. Bank of Qatar in mid-2010; cap. 3,600m., res 1,689m., dep. 16,175m. (Dec. 2011); Chair. and Man. Dir HAMAD BIN FAISAL BIN THANI AL THANI; Group CEO ROBIN McCALL.

Masraf Al Rayan: POB 28888, Doha; tel. 44253333; fax 44253312; e-mail info@alrayan.com; internet www.alrayan.com; f. 2006; offers *Shari'a*-compliant banking services; cap. 7,500m., res 975m., dep. 46,263m. (Dec. 2011); Chair. and Man. Dir Dr HUSSAIN ALI AL-ABDULLA; Group CEO ADEL MUSTAFAWI; 5 brs.

Qatar Development Bank (QDB): POB 22789, Doha; tel. 44596666; fax 44350433; e-mail contact@qdb.org.qa; internet www .qidb.com.qa; f. 1996 as Qatar Industrial Devt Bank; inaugurated Oct. 1997; relaunched under above name in April 2007 with expanded capital provision to facilitate private sector involvement in national economic devt; state-owned; provides long-term low-interest industrial loans; finances wide range of industrial and social projects; broadened consultancy services following relaunch; cap. 2,900m., res 200m., dep. 555m. (Dec. 2010); Chair. ABDULLAH BIN SA'UD AL THANI; CEO MANSOUR IBRAHIM AL-MAHMOUD.

Qatar First Investment Bank: POB 28028, Suhaim bin Hamad St, Doha; tel. 44483333; fax 44483560; e-mail information@qfib.com.qa; internet www.qfib.com.qa; f. 2008; offers *Shari'a*-compliant invest-ment banking services; Chair. ABDULLA BIN FAHAD BIN GHORAB AL-MARRI; CEO EMAD MANSOUR.

Qatar International Islamic Bank: POB 664, Grand Hamad St, Doha; tel. 44385555; fax 44444101; e-mail qiibit@qiib.com.qa; internet www.qiib.com.qa; f. 1990; cap. 1,513m., res 3,279m., dep. 18,106m. (Dec. 2011); Chair. and Man. Dir KHALID BIN THANI BIN ABDULLAH AL THANI; CEO ABD AL-BASIT AL-SHAIBEI; 5 brs.

Qatar Islamic Bank SAQ (QIB): POB 559, Grand Hamad St, Doha; tel. 44409409; fax 44412700; e-mail info@qib.com.qa; internet www .qib.com.qa; f. 1982; cap. 2,362m., res 8,459m., dep. 41,087m. (Dec. 2011); Chair. Sheikh JASIM BIN HAMAD BIN JASIM BIN JABER AL THANI; CEO AHMAD MESHARI (acting); 25 brs.

Qatar National Bank SAQ: POB 1000, Doha; tel. 44407777; fax 44413753; e-mail ccsupport@qnb.com.qa; internet www.qnb.com.qa; f. 1964; owned 50% by Govt of Qatar and 50% by Qatari nationals; cap. 6,361m., res 28,689m., dep. 237,784m. (Dec. 2011); Chair. YOUSUF HUSSAIN KAMAL (Minister of Economy and Finance); Group CEO ALI SHAREEF AL-EMADI; 32 brs in Qatar, 3 abroad.

SOVEREIGN WEALTH FUND

Qatar Investment Authority (QIA): POB 23224, Doha; tel. 44995900; fax 44995991; e-mail info@qia.qa; internet www.qia.qa; f. 2005 to develop, invest and manage state reserve funds; Chair. Heir Apparent Sheikh TAMIM BIN HAMAD BIN KHALIFA AL THANI; CEO Sheikh HAMAD BIN JASIM BIN JABER AL THANI (Prime Minister and Minister of Foreign Affairs).

STOCK EXCHANGE

Qatar Exchange (QE): POB 22114, Grand Hamad St, Doha; tel. 44333666; fax 44319233; e-mail dsm@dsm.com.qa; internet www .dsm.com.qa; f. 2009 to replace fmr Doha Securities Market (f. 1997); 80% stake owned by Qatar Holding, 20% owned by NYSE Euronext; 42 cos listed in June 2009; Chair. Dr KHALID BIN MUHAMMAD AL-ATTIYA; CEO ANDRE WENT.

INSURANCE

Doha Insurance Co: POB 7171, Doha; tel. 44335000; fax 44657777; e-mail dohainsco@qatar.net.qa; internet www.dicqatar.com; f. 1999 as public shareholding co; cap. 127.2m., total assets 518.3m. (Dec. 2007); Chair. Sheikh NAWAF BIN NASSER BIN KHALID AL THANI; Gen. Man. BASSAM HUSSAIN.

Al-Khaleej Insurance and Reinsurance Co QSC (SAQ): POB 4555, Doha; tel. 44414151; fax 44430530; e-mail alkhalej@qatar.net .qa; internet www.alkhaleej.com; f. 1978; cap. and res 568.4m. (2007); all classes except life; Chair. ABDULLAH BIN MUHAMMAD JABER AL THANI; Gen. Man. KARAM AHMAD MAHMOUD.

Qatar General Insurance and Reinsurance Co SAQ: POB 4500, A Ring Rd, al-Asmakh Area, Doha; tel. 44282222; fax 44437302; e-mail qgirc-tec@qatar.net.qa; internet www.qgirco.com; f. 1979; total assets 1,729.7m. (2007); all classes; Chair. and Man. Dir Sheikh NASSER BIN ALI AL THANI; Gen. Man. GHAZI ABU NAHL.

Qatar Insurance Co SAQ: POB 666, Tamin St, West Bay, Doha; tel. 44962222; fax 44831569; e-mail qatarins@qic.com.qa; internet www .qatarinsurance.com; f. 1964; cap. 424.7m., total assets 5,860.7m. (Dec. 2007); all classes; the Govt has a majority share; Chair. and Man. Dir Sheikh KHALID BIN MUHAMMAD ALI AL THANI; Pres. and CEO KHALIFA A. AL-SUBAEY; brs in Qatar, Dubai and Abu Dhabi (UAE), Kuwait and Oman.

Qatar Insurance Services LLC (Qatarlyst): 6th Floor, QFC Tower, POB 23245, Doha; tel. 44968301; fax 44968310; e-mail enquiries@qatarlyst.com; internet www.qatarlyst.com; f. 2008 by the QFCA, with the aim of establishing Qatar as a regional hub for the insurance industry; launched internet-based insurance-trading and -processing service (Qatarlyst) June 2009; CEO KHALID AL-MUGHESIB; Chair. ABD AL-RAHMAN AHMAD AL-SHAIBI.

Qatar Islamic Insurance Co: POB 22676, Doha; tel. 44658888; fax 44550111; e-mail qiic@qatar.net.qa; internet www.qiic.net.qa; f. 1993; cap. 150.0m., res 137.0m. (Dec. 2007); Chair. Sheikh ABDULLAH BIN THANI AL THANI; Gen. Man. JASSIM A. AL-SADI.

Trade and Industry

DEVELOPMENT ORGANIZATIONS

Department of Industrial Development: POB 2599, Doha; tel. 44846444; fax 44832024; e-mail did@mei.gov.qa; a div. of the Ministry of Energy and Industry; conducts research, licensing, devt and supervision of new industrial projects; Dir-Gen. SAID MUBARAK AL-KUWAIRI.

General Secretariat for Development Planning: POB 1588, Doha; tel. 44958888; e-mail webmaster@planning.gov.qa; internet www.gsdp.gov.qa; f. 2006; responsible for co-ordination of the emirate's long-term devt strategy; monitors progress of Qatar's Nat. Vision 2030 and Nat. Devt Strategy; Sec.-Gen. Dr SALIH MUHAMMAD AL-NABIT; Dir-Gen. Sheikh HAMAD BIN JASIM BIN JABER AL THANI (Prime Minister and Minister of Foreign Affairs).

Public Works Authority (Ashghal): POB 22188, Doha; tel. 44950000; fax 44950999; e-mail info@ashghal.gov.qa; internet www.ashghal.com; f. 2004; responsible for the management and devt of public infrastructure projects; Chair. Sheikh ABD AL-RAHMAN BIN KHALIFA BIN ABD AL-AZIZ AL THANI (Minister of Municipal Affairs and Urban Planning); Pres. NASSER ALI ABDULLAH AL-MAWLAWI.

Urban Planning and Development Authority: POB 22423, Doha; tel. 44955549; fax 44955594; e-mail general@up.org.qa; internet www.up.org.qa; f. 2005; planning, co-ordination and man-agement of urban devt projects; oversees devt of the Master Plan for the State of Qatar; Dir-Gen. ALI ABDULLAH AL-ABDULLAH.

CHAMBER OF COMMERCE

Qatar Chamber of Commerce and Industry: POB 402, Doha; tel. 44559111; fax 44661693; e-mail info@qcci.org; internet www.qcci .org; f. 1963; 17 elected mems; Chair. Sheikh KHALIFA BIN JASIM BIN MUHAMMAD AL THANI; Gen. Man. KHALID AL-HAJRI.

STATE HYDROCARBONS COMPANIES

Qatar International Petroleum Marketing Co (Tasweeq): POB 24183, Doha; tel. 44976111; fax 44976276; e-mail info@tasweeq.com.qa; internet www.tasweeq.com.qa; f. 2007 to take sole responsibility for all exports of natural gas and oil products; wholly govt-owned; CEO ALI AL-HAMADI.

Qatar Petrochemical Co SAQ (QAPCO): POB 756, Doha; tel. 44242444; fax 44324700; e-mail information@qapco.com.qa; internet www.qapco.com.qa; f. 1974; 80% owned by Industries Qatar, 20% by Total Petrochemicals (France); total assets QR 5,090.7m. (2006); operation of petrochemical plant at Mesaieed; produced 549,928 metric tons of ethylene, 359,460 tons of low-density polyethylene, and 32,297 tons of solid sulphur in 2007; Chair. HAMAD RASHID AL-MOHANNADI; Gen. Man. MUHAMMAD YOUSUF AL-MULLA; 879 employees (2004).

Qatofin Co Ltd: POB 55013, Doha; tel. 44242555; fax 44325936; e-mail info@qatofin.com.qa; internet www.qatofin.com.qa; f. 2009; 63% owned by Qatar Petrochemical Co, 36% by Total and 1% by Qatar Petroleum; capacity to produce 450,000 metric tons of low-density polyethylene; Chair. HAMAD RASHID AL-MOHANNADI; Vice-Chair. MUHAMMAD YOUSUF AL-MULLA.

Qatar Petroleum (QP): POB 3212, Doha; tel. 44402000; fax 44831125; e-mail webmaster@qp.com.qa; internet www.qp.com.qa; f. 1974 as Qatar Gen. Petroleum Corpn (QGPC), name changed 2001; total assets QR 137,851m. (2006); sales QR 2,243m. (2006); oil production 850,000 b/d (2006); the State of Qatar's interest in cos active in petroleum and related industries has passed to QP; has responsibility for all phases of oil and gas industry both on shore and off shore, incl. exploration, drilling, production, refining, transport and storage, distribution, sale and export of oil, natural gas and other hydrocarbons; Oryx gas to liquids (GTL) plant became operational in 2006, with capacity for 34,000 b/d of GTL products; Chair. and Man. Dir MUHAMMAD SALEH AL-SADA (Minister of Energy and Industry); Dep. Chair. HAMAD RASHID AL-MOHANNADI; 5,500 employees.

Qatar Liquefied Gas Co (Qatargas): POB 22666, Doha; tel. 44736000; fax 44736666; e-mail infos@qatargas.com.qa; internet www.qatargas.com; f. 1984 to develop the North Field of unassociated gas; cap. QR 500m.; 65% owned by Qatar Petroleum, 10% each by ExxonMobil (USA) and Total, and 7.5% each by Marubeni Corpn and Mitsui & Co of Japan; production capacity 42m. metric tons of LNG; Chair. MUHAMMAD SALEH AL-SADA (Minister of Energy and Industry); CEO KHALID BIN KHALIFA AL THANI.

Ras Laffan LNG Co Ltd (RasGas): POB 24200, Doha; tel. 44738000; fax 44738480; e-mail site-admin@rasgas.com.qa; internet www.rasgas.com; f. 1993; 70% owned by Qatar Petroleum, 30% by ExxonMobil; operates five LNG trains, which had a production capacity of 20.7m. metric tons per year in 2007; CEO HAMAD RASHID AL-MOHANNADI.

Qatar Petroleum also wholly or partly owns: Industries Qatar (IQ) and its subsidiaries, Qatar Gas Transport Co (Nakilat), Gulf Helicopters Co Ltd (GHC), Qatar Vinyl Co (QVC), Qatar Chemical Co (Q-Chem), Qatar Clean Energy Co (QACENCO), Qatar Electricity and Water Co (QEWC), Qatar Shipping Co (Q-Ship), Arab Maritime Petroleum Transport Co (AMPTC), Arab Petroleum Pipelines Co (SUMED), Arab Shipbuilding and Repair Yard Co (ASRY), Arab Petroleum Services Co (APSC) and Arab Petroleum Investments Corpn (APICORP).

UTILITIES

Qatar General Electricity and Water Corpn (Kahramaa): POB 41, Doha; tel. 44845555; fax 44845496; e-mail kmcontact@km.com.qa; internet www.km.com.qa; f. 2000; state authority for planning, implementation, operation and maintenance of electricity and water sectors; Chair. ISSA HILAL AL-KUWARI.

Qatar Electricity and Water Co (QEWC): POB 22046, Doha; tel. 44858585; fax 44831116; e-mail welcome@qewc.com; internet www.qewc.com; f. 1990; 57% privately owned; devt and operation of power generation and water desalination facilities; Chair. ABDULLAH BIN HAMAD AL-ATTIYA (Deputy Prime Minister and Chair. of the Emiri Diwan); Gen. Man. FAHAD HAMAD AL-MOHANNADI.

Transport

RAILWAYS

In 2009 the Qatar Railways Development Co (QRDC), a joint venture comprising Qatari Diar Real Estate Investment Co and Deutsche Bahn AG (Germany), was established to supervise the development of a national rail network, which would be linked to a regional rail network, connecting Qatar with member countries of the Cooperation Council for the Arab States of the Gulf (Gulf Cooperation Council—GCC). In 2011 QRDC established the Qatar Railways Co

(QRail) to oversee the implementation of plans to develop a national rail network in Qatar. In February 2012 QRail awarded a US $535.4m. contract for work on a light rail network serving the new, planned city of Lusail to Qatari Diar Vinci Construction. The project, which eventually would comprise a 30-km, four-line network, was expected to be completed in 2016. QRail awarded three contracts in August 2012 for phase one of construction work on a planned 300-km, four-line metro system in Doha, the first line of which was due to be operational by 2019.

Qatar Railways Co (QRail): Doha; tel. 44977886; f. 2011; fully owned by Qatar Railways Development Co (QRDC); CEO SAAD AHMED AL-MOHANNADI.

ROADS

The total road network in 2010 was estimated to be 9,830 km. A major upgrading of the national road network was planned for the first years of the 21st century. Work on the QR 8,000m., 13-phase Doha Expressway project, which involves the construction of a dual carriageway linking the north and south of the country and a Doha ring road, commenced in late 2007. A project to construct a causeway (the Friendship Bridge) linking Qatar with Bahrain was approved by both Governments in 2004. After protracted discussions and numerous delays, in May 2008 the contract to design and build the causeway, at a cost of some US $3,000m., was awarded to a France-based consortium. The decision, in late 2008, to incorporate a railway line into the project necessitated substantial design revisions that were expected to add up to $1,000m. to the cost of the causeway. Construction had yet to commence at early 2013.

SHIPPING

Doha Port has nine general cargo berths of 7.5 m–9.0 m depth. The total length of the berths is 1,699 m. In addition, there is a flour mill berth, and a container terminal (with a depth of 12.0 m and a length of 600 m) with a roll-on roll-off (ro-ro) berth at the north end currently under construction. Cold-storage facilities exist for cargo of up to 500 metric tons. The North Field gas project has increased the demand for shipping facilities. A major new industrial port was completed at Ras Laffan in 1995, providing facilities for LNG and condensate carriers and ro-ro vessels. Qatar Petroleum initiated a US $1,000m. expansion of Ras Laffan port in 2005. Further expansion plans at Ras Laffan, to accommodate the shipping requirements of the burgeoning LNG and associated industries, were finalized in 2008; completion of the project would render Ras Laffan the largest man-made harbour in the world, bounded by 26 km of breakwaters. In October 2007 Sheikh Hamad issued a decree announcing that the New Doha Port development would be located at Mesaieed industrial city. On completion of its first phase (scheduled for 2014), at a projected cost of some $5,500m., the port was expected to have annual handling capacity of 2m. 20-ft equivalent units (TEUs), with capacity projected to increase to 6m. TEUs by 2025. Capacity at Doha's existing port, which was to be decommissioned on completion of the new port, was 400,000 TEUs.

At 31 December 2012 Qatar's flag registered fleet totalled 152 vessels, with an aggregate displacement of 860,605 grt, of which three were bulk carriers, six were gas tankers and two were general cargo ships.

Port Authority

Customs and Ports General Authority (CPGA): POB 81, Doha; tel. and fax 44457457; e-mail comments@customs.gov.qa; internet www.customs.gov.qa; Chair. AHMAD ALI MUHAMMAD AL-MOHANNADI.

Principal Shipping Companies

Qatar Gas Transport Co Ltd (Nakilat): Royal Plaza, al-Sadd St, POB 22271, Doha; tel. 44998111; fax 44483111; e-mail info@qgtc.com.qa; internet www.nakilat.com.qa; f. 2004; 50% owned by founding shareholders and 50% owned by public; specializes in the shipment of LNG, LPG and petroleum products; owns 54 vessels; Chair. HAMAD RASHID AL-MOHANNADI; Man. Dir MUHAMMAD GHANNAM; 220 employees.

Qatar Navigation QSC: POB 153, 60 al-Tameen St, West Bay, Doha; tel. 44468666; fax 44468777; e-mail info@qatarnavigation.com; internet www.qatarnav.com; f. 1957 as Qatar Nat. Navigation and Transport Co Ltd; acquired Qatar Shipping Co in 2010; 100% owned by Qatari nationals; shipping agents, stevedoring, chandlers, forwarding, ship-owning, repair, construction, etc.; Chief Exec. KHALIFA BIN ALI AL-HITMI; Chair. and Man. Dir Sheikh ALI BIN JASSIM BIN MUHAMMAD AL THANI.

Qatar Shipping Co QSC (Q-Ship): POB 22180, al-Jazeera Tower, 61, Conference Center St, West Bay, Doha; tel. and fax 44191760; e-mail rahul@qship.com; internet www.qship.com; f. 1992; subsidiary of Qatar Navigation QSC; oil and bulk cargo shipping; wholly owns 7 vessels; Chair. and Man. Dir SALEM BIN BUTTI AL-NAIMI; CEO K. K. KOTHARI.

CIVIL AVIATION

A substantial redevelopment of Doha International Airport (to be known upon completion of the project as Hamad International Airport), 4 km to the east of the existing site, is currently under way. Phase one of the project, which was expected to cost some QR 9,500m., involved the construction of two runways and a new terminal building and was set to increase annual passenger-handling capacity to 24m. After delays to the original schedule, phase one was expected to be completed by April 2013. However, the opening was postponed until at least the end of the year, owing to concerns over safety. Upon completion of the third, and final, phase of the expansion, scheduled for 2015, passenger-handling capacity was to reach 50m.

Civil Aviation Authority: POB 3000, Doha; tel. 44557333; fax 44557105; e-mail info@caa.gov.qa; internet www.caa.gov.qa; Chair. and Man. Dir Abd al-Aziz Muhammad al-Noaimi.

Doha International Airport: POB 24659, Doha; tel. 44656666; fax 44622044; e-mail diainfo@qatarairways.com.qa; internet www.dohaairport.com; CEO Akbar al-Baker.

Gulf Helicopters Co (GHC): POB 811, al-Areesh St, Ras Abu Aboud Rd, Doha; tel. 44333888; fax 44411004; e-mail enquiries@gulfhelicopters.com; internet www.gulfhelicopters.com; f. 1970; owned by Qatar Petroleum; owns a fleet of 32 helicopters; CEO Muhammad al-Mohannadi.

Qatar Airways: POB 22550, Airport Rd, Doha; tel. 44496666; fax 44621792; e-mail infodesk@qatarairways.com; internet www.qatarairways.com; f. 1993; state-owned; services to more than 80 international destinations; operated a fleet of 87 aircraft at August 2010; planned fleet expansion to 110 aircraft by 2013; CEO Akbar al-Baker.

Tourism

Since 2000 the tourism industry has been undergoing a programme of expansion and development, and Qatar's reputation as a venue for international conferences and sporting events has grown. The 15th Asian Games, held in Doha in December 2006, provided a substantial impetus for increased hotel construction from 2004. In December 2010 Qatar was awarded the right to host the 2022 International Federation of Association Football (Fédération internationale de football association—FIFA) World Cup, an event that was expected to promote extensive development of the country's tourism infrastructure. A new Museum of Islamic Art opened in Doha in 2008, and several other new museums and cultural establishments were planned. Notable tourist attractions outside the capital include the historic forts and archaeological sites at al-Zubarah, and the natural beauty of the Khor al-Udaid, or Inland Sea, region. There were 1.9m. tourist arrivals in 2010; receipts from tourism (excluding passenger transport) were provisionally estimated at US $1,170m. in 2011.

Qatar National Hotels Co: POB 2977, Doha; tel. 44237777; fax 44270707; internet www.qnhc.com; f. 1993; develops and manages hotels and other tourist facilities; govt-owned; Chair. Sheikh Nawaf bin Jasim bin Jaber Al Thani; CEO Jan Poul N. De Boer.

Qatar Tourism Authority (QTEA): POB 24624, Doha; tel. 44997499; fax 44991919; e-mail soha@qatartourism.gov.qa; internet www.qatartourism.gov.qa; f. 2000; affiliated with the Ministry of Business and Trade; Chair. Ahmed Abdullah al-Nuaimi; Head of Promotions Soha Moussa.

Defence

Chief of Staff: Maj.-Gen. Hamad bin Ali al-Attiya.

Defence Expenditure (2011): QR 12,600m.

Total armed forces (as assessed at November 2012): 11,800: army 8,500; navy 1,800 (incl. marine police); air force 1,500.

Education

All education within Qatar is provided free of charge, although it is not compulsory, and numerous scholarships are awarded for study overseas. In the academic year 2010/11 there were 90,671 students at pre-primary, primary, preparatory and secondary levels of government-funded, regular education in Qatar; there were 106,584 students in private schools in the same year. In that year there were 23,932 children enrolled in pre-primary education. Primary schooling begins at six years of age and lasts for six years. In 2009/10 state primary schools were attended by 12,204 pupils. The next level of education, beginning at 12 years of age, is divided between a three-year preparatory stage and a further three-year secondary stage, with a total of 18,912 pupils at government schools in 2009/10. In that year there were 136 independent schools, which were attended by 27,306 pupils at primary level and 35,609 at preparatory and secondary levels. There are specialized religious, industrial, commercial and technical secondary schools for boys; the technical school admitted its first students in 1999/2000, as did two scientific secondary schools (one for girls). According to UNESCO estimates, enrolment at primary schools in 2009/10 included 92% of children in the relevant age-group; the comparable ratio for secondary enrolment was 83%. The University of Qatar was established in 1977. In 2010/11 there were 9,793 students enrolled at the university (including Qatar Community College). The Qatar Foundation for Education, Science and Community Development, established in 1995, is involved in various programmes to develop educational and research facilities, including through partnerships with international institutions. Education City Qatar, the foundation's flagship project, which opened in October 2003, hosts branch campuses of five US universities and numerous other educational and research institutions. In 2011/12 government expenditure on education amounted to QR 6,040m., equivalent to 14% of total government spending.

ROMANIA

Introductory Survey

LOCATION, CLIMATE, LANGUAGE, RELIGION, FLAG, CAPITAL

Romania lies in south-eastern Europe, bounded to the north and east by Ukraine, to the north-east by Moldova, to the north-west by Hungary, to the south-west by Serbia and to the south by Bulgaria. The south-east coast is washed by the Black Sea. Romania has hot summers and cold winters, with moderate rainfall. The average summer temperature is 23°C (73°F) and the winter average is −3°C (27°F). The official language is Romanian, although minority groups speak Hungarian (Magyar), German and other languages. Most of the inhabitants profess Christianity, and about 87% of the population are adherents of the Romanian Orthodox Church. The national flag (proportions 3 by 5) consists of three equal vertical stripes, of blue, yellow and red. The capital is Bucharest (Bucureşti).

CONTEMPORARY POLITICAL HISTORY

Historical Context

Formerly part of Turkey's Ottoman Empire, Romania became an independent kingdom in 1881. During the dictatorship of the Fascist 'Iron Guard' movement, Romania entered the Second World War as an ally of Nazi Germany. However, Soviet forces entered Romania in 1944, when the pro-Nazi regime was overthrown. Under Soviet pressure, King Michael (Mihail) I accepted the appointment of a communist-led coalition Government in March 1945. At elections in November 1946 a communist-dominated bloc claimed 89% of the votes cast, but the results were widely believed to have been fraudulent. In 1947 the small Romanian Communist Party (RCP) merged with the Social Democratic Party to become the Romanian Workers' Party (RWP). King Michael was forced to abdicate on 30 December 1947, when the Romanian People's Republic was proclaimed. The republic's first Constitution was adopted in 1948, and in the same year the nationalization of the main industrial and financial institutions began. The implementation of Soviet-style economic policies was accompanied by the establishment of full political control by the RWP.

In 1952, following a purge of the RWP membership, a new Constitution, closer to the Soviet model, was adopted. Gheorghe Gheorghiu-Dej, the First Secretary of the RWP, became Romania's unchallenged leader and proceeded to implement large-scale plans for industrialization. Gheorghiu-Dej died in 1965; he was succeeded as First Secretary of the RWP by Nicolae Ceauşescu, a Secretary of the RWP Central Committee since 1954. In June 1965 the RWP again became the RCP, and Ceauşescu's post of First Secretary was restyled General Secretary. A new Constitution, adopted in August, changed the country's name to the Socialist Republic of Romania.

Ceauşescu continued his predecessor's relatively independent foreign policy, establishing links with Western states and institutions. In order to strengthen his position, Ceauşescu (who had become President of the Republic in 1974) implemented frequent changes in the RCP leadership and the Government. In March 1980 his wife, Elena, became a First Deputy Chairman of the Council of Ministers, and numerous other family members held government and party posts.

In late 1985 an energy crisis resulted in a declaration of a state of emergency in the electric power industry and the dismissal of ministers and senior officials. In November 1987 demonstrators stormed the local RCP headquarters in the city of Braşov, protesting against declining living standards and working conditions. Hundreds of arrests were made, and similar protests followed in other cities. In March 1988 Ceauşescu announced details of a rural urbanization programme, to entail the demolition of some 8,000 villages, and the resettlement of their residents (mostly ethnic Hungarians) in new 'agro-industrial centres'. Despite domestic and international criticism, Ceauşescu maintained that the programme would raise living standards and ensure social equality.

In December 1989 there was unrest in the western city of Timişoara as supporters of László Tökés, a Protestant clergyman (an ethnic Hungarian who had repeatedly criticized the Government's policies), demonstrated their opposition to his eviction from his church. Security forces opened fire on protesters, reportedly killing several hundred people. There were reports of protests in other towns, and the country's borders were closed.

On 21 December 1989 President Ceauşescu attended a mass rally in Bucharest, intended to demonstrate popular support. However, anti-Government demonstrations followed later in the day, leading to clashes between protesters and members of the Securitate (the secret police force), during which many civilians were killed. The disturbances quickly spread to other parts of the country, and on the following day Ceauşescu declared a state of emergency; however, soldiers of the regular army declared their support for the protesters. Nicolae and Elena Ceauşescu escaped from the RCP Central Committee headquarters by helicopter as demonstrators stormed the building. The Ceauşescus were captured near Târgovişte and, on 25 December, after a summary trial, were executed by firing squad. Fighting continued for several days, mainly between Securitate forces and regular soldiers.

Meanwhile, a 145-member National Salvation Front (NSF) was formed, and a provisional Government was established. Ion Iliescu, a former Secretary of the RCP Central Committee, became interim President, and Petre Roman, an academic, was appointed Prime Minister. The new Government immediately decreed an end to the RCP's constitutional monopoly of power, and cancelled the rural urbanization programme. The RCP was banned, it was announced that free elections would be held in 1990, and the designation of Socialist Republic was abandoned. By early January 1990 the army had restored order, and the Securitate was abolished. According to official figures, 689 people were killed during the revolution.

Special military tribunals were established to try Ceauşescu's former associates. In February 1990 four senior RCP officials were found guilty of responsibility for the shootings in Timişoara and Bucharest and were sentenced to life imprisonment. Numerous other former government and RCP members were similarly charged. In September Ceauşescu's son, Nicu, who was found to have ordered security forces to open fire on demonstrators in Sibiu in December 1989, received a 20-year prison sentence. (He was released in 1992 on the grounds of ill health, and died in 1996.) Gen. Iulian Vlad, the former head of the Securitate, was sentenced to 12 years' imprisonment in 1991; in January 1994, however, he was released as part of a general amnesty. In December 1991 eight associates of the former President were sentenced to prison terms of up to 25 years for their part in the shootings in Timişoara.

Domestic Political Affairs

Despite the widespread jubilation that followed the downfall of Ceauşescu, the NSF did not enjoy total public support, largely owing to the widely held perception that the Front's leadership was too closely linked with the Ceauşescu regime. Furthermore, the NSF's announcement, in January 1990, that it was to contest the forthcoming elections, and its reversal of the prohibition of the RCP, increased fears that members of the disgraced regime were attempting to regain power. In January the offices of two opposition parties, the National Liberal Party (NLP) and the National Peasants' Party, were attacked by NSF supporters. In February, after negotiations among representatives of 29 political parties, the NSF agreed to share power with the opposition, pending the elections, in a 180-member Provisional National Unity Council (PNUC). Each of the political parties represented in the talks was allocated three seats on the Council, and the PNUC was subsequently expanded to 253 members to permit representation by other political parties; nevertheless, NSF members and supporters occupied 111 seats in the Council. The PNUC elected an Executive Bureau, with Iliescu as its President. Opposition to the NSF persisted, particularly in the armed forces. The Minister of National Defence was replaced in compliance with demands from within the military, but shortly afterwards thousands of anti-Government demonstrators demanded the resignation of Iliescu, and some 250 protesters forcibly entered the NSF headquarters.

As the elections approached, mass anti-communist demonstrations were staged in Bucharest. The election campaign was acrimonious, and there were widespread accusations of systematic intimidation and harassment of the NSF's opponents. On 20 May 1990 Iliescu won 85.1% of the votes cast in the presidential poll. In the concurrent elections to the bicameral legislature, the NSF won 65% of the votes cast, securing 263 of the 387 seats in the Camera Deputaților (Chamber of Deputies) and 91 of the 119 seats in Senatul (the Senate).

In June 1990 a protest in Bucharest was forcibly broken up by the police, provoking renewed clashes, in which the armed forces opened fire on rioters. Following an appeal for support by Iliescu, some 7,000 miners and other workers were transported to the capital, where they swiftly seized control of the streets. The disturbances resulted in several deaths and hundreds of injuries. Following President Iliescu's inauguration in late June, Roman was reappointed Prime Minister, and a new Council of Ministers was formed, in which nearly all the members of the interim administration were replaced. In the following months, as popular discontent at the deteriorating economic situation intensified, there was widespread strike action. In November price increases, as part of economic reforms, led to demonstrations in Bucharest, including a protest organized by a new opposition grouping, the Civic Alliance. In April 1991 Roman allocated three government portfolios to opposition politicians.

In September 1991 miners, by this time opposed to President Iliescu, began a strike in support of demands for pay increases and the resignation of the Government. Thousands of miners travelled to Bucharest, where they attacked government offices and ransacked the parliament building. Four people were killed and hundreds injured during violent clashes with the security forces, as a result of which the Council of Ministers was obliged to resign. Theodor Stolojan, a former Minister of Finance, was appointed as Prime Minister, leading a coalition Government formed in October, comprising members of the NSF, the NLP, the Agrarian Democratic Party of Romania (ADPR) and the Romanian Ecological Movement.

A new Constitution, enshrining a multi-party system, a free-market economy and guarantees of the respect of human rights, was approved by the legislature in November 1991 and was endorsed by some 77.3% of voters in a referendum in December. The results of local elections, which took place between February and April 1992, confirmed the decline in support for the NSF. Many seats were won by the centre-right Democratic Convention of Romania (DCR), an alliance of 18 parties and organizations, including the Christian-Democratic National Peasants' Party (CDNPP) and the Party of the Civic Alliance. The NSF divided into two factions, and in April the faction loyal to Iliescu, which favoured only limited reforms, was registered as the Democratic National Salvation Front (DNSF).

Legislative and presidential elections took place on 27 September 1992. The DNSF won 117 of the 328 elective seats in the Camera Deputaților and 49 of the 143 seats in Senatul, making it the largest party in the new Parlamentul (Parliament). Its closest rival was the DCR, with 82 seats in the Camera Deputaților and 34 in Senatul. The NSF secured only 43 and 18 seats, respectively. In the presidential election, the two leading candidates, Iliescu and Emil Constantinescu, representing the DCR, proceeded to a second round of voting on 11 October, at which Iliescu won 61.4% of the votes cast. In November Nicolae Văcăroiu, an economist with no professed political party affiliation, formed a Government comprising equal numbers of DNSF members and independents.

The abolition of price subsidies for many basic commodities and services, from May 1993, precipitated renewed labour unrest. The Government's position was also undermined by successive confidence motions. Meanwhile, the DNSF had changed its name to the Party of Social Democracy of Romania (PSDR) in July and absorbed three other parties. In May, in an apparently similar attempt to distance itself from the events of 1989–90, Roman's NSF renamed itself the Democratic Party—National Salvation Front (DP—NSF). In November 1993 a protest march in Bucharest, demanding rapid economic reforms, was the largest public demonstration in the country since the overthrow of the Ceaușescu regime. A government reorganization in March continued the pattern of single-party (PSDR) rule supplemented by independent 'technocrats' (although later in the year two members of the Romanian National Unity Party—RNUP—were appointed to the Council of Ministers). In November 1995 Iliescu approved legislation providing for the restitution of property confiscated by the communist regime in the late 1940s and 1950s.

In May 1996 the PSDR terminated its parliamentary co-operation with the RNUP. Although the PSDR secured the largest number of mayoral and council seats at the local elections in June, the results indicated a decline in support for the party. The DCR and the Social Democratic Union (SDU), formed by the DP—NSF and the Romanian Social Democratic Party (RSDP) in January, won control of many major cities, including Bucharest. In September the RNUP ministers were dismissed from the Government, after conflict with the PSDR had been exacerbated by the RNUP's opposition to the signing of a treaty with Hungary (see Minority Ethnic Groups).

The legislative and presidential elections of 1996

Legislative and presidential elections took place on 3 November 1996. The DCR won the largest number of parliamentary seats, with 122 of the 328 seats in the Camera Deputaților and 53 of the 143 seats in Senatul. The PSDR took 91 and 41 seats in the respective chambers, and the SDU 53 and 23. An agreement on political co-operation was subsequently reached between the DCR and the SDU. In the first round of the presidential election, which was contested by 16 candidates, Iliescu won 32.3% of the valid votes cast, and Constantinescu took 28.2%. With the support of nearly all the opposition parties, Constantinescu was duly elected in a second round on 17 November, with 54.4% of the votes cast. At the end of November Victor Ciorbea of the DCR, the Mayor of Bucharest, was nominated as Prime Minister, and in mid-December a new coalition Government, comprising the DCR, the SDU and the Democratic Alliance of Hungarians in Romania (DAHR), took office.

Despite protests from opposition parties, the Government restored citizenship to former King Michael, who visited Romania in February 1997. Meanwhile, in January a National Council for Action against Corruption and Organized Crime, headed by Constantinescu, was established; a number of leading bankers were subsequently arrested, principally on charges of fraud, and several senior members of the security forces were dismissed. The arrest, in February, of Miron Cozma, the leader of the miners' demonstrations in Bucharest in June 1990 and September 1991, prompted protests from miners and their trade union leaders.

Several prominent members of the PSDR resigned from the party in June 1997, and formed a new party, the Alliance for Romania (AFR). Adrian Severin, Minister of State and Minister of Foreign Affairs, and a member of the DP (as the DP—NSF had been renamed), resigned in December, after a judicial investigation failed to confirm his allegations that certain political leaders and newspaper editors were working with foreign intelligence services. In January 1998 the resignation of the Minister of Transport, Traian Băsescu of the DP, owing to his criticism of Ciorbea's Government, led the DP to demand his reinstatement, and DP ministers eventually withdrew from the Government.

In March 1998, in response to increasing pressure within the coalition, Ciorbea and his Government resigned. Radu Vasile, the Secretary-General of the CDNPP and a Deputy Chairman of Senatul, was designated Prime Minister in April. A new Council of Ministers was endorsed by Parlamentul in mid-April. As Romania's economic situation worsened, the Minister of Finance, Daniel Dăianu, was dismissed in September; he was replaced by Decebal Trăian Remeș. In October Sorin Dimitriu resigned as Minister of Privatization and head of the State Ownership Fund. Meanwhile, in September, after the DAHR threatened to leave the ruling coalition unless Parlamentul adopted legislation providing for the establishment of a minority-language university, the Government agreed to create an independent university in Cluj-Napoca for Hungarian and German minorities.

In January 1999 a strike by miners escalated when Vasile refused to negotiate with Cozma, who had been released from prison in mid-1998, after serving an 18-month sentence for the possession of firearms and ammunition. Encouraged by nationalist politicians (notably from the Greater Romania Party— GRP), 10,000–20,000 miners marched towards Bucharest, and in Costești, some 190 km north-west of Bucharest, violent clashes broke out with the security forces. Following emergency talks between the Prime Minister and miners' leaders, a temporary agreement was reached. The Minister of the Interior, Gavril Dejeu, resigned, amid severe criticism of the security forces' failure to halt the march; he was replaced by Constantin Dudu Ionescu. In February the Supreme Court of Justice sentenced Cozma, *in absentia*, to 18 years' imprisonment for undermining state authority. In protest, approximately 2,000–4,000 miners, led by Cozma, again marched towards Bucharest. The miners were stopped by the security forces some 160 km west of Bucharest, where more than 100 people were injured and one miner died during the violence that ensued; Cozma and several hundred miners were arrested. (In June 2002 Cozma was sentenced to an additional 12 years' imprisonment—to be served concurrently—for his involvement in the 1999 violence; in January 2007, however, it was reported that he had been granted early release.)

In early June 1999 the Camera Deputaţilor approved amendments to the electoral law, increasing the threshold for parliamentary representation from 3% to 5%, with alliances required to secure a further 3% for each member party. Later that month the Camera Deputaţilor voted in favour of providing public access to the files of the Securitate (although many documents were believed to have been destroyed); the President promulgated the legislation in December. In July Gen. Victor Stănculescu and Gen. Mihai Chiţac were sentenced to 15 years' imprisonment, having been found guilty of the murders of 72 people, by ordering the security forces to open fire on protesters during the Timişoara uprising in December 1989. The ruling was severely criticized by Victor Babiuc, the Minister of National Defence, whose ministry was ordered to pay damages to those wounded in the shootings and the relatives of the dead. (Babiuc resigned from the Government and from his party several months later.)

In November 1999 students undertook strike action, and some 10,000 trade union members participated in protest rallies to demand the resignation of the Government. In mid-December, as labour unrest continued, Constantinescu dismissed Vasile, after all seven CDNPP government ministers, followed by the three NLP ministers, resigned from the Government. Constantinescu nominated Mugur Isărescu, hitherto Governor of the National Bank of Romania (and without affiliation to any political party), as Prime Minister. The legislature subsequently approved the appointment of Isărescu and his Council of Ministers, which remained largely unchanged, although Roman joined the new Government as Minister of State and Minister of Foreign Affairs. Vasile was expelled from the CDNPP later that month.

In local elections, held on 4 June 2000, the PSDR won the largest proportion of the votes cast (36.7%). Băsescu left the Government, after being elected as Mayor of Bucharest. In July President Constantinescu unexpectedly announced that he would not stand for re-election at the forthcoming presidential election. In September the RSDP withdrew from the governing coalition, announcing that it was to merge with the main opposition party, the PSDR.

The legislative and presidential elections of 2000

Legislative and presidential elections took place concurrently on 26 November 2000. The PSDR secured 155 seats in the Camera Deputaţilor and 65 in Senatul, while the GRP obtained 84 and 37 seats, respectively. The rate of voter participation was the lowest recorded since the collapse of communism, at 57.5%. In the presidential election, former President Iliescu obtained 36.4% of the votes cast and Corneliu Vadim Tudor of the GRP won 28.3%. A second round was held on 10 December, in which Iliescu won 66.8% of the votes cast. Later in December Iliescu nominated Adrian Năstase of the PSDR as Prime Minister. Năstase subsequently signed a joint statement on priorities for the development of Romania with the leaders of the DAHR, the NLP and the DP. Although Năstase insisted that the declaration did not represent a coalition agreement, the support of those parties enabled the PSDR to form a minority Government. The new, expanded Council of Ministers was sworn in on 28 December.

In February 2001 President Iliescu endorsed a law, which provided for the return of some 300,000 properties nationalized during the communist era to their original owners; it superseded legislation on the restitution of property that had been approved in 1995. In mid-June the PSDR and the RSDP formally merged, creating the Social Democratic Party (SDP), under the leadership of Prime Minister Năstase. In November some 15,000 people took part in a demonstration in Bucharest against poverty and the Government's austerity programme. A further large-scale protest took place in December.

In March 2002 the Government announced the establishment of a new National Anti-corruption Prosecution Office. Also in March the Government sought to moderate the power of labour organizations through the signature of a 'social pact' with three of the five largest trade unions, which provided for an increased minimum wage and the creation of 10,000 jobs. In September

Senatul approved a new law on political parties, which required all parties to re-register by 31 December, and to be composed of a minimum of 10,000 members from at least 21 of Romania's 41 administrative sub-divisions. On 10 November local elections took place in 21 counties, in which the SDP was the most successful party. In early 2003 a number of prominent CDNPP members were expelled from the party after participating in the foundation of the new Popular Action civic movement, led by former President Constantinescu; in February it was confirmed that the movement was to become a political party.

In June 2003 Năstase reorganized the Council of Ministers, reducing the number of portfolios from 23 to 14. In a referendum held on 18–19 October some 90% of votes cast by 55.7% of the electorate approved 79 proposed amendments to the Constitution, which aimed to bring it into conformity with EU requirements (by, *inter alia*, guaranteeing the right to private property, strengthening legal rights for ethnic minorities and limiting the powers of the executive branch of government). The revised Constitution entered into force on 29 October.

In local elections held on 6 and 20 June 2004 the SDP received the greatest number of mayoral mandates, closely followed by the NLP. In August charges of abuse of office and embezzlement were brought against 79 people, including Băsescu (who had been re-elected Mayor of Bucharest), relating to responsibility in his former capacity as Minister of Transport for the alleged illegal sale of 16 ships from the national maritime fleet in 1991–2000. In September 2004 the SDP and the Humanist Party of Romania (HPR) formed an electoral alliance, the National Union. Meanwhile, the NLP and the DP announced their intention to contest the forthcoming legislative elections as the Justice and Truth Alliance.

The legislative and presidential elections of 2004

Legislative and presidential elections were held on 28 November 2004. The National Union emerged as the largest bloc in both chambers, with 132 seats (of a total of 332) in the Camera Deputaţilor and 57 (of a total of 137) in Senatul. The Justice and Truth Alliance received 112 seats in the Camera Deputaţilor and 49 in Senatul. The representation of the GRP was markedly reduced in both chambers, to 48 deputies in the lower chamber, and 21 senators. Following the presidential ballot, Năstase (with 40.9%) and Traian Băsescu (with 33.9%) proceeded to a second round of voting on 12 December. In the run-off election, Băsescu achieved a narrow victory, with 51.2% of the votes cast. Băsescu was inaugurated as President on 20 December (thus gaining immunity from prosecution). Năstase was elected as Chairman of the Camera Deputaţilor, and Văcăroiu, a Deputy Chairman of the SDP, was elected as Chairman of Senatul in a vote that was boycotted by senators of the Justice and Truth Alliance and the DAHR. Băsescu nominated Călin Popescu-Tăriceanu to form a government. The HPR was persuaded to abandon its electoral partner, the SDP, to form a coalition with the NLP, the DP and the DAHR, although the parties only held one more seat than the requisite quorum in the bicameral legislature. On 28 December the new coalition Council of Ministers was approved by both chambers of the legislature. In February 2005 Popescu-Tăriceanu was elected as President of the NLP.

The HPR was renamed the Conservative Party (CP) in May 2005. In June Emil Boc was elected President of the DP. In July the Constitutional Court rejected the Government's programme for judicial reform, prompting Popescu-Tăriceanu to announce that he intended to submit the resignation of his administration, in an attempt to precipitate early elections; however, an extraordinary session of Parlamentul approved amendments to the legislation, to accommodate the Court's objections. Popescu-Tăriceanu subsequently announced that his Government (which was reorganized) would remain in place in order to respond to severe flooding in central and eastern parts of the country.

In October 2005 the EU Commissioner responsible for Enlargement, Olli Rehn, warned Romania that its planned accession to the European Union (EU, see p. 281) in 2007 could be subject to delay if measures were not taken to combat corruption and accelerate the pace of judicial reform. In early 2006 a number of political figures duly came under investigation as a result of allegations of fraud, and in January Năstase resigned from the leadership of the SDP, following concerns about the legitimacy of an inheritance received by his wife. In February Năstase was indicted on charges of bribery pertaining to the acquisition of land in 1998. Năstase resigned as Chairman of the Camera Deputaţilor in March, following a vote of no confidence by the SDP; he was succeeded by Bogdan Olteanu of the NLP. In December the CP announced its withdrawal from the coalition Government, prompting the resignation of two ministers and ending the parliamentary majority commanded by Popescu-Tăriceanu.

In January 2007 Băsescu accused Popescu-Tăriceanu of attempting to influence a criminal investigation against a close associate who was accused of financial misconduct. In February Mihai Ungureanu resigned as Minister of Foreign Affairs at the request of Popescu-Tăriceanu, after he had failed to inform the Government about the detention of two Romanian nationals by US forces in Iraq; Băsescu subsequently refused to endorse the Prime Minister's nomination of an NLP representative, Adrian Cioroianu, to the post. At the beginning of April Popescu-Tăriceanu accused Băsescu of provoking dissension within the Government and ended his party's coalition with the DP, thereby removing eight DP ministers. He formed a new minority Government, comprising 13 representatives of the NLP and four of the DAHR, which was approved by Parlamentul, with the support of the SDP, on 3 April (and endorsed by Băsescu on the following day). Cioroianu became Minister of Foreign Affairs, while Tudor Chiuariu of the NLP, who had hitherto headed the anti-corruption department in the Office of the Prime Minister, was appointed Minister of Justice. On 19 April a motion initiated by the SDP to suspend Băsescu from office on grounds of unconstitutional conduct (by creating political instability, pressurizing the judiciary and interfering in government affairs) was approved by Parlamentul, after receiving the support of the ruling coalition deputies. On 9 May, in accordance with EU requirements, Senatul approved legislation providing for the creation of a National Integrity Agency to monitor the activities of civil servants, including parliamentary deputies, in an effort to prevent corruption. At a national referendum, held on 19 May, Băsescu's removal from office was opposed by about 74.5% of those who voted. Băsescu was officially reinstated as President on 23 May.

On 25 November 2007 elections (postponed since May) to 35 seats in the European Parliament (see below) were conducted. The DP won 13 seats and the SDP 10 seats, while the NLP secured six seats and its coalition partner, the DAHR, two seats; the Liberal Democratic Party (formed in late 2006 by breakaway members of the NLP, and led by Theodor Stolojan) won three seats, and the remaining seat was obtained by an independent. In December the DP merged with the Liberal Democratic Party to form the Democratic Liberal Party (DLP), under the continued leadership of Boc.

In December 2007 Chiuariu resigned as Minister of Justice, following the initiation of a criminal investigation into his alleged abuse of office. In January 2008 Băsescu refused to endorse Popescu-Tăriceanu's selected candidate, demanding that the new minister be a representative of a party other than the NLP. After the Constitutional Court ruled in support of Băsescu, in March Cătălin Marian Predoiu, a lawyer with no political affiliation, was appointed as the new Minister of Justice. In March 2008 Senatul adopted legislation providing for the introduction of compromise electoral reforms: rather than the existing party list system, candidates were to be directly elected by an absolute majority of votes in single-member constituencies, while the overall distribution of seats in each chamber was to be determined by proportional representation among parties securing a minimum of 5% of votes cast nationally. Prior to local elections, Constantinescu's Popular Action party merged with the NLP. Local, county and municipal elections were conducted on 1 June, with a second round of voting held in mayoral elections, where required, on 15 June. Notably, Sorin Oprescu, an independent candidate who, none the less, was closely affiliated with the SDP, was elected as Mayor of Bucharest. In August Senatul voted in favour of investigating Paul Păcuraru, the Minister of Labour, the Family and Equal Opportunities, who was alleged to have accepted bribes. Năstase was finally indicted in May 2010.

The legislative and presidential elections of 2008–09

Elections to the bicameral legislature were conducted under the new, mixed-member system of proportional representation on 30 November 2008. The DLP marginally secured the greatest representation in both chambers, with 115 of the total 334 seats in the Camera Deputaţilor (32.4% of the votes cast), and 51 of 137 seats in Senatul (33.6% of the votes cast); the SDP, allied with the CP, won 114 seats (33.1% of votes) in the Camera Deputaţilor and 49 seats (34.2%) in Senatul, and the NLP 65 seats (18.6%) in the Camera Deputaţilor and 28 seats (18.7%) in Senatul. In early December Băsescu invited former Prime Minister Stolojan, of the DLP, to establish a new administration; however, Stolojan

unexpectedly ceded the nomination to Boc. Following a coalition agreement between the DLP and the SDP, a new Government comprising members of both parties was approved by the legislature on 22 December. The Vice-President of the SDP, Dan Nica, became Deputy Prime Minister. Crin Antonescu was elected President of the NLP at a party congress in March 2009, defeating the incumbent, Popescu-Tăriceanu.

At elections to the European Parliament, conducted on 7 June 2009, the SDP-CP alliance secured 11 of the country's 33 seats. The DLP obtained 10 seats, the NLP five seats, and the DAHR and the GRP three seats each. One independent candidate, Elena Băsescu, the daughter of the President, was elected. Some 27.7% of the electorate participated in the voting.

Nica was dismissed from the Government in late September 2009, after he made comments regarding the potential for fraud in the presidential election due to take place in November, prompting the SDP to withdraw from the ruling coalition at the beginning of October. The DLP remained in office as a minority Government, with the party's ministers assuming temporary responsibility for the portfolios previously allocated to the SDP. In mid-October, however, Parlamentul approved a motion of no confidence in Boc's Government. Băsescu subsequently failed to endorse the candidate jointly nominated by the SDP, the NLP and the DAHR, and instead designated economist Lucian Croitoru, an adviser to the National Bank of Romania, as Prime Minister; however, Croitoru's proposed Council of Ministers was rejected by Parlamentul in early November. Two days later, Băsescu designated Liviu Negoiţă of the DLP as Prime Minister, but his cabinet was also not approved prior to the election. Later in November the Court of Appeals ruled that Nica's dismissal from the Government in September had been illegal.

The first round of the presidential election, which was conducted on 22 November 2009 and contested by 12 candidates, was inconclusive: Băsescu secured 32.4% of the votes cast, followed by Mircea Geoană, the President of the SDP, with 31.2%, and NLP leader Antonescu, with 20.0%. A rate of voter participation of 54.4% was recorded. Băsescu narrowly defeated Geoană in a second round of presidential voting on 6 December, securing 50.3% of the votes cast; 58.0% of the electorate participated in the ballot. The SDP and the CP challenged the results, alleging that electoral violations had taken place, but the Constitutional Court rejected their appeal for an annulment. On 17 December Băsescu nominated acting Prime Minister Boc to form a new government, after Negoiţă stood down as Prime Minister-designate. Băsescu was inaugurated to serve a second term as President on 21 December. On 23 December Parlamentul approved Boc's new Council of Ministers, which comprised nine members of the DLP, four members of the DAHR and four independents. The President of the DAHR, Markó Béla, was appointed Deputy Prime Minister.

The second Government of Emil Boc

The coalition Government immediately pursued the adoption of austerity measures demanded by the IMF and other donors (see Economic Affairs). In February 2010, however, public-sector workers staged a two-hour 'warning' strike in protest against plans to reduce salaries and employment. Victor Ponta was elected President of the SDP at a party congress later that month, defeating Geoană. Despite criticism by the European Commission of Romania's lack of progress in combating corruption, in April the Constitutional Court made a decision to limit the powers of the National Integrity Agency established in 2007, declaring its main functions to be unconstitutional.

In May 2010 the Camera Deputaţilor passed legislation prohibiting former high-ranking communists from standing for public office for five years. (The Camera Deputaţilor adopted a Lustration Law in February 2012 following its approval by Senatul in 2006.) On 15 June 2010 the Government secured a narrow victory in a no confidence vote in parliament, initiated over proposed austerity measures. Opposition parties subsequently appealed to the Constitutional Court, which ruled in late June that a proposed reduction of 15% in pensions was unconstitutional. On the same day demonstrators attempted to storm the presidential palace.

On 2 September 2010 Prime Minister Boc replaced six members of the cabinet, including those responsible for finance and the economy, prompting demands for Boc's resignation from within the DLP. At the end of the month the Minister of Administration and the Interior, Vasile Blaga, resigned from his post following a protest by police against the proposed austerity measures. In October a vote of no confidence by opposition parties failed to secure the requisite number of votes in Parlamentul. Boc subsequently survived two further votes of no confidence in Parlamentul. In early December Parlamentul finally adopted a pensions law, which set the retirement age at 63 years for women and 65 years for men; this was subsequently approved by the Constitutional Court. None the less, opposition parties continued their campaign against austerity measures.

In February 2011 the Centre Right Alliance of the NLP and the CP signed an agreement with the SDP, formally establishing an alliance known as the Social-Liberal Union (SLU). In April the Minister of Labour, the Family and Social Welfare, Ioan Boţiş, resigned following an inquiry into his assets, and claims of a conflict of interest involving his wife's role as an adviser for an EU-funded programme. (He was replaced by Sebastian Lazariou in June.) In November SLU deputies sought to impeach Băsescu on the grounds of abuse of power; the President had also sought to apportion blame for Romania's failure in September to accede to the EU's Schengen area to the judiciary (see Regional relations). The following day Geoană was expelled from the SDP, after being accused of attempting to destabilize the opposition alliance; he was also removed from the post of Chairman of Senatul. Vasile Blaga of the DLP, a former interior minister, was subsequently elected as Chairman of Senatul.

SDP-led Government

Large-scale public protests took place throughout January 2012, with demonstrators accusing the Government of corruption and demanding early legislative elections. The Minister of Foreign Affairs, Teodor Baconschi, was dismissed, after making inflammatory comments that increased tensions. On 6 February Boc's Government resigned, in an effort to bring about an end to the increasingly violent protests. Băsescu nominated a former chief of the intelligence services, Mihai Răzvan Ungureanu, to form a new government, which retained just seven ministers from Boc's outgoing cabinet. Meanwhile, in January former Prime Minister Adrian Năstase had been gaoled after being found guilty of corruption charges relating to the use of public funds to pay for his 2004 election campaign; former ministers Decebal Trăian Remes and Ioan Avram Muresan were imprisoned in the following month, having also been found guilty of charges of corruption. (In July 2012 Năstase attempted suicide.)

In April 2012 Ungureanu's Government collapsed, following a number of defections from the ruling DLP to the opposition SLU alliance, and amid continuing public protests against austerity measures. A new Government, led by the President of the SDP, Victor Ponta, took office on 7 May, pending legislative elections later that year. Local elections, at which the SLU performed strongly, took place throughout the country on 10 June. On 3 July Senatul elected the leader of NLP, Crin Antonescu, as its Chairman, after Blaga of the DLP was removed, while on the same day Valeriu Zgonea of the SDP replaced Roberta Anastase of the DLP as Chairman of the Camera Deputaţilor.

On 6 July 2012 Parlamentul voted to suspend Băsescu from office for a period of 30 days (with 256 votes cast in favour of his suspension and 114 against), and announced that a referendum would take place to seek public approval for his impeachment, on the grounds of having exceeded his authority and violated the rule of separation of state powers. Antonescu became interim President. Two days earlier the Government had approved an emergency decree, restricting the powers of the Constitutional Court, which was thereby prevented from ruling on parliamentary decisions and allowed only to provide a consultative opinion on the impeachment proceedings. The referendum on Băsescu's impeachment was held on 29 July, as scheduled. Although about 89% of those voting supported impeachment, only 46.2% of the electorate participated in the plebiscite. Despite continuing efforts by Ponta's Government to remove Băsescu from office, the Constitutional Court confirmed in a ruling on 21 August that a rate of participation by the electorate of more than 50% was required for the vote to be considered valid. Meanwhile, in early August Ioan Rus of the SDP resigned as Minister of Administration and the Interior, accusing senior politicians of having placed pressure on him to violate legislation.

In September 2012 former premier Ungureanu was elected leader of the centre-right Civic Force, which later that month joined with the DLP and the CDNPP to form the Romanian Alliance of the Right (RAD), in preparation for legislative elections. The SDP also established a Centre Left Alliance with the National Union for the Progress of Romania (NUPR). Meanwhile, Bucharest University demanded that Prime Minister Ponta's doctorate be withdrawn after it emerged that he had plagiarized a large proportion of his thesis in 2003. In October

2012 the Minister of Health, Vasile Cepoi, resigned, following allegations of corruption relating to his management as head of the public health department in the eastern city of Iaşi.

Recent developments: the 2012 legislative elections

Elections to both parliamentary chambers on 9 December 2012 resulted in victory for the SLU (by this time also comprising the NUPR); the four coalition parties together secured 58.6% of the votes cast and 273 seats in the Camera Deputaţilor (which had been expanded to 412 seats) and 60.1% of the votes and 122 seats in Senatul (enlarged to 176 seats). The RAD received 16.5% of the votes and 56 seats in the Camera Deputaţilor and 16.7% of the votes and 24 seats in Senatul, and the People's Party—Dan Diaconescu (which Diaconescu, a journalist and businessman, had established in 2011) obtained 14.0% of the votes and 47 seats in the lower chamber and 14.7% and 21 seats in the upper chamber. The rate of participation by voters was just 41.8%. On 21 December Parlamentul approved a new coalition Government, again under the premiership of Ponta, which included representatives of the NUPR, as well as of the other three SLU parties.

Discord between Ponta's administration and President Băsescu continued; in January 2013 Băsescu refused to endorse Minister of Justice Mona Pivniceru's nomination of a new prosecutor and head of the National Anti-Corruption Directorate, owing to alleged procedural irregularities. Băsescu subsequently also failed to promulgate Parlamentul's approval of legislation that reduced the allowances of deputies, but also made the initiation of prosecution proceedings against them on corruption charges more difficult. Later in January the state regulatory authority suspended broadcasts of the OTV television station owned by Diaconescu, on the grounds that large fines imposed for a number of offences, including illegal political advertising and incitement to racial hatred, had not been paid. In February the Government announced the establishment of a commission tasked with revising the Constitution, particularly with regard to the authorities of the President. In late February Antonescu was re-elected as President of the NLP. Pivniceru resigned her ministerial post in late March, after being appointed a Constitutional Court judge. Ponta, who temporarily assumed the justice portfolio, nominated further candidates for the posts of prosecutor and head of the National Anti-Corruption Directorate in early April. In mid-April Robert-Marius Cazanciuc was appointed as the new Minister of Justice.

Minority Ethnic Groups

Romania experienced frequent occurrences of ethnic unrest after the fall of Ceauşescu. In January 2002 the Council of Europe (see p. 260) published a report condemning police brutality and widespread discrimination against Roma (Gypsy) communities in Romania, and the EU made the improvement of the treatment of the Roma minority a requirement for Romania to be declared eligible to accede to the Union. In February 2005 Romania was one of eight countries in the region to announce its adherence to a World Bank-financed 10-year plan to assist the Roma community.

Following the overthrow of Ceauşescu, ethnic Hungarians (a sizeable minority, numbering more than 7% of the total population at the 1992 census) sought to increase their cultural and linguistic autonomy in Transylvania. In March 1990 demonstrations by ethnic Hungarians demanding such rights were attacked by Romanian nationalists in Târgu Mureş. Tanks and troops were deployed to quell the unrest, in which several people were killed, and a state of emergency was declared in the town. An agreement on Hungarian minority rights was signed in July 1993, which included guarantees for the training of Hungarian-speaking schoolteachers and the use of bilingual street signs in areas with Hungarian populations of at least 30%. In May Romania ratified the Framework Convention of the Council of Europe on the general protection of national minorities. In September 1996 Romania and Hungary signed a treaty of friendship, as a result of which Romania agreed to safeguard the rights of ethnic Hungarians, and Hungary relinquished any claim to territory in Transylvania. Relations between Romania and Hungary improved further in February 1997 with the signature of a defence co-operation agreement. Proposals to amend legislation on education, in favour of ethnic minorities, provoked controversy in Romania in 1997 and 1998, although the amendments were finally approved in June 1999.

In January 2001 the Camera Deputaţilor approved a new public administration law, which made compulsory bilingual place names and signs, and the use of a given minority's language in local administration, in towns where that minority formed at least 20% of the population. In June the Government condemned Hungary's intention to introduce a new 'status law', which was to grant education, employment and medical rights to ethnic Hungarians living in neighbouring countries (including Romania) from January 2002. In December 2001 the Prime Ministers of the two countries signed a memorandum of understanding, which extended the short-term employment rights offered to ethnic Hungarians under the terms of the status law to all Romanian citizens. Finally, in September 2003 Prime Minister Năstase and his Hungarian counterpart, Péter Medgyessy, signed a bilateral agreement on the implementation of the status law in Romania. In October 2005 the first joint Romanian-Hungarian inter-governmental meeting was held in Bucharest, at which a treaty was concluded on the border regime, co-operation and mutual assistance. In February 2013 there was renewed ethnic tension when local Romanian officials in the central Covasna and Harghita counties prevented the hoisting of a flag representing the so-called Szekler region, in eastern Transylvania, on office buildings; the Hungarian ambassador and ethnic Hungarian government members subsequently expressed support for the use of the flag and associated demands for greater autonomy in Transylvania.

Foreign Affairs

Regional relations

Diplomatic relations with the former Soviet republic of Moldova (much of which formed part of Romania in 1918–40, and where a majority of the population are ethnic Romanians) were established in August 1991, and some political groups began to advocate the unification of the two states. The Romanian leadership opposed unification, but encouraged the development of closer cultural and economic ties with Moldova. In March 1994 a plebiscite was held in Moldova on the question of reunification with Romania; more than 95% of those who took part in the referendum voted for an independent state, effectively signalling the demise of the pro-unification movement. In 2000, as formal negotiations on Romania's accession to the EU commenced, hundreds of Moldovans applied for Romanian citizenship, in anticipation of the eventual tightening of border regulations. After Romania's accession to the EU on 1 January 2007 necessitated the possession of entry visas for Moldovan citizens wishing to visit Romania, the Moldovan Government strongly criticized Romania for granting Romanian citizenship to large numbers of Moldovan nationals, and in March reversed a decision to allow Romania to open two new consulates in the country. Violent protests in Moldova, which erupted in April 2009 following legislative elections, precipitated a breach in relations with Romania. The Moldovan President, Vladimir Voronin, accused the Romanian Government of organizing a coup attempt (since many of the protesters had exhibited pro-Romanian sentiments) and expelled the Romanian ambassador, recalled the Moldovan envoy in Bucharest, and introduced visa requirements for Romanians. Băsescu subsequently pledged that the Romanian Government would expedite the process of granting Romanian citizenship to Moldovans, claiming that some 1m. applications had been received. Bilateral relations improved in September, following Voronin's resignation as President of Moldova and the formation of a pro-Western Government in that country; the new acting Moldovan President, Mihai Ghimpu, swiftly abolished the visa requirements imposed on Romanians in April. In November, moreover, the Romanian and Moldovan Prime Ministers signed a Convention on Small-Scale Border Traffic, allowing Moldovan citizens residing within 50 km of the joint border (an estimated 1.2m. people) to travel within an equivalent area in Romania without requiring a visa. In April 2010 Băsescu and his Moldovan counterpart signed a joint declaration urging a strategic partnership between the two countries to assist with Moldova's objective of accession to the EU. In November a long-delayed border treaty was finally signed.

A basic treaty between Romania and Ukraine, signed in June 1997, guaranteed the inviolability of their joint border, and provided for separate treaties to be established regarding the administration of the frontier and the disputed ownership of the Black Sea continental shelf. In June 2003 President Iliescu and President Leonid Kuchma of Ukraine signed an accord confirming the mutual land border of the two countries, as it was delineated in 1961, with the exception of the continental shelf. No further progress was made in resolving the disagreement over the disputed maritime area (comprising an islet, known as

Serpents' Island, and surrounding waters, which were believed to have significant petroleum and gas reserves). In 2004 both states agreed to refer the issue to the International Court of Justice (ICJ, see p. 26). In February 2009 the ICJ finally issued a ruling awarding some 79% of the maritime area under dispute to Romania.

An association agreement with the European Community (now EU) was signed in February 1993; in June 1995 Romania formally applied for full membership of the EU. In October 1993 Romania was admitted to the Council of Europe. In December 1999 Romania was one of six countries invited to begin negotiations on possible entry to the EU, and formal accession talks commenced in February 2000. In December the EU decided to impose conditions on Romania before granting its citizens the right to visa-free travel in Europe, partly in response to Romania's failure to combat illegal immigration. In December 2004 Romania concluded accession negotiations. In April 2005 members of the European Parliament voted to approve 2007 as the anticipated accession date for Romania. Formal accession agreements were signed by both Bulgaria and Romania on 25 April 2005. In May both chambers of the legislature unanimously ratified the EU Treaty of Accession.

In May 2006 the European Commission announced that a final decision on Romania's scheduled date of accession to the EU was to be postponed until October, and emphasized the need to implement further reform measures. In a report issued at the end of September, the Commission confirmed that Romania was sufficiently prepared to meet the accession criteria by 1 January 2007, but also identified issues requiring further attention; the Co-operation and Verification Mechanism (CVM) was to be established to further progress in the areas of judicial reform and measures against corruption. Romania's accession to the EU on 1 January 2007 was welcomed with mass celebrations in Bucharest. However, owing to restrictions on Romanian labour Romanians were unable to work in the majority of EU countries without an additional work permit (with the exception of Italy and the Czech Republic). Nine EU countries were to retain the restrictions until the beginning of 2014.

In January 2011 the admission of Romania (and Bulgaria) to the EU's Schengen area (which provides for free movement between EU member states and the strengthening of border controls with non-members), hitherto anticipated to take place in March, was postponed, owing to concern from some EU countries, particularly France and Germany, about the readiness of the two countries. In June the European Parliament voted in support of the admission of Romania and Bulgaria to the Schengen area. However, at a meeting of EU ministers of internal affairs in Brussels, Belgium, in September, Finland and the Netherlands vetoed membership of the area for the two states, owing to continuing concerns over issues including corruption and organized crime. In July an attempt by the Government to impeach the President (see Domestic Political Affairs) prompted the EU to express concern over the rule of law. In September a meeting of EU ministers responsible for internal affairs, which had been scheduled to vote on Romania's admission to the Schengen area, was postponed, owing to objections from the Netherlands and other member states. A January 2013 report presented by the European Commission, which had suspended the release of development funds late the previous year owing to misappropriation concerns, criticized the lack of independence of the judiciary and restrictions placed on anti-corruption prosecutors. (Some development funding was resumed in February.)

Other external relations

In early 1997 Romania appealed directly to member countries of the North Atlantic Treaty Organization (NATO, see p. 380) to support its candidacy for admittance to the Alliance. Following the large-scale suicide attacks against the USA on 11 September 2001, attributed by the USA to the Saudi-born Islamist fundamentalist Osama bin Laden, Romania immediately pledged full co-operation with US anti-terrorism efforts, made available basing facilities in the port city of Constanța, and offered the USA the use of its air bases. The Romanian intelligence services were restructured in January 2002, and Romania secured an invitation to join NATO at a summit meeting held in Prague, Czech Republic, in November, after which US President George W. Bush visited the country. Romania supported US-led military action in Iraq in early 2003, opening its airspace and offering other resources to the coalition. Romania was officially admitted to NATO on 29 March 2004, together with six other countries. In December 2005 the US Secretary of State signed an agreement with the Romanian Minister of Foreign Affairs, granting US troops access to military bases under the command of the Romanian army. Romania hosted a NATO summit meeting in Bucharest on 2–4 April 2008. In January 2010 the Romanian Supreme Defence Council decided to reinforce the 1,020-member Romanian contingent deployed in Afghanistan by a further 600 troops. In the following month the Council approved the deployment in Romania of elements of a proposed US missile defence system (prompting criticism from the Russian Government); negotiations were to be conducted on a detailed plan for the establishment of interceptors on Romanian territory, subject to the approval of Parlamentul. In September 2011 the Romanian President and Prime Minister met US President Barack Obama and US Secretary of State Hillary Clinton in Washington, DC, USA, to sign an agreement for the deployment of the anti-missile interceptors by 2015. In March 2013 the Romanian Government expressed concern at an announcement by the US Administration that the planned establishment of long-range anti-missile interceptors in Romania (and Poland) had been abandoned in favour of additional installations in Alaska, but insisted that it had received assurances that the development of defence sites in the country was to proceed as scheduled.

CONSTITUTION AND GOVERNMENT

Under the Constitution of 1991 (and as subsequently modified, most substantially in 2003), legislative power is vested in the bicameral Parlamentul (Parliament), comprising the Camera Deputaţilor (Chamber of Deputies, lower house) and Senatul (the Senate, upper house). Parlamentul is elected by universal adult suffrage for a term of four years. Executive power is vested in the President of the Republic, who may serve a maximum of two five-year terms and who is directly elected by universal adult suffrage. The President appoints the Prime Minister, who in turn appoints the Council of Ministers. Judicial power is exercised by the High Court of Cassation and Justice, as well as county and local courts.

For administrative purposes, Romania comprises 41 administrative divisions (counties) and the municipality of Bucharest.

REGIONAL AND INTERNATIONAL CO-OPERATION

Romania is a member of the European Bank for Reconstruction and Development (EBRD, see p. 276), of the Council of Europe (see p. 260) and of the Organization of the Black Sea Economic Cooperation (see p. 411). In 2007 Romania acceded to the European Union (see p. 281).

Romania became a member of the UN in 1955 and, as a contracting party to the General Agreement on Tariffs and Trade, joined the World Trade Organization (see p. 444) on its establishment in 1995. In 2004 Romania joined the North Atlantic Treaty Organization (see p. 380).

ECONOMIC AFFAIRS

In 2011, according to the World Bank, Romania's gross national income (GNI), measured at average 2009–11 prices, totalled US $169,192m., equivalent to $7,910 per head (or $15,140 per head on an international purchasing-power parity basis). During 2002–11, it was estimated, the population decreased at an average annual rate of 0.2%, while gross domestic product (GDP) per head increased, in real terms, at an average annual rate of 3.8%. Overall GDP increased, in real terms, by an average of 3.8% annually during 2002–11; real GDP declined by 0.4% in 2011.

Agriculture (including hunting, forestry and fishing) contributed 6.0% of GDP in 2012 and the sector employed 28.6% of the employed labour force in 2011. The principal crops are maize, wheat, potatoes, sunflower seeds, barley and grapes. Wine production plays a significant role. Forestry, the cropping of reeds (used as a raw material in the paper and cellulose industry) and the breeding of fish are also important. By 1999, according to the IMF, some 97.2% of agricultural land was privately owned. During 2002–11, according to the World Bank, agricultural GDP increased, in real terms, by an average of 6.3% per year; real agricultural GDP increased by 2.0% in 2011.

Industry (including mining, manufacturing, construction, power and water) accounted for 42.3% of GDP in 2012 and employed 28.8% of the working population in 2011. According to the World Bank, industrial GDP increased, in real terms, by an average of 5.4% annually in 2002–11; real industrial GDP increased by 4.0% in 2011.

The mining sector employed 0.9% of the employed labour force in 2011. Lignite (brown coal), hard coal, salt, iron ore, bauxite,

copper, lead and zinc are mined. Onshore production of crude petroleum began to increase in the early 1990s. At the end of 2010 Romania had proven reserves of 480m. barrels of petroleum, remaining the largest producer in central and eastern Europe, despite a dramatic decline in production. IMF figures indicated that mining output declined by 0.3% in 2005.

Manufacturing accounted for 21.1% of GDP in 2011, according to the World Bank, and engaged 18.3% of the employed labour force in 2011. The sector is based mainly on the metallurgical, mechanical engineering, chemical and timber-processing industries. However, many industries (particularly iron and steel) have been hampered by shortages of electricity and raw materials. According to the World Bank, manufacturing GDP increased, in real terms, by an average of 5.5% annually in 2005–09. Real sectoral GDP increased by some 5.0% in 2009.

In 2012 construction accounted for 9.8% of GDP, and the sector employed 7.5% of the working population in 2011.

According to the World Bank, in 2009 some 37.7% of gross electricity production was derived from coal, 26.9% from hydroelectric power, 13.2% from natural gas and 20.4% from nuclear power. The initial unit of Romania's first nuclear power station, at Cernavoda, became operational in December 1996; the second (700 MW) unit entered into operation in 2008. A further two units at the site were expected to commence operations by around 2016. A natural gas pipeline to connect the country with Hungary, and ultimately with a 'corridor' between Austria and Turkey (the Nabucco project), was under construction. In April 2008 Romania signed an agreement with Croatia and Serbia on a project that envisaged the construction of a pipeline linking the Romanian port city of Constanţa with Trieste, Italy, via Croatia, Serbia and Slovenia. According to official data, 36.1% of energy resources were imported in 2005. In that year mineral fuels accounted for 14.0% of total imports. In 2010 mineral fuels comprised 10.0% of total imports.

According to official figures, the services sector contributed 51.6% of GDP in 2012, and engaged 42.6% of the labour force in 2011. The GDP of the services sector increased, in real terms, by an average of 5.7% per year in 2002–11; the real GDP of the sector increased by 2.1% in 2011.

In 2011 Romania recorded a visible merchandise trade deficit of US $12,550m., and there was a deficit of $8,344m. on the current account of the balance of payments. In 2011 the principal source of imports was Germany, which provided 17.1% of the total. Other major suppliers were Italy, Hungary and France. Germany was also the main market for exports in that year (accounting for 18.6% of the total); other important purchasers were Italy, France, Turkey and Hungary. In 2010 the principal imports were machinery and transport equipment, basic manufactures, chemical products, mineral fuels and lubricants, miscellaneous manufactured articles and food and live animals. The major exports in that year were machinery and transport equipment, basic manufactures, miscellaneous manufactured articles, crude materials, chemical products, and mineral fuels.

In 2011 the overall budget deficit was estimated at 26,400.7m. new lei. Romania's general government gross debt was 163,023m. new lei in 2010, equivalent to 31.2% of GDP. Romania's total external debt in 2010 was US $121,505m., of which $20,557m. was public and publicly guaranteed debt. In that year the cost of servicing long-term public and publicly guaranteed debt and repayments to the IMF was equivalent to 31.2% of the value of exports of goods, services and income (excluding workers' remittances). The annual rate of inflation averaged 8.0% in 2002–12; the rate of inflation was 3.3% in 2012. In 2011 some 7.4% of the labour force were unemployed.

Romania's progress towards the development of a market economy proved slower than that of many other post-communist states of central and eastern Europe. None the less, the Romanian economy demonstrated considerable growth prior to European Union (EU, see p. 281) accession on 1 January 2007. However, after the onset of the global economic crisis, in March 2009 multilateral financial assistance amounting to €19,900m. was announced for Romania to support an IMF-supervised programme of reforms. Austerity measures introduced to meet IMF demands included a 25% reduction in public-sector wages and a 5% increase in value-added tax (VAT), to 24%. In December 2010 reforms to the pension system were adopted, in fulfilment of the requirements of international institutions. By 2012 the Government had succeeded in restraining the budget deficit to a projected 2.1% of GDP. However, GDP growth was adversely affected by the continued debt crisis in the eurozone, which resulted in reduced export revenue. In mid-2012 efforts by the centre-left Government of Victor Ponta to remove President Traian Băsescu from office resulted in a political crisis, with a dramatic decline in the value of the currency. Legislative elections in December produced a renewed parliamentary mandate for the Government headed by Ponta, who stated his intention to continue austerity reforms and to secure a further credit programme with the IMF in 2013. (Despite some political stabilization after the elections, tensions between the Government and President Băsescu remained.) Ponta's planned fiscal adjustment measures included a reduction in VAT to 19% and increases in public-sector wages to pre-crisis levels, as well as improvements to revenue collection, as part of which several fiscal authorities were to be amalgamated into a single structure. The Government began to implement retrenchment measures in the health sector in early 2013. In February the European Commission resumed some development funding (which had been suspended in late 2012, owing to alleged misappropriations), and the Romanian Government declared the restoration of further development programmes to be a priority. In late April the legislature approved the composition of a new Financial Supervision Authority, a single supervisory body to monitor the country's stock exchange, insurance and private pensions markets, the establishment of which had been demanded by the IMF.

PUBLIC HOLIDAYS

2014: 1–2 January (New Year), 6 January (Epiphany), 20–21 April (Orthodox Easter), 1 May (Labour Day), 9 June (Pentecost Monday), 15 August (Dormition of the Virgin Mary), 1 December (National Day), 25–26 December (Christmas).

Statistical Survey

Source (unless otherwise indicated): Institutul National de Statistică (National Institute of Statistics), 050706 Bucharest, Bd. Libertăţii 16; tel. (21) 3124875; fax (21) 3124873; e-mail romstat@insse.ro; internet www.insse.ro/cms/rw/pages/index.ro.do.

Area and Population

AREA, POPULATION AND DENSITY

Area (sq km)	238,391*
Population (census results)	
18–27 March 2002	10,568,741
20 October 2011 (preliminary)	
Males	9,279,756
Females	9,764,011
Total	19,043,767
Density (per sq km) at 2011 census	79.9

* 92,043 sq miles.

POPULATION BY AGE AND SEX
(official estimates at 1 January 2012)

	Males	Females	Total
0–14	1,649,305	1,562,132	3,211,437
15–64	7,454,481	7,484,063	14,938,544
65 and over	1,290,616	1,915,252	3,205,868
Total	10,394,402	10,961,447	21,355,849

Note: Estimates not adjusted to take account of the 2011 census results.

POPULATION BY ETHNIC GROUP
(2011 census, preliminary)

	Number	% of total
Romanian	17,263,561	90.6
Hungarian	1,268,444	6.7
Roma (Gypsy)	247,058	1.3
Others and unknown	264,704	1.4
Total	19,043,767	100.0

ADMINISTRATIVE DIVISIONS
(population at 2011 census, preliminary)

	Area (sq km)	Population	Density (per sq km)	Administrative capital
Counties . . .				
Alba	6,242	327,258	52.4	Alba Iulia
Arad	7,754	409,072	52.8	Arad
Argeş	6,826	591,353	86.6	Piteşti
Bacău	6,621	583,590	88.1	Bacău
Bihor	7,544	549,752	72.9	Oradea
Bistriţa-Năsăud .	5,355	277,861	51.9	Bistriţa
Botoşani . . .	4,986	398,932	80.0	Botoşani
Brăila	4,766	304,925	64.0	Brăila
Braşov . . .	5,363	505,442	94.2	Braşov

—continued	Area (sq km)	Population	Density (per sq km)	Administrative capital
Buzău . . .	6,103	432,050	70.8	Buzău
Călăraşi . . .	5,088	285,107	56.0	Călăraşi
Caraş-Severin .	8,520	274,277	32.2	Reşiţa
Cluj	6,674	659,370	98.8	Cluj-Napoca
Constanţa . .	7,071	630,679	89.2	Constanţa
Covasna . . .	3,710	206,261	55.6	Sfântu Gheorghe
Dâmboviţa . .	4,054	501,996	123.8	Târgovişte
Dolj	7,414	618,335	83.4	Craiova
Galaţi . . .	4,466	507,402	113.6	Galaţi
Giurgiu . . .	3,526	265,493	75.3	Giurgiu
Gorj	5,602	334,231	59.7	Târgu Jiu
Harghita . . .	6,639	304,969	45.9	Miercurea-Ciuc
Hunedoara . .	7,063	396,253	56.1	Deva
Ialomiţa . . .	4,453	258,669	58.1	Slobozia
Iaşi	5,476	723,553	132.1	Iaşi
Ilfov*	1,593	364,241	228.7	Bucharest
Maramureş . .	6,304	461,290	73.2	Baia Mare
Mehedinţi . .	4,933	254,570	51.6	Drobeta-Turnu Severin
Mureş . . .	6,714	531,380	79.1	Târgu Mureş
Neamţ . . .	5,896	452,900	76.8	Piatra Neamţ
Olt	5,498	415,530	75.6	Slatina
Prahova . . .	4,716	735,883	156.0	Ploieşti
Sălaj	3,864	217,895	56.4	Zalău
Satu Mare . .	4,418	329,079	74.5	Satu Mare
Sibiu	5,432	375,992	69.2	Sibiu
Suceava . . .	8,553	614,451	71.8	Suceava
Teleorman . .	5,790	360,178	62.2	Alexandria
Timiş . . .	8,697	650,544	74.8	Timişoara
Tulcea . . .	8,499	201,468	23.7	Tulcea
Vâlcea . . .	5,765	355,320	61.6	Râmnicu Vâlcea
Vaslui . . .	5,318	375,151	66.8	Vaslui
Vrancea . . .	4,857	323,080	66.5	Focşani
Capital City				
Bucharest* . .	228	1,677,985	7,359.6	Bucharest
Total . . .	238,391	19,043,767	79.9	

* Although Bucharest is a separate administrative division, the city is also the capital of the surrounding Ilfov County. The area and population given for Ilfov County do not include data for Bucharest.

PRINCIPAL TOWNS
(population at 2011 census, preliminary)

București (Bucharest, the capital) . . .	1,677,985	Brăila	168,389
Cluj-Napoca . .	309,136	Pitești	148,264
Timișoara . .	304,467	Arad	147,922
Iași	263,410	Sibiu	137,026
Constanța . .	254,693	Bacău	133,460
Craiova . . .	243,765	Târgu Mureș . .	127,849
Galați . . .	231,204	Baia Mare . . .	114,925
Brașov . . .	227,961	Buzău	108,384
Ploiești . . .	197,522	Botoșani . . .	100,890
Oradea . . .	183,123	Satu Mare . . .	94,948

BIRTHS, MARRIAGES AND DEATHS

	Registered live births		Registered marriages		Registered deaths	
	Number	Rate (per 1,000)	Number	Rate (per 1,000)	Number	Rate (per 1,000)
2005 . .	221,020	10.2	141,832	6.6	262,101	12.1
2006 . .	219,483	10.2	146,637	6.8	258,094	12.0
2007 . .	214,728	10.0	189,240	8.8	251,965	11.7
2008 . .	221,900	10.3	149,439	6.9	253,202	11.8
2009 . .	222,388	10.4	134,275	6.2	257,213	12.0
2010 . .	212,199	9.9	115,778	5.4	259,723	12.1
2011* .	196,373	10.3	105,587	5.5	251,370	13.2
2012 . .	198,770	9.3	107,716	5.0	255,457	12.0

* Rates adjusted in accordance with revised population data arising from 2011 census; not strictly comparable with previous years.

Life expectancy (years at birth): 73.5 (males 69.8; females 77.3) in 2010 (Source: World Bank, World Development Indicators database).

ECONOMICALLY ACTIVE POPULATION
(labour force surveys, '000 persons aged 15 years and over)

	2009	2010	2011
Agriculture, forestry and fishing	2,689	2,780	2,612
Mining and quarrying	100	96	85
Manufacturing	1,751	1,646	1,672
Electricity, gas and water . . .	197	202	194
Construction	726	705	681
Wholesale and retail trade; repair of motor vehicles, motorcycles, and personal and household goods	1,157	1,134	1,165
Hotels and restaurants . . .	165	180	185
Transport, storage and communications	578	570	562
Financial intermediation . . .	122	132	145
Real estate, renting and business services	314	332	345
Public administration	490	471	466
Education	386	385	392
Health and social assistance . .	395	403	402
Other services	173	204	232
Total employed	9,243	9,240	9,138
Unemployed	681	725	730
Total labour force	9,924	9,965	9,868
Males	5,524	5,549	5,457
Females	4,400	4,416	4,411

Health and Welfare

KEY INDICATORS

Total fertility rate (children per woman, 2010)	1.4
Under-5 mortality rate (per 1,000 live births, 2010) . .	14
HIV/AIDS (% of persons aged 15–49, 2009)	0.1
Physicians (per 1,000 head, 2006)	1.9
Hospital beds (per 1,000 head, 2006)	6.5
Health expenditure (2009): US $ per head (PPP)	818
Health expenditure (2009): % of GDP	5.6
Health expenditure (2009): public (% of total)	79.0
Access to water (% of persons, 2006)	88
Access to sanitation (% of persons, 2008)	72
Total carbon dioxide emissions ('000 metric tons, 2008) . .	94,659.9
Carbon dioxide emissions per head (metric tons, 2008) . .	4.4
Human Development Index (2011): ranking	50
Human Development Index (2011): value	0.781

For sources and definitions, see explanatory note on p. vi.

Agriculture

PRINCIPAL CROPS
('000 metric tons)

	2009	2010	2011
Wheat	5,202.5	5,811.8	7,131.6
Barley	1,182.1	1,311.0	1,329.7
Maize	7,973.3	9,042.0	11,717.6
Rye	33.0	34.3	31.4
Oats	295.8	304.5	375.9
Potatoes	4,004.0	3,283.9	4,076.6
Sugar beet	816.8	837.9	660.5
Beans, dry	22.3	21.1	21.4
Peas, dry	29.9	39.5	55.0
Walnuts, with shell	38.3	34.4	35.1
Soybeans (Soya beans)	84.3	149.9	142.6
Sunflower seed	1,098.0	1,262.9	1,789.3
Rapeseed	569.6	943.0	739.0
Cabbages and other brassicas .	1,004.2	983.6	1,027.8
Lettuce and chicory	1.9	2.7	2.7
Tomatoes	755.6	768.5	911.0
Pumpkins, squash and gourds .	96.5	81.6	98.8
Cucumbers and gherkins . . .	176.5	172.1	195.9
Chillies and peppers, green . .	245.7	243.5	253.5
Onions, dry	378.1	369.1	394.3
Garlic	63.2	67.2	66.6
Beans, green	55.9	55.7	60.3
Peas, green	20.5	23.3	26.7
Watermelons	602.8	610.6	592.2
Cantaloupes and other melons .	50.0	52.3	53.3
Apples	517.5	552.9	620.4
Pears	66.1	60.4	66.9
Cherries	67.9	70.3	81.8
Apricots	32.5	23.8	33.7
Plums and sloes	533.7	624.9	573.6
Grapes	990.2	740.1	879.5
Tobacco, unmanufactured . . .	1.6	3.0	2.6

Aggregate production ('000 metric tons, may include official, semi-official or estimated data): Total cereals 14,873.0 in 2009, 16,712.9 in 2010; 20,842.2 in 2011; Total roots and tubers 4,004.0 in 2009, 3,283.9 in 2010, 4,076.6 in 2011; Total vegetables (incl. melons) 3,902.4 in 2009, 3,864.1 in 2010, 4,176.9; Total fruits (excl. melons) 2,320.6 in 2009, 2,173.9 in 2010, 2,373.2 in 2011.

Source: FAO.

LIVESTOCK
('000 head, year ending September)

	2009	2010	2011
Horses	820	764	611
Cattle	2,684	2,512	2,001
Pigs	6,174	5,793	5,428
Sheep	8,882	9,142	8,417
Goats	898	917	1,241
Chickens	84,373	83,843	80,845

Source: FAO.

LIVESTOCK PRODUCTS
('000 metric tons)

	2009	2010	2011
Cattle meat	155.2	154.5	142.3
Sheep meat	63.8	62.6	62.4
Goat meat	7.1	7.3	7.1
Pig meat	470.6	428.9	454.4
Horse meat*	9.5	9.5	9.5
Chicken meat	371.4	349.0	327.0
Cows' milk	5,208.7	4,410.8	4,526.6
Sheep's milk	600.4	651.3	632.9
Hen eggs	297.3	297.5	304.3
Other poultry eggs	13.3	12.4	12.1
Honey	19.9	22.2	24.1
Wool, greasy*	18.0	17.6	17.6

* FAO estimates.

Source: FAO.

Forestry

ROUNDWOOD REMOVALS
('000 cubic metres, excluding bark)

	2009	2010	2011
Sawlogs, veneer logs and logs for sleepers	7,222	8,213	7,765
Pulpwood	489	1,809	1,839
Other industrial wood	877	526	741
Fuel wood	3,969	2,564	4,014
Total	12,557	13,112	14,359

Source: FAO.

SAWNWOOD PRODUCTION
('000 cubic metres, including railway sleepers)

	2009	2010	2011
Coniferous (softwood)	2,087	2,713	2,900
Broadleaved (hardwood)	1,510	1,610	1,541
Total	3,597	4,323	4,442

Source: FAO.

Fishing

(metric tons, live weight)

	2008	2009	2010
Capture	5,410	4,020	2,688
Freshwater bream	988	705	339
Goldfish	1,642	1,246	851
Pontic shad	601	297	422
European sprat	234	92	29
Aquaculture	12,532*	13,131	8,981*
Common carp	3,977	4,142	2,888
Goldfish	1,462	1,623	934
Silver carp	2,959	2,971	2,016
Bighead carp	2,228	2,352	1,020
Rainbow trout	268	320	480*
Total catch	17,942*	17,151	11,669*

* FAO estimate.

Source: FAO.

Mining

('000 metric tons unless otherwise indicated)

	2008	2009	2010
Brown coal (incl. lignite)*	35,000	30,000	30,000
Crude petroleum	4,798	4,494	4,490*
Copper concentrates*†	2.0	1.0	5.0
Salt (unrefined)*	2,450	2,040	2,500
Natural gas (million cu metres)	11,400*	10,860	10,800

* Estimate(s).
† Figures refer to the metal content of concentrates.

Source: US Geological Survey.

Industry

SELECTED PRODUCTS
('000 metric tons unless otherwise indicated)

	2007	2008	2009
Refined sugar	395	464	443
Margarine	60.2	60.3	56.7
Wine ('000 hectolitres)	5,404	1,545	1,442
Beer ('000 hectolitres)	18,865	19,518	17,891
Tobacco products	38	48	48
Cotton fabrics—pure and mixed (million sq metres)	77	54	36
Chemical wood pulp	119	253	10
Paper and paperboard	558	422	250
Rubber tyres ('000)	16,000	16,430	19,049
Motor spirit (petrol)	3,799	3,654	3,311
Kerosene	8	18	12
White spirit	40	42	40
Distillate fuel oils	4,660	4,841	4,422
Residual fuel oils	1,186	1,168	883
Petroleum bitumen (asphalt)	160	240	162
Liquefied petroleum gas	754	594	750
Coke	1,647	1,138	341
Cement	10,000	11,000	7,800
Pig-iron	3,923	2,945	1,575
Crude steel	6,261	5,035	2,761
Aluminium—unwrought	274	277	212
Electric energy (million kWh)	61,673	64,956	58,016

Electric energy (million kWh): 60,979 in 2010; 62,216 in 2011.

Sources: mainly UN Industrial Commodity Statistics Database; US Geological Survey; FAO.

Finance

CURRENCY AND EXCHANGE RATES

Monetary Units
100 bani (singular: ban) = 1 Romanian leu (plural: lei).

Sterling, Dollar and Euro Equivalents (31 December 2012)
£1 sterling = 5.298 lei;
US $1 = 3.358 lei;
€1 = 4.430 lei;
100 Romanian lei = £18.87 = $29.78 = €22.57.

Average Exchange Rate (lei per US $)
2010   3.1779
2011   3.0486
2012   3.4682

Note: On 1 July 2005 the leu was revalued at a rate of 10,000 old lei = 1 new leu.

STATE BUDGET
(million new lei)

Revenue	2009	2010	2011
Tax revenue	48,152.9	56,304.7	69,527.7
Tax on income, profit and capital earnings	15,539.7	14,454.2	15,601.3
Tax on profit	10,617.1	10,090.9	10,289.2
Tax on income	18,546.3	17,852.3	18,846.6
Taxes and duties on goods and services	31,789.8	41,222.1	53,227.9
Value-added tax	34,322.5	39,246.0	47,917.4
Excise duties	14,272.1	16,212.4	17,805.9
Taxes on international trade	655.5	574.0	673.6
Non-tax revenue (incl. insurance)	7,342.5	8,520.0	7,530.6
Capital revenue	39.4	282.6	275.6
Total (incl. others)	56,434.8	66,546.5	79,688.0

Expenditure	2009	2010	2011
General public services	25,064.4	33,369.3	37,968.8
Public authorities	8,803.5	8,324.2	9,546.6
Defence, public order and national security	14,690.1	14,686.0	15,566.0
Defence	4,093.2	3,929.3	4,293.7
Public order and safety	10,596.9	10,756.7	11,272.3
Social and cultural expenditure	29,537.3	30,607.5	26,421.9
Education	5,176.3	4,315.2	4,207.6
Health	2,063.9	2,076.9	2,435.1
Recreational, cultural and religious affairs	1,912.5	1,948.0	1,971.8
Social security and welfare	20,384.6	22,267.4	17,807.4
Community services, public development and housing	3,394.1	2,769.0	3,485.3
Economic activities	17,165.8	21,196.0	22,646.7
Agriculture and forestry	6,175.2	7,590.6	7,021.2
Industry	379.1	363.3	349.1
Transport and communications	9,583.9	9,954.1	12,366.2
Fuel and energy	1,357.5	1,291.8	820.8
Other economic activities	317.1	472.9	574.0
Total	89,851.7	102,627.8	106,088.7

INTERNATIONAL RESERVES
(US $ million at 31 December)

	2010	2011	2012
Gold (national valuation)	4,704	5,250	5,751
IMF special drawing rights	1,058	590	150
Foreign exchange	42,303	42,349	40,336
Total	48,065	48,189	46,237

Source: IMF, *International Financial Statistics.*

MONEY SUPPLY
('000 million new lei at 31 December)

	2009	2010	2011
Currency outside depository corporations	23.97	26.79	30.61
Transferable deposits	55.40	54.80	55.23
Other deposits	108.65	117.98	126.22
Securities other than shares	1.80	3.18	3.81
Broad money	189.81	202.75	215.87

Source: IMF, *International Financial Statistics.*

COST OF LIVING
(Consumer Price Index; base: 2000 = 100)

	2010	2011	2012
Food	266.2	282.2	287.5
All items (incl. others)	312.7	330.8	341.8

Source: ILO.

NATIONAL ACCOUNTS
(million new lei at current prices)

Expenditure on the Gross Domestic Product

	2010	2011	2012
Total final consumption	419,801.2	436,485.0	459,012.1
Changes in inventories	4,476.8	5,351.2	1,852.9
Gross fixed capital formation	129,421.8	144,558.2	156,927.6
Total domestic expenditure	553,699.8	586,394.4	617,792.6
Exports of goods and services	185,499.7	222,873.0	234,974.9
Less Imports of goods and services	215,506.2	252,559.0	265,268.1
GDP in purchasers' values	523,693.3	556,708.4	587,499.4

Gross Domestic Product by Economic Activity

	2010	2011	2012
Agriculture, hunting, forestry and fishing	29,874.2	36,438.7	30,897.7
Construction	47,762.3	47,563.3	50,448.9
Other industry*	148,553.1	160,928.0	167,081.0
Trade; hotels and restaurants; transport, storage and communications	87,552.2	80,681.6	90,710.9
Financial intermediation; real estate transactions, renting and business activities	82,648.7	92,219.8	98,268.1
Other services	70,006.5	69,495.4	76,396.2
Gross value added in basic prices	466,397.0	487,326.8	513,802.8
Taxes on products	59,475.3	70,208.9	74,790.7
Less Subsidies on products	2,179.0	827.3	1,094.1
GDP in market prices	523,693.3	556,708.4	587,499.4

*Comprising mining and quarrying, manufacturing, electricity, gas and water.

BALANCE OF PAYMENTS
(US $ million)

	2009	2010	2011
Exports of goods	33,707	43,367	55,808
Imports of goods	−45,745	−55,252	−68,358
Balance on goods	−12,038	−11,885	−12,550
Exports of services	11,789	10,362	12,086
Imports of services	−9,779	−7,966	−9,435
Balance on goods and services	−10,028	−9,489	−9,899
Primary income received	1,654	1,222	1,769
Primary income paid	−4,289	−3,748	−4,860
Balance on goods, services and primary income	−12,663	−12,015	−12,990
Secondary income received	9,278	7,951	7,938
Secondary income paid	−3,570	−3,194	−3,292
Current balance	−6,955	−7,258	−8,344
Capital account (net)	928	336	989
Direct investment assets	8	−241	—
Direct investment liabilities	4,926	3,204	2,557
Portfolio investment assets	−196	−512	−56
Portfolio investment liabilities	959	1,779	2,489
Financial derivatives and employee stock options (net)	−61	29	−99
Other investment assets	−2,916	299	910
Other investment liabilities	−1,294	1,532	883
Net errors and omissions	−1,769	−141	615
Reserves and related items	−6,369	−973	−56

Source: IMF, *International Financial Statistics.*

External Trade

PRINCIPAL COMMODITIES
(distribution by SITC, US $ million)

Imports c.i.f.	2008	2009	2010
Food and live animals . . .	4,746.9	4,113.0	3,857.9
Crude materials (inedible) except fuels	2,237.5	1,223.9	1,840.6
Mineral fuels, lubricants, etc. .	10,460.6	5,059.2	6,216.1
Petroleum, petroleum products, etc.	7,374.4	4,013.2	4,826.9
Gas, natural and manufactured .	2,048.4	722.4	903.9
Chemicals and related products	8,798.0	7,437.2	7,994.6
Medicinal and pharmaceutical products	2,649.4	2,649.7	2,815.7
Basic manufactures	17,768.4	11,326.6	13,124.0
Textiles and textile articles . .	3,524.1	2,634.4	2,808.3
Iron and steel	4,650.0	2,089.3	2,848.9
Manufactures of metals . . .	3,179.2	2,201.3	2,470.3
Machinery and transport equipment	29,147.8	17,850.6	21,349.3
Machinery specialized for particular industries . . .	2,928.8	1,629.0	1,577.9
General industrial machinery and parts	4,058.9	2,587.1	2,946.9
Telecommunications, sound-recording and -reproducing equipment	3,132.1	2,951.8	3,757.7
Electric machinery, apparatus, etc.	5,724.9	4,422.7	5,745.5
Road vehicles	9,323.5	3,335.5	3,922.1
Miscellaneous manufactured articles	7,055.6	4,978.9	5,264.7
Total (incl. others)	82,965.0	54,256.3	62,006.6

Exports f.o.b.	2008	2009	2010
Crude materials (inedible) except fuels	2,783.2	2,236.0	3,155.8
Cork and wood	653.2	632.1	827.7
Mineral fuels, lubricants, etc. .	4,535.0	2,394.3	2,619.0
Petroleum, petroleum products, etc.	3,971.3	2,046.7	2,234.6
Chemicals and related products	2,996.4	2,029.0	2,829.9
Basic manufactures	9,488.2	6,146.5	8,344.3
Iron and steel	3,603.5	1,591.8	2,569.5
Non-ferrous metals	1,013.9	497.9	697.2
Machinery and transport equipment	17,539.7	17,308.6	20,715.9
Telecommunications, sound-recording and -reproducing equipment	1,098.8	2,399.2	3,574.3
Electrical machinery, apparatus, etc.	5,366.7	4,469.0	5,435.1
Road vehicles	4,081.6	4,910.6	6,099.1
Miscellaneous manufactured articles	8,890.6	7,114.3	7,574.1
Furniture and parts . . .	1,612.1	1,394.0	1,520.4
Clothing and accessories (excl. footwear)	4,090.7	3,041.6	3,020.3
Footwear	1,749.2	1,359.8	1,475.8
Total (incl. others)	49,538.9	40,620.9	49,413.4

Source: UN, *International Trade Statistics Yearbook*.

2011 (US $ million): Total imports 76,535.6; Total exports 63,017.9.

PRINCIPAL TRADING PARTNERS
(US $ million)*

Imports c.i.f.	2008	2009	2010
Austria	4,045.8	2,581.5	2,539.2
Belgium	1,649.0	1,129.3	1,312.6
Bulgaria	1,433.9	1,313.4	1,900.1
China, People's Republic . .	3,505.1	2,646.1	3,381.5
Czech Republic	2,076.2	1,285.5	1,475.3
France (incl. Monaco) . . .	4,738.3	3,339.6	3,674.4
Germany	13,573.4	9,411.0	10,361.4
Greece	1,186.8	820.8	826.6
Hungary	6,131.8	4,548.2	5,382.7
India	608.9	560.1	689.4
Italy	9,438.7	6,382.5	7,171.3
Kazakhstan	3,800.9	1,910.5	1,799.7
Korea, Republic	765.3	478.2	536.6
Netherlands	3,091.6	2,087.9	2,181.3
Poland	2,843.2	1,934.7	2,318.4
Russia	4,950.3	2,094.6	2,701.3
Slovakia	1,232.7	752.4	959.1
Spain	1,622.7	1,044.8	1,303.4
Turkey	4,081.0	2,024.8	2,280.1
Ukraine	771.5	325.9	720.0
United Kingdom	1,616.3	1,202.8	1,420.3
USA	1,201.4	690.3	750.4
Total (incl. others)	82,965.0	54,256.3	62,006.6

Exports f.o.b.	2008	2009	2010
Austria	1,123.2	958.4	1,140.7
Belgium	812.2	725.7	963.3
Bulgaria	2,062.6	1,534.5	1,771.0
Czech Republic	775.1	671.3	758.8
France (incl. Monaco) . . .	3,656.4	3,338.4	4,115.4
Germany	8,176.0	7,641.9	8,928.7
Greece	898.9	768.9	744.0
Hungary	2,530.6	1,765.5	2,364.3
Italy	7,658.8	6,237.5	6,838.7
Moldova	824.4	520.9	611.9
Netherlands	1,430.4	1,329.8	1,363.7
Norway	461.8	558.5	413.8
Poland	986.7	901.5	1,302.0
Russia	897.7	716.3	1,096.7
Serbia	700.6	576.9	713.7
Slovakia	653.8	433.1	612.5
Spain	1,144.1	1,224.7	1,498.3
Turkey	3,276.0	2,008.7	3,391.3
Ukraine	1,220.2	487.2	706.7
United Arab Emirates . . .	462.3	241.7	302.3
United Kingdom	1,628.2	1,364.0	1,788.4
USA	838.5	475.7	734.0
Total (incl. others)	49,538.9	40,620.9	49,413.4

* Imports by country of production; exports by country of last consignment.

Source: UN, *International Trade Statistics Yearbook*.

2011 (US $ million): *Imports:* Austria 3,059.5; Belgium 1,581.8; Bulgaria 2,203.0; China, People's Republic 3,524.9; Czech Republic 1,877.0; France 4,420.4; Germany 13,095.5; Greece 834.7; Hungary 6,655.9; Italy 8,716.4; Kazakhstan 3,187.0; Netherlands 2,446.5; Poland 3,026.0; Russia 2,926.9; Spain 1,758.9; Turkey 2,646.7; United Kingdom 1,787.9; Total (incl. others) 76,535.6. *Exports:* Austria 1,389.6; Belgium 1,255.1; Bulgaria 2,276.4; France 4,699.1; Germany 11,735.2; Hungary 3,573.0; Italy 8,078.5; Netherlands 1,948.7; Poland 1,497.2; Russia 1,416.8; Spain 1,531.1; Turkey 3,870.3; Ukraine 1,176.0; United Kingdom 2,016.4; Total (incl. others) 63,017.9.

Transport

RAILWAYS
(traffic)

	2009	2010	2011*
Passenger journeys (million) . .	70	64	61
Passenger-km (million) . . .	6,128	5,437	5,073
Freight transported (million metric tons)	51	53	61
Freight ton-km (million) . . .	11,000	12,000	15,000

* Provisional.

ROAD TRAFFIC
('000 motor vehicles in use at 31 December)

	2009	2010	2011*
Passenger cars	4,245	4,320	4,335
Buses and coaches	41	41	41
Lorries and vans	662	667	696
Motorcycles and mopeds . .	80	85	90

* Provisional.

INLAND WATERWAYS
(traffic)

	2009	2010	2011*
Passenger journeys ('000) . .	500	500	500
Passenger-km (million) . . .	20	15	18
Freight transported (million metric tons)	25	32	29
Freight ton-km ('000 million) .	12	14	11

* Provisional.

SHIPPING

Flag Registered Fleet
(at 31 December)

	2010	2011	2012
Number of vessels	162	160	161
Total displacement ('000 grt) . .	261.8	222.1	220.4

Source: Lloyd's List Intelligence (www.lloydslistintelligence.com).

International Sea-borne Freight Traffic
('000 metric tons)

	2009	2010	2011
Goods loaded	19,687	21,181	20,743
Goods unloaded	16,407	16,941	18,175

CIVIL AVIATION
(traffic)

	2008	2009	2010
Passengers carried ('000) . . .	9,000	9,000	10,000
Passenger-km (million) . . .	4,347	n.a.	n.a.
Freight transported ('000 metric tons)	27	25	26
Freight ton-km (million) . . .	8	n.a.	n.a.

2011: Passengers carried ('000) 11,000 (provisional); Freight transported ('000 metric tons) 27 (provisional).

Tourism

FOREIGN VISITOR ARRIVALS
('000)*

Country of origin	2008	2009	2010
Austria	210.1	180.6	177.5
Bulgaria	1,114.1	877.3	786.5
France	183.4	150.1	131.1
Germany	521.7	442.8	394.4
Hungary	1,950.4	1,836.3	1,734.8
Italy	433.2	374.7	330.9
Moldova	1,428.6	1,042.9	1,216.1
Poland	276.5	222.8	237.9
Serbia and Montenegro . . .	183.8	170.0	243.8
Slovakia	148.4	114.0	97.7
Turkey	302.5	257.5	264.9
Ukraine	729.8	723.8	672.1
USA	137.3	119.1	116.9
Total (incl. others)	8,862.1	7,575.3	7,498.3

* Figures refer to arrivals at frontiers of visitors from abroad, including same-day visitors (excursionists).

Tourism receipts (US $ million, excl. passenger transport): 1,234 in 2009; 1,140 in 2010; 1,417 in 2011.

Source: World Tourism Organization.

Communications Media

	2009	2010	2011
Telephones ('000 main lines in use)	4,730	4,500	4,680
Mobile cellular telephones ('000 subscribers)	25,380	24,640	23,400
Internet subscribers ('000) . .	2,800	3,000	3,260
Broadband subscribers ('000) . .	2,790	2,980	3,260
Book production (incl. pamphlets):			
titles	8,563	11,143	5,164
copies ('000)	6,132	13,889	3,425
Daily newspapers	51	45	66
Other periodicals	2,657	3,046	3,978

Source: partly International Telecommunication Union.

Education

(2011/12 unless otherwise indicated)

	Institutions	Teachers	Pupils ('000)
Kindergartens	1,367	37,391	674
Primary and gymnasium schools	4,022	120,927	1,629
Secondary schools . . .	1,615	59,380	889
Vocational schools . . .	6	64	12
Specialized technical schools	86	1,360	80
Higher education . . .	108	28,365	540

Pupil-teacher ratio (primary education, UNESCO estimate): 16.1 in 2009/10 (Source: UNESCO Institute for Statistics).

Adult literacy rate (UNESCO estimates): 97.7% (males 98.3%; females 97.1%) in 2010 (Source: UNESCO Institute for Statistics).

Directory

The Government

HEAD OF STATE

President: Traian Băsescu.

COUNCIL OF MINISTERS
(May 2013)

A coalition Government comprising members of the Social Democratic Party (SDP), the National Liberal Party (NLP), the Conservative Party (CP) and the National Union for the Progress of Romania (UNPR).

Prime Minister: Victor Ponta (SDP).

Deputy Prime Minister and Minister of Regional Development and Public Administration: Liviu Dragnea (SDP).

Deputy Prime Minister and Minister of Public Finance: Daniel Chiţoiu (NLP).

Deputy Prime Minister: Gabriel Oprea (UNPR).

Minister of Agriculture and Rural Development: Daniel Constantin (CP).

Minister of Foreign Affairs: Titus Corlăţean (SDP).

Minister of Internal Affairs: Radu Stroe (NLP).

Minister of National Defence: Mircea Duşa (SDP).

Minister of Justice: Robert-Marius Cazanciuc (Independent).

Minister of the Environment and Climate Change: Rovana Plumb (SDP).

Minister of the Economy, Trade and the Business Environment: Varujan Vosganian (NLP).

Minister of Communications and the Information Society: Dan Nica (SDP).

Minister of Health: Eugen Gheorghe Nicolăescu (NLP).

Minister of National Education: Remus Pricopie (SDP).

Minister of Labour, the Family and Social Welfare: Mariana Câmpeanu (NLP).

Minister of European Affairs: Eugene Teodorovici (Independent).

Minister of Transport and Infrastructure: Relu Fenechiu (NLP).

Minister of Culture and National Heritage: Daniel Barbu (CP).

Minister of Youth and Sports: Nicolae Bănicioiu (SDP).

Minister-delegate, responsible for the Budget: Liviu Voinea (SDP).

Minister for Water Management, Forests and Fisheries: Lucia Varga (NLP).

Minister-delegate, responsible for Infrastructure Projects: Dan Sova (SDP).

Minister-delegate, responsible for Business Environment and Tourism: Maria Grapini (CP).

Minister-delegate, responsible for Energy: Constantin Nita.

Minister-delegate, responsible for Higher Education, Scientific Research and Technological Development: Mihnea Costoiu.

Minister for Relations with Parliament: Mihai Voicu (NLP).

Minister-delegate, responsible for the Diaspora: Cristian David (NLP).

Minister-delegate, responsible for Social Dialogue: Doina Adriana Pană (SDP).

MINISTRIES

Office of the President: 060116 Bucharest 5, Palatul Cotroceni, Str. Geniuliu 1–3; tel. (21) 4100581; fax (21) 4103858; e-mail procetatean@presidency.ro; internet www.presidency.ro.

Office of the Prime Minister: 011791 Bucharest 1, Piaţa Victoriei 1; tel. (21) 3143400; fax (21) 3139846; e-mail drp@gov.ro; internet www.guv.ro.

Ministry of Agriculture and Rural Development: 020921 Bucharest 3, Bd. Carol I 2–4, POB 37; tel. (21) 3072300; fax (21) 3078554; e-mail relatii.publice@madr.ro; internet www.madr.ro.

Ministry of Communications and the Information Society: 050706 Bucharest 5, Bd. Libertăţii 14; tel. (21) 4001190; fax (21) 3114131; e-mail cabinetministru@mcsi.ro; internet www.mcsi.ro.

Ministry of Culture and National Heritage: 030833 Bucharest 3, Bd Unirii 22; tel. (21) 2242510; fax (21) 2234951; e-mail cabinet .ministru@cultura.ro; internet www.cultura.ro.

Ministry of the Economy, Trade and the Business Environment: 010096 Bucharest 1, Calea Victoriei 152; tel. (21) 2025426; fax (21) 2025108; e-mail dezbateri_publice@minind.ro; internet www .minind.ro.

Ministry of the Environment and Climate Change: 040129 Bucharest 5, Bd. Libertăţii 12; tel. (21) 4089523; fax (21) 3124227; e-mail srp@mmediu.ro.

Ministry of European Affairs: 050741 Bucharest, Bd Aviatorilor 50A, Sector 1; tel. (21) 3085319; fax (374) 104500; e-mail contact@ maeur.ro; internet www.dae.gov.ro.

Ministry of Foreign Affairs: 011822 Bucharest, Al. Alexandru 31; tel. (21) 3192108; fax (21) 3196862; e-mail opinia_ta@mae.ro; internet www.mae.ro.

Ministry of Health: 010024 Bucharest 1, Str. Cristian Popişteanu 1–3; tel. (21) 3072500; fax (21) 3072671; e-mail dirrp@ms.ro; internet www.ms.ro.

Ministry of Internal Affairs: 010086 Bucharest 1, Piaţa Revoluţiei 1A; tel. (21) 3037080; fax (21) 3103072; e-mail petitii@mai.gov.ro; internet www.mai.gov.ro.

Ministry of Justice: 050741 Bucharest 5, Str. Apolodor 17; tel. (37) 2041999; fax (37) 2041226; e-mail relatiipublice@just.ro; internet www.just.ro.

Ministry of Labour, the Family and Social Welfare: 010026 Bucharest 1, Str. Demetru I. Dobrescu 2–4; tel. (21) 3136267; fax (21) 3158812; e-mail relatiicupublicul@mmuncii.ro; internet www .mmuncii.ro.

Ministry of National Defence: 050561 Bucharest 5, Str. Izvor 3–5; tel. (21) 3195660; fax (21) 3195864; e-mail secretariat_general@ mapn.ro; internet www.mapn.ro.

Ministry of National Education: 010168 Bucharest 1, Str. Gen. Berthelot 28–30; tel. (21) 4056200; fax (21) 3124719; e-mail public@ min.edu.ro; internet www.edu.ro.

Ministry of Public Finance: 050741 Bucharest 5, Str. Apolodor 17; tel. (21) 3199759; fax (21) 3122509; e-mail publicinfo@mfinante.gov .ro; internet www.mfinante.gov.ro.

Ministry of Regional Development and Public Administration: 050741 Bucharest 5, Str. Apolodor 17; tel. (37) 2111409; fax (37) 2111601; e-mail info@mdrt.ro; internet www.mdrt.ro.

Ministry of Transport and Infrastructure: 010873 Bucharest 1, Bd. Dinicu Golescu 38; tel. (21) 3196124; fax (21) 3138869; e-mail relpub@mt.ro; internet www.mt.ro.

Ministry of Youth and Sports: Bucharest.

President

Presidential Election, First Ballot, 22 November 2009

Candidates	Votes	%
Traian Băsescu (Democratic Liberal Party)	3,153,640	32.45
Mircea Dan Geoană (Social Democratic Party-Conservative Party alliance) . .	3,027,838	31.15
Crin Antonescu (National Liberal Party) .	1,945,831	20.02
Corneliu Vadim Tudor (Greater Romania Party)	540,380	5.56
Kelemen Hunor (Democratic Alliance of Hungarians in Romania)	372,764	3.84
Sorin Mircea Oprescu (Independent) . .	309,764	3.19
Gheorghe Becali (New Generation—Christian Democratic Party)	186,390	1.92
Others	182,233	1.88
Total	9,718,840	100.00

Second Ballot, 6 December 2009

Candidates	Votes	%
Traian Băsescu (Democratic Liberal Party)	5,275,808	50.33
Mircea Dan Geoană (Social Democratic Party-Conservative Party alliance) . .	5,205,760	49.67
Total	10,481,568	100.00

Legislature

PARLAMENTUL ROMÂNIEI
(The Romanian Parliament)

The bicameral Parlamentul României comprises the 334-member lower chamber, the Camera Deputaţilor (Chamber of Deputies), and the 137-member upper chamber, Senatul (the Senate). Members of both chambers are directly elected, for a term of four years.

Camera Deputaţilor
(Chamber of Deputies)

050563 Bucharest, Palatul Parlamentului, Str. Izvor 2–4, Sector 5; tel. (21) 3160300; fax (21) 4141417; e-mail secretar.general@cdep.ro; internet www.cdep.ro.

Chairman: VALERIU ZGONEA (SDP).

General Election, 9 December 2012

Parties	Votes	% of votes	Seats
Social Liberal Union*	4,344,288	58.63	273
Romanian Alliance of the Right†	1,223,189	16.51	56
People's Party—Dan Diaconescu	1,036,730	13.99	47
Democratic Alliance of Hungarians in Romania	380,656	5.14	18
Parties representing minority ethnic groups§	n.a.	n.a.	18
Others	424,763	5.75	—
Total	**7,409,626**	**100.00**	**412**

* Comprising the Centre Left Alliance of the Social Democratic Party and the National Union for the Progress of Romania, and the Centre Right Alliance of the National Liberal Party and the Conservative Party.
† Comprising the Democratic Liberal Party, the Civic Force and the Christian-Democratic National Peasants' Party.
§ One deputy was elected from each of the following parties: the Albanian League Association of Romania; the Armenian Union of Romania; the Bulgarian Union of the Banat-Romania; the Croat Union of Romania; the Cultural Union of Ruthenians of Romania; the Democratic Forum of Germans of Romania; the Democratic Turkish Union of Romania; the Democratic Union of Slovaks and Czechs of Romania; the Democratic Union of Turkic-Muslim Tatars of Romania; the Federation of Jewish Communities of Romania; the Greek Union of Romania; the Italian Association of Romania; the Macedonian Association of Romania; the Polish Union of Romania; the Pro-Europe Roma Party; the Rusyn-Lipovan Community of Romania; the Serb Union of Romania; and the Ukrainian Union of Romania.

Senatul
(The Senate)

050711 Bucharest 5, Calea 13 Septembrie 1–3; tel. (21) 4141111; fax (21) 4012721; e-mail infopub@senat.ro; internet www.senat.ro.

Chairman: GEORGE CRIN ANTONESCU (NLP).

General Election, 9 December 2012

Parties	Votes	% of votes	Seats
Social Liberal Union*	4,457,526	60.10	122
Romanian Alliance of the Right†	1,239,318	16.71	24
People's Party—Dan Diaconescu	1,086,822	14.65	21
Democratic Alliance of Hungarians in Romania	388,528	5.24	9
Greater Romania Party	109,142	1.47	—
Others	135,292	1.82	—
Total	**7,416,628**	**100.00**	**176**

* Comprising the Centre Left Alliance of the Social Democratic Party and the National Union for the Progress of Romania, and the Centre Right Alliance of the National Liberal Party and the Conservative Party.
† Comprising the Democratic Liberal Party, the Civic Force and the Christian-Democratic National Peasants' Party.

Election Commission

Central Electoral Office (Biroul Electoral Central): Bucharest 1, Str. Piaţa Presei Libere 1; tel. (21) 3140761; fax (21) 3140763; e-mail secretariat@becparlamentare2012.ro; internet www.becparlamentare2012.ro; Pres. ANA-MARIA PĂTRU.

Political Organizations

Christian-Democratic National Peasants' Party (CDNPP) (Partidul Naţional Ţărănesc Creştin Democrat): 020912 Bucharest, Str. Romulus 36, Sector 3; tel. and fax (21) 3235879; e-mail comunicare@pntcd.eu; internet www.pntcd.eu; f. 1989 by merger of centre-right Christian Democratic Party and traditional National Peasant Party, as revival of party originally founded in 1869 and banned in 1947; contested legislative elections in 2012 as member of the Romanian Alliance of the Right; absorbed the Union for the Reconstruction of Romania in March 2005; supports pluralist democracy and the restoration of peasant property; Pres. VICTOR CIORBEA.

Civic Force (Forţa Civică): Bucharest; f. 2004 as Christian Party; current name adopted in 2008; contested legislative elections in 2012 as member of the Romanian Alliance of the Right; liberal conservatism; Pres. MIHAI RĂZVAN UNGUREANU.

Conservative Party (CP) (Partidul Conservator—PC): 010093 Bucharest, Str. Muzeul Zambaccian 17, Sector 1; tel. (21) 4251100; fax (21) 2304776; e-mail secretariat@partidulconservator.ro; internet www.partidulconservator.ro; f. 1991 as the Humanist Party of Romania; contested legislative elections in 2012 as member of the Social Liberal Union; renamed in May 2005; absorbed the Romanian National Unity Party in Feb. 2006; Pres. DANIEL CONSTANTIN.

Democratic Alliance of Hungarians in Romania (DAHR) (Uniunea Democrată Maghiară din România/Romániai Magyar Demokrata Szövetség—UDMR/RMDSZ): 400489 Kolozsvár, Str. Majális 60; tel. and fax (264) 590758; e-mail office@rmdsz.ro; internet www.rmdsz.ro; f. 1990; supports the rights of ethnic Hungarians in Romania; Pres. KELEMEN HUNOR.

Democratic Liberal Party (DLP) (Partidul Democrat Liberal—PD-L): 011825 Bucharest, Al. Modrogan 1, Sector 1; tel. (21) 2303701; fax (21) 2302262; e-mail office@pd.ro; internet www.pdl.org.ro; f. 1990; fmrly Democratic Party—National Salvation Front, then Democratic Party; present name adopted 2008, following merger with Liberal Democratic Party; contested legislative elections in 2012 as member of the Romanian Alliance of the Right; Pres. VASILE BLAGA.

Greater Romania Party (GRP) (Partidul România Mare—PRM): 010296 Bucharest, Str. Vasile Lascăr 16; tel. and fax (21) 3149369; e-mail prm_central@yahoo.com; internet www.prm-central.ro; f. 1991; known as the Popular Greater Romania Party (under the chairmanship of Corneliu Ciontu) in March–June 2005; nationalist; splinter group formed under Ciontu in mid-2005 (People's Party), which subsequently merged with the New Generation—Christian Democratic Party; Chair. CORNELIU VADIM TUDOR.

National Liberal Party (NLP) (Partidul Naţional Liberal—PNL): 011866 Bucharest, Bd. Aviatorilor 86, Sector 1; tel. (21) 2310795; fax (21) 2310796; e-mail dre@pnl.ro; internet www.pnl.ro; f. 1990 as revival of party originally founded in 1869 and banned in 1947; merged with Liberal Party in 1993, and with Party of the Civic Alliance and Liberal Party of Romania in 1998, absorbed Alliance for Romania in 2002 and the Union of Rightist Forces in 2003; contested legislative elections in 2012 as member of the Social Liberal Union; supports the integration of Romania into the European Union and the North Atlantic Treaty Organization, advocates freedom of expression and religion, a market economy and the decentralization of state powers; Pres. GEORGE CRIN LAURENŢIU ANTONESCU; Sec.-Gen. EDUARD HELLVIG.

National Union for the Progress of Romania (Uniunea Naţională pentru Progresul Românie—UNPR): Bucharest; f. 2010; contested legislative elections in 2012 as member of the Social Liberal Union; Pres. MARIAN SÂRBU.

New Generation—Christian Democratic Party (Partidul Noua Generatie—Crestin Democrat—PNG): 030061 Bucharest 3, Str. Blănari 21–23; tel. (21) 3149360; fax (21) 3131203; e-mail secretariat@png.ro; internet www.png.ro; f. 2003; Chair. GHEORGHE BECALI.

People's Party—Dan Diaconescu (Partidul Poporului—Dan Diaconescu—PP—DD): Bucharest,; tel. (21) 3114199; e-mail mansimona@partidul.poporului.ro; internet www.partidul.poporului.ro; f. 2011; Pres. SIMONA MANN.

Romanian Ecologist Party (Partidul Ecologist Român): 010067 Bucharest 1, Calea Victoriei 91-93; tel. (21) 3168237; e-mail secretariat@per.ro; internet www.per.ro; f. 1990; Chair. DĂNUŢ POP.

Social Democratic Party (SDP) (Partidul Social Democrat—PSD): 011346 Bucharest 1, Şos. Kiseleff 10; tel. (21) 2222953; fax (21) 2223171; e-mail psd@psd.ro; internet www.psd.ro; f. 2001 by the merger of the Romanian Social Democratic Party and the Party of Social Democracy of Romania; contested legislative elections in 2008 as member of Social Liberal Union; Pres. VICTOR PONTA; Sec.-Gen. LIVIU DRAGNEA.

Diplomatic Representation

EMBASSIES IN ROMANIA

Albania: 712012 Bucharest, Str. Duiliu Zamfirescu 7, Sector 1; tel. (21) 2119829; fax (21) 2108039; e-mail embassy.bucharest@mfa.gov.al; Ambassador SAMI SHIBA.

Algeria: 010778 Bucharest, Str. Theodor Aman 4, Sector 1; tel. (21) 2124185; fax (31) 6208213; e-mail ambalgeria@ambasada-algeriei.ro; internet www.ambasada-algeriei.ro; Ambassador HAMRAOUI HABIB CHAWKI.

Argentina: 010031 Bucharest, Union International Centre, Str. Ion Campineanu 11, 3rd Floor, Rm 301; tel. (21) 3122626; fax (21) 3120116; e-mail eruma@mrecic.gov.ar; Ambassador CLAUDIO PÉREZ PALADINO.

Armenia: 014136 Bucharest, Str. Poiana 27, Sector 1; tel. (21) 2332452; fax (21) 2332725; e-mail armembro@cinor.ro; Ambassador HAMLET GASPARIAN.

Austria: 020461 Bucharest, Str. Dumbrava Roşie 7, Sector 2; tel. (21) 2015612; fax (21) 2100885; e-mail bukarest-ob@bmeia.gv.at; internet www.aussenministerium.at/bukarest; Ambassador MICHAEL SCHWARZINGER.

Azerbaijan: 014132 Bucharest 1, Str. Grigore Gafencu 10, Sector 1; tel. (21) 2332484; fax (21) 2332465; e-mail azsefroman@azembassy.ro; internet www.azembassy.ro; Ambassador ELDAR HASANOV.

Belarus: 011411 Bucharest, Str. Tuberozelor 6, Sector 1; tel. (21) 2231776; fax (21) 2231763; e-mail romania@mfa.gov.by; internet www.romania.mfa.gov.by; Chargé d'affaires a.i. SERGEI MOLUNOV.

Belgium: 020061 Bucharest, Bd. Dacia 58, Sector 2; tel. (21) 2102970; fax (21) 2102803; e-mail ambabuc@clicknet.ro; internet www.diplomatie.be/bucharest; Ambassador PHILIPPE BEKE.

Bosnia and Herzegovina: 011786 Bucharest 1, Str. Stockholm 12; tel. (21) 4092601; fax (21) 4092603; e-mail amb.bukurest@mvp.gov.ba; Ambassador DUSKO KOVAČEVIĆ.

Brazil: 011863 Bucharest, Bd. Aviatorilor 40, Sector 1; tel. (21) 2301130; fax (21) 2301599; e-mail ambassador.bucareste@itamaraty.gov; Ambassador RAYMUNDO SANTOS ROCHA MAGNO.

Bulgaria: 011835 Bucharest, Str. Rabat 5; tel. (21) 2302159; fax (21) 2307654; e-mail embassy.bucharest@mfa.bg; internet www.bgembassy-romania.org; Ambassador ALEKSANDAR FILIPOV.

Canada: 011411 Bucharest, Str. Tuberozelor 1–3, Sector 1; tel. (21) 3075000; fax (21) 3075010; e-mail bucst@international.gc.ca; internet www.canadainternational.gc.ca/romania-roumanie; Ambassador PHILIPPE BEAULNE.

Chile: 010732 Bucharest, Calea Griviței 24; tel. (21) 3127239; fax (21) 3127246; e-mail info@chile.ro; internet chileabroad.gov.cl/rumania; Ambassador MARÍA ELIANA CUEVAS BERNALES.

China, People's Republic: 014103 Bucharest, Şos. Nordului 2, Sector 1; tel. (21) 2328858; fax (21) 2330684; e-mail chinaemb_ro@mfa.gov.cn; internet www.chinaembassy.org.ro; Ambassador HUO YUZHEN.

Congo, Democratic Republic: 010517 Bucharest, Calea Victoriei nr 122, Sector 1; tel. and fax (21) 2105498; e-mail ambardcbuc@yahoo.fr; Chargé d'affaires a.i. PHOBA-KI-KUMBU.

Croatia: 024031 Bucharest, Str. Dr Burghelea 1, Sector 2; tel. (21) 3130457; fax (21) 3130384; e-mail croemb.bucharest@mvp.hr; internet ro.mfa.hr; Ambassador ANDREA GUSTOVIĆ ERCEGOVAC.

Cuba: 010516 Bucharest, Str. Nicolae Caramfil 73; tel. (21) 2118739; fax (21) 2118916; e-mail embacuba@embacuba.ro; Ambassador MARTA CARIDAD FAJARDO PALET.

Cyprus: 011406 Bucharest, Str. Petofi Sandor 2; tel. (21) 2230455; fax (21) 2230456; e-mail ambasada@ambacipru.ro; Ambassador KALLIOPI AVRAAM.

Czech Republic: 030045 Bucharest, Str. Ion Ghica 11, Sector 3; tel. (21) 3039230; fax (21) 3122539; e-mail bucharest@embassy.mzv.cz; internet www.mzv.cz/bucharest; Ambassador JIŘI ŠITLER.

Denmark: 024031 Bucharest, Str. Dr Burghelea 3, Sector 2; tel. (21) 3000800; fax (21) 3120358; e-mail buhamb@um.dk; internet www.rumaenien.um.dk; Ambassador MICHAEL STERNBERG.

Egypt: 010407 Bucharest 1, Bd. Dacia 67, Sector 1; tel. (21) 2110938; fax (21) 2100337; e-mail embassy.bucharest@mfa.gov.eg; Ambassador LAILA AHMED BAHAA ELDIN.

Finland: 011832 Bucharest, Str. Atena 2 bis; tel. (21) 2307504; fax (21) 2307505; e-mail sanomat.buk@formin.fi; internet www.finland.ro; Ambassador ULLA VÄISTÖ.

France: 010392 Bucharest, Str. Biserica Amzei 13–15, Sector 1; tel. (21) 3031000; fax (21) 3031090; e-mail chancellerie.bucarest-amba@diplomatie.gouv.fr; internet www.ambafrance-ro.org; Ambassador PHILIPPE GUSTIN.

Georgia: 011981 Bucharest 1, Str. Herăstrău 16, Sector 1; tel. (21) 2100602; fax (21) 2113999; e-mail romania.emb@mfa.gov.ge; internet www.romania.mfa.gov.ge; Ambassador ILIA GIORGADZE.

Germany: 011849 Bucharest, Str. Capt. Aviator Gh. Demetriade 6–8, Sector 1; tel. (21) 2029830; fax (21) 2029731; e-mail info@bukarest.diplo.de; internet www.bukarest.diplo.de; Ambassador ANDREAS VON METTENHEIM.

Greece: 021403 Bucharest, Bd. Pache Protopopescu 1–3, Sector 2; tel. (21) 2094170; fax (21) 2094175; e-mail gremb.buc@mfa.gr; internet www.mfa.gr/bucharest; Ambassador GEORGIOS POUKAMISSAS.

Holy See: 010187 Bucharest, Str. Pictor Stahi 5–7; tel. (21) 3123883; fax (21) 3120316; e-mail nuntius@clicknet.ro; Apostolic Nuncio Monsignor FRANCISCO-JAVIER LOZANO (Titular Archbishop of Penafiel).

Hungary: 020034 Bucharest, Str. Dimitrie Gerotă 63–65; tel. (21) 6204303; fax (21) 6204326; e-mail mission.buc@kum.hu; internet www.mfa.gov.hu/kulkepviselet/ro; Ambassador OSZKÁR LÁSZLÓ FÜZES.

India: 020078 Bucharest, Str. Mihai Eminescu 183, Sector 2; tel. (21) 2115451; fax (21) 2110614; e-mail office@embassyofindia.ro; internet www.embassyofindia.ro; Ambassador MANIMEKALAI MURUGESAN.

Indonesia: 010488 Bucharest 1, Str. Orlando 10, Sector 1; tel. (21) 3120742; fax (21) 3120214; e-mail indobuch@indonezia.ro; internet www.indonezia.ro; Ambassador MARIANNA SUTADI.

Iran: 010633 Bucharest, Bd. Lascăr Catargiu 39, Sector 1; tel. (21) 3120495; fax (21) 3120496; e-mail ambassador@iranembassy.ro; internet www.iranembassy.ro; Ambassador BAHADOR AMINIAN JAZI.

Iraq: 011834 Bucharest 1, Str. Venezuela 6–8, Sector 1; tel. (21) 2339008; fax (21) 2339007; e-mail iraqbuchrest@yahoo.com; Ambassador MOHAMMED SAED AL-SHAKARCHI.

Ireland: 011015 Bucharest 1, Str. Buzeşti 50–52, 3rd Floor; tel. (21) 3102131; fax (21) 3102181; e-mail bucharestembassy@dfa.ie; internet www.embassyofireland.ro; Ambassador OLIVER GROGAN.

Israel: 040231 Bucharest 4, Bd. Dimitrie Cantemir 1, tronson 2 & 3, B2, 5th Floor; tel. (21) 3028500; fax (21) 3028555; e-mail info@bucharest.mfa.gov.il; internet bucharest.mfa.gov.il; Ambassador DAN BEN-ELIEZER.

Italy: 010667 Bucharest, Str. Henri Coandă 7–9, Sector 1; tel. (21) 3052100; fax (21) 3120422; e-mail ambasciata.bucarest@esteri.it; internet www.ambbucarest.esteri.it; Ambassador MARIO COSPITO.

Japan: 011141 Bucharest 1, Şos. Nicolae Titulescu 4–8, Sector 1; tel. (21) 3191890; fax (21) 3191895; e-mail embassy@bu.mofa.go.jp; internet www.ro.emb-japan.go.jp; Ambassador KEIJI YAMAMOTO.

Jordan: 020461 Bucharest 2, Str. Dumbrava Roşie 1; tel. (21) 2104705; fax (21) 2100320; e-mail embassy@jordanembassy.ro; Ambassador MAEN MASADEH.

Kazakhstan: 14104 Bucharest, Şos. Nordului 60G, Sector 1; tel. (21) 2300865; fax (21) 2300866; e-mail bucharest@mfa.kz; internet www.kazembro.kz; Chargé d'affaires a.i. TALGAT KALIEV.

Korea, Democratic People's Republic: 014103 Bucharest, Şos. Nordului 6, Sector 1; tel. (21) 2321994; fax (21) 2321992; e-mail ambasadarpdc@yahoo.com; Ambassador KIM SON GYONG.

Korea, Republic: 012013 Bucharest, Bd. Mircea Eliade 14; tel. (21) 2307198; fax (21) 2307629; e-mail romania@mofat.go.kr; internet romania@mofat.go.kr; Ambassador IM HAN-TAEK.

Kuwait: 011751 Bucharest 1, Str. Louis Blanc 19A-B; tel. (21) 3154444; fax (21) 3159992; e-mail kuwaitstampa@tiscalinet.it; internet www.kuwaitembassy.ro; Ambassador FAHD HAJAR SHAOUF AL-MUTAIRI.

Lebanon: 011817 Bucharest 1, Str. Andrei Mureşanu 16, Sector 1; tel. (21) 2308175; fax (21) 2308179; e-mail ambasada.liban@gmail.com; Ambassador MUHAMMAD EL-DIB.

Lithuania: 011973 Bucharest 1, Bd. Primăverii 51/2, Sector 1; tel. (21) 3115997; fax (21) 3115919; e-mail amb.ro@urm.lt; internet ro.mfa.lt; Ambassador VLADIMIR JARMOLENKO.

Macedonia, former Yugoslav Republic: 020083 Bucharest, Str. Mihai Eminescu 144, Sector 2; tel. (21) 2100880; fax (21) 2117295; e-mail bucharest@mfa.gov.mk; internet www.missions.gov.mk/bucharest; Ambassador PANDE LAZAREVSKI.

Malaysia: 020521 Bucharest, Str. Drobeta 11, Sector 2; tel. (21) 2113801; fax (21) 2100270; e-mail mwbucrst@itcnet.ro; internet www.kln.gov.my/web/rou_bucharest; Ambassador Dato NIK MUSTAFA KAMAL BIN NIK AHMAD.

Mexico: 020082 Bucharest, Str. Mihai Eminescu 124C /13–14, Sector 2; tel. (21) 2104577; fax (21) 2104713; e-mail embamex@xnet.ro; internet www.embamex.ro; Ambassador MARÍA CRISTINA DE LA GARZA SANDOVAL.

Moldova: 712732 Bucharest 1, Al. Alexandru 40, Sector 1; tel. (21) 2300474; fax (21) 2307790; e-mail bucuresti@mfa.md; internet www.romania.mfa.gov.md; Ambassador IURIE RENIŢĂ.

Morocco: 010459 Bucharest 1, Str. Dionisie Lupu 78, Sector 1; tel. (21) 3174124; fax (21) 3174144; e-mail office@ambasadamaroc.ro; internet www.ambasadamaroc.ro; Ambassador FAOUZE AL-AACHABI.

Netherlands: 011832 Bucharest, Al. Alexandru 20; tel. (21) 2086030; fax (21) 2307620; e-mail bkr@minbuza.nl; internet www .netherlandsemb.ro; Ambassador JOHANNES HENDRIK MATTHEUS VAN BONZEL.

Nigeria: Str. Argentina 41, Sector 1; tel. (21) 3128685; fax (21) 3120622; e-mail nigerembinro@yahoo.com; Ambassador ABBA TIJANI.

Norway: 011832 Bucharest, Str. Atena 18; tel. (21) 3069800; fax (21) 3069890; e-mail emb.bucharest@mfa.no; internet www.norvegia.ro; Ambassador ØYSTEIN HOVDKINN.

Pakistan: 011352 Bucharest 1, Str. Barbu Delavrancea 22, Sector 1; tel. (21) 3187873; fax (21) 3187874; e-mail parepbucharest@live.com; internet www.mofa.gov.pk/romania; Ambassador RAB NAWAZ KHAN.

Peru: 020372 Bucharest, Bd. Lacul Tei 29/4, Sector 2; tel. (21) 2111816; fax (21) 2111818; e-mail embajadaperu@embajadaperu .ro; Ambassador JOSÉ ANTONIO ARROSPIDE DEL BUSTO.

Philippines: 050453 Bucharest 5, Str. Carol Davila 105–107, 5th Floor, Rm 10–11; tel. (21) 3198252; fax (21) 3198253; e-mail bucharestpe@rdsmail.ro; Chargé d'affaires a.i. MARIA PANGILIAN.

Poland: 011821 Bucharest 1, Al. Alexandru 23, Sector 1; tel. (21) 3082200; fax (21) 2307832; e-mail bukareszt.wpe@msz.gov.pl; internet www.bukareszt.polemb.net; Ambassador MAREK SZCZYGIEŁ.

Portugal: 011815 Bucharest 1, Str. Paris 55, POB 63-91; tel. (21) 2304136; fax (21) 2304117; e-mail secretariat@embportugal.ro; internet www.embportugal.ro; Chargé d'affaires a.i. RICARDO PRA-CANA.

Qatar: 011834 Bucharest, Str. Venezuela 10A, Sector 1; tel. (21) 2304741; fax (21) 2305446; e-mail qtr_embassy@b.astral.ro; internet www.qatarembassy.ro; Ambassador SAAD MOHAMED SAAD AL-KOBAISI.

Russia: 011341 Bucharest 1, Şos. Kiseleff 6, Sector 1; tel. (21) 2221652; fax (21) 2229450; e-mail ambasadarusiei@mail.ru; internet www.romania.mid.ru; Ambassador OLEG S. MALGINOV.

Saudi Arabia: 010501 Bucharest 1, Str. Polonă 6, Sector 1; tel. (21) 2109109; fax (21) 2107093; e-mail ksa_embassy@yahoo.com; Ambassador ABD AL-RAHMAN BIN IBRAHIM AL-RESI.

Serbia: 010573 Bucharest 1, Calea Dorobanţilor 34, Sector 1; tel. (21) 2119871; fax (21) 2100175; e-mail info@ambserbia.ro; internet www.bucharest.mfa.gov.rs; Ambassador ZORAN S. POPOVIĆ.

Slovakia: 020977 Bucharest 2, Str. Oţetari 3, Sector 2; tel. (21) 3006107; fax (21) 3006101; e-mail emb.bucharest@mzv.sk; internet www.mzv.sk/bukurest; Ambassador JÁN GÁBOR.

Slovenia: 011995 Bucharest, Str. Puşkin 10, Sector 1; tel. (21) 3002780; fax (21) 3150927; e-mail vbk@gov.si; internet www .bukaresta.veleposlanistvo.si; Ambassador JADRANKA STURM KOC-JAN.

South Africa: 010113 Bucharest, Str. Ştirbei Vodă 26–28, Sector 1; tel. (21) 3133725; fax (21) 3133795; e-mail sifubabucharest@yahoo .com; Ambassador PIETER ANDRIES SWANEPOEL.

Spain: 011822 Bucharest, Str. Al. Alexandru 43, Sector 1; tel. (21) 3181077; fax (21) 3181072; e-mail emb.bucarest@maec.es; internet www.maec.es/embajadas/bucarest; Ambassador ESTANISLAO DE GRANDES PASCUAL.

Sudan: 011941 Bucharest 1, Str. Pictor Ion Negulici 12-14, Sector 1; tel. (21) 2339181; fax (21) 2339188; e-mail sudanirom@yahoo.com; Ambassador YASIR ABDELSALAM AHMED.

Sweden: 011343 Bucharest, Şos. Kiseleff 43, Sector 1; tel. (21) 4067100; fax (21) 4067124; e-mail ambassaden.bukarest@ gov.se; internet www.swedenabroad.com/bukarest; Ambassador ANDERS BENGTCÉN.

Switzerland: 010626 Bucharest, Str. Grigore Alexandrescu 16–20, Sector 1; tel. (21) 2061600; fax (21) 2061620; e-mail buc.vertretung@ eda.admin.ch; internet www.eda.admin.ch/bucarest; Ambassador JEAN-HUBERT LEBET.

Syria: 010673 Bucharest, Bd. Lascăr Catargiu 50, Sector 1; tel. (21) 3192467; fax (21) 3129554; e-mail syrambro@yahoo.com; Ambassador WALID OTHMAN.

Thailand: 020953 Bucharest, Str. Vasile Conta 12, Sector 2; tel. (21) 3110078; fax (21) 3110044; e-mail thaibuh@speedmail.ro; internet www.thaiembassy.org/bucharest; Ambassador TASANAWADEE MIAN-CHAROEN.

Tunisia: 010517 Bucharest 1, Str. Clucerului 48/1; tel. (21) 2101197; fax (21) 2101114; e-mail at.bucarest@b.astral.ro; Ambassador MAHBOUBA CHEBBI.

Turkey: 010575 Bucharest, Calea Dorobanţilor 72, Sector 1; tel. (21) 2063700; fax (21) 2063737; e-mail embassy.bucharest@mfa.gov.tr; internet bucharest.emb.mfa.gov.tr; Ambassador ÖMÜR ŞÖLENDIL.

Turkmenistan: 012582 Bucharest, Str. Crinului 5, Sector 1; tel. (21) 3169066; fax (21) 3169046; e-mail tmembassy@clicknet.ro; Ambassador SHOHRAT JUMAYEV.

Ukraine: 010572 Bucharest, Bd. Aviatorilor 24, Sector 1; tel. (21) 2303660; fax (21) 2303661; e-mail emb_ro@mfa.gov.ua; internet www.ucraina.ro; Ambassador THEOPHILUS YOZYFOVYCH BAUER.

United Arab Emirates: 011825 Aleea Modrogan 4; tel. (21) 2317676; fax (21) 2315588; e-mail amb@uaeembassy.ro; Ambassador YACUB YUSUF AL-HOSANI.

United Kingdom: 010463 Bucharest, Str. Jules Michelet 24, Sector 1; tel. (21) 2017200; fax (21) 2017299; e-mail press@bucharest.mail .fco.gov.uk; internet ukinromania.fco.gov.uk; Ambassador MARTIN HARRIS.

USA: 015118 Bucharest, Str. Dr Liviu Librescu 4-6; tel. (21) 2003300; fax (21) 2003442; e-mail acsbucharest@state.gov; internet romania .usembassy.gov; Chargé d'affaires a.i. DUANE C. BUTCHER.

Uruguay: 011972 Bucharest, Str. Primaverii 19-21, Sector 1; tel. and fax (21) 3138129; e-mail ururumania@embadeuruguay.ro; internet www.embadeuruguay.ro; Ambassador PEDRO MO AMARO.

Venezuela: 011396 Bucharest 1, Str. Pictor Mirea 18, Sector 1; tel. (21) 2225874; fax (21) 2225073; e-mail embavero@clicknet.ro; Chargé d'affaires a.i. MARGOT JULY MÁRQUEZ GARCÍA.

Viet Nam: 020011 Bucharest, Str. C. A. Rosetti 35; tel. (21) 3110334; fax (21) 3121626; e-mail vnemb.ro@mofa.gov.vn; internet www .vietnamembassy-romania.org; Ambassador TRAN XUAN THUY.

Judicial System

In preparation for its entry into the European Union on 1 January 2007, Romania implemented a programme of judicial reform, with a particular emphasis on guaranteeing the independence of the judiciary.

High Court of Cassation and Justice (Înalte Curte de Casaţie şi Justiţie a României): 020934 Bucharest 2, Str. Batişte 25; tel. (21) 3103908; fax (21) 3147618; e-mail relatii.publice@scj.ro; internet www.scj.ro; reorganized in June 2004; exercises control over the judicial activity of all courts and ensures the correct and uniform application of the law. The Court includes sections dealing with: civil and intellectual property law; criminal law; commercial law; and administrative and fiscal regulations; Pres. LIVIA DOINA STANCIU.

Constitutional Court of Romania (Curtea Constituţională a României): 050725 Bucharest, Palatul Parlamentului, Calea 13 Septembrie 2, Sector 5; tel. (21) 4142121; fax (21) 3124359; e-mail ccr@ccr.ro; internet www.ccr.ro; f. 1992; comprises nine members, who serve nine-year terms; Pres. AUGUSTIN ZEGREAN.

Office of the Prosecutor-General: 050706 Bucharest 5, Bd. Libertăţii 12; tel. (21) 3193833; e-mail sesizare@mpublic.ro; internet www.mpublic.ro; Prosecutor-General (vacant).

COUNTY COURTS AND LOCAL COURTS

The judicial organization of courts at the county and local levels was established by Law 92 of 4 August 1992. In each of the 41 counties, there is a county court and between three and six local courts. The county courts also form 15 circuits of appeal courts, where appeals against sentences passed by local courts are heard, which are generally considered courts of first instance. There is also a right of appeal from the appeal courts to the Supreme Court. In both county courts and local courts, the judges are professional magistrates.

Religion

In Romania there are 15 religious denominations and more than 400 religious associations recognized by the state. According to census figures, about 87% of the population belonged to the Romanian Orthodox Church in January 1992.

State Secretariat for Religious Affairs: 020962 Bucharest, Str. Nicolae Filipescu 40; tel. (21) 2118116; fax (21) 2109471; e-mail ssc@ mediasat.ro; f. 1990; State Sec. LAURENŢIU TĂNASE.

CHRISTIANITY

The Romanian Orthodox Church

The Romanian Orthodox Church is the major religious organization in Romania (with more than 19m. believers) and is organized as an autocephalous patriarchate, led by the Holy Synod and headed by a patriarch. The Patriarchate comprises five metropolitanates, 10 archdioceses and 13 dioceses.

Romanian Patriarchate
(Patriarhia Română)

040163 Bucharest, Al. Dealul Mitropoliei 25; tel. (21) 3374035; fax (21) 3370097; e-mail externe@patriarhia.ro; internet www .patriarhia.ro.

Patriarch, Metropolitan of Muntênia and Dobrogea and Archbishop of Bucharest: DANIEL (CIOBOTEA), 040161 Bucharest, Str. Patriarhiei 21; tel. (21) 3372776.

Metropolitan of Banat and Archbishop of Timişoara and Caransebeş: Dr NICOLAE (CORNEANU), 300021 jud. Timiş, Timişoara, Bd. Constantin Diaconovici Loga 7; tel. (256) 190960; internet www.mitropolia-banatului.home.ro.

Metropolitan of Cluj, Alba, Crişana and Maramureş and Archbishop of Vad, Feleac and Cluj: BARTOLOMEU (ANANIA), 400117 jud. Cluj, Cluj-Napoca, Piaţa Avram Iancu 18; tel. (264) 593944; fax (264) 595184; e-mail bartolomeu@arhiepiscopia-ort-cluj .org; internet www.arhiepiscopia-ort-cluj.org.

Metropolitan of Moldova and Bucovina and Archbishop of Iaşi: TEOFAN (SAVU), 700064 jud. Iaşi, Iaşi, Bd. Ştefan cel Mare şi Sfânt 16; tel. (232) 214771; fax (232) 212656; e-mail iecum@mail .dntis.ro; internet www.mmb.ro.

Metropolitan of Oltenia and Archbishop of Craiova: IRINEU (POPA), 200381 jud. Dolj, Craiova, Str. Mitropolit Firmilian 3; tel. (251) 415054; fax (251) 418369; e-mail secretariat@m-ol.ro; internet www.mitropoliaolteniei.ro.

Metropolitan of Transylvania and Archbishop of Sibiu: LAURENŢIU (STREZA), 550179 jud. Sibiu, Sibiu, Str. Mitropoliei 24; tel. (269) 412867.

The Roman Catholic Church

Catholics in Romania include adherents of the Armenian, Latin and Romanian (Byzantine) Rites.

Bishops' Conference: 031555 Bucharest, Str. Diligenţei 24, Sector 3; tel. and fax (31) 4361250; e-mail secretariat@episcopat.ro; internet www.catholica.ro; f. 1990; Pres. Cardinal LUCIAN MURESAN (Archbishop Major of Blaj).

Latin Rite

There are two archdioceses (including one directly subordinate to the Holy See) and four dioceses. At 31 December 2007 there were 1,106,783 adherents of the Latin Rite (about 5.1% of the total population).

Archbishop of Alba Iulia: Most Rev. GYÖRGY-MIKLÓS JAKUBÍNYI, 510010 jud. Alba, Alba Iulia, Str. Mihai Viteazul 21; tel. (258) 811689; fax (258) 811454; e-mail albapress@gyrke.uab.ro.

Archbishop of Bucharest: Most Rev. IOAN ROBU, 010164 Bucharest, Str. Gen. Berthelot 19; tel. (21) 3158349; fax (21) 3121208; e-mail secretariat@arcb.ro.

Romanian Rite

There is one archbishopric-major and four dioceses. At 31 December 2007 there were 718,341 adherents of the Romanian Rite (about 3.3% of the total population).

Archbishop-Major of Făgăraş and Alba Iulia: Most Rev. LUCIAN MUREŞAN, 515400 jud. Alba, Blaj, Str. Petru Pavel Aron 2; tel. (258) 712057; fax (258) 713602; e-mail mitropolia@bru.ro.

Armenian Rite

There are 803 adherents of the Armenian Rite in Romania at 31 December 2007, represented by an Ordinariate.

Reformed (Calvinist) Church

The Reformed (Calvinist) Church has some 700,000 members. There are two bishoprics.

Bishop of Oradea: 410210 jud. Bihor, Oradea, Str. J. Calvin 1; tel. (259) 431710; e-mail krekpht@partium.ro; internet www .kiralyhagomellek.ro; Bishop LÁSZLÓ TŐKÉS.

Transylvanian Reformed Church District: 400079 jud. Cluj, Cluj-Napoca, Str. I. C. Brătianu 51; tel. (264) 597472; fax (264) 595104; e-mail office@reformatus.ro; internet www.reformatus.ro; f. 1564; Bishop Rev. BÉLA KATÓ.

Other Protestant Churches

Evangelical Church of the Augsburg Confession in Romania: 550185 Sibiu, Str. Gen. Magheru; tel. and fax (269) 217864; e-mail bischofsamt@evlk.artelecom.net; internet www.evang.ro; 13,271 mems (2010); Bishop REINHART GUIB.

Evangelical-Lutheran Church in Romania: 400105 jud. Cluj, Cluj-Napoca, Bd. 21 Decembrie 1989 1; tel. (264) 596614; fax (264) 593897; internet www.lutheran.ro; 30,720 mems (2010); Superintendent Bishop ZOLTÁN ADORJANI DEZSŐ.

Romanian Evangelical Church (Biserica Evanghelica România): 050454 Bucharest, Str. Carol Davila 48; tel. (21) 4119622; fax (21) 4103652; e-mail ber@rdsmail.ro; internet www.ber.ro.

Unitarian Church in Transylvania: 400105 jud. Cluj, Cluj-Napoca, Str. 21 Decembrie 1989 9; tel. (264) 593236; fax (264) 595927; e-mail ekt@unitarius.com; internet www.unitarius.com; f. 1568; comprises about 75,000 mems, principally of Hungarian ethnicity; 125 churches and 30 fellowships; Bishop ÁRPÁD SZABÓ.

Other Christian Churches

Belaya Krinitsa Old Believers' Orthodox Church: 810140 jud. Brăila, Brăila, Str. Zidari 5; tel. (239) 647023; Metropolitan LEONTY IZOTOV.

Pentecostal Church: 050453 Bucharest, Str. Carol Davila 81; tel. (21) 2126419; fax (21) 2204303; e-mail cuvadev@fx.ro; f. 1922; 2,455 churches, 525 pastors (Dec. 2001); 450,000 mems; Pres. Rev. RIVIS TIPEI PAVEL; Gen. Sec. Rev. IOAN GURĂU.

Seventh-day Adventist Church: 077190 jud. Ilfov, Voluntari, Str. Erou Iancu Nicolae 38; tel. (21) 4908590; fax (21) 4908570; e-mail communicatii@adventist.ro; internet www.adventist.ro; f. 1920; 67,000 mems; Pres. of the Union Rev. ADRIAN BOCANEANU; Sec.-Gen. TEODOR HUTANU.

ISLAM

There are an estimated 55,000 Muslims in Romania, mostly of Turkish or Tatar origin.

Muftiatul Cultului Musulman din Romania: Grand Mufti OSMAN NEGEAT, 900742 jud. Constanţa, Constanţa, Bd. Tomis 41; tel. (241) 611390.

JUDAISM

In 1999 there were about 14,000 Jews, organized in some 70 communities, in Romania.

Federation of Jewish Communities (Federatia Comunitatilor Evreiesti din Romania): 030202 Bucharest 3, Str. Sf. Vineri 9–11; tel. (21) 3132538; fax (21) 3120869; e-mail vainer@jewishfed.ro; internet www.jewish.ro; Pres. AUREL VAINER; Chief Rabbi MENACHEM HACOHEN.

The Press

The Romanian press is highly regionalized. In 2011 there were 66 daily newspapers and 3,978 periodicals in circulation. In 2002 some 10 newspapers and 207 periodicals were published in the languages of minority ethnic groups in Romania, including Hungarian, German, Serbian, Ukrainian, Armenian and Yiddish.

The publications listed below are in Romanian, unless otherwise indicated.

PRINCIPAL DAILY NEWSPAPERS

Adevărul (The Truth): 013701 Bucharest, Piaţa Presei Libere 1; tel. (21) 2240067; fax (21) 2243612; e-mail redactia@adevarul.kappa.ro; internet www.adevarul.ro; f. 1888; daily except Sun.; independent; Editor-in-Chief GRIGORE CARTIANU; circ. 91,006 (Jan. 2011).

Azi (Today): 010062 Bucharest, Calea Victoriei 39A, CP 45–49; tel. (21) 3141998; fax (21) 3144378; e-mail redactie@azi.ro; internet www .azi.ro; f. 1990; independent; Editor RUXANDRA NEGREA.

Cotidianul (The Daily): 020922 Bucharest 2, Bd. Carol I 34–36; tel. (21) 3173192; fax (21) 3173124; e-mail office@cotidianul.ro; internet www.cotidianul.ro; f. 1927; revived in 1991; daily except Sun.; online only; 50% owned by *Academia Caţavencu*; Editorial Dir DORU BUŞCU; Editor-in-Chief CORNEL NISTORESCU; circ. 120,000.

Cronica Română: 013701 Bucharest 1, POB 33, Piaţa Presei Libere 1, corp. C, etaj 1, camera 31; tel. (21) 3179165; fax (21) 3179169; e-mail cronica@rdsmail.ro; internet www.cronicaromana.ro; f. 1992; daily; Editor-in-Chief IULIAN BADEA; circ. 29,000.

Curierul Naţional (The National Courier): 010024 Bucharest, Str. Cristian Popişteanu 2–4; tel. (21) 5995500; fax (21) 3121300; e-mail office@curierulnational.ro; internet www.curierulnational.ro; f. 1991; Man. Editor ADRIAN VOINEA; circ. 3,206 (Sept. 2010).

Economistul (The Economist): 010702 Bucharest 1, Calea Grivitei 21, 8th Floor; tel. (21) 3122248; fax (21) 3129717; e-mail eredactie@ economistul.ro; internet www.economistul.ro; f. 1990; daily; Editor-in-Chief OCTAVIAN DRAGOMIR JORA.

Evenimentul Zilei (The Event of the Day): 020337 Bucharest 2, Bd. Dimitrie Pompeiu 6; tel. (21) 2022099; fax (21) 2022001; e-mail online@evz.ro; internet www.evz.ro; f. 1991; owned by Ringier (Switzerland); tabloid; Bucharest, Transylvania and western regional editions; Editor-in-Chief VLAD MACOVEI; circ. 20,003 (Sept. 2010).

Gândul (The Thought): 020097 Bucharest, Str. Aurel Vlaicu 62–64, Sector 2; tel. (31) 8257125; fax (31) 8257188; e-mail redactia@gandul .info; internet www.gandul.info; f. 2005; independent; Editor-in-Chief CLAUDIU PÂNDARU; circ. 12,238 (Jan. 2011).

Gazeta Sporturilor (Sports Gazette): 051431 Bucharest 1, Şos. Dionisie Lupu 64–66; tel. (21) 4066507; fax (21) 2087484; e-mail contact@gsp.ro; internet www.gsp.ro; f. 1924; daily except Sun.; independent; Editor-in-Chief CĂTĂLIN TOLONTAN; circ. 44,524 (Jan. 2011).

Jurnalul National (The National Journal): 013701 Bucharest 1, Piaţa Presei Libere 1, Corp. D, etaj 8; tel. (21) 3182029; fax (21) 3182027; e-mail dan.constantin@jurnalul.ro; internet www.jurnalul .ro; f. 1993; Editor-in-Chief DAN CONSTANTIN; circ. 46,074 (Jan. 2011).

Libertatea (Freedom): 020337 Bucharest, Bd. Dimitrie Pompeiu 6, Sector 2; tel. (21) 2030804; fax (21) 2030832; internet www.libertatea .ro; f. 1989; owned by Ringier (Switzerland); daily; Sunday edition, *Libertatea de Duminica*, launched in 2002; tabloid; morning paper; Editor-in-Chief ANA NITA; circ. 126,475 (Jan. 2011).

ProSport: 020337 Bucharest 2, Bd. Dimitrie Pompeiu 6, Novo Parc; tel. (21) 2030803; fax (21) 2030836; e-mail contact@prosport.ro; internet www.prosport.ro; f. 1997; owned by Ringier (Switzerland); sports news; circ. 39,039 (Jan. 2011).

România Libera (Free Romania): 031041 Bucharest 3, Str. Nerva Traian 3/101M, etaj 4; tel. (21) 2028290; fax (21) 2028143; e-mail redactia@romanialibera.ro; internet www.romanialibera.ro; f. 1877; daily except Sun.; independent; Editor-in-Chief DAN CRISTIAN TRUTURICĂ; circ. 40,308 (Jan. 2011).

Ziarul Financiar: 020097 Bucharest, Str. Aurel Vlaicu 62-64, Sector 2; tel. (31) 8256288; fax (31) 8256285; e-mail zf@zf.ro; internet www.zf.ro; Editor SORIN PISLARU; circ. 12,223 (Jan. 2011).

DISTRICT NEWSPAPERS

Adevărul (The Truth): 310130 jud. Arad, Arad, Bd. Revoluţiei 81; tel. (257) 281802; fax (257) 280904; e-mail adevarul@arad.ro; internet www.adevarul.arad.ro; f. 1989; independent; daily; Dir DOREL ZAVOIANU; circ. 25,900.

Adevărul Harghitei (Harghita Truth): 530190 jud. Harghita, Miercurea-Ciuc, Str. Leliceni 45; tel. (266) 371805; fax (266) 172065; f. 1990; independent; daily; Editor-in-Chief MIHAI GROZA.

Argeşul Liber (Free Argeş): 110177 jud. Argeş, Piteşti, Str. Republicii 88; tel. (24) 8217704; fax (24) 8210060; e-mail argesul@gmail .com; internet www.ziarulargesul.ro; f. 1990; independent; daily; Editor-in-Chief GABRIEL LIXANDRU.

Bună Ziua Braşov (Good Afternoon Braşov): 500090 jud. Braşov, Braşov, Str. Mihai Kogalniceanu 19, etaj 7; tel. (268) 547780; fax (268) 547780; e-mail bzb@bzb.ro; internet www.bzb.ro; f. 1995; Dir MIRELA LEONTICĂ; circ. 30,000.

Ceahlăul: 610263 jud. Neamţ, Piatra-Neamţ, Al. Tiparului 14; tel. (233) 225282; fax (233) 225282; e-mail redactie@ziarulceahlaul.ro; internet www.ziarulceahlaul.ro; f. 1989; daily; Editor-in-Chief CORNELIU LĂMĂTIC; circ. 20,000.

Crai nou: 720059 jud. Suceava, Suceava, Str. Mihai Viteazul 32; tel. (230) 215996; fax (230) 214723; e-mail redactie@crainou.ro; internet www.crainou.ro; f. 1990; daily; Editor-in-Chief L. D. CLEMENT.

Cuget Liber (Free Thinking): 900711 jud. Constanţa, Constanţa, Şos. I. C. Brătianu 5; tel. (241) 582100; fax (241) 619524; e-mail office@cugetliber.ro; internet www.cugetliber.ro; f. 1989; independent; Editor-in-Chief COSMIN ZAPOROJAN.

Curierul de Vâlcea (Courier of Vâlcea): 240591 jud. Vâlcea, Râmnicu Vâlcea, Carol I/19; tel. (250) 732325; fax (250) 732326; e-mail office@curierul.ro; internet www.curierul.ro; f. 1990; independent; daily except Sat. and Sun.; commerce; Editor-in-Chief SORIN ALEXANDRU BARBU.

Cuvântul Liber (The Free Word): 540015 jud. Mureş, Târgu Mureş, Str. Gh. Doja 9; tel. and fax (265) 266629; internet www .cuvantul-liber.ro; f. 1989; independent; daily; Editor-in-Chief LAZĂR LADARIU; circ. 10,000 (2009).

Cuvântul Libertăţii (The Word of Liberty): 200020 jud. Dolj, Craiova, Str. Nicolăescu Plopşor. 22A; tel. (251) 412457; fax (251) 414141; e-mail mediafax@cvl.homeip.net; internet www.cvlpress.ro; f. 1989; daily except Sun.; Editor-in-Chief MIRCEA CANŢĂR; circ. 10,000 (2010).

Cuvântul nou (The New Word): 520064 jud. Covasna, Sfântu Gheorghe, Str. Pieţei 8A; tel. and fax (240) 2311388; e-mail cuvnou@znet.ro; f. 1968; new series 1990; daily except Mon.; Editor-in-Chief DUMITRU MÂNOLĂCHESCU.

Dâmboviţa: 130082 jud. Dâmboviţa, Târgovişte, Bul. Unirii 32; tel. and fax (245) 634017; e-mail ziar_dambovita@yahoo.com; internet www.ziardambovita.ro; f. 1990; independent; Editor-in-Chief ALEXANDRU ILIE.

Datina (Tradition): 220016 jud. Mehedinţi, Drobeta-Turnu Severin, Str. Tabla-Buţii 74 A; tel. (252) 311995; fax (252) 326052; f. 1990; independent; Editor-in-Chief GHEORGHE BUREŢEA.

Delta (The Delta): 820180 jud. Tulcea, Tulcea, Str. Spitalului 4; tel. (2405) 12406; fax (2405) 16616; f. 1885; new series 1990; daily except Mon.; Editor-in-Chief NECULAI AMIHULESEI.

Deşteptarea (The Awakening): 600010 jud. Bacău, Bacău, Str. Vasile Alecsandri 41; tel. (234) 511272; fax (234) 523515; e-mail redactie@desteptarea.ro; internet www.desteptarea.ro; f. 1989; Editor-in-Chief DORIAN POCOVNICU; circ. 50,000.

Erdélyi Napló: 400009 jud. Kolozsvár, Str. Gen. Eremia Grigorescu 52, POB 1320; tel. (36) 4142301; fax (36) 4109836; e-mail office@ erdelyinaplo.ro; internet www.erdelyinaplo.ro; f. 1991; in Hungarian; weekly; Man. Editor SAMU CSINTA.

Evenimentul: 700497 jud. Iaşi, Str. Crişan 14; tel. (232) 246000; fax (232) 246002; e-mail contact@evenimentul.ro; internet www .evenimentul.ro; f. 1991; daily; Editor-in-Chief DAN N. DOBOŞ; circ. 3,868 (Jan. 2011).

Făclia de Cluj (Cluj Torch): 401050 jud. Cluj, Cluj-Napoca, Str. Napoca 16; tel. (264) 591681; fax (264) 592828; e-mail redactia@ ziarulfaclia.ro; internet www.ziarulfaclia.ro; f. 1989; fmrly Adevărul de Cluj (Cluj Truth); present name adopted 2007; independent; Editor-in-Chief ILIE CĂLIAN; circ. 200,000.

Gazeta de Transilvania (Transylvanian Gazette): 500030 jud. Braşov, Braşov, Str. M. Sadoveanu 3; tel. (268) 472099; fax (268) 475604; e-mail gazeta.transilvania@brasovia.ro; internet www.gtbv .ro; f. 1838; ceased publication 1946, re-established 1989; daily except Mon.; independent; Editor-in-Chief ADRIAN TEACĂ.

Gorjanul: 210192 jud. Gorj, Târgu Jiu, Str. Constantin Brâncuşi 15; tel. (253) 217464; fax (253) 212072; e-mail redactie@gorjeanul.ro; internet www.gorjeanul.ro; f. 1990; Editor-in-Chief ANAMARIA STOICA.

Graiul Maramureşului (The Voice of Maramureş): 430051 jud. Maramureş, Baia Mare, Bd. Bucureşti 25; tel. (262) 221017; fax (262) 224871; e-mail graiul@graiul.ro; internet www.graiul.ro; f. 1989; independent; daily except Sun.; Editor-in-Chief AUGUSTIN COZMUŢA; circ. 10,000.

Graiul Sălajului (Voice of Sălaj): 450042 jud. Sălaj, Zalău, Str. Mihai Viteazul 14; tel. (260) 611320; fax (260) 612479; e-mail graiulsj@unisys.ro; internet www.graiulsalajului.ro; f. 1990; Editor-in-Chief DANIEL MUNTEANU.

Hargita Népe (People of Hargita): 530190 jud. Harghita, Miercurea-Ciuc, Str. Leliceni 45; tel. (266) 372633; e-mail office@ hargitanepe.ro; internet www.topnet.ro/hargitanepe; daily; in Hungarian; Dir ISTVÁN CSONGOR ISAN; circ. 7,691 (Jan. 2011).

Háromszék (Three Chairs): 520003 jud. Covasna, Sfântu Gheorghe, Str. Gábor Áron 2; tel. (267) 351504; fax (367) 405264; e-mail hpress@ 3szek.ro; internet www.3szek.ro; f. 1989; socio-political; daily; in Hungarian; Editor-in-Chief BOTOND FARCÁDI.

Mesagerul de Bistriţa-Năsăud: 420074 jud. Bistriţa-Năsăud, Bistriţa, Str. Ursului 14; tel. (402) 63234688; fax (402) 63234689; e-mail mesagerul@mesagerul.ro; internet www.mesagerul.ro; daily.

Milcovul Liber (Free Milcov): 620095 jud. Vrancea, Focşani, Bd. Unirii 18; tel. (237) 614579; fax (237) 613588; f. 1989; weekly; Dir OVIDIU BUTUC.

Monitorul de Botoşani: 710210 jud. Botoşani, Botoşani, Str. Mihail Kogălniceanu 4; tel. (231) 515053; fax (231) 515130; e-mail monitorul@monitorulbt.ro; internet www.monitorulbt.ro; Editor-in-Chief CĂTĂLIN MORARU; circ. 6,685 (Jan. 2011).

Monitorul de Iaşi (Iaşi Monitor): 700237 jud. Iaşi, Iaşi, Şos. Naţională 45; tel. (332) 430806; fax (332) 430807; e-mail redactia@ monitorul.com.ro; internet www.monitorul.com.ro; f. 1991; daily; Editor-in-Chief LAURA MUSINA.

Népújság (People's Journal): 540015 jud. Mureş, Târgu Mureş, Str. Gh. Doja 9; tel. (265) 266780; fax (265) 266270; e-mail nepujsag@ e-nepujsag.ro; internet www.hhrf.org/nepujsag; f. 1990; daily; in Hungarian; Editor-in-Chief MIKLÓS NAGY KUND.

Opinia (Opinion): 120024 jud. Buzău, Buzău, Str. Chiristigii 3; tel. (238) 711063; fax (238) 412764; e-mail opinia@buzau.ro; internet ziarul.opiniabuzau.ro; f. 1990; independent; daily; Editor-in-Chief GABRIEL COSTIANU.

Pământul (Free Earth): 991048 jud. Călăraşi, Călăraşi, Str. Bucureşti 187; tel. (2911) 15840; fax (2911) 313630; f. 1990; socio-political; weekly; Editor-in-Chief GHEORGHE FRANGULEA.

Prahova: 100066 jud. Prahova, Ploieşti, Bd. Republicii 2; tel. (244) 515691; fax (244) 407399; e-mail edprahova@asesoft.ro; internet www.ziarulprahova.ro; f. 1870; Editor-in-Chief LUIZA RADULESCU-PINTILIE; circ. 17,000.

Renaşterea Bănăţeană (The Banat Renaissance): 300024 jud. Timiş, Timişoara, Bd. Revoluţiei 1989 8; tel. (256) 490145; fax (256) 490370; e-mail renasterea@renasterea.ro; internet www

.renasterea.ro; f. 1990; daily; independent; tabloid; Editor-in-Chief OCTAVIAN ROŞA; circ. 11,623 (Jan. 2011).

Szabadság (Freedom): 400009 jud. Cluj, Cluj-Napoca, Str. Napoca 16, POB 340; tel. (264) 596408; fax (264) 597206; e-mail office@ szabadsag.ro; internet www.szabadsag.ro; f. 1989; organ of Minerva Cultural Asscn (non-governmental org.); daily except Sun.; in Hungarian; online edition in parallel since 1995 (up to 5,000 readers); covers five counties; Editor-in-Chief ILDIKÓ ÚJVÁRI; circ. 10,000.

Szatmári Friss Újság: 440026 jud. Satu Mare, Satu Mare, Str. Mihai Viteazul 32; tel. (261) 714654; fax (261) 712024; e-mail marta .antal@informmedia.ro; internet www.frissujsag.ro; f. 1990; daily except Sun.; in Hungarian; Editor-in-Chief ELEK ANIKÓ; circ. 7,509 (Jan. 2011).

Szilágyaság (Word from Sălaj): 450042 jud. Sălaj, Zalău, Piaţa Libertăţii 9, POB 68; tel. (299) 633736; e-mail szilagysag@ zappmobile.ro; f. 1990; organ of Democratic Alliance of Hungarians in Romania; weekly; Editor-in-Chief JÁNOS KUI.

Teleormanul Liber (Free Teleorman): 140033 jud. Teleorman, Alexandria, Str. Ion Creangă 63; tel. (247) 311950; fax (247) 323871; e-mail etl@starnets.ro; f. 1990; daily; Editor-in-Chief GHEORGHE FILIP.

Timişoara: 300012 jud. Timiş, Timişoara, Str. Brediceanu 37A; tel. (256) 264546; fax (256) 146170; e-mail timisoara@rdstm.ro; internet www.cotidianultimisoara.ro; f. 1990; daily; Editor-in-Chief OSCAR BERGER.

Tribuna: 550013 jud. Sibiu, Sibiu, Str. Gheorghe Coşbuc 38; tel. (269) 211318; fax (269) 214141; e-mail red@tribuna.ro; internet www .tribuna.ro; f. 1884; daily; independent; Man. Editor FLORIN STAICU; circ. 17,000.

Tribuna Ialomiţei (Ialomiţa Tribune): 920033 jud. Ialomiţa, Slobozia, Str. Dobrogeanu-Gherea 2; f. 1969; weekly; Editor-in-Chief TITUS NIŢU.

Unirea (The Union): 510093 jud. Alba, Alba Iulia, Str. Decebal 27; tel. (258) 811419; fax (258) 812464; e-mail unirea@unirea-pres.ro; internet www.ziarulunirea.ro; f. 1891; independent; daily except Sun.; Gen. Man. GHEORGHE CIUL; Editor-in-Chief MARIA LUCIA MUNTEANU; circ. 17,577 (Jan. 2011).

Viaţa Libera (Free Life): 800215 jud. Galaţi, Galaţi, Str. Domnească 68; tel. (23) 460620; fax (23) 471028; e-mail sec@viata-libera.ro; internet www.viata-libera.ro; f. 1989; independent; daily; Editor-in-Chief COSTEL CRÂNGAN; circ. 7,648 (Jan. 2011).

Ziarul de Iaşi: 700399 jud. Iaşi, Iaşi, Str. Smârdan 5; tel. (232) 271333; fax (232) 270415; e-mail redactie@ziaruldeiasi.ro; internet www.ziaruldeiasi.ro; daily; Editor-in-Chief TONI HRITAC; circ. 5,798 (Jan. 2011).

PRINCIPAL PERIODICALS

22: 010093 Bucharest, Calea Victoriei 120; tel. (21) 3112208; fax (21) 3141776; e-mail redactia@revista22.ro; internet www.revista22.ro; f. 1990; weekly; Editor-in-Chief RODICA PALADE; circ. 10,000 (2008).

Academia Caţavencu (Caţavencu Academy): 030016 Bucharest 2, Bd. Regina Elisabeta 7–9, et. 6; tel. (21) 3140235; fax (21) 3140258; e-mail office@catavencu.ro; internet www.catavencu.ro; f. 1991; weekly; satirical; Dir MARCELA PETRACHE; circ. 22,111 (Jan. 2011).

Bursa: 010804 Bucharest 1, Str. Popa Tatu 71; tel. (21) 3154356; fax (21) 3124556; e-mail marketing@bursa.ro; internet www.bursa.ro; f. 1990; finance; Editor-in-Chief FLORIAN GOLDSTEIN; circ. 35,000.

Capital: 020337 Bucharest 2, Bd. Dimitrie Pompeiu 6, Novo Park; tel. (21) 2030802; fax (21) 2030902; e-mail secretariat@capital.ro; internet www.capital.ro; f. 1992; owned by Ringier (Switzerland); weekly; economic and financial magazine; Editor-in-Chief IULIAN BORTOS; circ. 12,250 (Jan. 2011).

Contemporanul—Ideea Europeană (The Contemporary—The European Idea): 014780 Bucharest 1, Piaţa Amzei, Asociaţia Contemporanul, POB 113, Of. p. 22; tel. (21) 2125692; fax (21) 3106618; e-mail office@contemporanul.ro; internet www.ideeaeuropeana.ro/ revista-contemporanul.php; f. 1881; monthly; cultural, political and scientific review; published by the European Idea Cultural Foundation; Editor-in-Chief AURA CHRISTI.

Cronica: 700037 jud. Iaşi, Iaşi, Str. I. C. Brătianu 22; tel. and fax (232) 262140; e-mail cronica_iasi@yahoo.com; internet www .revistacronica.wordpress.com; f. 1966; monthly; cultural review; Editor-in-Chief VALERIU STANCU; circ. 5,000.

Erdélyi Figyelö (Transylvanian Observer): 540026 jud. Mureş, Târgu Mureş, Str. Primăriei 1; tel. (265) 166910; fax (265) 168688; f. 1958; fmrly Új Élet; quarterly; illustrated magazine; in Hungarian; Editor-in-Chief JÁNOS LÁZOK.

Femeia Moderna (Modern Woman): 011013 Bucharest, Buzesti 85, et. 4, Sector 1; tel. (31) 2258700; fax (31) 2258715; e-mail revistafemeia@sanomahearst.ro; internet www.femeia.ro; f. 1868; monthly; Editor-in-Chief LUANA MURESAN; circ. 15,164 (Jan. 2011).

Flacăra (The Flame): 013701 Bucharest 1, Piaţa Presei Libere 1; tel. (21) 3179142; fax (21) 3179143; e-mail office@publicatiileflacara.ro; internet www.revistaflacara.ro; f. 1911; monthly; Editor-in-Chief LILIANA PETRUŞ; circ. 1,847 (Jan. 2011).

Jurnalul Afacerilor (Romanian Business Journal): 013701 Bucharest 1, Piaţa Presei Libere 1, Corp. 3, 3rd Floor, Rm 317–321; tel. (21) 2246897; fax (21) 2246896; e-mail rbj@euroweb.ro; f. 1990; Dir MARCEL BARBU; circ. 25,000.

Korunk (Our Time): 400304 jud. Cluj, Cluj-Napoca, Str. Gen. Eremia Grigorescu 52; tel. (264) 375035; fax (264) 375093; e-mail korunk@gmail.com; internet www.korunk.org; f. 1926; monthly; social review; in Hungarian; Editor-in-Chief KOVÁCS KISS GYÖNGY; circ. 1,200 (2012).

Magazin Istoric (Historical Magazine): 010155 Bucharest, Piaţa Valter Mărăcineanu 1–3, POB 15-702; tel. (21) 3126877; fax (21) 3150991; e-mail mistoric@gmail.com; internet www.magazinistoric .ro; f. 1967; monthly; review of historical culture; Chief Editor DORIN MATEI; circ. 18,000 (2013).

Napsugár (Sun Ray): 400462 jud. Cluj, Constantin Brâncuşi 202/ 101, POB 137; tel. and fax (264) 418001; e-mail naps.sziv@napsugar .ro; internet www.napsugar.ro; f. 1956; monthly; illustrated literary magazine for children aged 7–12 years; in Hungarian; Editor-in-Chief EMESE ZSIGMOND; circ. 13,500 (2011).

Orizont (Horizon): 300085 jud. Timiş, Timişoara, Piaţa St Gheorghe 3; tel. and fax (256) 294893; e-mail fundatia@3europe.org; internet www.revistaorizont.ro; f. 1949; monthly; review of the Writers' Union (Timişoara br.); Editor-in-Chief MIRCEA MIHĂIEŞ.

Panoramic Radio-TV: 011964 Bucharest, Str. Jean Baptiste Molière dramaturg 2–4; tel. (21) 2307501; fax (21) 156992; e-mail micara.dumutrescu@tvr.ro; f. 1990; weekly; Dir STEFAN DIMITRIU; Editor-in-Chief ADRIAN IONESCU; circ. 50,000.

PC World Romania: 011455 Bucharest, Pl. Independentei 202A, Sector 1; tel. (21) 3144102; fax (21) 3144120; e-mail pcworld@idg.ro; internet www.pcworld.ro; f. 1993; monthly; computing; Editor-in-Chief STEFANIA MIHALCEA; circ. 15,000.

Practic in bucătărie: 020912 Bucharest, Str. Carol I 31–33, Complexul Asirom, Sector 2; tel. (37) 2106000; fax (37) 2106055; e-mail publicitate@burda.ro; owned by Hubert Burda Media (Germany); monthly; cookery and kitchen-design magazine; Man. Editor VALENTIN IORDACHE; circ. 178,389 (Jan. 2011).

Revista Română de Statistică (Romanian Statistical Review): 050706 Bucharest, Bd. Libertăţii 16; tel. and fax (21) 3171110; e-mail rrs@insse.ro; internet www.revistadestatistica.ro; f. 1952; monthly; organ of Romanian National Institute of Statistics; Dir CRISTINA SACALĂ.

România Literară (Literary Romania): 010071 Bucharest, Calea Victoriei 133, Sector 1; tel. (21) 2127986; fax (21) 2127981; e-mail revistaromanialiterara@gmail.com; internet www.romlit.ro; f. 1968; weekly; literary, artistic and political magazine; published by the Fundation România Literară (Writers' Union); Dir NICOLAE MANOLESCU; Gen. Editor IONELA STANCIU.

România Mare (Greater Romania): 010062 Bucharest, Calea Victoriei 39A; tel. (21) 6156093; fax (21) 3125396; internet www.romare .ro; f. 1990; weekly; nationalist; Editor-in-Chief CORNELIU VADIM TUDOR; circ. 90,000.

Super Magazin: 013701 Bucharest, Piaţa Presei Libere 1; tel. (21) 2223323; fax (21) 2226382; f. 1993; Editor-in-Chief GHEORGHE VOICU; circ. 200,000.

Szivárvány (Rainbow): 400462 jud. Cluj, Cluj-Napoca, Bd. Constantin Brancusi 202/101; tel. and fax (264) 418001; e-mail naps .sziv@napsugar.ro; internet www.napsugar.ro; f. 1980; monthly; illustrated literary magazine for children aged 6–16 years; in Hungarian; Editor-in-Chief EMESE ZSIGMOND; circ. 16,500 (2012).

Tehnium: 013701 Bucharest, Piaţa Presei Libere 1; tel. (21) 2223374; f. 1970; monthly; hobbies; Editor-in-Chief ILIE MIHĂESCU; circ. 100,000.

Tribuna: 400091 jud. Cluj, Cluj-Napoca, Str. Universităţii 1; tel. (264) 117548; f. 1884; weekly; cultural review; Editor-in-Chief AUGUSTIN BUZURA.

Tribuna economică (Economic Tribune): 010336 Bucharest, Bd. Magheru 28–30, Sector 1; tel. (21) 3165544; fax (21) 3103833; e-mail tribunae@tribuneconomica.ro; internet www.tribuneconomica.ro; f. 1899; weekly; Editor-in-Chief Dr GH. N. IOSIF; circ. 10,000.

Vânatorul şi Pescarul Român (The Romanian Hunter and Angler): 020882 Bucharest, Calea Moşilor 128; tel. (21) 3133363; fax (21) 3136804; f. 1948; monthly review; Editor-in-Chief GABRIEL CHEROIU.

NEWS AGENCIES

Agerpres (Agenţia Română de Presă): 013701 Bucharest, Piaţa Presei Libere 1; tel. (21) 2076110; fax (21) 3170707; e-mail office@ agerpres.ro; internet www.agerpres.ro; f. 1889; renamed as Rom-press in 1989, and as above in 2008; provides news and photo services; in English and French; Dir-Gen. IOAN ROSCA.

Mediafax: 020097 Bucharest 2, Str. Aurel Vlaicu 62–64; tel. (31) 8256100; fax (31) 8256140; e-mail credactie.online@mediafax.ro; internet www.mediafax.ro; f. 1995; general and business news; Chief Exec. CRISTIAN DIMITRIU.

PRESS ASSOCIATION

Society of Romanian Journalists—Federation of All Press Unions (Societatea Ziariştilor din România—Federaţia Sindicatelor din Întreaga Presă): 013701 Bucharest, Piaţa Presei Libere 1; tel. (21) 2228351; fax (21) 3179796; e-mail szrpress@moon.ro; f. 1990; affiliated to International Organization of Journalists and to International Federation of Journalists; Pres. CORNELIUS POPA; 5,000 mems.

Publishers

Editura Academiei Române (Publishing House of the Romanian Academy): 050711 Bucharest, Calea 13 Septembrie 13; tel. (21) 4119008; fax (21) 4103983; e-mail edacad@ear.ro; internet www.ear.ro; f. 1948; books and periodicals on original scientific work; 80 periodicals in Romanian and foreign languages; Gen. Man. DUMITRU RADU POPESCU.

Editura Albatros: 013701 Bucharest, Piaţa Presei Libere 1, Of. 33; tel. and fax (21) 2228493; f. 1969; Romanian literature and culture; Editor-in-Chief GEORGETA DIMISIANO.

Editura Artemis (Artemis Publishing House): 013701 Bucharest, Piaţa Presei Libere 1; tel. (21) 2226661; f. 1991; fine arts, fiction, children's literature, history; Dir MIRELLA ACSENTE.

Editura Cartea Românească (Publishing House of the Romanian Book): 010071 Bucharest 1, Calea Victoriei 115; tel. (21) 3196599; fax (23) 2214100; e-mail ecr@cartearomaneasca.ro; internet www.cartearomaneasca.ro; f. 1969; Romanian contemporary literature; Dir SILVIU LUPESCU.

Editura Ceres: 013701 Bucharest, Piaţa Presei Libere 1; tel. (21) 2224836; f. 1953; books on agriculture and forestry; Dir MARIA DAMIAN.

Editura Dacia (Dacia Publishing House): 400660 jud. Cluj, Cluj-Napoca, Str. Ospatariei 4; tel. and fax (264) 429675; e-mail office@edituradacia.ro; internet www.edituradacia.ro; f. 1969; classical and contemporary literature, science fiction, academic, technical, philosophical and scientific books; in Romanian and Hungarian; Gen. Man. IOAN VĂDAN.

Editura Didactică şi Pedagogică (Educational Publishing House): 010176 Bucharest, Str. Spiru Haret 12; tel. and fax (21) 3122885; internet www.edituradp.ro; f. 1951; school, university, technical and vocational textbooks, pedagogic literature and methodology, teaching materials; Gen. Man. Prof. MIHAELA ZĂRNESCU-ENCEANU.

Editura Eminescu (Eminescu Publishing House): 020982 Bucharest 2, Str. Sfantul Spiridon 8; tel. and fax (21) 2123588; e-mail info@edituraeminescu.ro; internet www.edituraeminescu.ro; f. 1969; contemporary original literary works and translations of world literature; Dir SILVIA CINCA.

Editura Enciclopedică (Encyclopedia Publishing House): 013701 Bucharest, Piaţa Presei Libere 1; tel. and fax (21) 3179035; e-mail enciclopedica2006@yahoo.com; f. 1968; encyclopedias, dictionaries, monographs, reference books and children's books; Dir MARCEL POPA.

Editura Humanitas (Humanitas Publishing House): 013701 Bucharest, Piaţa Presei Libere 1; tel. (21) 4088350; fax (21) 4088351; e-mail secretariat@humanitas.ro; internet www.humanitas.ro; f. 1990; philosophy, religion, political and social sciences, economics, history, fiction, textbooks, art, literature, practical books; Dir GABRIEL LIICEANU.

Editura Litera Internaţional (International Letter Publishing House): 011422 Bucharest, Str. Emanoil Porumbaru 31A, et. 1, ap. 3; tel. (21) 3196393; fax (21) 3196390; e-mail info@litera.ro; internet www.litera.ro; f. 1989; original literature; Dir-Gen. DAN VIDRASCU.

Editura Medicală SA (Medical Publishing House): 020751 Bucharest 2, Episcop Radu 15A; tel. (21) 2525188; fax (21) 2525189; e-mail office@ed-medicala.ro; internet www.ed-medicala.ro; f. 1954; medical literature; Dir Prof. AL I. OPROIU.

Editura Militară (Military Publishing House): 061074 Bucharest 6, Iuliu Maniu 13; tel. and fax (21) 3149161; e-mail adrian.pandea@edituramilitara.ro; internet www.edituramilitara.ro; f. 1950; military history, theory, science, technology, medicine and fiction; Dir ADRIAN PANDEA.

Editura Muzicală (Musical Publishing House): 010071 Bucharest, Calea Victoriei 141; tel. and fax (21) 3129867; e-mail em@edituramuzicala.ro; internet www.edituramuzicala.ro; f. 1957;

books on music, musicology and musical scores; Dir MARIUS VASILEANU.

Editura Polirom: 700505 jud. Iaşi, Iaşi, Bd. Carol I 4, etaj 4, POB 266; tel. (232) 214100; fax (232) 214111; e-mail office@polirom.ro; internet www.polirom.ro; f. 1995; Dir SILVIU LUPESCU.

Editura Tehnică (Technical Publishing House): 024056 Bucharest 2, Str. Olari 213; tel. (21) 2522366; fax (21) 2525077; e-mail tehnica@edituratehnica.ro; internet www.edituratehnica.ro; f. 1950; technical and scientific books, technical dictionaries; Dir ROMAN CHIRILĂ.

Editura Univers: 010209 Bucharest, Str. Mircea Vulcănescu 2; tel. (21) 3153307; fax (21) 3153308; e-mail office@edituraunivers.ro; internet www.edituraunivers.ro; f. 1961; translations from world literature, criticism, essays, literary history, philosophy of culture, educational; Man. Dir SERGIU CRUPENSCHI.

Editura de Vest (Publishing House of the West): 300085 jud. Timiş, Timişoara, Piaţa Sfântul Gheorghe 2; tel. and fax (256) 434382; f. 1972 as Editura Facla; socio-political, technical, scientific and literary works; in Romanian, Hungarian, German and Serbian; Dir VASILE POPOVICI.

PUBLISHERS' ASSOCIATION

Romanian Publishers' Asscn (Asociaţia Editorilor din România): 011035 Bucharest, Str. Dr Iacob Felix 97, etaj 1, ap. 7; tel. (21) 3110650; fax (21) 3115941; e-mail info@aer.ro; internet www.aer.ro; f. 1993; 66 mems; Pres. GRIGORE ARSENE.

Broadcasting and Communications
TELECOMMUNICATIONS

Forty-eight fixed-line telephony services providers and five main mobile telephony operators were active in the telecommunications market in 2010. There were 4.5m. main lines in use and 24.6m. cellular phone users at that time.

Cosmote Romanian Mobile Telecommunications SA: 011141 Bucharest 1, Şos. Nicolae Titulescu 4–8; tel. (21) 4041234; fax (21) 4137530; e-mail info@cosmote.ro; internet www.cosmote.ro; f. 2000; fmrly CosmoROM; owned by COSMOTE (Greece); mobile cellular telecommunications services; Dir-Gen. STEFANOS THEOCHAROPOULOS.

Orange Romania SA: 010665 Bucharest 1, Bd. Lascar Catargiu 51–53, Europe House; tel. (21) 2033030; fax (21) 2033413; e-mail infocorporate@orange.ro; internet www.orange.ro; f. 1996; fmrly Mobil-Rom; owned by Orange (France); mobile cellular telecommunications services; CEO JEAN FRANCOIS FALLACHER.

Romtelecom SA: 013702 Bucharest 1, Piaţa Presei Libere 3–5; tel. (21) 4001212; fax (21) 4105581; e-mail contact@romtelecom.ro; internet www.romtelecom.ro; f. 1933; fmr state monopoly; 54% owned by Hellenic Telecommunications Organization (Greece); fixed line telecommunications, internet and digital TV services; Dir-Gen. GEORGIOS IOANNIDIS.

Telemobil SA (Zapp): 077015 jud. Ilfov, Baloteşti, Str. Bucureşti 2 bis; tel. (21) 4024444; fax (21) 4024456; internet www.telemobil.ro; f. 1999; operates mobile cellular telephone network; Man. Dir and Chief Exec. DIWAKER SINGH.

Vodafone Romania: 061344 Bucharest 6, Bd. Vasile Milea 4A; tel. (21) 3021111; fax (21) 3021413; e-mail contact@connex.ro; internet www.vodafone.ro; f. 1997; fmrly Connex (Mobifon); operates mobile cellular telephone network and third-generation (GSM) services, and provides internet services; 99% owned by Vodafone Group PLC (United Kingdom); Pres. INAKI BERROETA.

Regulatory Authority

National Authority for Management and Regulation in Communications (Autoritatea Naţională pentru Administrare şi Reglementare în Comunicaţii—ANCOM): 030925 Bucharest 3, Str. Delea Nouă 2; tel. (37) 2845845; fax (21) 2845404; e-mail ancom@ancom.org.ro; internet www.ancom.org.ro; f. 2002; as National Regulatory Authority for Communications (Autoritatea Naţională de Reglementare in Comunicaţii); name changed as above in 2009; Pres. CATALIN MARINESCU.

BROADCASTING

In 2010 there were 387 television and 704 radio licenses granted by the National Council of Broadcasting.

Radio

Societatea Romana de Radiodifuziune (SRR) (Romanian Radio Corpn): 010171 Bucharest, Str. Gen. Berthelot 60–64, POB 63-1200; tel. (21) 3031777; fax (21) 3121057; e-mail communication@radioromania.ro; internet www.srr.ro; f. 1928; 39 transmitters on medium-wave, 69 transmitters on VHF; 114 relays; operates the Radio Romania and Radio Romania International stations: news, cultural, youth and music programmes, plus two local and six regional programmes; foreign broadcasts on one medium-wave and eight short-wave transmitters in Arabic, Bulgarian, Chinese, English, German, Greek, Hungarian, Italian, Portuguese, Romanian, Russian, Serbian, Spanish, Turkish and Ukrainian; Pres. ANDRÁS I DEMETER.

Kiss FM: Bucharest 6, Spl. Independenţei 202A; tel. (21) 2233340; fax (21) 3125346; e-mail kissfm@kissfm.ro; internet www.kissfm.ro; owned by SBS Broadcasting S.a.r.l.

Pro FM: 021409 Bucharest 2, Bd. Protopopescu Pache 109; tel. (21) 2522642; fax (21) 8250515; e-mail profm@profm.ro; internet www.profm.ro; f. 1993; owned by Central European Media Enterprises Ltd (Bermuda); Gen. Dir COSTI MOCANU.

Radio Europa FM: 010541 Bucharest 1, Str. Horia Măcelariu 36–38; tel. (37) 2069500; fax (37) 2069502; e-mail webmaster@europafm.ro; internet www.europafm.ro; Gen. Dir ILIE NĂSTASE.

Radio Nord-Est: 700479 jud. Iaşi, Iaşi, Str. Codrescu 1; tel. and fax (232) 211550; fax (232) 211570; e-mail stiri@nordestfm.ro; internet www.nordestfm.ro; f. 1992; independent; Man. MIHAI GRETY.

Societatea Naţională de Radiocommunicaţii, SA (National Radiocommunications Co—Radiocom): 041303 Bucharest 4, Şos. Oltenitei 103; tel. (31) 5003131; fax (31) 5003631; e-mail telemarketing@radiocom.ro; internet www.radiocom.ro; f. 1991 through the reorganization of Rom Post Telecom; state-owned; radio and television broadcasting (including digital), high-speed internet and broadband services, satellite communications; 2,445 employees; Dir-Gen. CRISTIAN NIŢU.

Television

In addition to the publicly owned Televiziunea Română, which runs six television channels, there are 15 main, privately owned television stations, of which four are news channels and three are sports-orientated stations.

Televiziunea Română (TVR) (Romanian Television): Bucharest 1, Calea Dorobanţilor 191; tel. (21) 3199008; fax (21) 2307514; e-mail tvr@tvr.ro; internet www.tvr.ro; f. 1956; state-owned; public broadcasting service; six channels broadcasting 24 hours; Pres. and Dir-Gen. CLAUDIU SAFTOIU.

Antena 1: Bucharest, Şos. Bucureşti-Ploieşti 25–27; tel. (21) 2303202; fax (21) 2307946; e-mail relatii@antena1.ro; internet www.antena1.ro; f. 1993; independent commercial television station.

Prima TV: Bucharest 2, Bd. Dimitrie Pompeiu 9–9A; tel. (21) 5895000; fax (21) 2048489; e-mail focus@primatv.ro; internet www.primatv.ro; f. 1994; owned by SBS Broadcasting SA; Man. Dir MIHAELA DUMITRU.

Pro TV: 021409 Bucharest 2, Bd. Protopopescu Pache 109; tel. (21) 2505063; fax (21) 2524219; e-mail info@protv.ro; internet www.protv.ro; f. 1995; owned by Central European Media Enterprises Ltd (CME), Bermuda; commercial station; Gen. Dir COSTI MOCANU.

Finance

(cap. = capital; res = reserves; dep. = deposits; m. = million; brs = branches; amounts in new lei)

BANKING

Central Bank

National Bank of Romania (Banca Naţională a României): 030031 Bucharest 3, Str. Lipscani 25; tel. (21) 3130410; fax (21) 3123831; e-mail info@bnro.ro; internet www.bnro.ro; f. 1880; central bank and bank of issue; manages monetary policy; supervises commercial banks and credit business; cap. 30.0m., res 12,885.5m., dep. 24,593.2m. (Dec. 2008); Gov. MUGUR CONSTANTIN ISĂRESCU; 22 brs.

Other Banks

Alpha Bank Romania SA: 010566 Bucharest 1, Calea Dorobanţilor 237B; tel. (21) 2092100; fax (21) 2316570; e-mail info@alphabank.ro; internet www.alphabank.ro; f. 1994; present name adopted 2000; 99.92% owned by Alpha Bank AE (Greece) (q.v.); cap. 983.1m., res 136.8m., dep. 14,157.4m. (Dec. 2011); Chair. CHRISTOS GIAMPANAS.

Banca Comercială Carpatica SA (BCC): 550135 jud. Sibiu, Sibiu, Str. Autogarii 1; tel. (269) 233985; fax (269) 233371; e-mail centrala@carpatica.ro; internet www.carpatica.ro; f. 1999; cap. 314.6m., res 117.8m., dep. 2,491.1m. (Dec. 2011); Dir ION DOBRICA.

Banca Comercială Română SA—BCR (Romanian Commercial Bank): 030016 Bucharest 3, Bd. Regina Elisabeta 5; tel. (21) 3126185; fax (21) 3122096; e-mail contact.center@bcr.ro; internet www.bcr.ro; f. 1990; 93.26% owned by Erste Bank (Austria) (q.v.); cap. 2,880.7m., res 1,079.0m., dep. 58,826.1m. (Dec. 2011); Pres. TOMAS SPURNY; 372 brs and sub-brs.

Banca de Export-Import a României (Eximbank Romania): 050092 Bucharest 5, Str. Splaiul Independenţei 15; tel. (21) 4053096; fax (21) 4053388; e-mail informatii@eximbank.ro; internet www.eximbank.ro; f. 1992; 95.37% state-owned; cap. 800.8m., res 924.7m., dep. 1,085.5m. (Dec. 2011); Pres. TRAIAN HALALAI; 7 brs.

Banca Românească SA (Romanian Bank): 030822 Bucharest 3, Bd. Unirii 35, Bloc A3; tel. (21) 3059300; fax (21) 3059191; e-mail office@brom.ro; internet www.brom.ro; f. 1993; 99.28% owned by National Bank of Greece SA (NBG) (q.v.); cap. 835.3m., res 50.3m., dep. 6,141.0m (Dec. 2011); CEO MARINIS STRATOPOULOS.

Banca Transilvania SA (Transylvanian Bank): 400027 jud. Cluj, Cluj-Napoca, Str. G. Baritiu 8; tel. (264) 407150; fax (264) 407179; e-mail piatacapital@bancatransilvania.ro; internet www.bancatransilvania.ro; f. 1994; cap. 1,860.2m., res 226.4m., dep. 20,508.4m. (Dec. 2011); Chair. HORIA CIORCILA; CEO PETER FRANKLIN (acting).

Bancpost SA: 020337 Bucharest 3, Dimitrie Pompeiu 6A; tel. (21) 3084666; fax (21) 3233868; e-mail suportcomercianti@bancpost.ro; internet www.bancpost.ro; f. 1991; 99.11% owned by EFG Eurobank Ergasias SA (Greece) (q.v.); cap. 1,178.9m., res 404.1m., dep. 9,346.1m. (Dec. 2011); CEO ANTHONY C. HASSIOTIS; Gen. Man. MIHAI BOGZA.

BRD-Groupe Société Générale SA (Romanian Bank for Development): 011171 Bucharest 1, Bd. Ion Mihalache 1–7; tel. (21) 3014000; fax (21) 3014004; e-mail vocalis@brd.ro; internet www.brd.ro; f. 1990 to replace Investment Bank of Romania (f. 1923); present name adopted 2004; financial and banking services and operations to individuals and private and small cos; 60.17% owned by Société Générale (France) (q.v.); cap. 2,515.6m., res –15.4m., dep. 34,486.9m. (Dec. 2011); Pres. and CEO GUY POUPET; 191 brs.

CEC Bank SA: 030022 Bucharest 3, Calea Victoriei 11–13; tel. (21) 3111119; fax (21) 3125425; e-mail office@cec.ro; internet www.cec.ro; f. 1864; fmrly Casa de Economii şi Consemnaţiuni; present name adopted 2008; state-owned; handles private savings, loans for the inter-banking market and mortgages; cap. 1,047.7m., res 596.0m., dep. 19,054.7m. (Dec. 2011); Chair. and Chief Exec. RADU GRATIAN GHETEA; 42 brs.

Citibank Romania SA: 011742 Bucharest 1, Str. Calea Victoriei 145; tel. (21) 2035550; fax (21) 2035565; internet www.citibank.ro; f. 1996; owned by Citibank Europe (Ireland); Dir-Gen. SHAHMIR KHALIQ; 40 brs.

Credit Europe Bank (Romania) SA: 061331 Bucharest 6, Timişoara 26z, Clădirea Anchor Plaza; tel. (21) 4064000; fax (21) 3172066; e-mail office@crediteurope.ro; internet www.crediteurope.ro; f. 1993; fmrly Finansbank (Romania) in 2000; present name adopted 2007; 98.39% owned by Credit Europe Bank NV (Netherlands); cap. 675.0m., res 27.4m., dep. 2,481.0m. (Dec. 2011); CEO OMER TETIK; 86 brs.

Marfin Bank (Romania) SA: 010775 Bucharest 1, Str. Emanoil Porumbaru 90-92, BP 22-155; tel. (21) 2064200; fax (21) 2064281; e-mail office@marfinbank.ro; internet www.marfinbank.ro; f. 1998; fmrly Egnatia Bank (Romania); present name adopted 2008; 99.32% owned by Bank of Cyprus (Cyprus); cap. 243.9m., dep. 2,134.1m., total assets 2,580.1m. (Dec. 2010); Gen. Man. STYLIANOS SOFIANOS.

Nextebank SA: Bucharest 5, Str. Elefterie 18, Elefterie Business Center; tel. (21) 4051754; fax (21) 3178217; e-mail info@romexterra.ro; internet www.nextebank.ro; f. 1993; 94.98% owned by MKB Bank Nyrt (Hungary) (q.v.); name changed to MKB Romexterra Bank SA in 2007; present name adopted April 2012; cap. 145.2m., res 58.9m., dep. 966.0m. (Dec. 2011); CEO DAN SANDU; 68 brs.

OTP Bank Romania SA: 011017 Bucharest 3, Str. Buzesti 66–68; tel. (21) 3075700; fax (21) 3075730; e-mail office@otpbank.ro; internet www.otpbank.ro; f. 1995; present name adopted 2005; 99.99% owned by OTP Bank Ltd (Hungary); cap. 542.9m., res 42.8m., dep. 2,841.4m. (Dec. 2011); Chair. of Bd Dr ANTAL PONGRACZ.

Piraeus Bank Romania SA: 011132 Bucharest, Şos. Nicolae Titulescu 29-31, Sector 1; tel. (21) 3036969; fax (21) 3036968; e-mail office@piraeusbank.ro; internet www.piraeusbank.ro; f. 1995; present name adopted 2000; 99.99% owned by Piraeus Bank (Greece) (q.v.); cap. 1,000.2m., res 89.5m., dep. 5,014.1m. (Dec. 2011); CEO CĂTĂLIN PARVU; 3 brs.

Raiffeisen Bank SA: 011857 Bucharest 1, Piaţa Charles de Gaulle 15; tel. (21) 3061000; fax (21) 2300700; e-mail centrala@rzb.ro; internet www.raiffeisen.ro; f. 1968; present name adopted 2002; 99.49% owned by Raiffeisen International Beteiligungs AG (Austria); cap. 1,200.0m., res 117.9m., dep. 18,424.4m. (Dec. 2011); Pres. STEVEN VAN GRONIGEN; 329 brs.

UniCredit Tiriac Bank SA: 014106 Bucharest, Str. Ghetarilor 23–25, Sector 1; tel. (21) 2002020; fax (21) 2002022; e-mail office@unicredit.ro; internet www.unicredit-tiriac.ro; f. 1991; present name adopted 2007; cap. 1,101.6m., res 165.7m., dep. 15,203.4m. (Dec. 2011); Chair. CORNELIU DAN PASCARIU; Chief Exec. CĂTĂLIN RASVAN RADU; 50 brs.

Volksbank România SA: 021323 Bucharest 2, Şos. Mihai Bravu 171; tel. (21) 2094400; fax (21) 2094490; e-mail marketing@ volksbank.com.ro; internet www.volksbank.com.ro; f. 2000; 97.9% owned by Volksbank International AG (Austria); cap. 932.7m., res 1,518.0m., dep. 4,220.2m. (Dec. 2011); Pres. BENOIT CATEL.

BANKING ASSOCIATION

Romanian Banking Association (Asociaţia Română a Băncilor): 030205 Bucharest 3, Aleea Negru Voda 4–6, Bloc C3; tel. (21) 3212078; fax (21) 3212095; e-mail arb@arb.ro; internet www.arb .ro; f. 1991; 39 mems; Chair. RADU GRAŢIAN GHEŢEA; Sec.-Gen. RADU NEGREA.

STOCK EXCHANGE

Bucharest Stock Exchange (Bursa de Valori Bucureşti): 020922 Bucharest 2, Bd. Carol I 34–36, 14th Floor; tel. (21) 3079500; fax (21) 3079519; e-mail bvb@bvb.ro; internet www.bvb.ro; f. 1882; reopened 1995 (ceased operations 1948); 79 listed cos; Pres. of the Bd LUCIAN ANGHEL.

COMMODITIES EXCHANGE

Romanian Commodities Exchange (Bursa Română de Mărfuri): 011015 Bucharest, Str. Buzesti 50-52; tel. (21) 3174560; fax (21) 3172878; e-mail bursa@brm.ro; internet www.brm.ro; Pres. and CEO GABRIEL PURICE.

INSURANCE

In 2003 there were 46 insurance companies.

Allianz-Tiriac Asigurări: 010616 Bucharest, Str. Căderea Bastiliei 80–84; tel. (21) 2082222; fax (21) 2082211; e-mail relatii.publice@ allianztiriac.ro; internet www.allianztiriac.ro; CEO CRISTIAN CONSTANTINESCU.

Asigurarea Româneasca SA (ASIROM) (Romanian Insurance): 020912 Bucharest 2, Bd. Carol I 31–33; tel. (21) 6011289; fax (21) 6011288; internet www.asirom.com.ro; f. 1991; life and non-life; Chair. of Bd PETER HÖFINGER; 41 brs.

Astra SA: 031041 Bucharest 3, Str. Nerva Traian 3/101M; tel. (21) 3188080; fax (21) 3188074; e-mail office@astrasig.ro; internet www .astrasig.ro; f. 1991; Pres. RADU MUSTATEA.

ING Asigurări de Viăţa SA: 050552 Bucharest 3, Str. Costache Negri 1–5, Opera Centre; tel. (21) 4028391; fax (21) 4028581; e-mail asigurari@ing.ro; internet www.ingasigurari.ro; f. 1997; life; CEO CORNELIA AURELIA COMAN.

Omniasig SA: 011862 Bucharest 1, Bd. Aviatorilor 28; tel. (21) 2315040; fax (21) 2315029; e-mail secretary@omniasig.ro; internet www.omniasig.ro; f. 1994; insurance and reinsurance co; 98.9% owned by Vienna Insurance Group (Austria); Chair. CONSTANTIN TOMA.

Unita: 010413 Bucharest 1, Bd. Dacia 30; tel. (21) 2120882; fax (21) 2120843; e-mail unita@unita.ro; internet www.unita.ro; f. 1990; mem. of Uniqa Group (Austria); Dir IULIAN DUMITRU.

Insurance Association

Uniunea Naţională a Societăţilor de Asigurare şi Reasigurare din România (National Association of Insurance and Re-insurance Companies of Romania): 040129 Bucharest 4, Bd. Libertăţii 12, Bloc 114, sc. 3, 4th Floor, ap. 68; tel. (31) 4057328; fax (21) 3177832; e-mail office@unsar.ro; internet www.unsar.ro; f. 1994; 26 mems; Pres. CRISTIAN CONSTANTINESCU; Dir-Gen. FLORENTINA ALMAJANU.

Trade and Industry

GOVERNMENT AGENCIES

Agency for Small and Medium Enterprises and Co-operatives (Agenţia Naţională pentru Întreprinderi Mici şi Mijlocii şi Cooperaţie): 040263 Bucharest 4, Str. Poteraşi 11; tel. (21) 3352620; fax (21) 3361843; e-mail mariana.spranceana@mimmc.ro; internet www .mimmc.ro; Pres. (vacant).

Authority for the Recovery of State Assets (Autoritatea pentru Valorificarea Activelor Statului—AVAS): 715151 Bucharest 1, Str. Capt. A. Şerbănescu 50; tel. (21) 3036122; fax (21) 3036680; e-mail infopublic@avas.gov.ro; internet www.avas.gov.ro; created by merger of the Banking Assets Resolution Agency (AVAB) and the Authority for Privatization and Management of State Ownership (APAPS); successor org. to the State Ownership Fund; Pres. TEODOR ATANASIU.

Romanian Agency for Foreign Investment: 011974 Bucharest 1, Bd. Primaverii 22; tel. (21) 2339103; fax (21) 2339104; e-mail aris@ arisinvest.ro; internet www.arisinvest.ro; f. 2002; Sec.-Gen. FLORIN VASILACHE.

Romanian Trade Promotion Centre (Centrul Român pentru Promovarea Comertului—CRPC): 050741 Bucharest 5, Str. Apolodor 17, POB 1/756; tel. (21) 3185050; fax (21) 3111491; e-mail office@ traderom.ro; internet www.traderom.ro; f. 1995; Dir-Gen. SANDOR NEMES.

CHAMBER OF COMMERCE

Chamber of Commerce and Industry of Romania: 030982 Bucharest 3, Bd. Octavian Goga 2; tel. (21) 3190114; e-mail ccir@ ccir.ro; internet www.ccir.ro; f. 1868; Pres. MIHAIL VLASOV.

EMPLOYERS' ASSOCIATIONS

Alliance of Employers' Confederations of Romania (ACPR) (Alianţa Confederaţiilor Patronale din România): 030982 Bucharest 3, Str. Octavian Goga 2, floor 10; tel. (21) 3211381; fax (21) 3211443; internet www.acpr.ro; f. 2004; includes the National Confederation of Romanian Employers (CNPR), the Employer Confederation of Romanian Industry (CONPIROM) and four others; Pres. GHEORGHE COPOS.

National Confederation of Romanian Employers (Confederaţia Naţională a Patronatului Român—CNPR): 020982 Bucharest 3, Bd. Octavian Goga 2; tel. (21) 3212074; fax (21) 3212075; e-mail cnpr@untrr.ro; internet www.cnpr.org.ro; Pres. DINU PATRICIU; Dir-Gen. CRISTIAN PARVAN.

Romanian Private Farmers' Federation (Federaţia agricultorilor privatizaţi din România): 010043 Bucharest 1, Bd. Nicolae Bălcescu 17–19; tel. (21) 6131869; fax (21) 6133043; f. 1991; represents 4,000 farming co-operatives and 41 district unions; Pres. GHEORGHE PREDILA.

Union of Romanian Employers (Uniunea Patronatelor din România—UPR): 020361 Bucharest 2, Str. Luigi Galvani 17–19, c/o Romanian Employers' Organization (PR); tel. (21) 2111246; fax (21) 2103075; e-mail office@patronatulroman.ro; internet www .patronatulroman.ro; f. 2004; consists of 6 nationally representative employers' organizations; Pres. OVIDIU TENDER.

UTILITIES

Regulatory Authorities

National Energy Regulatory Authority (Autoritatea Naţională de Reglementare in domeniul Energiei—ANRE): 020995 Bucharest 2, Str. Constantin Nacu 3; tel. (21) 3112244; fax (21) 3124365; internet www.anre.ro; f. 1999; Pres. NICOLAE OPRIS.

National Regulatory Authority for the Natural Gas Sector (Autoritatea Naţională de Reglementare in domeniul Gazelor Naturala—ANRGN): 060114 Bucharest 6, Şos. Cotroceni 4; tel. (21) 3033800; fax (21) 3033808; e-mail anrgn@anrgn.ro; internet www .anrgn.ro; f. 2000; Pres. STEFAN COSMEANU.

Electricity

Electrica SA: 010621 Bucharest, Str. Grigore Alexandrescu 9, Sector 1; tel. (21) 2085999; fax (21) 2085998; internet www .electrica.ro; f. 2002; electricity distributor and supplier; 3 regional generating and 4 regional distribution branches, based in Cluj-Napoca (Transilvania Nord), Transilvania Sud (Braşov), Muntenia Nord (Ploieşti) and Muntenia (Bucharest), 1 national servicing branch; Chair. CRISTIAN ISTODORESCU.

Hidroelectrica SA: 020995 Bucharest, Str. Constantin Nacu 3, Sector 2; tel. (21) 3112231; fax (21) 3111174; e-mail generala@ hidroelectrica.ro; internet www.hidroelectrica.ro; state-owned; administers 120 hydropower plants and 4 pumping stations through 10 regional subsidiaries; Gen. Man. EUGEN PENA.

Nuclearelectrica SA: 010494 Bucharest 1, POB 22–102, Str. Polonă 65; tel. (21) 2038200; fax (21) 3169400; e-mail office@ nuclearelectrica.ro; internet www.nuclearelectrica.ro; f. 1998; electrical and thermal power generation; production of nuclear fuel; Gen. Dir Dr POMPILIU BUDULAN; 2,308 employees (2003).

Transelectrica SA: 030786 Bucharest 2, Str. Olteni 2–4; tel. (21) 3035611; fax (21) 3035820; e-mail office@transelectrica.ro; internet www.transelectrica.ro; f. 2000; 73.7% state-owned; transmission system operator; includes 9 brs and 6 subsidiaries; Gen. Dir OCTAVIAN LOHAN; 2,188 employees.

Gas

E.ON Gaz România: 540069 jud. Mureş, Tîrgu Mureş, Justiţiei 12; tel. (365) 403836; fax (365) 403807; e-mail office@eon-gaz-romania .ro; internet www.eon-gaz-romania.ro; f. 1975; fmrly DistriGaz Nord SA; 51% owned by E.ON Ruhrgas (Germany); natural gas distributor; Dir-Gen. VIRGIL METEA; 500 employees.

GDF SUEZ Energy România SA: 040254 Bucharest 4, Bd. Mărăşeşti 4–6; tel. (21) 9366; fax (21) 3012116; e-mail contact@gdfsuez .ro; internet www.gdfsuez-energy.ro; privatized 2004/05; a subsidiary of GDF Suez (France); natural gas distributor.

SNTGN Transgaz SA (Societatea Naţională de transport Gaze Naturale Transgaz SA): 551130 jud. Sibiu, Mediaş, Piaţa Constantin I. Moţaş 1; tel. (269) 803333; fax (269) 839031; e-mail cabinet@ transgaz.ro; internet www.transgaz.ro; 60.5% state-owned; 15% of state-owned shares divested to private ownership in 2013; exploration, transmission and distribution of natural gas; Gen. Dir FLORIN COSMA.

TRADE UNIONS

Cartel Alfa National Trade Union Confederation (Confederaţia Naţională Sindicală Cartel Alfa—CNS Cartel Alfa): 060041 Bucharest 6, Spl. Independenţiei 202A, 2nd Floor; tel. (21) 3171045; fax (21) 3123481; e-mail alfa@cartel-alfa.ro; internet www.cartel-alfa.ro; f. 1990; 750,000 mems (2008); 46 professional affiliations; Pres. BOGDAN IULIU HOSSU.

Confederation of Democratic Trade Unions of Romania (Confederaţia Sindicatelor Democratice din România—CSDR): 010155 Bucharest 1, Piaţa Walter Maracineanu 1–3; tel. (21) 3156542; e-mail csdr@b.astral.ro; f. 1994; 20 professional federations; 101,000 mems (2007); Pres. IACOB BACIU.

Frăţia (Brotherhood) National Confederation of Free Trade Unions of Romania (Confederaţia Naţională a Sindicatelor Libere din România Frăţia—CNSLR Frăţia): 010024 Bucharest 1, Str. Cristian Popisteanu 1–3; tel. and fax (21) 3151632; e-mail biroupresa@cnslr-fratia.ro; internet www.cnslr-fratia.ro; merged with the National Trade Union Bloc (Blocul Naţional Sindical—f. 1991) in 2004; 520,000 mems (2007); 44 professional federations; Pres. MARIUS PETCU.

Meridian National Trade Union Confederation (MNTUC) (Confederaţia Sindicala Naţională Meridian): 010366 Bucharest 1, Str. D. I. Mendeleev 36–38; tel. (21) 3168017; fax (21) 3168018; e-mail csnmeridian@csnmeridian.ro; internet www.csnmeridian.ro; f. 1994; 27 br. federations; Pres. ION POPESCU.

Transport

RAILWAYS

In 2009 there were 10,776 km of track in operation (of which some 4,200 km were electrified).

Romanian Railway Authority (Autoritatea Feroviara Româna— AFER): 010719 Bucharest 1, Calea Grivitei 393; tel. (21) 3077900; fax (21) 2241832; e-mail secretariat@afer.ro; internet www.afer.ro; f. 1998; under the jurisdiction of the Ministry of Transport and Infrastructure; Gen. Dir VASILE BELIBOU.

National Freight Railway Transport Co (Societatea Naţională de Transport Feroviar de Marfă) (CFR Marfă SA): 010873 Bucharest, Bd. Dinicu Golescu 38; tel. (21) 2249336; fax (21) 3124700; e-mail vtulbure@marfa.cfr.ro; internet www.cfrmarfa.cfr.ro; f. 1998 after the reorganization of the SNCFR; main railway freight transport operator in Romania; Gen. Man. LIVIU BOBAR.

National Passenger Railway Transport Co (Societatea Naţională de Transport Feroviar de Călători—CFR Călători SA): 010873 Bucharest, Bd. Dinicu Golescu 38; tel. (21) 3190322; fax (21) 4112054; e-mail marketing.calatori@cfr.ro; internet www.cfr.ro/calatori; f. 1998; divided into eight regional administrations since 1999; reorganized in Feb. 2001 and merged with eight regional companies; operates all local, regional, long-distance and international passenger rail services; Chair. and Chief Exec. ALEXANDRU NOAPTES.

National Railways Company (CFR SA): 010873 Bucharest, Bd. Dinicu Golescu 38; tel. (21) 3192400; fax (21) 3192401; e-mail virgil .daschievici@cfr.ro; internet www.cfr.ro; f. 1998; management of railway infrastructure; Gen. Dir VIOREL SCURTU.

City Underground Railway

The Bucharest underground railway network totals 69.2 km in length.

Metrorex SA—Societatea Comercială de Transport cu Metroul Bucureşti: 010873 Bucharest 1, Bd. Dinicu Golescu 38; tel. (21) 2248975; fax (21) 3125149; e-mail contact@metrorex.ro; internet www.metrorex.ro; f. 1977; Gen. Man. MARIUS IONEL LĂPĂDAT.

ROADS

In 2010 the total length of the national road network was 82,718 km, of which only 56.51% was paved; there were 16,552 km of highways and 65,834 km of secondary roads.

National Administration of Roads (Administraţia Naţională a Drumurilor RA—AND): Ministerul Transporturilor, 010873 Bucharest 1, Bd. Dinicu Golescu 38; tel. (21) 2232606; fax (21) 3120984; e-mail and@andnet.ro; internet www.andnet.ro; Gen. Dir MIHAI GRECU.

INLAND AND OCEAN SHIPPING

The Danube–Black Sea Canal was officially opened to traffic in 1984, and has an annual handling capacity of 80m. metric tons. Romania's principal ports are at Constanţa, on the Black Sea; and Tulcea, Galaţi, Brăila and Giurgiu, on the Danube. At 31 December 2012 Romania's flag registered fleet comprised 161 vessels, totalling 220,404 grt.

Administration of Navigable Canals SH (Administraţia Canalelor Navigabile SA): 907015 jud. Constanţa, Agigea, Str. Écluzei nr 1; tel. (241) 702705; fax (241) 737711; e-mail compania@acn.ro; internet www.acn.ro; f. 1984; Gen. Man. GEORGESCU DANIEL.

Maritime Port Administration of Constanţa SA (NC MPA SA): 900900 jud. Constanţa, Constanţa, Portului Incinta, Gara Maritima; tel. (241) 611540; fax (241) 619512; e-mail apmc@constantza-port.ro; internet www.portofconstantza.com; f. 1991; also administrates Midia and Mangalia ports, and Tomis marina; Gen. Man. IOAN BALAN.

National Co for the Administration of Maritime Ports on the Danube (CN APDM SA) (CN Administraţia Porturilor Dunării Maritime SA—Galaţi): 800025 jud. Galaţi, Galaţi, Str. Portului 34; tel. (236) 460660; fax (236) 460140; e-mail apdm@apdm.galati.ro; internet apdm.galati.ro; f. 1998; manages ports at Galaţi, Brăila, Tulcea, Chilia, Sulina and Sf. Gheorghe; Gen. Man. CARMEN COSTACHE.

National Co for the Administration of River Ports on the Danube (CN Administraţia Porturilor Dunării Fluviale SA—APDF SA): 080011 jud. Giurgiu, Giurgiu, Şos. Portului 1; tel. (246) 213003; fax (21) 3110521; internet www.apdf.ro; f. 1998; Gen. Man. CRISTIAN NEMTESCU.

NAVROM—Romanian River Navigation Co (Compania de Navigatie Fluviala Romana SA—NAVROM): 800025 jud. Galaţi, Galaţi, Str. Portului 34; tel. (236) 460706; fax (236) 460190; e-mail navrom@rls.roknet.ro; fleet of over 400 barges and tugs on the River Danube.

Petromin Shipping Co (CNM Petromin SA): 900125 jud. Constanţa, Constanţa, Portului Incinta, Poarta 2; tel. (241) 617802; fax (241) 619690; e-mail office@petromin.cunet.ro; merchant fleet of 30 ships and tankers; Chair. ANDREI CARAIANI.

River Administration of the Lower Danube–Galaţi (Administraţia Fluvială a Dunării de Jos RA–Galaţi): 800025 jud. Galaţi, Galaţi, Str. Portului 28–30; tel. (236) 460812; fax (236) 460847; e-mail secretariat@afdj.ro; internet www.afdj.ro; 2 brs and 3 agencies; Gen. Man. MIHAI OCHIALBESCU.

CIVIL AVIATION

There are two international airports at Bucharest: Aurel Vlaicu International (Băneasa) and the larger Henri Coandă International (Otopeni). There are other international airports at Constanţa (M. Kogălniceanu), Timişoara, Sibiu and Cluj-Napoca. Domestic airports include those at Arad, Bacău, Iaşi and Oradea.

Romanian Civil Aeronautic Authority (Regia Autonomă Autoritatea Aeronautică Civilă Română): 715621 Bucharest, District 1, Şos. Bucureşti-Ploieşti 38–40; tel. (21) 2081508; fax (21) 2081572; e-mail dir.gen@caa.ro; internet www.caa.ro; f. 1993; Dir-Gen. CLAUDIA VIRLAN.

Blue Air Transport Aerian: 013695 Bucharest, Şos. Bucureşti– Ploieşti 40, Aeroport Bucureşti-Băneasa-Aurel Vlaicu International; tel. (21) 2088686; e-mail info@blue-air.ro; internet www.blueairweb .com; f. 2004; low-cost airline operating flights to domestic and European destinations; Gen. Dir GHEORGHE RACARU.

Carpatair: 307201 jud. Timiş, Timişoara, Timişoara International Airport; tel. (256) 306933; fax (256) 306962; e-mail timisoara@ carpatair.com; internet www.carpatair.com; f. 1999 as Veg Air; assumed present name in 1999; scheduled domestic and international flights and charter services; Pres. NICOLAE PETROV.

Tarom—Compania Naţională de Transporturi Aeriene Române SA (TAROM): 013697 Bucharest, Şos. Bucureşti–Ploieşti, km 16.5, Henri Coandă International (Otopeni) Airport; tel. (21) 2322494; fax (21) 3125686; e-mail secrgen@tarom.ro; internet www .tarom.ro; f. 1954; joint-stock co; services throughout Europe, the Middle East, Asia, the USA and domestically; Pres. GHEORGHE RACARU.

Tourism

The Carpathian Mountains, with their numerous painted monasteries, the Danube delta and the Black Sea resorts (Mamaia, Eforie, Mangalia and others) are the principal attractions. There were 7.5m. foreign tourist arrivals in 2010. Receipts from tourism (including passenger transport) totalled US $1,417m. in 2011.

National Tourism Authority: 010873 Bucharest 1, Bd. Dinicu Golescu 38; tel. (21) 3149957; fax (21) 3149960; e-mail promovare@mturism.ro; govt org.; Pres. IULIU MARIAN OVIDIU.

Defence

As assessed at November 2012, active forces totalled 71,400: army 42,600, navy 6,900, air force 8,400 and a joint force of 13,500. Reserves totalled 45,000. There were also 22,900 border guards and a gendarmerie of an estimated 57,000. Conscription was officially abolished in October 2006. In January 1994 Romania became the first former Warsaw Pact state to join the North Atlantic Treaty Organization's (NATO) 'Partnership for Peace' programme, and it became a full member of NATO on 29 March 2004.

Defence Expenditure: Budgeted at an estimated 8,280m. lei in 2013.

Chief of General Staff of the Armed Forces: Lt-Gen. ŞTEFAN DĂNILĂ.

Education

Education is free and compulsory between the ages of six and 16 years. Before reaching the age of six years, children may attend crèches (creşe) and kindergartens (grădiniţe de copii); in 2002/03 76.5% of pre-school age children were attending kindergarten. Between the ages of six and 16 years children attend the general education school (şcoală de cultură generală de zece ani). In 2009/10 primary enrolment included 88% of children in the relevant age-group, while the comparable ratios for secondary education were equivalent to 97%. The general secondary school (liceul), for which there is an entrance examination, provides a specialized education suitable for preparation of students for admission to university or college. There are also specialized secondary schools, where the emphasis is on industrial, agricultural and teacher-training, and art schools, which correspond to secondary schools, but cover several years of general education. Vocational secondary schools (şcoli profesionale de ucenici) train pupils for a particular career. Tuition in minority languages, particularly Hungarian and German, is available. In June 1999 legislation providing for the establishment of a minority-language university was approved. In 2011/12 there were 108 higher educational institutes in Romania. In 2011 the state budget allocated an estimated 4,207.6m. new lei to education, equivalent to 3.97% of total expenditure in that year.

THE RUSSIAN FEDERATION

Introductory Survey

LOCATION, CLIMATE, LANGUAGE, RELIGION, FLAG, CAPITAL

The Russian Federation, or Russia, constituted the major part of the USSR, providing some 76% of its area and approximately 51% of its population in 1989. It is bounded by Norway, Finland, Estonia and Latvia to the north-west, and by Belarus and Ukraine to the west. The southern borders of European Russia are with the Black Sea, Georgia, Azerbaijan, the Caspian Sea and Kazakhstan. The Siberian and Far Eastern regions have southern frontiers with the People's Republic of China, Mongolia and the Democratic People's Republic of Korea. The eastern coastline is on the Sea of Japan, the Sea of Okhotsk, the Pacific Ocean and the Barents Sea, and the northern coastline is on the Arctic Ocean. The region around Kaliningrad (formerly Königsberg in East Prussia), on the Baltic Sea, became part of the Russian Federation in 1945. Separated from the rest of Russia by Lithuania and Belarus, it borders Poland to the south, Lithuania to the north and east, and has a coastline on the Baltic Sea. The climate of Russia is extremely varied, ranging from extreme Arctic conditions in northern areas and much of Siberia to generally temperate weather in the south. The average temperature in Moscow in July is 19°C (66°F); the average for January is −9°C (15°F). Average annual rainfall in Moscow is 575 mm (23 ins). The official language is Russian, but many other languages are also used. Christianity is the major religion, with the Russian Orthodox Church (Moscow Patriarchate) the largest denomination. The main concentrations of adherents of Islam are among the Tatar, Bashkir and Chuvash peoples of the middle Volga, and the peoples of the northern Caucasus, including the Chechen, Ingush, Kabardins and the peoples of Dagestan. Buddhism is the main religion of the Buryats, the Tyvans and the Kalmyks. The large pre-1917 Jewish population has been depleted by war and emigration, but some 230,000 Jews remained in the Russian Federation in 2002, according to census results. The national flag (proportions 2 by 3) consists of three equal horizontal stripes of (from top to bottom) white, blue and red. The capital is Moscow (Moskva).

CONTEMPORARY POLITICAL HISTORY

Historical Context

By the late 19th century the Russian Empire extended throughout vast territories in eastern Europe, and included much of northern and central Asia, a result of the territorial expansionism of the Romanov dynasty, which had ruled Russia as an autocracy since 1613. Growing dissatisfaction with economic conditions in urban areas, combined with the adverse effect of defeats in the Russo–Japanese War (1904–05), led Tsar Nicholas (Nikolai) II (1894–1917) to issue a manifesto in October 1905, which promised respect for civil liberties and the introduction of some constitutional order, although the ensuing attempt at reforms failed to placate the increasingly restive workers and peasants. In 1917 there were strikes and demonstrations in the capital, Petrograd (as St Petersburg had been renamed in 1914). In March 1917 the Tsar was forced to abdicate and a liberal Provisional Government, composed mainly of landowners, took power. However, most real authority lay with the soviets (councils), composed largely of workers and soldiers, which were attracted to socialist ideas.

The inability of the Provisional Government, led first by Prince Georgii Lvov and then by the moderate socialist Aleksandr Kerenskii, to implement land reforms, or to effect a withdrawal from the First World War, allowed more extreme groups, such as the Bolshevik faction of the Russian Social Democratic Labour Party (RSDLP) led by Vladimir Ulyanov (Lenin), to attain prominence. On 7 November 1917 (25 October in the Old Style calendar, which remained in use until February 1918) the Bolsheviks, who had come to dominate the Petrograd Soviet, seized power in the capital, with minimal use of force, and proclaimed the Russian Soviet Federative Socialist Republic (RSFSR or Russian Federation). The Bolsheviks subsequently adopted the name All-Russian Communist Party (Bolsheviks).

The Bolsheviks asserted that they would respect the self-determination of the former Empire's many nations. Poland, Finland, and the Baltic states of Estonia, Latvia and Lithuania achieved independence, but other independent states established in 1917–18 were forced, militarily, to declare themselves Soviet Republics. These were proclaimed as independent republics, in alliance with the RSFSR, but the laws, Constitution and Government of the Federation were supreme in all of them. However, in 1922 the RSFSR joined the Belarusian, Ukrainian and Transcaucasian republics as constitutionally equal partners in a Union of Soviet Socialist Republics (USSR, or Soviet Union), and institutions of the RSFSR were re-formed as institutions of the new Union. The USSR eventually numbered 15 constituent Soviet Socialist Republics (SSRs). Moscow, the RSFSR's seat of government since 1918, became the capital of the USSR.

The RSFSR, in common with the other republics, experienced hardship as a result of the collectivization campaign of the early 1930s and the widespread repression under Iosif Dzhugashvili (Stalin), who established a brutal dictatorship after the death of Lenin in 1924. The Five-Year Plans, introduced in the late 1920s, effected rapid industrialization, a process that was reinforced by the removal of strategic industries from the west of the republic to the Ural regions during the Second World War ('Great Patriotic War'), which the USSR was drawn into in 1941. Under the Nazi German–Soviet Treaty of Non-Aggression (the 'Molotov-Ribbentrop Pact') of August 1939, the USSR annexed the Baltic states as well as other territories. Victory in the war in 1945 led to further territorial gains for the Russian Federation. In the west it gained part of East Prussia around Königsberg (now Kaliningrad) from Germany, a small amount of territory from Estonia and Latvia, and those parts of Finland annexed during the Soviet–Finnish War (1939–40). In the east it acquired the Kurile Islands from Japan. The nominally independent People's Republic of Tuva (Tyva), situated between the USSR and Mongolia, was annexed in 1944. In 1954 the peninsula of Crimea was ceded by the Russian Federation to the Ukrainian SSR.

Shortly after the death of Stalin in 1953, Nikita Khrushchev became First Secretary of the Communist Party of the Soviet Union (CPSU—as the Communist Party had been renamed in 1952), and gradually assumed predominance over his rivals. The most brutal aspects of the regime were ended, and in 1956 Khrushchev admitted the existence of large-scale repression under Stalin. Khrushchev was dismissed in 1964. He was replaced as First Secretary (later General Secretary) of the CPSU by Leonid Brezhnev. During the 1970s relations with the West, which had, since the late 1940s, been generally characterized by the intense mutual hostility of the 'Cold War', experienced a considerable *détente*; however, this was ended by the Soviet invasion of Afghanistan in 1979. Brezhnev's successor as CPSU General Secretary, following his death in 1982, was Yurii Andropov. He was succeeded upon his death, in February 1984, by Konstantin Chernenko, who, in turn, died in March 1985.

Chernenko's successor as General Secretary was Mikhail Gorbachev. A policy of glasnost (openness) provided a greater degree of freedom for the mass media. In November 1987, however, supporters of perestroika (restructuring), as Gorbachev's reform programme was known, seemed to suffer a reverse, with the dismissal from the Politburo (the executive committee of the CPSU) of Boris Yeltsin. In June 1988 Gorbachev announced plans for the introduction of a two-tier legislature, elected largely by competitive elections. In elections to the new USSR Congress of People's Deputies, held in March 1989, many reformist politicians, including Yeltsin, were successful in achieving election. In May the Congress elected Gorbachev to the new post of executive President of the USSR.

Within the USSR, the RSFSR was clearly pre-eminent, both economically and politically, and ethnic Russians dominated the Soviet élite. However, this prominence meant that Russia developed few autonomous institutions. The initial stage in the process of instituting Russian sovereignty was the election of the RSFSR Congress of People's Deputies in March 1990 by largely free and competitive elections. In May the Congress elected Yeltsin to the highest state post in the RSFSR, the Chairman of the Supreme Soviet (the permanent working body of the Congress). On 12 June the Congress adopted a declaration asserting the sovereignty of the RSFSR in which the federation laws had primacy over all-Union legislation. In March 1991, when a referendum was held in nine republics to determine whether a restructured USSR should be retained, voters in the RSFSR also approved an additional question on the introduction of a Russian presidency. A direct presidential election, held in June, was won by Yeltsin and his Vice-President, Aleksandr Rutskoi, with 57.3% of the votes cast.

Domestic Political Affairs

On 19 August 1991, one day before the new union treaty was due to be signed, the conservative communist 'State Committee for the State of Emergency' (SCSE), led by the Soviet Vice-President, Gennadii Yanayev, seized power in Moscow, taking advantage of Gorbachev's absence from the city. The attempted coup collapsed within three days, and Yeltsin asserted control over all-Union bodies, appointing RSFSR ministers to head central institutions.

In October 1991 Yeltsin announced a programme of radical economic reforms. In November a new Government was announced, with Yeltsin as Chairman (Prime Minister). The CPSU was banned. In the same month the Congress granted Yeltsin special powers for one year, including the right to issue decrees with legislative force and to appoint government ministers without parliamentary approval, and elected Ruslan Khasbulatov, hitherto First Deputy Chairman of the Supreme Soviet, to succeed Yeltsin as Chairman.

On 8 December 1991 the leaders of Belarus, Ukraine and Russia announced the annulment of the 1922 Union Treaty creating the USSR; the Commonwealth of Independent States (CIS, see p. 251), defined as a co-ordinating organization, was created in its place. The CIS was formally established by the Almatı (Alma-Ata) Declaration, signed on 21 December 1991. Of the former Soviet republics, only Georgia, Estonia, Latvia and Lithuania remained outside the new body. (Georgia joined the CIS in December 1993.) On 25 December 1991 Gorbachev resigned as President of the USSR, and the Russian Supreme Soviet formally changed the name of the RSFSR to the Russian Federation.

In June 1992 Yeltsin appointed Yegor Gaidar, an advocate of radical economic reform, as acting Chairman, and in the same month the Supreme Soviet adopted legislation permitting large-scale privatization. In December the Congress of People's Deputies refused to endorse Gaidar's nomination, and Yeltsin was forced to appoint a new, less reformist, premier, Viktor Chernomyrdin. Following the annulment, in March 1993, of an agreement on constitutional reform by the Congress, Yeltsin announced that he would rule by decree prior to the holding of a referendum on a draft constitution, which was held on 25 April 1993. A question on confidence in Yeltsin as President received a positive response from 57.4% of voters, while 53.7% of voters expressed support for Yeltsin's socio-economic policies. Support for an early presidential election was only 49.1%, but 70.6% of voters favoured early elections to the Congress of People's Deputies.

In July 1993 the Constitutional Conference approved a draft that provided for a presidential system with a bicameral parliament—the Federalnoye Sobraniye (Federal Assembly)—comprising a lower chamber (Gosudarstvennaya Duma—State Duma) and an upper chamber (Sovet Federatsii—Federation Council); however, the Congress of People's Deputies rejected this draft. The long-standing impasse between the presidential administration and the legislature eventually resulted in violent confrontation. On 21 September Yeltsin suspended the Congress of People's Deputies and the Supreme Soviet, and scheduled elections to the Federalnoye Sobraniye for December. The Supreme Soviet consequently voted to dismiss Yeltsin as President, announcing the appointment of Rutskoi in his place; an emergency session of the Congress of People's Deputies confirmed this appointment, and voted to impeach Yeltsin. On 27 September government troops surrounded the parliament building: some 180 deputies remained inside, with armed supporters. Conflict erupted in early October, as supporters of the rebel deputies attempted to seize control of strategic buildings in Moscow, and Yeltsin declared a state of emergency in the capital. On 4 October army tanks bombarded the parliament building, forcing the surrender of the rebels. The leaders of the rebellion were imprisoned and charged with inciting mass disorder. According to official figures, 160 people were killed in the fighting.

The new draft constitution, which strengthened the powers of the President, was submitted to a referendum on 12 December 1993, held concurrently with elections to the Federalnoye Sobraniye. Of the 54.8% of the registered electorate that participated in the plebiscite, 58.4% endorsed the draft. In the elections to the Duma, Vladimir Zhirinovskii's nationalist Liberal Democratic Party of Russia (LDPR) secured a total of 64 seats, the largest number obtained by any single party or alliance. (Of the 450 members of the lower chamber, 225 were elected by proportional representation on the basis of party lists, and 225 within single-member constituencies.) Russia's Choice, an alliance of pro-reform groups, led by Gaidar, secured 58 seats. The Communist Party of the Russian Federation (CPRF), which had been founded earlier in the year, took 48 seats, while the Agrarian Party of Russia (APR) won 33 seats, and 130 independent candidates were elected. Russia's Choice emerged as the largest group in the Duma, although no coherent pro-Government majority was established. Direct elections were held concurrently to the Sovet Federatsii, which comprised two representatives from each of Russia's 89 federal subjects (as the constituent territories of the Federation were known). The majority of the Council's members were non-partisan regional leaders. A new Government was appointed in January 1994. In February the Duma voted in favour of granting amnesties to Rutskoi, Khasbulatov and other leaders of the 1993 rebellion, as well as to the SCSE.

In October 1994 a sudden decline in the value of the rouble prompted the resignation or dismissal of government members and the Chairman of the Central Bank, Viktor Gerashchenko. In November the reformist Anatolii Chubais was promoted to the post of First Deputy Chairman, although other government appointments appeared to advance those opposed to further economic liberalization.

In late 1994 Russia commenced military intervention in the separatist Chechen Republic (Chechnya); an apparent lack of progress there, together with the continued deterioration of the economy, were instrumental in the approval by the Duma, in June 1995, of a motion expressing no confidence in the Government. Yeltsin subsequently dismissed a number of ministers, and in July a second vote of no confidence (as required by the Constitution) failed to secure the necessary majority.

Yeltsin's second term as President

Elections to the Duma took place on 17 December 1995. In accordance with a new electoral law, which introduced a minimum requirement of 5% of the votes cast for seats allocated on the basis of party lists, only four parties—the CPRF, the LDPR, Chernomyrdin's Our Home is Russia (OHR) and the liberal Yabloko—secured representation on this basis, while an additional 10 parties and 77 independent candidates obtained seats through voting in single-member constituencies. The CPRF emerged as the largest party in the Duma, with 157 of the 450 deputies. OHR won 55 seats, the LDPR 51 and Yabloko 45.

In January 1996 Yeltsin dismissed Chubais as First Deputy Chairman. In the same month the Duma elected Gennadii Seleznev, a CPRF deputy, as its Chairman. In the same month the Sovet Federatsii was reconstituted, with the elected senators being replaced by regional governors and the heads of regional legislative bodies. In the first round of presidential voting, held on 16 June, and contested by 10 candidates, Yeltsin, with 35.8% of the votes cast, narrowly defeated Gennadii Zyuganov (of the CPRF), with 32.5%. Gen. Aleksandr Lebed, who had until recently commanded Russian forces in the separatist Transnistria (Pridnistrovie) region of Moldova, was placed third, with 14.7%. Yeltsin and Zyuganov duly proceeded to a second round of voting. Meanwhile, Yeltsin appointed Lebed Secretary of the Security Council and National Security Adviser, granting him particular responsibility for resolving the crisis in Chechnya. Despite increasingly infrequent public appearances, apparently a result of poor health, Yeltsin was re-elected as President in the second ballot, on 3 July, with 54% of the total votes cast. Chernomyrdin was subsequently reappointed as premier, and Chubais was promoted to head the Presidential Administration. Despite having negotiated a cease-fire with the Chechen rebels, in October Lebed was dismissed by Yeltsin. In November Yeltsin underwent heart surgery, and was again hospitalized in December, prompting growing pressure for his resignation.

Although Yeltsin delivered a vehement criticism of the Government in his annual address to the Federalnoye Sobraniye in March 1997, Chernomyrdin retained his post in a subsequent government reorganization. Chubais was appointed First Deputy Chairman and Minister of Finance, and Boris Nemtsov was appointed as First Deputy Chairman, with responsibility for dismantling state monopolies, particularly in the areas of fuel and energy. In November Nemtsov lost the fuel and energy portfolio, and Chubais was dismissed as Minister of Finance, although both retained their posts as First Deputy Chairmen.

In March 1998 Yeltsin removed Chernomyrdin from office. The Duma confirmed the appointment of Sergei Kiriyenko, hitherto Minister of Fuel and Energy, as Chairman in mid-April. Several ministers, including Nemtsov, retained their portfolios in the ensuing new Government. Chubais, meanwhile, was appointed Chairman of the electricity monopoly, Unified Energy System of Russia. An attempt by the CPRF to initiate impeachment charges against Yeltsin was ruled unconstitutional by a parliamentary commission in July. In mid-August, however, the Duma succeeded in approving a resolution urging that Yeltsin resign voluntarily.

In August 1998 political instability was exacerbated by severe economic difficulties. Yeltsin dismissed Kiriyenko and his Government, reappointing Chernomyrdin as Chairman. However, Chernomyrdin's candidacy to the premiership was twice rejected by the Duma. In mid-September Yeltsin (aware that should his candidate be rejected for a third time he would be constitutionally obliged to dissolve the Duma) nominated Yevgenii Primakov (Minister of Foreign Affairs since 1996, and a former Director of the Foreign Intelligence Service) as Chairman; his candidacy was endorsed by a large majority. In May 1999 Yeltsin dismissed Primakov. Sergei Stepashin, hitherto First Deputy Chairman and Minister of Internal Affairs, was appointed as Chairman, and a new Government was formed later in the month.

Yeltsin dismissed Stepashin as Chairman of the Government in August 1999. Later in the month the Duma endorsed the appointment in his place of Vladimir Putin, hitherto head of the Federal Security Service (FSB) and Secretary of the Security Council.

Following a number of incursions by Chechen militants into the neighbouring Republic of Dagestan in August 1999, tensions resurfaced relating to the unresolved status of Chechnya and the emergence there of militant Islamist groups. Putin attributed to Chechen militant groups a series of bomb explosions in Moscow, in Dagestan and in Rostov Oblast, which took place in August–September, killing more than 300 people. Putin announced that military action in Chechnya was to recommence, and, prior to the large-scale deployment of ground troops, the aerial bombardment of Chechnya began on 23 September 1999.

In the months preceding the Duma elections scheduled for December 1999 several new political alliances were established, notably the centrist Fatherland-All Russia (FAR), which was formed in August by the merger of the party of the Mayor of Moscow, Yurii Luzhkov, with a grouping of regional governors. In September a further centrist bloc, Unity, supportive of Putin, was formed under the leadership of Sergei Shoigu, the civil defence and emergencies minister, while Kiriyenko and Nemtsov were among the leaders of a new pro-market bloc, the Union of Rightist Forces (URF).

Some 62% of the electorate participated in the elections to the Duma on 19 December 1999. Six parties obtained representation on the basis of party lists; a further eight parties and blocs, and 106 independent candidates, secured representation from single-member constituency ballots. The CPRF, with 24.3% of the votes, again won the largest number of seats (113). Unity, which received 23.3% of the votes cast, was the second largest party in the Duma, with 72 seats; FAR won 67, the URF 29, Yabloko 21 and the Zhirinovskii bloc (chiefly comprising the LDPR) 17.

On 31 December 1999 Boris Yeltsin unexpectedly resigned as President. Putin assumed the presidency in an acting capacity. He granted Yeltsin immunity from prosecution, and removed from office principal members of Yeltsin's administration. When the new Duma convened in mid-January 2000, the CPRF and Unity factions formed an alliance; thus, for the first time since the dissolution of the USSR, pro-Government forces held a majority in the legislature.

Vladimir Putin elected President

Putin received 52.9% of the votes cast in the presidential election held on 26 March 2000, having received the support of FAR, as well as Unity. His closest rival was Zyuganov, with 29.2%. Putin was inaugurated as President on 7 May. In mid-May Mikhail Kasyanov, hitherto First Deputy Chairman and Minister of Finance, was approved as Chairman of the Council of Ministers. A new Government was appointed shortly afterwards.

In June 2000 Vladimir Gusinskii, the owner of the Mediya-Most holding company (which operated Russia's only wholly independent federation-wide television broadcaster, NTV), was arrested in June and charged with fraud. After being released on bail, Gusinskii fled to Spain. In September the state-controlled gas monopoly, Gazprom (to which Mediya-Most was heavily indebted), brought charges of criminal embezzlement against Mediya-Most's management. Gusinskii lost control of the company in November, and the deal reached with a Gazprom subsidiary, Gazprom-Mediya, effectively gave the state a controlling stake in all Mediya-Most enterprises, with the exception of NTV. In December the Moscow fiscal authorities demanded that Mediya-Most be closed, on grounds of insolvency. Following the refusal of the Spanish authorities to extradite Gusinskii to Russia, in April 2001 he took up residence in Israel (where he held dual citizenship). In August 2003 Gusinskii was arrested in Greece, but a Greek court subsequently ruled against his extradition to Russia.

Meanwhile, other prominent businessmen were subjected to examinations of their business affairs, in what was interpreted as an attempt by the Government to reduce the powers of the 'oligarchs' (a number of wealthy businessmen, who in many cases had acquired control of formerly nationalized industries in the 1990s). In July 2000 Boris Berezovskii, a prominent oligarch and former Deputy of the Security Council and Executive Secretary of the CIS (who had played a major role in promoting Putin's candidacy as President), relinquished his seat in the Duma, accusing Putin of having adopted an increasingly authoritarian style of governance. In September Berezovskii announced his intention to relinquish his 49% stake in the state-controlled television station, ORT, claiming that he had been ordered to surrender his holding to the state or risk imprisonment; the sale took place in February 2001. None the less, a warrant for Berezovskii's arrest was issued in November 2000, after he failed to return to Russia from France to answer questions relating to charges of money-laundering and illegal entrepreneurship.

Meanwhile, in May 2000, as part of measures intended to facilitate what Putin termed 'vertical power', seven Federal Okrugs (Districts) were created, each of which was headed by a presidential appointee, to whom regional governments and governors were to be answerable. A new consultative body, the State Council, comprising the heads of the federal subjects (who were no longer to sit in the Sovet Federatsii), was created by presidential decree in September.

In March 2001 Putin implemented a minor ministerial reorganization, appointing Boris Gryzlov, the head of the Unity faction in the Duma, as Minister of Internal Affairs, and Sergei Ivanov (hitherto Secretary of the Security Council and a former deputy head of the FSB) as Minister of Defence. In April it was announced that the Unity faction in the Duma was to form an alliance with FAR, ending its support for the CPRF. Gazprom-Mediya acquired NTV in the same month. Following the dismissal of NTV's management, Yevgenii Kiselyev, the company's former Director-General and Editor-in-Chief, was appointed to head a small television channel owned by Berezovskii, TV6, to which the majority of the former NTV journalists transferred. Meanwhile, in July the legislature approved a law banning foreign citizens, as well as Russians holding dual citizenship, from acquiring a majority stake in Russian television channels.

In July 2001 Putin signed a law imposing new conditions on political parties, which were henceforth required to have a minimum of 10,000 members, including no fewer than 100 members in at least 50 of the 89 federal subjects, in order to be permitted to participate in elections. At the beginning of December the first congress of Unity and Fatherland-United Russia (later known simply as United Russia—UR), formed by the merger of FAR and Unity, marked the formal establishment of the party, which enjoyed a majority in both parliamentary houses. The Sovet Federatsii, chaired by Sergei Mironov, an ally of Putin, was convened in January 2002 with a reformed composition. In place of regional leaders and chairmen of regional legislative assemblies, the Council comprised their full-time appointees; the formation of political factions and groups in the Council was prohibited.

In January 2002 TV6 ceased transmissions, following a court case brought by a minority shareholder, which had demanded the television company's liquidation on the grounds of unprofitability. In March a new, non-profit organization, Mediya-Sotsium, associated with Primakov, was awarded the contract to broadcast formerly held by TV6; Kiselyev and many TV6 journalists transferred to the new channel, which commenced operations as TVS. Meanwhile, Berezovskii presented a video-recording in London, United Kingdom, which purported to demonstrate the FSB's involvement, and Putin's acquiescence, in the bombings of mid-1999. In October 2002 Berezovskii was charged, *in absentia*, with defrauding the state. Later that month, following the publication of an interview in a nationalist journal in which he spoke in support of formation of a united opposition front combining liberal and left-wing forces, Berezovskii was suspended from the political party he had founded in late 2001, Liberal Russia; one week later the Ministry of Justice agreed to register the party. Berezovskii was arrested in the United Kingdom, where he was resident, in March 2003 in response to an extradition request by Russia, but was granted political asylum in September, and the extradition proceedings were dismissed.

In October 2002, following the deaths of at least 129 people as the result of an armed siege at a Moscow theatre by heavily armed militants linked to Chechen extremists, the Government implemented a number of personnel changes in Chechnya. In November Stanislav Ilyasov, hitherto the Prime Minister of Chechnya, was appointed to the federal Government as Minister without Portfolio, responsible for the Social and Economic Development of the Chechen Republic.

In June 2003 the Ministry of the Press, Broadcasting and Mass Media ordered the closure of TVS, purportedly as a result of financial difficulties experienced by the station; its broadcasts were replaced by a newly established, state-controlled sports channel.

Meanwhile, attacks against civilian targets by militants associated with Chechen separatist, or Islamist, rebels continued to occur, particularly in regions of southern Russia near Chechnya and in Moscow. In July 2003 at least 18 people were killed in two suicide bombings at a music festival near Moscow. A suicide bombing, in early December, on a train in southern Russia killed at least 42 people, and injured some 200 others. On 9 December, two days after the legislative elections (see below), a suicide bombing in central Moscow resulted in at least six deaths. In early February 2004 at least 39 people were killed and more than 100 injured in a further bomb attack on a train on the Moscow Metro.

In late 2003 several court cases and judicial investigations were instigated against senior officials of the prominent privately owned petroleum company Yukos, and its subsidiary companies. The chief executive of the company, Mikhail Khodorkovskii (who was reported to be the wealthiest person in Russia), had recently announced that he was providing financial support to Yabloko and the URF; it was reported that in undertaking such action, Khodorkovskii was breaching an informal agreement reported to have been reached between Putin and several prominent oligarchs in 2000, to the effect that the latter would refrain from engaging in overt political activity. On 25 October Khodorkovskii was arrested by FSB officers at an airport in Siberia; he was subsequently charged with tax evasion and fraud, and imprisoned pending further investigations.

Putin re-elected for a second presidential term

Some 32 parties and blocs contested the elections to the Duma held on 7 December 2003. Only four of these groupings received the minimum 5% share of votes cast required to obtain representation on the basis of federal party lists: UR won an absolute majority of seats in the new legislature, with 226 seats, while the representation of the CPRF was substantially reduced, to 53 seats. The LDPR secured 38 seats, while a recently formed electoral bloc, Motherland—People's Patriotic Union (Motherland), comprising several communist and nationalist groups, received 37 seats. Nine other groups and 57 independent deputies achieved representation in the new Duma in constituency voting. The URF, Yabloko and the CPRF alleged that electoral fraud had been perpetrated, and electoral observers of the Organization for Security and Co-operation in Europe (OSCE, see p. 397) expressed concern that UR had benefited from the use of state administrative resources in support of the party. Moreover, several government members held senior positions in UR, in apparent defiance of a constitutional clause prohibiting ministers from holding membership of political parties. Gryzlov, the Chairman of the Supreme Council of UR, was elected as the Chairman of the Duma on 24 December. He was succeeded as Minister of Internal Affairs by Col-Gen. Rashid Nurgaliyev.

Campaigning for the presidential election held on 14 March 2004 was characterized by an absence of prominent or credible challengers to Putin, who contested the election as an independent candidate, and refused to participate in televised debates with other candidates. The CPRF and LDPR nominated relatively obscure figures, Nikolai Kharitonov and Oleg Malyshkin, respectively, as their candidates. The URF's refusal to endorse the candidacy of one of its leading members, Irina Khakamada, obliged her to campaign as an independent candidate. Mironov contested the election as the candidate of his party, the Russian Party of Life (RPL), while none the less expressing support for Putin. Yabloko boycotted the election. After dismissing the Government on 24 February, on 1 March Putin announced the nomination of Mikhail Fradkov, hitherto the permanent representative of Russia to the European Communities, as the new Chairman of the Government. Following the approval of his appointment by the Duma, the formation of a new Government was announced on 9 March. Although most of the principal positions within the Government (which was reduced from 31 to 17 ministers) remained unchanged, a new Minister of Foreign Affairs, Sergei Lavrov, hitherto ambassador to the UN, was appointed.

On 14 March 2004 Putin was re-elected, as had been widely anticipated, for a second, and under the terms of the Constitution, final consecutive term of office, receiving 71.3% of the votes cast. His nearest rival, Kharitonov, took 13.7%. The rate of participation was 64.4%. Putin's second term formally commenced on 7 May.

In June 2004 the trial of Khodorkovskii and his business associate, Platon Lebedev, began in Moscow, on seven charges, including tax evasion, forgery and fraud. While the trial was in progress, the state authorities presented Yukos with a series of demands for unpaid taxes totalling some US $27,500m., and demanded that the principal production subsidiary of Yukos, Yuganskneftegaz, be brought to auction. In December Yuganskneftegaz was sold to a previously unknown company, Baikalfinansgrup, which was acquired by the state-owned petroleum company Rosneft shortly after the auction. In May 2005 Khodorkovskii and Lebedev were each sentenced to nine years' imprisonment. (In December 2010 Khodorkovskii and Lebedev were found guilty on further charges of embezzlement and money-laundering, and were each sentenced to 14 years' imprisonment, to run concurrently with the sentences that they had begun serving in 2005; in December 2012 the terms of both men were reduced by two years.) Meanwhile, opposition to the Putin administration was increasingly expressed by a grouping known as the United Civil Front, led by the former international chess champion Garri Kasparov, and incorporating both liberal democratic and radical nationalist groups.

Violent attacks on Russian civilians, attributed to extremist Chechen separatists intensified following the assassination of the President of Chechnya in May 2004. On 24 August two passenger planes flying from Moscow's Domodedovo airport, crashed, killing all 89 people on board. Both crashes were subsequently attributed to Chechen suicide bombers. On 1 September, the first day of the school year, armed militants occupied a school in Beslan, in the Republic of North Osetiya—Alaniya, taking at least 1,100 children, parents and teachers hostage. On 3 September troops stormed the building, reportedly in reaction to a series of explosions. Some 350 hostages, including 186 children, died in the ensuing battle, according to official figures. The militant Chechen leader, Shamil Basayev, subsequently claimed responsibility for the hostage-taking operation.

Apparently in reaction to this event, President Putin proposed a series of political reforms, including the introduction of a system whereby all regional governors would be appointed by the federal President, subject to the approval of the regional legislature, rather than being directly elected as had been the case in most territories since the second half of the 1990s. Putin signed legislation to this end on 12 December 2004, following its approval by both chambers of the Federalnoye Sobraniye. The final gubernatorial election took place in February 2005. Putin also announced proposals that all 450 members of the Duma be elected on the basis of proportional representation and party lists. Moreover, the minimum membership required of a registered political party was increased from 10,000 to 50,000, with effect from January 2006. The quota for representation in the Duma on the basis of federal party lists was also increased from 5% of the total votes cast to 7%.

On 14 November 2005 President Putin announced a government reorganization. Dmitrii Medvedev, the Chairman of the Board of Directors of Gazprom and hitherto Chief of the Presidential Staff, was appointed First Deputy Chairman, while retaining his post at Gazprom. Sergei Ivanov, while retaining the defence portfolio, was also to serve as one of two Deputy Chairmen of the Government.

The further consolidation of power

A major focus of parliamentary activity during the second half of 2005 was the development of measures intended to result in greater government supervision and regulation of non-governmental organizations (NGOs). Legislation that, *inter alia*, permitted the authorities to close NGOs deemed to infringe Russia's sovereignty, unity or cultural heritage was signed into law by President Putin in January 2006. On 12 March, after the restrictions on party registration entered into effect on 1 January, the first 'unified election day' (for elections to various levels of government, or to certain local and regional assemblies in the Federation, which had hitherto taken place throughout the year) took place. (Henceforth, the overwhelming majority of such elections were to take place in March and October each year.) UR won control of the overwhelming majority of regional assemblies to which elections were conducted (a pattern that was repeated at subsequent unified election days), although the rate of voter participation was relatively low. In June Putin nominated the Minister of Justice, Yurii Chaika, as Prosecutor-General; Chaika was succeeded as Minister of Justice by Vladimir Ustinov, the previous Prosecutor-General. In October Motherland, the RPL and the Russian Pensioners' Party united to form a new political party, A Just Russia (AJR), chaired by Mironov.

In October 2006 a journalist of the independent newspaper *Novaya Gazeta*, Anna Politkovskaya, a leading critic of the Russian military campaigns in Chechnya and the official Chechen leadership, was shot dead at her apartment building in Moscow. Her death attracted international attention, and speculation that the Chechen authorities may have been involved in her killing. (According to independent estimates, at least 13 journalists had been murdered in Russia since 2000; a substantially greater number of journalists had been killed in suspicious circumstances during the 1990s.) In November Aleksandr Litvinenko, a former officer in the FSB and exile to the United Kingdom, died in a London hospital as a result of radiation-poisoning, having publicly accused Putin of responsibility for his sickness. Medical tests concluded that Litvinenko had been exposed to the radioactive substance Polonium-210. Police investigations into the killing of Litvinenko, who had been a close associate of Berezovskii, and who was subsequently revealed to be working for the British Secret Intelligence Service, commenced in both the United Kingdom and Russia. The Russian authorities subsequently refused to accede to a request by the British Government for the extradition of the principal suspect, Andrei Lugovoi. (In December 2007 Lugovoi was elected to the Duma, thereby securing immunity from prosecution within Russia.)

In December 2006 the Central Electoral Commission (CEC) announced that the forthcoming presidential election would take place on 9 March 2008. On 15 February 2007 Putin reorganized the Government, appointing Sergei Ivanov First Deputy Chairman (thereby granting him equal status to Medvedev). Anatolii Serdyukov, hitherto the head of the Federal Tax Service, replaced Ivanov as Minister of Defence, becoming the first appointee to that position not to have a background in the military or security services. In early March a mass opposition rally was organized in St Petersburg by the Another Russia coalition, the leaders of which included Kasparov, Kasyanov and the leader of the extremist and prohibited National Bolshevik Party, Eduard Limonov. In April Another Russia organized anti-Government demonstrations in Moscow and St Petersburg, which were violently suppressed by OMON troops associated with the Ministry of Internal Affairs.

In April 2007, after Berezovskii declared to the British newspaper, *The Guardian*, that he planned the forcible ousting of the Putin administration, Minister of Foreign Affairs Lavrov reiterated demands for his extradition from the United Kingdom and announced further criminal proceedings against him. The insistence of the British authorities that Berezovskii's asylum status made him immune from extradition further exacerbated tensions between the two countries. (In November Berezovskii was sentenced *in absentia* by a Moscow district court to six years' imprisonment for embezzlement; in June 2009 he was sentenced to a further term of 13 years' imprisonment on further charges of embezzlement.)

On 14 September 2007, following the resignation of Fradkov and his Government, the Duma approved Putin's nomination of Viktor Zubkov, hitherto head of the Federal Financial Monitor-ing Service, as Chairman. Later that month Putin announced a government reorganization; notably, the Minister of Finance, Aleksei Kudrin, also became a Deputy Chairman. In October Putin announced, in a statement made at UR's party congress, that he would head the party's list of candidates in the forthcoming legislative elections on 2 December and that he viewed favourably a proposal by delegates that he, eventually, become Chairman of the Government. In November the Office for Democratic Institutions and Human Rights (ODIHR) of the OSCE announced the abandonment of plans to monitor the elections, after Russia imposed restrictions on the number of observers that would be invited; however, the Parliamentary Assemblies of the OSCE and Council of Europe (see p. 260) dispatched small monitoring missions.

At the elections to the Duma on 2 December 2007, UR won a substantial majority, securing 64.3% of the votes cast, according to official results, and 315 seats; the CPRF received 11.6% of votes and 57 seats, the LDPR 8.1% and 40 seats, and AJR 7.7% and 38 seats. Voter turn-out was 63.7% of the electorate. Reports emerged that students and public sector workers had been placed under pressure by the authorities to vote for UR. The Russian Government dismissed a subsequent joint statement by the OSCE and the Council of Europe that the conduct of the elections had failed to meet international standards for democracy. (A report by CIS observers, in contrast, upheld the organization of the elections.) On 10 December Putin announced his support for the nomination by UR and three other parties of Medvedev as a candidate in the forthcoming presidential election on 2 March 2008. In January 2008 the CEC rejected the presidential candidacy of Kasyanov, ruling that a number of the signatures collected in his support were invalid; he subsequently urged a boycott of the poll.

The Medvedev-Putin duumvirate

On 2 March 2008 Medvedev was elected to the presidency, with some 70.3% of the votes cast, according to final official results; Zyuganov of the CPRF received 17.7% of the votes, and Zhirinovskii of the LDPR 9.4%. The official rate of participation was 69.8%. Observers from the Parliamentary Assembly of the Council of Europe (PACE) acknowledged popular support for Medvedev, but reported that aspects of the electoral campaign had failed to meet democratic standards. At a UR congress in April, Putin accepted an invitation to assume the new post of Chairman of the party, although it was confirmed that he would not formally become a member of the party. Medvedev was inaugurated as President on 7 May. Shortly afterwards Medvedev nominated Putin as Chairman of the Government; on 8 May the Duma approved his nomination to the office by an overwhelming majority (with only CPRF deputies opposing it). On 12 May Putin announced a government reorganization, in which an additional three ministries were created. Zubkov became First Deputy Chairman, with particular responsibility for the agricultural sector, while a senior presidential aide, Igor Shuvalov, was also accorded the post of First Deputy Chairman. Igor Sechin, the Chairman of Rosneft and hitherto deputy head of the presidential administration, was appointed to the Government as a Deputy Chairman and was to supervise industrial development programmes.

In his first annual address as President on 5 November 2008, Medvedev announced proposed amendments to the Constitution, extending the term of office of the President from four to six years and that of the deputies of the Duma from four to five years. The constitutional amendments were adopted by both parliamentary chambers later in November. On 12 December opposition leaders from many organizations, including Nemtsov and Kasparov, officially established an opposition movement, Solidarity. Protest demonstrations were organized by Another Russia in Moscow and St Petersburg, who criticized the Government's failure to address the economic crisis and against the extension of the presidential and legislative mandates. The constitutional amendments were signed into law by Medvedev on 30 December.

In January 2009 a prominent human rights lawyer, Stanislav Markelov, who had represented the relatives of a Chechen woman murdered by a Russian officer in 2000, and a journalist were shot and killed in Moscow. (In November 2009 two members of an extreme nationalist group were arrested on suspicion of their killings.) In February three suspects charged with involvement in the killing of Anna Politkovskaya in 2006 (of whom two were Chechen nationals and one was a former senior police officer, Dmitrii Pavlyuchenkov) were acquitted by a Moscow court. In April 2009 Medvedev dismissed the head of the Main

Intelligence Directorate, Gen. Valentin Korabelnikov (who had been appointed to the post in 1997), and two other senior defence officials. In May acute economic difficulties in the town of Pikalevo, near St Petersburg, including mass unemployment resulting from the closure of three local factories, and the suspension of power supplies to the town, led to substantial civil disorder there. Putin visited the town and, publicly rebuking the owner of one of the closed factories, the prominent oligarch Oleg Deripaska, ordered that production be resumed at the factory. In June the Supreme Court overturned the acquittal of the three suspects charged with killing Politkovskaya, on grounds of procedural irregularities, and ordered a retrial. In September the Supreme Court additionally ordered a further investigation into the murder of Politkovskaya, reversing an earlier decision by a lower military court. (In December 2012 Pavlyuchenkov was sentenced to 11 years' imprisonment for organizing the killing of Politkovskaya.)

On 11 October 2009 elections were conducted to local and municipal authorities in 76 federal subjects, together with elections to three regional legislatures; UR won decisively in nearly every poll. Opposition leaders accused the authorities of mass falsification of the elections, notably in those to the Moscow Municipal Duma. Deputies belonging to AJR, the CPRF and the LDPR temporarily suspended participation in the State Duma, to protest against alleged widespread electoral malpractice. In the following month the bombing of an express train travelling from Moscow to St Petersburg was believed to have targeted prominent St Petersburg officials on board the train; some 26 people were killed, including a former Deputy Governor of the city, Sergei Tarasov, and the head of the federal agency for state reserves. The Chechen militant leader, Doku Umarov claimed responsibility for the attack. In January 2010 Medvedev announced the creation of a new North Caucasus Federal Okrug in a restructuring of regional government, as part of efforts to strengthen federal control over the North Caucasus region. The Presidential Representative of the new district, Aleksandr Khloponin, was also appointed as a Deputy Chairman of the Government. Later in January protest marches (which had taken place on several occasions during 2009) were again organized by opposition leaders in Moscow and St Petersburg.

Suicide bomb attacks in Moscow

In February 2009 Medvedev dismissed two deputy internal affairs ministers and 16 senior police officials, as part of an anti-corruption campaign in law enforcement bodies. On a further 'unified election day' on 14 March, local, municipal and regional elections took place in 76 federal subjects. An independent monitoring organization, GOLOS, reported widespread irregularities in many polls. The election results demonstrated a decline in support in some regions for UR, which had, unusually, secured less than 50% of votes cast to four of eight contested regional legislatures. In late March unauthorized demonstrations demanding the resignation of Putin, in response to continuing economic difficulties, took place in cities across Russia, and were violently suppressed in Moscow. In addition, opposition groups had, from July 2009, organized 'Strategy 31' marches nation-wide on the last day of every month with 31 days, in reference to Article 31 of the Russian Constitution that permits peaceful demonstrations.

On 29 March 2010 some 40 people were killed and more than 100 injured in two suicide bomb attacks on the Moscow Metro (the first explosion occurring at a station located beneath FSB headquarters). Umarov subsequently released a video recording in which he stated that the bombings had been undertaken on his orders, and that more attacks would follow. In May the head of the FSB officially announced that three organizers of the Metro bombings had been shot dead by security agents during an attempt to arrest them.

From July 2010 a prolonged drought and unusually high temperatures resulted in thousands of forest fires breaking out across the country, destroying many villages, and causing a noxious smog in Moscow and other nearby urban areas. By mid-August the fires had killed 54 people and left thousands homeless. On 2 August President Medvedev declared a state of emergency in several regions, and ordered an investigation into the fires. Later that month the head of the Federal Forestry Agency was replaced.

On 28 September 2010 President Medvedev dismissed Luzhkov (regarded as a close ally of Putin) as Mayor of Moscow, stating that he had lost his confidence. Luzhkov's removal, which followed that of several other long-serving regional leaders, was reportedly prompted by a newspaper article in which Luzhkov

had expressed opposition to Medvedev's decision to suspend the construction project of a new highway between Moscow and St Petersburg. Prior to his dismissal, Luzhkov had been subject to criticism on state-controlled television, where he had been accused of corruption and extreme incompetence. Luzhkov also resigned from UR. (In February 2011 the federal Audit Chamber announced that investigations into the finances of the Moscow City Government under Luzhkov had revealed violations amounting to 230,000m. roubles in 2009–10, while the Ministry of Internal Affairs was undertaking an investigation into an alleged malpractice scheme that involved several companies associated with Luzhkov and his wife, Yelena Baturina.

On 10 October 2010 local and municipal elections were held in 77 territories, together with elections to three regional legislatures: UR secured about 60% of votes cast overall. GOLOS again noted widespread violations, both during the electoral campaign and the voting process. On 21 October Sergei Sobyanin, a hitherto Deputy Chairman of the federal Government and Head of the Government Staff, was inaugurated as Mayor of Moscow, after the Municipal Duma voted in support of his nomination by President Medvedev. A Deputy Chairman of the Gosudarstvennaya Duma, Vyacheslav Volodin, was appointed to succeed Sobyanin in his government posts. Sobyanin immediately relaxed the stance of the municipal authorities towards the holding of opposition protests in the capital, granting permission for a limited 'Strategy 31' demonstration to be staged in central Moscow at the end of October, although large numbers of participants in similar gatherings in other major cities were again arrested.

In early December 2010 clashes erupted between extreme nationalists and police in Moscow after a rally, organized to protest against the killing earlier in the month of a football supporter during a fight with a group of men from the North Caucasus. Disturbances continued across Moscow, and numerous people originating from Central Asia and the Caucasus were attacked; at least two people from minority ethnic groups died as a result. Nationalist demonstrations and protests subsequently spread to other cities across Russia. On 21 December the Duma approved legislation, to enter into effect in 2015, prohibiting regional leaders from using the designation 'President' (as used by the leaders of several republics within the Federation). At the end of December 2010 some 60 people were arrested during a 'Strategy 31' rally in Moscow, despite it having been officially authorized. Nemtsov, who was among those detained, was sentenced to 15 days' imprisonment, prompting further protests by his supporters.

On 24 January 2011 a suicide bomb attack was carried out at Domodedovo international airport in Moscow, killing 36 people and injuring a further 168. The authorities announced that they had identified the perpetrator and named a further six suspects, of whom three were arrested. In March, following an investigation, Umarov (who had claimed direct responsibility for the attack) was officially charged with organizing the bombing.

Elections conducted to local and municipal authorities in 74 federal subjects, together with elections to 12 regional legislatures, on 13 March 2011 were viewed as illustrative of public opinion prior to the federal parliamentary elections due to be held in December. Although UR secured an estimated 68% of the contested legislative seats, according to preliminary results, it received only about 46% of the votes cast overall (significantly lower than the support it had received in the 2007 federal elections). Opposition parties again complained of numerous electoral violations. Later in the month speculation of dissent between Medvedev and Putin increased, when the President publicly rebuked Putin for having denounced a UN Security Council resolution that authorized military intervention in the civil conflict in Libya (see Libya); Medvedev openly favoured the resolution, which Russia consequently did not oppose in the Security Council. Medvedev subsequently dismissed the Russian ambassador in Libya, who had accused Medvedev of jeopardizing Russian interests in the country. At the end of March Medvedev ordered government officials who also held directorships of state companies to resign from these positions no later than 1 October, so as to reduce state influence (and, in particular, that of close allies of Putin) over the business sector. Accordingly, in April Sechin resigned from the chairmanship of Rosneft; prominent officials also relinquished posts in state banks. (However, Zubkov was permitted to retain the post of Chairman of the Board of Directors of Gazprom.)

In early May 2011 Putin announced the creation of an All-Russia National Front, an umbrella grouping of organizations supportive of him, including UR. On 18 May Mironov was removed as Chairman of the St Petersburg City Duma, and was consequently obliged to resign from the chairmanship of the Sovet Federatsii. (Later in the year he became a deputy in the Duma.) In late August President Medvedev appointed the hitherto Presidential Representative to the Central Federal Okrug, Georgii Poltavchenko, as Governor of St Petersburg, following the resignation from that post of Valentina Matviyenko, one day after she had been elected to a post on St Petersburg City Council, thereby granting her eligibility for nomination to the Sovet Federatsii. In early September Poltavchenko duly nominated Matviyenko as the representative of the City's Government to the upper chamber of the federal legislature, and later in the month she was elected Chairman of the Sovet Federatsii.

Putin's return to the presidency

During a UR party congress, held in Moscow in September 2011, Putin accepted Medvedev's proposal that he contest the presidential election of 2012, and indicated that, should he become President, he would offer Medvedev the post of Chairman of the Government. Two days later Kudrin tendered his resignation as a Deputy Chairman of the Government and Minister of Finance, after he criticized various decisions of Medvedev, and stated that he would be unwilling to serve in a future Government headed by him. He was succeeded as Minister of Finance by Anton Siluanov. In late November Medvedev formally nominated Putin as UR's presidential candidate. Meanwhile, in late 2011 unprecedented popular disaffection with UR and Putin's leadership began to emerge, particularly in view of his anticipated return to the presidency.

Elections were held to the Gosudarstvennaya Duma on 4 December 2011. According to the official results issued later in the month, UR won 49.3% of the votes cast and a total of 238 deputies (demonstrating a significant loss in support, while retaining an overall majority, albeit short of the two-thirds' majority required for the approval of constitutional amendments). The other three parties in the outgoing legislature all increased their representation: the CPRF, with 19.2% of the votes, received 92 seats; AJR, with 13.2%, 64 seats; and the LDPR, with 11.7%, 56 seats. On the same day elections were held to regional legislatures in 27 territories. Public protests against alleged electoral fraud took place in Moscow and other cities after the closure of polling stations, and international observers reported that serious violations of democratic norms had occurred, while campaigners published videos online apparently demonstrating malpractice. Opposition supporters and pro-Putin groups staged rival demonstrations in Moscow in the following days, and large numbers of troops and police were deployed in the capital; more than 400 people were reported to have been arrested, including Nemtsov, Limonov and prominent anti-corruption campaigner Aleksei Navalnyi, who was sentenced to 14 days' detention. On 10 December large demonstrations were staged in Moscow and other cities to demand the annulment of the election results, the dismissal of the head of the federal electoral commission, Vladimir Churov, and the registration of various opposition groups that had not been allowed to participate in the elections. Further mass protests, with broad-based support, took place in major cities on 24 December.

Meanwhile, on 21 December 2011 the hitherto head of the presidential administration, Sergei Naryshkin, was elected Chairman of the Duma, following Grzylov's resignation. One day later Medvedev proposed a number of reforms at a plenary session of the Federal Assembly, including the reintroduction of gubernatorial elections (Putin had also expressed support for such a proposal, subject to the list of potential candidates being 'filtered' by the President), the reintroduction of regional constituency mandates in the Duma, and an easing of the conditions for the registration of political parties. On 16 January 2012 Medvedev submitted draft legislation to the Duma providing for the introduction of the reforms. Meanwhile, on 23 December 2011 Dmitrii Rogozin, hitherto Permanent Representative of Russia to the North Atlantic Treaty Organization (and the former Co-chairman of the nationalist Motherland party) was appointed a Deputy Chairman of the Government, with specific responsibilities relating to defence. On 27 December Vladislav Surkov, a close ally of Putin, who was widely regarded as the principal ideologist of UR and the doctrine of 'sovereign democracy', was appointed as another Deputy Chairman. At the end of January 2012 Viktor Khristenko resigned as Minister of Industry and Trade following his appointment to head a new Eurasian Economic Commission (see Regional relations).

On 29 January 2012 it was announced that five candidates had been granted registration to contest the presidential election scheduled for 4 March; these included an independent candidate, wealthy businessman Mikhail Prokhorov, while Yabloko leader Grigorii Yavlinskii was one of several nominees to have been denied registration. On 4 February a further demonstration, attended by more than 100,000 supporters according to opposition estimates, was staged in Moscow to protest against Putin's expected return to the presidential office. On 23 February, during the national holiday Defenders of the Fatherland Day, Putin addressed a large rally in central Moscow, which was organized to support his campaign for the presidency. The presidential election on 4 March proceeded amid reports of voting irregularities; on the following day the CEC declared Putin to have won the poll, with 63.6% of votes cast, according to (subsequently confirmed) preliminary results. Zyuganov was second placed, with 17.2%, followed by Prokhorov, Zhirinovskii and Mironov. The rate of participation was reported at 65.3% of the electorate. International monitors from OSCE/ODIHR and PACE immediately stated that the campaign conditions and organization of the election had been biased towards Putin and urged an investigation into opposition allegations of widespread violations (included the casting of multiple ballots at numerous polling stations—so-called 'carousel voting'—by supporters of Putin). Also on 5 March OMON forces violently dispersed popular demonstrations staged in Moscow and St Petersburg against Putin's election, and more than 500 protesters were arrested. Further protests in support of demands for a new presidential poll were organized on 10 March. Following its approval by both parliamentary chambers in late March, on 3 April Medvedev signed into law the bill on party registration, which reduced the minimum number of party members from 40,000 (which itself had been reduced in stages since 2010 from the former level of 50,000) to 500, as well as lowering the required minimum strength of regional branches. On 1 May he enacted the legislation providing for the restoration of gubernatorial elections (which was to enter into effect on 1 June, with the first such elections to be held in October). Putin was inaugurated to a new, six-year term on 7 May; opposition protests continued in central Moscow, following a mass rally on the previous day which had resulted in violent clashes with police. The Duma approved Putin's nomination of Medvedev to the office of Chairman of the Government on 8 May. The long-standing Minister of Civil Defence, Emergencies and Clean-up Operations, Shoigu, subsequently resigned to take up the post of Governor of Moscow Oblast, to which his appointment had been approved in April. A new Government was appointed on 21 May.

Recent developments: consolidation of power

Legislation that increased fines for people participating in unauthorized protests (or for participating in authorized protests that were considered to have violated law and order) to 300,000 roubles, and for the organizers of unsanctioned demonstrations to 1m. roubles was approved by the Sovet Federatsii on 6 June 2012, and signed into effect by Putin on the following day. An authorized opposition protest was staged in central Moscow on 12 June. Shortly beforehand, the homes of several prominent opposition figures, including Navalnyi and Nemtsov, were raided by police, and the leaders were detained on the day of the rally. (Criminal charges of embezzlement relating to three separate cases were subsequently brought against Navalnyi.) In July Putin signed into force legislation classifying libel and slander as criminal offences (thereby reversing legislation implemented by Medvedev in late 2011, which had deemed libel to be an administrative offence), punishable by fines of up to 5m. roubles, and providing for the establishment of official state registers of internet sites containing allegedly criminal material, access to which could then be banned nation-wide. In the same month both parliamentary chambers adopted legislation (which entered into effect in November 2012) requiring NGOs engaging in political activity and receiving funding from abroad to register as 'foreign agents'. On 17 August three members of a group of musicians, known as Pussy Riot, were sentenced to two years' imprisonment, having been found guilty of 'hooliganism motivated by religious hatred', after they had created a disturbance in the Christ the Saviour Cathedral in Moscow in February, and had subsequently published online a video of the group's actions in the cathedral, over which had been overlaid a soundtrack of the group performing a song critical of Putin and the Patriarch of Moscow and All Rus. Western human rights organizations and governments described the trial as politically motivated and condemned the verdict, while several international celebrities also urged their release. (In October the sentence of one member of the group was suspended, and she was released from prison, although the appeals of the other two members were rejected.) A further authorized protest march, albeit with a much reduced attendance compared with similar recent rallies, took place in Moscow in mid-September. In the same month the parliamentary mandate of an AJR deputy who was also a prominent critic of the Government, Gennadii Gudkov, was removed following allegations that he had illegally conducted business activities.

On 14 October 2012 the first gubernatorial elections to be held since 2005 were conducted in five territories. In each case, the pro-Government incumbent was returned to office, after the participation of opposition candidates was obstructed, due in part to the introduction of a 'municipal filter', under the new gubernatorial electoral legislation, which required candidates to obtain supporting signatures of 5%–10% of municipal deputies, or 75% of heads of local administrations. Polls to six regional legislatures and numerous local government posts took place on the same day. Also in October President Putin dismissed Oleg Govorun as Minister of Regional Development, appointing a former regional governor, Igor Slyunyayev, in his place. On 6 November Sergei Shoigu, a former long-serving Minister of Civil Defence, Emergencies and Clean-up Operations, prior to his appointment as Governor of Moscow Oblast earlier in the year, was appointed Minister of Defence, replacing Serdyukov, who had been dismissed after several criminal investigations into corruption in the ministry began. At the end of October the Sovet Federatsii adopted legislation that expanded the legal definition of treason and introduced penalties of up to eight years' imprisonment for possession of information deemed secret; the legislation entered into effect shortly afterwards, on 14 November. On 1 March 2013 Putin submitted amendments to electoral legislation, under which voters would select individual candidates for one-half of the seats in the Duma (rather than electing all deputies on a party basis as previously). Opposition figures protested that the proposed changes would significantly benefit UR, following the party's declining share of the vote in successive elections. Following approval by both legislative chambers during March, on 2 April Putin signed into force further legislation that permitted regions to abolish direct gubernatorial elections in favour of a system whereby the regional legislature would elect the governor from three candidates nominated by the President. The Government had proposed the measure owing to purported concerns that direct elections would exacerbate ethnic violence in the North Caucasus territories. (In mid-April Dagestan became the first federal subject to approve legislation according to which its Head would be indirectly elected on this basis; similar arrangements for Ingushetiya were announced later in the month.) Also on 2 April Putin issued a presidential decree prohibiting state officials from holding assets abroad after 1 July, in an initiative that was widely regarded as an effort to increase his control over the political élite. Navalnyi's trial on charges of embezzlement from a timber company while he was adviser to the Governor of Kirov Oblast began in mid-April. On 8 May it was announced that Putin had accepted the resignation of Surkov from the post of Deputy Chairman of the Government and Head of the Government Administration.

Regional Government

In the early 1990s the Russian Federation encountered difficulties in meeting the aspirations of its many minority ethnic groups for self-determination. In March 1992 some 18 of Russia's 20 nominally autonomous republics signed a federation treaty. The dissenting regions, both predominantly Islamic and petroleum-producing, were Tatarstan, which had voted for self-rule earlier in the month, and the Checheno-Ingush Republic, which had declared independence from Russia in November 1991 (as the Chechen Republic—Chechnya). The new treaty granted the republics greater authority, including control of natural resources and formal borders, and allowed them to conduct their own foreign trade. An agreement signed with the Russian Government in February 1994 accorded Tatarstan a considerable measure of sovereignty. Other power-sharing agreements, granting varying degrees of sovereignty, were eventually signed by some 42 of the 89 federal subjects during Yeltsin's presidency; however, from 2000 President Putin implemented a number of measures intended to curtail the power of regional governors, which led to the rescission of the vast majority of the power-sharing treaties by mid-2002. In May 2000 the Gosudarstvennaya Duma approved legislation according the President the right to dismiss regional governors. As a result of legislation

approved in December 2004, regional governors were appointed by the federal President, subject to the approval of regional legislatures, from early 2005. In the mid-2000s the negotiation of new power-sharing treaties between the federal authorities and Chechnya and Tatarstan was undertaken. However, the Chechen authorities subsequently expressed opposition to the signature of any such document, while the treaty agreed with Tatarstan, ratified by the federal legislature in mid-2007, granted only limited privileges to the Republic.

On 19 January 2010 Medvedev announced the restructuring of the system of federal okrugs. A new North Caucasus Federal Okrug was created, comprising seven territories (six of which were ethnically defined republics formerly included within the Southern Federal Okrug). Aleksandr Khloponin, hitherto the Governor of Krasnoyarsk Krai in Siberia, was appointed as the Presidential Representative to the new federal district. In accordance with legislation approved in December 2011, on 1 July 2012 the territory governed as Moscow city was substantially expanded to incorporate numerous towns south-west of the capital. The system of direct gubernatorial elections was officially restored in May 2012, and the first such elections (in which those candidates supported by the federal authorities were victorious in each case) occured in October. However further legislation allowing regional legislatures to abolish direct elections to the regional governorship entered into force in April 2013 (see Recent developments).

The North Caucasus

In March 1992, in response to the unilateral declaration of independence from Russia by Chechnya, the Ingush inhabitants of the former Checheno-Ingush Republic demanded the establishment of a separate republic. The federal Supreme Council approved the formation of an Ingush Republic (later renamed Ingushetiya) in June. Ingush activists also claimed territories in neighbouring North Osetiya, which had formed part of designated Ingush territories prior to the Second World War, when the Ingush (and Chechens, in common with several other nationalities of the USSR) were deported *en masse* to Central Asia. In October 1992 violent conflict broke out in the disputed Prigorodnyi district in North Osetiya. By November more than 300 people had died in the conflict and some 50,000 Ingush had fled the region. In September 1997, following mediation by Yeltsin, a treaty on normalizing relations was signed by the Governments of North Osetiya and Ingushetiya.

In late 1993 armed hostilities commenced in Chechnya between forces loyal to the republican authorities and those of the separatist leader, Gen. Dzhokhar Dudayev (who had been elected President of the Republic in October 1991, following a coup against the republic's communist Government, led by Doku Zavgayev). In August 1994 an unsuccessful attempt to overthrow the Dudayev regime was reportedly aided by the federal security services. Following the defeat of a further offensive in November, federal troops entered Chechnya in December, and rapidly gained control of northern areas of the republic. Dudayev's forces, estimated to number some 15,000, were concentrated in the Chechen capital, Groznyi, against which federal troops launched an assault in late December, following heavy air bombardments. Federal troops gradually took control of the city and seized the presidential palace (the headquarters of Dudayev's forces) in January 1995. Groznyi suffered great devastation during the assault, and there were reported to be thousands of civilian casualties. In June Chechen gunmen engaged local security forces in Budennovsk, some 200 km from the border with Chechnya, and took hostage more than 1,000 people in the city hospital, demanding the immediate withdrawal of troops from Chechnya. Following the failure of attempts to free the hostages, telephone negotiations were conducted between the rebel leader, Shamil Basayev, and federal premier Chernomyrdin, by which time some 100 people had reportedly been killed. Subsequently, as a cease-fire took effect in Chechnya, the rebels began gradually to release hostages. Peace talks between a delegation from the federal Government and the Chechen leadership commenced in Groznyi in late June, and a cease-fire agreement was formalized in July, although the agreement did not endure. In December elections took place in Chechnya, to both the republican Duma and presidency. Zavgayev was elected republican President, reportedly receiving some 93% of the votes cast in elections that Dudayev rejected as invalid.

In January 1996 Chechen militants seized about 2,000 civilians in Kizlyar, Dagestan, and held them hostage in a hospital. Following negotiations, most were released, although 150 hostages were taken to Chechnya. Federal troops halted the rebels in the border village of Pervomaiskoye, and captured the village. Although the rebels' leader, Salman Raduyev, escaped to Chechnya with some of his forces and around 40 hostages, some 150 rebels and a number of their captives were killed in the assault. In April Dudayev was killed in a missile attack. He was succeeded as leader of the separatists by Zemlikhan Yandarbiyev, who reached a new cease-fire agreement with the federal authorities in May. In August, however, forces led by Basayev, launched a sustained offensive against Groznyi. Yeltsin granted Gen. Lebed, the recently appointed Secretary of the Security Council, extensive powers to co-ordinate federal operations in Chechnya and to conduct a negotiated settlement. Following discussions involving Yandarbiyev and the Chechen military leader, Gen. Khalid ('Aslan') Maskhadov, a fresh cease-fire was brokered in mid-August. The withdrawal of troops commenced, and on 31 August Lebed and Maskhadov signed a conclusive peace agreement (the Khasavyurt Accords) in Dagestan, according to which any decision regarding Chechnya's future political status was to be deferred until December 2001. The withdrawal of federal troops and the exchange of prisoners of war began, and the cease-fire was largely respected. In September 1996 a Chechen Government was created, with Maskhadov as Prime Minister, and Yandarbiyev as Chairman of the cabinet. Nevertheless, sporadic violence continued: by early 1997 it was estimated that the conflict had caused some 80,000 deaths, and resulted in the displacement of 415,000 people.

All federal troops were withdrawn before the republican presidential and legislative elections, held on 27 January 1997. Maskhadov was elected President, with some 59.3% of the total votes cast. The rate of voter participation was reported to be 79.4%. Maskhadov declined his seat in the Sovet Federatsii, and affirmed his support for Chechen independence. On 12 May Yeltsin and Maskhadov signed a formal peace treaty. The treaty, however, did not address Chechnya's constitutional status and, moreover, was refused ratification by the Gosudarstvennaya Duma.

Rebels opposed to the peace agreement continued to conduct attacks and, in particular, hostage-taking, while the federal authorities strongly opposed Chechnya's introduction of elements of *Shari'a* (Islamic religious) law in 1997, in particular the holding of public executions. In January 1998 Maskhadov dismissed his cabinet and appointed First Deputy Prime Minister Basayev (who had been indicted by the federal authorities on charges of terrorism), as acting Prime Minister. In March the republican parliament announced that the territory was henceforth to be known as the 'Chechen Republic of Ichkeriya'. In May Chechen rebels kidnapped Yeltsin's special representative to Chechnya, Vladimir Vlasov; he was freed in November by interior ministry troops. As lawlessness and militancy increased, Maskhadov dismissed the entire Chechen administration in October, and in December declared a state of emergency.

From August 1999 Islamist factions associated with Basayev launched a series of attacks on Dagestan, with the aim of protecting and extending the jurisdiction of a 'separate Islamic territory' in Dagestan proclaimed in the previous year. (The territory was returned to federal rule in mid-September.) A series of bomb explosions in August and September in Moscow, Dagestan and Volgodonsk (Rostov Oblast), including two that destroyed entire apartment blocks, officially attributed by the Government to Chechen separatists, killed almost 300 people, prompting the redeployment of federal armed forces in the republic in what the recently inaugurated premier, Putin, termed an 'anti-terrorist operation'. Allegations persisted that sources associated with the FSB had ordered the attacks, in order to justify a renewed military campaign in Chechnya. (In January 2004 two men were sentenced to life imprisonment for their part in the attacks.) In February 2000, following concerted air and ground offensives, federal forces obtained control of Groznyi; many republican and federal administrative bodies were relocated to Gudermes, Chechnya's second city.

In May 2000 President Putin decreed that, henceforth, Chechnya would be governed federally. Akhmad haji Kadyrov, a former senior mufti and former ally of Maskhadov, was inaugurated as administrative leader (Governor) of the republic in June. In January 2001 Putin signed a decree transferring control of operations in Chechnya from the Ministry of Defence to the FSB, and announced the intention of withdrawing the majority of the 80,000-strong federal forces from the region, leaving a 15,000-strong infantry division and 7,000 interior ministry troops. The local administration in Chechnya was restructured,

and Stanislav Ilyasov, a former Governor of Stavropol Krai, was appointed as the Chechen premier. In early 2001 a number of violent incidents outside Chechnya were staged by rebels, with the intention of drawing attention to the ongoing conflict. In May it was announced that the planned withdrawal of federal troops from the province had been halted. In December Raduyev, the only prominent Chechen rebel leader to have been captured by federal forces, was sentenced to life imprisonment, having been found guilty of 10 charges, including murder, terrorism and hostage-taking. (Raduyev died in prison in December 2002.)

Rebel activity increased markedly in mid-2002; although the political authority of Maskhadov had dwindled, his leadership of the military 'state defence committee' (to which Basayev was reportedly appointed to a senior position in July) became increasingly prominent. In August rebels shot down a military helicopter in Groznyi, killing 118 federal troops, their single largest loss of life since the recommencement of operations in 1999.

On 23–26 October 2002 over 40 heavily armed rebels took hostage more than 800 people in a Moscow theatre, demanding the withdrawal of federal troops from Chechnya. The siege ended when élite troops stormed the theatre, having filled the building with an incapacitating gas. The rebels were killed, and it subsequently emerged that at least 129 hostages had also died, in almost all cases owing to the toxic effects of the gas. Maskhadov issued a statement condemning the rebels' use of terrorist methods, although his deputy, Akhmed Zakayev, was arrested in late October, reportedly on the orders of the federal Government, in Denmark. In December the Danish authorities refused to extradite Zakayev to Russia, citing a lack of credible evidence of his involvement in terrorist activities. Zakayev subsequently fled to the United Kingdom, where, in November 2003, he was granted political asylum.

In November 2002 Ilyasov was appointed to the federal Government; he was succeeded as Chechen premier by Capt. (retd) Mikhail Babich. Later that month it was announced that a referendum on a new Chechen constitution was to be held in March 2003. At the end of December 2002 at least 83 people died, and more than 150 others were injured, when suicide bombers detonated bombs in two vehicles stationed outside the headquarters of the republican Government in Groznyi. (Basayev subsequently claimed responsibility for the attack.) By late December 2002 federal losses during the campaign were officially recorded at 4,572 dead and 15,549 wounded, although Chechen estimates were considerably higher. (It was also estimated that more than 14,000 rebel fighters had been killed since September 1999.) In February 2003, following Babich's resignation, Anatolii Popov, the hitherto deputy chairman of the state commission for the reconstruction of Chechnya, was appointed republican premier.

The referendum on the draft constitution for Chechnya, which described the republic as both a sovereign entity and as an integral part of the Russian Federation, and provided for the organization of elections to a strengthened republican presidency and legislature, proceeded on 23 March 2003. According to the official results, some 88.4% of the electorate participated in the plebiscite, of whom 96.0% supported the Constitution. Two further questions, on the method of electing the President and the Parliament of Chechnya, were supported by 95.4% and 96.1% of participants, respectively. However, independent observers claimed that the rate of participation had been much lower than officially reported.

Political violence continued to dominate Chechen affairs after the referendum. In May 2003 at least 59 people were killed when suicide bombers attacked government offices in the north of Chechnya. Two days later a suicide bombing at a religious festival attended by Kadyrov resulted in at least 14 deaths; Basayev claimed responsibility for the organization of both attacks. On 21 June Kadyrov inaugurated an interim legislative body, the State Council, formed of appointees. In July Putin announced that a presidential election in Chechnya would be held in October. None the less, clashes continued, and in August at least 50 people were killed in an attack on a military hospital in neighbouring North Osetiya.

From 1 September 2003 control of military operations in Chechnya was transferred from the FSB to the federal Ministry of Internal Affairs; such operations were no longer regarded as having an 'anti-terrorist' character but were, rather, to form part of an 'operation to protect law and constitutional order'. Meanwhile, campaigning for the presidential election commenced, and by mid-August 11 candidates had registered. However, the withdrawal and debarring of other potential candidates effectively removed any major challenges to Kadyrov's candidacy, and he was duly elected on 5 October, receiving 87.7% of the votes cast, according to official figures. The rate of participation by the electorate was stated to be 82.6%. An explosion in a Moscow Metro train on 6 February 2004, which resulted in the deaths of at least 39 people, was attributed to Chechen militants.

In February 2004 Yandarbiyev was killed by a car bomb in Doha, Qatar. (Two Russian intelligence agents were subsequently sentenced to life imprisonment for Yandarbiyev's murder by a Qatari court; although they were returned to Russia to serve out their sentences in December, they were released from detention in early 2005.) In March 2004 Popov was dismissed as Chechen premier, following a period of ill health; he was replaced by Sergei Abramov, who had previously worked in the republican Ministry of Finance.

An explosion in Groznyi on 9 May 2004 for which Basayev subsequently claimed responsibility, resulted in the deaths of several senior officials, including Kadyrov and the head of the republican legislature. Abramov became acting President, while Ramzan Kadyrov, the son of the assassinated President and the leader of the presidential security service (often known as the *Kadyrovtsi* and which was widely believed to have been involved in several unexplained 'disappearances'), was appointed as First Deputy Prime Minister. In the presidential election held on 29 August, Maj.-Gen. Alu Alkhanov, an officer in the interior ministry troops, and generally acknowledged to be the candidate favoured by the federal Government, was elected Chechen President, receiving 73.5% of the votes cast, according to official figures, which evaluated the rate of participation at 85.2%. The Council of Europe described the elections as undemocratic. Alkhanov retained Abramov as Prime Minister, while Ramzan Kadyrov continued as both First Deputy Prime Minister and head of the presidential security service. During the election period attacks on Russian civilians, attributed to extremist Chechen separatists, intensified, with the destruction, apparently by suicide bombers, of two passenger planes, the explosion of a bomb outside a Moscow Metro station, and the occupation of a school in Beslan, in the Republic of North Osetiya—Alaniya, on 1–3 September (see Domestic Political Affairs). Basayev subsequently released a statement claiming that the attacks had occurred under his orchestration, and describing the demands of the Beslan hostage-takers as the complete withdrawal of federal troops from Chechnya and the resignation of President Putin.

On 8 March 2005 Maskhadov was killed during a special operation by FSB forces north of Groznyi. He was replaced as leader of the State Defence Committee by Abdul-Khalim Sadulayev, who in June issued a decree appointing Doku Umarov, a close associate of Basayev, as vice-president of the rebel leadership, and issued a statement threatening military operations in other regions of Russia, in vengeance for the actions of federal forces in Chechnya. Earlier in the year, Basayev had announced the formation of a 'Caucasus Front' that would launch large-scale operations in other regions of Russia. In mid-August Sadulayev dismissed the rebel Chechen 'parliament-in-exile' and its international representatives; in the new rebel 'Government' appointed at the end of the month, Basayev became 'First Deputy Prime Minister', while Zakayev was appointed to represent the rebel authorities internationally. In early October a co-ordinated series of attacks by some 100 militants against law-enforcement bodies in Nalchik, the capital of the Kabardino-Balkar Republic, in the western North Caucasus, resulted in the deaths of at least 130 people; Basayev claimed responsibility for the organization of the attack.

On 27 November 2005 elections were held in Chechnya to a new, bicameral legislature. The federal Government cited the ballot as evidence that normality was returning to Chechnya, although no candidates advocating Chechen independence were allowed to stand. The official rate of voter participation was some 60%, well above the 25% required to validate the election; however, international observers expressed doubt that the vote was free and fair. The majority of representatives elected (33 out of 58) were from UR. Thus, the position of Kadyrov, a member of UR, was consolidated; furthermore, Kadyrov at this time held the position of acting premier, after Abramov sustained injuries in an automobile accident earlier in the month.

On 28 February 2006 Abramov resigned as Prime Minister of Chechnya, and on 4 March the republican legislature unanimously approved the appointment of Kadyrov as his successor. In June Sadulayev was killed in an operation by special forces in Chechnya. He was succeeded as leader of the separatist Chechen

rebels by Umarov, who appointed Basayev as his deputy. In July, however, Basayev was killed in an explosion in Ingushetiya for which the FSB claimed responsibility. In October Kadyrov reached 30 years of age, thereby attaining the minimum age for eligibility to serve as Chechen President. In February 2007 Putin transferred Alkhanov to the position of Deputy Minister of Justice in the federal Government, thereby allowing Kadyrov to assume the duties of President, in an acting capacity. Later in the month it was confirmed that he was the federal authorities' preferred nominee to become President; the Chechen legislature endorsed his appointment on 2 March.

On 21 June 2007 the Chechen Constitutional Assembly approved amendments to the republican Constitution, proposed by Kadyrov, which included the reconstitution of the legislature on a unicameral basis, confirming the abolition of direct elections to the republican presidency, and providing for the extension of the presidential term from four to five years, and the adoption of Chechen as a state language, in addition to Russian; the changes were endorsed by 96.9% of the votes cast in a referendum in December. Meanwhile, in October Umarov issued a statement proclaiming himself emir of 'the Caucasus Emirate', which sought to establish an Islamic state across the North Caucasus, thereby precipitating a split in the separatist movement between Islamist and nationalist elements. In November the rebel Chechen 'parliament-in-exile' announced that Umarov's title of 'President' of the 'Chechen Republic of Ichkeriya' had been formally removed. Zakayev, speaking from the United Kingdom, condemned Umarov's statement, precipitating a further split in the rebel movement, as the chairman of the 'parliament-in-exile' issued a decree appointing Zakayev as 'Prime Minister'.

Legislative elections were conducted in Chechnya on 12 October 2008; according to official results, UR secured some 88.4% of the votes cast and 37 of the 41 seats in the new unicameral Parliament. Following the completion of the post-conflict reconstruction of much of Groznyi, in April 2009 Medvedev issued a decree formally ending the counter-terrorism operation in Chechnya and providing for the withdrawal of some 20,000 of the 50,000 Russian troops deployed in the republic at that time. In July an employee of human rights organization Memorial and outspoken critic of the Chechen authorities, Natalya Estemirova, was discovered dead in Ingushetiya, after her abduction in Groznyi. The Chairman of Memorial subsequently accused Kadyrov of ordering her killing, and the organization subsequently suspended its activities in Chechnya. In August a further two prominent human rights activists were discovered dead in Groznyi. Meanwhile, a sharp increase in suicide bomb attacks was reported in the North Caucasus region, notably including an attack in Nazran, Ingushetiya, in June, in which the President of the Republic, Yunus-bek Yevkurov, was severely injured. On 10 October direct elections to municipal authorities took place in Chechnya (and in Ingushetiya) for the first time since 1990. In the mayoral poll in Groznyi, the incumbent Head of the City Administration, who was a close ally of Kadyrov, was returned to the post, with 87.4% of votes cast.

In January 2010 Chechnya became part of a new North Caucasus Federal Okrug, which was created by Medvedev in an effort to strengthen federal control over the region. Also in January Umarov issued a statement that Islamist forces under his control would stage attacks in Russian cities. He subsequently declared that he had personally ordered two suicide bomb attacks on the Moscow Metro in March (see Domestic Political Affairs), having also claimed responsibility for the bombing of an express train travelling from Moscow to St Petersburg in November 2009, in an apparent revival of the terrorist strategy pursued in Russia in the early 2000s under the command of Basayev. Nevertheless, in March 2010 Kadyrov announced that he had issued a request to the federal authorities to end the deployment in Chechnya of police and FSB personnel from elsewhere in Russia. At the end of March the Chechen parliament adopted a statement criticizing the Presidential Representative of the new Federal Okrug, Aleksandr Khloponin, for alleged lack of commitment to the republic. In April Arkadii Yedelov, a former federal Deputy Minister of Internal Affairs and a close associate of Kadyrov, was appointed as a deputy to Khloponin. On 1 August it was reported that, for health reasons, Umarov was to resign as leader of the 'Caucasus Emirate', although this decision was rescinded several days later. Speculation regarding a division in the insurgent leadership was confirmed later in August, when numerous Chechen field commanders announced that they had withdrawn their support for Umarov, instead pledging allegiance to another Chechen militant leader, Khusein Gakayev (Emir Hussein). In the same month the Chechen parliament voted to change Kadryov's title to 'Head of the Republic', with effect from 2 September. In October at least six people were killed as the result of an attack on the Chechen parliamentary building. In February 2011 Umarov claimed responsibility for a suicide bomb attack perpetrated at Domodedovo international airport in Moscow.

Although by 2012 the political situation in Chechnya had become relatively more stable, in part as a result of the strict control exercised by the administration of Kadyrov, which had also undertaken a substantial reconstruction of Groznyi, nationalist and Islamist insurgencies continued to result in loss of life across the North Caucasus, including in Chechnya. According to figures published by the independent newspaper, *Kavkazskii Uzel*, at least 700 people were killed in armed conflict in the North Caucasus during 2012, and at least a further 634 were injured; a similar number of casualties had been recorded in the previous year. The territory in which the highest number of casualties was recorded in each year in 2010–12 was Dagestan.

During the second half of 2012 acrimony increased between Kadyrov and Ingushetiyan President Yevkurov, who were preparing to enter into negotiations on the formal demarcation of the Chechen–Ingush border that would resolve the status of the disputed Sunzha and Malgobek regions. Kadyrov accused Ingushetiya of seizing Chechen territory, announced claims for the restoration of a pre-1934 border that would dramatically reduce Ingushetiya's territory, and presented himself as the leader of the Vainakh people (the collective term for the Chechens and the Ingush). In September Khloponin issued an order (which was widely interpreted as being a particular rebuke to Kadyrov) for both leaders to cease their public dispute. Nevertheless, in October the Chechen parliament adopted an amendment to legislation on boundaries (which was only made public in early 2013) providing for the incorporation of the Sunzha region into Chechnya. In January President Putin dismissed the President of Dagestan, Magomedsalam Magomedov; although no reason for his removal was announced, it was widely attributed to official concerns over the concentration of violence in Dagestan, where several prominent members of Sufi Islamic communities had been assassinated in recent months, seemingly by Salafi militants. In mid-April Dagestan became the first federal subject to announce that it would take advantage of new federal legislation permitting the abolition of (recently reintroduced) elections to the regional leadership; Ingushetiya followed suit shortly afterwards.

Foreign Affairs

Regional relations

Following the dissolution of the USSR in December 1991, Russia's most immediate foreign policy concerns were with the other former Soviet republics. Relations with Ukraine were, initially, dominated by a dispute over the division of the former Soviet Black Sea Fleet, based mainly in Sevastopol, on the Crimean peninsula (Ukraine). Russia and Ukraine signed an agreement on the division of the Fleet in June 1995, but Russia subsequently refused to implement the accord, owing to continued disagreement concerning the status of Sevastopol. In May 1997 an agreement was concluded with Ukraine, whereby Russia was to lease part of the city's naval base for 20 years. A Treaty on Friendship, Co-operation and Partnership was signed by the two countries in that month.

Relations with Ukraine were damaged by the circumstances of the disputed 2004 presidential election in that country (see Ukraine). Notably, Putin visited Ukraine twice during the campaign, appearing publicly with his preferred candidate, Viktor Yanukovych,; he also telephoned Yanukovych to congratulate him on his reported victory in the subsequently annulled second round of voting before the official (and later discredited) results had been announced. Putin also described the protests that led to the election being repeated (and Yanukovych's rival, Viktor Yushchenko, becoming President), and which became known as the 'orange revolution', as a violation of constitutional order. Relations between the two countries were again strained in 2005, following the announcement by the Russian state-controlled company, Gazprom, that it intended to charge Ukraine market prices for the supply of natural gas, which had hitherto been supplied at a subsidized rate. After failing to negotiate new terms, on 1 January 2006 Gazprom halted supplies to Ukraine, thereby causing a reduced output of gas in several countries in central and western Europe supplied by pipelines crossing Ukraine. Supplies were restored on 4 January, following agree-

ment on new terms of supply less favourable to Ukraine. Further disputes owing to Ukraine's non-payment of debts to Gazprom occurred in late 2007 and early 2008.

A further acrimonious dispute over the price Ukraine would pay for Russian gas and the level of transit fees to be paid by Gazprom resulted in Russia's suspension of gas supplies to Ukraine on 1 January 2009. After accusing Ukraine of abstracting gas flowing through its pipelines intended for export to Europe, Russia also halted supplies to Europe via Ukraine on 7 January (during a period of extremely cold weather). Following intensive European Union (EU, see p. 281) mediation and emergency discussions between Gazprom and Ukrainian state utility Naftogaz, on 19 January Putin and the Ukrainian Prime Minister, Yuliya Tymoshenko, signed an agreement in Moscow, whereby Ukraine would pay an average price for Russian gas in 2009 that would be 20% lower than the European price, while the transit price would remain unchanged; Ukraine was obliged to purchase 40,000m. cu m of Russian gas in that year. Gas supplies to Europe were finally restored on 21 January, and European energy officials urged measures to address the EU's overdependence on Russian gas. Following further discussions between Putin and Tymoshenko, it was agreed that Gazprom would not penalize Ukraine for failure to accept the contracted amount of gas in 2009 and would assist in payment of the transit fee to ensure supply.

In a highly critical open letter to Yushchenko in August 2009, Medvedev accused his counterpart of pursuing 'anti-Russian' policies and of supplying Ukrainian weapons to Georgian forces in the previous year's conflict (see below), and stated that he would delay sending a new Russian ambassador to Ukraine (the previous ambassador, former Russian premier Chernomyrdin, having been recalled in June). After Yanukovych was elected President of Ukraine in early 2010, relations between Ukraine and Russia improved markedly, and Tymoshenko was imprisoned on charges (widely considered to be politically motivated) of having entered into an illegal agreement with Russia in connection with the January 2009 pact. In February 2010 Medvedev invited Yanukovych to Moscow. In March the new Ukrainian Prime Minister, Mykola Azarov, met Putin and Gazprom officials for discussions in Moscow. In April Medvedev and Yanukovych reached an agreement whereby Russia was to grant Ukraine a significant discount on the price of Russian gas, while Ukraine was to extend the lease on the base of the Black Sea Fleet in the Crimean peninsula (due to expire in 2017) for a further 25 years. (The Gosudarstvennaya Duma ratified the agreement on 27 April.) However, in April 2011 it was reported that Ukraine had failed to respond to an invitation, extended by Putin, to join Russia's customs union with Belarus and Kazakhstan (see below), although further discussions on Ukraine's possible admission to the union were held between Yanukovych and Putin following the latter's return to the Russian presidency in 2012 and in 2013.

In April 1996 Russia and Belarus signed an agreement creating a 'Community of Russia and Belarus', according to which the two countries would pursue economic integration and close co-ordination of foreign and defence policies. In May 1997 a 'Charter of the Union of Belarus and Russia' was concluded, which moved away from advocating full union, although in June the first official session of the Union's joint Parliamentary Assembly was convened. During 1998 the Union was strengthened by the decision to grant joint citizenship to residents, and the establishment of a joint legislative and representative body to deal with union issues. A treaty on unification entered into force on 26 January 2000, when the President of Belarus, Alyaksandr Lukashenka, was appointed Chairman of the High State Council of the Union. A union budget was approved at a session of the Parliamentary Assembly (established under the 1996 Treaty, and comprising 36 members from the legislature of each country) in May. In 2009 Belarus and Kazakhstan agreed to enter into a customs union with Russia; this entered into force in July 2010. Relations with Belarus deteriorated in mid-2010, and a Russian state-owned television channel broadcast a series of programmes portraying Lukashenka in extremely unfavourable terms. However, in December (shortly before a pre-term presidential election in Belarus), Lukashenka visited Medvedev in Moscow, and terms were agreed on a reduction in the duties paid by Belarus on imports of Russian petroleum, and for Belarus to pay to Russia the duties that it received from re-exporting Russian oil products. Following a severe economic crisis in Belarus during 2011, in November an agreement was announced under which Gazprom acquired the remaining 50% of Belarus's gas transport network, in exchange for a substantial discount granted to Belarus in the price of natural gas supplied. In January 2013 Russia completed ratification of the accord.

In April 2010 premier Putin strenuously denied any Russian involvement in a popular uprising in Kyrgyzstan, which resulted in the overthrow of Kyrgyzstani President Kurmanbek Bakiyev (who went into exile in Belarus) and the establishment of an Interim Government of National Trust. Some 150 Russian troops were dispatched to Kyrgyzstan to protect the Russian air base and military personnel based at Kant. Putin, who had met Kyrgyzstani opposition leaders shortly before the uprising, rapidly indicated recognition of the legitimacy of the interim administration. In February 2012 the new Kyrgyzstani President, Almazbek Atambayev, made an official visit to Moscow; he failed on that occasion to secure economic assistance from Russia and tensions were subsequently reported. During a visit to Kyrgyzstan by Putin (who had returned to the presidency) in September, however, a significant agreement was reached under which Russia was to waive a total of US $489m. owed by the Kyrgyzstani Government and would invest substantially in the reconstruction of two hydroelectric installations in the country, while Russia's lease of the military air base at Kant was to be extended by 15 years from 2017. It was additionally announced in March 2013 that an agreement on the acquisition of chronically loss-making gas distribution network Kyrgyzgaz by Gazprom would be finalized.

Concern at the treatment and status of ethnic Russians in Estonia and Latvia remained a particular source of tension, and the demarcation of mutual frontiers also created difficulties. In the early 2000s Russia expressed particular concern for its citizens in the Russian exclave of Kaliningrad, which is separated from the remainder of the Russian Federation by Belarus and Lithuania. The Russian Government attempted to ensure that residents of the exclave would be exempted from visa requirements that were to be imposed by Lithuania and Poland prior to the two countries' accession to the EU (which took effect on 1 May 2004). In November 2002, at an EU-Russia summit meeting, held in Brussels, Belgium, Russia finally agreed to an EU proposal for simplified visa arrangements. According to the compromise accord, multiple-transit travel documentation would be made available to residents of the exclave travelling by motor vehicle; the new regulations came into effect on 1 July 2003. In 2006 President Putin inaugurated a railway ferry service, initially servicing only cargo, connecting the exclave to metropolitan Russia.

Following the dissolution of the USSR, Russia maintained significant political and military influence in many former Soviet republics, especially in those areas involved in civil or ethnic conflicts. Russian troops were deployed in Tajikistan to support the Tajikistani Government against rebel forces during the civil war of 1992–97, and remained thereafter to ensure the security of the Tajikistani–Afghan border. In 2004 it was announced that Russian troops were to transfer responsibility for border security to the Tajikistani military, but that October Russia was formally granted a permanent military base in Tajikistan. In October 2003 a Russian military base commenced operations in Kyrgyzstan, the first to be established outside Russia after the dissolution of the USSR; the base was intended to meet the requirements of the Collective Security Treaty Organization (CSTO, see p. 474), inaugurated in April to succeed the CIS Collective Security Treaty. In November 2005 Putin and President Islam Karimov of Uzbekistan signed a defence pact, which provided for mutual support in the event that one of the countries came under attack. Russia, together with Belarus, Kazakhstan, Kyrgyzstan and Tajikistan, was a founding member of the Eurasian Economic Community (EURASEC, see p. 461), which was formally established in 2001. In October 2007 EURASEC leaders approved the legal basis for the establishment of a new customs union that was initially to comprise Belarus, Kazakhstan and Russia. In November 2009 the Presidents of Russia, Kazakhstan and Belarus signed agreements finalizing plans for the establishment of a customs union, which officially entered into effect in July 2010. In October 2011 Putin proposed the formation of a 'Eurasian Union' to bring about greater economic integration between the post-Soviet states, initially being based upon the customs union of Russia, Belarus and Kazakhstan. In November Lukashenka, Medvedev and President Nursultan Nazarbaev of Kazakhstan signed an accord in Moscow that provided for the creation of a Eurasian Economic Commission, with the stated aim of establishing the Eurasian Union by 2015. In October 2012 Kyrgyzstan announced that it intended to join the customs union, while later that year negotiations were underway between Russia and Tajikistan on the latter country's prospective entry to the union.

Separatist conflicts in Moldova and Georgia

Considerable controversy arose in the 1990s because of Russian support for separatist factions in Moldova and Georgia. In 1999 it was announced that all Russian troops in the separatist Transnistria region of Moldova were to be withdrawn by the end of 2002; however, the withdrawal was subsequently postponed, and in February 2004 the Russian Minister of Defence, Sergei Ivanov, indicated that Russia intended to maintain a military presence in the region. (The Moldovan Government continued to demand that the Russian force be reconstituted as a civil mission.) Meanwhile, in December 1998 Russia and Georgia signed an agreement that provided for the gradual transfer of control of their mutual frontiers, from Russian to Georgian guards. (Control of the frontier was, however, complicated by the existence of separatist and rebel-controlled regions on both sides of the border—Chechnya within Russia, and Abkhazia and South Ossetia within Georgia). In November 1999 it was agreed that two of the four Russian bases on Georgian territory would be closed by mid-2001. Russian troops had left the two bases in Georgia by November 2001. (An agreement signed between Russia and Georgia in March 2006 provided for a Russian withdrawal from the military base that it maintained at Akhalkalaki and headquarters at Tbilisi by the end of 2007, and from the second base at Batumi in 2008; in the event, the withdrawal of Russian forces from the military bases was completed in November 2007, earlier than scheduled.) In October 2002, after the Russian authorities accused Georgia of permitting Chechen rebels to operate from bases within its territory, and stated that they reserved the right to instigate 'pre-emptive' military action, in self-defence, should the situation persist, Russia and Georgia agreed to commence joint patrols of their common border.

Relations with Georgia deteriorated significantly after the 'rose revolution' of late 2003 that led to the reformist, pro-Western Mikheil Saakashvili becoming President of Georgia. In October 2006 Russia temporarily withdrew its ambassador from Georgia and closed all transport, postal and banking communications with the country, in response to the detention by the Georgian authorities of four Russian military officers on charges of espionage. In August 2007 the Georgian authorities protested against an incident, in which two military jets had entered Georgia's airspace from Russia and launched a missile on its territory near South Ossetia. In April 2008 a Russian presidential decree providing for increased co-operation in trade and culture with Abkhazia and South Ossetia, and protection to Russian citizens living in those regions, was strongly criticized by the international community. Despite the resumption of direct air links with Georgia in March, tension between the two countries increased later in April, after a Georgian reconnaissance aeroplane was shot down over Abkhazia, allegedly by a Russian military aircraft; although Russia denied involvement in the incident, the Georgian Government condemned it as an act of aggression. Meanwhile, at a summit meeting of the North Atlantic Treaty Organization (NATO, see p. 380), which was convened in Bucharest, Romania, on 2 April, leaders indicated that Ukraine and Georgia would be offered Membership Action Plans in the future, but not, as the Georgian Government had hoped, in the immediate term; Russia's permanent representative at NATO had criticized US support for the aspirations towards NATO accession of those countries.

On 8 August 2008, following an offensive by Georgia against the Russian-supported separatist region of South Ossetia, Russia launched an intensive counter-attack, dispatching large numbers of troops to South Ossetia, where they engaged in hostilities with Georgian forces; the Russian authorities alleged that Georgia intended to commit 'genocide' against the South Ossetian population, stating that it sought to protect its citizens and peace-keeping troops present in the region. (Many South Ossetians had been issued with Russian passports by the separatist authorities since the mid-2000s.) Russian aircraft commenced bombardment of Georgian targets beyond the separatist territory, while Russian forces rapidly gained control of South Ossetia's principal city, Tskhinvali, and also advanced into Abkhazia. On 12 August Medvedev ordered an end to Russia's military operation in Georgia. Georgia and Russia agreed to a peace plan, mediated by French President Nicolas Sarkozy on behalf of the EU, providing for an immediate cease-fire, humanitarian assistance, and the withdrawal of Russian troops to pre-conflict positions. On 19 August, after Russia failed to implement fully the withdrawal of troops as stipulated, NATO foreign ministers decided to suspend meetings of the NATO-Russia Council (see Other external relations) until Russia was considered to have observed the terms of the peace plan. Two days later Russia announced its suspension of military co-operation with NATO. On 26 August President Medvedev endorsed a resolution, which had been approved in both chambers of the Russian legislature, officially recognizing South Ossetia and Abkhazia as independent, sovereign states. Georgia, the USA and the EU condemned the decision (which was subsequently followed by only a very small number of states). On 29 August Georgia formally suspended diplomatic relations with Russia.

In September 2008, following further negotiations with an EU delegation led by President Sarkozy in Moscow, Russia agreed on additional measures for the implementation of the August cease-fire plan, principally the withdrawal of all remaining forces from Georgian territory (outside South Ossetia and Abkhazia). On 17 September Russia signed friendship and co-operation treaties with the leaders of South Ossetia and Abkhazia, pledging to support the two regions militarily and economically. EU monitors were deployed in Georgia, and the withdrawal of the remaining Russian troops from areas adjacent to South Ossetia and Abkhazia was verified by 10 October. However, Georgia claimed that Russia continued to be in violation of the cease-fire agreement until it reduced the number of troops it deployed within South Ossetia and Abkhazia to pre-conflict levels and also withdrew from areas previously held by Georgian forces. (Russia had confirmed its intention to maintain a total of at least 7,600 troops within the two regions.) From October a series of discussions between Russian and Georgian delegations, which were also attended by South Ossetian and Abkhazian officials, held in Geneva, Switzerland, under the aegises of the UN, the EU and the OSCE, failed to result in any further agreement. In December the mandate of the OSCE mission in Georgia (deployed in South Ossetia since 1992) expired, owing to Russia's refusal to approve a further extension.

NATO resumed formal discussions with Russia at ambassadorial level on 29 April; however, later that day NATO ordered the expulsion of two Russian diplomats (one of whom was the son of Russia's ambassador to the EU) attached to the Russian mission at NATO headquarters on suspicion of espionage. (NATO's action followed the imprisonment of the head of the security department at the Estonian Ministry of Defence during 2000–06, on charges of having passed classified Estonian and NATO military documents to the Russian Foreign Intelligence Service.) The Russian Government protested vehemently against the expulsion of the two diplomats. On 30 April Medvedev signed agreements with the leaders of the separatist authorities of South Ossetia and Abkhazia, under which Russia was to assist in securing and patrolling the borders of the two regions with Georgia for an initial period of five years, pending the establishment of their own border services. NATO criticized the accords as being in contravention of Russian commitments under the EU-mediated peace agreements.

In May 2009 the separatist Abkhazian authorities granted management rights over the territory's airport and railways to Russia for 10 years. Later that month Abkhazia signed a five-year agreement according Rosneft the right to prospect for petroleum and natural gas off the territory's Black Sea coast. In June Russia vetoed the extension of the mandate of the UN Observer Mission in Georgia, which had been created in 1993 for deployment in Abkhazia. On 27 June, at the first ministerial meeting of the NATO-Russia Council to take place since the conflict, it was agreed to resume military co-operation. In late June Russia commenced several days of military exercises near the Georgian border; the Georgian Government denounced the manoeuvres, involving 8,500 troops, as a provocation. In August it was announced that Russia had reduced the number of its troops in Abkhazia and South Ossetia to 1,700 in each. In September the Russian Government signed further defence agreements with Abkhazia and South Ossetia, allowing it to maintain military bases in the territories for an initial period of 49 years (with the subsequent possibility of five-year renewals). The first high-level military meeting between representatives of NATO and Russia since the conflict was held in Brussels in January 2010. In August Russia announced that it had deployed anti-aircraft missiles in Abkhazia, and that an air defence system had also been established in South Ossetia. In June 2011 a Russian military officer who had been based in Abkhazia, Yevgenii Borisov, was sentenced to 30 years' imprisonment *in*

absentia for organizing a series of bomb attacks and attempted bomb attacks in Georgia, including one against the US embassy in Tbilisi; Borisov's deputy received a life sentence *in absentia* and a further four defendants were sentenced to terms of 30 years (one *in absentia*), while lesser sentences were imposed on the remaining eight.

Discussions between Georgian and Russian representatives in Bern, Switzerland, began in March 2011, in an effort to resolve Georgia's obstruction of Russia's longstanding application to join the World Trade Organization (WTO, see p. 444). In November Russia and Georgia signed a bilateral agreement allowing Russia's entry to the WTO; under a compromise arrangement, trade between Russia and Abkhazia and South Ossetia was to be controlled by Swiss monitors. (Russia's application to join the WTO was formally accepted on 16 December.) After President Saakashvili ended visa restrictions on Russian citizens travelling to Georgia in February 2012 (having previously lifted them for Russian citizens resident in certain regions of the North Caucasus), the Russian Ministry of Foreign Affairs announced in early March that it was prepared to consider the introduction of reciprocal arrangements for Georgian citizens who wished to visit Russia. In mid-March President Medvedev appointed special presidential representatives to the two separatist territories within Georgia; in both cases the representatives were the governors of Russian federal subjects neighbouring those territories: Aleksandr Tkachev, the head of the Provincial Administration of Krasnodar Krai, was additionally to serve as the Presidential Special Representative to Abkhazia, while Taimuraz Mamsurov, the Head of the Republic of North Osetiya—Alaniya, was to serve in the same capacity to South Ossetia. The simultaneous nomination of Rogozin in an equivalent role to Transnistria was a cause of some controversy in Moldova, owing to his reputation as a populist nationalist.

In September 2012 the Moldovan Prime Minister, Vladimir Filat, made an official visit to Russia, when negotiations on a new gas supply contract were conducted with government officials in Moscow and Sochi. However, the Moldovan authorities failed to accept a reported Russian offer of a number of financial concessions on condition that Moldova renounced plans to enter into the EU's Third Energy Package, while an initiative by some political parties in Moldova for the country to join the Russian-led customs union was also rejected. In Georgia, meanwhile, a new Government headed by Bidzina Ivanishvili, who had pledged to improve bilateral relations with Russia, was installed following elections in October, although it was subsequently confirmed that Georgia would not restore diplomatic relations until Russia ended its presence in South Ossetia and Abkhazia. In December the first direct discussions between Georgian and Russian officials since the August 2008 conflict were conducted in Geneva, when a plan for a partial normalization in bilateral relations was agreed. The Georgian Government denounced discussions between Putin and the President of Abkhazia, Aleksandr Ankvab, which took place in Moscow in March 2013. Later that month Russia (which had objected to ongoing joint US-Georgian military exercises) staged previously unannounced large-scale military manoeuvres on the Black Sea, prompting critical statements from Georgia.

Other external relations

After December 1991 the Russian Federation was recognized as the successor to the USSR. It was granted the USSR's permanent seat on the UN Security Council and, additionally, was to be responsible for the receipt and destruction of all nuclear weapons of the former USSR located in other newly independent republics (Belarus, Kazakhstan and Ukraine), a process that was successfully completed by the mid-1990s. In January 1993 Russia and the USA signed the second Strategic Arms Reduction Treaty (START II), which envisaged a reduction in the strategic nuclear weapons of both powers. The Russian legislature ratified START II in April 2000; however, as enactment of the treaty was contingent on the continuation of the Anti-Ballistic Missile (ABM) treaty (signed with the USSR in 1972), the announcement, in December 2001 by US President George W. Bush, that the USA's withdrawal from the ABM Treaty after a six-month notice period, meant that START II was effectively defunct.

Meanwhile, Russia offered assistance and gave support to the USA in its attempts to form a global coalition against militant Islamist terrorism, after the suicide air attacks against the USA on 11 September 2001 (see the USA). Although Russia refused to commit troops to participate in the military campaign against targets of the Taliban regime in Afghanistan, which commenced in October, it provided military intelligence and allowed access to its airspace. In May 2002 Russia and the USA announced that agreement had been reached on the reduction of their nuclear arsenals by approximately two-thirds, and a nuclear accord and a declaration on strategic partnership, the Strategic Offensive Reductions Treaty (SORT), which notably lacked the verification requirements of previous arms control treaties, were duly signed by Presidents Putin and Bush on 24 May. The USA withdrew from the ABM treaty on 13 June, and the following day Russia withdrew from START II, and SORT formally entered into effect on 1 June 2003.

The Russian Government consistently condemned intermittent US-led missile attacks on Iraq during the 1990s and early 2000s; additionally, in 1996, in contravention of a UN embargo, Russia concluded an agreement with Iraq on the development of oilfields in that country. In late 1997, following Iraq's refusal to permit weapons inspectors of the UN Special Commission (UNSCOM) access to contentious sites, the Russian Government intervened in an attempt to avert a renewal of hostilities, and the conclusion of an agreement between the UN and Iraq in February 1998 was regarded by Russia as a significant diplomatic success. In mid-2001 Russia, which supported Iraq in its demands that the sanctions regime in force since 1990 be revoked, obstructed a British-drafted proposal before the Security Council for the introduction of a new, US-advocated programme of 'smart' sanctions. From the second half of 2002, Russia urged the US Administration of George W. Bush to avoid the use of unilateral force, and encouraged Iraq's compliance with UN demands regarding weapons inspections. Although Russia voted to support UN Security Council Resolution 1441, approved in November, which provided for the expedited return of weapons inspectors to Iraq under the auspices of the UN Monitoring, Verification and Inspection Commission (UNMOVIC), it was a leading opponent of attempts, led by the USA and the United Kingdom in February–March 2003, to approve a further Security Council resolution explicitly to endorse military action in Iraq, and President Putin described the conflict, which commenced in mid-March, as a 'political mistake'.

In early 2007 the Russian Government declared emphatically its opposition to the establishment of a radar installation in the Czech Republic and missile interceptors in Poland as part of the USA's proposed National Missile Defence programme, despite repeated US assurances that the plan was not intended to threaten Russian interests. Russia warned that it would take retaliatory measures against the US programme, including withdrawal from the Conventional Forces in Europe (CFE) Treaty, prompting the Czech Republic and Poland to demand security and legal guarantees from the USA and further exacerbating strained relations with the West. Legislation providing for Russia's suspension of the CFE Treaty was formally adopted by both parliamentary chambers in November 2007, and, after its endorsement by Putin, entered into effect in December. A formal treaty signed between Poland and the USA in August 2008, providing for the installation of 10 US anti-missile interceptors, and guaranteeing the permanent stationing of missiles on Polish territory, prompted strenuous protests by the Russian Government. (A provisional accord providing for the installation of a US anti-missile radar system in the Czech Republic had also been signed in July.) However, following the election of US President Barack Obama in November, Russia welcomed an announcement by the new US Administration in early 2009 that it would review security policy, including the planned missile defence system. (In June 2011 the Czech Government announced the country's withdrawal from the US missile defence system, owing to dissatisfaction with the revised proposals.) Lavrov and US Secretary of State Hillary Clinton, meeting in Geneva, Switzerland, in early March 2009, affirmed commitment to the revision of US-Russian relations. Medvedev and Obama met for the first time at a summit of the heads of state and of government of the Group of 20 (G20) leading economies, which took place in London, United Kingdom, in April, and issued a joint statement agreeing to replace the START I treaty (which had entered into force in 1994 and was due to expire at the end of 2009) with a new treaty. Later in 2009 Russian and US officials signed a new strategic framework for military co-operation, which had been suspended since August 2008, and an agreement to allow the USA to transport military personnel and equipment across Russia to support its operations in Afghanistan.

A series of formal negotiations between Russian and US officials failed to result in agreement by the expiry of START I on 5 December 2009. Following further negotiations in Geneva in early 2010 and a meeting between Lavrov and Clinton in Moscow in March, the Russian and US Governments announced on 26 March that agreement had been reached on a new treaty limiting strategic offensive weapons. On 8 April Medvedev and Obama, meeting in the Czech capital, Prague, signed the New START Treaty, whereby both states, within seven years of its ratification by their respective legislatures, were each to reduce their operationally deployed nuclear warheads to 1,550, while the number of deployed ballistic missiles and heavy bombers on each side was to be restricted to 700, and the number of deployed and non-deployed launchers and heavy bombers equipped for nuclear armaments to 800 each. (At that time Russia was believed to have 2,600 and the USA 2,252 nuclear warheads.) In common with the previous START treaties, but unlike SORT, New START provided for inspection and verification procedures. Following its approval by the US and Russian legislatures, and ratification by Medvedev on 28 January 2011, the New START Treaty entered into force on 5 February. In November Medvedev issued renewed warnings that the Russian Government would deploy missiles, including in Kaliningrad (bordering Poland), against US missile defence bases in Europe unless it received legally binding guarantees that the US defence system was not aimed against Russia.

In June 2010 Medvedev visited the USA, meeting Obama in Washington, DC, and attending discussions in the high-technology business centre of 'Silicon Valley' in California. Later that month, however, the US Administration announced the detention, as a result of the findings of the Federal Bureau of Investigation, of 10 suspected Russian agents, who had been resident in the USA since the 1990s. In early July the 10 defendants pleaded guilty in a New York court to charges of conspiring to act as unregistered agents; they were immediately deported to Russia, in exchange for the pardoning and release of four Russian nationals, three of whom had been convicted and imprisoned on espionage charges. In March 2011 US Vice-President Joe Biden made an official visit to Moscow, where he confirmed US support for Russia's accession to the WTO.

Russia finally acceded to membership of the WTO (following lengthy negotiations with Georgia—see above) on 22 August 2012. In October, after undertaking a number of measures to suppress opposition activities, the Russian Government ordered the US Agency for International Development to cease operations in Russia, accusing the organization of political interference. On 14 December US legislation normalizing trade relations with Russia was adopted, as the Jackson-Vanik amendment, which placed trading restrictions on countries with non-market economies that restricted emigration, initially imposed against the USSR in 1974, was repealed. (Russia had been granted a waiver from the restrictions annually since 1992.) However, the new legislation also imposed entry visa bans and asset freezes on certain Russian officials accused of human rights abuses (the so-called 'Magnitsky list'. The new legislation followed particular international condemnation surrounding the death in custody, in November 2009, of lawyer Sergei Magnitskii, who had been detained after implicating a number of Russian interior ministry officials in a legal case relating to a fraudulent tax rebate claim. (In October the European Parliament had adopted a non-binding resolution for EU member states to impose similar sanctions against Russia.) On 28 December, in a measure that was widely regarded as retaliatory, Putin enacted legislation that imposed sanctions on US citizens deemed guilty of violating the human rights of Russian citizens. In response to the widely publicized death of an adopted Russian child in the USA in 2008, US parents were banned from further Russian adoptions, while people with US citizenship were also excluded from membership in political pressure groups in Russia, and US funding of political groups was prohibited. In January 2013 Russia ended a co-operation agreement under which the USA had provided financial assistance for Russian law enforcement and drugs control programmes. Despite continued allegations by international investment company Hermitage Capital Management, for which Magnitskii had worked, that he had died in detention as a result of torture, in March a government investigation into his death was ended, citing lack of evidence that a crime had been committed. After the Russian authorities had charged Magnitskii posthumously with tax evasion, his trial officially began later in March, amid continued international protests. Meanwhile, the Russian Government reacted cautiously to an announcement by the US Administration in March that continued plans for the establishment of anti-missile interceptors in Poland and Romania had been abandoned in favour of additional installations in

Alaska to counter a perceived threat from the Democratic People's Republic of Korea (North Korea). The Russian Minister of Defence, Sergei Shoigu, and his US counterpart subsequently declared their intention to resume missile defence negotiations, while Deputy Prime Minister, Dmitrii Rogozin, stated that the US proposals did not represent any threat to Russia. In April the names of 18 Russian citizens prohibited from entering the USA included on the 'Magnitsky list' were made available publicly. As a retaliatory measure Russia announced that 18 US officials, which it accused of human rights abuses, were prohibited from entering Russia.

Continuing strains in Russia's relations with the United Kingdom, principally following the death of Aleksandr Litvinenko in London in November 2006 (see Domestic Political Affairs) and attempts by the Russian authorities to close British Council offices in Russia in early 2008, intensified when a British Member of Parliament confirmed in December 2010 that his Russian aide had been detained and served with a deportation order. Tensions between Russia and the United Kingdom increased with the expulsion of a Russian diplomat from London for alleged espionage, which was followed by the reciprocal expulsion of a British diplomat from Moscow. In February 2011 Russian Minister of Foreign Affairs Lavrov visited the United Kingdom for discussions with Prime Minister David Cameron. In September Cameron visited Moscow, where he met government leaders, despite continuing tensions in the countries' relationship (particularly with regard to the refusal of the United Kingdom to permit the extradition of Berezovskii or Zakayev to Russia, and concerning the death of Litvinenko). Following campaigning by Litvinenko's wife, in October it was announced that a full public inquest into his death would take place in London; the British Government subsequently ordered that some of the information concerned be undisclosed at the inquest, which was scheduled to begin in May 2013. In August 2012 President Putin made his first official visit to the United Kingdom since 2005, attending judo matches in London (which was hosting the summer Olympic Games) with Cameron. In April 2013 Berezovskii was discovered dead at his British residence; initial police investigations concluded that he had died as a result of hanging, in an apparent suicide.

In February 2010 premier Putin invited his Polish counterpart, Donald Tusk, to attend a ceremony in Russia marking the 70th anniversary of a massacre of some 20,000 Polish officers by Soviet secret police at Katyń during the Second World War. (While the Soviet administration under Gorbachev had, belatedly, admitted Soviet responsibility for the massacre in 1990, the issue continued to strain relations between Russia and Poland.) A joint ceremony to commemorate the massacre, attended by the Russian and Polish premiers, took place at Katyń on 7 April, and was regarded as significant in furthering good bilateral relations. On 10 April Polish President Lech Kaczyński and 95 other senior Polish government, military and cultural personnel, who had been travelling to Katyń to attend a further commemoration of the massacre, were killed when their aeroplane crashed in adverse weather conditions near Smolensk airport. Putin, who visited the crash site with Tusk, was appointed by Medvedev to supervise a special commission to investigate the crash. (Following the crash, a Russian state-controlled federal TV channel broadcast a Polish film about the Katyń massacre, giving unprecedented prominence in Russia to the acknowledgement of Soviet responsibility for the killings.) In November the Gosudarstvennaya Duma formally acknowledged that Stalin had directly ordered the Katyń massacre. In December Medvedev made an official visit to Warsaw, where he signed agreements intended to strengthen bilateral co-operation.

In June 1994 Russia joined NATO's 'Partnership for Peace' (see p. 383) programme of military co-operation with former Eastern bloc states. A 'Founding Act on Mutual Relations, Co-operation and Security between NATO and the Russian Federation' was signed in May 1997. The Act provided for enhanced Russian participation in all NATO decision-making activities, equal status in peace-keeping operations and representation at the Alliance headquarters at ambassadorial level. A NATO-Russian Permanent Joint Council was established. The air offensive conducted by NATO forces against Yugoslav targets in March–June 1999 to enforce the withdrawal of Serbian forces from its province of Kosovo and Metohija (see Kosovo and Serbia) was strongly condemned by Russia, which suspended its relations with the Alliance. Following the acceptance of a peace plan on 3 June, and Serbian withdrawal from Kosovo, the entry of Russian troops into the territory shortly before NATO forces prompted fears of a military confrontation. Contacts were resumed between Russia and NATO in February 2000, and on 28 May 2002 Putin and the heads of state and of government of the 19 NATO member states, meeting in Italy, signed the Rome Declaration, inaugurating a new NATO-Russia Council to replace the Permanent Joint Council. The new Council was intended to enable Russia to enter into negotiations with its members on a range of issues, including terrorism, non-proliferation, defence and peace-keeping. At the NATO summit meeting in April 2008, Russia demonstrated strenuous opposition to the aspirations of Georgia and Ukraine for NATO membership. NATO suspended relations with Russia in August, in response to Russian military action in Georgia; relations were formally restored in March 2009, but remained strained. In April 2011 Russian Minister of Foreign Affairs Lavrov criticized NATO for exceeding the UN Security Council mandate for military intervention in Libya, and urged a political settlement to the conflict (see Libya).

In January 1996 Russia was admitted as a member of the Council of Europe. As a condition of membership, Russia was to abolish the death penalty by the end of February 1999. However, by 2013 the Duma had yet to approve its abolition, although capital punishment has been subject to a moratorium since Russia's admission to the organization. In February 2005 the European Court of Human Rights (ECHR), in a ruling on cases brought by six Chechens, concluded that serious human rights abuses had been committed by the Russian military in Chechnya and ordered the Russian Government to pay compensation to the victims' relatives. In June 2010 the ECHR, finding Russia to be in violation of the European Convention on Human Rights, ordered the authorities to pay a total of €473,800 to the families of eight Chechen men who had disappeared in 2001 and 2002. In the same month a resolution by PACE urging Russia to co-operate in implementing ECHR rulings relevant to the North Caucasus was for the first time approved by the Russian delegation to the Council of Europe.

Russia's relations with Iran in the late 1990s and early 2000s were a cause of concern for the USA. In December 2000 Igor Sergeyev, the Russian Minister of Defence, made the first official visit to Iran by a Russian official since the Islamic Revolution in that country of 1979. In March 2001, during a visit to Moscow by the Iranian President, Muhammad Khatami, Russia agreed to resume the sale of conventional weapons to Iran and to assist with the construction of a nuclear power plant in Bushehr; an agreement for arms sales worth some US $300m. was signed in October. Although in December 2002 it was announced that Russia was to increase its nuclear co-operation with Iran, the Russian Government reiterated that Russia remained opposed to Iran's potential development of nuclear weapons. In mid-2003 Russia announced that it was to suspend exports of nuclear fuel to Iran; however, in February 2005 a new agreement was reached between the two countries on the provision of nuclear fuel. In February 2006 Russia was one of 27 countries represented on the 35-member Board of Governors of the International Atomic Energy Agency (IAEA) to vote in favour of Iran's referral to the UN Security Council, after it was discovered not to have complied with the conditions of an agreement reached with the IAEA; none the less, Russia remained opposed to the use of military force against Iran to bring it into compliance. In June 2010 the Russian and Iranian Governments signed an agreement for increased energy co-operation. Following the adoption of further UN sanctions against Iran, however, in September Russian President Medvedev cancelled the planned delivery of an air defence missile system to Iran, and announced the virtual suspension of military exports to the country. In July 2012 it was announced that the Iranian authorities had presented a case against Russia at the International Court of Arbitration in Geneva, seeking compensation of US $4,000m. The Russian Government subsequently warned that it would withdraw diplomatic support for Iran over its nuclear programme unless Iran ended the legal proceedings.

Under a 1971 agreement, Russia maintains a naval facility at the Syrian port of Tartous (which Russia was further developing from 2008), and is a long-term supplier of armaments to Syria. From 2011 Russia continued to support the regime of Syrian President Bashar al-Assad following its sustained use of military force to repress opposition protests (see Syria). Russia, together with the People's Republic of China, vetoed a UN Security Council resolution condemning Assad's Government in October, and subsequently expressed strenuous opposition to the impos-

Introductory Survey

ition of sanctions against Syria. In January 2012 Russia was criticized by US, French and British representatives at the UN for continuing to supply armaments to the Syrian Government. Russia and China vetoed a further UN Security Council resolution on Syria in February, while the Russian Government repeatedly offered to mediate in negotiations between the Syrian Government and opposition. The Russian Government, in conflict with the USA, continued to support Assad, who refused to comply with Syrian opposition demands to relinquish office as a precondition to dialogue, and in early 2013 Minister of Foreign Affairs Lavrov urged a negotiated end to the conflict.

Relations with Japan were complicated by a continuing dispute over the status of the Kurile Islands (known in Japan as the Northern Territories), which became part of the USSR at the end of the Second World War; Japan maintained its long-standing demand that four of the islands be returned to Japanese sovereignty. Discussions on the territorial dispute between the leaderships of Russia and Japan were ongoing from the late 1990s, but resulted in little progress. Despite Russian President Vladimir Putin's repudiation of Japan's claim to any of the islands during his first official visit to Tokyo in September 2000, Russia subsequently offered to abide by a 1956 declaration that it would relinquish two of the islands after the signature of a peace treaty, a proposal rejected by Japan. The revocation, in September 2006, of an environmental permit associated with the Sakhalin-2 natural gas project, and the subsequent enforced reduction of the share held in the project by Japanese companies, was a further cause of heightened tensions between Russia and Japan. In April 2008, during an official visit by Japanese Prime Minister Yasuo Fukuda to Russia, he and President Putin agreed that further discussions would be conducted, in an effort to resolve the territorial dispute; pledges for increased bilateral co-operation were also made. However, in July the Russian Government criticized Japanese plans to introduce school textbooks depicting the Kurile Islands as part of Japanese territory. In January 2010 Japan formally protested to Russia, after two Japanese fishing vessels were shot at by Russian coastal guards near the disputed islands. In February 2013 Japan formally complained that two Russian fighter aircraft had entered Japanese airspace near the disputed islands; the Russian Government (which had been conducting military manoeuvres in the region) denied the accusations. Nevertheless, the Japanese Prime Minister, Shinzo Abe, subsequently declared his intention to visit Russia in April, in an effort to improve bilateral relations.

Relations with the People's Republic of China improved significantly during the 1990s. In 1999 several agreements on bilateral economic and trade co-operation, and a final accord on the demarcation of a common border between the two countries, were signed. Meanwhile, negotiations in the mid-1990s that initially focused on defining the mutual borders of China, Kazakhstan, Kyrgyzstan, Russia and Tajikistan appeared to be instrumental in bringing about closer co-operation between these countries, which in 1996 formed the so-called Shanghai Five group. The group subsequently broadened its areas of activity to include trade, cultural, military and security co-operation; in June 2001 Uzbekistan joined the grouping, which was renamed the Shanghai Co-operation Organization (see p. 478). Putin visited China in December 2002, when he met President Jiang Zemin and his appointed successor, Hu Jintao. In October 2004 a treaty was signed by Presidents Putin and Hu settling a long-standing dispute over the border between the two states. In 2005 Russia and China conducted joint military manoeuvres for the first time. During a visit by Putin to China in March 2006, a memorandum of understanding was signed for an arrangement under which Russia would supply China with up to 68,000 cu m of gas annually over a period of 30 years. (However, finalization of the agreement was subsequently delayed over pricing disagreements.) In October 2011 Putin signed bilateral trade accords worth US $7,000m. with China. In February 2013 Russian Deputy Chairman Arkadii Dvorkovich visited Beijing, the Chinese capital, to attend the first meeting of a bilateral intergovernmental commission on energy co-operation. In March the new Chinese President, Xi Jinping, made his first official visit to Moscow, when an agreement was announced for a gradual increase, to 45m.–50m. tons, in Russian oil supplies to China (although no conclusion to the gas accord was reached), while Russia secured Chinese loan and investment commitments.

CONSTITUTION AND GOVERNMENT

Under the Constitution of December 1993, the Russian Federation is a democratic, federal, multi-ethnic republic, in which state power is divided between the legislature, executive and judiciary, which are independent of one another. The President of the Russian Federation is Head of State and Commander-in-Chief of the Armed Forces, and also holds broad executive powers. The President, who is elected for a term of six years, renewable once, by universal direct suffrage, appoints the Chairman of the Government (Prime Minister). Supreme legislative power is vested in the bicameral Federalnoye Sobraniye (Federal Assembly). The upper chamber is the Sovet Federatsii (Federation Council), which comprises two representatives from each of the country's federal territorial units (appointed by the legislature and the executive in each region); its lower chamber is the 450-member Gosudarstvennaya Duma (State Duma), which is elected by direct universal suffrage for a period of five years. The Supreme Court is the highest judicial authority on civil, criminal, administrative and other cases within the jurisdiction of the common plea courts. The Supreme Arbitration Court is the highest authority in settling economic and other disputes within the jurisdiction of the courts of arbitration. The judges of the three higher courts (including the Constitutional Court) are appointed by the Federation Council on the recommendation of the President. Judges of other federal courts are appointed by the President. The majority of Russia's regions introduced jury trials, in many cases only for the most serious crimes, during 2003. The Russian Federation comprises 83 territorial 'subjects', comprising 21 republics, nine krais (provinces), 46 oblasts (regions), two cities of federal status, one autonomous oblast and four autonomous okrugs (districts). The republics and the autonomous oblast and okrugs are nominally representative of ethnic groups, and the administrative oblasts and krais of geographic regions. These territories are grouped into eight federal okrugs, each of which is headed by a Presidential Representative.

REGIONAL AND INTERNATIONAL CO-OPERATION

Russia is a founder member of the Commonwealth of Independent States (CIS, see p. 251), and a member of the Collective Security Treaty Organization (CSTO, see p. 474), the Eurasian Economic Community (EURASEC, see p. 461), the Asia-Pacific Economic Cooperation forum (APEC, see p. 208), the Shanghai Cooperation Organization (see p. 478), the Organization of the Black Sea Economic Cooperation (BSEC, see p. 411), the Council of the Baltic Sea States (see p. 258), the Organization for Security and Co-operation in Europe (OSCE, see p. 397), the Council of Europe (see p. 260) and the Organization of the Petroleum Exporting Countries (OPEC, see p. 418). The customs union of Belarus, Russia and Kazakhstan entered into effect in July 2010.

Russia is a member of the UN and permanent member of the UN Security Council (having been recognized as the successor to the USSR, a founder member of the UN). Russia participates in the Group of Eight major industrialized nations (G8, see p. 475) and the Group of 20 major industrialized and systemically important emerging market nations (G20). Russia acceded to membership of the World Trade Organization (WTO, see p. 444) in August 2012.

ECONOMIC AFFAIRS

In 2011, according to estimates by the World Bank, Russia's gross national income (GNI), measured at average 2009–11 prices, was US $1,476,086m., equivalent to $10,400 per head (or $19,940 per head on an international purchasing-power parity basis). In 2002–11, it was estimated, the population declined at an average annual rate of 0.3%, while gross domestic product (GDP) per head increased, in real terms, at an average annual rate of 5.0%. Overall GDP increased, in real terms, at an average annual rate of 4.6% in 2002–12; real GDP increased by 3.1% in 2012.

Agriculture (including forestry and fishing) contributed 3.9% of GDP in 2012. In 2008, according to ILO, 8.6% of the employed labour force were engaged in the agricultural sector. The principal agricultural products are grain, potatoes and livestock. In 1990 the Russian Government began a programme to encourage the development of private farming, to replace the state and collective farms. Legislation to permit the sale and purchase of agricultural land from 2003 was approved by the State Duma in June 2002. Widespread forest fires in August 2010 (following severe drought conditions) resulted in the destruction of large areas of arable land and the loss of about one-third of the crops;

the Government announced a ban on grain exports (which was subsequently extended until the end of 2011), and pledged some US $1,150m. in emergency assistance for farmers. Real agricultural GDP increased at an average annual rate of 0.9% in 2002–12; the GDP of the sector increased by 16.3% in 2011, but declined by 3.6% in 2012.

Industry contributed 36.0% of GDP in 2012. In 2008 the industrial sector (including mining, manufacturing, construction and utilities) provided 28.9% of employment. Industrial GDP increased, in real terms, at an average annual rate of 3.4% in 2002–12; industrial GDP increased by 2.1% in 2012.

Mining and quarrying contributed 10.9% of GDP in 2012, and employed 1.9% of the employed labour force in 2008. Russia has considerable reserves of energy-bearing minerals, including one-third of the world's natural gas reserves and substantial deposits of petroleum, coal and peat. It also has large supplies of palladium, platinum and rhodium. Other minerals exploited include bauxite, cobalt, copper, diamonds, gold, iron ore, mica, nickel and tin. The GDP of the mining sector increased, in real terms, at an average annual rate of 2.7% in 2002–12; mining GDP increased by 0.9% in 2012.

The manufacturing sector contributed 15.2% of GDP in 2012, and provided 16.4% of employment in 2008. Manufacturing GDP increased, in real terms, at an average annual rate of 3.4% in 2002–12; manufacturing GDP increased by 3.2% in 2012.

The construction sector contributed 6.5% of GDP in 2012, and provided 7.6% of employment in 2008. In 2002–12, the GDP of the construction sector increased, in real terms, at an average annual rate of 6.2%; construction GDP increased by 2.0% in 2012.

Electric energy is derived from petroleum-, gas- and coal-fired power stations, nuclear power stations, and hydroelectric installations. In 2009 nuclear reactors supplied some 16.5% of total electricity generation, while coal also accounted for some 16.5% of Russia's generating capacity; hydroelectric power accounted for 17.6% of electricity production, and 47.4% of the country's generating capacity originated from natural gas. Russia is a major exporter of natural gas and crude petroleum, and Russia's largest company, Gazprom, is also the world's largest producer of natural gas. Since the early 2000s Russia has also consistently been, with Saudi Arabia, one of the two largest producers of oil. From the late 1990s Russia sought to increase its exports of mineral fuels, particularly to central and western Europe. The construction of the 'Blue Stream' pipeline, which was to carry natural gas from Novorossiisk, Krasnodar Krai, in southern Russia, to Ankara, Turkey, was completed in 2002. In early 2005 it was announced that a pipeline would be constructed from eastern Siberia to Nakhodka on the Pacific Coast, enabling exports to Japan and the wider Pacific region. In November 2007 Gazprom and Italian energy company Eni signed an agreement creating the South Stream joint venture for the construction of a pipeline to transport Russian natural gas to Italy; Bulgaria, Hungary, Serbia and Greece subsequently agreed to participate in the project. Work on the pipeline was scheduled to be completed by 2015. Imports of mineral products (including fuels) comprised just 2.1% of the value of Russia's total merchandise imports in 2011.

The services sector contributed 60.1% of GDP in 2012, and provided 62.4% of employment in 2008. The GDP of the services sector increased, in real terms, at an average annual rate of 5.3% in 2002–12; the GDP of the sector increased by 4.9% in 2012.

In 2011 Russia recorded a visible merchandise trade surplus of US $197,115m., and there was a surplus of $98,834m. on the current account of the balance of payments. In 2011 the largest source of imports was the People's Republic of China (accounting for 15.8% of total imports). Other major suppliers were Germany and Ukraine. The largest market for Russian exports in that year was the Netherlands (accounting for 12.1% of total exports), followed by the People's Republic of China, Germany, Italy and Ukraine. The principal imports in 2011 were machinery, vehicles and transport equipment, followed by chemical products and rubber, foodstuffs and agricultural raw materials, metals and precious stones, and textile articles and footwear. The principal

exports in that year were mineral fuels, followed by metals and precious stones, and chemical products and rubber.

In 2012 Russia recorded a deficit on the federal budget of 37,000m. roubles, equivalent to 0.1% of GDP. Russia's general government gross debt was 6,503,238m. roubles in 2011, equivalent to 11.7% of GDP. At the end of 2010 the country's total external debt was US $384,740m., of which $162,924m. was public and publicly guaranteed debt. In that year, the cost of servicing long-term public and publicly guaranteed debt and repayments to the IMF was equivalent to 12.8% of the value of exports of goods, services and income (excluding workers' remittances). In 2002–10 the average annual rate of inflation was 11.1%, according to estimates by ILO. According to official data, the rate of inflation was 6.6% in 2012. In November 2011 some 5.0m. people (6.6% of the labour force) were unemployed.

After the dissolution of the USSR, a programme of economic reforms was initiated to effect the transition to a market-orientated system. However, the dismantling, in late 2004, of the privately owned petroleum company, Yukos, and the effective renationalization of its most productive subsidiary, Yuganskneftegaz (see Domestic Political Affairs), demonstrated a reverse from free market principles. Russia began to expand its network of international pipelines to east Asia and eastern, northern and southern Europe. Nevertheless, the successes of the fossil fuel sector were widely considered to obscure the relative lack of innovation in the wider economy. A privatization programme, which was intended to raise funds to cover high budget deficits, began in February 2011, with the sale of a share of VTB Bank. Following his re-election as President in March 2012, Vladimir Putin issued a decree supporting the sale of all state holdings in companies outside the defence and energy industries by 2016. Despite a public offering in state savings bank Sberbank in September 2012, however, implementation of privatization plans proved slow. An agreement announced in October, and which entered into effect in March 2013, moreover, provided for the acquisition by the state-owned company Rosneft of the remaining 50% share held by the British company BP in the TNK-BP joint venture that was one of Russia's major petroleum producers. Meanwhile, Russia sought to expand its customs union with Belarus and Kazakhstan, which had entered into force in July 2010. The enactment of a Russian-initiated free trade agreement, which had been signed in October 2011 by Russia and seven other member states of the Commonwealth of Independent States (see p. 251), was delayed pending ratification by all signatory countries. Russia's application to join the World Trade Organization (WTO, see p. 444), submitted in 1993, was finally approved in December 2011. Russia was expected to benefit significantly from membership of the WTO, to which it formally acceded in August 2012, and from the consequent decision of the US legislature in December to end longstanding trade restrictions on the country. Construction of the South Stream gas pipeline, which was to transport Russian natural gas to Italy, officially began in December, and the project was due to enter into production in late 2015. Following a recovery from the international economic crisis during 2010–11, GDP growth began to slow in 2012, and Russia was deemed continuously vulnerable to the negative impact of further global downturn, owing to the high level of the non-oil budget deficit and depreciation of the Oil Reserve Fund. Endemic corruption remained a source of concern, although large capital outflows since the crisis were estimated to have lessened somewhat.

PUBLIC HOLIDAYS

2014: 1–8 January (New Year and Christmas), 23 February (Defenders of the Fatherland Day), 8 March (International Women's Day), 1 May (Spring Holiday and Labour Day), 9 May (Victory Day), 11 June (Russia Day), 28 June (Baptism of Rus'), 4 November (National Unity Day).

Note: In addition to those listed above, the dates of two additional public holidays for 2014 were to be declared by the Gosudarstvennaya Duma no later than 1 December 2013.

Statistical Survey

Source (unless otherwise indicated): Federal Service of State Statistics,103450 Moscow, ul. Myasnitskaya 39; tel. (495) 207-49-02; fax (495) 207-40-87; e-mail stat@gks.ru; internet www.gks.ru.

Area and Population

AREA, POPULATION AND DENSITY

Area (sq km)	17,098,200*
Population (census results)	
9–16 October 2002	145,166,731
14–25 October 2010	
Males	66,046,579
Females	76,809,957
Total	142,856,536
Population (official estimates at 1 January)	
2011	142,865,433
2012	143,056,383
2013	143,356,941
Density (per sq km) at 1 January 2013	8.4

* 6,601,700 sq miles.

POPULATION BY AGE AND SEX
(official estimates at 1 January 2012)

	Males	Females	Total
0–14	11,378,555	10,828,681	22,207,236
15–64	49,055,897	53,517,212	102,573,109
65 and over	5,741,831	12,534,207	18,276,038
Total	66,176,283	76,880,100	143,056,383

POPULATION BY ETHNIC GROUP
(census of 14–25 October 2010)

	'000	%
Russian*	111,087.6	80.95
Tatar†	5,310.6	3.87
Ukrainian	1,928.0	1.40
Bashkir	1,584.6	1.15
Chuvash	1,435.9	1.05
Chechen‡	1,431.4	1.04
Armenian	1,182.4	0.86
Avar‖	912.0	0.66
Mordovian§	806.0	0.58
Belarusian	521.4	0.38
Others¶	16,656.6	8.06
Total	142,856.5	100.00

* Including Cossacks and Pomors.
† Including Astrakhan Tatars, Kryashens (Christian Tatars) and Siberian Tatars, but excluding Crimean Tatars.
‡ Including Chechen-akkintsy.
‖ Including Akhvakhtsy, Andiitsy, Bezhtintsy, Didoitsy, Karatintsy, and nine other ethnic groups with a declared population of under 1,000 each.
§ Including Erzya-Mordovians and Moksha-Mordovians.
¶ Including 5,629,429 respondents (4.10% of the total) who did not state their nationality or ethnic group.

ADMINISTRATIVE DIVISIONS
(2010 census, preliminary)

Federal territory	Area ('000 sq km)	Population ('000)	Density (per sq km)	Capital (with population, '000)
Central Federal Okrug	650.2	38,537.6	59.3	Moscow
Moscow City*	1.1	11,612.9	10,557.2	Moscow (11,612.9)
Belgorod Oblast	27.1	1,536.1	56.7	Belgorod (366.1)
Bryansk Oblast	34.9	1,264.4	36.2	Bryansk (412.8)
Ivanovo Oblast	21.4	1,054.4	49.3	Ivanovo (408.8)
Kaluga Oblast	29.8	1,008.2	33.8	Kaluga (326.4)
Kostroma Oblast	60.2	661.8	11.0	Kostroma (269.3)
Kursk Oblast	30.0	1,121.6	37.4	Kursk (423.2)
Lipetsk Oblast	24.0	1,165.9	48.6	Lipetsk (508.1)
Moscow Oblast*	45.8	7,198.7	157.2	Moscow†
Orel Oblast	24.7	781.3	31.6	Orel (319.1)
Ryazan Oblast	39.6	1,148.5	29.0	Ryazan (525.9)
Smolensk Oblast	49.8	980.5	19.7	Smolensk (329.9)
Tambov Oblast	34.5	1,082.5	31.4	Tambov (280.9)
Tula Oblast	25.7	1,554.5	60.1	Tula (499.5)
Tver Oblast	84.2	1,342.2	15.9	Tver (406.9)
Vladimir Oblast	29.1	1,431.9	49.2	Vladimir (345.9)
Voronezh Oblast	52.2	2,331.5	44.7	Voronezh (991.3)
Yaroslavl Oblast	36.2	1,271.0	35.1	Yaroslavl (595.2)
North-Western Federal Okrug . .	1,687.0	13,660.1	8.1	St Petersburg
St Petersburg City	1.4	4,953.2	3,538.0	St Petersburg (4,953.2)
Republic of Kareliya	180.5	639.7	3.5	Petrozavodsk (265.3)
Republic of Komi	416.8	889.8	2.1	Syktyvkar (238.6)
Archangel Oblast	589.9	1,213.5	2.1	Archangel (349.5)
Nenets Autonomous Okrug . .	176.8	42.4	0.2	Naryn-Mar (22.4)
Kaliningrad Oblast	15.1	946.8	62.7	Kaliningrad (433.5)
Leningrad Oblast	83.9	1,733.9	20.7	St Petersburg†
Murmansk Oblast	144.9	787.9	5.4	Murmansk (305.0)
Novgorod Oblast	54.5	629.7	11.6	Velikii Novgorod (219.9)
Pskov Oblast	55.4	666.9	12.0	Pskov (204.0)
Vologda Oblast	144.5	1,198.5	8.3	Vologda (304.3)
Southern Federal Okrug	420.9	13,884.0	33.0	Rostov-on-Don
Republic of Adygeya	7.8	442.5	56.7	Maikop (144.5)
Republic of Kalmykiya	74.7	286.7	3.8	Elista (104.1)
Krasnodar Krai	75.5	5,284.5	70.0	Krasnodar (764.0)
Astrakhan Oblast	49.0	1,015.0	20.7	Astrakhan (525.4)
Rostov Oblast	101.0	4,260.6	42.2	Rostov-on-Don (1,096.4)
Volgograd Oblast	112.9	2,594.8	23.0	Volgograd (1,018.7)

Federal territory—*continued*	Area ('000 sq km)	Population ('000)	Density (per sq km)	Capital (with population, '000)
North Caucasus Federal Okrug .	170.4	9,492.9	55.7	Pyatigorsk (143.8)
Chechen Republic	15.6	1,302.2	83.5	Groznyi (275.6)
Republic of Dagestan	50.3	2,930.4	58.3	Makhachkala (574.3)
Republic of Ingushetiya	3.6	430.5	119.6	Magas (3.4)
Kabardino-Balkar Republic	12.5	859.1	68.7	Nalchik (239.3)
Karachai-Cherkess Republic . . .	14.3	474.7	33.2	Cherkessk (127.6)
Republic of North Osetiya—Alaniya .	8.0	709.0	88.6	Vladikavkaz (310.1)
Stavropol Krai	66.2	2,787.0	42.1	Stavropol (404.6)
Volga Federal Okrug . . .	1,037.0	29,811.5	28.7	Nizhnii Novgorod
Republic of Bashkortostan . . .	142.9	4,064.2	28.4	Ufa (1,072.3)
Chuvash Republic	18.3	1,247.0	68.1	Cheboksary (460.4)
Republic of Marii-El	23.4	692.4	29.6	Yoshkar-Ola (252.9)
Republic of Mordoviya	26.1	825.5	31.6	Saransk (297.9)
Republic of Tatarstan	67.8	3,803.2	56.1	Kazan (1,161.3)
Udmurt Republic	42.1	1,518.1	36.1	Izhevsk (629.5)
Perm Krai	160.2	2,631.1	16.4	Perm (1,000.7)
Kirov Oblast	120.4	1,327.9	11.0	Kirov (478.0)
Nizhnii Novgorod Oblast . . .	76.6	3,296.9	43.0	Nizhnii Novgorod (1,254.6)
Orenburg Oblast	123.7	2,023.7	16.4	Orenburg (554.7)
Penza Oblast	43.4	1,366.5	31.7	Penza (520.0)
Samara Oblast	53.6	3,214.1	60.0	Samara (1,169.2)
Saratov Oblast	101.2	2,508.8	24.8	Saratov (836.9)
Ulyanovsk Oblast	37.2	1,282.1	34.5	Ulyanovsk (614.4)
Urals Federal Okrug	1,818.5	12,143.4	6.7	Yekaterinburg
Chelyabinsk Oblast	88.5	3,480.1	39.3	Chelyabinsk (1,143.5)
Kurgan Oblast	71.5	896.3	12.5	Kurgan (327.9)
Sverdlovsk Oblast	194.3	4,307.6	22.2	Yekaterinburg (1,377.7)
Tyumen Oblast	1,464.2	3,459.4	2.4	Tyumen (609.7)
Khanty-Mansii Autonomous Okrug— Yugra	534.8	1,561.2	2.9	Khanty-Mansiisk (85.0)
Yamalo-Nenets Autonomous Okrug .	769.3	536.6	0.7	Salekhard (44.3)
Siberian Federal Okrug . . .	5,145.0	19,260.9	3.7	Novosibirsk
Altai Republic	92.6	208.4	2.2	Gorno-Altaisk (59.7)
Republic of Buryatiya	351.3	971.4	2.8	Ulan-Ude (411.6)
Republic of Khakasiya	61.6	532.2	8.6	Abakan (167.6)
Republic of Tyva	168.6	309.4	1.8	Kyzyl (112.0)
Altai Krai	168.0	2,407.2	14.3	Barnaul (621.7)
Krasnoyarsk Krai	2,366.8	2,838.4	1.2	Krasnoyarsk (997.3)
Transbaikal Krai	431.9	1,099.4	2.5	Chita (327.4)
Irkutsk Oblast	774.8	2,424.4	3.1	Irkutsk (597.8)
Kemerovo Oblast	95.7	2,750.8	28.7	Kemerovo (536.3)
Novosibirsk Oblast	177.8	2,686.9	15.1	Novosibirsk (1,498.9)
Omsk Oblast	141.1	1,974.8	14.0	Omsk (1,156.6)
Tomsk Oblast	314.4	1,057.7	3.4	Tomsk (539.2)
Far Eastern Federal Okrug . .	6,169.3	6,265.8	1.0	Khabarovsk
Republic of Sakha (Yakutiya) . . .	3,083.5	955.9	0.3	Yakutsk (278.4)
Kamchatka Krai	464.3	320.2	0.7	Petropavlovsk-Kamchatskii (179.8)
Khabarovsk Krai	787.6	1,342.5	1.7	Khabarovsk (585.6)
Maritime (Primorskii) Krai . . .	164.7	1,950.5	11.8	Vladivostok (597.5)
Amur Oblast	361.9	821.6	2.3	Blagoveshchensk (215.7)
Magadan Oblast	462.5	154.5	0.3	Magadan (95.5)
Sakhalin Oblast	87.1	495.4	5.7	Yuzhno-Sakhalinsk (186.3)
Jewish Autonomous Oblast . . .	36.3	174.4	4.8	Birobidzhan (76.2)
Chukot Autonomous Okrug . . .	721.5	51.0	0.1	Anadyr (13.5)
Russian Federation	17,098.2	143,056.4	8.4	Moscow

* Data for Moscow City and Moscow Oblast refer to the territories as constituted prior to 1 July 2012, when several districts formerly located in the Oblast were transferred to the jurisdiction of the City.

† Although Moscow and St Petersburg are the administrative centres of Moscow and Leningrad Oblasts, respectively, the cities themselves do not form part of the oblasts.

PRINCIPAL TOWNS
(official estimates at 1 January 2012)

Moskva (Moscow, the capital)	11,612,943	Astrakhan	525,387
Sankt-Peterburg (St Petersburg)	4,953,219	Penza	519,992
		Naberezhnye	
Novosibirsk	1,498,921	Chelnyi	516,637
Yekaterinburg	1,377,738	Lipetsk	508,066
Nizhnii Novgorod	1,254,592	Tula	499,511
Samara	1,169,184	Kirov	478,012
Kazan	1,161,308	Cheboksary	460,383
Omsk	1,156,583	Kaliningrad	433,532
Chelyabinsk	1,143,458	Kursk	423,181
Rostov-na-Donu (Rostov-on-Don)	1,096,448	Bryansk	412,753
Ufa	1,072,291	Ulan-Ude	411,646
Volgograd	1,018,739	Magnitogorsk	409,593
Perm	1,000,672	Ivanovo	408,826
Krasnoyarsk	997,316	Tver	406,918
Voronezh	991,269	Stavropol	404,606
Saratov	836,892	Belgorod	366,110
Krasnodar	763,899	Sochi	360,324
Tolyatti	719,596	Nizhnii Tagil	358,917
		Arkhangelsk	
Izhevsk	629,455	(Archangel)	349,533
Barnaul	621,669	Vladimir	345,907
Ulyanovsk	614,444	Smolensk	329,944
Tyumen	609,650	Kurgan	327,898
Irkutsk	597,846	Chita	327,423
Vladivostok	597,476	Kaluga	326,400
Yaroslavl	595,155	Orel	319,138
Khabarovsk	585,556	Surgut	316,624
Makhachkala	574,277	Cherepovets	314,646
Orenburg	554,723	Volzhskii	314,169
Novokuznetsk	549,589	Vladikavkaz	310,070
Tomsk	539,205	Murmansk	305,034
Kemerovo	536,270	Vologda	304,301
Ryazan	525,929		

BIRTHS, MARRIAGES AND DEATHS

	Registered live births		Registered marriages		Registered deaths	
	Number	Rate (per 1,000)	Number	Rate (per 1,000)	Number	Rate (per 1,000)
2004	1,502,477	10.4	979,667	6.8	2,295,402	16.0
2005	1,457,376	10.2	1,066,366	7.5	2,303,935	16.1
2006	1,479,637	10.4	1,113,562	7.8	2,166,703	15.2
2007	1,610,122	11.3	1,262,500	8.9	2,080,445	14.6
2008	1,713,947	12.1	1,179,007	8.3	2,075,954	14.6
2009	1,761,687	12.4	1,199,446	8.5	2,010,543	14.2
2010	1,788,948	12.5	1,215,066	8.5	2,028,516	14.2
2011	1,796,629	12.6	1,316,011	9.2	1,925,720	13.5

Life expectancy (years at birth): 68.8 (males 63.0; females 74.9) in 2010 (Source: World Bank, World Development Indicators database).

IMMIGRATION AND EMIGRATION

	2010	2011	2012
Immigrants	191,656	356,520	417,681
Emigrants	33,578	36,478	122,751

ECONOMICALLY ACTIVE POPULATION
(sample surveys, '000 persons aged 15 to 72 years, at November, excl. Chechen Republic)

	2006	2007	2008
Agriculture, hunting and forestry	6,691	6,155	5,994
Fishing	176	192	141
Mining and quarrying	1,198	1,324	1,350
Manufacturing	12,472	12,324	11,663
Electricity, gas and water supply	2,063	2,017	2,116
Construction	4,462	4,933	5,413
Wholesale and retail trade; repair of motor vehicles and motorcycles and personal and household goods	10,599	11,096	10,774
Restaurants and hotels	1,392	1,344	1,467
Transport, storage and communications	6,211	6,573	6,560
Financial intermediation	1,060	1,249	1,316
Real estate, renting and business activities	4,148	4,410	4,448
Public administration and defence; compulsory social security	4,876	4,903	5,409
Education	6,198	6,420	6,442
Health and social work	4,896	5,177	5,243
Other community, social and personal service activities	2,388	2,439	2,580
Private households with employed persons	21	16	43
Extra-territorial organizations and bodies	4	—	5
Total employed	68,855	70,570	70,965
Unemployed	5,312	4,588	4,791
Total labour force	74,167	75,158	75,756
Males	37,506	38,103	38,681
Females	36,661	37,056	37,076

Source: ILO.

2010 (sample surveys, '000 persons aged 15 to 72 years, at November, incl. Chechen Republic): Total employed 69,803; Unemployed 5,645; Total labour force 75,448 (males 38,578, females 36,870).

2011 (sample surveys, '000 persons aged 15 to 72 years, at November, incl. Chechen Republic): Total employed 70,732; Unemployed 5,020; Total labour force 75,752.

Health and Welfare

KEY INDICATORS

Total fertility rate (children per woman, 2010)	1.5
Under-5 mortality rate (per 1,000 live births, 2010)	12
HIV/AIDS (% of persons aged 15–49, 2009)	1.0
Physicians (per 1,000 head, 2006)	4.3
Hospital beds (per 1,000 head, 2006)	9.7
Health expenditure (2009): US $ per head (PPP)	1,043
Health expenditure (2009): % of GDP	5.6
Health expenditure (2009): public (% of total)	63.4
Access to water (% of persons, 2010)	97
Access to sanitation (% of persons, 2010)	70
Total carbon dioxide emissions ('000 metric tons, 2008)	1,708,653.3
Carbon dioxide emissions per head (metric tons, 2008)	12.0
Human Development Index (2011): ranking	66
Human Development Index (2011): value	0.755

For sources and definitions, see explanatory note on p. vi.

Agriculture

PRINCIPAL CROPS
('000 metric tons)

	2009	2010	2011
Wheat	61,739.8	41,507.6	56,240.0
Rice, paddy	913.0	1,060.7	1,055.6
Barley	17,880.8	8,350.0	16,938.0
Maize	3,963.4	3,084.4	6,962.4
Rye	4,333.1	1,635.6	2,970.8
Oats	5,401.2	3,219.8	5,332.1
Millet	264.7	133.6	878.3
Buckwheat	564.0	339.3	800.4
Potatoes	31,134.0	21,140.5	32,681.5
Sugar beet	24,892.0	22,255.9	47,643.3
Peas, dry	1,348.9	1,217.8	2,021.0
Soybeans (Soya beans)	943.7	1,222.4	1,756.0
Sunflower seed	6,454.3	5,344.8	9,697.5
Rapeseed	666.8	670.1	1,056.1
Cabbages and other brassicas	3,312.1	2,732.5	3,527.6
Tomatoes	2,170.4	2,049.6	2,200.6
Cucumbers and gherkins	1,132.7	1,161.9	1,204.4
Onions, dry	1,601.6	1,536.3	2,122.7
Garlic	227.3	213.5	234.0
Carrots and turnips	1,518.7	1,303.3	1,735.0
Watermelons	1,419.0	1,151.6	1,574.6
Apples*	1,441	992	1,200
Sweet cherries*	76	67	76
Sour (Morello) cherries*	190	165	191
Plums and sloes*	138	120	137
Strawberries*	185.0	165.0	184.0
Currants*	367.0	327.0	364.5
Grapes	298.7	324.3	412.4

* Unofficial figures.

Aggregate production ('000 metric tons, may include official, semi-official or estimated data): Total cereals 95,616.0 in 2009, 59,624.3 in 2010, 91,825.2 in 2011; Total roots and tubers 31,134.0 in 2009, 21,140.5 in 2010, 32,681.5 in 2011; Total primary oilcrops 3,115.1 in 2009, 2,744.6 in 2010, 4,816.4 in 2011; Total pulses 1,579.0 in 2009, 1,400.6 in 2010, 25,067.1; Total vegetables (incl. melons) 14,827.1 in 2009, 13,283.5 in 2010, 16,275.3 in 2011; Total fruits (excl. melons) 3,055.4 in 2009,2,463.8 in 2010, 2,916.5 in 2011.

Source: FAO.

LIVESTOCK
('000 head at 1 January)

	2009	2010	2011
Horses	1,353	1,375	1,341
Cattle	21,038	20,671	19,968
Pigs	16,162	17,231	17,218
Sheep	19,602	19,850	19,761
Goats	2,168	2,137	2,059
Chickens	366,282	390,534	406,007
Turkeys	11,360	12,245	12,520

Source: FAO.

LIVESTOCK PRODUCTS
('000 metric tons)

	2009	2010	2011
Cattle meat	1,740.6	1,727.3	1,625.5
Sheep meat	164.5	166.7	170.7
Pig meat	2,169.5	2,330.8	2,427.6
Chicken meat	2,313.4	2,563.5	2,909.4
Cows' milk	32,325.8	31,585.2	31,385.7
Goats' milk	238.5	255.2	252.9
Hen eggs*	2,194.5	2,260.6	2,283.6
Honey	53.6	51.5	60.0
Wool, greasy	54.7	53.5	52.6

* Unofficial figures.

Source: FAO.

Forestry

ROUNDWOOD REMOVALS
('000 cubic metres, excl. bark; figures are rounded)

	2009	2010*	2011*
Sawlogs, veneer logs and logs for sleepers	62,800	77,968	87,770
Pulpwood	38,100	41,202	46,382
Other industrial wood	12,000	16,906	19,031
Fuel wood	38,500	38,924	43,817
Total	151,400	175,000	197,000

* Unofficial figures.

Source: FAO.

SAWNWOOD PRODUCTION
('000 cubic metres, incl. railway sleepers)

	2009	2010*	2011*
Coniferous (softwood)*	25,388	26,412	29,055
Broadleaved (hardwood)	1,905	2,458	2,637
Total	27,293	28,870	31,692

* Unofficial figures.

Source: FAO.

Fishing

('000 metric tons, live weight)

	2008	2009	2010
Capture	3,383.7	3,826.1	4,069.6
Pink (humpback) salmon	164.2	426.5	199.8
Atlantic cod	194.6	234.1	272.8
Alaska (Walleye) pollock	1,318.7	1,326.5	1,584.5
Blue whiting (Poutassou)	225.2	149.6	128.0
Atlantic herring	202.2	222.3	208.7
Pacific herring	158.1	190.9	222.0
Aquaculture	115.4	116.6	120.4
Total catch	3,499.1	3,942.7	4,190.0

Note: Figures exclude seaweeds and other aquatic plants ('000 metric tons): 10.5 (capture 10.2, aquaculture 0.3) in 2008; 6.5 (capture 5.8, aquaculture 0.7) in 2009; 6.5 (capture 5.9, aquaculture 0.6) in 2010. Also excluded are aquatic mammals, recorded by number rather than weight. The number of whales caught was: 147 in 2008; 116 in 2009; 8 in 2010. The number of seals (incl. walrus) caught was: 17,623 in 2008; 6,472 in 2009; 5,288 in 2010.

Source: FAO.

Mining

('000 metric tons unless otherwise indicated)

	2008	2009	2010
Iron ore: gross weight	99,900	92,000	95,500
Copper ore*†	750	676	703
Nickel ore†	267	262	270
Bauxite	5,675	5,775	5,475
Lead ore*†	60.0	70.0	97
Zinc ore*†	204	225	269
Tin (metric tons)*†	1,500	1,200	160
Manganese ore*†	9.2	9.2	9.2
Chromium ore	913.0	416.2	400.0*
Tungsten concentrates (metric tons)†	3,000	2,300	2,800
Molybdenum (metric tons)*	3,600	3,800	3,800
Cobalt ore (metric tons)*†	2,500	2,352	2,460
Mercury (metric tons)*	50	50	50
Silver (metric tons)†	1,132	1,313	1,356
Uranium concentrate (metric tons)†	3,521	3,564	3,562
Gold (metric tons)†	172.0	192.8	189.0
Platinum (metric tons)	25	25	25*

—*continued*			2008	2009	2010
Palladium (metric tons)*	.	. .	88	83	85
Kaolin (concentrate)*	.	. .	45	45	45
Magnesite*	. . .	. .	1,200	1,000	1,200
Phosphate rock (Apatite)‡		.	3,800	3,500	4,000*
Potash§	. . .	. .	5,992	3,727	6,283
Native sulphur*	. .	. .	50	50	50
Fluorspar (concentrate)*	.	.	269	240	250
Barite (Barytes)*	. .	. .	63	63	60
Salt (unrefined)*	. .	. .	2,200	2,200	2,200
Diamonds: gems ('000 metric carats):					
gem	. . .	. .	21,925	17,791	17,800*
industrial*	. .	. .	15,000	15,000	15,000
Gypsum (crude)	. .	. .	3,600*	2,900	2,900*
Asbestos	. . .	. .	1,017	1,000*	1,000*
Mica*	. . . .	. .	100	100	100
Talc*	. . . .	. .	160	160	160
Feldspar*	. . .	. .	45	45	45
Peat (horticulture and fuel use)	.		1,300	1,300	1,300

* Estimated production.

† Figures refer to the metal content of ores.

‡ Figures refer to the phosphoric acid content. The data exclude sedimentary rock (estimates, '000 metric tons): 375 in 2007, 700 in 2008 and 850 in 2009 (estimate).

§ Figures refer to the potassium oxide content.

Source: US Geological Survey.

Crude petroleum (million metric tons): 494,247 in 2009; 505,130 in 2010; 511,420 in 2011 (Source: BP, *Statistical Review of World Energy*).

Natural gas (excl. flared or recycled, million cu m): 527,654 in 2009; 588,946 in 2010; 607,009 in 2011 (Source: BP, *Statistical Review of World Energy*).

Coal (commercial solid fuels only, million metric tons): 301.3 in 2009; 321.6 in 2010; 333.5 in 2011 (Source: BP, *Statistical Review of World Energy*).

Industry

SELECTED PRODUCTS

('000 metric tons unless otherwise indicated)

	2009	2010	2011
Flour	10,145	9,823	9,858
Granulated sugar . . .	5,070	4,751	7,124
Cotton fabrics (million sq m) .	1,427	1,542	1,237
Woollen fabrics (million sq m) .	17.5	15.8	14.4
Linen fabrics (million sq m) . .	46.5	52.5	46.9
Footwear ('000 pairs) . . .	81,200	103,000	107,000
Plywood ('000 cu m) . . .	2,128	2,687	3,003
Particle board ('000 cu m) . .	4,600	n.a.	n.a.
Newspapers (million units) . .	17,088	18,512	19,063
Cardboard	2,828	2,908	2,930
Paper	4,480	4,675	4,672
Sulphuric acid	8,493	10,226	10,704
Soda ash (sodium carbonate) .	2,259	2,670	2,822
Mineral fertilizers	14,640	17,889	18,791
Synthetic ammonia . . .	12,942	13,295	13,918
Gasoline	35.8	36.0	36.8
Rubber tyres ('000) . . .	32,597	43,579	50,273
Rubber footwear ('000 pairs) .	21,500	n.a.	n.a.
Cement	44,300	50,400	56,100
Pig-iron	44,046	48,003	48,163
Steel	59,178	66,792	68,398
Steel pipes	6,738	9,188	10,017
Rolled metal products . . .	52,449	57,633	59,474
Tractors (number)	5,600	6,900	12,700
Refrigerators and freezers ('000) .	2,815	3,557	4,102
Domestic washing machines ('000)	2,244	2,758	3,030
Televisions ('000)	4,714	11,876	14,186
Electric vacuum cleaners ('000) .	203	225	111
Passenger motor cars ('000) .	600	1,210	1,737
Electric energy (million kWh)*	992,000	1,038,000	1,055,000

* Figures are rounded to nearest '000 million kWh.

2012 ('000 metric tons unless otherwise indicated): Flour 9,700 (rounded figure); Granulated sugar 5,324; Cotton fabrics (million sq m) 1,385; Woollen fabrics (million sq m) 14.2; Steel 70,400; Refrigerators and freezers ('000) 4,300; Passenger motor cars ('000) 2,000; Electric energy (million kWh) 1,064,000 (rounded figure).

Finance

CURRENCY AND EXCHANGE RATES

Monetary Units

100 kopeks = 1 Russian rubl (ruble or rouble).

Sterling, Dollar and Euro Equivalents (31 December 2012)

£1 sterling = 47.928 roubles;

US $1 = 30.373 roubles;

€1 = 40.074 roubles;

1,000 roubles = £20.86 = $32.92 = €24.95.

Average Exchange Rate (roubles per US dollar)

2010	30.3679
2011	29.3823
2012	30.8398

FEDERAL BUDGET

('000 million roubles)

Revenue	2009	2010	2011
Tax revenue	3,863.9	4,338.8	5,919.4
Profit tax	195.4	255.0	342.6
Value-added tax . . .	2,050.0	2,498.2	3,250.4
Excise duties . . .	101.5	144.0	278.4
Social tax revenues . .	509.8	—	—
Other	1,007.2	1,441.6	2,048.0
Non-tax revenue	3,168.1	3,708.8	5,129.7
Customs duties . . .	2,683.3	3,227.7	4,664.7
Other non-tax revenue . .	484.8	481.1	465
Total (incl. others)	7,337.8	8,305.4	11,367.7

Expenditure	2009	2010	2011
General government . . .	853.1	887.9	777.8
Debt service	176.2	195.0	262.7
National defence and national security and militia . . .	2,192.7	2,361.9	2,775.8
National economy	1,650.7	1,222.7	1,790.2
Fuel and electric power . .	34.9	18.0	41.0
Agriculture and fishing . .	83.1	35.3	141.4
Transport	444.1	584.2	640.5
Communication and informatics	26.9	39.3	42.6
Housing and communal utilities .	151.6	234.9	279.8
Social and cultural activities . .	1,205.5	1,260.7	4,370.6
Transfers to non-budget funds .	2,113.2	2,757.6	—
Total (incl. others)	9,660.1	10,117.5	10,925.6

2012 ('000 million roubles): Total revenue 12,853.7; Total expenditure 12,890.7.

Source: Ministry of Finance, Moscow.

INTERNATIONAL RESERVES

(US $ million at 31 December)

	2009	2010	2011
Gold (national valuation) . .	22,797.7	35,788.1	44,696.7
IMF special drawing rights . .	8,896.9	8,744.0	8,726.2
Reserve position in IMF . .	1,927.0	1,893.4	4,060.4
Foreign exchange	405,824.9	432,948.5	441,161.7
Total	439,446.5	479,374.0	498,645.0

Source: IMF, *International Financial Statistics*.

MONEY SUPPLY

('000 million roubles at 31 December)

	2009	2010	2011
Currency outside depository corporations	4,038.0	5,062.8	5,938.5
Transferable deposits . . .	4,247.6	5,762.6	6,921.6
Other deposits	10,810.1	12,965.9	15,954.8
Broad money	19,095.7	23,791.3	28,814.9

Source: IMF, *International Financial Statistics*.

COST OF LIVING
(Consumer Price Index; base: previous year = 100)

	2010	2011	2012
Food and beverages	112.9	103.9	107.5
Other consumer goods	105.0	106.7	105.2
Services	108.1	108.7	107.3
All items	108.8	106.1	106.6

NATIONAL ACCOUNTS
('000 million roubles at current prices)

Expenditure on the Gross Domestic Product

	2010	2011	2012
Final consumption expenditure.	32,514.7	37,442.9	42,458.0
Households	23,617.7	27,168.1	30,518.4
Non-profit institutions serving households	225.7	234.1	264.0
General government . . .	8,671.3	10,040.7	11,675.6
Gross capital formation . . .	10,472.6	14,207.8	16,018.9
Gross fixed capital formation . Acquisitions, less disposals, of valuables	10,014.3	12,075.8	13,767.4
Changes in inventories . .	458.3	2,132.0	2,251.5
Total domestic expenditure .	42,987.3	51,560.7	58,476.9
Exports of goods and services .	13,529.3	16,940.9	18,484.8
Less Imports of goods and services	9,789.6	12,164.4	13,795.7
Sub-total	46,727.0	56,427.2	63,166.0
Statistical discrepancy* . .	−405.2	−628.5	−809.1
GDP in market prices . .	46,321.8	55,798.7	62,356.9
GDP at constant 2008 prices	39,775.6	41,469.7	42,899.2

* Referring to the difference between the sum of the expenditure components and official estimates of GDP, compiled from the production approach.

Gross Domestic Product by Economic Activity

	2010	2011	2012
Agriculture, hunting and forestry.	1,451.5	1,973.7	1,954.2
Fishing	97.0	98.9	109.0
Mining and quarrying	3,842.8	5,157.3	5,802.5
Manufacturing	5,934.7	7,385.5	8,099.6
Electricity, gas and water supply .	1,527.1	1,814.5	1,847.1
Construction	2,587.9	3,101.9	3,447.2
Wholesale and retail trade; repair of motor vehicles, motorcycles and personal and household goods	8,021.0	9,329.7	10,518.4
Hotels and restaurants . . .	403.3	462.0	514.8
Transport, storage and communications	3,662.5	3,971.5	4,352.8
Financial intermediation . . .	1,773.5	1,956.0	2,327.4
Real estate, renting and business activities	4,901.5	5,650.2	6,289.0
Public administration and defence; compulsory social security . .	2,436.9	2,686.1	3,520.8
Education	1,226.0	1,403.7	1,604.2
Health and social work . . .	1,487.0	1,750.5	2,072.0
Other community, social and personal services	700.6	763.0	844.6
Sub-total	40,053.3	47,504.6	53,303.6
Taxes, *less* subsidies, on products .	6,268.5	8,294.1	9,053.4
GDP in market prices . . .	46,321.8	55,798.7	62,356.9

BALANCE OF PAYMENTS
(US $ million)

	2009	2010	2011
Exports of goods	296,050	391,338	512,872
Imports of goods	−188,475	−244,411	−315,758
Balance on goods	107,575	146,927	197,115
Exports of services	45,947	50,385	58,160
Imports of services	−61,773	−74,017	−93,042
Balance on goods and services	91,750	123,294	162,233
Primary income received . . .	33,184	37,361	42,376
Primary income paid	−73,467	−85,976	−102,583
Balance on goods, services and primary income	51,467	74,680	102,026
Secondary income received . .	8,908	9,953	16,358
Secondary income paid . . .	−11,770	−13,552	−19,549
Current balance	48,605	71,080	98,834
Capital account (net)	−11,869	73	−120
Direct investment assets . . .	−43,665	−52,523	−67,283
Direct investment liabilities . .	36,500	43,288	52,878
Portfolio investment assets . .	−10,375	−3,470	−10,578
Portfolio investment liabilities .	8,195	1,810	−7,279
Financial derivatives and employee stock options (net)	−3,244	−1,841	−1,394
Other investment assets . . .	6,141	−23,392	−83,326
Other investment liabilities . .	−25,201	10,010	40,891
Net errors and omissions . . .	−1,724	−8,285	−9,986
Reserves and related items .	3,363	36,749	12,638

Source: IMF, *International Financial Statistics*.

External Trade

PRINCIPAL COMMODITIES
(US $ '000 million)

Imports	2009	2010	2011
Foodstuffs and agricultural raw materials (excl. textiles) . .	30.0	36.4	42.5
Mineral products	4.1	5.2	6.3
Chemical products and rubber .	27.9	36.9	45.4
Leather, fur, and articles thereof .	0.8	1.2	1.5
Wood, pulp and paper products .	5.1	5.9	6.7
Textiles, textile articles and footwear	9.5	14.2	16.6
Metals, precious stones, and articles thereof	11.3	16.9	21.8
Machinery, vehicles and transport equipment	72.7	102.0	147.0
Other	6.0	10.5	18.6
Total	167.0	229.0	306.0

Exports	2009	2010	2011
Foodstuffs and agricultural raw materials (excl. textiles) . .	10.0	8.8	12.0
Mineral products	203.0	271.0	363.0
Chemical products and rubber .	18.7	24.5	31.0
Leather, fur, and articles thereof .	0.2	0.3	0.4
Wood, pulp and paper products .	8.4	9.6	10.7
Textiles, textile articles and footwear	0.7	0.8	0.8
Metals, precious stones, and articles thereof	38.5	50.5	57.4
Machinery, vehicles and transport equipment	17.9	21.5	23.2
Other	3.8	9.6	18.5
Total	302.0	397.0	517.0

Note: Totals may not be equal to the sum of components, owing to rounding.

PRINCIPAL TRADING PARTNERS
(US $ million)

Imports	2009	2010	2011
Austria	2,060	2,463	3,118
Belarus	6,719	9,954	13,685
Belgium	2,538	3,265	4,121
Brazil	3,478	4,067	4,389
China, People's Republic	22,795	38,964	48,264
Czech Republic	2,319	2,918	4,504
Denmark	1,373	1,703	2,053
Finland	3,955	4,584	5,671
France	8,431	10,043	13,276
Germany	21,229	26,699	37,676
Hungary	2,631	3,141	3,337
India	1,525	2,143	2,799
Italy	7,891	10,043	13,401
Japan	7,252	10,260	15,004
Kazakhstan	3,697	4,449	6,859
Korea, Republic	4,866	7,287	11,593
Netherlands	3,589	4,442	5,924
Poland	4,214	5,826	6,651
Spain	2,274	3,042	4,305
Sweden	2,039	2,854	4,038
Turkey	3,216	4,867	6,374
Ukraine	9,131	14,047	20,121
United Kingdom	3,544	4,576	7,179
USA	9,170	11,097	14,601
Uzbekistan	847	1,557	1,860
Total (incl. others)	167,348	228,912	305,605

Exports	2009	2010	2011
Austria	1,625	1,022	1,757
Belarus	16,726	18,081	24,923
Belgium	4,045	4,927	7,480
China, People's Republic	16,687	20,326	35,241
Cyprus	792	1,641	1,424
Czech Republic	4,438	5,500	5,449
Finland	9,162	12,170	13,190
France	8,726	12,420	14,857
Germany	18,710	25,662	34,174
Greece	2,338	2,852	4,685
Hungary	3,899	5,355	7,693
India	5,936	6,392	6,094
Israel	1,044	1,763	1,765
Italy	25,100	27,476	32,582
Japan	7,251	12,829	14,701
Kazakhstan	9,147	10,690	12,907
Korea, Republic	5,664	10,439	13,386
Netherlands	36,407	53,974	62,567
Poland	12,503	14,936	21,369
Romania	1,559	2,025	1,828
Slovakia	2,971	4,576	7,065
Spain	2,892	4,048	6,165
Sweden	3,200	3,589	5,127
Switzerland	6,213	8,716	11,627
Taiwan	791	1,797	2,121
Turkey	16,377	20,317	25,429
Ukraine	13,836	23,148	30,510
United Kingdom	9,074	11,309	13,997
USA	9,132	12,320	16,604
Total (incl. others)	301,667	397,068	516,481

Transport

RAILWAYS
(traffic)

	2009	2010	2011
Paying passengers ('000 journeys)	1,137,000	947,000	993,000
Freight carried ('000 metric tons)	1,109,000	1,312,000	1,382,000
Passenger-km (million)	151,500	138,900	139,800
Freight ton-km (million)	1,865,000	2,011,000	2,128,000

ROAD TRAFFIC
(motor vehicles in use)

	2006	2007	2009*
Passenger cars	26,793,500	29,249,000	33,084,000
Lorries and vans (incl. buses and coaches)	5,752,800	5,591,000	5,388,000

* Data for 2008 were not available.

Motorcycles and mopeds: 7,165,900 in 1998; 6,328,600 in 1999.

Source: IRF, *World Road Statistics*.

SHIPPING

Flag Registered Fleet
(at 31 December)

	2010	2011	2012
Number of vessels	4,636	4,676	4,753
Total displacement ('000 grt)	9,687.3	9,723.9	9,911.9

Source: Lloyd's List Intelligence (www.lloydslistintelligence.com).

International Sea-borne Freight Traffic
('000 metric tons, rounded data)

	2009	2010	2011
Goods loaded	210,324	201,516	189,240
Goods unloaded	34,620	23,532	21,840

Note: Annual data extrapolated from monthly averages.

Source: UN, *Monthly Bulletin of Statistics*.

CIVIL AVIATION
(traffic on scheduled services)

	2009	2010	2011
Passengers carried ('000)	47,000	59,000	66,000
Freight carried (million metric tons)	0.9	1.1	1.2
Passenger-km (million)	112,500	147,100	166,800
Freight ton-km (million)	3.6	4.7	4.9

Kilometres flown (million): 868 in 2007; 931 in 2008; 836 in 2009 (Source: UN, *Statistical Yearbook*).

Tourism

FOREIGN VISITOR ARRIVALS
('000, incl. excursionists)

Country of origin	2008	2009	2010
Azerbaijan	989.5	892.4	979.8
China, People's Republic	815.5	718.6	747.6
Estonia	662.9	920.5	474.9
Finland	1,000.2	1,057.6	1,012.6
Germany	636.3	592.3	611.4
Kazakhstan	2,732.1	2,590.7	2,747.4
Kyrgyzstan	552.7	406.5	552.9
Latvia	423.1	516.8	569.3
Lithuania	680.5	600.8	760.7
Moldova	1,167.3	885.0	988.1
Poland	779.8	434.5	394.9
Tajikistan	900.7	674.6	830.2
Ukraine	6,415.4	5,604.4	5,574.1
Uzbekistan	1,556.2	1,212.8	1,584.1
Total (incl. others)	23,676.1	21,338.7	22,281.2

Total arrivals ('000): 22,686 in 2011 (provisional).

Receipts from tourism (US $ million, excl. passenger transport): 9,366 in 2009; 8,830 in 2010; 11,398 in 2011 (provisional).

Source: World Tourism Organization.

Communications Media

	2009	2010	2011
Telephones ('000 main lines in use)	45,379.6	44,915.8	44,151.5
Mobile cellular telephones ('000 subscribers)	230,500.0	237,689.2	256,116.6
Internet subscribers ('000) . .	59,700	n.a.	19,427
Broadband subscribers ('000) . .	12,900	15,700	18,775

Source: International Telecommunication Union.

Education

(2011/12 unless otherwise indicated)

	Institutions	Students*	Teachers*
Pre-primary	45,100†	5,388,000†	600,800‡
Primary and general secondary .	47,146	13,446,000	1,060,000
Vocational secondary	2,925	2,082,000	118,700
Higher	1,080	6,490,000	348,200

* Rounded figures.
† 2010/11.
‡ 2009/10.

Pupil-teacher ratio (primary education, UNESCO estimate): 18.1 in 2008/09 (Source: UNESCO Institute for Statistics).

Adult literacy rate (UNESCO estimates): 99.6% (males 99.7%; females 99.5%) in 2010 (Source: UNESCO Institute for Statistics).

Directory

The Government

HEAD OF STATE

President of the Russian Federation: VLADIMIR V. PUTIN (elected 4 March 2012; inaugurated 7 May).

THE GOVERNMENT
(May 2013)

Chairman: DMITRII A. MEDVEDEV.

First Deputy Chairman: IGOR I. SHUVALOV.

Deputy Chairman and Head of the Government Administration: (vacant).

Deputy Chairman, Presidential Representative to the North Caucasus Federal Okrug: ALEKSANDR G. KHLOPONIN.

Deputy Chairman: ARKADII V. DVORKOVICH.

Deputy Chairman: OLGA YU. GOLODETS.

Deputy Chairman: DMITRII N. KOZAK.

Deputy Chairman: DMITRII O. ROGOZIN.

Minister of Agriculture: NIKOLAI V. FEDOROV.

Minister of Civil Defence, Emergencies and Clean-up Operations: VLADIMIR A. PUCHKOV.

Minister of Communications and the Mass Media: NIKOLAI A. NIKIFOROV.

Minister of Culture: VLADIMIR R. MEDINSKII.

Minister of Defence: Col-Gen. SERGEI K. SHOIGU.

Minister of Development of the Russian Far East, Presidential Representative to the Far Eastern Federal Okrug: VIKTOR I. ISHAYEV.

Minister of Economic Development: ANDREI R. BELOUSOV.

Minister of Education and Science: DMITRII V. LIVANOV.

Minister of Energy: ALEKSANDR V. NOVAK.

Minister of Finance: ANTON G. SILUANOV.

Minister of Foreign Affairs: SERGEI V. LAVROV.

Minister of Health: VERONIKA I. SKVORTSOVA.

Minister of Industry and Trade: DENIS V. MANTUROV.

Minister of Internal Affairs: Lt-Gen. VLADIMIR A. KOLOKOLTSEV.

Minister of Justice: ALEKSANDR V. KONOVALOV.

Minister of Labour and Social Protection: MAKSIM A. TOPILIN.

Minister of Natural Resources and Ecology: SERGEI YE. DONSKOI.

Minister of Regional Development: IGOR N. SLYUNYAYEV.

Minister of Sport: VITALII L. MUTKO.

Minister of Transport: MAKSIM YU. SOKOLOV.

Minister without Portfolio: MIKHAIL A. ABYZOV.

MINISTRIES

Office of the President: 103132 Moscow, Staraya pl. 4; tel. (495) 625-35-81; fax (495) 606-07-66; e-mail president@gov.ru; internet www.kremlin.ru.

Office of the Government: 103274 Moscow, Krasnopresnenskaya nab. 2; tel. (495) 605-53-29; fax (495) 605-52-43; e-mail duty_press@aprf.gov.ru; internet www.government.ru.

Ministry of Agriculture: 107139 Moscow, Orlikov per. 1/11; tel. (495) 607-80-00; fax (495) 607-83-62; e-mail info@mcx.ru; internet www.mcx.ru.

Ministry of Civil Defence, Emergencies and Clean-up Operations: 109012 Moscow, Teatralnyi prozeyd 3; tel. (495) 449-99-99; fax (495) 624-19-46; e-mail info@mchs.gov.ru; internet www.mchs.gov.ru.

Ministry of Communications and the Mass Media: 125375 Moscow, ul. Tverskaya 7; tel. (495) 771-81-00; fax (495) 771-87-10; e-mail office@minsvyaz.ru; internet www.minsvyaz.ru.

Ministry of Culture: 125993 Moscow, M. Gnezdnikovskii per. 7/6; tel. (495) 629-89-01; fax (495) 629-72-69; e-mail pisma@mkrf.ru; internet www.mkrf.ru.

Ministry of Defence: 119169 Moscow, ul. Znamenka 19; tel. (495) 696-71-71; fax (495) 696-86-73; internet www.mil.ru.

Ministry of Development of the Russian Far East: 109544 Moscow, ul. Shkolnaya 25; 680000 Khabarovsk, ul. Muravyeva-Amurskogo 18; tel. (4212) 97-00-10; fax (4212) 97-00-11; e-mail info@minvostokrazvitia.ru; internet minvostokrazvitia.ru.

Ministry of Economic Development: 125993 Moscow, ul. 1-ya Tverskaya-Yamskaya 1/3; tel. (495) 694-03-53; fax (499) 251-69-65; e-mail mineconom@economy.gov.ru; internet www.economy.gov.ru.

Ministry of Education and Science: 125993 Moscow, ul. Tverskaya 11; tel. (495) 629-70-62; fax (495) 629-08-91; e-mail info@mon.gov.ru; internet www.mon.gov.ru.

Ministry of Energy: 107996 Moscow, ul. Shchepkin 42; tel. (495) 631-98-58; fax (495) 631-83-64; e-mail minenergo@minenergo.gov.ru; internet minenergo.gov.ru.

Ministry of Finance: 109097 Moscow, ul. Ilinka 9; tel. (495) 987-91-01; fax (495) 625-08-89; internet www.minfin.ru.

Ministry of Foreign Affairs: 119200 Moscow, Smolenskaya-Sennaya pl. 32/34; tel. (499) 244-16-06; fax (499) 244-34-48; e-mail ministry@mid.ru; internet www.mid.ru.

Ministry of Health: 127994 Moscow, Rakhmanovskii per. 3; tel. and fax (495) 628-44-53; fax (495) 606-18-62; internet www.rosminzdrav.ru.

Ministry of Industry and Trade: 109074 Moscow, Kitaigorodskii proyezd 7; tel. and fax (495) 539-21-87; fax (495) 539-21-72; e-mail info_admin@minprom.gov.ru; internet www.minpromtorg.gov.ru.

Ministry of Internal Affairs: 119049 Moscow, ul. Zhitnaya 16; tel. (495) 667-72-64; fax (495) 667-57-33; e-mail mvd12@mvdrf.ru; internet www.mvd.ru.

Ministry of Justice: 119991 Moscow, ul. Zhitnaya 14; tel. (495) 955-59-99; fax (495) 677-06-72; e-mail pr@minjust.ru; internet www.minjust.ru.

Ministry of Labour and Social Protection: 127994 Moscow, ul. Ilinka 21; tel. (495) 606-00-60; fax (495) 606-18-76; e-mail zabolotnayate@rosminzdrav.ru; internet www.rosmintrud.ru.

Ministry of Natural Resources and Ecology: 123995 Moscow, ul. B. Gruzinskaya 4/6; tel. (495) 254-48-00; fax (495) 254-43-10; e-mail admin@cbi-mpr.ru; internet www.mnr.gov.ru.

Ministry of Regional Development: 127994 Moscow, ul. Sadovaya-Samotechnaya 10/23/1; tel. (495) 980-25-47; fax (495) 699-38-41; e-mail info@minregion.ru; internet www.minregion.ru.

Ministry of Sport: 105064 Moscow, ul. Kazakova 18; tel. (495) 995-35-74; fax (495) 265-34-17; e-mail info@minstm.gov.ru; internet www.minsport.gov.ru.

Ministry of Transport: 109012 Moscow, ul. Rozhdestvenka 1/1; tel. (495) 626-10-00; fax (495) 626-91-28; e-mail info@mintrans.ru; internet www.mintrans.ru.

President

Presidential Election, 4 March 2012

Candidates	Votes	%
Vladimir V. Putin (United Russia) . .	45,602,075	63.60
Gennadii A. Zyuganov (Communist Party of the Russian Federation) .	12,318,353	17.18
Mikhail D. Prokhorov (Independent) .	5,722,508	7.98
Vladimir V. Zhirinovskii (Liberal Democratic Party of Russia) . . .	4,458,103	6.22
Sergei M. Mironov (A Just Russia) .	2,763,935	3.85
Total*	71,701,665	100.00

* Including 836,691 invalid votes, equivalent to 1.17% of the total.

Legislature

The Federalnoye Sobraniye (Federal Assembly) is a bicameral legislative body, comprising the Sovet Federatsii (Federation Council) and the Gosudarstvennaya Duma (State Duma).

Sovet Federatsii
(Federation Council)

103426 Moscow, ul. B. Dmitrovka 26; tel. (495) 692-11-50; fax (495) 692-43-05; e-mail post_sf@gov.ru; internet www.council.gov.ru.

The Sovet Federatsii is the upper chamber of the Federalnoye Sobraniye. It comprises two deputies appointed from each of the constituent members (federal territorial units) of the Russian Federation, representing the legislative and executive branches of power in each republic and region.

Chairman: VALENTINA I. MATVIYENKO.

Gosudarstvennaya Duma
(State Duma)

103265 Moscow, Okhotnyi ryad 1; tel. (495) 692-62-66; fax (495) 697-42-58; e-mail stateduma@duma.ru; internet www.duma.gov.ru.

Chairman: SERGEI YE. NARYSHKIN.

General Election, 4 December 2011

Parties and blocs	Votes	%	Seats
United Russia	32,379,135	49.32	238
Communist Party of the Russian Federation	12,599,507	19.19	92
A Just Russia	8,695,522	13.24	64
Liberal Democratic Party of Russia .	7,664,570	11.67	56
Yabloko Russian United Democratic Party	2,252,403	3.43	—
Patriots of Russia	639,119	0.97	—
The Right Cause	392,806	0.60	—
Total*	65,656,526	100.00	450

* Excluding 1,033,464 invalid votes (1.57% of the total).

Election Commission

Central Electoral Commission of the Russian Federation (Tsentralnaya izbiratelnaya komissiya Rossiiskoi Federatsii): 109012 Moscow, B. Cherkasskii per. 9; tel. (495) 606-79-57; fax (495) 606-97-69; e-mail info@cikrf.ru; internet www.cikrf.ru; Chair. VLADIMIR YE. CHUROV.

Political Organizations

Legislation approved in late 2004 required each political party to have at least 50,000 members in order to obtain registration and to contest elections. Although a revision to electoral law, approved in 2009, reduced the minimum membership figure, initially to 45,000 (with effect from January 2010) and then to 40,000 (from January 2012), the number of registered political parties remained low, and only seven parties were registered to contest the elections to the Gosudarstvennaya Duma held in December 2011 (compared with 11 parties registered at the elections in 2007). A major revision to electoral law, adopted in 2012, reduced the minimum permissible number of party members to just 500. A large number of parties sought registration subsequently, and by early May 2013 a total of 65 parties were officially registered with the Ministry of Justice, including the following:

Agrarian Party of Russia (APR) (Agrarnaya partiya Rossii): 107078 Moscow, per. B. Kharitonevskii 21/6; tel. (495) 982-53-24; f. 2012 as revival of party in existence in 2003-08 that subsequently merged into United Russia (q.v.); left-wing, supports the agricultural sector; Chair. OLGA V. BASHMACHNIKOVA.

Citizens' Union (Soyuz Gorozhan): 119619 Moscow, ul. Proizvodstvennaya 2/1/157; tel. (929) 623-26-21; f. 2012; Chair. of Bd ILDAR F. GAIFUTDINOV.

Civic Force (Grazhdanskaya sila): 101000 Moscow, ul. Myasnitskaya 16; tel. (495) 777-27-93; fax (495) 777-27-62; internet www.gr-sila.ru; f. 2004 by fmr mems of the Union of Rightist Forces; fmrly Free Russia (Svobodnaya Rossiya); name changed as above 2007; Chair. ALEKSANDR YU. RYAVKIN.

Civic Platform (Grazhdanskaya Platforma): 123104 Moscow, bul. Tverskoi 13; tel. (495) 787-11-10; e-mail feedback@civilplatform.ru; internet www.civilplatform.ru; f. 2012; Chair. of Executive Cttee NIKOLAI V. MOROZOV; Leader MIKHAIL D. PROKHOROV; 500 mems (2012).

Communist Party of the Russian Federation (CPRF) (Kommunisticheskaya partiya Rossiiskoi Federatsii—KPRF): 103051 Moscow, per. M. Sukharevskii 3/1; tel. (495) 692-87-44; fax (495) 692-68-54; e-mail ck@kprf.ru; internet www.kprf.ru; f. 1993; claims succession to the Russian Communist Party, which was banned in 1991; Chair. of Central Committee GENNADII A. ZYUGANOV; 156,528 mems (Jan. 2012).

Communist Party of Social Justice (Kommunisticheskaya partiya sotsialnoi spravedlivosti): 117628 Moscow, ul. Starobitsevskaya 15; tel. (926) 451-69-46; f. 2012; Chair. VLADIMIR V. ARTEMOV.

Communists of Russia (Kommunisty Rossii): 125167 Moscow, Leningradskii per. 47/1/132; tel. (499) 963-01-11; e-mail komros@bk.ru; internet www.komros.info; f. 2009; Marxist-Leninist; Chair. MAKSIM A. SURAIKIN.

Democratic Party of Russia (Demokraticheskaya partiya Rossiya): 127287 Moscow, ul. Poltavskaya 18; tel. (495) 611-30-11; fax (495) 611-56-70; e-mail prav.delo@gmail.com; f. 1990; liberal-conservative; Chair. TIMUR V. BOGDANOV.

Green Alliance—People's Party (Aliyans Zelenykh—Narodnaya Partiya): 115093 Moscow, Partiinyi per. 1/3; tel. (495) 258-67-94; fax (495) 258-67-95; e-mail info@russian-greens.com; internet russian-greens.ru; f. 2012; Chair. GLEB G. FETISOV.

A Just Russia (AJR) (Spravedlivaya Rossiya): 123104 Moscow, ul. M. Dmitrovka 12/1; tel. (495) 787-85-15; fax (495) 787-85-20; e-mail info@spravedlivo.ru; internet www.spravedlivo.ru; f. 2006 by merger of Motherland, Russian Party of Life and Russian Pensioners' Party; absorbed People's Party of the Russian Federation in Apr. 2007; statist, patriotic party; Chair. NIKOLAI V. LEVICHEV; Leader SERGEI M. MIRONOV; 381,650 mems (Jan. 2012).

Liberal Democratic Party of Russia (LDPR) (Liberalno-demokraticheskaya partiya Rossii): 103045 Moscow, Lukov per. 9; tel. (495) 623-02-44; fax (495) 692-92-42; e-mail info@ldpr.ru; internet www.ldpr.ru; f. 1988; nationalist; Chair. VLADIMIR V. ZHIRINOVSKII; 204,693 mems (Jan. 2012).

Native Country (Rodnaya Strana): 125581 Moscow, ul. Festivalnaya 24/88; tel. (967) 132-28-60; f. 2012; Chair. DMITRII A. ISAYEV.

Party for Justice! (Partiya za spravedlivost!): 101000 Moscow, bul. Sretenskii 6/1; tel. (926) 101-20-22; e-mail info@parzs.ru; internet parzs.ru; Chair. VLADIMIR S. PONOMARENKO.

Party of Free Citizens (Partiya svobodiykh grazhdan): 115088 Moscow, ul. Sharikopodshipinikovskaya 13/1; f. 2012; Chair. PAVEL D. SKLYANCHUK.

Patriots of Russia (Patrioty Rossii): 119121 Moscow, Smolenskii bulv. 11/2; tel. (495) 604-42-71; fax (495) 692-15-50; e-mail patriot-rus@bk.ru; internet www.patriot-rus.ru; f. 2002; fmrly Russian Party of Labour; Leader GENNADII YU. SEMIGIN; 84,075 mems (Jan. 2010).

Peace and Unity Party (Partiya Mira i Yedinstva): 125009 Moscow, ul. B. Dmitrovka 7/5/3/43; tel. (495) 629-85-40; e-mail info@dppp

.su; internet www.pmerf.ru; socialist, nationalist; Chair. SAZHI Z. UMALATOVA.

Pensioners' Party of Russia (Partiya pensionerov Rossii): 105613 Moscow, Izmailovskoye shosse 71/4G–D; tel. and fax (499) 166-64-06; internet www.vppppr.ru; f. 2012; Chair. NIKOLAI V. CHEBOTAREV.

People's Party of Russia (Narodnaya partiya Rossii): 119517 Moscow, ul. Nezhinskaya 13/92; tel. (495) 628-99-42; f. 2012; Pres. ALEKSANDR V. VASENIN.

Republican Party of Russia—Party of People's Freedom (RPR-PARNAS) (Respublikanskaya partiya Rossii—Partiya narodnoy svobody): 119017 Moscow, per. Klimentovskii 9/1; tel. (495) 959-48-04; internet svobodanaroda.org; f. 1990; liberalism, liberal democracy; campaigns against corruption and the arbitrary application of the law; Responsible Sec. of the Federal Political Council VLADIMIR A. RYZHKOV; Exec. Dir MIKHAIL YA. SHNEIDER; Leaders MIKHAIL KASYANOV, BORIS NEMTSOV.

The Right Cause (Pravoye Delo): 127006 Moscow, Veskovskii per. 2; tel. (495) 276-09-65; fax (495) 276-09-67; e-mail info@pravoedelo .ru; internet www.pravoedelo.ru; f. 2008, registered 2009 by fmr mems of Union of Rightist Forces, Civic Force and the Democratic Party of Russia; economically liberal; Chair. ANDREI G. DUNAYEV; Chair. of the Party Apparatus DENIS V. PAKHMUTOV; 57,348 mems (Jan. 2012).

Russian Ecological Party 'The Greens' (Rossiiskaya Ekologicheskaya Partiya 'Zelenyye'): 119049 Moscow, ul. B. Yakimanka 38; tel. (495) 231-31-29; fax (495) 737–54-28; e-mail info@greenparty.ru; internet www.greenparty.ru; f. 1992 as 'Pine Tree' Constructive Ecological Party (Kedr); current name adopted in 2002; Chair. ANATOLII A. PANFILOV; 12,000 mems (2012).

Russian Party of Pensioners for Justice (Rossiiskaya partiya pensionerov za spravedlivost): 101000 Moscow, per. Ulanskii 14; tel. (495) 607-55-56; f. 1997; Chair. IGOR L. ZOTOV.

Russian People's Union (Rossiiskii obshchenarodnyi soyuz): 123056 Moscow, ul. Vasilevskaya 4; tel. (495) 605-62-88; fax (499) 255-68-75; e-mail ros910@yandex.ru; internet www.partia-nv.ru; f. 2001; dissolved in 2008, revived in 2012; nationalism and conservatism; Chair. SERGEI N. BABURIN.

Smart Russia (Umnaya Rossiya): 125062 Moscow, per. Podsosenskii 23; tel. (903) 001-68-89; internet xn–l1adffk.xn–p1ai; f. 2012; nationalist; Chair. NIKITA S. BOROVIKOV.

Social Democratic Party of Russia (Sotsial-demokraticheskaya partiya Rossii—SDPR): 115162 Moscow, ul. Gorodskaya 1; tel. (916) 406-89-41; f. 2001; dissolved in 2007; revived in 2012; Chair. TIMUR V. BOGDANOV.

Social Security Political Party (Politicheskaya Partiya Sotsialnoi Zashchity): 101000 Moscow, bul. Sretenskii 6/1/2/101; tel. (495) 628-36-90; Chair. VIKTOR D. SVIRIDOV.

United Russia (UR) (Yedinaya Rossiya): 129110 Moscow, Bannyi per. 3; tel. (495) 86-86-41; fax (495) 975-30-98; e-mail press@edinros .ru; internet www.er.ru; f. 2001 as Unity and Fatherland—United Russia, on the basis of Unity (f. 1999, incorporating Our Home is Russia), Fatherland (f. 1999, and led by Mayor of Moscow YURII LUZHKOV) and the All Russia grouping of regional governors; pragmatic centrist grouping that promotes moderate economic reforms and a strong state; absorbed Agrarian Party of Russia in Oct. 2008; Chair. DMITRII A. MEDVEDEV; Chair. of Supreme Council BORIS V. GRYZLOV; Sec. of General Council SERGEI I. NEVEROV; 2.1m. mems (Jan. 2012).

Yabloko Russian United Democratic Party (Rossiiskaya obyedinennaya demokraticheskaya partiya 'Yabloko'): 119034 Moscow, M. Levshinskii per. 7/3; tel. (495) 780-30-10; fax (495) 780-30-12; e-mail info@yabloko.ru; internet www.yabloko.ru; f. 1993 on the basis of the Yavlinskii-Boldyrev-Lukin electoral bloc; present name adopted 2008; democratic, politically and socially liberal; Chair. SERGEI S. MITROKHIN; 53,012 mems (Apr. 2012).

Young Russia (Molodaya Rossiya): 121069 Moscow, Novinskii bulv. 22/1; tel. (495) 973-15-96; internet molross.ru; f. 2012; liberal; Chair. NIKOLAI N. STOLYARCHUK.

UNREGISTERED POLITICAL ORGANIZATIONS

The following political organizations were unregistered, and, as such, not permitted to participate in elections.

All-Russia National Front (RNF) (Obshcherossii Narodni Front—ONF): 142703 Moscow, ul. Shkolnaya 24A; tel. (495) 786-86-79; fax (498) 547-34-35; internet www.narodfront.ru; f. 2011; seeks to build Russia as a strong 'sovereign democracy' with small enterprises and a market economy; Chair. of Coordinating Council VLADIMIR V. PUTIN.

Another Russia (Drugaya Rossiya): Moscow; tel. (495) 761-12-29; e-mail drugros@gmail.com; internet www.drugros.ru; f. 2010; direct successor of the National Bolshevik Party; Leader EDUARD LIMONOV.

Motherland—Congress of Russian Communities (CRC) (Rodina—Kongress Russkikh Obshchin—KRO): 103062 Moscow, Lyalin per. 21/2; tel. (916) 662-77-70; e-mail rodinakro@gmail.com; internet www.kro.su; f. 1993; nationalist; Leader ALEKSEI A. ZHURAVLEV; 100,000 mems.

Russian People's Democratic Union (Rossiyskiy Narodno-Demokraticheskiy Soyuz—RNDS): 119435 Moscow, ul. M. Pirogovskaya 14; tel. (495) 953-58-24; fax (495) 953-46-80; e-mail newtypeparty@mail.ru; internet www.nardemsoyuz.ru; f. 2006; liberal opposition party; Leader MIKHAIL M. KASYANOV.

Solidarity (Solidarnost): 101000 Moscow, POB 565; e-mail secretsolfed@gmail.com; internet www.rusolidarnost.ru; f. 2008; liberal, social democratic; Leader BORIS NEMTSOV.

United Civil Front (Obyedinennyi Grazhdanskii Front): 119002 Moscow, Gagarinskii per. 26/12; tel. (499) 241-82-80; fax (499) 241-95-96; e-mail info@rufront.ru; internet www.rufront.ru; f. 2005; Leader GARRI K. KASPAROV.

Diplomatic Representation

EMBASSIES IN RUSSIA

Afghanistan: 121069 Moscow, ul. Povarskaya 42; tel. (495) 690-16-80; fax (495) 690-01-46; e-mail safarat_moscow@yahoo.com; Ambassador AZIZULLAH KARZAI.

Albania: 119049 Moscow, ul. Mytnaya 3/8; tel. (495) 982-38-52; fax (495) 982-38-54; e-mail embassy.moscow@mfa.gov.al; Ambassador SOKOL GJOKA.

Algeria: 115127 Moscow, Krapivinskii per. 1A; tel. (495) 937-46-00; fax (495) 937-46-25; e-mail embalg@mail.ru; internet www .algerianembassy.ru; Ambassador SMAIL CHERGUI.

Angola: 119590 Moscow, ul. U. Palme 6; tel. (499) 143-63-24; fax (495) 956-18-80; e-mail angomosc@col.ru; internet www .angolarussia.ru; Ambassador JOAQUIM AUGUSTO DE LEMOS.

Argentina: 119017 Moscow, ul. B. Ordynka 72; tel. (495) 502-10-20; fax (495) 755-58-00; e-mail efrus@co.ru; internet www.efrus.mrecic .gov.ar; Ambassador JUAN CARLOS KRECKLER.

Armenia: 101990 Moscow, Armyanskii per. 2; tel. (495) 624-12-69; fax (495) 624-45-35; e-mail info@armem.ru; internet www .armenianembassy.ru; Ambassador OLEG YESAIAN.

Australia: 109028 Moscow, Podkolokolnyi per. 10A/2; tel. (495) 956-60-70; fax (495) 956-61-70; e-mail austembmos@dfat.gov.au; internet www.russia.embassy.gov.au; Ambassador PAUL MYLER.

Austria: 119034 Moscow, Starokonyushennyi per. 1; tel. (495) 780-60-66; fax (495) 937-42-69; e-mail moskau-ob@bmeia.gv.at; internet www.aussenministerium.at/moskau; Ambassador Dr MARGOT KLESTIL-LÖFFLER.

Azerbaijan: 125009 Moscow, Leontyevskii per. 16; tel. (495) 629-43-32; fax (495) 202-50-72; e-mail embassy@azembassy.msk.ru; internet www.azembassy.ru; Ambassador POLAD BÜLBÜLOĞLU.

Bahrain: 109017 Moscow, ul. B. Ordynka 18/1; tel. (495) 953-00-22; fax (495) 953-74-74; e-mail moscowbah@yahoo.com; internet www .mofa.gov.bh/default.aspx?tabid=5445; Ambassador Dr HASHIM HASAN AL-BASH.

Bangladesh: 119121 Moscow, Zemledelcheskii per. 6; tel. (499) 246-78-04; fax (499) 766-43-00; e-mail bdoot.moscow@mail.ru; internet www.bangladeshembassy.ru; Ambassador S. M. SAIFUL HOQUE.

Belarus: 101990 Moscow, ul. Maroseika 17/6; tel. (495) 777-66-44; fax (495) 777-66-33; e-mail mail@embassybel.ru; internet www .embassybel.ru; Ambassador IHOR PETRISHENKO.

Belgium: 121069 Moscow, ul. M. Molchanovka 7; tel. (495) 780-03-31; fax (495) 780-03-32; e-mail moscow@diplobel.fed.be; internet www.diplomatie.be/moscow; Ambassador GUY TROUVEROY.

Benin: 127006 Moscow, Uspenskii per. 7; tel. (495) 699-23-60; fax (495) 694-02-26; e-mail amba_beninmos@yahoo.fr; Ambassador ANICET GABRIEL KOTCHOFA.

Bolivia: 115191 Moscow, ul. Serpukhovskii val 8/135–137; tel. (495) 954-06-30; fax (495) 958-07-55; e-mail embolrus@online.ru; internet emborus.com; Ambassador MARÍA LUISA RAMOS URZAGASTE.

Bosnia and Herzegovina: 119590 Moscow, ul. Mosfilmovskaya 50/1; tel. (495) 147-64-88; fax (495) 147-64-89; e-mail embassybih@mail .ru; internet www.rf-bih.ru; Ambassador IVAN BARBALIĆ.

Brazil: 121069 Moscow, ul. B. Nikitskaya 54; tel. (495) 363-03-66; fax (495) 291-15-91; e-mail embaixador.moscou@itamaraty.gov.br; internet www.brasemb.ru; Ambassador CARLOS ANTONIO DA ROCHA PARANHOS.

Brunei: 119180 Moscow, ul. B. Yakimanka 12; tel. (495) 783-19-27; fax (495) 941-82-14; e-mail moscow.russia@mfa.gov.bn; Ambassador HAINI HASHIM.

Bulgaria: 119590 Moscow, ul. Mosfilmovskaya 66; tel. (495) 143-90-22; fax (495) 232-33-02; e-mail embassy.moscow@mfa.bg; internet www.mfa.bg/embassies/russia; Ambassador BOYKO KOTZEV.

Burundi: 119049 Moscow, Kaluzhskaya pl. 1/226–227; tel. (495) 230-25-64; fax (495) 230-20-09; e-mail bdiamb@yahoo.fr; Ambassador (vacant).

Cambodia: 121002 Moscow, Starokonyushennyi per. 16; tel. (495) 637-47-36; fax (495) 956-65-73; e-mail cambemoscow@stream.ru; Ambassador VANNA THAY.

Cameroon: 121069 Moscow, ul. Povarskaya 40; tel. (495) 690-65-49; fax (495) 690-61-16; e-mail ambacamos@yahoo.fr; Ambassador MAHAMAT PABA SALÉ.

Canada: 119002 Moscow, Starokonyushennyi per. 23; tel. (495) 925-60-00; fax (495) 925-60-25; e-mail mosco@international.gc.ca; internet www.canadainternational.gc.ca/russia-russie; Ambassador JOHN C. SLOAN.

Central African Republic: 117571 Moscow, ul. 26-i Bakinskikh Kommissarov 9/124–125; tel. (495) 434-45-20; fax (495) 933-28-99; Ambassador (vacant).

Chad: 119049 Moscow, ul. Korovii val 7; tel. (495) 936-17-63; fax (495) 936-11-01; e-mail ambatchamo@yahoo.fr; Ambassador ABAS-SALAH YUSSUF.

Chile: 119002 Moscow, Denezhnii per. 7, str. 1; tel. (499) 241-01-45; fax (499) 241-68-67; e-mail echile@col.ru; Ambassador JUAN EDUARDO EGUIGUREN.

China, People's Republic: 117330 Moscow, ul. Druzhby 6; tel. (495) 783-08-67; fax (499) 956-11-69; e-mail chiemb@microdin.ru; internet ru.china-embassy.org; Ambassador LI HUI.

Colombia: 119121 Moscow, ul. Burdenko 20/2; tel. (499) 248-30-42; fax (499) 248-30-25; e-mail colombia@colombia.ru; internet www.colombia.ru; Ambassador RAFAEL FRANCISCO AMADOR CAMPOS.

Congo, Democratic Republic: 119571 Moscow, Leninskii pr. 148; tel. and fax (499) 514-18-03; e-mail ambamoscourde@yahoo.fr; Ambassador MOÏSE KABAKU MUTSHALL.

Congo, Republic: 119049 Moscow, ul. Korovii val 7/1/10–12; tel. (495) 236-33-68; fax (495) 236-41-16; e-mail ambacoru@yahoo.fr; Ambassador ZME CLOVIS GIION.

Costa Rica: 121615 Moscow, Rublevskoye shosse 26/1/150–151; tel. (495) 415-40-14; fax (495) 415-40-42; e-mail embaric2@rol.ru; Ambassador MARIO FERNANDEZ SILVA.

Côte d'Ivoire: 119034 Moscow, Korobeinikov per. 14/9; tel. (495) 637-24-00; fax (495) 230-20-45; e-mail ambacimow@hotmail.com; internet ambaci-russie.org; Ambassador GBERNARD TANOH BOUTCH-OUÉ.

Croatia: 119034 Moscow, Korobeinikov per. 16/10; tel. (495) 785-40-70; fax (495) 637-29-88; e-mail crorus@mvep.hr; internet www.ru.mfa.hr; Ambassador IGOR POKAZ.

Cuba: 119017 Moscow, ul. B. Ordynka 66; tel. and fax (495) 933-79-50; e-mail rusiasegundomision@embacuba.ru; internet www.cubadiplomatica.cu/rusia/en/home.aspx; Ambassador EMILIO LOZADA.

Cyprus: 121069 Moscow, ul. Povarskaya 9; tel. (495) 575-03-10; fax (495) 575-03-11; e-mail moscowembassy@mfa.gov.cy; internet www.mfa.gov.cy/embassymoscow; Ambassador PETROS KESTORAS.

Czech Republic: 115127 Moscow, ul. Yu. Fuchika 12/14; tel. (495) 276-07-01; fax (045) 250-15-23; e-mail moscow@embassy.mzv.cz; internet www.mfa.cz/moscow; Chargé d'affaires a.i. MARTIN KLUČAR.

Denmark: 119034 Moscow, Prechistenskii per. 9; tel. (495) 642-68-00; fax (495) 775-01-91; e-mail mowamb@um.dk; internet www.ambmoskva.um.dk; Ambassador TOM RISDAHL JENSEN.

Dominican Republic: 121615 Moscow, Rublevskoye shosse 26, korp. 1, podyezd 4, of. 211; tel. (495) 415-25-96; fax (495) 415-36-01; e-mail embadomru@gmail.com; Ambassador JORGE LUIS PÉREZ ALVARADO.

Ecuador: 103064 Moscow, Gorokhovskii per. 12; tel. (499) 261-55-27; fax (499) 267-70-79; e-mail embajada@embajada-ecuador.ru; internet www.embajada-ecuador.ru; Ambassador PATRICIO ALBERTO CHÁVEZ ZAVALA.

Egypt: 119034 Moscow, Kropotkinskii per. 12; tel. (495) 246-02-34; fax (495) 246-10-64; e-mail egyemb_moscow@yahoo.com; Ambassador MAHMOUD GAMIL AHMED EL-DIEB.

El Salvador: 119049 Moscow, ul. Mytnaya 3; tel. (499) 238-00-62; e-mail embelsalvadorrusia@rree.gob.sv; Ambassador CLAUDIA IVETTE CANJURA DE CENTENO.

Equatorial Guinea: 119017 Moscow, Pogorelskii per. 7/1; tel. (495) 953-27-66; fax (495) 953-20-84; e-mail embajada1968@mail.ru; Ambassador FILIBERTO TOMO NGUEMA.

Eritrea: 119049 Moscow, ul. Kirovii val 7/31; tel. (499) 238-30-25; fax (499) 238-18-68; e-mail erembassy@yandex.ru; Ambassador TEKLAY MINASSIE ASGEDOM.

Estonia: 125009 Moscow, M. Kislovskii per. 5; tel. (495) 737-36-40; fax (495) 737-36-46; e-mail embassy.moskva@mfa.ee; internet www.estemb.ru; Ambassador JÜRI LUIK.

Ethiopia: 129041 Moscow, Orlovo-Davydovskii per. 6; tel. (495) 680-16-16; fax (495) 680-66-08; e-mail eth-emb@col.ru; Ambassador MELES KASAHUN DENDER.

Finland: 119034 Moscow, Kropotkinskii per. 15/17; tel. (495) 787-41-74; fax (495) 247-33-80; e-mail sanomat.mos@formin.fi; internet www.finland.org.ru; Ambassador HANNU HIMANEN.

France: 115127 Moscow, ul. B. Yakimanka 45; tel. (495) 937-15-00; fax (495) 937-14-30; e-mail amba@ambafrance.ru; internet www.ambafrance.ru; Ambassador JEAN DE GLINIASTY.

Gabon: 119002 Moscow, Denezhnyi per. 16; tel. (499) 241-00-80; fax (499) 241-15-85; e-mail ambgab-ru@mail.ru; Ambassador PAUL BIE-EYENE.

The Gambia: 115035 Moscow, Kadashevskaya nab. 32/2/3; tel. and fax 258-36-82; Ambassador (vacant).

Germany: 119285 Moscow, ul. Mosfilmovskaya 56; tel. (495) 937-95-00; fax (495) 783-08-75; e-mail germanmo@aha.ru; internet www.moskau.diplo.de; Ambassador ULRICH BRANDENBURG.

Ghana: 121069 Moscow, Skatertnyi per. 14; tel. (495) 690-19-69; fax (495) 690-21-98; e-mail missionsecretary@ghanaemb-mos.ru; internet www.ghanaemb-mos.ru; Ambassador Dr SETH KORANG-TENG.

Greece: 115127 Moscow, Leontiyevskii per. 4; tel. (495) 539-29-40; fax (495) 539-29-50; e-mail gremb.mow@mfa.gr; internet www.mfa.gr/moscow; Ambassador MICHEL SPINELLIS.

Guatemala: 119049 Moscow, ul. Korovii val 7/98; tel. (499) 238-22-14; fax (499) 238-14-46; e-mail embrusia@minex.gob.gt; Ambassador HERBERT ESTUARDO MENESES CORONADO.

Guinea: 119034 Moscow, ul. ul. Prechistenka 35; tel. (499) 238-10-85; fax (499) 238-97-68; e-mail ambaguineemoscou@yahoo.fr; Ambassador MOHAMED KEITA.

Guinea-Bissau: 117556 Moscow, Simferopolskii bulv. 7A/180; tel. and fax (499) 317-95-82; e-mail embaixadgb.ru@gmail.com; Ambassador SECO INTCHASSO.

Holy See: 103555 Moscow, Vadkovskii per. 7/37; tel. (495) 726-59-30; fax (495) 726-59-32; e-mail nuntius@inbox.ru; Apostolic Nuncio Most Rev. IVAN JURKOVIČ (Titular Archbishop of Corbavia).

Hungary: 115127 Moscow, ul. Mosfilmovskaya 62; tel. (495) 641-75-00; fax (495) 641-75-20; e-mail mission.mow@mfa.gov.hu; internet www.mfa.gov.hu/emb/moscow; Ambassador ISTVÁN IJGYÁRTÓ.

Iceland: 115127 Moscow, Skatertnyi per. 34/4; tel. (495) 956-76-04; fax (495) 956-76-12; e-mail icemb.moscow@utn.stjr.is; internet www.iceland.org/ru; Ambassador ALBERT JÓNSSON.

India: 101000 Moscow, ul. Vorontsovo Pole 6–8; tel. (495) 783-75-35; fax (495) 917-22-85; e-mail fshoc@indianembassy.ru; internet www.indianembassy.ru; Ambassador AJAI MALHOTRA.

Indonesia: 109017 Moscow, ul. Novokuznetskaya 12; tel. (495) 951-95-50; fax (495) 230-64-31; e-mail kbrimos@rol.ru; Ambassador DJAUHARI ORATMANGUN.

Iran: 109028 Moscow, Pokrovskii bulv. 7; tel. (495) 917-72-82; fax (495) 230-96-83; e-mail info@iranembassy.ru; internet www.iranembassy.ru; Ambassador SAYED MAHMOUD REZA SAJJADI.

Iraq: 119121 Moscow, ul. Pogodinskaya 12; tel. (499) 246-55-07; fax (499) 246-27-34; e-mail mosemb@iraqmfamail.com; Ambassador FAEK FAREEK ABD AL-AZIZ NEROYI.

Ireland: 115127 Moscow, Grokholskii per. 5; tel. (495) 937-59-11; fax (495) 680-06-23; e-mail moscowembassy@dfa.ie; internet www.embassyofireland.ru; Ambassador PHILIP MCDONAGH.

Israel: 119017 Moscow, ul. B. Ordynka 56; tel. (495) 660-27-00; fax (495) 660-27-68; e-mail info@moscow.mfa.gov.il; internet moscow.mfa.gov.il; Ambassador DORIT GOLENDER.

Italy: 121002 Moscow, Denezhnyi per. 5; tel. (495) 956-60-93; fax (495) 241-03-30; e-mail embitaly.mosca@esteri.it; internet www.ambmosca.esteri.it; Ambassador ANTONIO ZANARDI LANDI.

Japan: 129090 Moscow, Grokholskii per. 27; tel. (495) 229-25-50; fax (495) 229-25-55; e-mail japan-info@japan.orc.ru; internet www.ru.emb-japan.go.jp; Ambassador TIKAHITO HARADA.

Jordan: 123001 Moscow, Mamonovskii per. 3; tel. (495) 699-43-44; fax (495) 699-43-54; e-mail emjordan@umail.ru; Ambassador AHMAD S. AL-HASSAN.

Kazakhstan: 101000 Moscow, Chistoprudnyi bulv. 3A; tel. (495) 627-17-01; fax (495) 608-08-32; e-mail pressa@kazembassy.ru; internet www.kazembassy.ru; Ambassador GALYM I. ORAZBAKOV.

Kenya: 119034 Moscow, Lopukhinskii per. 5; tel. (495) 637-21-86; fax (495) 637-54-63; e-mail kenemb@kenemb.ru; internet www.kenemb.ru; Ambassador PAUL KIBIWOTT KURGAT.

Korea, Democratic People's Republic: 107140 Moscow, ul. Mosfilmovskaya 72; tel. (499) 143-62-31; fax (499) 143-63-12; e-mail dprk_embassy@mail.ru; Ambassador KIM YONG JAE.

Korea, Republic: 119121 Moscow, ul. Plyushchikha 56/1; tel. (495) 783-27-27; fax (495) 783-27-77; e-mail embru@mofat.go.kr; Ambassador WI SUNG-LAC.

Kuwait: 119285 Moscow, ul. Mosfilmovskaya 44A; tel. (495) 147-00-40; fax (495) 956-60-32; e-mail kuwaitmoscow@yahoo.com; internet kuwaitembassy-russia.com; Ambassador NASSER Haji IBRAHIM AL-MUZAYYAN.

Kyrgyzstan: 119017 Moscow, ul. B. Ordynka 64; tel. (495) 237-48-82; fax (495) 951-60-62; e-mail info@kyrgyzembassy.ru; internet www.kyrgyzembassy.ru; Ambassador BOLOT JUNUSOV.

Laos: 121069 Moscow, ul. M. Nikitskaya 18; tel. (495) 690-25-60; fax (495) 203-49-24; e-mail laoembassy@mail.ru; internet www .laoembassy.ru; Ambassador THIENG BOUPHA.

Latvia: 105062 Moscow, ul. Chaplygina 3; tel. (495) 232-97-60; fax (495) 232-97-50; e-mail embassy.russia@am.gov.lv; internet www .am.gov.lv/lv/moscow; Ambassador EDGARS SKUJA.

Lebanon: 115127 Moscow, ul. Sadovaya-Samotechnaya 14; tel. (495) 694-13-20; fax (495) 694-32-22; e-mail leb.emb.moscow@ mtu-net.ru; Ambassador SHAUKI BU HASSAR.

Libya: 131940 Moscow, ul. Mosfilmovskaya 38; tel. (495) 143-03-54; fax (495) 938-21-62; e-mail libyanbureau@mail.ru; Ambassador AMIR AL-ARABI ALI GHARIB.

Lithuania: 121069 Moscow, Borisoglebskii per. 10; tel. (495) 785-86-05; fax (495) 785-86-00; e-mail amb.ru@urm.lt; internet ru.mfa.lt; Ambassador RENATAS NORKUS.

Luxembourg: 119034 Moscow, Ostozhenka 23; tel. (495) 786-66-63; fax (495) 786-66-69; e-mail moscou.amb@mae.etat.lu; internet www .moscou.mae.lu; Ambassador PIERRE FERRING.

Macedonia, former Yugoslav republic: 117292 Moscow, ul. D. Ulyanova 16, korp. 2/509–510; tel. (495) 124-33-57; fax (495) 982-36-34; e-mail moscow@mfa.gov.mk; internet www.missions.gov .mk/moscow; Ambassador ILIJA ISAJLOVSKI.

Madagascar: 119034 Moscow, Kursovoi per. 5; tel. (495) 695-28-92; fax (495) 695-28-54; e-mail info@ambamadagascar.ru; internet www .ambamadagascar.ru; Ambassador ELOI ALPHONSE MAXIME DOVO.

Malaysia: 119192 Moscow, ul. Mosfilmovskaya 50; tel. (499) 147-15-14; fax (495) 937-96-02; e-mail malmoscow@kln.gov.my; internet www.kln.gov.my/perwakilan/moscow; Ambassador ZAINOL ABIDIN BIN OMAR.

Mali: 113184 Moscow, ul. Novokuznetskaya 11; tel. (495) 951-06-55; fax (495) 951-27-84; e-mail amaliru@mail.ru; Ambassador Gen. BRAHIMA COULIBALY.

Malta: 119049 Moscow, ul. Korovii Val 7/219; tel. (495) 237-19-39; fax (495) 237-21-58; e-mail maltaembassy.moscow@gov.mt; Ambassador RAYMOND J. SARSERO.

Mauritania: 119121 Moscow, B. Sabbinskii per. 21; tel. (499) 245-11-76; fax (499) 246-25-19; e-mail mauritanie@redline.ru; Ambassador SIDI MOHAMED OULD TALEB AMAR.

Mauritius: 109240 Moscow, ul. Nikolo-Yamskaya 8; tel. (495) 915-76-17; fax (495) 915-76-65; e-mail moscow_emb@mail.gov.mu; internet www.moscow.mauritius.gov.mu; Chargé d'affaires a.i. G. MOOTOOSAMY.

Mexico: 119034 Moscow, B. Levshinskii per. 4; tel. (495) 969-28-79; fax (495) 969-28-77; e-mail info@embamex.ru; internet portal.sre .gob.mx/rusia; Ambassador RUBÉN BELTRÁN GUERRERO.

Moldova: 107031 Moscow, ul. Kuznetskii most 18; tel. (495) 624-53-53; fax (495) 624-95-90; e-mail moscova@mfa.md; internet www .moldembassy.ru; Ambassador ANDREI GALBUR.

Mongolia: 115127 Moscow, Borisoglebskii per. 11; tel. (495) 290-67-92; fax (495) 291-46-36; e-mail moscow@mfat.gov.mn; Ambassador DOLOONZHIN IDEVHTEN.

Montenegro: 119049 Moscow, ul. Mytnaya 3/23–25; tel. (499) 230-18-65; fax (499) 230-18-86; e-mail russianfederation@mfa.gov.me; Ambassador ZORAN JOCOVIĆ.

Morocco: 121069 Moscow, ul. B. Nikitskaya 51; tel. (495) 291-17-62; fax (495) 609-94-93; e-mail sifmamos@gmail.com; internet www .ambmaroc.ru; Ambassador ABDELKADER LECHEHEB.

Mozambique: Moscow, ul. Krutitskii Val 3; tel. (495) 786-30-05; fax (495) 786-30-06; e-mail embamocru@hotmail.com; Ambassador BERNARDO MARCELINO CHERINDA.

Myanmar: 119049 Moscow, ul. B. Nikitskaya 41; tel. (495) 291-56-14; fax (495) 956-18-78; e-mail mofa.aung@mptmail.net.mm; Ambassador TIN YU.

Namibia: 113096 Moscow, 2-i Kazachii per. 7; tel. (495) 230-32-75; fax (495) 230-22-74; e-mail info@namibianembassy.ru; Ambassador SAMUEL KAVETO MBAMBO.

Nepal: 119121 Moscow, 2-i Neopalimovskii per. 14/7; tel. (499) 252-82-15; fax (499) 252-80-00; e-mail nepalemb@mtu-net.ru; internet www.nepalembassyrus.ru; Ambassador RAVI MOHAN SAPKOTA KOPILA.

Netherlands: 115127 Moscow, Kalashnyi per. 6; tel. (495) 797-29-00; fax (495) 797-29-04; e-mail mos@minbuza.nl; internet www .netherlands-embassy.ru; Ambassador RON KELLER.

New Zealand: 121069 Moscow, ul. Povarskaya 44; tel. (495) 956-35-79; fax (495) 956-35-83; e-mail nzembmoscow@mft.net.nz; internet www.nzembassy.com/russia; Ambassador HAMISH COOPER.

Nicaragua: 117330 Moscow, ul. Mosfilmovskaya 50, korp. 1; tel. (499) 783-08-64; fax (499) 783-08-53; e-mail embanicaragua@hotmail .com; Ambassador LUIS ALBERTO MOLINA CUADRA.

Nigeria: 121069 Moscow, Mamonovskii per. 5; tel. (495) 690-37-83; fax (495) 956-28-25; e-mail info@nigerianembassy.ru; internet www .nigerianembassy.ru; Ambassador ASSAM EKANEM ASSAM.

Norway: 131940 Moscow, ul. Povarskaya 7; tel. (499) 951-10-00; fax (499) 951-10-01; e-mail emb.moscow@mfa.no; internet www .norvegia.ru; Ambassador KNUT HAUGE.

Oman: 109180 Moscow, Staromonetnyi per. 14, str. 1; tel. (495) 230-15-87; fax (495) 230-15-44; e-mail embomn-mos@rambler.ru; Ambassador YUSUF BIN ISSA BIN ALI AL-ZIDJALI.

Pakistan: 123001 Moscow, ul. Sadovaya-Kudrinskaya 17; tel. (499) 254-97-91; fax (495) 956-90-97; e-mail parepmoscow@yahoo.com; internet www.pakistanembassy.ru; Ambassador ALAMGIR KHAN BABAR.

Panama: 119590 Moscow, ul. Mosfilmovskaya 50, korp. 1; tel. (495) 956-07-29; fax (495) 956-07-30; e-mail empanrus@aha.ru; Ambassador JULIO ERNESTO CÓRDOBA DE LEÓN.

Paraguay: 119049 Moscow, ul. Korovii val 7/142; tel. and fax (499) 230-18-10; e-mail embajada@embapar.ru; internet www.embapar .ru; Ambassador MARCIAL BOBADILLA GUILLÉN.

Peru: 121002 Moscow, Smolenskii bulv. 22/14/15; tel. (499) 650-07-56; fax (499) 248-00-72; e-mail leprumoscu@mtu-net.ru; Ambassador GUSTAVO ANTONIO OTERO ZAPATA.

Philippines: 121099 Moscow, Karmanitskii per. 6; tel. (499) 241-05-63; fax (499) 241-26-30; e-mail moscowpe@stream.ru; internet www .phil-embassy.ru; Ambassador ALEJANDRO B. MOSQUERA.

Poland: 123557 Moscow, ul. Klimashkina 4; tel. (495) 231-15-00; fax (495) 231-15-15; e-mail moskwa.amb.sekretariat@msz.gov.pl; internet www.moskwa.polemb.net; Ambassador WOJCIECH JACEK ZAJĄCZKOWSKI.

Portugal: 129090 Moscow, Botanicheskii per. 1; tel. (495) 981-34-10; fax (495) 981-34-16; e-mail embptrus@moscovo.dgaccp.pt; Ambassador PEDRO NUNO DE ABREU E MELO BÁRTOLO.

Qatar: 117049 Moscow, ul. Korovii Val 7/196–198; tel. (495) 980-69-18; fax (495) 980-69-17; e-mail moscow@mofa.gov.qa; Ambassador AHMAD SAIF KHALAF AL-MIDHADI.

Romania: 119590 Moscow, ul. Mosfilmovskaya 64; tel. (499) 143-04-24; fax (499) 143-04-49; e-mail ambasada@orc.ru; internet moscova .mae.ro; Ambassador CONSTANTIN MIHAIL GRIGORIE.

Saudi Arabia: 119121 Moscow, 3-i Neopalimovskii per. 3; tel. (495) 245-37-90; fax (495) 246-94-71; e-mail ruemb@mofa.gov.sa; Ambassador ALI HASSAN JAAFAR.

Senegal: 119049 Moscow, ul. Korovii val 7/1/193–194; tel. (495) 230-21-02; fax (495) 230-20-63; internet www.ambassen.ru; Ambassador MAMADOU SALIOU DIOUF.

Serbia: 119285 Moscow, ul. Mosfilmovskaya 46; tel. (499) 988-66-45; fax (499) 988-66-46; e-mail ambasada.moskva@mfa.rs; internet www .moskva.mfa.rs; Ambassador SLAVENKO TERZIĆ.

Sierra Leone: 121615 Moscow, Rublevskoye shosse 26, korp. 1/58–59; tel. (495) 415-41-66; fax (495) 415-41-24; e-mail slembassymoscow@yahoo.com; internet www.sierraleoneembassy .ru; Ambassador Dr JOHN YAMBASU.

Singapore: 121099 Moscow, per. Kamennoi slobody 5; tel. (499) 241-39-14; fax (499) 241-78-95; e-mail singemb_mow@sgmfa.gov.sg; internet www.mfa.gov.sg/content/mfa/overseasmission/moscow .html; Ambassador LIM KHENG HUA.

Slovakia: 115127 Moscow, ul. Yu. Fuchika 17/19; tel. (495) 956-49-20; fax (495) 791-20-65; e-mail emb.moscow@mzv.sk; internet www .mzv.sk/moskva; Ambassador Dr JOZEF MIGAŠ.

Slovenia: 127006 Moscow, ul. M. Dmitrovka 14/1; tel. (495) 737-63-55; fax (495) 694-15-68; e-mail vmo@gov.si; internet moscow .embassy.si; Ambassador ADA FILIP-SLIVNIK.

Somalia: 117556 Moscow, Simferopolskii bulv. 7A/145; tel. (499) 317-15-72; fax (499) 317-06-22; e-mail somembassy@nabad.org; internet www.russia.somaligov.net; Ambassador MOHAMED MOHAMOUD HANDULLE.

South Africa: 123001 Moscow, Granatnyi per. 1, str. 9; tel. (495) 926-11-77; fax (495) 926-11-78; e-mail moscow.ambassador@foreign

.gov.za; internet saembassy.ru; Ambassador MANDISI BONGANI MABUTO MPAHLWA.

South Sudan: Moscow, Khvostov per. 12; tel. (925) 132-60-09; fax (929) 985-40-23; e-mail rssembassymoscow@gmail.com; Ambassador SHOL DENG ALAK.

Spain: 115127 Moscow, ul. B. Nikitskaya 50/8; tel. (495) 690-29-93; fax (495) 691-91-71; e-mail emb.moscu@maec.es; internet www.maec.es/embajadas/moscu; Ambassador JOSÉ IGNACIO CARBAJAL GÁRATE.

Sri Lanka: 129090 Moscow, ul. Shchepkina 24; tel. (495) 688-16-20; fax (495) 688-17-57; e-mail moscow@srilankaembassy.org; internet www.srilankaembassy.org; Ambassador UDAYANGA WEERATUNGA.

Sudan: 127006 Moscow, Uspenskii per. 4A; tel. (495) 699-54-61; fax (495) 699-33-42; e-mail sudmos@cityline.ru; Ambassador OMAR DAHAB MOHAMED.

Swaziland: Moscow; Ambassador TEMBAYENA ANNASTASIA DLAMINI.

Sweden: 119590 Moscow, ul. Mosfilmovskaya 60; tel. (495) 937-92-00; fax (495) 937-92-02; e-mail moscow.sweinfo@gov.se; internet www.swedenabroad.com/moscow; Ambassador VERONIKA BARD BRINGÉUS.

Switzerland: 101000 Moscow, per. Ogorodnoi slobody 2/5; tel. (495) 258-38-30; fax (495) 621-21-83; e-mail mos.vertretung@eda.admin.ch; internet www.eda.admin.ch/moscow; Ambassador PIERRE HELG.

Syria: 119034 Moscow, Mansurovskii per. 4; tel. (499) 766-95-28; fax (495) 956-31-91; Ambassador RIAD HADDAD.

Tajikistan: 103001 Moscow, Granatnyi per. 13; tel. (495) 690-61-02; fax (495) 291-89-98; e-mail info@tajembassy.ru; internet www.tajembassy.ru; Ambassador ABDULMAJID S. DOSTIYEV.

Tanzania: 109017 Moscow, ul. Pyatnitskaya 33; tel. (495) 953-82-21; fax (495) 690-22-51; e-mail info@tanzania.ru; internet www.tanzania.ru; Ambassador JAKA MGWABI MWAMBI.

Thailand: 129090 Moscow, ul. B. Spasskaya 9; tel. (495) 608-08-17; fax (495) 290-96-59; e-mail thaiemb@nnt.ru; internet www.thaiembassymoscow.com; Ambassador Dr ITTI DITBANJONG.

Tunisia: 115127 Moscow, ul. M. Nikitskaya 28/1; tel. (495) 691-28-58; fax (495) 691-75-88; e-mail atmos@post.ru; Ambassador ALI GOUTALI.

Turkey: 119121 Moscow, 7-i Rostovskii per. 12; tel. (495) 246-14-89; fax (495) 246-49-89; e-mail dtmos@dtmos.ru; internet www.moscow.emb.mfa.gov.tr; Ambassador AYDIN ADNAN SEZGIN.

Turkmenistan: 119019 Moscow, Filippovskii per. 22; tel. (495) 691-65-93; fax (495) 291-09-35; e-mail emb-turkmenistan@mtu-net.ru; internet www.turkmenembassy.ru; Ambassador BERDIMYRAT REJEPOV.

Uganda: 119049 Moscow, ul. Mytnaya 3; tel. (499) 230-22-76; fax (499) 230-21-31; e-mail info@uganda.ru; internet www.uganda.ru; Ambassador Dr MOSES EBUK.

Ukraine: 103009 Moscow, Leontiyevskii per. 18; tel. (495) 629-35-42; fax (495) 629-46-81; e-mail emb_ru@mfa.gov.ua; internet www.mfa.gov.ua/russia; Ambassador VLADIMIR YELCHENKO.

United Arab Emirates: 101000 Moscow, ul. U. Palme 4; tel. (499) 234-40-60; fax (495) 234-40-70; e-mail uaemirates@mtu-net.ru; Ambassador OMAR SAIF GHOBASH.

United Kingdom: 121099 Moscow, Smolenskaya nab. 10; tel. (495) 956-72-00; fax (495) 956-72-01; e-mail ukinrussia@fco.gov.uk; internet ukinrussia.fco.gov.uk; Ambassador TIM BARROW.

USA: 121099 Moscow, B. Devyatinskii per. 8; tel. (495) 728-50-00; fax (495) 728-50-90; e-mail consulmo@state.gov; internet moscow.usembassy.gov; Ambassador MICHAEL A. MCFAUL.

Uruguay: 117330 Moscow, ul. Lomonosovskii per. 38; tel. (495) 143-04-01; fax (495) 938-20-45; e-mail ururus@uruguay.org.ru; Ambassador ANÍBAL FERNANDO CABRAL SEGALERBA.

Uzbekistan: 109017 Moscow, Pogorelskii per. 12; tel. (495) 230-00-76; fax (495) 238-89-18; e-mail info@uzembassy.ru; internet www.uzembassy.ru; Ambassador ZIYADULLA S. PULATXOJAYEV.

Venezuela: 115127 Moscow, B. Karetnyi per. 13/15; tel. (495) 699-40-42; fax (495) 956-61-08; Ambassador HUGO JOSÉ GARCIA HERNÁNDEZ.

Viet Nam: 119021 Moscow, ul. B. Pirogovskaya 13; tel. (495) 245-09-25; fax (495) 246-31-21; e-mail dsqvn@com2com.ru; Ambassador PHAM XUAN SON.

Yemen: 131000 Moscow, 2-i Neopalimovskii per. 6; tel. (499) 246-06-48; fax (495) 230-23-05; e-mail yemen-em@mail.ru; Ambassador MUHAMMAD SALEH AHMED AL-HELALI.

Zambia: 129041 Moscow, pr. Mira 52A; tel. (495) 688-50-01; fax (499) 763-12-92; e-mail ambassador@zambia-embassy.ru; internet www.zambia-embassy.ru; Ambassador PATRIK N. SINYINZA.

Zimbabwe: 119049 Moscow, ul. Mytnaya 3/29–31; tel. (499) 230-17-87; fax (499) 230-76-46; e-mail zimbabwe@msk.org.ru; internet www.zimmoscow.ru; Ambassador BONIFACE GUHWA CHIDYAUSIKU.

Judicial System

In January 1995 the first section of a new code of civil law came into effect. It included new rules on commercial and financial operations, and on ownership issues. The second part of the code was published in January 1996. The Constitutional Court rules on the conformity of government policies, federal laws, international treaties and presidential enactments with the Constitution. The Supreme Arbitration Court rules on disputes between commercial bodies. The Supreme Court (which was relocated from Moscow to St Petersburg in 2008) oversees all criminal and civil law, and is the final court of appeal from lower courts. A system of Justices of the Peace, to deal with certain civil cases, and with criminal cases punishable by a maximum of two years' imprisonment, was established in 1998. The majority of Russia's regions introduced jury trials, in many cases only for the most serious crimes, during 2003.

Constitutional Court of the Russian Federation (Konstitutsionnyi Sud Rossiiskoi Federatsii): 190000 St Petersburg, pl. Dekabristov 1; tel. (812) 404-33-11; e-mail ksrf@krsf.ru; internet www.ksrf.ru; f. 1991; Chair. VALERII D. ZORKIN; Sec.-Gen. YELENA V. KRAVCHENKO.

Office of the Prosecutor-General: 125993 Moscow, ul. B. Dmitrovka 15A; tel. (495) 987-56-56; fax (495) 292-88-48; internet www.genproc.gov.ru; Prosecutor-Gen. YURII YA. CHAIKA.

Supreme Arbitration Court of the Russian Federation (Vysshii Arbitrazhnyi Sud Rossiiskoi Federatsii): 101000 Moscow, M. Kharitonevskii per. 12; tel. (495) 608-11-97; fax (495) 208-11-62; e-mail vasrf@arbitr.ru; internet www.arbitr.ru; f. 1993; Chair. ANTON A. IVANOV.

Supreme Court of the Russian Federation (Verkhovnyi Sud Rossiiskoi Federatsii): 121260 Moscow, ul. Povarskaya 15; tel. (495) 627-92-68; fax (495) 691-98-77; e-mail gastello@ilinka.supcourt.ru; internet www.supcourt.ru; Chair. VYACHESLAV M. LEBEDEV.

Religion

The majority of the population of the Russian Federation are adherents of Christianity, but there are significant Islamic, Buddhist and Jewish minorities.

In 1997 legislation restricted the operation of religious groups to those that were able to prove that they had been established in Russia for a minimum of 15 years. Russian Orthodoxy, Islam, Buddhism and Judaism, together with some other Christian denominations, were deemed to comply with the legislation. Religious organizations failing to satisfy this requirement were, henceforth, obliged to register annually for 15 years, before being permitted to publish literature, hold public services or invite foreign preachers into Russia. Moreover, foreign religious groups were additionally obliged to affiliate themselves to Russian organizations.

CHRISTIANITY

The Russian Orthodox Church (Moscow Patriarchate)

The Russian Orthodox Church (Moscow Patriarchate) is the dominant religious organization in the Russian Federation, with an estimated 75m. adherents. In 2004 there were 12,638 parishes operating under the auspices of the Patriarchate in Russia.

Moscow Patriarchate: 115191 Moscow, Danilov Monastery, ul. Danilovskii Val 22; tel. (495) 954-04-54; fax (495) 633-72-81; e-mail cs@mospatr.ru; internet www.mospat.ru; Patriarch of Moscow and All Rus KIRILL (GUNDYAYEV).

The Roman Catholic Church

At 31 December 2007 there were an estimated 774,500 Catholics in the Russian Federation. In 1991 administrative structures of the Catholic Church in Russia were restored. The organization of the Church in Russia comprises one archdiocese, three dioceses, one apostolic prefecture, and an apostolic exarchate for adherents of the Byzantine Rite.

Conference of Catholic Bishops of the Russian Federation: 101031 Moscow, ul. Petrovka 19/5/35; tel. and fax (495) 923-16-97; e-mail ostastop@glasnet.ru; internet www.catholic.ru; f. 1999; Pres. Most Rev. JOSEPH WERTH (Bishop of the Diocese of the Transfiguration at Novosibirsk).

Archbishop of the Archdiocese of the Mother of God at Moscow: Most Rev. PAOLO PEZZI, 123557 Moscow, ul. M. Gruzinskaya 27/2; tel. (495) 785-54-34; fax (495) 785-54-70; e-mail p.pezzi@fscb.org.

Apostolic Prefect of Yuzhno-Sakhalinsk and Bishop of St Joseph at Irkutsk: Most Rev. CYRYL KLIMOWICZ, 664074 Irkutsk, ul. Gryboyedova 110, POB 4; tel. (3952) 41-03-10; fax (3952) 41-04-14; e-mail curiocat@curiocat.irk.ru.

Apostolic Exarch for Catholics of the Byzantine Rite in Russia: (vacant).

Protestant Churches

Russian Church of Christians of the Evangelical Faith: 123363 Moscow, ul. Fabritsiusa 31A; tel. (495) 493-57-88; internet hve.ru; f. 1907, re-established 1990; fmrly known as Union of Christians of the Evangelical Faith-Pentecostalists in Russia; 1,600 parishes and more than 300,000 adherents in 2005; Elder NAZAR P. RESHCHIKOVETS.

Russian Union of Evangelical Christians-Baptists: 117015 Moscow, Varshavskoye shosse 29/2; tel. (495) 958-13-36; fax (495) 975-23-67; e-mail bapt.un@g23.relcom.ru; internet baptist.org.ru; affiliated to the Euro-Asiatic Federation of Evangelical Christians-Baptists; Exec. Sec. YURII APATOV.

Other Christian Churches

Armenian Apostolic Church: 123022 Moscow, ul. S. Makeyeva 10; tel. (495) 255-50-19.

Russian Autonomous Orthodox Church: 125212 Moscow, Church of the New Martyrs and Confessors of Russia, Golovinskoye shosse 13 A; tel. (495) 152-50-76; formally established in 1990 as the Free Russian Orthodox Church; re-registered in 1998 under above name following opposition by local, 'catacomb' priests to moves of reconciliation between the Russian Orthodox Church Abroad and the Moscow Patriarchate; 100 parishes in 2001; First Hierarch Metropolitan of Suzdal and Vladimir VALENTIN (RUSANTSOV).

Russian Orthodox Old Belief (Old Ritual) Church (Russkaya Pravoslavnaya Staroobryadcheskaya Tserkov): 109052 Moscow, ul. Rogozhskii pos. 1B/3; tel. (495) 361-51-92; e-mail mitropolia@mail.ru; internet rpsc.ru; f. 1666 by separation from the Moscow Patriarchate; some 300 groups registered in 2005; divided into two main branches: the *popovtsi* (which have priests) and the *bespopovtsi* (which reject the notion of ordained priests and the use of all sacraments, other than that of baptism). Both branches are further divided into various groupings. The largest group of *popovtsi* are those of the Belokrinitskii Concord, under the Archbishop of Novozybkov, Moscow and All Rus, KORNILII (TITOV); c. 250 parishes, seven bishops in Russia, Ukraine and Moldova; a further significant group of *popovtsi* Old Believers are those of the Beglopopovtsyi Concord.

ISLAM

Most Muslims in the Russian Federation are adherents of the Sunni sect. Islam is the predominant religion among many peoples of the North Caucasus, such as the Chechens, the Ingush and many smaller groups, and also in the Central Volga region, among them the Tatars, Chuvash and Bashkirs.

Central Muslim Spiritual Board for Russia and European Countries of the CIS: 450057 Bashkortostan, Ufa, ul. Tukaya 50; tel. (3472) 50-80-86; f. 1789; 27 regional branches in the Russian Federation, and one branch in Ukraine; Chair. (vacant).

Council of Muftis of Russia: 129090 Moscow, per. Vypolzov 7; tel. and fax (495) 681-49-04; e-mail mufty@muslim.ru; internet www.muslim.ru; Chair. Mufti Sheikh RAVIL KHAZRAT GAINUTDIN.

JUDAISM

At the beginning of the 20th century approximately one-half of the world's Jews lived in the Russian Empire. Although many Jews emigrated from the USSR in the 1970s and 1980s, there is still a significant Jewish population (230,000 in late 2002, according to the official results of the census, although some estimates were considerably higher) in the Russian Federation.

Congress of Jewish Religious Communities and Organizations of Russia: 101000 Moscow, B. Spasoglinishevskii per. 10, Moscow Choral Synagogue; tel. (495) 917-95-92; fax (495) 740-12-18; e-mail keroor@mail.ru; f. 1996; co-ordinates activities of 120 Jewish communities throughout Russia; Chief Rabbi ADOLF SHAYEVICH; Dir ZINOVY KOGAN.

Federation of the Jewish Communities of Russia: 121099 Moscow, ul. Novyi Arbat 36/9/2; tel. (495) 290-75-18; fax (495) 290-86-49; e-mail office@fjc.ru; internet www.fjc.ru; unites 179 communities in Russia; affiliated to Federation of the Jewish Communities of the CIS and the Baltic States; Chief Rabbi of Russia, Chair. of Rabbinical Alliance of Russia and the CIS BEREL LAZAR.

Russian Jewish Congress: 101000 Moscow, B. Spasoglinishchevskii per. 9/1/936; tel. (495) 780-61-00; fax (495) 780-60-90; e-mail rjc@rjc.ru; internet www.rjc.ru; Pres. VYACHESLAV KANTOR.

BUDDHISM

Buddhism (established as an official religion in Russia in 1741) is most widespread in the Republic of Buryatiya, where the Buddhist Traditional Sangkha of Russia has its seat, in the Republics of Kalmykiya and Tyva, in Transbaikal Krai (formerly Chita Oblast), and in Irkutsk Oblast.

Buddhist Traditional Sangkha of Russia (Buddiiskaya Traditsionnaya Sangkha Rossii): 670000 Buryatiya, Ulan-Ude, Ivolginskii datsan; e-mail buddhism@buryatia.ru; internet www.sangharussia.ru; Head Pandito Khambo Lama DAMBA AYUSHEYEV.

The Press

In 2004 there were 46,000 officially registered printed media, including some 26,000 newspapers. However, the number of titles in circulation was only around one-half of the total. The total print run of Russian newspapers in that year was 8,500m. copies, and that of magazines was around 600m. copies. At that time *Moskovskii Komsomolets*, with a circulation of 2.2m., was the best-selling daily, while the weekly *Argumenty i Fakty*, which had a circulation of 2.9m. in 2007, was the best-selling newspaper overall.

REGULATORY AUTHORITY

Federal Agency for the Press and the Mass Media (Federalnoye Agentstvo po pechati i massovym kommunikatsiyam): 127994 Moscow, Strastnoi bulv. 5; tel. (495) 650-39-86; fax (495) 650-52-03; e-mail info@fapmc.ru; internet www.fapmc.ru; f. 2004; Chair. MIKHAIL V. SESLAVINSKII.

PRINCIPAL NEWSPAPERS

Moscow

Argumenty i Fakty (Arguments and Facts): 101000 Moscow, ul. Myasnitskaya 42; tel. (495) 735-44-47; e-mail n-boris@aif.ru; internet www.aif.ru; f. 1978; weekly; Editor-in-Chief NIKOLAI ZYATKOV; circ. 2.9m. (2007).

Gazeta.ru: 121059 Moscow, Berezhkovskaya nab. 16A/2; tel. (495) 980-80-28; fax (495) 980-90-73; internet www.gazeta.ru; online only; has no asscn with *Gazeta* newspaper; Editor-in-Chief ALEKSANDR PISAREV.

Grani.ru: Moscow; tel. (495) 585-84-11; e-mail info@grani.ru; internet grani.ru; f. 2000; online only; Dir-Gen. YULIYA BEREZOVSKAYA; Editor-in-Chief VLADIMIR KORSUNSKII.

Gudok (The Horn): 105066 Moscow, ul. Staraya Basmannaya 38/2/3; tel. (495) 262-26-53; fax (495) 624-78-53; e-mail gudok@css-rzd.ru; internet www.gudok.ru; f. 1917 as newspaper of railway workers; daily; Editor-in-Chief ALEKSANDR RETYUNIN; circ. 214,000 (2007).

Izvestiya (News): 127994 Moscow, ul. Tverskaya 18/1, POB 4; tel. (495) 209-05-81; fax (495) 933-64-62; e-mail izv@izvestia.ru; internet www.izvestia.ru; f. 1917; 50.19% owned by Gazprom Mediya, 49.81% by Prof-Mediya; Editor VITALY ABRAMOV; circ. 130,000 (2007).

Kavkazskii uzel (Caucasian Knot): Moscow; tel. and fax (495) 640-05-27; internet www.kavkaz-uzel.ru; f. 2001 as project of Memorial human rights NGO; independent; online only; news, features, analyses and reference data on the countries and territories in the North and South Caucasus regions; Editor-in-Chief GRIGORII SHVEDOV.

Kommersant (Businessman): 125080 Moscow, ul. Vrubelya 4/1; tel. (499) 943-97-71; fax (499) 943-97-28; e-mail kommersant@kommersant.ru; internet www.kommersant.com; f. 1989; daily; Chief Editor AZER MURSALIYEV; circ. 119,322 (2007).

Komsomolskaya Pravda (Young Communist League Truth): 103287 Moscow, Staryi Petrovsko-Razumovskii proyezd 1/23/1; tel. (495) 777-02-84; fax (495) 200-22-93; e-mail kp@kp.ru; internet www.kp.ru; f. 1925; fmrly organ of the Lenin Young Communist League (Komsomol); independent; weekly supplements *KP-Tolstushka* (KP-Fat volume), *KP-Ponedelnik* (KP-Monday); managed by Prof-Mediya; Chair. OLEG RUDNOV; Editor-in-Chief VLADIMIR SUNGORKIN; circ. 700,000.

Krasnaya Zvezda (Red Star): 123007 Moscow, Khoroshevskoye shosse 38; tel. (495) 941-21-58; fax (495) 941-40-57; e-mail mail@redstar.ru; internet www.redstar.ru; f. 1924; organ of the Ministry of Defence; Editor N. N. YEFIMOV; circ. 80,000 (2000).

The Moscow News: 119021 Moscow, Zubovskii bulv. 4; tel. (495) 645-65-65; fax (495) 637-40-40; e-mail info@moscownews.ru; internet www.themoscownews.com; f. 1930; twice a week; in English; democratic, liberal; Editor-in-Chief TIM WALL; circ. c. 41,000 (2012).

Moscow Times: 127018 Moscow, ul. Polkovaya 3/1; tel. (495) 232-47-74; fax (495) 232-65-28; e-mail moscowtimes.editors@imedia.ru; internet www.themoscowtimes.com; f. 1992; daily; in English; Publr MAXINE MATERS; Editor ANDREW McCHESNEY.

Moskovskaya Pravda (The Moscow Truth): 123846 Moscow, ul. 1905 Goda 7, POB D-22; tel. (495) 259-82-33; fax (495) 259-63-60; e-mail newspaper@mospravda.ru; internet www.mospravda.ru; f. 1918; fmrly organ of the Moscow city committee of the CPSU and the Moscow City Council; 5 a week; independent; Editor-in-Chief SHOD S. MULADZHANOV; circ. 400,000 (2007).

Moskovskii Komsomolets (MK): 123995 Moscow, ul. 1905 Goda 7; tel. (495) 250-72-72; fax (495) 259-46-39; e-mail info@mk.ru; internet www.mk.ru; f. 1919 as *Moskovskii Komsomolets* (The Moscow Young Communist); 6 a week; independent; Editor-in-Chief PAVEL GUSEV; circ. 800,000 in Moscow, 2.2m. nation-wide (2004).

Nezavisimaya Gazeta (NG) (Independent Newspaper): 101000 Moscow, ul. Myasnitskaya 13; tel. (495) 645-54-28; e-mail info@ng.ru; internet www.ng.ru; f. 1990; 5 a week; regular supplements include *NG-Nauka* (NG-Science), *NG-Regiony* (NG-Regions), *NG-Politekonomiya* (NG-Political Economy), *NG-Dipkuryer* (NG-Diplomatic Courier); Gen. Man. and Editor-in-Chief KONSTANTIN REMCHUKOV; circ. 53,000 (2005).

Novaya Gazeta (New Newspaper): 101990 Moscow, Potapovskii per. 3; tel. and fax (495) 623-68-88; e-mail pr@novayagazeta.ru; internet www.novayagazeta.ru; f. 1993; weekly; Editor DMITRII A. MURATOV; circ. 60,437 (March 2010).

Novye Izvestiya (New News): 107076 Moscow, ul. Elektrozavodskaya 33; tel. (495) 783-06-36; fax (495) 783-06-37; e-mail webmaster@newizv.ru; internet www.newizv.ru; f. 2003 following the closure of the fmr *Novye Izvestiya* (f. 1997); daily; Editor-in-Chief VALERII YAKOV.

Parlamentskaya Gazeta (Parliamentary Newspaper): 125993 Moscow, ul. 1-ya Yamskogo Polya 28; tel. (495) 257-50-90; fax (495) 257-50-82; e-mail pg@pnp.ru; internet www.pnp.ru; f. 1998; 5 a week; organ of the Federalnoye Sobraniye; Editor-in-Chief ANDREI B. FEDOTKIN; circ. 50,000 (2005).

Polit.ru: 101000 Moscow, Krivokolennyi per. 10/6A; tel. (495) 624-80-09; e-mail edit@polit.ru; internet www.polit.ru; f. 1998; independent; online only; Editor-in-Chief ANDREI LEVKIN.

Pravda (Truth): 125993 Moscow, ul. Pravdy 24; tel. and fax (499) 257-11-08; e-mail pravda2@cnt.ru; internet www.gazeta-pravda.ru; f. 1912; fmrly organ of the Cen. Cttee of the CPSU; independent; communist; Editor-in-Chief VALENTIN S. SHURCHANOV; circ. 100,300 (2007).

Pravda.ru: Moscow, ul. Staraya Basmannaya 16/1 A; 105066 Moscow, POB 26; tel. (495) 287-41-69; fax (495) 287-41-69; e-mail home@pravda.ru; internet pravda.ru; f. 1999; online only, in Russian, English and Portuguese; has no asscn with the newspaper *Pravda*; Dir-Gen. INNA S. NOVIKOVA.

Rossiiskaya Gazeta (Russian Newspaper): 125993 Moscow, ul. Pravdy 24, POB 40; tel. (499) 257-56-50; fax (495) 973-22-56; e-mail office@rg.ru; internet www.rg.ru; f. 1990; organ of the Russian Govt; 6 a week; Gen. Man. ALEKSANDR N. GORBENKO; Editor-in-Chief VLADISLAV A. FRONIN; circ. 373,820 (2004).

Rossiiskiye Vesti (Russian News): 105086 Moscow, ul. Bakuninskaya 74–76; tel. and fax (495) 641-04-57; e-mail rosvesty@yandex.ru; internet www.rosvesty.ru; f. 1991; weekly; Editor-in-Chief MIKHAIL PALIEVSKY; circ. 2,500 (2009).

Russkii Zhurnal (Russian Journal): 125009 Moscow, per. M. Gnezdnikovski 9/8/3A; tel. and fax (495) 745-52-25; e-mail russ@russ.ru; internet www.russ.ru; f. 1997; online only; culture, politics, society; Editor-in-Chief and Publr GLEB PAVLOVSKII.

Selskaya Zhizn (Country Life): 125993 Moscow, ul. Pravdy 24; tel. (495) 257-51-51; fax (495) 257-58-39; e-mail sg@sgazeta.ru; internet www.sgazeta.ru; f. 1918 as *Bednota* (Poverty), present name adopted in 1960; 2 a week; fmrly organ of the Cen. Cttee of the CPSU; independent; Editor-in-Chief and Gen. Man. SHAMUN M. KAGERMANOV; circ. 94,500.

Tribuna (Tribune): 127015 Moscow, Bumazhnii proyezd 14/1; tel. (499) 257-59-13; fax (499) 257-07-04; e-mail tribuna@tribuna.ru; internet www.tribuna.ru; f. 1969; national industrial daily; Editor-in-Chief OLEG KUZIN; circ. 57,500 (2010).

Trud (Labour): 125993 Moscow, ul. Elektrozavodskaya 27; tel. (495) 646-57-72; e-mail letter@trud.ru; internet www.trud.ru; f. 1921; 5 a week; Editor-in-Chief TATYANA KUZNETSOVA.

Vechernyaya Moskva (Evening Moscow): 123995 Moscow, ul. 1905 Goda 7, POB 5/22; tel. (499) 259-81-87; fax (499) 259-55-50; e-mail post@vm.ru; internet www.vm.ru; f. 1923; Chair. VLADIMIR V. ZUBKOV.

Vedomosti (Gazette): 127018 Moscow, ul. Polkovaya 3/1; tel. (495) 956-34-58; fax (495) 956-07-16; e-mail lys@vedomosti.ru; internet www.vedomosti.ru; f. 1999; independent business newspaper, publ. jointly with the *Financial Times* (United Kingdom) and *The Wall Street Journal* (USA); Editor-in-Chief LYSOVA TATIANA.

Zhizn (Life): 125212 Moscow, ul. Vyborgskaya 16/1; tel. (495) 510-29-84; fax (495) 510-29-81; e-mail info@zhizn.ru; internet www.zhizn.ru; weekly; Editor-in-Chief RUSLAN SAGAYEV; circ. 2.2m. within Russia (2007).

St Petersburg

Novosti Peterburga (Petersburg News): 197101 St Petersburg, ul. B. Monetnaya 16; tel. (812) 313-82-26; e-mail info@novostispb.ru; internet www.novostispb.ru; f. 1997; independent; Editor-in-Chief BORIS SUDAKOV.

Peterburgskii Chas Pik (Petersburg Rush Hour): 191040 St Petersburg, Nevskii pr. 81; tel. (812) 579-25-65; fax (812) 579-19-12; e-mail nabor@chaspik.spb.ru; internet www.chaspik.spb.ru; f. 1988; weekly; owned by Gazprom-Mediya; Editor-in-Chief LARISA AFONINA; circ. 30,000 (2010).

Sankt-Peterburgskiye Vedomosti (St Petersburg Gazette): 191025 St Petersburg, ul. Marata 25; tel. (812) 325-31-00; fax (812) 764-48-40; e-mail post@spbvedomosti.ru; internet www.spbvedomosti.ru; f. 1991 as revival of 1728–1917 title; Editor-in-Chief and Gen. Man. SERGEI A. SLOBODSKOI.

Smena (The Rising Generation): 191119 St Petersburg, ul. Marata 69; tel. (812) 315-04-76; fax (812) 315-03-53; e-mail info@smena.ru; internet www.smena.ru; f. 1919; 6 a week; controlled by Sistema Mass-Mediya; Editor-in-Chief LEONID DAVYDOV; circ. 80,000 (2002).

The St Petersburg Times: 190000 St Petersburg, Isaakevskaya pl. 4; tel. and fax (812) 325-60-80; e-mail letters@sptimes.ru; internet www.sptimes.ru; f. 1993; 2 a week; in English; independent; Editor TOBIN AUBER.

Vechernii Peterburg (Evening Petersburg): 197101 St Petersburg, ul. Mira 34; tel. (812) 334-35-64; fax (812) 314-31-05; e-mail gazeta@vspb.spb.ru; internet vppress.ru; f. 1917; Editor-in-Chief KONSTANTIN V. MIKOV.

REGIONAL NEWSPAPERS

Chelyabinskii Rabochii (The Chelyabinsk Worker): 454091 Chelyabinsk, ul. Pushkina 12; tel. and fax (351) 263-26-22; e-mail common@chelrabochy.ru; internet www.mediazavod.ru/newspapers/rabochy; f. 1908; 5 a week; Editor-in-Chief BORIS N. KIRSHIN; circ. 23,000 (2010).

Dagestanskaya Pravda (The Dagestan Truth): 367018 Dagestan, Makhachkala, pr. Petra I 61; tel. (8722) 65-00-10; fax (8722) 65-00-12; e-mail pravda@dagpravda.ru; internet www.dagpravda.ru; f. 1918; daily; Editor-in-Chief RADZHAB M. IDRISOV; circ. 22,000 (2003).

Kaliningradskaya Pravda (The Kaliningrad Truth): 236000 Kaliningrad, ul. Karla Marksa 18; tel. (4012) 21-14-87; fax (4012) 21-77-33; e-mail info@kaliningradka.ru; internet www.kaliningradka.ru; f. 1946; 5 a week; Editor-in-Chief DAMIR BATYRSHIN; circ. 13,066 (July 2010).

Kommuna (The Commune): 394036 Voronezh, ul. Komissarzhevskoi 4A; tel. and fax (4732) 51-24-87; e-mail mail@kommuna.ru; internet www.communa.ru; f. 1917; social-political; 4 a week; Editor-in-Chief VIKTOR G. RUDENKO; circ. 17,300 (June 2009).

Krasnoyarskii Rabochii (The Krasnoyarsk Worker): 660075 Krasnoyarsk, ul. Respubliki 51; tel. and fax (391) 211-77-17; e-mail redaktor@krasrab.krsn.ru; internet www.krasrab.com; f. 1905; 5 a week; Editor-in-Chief VLADIMIR YE. PAVLOVSKII; circ. 11,000 (2010).

Krasnyi Sever (The Red North): 160001 Vologda, ul. Maltsev 52/4; tel. (8202) 72-00-33; fax (8202) 72-04-61; e-mail reklama@krassever.ru; internet www.krassever.ru; f. 1917; 3 a week; publishes official documentation on behalf of the Governor and Legislative Assembly of Vologda Oblast on Tuesdays and Saturdays, and a full-colour edn, with various supplements, on Thursdays covering politics, culture, sport, etc.; daily; Editor-in-Chief NADEZHDA A. KUZMINSKAYA; circ. 42,100 (Thursdays, 2010).

Kubanskiye Novosti (Kuban News): 350000 Krasnodar, ul. Pashkovskaya 2; tel. (861) 259-30-49; fax (861) 259-60-27; e-mail redaktor@kubnews.ru; internet www.kubnews.ru; f. 1991; organ of the Governor and Legislative Assembly of Krasnodar Krai; 4 a week; Editor-in-Chief YEVGENII V. KHOMUTOV; circ. 55,000 (2010).

Mestnoye Vremya (Local Time): 614000 Perm, ul. Lenina 38/307; tel. (342) 200-01-53; fax (342) 200-01-57; e-mail vremya@permv.ru; internet www.permv.ru; f. 1992; socio-political, weekly; Editor-in-Chief YELENA V. TRETYAKOVA; circ. 250,000 (2010).

Nizhegorodskaya Pravda (The Nizhnii Novgorod Truth): 603006 Nizhnii Novgorod, ul. Varvarskaya 32, POB 417; tel. (831) 419-63-11; internet www.pravda-nn.ru; f. 1918; organ of the Governor and Legislative Assembly of Nizhnii Novgorod Oblast; 3 a week; Editor-in-Chief TATYANA V. METELKINA; circ. 17,000 (2007).

Novaya Sibir (Molodaya Sibir—Novaya Sibir) (New Siberia—A Young Siberia Is A New Siberia): 630048 Novosibirsk, ul. N. Danchenko 104; tel. (383) 240-89-80; e-mail newsib2005@yandex.ru; internet www.newsib.net; f. 1993; socio-political; weekly; Editor-in-Chief VYACHESLAV DOSYCHEV.

Oblastnaya Gazeta (Regional Newspaper): 620004 Sverdlovsk obl., Yekaterinburg, ul. Malysheva 101; tel. (343) 355-29-46; e-mail reklama@oblgazeta.ru; internet www.oblgazeta.ru; f. 1990; 5 a week;

organ of the Governor and Legislative Assembly of Sverdlovsk Oblast; circ. 71,000 (2010).

Pravda Severa (Truth of the North): 163002 Archangel, Novgorodskii pr. 32/507; tel. (8182) 20-37-98; fax (8182) 29-15-33; e-mail info@pravdasevera.ru; internet www.pravdasevera.ru; f. 1917; 3 a week; Editor SVETLANA N. LOICHENKO; circ. 8,000 (Tuesdays and Saturdays, 2010), 20,050 (Wednesdays, 2010).

Respublika Tatarstan (Republic of Tatarstan): 420066 Tatarstan, Kazan, ul. Dekabristov 2, POB 41; tel. (843) 562-11-02; fax (843) 292-37-00; e-mail info@rt-online.ru; internet www.rt-online.ru; f. 1917; organ of the Government and Parliament of the Republic of Tatarstan; 5 a week; Editor-in-Chief ALEKSANDR N. LATYSHEV; circ. 31,000 (2007).

Severnyi Kavkaz (The North Caucasus): 360000 Kabardino-Balkar Rep., Nalchik, ul. Molodogvardeiskaya 17; tel. (8662) 77-49-50; internet www.sknews.ru; f. 1990; independent; news coverage of various regions of the North Caucasus, and also the countries of the South Caucasus, and Turkey, Iran and Lebanon; weekly; Editor-in-Chief ALI M. KAZIKHANOV.

Sloboda: 300026 Tula, pr. Lenina 116, 1st Floor; tel. (4872) 35-14-51; fax (4872) 23-55-99; e-mail info@myslo.ru; internet www.tula.rodgor.ru; f. 1994; weekly; Editor-in-Chief TATYANA ALEKSEEVA; circ. 102,000 (2002).

Stavropolskaya Pravda (The Stavropol Truth): 355035 Stavropol, ul. Spartaka 8; tel. (8652) 94-05-09; fax (8652) 94-17-08; e-mail gazeta@stapravda.ru; internet www.stapravda.ru; f. 1917; 5 a week; Editor-in-Chief MIKHAIL L. TSYBULKO; circ. 20,135 (Jan. 2007).

Tyumenskaya Pravda (The Tyumen Truth): 625002 Tyumen, ul. Osipenko 81; tel. (3452) 22-74-12; fax (3452) 22-73-93; e-mail redaktortp@yandex.ru; internet pravda.port72.ru; f. 1963; social-political; 5 a week; Editor-in-Chief LARISA N. VOKHMINA.

Vladivostok: 690014 Maritime Krai, Vladivostok, ul. Narodnyi pr. 13, POB 35–47; tel. (4232) 41-56-00; fax (4232) 41-56-15; e-mail salova@vladnews.ru; internet vladnews.ru; f. 1992; daily; Editor-in-Chief YELENA V. VLADIMIROVNA.

PRINCIPAL PERIODICALS

Agriculture, Forestry, etc.

Ekologiya i Promlyshlennost Rossii (The Ecology and Industry of Russia): 119049 Moscow, Leninskii pr. 4; tel. (495) 913-80-94; e-mail info@kalvis.ru; internet www.ecip-kalvis.ru; f. 1996; monthly; environmental protection; Editor-in-Chief Prof. Dr V. D. KALNER.

Zashchita i Karantin Rastenii (Plant Protection and Quarantine): 107140 Moscow, Krasnoselskii per. 21; tel. and fax (495) 607-39-30; e-mail fitopress@ropnet.ru; internet www.z-i-k-r.ru; f. 1932; monthly; Editor-in-Chief YURII N. NEIPERT; circ. 5,000 (2009).

For Children

Koster (Campfire): 193024 St Petersburg, ul. Mytninskaya 1/20; tel. (812) 274-15-72; fax (812) 274-46-26; e-mail root@kostyor.spb.org; internet www.kostyor.ru; f. 1936; monthly; journal of the International Union of Children's Organizations (UPO-FCO); fiction, poetry, sport, reports and popular science; for ages 10–14 years; Editor-in-Chief N. B. KHARLAMPIYEV; circ. 7,500 (2000).

Murzilka: 127015 Moscow, ul. Novodmitrovskaya 5A; tel. and fax (495) 685-18-81; e-mail red-murzilka@yandex.ru; internet www.murzilka.org; f. 1924; monthly; illustrated; for first grades of school; Editor TATYANA ANDROSENKO; circ. 85,000 (2010).

Pionerskaya Pravda (Pioneers' Truth): 127994 Moscow, ul. Sushchevskaya 21; tel. and fax (495) 698-61-50; e-mail info@pionerka.ru; internet www.pionerka.ru; f. 1925; 4 a month; Editor-in-Chief MIKHAIL N. BARANNIKOV.

Yunyi Naturalist (Young Naturalist): 125015 Moscow, ul. Novodmitrovskaya 5A; tel. (495) 685-39-31; e-mail unnat1@mail.ru; internet www.unnaturalist.ru; f. 1928; monthly; popular science for children of fourth–10th grades, who are interested in biology; Editor L. V. SAMSONOVA.

Yunyi Tekhnik (Young Technician): 127015 Moscow, ul. Novodmitrovskaya 5A; tel. (495) 685-44-80; fax (495) 787-35-58; e-mail yut.magazine@gmail.com; internet www.utechnik.ru; f. 1956; monthly; popular science for children and youth; Chief Editor ALEKSANDR A. FIN.

Culture and Arts

Ex Libris-NG: 113935 Moscow, ul. Myasnitskaya 13; tel. (495) 928-48-50; fax (495) 975-23-46; e-mail exlibris@ng.ru; internet exlibris.ng.ru; weekly; literature; Editor-in-Chief IGOR ZOTOV.

Iskusstvo Kino (The Art of the Cinema): 125319 Moscow, ul. Arbat 35; tel. (499) 248-28-22; fax (499) 241-08-52; e-mail filmfilm@yandex.ru; internet www.kinoart.ru; f. 1931; monthly; journal of the Russian Film-makers' Union; Editor DANIIL B. DONDUREI; circ. 5,000 (2004).

Knizhnoye Obozreniye (Literary Review): 115054 Moscow, ul. Pyatnitskaya 71/5/2/9; tel. and fax (495) 955-79-70; e-mail all@knigoboz.ru; internet www.knigoboz.ru; f. 1966; weekly; summaries of newly published books; Editor-in-Chief ALEKSANDR M. NABOKOV; circ. 10,500 (2003).

Kultura (Culture): 101484 Moscow, ul. Novoslobodskaya 73; tel. (495) 685-06-40; fax (496) 685-31-50; e-mail kultura@dol.ru; internet www.kulturagz.ru; f. 1929; controlled by Sistema Mass-Mediya; weekly; Editor-in-Chief YURII I. BELYAVSKII; circ. 30,000 (2008).

Literaturnaya Gazeta (Literary Newspaper): 109028 Moscow, Khokhlovskii per. 10/6; tel. and fax (499) 788-02-10; e-mail litgazeta@lgz.ru; internet www.lgz.ru; f. 1831; publ. restored 1929; weekly; literature, politics, society; controlled by Sistema Mass-Mediya; Editor-in-Chief YU. M. POLYAKOV.

Literaturnaya Rossiya (Literary Russia): 103051 Moscow, Tsvetnoi bulv. 32/3; tel. (495) 694-03-65; fax (495) 694-50-10; e-mail litrossia@litrossia.ru; internet www.litrossia.ru; f. 1958; weekly; essays, verse, literary criticism; Editor VYACHESLAV OGRYZKO; circ. 10,000 (2010).

Nash Sovremennik (Our Contemporary): 127051 Moscow, Tsvetnoi bulv. 32/2; tel. (495) 621-48-71; fax (495) 200-24-12; e-mail n-sovrem@yandex.ru; internet www.nash-sovremennik.ru; f. 1956; monthly; publ. by the Union of Writers of Russia; contemporary prose and 'patriotic polemics'; Editor STANISLAV KUNAYEV; circ. 9,000 (2010).

Snob (Snob): 105064 Moscow, Nizhnii Susalnyi per. 5/19; tel. and fax (495) 785-65-85; e-mail snob@snob.ru; internet www.snob.ru; f. 2009; 10 a year; history, literature, culture, intended for élite international audience; Chief Editor VLADIMIR YAKOVLEV.

Znamya (Banner): 103001 Moscow, ul. B. Sadovaya 2/46; tel. (495) 299-52-38; e-mail info@znamlit.ru; internet magazines.russ.ru/znamia; f. 1931; monthly; independent; novels, poetry, essays; Editor-in-Chief SERGEI I. CHUPRININ; circ. 5,300 (2004).

Economics and Finance

Chelovek i Trud (Man and Labour): 105064 Moscow, Yakovoapostolskii per. 6/3; tel. and fax (495) 917-76-36; e-mail chelt@yandex.ru; internet www.chelt.ru; monthly; f. 1956 as *Sotsialisticheskii trud* (Socialist Labour); present name adopted 1992; employment issues, unemployment, social policy, pensions, personnel management; Editor-in-Chief M. A. BARINOVA; circ. 10,000 (2005).

Dengi (Money): 125080 Moscow, ul. Vrubelya 4/1; tel. (499) 943-97-71; fax (499) 943-97-28; e-mail dengi@kommersant.ru; internet www.kommersant.ru/money; weekly; publ. by the Kommersant Publishing House; Chief Editor SERGEI YAKOVLEV.

Ekonomika i Zhizn (Economics and Life): 125319 Moscow, ul. Chernyakhovskogo 16; tel. and fax (499) 152-68-65; e-mail eg@ekonomika.ru; internet www.eg-online.ru; f. 1918; weekly; fmrly *Ekonomicheskaya gazeta*; news and information about the economy and business; Editor TATYANA A. IVANOVA; circ. 150,000 (2005).

Ekspert (Expert): 125866 Moscow, ul. Pravdy 24, Novyi Gazetnyi kor., POB 33; tel. (495) 789-44-65; fax (495) 228-00-78; e-mail ask@expert.ru; internet www.expert.ru; f. 1995; weekly; business and economics; financial and share markets; policy and culture; regional edns: *Ekspert Severo-Zapad* (St Petersburg and North-Western Russia), *Ekspert Sibir* (Siberia), *Ekspert Ural* (Urals), *Ekspert Volga* (The Volga region), *Ekspert Yug* (Southern Russia), and edns for Kazakhstan and Ukraine; Editor-in-Chief VALERII FADEYEV.

Finansovaya Gazeta (Financial Newspaper): 101000 Moscow, ul. Tkatskaya 5D/3/202, POB 589; tel. and fax (499) 166-03-95; e-mail fingazeta@fingazeta.ru; internet www.fingazeta.ru; f. 1991; accounting, auditing, taxation and finance; official publ. of the Ministry of Finance (q.v.).

Finansy (Finance): 125009 Moscow, ul. Tverskaya 22B; tel. (495) 699-44-27; fax (495) 699-96-16; e-mail finance-journal@mail.ru; internet www.finance-journal.ru; f. 1926; monthly; theory and information on finance; compilation and execution of the state budget, insurance, lending, taxation, etc.; Editor YU. M. ARTEMOV; circ. 10,000 (2004).

Glavukh (Chief Accountant): 127015 Moscow, ul. Novodmitrovskaya 5A/8, POB 100; tel. (495) 788-53-16; fax (495) 788-53-17; e-mail glavred@glavbukh.ru; internet www.glavbukh.ru; f. 1994; taxation and accounting; Editor-in-Chief DMITRII A. VOLOSHIN; circ. 162,000.

Kompaniya (The Firm): 109544 Moscow, ul. B. Andronyevskaya 17; tel. (495) 745-84-10; e-mail ko@idr.ru; internet www.ko.ru; f. 1997; weekly; politics, economics, finance; Editor-in-Chief ALEKSANDR ZOTIKOV; circ. 63,400 (2010).

Rossiiskii Ekonomicheskii Zhurnal (Russian Economic Journal): 109542 Moscow, Ryazanskii pr. 99; tel. and fax (495) 377-25-56;

internet www.e-rej.ru; f. 1958; monthly; economics; Editor A. YU. MELENTEV; circ. 6,100 (2004).

Voprosy Ekonomiki (Questions of Economics): 117218 Moscow, Nakhimovskii pr. 32; tel. and fax (499) 124-52-28; e-mail mail@ vopreco.ru; internet www.vopreco.ru; f. 1929; monthly; journal of the Institute of Economics of the Russian Academy of Sciences; theoretical problems of economic devt, market relations, social aspects of transition to a market economy, international economics, etc.; Editor LEONID I. ABALKIN; circ. 5,300 (2009).

International Affairs

Ekho Planety (Echo of the Planet): 103860 Moscow, Tverskoi bulv. 12; tel. (499) 791-04-04; fax (499) 791-04-09; e-mail ekho@ekhoplanet .ru; internet www.ekhoplanet.ru; f. 1988; weekly; publ. by ITAR—TASS; international affairs, economic, social and cultural; Editor-in-Chief VALENTIN VASILETS.

Mezhdunarodnaya Zhizn (International Life): 105064 Moscow, Gorokhovskii per. 14; tel. (499) 265-37-81; fax (499) 265-37-71; e-mail journal@interaffairs.ru; internet www.interaffairs.ru; f. 1954; monthly; Russian and English; publ. by the Pressa Publishing House; foreign policy and diplomacy; Editor-in-Chief O. G. OGANE-YAN; circ. 70,000.

Novoye Vremya—The New Times: 125009 Moscow, Tverskoi bulv. 14/1; tel. (495) 648-07-60; fax (495) 648-07-61; e-mail info@ newtimes.ru; internet www.newtimes.ru; f. 1943; weekly; foreign and Russian affairs; Editor-in-Chief IRENA LESNEVSKAYA.

Russkii Reporter (Russian Reporter): 125866 Moscow, Bumazhnyi proyezd 14/1; tel. (495) 609-66-74; e-mail reporter@expert.ru; internet www.rusrep.ru; f. 2007; monthly; domestic and international affairs and culture; Chief Editor VITALII LEIBIN.

Leisure, Sport and General

Afisha (Poster): 103009 Moscow, B. Gnezdnikovskii per. 7/28/1; tel. (495) 785-17-00; fax (495) 785-12-00; e-mail info@afisha.ru; internet www.afisha.ru; f. 1999; every 2 weeks; listings and reviews of events; 3 edns, for Moscow, St Petersburg, and the rest of Russia; Chief Editor ILYA KRASILSHIK.

Bolshoi Gorod (Big City): 125009 Moscow, Bersenevskaya nab. 2/1; tel. (495) 744-01-77; fax (495) 785-17-01; e-mail info@bg.ru; internet www.bg.ru; f. 2001; every 2 weeks; Moscow and St Petersburg edns; culture, travel, technology; Chief Editor FILIPP DZYADKO.

Moya Lyubimaya Dacha (My Favourite Cottage): 105082 Moscow, ul. Bakuninskaya 71/10, POB 5; tel. (495) 775-14-35; fax (495) 775-14-36; internet www.ldacha.ru; publ. by Edipress-Konliga; monthly; gardening, landscape designing; Chief Editor YELENA FESTA.

Ogonek (Beacon): c/o Kommersant, 125080 Moscow, ul. Vrubelya 4 D; tel. (495) 960-31-18; fax (499) 973-14-30; e-mail ogoniok@ kommersant.ru; internet www.kommersant.ru/ogoniok; f. 1899; weekly; politics, popular science, economics, literature; Editor VIKTOR LOSHAK; circ. 69,000 (2007).

Rossiiskaya Okhotnichya Gazeta (Russian Hunters' Magazine): 123995 Moscow, ul. 1905 Goda 7; tel. (495) 250-72-72; e-mail rog@mk .ru; internet www.ohotniki.ru; weekly; hunting, shooting, fishing; Editor-in-Chief PAVEL GUSEV.

Russkii Vestnik (Russian Herald): 115035 Moscow, Chernigovskii per. 19/13; tel. (495) 953-70-10; fax (495) 953-68-36; e-mail rusvest@ rv.ru; internet www.rv.ru; f. 1991; socio-political; every 2 weeks; Editor-in-Chief ALEKSEI SENIN.

Sovetskii Sport (Soviet Sport): 125993 Moscow, Staryi Petrovsko-Razumovskii proyezd 1/23/1; tel. (495) 637-64-33; fax (495) 637-64-24; e-mail info@sovietsport.ru; internet www.sovsport.ru; f. 1924; weekly; Editor-in-Chief IGOR KOTS.

Speed-Info: 125284 Moscow, POB 42; tel. (495) 255-02-99; fax (495) 252-09-20; e-mail s-info@si.ru; internet www.s-info.ru; f. 1991; two a month; popular; Editor-in-Chief OLGA BELAN; Gen. Dir IGOR SAZONOV; circ. 850,000 (2008).

Sport Ekspress (Sport Express): 123056 Moscow, ul. Krasina 27/2; tel. (495) 254-47-87; fax (495) 733-93-08; e-mail sport@sport-express .ru; internet www.sport-express.ru; f. 1991; daily; sport; Editor-in-Chief VLADIMIR TITORENKO; circ. in Moscow and St Petersburg 190,000 (2004).

Vokrug Sveta (Around the World): 125362 Moscow, ul. Mescheryakova 5/1; tel. (495) 490-56-55; fax (495) 491-18-28; e-mail vokrugsveta@vokrugsveta.ru; internet www.vokrugsveta.ru; f. 1861; monthly; geographical, travel and adventure; illustrated; Chief Editor YELENA KNYAZEVA (acting).

Politics, History and Military Affairs

Nezavisimoye Voyennoye Obozreniye (Independent Military Review): 101000 Moscow, ul. Myasnitskaya 13/10; tel. (495) 645-54-28; e-mail info@ng.ru; internet nvo.ng.ru; f. 1990; Editor KONSTANTIN REMCHUKOV; circ. 20,140 (2004).

Rodina (Motherland): 127025 Moscow, ul. Novyi Arbat 19; tel. (495) 203-75-98; fax (495) 203-47-45; e-mail istrodina@mail.ru; internet www.istrodina.com; f. 1989 as revival of 1879–1917 publication; monthly; publ. by Administration of the President of the Russian Federation and Government of the Russian Federation; popular historical; supplement *Istochnik* (Source), every 2 months, documents state archives; Chief Editor YURII BORISENOK; circ. 20,000 (2003).

Rodnaya Gazeta (Native Gazette): 119121 Moscow, Smolenskii bulv. 11/2; tel. and fax (499) 248-42-36; e-mail mail@rodgaz.ru; internet www.rodgaz.ru; f. 2003; weekly; politics, culture, nationalist, left-wing; Dir-Gen. and Chief Editor KONSTANTIN PATRIN.

Rossiiskaya Federatsiya Segodnya (The Russian Federation Today): 127994 Moscow, ul. M. Dmitrovka 3/10; tel. (495) 933-54-79; fax (495) 933-54-74; e-mail rfs@russia-today.ru; internet www .russia-today.ru; f. 1994; journal of the Gosudarstvennaya Duma; Editor YURII A. KHRENOV.

Rossiya v Globalnoi Politike/ Russia in Global Affairs: 125009 Moscow, Zubovskii bulv. 4; tel. (495) 980-73-53; fax (495) 937-76-11; e-mail info@globalaffairs.ru; internet www.globalaffairs.ru; f. 2002; co-founded by the Russian Union of Industrialists and Entrepreneurs, the Council for Foreign and Defence Politics, and the newspaper *Izvestiya*, in collaboration with the US journal *Foreign Affairs*; 6 a year (Russian); 4 a year (English); online edns in Czech and Polish; Chair. of Editorial Bd SERGEI A. KARAGANOV; Editor-in-Chief FEDOR A. LUKYANOV.

Russia Profile: 119021 Moscow, Zubovskii bulv. 4; tel. (495) 981-64-86; fax (495) 201-30-71; e-mail info@russiaprofile.org; internet www .russiaprofile.org; f. 1966; monthly; in English; publ. by Independent Media for RIA-Novosti in association with the International Relations and Security Network (Zurich, Switzerland) and the Center for Defense Information (Washington, DC, USA); Editor ANDREI ZOLOTOV, Jr.

Shchit i Mech (Shield and Sword): 127434 Moscow, Ivanovskii pr. 18; tel. (495) 976-66-44; fax (495) 619-80-90; e-mail gazeta@simech .ru; internet www.simech.ru; f. 1989; weekly; military, security, geopolitical concerns; publ. by the Ministry of Internal Affairs; Editor-in-Chief VALERII KULIK; circ. 50,000 (2004).

Vlast (Power): 125080 Moscow, ul. Vrubelya 4/1; tel. (499) 195-96-36; fax (499) 943-97-28; e-mail vlast@kommersant.ru; internet www .kommersant.ru/k-vlast; f. 1997; weekly; Chief Editor (vacant).

Yezhenedelnyi Zhurnal (Weekly Magazine): 129110 Moscow, Pereyaslavskii per. 4; tel. (495) 785-82-50; fax (495) 785-82-51; e-mail info@ej.ru; internet www.ej.ru; f. 2001; Editor-in-Chief ALEKSANDR RYKLIN.

Zavtra (Tomorrow): 119146 Moscow, Frunzenskaya nab. 18/60; tel. (495) 726-54-83; e-mail zavtra@zavtra.ru; internet www.zavtra.ru; extreme left, nationalist; Editor-in-Chief ALEKSANDR A. PROGANOV; circ. 100,000.

Popular Scientific

Meditsinskaya Gazeta (Medical Gazette): 129090 Moscow, B. Sukharevskaya pl. 1/2; tel. (495) 608-86-95; fax (495) 208-69-80; e-mail mggazeta@post.ru; internet www.mgzt.ru; f. 1938; 2 a week; professional international periodical; Editor ANDREI POLTORAK.

Nauka i Zhizn (Science and Life): 101990 Moscow, ul. Myasnitskaya 24; tel. (495) 624-18-35; fax (495) 625-05-90; e-mail mail@nkj .ru; internet www.nkj.ru; f. 1890, resumed 1934; monthly; recent developments in all branches of science and technology; Editor-in-Chief YELENA LOZOVSKAYA; circ. 44,000 (2009).

PC Week: 109047 Moscow, ul. Marksistskaya 34/10; tel. (495) 974-22-60; fax (495) 974-22-63; e-mail editorial@pcweek.ru; internet www.pcweek.ru; f. 1995; 48 a year; Editor-in-Chief ALEKSEI MAKSIMOV.

Tekhnika-Molodezhi (Engineering is for Youth): 127055 Moscow, ul. Lesnaya 39/307; tel. (499) 972-63-11; fax (495) 628-34-79; e-mail real@tm-magazin.ru; internet www.tm-magazin.ru; f. 1933; monthly; engineering and science; Editor A. N. PEREVOZCHIKOV.

Vestnik Svyazi (Herald of Communications): 101000 Moscow, Krivokolennyi per. 14/1; tel. (495) 625-42-57; fax (495) 621-27-97; e-mail vs@vestnik-sviazy.ru; internet www.vestnik-sviazy.ru; f. 1917; monthly; telecommunications; Editor E. B. KONSTANTINOV.

Zdorovye (Health): 127994 Moscow, Bumazhnyi proyezd 14/1; tel. and fax (499) 257-32-51; e-mail zdorovie@zdr.ru; internet www.zdr .ru; f. 1955; monthly; Editor TATYANA YEFIMOVA; circ. 170,000 (2006).

Religion

Foma (Thomas): 123242 Moscow, ul. Druzhinnikovskaya 15, POB 46; tel. (495) 775-73-61; e-mail info@foma.ru; internet www.foma.ru; f. 1998; Orthodox and the relation of Orthodoxy to social and cultural life; monthly; Chief Editor VLADIMIR R. LEGOIDA; circ. 30,000.

Mezhdunarodnaya Yevreyskaya Gazeta (International Jewish Newspaper): 107005 Moscow, Pleteshkovskii per. 3A; tel. and fax (495) 265-08-69; e-mail info@jig.ru; internet www.jig.ru; f. 1989; weekly; Editor YELENA SATAROVA; circ. 15,000 (2002).

NG-Religii (The Independent-Religions): 101000 Moscow, ul. Myasnitskaya 13; tel. (495) 923-42-40; fax (495) 921-58-47; e-mail ngr@ng .ru; internet religion.ng.ru; f. 1997; analysis of religious affairs and their domestic and global social and political implications; 2 a month; Editor-in-Chief MAKSIM SHEVCHENKO.

Tserkovnyi Vestnik (Church Herald): 119435 Moscow, ul. Pogodinskaya 20/2; tel. and fax (495) 246-01-65; e-mail info03@rop.ru; internet www.e-vestnik.ru; f. 1989; 24 a year; organ of the Russian Orthodox Church (Moscow Patriarchate); Editor-in-Chief Protohierarch VLADIMIR SILOVYEV; circ. 20,000 (2007).

Yevreiskoye Slovo (The Jewish Word): 127018 Moscow, 2-i Vysheslavtsev per. 5A; tel. (495) 710-99-48; e-mail redaktor@e-slovo.ru; internet www.e-slovo.ru; f. 2000; Editor-in-Chief VLADIMIR DYNKIN.

Zhurnal Moskovskoi Patriarkhii (Journal of the Moscow Patriarchate): 119435 Moscow, ul. Pogodinskaya 20/2; tel. (499) 246-98-48; fax (499) (499) 246-01-65; e-mail info03@rop.ru; internet www .rop.ru; f. 1934; monthly; official publication of the Russian Orthodox Church (Moscow Patriarchate); Editor Archpriest VLADIMIR SILOVYEV.

Women's Interest

Cosmopolitan Beauty: 127018 Moscow, ul. Polkovaya 3/1; tel. (495) 232-32-00; fax (495) 232-17-61; internet www.cosmobeauty.ru; f. 2003; quarterly; health and beauty; Editor-in-Chief NATALIYA SHERSTYUK; circ. 195,000.

Domashnii Ochag (The Domestic Hearth): 127018 Moscow, ul. Polkovaya 3D/1; tel. (495) 232-32-00; e-mail goodhouse@imedia.ru; internet www.goodhouse.ru; fashion; Editor-in-Chief MARIYA VINOGRADOVA.

Domovoi (House-Sprite): 109544 Moscow, ul. B. Andronyevskaya 17; tel. (495) 745-84-43; fax (495) 678-52-05; e-mail domovoy@idr.ru; internet www.domovoy.ru; f. 1993; monthly; Chief Editor ANASTASIYA RAKHLINA; circ. 105,000.

Elle: 115162 Moscow, ul. Shabolovka 31B; tel. (495) 891-39-10; fax (495) 981-39-11; e-mail editor@elle.ru; internet www.elle.ru; f. 1996; monthly; fashion; Editor-in-Chief YELENA SOTNIKOVA.

Krestyanka (Peasant Woman): 127994 Moscow, ul. B. Andronyevskaya 17; tel. (495) 257-39-39; fax (495) 257-39-63; e-mail mail@ krestyanka.ru; f. 1922; monthly; popular; Chief Editor TAMARA VIRKUNEN; circ. 85,000 (2004).

NEWS AGENCIES

ANP—Agentstvo novostei i prognozy (News and Forecasting Agency): 103009 Moscow, Kalashnyi per. 10/2; tel. (495) 782-33-71; fax (495) 153-57-45; e-mail aninons@online.ru; f. 2001 on basis of ANI News and Information Agency (f. 1991); Editor-in-Chief ALEKSEI SHCHAVELEV.

Interfax: 127006 Moscow, ul. 1-aya Tverskaya-Yamskaya 2; tel. (495) 250-98-40; fax (495) 250-97-27; e-mail info@interfax.ru; internet www.interfax.ru; f. 1989; independent information agency; Chief Exec. MIKHAIL KOMISSAR.

ITAR—TASS (Information Telegraphic Agency of Russia— Telegraphic Agency of the Sovereign Countries): 125993 Moscow, Tverskoi bulv. 10/12; tel. (495) 202-29-81; fax (495) 202-54-74; e-mail worldmarket@itar-tass.com; internet www.itar-tass.com; f. 1904 as St Petersburg Telegraph Agency, renamed as TASS (Telegraph Agency of the Soviet Union) in 1925; present name adopted 1992; state information agency; 74 bureaux in Russia and the states of the former USSR, 65 foreign bureaux outside the former USSR; Dir-Gen. VITALII N. IGNATENKO.

Prima Human Rights News Agency: 111399 Moscow, POB 5; tel. and fax (495) 455-30-11; e-mail prima@prima-news.ru; internet www.prima-news.ru; f. 2000; Editor-in-Chief ALEKSANDR PODRABINEK.

RIA—Novosti (Russian Information Agency—News): 119021 Moscow, Zubovskii bulv. 4; tel. (495) 637-24-24; fax (495) 201-45-45; e-mail marketing@rian.ru; internet www.rian.ru; f. 1961 as Agenstvo Pechati 'Novosti' (APN); present name adopted 1991; network covers over 45 countries; provider of Russian news features and photographs; Dir-Gen. NIKOLAI BIRYUKOV; Editor-in-Chief SVETLANA MIRONYUK.

RosBalt Information Agency: 190000 St Petersburg, Konnogvardeiskii bulv. 7; tel. (812) 320-50-30; fax (812) 320-50-31; e-mail rosbalt@rosbalt.ru; internet www.rosbalt.ru; news coverage of European Russia and other countries in northern Europe; Chair. NATALIYA CHERKESOVA.

Rossiiskoye Informatsionnoye Agentstvo 'Oreanda' (RIA 'Oreanda'): 117342 Moscow, Sadovnicheskii per. 82/2; tel. (495)

995-82-21; fax (495) 23-04-39; e-mail info@oreanda.ru; internet www.oreanda.ru; f. 1994.

PRESS ASSOCIATIONS

Russian Guild of Publishers of Periodical Press: 125047 Moscow, ul. Lesnaya 20/6-211; tel. and fax (495) 978-41-89.

Union of Journalists of Russia: 119021 Moscow, Zubovskii bulv. 4; tel. (495) 201-51-01; fax (495) 201-35-47; f. 1991; Sec.-Gen. IGOR YAKOVENKO.

Publishers

Ad Marginem-Ad Patres: 105082 Moscow, Perevedenovskii per. 18; tel. and fax (495) 988-15-32; e-mail admarginem@admarginem.ru; internet admarginem.ru; f. 1993; fiction, philosophy, artistic and literary criticism; Dir ALEKSANDR IVANOV.

AST: 129085 Moscow, Zvezdnyi bulv. 21; tel. (495) 215-01-01; fax (495) 215-51-10; e-mail astpub@aha.ru; internet www.ast.ru; original and translated fiction and non-fiction, children's and schoolbooks.

Azbuka (Alphabet): 191014 St Petersburg, ul. Chekhova 9, POB 192; tel. (812) 327-04-55; fax (812) 327-01-60; e-mail assistant@azbooka .spb.ru; internet www.azbooka.ru; f. 1995; literary fiction, including translations; Dir-Gen. GENNADII MOLCHANOV.

Bolshaya Rossiiskaya Entsiklopediya (The Great Russian Encyclopedia): 109028 Moscow, Pokrovskii bulv. 8; tel. (495) 917-90-00; fax (495) 916-01-22; e-mail secretar@greatbook.ru; internet www .greatbook.ru; f. 1925; encyclopedias and reference; Dir-Gen. NIKOLAI S. ARTEMOV.

Detektiv-Press: 119049 Moscow, Leninskii per. 1; tel. (495) 237-53-59; e-mail office@detektiv-press.ru; internet www.detektiv-press.ru; f. 1997; history, memoirs and historical fiction; Dir VALERII A. STRELETSKII.

Drofa: 127018 Moscow, ul. Sushchevskii Val 49; tel. (495) 795-05-50; fax (495) 795-05-44; e-mail info@drofa.ru; internet www.drofa.ru; f. 1991; school textbooks, children's fiction; Dir-Gen. ALEKSANDR F. KISELEV.

Ekonomika (Economy): 123955 Moscow, Berezhkovskaya nab. 6; tel. (499) 240-58-18; fax (499) 240-48-178; e-mail info@economizdat .ru; internet www.economizdat.ru; f. 1963; various aspects of economics, management and marketing; Dir YELIZABETA V. POLIYEVKTOVA.

Eksmo: 127299 Moscow, ul. K. Tsetkina 18/5; tel. and fax (495) 411-68-86; e-mail info@eksmo.ru; internet www.eksmo.ru; f. 1991; fiction; Gen. Dir OLEG YE. NOVIKOV.

Finansy i Statistika (Finance and Statistics): 101000 Moscow, ul. Pokrovka 7; tel. (495) 625-47-08; fax (495) 625-09-57; e-mail mail@ finstat.ru; internet www.finstat.ru; f. 1924; education, economics, tourism, finance, statistics, banking, insurance, accounting, computer science; Dir Dr ALEVTINA N. ZVONOVA.

Forum: 101000 Moscow, Kolpachnyi per. 9A; tel. and fax (495) 625-52-43; e-mail mail@forum-books.ru; internet www.forum-books.ru; f. 2001; general and professional educational textbooks; Gen. Man. SVETLANA P. SILVANOVICH.

Galart: 125319 Moscow, ul. Chernyakhovskogo 4; tel. and fax (495) 151-25-02; e-mail galart@m9com.ru; internet www.galart-moscow .ru; f. 1969; fmrly Sovetskii Khudozhnik (Soviet Artist); art reproduction, art history and criticism; Gen. Dir A. D. SARABYANOV.

INFRA-M: 127282 Moscow, ul. Polyarnara 31B; tel. and fax (495) 363-42-60; e-mail books@infra-m.ru; internet www.infra-m.ru; f. 1992; economics, law, computing, history, reference works, encyclopedias; Man. Dir VADIM D. SINYANSKII.

Khimiya (Chemistry): 107976 Moscow, ul. Strominka 21/2; tel. (495) 268-29-76; f. 1963; chemistry and the chemical industry; Dir BORIS S. KRASNOPEVTSEV.

Khudozhestvennaya Literatura (Fiction): 107078 Moscow, ul. Novobasmannaya 19; tel. (499) 261-88-65; fax (499) 261-83-00; fiction and works of literary criticism, history of literature, etc.; Dir A. N. PETROV; Editor-in-Chief V. S. MODESTOV.

Kompozitor (Composer): 119034 Moscow, M. Levshinskii per. 7/2; tel. (495) 955-19-66; fax (495) 209-54-98; e-mail komp@kompubl.com; internet www.idk.su; f. 1957; music and music criticism; Dir GRIGORII A. VORONOV.

Meditsina (Medicine): 101838 Moscow, Petroverigskii per. 6/8; tel. (495) 924-87-85; fax (495) 928-60-03; e-mail meditsina@iname.com; internet www.medlit.ru; f. 1918; state-owned; imprint of Association for Medical Literature; books and journals on medicine and health; Dir A. M. STOCHIK.

Mezhdunarodnye Otnosheniya (International Relations): 107078 Moscow, ul. Sadovaya-Spasskaya 18/709; tel. (495) 207-67-

93; fax (495) 200-22-04; e-mail info@inter-rel.ru; internet www .inter-rel.ru; f. 1957; international relations, economics and politics of foreign countries, foreign trade, international law, foreign-language textbooks and dictionaries, translations and publications for the UN and other international organizations; Dir B. P. LIKHACHEV.

Muzyka (Music): 127051 Moscow, ul. Petrovka 26; tel. (495) 921-51-70; fax (495) 928-33-04; e-mail muz-sekretar@yandex.ru; f. 1861; sheet music, music scores and related literature; Dir MARK ZILBERQUIT.

M. V. Lomonosov Moscow State University Press: 125009 Moscow, ul. B. Nikitskaya 5/7; tel. (495) 939-33-23; fax (495) 697-66-71; e-mail secretary@msupublishing.ru; internet www .msupublishing.ru; f. 1756; scientific, educational and reference books and journals; Dir ALLA N. MATVEYEVA.

Mysl (Thought): 117071 Moscow, Leninskii pr. 15; tel. (495) 955-04-58; f. 1963; science, popular science, philosophy, history, political science, geography; Dir YEVGENYI A. TIMOFEYEV.

Nauka (Science): 117997 Moscow, ul. Profsoyuznaya 90; tel. (495) 334-71-51; fax (495) 420-22-20; e-mail secret@naukaran.ru; internet www.naukaran.ru; f. 1923; publishing house of the Academy of Sciences; general and social science, mathematics, physics, chemistry, biology, earth sciences, oriental studies, books in foreign languages, university textbooks, scientific journals, translation, export, distribution, typesetting and printing services; Dir-Gen. V. VASILIYEV.

Nauka i Tekhnologiya (Science and Technology): 107076 Moscow, Stromynskii per. 4; tel. (495) 164-47-74; fax (495) 164-47-74; e-mail admin@nait.ru; internet www.nait.ru; f. 2000; journals on chemistry, electronics and telecommunications; Gen. Dir MAKSIM A. KOVALEVSKII.

Nedra Biznestsentr (Natural Resources Business Centre): 125047 Moscow, pl. Tverskoi Zastavy 3; tel. (495) 251-31-77; fax (495) 250-27-72; e-mail business@nedrainform.ru; internet www.nedrainform.ru; f. 1964; geology, natural resources, mining and coal industry, petroleum and gas industry; Dir V. D. MENSHIKOV.

Nezavisimaya Gazeta ('Independent Newspaper' Publishing House): 101000 Moscow, ul. Myasnitskaya 13/10; tel. and fax (495) 981-61-53; e-mail ngbooks@ng.ru; internet www.ng.ru/izdatelstvo; f. 1991; books on history, literary essays, poetry, history of literature and of art, biography, dictionaries, encyclopaedias; Dir VIKTOR A. OBUKHOV.

Pedagogika Press (Pedagogy Press): 119034 Moscow, Smolenskii bulv. 4; tel. and fax (495) 246-59-69; f. 1969; scientific and popular books on pedagogics, didactics, psychology, developmental physiology; young people's encyclopaedias, dictionaries; Dir I. KOLESNIKOVA.

Pressa (The Press): 127137 Moscow, ul. Pravdy 24; tel. (499) 257-46-22; fax (499) 257-09-38; e-mail adm@media-pressa.ru; internet www .media-pressa.ru; f. 1934 as Pravda (Truth) Publishing House; booklets, newspapers and periodicals; Dir I. V. POLTAVTSEV.

Profizdat (Professional Publishers): 101000 Moscow, ul. Myasnitskaya 13/18; tel. (495) 924-57-40; fax (495) 975-23-29; e-mail profizdat@profizdat.ru; f. 1930; books and magazines; Gen. Dir VLADIMIR SOLOVYEV.

Prosveshcheniye (Enlightenment): 127521 Moscow, 3-i proyezd Maryinoi roshchi 41; tel. (495) 789-30-40; fax (495) 789-30-41; e-mail prosv@prosv.ru; internet www.prosv.ru; f. 1930; school textbooks, dictionaries, atlases, reference and scientific books, educational materials; Dir ALEKSANDR M. KONDAKOV.

Raduga (Rainbow): 129090 Moscow, Grokholskii per. 32/2; tel. and fax (495) 680-12-39; e-mail radugarel@sumail.ru; internet www .raduga-publ.ru; f. 1982; translations of Russian fiction into foreign languages and of foreign authors into Russian; Gen. Dir KSENIYA ATAROVA.

Respublika (Republic): 125811 Moscow, Miusskaya pl. 7; tel. and fax (495) 656-09-70; e-mail respublik@dataforce.net; internet www .republik.ru; f. 1918; fmrly Politizdat (Political Publishing House); dictionaries, books on politics, human rights, philosophy, history, economics, religion, fiction, arts, reference; Dir VLADIMIR V. AKIMOV.

Rosmen (Rosman): 127018 Moscow, ul. Oktyabskaya 4/2; tel. (495) 933-70-70; fax (495) 933-71-36; e-mail rosman@rosman.ru; internet www.rosman.ru; children's literature, general, popular science; Dir-Gen. OLEG V. ZHIVYKH.

Rosspen Publishing House—Russian Political Encylopedia: 117393 Moscow, ul. Profsoyuznaya 82; tel. and fax (495) 334-81-62; e-mail rosspen@rosspen.su; internet www.rosspen.su; f. 1992; politics, history, other academic and reference publishing; Dir-Gen. A. K. SOROKIN.

Shkola-Press (School-Press): 127254 Moscow, ul. Sh. Rustaveli 10/3; tel. and fax (495) 219-83-80; e-mail marketing@schoolpress.ru; internet www.schoolpress.ru; books on psychology, pedagogy, magazines.

Slovo (Word): 109147 Moscow, ul. Vorontsovskaya 41; tel. and fax (495) 911-61-33; internet www.slovo-online.ru; f. 1989; illustrated books on art, world literature in translation; Dir-Gen. NATALIYA AVETISYAN.

Stroyizdat (Construction Publishing House): 101442 Moscow, ul. Kalyayevskaya 23a; tel. (495) 251-69-67; f. 1932; building, architecture, environmental protection, fire protection and building materials; Dir V. A. KASATKIN.

Tekst (Text): 127299 Moscow, ul. Kosmonavta Volkova 7; tel. and fax (495) 150-0472; e-mail textpubl@yandex.ru; internet www.textpubl .ru; f. 1988; foreign poetry and prose fiction in translation, Russian poetry and prose, children's literature, social sciences, history, law; Dir OLGET M. LIBKIN.

Vagrius: 125993 Moscow, ul. Nikoloyamskaya 1; tel. (495) 221-61-80; fax (495) 510-56-10; e-mail vagrius@vagrius.com; internet www .vagrius.ru; f. 1992; fiction, politics, history; Pres. and Dir-Gen. GLEB USPENSKII.

Ves Mir (The Whole World): 125009 Moscow, ul. Mokhovaya 11/3 v; tel. and fax (495) 276-02-92; e-mail info@vesmirbooks.ru; internet www.vesmirbooks.ru; f. 1994; university textbooks, scholarly works in social sciences and humanities; Dir Dr OLEG A. ZIMARIN.

Vysshaya Shkola (Higher School): 127994 Moscow, ul. Neglinnaya 29/14; tel. (495) 200-04-56; fax (495) 200-34-86; e-mail info_vshkola@ mail.ru; internet www.vshkola.ru; f. 1939; textbooks for higher-education institutions; Dir MIKHAIL L. ZORIN.

Yuridicheskaya Literatura (Legal Literature): 121069 Moscow, ul. M. Nikitskaya 14; tel. (495) 203-83-84; fax (495) 291-98-83; internet www.jurizdat.ru; f. 1917; legal; official publishers of enactments of the Russian President and Govt; Dir IVAN A. BUNIN.

Znaniye (Knowledge): 101835 Moscow, proyezd Serova 4; tel. (495) 928-15-31; f. 1951; popular books and brochures on politics and science; Dir V. K. BELYAKOV.

Broadcasting and Communications

TELECOMMUNICATIONS

In 2011 there were 44.2m. fixed telephone lines and 256.1m. subscriptions to mobile telephone services in the country.

Golden Telecom: 115114 Moscow, Kozhevnicheskii proyezd 1; tel. (495) 799-98-98; fax (495) 797-93-32; e-mail info@mosreg.golden.ru; internet www.goldentelecom.ru; f. 1996; operates mobile cellular telecommunications network and provides internet services in cities across the Russian Federation, and in Almatı (Kazakhstan) and Kyiv (Ukraine); Chief Exec. JEAN-PIERRE VANDROMME.

Megafon: 115035 Moscow, Kadashevskaya nab. 30; tel. (495) 980-19-70; fax (495) 980-19-49; e-mail info@megafon.ru; internet www .megafon.ru; f. 2002; operates mobile cellular communications networks across Russia; 6 regional cos; 57m. subscribers (2011); Gen. Dir SERGEI SOLDATENKOV.

Mobilnye TeleSistemi/Mobile TeleSystems (MTS): 109147 Moscow, ul. Marksistskaya 4; tel. (495) 766-01-77; e-mail info@mts.ru; internet www.mts.ru; f. 1993; provides mobile cellular telecommunications in 82 regions of Russia; majority-owned by Sistema Telecom; 35.1% owned by Deutsche Telekom (Germany); over 85m. subscribers, incl. subsidiary cos in Armenia, Belarus, Ukraine and Uzbekistan (2008); Pres. ANDREI DUBOVSKOV.

Moscow City Telephone Network (MGTS—Moskovskaya Gorodskaya Telefonnaya Set): 119991 Moscow, ul. B. Ordynka 25/1; tel. (495) 636-06-36; fax (495) 950-06-18; e-mail mgts@mgts.ru; internet www.mgts.ru; f. 1882; provides telecommunications services in Moscow City; Gen. Dir SERGEI V. IVANOV.

Petersburg Telephone Network (PTS—Peterburgskaya Telefonnaya Set): 119186 St Petersburg, ul. B. Morskaya 24; tel. (812) 314-15-50; fax (812) 110-68-34; e-mail office@sp.nw.rt.ru; internet www.ptn.ru; f. 1993; Dir IGOR N. SAMYLIN.

Relkom (Relcom): ; tel. (495) 947-20-99; fax (495) 739-93-23; e-mail info@relcom.org; internet www.relcom.ru; f. 1990; provides commercial internet services.

Rostelekom (Rostelecom): 125047 Moscow, ul. 1-aya Tverskaya-Yamskaya 14; tel. (499) 999-82-83; fax (499) 999-82-22; e-mail info@ rostelecom.ru; internet www.rt.ru; 53.2% owned by Svyazinvest; dominant long-distance and international telecommunications service provider; 7 regional cos based in St Petersburg, Samara, Novosibirsk, Yekaterinburg, Khabarovsk, Moscow and Rostov-on-Don; Chair. of Bd IVAN I. RODIONOV.

Svyazinvest: 119121 Moscow, ul. Plyushchikha 55/2; tel. (495) 727-03-00; fax (495) 727-03-99; e-mail office@svyazinvest.ru; internet www.sinvest.ru; f. 1995; 75% state-owned; holds controlling stakes in 7 'mega-regional' telecommunications operators, 1 international and domestic long-distance operator, and 2 local telecommunications cos, and non-controlling stakes in 2 city telecommunications cos; Gen. Dir VADIM V. SEMENOV.

VympelKom-Bilain (Vimpelcom-Beeline): 127006 Moscow, ul. Krasnoproletarskaya 4; tel. (495) 974-88-88; fax (495) 991-79-03; e-mail info@beeline.ru; internet www.beeline.ru; provides internet services and operates mobile cellular telecommunications across the Russian Federation, and in Armenia, Georgia, Kazakhstan, Tajikistan, Ukraine and Uzbekistan; 26.6% owned by Telenor (Norway); Dir-Gen. YELENA A. SHMATOVA; 186m. subscribers (March 2011).

BROADCASTING

Pervyi Kanal (First Channel), operated by Public Russian Television (ORT), is received throughout Russia and many parts of the CIS. The All-Russian State Television and Radio Company (VGTRK) broadcasts Telekanal 'Rossiya', which reaches some 92% of the Russian population, and Telekanal 'Kultura' and Telekanal 'Sport'. In addition to the nation-wide television channels, there are local channels, and the NTV (Independent Television) channel (65% owned by the gas utility Gazprom, in which the Government holds a majority stake) is broadcast in most of Russia. In the regions, part of Rossiya's programming is devoted to local affairs, with broadcasts in minority languages. A state-supported, international, English-language television station, Russia Today (later RT), commenced broadcasts in 2006. In mid-2005 there were four nation-wide radio stations, as well as 11 urban radio networks and more than 200 regional stations. At that time Radio Rossiya had more listeners than any other state-run channel, but the commercial music station Russkoye Radio was the most popular station overall.

Association of Regional State Television and Radio Broadcasters: 113326 Moscow, ul. Pyatnitskaya 25/226; tel. and fax (495) 950-60-28; e-mail fstratyv@rzn.rosmail.com; Chair. of Bd ALEKSANDR N. LEVCHENKO.

Regulatory Authority

Russian Television and Radio Broadcasting Network: 113326 Moscow, ul. Pyatnitskaya 25; tel. (495) 233-66-03; fax (495) 233-28-93; f. 2001; Gen. Man. GENNADII I. SKLYAR.

Radio

All-Russian State Television and Radio Broadcasting Company (VGTRK): 125040 Moscow, ul. 5-aya Yamskogo Polya 19/21; tel. (495) 745-39-78; fax (495) 975-26-11; e-mail lir@rfn.ru; internet www.vgtrk.com; f. 1991; broadcasts 'Rossiya', 'Kultura', 'Sport', 'Nauka' and 'Vesti' television channels, regional television and radio cos, and national radio stations 'Radio Rossiya', 'Radio Mayak', 'Radio Nostalzhi' and 'Vesti-FM'; Chair. OLEG DOBRODEYEV.

Radio Mayak (Radio Beacon): 125040 Moscow, ul. 5-aya Yamskogo Polya 19/21; tel. (495) 955-85-61; fax (495) 959-42-04; e-mail pr@radiomayak.ru; internet www.radiomayak.ru; f. 1964; state-owned; Chair. SERGEI KUROKHTIN.

Radio Nostalzhi (Radio Nostalgia): 113162 Moscow, ul. Shabolovka 37; tel. (495) 955-84-00; e-mail nostalgie@vimain.vitpc.com; f. 1993; Gen. Man. IRINA A. GERASIMOVA.

Radio Rossiya (Radio Russia): 125040 Moscow, ul. 5-aya Yamskogo Polya 19/21; tel. (495) 950-69-89; fax (495) 730-42-77; e-mail news@radiorus.ru; internet www.radiorus.ru; f. 1990; broadcasts information, social, political, musical, literary and investigative programming; Dir-Gen. ALEKSEI V. ABAKUMOV.

Ekho Moskvy (Moscow Echo): 119992 Moscow, ul. Novyi Arbat 11; tel. (495) 202-92-29; e-mail echo@echo.msk.ru; internet www.echo.msk.ru; f. 1990; stations in Moscow, St Petersburg, Rostov-on-Don and Vologda; also broadcasts from Moscow to Chelyabinsk, Krasnoyarsk, Novosibirsk, Omsk, Perm, Saratov and Yekaterinburg; 66% owned by Gazprom-Mediya, 34% staff-owned; Gen. Man. YURII FEDUTINOV.

Golos Rossii (The Voice of Russia): 115326 Moscow, ul. Pyatnitskaya 25; tel. (495) 950-63-31; fax (495) 951-20-17; e-mail letters@ruvr.ru; internet www.vor.ru; f. 1929; fmrly Radio Moscow International; international broadcasts in 38 languages; Man. Dir ARMEN G. OGANESIAN.

Russkoye Radio (Russian Radio): 105064 Moscow, ul. Kazakova 16; tel. (495) 232-16-36; fax (495) 956-13-60; e-mail region@rr.ru; internet www.rusradio.ru; f. 1995; owned by Russkaya Mediyagruppa (Russian Media Group); nation-wide commercial music station; broadcasts to more than 700 towns in Russia, Ukraine, Kazakhstan, Moldova, Kyrgyzstan, the Baltic Republics and the USA; also *Russkoye Radio 2*, principally news and talk programming, broadcast to Moscow; Dir-Gen. SERGEI KOZHEVNIKOV.

Serebryanyi Dozhd (Silver Rain): 127083 Moscow, Petrovsko-Razumovskaya alleya 12A; tel. (495) 925-10-01; e-mail silver@silver.ru; internet www.silver.ru; f. 1995; commercial station broadcasting information and entertainment programming; broad-

casts to 98 cities in Russia and the 'near abroad'; Dir-Gen. DMITRII SAVITSKII.

Yevropa Plyus (Europa Plus): 109004 Moscow, ul. Stanislavskogo 21; tel. (495) 799-97-97; fax (495) 627-11-56; e-mail main@europaplus.ru; internet www.europaplus.ru; FM station, broadcasting music, entertainment and information programmes to 500 cities; Pres. ZHORZH POLINSKI.

Television

All-Russian State Television and Radio Broadcasting Company (VGTRK): 125040 Moscow, ul. 5-aya Yamskogo Polya 19/21; tel. and fax (495) 234-86-09; e-mail lir@rfn.ru; internet www.vgtrk.com; f. 1991; broadcasts 'Rossiya', 'Kultura', 'Sport', 'Nauka' and 'Vesti' television channels, regional television and radio cos, and national radio stations 'Radio Rossiya', 'Radio Mayak', 'Radio Nostalzhi' and 'Vesti-FM'; Chair. OLEG DOBRODEYEV.

Telekanal 'Kultura' (Television Channel 'Culture'): 123995 Moscow, ul. M. Nikitskaya 24; tel. (495) 780-56-01; e-mail pr@tv-culture.ru; internet www.tvkultura.ru; f. 1997; Gen. Dir ALEKSANDR S. PONOMAREV.

Telekanal 'Rossiya' (Television Channel 'Russia'): 115162 Moscow, ul. Shabolovka 37; tel. (495) 232-63-33; fax (495) 234-87-71; e-mail info@rutv.ru; internet www.rutv.ru; fmrly RTR-TV; name changed as above in 2002; Dir-Gen. ALEKSANDR S. PONOMAREV.

Telekanal 'Sport' (Television Channel 'Sport'): 115162 Moscow, ul. Shabolovka 37; e-mail reception@sport.vgtek.com; internet sportbox.ru; f. 2003; Dir-Gen. VASILII KIKNADZE.

Dozhd (Rain): 109072 Moscow, Bersenevskaya nab. 2/1; tel. (495) 744-01-77; e-mail info@tvrain.ru; internet www.tvrain.ru; f. 2010; online only; independent; Gen. Dir NATALYA SINDEYEVA.

NTV—Independent Television: 127427 Moscow, ul. Akademika Koroleva 12; tel. (495) 725-54-03; fax (495) 725-54-01; e-mail info@ntv.ru; internet www.ntv.ru; f. 1993; 65% owned by Gazprom-Mediya; also NTV World (NTV Mir), broadcasting to Russian communities in Israel, Europe and the USA; Dir-Gen. NIKOLAI YU. SENKEVICH.

Pervyi Kanal—First Channel (Channel One): 127427 Moscow, ul. Akademika Koroleva 12; tel. (495) 617-73-87; fax (495) 215-82-47; e-mail ort_int@ortv.ru; internet www.1tv.ru; f. 1995; fmrly ORT—Public Russian Television; name changed as above in 2002; 51% state-owned; 49% owned by private shareholders; Chair. MIKHAIL PYATKOVSKII; Dir-Gen. KONSTANTIN ERNST.

Ren-TV Network: 119843 Moscow, Zubovskii bulv. 17/510; tel. (495) 246-25-06; fax (495) 245-09-98; e-mail site@rentv.dol.ru; internet www.ren-tv.com; f. 1991; network of more than 100 television stations in the Russian Federation and 60 stations in republics of the CIS; Chair. MIKHAIL KONTSEREV.

STS (CTC) Media Inc: 125284 Moscow, Monarch Business Center, Leningradskii pr. 31A; tel. (495) 785-63-47; fax (495) 785-63-43; e-mail pr@ctcmedia.ru; internet www.ctcmedia.ru; f. 1989; owned by StoryFirst Communications (USA); CEO BORIS PODOLSKII.

Telekanal 'Zvezda' (Television Channel 'Star'): 129110 Moscow, pr. Mira 126; tel. (495) 645-92-89; internet www.tvzvezda.ru; f. 2005; controlled by the Ministry of Defence; factual, analytical, and drama programming; Gen. Dir VLADIMIR B. ZHELONKIN.

TNT—Territory of Our Viewers—TV Network: 127427 Moscow, ul. Akademika Koroleva 19; tel. (495) 217-81-88; fax (495) 748-14-90; e-mail info@tnt-tv.ru; internet www.tnt-tv.ru; f. 1997; cable television network broadcasting to 582 cities in Russia; Chief Exec. ALEKSANDR DYBAL; Dir-Gen. ROMAN PETRENKO.

TV-Tsentr (TVTs—TV-Centre): 113184 Moscow, ul. B. Tatarskaya 33/1; tel. (495) 959-39-87; fax (495) 959-39-66; e-mail info@tvc.ru; internet www.tvc.ru; f. 1997; broadcasting consortium for terrestrial cable and satellite television; receives funding from Govt of Moscow City; Dir-Gen. ALEKSANDR S. PONOMAREV.

Finance

(cap. = capital; res = reserves; dep. = deposits; m. = million; brs = branches; amounts in new roubles, unless otherwise stated)

BANKING

Central Bank

Bank Rossii—Central Bank of the Russian Federation: 107016 Moscow, ul. Neglinnaya 12; tel. (495) 771-91-00; fax (495) 621-64-65; e-mail webmaster@www.cbr.ru; internet www.cbr.ru; f. 1990; cap. 3,000m., res 1,899,352m., dep. 10,250,052m. (Dec. 2008); Chair. SERGEI M. IGNATIYEV; 79 brs.

Major Banks

AK BARS Bank: 420066 Tatarstan, Kazan, ul. Dekabristov 1; tel. (843) 230-33-03; fax (843) 519-39-75; e-mail kanc@akbars.ru; internet www.akbars.ru; f. 1993; cap. 34,244.0m., res 349.6m., dep. 203,905.4m. (Dec. 2011); Chair. of Bd ROBERT MINNEGALIYEV; 22 brs.

Alfa-Bank: 107078 Moscow, ul. Kalanchevskaya 27; tel. (495) 620-91-91; fax (495) 788-03-89; e-mail mail@alfabank.ru; internet www.alfabank.ru; f. 1990; cap. US $1,265m., res –$310m., dep. $32,972m. (Dec. 2012); Chair. of Exec. Bd ANDREI SOKOLOV; Pres. PETR SHMIDA.

Bank of Moscow (Bank Moskvy): 107996 Moscow, ul. Rozhdestvenka 8/15/3; tel. (495) 925-80-00; fax (495) 795-26-00; e-mail info@mmbank.ru; internet www.bm.ru; f. 1995; present name adopted 2004; 60% owned by Govt of Moscow City; cap. 29,651.3m., res 149,945.8m., dep. 606,405.6m. (Dec. 2011); Pres. MIKHAIL KUZOVLEV.

Bank Petrocommerce (Bank Petrokommerts): 127051 Moscow, ul. Petrovka 24; tel. (495) 411-64-11; fax (495) 623-36-07; e-mail pr@pkb.ru; internet www.pkb.ru; f. 1992; cap. 8,454.3m., res 5,037.5m., dep. 158,602.4m. (Dec. 2011); Pres. and Chair. of Bd VLADIMIR N. NIKITENKO.

Bank Sankt-Peterburg/Bank Saint Petersburg: 195112 St Petersburg, Malookhtinskii pr. 64A; tel. (812) 329-50-50; fax (812) 329-50-70; e-mail cc@bspb.ru; internet www.bspb.ru; f. 1990; cap. 3,648.1m., res 23,676.6m., dep. 244,257.4m. (Dec. 2012); Chair. ALEKSANDR SAVELIYEV.

Bank Soyuz: 127055, Moscow, ul. Sushchevskaya 27/1; tel. (495) 729-55-55; fax (495) 729-55-05; e-mail info@banksoyuz.ru; internet www.banksoyuz.ru; f. 1993; cap. 5,000m., res –417m., dep. 44,726m. (Dec. 2011); Chair. SERGEI I. TISHCHENKO.

Bank Uralsib: 119048 Moscow, ul. Yefremova 8; tel. (495) 785-12-12; e-mail press@uralsib.ru; internet www.uralsib.ru; f. 1993; cap. 41,446m., res 4,037m., dep. 348,998m. (Dec. 2011); Chair. IKKA S. SALONEN.

Bank Vozrozhdeniye—V-Bank: 101999 Moscow, per. Luchnikov 7/4/1, POB 9; tel. (495) 620-19-35; fax (495) 620-90-65; e-mail vbank@co.voz.ru; internet www.vbank.ru; f. 1991; cap. 250m., res 7,433m., dep. 176,473m. (Dec. 2012); Chair. of Man. Bd ALEKSANDR V. DOLGOPOLOV; 170 brs.

Bank VTB 24: 101000 Moscow, ul. Myasnitskaya 35; tel. (495) 777-24-24; fax (495) 980-46-66; e-mail info@vtb24.ru; internet www.vtb24.ru; f. 1991; present name adopted 2006; cap. 55,687m., res 23,242m., dep. 1,028,782m. (Dec. 2011); Chair. of Bd ANDREI L. KOSTIN; 44 brs.

Bank Zenit: 129110 Moscow, Bannyi per. 9; tel. (495) 937-07-37; fax (495) 777-57-06; e-mail info@zenit.ru; internet www.zenit.ru; f. 1994; 24.6% owned by Tatneft (q.v.); cap. 12,698.1m., res 921.2m., dep. 183,658.9m. (Dec. 2012); Chair. of Bd ALEKSEI A. SOKOLOV; 4 brs.

Gazprombank: 117420 Moscow, ul. Nametkina 16/1; tel. (495) 913-74-74; fax (495) 913-73-19; e-mail mailbox@gazprombank.ru; internet www.gazprombank.ru; f. 1990; 41.7% owned by Gazprom (q.v.); cap. 36,370m., res 122,086m., dep. 1,974,115m. (Dec. 2012); Chair. of Management Bd ANDREI I. AKIMOV; 32 brs.

Home Credit & Finance Bank (Khoum Kredit end Finans Bank): 125040 Moscow, ul. Pravdy 8/1; tel. (495) 785-82-22; fax (495) 785-82-18; e-mail info@homecredit.ru; internet www.homecredit.ru; f. 1990; present name adopted 2003; cap. 4,406m., res 10,613m., dep. 178,359m. (Dec. 2012); Chair. IVAN SVITEK.

ING Bank (Eurasia): 127473 Moscow, ul. Krasnoproletarskaya 36; tel. (495) 755-54-00; fax (495) 755-54-99; e-mail mail.russia@ingbank.com; internet www.ing.ru; f. 1993; 99.9% owned by ING Bank NV (Netherlands); cap. 10,174.9m., res 6,158.3m., dep. 125,364.9m. (Dec. 2011); Dir-Gen. HENDRIK WILLEM TEN BOSCH.

Khanty-Mansiiskii Bank: 628012 Tyumen obl., Khanty-Mansii AOk—Yugra, Khanty-Mansiisk, ul. Mira 38; tel. (34673) 908-00; fax (34671) 302-19; e-mail hmbank@khmb.ru; internet www.khmb.ru; f. 1992; cap. 11,282.4m., res 5,664.8m., dep. 228,190.8m. (Dec. 2012); Pres. DMITRII MIZGULIN; 16 brs.

MDM Bank: 630004 Novosibirsk, ul. Lenina 18; tel. (383) 227-75-99; e-mail info@mdmbank.com; internet www.mdm.ru; f. 1993; merged with URSA Bank in 2009; cap. 4,207m., res 30,825m., dep. 240,526m. (Dec. 2011); Dir IGOR KIM.

MTS Bank: 119034 Moscow, Yeropkinskii per. 5; tel. (495) 921-28-00; fax (495) 232-27-54; e-mail mbrd@mbrd.ru; internet www.mbrd.ru; fmrly Moscow Bank for Reconstruction and Devt; 58.44% owned by Sistema; cap. 1,832.1m., res 14,392.4m., dep. 177,192.2m. (Dec. 2011); Chair. of Bd MIKHAIL M. CHAIKIN.

Nomos-Bank: 109240 Moscow, ul. Verkhnyaya Radishchevskaya 3/1; tel. (495) 721-80-80; fax (495) 797-32-50; e-mail info@nomos.ru; internet www.nomos.ru; f. 1992; cap. 6,504m., res 21,365m., dep. 633,980m. (Dec. 2012); Pres. DMITRII ROMAYEV.

Nordea Bank: 125040 Moscow, ul. 3-aya Yamskogo Polya 19/1; tel. (495) 777-34-77; fax (495) 921-25-03; e-mail all@nordea.ru; internet www.nordea.ru; f. 1994; fmrly Orgresbank; renamed as above in March 2009; cap. 11,233.6m., res 239,765.7m., dep 2,443.1m. (Dec. 2011); Chair. IGOR BULANTSEV.

Promsvyazbank: 109052 Moscow, ul. Smirnovskaya 10/22; tel. (495) 727-10-20; fax (495) 727-10-21; e-mail info@psbank.ru; internet www.psbank.ru; f. 1995; cap. 12,201.9m., res 23,633.9m., dep. 508,907.2m. (Dec. 2012); Chair. of Bd of Dirs ALEKSEI ANANIYEV; Pres. ARTEM KONSTANDYAN; 11 brs.

Raiffeisenbank ZAO: 129090 Moscow, ul. Troitskaya 17/1; tel. (495) 721-99-00; fax (495) 721-99-01; e-mail info@raiffeisen.ru; internet www.raiffeisen.ru; f. 1996; owned by Raiffeisenbank (Austria); cap. 43,268.9m., res 2,111.1m., dep. 429,396.8m. (Dec. 2011); Chair. of Man. Bd SERGEI MONIN; 7 brs and sub-brs.

Rosbank: 107078 Moscow, ul. M. Poryvayevoi 11, POB 208; tel. (495) 921-01-01; fax (495) 725-05-11; e-mail mailbox@rosbank.ru; internet www.rosbank.ru; f. 1993; 50% owned by Société Générale (France); cap. 17,587m., res 68,514m., dep. 554,771m. (Dec. 2011); Chair. of Bd of Dirs OLEG DIDE; Chief Exec. VLADIMIR YE. GOLUBKOV; 68 brs.

RosselkhozBank (Russian Agricultural Bank): 119034 Moscow, Gagarinskii per. 3; tel. and fax (495) 363-06-53; e-mail fininst@rshb.ru; internet www.rusagrobank.com; f. 2000; wholly state-owned; cap. 148,048m., res 902m., dep. 627,335m. (Dec. 2011); Chair. of Bd and CEO DMITRII N. PATRUSHEV.

Russkii Standart Bank: 105187 Moscow, ul. Tkacka 36; tel. (495) 748-07-48; fax (495) 797-84-40; e-mail bank@bank.rs.ru; internet www.rs.ru; f. 1993; cap. 1,565m., res 1,194m., dep. 114,790m. (Dec. 2011); Chair. RUSTAM V. TARIKO; Chief Exec. DMITRII O. LEVIN.

Sberbank—Savings Bank of the Russian Federation: 117997 Moscow, ul. Vavilova 19; tel. (495) 500-55-50; fax (495) 957-57-31; e-mail sbrf@sbrf.ru; internet www.sbrf.ru; f. 1841 as a deposit-taking institution, reorganized as a joint-stock commercial bank in 1991; 60.6% owned by Bank Rossii—Central Bank of the Russian Federation; cap. 87,700m., res 336,600m., dep. 11,468,500m. (Dec. 2012); Chair. of Bd and Chief Exec. GERMAN O. GREF; 17 regional head offices, 823 brs and 19,307 sub-brs.

Svyaz-Bank (Interregional Bank for Settlements of the Telecommunications and Postal Services): 125375 Moscow, ul. Tverskaya 7; tel. (495) 771-32-60; fax (495) 771-32-76; e-mail sviaz-bank@sviaz-bank.ru; internet www.sviaz-bank.ru; f. 1991; absorbed Russian Industrial Bank in 2008; 90.0% owned by Vneshekonombank; cap. 19,772m., res –3,956m., dep. 168,632m. (Dec. 2011); Chair. of Bd of Dirs ANATOLII V. TIKHONOV.

TransKreditBank (TransCreditBank): 105066 Moscow, ul. N. Basmannaya 37A/1; tel. (495) 788-08-80; fax (495) 788-08-79; e-mail info@bnk.ru; internet www.tcb.ru; f. 1992; 55.1% owned by Russian Railways; cap. 4,001.9m., res 4,585.8m., dep. 359,992.8m. (Dec. 2011); Pres. ALEKSEI V. KROKHIN.

UniCredit Bank ZAO: 119034 Moscow, Prechistenskaya nab. 9; tel. (495) 258-72-00; fax (495) 258-72-72; e-mail unicredit@unicreditgroup.ru; internet www.unicreditbank.ru; f. 1989; fmrly International Moscow Bank; present name adopted 2007; 100% owned by UniCredit Bank Austria AG (Austria); cap. 41,787.8m., res 4,198.1m., dep. 646,805.8m. (Dec. 2012); Chair. of Bd MIKHAIL ALEKSEYEV; 22 brs.

Vneshekonombank (State Corporation Bank for Development and Foreign Economic Affairs): 107996 Moscow, pr. Sakharova 9; tel. (499) 721-18-63; fax (499) 975-21-43; e-mail info@veb.ru; internet www.veb.ru; f. 1924; wholly state-owned; cap. 382,571m., res 120,440m., dep. 1,265,632m. (Dec. 2011); Chair. VLADIMIR A. DMITRIYEV.

VTB Bank: 190000 St Petersburg, ul. B. Morskaya 29; tel. (495) 739-77-99; fax (495) 258-47-81; e-mail info@vtb.ru; internet www.vtb.ru; f. 1990; fmrly Bank for Foreign Trade; present name adopted 2007; 77.5% owned by Govt of Russian Federation; cap. 113,100m., res 388,200m., dep. 4,163,400m. (Dec. 2011); Chair. of Bd and Chief Exec. ANDREI L. KOSTIN.

Bankers' Association

Association of Russian Banks (Assostiatsiya Rossiiskikh Bankov—ARB): 121069 Moscow, Skatertnyi per. 20/1; tel. (495) 691-66-30; fax (495) 691-66-66; e-mail arb@arb.ru; internet www.arb.ru; f. 1991; 832 mem. orgs, incl. 612 credit orgs (2012); Pres. GAREGIN A. TOSUNYAN.

INSURANCE

Agroinvest Insurance Co: 127422 Moscow, ul. Timiryazevskaya 26; tel. (495) 976-94-56; fax (495) 977-05-88; health, life and general insurance services; Pres. YURII I. MORDVINTSEV.

AIG Insurance and Reinsurance Co (AIG strakhovaya i perestrakhovochnaya kompaniya—ZAO Chartis): 125009 Moscow, ul. Tverskaya 16/1; tel. (495) 935-89-50; fax (495) 935-89-52; e-mail tverskaya.moscow@aig.com; internet www.aigirc.ru; f. 1994; wholly owned subsidiary of AIG Europe (France); fmrly AIG Russia; present name adopted 2009; personal and business property insurance, also marine, life, financial, etc.; Pres. E. J. STUKANOVA.

Allianz Insurance Co: 127473 Moscow, 3-i Samotechnii per. 3; tel. (495) 937-69-96; fax (495) 937-69-80; e-mail allianz@allianz.ru; internet www.allianz.ru; engineering, professional liability, life, medical, property, marine and private; Man. Dir MICHAEL HERGE-SELL.

Ingosstrakh Insurance Co: 115998 Moscow, ul. Pyatnitskaya 12/2; tel. (495) 956-55-55; fax (495) 959-44-05; e-mail ingos@ingos.ru; internet www.ingos.ru; f. 1947; undertakes all kinds of insurance and reinsurance; Chair. ALEKSANDR V. GRIGORYEV; Gen. Dir YEVGENII TUMANOV.

Medstrakh—Medical Insurance Fund of the Russian Federation: 107076 Moscow, pl. Preobrazhenskaya 7A/1; tel. (495) 964-84-27; fax (495) 964-84-21; e-mail mz@mcramn.ru; internet www.medstrah.ru; f. 1991; health, life, property, travel, liability; also provides compulsory medical insurance; Pres. PETR KUZNETSOV.

RESO-Garantiya Insurance Co: 117105 Moscow, Nagornyi pr. 6; tel. (495) 730-30-00; fax (495) 956-25-85; e-mail mail@reso.ru; internet www.reso.ru; f. 1991; Dir-Gen. DMITRII G. RAKOVSHCHIK.

Rosgosstrakh—Russian State Insurance: 127994 Moscow, ul. Novoslobodskaya 23; tel. (495) 781-24-00; fax (495) 978-27-64; e-mail pr@rgs.ru; internet www.gosstrah.ru; majority state-owned; 49% stake transferred to private ownership in 2001; undertakes domestic insurance; subsidiary cos in 80 federal subjects (territorial units) of the Russian Federation; Chair. VLADISLAV REZNIK; Gen. Dir D. E. MARKAROV.

ROSNO—Russian National Society Insurance Co: 115184 Moscow, Ozerkovskaya nab. 30; tel. (495) 232-33-33; fax (495) 232-00-14; e-mail info@rosno.ru; internet www.rosno.ru; f. 1992; 100 brs and 186 agencies; 47% owned by AFK Sistema; 45.3% owned by Allianz AG (Germany); CEO HANNES SHARIPUTRA CHOPRA.

Russkiye Strakhovye Traditsii (Russian Traditions Insurance Co): 129110 Moscow, pr. Mira 69/1; tel. and fax (495) 730-55-33; e-mail info@rustrad.ru; internet www.rustrad.ru; f. 1992; Pres. IVAN I. DAVYDOV.

SOGAZ—Insurance Co of the Gas Industry: 142770 Moscow obl., Leninskii raion, pos. Gazoprovod, Biznes-Tsentr; 115035 Moscow, ul. Bolotnaya 16/1; tel. (495) 428-57-27; fax (495) 739-21-40; e-mail sogaz@sogaz.ru; internet www.sogaz.ru; f. 1993; owned by gas industry interests; Chair. of Management Bd VADIM E. YANOV.

Soglasiye (Agreement) Insurance Co: 109017 Moscow, M. Tolmachevskii per. 8–11/3; tel. (495) 739-01-01; e-mail official@soglasie.ru; internet www.soglasie.ru; f. 1993 as Interros-Soglasiye; owned by Interros; Dir-Gen. LYUBOV YELTSOVA.

STOCK EXCHANGES

MICEX: 125009 Moscow, B. Kislovskii per. 13; tel. (495) 363-32-32; fax (495) 705-96-22; internet www.micex.ru; f. 1992; 29% owned by the Central Bank of the Russian Federation (q.v.); Pres. RUBEN A. AGANBEGYAN.

Moscow Stock Exchange (MSE) (Moskovskaya Fondovaya Birzha): 127422 Moscow, ul. Vsevoloda Vishnevskogo 4; tel. (495) 771-35-80; fax (495) 771-35-81; e-mail mse@mse.ru; internet www.mse.ru; f. 1997; Pres. ALEKSEI RYZHKOV.

RTS—Russian Trading System: 125009 Moscow, ul. Vozdvizhenka 4/7; tel. (495) 705-90-31; fax (495) 733-95-15; e-mail international@rts.ru; internet www.rts.ru; f. 1995; Chief Exec. ROMAN YU. GORYUNOV.

Siberian Stock Exchange: 630104 Novosibirsk, ul. Frunze 5, POB 233; tel. (3832) 21-60-67; fax (3832) 21-06-90; e-mail sibex@sibex.nsk.su; f. 1991; Pres. ALEKSANDR V. NOVIKOV.

COMMODITY EXCHANGES

Asiatic Commodity Exchange: 670000 Buryatiya, Ulan-Ude, ul. Sovetskaya 23/37; tel. and fax (3012) 22-26-81; f. 1991; Chair. ANDREI FIRSOV.

European-Asian Exchange (EAE): 101000 Moscow, ul. Myasnitskaya 26; tel. and fax (495) 787-58-93; e-mail info@eae.ru; internet www.eae.ru; f. 2000; Chair. of Council TATYANA S. SOKOLOVA; Gen. Man. ALEKSANDR B. YEREMIN.

Khabarovsk Commodity Exchange (KhCE): 680000 Khabarovsk; tel. and fax (4212) 33-65-60; f. 1991; Pres. YEVGENII V. PANASENKO.

Komi Commodity Exchange (KoCE): 167610 Komi, Syktyvkar, Oktyabrskii pr. 16; tel. (8212) 22-32-86; fax (8212) 23-84-43; f. 1991; Pres. PETR S. LUCHENKOV.

Kuzbass Commodity and Raw Materials Exchange (KECME): 650090 Kemerovo, ul. Novgorodskaya 19; tel. (3842) 23-45-40; fax (3842) 23-49-56; f. 1991; Gen. Man. FEDOR MASENKOV.

Moscow Commodity Exchange (MCE): 129223 Moscow, pr. Mira, Russian Exhibition Centre, Pavilion 69 (4); tel. (495) 187-86-14; fax (495) 187-88-76; f. 1990; organization of exchange trading (cash, stock and futures market); Pres. and Chair. of Bd YURII MILYUKOV.

Petrozavodsk Commodity Exchange (PCE): 185028 Kareliya, Petrozavodsk, ul. Krasnaya 31; tel. and fax (8142) 7-80-57; f. 1991; Gen. Man. VALERII SAKHAROV.

Russian Commodity Exchange of the Agro-Industrial Complex (RosAgroBirzha): 125080 Moscow, Volokolamskoye shosse 11; tel. (495) 209-52-25; f. 1990; Chair. of Exchange Cttee ALEKSANDR VASILIYEV.

Russian Exchange (RE): 101000 Moscow, ul. Myasnitskaya 26; tel. (495) 787-84-34; fax (495) 262-57-57; e-mail ic@ci.re.ru; internet www.re.ru; f. 1990; Pres. PAVEL PANOV.

St Petersburg Exchange: 199026 St Petersburg, Vasilyevskii Ostrov, 26-aya liniya 15; tel. (812) 322-44-11; fax (812) 322-73-90; e-mail spbex@spbex.ru; internet www.spbex.ru; f. 1991; Pres. and Chief Exec. VIKTOR V. NIKOLAYEV.

Udmurt Commodity Universal Exchange (UCUE): 426075 Udmurt Rep., Izhevsk, ul. Soyuznaya 107; tel. (3412) 37-08-88; fax (3412) 37-16-57; e-mail iger@udmnet.ru; f. 1991; Pres. N. F. LAZAREV.

Yekaterinburg Commodity Exchange (UCE): 620012 Sverdlovsk obl., Yekaterinburg, pr. Kosmonavtov 23; tel. (343) 234-43-01; fax (343) 251-53-64; f. 1991; Chair. of Exchange Cttee KONSTANTIN ZHUZHLOV.

Trade and Industry

GOVERNMENT AGENCY

Russian Federal Property Fund (Rossiiskii Fond Federalnogo Imushchestva): 119049 Moscow, Leninskii pr. 9; tel. (495) 236-71-15; fax (495) 956-27-80; e-mail rffi@dol.ru; internet www.fpf.ru; f. 1992 to ensure consistency in the privatization process and to implement privatization legislation; Chair. YURII A. PETROV.

NATIONAL CHAMBER OF COMMERCE

Chamber of Commerce and Industry of the Russian Federation (Torgovo-Promyshlennaya Palata RF): 109012 Moscow, ul. Ilinka 6; tel. (495) 929-00-09; fax (495) 929-03-60; e-mail dios-inform@tpprf.ru; internet www.tpprf.ru; f. 1991; Pres. YEVGENII M. PRIMAKOV.

REGIONAL CHAMBERS OF COMMERCE

In early 2011 there were 173 regional chambers of commerce. The following are among the most important:

Astrakhan Chamber of Commerce: 414040 Astrakhan, ul. Zhelyabova 50; tel. (8512) 25-58-44; fax (8512) 28-14-42; e-mail cci@mail.astrakhan.ru; internet astrcci.astrakhan.ru; f. 1992; Pres. ALEKSEI D. KANTEMIROV.

Bashkortostan Chamber of Commerce: 450007 Bashkortostan, Ufa, ul. Vorovskogo 22; tel. (3472) 23-23-80; fax (3472) 51-70-79; e-mail office@tpprb.ru; internet www.tpprb.ru; f. 1990; Chair. BORIS A. BONDARENKO.

Central Siberian Chamber of Commerce: 660049 Krasnoyarsk, ul. Kirova 26; tel. (3912) 68-15-85; fax (3912) 68-16-70; e-mail cstp@mail.ru; internet www.cstpp.ru; f. 1985; Chair. NIKOLAI P. KHUDIKH.

East Siberian Chamber of Commerce: 664003 Irkutsk, ul. Sukhe-Batora 16; tel. (3952) 33-50-60; fax (3952) 33-50-66; e-mail info@ccies.ru; internet www.ccies.ru; f. 1974; Pres. KONSTANTIN S. SHAVRIN.

Far East Chamber of Commerce: 680670 Khabarovsk, ul. Sheronova 113; tel. (4210) 30-47-70; fax (4210) 30-54-58; e-mail dvtpp@fecci.khv.ru; f. 1970; Pres. MIKHAIL V. KRUGLIKOV.

Kaliningrad Chamber of Commerce and Industry: 236010 Kaliningrad, ul. Vatutina 20; tel. (4012) 95-68-01; fax (4012) 95-47-88; e-mail kaliningrad_cci@baltnet.ru; internet www.kaliningrad-cci.ru; f. 1990; Pres. IGOR V. TSARKOV.

Kamchatka Chamber of Commerce: 683000 Kamchatka Krai, Petropavlovsk-Kamchatskii, ul. Leninskaya 38/208; tel. and fax (4152) 12-35-10; e-mail kamtpp@iks.ru; Pres. ALLA V. PARKHOMCHUK.

Krasnodar Chamber of Commerce: 350063 Krasnodar, ul. Kommunarov 8; tel. and fax (861) 268-22-13; e-mail tppkk@tppkuban.ru; internet www.tppkuban.ru; f. 1969; Chair. YURII N. TKACHENKO.

Kuzbass Chamber of Commerce: 650099 Kemerovo, pr. Sovetskii 63/407; tel. and fax (3842) 58-77-64; e-mail ktpp@mail.kuzbass.net; internet city.info.kuzbass.net/ktpp; f. 1991; Pres. TATYANA O. IVLEVA.

Maritime (Primorskii) Krai Chamber of Commerce: 690600 Maritime Krai, Vladivostok, Okeanskii pr. 13A; tel. (4232) 26-96-30;

fax (4232) 22-72-26; e-mail palata@online.vladivostok.ru; internet www.ptpp.ru; f. 1964; Pres. VLADIMIR B. BREZHNEV.

Moscow Chamber of Commerce: 117393 Moscow, ul. Akademika Pilyugina 22; tel. (495) 132-07-33; fax (495) 132-75-03; e-mail extern@mtpp.org; internet www.mtpp.org; f. 1991; Chair. YURII I. KOTOV; Pres. LEONID V. GOVOROV.

Nizhnii Novgorod Chamber of Commerce: 603005 Nizhnii Novgorod, pl. Oktyabrskaya 1; tel. (8312) 19-42-10; fax (8312) 19-40-09; e-mail tpp@rda.nnov.ru; internet www.tpp.nnov.ru; f. 1990; Pres. GENNADII M. KHODYRYEV.

Northern Chamber of Commerce and Industry: 183766 Murmansk, per. Rusanova 10; tel. (8152) 47-29-99; fax (8152) 47-39-78; e-mail ncci@online.ru; internet www.ncci.ru; f. 1990; Pres. ANATOLII M. GLUSHKOV.

Novosibirsk Chamber of Commerce: 630064 Novosibirsk, pr. K. Marksa 1; tel. and fax (383) 346-41-50; e-mail org@ntpp.ru; internet www.ntpp.ru; f. 1991; Chair. BORIS V. BRUSILOVSKII; 315 mems (2002).

Omsk Chamber of Commerce: 644007 Omsk, ul. Gertsena 51/53; tel. (3812) 25-43-50; fax (3812) 23-45-80; e-mail omtpp@omsknet.ru; internet www.omsktpp.ru; f. 1992; Pres. TATYANA A. KHOROSHAVINA.

Rostov Chamber of Commerce: 344022 Rostov-on-Don, ul. Pushkinskaya 176; tel. and fax (836) 264-45-47; e-mail tpp@rost.ru; internet www.tpp.tis.ru; f. 1992; Pres. NIKOLAI I. PRISYAZHNYUK.

Sakha (Yakutiya) Chamber of Commerce: 677000 Sakha (Yakutiya), Yakutsk, ul. Lenina 22/214; tel. (4112) 26-64-96; e-mail palata91@mail.ru; f. 1991; Chair. SERGEI G. BAKULIN.

Samara Chamber of Commerce: 443099 Samara, ul. A. Tolstogo 6; tel. (8462) 32-11-59; fax (8462) 70-48-96; e-mail ccisr@samara.ru; internet www.cci.samara.ru; f. 1988; Pres. BORIS V. ARDALIN.

Saratov Regional Chamber of Commerce and Industry: 410600 Saratov, ul. B. Kazachya 30; tel. (8452) 27-70-78; fax (8452) 27-70-82; e-mail srcci@sgtpp.ru; internet www.sgtpp.ru; f. 1986; Pres. MAKSIM A. FATEYEV.

Smolensk Chamber of Commerce: 214000 Smolensk, ul. Bakunina 10A; tel. and fax (481) 238-74-50; e-mail smolenskcci@keytown .com; internet www.smolcci.keytown.com; f. 1993; Pres. VLADIMIR P. ARKHIPENKOV.

South Urals Chamber of Commerce: 454080 Chelyabinsk, ul. S. Krivoi 56; tel. (351) 266-18-16; fax (351) 265-41-53; e-mail mail@ uralreg.ru; internet www.uralreg.ru; f. 1992; Pres. FEDOR L. DEGTYAREV; 550 mems (2007).

St Petersburg Chamber of Commerce: 191123 St Petersburg, ul. Chaikovskogo 46–48; tel. and fax (812) 273-48-96; e-mail spbcci@ spbcci.ru; internet www.spbcci.ru; f. 1921; Pres. VLADIMIR I. KATENEV.

Stavropol Chamber of Commerce and Industry: 355003 Stavropol, ul. Lenina 384; tel. (8652) 94-53-34; fax (8652) 34-05-10; e-mail stcci@statel.stavropol.ru; f. 1991; Pres. VITALII S. NABATNIKOV.

Tatarstan Republic Chamber of Commerce and Industry: 420111 Tatarstan, Kazan, ul. Pushkina 18; tel. (843) 264-62-07; fax (843) 236-09-66; e-mail tpprt@tpprt.ru; internet www.tpprt.ru; f. 1992; Gen. Dir SHAMIL R. AGEYEV; 1,200 mems (2007).

Ulyanovsk Chamber of Commerce: 432063 Ulyanovsk, ul. Engelsa 19; tel. (8422) 41-03-61; fax (8422) 41-02-31; e-mail info@ ultpp.ru; f. 1992; Pres. YEVGENII S. BALANDIN.

Urals Chamber of Commerce and Industry: 620027 Sverdlovsk obl., Yekaterinburg, ul. Vostochnaya 6; tel. (343) 353-04-49; fax (343) 353-58-63; e-mail ucci@ucci.ur.ru; internet ucci.ur.ru; f. 1959; Pres. YURII P. MATUSHKIN.

Volgograd Chamber of Commerce: 400005 Volgograd, ul. 7-aya Gvardeiskaya 2; tel. (8442) 93-61-35; fax (8442) 34-22-02; e-mail cci@ volgogradcci.ru; internet www.volgogradcci.ru; f. 1990; Pres. ALEKSANDR D. BELITSKII.

Vologda Chamber of Commerce and Industry: 160000 Vologda, ul. Lermontova 15; tel. and fax (8172) 72-46-87; e-mail grant@ vologda.ru; internet www.vologdatpp.ru; f. 1992; Pres. GALINA D. TELEGINA.

Voronezh Chamber of Commerce: 394030 Voronezh, 'Voronezh-vnesh-servis', POB 63; tel. and fax (473) 252-49-38; e-mail mail@ oootpp.vm.ru; f. 1991; fmrly Central-Black Earth Chamber of Commerce and Industry; Pres. VYACHESLAV A. KONDRATYEV.

EMPLOYERS' ORGANIZATIONS

Co-ordinating Council of Employers' Unions of Russia (Koordinatsionnyi Sovet Obyedinenii Rabotodatelei Rossii—KSORR): 109017 Moscow, per. M. Tolmachevskii 8–11; tel. (495) 232-55-77; fax (495) 959-46-06; e-mail official@ksorr.ru; internet www.ksorr.ru; f. 1994; co-ordinates and represents employers in relations with government bodies and trade unions, and represents Russian employers in the International Labour Organization (ILO) and the International Organization of Employers (IOE); Chair. OLEG V. YEREMEYEV; Gen. Dir SERGEI V. LUKONIN; unites 35 major employers' unions, incl. the following:

Agro-Industrial Union of Russia: 107139 Moscow, POB 139; tel. (495) 204-41-04; fax (495) 207-83-62; e-mail sva@gvs.aris.ru; Pres. VASILII A. STARODUBTSEV.

All-Russian Social Organization of Small and Medium-sized Businesses (OPORA Rossii) (Obshcherossiiskaya Obshchestvennaya Organizatsiya Malogo i Srednego Predprinimatelstva): 125047 Moscow, ul. 4-ya Tverskaya-Yamskaya 21/22/ 3; tel. (495) 775-81-11; fax (495) 775-81-91; internet www.opora.ru; f. 2002; Pres. SERGEI BORISOV.

Russian Union of Industrialists and Entrepreneurs (Employers) (RSPPR) (Rossiiskii Soyuz Promyshlennikov i Predprinimatelei): 103070 Moscow, Staraya pl. 10/4; tel. (495) 748-42-37; fax (495) 206-11-29; e-mail pr_dep@rspp.net; internet www.rspp.ru; f. 1991; Pres. ALEKSANDR SHOKHIN; Exec. Sec. NIKOLAI TONKOV.

UTILITIES

Electricity

Federal Energy Commission: 103074 Moscow, Kitaigorodskii proyezd 7; tel. (495) 220-40-15; fax (495) 206-81-08; e-mail fecrf@ orc.ru; regulatory authority for natural energy monopolies; sole responsibility for establishing tariff rates for energy, transportation, shipping, postal and telecommunications industries in the Russian Federation from Sept. 2001; Chair. ANDREI ZADERNYUK.

Irkutskenergo (Irkutsk Energy Co): 664000 Irkutsk, ul. Sukhe-Batora 3; tel. (3952) 21-73-00; fax (3952) 21-78-99; e-mail idkan@ irkutskenergo.ru; internet www.irkutskenergo.ru; f. 1954; generation and transmission of electrical and thermal energy; Dir-Gen. VLADIMIR V. KOLMOGOROV.

Mosenergo (Moscow Energy Co): 113035 Moscow, Raushskaya nab. 8; tel. (495) 957-35-30; fax (495) 957-34-70; e-mail press-centre@ mosenergo.ru; internet www.mosenergo.ru; f. 1887; 49% owned by Unified Energy System of Russia; power generator and distributor; Chair. YURII A. UDALTSOV.

Rosenergoatom (Russian Atomic Energy Concern): 119017 Moscow, ul. B. Ordynka 24/26; tel. (495) 239-24-22; fax (495) 239-46-03; e-mail npp@rosatom.ru; internet www.rosenergoatom.ru; f. 1992; electricity-generating co, manages Russia's 10 nuclear reactors; Dir-Gen. SERGEI OBOZOV.

Sverdlovenergo (Sverdlovsk Energy Co): 620219 Sverdlovsk obl., Yekaterinburg, pr. Lenina 38; tel. (343) 259-13-99; fax (343) 259-12-22; e-mail post@energo.pssr.ru; internet www.po.pssr.ru; f. 1942; Chair. of Bd ALEKSANDR V. CHIKUNOV; Gen. Man. VLADIMIR V. KALSIN.

Uralenergo (Ural Energy): 454006 Chelyabinsk, ul. Rossiiskaya 17; tel. (3512) 67-59-54; fax (3512) 67-59-48; e-mail info@uralenergo .com; internet www.uralenergo.com; manages 22 joint-stock cos; oversees 55 thermal power stations and 6 hydroelectric stations; total installed capacity of over 28,500m. kW; Dir ALEKSANDR S. NEMTSEV.

Gas

Gazprom: 117997 Moscow, ul. Nametkina 16; tel. (495) 719-30-01; fax (495) 719-83-33; e-mail gazprom@gazprom.ru; internet www .gazprom.ru; f. 1989 from assets of Soviet Ministry of Oil and Gas; became independent joint-stock co in 1992, privatized in 1994; 51% state-owned; Chair. of Bd of Dirs VIKTOR A. ZUBKOV; Chair. of Management Bd and Deputy Chair. of Bd of Dirs ALEKSEI B. MILLER.

Gazprom Mezhregiongaz (Interregional Gas Supply Company): 142770 Moscow obl., Leninskii raion, pos. Gazoprovod, dom 101; tel. (495) 817-55-55; fax (495) 817-52-10; e-mail pr@mrg.gazprom.ru; internet www.mrg.ru; f. 1996; gas-marketing co; subsidiary of Gazprom (q.v.); brs in more than 65 federal subjects; CEO KIRILL SELEZNEV.

Water

Mosvodokanal: 105005 Moscow, per. Pleteshkovskii 2; tel. (499) 763-34-34; fax (495) 265-22-01; e-mail post@mosvodokanal.ru; internet www.mosvodokanal.ru; f. 1937; open jt-stock co; provides water and sewerage services to Moscow and the surrounding region; Dir-Gen. ALEKSANDR PONOMARENKO.

Vodokanal: 191015 St Petersburg, ul. Kavalergardskaya 42; tel. (812) 305-09-09; fax (812) 274-13-61; e-mail office@vodokanal.spb.ru; internet www.vodokanal.spb.ru; water and sewerage utility; Dir-Gen. FELIKS V. KARMAZINOV.

TRADE UNIONS

In 1990 several branch unions of the All-Union Central Council of Trade Unions (ACCTU) established the Federation of Independent Trade Unions of Russia (FITUR), which took control of part of the property and other assets of the ACCTU. The ACCTU was re-formed as the General Confederation of Trade Unions of the USSR, which was, in turn, renamed the General Confederation of Trade Unions—International Organization in 1992, later becoming the General Confederation of Trade Unions.

Principal Trade Union Coalitions

All-Russian Labour Confederation: 103031 Moscow, ul. Rozhdestvenka 5/7; tel. (495) 785-21-30; fax (495) 915-83-67; e-mail vktrussia@online.ru; internet www.trud.org/guide/VKT.htm; f. 1995; unites five national trade unions and 40 regional orgs with 1,270,900 mems; Pres. ALEKSANDR N. BUGAYEV.

Federation of Independent Trade Unions of Russia (FITUR) (Federatsiya Nezavisimykh Profsoyuzov Rossii—FNPR): 119119 Moscow, Leninskii pr. 42; tel. (495) 938-73-12; fax (495) 137-06-94; e-mail korneev@fnpr.ru; internet www.fnpr.ru; f. 1990; unites 48 national trade unions and 78 regional orgs (with c. 40m. mems); affiliated to General Confederation of Trade Unions (q.v.); Pres. MIKHAIL V. SHMAKOV.

General Confederation of Trade Unions (VKP): 119119 Moscow, Leninskii pr. 42; tel. (495) 938-01-12; fax (495) 938-21-55; e-mail inter@vkp.ru; internet www.vkp.ru; f. 1992 to replace General Confederation of Trade Unions of the USSR; co-ordinating body for trade unions in CIS member states and Georgia; unites 10 national and 28 regional industrial orgs with 50m. mems; publishes *Profsoyuzy* (Trade Unions), weekly, *Vestnik profsoyuzov* (Herald of the Trade Unions), every two weeks, and *Inform-Contact*, in English and French, quarterly; Pres. MIKHAIL V. SHMAKOV; Sec.-Gen. VLADIMIR P. SCHERBAKOV.

Moscow Trade Unions Federation: 121205 Moscow, ul. Novyi Arbat 36/9; tel. (495) 290-82-62; fax (495) 202-92-70; e-mail main@mtuf.ru; f. 1990; largest regional branch of FITUR (q.v.); Chair. MIKHAIL D. NAGAITSEV; 2.2m. mems.

Transport

RAILWAYS

At the end of 2010 the total length of railway track in use was 85,292 km, around one-half of which was electrified.

Russian Railways OAO (RZhD) (Rossiiskiye zheleznyye dorogi): 107174 Moscow, ul. Novobasmannaya 2; tel. (495) 262-16-28; fax (495) 975-24-11; e-mail info@rzd.ru; internet www.rzd.ru; f. 2003; Pres. VLADIMIR YAKUNIN.

City Underground Railways

Moscow Metro: 129110 Moscow, pr. Mira 41/2; tel. (495) 622-10-01; fax (495) 631-37-44; e-mail info@mosmetro.ru; internet www.mosmetro.org; f. 1935; 12 lines (313 km) with 188 stations in 2013; Gen. Man. DMITRII V. GAYEV.

Nizhnii Novgorod Metro: 603002 Nizhnii Novgorod, pl. Revolutsii 7; tel. (8312) 44-17-60; fax (8312) 44-20-86; e-mail metro@sandy.ru; f. 1985; 19 km with 14 stations in 2013; Gen. Man. A. KUZMIN.

Novosibirsk Metro: 630099 Novosibirsk, ul. Serebrennikovskaya 34; tel. (3832) 90-81-10; fax (3832) 46-56-82; e-mail nsk@metro.snt.su; internet www.nsk.su/~metro/; f. 1986; 2 lines (16 km) with 13 stations in 2013; Gen. Man. V. I. DEMIN.

St Petersburg Metro: 190013 St Petersburg, Moskovskii pr. 28; tel. (812) 251-66-68; fax (812) 316-14-41; e-mail np@metro.spb.ru; internet www.metro.spb.ru; f. 1955; 5 lines (113 km) with 67 stations in 2013; Gen. Man. VLADIMIR A. GARYUGIN.

Short underground railways began to operate in Samara, Yekaterinburg and Kazan in 1987, 1991 and 2005, respectively. In 2013 the construction of underground railways was under way in Chelyabinsk, Krasnoyarsk and Omsk, and a light railway was scheduled to open in Sochi, prior to the holding of the Winter Olympics there in 2014.

ROADS

At the end of 2009 the total length of roads was 983,000 km. In Siberia and the Far East, there are few roads, and they are often impassable in winter, while the *rasputitsa*, or spring thaw, notoriously impedes rural road traffic, even in European Russia.

SHIPPING

The seaports of the Russian Federation provide access to the Pacific Ocean, in the east, the Baltic Sea and the Atlantic Ocean, in the west, and the Black Sea, in the south. Major eastern ports are at Vladivostok, Nakhodka, Vostochnyi, Magadan and Petropavlovsk. In the west, St Petersburg and Kaliningrad provide access to the Baltic Sea, and the northern ports of Murmansk and Archangel (Arkhangelsk) have access to the Atlantic Ocean, via the Barents Sea. Novorossiisk and Sochi are the principal Russian ports on the Black Sea. At

31 December 2012 Russia's flag registered fleet comprised 4,753 vessels, totalling 9,911,898 grt, of which three were gas tankers and 1,087 were general cargo ships.

Principal Ship-owning Companies

Baltic Shipping Co: 198035 St Petersburg, Mezhevoi kanal 5; tel. (812) 251-33-97; fax (812) 186-85-44; freight and passenger services; Chair. MIKHAIL A. ROMANOVSKII.

Baltic Transport Systems: 199106 St Petersburg, pl. Morskoi Slavy 1; tel. (812) 303-99-14; fax (812) 380-34-76; e-mail bts@baltics.ru; internet www.baltics.ru; f. 1994; freight and passenger services; Gen. Dir ALEKSEI E. SHUKLETSOV.

Far Eastern Shipping Co: 690019 Maritime (Primorskii) Krai, Vladivostok, ul. Aleutskaya 15; tel. (4232) 41-14-32; fax (4232) 52-15-51; e-mail 41401@41.fesco.ru; internet www.fesco.ru; f. 1880; Gen. Man. YEVGENII N. AMBROSOV.

Kamchatka Shipping Co: 683600 Kamchatka Krai, Petropavlovsk-Kamchatskii, ul. Radiosvyazi 65; tel. (41522) 2-82-21; fax (41522) 2-19-60; f. 1949; freight services; Pres. NIKOLAI M. ZABLOTSKII.

Murmansk Shipping Co: 183038 Murmansk, ul. Kominterna 15; tel. (8152) 48-10-48; fax (8152) 48-11-48; e-mail postmaster@msco.ru; f. 1939; shipping and ice-breaking services; Gen. Dir VYACHESLAV RUKSHA.

Northern Shipping Co (NSC Arkhangelsk) (Severnoye morskoye parokhodstvo OAO—SMP): 163000 Archangel, nab. Severnoi Dviny 36; tel. (8182) 63-72-03; fax (8182) 63-71-95; e-mail nsosnina@ansc.ru; internet www.ansc.ru; f. 1870; dry cargo-shipping, liner services; Gen. Dir VIKTOR A. IZBITSKII.

Novorossiisk Shipping Co: 353900 Krasnodar Krai, Novorossiisk, ul. Svobody 1; tel. (8617) 25-31-26; fax (8617) 25-11-43; e-mail novoship@novoship.ru; internet www.novoship.ru; f. 1992; Chair. V. I. YAKUNIN.

Primorsk Shipping Corpn: 692900 Maritime (Primorskii) Krai, Nakhodka-4, Administrativnyi Gorodok; tel. (4236) 69-45-05; fax (4236) 69-45-75; e-mail psc@prisco.ru; internet www.prisco.ru; f. 1972; Dir-Gen. ALEKSANDR MIGUNOV.

Sakhalin Shipping Co: 694620 Sakhalin obl., Kholmsk, ul. Pobedy 18A; tel. (42433) 6-62-07; fax (42433) 6-60-20; e-mail chief@sasco.ru; internet www.sasco.org; f. 1945; ship-owners and managers, carriage of cargo and passengers; Gen. Dir ALEKSANDR MATSUK.

Sovfrakht: 127944 Moscow, Rakhmanovskii per. 4, Morskoi Dom; tel. (495) 258-27-41; fax (495) 230-26-40; e-mail general@sovfracht.ru; internet www.sovfracht.ru; f. 1929; jt-stock co; chartering and broking of tanker, cargo and other ships; forwarding, booking and insurance agency; ship management; Dir-Gen. D. YU. PURIM; 120 employees (2003).

White Sea and Onega Shipping Co (Belomorsko-Onezhskoye parokhodstvo): 185005 Kareliya, Petrozavodsk, ul. Rigachina 7; tel. (8142) 71-12-01; fax (8142) 71-12-67; e-mail dir@bop.onego.ru; internet bop.onego.ru; f. 1940; cargo-shipping, cargo ship construction and repair; Gen. Dir STANISLAV ROZOLINSKII; Pres. ALEKSANDR LYALLYA.

CIVIL AVIATION

Until 1991 Aeroflot—Soviet Airlines was the only airline operating on domestic routes in the former USSR. In 1992–94 some 300 different independent airlines emerged on the basis of Aeroflot's former regional directorates. Several small private airlines were also established. In 2003 there were 451 airports in Russia.

Aeroflot-Don: 344009 Rostov-on-Don, pr. Sholokhova 272; tel. (863) 276-78-11; fax (863) 252-11-78; e-mail avia1@aeroflot-don.ru; internet www.aeroflot-don.ru; f. 1925; present name adopted 2000; 100% owned by Aeroflot—Russian Airlines; operates scheduled and chartered passenger and cargo flights to various domestic and international destinations (incl. Armenia, Austria, Egypt, Germany, Israel, Turkey, Ukraine and the United Arab Emirates) from Rostov-on-Don, Moscow and Sochi, and between Moscow and Groznyi; Dir-Gen. MIKHAIL S. KRITSKII.

Aeroflot—Russian Airlines: 125167 Moscow, Leningradskii pr. 37/9; tel. and fax (495) 223-55-55; e-mail presscentr@aeroflot.ru; internet www.aeroflot.ru; f. 1923; 51% state-owned; operates flights to 94 destinations in 49 countries; Chair. IGOR YE. LEVITIN; Gen. Dir VALERII M. OKULOV.

Gazpromavia: 117997 Moscow, ul. Novocheremushkinskaya 71/32; tel. (495) 719-18-32; fax (495) 719-11-85; e-mail gazpromavia@gazprom.ru; internet www.gazpromavia.ru; f. 1995; Dir-Gen. ANDREI S. OVCHARENKO.

KD Avia: 238315 Kaliningrad obl., Guryevskii raion, Khrabrovo, Aeroport; tel. (401) 235-51-75; e-mail info@kdavia.ru; internet www.kdavia.ru; f. 1945; present name adopted 2005; international and domestic flights from Kaliningrad; Dir-Gen. VALERII MIKHAILOV.

Kuban Airlines (Kubanskiye Avialinii): 350026 Krasnodar, Krasnodar—Pashkovskaya Airport; tel. (861) 237-06-00; fax (861) 237-38-11; e-mail info@kuban-airlines.com; internet www.kuban-airlines.de; f. 1932; regional and international flights.

Rossiya—Russian Airlines: 191025 St Petersburg, Nevskii pr. 61; tel. (812) 333-22-22; fax (812) 333-22-44; internet www.rossiya-airlines.ru; f. 1992; merged with Pulkovo Airlines in 2006; state-owned; operates scheduled and charter passenger flights from St Petersburg and Moscow to domestic and international destinations; Gen. Dir SERGEI MIKHALIENKO.

S7 Airlines (Siberia Airlines): 633115 Novosibirsk obl., gorod Ob-4; tel. (3832) 59-90-11; fax (3832) 59-90-64; e-mail pr@s7.ru; internet www.s7.ru; fmrly Sibir Airlines; scheduled and charter flights to domestic, Asian, European and Middle Eastern destinations; Gen. Dir VLADISLAV FILEV.

SkyExpress: 119027 Moscow, Vnukovo, ul. Tsentralnaya 2/2; tel. (495) 648-93-60; fax (495) 980-74-61; e-mail info@skyexpress.ru; internet www.skyexpress.ru; f. 2006; 'low-cost' airline operating passenger flights between Moscow (Vnukovo) and Murmansk, and Rostov-on-Don and Sochi (Krasnodar Krai); also international charter flights; Chief Exec. MARINA BUKALOVA.

Transaero Airlines: 127083 Moscow, Mishina 56/3; tel. (495) 788-80-80; fax (495) 937-84-64; e-mail info@transaero.ru; internet www.transaero.ru; f. 1991; Russia's largest privately owned airline; operates scheduled and charter passenger services to Europe, Asia and Central America; CEO OLGA PLESHAKOVA.

Ural Airlines (Uralskiye Aviyalinii): 620910 Sverdlovsk obl., Yekaterinburg, ul. Sputnikov 6; tel. (343) 226-81-26; fax (343) 226-82-49; e-mail margarita@uralairlines.ru; internet www.uralairlines.ru; f. 1993; flights from Yekaterinburg to domestic and international destinations; Gen. Dir SERGEI SKURATOV.

Vladivostok Avia: 692756 Maritime (Primorskii) Krai, Artem, ul. Portovaya 41, Vladivostok Airport; tel. (4232) 30-73-33; fax (4232) 30-73-43; e-mail office@vladavia.ru; internet www.vladavia.ru; f. 1994; freight and scheduled passenger services from Vladivostok and Moscow to domestic and international destinations; Gen. Dir VLADIMIR SAIBEL.

Tourism

In 2011, according to provisional data, there were 22,686,000 tourist arrivals in Russia, and receipts from tourism totalled US $11,398m.

Intourist: 129366 Moscow, pr. Mira 150; tel. (495) 730-19-19; fax (495) 956-42-02; e-mail info@intourist.ru; internet www.intourist.ru; f. 1929; brs throughout Russia and abroad; Chair. VYACHESLAV KOPIEV.

Defence

In May 1992 the Russian Federation established its own armed forces, on the basis of former Soviet forces on the territory of the Russian Federation, and former Soviet forces outside its territory not subordinate to other former republics of the USSR. As assessed at November 2012, the total Russian active armed forces numbered an estimated 845,000, comprising 250,000 members of the army, 35,000 airborne troops, a navy of 130,000, an air force of 150,000, the 80,000-strong Strategic Defence Forces, and 200,000 command and support troops. There were an estimated 20,000,000 reserves. There were a further estimated 519,000 paramilitary troops, including 160,000 members of the Federal Border Guard Service, which is directly subordinate to the President, 170,000 troops of the Ministry of Internal Affairs, and an estimated 4,000 active (armed) members of the Federal Security Service. Compulsory military service (for males over the age of 18 years) lasts for a period of one year.

Defence Expenditure: Budgeted at 2,350,000m. roubles in 2013.

Chief of the General Staff, First Deputy Minister of Defence: Gen. VALERII V. GERASIMOV.

Chief of Staff of the Internal Troops: Col-Gen. SERGEI BUNIN.

Commander-in-Chief of the Army: Col-Gen. ALEKSANDR POSTNIKOV.

Commander-in-Chief of the Navy: Adm. VIKTOR V. CHIRKOV.

Chief of Staff of the Air Force: Gen. VIKTOR BONDAREV.

Education

Education is compulsory for nine years, to be undertaken between the ages of six and 15 years. State education is generally provided free of charge, although in 1992 some higher education establishments began charging tuition fees. Students of selected courses in higher education receive a small stipend from the state. Primary education usually begins at six years of age and lasts for four years. Secondary education, beginning at 10 years of age, lasts for seven years, comprising a first cycle of five years and a second of two years. In 2008/09 enrolment at primary schools included 93% of children in the appropriate age-group, while the comparable ratio for secondary enrolment was equivalent to 89%.

In 2011/12 6.5m. students were enrolled at institutes of higher education. Although Russian is the principal language used in educational establishments, a number of local languages are also in use. Budgetary expenditure on education (excluding scientific research and technology) in 2005 was an estimated 1,665,500m. roubles (representing 11.9% of total expenditure).

In 2011/12 there were 47,146 independent primary and general secondary schools, 2,925 independent vocational secondary schools, and 1,080 independent higher education institutions.

RWANDA

Introductory Survey

LOCATION, CLIMATE, LANGUAGE, RELIGION, FLAG, CAPITAL

The Rwandan Republic is a land-locked country in eastern central Africa, just south of the Equator, bounded by the Democratic Republic of the Congo to the west, by Uganda to the north, by Tanzania to the east and by Burundi to the south. The climate is tropical, although tempered by altitude. It is hot and humid in the lowlands, but cooler in the highlands. The average annual rainfall is 785 mm (31 ins). The main rainy season is from February to May. The population is composed of three ethnic groups: Hutu (85%), Tutsi (14%) and Twa (1%). French, English and Kinyarwanda, the native language, are all in official use, and Kiswahili is widely spoken. About one-half of the population adhere to animist beliefs. Most of the remainder are Christians, mainly Roman Catholics. There are Protestant and Muslim minorities. The national flag (proportions 1 by 2) has three unequal horizontal stripes, of blue, yellow and green, with a blue-ringed, yellow disc (framed by 24 yellow rays) depicted near the fly end of the top stripe. The capital is Kigali.

CONTEMPORARY POLITICAL HISTORY

Historical Context

Rwanda, with the neighbouring state of Burundi, became part of German East Africa in 1899. In 1916, during the First World War, it was occupied by Belgian forces from the Congo. From 1920 Rwanda was part of Ruanda-Urundi, administered by Belgium under a League of Nations mandate and later as a UN Trust Territory. Long-standing dissension between the majority Hutu tribe and their former overlords, the Tutsi, caused a rebellion and the proclamation of a state of emergency in 1959. In September 1961 it was decided by referendum to abolish the monarchy and to establish a republic. Full independence followed on 1 July 1962. Serious tribal conflict erupted in December 1963, and massacres (of an estimated 20,000) were perpetrated by the Hutu against the Tutsi. During 1964–65 large numbers of displaced Rwandans were resettled in neighbouring countries. In 1969 Grégoire Kayibanda, the new Republic's first President, was re-elected, and all 47 seats in the legislature were retained by the governing party, the Mouvement Démocratique Républicain (MDR).

Tension between Hutu and Tutsi escalated again at the end of 1972 and continued throughout February 1973. In July the Minister of Defence and head of the National Guard, Maj.-Gen. Juvénal Habyarimana, led a bloodless coup against President Kayibanda, proclaimed a Second Republic and established a military administration. In August a new Council of Ministers, with Habyarimana as President, was formed. All political activity was banned until July 1975, when a new ruling party, the Mouvement Révolutionnaire National pour le Développement (MRND), was formed.

A national referendum in December 1978 approved a new Constitution, which was intended to return the country to democratically elected government (in accordance with an undertaking made by Habyarimana in 1973 to end the military regime within five years). Elections to the legislature, the Conseil National de Développement (CND), took place in December 1981 and in December 1983; also in December 1983 Habyarimana was re-elected President. In December 1988 Habyarimana was again elected (unopposed) to the presidency, securing 99.98% of the votes cast. Elections to the CND were conducted in the same month.

Domestic Political Affairs

In September 1990 a Commission was appointed to compile recommendations for a draft national charter, which was to provide for the establishment of a multi-party system. In April 1991, following the CND's revision of the Commission's proposals, a draft constitution was presented to an extraordinary congress of the MRND, at which the party was renamed the Mouvement Républicain National pour la Démocratie et le Développement (MRNDD). On 10 June the reforms were promulgated by Habyarimana, and legislation regulating the formation of political parties was adopted; parties were to be non-tribal and independent, while members of the security forces and the judiciary were to be banned from political activity. (By June 1992 15 parties, among them the MRNDD and a revived MDR, had officially registered.) In October 1991 Sylvestre Nsanzimana, hitherto Minister of Justice, was appointed to the new post of Prime Minister, and in December he formed a transitional Government, in which all but two portfolios (assigned to the Parti Démocrate Centriste—PDC) were allocated to members of the MRNDD. Opposition parties, which had been excluded from participation in the transitional Government for their rejection of an MRNDD Prime Minister, organized anti-Government demonstrations in late 1991 and early 1992, demanding the removal of Nsanzimana and the convening of a national conference. A series of negotiations between the Government and the major opposition parties was initiated in February 1992, and in April a protocol agreement was signed, providing for the establishment of a new transitional administration, with Dismas Nsengiyaremye of the MDR as Prime Minister. Habyarimana announced that multi-party elections would be conducted within one year of the installation of the new Government.

Relations with neighbouring Uganda were frequently strained, owing mainly to the presence of some 250,000 Rwandan refugees in Uganda (mainly members of Rwanda's Tutsi minority), who had fled their homeland following successive outbreaks of persecution by the Hutu regime. In October 1990 rebel forces, based in Uganda, invaded northern Rwanda, occupying several towns. The 4,000-strong rebel army, known as the Front Patriotique Rwandais (FPR), which mainly comprised Rwandan Tutsi refugees, aimed to overthrow the Habyarimana regime and secure the repatriation of all Rwandan refugees. The Rwandan Government accused the Ugandan leadership of supporting the rebel forces (many of whom had served in the Ugandan armed forces), although this accusation was strenuously denied. With the assistance of French, Belgian and Zairean troops, the Rwandan army succeeded in repelling the FPR before it could reach Kigali. In late October the Government declared a cease-fire, although hostilities continued in northern Rwanda.

Negotiations held in Arusha, Tanzania, in July 1992 resulted in an agreement on the implementation of a new cease-fire, and the creation of a military observer group (GOM), sponsored by the Organization of African Unity (OAU—now the African Union—AU, see p. 191), to comprise representatives from both sides, together with officers from the armed forces of Nigeria, Senegal, Zimbabwe and Mali. However, subsequent negotiations failed to resolve outstanding problems concerning the creation of a proposed 'neutral zone' between the Rwandan armed forces and the FPR, the incorporation of the FPR in a future combined Rwandan national force, the repatriation of refugees, and FPR demands for full participation in a transitional government and legislature.

A resurgence in violence followed the breakdown of negotiations in February 1993, and France dispatched reinforcements to join a small military contingent that had been stationed in Kigali to protect French nationals. Later in February the Government accepted FPR terms for a cease-fire, in return for an end to attacks against FPR positions and Tutsi communities, and the withdrawal of foreign troops. Although fighting continued, fresh peace negotiations were convened in Arusha in March, and France subsequently began to withdraw its troops. In April the five participating parties in the ruling coalition agreed to a three-month extension of the Government's mandate, in order to facilitate the successful conclusion of a peace accord. Significant progress was made during renewed talks between the Government and the FPR during May, when a timetable for the demobilization of the 19,000-strong security forces was agreed. In June the UN Security Council approved the creation of the UN Observer Mission Uganda-Rwanda (UNOMUR), to be deployed on the Ugandan side of the border, for an initial period of six months, in order to prevent the maintenance of a military supply line for the FPR.

In July 1993 President Habyarimana met with delegates from those political parties represented in the Government to seek a further extension of the coalition's mandate. However, the Prime Minister's insistence that the FPR should be represented in any new government exacerbated existing divisions within the MDR, prompting Habyarimana to conclude the agreement with a conciliatory group of MDR dissidents, including the Minister of Education, Agathe Uwilingiyimana, who was elected to the premiership.

In August 1993 a peace accord was formally signed in Arusha by Habyarimana and Col Alex Kanyarengwe of the FPR. A new transitional government, to be headed by a mutually approved Prime Minister, would be installed, and multi-party elections would be conducted after a 22-month period. In October the UN Security Council adopted Resolution 872, providing for the establishment of the UN Assistance Mission to Rwanda (UNAMIR), to be deployed in Rwanda for an initial period of six months, with a mandate to monitor observance of the cease-fire, to contribute to the security of the capital and to facilitate the repatriation of refugees. UNAMIR, which was to incorporate UNOMUR and GOM and to comprise some 2,500 personnel, was formally inaugurated on 1 November. In December the UN expressed the opinion that conditions had been sufficiently fulfilled to allow the inauguration of the transitional institutions.

On 5 January 1994 Habyarimana was invested as President of a transitional administration, for a 22-month period, under the terms of the Arusha accord. The inauguration of the transitional government and legislature was, however, repeatedly delayed, owing to political opposition to the proposed Council of Ministers, and to the insistence of Habyarimana that the list of proposed legislative deputies, presented in March, should be modified to include representatives of additional political parties, including the reactionary Coalition pour la Défense de la République (CDR). Meanwhile, political frustration had erupted into violence in February, with the murder of the Minister of Public Works and Energy, Félicien Gatabazi of the Parti Social-démocrate (PSD), who had been a prominent supporter of the Arusha accord and of the transitional administration. Within hours the CDR leader, Martin Bucyana, was killed in a retaliatory attack by PSD supporters, and a series of violent confrontations ensued.

Collapse of civil order and genocide

On 6 April 1994 the presidential aircraft was fired on, above Kigali airport, and exploded, killing all 10 passengers, including Habyarimana. (The President of Burundi, Cyprien Ntaryamira, two Burundian cabinet ministers and the Chief of Staff of the Rwandan armed forces were among the other victims.) In Kigali the presidential guard immediately initiated a campaign of retributive violence against Habyarimana's political opponents, although it remained unclear who had been responsible for the attack on the aircraft. As politicians and civilians fled the capital, the political assassinations were compounded by attacks on the clergy, UNAMIR personnel and members of the Tutsi tribe. Many Hutu civilians were reportedly forced to murder their Tutsi neighbours, and the mobilization of the Interahamwe unofficial militias (allegedly affiliated to the MRNDD and the CDR), committed to the massacre of Tutsi civilians and opponents of the Government, was encouraged by the presidential guard (with support from some factions of the armed forces) and by inflammatory radio broadcasts. The Prime Minister, the President of the Constitutional Court and the Ministers of Labour and Social Affairs and of Information were among the prominent politicians murdered (or declared missing and presumed dead) within hours of Habyarimana's death. On 8 April the Speaker of the CND, Dr Théodore Sindikubwabo, announced that he had assumed the office of interim President of the Republic, in accordance with the provisions of the 1991 Constitution. The five remaining participating political parties and factions of the Government selected a new Prime Minister, Jean Kambanda, and a new Council of Ministers (drawn largely from the MRNDD) from among their ranks. The legality of the new administration was immediately challenged by the FPR, which claimed that the terms of the Constitution regarding succession had been superseded by the terms of the Arusha accord. The legitimacy of the Government was subsequently rejected by several political parties and factions.

In mid-April 1994 the FPR resumed operations from its northern stronghold, with the stated aim of relieving its beleaguered battalion in Kigali, restoring order there and halting the massacre of civilians. Belgium's UNAMIR contingent of more than 400 troops was also withdrawn, having encountered increasing hostility as a result of persistent rumours of Belgian complicity in the attack on President Habyarimana's aircraft, and accusations that Belgian troops were providing logistical support to the FPR.

As the violent campaign initiated by the presidential guard and the estimated 30,000 Interahamwe gathered national momentum, the militia's identification of all Tutsi as political opponents of the State provoked tribal polarization and an effective pogrom. Reports of mass Tutsi graves and of unprovoked attacks on fleeing Tutsi refugees and those sheltering in schools, hospitals and churches provoked unqualified international outrage. By May 1994 attempts to assess the full scale of the humanitarian catastrophe in Rwanda were complicated by reports that the FPR (which claimed to control more than one-half of the territory) was perpetrating retaliatory atrocities against Hutu civilians.

In view of the deteriorating security situation, in late April 1994 the UN Security Council approved a resolution to reduce UNAMIR to just 270 personnel. This was condemned by the Rwandan authorities, and in mid-May, following intense international pressure and the disclosure of the vast scale of the humanitarian crisis in the region, the Security Council approved Resolution 917, providing for the eventual deployment of some 5,500 UN troops with a revised mandate, including the protection of refugees in designated 'safe areas'. In early June the UN Security Council extended the mandate of what was designated UNAMIR II until December. However, the UN Secretary-General continued to encounter considerable difficulty in securing equipment and armaments requested by those countries that had agreed to participate.

By mid-June 1994 the emergence of confirmed reports of retributive murders committed by FPR members and the collapse of an OAU-brokered truce prompted the French Government to announce its willingness to lead an armed police action, endorsed by the UN, in Rwanda. Despite French insistence that its force (expected to total 2,000 troops) would maintain strict political neutrality, and operate in a purely humanitarian capacity pending the arrival of a multinational UN force, the FPR was vehemently opposed to its deployment, citing political bias. The UN Secretary-General welcomed the French initiative; however, the OAU expressed serious reservations as to the appropriateness of the action. In late June a first contingent of 150 French marine commandos launched 'Operation Turquoise', entering the western town of Cyangugu, in preparation for a large-scale operation to protect refugees in the area. An estimated 1m. Rwandans sought refuge in the Zairean border town of Goma, while a similar number attempted to cross the border elsewhere in the south-west. The FPR, meanwhile, swiftly secured all major cities and strategic territorial positions, but halted its advance several kilometres from the boundaries of the French-controlled neutral zone, requesting the apprehension and return for trial of those responsible for the recent atrocities. (In early July the UN announced the creation of a commission of inquiry to investigate allegations of genocide, following an initial report that as many as 500,000 Rwandans had been killed since April.)

Refugee crisis

On 19 July 1994 Pasteur Bizimungu, a Hutu, was inaugurated as President for a five-year term. On the same day the FPR announced the composition of a new Government of National Unity, with the leader of the MDR moderate faction, Faustin Twagiramungu, as Prime Minister. The majority of cabinet posts were assigned to FPR members (including the FPR military chief, Maj.-Gen. Paul Kagame, who became Minister of Defence and also assumed the newly created post of Vice-President), while the remainder were divided among the MDR, the PSD, the Parti Libéral (PL) and the PDC. The new administration urged all refugees to return to Rwanda, and issued assurances that civilian Hutus could return safely to their homes. The new Government declared its intention to honour the terms of the Arusha accord within the context of an extended period of transition. The claims to legitimacy of the exiled former administration were seriously undermined by recognition by the European Union (EU, see p. 281) of the new Government of National Unity in September.

Amid persistent rumours that the Rwandan armed forces were attempting to regroup and rearm in Zaire, in preparation for a counter-offensive against the FPR, in late August 1994 the UN initiated the deployment of some 2,500 UNAMIR II forces in the security zone (redesignated 'zone four'). French troops began to withdraw from the area (the final contingent departed in late

September), prompting hundreds of thousands of internally displaced Hutu refugees within the zone to move to Zairean border areas. The UNAMIR II mandate was extended for a further six months. (In June 1995, at the request of the Rwandan Government, the six-month mandate of the force, which was reduced from 5,586 to 2,330 personnel, was again renewed.)

In November 1994 a number of amendments to the terms of the August 1993 Arusha accord were adopted under a multi-party protocol of understanding. The most notable of the new provisions was the exclusion from the legislative process of those parties implicated in alleged acts of genocide during 1994. A 70-member Transitional National Assembly was formally inaugurated in December, with a composition including five representatives of the armed forces and one member of the national police force. On 5 May 1995 this legislature adopted a new Constitution, which was based on selected articles of the 1991 Constitution, the terms of the Arusha accord, the FPR's victory declaration of July 1994 and the November multi-party protocol. Meanwhile, in late 1994 Hutu refugees within Rwanda were continuing to resist the exhortations of the UN and the new Rwandan administration to return to their homes, following persistent allegations that the Tutsi-dominated FPR armed forces (the Armée Patriotique Rwandaise—APR) were conducting a systematic campaign of reprisal attacks against returning Hutus.

A political crisis emerged in August 1995, after the Prime Minister expressed dissatisfaction with the Government's lack of adherence to the provisions of the Arusha accord regarding power-sharing, and with the security forces' repeated recourse to violence in their management of the refugee crisis. Twagiramungu and four other disaffected ministers were subsequently replaced. Pierre Célestin Rwigyema of the MDR, also Hutu and the former Minister of Primary and Secondary Education, was named as the new Prime Minister at the end of the month. The new Council of Ministers included representatives of both major ethnic groups and four political parties.

Also in August 1995, in response to requests made by the Rwandan Government, the UN Security Council voted to suspend the arms embargo to Rwanda (imposed in May 1994) for one year, in order to allow the Government to safeguard against the threat of a military offensive by Hutu extremists encamped in neighbouring countries. Meanwhile, the security situation in refugee camps along the Zairean border had deteriorated to such an extent that the Zairean Government initiated a programme of forcible repatriation, attracting widespread international concern. Despite a formal agreement between the office of the UN High Commissioner for Refugees (UNHCR) and the Zairean Government for a more regulated approach to the refugee crisis, APR attacks near the border with Zaire further deterred refugees. At a conference of the Great Lakes countries, convened in Cairo, Egypt, in late November President Mobutu Sese Seko of Zaire indicated that the forcible return of remaining refugees in early 1996 was no longer a realistic objective. The conference also accepted the Rwandan President's assertion that the participation of UNAMIR forces in peace-keeping operations in Rwanda was no longer necessary, but urged the Rwandan Government to accept the extension of a revised, three-month mandate for the forces to provide assistance in the refugee repatriation process. (A three-month mandate for a 1,200-strong force was thus renewed in December 1995, and the mission was formally terminated in April 1996.)

Post-genocide justice

In February 1995 the UN Security Council adopted Resolution 977, whereby Arusha was designated the seat for the International Criminal Tribunal for Rwanda (ICTR), which was to investigate allegations made against some 400 individuals of direct involvement in the planning and execution of crimes against humanity perpetrated in Rwanda during 1994. The six-member Tribunal, to be headed by a Senegalese lawyer, Laïty Kama, was inaugurated in June 1995 for a four-year term.

The ICTR began formal proceedings in November 1995. The first court session of the Tribunal was convened in September 1996, but hearings concerning the first two (of 21) individuals indicted on charges of crimes against humanity were almost immediately postponed. In contrast, in January 1997 regional courts within Rwanda passed death sentences on five individuals accused of acts of genocide. (Whereas capital punishment would not be invoked by the ICTR, legislation published by the Rwandan authorities in September 1996 regarding penalties for crimes committed during 1994 made provision for the application of the death penalty.) In July 1997 former Prime Minister

Jean Kambanda, two senior armed forces officers and a former government minister were arrested in Kenya and transferred for trial to Arusha.

Some 300 genocide suspects were tried by Rwandan courts during 1997, and an estimated 125,000 defendants were in detention awaiting trial; arrests reportedly continued at a rate of 1,000 per month. In late 1997, in an attempt to address the problem of severe overcrowding in prisons, the release was authorized of elderly, infirm or juvenile detainees. (This policy was denounced by organizations representing survivors of the 1994 massacres, and there were reports of attacks on freed genocide suspects.) The announcement that 23 people convicted of acts of genocide were to be publicly executed provoked international condemnation. Amnesty International and other human rights organizations expressed serious concerns that those convicted had been denied adequate opportunity to prepare a defence. The Rwandan authorities refuted such claims, and dismissed pleas for clemency. The public executions proceeded in April 1998.

Meanwhile, in August 1996, during a visit to Kigali by the Zairean Prime Minister, a bilateral agreement for the organized and unconditional repatriation of all Rwandan refugees in Zaire was concluded (without the participation of UNHCR officials). During September, however, relations between the two countries were placed under renewed strain, when the attempts of the Interahamwe and the Zairean armed forces to displace large numbers of Zairean Banyamulenge (ethnic Tutsis) from eastern Zaire encountered large-scale armed resistance from the Banyamulenge, resulting in Zairean accusations of Rwandan support for the Banyamulenge, and culminating in a cross-border exchange of fire later that month.

There was renewed international concern for the estimated 1m. refugees previously encamped in eastern Zaire, following widespread conflict in the country. The rebel army in Zaire (the Alliance des Forces Démocratiques pour la Libération du Congo-Zaïre—AFDL) declared a cease-fire for returning refugees and announced the creation of a humanitarian corridor to the Rwandan border. The large-scale return of refugees was finally prompted by an AFDL attack on Interahamwe units operating from the camp. By May 1997 the AFDL had gained control of most of Zaire, which was renamed the Democratic Republic of the Congo (DRC), and the movement's leader, Laurent-Désiré Kabila, assumed power as head of state. Continuing ethnic unrest and violence, particularly in north-western Rwanda, throughout the year were exacerbated by the return from the DRC of large numbers of Hutus. An extensive demobilization programme was undertaken from September, with the aim of reintegrating former combatants into civil society.

The trial of genocide suspects continued in 1998, both in Rwanda and at the ICTR, and in early September the ICTR reached its first verdict. A former mayor of Taba, Jean-Paul Akayesu, was convicted and sentenced to life imprisonment; Kambanda, who had pleaded guilty to six charges of genocide and crimes against humanity, was also given a life sentence. Rwandan courts convicted and sentenced some 1,000 genocide suspects during 1998 (the authorities had aimed to hear 5,000 cases during the year). By June about 5,000 suspects in Rwandan prisons had pleaded guilty to acts of genocide in order to lessen their sentences, apparently in response to the public executions in April. In October some controversy was caused by the decision to release at least 10,000 genocide suspects owing to lack of evidence against them. It was announced in November that 34,000 suspects had been freed since 1994.

In June 1998 the Transitional National Assembly approved draft legislation establishing a commission that was to prepare a new constitution and the period of political transition, originally set at five years in 1994, was extended by a further four years. Legislation establishing a national police force (which was to unify the existing national gendarmerie, and the communal and judicial police) was adopted in August 1998.

During 1999 a number of prominent Hutu, including three former government ministers, were arrested on suspicion of involvement in the 1994 genocide and extradited to the ICTR. In May 1999 a former Rwandan mayor (the first Rwandan to be tried abroad for genocide) was convicted by a Swiss court on charges of inciting the killing of Tutsi civilians, and sentenced to life imprisonment. In June Navanethem Pillay succeeded Kama as President of the ICTR, and in September Carla del Ponte became UN Chief Prosecutor.

Kagame appointed President

In February 2000 the National Assembly voted in favour of investigating alleged abuses of power by Rwigyema. On 28 February he resigned from the office of Prime Minister, citing differences with the legislature. Bernard Makuza, hitherto the Rwandan ambassador in Germany, was appointed Prime Minister in March, and subsequently announced a government reorganization, in which six ministers were replaced. The new Government was the first since 1994 in which the parties were not represented in accordance with the 1993 Arusha peace accords. At its inauguration, Kagame (who remained Vice-President and Minister of Defence and National Security) failed to swear allegiance to the President. On 23 March 2000 Bizimungu resigned from office, owing to disagreement over the composition of the new Government, and Kagame was subsequently appointed interim President by the Supreme Court. On 17 April he was formally elected President of Rwanda by members of the Transitional National Assembly and the Government, securing 81 of 86 votes cast. He was inaugurated on 22 April (becoming the first Tutsi head of state since 1959).

In July 2000 Rwigyema was removed from the leadership of the MDR by the party's political bureau, which accused him of acting contrary to its interests. In April 2001 an international warrant was issued for the arrest of Rwigyema, who had taken refuge in the USA, on suspicion of participating in the genocide of 1994. In December 2001 a new national flag, emblem and anthem officially replaced those adopted at independence in 1962.

In late 2001, when the number of prisoners awaiting trial had increased to some 115,000, it was announced that those suspected of lesser crimes relating to the genocide were to be tried in Rwanda by a community court system known as *gacaca* ('on the grass'). In April 2002 the trial of Col Theoneste Bagosora, who was considered to be the principal organizer of the genocide, commenced at the ICTR. Bagosora, who had been in custody since his arrest in Cameroon in 1996, had allegedly planned the massacre of Tutsi civilians by the militia and had personally ordered the assassination of prominent politicians. Later in April 2002 security forces arrested former President Bizimungu (who had attempted to form an opposition political party in May 2001), and searched his residence. The authorities subsequently announced that Bizimungu had continued to engage in illegal political activity, and would be charged with endangering state security. In August 2002 Gen. Augustin Bizimungu, the army Chief of Staff in 1994, who had been indicted by the ICTR jointly with four other former military commanders, was arrested in Angola and transferred to the Tribunal. Later that month he pleaded not guilty to 10 charges, including that of genocide. In November 2002 trials by the *gacaca* court system officially commenced in large parts of the country.

In January 2003, in an effort to reduce numbers in prisons, Kagame issued a decree providing for the provisional release of some 40,000 of those held in detention, including many who had pleaded guilty to charges related to the 1994 genocide. Although the Ministry of Justice maintained that legal proceedings against the released prisoners would continue, organizations representing survivors of the genocide criticized the measure. Most of the prisoners due for release were to be dispatched to 'solidarity camps', where they were to be prepared for reintegration into society. (By the end of 2003 some 25,000 suspects had been released.)

A new Constitution, providing for the establishment of a bicameral legislature (comprising an 80-member Chamber of Deputies and a 26-member Senate) and a President, who was to be elected by universal suffrage, was approved by 93.4% of the electorate at a national referendum, which took place on 26 May 2003. The new Constitution entered into effect on 4 June; under its provisions, political associations formed on the basis of ethnicity, tribal or regional affiliation, religion or any other grounds for discrimination were prohibited. (Some existing political organizations were restructured to end such affiliations.) The presidential election was subsequently scheduled for 25 August, and was to be followed by legislative elections in late September. Kagame announced his intention to seek re-election, while former Prime Minister Twagiramungu returned to Rwanda from exile in Belgium in order to contest the presidency.

Kagame's second term

The first presidential election to take place in Rwanda since the single candidate poll of 1988 was conducted on 25 August 2003 (thereby marking the end of the nine-year transitional period).

Kagame was returned to power, with 95.1% of votes cast, while Twagiramungu won 3.6%, and Jean-Népomuscène Nayinzira 1.3% of the votes. Kagame was officially inaugurated on 12 September. Four political parties subsequently agreed to contest the forthcoming legislative elections in alliance with the FPR. Following the dissolution of the MDR, many of its former members joined the newly emerged Parti du Progrès et de la Concorde. In addition to the FPR-led coalition, the PSD, the PL and a number of independent candidates registered to contest the legislative elections. Elections to the Chamber of Deputies commenced on 29 September, with voting for seats allocated to one disabled and two youth representatives. The poll for the 53 seats contested by political parties and independent candidates followed on 30 September; the FPR-led coalition, with 73.8% of votes cast, secured 40 seats, while the PSD (12.3% of votes) won seven seats, and the PL (10.6%) six seats. The remaining 24 female representatives were selected at provincial level on 2 October. Kagame formed a new Council of Ministers on 19 October; Makuza was reappointed to the office of Prime Minister and most principal ministers retained their portfolios. Twagiramungu left the country in early November, after claiming that he faced detention owing to his opposition to Kagame's Government.

In September 2003 a Gambian judge, Hassan Bubacar Jallow, was appointed Chief Prosecutor of the ICTR, replacing del Ponte. In December the owners of Radio Télévision Libre des Mille Collines and the Hutu extremist newspaper *Kangura* were sentenced to life imprisonment at the ICTR, on charges relating to public incitement to commit genocide. In February 2004 the Rwandan authorities urged those prisoners awaiting trial in connection with the genocide to qualify for a general amnesty by confessing to the charges against them. Meanwhile, at the ongoing trial of Bagosora at the ICTR, the testimony of a principal witness, a former Canadian UN commander, Gen. (retd) Romeo Dallaire, implicated French forces in failing to prevent the genocide.

In June 2004 former President Bizimungu (who had remained in detention since April 2002) was sentenced to a term of 15 years' imprisonment, after being convicted of corruption, inciting civil disobedience and criminal association; he was, however, acquitted of the principal charge of endangering state security through anti-Government activities. In July 2004 the Minister of Finance of the 1994 Government, Emmanuel Ndindabahizi, who had been arrested in Belgium in July 2001, received a sentence of life imprisonment at the ICTR on charges of genocide and crimes against humanity for his participation in the massacre of Tutsi refugees during that period. Proceedings for some of the large number of cases to be transferred from the ICTR to the *gacaca* courts commenced in early 2005. In March the serving Minister of Defence, Gen. Marcel Gatsinzi, appeared before a *gacaca* court, where he pleaded not guilty to charges of failing to prevent troops under his command from perpetrating massacres in Butare.

In October 2005 both legislative chambers approved a number of constitutional amendments, which principally provided for the reorganization of local government structures (reducing the number of provinces, formerly prefectures, from 12 to five) to allow greater decentralization; the territorial reforms entered into effect at the beginning of 2006. In February the Supreme Court upheld the 15-year sentence imposed on Bizimungu. (In April 2007, however, Bizimungu received a presidential pardon and was released from prison.) In July 2006 the second stage of the *gacaca* system began. While those charged with crimes related to the genocide were in prison in Rwanda, many of those suspected of issuing the orders had fled and were living in exile. However, an announcement was made in October that France, Belgium and the Netherlands had agreed to seek those who had taken up residence in those countries and bring them to trial. Frustrated at the slow progress being made by the ICTR—since 1997 only 29 of those responsible for the genocide had been convicted—the Rwandan Government demanded that suspects be transferred to face trial in Rwanda. Since the extradition of suspects to a country that maintained the death penalty was not permitted, in July 2007 legislation to abolish this was officially promulgated; it was reported that those who had been sentenced to death would instead be subjected to terms of life imprisonment. Proceedings began in August to seek extradition orders.

Nevertheless, there were continuing concerns that trials at the ICTR would not be completed before its envisaged closure (first instance trials were scheduled to be completed by December 2008), and that too few of the suspected key perpetrators of the genocide had been prosecuted. In May 2008 the USA announced that it was to re-establish a programme offering large financial rewards for information leading to the arrest of 13 genocide suspects still at large before the ICTR ceased operations, while in June legislation was approved granting *gacaca* courts the jurisdiction to try up to 90% of those suspects who would otherwise be required to be brought before the ICTR. In December the ICTR concluded the trial of several high-profile suspects: Bagosora, together with two other senior Rwandan army officers, was sentenced to life imprisonment for genocide, war crimes and crimes against humanity; and a former governor of Ruhengeri prefecture, Protais Zigiranyirazo, was sentenced to 20 years in prison on charges of genocide. (In December 2011 Bagosora's sentence was reduced on appeal to 35 years.) In July 2009, when the ICTR had concluded only 44 cases, the mandate of the tribunal was extended by the UN Security Council until December 2010. (This was subsequently further extended until December 2012.) In October 2009 former Hutu rebel leader Salfe Bizimungu Mahoro was convicted of genocide and related charges, and sentenced to life imprisonment; several more suspects were found and detained in France, Germany, Italy and Uganda. In November the ICTR overturned Zigiranyirazo's conviction and acquitted him of all charges, on the grounds that several inconsistencies in the trial and sentencing procedures had emerged. The Rwandan Government condemned the decision.

The 2008 legislative elections

On 15 September 2008 the FPR secured a resounding victory with 78.8% of the votes cast, winning 42 of the 53 directly elected seats; the PSD took seven seats and the PL four. Turn-out for the elections was estimated at over 98%. The following month Rose Mukantantabana was nominated as Speaker of the Chamber of Deputies, becoming the first ever woman to hold that position.

It was announced in September 2009 that a presidential election would be held in August 2010. President Kagame, who confirmed his intention to seek re-election to the presidency, was criticized by the opposition for making it difficult for parties to register their candidates. The Parti Socialiste Rwandais and the FPR both subsequently announced that they would not be presenting candidates in the election. President Kagame effected a cabinet reorganization in December 2009, appointing John Rwangombwa to replace James Musoni as Minister of Finance and Economic Planning; Louise Mushikiwabo replaced Rosemary Museminari as Minister of Foreign Affairs.

In January 2010 the findings of a two-year investigation into the assassination of President Habyarimana, which was carried out by the Rwandan Committee of Independent Experts under the chairmanship of Jean Mutsinzi, a Rwandan judge and the President of the African Court on Human and Peoples' Rights, were made public. The conclusions revealed little new information, but maintained that Hutu extremists led by Bagosora, who were opposed to Habyarimana's intention to implement the Arusha accord, were responsible for the attack and that the missiles that brought down the aircraft had been launched from the Kanombe military camp where members of the presidential guard were based. It was also stated that there appeared to be widespread knowledge that an assassination attempt on Habyarimana was imminent, and that there had been significant French involvement in the incident. (In January 2012 a French report appeared to corroborate these findings.)

As part of a major reorganization of senior defence staff, implemented by President Kagame in April 2010, Gen. Marcel Gatsinzi, was replaced as Minister of Defence by the hitherto Chief of Defence Staff, Gen. James Kabarebe, and was appointed Minister of Disaster Preparedness and Refugee Affairs. Days later the former Chief of Staff of the Air Force and another senior general were suspended from office and arrested following allegations of corruption and misuse of office, and immoral conduct, respectively. There were reports in the Rwandan press that the arrests were connected to a series of bomb attacks in Kigali in February and March in which over 30 people were injured and at least one person was killed.

The 2010 presidential election

The campaign period prior to the presidential election was marred by further grenade attacks, attributed to the Interahamwe, in Kigali and increased FPR measures against opposition politicians, journalists and dissident military officials. In April 2010 Victoire Ingabire, the leader of the Forces Démocratiques Unifiées—Inkingi party and Kagame's main prospective presidential opponent, was arrested and imprisoned on charges of genocide denial and of collaborating with Hutu rebels in the

DRC. In May her US lawyer, Peter Erlinder, was also arrested in Rwanda on charges of genocide denial (shortly after the US Administration had expressed concerns over the human rights situation in the country prior to the presidential election). Violent incidents included the murders of the editor of suspended publication *Umuvugizi*, Jean-Léonard Rugambage (who had claimed to have knowledge of government responsibility for the shooting of a former army chief of staff in South Africa), in June and of André Kagwa Rwisereka, Vice-President of the opposition Parti Démocratique Vert, in July; the FPR was widely suspected of involvement in the killings. The presidential election was conducted on 9 August: according to official results released by the National Electoral Commission, Kagame secured an overwhelming victory, winning 93.1% of the votes cast. The second-placed candidate, Dr Jean Damascene Ntawukuriryayo of the PSD, took only 5.2% of the votes. Some 97.5% of the registered electorate participated in the poll. Although the European Commission welcomed the successful organization of the election, the UN Security Council expressed concern at the incidents in the preceding period. A final report by the Commonwealth Observer Group concluded that the poll had proceeded peacefully, but cited a lack of transparency of the results consolidation, an absence of critical opposition and problems faced by some media outlets. On 6 September Kagame was inaugurated for a second seven-year term. His Government was reappointed unchanged on 14 September.

At the beginning of October 2010 the UN released a report listing the violations of human rights and international humanitarian law committed in the DRC in 1993–2003, which had been significantly modified after a leaked draft of the text prompted the Rwandan Government to threaten to withdraw its peacekeeping troops from all UN missions upon its publication. Nevertheless, the Government denounced the report, which implicated the Rwandan armed forces in massacres of Hutu refugees. Later in October Ingabire was again arrested, and charged with forming a terrorist organization; Human Rights Watch expressed concern at her detention and the hospitalization of another opposition leader, Bernard Ntaganda, who had staged a hunger strike after his arrest in June. (The trial of Ingabire, on six charges, including complicity in terrorist activities, began at the High Court in Kigali in August 2011.) In January 2011 the High Military Court sentenced two former senior army officers to 24 years' imprisonment *in absentia* and a further two former officials in Kagame's administration to 20 years *in absentia* for threatening state security, after they issued a document in September 2010 denouncing Kagame's Government as authoritarian, corrupt and repressive. Meanwhile, in December 2010 the UN Security Council established the International Residual Mechanism for Criminal Tribunals (IRMCT), which was to begin operations in July 2012 as part of the closure strategy for the ICTR.

President Kagame effected a reorganization of the Council of Ministers in May 2011; notable changes included the mergers of the Ministry of Environment and Lands with that of Forestry and Mines, and of the Ministry of Youth with that of Sports and Culture. Later in May former army Chief of Staff Augustin Bizimungu was sentenced to 30 years' imprisonment by the ICTR for genocide and crimes against humanity. The former head of the paramilitary police, Augustin Ndindiliyimana, was also convicted, but was released after having already served 11 years in prison. In June Pauline Nyiramasuhuko, a former Minister of Family and Women's Affairs of the 1994 Government, was sentenced by the ICTR to life imprisonment for conspiracy to commit genocide and crimes against humanity; her son and a former mayor also received life sentences, and a further four senior officials were given lengthy terms, on similar charges. In July a Hutu who had received asylum in the Netherlands in 1998 was sentenced to life imprisonment, in the first conviction imposed by a Dutch court on a Rwandan, for leading an attack against Tutsi families sheltering in a church compound in Muganero, Kibuye prefecture, in 1994. In September 2011 two former ministers of the 1994 Government, Justin Mugenzi and Prosper Mugiraneza, were each sentenced by the ICTR to 30 years' imprisonment (while a further two were acquitted) on charges of conspiracy to commit genocide, and public incitement to commit genocide. Also in September 2011 Jallow's mandate as Chief Prosecutor of the ICTR was extended until 31 December 2014. In December 2011 a former Chairman and Deputy Chairman of the MRNDD were sentenced to life imprisonment for crimes against humanity and war crimes.

On 7 October 2011 Kagame appointed Pierre Damien Habumuremyi, hitherto Minister of Education, as Prime Minister, after Makuza was nominated to the Senate. A new Government, in which the majority of ministers from the previous administration were retained, was subsequently established. In January 2012 two people were killed and 18 injured in a grenade attack in Kigali, which was attributed by the authorities to a Hutu rebel group based in the DRC, the Forces Démocratiques de Libération du Rwanda (FDLR). Later in January four senior officers in the armed forces, including the head of military intelligence, were arrested on charges of involvement in illegal business dealings in the DRC.

Recent developments: closure of the *gacaca* system
The Rwandan Government officially closed the *gacaca* courts on 18 June 2012, after nearly 2m. people had been tried under the system. The trial of Ingabire (who boycotted proceedings, accusing the presiding judge of bias) had been concluded in April, with the prosecution demanding a life sentence. On 1 July the IRMCT, which was to assume the remaining responsibilities of the ICTR by the end of 2014, duly commenced operations in Arusha. At the end of October 2012 the High Court sentenced Ingabire to eight years' imprisonment, having convicted her of conspiring to overthrow the Government through terrorist activities and of denying the 1994 genocide; she was acquitted of four other charges. Human Rights Watch condemned the trial as biased and politically motivated. On 20 December 2012 Augustin Ngirabatware, the Minister of Planning and Co-operation at the time of the 1994 genocide, was convicted by the ICTR of genocide, incitement to commit genocide, and of crimes against humanity, and sentenced to 35 years' imprisonment; the Tribunal (which had processed a total of 75 cases, with 12 acquittals) was henceforth only to hear appeals. In February 2013 the Appeals Chamber of the ICTR overturned the convictions of Mugenzi and Mugiraneza and ordered their release, prompting public protests.

Foreign Affairs
Regional relations
In July 1998 Laurent-Désiré Kabila (the President of the DRC since 31 May 1997) announced that military co-operation with both Rwanda and Uganda was to end, and demanded that all foreign forces leave the DRC. Kabila claimed that a rebellion, which commenced in the east of the DRC in August, constituted a Rwandan invasion; the Rwandan Government denied any involvement, but in late 1998 conceded that Rwandan troops were present in the DRC to provide logistical support to the rebel-led action. The Rwandan Government participated in a series of regional peace negotiations, at which Kabila refused to negotiate directly with the rebels. Rwanda later denied reports that it was maintaining a joint military command with Uganda in the DRC.

Rwandan action in the DRC continued in 1999, although Rwanda's alliance with Uganda became increasingly unstable during that year. At the end of April Uganda temporarily recalled its ambassador to Rwanda, following an incident in the DRC, in which Rwandan troops killed a number of members of the Ugandan armed forces. A split within the rebel movement in the DRC, the Rassemblement Congolais pour la Démocratie (RCD), resulted in the creation of two factions, one supported by Rwanda and one by Uganda. Following further clashes in the DRC between Rwandan and Ugandan troops in Kisangani in August, both armies agreed to leave the city. In June the DRC instituted proceedings against Burundi, Rwanda and Uganda at the International Court of Justice (ICJ) in The Hague, Netherlands, accusing these countries of acts of armed aggression. (In February 2001, however, the DRC abandoned proceedings against Burundi and Rwanda.)

In May 2000 Rwandan and Ugandan forces again clashed in the town of Kisangani (despite a cease-fire agreement, which had been reached by all forces involved in the conflict in April). After meeting a UN Security Council delegation, the Rwandan and Ugandan contingents agreed to the demilitarization of the town, and its transfer to the control of the UN Mission in the Democratic Republic of the Congo (MONUC, see p. 94) deployed in the country. Despite further fighting, it was confirmed at the end of June that all Rwandan and Ugandan forces had withdrawn from Kisangani. In December, however, the principal RCD faction, supported by Rwandan troops, succeeded in gaining control of the south-eastern town of Pweto. The Rwandan Government denied any involvement in the assassination of Kabila in January 2001. In February Kagame met the new DRC President,

Joseph Kabila (the son of Laurent-Désiré), in Washington, DC, USA, to discuss the ongoing conflict. Later that month the groups involved in the conflict, under the aegis of the UN Security Council, agreed to a disengagement of their forces by mid-March, followed by a complete withdrawal of foreign troops from the DRC by mid-May. Although some military disengagement of forces took place accordingly in March, factions subsequently refused to continue until MONUC guaranteed security in the region. In April the Governments of Burundi, Rwanda and Uganda rejected the claims of a UN report that the forces of these countries had exploited the natural resources of the DRC. In June it was reported that Interahamwe militia, led by former members of the Rwandan army, had intensified incursions into north-western Rwanda from the DRC. Despite continued pressure from the UN Security Council, in August Kagame insisted that Kabila fulfil pledges to demobilize the Interahamwe (who were supporting DRC government forces), as a precondition to the withdrawal of Rwandan forces from the DRC.

At the end of July 2002, after further discussions mediated by the South African Government, a peace agreement was signed by Kabila and Kagame in Pretoria, South Africa. Under the accord, Kabila pledged to arrest and disarm the Interahamwe militia in the DRC, while the Rwandan Government agreed to withdraw all troops from the country. In October it was announced that all 23,400 Rwandan troops had been withdrawn from the DRC. In September 2003 the Governments of Rwanda and the DRC agreed to re-establish diplomatic links, and the improvement in bilateral relations was further demonstrated by the visit to Rwanda of the DRC Minister of Foreign Affairs in October. In May 2009 the two countries exchanged ambassadors. In August Kabila met Kagame for the first bilateral negotiations in 13 years, and the two leaders pledged to increase economic and security co-operation.

In November 2001 Kagame and the Ugandan head of state, Lt-Gen. Yoweri Kaguta Museveni, met in London, United Kingdom, in an effort to resolve the increasing tension between the two nations, following the repeated clashes in the DRC. The Ugandan Government had accused Rwanda of supporting dissidents who intended to overthrow Museveni's administration, while Kagame claimed that Ugandan troops were amassing on the joint border between the two countries. In February 2002 further discussions between Kagame and Museveni, with mediation by the British Secretary of State for International Development, were conducted in Uganda. It was agreed that both Governments would urge the dissidents based in their respective countries to take refuge elsewhere, and the adoption of a mutual extradition treaty was envisaged. In July 2003 the Rwandan Government signed a tripartite agreement with the Ugandan authorities and UNHCR, providing for the voluntary repatriation of some 26,000 Rwandans resident in refugee camps in western Uganda. (Similar accords were signed between Rwanda and the Governments of Malawi, Togo, Zambia and Tanzania.) In February 2004 an improvement in diplomatic relations between Rwanda and Uganda was demonstrated by a bilateral agreement to strengthen co-operation in several fields.

In October 2008 the DRC accused Rwanda of military incursions into Nord-Kivu to support Laurent Nkunda's Tutsi rebels; UN peace-keepers intervened to investigate the claims and relations between Rwanda and the DRC deteriorated. However, an unexpected accord was concluded between Presidents Kagame and Kabila in January 2009, and on 22 January Rwandan forces detained Nkunda as he attempted to cross the border into Rwandan territory. Nkunda subsequently remained under house arrest in Rwanda (without being formally charged).

In June 2012 a report by a UN Group of Experts on the DRC stated that senior Rwandan military officials had financed and supported a mutiny in eastern DRC undertaken by a militia group known as M23, led by Bosco Ntaganda. President Kagame strongly denied the allegations; however, in October a further UN report, which was leaked to the media, concluded that M23 had received direct military orders from the Rwandan Chief of Defence Staff (who was responsible to the Minister of Defence). On 24 February 2013 Kagame and 10 other regional heads of state signed a UN-mediated Peace and Security Co-operation Framework for the DRC in Addis Ababa, Ethiopia, pledging not to support rebel operations in the DRC. Following the emergence of divisions within M23, in March Ntaganda unexpectedly surrendered at the US embassy in Kigali, and requested to be transferred to the International Criminal Court (ICC) in The Hague. Kagame subsequently issued assurances that he would expedite Ntaganda's transferral to the ICC.

Other external relations

Since 1994 the role of the international community in failing to avert the genocide has come under frequent scrutiny. In late 1997 the report of a Belgian Senate investigation concluded that the international community, and more specifically the UN and the Belgian authorities, was directly or indirectly responsible for certain aspects of the developments arising from the political violence from April 1994. In December 1998 a French parliamentary committee presented its report on French involvement in events prior to and at the time of the genocide. (Despite evidence to the contrary, the French authorities have persistently denied allegations that France continued to supply military equipment and support to Rwanda after the imposition of the UN arms embargo in May 1994.) The report cleared France of any direct complicity in the genocide, although it conceded that 'Operation Turquoise' both delayed the accession to power of the FPR, and facilitated the escape of Hutu extremist forces into the DRC. The report attributed responsibility for the genocide to the international community as a whole, particularly to the USA (which had failed to support UN peace-keeping operations in Rwanda).

In December 1999 a three-member commission of inquiry established by the UN Security Council presented its report after a six-month investigation. The report criticized the UN for failing in its mission to prevent the genocide and for ignoring the warnings of the head of the peace-keeping mission. It also cited the UN Security Council's failure to deploy sufficient peace-keepers at the end of 1993. Following the report, UN Secretary-General Kofi Annan issued a personal apology for UN inaction at the time. In March a Canadian newspaper published a UN memorandum, stating that the FPR was responsible for the attack on the aircraft on 6 April 1994, which killed President Juvénal Habyarimana, and that Kagame had been in overall command of the force that carried out the attack. Kagame subsequently dismissed the allegations, claiming that the report was part of a UN attempt to absolve itself of blame for the genocide of 1994.

In August 2001 the French Minister of Foreign Affairs made an official visit to Rwanda (the first by a senior French official since 1994), in an effort to normalize bilateral relations. (Diplomatic links were restored in 2002.) In March 2002 the French Government (which, within the UN Security Council, had placed increasing pressure on Rwanda to withdraw forces from the DRC) protested that Rwandan troops had launched a major offensive in the east of the DRC. In March 2004 the results of an official French investigation into the destruction of President Habyarimana's aircraft alleged that Kagame, as leader of the FPR, had ordered the missile attack. Kagame again denied any responsibility, and claimed that French forces had, by training and arming the Hutu militia, supported the mass killings. In early April the French Secretary of State for Foreign Affairs curtailed his visit to Rwanda, after Kagame repeated these accusations at an official ceremony in Kigali commemorating the 10th anniversary of the genocide. On the following anniversary in April 2005 the Rwandan Government reiterated demands that the UN instigate legal proceedings against French officials for complicity in the genocide. In December a French military tribunal began to investigate claims by survivors of the genocide that French forces had facilitated attacks against Tutsi in 1994 (by failing to prevent massacres and then by allowing the perpetrators of the genocide to evade capture).

In November 2006 Rwanda severed diplomatic relations with France, recalling the ambassador to that country and closing the French embassy. The move followed the order by the French judiciary to issue international arrest warrants against President Kagame and nine high-ranking Rwandan officials. In September 2007, for the first time since the severance of diplomatic ties, a delegation of French officials visited Kigali, with the aim of making progress towards the restoration of normal relations. Despite the abolition of the death penalty in Rwanda in July 2007, the French Government had refused to extradite genocide suspects; however, in November a French court approved the extradition of one of the suspects resident in France. In January 2008 French Minister of Foreign and European Affairs Bernard Kouchner met briefly with President Kagame to resume dialogue with Rwanda, and in a press conference Kouchner admitted that France had made a political mistake in its response to the 1994 genocide, although he denied any military responsibility. However, in August 2008 a Rwandan commission of inquiry issued a report accusing high-ranking French officials of involvement in the genocide; among them

former President François Mitterrand and former Prime Minister Dominique de Villepin. Rwanda demanded that the French officials named be brought to trial and submitted the findings of the report as the basis for issuing arrest warrants. France denied all accusations made by Rwanda but reiterated its commitment to rebuilding a relationship with the African country. In November Rose Kabuye, a senior presidential aide and former guerrilla fighter with the now ruling FPR, was detained in Frankfurt, Germany, and extradited to France on charges of involvement in the attack on President Habyarimana's aircraft. Kabuye denied the accusations against her and was subsequently released from custody under a supervision order. Relations between Rwanda and Germany were severed as a result of the arrest, but were restored in January 2009.

In November 2009 it was announced that, following extensive consultations and negotiations between the two countries, Rwanda and France were to restore diplomatic relations. In January 2010 a new French ambassador to Rwanda was appointed. Rwanda officially reopened its embassy in Paris in February, immediately prior to the visit of President Nicolas Sarkozy to Kigali, during which he admitted that France had made a number of 'serious errors of judgement' (although again no admission of responsibility was forthcoming) in the period following the assassination of President Habyarimana, and pledged to bring any person suspected of involvement in the genocide resident in France to justice. The decision taken in the previous month by the French authorities to create a special investigative unit as part of the Tribunal de Grande Instance in Paris to expedite the prosecution of genocide crimes was welcomed by the Rwandan Government. In September 2010 a trial against the Belgian state and three Belgian army officers formerly belonging to UNAMIR, who were accused of failing to protect refugees during the 1994 genocide, began in the Belgian capital, Brussels, following a case brought by two survivors of a massacre of more than 2,000 Tutsis in April 1994. In a demonstration of reconciliation, in September 2011 Kagame made his first visit to France since 1994. In January 2012 a report by French judges exonerated Kagame of responsibility for the assassination of President Habyarimana in April 1994, after an investigative mission to Rwanda concluded that his forces were unlikely to have fired the missile that destroyed the presidential aircraft.

Following the release of a UN report accusing Rwanda of direct involvement with a militia group in the DRC, from July 2012 the United Kingdom, Germany and other EU member states withheld funding to Rwanda, while the USA announced a suspension of military aid. The British Government released a payment of £16m. in September, but again suspended assistance in November. However, on 18 October Rwanda was elected unopposed to a non-permanent seat on the UN Security Council (effective from 1 January 2013). In December 2012 15 campaign groups and associations sent an open letter to US President Barack Obama, urging the imposition of sanctions against Rwanda owing to its alleged involvement in rebel activities in the DRC. In February 2013 Germany announced the resumption of aid to Rwanda.

CONSTITUTION AND GOVERNMENT

Under the terms of the Constitution, which entered into force on 4 June 2003, executive power is exercised by the President (head of state), assisted by an appointed Council of Ministers. The President is elected by universal suffrage for a seven-year term, and is restricted to two mandates. Legislative power is vested in a bicameral Parliament, comprising a Chamber of Deputies and a Senate. The Chamber of Deputies has 80 deputies, who are elected for a five-year term. In addition to 53 directly elected deputies, 27 seats are allocated, respectively, to two youth representatives, one disabilities representative, and 24 female representatives, who are indirectly elected. The Senate comprises 26 members, of whom 12 are elected by local government councils in the 12 provinces, and two by academic institutions, while the remaining 12 are nominated (eight by the President and four by a regulatory body, the Parties' Forum). Members of the Senate serve for eight years.

Following territorial reforms, which entered into effect at the beginning of 2006, the country is divided into five provinces and subdivided into 30 districts, each administered by an elected mayor.

REGIONAL AND INTERNATIONAL CO-OPERATION

Rwanda is a member of the African Union (AU, see p. 191), and, with Burundi and the DRC, is a founding member of the

Economic Community of the Great Lakes Countries (see p. 461) and of the Common Market for Eastern and Southern Africa (see p. 241). Rwanda joined the East African Community (EAC, see p. 460) in 2007 and was admitted to the Commonwealth in 2009.

Rwanda became a member of the UN in 1962 and was admitted to the World Trade Organization (WTO, see p. 444) in 1996. Rwanda participates in the Group of 77 (G77, see p. 461) developing countries. Rwanda is also a member of the International Coffee Organization (see p. 456).

ECONOMIC AFFAIRS

In 2011, according to estimates by the World Bank, Rwanda's gross national income (GNI), measured at average 2009–11 prices, was US $6,223m., equivalent to $570 per head (or $1,240 per head on an international purchasing-power parity basis). During 2002–11, it was estimated, the population increased at an average annual rate of 2.6%, while gross domestic product (GDP) per head rose, in real terms, by an average of 4.5% per year. According to official figures, overall GDP increased, in real terms, at an average annual rate of 8.2% in 2005–11; growth of 8.2% was recorded in 2011.

Agriculture (including forestry and fishing) contributed 34.0% of GDP in 2011 according to official figures. According to FAO, 88.8% of the employed labour force were estimated to be engaged in the sector (mainly at subsistence level) at mid-2013. The principal food crops are plantains, sweet potatoes, cassava, dry beans and sorghum. The principal cash crops are coffee (which contributed 24.6% of total export earnings in 2010) and tea (14.5%). Pyrethrum and quinquina are also cultivated for export. Goats and cattle are traditionally the principal livestock raised. According to official figures, agricultural GDP increased by an average of 4.9% per year during 2005–11; sectoral GDP grew by 4.7% in 2011.

Industry (including mining, manufacturing, power and construction) accounted for 17.4% of GDP in 2011, and the industrial sector engaged 2.9% of the employed labour force in 2002. According to official figures, industrial GDP increased at an average annual rate of 10.2% during 2005–11; the GDP of the industrial sector grew by 8.6% in 2010 and by 16.8% in 2011.

Mining and quarrying contributed 1.3% of GDP in 2011. Cassiterite (a tin-bearing ore) is Rwanda's principal mineral resource. Exports of tin ores and concentrates contributed 28.1% of the value of total merchandise exports in 2010. There are also reserves of wolframite (a tungsten-bearing ore), columbo-tantalite, gold and beryl, and work is under way to exploit natural methane gas reserves, estimated to total at least 55,000m. cu m, beneath Lake Kivu. Mining GDP increased at an estimated average annual rate of 1.2% in 2005–11, according to official figures. Mining GDP decreased by 9.1% in 2010, but increased by a massive 40.0% in 2011.

Manufacturing accounted for 7.0% of GDP in 2011, while production activities engaged 1.3% of the employed labour force in 2002. The principal branches of manufacturing are beverages and tobacco, food products and basic consumer goods, including soap, textiles and plastic products. According to official figures, manufacturing GDP increased by an average of 6.6% per year during 2005–11; the GDP of the sector grew by 7.9% in 2011.

The construction sector contributed 8.8% of GDP in 2011, and engaged 1.3% of the employed labour force in 2002. According to official figures, the GDP of the construction sector increased at an average annual rate of 14.6% during 2005–11; growth in the construction sector was 8.9% in 2010 and 23.4% in 2011.

Output of electricity is insufficient to meet domestic needs, and the rate of connection is low. In 1999 Rwanda imported 35.5% of its electricity, but subsequently benefited from the completion of the Ruzizi-II plant (a joint venture with Burundi and the Democratic Republic of the Congo—DRC). In March 2009 the Government of Rwanda signed an agreement with a US-based company for the development of an integrated extraction and generation facility to supply methane gas-fired electricity from the Lake Kivu resource to Rwanda and the East Africa region. (Rwanda's first pilot methane gas plant was inaugurated in late 2008, and subsequently began supplying the national grid.) Projects such as the Nyabarongo hydroelectric dam, construction of which was due for completion in 2014, and other planned 'micro-dams', are expected to reduce Rwanda's reliance on thermal energy sources. Imports of fuels and lubricants comprised 4.2% of the total value of merchandise imports in 2010.

The services sector contributed 48.6% of GDP in 2011, and engaged 6.5% of the employed labour force in 2002. According to official figures, the GDP of the services sector increased at an average annual rate of 10.6% during 2005–11; growth in the services sector was 8.2% in 2011.

In 2010 Rwanda recorded a visible trade deficit of US $787m. and there was a deficit of $421m. on the current account of the balance of payments. In 2010 the principal source of imports was the United Arab Emirates (UAE), which supplied 7.0% of merchandise imports in that year; other major suppliers were Kenya, the People's Republic of China and Tanzania. In the same year Switzerland (incl. Liechtenstein) was the principal market for exports (taking 22.9% of the total); other significant purchasers were Kenya, Belgium, Hong Kong, China and Swaziland. The principal exports in 2010 were metalliferous ores and metal scrap, coffee and tea. The main imports in that year were road vehicles, electric machinery, apparatus and appliances, iron and steel, medicinal and pharmaceutical products, and petroleum and petroleum products.

An overall budgetary surplus of 24.8m. Rwanda francs was recorded in 2010. A deficit of 76.3m. Rwanda francs was projected for the year 2012. Rwanda's general government gross debt was 755,909m. Rwanda francs in 2010, equivalent to 23.2% of GDP. At the end of 2010 Rwanda's external debt totalled US $795m., of which $766m. was public and publicly guaranteed debt. In that year, the cost of servicing long-term public and publicly guaranteed debt and repayments to the IMF was equivalent to 2.3% of the value of exports of goods, services and income (excluding workers' remittances). In 2002–11 the average annual rate of inflation was 8.9%. Consumer prices increased by 5.7% in 2011.

By the late 2000s, through a sustained programme of donor-funded assistance, the Government of Rwanda had achieved considerable success in its efforts towards economic recovery and restructuring. Considerable relief was provided under the heavily indebted poor countries and multilateral debt relief initiatives (for which Rwanda qualified in 2005 and 2006, respectively). Rwanda gained full membership of the East African Community (EAC, see p. 460) customs union in July 2009. A common market protocol, allowing the free movement of goods, services, people and capital within the EAC, was signed by member states in November and entered into force in July 2010. The IMF approved a new three-year economic programme supported by its Policy Support Instrument (PSI) for Rwanda in June. Following a slowdown in 2009 resulting from the global crisis, GDP growth of more than 8% was recorded in 2011 (the highest level in East Africa), owing to a resurgence in food production in that year, which was attributed in part to the Government's efforts to modernize the agricultural sector, and to rises in output of industrial and mineral products. A November 2012 IMF report on the financed economic programme commended Rwanda's sustained strong economic growth, relatively low inflation, and sharp reduction in poverty (according to official figures, from about 58.9% of the total population identified as below the poverty line in 2000/01 to 44.9% in 2010/11). Following the release of a UN report in mid-2012 that accused Rwanda of involvement with a militia group in the DRC, the USA, the African Development Bank, the United Kingdom, and other European Union (see p. 281) member states withheld budget support amounting to US $128.1m. Nevertheless, in early 2013 Rwanda's growth projection for 2012 was revised upwards, again to over 8%, to be generated by high levels of investment. In view of Rwanda's dependence on external assistance, however, there were concerns that the continued suspension of aid would significantly lower growth and affect fiscal stability in 2013.

PUBLIC HOLIDAYS

2014: 1 January (New Year), 28 January (Democracy Day), 7 April (National Mourning Day), 21 April (Easter Monday), 1 May (Labour Day), 9 May (Ascension Day), 1 July (Independence Day), 1 August (Harvest Festival), 15 August (Assumption), 8 September (Culture Day), 25 September (Kamarampaka Day, anniversary of 1961 referendum), 1 October (Armed Forces Day), 1 November (All Saints' Day), 25 December (Christmas).

Statistical Survey

Source (unless otherwise stated): National Institute of Statistics of Rwanda (NISR); tel. 250571037; e-mail info@statistics.gov.rw; internet www.statistics.gov.rw.

Area and Population

AREA, POPULATION AND DENSITY

Area (sq km)	26,338*
Population (census results)	
16 August 2002	8,128,553
16 August 2012 (provisional)	
Males	5,074,942
Females	5,462,280
Total	10,537,222
Population (UN estimate at mid-year)†	
2013	11,608,441
Density (per sq km) at mid-2013	440.7

* 10,169 sq miles.

† Source: UN, *World Population Prospects: The 2010 Revision*; estimate not adjusted to take account of results of 2012 census.

POPULATION BY AGE AND SEX
(UN estimates at mid-2013)

	Males	Females	Total
0–14	2,485,750	2,499,771	4,985,521
15–64	3,074,634	3,227,792	6,302,426
65 and over	144,834	175,660	320,494
Total	5,705,218	5,903,223	11,608,441

Source: UN, *World Population Prospects: The 2010 Revision*.

PREFECTURES
(population at 1991 census)

	Area (sq km)	Population*	Density (per sq km)
Butare	1,830	765,910	418.5
Byumba	4,987	779,365	159.2
Cyangugu	2,226	517,550	232.5
Gikongoro	2,192	462,635	211.1
Gisenyi	2,395	728,365	304.1
Gitarama	2,241	849,285	379.0
Kibungo	4,134	647,175	156.5
Kibuye	1,320	472,525	358.0
Kigali . . . . . }	3,251	{ 921,050 }	355.2
Kigali-Ville		233,640	
Ruhengeri	1,762	765,255	434.3
Total	26,338	7,142,755	271.2

* Source: UN, *Demographic Yearbook*.

2002 census (population): Butare 725,914; Byumba 707,786; Cyangugu 607,495; Gikongoro 489,729; Gisenyi 864,377; Gitarama 856,488; Kibungo 702,248; Kibuye 469,016; Kigali 789,330; Kigali-Ville 603,049; Ruhengeri 891,498; Umutara 421,623; *Total* 8,128,553.

PRINCIPAL TOWNS
(population at 1978 census)

Kigali (capital) . .	117,749	Ruhengeri . . .	16,025
Butare	21,691	Gisenyi	12,436

Mid-2011 (incl. suburbs, UN estimate): Kigali 1,003,570 (Source: UN, *World Urbanization Prospects: The 2011 Revision*).

BIRTHS AND DEATHS
(annual averages, UN estimates)

	1995–2000	2000–05	2005–10
Birth rate (per 1,000)	40.7	39.8	40.7
Death rate (per 1,000)	19.9	14.4	12.3

Source: UN, *World Population Prospects: The 2010 Revision*.

Life expectancy (years at birth): 55.4 (males 54.1; females 56.7) in 2011 (Source: World Bank, World Development Indicators database).

ECONOMICALLY ACTIVE POPULATION
(persons aged 14 years and over, at census of August 2002)

	Males	Females	Total
Agriculture	1,218,181	1,731,411	2,949,592
Fishing	3,374	94	3,468
Industrial activities	3,692	1,636	5,328
Production activities	32,994	10,649	43,643
Electricity and water	2,390	277	2,667
Construction	41,641	1,244	42,885
Trade reconstruction	56,869	32,830	89,699
Restaurants and hotels . .	4,525	2,311	6,836
Transport and communications .	29,574	1,988	31,562
Financial intermediaries . . .	1,560	840	2,400
Administration and defence . .	22,479	5,585	28,064
Education	22,688	17,046	39,734
Health and social services . . .	7,521	7,054	14,575
Sub-total	1,447,488	1,812,965	3,260,453
Activities not adequately defined .	69,042	39,458	108,500
Total employed	1,516,530	1,852,423	3,368,953

Source: IMF, *Rwanda: Selected Issues and Statistical Appendix* (December 2004).

Mid-2013 (estimates in '000): Agriculture, etc. 4,749; Total labour force 5,345 (Source: FAO).

Health and Welfare

KEY INDICATORS

Total fertility rate (children per woman, 2010) . . .	5.4
Under-5 mortality rate (per 1,000 live births, 2010) . . .	64
HIV/AIDS (% of persons aged 15–49, 2009)	2.9
Physicians (per 1,000 head, 2004)	0.05
Hospital beds (per 1,000 head, 2007)	1.6
Health expenditure (2009): US $ per head (PPP)	111
Health expenditure (2009): % of GDP	10.1
Health expenditure (2009): public (% of total)	48.6
Access to water (% of persons, 2010)	65
Access to sanitation (% of persons, 2010)	55
Total carbon dioxide emissions ('000 metric tons, 2008) . .	704.1
Carbon dioxide emissions per head (metric tons, 2008) . .	0.1
Human Development Index (2011): ranking	166
Human Development Index (2011): value	0.429

For sources and definitions, see explanatory note on p. vi.

Agriculture

PRINCIPAL CROPS
('000 metric tons)

	2009	2010	2011
Maize	285.5	432.4	525.7
Sorghum	174.5	161.2	151.8
Potatoes	1,287.4	1,789.4	2,171.5
Sweet potatoes	801.4	840.1	845.1
Cassava (Manioc)	2,019.7	2,377.2	2,579.4
Taro (Cocoyam)	136.8	186.0	168.5
Sugar cane	100.7	115.3	115.0*
Beans, dry	326.5	327.5	331.2
Peas, dry	33.8	38.0	33.9
Groundnuts, with shell	15.4	14.4	14.8
Pumpkins, squash and gourds*	209.3	226.9	234.7
Plantains	2,993.5	2,749.2	3,036.3
Coffee, green	19.4	0.9	21.8
Tea	20.5	22.2	24.1

* FAO estimate(s).

Aggregate production ('000 metric tons, may include official, semi-official or estimated data): Total cereals 622 in 2009, 746 in 2010, 857 in 2011; Total roots and tubers 4,265 in 2009, 5,213 in 2010, 5,783 in 2011; Total pulses 360 in 2009, 365 in 2010, 365 in 2011; Total vegetables (incl. melons) 624 in 2009, 658 in 2010, 640 in 2011; Total fruits (excl. melons) 3,339 in 2009, 3,081 in 2010, 3,403 in 2011.

Source: FAO.

LIVESTOCK
('000 head, year ending September)

	2009	2010	2011
Cattle	1,218.5	1,334.8	1,143.2
Pigs	639.4	684.7	706.5
Sheep	718.2	743.2	829.0
Goats	2,620.6	2,688.3	2,970.8
Chickens	3,273	3,538	4,421

Source: FAO.

LIVESTOCK PRODUCTS
('000 metric tons)

	2009	2010	2011
Cattle meat*	35.4	36.4	34.8
Goat meat*	7.2	7.3	7.4
Pig meat*	6.9	7.6	7.8
Chicken meat*	2.4	2.4	2.5
Game meat*	11.9	13.2	13.2
Cows' milk	145.0	183.7*	183.7*
Sheep's milk*	2.7	2.7	2.7
Goats' milk*	28.9	29.8	29.8
Hen eggs*	2.9	2.9	2.9

* FAO estimate(s).
Source: FAO.

Forestry

ROUNDWOOD REMOVALS
('000 cubic metres, excluding bark, FAO estimates)

	2007	2008	2009
Sawlogs, veneer logs and logs for sleepers	245	961	962
Other industrial wood	250	250	250
Fuel wood	5,000	5,000	5,000
Total	5,495	6,211	6,212

2010–11: Production assumed to be unchanged from 2009 (FAO estimates).
Source: FAO.

SAWNWOOD PRODUCTION
('000 cubic metres, including railway sleepers)

	2007	2008	2009
Coniferous (softwood)	22	40	50
Non-coniferous (hardwood)	57	81	85
Total	79	121	135

2010–11: Production assumed to be unchanged from 2009 (FAO estimates).
Source: FAO.

Fishing

(metric tons, live weight, FAO estimates)

	2008	2009	2010
Capture	9,050	9,050	9,050
Nile tilapia	3,950	3,950	3,950
Aquaculture	388	488	628
Nile tilapia	300	400	500
Total catch	9,438	9,538	9,678

Source: FAO.

Mining

(metric tons, estimates)

	2008	2009	2010
Tin concentrates*	1,500	1,700	2,500
Tungsten concentrates*	1,708	874	843
Columbo-tantalite†	600	480	380

* Figures refer to the metal content of ores and concentrates.
† Figures refer to the estimated production of mineral concentrates. The metal content (metric tons, estimates) was: Niobium (Columbium) 190 in 2008, 150 in 2009, 120 in 2010; Tantalum 150 in 2008, 120 in 2009, 93 in 2010.

Source: US Geological Survey.

Industry

SELECTED PRODUCTS

	2001	2002	2003
Beer ('000 hectolitres)	479	539	412
Soft drinks ('000 hectolitres)	228	n.a.	n.a.
Cigarettes (million)	278	391	402
Soap (metric tons)	7,056	5,571	4,456
Cement (metric tons)	83,024	100,568	105,105

Source: IMF, *Rwanda: Statistical Annex* (August 2002) and IMF, *Rwanda: Selected Issues and Statistical Appendix* (December 2004).

Cement ('000 metric tons): 103.2 in 2008; 92.1 in 2009; 95.1 in 2010 (Source: US Geological Survey).

Electric energy (million kWh): 165.0 in 2007; 192.0 in 2008; 248.0 in 2009 (Source: UN Industrial Commodity Statistics Database).

Finance

CURRENCY AND EXCHANGE RATES

Monetary Units
    100 centimes = 1 franc rwandais (Rwanda franc).

Sterling, Dollar and Euro Equivalents (31 December 2012)
    £1 sterling = 996.360 Rwanda francs;
    US \$1 = 631.407 Rwanda francs;
    €1 = 833.078 Rwanda francs;
    10,000 Rwanda francs = £10.04 = \$15.84 = €12.00.

Average Exchange Rate (Rwanda francs per US \$)
2010	583.131
2011	600.307
2012	614.295

Note: Since September 1983 the currency has been linked to the IMF special drawing right (SDR). Until November 1990 the mid-point exchange rate was SDR 1 = 102.71 Rwanda francs. In November 1990 a new rate of SDR 1 = 171.18 Rwanda francs was established. This remained in effect until June 1992, when the rate was adjusted to SDR 1 = 201.39 Rwanda francs. The latter parity was maintained until February 1994, since when the rate has been frequently adjusted. In March 1995 the Government introduced a market-determined exchange rate system.

BUDGET
('000 million Rwanda francs)

Revenue*	2009/10	2010/11†	2011/12‡
Tax revenue	376.4	463.8	519.7
Direct taxes	148.8	180.9	207.3
Taxes on goods and services .	195.0	245.1	271.4
Taxes on international trade .	32.6	37.8	41.0
Non-tax revenue	15.0	20.6	45.4
Total	391.4	484.4	565.1

Expenditure§	2009/10	2010/11†	2011/12‡
Current expenditure	459.2	527.0	596.3
Wages and salaries	106.9	122.0	131.2
Purchases of goods and services	106.3	124.1	148.3
Interest payments	14.7	15.6	16.0
Domestic debt	10.1	10.9	10.1
External debt	4.6	4.7	5.9
Transfers	179.6	197.2	223.9
Exceptional expenditure . .	51.6	68.1	76.9
Capital expenditure	316.7	438.6	508.6
Domestic	159.3	218.9	248.9
External	157.4	219.7	259.7
Total	775.9	965.6	1,104.9

* Excluding grants received ('000 million Rwanda francs): 409.3 in 2009/10; 379.0 in 2010/11 (preliminary); 463.5 in 2011/12 (projection).
† Preliminary.
‡ Projections.
§ Excluding lending minus repayments ('000 million Rwanda francs): 28.2 in 2009/10; 18.7 in 2010/11 (preliminary); 0.7 in 2011/12 (projection).

Source: IMF, *Rwanda: Fourth Review Under the Policy Support Instrument and Request for Modification of Assessment Criteria—Staff Report; Press Release* (June 2012).

INTERNATIONAL BANK RESERVES
(US \$ million at 31 December)

	2009	2010	2011
IMF special drawing rights . .	130.92	128.55	127.58
Foreign exchange	611.82	684.21	922.46
Total	742.74	812.76	1,050.04

Source: IMF, *International Financial Statistics*.

MONEY SUPPLY
(million Rwanda francs at 31 December)

	2003	2004	2005
Currency outside banks . .	29,246	36,512	46,277
Demand deposits at deposit money banks . .	52,220	62,604	82,524
Total money (incl. others) . .	82,305	99,941	129,326

2006: Currency outside banks 52,620.

Source: IMF, *International Financial Statistics*.

COST OF LIVING
(Consumer Price Index for Kigali; base: 2000 = 100)

	2009	2010	2011
Food (incl. non-alcoholic beverages)	250.2	254.3	271.0
All items (incl. others) . . .	209.1	214.1	226.1

Source: ILO.

NATIONAL ACCOUNTS
('000 million Rwanda francs at current prices)

Expenditure on the Gross Domestic Product

	2009	2010	2011
Government final consumption expenditure	454	524	580
Private final consumption expenditure	2,464	2,742	3,160
Changes in inventories . . .			
Gross fixed capital formation .	644	688	818
Total domestic expenditure .	3,562	3,954	4,558
Exports of goods and services .	303	329	514
Less Imports of goods and services	881	1,003	1,244
GDP in purchasers' values .	2,985	3,280	3,828
GDP in constant 2006 prices	2,182	2,339	2,540

Gross Domestic Product by Economic Activity

	2009	2010	2011
Agriculture, hunting, forestry and fishing	1,012	1,058	1,223
Mining and quarrying	16	21	48
Manufacturing	190	218	252
Electricity, gas and water . . .	6	7	8
Construction	218	244	317
Wholesale and retail trade, restaurants and hotels . . .	446	500	564
Finance, insurance, real estate and business services	346	373	415
Transport and communications .	223	256	288
Public administration and defence	128	151	181
Education	140	167	210
Health	44	51	53
Other personal services . . .	30	33	34
Sub-total	2,799	3,079	3,593
Less Imputed bank service charges	41	50	69
Indirect taxes, less subsidies . .	226	249	306
GDP in purchasers' values .	2,985	3,280	3,828

Note: Totals may not be equal to the sum of components, owing to rounding.

BALANCE OF PAYMENTS
(US $ million)

	2008	2009	2010
Exports of goods	257	188	297
Imports of goods	−880	−961	−1,084
Balance on goods	**−623**	**−772**	**−787**
Exports of services	408	341	310
Imports of services	−521	−519	−557
Balance on goods and services	**−736**	**−950**	**−1,033**
Primary income received	28	15	13
Primary income paid	−62	−52	−59
Balance on goods, services and primary income	**−771**	**−987**	**−1,079**
Secondary income received	558	655	714
Secondary income paid	−40	−51	−56
Current balance	**−252**	**−383**	**−421**
Capital account (net)	210	200	286
Direct investment liabilities	103	119	42
Portfolio investment assets	−19	—	—
Portfolio investment liabilities	—	—	21
Other investment assets	−88	−19	−28
Other investment liabilities	—	143	117
Net errors and omissions	−5	3	−6
Reserves and related items	**−51**	**63**	**10**

Source: IMF, *International Financial Statistics*.

External Trade

PRINCIPAL COMMODITIES
(US $ million)

Imports c.i.f.	2008	2009	2010
Food and live animals	78.5	97.4	133.3
Cereals and cereal preparations	37.3	55.8	66.8
Rice	6.9	11.8	16.7
Vegetables and fruit	3.9	4.2	7.1
Sugar, sugar preparations and honey	19.1	23.4	39.5
Crude materials, inedible, except fuels	45.9	34.2	51.4
Textile fibres and their wastes	22.0	13.8	11.4
Mineral fuels, lubricants and related materials	64.5	89.8	52.9
Petroleum, petroleum products and related materials	63.6	88.9	51.7
Animal and vegetable oils, fats and waxes	30.8	36.0	40.2
Chemicals and related products	133.3	187.6	170.3
Medicinal and pharmaceutical products	46.8	79.2	63.1
Basic manufactures	238.2	224.1	265.4
Iron and steel	85.4	56.5	64.7
Machinery and transport equipment	301.4	340.5	449.2
Telecommunications, sound recording and reproducing equipment	42.7	89.0	50.4
Electric machinery, apparatus and appliances, and parts	47.4	78.7	76.0
Road vehicles	73.9	66.0	178.6
Miscellaneous manufactured articles	37.0	34.8	37.7
Total (incl. others)	1,035.6	1,112.0	1,273.8

Exports f.o.b.	2008	2009	2010
Coffee, tea, cocoa, spices, and manufactures thereof	—	109.6	92.8
Coffee	—	33.9	58.4
Tea	—	75.6	34.4
Crude materials, inedible, except fuels	140.7	71.6	105.0
Metalliferous ores and metal scrap	136.3	67.9	98.6
Tin ores and concentrates	78.6	34.2	66.9
Ores and concentrates of other non-ferrous base metals	17.0	11.2	10.5
Ores of molybdenum, niobium and titanium	38.0	20.4	20.3
Total (incl. others)	250.2	260.7	237.8

Source: UN, *International Trade Statistics Yearbook*.

PRINCIPAL TRADING PARTNERS
(US $ million)

Imports	2008	2009	2010
Bahrain	11.3	4.6	2.4
Belgium	59.4	42.3	50.7
Burundi	3.5	3.3	26.0
China, People's Republic	99.5	92.0	76.0
Congo, Democratic Republic	6.1	6.0	63.0
Denmark	10.1	37.5	47.0
Egypt	13.6	16.0	25.0
France (incl. Monaco)	32.9	29.5	41.3
Germany	39.2	41.8	50.9
India	48.4	54.3	55.6
Italy	7.6	10.2	15.4
Japan	39.1	35.0	59.9
Kenya	128.4	123.9	79.6
Korea, Republic	9.2	34.0	40.0
Netherlands	11.5	22.8	8.3
Saudi Arabia	17.5	11.5	19.2
South Africa	39.2	36.6	43.0
Spain	14.1	2.5	13.0
Sweden	30.9	54.2	120.0
Switzerland-Liechtenstein	6.2	13.7	13.3
Tanzania	25.4	54.6	75.0
Uganda	148.5	143.0	52.6
UAE	84.4	69.5	89.4
United Kingdom	24.6	22.3	14.9
USA	36.5	43.3	31.8
Total (incl. others)	1,035.6	1,112.0	1,273.8

Exports	2008	2009	2010
Angola	—	3.6	—
Belgium	65.0	29.5	26.7
Burundi	6.2	5.4	4.7
China, People's Republic	5.9	7.7	17.6
Congo, Democratic Republic	17.5	12.7	16.4
Germany	7.9	3.3	3.7
Hong Kong	25.8	16.0	19.1
India	13.0	1.4	0.4
Italy	3.7	1.1	2.5
Kenya	31.7	83.1	39.3
South Africa	12.0	5.5	3.2
Swaziland	14.4	23.6	11.8
Switzerland-Liechtenstein	7.5	12.2	54.4
Tanzania	1.1	4.1	4.3
Uganda	6.8	5.6	6.8
United Kingdom	13.4	4.8	11.0
USA	4.9	3.9	7.6
Total (incl. others)	250.2	260.7	237.8

Source: UN, *International Trade Statistics Yearbook*.

Transport

ROAD TRAFFIC
(motor vehicles in use at 31 December)

	2008	2010*
Passenger cars	22,251	17,220
Buses and coaches	4,776	
Lorries and vans	10,827	32,880
Motorcycles and mopeds	24,013	38,521

* Data for 2009 were not available.

Source: IRF, *World Road Statistics*.

CIVIL AVIATION
(traffic on scheduled services)

	2009	2010	2011
Passengers carried	266,946	313,327	376,918
Freight carried (metric tons) . .	6,724	6,352	5,922

Tourism

FOREIGN VISITOR ARRIVALS*

	2008	2009	2010
Belgium	11,161	8,166	10,100
Burundi	74,686	97,154	72,316
Congo, Democratic Republic . .	280,297	301,649	242,976
India	17,111	13,085	16,178
Kenya	25,870	30,721	37,193
Tanzania	44,166	31,535	40,286
Uganda	113,267	111,210	133,089
United Kingdom	10,238	10,295	10,824
Total (incl. others)	668,524	693,608	666,001

* Figures refer to total arrivals (including same-day visitors), excluding Rwandan nationals residing abroad.

Tourism receipts (US $ million, excl. passenger transport): 174 in 2009; 202 in 2010; 252 in 2011 (provisional).

Source: World Tourism Organization.

Communications Media

	2009	2010	2011
Telephones ('000 main lines in use)	33.5	39.7	38.9
Mobile cellular telephones ('000 subscribers)	2,429.3	3,548.8	4,446.2
Internet subscribers ('000) . .	15.2	16.7	16.7
Broadband subscribers ('000) . .	2.2	2.6	3.7

Personal computers: 28,000 (3.0 per 1,000 persons) in 2006.

Source: International Telecommunication Union.

Education

(2009/10)

	Teachers	Students		
		Males	Females	Total
Pre-primary	4,107	47,034	49,900	96,934
Primary	35,583	1,132,556	1,166,770	2,299,326
Secondary	14,477	209,926	215,661	425,587
Tertiary	2,829	35,242	27,492	62,734

Source: UNESCO Institute for Statistics.

Pupil-teacher ratio (primary education, UNESCO estimate): 58.1 in 2010/11 (Source: UNESCO Institute for Statistics).

Adult literacy rate (UNESCO estimates): 71.1% (males 74.8%; females 67.5%) in 2010 (Source: UNESCO Institute for Statistics).

Directory

The Government

HEAD OF STATE

President: Maj.-Gen. PAUL KAGAME (took office 22 April 2000; re-elected 25 August 2003 and 9 August 2010).

COUNCIL OF MINISTERS
(May 2013)

Prime Minister: PIERRE DAMIEN HABUMUREMYI.

Minister of Agriculture and Animal Resources: Dr AGNES KALIBATA.

Minister of the East African Community: MONIQUE MUKARULIZA.

Minister of Health: Dr AGNES BINAGWAHO.

Minister of Internal Security: MUSSA FAZIL HERERIMANA.

Minister of Defence: Gen. JAMES KABAREBE.

Minister of Lands, the Environment, Forestry and Mines: STANISLAS KAMANZI.

Minister of Finance and Economic Planning: CLAVER GATETE.

Minister of Disaster Preparedness and Refugee Affairs: SERAPHIN MUKANTABANA.

Minister of Local Government: JAMES MUSONI.

Minister in the Office of the Prime Minister, in charge of Gender and Family Promotion: ODA GASINZIGWA.

Minister of Youth, Sports and Culture: PROTAIS MITALI KABANDA.

Minister of Justice and Attorney-General: THARCISSE KARUGARAMA.

Minister in the Office of the President: VENANTIA TUGIREYEZU.

Minister of Education: Dr VINCENT BIRUTA.

Minister of Public Service and Labour: ANASTASE MUREKEZI.

Minister of Foreign Affairs: LOUISE MUSHIKIWABO.

Minister in the Office of the President, in charge of ICT: Dr IGNACE GATARE.

Minister in the Office of the Prime Minister, in charge of Cabinet Affairs: PROTAIS MUSONI.

Minister of Trade and Industry: FRANCOIS KANIMBA.

Minister of Infrastructure: Prof. SILAS RWAKABAMBA.

Minister of State in the Ministry of Local Government, in charge of Social Affairs and Community Development: ALVERA MUKABARAMBA.

Minister of State in the Ministry of Infrastructure, in charge of Energy and Water: EMMA FRANÇOISE ISUMBINGABO.

Minister of State in the Ministry of Education, in charge of Primary and Secondary Education: Dr MATHIAS HABAMUNGU.

Minister of State in the Ministry of Health, in charge of Public Health and Primary Healthcare: Dr ANITA ASIIMWE.

Minister of State in the Ministry of Education, in charge of Technical and Vocational Education and Training: ALBERT NSENGIYUMVA.

Minister of State in the Ministry of Natural Resources, in charge of Mining: EVODE IMENA.

MINISTRIES

Office of the President: BP 15, Kigali; tel. 59062000; fax 572431; e-mail info@presidency.gov.rw; internet www.presidency.gov.rw.

Office of the Prime Minister: Kigali; tel. 252585444; fax 252583714; e-mail primature@gov.rw; internet www.primature .gov.rw.

Ministry of Agriculture and Animal Resources: BP 621, Kigali; tel. 250585008; fax 250585057; e-mail info@minagri.gov.rw; internet www.minagri.gov.rw.

Ministry of Defence: BP 23, Kigali; tel. 250577942; fax 250576969; e-mail info@mod.gov.rw; internet www.mod.gov.rw.

Ministry of Disaster Management and Refugee Affairs: POB 4386, Blue Star House, Kacyiru, Kigali; e-mail info@midimar.gov .rw; internet www.midimar.gov.rw.

Ministry of the East African Community: BP 267, Kigali; tel. 250599122; internet www.mineac.gov.rw.

Ministry of Education: BP 622, Kigali; tel. 250583051; fax 250582161; e-mail info@mineduc.gov.rw; internet www.mineduc .gov.rw.

Ministry of Finance and Economic Planning: blvd de la Révolution, opp. Kigali City Council, BP 158, Kigali; tel. 250576701; fax 250577581; e-mail mfin@minecofin.gov.rw; internet www.minecofin .gov.rw.

Ministry of Foreign Affairs: Kimihurura, 5th and 6th Floors, ave du lac Muhazi, BP 179, Kigali; tel. 250599128; fax 250599129; e-mail info@minaffet.gov.rw; internet www.minaffet.gov.rw.

Ministry of Gender and Family Promotion: Kigali; tel. 250577626; fax 250577543; internet www.migeprofe.gov.rw.

Ministry of Health: BP 84, Kigali; tel. 250577458; fax 250576853; e-mail info@moh.gov.rw; internet www.moh.gov.rw.

Ministry of Infrastructure: BP 24, Kigali; tel. 250585503; fax 250585755; e-mail info@mininfra.gov.rw; internet www.mininfra .gov.rw.

Ministry of Internal Affairs: BP 446, Kigali; tel. 250586708; e-mail sec_cent@mininter.gov.rw; internet www.mininter.gov.rw.

Ministry of Justice: BP 160, Kigali; tel. 250586561; fax 250586509; e-mail mjust@minijust.gov.rw; internet www.minijust.gov.rw.

Ministry of Lands, the Environment, Forestry and Mines: BP 3052, Kigali; tel. 250582628; fax 250582629; e-mail info@minirena .gov.rw; internet www.minirena.gov.rw.

Ministry of Local Government: BP 790, Kigali; tel. 250585406; fax 250582228; e-mail webmaster@minaloc.gov.rw; internet www .minaloc.gov.rw.

Ministry of Public Service and Labour: BP 403, Kigali; tel. 250585714; fax 250583621; e-mail mifotra@mifotra.gov.rw; internet www.mifotra.gov.rw.

Ministry of Trade and Industry: BP 73, Kigali; tel. 250599103; fax 250599101; e-mail albert.bizimana@minicom.gov.rw; internet www .minicom.gov.rw.

Ministry of Youth, Sports and Culture: BP 1044, Kigali; tel. 250583531; fax 250583518; e-mail info@minispoc.gov.rw; internet www.minispoc.gov.rw.

President and Legislature

PRESIDENT

Presidential Election, 9 August 2010

Candidate	Votes	% of votes
Paul Kagame	4,638,560	93.08
Jean Damascene Ntawukuriryayo	256,488	5.15
Prosper Higiro	68,235	1.37
Alivera Mukabaramba	20,107	0.40
Total	4,983,390	100.00

CHAMBER OF DEPUTIES

Speaker: ROSE MUKANTANTABANA.

General Election, 15 September 2008

Party	Votes	% of votes	Seats
Front Patriotique Rwandais*	3,655,956	78.76	42
Parti Social-démocrate	609,327	13.12	7
Parti Libéral	348,186	7.50	4
Independent	27,848	0.60	—
Total	4,641,317	100.00	80†

* Contested the elections in alliance with the Parti Démocrate Centriste, the Parti Démocrate Idéal, the Union Démocratique du Peuple Rwandais, the Parti de Prospérité et de Solidarité and the Parti Socialiste Rwandais.

† In addition to the 53 directly elected deputies, 27 seats are allocated, respectively, to two youth representatives, one disabilities representative and 24 female representatives, who are indirectly elected.

SENATE

Pres.: Dr JEAN DAMASCENE NTAWUKURIRYAYO.

The Senate comprises 26 members, of whom 12 are elected by local government councils in the 12 provinces and two by academic institutions, while the remaining 12 are nominated (eight by the President and four by a regulatory body, the Parties' Forum).

Election Commission

National Electoral Commission: BP 6449, Kigali; tel. 250597800; fax 250597851; e-mail comelena@rwanda1.com; internet www .comelena.gov.rw; f. 2000; independent; Chair. Prof. KALISA MBANDA.

Political Organizations

Under legislation adopted in June 2003, the formation of any political organization based on ethnic groups, religion or sex was prohibited.

Democratic Green Party: BP 6334, Kigali; tel. 788563039 (mobile); e-mail info@rwandagreendemocrats.org; internet www .rwandagreendemocrats.org; f. 2009; Pres. FRANK HABINEZA.

Front Patriotique Rwandais (FPR): internet www.rpfinkotanyi .org; f. 1990; also known as Inkotanyi; comprises mainly Tutsi exiles, but claims multi-ethnic support; commenced armed invasion of Rwanda from Uganda in Oct. 1990; took control of Rwanda in July 1994; Chair. Maj.-Gen. PAUL KAGAME; Vice-Chair. CHRISTOPHE BAZIVAMO; Sec.-Gen. FRANÇOIS NGARAMBE.

Parti Démocrate Centriste (PDC): BP 2348, Kigali; tel. 250576542; fax 250572237; f. 1990; established as Parti Démocrate Chrétien, name changed as above 2003; Chair. AGNES MUKABARANGA.

Parti Démocrate Idéal (PDI): Tresor Bldg, 2nd Floor, Kigali; internet www.pdi-rwanda.org; f. 1991; established as Parti Démocratique Islamique, renamed as above 2003; Leader SHEIKH HARERIMANA MUSSA FAZIL.

Parti Démocratique Rwandais (Pader): Kigali; f. 1992; Sec. JEAN NTAGUNGIRA.

Parti Libéral (PL): BP 1304, Kigali; tel. 252577916; fax 252577838; f. 1991; restructured 2003; Chair. PROTAIS K. MITALI.

Parti du Progrès et de la Concorde (PPC): f. 2003; incl. fmr mems of Mouvement Démocratique Républicain; Leader Dr CHRISTIAN MARARA.

Parti de Prospérité et de Solidarité (PSP): Kigali.

Parti Social-démocrate (PSD): Nyarugenge, Quartier Commercial, Kigali; tel. 252577452; e-mail psd200891@yahoo.fr; internet psd-rwanda.org; f. 1991 by a breakaway faction of fmr Mouvement Révolutionnaire National pour le Développement; Leader Dr VINCENT BIRUTA.

Parti Social Imberakuri (PS Imberakuri): Nyamirambo, Kigali; tel. 788307145 (mobile); e-mail ntagandab@yahoo.fr; internet www .imberakuri.org; f. 2009; Pres. BERNARD NTAGANDA; Sec.-Gen. IMMACULÉE UWIZEYE KANSIIME.

Parti Socialiste Rwandais (PSR): BP 827, Kigali; tel. 252576658; internet psr-rwanda.org; f. 1991; workers' rights; Chair. JEAN-BAPTISTE RUCIBIGANGO.

Other political organizations have been formed by exiled Rwandans and operate principally from abroad; these include:

Rassemblement Républicain pour la Démocratie au Rwanda (RDR): Postbus 3124, 2280 GC, Rijswijk, Netherlands; tel. (31) 623075674; fax (31) 847450374; e-mail info@rdrwanda.org; internet www.rdrwanda.org; f. 1995; principal opposition party representing Hutu refugees in exile; Pres. VICTOIRE UMUHOZA INGABIRE.

Diplomatic Representation

EMBASSIES AND HIGH COMMISSIONS IN RWANDA

Belgium: rue Nyarugenge, BP 81, Kigali; tel. 250575551; fax 250573995; e-mail kigali@diplobel.fed.be; internet www.diplomatie.be/kigali; Ambassador MARC PECSTEEN DE BUYTSWERVE.

Burundi: rue de Ntaruka, BP 714, Kigali; tel. 250575010; Ambassador Col REMY SINKAZI.

China, People's Republic: BP 1345, 44 blvd de la Revolution, Kigali; tel. 250570843; fax 250570848; e-mail chinaemb_rw@mfa.gov.cn; internet rw.chineseembassy.org; Ambassador SHU ZHAN.

Congo, Democratic Republic: 504 rue Longue, BP 169, Kigali; tel. 250575289; Ambassador NORBERT NKULU KILOMBO.

Egypt: BP 1069, Kigali; tel. and fax 28082686; e-mail egypt@rwanda1.com; Ambassador KHALED ABD AL-RAHMAN.

France: rue du Député Kamunzinzi, BP 441, Kigali; tel. 252551800; fax 252551820; e-mail ambafrance.kigali-amba@diplomatie.gouv.fr; internet www.ambafrance-rw.org; Ambassador MICHEL FLESCH.

Germany: 10 ave Paul VI, BP 355, Kigali; tel. 280575141; fax 280502087; e-mail info@kigali.diplo.de; internet www.kigali.diplo.de; Ambassador PETER FAHRENHOLTZ.

Holy See: 49 ave Paul VI, BP 261, Kigali (Apostolic Nunciature); tel. 252575293; fax 252575181; e-mail na.rwanda@diplomat.va; internet www.vatican.va; Apostolic Nuncio Mgr LUCIANO RUSSO.

Japan: 1236, Kacyiru South Gasabo, BP 874, Kigali; tel. 250500884; internet www.rw.emb-japan.go.jp; Ambassador KUNIO HATANAKA.

Kenya: BP 1215, Kigali; tel. 250583332; fax 250510919; e-mail kigali@mfa.go.ke; High Commissioner JOHN MWANGEMI.

Korea, Democratic People's Republic: Kigali; Ambassador JOY THAE YANG.

Libya: BP 1152, Kigali; tel. 250576470; Secretary of the People's Bureau MOUSTAPHA MASAND EL-GHAILUSHI.

The Netherlands: blvd de l'Umuganda, Kacyiru, BP 6613, Kigali; tel. 280280281; e-mail kig@minbuza.nl; Ambassador LEONI CUELENAERE.

Nigeria: Kigali; High Commissioner AYIBAKURO PETER OGIDI-OKE.

Russia: 19 ave de l'Armée, BP 40, Kigali; tel. 250575286; fax 250503322; e-mail ambruss@rwandatel1.rwanda1.com; internet www.rwanda.mid.ru; Ambassador MIRGAYAS M. SHIRINSKII.

South Africa: 1370 blvd de l'Umuganda, POB 6563, Kacyiru-Sud, Kigali; tel. 250583185; fax 250583191; e-mail kigali.admin@dirco.gov.za; High Commissioner GEORGE NKOSINATI TWALA.

Sweden: Aurore House, Kacyiru, 1st Floor, Kigali; tel. 252597400; fax 252597459; e-mail ambassaden.kigali@sida.se; internet www.swedenabroad.com/kigali; Chargé d'affaires MARIA HÅKANSSON.

Uganda: 31 ave de la Paix, BP 656, Kigali; tel. and fax 250503537; e-mail embassy@ugandaembassy.rw; internet www.ugandaembassy.rw; High Commissioner RICHARD KABONERO.

United Kingdom: Parcelle 1131, blvd de l'Umuganda, Kacyiru, BP 576, Kigali; tel. 250584098; fax 250582044; e-mail bhc.kigali@fco.gov.uk; internet ukinrwanda.fco.gov.uk/en; High Commissioner BENEDICT LLEWELLYN-JONES.

USA: 2657 ave de la Gendarmerie, Kacyiru, BP 28, Kigali; tel. 252596400; fax 252596771; e-mail irckigali@state.gov; internet rwanda.usembassy.gov; Ambassador DONALD W. KORAN.

Judicial System

The judicial system is composed of the Supreme Court, the High Court of the Republic, and provincial, district and municipal Tribunals. In addition, there are specialized judicial organs, comprising *gacaca* and military courts. The *gacaca* courts were established to try cases of genocide or other crimes against humanity committed between 1 October 1990 and 31 December 1994. Trials for categories of lesser genocide crimes were to be conducted by councils in the communities in which they were committed, with the aim of alleviating pressure on the existing judicial system. Trials under the *gacaca* court system formally commenced on 25 November 2002 and the system closed in June 2012, having tried almost 2m. suspects. Military courts (the Military Tribunal and the High Military Court) have jurisdiction in military cases. The President and Vice-President of the Supreme Court and the Prosecutor-General are elected by the Senate.

Supreme Court: BP 2197, Kigali; tel. 252517649; fax 252582276; e-mail info@judiciary.gov.rw; internet www.judiciary.gov.rw; the Supreme Court comprises five sections: the Department of Courts and Tribunals; the Court of Appeals; the Constitutional Court; the Council of State; and the Revenue Court; Pres. Prof. SAM RUGEGE; Vice-Pres. SYLVIE KAYITESI ZAINABU.

High Court: Kigali; Vice-Pres. JEAN MARIE VIANNEY HITIMAN.

Prosecutor-General: MARTIN NGOGAEU.

Religion

AFRICAN RELIGIONS

About one-half of the population hold traditional beliefs.

CHRISTIANITY

Union des Eglises Rwandaises: BP 79, Kigali; tel. 28085825; fax 28083554; f. 1963; fmrly Conseil Protestant du Rwanda.

The Roman Catholic Church

Rwanda comprises one archdiocese and eight dioceses. About 49% of the total population is Roman Catholic.

Bishops' Conference

Conférence Episcopale du Rwanda, BP 357, Kigali; tel. 250575439; fax 250578080; e-mail cerwanda@rwanda1.com.
f. 1980; Pres. Rt Rev. SMARAGDE MBONYINTEGE (Bishop of Kabgayi).

Archbishop of Kigali: Most Rev. THADDÉE NTIHINYURWA, Archevêché, BP 715, Kigali; tel. 250575769; fax 250572274; e-mail kigarchi@yahoo.fr.

The Anglican Communion

The Church of the Province of Rwanda, established in 1992, has nine dioceses.

Archbishop of the Province and Bishop of Gasabo: Most Rev. ONESPHORE RWAJE, BP 61, Kigali; tel. and fax 250576340; e-mail ek@rwanda1.com.

Provincial Secretary: Rev. EMMANUEL GATERA, BP 61, Kigali; tel. and fax 250576340; e-mail egapeer@yahoo.com.

Protestant Churches

Eglise Baptiste: Nyantanga, BP 59, Butare; Pres. Rev. DAVID BAZIGA; Gen. Sec. ELEAZAR ZIHERAMBERE.

Eglise Luthérienne du Rwanda: BP 3099, Kigali; tel. 755110035 (mobile); fax 250519734; e-mail luthchurchlcr@yahoo.com; Bishop GEORGE W. KALIISA; 40,000 mems (2010).

There are about 250,000 other Protestants, including a substantial minority of Seventh-day Adventists.

BAHÁ'Í FAITH

National Spiritual Assembly: BP 652, Kigali; tel. 250572550; e-mail asnbaha@rwanda1.com.

ISLAM

There is a small Islamic community.

The Press

REGULATORY AUTHORITY

Media High Council: Revolution Ave, POB 6929, Kigali; tel. 250570333; fax 250570334; e-mail info@mhc.gov.rw; internet www.mhc.gov.rw; f. 2002; Pres. ARTHUR ASIIMWE; Exec. Sec. EMMANUEL MUGISHA (acting).

DAILY

The New Times: Immeuble Aigle Blanc, BP 4953, Kigali; tel. 788301166 (mobile); fax 250574166; e-mail editorial@newtimes.co.rw; internet www.newtimes.co.rw; f. 1995; daily; English; CEO and Editor-in-Chief COLLIN HABA (acting).

PERIODICALS

Bulletin Agricole du Rwanda: OCIR—Café, BP 104, Kigali-Gikondo; f. 1968; quarterly; French; Pres. of Editorial Bd Dr AUGUSTIN NZINDUKIYIMANA; circ. 800.

Etudes Rwandaises: Université Nationale du Rwanda, Rectorat, BP 56, Butare; f. 1977; quarterly; pure and applied science, literature, human sciences; French; Pres. of Editorial Bd CHARLES NTAKIRUTINKA; circ. 1,000.

Hobe: BP 761, Kigali; f. 1955; monthly; children's interest; circ. 95,000.

Inkingi: BP 969, Kigali; tel. 250577626; fax 250577543; monthly.

Inkoramutima: Union des Eglises Rwandaises, BP 79, Kigali; quarterly; religious; circ. 5,000.

Kinyamateka: 5 blvd de l'OUA, BP 761, Kigali; tel. 250576164; e-mail km@rwanda1.com; internet www.kinyamateka.org.rw; f. 1933; fortnightly; economics; circ. 11,000; Dir Fr PIERRE CLAVER NKUSI.

La Nouvelle Relève: Office Rwandais d'Information, BP 83, Kigali; tel. 250575735; e-mail lnr2020@yahoo.fr; internet www.orinfor.gov .rw; f. 1963; bi-weekly; politics, economics, culture, education, sport, justice, health, society and environment; French; Dir GÉRARD RUGAMBWA; circ. 1,700.

Nouvelles du Rwanda: Université Nationale du Rwanda, BP 117, Butare; every 2 months.

Nyabarongo—Le Canard Déchaîné: BP 1585, Kigali; tel. 250576674; monthly.

Le Partisan: BP 1805, Kigali; tel. 250573923; fortnightly.

La Patrie—Urwatubyaye: BP 3125, Kigali; tel. 250572552; monthly.

Rwanda Herald: Kigali; f. 2000; owned by Rwanda Independent Media Group.

Rwanda Libération: BP 398, Kigali; tel. 250577710; monthly; Dir and Editor-in-Chief ANTOINE KAPITENI.

Rwanda Renaître: BP 426, Butare; fortnightly.

Rwanda Rushya: BP 83, Kigali; tel. 250572276; fortnightly.

Le Tribun du Peuple: BP 1960, Kigali; bi-monthly; Owner JEAN-PIERRE MUGABE.

Umucunguzi: Gisenyi; f. 1998; Kinyarwanda and French; Chief Editor EMILE NKUMBUYE.

Umuhinzi-Mworozi: OCIR—Thé, BP 1334, Kigali; tel. 250514797; fax 250514796; f. 1975; monthly; circ. 1,500.

Umusemburo—Le Levain: BP 117, Butare; monthly.

Umuseso: Kigali; independent; weekly; Kinyarwanda; publ. suspended in April 2010; Editor CHARLES KABONERO.

Umusingi: BP 4305, Kigali; tel. 788350847 (mobile); e-mail umusingi@yahoo.com; Kinyarwandan; Editor STANLEY GATERA.

Urunana: Grand Séminaire de Nyakibanda, BP 85, Butare; tel. 250530793; e-mail wellamahoro@yahoo.fr; f. 1967; 3 a year; religious; Pres. WELLAS UWAMAHORO; Editor-in-Chief DAMIEN NIYOYIREMERA.

NEWS AGENCIES

Office Rwandais d'Information (Orinfor): BP 83, Kigali; tel. 250575735; fax 250576539; internet www.orinfor.gov.rw; f. 1973; Dir JOSEPH BIDERI.

Rwanda News Agency (RNA): BP 453, Kigali; tel. 250587215; fax 250587216; internet www.rnanews.com; f. 1975.

PRESS ASSOCIATION

Association Rwandaise des Journalistes (ARJ): POB 4305, Kigali; e-mail safarigaspard@hotmail.com; Pres. COLLIN HABA; Sec.-Gen. JANE UWIMANA.

Publishers

Editions Rwandaises: Caritas Rwanda, BP 124, Kigali; tel. 250575786; fax 250574254; e-mail caritas1@rwanda1.com; Man. Dir Abbé CYRIAQUE MUNYANSANGA; Editorial Dir ALBERT NAMBAJE.

Implico: BP 721, Kigali; tel. 250573771.

Imprimerie de Kabgayi: BP 66, Gitarama; tel. 250562252; fax 250562345; e-mail imprikabgayi@yahoo.fr; f. 1932; Dir Abbé CYRILLE UWIZEYE.

Imprimerie de Kigali, SARL: 1 blvd de l'Umuganda, BP 956, Kigali; tel. 250582032; fax 250584047; e-mail impkig@rwandatel1 .rwanda1.com; f. 1980; Dir LÉONCE NSENGIMANA.

Pallotti-Presse: BP 863, Kigali; tel. 250574084.

GOVERNMENT PUBLISHING HOUSES

Imprimerie Nationale du Rwanda: BP 351, Kigali; tel. 250576214; fax 250575820; f. 1967; Dir JUVÉNAL NDISANZE.

Régie de l'Imprimerie Scolaire (IMPRISCO): BP 1347, Kigali; e-mail imprisco@rwandatel1.rwanda1.com; f. 1985; Dir JEAN DE DIEU GAKWANDI.

Broadcasting and Communications

TELECOMMUNICATIONS

At November 2011 there were 4,446,194 mobile subscribers and 38,901 fixed-line subscribers.

Airtel Rwanda: Airtel Head Office, nr Amahoro National Stadium, Kigali; tel. 730000456 (mobile); e-mail customer.care@rw.airtel.com; internet www.africa.airtel.com; f. 2011; commenced operations in April 2012; Country Man. MARCELLIN PALUKU.

MTN Rwandacell: BP 264, MTN Centre, Nyarutarama, Kigali; tel. 250586863; fax 250586865; e-mail customercare@mtn.co.rw; internet www.mtn.co.rw; f. 1998; provides mobile cellular and fixed-line telephone services; CEO KHALED MIKKAWI; 2,892,827 mobile subscribers and 10,014 fixed-line subscribers.

Rwandatel: Ecobank Bldg, 7th Floor, ave de La Paix, BP 1332, Kigali; tel. 252555555; fax 252582300; e-mail info@rwandatel.rw; internet www.rwandatel.rw; national telecommunications service; privatized 2007; licence for cellular services revoked in April 2011; liquidation pending; provides fixed-line telephone services.

Tigo Rwanda: 9801 Nyarutarama, POB 6979, Kigali; tel. 722123000 (mobile); internet www.tigo.co.rw; provides mobile cellular telephone and internet services; CEO DIEGO CAMBEROS.

REGULATORY AUTHORITY

Rwanda Utilities Regulatory Authority (RURA): POB 7289, Kigali; tel. 252584562; fax 252584563; e-mail info@rura.gov.rw; internet www.rura.gov.rw; f. 2001; also responsible for regulation of electricity, water, sanitation, gas and transportation sectors; Chair. EUGÈNE KAZIGE; Dir-Gen. REGIS FRANCOIS GATARAYIHA.

BROADCASTING
Radio

Radio Rwanda: BP 83, Kigali; tel. 250575665; fax 250576185; f. 1961; state-controlled; daily broadcasts in Kinyarwanda, Swahili, French and English; Dir of Programmes DAVID KABUYE.

Deutsche Welle Relay Station Africa: Kigali; daily broadcasts in German, English, French, Hausa, Swahili, Portuguese and Amharic.

Television

Télévision Rwandaise (TVR): Kigali; fax 250575024; f. 1992; transmissions reach more than 60% of national territory; broadcasts for 10 hours daily in Kinyarwanda, French and English.

TV10: blvd de l'aeroport Gishushu, Remera, POB 4307, Kigali; tel. 250786022804; internet www.tv10rwanda.com; f. 2012; privately owned commercial station; Man. Dir CEDRIC PIERRE-LOUIS.

Finance

(cap. = capital; res = reserves; dep. = deposits; m. = million; brs = branches; amounts in Rwanda francs)

BANKING

In 2010 there were 12 banks in Rwanda.

Central Bank

Banque Nationale du Rwanda (BNR): ave Paul VI, BP 531, Kigali; tel. 250575282; fax 250572551; e-mail info@bnr.rw; internet www.bnr.rw; f. 1964; bank of issue; cap. 7,000m., res 21,183.0m., dep. 297,242.9m. (Dec. 2009); Gov. JOHN RWANGOMBWA.

Commercial Banks

Following the privatization of two commercial banks, government control of the banking section was reduced from 45% in 2003 to 22% in 2005, although the three largest banks continued to control two-thirds of the system's assets, valued at US $365m. (equivalent to 34% of GDP).

Access Bank (Rwanda) Ltd: UTC Bldg, 3rd Floor, 1232 ave de la Paix, BP 2059, Kigali; tel. 250500091; fax 250575761; e-mail bancor@ rwanda1.com; internet www.accessbankplc.com/rw; f. 1995 as Banque à la Confiance d'Or; fmrly Bancor SA; name changed as above in 2009 when acquired by private investors; 75% owned by Access Bank (Nigeria); cap. and res 3,417.1m., total assets 34,549.3m. (Dec. 2005); Chair. NICHOLAS WATSON.

Banque Commerciale du Rwanda, SA: BP 354, 11 blvd de la Révolution, Kigali; tel. 250595200; fax 250573395; e-mail bcr@ rwanda1.com; internet www.bcr.co.rw; f. 1963; privatized Sept. 2004; cap. 5,000m., res 749m., dep. 74,559m. (Dec. 2009); Chair. Dr NKOSANA MOYO; Man. Dir DAVID KUWANA; 6 brs.

Banque de l'Habitat du Rwanda: ave de la Justice, BP 1034, Kigali; tel. 250573843; fax 250572799; e-mail bhr@rwanda1.com; internet www.bhr.co.rw; f. 1975 as Caisse Hypothécaire du Rwanda; name changed as above in 2005; 56% state-owned; cap. 778.2m., total assets 6,966.8m. (Dec. 2003); Pres. FRANÇOIS RUTISHASHA; Dir-Gen. GERVAIS NTAGANDA.

Banque de Kigali, SA: 63 ave du Commerce, BP 175, Kigali; tel. 250593100; fax 250573461; e-mail bk@bk.rw; internet www.bk.rw;

f. 1966; cap. 5,005.0m., res 10,892.3m., dep. 124,586.8m. (Dec. 2009); Chair. LADO GURGENIDZE; Man. Dir JAMES GATERA; 33 brs.

Compagnie Générale de Banque: blvd de l'Umuganda, BP 5230, Kigali; tel. 250597500; fax 250503336; e-mail cogebank@cogebank .com; internet www.cogebank.com; f. 1999; cap. and res 1,210.8m., total assets 7,297.4m. (Dec. 2003); Pres. ANDRÉ KATABARWA; 13 brs.

Ecobank Rwanda: ave de la Paix, BP 3268, Kigali; tel. 250503580; fax 250501319; e-mail contact@ecobank.com; internet www.ecobank .com; cap. and res 3,158.4m., total assets 45,950.9m. (Dec. 2003); Man. Dir DANIEL SACKEY.

Fina Bank SA: 20 blvd de la Révolution, BP 331, Kigali; tel. 250598600; fax 250573486; e-mail info@finabank.co.rw; internet www.finabank.com; f. 1983 as Banque Continentale Africaine (Rwanda); name changed 2005; cap. 5,000.6m., res 634.6m., dep. 40,885.6m. (Dec. 2009); privatized; Chair. ROBERT BINYON; Man. Dir STEPHEN CALEY; 5 brs.

Development Banks

Banque Rwandaise de Développement, SA (BRD): blvd de la Révolution, BP 1341, Kigali; tel. 250575079; fax 250573569; e-mail brd@brd.com.rw; internet www.brd.com.rw; f. 1967; 56% state-owned; cap. and res 4,104.6m., total assets 13,920.7m. (Dec. 2003); CEO JACK NKUSI KAYONGA.

Banques Populaires du Rwanda (Banki z'Abaturage mu Rwanda): BP 1348, Kigali; tel. 250573559; fax 250573579; e-mail info@bpr.rw; internet www.bpr.rw; f. 1975; cap. and res 1,180.5m., total assets 20,433.8m. (Dec. 2002); Pres. MANASSÉ TWAHIRWA; CEO HERMAN KLAASSEN; 145 brs.

STOCK EXCHANGE

Rwanda Stock Exchange (RSE): Kigali; f. 2011.

INSURANCE

In 2010 there were five insurance companies in Rwanda.

Compagnie Générale d'Assurances et de Réassurances au Rwanda (COGEAR): ave de l'Armée, BP 2753, Kigali; tel. 250576041; fax 250576082; Dir-Gen. ANASTASE MUNYANDAMUTSA.

Société Nationale d'Assurances du Rwanda (SONARWA): 2417 blvd de la Révolution, BP 1035, Kigali; tel. 250572101; fax 250572052; e-mail sonarwa@rwandatel1.rwanda1.com; internet www.sonarwa.co.rw; f. 1975; 35% owned by Industrial and General Insurance Co Ltd (Nigeria); cap. 500m.; Pres. FRANÇOIS NGARAMBE; Dir-Gen. HOPE MURERA.

SORAS Group Ltd: blvd de la Révolution, BP 4742, Kigali; tel. 788185300 (mobile); fax 250573362; e-mail infogroup@soras.co.rw; internet www.soras.co.rw; f. 1984; cap. 2,505m. (2012); Pres. CHARLES MHORANYI.

Trade and Industry

GOVERNMENT AGENCIES

Capital Markets Authority: Ecobank Bldg, 5th Floor, ave de la Paix, POB 6136, Kigali; tel. 250500335; e-mail info@cma.rw; internet www.cma.rw; f. 2007; Exec. Dir ROBERT MATHU.

National Agricultural Export Development Board (NAEB): POB 104, Kigali; tel. and fax 252575600; e-mail info@naeb.gov.rw; internet www.naeb.gov.rw; f. 2011; formulates policies and strategies for developing exports of agricultural and livestock products; Dir Gen. ALEX KANYANKOLE.

Rwanda Agricultural Development Authority (RADA): BP 538, Kigali; tel. 755102618 (mobile); e-mail infos@rada.gov.rw; internet www.rada.gov.rw; f. 2006; contributes towards the growth of agricultural production through the development of appropriate technologies, providing advisory, outreach and extension services to stakeholders in agriculture; Dir-Gen. NORBERT SENDEGE.

Rwanda Investment and Export Promotion Agency: Kimihurura, ave du Lac Muhazi, POB 6239, Kigali; tel. 250510248; fax 250510249; e-mail info@rwandainvest.com; internet www .rwandainvest.com; f. 1998 as Rwanda Investment Promotion Agency; Dir-Gen. FRANCIS GATARE.

Rwanda Public Procurement Authority: ave de la Paix, POB 4276, Kigali; tel. 250501403; fax 250501402; e-mail rppa1@rwanda1 .com; internet www.rppa.gov.rw; f. 2008 to replace the Nat. Tender Bd (f. 1998); organizes and monitors general public procurement; Chair. DAMIEN MUGABO; Dir AUGUSTUS SEMINEGA.

Rwanda Revenue Authority (RRA): ave du Lac Muhazi, POB 3987, Kimihurura, Kigali; tel. 250595520; fax 250578488; e-mail cg@ rra.gov.rw; internet www.rra.gov.rw; f. 1998 to maximize revenue collection; Commissioner-Gen. BEN KAGARAMA.

DEVELOPMENT ORGANIZATIONS

Coopérative de Promotion de l'Industrie Minière et Artisanale au Rwanda (COOPIMAR): BP 1139, Kigali; Dir DANY NZARAMBA.

Institut de Recherches Scientifiques et Technologiques (IRST): BP 227, Butare; tel. 250530395; fax 250530939; e-mail irst@irst.ac.rw; internet www.irst.ac.rw; Dir-Gen. Dr JEAN BAPTISTE NDUWAYEZU.

Institut des Sciences Agronomiques du Rwanda (ISAR): 47 rue du Député Kamunzinzi, POB, 5016 Kigali; tel. 250530642; fax 250530644; e-mail info@isar.rw; internet www.isar.rw; for the devt of subsistence and export agriculture; Dir DAPHROSE GAHAKWA; 12 centres.

Office National pour le Développement de la Commercialisation des Produits Vivriers et des Produits Animaux (OPROVIA): BP 953, Kigali; privatization pending; Dir DISMAS SEZIBERA.

Régie d'Exploitation et de Développement des Mines (REDEMI): BP 2195, Kigali; tel. 250573632; fax 250573625; e-mail ruzredem@yahoo.fr; f. 1988 as Régie des Mines du Rwanda; privatized in 2000; state org. for mining tin, columbo-tantalite and wolfram; Man. Dir JEAN-RUZINDANA MUNANA.

Rwanda Development Board: Gishushu, Nyarutarama Rd, POB 6239, Kigali; tel. 250580804; e-mail info@rdb.rw; internet www.rdb .rw; f. 2008 to replace eight govt agencies (RIEPA, ORTPN, Privatization Secretariat, Rwanda Commercial Registration Services Agency, Rwanda Information and Technology Authority, Centre for Support to Small and Medium Enterprises, Human Resource and Institutional Capacity Development Agency, and Rwanda Environmental Management Authority); CEO JOHN GARA.

Société de Pyrèthre au Rwanda (SOPYRWA): BP 79, Ruhengeri; tel. and fax 250546364; e-mail info@sopyrwa.com; internet www .sopyrwa.com; f. 1978; cultivation and processing of pyrethrum; post-war activities resumed in Oct. 1994; current production estimated at 80% pre-war capacity; Dir SYLVAIN NZABAGAMBA.

INDUSTRIAL ASSOCIATIONS

Association des Industriels du Rwanda: BP 39, Kigali; tel. and fax 250575430; Pres. YVES LAFAGE; Exec. Sec. MUGUNGA NDOBA.

Private Sector Federation (PSF): Gikonda Magerwa, POB 319, Kigali; tel. 250252570650; fax 250583574; e-mail info@rpsf.org.rw; internet psf.org.rw; f. 1999 to replace the Chambre de Commerce et d'Industrie de Rwanda; promotes and represents the interests of the Rwandan business community; CEO HANNINGTON NAMARA.

UTILITIES

Rwanda Utilities Regulatory Agency (RURA): see Telecommunications.

Rwanda Electricity Corpn and Rwanda Water and Sanitation Corpn (RECO & RWASCO): POB 537, Kigali; tel. 252598400; e-mail fgatanazi@electrogaz.co.rw; internet www.electrogaz.co.rw; f. 1976 as Electrogaz; changed name as above in 2009 after company was split, although it is managed as one institution; state-owned water and electricity supplier; Man. Dir YVES MUYANGE; Dir of Electricity CHARLES KANYAMIHIGO; Dir of Water THEONESTE MINANI.

TRADE UNIONS

Centrale des Syndicats des Travailleurs du Rwanda (CESTRAR): BP 1645, Kigali; tel. 783266262 (mobile); e-mail cestrar@ rwanda1.com; f. 1985; Sec.-Gen. ERIC MANZI.

Congrès du Travail et de la Fraternité au Rwanda: BP 1576, Kigali; tel. 788635536 (mobile); e-mail cotraf_rw@yahoo.fr; internet www.cotraf.org; f. 2003; Pres. DOMINIQUE BICAMIMPAKA.

Conseil National des Organisations Syndicales Libres (COSYLI): BP 4866, Kigali; tel. 725102374 (mobile); Pres. FLORIDA MUKARUGAMBWA.

Transport

Rwanda Transport Development Agency (RTDA): Kucukiro Pension Plaza, 4th Floor, African Union Blvd, POB 6674, Kigali; e-mail info@rtda.gov.rw; internet www.rtda.gov.rw; f. 2010; manages day-to-day aspects of the transport sector; Pres. ELIAS TWAGIRA MATHANIYA.

RAILWAYS

There are no railways in Rwanda, although plans exist for the construction of a line linking Kigali and Isaka in Tanzania, with possible extensions to Bujumbura in Burundi and the Democratic Republic of the Congo. Rwanda has access by road to the Tanzanian railways system. In 2011 the African Development Bank approved

US \$8.5m. in loans and grants to finance a multinational railway project study in Rwanda, Tanzania and Burundi.

ROADS

In 2004 there were an estimated 14,008 km of roads, of which 2,662 km were paved. There are road links with Uganda, Tanzania, Burundi and the Democratic Republic of the Congo.

Office National des Transports en Commun (ONATRACOM): BP 619, Kigali; tel. 250575411; fax 250576126; e-mail onatraco@ rwanda1.com; f. 1978; Dir-Gen. BENJAMIN NTAGANIRA.

INLAND WATERWAYS

There are services on Lake Kivu between Cyangugu, Gisenyi and Kibuye, including two vessels operated by ONATRACOM.

CIVIL AVIATION

Kanombe International Airport at Kigali can process up to 500,000 passengers annually. There is a second international airport at Kamembe, near the border with the Democratic Republic of the Congo. Bugesera International Airport, currently under construction, was expected to receive its first flight in 2016. There are airfields at Butare, Gabiro, Nemba, Ruhengeri and Gisenyi, servicing internal flights.

Rwandair: Kigali Int. Airport Bldg, Top Floor, BP 7275, Kigali; tel. 250503687; fax 250503686; e-mail info@rwandair.com; internet www.rwandair.com; f. 2002 as Rwandair Express; renamed 2009; international services; CEO JOHN MIRENGE.

Tourism

Attractions for tourists include the wildlife of the national parks (notably mountain gorillas), Lake Kivu and fine mountain scenery. Since the end of the transitional period in late 2003, the Government has increased efforts to develop the tourism industry. In 2010 666,001 tourists (incl. same-day visitors) visited Rwanda. Total receipts from tourism were estimated at US \$252m. in 2011.

Office Rwandais du Tourisme et des Parcs Nationaux (ORTPN): blvd de la Révolution 1, BP 905, Kigali; tel. 250576514; fax 250576515; e-mail info@rwandatourism.com; internet www .rwandatourism.com; f. 1973; govt agency; Dir-Gen. ROSETTE RUGAMBA.

Defence

As assessed at November 2012, the total strength of the Rwandan armed forces was estimated at 33,000, comprising an army of 32,000 and an air force of 1,000. In addition, there were an estimated 2,000 local defence forces. A programme to restructure the army, which was expected to be reduced in size to number about 25,000, was planned and a Rwanda Demobilization and Reintegration Commission was mandated to facilitate the reintegration of discharged military personnel into civilian life. In 2012 a total of 4,111 troops were stationed abroad, of which 14 were observers.

Defence Expenditure: Budgeted at 51,700m. Rwanda francs in 2013.

Chief of Defence Staff: Lt-Gen. CHARLES KAYONGA.

Chief of Staff, Land Forces: Lt-Gen. CAESAR KAYIZARI.

Chief of Staff of the Air Force: Col JOSEPH DEMALI (acting).

Education

Primary education, beginning at seven years of age and lasting for six years, is officially compulsory. Secondary education, which is not compulsory, begins at the age of 14 and lasts for a further six years, comprising two equal cycles of three years. In 2003, however, the Government announced plans to introduce a nine-year system of basic education, including three years of attendance at lower secondary schools. Schools are administered by the State and by Christian missions. In 2009/10 99% of children in the relevant age-group were enrolled in primary schools, according to UNESCO estimates, while secondary enrolment in 2010/11 was equivalent to 36% of children in the appropriate age-group (males 35%; females 37%). The Ministry of Education established 94 new secondary schools in 2003, and a further 58 in 2005. Rwanda has a university, with campuses at Butare and Ruhengeri, and several other institutions of higher education, but some students attend universities abroad, particularly in Belgium, France or Germany. In 2009/10 the number of students in tertiary education (there were six public higher education institutions and seven private higher institutions) was 62,734. At the beginning of the 2011 school year English became the language of instruction in all public Rwandan educational establishments. In 2010 spending on education represented 18.2% of total budgetary expenditure.

SAINT CHRISTOPHER* AND NEVIS

Introductory Survey

LOCATION, CLIMATE, LANGUAGE, RELIGION, FLAG, CAPITAL

The Federation of Saint Christopher and Nevis is situated at the northern end of the Leeward Islands chain of the West Indies, with Saba and St Eustatius (both in the Netherlands Antilles) to the north-west, Barbuda to the north-east and Antigua to the south-east. Nevis lies about 3 km (2 miles) to the south-east of Saint Christopher, separated by a narrow strait. The tropical heat, varying between 17°C (62°F) and 33°C (92°F), is tempered by constant sea winds, and annual rainfall averages 1,400 mm (55 ins) on Saint Christopher and 1,220 mm (48 ins) on Nevis. English is the official language. The majority of the population are Christians of the Anglican Communion, and other Christian denominations are represented. The national flag (proportions 2 by 3) comprises two triangles, one of green (with its base at the hoist and its apex in the upper fly) and the other of red (with its base in the fly and its apex in the lower hoist), separated by a broad, yellow-edged black diagonal stripe (from the lower hoist to the upper fly) bearing two five-pointed white stars. The capital is Basseterre, on Saint Christopher.

CONTEMPORARY POLITICAL HISTORY

Historical Context

Saint Christopher, settled in 1623, was Britain's first colony in the West Indies. The French settled part of the island a year later, and conflict over possession continued until 1783, when Saint Christopher was eventually ceded to Britain under the Treaty of Versailles. Nevis was settled by the British in 1628, and remained one of the most prosperous of the Antilles until the middle of the 19th century. The island of Anguilla was first joined to the territory in 1816. The St Kitts-Nevis-Anguilla Labour Party, formed in 1932, campaigned for independence for the islands. In 1958 Saint Christopher-Nevis-Anguilla became a member of the West Indies Federation, remaining so until the Federation's dissolution in 1962. A new Constitution, granted to each of the British territories in the Leeward Islands in 1960, provided for government through an Administrator and an enlarged Legislative Council. After an abortive attempt to form a smaller East Caribbean Federation, Saint Christopher-Nevis-Anguilla attained Associated Statehood in February 1967, as part of an arrangement that gave five of the colonies full internal autonomy, while the United Kingdom retained responsibility for defence and foreign relations. The House of Assembly replaced the Legislative Council, the Administrator became Governor, and the Chief Minister, Robert Bradshaw, became the state's first Premier. Three months later Anguilla rebelled against government from Saint Christopher, and in 1971 reverted to being a de facto British dependency. Anguilla was formally separated from the other islands in 1980.

Domestic Political Affairs

A general election in 1971 returned Robert Bradshaw to the premiership. In the 1975 election the Labour Party again won the largest number of seats, while the Nevis Reformation Party (NRP) once more took both the Nevis seats. Bradshaw died in 1978 and was succeeded as Premier by Paul Southwell, the Deputy Premier. Southwell died in 1979, and was replaced by the party's leader, Lee L. Moore.

In February 1980 the Labour Party was removed from government for the first time in nearly 30 years: a coalition Government comprising the People's Action Movement (PAM) and the NRP was formed under PAM leader Dr Kennedy A. Simmonds. The change of government led to the suspension of a timetable for independence, which had been scheduled for June. In 1982 proposals for a greater degree of autonomy for Nevis and for independence for the whole state were approved by the House of Assembly, although the Labour Party opposed the plans, arguing that the coalition Government did not have a mandate for its independence policy. Disagreements concerning the content of the proposed independence constitution led to civil dis-

turbances in 1982 and 1983. Nevertheless, Saint Christopher and Nevis became an independent state, under a federal Constitution, on 19 September 1983. The Labour Party denounced the special provisions for Nevis in the Constitution as giving the island a powerful role in government that was disproportionate to its size and population. Elections to the Nevis Island Assembly were held in August, at which the NRP won all five elective seats.

Early elections to an enlarged National Assembly (now with 11 elective seats) took place in 1984, at which the ruling PAM-NRP coalition was returned to power. At an election to the Nevis Island Assembly in 1987, the NRP retained four seats and the Concerned Citizens' Movement (CCM) secured one. The CCM increased its representation at the 1989 general election, however. Moore resigned as leader of the Labour Party and was succeeded by Denzil Douglas. The electoral success of the coalition Government under the leadership of Simmonds was attributed to its economic policies.

The CCM secured a majority in the Nevis Island Assembly at an election in 1992. The party's leader, Vance Amory, became Premier of the Island Administration.

At a general election in November 1993 neither the PAM nor the Labour Party managed to secure a legislative majority. Following the refusal of Amory to form a coalition government with either the PAM or the Labour Party, the Governor-General invited Simmonds to form a minority government with the support of the NRP. Douglas protested against the decision and appealed for a general strike to support his demands for a further general election. Serious disturbances ensued, and in December the Governor-General declared a 21-day state of emergency. Meanwhile, Simmonds withdrew from negotiations with Douglas, although an initial agreement to hold a further general election had been reached, in protest at Douglas's premature public revelation of the agreement.

In October 1994 six people were charged in connection with the murder of the head of the Saint Christopher special investigations police unit, Jude Matthew, who had been conducting an investigation into the recent disappearances of William Herbert, the country's Permanent Representative to the UN, and Vincent Morris, a son of the Deputy Prime Minister Sidney Morris. Preliminary investigations suggested that these events were connected to the discovery, at the same time as Morris's disappearance, of a large consignment of cocaine in Saint Christopher. In November Morris resigned following the arrest of two other sons on drugs and firearms charges.

Dominance of the Labour Party

An early general election, conducted in July 1995, was won decisively by the Labour Party, and Denzil Douglas became Prime Minister. Douglas resolved to address violent crime and announced plans to draft proposals for constitutional reform that would provide for the establishment of separate governments for the two islands.

In July 1997 the National Assembly approved legislation to restore a full-time defence force, to include the coastguard, with the principal aim of strengthening the islands' anti-drugs operations. (The army had been in 1981.) In 1998 a convicted murderer was executed—the first implementation of the death penalty in the country since 1985. The Attorney-General, Delano Bart, defended the reintroduction of capital punishment, as part of the Government's strategy to reduce crime rates.

In March 1999 a Constitutional Task Force began work on the drafting of a new constitution. In August the Task Force submitted its report to the Prime Minister, who appointed a seven-member select committee, comprising representatives of all the major parties, to review its recommendations and to draft proposals for constitutional change.

At a general election in March 2000 the Labour Party won all eight seats available on Saint Christopher, gaining the seat previously held by the PAM. There was no change in the position on Nevis, where the CCM retained its two seats and the NRP its one. The new Government again sought to address the increasing crime rate on the islands, which was affecting the tourism industry.

---

*While this island is officially called Saint Christopher as part of the state, the name is usually abbreviated to St Kitts.

The Labour Party was returned to office for a third consecutive term at a general election on 25 October 2004. The incumbent administration, which campaigned on its social development record, won seven of the eight seats on Saint Christopher; the PAM secured the other seat. The balance of power remained the same on Nevis, where the CCM secured two seats and the NRP secured one. Turn-out was 62.2% on Saint Christopher, but was less than 50% overall, reflecting the dissatisfaction of many Nevisians with the current system. Although the voter registration process was regarded as imperfect, the team of observers from the Caribbean Community and Common Market (CARICOM, see p. 231) monitoring the election reported the contest to be generally free and fair.

Remarks made by Commonwealth and CARICOM observers of the 2004 general election precipitated governmental discussions from that year towards electoral reform in an effort to achieve a more comprehensive and democratic system of voting and greater regulation of campaign practices. Amendments submitted to the National Assembly in August 2006 included: the supervision of campaign spending; the consideration of constitutional revisions to provide for more inclusive consultations, particularly with political organizations without parliamentary representation; and a review and possible redefinition of constituency boundaries to achieve more proportional representation of the electorate. It was also suggested that a national registration scheme be conducted to ensure that records of eligible voters were current and accurate, and proposals for a voter identification card initiative, first advanced by the Labour Party in 2000, were also resurrected. The Electoral Reform Consultative Committee conducted a public consultation and submitted a report of its findings on 1 February 2007. The Government began to implement new legislation in early 2008 when the National Identification Card was introduced for registered voters, who were to receive the card on re-registering at an electoral office. The opposition expressed dissatisfaction, claiming that there were a number of discrepancies with the process, including the opportunity for voters to confirm their addresses in multiple constituencies.

A fourth term for Labour

A general election was held on 25 January 2010. The Labour Party won an unprecedented fourth term in office, albeit with a slightly reduced majority. The ruling party secured six of the 11 elected seats in the National Assembly (all in St Kitts constituencies), while the opposition CCM retained two seats (both on Nevis). The PAM increased its parliamentary representation to two deputies (one on each island) and the NRP held onto its single Nevis seat. The PAM launched legal challenges to the outcome of ballots in three constituencies and claimed that its earlier challenges to changes to constituency boundaries had not received sufficient hearing by the National Advisory Electoral Reform and Boundaries Committee. A preliminary report by election observers from the Organization of American States recommended that outstanding boundary issues be addressed as soon as possible, but declared itself satisfied with the election process. Leader Denzil Douglas was reappointed Prime Minister. A new Cabinet was installed in early February.

In October 2010 the Government implemented a closed circuit television scheme, with 70 security cameras installed in high-crime areas of Basseterre and Charlestown (the capital of Nevis). However, the country's crime problems came under international scrutiny in the following month, when a tourist bus was ambushed by armed thieves; two cruise lines diverted their vessels to neighbouring Antigua in response. Douglas emphasized that combating crime was the Government's main priority and boosted funding for the ministry responsible for national security in the 2011 budget. A controversial bill granting the authorities permission to intercept telecommunications transmissions was approved by the National Assembly in February 2011; the Government argued that the new legislation would form an important part of its strategy to address crime. The murder rate declined from a record 27 in 2009 to 20 in 2010. In September 2011 Douglas assumed direct responsibility for defence and the police, areas hitherto under the control of Deputy Prime Minister Sam Condor, who in turn received the redesignated homeland security portfolio. Also in that month, Douglas created two anti-crime task forces, while the legislature adopted the Gang (Prohibition and Prevention) Act, which introduced tough penalties against those convicted of gang-related activities. A new evidence bill received legislative approval in October, facilitating the use of DNA and computer-based evidence in trials and also providing new wit-

ness-protection mechanisms. In spite of these measures, the number of recorded murders rose sharply in 2011, to a new record of 34, before declining to 18 in 2012.

Recent developments: opposition to Douglas

Divisions within the ruling Labour Party administration became evident in early 2013 after Douglas publicly criticized Deputy Prime Minister Condor and Minister International Trade, Industry, Commerce and Consumer Affairs, of Agriculture, Marine Resources and Co-operatives, and of Constituency Empowerment, Timothy Harris, for failing fully to support certain government policies, including a proposal to increase the number of senators in the National Assembly. Following the failure of Condor and Harris to attend a cabinet meeting on the budget, the latter was dismissed from his ministerial role by Douglas in late January 2013; four days later Condor resigned. Harris's ministerial portfolios were divided between Patrice Nisbett and Nigel Carty. Earl Asim Martin, the Minister of Housing and of Public Works, Energy and Public Utilities, was also appointed Deputy Prime Minister. Condor and Harris withdrew their legislative support for the Government in March, depriving the Labour Party of a majority in the National Assembly. Both former ministers also endorsed a pending motion of no confidence in the Douglas administration, which had been submitted by the PAM in December 2012. The no confidence motion had still not been debated by early May 2013, although following approval of the 2013/14 budget on 9 April, despite an opposition boycott, a vote on the Douglas premiership was expected.

Autonomy for Nevis?

In June 1996 Amory announced that the Nevis Island Assembly was initiating proceedings (as detailed in the Constitution—see below) for the secession of Nevis from the federation with Saint Christopher. The announcement was made as plans proceeded for the establishment of a federal government office on Nevis (which Amory considered to be unconstitutional) and as the National Assembly considered a financial services bill that proposed referring all potential investors in Nevis to the federal administration for approval. The Nevis Island Assembly was reported to have interpreted both measures as serious infringements of its administrative rights. Despite the prompt intervention of a number of regional diplomatic initiatives to preserve the federation, a secession bill for Nevis received its preliminary reading in the National Assembly in July. In October the NRP, while supportive of the right to secede, expressed concern at the precipitant nature of Amory's secession timetable, and in November the NRP representative in the National Assembly boycotted a second reading of the bill, forcing a postponement of the debate.

At elections to the Nevis Island Assembly in February 1997 Amory's CCM retained three of the five elective seats, while the NRP retained the remaining two. In October the Nevis Assembly voted unanimously in favour of secession; a referendum on the issue was held in August 1998, in which 61.7%, less than the two-thirds' majority required by the Constitution, voted for autonomy. The leaders of the two islands immediately announced that they would work to improve relations, and Douglas pledged to implement the principal recommendations of a constitutional review commission intended to augment inter-island affairs.

In elections to the Nevis Island Assembly in September 2001 the CCM strengthened its control of the legislature, gaining a total of four elective seats. The NRP, under the leadership of Joseph Parry, took the remaining seat.

In October 2002 Douglas, pronouncing on the recurring issue of greater autonomy for Nevis, said that, while he supported the constitutional right of Nevis to secede from the federation, the federal Government was willing to discuss ways to increase the autonomy of the Nevis Island Administration and Assembly. Amory, however, remained convinced that full autonomy and separate membership of the Organisation of Eastern Caribbean States (OECS, see p. 477) would be a better option for Nevis. In January 2004 an OECS Heads of Government meeting urged the Nevis administration to review its intention to campaign for independence in favour of preserving the status quo. CARICOM (see p. 231), in 2003, and the US Administration, earlier in January 2004, also indicated their support for the existing federation.

The NRP emerged from 15 years in opposition to secure a legislative majority at an election to the Nevis Island Assembly in July 2006. The party captured three of the five elective seats, while the CCM won the remaining two seats. Parry took office as Nevis Island Premier later in the same month. The issue of secession was again foregrounded, with the participating parties presenting opposing stances on a move towards greater autonomy; the outgoing CCM had campaigned for independence from Saint Christopher, while the NRP indicated a preference for constitutional reform. In January 2007 Prime Minister Douglas encouraged the pursuit of greater collaboration between the two islands; by this time the possibility of an imminent referendum on Nevis, promulgated by the former CCM Government, seemed, once again, to have receded.

Legislative elections were held on Nevis on 11 July 2011. The composition of the Nevis Island Assembly remained unaltered after the voting, with the NRP retaining its three seats and the CCM maintaining control of the remaining two. Parry was inaugurated as Nevis Island Premier on the following day. However, Organization of American States (OAS) monitors reported some procedural issues with the poll and also highlighted inadequacies in the island's electoral registration mechanisms. Moreover, owing to concerns about the composition of the electoral roll, the CCM launched a legal challenge against the results and commenced a boycott of the Assembly. The trial took place in January 2012, and in March the Circuit Court declared the results in one constituency, won by the NRP, to be null and void. The Court of Appeal upheld this judgment in August. A by-election to fill the vacant seat was due within 90 days, but in October Parry declared that a fresh general election would be organized instead. Voting took place on 22 January 2013 and resulted in a change of leadership on the island, with the CCM securing three legislative seats and the NRP winning two. Amory duly assumed the premiership on 27 January.

Foreign Affairs

Regional relations

In the late 1980s regional discussions were held on the issue of political unity in the East Caribbean. Saint Christopher and Nevis expressed interest in political unity only if the proposed merger included its Leeward Island neighbours and the Virgin Islands, where an estimated 10,000 Kittitians and Nevisians reside. From 1990 the OECS agreed to relax restrictions on travel between member states. Moreover, in February 2002 it was agreed, with effect from March, to allow nationals of member states to travel freely within the OECS area and to remain in the territory of any other member state for up to six months. A Caribbean Community and Common Market (CARICOM, see p. 231) passport, designed to enhance a sense of community and facilitate intra- and extra-regional travel for citizens of participating nations, was launched in January 2005 and implemented by Saint Christopher and Nevis in October of that year. In July 2006 the Government—together with those of five other Caribbean states—signed a declaration of participation in CARICOM's Caribbean Single Market and Economy (CSME), which was established by six founding member states on 1 January. The CSME was intended to enshrine the free movement of goods, services and labour throughout the CARICOM region.

Other external relations

In 2005 Douglas reiterated the Government's commitment to its lucrative diplomatic relationship with Taiwan. Saint Christopher and Nevis, along with Saint Vincent and the Grenadines, remained the only Caribbean countries still to recognize the statehood of Taiwan, which was losing a contest of so-called 'dollar diplomacy' in the region with the People's Republic of China. In 2008 Saint Christopher and Nevis opened an embassy in Taiwan, the first embassy of a Caribbean country to be located in Asia.

CONSTITUTION AND GOVERNMENT

Saint Christopher and Nevis is a constitutional monarchy. Executive power is vested in the British monarch, as head of state, and is exercised locally by the monarch's personal representative, the Governor-General, who acts in accordance with the advice of the Cabinet. Legislative power is vested in Parliament, comprising the monarch and the National Assembly. The National Assembly is composed of the Speaker, three (or, if a nominated member is Attorney-General, four) nominated members, known as Senators (two appointed on the advice of the Premier and one appointed on the advice of the Leader of the Opposition), and 11 elected members (Representatives), who are chosen from single-member constituencies for up to five years by universal adult suffrage. The Cabinet comprises the Prime Minister, who must be able to command the support of the majority of the members of the National Assembly, the Attorney-

General (ex officio) and four other ministers. The Prime Minister and the Cabinet are responsible to Parliament.

The Nevis Island legislature comprises the Nevis Island Assembly and the Nevis Island Administration, headed by the British monarch (who is represented on the island by the Deputy Governor-General). It operates similarly to the Saint Christopher and Nevis legislature but has power to secede from the federation, subject to certain restrictions.

REGIONAL AND INTERNATIONAL CO-OPERATION

Saint Christopher and Nevis is a member of the Caribbean Community and Common Market (CARICOM, see p. 231), of the Organisation of Eastern Caribbean States (OECS, see p. 477), of the Organization of American States (OAS, see p. 404), the Association of Caribbean States (see p. 459), and of the Community of Latin American and Caribbean States (see p. 475), which was formally inaugurated in December 2011. The Eastern Caribbean Central Bank (ECCB, see p. 465), of which Saint Christopher is a member, is based in Basseterre. In 2001 a regional stock exchange, the Eastern Caribbean Securities Exchange, opened in Basseterre. In June 2010 Saint Christopher and Nevis was a signatory to the Revised Treaty of Basseterre, establishing an Economic Union among OECS member states. The Economic Union, which involved the removal of barriers to trade and the movement of labour as a step towards a single financial and economic market, came into effect on 21 January 2011. Freedom of movement between the signatory states was granted to OECS nationals on 1 August.

Saint Christopher and Nevis joined the UN upon independence in 1983. It acceded to the World Trade Organization (WTO, see p. 444) in 1996. Upon independence, Saint Christopher and Nevis became a full member of the Commonwealth (see p. 244). The country is a party to the Cotonou Agreement (see p. 334), the successor agreement to the Lomé Convention, signed in June 2000 between the European Union (EU, see p. 281) and a group of developing countries. The country is a member of the Group of 77 (see p. 461) organization of developing states and acceded to the Non-aligned Movement in 2006.

ECONOMIC AFFAIRS

In 2011, according to estimates by the World Bank, Saint Kitts and Nevis's gross national income (GNI), measured at average 2009–11 prices, was US $662m., equivalent to $12,480 per head (or $14,490 per head on an international purchasing-power parity basis). During 2002–11 the population increased by an average of 1.4% per year, while over the same period, it was estimated, gross domestic product (GDP) per head decreased, in real terms, at an average annual rate of 0.4%. According to estimates by the Eastern Caribbean Central Bank (ECCB, see p. 465), overall GDP increased, in real terms, by an average of 1.6% annually in 2002–11; GDP declined by 1.8% in 2011.

Agriculture (including forestry and fishing) contributed 1.7% of GDP in 2011. According to FAO estimates, some 20.8% of the working population were employed in the agriculture sector (including sugar manufacturing) in mid-2013. Major crops include coconuts and sea-island cotton, although some vegetables are also exported. Sugar and sugar products had traditionally dominated the economy, but the industry survived in recent years only as a result of generous government subsidies, and closed in 2005. Large areas formerly used for sugar were redesignated for tourism, and the Government made provision for the retraining of sugar industry employees. Other important crops include yams, sweet potatoes, groundnuts, onions, sweet peppers, cabbages, carrots and bananas. Fishing is an increasingly important commercial activity. According to ECCB estimates, agricultural GDP decreased at an average annual rate of 1.3% in 2002–11. The real value of agricultural GDP increased by 11.4% in 2011, owing mainly to growth in the fishing sector.

Industry (including mining, manufacturing, construction and public utilities) provided 24.1% of GDP in 2011. Excluding sugar manufacturing, the sector employed 21.0% of the working population in 1994. According to ECCB estimates, real industrial GDP decreased at an average annual rate of 2.9% in 2002–11. In 2011 the GDP of the sector declined by 6.7%.

Manufacturing provided 9.6% of GDP in 2011, and the sector employed 7.8% of the working population in 1994. The principal manufactured products are garments, electrical components, food products, beer and other beverages. According to the ECCB, the sector declined by an average annual rate of 1.3% during 2002–11. In 2011 real manufacturing GDP decreased by an estimated 15.2%.

Construction contributed 12.8% of GDP in 2011, according to ECCB figures, and employed 10.5% of the working population in 1994. The sector declined by 4.4% in 2002–11. According to ECCB estimates, real construction GDP declined by 13.1% in 2010 and by a further 4.4% in 2011.

The islands are dependent upon imports of fuel and energy (2.8% of total imports in 2011) for their energy requirements. In 2005 the Government became one of 13 Caribbean administrations to sign the PetroCaribe accord, under which Saint Kitts and Nevis was allowed to purchase petroleum from Venezuela at reduced prices. The Government took steps to explore alternative energy sources and to thereby decrease its dependency on costly fuel imports; to this end a wind farm was inaugurated on Nevis in 2010, producing up to 10,000 MW of electricity per year. Geothermal potential was also explored on Nevis, although a drilling project was suspended in 2012.

The services sector contributed 74.3% of GDP in 2011, and employed 64.4% of the working population in 1994. Tourism is a major contributor to the economy. In 2011 tourism generated some EC $248.67m. in receipts. In the same year total visitor arrivals stood at 721,431, an 18.3% increase on the previous year's total. Stop-over visitors (who traditionally spend more money) fell to 91,561 in 2010, but increased to 97,949 in 2011. The real GDP of the services sector increased at an average annual rate of 3.4% in 2002–11. According to the ECCB, real services sector GDP increased by 4.0% in 2010, but declined by 0.5% in 2011.

In 2011 Saint Kitts and Nevis recorded a visible merchandise trade deficit of EC $462.38m. and there was a deficit of some $238.22m. on the current account of the balance of payments. The USA was the islands' principal trading partner in 2008, supplying 61.0% of imports and purchasing 83.6% of exports. Trade with the United Kingdom and with other Caribbean states is also important. The country's leading exports were machinery and transport equipment, miscellaneous manufactured articles, beverages and tobacco, and food and live animals. The principal imports were machinery and transport equipment, food and live animals, basic manufactures, miscellaneous manufactured articles, and chemicals.

In 2011 the central Government of Saint Kitts and Nevis recorded a budgetary surplus of EC $14.4m., equivalent to 0.7% of GDP, according to figures from the ECCB. Saint Kitts and Nevis' general government gross debt was EC $2,981m. in 2011, equivalent to 154.3% of GDP. The country's total external debt was estimated to be US $203m. at the end of 2011, of which US $198m. was long-term public and publicly guaranteed debt. In that year, the cost of servicing long-term public and publicly guaranteed debt and repayments to the IMF was equivalent to 23.2% of the value of exports of goods, services and income (excluding workers' remittances). According to IMF estimates, the annual rate of inflation averaged 4.5% in 2005–11; consumer prices increased by 6.6% in 2011. The rate of unemployment, reported to be around 10% in 2003, is mitigated by mass emigration, particularly from Nevis; remittances from abroad provide an important source of revenue.

The economy was dependent on tourism, which was forecast by the World Travel and Tourism Council to provide some 26.6% of the country's GDP and 25.2% of employment in 2013. The global economic downturn negatively affected the tourism and construction sectors, and the economy entered into recession in 2009. The economy remained depressed throughout 2010, with real GDP contracting by 0.1%. The slow economic recovery in the country's key tourist markets of the USA and the United Kingdom contributed to continuing stagnation within the industry. In an attempt to improve the fiscal position, the Government implemented a 17% value-added tax (10% for the tourism sector) from November 2010, and electricity tariffs were raised sharply in January 2011. The IMF authorized an US $84.5m. stand-by arrangement in July. The three-year programme was intended to stabilize public finances and bolster the Government's economic recovery plans. Saint Kitts and Nevis had one of the highest debt-to-GDP ratios in the world (put at 190.4% of GDP in 2011) and in May 2012 the Government reached a debt-restructuring agreement with the 'Paris Club' of creditor nations: over 60% of the country's debt was cancelled and the remaining balance was to be restructured over 20 years. Following a contraction of 1.8% in 2011, the IMF predicted further economic decline of 0.9% in 2012, but expected a resumption of growth in 2013 owing to increased activity in the tourism and construction sectors.

PUBLIC HOLIDAYS

2014: 1 January (New Year's Day), 2 January (Carnival Last Lap), 18 April (Good Friday), 21 April (Easter Monday), 5 May (May Day), 9 June (Whit Monday), 4 August (August Monday/Culturama), 5 August (August Tuesday/Culturama), 16 September (Heroes' Day), 19 September (Independence Day), 25–26 December (Christmas).

Statistical Survey

Source (unless otherwise stated): St Kitts and Nevis Information Service, Government Headquarters, Church St, POB 186, Basseterre; tel. 465-2521; fax 466-4504; e-mail skninfo@caribsurf.com; internet www.stkittsnevis.net.

AREA AND POPULATION

Area (sq km): 269.4 (Saint Christopher 176.1, Nevis 93.3).

Population: 40,618 at census of 12 May 1991; 45,841 (males 22,784, females 23,057) at census of 14 May 2001. *Mid-2013* (UN estimate): 54,338 (UN estimate). Sources: UN, *Population and Vital Statistics Report* and *World Population Prospects: The 2010 Revision*.

Density (mid-2013): 201.7 per sq km.

Population by Age and Sex (at mid-2000): *0–14:* 12,390 (males 6,390, females 6,000); *15–64:* 24,450 (males 12,340, females 12,110); *65 and over:* 3,570 (males 1,670, females 1,900); *Total* 40,410 (males 20,400, females 20,010) (Source: UN, *Demographic Yearbook*).

Principal Town (estimated population incl. suburbs, mid-2011): Basseterre (capital) 12,496. Source: UN, *World Urbanization Prospects: The 2011 Revision*.

Births and Deaths (2001): Registered live births 803 (birth rate 17.4 per 1,000); Registered deaths 352 (death rate 7.6 per 1,000). *2011:* Crude birth rate 14.1 per 1,000; Crude death rate 7.1 per 1,000 (Source: Pan American Health Organization).

Life Expectancy (years at birth): 74.6 (males 72.3; females 77.0) in 2011. Source: Pan American Health Organization.

Employment (labour force survey, 1994): Sugar cane production/manufacturing 1,525; Non-sugar agriculture 914; Mining and quarrying 29; Manufacturing (excl. sugar) 1,290; Electricity, gas and water 416; Construction 1,745; Trade (except tourism) 1,249; Tourism 2,118; Transport and communications 534; Business and general services 3,708; Government services 2,738; Other statutory bodies 342; *Total* 16,608 (Saint Christopher 12,516, Nevis 4,092). Source: IMF, *St Kitts and Nevis: Recent Economic Developments* (August 1997).

HEALTH AND WELFARE

Key Indicators

Total Fertility Rate (children per woman, 2010): 1.8.

Under-5 Mortality Rate (per 1,000 live births, 2010): 8.

Physicians (per 1,000 head, 2000): 1.1.

Hospital Beds (per 1,000 head, 2009): 6.0.

Health Expenditure (2009): US $ per head (PPP): 689.

Health Expenditure (2009): % of GDP: 5.1.

Health Expenditure (2009): public (% of total): 49.0.

Access to Water (% of persons, 2010): 99.

Access to Sanitation (% of persons, 2010): 96.

Total Carbon Dioxide Emissions ('000 metric tons, 2008): 249.4.

Carbon Dioxide Emissions Per Head (metric tons, 2008): 4.9.

Human Development Index (2011): ranking: 72.

Human Development Index (2011): value: 0.735.

Source: partly Pan American Health Organization; for other sources and definitions, see explanatory note on p. vi.

AGRICULTURE, ETC.

Principal Crops ('000 metric tons, 2011, unless otherwise indicated): Sugar cane 110.0 (2009) (FAO estimate); Coconuts 1.1 (FAO estimate). *Aggregate Production* ('000 metric tons, may include official, semi-official or estimated data): Roots and tubers 0.9; Vegetables (incl. melons) 1.0; Fruits (excl. melons) 2.1.

Livestock ('000 head, 2011): Cattle 7.0; Sheep 7.0; Goats 9.0; Pigs 7.0.

Livestock Products ('000 metric tons, 2011): Chicken meat 0.2 (FAO estimate); Hen eggs 0.3.

Fishing (metric tons, live weight, 2010): Groupers 24; Snappers 46; Grunts, sweetlips 11; Parrotfishes 22; Surgeonfishes 17; European pilchard 3,083; European anchovy 3,077; Sardinellas 4,197; Caribbean spiny lobster 33; Stromboid conchs 95; *Total catch* (incl. others) 21,099.

Source: FAO.

INDUSTRY

Production: Raw sugar 10,700 metric tons in 2005; Electric energy 228.4 million kWh in 2010 (provisional). Sources: IMF, *St Kitts and Nevis: Statistical Appendix* (April 2008) and Eastern Caribbean Central Bank.

FINANCE

Currency and Exchange Rates: 100 cents = 1 Eastern Caribbean dollar (EC $). *Sterling, US Dollar and Euro Equivalents* (31 December 2012): £1 sterling = EC $4.261; US $1 = EC $2.700; €1 = EC $3.562; EC $100 = £23.47 = US $37.04 = €28.07. *Exchange Rate*: Fixed at US $1 = EC $2.70 since July 1976.

Budget (EC $ million, 2011): *Revenue:* Revenue from taxation 408.2 (Taxes on income 87.3, Taxes on property 8.8, Taxes on domestic goods and services 207.8, Taxes on international trade and transactions 104.4); Other current revenue 241.9; Capital revenue 9.7; Foreign grants 80.4; Total 740.2. *Expenditure:* Current expenditure 641.9 (Personal emoluments and wages 222.0, Goods and services 210.2, Interest payments 113.5, Transfers and subsidies 96.2); Capital expenditure and net lending 83.9; Total 725.8. Source: Eastern Caribbean Central Bank.

International Reserves (US $ million at 31 December 2011): Reserve position in IMF 0.13; IMF special drawing rights 12.60; Foreign exchange 231.54; Total 244.27. Source: IMF, *International Financial Statistics*.

Money Supply (EC $ million at 31 December 2011): Currency outside depository corporations 101.99; Transferable deposits 755.22; Other deposits 1,745.86; *Broad money* 2,603.08. Source: IMF, *International Financial Statistics*.

Cost of Living (Consumer Price Index; base: 2005 = 100): All items 121.9 in 2009; 122.5 in 2010; 130.6 in 2011. Source: IMF, *International Financial Statistics*.

Gross Domestic Product (EC $ million at constant 2006 prices): 1,800.91 in 2009; 1,801.76 in 2010; 1,768.43 in 2011. Source: Eastern Caribbean Central Bank.

Expenditure on the Gross Domestic Product (EC $ million at current prices, 2010): Government final consumption expenditure 207.02; Private final consumption expenditure 1,273.43; Gross capital formation 678.39; *Total domestic expenditure* 2,158.84; Exports of goods and services 564.20; *Less* Imports of goods and services 905.39; *GDP at market prices* 1,817.65. Source: Eastern Caribbean Central Bank.

Gross Domestic Product by Economic Activity (EC $ million at current prices, 2011): Agriculture, hunting, forestry and fishing 29.22; Mining and quarrying 1.44; Manufacturing 167.62; Electricity and water 26.02; Construction 223.56; Wholesale and retail trade 130.29; Restaurants and hotels 95.37; Transport, storage and communications 225.07; Finance and insurance 205.45; Real estate and housing 286.23; Government services 163.53; Other community, social and personal services 186.13; *Sub-total* 1,739.94; *Less* Financial intermediation services indirectly measured 23.87; *Total in basic prices* 1,716.07; Taxes, less subsidies, on products 298.73; *GDP at market prices* 2,014.80. Source: Eastern Caribbean Central Bank.

Balance of Payments (EC $ million, 2011): Exports of goods 183.83; Imports of goods –646.21; *Trade balance* –462.38; Services (net) 177.48; *Balance on goods and services* –284.90; Other income received (net) –79.13; *Balance on goods, services and income*

–364.03; Current transfers received (net) 125.81; *Current balance* –238.22; Capital account (net) 183.87; Direct investment (net) 296.01; Portfolio investment (net) –41.74; Other investment (net) 51.81; Net errors and omissions –83.15; *Overall balance* 168.57. Source: Eastern Caribbean Central Bank.

EXTERNAL TRADE

Principal Commodities (EC $ million, 2011): *Imports c.i.f.:* Food and live animals 138.9; Mineral fuels, lubricants, etc. 18.6; Chemicals 55.0; Basic manufactures 125.1; Machinery and transport equipment 179.6; Miscellaneous manufactured articles 114.3; Total (incl. others) 669.7. *Exports f.o.b.* (incl. re-exports): Food and live animals 3.5; Beverages and tobacco 9.0; Basic manufactures 1.0; Machinery and transport equipment 121.9; Miscellaneous manufactures 24.8; Total (incl. others) 163.4. Source: Eastern Caribbean Central Bank.

Principal Trading Partners (US $ million, 2008): *Imports:* Antigua and Barbuda 0.8; Barbados 5.4; Canada 6.7; China, People's Rep. 3.7; Denmark 2.2; Dominican Republic 5.7; France 1.6; Germany 0.4; Grenada 2.0; Jamaica 3.4; Japan 9.8; Netherlands Antilles 6.2; Trinidad and Tobago 37.5; United Kingdom 14.6; USA 198.1; Total (incl. others) 324.8. *Exports* (excl. re-exports): Antigua and Barbuda 0.8; Dominica 0.2; Netherlands Antilles 1.2; Trinidad and Tobago 0.2; United Kingdom 2.3; USA 43.3; Total (incl. others) 51.2. Source: UN, *International Trade Statistics Yearbook*.

TRANSPORT

Road Traffic (registered motor vehicles): 11,352 in 1998; 12,432 in 1999; 12,917 in 2000.

Shipping: *Arrivals* (2000): 1,981 vessels. *International Sea-borne Freight Traffic* ('000 metric tons, 2000): Goods loaded 24.7; Goods unloaded 234.2. *Flag Registered Fleet* (at 31 December 2012): Number 348; Total displacement 1,616,973 grt (Source: Lloyd's List Intelligence—www.lloydslistintelligence.com).

Civil Aviation (aircraft arrivals): 24,800 in 1998; 23,500 in 1999; 19,400 in 2000.

TOURISM

Visitor Arrivals: 547,561 (93,081 stop-over visitors, 3,718 excursionists, 209 yacht passengers, 450,553 cruise ship passengers) in 2009; 610,084 (91,561 stop-over visitors, 3,419 excursionists, 279 yacht passengers, 514,825 cruise ship passengers) in 2010; 721,431 (97,949 stop-over visitors, 3,316 excursionists, 3,797 yacht passengers, 616,369 cruise ship passengers) in 2011. *Stop-over Visitors by Origin* (2011): Canada 5,688; Caribbean 18,765; United Kingdom 8,388; USA 61,629; Other 3,479.

Tourism Receipts (EC $ million): 225.41 in 2009; 232.02 in 2010; 248.67 in 2011.

Source: Eastern Caribbean Central Bank.

COMMUNICATIONS MEDIA

Telephones ('000 main lines in use, 2011): 20.7.

Mobile Cellular Telephones (subscribers, 2011): 51,000.

Personal Computers: 11,000 (234.1 per 1,000 persons) in 2004.

Internet Users (2009): 17,000.

Broadband Subscribers (2010): 14,600.

Source: International Telecommunication Union.

EDUCATION

Pre-primary (2009/10 unless otherwise indicated): 77 schools (2003/04); 84 teachers; 1,685 pupils.

Primary (2009/10 unless otherwise indicated): 23 schools (2003/04); 443 teachers; 6,255 pupils.

Secondary (2009/10 unless otherwise indicated): 7 schools (2003/04); 465 teachers; 4,308 pupils.

Tertiary (2007/08 unless otherwise indicated): 1 institution; 79 teachers (2003/04); 859 students.

Pupil-teacher Ratio (primary education, UNESCO estimate): 14.1 in 2009/10.

Adult Literacy Rate: 97.8% in 2004 (Source: UN Development Programme, *Human Development Report*).

Source: mostly UNESCO Institute for Statistics.

Directory

The Government

HEAD OF STATE

Queen: HM Queen ELIZABETH II.

Governor-General: Sir EDMUND LAWRENCE (took office 1 January 2013).

CABINET
(May 2013)

The Cabinet consists of members of the St Kitts-Nevis Labour Party and one member of the Nevis Reformation Party.

Prime Minister and Minister of Finance, Sustainable Development, Human Resources Development, Constituency Empowerment and Social Security: Dr DENZIL LLEWELLYN DOUGLAS.

Deputy Prime Minister and Minister of Housing and of Public Works, Energy and Public Utilities: Dr EARL ASIM MARTIN.

Minister of Justice and Legal Affairs, of Foreign Affairs, Homeland Security and of Labour: PATRICE NISBETT (NRP).

Minister of Health and Social Services, of Community Development and Gender Affairs and of Culture: MARCELLA A. LIBURD.

Minister of Youth Empowerment and Sports and of Information Technology, Telecommunications and Posts: GLENN F. PHILLIP.

Minister of Education and Information and of Agriculture, Marine Resource and Co-operatives: NIGEL ALEXIS CARTY.

Minister of Tourism, International Transport and of International Trade, Industry, Commerce and Consumer Affairs: RICHARD OLIVER SKERRITT.

MINISTRIES

Office of the Governor-General: Government House, Basseterre; tel. 465-2315.

Government Headquarters: Church St, POB 186, Basseterre; tel. 465-2521; fax 466-4505; e-mail infocom@sisterisles.kn; internet www.gov.kn.

Prime Minister's Office: Government Headquarters, Church St, POB 186, Basseterre; tel. 465-0299; fax 465-1001; e-mail sknpmpresssec@cuopm.com; internet www.cuopm.org.

All ministries are located at Government Headquarters.

NEVIS ISLAND ADMINISTRATION

Premier: VANCE WINKWORTH AMORY.

There are also two appointed members.

Administrative Centre: Main St, POB 689, Charlestown, Nevis; tel. 469-1469; fax 469-0039; e-mail info@niagov.com; internet www.nia.gov.kn.

Legislature

NATIONAL ASSEMBLY

Speaker: CURTIS MARTIN.

Elected members: 11. Nominated members: 3. Ex officio members: 1.

Election, 25 January 2010

Party	Seats
St Kitts-Nevis Labour Party (SKNLP) . . .	6
Concerned Citizens' Movement (CCM) . . .	2
People's Action Movement (PAM)	2
Nevis Reformation Party (NRP)	1
Total	**11**

NEVIS ISLAND ASSEMBLY

President: FARREL SMITHEN.

Elected members: 5. Nominated members: 3.

Elections to the Nevis Island Assembly took place on 22 January 2013. The Concerned Citizens' Movement took three seats and the Nevis Reformation Party secured the remaining two seats.

Election Commission

Office of the Supervisor of Elections: Basseterre; Supervisor of Elections RAPHAEL ARCHIBALD.

Political Organizations

Concerned Citizens' Movement (CCM): Charlestown, Nevis; tel. 469-3519; e-mail admin@myccmparty.com; internet myccmparty.com; f. 1986; Leader VANCE W. AMORY; Chair. STEDMOND TROSS.

Nevis Reformation Party (NRP): Government Rd, POB 480, Charlestown, Nevis; tel. 469-0630; e-mail info@nrpnevis.com; internet nrpnevis.com; f. 1970; Pres. JOSEPH W. PARRY; Gen. Sec. LLEWELYN PARRIS.

People's Action Movement (PAM): Lockhart St, POB 1294, Basseterre; tel. 662-2073; fax 466-3854; e-mail pam.publicrelations@gmail.com; internet pamforchange.com; f. 1965; Political Leader LINDSAY GRANT; Deputy Leaders SHAWN RICHARDS, EUGENE HAMILTON.

St Kitts-Nevis Labour Party (SKNLP): Masses House, Church St, POB 239, Basseterre; tel. 465-5347; fax 465-8328; e-mail wanda.connor@sknlabourparty.com; internet www.sknlabourparty.com; f. 1932; socialist party; Leader Dr DENZIL LLEWELLYN DOUGLAS.

Diplomatic Representation

EMBASSIES IN SAINT CHRISTOPHER AND NEVIS

Brazil: St Kitts Marriott, Suite 17-206, 858 Frigate Bay Rd, Frigate Bay, Basseterre; tel. 465-1054; fax 465-2015; e-mail info@brazilskn.org; internet www.brazilskn.org; Ambassador ANTONIO JOSÉ REZENDE DE CASTRO.

Cuba: 34 Bladen Housing Devt, POB 600, Basseterre; tel. 466-3374; fax 465-8072; e-mail embacubask@sisterisles.kn; internet www.cubadiplomatica.cu/saintkittsnevis; Ambassador HUGO RUIZ CABRERA.

Taiwan (Republic of China): Taylor's Range, POB 119, Basseterre; tel. 465-2421; fax 465-7921; e-mail rocemb@caribsurf.com; internet www.taiwanembassy.org/KN; Ambassador MIGUEL TSAO.

Venezuela: Delisle St, POB 435, Basseterre; tel. 465-2073; fax 465-5452; e-mail frontado@caribsurf.com; Ambassador ROMOLO CAMILO HENRÍQUEZ GONZÁLEZ.

Diplomatic relations with other countries are maintained at consular level, or with ambassadors and high commissioners resident in other countries of the region, or directly with the other country.

Judicial System

Justice is administered by the Eastern Caribbean Supreme Court (ECSC), based in Saint Lucia and consisting of a Court of Appeal and a High Court. Two judges of the High Court are responsible for Saint Christopher and Nevis and preside over the Court of Summary Jurisdiction. One of two ECSC Masters, chiefly responsible for procedural and interlocutory matters, is also resident in Saint Kitts. The Magistrates' Courts deal with summary offences and civil offences involving sums of not more than EC $5,000.

High Court Judges: IANTHEA LEIGERTWOOD-OCTAVE (acting), ERROL THOMAS (acting).

Master: PEARLETTA LANNS.

Registrar: JANINE HARRIS.

Magistrates' Office: Losack Rd, Basseterre; tel. 465-2170; fax 465-2482; Chief Magistrate JOSEPHINE MALLALIEU.

Attorney-General: JASON AKIL HAMILTON.

Religion

CHRISTIANITY

St Kitts Christian Council: Victoria Rd, POB 48, Basseterre; tel. 465-2167; e-mail stgeorgessk@hotmail.com; Chair. Archdeacon VALENTINE HODGE.

The Anglican Communion

Anglicans in Saint Christopher and Nevis are adherents of the Church in the Province of the West Indies. The islands form part of the diocese of the North Eastern Caribbean and Aruba. The Bishop is resident in The Valley, Anguilla.

The Roman Catholic Church

The diocese of Saint John's-Basseterre, suffragan to the archdiocese of Castries (Saint Lucia), includes Anguilla, Antigua and Barbuda, the British Virgin Islands, Montserrat and Saint Christopher and Nevis. The Bishop participates in the Antilles Episcopal Conference (currently based in Port of Spain, Trinidad and Tobago).

Bishop of Saint John's-Basseterre: Mgr KENNETH DAVID OSWIN RICHARDS, POB 836, St John's, Antigua; e-mail djr@candw.ag.

Other Churches

There are also communities of Methodists, Moravians, Seventh-day Adventists, Baptists, Pilgrim Holiness, the Church of God, Apostolic Faith and Plymouth Brethren.

The Press

The Democrat: Cayon St and Walwyn Ave, POB 30, Basseterre; tel. 466-2091; fax 465-0857; e-mail info@skndemocrat.com; internet www.skndemocrat.com; f. 1948; weekly (Sat.); organ of PAM; Man. Editor DENIECE ALLEYNE; circ. 3,000.

The Labour Spokesman: Masses House, Church St, POB 239, Basseterre; tel. 465-2229; fax 466-9866; e-mail sknunion@sisterisles .kn; internet www.labourspokesman.com; f. 1957; Wed. and Sat.; organ of St Kitts-Nevis Trades and Labour Union; Editor DAWUD ST LLOYD BYRON; Man. WALFORD GUMBS; circ. 6,000.

The Leewards Times: Pinneys Industrial Site, POB 146, Nevis; tel. 469-1049; fax 469-0662; e-mail hbramble@caribsurf.com; internet www.leewardstimes.net; weekly (Fri.); Editor HOWELL BRAMBLE.

The St Kitts and Nevis Observer: Cayon St, POB 657, Basseterre; tel. 466-4994; fax 466-4995; e-mail contact@thestkittsnevisobserver .com; internet www.thestkittsnevisobserver.com; weekly (Fri.); independent; Publr and Editor-in-Chief KENNETH A. WILLIAMS.

Publishers

Caribbean Publishing Co (St Kitts-Nevis) Ltd: Dr William Herbert Complex, Frigate Bay Rd, POB 745, Basseterre; tel. 465-5178; fax 466-0307; e-mail sbrisban@caribpub.com; internet stkittsyp.com.

MacPennies Publishing Co: 10A Cayon St East, POB 318, Basseterre; tel. 465-2274; fax 465-8668; e-mail mcpenltd@macpennies .com; internet www.macpennies.com; f. 1969; publr of magazines, books, tel. directories and cable TV guides.

St Kitts-Nevis Publishing Association Ltd: 1 Observer Plaza, Observer Dr., POB 510, Charlestown, Nevis; tel. 469-5907; fax 469-5891; e-mail observnv@sisterisles.kn; internet www .thestkittsnevisobserver.com; f. 1994; Publr and Editor-in-Chief KENNETH A. WILLIAMS.

Broadcasting and Communications

TELECOMMUNICATIONS

Caribbean Cable Communications (CCC): Charlestown, Nevis; tel. 469-5601; e-mail customersupport@caribcable.com; internet ccc2 .caribcable.com; provides internet and cable television services to Nevis; nationalized by Nevis Island Assembly in 2009 and ownership transferred to Nevis Cable Communications Corpn.

Digicel St Kitts and Nevis: Wireless Ventures (Saint Kitts and Nevis) Ltd, Bldg 16, Of. 4, POB 1033, Basseterre; tel. 762-4000; fax 466-4194; e-mail customercarestkittsandnevis@digicelgroup.com; internet www.digicelstkittsandnevis.com; acquired Cingular Wireless' Caribbean operations and licences in 2005; owned by an Irish consortium; Group CEO KEVIN WHITE; Gen. Man. (St Kitts and Nevis) SEAN LATTY.

LIME (St Kitts and Nevis): Cayon St, POB 86, Basseterre; tel. 465-1000; fax 465-1106; e-mail customerservice@lime.com; internet www .time4lime.com; f. 1985 as St Kitts and Nevis Telecommunications Co Ltd (SKANTEL); fmrly Cable & Wireless St Kitts and Nevis; name changed as above 2008; CEO TONY RICE; CEO (Barbados and Eastern Caribbean) GERARD BORELY GERARD BORELY.

Regulatory Authority

National Telecommunications Regulatory Commission (NTRC): Fortlands, POB 1958, Basseterre; tel. 466-8997; fax 466-8617; e-mail directorntrcskn@ectel.int; internet ntrc.kn; f. 2000; regulates the sector in conjunction with the Eastern Caribbean Telecommunications Authority (based in Saint Lucia); Chair CHRISTOPHER MCMAHON; Dir ERVIN WILLIAMS.

BROADCASTING

Radio

Radio One (SKNBC): Bakers Corner, POB 1773, Basseterre; tel. 466-0941; fax 465-1141; e-mail radio1941fm@yahoo.com; internet www.radioone941fm.com; owned by St Kitts & Nevis Broadcasting Corpn; music and commentary.

Radio Paradise: Bath Plains, POB 508, Charlestown, Nevis; tel. 469-1994; fax 469-1642; e-mail info@radioparadiseonline.com; internet www.radioparadiseonline.com; owned by Trinity Broadcasting Network (USA); Christian; Gen. Man. ANDRE GILBERT.

Sugar City Roc FM: Greenlands, Basseterre; tel. 466-1113; e-mail sugarcityroc903fm@hotmail.com; Gen. Man. VAL THOMAS.

Voice of Nevis (VON) Radio 895 AM: Bath Plains, POB 195, Charlestown, Nevis; tel. 469-1616; fax 469-5329; e-mail gmanager@ vonradio.com; internet www.vonradio.com; f. 1988; owned by Nevis Broadcasting Co Ltd; Gen. Man. MERRIT HERBERT.

WINN FM: Unit C24, The Sands, Newtown Bay Rd, Basseterre; tel. 466-9586; fax 466-7904; e-mail info@winnfm.com; internet www .winnfm.com; owned by Federation Media Group; Man. Dir CLIVE BACCHUS.

ZIZ Radio and Television: Springfield, POB 331, Basseterre; tel. 465-2622; fax 465-5624; e-mail info@zizonline.com; internet www .zizonline.com; f. 1961; television from 1972; commercial; govt-owned; Gen. Man. WINSTON MCMAHON.

Television

ZIZ Radio and Television: see Radio.

Finance

(cap. = capital; res = reserves; dep. = deposits; brs = branches; amounts in EC dollars)

REGULATORY AUTHORITY

Financial Services Department: Ministry of Finance, Pelican Mall, Bay Rd, POB 868, Basseterre; tel. 466-5048; fax 466-5317; e-mail skanfsd@sisterisles.kn; internet www.skbfinancialservices .com; regulatory authority for banks and insurance companies; Dir FIDELA CLARKE.

BANKING

Central Bank

Eastern Caribbean Central Bank (ECCB): Headquarters Bldg, Bird Rock, POB 89, Basseterre; tel. 465-2537; fax 465-9562; e-mail info@eccb-centralbank.org; internet www.eccb-centralbank.org; f. 1965 as East Caribbean Currency Authority; expanded responsibilities and changed name 1983; responsible for issue of currency in Anguilla, Antigua and Barbuda, Dominica, Grenada, Montserrat, Saint Christopher and Nevis, Saint Lucia and Saint Vincent and the Grenadines; res 248.3m., dep. 1,302.5m., total assets 2,383.0m. (March 2009); Gov. and Chair. Sir K. DWIGHT VENNER; Man. Dir JENNIFER NERO.

Other Banks

Bank of Nevis Ltd: Main St, POB 450, Charlestown, Nevis; tel. 469-5564; fax 469-5798; e-mail info@thebankofnevis.com; internet www .thebankofnevis.com; cap. 9.3m., res 27.8m., dep. 352.5m., total assets 414.8m. (June 2011); Chair. RAWLINSON ISAAC; Gen. Man. L. EVERETTE MARTIN.

FirstCaribbean International Bank (Barbados) Ltd: The Circus, POB 42, Basseterre; tel. 465-2449; fax 465-1041; internet www .firstcaribbeanbank.com; f. 2002 following merger of Caribbean operations of Barclays Bank PLC and CIBC; Barclays relinquished its stake to CIBC in 2006; res 0.8m. (March 2006); Exec. Chair. MICHAEL MANSOOR; CEO RIK PARKHILL.

RBTT Bank (SKN) Ltd: Chappel St, POB 673, Charlestown, Nevis; tel. 469-5277; fax 469-1493; internet www.rbtt.com; f. 1955 as Nevis Co-operative Banking Co Ltd; acquired by Royal Bank of Trinidad and Tobago (later known as RBTT) in 1996; Group CEO SURESH SOOKOO.

St Kitts-Nevis-Anguilla National Bank Ltd: Central St, POB 343, Basseterre; tel. 465-2204; fax 466-1050; e-mail webmaster@

sknanb.com; internet www.sknanb.com; f. 1971; Govt of St Kitts and Nevis owns 51%; cap. 135.0m., res 352.6m., dep. 1,527.1m. (June 2011); Chair. WALFORD GUMBS; Man. Dir EDMUND LAWRENCE; 5 brs.

Development Bank

Development Bank of St Kitts and Nevis: Church St, POB 249, Basseterre; tel. 465-2288; fax 465-4016; e-mail info@skndb.com; internet www.skndb.com; f. 1981; cap. 10.8m., res 6.8m., dep. 42.7m. (Dec. 2008); Chair. ELVIS NEWTON; Gen. Man. LENWORTH HARRIS.

STOCK EXCHANGE

Eastern Caribbean Securities Exchange: Bird Rock, POB 94, Basseterre; tel. 466-7192; fax 465-3798; e-mail info@ecseonline.com; internet www.ecseonline.com; f. 2001; regional securities market designed to facilitate the buying and selling of financial products for the eight member territories—Anguilla, Antigua and Barbuda, Dominica, Grenada, Montserrat, Saint Christopher and Nevis, Saint Lucia, and Saint Vincent and the Grenadines; Chair. Sir K. DWIGHT VENNER; Gen. Man. TREVOR E. BLAKE.

INSURANCE

National Caribbean Insurance Co Ltd: Central St, POB 374, Basseterre; tel. 465-2694; fax 465-3659; e-mail ncic@skanb.com; internet www.nci-biz.com; f. 1973; subsidiary of St Kitts-Nevis-Anguilla National Bank Ltd; Gen. Man. JUDITH ATTONG.

St Kitts-Nevis Insurance Co Ltd (SNIC): Central St, POB 142, Basseterre; tel. 465-2845; fax 465-5410; e-mail snic@tdcltd.com; internet www.tdclimited.com; subsidiary of St Kitts-Nevis-Anguilla Trading & Devt Co Ltd (TDC); Chair. DENNIS MICHAEL ARTHUR MORTON; Gen. Man. NESTA SEATON-CLARKE.

Several foreign companies also have offices in Saint Christopher and Nevis.

Trade and Industry

GOVERNMENT AGENCY

St Kitts Investment Promotion Agency (SKIPA): POB 1433, Basseterre; tel. 465-1153; fax 465-1154; e-mail info@stkittsipa.org; internet www.stkittsipa.org; f. 2007; CEO ROSALYN HAZELLE.

DEVELOPMENT ORGANIZATION

Foundation for National Development (St Kitts and Nevis) Ltd: Box 507, Bladen Commercial Development, Basseterre; tel. 465-2576; fax 465-9187; e-mail fndskbnev@thecable.net; internet www.carib-hotels.com/stkitts/fndskn; f. 1988; non-profit, non-governmental agency providing loans and technical assistance to small businesses; br. in Nevis.

CHAMBER OF COMMERCE

St Kitts-Nevis Chamber of Industry and Commerce: Horsford Rd, Fortlands, POB 332, Basseterre; tel. 465-2980; fax 465-4490; e-mail sknchamber@sisterisles.kn; internet www.stkittsnevis chamber.org; f. 1949; Pres. DAVID LAKE; Exec. Dir CALVIN CABLE.

UTILITIES

Nevis Electricity Company Ltd (Nevlec): POB 852, Charlestown, Nevis; tel. 469-7245; fax 469-7249; e-mail info@nevlec.com; internet www.nevlec.com; f. 2000; owned by the Nevis Island Administration; Pres. ERNIE STAPLETON; Gen. Man. CARTWRIGHT FARRELL.

St Kitts Electricity Company: Cnr Sprott and Central Sts, Basseterre; internet stkittselectricitycoltd.com; f. Aug. 2011 under present name, fmrly state-run Electricity Dept; govt-run autonomous co; generation and distribution of electricity.

West Indies Power (Nevis) Ltd: POB 368, Charlestown, Nevis; tel. 662-4032; fax 469-0792; e-mail l.diaz@westindiespower.com; internet www.westindiespower.com; subsidiary of West Indies Power Holdings (Bonaire); devt of geothermal energy; CEO KERRY McDONALD; Man. (Nevis) RAWLINSON A. ISAAC.

TRADE UNION

St Kitts-Nevis Trades and Labour Union (SKTLU): Masses House, Church St, POB 239, Basseterre; tel. 465-2229; fax 466-9866; e-mail sknunion@caribsurf.com; f. 1940; affiliated to Caribbean Maritime and Aviation Council, Caribbean Congress of Labour, International Federation of Plantation, Agricultural and Allied Workers, and International Trade Union Confederation; associated with St Kitts-Nevis Labour Party; Pres. CLIFFORD THOMAS; Gen. Sec. BATUMBA TAK; c. 3,000 mems.

Transport

RAILWAYS

There are 58 km (36 miles) of narrow-gauge light railway on Saint Christopher, serving the sugar plantations and tourist routes.

St Kitts Scenic Railway: Sands Unit A6, Bay Rd, POB 191, Basseterre; tel. 465-7263; fax 466-4815; e-mail scenic reservations@sisterisles.kn; internet www.stkittsscenicrailway .com; f. 2002; Exec. Vice-Pres. and Gen. Man. THOMAS A. WILLIAMS.

ROADS

There were 320 km (199 miles) of road in Saint Christopher and Nevis in 2000, of which approximately 136 km (84 miles) were paved. In 2009 the Caribbean Development Bank approved a loan of US $6.3m. to the Government to improve the West Basseterre Bypass Road.

SHIPPING

The Government maintains a commercial motorboat service between the islands, and numerous regional and international shipping lines call at the islands. There is also a deep-water port, Port Zante, at Basseterre, as well as a ferry dock. There are three ports in Nevis, at Charlestown, Long Point Port and New Castle. A ferry service operates between Charlestown and Basseterre.

Nevis Air and Sea Ports Authority: Nisbett Bldg, Main St, POB 741, Charlestown; tel. 469-2001; fax 469-2004; e-mail nevports@ sisterisles.kn; internet www.nevisports.com; f. 1995; Chair. LAURIE LAWRENCE; Gen. Man. SPENCER HANLEY; Airport Man. STEPHEN HANLEY; Sea Port Man. EVERETTE MASON.

St Christopher Air and Sea Ports Authority: Bird Rock, POB 963, Basseterre; tel. 465-8121; fax 465-8124; e-mail info@scaspa.com; internet www.scaspa.com; f. 1993 to combine St Kitts Port Authority and Airports Authority; Chair. CAROL EVELYN; CEO and Gen. Man. TERRENCE GROSSMAN; Airport Man. ELSWORTH WARNER (acting); Sea Port Man. ROSEVELT TROTMAN.

Shipping Companies

Delisle Walwyn and Co Ltd: Liverpool Row, POB 44, Basseterre; tel. 465-2631; fax 465-1125; e-mail info@delislewalwyn.com; internet www.delislewalwyn.com; f. 1951; shipping agents; represents Tropical Shipping; Chair. KISHU CHANDIRAMANI; Man. Dir DENZIL V. CROOKE.

Hobson Enterprises Ltd: POB 105, Basseterre; tel. 465-8753; fax 465-6154; e-mail contact@hobsonenterprises.com; internet www .hobsonenterprises.com; f. 1987; shipping agent, freight forwarders; CEO DAMION HOBSON.

Woodsrite Enterprises: Bird Rock Industrial Park, POB 92, Basseterre; tel. 465-2532; fax 465-3230; e-mail contact@woodsrite .com; internet www.woodsrite.com; f. 1975; shipping agent, freight forwarders; Man. Dir CUTHBERT WOODS.

CIVIL AVIATION

Robert Llewellyn Bradshaw (formerly Golden Rock) International Airport, 4 km from Basseterre, is equipped to handle jet aircraft and is served by scheduled links with most Caribbean destinations, the United Kingdom, the USA and Canada. A US $17m. expansion and development project at the airport, financed by Taiwan and the St Kitts-Nevis-Anguilla National Bank Ltd, was completed in 2006. Saint Kitts and Nevis is a shareholder in the regional airline LIAT (see Antigua and Barbuda). Vance W. Amory International Airport (formerly Newcastle Airfield), 11 km from Charlestown, Nevis, has regular scheduled services to St Kitts and other islands in the region.

Nevis Air and Sea Ports Authority: see Shipping.

St Christopher Air and Sea Ports Authority: see Shipping.

LIAT Airlines: Robert Llewellyn Bradshaw International Airport; tel. 465-5491; fax 465-7042; e-mail customerrelations@liatairline .com; internet www.liatairline.com; f. 1956 as Leeward Islands Air Transport Services; privatized in 1995; shares are held by the Govts of Antigua and Barbuda, Montserrat, Grenada, Barbados, Trinidad and Tobago, Jamaica, Guyana, Dominica, Saint Lucia, Saint Vincent and the Grenadines, and Saint Christopher and Nevis (30.8%), Caribbean Airlines (29.2%), LIAT employees (13.3%) and private investors (26.7%); acquired Caribbean Star Airlines in March 2007; scheduled passenger and cargo services to 19 destinations in the Caribbean; charter flights are also undertaken; Chair. JEAN STEWART HOLDER; CEO Capt. IAN ARTHUR BRUNTON; Country Man. AVENICE JEFFERS-THOMPSON.

Tourism

The introduction of regular air services to the US cities of Miami and New York has opened up the islands as a tourist destination. Visitors are attracted by the excellent beaches and the historical Brimstone Hill Fortress National Park on Saint Christopher, the spectacular mountain scenery of Nevis and the islands' associations with Lord Nelson and Alexander Hamilton. In 2011 there were 616,369 cruise ship passengers and 97,949 stop-over visitors. Receipts from tourism were EC $248.6m. in that year.

Nevis Tourism Authority: Main St, POB 184, Charlestown, Nevis; tel. 469-7550; fax 469-7551; e-mail info@nevisisland.com; internet www.nevisisland.com; f. 2001; Chair. KEISHA JONES; CEO JOHN HANLEY.

St Kitts-Nevis Hotel and Tourism Association: Unit C9, Sands Complex, POB 438, Basseterre; tel. 465-5304; fax 465-7746; e-mail info@stkittsnevishta.org; internet www.stkittsnevishta.org; f. 1972; Pres. NICK MENON; Man. MICHAEL HEAD.

St Kitts Tourism Authority: Pelican Mall, Bay Rd, POB 132, Basseterre; tel. 465-4040; fax 465-8794; e-mail ceo@stkittstourism .kn; internet www.stkittstourism.kn; Chair. ALFONSO O'GARRO; CEO CAROLYN JAMES (acting).

Defence

The small army was disbanded by the Government in 1981, and its duties were absorbed by the Volunteer Defence Force and a special tactical unit of the police. Saint Christopher and Nevis participates in the US-sponsored Regional Security System, comprising police, coastguards and army units, which was established by independent Eastern Caribbean states in 1982. According to the 2011 budget presentation, the Ministry of National Security, Immigration and Labour was to receive an allocation of EC $50.3m. in that year.

Education

Education is compulsory for 12 years between five and 17 years of age. Primary education begins at the age of five, and lasts for seven years. Secondary education, from the age of 12, generally comprises a first cycle of four years, followed by a second cycle of two years. In 2009/10 enrolment at primary schools included 83% of children in the relevant age-group, according to UNESCO estimates, while comparable enrolment at secondary schools included 88% of pupils. There are 30 state, eight private and five denominational schools. There is also a technical college. In September 2000 a privately financed 'offshore' medical college, the Medical University of the Americas, opened in Nevis with 40 students registered. The Ross University School of Veterinary Medicine and the International University of Nursing also operated on Saint Christopher. Budgetary expenditure on education and information by the central Government in 2012 was projected to total EC $61.8m.

SAINT LUCIA

Introductory Survey

LOCATION, CLIMATE, LANGUAGE, RELIGION, FLAG, CAPITAL

Saint Lucia is the second largest of the Windward Islands group of the West Indies, lying 40 km (25 miles) to the south of Martinique and 32 km (20 miles) to the north-east of Saint Vincent, in the Caribbean Sea. The island is volcanic, with spectacular mountain scenery; the Pitons, the island's twin, jungle-clad volcanic mountains, were designated a UNESCO (see p. 158) World Heritage Site in June 2004. The average annual temperature is 26°C (79°F), with a dry season from January to April, followed by a rainy season from May to August. The average annual rainfall is 1,500 mm (60 ins) in the low-lying areas, and 3,500 mm (138 ins) in the mountains. The official language is English, although a large proportion of the population speak a French-based patois. Almost all of the island's inhabitants profess Christianity, and 68% are adherents of the Roman Catholic Church. The national flag (proportions 1 by 2) is blue, bearing in its centre a white-edged black triangle partly covered by a gold triangle rising from a common base. The capital is Castries.

CONTEMPORARY POLITICAL HISTORY

Historical Context

British settlers made an unsuccessful attempt to colonize the island (originally inhabited by a Carib people) in 1605. A further British party arrived in 1638 but were killed by the indigenous Carib population. France claimed sovereignty in 1642, and fighting between French and Caribs continued until 1660, when a peace treaty was signed. Control of Saint Lucia was transferred 14 times before it was ceded by the French and became a British colony in 1814. It remained under British rule for the next 165 years.

Representative government was introduced in 1924. The colony was a member of the Windward Islands, under a federal system, until December 1959. It joined the newly formed West Indies Federation in January 1958, and remained a member until the Federation's dissolution in May 1962. From January 1960 Saint Lucia, in common with other British territories in the Windward Islands, was given a new Constitution, with its own Administrator and an enlarged Legislative Council.

Domestic Political Affairs

In 1951 the first elections under adult suffrage were won by the Saint Lucia Labour Party (SLP), which retained power until 1964, when John (later Sir John) Compton, of the newly formed conservative United Workers' Party (UWP), became Chief Minister. In 1967 Saint Lucia became one of the West Indies Associated States, gaining full autonomy in internal affairs, with the United Kingdom retaining responsibility for defence and foreign relations only. The Legislative Council was replaced by a House of Assembly, the Administrator was designated Governor, and the Chief Minister became Premier.

In 1975 the Associated States agreed that they would seek independence individually. After three years of negotiations, Saint Lucia became independent on 22 February 1979, remaining within the Commonwealth. Compton became the country's first Prime Minister.

A general election in 1979 returned the SLP to government with a clear majority, and its leader, Allan Louisy, succeeded Compton as Prime Minister. In February 1980 a new Governor-General, Boswell Williams, was appointed. This led to disputes within the Government and contributed to a split in the SLP. The controversy continued until April 1981, when Louisy was forced to resign after Deputy Prime Minister George Odlum and three other SLP members of the House voted with the opposition against the Government's budget. In May Winston Cenac took office as Prime Minister. In September the Cenac administration narrowly defeated a motion of no confidence, introduced jointly by UWP and Progressive Labour Party (PLP—formed by Odlum) members of the House, who accused the Government of political and economic mismanagement. In January 1982 a government proposal to alter legislation regarding the expenses of members of Parliament produced widespread accusations of corruption. Demands for the Government's resignation increased from all sectors of the community, culminating in a general strike. Cenac resigned, and an all-party interim administration was formed, under the deputy leader of the PLP, Michael Pilgrim. At an election in May the UWP was returned to power, and John Compton was re-elected Prime Minister. In December Sir Allen Lewis was reappointed Governor-General, following the dismissal of Boswell Williams because of his previous close association with the SLP.

The UWP won a one-seat majority at a general election in April 1987; a further election took place at the end of the month, in the hope of a more decisive result, but the distribution of seats remained unchanged. In June the UWP's majority was increased to three seats, when Cenac defected from the SLP. He was subsequently appointed Minister of Foreign Affairs.

The UWP won a further term in office at a general election in April 1992. The SLP attributed its defeat largely to a redefinition of constituency boundaries by the Government prior to the election.

The SLP in power

In August 1995 the report of a commission of inquiry into allegations of the Government's involvement in the misappropriation, for electoral purposes, of some US $100,000 in UN contributions concluded that the former Permanent Representative to the UN, Charles Flemming, had been the sole perpetrator of the fraud. Flemming, who insisted that he had acted with the knowledge and endorsement of senior members of the UWP (including the Prime Minister), failed to return from a visit to the USA undertaken during the commission's hearings. The Minister of State with Responsibility for Financial Services and the National Development Corporation, Rufus Bousquet (who claimed to have been an unwitting recipient of the funds), had been dismissed in May, after he publicly questioned whether it was appropriate that the Government remain in office pending investigation of the affair.

The UWP, in January 1996, appointed Vaughan Lewis, the former Director-General of the Organisation of Eastern Caribbean States (OECS, see p. 477), to the vacancy created by the Prime Minister's retirement from the party leadership. Lewis won the Central Castries parliamentary by-election in February, and was subsequently appointed Minister without Portfolio. SLP leader Julian Hunte resigned later in the month; Kenny Anthony, a former SLP education and culture minister, replaced him. In March Compton resigned from the premiership, and was succeeded by Lewis.

A general election in May 1997 was won decisively by the SLP, which was returned to power after 15 years, securing 16 of the 17 seats in the House of Assembly. Kenny Anthony was sworn in as the new Prime Minister. Among the nine ministers in his first Cabinet was George Odlum, who had rejoined the SLP. Following his electoral defeat Lewis announced his intention to resign from the leadership of the UWP; Sir John Compton (as he had become) replaced him in June 1998.

In August 1997 the Governor-General, Sir George Mallet, resigned. His appointment, in June 1996, had been opposed by the SLP, on the grounds that the post's tradition of neutrality would be compromised: Mallet had previously been Deputy Prime Minister, and his portfolio had included several influential ministries. Saint Lucia's first female Governor-General, Dr Pearlette Louisy, was appointed in September 1997.

In 1997 an inquiry was launched into allegations of corruption under the UWP. The commission of inquiry submitted its report to the Government in August 1999. The report cleared Compton and Lewis of corruption, but noted instances of impropriety and a 'high degree of maladministration' in their Governments.

In January 2001, following an increase in tourist cancellations, Prime Minister Anthony announced a series of measures intended to reduce the crime rate in Saint Lucia. These included the establishment of a National Anti-Crime Commission, the creation of a 10-member police 'rapid response unit', a review of the penal code, and reforms to the police service. In June

Anthony announced the creation of four more rapid response units, a special task force to target known criminals, plans for more severe penalties for gun crimes, an increase in police patrols and an amnesty for holders of illegal firearms.

In March 2001 George Odlum left the Government and the SLP to join a new opposition grouping, the National Alliance (NA), founded by former premier Sir John Compton and UWP leader Morella Joseph. In October the NA's assembly elected Compton to head the party. However, Odlum rejected the decision and claimed the voting process was flawed. Later the same month the UWP withdrew from the Alliance and announced it would contest the elections as a single party. Odlum chose to retain the National Alliance name for his group.

The ruling SLP achieved another convincing victory at the December 2001 general election, winning 14 of the 17 parliamentary seats. The remaining seats were taken by the UWP. Joseph and Odlum, leaders of the UWP and the NA, respectively, both lost their seats. Joseph resigned as UWP leader and was replaced by Vaughan Lewis.

In July 2003 Parliament approved a constitutional amendment abolishing the oath of allegiance to the British monarch; instead, elected members were to pledge loyalty to the Saint Lucian people. In November the Government announced the establishment of a Constitutional Review Commission. The development, which was supported by the opposition, was designed to expand public participation in Saint Lucia's democracy. Meanwhile, also in November the Government adopted a new Criminal Code, which included two particularly controversial clauses. The first provided for a two-year prison sentence for anyone convicted of spreading 'false news'. The clause provoked consternation among local media representatives and the UWP, whose parliamentary members absented themselves from the vote. The second controversial element of the Code allowed for the legalization of abortion, previously illegal in all circumstances, in cases of rape, incest and medical danger to the mother. The law prompted trenchant criticism from anti-abortion and religious groups, and in January 2004 led to the dismissal of Sarah Flood-Beaubrun from her post as Minister of Home Affairs and Gender Relations; she resigned from the SLP in March and later established a new political party, the Organization for National Empowerment.

Flood-Beaubrun's dismissal from the Government was part of a wider cabinet realignment in early 2004, which included the appointment of Calixte George as head of a new Ministry of Home Affairs and Internal Security. The new department was to oversee the police service, previously the responsibility of the Attorney-General's Office, and was charged with finding a solution to the island's spiralling crime rate. In November 2005 legislation granting extra powers to law enforcement authorities received senate approval. Despite the recruitment of 10 British police officers in 2006 and renewed pledges by the Government for more rigorous anti-crime initiatives and deterrents, the murder rate escalated to a record 39 by the end of that year.

A UWP Government

The UWP celebrated an unprecedented and decisive victory in the December 2006 general election: the party secured 11 of the 17 parliamentary seats contested, while the incumbent SLP secured the remaining six seats. Compton, who had replaced Lewis as party leader in the previous year, was sworn in as premier on 15 December.

Mindful of the significant public debt burden requiring the new Government's urgent attention, Compton announced in January 2007 that an audit commission was to investigate considerable ministerial overspending on public sector projects. The inquiry followed reports of widespread financial irregularities and unexplained delays in implementation. The new UWP administration also confirmed in January that proposals by the previous Government to grant an amnesty to Caribbean Community and Common Market (CARICOM, see p. 231) nationals residing illegally in Saint Lucia would be sustained, offering those concerned the opportunity to 'regularize' their citizenship status upon payment of a stipulated fee.

Following a period of ill health, Compton died in early September 2007. Stephenson King, who had been acting Prime Minister in Compton's absence was designated his permanent successor, and was duly sworn in as Prime Minister. The new premier announced a new Cabinet, in which he assumed the portfolios for finance, external affairs, home affairs and national security.

In May 2008 Minister of Economic Affairs, Economic Planning, National Development and Public Service Ausbert d'Auvergne tendered his resignation following criticism from UWP colleagues over an alleged business relationship with convicted criminals. His departure prompted King to execute a reallocation of cabinet portfolios. Notable in the reorganization was the reappointment of Rufus Bousquet to the Government, as trade and industry minister. Bousquet had been dismissed from the Cabinet in the previous June, reportedly after he re-established diplomatic relations with Taiwan (see below) without the knowledge of Compton. At the end of the year Bousquet was allocated the external affairs portfolio, in addition to his existing duties.

A commission of inquiry was appointed in early 2009 to investigate claims of mismanagement of public funds by the Anthony Government. Among the allegations to be examined was the authorization of a loan for the construction of the Hyatt Hotel in 1997. The High Court in 2003 had ruled the refinancing 'void and illegal', in part because the SLP administration had not sought parliamentary approval for the project. The Commission's report, published in October, found instances of irregularities and mismanagement by the Anthony Government, but no criminal activity. It recommended, *inter alia*, proper management, financial and accounting systems be put in place when awarding government contracts and an end to the time limit put on the recovery of public funds.

Fears over rising crime rates prompted the Government in early 2009 to announce its intention to resume capital punishment of convicted murderers. Although the law allowed for capital punishment, the last execution in Saint Lucia occurred in 1995. There were a record 44 murders in Saint Lucia in 2010, indicating a worrying rise in gang-related violence, although the homicide rate declined to 39 in 2011 and 37 in 2012. Anti-gang legislation was under consideration in early 2013.

King declared a state of emergency on 2 November 2010 following the widespread damage to infrastructure, housing and agriculture caused by Hurricane Tomas. Reconstruction costs were estimated at US $336m., and at least 14 people lost their lives in the disaster. The Prime Minister of Trinidad and Tobago, Kamla Persad-Bissessar, generated controversy by initially implying that assistance to Saint Lucia (and other Caribbean nations affected by Hurricane Tomas) would come only if companies in Trinidad and Tobago were to benefit financially from reconstruction contracts.

The resignations of two UWP deputies in February and August 2011, respectively, reduced the ruling party's representation in the House of Assembly to nine seats, although King dismissed rumours of divisions within the party. In September the minister responsible for housing, Richard Frederick, also resigned after the US authorities withdrew his visa for unspecified reasons. Frederick, who had previously been accused of involvement in the illegal drugs trade, denied any wrongdoing.

Recent developments: the SLP in office

The SLP triumphed in the general election that took place on 28 November 2011, gaining control of 11 seats in the House of Assembly; the UWP secured the remaining six seats. The voter participation rate was recorded at 56.8%. Election monitors declared the poll free and fair, although concern was expressed about unequal electoral boundaries and the lack of transparency in campaign-financing. Commentators argued that high levels of crime, ministerial scandals and the island's ongoing economic problems had contributed to the UWP's defeat. Kenny Anthony was sworn in as Prime Minister on 30 November, and he announced his new Cabinet in early December. Most notably, Alva Baptiste received the foreign affairs portfolio, Philip La Corbiniere was appointed as Minister for Legal Affairs, Home Affairs and National Security, and Anthony assumed responsibility for finance and economic affairs.

Embarrassment was caused in February 2013, when the country's voting privileges at the UN were revoked owing to non-payment of membership fees. Anthony pledged to resolve the matter, which he claimed had arisen because of an 'administrative deficiency', although King demanded an inquiry into the incident.

The Banana Sector

In October 1993 a three-day strike was organized by a new pressure group, the Banana Salvation Committee (BSC), in support of demands for an increase in the minimum price paid to local producers for bananas and for the dismissal of the board of directors of the Saint Lucia Banana Growers' Association (SLBGA). Following recommendations made by a government-appointed committee, the Government implemented price increases and dismissed the board of directors of the SLBGA. An announcement by the Government that the SLBGA was to be placed into receivership provoked a strike by the BSC in March 1994. The BSC organized further strikes by banana farmers that year and in 1995 in support of demands for an extraordinary meeting of the SLBGA, and for an inquiry into the deaths of two demonstrators during the 1993 strike. Further industrial action was undertaken by the BSC in February 1996, in protest at the monopoly on banana exports exercised by the state-run Windward Islands Banana Development and Exporting Co (Wibdeco). In September the House of Assembly approved legislation revising the selection procedure for members of the SLBGA and the responsibilities of its general manager. The new legislation effectively transferred control of the association from the Government to the banana growers, who would henceforth elect six members of the board of directors (while the Government would continue to nominate the remaining five). In October the BSC coordinated industrial action by banana growers in support of renewed demands for an end to the Wibdeco monopoly, and for reform of the industry's management and payment systems. Subsequent negotiations with a parliamentary review committee and with the Government (which promised to transfer some responsibility for the industry to the private sector) failed to appease the farmers.

In September 1997 the directors of the SLBGA resigned, at Anthony's request: the Government was reportedly concerned that divisions at boardroom level were damaging the association's operations. Such divisions became increasingly pronounced as plans proceeded for the privatization of the SLBGA, one of the stated aims of the SLP Government. The Concerned Farmers Group (CFG), formed in December and led by the ousted Chairman, Rupert Gajadhar, which grouped larger farmers, expressed concern that the more numerous smaller producers in the BSC (whose secretary, Patrick Joseph, was also a government senator) would unduly dominate the new company, since decision-making was to be on the basis of 'one member, one vote'. Members of the CFG threatened to establish their own company unless their concerns were addressed.

In July 1998 the SLBGA was privatized and the Saint Lucia Banana Corpn (SLBC) was created in its place. The Government agreed to assume the debts incurred by the dissolved SLBGA, equivalent to EC \$44m. The CFG, which had refused to participate in the process, subsequently established a rival company, the Tropical Quality Fruit Co (TQF). In October a court judgment ruled that the SLBC did not enjoy monopoly rights in the banana trade. This ruling followed complaints from the TQF that Wibdeco had been refusing to accept its fruit for shipment. The TQF alleged that this refusal was owing to pressure exerted by the SLBC Chairman, Patrick Joseph, in his capacity as a member of the Wibdeco board.

In January 1999 the SLBC announced that it had incurred losses of EC \$6m. in 1998 and would therefore be forced to reduce the price paid to farmers. The SLBC blamed its operating deficit primarily on the fact that, because banana production had been underestimated, Wibdeco had failed to obtain sufficient European Union (EU, see p. 281) licences, meaning that much of the fruit produced did not reach high-paying markets. The TQF also announced a deficit, but claimed that its lower operating costs had reduced its losses. The TQF further suggested that the SLBC had damaged its own profitability by keeping prices deliberately high in an attempt to force the TQF out of business.

In July 1999 the Government founded a Banana Industry Trust, which was to oversee the improvement of farming practices in the banana sector and manage the financial resources available to the industry, including EC \$21m. in funds provided by the EU. In August Wibdeco agreed to finance a temporary subsidy on prices in order to alleviate hardship among growers. In late 1999, however, the company encountered increasing pressure from the SLBC and from the Government to deliver increased returns to farmers, and in January 2000, following the expiry of its agreement to sell through Wibdeco, the SLBC announced plans to sell direct to Geest Bananas.

The SLBC entered into a dispute with Wibdeco when, in February 2008, the latter announced plans to terminate its contract with the SLBC as it had not been certified by the Fairtrade Labelling Organization of the United Kingdom. The SLBC claimed that it had not been given adequate notice to achieve fair trade status and instructed Wibdeco to withdraw its notice of termination. However, in March Wibdeco signed a sales and purchase agreement with two other companies to bring the supply chain of the island's bananas into line with fair trade

regulations. The SLBC, now faced with the threat of closure, was subsequently granted a court injunction preventing Wibdeco from effecting its termination notice.

Saint Lucia's most important export market is the United Kingdom, which receives most of the banana crop under the terms of the Cotonou Agreement (see p. 334). In July 1993 new regulations came into effect governing the level of imports of bananas by the European Community (now EU, of which the United Kingdom is a member). The regulations were introduced to protect traditional producers from competition from the expanding Latin American producers. At the instigation of the Latin American producers, consecutive dispute panels were appointed by the General Agreement on Tariffs and Trade (GATT, which was succeeded by the World Trade Organization—WTO, see p. 444) to rule on whether the EU's actions contravened GATT rules. Although the disputes panel ruled in favour of the Latin American producers, the rulings were not enforceable. In February 1996 the USA renewed consultations with the WTO concerning the EU's banana import quota regime. A WTO interim report in 1997 appeared to uphold many of the charges of unfair discrimination brought by the plaintiffs. The WTO Appellate Body rejected representations by the EU against the ruling in September, and ruled that the EU must formulate a new system for banana imports by early 1998; new arrangements were duly proposed by the EU, under which it would apply a system of quotas and tariffs to both groups of producers, while retaining an import-licensing system.

The EU's new banana import regime was implemented on 1 January 1999 in compliance with the WTO ruling, though the USA criticized the reforms as negligible. Further discussions on the issue broke down in late January 1999 when Saint Lucia, backed by other countries, objected to any discussion of US demands for sanctions on EU goods. On 1 February the USA introduced punitive import duties on various EU goods, and in March the WTO disputes panel was asked to consider whether the EU had done enough to amend its import regime and whether the USA could legally impose retaliatory import tariffs. In retaliation, the banana-exporting countries threatened to withdraw their co-operation with the US campaign against drugs-trafficking, while banana producers warned that they might switch to growing marijuana if they were forced out of business. On 6 April WTO arbitrators awarded damages against the EU, although at a lower level than the USA had been claiming, and a week later delivered a ruling criticizing aspects of the EU banana-importing regime, which gave the USA permission to impose retaliatory tariffs on certain European goods. In April 2001 the USA agreed to suspend these sanctions from July, after the dispute was resolved: following a transition period, a new, tariff-only regime was introduced from January 2006. Despite substantial government and EU assistance, augmented by the efforts of a Banana Emergency Recovery Unit and the Banana Industry Trust, the Saint Lucian banana industry continued to exhibit decline. Agreement on the structure of the tariff-only regime was finally reached in December 2009. Saint Lucia would continue to enjoy tariff-free access to the EU market, but tariffs imposed on Latin American producers would be reduced over the following seven years. The EU pledged some €200m. in compensation to Caribbean producers, to be disbursed in 2010–14. Nevertheless, the sector was expected to contract further following the final resolution of the dispute.

Foreign Affairs

Regional relations

Saint Lucia is a member of the OECS, and, since 1987, has been a prominent advocate of the creation of a unitary East Caribbean state. In 1988, however, Antigua and Barbuda expressed opposition to political union, thereby discouraging any participation by Montserrat or Saint Christopher and Nevis. The four English-speaking Windward Islands countries (Saint Lucia, Dominica, Grenada, and Saint Vincent and the Grenadines) thus announced plans to proceed independently towards a more limited union. In 1990 the leaders of the four countries established a Regional Constituent Assembly. Following a series of discussions, the Assembly issued its final report in 1992, in which it stated that the four countries were committed to the establishment of economic and political union under a federal system.

In September 2005 the Government signed the PetroCaribe accord, under which Saint Lucia would be allowed to purchase petroleum from Venezuela at reduced prices. However, owing to very limited storage facilities, Saint Lucia was unable to proceed further in accepting fuel shipments. Furthermore, the UWP

Government that came to power in 2006 indicated that implementation of the PetroCaribe initiative would not be a priority and the enterprise was abandoned indefinitely. However, following the SLP's election victory in November 2011, the new administration moved to reverse this policy, and Saint Lucia formally joined PetroCaribe in February 2013.

In November 2003 Parliament approved legislation enabling the Government to pledge US $2.5m. towards the establishment of the Caribbean Court of Justice (CCJ), to be headquartered in Trinidad. The CCJ, which was to replace the Privy Council in the United Kingdom as the region's highest court, was inaugurated in April 2005; however, in 2013 Saint Lucia's final court of appeal remained the Privy Council.

Other external relations

In 1997 the new SLP Government effected a significant reorientation of foreign policy when it was announced that diplomatic relations were to be established with the People's Republic of China. Taiwan subsequently severed relations with Saint Lucia. By 2004 it was estimated that China had provided Saint Lucia with funds worth US $100m. throughout the seven years of their association. In late 2005 Prime Minister Anthony accused the UWP of jeopardizing Saint Lucia's profitable relationship with China after allegations emerged that Sir John Compton had secretly met the President of Taiwan and sought to develop a relationship between the UWP and Taiwan. Such fears were partly allayed with the signing of a technical co-operation agreement with China in September 2006. In February 2007 the new foreign affairs minister, Rufus Bousquet, reiterated his Government's intention to maintain links with China, but in April he announced that the country would resume diplomatic relations with Taiwan; China subsequently suspended ambassadorial relations with Saint Lucia. During an official state visit to the island in January 2008, Taiwan's President Chen Shui-bian stated his commitment to provide aid and investment. The opposition SLP accused the Taiwanese ambassador on the island of interfering in political affairs in March 2009 after it emerged that Taiwan was funding the establishment of a computer-literacy centre in the constituency headquarters of a prominent UWP politician (the centre was subsequently moved to a more neutral location). A similar accusation of political interference was made in August 2010, when the SLP claimed that the Taiwanese ambassador had provided funding to a UWP constituency group for a sports programme. This allegation was rejected by the Government and by the Taiwanese embassy. In mid-2011 Anthony accused Taiwan of funding the UWP's re-election campaign and in September demanded the resignation of the Taiwanese ambassador. Taiwan denied the allegations. Anthony became Prime Minister in November and promised to review the island's foreign relations, prompting speculation that the new SLP administration would withdraw recognition of Taiwan and re-establish diplomatic ties with China. However, in September 2012 Anthony confirmed that official relations with Taiwan would be maintained.

CONSTITUTION AND GOVERNMENT

The Constitution came into force at the independence of Saint Lucia in 1979. The country is a constitutional monarchy. Executive power is vested in the British monarch, as Head of State, and is exercisable by the Governor-General, who represents the monarchy and is appointed on the advice of the Prime Minister. Legislative power is vested in Parliament, comprising the monarch, the 17-member House of Assembly, elected from single-member constituencies for up to five years by universal adult suffrage, and the Senate, composed of 11 members appointed by the Governor-General, including six appointed on the advice of the Prime Minister and three on the advice of the Leader of the Opposition. Government is effectively by the Cabinet. The Governor-General appoints the Prime Minister and, on the latter's recommendation, the other Ministers. The Prime Minister must have majority support in the House, to which the Cabinet is responsible. Judicial power is vested in the Eastern Caribbean Supreme Court.

REGIONAL AND INTERNATIONAL CO-OPERATION

Saint Lucia is a member of the Caribbean Community and Common Market (CARICOM, see p. 231). The country became a signatory to CARICOM's Caribbean Single Market and Economy (CSME) in July 2006. The CSME, which was established by six founding member states on 1 January 2006, was to enshrine the free movement of goods, services and labour throughout most of the CARICOM region. An intra-regional CARICOM passport

initiative, regarded as an integral component in the advance towards economic union and designed to facilitate travel for citizens of participating nations, was implemented in Saint Lucia in January 2007. Saint Lucia is a party to the Caribbean Basin Initiative (CBI). The country is a member of the Organisation of Eastern Caribbean States (OECS, see p. 477), of the Organization of American States (see p. 404), the Association of Caribbean States (see p. 459), the Eastern Caribbean Central Bank (see p. 465), and of the Community of Latin American and Caribbean States (see p. 475), which was formally inaugurated in December 2011. In June 2010 Saint Lucia was a signatory to the Revised Treaty of Basseterre, establishing an Economic Union among OECS member states. The Economic Union, which involved the removal of barriers to trade and the movement of labour as a step towards a single financial and economic market, came into effect in January 2011. Freedom of movement between the signatory states was granted to OECS nationals on 1 August.

Saint Lucia joined the UN soon after independence in 1979. As a contracting party to the General Agreement on Tariffs and Trade (GATT), Saint Lucia joined the World Trade Organization (see p. 444) on its establishment in 1995. Upon independence, Saint Lucia became a full member of the Commonwealth (see p. 244). Saint Lucia is a party to the Cotonou Agreement (see p. 334), the successor agreement to the Lomé Convention, signed in June 2000 between the European Union (see p. 281) and a group of developing countries. The country is a member of the Group of 77 (see p. 461) organization of developing states and acceded to the Non-aligned Movement in 2006.

ECONOMIC AFFAIRS

In 2011, according to estimates by the World Bank, Saint Lucia's gross national income (GNI), measured at average 2009–11 prices, was US $1,176m., equivalent to $6,680 per head (or $9,080 per head on an international purchasing-power parity basis). During 2002–11, it was estimated, the population increased at an average annual rate of 1.1%, while gross domestic product (GDP) per head remained constant during the same period. According to estimates by the Eastern Caribbean Central Bank (ECCB, see p. 465), overall GDP increased, in real terms, at an average annual rate of 3.0% in 2001–11; real GDP increased by 1.0% in 2011.

Agriculture (including hunting, forestry and fishing) accounted for 3.3% of GDP in 2011. The sector employed some 12.2% of the active working population in 2007. Despite the decline in the banana industry, the fruit remains Saint Lucia's principal cash crop, although in 2008 it accounted for 13% of the total value of merchandise exports, compared with 50% in 2002. Other important crops include coconuts, mangoes, citrus fruit, cocoa and spices. Commercial fishing was being developed. According to ECCB estimates, during 2002–11 real agricultural GDP decreased at an average annual rate of 3.7%. The agriculture sector's GDP declined by 18.2% in 2010, and by 6.5% in 2011 following an outbreak of black sigatoka disease in the banana sector.

Industry (including mining, manufacturing, public utilities and construction) accounted for 16.4% of GDP in 2011, and the sector engaged an estimated 19.9% of the active working population in 2007. According to ECCB estimates, during 2002–11 industrial GDP increased at an average annual rate of 3.1%. The sector's real GDP declined by 5.2% in 2010, but increased by 2.0% in 2011.

Manufacturing accounted for 3.7% of GDP in 2011, and employed 6.1% of the employed population in 2007. The principal manufacturing industries, which have been encouraged by the establishment of 'free zones', include the processing of agricultural products, the assembly of electronic components and the production of garments, plastics, paper and packaging, and beer, rum and other beverages. During 2002–11 the sector's real GDP increased at an average annual rate of 3.5%. Real manufacturing GDP declined by 3.0% in 2010, but increased by 2.5% in 2011.

Construction contributed 8.4% to GDP in 2011, and engaged 13.1% of the employed labour force in 2007. According to ECCB estimates, the sector's GDP increased at an average annual rate of 2.6% in 2002–11. Construction GDP contracted by 9.4% in 2010, but increased by 2.1% in 2011, owing mainly to government-funded projects. The construction stimulus programme was expanded in late 2012.

Energy is traditionally derived from imported hydrocarbon fuels (mineral fuels and lubricants comprised an estimated 15.5% of total imports in 2011). There is a petroleum storage and transshipment terminal on the island, although in 2012 its owners, Hess of the USA, announced plans to sell it. Saint Lucia was a signatory to the PetroCaribe accord, under which the country was allowed to purchase petroleum from Venezuela at reduced prices.

The services sector contributed 80.2% of GDP in 2011, and engaged an estimated 68.0% of those employed in 2007. Tourism is the most important of the service industries, and in 2011 tourist receipts totalled EC $799.8m. Stop-over visitors increased by 9.9% in 2010, but decreased by 5.3% in 2011. The real GDP of the hotels and restaurants sector increased by 2.4% in 2011. During 2002–11 the real GDP of the services sector increased at an average annual rate of 3.6%. Sectoral GDP increased by 1.0% in 2011.

In 2011 Saint Lucia recorded an estimated visible merchandise trade deficit of EC $1,145.49m., and a deficit of some EC $657.90m. on the current account of the balance of payments. The principal source of imports was the USA (42.6% of the total in 2008); other important markets were Trinidad and Tobago and Japan. The principal market for exports was also the USA (34.0% of the total in 2008); other major export markets were Trinidad and Tobago and the United Kingdom. Mineral fuels and lubricants were the principal export commodity in 2011, ahead of beverages and tobacco, machinery and transport equipment, miscellaneous manufactured articles, basic manufactures, and food and live animals. The principal imports in that year were machinery and transport equipment, food and live animals, mineral fuels and lubricants, miscellaneous manufactured articles, basic manufactures, and chemicals.

In 2011 there was an overall budgetary deficit of EC $238.6m, according to provisional figures, equivalent to 7.3% of GDP. Saint Lucia's general government gross debt was EC $2,328m. in 2011, equivalent to 69.7% of GDP. Saint Lucia's total external debt at the end of 2010 was US $464m., of which US $286m. was public and publicly guaranteed debt. In that year, the cost of servicing long-term public and publicly guaranteed debt and repayments to the IMF was equivalent to 7.1% of the value of exports of goods, services and income (excluding workers' remittances). The annual rate of inflation averaged 3.0% in 2005–11; inflation

averaged 4.3% in 2011. In 2007 the average rate of unemployment was 14.6%.

The Saint Lucian economy, which traditionally relied on the production of bananas for export, underwent considerable structural change at the end of the 20th century, with the emergence of service industries as the most important sector of the economy, while investment in the island's infrastructure also benefited the tourism industry, which became the principal source of foreign exchange. In 2013 the World Travel and Tourism Council estimated that the tourism sector accounted for about 40% of Saint Lucia's GDP and 43% of its employment. The agricultural sector, nevertheless, remained a significant source of employment, and the loss of Saint Lucia's preferential access to European markets was of considerable concern. The tourism and construction industries recovered from the effects of the global downturn during 2010, but the agricultural sector was badly affected by Hurricane Tomas, which completely destroyed the banana crop along with most of the island's other crops in October of that year. The IMF released US $8.2m. in funding in January 2011 to support the country's reconstruction programme in the aftermath of Tomas. The economy expanded by just 0.6% in 2010 and 1.0% in 2011. These low rates of growth prompted the Government to implement a programme of expansionary spending in mid-2012, focused on the construction sector. Moreover, a value-added tax was introduced in October in an attempt to boost revenues and stabilize the fiscal situation, although the most immediate effect was a rise in inflation. According to the IMF, real GDP contracted by 0.4% in 2012, with modest growth of 1.1% expected in 2013, supported by an upturn in the tourism and agricultural sectors.

PUBLIC HOLIDAYS

2014: 1 January (New Year), 22 February (Independence Day), 18 April (Good Friday), 21 April (Easter Monday), 5 May (Labour Day), 9 June (Whit Monday), 19 June (Corpus Christi), 1 August (Emancipation Day), 6 October (Thanksgiving Day), 13 December (National Day), 25–26 December (Christmas).

Statistical Survey

Source (unless otherwise indicated): St Lucian Government Statistics Department, Block A, Government Bldgs, Waterfront, Castries; tel. 452-7670; fax 451-8254; e-mail statsdept@candw.lc; internet www.stats.gov.lc.

AREA AND POPULATION

Area: 616.3 sq km (238 sq miles).

Population: 162,982 at census of 22 May 2001 (including estimate for underenumeration); 165,595 (males 82,194, females 83,401) at census of 10 May 2010 (preliminary). *By District* (population at 2010 census, preliminary): Castries 65,656; Anse La Raye 6,247; Canaries 2,044; Soufrière 8,472; Choiseul 6,098; Laborie 6,701; Vieux Fort 16,284; Micoud 16,284; Dennery 12,599; Gros Islet 25,210. *Mid-2013* (UN estimate): 179,516 (Source: UN, *World Population Prospects: The 2010 Revision*).

Density (at mid-2013): 291.3 per sq km.

Population by Age and Sex (UN estimates at mid-2013): *0–14:* 44,328 (males 22,367, females 21,961); *15–64:* 122,872 (males 59,756, females 63,116); *65 and over:* 12,316 (males 5,195, females 7,121); *Total* 179,516 (males 87,318, females 92,198) (Source: UN, *World Population Prospects: The 2010 Revision*).

Principal Town (incl. suburbs, population at 2010 census, preliminary): Castries (capital) 22,111.

Births, Marriages and Deaths (2006, unless otherwise indicated): Registered live births 2,209 (birth rate 13.3 per 1,000); Registered marriages 591 (2005, preliminary); Registered deaths 1,019 (death rate 6.1 per 1,000). *2011:* Crude birth rate 14.6 per 1,000; Crude death rate 7.0 per 1,000 (Source: Pan American Health Organization).

Life Expectancy (years at birth): 74.4 (males 71.8, females 77.2) in 2010. Source: World Bank, World Development Indicators database.

Economically Active Population (persons aged 15 years and over, labour survey for October–December 2007): Agriculture, hunting and forestry 7,670; Fishing 600; Manufacturing 4,160; Electricity, gas and water 420; Construction 8,940; Wholesale and retail trade, repair of motor vehicles, motorcycles and personal and household goods 11,210; Hotels and restaurants 8,870; Transport, storage and communications 4,370; Financial intermediation 1,090; Real estate, renting and business activities 2,950; Public administration and compulsory social security 12,200; Education 890; Health and social work 280; Other community, social and personal service activities 2,080; Private households with employed persons 2,280; *Subtotal* 68,010; Activities not adequately defined 420; Not reported 4,350; *Total employed* 72,780; Unemployed 12,480; *Total labour force* 85,260 (males 45,510, females 39,750).

HEALTH AND WELFARE
Key Indicators

Total Fertility Rate (children per woman, 2010): 1.8.

Under-5 Mortality Rate (per 1,000 live births, 2010): 16.

Physicians (per 1,000 head, 2009): 0.8.

Hospital Beds (per 1,000 head, 2009): 1.5.

Health Expenditure (2009): US $ per head (PPP): 798.

Health Expenditure (2009): % of GDP: 8.4.

Health Expenditure (2009): public (% of total): 63.0.

Access to Water (% of persons, 2010): 96.

Access to Sanitation (% of persons, 2010): 65.

Total Carbon Dioxide Emissions ('000 metric tons, 2008): 396.0.

Carbon Dioxide Emissions Per Head (metric tons, 2008): 2.3.

Human Development Index (2011): ranking: 82.

Human Development Index (2011): value: 0.723.

Source: partly Pan American Health Organization; for other sources and definitions, see explanatory note on p. vi.

AGRICULTURE, ETC.

Principal Crops ('000 metric tons, 2011, FAO estimates): Cassava 1.3; Yams 0.5; Coconuts 14.9; Bananas 23.8; Plantains 1.7; Citrus fruits 1.9. *Aggregate Production* ('000 metric tons, may include official, semi-official or estimated data): Roots and tubers 4.7; Vegetables (incl. melons) 3.0; Fruits (excl. melons) 34.4.

Livestock ('000 head, 2011, FAO estimates): Cattle 11.0; Sheep 10.0; Goats 9.5; Pigs 20.0; Horses 1.1; Poultry 450.

Livestock Products ('000 metric tons, 2011, FAO estimates): Pig meat 1.4; Chicken meat 1.6; Cows' milk 1.2; Hen eggs 1.2.

Fishing (metric tons, live weight, 2010): Capture 1,844 (Wahoo 199; Skipjack tuna 153; Blackfin tuna 203; Yellowfin tuna 223; Common dolphinfish 352; Stromboid conchs 28); Aquaculture 6; Total catch 1,850. Figures exclude aquatic plants.

Source: FAO.

INDUSTRY

Production (2007 unless otherwise indicated): Electric energy 380.9 million kWh (2010, provisional); Copra 1,094 metric tons (2004); Coconut oil (unrefined) 0.1m. litres; Coconut oil (refined) 118,100 litres; Coconut meal 389,500 kg; Rum 115,100 proof gallons (Source: partly Eastern Caribbean Central Bank).

FINANCE

Currency and Exchange Rates: 100 cents = 1 Eastern Caribbean dollar (EC $). *Sterling, US Dollar and Euro Equivalents* (31 December 2012): £1 sterling = EC $4.261; US $1 = EC $2.700; €1 = EC $3.562; EC $100 = £23.47 = US $37.04 = €28.07. *Exchange Rate:* Fixed at US $1 = EC $2.70 since July 1976.

Budget (EC $ million, 2011, provisional): *Revenue:* Tax revenue 762.8 (Taxes on income and profits 245.2, Taxes on property 4.0, Taxes on domestic goods and services 124.2, Taxes on international trade and transactions 389.4); Other current revenue 49.2; Capital revenue 0.5; Total 812.5 (excl. grants 34.7). *Expenditure:* Current expenditure 771.0 (Personal emoluments 344.8, Goods and services 166.4, Interest payments 102.1, Transfers and subsidies 157.6); Capital expenditure and net lending 314.8; Total 1,085.8. Source: Eastern Caribbean Central Bank.

International Reserves (US $ million at 31 December 2011): IMF special drawing rights 23.66; Reserve position in IMF 0.01; Foreign exchange 189.77; Total 213.43. Source: IMF, *International Financial Statistics.*

Money Supply (EC $ million at 31 December 2011): Currency outside depository corporations 165.24; Transferable deposits 674.67; Other deposits 2,262.69 *Broad money* 3,102.61. Source: IMF, *International Financial Statistics.*

Cost of Living (Consumer Price Index; base: 2005 = 100): All items 114.1 in 2009; 114.8 in 2010; 119.7 in 2011. Source: IMF, *International Financial Statistics.*

Gross Domestic Product (EC $ million at constant 2006 prices): 2,967.46 in 2009; 2,985.33 in 2010; 3,016.25 in 2011. Source: Eastern Caribbean Central Bank.

Expenditure on the Gross Domestic Product (EC $ million at current prices, 2010, preliminary): Government final consumption expenditure 548.06; Private final consumption expenditure 2,032.19; Gross capital formation 1,058.62; *Total domestic expenditure* 3,638.87; Exports of goods and services 1,698.18; *Less* Imports of goods and services 2,099.99; *GDP at market prices* 3,237.05. Source: Eastern Caribbean Central Bank.

Gross Domestic Product by Economic Activity (EC $ million in current prices, 2011): Agriculture, hunting, forestry and fishing 94.63; Mining and quarrying 6.95; Manufacturing 105.54; Electricity and water 117.09; Construction 238.32; Wholesale and retail trade 231.95; Restaurants and hotels 418.42; Transport 293.79; Communications 182.15; Banking and insurance 177.96; Real estate and housing 454.76; Government services 187.45; Other services 339.09; *Sub-total* 2,848.08; *Less* Imputed bank service charge 54.00; *Total in basic prices* 2,794.08; Taxes, less subsidies, on products 475.62; *GDP at market prices* 3,269.70. Source: Eastern Caribbean Central Bank.

Balance of Payments (EC $ million, 2011): Exports of goods 517.01; Imports of goods −1,662.50; *Trade balance* −1,145.49; Services (net) 475.81; *Balance on goods and services* −669.68; Other income received (net) − 42.04; *Balance on goods, services and income* −711.72; Current transfers received (net) 53.82; *Current balance* −657.90; Capital account (net) 89.73; Direct investment (net) 261.49; Portfolio investment (net) 112.88; Other investment 226.84; Net errors and omissions −13.39; *Overall balance* 19.65. Source: Eastern Caribbean Central Bank.

EXTERNAL TRADE

Principal Commodities (EC $ million, 2011): *Imports c.i.f.:* Food and live animals 355.5; Beverages and tobacco 80.6; Mineral fuels, lubricants, etc. 293.6; Chemicals 125.0; Basic manufactures 259.3;

Machinery and transport equipment 372.7; Miscellaneous manufactured articles 270.9; Total (incl. others) 1,889.2. *Exports f.o.b.* (incl. re-exports): Food and live animals 24.6; Beverages and tobacco 90.9; Mineral fuels, lubricants, etc. 121.0; Chemicals 18.8; Basic manufactures 28.5; Machinery and transport equipment 83.8; Miscellaneous manufactured articles 49.6; Total (incl. others) 435.8. Source: Eastern Caribbean Central Bank.

Principal Trading Partners (US $ million, 2008): *Imports c.i.f.:* Barbados 23.1; Canada 11.9; China, People's Repub. 7.1; Finland 0.4; France (incl. Monaco) 8.4; Germany 5.9; Japan 28.2; Netherlands 7.0; Panama 8.8; Saint Vincent and the Grenadines 5.4; Thailand 11.4; Trinidad and Tobago 156.0; United Kingdom 26.8; USA 279.1; Total (incl. others) 655.7. *Exports f.o.b.* (excl. re-exports): Antigua and Barbuda 3.7; Barbados 13.9; Dominica 4.6; France (incl. Monaco) 1.9; Grenada 3.0; Saint Vincent and the Grenadines 4.9; Trinidad and Tobago 38.1; United Kingdom 24.8; USA 55.8; Total (incl. others) 164.0. Source: UN, *International Trade Statistics Yearbook.*

TRANSPORT

Road Traffic (registered motor vehicles, 2002): Goods vehicles 9,554; Taxis and hired vehicles 1,880; Motorcycles 797; Private vehicles 21,421; Passenger vans 3,439; Total (incl. others) 38,572.

Shipping: *Arrivals* (2006): 1,557 vessels. *Flag Registered Fleet* (at 31 December 2012): 2 vessels (total displacement 639 grt) (Source: Lloyd's List Intelligence—www.lloydslistintelligence.com). *International Sea-borne Freight Traffic* (at Castries and Vieux Fort, metric tons, 2011): Goods loaded 90,606; Goods unloaded 497,137. Source: Saint Lucia Air and Sea Ports Authority.

Civil Aviation (traffic at George F. L. Charles and Hewanorra International airports, 2011): Aircraft movements 36,546; Passenger departures 397,148; Passenger arrivals 382,613; Cargo loaded (metric tons) 1,260.5; Cargo unloaded (metric tons) 1,517.3. Source: Saint Lucia Air and Sea Ports Authority.

TOURISM

Visitor Arrivals: 1,014,761 (278,491 stop-over visitors, 4,967 excursionists, 31,997 yacht passengers, 699,306 cruise ship passengers) in 2009; 1,026,212 (305,937 stop-over visitors, 7,613 excursionists, 42,619 yacht passengers, 670,043 cruise ship passengers) in 2010; 990,577 (289,692 stop-over visitors, 11,059 excursionists, 43,014 yacht passengers, 646,812 cruise ship passengers) in 2011. *Stop-over Visitors by Origin* (2011): Canada 33,164; Caribbean 49,620; United Kingdom 66,142; USA 119,480; Other 21,286.

Tourism Receipts (EC $ million): 799.7 in 2009; 888.1 in 2010; 799.8 in 2011.

Source: Eastern Caribbean Central Bank.

COMMUNICATIONS MEDIA

Telephones ('000 main lines in use, 2011): 35.9.

Mobile Cellular Telephones ('000 subscribers, 2011): 216.5.

Personal Computers: 26,000 (160.1 per 1,000 persons) in 2004.

Internet Subscribers ('000 subscribers, 2011): 21.7.

Broadband Subscribers (2011): 21.3.

Source: International Telecommunication Union.

EDUCATION

Pre-primary (state institutions only, 2005/06): 148 schools; 480 teachers; 5,062 pupils.

Primary (state institutions only, 2007/08): 75 schools; 922 teachers; 20,164 pupils.

General Secondary (state institutions only, 2007/08): 23 schools; 924 teachers; 15,630 pupils.

Special Education (state institutions only, 2007/08): 4 schools; 47 teachers; 227 students.

Adult Education (state institutions only, 2006/07 unless otherwise indicated): 13 centres; 70 facilitators; 1,395 learners.

Tertiary (state institutions, including part-time, 2000/01): 127 teachers; 1,403 students.

Source: partly Caribbean Development Bank, *Social and Economic Indicators.*

Pupil-teacher Ratio (primary education, UNESCO estimate): 18.5 in 2009/10. Source: UNESCO Institute for Statistics.

Adult Literacy Rate (UNESCO estimate): 94.8% in 2004. Source: UN Development Programme, *Human Development Report.*

Directory

The Government

HEAD OF STATE

Queen: HM Queen ELIZABETH II.

Governor-General: Dame PEARLETTE LOUISY (took office 17 September 1997).

CABINET
(May 2013)

The Government is formed by the Saint Lucia Labour Party.

Prime Minister and Minister for Finance and Economic Affairs: Dr KENNY DAVIS ANTHONY.

Deputy Prime Minister and Minister for Infrastructure, Port Services and Transport: PHILIP J. PIERRE.

Minister for External Affairs, International Trade and Civil Aviation: ALVA BAPTISTE.

Minister for Education, Human Resource Development and Labour: Dr ROBERT K. LEWIS.

Minister for Health, Wellness, Human Services and Gender Relations: ALVINA REYNOLDS.

Minister for Agriculture, Food Production, Fisheries and Rural Development: MOSES JEAN BAPTISTE.

Minister for Social Transformation, Local Government and Community Empowerment: HAROLD DALSON.

Minister of Commerce, Business Development, Investment and Consumer Affairs: EMMA HIPPOLYTE.

Minister for Legal Affairs, Home Affairs and National Security: VICTOR PHILIP LA CORBINIERE.

Minister for Tourism, Heritage and the Creative Industries: LORNE THEOPHILUS.

Minister for Youth Development and Sports: SHAWN EDWARD.

Minister for Public Service, Sustainable Development, Energy, Science and Technology: Dr JAMES FLETCHER.

Minister for Physical Development, Housing and Urban Renewal: STANLEY FELIX.

MINISTRIES

Office of the Prime Minister: Greaham Louisy Administrative Bldg, 5th Floor, Waterfront, Castries; tel. 468-2111; fax 453-7352; e-mail admin@pm.gov.lc; internet www.pm.gov.lc.

Ministry of Agriculture, Food Production, Fisheries and Rural Development: Sir Stanislaus James Bldg, 4th and 5th Floors, Waterfront, Castries; tel. 468-4173; fax 453-6314; e-mail adminag@candw.lc; internet www.maff.egov.lc.

Ministry of Commerce, Business Development, Investment and Consumer Affairs: Ives Heraldine Rock Bldg, 4th Floor, Block B, Waterfront, Castries; tel. 468-4202; fax 453-7347; e-mail mincommerce@gosl.gov.lc; internet www.commerce.gov.lc.

Ministry of Education, Human Resource Development and Labour: Francis Compton Bldg, 4th Floor, Waterfront, Castries; tel. 468-5203; fax 453-2299; e-mail mineduc@candw.lc; internet www.education.gov.lc.

Ministry of External Affairs, International Trade and Civil Aviation: Conway Business Centre, 7th Floor, Waterfront, Castries; tel. 452-1178; fax 452-7427; e-mail foreign@candw.lc.

Ministry of Finance and Economic Affairs: Financial Centre, 3rd Floor, Bridge St, Castries; tel. 468-5580; fax 451-9231; e-mail info@finance.gov.lc; internet finance.gov.lc.

Ministry of Health, Wellness, Human Services and Gender Relations: Sir Stanislaus James Bldg, 2nd Floor, Castries; tel. 453-6966; fax 452-5655; e-mail health@candw.lc.

Ministry of Infrastructure, Port Services and Transport: Union Office Complex, Castries; tel. 468-4300; fax 453-2769; e-mail min_com@gosl.gov.lc; internet mipst.com.

Ministry of Legal Affairs, Home Affairs and National Security: Sir Stanislaus James Bldg, 1st Floor, Waterfront, Castries; tel. 468-3600; fax 456-0228; e-mail pshans@gosl.gov.lc.

Ministry of Physical Development, Housing and Urban Renewal: Greaham Louisy Administrative Bldg, 3rd Floor, Waterfront, Castries; tel. 468-4419; fax 452-2506; e-mail econdept@candw.lc.

Ministry of Public Service, Sustainable Development, Energy, Science and Technology: Greaham Louisy Administrative Bldg, 2nd Floor, Waterfront, Castries; tel. 468-2234; fax 453-1305; e-mail minpet@candw.lc.

Ministry of Social Transformation, Local Government and Community Empowerment: Greaham Louisy Administrative Bldg, 4th Floor, Waterfront, Castries; tel. 468-5101; fax 453-7921; e-mail most@gosl.gov.lc.

Ministry of Tourism, Heritage and the Creative Industries: Sir Stanislaus James Bldg, 3rd Floor, Waterfront, Castries; tel. 453-6644; fax 451-7414; e-mail tpreville@gosl.gov.lc.

Ministry of Youth Development and Sports: Sir Stanislaus James Bldg, 2nd Floor, Castries; tel. 468-5300; fax 452-5655; e-mail health@candw.lc.

Legislature

PARLIAMENT

Senate

The Senate has nine nominated members and two independent members.

President: CLAUDIUS JAMES FRANCIS.

House of Assembly

Speaker: PETER FOSTER.

Clerk: KURT THOMAS.

Election, 28 November 2011

Party	Seats
Saint Lucia Labour Party	11
United Workers' Party	6
Total	**17**

Election Commission

Election Commission: St Lucia Electoral Dept, 23 High St, POB 1074, Castries; tel. 452-3725; fax 451-6513; e-mail electoral@candw.lc; internet www.electoral.gov.lc; Chief Elections Officer CARSON RAGGIE.

Political Organizations

Lucian People's Movement: Marie Therese St, Gros Islet, Castries; tel. 287-6814; internet www.lpmstlucia.com; f. 2010; Leader THEROLD PRUDENT.

Organization for National Empowerment (ONE): POB 1496, Castries; tel. 484-9424; fax 452-9574; e-mail aziea99@yahoo.com; f. 2004; Leader PETER ALEXANDER; Chair. ROSEMUND CLERY.

Saint Lucia Labour Party (SLP): Tom Walcott Bldg, 2nd Floor, Jeremie St, POB 427, Castries; tel. and fax 453-1470; internet www.voteslp.com; f. 1946; socialist party; Leader Dr KENNY DAVIS ANTHONY; Deputy Leader PHILIP J. PIERRE.

United Workers' Party (UWP): 9 Coral St, POB 1550, Castries; tel. 451-9103; fax 451-9207; e-mail unitworkers@netscape.net; internet www.uwpstlucia.com; f. 1964; right-wing; Chair. and Leader STEPHENSON KING.

Diplomatic Representation

EMBASSIES AND HIGH COMMISSION IN SAINT LUCIA

Brazil: 1 Bella Rosa Rd, 3rd Floor, POB 6136, Gros Islet; tel. 450-1671; fax 450-4733; e-mail brasemb.castries@itamaraty.gov.br; Ambassador JOAQUIM A. WHITAKER SALLES.

Cuba: Rodney Heights, Gros Islet, POB 2150, Castries; tel. 458-4665; fax 458-4666; e-mail embacubasantalucia@candw.lc; internet www.cubadiplomatica.cu/santalucia; Ambassador LYDIA GONZÁLEZ NAVARRO.

France: French Embassy to the OECS, GPO Private Box 937, Vigie, Castries; tel. 455-6060; fax 455-6056; e-mail frenchembassy@candw.lc; internet www.ambafrance-lc.org; Ambassador MICHEL PROM.

Mexico: Nelson Mandela Dr., POB 6096, Vigie, Castries; tel. 453-1250; fax 451-4252; e-mail mexicanembassy@candw.lc; internet www.sre.gob.mx/santalucia; Ambassador EDMUNDO FONT LÓPEZ.

Radio Saint Lucia Co Ltd (RSL97): Morne Fortune, POB 660, Castries; tel. 452-2337; fax 453-1568; e-mail info@rslonline.com; internet www.rslonline.com; f. 1972; govt-owned; English and Creole services; Man. Dir CLAUDE EMMANUEL.

Television

National Television Network (NTN): Greaham Louisy Administrative Bldg, Waterfront, Castries; tel. 468-2116; fax 453-1614; f. 2001; operated by the Government Information Service; provides information on the operations of the public sector.

Finance

(cap. = capital; res = reserves; dep. = deposits; m. = million; brs = branches)

REGULATORY AUTHORITY

Financial Sector Supervision Unit: Financial Centre, 3rd Floor, Bridge St, Castries; tel. 468-2991; fax 451-7655; e-mail cleon@gosl.gov.lc; Dir CALIXTE LEON.

BANKING

The Eastern Caribbean Central Bank, based in Saint Christopher, is the central issuing and monetary authority for Saint Lucia.

Eastern Caribbean Central Bank—Saint Lucia Office: Colony House, Unit 5, John Compton Hwy, POB 295, Castries; tel. 452-7449; fax 453-6022; e-mail eccbslu@candw.lc; internet www.eccb-centralbank.org; Country Dir ISAAC ANTHONY; Rep. GREGOR FRANKLIN.

Local Banks

1st National Bank Saint Lucia Ltd: 21 Bridge St, POB 168, Castries; tel. 455-7000; fax 453-1630; e-mail manager@1stnationalbankslu.com; internet www.1stnationalbankonline.com; inc. 1937 as Saint Lucia Co-operative Bank Ltd; name changed as above Jan. 2005; commercial bank; cap. EC $7.9m., res EC $13.5m., dep. EC $365.3m. (Dec. 2009); Chair. and Pres. CHARMAINE GARDNER; Man. Dir G. CARLTON GLASGOW; 4 brs.

Bank of Saint Lucia Ltd: Financial Centre, 5th Floor, 1 Bridge St, POB 1860, Castries; tel. 456-6000; fax 456-6702; e-mail info@bankofsaintlucia.com; internet www.bankofsaintlucia.com; f. 2001 by merger of National Commercial Bank of St Lucia Ltd and Saint Lucia Devt Bank; cap. EC $188.9m., res EC $71.2m., dep. EC $1,112.6m. (Dec. 2010); 35% state-owned; parent co is East Caribbean Financial Holding Co Ltd; Chair. VICTOR A. EUDOXIE; Gen. Man. ROBERT NORSTROM; 7 brs.

FirstCaribbean International Bank (Barbados) Ltd: Bridge St, POB 335, Castries; tel. 456-2422; fax 452-3735; internet www.firstcaribbeanbank.com; f. 2002 following merger of Caribbean operations of Barclays Bank PLC and CIBC; CIBC acquired Barclays' 43.7% stake in 2006; Exec. Chair. MICHAEL MANSOOR; CEO RIK PARKHILL.

RBTT Bank Caribbean Ltd: 22 Micoud St, POB 1531, Castries; tel. 452-2265; fax 452-1668; e-mail rbttslu.isd@candw.lc; internet www.rbtt.com; f. 1985 as Caribbean Banking Corpn Ltd, name changed as above in March 2002; owned by R and M Holdings Ltd; Chair. JIM WESTLAKE; CEO SURESH SOOKOO; 4 brs.

STOCK EXCHANGE

Eastern Caribbean Securities Exchange: based in Basseterre, Saint Christopher and Nevis; tel. 466-7192; fax 465-3798; e-mail info@ecseonline.com; internet www.ecseonline.com; f. 2001; regional securities market designed to facilitate the buying and selling of financial products for the 8 mem. territories—Anguilla, Antigua and Barbuda, Dominica, Grenada, Montserrat, Saint Christopher and Nevis, Saint Lucia and Saint Vincent and the Grenadines; Chair. Sir K. DWIGHT VENNER; Gen. Man. TREVOR E. BLAKE.

INSURANCE

Eastern Caribbean Insurance Ltd: Laborie St, POB 290, Castries; tel. 452-2410; fax 452-3393; e-mail cgi.ltd@candw.lc.

EC Global Insurance Company Ltd: 2 Bridge St, POB 1860, Castries; tel. 451-3244; fax 458-1222; e-mail ecglobal@ecfh.com; internet www.ecfh.com; CEO LEATHON KHAN.

Saint Lucia Insurances Ltd: 48 Micoud St, POB 1084, Castries; tel. 452-3240; fax 452-2240; e-mail info@stluciainsurances.com; internet www.stluciainsurances.com; principal agents of Caribbean Alliance Insurance Co Ltd.

Saint Lucia Motor and General Insurance Co Ltd: 38 Micoud St, POB 767, Castries; tel. 452-3323; fax 452-6072.

Trade and Industry

DEVELOPMENT ORGANIZATIONS

Invest Saint Lucia: Heraldine Rock Bldg, 1st Floor, The Waterfront, POB 495, Castries; tel. 452-3400; fax 452-1841; e-mail info@investstlucia.com; internet www.investstlucia.com; f. 1971 to stimulate, facilitate and promote investment opportunities for foreign and local investors and to promote the economic devt of Saint Lucia; owns and manages 7 industrial estates; br. in Miami, FL, USA; Chair. COSTELLO MICHEL; CEO MCHALE ANDREW.

Small Enterprise Development Unit (SEDU): Heraldine Rock Bldg, 4th Floor, Waterfront, Castries; tel. 468-4202; fax 453-7347; e-mail mincommerce@gosl.gov.lc; f. 1994; technical assistance and training for the development of the micro- and small business sectors; operates under the Ministry of Commerce, Business Development and Consumer Affairs; Officer-in-Charge BARBARA INNOCENT CHARLES.

CHAMBER OF COMMERCE

Saint Lucia Chamber of Commerce, Industry and Agriculture: American Drywall Bldg, 2nd Floor, Vide Bouteille, POB 482, Castries; tel. 452-3165; fax 453-6907; e-mail info@stluciachamber.org; internet www.stluciachamber.org; f. 1884; Pres. GERARD BERGASSE; Exec. Dir BRIAN LOUISY; 150 mems.

EMPLOYERS' ASSOCIATIONS

Saint Lucia Agriculturists' Association Ltd: Mongiraud St, POB 153, Castries; tel. 452-2494; fax 453-2693; distributor and supplier of agricultural, industrial and organic products; exporter of cocoa; Chair. CUTHBERT PHILLIPS; CEO KERDE M. SEVERIN.

Saint Lucia Coconut Growers' Association Ltd: Palmiste Rd, POB 269, Soufrière; tel. 459-7227; fax 459-7216; f. 1939; Gen. Man. GERALD MORRIS.

Saint Lucia Employers' Federation: c/o The Morgan Bldg, L'Anse Rd, POB 160, Castries; tel. 452-2190; fax 452-7335; e-mail slefslu@candw.lc; internet www.slef-slu.org; Pres. CALLISTUS VERN GILL.

Saint Lucia Fish Marketing Corpn: POB 891, Sans Souci, Castries; tel. 452-1341; fax 451-7073; e-mail slfmc@candw.lc; Gen. Man. GREGORY ST HELENE.

Saint Lucia Industrial and Small Business Association: POB 585, La Panse, Castries; tel. 452-1608; fax 453-1023; e-mail slisbaslu@gmail.com; internet www.slisbastlucia.com; Pres. FLAVIA CHERRY.

Windward Islands Banana Development and Exporting Co (Wibdeco): Manoel St, POB 115, Castries; tel. 452-2411; fax 453-1638; e-mail wibdeco@candw.lc; internet www.wibdeco.com; f. 1994 in succession to the Windward Islands Banana Growers' Asscn (WINBAN); regional org. dealing with banana devt and marketing; jtly owned by the Windward govts and island banana asscns; CEO BERNARD CORNIBERT.

UTILITIES

Electricity

Caribbean Electric Utility Services Corpn (CARILEC): Desir Ave, Sans Soucis, POB 5907, Castries; tel. 452-0140; fax 452-0142; e-mail info@carilec.org; internet www.carilec.com; f. 1989; Exec. Dir. GRAY JACKSON.

St Lucia Electricity Services Ltd (LUCELEC): Sans Soucis, POB 230, Castries; tel. 457-4400; fax 457-4409; e-mail lucelec@candw.lc; internet www.lucelec.com; f. 1964; majority owned by Emera Inc of Canada; Chair. MARIUS ST ROSE; Man. Dir TREVOR LOUISY.

Water

Water and Sewerage Company (WASCO): L'Anse Rd, POB 1481, Castries; tel. 452-5344; fax 452-6844; e-mail wasco@candw.lc; f. 1999 as the Water and Sewerage Authority (WASA); planned privatization under review; Chair. TRESCOTT AUGUSTIN; Man. Dir EGBERT LOUIS.

TRADE UNION

Saint Lucia Trade Union Federation: c/o Saint Lucia Teachers' Union, La Clery, POB 821, Castries; tel. 452-4469; fax 453-6668; e-mail cumbatch42@gmail.com; f. 2005; comprises 9 trade unions of Saint Lucia, including the Saint Lucia Civil Service Asscn, Saint Lucia Teachers' Union, Saint Lucia Medical and Dental Asscn, Saint Lucia Nurses' Asscn, Saint Lucia Seamen and Waterfront General Workers' Union, National Farmers' Asscn, Police Welfare Asscn, Saint Lucia Fire Service Asscn and Vieux Fort General and Dock

Workers' Union; Pres. JULIAN MONROSE; Gen. Sec. WAYNE CUMBER-BATCH.

Transport

RAILWAYS

There are no railways in Saint Lucia.

ROADS

In 2000 there was an estimated total road network of 910 km, of which 150 km were main roads and 127 km were secondary roads. In that year only 5.2% of roads were paved. The main highway passes through every town and village on the island. There is also a coastal highway linking Castries with Cul de Sac Bay. The 2010/11 budget allocated EC $48.1m. to road improvement, including the 22 km West Coast Road Overlay between Roseau and Soufrière and the rehabilitation of 60 small road and bridge projects around the island. The estimated budget for the Ministry of Infrastructure, Port Services and Transport in the 2012/13 financial year was $125.4m.

SHIPPING

The ports at Castries and Vieux Fort have been fully mechanized. Castries has six berths with a total length of 2,470 ft (753 m). The port of Soufrière has a deep-water anchorage, but no alongside berth for ocean-going vessels. The Rodney Bay marina was upgraded in 2009. There is a petroleum transshipment terminal at Cul de Sac Bay. In 2011 646,812 cruise ship passengers called at Saint Lucia. Regular services are provided by a number of shipping lines, including ferry services to neighbouring islands. There were plans to develop the waterfront area at Castries in order for it to become a dedicated cruise ship port; the port at Vieux Fort was also to be expanded in order to handle all commercial cargo.

Saint Lucia Air and Sea Ports Authority (SLASPA): Manoel St, POB 651, Castries; tel. 452-2893; fax 452-2062; e-mail info@slaspa.com; internet www.slaspa.com; f. 1983; Chair. ISAAC ANTHONY; Gen. Man. SEAN MATTHEW; Dir of Airports PETER FERGUSON JEAN; Dir of Sea Ports ADRIAN HILAIRE.

Saint Lucia Marine Terminals Ltd (SLMTL): POB VF 355, Vieux Fort; tel. 454-8738; fax 454-8745; e-mail info@slmtl.com; internet www.slmtl.com; f. 1995; wholly owned subsidiary of the Saint Lucia Air and Sea Ports Authority; private port management co; manages Port Vieux Fort; Chair MICHAEL CHITOLIE; Gen. Man. LENIUS LENDOR.

CIVIL AVIATION

There are two airports: Hewanorra International (formerly Beane Field near Vieux Fort), 64 km from Castries, which is equipped to handle large jet aircraft, and George F. L. Charles Airport, which is at Vigie, in Castries, and which is capable of handling medium-range jets. Saint Lucia is served by scheduled flights to the USA, Canada, Europe and most destinations in the Caribbean. The country is a shareholder in the regional airline LIAT (see Antigua and Barbuda).

Saint Lucia Air and Sea Ports Authority: see Shipping.

LIAT Airlines: Brazil St, POB 416, Castries; tel. 452-3051; fax 453-6563; e-mail slu@liatairline.com; internet www.liatairline.com; Man. JOSSE MESMIN; Chair. Dr JEAN HOLDER; CEO Capt. IAN ARTHUR BRUNTON.

Tourism

Saint Lucia possesses spectacular mountain scenery, a tropical climate and sandy beaches. Historical sites, rich birdlife and the sulphur baths at Soufrière are other attractions. Visitor arrivals totalled 990,577 in 2011. Tourism receipts in that year were EC $799.8m. The USA is the principal market (41% of total stop-over visitors in 2011), followed by the United Kingdom (with 23%).

Saint Lucia Hotel and Tourism Association (SLHTA): 2 Alfiona Plaza, Rodney Heights, POB 545, Gros Islet; tel. 453-1811; fax 452-7967; e-mail slhta@candw.lc; internet www.slhta.com; f. 1963; Pres. KAROLIN TROUBETZKOY.

Saint Lucia Tourist Board: Sureline Bldg, Top Floor, Vide Bouteille, POB 221, Castries; tel. 452-4094; fax 453-1121; e-mail slutour@candw.lc; internet www.stlucia.org; f. 1981; 5 brs overseas; Chair. MATTHEW BEAUBRUN; Dir LOUIS LEWIS.

Defence

The Royal Saint Lucia Police Force, which numbers about 300 men, includes a 100-strong Special Service Unit for purposes of defence. Saint Lucia participates in the US-sponsored Regional Security System, comprising police, coastguards and army units, which was established by independent East Caribbean states in 1982. There are also two patrol vessels for coastguard duties. Some EC $113.7m. (equivalent to 7.8%) of the total expenditure was allocated to the departments of Home Affairs and National Security in the 2012/13 budget.

Education

Education is compulsory for 10 years between five and 15 years of age. Primary education begins at the age of five and lasts for seven years. Secondary education, beginning at 12 years of age, lasts for five years, comprising a first cycle of three years and a second cycle of two years. Enrolment at primary schools in 2009/10 included 88% of children in the relevant age-group, while comparable enrolment in secondary level education, according to UNESCO estimates, was equivalent to 85% of pupils in the relevant age category. Free education is provided in more than 90 government-assisted schools. Facilities for industrial, technical and teacher-training are available at the Sir Arthur Lewis Community College at Morne Fortune, which also houses an extra-mural branch of the University of the West Indies. Some EC $211.6m. of government expenditure was allocated to the Ministry of Education, Human Resource Development and Labour in the 2012/13 budget (equivalent to 14.5% of total planned recurrent expenditure).

SAINT VINCENT AND THE GRENADINES

Introductory Survey

LOCATION, CLIMATE, LANGUAGE, RELIGION, FLAG, CAPITAL

Saint Vincent and the Grenadines is situated in the Windward Islands group, approximately 160 km (100 miles) west of Barbados, in the West Indies. The nearest neighbouring countries are Saint Lucia, some 34 km (21 miles) to the north-east, and Grenada, to the south. As well as the main volcanic island of Saint Vincent, the state includes the 32 smaller islands and cayes known as the Saint Vincent Grenadines, the northerly part of an island chain stretching between Saint Vincent and Grenada. The principal islands in that part of the group are Bequia, Canouan, Mustique, Mayreau, Isle D'Quatre and Union Island. The climate is tropical, with average temperatures of between 18°C and 32°C (64°F–90°F). Annual rainfall ranges from 1,500 mm (60 ins) in the extreme south, to 3,750 mm (150 ins) in the mountainous interior of the main island. English is the official language. Most of the inhabitants profess Christianity. The national flag (proportions 2 by 3) has three unequal vertical stripes, of blue (at the hoist), yellow and green (at the fly), with three lozenges in green, in a 'V' formation, superimposed on the broad central yellow stripe. The capital is Kingstown, on the island of Saint Vincent.

CONTEMPORARY POLITICAL HISTORY

Historical Context

The islands were first settled by an Arawak people, who were subsequently conquered by the Caribs. The arrival of ship-wrecked and escaped African slaves resulted in the increase of a so-called 'Black Carib' population, some of whose descendants still remain. Under the collective name of Saint Vincent, and despite the opposition of the French and the indigenous population, the islands finally became a British possession during the 18th century. With other nearby British territories, the Governor of the Windward Islands administered Saint Vincent, under a federal system, until December 1959. The first elections under universal adult suffrage took place in 1951. The islands participated in the West Indies Federation from its foundation in January 1958 until its dissolution in May 1962. From January 1960, Saint Vincent, in common with the other Windward Islands, had a new Constitution, with its own Administrator and an enlarged Legislative Council.

Domestic Political Affairs

After the failure of negotiations to form a smaller East Caribbean Federation, most of the British colonies in the Leeward and Windward Islands became Associated States, with full internal self-government, in 1967. This change of status was delayed in Saint Vincent because of local political differences. At controversial elections to the Legislative Council in 1966, the ruling People's Political Party (PPP) was returned with a majority of only one seat. Further elections took place in May 1967, when the Saint Vincent Labour Party (SVLP) secured a majority in the Council. Milton Cato, leader of the SVLP, became Chief Minister. On 27 October 1969, despite objections from the PPP, Saint Vincent became an Associated State, with the United Kingdom retaining responsibility for defence and foreign relations only. The Legislative Council was renamed the House of Assembly, the Administrator was designated Governor, and the Chief Minister became Premier.

Elections were held in April 1972 for an enlarged, 13-seat House of Assembly. The PPP and the SVLP each obtained six seats, while James Mitchell, formerly a minister in the SVLP Government and standing as an independent, secured the remaining one. The PPP agreed to form a Government with Mitchell as Premier. In September 1974 a motion expressing no confidence in Mitchell's Government was approved, and the House was dissolved. In the ensuing election in December the SVLP secured a majority of seats. Cato became Premier again, at the head of a coalition with the PPP, and committed his Government to attaining full independence from the United Kingdom.

After a constitutional conference in 1978, the colony became fully independent, within the Commonwealth, on 27 October 1979. The Governor became Governor-General, while Cato took office as the country's first Prime Minister.

Cato's position was reinforced in the general election of December 1979, when the SVLP obtained a majority of seats. In 1982 the leader of the opposition United People's Movement (UPM), Dr Ralph Gonsalves, resigned, accusing the UPM of harbouring Marxist tendencies, and founded a new party, the Movement for National Unity (MNU). In June 1984 Cato announced an early general election, hoping to take advantage of divisions within the opposition. However, scandals surrounding the Government, and the economic and taxation policies of the SVLP, contributed to an unexpected victory for the centrist New Democratic Party (NDP) at the election in July. The NDP leader, James Mitchell, became Prime Minister.

At a general election in May 1989 the NDP won all 15 elective seats in the newly enlarged House of Assembly. Mitchell remained as Prime Minister and formed a new Cabinet. The NDP secured its third consecutive term of office at a general election in February 1994. In September the MNU and the SVLP formally merged to form the Unity Labour Party (ULP).

Opposition charges that the Government had failed to address problems presented by a marked decline in banana production, a crisis in the health and education sectors and persistent allegations that drugs-related activities were being conducted on the islands culminated in the defeat of a motion of no confidence in the Government in August 1994.

At a general election in June 1998 the NDP suffered a reverse, attributed to voter dissatisfaction with the state of the economy. Although the ULP had obtained around 55% of the vote, Mitchell claimed that the result was a mandate for his Government to undertake a record fourth term of office. The ULP leader, Vincent Beache, called on the NDP to hold fresh elections within nine months, and not to govern on the basis of a minority vote. The ULP also claimed to have obtained evidence of irregularities during the elections. In July, at the opening of the first session of the House of Assembly, several hundred protesters demonstrated against the new Government and two ministers were attacked.

In November 1998 members of the public and of the opposition demonstrated outside government offices to demand the resignation of Mitchell and Arnhim Eustace, the Minister of Finance and Public Services. The protests followed the announcement of the details of an agreement reached by the Government with the Government of Italy and a consortium of European financial institutions on the repayment of US $67m., incurred because the Government had guaranteed a loan of $50m. made to an Italian firm that subsequently went into liquidation. The loan had been made to finance the failed Ottley Hall marina and shipyard project, valued at only $5m. The new agreement stipulated that the shipyard should be sold and that repayments of $32m. of debt should begin immediately.

In November 1998 marijuana growers demonstrated outside the Prime Minister's office against plans to use regional and US troops to destroy the marijuana crop in the highlands of Saint Vincent. Mitchell refused to meet representatives of the protesters, telling them to take advantage of government schemes to promote economic diversification. In December US marines and troops provided by the Regional Security System destroyed crops during a two-week operation. Mitchell subsequently warned the USA that, if Saint Vincent's banana producers were bankrupted by the US initiative to challenge the preferential treatment accorded by the European Union (EU, see p. 281) to banana exports from Caribbean and African states, it was likely that producers would turn instead to the cultivation of marijuana. In March 1999 Saint Vincent and the Grenadines was one of a number of Caribbean states to warn that, if the USA continued to threaten their economic stability by pursuing its case against the EU banana import regime at the World Trade Organization (see p. 444), they would withdraw co-operation with US-sponsored anti-drugs initiatives. (See Saint Lucia for further details of the trade dispute over bananas between the USA and the EU.) In December, nevertheless, a large-scale marijuana eradication exercise took place in Saint Vincent with backing from US marines.

In December 1999 a proposed increase in salaries of members of the House of Assembly was opposed by the ULP. The Government's subsequent introduction in April 2000 of legislation increasing the salaries and benefits of legislative members provoked protests throughout the islands. In May the Government and the demonstrators reached an agreement, the Grand Beach Accord, whereby fresh legislative elections were to be called before March 2001.

In October 2000 Arnhim Eustace succeeded Mitchell as Prime Minister, following the latter's retirement. Mitchell remained in the Cabinet as Senior Minister.

The ULP in power

The ULP secured an overwhelming victory in the general election of March 2001, winning 12 of the 15 parliamentary seats. The new Government took office in April, led by Dr Ralph Gonsalves. In December 2002 Gonsalves established a 25-member Constitutional Review Commission, the first report of which was presented in March 2004. Among the issues to be addressed were local government organization and finance, civil service reform and the electoral system.

In March 2004 the opposition boycotted the House of Assembly and established an 'alternative parliament' at the NDP's headquarters; Eustace claimed that the parliamentary Speaker, Hendrick Alexander, had consistently demonstrated a pro-Government bias. The opposition again boycotted the House of Assembly and re-established its 'alternative parliament' in March 2005. On this occasion, the NDP was particularly unhappy about constituency boundaries and the registration of voters before the next elections.

Despite the concerns of the opposition, Gonsalves' Government maintained its popularity; however, during its first term in office violent crime became an increasingly prominent issue and it was widely held that the Government had devoted insufficient funds to attempting to resolve the problem. Moreover, Saint Vincent remained one of the largest cultivators of marijuana in the region. In November 2004 Gonsalves, who had previously expressed severe reservations about capital punishment, claimed that the use of the death penalty was necessary to reduce the influence of criminal gangs in the country. The comments were made in the House of Assembly, during the passage of the Firearm Amendment Act, which was to introduce stricter penalties for illegal possession of weapons.

The ULP secured a further term in office following legislative elections, held on 7 December 2005. The party again secured 12 of the 15 seats in the House of Assembly, while the NDP secured the remaining three seats. Registered votes were cast by 63.7% of the electorate. Following his party's re-election, Gonsalves pledged to introduce constitutional reform after popular consultation via referendums. In addition, the Prime Minister announced his intention to ask the House of Assembly to approve legislation making the Caribbean Court of Justice (CCJ—which had been inaugurated in Trinidad and Tobago in April 2005) the country's senior court of appeal, in place of the Privy Council in the United Kingdom.

Prime Minister Gonsalves and his ULP Government suffered a significant threat in February 2007 when the NDP marshalled a demonstration in Kingstown demanding the removal of the premier from office and requisitioning a general election. Public and opposition unrest had escalated during the preceding months following increased public concerns over crime, despite the fact that the overall crime rate had declined during that year and that a sustained decline had been recorded from 2001. Eustace suggested that the increasing prevalence of drugs-related and violent crime in the country was directly attributable to Gonsalves' inadequate enforcement of penal law, and that the Government was implicated in the alleged engagement of drugs magnates in the financing of political campaigns. Meanwhile, an inquiry into the failed Ottley Hall marina and shipyard development project, begun in 2003, remained stalled; the losses incurred under the scheme, according to some reports, accounted for more than one-quarter of Saint Vincent's total external debt.

A referendum on adopting a new constitution was held on 25 November 2009. The proposed new constitution would increase autonomy in the country, replacing the Queen as Head of State with an indirectly elected president, introducing electoral reform, and superseding the Privy Council as the country's final appellate body with the Trinidad-based CCJ. This last proposal, argued Gonsalves, would allow Saint Vincent greater power in carrying out death sentences without interference from the London-based (UK) appeal court. Although the opposition NDP supported Saint Vincent becoming a republic, the party campaigned against the new bill of rights, claiming that it did not reduce enough the powers of the Prime Minister, and that the House of Assembly, rather than the public, would be given more influence. Only 43.7% of voters were in favour of the Government's proposals, far short of the two-thirds' majority necessary.

Recent developments: a third term for the ULP

The ULP secured a narrow victory at the general election held on 13 December 2010, winning 51.1% of the valid votes cast and eight seats in the House of Assembly. The NDP gained 48.7% of the votes and the remaining seven legislative seats. Turn-out was 62.3%. Observers from the Organization of American States declared the election free and fair, although Eustace claimed that there had been extensive voting irregularities. After being sworn in as Prime Minister on 15 December, Gonsalves effected a cabinet reorganization. Most notably, Girlyn Miguel became Deputy Prime Minister, while retaining responsibility for education, and Douglas Slater was appointed as Minister of Foreign Affairs, Foreign Trade, and Consumer Affairs.

Gonsalves announced in January 2011 that police had foiled an alleged plot by 'two major drugs-trafficking and money-laundering entities' to assassinate him. Gonsalves claimed that these criminal organizations targeted him because of his uncompromising stance on the illegal drugs trade. He also made vague intimations that the NDP might have been involved in the alleged conspiracy, a charge vehemently denied by Eustace. According to a leaked US diplomatic cable released in August 2011, officials at the US embassy in Barbados had received information suggesting that the ULP had paid voters in return for supporting the party at the 2005 general election. The cable also detailed the use of money obtained from drugs-trafficking within political circles in Saint Vincent. The ULP denied the allegations.

Gonsalves effected another cabinet reorganization in February 2012. Saboto Caesar was given responsibility for agriculture, Cecil McKie was appointed as Minister of Tourism, Sports and Culture, Montgomery Daniel received the housing portfolio, and Clayton Burgin became Minister of Health, Wellness and the Environment. Gonsalves revealed in May that he intended to contest the next general election, which was scheduled to take place in 2015.

Foreign Affairs

Regional relations

There was some public unease over Saint Vincent and the Grenadines' burgeoning economic relations with Venezuela. Gonsalves maintained that relations with Venezuela and the USA were not mutually exclusive and emphasized the importance of Venezuela's influence upon the progress of national development, citing the benefits of the PetroCaribe initiative (under which the country could purchase petroleum from Venezuela at discounted prices) and the Venezuelan Government's contribution to the construction of an international airport. In April 2009 the country became a member of Venezuela's Bolivarian Alliance for the Peoples of our America (Alianza Bolivariana para los Pueblos de Nuestra América—ALBA, see p. 474), an economic integration initiative to rival the stagnant Free Trade Areas of the Americas proposed by the USA. In August 2012 the USA presented Saint Vincent and the Grenadines with security equipment, valued at almost US $2m., to combat drugs-smuggling within the islands' territorial waters. Gonsalves emphasized the strength of the bilateral relationship, but admitted that the two countries held differing views on some key issues.

Other external relations

In 2001 Libya granted the islands, in common with other eastern Caribbean countries, access to a US $2,000m. development fund. It was also reported that Libya had agreed to provide Saint Vincent and the Grenadines with a grant of $4.5m., following Gonsalves' controversial visit to the Libyan capital, Tripoli, earlier in the month. In February 2011, with international outrage growing at the deadly suppression of anti-Government protests in Libya, the opposition NDP condemned as 'blood money' $250,000 of aid provided by the Libyan authorities in the aftermath of Hurricane Tomas, which had caused extensive damage to the islands in October 2010. Gonsalves attempted to justify his Government's acceptance of the funds by arguing that the financing had been arranged prior to the outbreak of violence in Libya.

Controversy arose in 2001 after Japan pledged to provide $6m. for the construction of a fish market. It was claimed that, in return for Japanese financial aid, Saint Vincent and the Grenadines would support the pro-whaling bloc at meetings of the International Whaling Commission (IWC); Gonsalves refuted the allegation. However, the controversy re-emerged at the IWC meeting in June 2006 when Saint Vincent and the Grenadines endorsed Japan's proposal to end a 20-year moratorium on commercial whaling, invoking the vehement criticism of prominent international trading partners. Moreover, the subsequent announcement of a new EC $33m. fisheries complex to be financed by the Japanese Government provoked allegations of diplomacy motivated by economic incentive.

Saint Vincent and the Grenadines has maintained diplomatic relations with Taiwan since 1981; in 2006 the Taiwanese Government announced the donation of US $15m. and extension of a $10m. loan towards the construction of an international airport on the islands, while reiterating its commitment to assisting in Saint Vincent's infrastructural and human resource development. Following a visit to the Taiwanese capital, Taipei, in 2008, Gonsalves announced that the Taiwanese Government had agreed to increase funding for development projects in Saint Vincent and the Grenadines. Further talks on funding from Taiwan took place in 2011.

It was announced in August 2008 that Saint Vincent and the Grenadines was to establish diplomatic relations with Iran, with Iran providing US $7m. in development loans and grants for the airport construction project. The US Ambassador to the Eastern Caribbean expressed concern at the decision at a time when there were US anxieties at Iran's nuclear activities. According to a leaked US diplomatic cable released in August 2011, US officials suspected that, in an attempt to obtain Iranian funding for the airport, Saint Vincent and the Grenadines had abstained from a 2009 UN vote censuring the Iranian authorities for committing human rights abuses. Gonsalves met with Iranian President Mahmoud Ahmadinejad for further talks in 2011 and 2012.

CONSTITUTION AND GOVERNMENT

The Consitution came into force at independence, in October 1979. Saint Vincent and the Grenadines is a constitutional monarchy. Executive power is vested in the British monarch, as Head of State, and is exercisable by the Governor-General, who represents the British monarch locally and who is appointed on the advice of the Prime Minister. Legislative power is vested in Parliament, comprising the Governor-General and the House of Assembly (composed of 21 members: six nominated Senators and 15 Representatives, elected for five years by universal adult suffrage). Senators are appointed by the Governor-General: four on the advice of the Prime Minister and two on the advice of the Leader of the Opposition. Government is effectively by the Cabinet. The Governor-General appoints the Prime Minister and, on the latter's recommendation, selects the other Ministers. The Prime Minister must be able to command the support of the majority of the House, to which the Cabinet is responsible. Judicial power is invested in the Eastern Caribbean Supreme Court, based in Saint Lucia. The country's final appellate body is the Privy Council, based in the United Kingdom.

REGIONAL AND INTERNATIONAL CO-OPERATION

Saint Vincent and the Grenadines is a member of the Caribbean Community and Common Market (CARICOM, see p. 231) and of the Organisation of Eastern Caribbean States (OECS, see p. 477). In June 2010 Saint Vincent and the Grenadines was a signatory to the Revised Treaty of Basseterre, establishing an Economic Union among OECS member states. The Economic Union, which involved the removal of barriers to trade and the movement of labour as a step towards a single financial and economic market, came into effect in January 2011. Freedom of movement between the signatory states was granted to OECS nationals on 1 August. Saint Vincent and the Grenadines implemented CARICOM's intra-regional common passport initiative, regarded as an integral component in the advance towards economic union, in April 2006. Saint Vincent and the Grena-

dines, together with five other Caribbean states, became a signatory to CARICOM's Caribbean Single Market and Economy (CSME) in July, which had been established by six founding member states on 1 January of that year. The CSME was intended to enshrine the free movement of goods, services and labour throughout the CARICOM region. Two phases of implementation were to ensue: the first would be consolidation of the single market and initiation of the single economy by 1 January 2009; while the second phase, spanning 2010–15, would define and institute the single economy and regional monetary union. The country is a member of the Community of Latin American and Caribbean States (see p. 475), which was formally inaugurated in December 2011.

Saint Vincent and the Grenadines became a member of the UN in 1980, shortly after independence. As a contracting party to the General Agreement on Tariffs and Trade (GATT), Saint Vincent and the Grenadines joined the World Trade Organization (see p. 444) on its establishment in 1995. Upon independence, Saint Vincent became a full member of the Commonwealth (see p. 244). The country is a signatory of the Cotonou Agreement (see p. 334), the successor agreement to the Lomé Convention. In 2003 Saint Vincent and the Grenadines was admitted to the Non-Aligned Movement (see p. 477).

ECONOMIC AFFAIRS

In 2011, according to estimates by the World Bank, Saint Vincent and the Grenadines' gross national income (GNI), measured at average 2009–11 prices, was US $667m., equivalent to $6,100 per head (or $10,560 per head on an international purchasing-power parity basis). During 2002–11, it was estimated, the population increased at an average annual rate of 0.1%, while gross domestic product (GDP) per head increased, in real terms, by an average of 2.0% per year. According to the Eastern Caribbean Central Bank (ECCB, see p. 465), overall GDP increased, in real terms, at an average annual rate of 3.1% in 2002–11; however, real GDP decreased by 3.4% in 2010, and by a further 0.7% in 2011.

Agriculture (including forestry and fishing) contributed 7.2% of GDP in 2011 and engaged 15.4% of the economically active population in 2001. Agricultural products account for the largest share of export revenue (54.2% in 2011). The banana sector was in decline, although in 2010 the sector still contributed an estimated 14.2% of the value of total exports. This fell to 3.1% in 2011 after the crop was destroyed by Hurricane Tomas in late 2010. Other important crops are arrowroot, sweet potatoes, tannias, taro, plantains and coconuts. In 2011 the Government signed an agreement with cocoa trader Armajaro for the production of cocoa on the islands. According to the ECCB, during 2002–11 real agricultural GDP decreased at an annual average rate of 0.4%; sectoral GDP decreased by 18.2% in 2010, owing to Hurricane Tomas in that year, and by a further 0.6% in 2011.

Industry (including mining, manufacturing, electricity, water and construction) employed 19.7% of the working population in 2001, and contributed 19.8% of GDP in 2011. During 2002–11 real industrial GDP increased at an average annual rate of 1.9%, according to the ECCB; the sector's GDP declined by 3.3% in 2010 and by a further 0.5% in 2011.

The manufacturing sector contributed a preliminary 6.4% of GDP in 2011, and engaged 7.1% of the employed labour force in 2001. Apart from a garment industry and the assembling of electrical components, the most important activities involve the processing of agricultural products, including flour- and rice-milling, brewing, rum distillation, and processing dairy products. During 2002–11 real manufacturing GDP decreased by an average annual rate of 0.5%, according to ECCB figures; the sector's GDP declined by 2.7% in 2010, but increased by 8.3% in 2011.

Construction employed 10.6% of the working population in 2001, and contributed 8.5% of GDP in 2011. During 2002–11 construction GDP increased at an average annual rate of 2.6%, according to the ECCB; the sector's GDP declined by 2.2% in 2010 and by a further 3.4% in 2011.

Energy is derived principally from the use of hydrocarbon fuels (mineral fuels and lubricants accounted for around 30.0% of total imports in 2011). The islands imported most of their energy requirements. However, there is, an important hydroelectric plant in Cumberland. Saint Vincent and the Grenadines was a signatory to the PetroCaribe accord, under which the country is allowed to purchase petroleum from Venezuela at reduced prices.

The services sector contributed 73.0% of GDP in 2011 and engaged 64.9% of the employed population in 2001. Tourism is the most important activity within the sector, but is smaller in scale than in most other Caribbean islands. Total arrivals in 2011 decreased by 10.0% on the previous year; however, this was mainly owing to a 20.0% fall in cruise ship visitors. The number of stop-over visitors (traditionally a more lucrative sector) increased by 1.9%. Tourism generated EC $248m. in revenue in 2011, compared with $237m. in the previous year. Aside from tourism, a small 'offshore' financial sector also contributes to the services sector. Following its inclusion, in 2009, on the Organisation for Economic Co-operation and Development's (OECD) so-called 'grey list' of territories that had yet substantially to implement reform of the sector, the country made significant efforts to reach international financial standards: by mid-2012 the Government had signed 22 tax information-sharing agreements with other jurisdictions. OECD declared itself satisfied with these efforts, although it noted a lack of accounting information for International Business Companies on the islands. During 2002–11 the real GDP of the services sector as a whole increased by an average annual rate of 2.4%, according to the ECCB; there was a decline of 0.5% in the sector in 2010, but a growth of 0.6% was recorded in 2011.

In 2011 Saint Vincent and the Grenadines recorded an estimated visible trade deficit of EC $671.91m., and there was a deficit of $536.97m. on the current account of the balance of payments. The principal source of imports is the USA (accounting for an estimated 34.3% of the total in 2011). Trinidad and Tobago was another important supplier in that year. Saint Lucia is the principal market for exports (accounting for an estimated 22.2% of total exports in 2011). Other important markets in that year were Trinidad and Tobago, Barbados, Antigua and Barbuda, Dominica and Saint Kitts and Nevis. The principal exports in 2011 were vegetables products, while the principal imports were mineral fuels and lubricants, followed by machinery and mechanical appliances and food and live animals.

In 2011 there was a provisional budget deficit of EC $68.5m., equivalent to 3.7% of GDP. Saint Vincent and the Grenadines' general government gross debt was EC $1,266m. in 2011, equivalent to 68.1% of GDP. Saint Vincent and the Grenadines' total external debt was US $261m. at the end of 2010, of which US $255m. was public and publicly guaranteed debt. In that year, the cost of servicing long-term public and publicly guaranteed debt and repayments to the IMF was equivalent to 16.4% of the value of exports of goods, services and income (excluding workers' remittances). The average annual rate of inflation was 3.9% in 2005–11, and consumer prices increased by 1.9% in 2011. At the 2001 census 21.1% of the labour force were unemployed.

Two of Saint Vincent and the Grenadines' most important economic sectors—bananas and tourism—suffered reverses in the late 2000s. The banana sector had been declining from the 1990s and, more recently, the erosion of the islands' preferential access to European markets, together with lower prices and the onset of Hurricane Tomas in 2010, proved disastrous for the sector. The increasingly important tourism sector was affected by the global economic downturn from 2008. Expansion of this sector had been inhibited by the absence of an international airport, but construction of such a facility at Argyle, partially financed by the Governments of Venezuela, Cuba and Taiwan, was expected to be completed by the end of 2013. It was hoped that the new facility would increase overall capacity and attract a greater number of stop-over arrivals, a more lucrative market than cruise ship passengers. Hurricane Tomas not only destroyed the 2010 crop but also caused extensive devastation to infrastructure and housing: reconstruction spending placed added pressure on the already strained fiscal account. To support the reconstruction programme, the World Bank approved a US $5m. credit in January 2011 and the IMF released $3.3m. in the following month. The crisis was compounded in April by heavy rains and flooding, which caused further damage to infrastructure and agriculture. Additional reconstruction funding was subsequently provided by, *inter alia*, the IMF and Taiwan. The economy contracted by 0.7% in 2011, a fourth consecutive year of recession. ECCB estimates put real GDP growth at 1.5% in 2012, supported by a modest recovery in the tourism and manufacturing sectors. However, Moody's Investors Service downgraded Saint Vincent and the Grenadines' credit rating in October owing to concerns about the country's undiversified economy and weak fiscal position. Several tax raises were introduced in January 2013 in an attempt to increase revenues. The ECCB expected real GDP to rise by a further 1.5% in 2013.

PUBLIC HOLIDAYS

2014: 1 January (New Year's Day), 14 March (National Heroes' Day), 18 April (Good Friday), 21 April (Easter Monday), 5 May (Labour Day), 9 June (Whit Monday), 7 July (CARICOM Day), 8 July (Carnival Tuesday), 1 August (Emancipation Day), 27 October (Independence Day), 25–26 December (Christmas).

Statistical Survey

Source (unless otherwise stated): Statistical Office, Ministry of Finance and Economic Planning, Administrative Centre, Bay St, Kingstown; tel. 456-1111; e-mail statssvg@vincysurf.com; internet www.stats.gov.vc.

AREA AND POPULATION

Area: 389.3 sq km (150.3 sq miles). The island of Saint Vincent covers 344 sq km (133 sq miles).

Population: 97,914 at census of 12 May 1980; 106,499 at census of 12 May 1991; 106,253 (males 53,626, females 52,627) at census of 12 June 2001. *Mid-2013* (UN estimate): 109,355. Source: UN, *World Population Prospects: The 2010 Revision*.

Density (at mid-2013): 317.9 per sq km.

Population by Age and Sex (UN estimates at mid-2013): *0–14:* 27,649 (males 13,976, females 13,673); *15–64:* 74,211 (males 37,821, females 36,390); *65 and over:* 7,495 (males 3,392, females 4,103); *Total* 109,355 (males 55,189, females 54,166) (Source: UN, *World Population Prospects: The 2010 Revision*).

Principal Town: Kingstown (capital) population 13,212 at 2001 census. *Mid-2011* (population incl. suburbs, UN estimate): Kingstown 30,863. Source: UN, *World Urbanization Prospects: The 2011 Revision*.

Births, Marriages and Deaths (registrations, 2009): Live births 1,905 (birth rate 18.9 per 1,000); Marriages 573 (marriage rate 5.7 per 1,000); Deaths 765 (death rate 7.6 per 1,000). Source: UN, *Demographic Yearbook*.

Life Expectancy (years at birth): 72.3 (males 70.2; females 74.5) in 2011. Source: World Bank, World Development Indicators database.

Economically Active Population (persons aged 15 years and over, 2001 census): Agriculture, hunting, forestry and fishing 5,303; Mining and quarrying 104; Manufacturing 2,444; Electricity, gas and water 596; Construction 3,659; Trade, restaurants and hotels 8,271; Transport, storage and communications 2,594; Financing, insurance, real estate and business services 1,905; Public administration and defence 2,151; Education 2,500; Health and social work 743; Community, social and personal services 4,251; *Total employed* 34,521 (males 21,274, females 13,247); Unemployed 9,258 (males 6,229, females 3,029); *Total labour force* 43,779 (males 27,503, females 16,276).

HEALTH AND WELFARE

Key Indicators

Total Fertility Rate (children per woman, 2011): 1.9.

Under-5 Mortality Rate (per 1,000 live births, 2010): 25.4.

Physicians (per 1,000 head, 2009): 0.6.

Hospital Beds (per 1,000 head, 2010): 2.6.

Health Expenditure (2009): US $ per head (PPP): 487.

Health Expenditure (2009): % of GDP: 4.6.

Health Expenditure (2009): public (% of total): 84.3.

Access to Water (% of persons, 2000): 93.

Access to Sanitation (% of persons, 2000): 96.

Total Carbon Dioxide Emissions ('000 metric tons, 2008): 201.7.

Carbon Dioxide Emissions Per Head (metric tons, 2008): 1.8.

Human Development Index (2011): ranking: 85.

Human Development Index (2011): value: 0.717.

Source: partly Pan American Health Organization; for other sources and definitions, see explanatory note on p. vi.

AGRICULTURE, ETC.

Principal Crops ('000 metric tons, 2011, FAO estimates): Maize 0.8; Cassava 1.1; Sweet potatoes 2.2; Yams 2.9; Sugar cane 18.0; Coconuts 6.2; Bananas 67.1; Plaintains 2.8; Oranges 1.2; Lemons and limes 1.3; Apples 1.8; Mangoes 1.2. *Aggregate Production* ('000 metric tons, may include official, semi-official or estimated data): Roots and tubers 22.1; Vegetables (incl. melons) 5.9; Fruits (excl. melons) 76.4.

Livestock ('000 head, year ending September 2011, FAO estimates): Cattle 5.2; Sheep 13.5; Goats 7.5; Pigs 9.3; Chickens 250.

Livestock Products ('000 metric tons, 2011, FAO estimates): Pig meat 0.6; Chicken meat 0.5; Cows' milk 1.4; Hen eggs 0.8.

Fishing (metric tons, live weight of capture, 2010): Albacore 207; Skipjack tuna 46; Wahoo 40; Yellowfin tuna 882; Other tuna-like fishes 71; Other marine fishes 702; Total catch (incl. others) 65,626.

Source: FAO.

INDUSTRY

Selected Products ('000 metric tons, 2005 unless otherwise stated): Copra 2 (FAO estimate); Raw sugar 1.6 (2002); Rum 9,000 hl (2003); Electric energy 143.3 million kWh (2009). Sources: FAO, Eastern Caribbean Central Bank and UN Industrial Commodity Statistics Database.

FINANCE

Currency and Exchange Rates: 100 cents = 1 Eastern Caribbean dollar (EC $). *Sterling, US Dollar and Euro Equivalents* (31 December 2012): £1 sterling = EC $4.261; US $1 = EC $2.700; €1 = EC $3.562; EC $100 = £23.47 = US $37.04 = €28.07. *Exchange Rate:* Fixed at US $1 = EC $2.70 since July 1976.

Budget (EC $ million, 2011, provisional): *Revenue:* Revenue from taxation 411.7 (Taxes on income 114.4, Taxes on goods and services 213.5, Taxes on property 2.7, Taxes on international trade and transactions 81.2); Other current revenue 42.9; Capital revenue 8.8; Foreign grants 29.5; Total 492.9. *Expenditure:* Current expenditure 498.4 (Personal emoluments 231.2, Other goods and services 73.6, Interest payments 45.5, Transfers and subsidies 148.2); Capital expenditure and net lending 63.0; Total 561.4. Source: Eastern Caribbean Central Bank.

International Reserves (US $ million at 31 December 2011): IMF special drawing rights 1.09; Reserve position in IMF 0.77; Foreign exchange 87.76; *Total* 89.63. Source: IMF, *International Financial Statistics*.

Money Supply (EC $ million at 31 December 2011): Currency outside depository corporations 46.51; Transferable deposits 370.94; Other deposits 841.12; *Broad money* 1,258.57. Source: IMF, *International Financial Statistics*.

Cost of Living (Consumer Price Index; base: 2005 = 100): All items 121.8 in 2009; 123.6 in 2010; 126.0 in 2011. Source: IMF, *International Financial Statistics*.

Gross Domestic Product (EC $ million at constant 2006 prices): 1,691.33 in 2009; 1,634.62 in 2010; 1,623.69 in 2011. Source: Eastern Caribbean Central Bank.

Expenditure on the Gross Domestic Product (EC $ million at current prices, 2010, preliminary): Government final consumption expenditure 295.32; Private final consumption expenditure 1,617.64; Gross capital formation 463.97; *Total domestic expenditure* 2,376.92; Exports of goods and services 495.66; *Less* Imports of goods and services 1,050.71; *GDP at market prices* 1,821.88.

Gross Domestic Product by Economic Activity (EC $ million at current prices, 2011): Agriculture, hunting, forestry and fishing 116.15; Mining and quarrying 3.22; Manufacturing 103.19; Electricity and water 76.09; Construction 137.18; Wholesale and retail trade 224.99; Restaurants and hotels 31.85; Transport 148.60; Communications 71.64; Banking and insurance 104.91; Real estate, renting and business activities 242.39; Public administration and defence 170.97; Other services 184.94; *Sub-total* 1,616.12; *Less* Financial intermediation services indirectly measured 19.98; *Total in basic prices* 1,596.14; Taxes, less subsidies, on products 269.89; *GDP at market prices* 1,866.02. Source: Eastern Caribbean Central Bank.

Balance of Payments (EC $ million, 2011): Exports of goods 117.26; Imports of goods −789.17; *Trade balance* −671.91; Services (net) 148.58; *Balance on goods and services* −523.33 Other income received (net) −34.94; *Balance on goods, services and income* −558.27; Current transfers (net) 21.30; *Current balance* −536.97; Capital account (net) 104.31; Direct investment (net) 231.18; Portfolio investment (net) −8.57; Other investment (net) 152.88; Net errors and omissions −5.00; Overall balance −62.16. Source: Eastern Caribbean Central Bank.

EXTERNAL TRADE

Principal Commodities (US $ million, 2011): *Imports c.i.f.:* Live animals and animal products 23.1; Vegetable products 23.8; Prepared foodstuffs, beverages and tobacco 42.8; Mineral fuels, lubricants, etc. 115.0; Chemicals and related products 23.1; Plastic, rubber and articles thereof 12.9; Iron and steel, base metals and articles thereof 23.5; Machinery and mechanical appliances 44.5; Transport and transport equipment 16.6; Miscellaneous manufactured articles 12.4; Total (incl. others) 383.5. *Exports f.o.b.:* Vegetable products 20.8; Prepared foodstuffs, beverages and tobacco 6.3; Paper and paperboard 2.1; Iron and steel, base metals and articles thereof 3.7 (Iron and steel 2.3); Machinery and mechanical appliances 2.2; Total (incl. others) 38.4. Source: Trade Map-Trade Competitiveness Map, International Trade Centre, www.intracen.org/marketanalysis.

Principal Trading Partners (US $ million, 2011): *Imports c.i.f.:* Antigua and Barbuda 11.4; Barbados 9.2; Canada 9.9; China, People's Rep. 13.0; Colombia 4.9; Japan 5.8; Trinidad and Tobago 119.4; United Kingdom 19.8; USA 131.4; Venezuela 6.4; Total (incl. others) 383.5. *Exports f.o.b.:* Antigua and Barbuda 4.5; Barbados 4.6; Dominica 3.2; Grenada 1.4; Guyana 1.1; Jamaica 0.8; Saint Christopher and Nevis 2.6; Saint Lucia 8.5; Suriname 1.0; Trinidad and Tobago 5.9; United Kingdom 0.9; USA 1.8; Total (incl. others) 38.4. Source: Trade Map-Trade Competitiveness Map, International Trade Centre, www.intracen.org/marketanalysis.

TRANSPORT

Road Traffic (motor vehicles in use, 2008): Private cars 9,247; Buses and coaches 122; Lorries and vans 12,897; Motorcycles 1,217. Source: International Road Federation, *World Road Statistics*.

Shipping: *Arrivals* (2000): Vessels 1,007. *International Sea-borne Freight Traffic* ('000 metric tons, 2000): Goods loaded 54; Goods unloaded 156. *Flag Registered Fleet* (at 31 December 2012): Number of vessels 1,605; Total displacement 4,313,653 grt (Source: Lloyd's List Intelligence—www.lloydslistintelligence.com).

Civil Aviation (visitor arrivals): 99,657 in 2004; 104,432 in 2005; 106,466 in 2006 (estimate). Source: IMF, *St Vincent and the Grenadines: Statistical Appendix* (April 2009).

TOURISM

Visitor Arrivals: 270,952 (75,446 stop-over visitors, 5,185 excursionists, 40,859 yacht passengers, 149,462 cruise ship passengers) in 2009; 231,121 (72,478 stop-over visitors, 5,086 excursionists, 42,603 yacht passengers, 110,954 cruise ship passengers) in 2010; 207,997 (73,866 stop-over visitors, 3,941 excursionists, 41,266 yacht passengers, 88,924 cruise ship passengers) in 2011. *Stop-over Visitors by Origin* (2011): Canada 6,719; Caribbean 23,272; United Kingdom 14,895; USA 21,164; Other 7,816.

Tourism Receipts (EC $ million): 236.4 in 2009; 232.7 in 2010; 247.6 in 2011.

Source: Eastern Caribbean Central Bank.

COMMUNICATIONS MEDIA

Telephones ('000 main lines in use, 2011): 22.7.

Mobile Cellular Telephones (subscribers, 2011): 131,800.

Personal Computers: 16,500 (151.8 per 1,000 persons) in 2005.

Fixed Internet Subscribers ('000, 2010): 14.2.

Broadband Subscribers ('000, 2011): 14.1.

Source: International Telecommunication Union.

EDUCATION

Pre-primary (2008/09 unless otherwise indicated): 97 schools (1993/94); 378 teachers; 2,925 pupils.

Primary (2009/10 unless otherwise indicated): 60 schools (2000); 879 teachers; 14,435 pupils.

Secondary (2009/10 unless otherwise indicated): 21 schools (2000); 886 teachers; 11,426 pupils.

Teacher Training (2000): 1 institution; 10 teachers; 107 students.

Technical College (2000): 1 institution; 19 teachers; 187 students.

Community College (2000): 1 institution; 13 teachers; 550 students.

Nursing College (2000): 1 institution; 6 teachers; 60 students.

Pupil-teacher Ratio (primary education, UNESCO estimate): 16.3 in 2009/10.

Sources: partly Caribbean Development Bank, *Social and Economic Indicators*, and UNESCO Institute for Statistics.

Adult Literacy Rate: 88.1% in 2004. Source: UN Development Programme, *Human Development Report*.

Directory

The Government

HEAD OF STATE

Queen: HM Queen ELIZABETH II.

Governor-General: Sir FREDERICK NATHANIEL BALLANTYNE (took office 2 September 2002).

CABINET
(May 2013)

The Government was formed by the Unity Labour Party.

Prime Minister and Minister of Finance, National Security, Grenadines Affairs and Legal Affairs: Dr RALPH E. GONSALVES.

Deputy Prime Minister and Minister of Education: GIRLYN MIGUEL.

Minister of Foreign Affairs, Foreign Trade and Consumer Affairs: DOUGLAS SLATER.

Minister of Housing, Informal Human Settlements, Physical Planning, and Lands and Surveys: MONTGOMERY DANIEL.

Minister of Agriculture, Rural Transformation, Forestry, Fisheries and Industry: SABOTO CAESAR.

Minister of Tourism, Sports and Culture: CECIL McKIE.

Minister of National Reconciliation, Public Service, Information, Labour and Ecclesiastical Affairs: MAXWELL CHARLES.

Minister of Health, Wellness and the Environment: CLAYTON BURGIN.

Minister of Transport, Works, Urban Development and Local Government: JULIAN FRANCIS.

Minister of National Mobilization, Social Development, Family, Gender Affairs, Persons with Disabilities, and Youth: FREDERICK A. STEPHENSON.

Attorney-General: JUDITH S. JONES-MORGAN.

MINISTRIES

Office of the Governor-General: Government House, Kingstown; tel. 456-1401; fax 457-9701.

Office of the Prime Minister: Administrative Bldg, 4th Floor, Bay St, Kingstown; tel. 456-1703; fax 457-2152; e-mail pmosvg@vincysurf.com.

Office of the Attorney-General and Ministry of Legal Affairs: New Methodist Church Bldg, 3rd Floor, Granby St, Kingstown; tel. 457-2807; fax 457-2898; e-mail ag.gov.vc@gmail.com; internet www.legal.gov.vc.

Ministry of Agriculture, Rural Transformation, Forestry, Fisheries and Industry: Richmond Hill, Kingstown; tel. 456-1410; fax 457-1688; e-mail agriculture@gov.vc; internet www.agriculture.gov.vc.

Ministry of Education: Halifax St, Kingstown; tel. 457-1104; fax 457-1114; e-mail office.education@mail.gov.vc; internet www.education.gov.vc.

Ministry of Finance and Economic Planning: Halifax St, Kingstown; tel. 457-1343; fax 457-2943; e-mail office.finance@mail.gov.vc.

Ministry of Foreign Affairs, Foreign Trade and Consumer Affairs: Administrative Bldg, 3rd Floor, Bay St, Kingstown; tel. 456-2060; fax 456-2610; e-mail office.foreignaffairs@mail.gov.vc; internet www.foreign.gov.vc.

Ministry of Health, Wellness and the Environment: Ministerial Bldg, 1st Floor, Bay St, Kingstown; tel. 457-2586; fax 457-2684; e-mail office.health@mail.gov.vc; internet www.health.gov.vc.

Ministry of Housing, Informal Human Settlements, Physical Planning, and Lands and Surveys: Methodist Church Bldg, Granby St, Kingstown; tel. 456-1111; fax 451-2479; e-mail office.housing@mail.gov.vc; internet www.housing.gov.vc.

Ministry of National Mobilization, Social Development, Family, Gender Affairs, Persons with Disabilities, and Youth: DMG Bldg, 2nd and 3rd Floors, Halifax St, Kingstown; tel. 450-0395; fax 457-2476; e-mail office.socialdevelopment@mail.gov.vc; internet www.mobilization.gov.vc.

Ministry of National Reconciliation, Public Service, Information, Labour and Ecclesiastical Affairs: Ministerial Bldg, 2nd Floor, Halifax St, Kingstown; tel. 451-2707; fax 451-2820; e-mail office.reconciliation@gov.vc; internet www.reconciliation.gov.vc.

Ministry of National Security, Airport and Seaport Development: Ministerial Bldg, 2nd Floor, Halifax St, Kingstown; tel. 456-1111; fax 457-2152; e-mail office.natsec@mail.gov.vc; internet www.security.gov.vc.

Ministry of Tourism, Sports and Culture: NIS Bldg, 2nd Floor, Upper Bay St, POB 834, Kingstown; tel. 457-1502; fax 451-2425; e-mail tourism@vincysurf.com; internet www.tourism.gov.vc.

Ministry of Transport, Works, Urban Development and Local Government: Halifax St, Kingstown; tel. 457-2031; fax 457-1289; e-mail ps.mtw@gov.vc; internet www.transport.gov.vc.

Legislature

HOUSE OF ASSEMBLY

Senators: 6.

Elected Members: 15.

Speaker: HENDRICK ALEXANDER.

Clerk: NICOLE HERBERT, House of Assembly, Court House, Halifax St, Kingstown; tel. 457-1872; fax 457-1825; internet www.assembly.gov.vc.

Election, 13 December 2010

Party	Valid votes	% of votes	Seats
Unity Labour Party (ULP) .	32,099	51.11	8
New Democratic Party (NDP) .	30,568	48.67	7
Saint Vincent and the Grenadines Green Party .	138	0.22	—
Total	62,805	100.00	15

Election Commission

Electoral Office: Glenville St, Kingstown; tel. 457-1762; fax 485-6844; e-mail electoraloffice@gov.vc; Supervisor of Elections SYLVIA FINDLAY SCRUBB.

Political Organizations

New Democratic Party (NDP): Democrat House, Murray Rd, POB 1300, Kingstown; tel. 451-2845; fax 457-2647; e-mail info@ndpsvg.org; internet www.ndpsvg.org; f. 1975; democratic party supporting political unity in the Caribbean, social devt and free enterprise; Chair. LINTON LEWIS; Leader ARNHIM ULRIC EUSTACE; Gen. Sec. ALLAN CRUICKSHANK; 7,000 mems.

Saint Vincent and the Grenadines Green Party: POB 1707, Kingstown; tel. and fax 456-9579; e-mail mail@svggreenparty.org; internet www.svggreenparty.org; f. 2005; Leader IVAN O'NEAL; Gen. Sec. ORDAN O. GRAHAM.

Unity Labour Party (ULP): Tennis Court Cnr, Murrays Rd, POB 1651, Kingstown; tel. 457-2761; fax 457-1292; e-mail info@voteulp.com; internet voteulp.com; f. 1994 by merger of Movement for National Unity and the Saint Vincent Labour Party; moderate, social democratic party; Chair. EDWIN SNAGG; Political Leader Dr RALPH E. GONSALVES; Gen. Sec. JULIAN FRANCIS.

Diplomatic Representation

EMBASSIES IN SAINT VINCENT AND THE GRENADINES

Brazil: Hotel-Beaccombers, Kingstown; tel. and fax 457-4021; Ambassador RENATO XAVIER.

Cuba: Ratho Mill, Kingstown; tel. 458-5844; fax 456-9344; e-mail embajador@vc.embacuba.cu; internet www.cubadiplomatica.cu/sanvicentegranadinas; Ambassador PABLO ANTONIO RODRÍGUEZ VIDAL.

Taiwan (Republic of China): Murray Rd, POB 878, Kingstown; tel. 456-2431; fax 456-2913; e-mail rocemsvg@caribsurf.com; Ambassador WEBER SHIH.

Venezuela: Baynes Bros Bldg, Granby St, POB 852, Kingstown; tel. 456-1374; fax 457-1934; e-mail embavenezsanvicente@vincysurf.com; Ambassador YOEL PÉREZ MARCANO.

Judicial System

Justice is administered by the Eastern Caribbean Supreme Court, based in Saint Lucia and consisting of a Court of Appeal and a High Court. Three High Court Judges are resident in Saint Vincent and the Grenadines. There are five Magistrates, including the Registrar of the Supreme Court, who acts as an additional Magistrate.

High Court Judges: FREDERICK VICTOR BRUCE-LYLE, GERTEL THOM.

Registrar: TAMARA GIBSON-MARKS.

Religion

CHRISTIANITY

Saint Vincent Christian Council: Melville St, POB 445, Kingstown; tel. 456-1408; f. 1969; four mem. churches; Chair. Rt Rev. CALVERT LEOPOLD FRIDAY.

The Anglican Communion

Anglicans in Saint Vincent and the Grenadines are adherents of the Church in the Province of the West Indies, comprising eight dioceses. The Archbishop of the West Indies is the Bishop of Nassau and the Bahamas, and is resident in Nassau, Bahamas. The diocese of the Windward Islands includes Grenada, Saint Lucia and Saint Vincent and the Grenadines.

Bishop of the Windward Islands: Rt Rev. CALVERT LEOPOLD FRIDAY, Bishop's Court, POB 502, Kingstown; tel. 456-1895; fax 456-2591; e-mail diocesewi@vincysurf.com.

The Roman Catholic Church

Saint Vincent and the Grenadines comprises a single diocese (formed when the diocese of Bridgetown-Kingstown was divided in 1989), which is suffragan to the archdiocese of Port of Spain (Trinidad and Tobago). The Bishop participates in the Antilles Episcopal Conference, currently based in Port of Spain. Some 13% of the population are Roman Catholics.

Bishop of Kingstown: CHARLES JASON GORDON, Bishop's Office, POB 862, Edinboro, Kingstown; tel. 457-2363; fax 457-1903; e-mail rcdok@caribsurf.com.

Other Christian Churches

Methodists, Seventh-day Adventists, Baptists and other denominations also have places of worship.

BAHÁ'Í FAITH

National Spiritual Assembly: POB 1043, Kingstown; tel. 456-4717.

The Press

SELECTED WEEKLIES

Searchlight: Interactive Media Ltd, POB 152, Kingstown; tel. 456-1558; fax 457-2250; e-mail search@caribsurf.com; internet searchlight.vc; weekly on Fri.; Chair. CORLETHA OLLIVERRE; CEO and Acting Man. Editor CLARE KEIZER.

The Vincentian: St George's Pl., Kingstown; tel. 456-1123; fax 457-2821; e-mail info@thevincentian.com; internet www.thevincentian.com; f. 1899; weekly on Fri.; owned by the Vincentian Publishing Co; Man. Dir EGERTON M. RICHARDS; Editor-in-Chief TERRANCE PARRIS; circ. 6,000.

The Westindian Crusader: Kingstown; tel. and fax 458-0073; e-mail crusader@caribsurf.com; weekly; Editor ESLEE CARBERRY; Man. Editor LINA CLARKE.

SELECTED PERIODICALS

Caribbean Compass: Compass Publishing Ltd, POB 175, Bequia; tel. 457-3409; fax 457-3410; e-mail tom@caribbeancompass.com; internet www.caribbeancompass.com; f. 1995; marine news; monthly; free distribution in the Caribbean from Puerto Rico to Panama; circ. 11,000; Man. Dir TOM HOPMAN; Editor SALLY ERDLE.

Government Gazette: Govt Printery, Campden Park St, POB 12, Kingstown; tel. 457-1840; fax 453-3240; e-mail govprint@vincysurf.com; f. 1844; Govt Printer OTHNIEL WHITE; circ. 492.

Publishers

Interactive Media Ltd: Lower Kingstown Park, POB 152, Kingstown; tel. 456-1558; fax 457-2250; e-mail search@vincysurf.com; internet searchlight.vc; f. 1995; Chair. CORLETHA OLLIVIERRE; CEO CLARE KEIZER (acting).

SVG Publishers Inc: Campden Park Industrial Estate, POB 1609, Kinstown; tel. 453-3166; fax 453-3538; e-mail info@svgpublishers.com; internet www.svgpublishers.com; f. 2005; Dir CLARE KEIZER; Gen. Man. CARL JAMES.

The Vincentian Publishing Co Ltd: St George's Pl., Kingstown; tel. 456-1123; fax 457-2821; e-mail info@thevincentian.com; internet www.thevincentian.com; Man. Dir EGERTON M. RICHARDS; CEO DESIREE RICHARDS.

Broadcasting and Communications

TELECOMMUNICATIONS

Digicel: Suite KO59, cnr Granby and Sharpe Sts, Kingstown; tel. 453-3000; fax 453-3010; e-mail customercaresvg@digicelgroup.com; internet www.digicelsvg.com; f. 2003; mobile cellular phone operator; owned by an Irish consortium; Group CEO and Dir COLM DELVES; Gen. Man. SEAN LATTY.

KaribCable: Frenches Gate, POB 1684, Kingstown; tel. 570-1600; fax 570-1666; e-mail info@karibcable.com; internet www.karibcable.com/vc; internet service provider; Man. Dir KELLY GLASS.

LIME: Halifax St, POB 103, Kingstown; tel. 457-1901; fax 457-2777; e-mail support@vincysurf.com; internet www.time4lime.com; fmrly Cable & Wireless (St Vincent and the Grenadines) Ltd; name changed as above 2008; CEO TONY RICE; CEO, Eastern Caribbean GERARD BORELY.

Regulatory Authorities

Eastern Caribbean Telecommunications Authority (ECTEL): based in Castries, Saint Lucia; f. 2000 to regulate telecommunications in Saint Vincent and the Grenadines, Dominica, Grenada, Saint Christopher and Nevis, and Saint Lucia.

National Telecom Regulatory Commission (NTRC): NIS Bldg, 2nd Floor, Upper Bay St, Kingstown; tel. 457-2279; fax 457-2834; e-mail ntrc@ntrc.vc; internet www.ntrc.vc; f. 2001 by the Telecommunications Act to regulate the sector in collaboration with ECTEL; Chair S. MARSHALL.

BROADCASTING

National Broadcasting Corporation of Saint Vincent and the Grenadines (NBC): Richmond Hill, POB 705, Kingstown; tel. 457-1111; fax 456-2749; e-mail nbcsvgadmin@nbcsvg.com; internet www.nbcsvg.com; govt-owned; Chair. ELSON CRICK; Gen. Man. CORLITA OLLIVERRE.

Radio

NBC Radio: National Broadcasting Corpn, Richmond Hill, POB 705, Kingstown; tel. 457-1111; fax 456-2749; e-mail nbcsvgadmin@nbcsvg.com; internet www.nbcsvg.com; commercial; broadcasts BBC World Service (United Kingdom) and local programmes.

Nice Radio FM: BDS Company Ltd, Dorsetshire Hill, POB 324, Kingstown; tel. 458-1013; fax 456-5556; e-mail bdsnice@caribsurf.com; internet www.niceradio.org; Man. Dir DOUGLAS DE FREITAS.

Television

National Broadcasting Corporation of Saint Vincent and the Grenadines: see above

SVG Television (SVGTV): Dorsetshire Hill, POB 617, Kingstown; tel. 456-1078; fax 456-1015; e-mail svgbc@vincysurf.com;

internet www.svgbc.com/svgtv.htm; f. 1980; broadcasts local, regional and international programmes; Man. Dir R. PAUL MACLEISH.

Television services from Barbados can be received in parts of the islands.

Finance

(cap. = capital; res = reserves; dep. = deposits; m. = million; br. = branch)

BANKING

The Eastern Caribbean Central Bank, based in Saint Christopher, is the central issuing and monetary authority for Saint Vincent and the Grenadines.

Eastern Caribbean Central Bank—Saint Vincent and the Grenadines Office: Frenches House, POB 839, Frenches; tel. 456-1413; fax 456-1412; e-mail eccbnetwork@vincysurf.com; Country Dir ELRITHA DICK.

Regulatory Authority

Financial Services Authority (FSA): Upper Bay St, POB 356, Kingstown; tel. 456-2577; fax 457-2568; e-mail info@svgfsa.com; internet www.svgfsa.com; f. 1996 as International Financial Services Authority; Chair. LEON SNAGG; Exec. Dir SHARDA SINANAN-BOLLERS.

Financial Intelligence Unit (FIU): POB 1826, Kingstown; tel. 451-2070; fax 457-2014; e-mail svgfiu@vincysurf.com; internet www.svgfiu.com; f. 2002; Dir GRENVILLE WILLIAMS.

Local Banks

Bank of Nova Scotia Ltd (Canada): 76 Halifax St, POB 237, Kingstown; tel. 457-1601; fax 457-2623; e-mail bruce.sali@scotiabank.com; Country Man. BASIL ALEXANDER.

Bank of St Vincent and the Grenadines Ltd: Cnr Halifax and Egmont Sts, POB 880, Kingstown; tel. 457-1844; fax 456-2612; e-mail natbank@caribsurf.com; internet www.bosvg.com; f. 1977 as National Commercial Bank (SVG) Ltd, name changed 2010; govt-owned until 2010 when 51% stake sold to East Caribbean Financial Holding Ltd (St Lucia); cap. EC $14.8m., res EC $20.8m., dep. EC $624.4m. (June 2010); Man. Dir DERRY WILLIAMS; Chair. ERROL ALLEN.

FirstCaribbean International Bank: Halifax St, POB 604, Kingstown; tel. 457-1706; fax 457-2985; e-mail Earl.Crichton@firstcaribbeanbank.com; internet www.firstcaribbeanbank.com; f. 2002 following merger of Caribbean operations of Barclays Bank PLC and CIBC; CIBC acquired Barclays' 43.7% stake in 2006; Exec. Chair. MICHAEL MANSOOR; CEO RIK PARKHILL.

RBTT Bank Caribbean Ltd: 81 South River Rd, POB 81, Kingstown; tel. 456-1501; fax 456-2141; internet www.rbtt.com; f. 1985 as Caribbean Banking Corpn Ltd, name changed as above in 2002; Group CEO SURESH SOOKOO.

'OFFSHORE' FINANCIAL SECTOR

Legislation permitting the development of an 'offshore' financial sector was introduced in 1976 and revised in 1996 and 1998. International banks are required to have a place of business on the islands and to designate a licensed registered agent. International Business Companies registered in Saint Vincent and the Grenadines are exempt from taxation for 25 years. Legislation also guarantees total confidentiality. In 2010 the 'offshore' financial sector included 9,584 International Business Companies, 123 trusts and six banks.

Saint Vincent Trust Service: Trust House, 112 Bonadie St, POB 613, Kingstown; tel. 457-1027; fax 457-1961; e-mail info@st-vincent-trust.com; internet www.jeeves-group.com; br. in Liechtenstein; Chair. BRYAN JEEVES.

'Offshore' Banks

Commercial Holding Bank Ltd: The Jaycees Bldg, 2nd Floor, Stoney Ground, POB 1823, Kingstown; tel. 453-1950; e-mail joan.p.daniel@chbankltd.com; internet www.chbankltd.com; Contact JOAN DANIEL.

Euro Pacific Bank Ltd: 111 Euro House, Financial Services Centre, Stoney Ground, Kingstown; tel. 453-2086; fax 453-2085; e-mail info@europacbank.com; internet www.europacbank.com; Pres. GORDON MCBEAN; CEO PETER SCHIFF.

Loyal Bank Ltd: Cedar Hill Crest, POB 1825, Kingstown; tel. 485-6705; fax 451-2757; e-mail ceo@loyalbank.com; internet www.loyalbank.com; f. 1997; owned by Ost West Stiftung; cap. 5.0m., dep. EC $211.2m. (Dec. 2012); CEO ADRIAN BARON.

STOCK EXCHANGE

Eastern Caribbean Securities Exchange: based in Basseterre, Saint Christopher and Nevis; tel. (869) 466-7192; fax (869) 465-3798; e-mail info@ecseonline.com; internet www.ecseonline.com; f. 2001; regional securities market designed to facilitate the buying and selling of financial products for the 8 mem. territories—Anguilla, Antigua and Barbuda, Dominica, Grenada, Montserrat, Saint Christopher and Nevis, Saint Lucia, and Saint Vincent and the Grenadines; Chair. Sir K. DWIGHT VENNER; Gen. Man. TREVOR E. BLAKE.

INSURANCE

A number of foreign insurance companies have offices in Kingstown. Local companies include the following:

Haydock Insurances Ltd: Granby St, POB 1179, Kingstown; tel. 457-2903; fax 456-2952; e-mail haydock@vincysurf.com; internet www.caribbeanalliance.com.

Metrocint General Insurance Co Ltd: St George's Pl., POB 692, Kingstown; tel. 456-1821; fax 457-2821; e-mail metrocint@vincysurf.com; internet metrocintsvg.com.

Saint Vincent Insurances Ltd: Lot 69, Grenville St, POB 210, Kingstown; tel. 456-1733; fax 456-2225; e-mail admin@stvincentinsurances.com; internet www.stvincentinsurances.com.

Trade and Industry

DEVELOPMENT ORGANIZATION

Invest SVG: Administrative Bldg, 2nd Floor, Bay St, POB 2442, Kingstown; tel. 457-2159; fax 456-2688; e-mail info@investsvg.com; internet www.investsvg.com; f. 2003 as National Investment Promotions Inc; assumed DEVCO's responsibilities for investment promotion and foreign direct investment; reports to the Office of the Prime Minister; board mems appointed from both public and private sectors by the Cabinet; Chair. RHONDA KING; Exec. Dir CLEO HUGGINS.

CHAMBER OF COMMERCE

Saint Vincent and the Grenadines Chamber of Industry and Commerce (Inc): Corea's Bldg, 3rd Floor, Halifax and Hillsborough Sts, POB 134, Kingstown; tel. 457-1464; fax 456-2944; e-mail svgchamber@svg-cic.org; internet svg-cic.org; f. 1925; Pres. ANDREW WOODROFFE.

EMPLOYERS' ORGANIZATIONS

Saint Vincent Banana Growers' Association: Sharpe St, POB 10, Kingstown; tel. 457-1605; fax 456-2585; f. 1954; over 7,000 mems; Chair. LESLINE BEST; Gen. Man. HENRY KEIZER.

Saint Vincent Employers' Federation: Corea's Bldg, 3rd Floor, Middle St, POB 348, Kingstown; tel. 456-1269; fax 457-2777; e-mail svef@caribsurf.com; Pres. NOEL DICKSON; Exec. Dir PHYLLIS JOHN-PRIMUS.

Windward Islands Farmers' Association (WINFA): Paul's Ave, POB 817, Kingstown; tel. 456-2704; fax 456-1383; e-mail winfa@winfacaribbean.org; internet www.winfacaribbean.org; f. 1982; Chair. JULIUS POLIUS; Co-ordinator RENWICK ROSE.

UTILITIES

Electricity

Saint Vincent Electricity Services Ltd (VINLEC): Paul's Ave, POB 865, Kingstown; tel. 456-1701; fax 456-2436; e-mail vinlec@vinlec.com; internet www.vinlec.com; f. 1931; 100% state-owned; country's sole electricity supplier; Chair. DOUGLAS COLE; CEO THORNLEY O. A. O. MYERS; 280 employees.

Water

Central Water and Sewerage Authority (CWSA): New Montrose, POB 363, Kingstown; tel. 456-2946; fax 456-2552; e-mail cwsa@vincysurf.com; internet www.cwsasvg.com; f. 1970; Chair. RICHARD MACLEISH; Gen. Man. GARTH SAUNDERS.

TRADE UNION

National Labour Congress: POB 875, Kingstown; tel. 457-1062; fax 457-1705; e-mail svgtu@vincysurf.com; 5 affiliated unions; Pres. NOEL JACKSON.

Transport

RAILWAYS

There are no railways in the islands.

ROADS

In 2009 there was an estimated total road network of 1,033 km, of which 70% were paved. The first stage of a three-phase project to link Troumaca with Fergusson Gap was completed in 2007, at a cost of EC $2.5m. Extension of the Windward Highway was completed in 2010. In the 2010 budget EC $3m. was allocated for road and bridge improvement.

SHIPPING

The deep-water harbour at Kingstown can accommodate two ocean-going vessels and about five motor vessels. In addition, a cruise terminal allows two cruise ships to berth at the same time. There are regular motor-vessel services between the Grenadines and Saint Vincent. Geest Industries, formerly the major banana purchaser, operated a weekly service to the United Kingdom. Numerous shipping lines also call at Kingstown harbour. Some exports are flown to Barbados to link up with international shipping lines.

Saint Vincent and the Grenadines Port Authority: Upper Bay St, POB 1237, Kingstown; tel. 456-1830; fax 456-2732; e-mail bjohn@ svgpa.com; internet www.svgpa.com; CEO and Port Man. BISHEN JOHN.

CIVIL AVIATION

There is a civilian airport, E. T. Joshua Airport, at Arnos Vale, situated about 3 km (2 miles) south-east of Kingstown, that does not accommodate long-haul jet aircraft. Construction of an international airport at Argyle, 13 miles east of Kingstown, was due to be completed in December 2013. The new airport would be able to accommodate international jet services and would have facilities for 1.4m. passengers per year, more than five times the capacity at the existing airport. The project was estimated to cost EC $652m. The island of Canouan has a small airport with a runway and passenger terminal; construction of a jet airport was completed in 2008. In 2009 LIAT (in which Saint Vincent and the Grenadines is a shareholder) began scheduled flights from Grenada and Barbados to Canouan. Other airports include the J. F. Mitchell Airport in Bequia, Union Island Airport and one in Mustique island, which has a landing strip for light aircraft only.

LIAT Airlines: tel. 456-6333; fax 456-6111; e-mail pattersond@ liatairline.com; internet www.liatairline.com; f. 2009; Station Man. DOMINIQUE PATTERSON; Dir ISAAC SOLOMON.

Mustique Airways: POB 1232, E. T. Joshua Airport, Arnos Vale; tel. 458-4380; fax 456-4586; e-mail info@mustique.com; internet www.mustique.com; f. 1979; charter and scheduled flights; Chair. JONATHAN PALMER.

Saint Vincent and the Grenadines Air Ltd (SVG Air): POB 39, Arnos Vale; tel. 457-5124; fax 457-5077; e-mail info@svgair.com; internet www.svgair.com; f. 1990; charter and scheduled flights; CEO MARTIN BARNARD.

Tourism

The island chain of the Grenadines is the country's main tourism asset. There are superior yachting facilities, but the lack of major air links with countries outside the region has resulted in a relatively slow development for tourism. In 2011 Saint Vincent and the Grenadines received 88,924 cruise ship passengers and 73,886 stop-over tourists. Tourism receipts totalled EC $247.6m. in that year.

Saint Vincent and the Grenadines Hotel and Tourism Association (SVGHTA): E. T. Joshua International Airport, Arnos Vale; tel. 458-4379; fax 456-4456; e-mail svghotels@vincysurf.com; internet www.svghotels.com; f. 1968 as Saint Vincent Hotel Asscn; renamed as above in 1999; non-profit org.; mem. of the Caribbean Hotels Asscn; Pres. KIM HAILBICH; Asst Exec. Dir FRANCELIA MARKSMAN; 75 mems.

St Vincent and the Grenadines Tourism Authority (SVGTA): NIS Bldg, Upper Bay St, POB 834, Kingstown; tel. 456-6222; fax 485-6020; e-mail svgta@discoversvg.com; internet www.discoversvg .com; f. 2009; CEO GLEN BEACHE.

Defence

Saint Vincent and the Grenadines participates in the US-sponsored Regional Security System, comprising police, coastguards and army units, which was established by independent Eastern Caribbean states in 1982. The recurrent budget for 2008 allocated some 10.3% of total expenditure (projected at EC $423m.) for defence purposes.

Education

Free primary education, beginning at five years of age and lasting for seven years, is available to all children in government schools, although it is not compulsory and attendance is low. There are 61 government, and five private, primary schools. Secondary education, beginning at 12 years of age, comprises a first cycle of five years and a second, two-year cycle. However, government facilities at this level are limited, and much secondary education is provided in schools administered by religious organizations, with government assistance. There are also a number of junior secondary schools. Enrolment at primary schools during the 2009/10 academic year included 94% of children in the relevant age-group, while comparable enrolment in secondary schools in 2007/08 included 90% of pupils. There is a teacher-training college and a technical college. Total budgetary expenditure on education by the central Government was a projected EC $147.5m. in 2012 (18.6% of the total budget). The Government announced in 2005 that it had achieved its objective of instituting universal secondary education.

SAMOA

Introductory Survey

LOCATION, CLIMATE, LANGUAGE, RELIGION, FLAG, CAPITAL

The Independent State of Samoa (formerly Western Samoa) lies in the southern Pacific Ocean, about 2,400 km (1,500 miles) north of New Zealand. Its nearest neighbour is American Samoa, to the east. The country comprises two large and seven small islands, of which five are uninhabited. The climate is tropical, with temperatures generally between 23°C (73°F) and 30°C (86°F). The rainy season is from November to April. The languages spoken are Samoan (a Polynesian language) and English. Almost all of the inhabitants profess Christianity, and the major denominations are the Congregational, Roman Catholic and Methodist Churches. The national flag (proportions 1 by 2) is red, with a rectangular dark blue canton, containing five differently sized white five-pointed stars in the form of the Southern Cross constellation, in the upper hoist. The capital is Apia.

CONTEMPORARY POLITICAL HISTORY

Historical Context

The islands became a German protectorate in 1899. During the First World War (1914–18) they were occupied by New Zealand forces, which overthrew the German administration. In 1919 New Zealand was granted a League of Nations mandate to govern the islands. In 1946 Western Samoa (as it was known until July 1997) was made a UN Trust Territory, with New Zealand continuing as the administering power. From 1954 measures of internal self-government were gradually introduced, culminating in the adoption of an independence Constitution in October 1960. This was approved by a UN-supervised plebiscite in May 1961, and the islands became independent on 1 January 1962. The office of head of state was held jointly by two traditional rulers until April 1963 when, upon the death of his colleague, Malietoa Tanumafili II became sole head of state for life, performing the duties of a constitutional monarch.

Fiame Mata'afa Mulinu'u, Prime Minister since 1959, lost the general election in 1970, and a new Cabinet, led by Tupua Tamasese Lealofi, was formed. Mata'afa regained power in 1973, following another general election, and remained in office until his death in May 1975. He was again succeeded by Tamasese, who, in turn, lost the general election in March 1976 to his cousin, Tupuola Efi. The previously unorganized opposition members formed the Human Rights Protection Party (HRPP) in 1979, and won the elections in February 1982, taking 24 of the 47 seats in the Fono (Legislative Assembly). Va'ai Kolone was appointed Prime Minister, but in September he was removed from office as a result of previous electoral malpractice. Tupuola Efi returned to the premiership and, with much popular support, sought to nullify an earlier agreement between Kolone and the New Zealand Government which, in defiance of a ruling by the British Privy Council, denied automatic New Zealand citizenship to all Western Samoans except those already living in New Zealand. However, Tupuola Efi resigned in December 1982, after the Fono had rejected his budget, and was replaced by the new HRPP leader, Tofilau Eti Alesana.

Domestic Political Affairs

At elections in February 1985 the HRPP won 31 of the 47 seats, increasing its majority in the Fono from one to 15 seats; the newly formed Christian Democratic Party (CDP), led by Tupuola Efi, obtained the remaining 16 seats. In December Tofilau Eti resigned, following the rejection of the proposed budget by the Fono and the head of state's refusal to call another general election. Va'ai Kolone, with the support of a number of CDP members and HRPP defectors, was appointed Prime Minister of a coalition Government in January 1986.

At the February 1988 general election the HRPP and an alliance composed of independents and the CDP (later known as the Samoa National Development Party—SNDP) both initially gained 23 seats, with votes in the remaining constituency being tied. Following two inconclusive recounts, a judge from New Zealand presided over a third and declared the CDP candidate the winner. However, before a new government could be formed, a newly elected member of the Fono defected from the SNDP to the HRPP. Tofilau Eti was elected Prime Minister in April, appointing a new HRPP Government.

In early 1990 proposed legislation to permit local village councils to fine, or to impose forced labour or exile on, individuals accused of offending communal rules was widely perceived as an attempt by the Government to ensure the support of the Matai (elected clan chiefs) at the next general election. Of the 47 seats in the Fono, 45 were traditionally elected by holders of Matai titles. However, the political importance of the Matai had been increasingly diminished by the procurement of Matai titles by those seeking election to the Fono. This practice was believed to have undermined the system of chief leadership to such an extent that universal suffrage would have to be introduced to decide all of the seats in the Fono. A referendum was conducted in October 1990, at which voters narrowly accepted government proposals for the introduction of universal suffrage. A second proposal, to create an upper legislative chamber composed of the Matai, was rejected. A bill to implement universal adult suffrage was approved by the Fono in December, despite strong opposition from the SNDP.

Tofilau Eti Alesana's final two terms as Prime Minister

A general election was held in April 1991. Following the poll petitions were filed with the Supreme Court against 11 newly elected members of the Fono who were accused of corrupt or illegal electoral practices. Moreover, subsequent political manoeuvring resulted in the HRPP increasing its parliamentary representation from an initial 26 to 30 seats, while the SNDP ultimately secured only 16 seats in the Fono, and the remaining seat was retained by an independent. At the new Fono's first meeting in May Tofilau Eti was re-elected to the premiership. In November the Fono approved legislation to increase the parliamentary term from three to five years and to create an additional two seats in the Fono. These seats were contested in early 1992 and won by the HRPP.

The introduction of a value-added tax (VAT) on goods and services in January 1994 (which greatly increased the price of food and fuel) provoked a series of demonstrations and protest rallies, as well as demands for the resignation of the Prime Minister. In March, therefore, the Government agreed to amend the most controversial aspects of the tax. Meanwhile, four members of the Fono (including three recently expelled HRPP members), who had opposed the financial reforms, established a new political organization, the Samoa Liberal Party, under the leadership of the former Speaker, Nonumalo Leulumoega Sofara.

Protests against VAT continued in early 1995, following the Government's decision to charge two prominent members of the Tumua ma Pule group of traditional leaders with sedition, for organizing demonstrations against the tax during 1994. In March 1995 some 3,000 people delivered a petition to the Prime Minister, bearing the signatures of 120,000 people (around 75% of the population), which demanded that the tax be revoked. The Prime Minister questioned the authenticity of the signatures and appointed a 14-member committee to investigate the matter. In late June the case against the two members of Tumua ma Pule was dismissed on the grounds of insufficient evidence.

In December 1995 the HRPP unanimously re-elected Tofilau Eti as the leader of the party. Legislation introduced in April 1996 attempted to distinguish between the traditional Samoan practice of exchanging gifts and acts of bribery, amid numerous reports that voters were demanding gifts and favours from electoral candidates in return for their support.

Following a general election on 26 April 1996, the opposition was highly critical of the protracted counting of votes, claiming that the delay allowed the HRPP to recruit successful independent candidates in an attempt to gain a majority of seats in the Fono. It was eventually announced that the HRPP had secured a total of 28 of the 49 seats (with the recruitment of several independent members to their ranks), the SNDP had won 14 seats and independent candidates had secured seven. Tofilau Eti was subsequently re-elected as Prime Minister, defeating the

Leader of the Opposition, Tuiatua Tupua Tamasese, by 34 votes to 14.

In July 1997 the Fono voted by 41 votes to one to approve a constitutional amendment changing the country's name to Samoa. (The country has been known simply as Samoa at the UN since its admission to the organization in 1976.) However, the neighbouring US territory of American Samoa expressed dissatisfaction with the change (which it believed undermined its own Samoan identity), and in September introduced legislation to prohibit recognition of the new name within the territory. In March 1998 the House of Representatives in American Samoa voted against legislation that proposed not to recognize Samoan passports, but decided to continue to refer to the country as Western Samoa and to its inhabitants as Western Samoans.

A series of reports in *The Samoa Observer*, an independent newspaper, in mid-1997 alleged that a serious financial scandal involving the disappearance of some 500 blank passports, and their subsequent sale to Hong Kong Chinese purchasers for up to US $26,000 each, had occurred. The Government refused to comment on the newspaper's allegations, beyond confirming that several senior immigration officials had been suspended pending the outcome of an investigation into the affair. Moreover, the Government subsequently brought charges of defamatory libel against the editor, Savea Sano Malifa, for publishing a letter criticizing the Prime Minister (who was reported to have told the Fono of his intention to change legislation governing business licences, such that publications could have their licences withdrawn for publishing dissenting material). The regional Pacific Islands News Association also condemned the Prime Minister's comments as an attack on freedom of information and expression. Savea Sano Malifa was found guilty of defaming the Prime Minister in two libel cases in July and September 1998, and was ordered to pay a total of some $17,000 in costs. The newspaper had alleged that public funds had been used to construct a hotel owned by the Prime Minister and had criticized the allocation of $0.25m. in the 1998 budget to Tofilau Eti's legal costs. The Government's increasingly autocratic style, coupled with its poor economic record, resulted in frequent expressions of popular discontent during 1997. A series of protest marches in late 1997 and early 1998, organized by the Tumua ma Pule group of chiefs and attended by several thousand people, aimed to increase pressure on the Prime Minister to resign.

A long-standing dispute over land rights near Faleolo airport appeared to be the cause of violent activity in June 1998, when villagers shot a government official, burned buildings and slaughtered or stole hundreds of cattle on a government estate. However, it was subsequently revealed that the incidents had been perpetrated by members of a gang styling themselves as Japanese Ninja warriors, who were believed to be involved in the cultivation of marijuana and cattle theft. Some 38 men, thought to be members of the gang, were later arrested. The dispute, which originated in a land survey carried out in 1871, re-emerged in January 2003 when villagers presented the Government with a petition and a list of demands relating to land rights and revenue from the airport. In July 2005 the Government stated that it wanted all families living on the disputed land to vacate the area (covering about 22 acres) and move to a nearby, larger plot of government land, ostensibly in order to comply with health and safety regulations. However, the villagers rejected the Government's request, restating their original demand for the return of 6,000 acres close to the airport, which they claimed had been wrongfully taken from them at the end of the 19th century. They were led in their resistance by senior Matai and the former Minister of Civil Aviation, Toalepaiali'i Toeolesulu-sulu Suafaiga Siueva Pose Salesa III.

The premiership of Tuila'epa Sailele Malielegaoi

In November 1998 Tofilau Eti resigned as Prime Minister, owing to ill health. He was replaced by the Deputy Prime Minister, Tuila'epa Sailele Malielegaoi, and the Cabinet was reorganized. In July 1999 the Minister of Public Works, Luagalau Levaula Kamu, was shot dead while attending an event commemorating the 20th anniversary of the foundation of the HRPP. In August Eletise Leafa, the son of the Minister of Women's Affairs, Leafa Vitale, was convicted of the murder and sentenced to death (subsequently commuted to a life sentence). In April 2000 Leafa Vitale and the former Minister of Telecommunications, Toi Akuso, were found guilty of murdering Luagalau and were sentenced to death, which was similarly commuted to life imprisonment. It later emerged that Luagalau had been killed in an attempt to prevent him from uncovering cases of corruption and bribery in which the two ministers had become involved. Toi

Akuso died in prison in April 2009. Eletise Leafa and Leafa Vitale were granted parole and released in May and June 2010, respectively.

Meanwhile, in November 1999 the ruling HRPP increased its number of seats in the Fono to 34, following the defection of an independent candidate to the HRPP. At by-elections for the two imprisoned former ministers' seats in June 2000 HRPP candidates were successful in both constituencies. In August a supreme court ruling ordered the Government to allow opposition politicians access to the state-controlled media, which for several years had been denied.

At a general election in March 2001 the HRPP won 22 of the 49 parliamentary seats, the SNDP secured 13 seats and independent candidates took 14 seats. Tuila'epa Sailele won 28 votes in the Fono to be re-elected Prime Minister, although the opposition subsequently mounted a number of legal challenges to his election. In August charges of electoral malpractice against eight elected members of the Fono, including three cabinet ministers, were brought to the Supreme Court. None of the ministers was found guilty. By-elections for four vacant parliamentary seats in October and November were won by the HRPP.

In mid-2003 concerns were raised with regard to the increasing numbers of qualified medical staff choosing to emigrate or to leave the profession. It was estimated that one-third of Samoa's nurses had left the profession between 2002 and 2003, while one-half of all doctors' positions remained vacant. In September 2005 Samoan doctors went on strike in protest against low rates of pay and working conditions. In November some 1,500 people marched through the streets of Apia in support of 23 doctors who had resigned in protest. A petition was presented to the Prime Minister's Department, and a subsequent commission of inquiry made recommendations for changes, to which the Government then agreed, but no increase in doctors' starting salaries, as demanded by protesters, was forthcoming.

The general election held on 31 March 2006 was contested by a total of 211 candidates, including 18 women. The ruling HRPP regained power, securing 33 parliamentary seats, decisively defeating the Samoa Democratic United Party (SDUP, formed upon the merger of the SNDP and the Samoa Independent Party), which won 10 seats. Independent candidates won the remaining seats. Following the departure of several elected members from the party, the SDUP was unable to command the requisite eight seats for continued recognition in the chamber, and by the end of 2006 all SDUP members of the Fono had become independent legislators.

The Samoan head of state, Malietoa Tanumafili II, died in May 2007 at the age of 95. He had served as sole head of state, for life, since 1963. In June 2007 Tuiatua Tupua Tamasese Efi, Prime Minister in 1976–82 (when he was known as Tupuola Efi), was unanimously elected as head of state by the Fono, for a term of five years.

In May 2009 nine members of the Fono were disqualified by the Speaker on account of their formation in 2008 of a new political organization, the Tautua Samoa Party (TSP). Electoral law prohibited legislators from transferring allegiance from one party to another during the course of the parliamentary term. Among the nine legislators was Palusalue Faapo, a former cabinet minister, who had left the HRPP in 2008 (together with another HRPP member of the Fono) as a result of his disagreement with the Government's controversial plan for Samoan drivers to switch to using the left-hand side of the road (see below). In July 2009, however, the Supreme Court overruled the Speaker's decision, and the nine opposition members were reinstated in the Fono. In response to the ruling, the Government introduced legislation to amend the electoral law, which was approved in October, followed by the requisite revision of the Constitution in February 2010. In protest against the Government's use of intimidatory tactics, in March three opposition members resigned from the Fono, having deliberately refused to dissociate themselves from the TSP. At the resultant by-elections in May one TSP legislator was returned unopposed and another seat was taken by the HRPP.

A state of disaster was declared at the end of September 2009, when Samoa was devastated by a tsunami, which resulted in 143 deaths and displaced thousands of islanders. Substantial damage was sustained, estimated at some US $38m. Emergency assistance and relief supplies were provided by Australia and New Zealand. In May 2010 concern was raised by reports that a number of those whose homes had been destroyed were still awaiting permanent shelter some eight months after the tsunami. It was announced in September that the UN had agreed to delay Samoa's transition from the UN list of Least Developed Countries to that of Developing Countries, which had been scheduled to take effect in 2011, until January 2014, as a result of the difficulties posed by the post-tsunami recovery efforts. In October 2010 a report broadcast on New Zealand television claimed that up to $45m. of tsunami recovery funding had been misappropriated, a claim that was strongly refuted by the Prime Minister, who argued that of the $80m. pledged by foreign donors, Samoa had received just $15m. to date.

Meanwhile, following an unsuccessful lawsuit against the decision, the Government's plan for vehicles to drive on the left side of Samoa's roads, instead of the right as hitherto, was implemented in September 2009. The switch was apparently intended to encourage expatriate Samoans resident in Australia and New Zealand to dispatch used right-hand-drive cars to their families in Samoa, thereby reducing the country's need to import costly left-hand-drive vehicles from the USA and allowing more Samoans to own a motor vehicle.

In December 2010 it was revealed that an alleged plot to assassinate both the Prime Minister and the Chief Justice of the Supreme Court, Patu Tiava'asu'e Falefatu, was being investigated; the apparent plot was reported to be linked to the assassination in 1999 of Minister of Public Works Luagalau Levaula Kamu. Also in December 2010 Papalii Panoa Tavita Moala resigned as Leader of the TSP; Va'ai Papu was elected to replace him later in the month. Shortly before the legislative elections scheduled for March 2011 the Supreme Court disqualified three candidates (two TSP members and an independent candidate), owing to a provision in legislation requiring electoral nominees to secure the approval of Matai on the basis of service to the community. The decision was received with concern by many observers, and the TSP pledged to revoke the provision should it be elected to power.

Recent developments

The legislative election, held on 4 March 2011, was contested by a total of 158 candidates, of whom 102 were members of the HRPP. As a result of the disqualifications by the Supreme Court, Prime Minister Tuila'epa Sailele Malielegaoi secured re-election to his seat uncontested. Turn-out was recorded at 87.1%. The HRPP secured 29 of the 49 parliamentary seats, but was bolstered by the election of seven nominally independent candidates who supported the ruling party. Notably, three cabinet ministers lost their seats. The TSP increased its representation to 13 seats.

Following the polls, 10 challenges to the election results, including petitions against the Ministers of Education, Sport and Culture, of Finance, and of Works, Transport and Infrastructure, were lodged with the Supreme Court, although two were subsequently withdrawn. The first ruling, delivered in late April 2011, found the accused guilty on three allegations of vote-buying; however, the petitioner (of the HRPP) was found to have committed five acts of vote-buying himself. The Court declared the seat vacant and both men were disqualified from participating in elections for five years. In May, having been found guilty of bribery and so-called 'treating' (gift-giving), and thus disqualified from holding his parliamentary seat, Va'ai Papu was replaced as Leader of the TSP by his deputy, Palusalue Faapo. Two other parliamentarians were also disqualified as a result of election petitions. The four seats declared vacant by the Supreme Court were all won by HRPP candidates in by-elections held in late July, giving the party control of a total of 37 seats, while the TSP held 12. The post-electoral legal challenges and the resultant period of political upheaval appeared to illustrate, once again, the clash between the traditional Samoan practice of gift-giving and the strict code of conduct relating to candidates as stipulated in electoral law. Members of the TSP stated that they would seek clarification from the electoral authority in order to address this perennial problem.

Samoa transferred to the western side of the International Date Line on 29 December 2011 in a bid to facilitate the conduct of business with Australia and New Zealand (increasingly its most significant trading partners). The transition—following which Samoa was three hours ahead of, rather than 21 hours behind, the Australian business and financial hub of Sydney—reversed an earlier transfer, in 1892, to the eastern side of the dateline, which had been made to ease trade with merchant ships from the USA.

In March 2012 the Government proposed a constitutional amendment seeking to introduce a 10% quota for female representatives in the Fono, which would result in five seats being reserved for women. At that time there were only two female members of the Fono, and Prime Minister Tuila'epa Sailele

Malielegaoi had previously stated his desire that Samoa should be a role model for other Pacific islands by increasing the representation of women in the legislature. However, at March 2013 the bill had yet to be approved by the Fono.

Unresolved tensions relating to customary land rights re-emerged in 2012, following the announcement of government plans to build a hospital on some 4 ha of disputed land adjacent to Faleolo international airport. Residents and leaders of the village of Satapuala claimed that the land had been sold unlawfully during the German and New Zealand colonial administrations. Following the rejection of their claim for the return of the land by the Supreme Court in April, the villagers began a series of protests, which culminated in August in a brief armed blockade of the road from the airport to Apia. In the same month the villagers presented a petition demanding the return of the land to New Zealand Prime Minister John Key, during his official visit to celebrate the 50th anniversary of Samoa's independence.

Meanwhile, Tuiatua Tupua Tamasese Efi was re-elected unopposed by the Fono in July 2012 to serve a second term as head of state.

In mid-December 2012 Samoa was struck by Cyclone Evan, resulting in the deaths of 15 people and widespread damage to infrastructure, power and water supplies, and crops. Some 4,500 people were left homeless by the unexpectedly powerful storm, and the Government declared a 30-day state of emergency in order to assist its recovery programme. Scientists from the Pacific Climate Change Science Programme had stated earlier in the year that Samoa, in common with the entire South Pacific region, could expect a pattern of increasingly intense cyclones and episodes of extreme rainfall as a result of climate change.

Foreign Affairs
Regional relations

Samoa maintains strong links with New Zealand, where many Samoans live and many more receive secondary and tertiary education. In June 2002 New Zealand formally apologized for injustices that it had committed against its former colony during its administration between 1914 and 1962. These included allowing the 1918 influenza pandemic to kill 22% of Samoa's population (the virus having been brought in on a ship from New Zealand); the murder of a Samoan paramount chief and independence leader, Tupua Tamasese Lealofi III, and the killing of nine other supporters of the pacifist Mau movement during a non-violent protest in 1929; and the banishment of native leaders, who were also stripped of their chiefly titles. The apology, while accepted, drew mixed reactions from Samoans, many of whom were more concerned with the issue of the restoration of their rights to New Zealand citizenship (which had been severely curtailed by the Citizenship Western Samoa Act of 1982). In March 2003 large protest marches took place in Samoa and New Zealand demanding the repeal of the 1982 law. In May 2004 a parliamentary select committee rejected a 100,000-signature petition seeking a repeal of the law and upheld the principles of the 1982 ruling. The number of Samoans applying for New Zealand citizenship under a quota scheme increased by more than 50% in 2004 to reach 8,600. New Zealand Prime Minister John Key visited Samoa in July 2009, pledging to expand development aid to Samoa; the funding was to be focused on education, health, and public and private sector development. Development aid to Samoa was further increased in 2010/11 and 2011/12 (see Economic Affairs). Relations between the two countries were strained by changes to immigration regulations introduced by the New Zealand Government in 2012. Under the new rules, those seeking residency in New Zealand were required to have substantial private funds. The changes were widely criticized by Samoans and by human rights groups in New Zealand on the grounds that they would split families by discriminating against less wealthy Samoans.

In April 2009 Samoa and Australia renewed their bilateral Defence Co-operation Programme. Following the tsunami that caused widespread damage in Samoa in September 2009 (see Domestic Political Affairs), Australia donated US $24m. to the Samoan Government to assist in its recovery operations. In February 2010, as part of the Samoa-Australia Partnership for Development, the Australian Government provided $A1.15m., the first allocation within a six-year programme of support for the purposes of addressing the impact of climate change on health, agriculture and food security in the islands. During a visit to Samoa in October, Australia's Parliamentary Secretary for Pacific Island Affairs, Richard Marles, commended the Samoan Government for the manner in which it had deployed

Australian aid and announced the provision of US $700,000 to help Samoa establish an emergency response team to deal with natural disasters akin to the tsunami in the previous year. Along with New Zealand, Australia was also providing support for the introduction of free education in Samoa. The two countries provided a total of $NZ50,000 in emergency funding in response to the destruction wreaked by Cyclone Evan in December 2012.

In September 2004 the Samoan Government announced that it was seeking to formalize its maritime boundary with American Samoa, owing to a number of recent, unspecified incidents, and discussions began in Apia in the following year. In October 2012 the Samoan and American Samoan Governments announced that they had agreed to exchange a plot of land in each other's capitals in order to establish permanent consular premises. They were also to ease restrictions on their citizens travelling between Samoa and American Samoa.

In November 2011 the Samoan Prime Minister hosted a meeting of leaders from French Polynesia, Niue, Tokelau, the Cook Islands, Tonga, Tuvalu and American Samoa, which led to the creation of the Polynesian Leaders Group (see p. 478). The organization, which stated that its primary aims were the development, promotion and protection of common Polynesian interests, particularly with regard to culture, traditions, languages, sustainable economic development, democracy and human rights, intended to meet annually in conjunction with the Pacific Islands Forum (see p. 426).

Other external relations

Samoa hosted the 13th South Pacific Games in August–September 2007, in which 22 Pacific island nations participated. The Government of the People's Republic of China financed much of the preparations, including a US $12.7m. aquatic centre and the reconstruction of Apia Park Stadium, at a cost of $6.9m. (However, the total cost of approximately $92m. left Samoa in debt.) Burgeoning bilateral relations were reflected in the opening of a Samoan embassy in China in January 2009. (Samoa also opened an embassy in Japan in the same month.) Under the terms of an agreement signed in May 2010, trade duties were to be exempted on 472 of Samoa's exports to China, about 60% of its total exports to that country; eventually, some 95% of Samoa's exports to China were to be tariff-free. A visit to Samoa by a Chinese delegation headed by Jia Qinglin, Chairman of the National Committee of the Chinese People's Political Consultative Conference, attracted considerable attention in April 2011; Jia was the highest-ranking Chinese official ever to visit Samoa. During talks with Prime Minister Tuila'epa Sailele Malielegaoi and head of state Tuiatua Tupua Tamasese Efi, Jia expressed gratitude for Samoa's continued 'firm support' of the 'one China policy'. Samoa's Prime Minister commended China in a public statement in mid-2012 for its 'flexible' approach to aid and financial assistance.

The European Union (EU, see p. 281) has supported development programmes in Samoa since the 1970s. In May 2010 the EU allocated the sum of €16.7m. over the period 2010–13 for the purposes of upgrading water and sanitation facilities in the islands. In March 2011 the EU allocated €5.5m. to Samoa's budgetary support programme for 2011/12, to assist recovery from the global financial crisis of 2008–09. At the same time the EU granted an additional €3m. for Samoa's Civil Society Support Programme, a four-year programme intended to help eradicate poverty through sustainable development.

Samoa has sought to establish diplomatic relations with a number of new countries in recent years. Diplomatic relations were established with Brunei in February 2006, with Cuba in October 2007, with Estonia in January 2009, with Bosnia and Herzegovina in March 2009, with Georgia and Botswana in March 2010, with the United Arab Emirates in May 2010, and with Morocco in February 2011.

CONSTITUTION AND GOVERNMENT

The country's Constitution, which took effect in 1962, provides for the head of state to be elected by the Legislative Assembly for a term of five years. Until 2007 the head of state held office for life. The Legislative Assembly is composed of 49 members, all of whom are elected by universal suffrage. A total of 47 members are elected from among holders of Matai titles (elected clan chiefs), and two are selected from non-Samoan candidates. Members hold office for five years. Executive power is held by the Cabinet, comprising the Prime Minister and other selected members of the Assembly. The Prime Minister is appointed by the head of state with the necessary approval of the Assembly.

Judicial power is exercised by two district courts, the Land and Titles Court, the Supreme Court and the Court of Appeal.

REGIONAL AND INTERNATIONAL CO-OPERATION

Samoa is a member of the Pacific Islands Forum (see p. 426), the Pacific Community (see p. 422), the Asian Development Bank (ADB, see p. 214) and the UN's Economic and Social Commission for Asia and the Pacific (ESCAP, see p. 31). It is also a signatory to the Lomé Conventions and the successor Cotonou Agreement (see p. 334) with the European Union (EU, see p. 281). In November 2011 Samoa was one of eight founding members of the Polynesian Leaders Group (see p. 478).

Samoa joined the UN in 1976. The country is also a member of the Commonwealth. Samoa became a full member of the World Trade Organization (see p. 444) in May 2012.

ECONOMIC AFFAIRS

In 2011, according to estimates by the World Bank, Samoa's gross national income (GNI), measured at average 2009–11 prices, was US $587m., equivalent to $3,190 per head (or $4,430 per head on an international purchasing-power parity basis). During 2002–11, it was estimated, the population increased at an average annual rate of 0.3%, while gross domestic product (GDP) per head increased, in real terms, by an average of 1.9% per year. Overall GDP increased, in real terms, at an average annual rate of 2.2% in 2002–11. According to official figures, real GDP increased by 1.2% in the fiscal year ending 30 June 2012.

Agriculture (including hunting, forestry and fishing) accounted for 9.9% of GDP in 2011 and engaged some 37.0% of the employed labour force at the 2011 census. The principal cash crops are coconuts and taro (also the country's primary staple food). Breadfruit, yams, maize, passion fruit, papaya, pineapples and mangoes are also cultivated, some of which are exported. Pigs, cattle, poultry and goats are raised, mainly for local consumption. The country's commercial fishing industry expanded considerably from the late 1990s; revenue from exports of fresh fish totalled 20.0m. tala in 2007. Exports of food and live animals earned 23.3m. tala (15.2% of total export receipts) in 2012. Between 2002 and 2011, according to figures from the Asian Development Bank (ADB), the GDP of the agricultural sector contracted, in real terms, at an average annual rate of 2.8%. Agricultural GDP decreased by 5.1% in 2011/12, according to official figures.

Industry (comprising manufacturing, mining, construction and power) employed 12.3% of the employed labour force at the 2011 census and provided 26.7% of GDP in 2011. According to ADB figures, between 2002 and 2011 industrial GDP increased, in real terms, at an average annual rate of 1.7%. The GDP of the industrial sector expanded by 1.6% in 2011/12, according to official figures.

Manufacturing provided 8.2% of GDP in 2011 and, together with mining, engaged 5.5% of the employed labour force at the 2011 census. The manufacturing sector expanded considerably in the early 1990s with the establishment of a Japanese-owned factory producing electrical components for road vehicles. The Yazaki EDS Samoa factory, which assembles wire harnessing systems for export to car-manufacturing plants, is the major employer in the private sector, although operations at the plant were scaled back in 2011 in response to the tsunami catastrophe in Japan (the base of the parent company) and to the decrease in demand for wire harnessing from Toyota Australia. Other products of the manufacturing sector include coconut-based products, cigarettes and beverages. Beer accounted for 8.6% of exports in 2007. Soft drinks are also manufactured, mainly for local consumption. A major water-bottling plant, which hoped to sell its product to the US market, opened in 2008. Between 2002 and 2011, according to figures from the ADB, manufacturing GDP decreased, in real terms, at an average annual rate of 4.8%. The GDP of the manufacturing sector declined by 1.7% in 2011/12, according to official figures.

Construction employed 4.2% of the employed labour force at the 2011 census and provided 13.5% of GDP in 2011. According to ADB figures, between 2002 and 2011 construction GDP increased, in real terms, at an average annual rate of 9.5%. The GDP of the sector grew by 5.5% in 2011/12, according to official figures.

Energy is derived principally from hydroelectric power and thermal power stations. A programme for the generation of electricity from coconut oil commenced in early 2009. A project aimed at producing 4 MW of solar power commenced in mid-2012 and was scheduled to take some two years to complete. Imports of mineral fuels accounted for 22.7% of the value of total imports in 2012.

The services sector provided 63.4% of GDP in 2011 and engaged 50.7% of the employed labour force at the 2011 census. Tourism makes a significant contribution to the economy, with revenue from this source (excluding passenger transport) rising to US $124m. in 2010. Tourist arrivals reached 134,660 in 2012. 'Offshore' banking was introduced to the islands in 1989, and by July of that year more than 30 companies had registered in Apia. A large proportion of the islands' revenue is provided by remittances from nationals working abroad, which were equivalent to 24.5% of GDP in 2010/11. Between 2002 and 2011, according to ADB figures, the services sector's GDP increased at an average annual rate of 3.9%. Sectoral GDP increased by 1.5% in 2011/12, according to official figures.

In 2011 the country recorded a visible merchandise trade deficit of US $307.3m. and a deficit of $78.2m. on the current account of the balance of payments. In 2012 New Zealand was Samoa's principal supplier of imports, providing 27.2% of the total, other important suppliers were the USA, Australia and the People's Republic of China. Australia was the dominant buyer of Samoan goods, accounting for 62.5% of exports; New Zealand was also an important purchaser. The principal exports, including re-exports, in 2012 were machinery and transport equipment, food and live animals, beverages and tobacco, basic manufactures, and animal and vegetable oils. The main imports were food and live animals, mineral fuels, machinery and transport equipment, basic manufactures, miscellaneous manufactured articles and chemicals and related products.

In the fiscal year ending 30 June 2012 an overall budget deficit, including external funding, of 93.3m. tala was recorded, equivalent to 6.0% of GDP. Aid from Australia and New Zealand is a major source of finance. In 2012/13 an estimated $A43.5m. was to be provided by Australia, with $NZ17.0m. to be supplied by New Zealand in 2011/12. Assistance from China is of increasing significance (see Foreign Affairs). The European Union (EU, see p. 281) has also provided substantial aid for various development projects. The EU provided €5.5m. for the purposes of budgetary support in 2011/12. At the end of 2012 the country's total external debt was estimated by the ADB at US $278m. The cost of debt-servicing in 2010 was equivalent to 75.8% of the value of exports of goods and services. In 2001–10 the annual rate of inflation (excluding rents) averaged 5.9%. According to the ADB, consumer prices increased by 2.9% in 2010/11 and by 6.2%

in 2011/12. The rate of unemployment was 5.7% of the labour force at the 2011 census.

The economy of Samoa has remained vulnerable to external factors, notably fluctuations in world commodity prices and variations in global demand for Samoa's export items. The global recession of 2008/09 led to a temporary reduction in remittances (a vital source of income for many) from Samoan workers employed overseas, while the tsunami disaster of September 2009 also caused considerable economic hardship for the islands. To assist the country's recovery from the disaster, in November the World Bank announced that it was to double its aid to Samoa, to US $40m., and the IMF approved the release of SDR 5.8m. Moreover, the ADB approved a loan of $11m. in 2011 under its Economic Recovery Support Program, which aimed to provide assistance to Samoa in the wake of the global financial crisis and the tsunami. Following two consecutive years of weak economic performance, GDP expanded by 2.0% in 2010/11, but growth slowed to 1.2% in 2011/12, as post-tsunami reconstruction activities were completed. Cyclone Evan, which struck in December 2012, caused damage estimated at $210m., equivalent to some 30% of GDP, particularly affecting the agriculture and tourism sectors. As a result, the ADB forecast GDP growth of only 0.9% in 2012/13. It was hoped that a major expansion of Samoa's fish-processing capacity, with the construction of a new facility in 2012, would lead to increased employment opportunities and greater export revenue. Plans to develop the commercial production of rice, announced in that year, aimed to reduce import costs of the crop. A report by the IMF published in late 2012 claimed that Samoa's currency was overvalued and recommended a gradual realignment of the exchange rate in order to improve the competitiveness of the country's exports and prevent further losses of reserves. The World Bank offered $100m. in concessional finance for the period 2012–17 to assist Samoa's development efforts, to guard against future shocks (including natural disasters or increases in food and fuel prices) and to control rising debt, which had reached more than 50% of GDP in 2012.

PUBLIC HOLIDAYS

2014: 1–2 January (New Year), 18–21 April (Easter), 12 May (Mother's Day), 2 June (for Independence Day), 11 August (Father's Day), 13 October (Day after Lotu a Tamaiti—White Sunday), 25–26 December (Christmas).

Statistical Survey

Source (unless otherwise indicated): Samoa Bureau of Statistics, Ministry of Finance, Government Building (MFMII), POB 1151, Apia; tel. 24384; fax 24675; e-mail info.stats@sbs.gov.ws; internet www.sbs.gov.ws.

AREA AND POPULATION

Area: Savai'i and adjacent small islands 1,694 sq km; Upolu and adjacent small islands 1,091 sq km; Total 2,785 sq km (1,075 sq miles).

Population: 180,741 at census of 5 November 2006; 187,820 (males 96,990, females 90,830) at census of 7 November 2011. *By Island* (2011 census): Savai'i 44,402; Upolu 143,418 (Apia Urban Area 36,735, North West Upolu 62,390, Rest of Upolu 44,293).

Density (at 2011 census): 67.4 per sq km.

Population by Age and Sex (Secretariat of the Pacific Community estimates at mid-2013): *0–14:* 68,090 (males 35,411, females 32,679); *15–64:* 106,884 (males 56,236, females 50,648); *65 and over:* 9,547 (males 4,353, females 5,194); *Total* 184,521 (males 96,001, females 88,520). Note: Estimates not adjusted to take account of 2011 census. Source: Pacific Regional Information System.

Principal Towns (population at 2011 census): Apia (capital) 36,735 (urban area); Vaitele 7,182; Faleasi'u 3,745; Vailele 3,647; Le'auva'a 3,168.

Births, Marriages and Deaths (registrations, 2001): Live births 3,516; Marriages 821; Deaths 339. *2004:* Live births 1,679; Deaths 547. Note: Registration is incomplete. *2006 Census:* Crude birth rate 27.3; Crude death rate 4.0. *2005–10* (annual averages, UN estimates): Birth rate 25.9 per 1,000; Death rate 5.5 per 1,000. Source: UN, *World Population Prospects: The 2010 Revision*.

Life Expectancy (years at birth): 72.5 (males 69.5; females 75.7) in 2011. Source: World Bank, World Development Indicators database.

Economically Active Population (persons aged 15 years and over, 2011 census): Agriculture, hunting and forestry 14,753; Fishing 1,895; Manufacturing and handicrafts (incl. mining) 2,489; Electricity, gas and water supply 1,137; Construction 1,899; Wholesale and retail trade; repair of motor vehicles, motorcycles and personal and household goods 3,529; Hotels and restaurants 2,471; Transport, storage and communications 3,116; Financial intermediation 1,081; Real estate, renting and business activities 1,236; Public administration and defence; compulsory social security 2,370; Education 3,217; Health and social work 960; Consultancy services 534; Other community, social and personal service activities 4,270; *Sub-total* 44,957; Activities not adequately defined 220; *Total employed* 45,177 (males 32,949, females 12,228); Unemployed 2,750 (males 1,843, females 907); *Total labour force* 47,927 (males 34,792, females 13,135).

HEALTH AND WELFARE

Key Indicators

Total Fertility Rate (children per woman, 2010): 3.9.

Under-5 Mortality Rate (per 1,000 live births, 2009): 25.

Physicians (per 1,000 head, 2008): 0.5.

Hospital Beds (per 1,000 head, 2005): 1.0.

Health Expenditure (2009): US $ per head (PPP): 234.

Health Expenditure (2009): % of GDP: 5.4.

Health Expenditure (2009): public (% of total): 85.3.

Total Carbon Dioxide Emissions ('000 metric tons, 2008): 161.3.

Carbon Dioxide Emissions Per Head (metric tons, 2008): 0.9.

Human Development Index (2011): ranking 99.

Human Development Index (2011): value 0.688.

For sources and definitions, see explanatory note on p. vi.

AGRICULTURE, ETC.

Principal Crops ('000 metric tons, 2011, FAO estimates): Taro 18.6; Yams 3.0; Other roots and tubers 2.7; Coconuts 178.0 (unofficial figure); Bananas 18.7; Papayas 3.3; Pineapples 4.3; Guavas, mangoes and mangosteens 3.6; Avocados 1.1; Other fruits 8.7; Vegetables 1.1; Cocoa beans 0.4.

Livestock ('000 head, year ending September 2011, FAO estimates): Pigs 204; Cattle 30; Horses 1.9; Chickens 620.

Livestock Products (metric tons, 2011, FAO estimates): Cattle meat 1,100; Pig meat 4,120; Chicken meat 630; Cows' milk 1,500; Hen eggs 365; Honey 220.

Forestry ('000 cu m, 2006): *Roundwood Removals* (excl. bark): Sawlogs and veneer logs 3; Other industrial roundwood 3; Fuel wood 70; Total 76. *Sawnwood Production* (incl. sleepers): 1. *2007–11* (FAO estimates): Annual output as in 2006.

Fishing (metric tons, live weight, 2010): Albacore 2,529; Yellowfin tuna 386; Other marine fishes 6,280 (FAO estimate); Marine crustaceans 408 (FAO estimate); Marine molluscs 2,200 (FAO estimate); Sea urchins and other echinoderms 7 (FAO estimate); Total capture (incl. others) 13,000 (FAO estimate); Aquaculture 5 (FAO estimate); *Total catch* 13,005 (FAO estimate).

Source: FAO.

INDUSTRY

Electric Energy (production, million kWh): 113.5 in 2006; 119.6 in 2007; 109.9 in 2008. Note: Figures relate only to government-owned power schemes (Source: Treasury Department of Samoa). *2011* (production, million kWh): 112 (Source: Asian Development Bank).

FINANCE

Currency and Exchange Rates: 100 sene (cents) = 1 tala (Samoan dollar). *Sterling, US Dollar and Euro Equivalents* (31 December 2012): £1 sterling = 3.599 tala; US $1 = 2.281 tala; €1 = 3.010 tala; 100 tala = £27.78 = US $43.84 = €33.23. *Average Exchange Rate* (tala per US $): 2.4847 in 2010; 2.3175 in 2011; 2.2923 in 2012.

Budget (million tala, year ending 30 June 2010): *Revenue:* Tax revenue 324.8 (Income tax 76.3; Excise tax 90.9; Taxes on international trade 35.8; Value-added gross receipts and services tax 116.9); Other revenue 48.1; Total 372.9, excl. external grants received (152.8). *Expenditure:* Current expenditure 349.1 (Salaries and wages 115.0, External interest payments 10.9, Domestic interest payments 4.2, Other current expenditure 219.0); Development expenditure 273.8; Total 622.9, excl. net lending (10.9). *2010/11* (million tala): Total revenue 567.2 (Domestic receipts 423.8, External grants 143.4); Total expenditure 664.6 (Domestically financed 374.8). *2011/12* (million tala, budget figures): Total revenue 549.0 (Domestic receipts 415.7, External grants 133.3); Total expenditure 642.3 (Domestically financed 440.6). (Source: Ministry of Finance, *Quarterly Economic Review*).

International Reserves (US $ million at 31 December 2011): IMF special drawing rights 19.36; Reserve position in IMF 1.06; Foreign exchange 146.37; *Total* 166.79. Source: IMF, *International Financial Statistics*.

Money Supply (million tala at 31 December 2011): Currency outside banks 64.04; Transferable deposits 189.55; Other deposits 460.34. *Broad money* 713.92. Source: IMF, *International Financial Statistics*.

Cost of Living (Consumer Price Index, excluding rent; base: 2005 = 100): All items 129.9 in 2009; 130.9 in 2010; 137.7 in 2011. Source: IMF, *International Financial Statistics*.

Gross Domestic Product (million tala at constant 2002 prices, year ending 31 December): 1,046.5 in 2009; 1,065.7 in 2010; 1,080.3 in 2011.

Expenditure on the Gross Domestic Product (million tala in current prices, fiscal year ending 30 June 2010): Final consumption expenditure 1,466.8 (Households 1,050.9, Non-profit institutions serving households 69.3, General government 346.6); Gross fixed capital formation 393.1; Changes in inventories 29.7; *Total domestic expenditure* 1,889.6; Exports of goods and services 471.2; *Less* Imports of goods and services 762.6; Statistical discrepancy –151.6; *GDP in market prices* 1,446.6.

Gross Domestic Product by Economic Activity (million tala in current prices, year ending 31 December 2011): Agriculture and fishing 155.1; Manufacturing 127.8; Electricity, gas and water 78.6; Construction 212.2; Trade 319.2; Hotels and restaurants 54.5; Transport and communications 216.6; Finance and business services 141.1; Public administration 146.6; Ownership of dwellings 51.3; Other services 64.7; *Sub-total* 1,567.8; *Less* Financial intermediation services indirectly measured 21.2; *Total* 1,546.5.

Balance of Payments (US $ million, 2011): Exports of goods 11.4; Imports of goods –318.7; *Balance on goods* –307.3; Exports of services 186.6; Imports of services –76.4; *Balance on goods and services* –197.2; Primary income received 5.8; Primary income paid –37.6; *Balance on goods, services and primary income* –229.0; Secondary income received 161.7; Secondary income paid –10.9; *Current balance* –78.2; Capital account (net) 77.3; Direct investment assets 9.6; Direct investment liabilities 14.9; Portfolio investment assets –0.4; Portfolio investment liabilities 0.0; Other investments assets –66.8; Other investment liabilities 28.3; Net errors and omissions –26.5; *Reserves and related items* –41.8. Source: IMF, *International Financial Statistics*.

EXTERNAL TRADE

Principal Commodities (million tala, 2012): *Imports c.i.f.:* Food and live animals 202.0; Beverages and tobacco 11.0; Crude materials (excl. fuels) 23.9; Mineral fuels, etc. 179.8; Chemicals and related products 48.5; Basic manufactures 122.6; Machinery and transport equipment 132.7; Miscellaneous manufactured articles 65.8; Total (incl. others) 792.0. *Exports (incl. re-exports) f.o.b.:* Food and live animals 23.3; Beverages and tobacco 13.2; Basic manufactures 9.9; Crude materials (excl. fuels) 1.0; Mineral fuels and lubricants 2.0; Machinery and transport equipment 84.1; Animal and vegetable oils (incl. fats and waxes) 8.8; Total (incl. others) 153.4.

Principal Trading Partners (million tala, 2012): *Imports:* Australia 72.8; China, People's Republic 62.5; Japan 32.2; New Zealand 215.2; USA 100.8; Total (incl. others) 792.0. *Exports (incl. re-exports):* Australia 95.8; New Zealand 20.1; USA 5.2; Total (incl. others) 153.4.

TRANSPORT

Road Traffic (motor vehicles registered, 2007): Private cars 5,189; Pick-ups 4,136; Taxis 1,916; Trucks 2,375; Buses 251; Motorcycles 104; Tractors 45; Total (incl. others) 16,215.

International Shipping (freight traffic, '000 metric tons, 2009): Goods loaded 207.2; Goods unloaded 45.6. *Flag Registered Fleet* (at 31 December 2012): Vessels 12; Total displacement ('000 grt) 12.2 (Source: Lloyd's List Intelligence—www.lloydslistintelligence.com).

Civil Aviation (traffic on scheduled services, 2009): Kilometres flown 6 million; Passengers carried 402,000; Passenger-km 532 million; Total ton-km 56 million. Source: UN, *Statistical Yearbook*.

TOURISM

Visitor Arrivals: 129,500 in 2010; 127,603 in 2011; 134,660 in 2012.

Visitor Arrivals by Country (2011): American Samoa 24,582; Australia 25,197; Fiji 2,646; New Zealand 54,924; USA 7,425; Total (incl. others) 127,603.

Tourism Receipts (US $ million, excl. passenger transport): 116 in 2009; 124 in 2010. Source: World Tourism Organization.

COMMUNICATIONS MEDIA

Telephones (2010): 35,300 main lines in use.

Internet Users (2009): 9,000.

Broadband Subscribers (2010): 200.

Mobile Cellular Telephones (2010): 167,400 subscribers.

Source: International Telecommunication Union.

EDUCATION

Pre-primary (2009/10): 303 teachers; 3,514 pupils.

Primary (2010/11): 162 schools; 1,426 teachers; 39,114 pupils.

Secondary (2010/11): 36 schools; 782 teachers; 16,386 pupils.

Universities and other Higher (2001): 140 teachers; 1,179 students.

Pupil-teacher Ratio (primary education): 24.0 in 2011.

Adult Literacy Rate (UNESCO estimates): 98.8% (males 99.0%; females 98.6%) in 2010.

Sources: Ministry of Education, Sports and Culture, Apia; UNESCO Institute for Statistics.

Directory

The Government

HEAD OF STATE

O le Ao o le Malo: TUIATUA TUPUA TAMASESE EFI (elected by the Fono 15 June 2007; re-elected 20 July 2012).

CABINET
(May 2013)

The Government is formed by the Human Rights Protection Party.

Prime Minister and Minister of Foreign Affairs, Immigration and Tourism: TUILA'EPA SAILELE MALIELEGAOI.

Deputy Prime Minister and Minister of Trade, Commerce, Industry and Labour: FONOTOE PIERRE LAUOFO.

Minister of Women, Community and Social Development: TOLOFUAIVALELEI FALEMOE LEI'ATAUA.

Minister of Police and Prisons: SALA FATA PINATI.

Minister of Works, Transport and Infrastructure: MANU'ALE-SAGALALA POSALA ENOKATI .

Minister of Natural Resources and Environment: FA'AMOETAU-LOA FA'ALE TU'UMALI'I.

Minister of Finance: FAUMUINA TIATIA LIUGA.

Minister of Revenue: TUILOMA PULE LAMEKO.

Minister of Health: Dr TUITAMA TALALELEI TUITAMA.

Minister of Communications and Information Technology: TUISUGALETAUA SOFARA AVEAU.

Minister of Education, Sports and Culture: MAGELE MAUILIU MAGELE.

Minister for Justice and Courts Administration: FIAME NAOMI MATA'AFA.

Minister of Agriculture and Fisheries: LE MAMEA ROPATI.

MINISTRIES

Prime Minister's Department: POB L 1861, Apia; tel. 63222; fax 26322; e-mail presssecretariat@samoa.ws; internet www.govt.ws.

Ministry of Agriculture and Fisheries: POB 1874, Apia; tel. 22561; fax 24576; e-mail fono@maf.gov.ws; internet www.maf.gov.ws.

Ministry of Commerce, Industry and Labour: Apia; tel. 20441; fax 20443; e-mail mpal@mcil.gov.ws; internet www.mcil.gov.ws.

Ministry of Communications and Information Technology: Private Bag, Apia; tel. 26117; fax 24671; e-mail mcit@mcit.gov.ws; internet www.mcit.gov.ws.

Ministry of Education, Sports and Culture: POB 1869, Apia; tel. 64602; fax 64664; e-mail education@mesc.gov.ws; internet www.mesc.gov.ws.

Ministry of Finance: Private Bag, Apia; tel. 34333; fax 21312; e-mail helpdesk@mof.gov.ws; internet www.mof.gov.ws.

Ministry of Foreign Affairs and Trade: POB L 1859, Apia; tel. 21171; fax 21504; e-mail mfat@mfat.gov.ws; internet www.mfat.gov.ws.

Ministry of Health: Private Bag, Apia; tel. 68100; fax 24496; e-mail EteuatiI@health.gov.ws; internet www.health.gov.ws.

Ministry of Justice and Courts Administration: POB 49, Apia; tel. 22671; fax 21050; e-mail info@mjca.gov.ws; internet www.mjca.gov.ws.

Ministry of Natural Resources and Environment: Private Bag, Apia; tel. 67200; fax 23176; e-mail info@bowthemes.com; internet www.mnre.gov.ws.

Ministry of Police: Apia; tel. 28055; fax 21319; e-mail anisi.tua@police.gov.ws; internet www.police.gov.ws.

Ministry of Revenue: POB 1877, Apia; tel. 20411; fax 20414; e-mail info_services@revenue.gov.ws; internet www.revenue.gov.ws.

Ministry of Women, Community and Social Development: Private Bag, Apia; tel. 20854; fax 23665; e-mail tolofua@lesamoa.net; internet www.mwcsd.gov.ws.

Ministry of Works, Transport and Infrastructure: Private Bag, Apia; tel. 21611; fax 21990; e-mail enquiries@mwti.gov.ws; internet www.mwti.gov.ws.

Election Commission

Office of the Electoral Commissioner: POB 219, Apia; tel. 25967; fax 24309; internet www.oec.gov.ws; Electoral Commr PAPALII MALIETAU MALIETOA.

Legislature

FONO
(Legislative Assembly)

The Assembly has 47 Matai members, representing 41 territorial constituencies, and two individual members. Elections are held every five years. A total of 158 candidates contested the general election of 4 March 2011. The ruling Human Rights Protection Party (HRPP) was returned to office, winning the support of 36 newly elected legislators, including seven independent members of the Fono. In June 2011 four parliamentarians were disqualified. The HRPP won all four by-elections in July, consequently holding 37 seats and thus maintaining its majority. The Tautua Samoa Party held 12 seats.

Speaker: LA'AULIALEMALIETOA LEUATEA POLATAIVAO FOSI.

Political Organizations

Human Rights Protection Party (HRPP): c/o The Fono, Apia; f. 1979; Western Samoa's first formal political party; Leader TUILA'EPA SAILELE MALIELEGAOI; Gen. Sec. LAULU DAN STANLEY.

The People's Party (TPP): f. 2008; Leader SOLOMONA TOAILOA.

Samoa Christian Party: Leader TUALA TIRESA MALIETOA.

Samoa Democratic United Party (SDUP): POB 1233, Apia; tel. 23543; fax 20536; f. 1988; est. as Samoa National Development Party (SNDP); coalition party comprising Christian Democratic Party (CDP) and several independents; assumed present name after 2001 election, following merger of SNDP and Samoa Independent Party; Leader LE MAMEA ROPATI; Sec. VALASI TAFITO.

Samoa Progressive Political Party: Leader TOEOLESULUSULU SIUEVA.

Tautua Samoa Party (TSP): Apia; f. 2008; Leader PALUSALUE FAAPO; Pres. LEATINU'U SALOTE.

Diplomatic Representation

EMBASSIES AND HIGH COMMISSIONS IN SAMOA

Australia: Beach Rd, POB 704, Apia; tel. 23411; fax 23159; internet www.samoa.embassy.gov.au; High Commissioner Dr STEPHEN HENNINGHAM.

China, People's Republic: Vailima, Private Bag, Apia; tel. 22474; fax 21115; e-mail tce@samoa.net; Ambassador ZHAO WEIPING .

New Zealand: Beach Rd, POB 1876, Apia; tel. 21711; fax 20086; e-mail nzhcapia@samoa.ws; High Commissioner NICHOLAS JOHN HURLEY.

USA: Matafele, POB 3430, Apia; tel. 21631; fax 22030; e-mail AmEmbApia@state.gov; internet samoa.usembassy.gov; Ambassador DAVID HUEBNER (resident in New Zealand); Chargé d'affaires CHAD JONATHAN BERBERT (resident in Samoa).

Judicial System

The Supreme Court, which is composed of six local judges and presided over by the Chief Justice, has full jurisdiction for both criminal and civil cases. Appeals lie with the Court of Appeal, which sits twice a year and is presided over by three overseas judges. The Magistrates' Court was replaced by two District Courts in 1998. The Land and Titles Court has jurisdiction in respect of disputes over land ownership and Samoan titles. It consists of the President and two Samoan judges appointed by the President.

Attorney-General: MING LEUNG WAI.

Chief Justice of the Supreme Court: PATU TIAVA'ASU'E FALEFATU SAPOLU.

President of the Court of Appeal: WILLIAM DAVID BARAGWANATH (non-resident).

President of the Land and Titles Court: TAGALOA KERSLAKE.

Religion

Almost all of Samoa's inhabitants profess Christianity.

CHRISTIANITY

Fono a Ekalesia i Samoa (Samoa Council of Churches): POB 574, Apia; f. 1967; 4 mem. churches; Sec. Rev. EFEPAI KOLIA.

The Anglican Communion

Samoa lies within the diocese of Polynesia, part of the Church of the Province of New Zealand. The Bishop of Polynesia is resident in Fiji, while the Archdeacon of Tonga and Samoa is resident in Tonga.

Anglican Church: POB 16, Apia; tel. 20500; fax 24663; Rev. PETER E. BENTLEY.

The Roman Catholic Church

The islands of Samoa constitute the archdiocese of Samoa-Apia. At 31 December 2007 there were an estimated 40,500 adherents in the country. The Archbishop participates in the Catholic Bishops' Conference of the Pacific, based in Fiji.

Archbishop of Samoa-Apia: Cardinal ALAPATI L. MATA'ELIGA, Archbishop's House, Fetuolemoana, POB 532, Apia; tel. 20400; fax 20402; e-mail archdiocese@samoa.ws.

Other Churches

Church of Jesus Christ of Latter-day Saints (Mormon): Samoa Apia Mission, POB 1621, Apia; tel. 64230; fax 64241; f. 1888; Pres. ALEMA S. FITISEMANU; f. 1888; 65,000 mems.

Congregational Christian Church in Samoa: Tamaligi, POB 468, Apia; tel. 22279; fax 20429; e-mail cccsgsec@lesamoa.net; f. 1830; 100,000 mems; Gen. Sec. Rev. MAONE F. LEAUSA.

Congregational Church of Jesus in Samoa: 505 Borie St, Honolulu, HI 96818, USA; Rev. NAITULI MALEPEAI.

Methodist Church in Samoa (Ekalesia Metotisi i Samoa): POB 1867, Apia; tel. 22283; fax 22203; e-mail afereti@samoa.ws; f. 1828; 37,000 mems; Pres. Rev. TUPU FOLASA, II; Gen. Sec. Rev. ELISAIA TUITOLOVA'A.

Seventh-day Adventist Church: POB 600, Apia; tel. 20451; f. 1895; covers Samoa and American Samoa; 5,000 mems; Pres. Pastor SAMUELU AFAMASAGA; Sec. UILI SOLOFA.

BAHÁ'Í FAITH

National Spiritual Assembly: POB 1117, Apia; tel. 23348; e-mail secretariat@bahaisamoa.ws.

The Press

Newsline: POB 2441, Apia; tel. 24216; fax 23623; twice a week; Editor PIO SIOA.

Samoa News: POB 1160, Apia; daily; merged with the weekly *Samoa Times* (f. 1967) in Sept. 1994; Publr RHONA ANNESLEY.

The Samoa Observer: POB 1572, Apia; tel. 21099; fax 21195; e-mail samoaobserver@yahoo.com; internet www.samoaobserver .ws; f. 1979; 5 a week; independent; English and Samoan; also publ. in New Zealand twice a week; Editor-in-Chief SAVEA SANO MALIFA; Editor KENI LESA; circ. 4,500.

Samoa Weekly: Saleufi, Apia; f. 1977; weekly; independent; bilingual; Editor LANCE POLU; circ. 4,000.

Savali: POB L 1861, Apia; tel. 26938; fax 21339; e-mail savalinews@ samoa.ws; publ. of Lands and Titles Court; monthly; govt-owned; Samoan edn f. 1904; Editor FALESEU L. FUA; circ. 6,000; English edn f. 1977; circ. 500; bilingual commercial edn f. 1993; circ. 1,500; Editor TUPUOLA TERRY TAVITA.

South Seas Star: POB 800, Apia; tel. 23684; weekly.

PRESS ASSOCIATION

Journalists' Association of Samoa (JAWS): Apia; tel. 7773776; e-mail jawsexec@yahoo.com; internet jawsamoa.blogspot.com; f. 1980; Pres. UALE PAPALII TAIMALELAGI.

Broadcasting and Communications

TELECOMMUNICATIONS

BlueSky Samoa: Maluafou, Private Bag, Apia; tel. 67788; fax 24123; e-mail info@blueskysamoa.com; internet www .blueskysamoa.ws; fmrly SamoaTel; name changed as above following privatization in 2011; 25% owned by Unit Trust of Samoa and

75% owned by BlueSky Communications; telecommunications and internet services provider; CEO ADOLFO MONTENEGRO.

Digicel Samoa Ltd: Vaimea, Apia; tel. 28003; fax 28005; e-mail customercaresamoa@digicelgroup.com; internet www.digicelsamoa .com; f. 2006; est. following acquisition of Telecom Samoa by Digicel Group; 90% owned by Digicel Group, 10% govt-owned; CEO PEPE CHRISTIAN FRUEAN.

Lesamoa.net: Tamaligi, Apia; tel. 20181; fax 24619; internet www .lesamoa.net; f. 1996; a subsidiary of Lesa's Telephone Services Ltd; provider of dial-up and broadband internet services.

Samoa.ws: SLAC Bldg, Apia; tel. 20926; e-mail helpdesk@samoa .ws; internet www.samoa.ws; f. 1977; private co; locally owned internet service provider; CEO LAEIMAU OKETEVI TANUVASA.

BROADCASTING

Radio and Television

Samoa Broadcasting Corpn: Apia; tel. 21420; fax 21072; f. 1948; govt-controlled, with commercial sponsorship; operates SBC Radio 1 and SBC Television 1; CEO FAIASEA LEI SAM MATAFEO.

Graceland Broadcasting Network: POB 3444, Apia; tel. 20197; fax 25487; e-mail gbn@lesamoa.net; internet www.welcome.to/gbn; f. 1992; telecommunications, television and radio.

Radio Polynesia Ltd: POB 762, Apia; tel. 25148; fax 2514; internet www.fmradio.ws; f. 1989; operates 4 radio stations: Magik FM 98.1, Talofa FM 88.5/91.5/99.9, Star FM 96.1 and K-Lite FM 101.1.

Star Television: Apia; f. 2009; Man. Dir APULU LANCE POLU.

Finance

(cap. = capital; res = reserves; dep. = deposits; m. = million; brs = branches; amounts in tala, unless otherwise indicated)

BANKING

Central Bank

Central Bank of Samoa: Private Bag, Apia; tel. 34100; fax 20293; e-mail centralbank@cbs.gov.ws; internet www.cbs.gov.ws; f. 1984; cap. 10.0m., res 18.2m. (June 2010); Gov. ATELINA EMMA ENARI.

Commercial Banks

ANZ Bank (Samoa) Ltd: Beach Rd, POB L1885, Apia; tel. 69999; fax 69972; e-mail samoa@anz.com; internet www.anz.com/samoa; f. 1959; est. as Bank of Western Samoa, name changed 1997; 100% owned by ANZ Funds Pty Ltd; Man. Dir PETER JOHNSON; 5 brs.

National Bank of Samoa: ACB Bldg, Ground Floor, Beach Rd, Apia 00685; tel. 26766; fax 23477; internet www.nbs.ws; f. 1995; owned by consortium of private interests in Samoa, American Samoa and the USA; Chair. SALA EPA TUIOTI; CEO MALCOLM JOHNSTON; 15 agencies; 5 brs.

Samoa Commercial Bank: POB L 602, Apia; tel. 31233; fax 30250; e-mail info@scbl.ws; internet www.scbl.ws; f. 2003; CEO RAY AH LIKI; 7 brs.

Westpac Bank Samoa Ltd: Beach Rd, POB 1860, Apia; tel. 20000; fax 22848; e-mail westpacsamoa@westpac.com.au; internet www .westpac.com.ws; f. 1977; est. as Pacific Commercial Bank Ltd, current name adopted 2001; first independent bank; 93.5% owned by Westpac Banking Corpn (Australia); cap. 1.2m., res 1.1m., dep. 215.7m. (Sept. 2009); Chair. ALAN WALTER; Gen. Man. JASON GREEN; 2 brs.

Development Bank

Development Bank of Samoa: POB 1232, Apia; tel. 22861; fax 23888; e-mail info@dbsamoa.ws; internet www.dbsamoa.ws; f. 1974; est. by Govt to foster economic and social development; Chair. TUPAIMATUNA LULAI LAVEA; CEO TUIASAU SAUMANI WONGSIN.

INSURANCE

National Pacific Insurance Ltd: DBS Bldg, Level 5, Beach Rd, Apia; tel. 20481; fax 23374; e-mail NationalPacificInsurance@ npisamoa.ws; internet www.nationalpacificinsurance.com; f. 1977; Gen. Man. DARRYL WILLIAMSON.

Progressive Insurance Company: Lotemau Centre, POB 620, Apia; tel. 26110; fax 26112; e-mail progins@samoa.ws; f. 1993; Gen. Man. I. O. FILEMU.

Samoa Life Assurance Corporation: POB 494, Apia; tel. 23360; fax 23024; e-mail info@samoalife.ws; internet www.samoalife.ws; f. 1977; Gen. Man. A. S. CHAN TING.

Trade and Industry

CHAMBER OF COMMERCE

Samoa Chamber of Commerce and Industry: Le Sanalele Complex, 1st Floor, Saleufi, POB 2014, Apia; tel. 31090; fax 31089; e-mail chamber@samoa.ws; internet www.samoachamber.ws; f. 1938; represents the interests of the private sector; Pres. NAMULAUULU SAMI LEOTA.

INDUSTRIAL AND TRADE ASSOCIATIONS

Samoa Coconut Products: Apia.

Samoa Forest Corporation: Apia.

UTILITIES
Electricity

Electric Power Corporation: POB 2011, Apia; tel. 65426; fax 23748; e-mail epc.info@epc.ws; internet www.epc.ws; f. 1972; autonomous govt-owned corpn; part of Public Works Dept, known as Electric Power Scheme, until 1972; Gen. Man. TOLOGATA G. L. TAGALOATELE TILE LEI'A.

Water

Samoa Water Authority: POB 245, Apia; tel. 20409; fax 21298; e-mail taputoa@swa.gov.ws; internet www.swa.gov.ws; Chair. AFIOGA TUISUGALETAUA AVEAU SOFARA AVEAU.

TRADE UNIONS

Samoa Trade Union Congress (STUC): POB 1515, Apia; tel. 24134; fax 20014; f. 1981; affiliate of ITUC; Pres. FALEFATA TUANIU PETAIA; Dir MATAFEO R. MATAFEO; 5,000 mems.

Transport

Public Works Department: Private Bag, Apia; tel. 20865; fax 21927; e-mail pwdir@lesamoa.net; Dir of Works ISIKUKI PUNIVALU.

ROADS

In 2001 there were 2,337 km of roads on the islands, of which some 847 km were highways and 1,480 km were secondary roads. In 2004 the Government announced a programme of road-building, including new roads from Apia to the airport and to the inter-island wharves.

SHIPPING

There are deep-water wharves at Apia and Asau. Regular cargo services link Samoa with Australia, New Zealand, American Samoa, Fiji, New Caledonia, Solomon Islands, Tonga, US Pacific coast ports and various ports in Europe.

Samoa Ports Authority: POB 2279, Apia; tel. 64400; fax 25870; e-mail spa@spasamoa.ws; internet www.spasamoa.ws; f. 1999; Gen. Man. TAULAPAPA TOMINIKO.

Samoa Shipping Corporation Ltd: Shipping House Matautu-tai, Private Bag, Apia; tel. 20935; fax 22352; e-mail info@samoashipping .com; internet www.samoashipping.com; Man. Dir PAPALI'I WILLIE NANSEN.

Samoa Shipping Services Ltd: POB 1884, Apia; tel. 20790; fax 20026; e-mail sss@lesamoa.net; internet www.sssl.ws; Gen. Man. SALA THEODORE TOALEPAI.

CIVIL AVIATION

There is an international airport at Faleolo, about 35 km from Apia, and an airstrip at Fagali'i, 4 km east of Apia Wharf, which receives light aircraft from American Samoa.

Polynesian Ltd: SNPF Bldg, 2nd Floor, Beach Rd, POB 599, Apia; tel. 21261; fax 20023; e-mail enquiries@polynesianairlines.com; internet www.polynesianairlines.com; f. 1959; 100% govt-owned; operates service to American Samoa and offers charter services between the islands of Upolu and Savai'i; Chair. FEESAGO SIAOSI FEPULEA'I; CEO TAUA FATU TIELU.

Samoa Air: POB 2894, Apia; tel. 27955; fax 27905; e-mail admin@ samoaair.ws; internet www.samoaair.ws; f. 2012; operates a daily scheduled service between the islands of Savai'i and Upolu; CEO CHRIS LANGTON.

Virgin Samoa: internet www.virginsamoa.com; f. 2005; 49% govt-owned, 49% owned by Virgin Australia, 2% owned by independent Samoan shareholder; flies between Samoa, Australia and New Zealand; fmrly known as Polynesian Blue; CEO MARK PITT.

Tourism

The principal attractions are the scenery and the pleasant climate. Samoa has traditionally maintained a cautious attitude towards tourism, fearing that the Samoan way of life might be disrupted by an influx of foreign visitors. Visitor arrivals increased from 127,603 in 2011 to 134,660 in 2012. Most visitors come from New Zealand, Australia, American Samoa and the USA. Tourism receipts (excluding passenger transport) totalled US $124m. in 2010.

Samoa Tourism Authority: POB 2272, Apia; tel. 63500; fax 20886; e-mail info@samoa.travel; internet www.samoa.travel; f. 1986; CEO MATATAMALI'I SONJA HUNTER.

Samoa Hotel Association: POB 3973, Apia; tel. 30160; fax 30161; e-mail info@samoa-hotels.ws; internet www.samoa-hotels.ws; f. 1999; owned by Asscn of Accommodation Providers; Pres. TUALA OLI AH HIM.

Defence

In August 1962 Western Samoa (as it was then known) and New Zealand signed a Treaty of Friendship, whereby the New Zealand Government, on request, acts as the sole agent of the Samoan Government in its dealings with other countries and international organizations. In April 2009 Samoa and Australia renewed a bilateral programme of defence co-operation. In the year ending June 2011 current central government expenditure on defence amounted to 30.4m. tala (equivalent to 8.1% of total current expenditure).

Education

The education system is divided into pre-primary, primary, intermediate and secondary and is based on the New Zealand system. In 2009/10 there were 3,514 pupils at pre-primary schools. In 2010/11 there were 39,114 pupils at primary schools and 16,386 pupils undergoing secondary-level education. Enrolment in primary schools in that year included 95% of all students in the relevant age-groups, while the comparable ratio for secondary schools was 76%. Teaching staff at pre-primary level numbered 303 in 2009/10. There were 1,426 primary teachers and 782 secondary school teachers in 2010/11. There are also a trades training institute, a teacher-training college and a college for tropical agriculture. About 99% of the adult population are literate. The National University of Samoa was founded in 1988, and had an initial intake of 328 students. By 2001 some 1,179 students were enrolled at universities and other higher education institutes. Samoa joined other governments in the region in establishing the University of the South Pacific, based in Fiji, in 1977. Current central government expenditure on education in the year ending 30 June 2011 was an estimated 74.3m. tala (19.8% of total current expenditure). With support from Australia and New Zealand, the Government introduced a programme of free primary education in 2010; a similar programme for secondary education was announced in August 2012, supported by New Zealand.

SAN MARINO

Introductory Survey

LOCATION, CLIMATE, LANGUAGE, RELIGION, FLAG, CAPITAL

The Republic of San Marino is in southern Europe, entirely surrounded by Italy. The country is situated on the slopes of Mount Titano, in the Apennines, bordered by the central Italian region of Emilia-Romagna to the north, and the Marches region to the south. San Marino has cool winters and warm summers, with temperatures generally between $-2°C$ ($28°F$) and $30°C$ ($86°F$). Average annual rainfall totals 880 mm (35 ins). The language is Italian. Almost all of the inhabitants profess Christianity, and the state religion is Roman Catholicism. The civil flag (proportions 3 by 4) has two equal horizontal stripes, of white and light blue. The state flag has, in addition, the national coat of arms (a shield, framed by a yellow cartouche, bearing three green mountains—each with a white tower, surmounted by a stylized ostrich feather, at the summit—the shield being surmounted by a bejewelled crown and framed by branches of laurel and oak, and surmounting a white ribbon bearing, in black, the word 'libertas') in the centre. The capital is San Marino.

CONTEMPORARY POLITICAL HISTORY

San Marino evolved as a city-state in the early Middle Ages and is the sole survivor of the numerous independent states that existed in Italy prior to its unification in the 19th century. A treaty of friendship and co-operation with Italy was signed in 1862, renewed in March 1939 and revised in September 1971.

From 1945 to 1957 San Marino was ruled by a left-wing coalition of the Partito Comunista Sammarinese (PCS) and the Partito Socialista Sammarinese (PSS). Defections from the PCS in 1957 led to a bloodless revolution, after which a coalition of the Partito Democratico Cristiano Sammarinese (PDCS) and the Partito di Democrazia Socialista came to power. In early 1973 an internal dispute over economic policy led to the resignation of the Government, and a new administration was formed by an alliance between the PDCS and the PSS. The PSS withdrew from the coalition in November 1975, and the Captains-Regent (Capitani Reggenti) took over government until March 1976, when a new coalition between the PDCS and the PSS was formed. This Government collapsed in late 1977 but continued in an interim capacity pending the formation of a new administration. Attempts by the PCS to form a government were frustrated by the lack of a clear majority in the unicameral legislature, the Great and General Council (Consiglio Grande e Generale). Eventually the Council agreed to a dissolution and fresh elections were held in May 1978, when the PDCS secured 26 of the 60 seats. However, it was also unable to form an administration and the three left-wing parties, the PCS, PSS and the Partito Socialista Unitario, which together held 31 seats, agreed to form a coalition Government led by the PCS. San Marino thus became the only Western European country with a communist-led government. A left-wing coalition again formed the administration following the May 1983 elections.

In 1986 a political crisis, resulting from a financial scandal which allegedly involved several prominent PSS members, led to the formation of a new coalition Government, the first to be composed of the PDCS and the PCS. The coalition was renewed in June 1988, following a general election in May. In 1990 the PCS was renamed the Partito Progressista Democratico Sammarinese (PPDS). In 1992 the PDCS negotiated the formation of a coalition Government with the PSS.

At the general election of May 1993 the PDCS and the PSS obtained 26 and 14 seats, respectively. The PPDS secured only 11 seats. Seats were also won by three recently formed parties, the Alleanza Popolare dei Democratici Sammarinesi (known as the Alleanza Popolare—AP), the Movimento Democratico and the Rifondazione Comunista Sammarinese (RCS). In June the PDCS and the PSS agreed to form a coalition Government. The two parties were again dominant at the general election of May 1998, winning 25 and 14 seats, respectively. The PPDS, in an electoral alliance with Idee in Movimento, as the Movimento Democratico had been renamed, won 11 seats, the AP six, and the RCS two.

The remaining two seats were secured by a new grouping, Socialisti per le Riforme, which had been founded in 1997. A coalition Government was formed by the PDCS and the PSS in July 1998. In February 2000 the PSS left the Government, and in March a new coalition was formed, comprising six members of the PDCS, three members of the PPDS and one member of Socialisti per le Riforme; the new Government also had parliamentary support from Idee in Movimento. In March 2001 the Partito dei Democratici Sammarinese (PdD) was formed, following the merger of Idee in Movimento, the PPDS and the Socialisti per le Riforme. At legislative elections held in June the PDCS won 25 seats and the PSS obtained 15. The two parties subsequently formed a coalition Government. The PdD won 12 seats, while the AP secured five, the RCS two and the Alleanza Nazionale Sammarinese one.

In June 2002 the PDCS-PSS coalition Government collapsed after the PSS withdrew its support, ending the long-term domination of Sammarinese politics by the PDCS. A new coalition was formed later in June, incorporating five members of the PSS, three of the PdD and two members of the AP. By December, however, the PDCS-PSS alliance had been renewed, and a new coalition Government was instituted on 17 December, with five members from each party. In January 2003 a new political party, Sammarinesi per la Libertà, was formed. In December, following disagreements between the two ruling parties, a new coalition comprising four PDCS members and two each from the PSS and the PdD was installed. In early 2005 the PSS and the PdD merged to form the Partito dei Socialisti e dei Democratici (PSD). Former members of the PSS founded a new party, the Nuovo Partito Socialista, in November.

At a general election in June 2006 the PDCS won 21 of the 60 seats in the Great and General Council. However, the PSD, which secured 20 seats, subsequently formed a coalition Government with the AP and the Sinistra Unita (SU, an alliance of the RCS and Zona Franca), which received seven and five seats, respectively. The new Government, comprising six members of the PSD and two each from the AP and the SU, took office in July. In October a government bill regarding judicial reform was narrowly rejected by the Great and General Council. In November a new four-party coalition Government was formed, comprising the PSD (five members), the AP, the SU (two each) and a new party, the Democratici di Centro (DdC), which had been established by disaffected former members of the PDCS and which took the remaining post.

In June 2008 the coalition once again collapsed due to disagreements between the AP and the other ruling parties; an early general election was held on 9 November. Under new regulations approved earlier in the year, which had aligned the country's electoral system more closely to that of the Italian model, the parties contested the election in two major electoral coalitions: the Patto per San Marino (including the PDCS, the AP, the Lista della Libertà, Europopolari per San Marino, Arengo e Libertà and the Unione Sammarinesi dei Moderati); and Riforme e Libertà (including the PSD, Sammarinesi per la Libertà, the SU and the DdC). The Patto per San Marino won 54.2% of the valid votes cast and 35 seats, while Riforme e Libertà won 45.8% of the votes and 25 seats. The rate of participation by eligible voters was 68.5%. A new coalition Government was sworn in at the beginning of December, comprising three members of the PDCS, two each from the AP and the Lista della Libertà, and a sole representative each from the Unione Sammarinesi dei Moderati and Arengo e Libertà.

The general election of 11 November 2012, which attracted a turn-out of 63.9%, was contested by three major electoral coalitions: the San Marino Bene Comune (comprising the PDCS/Noi Sammarinesi (NS), the PSD and the AP), the Intesa per il Paese (comprising the Partito Socialista, the Unione per la Repubblica and the Moderati Sammarinesi) and the Cittadinanza Attiva (comprising the SU and the Movimento Civico Dieci). The San Marino Bene Comune won 50.7% of the valid votes cast and 35 seats, the Intesa per il Paese obtained 22.3% of votes and 12 seats, and the Cittadinanza Attiva 16.1% of votes and 9 seats. The four remaining seats were secured by the stand-alone Movimento Civico Rete, with 6.3% of votes. Two other parties each ran alone in the election, but failed to win representation in the legislature. A new coalition Government, composed of four PDCS members, three PSD members, and one member each from the NC and the AP, was appointed at the end of the month.

San Marino's tradition of banking secrecy gave rise to concerns—particularly within Italy—that the country's banks might be used for tax avoidance, money-laundering and the financing of terrorism. An Italian judicial investigation into money-laundering, involving San Marino's largest bank, the Cassa di Risparmio della Repubblica de San Marino, and an Italian subsidiary, resulted in the arrest of five senior executives in May 2009. An investigation by the Italian Guardia di Finanzia (financial police) into value-added tax (VAT) fraud in early 2010 revealed that large quantities of goods were being traded between San Marino and Italy without payment of VAT. Meanwhile, in September 2009 San Marino was listed by the Organisation for Economic Co-operation and Development (OECD, see p. 388) as conforming to the OECD's international standards for the exchange of financial information, allowing the disclosure of account details to the relevant authorities where fraud or tax evasion were suspected; San Marino was thereby removed from the OECD's 'grey list' of unco-operative tax havens (having been taken off the blacklist in 2002). By June 2010 San Marino had concluded bilateral tax information exchange agreements with 25 countries. However, an agreement with Italy concerning double taxation, signed in 2002, had still not been ratified by Italy; as a result, under a 'tax amnesty' announced by the Italian Government in July 2009, repatriation of funds was the only way that Italians wishing to declare deposits held in San Marino could avail themselves of the amnesty, and by July 2010 about €5,800m., more than one-third of total deposits, had been withdrawn from San Marino banks. The withdrawal contributed to the economic recession experienced by San Marino from 2008, accompanied by increasing unemployment. In December 2010 local trade unions organized a one-day general strike and demonstrations against the budget for 2011, which envisaged a temporary increase in income tax, a tax on higher pensions and the non-replacement of retiring public sector employees; it also, controversially, imposed extra taxation on Italian cross-border workers in San Marino, who numbered about 6,000. A 'freeze' on public sector salaries was also imposed in 2011 and continued in the budget for 2012, which, in addition, retained the previous year's income tax increase and introduced a property tax. In December 2012 the Italian Government finally approved the ratification of the 2002 double taxation agreement (DTA) with San Marino, which also included a protocol for the exchange of tax information (signed by the two countries in June); however, the DTA awaited further ratification, by the Italian President and both houses of parliament, and San Marino remained on Italy's blacklist of tax haven countries.

In September 2011 Antonella Mularoni, since 2008 the Secretary of State for Foreign and Political Affairs, Telecommunications and Transport (a post regarded as equivalent to that of prime minister) held discussions with the President of the European Council, Herman Van Rompuy, on strengthening San Marino's relations with the European Union (EU, see p. 281), in particular the possibility of further integration into the EU's internal market. In March 2012 a new monetary agreement was signed between the EU and San Marino, whereby the latter agreed to adopt relevant EU legislation concerning the prevention of fraud, counterfeiting and money-laundering, and to comply with statistical reporting requirements. In December the European Commission published a report outlining options for the further integration of the European microstates, Andorra, Monaco and San Marino, into the EU. The report dismissed EU membership for the three states in the near future, but recommended either membership of the European Economic Area or the drawing up of a comprehensive, multilateral Framework Association Agreement with each of the states.

CONSTITUTION AND GOVERNMENT

The *Leges Statutae Republicae Sancti Marini* date back to the late 16th century and outline the main administrative posts and legal basis of the republic. Electoral legislation dates from 1926. Legislative power is vested in the unicameral Great and General Council (Consiglio Grande e Generale), with 60 members elected by universal adult suffrage, under a system of proportional representation, for five years (subject to dissolution). The Council elects two of its members (from opposing political parties) to act jointly as Captains-Regent (Capitani Reggenti), with the functions of Head of State and Government, for six months at a time (ending in March and September). Executive power is held by the Congress of State (Congresso di Stato), with up to 10 members elected by the Council for the duration of its term. The Congress is presided over by the Captains-Regent.

For the purposes of local administration, San Marino is divided into nine 'Castles' (Castelli) corresponding to the original parishes of the Republic. Each 'Castle' is governed by a Castle Captain (Capitano di Castello), who holds office for two years, and a Castle Board (Giunta di Castello), which holds office for five years.

REGIONAL AND INTERNATIONAL CO-OPERATION

San Marino is a member of the Council of Europe (see p. 260) and the Organization for Security and Co-operation in Europe (OSCE, see p. 397). It joined the UN in 1990. San Marino is closely linked to the European Union (EU, see p. 281) through a Co-operation and Customs Union Agreement, originally concluded in 1991, and an agreement on monetary relations, concluded in 2000 (and expanded in 2012: see Contemporary Political History), which allowed San Marino to adopt the single European currency, the euro, in 2002.

ECONOMIC AFFAIRS

San Marino's gross national product (GNP) was €824m. in 2009, equivalent to €24,990 per head. According to UN figures, annual gross domestic product (GDP) declined, in real terms, at an average annual rate of 0.8% in 2002–11; GDP contracted by 2.6% in 2011.

Agriculture contributed only 0.1% of GDP in 2009, and engaged 0.2% of the employed population (excluding the self-employed) in 2012. The principal crops are wheat, barley, maize, olives and grapes. Livestock-rearing (notably of pigs) and dairy farming are also significant. Olive oil and wine are produced for export. In 2010 there were 80 agricultural businesses.

Industry (including manufacturing and construction) contributed 39.2% of GDP in 2009, and engaged 33.3% of the employed population (excluding the self-employed) in 2012. Stone-quarrying is the only mining activity in San Marino, and is an important export industry. Manufacturing contributed 33.3% of GDP in 2009, and engaged 27.4% of the employed population (excluding the self-employed) in 2012. The most important branches of manufacturing are the production of cement, synthetic rubber, leather, textiles and ceramics. The sector is largely export-orientated, owing to integration with firms in Italy.

Energy is derived principally from gas (more than 75%). San Marino is dependent on the Italian state energy companies for much of its energy requirements.

The services sector contributed 60.7% of GDP in 2009, and engaged 66.5% of the employed population (excluding the self-employed) in 2012. Tourism is a significant source of government revenue. In 2004 the number of visitor arrivals was 2,127,573; however, of that number, only 41,546 stayed at least one night. Total visitor arrivals numbered 1,869,393 in 2012. The sale of coins and postage stamps, mainly to foreign collectors, is also a significant source of foreign exchange. San Marino was granted special dispensation to mint its own euro coins in 2002, with a view to providing for this specialist market. The sale of uncirculated minted coins to collectors plays a significant role in San Marino's economy and it was permitted to continue to mint gold scudi as a legal tender for San Marino only. The financial sector is important, with the credit and insurance sectors contributing 17.6% of GDP in 2009. San Marino's banks suffered a significant loss of deposits as a result of a 'tax amnesty' declared by Italy in October 2009 to encourage the repatriation of undeclared funds held abroad. Consequently, in the early 2010s the country's financial sector was seeking to develop a new business model that would allow it to maintain its prosperity without relying on banking secrecy.

In 2002, according to official figures, San Marino recorded a trade deficit of €96.2m. In the same year, according to the IMF, there was a deficit of €302.5m. on the current account of the balance of payments. Data concerning imports and exports are included in those of Italy, with which San Marino maintains a customs union. A customs union is also maintained with the

EU. The principal source of imports (estimated at around 87%) is Italy, upon which the country is dependent for its supply of raw materials. The major exports are wine, woollen goods, furniture, ceramics, building stone and artisan- and hand-made goods.

San Marino receives a subsidy from the Italian Government, under the *Canone Doganale*, amounting to about €11m. annually, in exchange for the Republic's acceptance of Italian rules concerning exchange controls and the renunciation of customs duties. The European single currency, the euro, became the sole currency in circulation at the start of 2002.

No consolidated general government accounts are published by San Marino, and separate accounts and budgets are prepared by the central administration, the Social Security Institute, and each of the public enterprises, on an accrual basis. After recording budgetary surpluses in 2003–07 and a balanced budget in 2008, San Marino recorded a deficit equivalent to 3.4% of GDP in 2009. Figures published by the IMF, on a cash basis, for the budget of the central administration indicated a deficit equivalent to some 3.3% of GDP in 2011. The annual rate of inflation averaged 2.5% in 2003–11; consumer prices increased by 2.9% in 2011. In 2012 1,145 people were unemployed—equivalent to 5.7% of the total labour force (excluding the self-employed). A large proportion of the work-force (32.0% of the employed labour force, excluding the self-employed, in 2010, compared with 10.8% in 1991) are cross-border workers, mainly Italians from the surrounding regions.

San Marino's economy is linked to that of its neighbour, Italy, with which it shares a monetary and customs union. Owing to its size, it is extremely vulnerable to economic developments in Italy and the wider EU. Although traditionally manufacturing was the principal sector of the economy, its contribution to GDP declined while that of services increased, particularly the financial sector (which benefited from alternative taxation and regulation structures) and tourism. Growth in the financial sector was stimulated by advantageous banking confidentiality, which aroused concern from the Italian Government and the Organisation for Economic Co-operation and Development (OECD, see p. 388) that this encouraged tax fraud, money-laundering and the possible financing of terrorism. New legislation was adopted in 2008 (and expanded in March 2012) to combat money-laundering and the financing of terrorism, in accordance with EU directives, and agreements were signed with a number of countries on the exchange of tax information. From late 2008 the international financial crisis placed severe strains on the financial sector and on the economy as a whole, which entered into recession at the end of the year. An amnesty offered to tax evaders by the Italian Government resulted in a massive outflow of deposits from San Marino banks in 2009 and 2010 (see Contemporary Political History). The Government allocated significant funds in the 2009 budget to mitigate the effects of the economic downturn and encourage economic diversification, including increased investment in infrastructure projects and renewable energy sources. According to estimates by the IMF, San Marino's budget deficit was equivalent to 2.2% of GDP in 2010 and 3.3% in 2011, and was expected to be about 3.5% in 2012, despite increases in taxation, pension reforms, and reductions in public sector employment. After four successive years of contraction in GDP from 2008 onwards, a further decline of around 2% was forecast by the IMF for 2012. According to an IMF report published in March 2013, the San Marino economy was expected to remain in recession in 2013 (with GDP contracting by a further 3%–4%), as a result of a decrease in tourist arrivals, rising unemployment, the country's continued place on Italy's blacklist of tax haven states, weak external demand arising from the persistent fiscal crisis in the eurozone, and increased government expenditure on social security. The IMF noted the progress that San Marino had made in recent years in achieving greater transparency and more stringent regulation within its financial sector, but stressed that the country could only return to strong growth through the attainment of full normalization of economic relations with Italy.

PUBLIC HOLIDAYS

2014: 1 January (New Year's Day), 6 January (Epiphany), 5 February (Liberation Day), 25 March (Anniversary of the Arengo), 1 April (Investiture of the new Captains-Regent), 21 April (Easter Monday), 1 May (Labour Day), 19 June (Corpus Christi), 28 July (Fall of Fascism), 15 August (Assumption), 3 September (San Marino Day and Republic Day), 1 October (Investiture of the new Captains-Regent), 1 November (All Saints' Day), 2 November (Commemoration of the Dead), 8 December (Immaculate Conception), 25 December (Christmas Day), 26 December (St Stephen's Day), 31 December (New Year's Eve).

Statistical Survey

Source (unless otherwise stated): Ufficio Programmazione Economica e Centro Elaborazione Dati e Statistica, Viale Antonio Onofri 109, 47890 San Marino; tel. 0549 885150; fax 0549 885154; e-mail statistica.upeceds@pa.sm; internet www.upeceds.sm.

AREA AND POPULATION

Area: 61.2 sq km (23.6 sq miles).

Population: 32,471 (males 15,965, females 16,506) at 31 December 2012 (*of whom* Sammarinese 27,450, Others 5,021).

Density (at 31 December 2012): 530.6 per sq km.

Population by Age and Sex (official estimates at 31 December 2012): *0–14:* 4,986 (males 2,607, females 2,379); *15–64:* 21,562 (males 10,705, females 10,857); *65 and over:* 5,923 (males 2,653, females 3,270); *Total* 32,471 (males 15,965, females 16,506).

Principal Towns (population at 31 December 2012): Serravalle 10,571; Borgo Maggiore 6,609; San Marino (capital) 4,214.

Births, Marriages and Deaths (registrations, 2012): Live births 292 (birth rate 9.0 per 1,000); Marriages 203 (marriage rate 6.3 per 1,000); Deaths 237 (death rate 7.3 per 1,000).

Life Expectancy (years at birth, official estimates, 2012): Males 81.5; females 86.1.

Migration (2012): Immigrants 364; Emigrants 141.

Economically Active Population (2012): Agriculture 34; Manufacturing 5,204; Construction 1,132; Trade and hospitality 3,361; Communication and transport 546; Finance 965; Real estate, information technology and business services 2,268; Health 231; Education 50; Public sector 4,100; Other services 1,118; *Sub-total* 19,009; Activities not classified 2; *Total employed* 19,011 (males 10,527, females 8,484); Unemployed 1,145 (males 412, females 733); *Total labour force* 20,156 (males 10,939, females 9,217). Note: Figures exclude self-employed (1,914).

HEALTH AND WELFARE

Key Indicators

Total Fertility Rate (children per woman, 2010): 1.5.

Under-5 Mortality Rate (per 1,000 live births, 2010): 2.

Physicians (per 1,000 head, 1990): 47.35.

Hospital Beds (per 1,000 head, 1990): 7.2.

Health Expenditure (2009): US $ per head (PPP): 2,838.

Health Expenditure (2009): % of GDP: 7.1.

Health Expenditure (2009): public (% of total): 85.2.

For sources and definitions, see explanatory note on p. vi.

FINANCE

Currency and Exchange Rates: Italian currency: 100 cent = 1 euro (€). *Sterling and Dollar Equivalents* 31 December 2012: £1 sterling = 1.196 euros; US $1 = 0.758 euros; €10 = £8.36 = $13.19. *Average Exchange Rates* (euros per US $): 0.7550 in 2010; 0.7194 in 2011; 0.7779 in 2012. Note: The local currency was formerly the Italian lira (plural = lire). From the introduction of the euro, with Italian participation, on 1 January 1999, a fixed exchange rate of €1 = 1,936.27 lire was in operation. Euro notes and coins were introduced on 1 January 2002. The euro and local currency circulated alongside each other until 28 February, after which the euro became the sole legal tender.

General Budget (€ million, 2009): *Revenue:* Tax revenue 250.7 (Taxation on individuals 98.0; Taxes on goods and services 116.8);

Social contributions 167.7; Grants 17.5; Other revenue 147.1; Total revenue 583.0. *Expenditure:* Compensation of employees 177.2; Use of goods and services 143.7; Consumption of fixed capital 19.9; Interest 6.4; Subsidies 7.3; Grants 4.6; Social benefits 219.4; Other expense 20.0; Total expenditure 598.5. Source: IMF, *Government Finance Statistics Yearbook*.

International Reserves (excl. gold, US $ million at 31 December 2011): IMF special drawing rights 23.60; Reserve position in IMF 8.37; Foreign exchange 309.90; *Total* 341.86. Source: IMF, *International Financial Statistics*.

Money Supply (€ '000 at 31 December 2011): Demand deposits at banks 1,113,960. Source: IMF, *International Financial Statistics*.

Cost of Living (Consumer Price Index; base: 2003 = 100): All items 115.0 in 2009; 118.0 in 2010; 121.4 in 2011. Source: ILO.

Gross Domestic Product (€ million at constant 1995 prices): 948 in 2007; 938 in 2008; 816 in 2009.

Expenditure on the Gross Domestic Product (€ million at current prices, 2009): Final consumption expenditure 601; Increase in stocks −35; Gross fixed capital formation 272; *Total domestic expenditure* 838; Exports of goods and services 2,362; *Less* Imports of goods and services 2,098; *GDP in purchasers' values* 1,102.

Gross Domestic Product by Economic Activity (€ million at current prices, 2009): Agriculture 1.1; Manufacturing 367.0; Construction 65.0; Services 668.9 (Trade 148.8, Transport and communications 26.4, Finance and insurance 194.0, Public sector 149.8, Other services 149.9); Total 1,102.0.

Balance of Payments (US $ million, 1996, estimates): Merchandise exports f.o.b. 1,741,9; Merchandise imports c.i.f. −1,719.3; *Trade balance* 22.6; Exports of services 120.4; Imports of services −102.2; *Balance on goods and services* 40.9; Interest payments 63.5; Net labour income −57.9; Other capital income −45.5; *Balance on goods, services and income* 1.0; Net transfers 9.7; *Current balance* 10.7; Capital account (net) 218.5; Errors and omissions −219.8; *Overall balance* 9.4. Source: IMF, *San Marino: Recent Economic Developments* (April 1999).

EXTERNAL TRADE

Data concerning imports and exports are included in those of Italy, with which San Marino maintains a customs union.

TRANSPORT

Road Traffic (registered motor vehicles, 2012): Motorcycles 13,149; Passenger cars 36,171; Buses and coaches 4,038; Agricultural vehicles 1,109; Total (incl. others) 56,119.

TOURISM

Visitor Arrivals (incl. excursionists): 1,976,481 in 2010; 2,038,359 in 2011; 1,869,393 in 2012.

Tourist Arrivals (staying at least one night): 45,508 in 2002; 40,686 in 2003; 41,546 in 2004.

COMMUNICATIONS MEDIA

Telephones (2011): 18,700 main lines in use.

Mobile Cellular Telephones (subscribers, 2011): 35,500.

Internet Users (2009): 17,000.

Broadband Subscribers (2011): 6,500.

Sources: International Telecommunication Union.

EDUCATION

Pre-primary (2011/12): 14 schools; 142 teachers; 1,102 pupils.

Primary (2011/12): 14 schools; 251 teachers; 1,574 pupils.

Secondary (Scuola Media) (2011/12): 3 schools; 150 teachers; 949 pupils.

Secondary and Vocational (Scuola Secondaria Superiore e Formazione Professionale): 4 schools (2004/05); 90 teachers (2009/10); 684 pupils (2011/12—a further 774 pupils were studying outside San Marino).

University (2011/12): 1 university, 42 students (a further 830 students were attending courses outside San Marino).

Pupil-teacher Ratio (primary education, UNESCO estimate): 6.5 in 2009/10 (Source: UNESCO Institute for Statistics).

Directory

The Government

HEADS OF STATE

Capitani Reggenti (Captains-Regent): ANTONELLA MULARONI (AP), DENIS AMICI (PDCS) (1 April 2013–1 October 2013).

CONGRESSO DI STATO
(Congress of State)
(May 2013)

A coalition of the Partito Democratico Cristiano Sammarinese (PDCS)/Noi Sammarinesi (NS), the Partito dei Socialisti e dei Democratici (PSD) and the Alleanza Popolare (AP).

Secretary of State for Foreign and Political Affairs: PASQUALE VALENTINI (PDCS).

Secretary of State for Internal Affairs Public Administration, Justice and Relations with the Castle Boards: GIANCARLO VENTURINI (PDCS).

Secretary of State for Finance, the Budget, Postal Services and Relations with the Azienda Autonoma di Stato Filatelica e Numismatica (AASFN): CLAUDIO FELICI (PSD).

Secretary of State for Education, Culture, the University, Scientific Research, Social Affairs and Equal Opportunities: GIUSEPPE MARIA MORGANTI (PSD).

Secretary of State for Health, Social Security, Family Retirement and Economic Planning: FRANCESCO MUSSONI (PDCS).

Secretary of State for Land and Environment, Agriculture, Telecommunications, Youth, Sport, Civil Defence and Relations with the Azienda Autonoma di Stato di Produzione (AASP): MATTEO FIORINI (AP).

Secretary of State for Labour, Co-operation and Information: IRO BELLUZZI (PSD).

Secretary of State for Industry, Handicrafts, Trade, Commerce, Transport and Technological Research: MARCO ARZILLI (NS).

Secretary of State for Tourism and Relations with the Azienda Autonoma di Stato per i Servizi Pubblici (AASS): TEODORO LONFERNINI (PDCS).

MINISTRIES

Secretariat of State for Education, Culture and the University: Via Napoleone Bonaparte 3, 47890 San Marino; tel. 0549 882425; fax 0549 882554; e-mail segreteria.ic@gov.sm; internet www.educazione.sm.

Secretariat of State for Finance, the Budget and Relations with the Azienda Autonoma di Stato Filatelica e Numismatica (AASFN): Palazzo Begni, Contrada Omerelli, 47890 San Marino; tel. 0549 882661; fax 0549 882244; e-mail lbeccari@finanze.sm; internet www.finanze.sm.

Secretariat of State for Foreign and Political Affairs, Tourism and Relations with the Azienda Autonoma di Stato per i Servizi Pubblici (AASS): Palazzo Begni, Contrada Omerelli, 47890 San Marino; tel. 0549 882431; fax 0549 882422; e-mail dipartimentoaffariesteri@pa.sm; internet www.esteri.sm.

Secretariat of State for Health, Social Security, Welfare, Family and Social Affairs and Equal Opportunities: Via V. Scialoia, 47895 Cailungo; tel. 0549 883040; fax 0549 883044; e-mail info.sanita@gov.sm; internet www.sanita.sm.

Secretariat of State for Industry, Handicrafts and Trade: Palazzo Mercuri, Contrada del Collegio, 47890 San Marino; tel. 0549 882924; fax 0549 882529; e-mail uff.iac@omniway.sm; internet www.industria.sm.

Secretariat of State for Internal Affairs, Justice, Civil Affairs and Relations with the Castle Boards: Parva Domus, Piazza della Libertà 2, 47890 San Marino; tel. 0549 882425; fax 0549 885080;

e-mail segreteria.interni@gov.sm; internet www.interni.segreteria .sm.

Secretariat of State for Labour, Co-operation and the Postal Service: Palazzo Mercuri, Contrada del Collegio 38, 47890 San Marino; tel. 0549 882532; fax 0549 882535; e-mail segreteria.lavoro@ gov.sm; internet www.lavoro.sm.

Secretariat of State for Territory, Environment, Agriculture, Telecommunications, Youth, Sport, Civil Defence and Relations with the Azienda Autonoma di Stato per i Lavori Pubblici (AASLP): Contrada Omerelli 43, 47890 San Marino; tel. 0549 882474; fax 0549 885265; e-mail segreteria.territorio@gov.sm; internet www.segreteriaterritorio.sm.

Legislature

Consiglio Grande e Generale
(Great and General Council)

Palazzo Pubblico, Piazza della Libertà, 47890 San Marino; tel. 0549 882273; fax 0549 882389; e-mail info.segristituzionale@pa.sm; internet www.consigliograndeegenerale.sm.

Election, 11 November 2012

Party	Votes	% of votes	Seats
San Marino Bene Comune	10,028	50.70	35
Partito Democratico Cristiano Sammarinese (PDCS)/Noi Sammarinesi (NS)	5,828	29.47	21
Partito dei Socialisti e dei Democratici (PSD)	2,832	14.32	10
Alleanza Popolare (AP)	1,319	6.67	4
Intesa per il Paese	4,407	22.28	12
Partito Socialista (PS)	2,393	12.10	7
Unione per la Repubblica (UPR)	1,651	8.35	5
Moderati Sammarinesi (MOD)	340	1.72	—
Cittadinanza Attiva	3,179	16.07	9
Sinistra Unita (SU)	1,808	9.14	5
Movimento Civico Dieci (CI10)	1,325	6.70	4
Movimento Civico Rete (RETE)	1,244	6.29	4
per San Marino	556	2.81	—
San Marino 3.0 (SM3.0)	364	1.84	—
Total	**19,778**	**100.00**	**60**

Political Organizations

Alleanza Nazionale Sammarinese (ANS) (San Marino National Alliance): Via XXVIII Luglio 148, 47893 Borgo Maggiore; tel. 0549 907815; fax 0549 875203; e-mail anrsm@omniway.sm; right-wing; formed a coalition, the Unione Sammarinese dei Moderati, with the Popolari Sammarinesi in early 2008 in order to contest the Nov. 2008 general election; Pres. ENNIO VITTORIO PELLANDRA; Political Sec. GLAUCO SANSOVINI.

Alleanza Popolare (AP) (Popular Alliance): Strada VI, Gualdaria 14A, 47893 Borgo Maggiore; tel. 0549 887427; fax 0549 907080; e-mail ap@alleanzapopolare.net; internet www.alleanzapopolare .net; f. 1993 as Alleanza Popolare Democratici Sammarinesi; advocates a constitution and institutional reform; Pres. ANTONELLA MULARONI; Co-ordinator NICOLA RENZI.

Cittadinanza Attiva (Active Citizenship): f. 2012 as a coalition of Sinistra Unita and Movimento Civico Dieci to contest the Nov. 2012 general election.

Intesa per il Paese (Agreement for the Country): f. 2012; coalition of Partito Socialista, Unione per la Repubblica and Moderati Sammarinesi to contest the Nov. 2012 general election.

Movimento Civico Dieci (CI10) (Citizens' Movement 10): Via Ca' dei Lunghi 4, 47893 Borgo Maggiore; tel. and fax 0549 909833; e-mail info@civico10.org; internet www.civico10.org; f. 2012.

Movimento Civico Rete (RETE): Via dei Pini 1, Domagnano; tel. 0549 907777; e-mail rete@movimentorete.org; internet www .movimentorete.org; Pres. GRAZIA ZAFFERANI.

Noi Sammarinesi (We Sammarinesi): Via XXVIII Luglio 160, 47893 Borgo Maggiore; tel. and fax 0549 907101; e-mail info@ noisammarinesi.com; internet www.noisammarinesi.com; f. 2006; contested Nov. 2012 general election with Partito Democratico Cristiano Sammarinese (PDCS) as part of San Marino Bene Comune; Spokesman MARCO ARZILLI.

Partito Democratico Cristiano Sammarinese (PDCS) (San Marino Christian Democrat Party): Via delle Scalette 6, 47890 San Marino; tel. 0549 991193; fax 0549 992694; e-mail pdcs@

omniway.sm; internet www.pdcs.sm; f. 1948; Pres. TEODORO LONFERNINI; Political Sec. MARCO GATTI; 2,400 mems.

Partito dei Socialisti e dei Democratici (PSD) (Party of Socialists and Democrats): Via Ordelaffi 46, 47893 Borgo Maggiore; tel. 0549 903806; fax 0549 906438; e-mail info@psd.sm; internet www .psdsanmarino.org; f. 2005 by merger of the Partito dei Democratici and the Partito Socialista Sammarinese; Pres. DENISE BRONZETTI; Sec.-Gen. GERARDO GIOVAGNOLI.

Partito Socialista (PS) (Socialist Party): Via XXVIII Luglio 212, 47893 Borgo Maggiore; tel. 0549 808008; fax 0549 808009; e-mail comunicazione@socialisti.sm; internet www.socialisti.sm; f. 2012 by the merger of Nuovo Partito Socialista and Partito Socialista Riformista Sammarinese; Pres. ANTONIO LAZZARO VOLPINARI; Sec. SIMONE CELLI.

per San Marino: Via 3 Settembre 99, 47891 Admiral Point Dogana; tel. 0549 909524; e-mail info@persanmarino.it; internet www .persanmarino.com.

San Marino Bene Comune (San Marino Common Good): coalition f. 2012 in order to contest the Nov. 2012 general election; comprises Partito Democratico Cristiano Sammarinese, Noi Sammarinesi, Partito dei Socialisti e dei Democratici and Alleanza Popolare.

Sinistra Unita (SU) (United Left): Via delle Tamerici 1, 47895 Domagnano; tel. 0549 907656; fax 0549 944397; e-mail sinistraunita@omniway.sm; internet www.sxun.org; f. 2005; left-wing coalition, comprising Rifondazione Comunista Sammarinese and Zona Franca, formed to contest 2006 general election.

Rifondazione Comunista Sammarinese (RCS) (San Marino Communist Refoundation): Strada delle Tamerici 1, 47895 Domagnano; tel. and fax 0549 907656; e-mail rcs@omniway.sm; f. 1992; communist.

Unione per la Repubblica (UPR) (Union for the Republic): Via Cà Franceschino 2, 47893 Borgo Maggiore; tel. 0549 909884; fax 0549 972855; e-mail info@upr.sm; internet www.upr.sm; f. 2011 by the merger of Democratici di Centro and Europopolari per San Marino; Pres. GIAN MARCO MARCUCCI; Co-ordinators PIER MARINO MULARONI, LORENZO LONFERNINI.

Other parties contesting the November 2012 election included the Moderati Sammarinesi (MOD) and San Marino 3.0 (SM3.0).

Diplomatic Representation

By December 2010 San Marino had established full diplomatic relations with 100 countries.

EMBASSIES IN SAN MARINO

Holy See: Domus Plebis 1, 47890 San Marino; tel. 0549 992448; Apostolic Nuncio Most Rev. ADRIANO BERNARDINI (Titular Archbishop of Falerii) (resident in Rome, Italy).

Italy: Viale Antonio Onofri 117, 47890 San Marino; tel. 0549 991146; fax 0549 992229; e-mail ambsanmar@omniway.sm; internet www .ambsanmarino.esteri.it; Ambassador BARBARA BREGATO.

Judicial System

The administration of justice is entrusted to foreign judges, with the exception of the Justice of the Peace, who must be of San Marino nationality, and who judges minor civil suits. The major judicial institutions are as follows:

Tribunale Commissariale Civile e Penale (Civil and Criminal Commissionary Tribunal): Via Luglio 28, 47893 Borgo Maggiore; tel. 0549 882626; fax 0549 8825980; e-mail tribunale@omniway.sm.

Commissario della Legge (Law Commissioner): deals with civil and criminal cases where the maximum sentence does not exceed three years' imprisonment.

Giudice Penale di Primo Grado (Criminal Judge of the Primary Court of Claims): deals with criminal cases that are above the competence of the Law Commissioner.

Giudice Amministrativo di Appello (Court of Appeal): two judges, who deal with civil and criminal proceedings.

Consiglio dei XII (Council of Twelve): has authority as a Supreme Court of Appeal, for civil proceedings only.

Religion

CHRISTIANITY

The Roman Catholic Church

Roman Catholicism is the official state religion of San Marino. The Republic forms part of the diocese of San Marino-Montefeltro (comprising mainly Italian territory), suffragan to the archdiocese of Ravenna-Cervia.

Bishop of San Marino-Montefeltro: (vacant), Curia Vescovile, Piazza Giovanni Paolo II 1, 47864 Pennabilli, Pesaro, Italy; tel. (0541) 913720; fax (0541) 928832; e-mail vescovo.negri@ diocesi-sanmarino-montefeltro.it; internet www.diocesi -sanmarino-montefeltro.it.

The Press

Argomenti: c/o CSdL, Via V Febbraio 17, Fiorina C-3, 47895 Domagnano; tel. 0549 962060; fax 0549 962075; organ of the Confederazione Sammarinese del Lavoro (CSdL); periodical; Dir ANDREA LEARDINI; circ. 5,000.

Corriere di Informazione Sammarinese: Via Piana, 47890 San Marino; tel. 0549 995147; fax 0549 879021; e-mail sanmarino@ corriereromagna.it; daily.

Il San Marino: Via delle Scalette 6, 47890 San Marino; tel. 0549 991193; fax 0549 992694; e-mail info@pdcs.sm; internet www.pdcs .sm; periodical; organ of the PDCS; quarterly; Dir TEODORO LONFERNINI.

San Marino Fixing: Via G. Giacomini 37, 47890 San Marino; tel. 0549 991719; fax 0549 879049; e-mail fixing@omniway.sm; internet www.sanmarinofixing.com; weekly; economics and politics; Dir LORIS PIRONI.

La Tribuna Sammarinese: Via Gino Giacomini 86A, 47890 San Marino; tel. 0549 990420; fax 0549 990398; e-mail redazione@ latribunasammarinese.net; internet www.latribunasammarinese .net; daily; Dir DAVIDE GRAZIOSI.

Publishers

AIEP Editore: Via Rancaglia 25, 47899 Serravalle; tel. 0549 941457; fax 0549 973164; e-mail info@aiepeditore.net; internet www.aiepeditore.net; f. 1980; general book publishing; Man. GIUSEPPE MARIA MORGANTI.

Guardigli Editore: Via Istriani 94, 47890 San Marino; tel. 0549 995144; fax 0549 990454; e-mail guardiglieditore@omniway.sm; internet www.guardiglieditore.com; f. 1991; book publishing; Man. Dir PIER PAOLO GUARDIGLI.

Broadcasting and Communications

TELECOMMUNICATIONS

Direzione Generale Poste e Telecomunicazioni: Contrada Omerelli 17, 47890 San Marino; tel. 0549 882555; fax 0549 992760; e-mail direttoregenerale.dirposte@pa.sm; state body responsible for telecommunications; Dir-Gen. Dott. ROSA ZAFFERANI.

San Marino Telecom: Piazza Tini 20, 47891 San Marino; tel. 0549 941502; fax 0549 942768; e-mail info@smt.sm; internet www.smt.sm; mobile services; Pres. SIMON MURRAY.

Telecom Italia San Marino, SpA: Strada degli Angariari 3, 47891 Falciano; tel. 0549 886111; fax 0549 886188; e-mail secretary@ telecomitalia.sm; internet www.telecomitalia.sm; f. 1992; provides international telecommunications services; CEO CESARE PISANI.

Telefonia Mobile Sammarinese, SpA (TMS): Via XXVIII Luglio 148, 47893 Borgo Maggiore; tel. 0549 980222; fax 0549 980044; e-mail info@tms.sm; internet www.tms.sm; f. 1999; mobile services.

BROADCASTING

In addition to the broadcasts of San Marino RTV, San Marino receives radio and television broadcasts from Italy.

San Marino RTV (Radiotelevisione della Repubblica di San Marino): Viale Kennedy 13, 47890 San Marino; tel. 0549 882000; fax 0549 882840; e-mail redazione@sanmarinortv.sm; internet www .sanmarinortv.sm; f. 1991; began broadcasting in 2003; jtly owned by the Italian state broadcaster, Rai—Radiotelevisione Italiana, and Ente per la Radiodiffusione Sammarinese; operates 1 television station and 2 radio stations, Radio San Marino and Radio San Marino Classic; Pres. STEFANO VALENTINO PIVA; Dir-Gen. Dott. CARMEN LASORELLA.

Finance

(cap. = capital; res = reserves; dep. = deposits; m. = million; brs = branches; amounts in euros)
In August 2010 there were 12 banks operating in San Marino.

BANKING

Central Bank

Banca Centrale della Repubblica di San Marino: Via del Voltone 120, 47890 San Marino; tel. 0549 882325; fax 0549 882328; e-mail info@bcsm.sm; internet www.bcsm.sm; f. 2003; formed by a merger between the Istituto di Credito Sammarinese and the Ispettorato per il Credito e le Valute; cap. 12.9m., res 11.8m., dep. 464.2m. (Dec. 2008); Chair. RENATO CLARIZIA; Vice-Chair. ORIETTA BERARDI; Dir-Gen. MARIO GIANNINI.

Commercial Banks

Banca CIS: Piazza Bertoldi 8, 47899 Serravalle; tel. 0549 874115; fax 0549 874116; e-mail info@cis.sm; internet www.cis.sm; f. 1933; fmrly Credito Industriale Sammarinese SpA; owned by Banca Carim (Italy); cap. 35.0m., res 14.7m., dep. 266.9m. (Dec. 2011); Chair. LORENZO STANGHELLINI; CEO ALBERTO MOCCHI; 3 brs.

Banca Commerciale Sammarinese: Via Cinque Febbraio 17, 47895 Domagnano; tel. 0549 904280; fax 0594 901356; e-mail info@bcs.sm; internet www.bcs.sm; cap. 19.0m., res 0.01m., dep. 150.2m. (Dec. 2010); Pres. Dott. EMILIO DELLA BALDA; Dir-Gen. Dott. PAOLO DROGHINI.

Banca di San Marino, SpA: Strada della Croce 39, 47896 Faetano; tel. 0549 873411; fax 0549 873401; e-mail info@bsm.sm; internet www.bsm.sm; f. 1920 as Cassa Rurale Depositi e Prestiti di Faetano, Scrl; changed name as above in 2001; cap. 114.6m., res 89.3m., dep. 935m. (Dec. 2011); Chair. FAUSTO MULARONI; Dir-Gen. Prof. VINCENZO TAGLIAFERRO; 9 brs.

Cassa di Risparmio della Repubblica di San Marino: Piazzetta del Titano 2, 47890 San Marino; tel. 0549 872301; fax 0549 872700; e-mail info@carisp.sm; internet www.carisp.sm; f. 1882; cap. 278.3m., res 16.2m., dep. 1,718.7m. (Dec. 2011); Pres. and CEO LEONE SIBANI; 16 brs.

Euro Commercial Bank SpA: Strada dei Censiti 21, 47891 Rovereta; tel. 0549 943711; fax 0549 943737; e-mail info@ecb.sm; internet www.ecb.sm; f. 2000; cap. 30.0m., res 1.8m., dep. 53.4m. (2011); Dir-Gen. GIUSEPPE GUIDI; 2 brs.

INSURANCE

Several major Italian insurance companies have agencies in San Marino.

Trade and Industry

GOVERNMENT AGENCIES

Azienda Autonoma di Stato Filatelica e Numismatica (AASFN): Piazza Garibaldi 5, 47890 San Marino; tel. 0549 882350; fax 0549 882363; e-mail info.ufn@pa.sm; internet www .aasfn.sm; autonomous public enterprise; responsible for production and distribution of postage stamps and coins; Pres. PIGNATTA ORAZIO; Dir-Gen. MARINO MANUZZI.

Azienda Autonoma di Stato di Produzione (AASP): Via Ventotto Luglio 50, 47031 Borgo Maggiore; tel. 0549 883600; fax 0549 883600; e-mail aasp@omniway.sm; civil engineering works, road works, land reclamation; Dir FABIO BERARDI.

Azienda Autonoma di Stato per la gestione della Centrale del Latte: Strada Genghe di Atto 71, 47031 Acquaviva; tel. 0549 999207; fax 0549 999606; operates state monopoly in production and distribution of dairy products; Pres. TIZIANO CANINI; Dir PAOLO MUSCI.

CHAMBER OF COMMERCE

Camera di Commercio, Industria, Artigianato e Agricoltura di San Marino (CCIAA): Strada di Paderna 2, 47895 San Marino; tel. 0549 980380; fax 0549 944554; e-mail info@cc.sm; internet www .cc.sm; f. 2004; Pres. SIMONA MICHELOTTI; Gen. Man. Dott. MASSIMO GHIOTTI.

INDUSTRIAL AND TRADE ASSOCIATIONS

Associazione Nazionale dell'Industria Sammarinese (ANIS) (National Association for Industry): Via Gino Giacomini 39, 47890 San Marino; tel. 0549 873911; fax 0549 992832; e-mail anis@ omniway.sm; internet www.anis.sm; Pres. EMANUEL COLOMBINI; Sec.-Gen. CARLO GIORGI.

Associazione Sammarinese Produttori Agricoli (ASPA): Serrabolino 42, 47893 Borgo Maggiore; tel. 0549 902617; agricultural producers' association.

Consorzio San Marino 2000 srl: Via Piana 103, 47890 San Marino; tel. 0549 995031; fax 0549 990573; e-mail info@sanmarino2000.sm; internet www.sanmarino2000.sm; f. 1998; fmrly Unione Sammarinese Operatori Turistici (USOT); hotels and restaurants association.

Organizzazione Sammarinese degli Imprenditori (OSLA): Via N. Bonaparte 75, 47890 San Marino; tel. 0549 992885; fax 0549 992620; e-mail ufficiosegreteria@osla.sm; internet www.osla.sm; f. 1985; organization for the self-employed; Pres. MIRKO DOLCINI.

Unione Nazionale Artigiani e PMI della Repubblica di San Marino (UNAS): Piazzale M. Giangi 2, San Marino; tel. 0549 992148; fax 0549 992837; e-mail info@unas.sm; f. 1968; artisans' association; Pres. LORETTA J. MENICUCCI.

Unione Sammarinese Commercianti (USC): Via Piana 111, 47890 San Marino; tel. 0549 992892; shopkeepers' association; Pres. CARLO LONFERNINI.

UTILITIES

All utilities are imported from Italy.

Azienda Autonoma di Stato per i Servizi Pubblici (AASS): Via Andrea di Superchio 16, 47893 Cailungo; tel. 0549 883700; fax 0549 883720; e-mail info@aass.sm; internet www.aass.sm; f. 1981; autonomous state service company; distributes electricity, gas and water within San Marino; Pres. ANTHONY BUCCI; Dir-Gen. EMANUELE VALLI.

TRADE UNIONS

Centrale Sindacale Unitaria (CSU): Via V Febbraio 17, 47895 Domagnano; tel. 0549 962011; fax 0549 962055; e-mail amministrazione@csu.sm; f. 1976; Pres. GIULIANO TAMAGNINI MARCO TURA.

Unione Sammarinese dei Lavoratori (USL): Via Ventotto Luglio 212, Centro Uffici Tavolucci, 47893 Borgo Maggiore; tel. 0549 907031; fax 0549 908978; e-mail info@usl.sm; internet www.usl.sm; f. 2008; affiliated to the Unione Italiana del Lavoro; Sec.-Gen. FRANCESCO BIORDI.

Transport

The capital, San Marino, is connected with Borgo Maggiore, about 1.5 km away, by funicular. There is also a bus service, and a highway down to the Italian coast at Rimini, about 24 km away. San Marino has an estimated 220 km of roads. The nearest airport to the Republic is at Rimini. There is also a heliport in Borgo Maggiore; a seasonal helicopter service is available between San Marino and Rimini, Italy. There are no frontier or customs formalities.

Azienda Autonoma di Stato per i Servizi Pubblici (AASS): (see Utilities); numerous responsibilities include public transport and funicular railway.

Tourism

The mild climate attracts many visitors to San Marino each year, as do the contrasting scenery and well-preserved medieval architecture. In 2012 San Marino received some 1.9m. visitors (including excursionists).

Ufficio di Stato per il Turismo (State Tourist Board): Contrada Omagnano 20, 47890 San Marino; tel. 0549 882420; fax 0549 885399; e-mail info@visitsanmarino.com; internet www.visitsanmarino.com; Dir ANTONIO MACINA.

Defence

There are combined Voluntary Military Forces, comprising the military police (Gendarmeria), a uniformed militia (Compagnia Uniformata delle Milizie) and two bodies of institutional guards (Guardia del Consiglio Grande e Generale and Guardia di Rocca). There is no obligatory military service, but citizens aged between 16 and 55 years may be enlisted, in certain circumstances, to defend the state.

High Commandant of the Militia: Gen. ROSOLINO MARTELLI.

Education

Education is compulsory for 10 years between the ages of six and 16 years. Primary education begins at six years of age and lasts for five years. Secondary education begins at the age of 11 and may last for up to eight years: a first cycle of three years, a second of two years and a third, non-compulsory, cycle of three years. There is one, state-run, university, the University of the Republic of San Marino. In 2011/12 1,102 pupils were attending pre-primary schools, 1,574 were attending primary schools, 949 were enrolled at lower secondary school, while 1,458 were undertaking upper secondary and vocational education (some 774 of whom were studying outside San Marino). In that year 42 university students were studying in San Marino, with a further 830 attending courses outside the country. In 2004, according to official figures, spending on education was €35.1m., equivalent to 8.1% of public spending.

SÃO TOMÉ AND PRÍNCIPE

Introductory Survey

LOCATION, CLIMATE, LANGUAGE, RELIGION, FLAG, CAPITAL

The Democratic Republic of São Tomé and Príncipe lies in the Gulf of Guinea, off the west coast of Africa. There are two main islands, São Tomé and Príncipe, and the country also includes the rocky islets of Caroço, Pedras and Tinhosas, off Príncipe, and Rôlas, off São Tomé. The climate is warm and humid, with average temperatures ranging between 22°C (72°F) and 30°C (86°F). The rainy season extends from October to May, and average annual rainfall varies from 500 mm (20 ins) in the southern highlands to 1,000 mm (39 ins) in the northern lowlands. Portuguese is the official language and native dialects are widely spoken. Almost all of the inhabitants profess Christianity, and the overwhelming majority (some 72.3%) are adherents of the Roman Catholic Church. The national flag (proportions 1 by 2) has three horizontal stripes, of green, yellow (one-half of the depth) and green, with a red triangle at the hoist and two five-pointed black stars on the yellow stripe. The capital is the town of São Tomé, on São Tomé island.

CONTEMPORARY POLITICAL HISTORY

Historical Context

A former Portuguese colony, São Tomé and Príncipe became an overseas province of Portugal in 1951 and received local autonomy in 1973. A nationalist group, the Comissão de Libertação de São Tomé e Príncipe, was formed in 1960 and became the Movimento de Libertação de São Tomé e Príncipe (MLSTP) in 1972, under the leadership of Dr Manuel Pinto da Costa. Based in Libreville, Gabon, the MLSTP was recognized by the Organization of African Unity (now the African Union—AU, see p. 191) in 1973.

Following the military coup in Portugal in April 1974, the Portuguese Government recognized the right of the islands to independence. Negotiations began in November, at which Portugal recognized the MLSTP as the sole representative of the people. On 12 July 1975 independence was achieved, with da Costa as the country's first President and Miguel dos Anjos da Cunha Lisboa Trovoada as Prime Minister. In December a legislative Assembleia Popular Nacional (National People's Assembly) was elected.

Worsening economic conditions, following a severe drought in 1982, prompted the Government to review the country's close ties with communist regimes and its consequent isolation from major Western aid sources. In late 1984 da Costa declared São Tomé and Príncipe to be politically non-aligned.

Domestic Political Affairs

In October 1987 the Central Committee of the MLSTP announced major constitutional reforms, including the election by universal adult suffrage of the President of the Republic and of members of the Assembleia Popular Nacional. The amended Constitution also allowed 'independent' candidates to contest legislative elections, although the President of the MLSTP, chosen by the MLSTP Congress from two candidates proposed by the Central Committee, would continue to be the sole candidate for the presidency of the Republic. In January 1988 the premiership was restored, and Celestino Rochas da Costa, hitherto Minister of Education, Labour and Social Security, was appointed as Prime Minister.

In March 1990 a joint meeting of the Assembleia Popular Nacional and the MLSTP Central Committee approved a new draft constitution, which provided for the establishment of a multi-party system, limited the President's tenure of office to two five-year terms, and permitted independent candidates to participate in legislative elections. On 22 August, in a national referendum, 72% of the electorate endorsed the new Constitution. In the following month new legislation on the formation of political parties came into effect. Delegates to the MLSTP Congress in October voted to replace da Costa as party President, appointing Carlos Alberto Monteiro Dias da Graça to the new post of Secretary-General. The party's name was amended to the Movimento de Libertação de São Tomé e Príncipe—Partido Social Democrata (MLSTP—PSD).

In January 1991 elections to the new Assembleia Nacional resulted in defeat for the MLSTP—PSD, which secured only 21 seats in the 55-member legislature, while the Partido de Convergência Democrática—Grupo de Reflexão (PCD—GR) won 33 seats. The Partido Democrático de São Tomé e Príncipe—Coligação Democrático da Oposição (PDSTP—CODO) took the remaining seat. In February a transitional Government, headed by the Secretary-General of the PCD—GR, Daniel Lima dos Santos Daio, was installed. In the same month President da Costa announced that he would not be contesting the presidential election, to be held in March. The MLSTP—PSD did not present an alternative candidate. In late February two of the three remaining presidential candidates withdrew from the election. Miguel Trovoada, who stood as an independent candidate (with the support of the PCD—GR), was thus the sole contender, and on 3 March he was elected President with the support of 81% of those who voted. He took office on 3 April.

In April 1992, following demonstrations demanding the resignation of the Government due to the unpopular imposition of stringent austerity measures, Trovoada dismissed the Daio administration. The PCD—GR was invited to designate a new Prime Minister, and in May Norberto Costa Alegre (hitherto Minister of Economy and Finance) was chosen as Prime Minister. A new Government was named shortly afterwards.

Meanwhile, relations between the Government and the presidency deteriorated, and in April 1994 Trovoada publicly dissociated himself from government policy. Political tension increased in June, when the PCD—GR accused Trovoada of systematic obstruction of the government programme. In July Trovoada dismissed the Alegre Government and appointed Evaristo do Espírito Santo de Carvalho (the Minister of Defence and Security in the outgoing administration) as Prime Minister. The PCD—GR, refusing to participate in an administration formed on presidential initiative, subsequently expelled Carvalho from the party. An interim Government, comprising principally technocrats and senior civil servants, was appointed. Shortly afterwards Trovoada dissolved the Assembleia Nacional, thus preventing the PCD—GR from using its parliamentary majority to declare the new Government unconstitutional.

Legislative elections were held on 2 October 1994, at which the MLSTP—PSD secured 27 seats, one short of an absolute majority. The PCD—GR and Acção Democrática Independente (ADI) each obtained 14 seats; da Graça was subsequently appointed Prime Minister. His Council of Ministers was dominated by members of the MLSTP—PSD.

In March 1995 the first elections to a new seven-member Assembleia Regional and five-member regional government were conducted on Príncipe, which had been granted local autonomy by the Assembleia Nacional in 1994. The elections resulted in an absolute majority for the MLSTP—PSD. The new regional Government began functioning in April 1995.

In mid-August 1995 a group of some 30 soldiers, led by five junior officers, seized control of the presidential palace in a bloodless coup. Trovoada was detained at the headquarters of the armed forces and da Graça was placed under house arrest. The legislature was disbanded, the Constitution suspended and a curfew imposed. Following talks mediated by an Angolan delegation, the insurgents and the Government signed a 'memorandum of understanding', providing for the reinstatement of Trovoada and the restoration of constitutional order. In return, the Government gave an undertaking to restructure the armed forces, and the Assembleia Nacional granted a general amnesty to all those involved in the coup.

The 1996 presidential election

In December 1995 Armindo Vaz d'Almeida was appointed Prime Minister, by presidential decree, to head a Government of National Unity. The new administration included six members of the MLSTP—PSD, four members of the ADI and one of the PDSTP—CODO. The three parties had signed a political pact, with the aim of ensuring political stability. In February 1996, at the request of the Comissão Eleitoral Nacional (National Elect-oral Commission), the forthcoming presidential election, which had been set for March, was postponed, pending the satisfactory completion of the electoral rolls. The date of the election was subsequently rescheduled for 30 June. In March Pinto da Costa was selected as the presidential candidate of the MLSTP—PSD and Francisco Fortunato Pires was appointed Secretary-General of the party, replacing the more moderate da Graça. In April Trovoada declared his candidacy for the presidential election, supported by the ADI and the PDSTP—CODO.

At the presidential election of 30 June 1996 no candidate secured an absolute majority. The two leading candidates thus proceeded to a second round of voting on 21 July, at which Trovoada won 52.7% of the votes, defeating Pinto da Costa. Although he did not command majority support in the Assem-bleia Nacional, Trovoada dismissed the possibility of new legis-lative elections, announcing instead his intention to seek a broadly based government of national consensus. Vaz d'Almeida remained as Prime Minister in an interim capacity until Novem-ber, when Raul Wagner da Conceição Bragança Neto, Assistant Secretary-General of the MLSTP—PSD, was appointed Prime Minister. A new coalition Government, including five members of the MLSTP—PSD, three members of the PCD—GR and one independent, was inaugurated later that month.

At an extraordinary congress of the MLSTP—PSD in May 1998, Pinto da Costa was elected unopposed as President of the party. (The ruling party of Angola, the Movimento Popular de Libertação de Angola (MPLA), had made the resumption of financial support for the MLSTP—PSD conditional on da Costa's election; following his defeat in the 1996 presidential election, the MPLA had ceased payments, creating serious problems for the MLSTP—PSD.) New party statutes were approved, creating the position of party President, together with three vice-presi-dential posts.

At legislative elections held on 8 November 1998 the MLSTP—PSD secured a majority, with 31 seats, while the ADI won 16 seats and the PCD—GR obtained the remaining eight seats. In December Guilherme Pósser da Costa (a Vice-President of the MLSTP—PSD and former Minister of Foreign Affairs and Co-operation) was appointed Prime Minister. A new Council of Ministers was installed in January 1999.

A presidential election took place on 29 July 2001. Among the five candidates to succeed Trovoada were former President Manuel Pinto da Costa, the leader of the MLSTP—PSD, and Fradique de Menezes, a businessman representing the ADI. In the event, de Menezes was elected to the presidency, winning 56.3% of the votes cast, while da Costa secured 38.7%. De Menezes was inaugurated as President on 3 September. A new Government of 'presidential initiative', which did not include any members of the MLSTP—PSD, was appointed in late September. The new Council of Ministers, led by Evaristo de Carvalho as Prime Minister, was composed of members of the ADI, the PCD (which had recently removed the suffix Grupo de Reflexão from its official name) and one independent. In Decem-ber de Menezes dissolved the Assembleia Nacional and announced that legislative elections would be held in March 2002, after which a new, more broadly based Government would be formed, according to an agreement reportedly signed by the President and representatives of political parties. In January 2002 the PCD formed an electoral alliance with the Movimento Democrático Força da Mudança (MDFM), which had been cre-ated in December by supporters of de Menezes.

At legislative elections held on 3 March 2002 no party obtained an absolute majority in the Assembleia Nacional. Provisional results indicated that the MLSTP—PSD and the MDFM-PCD alliance had each secured 23 of the 55 seats, while the remaining nine seats had been won by Uê Kédadji (UK), an alliance of the ADI and four minor parties. However, following a re-run of voting in one district, the MLSTP—PSD secured an extra seat, to the cost of the UK alliance, and was proclaimed victorious. Dr Gabriel Arcanjo Ferreira da Costa, the former ambassador to Portugal, was subsequently appointed as the nominally inde-pendent Prime Minister, and in April a new coalition Govern-ment of National Unity, which included representatives of the MLSTP—PSD, the MDFM-PCD and UK, as well as a number of independents, was installed.

In September 2002 da Costa's Government was dismissed by de Menezes, who appointed Maria das Neves de Souza, of the MLSTP—PSD, hitherto Minister of Trade, Industry and Tour-ism, as Prime Minister in October. A new Government of National Unity, with six representatives from the MLSTP—

PSD, five from the MDFM-PCD alliance, two from the UK alliance and one independent, was formed. In December the first MDFM congress elected Tomé Vera Cruz as Secretary-General of the party.

Constitutional reform

Meanwhile, in November 2002 the Assembleia Nacional approved a resolution for constitutional reform, altering the structure of the semi-presidential system to reduce presidential power. However, in January 2003 President de Menezes vetoed the draft constitution on the grounds that it should be endorsed by public referendum before coming into force. De Menezes dissolved the Assembleia Nacional by presidential decree later that month and called early elections for April. Prime Minister das Neves vowed to continue working and transferred the Gov-ernment of National Unity to the island of Príncipe. Following negotiations between the Government and the President, de Menezes reversed his decree, reinstating the Government, and a 'memorandum of understanding' was signed by de Menezes and the Assembleia Nacional, which provided for the immediate promulgation of the new Constitution.

The new Constitution, which took effect in March 2003, pro-vided for the establishment of an advisory Council of State and a Constitutional Tribunal, with jurisdiction over issues of consti-tutionality. The President's right to veto constitutional amend-ments was removed. The changes were regarded as significantly reducing the executive power of the President, although main-taining a semi-presidential system pending the referendum.

On 16 July 2003, while de Menezes was in Nigeria, Maj. Fernando Pereira 'Cobo', together with Sabino dos Santos and Alércio Costa, the leaders of a small political party, the Frente Democrata Cristã (FDC), took power in a bloodless coup. They formed a Junta Militar de Salvação Nacional and detained government ministers. The coup was condemned by the inter-national community, which demanded a return to civilian rule. Following successful regional mediation efforts, co-ordinated by Rodolphe Adada, the Republic of the Congo's Minister of Foreign Affairs, Co-operation and Francophone Affairs, on 22 July de Menezes returned to São Tomé. On the same day de Menezes, Pereira and Adada signed a 'memorandum of understanding', which provided for the restoration of de Menezes to the presi-dency, an amnesty for the coup leaders, a more transparent system of government finance, and the formation of a new Government. In accordance with the conditions of the memo-randum, Prime Minister das Neves resigned. She was subse-quently reappointed by de Menezes to head a new Government of National Unity, comprising representatives of the MLSTP—PSD, the MDFM and the ADI. Vera Cruz was appointed to the increasingly significant post of Minister of Natural Resources and the Environment.

In March 2004 tension increased between das Neves and de Menezes. Das Neves had repeatedly requested the dismissal of Vera Cruz and of Mateus Rita, the Minister of Foreign Affairs and Co-operation, claiming that she had not been appropriately consulted by either minister on government decisions. The sub-sequent resignations of Rita and Vera Cruz—both members of the MDFM—prompted the remaining two MDFM ministers, responsible for health and justice, to resign in protest. Agree-ments that Vera Cruz had signed with Canadian and South African mining companies were subsequently annulled. Later that month members of the ADI were appointed to head the ministries of health and of natural resources and the environ-ment, while Elsa Pinto of the MLSTP—PSD became Minister of Justice, State Reform and Public Administration, and an inde-pendent, Ovídio Manuel Barbossa Pequeno, was appointed Min-ister of Foreign Affairs and Co-operation.

In early September 2004 a report issued by the Auditor-General, Adelino Pereira, accused the das Neves Government of the embezzlement of funds provided by foreign donors and also revealed a series of financial irregularities during 2001–04, including illicit transfers of funds to the Ministry of Finance. Following requests by the MDFM and UK (the latter resigned from the Government in mid-September) for the removal of the das Neves Government, President de Menezes held a series of meetings with the main political parties in an attempt to estab-lish a consensus. Das Neves and her Council of Ministers were dismissed in September, and Damião Vaz de Almeida, hitherto Minister of Labour, Employment and Security and Vice-President of the MLSTP—PSD, was asked to form a new admin-istration. The new 14-member Government was a coalition of the MLSTP—PSD, the ADI and independents, and comprised six members of the previous administration.

In September 2004 Diógenes Moniz, the former Director of the Gabinete de Gestão das Ajudas (GGA—a department attached to the Ministry of Trade, Industry and Tourism responsible for the administration of food aid counterpart funds) was arrested on charges of embezzlement. In October das Neves was among a number of former ministers questioned by the Public Prosecutor about their involvement with the GGA.

In February 2005 the Assembleia voted to remove parliamentary immunity from the former Prime Minister, Pósser da Costa, in order that he be questioned regarding an alleged assault on Pereira in November 2004. (Pósser da Costa received a suspended sentence in March 2005.) A further four members of the Assembleia, including das Neves, also had their immunity lifted, thus providing for the possibility of them being tried in connection with the GGA case. In May das Neves and Arzemiro dos Prazeres, a former Minister of Trade, Industry and Tourism, were charged with embezzlement.

In April 2005 trade unions representing public sector workers demanded a significant increase in the minimum salaries of their members. The Government, however, citing budgetary constraints, was unable to accede to the unions' demands and in late May the unions commenced a five-day general strike. Following declarations by de Menezes that the Government was responsible for the action, Prime Minister Vaz de Almeida abruptly resigned, accusing the President of a lack of institutional solidarity with the Government. On 9 June a new MLSTP—PSD Council of Ministers, led by Maria do Carmo Silveira, hitherto the Governor of the central bank, took office, and in late July the Assembleia Nacional approved the new Government's budget and a preliminary agreement on a pay rise for public sector workers was reached. Relations between de Menezes and the Government remained strained, however.

Voting in the legislative elections began as scheduled on 26 March 2006; however, owing to boycotts and protests against continuing poor living conditions, voting at 26 polling stations was rescheduled for 2 April when it proceeded without incident. According to results released by the Constitutional Court on 18 April, the renewed MDFM-PCD alliance won 23 seats in the Assembleia Nacional, the MLSTP—PSD took 20 and the ADI 11, while a newly formed party, the Novo Rumo, secured the remaining seat. Vera Cruz (who remained Secretary-General of the MDFM), was subsequently appointed Prime Minister. The new Government took office on 21 April.

De Menezes re-elected

De Menezes was re-elected to the presidency on 30 July 2006, after securing 60.6% of the votes cast in a presidential election. His nearest rival, Patrice Emery Trovoada, of the ADI, received 38.8%. International observers deemed the election, at which voter turn-out was 64.9%, to have been transparent and fair. In late August, at the first local elections to be held on the islands since 1992, the MDFM-PCD alliance won six of the seven constituencies on São Tomé and secured an absolute majority in five of the six local assemblies. Supported by the ruling MDFM-PCD, the União para a Mudança e Progresso do Príncipe (UMPP) won all seven seats in the Assembleia Regional on Príncipe.

In February 2007 the MLSTP—PSD elected Joaquim Rafael Branco as party President. Prime Minister Vera Cruz was re-elected Secretary-General of the MDFM at a convention in May; at the same time President de Menezes was elected Chairman of that party, despite a provision in the Constitution preventing the Head of State from accepting other public roles. De Menezes stated that he would not assume the role publicly while he remained President.

Vera Cruz announced his resignation as Prime Minister on 7 February 2008, after the Assembleia Nacional failed to approve his Government's budget for 2008. He was replaced by Patrice Emery Trovoada, who was sworn in on 14 February. Trovoada's ADI had agreed to form a coalition government with the MDFM-PCD on the condition that his party was awarded, *inter alia*, the premiership and the natural resources and environment portfolio. Trovoada named a Council of Ministers, which included Raúl Cravid as Minister of Planning and Finance.

Although a revised national budget for 2008 was eventually approved by the Assembleia Nacional, in May the MLSTP—PSD presented a motion of no confidence in Trovoada's administration. The motion was adopted with the support of members of the PCD, who were critical of Trovoada, and the Government was dissolved. Following several weeks of negotiations, in late June Branco was sworn in as Prime Minister at the head of a new Council of Ministers (comprising members of the MLSTP—PSD, the PCD and the MDFM), in which Carlos Tiny assumed respon-

sibility for the foreign affairs, co-operation and communities portfolio, Elsa Pinto became the country's first female defence minister, and Cravid was appointed Minister of the Interior, Territorial Administration and Civil Protection. Minister of Natural Resources, Energy and the Environment Agostinho Rita was dismissed in October and was replaced by Carlos Fernandes Marques. After a series of electricity outages during late 2008, believed to be the result of a power generating deficit, Marques resigned in November, citing health concerns. Marques was succeeded by Cristina Dias, hitherto a senior official at the Agência Nacional do Petróleo de São Tomé e Príncipe.

An attempted coup was staged in February 2009, believed to have been led by a group of South African former mercenaries. It was subsequently announced that a number of the group had been detained, including Alércio Costa of the FDC. A trial commenced in September, and in November Costa was sentenced to five years' imprisonment; however, in January 2010 he received a presidential pardon and was released.

In December 2009 de Menezes was re-elected as President of the MDFM, prior to forthcoming legislative elections (which were subsequently postponed from February 2010 until August). In January de Menezes withdrew the four members of the MDFM who held government portfolios from the Council of Ministers, following criticism by the other parties represented in the coalition at his continued presidency of the MDFM while he remained national President. In the new Government formed by Prime Minister Branco, Pinto (of the MLSTP—PSD), assumed responsibility for the justice and parliamentary affairs portfolio in addition to that of defence, while the Minister of Agriculture, Rural Development and Fishing, Xavier Mendes (PCD), took on the natural resources and energy portfolio. An additional PCD member, Carlos Gomes, was appointed Minister of Labour, Solidarity and Family, while an independent, António Paquete, became Minister of the Interior, Territorial Administration and Civil Protection. Two days later, de Menezes unexpectedly retracted his acceptance of the MDFM leadership, but denied that his decision had been influenced by political pressure.

In local elections conducted on 25 July 2010 (originally scheduled for August 2009 but postponed owing to a lack of funding), the MLSTP—PSD obtained a majority in the four district councils of Lobata, Lembá, Cantagolo and Caué, while the ADI gained a majority in the two principal district councils of Agua Grande (with the capital São Tomé) and Mé-Zochi. The UMPP, led by José Cardoso Cassandra, won all seven seats of the Assembleia Regional of Príncipe. The ADI, with 42.2% of total votes cast and 26 seats, secured the greatest representation in the legislative elections on 1 August 2010 (but failed to obtain an absolute majority in the Assembleia Nacional). The MLSTP—PSD, with 32.1% of the votes, won 21 seats, while the PCD secured 13.6% and seven seats. The MDFM received only 7.1% of the votes and one seat, compared with 12 seats in the previous legislative elections. Trovoada was re-appointed Prime Minister on 10 August. On 14 August de Menezes approved the installation of a new minority Government, which included a number of independents in addition to ADI members.

Recent developments: the 2011 presidential election

A presidential election was held on 17 July 2011 to determine the successor to de Menezes, who, under the terms of the Constitution, was ineligible to stand for a third term in office. Former President Pinto da Costa, contesting the poll as an independent, secured 35.8% of the votes cast, while former Prime Ministers Evaristo Carvalho (representing the ADI) and Maria das Neves (running as an independent) won 21.8% and 14.0%, respectively. Pinto da Costa defeated Carvalho in the second round run-off vote on 7 August, receiving 52.9% of the ballot, and was inaugurated as President on 3 September. The rate of participation by the electorate was recorded at 68.4% in the first round and 74.1% in the second round. On assuming power, the new President pledged to address the high levels of corruption and poverty within the country, although some commentators questioned Pinto da Costa's democratic credentials, citing the autocratic nature of his previous presidency.

Anti-government demonstrations were organized in Príncipe during December 2011, in protest against the rising cost of living, inadequate power supplies and the failure of the central Government to approve a US $50m. tourism investment agreement, which had been signed by the Principean authorities and a South African company earlier in the year. Some demonstrators appealed for Principean independence and the national flag outside the regional assembly building was burned, prompting condemnation from the central Government. The Santomean authorities also expressed reservations about the tourism deal, arguing that the Príncipean administration did not have the authority to sign such an agreement and that implementation of the project would violate the terms of an existing arrangement (negotiated by the central Government) concerning an oil palm development. Inter-island relations were further strained by allegations that the authorities in São Tomé had reneged on earlier promises to invest in upgrading Príncipe's infrastructure. Nevertheless, following talks between Trovoada and Cassandra, the central Government approved the tourism project in early 2012.

In December 2011 PCD deputy Amândio Pinheiro, with the approval of the President of the Assembleia Nacional (Carvalho of the ADI), resigned from the opposition party and re-registered as an independent, thereby potentially allowing the ADI to form an absolute majority in the legislature. However, new regulations preventing elected representatives from changing party allegiance had recently come into force, and the PCD disputed the legality of Pinheiro's move. A constitutional crisis developed in February 2012, after the PCD (along with the MLSTP—PSD) refused to recognize Pinheiro as a member of the Assembleia Nacional, arguing that he had effectively resigned his mandate. The PCD appointed a replacement deputy, leaving the legislature with 56 members rather than the 55 stipulated in the Constitution. This impasse was resolved in August, when the legislature voted to terminate Pinheiro's mandate. Pinheiro immediately filed an appeal with the Supreme Court, arguing that the Assembleia had acted in violation of the Constitution. The case was pending in early 2013.

Jorge Amado was elected as MLSTP—PSD President in June 2012, and in the following month the party formed a political alliance with the PCD and the MDFM, leaving the now-unified opposition with a legislative majority. Later in July the MLSTP—PSD submitted a motion of censure against the Government, citing the administration's failure to address the rising cost of living and other alleged transgressions. However, this was promptly rejected by Carvalho, who regarded the motion as groundless. Nevertheless, in November the MLSTP—PSD, the PCD and the MDFM, dissatisfied with Trovoada's budget for 2013, introduced a further motion of censure, and later that month elected the MLSTP—PSD's Alcino Pinto to serve as the new President of the Assembleia Nacional. The opposition alliance approved the motion shortly thereafter, and in early December 2012 the President duly ordered the dissolution of the Government. The ADI, which had marshalled demonstrations to demand the organization of fresh elections, withdrew from negotiations with Pinto da Costa on the formation of a new government, obliging him to open discussions with the opposition. Former Prime Minister Dr Gabriel Arcanjo Ferreira da Costa (of the MDFM) was consequently named as the new premier, and his administration, consisting of members of the erstwhile opposition parties, was inaugurated on 12 December. The ADI refused to acknowledge the new Government, although in late December the Constitutional Court ruled that the legislature had acted lawfully.

Foreign Affairs

Regional relations

São Tomé and Príncipe has important trade links with the nearby mainland states of Angola, Gabon, Cameroon and Equatorial Guinea. In November 1999 São Tomé and Príncipe was a founder of the seven-member Gulf of Guinea Commission to assist in solving inter-state conflicts within the region.

In 2000 São Tomé and Príncipe and Nigeria agreed to establish a joint development zone (JDZ) for the exploitation of petroleum resources. A further accord, on the joint exploitation of a variety of mineral resources, was signed in February 2001; Nigeria was to receive 60% of revenues and São Tomé and Príncipe 40%. In January 2002 the Presidents of both countries inaugurated a development authority to oversee the affairs of the JDZ. Disagreements developed during 2002, however, over Nigeria's commitment to provide São Tomé and Príncipe with 60,000 barrels of petroleum per day (reduced to 40,000 in September, and to 10,000 in October) and the relative lack of Santomean representation in the development authority. In November de Menezes refused to continue with the proposed sale of oil blocks until the issue was resolved; he was supported in this by a report from the World Bank, which suggested that the division of profits was unfair to São Tomé and Príncipe. By 2003, however, issues had been resolved sufficiently for bids for exploration rights in

the first nine of the 25 blocks in the JDZ to open in October. In December 2009 a bilateral military commission was established jointly by the Nigerian and Santomean authorities to provide, inter alia, security for oil companies operating within the JDZ.

Other external relations

São Tomé and Príncipe maintains cordial relations with the other former Portuguese African colonies and with Portugal. In July 1996 São Tomé and Príncipe was among the five lusophone African countries that, together with Portugal and Brazil, formed the Comunidade dos Países de Língua Portuguesa (CPLP, see p. 475), a Portuguese-speaking commonwealth seeking to achieve collective benefits from co-operation in technical, cultural and social matters. São Tomé and Príncipe was a signatory to the 'Luanda Declaration' in November 2011, which pledged greater co-operation between the CPLP member states in areas such as security, crime prevention and immigration.

São Tomé and Príncipe has maintained diplomatic relations with Taiwan since 1997. The Taiwanese Government provides the islands with annual funding of approximately US $15m.

CONSTITUTION AND GOVERNMENT

Under the Constitution adopted on 4 March 2003, legislative power is vested in the Assembleia Nacional, which comprises 55 members, elected by universal adult suffrage for a term of four years. No limit is placed on the number of political parties permitted to operate. Executive power is vested in the President of the Republic, who is Head of State, and who governs with the assistance of an appointed Council of Ministers, led by the Prime Minister. The Council of State acts as an advisory body to the President, who is elected by universal suffrage for a term of five years. The President's tenure of office is limited to two successive terms. The Prime Minister, who is appointed by the President, is, in theory, nominated by the deputies of the Assembleia Nacional. Judicial power is exercised by the Supreme Court and all other competent tribunals and courts. The Supreme Court is the supreme judicial authority and is accountable only to the Assembleia Nacional. Its members are appointed by the Assembleia Nacional. The right to a defence is guaranteed.

In 1994 the Assembleia Nacional granted political and administrative autonomy to the island of Príncipe. Legislation was adopted establishing a seven-member Assembleia Regional and a five-member regional government; both are accountable to the Government of São Tomé and Príncipe.

REGIONAL AND INTERNATIONAL CO-OPERATION

São Tomé and Príncipe is a member of the African Union (see p. 191) and of the Communauté Economique des Etats de l'Afrique Centrale (see p. 460).

São Tomé and Príncipe became a member of the UN in 1975 and has observer status at the World Trade Organization (WTO, see p. 444). São Tomé and Príncipe participates in the Group of 77 (G77, see p. 461) developing countries and is a member of the International Cocoa Organization (see p. 456).

ECONOMIC AFFAIRS

In 2011, according to estimates by the World Bank, São Tomé and Príncipe's gross national product (GNI), measured at average 2009–11 prices, was US $229m., equivalent to $1,360 per head (or $2,080 per head on an international purchasing-power parity basis). During 2002–11, it was estimated, the population increased at an average annual rate of 1.6%, while gross domestic product (GDP) per head, in real terms, grew at an average annual rate of 0.8% in 1995–2005. Overall GDP increased, in real terms, at an average annual rate of 5.5% in 2002–11; growth of 4.9% was recorded in 2011.

Agriculture (including fishing) contributed an estimated 19.6% of GDP in 2011, and accounted for an estimated 54.8% of the labour force in mid-2013, according to FAO estimates. The principal cash crop is cocoa, which accounted for 89.8% of export earnings in 2011. Secondary cash crops include coconuts and coffee. Staple crops for local consumption include bananas, taro and cassava. Agricultural production is principally concentrated on export commodities, although smallholder agriculture has become increasingly important. An agricultural policy charter, the Carta de Política e Desenvolvimento Rural, which was introduced in 2000, aimed to emphasize private sector involvement and diversification into areas such as ylang ylang, pepper, vanilla, fruits, vegetables and flowers. Fishing is also a significant activity. The sale of fishing licences to foreign fleets is an important source of income. Agricultural GDP increased at an average annual rate of 2.6% in 2002–11, while growth in the sector was 2.0% in 2011.

Industry (including mining, manufacturing, construction and power) contributed an estimated 15.8% of GDP in 2011, and employed 17.0% of the employed population in 2001. Industrial GDP increased by an average of 4.3% per year in 2002–11; growth in 2011 was 3.6%.

In 2011 mining contributed an estimated 0.6% of GDP. There are no mineral resources on the islands, but offshore prospecting for hydrocarbons resulted in the discovery of significant quantities of petroleum in 1998, including an estimated 4,000m. barrels in the joint development zone (JDZ) with Nigeria, as well as higher-risk resources in São Tomé's exclusive economic zone (EEZ). In February 2005 a consortium led by ChevronTexaco was awarded a concession to exploit the first section of the JDZ. That company signed a production-sharing agreement with the joint development authority responsible for overseeing activities in the JDZ in 2005 and began drilling activities in January 2006. Inquiries into the subsequent award of a further five blocks to the Environmental Remedial Holding Corp (ERHC), resulted in the Attorney-General concluding that the procedures used in selecting petroleum companies were flawed. He recommended a restructuring of the procedures for future bidding rounds that would conform to international standards. The Attorney-General's report also demanded the re-examination of ERHC's preferential rights for Blocks 2–6 within the JDZ. The GDP of the mining sector increased by an average of 5.5% per year in 2002–11; the sector grew by 3.0% in 2011.

The manufacturing sector consists solely of small processing factories, producing soap, soft drinks, textiles and beer. Manufacturing contributed an estimated 6.4% of GDP in 2011. Manufacturing GDP increased at an average annual rate of 2.9% in 2002–11; the sector grew by 3.0% in 2011.

The construction sector contributed 7.2% of GDP in 2011 and employed 10.3% of the employed population in 2001. The GDP of the construction sector increased by 5.3% during 2002–11; sectoral GDP increased by 4.5% in 2011.

In 2000 some 74% of electricity generation was derived from thermal sources and 26% from hydroelectric sources. Imports of petroleum products comprised 15.3% of the value of merchandise imports in 2011. In 2006 it was announced that a thermal power plant, which would increase São Tomé's energy production by 70%, was to be built by a Nigerian company.

The services sector contributed an estimated 64.5% of GDP in 2011, and engaged 51.5% of the employed population in 2001. The GDP of the services sector increased by an average of 4.8% per year in 2002–11; growth in 2011 was 4.5%.

In 2011 São Tomé and Príncipe recorded a merchandise trade deficit of US $104.74m. and a deficit of $107.94m. on the current account of the balance of payments. In 2011 the principal source of imports was Portugal (providing 58.9% of total imports); the other major supplier was Angola. The principal market for exports in that year was the Netherlands (taking 37.3% of the total); other significant purchasers were Belgium and Portugal.

The principal export in 2011 was cocoa. The principal imports in that year were foodstuffs, machinery, petroleum and petroleum products, transport equipment, beverages and construction materials.

In 2011 there was an estimated budgetary deficit of 523,000m. dobras. São Tomé's general government gross debt was 3,540,703m. dobras in 2010, equivalent to 80.9% of GDP. São Tomé's total external debt was US $170m. at the end of 2010, of which $145m. was public and publicly guaranteed debt. In that year, the cost of servicing long-term public and publicly guaranteed debt and repayments to the IMF was equivalent to 6.5% of the value of exports of goods, services and income (excluding workers' remittances). Annual inflation averaged 16.1% in 2002–11. Consumer prices increased by an average 12.9% in 2010 and by 9.2% in 2011. According to official figures, 14.2% of the labour force were unemployed in 2006.

São Tomé and Príncipe's economy has traditionally been dominated by cocoa production and is therefore vulnerable to adverse weather conditions and to fluctuations in international prices for that commodity. While the discovery of petroleum in Santomean waters was a welcome development, concerns were raised by international institutions regarding the lack of transparency and accountability in the petroleum sector. Thus, in mid-2004 the Government agreed to establish a National Petroleum Fund into which all petroleum earnings were to be deposited, and which was to be subject to annual independent audits. Despite ongoing investigations into the misappropriation of donor funds, São Tomé and Príncipe continued to be a major recipient of external assistance. The rate of GDP growth slowed in 2009, largely owing to a sharp decline in foreign direct investment as a result of the global economic crisis. Although foreign investment continued to fall in 2010, an increase in externally financed public investment projects stimulated economic activity, and the IMF reported real GDP growth of 4.5% in that year. Economic expansion accelerated in 2011 to 4.9%, with rising exports and the recovering construction, agricultural and tourism industries contributing to this growth, although the high inflation rate (17% at mid-2011) proved a concern. In July 2012 the IMF authorized a three-year Extended Credit Facility arrangement, valued at US $3.9m., to support the Government's economic plans. Real GDP growth moderated to 4.0% in 2012 due to the weakness of the global economy, although inflation had declined to 10.5% by the end of that year. The IMF forecast that real GDP would increase by 4.5% in 2013, but warned that economic uncertainty in Europe had the potential to disrupt inflows of aid, investment and remittances. Nevertheless, the medium-term outlook appeared positive, primarily because of the announcement in November 2011 of a significant petroleum discovery in the JDZ. It was anticipated that production would commence by 2015.

PUBLIC HOLIDAYS

2014: 1 January (New Year), 3 February (Martyrs' Day), 1 May (Labour Day), 12 July (Independence Day), 6 September (Armed Forces Day), 30 September (Agricultural Reform Day), 21 December (São Tomé Day), 25 December (Christmas Day).

Statistical Survey

Source (unless otherwise stated): Instituto Nacional de Estatística, CP 256, São Tomé; tel. 221982; internet www.ine.st.

AREA AND POPULATION

Area: 1,001 sq km (386.5 sq miles); São Tomé 859 sq km (331.7 sq miles), Príncipe 142 sq km (54.8 sq miles).

Population: 137,599 at census of September 2001; 187,356 (males 93,735, females 93,621) at census of May 2012 (preliminary). *Mid-2013* (UN estimate): 175,380 (Source: UN, *World Population Prospects: The 2010 Revision*). Note: UN estimate not revised to take account of results of 2012 census.

Density (mid-2013): 175.2 per sq km.

Population by Age and Sex (UN estimates at mid-2013): *0–14:* 68,441 (males 34,569, females 33,872); *15–64:* 100,632 (males 49,680, females 50,952); *65 and over:* 6,307 (males 2,669, females 3,638); *Total* 175,380 (males 86,918, females 88,462) (Source: UN, *World Population Prospects: The 2010 Revision*).

Population by District (at 2012 census, preliminary): Água-Grande 73,091, Mé-Zochi 46,265, Cantagolo 18,194, Caué 6,887, Lembá 15,370, Lobata 20,007, Pagué (Príncipe) 7,542; *Total* 187,356.

Principal Towns (population at 2012 census, preliminary): São Tomé (capital) 69,581; Trindade 19,659; Neves 12,205; Santana 11,551; Bombom 10,028; Santo Amaro 7,842; Santo Antônio 7,542.

Births, Marriages and Deaths (2006): Registered live births 5,072 (birth rate 33.40 per 1,000); Registered marriages 171 (marriage rate 1.2 per 1,000) (2003); Registered deaths 1,111 (death rate 7.3 per 1,000). *2011:* Birth rate 30.7 per 1,000; Death rate 7.6 per 1,000 (Source: African Development Bank).

Life Expectancy (years at birth): 64.6 (males 63.2; females 66.1) in 2011. (Source: World Bank, World Development Indicators database).

Economically Active Population (census of 2001): Agriculture and fishing 13,518; Industry, electricity, gas and water 2,893; Public works and civil construction 4,403; Trade, restaurants and hotels 8,787; Transport, storage and communications 792; Public administration 3,307; Health 776; Education 1,373; Other activities 7,088; *Total employed* 42,937. *2006:* Total employed 53,725 (males 28,729, females 24,996); Unemployed 8,894 (males 4,276, females 4,618); Total labour force 62,619 (males 33,005, females 29,614). *Mid-2013* ('000, estimates): Agriculture, etc. 34; Total labour force 62 (Source: FAO).

HEALTH AND WELFARE

Key Indicators

Total Fertility Rate (children per woman, 2010): 3.7.

Under-5 Mortality Rate (per 1,000 live births, 2010): 80.

Physicians (per 1,000 head, 2004): 0.5.

Hospital Beds (per 1,000 head, 2006): 3.2.

Health Expenditure (2009): US $ per head (PPP): 144.

Health Expenditure (2009): % of GDP: 7.2.

Health Expenditure (2009): public (% of total): 40.1.

Access to Water (% of persons, 2010): 89.

Access to Sanitation (% of persons, 2010): 26.

Total Carbon Dioxide Emissions ('000 metric tons, 2008): 128.3.

Carbon Dioxide Emissions Per Head (metric tons, 2008): 0.8.

Human Development Index (2011): ranking: 144.

Human Development Index (2011): value: 0.509.

For sources and definitions, see explanatory note on p. vi.

AGRICULTURE, ETC.

Principal Crops (metric tons, 2011, FAO estimates): Bananas 34,100; Maize 3,900; Cassava (Manioc) 8,100; Taro 26,000; Yams 1,850; Cocoa beans 2,096; Coconuts 34,842; Oil palm fruit 16,100; Coffee, green 36; Cinnamon 51.

Livestock (head, 2011, FAO estimates): Cattle 5,100; Sheep 3,200; Goats 5,600; Pigs 2,900; Chickens 440,000.

Livestock Products (metric tons, 2011, FAO estimates): Cattle meat 137; Pig meat 115; Sheep meat 7; Goat meat 21; Chicken meat 728; Hen eggs 585; Cows' milk 175.

Forestry ('000 cubic metres, 2011): Roundwood removals 121.5; Sawnwood production 5.4.

Fishing (metric tons, live weight of capture, 2010, FAO estimates): Total catch 4,650 (Croakers and drums 170; Pandoras 200; Threadfins and tasselfishes 130; Wahoo 241; Little tunny 193; Atlantic sailfish 121; Flyingfishes 830; Jacks and crevalles 180; Sharks, rays and skates 102).

Source: FAO.

INDUSTRY

Production (metric tons, unless otherwise indicated): Bread and biscuits 3,768 (1995); Soap 261.1 (1995); Beer (litres) 529,400 (1995); Coconut oil 280 (2011, FAO estimate); Palm oil 3,300 (2011, FAO estimate); Electric energy (million kWh) 34 (2009). Sources: IMF, *Democratic Republic of São Tomé and Príncipe: Selected Issues and Statistical Appendix* (September 1998, February 2002, April 2004 and September 2006); UN Industrial Commodity Statistics Database; FAO.

FINANCE

Currency and Exchange Rates: 100 cêntimos = 1 dobra (Db). *Sterling, Dollar and Euro Equivalents* (31 December 2012): £1 sterling = 29,302.0 dobras; US $1 = 18,569.0 dobras; €1 = 24,500.0 dobras; 100,000 dobras = £3.41 = $5.39 = €4.08. *Average Exchange Rate* (dobras per US $): 18,498.6 in 2010; 17,622.9 in 2011; 19,058.3 in 2012.

Budget ('000 million dobras, 2010): *Revenue:* Taxation 617; Non-tax revenue 60; Grants 739; Total 1,417. *Expenditure:* Current expenditure 737 (Personnel costs 309, Goods and services 191, Interest on external debt 16, Transfers 192, Other current expenditure 29); Capital expenditure 1,066; HIPC-related social expenditure 21; Total 1,824. *2011* (estimates): Total revenue and grants 1,622; Total expenditure 2,145. Source: IMF, *Democratic Republic of São Tomé and Príncipe: Request for a Three-Year Arrangement Under the Extended Credit Facility* (August 2012).

International Reserves (US $ million at 31 December 2011): IMF special drawing rights 5.78; Foreign exchange 45.69; *Total* 51.47. Source: IMF, *International Financial Statistics*.

Money Supply ('000 million dobras at 31 December 2011): Currency outside depository corporations 177.1; Transferable deposits 918.8; Other deposits 435.6; *Broad money* 1,531.5. Source: IMF, *International Financial Statistics*.

Cost of Living (Consumer Price Index; base: 2000 = 100): 372.9 in 2009; 421.0 in 2010; 459.6 in 2011. Source: African Development Bank.

Gross Domestic Product ('000 million dobras at current prices): 3,185 in 2009; 3,719 in 2010; 4,376 in 2011.

Expenditure on the Gross Domestic Product ('000 million dobras at current prices, 2009, provisional): Government final consumption expenditure 446.9; Private final consumption expenditure 3,761.6; Gross capital formation 589.4; *Total domestic expenditure* 4,797.9; Exports of goods and services 288.5; *Less* Imports of goods and services 1,876.9; *GDP in purchasers' values* 3,209.5. Source: African Development Bank.

Gross Domestic Product by Economic Activity ('000 million dobras at current prices, 2011): Agriculture 865.5; Mining and quarrying 26.1; Manufacturing 280.5; Electricity, gas and water 74.3; Construction 315.9; Trade 1,051.8; Restaurants and hotels 63.4; Finance, insurance and real estate 721.0; Transport and communications 525.1; Public administration and defence 150.6; Other services 331.5; *Sub-total* 4,405.8; *Less* Financial intermediation services indirectly measured (FISIM) 477.7; *GDP at factor cost* 3,928.1; Taxes on products, less subsidies 447.5; *GDP at market prices* 4,375.5.

Balance of Payments (US $ million, 2011): Exports of goods 10.94; Imports of goods −115.68; *Balance on goods* −104.74; Exports of services 18.40; Imports of services −31.40; *Balance on goods and services* −117.74; Primary income received 1.87; Primary income paid −2.29; *Balance of goods, services and primary income* −118.16; Secondary income received 14.58; Secondary income paid −4.36; *Current balance* −107.94; Capital account (net) 46.48; Direct investment assets −0.30; Direct investment liabilities 35.00; Other investment assets 9.80; Other investment liabilities 22.56; Net errors and omissions −10.29; *Reserves and related items* −4.69. Source: IMF, *International Financial Statistics*.

EXTERNAL TRADE

Principal Commodities (US $ million, 2011): *Imports f.o.b.:* Foodstuffs 30.3; Beverages 11.6; Petroleum and petroleum products 20.2; Machinery 21.7; Transport equipment 12.0; Construction materials 8.7; Total (incl. others) 131.6. *Exports f.o.b.:* Cocoa 5.3; Total (incl. others) 5.9.

Principal Trading Partners (US $ million, 2011): *Imports c.i.f.:* Angola 12.6; Belgium 2.3; China, People's Republic 2.6; France 3.2; Gabon 2.7; Japan 3.3; Portugal 77.5; Spain 1.6; Thailand 1.8; Total (incl. others) 131.6. *Exports f.o.b.:* Angola 0.1; Belgium 1.7; France 0.1; Netherlands 2.2; Portugal 0.8; Spain 0.1; Total (incl. others) 5.9. Source: Banco Central de São Tomé e Príncipe.

TRANSPORT

Road Traffic (registered vehicles, 2007, estimates): Passenger cars 305; Lorries and vans 37. Source: IRF, *World Road Statistics*.

Shipping: *International Freight Traffic* (estimates, metric tons, 1992): Goods loaded 16,000; Goods unloaded 45,000. *Flag Registered Fleet* (at 31 December 2012): Number of vessels 31; Total displacement 42,920 grt (Source: Lloyd's List Intelligence—www.lloydslistintelligence.com).

Civil Aviation (traffic on scheduled services, 2009): Kilometres flown (million) 0.1; Passengers carried ('000) 51; Passenger-km (million) 20; Total ton-km (million) 2. Source: UN, *Statistical Yearbook*.

TOURISM

Foreign Tourist Arrivals: 14,456 in 2008; 15,200 in 2009 (rounded figure); 7,963 in 2010.

Arrivals by Country of Residence (2010): Angola 1,105; Brazil 139; Cape Verde 251; France 514; Gabon 144; Germany 193; Nigeria 198; Portugal 3,578; Spain 149; United Kingdom 229; USA 280; Total (incl. others) 7,963.

Tourism Receipts (US $ million, excl. passenger transport): 7.7 in 2008; 8.4 in 2009; 9.4 in 2010.

Source: World Tourism Organization.

COMMUNICATIONS MEDIA

Telephones ('000 main lines, 2011): 8.0 in use.

Mobile Cellular Telephones ('000 subscribers, 2011): 115.0.

Personal Computers: 6,000 (39.3 per 1,000 persons) in 2005.

Fixed Internet Subscribers (2011): 900.

Broadband Subscribers (2011): 700.

Source: International Telecommunication Union.

EDUCATION

Pre-primary (2010/11 unless otherwise indicated): 8,591 pupils (males 4,226, females 4,365); 330 teachers (2009/10).

Primary (2010/11): 35,250 pupils (males 18,045, females 17,205); 1,183 teachers.

Secondary (2010/11): 11,884 pupils (males 5,594, females 6,290); 601 teachers.

Tertiary (2009/10 unless otherwise indicated): 1 polytechnic (2000/01); 95 teachers; 766 pupils.

Source: UNESCO Institute for Statistics; *Carta Escolar de São Tomé e Príncipe,* Ministério de Educação de Portugal.

Pupil-teacher Ratio (primary education, UNESCO estimate): 29.8 in 2010/11. Source: UNESCO Institute for Statistics.

Adult Literacy Rate (UNESCO estimates): 89.2% (males 93.9; females 84.7) in 2010. Source: UNESCO Institute for Statistics.

Directory

The Government

HEAD OF STATE

President and Commander-in-Chief of the Armed Forces: Dr MANUEL PINTO DA COSTA (took office 3 September 2011).

COUNCIL OF MINISTERS
(May 2013)

The Government comprises members of the Movimento Democrático Força da Mudança (MDFM), the Movimento de Libertação de São Tomé e Príncipe—Partido Social Democrata (MLSTP—PSD), the Partido de Convergência Democrática (PCD) and an independent.

Prime Minister: Dr GABRIEL ARCANJO FERREIRA DA COSTA (MDFM).

Minister of Foreign Affairs, Co-operation and Communities: NATÁLIA PEDRO DA COSTA UMBELINA NETO (Ind.).

Minister of Defence and Internal Order: Col ÓSCAR AGUIAR SACRAMENTO E SOUSA (MDFM).

Minister of Justice, Public Administration and Parliamentary Affairs: EDITE RAMOS DA COSTA TENJUA (MLSTP—PSD).

Minister of Planning and Finance: HÉLIO SILVA VAZ DE ALMEIDA (MLSTP—PSD).

Minister of Trade, Industry and Tourism: DEMÓSTENES VASCONCELOS PIRES DOS SANTOS (PCD).

Minister of Public Works, Natural Resources and the Environment: OSVALDO CRAVID VIEGAS D'ABREU (MLSTP—PSD).

Minister of Health and Social Affairs: LEONEL PINTO DE ASSUNÇÃO PONTES (MDFM).

Minister of Education, Culture and Vocational Training: JORGE LOPES BOM JESUS (MLSTP—PSD).

Minister of Youth and Sports: ALBERTINO FRANCISCO BOA MORTE (PCD).

Provisional Government of the Autonomous Region of Príncipe
(May 2013)

President: JOSÉ CARDOSO CASSANDRA.

Secretary for Social and Cultural Affairs: FELÍCIA FONSECA DE OLIVEIRA E SILVA.

Secretary for Economic and Financial Affairs: HÉLIO LAVRES.

Secretary for Infrastructure and the Environment: TIAGO ROSAMONTE.

Secretary for Political, Organizational and Institutional Affairs: (vacant).

MINISTRIES

Office of the President: Palácio Presidêncial, São Tomé; internet www.presidencia.st.

Office of the Prime Minister: Rua do Município, CP 302, São Tomé; tel. 223913; fax 224679; e-mail gpm@cstome.net.

Ministry of Defence and Public Security: Av. 12 de Julho, CP 427, São Tomé; tel. 222041; e-mail midefesa@cstome.net.

Ministry of Education, Culture and Vocational Training: Rua Misericórdia, CP 41, São Tomé; tel. 222861; fax 221466; e-mail mineducal@cstome.net.

Ministry of Finance and International Co-operation: São Tomé.

Ministry of Foreign Affairs and Communities: Av. 12 de Julho, CP 111, São Tomé; tel. 222309; fax 223237; e-mail minecoop@cstome.net; internet www.mnecc.gov.st.

Ministry of Health and Social Affairs: Av. Patrice Lumumba, CP 23, São Tomé; tel. 241200; fax 221306; e-mail msaude@cstome.net; internet saude.gov-stp.net.

Ministry of Justice and State Reform: Av. 12 de Julho, CP 4, São Tomé; tel. 222318; fax 222256; e-mail emilioma@cstome.net.

Ministry of Parliamentary Affairs and Decentralization: São Tomé.

Ministry of Planning and Development: Largo Alfândega, CP 168, São Tomé; tel. 224173; fax 222683; e-mail mpfc@cstome.net.

Ministry of Public Works and Natural Resources: São Tomé.

Ministry of Youth and Sports: Rua Misericórdia, CP 41, São Tomé; tel. 222861; fax 221466.

President and Legislature

PRESIDENT

Presidential Election, First Round, 17 July 2011

Candidate	Votes	% of votes
Dr Manuel Pinto da Costa	20,960	35.82
Evaristo do Espírito Santo de Carvalho	12,767	21.82
Maria das Neves de Souza	8,208	14.03
Delfim Neves	8,127	13.89
Elsa Pinto	2,661	4.55
Aurélio Martins	2,431	4.15
Filinto Costa Alegre	2,420	4.14
Jorge Coelho	375	0.64
Helder Barros	369	0.63
Manuel de Deus Lima	204	0.35
Total	58,522	100.00

Presidential Election, Second Round, 7 August 2011

Candidate	Votes	% of votes
Dr Manuel Pinto da Costa	35,110	52.88
Evaristo do Espírito Santo de Carvalho	31,287	47.12
Total	66,397	100.00

ASSEMBLEIA NACIONAL

Assembleia Nacional: Palácio dos Congressos, CP 181, São Tomé; tel. 222986; fax 222835; e-mail romao.couto@parlamento.st; internet www.parlamento.st.

President: ALCINO MARTINHO DE BARROS PINTO.

General Election, 1 August 2010

Party	Seats
Acção Democrática Independente	26
Movimento de Libertação de São Tomé e Príncipe—Partido Social Democrata	21
Partido de Convergência Democrática	7
Movimento Democrático Força da Mudança	1
Total	55

Election Commission

Comissão Eleitoral Nacional (CEN): Av. Amílcar Cabral, São Tomé; tel. 225497; fax 224116; e-mail censtome@cstome.net; Pres. VICTOR CORREIA.

Political Organizations

Acção Democrática Independente (ADI): Av. Marginal 12 de Julho, Edif. C. Cassandra, São Tomé; tel. 222201; f. 1992; Pres. PATRICE TROVOADA.

Frente Democrata Cristã—Partido Social da Unidade (FDC—PSU): São Tomé; f. 1990; Pres. ALÉRCIO COSTA.

Movimento Democrático Força da Mudança (MDFM): São Tomé; f. 2001; Pres. FRADIQUE DE MENEZES; Sec.-Gen. RAUL CRAVID.

Movimento de Libertação de São Tomé e Príncipe—Partido Social Democrata (MLSTP—PSD): Estrada Riboque, Edif. Sede do MLSTP, São Tomé; tel. 222253; f. 1972 as MLSTP; adopted present name in 1990; sole legal party 1972–90; Pres. JORGE AMADO; Sec.-Gen. JOSÉ VIEGAS.

Novo Rumo: São Tomé; f. 2006 by citizens disaffected by current political parties; Leader JOÃO GOMES.

Partido de Coligação Democrática (CÓDÓ): São Tomé; f. 1990 as Partido Democrático de São Tomé e Príncipe—Coligação Democrática da Oposição; renamed as above June 1998; Leader MANUEL NEVES E SILVA.

Partido de Convergência Democrática (PCD): Av. Marginal 12 de Julho, CP 519, São Tomé; tel. and fax 223257; f. 1990 as Partido de Convergência—Grupo de Reflexão; formed alliance with MDFM to contest legislative elections in 2006; Pres. XAVIER MENDES; Sec.-Gen. DELFIM SANTIAGO DAS NEVES.

Partido Popular do Progresso (PPP): São Tomé; f. 1998; Leader FRANCISCO SILVA.

Partido de Renovação Democrática (PRD): São Tomé; tel. 903109; e-mail prd100@hotmail.com; f. 2001; Pres. ARMINDO GRAÇA.

Partido Social e Liberal (PSL): São Tomé; f. 2005; promotes devt and anti-corruption; Leader AGOSTINHO RITA.

Partido Social Renovado (PSR): São Tomé; f. 2004; Leader HAMILTON VAZ.

União para a Democracia e Desenvolvimento (UDD): São Tomé; f. 2005; Leader MANUEL DIOGO.

União Nacional para Democracia e Progresso (UNDP): São Tomé; f. 1998; Leader PAIXÃO LIMA.

The União para a Mudança e Progresso do Príncipe (UMPP), led by JOSÉ CARDOSO CASSANDRA, operates on the island of Príncipe and there is also a local civic group, O Renascimento de Água Grande, in the district of Água Grande, which includes the city of São Tomé.

Diplomatic Representation

EMBASSIES IN SÃO TOMÉ AND PRÍNCIPE

Angola: Av. Kwame Nkrumah 45, CP 133, São Tomé; tel. 222400; fax 221362; e-mail embrang@cstome.net; Ambassador ALFREDO EDUARDO MANUEL MINGAS.

Brazil: Av. Marginal de 12 de Julho 20, CP 217, São Tomé; tel. 226060; fax 226895; e-mail brasembsaotome@cstome.net; Ambassador JOSÉ CARLOS DE ARAÚJO LEITÃO.

Equatorial Guinea: Av. Kwame Nkrumah, São Tomé; tel. 225427; Ambassador ANTÓNIO EBADE AYINGONO.

Gabon: Rua Damão, CP 394, São Tomé; tel. 224434; fax 223531; e-mail ambagabon@cstome.net; Ambassador CORENTIN BERNARDIN MBOUROU HERVO AKENDENGUE.

Nigeria: Av. Kwame Nkrumah, CP 1000, São Tomé; tel. 225404; fax 225406; e-mail nigeria@cstome.net; Ambassador SUNDAY DOGONYARO OON.

Portugal: Av. Marginal de 12 de Julho, CP 173, São Tomé; tel. 221130; fax 221190; e-mail eporstp@cstome.net; Ambassador MARIA PAULA DA SILVA CEPEDA.

South Africa: Av. da Independencia, No. 7 Representanção da República da Africa de Sul, CP 555, São Tomé; tel. 227568; e-mail consuafricasul@cstome.net; Ambassador T. SHOPE-LINNEY.

Taiwan (Republic of China): Av. Marginal de 12 de Julho, CP 839, São Tomé; tel. 2228108; fax 2221376; e-mail taiwanstp@gmail.com; Ambassador JACK Y. T. CHENG.

Judicial System

Judicial power is exercised by the Supreme Court of Justice and the Courts of Primary Instance. The Supreme Court is the ultimate judicial authority. The Constitutional Court rules on election matters. There is also an Audit Court and tribunals of first instance.

Supremo Tribunal de Justiça (Supreme Court of Justice): Av. Marginal de 12 de Julho, CP 04, São Tomé; tel. 222615; fax 222329; e-mail info@stj.st; internet www.stj.st; Pres. SILVESTRE DA FONSECA LEITE.

Tribunal Constitucional (Constitutional Court): São Tomé.

Tribunal de Contas (Audit Court): São Tomé; Pres. JOSÉ ANTÓNIO DE MONTE CRISTO.

Attorney-General of the Republic: FREDERICO SAMBA VIEGAS D'ABREU.

Religion

According to the 2001 census more than 80% of the population are Christians, almost all of whom are Roman Catholics.

CHRISTIANITY

The Roman Catholic Church

São Tomé and Príncipe comprises a single diocese, directly responsible to the Holy See. An estimated 72% of the population are adherents. The bishop participates in the Episcopal Conference of Angola and São Tomé (based in Luanda, Angola).

Bishop of São Tomé and Príncipe: Rt Rev. MANUEL ANTÓNIO MENDES DOS SANTOS, Centro Diocesano, CP 104, Rua P. Pinto da Rocha 1, São Tomé; tel. 223455; fax 227348; e-mail diocese@cstome.net.

Other Churches

Igreja Adventista do 7° Dia (Seventh-Day Adventist Church): Rua Barão de Água Izé, São Tomé; tel. 2222270; e-mail sdastp@gmail.com; Pres. JOSÉ MARQUES.

Igreja Evangélica: Rua 3 de Fevereiro, São Tomé; tel. 221350.

Igreja Evangélica Assembléia de Deus: Rua 3 de Fevereiro, São Tomé; tel. and fax 222442; e-mail iead@cstome.net.

Igreja Maná: Av. Amílcar Cabral, São Tomé; tel. and fax 224654; e-mail imana@cstome.net.

Igreja do Nazareno: Vila Dolores, São Tomé; tel. 223943; e-mail nszst@cstome.net.

Igreja Nova Apostólica: CP 220, Vila Maria, São Tomé; tel. and fax 222797; e-mail j.cunha@ina-stp.org; internet ina-stp.org.

Igreja Universal do Reino de Deus: Travessa Imprensa, São Tomé; tel. 224047.

The Press

Correio da Semana: Av. Amílcar Cabral 382, São Tomé; tel. 225299; e-mail correiodasemana@cstome.net; f. 2005; weekly; Dir JUVENAL RODRIGUES; circ. 3,000.

Diário da República: Cooperativa de Artes Gráficas, Rua João Devs, CP 28, São Tomé; tel. 222661; internet dre.pt/stp; f. 1836; official gazette; Dir OSCAR FERREIRA.

Jornal Maravilha: São Tomé; tel. 911690; f. 2006; Dir NELSON SIGNO.

Jornal Tropical: Rua Padre Martinho Pinto da Rocha, São Tomé; tel. 923140; e-mail jornaltropical06@hotmail.com; internet www.jornaltropical.st; Dir OCTÁVIO SOARES.

O Parvo: CP 535, São Tomé; tel. 221031; f. 1994; weekly; Publr AMBRÓSIO QUARESMA; Editor ARMINDO CARDOSO.

Téla Nón: Largo Água Grande, Edif. Complexo Técnico da CST, São Tomé; tel. 225099; e-mail diario_digital@cstome.net; internet www.telanon.info; f. 2000; provides online daily news service; Chief Editor ABEL TAVARES DE VEIGA.

Online newspapers include the Jornal de São Tomé e Príncipe (www.jornal.st), Jornal Horizonte (www.cstome.net/jhorizonte) and Vitrina (www.vitrina.st).

PRESS ASSOCIATION

Associação Nacional de Imprensa (ANI): São Tomé; Pres. MANUEL BARRETO.

NEWS AGENCY

STP-Press: Av. Marginal de 12 de Julho, CP 12, São Tomé; tel. 2222087; e-mail stp-press@hotmail.com; internet www.stp-press.st; f. 1985; Dir MANUEL DEMDÉ.

Broadcasting and Communications

TELECOMMUNICATIONS

Companhia Santomense de Telecomunicações, SARL (CST): Av. Marginal 12 de Julho, CP 141, São Tomé; tel. 222226; fax 222500; e-mail webmaster@cstome.net; internet www.cstome.net; f. 1989 by Govt of São Tomé (49%) and Grupo Portugal Telecom (Portugal, 51%) to facilitate increased telecommunications links and television reception via satellite; in March 1997 CST introduced internet services; Rádio Marconi's shares subsequently assumed by Portugal Telecom SA; introduced mobile cellular telephone service in 2001; Pres. FELISBERTO AFONSO L. NETO; Sec. JORGE LIMA D'ALVA TORRES; 120,000 mobile subscribers (2010).

BROADCASTING

Portuguese technical and financial assistance in the establishment of a television service was announced in 1989. Transmissions commenced in 1992 and the service currently broadcasts seven days a week. In 1995 Radio France Internationale and Rádio Televisão Portuguesa Internacional began relaying radio and television broadcasts, respectively, to the archipelago. In 1997 Voice of America, which had been broadcasting throughout Africa since 1993 from a relay station installed on São Tomé, began local transmissions on FM. The liberalization of the sector was approved by the Government in early 2005 and Rádio Jubilar, Rádio Tropicana and Rádio Viva FM subsequently began broadcasting. The French television channel TV5 commenced broadcasting in December 2007.

Radio

Rádio Jubilar: Av. Kwam Kruman-Edifício da Catequese, CP 104, São Tomé; tel. 223868; e-mail radiojubilar@cstome.net; f. 2005; operated by the Roman Catholic Church; Dir LEONEL PEREIRA.

Rádio Nacional de São Tomé e Príncipe: Av. Marginal de 12 de Julho, CP 44, São Tomé; tel. 223293; fax 221973; e-mail rnstp@cstome.net; internet www.rnstp.st; f. 1958; state-controlled; home service in Portuguese and Creole; Dir MÁXIMO CARLOS.

Rádio Tropicana: Travessa João de Deus, CP 709, São Tomé; tel. 226856; f. 2005; Dir AGUINALDO SALVATERRA.

Television

Televisão Santomense (TVS): Bairro Quinta de Santo António, CP 393, São Tomé; tel. 221041; fax 2226392; e-mail medeiros450@hotmail.com; state-controlled; Dir ÓSCAR MEDEIROS.

Finance

(cap. = capital; res = reserves; dep. = deposits; m. = million; br(s). = branch(es); amounts in dobras, unless otherwise indicated)

BANKING

Central Bank

Banco Central de São Tomé e Príncipe (BCSTP): Praça da Independência, CP 13, São Tomé; tel. 243700; fax 222777; e-mail bcstp@bcstp.st; internet www.bcstp.st; f. 1992 to succeed fmr Banco Nacional de São Tomé e Príncipe; bank of issue; cap. 108,721.2m., res 175,726.5m., dep. 1,286,443.2m. (Dec. 2009); Gov. MARIA DO CARMO SILVEIRA.

Commercial Banks

Afriland First Bank/STP: Praça da Independência, CP 202, São Tomé; tel. 226749; fax 226747; e-mail stp@afrilandfirstbank.com; internet www.afrilandfirstbank.com; f. 2003; private bank; owned by Afriland First Bank, SA, Cameroon; cap. US $1.8m.; Gen. Man. AUGUSTIN DIAYO; Administrator-Delegate JOSEPH TINDJOU.

Banco Equador SARL: Rua de Moçambique 3B, CP 361, São Tomé; tel. 2241950; fax 2241959; e-mail be@bancoequador.st; internet www.bancoequador.st; f. 1995 as Banco Comercial do Equador; restructured and name changed to above in 2004; owned by Monbaka, Angola (40%) and Grupo António Mbakassi (40%); cap. US $7m.; Pres. DIONÍSIO MENDONÇA; Gen. Man. RUI MENDONÇA; 1 br.

Banco Internacional de São Tomé e Príncipe (BISTP) (International Bank of São Tomé and Príncipe): Praça da Independência 3, CP 536, São Tomé; tel. 243100; fax 222427; e-mail bistp@cstome.net; internet www.bistp.st; f. 1993; 48% govt-owned, 27% by Caixa Geral

de Depósitos (Portugal), 25% by Banco Africano de Investimentos SARL (Angola); cap. 12,546.0m., res 201,953.5m., dep. 689,557.5m. (2009); CEO JOÃO CARLOS AGUIAR CRISTÓVÃO; 3 brs.

Commercial Bank—São Tomé e Príncipe: Av. Marginal 12 de Julho, CP 1109, São Tomé; tel. 227678; fax 227676; e-mail cobstp@cstome.net; internet www.cbc-bank.com; f. 2005; 42% owned by Groupe FOTSO (Cameroon); cap. US $3m. (2005); Chair. YVES MICHEL FOTSO; Gen. Man. JAQUES PAUL WOUENDJI.

Ecobank São Tomé: Edifício HB, Traversa de Pelorinho, CP 316, São Tomé; tel. 222141; fax 222672; e-mail ecobankstp@cstome.net; f. 2007; cap. US $1.5m.

Island Bank, SA: Rua de Guiné, CP 1044, São Tomé; tel. 227484; fax 227490; e-mail ceo@islandbanksa.com; internet www.islandbanksa.com; f. 2005; cap. US $1.8m. (2005); Pres. MARC WABARA; Man. Dir EDWIN F. B. KRUKRUBO.

Oceanic Bank STP: Rua Dr Palma Carlos, CP 1175, São Tomé; tel. 222689; fax 222641; f. 2008; cap. US $5.0m. (Dec. 2008); Dir PETER NWACHUKWU.

INSURANCE

Instituto de Segurança Social: Rua Soldado Paulo Ferreira, São Tomé; tel. 221382; e-mail inss@cstome.net; f. as Caixa de Previdência dos Funcionários Públicos, adopted present name 1994; insurance fund for civil servants; Pres. of Admin. Bd ALBINO GRAÇA DA FONSECA; Dir JUVENAL DO ESPÍRITO SANTO.

NICON Seguros STP: Av. 12 de Julho 997, CP556, São Tomé; tel. and fax 227057; e-mail niconseguros@cstome.net; f. 2008; cap. US $1.3m.; Dir TOWOJO PIUS AGBOOLA.

SAT INSURANCE: Av. Amílcar Cabral, CP 293, São Tomé; tel. 226161; fax 226160; e-mail satinsuran@cstome.net; f. 2001; general insurance; cap. US $1.0m.; Dir MICHEL SOBGUI.

Trade and Industry

GOVERNMENT AGENCIES

Agência Nacional do Petróleo de São Tomé e Príncipe (ANP—STP): Av. Nações Unidas, CP 1048, São Tomé; tel. 226940; fax 226937; e-mail anp_geral@cstome.net; internet www.anp-stp.gov.st; f. 2004; manages and implements govt policies relating to the petroleum sector; Exec. Dir LUÍS PRAZERES.

Nigeria-São Tomé and Príncipe Joint Development Authority (JDA): Plot 1101, Aminu Kano Cres., Wuse II, Abuja, Nigeria; Praça da UCCLA, São Tomé; tel. (234) 95241069; fax (234) 95241061; e-mail enquiries@nigeriasaotomejda.com; internet www.nigeriasaotomejda.com; f. 2002; manages devt of petroleum and gas resources in Joint Development Zone; Exec. Dir Dr JORGE PEREIRA DOS SANTOS.

DEVELOPMENT ORGANIZATION

Instituto para o Desenvolvimento Económico e Social (INDES): Travessa do Pelourinho, CP 408, São Tomé; tel. 222491; fax 221931; e-mail indes@cstome.net; f. 1989 as Fundo Social e de Infrastructuras; adopted present name 1994; channels foreign funds to local economy; Dir HOMERO JERÓNIMO SALVATERRA.

CHAMBER OF COMMERCE

Câmara do Comércio, Indústria, Agricultura e Serviços (CCIAS): Av. Marginal de 12 de Julho, CP 527, São Tomé; tel. 222723; fax 221409; e-mail ccias@cstome.net; internet www2.cciastp.org; Pres. ABÍLIO AFONSO HENRIQUES.

UTILITIES

Electricity and Water

Empresa de Água e Electricidade (EMAE): Av. Água Grande, CP 46, São Tomé; tel. 222096; fax 222488; e-mail emae@cstome.net; f. 1979; state electricity and water co; privatized in 2004; Dir-Gen. Lt-Col ÓSCAR SOUSA.

TRADE UNIONS

Organização Nacional de Trabalhadores de São Tomé e Príncipe (ONTSTP): Rua Cabo Verde, São Tomé; tel. 222431; e-mail ontstpdis@cstome.net; Sec.-Gen. JOÃO TAVARES.

União Geral dos Trabalhadores de São Tomé e Príncipe (UGSTP): Av. Kwame Nkrumah, São Tomé; tel. 222443; e-mail ugtdis@cstome.net; Sec.-Gen. COSTA CARLOS.

Transport

RAILWAYS

There are no railways in São Tomé and Príncipe.

ROADS

In 1999 there were an estimated 320 km of roads, of which 218 km were asphalted. In 2005 the European Union granted €930,000 towards upgrading the road network.

SHIPPING

The principal ports are at São Tomé city and at Neves on São Tomé island. At 31 December 2012 São Tomé and Príncipe's flag registered fleet comprised 31 vessels, totalling 42,920 grt.

Companhia Santomense de Navegação, SA (CSN): CP 49, São Tomé; tel. 222657; fax 221311; e-mail csn@setgrcop.com; shipping and freight forwarding.

Empresa Nacional de Administração dos Portos (ENAPORT): Largo Alfândega, CP 437, São Tomé; tel. 221841; fax 224949; e-mail enaport@cstome.net; internet www.enaport.st; Pres. ANTERO DE OLIVEIRA.

Navetur-Equatour: CP 277, Rua Viriato da Cruz, São Tomé; tel. 223781; fax 222122; e-mail navequatur@cstome.net; internet www.navetur-equatour.st; Dir-Gen. LUÍS BEIRÃO.

Transportes e Serviços, Lda (TURIMAR): Rua da Caixa, CP 48, São Tomé; tel. 221869; fax 222162; e-mail turimar@cstome.net; Man. ALBERTO PEREIRA.

CIVIL AVIATION

There is an international airport at São Tomé.

Empresa Nacional de Aeroportos e Segurança Aérea (ENASA): Aeroporto, CP 703, São Tomé; tel. 221878; fax 221154; e-mail enasa@cstome.net; Dir ARISTIDES BAROS.

Linhas Aéreas São-tomenses (LAS): Rua Santo António do Príncipe, São Tomé; tel. 227282; fax 227281; e-mail hba.saotome@gmail.com; f. 2002; owned by Aerocontractors, Nigeria; Dir ANTÓNIO AGUIAR.

SCD-Aviation: Omali Lodge Luxury Hotel, São Tomé; tel. 222350; fax 221814.

STP-Airways: Av. Marginal 12 de Julho, São Tomé; tel. 221160; fax 223449; e-mail stp-airways@cstome.net; internet www.stpairways.st; f. 2006; 35% govt-owned; Dir FELISBERTO NETO.

Tourism

The islands benefit from spectacular mountain scenery, unspoilt beaches and unique species of flora and wildlife. Although still largely undeveloped, tourism is currently one of the sectors of the islands' economy attracting most foreign investment. However, the high level of rainfall during most of the year limits the duration of the tourist season, and the expense of reaching the islands by air is also an inhibiting factor. There were 7,963 tourist arrivals in 2010, and receipts totalled some US $9.4m.

Defence

In early 2005 the armed forces were estimated to number some 300. Military service, which is compulsory, lasts for 30 months. There is also a presidential guard numbering some 160. In 2000 Portugal and São Tomé renewed the military agreement for the stationing of the 'Aviocar' and a crew of the Portuguese Air Force in the country. Since April 1988 the aeroplane has provided humanitarian emergency flights from Príncipe to São Tomé, as well as rescue operations for local fishermen along the coast. In 2004 a paramilitary unit, trained by the Angolan Government and comprising 200 men, was created. In mid-2006 army recruitment was broadened to include women.

Defence Expenditure: Budgeted at 1,100m. dobras (excl. capital expenditure) in 2000.

Commander-in-Chief of the Armed Forces: MANUEL PINTO DA COSTA.

Chief of General Staff of the Armed Forces: Lt-Col IDALÉCIO PACHIRE.

Education

Education is officially compulsory between six and 14 years of age. It starts at the age of six and lasts for six years, comprising a first cycle of four years and a second of two years. Secondary education lasts for a further six years, comprising two cycles of three years each. According to UNESCO estimates, in 2009/10 enrolment at primary schools included 98% of children in the relevant age-group (males 97%; females 100%), while the comparable ratio for secondary enrolment in 2010/11 was 48% (males 44%; females52%). The country's first university, Universidade Lusíada, was inaugurated in October 2006. In 2000 public investment in education (including culture and sport) amounted to US $1.3m., equivalent to 6.7% of total public investment. The budget for 2005 allocated 13.4% of total government expenditure to education.

SAUDI ARABIA

Introductory Survey

LOCATION, CLIMATE, LANGUAGE, RELIGION, FLAG, CAPITAL

The Kingdom of Saudi Arabia occupies about four-fifths of the Arabian peninsula, in south-western Asia. It is bordered by Jordan, Iraq and Kuwait to the north, by Yemen to the south, by Oman to the south and east, and by Qatar and the United Arab Emirates to the north-east. Saudi Arabia has a long western coastline on the Red Sea, facing Egypt, Sudan and Eritrea, and a shorter coastline (between Kuwait and Qatar) on the Persian (Arabian) Gulf, with the Bahrain archipelago (to which Saudi Arabia is connected via a causeway) just off shore and Iran on the opposite coast. Much of the country is arid desert, and some places are without rain for years. In summer average temperatures in coastal regions range from 38°C to 49°C, and humidity is high. Temperatures sometimes reach 54°C in the interior. Winters are mild, except in the mountains. Annual rainfall averages between 100 mm and 200 mm in the north, and is even lower in the south. The official language is Arabic, which is spoken by almost all of the population. Except for the expatriate community (estimated to represent some 32% of the total population in 2011), virtually all of the inhabitants are adherents of Islam, the official religion. About 85% of the population are Sunni Muslims, and most of the indigenous inhabitants belong to the strictly orthodox Wahhabi sect. About 15% of the population are Shi'a Muslims, principally in the east of the country. The national flag (proportions 2 by 3) is green and bears, in white, an Arabic inscription ('There is no God but Allah and Muhammad is the Prophet of Allah') above a white sabre. The capital is Riyadh.

CONTEMPORARY POLITICAL HISTORY

Historical Context

The whole of the Arabian peninsula became part of Turkey's Ottoman Empire in the 16th century. Under the suzerainty of the Ottoman Sultan, the local tribal rulers enjoyed varying degrees of autonomy. The Wahhabi movement, dedicated to the reform of Islam, was launched in the Najd (Nejd) region of central Arabia in the 18th century. A Wahhabi kingdom, ruled by the House of Sa'ud from its capital at Riyadh, quickly expanded into the Hedjaz region on the west coast of Arabia. In 1890 the rival Rashidi family seized control of Riyadh, but in 1902 a member of the deposed Sa'udi family, Abd al-Aziz ibn Abd al-Rahman, expelled the Rashidi dynasty and proclaimed himself ruler of Najd. In subsequent years he recovered and consolidated the outlying provinces of the kingdom, defeating Turkish attempts to subjugate him. Having restored the House of Sa'ud as a ruling dynasty, Abd al-Aziz became known as Ibn Sa'ud. In order to strengthen his position, he instituted the formation of Wahhabi colonies, known as Ikhwan ('Brethren'), throughout the territory under his control.

During the First World War (1914–18), in which Turkey was allied with Germany, the Arabs under Ottoman rule rebelled. In 1915 the United Kingdom signed a treaty of friendship with Ibn Sa'ud, who was then master of central Arabia, securing his co-operation against Turkey. Relations subsequently deteriorated as a result of the British Government's decision to support Hussein ibn Ali, who proclaimed himself King of the Hedjaz in 1916, as its principal ally in Arabia. Hussein was also Sharif of Mecca (the holiest city of Islam), which had been governed since the 11th century by his Hashimi (Hashemite) family, rivals of the House of Sa'ud. At the end of the war, following Turkey's defeat, the Ottoman Empire was dissolved. Continuing his conquests, Ibn Sa'ud successfully campaigned against the rulers of four Arabian states (the Hedjaz, Asir, Hayil and Jauf) between 1919 and 1925. In September 1924 his forces captured Mecca, forcing Hussein to abdicate, and in 1925 they overran the whole of the Hedjaz. In January 1926 Ibn Sa'ud was proclaimed King of the Hedjaz and Sultan of Najd. On 23 September 1932 the dual monarchy ended when the two areas were merged as the unified Kingdom of Saudi Arabia.

Commercially exploitable deposits of petroleum (the basis of Saudi Arabia's modern prosperity) were discovered in the Eastern Province in 1938, and large-scale exploitation of the kingdom's huge reserves of petroleum began after the Second World War (1939–45). Petroleum royalties were used to develop and modernize the country's infrastructure and services.

Ibn Sa'ud remained in power until his death in November 1953; all subsequent rulers of Saudi Arabia have been sons of his. The kingdom has remained an absolute monarchy and a traditional Islamic society. The King is the supreme religious leader as well as the head of state, and governs by royal decree. In foreign affairs, Saudi Arabia has historically allied itself with the USA and other Western countries.

Domestic Political Affairs

Ibn Sa'ud was succeeded by the Crown Prince, Sa'ud ibn Abd al-Aziz. Another of the late King's sons, Faisal ibn Abd al-Aziz, replaced Sa'ud as Crown Prince and Prime Minister. In 1958, bowing to pressure from the royal family, King Sa'ud conferred on Crown Prince Faisal full powers over foreign, internal and economic affairs. In March 1964 King Sa'ud relinquished power to Crown Prince Faisal, and in November was forced by the royal family to abdicate in his favour. The new King Faisal retained the post of Prime Minister, and appointed his half-brother, Khalid ibn Abd al-Aziz, to be Crown Prince in 1965. In the Six-Day War of June 1967 Saudi Arabian forces collaborated with Iraqi and Jordanian troops in action against Israel. As a result of the Arab–Israeli War of October 1973, Saudi Arabia led a movement by Arab oil producers to exert pressure on Western countries by reducing supplies of crude petroleum.

In March 1975 King Faisal was assassinated by one of his nephews, and was immediately succeeded by Crown Prince Khalid. The new King also became Prime Minister, and appointed his brother, Fahd ibn Abd al-Aziz (Minister of the Interior since 1962), as Crown Prince and First Deputy Prime Minister.

The religious fervour that the Middle East experienced in the wake of the Iranian Revolution also arose in Saudi Arabia in late 1979, when an armed group of about 250 Sunni Muslim extremists attacked and occupied the Grand Mosque in Mecca, the most important centre of pilgrimage for Muslims. There was also a riot by Shi'a Muslims in the Eastern Province. In response to the unrest, Crown Prince Fahd announced in early 1980 that a consultative assembly would be formed to act as an advisory body, although the assembly was not inaugurated until December 1993.

The reign of King Fahd

King Khalid died in June 1982 and was succeeded by Crown Prince Fahd, who, following precedent, became Prime Minister and appointed a half-brother, Abdullah ibn Abd al-Aziz (Commander of the National Guard since 1962), to be Crown Prince and First Deputy Prime Minister.

As a result of its position as the world's leading exporter of petroleum, Saudi Arabia is a dominant member of the Organization of the Petroleum Exporting Countries (OPEC, see p. 418) and one of the most influential countries in the Arab world. In May 1981 the kingdom joined five neighbouring states in establishing the Cooperation Council for the Arab States of the Gulf (the Gulf Cooperation Council—GCC, see p. 255).

Widely held misgivings regarding national defence capabilities, and fears of Iraqi expansionist policy (a pact of non-aggression was signed with Iraq in March 1989), were exacerbated in August 1990, when Iraq invaded and annexed Kuwait and proceeded to deploy armed forces along the Kuwaiti–Saudi Arabian border. King Fahd requested that US forces be deployed in Saudi Arabia, as part of a multinational force, in order to deter a possible attack by Iraq. The dispatch of US combat troops and aircraft to Saudi Arabia signified the beginning of 'Operation Desert Shield' for the defence of Saudi Arabia, in accordance with Article 51 of the UN Charter. By the beginning of 1991 some 30 countries had contributed ground troops, aircraft and warships to the US-led multinational force based in Saudi Arabia and the Gulf region. The entire Saudi Arabian armed forces (numbering about 67,500 men) were mobilized. In January, following the failure of international diplomatic efforts to secure Iraq's withdrawal from Kuwait, the multinational force launched a military campaign ('Operation Desert Storm') to liberate Kuwait. Although Iraq responded by launching *Scud* missiles against targets in Saudi Arabia, fighting on Saudi Arabian territory was confined to a few minor incidents. In February Iraq formally severed diplomatic relations with Saudi Arabia.

Following the liberation of Kuwait in February 1991, the ministers responsible for foreign affairs of the GCC met their Syrian and Egyptian counterparts in Damascus, Syria, in March in order to discuss regional security issues. Diplomatic relations between Saudi Arabia and Iran were re-established in March, and Iranians resumed attendance of the *Hajj* (pilgrimage) to Mecca, their numbers regulated in accordance with the quota system.

In March 1992 King Fahd announced by royal decree the imminent creation of an advisory Consultative Council (Majlis al-Shura), with 60 members to be selected by the King every four years. Two further decrees provided for the establishment of regional authorities, and a 'basic law of government', equivalent to a written constitution. The Majlis was inaugurated by King Fahd at the end of 1993. (Its membership was increased to 90 in July 1997, to 120 in May 2001 and to 150 in April 2005.)

In May 1993 the Saudi authorities disbanded the Committee for the Defence of Legitimate Rights (CDLR), recently established by a group of six prominent Islamist scholars and lawyers. The organization's founders were also dismissed from their positions, and their spokesman, Muhammad al-Masari, was arrested. In April 1994 members of the CDLR, including al-Masari (who had recently been released from custody), relocated their organization to the United Kingdom.

More than 1,000 people, including clerics and academics, were reportedly detained in September 1994, after most of them had attended a demonstration in Buraidah, north-west of Riyadh, to protest against the arrest of two religious leaders who had allegedly been agitating for the stricter enforcement of *Shari'a* (Islamic) law. The Government announced in October that only 157 people had been arrested in September, 130 of whom had since been released. Also in October the King approved the creation of a Higher Council for Islamic Affairs, apparently to limit both the influence of militant clerics and the authority of the powerful 18-member Council of Senior Ulama (Saudi Arabia's most senior Islamic authority). In mid-1995 King Fahd replaced six of the seven university chancellors and more than one-half of the members of the Council of Senior Ulama, in an attempt to counter the perceived spread of Islamist fundamentalism. In August the King announced the most far-reaching reorganization of the Council of Ministers for two decades, although no changes were made to the portfolios held by members of the royal family.

A Supreme Economic Council, established by royal decree, convened for the first time in October 1997 under the chairmanship of the Crown Prince. A Supreme Petroleum and Minerals Council was established by royal decree in January 2000. The Government declared in May that ministers were to lose their right to hold company posts while in office, with the exception of employees of the state-owned Saudi Aramco petroleum corporation. In June the inaugural session was held of the newly formed Royal Family Council, an officially apolitical body to be chaired by Crown Prince Abdullah.

Saudi Arabia's human rights record has for many years been the focus of international scrutiny, particularly regarding the use of public beheading in the Saudi judicial system. A report issued by Amnesty International in March 2000 alleged that Saudi Arabia was guilty of widespread human rights abuses, including the use of torture and refusal to allow prisoners access to family members and lawyers. In September Amnesty accused the Saudi authorities of widespread discrimination against women and cited serious abuses of their human rights, including arbitrary detention and torture. The organization also criticized the Saudi judiciary for failing to conduct trials in compliance with internationally recognized standards. However, it was reported in late 2000 that Saudi Arabia had agreed to sign the UN Convention on the Elimination of All Forms of Discrimination against Women, although it would lodge reservations regarding any section deemed to contravene *Shari'a* law.

King Fahd announced a restructured Council of Ministers in April 2003; this was only the third reorganization of the Government in almost 30 years. Reformists were disappointed that most of the key positions were unchanged, and that all the senior ministers belonging to the ruling Al Sa'ud family remained in post.

At an unprecedented human rights conference held in Riyadh in October 2003, the Government disclosed plans to create municipal councils and hold local elections by October 2004. The decision by the authorities to introduce a degree of democracy to the kingdom came amid huge pressure both from inside and outside the country to implement social, economic, political and constitutional reforms. However, Saudi reformists noted that one-half of the councillors would be centrally appointed and that there had been no suggestion that suffrage would be extended to women. Several hundred protesters took part in an illegal demonstration, organized by the British-based Movement for Islamic Reform, outside the conference, demanding widespread reforms including the removal of the House of Sa'ud. Reports indicated that around 150 people were subsequently arrested. In November 2003 King Fahd issued a decree according to which the Majlis al-Shura was henceforth to be allowed to propose new laws and amendments to existing legislation without first asking permission from the King. In addition, the Council of Ministers was to be obliged to return laws to the Majlis for amendment should there be disagreement on an issue. (Under the previous system, whereby the Majlis was a purely advisory body, the matter would be resolved by the King.) In April 2005 a royal decree increased the membership of the Majlis to 150; the expansion prompted renewed demands for the introduction of a partially elected membership. In May the Government announced the establishment of a human rights supervision body, headed by Turki ibn Khalid al-Sudairi, who would be given the equivalent rank to that of a government minister.

The first stage of the elections for 178 municipal authorities in all 13 of the kingdom's provinces took place on 10 February 2005 in Riyadh, having been postponed from September 2004; however, suffrage was not extended to women. In excess of 1,800 candidates stood for the 592 contested seats in the 178 councils; reportedly only about one-quarter of eligible voters in the capital had registered for the elections. The second phase of the elections took place in the Eastern, Aseer, Jazan, Najran and al-Baha provinces on 3 March 2005. According to the local chamber of commerce, only around 12% of the local male population in the Eastern Province had registered to vote. The final phase, in the northern border provinces, was held on 21 April. Nationally, Islamist candidates secured a comfortable majority of the council seats. Later in the year two women secured elected positions on the 18-member board of the Jeddah Chamber of Commerce and Industry, and one on the 10-member board of the Saudi Engineers' Council.

Accession of King Abdullah

On 1 August 2005 it was announced that King Fahd had died. He was succeeded by his half-brother, Crown Prince Abdullah, also aged 84, who had been the de facto ruler of the kingdom since King Fahd suffered a stroke in 1995. The Second Deputy Prime Minister, Minister of Defence and Civil Aviation and Inspector General, Prince Sultan ibn Abd al-Aziz, a full brother of King Fahd and also in his eighties, was named as Crown Prince. In accordance with the Constitution, King Abdullah assumed the role of Prime Minister, while the Crown Prince was appointed Deputy Prime Minister. No replacement was named for the position of Second Deputy Prime Minister, which increased speculation surrounding the succession to the throne after Crown Prince Sultan. In October 2005 a National Security Council, chaired by King Abdullah, was established, with the power to declare states of emergency and war; control diplomatic relations; and combat public corruption and mismanagement.

The Ministry of the Interior announced in May 2006 that the authority of the national religious police force (the *mutawwa'in*)—under the control of the Commission for the Promotion of Virtue and the Prevention of Vice—was to be reduced: those arrested on suspicion of moral offences were henceforth to be tried by a public prosecutor. In October a constitutional amendment—first proposed by King Abdullah while he was still Crown Prince—was adopted that removed the monarch's power to choose his successor. Following the forthcoming accession to the throne of Crown Prince Sultan, subsequent heirs were to be elected by the Bay'ah Council (comprising senior members of the royal family). In May 2007 the Crown Prince stated that in the future it was intended that one-third of Saudi government posts would be allocated to women; however, the reform had not been implemented by early 2013 (see Recent developments). Following Saudi Arabia's accession to the World Trade Organization (WTO, see p. 444) in December 2005, in October 2007 King Abdullah issued a royal decree allowing for the creation of a supreme court in Riyadh and special tribunals intended to settle commercial and labour grievances, as well as the introduction of appeal courts in each of the country's 13 regions. The new Judiciary Law also included provision for the modernization of the judicial system.

In April 2008 a report by the US-based Human Rights Watch urged the Saudi authorities to reform their policies of sex segregation and male guardianship over women, noting that Saudi women required the consent of a male guardian in order to work, travel or avail of public services. In its annual report for 2010 the organization noted that the Saudi authorities had not adhered to a pledge made to the UN Human Rights Council in 2009 regarding reform of the system of male guardianship.

King Abdullah's patronage of several inter-faith and inter-cultural forums in 2008 was regarded by some observers as evidence of his commitment to gradual social and political reform. In June the King inaugurated the International Islamic Conference for Dialogue in Mecca. The conference, organized by the Muslim World League and attended by some 600 senior Muslim clerics and world leaders, was established to foster co-operation and understanding between Muslims world-wide, including between Sunnis and Shi'as. In a conciliatory gesture, King Abdullah (a Sunni Muslim) entered the opening ceremony hand-in-hand with the former Iranian President, Ali Akbar Hashemi Rafsanjani (a Shi'a Muslim). In July the King hosted a three-day inter-faith conference in Madrid, Spain, attended by almost 300 religious, political and cultural leaders from 50 countries, including Jews, Muslims, Christians, Hindus and Buddhists.

In September 2008, despite the recent conference promoting Sunni-Shi'a dialogue, Human Rights Watch published a report criticizing the 'systematic discrimination' experienced by Saudi Arabia's significant Shi'a minority, particularly in the areas of government employment, the judicial system, education and religious freedom. Evidence of sectarian tensions within the kingdom surfaced in February 2009, when violent clashes occurred between Shi'a pilgrims from the Eastern Province and members of the *mutawwa'in* near the tomb of the Prophet Muhammad in Medina; numerous injuries were reported and several pilgrims arrested. While each side accused the other of provoking the violence, two rallies protesting against the treatment of the pilgrims were held near Qatif in the Eastern Province. In March, after receiving a delegation of Shi'a leaders, King Abdullah announced the release from custody of 38 Shi'a detainees.

Social and political reform under King Abdullah

King Abdullah implemented his first government reorganization in February 2009, effecting wide-ranging changes at senior level throughout the kingdom's administrative, legal and education systems. Nora bint Abdullah al-Fayez became the first Saudi woman to achieve ministerial status when she was appointed Deputy Minister for Girls' Education. The outgoing Chairman of the Majlis, Dr Salih ibn Humayd, was installed as the new Chairman of the Supreme Council of Justice, the most senior post in the judiciary, replacing Sheikh Salih bin Muhammad al-Luhaidan, who had held the post since the mid-1980s. Sheikh al-Luhaidan, a staunchly conservative religious cleric, had provoked domestic and international dismay when he issued a *fatwa* (edict) in September 2008 that described as lawful the killing of the owners of satellite television channels that broadcast 'depraved' programmes, such as soap operas and game shows, during Ramadan; channels targeted by his disapproval included those owned by members of the Saudi royal family. In another notable change to the conservative establishment, Sheikh Ibrahim al-Ghaith, President of the Commission for the Promotion of Virtue and the Prevention of Vice, was replaced by a more moderate scholar, Sheikh Abd al-Aziz al-Humayun. Several clerics were appointed to a restructured Council of Senior Ulama, which, for the first time, included representatives of all four schools of Sunni religious thought; however, Shi'ite clerics were still excluded.

In March 2009 the King appointed his half-brother Prince Nayef ibn Abd al-Aziz Al Sa'ud, Minister of the Interior since 1975, as Second Deputy Prime Minister—a post which had been vacant since King Abdullah's accession in 2005. Observers suggested that the appointment had been precipitated by concerns about the ailing health of Crown Prince Sultan, now First Deputy Prime Minister, Minister of Defence and Civil Aviation and Inspector General, who had left Saudi Arabia in November 2008 to receive medical treatment in the USA and who did not return to the kingdom until December 2009.

Reports emerged in April 2009 that several members of the *mutawwa'in* had been indicted for an alleged assault on a young woman in Tabuk. Such forceful intervention by civil authorities into the activities of the religious police was considered unprecedented, and observers also noted the freedom with which the case had been reported in national newspapers. In April 2010, as part of the judicial reforms initiated in 2007, the Council of Senior Ulama endorsed a further change proposed by King Abdullah, which involved the codification of the *Shari'a*; however, the modernization of Saudi Arabia's legal system proceeded slowly, partly owing to the lack of support from Saudi Arabia's religious conservatives. Moreover, in August 2010, as a growing number of clerics and religious scholars were issuing their own *fatwas*, the King decreed that henceforth only members of the Council would have this right.

In mid-November 2010 King Abdullah appointed one of his sons, Prince Mitab ibn Abdullah Al Sa'ud, as Minister of State and Commander of the National Guard (the élite military force charged with protecting the royal family), after standing down from the post he had held since 1962. King Abdullah also requested that the First Deputy Prime Minister assume responsibility for supervising the annual *Hajj*, traditionally a role for the Saudi monarch. There was considerable speculation that the decision of the King to relinquish some of his duties to other family members indicated a deterioration in his health.

Response to domestic protests and regional unrest

As political and social unrest spread across large parts of the Middle East and North Africa in the early months of 2011, a number of illegal street protests were held in Saudi Arabia. However, these were relatively small demonstrations initially held mainly in the Shi'a Eastern Province, which lies adjacent to Bahrain, by protesters demanding the release of political prisoners who they claimed were being held without trial. The authorities warned that they would not tolerate any actions that posed a threat to Saudi Arabia's security and stability. Nevertheless, in late February King Abdullah—returning to the kingdom after a three-month absence to receive medical treatment in the USA and then to convalesce in Morocco—promised to increase social welfare payments by US $37,000m. and to raise the salaries of public sector workers by 15%. In the second week of February nine pro-reform campaigners sought the permission of the monarch to register a political party, the Islamic Umma Party, despite political organizations being illegal in Saudi Arabia; several of the party's founders were subsequently arrested.

In early March 2011 a small number of demonstrators in Riyadh and other cities took part in illegal rallies demanding political reforms; this led the Government to warn that the security forces had been granted permission to take 'all measures needed' to maintain law and order. On 9–10 March in Qatif, hundreds of Shi'a protesters demanded the release of nine prisoners who had been held without charge for at least 14 years on suspicion of involvement in the 1996 al-Khobar bombing (see Militant Islamism). Security forces were reported to have fired rubber bullets to disperse the crowds, and some of those in attendance described having witnessed beatings. Meanwhile, a group of young Saudis used a social networking website to urge people to join a 'day of rage' on 11 March 2011. One reason for the planned rally—the inspiration for which appeared to be similar events in Tunisia and Egypt—was said to be the arrest in February of a Shi'a cleric, Sheikh Tawfiq al-Amer, who had advocated the transformation of Saudi Arabia into a constitutional monarchy; al-Amer was released in the week before 11 March in an apparent attempt by the authorities to appease the demonstrators. In the event, the number of people who attended the protests was relatively small, apparently owing to the significant presence of Saudi security forces. Nevertheless, in mid-March police in the east of the country detained more than 100 Shi'a demonstrators, many of whom were protesting against Saudi Arabia's recent military intervention in Bahrain (see Regional relations); human rights groups alleged that some of the detainees were subsequently tortured.

King Abdullah gave a rare televised speech on 18 March 2011, in which he again warned those protesters who threatened national security. However, a number of royal decrees were subsequently announced which included pledges to: raise the minimum wage for public sector employees; improve benefits for students and the unemployed; expand the provision of affordable housing; and establish an anti-corruption commission which would report directly to the Saudi monarch. Muhammad bin Abdullah al-Sharif was appointed as President of the National

Commission to Combat Corruption (NCCC), with the rank of government minister; the NCCC was formally instituted in mid-May. In addition to King Abdullah's promised welfare payments, which amounted to an estimated US $91,000m., he also declared that the *mutawwa'in* was to be expanded, and that 60,000 new security posts were to be created within the Ministry of the Interior. Towards the end of March 2011 a new Ministry of Housing was created.

In a rare political concession, in late March 2011 officials from the Ministry of Municipal and Rural Affairs declared that voter registration for municipal elections postponed from October 2009—in order to consider whether to extend participation to Saudi women—would commence on 23 April 2011; the actual elections (the second municipal polls in the kingdom's history) were to take place on 29 September. However, it was reported in mid-April 2011 that the National Society for Human Rights, the organization charged with monitoring the forthcoming elections, had decided to withdraw its participation from the polls in protest against the failure of the Government to include female voters in the process. In an address to mark the opening of the annual session of the Majlis al-Shura on 25 September, King Abdullah unexpectedly announced that women would be given the right to participate in the Majlis from its sixth term (due to begin in 2013—see Recent developments), while also being allowed to vote and to seek election at the country's third staging of municipal polls (scheduled for 2015). In the event, turn-out at the municipal elections of September 2011, in which the voting system had been amended to allow voters to choose a single candidate rather than several, was reported to have been low. Voters elected councillors to serve one-half of the 285 councils, while the other half were chosen by the Government.

Saudi Arabia's ban on women driving became a focal point in the struggle between conservatives and reformists in mid-2011. In May a woman, Manal al-Sharif, released a video portraying herself driving around al-Khobar and encouraging other women, via the internet, to flout the ban; she was subsequently arrested by the *mutawwa'in*. Despite being released by the authorities a few days later, following a pledge to end her campaigning, al-Sharif's actions sparked widespread international support. In June a large number of Saudi women defied the ban by driving around Riyadh and Jeddah in the first such organized protest in the kingdom; the mass drive protest was essentially ignored by the security forces. The leaders of the protests emphasized the fact that the female driving ban was not determined by *Shari'a* law, but had arisen as a result of the Ministry of the Interior adhering to a clerical *fatwa* (which prevented men and women from mixing without a chaperone).

In late July 2011 Amnesty International published details of a new penal law ostensibly aimed at fighting the terrorist threat facing Saudi Arabia, which had recently been approved by the Saudi Government. The draft legislation appeared to represent a crackdown by the authorities against any large-scale protests taking place as had occurred elsewhere in the region since the start of the year. Among the increased powers granted to the security forces were the ability to hold detainees without trial for up to 12 months; conduct secret trials; imprison for 10 years those who questioned the integrity of the King or the Crown Prince; and search properties without prior authorization.

Crown Prince Sultan, the heir to the throne and First Deputy Prime Minister, Minister of Defence and Civil Aviation and Inspector General, died in the USA on 22 October 2011, after several years of ill health. On 27 October Prince Nayef succeeded him as Crown Prince and Deputy Prime Minister, while retaining responsibility for the interior portfolio. Prince Salman, King Abdullah's half-brother and the governor of Riyadh, was appointed as Crown Prince Sultan's replacement at the Ministry of Defence in early November. In mid-January 2012 Sheikh Abd al-Aziz al-Humayun, President of the Commission for the Promotion of Virtue and Prevention of Vice, was replaced by the more moderate Abd al-Latif Abd al-Aziz al-Sheikh. It was evident by late 2012 that al-Sheikh had taken a number of measures intended to limit the powers of the Commission and improve its reputation among the Saudi population.

Renewed unrest was evident in the Eastern Province from October 2011, when Shi'a protesters were reported to have clashed with security forces in Qatif. At least 20 were injured in the violence, which the Saudi Government implied had been instigated by the Iranian regime. In late November four people died as the result of exchanges of gunfire between Shi'as and the police. The authorities claimed, in response to reports that at least two protesters had been shot dead by security forces, that

armed militants had 'infiltrated' the funeral of another protester. By mid-January 2012, according to opposition activists, some 400 people had been detained in connection with the Shi'a-led protests in the Eastern Province since March 2011; however, all but about 70 had subsequently been released by the authorities. A young Shi'a protester was killed by security forces in al-Awamiya, in the Qatif region, in mid-January 2012, after their vehicle had reportedly been attacked. Another two protesters reportedly died during clashes with security forces in early February, after some of those taking part in a procession on the occasion of the Islamic festival of Ashoura began to demand political reform and the release of Shi'a prisoners. At least three demonstrators were killed by police amid further unrest in the Eastern Province during July and August; the Saudi authorities continued to allege Iranian involvement in the ongoing protest movement.

In late June 2012 the Saudi Arabian Olympic Committee publicly overturned its ban on sportswomen participating in the Olympic Games, reportedly following discussions between King Abdullah, the Crown Prince, other leading government officials and senior Muslim clerics. The issue of women competing in public sporting events such as the Olympics is controversial in the kingdom, and is strongly opposed by many adherents to a strict interpretation of Islamic law. However, the Committee's decision, which had reportedly been endorsed by the King, allowed two Saudi athletes to represent their country at the Games held in London, United Kingdom, between 27 July and 12 August.

Recent developments: death of Crown Prince and women appointed to the Majlis al-Shura

The Crown Prince, Deputy Prime Minister and Minister of the Interior, Prince Nayef, died in Geneva, Switzerland, on 16 June 2012. Two days later Prince Ahmad ibn Abd al-Aziz Al Sa'ud was named as Minister of the Interior; he formally assumed the post on 22 June. However, on 5 November Ahmad's nephew, Prince Muhammad ibn Nayef, was appointed to the role, after the former had reportedly asked to be relieved of his duties. Meanwhile, on 18 June 2012 the Minister of Defence, Prince Salman ibn Abd al-Aziz Al Sa'ud, was elevated to the role of Crown Prince. He retained responsibility for the defence portfolio, while concurrently assuming the title of Deputy Prime Minister.

In a major political development for Saudi Arabia (as had first been announced in September 2011), on 11 January 2013 King Abdullah appointed 30 women to the 150-member Majlis al-Shura; they were sworn into office at the start of the chamber's new four-year term on 19 February. Although the reform—which for the first time permitted women to hold political office—was hailed as a significant advance as far as women's rights were concerned, the female council members would be separated from their male counterparts in the Majlis building. Moreover, by early 2013 the Council of Ministers remained exclusively male, despite a pledge made by Crown Prince Sultan in May 2007 to introduce a quota for female cabinet ministers (see Accession of King Abdullah). The newly appointed Majlis al-Shura also contained four Shi'a members (one being female), compared with three in the previous chamber. Meanwhile, in early January 2013 the Office of the UN High Commissioner for Human Rights criticized the significant rise in the number of executions carried out by the Saudi authorities during 2012: in that year 79 people were reported to have been executed, compared with 27 in 2010.

King Abdullah appointed his younger half-brother, Prince Muqrin ibn Abd al-Aziz Al Sa'ud, as Second Deputy Prime Minister on 1 February 2013. The appointment to this highly influential position was considered surprising given that Prince Muqrin's mother originates from Yemen. Muqrin had become an adviser to the King in late July 2012, when he was succeeded as head of the Saudi intelligence agency by Prince Bandar bin Sultan ibn Abd al-Aziz Al Sa'ud. King Abdullah's decision to promote Prince Muqrin increased speculation that he was being prepared as the next successor to the throne after Crown Prince Salman.

After six months of trial proceedings, in mid-March 2013 two well-known Shi'a human rights campaigners, Muhammad al-Qahtani and Abdullah al-Hamid, were convicted of several offences, including undermining national security by encouraging pro-democracy protests, forming an illegal human rights organization and giving false information to foreign sources. Both men were sentenced to at least 10 years in prison (in al-Hamid's case, six years from a previous sentence were included);

they were additionally given 10- and five-year travel bans. However, international human rights groups described the verdicts as being politically motivated. In late March the Saudi authorities were reported to have detained 18 Shi'as (16 Saudis, an Iranian and a Lebanese) whom they accused of involvement in espionage; it was not disclosed for which country they were alleged to be spying.

Militant Islamism

From the mid-1990s numerous bombings and other terrorist attacks, often targeted against foreign civilians, took place in Saudi Arabia. In November 1995 a car bomb exploded outside the offices of the National Guard in Riyadh, which was being used by US civilian contractors to train Saudi personnel. Seven foreign nationals (including five US citizens) were killed in the explosion, responsibility for which was claimed by several organizations, including the Islamic Movement for Change, which earlier in the year had warned that it would initiate attacks if non-Muslim Western forces did not withdraw from the Gulf region. In May 1996 four Saudi nationals were executed, having been convicted of involvement in the attack.

In June 1996 19 US military personnel were killed, and as many as 400 others (mostly Saudi, Bangladeshi and US citizens) were injured, when an explosive device attached to a petroleum tanker was detonated outside a military housing complex in al-Khobar, near Dhahran. By late 1996 there was speculation that the investigating authorities were holding Saudi Shi'a groups with possible links to Iran responsible for the atrocity, rather than the Sunni extremist factions that were widely blamed for the November 1995 bombing. The Iranian Government, however, repeatedly denied any involvement in the incident. In March 1997 the Canadian intelligence service announced the detention of Hani Abd al-Rahim al-Sayegh, a Saudi Shi'a Muslim implicated in the al-Khobar attack, who was alleged to have links with the militant Saudi Hezbollah. Al-Sayegh was extradited from Canada to stand trial in the USA, but in September US officials announced that there was insufficient evidence to secure a conviction. In May 1998 Saudi Arabia's Minister of the Interior stated that there was no indication of a foreign role in the bombing, despite continuing US assertions of Iranian involvement. In October 1999 al-Sayegh was extradited from the USA to Saudi Arabia, where he remained in custody. Several Saudi nationals were arrested in January 2001 in connection with the bombing. In June US investigators indicted 14 individuals on charges relating to the explosion, although three of them remained at large in June 2002 when the Saudi authorities announced that sentences had been imposed on a number of the detainees.

Following the murders of a British defence contractor in February 2003 and of two North Americans in March, a series of co-ordinated suicide attacks on an expatriate housing compound in Riyadh killed 34 people on 12 May. The Minister of Foreign Affairs indicated that 19 people, including 17 Saudis, were believed to have been responsible for the attacks. The bombings, widely held to be the work of the militant Islamist al-Qa'ida network, provoked further US criticism of Saudi security measures, and led to the withdrawal of most of the US diplomats stationed in the kingdom. It emerged after the attacks that the Saudi authorities had made an unsuccessful attempt to apprehend the perpetrators in the week prior to 12 May. The Saudi leadership responded to the bombings by acknowledging more openly that the threat presented by al-Qa'ida was indeed serious, and pledged to take effective action against members and sympathizers of the organization. Between 12 May and late October at least 600 suspected militant Islamists were arrested, 70–90 of whom were charged, and more than 2,000 people were interrogated. In addition, in June some 1,000 Muslim clergy were suspended and ordered to undergo retraining aimed at eliminating Islamist militancy from the profession. However, despite these measures, on 8 November al-Qa'ida apparently struck again when 17 people were killed and more than 120 injured in a suicide attack on a housing complex, mostly populated by Arab expatriates, in Riyadh. In December the Government stated that two Saudi nationals had carried out the latest suicide bombing.

On 21 April 2004 a car bomb exploded close to one of the headquarters of Riyadh's security services, killing five people and wounding up to 150. A militant Islamist group called the al-Haramain Brigades (alleged to have links to al-Qa'ida) claimed responsibility for the attack, which was regarded as the first direct assault on the Saudi regime. On 1 May gunmen in the Red Sea port of Yanbu killed at least one Saudi and five Western petroleum industry workers. On 29 May an attack by militants against a compound housing oil workers at al-Khobar resulted in the deaths of three Saudis and 19 expatriate workers. Despite an attempt by security forces to storm the compound, three of the attackers managed to escape. It was alleged that the militants had agreed a deal with police officers sympathetic to al-Qa'ida, an accusation that was vehemently denied by the Saudi authorities. In early June two of those responsible for the atrocity were reported to have been killed by Saudi forces near Mecca. One of the men was believed to be Abd al-Rahman Muhammad Yazji, one of the kingdom's most wanted militants. In late June the Crown Prince announced that a dozen named individuals with alleged ties to al-Qa'ida would not face the death penalty should they surrender to the security forces within one month. The Saudi authorities were particularly keen to obtain the surrender of Saleh Muhammad al-Oufi, regarded as the overall leader of al-Qa'ida in the kingdom following the death of Abd al-Aziz al-Muqrin in a police raid in that month. It was, however, reported in November that al-Qa'ida had appointed Saud bin Hamoud al-Otaibi as the new leader of its Saudi network; some commentators presumed that this confirmed suspicions that al-Oufi had been killed by security forces in July. In February 2005 the Government launched a national awareness campaign to mobilize people against militant activity. In December seven expatriates and five Saudis died when gunmen attacked the US consulate in Jeddah.

It was announced in August 2006 that more than 700 alleged al-Qa'ida sympathizers had been released after undergoing a 'correction' programme intended to uproot their belief in Islamist fundamentalism. In October the Deputy Minister of the Interior announced that trials of suspected Islamist militants in Islamic courts had commenced, and that many defendants had already been sentenced; it was unclear as to whether some had been executed. In February 2007 three French nationals were shot dead near the town of Tabuk, reportedly while travelling on a pilgrimage to Mecca; a fourth died later in hospital from injuries sustained in the ambush. In April 172 people were arrested for allegedly plotting attacks against public figures, oil refineries and military targets in Saudi Arabia and other neighbouring countries; by late November at least 200 other suspected al-Qa'ida affiliates had been detained by the authorities. Meanwhile, it was revealed in August 2007 that the Government had begun to establish an Industrial Security Force of some 35,000 personnel specifically charged with providing security at the country's petroleum facilities; by mid-November an estimated 9,000 members had been deployed, and a further 8,000 were expected to be deployed each year thereafter. A reported 28 people, most of whom were Saudi citizens, were arrested in late December, on suspicion of preparing terrorist actions in the holy cities of Mecca and Medina during the *Hajj*. The detainees were alleged members of an organization taking its instructions from Ayman al-Zawahiri, believed to be the deputy leader of al-Qa'ida; by March 2008 Saudi security forces had reportedly dismantled the unit. The Ministry of the Interior announced in October that 991 detainees had been charged with involvement in more than 30 terrorist attacks in the kingdom over the preceding five years, in which 164 had been killed and more than 1,000 injured. During 2007–08 the frequency of violent attacks was clearly declining, and the Government's strategy of combining stronger security measures with the retraining of clerics and the re-education of convicted militants appeared to be having some success.

However, despite the apparent effectiveness of domestic counter-terrorism measures, the activities of Saudi militants outside the kingdom remained a source of considerable concern. In January 2009 two Saudi nationals appeared in a video posted on a jihadist website that announced the merger of al-Qa'ida's Saudi Arabian and Yemeni operations, forming an entity known as al-Qa'ida in the Arabian Peninsula (AQAP). Both men were former detainees at the US detention camp at Guantánamo Bay, Cuba, who had been released in 2007 and, despite undergoing the Saudi rehabilitation programme, had absconded to Yemen and allegedly resumed their jihadist activities. Saeed al-Shihri, who was suspected of involvement in the bombing of the US embassy in the Yemeni capital, San'a, in September 2008, was described in the video as the deputy leader of al-Qa'ida in Yemen; Muhammad al-Oufi was described as a field commander. In February 2009 the Saudi authorities released a list of 85 wanted alleged militants living abroad; 83 were Saudi nationals, two were Yemeni, and all were suspected of illegal activities with various al-Qa'ida-affiliated groups abroad and of plotting attacks against targets within Saudi Arabia. The list, which was subsequently distributed by the International Criminal Police Organization (INTERPOL), included several former Guantánamo detainees. Later that month al-Oufi reportedly surrendered to the security forces in Yemen and was handed over to the Saudi authorities.

In July 2009, following the conclusion of the first mass trial of suspected Islamist militants indicted on terrorism charges in October 2008, 330 suspects were convicted of membership of 'the deviant group', the customary Saudi term for al-Qa'ida; one suspect was sentenced to death, while the remaining 329 received sentences that ranged from house arrest to life imprisonment. In August 2009 the Ministry of the Interior announced the arrest of a network of 44 suspected militants and the seizure of several caches of armaments, following a series of operations in Riyadh and Qassim. None of those arrested had been included on the list of 85 wanted militants issued in February. Later that month Prince Muhammad ibn Nayef, the Deputy Minister of the Interior and the kingdom's chief counter-terrorism official, narrowly survived a suicide bomb attack at his home in Jeddah. Responsibility for the bombing, which was the first direct attack on a member of the royal family in decades, was subsequently claimed by AQAP.

In March 2010 security officials arrested 113 suspected Islamist militants, including 55 foreign nationals from countries including Yemen, Somalia and Eritrea, who, as members of three separate cells, had allegedly been planning attacks against oil facilities in the Eastern Province. Evidence of direct links between the cells and AQAP militants in Yemen was reported by the authorities. The Government declared towards the end of November that a further 149 alleged militants—124 Saudis and 25 foreign nationals, most of whom were members of al-Qa'ida—had been detained since March. The Ministry of the Interior claimed that by detaining the suspected militants, one of whom was reported to be female, 19 terrorist cells had been prevented from carrying out attacks against senior officials and journalists in Saudi Arabia. Trials of a large number of suspected Islamists charged with having plotted and carried out attacks against government and Western targets in the kingdom continued during 2011–12. These included, from April 2012, trial proceedings against 50 alleged al-Qa'ida affiliates, some of whom were accused of involvement in the suicide attacks on the expatriate housing compound in Riyadh in May 2003; other charges against the defendants—of whom 47 were Saudi, two Syrian and one Yemeni—included the plotting of attacks against the British and US embassies in the Saudi capital.

Foreign Affairs

Relations with the USA

Despite being one of only three countries (along with Pakistan and the United Arab Emirates—UAE) to have recognized the Taliban administration in Afghanistan, Saudi Arabia severed diplomatic relations with the regime in September 2001, following the suicide attacks on New York and Washington, DC, USA. Although the USA's principal suspect in the attacks, Osama bin Laden (who was at that time based in Afghanistan), was born to a wealthy Saudi Arabian family, the Saudi authorities emphasized that bin Laden had been exiled since 1991 and his nationality revoked because of his subversive activities against the royal family. It was later revealed that 15 of the 19 hijackers were also of Saudi descent (although many of their identities were forged or stolen). The Saudi Government immediately sought to assure US officials of its commitment to eliminating terrorism, and agreed to investigate alleged Saudi funding of bin Laden's al-Qa'ida network, said to be raised through certain charitable organizations and individual donations. However, the Saudi regime, under pressure from internal Islamist groups implacably opposed to the US military presence on Saudi territory and to any military action against another Islamic state, subsequently refused permission for the use of its airbases for military action against Afghanistan.

Following the launch of military attacks against Afghanistan by the US-led 'coalition against terror' in October 2001, the USA briefly closed its embassy in Saudi Arabia because of fear of reprisals. Later that month Crown Prince Abdullah accused the US media of conspiring to damage Saudi Arabia's reputation, following the publication of articles highly critical of Saudi Arabia's perceived lack of co-operation after the September attacks. In January 2002 the US authorities denied a request by their Saudi counterparts for the return of all Saudi citizens (reported to number more than 100 detainees), captured in

Afghanistan while apparently fighting for the Taliban, who were imprisoned at Guantánamo Bay. In August a group representing 900 relatives of victims of the September 2001 attacks filed a civil suit in Washington, DC, against senior Saudi ministers and institutions (and the Government of Sudan) seeking compensation amounting to US $1,000,000m. for their alleged funding of al-Qa'ida activities. Saudi investors responded by threatening to withdraw from the USA some $750,000m. in Saudi investments.

Despite the Saudi–US tensions, in September 2002, following intense pressure from the USA and the United Kingdom, the Saudi Minister of Foreign Affairs indicated that Saudi Arabia might be prepared to approve the use of military bases in Saudi Arabia for a future US-led attack on the regime of Saddam Hussein in Iraq. However, he emphasized that Saudi co-operation would only be forthcoming if the Iraqi authorities continued to reject UN resolutions demanding the unconditional return of weapons inspectors to Iraq and if such a military undertaking was to be conducted under UN auspices. It was established in December that the highly equipped Prince Sultan airbase would be made available to the US military, and that, although combat aircraft would not be allowed to fly offensive missions from the base with the primary aim of bombing Iraqi targets, aircraft launched from Saudi soil would be permitted to open fire or release bombs in self-defence. In January 2003 Saudi Arabia attempted to secure support for a plan to persuade Saddam Hussein to relinquish power and go into exile in order to avert a US-led war to oust his regime. In the following month, however, as conflict appeared increasingly inevitable, the Saudi authorities deployed warships, troops and military helicopters to Kuwait, in order to strengthen the emirate's defences. In late April, after most of the USA's principal military objectives in Iraq had been achieved, it was announced that all but 400 of the 5,000 US military personnel in the country were to be withdrawn from Saudi Arabia by the end of August. Those troops that remained were to assist in training the Saudi armed forces.

In February 2006, following the victory of the Islamic Resistance Movement (Hamas) in the Palestinian legislative elections of the previous month, the Saudi Government incurred US displeasure when it refused to support a US-led plan to deny regional aid to the new Hamas-led administration in the West Bank and Gaza Strip. During a tour of the Middle East in January 2008, US President Bush visited Riyadh, where he reiterated his intention to pursue a controversial arms agreement with the Saudi Government, at an estimated cost of US $20,000m.; the deal formed part of a broader package of US military aid to its allies in the Gulf region aimed at countering any increased Iranian military strength. Bush's visit to Riyadh was, however, marred by Saudi demands that the US Administration hand over to the kingdom 13 of its citizens currently being held at Guantánamo Bay, Cuba.

Saudi Arabia's status as a key regional ally of the USA was emphasized in June 2009, when US President Barack Obama, who had been inaugurated in January, began his first visit to the Middle East in Riyadh, where he held talks on regional affairs with King Abdullah. During a visit to the USA in June 2010, the King emphasized to President Obama that Saudi Arabia refused to normalize relations with Israel in the absence of 'genuine progress' in the Middle East peace process. It was confirmed in October that the US Congress was examining the terms of a massive weapons agreement between the US Government and its Saudi counterpart, reportedly involving the purchase by Saudi Arabia of some US $60,000m. of advanced weaponry (including fighter planes and helicopters) from the USA over a period of 15–20 years. The first part of the deal, to include the upgrading of 70 Saudi fighter planes and the purchase of 84 new planes, at a cost of $29,400m., was signed in December. Meanwhile, in that month the content of a series of leaked confidential US diplomatic cables published by the WikiLeaks organization apparently indicated that the US Administration remained extremely concerned about the private funding of international Sunni terrorist organizations, including al-Qa'ida, by certain Saudi individuals. Osama bin Laden was killed in a US military raid in Pakistan in May 2011; in June the ruling council of al-Qa'ida declared that Ayman al-Zawahiri was to succeed him as leader. Although US–Saudi relations remained uneasy in 2011, owing to a number of divergent viewpoints on developments in the region (including the Palestinian attempt to obtain UN membership), in August the two countries announced that they were soon to begin discussions concerning a nuclear co-operation accord; the talks commenced in Riyadh in January 2013.

Regional relations

In December 1994 Yemen accused Saudi Arabia of erecting monitoring posts and constructing roads on Yemeni territory. In January 1995 the two countries failed to renew the 1934 Ta'if agreement (renewable every 20 years), delineating their de facto frontier. Following military clashes between Saudi and Yemeni forces, and intense mediation by Syria, the two sides undertook to halt all military activity in the disputed border area. In February the Saudi and Yemeni Governments signed a memorandum of understanding (MOU) that reaffirmed their commitment to the legitimacy of the Ta'if agreement and provided for the establishment of six joint committees to delineate the land and sea borders and to develop economic and commercial ties. A border security agreement was signed in July 1996. In May 1998, however, Saudi Arabia invaded the disputed island of Huraym in the Red Sea and was reported to have sent a memorandum to the UN stating that it did not recognize the 1992 border agreement between Yemen and Oman, claiming that parts of the area involved were Saudi Arabian territory. The Saudi objection to the accord was widely believed to be related to its attempts to gain land access to the Arabian Sea, via a corridor between Yemen and Oman, which it had thus far been denied in its negotiations with Yemen.

Yemen submitted a memorandum to the League of Arab States (the Arab League, see p. 372) in July 1998, refuting the Saudi claim to the land and stating that the Saudi protests contravened the Ta'if agreement signed by that country. Further clashes were reported close to the land and sea border between Yemen and Saudi Arabia in June, and in July three Yemeni troops were killed during fighting with a Saudi border patrol on the disputed island of Duwaima in the Red Sea; Saudi Arabia claimed its actions there were in self-defence and that, under the Ta'if agreement, three-quarters of the island was Saudi territory. Nevertheless, in June 2000, during a visit to Saudi Arabia by Yemeni President Ali Abdullah Saleh, a final agreement delineating land and sea borders was signed. As part of the accord, which incorporated the 1934 Ta'if agreement and much of the 1995 MOU, both sides agreed to promote economic, commercial and cultural relations, and each undertook not to permit on its territory activities against the other by opposition groups. The agreement did not demarcate sections of the eastern border, however, and in August 2000 three Saudi border guards and one Yemeni soldier were reportedly killed in border clashes. The first meeting of the Saudi-Yemeni Co-ordination Council for more than a decade took place in December, by which time the withdrawal from the border region of troops of both countries' troops was almost complete. However, relations deteriorated again in early 2004, after the Saudi Government began construction of a 'security fence' along the border that risked violating the border demarcation treaty signed in June 2000. In June 2006 the Saudi and Yemeni ministers responsible for internal affairs signed an agreement on the final demarcation of their shared border.

Following the formation of al-Qa'ida in the Arabian Peninsula (AQAP) in early 2009, the Saudi Arabian authorities became increasingly concerned about the concentration of militant Islamist activity in ungoverned areas of Yemen. The growing lawlessness in Yemen's northern border region, exacerbated by a violent conflict between government forces and the Shi'ite al-Houthi movement, led to a significant expansion of Saudi military capacity in the region. In early November, following an exchange of gunfire between al-Houthi militants and Saudi border guards, Saudi Arabia launched a campaign of air-strikes and ground offensives against rebel targets in the Saudi-Yemeni border region. The Saudi authorities insisted that their operations were limited to clearing al-Houthi 'infiltrators' from its territory; however, there were reports of Saudi air-strikes inside Yemeni territory. Al-Houthi sources claimed that 54 civilians had been killed in one air-strike. Although Saudi Arabia announced that full control of the border region had been regained by late December, sporadic fighting between Saudi forces and al-Houthi militants continued. In late January 2010 the al-Houthi rebels, in preparation for cease-fire negotiations with the Yemeni Government, offered a truce to the Saudi authorities, stating that all fighters had been withdrawn from the kingdom's territory. At that time, 133 Saudi troops had been killed in the recent military campaign, while thousands of Saudi citizens had been displaced by the conflict. Following a meeting of the Saudi-Yemeni Co-ordination Council in Riyadh in March

2010, a number of agreements were signed concerning Saudi-funded energy, health, education and humanitarian projects in Yemen.

After a series of anti-Government demonstrations had been held in Yemen since February 2011, with protesters demanding the removal from office of President Saleh and government troops using considerable force against them, Saudi Arabia played a key role in efforts to formulate a Cooperation Council for the Arab States of the Gulf (Gulf Cooperation Council—GCC, see p. 255) plan designed to end the increasingly violent situation in that country. Following further mediation by the UN, Saleh finally signed the GCC-brokered agreement between the Yemeni Government and opposition on 23 November at a ceremony in Riyadh, which was hosted by King Abdullah. Under the terms of the deal, the Yemeni leader agreed to step down, hand over power to his deputy and accept the staging of a presidential election two months later, on condition that he and his family were given immunity from prosecution. A national unity government was duly formed in Yemen and, at a presidential election held in February 2012, Abd al-Rabbuh Mansur al-Hadi was elected as President. Following the change of leadership, security in the Saudi-Yemeni border region was reported to have deteriorated considerably, with many Islamist militants and other criminals including drugs-smugglers using the area as a base for their activities. In early 2013 the Saudi Government emphasized that it was proceeding with its construction of the 'security fence', so that the barrier would eventually run along the entire border.

In September 1992 Qatar accused a Saudi force of attacking a Qatari border post, killing two border guards and capturing a third. As a result, Qatar suspended a 1965 border agreement with Saudi Arabia, which had never been fully ratified. In December 1992, following mediation by President Hosni Mubarak of Egypt, the Amir of Qatar, Sheikh Khalifa Al Thani, signed an agreement in Medina with King Fahd to establish a committee to demarcate the disputed border. In June 1999 officials of the two countries met in Riyadh to sign maps defining their joint border, and an apparently final land and maritime demarcation agreement was signed in Doha, Qatar, in March 2001. The border agreement provided for a joint Saudi-Qatari committee, charged with ensuring full implementation of the 1965 accord.

The Saudi ambassador to Qatar was recalled in October 2002, following broadcasts by the Qatar-based satellite television broadcaster *Al Jazeera* that were deemed to be critical of the Saudi regime. Despite the 2001 agreement, the border dispute was revived in July 2007, when Saudi Arabia threatened to block a US $3,500m. gas pipeline between Qatar and the UAE, claiming that sections of the undersea pipeline ran through Saudi territory. In September the Qatari Amir, Sheikh Hamad bin Khalifa Al Thani, during a visit to Jeddah, gave an assurance that *Al Jazeera* would not broadcast material that could be regarded as defamatory in respect of Saudi Arabia; in return *Al Jazeera* would be permitted to establish a presence in the kingdom. Saudi Arabia confirmed the return of its diplomatic envoy to Qatar, and King Abdullah agreed to attend the forthcoming GCC summit in Doha (having refused such an invitation in 2002). Saudi objections to the Qatar-UAE gas pipeline were also resolved.

The new Saudi ambassador to Qatar acceded to his position in March 2008. In July the respective Governments agreed to resolve the issue of border demarcation and to establish a Joint Co-ordination Council to encourage co-operation in military, industrial, agricultural and energy affairs. A definitive Land and Maritime Border Delimitation Agreement was signed in December, together with various other bilateral agreements, at the first meeting of the Saudi-Qatari Joint Co-ordination Council, and was registered with the UN in March 2009. In June the UAE Government lodged an official complaint to the UN concerning the signing of the Saudi-Qatari agreement, claiming that it ran contrary to a border accord it had signed with Qatar in 1969, as well as to a 2004 agreement between the UAE and Qatar concerning the Dolphin gas pipeline. In July 2011 the Saudi authorities formally granted permission for *Al Jazeera* to open a bureau in the kingdom.

Officials from Saudi Arabia and Oman signed documents to demarcate their joint border in July 1995. In March 1999 Saudi Arabia held talks with Iran in an effort to mediate in its dispute with the UAE over the Tunb islands. Following a statement by the GCC condemning both Iran's recent military exercises near the islands and its claim to them, and emphasizing UAE sovereignty of the islands, the Iranian President temporarily cancelled a planned visit to Saudi Arabia. Saudi Arabia's rapprochement with Iran had resulted in a deterioration in its relations with the UAE, and in March the UAE boycotted a meeting of GCC ministers responsible for petroleum production in protest against Saudi exploration of an oilfield in disputed territory prior to an agreement being reached. In September 2000 the Saudi Government approved an agreement, signed in July, which ended the long-standing dispute with Kuwait regarding their mutual sea border. Final maps delineating that border were signed by officials from both sides in January 2001.

In 2005 relations deteriorated between Saudi Arabia and three of its Gulf neighbours: Bahrain, Oman and the UAE. Bahrain and Oman had signed free trade agreements with the USA in September 2004 and October 2005, respectively, and in April 2006 the UAE was involved in negotiations with a view to signing a similar accord. Saudi Arabia, which argued that the GCC should negotiate a trade deal as a single body, claimed that the agreements contravened the GCC's external tariff treaty. In December relations with the UAE were further strained by a border dispute relating to the Shaybah oilfield in the Rub al-Khali desert region, which dated back to the 1970s and which formed the focal point of discussions between the UAE President, Sheikh Khalifa bin Zayed Al Nahyan, and the Saudi Minister of the Interior, Prince Nayef ibn Abd al-Aziz Al Sa'ud, in June 2006. In March 2011 Saudi Arabia sent 1,000 of its armed forces to Bahrain as the largest contingent of a GCC Peninsula Shield force (500 UAE police officers were also deployed) to assist that country's military in preventing the escalating pro-democracy protests there from turning into a full-scale rebellion against the ruling Sunni monarchy. Bahrain's Shi'a opposition described the deployment as an 'overt occupation'. There were allegations in April that Bahraini security forces, with Saudi backing, had destroyed or desecrated a number of Shi'a mosques and shrines in that country. At the GCC summit meeting held in Riyadh in mid-May 2012, the much talked about proposals for a unification of Saudi Arabia with Bahrain did not materialize.

In September 2000 Iraq accused Saudi Arabia and Kuwait of inflicting (through the maintenance of the sanctions regime) suffering on the Iraqi population, and alleged that Saudi Arabia was appropriating Iraqi petroleum transported under the oil-for-food programme. Nevertheless, Saudi Arabia, encouraged by the mediation of the Arab League, indicated at the beginning of 2002 that it was ready for a cautious rapprochement with Iraq. In October the border crossing from Saudi Arabia to Iraq was reopened, providing a fifth land route for Iraqi trade under the UN oil-for-food arrangement. In July 2004, following the US-led military campaign to remove Saddam Hussain's regime in Iraq in 2003, Saudi Arabia and Iraq restored diplomatic relations; these had been severed in 1991, after Iraq's invasion of Kuwait. The two countries announced that their embassies in Baghdad and Riyadh, respectively, would be reopened. However, although the Iraqi embassy in Riyadh was opened in February 2007, the opening of the Saudi embassy in Baghdad was subsequently delayed owing to security concerns; it remained closed as of early 2013. A contract to construct a 900-km 'security fence' along Saudi Arabia's border with Iraq, at a cost of some US $900m., was awarded to a joint Saudi-European consortium in June 2008. The fence, which would incorporate sophisticated surveillance equipment, represented the first phase of a planned 6,500-km barrier along all the kingdom's borders. The contract for the second and final phase of the project was awarded to the same consortium in February 2009 and was estimated to be worth $2,200m. In February 2012 Saudi Arabia finally named its ambassador to Jordan as the non-resident ambassador in Baghdad, although the improvement in Iraqi-Saudi relations was hindered in April when the Iraqi Prime Minister, Nuri al-Maliki, strongly criticized demands by officials of both Saudi Arabia and Qatar for anti-Government rebels in Syria to be provided with weapons. The rebels did begin to receive Saudi military assistance from early 2012.

Relations between Saudi Arabia and Iran, which were particularly strained by suspicions of Iranian involvement in the 1996 al-Khobar bombing (see Militant Islamism), improved considerably following the election of Muhammad Khatami to the Iranian presidency in 1997. Co-operation was notably strengthened following the September 2001 attacks on New York and Washington, DC, USA, as Saudi Arabia and Iran sought to counter the emergence of anti-Islamic sentiment in the West. The election of Mahmoud Ahmadinejad to the Iranian

presidency in June 2005 proved somewhat damaging to bilateral relations, however, with the Saudi Government becoming increasingly concerned by what it perceived to be Ahmadinejad's destabilizing effect on the region. Nevertheless, in January 2007 the two states were reported to be conducting negotiations to seek an end to the political impasse in Lebanon (q.v.). Furthermore, President Ahmadinejad was unexpectedly granted an audience with King Abdullah in Riyadh in March, which was widely seen as an implicit snub by the Saudi monarch of the US policy of exclusion towards Iran. The two leaders also apparently sought to demonstrate unity between the Sunni and Shi'ite factions of Islam. Ahmadinejad returned to Saudi Arabia in December to participate, at the King's invitation, in the *Hajj* to Mecca, becoming the first Iranian President to do so.

Notwithstanding public displays of harmony, Saudi-Iranian relations remained somewhat adversarial during 2008–09. In May 2008 Saudi Minister of Foreign Affairs Prince Sa'ud al-Faisal, referring to Iran's support for the militant Lebanese organization Hezbollah's recent military clashes with government forces in that country, accused Iran of inciting sectarian conflict and interfering in the affairs of an independent state. In March 2009, at a meeting of Arab ministers of foreign affairs, Prince al-Faisal appealed for a unified Arab strategy in dealing with what he described as the 'Iranian challenge'. Meanwhile, President Ahmadinejad, in January 2009, appeared to accuse Saudi Arabia of complicity in the killing of Palestinians in the Israeli military operation in Gaza in late December 2008 and early January 2009, alleging that the kingdom was silent in the face of Israel's aggression and urging Saudi Arabia to end its trade ties with the Jewish state.

Saudi Arabia's decision to assist the Bahraini Government in quelling popular unrest by sending 1,000 troops to Bahrain in March 2011 led to a deterioration in relations with Iran, which had issued a formal complaint to the UN regarding the tough measures being taken by the Bahrain security forces against anti-Government demonstrators. In April, following a meeting of the GCC in Riyadh, member states urged the UN Security Council to prevent Iran's 'interference, provocation and threats', which they said risked destabilizing the entire Gulf region. It was reported in May that Saudi officials had refused to hold talks with Iran's Minister of Foreign Affairs, Ali Akbar Salehi, who was on a tour of the Gulf, unless the Iranian Government issued a formal apology for recent attacks on Saudi diplomatic buildings in Iran. A request by Salehi for Qatar to mediate in the two countries' ongoing dispute had apparently been turned down by the emirate. In October the US Administration revealed details of an alleged plot by Iranian militants linked to that country's Revolutionary Guards to assassinate the Saudi ambassador in Washington, DC. President Ahmadinejad claimed that the US allegations were intended to increase pressure on the Islamic regime; however, the Saudi Government asked the UN Security Council to investigate the matter. It was reported by *The Times* newspaper in February 2012 that sources within the kingdom indicated that Saudi Arabia would respond to any future announcement that Iran had succeeded in manufacturing a nuclear weapon by swiftly pursuing its own nuclear weapons programme.

In February 2002 Crown Prince Abdullah put forward a proposal, based on the 1981 Fahd Plan, to end the escalating conflict between Israel and the Palestinians based on the principle of 'land for peace'. In return for a collective Arab recognition of the State of Israel, the Plan insisted on Israel's complete withdrawal from Arab territories occupied since 1967. The Crown Prince also urged the US Administration to exert pressure on Israel to withdraw its forces from the West Bank. The Saudi peace initiative was unanimously endorsed at a summit conference of the Arab League Council held in March 2002 in Beirut, Lebanon, but was rejected by Israel. In March 2007 Riyadh hosted the annual summit meeting of the Arab League Council, at which negotiations were dominated by the Israeli–Palestinian conflict, as well as by the situations in Iraq and Lebanon. The Council reaffirmed its endorsement of the 'land-for-peace' proposal, which had been amassing increasing levels of support, and which Israeli Prime Minister Ehud Olmert had conceded might provide an initial basis for the renewal of formal peace discussions with Arab leaders. Saudi Arabia participated in the US-sponsored international peace meeting held at Annapolis, Maryland, USA, in November, at which negotiations towards a resolution of the Israeli–Palestinian conflict were officially relaunched.

In response to the military offensive launched by Israel against Hamas targets in the Gaza Strip in late December 2008, King Abdullah hosted an emergency GCC summit in Riyadh on 15 January 2009, which focused on seeking an end to the hostilities and on the provision of aid. Meanwhile, Sheikh Hamad of Qatar planned to convene an emergency Arab League summit in the Qatari capital, Doha, to formulate a unified Arab response to the conflict in Gaza, which by mid-January had reportedly resulted in more than 1,400 Palestinians deaths, with some 5,000 wounded. However, the Saudi King did not send a delegation to the Doha meeting, which was held on 16 January, stating his preference for the forthcoming Arab Economic, Social and Development Summit in Kuwait as a forum for pan-Arab discussions. As a result of the absence of Saudi Arabia, Egypt and others, the Doha summit failed to attain the quorum required to grant the meeting official status. In 2011 the Saudi Government supported efforts by the Palestinian (National) Authority, as part of its desire to achieve statehood, to be granted membership of the UN; this led to a disagreement with the US Administration, which advocated a postponement of any such vote. Saudi Arabia argued that the Israeli-Palestinian peace process sponsored by international actors, including the USA, had thus far been unsuccessful.

Following the transfer of its ambassador in Damascus to Doha in early 2008, Saudi Arabia declined to appoint a new ambassador to Syria, demonstrating its disapproval at Syria's role in the ongoing political crisis in Lebanon. The conflicting interests of Saudi Arabia and Syria in the region were highlighted by their divergent responses to the Israeli military offensive in Gaza launched in December 2008. However, there were hopes of a rapprochement after Syria and other Arab states held private talks with King Abdullah during the Arab Economic, Social and Development Summit in Kuwait in January 2009. In early March Saudi Minister of Foreign Affairs Prince Sa'ud al-Faisal held constructive talks with Syrian President Bashar al-Assad in Damascus on Arab reconciliation and other regional issues. On 11 March the King hosted a one-day summit on regional affairs, which was attended by Assad, President Mubarak of Egypt and the Kuwaiti Amir, Sheikh Sabah al-Ahmad al-Jaber al-Sabah. A key objective of the summit was support for Egyptian-brokered reconciliation talks between the rival Palestinian factions, Fatah and Hamas.

The appointment, in July 2009, of a new Saudi ambassador to Syria confirmed the positive trend in bilateral relations. In October King Abdullah completed his first official visit to Syria since acceding to the throne in 2005. He held two rounds of talks with President Assad on bilateral relations and regional issues, and an agreement on taxation was signed by the respective Ministers of Finance. Analysts regarded the summit as highly significant, given the important, and often antagonistic, influence exerted by both powers in the region. At the summit's conclusion the leaders issued a statement confirming their joint support for the establishment of a government of national unity in Lebanon (this was achieved in November 2009); joint Arab measures in support of the Palestinian cause; and the safeguarding of stability and national unity in Yemen. Assad made a reciprocal visit to Riyadh in January 2010, during which discussions continued on a range of key regional issues. In July King Abdullah and President Assad held a tripartite summit meeting with the Lebanese President, Michel Suleiman, in Beirut, in an effort to prevent the tensions between Lebanon's rival Sunni and Shi'ite factions from descending into violence. This was the first visit to Lebanon by a Saudi monarch since 1957. The meeting was convened amid reports, later substantiated, that the UN Special Tribunal established to investigate the 2005 assassination of former premier Rafiq Hariri was likely to implicate members of the Shi'ite Hezbollah—part of the governing coalition—in the crime. However, in mid-January 2011, with the issuing of the first tribunal indictments imminent, the Lebanese Government collapsed, following the withdrawal of Hezbollah-allied ministers. The previous day the Saudi and Syrian Governments were reported to have failed in their efforts to secure a compromise agreement for Lebanon.

The Saudi leadership initially gave strong backing to the Syrian regime of President Assad, which persistently claimed that protesters leading a popular uprising against his rule from early 2011 were 'armed terrorist gangs'. However, as the Syrian armed forces intensified their military crackdown against the opposition activists and the death toll arising from the unrest rose, in August King Abdullah launched a strong condemnation of the regime's actions, urging the Syrian President to 'stop the

killing machine'. The Saudi ambassador to Damascus was recalled in protest at the crackdown. In November a group of Syrians attacked the Saudi embassy in the Syrian capital; their action followed the decision by the Arab League to suspend Syria from the organization in protest against the Syrian Government's harsh repression of pro-democracy demonstrators. In mid-March 2012, by which time more than 9,000 people were reported to have been killed since the start of the Syrian uprising, Saudi Arabia announced the closure of its embassy in Damascus. Meanwhile, the Syrian Minister of Information, Dr Adnan Mahmoud, accused both the Saudi and Qatari Governments of providing military assistance to the Free Syrian Army, a group of opposition forces formed by defecting soldiers from President Assad's armed forces.

After the Tunisian revolution of January 2011, ousted President Zine al-Abidine Ben Ali fled the country and was given refuge in Saudi Arabia. The Saudi Government did, however, recognize the interim Government formed immediately following Ben Ali's ouster, as it did the new administration in Egypt, following the removal from power of its erstwhile ally, President Hosni Mubarak, in February. Efforts made by the new Tunisian leadership to extradite Ben Ali—who in June, along with his wife, was found guilty of the embezzlement of state funds during his time in office and sentenced *in absentia* to 35 years in prison—had not succeeded by early 2013. Ben Ali was also convicted of abuse of power, and other trial proceedings were ongoing, including those accusing him of having been responsible for the deaths of anti-Government protesters during the Tunisian revolution. Relations with the new administration in Egypt appeared to deteriorate in early 2012, amid growing public criticism in Egypt of the treatment of Egyptian expatriate workers in Saudi Arabia. In April the Saudi Government announced that it had closed the country's embassy in Cairo and recalled the ambassador for consultations, following protests outside the building earlier that month. The protests followed the arrest in Jeddah of a prominent Egyptian human rights lawyer, Ahmad al-Gizawi, ostensibly on charges of drugs-smuggling; al-Gizawi had previously sought to bring legal proceedings against King Abdullah in an Egyptian court over the alleged detention without trial of Egyptian citizens in the kingdom. It was reported that al-Gizawi had been sentenced *in absentia* by a Saudi court to one year's imprisonment for insulting the King, prior to his arrival in Saudi Arabia.

Other external relations

King Abdullah visited the People's Republic of China in January 2006—the first such visit by a Saudi monarch since the formal establishment of diplomatic relations in 1990—whereupon he signed a bilateral agreement to co-operate in the petroleum and natural gas sectors. With the deterioration in Saudi–US relations, the kingdom was keen to diversify its international trade, and China, as the world's second largest petroleum consumer, was an ideal candidate for partnership. In the same month Abdullah also became the first Saudi monarch to visit India since 1955. In February 2006 a visit to Pakistan further bolstered traditionally strong bilateral relations, with the signing of five agreements aimed at increasing co-operation on the economy, education, investment, science and technology. In April Crown Prince Sultan embarked upon a tour of the Far East, visiting Japan, Singapore and China. This 'look east' policy was adopted principally for economic gain, but it also served as a demonstration of Saudi independence from the USA.

In September 2007 an agreement with the United Kingdom reached in 2006 regarding the purchase of 72 *Eurofighter Typhoon* military aircraft as part of efforts to establish 'a greater partnership to modernize the Saudi Arabian armed forces' was confirmed by the Saudi authorities. A further agreement concerning the purchase of British trainer aircraft was announced in May 2012. King Abdullah, accompanied by a large delegation of senior Saudi officials, began a high-profile state visit to the United Kingdom in October 2007, during which protests were held by those angered at what they deemed to be Saudi Arabia's poor record on human rights and curbing Islamist extremism. In the following month King Abdullah undertook a landmark visit to the Vatican City, where he became the first Saudi monarch to hold discussions with a Supreme Pontiff of the Roman Catholic Church; the talks with Pope Benedict XVI were reported to have focused on how to promote peace between Christians, Muslims and Jews world-wide and to achieve a just solution to the Israeli–Palestinian conflict. Although in 2008 discussions were said to be taking place between Saudi and Vatican officials concerning the possibility of the first Catholic church being built in the kingdom, the Saudi Government confirmed in April 2013 that the construction of non-Muslim places of worship would remain prohibited.

CONSTITUTION AND GOVERNMENT

Saudi Arabia is an absolute monarchy, with no legislature or political parties. Constitutionally, the King rules in accordance with the *Shari'a*, the sacred law of Islam. He appoints and leads a Council of Ministers, which serves as the instrument of royal authority in both legislative and executive matters. Decisions of the Council are reached by majority vote, but require royal sanction. A Consultative Council (Majlis al-Shura) was officially inaugurated in December 1993. Members of the Majlis are chosen by the King. Membership of the Majlis was increased from 60 to 90 in July 1997, to 120 in May 2001 and to 150 in April 2005. In September 2011 King Abdullah announced that women would be allowed to participate in the Majlis from the beginning of its next term, and would be permitted to vote and to seek election at the municipal elections scheduled for 2015. In January 2013 King Abdullah issued two decrees, the first stipulating that at least 20% of seats in the Majlis must be allocated to women and the second appointing 30 women to the council.

The organs of local government are the General Municipal Councils and the tribal and village councils. A General Municipal Council is established in the towns of Mecca, Medina and Jeddah. Its members are proposed by the inhabitants and must be approved by the King. Functioning concurrently with each General Municipal Council is a General Administration Committee, which investigates ways and means of executing resolutions passed by the Council. Every village and tribe has a council with the power to enforce regulations; it is composed of the presiding sheikh, his legal advisers and two other prominent personages. A system of provincial government was announced in late 1993 by royal decree: this defined the nature of government for 13 newly created regions, as well as the rights and responsibilities of their governors, and appointed councils of prominent citizens for each region to monitor development and advise the government. Each council was to meet four times a year under the chairmanship of a governor, who would be an emir with ministerial rank. A royal decree, issued in April 1994, further divided the 13 regions into 103 governorates. In October 2003 it was announced that new municipal councils, of which one-half of the membership would be elected by universal suffrage and one-half appointed by the central Government, would be introduced. Municipal elections took place in 2005 and in 2011.

REGIONAL AND INTERNATIONAL CO-OPERATION

Saudi Arabia is a member of the Cooperation Council for the Arab States of the Gulf (the Gulf Cooperation Council—GCC, see p. 255), which created a unified regional customs tariff in January 2003 and agreed to establish a single market and currency. The economic convergence criteria for the proposed monetary union were agreed at a heads of state meeting in Abu Dhabi, United Arab Emirates, in December 2005, and in January 2008 the GCC launched its common market. However, the introduction of a single currency, originally scheduled for 1 January 2010, was subsequently postponed until at least 2015. Saudi Arabia is also a member of the League of Arab States (the Arab League, see p. 372), and the Organization of Arab Petroleum Exporting Countries (OAPEC, see p. 410).

The kingdom was a founder member of the UN on that organization's establishment in October 1945, and acceded to the World Trade Organization (WTO, see p. 444) in December 2005. Saudi Arabia also participates in the Organization of the Petroleum Exporting Countries (OPEC, see p. 418). The Organization of Islamic Cooperation (OIC, see p. 413) maintains its permanent headquarters in Jeddah.

ECONOMIC AFFAIRS

In 2011, according to estimates by the World Bank, Saudi Arabia's gross national income (GNI), measured at average 2009–11 prices, was US $500,543m., equivalent to $17,820 per head (or $24,870 per head on an international purchasing-power parity basis). During 2002–11, it was estimated, the population increased at an average annual rate of 3.0%, while gross domestic product (GDP) per head increased, in real terms, by an average of 1.3% per year. According to official figures, overall GDP increased, in real terms, at an average annual rate of 6.9% in 2002–11; real GDP increased by a preliminary 6.8% in 2012.

Agriculture (including forestry and fishing) contributed a preliminary 1.8% of GDP in 2012 and employed 4.3% of the economically active population in 2011. The principal crop is wheat, the production of which depends almost entirely on irrigation. Saudi Arabia has exported a large wheat surplus since the late 1980s; however, the kingdom planned gradually to reduce output of the crop (with production scheduled to cease entirely by 2016), owing to the increasing scarcity of water resources. Sorghum, barley, potatoes, tomatoes, watermelons and dates are also significant crops. Saudi Arabia is self-sufficient in many dairy products, and in eggs and broiler chickens. Agricultural GDP increased by an average of 1.6% per year in 2002–11; the sector's GDP increased by a preliminary 2.6% in 2012.

Industry (including mining, manufacturing, construction and power) provided a preliminary 63.1% of GDP in 2012 and employed 22.5% of the active labour force in 2011. During 2002–11, it was estimated, industrial GDP increased at an average annual rate of 6.2%; the sector expanded by a preliminary 7.1% in 2012.

Mining and quarrying contributed a preliminary 47.2% of GDP in 2012, while it engaged only 1.3% of the employed population in 2011. The sector is dominated by petroleum and natural gas, which provided a preliminary 46.8% of GDP in that year. Saudi Arabia was the world's largest petroleum producer in 2011, and mineral products provided 87.2% of total export revenue in that year. At the end of 2011 Saudi Arabia's proven recoverable reserves of petroleum were 265,405m. barrels, equivalent to 16.1% of the world's proven oil reserves. Crude petroleum production averaged 11.2m. barrels per day (b/d) in 2011. As a member of the Organization of the Petroleum Exporting Countries (OPEC, see p. 418), Saudi Arabia is subject to production quotas agreed by the Organization's Conference. Government sources reported oil production capacity to be around 12.5m. b/d in mid-2012. Demand for energy in the kingdom was forecast to almost double between 2013 and 2030, from 4.3m. b/d of oil to 8.0m. b/d. The Saudi Government has denied suggestions by some observers that information pertaining to the country's recoverable reserves has been inaccurate, and that it might not possess sufficient petroleum to meet demand in the long term. In February 2011, after the popular uprising and subsequent conflict in Libya had virtually halted that country's oil production, the Saudi authorities agreed to increase oil output by 700,000 b/d in order to make up the shortfall. In March 2012, with oil exports from Iran under threat as a result of international sanctions, Saudi Arabia declared its willingness to increase production further. Gas reserves, mostly associated with petroleum, totalled 8,150,212m. cu m at the end of 2011. In 2002 the world's largest natural gas plant was opened at Hawiya; the plant, which was the first Saudi project to produce gas not associated with petroleum, was expected to increase the country's production of gas by more than 30%. Further non-associated gas reserves are yet to be fully exploited. Other minerals produced include limestone, gypsum, marble, clay and salt, while there are substantial deposits of phosphates, bauxite, gold and other metals. The GDP of the mining sector increased at an average annual rate of 3.5% in 2002–11; the rate of growth increased by a preliminary 5.6% in 2012.

Manufacturing contributed a preliminary 10.2% of GDP in 2012 and provided 7.1% of employment in 2011. The most important activity is the refining of petroleum, which contributed a preliminary 2.6% of GDP in 2012. The production of petrochemicals, fertilizers, construction materials (particularly steel and cement), and food- and drink-processing are also important activities. Manufacturing GDP increased by an average of 9.5% per year in 2002–11; the GDP of the sector increased by a preliminary 7.6% in 2012.

According to preliminary figures, construction contributed 4.6% of GDP in 2012, while it engaged 13.0% of the employed labour force in 2011. Construction GDP increased by an average of 7.6% per year in 2002–11; the GDP of the sector increased by a preliminary 10.3% in 2012.

Electrical energy is generated by thermal power stations, using Saudi Arabia's own petroleum resources, although an increasing amount of electricity is now produced in association with sea-water desalination. Electricity expansion projects were being planned in 2011 to satisfy domestic demand, which was increasing by around 8% per year. In addition to building new electric power stations, the Government was also planning a civil nuclear energy programme, involving the construction of 16 nuclear reactors over a 20-year period, at a cost of SR 300,000m.

Bilateral co-operation accords have been signed with a number of countries in recent years, including the USA, France and the Republic of Korea (South Korea). A regional electricity grid, linking countries of the Cooperation Council for the Arab States of the Gulf (the Gulf Cooperation Council, see p. 255), became fully operational in November 2012, and was eventually to achieve regional self-sufficiency up to 2058.

The services sector contributed a preliminary 35.1% of GDP in 2012. The sector engaged 73.2% of the employed labour force in 2011. The GDP of the services sector increased by an average of 7.8% per year in 2002–11; the rate of growth was 6.7% in 2012, according to preliminary figures.

In 2011 Saudi Arabia recorded a visible merchandise trade surplus of US $244,775m., and a surplus of $158,545m. on the current account of the balance of payments. In that year the principal source of imports (13.1%) was the People's Republic of China; other important suppliers were the USA, Germany, Japan and South Korea. According to official provisional figures, the USA was the principal market for exports (13.7%) in that year; other major markets were Japan, China, South Korea and India. In 2011 the dominant exports were mineral products (particularly crude petroleum) and chemical products. The principal imports in that year were machinery and transport equipment, base metals and their articles, food and live animals, and chemicals and related products.

A budgetary surplus of SR 291,092m. was recorded in 2011. Saudi Arabia's general government gross debt was SR 135,500m. in 2011, equivalent to 6.1% of GDP. Consumer prices increased by an annual average of 3.7% in 2002–12, and by 4.5% in 2012. The overall unemployment rate was 5.5% in 2012, although for Saudi nationals the rate was considerably higher, at 12.1%. In 2011 non-Saudi nationals comprised 55.2% of the total labour force, according to official figures. The Government approved legislation in 2005 to reduce the number of foreign workers to 20% of the population by 2015; the new law was also to provide maternity leave rights and childcare facilities, in order to encourage greater female participation in the work-force. Women, including non-Saudi nationals, comprised 15.3% of the total labour force in 2011, with Saudi women comprising only 8.6% of the total.

Saudi Arabia's prosperity is based on exploitation of its petroleum reserves. Although during 2009–10 the country was overtaken as the world's largest oil producer by Russia, in 2011 Saudi Arabia regained the leading position. The kingdom remained the biggest exporter of oil world-wide and it continued to play a crucial role in determining OPEC production levels and, thus, world prices. Since 2000 the Saudi authorities have aimed to increase private investment and growth in the private and non-oil sectors, and sought to expand employment opportunities and housing provision for the rapidly expanding Saudi population. The construction of the new King Abdullah Economic City, situated on the west coast between Jeddah and Rabigh, commenced in 2006 and was projected to be completed by 2025. A further five 'economic cities' were planned in order to establish new industries and create at least 1.3m. jobs by 2020. In 2009 the kingdom recorded its first fiscal deficit since 2002, equivalent to 6.1% of GDP, owing to reduced petroleum revenues and high public expenditure. However, following a significant increase in oil revenues, a budget surplus of some 17% of GDP was recorded in 2010. As regional instability pushed international oil prices still higher, large fiscal surpluses were recorded in both 2011 and 2012. Nevertheless, in September 2012 the IMF warned that, unless further measures were taken to diversify the economy and reduce state spending, such surpluses could become deficits by 2016. In October 2010 the Council of Ministers endorsed the Ninth Development Plan for 2010–14, which sought to continue the process of economic diversification and to base growth on the principal of sustainable development. Amid rare street protests in parts of Saudi Arabia in early 2011, caused in part by frustration over rising food prices and high youth unemployment (at least 28% at the end of 2011), the King announced a range of economic measures—including the introduction of unemployment benefit, the creation of additional public sector jobs and the expansion of housing provision. By January 2013 official figures showed that the authorities' US $130,000m. stimulus package had increased growth in both the non-oil and private sectors; the latter sector now contributed 58% of GDP.

PUBLIC HOLIDAYS

2014: 23 July–5 August* (Id al-Fitr, end of Ramadan), 23 September (National Day), 30 September–8 October* (Id al-Adha, Feast of the Sacrifice).

* These holidays are dependent on the Islamic lunar calendar and may vary by one or two days from the dates given.

Statistical Survey

Sources (unless otherwise indicated): Central Department of Statistics, Ministry of Economy and Planning, POB 358, University St, Riyadh 11182; tel. (1) 401-3333; fax (1) 401-9300; e-mail info@cds.gov.sa; internet www.cdsi.gov.sa; Saudi Arabian Monetary Agency, *Annual Report* and *Statistical Summary*.

Area and Population

AREA, POPULATION AND DENSITY

Area (sq km)	2,240,000*
Population (census results)	
15 September 2004	22,678,262
28 April 2010†	
Males	15,460,147
Females	11,676,830
Total	27,136,977
Population (official estimates at mid-year)	
2011	28,376,355
2012‡	29,195,895
Density (per sq km) at mid-2012	13.0

* 864,869 sq miles.

† Of the total population at the 2010 census, 18,707,576 (males 9,527,173, females 9,180,403) were nationals of Saudi Arabia, while 8,429,401 (males 5,932,974, females 2,496,427) were foreign nationals.

‡ Population comprised of 19,838,448 Saudi nationals and 9,357,447 foreign nationals.

Saudi Arabia-Iraq Neutral Zone: The Najdi (Saudi Arabian) frontier with Iraq was defined in the Treaty of Mohammara in May 1922. Later a Neutral Zone of 7,044 sq km was established adjacent to the western tip of the Kuwait frontier. No military or permanent buildings were to be erected in the zone and the nomads of both countries were to have unimpeded access to its pastures and wells. A further agreement concerning the administration of this zone was signed between Iraq and Saudi Arabia in May 1938. In July 1975 Iraq and Saudi Arabia signed an agreement providing for an equal division of the diamond-shaped zone between the two countries, with the border following a straight line through the zone.

Saudi Arabia-Kuwait Neutral Zone: A Convention signed at Uqair in December 1922 fixed the Najdi (Saudi Arabian) boundary with Kuwait. The Convention also established a Neutral Zone of 5,770 sq km immediately to the south of Kuwait in which Saudi Arabia and Kuwait held equal rights. The final agreement on this matter was signed in 1963. Since 1966 the Neutral Zone, or Partitioned Zone as it is sometimes known, has been divided between the two countries and each administers its own half, in practice as an integral part of the state. However, the petroleum deposits in the Zone remain undivided and production from the onshore oil concessions in the Zone is shared equally between the two states' concessionaires.

POPULATION BY AGE AND SEX
(official demographic survey, 2007)

	Males	Females	Total
0–14	3,926,920	3,856,076	7,782,996
15–64	9,024,995	6,496,928	15,521,923
65 and over	349,254	326,661	675,915
Total	13,301,169	10,679,665	23,980,834

ADMINISTRATIVE REGIONS
(population at 2010 census)

Aseer	. . .	1,913,392	Makkah . . .	6,915,006
Al-Baha	. .	411,888	Najran . . .	505,652
Eastern	. .	4,105,780	Northern Borders.	320,524
Ha'il	. . .	597,144	Qassim . . .	1,215,858
Jazan	. . .	1,365,110	Riyadh . . .	6,777,146
Al-Jouf	. .	440,009	Tabouk . . .	791,535
Al-Madinah	. .	1,777,933	**Total** . . .	27,136,977

PRINCIPAL TOWNS
(population at 2010 census)

Riyadh (royal capital) . .	5,188,286	Jubail	337,778
Jeddah (administrative capital) . .	3,430,697	Ha'il (Hayil) . .	310,897
Makkah (Mecca)	1,534,731	Najran	298,288
Al-Madinah (Medina) . .	1,100,093	Hafar al-Batin . .	271,642
Dammam . .	903,312	Al-Thuqbah . . .	238,066
Hufuf* . . .	660,788	Abha	236,157
Al-Ta'if . . .	579,970	Al-Saih	234,607
Tabouk . . .	512,629	Yanbu	233,236
Buraidah . .	467,410	Al-Khubar . . .	219,679
Khamis-Mushait .	430,828		

* Includes population of Al-Mobarraz city.

BIRTHS AND DEATHS
(UN estimates, annual averages)

	1995–2000	2000–05	2005–10
Birth rate (per 1,000)	29.7	24.7	22.1
Death rate (per 1,000)	4.5	4.1	3.8

Source: UN, *World Population Prospects: The 2010 Revision*.

Crude birth rate (per 1,000): 23.3 in 2010; 22.9 in 2011; 22.5 in 2012.

Crude death rate (per 1,000): 3.9 in 2010–11; 3.8 in 2012.

Life expectancy (years at birth): 73.9 (males 72.8; females 75.0) in 2010 (Source: World Bank, World Development Indicators database).

ECONOMICALLY ACTIVE POPULATION
(persons aged 15 years and over, labour force survey, 2011)

	Males	Females	Total
Agriculture, hunting, forestry and fishing	425,891	2,660	428,551
Mining and quarrying	123,641	1,242	124,883
Manufacturing	689,007	15,424	704,431
Electricity, gas and water . . .	111,574	318	111,892
Construction	1,284,061	9,686	1,293,747
Wholesale and retail trade . .	1,760,330	12,912	1,773,242
Restaurants and hotels . . .	288,366	6,727	295,093
Transport and communications .	459,597	4,391	463,988
Financial intermediation . .	92,846	7,005	99,851
Real estate, renting and business activities	325,645	7,145	332,790
Public administration and defence	1,559,468	35,798	1,595,266
Education	674,234	484,242	1,158,476
Health and social work . . .	302,381	126,692	429,073
Other community and personal services	158,402	15,949	174,351
Private households with employed persons	368,638	570,505	939,143
Extra-territorial organizations .	9,359	1,398	10,757
Total employed	8,633,440	1,302,094	9,935,534
Unemployed	298,927	309,628	608,555
Total labour force	8,932,367	1,611,722	10,544,089

Health and Welfare

KEY INDICATORS

Total fertility rate (children per woman, 2010)	2.8
Under-5 mortality rate (per 1,000 live births, 2010) . . .	18
Physicians (per 1,000 head, 2008)	0.9
Hospital beds (per 1,000 head, 2009)	2.2
Health expenditure (2009): US $ per head (PPP)	964
Health expenditure (2009): % of GDP	4.4
Health expenditure (2009): public (% of total)	62.4
Total carbon dioxide emissions ('000 metric tons, 2008) . .	433,556.7
Carbon dioxide emissions per head (metric tons, 2008) . .	16.6
Human Development Index (2011): ranking	56
Human Development Index (2011): value	0.770

For sources and definitions, see explanatory note on p. vi.

Agriculture

PRINCIPAL CROPS
('000 metric tons)

	2009	2010*	2011*
Wheat . . .	1,152	1,300	1,364
Barley	20	18	17
Maize	161	182	182
Millet	8	9	10
Sorghum	244	275	327
Potatoes	444	490	594
Tomatoes	543	500	484
Pumpkins, squash and gourds .	117	120	122
Cucumbers and gherkins . .	326	367	400
Aubergines (Eggplants) . .	57	56	56
Onions, dry	62	69	73
Carrots and turnips . . .	49	47	54
Okra	61	56	58
Watermelons	338	296	294
Cantaloupes and other melons .	211	194	191
Grapes	160	160	160
Dates	992	1,089	1,123

* FAO estimates.

Aggregate production ('000 metric tons, may include official, semi-official or estimated data): Total cereals 1,586 in 2009, 1,784 in 2010, 1,900 in 2011; Total roots and tubers 444 in 2009, 490 in 2010, 594 in 2011; Total vegetables (incl. melons) 2,240 2009, 2,236 in 2010, 2,439 in 2011; Total fruits (excl. melons) 1,619 in 2009, 1,744 in 2010, 1,842 in 2011.

Source: FAO.

LIVESTOCK
('000 head, year ending September)

	2009	2010	2011*
Asses*	100	100	100
Camels	230	230*	240
Cattle	424	404*	400
Sheep	5,886	5,245†	5,000
Goats	3,809	3,408†	3,200
Chickens*	146,000	146,000	147,000

* FAO estimate(s).
† Unofficial figure.

Source: FAO.

LIVESTOCK PRODUCTS
('000 metric tons)

	2009	2010	2011
Cattle meat*	31.6	44.0	43.6
Sheep meat*	64.0	63.0	61.0
Goat meat*	18.4	24.0	26.5
Chicken meat	570.0†	575.0†	580.0*
Camel meat*	42.0	43.0	44.0
Cows' milk	1,508.4	1,670.0*	1,670.0*
Sheep's milk*	68.0	66.9	66.9
Goats' milk*	65.0	75.0	75.0
Camels' milk*	80.5	97.8	97.8
Hen eggs	191.0	193.0*	193.0*
Wool, greasy*	9.0	10.5	10.5

* FAO estimate(s).
† Unofficial figure.

Source: FAO.

Fishing

(metric tons, live weight)

	2008	2009	2010
Capture	68,898	67,664	65,142
Pink ear emperors . . .	2,297	2,990	2,460
Emperors (Scavengers) . .	4,113	4,386	4,224
Spinefeet (Rabbitfishes) . .	1,890	2,075	2,170
Narrow-barred Spanish mackerel	4,356	4,802	3,728
Indian mackerel	3,914	3,950	3,950
Green tiger prawns . . .	10,551	9,083	7,571
Aquaculture	22,353	26,120*	26,374*
Nile tilapia	3,673	3,837	3,382
Indian white prawn	17,912	20,781	20,652
Total catch	90,874	93,784*	91,516*

* FAO estimate.

Source: FAO.

Mining

('000 metric tons unless otherwise indicated)

	2009	2010	2011
Crude petroleum (million barrels)*	2,987	2,980	n.a.
Silver (kg)†	8,527	7,670	7,900‡
Gold (kg)†	4,857	4,476	4,611
Salt (unrefined)	1,640	1,800	1,800‡
Gypsum (crude)	2,000	2,100	2,300‡
Pozzolan	802	915	1,000‡

* Including 50% of the total output of the Neutral (Partitioned) Zone, shared with Kuwait (Source: Saudi Arabian Monetary Agency).
† Figures refer to the metal content of concentrate and bullion.
‡ Estimated figure.

Source: mainly US Geological Survey.

Natural gas (excluding flared and recycled, million cu m): 78,450 in 2009; 87,660 in 2010; 99,231 in 2011 (Source: BP, *Statistical Review of World Energy*).

Industry

SELECTED PRODUCTS
(including 50% of the total output of the Neutral Zone; '000 barrels unless otherwise indicated)

	2008	2009	2010
Phosphatic fertilizers ('000 metric tons)*†	300	300	300
Motor spirit (petrol) and naphtha .	200,606	194,983	208,770
Jet fuel and kerosene	69,677	63,502	58,112
Gas-diesel (distillate fuel) oils .	247,438	227,686	231,212
Residual fuel oils	174,381	181,613	162,575
Petroleum bitumen (asphalt) . .	17,960	17,035	18,212
Liquefied petroleum gas . . .	11,303	12,692	12,228
Cement ('000 metric tons) . .	31,823	36,500	42,300
Crude steel ('000 metric tons) .	4,670	4,700	5,000
Electric energy (million kWh sold)	181,097	193,472	212,263

* Production in terms of phosphoric acid.
† Estimates.
‡ Preliminary figure.

2011 ('000 metric tons unless otherwise indicated): Cement 48,000 (estimate); Crude steel 5,300 (estimate); Electric energy (million kWh sold) 219,662.

Sources: Saudi Arabian Monetary Agency; US Geological Survey.

Finance

CURRENCY AND EXCHANGE RATES

Monetary Units:
100 halalah = 20 qurush = 1 Saudi riyal (SR).

Sterling, Dollar and Euro Equivalents (31 December 2012):
£1 sterling = 5.918 riyals;
US $1 = 3.750 riyals;
€1 = 4.948 riyals;
100 Saudi riyals = £16.90 = $26.67 = €20.21.

Exchange Rate: Since June 1986 the official mid-point rate has been fixed at US $1 = 3.75 riyals.

BUDGET ESTIMATES
(million riyals)

Revenue	2010	2011	2012
Petroleum revenues	400,000	468,000	621,000
Other revenues	70,000	72,000	81,000
Total	470,000	540,000	702,000

Expenditure	2010	2011	2012
Human resource development .	137,440	148,307	167,933
Transport and communications .	16,442	17,334	20,566
Economic resource development .	29,288	32,938	36,048
Health and social development .	46,600	52,447	61,009
Infrastructure development . .	8,438	8,918	11,211
Municipal services	18,748	21,201	25,460
Defence and security	169,667	181,991	212,715
Public administration and other government spending . . .	92,017	93,820	111,434
Government lending institutions*.	596	635	10,785
Local subsidies	20,764	22,410	32,839
Total	540,000	580,000	690,000

* Including transfers to the Saudi Fund for Development (SFD).

2010 (revised figures, million riyals): Total revenue 741,616 (Petroleum revenue 670,265, Other revenue 71,351); Total expenditure 653,885.

2011 (revised figures, million riyals): Total revenue 1,117,792 (Petroleum revenue 1,034,360, Other revenue 83,432); Total expenditure 826,700.

INTERNATIONAL RESERVES
(US $ million in December)

	2009	2010	2011
Gold*	415	415	415
IMF special drawing rights . .	10,928	10,646	10,293
Reserve position in IMF . . .	2,017	1,981	4,862
Foreign exchange	396,748	432,094	525,521
Total	410,108	445,136	541,091

* Valued at US $40 per troy ounce at 31 December 2010.

Source: IMF, *International Financial Statistics.*

MONEY SUPPLY
('000 million riyals in December)

	2009	2010	2011
Currency outside banks . . .	88.40	95.52	119.93
Demand deposits at commercial banks	433.48	530.39	641.51
Total money	521.88	625.91	761.44

Source: IMF, *International Financial Statistics.*

COST OF LIVING
(Consumer Price Index for all cities; base: 1999 = 100)

	2010	2011	2012
Food and beverages	148.4	156.1	163.0
Housing, fuel and water . . .	160.3	172.7	186.7
Textiles and clothing (incl. footwear)	85.7	86.0	88.5
House furnishing	115.7	116.4	120.4
Medical care	113.7	114.6	114.7
Transport and communications .	90.2	92.1	93.8
Entertainment and education .	103.2	104.8	108.0
All items (incl. others) . . .	128.9	135.4	141.5

NATIONAL ACCOUNTS
(million riyals at current prices)

Expenditure on the Gross Domestic Product

	2010	2011	2012*
Government final consumption expenditure	400,173	489,846	537,583
Private final consumption expenditure	639,417	674,143	718,725
Increase in stocks	123,426	103,714	116,852
Gross fixed capital formation .	483,921	574,660	609,932
Total domestic expenditure .	1,646,937	1,842,363	1,983,092
Exports of goods and services .	981,867	1,410,702	1,525,587
Less Imports of goods and services	653,261	742,415	781,279
GDP in purchasers' values .	1,975,543	2,510,650	2,727,400
GDP at constant 1999 prices .	1,067,092	1,157,572	1,236,357

Gross Domestic Product by Economic Activity

	2010	2011	2012*
Agriculture, forestry and fishing .	47,063	48,163	49,903
Mining and quarrying:			
crude petroleum and natural gas	813,147	1,206,751	1,277,376
other	8,081	8,767	9,428
Manufacturing:			
petroleum refining	63,771	64,216	70,084
other	154,400	187,787	209,454
Electricity, gas and water . .	26,281	28,285	30,670
Construction	90,780	107,021	124,658
Trade, restaurants and hotels .	174,506	197,926	219,073

—*continued*	2010	2011	2012*
Transport, storage and communications	101,205	115,272	129,278
Finance, insurance, real estate and business services:			
ownership of dwellings . . .	88,276	96,715	106,108
other	94,328	98,339	110,651
Government services	280,863	312,308	344,723
Other community, social and personal services	37,768	41,892	46,509
Sub-total	1,980,469	2,513,442	2,727,915
Import duties	14,669	17,285	20,101
Less Imputed bank service charge	19,595	20,077	20,616
GDP in purchasers' values .	1,975,543	2,510,650	2,727,400

* Preliminary.

BALANCE OF PAYMENTS
(US $ million)

	2009	2010	2011
Exports of goods	192,307.2	251,142.7	364,735.5
Imports of goods	−87,077.6	−97,431.1	−119,960.7
Balance on goods	105,229.6	153,711.5	244,774.8
Exports of services	9,749.3	10,688.5	11,488.7
Imports of services	−74,991.4	−76,772.1	−78,016.6
Balance on goods and services	39,987.6	87,628.0	178,246.9
Primary income received . .	19,752.0	18,171.5	19,765.7
Primary income paid	−11,112.5	−11,127.6	−10,081.6
Balance on goods, services and Primary income	48,627.2	94,671.9	187,931.0
Secondary income received . .	—	—	34.7
Secondary income paid . . .	−27,672.6	−27,920.9	−29,420.5
Current balance	20,954.6	66,751.0	158,545.2
Direct investment assets . . .	−2,177.3	−3,906.8	−3,429.9
Direct investment from liabilities .	36,457.7	29,232.7	16,308.3
Portfolio investment assets . . .	−20,133.5	−16,656.9	−15,423.9
Portfolio investment liabilities .	−5.2	1,502.7	−623.7
Other investment assets . . .	−9,542.4	−6,523.2	−7,249.5
Other investment liabilities . .	2,644.5	−991.4	−3,993.9
Net errors and omissions . . .	−60,836.6	−34,152.7	−48,075.2
Reserves and related items .	−32,638.2	35,255.4	96,057.3

Source: IMF, *International Financial Statistics*.

External Trade

PRINCIPAL COMMODITIES
(distribution by SITC, US $ million)

Imports c.i.f.	2008	2009	2010
Food and live animals . .	11,475.7	12,543.7	14,881.1
Cereals and cereal preparations .	5,361.1	4,029.0	4,605.7
Chemicals and related products	3,828.1	9,485.0	10,804.8
Medicinal and pharmaceutical products	1,777.6	3,233.1	3,424.8
Basic manufactures . . .	10,824.4	16,290.2	19,720.3
Iron and steel	5,561.4	4,848.7	6,728.4
Machinery and transport equipment	27,676.2	43,614.3	45,344.5
General industrial machinery equipment and parts . .	3,368.5	7,891.4	7,067.3
Electrical machinery, apparatus, etc.	964.4	4,749.5	4,899.4
Road vehicles and parts . .	12,357.8	12,781.9	15,583.7
Passenger motor cars (excl. buses)	9,016.9	8,259.9	10,639.9
Miscellaneous manufactured articles	2,105.4	9,432.9	8,852.7
Total (incl. others)	115,133.9	95,552.2	106,863.0

Exports f.o.b.	2008	2009	2010
Mineral fuels, lubricants, etc. .	280,623.5	163,073.5	215,248.7
Petroleum, petroleum products and related materials	270,337.2	157,821.4	208,198.0
Crude petroleum (bituminous) .	247,097.2	142,194.2	189,433.6
Natural gas, manufactured . .	10,286.3	5,252.1	7,050.6
Chemicals and related products	14,651.6	14,016.5	21,851.8
Organic chemicals	5,756.5	4,998.8	7,440.7
Basic manufactures	1,993.9	4,048.1	4,317.0
Machinery and transport equipment	4,333.9	6,272.6	4,736.7
Total (incl. others)	313,462.2	192,314.1	251,143.0

Source: UN, *International Trade Statistics Yearbook*.

2011 (million riyals, preliminary): *Imports:* Animals and animal products 20,192; Vegetable products 28,008; Foodstuff, beverages and tobacco 22,620; Chemicals and related products 41,952; Textiles and related articles 16,938; Base metals and articles thereof 66,225; Machinery, mechanical appliances, electrical equipment and parts thereof 131,988; Transport equipment 77,141; Total (incl. others) 493,450. *Exports:* Mineral products 1,192,165; Chemical products 62,005; Plastic products 54,622; Total (incl. others and re-exports) 1,367,620.

PRINCIPAL TRADING PARTNERS
(US $ million)

Imports c.i.f.	2008	2009	2010
Australia	2,473.1	1,643.3	1,641.8
Austria	1,127.2	1,172.6	n.a.
Bahrain	1,181.1	932.4	1,071.0
Belgium	1,509.3	1,312.5	1,010.0
Brazil	2,893.6	2,370.7	3,107.1
Canada	1,812.4	1,345.0	1,435.3
China, People's Republic . . .	12,677.7	10,736.3	12,425.3
Egypt	1,496.5	1,388.9	1,596.4
Finland	1,208.8	688.9	n.a.
France (incl. Monaco)	4,065.5	3,763.4	3,616.8
Germany	8,545.9	7,546.4	8,223.7
India	4,803.1	3,402.4	3,981.0
Italy	4,610.3	3,458.9	3,339.4
Japan	9,400.2	7,191.4	7,962.2
Korea, Republic	5,124.8	4,201.1	4,710.6
Malaysia	1,220.4	910.1	1,162.8
Netherlands	1,461.0	1,150.8	1,193.1
Spain	1,350.3	1,176.7	1,219.5
Sweden	1,561.0	1,373.7	1,353.9
Switzerland (incl. Liechtenstein) .	2,065.4	1,641.0	2,189.9
Thailand	2,088.5	2,027.4	2,310.0
Turkey	1,914.9	1,624.1	2,137.4
United Arab Emirates	2,883.9	2,830.1	3,754.1
United Kingdom	4,060.0	3,353.9	3,254.3
USA	15,774.3	13,539.3	13,955.5
Total (incl. others)	115,133.9	95,552.2	106,863.0

Exports (incl. re-exports)	2005	2006	2007*
Bahrain	4,974.4	6,065.9	1,205.7
Belgium	2,276.3	2,869.5	905.4
China, People's Republic . . .	10,814.9	13,232.7	2,667.3
Egypt	2,046.2	2,755.7	2,818.7
France (incl. Monaco) . . .	4,297.7	4,117.7	2,922.1
India	10,739.7	12,956.1	3,387.4
Indonesia	2,447.6	3,066.6	683.6
Italy	5,377.0	5,169.3	3,376.6
Japan	28,180.5	34,811.5	62,970.9
Korea, Republic	15,312.1	19,377.8	1,624.2
Netherlands	6,488.1	6,497.0	3,855.1
Singapore	9,472.2	9,988.1	2,889.0
South Africa	3,065.9	3,220.3	694.1
Spain	2,971.9	3,582.7	2,826.0
Thailand	3,207.2	3,541.8	604.7
United Arab Emirates	4,811.7	6,805.9	8,404.7
USA	27,958.5	31,842.2	41,033.0
Total (incl. others)	180,737.2	211,305.8	234,950.8

* Data for many countries assumed to exclude petroleum exports.

2008: Total exports 313,462.2.

2009: Total exports 192,314.1.

2010: Total exports 251,143.0.

Source: UN, *International Trade Statistics Yearbook.*

2011 (million riyals, preliminary): *Imports:* Australia 6,567; Brazil 14,222; China, People's Republic 14,469; France 18,178; Germany 33,469; India 16,191; Italy 17,290; Japan 31,065; Korea, Republic 29,076; Switzerland 12,264; Thailand 10,149; Turkey 9,192; United Arab Emirates 20,426; United Kingdom 14,313; USA 61,943; Total (incl. others) 493,450. *Exports:* Bahrain 36,935; China, People's Republic 170,500; India 103,272; Japan 180,828; Korea, Republic 137,392; Singapore 60,398; Taiwan 46,848; Thailand 24,641; United Arab Emirates 37,881; USA 187,522; Total (incl. others and re-exports) 1,367,620.

Transport

RAILWAYS
(traffic)

	2008	2009	2010
Passenger journeys ('000) . . .	1,106	1,124	1,231
Passenger-km (million) . . .	338	338	375
Freight carried ('000 metric tons) .	3,395	3,516	3,826
Net freight ton-km (million) . .	1,691	1,718	1,786

ROAD TRAFFIC
(motor vehicles in use at 31 December)

	1989	1990	1991
Passenger cars	2,550,465	2,664,028	2,762,132
Buses and coaches	50,856	52,136	54,089
Goods vehicles	2,153,297	2,220,658	2,286,541
Total	4,754,618	4,936,822	5,103,205

2005 (motor vehicles in use at 31 December): Passenger cars 3,206,000; Buses and coaches 113,073; Vans and lorries 1,127,900; Motorcycles and mopeds 16,250; Total (incl. others) 4,446,973 (Source: IRF, *World Road Statistics*).

SHIPPING

Flag Registered Fleet
(at 31 December)

	2010	2011	2012
Number of vessels	376	384	403
Total displacement ('000 grt) . .	1,742.6	1,860.2	2,306.9

Source: Lloyd's List Intelligence (www.lloydslistintelligence.com).

International Sea-borne Freight Traffic
('000 metric tons, excluding crude oil)

	2008	2009	2010
Goods loaded	70,740	81,476	75,636
Goods unloaded	65,233	56,499	64,523

CIVIL AVIATION
(traffic on scheduled services)

	2007	2008	2009
Kilometres flown (million) . .	179	191	196
Passengers carried ('000) . . .	17,141	16,708	17,508
Passenger-km (million) . . .	26,904	27,736	28,891
Total ton-km (million) . . .	3,659	3,888	3,746

Source: UN, *Statistical Yearbook.*

2010 (Saudi Arabian airlines): Passengers carried ('000) 18,890; Number of flights 155,895; Cargo carried ('000 metric tons) 382.

2011 (Saudi Arabian airlines): Passengers carried ('000) 21,472; Number of flights 162,460; Cargo carried ('000 metric tons) 445.

Tourism

Country of nationality	2008	2009	2010
Algeria	393,609	64,015	96,097
Bahrain	594,188	624,793	820,132
Bangladesh	34,187	23,698	188,584
Egypt	1,853,663	538,287	763,901
India	601,922	247,075	389,116
Indonesia	501,758	205,378	235,636
Iran	349,848	413,656	220,051
Iraq	24,282	64,138	171,913
Jordan	501,269	517,318	451,099
Kuwait	2,589,988	2,475,318	2,507,813
Lebanon	307,492	58,337	116,129
Malaysia	141,778	62,749	152,396
Oman	125,552	165,875	176,687
Pakistan	817,550	336,255	465,571
Qatar	808,072	1,470,382	843,762
Sudan	398,607	88,269	65,352
Syria	708,034	730,306	254,140
Turkey	248,500	154,011	128,927
United Arab Emirates	1,613,574	1,889,187	1,957,613
United Kingdom	284,685	170,467	98,114
Yemen	197,652	101,576	112,472
Total (incl. others)	14,757,444	10,896,712	10,850,187

Total tourist arrivals ('000): 17,336 in 2011 (provisional).

Tourism receipts (US $ million, excl. passenger transport): 5,995 in 2009; 6,712 in 2010; 8,459 in 2011 (provisional).

Source: World Tourism Organization.

PILGRIMS TO MECCA FROM ABROAD

	2010*	2011†	2012‡
Total	1,799,601	1,828,195	1,752,932

* Figures for Islamic year 1431 (18 December 2009 to 06 December 2010).
† Figures for Islamic year 1432 (07 December 2010 to 26 November 2011).
‡ Figures for Islamic year 1433 (27 November 2011 to 14 November 2012).

Communications Media

	2009	2010	2011
Telephones ('000 main lines in use)	4,171	4,166	4,633
Mobile cellular telephones ('000 subscribers)	44,864	51,564	53,706
Internet subscribers ('000) . .	1,881.8	1,898.0	1,871.4
Broadband subscribers ('000) . .	1,342.8	1,496.6	1,577.0

Personal computers: 17,200,000 (697.9 per 1,000 persons) in 2008.

Source: International Telecommunication Union.

Education

(2011/12)

	Institutions	Teachers	Students
Pre-primary	2,323	12,705	141,422
Primary	13,845	232,453	2,530,744
Intermediate	8,241	125,355	1,212,029
Secondary (general)	5,658	114,625	1,226,205
Special	1,703	8,074	27,439
Adult education	2979	7,899	49,659
Technical and vocational* . . .	112	7,845	81,283
Higher*	n.a.	47,997	925,027

* 2010/11 figures.

Source: Ministry of Education, Riyadh.

Pupil-teacher ratio (primary education, UNESCO estimate): 11.2 in 2009/10 (Source: UNESCO Institute for Statistics).

Adult literacy rate (UNESCO estimates): 86.6% (males 90.4%; females 81.3%) in 2010 (Source: UNESCO Institute for Statistics).

Directory

The Government

HEAD OF STATE

King: HM King ABDULLAH IBN ABD AL-AZIZ AL SA'UD (acceded to the throne 1 August 2005).

COUNCIL OF MINISTERS
(May 2013)

Prime Minister: King ABDULLAH IBN ABD AL-AZIZ AL SA'UD.

First Deputy Prime Minister and Minister of Defence: Crown Prince SALMAN IBN ABD AL-AZIZ AL SA'UD.

Second Deputy Prime Minister: Prince MUQRIN IBN ABD AL-AZIZ AL SA'UD.

Minister of the Interior: Prince MUHAMMAD IBN NAYEF IBN ABD AL-AZIZ AL SA'UD.

Minister of Municipal and Rural Affairs: Prince MANSOUR IBN MUTAIB IBN ABD AL-AZIZ AL SA'UD.

Minister of Foreign Affairs: Prince SA'UD AL-FAISAL AL SA'UD.

Minister of Petroleum and Mineral Resources: Eng. ALI IBN IBRAHIM AL-NUAIMI.

Minister of Labour: Eng. ADEL BIN MUHAMMAD ABD AL-KADER FAKIEH.

Minister of Social Affairs: Dr YOUSUF ABDULLAH AL-OTHMAN.

Minister of Agriculture: Dr FAHD IBN ABD AL-RAHMAN IBN SULAIMAN BALGHUNAIM.

Minister of Water and Electricity: ABDULLAH IBN ABD AL-RAHMAN AL-HUSSEIN.

Minister of Education: Prince FAISAL IBN ABDULLAH IBN MUHAMMAD AL SA'UD.

Minister of Higher Education: Dr KHALID IBN MUHAMMAD AL-ANGARI.

Minister of Communications and Information Technology: MUHAMMAD IBN JABIL IBN AHMAD MULLA.

Minister of Finance: Dr IBRAHIM IBN ABD AL-AZIZ AL-ASSAF.

Minister of Economy and Planning: MUHAMMAD IBN SULAYMAN AL-JASSER.

Minister of Culture and Information: Dr ABD AL-AZIZ IBN MOHI EL-DIN KHOJA.

Minister of Commerce and Industry: TAWFIQ AL-RABEEAH.

Minister of Justice: Dr MUHAMMAD IBN ABD AL-KARIM IBN ABD AL-AZIZ AL-EISSA.

Minister of Pilgrimage (Hajj) Affairs: BANDAR AL-HAJJAR.

Minister of Awqaf (Religious Endowments), Dawa, Mosques and Guidance Affairs: SALEH IBN ABD AL-AZIZ MUHAMMAD IBN IBRAHIM AL-SHEIKH.

Minister of Health: Dr ABDULLAH IBN ABD AL-AZIZ AL-RABEA.

Minister of the Civil Service: Dr ABDULLAH AL-BARRAK.

Minister of Transport: Dr JUBARAH IBN EID AL-SURAISERI.

Minister of Housing: SHUWAISH AL-DUWAIHI.

Minister of State and Commander of the National Guard: Prince MITAB IBN ABDULLAH AL SA'UD.

Minister of State for Foreign Affairs: NIZAR IBN UBAYD MADANI.

Minister of State for Consultative Council Affairs: Dr SAUD IBN SAEED IBN ABD AL-AZIZ AL-MATHAMI.

Ministers of State: Prince ABD AL-AZIZ IBN ABDULLAH IBN ABD AL-AZIZ AL SA'UD, Dr ABD AL-AZIZ IBN ABDULLAH AL-KHUWEITER, Dr MUTLIB IBN ABDULLAH AL-NAFISA, Dr MUSAID IBN MUHAMMAD AL-AYBAN, Prince ABD AL-AZIZ IBN FAHD AL SA'UD.

MINISTRIES

Most ministries have regional offices in Jeddah.

Council of Ministers: Murabba, Riyadh 11121; tel. (1) 488-2444.

Ministry of Agriculture: Airport Rd, Riyadh 11195; tel. (1) 401-6666; fax (1) 403-1415; e-mail pubrel@moa.gov.sa; internet www .moa.gov.sa.

Ministry of Awqaf (Religious Endowments), Dawa, Mosques and Guidance Affairs: Riyadh 11232; tel. (1) 473-0401; fax 477-2938; internet www.al-islam.com.

Ministry of the Civil Service: POB 18367, Riyadh 11114; tel. (1) 402-6900; fax (1) 405-6258; e-mail mcswebmaster@mcs.gov.sa; internet www.mcs.gov.sa.

Ministry of Commerce and Industry: POB 1774, Airport Rd, Riyadh 11162; tel. (1) 405-6292; fax (1) 403-5567; e-mail public-relation@commerce.gov.sa; internet www.commerce.gov.sa.

Ministry of Communications and Information Technology: Intercontinental Rd, Riyadh 11112; tel. (1) 452-2222; fax (1) 452-2220; e-mail info@mcit.gov.sa; internet www.mcit.gov.sa.

Ministry of Culture and Information: Intercontinental Rd, Riyadh 11112; tel. (1) 401-4440; fax (1) 402-3570; internet www .moci.gov.sa.

Ministry of Defence: POB 26731, Airport Rd, Riyadh 11165; tel. (1) 478-9000; fax (1) 401-1336; internet www.moda.gov.sa.

Ministry of Economy and Planning: POB 358, 44 University St, Riyadh 11182; tel. (1) 401-1444; fax (1) 405-2051; e-mail ministry@ planning.gov.sa; internet www.mep.gov.sa.

Ministry of Education: POB 3734, Airport Rd, Riyadh 11148; tel. (1) 404-2888; fax (1) 401-2365; internet www.moe.gov.sa.

Ministry of Finance: Airport Rd, Riyadh 11177; tel. (1) 405-0000; fax (1) 403-3130; e-mail info@mof.gov.sa; internet www.mof.gov.sa.

Ministry of Foreign Affairs: POB 55937, Riyadh 11544; tel. (1) 405-5000; fax (1) 403-0645; e-mail info@mofa.gov.sa; internet www .mofa.gov.sa.

Ministry of Health: Airport Rd, Riyadh 11176; tel. (1) 212-5555; fax (1) 402-9876; e-mail f_otaibi@moh.gov.sa; internet www.moh.gov.sa.

Ministry of Higher Education: POB 225085, Riyadh 11324; tel. (1) 441-5555; fax (1) 441-9004; e-mail contact@mohe.gov.sa; internet www.mohe.gov.sa.

Ministry of Housing: Riyadh.

Ministry of the Interior: POB 2933, Airport Rd, Riyadh 11134; tel. (1) 401-1111; fax (1) 403-3125; internet www.moi.gov.sa.

Ministry of Justice: POB 7775, University St, Riyadh 11137; tel. (1) 405-7777; fax (1) 405-5399; internet www.moj.gov.sa.

Ministry of Labour: POB 21110, King Abd al-Aziz Rd, Riyadh 11475; tel. (1) 200-6666; fax (1) 478-9175; e-mail info@mol.gov.sa; internet www.mol.gov.sa.

Ministry of Municipal and Rural Affairs: POB 955, Nasseriya St, Riyadh 11136; tel. (1) 456-9999; fax (1) 456-3196; e-mail info@momra .gov.sa; internet www.momra.gov.sa.

Ministry of Petroleum and Mineral Resources: POB 247, Al Ma'ather St, Riyadh 11191; tel. (1) 478-1661; fax (1) 479-3596; e-mail info@mopm.gov.sa; internet www.mopm.gov.sa.

Ministry of Pilgrimage (Hajj) Affairs: al-Maazar St, Riyadh 11183; tel. (1) 404-3003; fax (1) 402-2555; internet www .hajinformation.com.

Ministry of Social Affairs: Riyadh 11157; tel. (1) 477-8888; fax (1) 477-7336; e-mail info@mosa.gov.sa; internet www.mosa.gov.sa.

Ministry of Transport: Airport Rd, Riyadh 11178; tel. (1) 874-4444; fax (1) 874-4588; e-mail info@mot.gov.sa; internet www.mot.gov.sa.

Ministry of Water and Electricity: King Fahd Rd, Riyadh 11233; tel. (1) 205-6666; fax (1) 205-2749; e-mail info@mowe.gov.sa; internet www.mowe.gov.sa.

Majlis al-Shura
(Consultative Council)

Al-Yamamh Palace, Riyadh 11212; tel. (1) 4821666; fax (1) 4816985; e-mail webmaster@shura.gov.sa; internet www.shura.gov.sa.

In March 1992 King Fahd issued a decree to establish a Consultative Council of 60 members, whose powers include the right to summon and question ministers. The composition of the Council was announced by King Fahd in August 1993, and it was officially inaugurated in December. Each member serves a term of four years. The Council's membership was increased to 90 when its second term began in July 1997; it was expanded further, to 120, in May 2001, and to 150 in April 2005. King Fahd issued a decree extending the legislative powers of the Council in November 2003, including the right to propose new legislation.

Chairman: Dr ABDULLAH IBN MUHAMMAD IBN IBRAHIM AL-SHEIKH.

Vice-Chairman: Dr MUHAMMAD AMIN AHMAD JEFRI.

Secretary-General: Dr MUHAMMAD ABDULLAH AL-AMER.

Political Organizations

There are no political organizations in Saudi Arabia.

Diplomatic Representation

EMBASSIES IN SAUDI ARABIA

Afghanistan: POB 93337, Riyadh 11673; tel. (1) 480-3459; fax (1) 480-3451; e-mail afgembriyad@hotmail.com; Ambassador SAYED AHMAD UMERKHIL.

Albania: POB 94004, Riyadh 11693; tel. (1) 281-6534; fax (1) 281-6535; e-mail embassy.riyadh@mfa.gov.al; Ambassador ADMIRIM BANAJ.

Algeria: POB 94388, Riyadh 11693; tel. (1) 488-7171; fax (1) 482-1703; e-mail Mail@algerianembassy-saudi.com; internet algerianembassy-saudi.com; Ambassador ABD AL-WAHAB DERBAL.

Argentina: POB 94369, Riyadh 11693; tel. (1) 465-2600; fax (1) 465-3075; e-mail earab@mrecic.gov.ar; internet earab.mrecic.gov.ar; Ambassador JAIME SERGIO CERDA.

Australia: POB 94400, Riyadh 11693; tel. (1) 488-7788; fax (1) 488-7973; internet www.saudiarabia.embassy.gov.au; Ambassador NEIL HAWKINS.

Austria: POB 94373, Riyadh 11693; tel. (1) 480-1217; fax (1) 480-1526; e-mail riyadh-ob@bmeia.gv.at; internet www.bmeia.gv.at/riyadh; Ambassador GREGOR W. KOESSLER.

Azerbaijan: 59 al-Worood Quarter St, off Amir Failsal bin Sa'ud Abd al-Rahman, Aloroba Rd, Riyadh; tel. (1) 419-2382; fax (1) 419-2260; e-mail riyadh@mission.mfa.gov.az; internet www.azembassy.org.sa; Ambassador RASIM SHAMSADDIN OGLU RZAYEV.

Bahrain: POB 94371, Riyadh 11693; tel. (1) 488-0044; fax (1) 488-0208; e-mail riyadh.mission@mofa.gov.bh; Ambassador Sheikh HAMOUD BIN ABDULLAH AL KHALIFA.

Bangladesh: POB 94395, Riyadh 11693; tel. (1) 419-5300; fax (1) 419-3555; e-mail info@bangladeshembassy.org.sa; internet www .bangladeshembassy.org.sa; Ambassador MUHAMMAD SHAHIDUL ISLAM.

Belgium: POB 94396, Riyadh 11693; tel. (1) 488-2888; fax (1) 488-2033; e-mail riyadh@diplobel.fed.be; internet www.diplomatie.be/riyadh; Ambassador MARC VINCK.

Bosnia and Herzegovina: POB 94301, Riyadh 11693; tel. (1) 456-7914; fax (1) 454-4360; e-mail baembsaruh@awalnet.net.sa; Ambassador (vacant).

Brazil: POB 94348, Riyadh 11693; tel. (1) 488-0018; fax (1) 488-1073; e-mail embaixada@brazemb-ksa.org; internet www.brazemb-ksa .org; Ambassador SERGIO LUIZ CANAES.

Brunei: POB 94314, al-Warood, Area 29, al-Fujairah St, Riyadh 11693; tel. (1) 456-0814; fax (1) 456-1594; e-mail riyadh.arabsaudi@ mfa.gov.bn; Ambassador (vacant).

Burkina Faso: POB 94330, Riyadh 11693; tel. (1) 465-2244; fax (1) 465-3397; e-mail burkinafaso.ksa@arab.net.sa; Ambassador OUNTANA MANSA.

Cameroon: POB 94336, Riyadh 11693; tel. (1) 488-0022; fax (1) 488-1463; e-mail ambacamriyad@ifrance.com; internet www .ambacamriyad.org.sa; Ambassador IYA TIDJANI.

Canada: POB 94321, Riyadh 11693; tel. (1) 488-2288; fax (1) 488-1997; e-mail ryadh@international.gc.ca; internet www .canadainternational.gc.ca/saudi_arabia-arabie_saoudite; Ambassador TOM MACDONALD.

Chad: POB 94374, Riyadh 11693; tel. and fax (1) 465-7702; Ambassador SAQR YOUSUF ANTO.

China, People's Republic: POB 75231, Riyadh 11578; tel. (1) 483-2126; fax (1) 281-2070; e-mail chinaemb_sa@mfa.gov.cn; internet www.chinaembassy.org.sa; Ambassador LI CHENGWEN.

Comoros: Riyadh; tel. (1) 293-4697; fax (1) 293-4797; Ambassador ASSIANDI ABDOU RAHMANE AMIR.

Côte d'Ivoire: POB 94303, Riyadh 11693; tel. (1) 482-5582; fax (1) 482-9626; e-mail acisa@ambaci-riyadh.org; Ambassador VAZOUMANA TORRE.

Denmark: POB 94398, Riyadh 11693; tel. (1) 488-0101; fax (1) 488-1366; e-mail ruhamb@um.dk; internet www.ambriyadh.um.dk; Ambassador CHRISTIAN KØNIGSFELDT.

Djibouti: POB 94340, Riyadh 11693; tel. (1) 454-3182; fax (1) 456-9168; e-mail dya_bamakhrama@hotmail.com; Ambassador DYA-EDDINE SAID BAMAKHRAMA.

Egypt: POB 94333, Riyadh 11693; tel. (1) 481-0464; fax (1) 481-0463; Ambassador AFIF ABD AL-WAHAB.

Eritrea: POB 94002, Riyadh; tel. (1) 480-1726; fax (1) 482-7537; Ambassador MOHAMMED OMAR MAHMOUD.

Ethiopia: POB 94341, Riyadh 11693; tel. (1) 482-3919; fax (1) 483-3281; e-mail ethiopian@awalnet.net.sa; Ambassador Dr MUHAMMAD HASEN.

Finland: POB 94363, Riyadh 11693; tel. (1) 488-1515; fax (1) 488-2520; e-mail sanomat.ria@formin.fi; internet www.finland.org.sa; Ambassador JARNO SYRJÄLÄ.

France: POB 94367, Riyadh 11693; tel. (1) 488-1255; fax (1) 488-2882; e-mail diplomatie@ambafrance.org.sa; internet www .ambafrance-sa.org; Ambassador BERTRAND BESANCENOT.

Gabon: POB 94325, Riyadh 11693; tel. (1) 456-7171; fax (1) 453-6121; e-mail ambagabonriyad@yahoo.com; Ambassador ISMAIL GHALAMA LINGONGO.

The Gambia: POB 94322, Riyadh 11693; tel. (1) 205-2158; fax (1) 456-2024; e-mail gamextriyadh@yahoo.com; Ambassador OMAR GIBRIL SALLAH.

Germany: POB 94001, Riyadh 11693; tel. (1) 488-0700; fax (1) 488-0660; e-mail info@riad.diplo.de; internet www.riad.diplo.de; Ambassador DIETER W. HALLER.

Ghana: POB 94339, Riyadh 11693; tel. (1) 454-5126; fax (1) 225-2771; e-mail ghanaembrym@yahoo.com; internet www .ghanaembassyksa.com; Ambassador Alhaji ABDULAI SALIFU.

Greece: POB 94375, Riyadh 11693; tel. (1) 480-1975; fax (1) 480-1969; e-mail gremb.ria@mfa.gr; internet www.mfa.gr/saoudi-arabia; Ambassador DIMITRIOS LETSIOS.

Guinea: POB 94326, Riyadh 11693; tel. (1) 488-1101; fax (1) 482-6757; e-mail riydambagunee@yahoo.fr; Ambassador el-Hadj CANDIDO RIVAS.

Hungary: POB 94014, al-Waha District, Ahmad Tonsy St 23, Riyadh 11693; tel. (1) 454-6707; fax (1) 456-0834; e-mail mission .ryd@mfa.gov.hu; internet www.mfa.gov.hu/emb/riyadh; Ambassador MIKLÓS KÁLLAY.

India: POB 94387, Riyadh 11693; tel. (1) 488-4144; fax (1) 488-4189; e-mail info@indianembassy.org.sa; internet www.indianembassy .org.sa; Ambassador HAMID ALI RAO.

Indonesia: POB 94343, Riyadh 11693; tel. (1) 488-2800; fax (1) 488-2966; e-mail kbri.riyadh@gmail.com; internet riyadh.kemlu.go.id; Ambassador GATOT ABDULLAH MANSYUR.

Iran: POB 94394, Riyadh 11693; tel. (1) 488-1916; fax (1) 488-1890; Ambassador JAVAD RASOULI MAHALLATI.

Iraq: Riyadh; tel. (1) 480-6514; e-mail rydemt@iraqmfamail.com; Ambassador Dr GHANIM ALWAN JAWAD AL-JUMAILI.

Ireland: POB 94349, Riyadh 11693; tel. (1) 488-2300; fax (1) 488-0927; e-mail riyadhembassy@dfa.ie; internet www.embassyofireland.org.sa; Ambassador Dr NIALL HOLOHAN.

Italy: POB 94389, Riyadh 11693; tel. (1) 488-1212; fax (1) 480-6964; e-mail segreteria1.riad@esteri.it; internet www.ambriad.esteri.it; Ambassador MARIO BUFFO.

Japan: POB 4095, Riyadh 11491; tel. (1) 488-1100; fax (1) 488-0189; e-mail info@jpn-emb-sa.com; internet www.ksa.emb-japan.go.jp; Ambassador JIRO KODERA.

Jordan: POB 94316, Riyadh 11693; tel. (1) 488-0051; fax (1) 488-0072; e-mail jordan.embassy@nesma.net.sa; Ambassador JAMAL HAMID AL-SHAMAYLEH.

Kazakhstan: POB 94012, Riyadh 11693; tel. (1) 480-6406; fax (1) 480-9106; e-mail office@kazembgulf.net; internet www.kazembsaudi.com; Ambassador BAKHTIYAR TASSYMOV.

Kenya: POB 94358, Riyadh 11693; tel. (1) 488-1238; fax (1) 488-2629; e-mail riyadh@mfa.go.ke; internet www.kenyaembassyriyadh.com; Ambassador MAHMOUD ALI SALEH.

Korea, Republic: POB 94399, Riyadh 11693; tel. (1) 488-2211; fax (1) 488-1317; e-mail emsau@mofat.go.kr; internet sau.mofat.go.kr; Ambassador KIM JONG-YONG.

Kuwait: POB 94304, Riyadh 11693; tel. (1) 488-3201; fax (1) 488-3682; Ambassador Sheikh THAMER JABER AL-AHMED AL-JABER AL-SABAH.

Kyrgyzstan: POB 94383, Riyadh 11693; tel. (1) 229-3272; fax (1) 229-3274; e-mail info@kyrgyzembarabia.kg; internet www.kyrgyzembarabia.kg; Ambassador JUSUPBEK SHARIPOV.

Lebanon: POB 94350, Riyadh 11693; tel. (1) 480-4060; fax (1) 480-4703; e-mail embassy@lebanon.org.sa; internet www.lebanon.org.sa; Chargé d'affaires a.i. MUNIR ANOUTI.

Libya: POB 94365, Riyadh 11693; tel. (1) 488-9757; fax (1) 488-3252; e-mail libianembassy@yahoo.com; Ambassador MUHAMMAD ABDULLAH AL-SHAKAL.

Malaysia: POB 94335, Riyadh 11693; tel. (1) 488-7100; fax (1) 482-4177; e-mail malriyadh@kln.gov.my; internet www.kln.gov.my/perwakilan/riyadh; Ambassador Datuk Syed OMAR MUHAMMAD AL-SAGGAF.

Maldives: POB 2228, Riyadh 11451; tel. (1) 462-6787; fax (1) 464-3725; e-mail admin@maldivesembassy.org.sa; Ambassador ADAM HASSAN.

Mali: POB 94331, Riyadh 11693; tel. (1) 464-5640; fax (1) 419-5016; e-mail consulat@sbm.net.sa; Ambassador MUHAMMAD MAHMOUD BEN LABAT.

Malta: POB 94361, Riyadh 11693; tel. (1) 463-2345; fax (1) 463-3993; e-mail maltaembassy.riyadh@gov.mt; internet www.foreign.gov.mt/saudi_arabia; Ambassador STEPHEN BORG.

Mauritania: POB 94354, Riyadh 11693; tel. (1) 464-6749; fax (1) 465-8355; Ambassador MUHAMMAD MAHMOUD OULD ABDULLAH.

Mexico: POB 94391, Riyadh 11693; tel. (1) 480-8822; fax (1) 480-8833; e-mail embassyofmexico@embamex.org.sa; internet www.embamex.org.sa; Ambassador ARTURO TREJO.

Morocco: POB 94392, Riyadh 11693; tel. (1) 481-1858; fax (1) 482-7016; e-mail ambassaderiyad@maec.gov.ma; Ambassador ABDESLAM BARAKA.

Myanmar: Villa No. 5, al-Kadi St, King Fahd Area, Riyadh; tel. (1) 229-3306; e-mail meriyadh@gmail.com; Ambassador KHIN ZAW WIN.

Nepal: POB 94384, Riyadh 11693; tel. (1) 461-1108; fax (1) 464-0690; e-mail info@neksa.org; internet www.neksa.org; Ambassador UDAYA RAJ PANDEY.

Netherlands: POB 94307, Riyadh 11693; tel. (1) 488-0011; fax (1) 488-0544; e-mail riy@minbuza.nl; internet saudiarabia.nlembassy.org; Ambassador J. L. WESTHOFF.

New Zealand: POB 94397, Riyadh 11693; tel. (1) 488-7988; fax (1) 488-7911; e-mail info@nzembassy.org.sa; internet www.nzembassy.com/saudiarabia; Ambassador ROD HARRIS.

Niger: POB 94334, Riyadh 11693; tel. and fax (1) 470-8698; fax (1) 205-4323; e-mail ambassadeduniger_riyadh@yahoo.com; Ambassador IBRAHIM KATCHALLOU MUHAMMAD.

Nigeria: POB 94386, Riyadh 11693; tel. (1) 482-3024; fax (1) 482-4134; e-mail nigeria@nigeria.org.sa; internet www.nigeria.org.sa; Ambassador ABUBAKAR SHEHU BUNU.

Norway: POB 94380, Riyadh 11693; tel. (1) 488-1904; fax (1) 488-0854; e-mail emb.riyadh@mfa.no; internet www.al-norwige.org.sa; Ambassador CARL SCHIÖTZ WIBYE.

Oman: POB 94381, Riyadh 11693; tel. (1) 482-3120; fax (1) 482-3738; e-mail riyadh@mofa.gov.om; Ambassador Dr SAEED AHMAD BIN HILAL BIN SAUD AL-BUSAIDI.

Pakistan: POB 94007, Riyadh 11693; tel. (1) 488-4111; fax (1) 488-7953; e-mail parep_riyadh@yahoo.com; internet www.mofa.gov.pk/saudiarabia; Ambassador MUHAMMAD NAEEM KHAN.

Peru: POB 94433, Riyadh 11693; tel. (1) 482-2474; fax (1) 483-0474; e-mail lepru.riyadh@gmail.com; Ambassador JULIO EDUARDO MARTINETTI MACEDO.

Philippines: POB 94366, Riyadh 11693; tel. (1) 482-0507; fax (1) 488-3945; e-mail filembry@sbm.net.sa; internet www.philembassy-riyadh.org; Ambassador EZZEDIN H. TAGO.

Poland: POB 94016, Riyadh 11693; tel. (1) 454-9274; fax (1) 454-9210; e-mail riyadh@msz.gov.pl; internet www.rijad.polemb.net; Ambassador WITOLD SMIDOWSKI.

Portugal: POB 94328, Riyadh 11693; tel. (1) 482-9042; fax (1) 482-6981; e-mail portriade@nesma.net.sa; Ambassador Dr ANTONIO MARIA DE SOUSA.

Qatar: POB 94353, Riyadh 11461; tel. (1) 482-5544; fax (1) 482-5394; e-mail riyadh@mofa.gov.qa; Ambassador ALI ABDULLAH AL-MAHMOUD.

Romania: POB 94319, Riyadh 11693; tel. (1) 263-0456; fax (1) 456-9985; e-mail office@embrom.org.sa; Chargé d'affaires a.i. MIHAIL-CONSTANTIN COMAN.

Russia: POB 94308, Riyadh 11693; tel. (1) 481-1875; fax (1) 481-1890; e-mail rusembass@mail.ru; internet www.rfemb-ksa.mid.ru; Ambassador OLEG OZEROV.

Rwanda: POB 94383, Riyadh 11693; tel. (1) 454-0808; fax (1) 456-1769; Ambassador SIMON INSONERE.

Senegal: POB 94352, Riyadh 11693; tel. (1) 488-0146; fax (1) 488-3804; Ambassador MOUHAMADOU DOUDOU LO.

Sierra Leone: POB 94329, Riyadh 11693; tel. (1) 465-6204; fax (1) 464-3662; e-mail slembrdh@zajil.net; Ambassador Alhaji WUSU MUNU.

Singapore: POB 94378, Riyadh 11693; tel. (1) 480-3855; fax (1) 483-0632; e-mail singemb_ruh@sgmfa.gov.sg; internet www.mfa.gov.sg/riyadh; Ambassador LAWRENCE ANDERSON.

Somalia: POB 94372, Riyadh 11693; tel. (1) 464-3456; fax (1) 464-9705; Ambassador AHMED ABDULLAH MOHAMED.

South Africa: POB 94006, Riyadh 11693; tel. (1) 442-9716; fax (1) 442-9708; e-mail riyadh.info@foreign.gov.za; Ambassador MUHAMMAD SADIQ JAAFAR.

Spain: POB 94347, Riyadh 11693; tel. (1) 488-0606; fax (1) 488-0420; e-mail emb.riad.info@maec.es; Ambassador JOAQUIN PERTH.

Sri Lanka: POB 94360, Riyadh 11693; tel. (1) 460-8232; fax (1) 460-8846; e-mail mail@srilankaembassyriyadh.com; internet www.lankaemb-riyadh.org; Ambassador AHMED A. JAWAD.

Sudan: POB 94337, Riyadh 11693; tel. (1) 488-7979; fax (1) 488-7729; Ambassador ABD AL-HAFEZ IBRAHIM MUHAMMAD.

Sweden: POB 94382, Riyadh 11693; tel. (1) 482-7796; fax (1) 488-0604; e-mail ambassaden.riyadh@gov.se; internet www.swedenabroad.com/riyadh; Ambassador DAG JUHLIN-DANNFELT.

Switzerland: POB 94311, Riyadh 11693; tel. (1) 488-1291; fax (1) 488-0632; e-mail rya.vertretung@eda.admin.ch; internet www.eda.admin.ch/riad; Ambassador PETER REINHARDT.

Syria: POB 94323, Riyadh 11693; tel. (1) 482-6191; fax (1) 482-6196; Ambassador MAHDI DAKHLALLAH.

Tajikistan: Riyadh; Ambassador Dr ABDULLAH YULDASHEV.

Tanzania: POB 94320, Riyadh 11693; tel. (1) 454-2839; fax (1) 454-9660; e-mail tzriyad@deltasa.com; Ambassador Prof ABDULLAH H. OMARI.

Thailand: POB 94359, Riyadh 11693; tel. (1) 488-1174; fax (1) 488-1179; e-mail thaiemryadsl@awalnet.net.sa; internet www.thaiembassy.org/riyadh; Chargé d'affaires a.i. CHARN JULLAMON.

Tunisia: POB 94368, Riyadh 11693; tel. (1) 488-7900; fax (1) 488-7641; e-mail amb.tunisie.riyadh@saudi.net.sa; Ambassador NAJIB AL-MUNIF.

Turkey: POB 94390, Riyadh 11693; tel. (1) 482-0101; fax (1) 488-7823; e-mail embassy.riyadh@mfa.gov.tr; internet riyadh.emb.mfa.gov.tr; Ambassador AHMET MUHTAR GÜN.

Turkmenistan: POB 94019, Riyadh 11693; tel. (1) 205-4898; fax (1) 205-2990; e-mail info@turkmenemb-sa.org; internet www.turkmenemb-sa.org; Ambassador NAZARGULY SHAGULYEV.

Uganda: POB 94344, Riyadh 11693; tel. (1) 454-4910; fax (1) 454-9264; e-mail ugariyadh@hotmail.com; Ambassador AZIZ KALUNGI KASUJJA.

Ukraine: POB 94010, Riyadh 11693; tel. (1) 450-8536; fax (1) 450-8534; e-mail emb_sa@mfa.gov.ua; internet saudiarabia.mfa.gov.ua; Ambassador PETRO KOLOS.

United Arab Emirates: POB 94385, Riyadh 11693; tel. (1) 488-1227; fax (1) 482-7504; e-mail riyadh@mofa.gov.ae; internet uae-embassy.ae/embassies/sa; Ambassador MUHAMMAD SAEED MUHAMMAD AL-DHAHIRI.

United Kingdom: POB 94351, Riyadh 11693; tel. (1) 481-9100; fax (1) 481-9350; e-mail pressoffice.riyadh@fco.gov.uk; internet ukinsaudiarabia.fco.gov.uk; Ambassador JOHN JENKINS.

USA: POB 94309, Riyadh 11693; tel. (1) 488-3800; fax (1) 488-7360; e-mail usembriyadhwebsite@state.gov; internet riyadh.usembassy .gov; Ambassador JAMES B. SMITH.

Uruguay: POB 94346, Riyadh 11693; tel. (1) 462-0739; fax (1) 462-0638; e-mail uruarabia@mrree.gub.uy; Ambassador RODOLFO INVERNIZZI ARENA.

Uzbekistan: POB 94008, Riyadh 11693; tel. (1) 263-5223; fax (1) 263-5105; Ambassador ALISHER QADIROV.

Venezuela: POB 94364, Riyadh 11693; tel. (1) 480-7141; fax (1) 480-0901; e-mail embvenar@embvenar.org.sa; Ambassador JOSEBA ACHUTEGUI.

Yemen: POB 94356, Riyadh 11693; tel. (1) 488-1769; fax (1) 488-1562; Ambassador MUHAMMAD ALI MOHSEN AL-AHWAL.

Judicial System

Judges are independent and governed by the rules of Islamic *Shari'a*. A new Judicial Law approved in May 2007 provided for a number of significant changes to the courts system. The new legislation called for the establishment of appeal courts, criminal courts and specialized courts. A Supreme Court was to be established in Riyadh, and new appeals courts were planned for each of the kingdom's 13 regions. There were to be general courts to deal with all conflicts except labour, commercial and family disputes, and criminal courts to address crimes. Family and personal conflicts were to be handled by civil courts. However, by 2013 few of these proposed amendments had yet to be implemented and the following courts were in operation:

Supreme Judicial Council: comprises 11 mems; supervises work of the courts; reviews legal questions referred to it by the Minister of Justice and expresses opinions on judicial questions; reviews sentences of death, cutting and stoning; Chair. Dr MUHAMMAD IBN ABD AL-KARIM IBN ABD AL-AZIZ AL-EISSA.

Court of Cassation: consists of Chief Justice and an adequate number of judges; includes department for penal suits, department for personal status and department for other suits.

General (Public) Courts: consist of one or more judges; sentences are issued by a single judge, with the exception of death, stoning and cutting, which require the decision of three judges.

Summary Courts: consist of one or more judges; sentences are issued by a single judge.

Specialized Courts: the setting up of specialized courts is permissible by Royal Decree on a proposal from the Supreme Council of Justice.

Religion

ISLAM

Arabia is the centre of the Islamic faith, and Saudi Arabia includes the holy cities of Mecca and Medina. Except in the Eastern region, where a large number of people follow Shi'a rites, the majority of the population are Sunni Muslims, and most of the indigenous inhabitants belong to the strictly orthodox Wahhabi sect. The Wahhabis originated in the 18th century, but first became unified and influential under Abd al-Aziz (Ibn Sa'ud), who became the first King of Saudi Arabia. They are now the keepers of the holy places and control the pilgrimage to Mecca. In 1986 King Fahd adopted the title of Custodian of the Two Holy Mosques; the title passed to King Abdullah upon his accession to the throne in August 2005. The country's most senior Islamic authority is the Council of Senior Ulama.

Mecca: Birthplace of the Prophet Muhammad, seat of the Grand Mosque and Shrine of Ka'ba, visited by 1,828,195 Muslims from abroad in the Islamic year 1432 (2010/11).

Medina: Burial place of Muhammad, second sacred city of Islam.

Grand Mufti and Chairman of Council of Senior Ulama: Sheikh ABD AL-AZIZ IBN ABDULLAH AL-SHEIKH.

CHRISTIANITY

The Roman Catholic Church

A small number of adherents, mainly expatriates, form part of the Apostolic Vicariate of Northern Arabia. The Vicar Apostolic is resident in Kuwait.

The Anglican Communion

Within the Episcopal Church in Jerusalem and the Middle East, Saudi Arabia forms part of the diocese of Cyprus and the Gulf. The Anglican congregations in the country are entirely expatriate. The Bishop in Cyprus and the Gulf is resident in Cyprus, while the Archdeacon in the Gulf is resident in Bahrain.

Other Denominations

The Greek Orthodox Church is also represented.

The Press

Since 1964 most newspapers and periodicals have been published by press organizations, administered by boards of directors with full autonomous powers, in accordance with the provisions of the Press Law. These organizations, which took over from small private firms, are privately owned by groups of individuals experienced in newspaper publishing and administration (see Publishers).

There are also a number of popular periodicals published by the Government and by the Saudi Arabian Oil Co, and distributed free of charge. The press is subject to no legal restriction affecting freedom of expression or the coverage of news.

DAILIES

Arab News: POB 10452, SRP Bldg, Madinah Rd, Jeddah 21433; tel. (2) 639-1888; fax (2) 639-3223; e-mail arabnews@arabnews.com; internet www.arabnews.com; f. 1975; English; publ. by Saudi Research and Publishing Co; Editor-in-Chief KHALED AL-MAEENA; circ. 110,000.

Al-Bilad (The Country): POB 6340, Jeddah 21442; tel. (2) 672-3000; fax (2) 671-2545; internet www.albilad-daily.com; f. 1934; Arabic; publ. by Al-Bilad Publishing Org; Editor-in-Chief QUINAN AL-GHOMDI; circ. 66,210.

Al-Eqtisadiah: POB 10452, Jeddah 21433; tel. (2) 651-1333; fax (2) 667-6212; internet www.aleqt.com; f. 1992; business and finance; publ. by Saudi Research and Publishing Co; Editor-in-Chief SALMAN IBN YUSUF DOSARI; circ. 81,000.

Al-Jazirah (The Peninsula): POB 354, Riyadh 11411; tel. (1) 487-0911; fax (1) 487-1063; e-mail ccs@al-jazirah.com.sa; internet www .al-jazirah.com; f. 1972; Arabic; publ. by Al-Jazirah Corpn for Press, Printing and Publishing; Dir-Gen. ABD AL-LATIF BIN SAAD; Editor-in-Chief KHALID BIN HAMAD AL-MALIK; circ. 110,000.

Al-Madina al-Munawara (Medina—The Enlightened City): POB 807, Makkah Rd, Jeddah 21421; tel. (2) 671-2100; fax (2) 671-1877; e-mail webmaster@al-madina.com; internet al-madina.com; f. 1937; Arabic; publ. by Al-Madina Press Establishment; Chief Editor FAHD HASSAN AL-AQRAN; circ. 46,370.

Al-Nadwah (The Council): POB 5803, Jarwal Sheikh Sayed Halabi Bldg, Mecca; tel. (2) 520-0111; fax (2) 520-3055; e-mail info@ al-nadwah.com; internet www.alnadwah.com.sa; f. 1958; Arabic; publ. by Makkah Printing and Information Establishment; Editor AHMAD BIN SALEH BAYUSUF; circ. 35,000.

Okaz: POB 1508, Seaport Rd, Jeddah 21441; tel. (2) 672-7621; fax (2) 672-4297; e-mail 104127.266@compuserve.com; internet www.okaz .com.sa; f. 1948; Arabic; publ. by Okaz Org. for Press and Publication; Editor-in-Chief MUHAMMAD AL-TUNISI; circ. 110,000.

Al-Riyadh: POB 2943, Riyadh 11476; tel. (1) 487-1000; fax (1) 441-7417; internet www.alriyadh.com; f. 1965; Arabic; publ. by Al-Yamama Press Establishment; Editor TURKI A. AL-SUDARI; circ. 150,000 (Sat.–Thurs.), 90,000 (Fri.).

Saudi Gazette: POB 5576, Jeddah 21432; tel. (2) 676-0000; fax (2) 672-7621; e-mail news@saudigazette.com.sa; internet www .saudigazette.com.sa; f. 1976; English; publ. by Okaz Org. for Press and Publication; Editor-in-Chief MUHAMMAD NASIR SHOUKANI; circ. 15,000.

Al-Watan: POB 15156, Airport Road, Abha; tel. (7) 227-3333; fax (7) 227-3756; e-mail editor@alwatan.com.sa; internet www.alwatan .com.sa; f. 1998; publ. by Assir Establishment for Press and Publishing; Dir-Gen. HATEM HAMID; circ. 150,000.

Al-Yaum (Today): POB 565, Dammam 31421; tel. (3) 858-0800; fax (3) 858-8777; e-mail mail@alyaum.com; internet www.alyaum.com; f. 1965; publ. by Dar al-Yaum Press, Printing and Publishing Ltd; Dir-Gen. SALEH ALI HAMID; Editor-in-Chief MUHAMMAD ABDULLAH AL-WAEEL; circ. 40,000.

WEEKLIES

Al-Muslimoon (The Muslims): POB 13195, Jeddah 21493; tel. (2) 669-1888; fax (2) 669-5549; f. 1985; Arabic; cultural and religious affairs; publ. by Saudi Research and Publishing Co; Editor-in-Chief Dr ABDULLAH AL-RIFA'E; circ. 68,665.

Saudi Economic Survey: POB 1989, Jeddah 21441; tel. (2) 657-8551; fax (2) 657-8553; e-mail info@saudieconomicsurvey.com;

internet www.saudieconomicsurvey.com; f. 1967; English; review of Saudi Arabian economic and business activity; Publr SAIFUDDIN A. ASHOOR; Gen. Man. WALID S. ASHOOR.

Sayidaty (My Lady): POB 4556, Madina Rd, Jeddah 21412; tel. (2) 639-1888; fax (2) 669-5549; internet www.sayidaty.net; f. 1981; publ. in Arabic and English edns; women's magazine; publ. by Saudi Research and Publishing Co; Editor-in-Chief MUHAMMAD FAHAD AL-HARTHI.

Al-Shams (The Sun): Riyadh; internet shms.pressera.com; f. 2005; tabloid format; sports, culture, entertainment; publishing licence revoked by the Govt in Feb. 2006, but restored after some 6 weeks; Editor-in-Chief KHALAF AL-HARBI.

Al-Yamama: POB 851, Riyadh 11421; tel. (1) 442-0000; fax (1) 441-7114; f. 1952; literary magazine; Editor-in-Chief ABDULLAH AL-JAH-LAN; circ. 35,000.

OTHER PERIODICALS

Ahlan Wasahlan (Welcome): POB 8013, Jeddah 21482; tel. (2) 686-2349; fax (2) 686-2006; internet pr.sv.net/aw; monthly; flight journal of Saudi Arabian Airlines; Gen. Man. and Editor-in-Chief YARUB A. BALKHAIR; circ. 150,000.

Al-Daragh: POB 2945, Riyadh 11461; tel. (1) 401-1999; fax (1) 401-3597; e-mail info@aldarahmagazine.com; internet aldarahmagazine .com; history journal; publ. by King Abd al-Aziz Foundation for Research and Archives.

Al-Faysal: POB 3, Riyadh 11411; tel. (1) 465-3027; fax (1) 464-7851; monthly; f. 1976; Arabic; culture, education, health, interviews; Man. Editor ABDULLAH Y. AL-KOWAILEET.

Majallat al-Iqtisad wal-Idara (Journal of Economics and Administration): King Abd al-Aziz University, POB 9031, Jeddah 21413; 2 a year; Chief Editor Prof. ABD AL-AZIZ A. DIYAB.

Al-Manhal (The Spring): POB 2925, Jeddah; tel. (2) 643-2124; fax (2) 642-8853; e-mail info@manhalmagazine.com; f. 1937; monthly; Arabic; cultural, literary, political and scientific; Editor ZUHAIR N. AL-ANSARI.

The MWL Journal: Press and Publications Department, Rabitat al-Alam al-Islami, POB 537, Mecca; fax (2) 544-1622; e-mail info@ themwl.org; internet www.themwl.org; monthly; English; Dir MURAD SULAIMAN IRQISOUS.

Al-Rabita: POB 537, Mecca; tel. (2) 560-0919; fax (2) 543-1488; e-mail info@themwl.org; internet www.themwl.org; Arabic; Chief Editor Dr OSMAN ABUZAID.

Saudi Review: POB 4288, Jeddah 21491; tel. (2) 651-7442; fax (2) 653-0693; f. 1966; English; monthly; newsletter from Saudi newspapers and broadcasting service; publ. by Int. Communications Co; Chief Editor SAAD AL-MABROUK; circ. 5,000.

Al-Sharkiah-Elle (Oriental Elle): POB 6, Riyadh; monthly; Arabic; women's magazine; Editor SAMIRA M. KHASHAGGI.

Al-Soqoor (Falcons): POB 2973, Riyadh 11461; tel. (1) 476-6566; f. 1978; 2 a year; air force journal; cultural activities; Editor HAMAD A. AL-SALEH.

Al-Tadhamon al-Islami (Islamic Solidarity): Ministry of Pilgrimage (Hajj) Affairs, Omar bin al-Khatab St, Riyadh 11183; monthly; Editor Dr MUSTAFA ABD AL-WAHID.

Al-Tijarah (Commerce): POB 1264, Jeddah 21431; tel. (2) 651-5111; fax (2) 651-7373; e-mail jcci@mail.gcc.com.bh; f. 1960; monthly; publ. by Jeddah Chamber of Commerce and Industry; Chair. Sheikh ISMAIL ABU DAUD; circ. 8,000.

NEWS AGENCIES

International Islamic News Agency (IINA): POB 5054, Jeddah 21422; tel. (2) 665-2056; fax (2) 665-9358; e-mail iina@islamicnews .org.sa; internet www.islamicnews.org.sa; f. 1972; operates under the auspices of the Org. of the Islamic Conference; Dir-Gen. ABD AL-WAHAB KASHIF.

Saudi Press Agency (SPA): POB 7186, King Fahd Rd, Riyadh 11171; tel. (1) 419-5485; fax (1) 419-5685; e-mail wass@spa.gov.sa; internet www.spa.gov.sa; f. 1970; Dir-Gen. ABDULLAH BIN FAHD AL-HUSSAIN.

Publishers

Assir Establishment for Press and Publishing: POB 15156, Abha; tel. (7) 227-3333; fax (7) 227-3590; f. 1998; publishes *Al-Watan*; Gen. Man. HATEM HAMED MOUMINAH.

Al-Bilad Publishing Organization: POB 6340, al-Sahafa St, Jeddah 21442; tel. (2) 672-3000; fax (2) 671-2545; publishes *Al-Bilad* and *Iqra'a*; Dir-Gen. AMIN ABDULLAH AL-QARQOURI.

Dar al-Maiman Publishers and Distributors: POB 90020, Riyadh 11613; tel. and fax (1) 4627336; fax (1) 2800587.

Dar al-Shareff for Publishing and Distribution: POB 58287, Riyadh 11594; tel. (1) 403-4931; fax (1) 405-2234; f. 1992; fiction, religion, science and social sciences; Pres. IBRAHIM AL-HAZEMI.

Dar al-Yaum Press, Printing and Publishing Ltd: POB 565, Dammam 31421; tel. (3) 858-0800; fax (3) 858-8777; e-mail mail@ alyaum.com; internet www.alyaum.com; f. 1964; publishes *Al-Yaum*; Chair. ABD AL-AZIZ MUHAMMAD AL-HUGAIL; Gen. Man. SALIH ALI AL-HUMAIDAN.

International Publications Agency (IPA): POB 70, Dhahran 31942; tel. and fax (3) 895-4925; publishes material of local interest; Man. SAID SALAH.

Al-Jazirah Corpn for Press, Printing and Publishing: POB 354, Riyadh 11411; tel. (1) 487-0911; fax (1) 487-1175; e-mail ccs@ al-jazirah.com.sa; internet www.al-jazirah.com.sa; f. 1964; 42 mems; publishes *Al-Jazirah* daily newspaper; Chair. ABD AL-LATIF BIN SAAD AL-ATEEQ; Editor-in-Chief KHALID EL-MALEK.

Al-Madina Press Establishment: POB 807, Jeddah 21421; tel. (2) 671-2100; fax (2) 671-1877; f. 1937; publishes *Al-Madina al-Munawara*; Gen. Man. AHMAD SALAH JAMJOUM.

Makkah Printing and Information Establishment: POB 5803, Jarwal Sheikh Sayed Halabi Bldg, Mecca; tel. (2) 542-7868; publishes *Al-Nadwah* daily newspaper; Chair. MUHAMMAD ABDOU YAMANI.

Okaz Organization for Press and Publication: POB 1508, Jeddah 21441; tel. (2) 672-2630; fax (2) 672-8150; publishes *Okaz* and *Saudi Gazette*; Chair. SAEED AL-HARTHI.

Al-Rushd Publishers: POB 17522, Riyadh 11494; tel. (1) 459-3451; fax (1) 457-3381; e-mail alrushd@alrushdryh.com; internet www .rushd.com.sa; scientific and academic publs.

Saudi Publishing and Distributing House: Umm Aslam District, nr Muslaq, POB 2043, Jeddah 21451; tel. (2) 629-4278; fax (2) 629-4290; e-mail info@spdh-sa.com; internet www.spdh-sa.com; f. 1966; publishers, importers and distributors of English and Arabic books; Chair. MUHAMMAD SALAHUDDIN.

Saudi Research and Publishing Co: POB 478, Riyadh 11411; tel. (1) 441-9933; fax (1) 442-9555; internet www.srpc.com; publs include *Arab News*, *Asharq al-Awsat*, *Al-Majalla*, *Al-Muslimoon* and *Sayidati*; Dep. Gen. Man. SALEH AL-DOWAIS.

Al-Yamama Press Establishment: POB 851, Al Sahafa Qtr, Riyadh 11421; tel. (1) 441-6611; fax (1) 441-7580; publishes *Al-Riyadh* and *Al-Yamama*; Dir-Gen. SAKHAL MAIDAN.

Broadcasting and Communications

TELECOMMUNICATIONS

Ettihad Etisalat: POB 9979, Riyadh 11423; tel. (1) 211-8015; fax (1) 211-8029; e-mail info@mobily.com.sa; internet www.mobily.com.sa; f. 2004; owned by consortium led by Emirates Telecommunications Corpn (United Arab Emirates); awarded the second licence to provide mobile telephone services in 2004; operates under the brand name *Mobily* (launched 2005); 14.8m. subscribers (Dec. 2008); Chair. ABD AL-AZIZ BIN SALEH AL-SUGHAYIR; CEO KHALID AL-KAF.

Saudi Telecommunications Co—Saudi Telecom (STC): POB 87912, Riyadh 11652; tel. (1) 215-3030; fax (1) 215-2734; e-mail contactus@stc.com.sa; internet www.stc.com.sa; f. 1998; partially privatized in 2002; provides telecommunications services in Saudi Arabia; Chair. Eng. ABD AL-AZIZ A. AL-SUGAIR; CEO Dr KHALED BIN ABD AL-AZIZ AL-GHONEIM.

Zain Saudi Arabia: POB 295814, Riyadh 11351; tel. (1) 216-1800; e-mail corporate.communications@sa.zain.com; internet www.sa .zain.com; f. 2007; wholly owned by Mobile Telecommunications Co KSC (Zain Kuwait); awarded the third licence to provide mobile telephone services in 2007; Chair. Prince HUSSAM IBN SA'UD IBN ABD AL-AZIZ AL SA'UD; CEO SAAD AL-BARRAK.

Regulatory Authority

Communications and Information Technology Commission (CITC): POB 75606, Riyadh; tel. (1) 461-8000; fax (1) 461-8002; internet www.citc.gov.sa; f. 2001 under the name Saudi Communications Comm.; present name adopted 2003; independent regulatory authority; Gov. ABDULLAH ABD AL-AZIZ AL-DARRAB.

BROADCASTING

Radio

Saudi Arabian Broadcasting Service: c/o Ministry of Information and Culture, POB 60059, Riyadh 11545; tel. (1) 401-4440; fax (1) 403-8177; e-mail saudi-radio@saudiradio.net.sa; internet www .saudiradio.net; 24 medium- and short-wave stations, incl. Jeddah, Riyadh, Dammam and Abha, broadcast programmes in Arabic and English; 23 FM stations; overseas service in Bengali, English, Farsi, French, Hausa, Indonesian, Somali, Swahili, Turkestani, Turkish and Urdu; Dir-Gen. MUHAMMAD AL-MANSOOR.

Saudi Aramco FM Radio: Bldg 3030 LIP, Dhahran 31311; tel. (3) 876-1845; fax (3) 876-1608; f. 1948; English; private; for employees of Saudi Aramco; Man. ESSAM Z. TAWFIQ.

Television

Saudi Arabian Government Television Service: POB 7971, Riyadh 11472; tel. (1) 401-4440; fax (1) 404-4192; e-mail satepjeng@moci.gov.sa; began transmission 1965; 112 stations, incl. 6 main stations at Riyadh, Jeddah, Medina, Dammam, Qassim and Abha, transmit programmes in Arabic and English; operates 4 channels: Channel 1 (Arabic); Channel 2 (English and French); Channel 3 (sport); Al-Ekhbariya (news); Dir-Gen. ABD AL-AZIZ AL-HASSAN (Channel 1).

Finance

(cap. = capital; res = reserves; dep. = deposits; m. = million; br(s) = branch(es); amounts in Saudi riyals, unless otherwise stated)

BANKING

Central Bank

Saudi Arabian Monetary Agency (SAMA): POB 2992, Riyadh 11169; tel. (1) 463-3000; fax (1) 466-2966; e-mail info@sama.gov.sa; internet www.sama.gov.sa; f. 1952; functions include stabilization of currency, administration of monetary reserves, regulation of banking and insurance sectors, and issue of notes and coins; dep. 962,808m., total assets 1,393,080m. (June 2009); Gov. Dr FAHD IBN ABDULLAH AL-MUBARAK; 10 brs.

National Banks

Alinma Bank: POB 66674, al-Anoud Tower, King Fahad Rd, Riyadh 11586; e-mail info@alinma.com; internet www.alinma.com; f. 2006; cap. 15,000m., res 105m., dep. 17,984m. (Dec. 2011); Chair. ABD AL-AZIZ ABDULLAH AL-ZAMIL; 15 brs.

National Commercial Bank (NCB): POB 3555, King Abd al-Aziz St, Jeddah 21481; tel. (2) 649-3333; fax (2) 644-6468; e-mail contact@alahli.com; internet www.alahli.com; f. 1950; 69.3% govt-owned; cap. 15,000m., res 13,938m., dep. 241,668m. (Dec. 2011); Chair. MANSOUR S. AL-MAIMAN; 258 domestic brs, 2 abroad.

Al-Rajhi Banking and Investment Corpn (Al-Rajhi Bank): POB 28, al-Akariya Bldg, Oleya St, Riyadh 11411; tel. (1) 211-6000; fax (1) 460-0922; e-mail contactus@alrajhibank.com.sa; internet www.alrajhibank.com.sa; f. 1988; operates according to Islamic financial principles; cap. 15,000m., res 17,706m., dep. 180,450m. (Dec. 2011); Chair. Sheikh SULAIMAN BIN ABD AL-AZIZ AL-RAJHI; 700 brs.

Riyad Bank Ltd: POB 22601, King Abd al-Aziz St, Riyadh 11416; tel. (1) 401-3030; fax (1) 404-1255; internet www.riyadbank.com.sa; f. 1957; cap. 15,000m., res 14,285m., dep. 146,064m. (Dec. 2011); Chair. RASHED A. AL-RASHED; Pres. and CEO TALAL I. AL-QUDAIBI; 201 domestic brs, 1 abroad.

Specialist Bank

Arab Investment Co SAA (TAIC): POB 4009, King Abd al-Aziz St, Riyadh 11491; tel. (1) 476-0601; fax (1) 476-0514; e-mail taic@taic.com; internet www.taic.com; f. 1974 by 17 Arab countries for investment and banking; cap. US $700m., res $141m., dep. $1,184m. (Dec. 2011); Chair. YOUSUF IBN IBRAHIM AL-BASSAM; CEO IBRAHIM H. AL-MAZYAD; 1 br.

Banks with Foreign Interests

Arab National Bank (ANB): POB 56921, King Faisal St, North Murabba, Riyadh 11564; tel. (1) 402-9000; fax (1) 402-7747; e-mail info@anb.com.sa; internet www.anb.com.sa; f. 1980; Arab Bank PLC, Jordan, 40%, Saudi shareholders 60%; cap. 8,500m., res 7,057m., dep. 96,683m. (Dec. 2011); Chair. ABD AL-LATIF HAMAD AL-JABR; Man. Dir Dr ROBERT EID; 117 domestic brs, 1 abroad.

Bank al-Jazira: POB 6277, Khalid bin al-Waleed St, Jeddah 21442; tel. (2) 651-8070; fax (2) 653-2478; e-mail info@baj.com.sa; internet www.baj.com.sa; 94.17% Saudi-owned; cap. 3,000m., res 1,726m., dep. 32,464m. (Dec. 2011); Chair. TAHA ABDULLAH AL-KUWAIZ; CEO NABIL AL-HOSHAN; 23 brs.

Banque Saudi Fransi (Saudi French Bank): POB 56006, Ma'ather Rd, Riyadh 11554; tel. (1) 404-2222; fax (1) 289-9999; e-mail communications@alfransi.com.sa; internet www.alfransi.com.sa; f. 1977; present name adopted 2002; Saudi shareholders 68.9%, Calyon, Paris La Défense 31.1%; cap. 7,232m., res 8,601m., dep. 95,842m. (Dec. 2010); Chair. Dr SALEH A. AL-OMAIR; Man. Dir PATRICE COUVEGNES; 79 brs.

SAMBA Financial Group: POB 833, Riyadh 11421; tel. and fax (1) 477-4770; e-mail sambacare@samba.com; internet www.samba.com.sa; f. 1980; merged with United Saudi Bank in 1999; 96.4% owned by Saudi nationals; cap. 9,000m., res 8,078m., dep. 157,885m. (Dec. 2011); Chair. EISA AL-EISA; 66 domestic brs, 2 abroad.

Saudi British Bank (SABB): POB 9084, Prince Abd al-Aziz bin Mossaid bin Jalawi St, Riyadh 11413; tel. (1) 405-0677; fax (1) 405-0660; e-mail sabb@sabb.com; internet www.sabb.com.sa; f. 1978; 60% owned by Saudi nationals, 40% by HSBC Holdings BV; cap. 7,500m., res 6,517m., dep. 111,470m. (Dec. 2011); Chair. KHALED SULIMAN OLAYAN; Man. Dir DAVID DEW; 78 domestic brs, 1 abroad.

Saudi Hollandi Bank (Saudi Dutch Bank): POB 1467, Head Office Bldg, al-Dhabab St, Riyadh 11431; tel. (1) 406-7888; fax (1) 403-1104; e-mail csc@shb.com.sa; internet www.shb.com.sa; f. 1977 to assume activities of Algemene Bank Nederland NV in Saudi Arabia; jt stock co; ABN AMRO Bank (Netherlands) 40%, Saudi citizens 60%; cap. 3,307m., res 3,544m., dep. 44,572m. (Dec. 2011); Chair. Sheikh MUBARAK ABDULLAH AL-KHAFRAH; Man. Dir BERND VAN LINDER; 40 brs.

Saudi Investment Bank (SAIB): POB 3533, Riyadh 11481; tel. (1) 478-6000; fax (1) 477-6781; e-mail info@saib.com.sa; internet www.saib.com.sa; f. 1976; provides a comprehensive range of traditional and specialized banking services; cap. 5,500m., res 2,726m., dep. 37,957m. (Dec. 2011); Chair. Dr ABD AL-AZIZ O'HALI; Gen. Man. MUSAED AL-MINEEFI; 30 brs.

Government Specialized Credit Institutions

Real Estate Development Fund (REDF): POB 5591, Riyadh 11139; tel. (1) 479-2222; fax (1) 479-0148; f. 1974; provides interest-free loans to Saudi individuals and cos for private or commercial housing projects; loans granted amounted to 5,264m. in 2002; Chair. Dr IBRAHIM IBN ABD AL-AZIZ AL-ASSAF (Minister of Finance); Dir-Gen. MUHAMMAD AL-ABDANI; 24 brs.

Saudi Arabian Agricultural Bank (SAAB): POB 1811, Riyadh 11126; tel. (1) 402-3911; fax (1) 402-2359; f. 1963; provides loans to farmers for industry-specific use; loans disbursed amounted to 1,320.0m. in 2002; Controller-Gen. ABDULLAH SAAD AL-MENGASH; Gen. Man. ABD AL-AZIZ MUHAMMAD AL-MANQUR; 70 brs.

Saudi Credit Bank: POB 3401, Riyadh 11471; tel. (1) 402-9128; f. 1973; provides interest-free loans for specific purposes to Saudi citizens of moderate means; loans disbursed amounted to 348.0m. in 2002; Man. IBRAHIM AL-HINAISHIL; 25 brs.

STOCK EXCHANGE

The Electronic Securities Information System (ESIS) was formed in 1990 and operated by the Saudi Arabian Monetary Agency (see Central Bank). The ESIS was superseded by a new market system, Tadawul, in 2001. Since 2003 Tadawul has been supervised by the Capital Market Authority. A total of 57,269m. shares were traded in 2009, amounting to SR 1,262,148.8m.

Saudi Stock Exchange (Tadawul): NCCI Bldg, North Tower, King Fahd Rd, POB 60612, Riyadh 11555; tel. (1) 218-9999; e-mail webinfo@tadawul.com.sa; internet www.tadawul.com.sa; f. 2001; restructured as a jt stock co in 2007; 146 listed cos in 2010; Chair. TAHA A. AL-KUWAIZ.

Regulatory Authority

Capital Market Authority: Faisaliah Tower, King Fahd Rd, POB 220022, Riyadh 11311; fax (1) 279-7770; e-mail info@cma.org.sa; internet www.cma.org.sa; f. 2003 to regulate and develop the Saudi Arabian capital market; Chair. MUHAMMAD IBN ABD AL-MALIK AL-SHEIKH.

INSURANCE

A new Co-operative Insurance Law, promulgated in 2004, required all companies operating in the kingdom to be locally registered and brought the sector under the supervision of the Saudi Arabian Monetary Agency (see Central Bank). In March 2009 some 29 insurance companies were operating in Saudi Arabia.

Ace Arabia Insurance Co Ltd (E.C.): 7th and 8th Floors, Southern Tower, Khobar Business Gate, King Faisal Bin Abd al-Aziz St (Coastal Rd), al-Khobar; tel. (3) 849-3633; fax (3) 849-3660; e-mail ace@ace-arabia.com; internet www.ace-arabia.com; f. 1974; cap. US $1m.; Chair. Sheikh ABD AL-KARIM EL-KHEREIJI; CEO BRUCE C. AITKEN.

Allied Cooperative Insurance Group: POB 7076, Jeddah 21462; tel. (2) 663-3222; fax (2) 661-7421; e-mail csc@acig.com.sa; internet www.acig.com.sa; Chair. KHALID AL-BASSAM; CEO HESHAM AL-SHAREEF.

Bank Al-Jazira Takaful Ta'awuni: POB 6277, Jeddah 21442; tel. and fax (2) 683-6364; e-mail infotakaful@baj.com.sa; internet www.takaful.com.sa; Islamic life insurance; Gen. Man. DAWOOD Y. TAYLOR.

Mediterranean and Gulf Cooperative Insurance and Reinsurance Co (MEDGULF): POB 2302, Riyadh 11451; tel. (1) 405-5550; fax (1) 478-9219; e-mail riyadh@medgulf.com; internet www.medgulf.com.sa; Chair. SALEH A. S. AL-SAGRI; Exec. Pres. and Man. Dir LUTFI F. EL-ZEIN.

Al-Rajhi Co for Co-operative Insurance: Platinum Centre, 3rd Floor, Setteen St, POB 67791, Riyadh 11517; tel. (1) 475-2211; fax (1) 475-5017; e-mail info@alrajhitakaful.com; internet www .alrajhiinsurance.com.sa; f. 1990 as Al-Rajhi Insurance Co; renamed as above 2006; cap. 200m.; Chair. ABDULLAH SULAIMAN AL-RAJHI; CEO ABD AL-AZIZ M. AL-SEDEAS.

Red Sea Insurance Group of Cos: POB 5627, Jeddah 21432; tel. (2) 660-3538; fax (2) 665-5418; e-mail redsea@anet.net.sa; f. 1974; insurance, devt and reinsurance; Chair. KHALDOUN B. BARAKAT.

RSA Saudi Arabia—Al-Alamiya: 1st Floor, Obekan Bldg, Prince Sultan St, POB 2374, Jeddah 21451; tel. (2) 692-7085; fax (2) 692-7125; e-mail alamiya.insurance@sa.rsagroup.com; internet www .alamiyainsurance.com.sa; part of the Royal & Sun Alliance (RSA) Group; total assets US $73.0m. (2002); CEO STUART PURDY.

SABB Takaful Co: POB 9086, Riyadh 11413; tel. (1) 403-0087; fax (1) 402-5832; internet www.sabbtakaful.com; f. 2007; 32.5% owned by Saudi British Bank (SABB), 32.5% by HSBC, 35% by private investors; cap. 100m.; Chair. FOUAD ABD AL-WAHAB BAHRAWI; Man. Dir DAVID ROBERT HUNT.

Sanad Cooperative Insurance and Reinsurance JSC: 3rd Floor, Dareen Centre, Alahsa St, POB 27477, Riyadh 11417; tel. (1) 292-7111; fax 292-7888; e-mail info@sanad.com.sa; internet www .sanad.com.sa; f. 2007; Chair. AHMAD AL-ABDULLAH AL-AKEIL; CEO PHILIP WILLIAM.

Saudi IAIC Cooperative Insurance Co (SALAMA): POB 122392, Jeddah 21332; tel. (2) 664-7877; fax (2) 664-7387; e-mail customers.relation@salama.com.sa; internet www.salama.com.sa; Chair. Dr SALEH J. MALAIKAH.

Saudi National Insurance Co (E.C.): POB 5832, Jeddah 21432; tel. (2) 660-6200; fax (2) 667-4530; e-mail snic@eajb.com.sa; internet www.snic.com.sa; f. 1974; Chair. Sheikh HATEM ALI JUFFALI; Gen. Man. OMAR S. BILANI.

Tawuniya (NCCI): POB 86959, Riyadh 11632; tel. and fax (1) 218-0100; e-mail info@tawuniya.com.sa; internet tawuniya.com.sa; f. 1985 by royal decree as Nat. Co for Co-operative Insurance; name changed as above 2007; owned by 3 govt agencies; proposed privatization approved by the Supreme Economic Council in May 2004; initial public offering of shares in Dec. 2004; auth. cap. 500m.; Chair. SULAYMAN AL-HUMMAYYD; Man. Dir and Gen. Man. ALI A. AL-SUBAIHIN; 13 brs.

United Cooperative Assurance Co (UCA): POB 5019, Medina Rd, Jeddah 21422; tel. (2) 653-0068; fax (2) 651-1936; e-mail jeddah@ uca.com.sa; internet www.uca.com.sa; f. 1974 as United Commercial Agencies Ltd; name changed as above 2007; all classes of insurance; cap. 200m.; Chair. HASSAN M. MAHASSINI; CEO MACHAAL A. KARAM.

Wala'a Insurance: POB 31616, al-Khobar 31952; tel. (3) 865-1866; fax (3) 865-1944; e-mail khobar@walaa.com; internet www.walaa .com; f. 1976; fmrly Saudi United Insurance; operated by Saudi United Cooperative Insurance Co; provides all classes of insurance for businesses and govt agencies; majority shareholding held by Ahmad Hamad al-Gosaibi & Bros; cap. US $5m.; Chair. SULAYMAN AL-KADI; CEO JOHNSON VARUGHESE; 6 brs.

Trade and Industry
(Figures for weight are in metric tons)
DEVELOPMENT ORGANIZATIONS

Arab Petroleum Investments Corpn: POB 9599, Dammam 31423; tel. (3) 847-0444; fax (3) 847-0011; e-mail apicorp@ apicorp-arabia.com; internet www.apicorp-arabia.com; f. 1975; affiliated to the Org. of Arab Petroleum Exporting Countries; specializes in financing petroleum and petrochemical projects and related industries in the Arab world and in other developing countries; shareholders: Kuwait, Saudi Arabia and the United Arab Emirates (17% each), Libya (15%), Iraq and Qatar (10% each), Algeria (5%), Bahrain, Egypt and Syria (3% each); auth. cap. US $1,200m.; cap. $550m. (Dec. 2006). Chair. ABDULLAH A. AL-ZAID; Gen. Man. and CEO AHMAD BIN HAMAD AL-NUAIMI.

National Agricultural Development Co (NADEC): POB 2557, Riyadh 11461; tel. (1) 404-0000; fax (1) 405-5522; e-mail info@nadec .com.sa; internet www.nadec.com.sa; f. 1981; interests include 6 dairy farms, 2 dairy processing plants and 40,000 ha of land for cultivation of wheat, barley, forage and vegetables, and processing of dates; the Govt has a 20% share; chief agency for agricultural devt; cap. SR 400m.; Chair. SULAYMAN ABD AL-AZIZ AL-RAJHI; Man. Dir ABD AL-AZIZ AL-BABTAIN.

Public Investment Fund: POB 6847, Riyadh 11452; tel. (1) 477-4488; fax (1) 474-2693; e-mail info@mof.gov.sa; internet www.mof .gov.sa/en/docs/ests/sub_invbox.htm; f. 1971 to facilitate devt of the nat. economy; 100% state-owned; under the control of the Ministry of Finance; provides the Govt's share of capital to mixed capital cos; has managed Sanabil al-Saudia, a sovereign wealth fund with cap. of US $5,300m., since 2008; Chair. Dr IBRAHIM IBN ABD AL-AZIZ AL-ASSAF (Minister of Finance); Sec.-Gen. MANSOUR AL-MAIMAN.

Saudi Arabian General Investment Authority (SAGIA): POB 5927, Riyadh 11432; tel. (1) 203-5555; fax (1) 263-2894; e-mail marketing_dept@sagia.gov.sa; internet www.sagia.gov.sa; f. 2000 to promote foreign investment; Gov. ABD AL-LATIF IBN AHMAD AL-UTHMAN.

Saudi Fund for Development (SFD): POB 50483, Riyadh 11523; tel. (1) 279-4000; fax (1) 464-7450; e-mail info@sfd.gov.sa; internet www.sfd.gov.sa; f. 1974 to help finance projects in developing countries; state-owned; had financed 511 projects by 2011; total commitments amounted to SR 35,651.49m; Chair. Dr IBRAHIM IBN ABD AL-AZIZ AL-ASSAF (Minister of Finance); Vice-Chair. and Man. Dir E. YOUSUF I. AL-BASSAM.

Saudi Industrial Development Fund (SIDF): POB 4143, Riyadh 11149; tel. (1) 477-4002; fax (1) 479-0165; e-mail sidf@sidf.gov.sa; internet www.sidf.gov.sa; f. 1974; supports and promotes local industrial devt, providing medium-term interest-free loans; also offers marketing, technical, financial and administrative advice; loans disbursed amounted to SR 8,544m. in 2007; cap. SR 20,000m. (2007). Chair. YOUSUF BIN IBRAHIM AL-BASSAM; Dir-Gen. ABDULLAH MUHAMMAD AL-OBOUDI.

TASNEE: POB 26707, Riyadh 11496; tel. (1) 476-7166; fax (1) 477-0898; e-mail general@tasnee.com; internet www.tasnee.com; f. 1985 as Nat. Industrialization Co to promote and establish industrial projects in Saudi Arabia; cap. SR 785m.; 100% owned by Saudi nationals; Chair. MUBARAK BIN ABDULLAH AL-KHAFRAH; CEO MOAYYED BIN ISSA AL-QURTAS.

CHAMBERS OF COMMERCE

Council of Saudi Chambers of Commerce and Industry: POB 16683, Riyadh 11474; tel. (1) 218-2222; fax (1) 218-2111; e-mail council@saudichambers.org.sa; internet www.saudichambers.org .sa; comprises one delegate from each of the chambers of commerce in the kingdom; Chair. MUHAMMAD ABD AL-QADER AL-FADEL; Sec.-Gen. Dr FAHD AL-SULTAN.

Abha Chamber of Commerce and Industry: POB 722, Abha; tel. (7) 227-1818; fax (7) 227-1919; e-mail info@abhacci.org.sa; internet www.abhacci.org.sa; Pres. ABDULLAH SAID AL-MOBTY; Sec.-Gen. Dr HAMDI ALI AL-MALIKI.

Al-Ahsa Chamber of Commerce and Industry: POB 1519, al-Ahsa 31982; tel. (3) 582-0458; fax (3) 587-5274; internet www.hcci .org.sa; Pres. SULAYMAN A. AL-HAMAAD.

Ar'ar Chamber of Commerce and Industry: POB 440, Ar'ar; tel. (4) 662-6544; fax (4) 662-4581; Sec.-Gen. THANI B. AL-ANEZI.

Al-Baha Chamber of Commerce and Industry: POB 311, al-Baha; tel. (7) 727-0291; fax (7) 828-0146; Pres. ABDULLAH M. AL-MOAGEB; Sec.-Gen. YAHYA AL-ZAHRANI.

Eastern Province Chamber of Commerce and Industry (Asharqia Chamber): POB 719, Dammam 31421; tel. (3) 857-1111; fax (3) 857-0607; e-mail info@chamber.org.sa; internet www .chamber.org.sa; f. 1952; Pres. ABD AL-RAHMAN RASHID AL-RASHID; Sec.-Gen. IBRAHIM ABDULLAH AL-OLAYAN.

Federation of Gulf Co-operation Council Chambers (FGCCC): POB 2198, Dammam 31451; tel. (3) 826-5943; fax (3) 826-6794; e-mail fgccc@zajil.net; internet www.fgccc.org; Pres. SALIM H. ALKHALILI; Sec.-Gen. MUHAMMAD A. AL-MULLA.

Ha'il Chamber of Commerce and Industry: POB 1291, Ha'il; tel. (6) 532-1060; fax (6) 533-1366; e-mail hussa_mk@yahoo.com; internet www.hcc.org.sa; Pres. KHALID A. AL-SAIF.

Jeddah Chamber of Commerce and Industry: POB 1264, Jeddah 21431; tel. (2) 651-5111; fax (2) 651-7373; e-mail customerservice@jcci.org.sa; internet www.jcci.org.sa; f. 1946; 26,000 mems; Chair. Sheikh SALEH KAMEL; Sec.-Gen. Dr HANI M. ABURAS.

Jizan Chamber of Commerce and Industry: POB 201, Jizan; tel. (7) 322-5155; fax (7) 322-3635; Pres. Eng. FAHD A. QALM.

Al-Jouf Chamber of Commerce and Industry: POB 585, al-Jouf; tel. (4) 624-9060; fax (4) 624-0108; Pres. MARZOUK S. AL-RASHID; Sec.-Gen. AHMAD KHALIFA AL-MUSALLAM.

Al-Majma' Chamber of Commerce and Industry: POB 165, al-Majma' 11952; tel. (6) 432-0268; fax (6) 432-2655; Pres. FAHD MUHAMMAD AL-RABIAH; Sec.-Gen. ABDULLAH IBRAHIM AL-JAAWAN.

Mecca Chamber of Commerce and Industry: POB 1086, Mecca; tel. (2) 534-3838; fax (2) 534-2904; f. 1947; Pres. ADEL ABDULLAH KA'AKI; Sec.-Gen. YASSER ABDULLAH AWAN.

Medina Chamber of Commerce and Industry: POB 443, King Abd al-Aziz Rd, Medina; tel. (4) 838-8909; fax (4) 838-8905; e-mail info@mcci.org.sa; internet www.mcci.org.sa; Pres. MUHAMMAD AL-GHAMDI; Sec.-Gen. Dr AMIR ABDULLAH SLEHM.

Najran Chamber of Commerce and Industry: POB 1138, Najran; tel. (7) 522-2216; fax (7) 522-3926; e-mail ywadidi@najcci.org.sa; internet www.najcci.org.sa; Pres. ALI BIN HAMAD HAMROUR AL-ABAAS; Sec.-Gen. ALI BIN SALEH AL-QUMAISH.

Al-Qassim Chamber of Commerce and Industry: POB 444, Buraydah, al-Qassim 51411; tel. (6) 381-4000; fax (6) 381-2231; e-mail info@qcc.org.sa; internet www.qcc.org.sa; Sec.-Gen. Dr FAISAL AL-KHAMIS.

Al-Qurayat Chamber of Commerce and Industry: POB 416, al-Qurayat; tel. (4) 642-6200; fax (4) 642-3172; Pres. OTHMAN ABDULLAH AL-YOUSUF; Sec.-Gen. JAMAL ALI AL-GHAMDI.

Riyadh Chamber of Commerce and Industry: POB 596, Riyadh 11421; tel. (1) 404-0044; fax (1) 402-1103; e-mail info@rdcci.org.sa; internet www.riyadhchamber.org.sa; f. 1961; acts as arbitrator in business disputes, information centre; Pres. ABD AL-RAHMAN ALI AL-JERAISY; Sec.-Gen. HUSSEIN ABD AL-RAHMAN AL-AZAL; 70,000 mems.

Tabouk Chamber of Commerce and Industry: POB 567, Tabouk; tel. (4) 422-2736; fax (4) 422-7387; internet www.tcci.org.sa; Pres. MUHAMMAD H. AL-WABSI; Sec.-Gen. AWADH AL-BALAWI.

Ta'if Chamber of Commerce and Industry: POB 1005, Ta'if; tel. (2) 736-6800; fax (2) 738-0040; e-mail info@taifchamber.org.sa; internet www.taifcci.com; Pres. NAIF A. AL-ADWANI; Sec.-Gen. Eng. YOUSUF MUHAMMAD AL-SHAFI.

Yanbu Chamber of Commerce and Industry: POB 58, Yanbu; tel. (4) 322-7878; fax (4) 322-6800; f. 1979; publishes quarterly magazine; 5,000 members; Pres. Dr MANSOUR M. AL-ANSARI; Sec.-Gen. KHALED SALMAN AL-SAHALI.

STATE HYDROCARBONS COMPANIES

Saudi Arabian Oil Co (Saudi Aramco): POB 5000, Dhahran 31311; tel. (3) 872-0115; fax (3) 873-8190; e-mail webmaster@aramco.com.sa; internet www.saudiaramco.com; f. 1933; previously known as Arabian-American Oil Co (Aramco); in 1993 incorporated the Saudi Arabian Marketing and Refining Co (SAMAREC, f. 1988) by merger of operations; holds the principal working concessions in Saudi Arabia; operates 5 wholly owned refineries (at Jeddah, Rabigh, Ras Tanura, Riyadh and Yanbu); Pres. and CEO KHALID A. AL-FALIH.

Aramco Gulf Operations Co (AGOC): POB 688, Khafji City 31971; tel. (3) 766-4024; fax (3) 767-5514; e-mail alsultanbf@kjo.com.sa; internet www.agoc.com.sa; f. 2000; wholly owned by Saudi Aramco; holds concession for offshore exploitation of Saudi Arabia's half-interest in the Saudi Arabia-Kuwait Neutral Zone; Pres. and CEO MUHAMMAD A. AL-SHAMMARY.

Petromin Corporation (Petromin Oils): POB 1432, Jeddah 21431; tel. (2) 215-7000; fax (2) 215-7111; e-mail info@petromin.com; internet www.petromin.com; f. 1968; 71% owned by Saudi Aramco, 29% by Mobil; manufacture and marketing of lubricating oils and other related products; production 140m. litres (2002); cap. 110m. riyals; Exec. Dir WAHEED A. SHAIKH; Pres. and CEO SAMIR M. NAWAR.

Rabigh Refining and Petrochemical Co (Petro Rabigh): POB 666, Rabigh 21911; tel. (2) 425-1855; fax (2) 425-2732; internet www.petrorabigh.com; f. 2005; jt venture between Saudi Aramco and Sumitomo Chemical (Japan); operation of integrated oil-refining and petrochemical production facilities at Rabigh; initial public offering of 20% of shares announced in Jan. 2008; Chair. ABD AL-AZIZ F. AL-KHAYYAL; Pres. and CEO SAAD FAHAD AL-DOSARI.

Saudi Aramco Lubricating Oil Refining Co (LUBEREF): POB 5518, Jeddah 21432; tel. (2) 427-5497; fax (2) 636-6933; e-mail webmaster@luberef.com; internet www.luberef.com; f. 1975; owned 70% by Saudi Aramco and 30% by Jadwa Industrial Investment Co; Pres. and CEO ABDULLAH O. AL-BAIZ.

Saudi Aramco Mobil Refinery Co Ltd (SAMREF): POB 30078, Yanbu; tel. (4) 396-4443; fax (4) 396-0942; e-mail amrihh@samref.com.sa; internet www.samref.com.sa; f. 1981; operation of oil-refining facilities at Yanbu; operated by Saudi Aramco and Mobil, capacity 360,000 b/d; Pres. and CEO FAWWAZ I. NAWWAB.

Saudi Aramco Shell Refinery Co (SASREF): POB 10088, Madinat al-Jubail, al-Sinaiyah 31961; tel. (3) 357-2000; fax (3) 357-2525; e-mail info@sasref.com.sa; internet www.sasref.com.sa; operation of oil-refining facilities at Jubail; operated by Saudi Aramco and Shell; capacity 300,000 b/d; exports began in 1985; Chair. HAMID T. AL-SAUDOON.

Saudi Basic Industries Corpn (SABIC): POB 5101, Riyadh 11422; tel. (1) 225-8000; fax (1) 225-9000; e-mail info@sabic.com; internet www.sabic.com; f. 1976 to foster the petrochemical industry and other hydrocarbon-based industries through jt ventures with foreign partners, and to market their products; 70% state-owned; production 55m. tons (2007); Chair. Prince SA'UD BIN THUNAYAN AL SA'UD; Vice-Chair. and CEO MUHAMMAD AL-MADY.

Projects include:

Arabian Petrochemical Co (Petrokemya): POB 10002, Jubail 31961; tel. (3) 358-7000; fax (3) 358-4480; e-mail petrokemya@petrokemya.sabic.com; f. 1981; wholly owned subsidiary of SABIC; produced 2.4m. tons of ethylene, 135,000 tons of polystyrene, 100,000 tons of butene-1, 570,000 tons of propylene, 100,000 tons of butadiene and 150,000 tons of benzene in 2001; owns 50% interest in ethylene glycol plant producing 610,000 tons per year of monoethylene glycol, 65,000 tons per year of diethylene glycol and 3,900 tons per year of triethylene glycol; Pres. SAMI A. AL-SUWAIGH.

Eastern Petrochemical Co (Sharq): POB 10035, Jubail 31961; tel. (3) 357-5000; fax (3) 358-0383; e-mail sharq@sharq.sabic.com; f. 1981 to produce linear low-density polyethylene, ethylene glycol; a SABIC jt venture with Japanese cos led by Mitsubishi Corpn; total capacity 660,000 tons of ethylene glycol and 280,000 tons of polyethylene per year; Chair. ABD AL-AZIZ AL-JARBOOA.

Al-Jubail Petrochemical Co (Kemya): POB 10084, Jubail 31961; tel. (3) 357-6000; fax (3) 358-7858; e-mail kemya@kemya.sabic.com; f. 1980; began production of linear low-density polyethylene in 1984, of high-density polyethylene in 1985, and of high alfa olefins in 1986, capacity of 330,000 tons per year of polyethylene; jt venture with Exxon Corpn (USA) and SABIC; Chair. HOMOOD AL-TUWAIJRI; Pres. ABD AL-AZIZ SULAYMAN AL-HAMAAD.

National Industrial Gases Co (Gas): POB 10110, Jubail 31961; tel. (3) 357-5738; fax (3) 358-8880; e-mail hussainaa@gas.sabic.com; 70% SABIC-owned jt venture with Saudi private sector; total capacity of 876,000 tons of oxygen and 492,750 tons of nitrogen per year; Pres. ALI AL-GHAMDI.

National Plastic Co (Ibn Hayyan): POB 10002, Jubail 31961; tel. (3) 358-7000; fax (3) 358-4736; f. 1984; 86.5% owned by SABIC; produces 390,000 tons per year of vinylchloride monomer and 324,000 tons per year of polyvinylchloride; Pres. KHALED AL-RAWAF.

Saudi-European Petrochemical Co (Ibn Zahr): POB 10330, Jubail 31961; tel. (3) 341-5060; fax (3) 341-2966; e-mail info@ibnzahr.sabic.com; f. 1985; annual capacity 1.4m. tons of methyl-tertiary-butyl ether (MTBE), 0.3m. tons of propylene; SABIC has an 80% share, Ecofuel and APICORP each have 10%; Chair. Dr ABD AL-RAHMAN S. AL-UBAID.

Saudi Kayan Petrochemical Co: POB 10302, Jubail Industrial City 31961; tel. (3) 359-3000; fax (3) 359-3111; e-mail shares@saudikayan.sabic.com; internet www.saudikayan.com; f. 2006; jt venture between SABIC and Al-Kayan Petrochemical Co; initial public offering of 45% of shares in 2008; production of ethylene, propylene, polypropylene, ethylene glycol, butene-1 and specialized products incl. aminomethyls, dimethylformamide and choline chloride; Chair. MUTLAQ HAMAD AL-MORISHED.

Saudi Methanol Co (ar-Razi): POB 10065, Jubail Industrial City 31961; tel. (3) 357-7800; fax (3) 358-5552; e-mail arrazi@arrazi.sabic.com; f. 1979; jt venture with a consortium of Japanese cos; capacity of 3.2m. tons per year of chemical-grade methanol; total methanol exports in 2001 were 3.2m. tons; Pres. NABIL A. MANSOURI; Exec. Vice-Pres. H. MIZUNO.

Saudi Petrochemical Co (Sadaf): POB 10025, Jubail 31961; tel. (3) 357-3000; fax (3) 357-3343; e-mail info@sadaf.sabic.com; f. 1980 to produce ethylene, ethylene dichloride, styrene, crude industrial ethanol, caustic soda and methyl-tertiary-butyl-ether (MTBE); total capacity of 4.3m. tons per year; Shell Chemicals Arabia has a 50% share; Pres. MOSAED S. AL-OHALI.

Saudi Yanbu Petrochemical Co (Yanpet): POB 30333, Yanbu 21441; tel. (4) 396-5000; fax (4) 396-5006; e-mail info@yanpet.sabic.com; f. 1980 to produce 820,000 tons per year of ethylene, 600,000 tons per year of high-density polyethylene and 340,000 tons per year of ethylene glycol; total capacity 1.7m. tons per year by 1990; ExxonMobil and SABIC each have a 50% share; Pres. SULAYMAN AL-HUSSAIN.

Yanbu National Petrochemical Co (Yansab): POB 31396, Yanbu Industrial City 21477; tel. (4) 325-9000; fax (4) 325-6666; e-mail shares@yansab.sabic.com; internet www.yansab.com.sa; f. 2006; 55% owned by SABIC; projected total capacity of over 4.0m. tons per year, incl. 1.3m. tons of ethylene; Chair. MUTLAQ HAMAD AL-MORISHED.

Foreign Concessionaire

Saudi Arabian Chevron: POB 363, Riyadh; tel. (1) 462-7274; fax (1) 464-1992; internet www.sachevron.com; also office in Kuwait; f. 1928; fmrly Getty Oil Co; renamed Saudi Arabian Texaco Inc. 1993, renamed as above 2007; holds concession (5,200 sq km at Dec. 1987) for exploitation of Saudi Arabia's half-interest in the Saudi Arabia-Kuwait Neutral (Partitioned) Zone; Pres. AHMAD AL-OMAR.

UTILITIES

Power and Water Utility Company for Jubail and Yanbu (MARAFIQ): POB 11133, Jubail 31961; tel. (3) 340-1111; fax (3) 340-1168; e-mail marafiqworld@marafiq.com.sa; internet www.marafiq.com.sa; f. 2003; equal ownership held by the Royal Comm.

for Jubail and Yanbu, Saudi Aramco, Saudi Basic Industries Corpn and the Public Investment Fund; operation and devt of utility services; Chair. Prince SA'UD IBN ABDULLAH IBN THUNAYAN AL SA'UD; CEO THAMIR S. AL-SHARHAN.

Water and Electricity Co: POB 300091, Riyadh 11372; tel. (1) 211-3362; fax (1) 211-3313; e-mail info@wec.com.sa; internet www.wec.com.sa; f. 2003; jointly owned by Saline Water Conversion Corpn and Saudi Electricity Co; responsible for managing supply and demand of electricity and water; Chair. FAHID AL-SHARIF; CEO OMAR AL-GHAMDI.

Electricity

Electricity and Co-generation Regulatory Authority (ECRA): PO Box 4540, Riyadh 11412; tel. (1) 201-9045; e-mail public@ecra.gov.sa; internet www.ecra.gov.sa; f. 2001 to regulate the power industry and to recommend tariffs for the sector; Gov. Dr FAREED M. ZEDAN.

ACWA Power International: POB 22616, Riyadh 11416; tel. (1) 473-4400; fax (1) 474-9215; e-mail info@acwapower.com; internet www.acwapowerprojects.com; f. 2008; develops privately financed power and water projects; Exec. Chair. MUHAMMAD ABUNAYYAN.

Saudi Electricity Co (SEC): POB 57, Riyadh 11411; tel. (1) 403-2222; fax (1) 405-1191; internet www.se.com.sa; f. 1999 following merger of 10 regional cos, to organize the generation, transmission and distribution of electricity into separate operating cos; jt stock co; cap. SR 33,758m.; Chair. Dr SALEH HUSSEIN AL-AWAJI.

Water

National Water Co: POB 676, Riyadh 11421; tel. (1) 211-3014; fax (1) 211-3016; e-mail info@nwc.com.sa; internet www.nwc.com.sa; f. 2008 to consolidate all govt-run water and wastewater management services and to facilitate the gradual privatization of the sector; Chair. ABDULLAH IBN ABD AL-RAHMAN AL-HUSSEIN (Minister of Water and Electricity); CEO LOAY A. AL-MUSALLAM.

Saline Water Conversion Corpn (SWCC): POB 4931, 21412 Jeddah; tel. (2) 682-1240; fax (2) 682-0415; e-mail computerdirector@swcc.gov.sa; internet www.swcc.gov.sa; f. 1974; provides desalinated water; 24 plants; Gov. FAHID AL-SHARIF; Dir-Gen. ABD AL-AZIZ OMAR NASSIEF.

TRADE UNIONS

Trade unions are illegal in Saudi Arabia.

Transport

RAILWAYS

Saudi Arabia has the only rail system in the Arabian peninsula. The Saudi Government Railroad comprises 719 km of single and 157 km of double track. The main line is 570 km in length and connects Dammam port, on the Gulf coast, with Riyadh, via Dhahran, Abqaiq, Hufuf, Harad and al-Kharj. New 950-km and 115-km lines, connecting Riyadh with Jeddah and Dammam with Jubail, respectively, known as the Saudi Landbridge Project, were planned. The revamped network was to connect the Red Sea with the Persian (Arabian) Gulf and was to be closely linked with Jeddah Islamic Port and King Abd al-Aziz Port (at Dammam). Bidding for the build-operate-transfer contract was opened in February 2008, but was subsequently delayed owing to developments in the global economic climate. In October 2011 the Government announced that it would carry out the project. In March 2009 a SR 6,900m. contract was awarded for the part one of the first phase of the Haramain High-Speed Rail Project, a proposed 450-km line that would connect the west-coast centres of Mecca, Medina and Jeddah, and provide a passenger service for millions of *Umrah* and *Hajj* pilgrims every year. Contracts for part two were awarded to eight companies, including Saudi Binladin Group and Saudi Oger, in February 2011. Completion of the entire project was anticipated by 2014. The concession for a 2,400-km North–South line, connecting Riyadh, Qassim, Ha'il, al-Zubayrah and al-Jalamid, to be mainly utilized for transporting minerals, was tendered, in several stages, from September 2007 to September 2009.

An 18-km elevated metro system linking the holy sites in Mecca was opened in November 2010. Plans for the construction of a metro system in Jeddah, with 200 stations, at a cost of some US $5,600m., were announced in April 2009, while construction work on a two-line urban light-rail system in Riyadh was reportedly under way in 2012. A total of 1.1m. passengers travelled by rail in the kingdom in 2009. In 2010 the total length of Saudi Arabia's railways was 1,020 route-km.

Saudi Railway Co (SAR): Diplomatic Quarter Bldg S-24, POB 64447, Riyadh 11452; tel. (1) 250-1111; fax (1) 480-7517; e-mail info@sar.com.sa; internet www.sar.com.sa; f. 2006; manages North–South Railway project; CEO RUMAIH AL-RUMAIH; Chair. MANSOUR IBN SALEH AL-MAYMAN.

Saudi Railways Organization (SRO): POB 36, Dammam 31241; tel. (3) 871-3000; fax (3) 827-1130; e-mail sro@sro.org.sa; internet www.saudirailways.org; Pres. ABD AL-AZIZ IBN MUHAMMAD AL-HOQAIL.

ROADS

Asphalted roads link Jeddah to Mecca, Jeddah to Medina, Medina to Yanbu, al-Ta'if to Mecca, Riyadh to al-Kharj, and Dammam to Hufuf, as well as the principal communities and certain outlying points in Saudi Aramco's area of operations. The trans-Arabian highway links Dammam, Riyadh, al-Ta'if, Mecca and Jeddah. In 2007 there were 221,372 km of roads, of which 13,596 km were main roads (including motorways) and 33,924 km were secondary roads. Metalled roads link all the main population centres.

Saudi Public Transport Co (SAPTCO): POB 10667, Riyadh 11443; tel. (1) 2884400; fax (1) 2884411; e-mail info@saptco.com.sa; internet www.saptco.com.sa; f. 1979; operates a public bus service throughout Saudi Arabia and to neighbouring countries; the Govt holds a 30% share; Chair. ABDULLAH AL-MUGHBIL; CEO Eng. KHALID AL-HOGAIL.

SHIPPING

On average over 95% of Saudi Arabia's imports and exports pass through the country's sea ports. Responsibility for the management, operation and maintenance of a number of ports began to be transferred to the private sector from 1997, but all ports remain subject to regulation and scrutiny by the Ports Authority. In January 2008 the Ports Authority announced the signing of a US $586m. contract with the China Harbour Engineering Co Ltd to build a new port at Ras Azzawr.

Jeddah is the principal commercial port and the main point of entry for pilgrims bound for Mecca. It has 58 berths for general cargo, container traffic, roll-on roll-off (ro-ro) traffic, livestock and bulk grain shipments, with draughts ranging from 8 m to 16 m. The port also has a 200-metric ton floating crane, cold storage facilities and a fully equipped ship-repair yard. Dammam is the second largest commercial port and has general cargo, container, ro-ro, dangerous cargo and bulk grain berths. Draughts range from 8 m to 13.5 m. It has a 200-metric ton floating crane and a fully equipped ship-repair yard.

The other three important ports are Jubail, Yanbu and Jazan. Jubail has one commercial and one industrial port. Yanbu, which comprises one commercial and one industrial port, is Saudi Arabia's nearest major port to Europe and North America, and is the focal point of the most rapidly growing area, in the west of Saudi Arabia. Jazan is the main port for the southern part of the country.

At 31 December 2012 Saudi Arabia's flag registered fleet totalled 403 vessels, with an aggregate displacement of 2,306,943 grt, of which 11 were fish carriers, two were gas tankers and six were general cargo ships.

Port Authorities

Saudi Ports Authority: POB 5162, Riyadh 11422; tel. (1) 405-0005; fax (1) 405-3508; e-mail info@ports.gov.sa; internet www.ports.gov.sa; f. 1976; regulatory authority; Pres. Dr ABD AL-AZIZ BIN MUHAMMAD AL-TUWAIJRI; Chair. Dr JUBARAH IBN EID AL-SURAISERI (Minister of Transport).

Dammam: POB 28062, Dammam 31188; tel. (3) 858-3199; fax (3) 857-1727; Dir-Gen. NAEEM IBRAHIM AL-NAEEM.

Dhiba: POB 190, Dhiba; tel. (4) 432-1060; fax (4) 432-2679; Dir-Gen. MAHMOUD AL-HARBI.

Jazan: POB 16, Jazan; tel. (7) 317-1000; fax (7) 317-0777; Dir-Gen. ABD AL-HAMEED SOURI.

Jeddah: POB 9285, Jeddah 21188; tel. (2) 647-1200; fax (2) 647-7411; Dir-Gen. SAHIR M. TAHLAWI.

Jubail Commercial Port: POB 276, Jubail 31951; tel. (3) 362-0600; fax (3) 362-3340; e-mail Jubail@ports.gov.sa; Dir-Gen. Capt. FAHD A. AL-AMER.

Jubail Industrial Port: POB 547, Jubail 31951; tel. (3) 357-8000; fax (3) 357-8011; Dir-Gen. ABDULLAH NASIR AL-TWAIJRI.

Yanbu Commercial Port: POB 1019, Yanbu al-Bahar; tel. (4) 322-2100; fax (4) 322-7643; Dir-Gen. ABDULLAH BIN AWAD AL-ZAIMI.

Yanbu Industrial Port: POB 30325, Yanbu; tel. (4) 396-7048; fax (4) 396-7037; Dir-Gen. ABDULLAH BIN AWAD AL-ZAIMI.

Principal Shipping Companies

Arabian Establishment for Trade and Shipping (AET): POB 832, 2nd Floor, Al-Matbouli Plaza, al-Ruwaiz District, Jeddah 21421; tel. (2) 652-5500; fax (2) 657-1148; e-mail aetjed@aetshipping.com; internet www.aetshipping.com; f. 1963; shipping agency; Gen. Man. ANTHONY ROBINSON.

Arabian Petroleum Supply Co Ltd (APSCO): POB 1408, Al-Qurayat St, Jeddah 21431; tel. (2) 608-1171; fax (2) 637-0966; e-mail marine@apsco-ksa.com; internet www.apsco.com.sa; f. 1961; Chair. Sheikh MUHAMMAD YOUSSUF ALI AL-REZA; Man. Dir MUHAMMAD ALI IBRAHIM ALIREZA.

Baaboud Trading and Shipping Agencies: POB 7262, Jeddah 21462; tel. (2) 627-0000; fax (2) 627-1111; e-mail info@baaboud.net; internet www.baaboud.net; Man. Dir AHMAD M. BAABOUD.

Bakri Navigation Co Ltd: POB 3757, Jeddah 21481; tel. (2) 652-4298; fax (2) 652-4297; e-mail info@bakrinavigation.com; internet www.bakrinavigation.com; f. 1973; owns and operates a fleet of oil tankers, tug boats and utility vessels; Chair. Sheikh A. K. AL-BAKRY; Man. Dir G. A. K. AL-BAKRY.

National Shipping Co of Saudi Arabia (Bahri): POB 8931, NSCSA Bldg No. 569, Sitteen St, Malaz Area, Riyadh 11492; tel. (1) 478-5454; fax (1) 477-8036; e-mail info@bahri.sa; internet www.bahri.sa; f. 1979; transportation of crude petroleum and petrochemical products; routes through Red Sea and Mediterranean to USA and Canada; operates a fleet of 42 ships; due to merge with Vela International Marine Ltd in 2013; Chair. ABDULLAH SULAIMAN AL-RUBAIAN; CEO SALEH AL-JASSER.

Saudi Shipping and Maritime Services Co Ltd (TRANSHIP): POB 7522, Jeddah 21472; tel. (2) 642-4255; fax (2) 643-2821; e-mail bunker@tranship.com; internet www.ssmsc.com; Chair. Prince SA'UD IBN NAYEF IBN ABD AL-AZIZ; Dir Eng. SULAIMAN AL-HUDAIRI.

Shipping Corpn of Saudi Arabia Ltd: POB 1691, Arab Maritime Center, Malik Khalid St, Jeddah 21441; tel. (2) 647-1137; fax (2) 647-8222; e-mail arablines@arabjeddah.com; Pres. and Man. Dir ABD AL-AZIZ AHMAD ARAB.

CIVIL AVIATION

There are 27 commercial airports, which handled some 42m. passengers in 2008. Plans to privatize the kingdom's airports were first announced in 2003. In 2008 concessions were awarded to two foreign companies for the management of the three main airports—King Abd al-Aziz International Airport (KAIA, in Jeddah), King Khalid International Airport (KKIA, in Riyadh) and King Fahd International Airport (KFIA, in the Eastern region, near Dammam). Construction of a new passenger terminal at KAIA, with an annual passenger capacity of 30m., commenced in February 2011 and was expected to be completed by 2013 or 2014. A further two expansion phases, which would increase annual passenger capacity to about 80m. by 2035, were also planned. Prince Muhammad Bin Abd al-Aziz Airport in Medina, which opened in 1972, began handling international flights in 2006. Plans to build two new terminals, thus increasing capacity to around 12m. passengers per year by 2019, were at an advanced planning stage in 2012.

General Authority of Civil Aviation (GACA): POB 887, Jeddah 21165; tel. (2) 640-5000; fax (2) 640-1477; e-mail gaca-info@gaca.gov.sa; internet www.gaca.gov.sa; f. 1934; as the Presidency of Civil Aviation; name changed as above 1977; regulatory authority; Pres. FAISAL IBN HAMAD AL-SUGAIR.

National Air Services (NAS): POB 18118, 2nd Floor, Al-Jirasi Bldg, Madinah Rd, Jeddah 21415; tel. (2) 6910122; fax (2) 6520394; e-mail info@nasaviation.com; internet www.nasaviation.com; f. 1999; privately owned; also operates low-cost air carrier, Nas Air; CEO SULAIMAN AL-HAMDAN.

Saudi Arabian Airlines (SAUDIA): POB 620, Jeddah 21231; tel. (2) 686-4588; fax (2) 686-4587; e-mail webmaster@saudiairlines.com.sa; internet www.saudiairlines.com; f. 1945; began operations in 1947; carried 18.9m. passengers in 2010; regular services to 25 domestic and 52 international destinations; catering and cargo divisions part-privatized in 2008; further divestment of shares in technical services and training divisions finalized in March 2010; Chair. Prince SULTAN IBN ABD AL-AZIZ; Dir-Gen. KHALID ABDULLAH AL-MULHIM.

Tourism

The vast majority of devout Muslims try to make at least one visit to the holy cities of Medina, the burial place of Muhammad, and Mecca, his birthplace. In 2000 the Government decided to issue tourist visas for the first time. A Supreme Commission for Tourism (now Saudi Commission for Tourism and Antiquities—SCTA) was subsequently established to develop the tourism industry in Saudi Arabia. According to the SCTA, at the end of 2008 there were 1,006 hotels operating in the kingdom, providing more than 270,000 hotel rooms. It was reported in 2008 that the SCTA planned to invest almost US $40,000m. to develop 19 tourism resorts on the Red Sea coast. According to provisional data, tourist arrivals were recorded at some 17.3m. in 2011, while receipts from tourism totalled $8,459m. An estimated 1.8m. foreign pilgrims visited Mecca in 2012.

Saudi Commission for Tourism and Antiquities (SCTA): POB 66680, Riyadh 11586; tel. (1) 880-8855; fax (1) 880-8844; internet www.scta.gov.sa; f. 2001 as Supreme Comm. for Tourism, renamed as above 2008; Pres. Prince SULTAN IBN SALMAN IBN ABD AL-AZIZ AL SA'UD.

Saudi Hotels and Resort Areas Co (SHARACO): POB 5500, Riyadh 11422; tel. (1) 481-6666; fax (1) 480-1666; e-mail info@saudi-hotels.com.sa; internet www.saudi-hotels.com.sa; f. 1975; construction and management of hotels, resorts and other tourism facilities; Saudi Govt has a 40% interest; Chair. MUSAAD AL-SENANY; Dir-Gen. ABD AL-AZIZ AL-AMBAR.

Defence

Chief of the General Staff: Gen. HUSSAIN IBN ABDULLAH IBN HUSSAIN AL-GABEEL.

Director-General of Public Security Forces: Gen. SAEED IBN ABDULLAH AL-QAHTANI.

Commander of Land Forces: Lt-Gen. EID IBN AWADH AL-SHALAWI.

Commander of Air Force: Gen. FAYYAD IBN HAMID IBN RAGAD AL-RUWAILI.

Commander of the Navy: Lt-Gen. DHAKHAIL ALLAH IBN AHMAD IBN MUHAMMAD AL-WAQDANI.

Defence Budget (2011): SR 182,000m.

Total Armed Forces (as assessed at November 2012): 233,500 (army 75,000; navy 13,500; air force 20,000; air defence forces 16,000; national guard 100,000—75,000 active personnel and 25,000 tribal levies); industrial security force 9,000).

Paramilitary Forces (as assessed at November 2012): 15,500: 10,500 frontier force; 4,500 coastguard; and 500 special security force.

Education

The educational system in Saudi Arabia resembles that of other Arab countries. Educational institutions are administered mainly by the Government. The private sector plays a significant role at the first and second levels, but its total contribution is relatively small compared with that of the public sector.

Pre-elementary education is provided on a small scale, mainly in urban areas. Elementary or primary education is of six years' duration and the normal entrance age is six. The total number of pupils at this stage in 2011/12 was estimated at 2,530,744, with 232,453 teachers. Intermediate education begins at 12 and lasts for three years. The total number of pupils at this stage in 2011/12 was estimated at 1,212,029, with teachers numbering 125,355. Secondary education begins at 15 and extends for three years. After the first year, successful pupils branch into science or arts groups. The total number of pupils at this stage in 2011/12 was estimated at 1,226,205, with 114,625 teachers. According to UNESCO estimates, enrolment of children in the primary age-group increased from 32% in 1970 to 90% in 2008/09. Between 1970 and 2009/10 enrolment at the secondary level rose from 9% to 81%. The proportion of females enrolled in Saudi Arabian schools increased from 25% of the total number of pupils in 1970 to 47.7% in 2007. Vocational and technical education programmes can be entered after completion of the intermediate stage. In 2010/11 a total of 81,283 students attended 112 technical and vocational institutes.

In 2010/11 an estimated 925,027 students were enrolled in higher education. In 2008/09 the number of new students admitted to universities increased to 242,835, compared with 68,000 in 2003. In 2006 tertiary institutions included 110 university colleges and 87 colleges exclusively for women. In early 2012 there were 24 Government and nine private universities in the country. Princess Nora bint Abdulrahman University, established as Riyadh University for Women in 1970, moved to a new campus within the capital in May 2011. A planned increase in capacity from 26,000 to 50,000 students would make it the largest women's university in the world. The Imam Muhammad bin Sa'ud Islamic University comprises 11 colleges. It also includes six institutes abroad for teaching Islamic and Arab knowledge in the United Arab Emirates, Mauritania, Djibouti, Indonesia, the USA and Japan. Early in 2006 the Ministry of Higher Education announced that foreign universities would be permitted to establish campuses in the kingdom for the first time. The Government's budget for 2012 envisaged expenditure on education and training of SR 165,000m., equivalent to 24% of total spending.

SENEGAL

Introductory Survey

LOCATION, CLIMATE, LANGUAGE, RELIGION, FLAG, CAPITAL

The Republic of Senegal lies on the west coast of Africa, bordered to the north by Mauritania, to the east by Mali, and to the south by Guinea and Guinea-Bissau. In the southern part of the country The Gambia forms a narrow enclave extending some 320 km (200 miles) inland. The climate is tropical, with a long dry season followed by a short wet season—from June to September in the north, and from June to October in the south. Average annual temperatures range from 22°C (72°F) to 28°C (82°F). French is the official language, although use of Arabic has increased since the 1980s; the most widely spoken national languages at the time of the 2002 census were Wolof, Pulaar and Sereer. At the 1988 census almost 94% of the population were Muslims, and some 4% Christians, mostly Roman Catholics; a small number followed traditional beliefs. The national flag (proportions 2 by 3) has three equal vertical stripes, of green, yellow and red, with a five-pointed green star in the centre of the yellow stripe. The capital is Dakar. In July 2005 the Assemblée nationale approved legislation providing for the creation of a new administrative capital, near Kébèmer, on the Atlantic littoral.

CONTEMPORARY POLITICAL HISTORY

Historical Context

After 300 years as a French colony, Senegal became a self-governing member of the French Community in November 1958. The Mali Federation, linking Senegal with Soudan (later the Republic of Mali), had only two months of independence before being dissolved when Senegal seceded, to become a separate independent state, on 20 August 1960. The Republic of Senegal was proclaimed on 5 September, with Léopold Sédar Senghor, leader of the Union Progressiste Sénégalaise (UPS), as the country's first President.

In late 1962, following the discovery of a coup attempt led by the Prime Minister, Mamadou Dia, Senghor assumed the premiership; other political parties were gradually absorbed into the UPS or outlawed, effectively creating a one-party state by 1966. In 1970 the office of Prime Minister was restored and assigned to a provincial administrator, Abdou Diouf, who in 1976 was made Senghor's constitutional successor. In 1973 Senghor, the sole candidate, was re-elected President. Senghor amended the Constitution in March 1976 to allow three parties to contest elections—the UPS, renamed the Parti Socialiste (PS), the Parti Démocratique Sénégalais (PDS) and the Parti Africain de l'Indépendance (PAI). The first national elections under the three-party system took place in February 1978; the PS won 83 of the 100 seats in the Assemblée nationale, the remainder being won by the PDS. In the concurrent presidential election, Senghor overwhelmingly defeated the leader of the PDS, Abdoulaye Wade.

Domestic Political Affairs

Senghor was succeeded as President by Diouf in January 1981, and the Constitution was amended to allow the existence of an unlimited number of political parties. At elections in February 1983 Diouf received 83.5% of the presidential vote (compared with 14.8% for his nearest rival, Wade), while in legislative elections the PS won 111 of the 120 seats. In April Diouf abolished the post of Prime Minister, which had latterly been held by Habib Thiam.

When preliminary results of the February 1988 presidential and legislative elections indicated clear victories for both Diouf and the PS, opposition parties alleged fraud on the part of the ruling party, and, following the outbreak of rioting in Dakar, a state of emergency was imposed. According to the official results of the presidential election, contested by four candidates, Diouf obtained 73.2% of the votes cast and Wade 25.8%. In the legislative elections, the PS won 103 seats and the PDS the remaining 17.

In March 1991 the legislature approved several amendments to the Constitution, notably the restoration of the post of Prime Minister, to which post Thiam was again named in the following month. Thiam's Government included four representatives of the PDS (including Wade, as Minister of State, effectively the most senior post in the Government other than the Prime Minister). In September the Assemblée nationale adopted amendments to the electoral code. Presidential elections would henceforth take place, in two rounds if necessary (to ensure that the President would be elected by an absolute majority of votes cast), every seven years, with a mandate that would be renewable only once.

In October 1992 Wade and his three PDS colleagues resigned from the Council of Ministers, protesting that they had been excluded from the governmental process. Eight candidates contested the presidential election, which took place in February 1993. The opposition denounced the preliminary results, which indicated that Diouf had won a clear majority. In March the Constitutional Council announced that Diouf had been re-elected with 58.4% of the votes cast (51.6% of the electorate had voted); Wade secured 32.0% of the votes.

Elections to the Assemblée nationale took place in May 1993; the PS won 84 of the 120 elective seats and the PDS 27. Shortly after the announcement of the results the Vice-President of the Constitutional Council, Babacar Sèye, was assassinated. Wade and three other PDS leaders were detained for three days in connection with the killing, and in October Wade was charged with complicity in the assassination; Wade's wife and a PDS deputy were also charged in connection with the murder. In November Ousmane Ngom, the PDS parliamentary leader, and Landing Savané, the leader of And Jëf—Parti Africain pour la Démocratie et le Socialisme (AJ—PADS), were among those detained following a protest in Dakar to demand the cancellation of austerity measures. Ngom, Savané and some 87 others were convicted of participating in an unauthorized demonstration, and received suspended prison sentences.

Following the devaluation of the CFA franc in January 1994, emergency measures were adopted to offset the immediate adverse economic effects. In February a demonstration in Dakar to denounce the devaluation degenerated into serious rioting, as a result of which eight people were killed. Wade and Savané were among those subsequently charged in association with the unrest. Charges against Wade and his opposition associates in connection with the murder of Sèye were dismissed in May, although Wade and Savané remained in custody until July, in connection with the post-devaluation violence. In October three of Sèye's alleged assassins were convicted and sentenced to 18–20 years' imprisonment.

In January 1996 Diouf announced that a second legislative chamber, the Sénat, was to be established. In February 1998 Wade (who had rejoined the Council of Ministers in March 1995 as Minister of State at the Presidency) appealed to the Constitutional Council to reject an amendment to the electoral code whereby the number of deputies in the Assemblée nationale was to be increased to 140; later in February 1998 the Council annulled the proposed increase, the first occasion on which the Council had ruled against a decision of the legislature. In March, however, the Assemblée nationale again voted to increase the number of deputies.

Some 18 parties and coalitions contested the legislative elections on 24 May 1998. The PS obtained 93 seats in the enlarged assembly, while the number of PDS deputies was reduced to 23. Voter turn-out was 39% of the registered electorate. In July Thiam resigned as Prime Minister, and was replaced by Mamadou Lamine Loum. A new Council of Ministers was named shortly afterwards, in which Serigne Diop, the leader of the Parti Démocratique Sénégalais—Rénovation (which had broken away from the PDS in 1997), was the only non-PS member.

In August 1998 the Assemblée nationale voted to revise the Constitution to remove the clause restricting the Head of State to a maximum of two terms of office, thus permitting Diouf to contest the next presidential election, in 2000. A requirement that the President be elected by more than 25% of all registered voters was also abandoned. The opposition parties, condemning the amendments, boycotted the vote.

The PS won all 45 elective seats in the first, indirect, elections to the Sénat in January 1999; these 45 members were chosen by an electoral college of deputies, local, municipal and regional councillors. Only the PS, the Parti Libéral du Sénégal (formed in 1998 by Ngom, leading a breakaway movement from the PDS), and a coalition of the Parti de l'Indépendance et du Travail (PIT) and AJ—PADS contested the elections; the PDS and other opposition parties were opposed to the introduction of an additional parliamentary chamber. A further 12 senators were appointed by the President of the Republic, including two opposition figures, and three were elected by Senegalese resident abroad.

In March 1999 an alliance of AJ—PADS, the PIT, the PDS and the Ligue Démocratique—Mouvement pour le Parti du Travail (LD—MPT) agreed to nominate Wade, who had resigned from the Assemblée nationale in mid-1998, as their joint candidate in the presidential election scheduled for 2000. In June 1999 former Minister of Foreign Affairs Moustapha Niasse announced his intention of contesting the presidential election, and published a document accusing Diouf and the PS of corruption; Niasse was consequently expelled from the PS and subsequently formed the Alliance des Forces de Progrès (AFP).

Although Diouf won the largest proportion of the votes cast (41.3%) at the election, held on 27 February 2000, his failure to secure an absolute majority necessitated a second round of voting between Diouf and Wade (who had secured 31.0% of the votes cast). Prior to the second round, Wade received the endorsement of the majority of the candidates defeated in the first round, including Niasse, who had been placed third with 16.8% of the votes. At the second round, held on 19 March, Wade won 58.5% of the total votes cast, thus taking the presidency from the PS for the first time. Turn-out in the second round was estimated at 60.1%, marginally lower than in the first round.

The new Constitution

Wade was sworn in as President on 1 April 2000 and named Niasse as Prime Minister. The new Council of Ministers incorporated several other opposition leaders, including Savané of AJ—PADS and Abdoulaye Bathily of the LD—MPT. Wade announced that he did not envisage governing alongside an Assemblée nationale dominated by the PS, and that he therefore intended to hold fresh legislative elections, following a constitutional referendum. Among the proposed changes, the President would gain the power to dissolve the Assemblée nationale, while other presidential powers would be transferred to the Prime Minister; the presidential mandate would again be reduced from seven to five years, renewable only once. Furthermore, the Sénat was to be abolished.

The constitutional referendum was held on 7 January 2001. Some 94.0% of the votes cast in the plebiscite supported the new Constitution; 65.8% of the registered electorate voted. Most provisions of the Constitution, including the abolition of the Sénat, took immediate effect, with only those sections relating to the legislature necessitating new elections before their implementation. Future presidential mandates would be reduced from seven to five years, and the number of deputies in the Assemblée nationale was lowered from 140 to 120.

The President dissolved the Assemblée nationale in February 2001 and announced that the new legislature, which was to be elected in April, would consist of 65 seats elected by majority voting in departments, and 55 by proportional representation using national lists. In March Wade appointed Mame Madior Boye, a politically unaffiliated magistrate, and hitherto Minister of Justice, as Prime Minister. In the ensuing reshuffle Niasse and other members of the AFP were removed from office, in what was regarded as an attempt by Wade to create a more unified Government, which incorporated greater representation for the PDS and its allies, prior to the legislative elections.

Legislative elections duly took place on 29 April 2001, contested by 25 parties. The pro-Wade Sopi (Change) coalition won 89 of the 120 seats in the Assemblée nationale, the AFP 11 and the PS only 10. The rate of electoral participation was 67.5%. Boye was reappointed as Prime Minister on 10 May. The new 24-member Government comprised 11 members of the PDS (which obtained most principal posts), nine representatives of civil society, and two members each of AJ—PADS and the LD—MPT.

In August 2001 some 25 parties, led by the PDS, formed a pro-presidential electoral alliance, the Convergence des Actions autour du Président en Perspective du 21ème Siècle (CAP-21), in advance of local and municipal elections. In February 2002 the three men convicted of the assassination of Babacar Sèye in 1993 were granted presidential pardons and subsequently released

from prison, provoking renewed controversy about the case. In the local and municipal elections, which were held on 12 May 2002, CAP-21 won control of nine of the 11 regional governments, as well as a majority of municipal and communal seats.

The sinking of a state-owned passenger ferry, the MV *Joola*, in September 2002, en route from Ziguinchor, the principal city of Casamance, to Dakar led to a national political crisis, even before the final death toll of the accident, subsequently enumerated at more than 1,800 people, became apparent. In early October the Minister of Equipment and Transport, Youssouph Sakho, and the Minister of the Armed Forces, Yoba Sambou, resigned in response to the tragedy, as it became clear that the vessel had been severely overloaded; only 64 survivors were reported. Later in the month the head of the navy was dismissed, and Wade announced that the Government accepted responsibility for the disaster. In early November Wade dismissed Boye and her Government; the dismissal was widely believed to have been prompted by the Government's response to the disaster. Shortly after Boye's dismissal, an inquiry into the incident found that safety regulations had been widely violated on the *Joola*, and that the dispatch of rescue equipment and staff to the ship by the armed forces had been inexplicably delayed. Idrissa Seck, the Mayor of Thiès, a close ally of Wade and previously a senior official in the PDS, was appointed as the new Prime Minister. In August 2003 the Chief of Staff of the Armed Forces and the Chief of Staff of the Air Force were dismissed as a result of disciplinary action related to the response to the sinking of the *Joola*.

Political tensions intensified in early 2004 as several parties that had supported Wade's candidacy in the presidential election of 2000 and had ministerial representation in the Government, including the LD—MPT and AJ—PADS, declined to participate in celebrations organized to mark the fourth anniversary of Wade's accession to power. In April Wade dismissed Seck's Government, appointing Macky Sall, hitherto Minister of State, Minister of the Interior and Local Communities, Government Spokesperson, as Prime Minister.

A series of government reorganizations in March and May 2005 left AJ—PADS as the only party (other than the PDS) to retain ministerial representation from the alliance that supported Wade's presidential candidacy in 2000, and were interpreted as an attempt to strengthen support for the President following sustained criticism from the LD—MPT. Wade also appointed members to a new Commission Électorale Nationale Autonome (CENA) in June; however, the opposition expressed concern at the composition of the body.

Seck was questioned by police in July 2005, after he was accused by President Wade of overspending on work to upgrade roads in Thiès, where he served as mayor. The former Prime Minister refuted any suggestion that he had embezzled government funds from the project. Later in July Seck was formally charged with endangering national security; there was no immediate explanation of the charges, which Seck's defence lawyers claimed to be politically motivated. In September the Assemblée nationale ruled that Seck should be brought to trial on charges of embezzlement at the High Court of Justice, which was reserved for cases concerning crimes committed by members of the Government in the exercise of their duties. Meanwhile, the Assemblée nationale adopted legislation providing for the eventual creation of a new administrative and political capital some 150 km north-east of Dakar, near Kébèmer.

In December 2005 the Assemblée nationale approved legislation, supported by President Wade, that delayed the legislative elections, which had been scheduled for mid-2006, until February 2007, when they were to be held concurrently with presidential voting. Wade justified this postponement (which was condemned by the parliamentary opposition) on financial grounds. (The legislative elections were later postponed further until June 2007.)

Seck was released from detention in February 2006, following the partial dismissal of the charges of corruption and embezzlement against him (some minor charges remained); the charges of endangering state security had been dropped in the previous month.

In November 2006, prior to the forthcoming presidential election, the Assemblée nationale adopted new legislation ending the obligation for a candidate to receive votes from one-quarter of the total registered electorate to be elected in the first round. Under the new law it became possible for a candidate to secure victory in the first round by obtaining a majority of more than 50% of recorded votes.

Wade's second term

The presidential election took place on 25 February 2007. President Wade secured a second term of office in the first round, winning 55.9% of the votes cast; his closest rival, with 14.9% of the votes, was Seck. Two days after the election five ministers resigned and a government reorganization was implemented. Those who left the Government were members of AJ—PADS, hitherto an ally of the ruling PDS, and cited changes in the relationship with the ruling party as reasons for their resignations.

Legislative elections were held on 3 June 2007, at which President Wade's Sopi coalition (comprising some 40 parties and movements, led by the PDS) secured 131 of the 150 available seats. However, many of the principal opposition parties chose to boycott the ballot when their demands for the establishment of an independent electoral commission were not met, and voter turn-out was estimated at just 34.7%. Later that month Prime Minister Sall resigned and was replaced by Cheikh Hadjibou Soumaré, hitherto Minister-delegate at the Office of the Minister of State of the Economy and Finance, responsible for the Budget. Soumaré subsequently named a new Government, which included 13 new appointees, eight of whom were women; the key portfolios remained unaltered.

Meanwhile, in May 2007 the Assemblée nationale voted to reinstate the Sénat. On 19 August parliamentarians and local officials elected 35 of the 100 senators; 34 of those seats were secured by PDS members. President Wade appointed the remaining 65 members. The Sénat was officially installed in September; Pape Diop was elected President of that body and was replaced as President of the Assemblée nationale by former Prime Minister Sall.

In May 2008 President Wade proposed an amendment to the Constitution, approved by the Council of Ministers, that would result in the extension of the presidential term of office from five to seven years. Wade suggested that the current mandate did not allow sufficient time to develop long-term policies, although it was stated that the new legislation would only enter into force after the next presidential election, which was due to be held in 2012. Wade promulgated the amendment in October 2008. Also that month the Sénat approved the amendment of the mandate of the President of the Assemblée nationale, from five years to a renewable term of one year. The move was regarded as preparation for removing Sall from office and the following month he was dismissed; Mamadou Seck, a former finance minister, was appointed in Sall's place. Sall subsequently announced that he had left the PDS to establish his own party, the Alliance pour la République (APR—Yaakaar).

In April 2009 Prime Minister Soumaré tendered his resignation and that of the Government. The announcement followed local elections, held the previous month, in which opposition parties had secured the majority of the seats available for the first time since 2000. In May 2009 President Wade nominated Souleymane Ndéné Ndiaye, hitherto Minister of State, Minister of the Maritime Economy, Maritime Transport, Fisheries and Fishbreeding, as Prime Minister and a new Council of Ministers was announced. Although the key portfolios remained unchanged, Karim Wade, son of the President, entered the administration as Minister of State, Minister of International Co-operation, Land Settlement, Air Transport and Infrastructure. Countering speculation that Wade was opening the way for his son to stand in the next presidential election, in August Abdoulaye Wade confirmed that he would be the party's presidential candidate in 2012.

In October 2009 President Wade carried out a ministerial reorganization in which the Minister of State, Minister of Foreign Affairs, Cheikh Tidiane Gadio, who had been in office since Wade came to power, was replaced by Madické Niang, hitherto Minister of State, Minister of Justice. It was widely believed that Niang had been appointed in order to mediate in a diplomatic crisis caused by Wade's support of the junta leader, Capt. Moussa Dadis Camara, in neighbouring Guinea. The interior and defence portfolios were allocated to new appointees, with both new ministers originating from Casamance, where renewed unrest had been experienced (see Separatism in Casamance).

In January 2010 Wade appointed close ally and former magistrate Doudou Ndir as President of the CENA, following the resignation of the incumbent, Mamadou Moustapha Touré, apparently at Wade's request. In June a series of government reorganizations took place; a number of additional women entered the Council of Ministers, bringing their number to 12 out of 41 ministers.

In August 2010 the opposition denounced a move to appoint further presidential allies to strategic posts ahead of the 2012 elections, when Wade nominated Cheikh Tidiane Diakhaté as President of the Constitutional Council, the body that would be responsible for considering any challenge to the legality of a third presidential mandate for Wade should he formally register his candidacy. In September 2010 three ministerial portfolios were reshuffled: Ngom, hitherto Minister of Mines, Industry, Agro-industry and Small and Medium-sized Enterprises became Minister of the Interior, replacing Bécaye Diop, who was appointed as Minister of the Armed Forces, succeeding Abdoulaye Baldé, who was allocated the mines portfolio. Meanwhile, there had been angry protests in Dakar against recurring power cuts, and in late September an IMF mission noted that electricity outages were one of the major factors negatively affecting economic growth. In response, in October President Wade dismissed the Minister of State, Minister of Energy, Samuel Sarr, and ordered an audit of the state electricity company, the Société Nationale d'Electricité. Karim Wade assumed additional responsibility for energy, becoming Minister of State, Minister of International Co-operation, Air Transport, Infrastructure and Energy. In November President Wade issued a decree scheduling the presidential election for 26 February 2012, and a few days later a committee of the ruling PDS endorsed his candidacy, rejecting claims from the opposition that such a move was unconstitutional.

In May 2011 Wade carried out a minor reorganization of the Council of Ministers. Notably, Cheikh Tidiane Sy was reappointed to the post of Minister of Justice, from which he had resigned six days previously. In March Sy had publicly accused opposition groups of planning a coup to overthrow the Government, a claim the Government had subsequently refuted. In mid-June the Cabinet approved a proposed constitutional change that would create the post of Vice-President. The opposition criticized the proposal, suggesting that Wade would seek to guarantee the succession of Karim Wade by appointing him to the post, since the Vice-President would, under the proposed change, succeed the incumbent President in the event of his death. A further amendment was proposed later that month, whereby a presidential candidate could win an election by receiving over 25% of votes cast in the first round, as opposed to the previous threshold of 50%. This proposal was also denounced by the opposition as a virtual guarantee of Wade's re-election. Following violent protests in Dakar and nation-wide on 23 June, in which more than 100 people were reportedly injured, both proposals were ultimately withdrawn. Days later riots occurred across the country in apparent protest at continuing power shortages, prompting the Government to deploy the army. Despite these disturbances, in July Wade confirmed his intention to seek a third term. Later that month, shortly before a planned opposition demonstration against Wade's candidacy, the Ministry of the Interior banned political rallies in the main squares and roads of central Dakar. None the less, a large and peaceful opposition rally was held, followed shortly afterwards by a larger demonstration in support of Wade.

In October 2011 an opposition activist, Malick Noel Seck, was imprisoned after a letter he had written which demanded that Wade not stand for a third term was adjudicated to contain death threats directed at members of the Constitutional Council. In November Wade used an appearance on state television to offer two opposition politicians, Moustapha Niasse of the AFP and Ousmane Tanor Dieng of the PS, ministerial positions in a future cabinet, should Wade gain re-election. Both Niasse and Dieng, who rejected this offer of co-operation, subsequently declared that they would stand as candidates in the presidential election, after a meeting of the umbrella opposition grouping Bennoo Siggil Senegaal in early December failed to agree on a single opposition candidate. In November prominent Senegalese musician Youssou N'Dour announced that he would be abandoning performances in 2012 to concentrate on politics; in January 2012 N'Dour confirmed that he would stand in the presidential election. In late December 2011, meanwhile, Wade was officially nominated as the PDS's electoral candidate.

The constitutionality of Wade's candidacy was finally confirmed by the Constitutional Council in January 2012, whereas the candidacy of N'Dour was rejected, on the grounds that he had not collected enough valid signatures to be nominated. In addition to Niasse and Dieng, former Prime Ministers Macky Sall and Idrissa Seck were also registered among a total of 14 candidates. Protests against Wade's candidacy took place in Dakar and elsewhere in the days following the ruling. Opposition politicians, operating under the auspices of the Mouvement Juin 23 (M23)—named in memory of the protests that took place in June 2011—played a key role in organizing these protests, which continued into February, in spite of an official ban on demonstrations; six people were reported to have died during the protests.

Recent developments: the 2012 elections

At the first round of voting in the presidential election, held on 26 February 2012, no single candidate secured the 50% of votes cast required for an outright victory. Wade received 34.8% of the votes cast, while Sall took 26.6% of the votes and Niasse 13.2%. Consequently, a second round of voting between Wade and Sall was scheduled for 25 March. All 12 of the remaining candidates subsequently declared their support for Sall, as did other prominent opposition figures, including N'Dour and the leaders of M23. At the second round of voting, which took place as scheduled, Sall was victorious, receiving 65.8% of votes cast as against 34.2% for Wade, who conceded defeat. A European Union (EU, see p. 281) observer mission affirmed the credibility of the vote. Sall was sworn in as President on 2 April and on the following day nominated Abdoul Mbaye, a former banker without party affiliation, as Prime Minister. A new Government in which, notably, the finance portfolio passed to another former banker, Amadou Kane, was installed on 4 April. Alioune Badara Cissé became Minister of Foreign Affairs, and N'Dour was appointed to the post of Minister of Culture and Tourism.

Elections to the Assemblée nationale were held on 1 July 2012 and resulted in a comprehensive victory for Benno Bokk Yaakaar (BBY), a recently formed coalition supportive of President Sall. BBY secured 119 legislative seats, compared with 12 for the PDS, while the remaining 19 seats were distributed among 11 smaller political groupings. The voter participation rate was only 36.7%. In September the legislature approved the abolition of the PDS-dominated Sénat, which Sall argued was too costly to maintain; he pledged to use the money saved to fund a flood prevention programme. The vice-presidency was also abrogated.

Mbaye reorganized the Council of Ministers in October 2012. Among other changes, Pathé Seck became Minister of the Interior, Mankeur Ndiaye received the foreign affairs portfolio and Abdou Latif Coulibaly was appointed to lead the newly established Ministry of Good Governance.

Meanwhile, in April 2012 the new administration claimed that evidence of embezzlement by members of the previous PDS Government had been uncovered. Investigations were conducted into the matter, with several Wade-era ministers and officials questioned during that year, and in April 2013 Karim Wade was arrested and charged with illegal enrichment. The French authorities were also investigating the Wade family's assets in early 2013.

Separatism in Casamance

Long-standing resentment against the Government of Senegal in the southern province of Casamance (which is virtually cut off from the rest of the country by the enclave of The Gambia) was embodied from the early 1980s by the separatist Mouvement des Forces Démocratiques de la Casamance (MFDC). The announcement in May 1991 of the imminent release of more than 340 detainees (including the Secretary-General and executive leader of the MFDC, Fr Augustin Diamacouné Senghor) who had been arrested in connection with unrest in Casamance facilitated the conclusion, shortly afterwards in Guinea-Bissau, of a cease-fire agreement by representatives of the Senegalese Government and of the MFDC. An amnesty was approved by the Assemblée nationale later in June, and some 400 detainees were released. A period of relative calm ensued.

In January 1992 a peace commission, comprising government representatives and members of the MFDC, was established, with mediation by Guinea-Bissau. A resurgence of violence in Casamance from July prompted the Government to redeploy armed forces in the region, giving rise to MFDC protests that the 'remilitarization' of Casamance contravened the truce. Contradictory statements made by MFDC leaders regarding their commitment to the peace accord evidenced a split within the movement. The 'Front Nord' and the MFDC Vice-President, Sidi Badji, appealed to the rebels to disarm, while the 'Front Sud', led by Diamacouné Senghor (who was now based in Guinea-Bissau), appeared determined to continue the armed struggle. After an escalation of the conflict in late 1992 and early 1993, a new round of negotiations resulted in the signing, in July 1993, of a cease-fire agreement, the Ziguinchor Accord, between the Government and Diamacouné Senghor (who had returned to Ziguinchor in

March). Guinea-Bissau was to act as a guarantor of the agreement, and the Government of France was to be asked to submit an historical arbitration regarding the Casamance issue. In December France issued its judgment that Casamance had not existed as an autonomous territory prior to the colonial period, and that independence for the region had been neither demanded nor considered at the time of decolonization.

In September 1995 a Commission Nationale de Paix (CNP) was established and members of the commission reportedly sought a dialogue with Diamacouné Senghor and the MFDC's four other political leaders (all of whom remained under house arrest). During October renewed rebel attacks on government forces were accompanied by a major army offensive in the southwest. By the end of November it was reported that about 150 separatists and 15 members of the armed forces had been killed in clashes.

While both the Senegalese authorities and the MFDC leadership appeared committed to reviving the peace process, the deaths of 25 soldiers in August 1997 near Ziguinchor prompted fears of a revival of the conflict. In September the armed forces launched a new offensive, in which rebel forces were reported to have sustained heavy losses. A further armed forces offensive in October involved as many as 3,000 troops and resulted in the deaths of 12 soldiers and 80 rebels in clashes near the border with Guinea-Bissau, according to Senegalese military sources. Salif Sadio, the MFDC's military leader, stated that the organization remained committed to the peace process, but maintained that its forces were justified in defending themselves against armed attack.

In January 1998 Diamacouné Senghor appealed for a cease-fire, indicating that his organization would be prepared to abandon its demand for independence, subject to the Government instituting measures to ensure greater economic and social development in Casamance. Nevertheless, rebel violence continued intermittently throughout the second half of 1998.

In June 1999 talks between several MFDC factions began in Banjul, The Gambia, although many leaders of military and exiled factions of the MFDC did not attend, claiming that Diamacouné Senghor was effectively a hostage of the Senegalese Government. At the meeting, Léopold Sagna was confirmed as the head of the armed forces of the MFDC, replacing Sadio, who was reportedly less prepared to compromise with government demands. The Senegalese authorities subsequently acceded to the MFDC's demand that Diamacouné Senghor be released from house arrest; his movements were, however, to remain restricted.

In November 1999 Diamacouné Senghor agreed to recommence negotiations with the Government. At the meeting, held in Banjul in December, the Government and the MFDC agreed to an immediate cease-fire, and to create the conditions necessary to bring about lasting peace; the Governments of The Gambia and of Guinea-Bissau were to monitor the situation in the region. In February 2000 a joint mission of the Senegalese Government and the MFDC was established to oversee the cease-fire. Following his election as President in March, Abdoulaye Wade announced that he was to continue the process of negotiations, but that his preference was to conduct direct dialogue with the MFDC. Wade further announced that Diamacouné Senghor would be permitted total freedom of movement.

The overwhelming support in Casamance for the new Constitution, which was endorsed by 96% of voters in the region at the referendum in January 2001, prompted Wade to announce that Casamance had definitively voted to remain part of Senegal. In mid-January the Guinea-Bissau armed forces reportedly destroyed all the Casamance rebel bases in that country, in response to clashes between rival MFDC factions there. Continued unrest in the region south-west of Ziguinchor further delayed the signature of a cease-fire agreement, originally intended to take place at the meeting of mid-December 2000, which had been rescheduled to occur in Dakar in early February 2001.

In February 2001 Diamacouné Senghor announced that, in order to accelerate the peace process in Casamance, several senior members of the MFDC, including Sidi Badji and Djiba, had been removed from their positions. However, Sidi Badji, who had served as Military Affairs Adviser to Diamacouné Senghor, rejected the legitimacy of his dismissal. Also in mid-February, in what was reportedly the most serious attack on civilian targets in Casamance for several years, separatist rebels killed some 13 civilians in an ambush. Both Sidi Badji and Diamacouné Senghor denied any knowledge of their supporters' involvement and condemned the attack, into which Wade announced the opening of a judicial inquiry.

In mid-March 2001 Minister of the Interior Mamadou Niang and Diamacouné Senghor signed a cease-fire agreement at a meeting in Ziguinchor, which provided for the release of detainees, the return of refugees, the removal of landmines (which had been utilized in the region since 1998) and for economic aid to reintegrate rebels and to ameliorate the infrastructure of Casamance. Some 16 prisoners were released several days after the accord was signed. The Gambian Government issued a communiqué in mid-March, in which it promised to prevent armed rebel groups from operating on Gambian territory; it was suspected that the renewed violence had been co-ordinated by groups based in The Gambia. Later in March Niang and Diamacouné Senghor signed a further agreement, which provided for the disarmament of rebel groups and the confinement to barracks of military forces in Casamance. In April Wade and Minister of the Armed Forces Yoba Sambou participated in negotiations with Diamacouné Senghor, at which other MFDC leaders, including Sidi Badji, were also present.

As a result of the renewed conflict, Diamacouné Senghor announced, in May 2001, that a proposed reconciliation forum, intended to unite the various factions of the MFDC, had been postponed indefinitely, and a number of members of the movement, including Djiba, were reportedly expelled. None the less, Diamacouné Senghor and Sidi Badji attended a meeting convened by the Gambian Government in Banjul in early June, in an attempt to overcome the impasse. As tensions between factions within the MFDC intensified, with further clashes reported in June and July, Diamacouné Senghor was removed from the position of Secretary-General of the MFDC in August, at the much-delayed reconciliation forum, and appointed as honorary President. Jean-Marie François Biagui, who had previously been involved in the French-based section of the MFDC, became Secretary-General and de facto leader. Sidi Badji, who continued to question the tactics of Diamacouné Senghor, was appointed as the organization's head of military affairs. Biagui not only demonstrated considerable reluctance to play a leadership role, but was also apparently unable to prevent Sidi Badji, who was reputed to have support from the authorities in The Gambia, from becoming the dominant force in the movement.

Despite these personnel changes within the MFDC, President Wade met Diamacouné Senghor at the presidential palace in Dakar in September 2001; both leaders reiterated the importance of implementing the cease-fire agreement. In response to this meeting, it was reported that the new leadership of the MFDC had suspended all further negotiations with the Government. Following further attacks by rebels, Biagui resigned as Secretary-General of the MFDC in early November. Sidi Badji was announced as Biagui's successor, in an acting capacity, although Diamacouné Senghor rejected this appointment, and reappointed Biagui as Secretary-General.

In August 2002, following a joint declaration signed by Diamacouné Senghor and Sidi Badji urging the resumption of peace talks between the rebels and the Government, Wade appointed an official delegation, chaired by the Second Vice-President of the Assemblée nationale and President of Ziguinchor Regional Council, Abdoulaye Faye, and including among its membership Niang and Sambou, to undertake negotiations with the MFDC. Meanwhile, the holding of an intra-Casamance conference, in early September, appeared to indicate a decline in support for separatist aspirations, as the conference produced a declaration, signed by representatives of 10 ethnic groups resident in the region, in favour of a 'definitive peace in Casamance', and which referred to the region as 'belonging to the great and single territory of Senegal'. However, the absence from the meeting of the MFDC faction loyal to Sidi Badji appeared to refute reports that the various wings of the MFDC had effectively reunited. In late September five civilians, including the brother of Sambou, were killed in an attack attributed to separatist rebels north of Ziguinchor. The internal disunity of the MFDC was emphasized in October, when Biagui, announcing that the conflict had definitively ended, publicly demanded forgiveness from the people of Casamance and Senegal for the actions of the organization; this statement was emphatically rejected by Sidi Badji.

In May 2003 President Wade announced that several substantive measures towards the normalization of the political and economic situation in Casamance were to be implemented, notably major infrastructural projects and the rehabilitation of damaged villages. Also in that month, Diamacouné Senghor announced that an MFDC convention, comprising 460 partici-

pants from the various factions of the organization, was to be held in Guinea-Bissau in June. Following the death of Sidi Badji, from natural causes, in late May, the convention was postponed, initially to July. However, the Guinea-Bissau authorities announced that they would be unable to provide sufficient guarantees of security for participants, and the meeting was again postponed, until October, when the gathering was held in Ziguinchor. On this occasion both Diamacouné Senghor and Biagui issued statements confirming that the conflict had ended, and announced that what was termed the emancipation of Casamance did not, as a matter of course, necessarily entail its independence from Senegal. Following the restoration of peace in Casamance, it was anticipated that some 15,000 displaced persons would return to their home villages in the Ziguinchor administrative region, while de-mining operations commenced in July 2004.

In September 2004 it was reported that an extraordinary general assembly of the MFDC had dismissed Diamacouné Senghor as the organization's leader and, as in 2001, appointed him Honorary President, while Biagui was reappointed Secretary-General and de facto leader. Biagui subsequently announced that the MFDC intended to transform itself into a legitimate political party and contest national elections; however, his status as leader was rejected by the MFDC's military wing, which issued a statement declaring its continuing recognition of Diamacouné Senghor as the movement's leader, while also reaffirming its commitment to full independence for Casamance. (The Senegalese Government was also reported to regard Diamacouné Senghor as remaining the MFDC's legitimate leader for the purposes of negotiations.) Following talks in Paris, France, between representatives of the Government and the external wing of the MFDC, plans were announced for the signing of a cease-fire between the two parties in December 2004, to be followed by detailed negotiations towards a peaceful political settlement. Concerns persisted, however, over internal divisions within the MFDC: Diamacouné Senghor's appeal for a general assembly of the movement in November, intended to reconcile the various factions in advance of the signing of the cease-fire, was reportedly rejected by his rivals in the movement's political wing, while Abdoulaye Diédhiou, leader of the military wing Atika ('arrow'), insisted that independence remained the MFDC's primary aim and criticized Diamacouné Senghor for making excessive concessions to the Senegalese Government.

On 30 December 2004 a 'General Peace Accord' was signed in Ziguinchor by the Minister of the Interior, on behalf of the Government, and Diamacouné Senghor, representing the MFDC. President Wade also signed the accord, which was, however, rejected by several factions of the MFDC, including Atika, the Front Nord, and elements of the movement's international wing. Negotiations aimed at achieving a definitive resolution of the conflict in Casamance were opened by Prime Minister Sall in February 2005, but were boycotted by Biagui and Diédhiou, who reportedly favoured further dialogue within the MFDC before engaging in talks with the Government. Both sides agreed to establish joint technical commissions to address reconstruction, economic and social development, and disarmament, demobilization and de-mining. Meanwhile, Diamacouné Senghor appointed Ansoumana Badji, formerly the MFDC's representative in Portugal, as Secretary-General of the movement; Badji stated that he aimed to persuade as many MFDC members as possible to join the peace process. Biagui rejected the legitimacy of Badji's appointment.

Since the signing of the 2004 peace agreement, outbreaks of violence had been sporadic. However, in August 2006 violent incidents between the Senegalese armed forces and the MFDC in Casamance began to escalate and by mid-August fighting had resumed in earnest. Although the fighting spread north towards The Gambia, there were no reports of the conflict crossing the border. Nevertheless, many civilians fled to that country, seeking refuge and medical treatment. By October the violence began to subside as the army took control of the rebels' base. However, many civilians refused to return to the region until the security forces had departed. In 2007 small-scale operations were conducted to clear the region of landmines and the people of Casamance slowly began to return to their homes. However, having been abandoned for over a decade, many of the villages were uninhabitable. Tensions persisted between the MFDC and the Government and a rebel faction of the MFDC was blamed for sabotaging mine-clearing efforts. Minor conflicts continued and in December the presidential envoy to the region was killed, an incident that threatened to destabilize the reconstruction process.

Renewed violence was reported in Casamance in 2009 as armed groups to the north-west of Ziguinchor attacked Senegalese military positions along the Gambian border. In September, in retaliation for the killing of a government soldier, a Senegalese military jet bombed MFDC bases. At least 600 people fled their homes on the outskirts of Ziguinchor, according to human rights organizations. In mid-March 2010 Senegalese troops shelled MFDC positions in Casamance, just days after capturing two rebel combatants. Earlier that month hostilities had again escalated, following the killing of a Senegalese soldier in an MFDC rocket attack.

In December 2010, on the anniversary of the beginning of the rebellion (in 1982), renewed violence broke out in Casamance. Senegalese military forces that had been dispatched to deal with armed robberies around the town of Bignona faced strong resistance and were forced to retreat. Seven Senegalese soldiers were killed in an ambush some 35 km from Ziguinchor, while unconfirmed reports suggested that there had also been casualties on the side of the rebels. A MFDC council that had been due to meet in January 2011 to harmonize the different rebel positions was postponed, and more than 1,000 women marched on Ziguinchor, demanding an immediate end to violence and a resumption of peace negotiations. A further three government soldiers were killed in February, when MFDC rebels reportedly attacked a Senegalese military convoy some 75 km north of Ziguinchor, while in March at least 10 Senegalese soldiers were injured when their vehicle struck a mine near the Gambian border. In February 2012 four Senegalese soldiers were killed in fighting some 60 km north of Ziguinchor.

Although suspected MFDC attacks continued sporadically during 2012–13, the election of Sall to the presidency in March 2012 raised hopes that peace talks would be reconvened. The leaders of the various MFDC factions confirmed in mid-2012 that they would be willing to enter negotiations with the new administration, and a first round of discussions was duly held in Rome, Italy, in October. As a expression of goodwill, in December the MFDC released eight hostages (mostly security personnel), whom they had seized approximately one year previously.

Foreign Affairs

Regional relations

From 1989 Senegal's regional relations underwent a period of considerable strain. A long-standing border dispute with Mauritania, which also involved ethnic and economic rivalries, was exacerbated by the deaths, in April of that year, of two Senegalese farmers, who had been involved in a dispute regarding grazing rights with Mauritanian livestock-breeders. Mauritanian nationals residing in Senegal were attacked, and their businesses looted, while Senegalese nationals in Mauritania suffered similar aggression. By early May it was believed that several hundred people, mostly Senegalese, had been killed. Operations to repatriate nationals of both countries commenced, with international assistance. Diplomatic relations, which had been suspended in August 1989, were fully restored in April 1992, and the process of reopening the border began in May. In December 1994 the Governments of Senegal and Mauritania agreed new co-operation measures, including efforts to facilitate the free movement of goods and people between the two countries.

In January 1995 the Governments of Senegal, Mauritania and Mali undertook to co-operate in resolving joint border issues and in combating extremism, arms-smuggling and drugs-trafficking. In July the office of the UN High Commissioner for Refugees (UNHCR) began a census of Mauritanian refugees in Senegal, estimated to number some 66,000, as part of initiatives for their eventual repatriation. In May 1998 the Ministers of the Interior of Mauritania, Mali and Senegal met to discuss border security, following reports of increased cross-border banditry, particularly in eastern Senegal. The unrest in the region was blamed by the Senegalese press on the continued presence there of Mauritanian refugees; in September it was reported that the Senegalese authorities had ceased to issue the refugees with travel documents. In May 1999 the two countries signed an agreement on the joint exploitation of fisheries. In mid-2000, however, a dispute over water rights resulted in a period of substantial tension between Senegal and Mauritania. Following renewed negotiations, the visit of President Taya of Mauritania to Dakar in 2001, as the guest of honour at a ceremony to commemorate the 41st anniversary of the independence of Senegal, was widely

regarded as indicating an improvement in relations between the countries. Presidents Taya and Wade met again in July 2003, when negotiations were conducted on a range of bilateral and international issues; Wade reiterated his support for Taya's administration, following an attempted coup in Mauritania in the previous month. The extradition of one of the suspected coup plotters from Senegal to Mauritania was also interpreted as an indication of improved relations between the countries, as was the Mauritanian Government's decision to accord 270 temporary fishing licences to Senegalese fishermen in June 2004. The UNHCR initiated a programme of voluntary repatriation for Mauritanian refugees in Senegal in 2008. By 2012 over 24,000 Mauritanian refugees had reportedly been repatriated under the programme, while some 14,000 chose to remain in Senegal under a UNHCR-assisted local integration programme.

In October 1993 Senegal and Guinea-Bissau signed an agreement regarding the joint exploitation and management of fishing and petroleum resources in their maritime zones. This treaty was ratified in December 1995, to the effect that fishing resources were to be shared equally between the two countries, while Senegal was to benefit from an 85% share of revenue obtained from petroleum deposits. During bilateral contacts in 1995–97 Senegal and Guinea-Bissau pledged co-operation in matters of joint defence and security. It was hoped that the movement of refugees from the conflict in Casamance to Guinea-Bissau, which began, under the auspices of UNHCR, in February 1996, would expedite efforts to restore security in the border region between the countries. In January 1998 it was announced that the authorities in Guinea-Bissau had intercepted a consignment of armaments destined for MFDC rebels, and that some 15 officers of the Guinea-Bissau armed forces had been arrested and suspended from duty, including the head of the armed forces, Brig. (later Gen.) Ansumane Mané. In June, however, troops loyal to Mané rebelled against President Commdr João Vieira of Guinea-Bissau, and civil war broke out in that country. Senegalese troops intervened in support of the armed forces loyal to Vieira. By the end of the month refugees from the conflict were crossing into Casamance, exacerbating security concerns in the province, while it was also reported that members of the MFDC were fighting alongside the rebels against the Government of Guinea-Bissau and Senegalese forces. From December, as a result of a peace-keeping agreement brokered by the Economic Community of West African States (ECOWAS, see p. 268), Senegalese troops began to depart from Guinea-Bissau, but strengthened their presence in the border area, while the ECOWAS peace-keeping force, ECOMOG (see p. 000), assumed positions on the Guinea-Bissau side of the frontier with Casamance.

Tensions between Guinea-Bissau and Senegal resurfaced in April 2000, when an armed group, reportedly composed of members of the MFDC operating from within Guinea-Bissau, attacked a Senegalese border post, killing three soldiers, and later that month the border between the two countries was temporarily closed. In August the terms of the agreement concerning the joint exploitation of maritime resources by the two countries was revised; henceforth, Guinea-Bissau was to receive 20%, rather than 15%, of the revenue generated from petroleum deposits. In early September, following clashes near the border in Guinea-Bissau, attributed to an armed faction of the MFDC, the Senegalese Government closed all border posts between the two countries. Following the killing of Mané in November 2000, during an attempted coup, relations between Senegal and Guinea-Bissau improved significantly.

In October 2009 Guinea-Bissau placed its troops on alert following a renewed border dispute over the allocation by Senegalese authorities of plots of land along the coast between Cabrouse (a Senegalese town in southern Casamance) and Tcheda in Guinea-Bissau. The area, which has potential to be developed for tourism, is claimed by Guinea-Bissau as an integral part of its territory. In April 2012 Senegal's border with Guinea-Bissau was temporarily sealed following a military coup in that country.

In August 1989 Diouf announced the withdrawal of Senegalese troops from The Gambia, in protest at a request by President Jawara of that country that The Gambia be accorded more power within the confederal agreement of Senegambia that had been formed by the two countries in 1982. Diouf subsequently stated that, in view of The Gambia's reluctance to proceed towards full political and economic integration with Senegal, the functions of the Confederation would be suspended. The Confederation was dissolved in September. In January 1991 the two countries signed a bilateral treaty of friendship and co-operation. Senegal's abrupt decision to close the Senegalese–Gambian border in September 1993, apparently to reduce smuggling between the two countries, again strained relations, although subsequent negotiations sought to minimize the adverse effects of the closure on The Gambia's regional trading links. Since the coup in The Gambia in July 1994 Senegal has fostered cordial relations with the Government of President Jammeh and in June 1996 the two countries agreed to adopt joint measures to combat insecurity, illegal immigration, arms-trafficking and drugs-smuggling. In early 1998 Jammeh offered to act as a mediator between the Senegalese Government and the MFDC, and subsequently held regular meetings with MFDC representatives. None the less, intermittent disputes relating to transportation issues between the two countries have occurred, and tensions between the two countries again heightened in mid-2005, following a 100% increase in transportation fees for the ferry across the Gambia river by the Gambian port authorities. Senegalese trade unionists blockaded border crossings between Senegal and The Gambia to protest at the increase, and the Senegalese Government granted fuel subsidies to drivers who used a longer, alternative route between the southern and northern parts of Senegal, avoiding The Gambia. Although tensions lessened later in the year, when the port authority reduced the ferry charges by 15%, in what was described as a gesture of goodwill, there was increasing speculation that the Senegalese authorities were considering the construction of a tunnel to link the southern and northern parts of Senegal. Bilateral relations were again strained in March 2006 following allegations of Senegalese complicity in an abortive coup in The Gambia. One of those arrested in connection with the plot reportedly claimed to have been instructed by the alleged leader of the coup (who was believed to have fled to Senegal) to liaise with the Senegalese embassy in The Gambia. The Senegalese Government denied any involvement in the plot, which it condemned, and recalled its ambassador to The Gambia for consultations; a new ambassador was appointed in June. In February 2011 Senegal and The Gambia agreed to establish a boundary management commission to address matters relating to their common border. In August, during an official state visit to The Gambia, President Wade reiterated the hope that Gambian President Yahya Jammeh would assist in enabling a peaceful resolution to the situation in Casamance, a sentiment that was echoed by President Sall in April 2012. However, relations were strained in August, when Jammeh ordered the execution of all 47 'death row' prisoners in The Gambia; nine of the detainees, including two Senegalese citizens, were executed later that month before international pressure forced Jammeh to suspend the process in September.

In September 2011 the President of Guinea, Alpha Condé, accused the Government of Senegal, alongside that of The Gambia, of complicity in an assassination attempt made against him that July. Condé asserted that the attack had been planned in a hotel in Senegal, arguing that this could not have happened without the Senegalese Government's knowledge. The Senegalese Government denied the charges. In November Senegal banned flights to or from Guinea from travelling through its airspace, after a Senegalese commercial aircraft was detained by Guinean authorities.

Since his election in March 2000, President Wade has on several occasions promoted greater democratization in other West African countries and encouraged an expansion in the international political engagement of African countries. Notably, Wade's well-publicized condemnation, at an international conference on racism and xenophobia held under the auspices of the office of the UN High Commissioner for Human Rights in Dakar in January 2001, of the increasing importance of ethnically based politics in Côte d'Ivoire prompted violent demonstrations across Côte d'Ivoire. At the UN World Conference against Racism, Racial Discrimination, Xenophobia and Related Intolerance, held in Durban, South Africa, in August–September, Wade, notably among African leaders, condemned the notion that reparations should be paid by Western nations to the descendants of slaves. In February 2010 Wade was appointed by ECOWAS to mediate in the ongoing Nigerien political crisis, while in April he was also invited to participate in attempts to resolve the continued deadlock between the Government and the Forces Nouvelles in Côte d'Ivoire. In early November, however, Côte d'Ivoire recalled its ambassador from Dakar, accusing the Senegalese Government of seeking to interfere in the forthcoming second round of its presidential election, after Wade met with the opposition candidate, Alassane Ouattara.

Other external relations

Relations with France have remained particularly strong since independence, and the existing defence arrangements between France and Senegal remained substantially unaltered following the major restructuring of the French armed forces undertaken by the administration of Jacques Chirac in the late 1990s and early 2000s. However, in April 2010, on the occasion of Senegal's 50th anniversary of independence from France, President Wade declared that Senegal would commence the reclamation of all military bases in the country previously held by France. The two countries had agreed in February to reduce the number of French troops stationed in Dakar from 1,200 to just 300 (non-combat troops) by the end of the year, and Wade indicated in his speech that discussions would swiftly commence regarding the logistics of the handover. Following a number of delays, the French withdrawal finally commenced in June 2011. A new defence co-operation agreement was signed by both countries in April 2012, and France also provided Senegal with a €130m. credit.

In late 2005 Senegal announced that it was to terminate its diplomatic relations with Taiwan in order to resume relations with the People's Republic of China. The respective embassies in Dakar and Beijing were reopened, and ambassadors were exchanged between the two countries in early 2006.

Senegal's previously strong relations with Iran were strained from October 2010, when an Iranian ship en route to The Gambia docked at the port of Lagos, Nigeria, and was found to be carrying 13 containers of arms, including rocket launchers and grenades. It was widely suspected that the weapons were intended for Casamance separatist rebels (see Separatism in Casamance). The Senegalese ambassador to Iran was recalled in December, but in January 2011, following mediation by Turkey, President Wade held talks with the Iranian Minister of Foreign Affairs, Ali Akbar Salehi, in Dakar and subsequently reinstated his envoy to Iran. Investments in Senegal worth US $200m. were announced by Salehi during his visit. In February, however, the Senegalese Government again severed diplomatic relations with Iran, citing further evidence that MFDC rebels were in possession of arms supplied by that country. Diplomatic ties were restored in February 2013.

Senegal is an active participant in regional and international peace-keeping operations. In February 1998 Senegal, with Mali and Mauritania, was among the principal participants in multinational military exercises conducted in eastern Senegal under the auspices of the UN and the Organization of African Unity (now the African Union—AU), as part of efforts to establish a regional crisis-intervention force. The exercise was organized by France and involved almost 3,500 troops from eight West African countries, as well as units from the USA, the United Kingdom and Belgium. Senegal is a member of the Accord de Non-Agression et d'Assistance en Matière de Défense, which in April 1999 adopted a draft protocol on the setting up of a peace-keeping force in the region. In September a Senegalese contingent joined the international peace-keeping operation in the Kosovo and Metohija province of Yugoslavia (now Serbia and Montenegro). In April 2001 more than 500 Senegalese soldiers joined UN observer missions in the Democratic Republic of the Congo. In early 2003 it was announced that Senegal was to contribute some 650 troops to the Economic Community of West African States (ECOWAS, see p. 268) military mission in Côte d'Ivoire (ECO-MICI); Senegalese troops also played a prominent role in the UN Operation in Côte d'Ivoire (UNOCI, see p. 92), which assumed the responsibilities of ECOMICI from April 2004. Meanwhile, in August 2003 some 260 Senegalese troops were dispatched to serve in the ECOWAS Mission in Liberia (ECOMIL), which was replaced by the UN Mission in Liberia (UNMIL, see p. 90) in October. In 2007 Senegal agreed to contribute 1,600 peace-keeping troops to the AU/UN Hybrid Operation in Darfur, which was deployed in Sudan. Senegalese military personnel began to arrive in Mali during January 2013 as part of the UN's African-led International Support Mission in Mali (AFISMA); the Senegalese Government had pledged to deploy a total of 500 soldiers.

CONSTITUTION AND GOVERNMENT

The Constitution of the Republic of Senegal was promulgated following its approval by popular referendum on 7 January 2001, and entered into force thereafter, with the exception of those sections relating to the Assemblée nationale and the relations between the executive and legislative powers, which took effect following legislative elections on 29 April 2001. Executive power is held by the President, who is directly elected for a mandate of seven years, which is renewable only once. Legislative power rests with the Assemblée nationale, with 150 members elected for five years by universal adult suffrage. The judiciary is independent of the legislature and the executive. The formation of parties on an ethnic, religious or geographical basis is prohibited. The President appoints the Prime Minister, who, in consultation with the President, appoints the Council of Ministers. Senegal comprises 14 regions, each with an appointed governor or Regional Council president, an elected local assembly and a separate budget.

REGIONAL AND INTERNATIONAL CO-OPERATION

Senegal is a member of the African Union (see p. 191), of the Economic Community of West African States (ECOWAS, see p. 268) and of the West African organs of the Franc Zone (see p. 339). Senegal is also a member of the African Groundnut Council (see p. 455), of the Africa Rice Center (see p. 455), of the Gambia River Basin Development Organization (see p. 461) and of the Organisation pour la Mise en Valeur du Fleuve Sénégal (see p. 463).

Senegal became a member of the UN in 1960. As a contracting party to the General Agreement on Tariffs and Trade, Senegal joined the World Trade Organization (WTO, see p. 444) on its establishment in 1995. Senegal participates in the Group of 15 (G15, see p. 461) and the Group of 77 (G77, see p. 461) developing countries.

ECONOMIC AFFAIRS

In 2011, according to estimates by the World Bank, Senegal's gross national income (GNI), measured at average 2009–11 prices, was US $13,716m., equivalent to $1,070 per head (or $1,960 on an international purchasing-power parity basis). During 2002–11, it was estimated, the population increased at an average annual rate of 2.7%, while gross domestic product (GDP) per head increased by an average of 1.4% per year. Overall GDP increased, in real terms, at an average annual rate of 4.2% per year in 2002–11; growth in 2011 was 2.6%.

According to provisional official figures, agriculture (including forestry and fishing) contributed 17.0% of GDP in 2011. According to FAO, some 69.2% of the labour force were estimated to be employed in the sector in mid-2013. The principal cash crops are groundnuts and cotton. Senegal also exports fruit and vegetables to European markets. Groundnuts, millet, sorghum, rice, maize and vegetables are produced for domestic consumption, although Senegal has yet to achieve self-sufficiency in basic foodstuffs. The fishing sector makes an important contribution to both the domestic food supply and export revenue: fish and fish products are one of Senegal's principal export commodities, contributing 12.5% of export earnings in 2011. The sale of fishing licences to the EU has been an important source of revenue. However, despite the inclusion of safeguards intended to preserve stocks, the Senegalese Government and the domestic fishing industry have expressed concerns regarding the impact of fishing by EU vessels on supplies in easily attainable waters, and negotiations for a new agreement with the EU, following the expiry of the 2002–06 accord, remained suspended in early 2013. According to the World Bank, during 2002–11 agricultural GDP increased by an average of 6.3% per year; agricultural GDP rose by 4.5% in 2011.

According to provisional official figures, industry (including mining, manufacturing, construction and power) contributed 23.6% of GDP in 2011. Some 17.5% of the employed labour force were engaged in the sector in 2006. During 2002–11, according to the World Bank, industrial GDP increased at an average annual rate of 3.5%. Industrial GDP grew by 5.1% in 2011.

Mining contributed just 2.5% of GDP in 2011, according to provisional official figures, and the sector engaged only 0.5% of the employed labour force in 2006. The principal mining activity is the extraction of calcium phosphates (aluminium phosphates are also mined in smaller quantities). Deposits of salt, fuller's earth (attapulgite), clinker, petroleum and natural gas are also exploited, and investigations are under way into the feasibility of mining copper, alluvial diamonds, uranium and iron ore. Explorations at Sabodala, in the south-east, have revealed gold reserves estimated at 1.6m. oz; the first gold pour was made in March 2009. According to the African Development Bank (AfDB), mining GDP increased by 5.0% in 2010 and by 16.4% in 2011.

Manufacturing contributed 13.8% of GDP in 2011, according to provisional official figures. The sector engaged 9.2% of the employed labour force in 2006. The most important manufacturing activities are food-processing (notably fish, groundnuts and sugar), chemicals, textiles and petroleum-refining (using

imported crude petroleum). Exports of petroleum products contributed 15.1% of the value of total exports in 2012. According to the World Bank, manufacturing GDP increased at an average annual rate of 2.2% in 2002–11; GDP of the sector increased by 5.4% in 2011.

Construction contributed 4.4% of GDP in 2011, according to provisional official figures. Some 7.0% of the employed labour force were engaged in the sector in 2006. According to the AfDB, construction GDP increased by 5.4% in 2011.

In 2009 Senegal derived 86.4% of its electrical energy from petroleum sources. Senegal also receives supplies from the Manantali hydroelectric power installation (constructed under the auspices of the Organisation pour la Mise en Valeur du Fleuve Sénégal): 9.5% of Senegal's electricity was derived from hydropower in the same year. Imports of fuels (including petroleum for refining) accounted for 25.0% of the value of merchandise imports in 2012.

The services sector contributed 59.4% of GDP in 2011, according to provisional official figures. Some 42.6% of the employed labour force were engaged in the sector in 2006. Tourism is a major source of foreign exchange, with receipts totalling US $453m. in 2010. Dakar's port is of considerable importance as a centre for regional trade. According to the World Bank, the GDP of the services sector increased by an average of 4.6% per year in 2002–11. The GDP of the sector grew by 2.5% in 2010, but declined by 0.4% in 2011.

In 2010 Senegal recorded a visible merchandise trade deficit of US $1,929.1m. and there was a deficit of $600.0m. on the current account of the balance of payments. In 2012 the principal source of imports was France, which supplied 16.2% of total imports; other major suppliers were Nigeria, India and the People's Republic of China. Mali was the principal market for exports in that year, taking 14.3% of the total; Switzerland and India were also important purchasers. The principal exports in 2012 were petroleum products, phosphoric acid, hydraulic cement, and fish and fish products. The principal imports in that year were petroleum and petroleum products, agricultural and industrial machinery, and rice.

Senegal's overall fiscal deficit was estimated at 454,000m. francs CFA in 2011 (equivalent to 6.6% of GDP). Senegal's general government gross debt was 2,780,818m. francs CFA in 2011, equivalent to 40.8% of GDP. Total external debt in 2010 was US $3,677m., of which $3,155m. was public and publicly guaranteed debt. In 2009, the cost of servicing long-term public and publicly guaranteed debt and repayments to the IMF was equivalent to 3.7% of the value of exports of goods, services and income (excluding workers' remittances). The average annual rate of inflation in 2002–12 was 1.9%. Consumer prices increased by 1.4% in 2012. Some 10.0% of the economically active population were unemployed in 2006.

The attainment of sustained economic growth has been impeded by Senegal's dependence on revenue from a narrow export base, and by the country's consequent vulnerability to fluctuations in international prices for its principal commodities. Plans were announced to transform Senegal into a regional transportation hub and to encourage foreign and domestic partnerships in infrastructural development. Recurrent electricity shortages, however, were considered to be the main impediment to economic development. The Société Nationale d'Electricité du Sénégal continued its policy of rationing electricity in 2011, exacerbating a long-standing shortfall of national capacity. In early 2011 the Government initiated Plan Takkal, a three-year programme aimed at addressing the power shortages by restructuring the energy sector. In mid-2011, as ongoing power shortages provoked protests across the country (see Domestic Political Affairs), the Banque Ouest Africaine de Développement announced that it would be granting Senegal a loan to the value of 57,000,000m. francs CFA to assist with the financing of energy projects, while the Islamic Development Bank pledged €67m. in loans towards the construction of a power plant. Meanwhile, a Saudi Arabian conglomerate acquired a 34% share in the national petroleum refinery, Société Africaine de Raffinage, in April 2010; the expansion of the refinery's capacity from 27,000 barrels per day to 130,000, at a cost of €350m., was planned. The Republic of Korea also agreed to increase its investment in Senegal, particularly in the energy sector, most notably through the construction of a coal-fired power plant with a capacity of 250 MW. A scheme to upgrade the country's electricity grid at a cost of US $85m. received World Bank approval in July 2012; the Government pledged to provide a further $8.5m. of funding for the project. The overall rate of economic growth increased to

4.1% in 2010, from a depressed 2.1% in 2009. However, the vital agricultural sector was adversely affected by drought in 2011, and the rate of growth of real GDP decelerated to 2.6% in that year. Economic growth rose to 3.5% in 2012 as agricultural output recovered and the Government continued to fund large-scale infrastructural projects. The fiscal position remained under pressure in 2012 due to costly electricity and fuel subsidies, as well as additional spending on the elections and drought relief measures. The IMF forecast that the economy would expand by 4.0% in 2013, again supported by agricultural growth and infrastructural expenditure.

PUBLIC HOLIDAYS

2014: 1 January (New Year's Day), 13 January* (Mouloud, Birth of the Prophet), 4 April (National Day), 18 April (Good Friday), 21 April (Easter Monday), 1 May (Labour Day), 29 May (Ascension Day), 9 June (Whit Monday), 14 July (Day of Association), 28 July* (Korité, end of Ramadan), 15 August (Assumption), 4 October* (Tabaski, Feast of the Sacrifice), 1 November (All Saints' Day), 3 November* (Ashoura), 25 December (Christmas).

* These holidays are determined by the Islamic lunar calendar and may vary by one or two days from the dates given.

Statistical Survey

Source (unless otherwise stated): Agence nationale de la Statistique et de la Démographie, blvd de l'Est, Point E, BP 116, Dakar; tel. 33-824-0301; fax 33-824-9004; e-mail statsenegal@yahoo.fr; internet www.ansd.sn.

Area and Population

AREA, POPULATION AND DENSITY

Area (sq km)	196,722*
Population (census results)†	
27 May 1988	6,896,808
8 December 2002	
Males	4,846,126
Females	5,009,212
Total	9,855,338
Population (UN estimates at mid-year)	
2011	12,767,553
2012	13,107,943
2013	13,454,191
Density (per sq km) at mid-2013	68.0

* 75,955 sq miles.

† Figures for 1988 and 2002 refer to the *de jure* population. The de facto population at the 1988 census was 6,773,417, and at the 2002 census was 9,552,442.

POPULATION BY AGE AND SEX
(UN estimates at mid-2013)

	Males	Females	Total
0–14	2,931,603	2,864,732	5,796,335
15–64	3,593,324	3,746,569	7,339,893
65 and over	148,474	169,489	317,963
Total	6,673,401	6,780,790	13,454,191

Source: UN, *World Population Prospects: The 2010 Revision.*

POPULATION BY ETHNIC GROUP
(at 1988 census)

Ethnic group	Number	%
Wolof	2,890,402	42.67
Serere	1,009,921	14.91
Peul	978,366	14.44
Toucouleur	631,892	9.33
Diola	357,672	5.28
Mandingue	245,651	3.63
Rural-Rurale	113,184	1.67
Bambara	91,071	1.34
Maure	67,726	1.00
Manjaag	66,605	0.98
Others	320,927	4.74
Total	6,773,417	100.00

Source: UN, *Demographic Yearbook.*

REGIONS
(official population estimates, 2011)

	Area (sq km)	Population	Density (per sq km)
Dakar	546	2,647,751	4,849.4
Diourbel	4,862	1,399,219	287.8
Fatick	7,049	770,193	109.3
Kaffrine*	11,041	572,735	51.9
Kaolack	5,265	816,855	155.1
Kedougou*	16,825	133,459	7.9
Kolda	13,721	620,013	45.2
Louga	25,644	880,482	34.3
Matam	28,852	556,866	19.3
Saint-Louis	18,981	918,700	48.4
Sedhiou*	7,346	442,700	60.3
Tambacounda	42,638	668,804	15.7
Thiès	6,597	1,698,412	257.5
Ziguinchor	7,355	728,964	99.1
Total	196,722	12,855,153	65.3

* Region created in March 2008.

PRINCIPAL TOWNS
(2002 census, provisional results)

Dakar (capital) . .	955,897	Mbour	153,503
Pikine	768,826	Diourbel	95,984
Rufisque . . .	284,263	Louga	73,662
Guediawaye . . .	258,370	Tambacounda . .	67,543
Thiès	237,849	Kolda	53,921
Kaolack	172,305	Mbacké	51,124
Saint-Louis . . .	154,555		

Note: Data given pertain to communes, except for Dakar, Pikine, Rufisque and Guediawaye, where the population figure given is that of the département.

Mid-2011 (incl. suburbs, UN estimate): Dakar 3,035,470 (Source: UN, *World Urbanization Prospects: The 2011 Revision*).

BIRTHS AND DEATHS
(annual averages, UN estimates)

	1995–2000	2000–05	2005–10
Birth rate (per 1,000)	40.8	39.8	38.6
Death rate (per 1,000)	11.6	10.6	9.5

Source: UN, *World Population Prospects: The 2010 Revision.*

2011: Birth rate 36.8 per 1,000; Death rate 8.8 per 1,000 (Source: African Development Bank).

Life expectancy (years at birth): 59.3 (males 58.2; females 60.4) in 2011 (Source: World Bank, World Development Indicators database).

ECONOMICALLY ACTIVE POPULATION
('000 persons, 2006)

	Males	Females	Total
Agriculture, hunting and forestry .	631.9	354.6	986.5
Fishing	66.5	10.4	76.9
Mining and quarrying	11.5	2.6	14.1
Manufacturing	203.7	41.7	245.4
Electricity, gas and water supply .	18.5	3.3	21.8
Construction	179.7	6.9	186.6
Wholesale and retail trade; repair of motor vehicles, motorcycles and personal household goods	388.0	397.9	785.9
Hotels and restaurants	12.2	16.4	28.6
Transport, storage and communication	135.9	5.8	141.7
Financial intermediation	11.8	4.9	16.7
Public administration and defence; compulsory social security; education; health and social work	118.7	39.0	157.7
Extra-territorial organizations and bodies	3.3	3.7	7.0
Sub-total	1,781.7	887.2	2,668.9
Not classified by economic activity	266.5	217.5	484.0
Total	2,048.1	1,104.8	3,152.9
Unemployed	174.5	176.8	351.4
Total labour force	2,222.6	1,281.6	3,504.3

Source: ILO.

Mid-2013 (estimates in '000): Agriculture, etc. 4,165; Total labour force 6,020 (Source: FAO).

Health and Welfare

KEY INDICATORS

Total fertility rate (children per woman, 2010)	4.8
Under-5 mortality rate (per 1,000 live births, 2010)	75
HIV/AIDS (% of persons aged 15–49, 2009)	0.9
Physicians (per 1,000 head, 2008)	0.06
Hospital beds (per 1,000 head, 2008)	0.3
Health expenditure (2009): US $ per head (PPP)	106
Health expenditure (2009): % of GDP	5.7
Health expenditure (2009): public (% of total)	54.5
Access to water (% of persons, 2010)	72
Access to sanitation (% of persons, 2010)	52
Total carbon dioxide emissions ('000 metric tons, 2008)	4,976.1
Carbon dioxide emissions per head (metric tons, 2008)	0.4
Human Development Index (2011): ranking	155
Human Development Index (2011): value	0.459

For sources and definitions, see explanatory note on p. vi.

Agriculture

PRINCIPAL CROPS
('000 metric tons)

	2009	2010	2011
Rice, paddy	502.1	604.0	405.8
Maize	328.6	186.5	124.1
Millet	810.1	813.3	480.8
Sorghum	225.0	162.6	86.9
Cassava (Manioc)	265.5	181.2	154.9
Sugar cane*	836	850	860
Cashew nuts*	5.4	5.9	7.0
Groundnuts, with shell	1,032.7	1,286.9	527.5
Oil palm fruit*	93	120	120

—*continued*	2009	2010	2011
Tomatoes	150	165	180
Onions, dry	160	160	190
Watermelons	190.6	240.8	148.7
Oranges	40	40	50
Guavas, mangoes and mangosteens	100	100	120

* FAO estimates.

Aggregate production ('000 metric tons, may include official, semi-official or estimated data): Total cereals 1872.0 in 2009, 1,769.2 in 2010, 1,101.0 in 2011; Total pulses 86.7 in 2009, 49.0 in 2010, 28.2 in 2011; Total roots and tubers 340.5 in 2009, 266.2 in 2010, 208.0 in 2011; Total vegetables (incl. melons) 642.8 in 2009, 726.0 in 2010, 665.9 in 2011; Total fruits (excl. melons) 210.1 in 2009, 195.6 in 2010; 228.9 in 2011.

Source: FAO.

LIVESTOCK
('000 head, year ending September)

	2009	2010	2011
Cattle	3,261	3,313	3,346
Sheep	5,383	5,571	5,516
Goats	4,598	4,755	4,887
Pigs	344	354	364
Horses	518	523	520
Asses	446	450	453
Camels	5	5	5
Chickens	35,472	40,449	44,171

Source: FAO.

LIVESTOCK PRODUCTS
('000 metric tons)

	2009	2010	2011
Cattle meat	59.5	61.1	65.1
Sheep meat	19.5	20.5	23.2
Goat meat	12.5	12.9	15.1
Pig meat	9.9	10.6	11.1
Horse meat*	7.2	7.3	7.3
Chicken meat	39.4	45.5	55.8
Cows' milk	146.6	160.7	163.3
Sheep's milk	11.6	11.8	12.3
Goats' milk	13.6	13.9	14.4
Hen eggs*	27	30	30

* FAO estimates.

Source: FAO.

Forestry

ROUNDWOOD REMOVALS
('000 cubic metres, excl. bark, FAO estimates)

	2009	2010	2011
Sawlogs, veneer logs and logs for sleepers	40	34	50
Other industrial wood*	754	754	754
Fuel wood	5,396	5,427	5,453
Total	6,190	6,215	6,257

* Annual output assumed to be unchanged since 1999 (FAO estimates).

Source: FAO.

SAWNWOOD PRODUCTION
('000 cubic metres, incl. railway sleepers, FAO estimates)

	2009	2010	2011
Total (all broadleaved)	23	17	25

Source: FAO.

Fishing

('000 metric tons, live weight)

	2008	2009	2010
Capture	425.8	442.3*	409.6*
Freshwater fishes	7.4	14.0*	20.0*
Sea catfishes	10.2	13.3	8.8
Round sardinella	165.1	143.0	126.0
Madeiran sardinella	86.0	93.5	83.0
Bonga shad	17.6	12.7	19.2
Octopuses	3.7	3.8	3.3
Aquaculture	0.1	0.1	0.1
Total catch	425.9	442.4*	409.7*

* FAO estimate.

Source: FAO.

Mining

('000 metric tons unless otherwise stated)

	2008	2009	2010
Crude petroleum ('000 barrels)	99	249	398
Gold (kg)	600*	5,354	4,381
Cement, hydraulic	3,084	3,320	4,066
Calcium phosphates	645	948	976
Aluminium phosphates	4	4†	n.a.
Fuller's earth (attapulgite)	167	181	204
Salt (unrefined)	241	222	231

* Government estimate of unreported production of artisanal gold.
† Estimate.

Source: US Geological Survey.

Industry

PETROLEUM PRODUCTS
('000 metric tons)

	2007	2008	2009
Jet fuels	48	99	68
Motor gasoline (petrol)	77	68	83
Kerosene	5	4	3
Gas-diesel (distillate fuel) oils	339	409	n.a.
Residual fuel (Mazout) oils	188	243	191

Source: UN, *Industrial Commodity Statistics Yearbook* and Database.

SELECTED OTHER PRODUCTS
('000 metric tons unless otherwise indicated)

	2010	2011	2012
Wheat flour	305.7	350.8	334.2
Sugar cubes	18.1	12.1	13.0
Salt	231.6	258.3	237.3
Soap	17.9	19.3	n.a.
Phosphates	1,079.2	1,437.2	1,416.7
Fertilizers	44.9	37.0	57.7
Cement	4,065.8	4,722.3	4,689.2
Electric energy (million kWh)	2,783.2	2,730.5	2,935.2

Finance

CURRENCY AND EXCHANGE RATES

Monetary Units
100 centimes = 1 franc de la Communauté Financière Africaine (CFA).

Sterling, Dollar and Euro Equivalents (31 December 2012)
£1 sterling = 784.523 francs CFA;
US $1 = 497.163 francs CFA;
€1 = 655.957 francs CFA;
10,000 francs CFA = £12.75 = $20.11 = €15.24.

Average Exchange Rate (francs CFA per US $)
2010   495.28
2011   471.87
2012   510.29

Note: An exchange rate of 1 French franc = 50 francs CFA, established in 1948, remained in force until January 1994, when the CFA franc was devalued by 50%, with the exchange rate adjusted to 1 French franc = 100 francs CFA. This relationship to French currency remained in effect with the introduction of the euro on 1 January 1999. From that date, accordingly, a fixed exchange rate of €1 = 655.957 francs CFA has been in operation.

BUDGET
('000 million francs CFA)

Revenue*	2011	2012†	2013†
Tax revenue	1,287	1,421	1,492
Income tax	346	379	382
Taxes on goods and services (excl. petroleum)	729	817	835
Taxes on petroleum products	212	225	276
Non-tax revenue	50	50	77
Energy sector support fund operations	39	40	35
Total	1,376	1,511	1,605

Expenditure‡	2011	2012†	2013†
Current expenditure	1,233	1,282	1,278
Wages and salaries	428	454	467
Other operational expenses	702	706	665
Transfers and subsidies	335	328	291
Goods and services	356	366	363
Capital expenditure	718	875	912
Domestically financed	475	504	515
Externally financed	244	370	397
Total	1,952	2,157	2,190

* Excluding grants received ('000 million francs CFA): 150 in 2011; 212 in 2012 (projection); 208 in 2013 (projection).
† Projections.
‡ Excluding net lending ('000 million francs CFA): 28 in 2011; −8 in 2012 (projection); 0 in 2013 (projection).

Source: IMF, *Senegal: Staff Report for the 2012 Article IV Consultation, Fourth Review Under the Policy Support Instrument, and Request for Modification of an Assessment Criterion—Staff Report; Staff Supplements; Public Information Notice and Press Release on the Executive Board Discussion; and Statement by the Executive Director for Senegal* (November 2012).

INTERNATIONAL RESERVES
(excluding gold, US $ million at 31 December)

	2009	2010	2011
IMF special drawing rights	204.4	200.7	199.9
Reserve position in IMF	2.7	2.8	2.8
Foreign exchange	1,916.1	1,844.0	1,742.9
Total	2,123.2	2,047.5	1,945.7

Source: IMF, *International Financial Statistics*.

MONEY SUPPLY
('000 million francs CFA at 31 December)

	2009	2010	2011
Currency outside banks . . .	494.8	561.8	589.4
Demand deposits at deposit money banks . . .	856.6	980.3	1,051.0
Checking deposits at post office .	14.6	6.1	7.9
Total money (incl. others) . .	1,366.9	1,549.2	1,649.7

Source: IMF, *International Financial Statistics*.

COST OF LIVING
(Consumer Price Index; base: 2000 = 100)

	2006	2007	2008
Food (incl. tobacco)	116.0	124.5	136.4
Clothing	85.9	88.4	86.3
Electricity, gas and other fuels .	112.0	123.2	n.a.
Rent	108.2	119.1	120.8
All items (incl. others) . . .	110.0	116.4	123.1

2009: Food (incl. tobacco) 132.3; All items (incl. others) 121.8.

2010: All items 121.9.

2011: All items 126.0.

2012: All items 127.8.

Source: ILO.

NATIONAL ACCOUNTS
(million francs CFA at current prices)

Expenditure on the Gross Domestic Product

	2009	2010	2011
Government final consumption expenditure	871,000	944,000	1,007,500
Private final consumption expenditure	4,843,523	4,980,518	5,312,500
Gross fixed capital formation . .	1,388,000	1,414,000	1,540,100
Changes in inventories . . .	−56,000	29,000	92,700
Total domestic expenditure .	7,046,523	7,367,518	7,952,800
Exports of goods and services . .	1,472,000	1,538,000	1,611,600
Less Imports of goods and services	2,490,000	2,536,000	2,724,800
Statistical discrepancy	—	−400	140
GDP at purchasers' values .	6,028,523	6,369,118	6,839,740

Gross Domestic Product by Economic Activity

	2009	2010	2011
Agriculture, hunting, forestry and fishing	907,000	971,000	1,041,900
Mining and quarrying . . .	106,000	123,000	154,100
Manufacturing	740,000	781,000	847,700
Electricity, gas and water . . .	153,000	171,000	173,800
Construction	244,000	246,000	267,800
Trade, restaurants and hotels .	1,002,580	1,036,518	1,093,000
Finance, insurance and real estate	524,849	553,194	580,000
Transport and communications .	635,541	646,486	696,100
Public administration and defence	613,382	652,736	693,861
Other services	514,670	539,583	573,579
Sub-total	5,441,022	5,720,517	6,121,840
Indirect taxes	722,000	791,600	868,300
Less imputed bank service charge .	134,500	143,000	150,400
GDP at purchasers' values .	6,028,523	6,369,118	6,839,740

Source: African Development Bank.

BALANCE OF PAYMENTS
(US $ million)

	2008	2009	2010
Exports of goods	2,208.4	2,096.9	2,153.2
Imports of goods	−5,595.3	−4,122.9	−4,082.3
Balance on goods	−3,387.0	−2,026.0	−1,929.1
Exports of services	1,285.6	1,017.7	1,048.3
Imports of services	−1,419.0	−1,149.0	−1,118.9
Balance on goods and services	−3,520.4	−2,157.2	−1,999.7
Primary income received . . .	290.6	171.3	205.5
Primary income paid	−338.5	−341.0	−355.5
Balance on goods, services and primary income	−3,568.3	−2,327.0	−2,149.7
Secondary income received . .	1,985.9	1,756.8	1,873.7
Secondary income paid . . .	−301.3	−283.6	−324.0
Current balance	−1,883.7	−853.8	−600.0
Capital account (net)	239.5	305.1	301.9
Direct investment assets . . .	−182.5	−87.2	−11.0
Direct investment liabilities . .	453.9	330.1	274.9
Portfolio investment assets . .	51.6	−91.3	−125.4
Portfolio investment liabilities .	20.9	−1.6	43.5
Financial derivatives and employee stock options (net)	—	—	0.1
Other investment assets . . .	147.7	−128.2	−187.4
Other investment liabilities . .	599.7	451.4	−221.9
Net errors and omissions . . .	−13.5	−171.3	−4.0
Reserves and related items .	−566.5	−246.8	−529.4

Source: IMF, *International Financial Statistics*.

External Trade

PRINCIPAL COMMODITIES
('000 million francs CFA)

Imports c.i.f.	2010	2011	2012
Rice	130.8	175.7	207.6
Animal and vegetable oils and fats	59.9	79.8	99.3
Crude petroleum	224.4	255.1	385.7
Other petroleum products . . .	312.9	389.4	364.2
Pharmaceutical products . . .	62.6	71.6	82.8
Artificial plastic materials . .	52.1	77.0	95.4
Common metals	101.5	122.4	127.8
Agricultural and industrial machinery	271.3	307.4	333.1
Vehicles	69.7	71.1	89.6
Total (incl. others)	2,196.3	2,544.2	3,005.5

Exports f.o.b.	2010	2011	2012
Fresh fish	78.8	89.5	87.3
Crustaceans, molluscs and other shellfish	35.2	51.1	44.9
Frozen fish	2.0	1.5	1.6
Peanut oil	28.4	36.9	13.7
Hydraulic cement	99.7	112.2	111.9
Petroleum products	215.9	176.5	184.0
Phosphoric acid	98.5	160.7	140.4
Total (incl. others)	978.2	1,138.8	1,216.3

PRINCIPAL TRADING PARTNERS
('000 million francs CFA)

Imports c.i.f.	2010	2011	2012
Argentina	48.2	47.6	55.2
Belgium-Luxembourg . . .	46.5	40.6	71.2
Brazil	54.3	87.2	61.9
China, People's Republic . . .	195.1	177.9	188.0
Côte d'Ivoire	50.9	74.0	86.1
France (incl. Monaco) . . .	441.4	460.3	486.1
Germany	54.8	48.5	61.0
India	59.1	50.9	188.6
Ireland	12.3	10.7	7.9
Italy	47.3	80.1	63.2
Japan	52.0	40.5	55.4
Morocco	27.8	26.2	33.8
Netherlands	96.1	122.3	59.9
Nigeria	230.8	256.3	388.1
South Africa	40.1	47.7	47.7
Spain	84.9	93.7	103.1
Thailand	73.9	96.8	54.8
Turkey	40.5	94.3	73.6
Ukraine	57.4	37.1	40.8
United Kingdom	58.4	87.2	139.3
USA	61.5	121.2	81.3
Viet Nam	27.8	54.0	10.3
Total (incl. others)	2,196.3	2,544.2	3,005.5

Exports f.o.b.	2010	2011	2012
Benin	10.2	9.8	8.6
Burkina Faso	12.4	19.0	30.3
Cameroon	15.6	22.8	25.5
Côte d'Ivoire	25.5	24.9	32.6
France (incl. Monaco) . . .	47.2	53.0	56.8
The Gambia	33.7	37.5	41.0
Greece	8.1	8.3	7.0
Guinea	34.6	55.1	51.1
Guinea-Bissau	20.6	23.7	28.6
India	103.8	168.2	148.3
Italy	23.2	32.6	29.3
Japan	2.0	4.9	5.4
Mali	247.7	181.0	174.0
Mauritania	23.4	31.4	33.4
Netherlands	10.9	11.8	11.5
Spain	28.9	35.0	29.2
Switzerland	82.0	104.4	170.6
Togo	10.0	13.2	14.7
United Arab Emirates . . .	18.0	15.5	19.0
Total (incl. others)	978.2	1,138.8	1,216.3

Transport

RAILWAYS
(traffic)

	2002	2003	2004
Passenger-km (million) . . .	105	129	122
Net ton-km (million) . . .	345	375	358

Passengers ('000): 4,789 in 1999.

Freight carried ('000 metric tons): 2,017 in 1999.

ROAD TRAFFIC
(motor vehicles in use)

	2007	2008	2010*
Passenger cars	187,838	196,074	210,774
Buses and coaches	14,110	15,969	n.a.
Lorries and vans	33,212	53,852	59,454
Motorcycles and mopeds . . .	10,656	12,403	19,806

* Data for 2009 were not available.

Source: IRF, *World Road Statistics*.

SHIPPING

Flag Registered Fleet
(at 31 December)

	2010	2011	2012
Number of vessels	88	88	88
Total displacement ('000 grt) . .	27.9	27.9	27.5

Source: Lloyd's List Intelligence (www.lloydslistintelligence.com).

International Sea-borne Freight Traffic
('000 metric tons)

	2006	2007	2008
Goods loaded	2,279	2,322	2,232
Goods unloaded	7,651	8,787	8,358

Source: Port Autonome de Dakar.

CIVIL AVIATION
(traffic on scheduled services)*

	2007	2008	2009
Kilometres flown (million) . .	13	20	19
Passengers carried ('000) . .	539	567	573
Passenger-km (million) . . .	993	1,017	985
Total ton-km (million) . . .	97	103	101

* Including an apportionment of the traffic of Air Afrique.

Source: UN, *Statistical Yearbook*.

Tourism

FOREIGN TOURIST ARRIVALS BY NATIONALITY*

	2005	2006	2007
African states	87,565	106,396	97,398
Belgium, Luxembourg and the Netherlands	21,712	23,896	17,717
East Asian and Pacific states . .	3,837	3,846	3,620
France	191,580	184,376	171,452
Germany	9,615	8,708	6,973
Italy	11,493	13,705	13,953
Spain	15,353	17,021	19,039
United Kingdom	4,380	5,582	5,416
USA	11,080	12,404	20,482
Total (incl. others)	386,565	405,827	386,793

* Figures refer to arrivals at hotels and similar establishments.

Total tourist arrivals ('000): 810 in 2009; 900 in 2010.

Receipts from tourism (US $ million, excl. passenger transport): 463 in 2009; 453 in 2010.

Source: World Tourism Organization.

Communications Media

	2009	2010	2011
Telephones ('000 main lines in use)	278.8	341.9	346.4
Mobile cellular telephones ('000 subscribers)	6,901.5	8,343.7	9,352.9
Internet subscribers ('000) . .	59.7	78.6	92.7
Broadband subscribers ('000) . .	58.7	78.6	92.7

Source: International Telecommunication Union.

Education

(2009/10 unless otherwise indicated)

	Institutions*	Teachers	Students ('000)		
			Males	Females	Total
Pre-primary .	1,725	6,009	70.1	76.7	146.8
Primary . .	7,939	50,369	832.1	862.9	1,695.0
Secondary .	1,122	22,437	389.5	335.7	725.2
Tertiary . . .	n.a.	n.a.	57.8	34.3	92.1

* 2008/09 (Source: Ministry of Education, Dakar).

Source: UNESCO Institute for Statistics.

Pupil-teacher ratio (primary education, UNESCO estimate): 33.7 in 2009/10 (Source: UNESCO Institute for Statistics).

Adult literacy rate (UNESCO estimates): 49.7% (males 61.8%; females 38.7%) in 2009 (Source: UNESCO Institute for Statistics).

Directory

The Government

HEAD OF STATE

President: MACKY SALL (took office 2 April 2012).

COUNCIL OF MINISTERS
(May 2013)

Prime Minister: ABDOUL MBAYE.

Minister of the Armed Forces: AUGUSTIN TINE.

Minister of Justice, Keeper of the Seals: AMINATA TOURÉ.

Minister of Health and Social Action: AWA MARIE COLL SECK.

Minister of the Interior: PATHÉ SECK.

Minister of Foreign Affairs and Senegalese Nationals Abroad: MANKEUR NDIAYE.

Minister of the Economy and Finance: AMADOU KANE.

Minister of Infrastructure and Transport: THIERNO ALASSANE SALL.

Minister of Tourism and Leisure: YOUSSOU N'DOUR.

Minister of Women, Childhood and Female Entrepreneurship: MARIAMA SARR.

Minister of Culture: ABDOUL AZIZ MBAYE.

Minister of Communication, Telecommunications and the Digital Economy: CHEIKH MAMADOU ABIBOULAYE DIÈYE.

Minister of National Education: SERIGNE MBAYE THIAM.

Minister of Agriculture and Rural Equipment: ABDOULAYE BALDÉ.

Minister of Land Settlement and Local Communities: ARAME NDOYE.

Minister of Trade, Industry and the Informal Sector: ALIOUNE SARR.

Minister of Stockbreeding: AMINATA MBENGUE NDIAYE.

Minister of Fishing and Maritime Affairs: PAPE DIOUF.

Minister of Energy and Mines: ALY NGOUILLE NDIAYE.

Minister of Youth, Employment and the Promotion of Civic Values: BENOÎT SAMBOU.

Minister of Good Governance and Government Spokesperson: ABDOU LATIF COULIBALY.

Minister of Sport: MBAGNICK NDIAYE.

Minister of Town Planning and Housing: KHOUDIA MBAYE.

Minister of Higher Education and Research: MARY TEUW NIANE.

Minister of the Environment and Sustainable Development: HAYDAR EL ALI.

Minister of the Civil Service, Labour and Relations with the Institutions: MANSOUR SY.

Minister of Hydraulics and Sanitation: OUMAR GUÈYE.

Minister of Professional Training, Apprenticeships and Handicrafts: MAMADOU TALLA.

Minister of Rebuilding and Reconstruction in Flooded Zones: KHADIM DIOP.

Minister-delegate to the Minister of the Economy and Finance, in charge of the Budget: ABDOULAYE DAOUDA DIALLO.

Minister-delegate to the Minister of Foreign Affairs and Senegalese Nationals Abroad: SEYNABOU GAYE TOURÉ.

MINISTRIES

Office of the President: ave Léopold Sédar Senghor, BP 168, Dakar; tel. 33-880-8080; internet www.presidence.sn.

Office of the Prime Minister: Bldg Administratif, 9e étage, ave Léopold Sédar Senghor, BP 4029, Dakar; tel. 33-889-6969; fax 33-823-4479; internet www.gouv.sn.

Ministry of Agriculture and Rural Equipment: Bldg Administratif, 3e étage, BP 4005, Dakar; tel. 33-849-7000; fax 33-823-3268; internet www.agriculture.gouv.sn.

Ministry of the Armed Forces: Bldg Administratif, 8e étage, ave Léopold Sédar Senghor, BP 4041, Dakar; tel. 33-849-7612; fax 33-823-6338; internet www.forcesarmees.gouv.sn.

Ministry of the Civil Service, Labour and Relations with the Institutions: Bldg Administratif, 1er étage, BP 4007, Dakar; tel. 33-849-7000; fax 33-823-7429; e-mail mineladiallo@yahoo.fr; internet www.fonctionpublique.gouv.sn.

Ministry of Communication, Telecommunications and the Digital Economy: 2 rue Béranger Ferraud, angle Assane Ndoye, BP 4027, Dakar; tel. 33-889-1715; fax 33-842-1291; internet www.telecom.gouv.sn.

Ministry of Culture: Bldg Administratif, 3e étage, Dakar; tel. 33-849-7000.

Ministry of the Economy and Finance: rue René Ndiaye, BP 4017, Dakar; tel. 33-889-2100; fax 33-822-4195; e-mail i_diouf@minfinances.sn; internet www.finances.gouv.sn.

Ministry of Energy and Mines: 122 bis ave André Peytavin, BP 4021, Dakar; tel. 33-849-7300; fax 33-823-4470; e-mail mindpme@msn.com; internet www.industrie.gouv.sn.

Ministry of the Environment and Sustainable Development: Bldg Administratif, 2e étage, BP 4055, Dakar; tel. 33-889-0234; fax 33-822-2180; e-mail ministereenvironnement@gmail.com; internet www.environnement.gouv.sn.

Ministry of Fishing and Maritime Affairs: Bldg Administratif, 4e étage, BP 4050, Dakar; tel. 33-849-5073; fax 33-823-8720; e-mail abdoumbodj@yahoo.fr.

Ministry of Foreign Affairs and Senegalese Nationals Abroad: pl. de l'Indépendance, BP 4044, Dakar; tel. 33-889-1300; fax 33-823-5496; e-mail webmaster@diplomatie.gouv.sn; internet www.diplomatie.gouv.sn.

Ministry of Good Governance: rue Parchappe, Immeuble Fayçal, 3e étage, Dakar; tel. 33-842-3053.

Ministry of Health and Social Action: Fann Résidence, rue Aimé Césaire, BP 4024, Dakar; tel. 33-869-4242; fax 33-869-4269; e-mail mdseck@minsante.sn; internet www.sante.gouv.sn.

Ministry of Higher Education and Research: Bldg Administratif, 5e étage, aile droite, BP 4025, Dakar; tel. 33-849-7552; fax 33-822-4563; internet www.recherche.gouv.sn.

Ministry of Hydraulics and Sanitation: Bldg Administratif, 2e étage, BP 2372, Dakar; tel. 33-889-0234; fax 33-822-2180.

Ministry of Infrastructure and Transport: Bldg Administratif, Dakar; tel. 33-849-7000; fax 33-842-0292.

Ministry of the Interior: pl. Washington, BP 4002, Dakar; tel. 33-889-9100; fax 33-821-0542; e-mail mint@primature.sn; internet www.interieur.gouv.sn.

Ministry of Justice: Bldg Administratif, 7e étage, ave Léopold Sédar Senghor, BP 4030, Dakar; tel. 33-849-7000; fax 33-823-2727; e-mail justice@justice.gouv.sn; internet www.justice.gouv.sn.

Ministry of Land Settlement and Local Communities: Dieuppeul Derklé, rue DD, 142 BP 4002, Dakar; tel. 33-869-4700; fax 33-869-4713.

Ministry of National Education: 56 ave Lamine Gueye, Dakar; tel. 33-849-5402; fax 33-821-8930; internet www.education.gouv.sn.

Ministry of Professional Training, Apprenticeships and Handicrafts: Dakar.

Ministry of Sport: Bldg Administratif, 6e étage, Dakar; tel. 33-849-1299; fax 33-842-0292.

Ministry of Rebuilding and Reconstruction in Flooded Zones: Sacré coeur, Cité Sicap Keur Gorgui, Immeuble Elysée 4e étage, Dakar; tel. 33-824-6031; fax 33-824-6031.

Ministry of Stockbreeding: VDN, blvd du Koweit, BP 45677, Dakar; tel. 33-859-0630; fax 33-864-6311.

Ministry of Tourism and Leisure: Bldg Administratif, 3e étage, ave Léopold Sédar Senghor, BP 4001, Dakar; tel. 33-822-4303; fax 33-822-1638; internet www.culture.gouv.sn.

Ministry of Town Planning and Housing: en face du Lycée Blaise Diagne, Dakar; tel. 33-869-1526; e-mail minurbas@orange.sn.

Ministry of Trade, Industry and the Informal Sector: 122 bis, ave André Peytavin, BP 4037, Dakar; tel. 33-889-5757; fax 33-822-5594; internet www.commerce.gouv.sn.

Ministry of Women, Childhood and Female Entrepreneurship: Bldg Administratif, 6e étage, BP 4050, Dakar; tel. 33-849-7061; fax 33-822-9490; e-mail communication@famille.gouv.sn; internet www.famille.gouv.sn.

Ministry of Youth, Employment and the Promotion of Civic Values: Bldg Administratif, 5e étage, Dakar; tel. 33-821-9457; fax 33-822-9542; internet www.jeunesse.gouv.sn.

President and Legislature

PRESIDENT

Presidential Election, First Round, 26 February 2012

Candidate	Valid votes	% of valid votes
Abdoulaye Wade	942,546	34.82
Macky Sall	719,369	26.57
Moustapha Niasse	357,347	13.20
Ousmane Tanor Dieng	305,980	11.30
Idrissa Seck	212,848	7.86
Cheikh Mamadou Abiboulah Dièye . .	52,196	1.93
Ibrahima Fall	48,950	1.81
Others*	67,820	2.51
Total	**2,707,056†**	**100.00**

* There were seven other candidates.

† In addition, there were 28,350 invalid votes.

Presidential Election, Second Round, 25 March 2012

Candidate	Valid votes	% of valid votes
Macky Sall	1,909,244	65.80
Abdoulaye Wade	992,556	34.20
Total	**2,901,800***	**100.00**

* In addition, there were 14,093 invalid votes.

LEGISLATURE

Assemblée nationale

pl. Soweto, BP 86, Dakar; tel. 33-823-1099; fax 33-823-6708; e-mail assnat@assemblee-nationale.sn; internet www.assemblee-nationale.sn.

President: MOUSTAPHA NIASSE.

General Election, 1 July 2012

Party	Votes	% of votes	Seats
Benno Bokk Yaakaar (BBY) .	1,040,899	53.06	119
Parti Démocratique Sénégalais (PDS)	298,846	15.23	12
Bokk Gis Gis (BGG) . . .	143,180	7.30	4
Bës du Niak	113,321	5.78	4
Mouvement de la Réforme pour le Développement Social (MRDS)	70,655	3.60	2
Parti de la Vérité pour le Développement (PVD) . .	48,553	2.47	2
Union pour le Renouveau Démocratique (URD) . .	21,964	1.12	1
Mouvement Patriotique du Sénégal/Faxas	21,868	1.11	1
Convergence Patriotique pour la Justice et l'Équité/Nay Leer	20,762	1.06	1
Tekki 2012	20,671	1.05	1
Deggo Soxali Transport Ak Commerce	18,859	0.96	1
Leeral	17,791	0.91	1
And Jëf—Parti Africain pour la Démocratie et le Socialisme (AJ—PADS)	15,889	0.81	1
Others	108,518	5.53	—
Total	**1,961,776**	**·100.00**	**150**

Sénat

President: PAPE DIOP.

Election, 19 August 2007

Party	Seats
Parti Démocratique Sénégalais (PDS) . .	34
And Jëf—Parti Africain pour la Démocratie et le Socialisme (AJ—PADS)	1
Total	**100***

* The remaining 65 members are appointed by the President.

Election Commission

Commission Electorale Nationale Autonome (CENA): Immeuble Fonds de Garantie Automobile, ave Malick Sy, angle Impasse Cosec, BP 28900, Dakar; tel. 33-889-66-00; fax 33-823-4204; internet www.cena.sn; f. 2005; Pres. DOUDOU NDIR.

Political Organizations

A total of 24 parties and coalitions contested the legislative elections held in July 2012.

Alliance des Forces de Progrès (AFP): rue 1, angle rue A, point E, BP 5825, Dakar; tel. 33-869-7595; fax 33-825-7770; e-mail afp.net@yahoo.fr; internet www.afp-senegal.org; f. 1999; Sec.-Gen. MOUSTAPHA NIASSE.

Alliance Jëf-Jël: Villa 5, rue 1, Castors Front de Terre, Dakar; tel. 77-652-2232 (mobile); e-mail tallasylla@hotmail.com; f. 1997; Pres. PAPA AMETH KEÏTA.

And Jëf—Parti Africain pour la Démocratie et le Socialisme (AJ—PADS): Villa 1, Zone B, BP 12136, Dakar; tel. and fax 33-864-4130; e-mail webmaster@ajpads.org; internet ajpads.com; f. 1992; Sec.-Gen. LANDING SAVANÉ.

Benno Bokk Yaakaar (BBY): Dakar; coalition comprising 80 political organizations.

   Alliance pour la République (APR—Yaakaar): Dakar; f. 2008; Leader MACKY SALL.

Bës du Niak: Leader SERIGNE MANSOUR MANSOUR SY DJAMIL.

Bokk Gis Gis (BGG): Dakar; coalition of political organizations.

Bloc des Centristes Gaïndé (BCG): Villa 734, Sicap Baobabs, Dakar; tel. 33-825-3764; e-mail issa_dias@sentoo.sn; f. 1996; Pres. and Sec.-Gen. JEAN-PAUL DIAS.

Convergence Patriotique pour la Justice et l'Équité/Nay Leer: Dakar; Leader DEMBA DIOP.

Convergence pour le Renouveau et la Citoyenneté (CRC): 7 ave Bourguiba, Industrial Zone, Sodida, Dakar; tel. 33-824-4900; e-mail info@crc-sn.org; Sec.-Gen. ALIOU DIA.

Deggo Soxali Transport Ak Commerce: Dakar; Leader ALASSANE NDOYE.

Front pour le Socialisme et la Démocratie—Benno Jubël (FSD—BJ): contested 2001 election as mem. of Sopi Coalition; Sec.-Gen. BAMBA DIÈYE.

Leeral: Dakar; Leader EL HADJI DIOUF.

Ligue Démocratique—Mouvement pour le Parti du Travail (LD—MPT): ave Bourguiba, Dieuppeul 2, Villa 2566, BP 10172, Dakar Liberté; tel. 33-825-6706; fax 33-827-4300; e-mail jallarbi@sentoo.sn; internet www.ldmpt.sn; regd 1981; social-democrat; Sec.-Gen. ABDOULAYE BATHILY.

Mouvement pour la Démocratie et le Socialisme—Naxx Jarinu (MDS—NJ): Unité 20, Parcelles Assainies, Villa 528, Dakar; tel. 33-869-5049; f. 2000; Leader OUMAR KHASSIMOU DAI.

Mouvement Patriotique du Sénégal/Faxas (MPS/Faxas): Ouest Foire, en face du CICES, prés de la Station Shell, Dakar; tel. 77-568-2787 (mobile); e-mail info@mpsfaxas.com; internet www.mpsfaxas.com; Leader SERIGNE KHADIM THIOUNE.

Mouvement de la Réforme pour le Développement Social (MRDS): HLM 4, Villa 858, Dakar; e-mail sgmrds@mrds.sn; internet www.mrds.sn; f. 2000; Pres. IMAM MBAYE NIANG; Sec.-Gen. Imam IYANE SOW.

Mouvement Républicain Sénégalais (MRS): Résidence du Cap-Vert, 10e étage, 5 pl. de l'Indépendance, BP 4193, Dakar; tel. 33-822-0319; fax 33-822-0700; e-mail agaz@omnet.sn; Sec.-Gen. ABDOUL AZIZ PAYE.

Mouvement pour le Socialisme et l'Unité (MSU): HLM 1, Villa 86, Dakar; tel. 33-825-8544; f. 1981 as Mouvement Démocratique Populaire; National Co-ordinator-Gen. MOUHAMADOU BAMBA N'DIAYE.

Parti Africain de l'Indépendance (PAI): Maison du Peuple, Guediewaye, BP 820, Dakar; tel. 33-837-0136; f. 1957; reorg. 1976; Marxist; Sec.-Gen. MAJMOUT DIOP.

Parti Démocratique Sénégalais (PDS): blvd Dial Diop, Immeuble Serigne Mourtada Mbacké, Dakar; tel. 33-823-5027; fax 33-823-1702; e-mail cedobe@aol.com; f. 1974; liberal democratic; Sec.-Gen. Me ABDOULAYE WADE.

Parti de l'Indépendance et du Travail (PIT): route front de terre, BP 10470, Dakar; tel. 33-827-2907; fax 33-820-9000; regd 1981; Marxist-Leninist; Sec.-Gen. AMATH DANSOKHO.

Parti Populaire Sénégalais (PPS): Quartier Escale, BP 212, Diourbel; tel. 33-971-1171; regd 1981; populist; Sec.-Gen. Dr OUMAR WANE.

Parti pour le Progrès et la Citoyenneté (PPC): Quartier Merina, Rufique; tel. 33-836-1868; Sec.-Gen. Me MBAYE JACQUES DIOP.

Parti pour la Renaissance Africaine—Sénégal (PARENA): Sicap Dieuppeul, Villa 2685/B, Dakar; tel. 77-636-8788 (mobile); fax 33-823-5721; e-mail mariamwane@yahoo.fr; f. 2000; Sec.-Gen. MARIAM MAMADOU WANE LY.

Parti de la Renaissance et de la Citoyenneté: Liberté 6, Villa 7909, Dakar; tel. 33-827-8568; f. 2000; Sec.-Gen. SAMBA DIOULDÉ THIAM.

Parti Social-démocrate—Jant Bi (PSD—JB): Leader MAMOUR CISSÉ.

Parti Socialiste Authentique (PSA): internet psa-senegal.org; Leader SOUTY TOURRE.

Parti Socialiste du Sénégal (PS): Maison du Parti Socialiste Léopold Sédar Senghor, Colobane, BP 12010, Dakar; tel. and fax 33-824-7744; e-mail senegalpartisocialiste@gmail.com; internet www.ps-senegal.com; f. 1958 as Union Progressiste Sénégalaise; Sec.-Gen. OUSMANE TANOR DIENG.

Parti de la Vérité pour le Développement (PVD): Dakar; f. 2004; Leader SOKHNA DIENG MBACKÉ.

Rassemblement des Écologistes du Sénégal—Les Verts (RES): rue 67, angle rue 52, Gueule Tapée, BP 25226, Dakar-Fann; tel. and fax 33-842-3442; f. 1999; Sec.-Gen. MAMADOU BERTHÉ.

Rassemblement National Démocratique (RND): Sacré-Coeur III, Villa no 9721, Dakar; tel. 76-580-86-17 (mobile); f. 1976; legalized 1981; mem. of opposition Bennoo Siggil Senegal (f. 2009); Sec.-Gen. MADIOR DIOUF.

Rassemblement Patriotique Sénégalais—Jammi Rewmi (RPS—JR): Leader ELY MADIODO FALL FALL.

Rassemblement des Travailleurs Africains—Sénégal/Péncoo Réew (RTA—S/PENCOO REEW): Immeuble Seydou Nourou Tall, Apt. B6, 2ème étage, 12 rue 14 angle P, BP 13725, Derklé, Grand-Yoff, Dakar; tel. 33-827-1579; e-mail rtas@rtasenegal.org; internet www.rtasenegal.org; f. 1997; Sec.-Gen. El Hadji MOMAR SAMBE.

Takku Defaraat Sénégal Coalition: VDN à côté de la Poste; tel. 33-860-5019; fax 33-860-5020; f. 2000; Leader ROBERT SAGNA.

Tekki 2012: Zone B, Villa 23A, Bis, Dakar; tel. 33-868-4333; e-mail tekki@sentoo.sn; internet www.tekki.org; Leader MAMADOU LAMINE DIALLO.

Union Nationale Patriotique (UNP): Leader NDÈYE FATOU TOURÉ.

Union pour le Renouveau Démocratique (URD): Bopp Villa 234, rue 7, Dakar; tel. 33-864-7431; fax 33-820-7317; e-mail urd@urdsenegal.sn; internet www.urdsenegal.sn; f. 1998 by breakaway faction of PS; Sec.-Gen. DJIBO LEÏTY KÂ.

The **Mouvement des Forces Démocratiques de la Casamance (MFDC)** was founded in 1947; it had paramilitary and political wings and formerly sought the independence of the Casamance region of southern Senegal. The MFDC is not officially recognized as a political party (the Constitution of 2001 forbids the formation of parties on a geographic basis) and waged a campaign of guerrilla warfare in the region from the early 1980s. Representatives of the MFDC have participated in extensive negotiations with the Senegalese Government on the restoration of peace and the granting of greater autonomy to Casamance, and in December 2004 a cease-fire agreement was signed between the two sides, pending further peace negotiations. The Honorary President of the MFDC, Fr AUGUSTIN DIAMACOUNÉ SENGHOR, died in January 2007; the post of Secretary-General was disputed between JEAN-MARIE FRANÇOIS BIAGUI and ANSOUMANA BADJI.

Diplomatic Representation
EMBASSIES IN SENEGAL

Algeria: 5 rue Mermoz, Plateau, POB 3233, Dakar; tel. 33-849-5700; fax 33-849-5701; e-mail ambalgdak@orange.sn; internet ambalgdakar.org; f. 1963; Ambassador ABDERRAHMANE BENGUERAH.

Austria: 18 rue Emile Zola, BP 3247, Dakar; tel. 33-849-4000; fax 33-849-4370; e-mail dakar-ob@bmaa.gv.at; Ambassador Dr GERHARD DEISS.

Belgium: ave des Jambaars, BP 524, Dakar; tel. 33-889-4390; fax 33-889-4398; e-mail dakar@diplobel.fed.be; internet diplomatie.belgium.be/senegal; Ambassador JOHAN VERKAMMEN.

Brazil: Immeuble Fondation Fahd, 4e étage, blvd Djily Mbaye, angle rue Macodou Ndiaye, BP 136, Dakar; tel. 33-823-1492; fax 33-823-7181; e-mail embdakar@sentoo.sn; Ambassador MARIA ELISA THÉÔFILO DE LUNA.

Burkina Faso: Sicap Sacré Coeur III, Extension VDN No. 10628B, BP 11601, Dakar; tel. 33-864-5824; fax 33-864-5823; e-mail ambabf@sentoo.sn; Ambassador HIPPOLYTE OUÉDRAOGO.

Cameroon: 157–9 rue Joseph Gomis, BP 4165, Dakar; tel. 33-849-0292; fax 33-823-3396; Ambassador JEAN KOE NTONGA.

Canada: rue Galliéni angle rue Amadou Cissé Dia, BP 3373, Dakar; tel. 33-889-4700; fax 33-889-4720; e-mail dakar@international.gc.ca; internet www.canadainternational.gc.ca/senegal; Ambassador PERRY CALDERWOOD.

Cape Verde: 3 blvd El-Hadji Djilly M'Baye, BP 11269, Dakar; tel. 33-822-4285; fax 33-821-0697; e-mail acvc.sen@metissacana.sn; Ambassador FRANCISCO PEREIRA DA VEIGA.

China, People's Republic: rue 18 prolongée, Fann Résidence, BP 342, Dakar; tel. 33-864-7775; fax 33-864-7780; Ambassador XIA HUANG.

Congo, Democratic Republic: 16 rue Léo Frobénus, Fann Résidence, Dakar; tel. 33-824-6574; fax 33-864-6576; Chargé d'affaires a.i. FATAKI NICOLAS LUNGUELE MUSAMBYA.

Congo, Republic: Statut Mermoz, Pyrotechnie, BP 5242, Fann Résidence, Dakar; tel. 33-824-8398; fax 33-825-7856; Ambassador VALENTIN OLLESSONGO.

Côte d'Ivoire: ave Birago Diop, BP 359, Dakar; tel. 33-869-0270; fax 33-825-2115; e-mail cmrci@ambaci-dakar.org; internet www.ambaci-dakar.org; Ambassador EDOUARD TIAPÉ KASSARATÉ.

Cuba: 9 rue 208, BP 4510, Mermoz-Sotrac, Dakar; tel. 33-869-08319; fax 860-9219; e-mail embacubasen@sentoo.sn; Ambassador VILMA REYES VALDESPINO.

Egypt: 22 rue à Brière de l'Isle, Plateau, BP 474, Dakar; tel. 33-889-2474; fax 33-821-8993; e-mail ambegydk@telecomplus.sn; Ambassador HESHAM MUHAMMAD MAHER.

Ethiopia: 18 blvd de la République, BP 379, Dakar; tel. 33-821-9896; fax 33-821-9895; e-mail ethembas@sentoo.sn; Ambassador ATO HASSEN ABDULKADIK.

France: 1 rue El Hadj Amadou Assane Ndoye, BP 4035, Dakar; tel. 33-839-5100; fax 33-839-5181; internet www.ambafrance-sn.org; Ambassador JEAN FÉLIX-PAGANON.

Gabon: ave Cheikh Anta Diop, cnr Fann Résidence, BP 436, Dakar; tel. 33-865-2234; fax 33-864-3145; e-mail ambgabon@refer.sn; Ambassador GUY BLAISE NAMBO-WEZET.

The Gambia: 11 rue Elhadji Ismaïla Guèye (Thiong), BP 3248, Dakar; tel. 33-821-4416; fax 33-821-6279; e-mail gambit.high .commission@gmail.com; Ambassador OUSMAN BADJIE.

Germany: 20 ave Pasteur, angle rue Mermoz, BP 2100, Dakar; tel. 33-889-4884; fax 33-822-5299; e-mail info@daka.diplo.de; internet www.dakar.diplo.de; Ambassador CHRISTIAN CLAGES.

Ghana: Lot 27, Parcelle B, Almadies, BP 25370, Dakar; tel. 33-869-1990; fax 33-820-1950; e-mail info@ghembsen.org; Ambassador ABDULAI YAKUBU.

Guinea: rue 7, angle B&D, point E, BP 7123, Dakar; tel. 33-824-8606; fax 33-825-5946; Ambassador Elhadj MADIFING DIANÉ.

Guinea-Bissau: rue 6, angle B, point E, BP 2319, Dakar; tel. 33-824-5922; fax 33-825-9089; e-mail ambgb@orange.sn; Ambassador MARIO CABRAL.

Holy See: rue Aimé Césaire, angle Corniche-Ouest, Fann Résidence, BP 5076, Dakar; tel. 33-824-2674; fax 33-824-1931; e-mail vatemb@ orange.sn; Apostolic Nuncio Most Rev. LUIS MARIANO MONTEMAYOR (Titular Archbishop of Illici).

India: 5 rue Carde, BP 398, Dakar; tel. 33-849-5875; fax 33-822-3585; e-mail indiacom@orange.sn; internet www.ambassadeinde.sn; Ambassador NAGESHA RAO PARTHASARATHI.

Indonesia: ave Cheikh Anta Diop, BP 5859, Dakar; tel. 33-825-7316; fax 33-825-5896; e-mail kbri@sentoo.sn; Ambassador ANDRADJATI.

Iran: 17 ave des Ambassadeurs, Fann Résidence, BP 735, Dakar; tel. 33-825-2528; fax 33-824-2314; e-mail ambiiran@telecomplus.sn; Ambassador JAHAN BAKHSHE HASANZADE.

Iraq: point E, rue 6, angle B, à coté de la Croix Rouge Internationale, BP45448, Dakar; tel. 33-869-7799; fax 33-824-0909; e-mail dkremb@ iraqmfamail.com; Ambassador MOHAMMED HAKIM AL-ROBAI'EE.

Israel: Immeuble SDIH, 3 pl. de l'indépendance, BP 2096, Dakar; tel. 33-823-7965; fax 33-823-6490; e-mail info@dakar.mfa.gov.il; internet embassies.gov.il/dakar; Ambassador Dr ELI BEN-TURA.

Italy: rue Alpha Achamiyou Tall, BP 348, Dakar; tel. 33-889-2636; fax 33-821-7580; e-mail ambasciata.dakar@esteri.it; internet www .ambdakar.esteri.it; Ambassador ARTURO LUZZI.

Japan: blvd Martin Luther King, Corniche-Ouest, BP 3140, Dakar; tel. 33-849-5500; fax 33-849-5555; internet www.sn.emb-japan.go.jp; Ambassador HIROSHI FUKADA.

Korea, Republic: Villa Hamoudy, rue Aime Cesaire, Fann Résidence, BP 5850, Dakar; tel. 33-824-0672; fax 33-824-0695; e-mail senegal@mofat.go.kr; internet sen.mofat.go.kr; Ambassador CHONG-WEON SHIN.

Kuwait: blvd Martin Luther King, Dakar; tel. 33-824-1723; fax 33-825-0899; e-mail q8embassydkr@sentoo.sn; Ambassador HAMAD BURAHAMAH.

Lebanon: 56 ave Jean XXIII, BP 6700 Dakar-Etoile, Dakar; tel. 33-822-0255; fax 33-823-5899; e-mail ambaliban@orange.sn; internet www.ambaliban.org; Ambassador MICHEL HADDAD.

Liberia: 146 Ouest-Foire, BP 5845, Dakar-Fann; tel. 33-869-4019; fax 33-820-8223; e-mail libembdkr1@yahoo.com; Ambassador JOHNNY A. MCCLAIN.

Libya: route de Ouakam, BP 16449, Dakar; tel. 33-824-5710; fax 33-824-5722; Ambassador MASSOUD MOHAMED SHALGAM.

Madagascar: Villa numero 104, Mermoz Sotrac, BP 25395, Dakar; tel. 33-860-2987; fax 33-860-2995; e-mail ambadak@yahoo.fr; internet www.ambamad.sn; Ambassador RICHARD AUGUSTE PARAINA.

Malaysia: 7 Extension VDN, Fann Mermoz, BP 15057, Dakar; tel. 33-825-8935; fax 33-825-4719; e-mail maldakar@kln.gov.my; internet www.kln.gov.my/web/sen_dakar/home; Ambassador (vacant).

Mali: Fann Résidence, Corniche-Ouest, rue 23, BP 478, Dakar; tel. 33-824-6252; fax 33-825-9471; e-mail ambamali@orange.sn; Ambassador MOULAYE ALI KHALIL ASCOFARÉ.

Mauritania: 37 blvd Charles de Gaulle, Dakar; tel. 33-823-5344; fax 33-823-5311; Ambassador SIDI ALI OULD HAIBA.

Morocco: 73 ave Cheikh Anta Diop, BP 490, Dakar; tel. 33-824-6927; fax 33-825-7021; e-mail ambmadk@sentoo.sn; Ambassador TALEB BERRADA.

Netherlands: 37 rue Jaques Bugnicourt, BP 3262, Dakar; tel. 33-849-0360; fax 33-821-7084; e-mail dak@minbuza.nl; internet www .nlambassadedakar.org; Ambassador PIETER JAN KLEIWEG DE ZWAAN.

Niger: ave Cheikh Anta Diop, Dakar; tel. 33-824-1226; fax 33-824-1251; Ambassador MALÉMI HASSANE CHETIMA.

Nigeria: 8 ave Cheikh Anta Diop, BP 3129, Dakar; tel. 33-869-8600; fax 33-825-8136; e-mail info@nigeriandakar.sn; internet www .nigeriandakar.sn; Ambassador KAYTEN CATHERINE JACKDEN.

Oman: Villa 7062, Stéle Mermoz, BP 2635; tel. 33-824-6136; e-mail dakar@mofa.gov.om; Ambassador AHMED BARAKAT ABDULLAH AL-IBRAHIM.

Pakistan: Stèle Mermoz, Villa 7602, BP 2635, Dakar; tel. 33-824-6135; fax 33-824-6136; e-mail parepdakar@gmail.com; internet www .mofa.gov.pk/senegal; Ambassador MOHAMMAD ABDUL MATEEN KHAN.

Portugal: Villa Martha, ave des Ambassadeurs 6, Fann Résidence, BP 281, Dakar; tel. 33-864-0317; fax 33-864-0322; e-mail ambportdakar@sentoo.sn; Ambassador RUI ALBERTO MANUPPELLA TERENO.

Qatar: 25 blvd Martin Luther King, BP 5150, Dakar; tel. 33-820-9559; fax 33-869-1012; Ambassador ALI ABDUL LATIF AHMED AL-MASALAMANI.

Romania: rue A prolongée, point E, BP 3171, Dakar; tel. 33-825-2068; fax 33-824-9190; e-mail romania.consul@orange.sn; internet dakar.mae.ro; Ambassador CIPRIAN MIHALI.

Russia: ave Jean Jaurès, angle rue Carnot, BP 3180, Dakar; tel. 33-822-4821; fax 33-821-1372; e-mail ambrus@orange.sn; internet www .senegal.mid.ru; Ambassador VALERY NESTERUSHKIN.

Rwanda: route du Méridien, Dakar; Ambassador GÉRARD NTWARI.

Saudi Arabia: 10 route de Ngor n° 10, BP 15150, Dakar; tel. 33-869-8390; fax 33-820-6553; e-mail snemb@mofa.gov.sa; Ambassador ABDULAZIZ M. A. AL-AIFAN.

Sierra Leone: Immeuble FAHD, 13e étage, blvd El Hadji Djily Mbaye, Dakar; tel. 33-842-3120; Ambassador KHADIJATU BASSIR.

South Africa: Memoz SUD, Lotissement Ecole de Police, BP 21010, Dakar-Ponty; tel. 33-865-1959; fax 33-864-2359; e-mail ambafsud@ orange.sn; internet www.saesenegal.info; Ambassador SEGOGWANE SAM KOTANE.

Spain: 18–20 ave Nelson Mandela, BP 2091, Dakar; tel. 33-821-1178; fax 33-821-6845; e-mail emb.dakar@mae.es; Ambassador CRISTINA DIAZ FERNANDEZ-GIL.

Sudan: 31 route de la Pyrotechnie, Mermoz, Fann-Résidence, BP 15033, Dakar; tel. 33-824-9853; fax 33-824-9852; e-mail sudembse@ sentoo.sn; Ambassador EL-OBEID MOHAMED EL-OBEID RAHMA.

Switzerland: rue René N'Diaye, angle rue Seydou, BP 1772, Dakar; tel. 33-823-0590; fax 33-822-3657; e-mail dak.vertretung@eda .admin.ch; internet www.eda.admin.ch/dakar; Ambassador MURIEL BERSET KOHEN.

Syria: rue 1, point E, angle blvd de l'Est, BP 498, Dakar; tel. 33-824-6277; fax 33-824-9007; e-mail syrdak@orange.sn; Ambassador (vacant).

Thailand: 10 rue Léon Gontran Damas, Angle F, Fann Résidence BP 3721, Dakar; tel. 33-869-3290; fax 33-824-8458; e-mail thaidkr@ sentoo.sn; internet www.mfa.go.th/web/2366.php; Ambassador BUSAYA MATHELIN.

Tunisia: rue Alpha Hachamiyou Tall, BP 3127, Dakar; tel. 33-823-4747; fax 33-823-7204; e-mail at.dakar@sentoo.sn; Ambassador CHOUKRI HERMASSI.

Turkey: ave des Ambassadeurs, Fann Résidence, BP 6060, Etoile, Dakar; tel. 33-869-2542; fax 33-825-6977; e-mail trambdkr@sentoo .sn; Ambassador ASLI UĞDÜL.

United Arab Emirates: Corniche Ouest Mermoz, BP 15150, Dakar; tel. 33-869-8390; Ambassador HAMAD SAEED AL-ZAABI.

United Kingdom: 20 rue du Dr Guillet, BP 6025, Dakar; tel. 33-823-7392; fax 33-823-2766; e-mail britembe@orange.sn; internet ukinsenegal.fco.gov.uk; Ambassador JOHN MARSHALL.

USA: ave Jean XXIII, angle rue Kleber, BP 49, Dakar; tel. 33-829-2100; fax 33-822-2991; e-mail usadakar@state.gov; internet dakar .usembassy.gov; Ambassador LEWIS LUKENS.

Venezuela: rue 11, angle 6, Fann Mermoz, BP 45287, Dakar; tel. 33-864-1515; fax 33-864-7935; e-mail embavenez_senegal@yahoo.com; Ambassador EDDY JOSÉ CORDOBA CORCEGA.

Zimbabwe: rue de Louga, angle rue 31, Point E, BP 25342, Fann, Dakar; tel. 33-825-4131; fax 33-825-4016; e-mail zimdakar@yahoo .com; Ambassador TRUDY STEVENSON.

Judicial System

The Supreme Court was re-established in 2008, replacing the Court of Cassation and the Council of State. The Supreme Court is the highest court of appeal, and regulates the activities of subordinate courts and tribunals. It also judges complaints brought against the Executive and resolves electoral disputes. The Constitutional Council verifies that legislation and international agreements are in accordance with the Constitution, and decides disputes between the Executive and the Legislature. The Revenue Court supervises the public accounts.

Supreme Court (Cour Suprême): blvd Martin Luther King, BP 15184, Dakar; tel. 33-889-1010; fax 33-823-7894; internet www .coursupreme.sn; f. 2008; Pres. PAPE OMAR SAKHO.

Constitutional Council (Conseil Constitutionnel): BP 45732, Dakar; tel. 33-822-5252; fax 33-822-8187; e-mail magou_51@hotmail.com; 5 mems; Pres. CHEIKH TIDIANE DIAKHATÉ.

Courts of Appeal (Cours d'Appel): ; Dakar: Pres. DEMBA KANDJI; Kaolack: Pres. HENRI GRÉGOIRE DIOP; Saint-Louis: Pres. BARANE THIAM; Thiès: Pres. EL HADJI MANSOUR TALL.

Revenue Court (Cour des Comptes): 15 ave Franklin Roosevelt, BP 9097, Peytavin, Dakar; tel. 33-859-96-97; fax 33-859-90-40; e-mail ccomptes@courdescomptes.sn; internet www.courdescomptes.sn; f. 1999; Pres. MAMADOU HADY SARR; Sec.-Gen. El Hadji ABDOUL MADJIB GUEYE.

High Court of Justice (Haute Cour de Justice): Dakar; competent to try the Prime Minister and other members of the Government for crimes committed in the exercise of their duties; the President of the Republic may only be brought to trial in the case of high treason; mems elected by the Assemblée nationale.

Religion

At the time of the 1988 census almost 94% of the population were Muslims, while some 5% professed Christianity (the dominant faith being Roman Catholicism); a small number, mostly in the south, followed traditional beliefs.

ISLAM

There are four main Islamic brotherhoods active in Senegal: the Tidjanes, the Mourides, the Layennes and the Qadiriyas.

Association pour la Coopération Islamique (ACIS): Dakar; f. 1988; Pres. Dr THIERNAO KÂ.

Grande Mosquée de Dakar: Dakar; tel. 33-822-5648; Grand Imam El Hadj ALIOUNE MOUSSA SAMB.

CHRISTIANITY

The Roman Catholic Church

Senegal comprises one archdiocese and six dioceses. Roman Catholics represent about 5% of the total population.

Bishops' Conference

Conférence des Evêques du Sénégal, de la Mauritanie, du Cap-Vert et de Guinée-Bissau, BP 941, Dakar; tel. 33-836-3309; fax 33-836-1617; e-mail archevchedkr@sentoo.sn.

f. 1973; Pres. Most Rev. JEAN-NOËL DIOUF (Bishop of Tambacounda).

Archbishop of Dakar: Cardinal THÉODORE-ADRIEN SARR, Archevêché, ave Jean XXIII, BP 1908, Dakar; tel. 33-889-0600; fax 33-823-4875; e-mail archevechedkr@sentoo.sn.

The Anglican Communion

The Anglican diocese of The Gambia, part of the Church of the Province of West Africa, includes Senegal and Cape Verde. The Bishop is resident in Banjul, The Gambia.

Protestant Church

Église Luthérienne du Sénégal: BP 9, Fatick, Niakhar; tel. 33-949-1171; fax 33-949-1385; e-mail elsfk@orange.sn; Pres. Rev. ABDOU THIAM.

Eglise Protestante du Sénégal: 65 rue Wagane Diouf, BP 22390, Dakar; tel. 33-821-5564; fax 33-821-7132; internet www.epsenegal.org; f. 1862; Pastor JUPITER GUEYE; Sec.-Gen. SANDRA FONKUI.

BAHÁ'Í FAITH

National Spiritual Assembly: Point E, rue des Ecrivains, impasse 2 à droite après la Direction de la Statistique, BP 1662, Dakar; tel. 77-576-0471 (mobile); e-mail bahai@sentoo.sn; internet www.sn.bahai.org; regd 1975; Sec. ABOUBAKRINE BA.

The Press

DAILY NEWSPAPERS

L'Actuel: route du Front de Terre, angle ave Bourguiba, Immeuble Dramé, BP 11874, Dakar; tel. 33-864-2601; fax 33-864-2602; e-mail lactuel@sentoo.sn; Editor-in-Chief ABDOURAHMANE SY.

Dakar Soir: Point Presse Sarl, 3e étage, 108 Hann Maristes, BP 21548, Dakar; tel. and fax 33-832-1093; f. 2000; Editor-in-Chief ALAIN NDIAYE.

Frasques Quotidiennes: 51 rue du Docteur Thèze, BP 879, Dakar; tel. 33-842-4226; fax 33-842-4277; e-mail frasques@arc.sn.

L'Info 7: Sicap rue 10, BP 11357, Dakar; tel. and fax 33-864-2658; e-mail comsept@sentoo.sn; f. 1999.

Le Matin: route de l'Aéroport Léopold Sédar Senghor, Yoff, BP 6472, Dakar; tel. 33-869-1270; fax 33-820-1181; e-mail lematin@metissacana.sn; internet www.lematindelafrique.com; daily; independent; Editor-in-Chief ALIOUNE FALL.

L'Observateur: Immeuble Elimane Ndour, rue 15, angle Corniche, Dakar; tel. 33-849-1644; fax 33-849-1645; e-mail info@futursmedias.net; internet www.lobservateur.sn; Editor-in-Chief SERIGNE SALIOU SAMB.

L'Office: 9 rue de Thann, Dakar; tel. 33-824-2115; fax 33-824-2108; e-mail loffice@loffice.sn; internet www.loffice.sn; Editor-in-Chief LAMINE NDOUR.

Le Populaire: ave Bourguiba, Immeuble Baye Ndama, BP 11357, Dakar; tel. 33-869-6363; fax 33-824-2446; e-mail popxibaar@yahoo.fr; internet www.popxibaar.com; f. 2000; Dir of Publication DAOUDA DIARRA; Editor-in-Chief HAROUNA DÈME.

Le Quotidien: 12 Cité Adama Diop, Yoff Routes de Cimétieres, BP 25221, Dakar; tel. 33-869-8484; fax 33-820-7297; e-mail lequotidien@lequotidien.sn; internet www.lequotidien.sn; f. 2003; Dir MAMADOU BIAYE.

Le Soleil: Société Sénégalaise de Presse et de Publications, route du Service Géographique, Hann, BP 92, Dakar; tel. 33-859-5959; fax 33-832-0886; e-mail lesoleil@lesoleil.sn; internet www.lesoleilmultimedia.com; f. 1970; Editors-in-Chief HABIB DEMBA FALL, SIDY DIOP; circ. 25,000 (2009).

Sud Quotidien: Amitié II, angle blvd Bourguiba, BP 4130, Dakar; tel. 33-824-3306; fax 33-824-3322; e-mail info@sudonline.sn; internet www.sudonline.sn; independent; Dir ABDOULAYE NDIAGA SYLLA; circ. 30,000.

Tract: 13 rue de Thann, BP 3683, Dakar; tel. and fax 33-823-4725; e-mail tract.sn@laposte.net; f. 2000.

Wal Fadjri/L'Aurore (The Dawn): Sicap Sacré-Coeur 8542, BP 576, Dakar; tel. 33-824-2343; fax 33-824-2346; e-mail walf@walf.sn; internet www.walf.sn; f. 1984; Exec. Dir MBAYE SIDY MBAYE; circ. 15,000.

24 Heures Chrono: Sacré coeur 3, Villa 10595; tel. 77-576-0358 (mobile); internet www.24sn.com; Editor SAMBA BIAGUI.

PERIODICALS

Le Cafard Libéré: 10 rue Tolbiac, angle Autoroute, Soumédioune, BP 7292, Dakar; tel. 33-822-4383; fax 33-822-0891; f. 1987; weekly; satirical; Editor PAPE SAMBA KANE; circ. 12,000.

Le Courrier du Sud: BP 190, Ziguinchor; tel. 33-991-1166; weekly.

Dakar Life: Dakar; tel. 77-638-8585 (mobile); Dir of Publication MASSAMBA MBAYE; circ. 15,000.

Démocratie: Liberté V, 5375 M, 71 rue du rond-point Liberté V et VI, Dakar; tel. 33-824-8669; fax 33-825-1879.

Eco Hebdo: rue 22, Médina, BP 11451, Dakar; tel. and fax 33-837-1414; weekly.

Emergence Plus: Dakar; tel. 33-867-67-05; fax 33-867-46-99; e-mail emergencemag@orange.sn; Dir of Publication MOUMINA AÏDA KANE.

Ethiopiques: BP 2035, Dakar; tel. 33-849-1414; fax 33-822-1914; e-mail senghorf@orange.sn; internet www.refer.sn/ethiopiques; f. 1974; literary and philosophical review; publ. by Fondation Léopold Sédar Senghor; Editor BASSIROU DIENG.

Icone: Dakar; monthly; Dir of Publication MANSOUR DIENG.

Le Journal de l'Economie: 15 rue Jules Ferry, BP 2851, Dakar; tel. 33-823-8733; fax 33-823-6007; e-mail lejeco@sentoo.sn; weekly.

Journal Officiel de la République du Sénégal: Rufisque; tel. 33-849-1817; internet www.jo.gouv.sn; f. 1856; weekly; govt journal.

Nord Ouest: Immeuble Lonase, BP 459, Louga; tel. 76-680-7943 (mobile); e-mail lenordouest@yahoo.fr; f. 2000; regional monthly; Dir of Publication PAPE MOMAR CISSÉ.

Nouvel Horizon: Liberté II, Villa 1589, BP 10037, Dakar; tel. 33-864-1152; fax 33-864-1150; e-mail nh-thiof@sentoo.sn; weekly; Editor-in-Chief ISSA SALL.

Le Politicien: 8123 Terminus Liberté VI, BP 11018, Dakar; tel. and fax 33-827-6396; f. 1977; weekly; satirical.

Promotion: BP 1676, Dakar; tel. 33-825-6969; fax 33-825-6950; e-mail giepromo@telecomplus.sn; f. 1972; fortnightly; Dir BOUBACAR DIOP; circ. 5,000.

République: BP 21740, Dakar; tel. 33-822-7373; fax 33-822-5039; e-mail republike@yahoo.fr; f. 1994; weekly.

Sopi (Change): 5 blvd Dial Diop, Dakar; tel. 33-824-4950; fax 33-824-4700; f. 1988; weekly; publ. by PDS; Editor CHEIKH KOUREYSSI BA.

Station One: Immeuble Cheikh Tall Dioum, 5éme étage, 58 ave Bourguiba, Dakar; tel. 77-633-5040 (mobile); f. 2008; monthly; Dir of Publication MOUSTAPHA SOW; 20,000.

Le Témoin: Gibraltar II, Villa 310, Dakar; tel. 33-822-3269; fax 33-821-7838; f. 1990; weekly; Editor-in-Chief MAMADOU OUMAR NDIAYE; circ. 5,000.

Thiof: BP 10037, Dakar; tel. 33-864-11-51; monthly; Editor-in-Chief SOULEYMANE THIAM; circ. 15,000.

Le 221: BP 11600, Dakar; tel. 33-860-45-15; fax 33-867-67-79; internet agenda.au-senegal.com; Editor-in-Chief SELLY WANE; circ. 25,000.

Vive La République: Sicap Amitié III, Villa 4057, Dakar; tel. 33-864-0631; weekly.

Weekend Magazine: 12 Cité Adama Diop, Yoff Routes de Cimétieres, BP 25221, Dakar; tel. 33-869-8484; fax 33-869-8499; e-mail weekend@weekend.sn; internet www.weekend.sn; f. 2007; publ. by Groupe Avenir Communication, which also publishes the daily Le Quotidien; Dir of Publication PAPA SAMBA DIARRA; circ. 9,000.

Xareli (Struggle): BP 12136, Dakar; tel. 33-822-5463; fortnightly; publ. by AJ—PADS; circ. 7,000.

NEWS AGENCIES

Agence Panafricaine d'Information—PANA-Presse SA: ave Bourjuiba, BP 4056, Dakar; tel. 33-869-1234; fax 33-824-1390; e-mail marketing@panapress.com; internet www.panapress.com; f. 1979 as Pan-African News Agency (under the auspices of the Organization of African Unity), restructured as 75% privately owned co in 1997; Dir-Gen. BABACAR FALL.

Agence de Presse Sénégalaise: 58 blvd de la République, BP 117, Dakar; tel. 33-823-1667; fax 33-822-0767; e-mail aps@aps.sn; internet www.aps.sn; f. 1959; govt-controlled; Dir-Gen. DOUDOU SARR NIANG.

PRESS ORGANIZATION

Syndicat des Professionnels de l'Information et de la Communication du Sénégal (SYNPICS): BP 21722, Dakar; tel. 33-842-4256; fax 33-842-0269; e-mail synpics@yahoo.fr; Sec.-Gen. DIATA CISSÉ.

Publishers

Africa Editions: BP 1826, Dakar; tel. 33-823-4880; fax 33-822-5630; f. 1958; general, reference; Man. Dir JOËL DECUPPER.

Agence de Distribution de Presse: km 2.5, blvd du Centenaire de la Commune de Dakar, BP 374, Dakar; tel. 33-832-0278; fax 33-832-4915; e-mail adpresse@telecomplus.sn; f. 1943; general, reference; Man. Dir PHILIPPE SCHORP.

Centre Africain d'Animation et d'Echanges Culturels Editions Khoudia: BP 5332, Dakar-Fann; tel. 33-821-1023; fax 33-821-5109; f. 1989; fiction, education, anthropology; Dir AISSATOU DIA.

Editions Clairafrique: 2 rue El Hadji Mbaye Guèye, BP 2005, Dakar; tel. 33-822-2169; fax 33-821-8409; f. 1951; politics, law, sociology, anthropology, literature, economics, devt, religion, school books.

Editions des Ecoles Nouvelles Africaines: ave Cheikh Anta Diop, angle rue Pyrotechnie, Stèle Mermoz, BP 581, Dakar; tel. 33-864-0544; fax 33-864-1352; e-mail eenas@sentoo.sn; youth and adult education, in French.

Editions Juridiques Africaines (EDJA): 18 rue Raffenel, BP 22420, Dakar-Ponty; tel. 33 821-6689; fax 33 823-2753; e-mail edja.ed@orange.sn; internet www.edja.sn; f. 1987; law; Dir NDÉYE NGONÉ GUÉYE.

Editions des Trois Fleuves: blvd de l'Est, angle Cheikh Anta Diop, BP 123, Dakar; tel. 33-825-7923; fax 33-825-5937; f. 1972; general non-fiction; luxury edns; Dir GÉRARD RAZIMOWSKY; Gen. Man. BERTRAND DE BOISTEL.

Enda—Tiers Monde Editions (Environmental Development Action in the Third World): 54 rue Carnot, BP 3370, Dakar; tel. 33-822-9890; fax 33-823-5157; e-mail editions@enda.sn; internet www.enda.sn; f. 1972; Third-World environment and devt; Dir RAPHAËL NDIAYE; Exec. Sec. JOSÉPHINE OUÉDRAOGO.

Grande Imprimerie Africaine (GIA): 9 rue Amadou Assane Ndoye, Dakar; tel. 33-822-1408; fax 33-822-3927; f. 1917; law, administration; Man. Dir CHEIKH ALIMA TOURÉ.

Institut Fondamental d'Afrique Noire (IFAN)—Cheikh Anta Diop: BP 206, Campus universitaire, Dakar; tel. 33-825-9890; fax 33-824-4918; internet www.afrique-ouest.auf.org; f. 1936; scientific and humanistic studies of Black Africa, for specialist and general public.

Nouvelles Editions Africaines du Sénégal (NEAS): 10 rue Amadou Assane Ndoye, BP 260, Dakar; tel. 33-822-1580; fax 33-822-3604; e-mail neas@orange.sn; f. 1972; literary fiction, school-books; Dir-Gen. SEYDOU SOW.

Per Ankh: BP 2, Popenguine; e-mail perankheditions@arc.sn; internet www.perankhbooks.com; history.

Société Africaine d'Édition: 16 bis rue de Thiong, BP 1877, Dakar; tel. 33-821-7977; f. 1961; African politics and economics; Man. Dir PIERRE BIARNES.

Société d'Édition 'Afrique Nouvelle': 9 rue Paul Holle, BP 283, Dakar; tel. 33-822-3825; f. 1947; information, statistics and analyses of African affairs; Man. Dir ATHANASE NDONG.

Société Nationale de Presse, d'Édition et de Publicité (SONA-PRESS): Dakar; f. 1972; Pres. OBEYE DIOP.

Sud-Communication: BP 4100, Dakar; operated by a journalists' co-operative; periodicals.

Xamal, SA: BP 380, Saint-Louis; tel. 33-961-1722; fax 33-961-1519; general literature, social sciences, in national languages and in French; Dir ABOUBAKAR DIOP.

GOVERNMENT PUBLISHING HOUSE

Société Sénégalaise de Presse et de Publications—Imprimerie nationale (SSPP): route du Service géographique, BP 92, Dakar; tel. 33-832-4692; fax 33-832-0381; f. 1970; 62% govt-owned; Dir SALIOU DIAGNE.

Broadcasting and Communications

TELECOMMUNICATIONS

At the end of 2012 there were three providers of mobile cellular telephone services in Senegal. Two of them also provided fixed-line services. At September 2012 there were 339,697 subscribers to fixed-line telephone services and 10.8m. subscribers to mobile telephone services.

Excaf Telecom: Domaine Industriel SODIDA, rue 14 Prolongée, BP 1656, Dakar; tel. 33-824-2424; fax 33-824-2191; e-mail dunyaa@excaf.com; internet www.excaf.com; f. 1972 as L'Agence Africaine de Commercialisation Artistique; name changed as above in 1992; Pres. and Dir-Gen. IBRAHIMA DIAGNE.

Expresso Sénégal: Dakar; internet www.expressotelecom.com; f. 2007; Pres. and Dir-Gen. EL AMIR AHMED EL AMIR YOUSIF.

Société Nationale des Télécommunications du Sénégal (SONATEL): 46 blvd de la République, BP 69, Dakar; tel. 33-839-1118; fax 33-823-6037; internet www.sonatel.sn; f. 1985; 52.2% owned by France Câbles et Radio (France Télécom, France), 27.67% owned by Govt; Pres. MICHEL HIRSCH; Man. Dir ALIOUME N'DIAYE; 2,340 employees (2007).

Orange Sénégal: 46 ave de la République, en face de la Cathédrale, BP 2352, Dakar; tel. 33-839-1771; fax 33-839-1754; internet www.orange.sn; f. 1996 as Sonatel Mobiles; fmrly known as Alizé.

Télécom Plus SARL: 20 rue Amadou Assane Ndoye, BP 21100, Dakar; tel. 33-839-9700; fax 33-823-4632; telecommunications products and services.

Tigo: 15 route de Ngor, BP 146, Dakar; tel. 33-869-7420; fax 33-820-6788; internet www.tigo.sn; fmrly Sentel Sénégal GSM; name changed as above in 2005; mobile cellular telephone operator in Dakar, most western regions, and in selected localities nation-wide; 75% owned by Millicom International Cellular (Luxembourg), 25% by Senegalese private investors; Gen. Man. YOUVAL ROSH; 250,000 subscribers (2003).

Regulatory Authority

Agence de Régulation des Télécommunications et des Postes (ARTP): route des Almadies Angle Dioulikayes, BP 14130, Dakar-Peytavin; tel. 33-869-0369; fax 33-869-0370; e-mail contact@artp.sn; internet www.artp.sn; f. 2001; Pres. Prof. ABDOULAYE SAKHO; Dir-Gen. NDONGO DIAO.

BROADCASTING

Regulatory Authority

Haut Conseil de l'Audiovisuel: Immeuble Fahd, Dakar; tel. and fax 33-823-4784; f. 1991; Pres. AMINATA CISSÉ NIANG.

Radio

Radiodiffusion-Télévision Sénégalaise (RTS): Triangle sud, angle ave Malick Sy, BP 1765, Dakar; tel. 33-849-1212; fax 33-822-3490; e-mail rts@rts.sn; internet www.rts.sn; f. 1992; state broadcasting co; broadcasts 2 national and 8 regional stations; Dir-Gen. RACINE TALLA.

Radio Sénégal Internationale: Triangle sud, angle ave El Hadj Malick Sy, BP 1765, Dakar; tel. 33-849-1212; fax 33-822-3490; f. 2001; broadcasts news and information programmes in French, English, Arabic, Portuguese, Spanish, Italian, Soninké, Pulaar and Wolof from 14 transmitters across Senegal and on cable; Dir CHÉRIF THIAM.

RST1: Triangle sud, angle ave El Hadj Malick Sy, BP 1765, Dakar; tel. 33-849-1212; fax 33-822-3490; f. 1992; broadcasts in French, Arabic and 6 vernacular languages from 16 transmitters across Senegal; Dir MANSOUR SOW.

JDP FM (Jeunesse, Développement, Paix): Dakar; tel. 33-991-4813; e-mail abdousarr@orange.sn; Dir ABDOU SARR.

Oxy-Jeunes: Fojes BP 18303, Pikine, Dakar; tel. 33-834-4919; fax 33-827-3215; e-mail cheikh_seck@eudoramail.com; f. 1999; youth and community radio station supported by the World Asscn of Community Radio Stations and the Catholic Organization for Development and Peace.

Radio Nostalgie Dakar: BP 21021, Dakar; tel. 33-821-2121; fax 33-822-2222; e-mail nostafric@globeaccess.net; f. 1995; music; broadcasts in French and Wolof; Gen. Man. SAUL SAVÎOTE.

Radio PENC-MI: BP 51, Khombole; tel. 33-957-9103; fax 33-824-5898; e-mail rdoucoure@oxfam.org.uk.

Radio Rurale FM Awagna de Bignona: BP 72, Bignona; tel. 33-994-1021; fax 33-994-1909; e-mail mksonko2000@yahoo.fr.

Sud FM: Immeuble Fahd, 5e étage, BP 4130, Dakar; tel. 33-865-0888; fax 33-822-5290; e-mail info@sudonline.sn; internet www.sudfm.net; f. 1994; operated by Sud-Communication; regional stations in Saint-Louis, Kaolack, Louga, Thiès, Ziguinchor and Diourbel; Dir-Gen. OUMAR-DIOUF FALL.

Wal Fadjri FM: Sicap Sacré-Coeur no 8542, BP 576, Dakar; tel. 33-824-2343; fax 33-824-2346; internet www.walf.sn/radio; f. 1997; Islamic broadcaster; Exec. Dir MBAYE SIDY MBAYE.

Senegal also receives broadcasts from Radio France Internationale (RFI), the French-language service of the British Broadcasting Corporation (BBC) and Radio Chine Internationale.

Television

Radiodiffusion-Télévision Sénégalaise (RTS): see Radio; Dir of Television RACINE TALLA.

Canal Horizons Sénégal: 31 ave Albert Sarrault, BP 1390, Dakar; tel. 33-889-5050; fax 33-823-3030; e-mail infos@canalhorizons.sn; internet www.canalhorizons.com; f. 1990; private encrypted channel; 18.8% owned by RTS and Société Nationale des Télécommunications du Sénégal, 15% by Canal Horizons (France); Man. Dir BÉNÉDICTE CHENUET.

Réseau MMDS-EXCAF Télécom: rue 14 prolongée, HLM 1, Domaine Industriel SODIDA, BP 1656, Dakar; tel. 33-824-2424; fax 33-824-2191; broadcasts selection of African, US, European and Saudi Arabian channels.

The French television stations France-2, TV5 and Arte France are also broadcast to Senegal.

Finance

(cap. = capital; res = reserves; dep. = deposits; m. = million; br(s). = branch(es); amounts in francs CFA)

BANKING

In 2009 there were 18 commercial banks and three other financial institutions in Senegal.

Central Bank

Banque Centrale des Etats de l'Afrique de l'Ouest (BCEAO): blvd du Général de Gaulle, angle rue 11, BP 3159, Dakar; tel. 33-889-4545; fax 33-823-5757; e-mail akangni@bceao.int; internet www.bceao.int; f. 1962; bank of issue for mem. states of the Union Economique et Monétaire Ouest-Africaine (UEMOA, comprising Benin, Burkina Faso, Côte d'Ivoire, Guinea-Bissau, Mali, Niger, Senegal and Togo); cap. 134,120m., res 1,474,195m., dep. 2,124,051m. (Dec. 2009); Gov. KONÉ TIÉMOKO MEYLIET; Dir in Senegal FATIMATIOU ZAHRA DIOP; brs at Kaolack and Ziguinchor.

Commercial Banks

Bank of Africa—Sénégal: Résidence Excellence, 4 ave Léopold Sédar Senghor, BP 1992, Dakar; tel. 33-849-6240; fax 33-842-1667; e-mail information@boasenegal.com; internet www.boasenegal.com; f. 2001; cap. 2,750m., res 82,011m., dep. 48,703m. (Dec. 2007); Pres. PAUL DERREUMAUX; Dir-Gen. FAUSTIN AMOUSSOU; 8 brs.

Banque Internationale pour le Commerce et l'Industrie du Sénégal (BICIS): 2 ave Léopold Sédar Senghor, BP 392, Dakar; tel. 33-839-0390; fax 33-823-0737; e-mail bicis@africa.bnpparibas.com; internet www.bicis.sn; f. 1962; 54.11% owned by Groupe BNP Paribas (France); cap. 5,000m., res 21,473m., dep. 272,099m. (Dec. 2008); Chair. LANDING SANÉ; Dir-Gen. AMADOU KANE; 17 brs.

CBAO Groupe Attijariwafa bank: 1 pl. de l'Indépendance, BP 129, Dakar; tel. 33-849-9696; fax 33-823-2005; e-mail cbao@cbao.sn; internet www.cbao.sn; fmrly Compagnie Bancaire de l'Afrique Occidentale (CBAO), name changed as above in 2008 following merger with Attijari bank Sénégal; 100% owned by Attijariwafa Bank Group (Morocco); cap. 11,450m., res 48,171m., dep. 551,272m. (Dec. 2008); Pres. BOUBKER JAÏ; Dir-Gen. ABDELKRIM RAGHNI.

Citibank Senegal SA: Immeuble SDIH, 4e étage, 2 pl. de l'Indépendance, BP 3391, Dakar; tel. 33-849-1104; fax 33-823-8817; e-mail thioro.ba@citicorp.com; f. 1975; wholly owned subsidiary of Citibank NA (USA); cap. 1,626m., total assets 84,864m. (Dec. 2001); Pres. JOHN REED; Man. KEVIN A. MURRAY; 1 br.

Compagnie Ouest Africaine de Crédit Bail (LOCAFRIQUE): Immeuble Coumaba Castel, 11 rue Galandou Diouf, BP 292, Dakar; tel. 33-849-8100; fax 33-822-0894; e-mail locafrique@arc.sn; f. 1977; cap. 579m., total assets 1,241m. (Dec. 2003); Dir-Gen. AMADOU SY.

Crédit du Sénégal (CLS): blvd El Hadji Djily Mbaye, angle rue Huart, BP 56, Dakar; tel. 33-849-0000; fax 33-823-8430; e-mail cl_senegal@creditdusenegal.com; internet www.creditdusenegal.com; f. 1989 by acquisition of USB by Crédit Lyonnais (France); name changed as above in 2007 following merger with Crédit Agricole (France); 95% owned by Attijariwafa Bank Group (Morocco); cap. 2,000m., res 9,099m., dep. 107,497m. (Dec. 2009); Pres. and Chair. BOUBKER JAÏ; Dir-Gen. MOHAMED EL-GHAZI; 5 brs.

Ecobank Sénégal: 8 ave Léopold Sédar Senghor, BP 9095, Dakar; tel. 33-849-2000; fax 33-823-4707; e-mail ecobanksn@ecobank.com; internet www.ecobank.com; 41.45% owned by Ecobank Transnational Inc (Togo, operating under the auspices of the Economic Community of West African States), 17.0% by Ecobank Bénin, 12.43% by Ecobank Côte d'Ivoire, 4.56% by Ecobank Niger, 4.56% by Ecobank Togo; cap. 10,463m., res 3,351m., dep. 229,122m. (Dec. 2009); Pres. MAHENTA BIRIMA FALL; Dir-Gen. BOATIN KWASI.

International Commercial Bank (Senegal) SA: 18 ave Léopold Sédar Senghor, BP 32310, Dakar; tel. 33-823-5647; fax 33-842-2585; e-mail mail@icbank-senegal.com; internet www.icbank-senegal.com; f. 2006; CEO S. GANESH KUMAR; 1 br.

Société Générale de Banques au Sénégal (SGBS): 19 ave Léopold Sédar Senghor, BP 323, Dakar; tel. 33-839-5500; fax 33-823-9036; e-mail sgbs@sentoo.sn; internet www.sgbs.sn; f. 1962; 57.72% owned by Société Générale (France), 35.23% owned by private Senegalese investors; cap. 4,527m., res 28,301m., dep. 366,361m. (Dec. 2006); Pres. PAPA-DEMBA DIALLO; Dir-Gen. DANIEL TERUIN; 30 brs and sub-brs.

Development Banks

Banque de l'Habitat du Sénégal (BHS): 69 blvd du Général de Gaulle, BP 229, Dakar; tel. 33-839-3333; fax 33-823-8043; e-mail bdld10@calva.com; internet www.bhs.sn; f. 1979; cap. and res 19,661.0m., total assets 132,554.6m. (Dec. 2003); Pres. AHMED YÉRO DIALLO; Dir-Gen. BOCAR SY; 5 brs in Senegal and 5 brs abroad.

Caisse Nationale de Crédit Agricole du Sénégal (CNCAS): pl. de l'Indépendance, Immeuble ex-Air Afrique, 31–33 rue El Hadji Asmadou Assane Ndoye, angle ave Colbert, BP 3890, Dakar; tel. 33-839-3636; fax 33-821-2606; e-mail cncas@cncas.sn; internet www.cncas.sn; f. 1984; 23.8% state-owned; cap. 5,500m., res 2,065m., dep. 101,944m. (Dec. 2009); Pres. ABDOULAYE DIACK; Dir-Gen. ARFANG BOUBACAR DAFFE; 13 brs.

Société Financière d'Equipement (SFE): 2e étage, Immeuble Sokhna Anta, rue Dr Thèze, BP 252, Dakar; tel. 33-823-6626; fax 33-823-4337; 59% owned by Compagnie Bancaire de l'Afrique Occidentale; cap. and res 388m., total assets 6,653m. (Dec. 1999); Pres. ARISTIDE ORSET ALCANTARA; Dir-Gen. MOHAMED A. WILSON.

Islamic Bank

Banque Islamique du Sénégal (BIS): Immeuble Abdallah Fayçal, rue Huart, angle rue Amadou Ndoye, BP 3381, 18524 Dakar; tel. 33-849-6262; fax 33-822-4948; e-mail contact@bis-bank.com; internet www.bis-bank.com; f. 1983; 44.5% owned by Dar al-Maal al-Islami (Switzerland), 33.3% by Islamic Development Bank (Saudi Arabia), 22.2% state-owned; cap. 2,706m., res 1,335m., dep. 44,798m. (Dec. 2007); Pres. of Bd of Administration BADER EDDINE NOUIOUA; Dir-Gen. AZHAR S. KHAN; 4 brs.

Banking Association

Association Professionnelle des Banques et des Etablissements Financiers du Sénégal (APBEF): 5 rue Calmette, angle A. Assane Ndoye, BP 6403, Dakar; tel. 33-823-6093; fax 33-823-8596; e-mail apbef@orange.sn; Pres. ARFANG BOUBACAR DAFFE.

STOCK EXCHANGE

Bourse Régionale des Valeurs Mobilières (BRVM): BP 22500, Dakar; tel. 33-821-1518; fax 33-821-1506; e-mail nksy@brvm.org; internet www.brvm.org; f. 1998; national branch of BRVM (regional stock exchange based in Abidjan, Côte d'Ivoire, serving the member states of UEMOA); Man. NDÈYE KHADY SY.

INSURANCE

In 2010 the insurance sector comprised 22 companies: 13 non-life insurance companies, seven life insurance companies, one reinsurance company and one agricultural insurance company.

Allianz Sénégal Assurances: rue de Thann, angle ave Abdoulaye Fadiga, BP 2610, Dakar; tel. 33-849-4400; fax 33-823-1078; e-mail allianz.senegal@allianz-sn.com; internet www.allianz-senegal.com; name changed as above in 2009; Dir-Gen. OLIVIER MALÂTRE; also **Allianz Sénégal Assurances Vie**; life insurance.

AMSA Assurances: 43 ave ave Hassan II, BP 225, Dakar; tel. 33-839-3600; fax 33-823-3701; e-mail amsa-sn@amsa-group.com; internet amsa-group.com; f. 1977; fmrly Assurances Générales Sénégalaises (AGS); cap. 2,990m.; Dir-Gen. AÏDA DJIGO WANE; also **AMSA Assurances Vie**; life insurance.

Assurances La Sécurité Sénégalaise (ASS): BP 2623, Dakar; tel. 33-849-0599; fax 33-821-2581; e-mail ass.dk@orange.sn; internet ass-assurances.com; f. 1984; cap. 1,000m. (2007); Pres. MOUSSA SOW; Man. Dir MBACKÉ SENE.

AXA Sénégal: 5 pl. de l'Indépendance, BP 182, Dakar; tel. 33-849-1010; fax 33-823-4672; internet www.axa.sn; e-mail info@axa.sn; f. 1977; fmrly Csar Assurances; 51.5% owned by AXA (France); cap. 2,116m. (June 2011); Dir-Gen. ALIOUNE DIAGNE.

Compagnie d'Assurances-Vie et de Capitalisation (La Nationale d'Assurances-Vie): 7 blvd de la République, BP 3853, Dakar; tel. 33-822-1181; fax 33-821-2820; f. 1982; cap. 80m.; Pres. MOUSSA DIOUF; Man. Dir BASSIROU DIOP.

Compagnie Générale d'Assurances (CGA): 10 ave Léopold Sédar Senghor, angle rue Félix Faure, BP 50184, Dakar; tel. 33-889-6200; fax 33-821-3363; e-mail cgasen@orange.sn; internet www.cga.sn; f. 2007; Pres. MAMADOU LAMINE LOUM; Dir-Gen. MAMADOU MOUSTAPHA NOBA.

Compagnie Nationale d'Assurance Agricole du Sénégal: BP 15297, Dakar; tel. 33-869-7800; fax 33-860-6880; e-mail cnaas@cnaas.sn; internet www.cnaas.sn; f. 2008; agricultural insurance; Dir-Gen. AMADOU NDIAYE.

Compagnie Nationale d'Assurance et de Réassurance des Transporteurs: Rocade Fann Bel-Air, pl. Bakou, BP 22545, Dakar; tel. 33-831-0606; fax 33-832-1205; e-mail cnart@cnart.sn; internet www.cnart.sn; f. 2000; Dir-Gen. MOR ADJ.

Compagnie Sénégalaise d'Assurances et de Réassurances (CSAR): 5 pl. de l'Indépendance, BP 182, Dakar; tel. 33-823-2776; fax 33-823-4672; f. 1972; cap. 945m.; 49.8% state-owned; Pres. MOUSTAPHA CISSÉ; Man. Dir MAMADOU ABBAS BA.

Gras Savoye Sénégal: Immeuble Isocèle au Point E, rue de Diourbel, angle Rond-Point de l'Ellipse, BP 9, Dakar; tel. 33-859-4051; fax 33-824-9392; e-mail gs.senegal@sn.grassavoye.com; Man. THIERRY LABBÉ.

Intercontinental Life Insurance Co (ILICO): 16 rue de Thing, angle rue Moussé Diop, BP 1359, Dakar; tel. 33-889-8787; fax 33-822-0449; e-mail dakar@ilico.sn; internet www.ilico.sn; f. 1993; life insurance; fmrly American Life Insurance Co; Dir-Gen. YACINE DIOP DJIBO.

La Nationale d'Assurances: 5 ave Albert Sarrault, BP 3328, Dakar; tel. 33-822-1027; fax 33-821-2820; f. 1976; fire, marine, travel and accident insurance; Pres. AMSATA DIOUF; also **La Nationale d'Assurances—Vie**; life insurance.

Nouvelle Société Interafricaine d'Assurances Sénégal (NSIA): 18–20 ave Léopold Sédar Senghor, BP 18524, Dakar; tel. 33-889-6060; fax 33-842-6464; e-mail nsiasenegal@orange.sn; f. 2002; Dir-Gen. SIDY FAYE; also **Nouvelle Société Interafricaine d'Assurances Vie Sénégal**; Dir-Gen. RAMATOULAYE NDIAYE.

Salama Assurances Sénégal: 67 blvd de la République, BP 21022, Dakar; tel. 33-849-4800; fax 33-822-9446; e-mail salama@orange.sn; internet www.salama.sn; f. 1987; fmrly Sosar al amane, name changed as above in 2008; Dir-Gen. MAMADOU FAYE.

Société Africaine d'Assurances: Dakar; tel. 33-823-6475; fax 33-823-4472; f. 1945; cap. 9m.; Dir CLAUDE GERMAIN.

Société Nationale d'Assurance Mutuelle Vie (SONAM Vie): 6 ave Léopold Sédar Senghor, angle Carnot, BP 210, Dakar; tel. 33-889-8900; fax 33-823-6315; e-mail sonam@sonam.sn; f. 1973; Dir-Gen. SOULEYMANE NIANE; also **Société Nationale d'Assurance Mutuelle Assurances**; Dir-Gen. MAMADOU DIOP.

Société Sénégalaise de Courtage et d'Assurances (SOSE-CODA): 16 ave Léopold Sédar Senghor, BP 9, Dakar; tel. 33-823-5481; fax 33-821-5462; f. 1963; cap. 10m.; 55% owned by SONAM; Man. Dir A. AZIZ NDAW.

Société Sénégalaise de Réassurances SA (SENRE): 39 ave Georges Pompidou, BP 386, Dakar; tel. 33-822-8089; fax 33-821-5652; e-mail moussadiaw@senre.sn; internet www.senre.sn; cap. 600m; Pres. MAREME MBENGUE; Dir-Gen. MOUSSA DIAW.

Union des Assurances du Sénégal Vie (UASen-Vie): 4 ave Léopold Sédar Senghor, BP 182, Dakar; tel. 33-889-0040; fax 33-823-1108; e-mail uasenvie@uasen.com; Dir-Gen. ADJARATOU KHADY N'DAW SY.

Insurance Association

Fédération Sénégalaise des Sociétés d'Assurances (FSSA): 43 ave Hassan II, BP 1766, Dakar; tel. 33-889-4864; fax 33-821-4954; e-mail fssa@orange.sn; internet www.fssa.sn; f. 1967; fmrly Comité des Sociétés d'Assurances du Sénégal; Pres. MOR ADJ; Sec.-Gen. VADIOUROU DIALLO; 24 mems.

Trade and Industry

GOVERNMENT AGENCIES

Agence de Développement et d'Encadrement des Petites et Moyennes Entreprises (ADEPME): 9 Fenêtre Mermoz, ave Cheikh Anta Diop, BP 333, Dakar-Fann; tel. 33-869-7071; fax 33-860-1363; e-mail adepme@orange.sn; internet www.adepme.sn; f. 2001; assists in the formation and operation of small and medium-sized enterprises; Dir-Gen. MARIE THÉRÈSE DIEDHIOU.

Agence Nationale Chargée de la Promotion de l'Investissement et des Grands Travaux (APIX): 52–54 rue Mohamed V, BP 430, 18524 Dakar; tel. 33-849-0555; fax 33-823-9489; e-mail contact@apix.sn; internet www.investinsenegal.com; f. 2000; promotes investment and major projects; Dir-Gen. AMINATA NIANE.

Agence Sénégalaise de Promotion des Exportations (ASE-PEX): Amitié 3, No. 4426, Sotrac Mermoz, BP 14709, Dakar; tel. 33-869-2021; fax 33-869-6022; e-mail asepex@asepex.sn; internet www.asepex.sn; f. 2005; promotes exports; Dir-Gen. SAGAR DIOUF TRAORÉ.

Société de Développement Agricole et Industriel (SODAGRI): Immeuble King Fahd, 9e étage, BP 222, Dakar; tel. 33-821-0426; fax 33-822-5406; e-mail contats@sodagri.net; internet www.sodagri.net; f. 1974; cap. 120m. francs CFA; agricultural and industrial projects; Dir-Gen. BOUBACAR SY.

Société de Gestion des Abattoirs du Sénégal (SOGAS): BP 14, Dakar; tel. 33-854-0740; fax 33-834-2365; e-mail sogas@sentoo.sn; f. 1962; cap. 619.2m. francs CFA; 28% state-owned; livestock farming; Dir-Gen. TALLA CISSÉ.

Société Internationale des Etudes de Développement en Afrique (SONED—AFRIQUE): Parc à Mazout, Immeuble Ndiaga Diop, Colobane, BP 2084, Dakar; tel. 33-825-8802; fax 33-825-8881; e-mail sonedaf@orange.sn; internet www.soned-afrique.org; f. 1974; cap. 150m. francs CFA; Pres. ABDOUL EL MAZIDE NDIAYE.

Société Nationale d'Aménagement et d'Exploitation des Terres du Delta du Fleuve Sénégal et des Vallées du Fleuve Sénégal et de la Falémé (SAED): 200 ave Insa Coulibaly-Sor, BP 74, Saint-Louis; tel. 33-961-1533; fax 33-961-1463; e-mail saed@orange.sn; internet www.saed.sn; f. 1965; cap. 2,500m. francs CFA; 100% state-owned; controls the agricultural devt of more than 40,000 ha around the Senegal river delta; Dir-Gen. MAMOUDOU DEME.

DEVELOPMENT ORGANIZATIONS

Agence Française de Développement (AFD): 15 ave Nelson Mandela, BP 475, Dakar; tel. 33-849-1999; fax 33-823-4010; e-mail afddakar@groupe-afd.org; internet www.afd.fr; Country Dir DENIS CASTAING.

Centre International du Commerce Extérieur du Sénégal (CICES): route de l'Aéroport, BP 8166, Dakar-Yoff, Dakar; tel. 33-827-5414; fax 33-827-5275; e-mail cices@sn.ecobiz.ecowas.com; internet cicesfidak.com; Pres. MATAR GUEYE; Dir-Gen. BAÏDY SOULEYMANE NDIAYE.

Conseil des Investisseurs Européens au Sénégal (CIES): 2 pl. de l'Indépendance, BP 130, Dakar; tel. 33-823-6272; fax 33-823-8512; e-mail cies@orange.sn; f. 1993; Pres. GÉRARD SENAC.

France Volontaires: BP 1010, route de la VDN, Sacré coeur 3, Villa no 8908, Dakar; tel. 33-824-5295; fax 33-824-5390; e-mail afvp.dn@sentoo.sn; internet www.france-volontaires.org; f. 1972; name changed as above in 2009; Regional Delegate for Senegal, Cape Verde, Guinea, Guinea-Bissau, Mali and Mauritania JEAN-LOUP CAPDEVILLE; Nat. Delegate MAMADOU NDOUR CAMARA.

Groupements Economiques du Sénégal (GES): 21 ave Faidherbe, BP 282, Dakar; tel. 33-822-2821; Pres. MOR MATY SARR.

Service de Coopération et d'Action Culturelle: BP 2014, Dakar; tel. 33-839-5100; fax 33-839-5359; administers bilateral aid from France; fmrly Mission Française de Coopération et d'Action Culturelle; Dir JEAN-LUC LE BRAS.

Directory

CHAMBERS OF COMMERCE

Union Nationale des Chambres de Commerce, d'Industrie et d'Agriculture du Sénégal (UNCCIA): 1 pl. de l'Indépendance, BP 118, Dakar; tel. 33-823-7169; fax 33-823-9363; f. 1888; restructured 2002; Pres. MAMADOU LAMINE NIANG.

Chambre de Commerce, d'Industrie et d'Agriculture de Dakar (CCIAD): 1 pl. de l'Indépendance, BP 118, Dakar; tel. 33-823-7189; fax 33-823-9363; e-mail cciad@orange.sn; internet www.cciad.sn; f. 1888; Pres. MAMADOU LAMINE NIANG; Sec.-Gen. ALY MBOUP.

Chambre de Commerce, d'Industrie et d'Agriculture de Diourbel: 744 ave Léopold Sédar Senghor, BP 7, Diourbel; tel. 33-971-1203; fax 33-971-3849; e-mail mamandiaye@hotmail.com; f. 1969; Pres. MOUSTAPHA CISSÉ LO; Sec.-Gen. MAMADOU NDIAYE.

Chambre de Commerce, d'Industrie et d'Agriculture de Fatick: BP 66, Fatick; tel. and fax 33-949-1425; e-mail ccfatick@cosec.sn; Pres. BABOUCAR BOP; Sec.-Gen. SEYDOU NOUROU LY.

Chambre de Commerce, d'Industrie et d'Agriculture de Kaolack: BP 203, Kaolack; tel. 33-941-2052; fax 33-941-2291; e-mail cciak@netcourrier.com; internet www.cciak.fr.st; Pres. IDRISSA GUÈYE; Sec.-Gen. SALIMATA S. DIAKHATÉ.

Chambre de Commerce, d'Industrie et d'Agriculture de Kolda: BP 23, Quartier Escale, Kolda; tel. 33-996-1230; fax 33-996-1068; Pres. AMADOU MOUNIROU DIALLO; Sec.-Gen. YAYA CAMARA.

Chambre de Commerce, d'Industrie et d'Agriculture de Louga: 2 rue Glozel, BP 26, Louga; tel. 33-967-1114; fax 33-967-0825; e-mail ccial@orange.sn; Pres. CHEIKH MACKÉ FAYE; Sec.-Gen. CHEIKH SENE.

Chambre de Commerce, d'Industrie et d'Agriculture de Matam: BP 95, Matam; tel. and fax 33-966-6591; Pres. MAMADOU NDIADE; Sec.-Gen. BOCAR BA.

Chambre de Commerce, d'Industrie et d'Agriculture de Saint-Louis: 10 rue Blanchot, BP 19, Saint-Louis; tel. 33-961-1088; fax 33-961-2980; f. 1879; Pres. El Hadj ABIBOU DIEYE; Sec.-Gen. MOUSSA NDIAYE.

Chambre de Commerce, d'Industrie et d'Agriculture de Tambacounda: 120 blvd Diogoye, BP 127, Tambacounda; tel. 33-981-1014; fax 33-981-2995; Pres. DJIBY CISSÉ; Sec.-Gen. TENGUELLA BA.

Chambre de Commerce, d'Industrie et d'Agriculture de Thiès: 96 ave Lamine Guèye, BP 3020, Thiès; tel. 33-951-1002; fax 33-951-1397; e-mail ccthies@cosec.sn; f. 1883; 38 mems; Pres. ATTOU NDIAYE; Sec.-Gen. ABDOULKHADRE CAMARA.

Chambre de Commerce, d'Industrie et d'Agriculture de Ziguinchor: rue du Gen. de Gaulle, BP 26, Ziguinchor; tel. 33-991-1310; fax 33-991-5238; f. 1908; Pres. JEAN PASCAL EHEMBA; Sec.-Gen. MAMADOU LAMINE SANE.

EMPLOYERS' ASSOCIATIONS

Association des Industries et Prestataires de Services de la Zone Franche Industrielle de Dakar: km 18, route de Rufisque, BP 3857, Dakar; tel. 33-839-8484; fax 33-821-2609; Pres. MANSOUR GUEYE.

Chambre des Métiers de Dakar: route de la Corniche-Ouest, Soumbedioune, Dakar; tel. 33-821-7908; e-mail dakarmetiers@orange.sn; Pres. MAGATTE MBOW; Sec.-Gen. MBAYE GAYE.

Confédération Nationale des Employeurs du Sénégal: 5 ave Carde, Rez de Chaussée, BP 3819, Dakar; tel. 33-823-0974; fax 33-822-9658; e-mail cnes@sentoo.sn; internet www.cnes.sn; Pres. MANSOUR KAMA.

Conseil National du Patronat du Sénégal (CNP): 7 rue Jean Mermoz, BP 3537, Dakar; tel. 33-889-6565; fax 33-822-2842; e-mail cnp@orange.sn; internet www.cnp.sn; Pres. BAÏDY AGNE; Sec.-Gen. HAMIDOU DIOP.

Groupement Professionnel de l'Industrie du Pétrole au Sénégal (GPP): rue 6, km 4.5, blvd du Centenaire de la Commune de Dakar, BP 479, Dakar; tel. 33-849-3115; fax 33-832-5212; e-mail noeljp@orange.sn; Pres. BERNARD LACAZE; Sec.-Gen. JEAN-PIERRE NOËL.

Organisation des Commerçants, Agriculteurs, Artisans et Industriels: 52 rue Paul Holl, angle rue Tolbiac, Dakar; tel. 33-823-6794; fax 33-823-6550; Pres. ALASSANE SECK.

Rassemblement des Opérateurs Economiques du Sénégal (ROES): BP 5001/2, Dakar; tel. 33-825-5717; fax 33-825-5713; Pres. KHADIM BOUSSO.

Syndicat des Commerçants Importateurs, Prestataires de Services et Exportateurs de la République du Sénégal (SCIM-PEX): 7 rue Jean Mermoz, BP 806, Dakar; tel. 33-821-3662; fax 33-842-9648; e-mail scimpex@orange.sn; f. 1943; Pres. PAPA ALSASSANE DIENG; Sec.-Gen. MAURICE SARR.

Syndicat Patronal de l'Ouest Africain des Petites et Moyennes Entreprises et des Petites et Moyennes Industries: BP 3255, 41 blvd Djily M'Baye, Dakar; tel. 33-823-3732; e-mail mactarniang@yahoo.fr; f. 1937; Pres. MACTAR NIANG.

Syndicat Professionnel des Entrepreneurs de Bâtiments et de Travaux Publics du Sénégal: ave Abdoulaye Fadiga, BP 1520, Dakar; tel. 33-832-4708; fax 33-832-5071; f. 1930; 130 mems; Pres. OUMAR SOW.

Syndicat Professionnel des Industries du Sénégal (SPIDS): BP 593, Dakar; tel. 33-823-4324; fax 33-822-0884; e-mail spids@spids.sn; internet www.spids.sn; f. 1944; 110 mems; Pres. CHRISTIAN BASSE.

Union des Entreprises du Domaine Industriel de Dakar: BP 10288, Dakar-Liberté; tel. 33-825-0786; fax 33-825-0870; e-mail snisa@orange.sn; Pres. ARISTIDE TINO ADEDIRAN.

Union Nationale des Chambres de Métiers: Domaine Industriel SODIDA, ave Bourguiba, BP 30040, Dakar; tel. 33-825-0588; fax 33-824-5432; e-mail uncm@orange.sn; internet www.artisanat-senegal.org; f. 1981; Pres. El Hadj SEYNI SECK; Sec.-Gen. BABOUCAR DIOUF.

Union Nationale des Commerçants et Industriels du Sénégal (UNACOIS): ave Cheikh Ahmadou Bamba 3780, BP 3698, Dakar; tel. 33-821-6080; fax 33-822-0185; e-mail unacois.as@orange.sn; internet www.unacois.org; Pres. IDY THIAM; Sec.-Gen MAME BOU DIOP.

UTILITIES

Electricity

Commission de Régulation du Secteur de l'Electricité: Ex-Camp Lat Dior, BP 11701, Dakar; tel. 33-849-0459; fax 33-849-0459; e-mail crse@orange.sn; internet www.crse.sn; f. 1998; regulatory authority; Pres. MAÏMOUNA NDOYE SECK.

Agence Sénégalaise d'Électrification Rurale (ASER): Ex-Camp Lat Dior, BP 11131, Dakar; tel. 33-849-4717; fax 33-849-4720; internet www.aser.sn; Dir-Gen. ALIOU NIANG.

Société Nationale d'Electricité (SENELEC): 28 rue Vincent, BP 93, Dakar; tel. 33-839-3030; fax 33-823-1267; e-mail webmaster@senelec.sn; internet www.senelec.sn; f. 1983; 100% state-owned; Pres. CHEIKH TIDIANE MBAYE; Dir-Gen. SEYDINA KANE.

Water

Société Nationale des Eaux du Sénégal (SONES): route de Front de Terre, BP 400, Dakar; tel. 33-839-7800; fax 33-832-2038; e-mail sones@sones.sn; internet www.sones.sn; f. 1995; water works and supply; state-owned; Pres. ABDOUL ALY KANE; Dir-Gen. Dr IBRAHIMA DIALLO.

Sénégalaise des Eaux (SDE): Centre de Hann-Route du Front de Terre, BP 224, Dakar; tel. 33-839-3737; fax 33-839-3705; e-mail eau@sde.sn; internet www.sde.sn; f. 1996; subsidiary of Groupe Saur International (France); water distribution services; Pres. ABDOULAYE BOUNA FALL; Dir-Gen. MAMADOU DIA.

TRADE UNIONS

Confédération Nationale des Travailleurs du Sénégal (CNTS): 7 ave du Président Laminé Gueye, BP 937, Dakar; tel. 33-821-0491; fax 33-821-7771; e-mail cnts@orange.sn; internet cnts-senegal.net; f. 1969; affiliated to PS; Sec.-Gen. MODY GUIRO.

Confédération Nationale des Travailleurs du Sénégal—Forces de Changement (CNTS—FC): Dakar; f. 2002 following split from CNTS; Sec.-Gen CHEIKH DIOP; 31 affiliated asscns.

Confédération des Syndicats Autonomes (CSA): BP 10224, Dakar; tel. 33-835-0951; fax 33-893-5299; e-mail csasenegal@yahoo.com; organization of independent trade unions; Sec.-Gen. MAMADOU DIOUF.

Union Démocratique des Travailleurs du Sénégal (UDTS): BP 7124, Médina, Dakar; tel. 33-835-3897; fax 33-854-1070; 18 affiliated unions; Sec.-Gen. MALAMINE NDIAYE.

Union Nationale des Syndicats Autonomes du Sénégal (UNSAS): BP 10841, HLM, Dakar; fax 33-824-8013; Sec.-Gen. MADEMBA SOCK.

Transport

RAILWAYS

There are 922 km of main line, including 70 km of double track. One line runs from Dakar north to Saint-Louis (262 km), and the main line runs to Bamako (Mali). All the locomotives are diesel-driven. In

2009 plans were announced for the construction of a 4,000-km transcontinental railway linking Dakar with Port Sudan (Sudan).

Société Nationale des Chemins de Fer du Sénégal (SNCS): BP 175A, Thiès; tel. 33-939-5300; fax 33-951-1393; f. 1905; state-owned; operates passenger and freight services on Dakar–Thiès and Djour-bel–Kaoulack lines, following transfer of principal Dakar–Bamako (Mali) line to private management in 2003; suburban trains operate on Dakar–Thiès route as 'Le Petit Train Bleu'; Pres. DRAME ALIA DIENE; Man. Dir DIOUF MBAYE.

ROADS

In 2010 there were 14,785 km of roads, of which some 5,249 km were paved. A 162.5-km road between Dialakoto and Kédougou, the construction of which (at a cost of some 23,000m. francs CFA) was largely financed by regional donor organizations, was inaugurated in 1996. The road was to form part of an eventual transcontinental highway linking Cairo (Egypt) with the Atlantic coast, via N'Dja-mena (Chad), Bamako (Mali) and Dakar. In 1999 new highways were completed in the east of Senegal, linking Tambacounda, Kidira and Bakel.

Comité Executif des Transports Urbains de Dakar (CETUD): Résidence Fann, route du Front de Terre Hann, BP 17265 Dakar; tel. 33-859-4720; fax 33-832-5686; e-mail cetud@cetud.sn; internet www .cetud.sn; f. 1997; regulates the provision of urban transport in Dakar; Pres. OUSMANE THIAM.

Dakar-Bus: Dakar; f. 1999; operates public transport services within the city of Dakar; owned by RATP (France), Transdev (France), Eurafric-Equipment (Senegal), Mboup Travel (Senegal) and Senegal Tours (Senegal).

Dakar Dem Dikk: km 4.5, ave Cheikh Anta Diop, Dakar; tel. 33-865-1555; fax 33-860-3193; internet www.demdikk.com; f. 2001; Dir-Gen. MOUSSA DIAGNE.

Fonds d'Entretien Routier Autonome (FERA): Dakar; f. 2007.

INLAND WATERWAYS

Senegal has three navigable rivers: the Senegal, navigable for three months of the year as far as Kayes (Mali), for six months as far as Kaédi (Mauritania) and all year as far as Rosso and Podor, and the Saloun and the Casamance. Senegal is a member of the Organisation pour la Mise en Valeur du Fleuve Gambie and of the Organisation pour la Mise en Valeur du Fleuve Sénégal, both based in Dakar. These organizations aim to develop navigational facilities, irrigation and hydroelectric power in the basins of the Gambia and Senegal rivers, respectively.

SHIPPING

The port of Dakar is the second largest in West Africa, after Abidjan (Côte d'Ivoire), and the largest deepwater port in the region, serving Senegal, Mauritania, The Gambia and Mali. It handled more than 10m. metric tons of international freight in 2008. The port's facilities include 40 berths, 10 km of quays, and also 53,000 sq m of ware-housing and 65,000 sq m of open stocking areas. In addition, there is a container terminal with facilities for vessels with a draught of up to 11 m. In March 2005 the Governments of Mauritania, Morocco and Senegal agreed that a shipping line linking the three countries and to transport merchandise was to commence operations, following the completion of a tendering process. At 31 December 2012 Senegal's flag registered fleet numbered 88 vessels and amounted to 27,470 gross registered tons.

Dakarnave: blvd du Centenaire de la Commune, 2POB 438, Dakar; tel. 33-849-1001; fax 33-823-8399; e-mail commercial@dakarnave .sn; internet www.dakarnave.com; responsible for Senegalese ship-yards; owned by Chantier Navals de Dakar, SA (Dakarnave), a subsidiary of Lisnave International, Portugal; CEO FREDERICO J. SPRANGER.

Maersk Sénégal: route de Rufisque, BP 3836, Dakar; tel. 33-859-1111; fax 33-832-1331; e-mail senmkt@maersk.com; internet www .maersksealand.com/senegal; f. 1986.

SDV Sénégal: 47 ave Albert Sarrault, BP 233, Dakar; tel. 33-839-0000; fax 33-839-0069; e-mail sdv.shipping@sn.dti.bollore.com; f. 1936; 51.6% owned by Groupe Bolloré (France); shipping agents, warehousing; Pres. ANDRÉ GUILLABERT; Dir-Gen. BERNARD FRAUD.

Société Maritime de l'Atlantique (SOMAT): c/o Port Autonome de Dakar, BP 3195, Dakar; internet www.somat.sn; f. 2005; 51% owned by Compagnie Marocaine de Navigation, COMANAV (Morocco), 24.5% by Conseil Sénégalais des Chargeurs, COSEC, 24.5% by Société Nationale de Port Autonome de Dakar, PAD; operates foot passenger and freight ferry service between Dakar and Ziguinchor (Casamance).

Société Nationale de Port Autonome de Dakar (PAD): 21 blvd de la Libération, BP 3195, Dakar; tel. 33-823-4545; fax 33-823-3606; e-mail pad@portdakar.sn; internet www.portdakar.sn; f. 1865; state-owned port authority; Pres. and Dir-Gen. BARA SADY.

SOCOPAO-Sénégal: BP 233, Dakar; tel. 33-823-1001; fax 33-823-5614; e-mail socopao@sn.dti.bollore.com; f. 1926; warehousing, shipping agents, sea and air freight transport; Man. Dir GILLES CUCHE.

TransSene: 1 blvd de l'Arsenal, face à la gare ferroviaire, Dakar; tel. 33-823-0290; fax 33-821-1431; e-mail transsene@transsene.com; internet www.transsene.com; f. 1978; CEO CHEIKH DIOP.

CIVIL AVIATION

The international airport is Dakar-Léopold Sédar Senghor. There are other major airports at Saint-Louis, Ziguinchor and Tamba-counda, in addition to about 15 smaller airfields. A new international airport (Blaise Diagne), near Ndiass, some 45 km south-east of Dakar, was expected to be operational in early 2014.

Agence Nationale de l'Aviation Civile du Sénégal (ANACS): BP 8184, Dakar; tel. 33-869-5335; fax 33-820-0403; e-mail daviacivile@sentoo.sn; internet www.anacs.sn; civil aviation author-ity; Dir-Gen. MATHIACO BESSANE.

Sénégal Airlines: Immeuble La Rotonde, rue Amadou Assane Ndoye, Dakar; e-mail contact@senegalairlines.aero; internet www .senegalairlines.aero; f. 2010; 36% state-owned; domestic and regional services; Dir-Gen. EDGARDO BADIALI.

Tourism

Senegal's attractions for tourists include six national parks (one of which, Djoudj, is listed by UNESCO as a World Heritage Site) and its fine beaches. The island of Gorée, near Dakar, is of considerable historic interest as a former centre for the slave trade. In 2010 some 900,000 visitor arrivals were recorded; receipts from tourism in that year were US \$453m.

Ministry of Culture and Tourism: Bldg Administratif, 3e étage, ave Léopold Sédar Senghor, BP 4001, Dakar; tel. 33-822-4303; fax 33-822-1638; internet www.culture.gouv.sn.

Defence

As assessed at November 2012, Senegal's active armed forces com-prised a land army of 11,900, a navy of 950, and an air force of 770. There was also a 5,000-strong paramilitary gendarmerie. Military service is by selective conscription and lasts for two years. France and the USA provide technical and material aid. In April 2010 President Abdoulaye Wade announced that Senegal was to reclaim all military bases held by France and that 900 of the 1,200 French troops currently stationed in Senegal were to be withdrawn; the 300 troops who remained in the country were to comprise non-combat forces. The withdrawal of the French military finally commenced in June 2011. In 2012 a total of 1,603 Senegalese troops were deployed abroad, of which 47 were observers.

Defence Expenditure: Estimated at 98,800m. francs CFA in 2011.

Chief of Staff of the Armed Forces: Gen. ABDOULAYE FALL.

Education

Primary education, which usually begins at seven years of age, lasts for six years and is officially compulsory. In 2009/10 primary enrol-ment included 75% of children in the relevant age-group (males 73%; females 78%), according to UNESCO estimates. Secondary educa-tion usually begins at the age of 13, and comprises a first cycle of four years (also referred to as 'middle school') and a further cycle of three years. According to UNESCO estimates, in 2009/10 secondary enrolment was equivalent to 37% of children in the relevant age-group (males 40%; females 35%). There are three universities in Senegal: the Université Cheikh Anta Diop and the Université du Sahel in Dakar, and the Université Gaston Berger in Saint-Louis. Some 92,100 students were enrolled in tertiary education in 2009/10. Since 1981 the reading and writing of national languages has been actively promoted, and is expressly encouraged in the 2001 Consti-tution. According to official figures, in 2010 spending on education represented 40% of total government budgetary expenditure, a rise of some 202% since 2000. However, the World Bank disputed these figures and estimated the level of spending at 32%.

SERBIA

Introductory Survey

LOCATION, CLIMATE, LANGUAGE, RELIGION, FLAG, CAPITAL

The Republic of Serbia is situated in the central Balkan Peninsula, in south-eastern Europe, and is landlocked. There are western borders (from south to north) with Montenegro, Bosnia and Herzegovina, and Croatia, a border with Hungary to the north, with Romania and Bulgaria to the east, and with the former Yugoslav republic of Macedonia to the south. Kosovo (a former Serbian autonomous province, which made a declaration of independence in February 2008) also lies to the south. Serbia includes the Autonomous Province of Vojvodina. The climate is continental, with steady rainfall throughout the year. The average summer temperature in Belgrade is 22°C (71°F), the winter average being 0°C (32°F). The official language is Serbian, which is officially written in the Cyrillic script. Orthodox Christianity is predominant, the Serbian Orthodox Church being the largest denomination. There are small Jewish and Roman Catholic communities, the latter principally in Vojvodina. The national flag (proportions 1 by 2) has three equal horizontal stripes, of blue, white and red. The capital is Belgrade (Beograd).

CONTEMPORARY POLITICAL HISTORY

Historical Context

A pact between Serbia (which was under Ottoman Turkish rule until the 19th century) and the other South Slavs was signed in July 1917, declaring the intention to merge all the territories in a united state under the Serbian monarchy. Accordingly, when the First World War ended, the Kingdom of Serbs, Croats and Slovenes was proclaimed on 4 December 1918.

Prince Aleksandar, Regent of Serbia since 1914, became King in August 1921. Following bitter disputes between Serbs and Croats, King Aleksandar assumed dictatorial powers in January 1929. He formally changed the country's name to Yugoslavia in October. Aleksandar's regime was Serb-dominated, and in 1934 he was assassinated in France by Croat extremists. His brother, Prince Pavle, assumed power as Regent. An anti-Government group, the Communist Party of Yugoslavia (CPY), had been officially banned in 1921, but continued to operate clandestinely. In 1937 the CPY appointed a new General Secretary, Josip Broz (Tito).

In March 1941 the increasingly pro-German regime of Prince Pavle was overthrown in a coup, and a Government that supported the Allied Powers of the Second World War was installed, with King Petar II as head of state. In April, however, German and Italian forces invaded, forcing the royal family and Government into exile. Resistance to the occupation forces was initially divided between two rival groups. The Yugoslav Army of the Fatherland (Četniks) operated mainly in Serbia and represented the exiled Government, while the National Liberation Army (Partisans), led by the CPY, under Gen. (later Marshal) Tito, recruited supporters from Bosnia, Croatia, Montenegro and Slovenia. Rivalry between the two groups led to civil war, eventually won by the communist Partisans. On 29 November 1943 the Partisans proclaimed their own government in liberated areas. King Petar II was deposed in 1944.

After the war ended, elections were held, under communist supervision, for a Provisional Assembly. The Federative People's Republic of Yugoslavia was proclaimed on 29 November 1945, with Tito as Prime Minister. A Soviet-style Constitution, establishing a federation of six republics (Serbia, Montenegro, Croatia, Slovenia, Macedonia, and Bosnia and Herzegovina) and two autonomous provinces, both within Serbia, was adopted in January 1946. The two autonomous provinces were Kosovo and Metohija, with a substantial Albanian population, but also the location of the seat of the Serbian Orthodox Patriarchate, and Vojvodina, with a large Hungarian population. In 1948 Yugoslavia was expelled from the Soviet-dominated Cominform (the official forum of the international communist movement). The CPY was renamed the League of Communists of Yugoslavia (LCY) in November 1952, by which time it had established exclusive political control. A new Constitution was adopted in January 1953, and Tito became President of the

Republic. Another Constitution, promulgated in April 1963, changed the country's name to the Socialist Federal Republic of Yugoslavia (SFRY). Although links with the USSR were resumed in 1955, Yugoslavia largely pursued a policy of non-alignment, the first conference of the Non-aligned Movement (see p. 477) being held in the Serbian and federal capital, Belgrade, in 1961.

In July 1971 President Tito introduced a system of collective leadership and regular rotation of personnel between posts. A collective federal Presidency, headed by Tito, was established. A new Constitution introduced in February 1974 granted the two autonomous provinces within Serbia substantially the same powers, with regard to representation at federal level, as the six republics, as a result of which three of the eight members of the rotating collective presidency represented Serbia and its provinces. In May Tito became Life President of the LCY. Tito died in 1980, and his responsibilities were transferred to the collective federal Presidency and to the Presidium of the LCY.

Inter-ethnic tensions, largely suppressed or managed during Tito's period in power, became increasingly evident after his death. This was particularly the case in Kosovo, where a state of emergency was declared in 1981, following widespread demonstrations by ethnic Albanian nationalists, in support of demands for the province to be granted the status of a republic within Yugoslavia. Tensions were exacerbated in April 1987, when thousands of Serbs and Montenegrins gathered at Kosovo Polje (Fushë Kosovë, the site of a renowned battle between Serbian forces and Osmanlı—Ottoman Turkish troops in 1389) to protest against harassment by the Albanian majority population, clashing violently with the security forces. The perceived failure of the Serbian and federal leadership to curb Albanian nationalism led to the dismissal in September of the First Secretary of the League of Communists of Serbia (LCS—the Serbian branch of the LCY), Ivan Stambolić. His replacement, Slobodan Milošević, had denounced the Serbian leadership's policy on Kosovo (which he regarded as being too sympathetic to the demands of ethnic Albanians) and promised to reverse the emigration of Serbs from the area.

During 1988 and 1989 ethnic unrest increased. Proposals to amend the Serbian Constitution to reduce the level of autonomy of Vojvodina and Kosovo were supported by regular demonstrations by Serbs. Protests against the local party leadership were organized by Milošević and his supporters in Vojvodina. In October 1988 rallies attended by some 100,000 demonstrators in Novi Sad, the administrative centre of Vojvodina, forced the resignation of the Presidium of the League of Communists of Vojvodina. Tension between the party leaderships of Kosovo and Serbia increased, and in November, following the resignation of several members of the Kosovo leadership, some 100,000 ethnic Albanians demonstrated in Prishtina (Prishtinë/Priština—the administrative capital of Kosovo) to demand their reinstatement. Public demonstrations in Kosovo were banned in late November. In May 1989 Milošević was elected President of the Serbian Presidency.

In January 1990 the abolition of the LCY's constitutional monopoly of power was formally approved. In May Borisav Jović of Serbia replaced Janez Drnovšek of Slovenia as President of the federal Presidency. In June the Serbian authorities dissolved the Kosovo Provincial Assembly. In response, a group of 114 ethnic Albanian deputies from the disbanded Assembly attempted to declare Kosovo's independence from Serbia. A new Serbian Constitution entered into effect in September, including provisions removing the autonomous status of Kosovo (which was officially renamed Kosovo and Metohija, the name used in 1946–74) and Vojvodina. In the same month a general strike was organized to protest against the mass dismissals of ethnic Albanian officials by the Serbian authorities. During November and December multi-party elections were held in four republics. In Serbia, amid allegations of widespread irregularities, Milošević was re-elected President, overcoming a challenge by Vuk Drašković of the nationalist and anti-communist Serbian Renewal Movement (SRM). In the Narodna skupština Republike Srbije (National Assembly of the Republic of Serbia—as the republican legislature had been renamed) 194 of the 250 seats were won by the Socialist Party of Serbia (SPS), led by Milošević, which had been formed by the LCS and a smaller left-wing faction.

Tensions between the republics following disagreement over the reconstitution of Yugoslavia increased in December 1990, when Croatia adopted a new Constitution, giving the republic the right to secede from the federation, while in Slovenia (following constitutional amendments in September 1989) a majority voted in favour of secession at a referendum. In January 1991 Macedonia declared its sovereignty and right to secede. In February Slovenia formally initiated its process of 'dissociation' from Yugoslavia, and Croatia asserted the primacy of its Constitution and laws over those of the federation. Later that month the self-proclaimed 'Serb Autonomous Region (SAR) of Krajina'—which subsequently formed part of a self-styled 'Republic of the Serb Krajina' (RSK)—declared its separation from Croatia and its intention to unite with Serbia. In May the population of Croatia voted in favour of independence at a referendum that was largely boycotted by the Serb minority, and armed clashes between Serbs and Croats ensued. On 25 June Slovenia and Croatia declared independence, after which federal troops attacked a number of targets in Slovenia, including Ljubljana airport, resulting in 79 deaths, according to official figures. Following mediation by the European Community (EC—now European Union—EU, see p. 281), in July agreement was reached on the immediate cessation of hostilities and on a three-month suspension in the implementation of dissociation by Croatia and Slovenia. The withdrawal of federal troops from Slovenia began almost immediately, but fighting intensified in Croatia, where federal troops increasingly identified openly with local Serb forces. By September Serb forces controlled almost one-third of Croatia's territory, and successive cease-fire agreements failed to end the conflict. In the same month, at a referendum in Macedonia, voters approved the establishment of an independent republic.

In October 1991 Croatia and Slovenia formally ended their association with Yugoslavia, the moratoriums on independence (agreed in July) having expired. In the same month the Assembly of Bosnia and Herzegovina declared the republic's sovereignty, despite the objections of ethnic Serb deputies. The federal Prime Minister, Ante Marković, resigned, having been defeated in a vote of no confidence in the bicameral Savezna skupština (Federal Assembly, comprising the directly elected Veće građana—Chamber of Citizens—and the indirectly elected Veće Republika—Chamber of Republics). In December, declaring that Yugoslavia had ceased to exist, Stipe Mesić resigned as President of the federal Presidency.

After the independence of Croatia and Slovenia

Following the international recognition of the independence of Croatia and Slovenia, Serbia and Montenegro agreed to uphold the Yugoslav state. Macedonia's representative to the federal Presidency resigned in January 1992. In March Bosnia and Herzegovina declared its independence, the decision having been approved in a referendum that was largely boycotted by the Republic's Serb population. Later that month a severe escalation in the Bosnian conflict ensued, after the 'Serb Republic (Republika Srpska) of Bosnia and Herzegovina' was proclaimed.

In April 1992 the Savezna skupština adopted a new Constitution, formally establishing the Federal Republic of Yugoslavia, which comprised Serbia—including the provinces of Kosovo and Metohija, and Vojvodina—and Montenegro, thereby effectively acknowledging the secession of the four other former Yugoslav republics. (The Constitution was formally promulgated on 28 September.) In May elections to the Savezna skupština were held, the SPS enjoying considerable success as a result of an opposition boycott. In June Dobrica Ćosić became President of Yugoslavia, and the collective federal Presidency ceased to exist. In that month an alliance of opposition parties formed the Democratic Movement of Serbia (Depos), led by Drašković.

In May 1992 legislative elections, declared to be illegal by the Serbian authorities, were held in Kosovo for an Assembly of the self-proclaimed 'Republic of Kosovo'. In July the Savezna skupština elected Milan Panić federal Prime Minister. At a conference on the former Yugoslavia, which took place in London, United Kingdom, in August, Panić condemned the policy of 'ethnic cleansing', following the discovery of Serb-run concentration camps in Bosnia and Herzegovina, and reiterated the claim that there was no federal military involvement in the republic. The federal Minister of Foreign Affairs resigned in September, in

protest against Panić's policies; in November a further three federal ministers resigned.

Presidential and parliamentary elections, at both federal and republican levels, took place on 20 December 1992. Ćosić was overwhelmingly re-elected federal President. Milošević was re-elected President of Serbia, and the SPS secured 47 of the 138 seats in the Veće građana. Panić was removed as federal Prime Minister on 29 December, after losing a third vote of no confidence. The SPS won 101 seats in the 250-member Narodna skupština Republike Srbije, while the extreme nationalist Serbian Radical Party (SRP) secured 73. In February 1993 a new federal Government, comprising the SPS and the Democratic Party of Socialists of Montenegro (DPMS), was established, with Radoje Kontić as Prime Minister. In the same month the SPS formed a new Serbian Government, headed by Nikola Šainović. Depos, which had obtained 49 seats in the Narodna skupština, commenced a legislative boycott, claiming that the elections had been fraudulent.

On 1 June 1993 Ćosić was removed from office by a vote of no confidence in the Savezna skupština. Later that month the Savezna skupština appointed Zoran Lilić of the SPS as federal President. In October an attempt by the SRP to force a parliamentary vote expressing no confidence in the Šainović Government prompted Milošević to dissolve the Narodna skupština Republike Srbije.

In elections to the Narodna skupština Republike Srbije, held on 19 December 1993, the SPS obtained 123 deputies, winning 36.7% of the votes cast. Depos secured 45 seats, and the SRP 39. In February 1994 a new Serbian Government was formed, with the support of the six deputies of the New Democracy (ND) party. Mirko Marjanović was appointed Prime Minister, replacing Šainović, who became a Deputy Prime Minister in the federal Government. In September a new federal Government, in which Kontić remained Prime Minister, was appointed. The results of the elections in Serbia and the defection of the ND to support the Government permitted Milošević to consolidate his political control in Yugoslavia. The position of the already controversial SRP leader Vojislav Šešelj was further damaged when he was sentenced to a term of imprisonment in September for assaulting the parliamentary Speaker.

In August 1995, following a military offensive, Croatian troops took control of the RSK. The Yugoslav leadership protested strongly against the Croatian action, demanding UN intervention. The Croatian offensive resulted in the exodus of some 150,000 Serb refugees to Yugoslavia and Serb-controlled areas of Bosnia and Herzegovina. Many were settled in Vojvodina, prompting protests from ethnic Hungarians in that region.

In November 1995 peace negotiations were convened in Dayton, Ohio, USA. The conference, at which Milošević represented not only Yugoslavia, but also the Bosnian Serbs, resulted in an agreement on the future territorial and constitutional structure of Bosnia and Herzegovina, including the recognition of Republika Srpska as one of two constituent entities within the country. All UN sanctions against Yugoslavia were suspended later in the month. The SRP denounced the Dayton agreement, which was also criticized by the Democratic Party (DP), the Democratic Party of Serbia (DPS—founded in 1992 by former members of the DP) and the leadership of the Serbian Orthodox Church.

In June 1996 members of the increasingly influential Yugoslav United Left (YUL), led by Milošević's wife, Mirjana Marković, were appointed to the Serbian Government as part of a reorganization. A number of new coalitions were formed prior to elections, notably the Together (Zajedno) grouping, comprising the SRM, the DP, the DPS and the Civic Alliance of Serbia, and the United List, an alliance of the SPS, the YUL and the ND. On 3 November municipal elections, and elections to the Veće građana and the Skupština Republike Crne Gore (the Republican Assembly of Montenegro), were held. At the elections to the Veće građana, the United List secured 64 seats, Together took 22, the DPMS 20 and the SRP 16; of the 138 elected deputies, 108 were from Serbia and 30 from Montenegro. Following a second round of voting in the Serbian municipal elections, provisional results indicated that Together had obtained control of 14 principal towns, including Belgrade. However, most of the opposition victories were annulled by (SPS-dominated) municipal courts and electoral commissions, precipitating a series of demonstrations in Belgrade and other towns, which by December had developed into general protests against the Milošević Government. In late December the demonstrations degenerated into violent clashes with members of the security forces in Belgrade, in which two people were reportedly killed. Despite a ban ordered by the Ministry of Internal Affairs, anti-Government rallies continued. In early February 1997 the violent suppression of anti-Government demonstrations attracted further international criticism. On 11 February the Narodna skupština Republike Srbije voted in favour of reinstating the annulled results; Together consequently obtained control of the municipal assemblies in Belgrade and 13 other towns. At the same time seven ministers were replaced in a reorganization of the Serbian Government. Later in February Zoran Đinđić, the leader of the DP, was elected Mayor of Belgrade by Together members, who controlled 69 of the 110 seats in the city's municipal council.

In June 1997 the SRM withdrew from the Together coalition. The SPS nominated Milošević as a candidate for the federal Presidency. Later that month a DPMS committee declared its support for Milošević's candidature. On 25 June Lilić relinquished office. In July supporters of the Montenegrin Prime Minister, Milo Đukanović, voted to remove the Republic's President, Momir Bulatović, from the DPMS leadership. In mid-July the Savezna skupština elected Milošević to the federal Presidency. On 23 July Milošević resigned from the office of President of Serbia and was inaugurated as federal President.

In September 1997 students demonstrated in Belgrade in support of Đinđić, who, following the dissolution of Together, urged a boycott of the forthcoming Serbian presidential and legislative elections. At the elections to the Narodna skupština Republike Srbije, held on 21 September, the United List coalition won 110 seats, failing to secure an outright majority); the SRP received 82 seats and the SRM 45. In the concurrent presidential election, Lilić, the candidate of the United List, received 35.7% of the votes cast, while Šešelj, contesting the election for the SRP, won 27.3% of the votes, ahead of Drašković, with 20.6%. Some 62% of the electorate participated in the first round of presidential voting. In early October SPS and SRP councillors in the Belgrade municipal assembly voted in support of an SRM initiative to remove Đinđić from the office of Mayor of Belgrade. Security forces subsequently suppressed protests in Belgrade by supporters of the DP. In the second round of voting in the presidential election on 5 October, Šešelj won 49.1% and Lilić 47.9% of the votes cast. However, since less than 50% of the electorate had participated, the poll was invalid, and a new presidential election was scheduled.

In the Serbian presidential election, contested by seven candidates on 7 December 1997, the United List coalition was represented by the federal Minister of Foreign Affairs, Milan Milutinović, who secured 43.7% of the votes cast; Šešelj received 32.2% of the votes. In the second round, held on 21 December, Milutinović won 59.2% of the votes cast, defeating Šešelj. An official voter turn-out of about 50.1% was recorded. Šešelj claimed that the Serbian authorities had perpetrated electoral malpractice, while Organization for Security and Co-operation in Europe (OSCE, see p. 397) observers reported that severe irregularities had taken place. None the less, on 29 December Milutinović was inaugurated as President of Serbia.

In February 1998 Milutinović reappointed Marjanović as Serbian Prime Minister. Marjanović subsequently formed a new coalition Government, comprising 15 representatives of the SRP (including Šešelj, who became a Deputy Prime Minister), 13 representatives of the SPS, and four of the YUL. In May the Savezna skupština adopted a motion expressing no confidence in Kontić, which had apparently been initiated by DPMS deputies. Milošević's subsequent nomination of Bulatović as federal Prime Minister was approved by the Savezna skupština, and a new federal Government was established. Đukanović, however, declared Bulatović's Government to be illegitimate, and in June the Montenegrin legislature withdrew the 20 deputies representing Montenegro from the Veće Republika, to ensure that Milošević would not command the requisite two-thirds' majority for constitutional amendments. In August a new Montenegrin Government, headed by Filip Vujanović of the DPMS, announced that it had suspended links with the federal Government until Bulatović agreed to resign as Prime Minister.

During 1998 and early 1999 inter-ethnic hostilities in Kosovo intensified, and, following the failure of internationally sponsored negotiations, culminated in the aerial bombardment of military, and subsequently certain civilian, targets in Serbia and Montenegro in March–June 1999 by North Atlantic Treaty Organization (NATO, see p. 380) forces, which sought to defend Kosovo Albanians from the Serbian security forces (see Foreign Affairs). In late April Drašković was dismissed as Deputy Prime Minister of Yugoslavia, after he publicly opposed Milošević's refusal to comply with NATO demands.

In May 1999 the International Criminal Tribunal for the former Yugoslavia (ICTY, see p. 23) indicted Milošević, together with Milutinović, Sainović, the former Serbian Minister of the Interior, Vlajko Stojiljković, and the Yugoslav Army Chief of Staff, Gen. (retd) Dragoljub Ojdanić, for crimes against humanity. In June SRP ministers and legislative deputies temporarily suspended participation in the Serbian Government, in protest against Milošević's acceptance of the peace plan for Kosovo. From July a series of demonstrations was conducted by a grouping of opposition associations, known as Alliance for Change, in support of demands for Milošević's resignation. In August, meanwhile, the Montenegrin Government presented demands for the dissolution of Yugoslavia, and its replacement with an 'Association of States'.

In January 2000 a notorious Serbian paramilitary leader and war crimes suspect, Željko Ražnatović ('Arkan'), was shot dead in Belgrade. In February the federal Minister of Defence, Pavle Bulatović, was also killed. Milošević subsequently appointed Ojdanić to the post. In July the Savezna skupština approved constitutional amendments removing presidential term limits, providing for direct election to the presidency and the Veće Republika, and reducing Montenegro's status within Yugoslavia. At the end of July Milošević announced that federal presidential and legislative elections were to take place on 24 September. The Montenegrin Government announced that the republic would not participate in the forthcoming elections, in protest against the amendments, which the Skupština Republike Crne Gore had voted to reject. In August an alliance of 18 opposition parties, the Democratic Opposition of Serbia (DOS), presented the leader of the DPS, Vojislav Koštunica, as their joint candidate to oppose Milošević in the presidential election.

Domestic Political Affairs

Numerous allegations of electoral malpractice and intimidation surrounded the elections to the federal Presidency and legislature on 24 September 2000. Preliminary results released by the Federal Election Commission indicated that Koštunica had won 48% of the votes cast, compared with the 40% of the votes received by Milošević, and had thereby failed to obtain the 50% majority required to secure the presidency. Milošević subsequently insisted that a second round of voting be conducted on 8 October, while Koštunica rejected the results, claiming to have won the election outright. The international community declared its support for Koštunica and urged Milošević to accept defeat. The Yugoslav Army announced that it would not intervene on Milošević's behalf, while Serbian parties in Montenegro and the SRP acknowledged Koštunica's victory. Opposition supporters commenced a campaign of peaceful protest in Serbia (including a widely observed general strike), in an effort to compel Milošević to resign. On 5 October protesters at a mass rally in Belgrade overpowered security forces and seized control of the parliament building, the state television station and the official news agency, declaring Koštunica to be the elected President. One day later Milošević relinquished the presidency. Koštunica was inaugurated as President on 7 October. According to the final election results, Koštunica received 51.7% of the votes cast and Milošević 38.2%; in the concurrent legislative polls, the DOS secured 58 seats in the 138-member Veće građana, and the SPS 44. After the DOS negotiated an agreement with the SPS in mid-October, the Narodna skupština Republike Srbije was dissolved, and a transitional Government, in which the SPS retained the premiership, was installed, pending legislative elections in December. Since only about 30% of the Montenegrin electorate had participated in the voting, as a result of Đukanović's boycott, Koštunica was obliged to form an administration with the Socialist People's Party of Montenegro (SPPM), the only Montenegrin party to be represented in the legislature. A member of that party, Zoran Žižić, was nominated as Prime Minister, and a new federal Government, comprising representatives of the DOS and the SPPM, was established. The normalization of relations between Yugoslavia and the international community proceeded rapidly thereafter, and the country was formally admitted to the UN (from which it had been absent since the dissolution of the SFRY) on 1 November. In December Koštunica reorganized the armed forces, removing officers loyal to Milošević.

In the elections to the 250-member Narodna skupština Republike Srbije, held on 23 December 2000, the DOS secured a substantial majority, with 176 seats, while the SPS won 37 seats and the SRP 23. Later that month Đukanović announced proposals that Yugoslavia become a loose union of two separate, internationally recognized states. In January Đinđić was elected to the Serbian premiership, and a new Serbian Government, comprising members of the DOS, was installed later that month.

In early 2001 the federal Government came under increasing pressure from the EU and the USA to arrest Milošević and other war crimes suspects; Koštunica maintained that their extradition would contravene the Constitution. Following a warning by the USA that it would end financial aid to Yugoslavia unless it fully co-operated with the ICTY, Milošević was taken into custody on 1 April. The federal Public Prosecutor issued a series of charges against Milošević for abuses of power during his term of office (principally extensive embezzlement from state funds, and involvement in political assassinations, electoral malpractice and organized crime). Koštunica, however, refused to comply with international demands that Milošević be dispatched for trial at the ICTY, apparently owing to concern that his extradition might prompt political unrest. Meanwhile, the Montenegrin pro-independence alliance, led by the DPMS, won elections to the Skupština Republike Crne Gore on 22 April.

Milošević extradited to The Hague

In June 2001, following continued international pressure, the Serbian Government approved a decree providing for the extradition of Milošević and other indicted war criminals to the ICTY; supporters of Milošević subsequently staged a large demonstration in Belgrade. On 29 June Milošević was extradited to the ICTY. On the following day Žižić resigned as office of federal Prime Minister, in protest against the extradition. In July Koštunica appointed Dragiša Pešić, also a member of the SPPM, to the post. Later that month a reorganized federal Government was approved in the legislature. In August the division between Koštunica and Đinđić resulting from the Serbian Government's decision to extradite Milošević increased following the killing in Belgrade of a security agent, who had reportedly been investigating alleged connections of state officials to organized crime. Koštunica accused Đinđić's administration of failing to address widespread crime, and withdrew the DPS ministers from the Government.

In October 2001 the initial indictment against Milošević relating to Kosovo was amended, to read that he had organized security force operations against Kosovo Albanians, which had resulted in the expulsion of 80,000 civilians from the province. Also in October Milošević was further indicted in connection with war crimes perpetrated in Croatia in 1991–92; he was accused of ordering the forcible removal of the majority of the non-Serb population from one-third of the territory of Croatia. Four former naval officers were indicted for participation in an offensive against Dubrovnik, in Croatia, in late 1991. The former Commander of the Yugoslav Navy, Pavle Strugar, surrendered to the ICTY later in October 2001. (He was sentenced to eight years' imprisonment in January 2005, but was released owing to ill health in February 2009.) In November 2001 Milošević (hitherto indicted for crimes against humanity, breaches of the 1949 Geneva Convention, and violations of the laws or customs of war) was charged with genocide, in connection with the atrocities perpetrated by Serb forces in Bosnia and Herzegovina in 1992–95. He continued to refuse to recognize the authority of the ICTY, and 'not guilty' pleas were submitted on his behalf for all three indictments. The trial of Milošević, who had decided to conduct his own defence, officially commenced on 12 February 2002.

In December 2001 the Speaker of the Narodna skupština Republike Srbije, Dragan Maršićanin, the deputy leader of the DPS and a close associate of Koštunica, resigned, having accused parties belonging to the DOS coalition of electoral malpractice. In January 2002 the Narodna skupština Republike Srbije voted to partially restore the autonomous status of Vojvodina. In March a Serbian Deputy Prime Ministers, Momčilo Perišić, was arrested, after military intelligence sources claimed that he had given classified information to a US diplomat. He subsequently resigned from the Government. Đinđić rejected demands by Koštunica that he submit his resignation over the issue, and requested the dismissal of the head of the military security service responsible for Perišić's arrest. In June the DPS withdrew from the Narodna skupština Republike Srbije, in protest against the expulsion of 21 DPS deputies. The Serbian Government was reorganized in the same month.

Following protracted negotiations on the status of Montenegro, mediated by the EU from November 2001, the leaders of the Governments of Yugoslavia and its two republics signed a framework agreement on 14 March 2002, providing for the establishment of a State Union of Serbia and Montenegro. Under the accord, the two republics were to maintain separate economies, but were to have joint foreign and defence ministries, and

a joint presidency and legislature. Montenegro was to retain the right to refer the issue of independence to a referendum after a period of three years. Later in March the Liberal Alliance of Montenegro (LAM) withdrew from Đukanović's coalition in protest against the agreement, thereby ending the governing majority in the Skupština Republike Crne Gore.

Meanwhile, the USA renewed pressure on the federal Government to demonstrate co-operation with the ICTY. Following the expiry of a deadline for Yugoslav compliance with these demands, economic aid to Yugoslavia was suspended at the end of March 2002. In April the Savezna skupština finally approved legislation providing for the extradition of indicted war crimes suspects, and the issue of arrest warrants for those who did not surrender to the ICTY. Shortly afterwards one of the indictees, Stojiljković, committed suicide. Of 10 former Yugoslav state officials indicted, six (including Ojdanić and Šainović) agreed to surrender to the Tribunal. In early May 2002 Šainović was voluntarily transferred to the ICTY.

In late May 2002 the Savezna skupština officially approved the agreement on the creation of a State Union (which had been ratified by the legislatures of both republics in April). In July Lilić was arrested and extradited to the ICTY, having been subpoenaed as a prosecution witness in the trial of Milošević. It was announced that the presidential election in Serbia would be brought forward to 29 September, to allow the extradition of Milutinović to the ICTY.

At the Serbian presidential election, held on 29 September 2002, Koštunica won some 30.9% of the votes cast, while Miroljub Labus (the incumbent federal Deputy Prime Minister and Minister of Foreign Trade, who was supported by Đinđić) received 27.4% and Šešelj 23.2%; some 55.5% of the registered electorate voted. A second round of voting took place on 13 October between Koštunica and Labus, at which Koštunica secured some 68.4% of the votes cast. However, the election was declared invalid, owing to the participation of only 44.0% of the electorate, lower than the required minimum level of 50%.

State Union of Serbia and Montenegro

On 6 December 2002 a 27-member commission on constitutional reform, comprising representatives of the principal parties of the two republics, submitted a draft of the new Constitutional Charter for the proposed State Union. A third presidential poll in Serbia on 8 December (in which Koštunica won just 57.7% of the votes) was again annulled, owing to a rate of participation of 45.0%. On 30 December Milutinović was replaced as Serbian President, on an interim basis, by the President of the Narodna skupština Republike Srbije, Nataša Mićić. (Đukanović's pro-independence coalition, now known as the Democratic List for a European Montenegro, had obtained an overall majority in the republican legislature at elections held in Montenegro in October.)

In January 2003 Milutinović was voluntarily transferred to the ICTY, where he pleaded not guilty to charges relating to the 1999 conflict in Kosovo. In February 2003 Šešelj surrendered to the ICTY, where he was charged in connection with the forcible removal of the non-Serb population from Vojvodina and various regions of Bosnia and Herzegovina and Croatia in 1991–95. Meanwhile, the new Constitutional Charter, providing for the creation of the State Union of Serbia and Montenegro, was approved by the Narodna skupština Republike Srbije on 27 January 2003 and by the Skupština Republike Crne Gore on 29 January. On 4 February both chambers of the Savezna skupština approved the Constitutional Charter, thereby officially replacing Yugoslavia with the State Union of Serbia and Montenegro. On 25 February, in accordance with the Charter, the existing federal and republican legislatures elected a 126-member Skupština Srbije i Crne Gore (Assembly of Serbia and Montenegro), comprising 91 Serbian and 35 Montenegrin deputies. On 7 March a former Speaker of the Montenegrin legislature, Svetozar Marović, was elected unopposed as President of Serbia and Montenegro by the Skupština Srbije i Crne Gore. The President was also to chair a five-member Council of Ministers, which was approved by the Skupština Srbije i Crne Gore on 18 March.

On 12 March 2003 Đinđić, who had survived an assassination attempt in the previous month, was shot dead in Belgrade. Mićić imposed a state of emergency in Serbia, and on 18 March the Narodna skupština Republike Srbije approved the nomination of former federal Minister of Internal Affairs Zoran Živković to replace Đinđić as Serbian Prime Minister. At the end of March security forces discovered the remains of Ivan Stambolić, who had been abducted in August 2000. The Serbian authorities issued an international arrest warrant for Mirjana Marković and her son (who were in hiding in Russia), in connection with the killing of Stambolić; Milošević was subsequently also charged. In April the Skupština Srbije i Crne Gore voted in favour of extending co-operation with the ICTY, ending a stipulation that all war crimes suspects indicted by the Tribunal from that month be tried by domestic courts. Later in April the state of emergency in Serbia was ended.

In May 2003 Filip Vujanović was elected as President of Montenegro; he subsequently pledged to hold a referendum on Montenegrin independence within three years. In September the Serbian Government announced that Milošević would be arraigned at a special court on charges of ordering the killing of Stambolić. In October the ICTY issued indictments against four senior Serbian military and security officials, including the former Chief of General Staff of the Yugoslav Army, Col-Gen. (retd) Nebojša Pavković (whom Koštunica had removed in 2002), for war crimes perpetrated in Kosovo.

In November 2003 two small parties withdrew from the DOS coalition, thereby ending its parliamentary majority. The DOS subsequently dissolved, and Živković scheduled fresh elections to the Narodna skupština Republike Srbije. Meanwhile, on 16 November a further presidential poll in Serbia (at which the acting leader of the SRP, Tomislav Nikolić, secured 47.9% of the votes cast) was declared invalid, owing to a rate of electoral participation of only 38.8%. In December the trial began of 36 suspects charged in connection with Đinđić's assassination (15 of them—including Milorad 'Legija' Ulemek, the leader of an organized criminal group and a prominent member of a para-military unit of Milošević's regime—*in absentia*). At the elections to the Narodna skupština Republike Srbije, held on 28 December, the SRP, with 28.0% of the votes cast, secured 82 seats, the DPS (18.0%) 53 seats, the DP (12.8%) 37 seats, a newly emerged reformist grouping known as G17 Plus (11.6%) 34 seats, an alliance of the SRM and New Serbia (NS—7.8%) 22 seats, and the SPS (7.7%) 22 seats. Following lengthy inter-party discussions, the DPS formed a minority coalition with G17 Plus and the SRM-NS alliance, which would also be reliant on the support of the SPS. On 4 February 2004 Maršićanin was elected President of the Narodna skupština Republike Srbije, and thereby replaced Mićić as the Republic's acting President. In that month, so as to end the protracted political impasse, the Narodna skupština abolished the minimum rate of participation in republican presidential elections. A new Serbian Council of Ministers, headed by Koštunica, was formed in March; owing to Maršićanin's inclusion in the administration as Minister of the Economy, he was replaced as President of the Narodna skupština Republike Srbije (and therefore acting President of Serbia) by the hitherto deputy speaker, Predrag Marković. In April the Skupština Srbije i Crne Gore approved a reorganization of the State Union's Council of Ministers; Drašković received the foreign affairs portfolio, while Prvoslav Davinić of G17 Plus replaced Boris Tadić, the leader of the DP, as Minister of Defence. Ulemek surrendered to the Serbian authorities in early May.

Tadić elected President

Some 15 candidates contested the election to the presidency of Serbia, held on 13 June 2004. Nikolić secured 30.1% of the votes cast, while Tadić won 27.7%. Bogoljub Karić, a prominent businessman, won 18.5% of the votes, and Maršićanin (having resigned his ministerial post, and contesting the election for a DPS-led coalition) 13.5%. A second round between Nikolić and Tadić was conducted on 27 June; Tadić, who benefited from the transferred support of the governing coalition parties, was elected to the presidency, receiving 54.0% of the votes. At his inauguration on 17 July, Tadić spoke in support of the eventual integration of Serbia into the EU.

In December 2004 a former Yugoslav Army officer, Gen. (retd) Dragoljub Milošević, surrendered to the Serbian authorities and was extradited to the ICTY, where he was charged with crimes relating to the blockade and bombardment of the capital of Bosnia and Herzegovina, Sarajevo, in 1994. In January 2005, however, the USA expressed dissatisfaction with Serbia and Montenegro's co-operation with the ICTY, and announced a reduction in financial aid and the withdrawal of US technical advisers from Serbian ministries. Representatives of the international community accused the Serbian authorities of aiding the continuing evasion from the Tribunal of former Bosnian Serb military commander Gen. (retd) Ratko Mladić (who had originally been indicted in 1995 on a number of counts, including two of genocide), and cited his extradition as essential for Serbia and Montenegro's accession to NATO's 'Partnership for Peace' (PfP) programme. In February 2005 one of those indicted, a former

military commander in Prishtina, Gen. (retd) Vladimir Lazarević, agreed to surrender to the ICTY after meeting with Koštunica, and was subsequently extradited. Following further surrenders of a number of Serbian and Bosnian Serb war crime suspects mediated by the Koštunica Government, notably including that of Pavković in early April, EU officials commended Serbia's improved co-operation with the ICTY. On 12 April the European Commission indicated that sufficient progress had been made for Serbia and Montenegro to commence negotiations on a Stabilization and Association Agreement (SAA) with the EU.

In July 2005 Ulemek was sentenced to 40 years' imprisonment for involvement in the murder of Stambolić; the head of Milošević's secret service, Radomir Marković, received a 15-year term, while six former secret service officers received custodial terms. In September a further international arrest warrant was issued for Mirjana Marković, who remained in Russia. On 10 October negotiations on the SAA officially commenced between Serbia and Montenegro and the EU. In February 2006 the Montenegrin Government and opposition agreed that the planned referendum on Montenegrin's secession from the State Union would take place on 21 May.

On 11 March 2006 Milošević (whose trial had repeatedly been adjourned on grounds of ill health) died of a heart attack while in custody at the ICTY. Supporters of Milošević immediately criticized the medical treatment that he had received in detention and the Tribunal's refusal in late February to grant a request for his transfer to hospital in Russia.

Negotiations on the SAA with the EU were suspended on 3 May 2006, after the Serbia failed to meet a deadline for Mladić's extradition to the ICTY. Labus resigned from the post of Deputy Prime Minister of Serbia in protest at the failure of the authorities to apprehend Mladić, and also resigned from the leadership of G17 Plus, after the party refused to withdraw other representatives from the Government. Ivana Dulić-Marković (hitherto Minister of Agriculture) was appointed Deputy Prime Minister in June.

Montenegro's secession

At the referendum held in Montenegro on 21 May 2006, some 55.5% of votes were cast in favour of independence, narrowly exceeding the minimum requirement of 55% stipulated by the EU. Following Montenegro's declaration of independence two days earlier, on 5 June the Narodna skupština Republike Srbije officially declared Serbia as the successor state to the State Union of Serbia and Montenegro. In mid-June the Serbian Government adopted a decision recognizing Montenegro's independence, and the Ministers of Foreign Affairs of the two countries signed a protocol on the establishment of diplomatic relations on 22 June. At the end of the month Tadić made an official visit to independent Montenegro.

In July 2006 the trial of six formerly senior Serbian officials began at the ICTY: Milutinović, Sainović, Ojdanić, Pavković, Lazarević and Gen. (retd) Sreten Lukić (the former head of police in Kosovo) were charged with crimes relating to human rights violations committed in Kosovo. On 30 September the Narodna skupština Republike Srbije adopted a new draft Constitution by a unanimous vote (with 242 deputies attending). The new Constitution, which included increased provisions for the guarantee of human and minority rights, and which referred to Kosovo and Metohija as an integral part of the Republic, was approved by 53.0% of votes cast at a national referendum on 29 October and entered into effect on 8 November. At the end of November NATO invited Serbia to join the PfP programme; Del Ponte strongly criticized Serbia's admission to the programme (which officially took place on 14 December), in view of the authorities' continued failure to extradite Mladić. In December an SPS congress elected Ivica Dačić to replace Milošević as party leader.

At the elections to the Narodna skupština Republike Srbije, contested by 20 political parties and alliances on 21 January 2007, the SRP, with 29.1% of votes cast, obtained the largest number of seats (81), while the DP secured 23.1% (64 seats), and an alliance led by the DPS won 16.8% (47 seats). G17 Plus received 6.9% (19 seats) and the SPS 5.7% (16 seats), while a new reformist alliance led by the Liberal Democratic Party won 5.4% (15 seats). After smaller parliamentary parties declared reluctance to enter into a minority administration with the SRP, Tadić engaged in consultations on the establishment of a DP-led coalition government. EU officials urged the formation of an administration that supported democratic reforms, which would allow negotiations on an SAA to proceed (thereby abandoning the previous stipulation for the prior extradition of Mladić).

On 8 May 2007 Nikolić was elected President of the Narodna skupština Republike Srbije, after Koštunica instructed DPS deputies to support his nomination, prompting expressions of consternation from the international community. On 11 May Tadić announced that a coalition agreement had been reached between the DP, the DPS and New Serbia alliance, and G17 Plus, and that he had nominated Koštunica for a second term as Prime Minister. On 13 May Nikolić tendered his resignation from his new post. On 15 May, shortly before the expiry of the constitutional deadline, the formation of a coalition Government was approved in the Narodna skupština Republike Srbije; the administration notably included the new position of a Minister of Kosovo and Metohija. In the same month the Belgrade Special Court for Organized Crime convicted Ulemek and 11 others (five *in absentia*) for the assassination of Đinđić; Ulemek received a further sentence of 40 years' imprisonment. In early June the European Commission invited Serbia to resume negotiations on an SAA, citing the authorities' improved co-operation with the ICTY, following the arrest in Bosnia and Herzegovina of a former Bosnian Serb army officer, Zdravko Tolimir, who was regarded as a close associate of Mladić.

In December 2007 the Narodna skupština Republike Srbije approved legislation allowing a pre-term presidential election to be scheduled for early 2008. At the first round of the election, which was contested by nine candidates on 20 January, Nikolić won 40.0% of the votes cast and Tadić 35.4%. The second round was conducted on 3 February: Tadić was re-elected to the presidency, narrowly defeating Nikolić, with about 50.3% of the votes cast. The rate of participation by the electorate was estimated at some 67%. EU officials welcomed the election results. Tadić was inaugurated on 15 February.

Approval of Serbia's EU candidate status

In February 2008 Koštunica rejected Tadić's proposed political agreement with the EU, owing to his strenuous opposition to the EU's decision to establish EULEX Kosovo, a police and justice mission for the territory. Kosovo's declaration of independence on 17 February 2008, which was rapidly recognized by a number of EU nations, presented a further obstacle to prospects for EU integration, since the United Kingdom, France and Germany (principal supporters of Kosovo's independence) indicated that Serbia would be required to relinquish its territorial claim on Kosovo for accession. In early March Koštunica declared support for a draft resolution, proposed in the Narodna skupština Republike Srbije by the SRP, which made further progress towards EU accession conditional on the rejection of Kosovo's independence by the Union. However, on 8 March Koštunica resigned from the premiership, citing irreconcilable differences within the ruling coalition. On 13 March Tadić dissolved the Narodna skupština, at the request of the Government, and scheduled legislative elections for 11 May (when local elections and elections to the Vojvodina Assembly were also due to be conducted). In April EU foreign ministers reached a decision to sign the SAA with Serbia, an offer that was widely perceived as an effort to strengthen popular support for reformist parties contesting the forthcoming elections. On 29 April the EU signed the SAA; however, its implementation was to be suspended until EU member states agreed unanimously on Serbia's full co-operation with the ICTY.

At the legislative elections on 11 May 2008, an electoral coalition of parties supporting EU integration formed by Tadić, known as For a European Serbia—Boris Tadić, won 38.4% of the votes cast, according to official results, increasing the strength of the DP and its allied parties to 102 seats. The SRP secured 29.4% of the votes (78 seats), and the alliance between the DPS and New Serbia 11.6% of votes (30 seats); a coalition comprising the SPS, the Party of United Pensioners of Serbia (PUPS) and United Serbia obtained 7.6% (20 seats). The participation rate (including Serbs voting in Kosovo) was recorded at 60.1%. (Voting was repeated in three constituencies on 18 May, owing to irregularities.) At the poll to the Vojvodina Assembly, held in two rounds on 11 and 25 May, For a European Vojvodina (allied with Tadić) secured 64 seats and the SRP 24 seats in the 120-member Assembly.

In June 2008 Dačić announced that the SPS would enter into a coalition agreement the parties of Tadić's DP-led coalition. On 7 July a new Government, comprising representatives of For a European Serbia—Boris Tadić and the SPS-led alliance, narrowly secured approval in the Narodna skupština Republike Srbije. A former Minister of Finance, Mirko Cvetković (a member of the DP), became Prime Minister, while Dačić became First Deputy Prime Minister and Minister of Internal Affairs. Meanwhile, in June the Supreme Court (in a third retrial) sentenced

Radomir Marković and Ulemek to 40 years' imprisonment, and imposed lengthy custodial terms on five former state security and special police officers, for the attempted assassination of Vuk Drašković and the killing of four of his associates in 1999. On 21 July 2008 Tadić released a statement announcing that the former Bosnian Serb leader Radovan Karadžić, the most senior war crimes suspect indicted by the ICTY, had been located and apprehended in an operation by Serbian security officers. The arrest of Karadžić (who was transferred to the War Crimes Panel of the Belgrade District Court and subsequently extradited to the ICTY) was strongly welcomed by the international community.

In September 2008 the Narodna skupština Republike Srbije ratified the SAA; its implementation remained conditional on full co-operation with the ICTY, specifically the arrest of Mladić and the other remaining major war crimes suspect, Croatian Serb Goran Hadžić. Nikolić, who had accepted ratification of the SAA, resigned as acting leader of the SRP, owing to opposition to the Agreement from Šešelj, who was supported by more traditionalist elements of the party; Nikolić subsequently formed a breakaway organization, the Serbian Progressive Party (SPP). In October 2008 the trial began at the ICTY of Momčilo Perišić, the Chief of the General Staff of the Yugoslav Army in 1993–98, who had surrendered to the Tribunal in March 2005 after being indicted on 13 counts relating to war crimes committed in Sarajevo, the Croatian capital, Zagreb, and the Bosnian town of Srebrenica. In February 2009 the ICTY sentenced Sainović, Pavković and Milan Lukić to 22 years' imprisonment, while Lazarević and Ojdanić each received a term of 15 years, on charges relating to the killing and forced deportation of Kosovo Albanian civilians; Milutinović was acquitted on the grounds that he had not been directly responsible for the command of forces. In the same month the trial of Šešelj (who had repeatedly staged hunger strikes in protest at the proceedings) was suspended, owing to prosecution claims of witness intimidation. In June the war crimes chamber of Belgrade district court sentenced three former members of a Serb paramilitary unit to 20 years' imprisonment, and another member to 15 years, for killing a number of ethnic Albanian civilians in Kosovo in March 1999. In July 2009 the ICTY convicted Šešelj of being in contempt of the Tribunal, sentencing him to 15 months' imprisonment for disclosing personal details of three protected witnesses in a book that he had written and published on his website.

In November 2009 it was announced that Serbia had met EU requirements for the abolishment of visa requirements, which were thereby removed with effect from late December. The EU ended restrictions on the interim trade agreement with Serbia (which had been signed alongside the SAA) in December. On 22 December Serbia submitted an official application to join the EU. In March 2010 the Narodna skupština Republike Srbije adopted a resolution, submitted by the parties of the governing coalition, condemning the massacre of up to 8,000 Bosniak (Bosnian Muslim) males by Bosnian Serb forces at Srebrenica in July 1995. (At the reported insistence of the SPS, the term 'genocide' was not included in the resolution.) On 14 June 2010 the EU agreed to begin implementing the SAA with Serbia, following a favourable assessment of Serbia's co-operation with the ICTY.

Meanwhile, on 25 October 2010 the EU Council agreed to recommend Serbia's application for EU membership to the European Commission, but stipulated that further progress on the application would be dependent on Serbia's full co-operation with the ICTY.

In February 2011 Mlađan Dinkić, the leader of G17 Plus and the United Regions of Serbia (URS—a political grouping established in May 2010), was dismissed as Deputy Prime Minister and Minister of the Economy, after strongly criticizing dissent within the ruling coalition and Cvetković's leadership. Following popular protests against government economic policies, Cvetković announced an extensive reorganization of the Government, which was approved by the Narodna skupština Republike Srbije on 14 March. Notably, the number of ministries was reduced from 24 to 17, with Cvetković additionally assuming the finance portfolio; Verica Kalanović replaced Dinkić as Deputy Prime Minister, while Nebojša Ćirić was appointed Minister of the Economy and Regional Development.

On 26 May 2011 (shortly after the Chief Prosecutor of the ICTY, Serge Brammertz, presented a report to the UN Security Council criticizing Serbia's failure fully to co-operate with the Court) the Serbian authorities arrested Mladić in a village in northern Serbia, where he had resided under an assumed identity. The SRP organized a demonstration in Belgrade to denounce Mladić's arrest. Mladić was transferred to the ICTY on 31 May, after Serbia's war crimes court rejected his appeal against extradition on the grounds of ill health; his trial commenced on 3 June. The arrest of Hadžić, the final major war crimes suspect to be indicted by the ICTY, was announced by the Serbian authorities on 20 July; two days later, he was extradited to the ICTY to be brought to trial on 14 charges of war crimes and crimes against humanity. On 6 September Perišić was convicted by the ICTY and sentenced to 27 years' imprisonment. In October the European Commission issued a report stating that Serbia had made sufficient progress towards meeting EU criteria for a formal recommendation to be made that it become a candidate country. In December, nevertheless, Serbia failed to secure this status at an EU summit meeting in Brussels, Belgium, owing to the insistence of a number of EU leaders that the question of Serbia's refusal to recognize Kosovo (which was also unrecognized by five EU member states, including Greece, Romania and Spain) first be resolved. At the end of February 2012, shortly before a further EU summit meeting in Brussels, the Romanian Government unexpectedly presented objections to Serbia's candidacy relating to the treatment of the Vlach ethnic minority in Serbia (Vlachs being closely related to Romanians); these objections were subsequently withdrawn following an agreement between Serbian and Romanian officials. EU heads of state and government officially approved Serbia's candidate status on 1 March (following significant progress in dialogue between Serbian and Kosovo representatives in Brussels, although no date for the beginning of accession negotiations was announced.

Nikolić elected President

In March 2012 the Government scheduled legislative and local elections for 6 May. On 5 April Tadić formally resigned as President prior to an early presidential election (to take place concurrently with the legislative and local elections), at which he was to seek a second term; parliamentary speaker Slavica Đukić Dejanović assumed the presidency on an acting basis.

At the legislative elections on 6 May 2012 a grouping led by the SPP, Let's Get Serbia Moving—Tomislav Nikolić, secured 73 seats, with 24.0% of votes cast, while the DP-led coalition, Choice for a Better Life—Boris Tadić, received 67 seats, with 22.1% of the vote; Dačić's alliance of the SPS, the PUPS and United Serbia performed strongly, obtaining 44 seats (14.5% of the vote). At the presidential election, contested by 12 candidates, Tadić received 25.3% and Nikolić 25.1% of the vote; a second round was scheduled for 20 May. The DP-led coalition secured the highest number of votes at the elections to Belgrade's municipal council (although it failed to secure a majority of seats). Overall voter turn-out in the parliamentary and presidential elections was estimated at about 57.9% of the electorate. Despite complaints by opposition parties of irregularities, the OSCE endorsed the general conduct of the elections. The DP and the SPS subsequently reached an agreement on the establishment of a coalition, which was to support Tadić in the second round of the presidential election. Nevertheless, on 20 May Nikolić, with 49.5% of the votes cast, unexpectedly defeated Tadić (with 47.3%) in the second round of presidential voting, according to official results. Nikolić was inaugurated as President on 31 May.

On 28 June 2012 Nikolić nominated Dačić to form a new administration. Meanwhile, in June Serbia's war crimes court sentenced 14 former Serbian soldiers to prison terms of up to 20 years, after convicting them of involvement in the killing of 70 ethnic Croats in eastern Croatia in 1991. On 10 July 2012 the Constitutional Court ruled some 20 provisions of the self-proclaimed statute of Vojvodina (adopted in January 2010) to be unconstitutional, including one that named Novi Sad as the capital of the province. On 27 July the Narodna skupština Republike Srbije voted to approve the formation of a new coalition Government, headed by Dačić (who was to retain the internal affairs portfolio), and principally comprising members of the SPS, the SPP, the URS, the PUPS and the Social Democratic Party of Serbia (SDP). The Deputy President of the SPP, Aleksandar Vučić, was appointed as First Deputy Prime Minister, responsible for Defence, Security, the Fight against Corruption and Crime, and Minister of Defence, while leaders of the URS, the PUPS and the SDP became deputy premiers; other notable appointments included that of Dinkić as Minister of Finance and the Economy. Vučić was appointed head of the Council for National Security in August, and was elected as President of the SPP in September (following Nikolić's resignation from the post in late May). It was reported that Vučić had initiated investigations into alleged corrupt practices in state-owned companies, amid a further deterioration in the economy

(see Economic Affairs). As a consequence, in December Miroslav Mišković, a wealthy businessman who had served as a deputy premier under Milošević in 1990, was detained, together with his son and eight others, in connection with the alleged embezzlement of €30m. from state road-building contracts; he subsequently claimed to have financed some 20 Serbian politicians.

In February 2013 the Serbian media published leaked police surveillance material documenting meetings between Dačić (while he was Minister of the Interior in previous administrations) and a prominent member of a drugs-trafficking group. Dačić denounced the allegations as an attempt to discredit him and rejected DPS demands for his resignation, while the SPP also discounted the organization of early elections. The Government strongly welcomed a decision by the ICTY appeals chamber, on 28 February, to overturn the conviction and 27-year sentence imposed against Perišić in September 2011, on the grounds that he was not responsible for war crimes committed by the Republika Srpska army.

Recent developments: provisional agreement on Kosovo

On 7 February 2013 the European Parliament adopted a resolution in favour of the adoption of a date for the beginning of Serbia's EU accession negotiations, contingent on the Government's continued progress in the reform process and in dialogue with the Kosovo authorities in Brussels (see Foreign Affairs). On 19 April, with a decision on the opening of EU negotiations pending, Dačić signed a provisional accord with the Prime Minister of Kosovo, Hashim Thaçi. The agreement, which, *inter alia*, allowed both Serbia and Kosovo to seek EU accession without obstruction, was formally approved by the Serbian Government on 22 April. On the same day the European Commission issued a recommendation for the opening of Serbia's membership negotiations, which was to be discussed by EU foreign ministers in June.

Vojvodina

The Autonomous Province of Vojvodina comprises slightly more than one-quarter of the territory of Serbia (excluding Kosovo). The principal city is Novi Sad. Vojvodina had formerly been a Hungarian margraviate or banat (frontier province), in which the Habsburgs had settled other ethnic groups to defend Christendom against the Ottomans. A large Serb population had first settled there in 1690. In the 19th century the Habsburgs had created a province of Serbian Vojvodina, hoping to satisfy the aspirations of the Serb nationalists. At the end of the Second World War more Serbs had settled there and they became the dominant ethnic group, by 2002 constituting around 65% of the population. The Statute of Vojvodina, which is the constitutive act of the province, permits, in addition to the Serbian language, the official use of five other languages of the largest national minorities: Hungarian, Slovak, Romanian, Croatian and Pannonian Rusyn (Ruthenian).

Vojvodina (which had received the status of Autonomous Province in 1945) retained some autonomous powers until the late 1980s. In October 1988 demonstrations organized by supporters of the leader of the League of Communists of Serbia, Slobodan Milošević, secured a provincial leadership sympathetic to Serbian nationalist interests. The Hungarian Government expressed concern for the rights of the ethnic Hungarian minority (somewhat under one-third of the provincial population) during 1990 and 1991, particularly following the effective removal of Vojvodina's autonomous status by the 1990 Serbian Constitution. This change in the balance of powers was confirmed by the April 1992 Constitution of the Federal Republic of Yugoslavia (FRY). However, Vojvodina did retain a provincial Assembly, and the numerous minority ethnic groups of Vojvodina had political or social organizations to represent them.

In the mid- and late 1990s there were signs that opposition was increasing among the inhabitants of Vojvodina to the province's domination by the Serbian authorities. On 13 May 1996 a total of 17 political parties, associations and organizations signed a manifesto demanding the restoration of autonomy to Vojvodina. This move was the beginning of a campaign to amend the Serbian Constitution of 1990 and the federal Yugoslav Constitution of 1992 to restore the province's autonomous status, with full legislative, judicial and executive powers. Potential conflict emerged in May 2000, following the assassination of the President of the Executive Council (administration) of Vojvodina, Boško Perošević, for which opposition parties were blamed. Furthermore, in the same month the Serbian Government's decision to take control of the Studio B television station in Novi Sad, the administrative centre of Vojvodina, precipitated demonstrations and violent clashes that continued for several weeks. In early June opposition parties established a united Vojvodina Democratic Opposition. The governing coalition in Vojvodina opposed the constitutional changes instigated to the Constitution of the FRY (by then comprising only Serbia and Montenegro) by Milošević, as President of the FRY (to which position he had been elected in 1997), which, *inter alia*, removed limits on the federal President's tenure of office, provided for direct election to the presidency and the federal legislature, and reduced Montenegro's status within the FRY. In July 2000 Vojvodina threatened to declare independence in protest. Elections to the Vojvodina Assembly took place on 24 September, with a second round on 8 October. The Democratic Opposition of Serbia for Vojvodina secured 71.7% of votes cast, and 86 of the 120 elective seats. Pressures towards the centralization of power in Serbia and the FRY abated somewhat following the removal of Milošević from office in October.

Following the failure of the Coalition Vojvodina to secure representation in the Narodna skupština Republike Srbije in early legislative elections on 28 December 2003, its main constituent party, the Alliance of Vojvodina Hungarians, announced its withdrawal from the electoral coalition, and urged its supporters to campaign for the autonomy of the province. Nationalist violence in Vojvodina, with frequent attacks against members of the Croat and Hungarian communities, subsequently increased. The political leaders of Vojvodina's ethnic Hungarian community welcomed the victory of a reformist, Boris Tadić of the DP, in Serbia's presidential election in June 2004.

Elections to the 120-member Vojvodina Assembly took place, concurrently with local elections across Serbia, on 19 September 2004, with a second round conducted on 3 October. The SRP secured 36 seats, the DP 34 seats and the Alliance of Vojvodina Hungarians 11 seats. (A DP representative, Bojan Pajtić, subsequently became President of the Executive Council.) Maja Gojković, the SRP candidate, was elected Mayor of Novi Sad, after a second round of voting, attracting 49.9% of votes cast, narrowly defeating the DP candidate. In March 2005 the Executive Council adopted proposals (which were subsequently presented to the Serbian Government) on the province's future constitutional status, providing for full autonomy.

Following Serbia's declaration of independence from the State Union of Serbia and Montenegro (which had replaced the FRY in 2003) on 5 June 2006, a new Serbian Constitution, which was endorsed by national referendum on 28–29 October, granted Vojvodina powers of financial autonomy. Provisions were included for elections both to the Vojvodina Assembly and for deputies to the local self-government assemblies by the end of 2007. Pajtić welcomed the adoption of the new Constitution, which he regarded as facilitating the decentralization of power and regional development.

On 11 May 2008 elections to the Vojvodina Assembly took place concurrently with legislative and local government elections throughout Serbia; further rounds of voting followed on 18 May, 25 May, 1 June and 8 June. A DP-led alliance, For A European Vojvodina, secured a decisive victory with 65 of 120 seats in the Assembly. Support for the SRP was dramatically reduced, from 36 to 24 seats, while the Hungarian Coalition, led by the Alliance of Vojvodina Hungarians, won nine seats. In July Sándor Egeresi of the Alliance of Vojvodina Hungarians was elected as the new President of the Vojvodina Assembly, while Pajtić was re-elected President of the Executive Council with the support of 86 deputies in the Assembly. It was subsequently announced that the new Assembly would be required to adopt a new Statute of Vojvodina within 90 days of its inauguration.

In September 2008 it was announced that the governing coalition had agreed on the text of a new Statute of Vojvodina. On 15 October the Vojvodina Assembly adopted the draft Statute by 89 votes, and submitted it for the consent of the Narodna skupština Republike Srbije. Assembly deputies belonging to the SRP, the Democratic Party of Serbia (DPS) and New Serbia strenuously opposed the draft, particularly objecting to proposals that the Executive Council be renamed the Provincial Government and that the Assembly be granted the authority to adopt 'provincial legal acts'. Following the eventual ratification of the Statute by the Serbian legislature, it was to be returned to the Vojvodina Assembly for proclamation, whereupon it would officially take effect. A law on the transfer of certain powers from Serbia to Vojvodina was also to be adopted by the Narodna skupština Republike Srbije. However, the process of approval of the Statute in the Serbian legislature was subsequently obstructed by the parliamentary opposition parties, which com-

plained that it encouraged separatism and the creation of 'a state within a state'. In June 2009 the DPS adopted a declaration on Vojvodina, stating that, as an integral part of Serbia, its position should remain unchanged under the terms of the Serbian Constitution. In the same month it was reported that President Tadić, following a meeting with Pajtić, had agreed to submit the Statute to the Narodna skupština Republike Srbije for approval by August. At the beginning of December the Narodna skupština Republike Srbije adopted the Statute of Vojvodina, with some 137 votes cast in favour and 24 against. The Statute entered into force on 1 January 2010.

Elections to the Vojvodina Assembly took place on 6 and 20 May 2012, concurrently with presidential and legislative elections throughout Serbia. A DP-led alliance, Choice For A Better Vojvodina, obtained 57 of the 120 seats in the Assembly. An SPP-led coalition, Let's Get Vojvodina Moving, won 22 seats, while a coalition comprising the SPS, the PUPS, United Serbia and the SDP won 13 seats. A coalition Government by Bojan Pajtić of the DP was subsequently formed.

In July 2012 the Constitutional Court ruled some 20 provisions of the self-proclaimed Statute on Vojvodina to be unconstitutional, including that naming Novi Sad as the capital of the province, and that permitting Vojvodina to open a representative office in Brussels. Tensions between the provincial and national authorities subsequently intensified, in part reflecting the differing political complexions of the Governments in Serbia and Vojvodina. The publication, in early April 2013, by Pajtić of a Draft Declaration on the Protection of Constitutional and Legal Rights of Vojvodina, which was intended (following debate in the provincial Assembly) to protect the autonomous status of the province was a particular focus of discontent for Serbian nationalists. Later in the month around 30,000 protesters from across Serbia attended a rally outside the offices of the Vojvodina Government in Novi Sad to protest against what they claimed was support for separatism in the document and to demand the resignation of the provincial authorities; Pajtić alleged that the protests had been organized with the support of the Serbian Government.

Foreign Affairs
Kosovo

In 1996 a newly emerged ethnic Albanian paramilitary movement, the Kosovo Liberation Army (KLA), began to launch attacks against Serbian special forces operating in the province. In early 1998 the USA and the EU issued statements condemning the violent measures taken by the Serbian security forces in Kosovo to suppress the activities of the KLA, while also criticizing the means employed by the movement, which had announced its intention to achieve independence for the province through armed resistance. The US Government announced that it was to withdraw the concessions that it had granted to Yugoslavia in February, and threatened military intervention in Kosovo. A 'Contact Group', comprising the United Kingdom, France, Germany, Italy, Russia and the USA, was convened in London; member nations envisaged the imposition of further sanctions against Yugoslavia, unless the Serbian authorities acceded to a number of demands, including the withdrawal of security forces from Kosovo and the initiation of negotiations regarding the future status of the province. At the end of March the UN Security Council officially imposed an embargo on armaments against Yugoslavia. The members of the Contact Group (apart from Russia) announced in April that Yugoslav assets abroad were to be frozen and in May imposed a ban on foreign investment in Serbia.

In July 1998 Milošević agreed that diplomatic observers from the EU, the USA and Russia be allowed access to all regions of Kosovo to report on the activities of Serbian security forces. The Contact Group, meeting in Bonn, Germany, recognized for the first time that it would be necessary to include KLA representatives in future negotiations on the province. In September the UN Security Council adopted Resolution 1199, which demanded the immediate cessation of hostilities in Kosovo, the withdrawal of Serbian forces from the province, unrestricted access for humanitarian aid organizations, and the continuation of negotiations to determine the status of the province. Following reports of continued fighting south of Prishtina (Prishtinë/ Priština), NATO officially approved air bombardments against Yugoslavia, and issued an ultimatum to Milošević that attacks would commence unless he complied with UN demands by a stipulated date later that month. (Russia continued to oppose military intervention against Yugoslavia and indicated that it would veto a further Security Council resolution authorizing such action.) Following intensive discussions with the US special envoy, Richard Holbrooke, Milošević agreed to the presence in Kosovo of a 2,000-member OSCE 'verification force', and to NATO surveillance flights in Yugoslav airspace, to monitor the implementation of the Security Council's demands. It was subsequently reported that the majority of federal army units had been withdrawn from Kosovo, but that some 11,600 members of the special Serbian security forces remained in the province. NATO urged further progress in the withdrawal of Serbian forces from Kosovo, but at the end of October suspended the implementation of military action against Yugoslavia.

In November 1998 the deployment of OSCE observers in Kosovo commenced; however, intermittent violations of the cease-fire were reported. Following the outbreak of heavy fighting between the KLA and Serbian forces in northern Kosovo in December, it became evident that the OSCE monitoring force was inadequate (and had no mandate) for peace-keeping operations. In January 1999 the discovery that some 45 ethnic Albanian civilians had been killed at the village of Reçak (Račak) prompted international condemnation of the Serbian authorities. OSCE observers dismissed claims by the federal Government that those killed had been members of the KLA. At the end of January the Contact Group, meeting in London, decided that a peace conference should be convened in Rambouillet, France, with the participation of the KLA.

The peace conference began in Rambouillet on 6 February 1999. Under the Contact Group's proposed peace plan, the Serbian authorities would be required to withdraw most of the 14,000 armed and security forces from Kosovo, while the KLA would be required to disarm within a period of three months. It was envisaged that NATO troops would be deployed throughout the territory to enforce the peace agreement. Meanwhile, in early March it was reported that Serbian troops had forced several thousand ethnic Albanian civilians to flee from southern Kosovo, amid continued heavy fighting in the province. On 18 March the ethnic Albanian representatives signed the agreement in Rambouillet; however, the Serbian delegation continued to present objections and proposed amendments to the peace plan, which were rejected by the Contact Group. In the absence of a negotiated settlement to the conflict, the NATO Secretary-General ordered the commencement of air attacks against Yugoslavia, in a campaign, codenamed Operation Allied Force, which was designed to force Milošević's capitulation to the demands of the Contact Group.

On 24 March 1999 NATO forces commenced an aerial bombardment of air defences and military installations across Yugoslavia, notably in Belgrade, Novi Sad, Prishtina and Podgorica. The Yugoslav Government declared a state of war (which, however, the Montenegrin administration refused to recognize), suspended diplomatic relations with the USA, France, Germany and the United Kingdom (the countries directly involved in the attacks), and ordered foreign journalists to leave the country. The People's Republic of China and Russia immediately condemned the air offensive (which NATO justified on humanitarian grounds, despite the lack of endorsement by a UN Security Council resolution). The office of the UN High Commissioner for Refugees (UNHCR) reported that by early April some 390,000 ethnic Albanian refugees had fled from Kosovo to neighbouring countries since the NATO air campaign had commenced.

During April 1999 the NATO air offensive intensified. The increasing number of civilian casualties was condemned by opponents of the air offensive, particularly after NATO aircraft bombarded a convoy of ethnic Albanian refugees in Kosovo in mid-April, killing about 64. The Russian special envoy to the Balkans (and former premier), Viktor Chernomyrdin, became engaged in intensive mediation efforts with the Yugoslav Government, while urging a suspension of the NATO air offensive. NATO, however, continued to demand the full withdrawal of Serbian forces from Kosovo as a precondition to the suspension of air attacks. In early May the Group of Eight (G8—comprising seven Western industrialized nations and Russia), meeting in Bonn, agreed on general principles for a political solution to the conflict (which was referred to the UN Security Council). Shortly afterwards NATO forces bombarded the Chinese embassy in Belgrade, causing the Chinese Government to demand a cessation of the air offensive as a precondition to the discussion of the settlement at the UN Security Council. By 4 May UNHCR estimated that some 675,000 refugees had fled from Kosovo during the air bombardment (following an exodus of 360,000 in the previous 14 months).

On 3 June 1999 the Narodna skupština Republike Srbije formally approved a peace plan presented to the federal Government by EU and Russian envoys (based on the G8 principles). The peace agreement provided for the withdrawal of Serbian forces from Kosovo, and the deployment of a joint NATO-Russian peace-keeping force of about 50,000 personnel. Ethnic Albanian refugees were to be allowed to return to Kosovo, and the province was to be granted some autonomy under an interim administration. On 9 June a Military Technical Agreement, providing for the complete withdrawal of Serbian forces within 11 days, was signed by Yugoslav and NATO officials. On the following day the UN Security Council adopted Resolution 1244 approving the peace plan for Kosovo, and NATO announced the suspension of the air offensive, after it had been verified that the withdrawal of Serbian forces had commenced. NATO formally approved the establishment of a Kosovo Force (KFOR), and divided the province into five sectors (which were to be under the respective control of the United Kingdom, Germany, France, the USA and Italy). Shortly before NATO troops commenced deployment in Kosovo, however, about 200 Russian forces unexpectedly entered the province, and assumed control of the airport at Prishtina. An agreement was subsequently reached for a Russian contingent to participate in KFOR.

Under the terms of the UN Resolution, the UN Interim Administration Mission in Kosovo (UNMIK, see p. 86) was established as the supreme legal and executive authority in Kosovo, with responsibility for civil administration, and for facilitating the reconstruction of the province as an autonomous region. A 3,100-member international police unit (which constituted part of UNMIK) was to supervise the creation of a new security force in Kosovo. The OSCE was allocated primary responsibility for installing democratic institutions, organizing elections and monitoring human rights in the province. On 20 June 1999 NATO announced that the air campaign had officially ended, following the completion of the withdrawal of Serbian forces from Kosovo. The KLA subsequently signed an agreement with NATO, whereby the paramilitary organization was to disarm within a period of 90 days. On 24 June the Narodna skupština Republike Srbije formally ended the state of war in Serbia. Meanwhile, following the deployment of KFOR troops, nearly one-half of the ethnic Albanian refugees in neighbouring countries had returned to Kosovo by the end of the month, while an estimated 70,000 Serbian civilians had fled from the province, after reprisal attacks from KLA forces and members of the returning Albanian community. Under a programme to establish partial provisional self-government in the province, elections to a Kosovo Assembly (Kuvendi i Kosovës/Skupština Kosova) were conducted in 2001 (see the chapter on Kosovo).

The process towards an agreement on a future status for Kosovo was problematic, since the authorities of Serbia and Montenegro strongly favoured conditions of increased autonomy, but less than total independence, while the Kosovo Albanian population insisted on unconditional independence. In June 1995 UN Secretary-General Kofi Annan appointed the Norwegian ambassador to NATO, Kai Eide, as the special envoy responsible for assessing standards in Kosovo. On 24 October, after Eide submitted a favourable review on Kosovo, the UN Security Council endorsed the initiation of final status negotiations on Kosovo. In November the Serbian Government adopted a unanimous resolution rejecting any eventual proclamation of independence by Kosovo, while the Kosovo Assembly approved a motion stating that it would accept only independence as the final status of the territory. Later that month former Finnish President Martti Ahtisaari, who had been appointed by Annan as the Special Envoy for the negotiations of Kosovo's future status, commenced separate discussions with Serbian and Kosovo leaders.

The first round of final status negotiations on Kosovo was conducted in Vienna, Austria, in February 2006. At the instigation of Ahtisaari, direct high-level discussions, the first to involve the Presidents and Prime Ministers of Serbia and Kosovo since 1999, were conducted in Vienna in July 2006. The Kosovo delegation remained opposed to increased decentralization (including a Serbian proposal that a number of new Serb municipalities with autonomous powers be created), owing to concern that an effectively autonomous Serb polity would be established within the province. A new Serbian Constitution, which entered into effect in November, reaffirmed that Kosovo (again referred to as Kosovo and Metohija) was an integral part of the territory of Serbia, but was entitled to substantial autonomy. On 2 February 2007 Ahtisaari presented his proposal for the future status of

Kosovo to the Serbian and Kosovo authorities and invited the delegations to engage in consultations on the draft in Vienna. The discussions, which commenced on 21 February, ended on 10 March, with a meeting of the Serbian and Kosovo government leaders; Ahtisaari concluded that, in view of the failure of the delegations to compromise on previously stated positions, there was no further prospect of achieving a negotiated agreement. On 26 March Ahtisaari submitted to the UN Security Council the finalized Comprehensive Proposal for the Kosovo Status Settlement, which recommended independence, to be supervised and supported for an initial period by an international military and civilian presence. On 3 April, during a debate in the UN Security Council, Prime Minister Koštunica declared that Serbia rejected the Proposal (following a vote in the Serbian legislature in February). On 5 April Ahtisaari's plan was approved by 100 of 101 votes cast in the Kosovo Assembly. In August, after Russia obstructed the adoption of a resolution based on Ahtisaari's plan at the UN Security Council, a further series of negotiations began between Serbian and Kosovo delegations, with mediation by the USA, the EU and Russia. However, on 7 December it was announced that the negotiations had failed to result in an agreement.

In January 2008 Hashim Thaçi, the former leader of the KLA who had become Prime Minister of Kosovo, announced his intention to achieve independence for the territory. On 17 February the Kosovo Assembly adopted a declaration establishing the province as the Republic of Kosovo (Kosova), a sovereign state independent from Serbia, the resolution being based on Ahtisaari's Comprehensive Proposal for the Kosovo Status Settlement and in accordance with UN Security Council Resolution 1244. Serbia, with the continued support of Russia, immediately protested that the declaration of independence contravened international law and demanded that it be annulled. KFOR reinforced the border between Kosovo and Serbia, after the destruction of two border posts by Serb protesters. Several nations, including Albania, France, the USA and the United Kingdom, extended recognition to Kosovo on 18 February, followed by many others; Serbia immediately recalled its ambassadors based in those countries. On 21 February Serb protesters rioted in Belgrade, attacking several embassies, including those of the United Kingdom and the USA. In March the Serbian Government announced that it intended to submit a legal challenge against Kosovo's declaration of independence at the International Court of Justice (see p. 26) in The Hague, Netherlands, sand would also apply for international support at the UN General Assembly. After elections were conducted in predominantly Serb municipalities in Kosovo on 11 May, a parallel 'Assembly of the Community of Municipalities of the Autonomous Province of Kosovo and Metohija', unrecognized by the Kosovo Government, was established in June.

The deployment of an EU Rule of Law Mission in Kosovo (EULEX), which was scheduled to begin in June 2008 in accordance with a new Constitution, failed to proceed, owing to opposition from Kosovo Serbs and the Serbian Government (which was supported by Russia). In July the Serbian Government announced its decision to return its ambassadors to the EU nations that had recognized Kosovo, in order to further the country's EU integration aspirations. In October it was announced that the remaining ambassadors were to return to the countries from where they had been withdrawn (notably including the USA). On 8 October the UN General Assembly adopted a Serbian resolution requesting that the ICJ arbitrate on the validity under international law of Kosovo's unilateral declaration of independence from Serbia. Representatives of 77 countries (including the five of the 27 EU nations that had not recognized Kosovo) voted in favour of the Serbian resolution, while six opposed it and 74 abstained. In early November the UN Secretary-General presented an amended six-point plan on the reconfiguration of the international presence in Kosovo, under which officials in the Serb-majority areas would receive directives from UNMIK, while those in Albanian-majority areas would be the responsibility of EULEX. The UN Security Council unanimously endorsed the six-point plan on 26 November, and deployment of EULEX throughout Kosovo began in early December.

In March 2009 the Serbian War Crimes Prosecutor announced that he intended to request a reinvestigation into Serbia's claims that some 300 Serbs had been abducted and killed during the Kosovo conflict in connection with an international organ-trafficking group based in Albania. (In December 2010 a report by Swiss senator and Council of Europe rapporteur Dick Marty presented allegations of organ-trafficking, which implicated

Thaçi.) In December 2009 proceedings officially began at the ICJ to consider Serbia's challenge to the legality of Kosovo's declaration of independence. In January 2010 Serbia's Minister of Kosovo and Metohija, Goran Bogdanović, was expelled from Kosovo, shortly before meeting local Serb representatives, on the grounds that he had intended to conduct illicit political activities. On 22 July the ICJ issued a non-binding, advisory opinion that Kosovo's declaration of independence had not breached international law, UN Security Council Resolution 1244 or the constitutional framework. Serbia subsequently reaffirmed that it would continue to withhold recognition of independence for Kosovo.

In September 2010 the UN General Assembly adopted a resolution, supported by Serbia and the EU member states, urging a direct dialogue between Serbia and Kosovo on ensuing issues. Accordingly, in March 2011 EU-mediated discussions between Kosovo and Serbian delegations began in Brussels. In July it was announced that the discussions had resulted in agreement on free movement between the two states, the mutual recognition of university diplomas, and the establishment of a civil registry for Kosovo. Seeking to secure EU membership status for Serbia, in November President Tadić urged Kosovo Serbs to end their violent resistance to the authority of the Kosovo police, which had resulted in a series of clashes at Kosovo's border with Serbia (see the chapter on Kosovo); he also refused to endorse a referendum that was conducted in northern Kosovo in February 2012 (resulting in a vote not to accept Kosovo institutions). In March the Kosovo Government announced its intention to prevent the organization of ballots in northern Kosovo (which was requested by Kosovo Serb representatives) for Serbia's elections on 6 May. In April Bogdanović announced that the Serbian Government would not conduct local elections in Kosovo, in compliance with UN Security Council Resolution 1244; the Serbian authorities subsequently declared that a compromise agreement had been reached with the OSCE on the organization of presidential and legislative elections in northern Kosovo. Shortly before the elections, at least eight ethnic Albanians (one of whom was a candidate in the local polls) were arrested in southern Serbia on charges relating to armed clashes in the region in 2001.

The EU-mediated discussions were effectively suspended in mid-2012, following the election of President Nikolić, but resumed in October. In January 2013 local Serb leaders formally protested to Nikolić against a perceived relaxation in the stance of the Serbian Government, after it adopted a resolution reaffirming opposition to Kosovo's independence, but demanding a high level of territorial and political autonomy for Serb municipalities in Kosovo (thereby apparently implying disassociation from the Serb bodies). The DPS demanded the resignation of Prime Minister Dačić, following his remarks to journalists (which he later retracted) that Serbia could envisage Kosovo's admission to the UN as part of a compromise agreement. Later in January the Serbian police's removal of a war memorial to ethnic Albanian rebels in central Preševo, following increasing unrest in the region, prompted a mass rally in Prishtina. However, the discussions in Brussels resulted in Kosovo's appointment of a liaison officer to Serbia, the hitherto ambassador to Sweden, Lulzim Peci, on 23 January. On 4 February the Serbian Government reciprocated with the appointment of a senior negotiator, Dejan Pavićević, as its representative in Kosovo (to be based in EU offices in Prishtina). Nikolić and the President of Kosovo, Atifete Jahjaga, met for the first time, with EU mediation, in Brussels, on 6 February, after which both leaders pledged commitment to continued dialogue. Following further discussions, the two sides appeared close to agreement on the dismantling of a Serb 'Assembly', financed by Serbia, in northern Kosovo and the operation of a legitimate 'Association of Serbian Municipalities' in the territory. In early April, however, the Serbian Government rejected a proposed, EU-mediated accord, refusing to end opposition to Kosovo's accession to international organizations. Following increased pressure (with an imminent decision on the opening of Serbia's EU accession negotiations expected—see Domestic Political Affairs), on 19 April Dačić and Thaçi initialled an accord in Brussels; although Kosovo Serbs immediately rejected the agreement, it was approved by the Kosovo Assembly two days later.

Regional relations

On 27 February 2006 a case submitted to the ICJ at The Hague, Netherlands, in 1993 by Bosnia and Herzegovina against the Federal Republic of Yugoslavia (represented by Serbia, as its successor state and that of Serbia and Montenegro), claiming reparations for acts of genocide perpetrated against the Bosniak population in 1992–95, finally commenced. On 26 February 2007 the ICJ ruled that the Serbian state was not directly responsible for genocide or complicity in genocide in Bosnia and Herzegovina in 1992–95. However, the Court declared that Serbia was in violation of its obligation under international law by having failed to prevent the 1995 massacre in Srebrenica and to co-operate fully with the ICTY. In May 2007 the new Serbian Minister of Foreign Affairs, Vuk Jeremić, met his Bosnian counterpart for discussions in Sarajevo, in an effort to improve bilateral relations. Meanwhile, a 'special relations' agreement was signed by Republika Srpska and Serbia in September 2006; a number of economic co-operation accords were subsequently reached by the two Governments. In December 2009 direct rail connections between Belgrade and Sarajevo were restored. In February 2010 it was announced that, following Turkish mediation, Serbia had accepted the appointment of a new Bosnian ambassador (the post having remained vacant since 2007, owing to Serbia's rejection of the ambassadors nominated). On 1 March 2010 Ejup Ganić, the former President of the Federation of Bosnia and Herzegovina, was arrested at an airport in London, in response to a request issued by Serbia for his extradition on war crimes charges related to an attack on a Yugoslav army convoy near Sarajevo in May 1992. In July 2010 a court in London rejected the Serbian authorities' attempt to extradite Ganić from the United Kingdom, describing it as being politically motivated. In April Serbian President Boris Tadić met the Chairman of the Bosnian collective Presidency, Haris Silajdžić, in İstanbul, Turkey, with the mediation of the Turkish President, Abdullah Gül, after which Tadić and Silajdžić signed a declaration pledging to improve relations and resolve outstanding disputes. However, the Republika Srpska Government rejected the declaration, on the grounds that Silajdžić had failed to consult with the other members of the Bosnian presidency; the close relations between Serbia and Republika Srpska were also believed to have been strained following a resolution in March by the Serbian legislature condemning the Srebrenica massacre. In January 2013 Bosnian and Serbian prosecutors, meeting in Brussels, signed a protocol on co-operation in the prosecution of war crimes suspects.

During a visit to Zagreb for a regional energy summit meeting in June 2007, President Tadić issued an unprecedented apology to the Croatian people for atrocities committed by Serbs during the war. However, Croatia's relations with Serbia became strained after the Croatian Government recognized Kosovo's independence in March 2008. In November the ICJ ruled that it had jurisdiction to hear Croatia's case of genocide against Serbia, pertaining to crimes allegedly committed by Yugoslav forces in Croatia in 1991–95, which had been referred to the Court in 1999. In January 2010 Serbia submitted a genocide counter-case against Croatia for alleged war crimes committed during Operation Storm in 1995. In April 2010 the new Croatian President, Ivo Josipović, met Tadić and the Hungarian President for trilateral discussions in Budapest, Hungary, and subsequently visited Vojvodina; following the improvement in relations between Serbia and Croatia, it was reported that Tadić and Josipović favoured an out-of-court settlement of the two countries' reciprocal genocide cases submitted to the ICJ. In June the Serbian and Croatian Ministers of Defence signed a military co-operation agreement in Zagreb. Following the establishment of a new Croatian Government in December 2011, its Minister of Foreign Affairs indicated that Croatia might abandon its genocide case against Serbia at the ICJ, but later stipulated that the Serbian Government would first be required to meet conditions on missing persons, looted property and war crimes. Shortly before his election in May 2012, President Nikolić prompted protests from the Croatian Government after he referred to the Croatian town of Vukovar (a focal point of military activity by Serb forces in 1991, and which retained a substantial Serb population) as 'a Serbian town' during a media interview. In November Nikolić and other Serbian politicians reacted with outrage to the ICTY's reversal of guilty verdicts on retired generals Ante Gotovina and Mladen Markač, who in April 2011 had both been convicted on charges relating to the expulsion of ethnic Serbs from Croatia in 1995 (see Croatia). In January 2013 the Serbian Government requested the ICTY to consider reopening the case against Gotovina and Markač. In the same month an official visit by Croatian premier Zoran Milanović to Belgrade, where he met Prime Minister Dačić, was regarded as an initial move towards improving bilateral relations.

The decision of the former Yugoslav republic of Macedonia (FYRM) and Montenegro in October 2008 to extend recognition to Kosovo prompted strong protests from Serbia, which expelled the ambassadors of both countries (but in November invited the appointment of new envoys). In May 2009 Montenegrin President Filip Vujanović visited Belgrade, in an effort to improve bilateral relations, while President Tadić made a reciprocal visit to Montenegro in June. In October Serbia finally accepted Montenegro's nomination of a new ambassador. In January 2010 Serbia recalled its ambassador, in protest against Montenegro's decision to establish diplomatic relations with Kosovo; however, the Serbian ambassador returned to the Montenegrin capital of Podgorica in February. Following the EU accession aspirations of Serbia, in March 2013 the Governments of Serbia and the FYRM signed an agreement providing for improved bilateral relations and co-operation in the EU integration processes of both states.

Other external relations

Relations between Russia and Serbia were consolidated in early 2008, with the signature of an agreement whereby Serbia was to join Russia's 'South Stream' pipeline project (which was to supply natural gas from Russia to southern and eastern Europe) and Russian state-controlled energy producer Gazprom acquired a 51% share in the Serbian state-owned petroleum enterprise, Naftna Industrija Srbije. The sale of the majority share in Naftna Industrija Srbije was completed in February 2009; agreements with Serbia, together with Italy, Bulgaria and Greece, were signed in Sochi, Russia, in May. In October Russian President Dmitrii Medvedev made an official visit to Serbia (the first by a Russian head of state); he approved a loan of US $1,500m. to support Serbia's economy and signed a number of bilateral agreements with President Tadić. In March 2011 Russian Prime Minister Vladimir Putin visited Serbia, when he reiterated his commitment to the joint energy projects, and issued an offer to lend the Serbian Government $3,000m. for the purchase of Russian fighter aircraft and air defence systems. In November the Russian ambassador to Serbia, Aleksandr Konuzin, was strongly criticized by the ruling DP for perceived interference in Serbia's internal affairs, after he praised the nationalist SPP during a party rally in October; Konuzin had previously denounced the Serbian authorities at a security forum in Belgrade in September for failing to defend Serbian interests in Kosovo. In October 2012 a final investment agreement on the 'South Stream' gas pipeline was signed by Gazprom and the Serbian state-owned firm Srbijagas, allowing construction on the Serbian section (which was subsequently envisaged to begin in late 2013). In March Russia and Serbia signed a 10-year agreement that provided for increased exports of Russian natural gas to Serbia.

Having recalled all ambassadors from states that extended recognition to Kosovo following its declaration of independence in February 2008, the Serbian Government in July announced its decision to return its ambassadors to the EU member nations that had recognized Kosovo; the remaining Serbian ambassadors (including the ambassador to the USA) returned in October. Serbian Minister of Foreign Affairs Vuk Jeremić visited numerous states to urge their respective governments to withhold recognition of Kosovo. Following the arrest of former Bosnian Serb leader Radovan Karadžić in July, Serbia's relations with the EU and the USA improved significantly. During a visit to Serbia in May 2009, US Vice-President Joe Biden met President Tadić, and declared support for Serbia's aspirations for EU integration. In August Tadić made an official seven-day visit to the People's Republic of China, when he and Chinese President Hu Jintao signed a strategic partnership agreement, pledging to increase political, economic and trade co-operation. US Secretary of State Hillary Clinton visited Serbia in October 2010, and reiterated US support for the Serbian Government's objective of EU integration. In September 2011 Serbia hosted the 50th anniversary summit of the Non-aligned Movement (see p. 477).

CONSTITUTION AND GOVERNMENT

Under the terms of the Constitution, which officially entered into effect on 8 November 2006, legislative power is vested in the 250-member Narodna skupština Republike Srbije (National Assembly of the Republic of Serbia), which is directly elected for a period of four years. The President of the Republic, who is directly elected for a term of five years, nominates the Prime Minister for approval by the Narodna skupština. Executive power is vested in the Council of Ministers, which is proposed to the Narodna skupština by the designated Prime Minister. The Narodna skupština is to be dissolved if it fails to appoint a new Council of Ministers within 90 days of its inaugural session. The 11-member High Judicial Council ensures the independence of courts and judges, and is empowered to nominate or remove judges. Serbia formally comprises 24 administrative regions, including the seven regions of the province of Vojvodina, in the north of Serbia; the administrative regions are themselves divided into 170 municipalities.

REGIONAL AND INTERNATIONAL CO-OPERATION

Serbia is a member of the Organization for Security and Co-operation in Europe (OSCE, see p. 397) and the Council of Europe (see p. 260). In 2006 the North Atlantic Treaty Organization (NATO, see p. 380) invited Serbia to join its 'Partnership for Peace' programme. Serbia joined the Central European Free Trade Agreement (CEFTA, see p. 459) in 2007 and held its rotating chairmanship in 2010. On 22 December 2009 Serbia submitted an official application to join the EU.

Following Montenegro's achievement of independence on 3 June 2006, the membership of Serbia and Montenegro in the UN was inherited by Serbia as the successor state.

ECONOMIC AFFAIRS

In 2011, according to estimates by the World Bank, the gross national income (GNI) of Serbia, measured at 2009–11 prices, was US $41,237m., equivalent to $5,680 per head (or $11,640 per head on an international purchasing-power parity basis). During 2002–11, it was estimated, the population declined at an average annual rate of 0.4%, while gross domestic product (GDP) per head increased, in real terms, by an average of 3.6% per year. Overall GDP grew, in real terms, at an average annual rate of 3.2% in 2002–11; according to the World Bank, GDP increased by 1.8% in 2011.

Agriculture (including hunting, forestry and fishing) contributed 10.1% of GDP in 2012 and engaged 21.0% of the employed labour force in 2011. Serbia's principal crops are maize, wheat, sugar beet and potatoes. The cultivation of fruit and vegetables is also important. Agricultural GDP increased at an average annual rate of 0.7% during 2002–10, according to official figures; sectoral GDP rose by 0.8% in 2009 and declined by 0.5% in 2010.

Industry (including mining, manufacturing, construction and power) contributed 27.7% of GDP in 2012 and engaged 27.3% of the employed labour force in 2011. Industrial GDP increased at an average annual rate of 0.8% in 2002–10; sectoral GDP declined by 13.5% in 2009, and increased by 0.4% in 2010.

The mining and quarrying sector contributed 2.0% of GDP in 2012 and engaged 1.4% of the employed labour force in 2011. The principal minerals extracted are coal (mainly brown coal), copper ore and bauxite. Iron ore, crude petroleum, lead, zinc ore and natural gas are also produced. The GDP of the mining and quarrying sector increased at an average annual rate of 2.4% in 2002–10; mining GDP declined by an estimated 4.8% in 2009 and increased by 4.5% in 2010.

The manufacturing sector contributed 16.4% of GDP in 2012 and engaged 17.3% of the employed labour force in 2011. Manufacturing GDP increased at an average annual rate of 0.1% in 2002–10; the sector declined by 15.6% in 2009, but expanded by 3.2% in 2010.

The construction sector contributed 4.3% of GDP in 2012 and engaged 5.6% of the employed labour force in 2011. Construction GDP increased at an average annual rate of 4.0% in 2002–10; the sector declined by 19.7% in 2009 and by a further 7.1% in 2010.

Energy in Serbia (including Montenegro) is derived principally from coal (which provided about 71.9% of total electricity generated in 2009) and hydroelectric power (27.4%). Imports of mineral fuels accounted for 17.8% of the value of total imports in 2012.

Services contributed 62.1% of GDP in 2012 and engaged 51.8% of the employed labour force in 2011. Services GDP increased at an average annual rate of 5.8% in 2002–10; sectoral GDP grew by 3.4% in 2010.

In 2011 Serbia recorded a merchandise trade deficit of US $7,375.7m., and there was a deficit of $4,157.1m. on the current account of the balance of payments. In 2012 the principal source of imports to Serbia was Russia (amounting for 10.9% of the total); other major sources were Germany, Italy and the People's Republic of China. The principal market for exports in that year was Germany (taking 11.6% of all exports); other important purchasers were Italy, Bosnia and Herzegovina, Romania, Russia and Montenegro. (These figures excluded trade to or from Kosovo.) The main exports in 2012 were basic manufactures, machinery and transport equipment, food and live animals, miscellaneous manufactured articles, chemicals, and crude materials (except fuels). The principal imports in that year were machinery and transport equipment, basic manufactures, mineral fuels and lubricants, chemicals, miscellaneous manufactured articles, and food and live animals.

In 2010 Serbia recorded an overall budgetary deficit of 136,000m. dinars. In 2011 a budgetary deficit of 141,000m. dinars was forecast. Serbia's general government gross debt was €1,589,251m. in 2011, equivalent to 50.1% of GDP. At the end of 2010 the total external debt of Serbia was US $32,222m., of which $9,477m. was public and publicly guaranteed debt. In that year, the cost of servicing long-term public and publicly guaranteed debt and repayments to the IMF was equivalent to 30.9% of the value of exports of goods, services and income (excluding workers' remittances). According to the National Statistical Office, the annual rate of inflation averaged 10.4% in January 2002–January 2010. Consumer prices increased by an annual average of 5.6% in the 12 months to January 2012. The rate of unemployment was 24.8% in November 2011.

Serbia submitted an official application to join the European Union—EU (see p. 281) in December 2009, and an interim trade agreement with the Union was adopted. Implementation of an EU Stabilization and Association Agreement, which had been signed in 2007, was finally approved in June 2010. In April 2011 the Government reached a four-year agreement with the World Bank, under which it was able to draw funds of US $200m. each year. In September the IMF approved a precautionary, 18-month stand-by arrangement, totalling about $1,300m., for Serbia. In February 2012, however, the credit arrangement was suspended, after the authorities failed to meet fiscal performance criteria. Amid a continuing financial crisis in the euro area, with concomitant adverse effects on Serbia's trade and investment, GDP contracted by an estimated 1.7% in 2012, and by December of that year the budget deficit exceeded 6% of GDP, while public debt was equivalent to more than 60% of GDP, and the inflation rate had risen sharply. The IMF predicted that modest growth would resume in 2013, but considered a 2013 budget deficit target announced by the Serbian authorities to be over-ambitious. A new coalition Government that was installed in July 2012 sought the restoration of a precautionary credit agreement with the IMF (which would also benefit investment), and by early 2013 had succeeded in stabilizing the currency. After Eurobond sales generated revenue of some $1,750m. during 2012, the Government planned to finance its debt in 2013 through further Eurobond issues, and also to secure funding of $1,000m. from Russia. Meanwhile, prospects for greater economic integration with the countries of the EU was enhanced following the EU's approval, in March 2012, of Serbia's candidate status, and the issuing of a recommendation, in April 2013, by the European Commission, on the opening of negotiations with Serbia on the eventual accession of the country to the Union. Meanwhile, negotiations on Serbia's admission to the World Trade Organization (see p. 444) were ongoing in 2013; one impediment to Serbia's accession to the organization was legislation, adopted in 2008, that prohibited the import, production or sale, of genetically modified organisms.

PUBLIC HOLIDAYS

2014: 1–2 January (New Year), 7–8 January (Christmas), 15–16 February (National Day), 18–21 April (Orthodox Easter), 1–2 May (Labour Day), 9 May (Victory Day), 11 November (Armistice Day).

Statistical Survey

Source (unless otherwise indicated): Statistical Office of the Republic of Serbia, 11000 Belgrade, Milana Rakića 5; tel. (11) 2412922; fax (11) 2411260; internet webrzs.stat.gov.rs/WebSite.

Note: Except where otherwise stated, figures in this survey exclude data for Kosovo, which declared independence from Serbia on 17 February 2008.

Area and Population

AREA, POPULATION AND DENSITY

Area (sq km)	77,498*
Population (census results)	
31 March 2002	
Males	3,645,930
Females	3,852,071
Total	7,498,001
1–15 October 2011	7,120,666
Density (per sq km) at 2011 census	91.9

* 29,922 sq miles, according to 2002 census.

POPULATION BY AGE AND SEX
(official estimates at mid-2010)

	Males	Females	Total
0–14	566,616	535,644	1,102,260
15–64	2,460,410	2,495,354	4,955,764
65 and over	519,348	714,064	1,233,412
Total	**3,546,374**	**3,745,062**	**7,291,436**

Note: Estimates not adjusted to take account of 2011 census.

POPULATION BY ETHNIC GROUP
(2002 census)

Ethnic group	Population ('000)	%
Serbs	6,213	82.9
Hungarians	293	3.9
Bosniaks	136	1.8
Roma	108	1.4
Yugoslavs	81	1.1
Croats	71	0.9
Montenegrins	69	0.9
Others	527	7.0
Total	**7,498**	**100.0**

ADMINISTRATIVE DIVISIONS
(population at 2011 census)

	Area (sq km)	Population ('000)	Density (per sq km)	Principal city
Capital				
Belgrade . . .	3,224	1,639,121	508.4	—
Okruzi (Districts)				
Bor	3,507	123,848	35.3	Bor
Braničevo . .	3,865	180,480	46.7	Požarevac
Jablanica . .	2,769	215,463	77.8	Leskovac
Kolubara . .	2,474	174,228	70.4	Valjevo
Mačva . . .	3,268	297,778	91.1	Šabac
Moravica . .	3,016	212,149	70.3	Čačak
Nišava . . .	2,729	373,404	136.8	Niš
Pčinja . . .	3,520	158,717	45.1	Vranje
Pirot . . .	2,761	92,277	33.4	Pirot
Podunavlje . .	1,248	198,184	158.8	Smederevo
Pomoravlje . .	2,614	212,839	81.4	Jagodina
Rasina . . .	2,668	240,463	90.1	Kruševac
Raška . . .	3,918	300,102	76.6	Kraljevo
Šumadija . .	2,387	290,900	121.9	Kragujevac
Toplica . . .	2,231	90,600	40.6	Prokuplje
Zaječar . . .	3,623	118,295	32.7	Zaječar
Zlatibor . . .	6,140	284,929	46.4	Užice

—*continued*	Area (sq km)	Population ('000)	Density (per sq km)	Principal city
Province . . .				
Vojvodina . .	21,536	1,916,886	89.0	Novi Sad
Okruzi (Districts) within the Province of Vojvodina				
Central Banat .	3,256	186,851	57.4	Zrenjanin
North Bačka .	1,784	185,552	104.0	Subotica
North Banat .	2,329	146,690	63.0	Kikinda
South Bačka .	4,016	607,835	151.4	Novi Sad
South Banat .	4,245	291,327	68.6	Pančevo
Srem . . .	3,486	311,053	89.2	Sremska Mitrovica
West Bačka .	2,420	187,581	77.5	Sombor
Total	**77,498**	**7,120,666**	**91.9**	**—**

PRINCIPAL TOWNS
(population at 2011 census)

Beograd (Belgrade, the capital) . .	1,639,121	Šabac	115,347
Novi Sad . .	335,701	Čačak	114,809
Niš	257,867	Smederevo . . .	107,528
Kragujevac . .	177,468	Novi Pazar . .	92,766
Leskovac . .	143,962	Valjevo . . .	90,301
Subotica . . .	140,358	Sombor . . .	85,569
Kruševac . .	127,429	Vranje . . .	82,782
Kraljevo . .	124,554	Sremska Mitrovica .	79,773
Zrenjanin . .	122,714	Loznica . . .	78,788
Pančevo . . .	122,252	Užice	78,018

BIRTHS, MARRIAGES AND DEATHS

	Registered live births		Registered marriages		Registered deaths	
	Number	Rate (per 1,000)	Number	Rate (per 1,000)	Number	Rate (per 1,000)
2004	78,186	10.5	42,030	5.6	104,320	14.0
2005	72,180	9.7	38,846	5.2	106,771	14.3
2006	70,997	9.6	39,756	5.4	102,884	13.9
2007	68,102	9.2	41,083	5.6	102,805	13.9
2008	69,083	9.4	38,285	5.2	102,711	14.0
2009	70,299	9.6	36,853	5.0	104,000	14.2
2010	68,304	9.4	35,815	4.9	103,211	14.2
2011	65,598	9.0	35,808	4.9	102,935	14.2

Life expectancy (years at birth): 73.9 (males 71.4; females 76.6) in 2010 (Source: World Bank, World Development Indicators database).

ECONOMICALLY ACTIVE POPULATION
(labour force survey, persons aged 15 years and over, October 2009)

	Males	Females	Total
Agriculture, forestry, fishing and water works	366,711	255,474	622,185
Mining and quarrying	22,349	5,377	27,726
Manufacturing	293,798	147,674	441,472
Electricity, gas and water . . .	40,320	5,664	45,984
Construction	119,380	16,098	135,478
Wholesale and retail trade . . .	176,728	184,598	361,326
Hotels and restaurants . . .	34,829	41,304	76,133
Transport, storage and communications	120,395	34,250	154,646
Financial intermediation . . .	22,063	33,263	55,326
Real estate and property . . .	48,963	40,294	89,257
Public administration and social security	71,552	56,113	127,665
Education	57,626	92,895	150,522
Health and social work . . .	33,064	143,268	176,332
Other community, social and personal services	64,991	53,700	118,691
Households with employed persons	707	5,321	6,028
Extra-territorial organizations and bodies	538	877	1,415
Total employed	1,474,017	1,116,171	2,590,188
Unemployed	266,427	250,942	517,369
Total labour force	1,740,444	1,367,113	3,107,557

November 2011: Agriculture, forestry and fishing 466,219; Mining and quarrying 31,828; Manufacturing 384,203; Electricity, gas and water 66,348; Construction 124,046; Wholesale and retail trade 295,453; Hotels and restaurants 60,527; Transport, storage and communications 165,185; Financial intermediation 39,250; Real estate and property 103,066; Public administration and social security 119,842; Education 156,399; Health and social work 142,485; Other community, social and personal services 58,912; Households with employed persons 9,801; Extra-territorial organizations and bodies 943; *Total employed* 2,224,508; Unemployed 735,053; *Total labour force* 2,959,561.

Health and Welfare

KEY INDICATORS
(data for Serbia only, unless otherwise indicated)

Total fertility rate (children per woman, 2010)	1.6
Under-5 mortality rate (per 1,000 live births, 2010) . . .	7
HIV/AIDS (% of persons aged 15–49, 2009, Serbia and Montenegro)	0.1
Physicians (per 1,000 head, 2006)	2.0
Hospital beds (per 1,000 head, 2006)	5.4
Health expenditure (2009): US $ per head (PPP)	1,162
Health expenditure (2009): % of GDP	10.5
Health expenditure (2009): public (% of total)	61.9
Access to water (% of persons, 2010)	99
Access to sanitation (% of persons, 2010)	92
Total carbon dioxide emissions ('000 metric tons, 2008) . .	49,933.5
Carbon dioxide emissions per head (metric tons, 2008) . .	6.8
Human Development Index (2011): ranking	59
Human Development Index (2011): value	0.766

For sources and definitions, see explanatory note on p. vi.

Agriculture

PRINCIPAL CROPS
('000 metric tons; incl. Kosovo)

	2009	2010	2011
Wheat	2,067.6	1,630.4	2,076.2
Barley	302.5	244.3	279.2
Maize	6,396.3	7,207.2	6,479.6
Oats	73.6	67.6	71.3
Potatoes	898.3	887.4	891.5
Sugar beet	2,797.6	3,324.9	2,821.9
Beans, dry	46.3	43.2	39.5
Soybeans (Soya beans) . . .	349.2	540.9	440.8
Sunflower seed	377.5	378.4	432.0
Cabbages and other brassicas .	326.2	336.6	315.5
Tomatoes	189.4	189.4	198.7
Chillies and peppers, green . .	171.4	155.0	145.2
Onions, dry	131.2	144.1	139.6
Carrots and turnips . . .	67.8	101.2	60.3
Watermelons	230.1	197.5	224.5
Apples	281.9	239.9	265.6
Pears	67.8	47.5	65.3
Sour (Morello) cherries . . .	105.4	66.2	90.6
Peaches and nectarines . . .	77.2	68.6	75.2
Plums and sloes	662.6	426.8	581.9
Raspberries and other berries .	87.0	83.9	89.6
Grapes	431.3	330.1	324.9
Tobacco, unmanufactured . . .	9.9	10.4	10.4

Aggregate production ('000 metric tons, may include official, semi-official or estimated data): Total cereals 8,999.0 in 2009, 9,290.7 in 2010, 9,077.5 in 2011; Total roots and tubers 898.3 in 2009, 887.4 in 2010, 891.5 in 2011; Total vegetables (incl. melons) 1,326.1 in 2009, 1,327.1 in 2010, 1,287.5 in 2011; Total fruits (excl. melons) 1,828.0 in 2009, 1,355.7 in 2010, 1,608.6 in 2011.

Source: FAO.

LIVESTOCK
('000 head, year ending 30 September; incl. Kosovo)

	2009	2010	2011
Horses	14	14	12
Cattle	1,002	938	937
Pigs	3,631	3,489	3,287
Sheep	1,504	1,475	1,460
Goats	143	129	130
Chickens	22,400	19,725	18,726

Source: FAO.

LIVESTOCK PRODUCTS
('000 metric tons; incl. Kosovo)

	2009	2010	2011
Cattle meat	100	96	81
Sheep meat	24	23	24
Pig meat	252	269	271
Chicken meat	80	84	103
Cows' milk	1,505	1,485	1,462
Sheep's milk	10	10	11
Hen eggs	59	70	70
Honey	5	4	4

Source: FAO.

Forestry

ROUNDWOOD REMOVALS
('000 cu m, excl. bark; incl. Kosovo)

	2009	2010	2011
Sawlogs, veneer logs and logs for sleepers	1,175	1,222	1,173
Pulpwood	93	96	99
Other industrial roundwood	91	95	89
Fuel wood	1,778	6,223	6,345
Total	3,137	7,636	7,706

Source: FAO.

SAWNWOOD PRODUCTION
('000 cu m, including railway sleepers; incl. Kosovo)

	2009	2010	2011
Coniferous (softwood)	146	152	144
Non-coniferous (hardwood)	428	437	368
Total	574	589	512

Source: FAO.

Fishing

('000 metric tons, live weight, incl. Kosovo)

	2008	2009	2010
Capture	3.2	3.8	4.8
Freshwater fishes	1.3	6.6	13.7
Common carp	2.9	3.3	4.9
Aquaculture	7.5	7.4	8.2
Rainbow trout	0.1	0.1	0.1
Total catch	10.7	11.3	13.0

Source: FAO.

Mining

('000 metric tons unless otherwise indicated)

	2009	2010	2011
Coal	38,897	38,598	41,574
Lignite	38,828	38,490	41,440
Crude petroleum	663	865	1,020
Natural gas (million cu m)	283	427	616
Lead and zinc ore	225	219	220*
Copper ore	9,896	10,665	12,000*
Clay and kaolin	161	152	379

* Estimate.

Source: partly US Geological Survey.

Industry

SELECTED PRODUCTS
('000 metric tons unless otherwise indicated)

	2009	2010	2011
Refined vegetable oils	136.9	181.5	142.3
Fruit and vegetable juices	240.3	215.7	207.6
Beer ('000 hectolitres)	5,436	5,289	5,462
Cigarettes (million)	20,482	21,906	19,985
Cotton yarn (metric tons)	804	1,016	828
Wool yarn (metric tons)	265	33	24
Hosiery ('000 pairs)	191,087	200,746	226,395
Underwear ('000 units)	12,449	9,534	8,427
Leather footwear ('000 pairs)	2,225	2,250	2,480
Parquet wooden flooring and blinds ('000 sq metres)	180.9	145.1	n.a.
Paper and cardboard	101.0	128.0	139.4
Newsprint	45.2	56.2	47.5
Cement	2,232	2,130	2,095
Motor spirit (gasoline)*	570	n.a.	n.a.
Gas-diesel (distillate fuel) oil*	1,001	n.a.	n.a.
Residual fuel oil*	626	n.a.	n.a.
Nitrogenous fertilizers	220.7	395.2	482.9
Rubber tyres for vehicles ('000)	10,263	8,025	8,248
Pig-iron	964.6	1,158.8	1,197.7
Flat-rolled steel products	1,556.0	2,128.0	1,885.0
Alternating current motors (units)	29,993	213,503	6,455
Tractors (number)	3,625	2,153	1,736
Passenger cars (number)	16,512	14,955	10,593
Kitchen wooden furniture ('000 units)	66.2	160.0	108.0
Electric energy (million kWh)	38,376	38,105	38,441

* Source: UN Industrial Commodity Statistics Database.

Finance

CURRENCY AND EXCHANGE RATES

Monetary Units
100 para = 1 Serbian dinar.

Sterling, Dollar and Euro Equivalents (30 November 2012)
£1 sterling = 139.136 dinars;
US $1 = 86.651 dinars;
€1 = 112.525 dinars;
1,000 Serbian dinars = £7.19 = $11.54 = €8.89.

Average Exchange Rate (dinars per US $)
2009   67.581
2010   77.729
2011   73.333

CONSOLIDATED BUDGET
('000 million dinars; incl. Kosovo)

Revenue*	2009	2010	2011†
Tax revenue	1,000	1,057	1,153
Personal income tax	133	139	148
Social security contributions	319	324	345
Corporate income tax	31	33	38
Retail sales tax; value-added tax	297	319	356
Excises	135	152	179
Taxes on international trade and operations	48	44	40
Other taxes	37	46	48
Non-tax revenue	138	159	171
Total	1,140	1,218	1,323

Expenditure	2009	2010	2011†
Current expenditure	1,154	1,226	1,319
Wages and salaries . . .	302	310	329
Expenditure on goods and services	211	227	253
Interest payments	22	34	50
Subsidies and other current transfers	619	655	687
Capital expenditure	93	105	119
Lending minus repayments . .	20	30	28
Total	1,268	1,361	1,466

* Excluding grants received ('000 million dinars): 7 in 2009; 7 in 2010; 2 in 2011 (budget forecast).
† Budget forecasts.

Source: IMF, *Republic of Serbia: Request for Stand-by Arrangement—Staff Report; Staff Statement; Press Release; and Statement by the Executive Director for the Republic of Serbia* (October 2011).

INTERNATIONAL RESERVES
(US $ million at 31 December; incl. Kosovo)

	2009	2010	2011
Gold (national valuation) . .	465.7	594.9	725.9
IMF special drawing rights . .	19.3	3.0	2.6
Foreign exchange	14,749.9	12,711.7	14,874.6
Total	15,234.9	13,309.5	15,603.1

Source: IMF, *International Financial Statistics.*

MONEY SUPPLY
(million dinars at 31 December; incl. Kosovo)

	2009	2010	2011
Currency outside depository corporations	95,522	91,803	114,190
Transferable deposits . . .	288,661	304,809	353,425
Other deposits	819,797	964,913	1,032,829
Broad money	1,203,980	1,361,525	1,500,444

Source: IMF, *International Financial Statistics.*

COST OF LIVING
(Consumer Price Index at January; base: 2006 = 100)

	2010	2011	2012
Food and non-alcoholic beverages .	136.7	154.9	160.4
Tobacco and beverages . . .	179.7	207.7	223.6
Clothing (incl. footwear) . . .	122.1	129.4	133.4
Rent and fuels	115.2	124.6	124.2
All items (incl. others) . .	131.4	146.2	154.4

NATIONAL ACCOUNTS
('000 million dinars at current prices)

Expenditure on the Gross Domestic Product

	2010	2011	2012
Final consumption expenditure .	2,876.9	3,088.8	3,268.8
Households	2,282.8	2,438.2	2,552.5
Non-profit institutions serving households	27.3	31.2	33.7
General government	566.7	619.4	682.6
Gross fixed capital formation . .	512.3	592.8	604.3
Changes in inventories . . .	−15.6	53.5	116.4
Total domestic expenditure .	3,376.3	3,735.1	3,989.5
Exports of goods and services . .	1,036.9	1,173.4	1,349.6
Less Imports of goods and services	1,528.6	1,699.9	1,952.9
Gross domestic product at market prices	2,881.9	3,208.6	3,386.2

Gross Domestic Product by Economic Activity

	2010	2011	2012
Agriculture, hunting, forestry and fishing	245.1	292.9	296.9
Mining and quarrying	42.3	52.6	58.0
Manufacturing	389.9	449.8	480.5
Electricity, gas and water . . .	123.9	152.5	151.3
Construction	114.5	135.6	125.3
Wholesale and retail trade, and repairs	268.0	295.1	318.0
Restaurants and hotels . . .	27.5	32.6	36.0
Transport, storage and communications	256.4	282.8	313.4
Financial intermediation . . .	94.8	96.1	110.3
Real estate, renting and business activities	463.1	503.4	528.4
Public administration and defence; compulsory social security . .	100.1	112.0	116.7
Education	121.5	125.1	136.5
Health and social work . . .	151.0	179.8	191.8
Other community, social and personal services	75.9	66.3	72.3
Private households with employed persons	2.7	2.8	3.0
Sub-total	2,476.7	2,779.5	2,938.7
Less Financial intermediation services indirectly measured .	76.7	80.9	93.8
Gross value added in basic prices	2,400.0	2,698.6	2,844.9
Net taxes on products . . .	481.9	510.0	541.3
GDP in market prices . . .	2,881.9	3,208.6	3,386.2

BALANCE OF PAYMENTS
(US $ million; incl. Kosovo)

	2009	2010	2011
Exports of goods	8,361.3	9,818.5	11,748.1
Imports of goods	−15,490.8	−16,163.3	−19,123.7
Balance on goods	−7,129.5	−6,344.9	−7,375.7
Exports of services	3,487.9	3,531.2	4,217.8
Imports of services	−3,456.0	−3,524.1	−3,994.8
Balance on goods and services	−7,097.6	−6,337.8	−7,152.6
Primary income received . . .	695.2	581.1	595.1
Primary income paid	−1,401.4	−1,479.9	−1,654.9
Balance on goods, services and primary income	−7,803.9	−7,236.6	−8,212.5
Secondary income received . .	4,969.5	4,474.9	4,542.8
Secondary income paid . . .	−344.5	−353.4	−487.5
Current balance	−3,178.8	−3,115.1	−4,157.1
Capital account (net)	2.6	1.3	−3.4
Direct investment assets . . .	−54.8	−188.4	−167.7
Direct investment liabilities . .	1,935.6	1,340.2	2,700.4
Portfolio investment assets . .	−9.6	−41.7	58.2
Portfolio investment liabilities . .	−56.1	130.1	2,168.5
Financial derivatives and employee stock options (net)	−2.5	−35.8	35.2
Other investment assets . . .	94.8	−1,086.2	633.6
Other investment liabilities . .	2,824.1	765.3	567.1
Net errors and omissions . . .	−30.5	246.6	279.0
Reserves and related items .	1,524.7	−1,983.8	2,113.8

Source: IMF, *International Financial Statistics.*

External Trade

PRINCIPAL COMMODITY GROUPS
(US $ million, distribution by SITC)

Imports c.i.f.	2010	2011	2012
Food and live animals	875.2	1,055.2	1,084.8
Beverages and tobacco	170.4	197.9	191.8
Crude materials (inedible) except fuels	681.1	792.3	614.6
Mineral fuels, lubricants, etc.	3,254.3	3,963.4	3,338.1
Chemicals and related products	2,454.4	2,975.1	3,099.7
Basic manufactures	3,268.8	3,842.6	3,458.4
Machinery and transport equipment	3,460.0	4,526.4	4,405.9
Miscellaneous manufactured articles	1,300.1	1,510.2	1,349.4
Total (incl. others)	16,470.5	19,861.9	19,013.3

Exports f.o.b.	2010	2011	2012
Food and live animals	1,768.0	2,091.5	2,108.4
Crude materials (inedible) except fuels	464.6	656.0	589.9
Mineral fuels, lubricants, etc.	500.5	496.0	401.2
Chemicals and related products	877.5	1,002.2	924.2
Basic manufactures	2,841.0	3,481.2	2,634.0
Machinery and transport equipment	1,588.5	1,960.9	2,546.2
Miscellaneous manufactured articles	1,234.4	1,510.4	1,559.7
Total (incl. others)	9,794.5	11,779.5	11,353.6

PRINCIPAL TRADING PARTNERS
(US $ million)

Imports c.i.f.	2010	2011	2012
Austria	499.1	678.0	659.1
Belgium	232.0	311.0	337.2
Bosnia and Herzegovina	555.1	670.1	491.3
Bulgaria	579.6	480.1	501.2
China, People's Republic	1,172.9	1,488.5	1,386.7
Croatia	427.4	488.2	538.1
Czech Republic	311.4	423.2	389.3
France (incl. Monaco)	476.9	537.0	516.9
Germany	1,731.4	2,149.8	2,066.3
Greece	225.6	306.4	304.5
Hungary	788.6	909.7	936.9
Italy	1,389.4	1,771.4	1,840.5
Japan	130.1	165.6	186.2
Macedonia, former Yugoslav republic	266.8	320.5	297.5
Montenegro	164.2	130.9	122.1
Netherlands	247.0	281.1	280.8
Poland	404.9	453.6	526.8
Romania	593.6	883.0	825.4
Russia	2,156.1	2,654.2	2,078.6
Slovakia	396.4	268.6	253.2
Slovenia	500.3	588.6	592.0
Spain	154.9	210.8	238.4
Sweden	188.9	170.0	161.7
Switzerland	199.6	214.8	206.4
Turkey	322.8	405.1	439.2
Ukraine	284.6	384.0	173.3
United Kingdom	194.2	227.2	230.2
USA	251.8	288.2	317.0
Total (incl. others)	16,470.5	19,861.9	19,013.3

Exports f.o.b.	2010	2011	2012
Albania	131.2	126.6	87.3
Austria	338.4	371.6	283.6
Belgium	131.5	132.5	126.4
Bosnia and Herzegovina	1,088.8	1,191.4	1,082.5
Bulgaria	241.1	325.3	290.4
Croatia	307.0	468.1	397.2
Czech Republic	135.0	157.4	170.5
France (incl. Monaco)	276.7	309.1	285.2
Germany	1,008.1	1,330.7	1,315.7
Greece	182.0	201.0	165.5

Exports f.o.b.—*continued*	2010	2011	2012
Hungary	303.4	346.6	329.4
Iraq	46.9	53.9	37.8
Italy	1,118.4	1,306.2	1,201.0
Macedonia, former Yugoslav republic	476.7	524.7	482.1
Montenegro	803.6	891.0	798.9
Netherlands	157.0	132.3	145.6
Poland	113.1	182.4	180.8
Romania	650.7	812.5	935.9
Russia	534.7	792.3	867.1
Slovakia	173.4	216.0	253.7
Slovenia	425.8	526.1	428.8
Switzerland	61.1	82.7	92.1
Turkey	88.0	183.1	187.0
Ukraine	195.7	211.0	131.8
United Kingdom	155.4	185.2	144.1
Total (incl. others)	9,794.5	11,779.5	11,353.6

Transport

(data include Kosovo)

RAILWAYS
(traffic)

	2009	2010	2011
Passengers carried ('000)	5,358	5,269	6,123
Passenger-km (million)	521	522	541
Freight carried ('000 metric tons)	10,419	12,585	12,620
Freight ton-km (million)	2,967	3,522	3,612

ROAD TRAFFIC
(motor vehicles in use)

	2007	2008	2009
Passenger cars	1,476,642	1,486,608	1,641,352
Buses and coaches	8,887	8,557	8,853
Goods vehicles	129,877	139,331	148,252
Special-purpose passenger vehicles	14,574	13,574	13,475
Special-purpose goods vehicles	25,802	24,169	23,552
Road tractors	7,263	7,387	7,376
Trailers and semi-trailers	103,859	27,686	28,597
Motorcycles and mopeds	24,897	31,803	34,497

2010: Passenger cars 1,567,114; Buses 8,034; Lorries 162,877; Special purpose motor vehicles 1,020; Road tractors 228,637; Motor cultivators 286; Agricultural tractors and trailers 10,720; Trailers and semi-trailers 98,963; Motorcycles and mopeds 37,948.

2011: Passenger cars 1,677,510; Buses 8,805; Lorries 158,873; Special purpose motor vehicles 2,736; Road tractors 228,641; Motor cultivators 230; Agricultural tractors and trailers 18,490; Trailers and semi-trailers 124,111; Motorcycles and mopeds 39,456.

INLAND WATERWAYS

Traffic
('000 metric tons, national and international traffic at river ports, excl. transit)

	2009	2010	2011
Goods loaded	3,115	3,373	3,414
Goods unloaded	4,007	4,739	4,550

CIVIL AVIATION
(scheduled and non-scheduled services)

	2009	2010	2011
Km flown (million)	16	15	18
Passengers carried ('000)	1,054	1,088	1,285
Passenger-km (million)	1,123	1,145	1,399
Cargo carried (metric tons)	2,487	2,394	2,230
Total ton-ketres (million)	2.7	2.7	2.7

Tourism

FOREIGN TOURIST ARRIVALS
('000 at accommodation establishments)

Country of origin	2009	2010	2011
Bosnia and Herzegovina . . .	64	64	66
Bulgaria	24	25	28
Croatia	40	46	51
Germany	39	43	48
Greece	24	25	26
Italy	37	34	38
Macedonia, former Yugoslav republic	30	32	34
Montenegro	62	57	67
Slovenia	55	67	75
Total (incl. others)	645	683	764

Tourism receipts (Serbia and Montenegro, US $ million, excl. passenger transport): 989 in 2009; 798 in 2010; 992 in 2011 (provisional) (Source: World Tourism Organization).

Communications Media

(data include Kosovo)

	2009	2010	2011
Telephones (fixed network, '000 subscribers)	3,105.7	3,110.3	3,030.4
Mobile cellular telephones ('000 subscribers)	9,912.3	9,915.3	10,182.0
Internet subscribers ('000) . .	842.8	917.9	971.8
Broadband subscribers ('000) . .	590.6	801.6	916.7

Source: International Telecommunication Union.

Personal computers: 1,900,000 (258.5 per 1,000 persons) in 2008 (Source: International Telecommunication Union).

Education

(2010/11)

	Institutions	Teachers	Students
Pre-primary	2,384	22,501	179,865
Regular primary	3,470	50,700	573,274
Special primary	240	1,703	6,120
Primary education of adults .	16	272	3,204
Regular secondary . . .	497	} 30,479 {	281,605
Special secondary . . .	43		1,916
Accessory	99	n.a.	21,547
Higher	189	9,467	228,531

Pupil-teacher ratio (primary education, UNESCO estimate): 16.4 in 2009/10 (Source: UNESCO Institute for Statistics).

Adult literacy rate (UNESCO estimates): 97.9% (males 99.2%; females 96.7%) in 2010 (Source: UNESCO Institute for Statistics).

Directory

The Government

HEAD OF STATE

President: TOMISLAV NIKOLIĆ (elected 20 May 2012, inaugurated 31 May).

COUNCIL OF MINISTERS
(May 2013)

A coalition Government, comprising representatives of the Serbian Progressive Party, the Socialist Party of Serbia, the United Regions of Serbia, the Social Democratic Party of Serbia, and the Party of Democratic Action of Sandžak.

Prime Minister and Minister of Internal Affairs: IVICA DAČIĆ.

First Deputy Prime Minister, responsible for Defence, Security, the Fight against Corruption and Crime, and Minister of Defence: ALEKSANDAR VUČIĆ.

Deputy Prime Minister and Minister of Foreign and Domestic Trade and Telecommunications: RASIM LJAJIĆ.

Deputy Prime Minister and Minister of Labour, Employment and Social Policy: JOVAN KRKOBABIĆ.

Deputy Prime Minister, responsible for European Integration: SUZANA GRUBJEŠIĆ.

Minister of Finance and the Economy: MLAĐAN DINKIĆ.

Minister of Foreign Affairs: IVAN MRKIĆ.

Minister of Regional Development and Local Self-Government: VERICA KALANOVIĆ.

Minister of Transport: MILUTIN MRKONJIĆ.

Minister of Construction and Town Planning: VELIMIR ILIĆ.

Minister of Justice and Public Administration: NIKOLA SELAKOVIĆ.

Minister of Agriculture, Forestry and Water Management: GORAN KNEŽEVIĆ.

Minister of Education, Science and Technological Development: ŽARKO OBRADOVIĆ.

Minister of Health: SLAVICA ĐUKIĆ-DEJANOVIĆ.

Minister of Energy, Development and the Protection of the Environment: ZORANA MIHAJLOVIĆ.

Minister of Culture and Information: BRATISLAV PETKOVIĆ.

Minister of Natural Resources, Mining and Spatial Planning: MILAN BAČEVIĆ.

Minister of Youth and Sports: ALISA MARIĆ.

Minister without Portfolio: SULEJMAN UGLJANIN.

Secretary-General of the Government: VELJKO ODALOVIĆ.

MINISTRIES

Office of the President: 11000 Belgrade, Andrićev venac 1; tel. (11) 3043068; fax (11) 3030868; e-mail kontakt.predsednik@predsednik .rs; internet www.predsednik.rs.

Office of the Prime Minister: 11000 Belgrade, Nemanjina 11; tel. (11) 3617586; e-mail kabinetpremijera@gov.rs; internet www.srbija .gov.rs.

Ministry of Agriculture, Forestry and Water Management: 11070 Belgrade, Omladinskih brigada 1; tel. and fax (11) 2607961; e-mail office@minpolj.gov.rs; internet www.minpolj.gov.rs.

Ministry of Construction and Town Planning: 11000 Belgrade, Nemanjina 22–26; tel. (11) 3616518; fax (11) 3616521.

Ministry of Culture and Information: 11000 Belgrade, Vlajkovićeva 3; tel. (11) 3345701; e-mail kabinet@kultura.gov.rs; internet www.kultura.gov.rs.

Ministry of Defence: 11000 Belgrade, Birčaninova 5; tel. (11) 3006311; fax (11) 3006062; e-mail info@mod.gov.rs; internet www .mod.gov.rs.

Ministry of Education, Science and Technological Development: 11000 Belgrade, Nemanjina 24; tel. (11) 3616489; fax (11) 3616491; e-mail kabinet@mp.gov.rs; internet www.mp.gov.rs.

Ministry of Energy, Development and the Protection of the Environment: 11000 Belgrade, Nemanjina 22–26; tel. (11) 3617722; fax (11) 3617632; e-mail kabinet.min@merz.gov.rs; internet www.merz.gov.rs.

Ministry of Finance and the Economy: 11000 Belgrade, Kneza Miloša 20; tel. (11) 3642626; fax (11) 3618961; e-mail kabinet@mfp.gov.rs; internet www.mfp.gov.rs.

Ministry of Foreign Affairs: 11000 Belgrade, Kneza Miloša 24–26; tel. (11) 3616333; fax (11) 3618366; e-mail mfa@mfa.rs; internet www.mfa.gov.rs.

Ministry of Foreign and Domestic Trade and Telecommunications: Belgrade, bul. Mihaila Pupina 2; tel. (11) 3113432; fax (11) 3114650; e-mail kabinet@mtt.gov.rs; internet www.mtt.gov.rs.

Ministry of Health: 11000 Belgrade, Nemanjina 22–26; tel. (11) 3616596; fax (11) 2656548; e-mail kabinet@zdravlje.gov.rs; internet www.zdravlje.gov.rs.

Ministry of Internal Affairs: 11070 Belgrade, bul. Mihaila Pupina 2; tel. (11) 3112916; fax (11) 3114650; e-mail info@mup.gov.rs; internet www.mup.gov.rs.

Ministry of Justice and Public Administration: 11000 Belgrade, Nemanjina 22–26; tel. (11) 3622356; fax (11) 3616419; e-mail kabinet@mpravde.gov.rs; internet www.mpravde.gov.rs.

Ministry of Labour, Employment and Social Policy: 11000 Belgrade, bul. Nemanjina 11; tel. (11) 3614621; fax (11) 3617587; e-mail press@minrzs.gov.rs; internet www.minrzs.gov.rs.

Ministry of Natural Resources, Mining and Spatial Planning: 11000 Belgrade, Nemanjina 11; tel. (11) 3617717; fax (11) 3619828; e-mail kabinet@ekoplan.gov.rs; internet www.ekoplan.gov.rs.

Ministry of Regional Development and Local Self-Government: 11000 Belgrade, Vlajkovićeva 10; tel. (11) 3334118; fax (11) 3334181; e-mail kabinet@mrrls.gov.rs; internet www.mrrls.gov.rs.

Ministry of Transport: 11000 Belgrade, Nemanjina 22–26; tel. (11) 3616431; fax (11) 3617486.

Ministry of Youth and Sports: 11070 Belgrade, bul. Mihaila Pupina 2; tel. and fax (11) 2142564; e-mail sport@mos.gov.rs; internet www.mos.gov.rs.

President

Presidential Election, First Ballot, 6 May 2012

Candidate	Votes	% of votes
Boris Tadić	989,454	25.31
Tomislav Nikolić	979,216	25.05
Ivica Dačić	556,013	14.23
Vojislav Koštunica	290,861	7.44
Zoran Stanković	257,054	6.58
Čedomir Jovanović	196,668	5.03
Jadranka Šešelj	147,793	3.78
Others	316,933	8.11
Total*	3,908,652	100.00

* Including 174,660 invalid votes (4.47% of the total).

Second Ballot, 20 May 2012

Candidate	Votes	% of votes
Tomislav Nikolić	1,552,063	49.54
Boris Tadić	1,481,952	47.31
Total*	3,132,679	100.00

* Including 98,664 invalid votes (3.15% of the total).

Legislature

**Narodna skupština Republike Srbije
(National Assembly of the Republic of Serbia)**

11000 Belgrade, Nikole Pashića; tel. (11) 3026100; e-mail nsrs@parlament.rs; internet www.parlament.gov.rs.

President: NEBOŠJA STEFANOVIĆ.

Election, 6 May 2012

Parties and blocs	Votes	%	Seats
Let's Get Serbia Moving—Tomislav Nikolić*	940,659	24.04	73
Choice for a Better Life—Boris Tadić†	863,294	22.06	67
Ivica Dačić—Socialist Party of Serbia- Party of United Pensioners of Serbia- United Serbia coalition	567,689	14.51	44
Democratic Party of Serbia—Vojislav Koštunica	273,532	6.99	21
Čedomir Jovanović—Overturn‡	255,546	6.53	19
United Regions of Serbia—Mlađan Dinkić‖	215,666	5.51	16
Alliance of Vojvodina Hungarians—István Pásztor	68,323	1.75	5
Party of Democratic Action of Sandžak	27,708	0.71	2
All Together§	24,993	0.64	1
None of the Stated Options	22,905	0.59	1
Albanian Coalition from Preševo Valley	13,384	0.34	1
Others	465,618	11.90	—
Total¶	3,912,904	100.00	250

* A coalition led by the Serbian Progressive Party, and also including New Serbia, the Association of Small and Medium-sized Organizations and Entrepreneurs, the Coalition of Societies of Refugees in the Republic of Serbia, the Strength of Serbia Movement—BK, the People's Peasant Party, the Bosniak People's Party, the Democratic Party of Macedonians, the Roma Party, the United Vlach Movement, the Socialist Movement and the Movement for the Economic Renewal of Serbia.

† A coalition led by the Democratic Party, and also including the Social Democratic Party of Serbia, the League of Social Democrats of Vojvodina, the Greens of Serbia, the Democratic Union of Vojvodina Croats and the Democratic Christian Party of Serbia.

‡ A coalition led by the Liberal Democratic Party, and also including the Serbian Renewal Movement, the Social Democratic Union, Rich Serbia, the Vojvodina Party, the Democratic Party of Sandžak, the Green Ecological Party—Greens and the Party of Bulgarians of Serbia.

‖ A coalition of G17 Plus, Together for Šumadija, the People's Party, four regional parties and numerous civic associations.

§ A coalition of the Bosniak Democratic Union, the Civil Alliance of Hungarians, the Democratic Union of Croats, the Democratic Association of Vojvodina Hungarians and the Slovak Party.

¶ Including 173,587 invalid votes (representing 4.44% of the total).

Election Commission

Electoral Commission of the Republic of Serbia: 11000 Belgrade, Kralja Milana 14; tel. (11) 3026000; fax (11) 3221029; e-mail izbori@parlament.rs; internet www.rik.parlament.gov.rs; Chair. Prof. Dr DEJAN ĐURĐEVIĆ.

Political Organizations

Political parties are required to have at least 10,000 members (or 1,000 members in the case of those representing minority ethnic groups) to obtain registration. At March 2012 there were 87 registered parties in the country.

Alliance of Vojvodina Hungarians—István Pásztor (Vajdasági Magyar Szövetség—Pásztor István/Savez Vojvođanskih Mađara—István Pásztor): 24000 Subotica, Age Mamužića 11/I; tel. and fax (24) 553801; e-mail office@vmsz.org.rs; internet www.vmsz.org.rs; f. 1994; supports autonomous status for Vojvodina; Chair. IŠTVAN PÁSZTOR.

Democratic Party (DP) (Demokratska Stranka—DS): 11000 Belgrade, Krunska 69; tel. (11) 3443003; fax (11) 2444864; e-mail info@ds.org.rs; internet www.ds.org.rs; f. 1990; contested 2012 legislative elections as leading mem. of Choice for a Better Life—Boris Tadić coalition; Pres. DRAGAN ĐILAS.

Democratic Party of Serbia (DPS) (Demokratska stranka Srbije—DSS): 11000 Belgrade, Pariska 13; tel. (11) 3204719; fax (11) 3204743; e-mail info@dss.rs; internet www.dss.rs; f. 1992 following split from Democratic Party; Leader Dr VOJISLAV KOŠTUNICA.

G17 Plus: 11000 Belgrade, trg Republike 5; tel. (11) 3210355; fax (11) 3284054; e-mail office@g17plus.rs; internet www.g17plus.rs; f. 2003;

contested 2012 legislative elections as leading mem. of the United Regions of Serbia—Mlađan Dinkić coalition; Pres. MLAĐAN DINKIĆ.

League of Social Democrats of Vojvodina (LSV) (Liga Socijaldemokrata Vojvodine): 21000 Novi Sad, trg Mladenaca 10; tel. (21) 529139; fax (21) 420628; e-mail info@lsv.org.rs; internet www.lsv.org.rs; contested 2012 legislative elections as mem. of Choice for a Better Life—Boris Tadić coalition, led by the Democratic Party; Pres. NENAD ČANAK.

Liberal Democratic Party (LDP) (Liberalno-demokratska Partija): 11000 Belgrade, Simina 41; tel. (11) 3208300; fax (11) 3208301; e-mail predsednik@ldp.rs; internet www.ldp.rs; f. 2005 by fmr mems of the Democratic Party; contested 2012 legislative elections as leading mem. of the Čedomir Jovanović—Overturn coalition; Pres. ČEDOMIR JOVANOVIĆ.

New Serbia (Nova Srbija): 11000 Belgrade, Obilićev venac 4/1; tel. (11) 3284766; fax (11) 2631748; e-mail nscentrala@gmail.com; internet www.nova-srbija.org; contested 2012 legislative elections as mem. of the Let's Get Serbia Moving—Tomislav Nikolić coalition, led by the Serbian Progressive Party; Pres. VELIMIR ILIĆ.

None of the Stated Options (Nijedan od ponuđenih odgovora): Belgrade; tel. (11) 2661436; e-mail javnost@nopo.org.rs; internet www.nopo.org.rs; f. 2008; reformist, democratic; Leader NIKOLA TULIMIROVIĆ.

Party of Democratic Action of Sandžak (Stranka Demokratske Akcije Sandžaka—SDA Sandžaka): 36300 Novi Pazar, S. Nemanje 25; tel. (20) 313032; fax (20) 313034; e-mail centrala@sda.rs; internet www.sda.rs; f. 1990; br. of the Party of Democratic Action (Bosnia and Herzegovina); represents the Bosniak ethnic minority in the Sandžak region; Pres. Dr SULEJMAN UGLJANIN.

Party of United Pensioners of Serbia (PUPS) (Partija Ujedinjenih Penzionera Srbije): 11000 Belgrade, Topličin venac 11/III; tel. (11) 2928205; fax (11) 2928216; e-mail office@pups.org.rs; internet www.pups.org.rs; contested 2012 legislative elections in coalition with the Socialist Party of Serbia and United Serbia; Pres. JOVAN KRKOBABIĆ.

Roma Party (Romska Partija): represents Roma ethnic minority; contested 2012 legislative elections as mem. of the Let's Get Serbia Moving—Tomislav Nikolić coalition, led by the Serbian Progressive Party; Leader SAJN SRĐAN.

Roma Union of Serbia (Unija Roma Srbije): 11000 Belgrade, Sarajevska 11; tel. and fax (11) 2681693; e-mail unijaromasrbije@hotmail.com; f. 2004; represents Roma ethnic minority; Pres. MILOŠ PAUNKOVIĆ.

Serbian Progressive Party (SPP) (Srpska napredna stranka): 11070 Belgrade, Palmira Toljatija 5/3; tel. (11) 6557486; fax (11) 6557491; e-mail informativna-sluzba@sns.org.rs; internet www.sns.org.rs; f. 2008 as breakaway party from the Serbian Radical Party; nationalist; contested 2012 legislative elections as leading mem. of the Let's Get Serbia Moving—Tomislav Nikolić coalition; Pres. ALEKSANDAR VUČIĆ.

Serbian Radical Party (SRP) (Srpska Radikalna Stranka—SRS): 11080 Belgrade, Zemun, Magistratski trg 3; tel. (11) 3164621; e-mail info@srpskaradikalnastranka.rs; internet www.srpskaradikalnastranka.org.rs; f. 1991; extreme nationalist; advocates a 'Greater Serbian' state of territories inhabited by Serbs within and outside Serbia; leader Dr Vojislav Šešelj in detention at the International Criminal Tribunal for the former Yugoslavia; Pres. Dr VOJISLAV ŠEŠELJ; Vice-Pres. DRAGAN TODOROVIĆ.

Serbian Renewal Movement (SRM) (Srpski pokret obnove—SPO): 11000 Belgrade, Kneza Mihailova 48; tel. (11) 3283620; fax (11) 2628170; e-mail vuk@spo.rs; internet www.spo.rs; f. 1990; nationalist; contested 2012 legislative elections as mem. of the Čedomir Jovanović—Overturn coalition, led by the Liberal Democratic Party; Pres. VUK DRAŠKOVIĆ.

Social Democratic Party of Serbia (SDP) (Socijaldemokratska Partija Srbije): 11000 Belgrade, Terazije 16; tel. (11) 2656442; fax (11) 2656333; e-mail info@sdpsrbije.org.rs; internet www.sdpsrbije.org.rs; f. 1997; contested 2012 legislative elections as mem. of Choice for a Better Life—Boris Tadić coalition, led by the Democratic Party; Pres. Dr RASIM LJAJIĆ.

Social Democratic Union (Socijaldemokratska Unija): 11000 Belgrade, Kralja Milana 34/1; tel. (11) 3613649; fax (11) 3620862; e-mail info@sdu.org.rs; internet www.sdu.org.rs; f. 1996; contested 2012 legislative elections as mem. of the Čedomir Jovanović—Overturn coalition, led by the Liberal Democratic Party; Pres. ŽARKO KORAĆ.

Socialist Party of Serbia (SPS) (Socijalistička partija Srbije): 11000 Belgrade, Studentski trg 15; tel. (11) 2627164; fax (11) 2654458; e-mail info@sps.org.rs; internet www.sps.org.rs; f. 1990 by merger of League of Communists of Serbia and Socialist Alliance of Working People of Serbia; contested 2012 legislative elections in coalition with the Party of United Pensioners of Serbia and United Serbia; Pres. IVICA DAČIĆ.

Strength of Serbia Movement—BK (Pokret snaga Srbije—BK): 11000 Belgrade, Vase Pelagića 23; tel. and fax (11) 4141054; e-mail pokret@snagasrbije.com; internet www.snagasrbije.com; f. 2004; contested 2012 legislative elections as mem. of the Let's Get Serbia Moving—Tomislav Nikolić coalition, led by the Serbian Progressive Party; Leader BOGOLJUB KARIĆ.

United Serbia (US) (Jedinstvena Srbija): 11000 Belgrade, Terazije 3; tel. (11) 3344313; fax (11) 3344230; e-mail info@jedinstvenasrbija.org.rs; internet www.jedinstvenasrbija.org.rs; contested 2012 legislative elections in coalition with the Socialist Party of Serbia and the Party of United Pensioners of Serbia; Pres. DRAGAN MARKOVIĆ.

Diplomatic Representation

EMBASSIES IN SERBIA

Albania: 11000 Belgrade, bul. Kneza Aleksandra Karađorđevića 25A; tel. (11) 3066642; fax (11) 2665439; e-mail embassy.belgrade@mfa.gov.al; Ambassador SHPËTIM ÇAUSHI.

Algeria: 11000 Belgrade, Maglajska 26 B; tel. (11) 3671211; fax (11) 2668200; e-mail ambalgerie-serbie@eunet.rs; internet www.ambalgserbia.rs; Ambassador ABDELKADER MESDOUA.

Angola: 11000 Belgrade, Vladete Kovačevića 14; tel. (11) 2653422; fax (11) 2653424; e-mail ambasada.angole@sbb.rs; internet www.angolaembassy.org.rs; Ambassador TOKO DIAKENGA SERÃO.

Argentina: 11000 Belgrade, Kneza Mihajlova 24/I; tel. (11) 2623569; fax (11) 2622630; e-mail eserb@mrecic.gov.ar; Ambassador RICARDO FERNANDEZ.

Australia: 11070 Belgrade, Vladimira Popovića 38–40, 8th Floor; tel. (11) 3303400; fax (11) 3303409; e-mail belgrade.embassy@dfat.gov.au; internet www.serbia.embassy.gov.au; Ambassador Dr HELENA STUDDERT.

Austria: 11000 Belgrade, Kneza Sime Markovića 2; tel. (11) 3336500; fax (11) 2635606; e-mail belgrade-ob@bmeia.gv.at; internet www.aussenministerium.at/belgrad; Ambassador Dr JOHANNES EIGNER.

Azerbaijan: 11000 Belgrade, Pere Velimirovića 25; tel. (11) 3515101; fax (11) 3515103; e-mail belgrade@mission.mfa.gov.az; internet www.azembassy.rs; Ambassador ELDAR HASANOV (resident in Bucharest, Romania).

Belarus: 11000 Belgrade, Deligradska 13; tel. (11) 3616938; fax (11) 3616836; e-mail serbia@mfa.gov.by; internet www.serbia.mfa.gov.by; Ambassador VLADIMIR N. CHUSHEV.

Belgium: 11000 Belgrade, Krunska 18; tel. (11) 3230018; fax (11) 3244394; e-mail belgrade@diplobel.fed.be; Ambassador ALAIN KUNDYCKI.

Bosnia and Herzegovina: 11000 Belgrade, Krunska 9; tel. (11) 3241170; fax (11) 3241057; e-mail bihambasada@sbb.rs; Ambassador BORIŠA ARNAUT.

Brazil: 11000 Belgrade, Krunska 14; tel. (11) 3239781; fax (11) 3230653; e-mail brasbelg@ambasadabrazila.org.rs; internet www.ambasadabrazila.org.rs; Ambassador ALEXANDRE ADDOR-NETO.

Bulgaria: 11000 Belgrade, Birčaninova 26; tel. (11) 3613980; fax 3611136; e-mail embassy.belgrade@mfa.bg; internet www.mfa.bg/embassies/serbia; Ambassador ANGEL DIMITROV.

Canada: 11000 Belgrade, Kneza Miloša 75; tel. (11) 3063000; fax (11) 3063042; e-mail bgrad@international.gc.ca; internet www.canadainternational.gc.ca/serbia-serbie; Ambassador ROMAN WASCHUK.

China, People's Republic: 11000 Belgrade, Užička 25; tel. (11) 3695057; fax (11) 3066001; e-mail chinaemb_yu@mfa.gov.cn; internet rs.chineseembassy.org; Ambassador ZHANG WANXUE.

Congo, Democratic Republic: 11000 Belgrade, Moravska 5; tel. and fax (11) 3446431; e-mail rdcongobelgrade@gmail.com; internet www.drcongo-embassy.rs; Chargé d'affaires a.i. Dr PAUL-EMILE TSHINGA AHUKA.

Croatia: 11000 Belgrade, Kneza Miloša 62; tel. (11) 3679150; fax (11) 3610032; e-mail croebg@mvep.hr; internet rs.mvp.hr; Ambassador ŽELJKO KUPREŠAK.

Cuba: 11000 Belgrade, Vukovarska 3; tel. (11) 3692441; fax (11) 3692442; e-mail recepcion@ambasadakube.org.rs; internet www.cubadiplomatica.cu/serbia; Ambassador MERCEDES MARTÍNEZ VALDÉS.

Cyprus: 11000 Belgrade, Generala Save Grujića 18; tel. (11) 3620002; fax (11) 3621122; e-mail belgradeembassy@mfa.gov.cy; Ambassador NAFSIKA KROUSTI.

Czech Republic: 125108 Belgrade, bul. Kralja Aleksandra 22; tel. (11) 3336200; fax (11) 3236448; e-mail belgrade@embassy.mzv.cz; internet www.mzv.cz/belgrade; Ambassador JAN SECHTER.

Denmark: 11040 Belgrade, Neznanog Junaka 9A; tel. (11) 3679500; fax (11) 3679502; e-mail begamb@um.dk; internet www.ambbeograd.um.dk; Ambassador METTE KJUEL NIELSEN.

Egypt: 11000 Belgrade, Andre Nikolića 12; tel. (11) 2650585; fax (11) 2652036; e-mail egemb@sbb.rs; Ambassador ALY GALAL BASSIOUNY.

Finland: 11001 Belgrade, Birčaninova 29, POB 926; tel. (11) 3065400; fax (11) 3065375; e-mail sanomat.beo@formin.fi; internet www.finska.co.rs; Ambassador PEKKA EINARI ORPANA.

France: 11000 Belgrade, Pariska 11, POB 283; tel. (11) 3023500; fax (11) 3023510; internet www.ambafrance-srb.org; Ambassador FRANÇOIS-XAVIER DENIAU.

Germany: 11040 Belgrade, Neznanog Junaka 1A; tel. (11) 3064300; fax (11) 3064303; e-mail germany@sbb.rs; internet www.belgrad.diplo.de; Ambassador HEINZ WILHELM.

Greece: 11000 Belgrade, Francuska 33; tel. (11) 3226523; fax (11) 3344746; e-mail gremb.bel@mfa.gr; internet www.mfa.gr/belgrade; Ambassador DIMOSTHENIS STOIDIS.

Guinea: 11000 Belgrade, Ohridska 4; tel. (11) 2451391; fax (11) 3444870; e-mail ambaguineebelgrade@eunet.rs; Chargé d'affaires a.i. LAMINE TOURE.

Holy See: 11000 Belgrade, Svetog Save 24; tel. (11) 3085356; fax (11) 3085216; e-mail nunbel@an.org.rs; Apostolic Nuncio Most Rev. ORLANDO ANTONINI (Titular Archbishop of Formiae).

Hungary: 11000 Belgrade, Krunska 72; tel. (11) 2443739; fax (11) 3441876; e-mail mission.blg@mfa.gov.hu; internet www.mfa.gov.hu/emb/belgrade; Ambassador OSZKÁR NIKOWITZ.

India: 11040 Belgrade, Ljutice Bogdana 8; tel. (11) 2666520; fax (11) 3674209; e-mail indemb@eunet.rs; internet www.embassyofindiabelgrade.org; Ambassador NENGCHA LHOUVUM MUKHOPADHAYA.

Indonesia: 11040 Belgrade, bul. Kneza Aleksandra Karađorđevića 18; tel. (11) 3635666; fax (11) 3672984; e-mail kbri.beograd@eunet.rs; internet www.deplu.go.id/belgrade; Ambassador SEMUEL SAMSON.

Iran: 11000 Belgrade, Ljutice Bogdana 40; tel. (11) 3674360; fax (11) 3674363; e-mail iran-emb@bitsyu.net; Ambassador ABOLQASEM DALAFI.

Iraq: 11000 Belgrade, Neznanog Junaka 27A; tel. (11) 2662681; fax (11) 2668068; e-mail bgremb@iraqmofamail.net; Ambassador FALAH ABDUL HASSAN ABDUL SADA.

Israel: 11000 Belgrade, bul. Kneza Aleksandra Karađorđevića 47; tel. (11) 3643500; fax (11) 3670304; e-mail info@belgrade.mfa.gov.il; internet belgrade.mfa.gov.il; Ambassador YOSSEF LEVY.

Italy: 11000 Belgrade, Birčaninova 11; tel. (11) 3066100; fax (11) 3249413; e-mail segreteria.belgrado@esteri.it; internet www.ambelgrado.esteri.it; Ambassador ARMANDO VARRICCHIO.

Japan: 11070 Belgrade, Vladimira Popovića 6; tel. (11) 3012800; fax (11) 3118258; internet www.yu.emb-japan.go.jp; Ambassador MASAFUMI KUROKI.

Korea, Republic: 11070 Belgrade, Užička 32; tel. (11) 3674225; fax (11) 3674229; e-mail koreanembsb@hotmail.co.kr; Ambassador KIM KWANG-KEUN.

Kuwait: 11000 Belgrade, Tolstojeva 42B; tel. (11) 2661414; fax (11) 2668436; e-mail belgrade@mofa.gov.kw; Ambassador FAWZI ABD AL-AZIZ AHMAD AL-JASEM.

Lebanon: 11000 Belgrade, Diplomatska kolonija 5; tel. (11) 3675153; fax (11) 3675156; e-mail ambaleb@sbb.rs; Chargé d'affaires a.i. GHASSAN ABDEL KHALEK.

Libya: 11000 Belgrade, Sime Lozanića 8; tel. (11) 2663445; fax (11) 3670805; e-mail libyaamb@open.telekom.rs; Chargé d'affaires a.i. TAJOURI TAJOURI.

Macedonia, former Yugoslav republic: 11000 Belgrade, Gospodar Jevremova 34; tel. (11) 3284924; fax (11) 3285076; e-mail belgrade@mfa.gov.mk; Ambassador LJUBIŠA GEORGIEVSKI.

Malaysia: 11040 Belgrade, Krajiška 2; tel. (11) 2662736; fax (11) 3679080; e-mail malbelgrade@kln.gov.my; internet www.kln.gov.my/web/srb_belgrade; Chargé d'affaires a.i. YUBAZLAN HAJI YUSOF.

Malta: 11070 Belgrade, Vladimira Popovića 6; tel. (11) 3121335; fax (11) 3121336; e-mail embassy@orderofmalta.org.rs; internet www.orderofmalta.org.rs; Ambassador ALBERTO DI LUCA.

Mexico: 11040 Belgrade, Ljutice Bogdana 5; tel. (11) 3674170; fax (11) 3675013; e-mail embamex@mexican-embassy.org.rs; Ambassador MERCEDES FELÍSITAS RUIZ ZAPATA.

Montenegro: Belgrade, Užička 1; tel. (11) 2662300; fax (11) 3699546; e-mail emb.belgrade@mfa.gov.me; Ambassador IGOR JOVOVIĆ.

Morocco: 11000 Belgrade, Sanje Živanović 4; tel. (11) 3691866; fax (11) 3690499; e-mail midi@ambasada-maroka.org.rs; Ambassador ABDELLAH ZAKOUR.

Myanmar: 11000 Belgrade, Kneza Miloša 72; tel. (11) 3617165; fax (11) 3614968; e-mail myanbel@sezampro.rs; Ambassador ZAW TUN.

Netherlands: 11000 Belgrade, Simina 29; tel. (11) 2023900; fax (11) 2023999; e-mail bel@minbuza.nl; internet www.nlembassy.rs; Ambassador LAURENT STOKVIS.

Norway: 11000 Belgrade, Užička 43; tel. (11) 3670404; fax (11) 3690158; e-mail emb.belgrade@mfa.no; internet www.norveska.org.rs; Ambassador NILS RAGNAR KAMSVÅG.

Pakistan: 11000 Belgrade, bul. Kneza Aleksandra Karađorđevića 62; tel. (11) 2661676; fax (11) 2661667; e-mail ambpakistana@sbb.rs; internet www.pakistanembassy.org.rs; Ambassador GHULAM FARID FARRUKH.

Poland: 11000 Belgrade, Kneza Miloša 38; tel. (11) 2065318; fax (11) 3617576; e-mail belgrad.amb.sekretariat@msz.gov.pl; internet www.belgrad.msz.gov.pl; Ambassador ANDRZEJ EDWARD JASIONOWSKI.

Portugal: 11040 Belgrade, Vladimira Gaćinovića 4; tel. (11) 2662894; fax (11) 2662892; e-mail portambs@verat.net; Chargé d'affaires a.i. JOSÉ DE CASTRO ATAÍDE AMARAL.

Romania: 11000 Belgrade, Užička 10; tel. (11) 3675772; fax (11) 3675771; e-mail embassy@romania.org.rs; internet www.belgrad.mae.ro; Ambassador DANIEL BANU.

Russia: 11000 Belgrade, Deligradska 32; tel. (11) 3611090; fax (11) 3611900; e-mail info@ambarusk.rs; internet www.ambasadarusije.rs; Ambassador ALEKSANDR V. CHEPURIN.

San Marino: 11000 Belgrade, bul. Despota Stefana 68C; tel. and fax (11) 3288040; e-mail ambasciata_rsm_in_serbia@gmail.it; Chargé d'affaires a.i. SCIPIONE CANEVA.

Slovakia: 11070 Belgrade, bul. Umetnosti 18; tel. (11) 2223800; fax (11) 2223820; e-mail emb.beograd@mzv.sk; internet www.belehrad.mfa.sk; Ambassador JÁN VARŠO.

Slovenia: 11000 Belgrade, Pariska 15; tel. (11) 3038470; fax (11) 3288657; e-mail vbg@gov.si; internet beograd.veleposlanistvo.si; Ambassador FRANCI BUT.

Spain: 11000 Belgrade, Prote Mateje 45; tel. (11) 3440231; fax (11) 3444203; e-mail emb.belgrado@maec.es; internet www.maec.es/subwebs/embajadas/belgrado; Ambassador ARTURO LACLAUSTRA BELTRÁN.

Sweden: 11040 Belgrade, Ledi Pedzet 2; tel. (11) 2069200; fax (11) 2069250; e-mail ambassaden.belgrad@foreign.ministry.se; internet www.swedenabroad.com/en-gb/embassies/belgrade; Ambassador BERTIL CHRISTER ASP.

Switzerland: 11000 Belgrade, bul. Oslobođenja 4; tel. (11) 3065820; fax (11) 2657253; e-mail bel.vertretung@eda.admin.ch; internet www.eda.admin.ch/belgrade; Ambassador JEAN-DANIEL RUCH.

Syria: 11000 Belgrade, Aleksandra Stamboliskog 13; tel. (11) 2666124; fax (11) 2660221; e-mail ambasada.sirije@open.telekom.rs; Chargé d'affaires a.i. SULEMAN ABO DIAB.

Tunisia: 11000 Belgrade, Vase Pelagića 19; tel. (11) 3691961; fax (11) 2651848; e-mail at.belgrade@sbb.rs; Ambassador MAJID HAMLAOUI.

Turkey: 11000 Belgrade, Krunska 1; tel. (11) 3232400; fax (11) 3332433; e-mail embassy.belgrade@mfa.gov.tr; internet belgrade.emb.mfa.gov.tr; Ambassador MEHMET KEMAL BOZAY.

Ukraine: 11040 Belgrade, Paje Adamova 4; tel. (11) 3672411; fax (11) 3672413; e-mail emb_sm@mfa.gov.ua; internet www.mfa.gov.ua/serbia; Ambassador VIKTOR NEDOPAS.

United Kingdom: 11000 Belgrade, Resavska 46; tel. (11) 3060900; fax (11) 2659651; e-mail belgrade.ppd@fco.gov.uk; internet ukinserbia.fco.gov.uk; Ambassador MICHAEL DAVENPORT.

USA: 11000 Belgrade, Kneza Miloša 50; tel. (11) 3619344; fax (11) 3615489; internet serbia.usembassy.gov; Ambassador MICHAEL KIRBY.

Judicial System

The judicial system in the Republic of Serbia comprises the courts of regular competence (138 municipal courts, 30 district courts and the Supreme Court of Serbia) and courts of special competence (17 commercial courts and the High Commercial Court). A new Constitution, which entered into effect on 8 November 2006, provided for an 11-member independent High Judicial Council, which was to guarantee the independence and autonomy of courts and judges. The legislature was to elect judges on the proposal of the High Judicial Council, while the High Judicial Council was to elect permanent judges. The Constitutional Court, comprising 15 judges, was to protect constitutionality and legality, as well as human and minority rights and freedoms.

Constitutional Court (Ustavni Sud Srbije): 11306 Belgrade, Nemanjina 26; tel. (11) 3616371; fax (11) 2681675; e-mail sekretar.us@ustavni.sud.rs; internet www.ustavni.sud.rs; f. 1963; Pres. DRAGISA SLIJEPČEVIĆ.

Supreme Court (Vrhovni Sud Srbije): 11000 Belgrade, Resavska 42; tel. (11) 3634207; fax (11) 3619376; e-mail vss@vrh.sud.rs; Pres. NATA MESAROVIĆ.

Office of the Public Prosecutor of Serbia: 11000 Belgrade, Nemanjina 22-26; tel. (11) 3631703; fax (11) 3616305; e-mail kabinetrjt@rjt.gov.rs; internet www.rjt.gov.rs; Public Prosecutor ZAGORKA DOLOVAC.

Religion

Most of the inhabitants of Serbia are Christian, but there is a significant Muslim minority. The main Christian denomination is Eastern Orthodox, but there is a strong Roman Catholic presence. There are also small minorities of Old Catholics, Protestants and Jews.

CHRISTIANITY

The Eastern Orthodox Church

Serbian Orthodox Church (Srpska Pravoslavna Crkva): 11001 Belgrade, Kralja Petra 5, POB 182; tel. (11) 3025112; e-mail info@spc .rs; internet www.spc.rs; 11m. adherents; Patriarch of Serbia, Archbishop of Peć and Metropolitan of Belgrade-Karlovci IRINEJ.

The Roman Catholic Church

Serbia comprises one archdiocese and three dioceses, including one, Srijem, responsible to the Croatian hierarchy. There is also an apostolic exarchate of Serbia and Montenegro for Byzantine rite Catholics.

International Bishops' Conference of SS Cyril and Methodius: 11000 Belgrade, Višegradska 23; tel. (11) 3032246; fax (11) 3032248; f. 2006; membership comprises Bishops of Montenegro and Serbia; Pres. Most Rev. STANISLAV HOČEVAR (Archbishop of Belgrade).

Archbishop of Belgrade: Most Rev. STANISLAV HOČEVAR, 11000 Belgrade, Svetozara Markovića 20; tel. (11) 3032246; fax (11) 3032248; e-mail nadbiskupija@kc.org.rs; internet www.kc.org.rs.

Apostolic Exarch to Serbia and Montenegro for Catholics of the Byzantine Rite: ĐURA DŽUDŽAR (Titular Archbishop of Acrasso), 21000 Novi Sad, D. Magaraševića 18; tel. (21) 6371609; fax (21) 6371613; 22,653 adherents (2006).

Protestant Churches

Christian Reformed Church: 24323 Feketić, Bratsva 26; tel. and fax (24) 738070; f. 1919; 22,000 mems; Bishop ISTVAN CSETE-SZEMESI.

Evangelical Christian Church of the Augsburg (Lutheran) Confession in Serbia-Vojvodina: 24000 Subotica, Braće Radića 17; tel. and fax (24) 527778; e-mail lutheran@stcable.net; internet www.lutheran.org.rs; Superintendent DOLINSZKY ÁRPÁD.

Slovak Evangelical Church of the Augsburg (Lutheran) Confession: 21000 Novi Sad, Karadžićeva 2; tel. (21) 6611882; 50,000 mems (2002); Bishop Dr SAMUEL VRBOVSKY.

Union of Baptist Churches in Serbia: 11000 Belgrade, Slobodanke D. Savić 33; tel. and fax (11) 410964; f. 1992; Gen. Sec. Rev. AVRAM DEGA.

ISLAM

There are ethnic Slav Muslims (Bosniaks) in the part of Sandžak located in south-western Serbia, in particular in and around the town of Novi Pazar. Most Muslims in the country are Sunni.

Islamic Community of Serbia: Belgrade, G. Jevremova 11; tel. (11) 2622428; e-mail reis@rijaset.rs; internet www.rijaset.rs; Reis-ul-ulema ADEM EF. ZILKIĆ.

Islamic Community of Vojvodina: 21000 Novi Sad, Futoška 61; tel. and fax (21) 6619444; internet www.islamvojvodina.com; Chair. ZIJA ZEKIR.

JUDAISM

Federation of Jewish Communities in Serbia: 11000 Belgrade, Kralja Petra 71A/III, POB 512; tel. (11) 2624359; fax (11) 2621837; e-mail office@savezscg.net; f. 1919, revived 1944; Pres. ALEKSANDAR NEĆAK.

The Press

PRINCIPAL DAILIES

Blic: 11000 Belgrade, Žorža Klemansoa 19; tel. (11) 3334559; fax (11) 3334556; e-mail redakcija@blic.rs; internet www.blic.rs; f. 1996; Editor-in-Chief VESLIN SIMONOVIĆ; circ. 230,000.

Borba: 11000 Belgrade, trg Nikole Pašića 7; tel. (11) 3398137; e-mail redakcija@borba.rs; internet www.borba.rs; f. 1922; morning; Editor-in-Chief OLIVERA ZEKIĆ.

Dnevnik (Daily News): 21000 Novi Sad, bul. Oslobođenja 81; tel. (21) 4806802; fax (21) 423761; e-mail redakcija@dnevnik.rs; internet www.dnevnik.rs; f. 1942 as *Slobodna Vojvodina* (Free Vojvodina); morning; Editor-in-Chief ALEKSANDAR DJIVULJSKIJ.

Glas Javnosti (Voice of the Public): 11000 Belgrade, Vlajkovićeva 8; tel. (11) 3240551; fax (11) 3240550; e-mail redakcija@glas-javnosti .rs; internet www.glas-javnosti.rs; f. 1874; Editor SONJA LAKIĆ.

Narodne Novine (The People's News): 18000 Niš, Gen. Bože Jankovića 9; tel. (18) 527595; fax (18) 527603; e-mail nn.edit@ pogled.net; internet www.narodne.com; morning; Editor-in-Chief TIMOŠENKO MILOSAVLJEVIĆ.

Politika: 11000 Belgrade, Makedonska 29; tel. (11) 3301682; fax (11) 3373419; e-mail redakcija@politika.rs; internet www.politika.rs; f. 1904; Dir-Gen. MIRA GLISIĆ-SIMIĆ; Editor-in-Chief DRAGAN BUJOŠEVIĆ; circ. 110,000.

Pregled: 11030 Belgrade, Jasenova 5; tel. (11) 2395089; fax (11) 2519106; e-mail pregled@pregled.com; internet www.pregled.com; f. 1950; business and economics; Dir and Chief Editor ALEKSANDAR JOVANOVIĆ.

Večernje novosti (Evening News): 11000 Belgrade, trg Nikole Pašića 7; tel. (11) 3028000; e-mail redakcija@novosti.rs; internet www.novosti.rs; f. 1953; Gen. Dir and Editor-in-Chief MANOJLO MANJO VUKOTIĆ; circ. 270,000.

PERIODICALS

Ekonomist: Belgrade, Kosovska 1/IV; tel. (11) 3284034; internet www.emportal.rs; f. 1948; quarterly; journal of the Yugoslav Association of Economists; Editor Dr HASAN HADŽIOMEROVIĆ.

Ekonomska Politika (Economic Policy): 11000 Belgrade, trg Nikole Pašića 7; tel. (11) 3398298; fax (11) 3398300; f. 1952; weekly; Dir ČEDOMIR ŠOŠKIĆ; Editor-in-Chief SLAVKA KOVAČ.

Ilustrovana Politika: 11000 Belgrade, Makedonska 35; tel. (11) 3301442; fax (11) 3373346; e-mail ilustrovana@politika-ad.com; internet www.ilustrovana.com; f. 1958; weekly illustrated review; Gen. Dir MILORAD GUŠAVAC; Editor-in-Chief SRĐJAN JAKANOVIĆ; circ. 90,000.

Jisa Info: 11000 Belgrade, Zmaj Jovina 4; tel. (11) 2620374; fax (11) 2626576; e-mail jisa@jisa.rs; internet www.jisa.rs; f. 1993; publ. by Jisa (Jedinstveni informatički savez Srbije—Union of ICT Societies of Serbia); computing, technology; Pres. ĐORĐE DUKIĆ.

Letopis Matice Srpske: 21000 Novi Sad, Matice srpske 1; tel. (21) 6613864; fax (21) 528901; e-mail letopis@maticasrpska.org.rs; internet www.maticasrpska.org.rs/pages/izdanja/letopis.htm; f. 1824; monthly; literary review; Editor-in-Chief SLOBODAN VLADUŠIĆ.

Međunarodni Problemi/International Problems: 11000 Belgrade, Institute of International Politics and Economics, Makedonska 25; tel. (11) 3373633; fax (11) 3373835; e-mail iipe@ diplomacy.bg.ac.rs; internet www.diplomacy.bg.ac.rs/mpro.htm; f. 1949; quarterly; in Serbian and English; Editor BRANA MARKOVIĆ; circ. 500 (2012).

Mikro/PC World: 11030 Belgrade, Požeška 81A; tel. (11) 3055010; fax (11) 3058034; internet www.mikro.rs; f. 1997; 11 a year; computing; Editorial Dir ALEKSANDAR SPASIĆ; circ. 23,000 (2007).

Nezavisna Svetlost: 34000 Kragujevac, Branka Radičevića 9; tel. (34) 336176; fax (34) 335218; e-mail urednik@svetlost.rs; internet www.svetlost.rs; f. 1995; weekly news; Dir and Editor-in-Chief RANKO MILOSAVLJEVIĆ.

NIN—Nedeljne informativne novine (Weekly Informative News): 11000 Belgrade, Zorza Klemansoa 19; tel. (11) 3373171; fax (11) 3334658; e-mail redakcija@nin.co.rs; internet www.nin.co.rs; f. 1935; politics, economics, culture; Dir JELENA DRAKULIĆ-PETROVIĆ; Editor-in-Chief NEBOJŠA SPASIĆ; circ. 35,000.

Odbrana (Defence): 11002 Belgrade, Brace Jugovića 19; tel. (11) 3201808; fax (11) 3241363; e-mail redakcija@odbrana.mod.gov.rs; internet www.odbrana.mod.gov.rs; f. 2005 to replace *Vojska* (Soldier); two a month; publ. by Ministry of Defence; Editor-in-Chief RADENKO MUTAVDŽIĆ.

Ošišani Jež (Trimmed Hedgehog): 11000 Belgrade, Resavska 28; tel. (11) 3232211; fax (11) 3232423; f. 1935 as *Jež* (Hedgehog); fortnightly; satirical; Editor RADIVOJE BOJIČIĆ; circ. 50,000.

Politikin Zabavnik: 11001 Belgrade, Cetinska 1; tel. (11) 3301452; fax (11) 3373319; e-mail politikin.zabavnik@politika-ad.com; internet www.politika-zabavnik.rs; f. 1939; weekly; comic; Editor-in-Chief ZEFIRINO GRASI; circ. 41,000.

Pravoslavlje (Orthodoxy): 11000 Belgrade, Kralja Petra 5; tel. (11) 3025116; fax (11) 3282588; e-mail pravoslavljespc@gmail.com; internet www.pravoslavlje.rs; f. 1967; fortnightly; Orthodox Christian; Editor-in-Chief ALEKSANDAR ĐAKOVAC.

Pregled Republika Srbija/Survey—Republic of Serbia: 11000 Belgrade, Dečanska 8, POB 677; tel. (11) 3233610; fax (11) 3240291; e-mail info@pregled-rs.rs; internet www.pregled-rs.rs; f. 1957 as *Jugoslovenski pregled/Yugoslav Survey*, renamed *Pregled SCG/Survey Serbia & Montenegro* in 2003, present name adopted 2006; quarterly; general reference publication of basic documentary information about Serbia; Serbian and English edns; Editor-in-Chief ILE KOVAČEVIĆ.

Viva: 11000 Belgrade, Cetinjska 1v; tel. (11) 3301501; fax (11) 3373099; e-mail viva@politika.rs; internet www.vivamagazin.info; monthly; health; Editor-in-Chief Dr GRADIMIR JOKSIMOVIĆ; circ. 25,000.

Vreme (Time): 11000 Belgrade, trg Republike 5/III; tel. (11) 3234774; fax (11) 3238662; e-mail redakcija@vreme.com; internet www.vreme.com; f. 1990; weekly; Editor-in-Chief DRAGOLJUB ŽARKOVIĆ.

NEWS AGENCIES

Beta News Agency: 11000 Belgrade, Kraljana Milana 4; tel. (11) 3602400; fax (11) 2642551; e-mail plasman@beta.co.rs; internet www.beta.rs; f. 1992; regional independent news service; Dir LJUBICA MARKOVIĆ; Editor-in-Chief IVAN CVEJIĆ.

Tanjug News Agency (Novinska Agencija Tanjug): 11001 Belgrade, Obilićev Venac 2, POB 439; tel. (11) 3281608; fax (11) 3282766; e-mail office@tanjug.rs; internet www.tanjug.rs; f. 1943; press and information agency; in Serbian, English, French and Spanish; Dir BRANKA ĐUKIĆ.

PRESS ASSOCIATIONS

Association of Journalists of Serbia (Udruženje novinara Srbije): 11000 Belgrade, Resavska 28/I; tel. (11) 3236337; fax (11) 3236493; e-mail ljiljana.smajlovic@uns.rs; internet www.uns.org.rs; f. 1881; Pres. LJILJANA SMAJLOVIĆ; Gen. Sec. NINO BRAJOVIĆ.

Independent Association of Journalists of Serbia (Nezavisno udruženje novinara Srbije): 11000 Belgrade, Resavska 28/II; tel. (11) 3343255; fax (11) 3343136; e-mail sekretar@nuns.rs; internet www.nuns.rs; Pres. VUKAŠIN OBRADOVIĆ.

Publishers

Alfa-Narodna (Alfa-People's Books) Publishing House: 11000 Belgrade, Višegradska 1A; tel. and fax (11) 3660349; internet www.narodnaknjigaskola.com; f. 1955; fiction, non-fiction, children's books and dictionaries; Gen. Man. MILIČKO MIJOVIĆ.

BIGZ (Beogradski izdavačko-grafički zavod) Publishing a.d. (Belgrade Publishing and Graphics Co): 11000 Belgrade, bul. Vojvode Mišića 17/III; tel. (11) 3691259; fax (11) 3690519; e-mail bigz@bigz-publishing.co.rs; internet www.bigz-publishing.co.rs; f. 1831; privately owned; literature and criticism, children's books, pocket books, popular science, philosophy, politics; Dir MIRJANA MILORADOVIĆ.

Dečje novine: 32300 Gornji Milanovac, T. Matijevića 4; tel. (32) 711195; fax (32) 711248; general literature, children's books, science, science fiction, textbooks; Gen. Dir MIROSLAV PETROVIĆ.

Forum Publishing Institute: 21000 Novi Sad, Vojvode Mišića 1, POB 200; tel. and fax (21) 457216; e-mail direktor@forumliber.rs; internet www.forumliber.rs; f. 1957; books and periodicals in Hungarian; Dir GÁBOR VIRÁG.

Građevinska Knjiga (Citizens' Books) Publishing House: 11000 Belgrade, trg Nikole Pašića 8/II; tel. (11) 3233565; fax (11) 3233563; f. 1948; technical, scientific and educational textbooks; Dir LJUBINKO ANDELIĆ.

Jugoslovenska knjiga (Yugoslav Books) Publishing House: 11000 Belgrade, trg Republike 5, POB 36; tel. (11) 621992; fax (11) 625970; art, economics and culture; Dir ZORAN NIKODIJEVIĆ.

Matice srpske Publishing House: 21000 Novi Sad, Matice Srpske 1; tel. (21) 528910; fax (21) 528574; e-mail bms@eunet.rs; internet www.maticasrpska.org.rs; f. 1826; domestic and foreign fiction and humanities; Man. Dir MIRO VUKSANOVIĆ.

Medicinska knjiga (Medical Books) Publishing House: 11001 Belgrade, Mata Vidakovića 24–26; tel. (11) 458165; f. 1947; medicine, pharmacology, stomatology, veterinary; Dir MILE MEDIĆ.

Minerva Publishing House: 24000 Subotica, trg 29 Novembra 3; tel. (24) 25712; fax (24) 23208; novels and general; Dir LADISLAV ŠEBEK.

Naučna knjiga (Scientific Books) Publishing House: 11000 Belgrade, Uzun Mirkova 5; tel. (11) 637220; f. 1947; school, college and university textbooks, publications of scientific bodies; Dir Dr BLAŽO PEROVIĆ.

Nolit: 11000 Belgrade, Terazije 27; tel. (11) 3245017; fax (11) 627285; f. 1928; belles-lettres, philosophy and fine art; scientific and popular literature; Dir-Gen. RADIVOJE NEŠIĆ; Editor-in-Chief RADIVOJE MIKIĆ.

Prosveta (Education) Publishing House: 11000 Belgrade, Čika Ljubina 1; tel. (11) 2629843; fax (11) 2627465; e-mail prosveta@prosveta.co.rs; internet www.prosveta.co.rs; f. 1944; general literature, art books, dictionaries, encyclopaedias, science, music; Dir ZOVICA MIŠIĆ.

Rad Publishing House: 11000 Belgrade, Dečanska 12; tel. (11) 3715000; fax (11) 3715001; e-mail vanja.tomic@ips.rs; f. 1949; politics, economics, sociology, psychology, literature, biographies; Man. Dir VANJA TOMIĆ; Editor-in-Chief DANKO JESIĆ.

Savremena administracija (Contemporary Administration) Publishing House: 11000 Belgrade, Crnotravska 7–9; tel. (11) 667633; fax (11) 667277; e-mail m.jovic@savremena-ad.com; internet www.savremena-ad.com; f. 1954; economy, law, science university textbooks, encyclopaedias and dictionaries; Dir MILUTIN PEJČIĆ.

Srpska književna zadruga (Serb Publishing Collective): 11000 Belgrade, Srpskih Vladara 19/I; tel. (11) 330305; fax (11) 626224; f. 1892; works of classical and modern Serb writers, and translations of works of foreign writers; Pres. RADOVAN SAMARDŽIĆ; Editor RADOMIR RADOVANAĆ.

Tehnička Knjiga (Technical Books) Publishing House: 11000 Belgrade, Vojvode Stepe 89; tel. (11) 468596; fax (11) 473442; f. 1948; technical works, popular science, reference books, hobbies; Dir RADIVOJE GRBOVIĆ.

Vuk Karadžič Publishing House: 11000 Belgrade, Kraljevića Marka 9, POB 762; tel. (11) 628066; fax (11) 623150; scientific and academic literature, popular science, children's books, general; Gen. Man. VOJIN ANČIĆ.

Zavod za udžbenike i nastavna sredstva (Institute for School Books and Teaching Aids): 11000 Belgrade, Obilićev Venac 5; tel. (11) 2637433; fax (11) 2637426; internet www.zavod.co.rs; f. 1957; textbooks and teaching aids; Dir and Editor-in-Chief MILOLJUB ALBIJANIĆ.

PUBLISHERS' ASSOCIATIONS

Asscn of Publishers and Booksellers of Serbia (Udruženje izdavača i knjižara Srbije): 11000 Belgrade, Kneza Miloša 25, POB 570; tel. (11) 642533; fax (11) 646339; f. 1954; organizes Belgrade International Book Fair; Dir OGNJEN LAKIĆEVIĆ; 116 mem. orgs.

Asscn of Publishers and Booksellers of Vojvodina (Poslovno udruženje izdavača i knjižara Vojvodine): 21000 Novi Sad; tel. and fax (21) 4720452; e-mail knjigaknjiga@gmail.com; internet www.knjigavoj.co.rs; f. 2001; Dir ROMAN VEHOVEĆ; Chair. of Council DJEZE BORDAŠ.

Broadcasting and Communications

TELECOMMUNICATIONS

In 2010 there were 3.1m. active land-lines and 9.9m. subscribers of mobile telephone communications services. Besides Telenor, the dominant fixed-line service provider, there were two other mobile network operators.

Telekom Srbija (Telecom Serbia): 11000 Belgrade, Takovska 2; tel. (11) 3335729; fax (11) 3237260; e-mail prsektor@telekom.rs; internet www.telekomsrbija.com; f. 1997; 20% owned by OTE (Greece); fixed-line and mobile cellular telecommunications services; Dir-Gen. PREDRAG ĆULIBRK.

Telenor d.o.o.: 11070 Belgrade, Omladinskih brigada 90; tel. (11) 0639000; e-mail pr@telenor.rs; internet www.telenor.co.rs; f. 1994 as Mobtel Srbija; present name adopted 2006, following acquisition by Telenor Group (Norway); fixed-line and mobile cellular telecommunications; CEO KJELL-MORTEN JOHNSEN.

VIP Mobile: 11070 Belgrade, Omladinskih brigada 21; e-mail komunikacije@vipmobile.rs; internet www.vipmobile.rs; f. 2007; mem. of Telekom Austria Group; mobile cellular telecommunications; Pres. THANASIS KATSIROUMPAS.

BROADCASTING

Association of Independent Electronic Media (ANEM): 11000 Belgrade, Takovska 9/16; tel. and fax (11) 3225852; e-mail anem@anem.org.rs; internet www.anem.org.rs; f. 1993; comprises 19 television and 32 radio stations, and 60 affiliated orgs; Chair. SAŠA MIRKOVIĆ.

Radiotelevizija Srbije (RTS) (Radio-Television of Serbia): 11000 Belgrade, Takovska 10; tel. (11) 3212000; fax (11) 3212211; e-mail kontaktcentar@rts.rs; internet www.rts.rs; f. 1929; comprises

Radiotelevizija Beograd (Radio-Television of Belgrade); Dir-Gen. ALEKSANDAR TIJANIĆ.

Radiotelevizija Vojvodina (RTV) (Radio-Television of Vojvodina): 21000 Novi Sad, Ignjata Pavlasa 3; tel. (21) 425588; fax (21) 423348; e-mail pr@rtv.rs; internet www.rtv.rs; f. 2006 to replace Radiotelevizija Novi Sad; Gen. Dir BLAŽO POPOVIĆ; Dir of TV ALEKSANDR DOTLIĆ.

Radio

In 2009 there were five national, 37 regional and 235 local radio stations in Serbia.

Međunarodni Radio Srbija (International Radio Serbia): 11000 Belgrade, Hilandarska 2, POB 200; tel. (11) 3244455; fax (11) 3232014; e-mail radioju@sbb.rs; internet www.glassrbije.org; f. 1951; fmrly Radio Jugoslavija (Radio Yugoslavia); state-owned short-wave station; broadcasts daily in Serbian, English, French, German, Russian, Spanish, Hungarian, Chinese, Albanian, Greek, Italian and Arabic; Dir MILORAD VUJOVIĆ.

Radio B92: 11000 Belgrade, bul. Zorana Đinđića 64; tel. (11) 3012000; fax (11) 3012001; internet www.b92.net; f. 1989; independent; Dir VERAN MATIĆ; Dir of Radio Programming GORICA NEŠOVIĆ.

Radio JAT: 11000 Belgrade, Svetog Save 1/XVI; tel. (11) 2440142; e-mail radio_jat@jat.com.

Radiotelevizija Košava: 11000 Belgrade, Aleksandra Dubčeka 14; tel. (11) 3061491; fax (11) 3612135; internet www.kosava.co.rs; f. 1994; radio station broadcasting popular music and talk programmes to most regions of Serbia; Editor-in-Chief MILOMIR MARIĆ.

Radio TV Bajina Basta: 31250 Bajina Basta, Svetosavska 34; tel. (31) 851688; fax (31) 853162; e-mail office@bajinabasta.org; internet www.bajinabasta.org; f. 1986; independent radio and television station; Dir BOBAN TOMIĆ.

Television

Many new TV stations were founded in Serbia in the 1990s and 2000s. In mid-2001 there were 253 television stations, and by 2008 licenses had been issued to a further 129 broadcasters, of which seven were national, 31 were regional and 91 were local.

B92 Televizija: 11000 Belgrade, bul. Zorana Đinđića 64; tel. (11) 3012000; fax (11) 3012001; internet www.b92.net; f. 2000; independent; Dir VERAN MATIĆ; Dir of Programming IVA IVANIŠEVIĆ.

BK Telecom (BK): 11070 Belgrade, Nikole Tesle 42A; tel. (11) 3013555; fax (11) 3013526; internet www.bktv.com; f. 1994; independent television station; Dir-Gen. Dr TIMOHIR SIMIĆ; Editor-in-Chief MILOMIR MARIĆ.

RTV Pink: 11000 Belgrade, Neznanog Junaka 1; tel. (11) 3063400; fax (11) 3063500; internet www.rtvpink.com; f. 1993; Pres. and CEO ŽELJKO MITROVIĆ.

Finance

(cap. = capital; res = reserves; dep. = deposits; m. = million; amounts in Serbian dinars, unless otherwise stated; brs = branches)

BANKING

Central Bank

In May 2009 there were 34 banks in Serbia, 21 of which were in majority foreign ownership, 10 in majority domestic private ownership and three in majority state ownership.

National Bank of Serbia (Narodna banka Srbije): 11000 Belgrade, Kralja Petra 12, POB 1010; tel. (11) 3027100; fax (11) 3027394; e-mail informativni.centar@nbs.rs; internet www.nbs.rs; f. 1884; present name adopted 2003; cap. 14,751m., res 7,692m., dep. 705,635m. (Dec. 2007); Gov. JORGOVANKA TABAKOVIĆ; 6 brs.

Other Banks

Alpha Bank Srbija a.d.: 11000 Belgrade, Kralja Milana 11; tel. (11) 3234931; fax (11) 3246840; e-mail alphabankserbia@alphabankserbia.com; internet www.alphabankserbia.com; f. 1956; 100% owned by Alpha Bank AE (Greece) (q.v.); present name adopted 2006; cap. 18,626.2m., res 25.6m., dep. 60,368.8m. (Dec. 2011); Pres. GEORGIOS PAPANASTASIOU; 23 brs.

Banca Intesa a.d. Beograd: 11070 Belgrade, Vladimira Popovića 8; tel. (11) 3108888; fax (11) 3108855; e-mail kontakt@bancaintesa.rs; internet www.bancaintesabeograd.com; f. 1991; present name adopted 2005; 77.79% owned by Intesa Sanpaolo Holding International SA (Luxembourg); absorbed Panonska Banka a.d. in Jan. 2008; cap. 21,315.9m., res 21,251.8m., dep. 261,680.0m. (Dec. 2012); Chief Exec. DRAGINJA ĐURIĆ; 196 brs.

Erste Bank a.d. Novi Sad: 21000 Novi Sad, bul. Oslobođenja 5; tel. (21) 4873510; fax (21) 4890651; e-mail info@erstebank.rs; internet www.erstebank.rs; f. 1864 as Novosadska Banka a.d.; present name adopted 2005; 74% owned by Erste Bank Group AG (Austria), and 26% owned by Steiermärkische Bank und Sparkassen AG, (Austria); cap. 10,040.0m., res 1,200.8m., dep. 39,054.5m. (Dec. 2011); Pres. SLAVKO CARIĆ.

Hypo Alpe-Adria-Bank a.d. Beograd: 11070 Belgrade, bul. Mihaila Pupina 6; tel. (11) 2226000; fax (11) 2226555; e-mail office@hypo-alpe-adria.rs; internet www.hypo-alpe-adria.rs; f. 1991 as Depositno-Kreditna Banka; merged with Hypo Alpe-Adria-Bank 2002; 99.99% owned by Hypo Alpe-Adria-Bank International AG (Austria); cap. 14,319.5m., res 9,798.4m., dep. 68,284.8m. (Dec. 2011); Chair. VLADIMIR ČUPIĆ.

Komercijalna Banka a.d. Beograd: 11000 Belgrade, Svetog Save 14; tel. (11) 3029582; fax (11) 3346810; e-mail posta@kombank.com; internet www.kombank.com; f. 1970; 42.6% state-owned, 25.0% owned by European Bank for Reconstruction and Development (United Kingdom); cap. 13,881.0m., res 28,332.4m., dep. 221,599.9m. (Dec. 2011); Pres. IVICA SMOLIĆ.

NLB Banka a.d. Beograd: 21000 Novi Sad, trg Mladenaca 1–3; tel. (21) 452144; fax (21) 6616560; e-mail info@nlb.rs; internet www.nlb.rs; f. 1991; fmrly NLB Continental Banka a.d. Novi Sad, renamed as above after merger with NLB LHB Banka Beograd a.d. in Jan. 2010; 99.98 owned by Nova Ljubljanska banka d.d. (Slovenia); cap. 5,290.3m., res 2,113.0m., dep. 28,128.1m. (Dec. 2011); Chair. MARKO JAZBEC.

OTP Banka a.d. Novi Sad: 21000 Novi Sad, bul. Oslobođenja 80; tel. (21) 4800000; fax (21) 4800032; e-mail office@otpbanka.rs; internet www.otpbanka.rs; f. 2007 by merger of Niška Banka a.d. Niš, Kulska Banka a.d. Novi Sad and Zepter banka a.d. Beograd; 93.17% owned by OTP Bank (Hungary); cap. 7,643.8m., res 2,797.6m., dep. 11,979.2m. (Dec. 2011); Pres. of Exec. Bd IMRE BERTALAN.

ProCredit Bank a.d. Beograd: 11000 Belgrade, bul. Milutina Milankovića 17; tel. (11) 2077906; fax (11) 2077905; e-mail info@procreditbank.rs; internet www.procreditbank.rs; f. 2001; owned by ProCredit Holding AG (Germany); cap. 3,663.0m., res 4,428.2m., dep. 37,563.9m. (Dec. 2011); Chair. of Exec. Bd SVETLANA TOLMAČEVA DINGARAC.

Raiffeisen Banka a.d. Beograd: 11000 Belgrade, bul. Zorana Đinđića 64A; tel. (11) 3202100; fax (11) 2207080; e-mail info@raiffeisenbank.rs; internet www.raiffeisenbank.rs; f. 2001 as Raiffeisenbank a.d. Beograd; name changed as above in 2006; 100% owned by Raiffeisenbank International Bank-Holding AG (Austria); cap. 27,466.2m., res 188.0m., dep. 131,607.9m. (Dec. 2011); Chair. and Gen. Man. OLIVER ROEGL.

UniCredit Bank Srbija a.d.: 11000 Belgrade, Rajićeva 27–29; tel. (11) 3777888; fax (11) 3342200; e-mail kontakt@unicreditbank.rs; internet www.unicreditbank.co.rs; f. 2001; present name adopted 2007; 100% owned by Unicredit Bank Austria AG (Austria); cap. 23,607.6m., res 520.4m., dep. 80,874.5m. (Dec. 2011); Chair. of Management Bd CLAUDIO CEZARIO.

Vojvodjanska Banka, a.d. Novi Sad: 21000 Novi Sad, POB 391, trg Slobode 7; tel. (21) 4886600; fax (21) 6624859; e-mail office@voban.groupnbg.com; internet www.voban.co.rs; f. 1962; 100% owned by National Bank of Greece SA (Greece); cap. 16,337.4m., res 4,657.9m., dep. 64,729.6m. (Dec. 2011); Pres. MARINIS STRATOPOULOS.

Banking Association

Association of Serbian Banks (Udruženje banaka Srbije): 11000 Belgrade, bul. Kralja Aleksandra 86; tel. (11) 3020760; fax (11) 3370179; e-mail ubs@ubs-asb.com; internet www.ubs-asb.com; f. 1955; association of business banks; works on improving interbank co-operation, organizes agreements of mutual interest for banks, gives expert assistance, establishes co-operation with foreign banks, other financial institutions and their associations, represents banks in relations with the Government and the National Bank of Serbia; Sec.-Gen. VEROLJUB DUGALIĆ.

STOCK EXCHANGE

Belgrade Stock Exchange (Beogradska Berza): 11070 Belgrade, Omladinskih brigada 1, POB 50; tel. (11) 3117297; fax (11) 2138242; e-mail info@belex.rs; internet www.belex.rs; CEO GORDANA DOSTANIĆ.

INSURANCE

AMS Osiguranje (AMS Insurance): 11000 Belgrade, Ruzveltova 16; tel. (11) 3084900; fax (11) 3084902; e-mail info@ams.co.rs; internet www.ams.co.rs; f. 1998; non-life; Gen. Dir VUČETA MANDIĆ.

DDOR Novi Sad: 21000 Novi Sad, bul. Mihaila Pupina 8; tel. (21) 4886000; internet www.ddor.co.rs; f. 1990; life and non-life insurance and reinsurance; Chair. of Exec. Bd CHRISTIAN OTTO NEU.

Delta Generali Osiguranje: 11070 Belgrade, Milentija Popovića 7B; tel. (11) 2220555; fax (11) 2011727; e-mail kontakt@deltagenerali

.rs; internet www.deltagenerali.rs; life and non-life insurance and reinsurance.

Dunav Osiguranje (Danube Insurance): 11000 Belgrade, Makedonska 4, POB 624; tel. (11) 3221214; fax (11) 3344936; e-mail info@ dunav.com; internet www.dunav.com; f. 1974; life and non-life insurance and reinsurance; Gen. Dir MIRKO PETROVIĆ.

Sava Osiguranje: 11000 Belgrade, bul. Vojvode Mišića 51; tel. (11) 3644888; fax (11) 3644899; e-mail info@sava-osiguranje.rs; internet www.sava-osiguranje.rs; subsidiary of Sava Re (Slovenia); Chair. of Managing Bd DUŠKO JOVANOVIĆ.

SIM Osiguranje (SIM Insurance): 11000 Belgrade, Oblakovska 28; tel. and fax (11) 3690110.

Uniqa Osiguranje: 11070 Belgrade, Milutina Milankovića 134G; tel. (11) 2024100; e-mail info@uniqa.rs; internet www.uniqa.rs; fmrly Zepter Osiguranje; present name adopted 2006, following acquisition by Uniqa (Austria); life and non-life insurance; Gen. Dir KONSTANTIN KLIJEN.

Trade and Industry

GOVERNMENT AGENCIES

Foreign Trade Institute (Institut za Spoljnu Trgovinu): 11000 Belgrade, Moše Pijade 8; tel. (11) 3235391; fax (11) 3235306; Dir Dr SLOBODAN MRKŠA.

Investment and Export Promotion Agency of the Republic of Serbia (Agencija za strana ulaganja i promociju izvoza Republike Srbije—SIEPA): 11000 Belgrade, Vlajkovićeva 3; tel. (11) 3398550; fax (11) 3398814; e-mail office@siepa.gov.rs; internet www.siepa.gov .rs; f. 2001; Dir VESNA PERIĆ.

CHAMBER OF COMMERCE

Chamber of Commerce of Serbia (Privredna Komora Srbije): 11000 Belgrade, Resavska 13–15; tel. (11) 3300900; fax (11) 3230949; internet pks.komora.net; Pres. MILOŠ BUGARIN.

UTILITIES

Electricity

Elektroprivreda Srbije (EPS) (Serbia Electricity Corpn): 11000 Belgrade, Balkanska 13; tel. (11) 3610580; fax (11) 3611908; e-mail dragomir.markovic@eps.rs; internet www.eps.rs; state-owned; production, transmission and distribution of electric power in Serbia (incl. Kosovo); Chair. ACA MARKOVIĆ; Gen. Man. DRAGOMIR MARKOVIĆ.

Gas

Naftna Industrija Srbije—NIS a.d. Novi Sad (Oil Industry of Serbia): 21000 Novi Sad, Narodnog fronta 12; tel. (21) 4811111; fax (21) 4814321; e-mail office@nis.rs; internet www.nis.rs; four principal subsidiaries: NIS-Naftagas (NIS Oil and Gas); NIS-Petrol Jugpetrol (NIS Petrol); NIS-TNG (liquid petroleum gas); NIS-Ogostiteljstvo i turizam (Hospitality and Tourism); owns oil refineries at Pančevo and Novi Sad; 51% owned by Gazprom (Russia); Pres. Dr PETAR ŠKUNDRIĆ; Gen. Dir KIRIL KRAVČENKO; 13,900 employees (2009).

Srbijagas: 21000 Novi Sad, Narodnog fronta 12; tel. (11) 4812703; fax (11) 4814305; internet www.srbijagas.com; f. 2005; transportation and distribution of natural gas and liquid petrol gas, civil engineering; Dir-Gen. DUŠAN BAJATOVIĆ.

TRADE UNIONS

Association of Free and Independent Trade Unions: 11000 Belgrade, Karađorđeva 71; tel. and fax (11) 2623671; e-mail asns@ asns.org.rs; internet www.asns.org.rs; Pres. RANKA SAVIĆ.

Confederation of Autonomous Trade Unions of Serbia (Savez Samostalnih Sindikata Srbije): 11000 Belgrade, trg Nikole Pašić 5; tel. (11) 3230922; fax (11) 3241911; 600,000 mems.

Transport

RAILWAYS

In 2010 there were 4,092 km of railway track in use in Serbia, excluding Kosovo, of which 1,724 km were electrified.

Železnice Srbije (Serbian Railways): 11000 Belgrade, Nemanjina 6; tel. (11) 3614811; fax (11) 3616722; internet www.zeleznicesrbije .com; Pres. ZORAN ANĐELKOVIĆ; Dir-Gen. MILOVAN MARKOVIĆ.

ROADS

In 2010 there were an estimated 44,248 km of roads in Serbia, of which 63.28% were paved; there were 5,020 km of highways and 10,400 km of secondary roads.

INLAND WATERWAYS

About 8.0m. metric tons of freight were carried on inland water transport in Serbia in 2011.

SHIPPING

At 31 December 2012 Serbia's flag registered fleet comprised one vessel, totalling 299 grt.

Jugoagent Pomorska-rečna Agencija (Yugo Maritime and Rivers Shipping Agency): 11070 Belgrade, bul. Mihaila Pupina 165A, POB 210; tel. (11) 2018700; fax (11) 3112070; e-mail office@ jugoagent.net; internet www.jugoagent.net; f. 1947; fmrly Jugoslovenska Pomorska Agencija (Yugoslav Maritime Agency); charter services, liner and container transport, port agency, passenger service, air cargo service; Gen. Man. ZORAN NETKOVIĆ.

CIVIL AVIATION

There is an international airport at Belgrade and several domestic airports.

Jat Airways: 11070 Belgrade, bul. Umetnosti 16A; tel. (11) 3114222; fax (11) 3112853; e-mail pr@jat.com; internet www.jat.com; f. 1927 as Aeroput; fmrly Jugoslovenski Aerotransport (JAT—Yugoslav Airlines); flights between Serbia and destinations in Central, Western, Eastern and Southern Europe and the Middle East; Dir-Gen. VLADIMIR OGNJENOVIĆ.

Tourism

In 2011 tourist arrivals in Serbia (excluding Kosovo) totalled some 764,000. Receipts from tourism to Serbia and Montenegro amounted to US $992m. in that year, according to provisional data.

National Tourism Organization of Serbia (Turistička Organizacija Srbije): 11000 Belgrade, Čika Ljubina 8, POB 90; tel. (11) 6557100; fax (11) 2626767; e-mail office@serbia.travel; internet www .serbia.travel; f. 1994; produces information and conducts market research and promotion in the field of tourism; Man. Dir GORDANA PLAMENAC.

Defence

Compulsory military service was abolished with effect from 1 January 2011. Voluntary military service for women was introduced in 1983. As assessed at November 2012, the estimated total strength of the armed forces was 28,150, of which the army accounted for 13,250 and the air force nd air defence 5,100. Reserves totalled 50,150 personnel. In December 2006 Serbia was admitted to the 'Partnership for Peace' programme of the North Atlantic Treaty Organization (NATO, see p. 383). The budget for 2013 allocated 76,600m. dinars to defence.

Chief of Staff of the Military: Lt-Gen. LJUBIŠA DIKOVIĆ.

Commander of the Ground Forces: Lt-Gen. ALEKSANDAR ŽIVKOVIĆ.

Commander of the Air Forces and Air Defence Forces: Brig.-Gen. RANKO ŽIVAK.

Education

Elementary education is free and compulsory for all children between the ages of seven and 15. Various types of secondary education are available, but the vocational and technical schools are the most popular. Alternatively, children may attend a general secondary school (gymnasium) where they follow a four-year course, prior to university entrance. In 2009/10 enrolment in primary education included 93% of children in the appropriate age-group. The corresponding ratio in secondary education in the same year was 90%. In 2010/11 some 228,531 students were enrolled in state and private higher education faculties. Serbia has seven state universities and seven private universities.

SEYCHELLES

Introductory Survey

LOCATION, CLIMATE, LANGUAGE, RELIGION, FLAG, CAPITAL

The Republic of Seychelles comprises about 115 islands, widely scattered over the western Indian Ocean. Apart from the Seychelles archipelago, the country includes several other island groups, the southernmost being about 210 km (130 miles) north of Madagascar. The climate is tropical, with small seasonal variations in temperature and rainfall. The average temperature in Victoria is nearly 27°C (80°F) and average annual rainfall 236 cm (93 ins). In 1981 Seselwa, a creole spoken by virtually all Seychellois, replaced English and French as the official language. Almost all of the inhabitants are Christians, of whom more than 85% belong to the Roman Catholic Church. The national flag (proportions 1 by 2) has five rays, extending from the lower hoist corner, of blue, yellow, red, white and green. The capital is Victoria, on the island of Mahé.

CONTEMPORARY POLITICAL HISTORY

Historical Context

Seychelles was uninhabited until colonized by France in 1770. It was ceded to the United Kingdom in 1814 and administered as a dependency of Mauritius until 1903, when it became a Crown Colony. A ministerial system of government was introduced in 1970, and Seychelles proceeded to full independence, as a sovereign republic within the Commonwealth, on 29 June 1976, under a coalition Government with James (later Sir James) Mancham as President and Albert René, the leader of the Seychelles People's United Party (SPUP), as Prime Minister. Under the independence agreement, the United Kingdom returned to Seychelles the islands of Aldabra, Farquhar and Desroches, detached in 1965 to form part of the British Indian Ocean Territory and subsequently leased to the USA.

In June 1977 the SPUP staged an armed coup while Mancham was absent from the islands. René was declared President, the National Assembly was dissolved and the Constitution suspended. In May 1978 the SPUP was renamed the Seychelles People's Progressive Front (SPPF). A new Constitution, proclaimed in March 1979, established a one-party state. René was re-elected to the presidency in 1979, 1984 and again in 1989 as sole candidate, for a third term of office, the maximum period permitted under the 1979 Constitution. During this period opponents of René's socialist Government made a number of attempts to overthrow the regime. The most serious assault took place in November 1981, when about 50 mercenaries, mainly South Africans posing as tourists, flew to join insurgents already on the islands. When the rebellion collapsed, most of the mercenaries escaped to South Africa, where several of their number were later tried and imprisoned. Further plots, discovered in October 1982 and November 1983, were ascribed to the same Seychellois exiles who had planned the 1981 coup attempt.

Domestic Political Affairs

Until the early 1990s exiled opposition to René remained split among a number of small groups based principally in London, United Kingdom. In July 1991 five of these parties formed a coalition, the United Democratic Movement (UDM), under the leadership of Dr Maxime Ferrari, a former political associate of René, while ex-President Mancham established a 'Crusade for Democracy'. René, meanwhile, came under increasing pressure from France and the United Kingdom, the islands' principal aid donors, to restore a democratic political system. Internally, open opposition to the SPPF was fostered by the newly formed Parti Seselwa, or Parti Seychellois (PS), led by an Anglican clergyman, Wavel Ramkalawan. In August 1991 Ferrari returned from exile to organize support for the UDM, and in November the Government invited all political dissidents to return to the islands.

In December 1991 the SPPF agreed to surrender the party's monopoly of power. It was announced that, from January 1992, political groups numbering at least 100 members would be granted official registration, and that multi-party elections would take place in July for a constituent assembly, whose proposals for constitutional reform would be submitted to a national referendum, with a view to holding multi-party parliamentary elections before the end of 1992. In April Mancham returned from exile to lead the New Democratic Party (NDP), subsequently the Democratic Party—DP).

After an initial draft Constitution, which required the approval of at least 60% of voters, was endorsed by only 53.7% at a referendum held in November 1992, work began in January 1993 on proposals for submission to a further referendum. A compromise was reached on the hitherto divisive electoral formula for a new National Assembly and with the joint endorsement of René and Mancham, the draft document was submitted to a national referendum in June, and approved by 73.9% of voters. At the presidential election that followed in July, René, who under the new Constitution was eligible to stand for a further three five-year terms, received 59.5% of the votes, against 36.7% for Mancham. In the concurrently held legislative elections, the SPPF secured 21 of the 22 directly elective seats, and the DP one seat. Of the 11 additional seats allocated on a proportional basis, the SPPF received a further seven seats, the DP three seats and the PS one seat. The new Government began to promote a gradual transition from socialism to free-market policies, aimed at maximizing the country's potential as an 'offshore' financial and business centre.

In July 1996 the SPPF introduced a series of constitutional amendments, creating the post of Vice-President, to which James Michel, the Minister of Finance, Communications and Defence and a long-standing political associate of René, was appointed in the following month. The constitutional changes also provided for revisions in constituency boundaries, which were generally interpreted as favouring SPPF candidates in future parliamentary elections, and an increase in the number of seats in the National Assembly (see Constitution and Government).

The outcome of the elections of March 1998 provided the SPPF with a decisive victory. René obtained 66.7% of the presidential ballot, while his party secured 30 of the 34 seats in the enlarged National Assembly. Ramkalawan took 19.5% of the votes cast in the presidential election, while Mancham received only 13.8%. In the National Assembly the United Opposition (UO, formed in 1995) increased its representation from one to three seats, with the DP losing three of the four seats previously held. Since the 1993 elections, effective opposition to the Government had increasingly been led by Ramkalawan's UO, as the DP opted to pursue a policy of 'reconciliation' with the SPPF. In mid-1998 the UO changed its name to the Seychelles National Party (SNP).

In July 2001 René declared a presidential election almost two years early, claiming that this was in order to reassure investors about the long-term stability of the country. On 31 August–2 September René was re-elected as President, but with a reduced mandate, securing 54.2% of the valid votes cast. Ramkalawan, the SNP candidate, won 45.0% of the votes. Legislative elections, which were due in 2003, took place early, on 4–6 December 2002. The SPPF retained its majority in the National Assembly, but with a reduced margin, securing 23 of the 34 seats, while the SNP won the remaining 11 seats. In March 2003 René indicated during the congress of the SPPF that he would progressively relinquish control of certain presidential duties to Vice-President Michel, who was also designated as the party's candidate for the next presidential election.

The Michel presidency

On 14 April 2004 President René formally retired, having spent almost 27 years in office. He was succeeded by Vice-President Michel, who was inaugurated as President on the same day. Joseph Belmont was subsequently appointed Vice-President, retaining responsibility for tourism and transport.

In the weeks prior to the 2006 presidential election, tensions increased between supporters of the leading political parties contesting the vote, and there were reports of numerous violent incidents. Nevertheless, the election proceeded as scheduled on 28–30 July, when Michel secured victory with 53.7% of the valid votes cast; Ramkalawan received 45.7%. A voter turn-out of 88.7% was recorded. In mid-August a new Government was installed. In October several high-ranking SNP officials, including Ramkalawan, were injured by security forces, after protesting outside the parliamentary building. The incident followed a speech made by Ramkalawan at the National Assembly denouncing a proposal to ban all political parties from establishing private radio stations. Ramkalawan was among three members of the SNP who were subsequently charged with attending an illegal demonstration. They were brought to trial that month; however, President Michel later suspended the charges in an attempt to quell rising violence among the political parties and their supporters. An independent inquiry into the incident was launched in March 2007, and in February 2008 the Government accepted responsibility for injuries caused during the protests.

In March 2007 President Michel dissolved the National Assembly and announced that early elections would be organized. At the legislative elections, which were conducted on 10–12 May, the SPPF retained 23 seats and its majority in the National Assembly, securing 56.2% of the votes cast. An alliance of the SNP and the DP received 43.8% of the votes, and took the 11 remaining seats. International observers praised the conduct of the elections, at which 85.9% of the registered electorate participated.

The ruling SPPF and the opposition DP both adopted new names in June 2009: the former was restyled the Parti Lepep (People's Party) and the latter, no longer in alliance with the SNP, became the New Democratic Party (NDP). Michel, hitherto Secretary-General of the SPPF, was elected President of the Parti Lepep (René being accorded the title Founding President), while Ralph Volcere was confirmed as leader of the NDP, having assumed the leadership of the DP in March, following the resignation of Paul Chow.

Meanwhile, in April 2008 President Michel established an 11-member committee, chaired by former Attorney-General Francis Chang-Sam, to review the Constitution; the committee held its first meeting in June, and in December 2009 presented its findings to the President. In March 2010 Michel confirmed that the review's conclusions had been considered, and requested that the Attorney-General, Ronny Govinden, commence the process of revising the Constitution.

President Michel announced a reorganization of the Council of Ministers in June 2010, prompted by the imminent retirement of Vice-President Belmont and by the resignation of the Minister of Social Development and Health, Marie-Pierre Lloyd. The changes included the appointment of three new ministers to the Government: Jean-Paul Adam as Minister of Foreign Affairs; Erna Athanasius as Minister of Health; and Peter Sinon, hitherto an Executive Director at the African Development Bank, as Minister of Investment, Natural Resources and Industry, a newly created post. Danny Faure, the Minister of Finance, succeeded Belmont as Vice-President on 1 July, retaining the finance portfolio and assuming additional responsibility for trade, information technology and public administration.

Recent developments: presidential and legislative elections

The presidential election took place on 19–21 May 2011. The election duly took place on those dates and, according to official results, Michel was re-elected to the presidency having secured 55.5% of the total votes cast. Ramkalawan again finished in second place, with 41.4%, while the independent candidate Philippe Boullé and Volcere, representing the NDP, took just 1.7% and 1.5%, respectively. Michel was inaugurated on 24 May and the following month the National Assembly approved the new Council of Ministers, which, with only one exception, was composed of members of the previous administration.

Legislative elections, originally scheduled to take place in May 2012, were held early, on 29 September–1 October 2011, following approval from the National Assembly for its dissolution. The SNP had boycotted sessions since late May, prompting the decision to bring forward the elections to the National Assembly, although the SNP also boycotted that poll. As a result, Parti Lepep secured all 31 seats in the legislature. Of those seats, 25 were filled by direct election and the remaining six were allocated on the basis of proportional representation (PR). On 9 December the Court of Appeal ruled that the number of PR seats be calculated based on the number of valid votes, rather than the number of actual votes (including invalid and spoiled votes, of which there were a substantial number), resulting in two further PR seats being awarded to Parti Lepep and one seat to the newly

registered Popular Democratic Movement. (Prior to the elections, another party—the Seychelles Freedom Party—had also been registered.) Parti Lepep declined to nominate additional members, and thus the total number of seats in the National Assembly increased to 32.

In March 2012 the Governor of the Central Bank of Seychelles, Pierre Laporte, was appointed to replace Faure as Minister of Finance, Trade and Investment. However, Faure retained his posts as Vice-President and Minister of Information Technology and Public Administration. President Michel announced that Faure would have a wider mandate as Vice-President following the reorganization, which also included, *inter alia*, new Ministers of Tourism and Culture (Alain St Ange), Health (Mitcy Larue), and Environment and Energy (Rolph Payet).

In March 2012 US authorities handed over to Seychelles 15 suspected Somali pirates accused of attacking an Iranian fishing vessel in the Arabian Sea. A further 17 were transferred into Seychellois custody at the end of the month. In May 11 more suspected Somali pirates were accepted by Seychelles authorities for prosecution. Representing some 20% of its prison population, Seychelles detained the highest percentage of Somali pirates in the world. Moreover, it was reported in September that the UN's Regional Anti-Piracy Prosecution and Intelligence Coordination Centre (RAPPICC) would be based in Seychelles. The centre would be tasked with collecting intelligence and evidence relating to the prosecution of suspected pirates.

Foreign Affairs

Seychelles has traditionally pursued a policy of non-alignment in international affairs, and supports movements for the creation of a 'zone of peace' in the Indian Ocean area. Until 1983 all naval warships wishing to dock at Seychelles had to provide a guarantee that they were not carrying nuclear weapons. The British and US Governments refused to agree to this condition, and their respective naval fleets were therefore effectively banned from using Seychelles port facilities. This requirement was withdrawn in September 1983, although Seychelles continued, in theory, to refuse entry to ships carrying nuclear weapons.

Since the late 1980s Seychelles has expanded the scope of its formal diplomatic contacts. Relations have been established with the Comoros and with Mauritius, and agreements have been made with the latter for co-operation in health and economic development matters. In 1989 diplomatic relations were established with Morocco, Madagascar and Côte d'Ivoire, and in 1990 with Kenya. During 1992 formal relations were established with Israel and South Africa, and in 1998 Seychelles proposed to establish a diplomatic mission in Malaysia to expand its relations in Asia and Oceania. Libya opened a diplomatic mission in Seychelles in January 2000, and diplomatic ties were established with Sudan in October. Following years of minimal interaction between France and Seychelles, owing to Seychelles' accumulated debt to the Agence Française de Développement, the French Minister for Co-operation was the first minister in over four years to visit Seychelles in February 2001. It was hoped that a resolution to the situation could be found and a new schedule for repayments negotiated. In 2001 relations were restored with Japan, which granted a subsidy for fishery development to Seychelles; this was said to be a consequence of the reversal of Seychelles' whaling policy. President Michel paid a state visit to Mauritius in March 2005, as guest of honour at that country's annual celebration of independence; various economic and co-operative agreements between the two countries were also signed. In December, as a result of the seventh session of the Seychelles-Mauritius Commission on Bilateral Co-operation, a further agreement was signed on the sharing of expertise in a wide range of fields. The Government also strengthened relations with the People's Republic of China, following a state visit to that country by Michel in November 2006.

CONSTITUTION AND GOVERNMENT

Under the 1993 Constitution, executive power is vested in the President, who is Head of State and Commander-in-Chief of the Armed Forces. The President, who is elected by direct popular vote, appoints and leads the Council of Ministers, which acts in an advisory capacity to him. The President also appoints the holders of certain public offices and the judiciary. The President may hold office for a maximum period of three five-year terms. The legislature is the unicameral National Assembly, presently comprising 32 members, of whom 25 were directly elected for five years and seven allocated on a proportional basis. Constitutional changes, introduced in July 1996, provide for an enlargement to 35 members: 25 directly elected and a maximum of 10 allocated on a proportional basis. A review of the Constitution commenced in the early 2010s (see Contemporary Political History).

REGIONAL AND INTERNATIONAL CO-OPERATION

Seychelles is a member of the African Union (see p. 191), of the Common Market for Eastern and Southern Africa (see p. 241) and of the Indian Ocean Commission (see p. 462), which aims to promote co-operation in the region. It was announced in December 1996 that Seychelles was to provide the headquarters of the Indian Ocean Tuna Commission.

Seychelles became a member of the UN in 1976 and currently has observer status at the World Trade Organization (WTO, see p. 444). Seychelles participates in the Group of 77 (G77, see p. 461) developing countries.

ECONOMIC AFFAIRS

In 2011, according to estimates by the World Bank, Seychelles' gross national income (GNI), measured at average 2009–11 prices, was US $957m., equivalent to $11,130 per head (or $25,320 per head on an international purchasing-power parity basis). During 2002–11, it was estimated, the population increased at an average annual rate of 0.3%, while gross domestic product (GDP) per head increased, in real terms, by an average of 2.8% per year. Overall GDP increased, in real terms, at an average annual rate of 3.1% in 2002–11. Real GDP grew by 5.0% in 2011.

Agriculture (including forestry and fishing) contributed 2.7% of GDP in 2011, according to provisional figures, and accounted for 1.0% of total employment in the same year. Seychelles' main agricultural crop is the coconut. Other cash crops include cinnamon bark, tea, patchouli, vanilla and limes. Tea, sweet potatoes, cassava, yams, sugar cane, bananas, eggs and poultry meat are produced for local consumption. However, imports of food and live animals constituted an estimated 19.3% of the value of total imports in 2011. Fishing has become increasingly important since the 1980s, and exports of canned tuna alone contributed an estimated 50.9% of the value of total exports in 2011. Licence fees from foreign fishing vessels, allowed to operate in Seychelles' waters, contribute significantly to foreign exchange. A fishing protocol, worth €5.6m. per year, was signed with the European Union (EU) in 2005 and was renewed for a three-year period commencing in January 2011. Under the agreement, EU vessels are permitted to catch a maximum of 52,000 metric tons of fish in Seychelles waters. Agricultural GDP decreased at an average annual rate of 1.9% during 2004–11; the sector's GDP decreased by 6.0% in 2010, but grew by 3.5% in 2011, according to provisional official figures.

Industry (including mining, manufacturing, construction and power) provisionally contributed 16.2% of GDP in 2011, and accounted for 23.8% of total employment in that year. Industrial GDP increased at an average annual rate of 4.7% during 2004–11; and by 5.4% in 2011, according to provisional official figures.

The mining sector is small (it accounted for less than 0.5% of total employment in 2008) and mineral production consists mainly of quantities of construction materials, such as clay, coral, stone and sand. There are deposits of natural gas, and during the 1980s concessions were sold to several foreign companies, allowing exploration for petroleum. Exploratory drilling has so far proved unsuccessful; however, an agreement to renew exploration was made in 2005. A survey of offshore areas, initiated in 1980, revealed the presence of nodules, containing deposits of various metals, on the sea-bed. The renewed commercial exploitation of Seychelles' granite reserves is under investigation and the future development of offshore petroleum reserves remains a possibility.

Manufacturing contributed 8.5% of GDP in 2011, according to provisional official figures, and accounted for 9.4% of total employment in that year. Apart from a tuna-canning plant (opened in 1987), the manufacturing sector consists mainly of small-scale activities, including boat-building, printing and furniture-making. Manufacturing GDP increased at an average annual rate of 1.0% during 2004–11; the sector's GDP increased by 6.5% in 2011, according to provisional official figures.

Construction contributed a provisional 7.2% of GDP in 2011, and, along with quarrying, accounted for 12.3% of total employment in that year. According to official estimates, the construction sector grew at an average annual rate of 11.7% in 2004–11. However, the GDP of the sector declined by 5.0% in 2010, before growing by 27.7% in 2011, according to provisional official figures.

Energy is derived principally from oil-fired power stations. In 2011 mineral fuels and lubricants accounted for an estimated 25.2% of the total value of imports. The vast majority of fuel imports are re-exported, mainly as bunker sales to visiting ships and aircraft—exports of refined petroleum products contributed 30.0% of total export earnings in 2004, and re-exports accounted for an estimated 44.5% of the value of total exports in 2011. It is envisaged that the proceeds from re-exports will eventually fully fund fuel imports.

Services provided 81.1% of GDP in 2011, according to provisional figures, and accounted for 75.1% of total employment in that year. In 2011 tourist arrivals totalled 194,476 and income from tourism amounted to SR $2,750m. in that year, according to central bank estimates. The majority of visitors were from Western Europe, notably from France, Germany, Italy and the United Kingdom. The GDP of the services sector increased at an average annual rate of 5.7% during 2004–11. Services GDP increased by 4.5% in 2011, according to provisional official figures.

In 2011 Seychelles recorded a visible merchandise trade deficit of US $401.6m. and there was a deficit of $226.3m. on the current account of the balance of payments. The principal source of imports (providing 32.6% of the total) in 2011 was the United Arab Emirates; other important suppliers were Spain, South Africa, Singapore, France and the United Kingdom. The principal market for domestic exports (excluding re-exports) in 2011 was France (taking 38.9% of the total); other significant purchasers were the United Kingdom and Italy. The principal export is canned tuna (following the expansion of the Indian Ocean Tuna Co in 1995 and increasing rates of production thereafter); in 2011 canned tuna represented 91.8% of domestic exports. The main imports in 2011 were mineral fuels, machinery and transport equipment, basic manufactures, and food and live animals.

In 2011 Seychelles recorded a budgetary surplus of SR 316.1m. (equivalent to 2.4% of GDP). Seychelles' general government gross debt was SR 9,746m. in 2011, equivalent to 77.4% of GDP. Seychelles' total external debt was US $1,510m. at the end of 2010, of which $498m. was public and publicly guaranteed debt. In that year, the cost of servicing long-term public and publicly guaranteed debt and repayments to the IMF was equivalent to 5.7% of the value of exports of goods, services and income (excluding workers' remittances). According to the IMF, the annual rate of inflation averaged 11.3% in 2005–11; consumer prices decreased by 2.4% in 2010, but increased by 2.6% in 2011. Some 8.3% of the labour force were registered as unemployed in 1993.

Since the early 1970s tourism has been the mainstay of the Seychelles economy, and despite measures introduced in 1995 to develop Seychelles as an 'offshore' financial services centre, and to establish the islands as a centre for transshipment and air freight in the Indian Ocean area, the continuing dependence of the economy on tourism leaves the country highly vulnerable to outside economic influences, while the cost of servicing the external debt remains an impediment to balanced growth. In November 2008 the rupee was allowed to float freely on foreign exchange markets, resulting in a depreciation in its value of some 48% and significantly higher inflation. According to the IMF in its sixth review of Seychelles' economic reform programme (released in January 2013), GDP growth had been sustained during 2012 in spite of a difficult economic situation in Europe—which provides Seychelles with most of its tourism arrivals—and the discontinuation of direct flights to and from that continent with the country's national carrier. Fewer tourist arrivals from France and Italy were offset by increases in arrivals from Germany, Russia and the Gulf states. The IMF expected growth of 2.7% in 2012, driven by the tourism and telecoms sectors; and forecast growth of 3.0% in 2013. The outlook for the economy in the medium term was positive, as tourism was expected to continue to expand into non-traditional markets and inflation was expected to return to more moderate levels. (It peaked at 8.9% in June 2012.) Meanwhile, public debt increased by 2.5% of GDP in the first half of 2012 following a restructuring agreement with Air Seychelles, but the increase was mitigated in the second half of the year by the Government's sale of d'Arros Island. The IMF projected a budget surplus of 5.9% of GDP for 2012.

PUBLIC HOLIDAYS
2014: 1–2 January (New Year), 18–21 April (Easter), 1 May (Labour Day), 5 June (Liberation Day, anniversary of 1977 coup), 18 June (National Day), 19 May (Corpus Christi), 29 June (Independence Day), 15 August (Assumption), 1 November (All Saints' Day), 8 December (Immaculate Conception), 25 December (Christmas Day).

Statistical Survey

Source (unless otherwise stated): Statistics and Database Administration Section, Management and Information Systems Division, POB 206, Victoria; e-mail misdstat@seychelles.net; internet www.nsb.gov.sc.

AREA AND POPULATION

Area: 455.3 sq km (175.8 sq miles), incl. Aldabra lagoon (145 sq km).

Population: 81,755 at census of 26 August 2002; 90,945 (males 46,912, females 44,033) at census of 26 August 2010. *Mid-2012* (official estimate): 88,303.

Density (at mid-2012): 193.9 per sq km.

Population by Age and Sex (official estimates at mid-2012): *0–14:* 19,689 (males 9,908, females 9,781); *15–64:* 61,625 (males 30,628, females 30,997); *65 and over:* 6,989 (males 2,777, females 4,212); *Total* 88,303 (males 43,313, females 44,990).

Principal Town: Victoria (capital), estimated population 60,000 (incl. suburbs) in 1994. *Mid-2011* (incl. suburbs, UN estimate): Victoria 26,609. (Source: UN, *World Urbanization Prospects: The 2011 Revision*).

Births, Marriages and Deaths (registrations, 2011): Live births 1,625 (birth rate 18.6 per 1,000); Marriages (of residents) 466 (marriage rate 5.3 per 1,000); Deaths 691 (death rate 7.9 per 1,000).

Life Expectancy (years at birth, official estimates): 72.6 (males 67.7; females 78.0) in 2011.

Employment (2011, averages): Agriculture, forestry and fishing 506; Manufacturing 4,670; Electricity and water 1,080; Construction (with quarrying) 6,147; Trade, restaurants and hotels 14,522; Transport, storage and communications 4,747; Other services 18,219; *Total* 49,891.

HEALTH AND WELFARE

Key Indicators

Total Fertility Rate (children per woman, 2010): 2.3.

Under-5 Mortality Rate (per 1,000 live births, 2010): 14.

Physicians (per 1,000 head, 2004): 1.51.

Hospital Beds (per 1,000 head, government establishments only, 2010): 3.6.

Health Expenditure (2009): US $ per head (PPP): 712.

Health Expenditure (2009): % of GDP: 3.3.

Health Expenditure (2009): public (% of total): 92.7.

Access to Water (% of persons, 2004): 88.

Total Carbon Dioxide Emissions ('000 metric tons, 2008): 682.1.

Carbon Dioxide Emissions Per Head (metric tons, 2008): 7.8.

Human Development Index (2011): ranking: 52.

Human Development Index (2011): value: 0.773.

For sources and definitions, see explanatory note on p. vi.

AGRICULTURE, ETC.

Principal Crops (metric tons, 2011): Coconuts 2,782*; Vegetables (incl. melons) 2,630*; Bananas 1,600*; Other fruits (excl. melons) 2,202*; Tea 38; Cinnamon 39.

*FAO estimate.

Livestock (head, 2011, FAO estimates unless otherwise indicated): Cattle 660; Pigs 6,000 (unofficial figure); Goats 5,400.

Livestock Products (metric tons, 2011, FAO estimates): Pig meat 328; Chicken meat 622; Hen eggs 1,280.

Fishing ('000 metric tons, live weight, 2010): Capture 87.1 (Skipjack tuna 43.8; Yellowfin tuna 26.0; Bigeye tuna 10.7); Aquaculture 0.3* (Giant tiger prawn 0.3*); *Total catch* 87.4*.

*FAO estimate.

Source: FAO.

INDUSTRY

Industrial Production (2011): Canned tuna 30,152 metric tons; Beer and stout ('000 litres) 5,400; Soft drinks ('000 litres) 6,984; Cigarettes 55m.; Electric energy 324m. kWh.

FINANCE

Currency and Exchange Rates: 100 cents = 1 Seychelles rupee (SR). *Sterling, Dollar and Euro Equivalents* (31 October 2012): £1 sterling = 20.971 rupees; US $1 = 13.013 rupees; €1 = 16.907 rupees; 100 Seychelles rupees = £4.77 = $7.68 = €5.91. *Average Exchange Rate* (Seychelles rupees per US $): 13.6099 in 2009; 12.0678 in 2010; 12.3810 in 2011. Note: In November 1979 the value of the Seychelles rupee was linked to the IMF's special drawing right (SDR). In March 1981 the mid-point exchange rate was set at SDR 1 = 7.2345 rupees. This remained in effect until February 1997, when the fixed link with the SDR was ended.

Budget (SR million, 2011): *Revenue:* Tax revenue 4,232.3 (Taxes on income, etc. 612.4; Domestic taxes on goods and services 1,208.4; Excise tax 420.9); Non tax revenue 570.0; Total 4,802.4, excl. grants received (278.9). *Expenditure:* Current expenditure 3,713.3 (Wages and salaries 891.2; Goods and services 994.2; Interest 383.5; Transfers 1,423.4); Capital expenditure 1,060.5; Total 4,773.8, excl. lending minus repayments (8.6). *2012* (budget estimates): Total revenue 4,985.2 (excl. grants 440.1); Total expenditure 5,172.6 (excl. lending minus repayment 8.5). Note: Figures represent the consolidated accounts of the central Government, covering the operations of the Recurrent and Capital Budgets and of the Social Security Fund (Source: Ministry of Finance, Victoria).

International Reserves (US $ million at 31 December 2011): IMF special drawing rights 10.39; Reserve position in IMF 0.81; Foreign exchange 241.11; Total 252.31. Source: IMF, *International Financial Statistics*.

Money Supply (SR million at 31 December 2011): Currency outside depository corporations 623.5; Transferable deposits 5,707.8; Other deposits 1,264.4; *Broad money* 7,595.7. Source: IMF, *International Financial Statistics*.

Cost of Living (Consumer Price Index; base: 2005 = 100): All items 189.4 in 2009; 184.8 in 2010; 189.6 in 2011. Source: IMF, *International Financial Statistics*.

Expenditure on the Gross Domestic Product (SR million at current prices, 2011): Government final consumption expenditure 3,697.7; Private final consumption expenditure 6,929.4; Gross capital formation 4,450.7; *Total domestic expenditure* 15,077.8; Exports of goods and services 13,523.7; *Less* Imports of goods and services 16,043.7; *GDP in purchasers' values* 12,557.8. Source: UN National Accounts Main Aggregates Database.

Gross Domestic Product by Economic Activity (SR million at current prices, 2011, provisional): Agriculture, forestry and fishing 293.1; Manufacturing 938.8; Electricity and water 56.8; Construction 787.6; Wholesale and retail trade, and repair of motor vehicles and motorcycles 838.4; Trade, restaurants and hotels 2,456.3; Transport, storage and communications 1,208.0; Finance, insurance, real estate and business services 3,018.5; Education 332.9; Public administration and defence, and social security 700.8; Other services 353.4; *Sub-total* 10,984.9; Import duties, less subsidies 2,339.3; *Less* Imputed bank service charge 205.3; *GDP in purchasers' values* 13,118.9.

Balance of Payments (US $ million, 2011): Exports of goods 478.0; Imports of goods –879.6; *Balance on goods* –401.6; Exports of services 614.3; Imports of services –422.8; *Balance on goods and services* –210.1; Primary income received 6.7; Primary income paid –57.6; *Balance on goods, services and primary income* –261.0; Secondary income received 52.3; Secondary income paid –17.6; *Current balance* –226.3; Capital account (net) 47.5; Direct investment assets –2.0; Direct investment liabilities 138.8; Portfolio investment assets –17.9; Other investment assets –46.3; Other investment liabilities 73.2; Net errors and omissions 55.5; *Reserves and related items* 22.4. Source: IMF, *International Financial Statistics*.

EXTERNAL TRADE

Principal Commodities (distribution by SITC, SR million, 2011, provisional): *Imports c.i.f.:* Food and live animals 2,466.1; Mineral fuels 3,224.4; Basic manufactures 2,437.2; Machinery and transport 2,831.1; Total (incl. others) 12,802.9. *Exports f.o.b.:* Canned tuna 3,001.3; Fish (fresh/frozen) 27.7; Frozen prawns 0.0; Fish meal 91.3; Medicaments, etc. 29.6; Total (incl. others) 5,893.0 (of which domestic exports SR 3,268.9m. and re-exports SR 2,624.1m.).

Principal Trading Partners (SR million, 2011, provisional): *Imports c.i.f.:* France 740.2; Italy 397.5; Singapore 747.6; South Africa 864.7; Spain 1,321.2; United Arab Emirates 4,171.8; United Kingdom 654.3; Total (incl. others) 12,802.9. *Exports f.o.b.:* France 1,270.3; Germany 59.9; Italy 480.3; Netherlands 74.0; Sri Lanka 44.6; United Kingdom 1,055.3; Total (incl. others) 5,893.0 (of which domestic exports SR 3,268.9m. and re-exports SR 2,624.1m.).

TRANSPORT

Road Traffic (registered motor vehicles, 2011): Private 9,974; Commercial 3,105; Taxis 305; Self-drive 1,823; Motorcycles 173; Omnibuses 473; *Total* 15,853.

Shipping: *Flag Registered Fleet* (at 31 December 2012): Vessels 42; Total displacement 364,448 grt (Source: Lloyd's List Intelligence—www.lloydslistintelligence.com); *International Sea-borne Freight Traffic* (2011): Freight ('000 metric tons): Imports 406; Exports 5,877; Transshipment (of fish) 153.

Civil Aviation (traffic on scheduled services, 2009): Kilometres flown 17m.; Passengers carried 565,000; Passenger-km 1,428m.; Total ton-km 165m. (Source: UN, *Statistical Yearbook*). *2011:* Aircraft movements 4,470; Passengers embarked 248,000; Passengers disembarked 247,000; Freight embarked 2,314 metric tons; Freight disembarked 7,299 metric tons.

TOURISM

Foreign Tourist Arrivals ('000): 157.5 in 2009; 174.5 in 2010; 194.5 in 2011.

Arrivals by Country of Residence (2011): France 39,370; Germany 23,706; Italy 25,674; Russia 8,840; South Africa 10,559; Switzerland 7,644; United Kingdom 13,291; Total (incl. others) 194,476.

Tourism Receipts (SR million, central bank estimates): 2,841 in 2009; 2,451 in 2010; 2,750 in 2011.

COMMUNICATIONS MEDIA

Telephones (2011): 27,900 main lines in use. Source: International Telecommunication Union.

Mobile Cellular Telephones (2011): 126,600 subscribers. Source: International Telecommunication Union.

Internet Subscribers (2011): 10,600 accounts. Source: International Telecommunication Union.

Broadband Subscribers (2011): 9,000. Source: International Telecommunication Union.

Daily Newspapers (2011): 3.

Non-daily Newspapers (2011): 3.

EDUCATION

Pre-primary (2012): 33 schools; 203 teachers; 2,916 pupils.

Primary (2012): 27 schools; 736 teachers (males 80, females 656); 8,695 pupils (males 4,339, females 4,356).

Secondary (2012): 13 schools; 581 teachers (males 236, females 345); 7,113 pupils (males 3,540, females 3,573).

Post-secondary (2012): 9 schools; 141 teachers; 2,021 pupils.

Special Education (2012): 2 institution; 25 teachers; 57 pupils.

Pupil-teacher Ratio (primary education): 13 in 2012.

Adult Literacy Rate (official estimate): 94% (males 94%; females 95%) in 2010.

Directory

The Government

HEAD OF STATE

President: JAMES ALIX MICHEL (took office 14 April 2004, elected 28–30 July 2006; re-elected 19–21 May 2011).
Vice-President: DANNY FAURE.

COUNCIL OF MINISTERS
(May 2013)

President, with additional responsibility for Defence, Legal Affairs, Youth and Hydrocarbons: JAMES ALIX MICHEL.

Vice-President, Minister of Information Technology and Public Administration: DANNY FAURE.

Minister of Community Development, Social Affairs and Sports: VINCENT MERITON (Designated Minister).

Minister of Home Affairs and Transport: JOEL MORGAN.

Minister of Education: MACSUZY MONDON.

Minister of Foreign Affairs: JEAN-PAUL ADAM.

Minister of Natural Resources and Industry: PETER SINON.

Minister of the Environment and Energy: Dr ROLPH PAYET.

Minister of Finance, Trade and Investment: PIERRE LAPORTE.

Minister of Tourism and Culture: ALAIN ST ANGE.

Minister of Health: MITCY LARUE.

Minister of Land Use and Housing: CHRISTIAN LIONNET.

Minister of Labour and Human Resource Development: IDITH ALEXANDER.

MINISTRIES

Office of the President: State House, POB 55, Victoria; tel. 4224155; fax 4224985; internet www.statehouse.gov.sc.

Office of the Vice-President: State House, POB 1303, Victoria; tel. 4286800; fax 4225152; e-mail jbelmont@statehouse.gov.sc.

Ministry of Community Development, Social Affairs and Sports: Oceangate House, POB 731, Victoria; tel. 4225477; fax 4224081; e-mail oplg@seychelles.net; internet www.localgovernment.gov.sc.

Ministry of Education: POB 48, Mont Fleuri; tel. 4283283; fax 4224859; e-mail ps@eduhq.edu.sc; internet www.education.gov.sc.

Ministry of the Environment and Energy: Victoria; f. .

Ministry of Finance, Trade and Investment: Liberty House, POB 113, Victoria; tel. 4382006; fax 4225265; e-mail psf@finance.gov.sc; internet www.finance.gov.sc.

Ministry of Foreign Affairs: Maison Quéau de Quinssy, POB 656, Mont Fleuri; tel. 4283500; fax 4224845; e-mail mfapesey@seychelles.net; internet www.mfa.gov.sc.

Ministry of Health: POB 52, Mont Fleuri; tel. 4388000; fax 4226042; internet www.moh.gov.sc.

Ministry of Home Affairs and Transport: Independence House, POB 199, Victoria; tel. 4670504; fax 4323651; internet www.env.gov.sc.

Ministry of Labour and Human Resource Development: Independence House, 1st Floor, POB 1097, Victoria; tel. 4297200; fax 4325326; e-mail contact@employment.gov.sc; internet www.employment.gov.sc.

Ministry of Land Use and Housing: Victoria; tel. 4284444; fax 4225187; e-mail mluh@mluh.gov.sc.

Ministry of Natural Resources and Industry: Victoria.

Ministry of Tourism and Culture: Victoria.

President and Legislature

PRESIDENT

Election, 19–21 May 2011

Candidate			Votes	% of votes
James Alix Michel (Parti Lepep)	.	.	31,966	55.46
Wavel Ramkalawan (SNP)	.	. .	23,878	41.43
Philippe Boullé (Independent)	.	. .	956	1.66
Ralph Volcere (NDP)	.	. . .	833	1.45
Total	. . . .		**57,633**	**100.00**

NATIONAL ASSEMBLY

Speaker: Dr PATRICK HERMINIE.

Election, 29 September–1 October 2011

Party	Valid votes cast	% of valid votes	Seats*
Parti Lepep	31,123	88.56	31
Popular Democratic Movement (PDM)	3,828	10.89	—
Independent	194	0.55	—
Total	**35,145†**	**100.0**	**31**

* Of the Assembly's 31 seats, 25 were filled by direct election and six by allocation on a proportional basis. The election was boycotted by the Seychelles National Party (SNP), the main opposition party of Seychelles. On 9 December 2011 the Court of Appeal directed the Election Commission to compute the number of proportional seats based on the number of valid votes (rather than the number of actual votes—including invalid or spoiled votes), and thus two further proportional seats were awarded to Parti Lepep and one seat was awarded to the PDM. Parti Lepep, however, declined to nominate additional members, and consequently the total number of seats in the National Assembly was increased to 32.

† Excludes 16,447 invalid votes (31.87% of the total votes cast).

Election Commission

Electoral Commission: Suite 203, Aarti Bldg, Mont Fleuri, POB 741, Victoria; tel. 4295555; fax 4225474; e-mail hendrick@seychelles.net; internet www.ecs.sc; f. 1993; Electoral Commissioner HENDRICK PAUL GAPPY.

Political Organizations

New Democratic Party (NDP): POB 169, Mont Fleuri; tel. 4224916; fax 4224302; e-mail management@dpseychelles.com; internet www.dpseychelles.com; f. 1992; successor to the Seychelles Democratic Party (governing party 1970–77); Leader RALPH VOLCERE.

Parti Lepep (People's Party): POB 1242, Victoria; tel. 4284900; fax 4225070; e-mail admin@sppf.sc; internet www.partilepep.com; fmrly the Seychelles People's United Party (f. 1964), which assumed power in 1977; renamed Seychelles People's Progressive Front in 1978; sole legal party 1978–91; assumed present name in 2009; Pres. JAMES ALIX MICHEL; Sec.-Gen. DANNY FAURE.

Seychelles National Party (SNP): Arpent Vert, Mont Fleuri, POB 81, Victoria; tel. 4224124; fax 4225151; e-mail secretariat@snpseychelles.sc; internet www.snpseychelles.sc; f. 1995 as the United Opposition, comprising the fmr mem. parties of a coalition formed to contest the 1993 elections; adopted present name in 1998; Leader Rev. WAVEL RAMKALAWAN; Sec.-Gen. NICHOLAS PREA.

Other political parties active in Seychelles include: the Popular Democratic Movement (f. 2011; Leader David Pierre) and the Seychelles Freedom Party (f. 2011; Leader Christopher Gill).

Diplomatic Representation

EMBASSIES AND HIGH COMMISSIONS IN SEYCHELLES

China, People's Republic: POB 680, St Louis; tel. 4671700; fax 4671730; e-mail china@seychelles.net; internet sc.china-embassy.org/eng; Ambassador SHI ZHONGJUN.

Cuba: Bel Eau, POB 730, Victoria; tel. 4224094; fax 4224376; e-mail cubasey@seychelles.net; internet emba.cubaminrex.cu/seychellesing; Ambassador MARIA AIDA NOGALES JIMÉNEZ.

France: La Ciotat Bldg, Mont Fleuri, POB 478, Victoria; tel. 4382500; fax 4382510; e-mail ambafrance@intelvision.net; internet www.ambafrance-sc.org; Ambassador PHILLIPE DELACROIX.

India: Le Chantier, POB 488, Francis Rachel St, Victoria; tel. 4610301; fax 4610308; e-mail hicomind@seychelles.net; internet www.seychelles.net/hicomind; High Commissioner ASIT KUMAR NAG.

Russia: Le Niol, POB 632, St Louis; tel. 4266590; fax 4266653; e-mail rfembsey@seychelles.net; Ambassador (vacant).

United Kingdom: 3rd Floor, Oliaji Trade Centre, Francis Rachel St, POB 161, Victoria; tel. 4283666; fax 4283657; e-mail bhcvictoria@fco.gov.uk; internet ukinseychelles.fco.gov.uk/en; High Commissioner LINDSAY SKOLL.

Judicial System

The legal system is derived from English Common Law and the French Code Napoléon. There are three Courts: the Court of Appeal, the Supreme Court and the Magistrates' Courts. The Court of Appeal hears appeals from the Supreme Court in both civil and criminal cases. The Supreme Court is also a Court of Appeal for the Magistrates' Courts as well as having jurisdiction at first instance. The Constitutional Court, a division of the Supreme Court, determines matters of a constitutional nature, and considers cases bearing on civil liberties. There is also a Family Tribunal and a Rent Control Board.

Court of Appeal: ex-National Library, State House Ave; tel. 4224131; fax 4226279; Pres. FRANCIS MACGREGOR.

Supreme Court: Victoria Clock Tower, Palais de Justice, POB 157, Victoria; tel. 4285800; fax 4224197; e-mail judiciary@seychelles.sc; Chief Justice FREDERICK EGONDE-ENTENDE.

Attorney-General: RONNY GOVINDEN.

Religion

The majority of the inhabitants are Christians, of whom more than 85% are Roman Catholics and about 8% Anglicans. Hinduism, Islam, and the Bahá'í Faith are also practised.

CHRISTIANITY

The Anglican Communion

The Church of the Province of the Indian Ocean comprises six dioceses: four in Madagascar, one in Mauritius and one in Seychelles. The Archbishop of the Province is the Bishop of Antananarivo, Madagascar.

Bishop of Seychelles: Rev. JAMES RICHARD WONG YIN SONG, POB 44, Victoria; tel. 4321977; fax 4323879; e-mail angdio@seychelles.net.

The Roman Catholic Church

Seychelles comprises a single diocese, directly responsible to the Holy See. An estimated 85% of the total population are Roman Catholics.

Bishop of Port Victoria: Rt Rev. DENIS WIEHE, Bishop's House-Evêché, Olivier Maradan St, POB 43, Victoria; tel. 4322152; fax 4324045; e-mail rcchurch@seychelles.net.

Other Christian Churches

Pentecostal Assemblies of Seychelles: Victoria; tel. 4224598; e-mail paos@seychelles.net; Pastor HERMITTE FREMINOT; 700 mems.

The Press

L'Echo des Iles: POB 12, Victoria; tel. 4322262; fax 4321464; e-mail echo@seychelles.net; bi-monthly; French, Creole and English; Roman Catholic; Editor Fr EDWIN MATHIOT; circ. 2,800.

The People: Maison du Peuple, Revolution Ave, Victoria; tel. 4224455; internet www.thepeople.sc; owned by Parti Lepep; monthly; Creole, French and English; circ. 1,000.

Seychelles Nation: Information Technology and Communication Division, POB 800, Victoria; tel. 4225775; fax 4321006; e-mail seynat@seychelles.net; internet www.nation.sc; f. 1976; govt-owned; Mon.–Sat.; English, French and Creole; the country's only daily newspaper; Dir DENIS ROSE; circ. 3,500.

Seychelles Review: POB 29, Victoria; tel. 4241881; fax 4241545; e-mail surmer@seychelles.net; internet www.seychellesreview.com; f. 1994; monthly; business, politics, real estate and tourism; Editor ROLAND HOARAU.

Seychelles Weekly: POB 308, Victoria; e-mail editor@seychellesweekly.com; internet www.seychellesweekly.com; supports democracy in Seychelles; Editor (vacant).

Seychellois: POB 32, Victoria; f. 1928; publ. by Seychelles Farmers Asscn; quarterly; circ. 1,800.

Vizyon: Arpent Vert, Mont Fleuri, Victoria; tel. 4224507; fax 4224987; internet www.snpseychelles.sc/vizyon.htm; f. 2007; political fortnightly magazine of the opposition SNP; successor to weekly Regar; Creole, English and French; Editor ROGER MANCIENNE.

Broadcasting and Communications

TELECOMMUNICATIONS

Cable and Wireless (Seychelles) Ltd: Mercury House, Francis Rachel St, POB 4, Victoria; tel. 4284000; fax 4322777; e-mail cws@seychelles.net; internet www.cwseychelles.com; f. 1990; Chief Exec. CHARLES HAMMOND.

Atlas Seychelles Ltd (XNET): POB 903, Victoria; tel. 4304060; fax 4324565; e-mail atlas@seychelles.net; internet www.seychelles.net; f. 1996 by a consortium of Space95, VCS and MBM; acquired by Cable and Wireless (Seychelles) Ltd in 2005; internet service provider; Gen. Man. ANTHONY DELORIE.

Telecom Seychelles Ltd (Airtel): POB 1358, Providence; tel. 4600609; fax 4601602; internet africa.airtel.com/seychelles; f. 1998; 100% owned by Bharti Airtel (India); provides fixed-line, mobile and satellite telephone and internet services; Chief Exec. VINOD SUD.

BROADCASTING

Radio

Seychelles Broadcasting Corpn (SBC): Hermitage, POB 321, Victoria; tel. 4289600; fax 4225641; e-mail sbcradtv@seychelles.sc; internet www.sbc.sc; f. 1983; reorg. as independent corpn in 1992; programmes in Creole, English and French; Man. Dir ANTOINE ONEZIME.

SBC Radio: Union Vale, POB 321, Victoria; tel. 4289600; fax 4289720; e-mail sbcradtv@seychelles.sc; internet www.sbc.sc; f. 1941; programmes in Creole, English and French; Man. Dir IBRAHIM AFIF.

Television

Seychelles Broadcasting Corpn (SBC): see Radio.

SBC TV: Hermitage, POB 321, Victoria; tel. 4224161; fax 4225641; e-mail sbcradtv@seychelles.sc; f. 1983; programmes in Creole, English and French; Head of TV Production JUDE LOUANGE.

Finance

(cap. = capital; res = reserves; dep. = deposits; m. = million; brs = branches; amounts in Seychelles rupees)

BANKING

In 2009 there were seven banks operating in Seychelles, of which two conducted 'offshore' business. Five of these seven banks were foreign-owned, whereas the Government of Seychelles had a majority stake in the other two banks.

Central Bank

Central Bank of Seychelles (CBS): Independence Ave, POB 701, Victoria; tel. 4282000; fax 4226104; e-mail enquiries@cbs.sc; internet www.cbs.sc; f. 1983; bank of issue; cap. 97.7m., res 172.0m., dep. 2,787.1m. (Dec. 2010); Gov. CAROLINE ABEL.

National Banks

Development Bank of Seychelles: Independence Ave, POB 217, Victoria; tel. 4294400; fax 4224274; e-mail devbank@dbs.sc; internet www.dbs.sc; f. 1977; 55.5% state-owned; cap. 39.2m., res 43.9m., dep. 137.4m. (Dec. 2009); Chair. ANTONIO LUCAS; Man. Dir ROGER TOUSSAINT.

Seychelles International Mercantile Banking Corporation Ltd (Nouvobanq) (SIMBC): Victoria House, State House Ave, POB 241, Victoria; tel. 4293000; fax 4224670; e-mail nvb@nouvobanq.sc; internet www.nouvobanq.sc; f. 1991; 78% state-owned, 22% by Standard Chartered Bank (UK); cap. 100.0m., res 103.0m., dep. 2,774.0m. (Dec. 2009); Chair. AHMED AFIF; Pres. AHMED SAEED; 2 brs.

Seychelles Savings Bank Ltd (SSB): Kingsgate House, POB 531, Victoria; tel. 4294000; fax 4224713; e-mail ssb@savingsbank.sc; f. 1902; state-owned; term deposits, savings and current accounts; cap. and res 7.8m. (Dec. 1992); Man. Dir MICHAEL BENSTRONG; 4 brs.

Foreign Banks

Bank of Baroda (India): Trinity House, Albert St, POB 124, Victoria; tel. 4610333; fax 4324057; e-mail ce.seychelles@bankofbaroda.com; internet www.bankofbaroda.com/seychelles.asp; f. 1978.

Barclays Bank (Seychelles) Ltd (UK): Independence Ave, POB 167, Victoria; tel. 4383838; fax 4324054; e-mail barclays@seychelles.sc; f. 1959; Seychelles Dir LOGANADEN SIDAMBARAM; 3 brs and 4 agencies.

Habib Bank Ltd (Pakistan): Frances Rachel St, POB 702, Victoria; tel. 4224371; fax 4225614; e-mail habibsez@seychelles.net; f. 1976; Vice-Pres. and Chief Man. SOHAIL ANWAR.

Mauritius Commercial Bank (Seychelles) Ltd (MCB Seychelles): POB 122, Manglier St, Victoria; tel. 4284555; fax 4322676; e-mail contact@mcbseychelles.com; internet www.mcbseychelles.com; f. 1978 as Banque Française Commerciale (BFCOI); changed name in 2003; cap. 20.0m., res 20.0m., dep. 1,232.6m. (Dec. 2009); Man. Dir JOCELYN AH-YU; 5 brs.

Offshore Bank

BMI Offshore Bank: Suite G-04, Capital City Bldg, POB 672, Victoria; tel. 4325660; fax 4325490; e-mail seychelles.enquiries@bmibank.com; internet www.bmibank.com; Dir-Gen. FRANK HOAREAU.

INSURANCE

In 2010 there were four domestic and three non-domestic insurance companies in Seychelles.

H. Savy Insurance Co Ltd (HSI): Maison de la Rosière, 2nd Floor, Palm St, POB 887, Victoria; tel. 4322272; fax 4321666; e-mail insurance@mail.seychelles.net; f. 1995; all classes; Gen. Dir JEAN WEELING-LEE.

Seychelles Assurance Co Ltd (SACL): Pirate's Arms Bldg, POB 636, Victoria; tel. 4225000; fax 4224495; e-mail sacos@sacos.sc; internet www.sacos.sc; f. 1980; 37% owned by Opportunity Investment Company, 20% state-owned; all classes of insurance; subsidiaries include SUN Investments (Seychelles) Ltd, property-development company; fmrly State Assurance Corporation of Seychelles—SACOS; current name adopted 2006; Chair. and Man. Dir ANTONIO A. LUCAS.

Trade and Industry

GOVERNMENT AGENCIES

National Economic Council: Victoria; f. 2012; advisory body comprising the President as Chairman, the Vice-President as Vice-Chairman and also ministers, the Governor of the Central Bank and the CEOs of several banks and govt organizations.

Seychelles Fishing Authority (SFA): POB 449, Fishing Port, Victoria; tel. 4670300; fax 4224508; e-mail management@sfa.sc; internet www.sfa.sc; f. 1984; assessment and management of fisheries resources; Chair. VÉRONIQUE HERMINIE; Man. Dir RONDOLPH PAYET.

Seychelles Trading Co Ltd (STC): Latanier Rd, POB 634, Victoria; tel. 4285000; fax 4224735; e-mail mail@stcl.sc; internet stcl.sc; f. 1984; replaced import and distribution arm of the fmr Seychelles Marketing Board (SMB) in 2008; manufacturing and marketing of products, retailing, trade; Chair. COLIN JEAN-LOUIS; CEO PATRICK VEL.

Small Business Financing Agency (SBFA): Victoria; Chair. DOREEN ARNEPHY; CEO ROSANDA ALCINDOR.

DEVELOPMENT ORGANIZATIONS

Indian Ocean Tuna Commission (IOTC) (Commission de Thons de l'Océan Indien): Le Chantier Mall, 2nd Floor, POB 1011, Victoria; tel. 4225494; fax 4224364; e-mail secretariat@iotc.org; internet www.iotc.org; f. 1996; an inter-governmental organization mandated to manage tuna and tuna-like species in the Indian Ocean and adjacent seas; to promote co-operation among its members with a view to ensuring, through appropriate management, the conservation and optimum utilization of fish stocks and encouraging sustainable development of fisheries; Exec. Sec. RONDOLPH PAYET; 31 mems.

Seychelles International Business Authority (SIBA): Industrial Trade Zone, Bois de Rose Ave, Roche Caiman, POB 991, Victoria; Bois de Rose Ave, Roche Caiman; tel. 4380800; fax 4380888; e-mail siba@seychelles.net; internet www.siba.net; f. 1995 to supervise registration of companies, transshipment and 'offshore' financial services in an international free-trade zone covering an area of 23 ha near Mahé International Airport; CEO WENDY PIERRE.

Seychelles Investment Board (SIB): POB 1167, Caravelle House, 2nd floor, Manglier St, Victoria; tel. 4295500; fax 4225125; e-mail info@sib.gov.sc; internet www.sib.gov.sc; f. 2004; CEO RUPERT SIMEON.

Small Enterprises Promotion Agency (SEnPA): Camion Hall Bldg, Victoria; tel. 4323151; fax 4324121; e-mail senpa@senpa.sc; internet www.senpa.sc; f. 2004; fmrly the Seychelles Industrial Development Corpn, f. 1988; promotes and develops small enterprises, crafts and cottage industries; CEO SYLVIANE VALMONT.

CHAMBER OF COMMERCE

Seychelles Chamber of Commerce and Industry: Ebrahim Bldg, 2nd Floor, POB 1399, Victoria; tel. 4323812; fax 4321422; e-mail scci@seychelles.int; Chair. (vacant); Sec.-Gen. NICHOLE TIRANT-GHÉRARDI.

EMPLOYERS' ORGANIZATION

Federation of Employers' Associations of Seychelles (FEAS): POB 214, Victoria; tel. 4324969; fax 4324996; Chair. BASIL SOUNDY.

UTILITIES

Electricity

Public Utilities Corporation (Electricity Division): Electricity House, POB 174, Roche Caiman; tel. 4678000; fax 4321020; e-mail pmorin@puc.sc; Man. Dir PHILIPPE MORIN.

Seychelles Energy Commission: Room 307-308, Unity House Block B, POB 1488, Victoria; tel. 4610822; e-mail mrazanajatovo@sec.sc; f. 2010; Chair. WILLS AGRICOLE.

Water

Public Utilities Corporation (Water and Sewerage Division): Unity House, POB 34, Victoria; tel. 4322444; fax 4325612; e-mail pucwater@seychelles.net; Man. Dir STEPHEN ROUSSEAU.

TRADE UNION

Seychelles Federation of Workers' Unions (SFWU): Maison du Peuple, Latanier Rd, POB 154, Victoria; tel. 4224455; fax 4225351; e-mail sfwu@seychelles.net; f. 1978 to amalgamate all existing trade unions; affiliated to Parti Lepep; 25,200 mems; Pres. OLIVIER CHARLES; Gen. Sec. ANTOINE ROBINSON.

Transport

RAILWAYS

There are no railways in Seychelles.

ROADS

In 2008 there were 508 km of roads, of which 490 km were surfaced. Most surfaced roads are on Mahé and Praslin.

Seychelles Public Transport Corpn (SPTC): POB 610, Mahé; tel. 4280280; fax 4322425; internet www.sptc.sc; f. 1977; covers 66 routes on Mahé; CEO GEFFY ZIALOR.

SHIPPING

Privately owned ferry services connect Victoria, on Mahé, with the islands of Praslin and La Digue. At 31 December 2012 Seychelles' flag registered fleet numbered 42 vessels, totalling 364,448 grt.

Seychelles Ports Authority (SPA): POB 47, Mahé Quay, Victoria; tel. 4224701; fax 4224004; e-mail enquiries@seychellesports.sc; internet www.spa.sc; Chair. Capt. GUY ADAM; CEO Lt Col ANDRÉ D. CISEAU.

Aquarius Shipping Agency Ltd: POB 865, Victoria; tel. 4225050; fax 4225043; e-mail aqua@seychelles.net; Gen. Man. ANTHONY SAVY.

Hunt, Deltel and Co Ltd: Trinity House, Albert St, POB 14, Victoria; tel. 4380300; fax 4225367; e-mail hundel@seychelles.net; internet www.hundel.sc; f. 1937; Man. Dir E. HOUAREAU.

Mahé Shipping Co Ltd: Maritime House, POB 336, Victoria; tel. 4380500; fax 4380538; e-mail mail@maheship.sc; internet www.maheship.sc; f. 1969; shipping agents; Chair. Capt. G. C. C. ADAM.

Seychelles Shipping Line Ltd: POB 977, Providence, Victoria; tel. 4373737; fax 4373647; e-mail ssl@gondwana.sc; f. 1994; operates freight services between Seychelles and Durban, South Africa; Chair. SELWYN GENDRON; Man. Dir HASSAN OMAR.

CIVIL AVIATION

Seychelles International Airport is located at Pointe Larue, 10 km from Victoria. A new international passenger terminal and aircraft parking apron were constructed in the mid-2000s on land reclaimed in 1990; the existing terminal (which underwent SR 3m. in renovations in 2002) was to be converted into a cargo terminal. The airport also serves as a refuelling point for aircraft traversing the Indian Ocean. There are airstrips on several outlying islands.

Seychelles Civil Aviation Authority (SCAA): POB 181, Victoria; tel. 4384000; fax 4384009; e-mail secretariat@scaa.sc; internet www.scaa.sc; f. 1970; formerly Directorate of Civil Aviation; responsible for the Flight Information Region of 2.6m. sq km of Indian Ocean airspace; Chair. Capt. DAVID SAVY; CEO GILBERT FAURE.

Air Seychelles: The Creole Spirit Bldg, Quincy St, POB 386, Victoria; tel. 4381002; fax 4224305; e-mail airseymd@seychelles.net; internet www.airseychelles.net; f. 1979; operates scheduled internal flights from Mahé to Praslin; also charter services to Bird, Desroches and Denis Islands and to outlying islands of the Amirantes group; international services to Europe were discontinued in Jan. 2012, but a twice-weekly service to Abu Dhabi, United Arab Emirates, commenced in March 2012 and flights to Hong Kong commenced in March 2013; Chair. JOEL MORGAN; CEO CRAMER BALL.

Tourism

Seychelles enjoys an equable climate, and is renowned for its fine beaches and attractive scenery. The islands are home to a unique endemic flora and fauna, including several rare species of birds. Most tourist activity is concentrated on the islands of Mahé, Praslin and La Digue, although the potential for ecological tourism of the outlying islands has received increased attention. It is government policy that the development of tourism should not blight the environment, and strict laws govern the location and construction of hotels. In 1998 the Government indicated that up to 200,000 visitors (although not more than 4,000 at any one time) could be accommodated annually without detriment to environmental quality. However, several new luxury resorts were constructed in the early 2000s, and the yachting sector was also under development. Receipts from tourism totalled an estimated SR 2,750m. in 2011. In that year there were 194,476 tourist arrivals; most visitors were from Europe.

Compagnie Seychelloise de Promotion Hotelière Ltd: POB 683, Victoria; tel. 4224694; fax 4225291; e-mail cosproh@seychelles.net; promotes govt-owned hotels.

Seychelles Tourism Board (STB): POB 1262, Victoria; tel. 4671300; fax 4620620; e-mail info@seychelles.travel; internet www.seychelles.travel; f. 1998 as Seychelles Tourism Marketing Authority; merged with Seychelles Tourism Office in 2005; Chair. BARRY FAURE; CEO ELSIA GRANDCOURT.

Defence

As assessed at November 2012, the army numbered 200 men, the coast guard 200 men and the air force 20 men. Seychelles contributes servicemen to the East African Stand-by Brigade, a part of the African Union stand-by peace-keeping force.

Defence Expenditure: Budgeted at SR 292m. in 2011 (including capital expenditure).

Commander-in-Chief of Seychelles Armed Forces: Brig. LÉOPOLD PAYET.

Education

Education is free and compulsory for children between six and 16 years of age. A programme of educational reform, based on the British comprehensive schools system, was introduced in 1980. The language of instruction in primary schools is English. The duration of primary education is six years, while that of general secondary education is five years (of which the first four years are compulsory), beginning at 12 years of age. Pre-primary and special education facilities are also available. According to UNESCO estimates, in 2008/09 enrolment at primary schools included 94% of children (males 93%; females 95%) in the relevant age-group, while the comparable ratio for secondary enrolment in that year was 97% (males 95%; females 99%). There were 2,198 students in post-secondary (non-tertiary) education in 2011. A number of students study abroad, principally in the United Kingdom. Government expenditure on education in 2009 was SR 229.2m., equivalent to about 6.0% of total spending.

SIERRA LEONE

Introductory Survey

LOCATION, CLIMATE, LANGUAGE, RELIGION, FLAG, CAPITAL

The Republic of Sierra Leone lies on the west coast of Africa, with Guinea to the north and east, and Liberia to the south. The climate is hot and humid, with an average annual temperature of 27°C (80°F). The rainy season lasts from May to October. The average annual rainfall is about 3,436 mm (13.5 ins). English is the official language, while Krio (Creole), Mende, Limba and Temne are also widely spoken. The majority of the population follow animist beliefs, but there are significant numbers of Islamic and Christian adherents. The national flag (proportions 2 by 3) has three equal horizontal stripes, of green, white and blue. The capital is Freetown.

CONTEMPORARY POLITICAL HISTORY

Historical Context

Sierra Leone, formerly a British colony and protectorate, achieved independence as a constitutional monarchy within the Commonwealth on 27 April 1961. The Prime Minister and leader of the Sierra Leone People's Party (SLPP), Dr (later Sir) Milton Margai, died in April 1964 and was succeeded by his half-brother, Dr (later Sir) Albert Margai, previously the Minister of Finance.

In March 1967 the army assumed control and established a ruling body, the National Reformation Council. In April 1968 a further coup was staged by army officers, and power was subsequently transferred to a civilian Government; Dr Siaka Stevens, the leader of the All-People's Congress (APC), was elected as Prime Minister. In April 1971 a republican Constitution was introduced and Stevens became executive President.

The general election in May 1973 was not contested by the SLPP, and in 1976 Stevens, the sole candidate, was unanimously re-elected to the presidency for a second five-year term of office. A new Constitution, which provided for a one-party system, was adopted by the House of Representatives in June. The APC thus became the sole legitimate political organization. Stevens was inaugurated as President for a seven-year term on 14 June 1978. He subsequently released political detainees and allocated ministerial posts to several former SLPP members (who had joined the APC).

Domestic Political Affairs

During the 1980s civil unrest, prompted by economic hardship, increased and in April 1985 Stevens announced that he would not seek re-election to the presidency upon the expiry, in June, of his existing mandate. Stevens' term of office was subsequently extended for six months, to allow time for registration of voters and the nomination of a presidential candidate. At a conference of the APC in August, Maj.-Gen. Joseph Momoh, a cabinet minister and the Commander of the Army, was the sole candidate for the leadership of the party and for the presidential nomination. Momoh was elected to the national presidency in October, with 99% of the votes cast, and was inaugurated on 28 November. Although retaining his military status, Momoh appointed a civilian Cabinet, which included several members of the previous administration. Elections to the House of Representatives took place in May 1986.

Momoh's administration failed to improve the economic situation, and popular discontent continued. In March 1987 the Government announced that it had suppressed an attempted coup; more than 60 people were subsequently arrested, including the First Vice-President, Francis Minah. In October Minah and 15 other defendants were sentenced to death for plotting to assassinate Momoh and to overthrow the Government. In October 1989 Minah and five others were executed, despite international appeals for clemency.

Following the outbreak of civil conflict in Liberia in December 1989, an estimated 125,000 Liberians took refuge in Sierra Leone. The Sierra Leonean Government contributed troops to the cease-fire monitoring group (ECOMOG) of the Economic Community of West African States (ECOWAS, see p. 268), which was dispatched to Liberia in August 1990. In November of that year Charles Taylor, the leader of the principal Liberian rebel faction, the National Patriotic Front of Liberia (NPFL), threatened to attack Freetown International Airport (alleged to be a base for ECOMOG offensives against rebel strongholds). In early April 1991, following repeated border incursions by members of the NPFL, government forces entered Liberian territory and launched a retaliatory attack against NPFL bases. The Momoh Government alleged that the rebel offensive had been instigated by Taylor, in an attempt to force Sierra Leone's withdrawal from ECOMOG, and also accused the Government of Burkina Faso of actively assisting the rebels. It was reported, however, that members of a Sierra Leonean resistance movement, the Revolutionary United Front (RUF), had joined the NPFL in attacks against government forces. In mid-1991 government troops, with the assistance of military units from Nigeria and Guinea, initiated a successful counter-offensive against the rebels.

On 29 April 1992 members of the armed forces, led by a five-member military junta, seized a radio station in Freetown and broadcast demands for improvements in conditions in the armed forces. The rebel troops later occupied the presidential offices, and the leader of the junta, Capt. Valentine E. M. Strasser, announced that the Government had been overthrown. On the following day Momoh fled to Guinea, and Strasser announced the establishment of a governing council, to be the National Provisional Ruling Council (NPRC). Strasser affirmed the NPRC's commitment to the introduction of a multi-party system (legislation that permitted the formation of political associations had been approved in September 1991), and pledged to end the conflict in the country. On the same day the Constitution was suspended, the House of Representatives was dissolved and a state of emergency was imposed. On 1 May 1992 the NPRC (which principally comprised military officers), chaired by Strasser, was formed. Shortly afterwards a new Cabinet, which included a number of members of the NPRC, was appointed, and the Commander of the Armed Forces and the head of the security forces were replaced. On 6 May Strasser was inaugurated as Head of State.

In July 1992 Strasser replaced the three members of the NPRC in the Cabinet with civilians, and removed all civilian cabinet ministers from the NPRC. Later that month he announced extensive structural changes, which were designed to reduce the direct involvement of the NPRC in government administration: the NPRC was officially designated the Supreme Council of State, while the Cabinet was reconstituted as the Council of Secretaries (headed by the Chief Secretary of State), which was to be responsible for government administration, subject to the authority of the NPRC. In December the Deputy Chairman of the NPRC, Capt. Solomon A. J. Musa, became Chief Secretary of State. Later in December the Government established a National Advisory Council, which comprised representatives of various non-governmental organizations, and was to draft a programme for transition to civilian rule.

At the end of December 1992 the Government announced that the security forces had suppressed a coup attempt. Shortly afterwards nine of those accused of involvement in the attempted coup were convicted by a special military tribunal, and, together with 17 prisoners who had been convicted in November on charges of treason, were executed. In January 1993 the United Kingdom announced the suspension of economic aid to Sierra Leone in protest against the executions (which were condemned by human rights organizations). In July Musa was replaced as Deputy Chairman of the NPRC and Chief Secretary of State by Capt. Julius Maada Bio. Musa (who was widely believed to be responsible for the repressive measures undertaken by the Government) took refuge in the Nigerian high commission in Freetown, and subsequently emigrated to the United Kingdom.

Transition to civilian rule

In November 1993 Strasser announced the details of a two-year transitional programme, which provided for the installation of a civilian government by January 1996. The registration of political parties was to take place in June 1995, prior to a presidential election in November and legislative elections in December of that year. In December 1993 an Interim National Electoral Commission was established to organize the registration of voters and the demarcation of constituency boundaries, in preparation for local government elections. In the same month the National Advisory Council submitted constitutional proposals, which were largely similar to the provisions of the 1991 Constitution, but stipulating that only Sierra Leonean nationals of more than 40 years of age were eligible to contest a presidential election (thereby precluding Strasser and the majority of NPRC members, on grounds of age). A draft Constitution was submitted to the NPRC in October 1994.

In January 1995 the RUF, which had been joined by disaffected members of the armed forces, seized the mining installations owned by the Sierra Leone Ore and Metal Company (SIEROMCO) and Sierra Rutile Ltd. In February the RUF leadership rejected appeals by the UN and the Organization of African Unity—now the African Union (AU, see p. 191)—that peace negotiations be initiated, and demanded that all troops that had been dispatched by foreign Governments to assist the Strasser administration be withdrawn as a precondition to discussions. Despite successful counter-offensives by government forces (which had regained control of the mining installations), by April the RUF had advanced towards Freetown and had initiated a series of attacks against towns in the vicinity (including Songo, which was situated only 35 km east of Freetown).

In March 1995 the Council of Secretaries was reorganized to allow principal military officials in the Government to assume active functions within the armed forces; Lt-Col Akim Gibril became Chief Secretary of State, replacing Bio, who was appointed Chief of Defence Staff. The ban on political activity was formally ended in June; some 15 parties were subsequently granted registration (although the RUF failed to respond to government efforts to include the movement in the electoral process).

In May 1995 government forces initiated a number of counter-attacks against the RUF, and succeeded in recapturing Songo, subsequently also regaining control of significant diamond-mining regions in the eastern Kono District and part of Bo District. In September, however, the RUF launched further offensives in Bo District, while increasing reports of massacres and other violations of human rights perpetrated by the rebels against the civilian population emerged.

In December 1995 it was announced that presidential and legislative elections were to take place concurrently on 26 February 1996. In January 1996, however, Strasser was deposed by military officers, led by Bio, in a bloodless coup. Bio, who assumed the office of Head of State, announced that the coup had been instigated in response to efforts by Strasser to remain in power. (It was reported that Strasser had intended to amend restrictions on the age of prospective candidates to enable himself to contest the election.) Strasser, who had been expelled to Guinea, claimed that the new military administration planned to delay the transition to civilian government. A reconstituted Supreme Council of State and Council of Secretaries were formed and it was announced that the elections were to take place as scheduled. In February the RUF launched a series of attacks in various parts of the country, in an apparent attempt to undermine the electoral process.

The 1996 elections

The presidential and legislative elections duly took place on 26–27 February 1996. The reconstituted SLPP secured 36.1% of votes cast in the legislative elections, while its presidential candidate, Ahmed Tejan Kabbah, also received most support, with 35.8% of votes. A second round of the presidential election, which took place on 15 March, was contested by Kabbah and the candidate of the United National People's Party (UNPP), John Karefa-Smart (who had obtained 22.6% of votes cast in the first round); Kabbah was elected President by 59.5% of the votes. Later in March seats in the new 80-member Parliament were allocated on a basis of proportional representation, with the SLPP securing 27, the UNPP 17, the People's Democratic Party 12 and the reconstituted APC only five seats; the 12 provincial districts were represented in the legislature by Paramount Chiefs. Kabbah was inaugurated on 29 March, when the military Government officially relinquished power to the new civilian administration. In April Kabbah appointed a new Cabinet, which was subsequently approved by the new Parliament.

Following the elections, the Government announced in March 1996 that the RUF had agreed to a cease-fire. After discussions between RUF leader Foday Sankoh and Kabbah in April, the Government and the RUF reaffirmed their commitment to a permanent cessation of hostilities, and announced the establishment of three joint committees, which would consider issues regarding the demobilization of rebel forces. Despite the official cease-fire, sporadic attacks by the RUF were subsequently reported and further clashes occurred later that year between government forces and the Kamajors (traditional fighters reconstituted as an auxiliary defence force).

In July 1996 the Parliament adopted legislation that formally reinstated the Constitution of 1991. In September 1996 Kabbah ordered the compulsory retirement of some 20 officers, including Strasser and Bio, from the armed forces. Shortly afterwards it was reported that a conspiracy to overthrow the Government had been thwarted by senior military officers. About 17 members of the armed forces were arrested, of whom nine were subsequently charged with involvement in the conspiracy.

In November 1996 Kabbah and Sankoh signed a peace agreement in Abidjan, Côte d'Ivoire, whereby RUF forces were to be demobilized and the movement was to be reconstituted as a political organization, while all foreign troops were to be withdrawn from the country and replaced with foreign observers. A National Commission for the Consolidation of Peace was subsequently established to monitor the peace settlement. By February 1997 all foreign mercenaries had left Sierra Leone in accordance with the agreement, while the repatriation of Sierra Leonean refugees from Liberia had commenced. However, at the end of that month (when the implementation of the peace agreement was scheduled for completion) it was reported that members of the RUF had repeatedly violated the peace agreement and had failed to report to designated centres for disarmament. In March members of the political wing of the RUF issued a declaration that Sankoh had been removed as leader of the organization, owing to his failure to implement the peace accord. Later that month, however, RUF forces loyal to Sankoh kidnapped members of the movement who had supported his replacement, together with the Sierra Leonean ambassador to Guinea; the faction issued demands for the release of Sankoh, who had been detained in Nigeria earlier that month (being reportedly in possession of armaments).

On 25 May 1997 dissident members of the armed forces, led by Maj. Johnny Paul Koroma, seized power, deposing Kabbah, who fled to Guinea. The new authorities imposed a curfew in Freetown, following widespread violent looting by armed factions, and most foreign nationals were evacuated. In early June Nigerian forces initiated a naval bombardment of Freetown in an effort to force the new military leaders to resign. However, forces loyal to the coup leaders, assisted by RUF members, succeeded in repelling Nigerian attacks. Koroma announced the establishment of a 20-member Armed Forces Revolutionary Council (AFRC), with himself as Chairman and Sankoh (who remained in detention in Nigeria) as Vice-Chairman. All political activity, the existing Constitution and government bodies were suspended, although Koroma pledged that democratic rule would be restored. Nigeria reiterated that it intended to reinstate the ousted Government with the support of ECOWAS, and a further two Nigerian warships were dispatched to the region; further clashes between Nigerian troops, who had been serving under the mandate of ECOMOG in neighbouring Liberia, and supporters of the new military leaders occurred at the international airport at Lungi. In mid-June the AFRC announced that it had suppressed a coup attempt, following the arrest of 15 people, including several senior military officers. On 17 June Koroma was formally inaugurated as the self-proclaimed Head of State. However, despite appeals from Koroma, a campaign of civil disobedience, organized by the labour congress in protest against the coup, continued.

By early July 1997 the new military Government had been completely isolated by the international community. The Commonwealth Ministerial Action Group on the Harare Declaration (CMAG—which had been established to ensure adherence to the principles of democracy by member states) suspended Sierra Leone from meetings of the Commonwealth, pending the restoration of constitutional order and the reinstatement of a democratically elected government. The UN Security Council also condemned the coup, and expressed support for ECOWAS efforts to resolve the situation. Meanwhile, a four-member ministerial committee, comprising representatives of Nigeria, Côte d'Ivoire, Guinea and Ghana, which had been established by ECOWAS, urged the Government to relinquish power during a series of negotiations with an AFRC delegation.

In July 1997 Koroma formed a cabinet, the Council of Secretaries, comprising representatives of the RUF and the army, together with a number of civilians. At the end of that month discussions between the ECOWAS committee and AFRC representatives in Abidjan were abandoned, after Koroma insisted that he retain power for a tenure of four years, and refused to restore the Constitution and to end the ban on political activity. Consequently, in August an ECOWAS conference, which was convened at Abuja, Nigeria, officially endorsed the imposition of sanctions against Sierra Leone, with the aim of obliging the AFRC to relinquish power. ECOMOG was granted a mandate to monitor the cease-fire and to enforce the economic embargo; it was also agreed that the ECOWAS monitoring committee would henceforth include Liberia (following the election of a democratic Government in that country).

The reinstatement of Kabbah

In September 1997 CMAG voted in support of the decision of the ECOWAS committee to effect the reinstatement of the Kabbah administration. In early October the UN Security Council imposed sanctions on the import of armaments and petroleum products to Sierra Leone. Following aerial bombardments of Freetown by ECOMOG troops, a mass demonstration was held in the capital to demand that the Nigerian Government withdraw its troops from Sierra Leone. Negotiations between the AFRC and the five-member committee continued, however, and later in October an agreement, which was signed in Conakry, Guinea, provided for an immediate cease-fire, and the reinstatement of Kabbah's Government by April 1998, together with immunity from prosecution for AFRC members; all troops loyal to the incumbent military administration and RUF members were to be demobilized.

In February 1998 further clashes erupted near Freetown between ECOMOG troops and supporters of the military junta. Nigerian troops belonging to ECOMOG subsequently launched an intensive bombardment against Freetown and succeeded in gaining control of the capital, after senior members of the AFRC, including Koroma, fled into hiding, or surrendered to the ECOMOG forces. About 50 members of the military junta were arrested in Monrovia, Liberia, prompting protests from the Liberian Government regarding the Nigerian military intervention. It was announced that the Government that had been ousted on 25 May 1997 was to be reinstated, and that all subsequent appointments were to be considered invalid. ECOMOG forces were to remain in the country to assist in the restructuring of the armed forces. Meanwhile, following reports that troops loyal to the former military junta, with the assistance of the RUF, had taken control of Bo, ECOMOG forces were deployed in the region to support the Kamajors, and rapidly succeeded in regaining control of most of the region.

On 10 March 1998 Kabbah returned from exile and was officially reinstated as President; he subsequently appointed a Cabinet (which included a number of members of his previous administration). The new Government declared a state of emergency under which members of the former military junta could be detained for a maximum of 30 days without being formally charged. It was announced that some 1,500 civilians and members of the armed forces (including Momoh) had been placed in detention and were to be charged for their alleged connections with the former military junta. Also in March the UN Security Council voted to end its embargo on imports of petroleum products to Sierra Leone (which had resulted in severe fuel shortages), although an embargo on the supply of armaments was maintained. In July the UN Security Council adopted a resolution establishing a UN Observer Mission in Sierra Leone (UNOMSIL), comprising 70 military observers. In the same month it was announced that the national army had been dissolved.

In late July 1998 the Nigerian Government returned Sankoh (who had been in detention in Nigeria since early 1997) to Sierra Leone, where he was charged with treason following his support for the military coup of May 1997. In August 1998 16 civilians, including five journalists, were sentenced to death, after being convicted of supporting the former military junta. In October 24 army officers were publicly executed, following their conviction for involvement with the military junta, provoking condemnation from many foreign Governments and human rights organizations. Death penalties imposed against a further 10 officers were commuted to terms of life imprisonment. In November a further 15 civilians, including several ministers who had served in the AFRC Government, were sentenced to death for their part in the May 1997 coup; Momoh received a custodial term of 10 years for colluding with the military junta.

Meanwhile, ECOMOG continued efforts to suppress rebel activity, particularly in the north and east of the country, and in October 1998 transferred its operational headquarters from the Liberian capital, Monrovia, to Freetown. In that month the RUF intensified hostilities, after it was announced that Sankoh had been sentenced to death by the High Court on charges of treason. In November ECOMOG forces commenced aerial bombardments of rebel bases. By late December, however, RUF forces, together with supporters of the former military junta, had advanced towards Freetown, and had seized control of the principal town of Makeni, 140 km north-east of Freetown. The Governments of Nigeria and Ghana dispatched additional troops to reinforce the ECOMOG contingent (which henceforth numbered about 15,000). At the end of December the acting Commander of the RUF, Sam Bockarie, rejected a government invitation to enter into peace negotiations.

On 6 January 1999 rebel forces attacked Freetown (where thousands of civilians from the surrounding area had taken refuge), releasing a number of supporters of the former junta from the capital's prison and seizing the Nigerian High Commission and government offices; Kabbah and a number of cabinet ministers were obliged to flee to ECOMOG headquarters. (It was subsequently discovered that two ministers had been killed by the rebels.) Bockarie announced that Freetown was under the control of the RUF, and demanded that Sankoh be released from detention. By late January ECOMOG forces claimed to have regained control of Freetown, and a cease-fire was agreed, pending peace negotiations, which were convened in Conakry, with mediation by the Governments of Guinea, Côte d'Ivoire and Togo. It was reported that Sankoh (who had been allowed by the Sierra Leonean authorities to attend the peace discussions) demanded his release and the official recognition of the RUF as a political movement as preconditions to the cessation of hostilities. Some 100 members of ECOMOG were arrested, following claims by a UN report (which were denied by ECOMOG) that suspected rebels had been summarily executed; the Kamajors were also implicated in summary killings.

Peace negotiations

Following the rebel offensive in January 1999, a number of West African Governments reiterated claims that the Liberian Government was supporting the RUF with mercenaries and illicit exports of armaments in exchange for diamonds. Charles Taylor (now the Liberian President) denied any connections with the RUF, dismissing the allegations as an attempt to destabilize his administration. In April the Nigerian President-elect, Olusegun Obasanjo, agreed that the Nigerian contingent (then numbering nearly 15,000) would remain in Sierra Leone until peace was restored; however, a gradual withdrawal of ECOMOG troops, to be completed by early 2000, was envisaged. Formal peace negotiations between the RUF and a government delegation commenced in April 1999 in the Togolese capital, Lomé, with mediation by President Gnassingbé Eyadéma of Togo. In early May the Government and the RUF signed a cease-fire agreement, which came into effect later that month. In July the Government and the RUF reached a power-sharing agreement, after government negotiators acceded to rebel demands that Sankoh be granted vice-presidential powers, with responsibility for the mineral resources industry, and the RUF be allocated a number of cabinet posts. The accord provided for the release of civilians who had been abducted by the rebels, and the disarmament and reintegration into the armed forces of former combatants; the RUF was to be reconstituted as a political organization. Following the completion of disarmament, legislative and presidential elections were to take place by February 2001.

In early October 1999 Sankoh (who had been conducting discussions with Taylor) and Koroma returned to Freetown from Monrovia, and pledged to co-operate with Kabbah in the implementation of the Lomé peace accord. Later that month the UN Security Council adopted Resolution 1270, establishing a 6,000-member force, the UN Mission in Sierra Leone (UNAMSIL), to succeed UNOMSIL; UNAMSIL was granted a six-month mandate to supervise the implementation of the peace agreement, and to assist in a programme for the disarmament and reintegration of the former rebel factions. The withdrawal of the ECOMOG contingent was to be completed following the deployment of UNAMSIL (although the new peace-keeping force would incorporate a number of the Nigerian forces belonging to ECOMOG). On 2 November a new coalition Cabinet was officially installed; four former members of the RUF and the AFRC junta were allocated ministerial posts. Sankoh became Chairman of a commission overseeing the reconstruction of the mineral resources industry, with vice-presidential status, while Koroma was nominated Chairman of the Commission for the Consolidation of Peace. In the same month the Government announced the establishment of a Truth and Reconciliation Commission (TRC), which was to make recommendations regarding compensation for victims of human rights violations. However, reports of atrocities perpetrated against the civilian population by rebels continued, and in November division between the AFRC and RUF leadership emerged, apparently as a result of the former junta's dissatisfaction with its cabinet posts.

In early 2000 reports emerged of RUF forces in the Kailahun District of eastern Sierra Leone (where illegal diamond-mining continued) resisting disarmament and the deployment of UNAMSIL troops. In February the UN Security Council adopted a resolution in favour of expanding UNAMSIL to number 11,100, and extended its mandate for six months. In March Kabbah established a commission to supervise the elections, which, under the terms of the peace agreement, were to take place following the disarmament of the former rebel factions. By the end of that month, however, only about 17,000 of the 45,000 former combatants had been disarmed.

Peace-keeping difficulties

In April 2000 UNAMSIL troops stationed in the eastern town of Kenema repulsed attacks from rebel forces. In early May, following a further dispute over disarmament, RUF forces attacked UNAMSIL troops in Makeni and the neighbouring town of Magburaka, killing at least four Kenyan members of the contingent, and seizing a number of UN personnel as hostages. Six civilian UN observers were subsequently released, following intervention by Taylor. However, rebel forces continued to hold about 300 members of UNAMSIL (principally Zambians) hostage, while a further Zambian contingent of the peace-keeping force, numbering about 200, was reported missing. The British Government dispatched a military task force to the region (stationing troops at the airport at Lungi, and in Senegal), which evacuated most European nationals. RUF supporters guarding Sankoh's residence in Freetown fired on civilian demonstrators, who were demanding that Sankoh comply with the peace agreement; some 20 protesters were killed. (UN officials were subsequently unable to contact Sankoh, who had fled from Freetown.) Sierra Leonean government forces, led by Koroma (who continued to support the Kabbah administration), were deployed to halt rebel advances, and claimed to have recaptured territory from the RUF. In late May Sankoh was arrested in Freetown by troops loyal to Kabbah and by the end of that month the hostages held by the RUF were released. In early June, however, 21 Indian members of UNAMSIL were seized by the RUF at the eastern town of Pendembu. By mid-June most of the British forces had withdrawn (with about 250 troops remaining in the country to train new members of the Sierra Leone armed forces).

In early July 2000 the UN Security Council adopted a resolution, proposed by the British Government, imposing an international embargo on the purchase of unauthenticated diamonds (in an effort to prevent illicit trade from RUF-held regions, thereby ending the rebels' principal source of funding for armaments); the Sierra Leonean Government was to implement a system whereby officially mined diamonds would be granted certification. In the same month government forces clashed with one of the most notorious militia groups, the West Side Boys (WSB), which had hitherto supported the former AFRC junta. In mid-July the battalion of (principally Indian) peace-keeping personnel, who had been besieged by the RUF at Kailahun, were rescued in a military operation by UNAMSIL; one member of the contingent was killed during the offensive. In early August the UN Security Council approved the establishment of an international tribunal, where Sankoh and others responsible for atrocities committed during the civil conflict would be placed on trial. The RUF leadership announced the nomination of Gen. Issa Sesay to replace Sankoh. Later in August the WSB abducted 11 British military personnel and one member of the Sierra Leonean armed forces, subsequently issuing a number of demands as a precondition to releasing the hostages. Five of the British personnel were freed after negotiations, but additional British troops were dispatched to Sierra Leone, following the failure of government officials to secure an agreement on the remaining hostages. In early September about 150 British troops attacked the main WSB base, 48 km east of Freetown, and

succeeded in rescuing the other seven hostages. One member of the British armed forces died during the military operation, while 25 members of the WSB were killed, and a further 18 (including the movement's leader, Foday Kallay) were captured.

In September 2000 the Indian Government announced that it was to withdraw its contingent (then numbering 3,073 troops) from UNAMSIL, despite a proposal by the UN SecretaryGeneral that the maximum strength of the peace-keeping force be increased. In October several nations, notably Bangladesh, Ghana and Kenya, pledged to dispatch additional troops to replace those of India. The number of British troops in the country had been increased to 400, while a 500-member naval task force was deployed off Freetown to provide additional support to the UN peace-keeping operations. On 10 November, following further negotiations mediated by ECOWAS, the Government and the RUF signed a cease-fire agreement in Abuja, providing for the demobilization and disarmament of all militia forces, and the deployment of UNAMSIL throughout the country.

In February 2001 the National Assembly unanimously approved a proposal by Kabbah that presidential and legislative elections, scheduled to take place in February and March, respectively, be postponed for six months, owing to the continued civil unrest in the country. At the end of March the UN Security Council adopted a resolution increasing the strength of UNAMSIL (which then numbered 9,500) to 17,500 troops. In June UNAMSIL and government forces regained control of part of the significant diamond-mining regions and the eastern border with Guinea and Sierra Leone (thereby forestalling renewed rebel activity originating from the neighbouring countries). The Government, the RUF and UNAMSIL subsequently agreed to a ban on diamond-mining in eastern regions still controlled by the rebels, in order to facilitate the demobilization of combatants.

Following a further postponement, in September 2001 the Government announced that presidential and legislative elections would take place, under the aegis of the UN, on 14 May 2002. In November 2001 representatives of the Government, the RUF and civil society agreed that parliamentary deputies in the forthcoming elections were to be elected by district (rather than under the previous system of proportional representation). In December the UN Security Council extended its ban on trade in uncertified diamonds for a further 11 months (effective from 5 January 2002).

In January 2002 the UN and the Government reached agreement on the establishment of a war crimes tribunal, to be known as the Special Court, which was to be based in Sierra Leone; the Special Court had a three-year mandate to prosecute crimes perpetrated from the end of November 1996. Meanwhile, the continuing rebel insurgency in northern Liberia, which had advanced rapidly towards Monrovia by early 2002, prompted concern that the resumption of civil conflict there would cause further instability in Sierra Leone. Despite UN pressure on the Liberian Government to end assistance for the RUF, it was reported that Bockarie, supported by 4,000 rebel forces, continued to be based in Liberia.

Following the completion of the disarmament of an estimated 45,000 former combatants in January 2002, the RUF announced its reconstitution as a political organization, the Revolutionary United Front Party (RUFP), with the aim of contesting the elections. In early March, however, Sankoh (who remained titular leader of the RUFP) was formally charged with murder, in connection with the killing of some 20 civilian protesters by his supporters in May 2000. (The trial of Sankoh, together with a further 49 former RUF members, commenced later in March 2002.) In mid-March Kabbah was elected unopposed as the presidential candidate of the SLPP. A total of 24 political parties had officially registered by this time, notably the Peace and Liberation Party (PLP), led by Koroma. However, after the collapse of an opposition alliance, which had been established in late 2001, no serious challenge to the SLPP had emerged. In early April 2002, after the authorities announced that Sankoh would not be permitted to contest the elections on behalf of the RUFP, the party's Secretary-General, Pallo Bangura, was nominated as its presidential candidate. By the end of that month an estimated 60,000 of the 150,000 Sierra Leonean refugees in Guinea and Liberia had returned voluntarily in order to participate in the elections.

Kabbah re-elected

Presidential and legislative elections took place peacefully on 14 May 2002. Kabbah was elected to a second term in office by 70.1% of the votes cast, while Ernest Bai Koroma of the APC received 22.4% of the votes. The SLPP also secured an outright majority in the expanded 124-member Parliament, with 83 seats, while the APC won 27 seats and the PLP two. Later that month Solomon Berewa (hitherto Minister of Justice) became the new Vice-President, and a reorganized Cabinet was installed.

In July 2002 the authorities announced that a seven-member TRC had been established. In August Pallo Bangura resigned his RUFP office, having secured less than 2% of votes cast in the presidential election. In September the UN Security Council adopted a resolution extending the mandate of UNAMSIL for a further six months, but also advocating that the contingent be reduced in size, while in December the UN embargo on illicit trade in diamonds was renewed for a further six months. In February 2003 some 300 British troops were deployed in Sierra Leone (in addition to the 100 British officers in the country at that time), owing to concern that the intensification of hostilities between government and rebel Liberians United for Reconciliation and Democracy (LURD) forces in Liberia might destabilize the country.

After the appointment of a British lawyer, Geoffrey Robertson, as President of the Special Court and a US lawyer, David Crane, as Chief Prosecutor, trial activities commenced at the end of 2002. In March 2003 the Special Court approved indictments for war crimes against seven former faction leaders, notably Sankoh, Koroma, the former RUF Commanders, Bockarie and Sesay, and the incumbent Minister of the Interior (and Kamajor leader), Sam Hinga Norman. Five of those indicted, including Hinga Norman, were taken into custody. Koroma went into hiding, following an attempt by the authorities to arrest him, while it was reported that Bockarie was supporting Liberian government forces against the LURD. In April Hinga Norman pleaded not guilty at the Special Court to charges relating to atrocities perpetrated during the civil war. Public hearings before the TRC commenced in mid-April. In early May the Liberian authorities announced that Bockarie had been killed near the border with Côte d'Ivoire, after clashing with Liberian troops attempting to arrest him, and ordered an investigation. Officials at the Special Court claimed that Bockarie and his immediate family had been captured and murdered by Liberian security forces, in an effort to prevent him from testifying against prominent regional figures.

On 4 June 2003 the Special Court officially indicted Taylor for crimes against humanity, owing to his alleged long-standing support for the RUF, and an international warrant was issued for his arrest. Having accepted an offer of asylum from the Nigerian Head of State, Olusegun Obasanjo, Taylor formally resigned his office and left for exile in Nigeria on 11 August, thereby evading arrest for the charges brought against him by the Special Court. Meanwhile, progress in the case against Sankoh was hindered by the deterioration of his state of health, and, after receiving medical treatment in hospital under UN custody from March, he died at the end of July. Also in July the UN Security Council adopted a resolution recommending the gradual withdrawal of UNAMSIL by the end of 2004, in view of improved security conditions.

In early February 2004 the five-year programme for 'disarmament, demobilization and reintegration' (in which 72,490 former combatants had been disarmed) officially ended. In March Robertson was removed from the office of President of the Special Court, after being accused of demonstrating bias against the RUF in a book that he had written concerning the atrocities committed during the civil conflict. At the end of that month, owing to renewed concern that the Sierra Leonean authorities would be unable to maintain stability, the UN Security Council approved a resolution in favour of maintaining a reduced UNAMSIL contingent in the country until the end of September, with further extensions possible. On 23 September UNAMSIL officially transferred primary responsibility for security in the remaining parts of the country where it was deployed, including Freetown, to government forces. The UN Security Council approved a further resolution in the same month, authorizing the contingent's continued presence in the country until the end of June 2005.

At the end of June 2005 the UN Security Council extended the mandate of UNAMSIL for a final six months, until the end of that year. In August a further resolution provided for the creation of the United Nations Integrated Office in Sierra Leone (UNIOSIL). Following the complete withdrawal of UNAMSIL as scheduled, UNIOSIL was established on 1 January 2006, for an initial period of one year; the mission was authorized to support the consolidation of peace and assist the Government in strengthening state institutions, the rule of law, human rights, and the security sector, and the organization of presidential and legislative elections, scheduled for July 2007. In December 2006 UNIOSIL's mandate was extended until 31 December 2007. In mid-December the UN Secretary-General recommended that UNIOSIL's mandate be extended for a further nine months, to assist the Government in conducting the forthcoming elections. A new, smaller office was to replace UNIOSIL after that time, which would continue to aid the Sierra Leonean authorities in consolidating peace in the country. At the end of December the UN Security Council approved the final, nine-month extension (until September 2008) of UNIOSIL's mandate.

Meanwhile, in February 2006 the trial of Hinga Norman officially commenced at the Special Court. In early February 2007 Hinga Norman was taken to a hospital in Dakar, Senegal, for what was termed a routine procedure. On 22 February it was reported that he had collapsed and died in hospital. An autopsy report released the following month concluded that he died of natural causes, although Hinga Norman's family voiced their suspicions at the verdict.

In March 2006 Nigeria announced that it had received a formal request from the new Liberian Government to extradite Taylor to the Special Court. Later that month Taylor fled from his residence in Nigeria in an attempt to evade custody, but was apprehended two days later, near the border with Cameroon, and dispatched to Liberia, from where he was immediately extradited by peace-keeping forces to the Special Court. In early April Taylor (who initially refused to accept the authority of the Court) pleaded not guilty to 11 charges relating to his involvement in the civil conflict in Sierra Leone. Tribunal officials subsequently requested that his trial be transferred to the International Criminal Court (see p. 349) at The Hague, Netherlands (while remaining under the jurisdiction of the Special Court), in the interests of regional stability. The Dutch authorities acceded to that request on the condition that any sentence handed down to Taylor was served in another country. The United Kingdom subsequently agreed to host Taylor should he be imprisoned and, following the unanimous approval of the UN Security Council, on 20 June Taylor was transferred to The Hague. His trial commenced in April 2007, but was repeatedly adjourned. (In April 2012 Taylor was found guilty of aiding and abetting war crimes, but acquitted of charges of ordering the crimes to be carried out; he was sentenced in May to 50 years' imprisonment, which he was to serve in the United Kingdom.) Meanwhile, in June 2007 the Special Court imposed its first verdicts, finding three former AFRC members guilty of war crimes and crimes against humanity. The following month two of those convicted were sentenced to 50 years' imprisonment, while the third defendant received a prison term of 45 years. (In February 2009 the last trials to be held at the Special Court in Sierra Leone concluded with the conviction of three former RUF members on charges of war crimes and crimes against humanity, and in April they were sentenced to terms of imprisonment ranging from 25 to 52 years.)

The presidency of Ernest Bai Koroma

Legislative and presidential elections, initially due to be held in July 2007, were postponed to allow more time for campaigning and logistical preparations, and voting eventually took place on 11 August. Official results indicated that the opposition APC had secured the largest representation in Parliament, taking 59 of the 124 available seats. The SLPP returned 43 deputies and the People's Movement for Democratic Change (PMDC), led by Charles Margai, the son of Sir Albert Margai, took 10 seats. In the presidential election Koroma, contesting the election on behalf of the APC, secured 44.3% of votes cast, while Berewa of the SLPP received 38.3% and Margai 13.9%. Koroma and Berewa proceeded to a second round on 8 September, at which Koroma won 60.2% of the votes. The elections were conducted in a largely peaceful manner, despite a small number of disturbances and opposition claims of procedural irregularities. In October President Koroma formed a new Cabinet, which included Zainab Hawa Bangura as Minister of Foreign Affairs, David Carew as Minister of Finance and Development, and Abdul Serry Kamal as Minister of Justice and Attorney-General.

In October 2008 UNIOSIL was succeeded by the United Nations Integrated Peacebuilding Office in Sierra Leone (UNIPSIL), which was granted an initial mandate of one year. (In September 2009 the UN Security Council approved the extension of UNIPSIL's mandate until the end of September 2010.) In December 2008 a court repealed the sentences of 11 former armed rebels convicted of treason, the first time that death sentences had been overturned in Sierra Leone. Meanwhile, in September Brig. Alfred Nelson Williams replaced Maj.-Gen. Sam Mboma as Chief of Staff of the Armed Forces.

President Koroma's pledge to address corruption resulted in a number of high-profile dismissals during 2009 and 2010. In November 2009 the Minister of State, Office of the Vice-President, Leonard Balogun Koroma, and the Minister of Health and Sanitation, Sheku Tejan Koroma, were both removed from office amid speculation of their involvement in fraud and corruption. Mohamed D. Koroma, hitherto Deputy Minister for Health and Sanitation, was named to replace Tejan Koroma, while Komba Kono replaced Balogun Koroma. The following month the Commissioner-General of the National Revenue Commission was suspended from office after allegations of financial irregularities were made against him. In January 2010 the President reiterated his intention to take action against those in public office who were found to have engaged in corrupt practices. In March Haja Afsatu Kabba, the Minister of Marine Resources and Fisheries, was charged with abuse of office and financial irregularities and was dismissed. She was replaced by Joseph Koroma, who had hitherto served as Minister of Presidential and Public Affairs.

On 15 September 2010 the UN Security Council unanimously adopted a resolution ending the arms embargo and international travel sanctions imposed against former rebels, in view of the restoration of government control in the country. The Council approved a further resolution extending the mandate of UNIPSIL for a further year. In December Koroma effected an extensive government reorganization, in which Kamal was dismissed as Minister of Justice and Attorney-General and replaced by Frank Kargbo; other principal changes included the reassignment of Bangura as Minister of Health and Sanitation, while a long-standing member of the SLPP, Joseph Bandabla Dauda, was appointed as the new Minister of Foreign Affairs and International Co-operation. In addition, a Ministry of Internal Affairs and a Ministry of Youth Employment and Sports were created. Dauda subsequently resigned from the SLPP, which had suspended his membership, and that of the new Deputy Minister of Health and Sanitation, Borbor Sawyer, after they accepted ministerial posts. In early 2011 it was reported that the SLPP had continued to lose support, with many senior members leaving the party to join the APC. In April Margai publicly declared the end of an alliance between the PMDC (which was represented in the Government) and the APC; some 50 senior members of the PMDC subsequently announced their resignation from the party, in protest against its leadership.

Recent developments: the 2012 elections

At a SLPP congress in July 2011, former member of the NPRC military junta and coup leader Julius Maada Bio was unexpectedly selected as the party's candidate to contest the next presidential election, which was due to take place in late 2012. The approval of Bio's nomination, defeating that of businessman Usman Boie Kamara, followed intensive intra-party negotiations and was regarded as particularly controversial in view of his possible implication in extrajudicial killings perpetrated by the NPRC. (Koroma had been nominated as the APC presidential candidate in April 2009.) In September 2011 the UN Security Council extended the mandate of UNIPSIL for a further year, amidst reports of violent incidents resulting from tensions between supporters of the APC and the SLPP. In November the National Electoral Commission announced that the presidential, legislative and local elections would take place on 17 November 2012. In September the mandate of UNIPSIL was extended until the end of March 2013.

In October 2012 clashes between supporters of rival political parties were reported in Kono District, prior to the elections. The presidential poll on 17 November was contested by a total of nine candidates; Koroma was decisively elected by 58.7% of votes cast, while Maada Bio took 37.4% of the votes. At the concurrent legislative elections, the APC secured 67 seats and the SLPP 42. (Three seats in the Parliament remained vacant, since two were subject to a court injunction and a candidate in the other constituency had died.) At the local elections, the APC and the SLPP each secured control of six district councils, and each party won three of six contested mayoralties (with the APC retaining control of the municipal council of Freetown). A high participation rate of 87.3% of the electorate was recorded. Maada Bio subsequently complained that the electoral process was fraudulent, although ECOWAS, European Union (EU) and other international observers endorsed the conduct of the elections. On 28 November the SLPP announced that its elected members

would boycott the Parliament and local councils until the party's demands concerning an investigation into alleged malpractice were met. Koroma, who was inaugurated for a second term on 23 November, pledged to address endemic corruption and poverty. His new Government, which was formed in January 2013, included Dr Keifala Marrah, hitherto Chief of Staff to the presidency, as Minister of Finance and Economic Development, replacing Samura Kamara, who became Minister of Foreign Affairs and International Co-operation. In March the country's Anti-Corruption Commission charged 29 state employees—most of them, including the Chief Medical Officer, attached to the Ministry of Health—in connection with the misappropriation of funds provided by a non-governmental organization for vaccinations.

Foreign Affairs

Following the intensive civil conflict in Sierra Leone, large numbers of civilians fled to neighbouring countries; in September 2000 the Guinean President, Gen. Lansana Conté, claimed that Liberian and Sierra Leonean refugees were supporting the activity of rebels attempting to overthrow his Government, and ordered them to leave the country. In March 2001 President Charles Taylor expelled the ambassadors of Guinea and Sierra Leone from Liberia, on the grounds that they had been engaged in activity incompatible with their office. The Sierra Leonean Government retaliated by ordering the Liberian chargé d'affaires to leave the country, and announced the closure of the joint border with Liberia. (Diplomatic links between Liberia and Sierra Leone and Guinea were normalized in August.)

Sierra Leone's relations with its neighbouring states improved significantly following the restoration of peace in the country in 2002 and the organization of democratic elections in August 2007. The newly elected President, Ernest Bai Koroma, visited Liberia in September 2007, where he signed a non-aggression pact with his Liberian counterpart, Ellen Johnson Sirleaf. The Mano River Union (see p. 462), which was originally formed in 1973 by Sierra Leone and Liberia to promote regional co-operation and joined by Guinea in 1980, was reactivated in 2004; Côte d'Ivoire announced its decision to join the body in 2008. Guinea and Sierra Leone concluded an agreement in March 2012 to delineate their maritime boundaries. Following a longstanding dispute over the ownership of the Sierra Leonean border town of Yenga (which had been occupied by Guinean troops in 1998), in August 2012 both countries pledged to withdraw all military personnel from Yenga and negotiate a peaceful settlement to the issue.

The British Government of Tony Blair intervened militarily to support UN forces in the civil conflict in 2000, and an International Military Assistance Training Team was established in Sierra Leone in 2002 to assist in the restructuring of its armed forces. Sierra Leone also received considerable development and security assistance from the USA. In early 2013 Sierra Leone participated in the UN-AU Hybrid operation in Darfur, was preparing a contingent for the AU Mission in Somalia, and had also pledged to contribute to an AU-led peace-keeping mission in Mali. Following his re-election in November 2012, President Koroma and other regional heads of state met US President Barack Obama in Washington, DC, in March 2013.

CONSTITUTION AND GOVERNMENT

Under the terms of the Constitution of 1991, executive power is vested in the President, who is directly elected by universal adult suffrage and must secure at least 25% of the votes cast in each of the four provinces. The President appoints the Cabinet (subject to approval by the legislature). The maximum duration of the President's tenure of office is limited to two five-year terms. Legislative power is vested in a unicameral Parliament, which is elected for a five-year term and comprises 112 members elected by a system of proportional representation in 14 constituencies, and 12 Paramount Chiefs, who represent the provincial districts. Members of the Parliament are not permitted concurrently to hold office in the Cabinet.

The country is divided into four regions: the Northern, Eastern and Southern Provinces, and the Western Area, which comprise 12 districts. There are 147 chiefdoms, each controlled by a Paramount Chief and a Council of Elders, known as the Tribal Authority.

REGIONAL AND INTERNATIONAL CO-OPERATION

Sierra Leone is a member of the African Union (see p. 191), of the Economic Community of West African States (see p. 268) and of the Mano River Union (see p. 462).

Sierra Leone became a member of the UN in 1961, and was admitted to the World Trade Organization (WTO, see p. 444) in 1995. Sierra Leone participates in the Group of 77 (G77, see p. 461) developing countries.

ECONOMIC AFFAIRS

In 2011, according to the World Bank, Sierra Leone's gross national income (GNI), measured at average 2009–11 prices, was US $2,069m., equivalent to $340 per head (or $850 per head on an international purchasing-power parity basis). During 2002–11, it was estimated, the population increased at an average annual rate of 3.2%, while gross domestic product (GDP) per head rose, in real terms, by an average of 3.0% per year. Overall GDP increased, in real terms, at an average annual rate of 6.4% in 2002–11; growth was 6.0% in 2011.

Agriculture (including forestry and fishing) contributed 60.1% of GDP in 2010, according to provisional figures from the African Development Bank (AfDB) and about 58.4% of the labour force were employed in the sector in 2013, according to FAO. The principal cash crops are cocoa beans and coffee. Staple food crops include rice, cassava, and citrus fruit. Chickens, cattle and goats are the principal livestock. In January 2010 the Sierra Leone Government issued a ban on the transport and export of logs, in an attempt to curb the largely uncontrolled logging industry that had been blamed for the depletion of the country's forests. According to the AfDB, during 2000–07 the GDP of the agricultural sector increased at an average annual rate of 5.1%; growth in agricultural GDP was 4.0% in 2010.

Industry (including mining, manufacturing, construction and power) contributed an estimated 5.4% of GDP in 2010, according to provisional figures from the AfDB. This sector employed 6.5% of the working population in 2004. According to the AfDB, the GDP of the industrial sector increased by an average of 11.9% per year in 2000–07; industrial GDP increased by 10.4% in 2007.

Mining and quarrying contributed 1.7% of GDP in 2010, according to provisional figures from the AfDB, and employed 3.6% of the working population in 2004. The principal mineral exports are diamonds (which, according to official figures, accounted for 21.7% of total export earnings in 2011), rutile (titanium dioxide) and bauxite. In 1995 increased rebel activity effectively suspended official mining operations (although illicit exports of diamonds by rebel forces continued). In October 2000 official exports of diamonds were resumed under a certification scheme. Following reinvestment in a major kimberlite diamond field at Koidu, production commenced at the end of 2003. The Sierra Rutile mines (the largest source of private sector employment and foreign exchange earnings prior to 1995) resumed full mining operations in early 2006, while rehabilitation of the country's bauxite mine was completed in 2005, also allowing production to recommence in early 2006. According to the AfDB, the mining sector's GDP decreased by 26.4% in 2009, but increased by 8.5% in 2010.

Manufacturing contributed an estimated 1.9% of GDP in 2010, according to provisional figures from the AfDB, and engaged 0.5% of the employed population in 2004. The manufacturing sector consists mainly of the production of palm oil and other agro-based industries, textiles and furniture-making. During 2000–07 the GDP of the manufacturing sector increased at an average annual rate of 6.5%, according to the AfDB. Manufacturing GDP declined by 1.4% in 2009, but increased by 11.0% in 2010.

The construction sector contributed 1.5% of GDP in 2010, according to provisional figures by the AfDB, and employed 2.0% of the engaged population in 2004. According to the AfDB, the sector declined by 2.6% in 2009, but grew by 14.0% in 2010.

Energy is derived principally from oil-fired thermal power stations. Following long-term energy shortages, a delayed hydroelectric project at Bumbuna, in the north of the country, entered into operation in late 2009. Imports of mineral fuels comprised 16.1% of the value of total imports in 2011.

The services sector contributed 34.6% of GDP in 2010, according to provisional figures by the AfDB, and employed 25.0% of the engaged population in 2004. According to the AfDB, the GDP of the services sector increased by an average of 21.5% per year in 2000–07; it grew by 3.7% in 2007.

In 2011 Sierra Leone recorded an estimated merchandise trade deficit of US $1,249.6m., and there was a deficit of $1,211.7m. on the current account of the balance of payments. In 2008, according to the AfDB, the principal source of imports (16.7%) was the People's Republic of China; the other major suppliers were the USA and Côte d'Ivoire. In that year, Belgium was the principal market for exports (taking 35.7% of the total); the other significant purchasers were the USA, India, France and Germany. The principal exports in 2011 were diamonds, cocoa beans, bauxite and rutile. The principal imports in that year were machinery and transport equipment, mineral fuels and lubricants, and food and live animals.

In 2011 the country recorded an overall budget deficit of Le 580,000m. The overall budget deficit was projected to be Le 285,000m. in 2012 and Le 491,000m. in 2013. Sierra Leone's general government gross debt was Le 4,972,488m. in 2010, equivalent to 48.9% of GDP. Sierra Leone's external debt totalled US $778m. at the end of 2010, of which $661m. was public and publicly guaranteed debt. In that year, the cost of servicing long-term public and publicly guaranteed debt and repayments to the IMF was equivalent to 2.6% of the value of exports of goods, services and income (excluding workers' remittances). The annual rate of inflation averaged 13.6% in 2003–11. Consumer prices increased by 16.1% in 2011. An estimated 68,252 people (3.5% of the total work-force) were unemployed, according to the 2004 census.

Since the end of the civil war in January 2002 Sierra Leone has experienced substantial real economic growth and declining inflation. Additionally, improvements in fiscal control and considerable support from international financial institutions have resulted in some progress in reconstruction. Sierra Leone's economic prospects improved further with the post-war resumption of the production and export of rutile and bauxite in early 2006. Furthermore, following the restoration of government control throughout the country, Sierra Leone again became popular as a tourism destination. The completion of a delayed hydroelectric project at Bumbuna, in the north of the country, in late 2009 partly resolved long-term electricity shortages in the capital (although further technical difficulties were reported). In June 2010 the IMF approved a three-year Extended Credit Facility (ECF) of about US $45.4m. Government expenditure continued to focus on increased investment in basic infrastructure, notably the expansion of the country's road network and modernization of the international airport, with the aim of further expanding the tourism industry. In January 2011 the Government announced new incentives for foreign businesses, which included exemption from an export licence requirement for the export of locally produced goods, except precious minerals. In September 2012 the IMF completed its fourth review of Sierra Leone's ECF-supported economic performance, and approved a disbursement of about $6.9m., raising total disbursements under the arrangement to date to $34.4m. With the conclusion of the first stage of an iron ore project in November of that year, involving the mining of large-scale deposits in the northern district of Tonkolili by a private, foreign company, African Minerals Limited, growth of about 21% was projected by the IMF for 2012 (up from about 6.0% in 2011, although less than the 51% level originally envisaged); more moderate growth of 7.5% was projected for 2013. Following his re-election in November 2012, President Ernest Bai Koroma pledged to address corruption, and to reduce continuing high levels of unemployment and poverty through the maximization of tax revenue from the expanding mining sector. Accordingly, in March 2013 the Government established a National Minerals Agency, with the stated aim of ensuring transparency and sustainable development in the mining sector, and it was announced that the country's existing contracts with foreign-owned mining corporations were to be reviewed.

PUBLIC HOLIDAYS

2014: 1 January (New Year's Day), 13 January* (Mouloud, Birth of the Prophet), 8 March (International Women's Day), 18–21 April (Easter), 27 April (Independence Day), 28 July* (Id al-Fitr, end of Ramadan), 4 October* (Id al-Adha, Feast of the Sacrifice), 25–26 December (Christmas and Boxing Day).

* These holidays are dependent on the Islamic lunar calendar and may vary by one or two days from the dates given.

Statistical Survey

Source (unless otherwise stated): Central Statistics Office, PMB 595, Tower Hill, Freetown; tel. (22) 223287; fax (22) 223897; internet www.sierra-leone.org/cso .html and www.statistics-sierra-leone.org.

Area and Population

AREA, POPULATION AND DENSITY

Area (sq km)	71,740*
Population (census results)†	
14 December 1985	3,515,812
4 December 2004	
Males	2,420,218
Females	2,556,653
Total	4,976,871
Population (UN estimates at mid-year)‡	
2011	5,997,487
2012	6,126,453
2013	6,255,163
Density (per sq km) at mid-2013	87.2

* 27,699 sq miles.
† Excluding adjustment for underenumeration, estimated to have been 9% in 1985.
‡ Source: UN, *World Population Prospects: The 2010 Revision.*

POPULATION BY AGE AND SEX
(UN estimates at mid-2013)

	Males	Females	Total
0–14	1,316,512	1,336,198	2,652,710
15–64	1,683,036	1,799,332	3,482,368
65 and over	61,283	58,802	120,085
Total	**3,060,831**	**3,194,332**	**6,255,163**

Source: UN, *World Population Prospects: The 2010 Revision.*

ADMINISTRATIVE DISTRICTS
(population at 2004 census)

	Population
Bo	463,668
Bombali	408,390
Bonthe	129,947
Kailahun	358,190
Kambia	270,462
Kenema	497,948
Koinadugu	265,758
Kono	335,401
Moyamba	260,910
Port Loko	453,746
Pujehun	228,392
Sherbo	9,740
Tonkolili	347,197
Western Area Rural District	174,2489
Western Area Urban District	772,873
Total	**4,976,871**

PRINCIPAL TOWNS
(population at 2004 census)

Freetown (capital) .	772,873*		Makeni	82,840
Bo	149,957		Koindu	80,025
Kenema	128,402			

* Western Area Urban District.

Mid-2011 (incl. suburbs, UN estimate): Freetown 940,683 (Source: UN, *World Urbanization Prospects: The 2011 Revision*).

BIRTHS AND DEATHS
(annual averages, UN estimates)

	1995–2000	2000–05	2005–10
Birth rate (per 1,000)	44.6	42.7	40.6
Death rate (per 1,000)	24.9	20.8	16.9

Source: UN, *World Population Prospects: The 2010 Revision.*

Life expectancy (years at birth): 47.8 (males 47.2; females 48.4) in 2011 (Source: World Bank, World Development Indicators database).

ECONOMICALLY ACTIVE POPULATION
(persons aged 10 years and over, 2004 census)

	Male	Female	Total
Agriculture, hunting and forestry .	617,928	654,306	1,272,234
Fishing	33,317	17,822	51,139
Mining and quarrying	59,311	9,663	68,974
Manufacturing	7,397	2,015	9,412
Electricity, gas and water supply .	7,104	1,243	8,347
Construction	28,239	10,829	39,068
Wholesale and retail trade; Repair of motor vehicles, motorcycles, and personal and household goods	102,212	167,283	269,495
Hotels and restaurants . . .	2,619	2,312	4,931
Transport, communications and storage	14,425	1,257	15,682
Financial intermediation . . .	3,993	2,941	6,934
Real estate, renting and business activities	5,475	5,310	10,785
Public administration and defence; compulsory social security . .	21,126	4,853	25,979
Education	23,254	11,326	34,580
Health and social work . . .	9,852	9,976	19,828
Other community, social and personal service activities . .	44,423	39,063	83,486
Households with employed persons	3,983	4,306	8,289
Extra-territorial organizations and bodies	2,508	1,338	3,846
Total employed	**987,166**	**945,843**	**1,933,009**
Unemployed	45,936	22,316	68,252
Total labour force	**1,033,102**	**968,159**	**2,001,261**

Source: ILO.

Mid-2013 (estimates in '000): Agriculture, etc. 1,377; Total labour force 2,359 (Source: FAO).

Health and Welfare

KEY INDICATORS

Total fertility rate (children per woman, 2010)	5.0
Under-5 mortality rate (per 1,000 live births, 2010) . .	174
HIV/AIDS (% of persons aged 15–49, 2009)	1.6
Physicians (per 1,000 head, 2008)	0.02
Hospital beds (per 1,000 head, 2006)	0.4
Health expenditure (2009): US $ per head (PPP) . . .	110
Health expenditure (2009): % of GDP	13.9
Health expenditure (2009): public (% of total) . . .	10.5
Access to water (% of persons, 2010)	55
Access to sanitation (% of persons, 2010)	13
Total carbon dioxide emissions ('000 metric tons, 2008) .	1,334.8
Carbon dioxide emissions per head (metric tons, 2008) . .	0.2
Human Development Index (2011): ranking	180
Human Development Index (2011): value	0.336

For sources and definitions, see explanatory note on p. vi.

Agriculture

PRINCIPAL CROPS
('000 metric tons)

	2009	2010	2011
Rice, paddy	888.4	1,026.7	1,078.0
Maize	29.6	51.4	41.6
Millet*	27.0	32.0	33.0
Sorghum*	30.1	35.3	36.7
Sweet potatoes*	35.0	34.5	39.5
Cassava (Manioc)*	390.0	434.7	512.9
Sugar cane*	70.0	76.0	77.0
Groundnuts, with shell	70.0	81.5	85.5
Oil palm fruit*	209.0	212.0	212.0
Tomatoes*	25.0	25.8	23.0
Plantains*	40.0	40.2	40.9
Citrus fruit*	98.0	99.2	101.3
Coffee, green*	22.0	30.8	33.5
Cocoa beans	10.0†	14.0†	15.2*

* FAO estimate(s).
† Unofficial figure.

Aggregate production ('000 metric tons, may include official, semi-official or estimated data): Total cereals 985.6 in 2009, 1,153.2 in 2010, 1,197.6 in 2011; Total roots and tubers 427.8 in 2009, 472.0 in 2010, 555.4 in 2011; Total vegetables (incl. melons) 290.0 in 2009, 364.7 in 2010, 339.6 in 2011; Total fruits (excl. melons) 232.9 in 2009, 232.5 in 2010, 245.2 in 2011.

Source: FAO.

LIVESTOCK
('000 head, year ending September)

	2009	2010	2011
Cattle	470	517	569
Pigs	43	47	52
Sheep	620	682	750
Goats	730	803	883
Chickens	8,600	9,460	10,406
Ducks	730	803	883

Source: FAO.

LIVESTOCK PRODUCTS
('000 metric tons, FAO estimates)

	2009	2010	2011
Chicken meat	11.9	13.1	13.7
Pig meat	2.1	2.1	2.1
Game meat	3.4	3.6	3.6
Cows' milk	20.9	21.1	21.1
Hen eggs	9.2	9.2	9.2

Source: FAO.

Forestry

ROUNDWOOD REMOVALS
('000 cubic metres, excl. bark, FAO estimates)

	2009	2010	2011
Sawlogs, veneer logs and logs for sleepers*	3.6	3.6	3.6
Other industrial wood†	120.0	120.0	120.0
Fuel wood	5,543.7	5,581.6	5,619.3
Total	5,667.3	5,705.2	5,742.9

* Annual output assumed to be unchanged since 1993.
† Annual output assumed to be unchanged since 1980.
Source: FAO.

SAWNWOOD PRODUCTION
('000 cubic metres, incl. railway sleepers)

	1991	1992	1993
Total (all broadleaved)	9.0	9.0*	5.3

* FAO estimate.
1994–2011: Annual production as in 1993 (FAO estimates).
Source: FAO.

Fishing
('000 metric tons, live weight of capture)

	2007	2008	2009*
Freshwater fishes*	14.0	14.0	14.0
West African ilisha	3.9	7.8	7.7
Tonguefishes	1.2	1.3	1.2
Bobo croaker	8.7	12.2	12.0
Sardinellas	16.6	20.2	19.8
Bonga shad	52.7	86.0	84.4
Tuna-like fishes	2.3	2.7	2.7
Penaeusus shrimps	1.4	1.0	1.0
Marine molluscs	0.9	0.8	0.8
Total catch (incl. others)*	144.5	203.6	200.0

* FAO estimates.
2010: Catch assumed to be unchanged from 2009 (FAO estimates).
Source: FAO.

Mining
(metric tons unless otherwise indicated)

	2009	2010	2011
Cement (hydraulic)	236,240	300,980	310,890
Bauxite ('000 metric tons)	757	1,090	1,457
Diamonds ('000 carats)	401	438	357
Ilmenite	15,161	18,206	15,946
Rutile	63,864	68,198	67,916

Source: US Geological Survey.

Industry

PETROLEUM PRODUCTS
('000 metric tons, estimates)

	2006	2007	2008
Jet fuels	22	22	22
Motor spirit (petrol)	33	33	33
Kerosene	11	11	12
Distillate fuel oils	60	60	60
Residual fuel oils	40	40	40

Source: UN Industrial Commodity Statistics Database.

SELECTED OTHER PRODUCTS
('000 metric tons unless otherwise indicated)

	2005	2006	2007
Beer and stout ('000 crates)	1,012	832	780
Soft drinks ('000 crates)	1,908	2,089	2,432
Confectionery ('000 kg)	2,074.3	2,329.9	3,141.0
Soap (metric tons)	417	n.a.	n.a.
Paint ('000 litres)	135	649	714

Source: mainly IMF, *Sierra Leone: Selected Issues and Statistical Appendix* (January 2009).

Finance

CURRENCY AND EXCHANGE RATES

Monetary Units
100 cents = 1 leone (Le).

Sterling, Dollar and Euro Equivalents (30 November 2012)
£1 sterling = 6,963.50 leones;
US $1 = 4,336.74 leones;
€1 = 5,631.69 leones;
10,000 leones = £1.44 = $2.31 = €1.78. .

Average Exchange Rate (leones per US $)
2009   3,385.65
2010   3,978.09
2011   4,349.16

CENTRAL GOVERNMENT BUDGET
(Le '000 million)

Revenue*	2011	2012†	2013†
Tax	1,383	1,746	1,729
Personal income tax . .	467	760	713
Goods and services tax . .	351	410	473
Import duties . . .	282	271	299
Excise duties	55	3	59
Non-tax revenue . . .	80	80	136
Total	1,463	1,826	1,865

Expenditure‡	2011	2012†	2013†
Current expenditure . . .	1,603	1,926	1,902
Wages and salaries . . .	681	878	958
Goods and services . . .	396	356	405
Transfer and subsidies . .	275	418	258
Interest	250	274	281
Capital expenditure . . .	1,149	981	1,056
Total	2,752	2,907	2,958

* Excluding grants received (Le '000 million): 709 in 2011; 701 in 2012 (projected); 602 in 2013 (projected).
† Projected.
‡ Excluding net lending (Le '000 million): 0 in 2011; −95 in 2012 (projected); 0 in 2013 (projected).

Source: IMF, *Sierra Leone: Fourth Review Under the Three-Year Arrangement Under the Extended Credit Facility, and Financing Assurances Review* (October 2012).

INTERNATIONAL RESERVES
(US $ million at 31 December)

	2009	2010	2011
IMF special drawing rights . .	189.6	184.2	178.7
Foreign exchange	215.3	224.8	260.4
Total	405.0	409.0	439.1

Source: IMF, *International Financial Statistics*.

MONEY SUPPLY
(Le million at 31 December)

	2009	2010	2011
Currency outside banks . .	420,921	557,262	641,832
Demand deposits at commercial banks	359,688	454,007	526,779
Total money (incl. others) . .	807,479	1,048,055	1,209,324

Source: IMF, *International Financial Statistics*.

COST OF LIVING
(Consumer Price Index; base: 2003 = 100)

	2009	2010	2011
Food (incl. beverages) . . .	203.2	243.1	295.7
All items (incl. others) . . .	199.0	238.8	277.2

Source: ILO.

NATIONAL ACCOUNTS
(Le million at current prices)

Expenditure on the Gross Domestic Product

	2008	2009	2010*
Government final consumption expenditure	941,478	1,103,894	1,798,606
Private final consumption expenditure	4,890,660	5,891,034	6,539,564
Gross fixed capital formation .	428,359	504,900	643,552
Changes in inventories . .	1,537,383	912,197	1,020,872
Total domestic expenditure	7,797,880	8,412,025	10,002,594
Exports of goods and services .	1,082,595	1,059,017	1,645,869
Less Imports of goods and services	2,342,461	2,130,118	3,082,034
GDP in purchasers' values .	6,538,014	7,340,924	8,566,429

Gross Domestic Product by Economic Activity

	2008	2009	2010*
Agriculture, hunting, forestry and fishing	3,721,762	4,306,282	4,904,307
Mining and quarrying . . .	171,161	132,382	142,111
Manufacturing	128,082	122,316	154,206
Electricity, gas and water . .	16,917	19,948	24,833
Construction	95,936	85,364	119,354
Wholesale and retail trade, restaurants and hotels . . .	583,990	584,236	680,114
Finance, insurance, real estate and business services	317,536	348,224	396,264
Transport and communications .	424,827	475,009	560,867
Public administration and defence	215,951	244,668	313,897
Other services	609,696	728,319	870,323
Sub-total	6,285,858	7,046,748	8,166,276
Less Imputed bank service charges	105,210	126,328	166,329
Indirect taxes, less subsidies . .	357,365	420,503	566,482
GDP in purchasers' values .	6,538,014	7,340,924	8,566,429

* Provisional figures.

Source: African Development Bank.

BALANCE OF PAYMENTS
(US $ million)

	2009	2010	2011
Exports of goods	267.7	360.2	381.5
Imports of goods	−617.5	−880.7	−1,631.1
Balance on goods	−349.9	−520.6	−1,249.6
Exports of services	100.7	56.7	156.7
Imports of services	−132.1	−154.0	−247.8
Balance on goods and services	−381.3	−617.9	−1,340.7
Primary income received . . .	11.3	9.7	9.4
Primary income paid	−46.9	−58.8	−44.7
Balance on goods, services and primary income	−417.0	−667.0	−1,376.0
Secondary income received . .	58.7	63.4	186.5
Secondary income paid . . .	−65.9	−50.1	−22.2
Current balance	−424.2	−653.7	−1,211.7
Capital account (net)	145.0	92.1	152.1
Direct investment (net) . . .	110.4	238.8	715.0
Portfolio investment assets . .	−26.0	−22.1	−13.3
Portfolio investment liabilities .	5.6	1.9	47.1
Other investment assets . .	21.7	−11.8	−29.2
Other investment liabilities . .	272.3	28.3	173.3
Net errors and omissions . . .	−201.4	7.6	24.9
Reserves and related items .	−96.1	−319.2	−141.9

Source: IMF, *International Financial Statistics*.

External Trade

PRINCIPAL COMMODITIES
(US $ '000)

Imports c.i.f.	2009	2010	2011
Food and live animals	104,509.7	104,894.0	245,883.5
Beverages and tobacco	25,255.6	19,487.5	33,141.5
Crude materials (inedible) except fuels	16,142.2	13,267.3	18,469.6
Mineral fuels, lubricants, etc. .	126,459.4	171,414.2	275,758.2
Chemicals	33,682.7	43,837.9	67,039.4
Basic manufactures	67,746.2	110,535.5	175,716.6
Machinery and transport equipment	95,085.7	248,698.2	756,262.4
Miscellaneous manufactured articles	43,659.2	18,217.6	31,261.5
Miscellaneous transactions and commodities	—	30,250.2	103,394.9
Total (incl. others)	520,304.8	770,037.5	1,716,557.6

Exports f.o.b.	2009	2010	2011
Bauxite	18,678.0	31,061.1	38,998.0
Coffee	13,123.6	1,698.2	2,000.8
Cocoa beans	20,544.6	37,051.2	44,022.0
Diamonds	78,374.0	113,514.7	129,766.2
Rutile	35,920.4	40,567.2	34,436.6
Total (incl. others)*	207,100.3	317,780.7	597,018.3

* Excluding re-exports: 23,561.9 in 2009; 23,445.7 in 2010; 33,199.0 in 2011.

Source: Bank of Sierra Leone.

PRINCIPAL TRADING PARTNERS
(Le million)

Imports c.i.f.	2006	2007	2008
China, People's Repub. . . .	115,451.1	174,865.4	233,933.1
Côte d'Ivoire	140,820.1	123,869.0	152,358.8
Germany	36,348.6	53,783.9	42,616.6
USA	116,243.5	165,403.2	176,288.8
Total (incl. others)	1,040,180.0	1,180,481.0	1,404,925.0

Exports	2006	2007	2008
Belgium	354 620.5	436,257.7	291,015.4
France	59,754.0	101,826.2	96,328.2
Germany	70,164.7	94,728.3	42,150.4
India	5,970.9	10,952.3	149,813.9
USA	129,994.1	174,698.0	168,149.9
Total (incl. others)	775,658.0	862,346.0	815,532.0

Source: African Development Bank.

Transport

ROAD TRAFFIC
(motor vehicles in use at 31 December)

	2000	2001	2002
Passenger cars	2,045	2,263	11,353
Buses and coaches	2,597	3,516	4,050
Goods vehicles	2,309	2,898	3,565
Motorcycles	1,398	1,532	1,657

2008 (motor vehicles in use at 31 December): Passenger cars 25,376; Buses and coaches 6,197; Vans and lorries 2,279; Motorcycles and mopeds 9,474.

Source: IRF, *World Road Statistics*.

Flag Registered Fleet
(at 31 December)

	2010	2011	2012
Number of vessels	426	509	537
Total displacement ('000 grt) . .	1,010.3	1,509.2	1,279.8

Source: Lloyd's List Intelligence (www.lloydslistintelligence.com).

International Sea-borne Freight Traffic
(estimates, '000 metric tons)

	1991	1992	1993
Goods loaded	1,930	2,190	2,310
Goods unloaded	562	579	589

Source: UN Economic Commission for Africa, *African Statistical Yearbook*.

CIVIL AVIATION
(traffic on scheduled services)

	2007	2008	2009
Kilometres flown (million) . .	2	2	2
Passengers carried ('000) . . .	20	21	22
Passenger-km (million) . . .	108	110	107
Total ton-km (million)	19	19	18

Source: UN, *Statistical Yearbook*.

Passengers carried ('000): 24 in 2010 (Source: World Bank, World Development Indicators database).

Tourism

TOURIST ARRIVALS BY REGION OF RESIDENCE

	2009	2010	2011
Africa	11,637	10,806	15,652
Americas	7,348	7,406	10,474
Asia	3,515	3,516	5,360
Europe	12,815	10,295	13,807
Middle East	948	2,667	3,485
Not specified	512	3,925	3,664
Total	36,775	38,615	52,442

Tourism receipts (US $ million, excl. passenger transport): 34 in 2008; 25 in 2009; 26 in 2010 (Source: World Tourism Organization).

Communications Media

	2008	2009	2010
Telephones ('000 main lines in use)	31.5	32.8	14.0
Mobile cellular telephones ('000 subscribers)	1,008.8	1,160.0	2,000.0
Internet users ('000)	13.9	14.9	n.a.

2011: Mobile cellular telephones ('000 subscribers) 2,137.0.

Source: International Telecommunication Union.

Education

(2010/11 unless otherwise indicated)

		Schools*	Teachers	Number of pupils		
				Males	Females	Total
Pre-primary	.	n.a.	2,167	18,247	19,104	37,351
Primary	.	2,704	38,125	582,899	611,604	1,194,503
Secondary	. .	246	10,024†	141,418†	98,161†	239,579†
Tertiary*	. .	n.a.	1,198	6,439	2,602	9,041

* 2001/02.
† 2006/07.

Source: mainly UNESCO Institute for Statistics.

Pupil-teacher ratio (primary education, UNESCO estimate): 31.3 in 2010/11 (Source: UNESCO Institute for Statistics).

Adult literacy rate (UNESCO estimates): 42.1% (males 53.6%; females 31.4%) in 2010 (Source: UNESCO Institute for Statistics).

Directory

The Government

HEAD OF STATE

President and Commander-in-Chief of the Armed Forces: ERNEST BAI KOROMA (elected 8 September 2007; inaugurated 15 November 2007; re-elected 17 November 2012).

Vice-President: SAHR SAM-SUMANA.

CABINET
(May 2013)

The Government is formed by members of the All-People's Congress.

Minister of Finance and Economic Development: Dr KEIFALA MARRAH.

Minister of Foreign Affairs and International Co-operation: SAMURA KAMARA.

Minister of Justice and Attorney-General: FRANKLYN BAI KARGBO.

Minister of Local Government and Rural Development: DIANA KONOMANI.

Minister of Internal Affairs: JOSEPH BANDABLA DAUDA.

Minister of Information and Communications: Alhaji ALPHA SAHID BAKAR KANU.

Minister of Trade and Industry: Alhaji OSMAN BOIE KAMARA.

Minister of Defence: Maj. (retd) ALFRED PALO CONTEH.

Minister of Education, Science and Technology: Dr MINKAILU BAH.

Minister of Health and Sanitation: MIATTA KARGBO.

Minister of Agriculture, Food Security and Forestry: Dr JOSEPH SAM SESAY.

Minister of Works, Housing and Infrastructure: ALIMAMY P. KOROMA.

Minister of Energy: OLUNIYI ROBBIN-COKER.

Minister of Water Resources: MOMODU MALIGI.

Minister of Mines and Mineral Resources: Alhaji MINKAILU MANSARAY.

Minister of Transport and Aviation: VANDI CHIDI MINAH.

Minister of Lands, Country Planning and the Environment: MUSA TARAWALLY.

Minister of Social Welfare, Gender and Children's Affairs: MOIJUEH KAIKAI.

Minister of Fisheries and Marine Resources: Capt. MOMODU ALLIEU PAT-SOWE.

Minister of Labour and Social Security: Dr MATTHEW TEAMBO.

Minister of Youth Affairs: ALIMAMY KAMARA.

Minister of Sports: PAUL KAMARA.

Minister of Political and Public Affairs: Alhaji IBRAHIM KEMOH SESAY.

Minister of Tourism and Culture: PETER BAYUKU KONTE.

Minister of State in the Office of the Vice-President: HARRIET TURAY.

Ministers of State in the Ministry of Finance and Economic Development: MOMODU KARGBO, Alhaji F. B. L. MANSARAY.

Resident Minister, Northern Region: ALIE D. KAMARA.

Resident Minister, Southern Region: MUCTARR CONTEH.

Resident Minister, Eastern Region: WILLIAM JUANA SMITH.

There were also 26 Deputy Ministers.

MINISTRIES

Office of the President: Freetown; tel. (22) 232101; fax (22) 231404; e-mail info@statehouse-sl.org; internet www.statehouse.gov.sl.

Ministry of Agriculture, Food Security and Forestry: Youyi Bldg, 3rd Floor, Brookfields, Freetown; tel. (22) 222242; fax (22) 241613.

Ministry of Defence: State Ave, Freetown; tel. (22) 227369; fax (22) 229380.

Ministry of Education, Science and Technology: New England, Freetown; tel. (22) 240881; fax (22) 240137.

Ministry of Energy: Electricity House, 4th Floor, Siaka Stevens St, Freetown; tel. (22) 226566; fax (22) 228199; e-mail info@energyandpower.gov.sl; internet www.energyandpower.gov.sl.

Ministry of Finance and Economic Development: Freetown.

Ministry of Fisheries and Marine Resources: Marine House, 11 Old Railway Line, Brookfields, Freetown; tel. (22) 242117.

Ministry of Foreign Affairs and International Co-operation: Gloucester St, Freetown; tel. (22) 223260; fax (22) 225615; e-mail mfaicsl@yahoo.com.

Ministry of Health and Sanitation: Youyi Bldg, 4th Floor, Brookfields, Freetown; tel. (22) 240187; e-mail info@health.sl; internet www.health.sl.

Ministry of Information and Communications: Youyi Bldg, 8th Floor, Brookfields, Freetown; tel. (22) 240339; fax (22) 241757.

Ministry of Internal Affairs: Liverpool St, Freetown; tel. (22) 226979; fax (22) 227727.

Ministry of Justice: Guma Bldg, Lamina Sankoh St, Freetown; tel. (22) 227444; fax (22) 229366.

Ministry of Labour and Social Security: New England Ville, Freetown; tel. 78341246 (mobile); fax (22) 228472.

Ministry of Lands, Country Planning and the Environment: Youyi Bldg, 4th Floor, Brookfields, Freetown; tel. (22) 242013.

Ministry of Local Government and Rural Development: New England, Freetown; tel. (22) 226589; fax (22) 222409.

Ministry of Mines and Mineral Resources: Youyi Bldg, 5th Floor, Brookfields, Freetown; tel. and fax (22) 240467; internet www.slminerals.org.

Ministry of Political and Public Affairs: State House, State Ave, Freetown; tel. (22) 228698; fax (22) 222781.

Ministry of Social Welfare, Gender and Children's Affairs: New England, Freetown; tel. (22) 241256; fax (22) 242076.

Ministry of Sports: Freetown.

Ministry of Tourism and Culture: Ministerial Bldg, George St, Freetown; tel. (22) 222588.

Ministry of Trade and Industry: Youyi Bldg, 6th Floor, Brookfields, Freetown; tel. (22) 225127; e-mail info@trade.gov.sl; internet www.trade.gov.sl.

Ministry of Transport and Aviation: Ministerial Bldg, George St, Freetown; tel. (22) 221245; fax (22) 227337.

Ministry of Water Resources: Freetown.

Ministry of Works, Housing and Infrastructure: New England, Freetown; tel. (22) 240937; fax (22) 240018.

Ministry of Youth Affairs: New England, Freetown; tel. (22) 240881; fax (22) 240137.

President and Legislature

PRESIDENT

Presidential Election, 17 November 2012

Candidate	Votes	% of votes
Ernest Bai Koroma (APC)	1,314,881	58.66
Julius Maada Bio (SLPP)	837,517	37.36
Charles Francis Margai (PMDC)	28,944	1.29
Joshua Albert Carew (CDP)	22,863	1.02
Others*	37,523	1.67
Total	2,241,728†	100.00

* There were five other candidates.
† In addition, there were 108,898 invalid votes.

PARLIAMENT

Speaker: ABEL NATHANIEL BANKOLE STRONGE.
General Election, 17 November 2012

Party	Seats
All-People's Congress (APC)	67
Sierra Leone People's Party (SLPP)	42
Total	109*

* The results in three constituencies had yet to be declared. A further 12 seats were allocated to Paramount Chiefs, who represented the 12 provincial districts.

Election Commission

National Electoral Commission (NEC): NEC Bldg, 15 Industrial Estate, Wellington, Freetown; tel. 76547299 (mobile); internet www.nec-sierraleone.org; f. 2000; Chair. Dr CHRISTIANA AYOKA MARY THORPE.

Political Organizations

The 2012 legislative and presidential elections were contested by the following parties:

All-People's Congress (APC): 11 Old Railway Line, Brookfields, Freetown; f. 1960; sole authorized political party 1978–91; merged with the Democratic People's Party in 1992; reconstituted in 1995; Leader ERNEST BAI KOROMA.

Citizens' Democratic Party (CDP): 21 Rowe St, off Mountain Cut, Freetown; internet www.citizensdemocraticparty.com; f. 2012; Chair. JOSHUA ALBERT CAREW.

National Democratic Alliance (NDA): 5 Duke St, off Circular Rd, Freetown.

Peace and Liberation Party (PLP): 60 Bai Bureh Rd, Kissy, Freetown; f. 2002; Nat. Chair. Rev. DARLINGTON MORRISON; Leader KANDEH BABA CONTEH.

People's Democratic Party (PDP): 2C Bismarck Johnson St, Freetown; Chair. Dr PRINCE COKER.

People's Movement for Democratic Change (PMDC): 12 Prince St, Freetown; e-mail karamohslylhorg@aol.com; internet www.pmdcsl.net; f. April 2006 by fmr mems of Sierra Leone People's Party; Leader CHARLES F. MARGAI; Sec.-Gen. AIAH ERICK JABBA (acting).

Sierra Leone People's Party (SLPP): 15 Wallace Johnson St, Freetown; tel. and fax (22) 2256341; e-mail info@slpp.ws; internet www.slpponline.com; f. 1951; Nat. Chair. JOHN BENJAMIN; Sec.-Gen. SULAIMAN BANJAN TEJAN-SIE.

United Democratic Movement: 112 Pademba Rd, Freetown; Chair. MOHAMED BANGURA.

United National People's Party (UNPP): 220 Bai Bureh Rd, Freetown; Leader Dr JOHN KAREFA-SMART.

Diplomatic Representation

EMBASSIES AND HIGH COMMISSIONS IN SIERRA LEONE

China, People's Republic: 29 Wilberforce Loop, POB 778, Freetown; tel. and fax (22) 231797; e-mail chinaemb_sl@mfa.gov.cn; internet sl.china-embassy.org; Ambassador KUANG WEILIN.

Egypt: 174C Wilkinson Rd, POB 652, Freetown; tel. (22) 231245; fax (22) 234297; Ambassador GAMAL TAWFIK ABDULLAH.

The Gambia: 6 Wilberforce St, Freetown; tel. (22) 225191; fax (22) 226846; High Commissioner DEMBO BADJIE.

Ghana: 13 Walpole St, Freetown; tel. (22) 223461; fax (22) 227043; High Commissioner ELIZABETH MILLS-ROBERTSON.

Guinea: 6 Wilkinson Rd, Freetown; tel. (22) 232584; fax (22) 232496; Ambassador MOHAMED LAMIN SOMPARE.

Lebanon: 22A Spur Rd, Wilberforce, Freetown; tel. (22) 222513; fax (22) 234665; Ambassador GHASSAN ABDEL SATER.

Liberia: 10 Motor Rd, Brookfields, POB 276, Freetown; tel. (22) 230991; Ambassador THOMAS N. BRIMA.

Libya: 1A and 1B P. Z. Compound, Wilberforce, Freetown; tel. (22) 235231; fax (22) 234514; Chargé d'affaires a.i. Dr AHMED ABUDABBOUS.

Nigeria: 37 Siaka Stevens St, Freetown; tel. (22) 224224; fax (22) 2242474; High Commissioner EYO ASUQUO.

United Kingdom: 6 Spur Rd, Wilberforce, Freetown; tel. 78200192 (mobile); fax (22) 232070; e-mail freetown.general.enquiries@fco.gov.uk; internet www.gov.uk/government/world/sierra-leone; High Commissioner PETER WEST.

USA: South Ridge, Hill Station, Freetown; tel. (22) 515000; fax (22) 515355; e-mail TaylorJB2@state.gov; internet freetown.usembassy.gov; Ambassador MICHAEL S. OWEN.

Judicial System

The judicial system of Sierra Leone is composed of a Supreme Court, a Court of Appeal, a High Court and Magistrates' Courts. The Supreme Court is the ultimate court of appeal in both civil and criminal cases. In addition to its appellate jurisdiction, the Court has supervisory jurisdiction over all other courts and over any adjudicating authority in Sierra Leone, and also original jurisdiction in constitutional issues. The Court of Appeal has jurisdiction to hear and determine appeals from decisions of the High Court in both criminal and civil matters, and also from certain statutory tribunals. Appeals against its decisions may be made to the Supreme Court. The High Court has unlimited original jurisdiction in all criminal and civil matters. It also has appellate jurisdiction against the decisions of Magistrates' Courts. However, in the countryside where the majority of the population lives the informal judicial system—based on customary law and comprising local courts, district appeal courts and local chiefs—plays a significant role, although their jurisdiction is limited to matters of marriage, divorce, succession and land tenure.

Supreme Court: Freetown; mainly consists of the Chief Justice and not fewer than four other judges; Chief Justice UMU HAWA TEJAN JALLOH.

Court of Appeal: Freetown; mainly consists of the Chief Justice and not fewer than seven other judges.

High Court: mainly consists of the Chief Justice and not fewer than nine other judges.

Magistrates' Courts: In criminal cases the jurisdiction of the Magistrates' Courts is limited to summary cases and to preliminary investigations to determine whether a person charged with an offence should be committed for trial.

Religion

A large proportion of the population holds animist beliefs, although there are significant numbers of Islamic and Christian adherents.

ISLAM

In 1990 Islamic adherents represented an estimated 30% of the total population.

Ahmadiyya Muslim Mission: 15 Bath St, Brookfields, POB 353, Freetown; Emir and Chief Missionary SAID UR-RAHMAN.

Kankaylay (Sierra Leone Muslim Men and Women's Association): 15 Blackhall Rd, Kissy, POB 1168, Freetown; tel. 33635205 (mobile); fax (22) 224439; e-mail kankaylay@yahoo.com; internet www.kankaylay.com; f. 1972; 500,000 mems; Pres. Alhaji IBRAHIM ALPHA TURAY; Lady Pres. Haja MARIAM TURAY.

Sierra Leone Muslim Congress: POB 875, Freetown; f. 1928; Pres. Alhaji MUHAMMAD SANUSI MUSTAPHA.

CHRISTIANITY

Council of Churches in Sierra Leone: 4A King Harman Rd, Brookfields, POB 404, Freetown; tel. (22) 240569; fax (22) 421109; f. 1924; 17 mem. churches; Pres. Rev. MOSES B. KHANU; Gen. Sec. ALIMAMY P. KOROMA.

The Anglican Communion

Anglicans in Sierra Leone are adherents of the Church of the Province of West Africa, comprising 12 dioceses, of which two are in Sierra Leone. The Archbishop of the Province is the Bishop of Koforidua, Ghana.

Bishop of Bo: Rt Rev. SAMUEL SAO GBONDA, MacRobert St, POB 21, Bo, Southern Province; e-mail bishop@sierratel.sl.

Bishop of Freetown: Rt Rev. JULIUS O. PRINCE LYNCH, Bishopscourt, Fourah Bay Rd, POB 537, Freetown; tel. (22) 251307; fax (22) 251306; e-mail bishop@sierratel.sl.

Baptist Churches

Sierra Leone Baptist Convention: POB 64, Lunsar; 119 mem. churches; 994 mems; Pres. Rev. JOSEPH S. MANS; Sec. Rev. N. T. DIXON.

The Nigerian Baptist Convention is also active.

Methodist Churches

Methodist Church Sierra Leone: Wesley House, George St, POB 64, Freetown; tel. (22) 222216; fax (22) 227539; e-mail mcsl@ymail.com; f. 1792; autonomous since 1967; Pres. of Conf. Rt Rev. ARNOLD C. TEMPLE; Sec. Rev. MUSA J. JAMBAWAI; 26,421 mems.

United Methodist Church: Freetown; tel. 76444100 (mobile); e-mail sierraleoneannualconference@yahoo.com; f. 1880; Presiding Bishop JOHN K. YAMBASU; 225,000 mems.

Other active Methodist bodies include the African Methodist Episcopal Church, the Wesleyan Church of Sierra Leone, the Countess of Huntingdon's Connexion and the West African Methodist Church.

The Roman Catholic Church

Sierra Leone comprises one archdiocese and three dioceses. An estimated 5% of the total population are Roman Catholics.

Inter-territorial Catholic Bishops' Conference of The Gambia and Sierra Leone
Santanno House, POB 893, Freetown; tel. (22) 228240; fax (22) 228252.
f. 1971; Pres. Rt Rev. GEORGE BIGUZZI (Bishop of Makeni).

Archbishop of Freetown: Most Rev. EDWARD TAMBA CHARLES, Santanno House, 10 Howe St, POB 893, Freetown; tel. (22) 224590; fax (22) 224075; e-mail jhg3271@sierratel.sl.

Other Christian Churches

The following are represented: the Christ Apostolic Church, the Church of the Lord (Aladura), the Evangelical Church, the Evangelical Lutheran Church in Sierra Leone, the Missionary Church of Africa, the Sierra Leone Church and the United Brethren in Christ.

AFRICAN RELIGIONS

There is a diverse range of beliefs, rites and practices, varying between ethnic and kinship groups.

The Press

DAILIES

For di People: Freetown; independent; Editor PAUL KAMARA.

The Sierra Leone Daily Mail: 29–31 Rawdon St, POB 53, Freetown; tel. (22) 223191; internet www.sierraleonedailymail.com; f. 1931; state-owned; currently online only; Editor-in-Chief CHRISTIAN F SESAY, Jr; circ. 10,000.

PERIODICALS

The Catalyst: Christian Literature Crusade Bookshop, 92 Circular Rd, POB 1465, Freetown; tel. (22) 224382; Editor JUSU-WAI SAWI.

Concord Times: 51 Krootown Rd, Freetown; tel. (22) 229199; e-mail info@concordtimessl.com; internet www.concordtimessl.com; 3 a week; Editor DOROTHY GORDON.

Leonean Sun: 49 Main Rd, Wellington, Freetown; tel. (22) 223363; f. 1974; monthly; Editor ROWLAND MARTYN.

Liberty Voice: 139 Pademba Rd, Freetown; tel. (22) 242100; Editor A. MAHDIEU SAVAGE.

The New Citizen: 7 Wellington St, Freetown; tel. (22) 228693; e-mail info@thenewcitizen-sl.com; internet www.thenewcitizen-sl.com; f. 1982; Man. Editor SAMUEL B. CONTEH.

The New Shaft: 60 Old Railway Line, Brookfields, Freetown; tel. (22) 241093; 2 a week; independent; Editor FRANKLIN BUNTING-DAVIES; circ. 10,000.

The Pool Newspaper: 1 Short St, 5th Floor, Freetown; tel. and fax (22) 220102; e-mail pool@justice.com; f. 1992; 3 a week; independent; Man. Dir CHERNOR OJUKU SESAY; circ. 3,000.

Progress: 1 Short St, Freetown; tel. (22) 223588; weekly; independent; Editor FODE KANDEH; circ. 7,000.

Sierra Leone Chamber of Commerce Journal: Sierra Leone Chamber of Commerce, Industry and Agriculture, Guma Bldg, 5th Floor, Lamina Sankoh St, POB 502, Freetown; tel. (22) 226305; fax (22) 228005; monthly.

The Vision: 60 Old Railway Line, Brookfields; tel. (22) 241273; Editor SIAKA MASSAQUOI.

Weekend Spark: 7 Lamina Sankoh St, Freetown; tel. (22) 223397; f. 1983; weekly; independent; Editor ROWLAND MARTYN; circ. 20,000.

NEWS AGENCY

Sierra Leone News Agency (SLENA): 15 Wallace Johnson St, PMB 445, Freetown; tel. (22) 224921; fax (22) 224439; f. 1980; Man. Dir AUGUSTUS KAMARA.

Publishers

Njala University Publishing Centre: Njala University College, PMB, Freetown; science and technology, university textbooks.

Sierra Leone University Press: Fourah Bay College, POB 87, Freetown; tel. (22) 22491; fax (22) 224439; f. 1965; biography, history, Africana, religion, social science, university textbooks; Chair. Prof. ERNEST H. WRIGHT.

United Christian Council Literature Bureau: Bunumbu Press, POB 28, Bo; tel. (32) 462; books in Mende, Temne, Susu; Man. Dir ROBERT SAM-KPAKRA.

Broadcasting and Communications

TELECOMMUNICATIONS

In early 2012 there were three GSM mobile cellular telephone operators in Sierra Leone, while state-owned SIERRATEL was the sole fixed-line operator. SIERRATEL also provided mobile telephone services using CDMA (code division multiple access) technology.

Africell: 1 Pivot St, Wilberforce, Freetown; tel. 77777777 (mobile); e-mail info@africell.sl; internet www.africell.sl; f. 2005; CEO SHADI AL-GERJAWI; 1.5m. subscribers (Aug. 2012).

Airtel Sierra Leone: Zain House, 42 Main Motor Rd, Wilberforce, Freetown; tel. (22) 233222; e-mail info.africa@airtel.com; internet africa.airtel.com/sierra; f. 2000; fmrly Zain Sierra Leone, present name adopted in 2010; Man. Dir RAJVARDHAN SINGH BHULLAR.

Comium (SL) Ltd: Comium Bldg, 30D Wilkinson Rd, Freetown; tel. 33333030 (mobile); fax 33333060 (mobile); e-mail info@comium.com.sl; internet www.comium.com.sl; f. 2005; mobile cellular telephone and broadband internet provider; CEO MIKE CAROLL.

Sierra Leone Telecommunications Co (SIERRATEL): 7 Wallace Johnson St, POB 80, Freetown; tel. (22) 222801; fax (22) 224439; internet www.sierratel.sl; state-owned telecommunications operator; Chair. Dr TOM OBALEH KARGBO; Man. Dir ALPHA SESAY.

Regulatory Authority

National Telecommunications Commission (NATCOM): Freetown; tel. 76604359 (mobile); e-mail its@natcomsl.com; internet www.natcom.gov.sl; f. 2006; manages radio spectrum; Chair. and Commissioner SIRAY A. TIMBO; Dir-Gen. MOHAMED BANGURA.

BROADCASTING

Sierra Leone Broadcasting Corpn (SBC): New England, Freetown; tel. (22) 240403; f. 1934; name changed as above in 2010 following merger of Sierra Leone Broadcasting Service and UN Radio in Sierra Leone; state-controlled; programmes mainly in English and the four main Sierra Leonean vernaculars: Mende, Limba, Temne and Krio; weekly broadcast in French; television service established 1963; Dir-Gen. ELVIS GBANABOM HALLOWELL.

Finance

(cap. = capital; res = reserves; dep. = deposits; m. = million; br(s). = branch(es); amounts in leones)

BANKING

In 2010 there were 12 commercial banks and six community banks in Sierra Leone.

Central Bank

Bank of Sierra Leone: Siaka Stevens St, POB 30, Freetown; tel. (22) 226501; fax (22) 224764; e-mail info@bankofsierraleone.com; internet www.bsl.gov.sl; f. 1964; cap. 50,000.0m., res −352,030.6m., dep. 419,113.6m. (Dec. 2009); Gov. Dr SHEKU S. SESAY; Dep. Gov. ANDRINA ROSA COKER; 1 br.

Other Banks

Access Bank Sierra Leone Ltd: 30 Siaka Stevens St, Freetown; internet www.accessbankplc.com/sl; f. 2007.

Ecobank Sierra Leone Ltd: 7 Lightfoot Boston St, POB 1007, Freetown; tel. (22) 221704; fax (22) 229450; e-mail info@ecobanksl.com; internet www.ecobank.com; Chair. KEILI ANDREW KARMOH; Man. Dir CLEMENT DODOO.

First International Bank (SL) Ltd: 2 Charlotte St, Freetown; tel. (22) 220038; fax (22) 221970; e-mail fib@sierratel.sl; internet fibsl.biz; f. 1998; Chair. CHRISTIAN J. SMITH; Man. Dir CHRIS UCHENDU.

Guaranty Trust Bank: Sparta Bldg, 12 Wilberforce St, POB 1168, Freetown; tel. (22) 228493; fax (22) 228318; internet www.gtb.sl; f. Feb. 2002 through the acquisition of 90% of shareholding of First Merchant Bank of Sierra Leone by Guaranty Trust Bank of Nigeria; cap. 2,261.0m., total assets 17,769.0m. (Dec. 2003); Chair. JIDE OGUNDARE; Man. Dir ADE BURAIMO; 3 brs.

International Commercial Bank (Sierra Leone) Ltd: 22 Rawdon St, POB 515, Freetown; tel. (22) 222877; fax (22) 220376; e-mail enquiry@icbank-sl.com; internet www.icbank-sl.com; f. 2004; 1 br.

National Development Bank Ltd: Leone House, 6th Floor, 21–23 Siaka Stevens St, Freetown; tel. (22) 226792; fax (22) 224468; f. 1968; 99% state-owned; provides medium- and long-term finance and tech. assistance to devt-orientated enterprises; cap. 1,604.3m., total assets 2,200m. (Dec. 2003); Chair. MURRAY E. S. LAMIN; Man. Dir MOHAMED M. TURAY; 3 brs.

Rokel Commercial Bank (Sierra Leone) Ltd: 25–27 Siaka Stevens St, POB 12, Freetown; tel. (22) 222501; fax (22) 222563; e-mail rokelsl@sierratel.sl; internet www.rokelsl.com; f. 1971; cap. 15,116.5m., res 29,772.8m., dep. 312,619.4m. (Dec. 2009); 51% govt-owned; Chair. BIRCH M. CONTE; Man. Dir HENRY AKINTOTA MACAULEY; 11 brs.

Sierra Leone Commercial Bank Ltd: Christian Smith Bldg, 29–31 Siaka Stevens St, Freetown; tel. (22) 225264; fax (22) 225292; e-mail slcb@slcb.biz; internet www.slcb.biz; f. 1973; state-owned; cap. 12,000.0m., res 22,891.9m., dep. 274,726.8m. (Dec. 2008); Chair. SHEIKI G. BANGURA; Gen. Man. PATRICK CONTEH (acting); 8 brs.

Skye Bank Sierra Leone Ltd: 31 Siaka Stevens St, Freetown; tel. (22) 220095; fax (22) 221773; internet www.skyebanksl.com; Chair. PATRICK COKER; Man. Dir OLUMIDE OLATUNJI.

Standard Chartered Bank Sierra Leone Ltd: 9–11 Lightfoot-Boston St, POB 1155, Freetown; tel. (22) 225021; fax (22) 225760; e-mail scbsl@sierratel.sl; internet www.standardchartered.com/sl; f. 1894; cap. 15,255.7m., res 18,399.8m., dep. 221,661.7m. (Dec. 2009); Chair. ALEX B. KAMARA; CEO and Man. Dir ALBERTO R. SALTSON; 3 brs.

Union Trust Bank Ltd: Lightfoot-Boston St, PMB 1237, Freetown; tel. (22) 226954; fax (22) 226214; e-mail info@utb.sl; internet www.utb.sl; fmrly Meridien BIAO Bank Sierra Leone Ltd; adopted present name in 1995; cap. 7,477.9m., res 8,275.1m., total assets 60,720.1m. (Dec. 2007); Chair. Alhaji Dr SHEKU TEJAN KAMARA; Man. Dir and CEO JAMES SANPHA KOROMA; 7 brs.

United Bank For Africa Sierra Leone Ltd: 15 Charlotte St, Freetown; tel. (22) 228099; fax (22) 225395; e-mail cicsl@ubagroup.com; internet www.ubagroup.com; f. 2008; 4 brs.

Zenith Bank Sierra Leone Ltd: 18–20 Rawdon St, Freetown; tel. (22) 225400; fax (22) 225070; e-mail enquiry@zenithbank.com.sl; f. 2007; Chair. EDDY MARTINS EGWUENU; Man. Dir ADEWALE ADENIYI.

INSURANCE

In 2010 there were nine insurance companies in Sierra Leone.

Aureol Insurance Co Ltd: Kissy House, 54 Siaka Stevens St, POB 647, Freetown; tel. (22) 223435; fax (22) 229336; e-mail info@aureolinsurance.com; internet aureolinsurance.com; f. 1986; Chair. Dr PATRICK E. COKER; Man. Dir SOLOMON J. SAMBA.

National Insurance Co Ltd: 18–20 Walpole St, PMB 84, Freetown; tel. (22) 224328; fax (22) 226097; e-mail info@sl-nic.com; internet www.sl-nic.com; f. 1972; state-owned; Chair. P. J. KUYEMBEH; CEO ARTHUR NATHANIEL YASKEY.

New India Assurance Co Ltd: 18 Wilberforce St, POB 340, Freetown; tel. (22) 226453; fax (22) 222494; e-mail niasl@sierratel.sl; Man. Dir A. CHOPRA.

Reliance Insurance Trust Corpn Ltd: 24 Siaka Stevens St, Freetown; tel. (22) 225115; fax (22) 228051; e-mail oonomake@yahoo.com; f. 1985; Chair. MOHAMED B. COLE; Man. Dir ALICE M. ONOMAKE.

Sierra Leone Insurance Co Ltd: 3 Howe St, POB 836, Freetown; tel. (22) 224920; fax (22) 222115; e-mail office@slico.com.sl; internet www.slico.com.sl; f. 1983; Man. Dir and CEO ALI-DAUSY MASSALLY.

Trade and Industry

GOVERNMENT AGENCIES

Government Gold and Diamond Office (GGDO): c/o Bank of Sierra Leone, Siaka Stevens St, Freetown; tel. (22) 222600; fax (22) 229064; f. 1985; govt regulatory agency for diamonds and gold; combats illicit trade; Chair. Alhaji M. S. DEEN.

National Commission for Privatisation: Lotto House, OAU Dr., Tower Hill, POB 56, Freetown; tel. (22) 227759; fax (22) 227935; e-mail info@ncp.gov.sl; internet ncp.gov.sl; f. 2001; Chair. ABU BANGURA.

National Minerals Agency (NMA): Coal Farm, 13 Wilkinson Road, Freetown; f. 2013; Chair. RAYMOND MOSHE ROBERTS; Dir-Gen. SAHR WONDAY.

CHAMBER OF COMMERCE

Sierra Leone Chamber of Commerce, Industry and Agriculture (SLCCIA): Guma Bldg, 5th Floor, Lamina Sankoh St, POB 502, Freetown; tel. 76483017 (mobile); e-mail info@chamberofcommerce.sl; internet www.chamberofcommerce.sl; f. 1961; 300 mems; Pres. GLADYS STRASSER-KING.

TRADE AND INDUSTRIAL ASSOCIATIONS

Sierra Leone Investment and Export Promotion Agency (SLIEPA): Standard Chartered Bank Bldg, 3rd Floor, Lightfoot-Boston St, Freetown; tel. (22) 220788; e-mail info@sliepa.org; internet www.sliepa.org; f. 2007; fmrly Sierra Leone Export Development and Investment Corporation; Man. Dir CHRIS JASABE.

Small-Medium Scale Businesses Association (Sierra Leone): OAU Dr., Tower Hill, PMB 575, Freetown; tel. (22) 222617; fax (22) 224439; Dir ABU CONTEH.

EMPLOYERS' ORGANIZATIONS

Sierra Leone Chamber of Mines: POB 456, Freetown; tel. (22) 226082; f. 1965; mems comprise the principal mining concerns; Pres. JOHN SISAY; Exec. Officer N. H. T. BOSTON.

Sierra Leone Employers' Federation: POB 562, Freetown; Chair. AMADU B. NDOEKA; Exec. Officer L. E. JOHNSON.

UTILITIES

Electricity

National Power Authority: Electricity House, 36 Siaka Stevens St, Freetown; tel. (22) 229868; fax (22) 227584; e-mail Sierra_Leone@iaeste.org; supplies all electricity in Sierra Leone.

Water

Guma Valley Water Co: Guma Bldg, 13/14 Lamina Sankoh St, POB 700, Freetown; tel. (22) 25887; e-mail gumasl@yahoo.co.uk; f. 1961; responsible for all existing water supplies in Freetown and surrounding villages, including the Guma dam and associated works.

TRADE UNION

Sierra Leone Labour Congress: 35 Wallace Johnson St, POB 1333, Freetown; tel. (22) 226869; f. 1966; 51,000 mems in 19 affiliated unions; Pres. MOHAMED A. DEEN; Sec.-Gen. Alhaji KANDEH YILLA; 25,000 mems (2007).

Transport

RAILWAYS

There are no passenger railways in Sierra Leone.

Marampa Mineral Railway: Delco House, POB 735, Freetown; tel. (22) 222556; 84 km of track linking iron ore mines at Marampa (inactive since 1985) with Pepel port; Gen. Man. SYL KHANU.

ROADS

In 2002 there were an estimated 11,300 km of classified roads, including 2,138 km of main roads and 1,950 km of secondary roads; about 904 km of the total network was paved.

Sierra Leone Road Transport Corpn (SLRTC): Blackhall Rd, POB 1008, Freetown; tel. (22) 250442; fax (22) 250000; f. 1965; state-owned; operates transport services throughout the country; Gen. Man. BOCKARIE LEWIS KAMARA.

Sierra Leone Road Transport Authority: Blackhall Rd, PMB 1324, Freetown.

INLAND WATERWAYS

Established routes for launches, which include the coastal routes from Freetown northward to the Great and Little Scarcies rivers and southward to Bonthe, total almost 800 km. Although some of the upper reaches of the rivers are navigable only between July and September, there is a considerable volume of river traffic.

SHIPPING

Freetown, the principal port, has full facilities for ocean-going vessels. At 31 December 2012 Sierra Leone's flag registered fleet numbered 537 vessels, totalling 1,279,825 grt.

Sierra Leone National Carrier: 45 Cline St, POB 935, Freetown; tel. (22) 229883; fax (22) 229513; f. 1972 as Sierra Leone National Shipping Co; 51% state-owned, 49% owned by Four Handy (United Kingdom); shipping, clearing and forwarding agency; representatives for foreign lines; Chair. Alhaji B. M. KOROMA; CEO STEFANO ROSINA.

Sierra Leone Ports Authority: Queen Elizabeth II Quay, PMB 386, Cline Town, Freetown; tel. (22) 226480; fax (22) 226443; e-mail sierraleoneports@yahoo.com; f. 1965; parastatal body, supervised by the Ministry of Transport and Aviation; operates the port of Freetown; Gen. Man. HUBERT A. BLOOMER (acting).

Sierra Leone Shipping Agencies Ltd: Deep Water Quay, Clinetown, POB 74, Freetown; tel. (22) 221709; fax (22) 293111; e-mail fna.otal@bollore.com; f. 1949; Man. Dir MICHEL MEYNARD.

CIVIL AVIATION

There is an international airport at Lungi.

Directorate of Civil Aviation: Ministry of Transport and Aviation, Ministerial Bldg, George St, Freetown; tel. (22) 222106; fax (22) 228488; Dir GEORGE GBONGBOR.

Sierra Leone Airports Authority: 15 Rawdon St, POB 927, Freetown; tel. (22) 223881; fax (22) 224653; Gen. Man. JOHN SESAY.

Sierra National Airlines: Leone House, 25 Pultney St, POB 285, Freetown; tel. (22) 222075; fax (22) 222026; f. 1982; state-owned; operates domestic and regional services, and a weekly flight to Paris, France; operations resumed, following civil conflict, in Nov. 2000; Chair. TAMBA MATTURI; Man. Dir ADAM CORMACK.

Tourism

The main attractions for tourists are the coastline, the mountains and the game reserves. Civil conflict throughout most of the 1990s effectively suspended tourist activity. By 2011, however, tourist arrivals had increased to 52,442, compared with 10,615 in 1999. Receipts from tourism totalled an estimated US $26m., according to the World Tourism Organization, in 2010.

Sierra Leone National Tourist Board: Cape Sierra Hotel, Room 100, Aberdeen, POB 1435, Freetown; tel. (22) 236620; fax (22) 236621; e-mail info@welcometosierraleone.org; internet www.welcometosierraleone.org; f. 1990; Gen. Man. CECIL J. WILLIAMS.

Defence

As assessed at November 2012, the armed forces of the Republic of Sierra Leone numbered about 10,500, with a navy of 200. In October 1999 the UN Security Council adopted a resolution establishing the UN Mission in Sierra Leone (UNAMSIL), which was to supervise the implementation of a peace agreement between the Government and rebel forces, signed in July of that year. Following the completion of disarmament in January 2002, a new army, restructured with British military assistance, was established. In September 2004 UNAMSIL transferred primary responsibility for security to the armed forces, but retained its own rapid intervention capacity. Some 100 British troops remained in the country to support peace-keeping operations and to continue reorganization of the Sierra Leone armed forces. The mandate of UNAMSIL (which had been reduced from nearly its maximum authorized strength of 17,500 to about 3,400) was completed at the end of 2005. Following a UN Security Council resolution in August, the United Nations Integrated Office in Sierra Leone (UNIOSIL) was established in the capital, Freetown, on 1 January 2006 for an initial period of one year, extended in December until the end of 2007. In December of that year, UNIOSIL's mandate was extended until September 2008. In October the United Nations Integrated Peacebuilding Office in Sierra Leone (UNIPSIL) officially replaced UNIOSIL with an initial mandate of one year. In March 2013 it was announced that UNIPSIL would end its operations in March 2014. Preparations were under way in the early 2010s to reduce the size of the armed forces.

Defence Expenditure: Estimated at Le 62,700m. in 2013.

Commander-in-Chief of the Armed Forces: Pres. ERNEST BAI KOROMA.

Chief of Defence Staff: Maj.-Gen. SAMUEL OMARU WILLIAMS.

Education

Primary education begins at five years of age and lasts for seven years. Secondary education, beginning at the age of 12, also lasts for a further seven years, comprising a first cycle of five years and a second cycle of two years. In 1987 tuition fees for government-funded primary and secondary schools were abolished. In 2000/01 primary enrolment was equivalent to 92.8% of children in the relevant age-group, while about 26% of children of the relevant age-group were enrolled at secondary schools (males 30%; females 20%) in 2006/07. There is one university, which comprises six colleges. A total of 9,041 students were enrolled in tertiary education in 2001/02. Budgetary expenditure on education by the central Government in 2010 was was 13.9% of total spending.

SINGAPORE

Introductory Survey

LOCATION, CLIMATE, LANGUAGE, RELIGION, FLAG, CAPITAL

The Republic of Singapore lies in South-East Asia. The country comprises one main island and some 64 offshore islands, situated approximately 137 km (85 miles) north of the Equator, off the southernmost tip of the Malay Peninsula, to which it is linked by a causeway. The climate is equatorial, with a uniformly high daily and annual temperature varying between 24°C and 27°C (75°F–80°F). Relative humidity is high (often exceeding 90%), and the average annual rainfall is 235 cm (93 ins). There are four official languages—Malay (the national language), Chinese (Mandarin), Tamil and English. The language of administration is English. Chinese dialects were spoken as a first language by 24% of the population in 2000. The principal religions are Daoism, Buddhism, Islam, Christianity and Hinduism. The national flag (proportions 2 by 3) has two equal horizontal stripes of red and white, with a white crescent moon and five white stars, arranged in a pentagram, in the upper hoist. The capital is Singapore City.

CONTEMPORARY POLITICAL HISTORY

Historical Context

In 1826 the East India Company formed the Straits Settlements by the union of Singapore and the dependencies of Penang and Malacca on the Malay Peninsula. They came under British rule in 1867 as a Crown Colony. Singapore was occupied by Japan for three years during the Second World War. At the end of the war in 1945, following Japan's defeat, Singapore was governed by a British military administration. When civil rule was restored in 1946, Singapore was detached from the other Straits Settlements and became a separate Crown Colony. A new Constitution, adopted in February 1955, introduced some measure of self-government, and in June 1959 the state achieved complete internal self-government, with Lee Kuan Yew as Prime Minister. The Federation of Malaysia came into being in September 1963, with Singapore as a constituent state. On 9 August 1965, following irreconcilable differences with the central Government in Malaysia, Singapore seceded from the federation and became an independent country. Singapore joined the UN in September and the Commonwealth in October. In December Singapore was proclaimed a republic, with a President as constitutional head of state. In May 1973 the last major links with Malaysia, concerning currency and finance, were renounced. In September 1972 Lee Kuan Yew's ruling People's Action Party (PAP) won all 65 parliamentary seats in a general election.

Domestic Political Affairs

At the general election in December 1976 and again in December 1980, the PAP won all 69 seats in the enlarged Parliament. However, the PAP's monopoly ended in October 1981, when the Secretary-General of the opposition Workers' Party, J. B. Jeyaretnam, won a by-election. This posed no direct threat, but, in order to reassert its authority, the Government increased its control over trade unions and restructured the ownership of major newspapers. The PAP was again returned to power in December 1984 with a large majority in Parliament (now expanded to 79 seats), but the party lost two seats to opposition parties, and its share of the total vote was reduced to 63% from 75% in 1980. A constitutional amendment approved in July 1984 provided for up to three 'non-constituency' parliamentary seats for the opposition (with restricted voting rights) if none was won in the election. One extra seat was subsequently offered to the losing opposition candidate with the highest percentage of votes. However, this seat was refused by the Workers' Party in January 1985. In March the state President, Devan Nair, resigned. Wee Kim Wee (hitherto Chairman of the Singapore Broadcasting Corporation) was elected as the new President by Parliament in August.

In August 1986 amendments to the Parliament (Privileges, Immunities and Powers) Act were adopted, enabling Parliament to fine, expel or imprison members who were deemed to have abused their parliamentary privileges. Parliament also approved a Newspaper and Printing Presses (Amendment) Act, which empowered the Government to restrict the distribution of foreign publications deemed to be interfering in domestic political affairs; the circulation of several foreign periodicals was subsequently restricted.

In November 1986 Jeyaretnam was sentenced to one month's imprisonment and fined S \$5,000 (enough, according to the Constitution, to deprive him of his parliamentary seat and prevent him from standing for election for five years), when the Supreme Court upheld a conviction for perjury in connection with bankruptcy proceedings brought against the Workers' Party four years previously. In February 1987 Jeyaretnam was also fined by a parliamentary committee for abuse of privilege, having made allegations of government interference in the judiciary; further fines were imposed on him for publishing 'distorted' accounts of an earlier hearing of the committee, and (in May) for alleged contempt of Parliament and abuse of parliamentary privilege. In October Jeyaretnam's removal from the Law Society register was ordered by a three-judge court. An appeal to the Judicial Committee of the Privy Council in the United Kingdom (then the highest court of appeal for Singapore) resulted, in October 1988, in his reinstatement as a practising lawyer. During the course of the appeal, investigations into Jeyaretnam's previous convictions found that they had been 'fatally flawed'. However, since the criminal case had been considered in the District Court, where there was no right of appeal to the Privy Council, the original convictions prevented Jeyaretnam from re-entering Parliament without a presidential pardon. This was refused by Wee Kim Wee in May 1989.

In May and June 1987 the Government detained 22 people (including 10 Roman Catholic church workers and four members of the Workers' Party) without trial, under the Internal Security Act (ISA), for their alleged involvement in a 'Marxist conspiracy' to subvert state organizations. In November the Government was criticized by international human rights groups, including Amnesty International, for its refusal to present evidence of such a conspiracy in court. By December most of the alleged conspirators had been released, but eight of them were rearrested in April 1988, after complaining that they had been tortured while in detention. Four prisoners were released by June, and in December a further four were released in accordance with a ruling by the Court of Appeal, based on a fault in their detention orders. They were immediately rearrested. However, the trial had established a precedent for the judicial review of cases brought under the ISA, including the acceptability to the courts of evidence used in warrants for the arrest of suspects. In January 1989 Parliament approved legislation ensuring that the judiciary could examine such detentions only on technical grounds, and abolishing the right of appeal to the Privy Council in cases brought under the ISA. In March three of the detainees were released. The two remaining prisoners (of the original 22) remained in detention until June 1990.

A general election was held in September 1988. The electoral system was altered so that 39 of the existing 79 constituencies were replaced by 13 'group representation constituencies', to be contested by teams of three representatives for each party, at least one of whom was to be a member of an ethnic minority (i.e. non-Chinese). The declared aim was to ensure the presence of racial minorities in Parliament; however, in practice, opposition parties with few resources were restricted by the difficulty of presenting three candidates. The PAP won 80 of the elective seats (which now totalled 81); one was secured by the leader of the Singapore Democratic Party (SDP), Chiam See Tong. Two non-constituency seats were offered, to Francis Seow (of the Workers' Party) and Lee Siew Choh (of the Socialist Front). In December, however, while Seow (who had already been detained in May under the ISA for organizing a meeting between a US diplomat and lawyers critical of the Government) was undergoing medical treatment in the USA, he was convicted *in absentia* for tax evasion and fined S \$19,000: he was thus debarred from taking his seat in Parliament.

In January 1989 Lee Kuan Yew began his eighth term as Prime Minister, and announced that he would retire from the premiership before the expiry of the term. This announcement was followed by a statement from the First Deputy Prime Minister, Goh Chok Tong (Lee's chosen successor), that Lee was adopting a secondary and more advisory role in the government of the country. In August Parliament unanimously re-elected Wee Kim Wee for a further four-year term as President. In early 1990 Parliament approved legislation enabling the Government to nominate as many as six unelected members of Parliament. The politically neutral nominated members would be appointed for two years, and would be able to vote on all legislative proposals except those concerning financial and constitutional affairs.

The premiership of Goh Chok Tong

On 28 November 1990 Lee Kuan Yew was duly replaced as Prime Minister by Goh Chok Tong. Lee remained in the Cabinet as Senior Minister in the Prime Minister's Office, and retained the position of Secretary-General of the PAP; Lee's son, Brig.-Gen. Lee Hsien Loong, was appointed as a Deputy Prime Minister.

In January 1991 the Constitution was amended to provide for a popularly elected presidency with extensive powers of veto on proposed financial legislation, a role as final arbiter in cases of detention for reasons of national security, and influence in civil and military appointments. Under the amendment, which had been initially proposed by Lee Kuan Yew in 1984, Wee Kim Wee was to continue in office until October 1993. Legislation empowering him with the authority of an elected President took effect from 30 November 1991. Candidates for the presidency were limited to those who had held the post of minister, chief justice or senior civil servant or who headed a large company. The candidates were to be scrutinized by a new Presidential Election Committee, which was to comprise the head of the Society of Accountants, the Chairman of the Public Service Commission and a member of the Presidential Council of Human Rights; the last two officials were government appointees. The constitutional amendment also included a clause increasing the number of candidates required to contest a 'group representation constituency' in a general election to a minimum of three and a maximum of four, one of whom was to be a member of an ethnic minority.

In early 1991 the Government promoted the acceptance of five 'shared values', based on Confucian philosophy, as the basis of a national ideology. Critics alleged that the ideology would be used to reinforce support for the PAP and to obviate opposition challenges. Goh attempted, in principle, to introduce a more 'open', consultative form of government. He instituted an extensive programme of community visits to assess popular opinion, showing solicitude for the views of the minority Malay and Indian communities. However, although film censorship was relaxed, the ISA and restrictions on the foreign press remained in force.

In early August 1991, seeking a popular mandate for his style of government, Goh announced that there would be a general election at the end of the month. Under a plan conceived by SDP leader Chiam See Tong, the opposition parties contested only 40 of the 81 seats, thus guaranteeing an absolute majority for the incumbent PAP. Goh indicated that a failure to receive a popular endorsement would result in a return to a more authoritarian and paternalistic form of government. At the election, held on 31 August, the PAP's share of the vote was 61.0% (compared with 63.2% in 1988), and the party won 77 seats (compared with 80 in 1988). The SDP secured three seats and the Workers' Party one seat. Jeyaretnam was unable to contest the election, as his disqualification remained in force until November. Prior to the convening of Parliament in September, the Government appointed the maximum of six nominated members.

In response to Jeyaretnam's accusations that he had been deliberately excluded from the election, and also because the election schedule had prevented the PAP from presenting enough new candidates, Goh had announced, prior to the polls, that he would organize by-elections within 12–18 months of the general election. In October 1991 Francis Seow, who had remained in exile in the USA since 1988, was convicted *in absentia* of a further 60 offences involving tax evasion, rendering him ineligible to contest any potential by-election. Later that month Jeyaretnam paid S $392,838 in legal costs to Lee Kuan Yew, thus avoiding bankruptcy, which would have prevented his candidacy. Lee had instituted a successful defamation suit against Jeyaretnam in 1990, over remarks made by the latter at a 1988 election rally.

Following the general election, Lee Kuan Yew, who had temporarily withdrawn from public attention after Goh's accession to the premiership, resumed a prominent role in domestic politics. He attributed the decline in PAP support to neglect of the Mandarin-educated ethnic Chinese majority, and advocated a greater emphasis on Chinese culture and language. In December 1992 Goh was unanimously elected to replace Lee Kuan Yew (who proposed his candidacy) as Secretary-General of the PAP.

In December 1992 Goh relinquished his parliamentary seat (which formed part of a four-member 'group representation constituency') in order to contest a by-election. Jeyaretnam was unable to contest the by-election as only three candidates from the Workers' Party registered with the authorities. The results of the by-election were regarded as an endorsement of Goh's leadership, as the four PAP candidates received 72.9% of the votes cast, while the opposition SDP secured 24.5%.

In March 1993 Chee Soon Juan, who contested the December by-election as a candidate for the SDP, was dismissed from his post as a lecturer at the National University of Singapore for 'dishonest conduct'. The Government denied that the dismissal was politically motivated. In June, following a rejection by the SDP Central Committee of a motion of censure proposed by Chiam See Tong against Chee for bringing the party into disrepute, Chiam resigned as Secretary-General of the party. Chee replaced him as acting Secretary-General, and was formally elected Secretary-General of the SDP in January 1995.

Meanwhile, in August 1993 Ong Teng Cheong was elected President with 58.7% of the votes cast. However, contrary to expectation, the only other candidate, Chua Kim Yeow, a former government official, who adopted an apolitical position, secured a substantial proportion (41.3%) of the vote. The candidacies of both Jeyaretnam and Tan Soo Phuan, also of the Workers' Party, were rejected by the Presidential Election Committee on the grounds that they were unsuitable 'in regard to integrity, good character and reputation'.

In October 1996 Parliament approved amendments to the Constitution that redefined the role of the President and partially reformed the voting system. The President's powers were restricted by new provisions empowering the Government to call a referendum if the President vetoed certain constitutional amendments, and also enabling Parliament to overrule (by a two-thirds' majority) a presidential veto on senior civil service appointments. A further amendment expanded the number of 'group representation constituencies' and increased the maximum number of group candidates from four to six. The electoral reforms were opposed by the opposition parties on the grounds that the amendments favoured large, well-established parties such as the PAP, while smaller parties would have difficulty in finding and funding large numbers of candidates.

Prior to the general election, which took place on 2 January 1997, the success of the PAP was predetermined by the opposition parties' decision to contest only 36 of the 83 seats. The party secured a resounding victory, winning 65.0% of the vote and 81 seats (including all nine single-member constituencies). The remaining two elective seats were won by Chiam See Tong, now representing the Singapore People's Party (SPP), and Low Thia Khiang of the Workers' Party. The Workers' Party, as the opposition party with the most votes but less than three seats, was also allocated a non-constituency seat; this was accepted by Jeyaretnam. The SDP lost the three seats that it had previously held.

Legislation introduced in May 1997 increased the number of nominated members of Parliament from six to nine; the Constitution was amended accordingly in September. In the same month Jeyaretnam was ordered to pay damages of S $20,000, after Goh and 10 senior PAP members had sued him for defamation following critical remarks that he was alleged to have made about the PAP at an election rally; however, the award represented only 10% of the amount sought by the PAP leadership, and the judge, who criticized Goh's lawyers for their handling of the case, ordered that Jeyaretnam pay only 60% of the legal costs. The Court of Appeal dismissed an appeal by Jeyaretnam in July 1998, increasing the damages to S $100,000, and awarding full costs against him.

During 1999 Lee Hsien Loong, who had been appointed Chairman of the Monetary Authority of Singapore (MAS) in December 1997, began to assume a more prominent political role. Brig.-Gen. (retd) George Yeo, hitherto the Minister for Information and the Arts, also gained prominence following his promotion to the trade and industry portfolio in June 1999. Singapore's second presidential election was scheduled to take place in August. Ong Teng Cheong, despite his PAP affiliation, had proved an independent President, whose determination to exercise the full powers of the elected presidency had resulted in strained relations with his former government colleagues. His allegations of government obstruction of his efforts to establish the details of the Republic's financial reserves (in order to fulfil his role of guardian of those reserves as specified in the constitutional amendments of 1991) had led to a rare display of disunity among senior PAP officials, involving public disputes with both Goh and Lee Kuan Yew. Despite a medical report confirming that Ong was in complete remission from cancer diagnosed in 1992, the PAP announced that, on the grounds of health, it would not support his candidacy should he choose to seek a second term of office. Ong, who was widely believed to command sufficient popular support to secure the presidency without a government endorsement, finally announced his decision not to contest the election in July 1999, but unexpectedly proceeded to enumerate the political difficulties he suffered while in office. Despite Goh's expressed support for a more consultative style of governance, in mid-August a government-appointed committee declared that only one of three potential presidential candidates, S. R. Nathan (a former Singaporean ambassador to the USA whose presidential candidature was supported by the Cabinet), had fulfilled the criteria set by the committee; Nathan was subsequently nominated as the new President of Singapore on 18 August, and was formally appointed to the position on 1 September, prompting criticism of the Government's autocratic approach.

Meanwhile, government suppression of expressions of opposition continued. In January 1999 Chee Soon Juan was charged twice under the Public Entertainment Act for making unlicensed public speeches. Chee had deliberately refused to apply for licences to make the two public speeches, in which he had criticized government policy, on the grounds that freedom of expression was guaranteed under the Constitution. Chee was found guilty of the first charge in February, and, owing to his refusal to pay a fine of S $1,400, was sentenced to seven days' imprisonment. Following his release, Chee appeared in court for a second time in February, and was sentenced, together with the Assistant Secretary-General of the SDP, Wong Hong Toy, who had reportedly assisted Chee at the speech, to 12 days' imprisonment (both defendants having refused to pay fines, of S $2,500 and S $2,400, respectively). However, following an appeal, the two had their fines reduced to S $1,900 each, below the S $2,000 level that would have automatically disqualified them from seeking political office for five years. The Government maintained that opposition politicians had adequate opportunity to expound their views in Parliament or in the media (although in February 1998 the Government had banned political parties from producing videos and from promoting their opinions on television). In March 1999 members of the PAP filed a petition to close the Workers' Party, owing to its inability to pay the damages and costs awarded against it in a defamation case. The party's closure would force the resignation of its two parliamentary representatives. It was subsequently reported that the party had lost a judicial appeal against the award.

In May 2000 Jeyaretnam was declared bankrupt by the High Court after he failed to pay libel damages of S $30,000 arising from a lawsuit concerning an article that appeared in the Workers' Party newspaper, *The Hammer*, in 1995. The bankruptcy ruling would have disqualified Jeyaretnam from serving in Parliament, but the orders were set aside after the outstanding debt was paid, and he was authorized to retain his non-constituency seat. In January 2001, however, Jeyaretnam was once again declared bankrupt by the High Court, with a S $235,000 debt as a result of a defamation claim against a Workers' Party newsletter. The appeal against the bankruptcy ruling was dismissed in February. In May Jeyaretnam was replaced as Secretary-General of the Workers' Party by Low Thia Khiang. In July Jeyaretnam finally lost his seat in Parliament when the Court of Appeal confirmed that it would not rescind the bankruptcy ruling against him.

In September 2000 the Government appeared to have relaxed its strict control over public speaking, with the opening of a 'Speakers' Corner', theoretically allowing a forum for any citizen to air issues of concern. However, in practice, speakers were obliged to register with the police beforehand, and to refrain from speaking on certain racial issues. In April 2001 the Government permitted a rare opposition political rally. The rally, intended as a pro-democracy fund-raising event for Jeyaretnam, was attended by over 1,000 people, and was the first authorized protest to be openly critical of the Government since independence.

In July 2001 four opposition parties—the SPP, the Pertubuhan Kebangsaan Melayu Singapura (PKMS—Singapore Malay National Organization), the National Solidarity Party and the Singapore Justice Party—formed the Singapore Democratic Alliance (SDA). The new coalition was chaired by Chiam See Tong, and it was hoped that its formation would strengthen the fragmented political opposition to the PAP.

In October 2001 President S. R. Nathan unexpectedly announced that a general election was to be held in November, significantly in advance of the August 2002 deadline. During the campaign the Government declared that the allocation of priority to public housing improvements would again be affected by levels of electoral support. Electoral boundaries were also redrawn, leading to the enlargement of 14 multi-member constituencies and to an increase in the number of parliamentary seats to 84. The opposition protested that it had been disadvantaged by the rearrangements. As in previous elections, the Government secured victory by default before the polls opened, with PAP candidates being unopposed for 55 of the 84 seats. Meanwhile, Goh announced that he would leave office upon the conclusion of his next term.

The legislative elections were held on 3 November 2001. The level of voter participation was low, owing to the large number of uncontested seats. The PAP increased its share of the vote and won 82 seats. The remaining two seats went to SDA Chairman Chiam See Tong and Low Thia Khiang of the Workers' Party. Steve Chia of the SDA was awarded a non-constituency seat.

Shortly after the general election it was reported that Lee Kuan Yew and Goh were suing Chee Soon Juan for defamation. Chee had alleged that the Government had lent more than S $17,000m. of public money to the Suharto administration in Indonesia during the 1997–98 financial crisis. Goh claimed that, while the loan had been offered to the Suharto administration, it had never been disbursed. In February 2002 Chee was the focus of further legal action after he contravened the rule banning the discussion of racial and religious issues at 'Speakers' Corner'. He had criticized the Government's policy of banning Muslim girls from wearing headscarves in public schools and urged the promotion of cultural diversity.

In April 2002 Jeyaretnam made a public apology in the High Court in an attempt to bring to an end the series of defamation suits that had been brought against him by the Government; seven outstanding lawsuits were subsequently abandoned. In the same month Chee Soon Juan stated that he intended to defend the lawsuits against him. In May Chee and the Vice-Chairman of the SDP, Gandhi Ambalam, led an unauthorized rally outside the presidential palace demanding workers' rights. Following the rally, Chee and Ambalam were both sentenced to brief prison terms, having chosen not to pay the fines imposed upon them. However, Ambalam's family subsequently paid his fine, in order to enable his release from prison on the grounds of ill health. In August the High Court ordered Chee to pay damages of S $500,000 to Goh and Lee Kuan Yew, after his request for a trial was rejected; the verdict was confirmed in January 2005. Meanwhile, a constitutional amendment was approved stipulating that any member of Parliament declared bankrupt or found guilty of a crime would be banned from speaking or voting in Parliament for the duration of any appeal. In February 2003 Ambalam's appeal against his fine (which was sufficient to prohibit him from standing for political office for five years) was rejected by the Chief Justice. In October 2004 Jeyaretnam again appealed for early discharge from bankruptcy in order to secure re-entry into the political arena. However, the Court of Appeal deemed him to have been dishonest about his assets, ruling that he had failed to declare property in Johor Baru worth more than S $350,000. Consequently, the Court's original decision was upheld and Jeyaretnam's application for clemency was denied. Jeyaretnam was discharged from bankruptcy in May 2007 after paying the damages that he owed.

In April 2003, meanwhile, Goh announced a cabinet reorganization, in which, *inter alia*, Deputy Prime Minister and erstwhile Minister for Defence Dr Tony Tan Keng Yam was appointed to the newly created position of Co-ordinating Minister for Security and Defence in the Prime Minister's Office (effective from August 2003). The defence portfolio was allocated to former Minister for Education Rear-Adm. (retd) Teo Chee Hean.

The premiership of Lee Hsien Loong

In August 2003 Prime Minister Goh Chok Tong announced that he intended to resign from his post at least two years prior to the country's next general election, scheduled to be held in 2007. He designated his deputy, Lee Hsien Loong, as his successor. In early 2004 Lee indicated that, following his accession to power, he would implement measures to reduce the control of the Government over Singaporean citizens and to promote a culture of political 'openness'.

On 12 August 2004 Lee Hsien Loong was formally sworn in as Prime Minister, amid claims that a dynastic succession had been contrived. Both former Prime Ministers were included within the new Cabinet: Goh was retained as Senior Minister, while Lee Kuan Yew was redesignated as Minister Mentor. Shanmugam Jayakumar became Singapore's first Deputy Minister of Indian origin. Lee Hsien Loong retained the finance portfolio but, in an unexpected development, relinquished the chairmanship of the MAS to Goh. George Yeo was named the new Minister for Foreign Affairs and Teo Chee Hean retained the defence portfolio. Two women were appointed as Ministers of State. Lee identified the reversal of the decline in Singapore's birth rate, which had decreased sharply since the 1960s, as a major government priority, adding responsibility for the revival of the country's population growth to the brief of the Minister for Home Affairs, Wong Kan Seng. Government bonuses were offered to parents producing a third or fourth child, maternity leave was lengthened and tax rebates were introduced for working mothers.

In April 2005 the Government legalized gambling on Singapore, ending a 40-year ban and allowing for the construction of two major casino resorts, at Marina Bay and on Sentosa Island, to be built at an estimated cost of US $3,000m. The decision encountered widespread disapproval, particularly from religious groups, which accused the Government of prioritizing profit over the country's moral standing. The first hotels at the Sentosa resort opened in January 2010, and the casino commenced operations in February. The Marina Bay resort was officially inaugurated in June, with the final stages of the resort being completed in September 2011. The resorts were expected significantly to boost the country's tourism industry, as well as allowing Singapore to retain the money of its nationals who had hitherto been obliged to travel abroad in order to engage in gambling activities. Furthermore, the two resorts were expected to create more than 20,000 new employment opportunities.

Meanwhile, of the four candidates who had applied for inclusion in the presidential contest due to be held in August 2005, only the incumbent, S. R. Nathan, was granted a certificate of eligibility, the other three candidates being deemed to be lacking in political experience. Consequently, Nathan was returned unopposed for a second term in office; he was formally sworn in on 1 September. Also in September Minister for Home Affairs Wong Kan Seng succeeded Dr Tan, upon the latter's resignation, to become Deputy Prime Minister (while retaining the home affairs portfolio), alongside Shanmugam Jayakumar.

In order to take advantage of Singapore's strong economic position, Prime Minister Lee Hsien Loong called early legislative elections for 6 May 2006 (they had not been due until June 2007). At the elections, opposition parties contested 47 of the 84 parliamentary seats. The PAP won 82 seats, as it had done at the 2001 poll, while the SDA and the Workers' Party secured one seat each. However, the PAP's share of the votes cast decreased to 66.6%, compared with 75.3% at the 2001 elections.

In February 2006, meanwhile, Chee Soon Juan was declared bankrupt by the High Court, having failed to pay the stipulated damages of S $500,000 to Lee Kuan Yew and Goh Chok Tong for the comments that he had made during the 2001 elections (see The premiership of Goh Chok Tong). Under the bankruptcy order, Chee was forbidden from contesting legislative elections for five years and was required to seek official permission to travel overseas. In the following month Chee was convicted of contempt of court for his criticism of Singapore's judiciary during the February court hearing, and was ordered to pay a fine of S $6,000. Upon his refusal to pay the fine, Chee was imprisoned for seven days, after which he again refused to pay and his imprisonment was subsequently extended for a further seven days. In April Chee and several other SDP officials were sued for defamation by Lee Kuan Yew and Lee Hsien Loong in connection with articles published in February in the party's newsletter, The New Democrat, which had compared the PAP Government's running of the country to the alleged mismanagement of the National Kidney Foundation, which was embroiled in a corruption scandal. Chee Soon Juan and his sister, Chee Siok Chin, were found guilty of defamation in September 2006 in a summary judgment by the High Court, their request for a trial having been rejected, and in October 2008 the High Court ordered Chee

to pay S $610,000 in defamation damages to Prime Minister Lee and his father. In November 2006 Chee was sentenced to five weeks' imprisonment for not paying a fine for speaking in public without a government permit during the 2006 election period.

The Government continued to seek to curb freedom of expression during 2006–07, attempting to restrict public gatherings, political demonstrations and views portrayed over the internet. The Government's decision to prevent five activists from attending the annual meeting of the IMF and the World Bank in September 2006, although it had originally yielded to international pressure by allowing access to 22 others, elicited criticism from the President of the World Bank; the Government claimed that the activists posed a security threat. In February 2007 the *Far Eastern Economic Review*, a Hong Kong-based journal, distribution of which had been banned by the Singapore Government in September 2006 on the grounds that it did not comply with media regulations, failed in its second attempt to have a defamation action dismissed after the publication in July 2006 of an article entitled 'Singapore's "Martyr" Chee Soon Juan'. The suit had been filed by Lee Hsien Loong and Lee Kuan Yew over alleged negative comments made by Chee about them and the Government. In its defence, the journal argued that, as it was published in Hong Kong and employed no Singaporean journalists, it was not bound by Singaporean law. In September 2008 the High Court of Singapore ruled that the *Review* had defamed the country's leaders; in October 2009 the Court of Appeal dismissed the publication's appeal against this ruling.

The application of the death penalty continued to be a contentious issue following the execution of two convicted drugs-smugglers, one from Nigeria and the other from South Africa, in January 2007. The case attracted widespread international condemnation, while the UN Special Rapporteur on extra-judicial, summary or arbitrary executions described it as failing to meet international legal standards for criminal prosecution.

In April 2007 it was revealed that cabinet ministers were to receive a salary increase of 60% by 2008. While the decision prompted large-scale public opposition, Prime Minister Lee argued that the rise was well deserved and a necessary precaution against corruption. Chee Soon Juan criticized the pay rises at an unauthorized forum on democracy in Asia and Europe organized by the SDP. In September 2007 the bankrupt Chee served a three-week prison sentence after failing to pay a fine for trying to leave Singapore without permission in April 2006. Chee was arrested again in October 2007, together with three other members of the SDP, as they attempted to stage a protest outside the presidential palace in support of their demands for the full disclosure of investments by Singaporean state-controlled companies in Myanmar, following the recent violent suppression of anti-Government marches in that country. In March 2008 Chee was among 18 activists arrested and charged with unlawful assembly, after taking part in an unauthorized demonstration in protest against the rising cost of living in Singapore. His trial, one of seven that Chee awaited over the coming months, began in October.

In December 2007 Lee Hsien Loong relinquished responsibility for the finance portfolio to the Minister for Education, Tharman Shanmugaratnam, a former Managing Director of the MAS. In a cabinet reorganization announced in March 2008, Tharman was retained as Minister for Finance, but relinquished the education portfolio to Ng Eng Hen, hitherto Minister of Manpower. From May K. Shanmugam, a senior lawyer, was to succeed Shanmugam Jayakumar as Minister of Law, while also being appointed Second Minister for Home Affairs. Jayakumar remained as Deputy Prime Minister and Co-ordinating Minister for National Security.

In April 2008 veteran opposition leader J. B. Jeyaretnam established the Reform Party, urging a restructuring of the electoral system and stating his intention to bring an end to the 'enslavement' of Singapore after nearly 50 years of rule by the PAP. However, Jeyaretnam died in September. The activist's son, Kenneth Jeyaretnam, was elected to replace his father as Secretary-General of the Reform Party in April 2009. In the same month Ng Teck Siong resigned as party Chairman following a vote of no confidence in his leadership; he was subsequently replaced by Edmund Ng.

In March 2009 Prime Minister Lee Hsien Loong announced a cabinet reorganization, which included the promotion, to the position of Senior Minister, of Shanmugam Jayakumar, who retained his position as Co-ordinating Minister for National Security, and the promotion, to the position of Deputy Prime

Minister, of Teo Chee Hean, who retained the defence portfolio. In April Parliament approved a new Public Order Act, imposing further restrictions on the right to peaceful assembly and enhancing the powers of the police. The Government claimed that the increasing threat from international terrorist activity had necessitated the enactment of the new legislation, particularly in advance of the summit meeting of Asia-Pacific Economic Cooperation (APEC, see p. 208) (which, in the event, was convened without incident in Singapore in November). Amnesty International urged the Government to amend the Act in order to meet global standards of human rights and to comply with the Singaporean Constitution, which provided for freedom of speech and expression.

In December 2009 Chee Soon Juan and Gandhi Ambalam were again imprisoned, for a period of one week, and fined S $1,000, after being convicted of distributing anti-PAP pamphlets without a permit during the 2006 elections.

In April 2010 two constitutional amendments were approved, whereby the maximum number of non-constituency seats was to be raised from six to nine at the next legislative elections, and the system whereby the Government was able to nominate up to nine unelected, politically neutral members of Parliament was made permanent, having previously been subject to parliamentary approval prior to each general election. Meanwhile, in March a new political party, the United Singapore Democrats (USD), was formally established by former members of the SDP, including Narayanasamy Gogelavany, subsequently named USD President, and Jaslyn Go, USD Secretary.

With many Singaporeans becoming increasingly vocal in their dissatisfaction with regard to the city-state's 'open-door' immigration policy for foreign workers (with about one-third of the total number of people resident in Singapore of foreign origin), Prime Minister Lee's National Day Rally speech in August 2010 focused primarily on the issue of immigration. Lee declared that Singapore should 'slow down the pace' of immigration, stating that present rates could not be sustained indefinitely. In September the Government announced a revision to Singapore's permanent residency regulations, including an increase, from S $1.0m. to S $2.5m., in the value of Singapore-based investments required to be made by foreigners aiming to become permanent residents, and the introduction of higher minimum income and residential requirements. During 2009 59,500 applications for permanent residency were approved, a significant decline on 2008, when some 79,200 such applications were endorsed.

In October 2010 former Reform Party Chairman Ng Teck Siong, together with Chia Ti Lik, a lawyer who had contested the 2006 legislative elections as a candidate of the Workers' Party, established a new political party, the Socialist Front.

A cabinet reorganization in November 2010 was widely interpreted as part of ongoing efforts to promulgate an image of political renewal in advance of the next legislative elections. Notable changes included the transfer of Deputy Prime Minister Wong from the home affairs portfolio to the position of Co-ordinating Minister for National Security, in place of Shanmugam Jayakumar. The latter remained Senior Minister in the Prime Minister's Office, but subsequently announced his intention to resign from political office. Wong was replaced as Minister for Home Affairs, a position that he had held for 17 years, by his deputy, K. Shanmugam, who concurrently retained the law portfolio, while Lui Tuck Yew, the acting Minister for Information, Communications and the Arts, was confirmed in the post on a permanent basis.

In December 2010 Edmund Ng resigned as Chairman of the Reform Party, and was replaced by Tan Tee Seng; Kenneth Jeyaretnam continued as party Secretary-General. In February 2011 at least nine members of the Reform Party, including five members of the party's central leadership, tendered their resignation from the party, citing difficulties in working with Jeyaretnam. Tan Tee Seng resigned as Chairman, also citing differences of opinion with the Secretary-General; he was succeeded by Andy Zhu Lai Cheng.

Meanwhile, following the conclusion of a three-year trial, in October 2010 Chee Soon Juan was convicted on charges of speaking in public without a permit and ordered to pay a fine of S $20,000, to the consternation of the political opposition and civil liberties organizations. An SDP-initiated internet appeal for donations raised the stipulated amount and Chee avoided a custodial term.

Recent developments: 2011 legislative and presidential elections

The PAP was returned to power at the general election conducted on 7 May 2011. Although the ruling party took 81 of the 87 parliamentary seats, it received only 60.1% of the votes cast (compared with 66.6% at the 2006 election)—its lowest ever share of the vote. Only five PAP candidates were unopposed, compared with 37 in 2006. The Workers' Party substantially improved its representation in Parliament, winning six seats, while the SDA lost its one seat.

In mid-May 2011 Minister Mentor Lee Kuan Yew and Senior Minister Goh Chok Tong unexpectedly announced their retirement from the Cabinet. In a joint statement, the two former premiers declared that they were removing themselves from the upper echelons of Singapore's leadership to allow Prime Minister Lee and a younger generation of leaders 'a fresh clean slate'. Both Lee and Goh remained as members of Parliament. In addition, Lee Kuan Yew was appointed Senior Advisor to the Government of Singapore Investment Corporation (GIC), having resigned from the GIC chairmanship (a position that was subsequently filled by the Prime Minister), and Goh, who was awarded the honorary title of Emeritus Senior Minister, was appointed Senior Advisor to the MAS. Deputy Prime Minister Wong Kan Seng, Minister for National Development Mah Bow Tan and Minister for Transport Raymond Lim Siang Keat also tendered their resignations. Senior Minister Shanmugam Jayakumar and Minister in the Prime Minister's Office Lim Boon Heng had announced their respective retirements prior to the polls; Lim also relinquished the chairmanship of the PAP, but remained a member of the party's Central Executive Committee. An extensive government reorganization followed. Tharman Shanmugaratnam was appointed Deputy Prime Minister, retaining the finance portfolio (and also becoming Chairman of the MAS, in place of Goh); in addition, Tharman was allocated the manpower portfolio. Teo Chee Hean remained as Deputy Prime Minister, also taking the post of Co-ordinating Minister for National Security and Minister for Home Affairs. George Yeo, who had lost his parliamentary seat in the election, was replaced as Minister for Foreign Affairs by K. Shanmugam, who retained the law portfolio. Responsibility for the defence portfolio was assumed by Ng Eng Hen, hitherto the Minister for Education, who was replaced in the latter position by Heng Swee Keat, one of three new cabinet members. Khaw Boon Wan was transferred from the health portfolio to head the Ministry of National Development, while Lui Tuck Yew was appointed Minister for Transport. In June Khaw Boon Wan was appointed as Lim Boon Heng's replacement as Chairman of the PAP. Prime Minister Lee remained Secretary-General of the party.

Prime Minister Lee's 2011 National Day Rally speech in August focused on addressing some of the causes of simmering popular discontent with the PAP and included a pledge to prioritize the needs of local Singaporeans, in an apparent attempt to assuage ongoing concerns about the high number of foreign workers in the city-state. Proposed measures included expanding the availability of affordable accommodation for Singaporeans, increasing the number of university places for local students, improving access to health care for the elderly, improving public transport and introducing new limitations on the entry of foreign workers.

Meanwhile, in July 2011 President S. R. Nathan announced that he was to relinquish office at the end of his second term. Four candidates were successfully nominated to contest the presidential election: former Deputy Prime Minister Tony Tan, Goh Chok Tong's former Principal Private Secretary, Tan Jee Say, former PAP member of Parliament Tan Cheng Bock, and a former chief executive of NTUC Income Insurance, Tan Kin Lian. The presidential election—the first to be conducted in Singapore since 1993—was held on 27 August 2011. In a close-run contest, Tony Tan emerged victorious with 35.2% of the ballot, narrowly defeating Tan Cheng Bock, who garnered 34.8%. Tan Jee Say and Tan Kin Lian polled 25.0% and 4.9% of the vote, respectively. Tony Tan was inaugurated as President on 1 September.

In September 2011 the Supreme Executive Council of the PKMS stripped party President Ali Asjadi of his party membership following his arrest, together with three other men, on charges of smuggling contraband cigarettes. In October Asjadi, who was replaced as party President by Abu bin Mohamed, was sentenced to 30 months' imprisonment and ordered to pay a fine of S $8,200. His three co-defendants also received prison terms. Meanwhile, the Government announced in September that three men had been arrested under the ISA between January and July;

two of those detained were suspected of being members of the regional militant organization Jemaah Islamiah, while the third was believed to be a member of the Moro Islamic Liberation Front, an Islamist fundamentalist grouping active in the southern Philippines.

In its annual report published in January 2012, US-based Human Rights Watch noted that the Singapore Government had eased restrictions on campaign rallies and online electioneering in advance of the May 2011 legislative elections, but had 'continued to effectively control television and print media'. The report also criticized the Singaporean authorities' continued recourse to the mandatory death penalty for some 20 drugs-related offences, despite widespread censure from human rights bodies, and its use of judicial caning as an 'inherently cruel' additional punishment for a wide range of crimes, including drugs-smuggling and immigration offences. In July 2011 the authorities had suspended executions as part of a year-long review of the death penalty. In November 2012 legislative amendments were approved that reduced the number of offences for which the death penalty was mandatory (discretionary measures being given to the presiding judge), although it was stressed that capital punishment would remain 'an integral part' of the country's criminal justice system.

Following the losses incurred by the PAP in the 2011 general election and amid increasing public anger over housing and transport costs and income inequality, the Government had appointed a special committee to review ministerial salaries. In January 2012 Prime Minister Lee announced that he had agreed to accept the committee's recommendation that his salary be reduced by 36%. In addition, the committee proposed that the President's salary be lowered by 51% and those of cabinet ministers by 37%, that the provision of pensions for government officials (including the President) should cease, that a national bonus scheme (linked to economic performance) for ministers should be introduced and that allowances for parliamentary deputies should be reduced. In September, following a three-day debate, Parliament voted to accept the committee's proposals and adopted legislation abolishing government pensions. However, even allowing for the salary reductions, the ministers of Singapore remained the highest paid in the world (with the Prime Minister on an annual salary of US $1.7m.).

Meanwhile, in a closely contested by-election in May 2012 the Workers' Party retained a parliamentary seat that had been vacated in February when the incumbent legislator was expelled from the party.

Singapore's first major strike action since 1986 was reported in November 2012 when around 170 employees of the state-controlled transport company SMRT (all of whom were recruited from the People's Republic of China) failed to attend work for two days; the bus drivers were protesting against their low level of pay in comparison to that of workers from other countries and against poor working conditions. In response, the authorities charged five of the drivers with inciting illegal strike action (strikes are illegal in Singapore for workers in services deemed essential, unless the employer is given 14 days' notice); in December one defendant was convicted and sentenced to six weeks' imprisonment, while 29 of the other strikers were deported. Despite pleas for clemency from human rights groups, which claimed that the strike did not cause serious disruption, in February 2013 the four other defendants received prison sentences of six to seven weeks.

In December 2012 the Speaker of Parliament, Michael Palmer, resigned from the post and left the PAP after admitting to an extramarital affair. He was replaced in January 2013 by Halimah Yacob, who thus became Singapore's first female parliamentary Speaker.

A government report published in January 2013 projected that Singapore's population would increase by 30%, to 6.5m.–6.9m., by 2030 (with non-residents accounting for around 36% of the total and foreigners who had been granted permanent residency a further 9%), largely as a result of the planned intake of 15,000–25,000 new young immigrants every year in an attempt to offset the decelerating birth rate and the ageing population. The Government's plans to allow more immigration prompted the staging of a rare demonstration at 'Speakers' Corner' in the following month, which was attended by more than 4,000 people, making it one of the country's largest ever protests. The demonstrators claimed that further rises in the number of immigrants and foreign workers would place greater strain on the city-state's already overstretched resources and would lead to higher property prices and lower wages.

Foreign Affairs
Regional relations

Singapore's foreign policy has been dominated by its membership of the Association of Southeast Asian Nations (ASEAN, see p. 218) (which comprised all 10 South-East Asian nations by mid-1999), although it has also maintained strong political and military links with more distant allies, including the USA (see Other external relations). In November 2000 the fourth informal summit meeting of the ASEAN + 3 group of leaders was convened in Singapore. The summit comprised the leaders of all 10 ASEAN members, as well as those of the People's Republic of China, Japan and the Republic of Korea. An outcome of the meeting was the commissioning of an East Asia Study Group to report on the feasibility of a larger East Asia political and economic grouping and free trade area. Singapore assumed the annually rotating chairmanship of the Association in 2007/08. Achievements of the 13th ASEAN summit meeting, held in Singapore in November 2007, included the adoption of a Declaration on Environmental Sustainability, which contained commitments related to environmental protection and management, climate change, and the conservation of natural resources; the approval of plans for the establishment of an Asian Economic Community by 2015; and the signature of an ASEAN Charter codifying the principles and purposes of the Association. In December 2007 Singapore became the first country to ratify the new Charter, which, having been ratified by the other nine members by October 2008, entered into force in January 2009. On 1 January 2010 a free trade agreement came into effect between the six core ASEAN members—namely Brunei, Indonesia, Malaysia, the Philippines, Singapore and Thailand—under the terms of which tariffs were to be removed on some 90% of goods traded. In April 2013 Singapore called for a review of ASEAN's institutions and processes, in order to make them more efficient, and proposed that the Secretariat of the grouping be strengthened in order to enhance community integration.

Since its inaugural meeting in 2002 the annual Asia Security Summit of the International Institute for Strategic Studies (see p. 476)—or, as it is more commonly known, the Shangri-La Dialogue—has been hosted by Singapore at the Shangri-La Hotel. The informal intergovernmental meetings, which provide a forum for negotiations, are attended by the senior defence and security government officials of 28 Asia-Pacific states (including the USA, China and Russia) in addition to around 200 non-government delegates.

In September 1994 Singapore and Malaysia agreed to settle a long-standing dispute over ownership of Pedra Branca Island (Batu Puteh) by referring the case to the International Court of Justice (ICJ) in The Hague, Netherlands. A decision was finally reached in May 2008 when the ICJ ruled in favour of Singapore, by 12 votes to four. In August 1995 Singapore and Malaysia agreed on the permanent boundary of their territorial waters after 15 years of negotiations.

In August 1998 the Malaysian Prime Minister condemned Singapore for requesting that Malaysia transfer its customs, immigration and quarantine facilities from Tanjung Pagar, a railway station in central Singapore situated on land owned by the Malaysian Government; Malaysia subsequently decided to continue using its facilities at Tanjung Pagar, while Singapore moved its customs office to a new location. In September Malaysia announced its decision to insist on prior clearance for Singaporean military aircraft wishing to enter its airspace; joint defence exercises within the context of the regional Five-Power Defence Arrangements were also terminated. An improvement in relations was perceived in November, when Goh Chok Tong visited Malaysia at the invitation of Malaysian Prime Minister Mahathir Mohamad. Joint defence exercises were resumed in April 1999. However, relations deteriorated again in August 2000, when Lee Kuan Yew publicly criticized Mahathir over his handling of the dismissal and detention of Anwar Ibrahim, Malaysia's former Deputy Prime Minister.

In September 2001 Lee Kuan Yew visited Malaysia and held talks with Mahathir to address outstanding bilateral issues. Disagreement persisted, however, over plans to construct a suspension bridge, which would enable the demolition of the causeway linking the two countries. (A twin-deck bridge—the Tuas Second Link—connecting Singapore and Johor, Malaysia, had been opened in 1998 to reduce traffic congestion on the causeway.) Tension was also prompted by the ongoing renegotiation of the terms upon which Malaysia would continue to supply water to Singapore (based upon two separate agreements concluded in 1961 and 1962 and due to expire in 2011 and 2061, respectively).

In March 2002 relations were further strained when Malaysia claimed that reclamation work being carried out by Singapore in the Tebrau Straits was too close to its border and was obstructing ships sailing into ports in Johor. Malaysia later applied to the International Tribunal for the Law of the Sea (see p. 363) for a suspension of the reclamation work. The tribunal ruled in October 2003 that Singapore's reclamation work was in accordance with international law and could, therefore, proceed. The protracted dispute was ostensibly resolved in January 2005 when the respective Governments of Singapore and Malaysia issued a joint statement declaring their agreement that the Tebrau Straits constituted a shared body of water. Meanwhile, in February 2003 Mahathir pledged that his country would continue to supply water to Singapore indefinitely. However, he stated that Malaysia would cease its provision of untreated water to the city-state upon the termination of the 1961 agreement in 2011 and provide filtered water instead, at what it considered to be a reasonable price. Singapore continued to insist that any proposed price was too high and that it received too little for the treated water that it supplied to Malaysia in return.

In Prime Minister Lee Hsien Loong's first National Day Rally speech, given in August 2004, the new premier stressed his deep commitment to working in close unison with Abdullah Badawi, who had acceded to the Malaysian premiership in October 2003, in order to consolidate Singapore's links with Malaysia. In January 2006 Malaysia unexpectedly announced that it was to commence construction of its section of a new bridge, also referred to as the 'scenic bridge', in the hope that Singapore would agree in due course to the construction of its part. Construction of the Malaysian section of the bridge began in March, but was halted in the following month by Abdullah, who announced that all negotiations with Singapore pertaining to the bridge were also to be abandoned. Prime Minister Lee visited Malaysia in May 2007 for two days of informal talks with Abdullah. The main outcome of the discussions was a decision to form a joint ministerial committee to oversee collaboration on Malaysia's plan to establish a 2,217-sq-km economic development zone in its southern state of Johor, to be known as the Iskandar Development Region (subsequently renamed Iskander Malaysia), with both leaders agreeing that outstanding issues of dispute, such as water sales to Singapore and the suspended construction of the new bridge, should not be allowed to impede bilateral co-operation in other areas.

During a meeting in May 2010 between Lee Hsien Loong and the Malaysian Prime Minister, Najib Tun Razak (who had replaced Abdullah in April 2009), the two leaders affirmed their commitment to enhancing bilateral co-operation, and agreed to the joint development of a rapid transit system (RTS) between Johor Baru and Singapore. In June 2011, in a development that was hailed as signalling the beginning of a new spirit of bilateral co-operation, a land swap agreement was finalized, under the terms of which Malaysia was to be awarded six parcels of land in Singapore in exchange for giving up land owned by Malayan Railways in the city-state. In addition, the two countries agreed to establish co-located customs, immigration and quarantine facilities in Singapore to ease the passage of customers using the RTS. Upon the expiry in August of the 1961 water-sharing agreement, the Singapore Government transferred ownership of water assets, including water treatment facilities and pump houses, to the Johor state government, and reaffirmed previous claims that Singapore would achieve water self-sufficiency before the scheduled expiry, in August 2061, of the 1962 agreement. During a visit to Singapore by Malaysian Prime Minister Najib in February 2013 plans were confirmed to construct a high-speed rail link between the two countries, with a target completion date of 2020.

Singapore's relations with Myanmar were threatened in June 2009 when Senior Minister Goh Chok Tong, during a visit to the Myanma city of Yangon, linked the future of Singaporean investment in Myanmar to the development of democracy therein and urged the Myanma ruling junta to ensure that the forthcoming 2010 legislative elections were free, fair and genuinely inclusive. Goh's comments angered the junta, which argued that the remarks constituted a breach of ASEAN's policy of non-interference in the domestic affairs of member states. The extension, by a further 18 months, of the house arrest of Myanma opposition leader Aung San Suu Kyi in August 2009 disappointed the Singaporean Government, which urged the holding of 'meaningful dialogue' between the junta and the opposition. The exclusion of Suu Kyi from the elections held in November 2010 elicited expressions of concern and disappointment from the Singaporean Government, as well as others within ASEAN. Following the installation of a nominally civilian Government in Myanmar, under the presidency of Thein Sein, in March 2011, an improvement in relations became evident. Singapore's Minister for Foreign Affairs and Law, K. Shanmugam, made an official visit to Myanmar in December, during which he held discussions with President Thein Sein and the Myanma Minister of Foreign Affairs, Wunna Maung Lwin, pledging to increase bilateral co-operation and affirming his Government's willingness to share its own development experience in order to assist Myanmar's progress. Shanmugam also met with Suu Kyi, who had been released from house arrest shortly after the November 2010 elections. In February 2012 a large Singaporean business delegation, representing more than 70 Singapore-based companies, visited Myanmar to discuss potential co-operation in the latter country's developing economy and emerging business opportunities; more such delegations visited Myanmar over the ensuing year. In April Shanmugam welcomed the conduct of by-elections in Myanmar in which Suu Kyi's National League for Democracy was allowed to participate and she herself was elected. Singaporean President Tony Tan paid a four-day visit to Myanmar in April 2013, during which he held a meeting with President Thein Sein, who highlighted the burgeoning economic co-operation between the two countries.

Singapore's relations with Indonesia, which had been strained during the presidency of Prof. Dr Ir B. J. Habibie, improved temporarily following Habibie's replacement as President by Abdurrahman Wahid in October 1999. In November 2000, however, Wahid jeopardized the relationship, as his predecessor had done, by accusing Singapore of discriminating against Malays, after Singapore rejected certain motions proposed by its neighbour at the ASEAN summit. Nevertheless, Singapore and Indonesia subsequently concluded a long-term agreement whereby Indonesia would supply the city-state with natural gas.

In February 2002 Singaporean-Indonesian relations deteriorated once more following the publication of an article in *The Straits Times* in which Lee Kuan Yew remarked that Singapore's national security was being compromised by the fact that terrorists remained at large in Indonesia. In response, the Indonesian Government summoned the Singaporean envoy to Jakarta and lodged an objection to the accusations, claiming that they were provocative and unsubstantiated. Meanwhile, Indonesian Islamic groups held protests outside Singapore's embassy in Jakarta. In February 2006 the Indonesian authorities agreed to the deportation to Singapore of Mas Selamat Kastari, the alleged leader of the Singaporean branch of Jemaah Islamiah (JI), following his rearrest in Indonesia on suspicion of immigration offences. Kastari, first arrested in Indonesia in 2003, also on charges of suspected illegal immigration, had been the subject of several previous extradition requests from Singapore, which accused Kastari of a central role in an alleged plot, thwarted in late 2001, to crash a hijacked aeroplane into Changi International Airport. The Indonesian Government had rejected those requests, on the grounds that Indonesia and Singapore had no formal extradition treaty; it was unclear why Indonesia subsequently chose to reverse its decision. In February 2008 Kastari escaped from a detention centre in Singapore, where he was being held under the ISA. In May 2009 it was reported that Kastari had been reapprehended in the previous month in the Malaysian state of Johor; his arrest and renewed detention under the Malaysian ISA were subsequently confirmed by the respective Governments of Singapore and Malaysia. In September 2010 the Malaysian authorities confirmed the second extradition to Singapore of Kastari.

Meanwhile, fires resulting from uncontrolled 'slash and burn' land-clearing practices in Indonesia caused a prolonged haze in late 2006, affecting Singapore and other countries in the region. Singapore was reported to have suffered US $50m. in economic losses. Relations between the two nations came under further pressure in February 2007 when Indonesia imposed an outright ban on all sand exports to Singapore after independent environmental experts highlighted the extensive damage caused to the environment by sand exports. (Singapore had been importing sand from Indonesia after Malaysia banned all exports in 1997.) Myanmar later offered to be Singapore's long-term supplier of sand, cement, granite and other construction materials. It was hoped that relations between Singapore and Indonesia would improve following the signature of an extradition treaty and a new agreement on defence co-operation in April 2007. However, differences emerged in May, when Indonesia sought amendments to the defence accord regarding arrangements for

Singaporean troops to use Indonesian military training facilities. With Singapore refusing to consider any revisions, the Indonesian legislature refused to ratify the defence and extradition agreements, owing to concerns that they favoured Singapore and could compromise Indonesia's national security. As a result, the two countries suspended further discussion of both agreements indefinitely. Following a visit to Indonesia in March 2012 by Prime Minister Lee Hsien Loong, Indonesian President Susilo Bambang Yudhoyono indicated that Lee had appeared willing to revive negotiations pertaining to the two agreements. However, in October the Singaporean Ministry of Foreign Affairs made it clear that it considered that the extradition treaty and defence co-operation agreement had already been negotiated, as a package, and that Singapore was ready to proceed with the implementation of both agreements once Indonesia had completed its ratification process. Meanwhile, in March 2009 the Governments of Singapore and Indonesia signed a maritime boundary agreement that redrew the border between the Singaporean island of Sultan Shoal and Pulau Nipah in Indonesia, successfully concluding four years of negotiations. The agreement was ratified by the two countries in May 2010, with both sides expressing their belief that the new, more clearly defined boundary would assist the economic development of border islands and increase Singapore's border security. However, a section of the maritime boundary between Singapore and Indonesia (known as the 'eastern segment') remained undefined pending further negotiations, which would necessitate the involvement of Malaysia.

Singapore and the People's Republic of China established diplomatic relations at ambassadorial level in October 1990. Nevertheless, Prime Minister Goh made his first official visit to Taiwan, with which Singapore enjoyed close military and economic links, in October 1993. In October 1996 Singapore and Australia issued a joint communiqué urging the integration of the People's Republic of China into the Asian regional security structure, and reaffirming their commitment to a co-operative dialogue with the People's Republic. However, a private visit to Singapore in January 1998 by the Taiwanese Vice-President, Lien Chan, during which he met with Goh and with Singaporean cabinet ministers, provoked the disapproval of the People's Republic, as did visits to Taiwan by Lee Kuan Yew, in September 2000 and September 2002, and by Lee Hsien Loong, in July 2004. The diplomatic furore caused by the 2004 visit served to delay the start of negotiations concerning a free trade pact between the People's Republic and Singapore, which had been due to commence in November that year, despite Lee's insistence that his visit in no way weakened his country's commitment to the 'one China' policy that denied recognition of Taiwan. In October 2005, at a meeting in the Chinese capital, Beijing, of Singaporean and Chinese delegates, led by Lee Hsien Loong and Chinese Premier Wen Jiabao, both countries affirmed their commitment to accelerating the holding of free trade negotiations. The two countries also agreed to work together to address the regional threats of terrorism and piracy in the Straits of Melaka. China and Singapore held their first round of free trade talks in October 2006; several further sessions took place in 2007, and final negotiations in October 2008 resulted in the signing of a free trade agreement that entered into force in January 2009.

Meanwhile, in early 2008 Singapore and China signed an agreement to increase defence and security co-operation, and in June 2009 the two countries conducted a week-long joint anti-terrorism exercise in China's Guangxi Zhuang autonomous region, China's first such exercise with foreign forces. During a visit by Prime Minister Lee to Beijing in August 2010, Chinese President Hu Jintao expressed appreciation for Singapore's continued adherence to the 'one China' policy, and both leaders pledged further to enhance bilateral relations. Amid mounting tensions between China and the Philippines in mid-2011 over their rival claims to the Spratly Islands in the South China Sea, in June the Singaporean Minister for Foreign Affairs and Law, K. Shanmugam, urged the Chinese Government more precisely to clarify its claims, ambiguity over which, he stated, had engendered 'serious concerns' among the international maritime community. Meeting on the sidelines of the East Asia Summit on Bali, Indonesia, in November, Prime Minister Lee and Chinese Premier Wen Jiabao pledged further to strengthen bilateral co-operation in a wide range of fields, including trade, the economy, culture and education. These pledges were reiterated during a visit by Lee to China in September 2012.

Other external relations

In November 1990 representatives of the Governments of the USA and Singapore signed an agreement providing the US navy and air force with increased access to existing bases in Singapore following the planned US withdrawal from military installations in the Philippines. In January 1992 the two countries reached an agreement, in principle, on the relocation of a naval logistic command headquarters from Subic Bay, in the Philippines. However, relations with the USA were occasionally strained by attacks on the authoritarian style of government in Singapore by the liberal US media.

Following the attacks on the USA in September 2001, Singapore affirmed its support for the US-led alliance against terrorism. In the aftermath of the attacks a number of suspects with alleged links to al-Qa'ida and its regional affiliates Abu Sayyaf and JI were arrested in Singapore under the ISA. In March 2003 the Government announced its support for the US-led military campaign to oust the regime of Saddam Hussain in Iraq. In November 2005 the Government reported that it had detained for a two-year period Mohammad Sharif Rahmat, an alleged member of JI. While JI's network seemed to have been severely damaged by the recent arrests, leading members of both JI and Abu Sayyaf remained at large in the region. In order to address the ensuing national security concerns, the Government announced the establishment of a national security secretariat, within the Ministry of Defence, intended to strengthen co-ordination between the security services of Singapore and the USA. In October 2007 Singapore's Parliament approved counter-terrorism legislation designed to give effect to the International Convention for the Suppression of Terrorist Bombings (adopted by the UN General Assembly in 1997). The new law provided for the extradition of those suspected of perpetrating terrorist bombings, even in the absence of an extradition treaty between Singapore and the other country, and gave Singapore the power to prosecute foreign nationals accused of committing terrorist offences within its territory.

Cordial relations with the USA remained largely stable following the inauguration of Barack Obama as the new US President in January 2009. A number of important bilateral visits were conducted during 2009–10, including that of Minister for Foreign Affairs George Yeo to Washington, DC, in April 2009, during which he met with several senior US officials, including US Secretary of State Hillary Clinton. In October Minister Mentor Lee Kuan Yew visited New York and Washington, DC, where he met with President Obama, who himself visited Singapore in the following month to attend the APEC summit meeting, along with Secretary of State Clinton and other leading US officials. Additional discussions between Prime Minister Lee and Obama, and between Yeo and Clinton, were reported further to have enhanced the close relations between Singapore and the USA. In April 2010 Prime Minister Lee visited Washington, DC, in order to attend the Nuclear Security Summit; during his visit Lee also met with members of the Obama Administration.

The removal of Singapore from the 'watch list' of the US Department of State's *Trafficking in Persons Report* for 2011, published in June of that year, and its elevation to the so-called Tier 2 list of countries that did not fully meet standards on human-trafficking but were making significant efforts to do so, was welcomed by the Singaporean Government. The city-state's inclusion on the 2010 list had provoked an angry reaction from the Lee Hsien Loong administration, which had responded by urging the US Government to examine its own record, including the treatment of illegal migrants within the USA. During a visit to Washington, DC, in February 2012, Singapore's Minister for Foreign Affairs and Law, K. Shanmugam, addressing a 'think tank' conference, cautioned the USA against 'anti-Chinese rhetoric'. Shanmugam's comments appeared to reveal Singapore's desire to mediate between the USA and China as part of efforts both to preserve its long-running warm relations with the former and to forge increasingly close political and economic ties with the latter. Prime Minister Lee visited the USA in April 2013, when he held a very cordial meeting with President Obama, who expressed gratitude for the close military co-operation between the two countries.

In October 2004 officials from Bahrain, Bangladesh, Egypt, Jordan, Kuwait, Malaysia, Singapore and Thailand convened in Singapore and agreed to hold the inaugural Asia-Middle East Dialogue (AMED) in mid-2005. This diplomatic initiative had been instigated by former Prime Minister Goh owing to concern that terrorism was being equated with Islam and also out of respect for Middle Eastern states' general suspicion of dialogues initiated by the USA or Europe. It was to focus on improving political, economic and business links between the two regions, as well as on promoting a greater level of mutual cultural understanding. The meeting was held in Singapore in June and was attended by representatives of approximately 50 Asian and Middle Eastern states. It was agreed that AMED would convene on a biennial basis, at venues alternating between Asia and the Middle East. In January 2008 Singapore concluded negotiations with the Cooperation Council for the Arab States of the Gulf (Gulf Cooperation Council, GCC, see p. 255) on its second free trade agreement in the Middle East, the first having been signed with Jordan in May 2004; at early 2012, however, the agreement with the GCC was still awaiting ratification by Saudi Arabia and Kuwait. An upsurge in senior-level visits to Middle Eastern countries, including visits to Oman and Bahrain by Senior Minister Goh in January and February 2010, respectively, and to Saudi Arabia by Minister for Foreign Affairs George Yeo in May of that year, reflected Singapore's increasingly deep political and economic engagement with the region.

Relations with the United Kingdom, generally cordial, were strained in November 2010 when a British author and resident of Malaysia, Alan Shadrake, was convicted of contempt by Singapore's High Court, after criticizing the use of capital punishment in Singapore and alleging a lack of impartiality within the country's judicial system in one of his books; Shadrake was sentenced to six weeks' imprisonment and fined S \$20,000. British Minister of State at the Foreign and Commonwealth Office Jeremy Browne expressed his 'dismay' at the author's conviction and stern sentence, appealing to Singapore to recognize 'the right to freedom of expression'. However, in May 2011 the Court of Appeal rejected Shadrake's formal challenge against his conviction, and the author commenced serving his sentence (which had been increased by an additional two weeks owing to his inability to pay the S \$20,000 fine). Human Rights Watch, which, together with a number of other rights groups, had urged the Singaporean authorities to exonerate Shadrake, criticized the Court's ruling as a setback for freedom of expression in Singapore. Shadrake was released from prison in July, after serving five weeks of his sentence, and was deported to the United Kingdom. In April 2012 the British Prime Minister, David Cameron, paid a brief visit to Singapore, where he met with Prime Minister Lee. In December Cameron described the successful completion in that month of negotiations regarding the establishment of a free trade agreement between Singapore and the European Union as 'a landmark moment'; a draft agreement was expected to be signed in the first half of 2013.

CONSTITUTION AND GOVERNMENT

Legislative power is vested in the unicameral Parliament, members of which are elected by universal adult suffrage for five years (subject to dissolution—within three months of which a general election must be held) in single-member and multi-member constituencies. At the May 2011 legislative elections there were 87 elected members. Up to nine 'non-constituency' seats can be offered to opposition parties (increased from six in a constitutional amendment approved in April 2010). In addition, the Government is able to nominate up to nine politically neutral members; nominated members have restricted voting rights. The President is directly elected by universal adult suffrage for a six-year term as a constitutional head of state, vested with limited powers of veto in financial matters, public appointments and detentions for reasons of national security. Effective executive authority rests with the Cabinet, led by the Prime Minister, who is appointed by the President and is responsible to Parliament.

REGIONAL AND INTERNATIONAL CO-OPERATION

Singapore is a member of the Association of Southeast Asian Nations (ASEAN, see p. 218), the Asia-Pacific Economic Cooperation (APEC, see p. 208) forum, the Asian Development Bank (ADB, see p. 214), the UN's Economic and Social Commission for Asia and the Pacific (ESCAP, see p. 31) and the Colombo Plan (see p. 460).

Singapore became a member of the UN in 1965. As a contracting party to the General Agreement on Tariffs and Trade, Singapore joined the World Trade Organization (WTO, see p. 444) on its establishment in 1995. Singapore is also a member of the International Labour Organization (ILO, see p. 142) and the Non-aligned Movement (see p. 477). Singapore hosts the Asia Security Summit of the International Institute for Strategic Studies (see p. 476), commonly known as the Shangri-La

Dialogue, an annual meeting of ministers responsible for defence and security.

ECONOMIC AFFAIRS

In 2011, according to estimates by the World Bank, Singapore's gross national income (GNI), measured at average 2009–11 prices, was US \$222,550m., equivalent to \$42,930 per head (or \$59,790 per head on an international purchasing-power parity basis). During 2002–11, it was estimated, the population increased at an average annual rate of 2.4%, while gross domestic product (GDP) per head increased, in real terms, by an average of 4.0% per year. Overall GDP increased, in real terms, at an average annual rate of 6.5% in 2002–11. According to official figures, GDP grew by 5.2% in 2011 and by a preliminary 1.3% in 2012.

In 2012 agriculture (including fishing and quarrying—mainly of granite) contributed less than 0.1% of GDP, according to preliminary figures, and, including utilities, engaged only 1.3% of the employed labour force. Vegetables, plants and orchid flowers are the principal crops. According to figures from the World Bank, agricultural GDP (again including fishing and quarrying) declined at an average annual rate of 1.2% during 2002–11. According to official figures, agricultural GDP (including fishing and quarrying) increased by 3.2% in 2011 and by a preliminary 1.2% in 2012.

Industry (including manufacturing, construction and utilities) contributed 26.7% of GDP in 2012, according to preliminary figures, and, excluding utilities, engaged 19.2% of the employed labour force. During 2002–11, according to figures from the World Bank, industrial GDP increased at an average annual rate of 7.1%. According to official figures, the GDP of the manufacturing and construction sectors combined expanded by 7.6% in 2011 and by a preliminary 1.1% in 2012.

Manufacturing contributed 20.7% of GDP in 2012, according to preliminary figures, and engaged 14.1% of the employed labour force. The principal branches of manufacturing in 2008 (measured in terms of value of output) were electronic products and components (which accounted for an estimated 26.3% of total manufacturing production), biomedical and pharmaceutical products, transport engineering (especially ship-building), chemicals and chemical products, and precision engineering. According to figures from the World Bank, manufacturing GDP increased at an average annual rate of 7.7% in 2002–11. According to official figures, manufacturing GDP expanded by 7.8% in 2011 and by a preliminary 0.1% in 2012.

In 2012 construction contributed 4.4% of GDP, according to preliminary figures, and engaged 5.1% of the employed labour force. According to official figures, the GDP of the sector expanded by 6.2% in 2011 and by a preliminary 8.3% in 2012.

Singapore relies on imports of hydrocarbons to fuel its three thermal power stations. In 2009 natural gas accounted for 81.0% of the total amount of electrical energy produced; petroleum accounted for 18.8%. In 2012 imports of mineral fuels accounted for 32.6% of total merchandise imports.

In 2012 the services sector contributed 73.2% of GDP, according to preliminary figures, and engaged 79.5% of the employed labour force. Financial and business services provided 26.4% of GDP in 2012. Singapore is a major regional foreign exchange dealing centre, and banking is an important sector. Tourism is also a significant source of foreign exchange, and receipts from tourism amounted to an estimated US \$17,990m. in 2011. The number of tourist arrivals rose from 13.2m. in 2011 to 14.4m. in 2012. Singapore is the world's busiest port in tonnage terms and has one of the largest merchant shipping registers in the world. According to figures from the World Bank, the GDP of the services sector increased at an average annual rate of 6.3% in 2002–11. According to official figures, the sector expanded by 4.4% in 2011 and by a preliminary 1.2% in 2012.

In 2011 Singapore recorded a visible merchandise trade surplus of US \$67,453m. and a surplus of \$56,989m. on the current account of the balance of payments. In 2012 the principal source of imports was Malaysia (which provided 10.6% of the total), followed by the People's Republic of China, the USA, the Republic of Korea, Taiwan and Japan. Malaysia was also the principal purchaser of exports in that year (taking 12.3% of the total); other major export markets included Hong Kong, China and the USA. Principal imports in 2012 included machinery and equipment (notably electronic components and parts), mineral fuels, miscellaneous manufactured articles, chemicals and basic manufactures. Principal exports included machinery and equipment (notably electronic components and parts), mineral fuels (mainly petroleum products), chemicals and miscellaneous manufactured articles. Singapore is an important entrepôt, and re-exports accounted for 44.1% of total exports in 2012.

The 2012 budget projected a surplus of S $7,013m., equivalent to 2.0% of GDP. According to the Asian Development Bank (ADB), at the end of 2012 Singapore's external debt totalled US $1,148,412m. The annual rate of inflation averaged 2.2% in 2002–11. According to official figures, consumer prices increased by 4.5% in 2012. The rate of unemployment declined to 3.7% of the labour force among Singapore citizens and permanent residents in mid-2012. The overall unemployment rate (including foreign workers) was estimated at 1.8% in December 2012.

Having sought to diversify economic activities, Singapore has in recent years recorded strong growth in areas such as biomedical manufacturing, financial services and oil-refining. However, the country's dependency on external demand was highlighted in 2008/09, when the deterioration in global economic conditions led to a steep decline in Singapore's exports. The economy entered recession in the third quarter of 2008, and, in comparison with the corresponding quarter of the previous year, GDP contracted by an unprecedented 11.5% in the first three months of 2009; for the year as a whole, however, GDP contracted at a slower rate than anticipated (0.8%), in part owing to the effects of a S $20,500m. fiscal stimulus plan announced in early 2009. Inflationary pressures re-emerged in 2010–11, mainly owing to the increasing costs of housing, transport and food. However, inflation decelerated during 2012, as a result of a decline in world food prices and measures undertaken by the Government during 2011 to address an ongoing shortage of accommodation, which helped to curb the continuing rise in housing prices. The ADBforecast a further moderation in inflation in 2013 and 2014. In 2012 the cost of imports increased by

3.2%, compared with 8.6% in the previous year, while exports decreased by 0.9%, compared with growth of 7.5% in 2011. The fall in exports contributed to a slight decline in the fiscal surplus to an estimated 0.7% of GDP in the fiscal year ending 31 March 2013. After slowing from 5.2% in 2011 to 1.3% in 2012, largely owing to a fall in external demand for manufactured goods (particularly in the USA and the eurozone), GDP growth was forecast by the ADB to accelerate to 2.6% in 2013, fuelled mainly by continuing strong domestic demand and a rise in exports to other Asian countries. The European sovereign debt crisis, which remained ongoing at early 2013, was a cause for considerable concern, given the Singapore economy's sizeable exposure to European banking systems. Meanwhile, as the Singaporean population continued to age, and with foreign workers estimated to account for one-third of the labour force, the Government renewed its efforts to encourage population growth and to increase the skills, innovation and productivity of the domestic labour force. A three-year package worth S $5,350m. was included in the 2012/13 budget to help small and medium-sized businesses to cope with rising costs.

PUBLIC HOLIDAYS

2014: 1 January (New Year's Day), 31 January–1 February (Chinese New Year), 18 April (Good Friday), 1 May (Labour Day), 13 May (Vesak Day), 28 July* (Hari Raya Puasa, end of Ramadan), 9 August (National Day), 6 October* (for Hari Raya Haji, Feast of the Sacrifice), 23 October (Deepavali), 25 December (Christmas Day).

* These holidays are dependent on the Islamic lunar calendar and may vary by one or two days from the dates given.

Statistical Survey

Source (unless otherwise stated): Department of Statistics, 100 High St, 05-01 The Treasury, Singapore 179434; tel. 63327686; fax 63327689; email info@singstat.gov.sg; internet www.singstat.gov.sg.

Area and Population

AREA, POPULATION AND DENSITY

Area (sq km)	714.3*
Population (census results)†	
30 June 2000	
Males	2,061,800‡
Females	1,955,900‡
Total	4,017,733
30 June 2010	5,076,700‡
Population (official estimates at mid-year)	
2011	5,183,700
2012	5,312,400
Density (per sq km) at mid-2012	7,437.2

* 275.8 sq miles.
† Includes non-residents, totalling 754,524 in 2000 and 1,305,000 in 2010; the resident population in 2010 was 3,771,721 (males 1,861,133, females 1,910,588).
‡ Rounded figure.

POPULATION BY AGE AND SEX
(official estimates at mid-2012)*

	Males	Females	Total
0–14	319,600	306,600	626,200
15–64	1,392,000	1,421,300	2,813,300
65 and over	168,600	210,100	378,700
Total	1,880,000	1,938,200	3,818,200

Note: Totals may not be equal to the sum of components, owing to rounding.

* Resident population of Singapore only; the total population was recorded at 5,312,400.

ETHNIC GROUPS
('000 persons at 30 June 2012)*

	Males	Females	Total
Chinese	1,385.6	1,446.4	2,832.0
Malays	253.6	255.9	509.5
Indians	180.9	170.1	351.0
Others	59.9	65.8	125.7
Total	1,880.0	1,938.2	3,818.2

* Figures refer to the resident population of Singapore only.

BIRTHS, MARRIAGES AND DEATHS*

	Registered live births Number	Rate (per 1,000)	Registered marriages Number	Rate (per 1,000)	Registered deaths Number	Rate (per 1,000)
2005	37,492	10.2	22,992	5.3	16,215	4.4
2006	38,317	10.3	23,706	6.5	16,393	4.4
2007	39,490	10.3	23,966	6.4	17,140	4.5
2008	39,826	10.2	24,596	6.5	17,127	4.4
2009	39,570	9.9	26,081	6.6	17,101	4.3
2010	37,967	9.3	24,363	6.1	17,610	4.4
2011	39,654	9.5	27,258	6.7	18,027	4.5
2012	42,600	10.1	27,936	n.a.	18,410	4.5

* Data are tabulated by year of registration, rather than by year of occurrence.

Life expectancy (years at birth): 81.6 (males 79.3; females 84.1) in 2010 (Source: World Bank, World Development Indicators database).

ECONOMICALLY ACTIVE POPULATION
('000 residents aged 15 years and over, at June of each year)*

	2010	2011	2012
Agriculture, fishing, mining and quarrying, utilities, sewage and waste management	37.6	23.5	26.5
Manufacturing	291.4	292.4	288.2
Construction	104.0	99.7	104.5
Wholesale and retail trade; repair of motor vehicles, motorcycles and personal and household goods	281.7	300.5	306.3
Hotels and restaurants . . .	128.9	135.2	129.3
Transport and storage . . .	191.3	192.0	189.5
Information and communications .	99.9	85.4	85.8
Financial intermediation . . .	126.0	145.5	150.6
Real estate, renting and business activities	253.4	271.6	289.8
Community, social and personal services	448.6	453.1	470.2
Total employed	1,962.9	1,998.9	2,040.6
Unemployed	84.4	81.2	79.0
Total labour force	2,047.3	2,080.1	2,119.6

* Data refer to Singapore citizens and permanent residents, but exclude foreign workers temporarily resident.

Health and Welfare

KEY INDICATORS

Total fertility rate (children per woman, 2010)	1.3
Under-5 mortality rate (per 1,000 live births, 2010) . . .	3
HIV/AIDS (% of persons aged 15–49, 2009)	0.1
Physicians (per 1,000 head, 2009)	1.8
Hospital beds (per 1,000 head, 2008)	3.1
Health expenditure (2009): US $ per head (PPP)	2,111
Health expenditure (2009): % of GDP	4.1
Health expenditure (2009): public (% of total)	36.1
Total carbon dioxide emissions ('000 metric tons, 2008) . .	32,295.3
Carbon dioxide emissions per head (metric tons, 2008) . .	6.7
Human Development Index (2011): ranking	26
Human Development Index (2011): value	0.866

For sources and definitions, see explanatory note on p. vi.

Agriculture

PRINCIPAL CROPS
('000 metric tons)

	2009	2010	2011
Groundnut oil*	1,935	1,885	1,885
Sesame oil*	2,958	2,754	2,754
Soybean oil*	3,113	3,350	3,350
Cabbages and other brassicas .	499	546	600†
Spinach	2,105	1,883	2,000†

* FAO estimates.
† Unofficial figure.

Total vegetables (incl. melons, '000 metric tons, may include official, semi-official or estimated data): 20.0 in 2009; 19.5 in 2010; 20.3 in 2011.

Source: FAO.

LIVESTOCK
('000 head, year ending September, FAO estimates)

	2009	2010	2011
Pigs	260	270	270
Chickens	3,200	3,300	3,300
Ducks	750	750	750

Source: FAO.

LIVESTOCK PRODUCTS
('000 metric tons)

	2009	2010	2011
Pig meat	17.5	18.8	19.0*
Chicken meat*	86.2	89.3	90.0
Hen eggs	20.0	20.4	22.1

* FAO estimate(s).
Source: FAO.

Forestry

SAWNWOOD PRODUCTION
('000 cubic metres, incl. railway sleepers, FAO estimates)

	1990	1991	1992
Coniferous (softwood)	5	10	5
Broadleaved (hardwood) . . .	50	20	20
Total	55	30	25

1993–2011: Annual production assumed to be unchanged since 1992 (FAO estimates).
Source: FAO.

Fishing

(metric tons, live weight)

	2008	2009	2010
Capture	1,623	2,121	1,732
Prawns and shrimps . . .	132	244	189
Aquaculture	3,518	3,567	3,499
Indonesian snakehead . . .	175	157	272
Milkfish	917	961	1,312
Green mussel	1,488	1,299	265
Total catch	5,141	5,688	5,231

Note: Figures exclude crocodiles, recorded by number rather than by weight. The number of estuarine crocodiles caught was: 1,877 in 2008; 1,086 in 2009; 1,217 in 2010.

Source: FAO.

Industry

SELECTED PRODUCTS
('000 metric tons unless otherwise indicated)

	2007	2008	2009
Liquefied petroleum gas . . .	673	608	608
Naphtha	4,490	4,405	3,864
Motor spirit (petrol)	8,405	9,300	9,627
Kerosene	584	573	503
Jet fuel	10,416	9,997	7,408
Gas-diesel (distillate fuel) oils .	14,364	14,968	13,309
Residual fuel oil	7,794	6,902	11,712
Lubricating oils	2,581	2,837	2,481
Petroleum bitumen (asphalt) . .	1,982	2,030	1,943
Electric energy (million kWh) .	41,134	41,717	41,801

Plywood ('000 cu m, estimates): 280 per year in 1991–2011. Source FAO.

Electric energy (million kWh): 45,367 in 2010; 45,999 in 2011.

Sources (unless otherwise indicated): UN Industrial Commodity Statistics Database; Asian Development Bank.

Finance

CURRENCY AND EXCHANGE RATES

Monetary Units
100 cents = 1 Singapore dollar (S $).

Sterling, US Dollar and Euro Equivalents (31 December 2012)
£1 sterling = S $1.9307;
US $1 = S $1.2235;
€1 = S $1.6143;
S $100 = £51.80 = US $81.73 = €61.95.

Average Exchange Rate (Singapore dollars per US $)
2010   1.3635
2011   1.2578
2012   1.2497

BUDGET
(S $ million)

Revenue*	2010	2011	2012
Tax revenue	40,662	46,172	48,755
Income tax	18,077	20,976	21,896
Corporate and personal income tax	17,206	18,907	20,059
Contributions by statutory board	420	892	514
Assets taxes	2,598	3,813	3,651
Taxes on motor vehicles . .	1,893	1,868	1,901
Customs and excise duties . .	2,090	2,108	2,145
Betting taxes	2,120	2,343	2,342
Stamp duty	3,097	3,259	3,968
Goods and services tax . . .	7,699	8,914	8,743
Others	2,889	2,891	4,109
Fees and charges	3,779	4,473	5,221
Total (incl. others)	44,581	50,986	54,284

Expenditure	2010	2011	2012
Operating expenditure . . .	32,755	35,011	34,810
Security and external relations .	14,311	13,728	13,645
Social development	15,400	17,720	17,475
Education	8,517	9,929	9,248
Health	3,070	3,501	3,899
Community development and sports	1,793	1,855	1,803
Environment and water resources	661	746	803
Economic development . . .	1,914	2,198	2,371
Trade and industry . . .	673	689	726
Transport	420	482	476
Government administration .	1,130	1,365	1,319
Development expenditure . . .	11,295	11,761	12,461
Total	44,050	46,772	47,271

* Figures refer to operating revenue only; the data exclude investment income and capital revenue.

INTERNATIONAL RESERVES
(US $ million at 31 December)

	2009	2010	2011
Gold and foreign exchange . .	186,005	223,890	235,709
IMF special drawing rights . .	1,537	1,527	1,332
Reserve position in the IMF . .	262	297	833
Total	187,803	225,714	237,874

Source: IMF, *International Financial Statistics*.

MONEY SUPPLY
(S $ million at 31 December)

	2009	2010	2011
Currency outside banks . . .	20,217	22,300	24,690
Demand deposits at commercial banks	73,255	90,166	104,429
Total money	93,472	112,466	129,119

Source: IMF, *International Financial Statistics*.

COST OF LIVING
(Consumer Price Index; base: 2009 = 100)

	2010	2011	2012
Food	101.3	104.4	106.9
Transport	110.3	123.5	132.2
Clothing and footwear	100.4	100.5	102.0
Housing	102.0	110.5	119.0
Education	102.7	105.7	109.3
Health	101.9	104.3	109.0
All items (incl. others) . . .	102.8	108.2	113.1

NATIONAL ACCOUNTS
(S $ million at current prices)

Expenditure on the Gross Domestic Product

	2010	2011	2012*
Government final consumption expenditure	33,000.7	33,995.5	33,370.4
Private final consumption expenditure	117,680.5	127,915.5	135,551.8
Change in inventories	−6,599.8	−3,894.0	9,927.5
Gross fixed capital formation .	74,254.1	78,029.2	83,368.5
Statistical discrepancy . . .	4,431.8	5,777.4	6,730.7
Total domestic expenditure .	222,767.3	241,823.6	268,948.9
Exports of goods and services .	643,167.8	692,206.8	693,393.1
Less Imports of goods and services	550,013.9	599,937.7	616,781.5
GDP in market prices . . .	315,921.2	334,092.7	345,560.5
GDP at constant 2005 prices .	286,446.7	301,228.4	305,201.5

Gross Domestic Product by Economic Activity

	2010	2011	2012*
Agriculture, fishing and quarrying	113.3	114.9	111.0
Manufacturing	64,459.8	65,361.7	67,189.7
Electricity, gas and water . .	4,781.2	5,206.6	5,329.7
Construction	12,584.4	13,186.3	14,231.2
Wholesale and retail trade . .	55,246.2	56,686.3	55,184.9
Hotels and restaurants . . .	6,606.8	7,640.3	8,170.2
Transport and storage . . .	25,546.5	23,733.7	25,104.5
Information and communications .	11,172.3	11,837.2	12,327.8
Financial services	33,558.9	37,113.5	38,485.5
Business services	40,559.1	44,478.7	47,224.4
Owner-occupied dwellings . .	11,710.3	13,715.1	15,416.6
Other services	31,633.8	35,139.4	35,753.7
Sub-total	297,972.6	314,213.7	324,529.2
Taxes on products (net) . . .	17,948.6	19,879.0	21,031.3
GDP in market prices . . .	315,921.2	334,092.7	345,560.5

* Preliminary figures.

BALANCE OF PAYMENTS
(US $ million)

	2009	2010	2011
Exports of goods	288,408	371,056	429,368
Imports of goods	−241,137	−307,958	−361,916
Balance on goods	47,270	63,097	67,453
Exports of services	80,185	100,012	113,588
Imports of services	−83,373	−98,484	−111,743
Balance on goods and services	44,082	64,626	69,297
Primary income received . . .	46,063	61,966	67,999
Primary income paid	−56,012	−65,920	−73,595
Balance on goods, services and primary income . . .	34,134	60,672	63,701
Secondary income received . .	2,407	4,054	3,623
Secondary income paid . . .	−6,403	−9,218	−10,335

—*continued*	2009	2010	2011
Current balance	30,138	55,509	56,989
Direct investment assets . . .	−17,704	−21,215	−25,228
Direct investment liabilities . .	24,418	48,637	64,003
Portfolio investment assets . .	−41,357	−28,109	−22,761
Portfolio investment liabilities .	1,183	1,189	−5,966
Financial derivatives and employee stock options (net)	−17,596	−9,618	−11,115
Other investment assets . . .	75,567	−38,776	−111,384
Other investment liabilities . .	−47,189	34,965	72,410
Net errors and omissions . .	3,854	−228	293
Reserves and related items .	11,314	42,353	17,243

Source: IMF, *International Financial Statistics*.

External Trade

PRINCIPAL COMMODITIES
(S $ million)

Imports c.i.f.	2010	2011	2012
Mineral fuels, lubricants, etc.	115,592	149,946	154,803
Chemicals and related products	28,630	31,882	32,403
Basic manufactures . . .	26,458	30,996	29,642
Machinery and equipment	196,106	188,268	196,288
Electronic components and parts	79,903	71,487	74,464
Miscellaneous manufactured articles	29,684	32,060	34,027
Total (incl. others)	423,221	459,655	474,554

Exports f.o.b.*	2010	2011	2012
Mineral fuels, lubricants, etc. .	103,511	136,774	130,900
Petroleum products . . .	76,886	101,485	93,936
Chemicals and related products	56,644	64,777	67,519
Basic manufactures . . .	18,861	20,124	19,145
Machinery and equipment .	244,128	235,346	230,885
Electronic components and parts .	118,962	106,090	103,470
Miscellaneous manufactured articles	33,775	36,187	40,002
Total (incl. others) . . .	478,840	514,741	510,329

* Including re-exports (S $ million); 230,231 in 2010; 233,392 in 2011; 225,183 in 2012.

PRINCIPAL TRADING PARTNERS
(S $ million)

Imports c.i.f.	2010	2011	2012
Australia	4,711	4,705	6,129
China, People's Republic . . .	45,844	47,748	48,950
France	10,119	10,663	11,344
Germany	12,125	13,081	13,204
Hong Kong	4,004	3,994	3,637
India	12,566	17,771	16,213
Italy	3,830	4,476	4,474
Japan	33,262	32,964	29,539
Korea, Republic	24,515	27,318	32,026
Kuwait	3,607	4,515	5,991
Malaysia	49,490	49,167	50,501
Netherlands	7,280	8,762	9,800
Philippines	12,523	7,793	7,547
Saudi Arabia	15,297	22,164	21,509
Switzerland	6,181	5,378	5,665
Taiwan	25,239	27,333	31,601
Thailand	14,001	14,270	12,675
United Arab Emirates . . .	8,693	14,545	19,604
United Kingdom	7,603	7,598	8,744
USA	47,515	49,050	48,201
Total (incl. others)	423,222	459,655	474,554

Exports f.o.b.*	2010	2011	2012
Australia	17,111	20,146	21,320
China, People's Republic . . .	49,468	53,651	54,873
France	7,531	7,690	7,815
Germany	8,370	8,417	7,442
Hong Kong	56,081	56,777	55,900
India	18,101	17,654	13,593
Japan	22,332	23,121	22,609
Korea, Republic	19,548	19,459	20,713
Malaysia	57,114	62,835	62,869
Netherlands	8,388	9,487	8,878
Philippines	9,775	8,506	7,920
Taiwan	17,442	18,356	18,058
Thailand	17,284	17,645	19,500
United Arab Emirates . . .	5,183	5,830	5,889
United Kingdom	8,334	8,328	7,716
USA	30,871	27,638	27,445
Viet Nam	10,061	12,835	12,944
Total (incl. others)	478,841	514,741	510,329

* Including re-exports (S $ million); 230,231 in 2010; 233,392 in 2011; 225,183 in 2012.

Transport

ROAD TRAFFIC
(registered vehicles)

	2010	2011	2012
Cars*	597,746	606,280	620,011
Motorcycles and scooters . . .	148,160	146,559	144,110
Motor buses	16,309	17,046	17,162
Taxis	26,073	27,051	28,210
Goods and other vehicles (incl. private)	157,541	159,768	160,417
Total	945,829	956,704	969,910

* Including private, company, tuition and private hire cars.

SHIPPING

Flag Registered Fleet
(at 31 December)

	2010	2011	2012
Number of vessels	4,468	4,579	4,656
Total displacement ('000 grt) . .	48,925.9	56,883.0	64,549.4

Source: Lloyd's List Intelligence (www.lloydslistintelligence.com).

International Sea-borne Shipping

	2010	2011	2012
Vessels entered	127,299	127,998	130,422
Total cargo ('000 metric tons) . .	503,342	531,176	537,588

Source: Maritime and Ports Authority of Singapore.

CIVIL AVIATION

	2010	2011	2012
Passengers:			
arrived	20,486,452	22,778,148	25,055,954
departed	20,437,264	22,651,114	24,853,644
in transit	1,115,061	1,114,582	1,272,205
Mail (metric tons):			
landed	11,165	14,361	15,789
dispatched	16,027	19,235	19,844
Freight (metric tons):			
discharged	941,403	983,110	964,533
loaded	872,406	882,142	841,692

Source: partly Civil Aviation Authority of Singapore.

Tourism

FOREIGN VISITOR ARRIVALS
(incl. excursionists)

Country of nationality	2009	2010	2011
Australia	830,299	880,558	956,039
China, People's Republic . . .	936,747	1,171,493	1,577,522
Germany	183,681	209,263	219,952
Hong Kong	294,420	387,579	464,375
India	725,624	828,994	868,991
Japan	489,987	528,951	656,417
Korea, Republic	271,987	360,703	414,879
Taiwan	156,761	191,186	238,488
United Kingdom	469,756	461,769	442,611
USA	370,704	417,195	440,576
Total (incl. others)	9,682,690	11,641,700	13,171,303

Total foreign visitor arrivals ('000): 14,369.2 in 2012.

Tourism receipts (US $ million, excl. passenger transport): 9,200 in 2009; 14,133 in 2010; 17,990 in 2011 (provisional) (Source: World Tourism Organization).

Communications Media

(at 31 December)

	2009	2010	2011
Telephones ('000 main lines in use)	1,925.6	1,996.1	2,018.1
Mobile cellular telephones ('000 subscribers)	6,879.8	7,384.6	7,794.3
Internet subscribers ('000) . .	1,247.2	1,333.6	1,386.3
Broadband subscribers ('000) . .	1,170.7	1,270.6	1,329.9

Source: International Telecommunication Union.

Education

(2011)

	Institutions	Teachers	Students
Primary	174	13,586	251,165
Secondary	154	12,936	189,735
Mixed levels*	15	2,483	37,513
Pre-university	13	1,810	20,150
Institute of Technical Education .	3	1,684	25,279
Polytechnics	5	5,013	85,111
National Institute of Education .	1	719	4,452
Universities†	4	4,553	75,655

* Referring to schools with multiple levels, encompassing full schools (P1–S4/5), sixth-form schools (S1–JC2) and JC-plus levels (S3–JC2).
† Student and teacher numbers are not available for Singapore's fourth university (SIM University), which opened in 2005.

Pupil-teacher ratio (primary education, UNESCO estimate): 17.4 in 2008/09 (Source: UNESCO Institute for Statistics).

Adult literacy rate (official estimate): 96.1% in 2011.

Directory

The Government

HEAD OF STATE

President: Dr TONY TAN KENG YAM (elected 27 August 2011).

CABINET
(May 2013)

The Cabinet comprises members of the People's Action Party.

Prime Minister: Brig.-Gen. (retd) LEE HSIEN LOONG.

Deputy Prime Minister, Co-ordinating Minister for National Security and Minister for Home Affairs: TEO CHEE HEAN.

Deputy Prime Minister and Minister for Finance: THARMAN SHANMUGARATNAM.

Minister for Trade and Industry: LIM HNG KIANG.

Minister in the Prime Minister's Office: LIM SWEE SAY.

Minister for Communications and Information: Dr YAACOB IBRAHIM.

Minister for National Development: KHAW BOON WAN.

Minister for Defence: Dr NG ENG HEN.

Minister for the Environment and Water Resources: Dr VIVIAN BALAKRISHNAN.

Minister for Foreign Affairs and Law: K. SHANMUGAM.

Minister for Health: GAN KIM YONG.

Minister for Transport: LUI TUCK YEW.

Minister in the Prime Minister's Office and Second Minister for Home Affairs, Trade and Industry: S. ISWARAN.

Minister for Education: HENG SWEE KEAT.

Minister in the Prime Minister's Office, Second Minister for the Environment and Water Resources and for Foreign Affairs: GRACE FU HAI YIEN.

Acting Minister for Social and Family Development and Senior Minister of State for Ministry of Defence: CHAN CHUN SING.

Acting Minister of Manpower and Senior Minister of State for Ministry of National Development: TAN CHUAN JIN.

Acting Minister for Culture, Community and Youth and Senior Minister of State, Ministry of Communications and Information: LAWRENCE WONG.

MINISTRIES

Office of the President: The Istana, Orchard Rd, Singapore 238823; e-mail istana_feedback@istana.gov.sg; internet www.istana.gov.sg.

Office of the Prime Minister: The Istana, Orchard Rd, Singapore 238823; tel. 62358577; fax 68356621; e-mail pmo_hq@pmo.gov.sg; internet www.pmo.gov.sg.

Ministry of Communications and Information: 4th Floor, 140 Hill St, Old Hill St Police Station, Singapore 179369; tel. 62707988; fax 68379480; e-mail mci@mci.gov.sg; internet www.mci.gov.sg.

Ministry of Culture, Community and Youth: 140 Hill St, 02-00/03-00, Singapore 179369; tel. 63383632; fax 68379459; e-mail contact@mccy.gov.sg; internet www.mccy.gov.sg.

Ministry of Defence: Gombak Dr., off Upper Bukit Timah Rd, Mindef Bldg, Singapore 669645; tel. 67608844; fax 67646119; e-mail contact@ns.sg; internet www.mindef.gov.sg.

Ministry of Education: 1 North Buona Vista Dr., MOE Bldg, Singapore 138675; tel. 68722220; fax 67755826; e-mail contact@moe.edu.sg; internet www.moe.gov.sg.

Ministry of the Environment and Water Resources: 40 Scotts Rd, 24-00 Environment Bldg, Singapore 228231; tel. 67319000; fax 67319456; e-mail mewr_feedback@mewr.gov.sg; internet www.mewr.gov.sg.

Ministry of Finance: 100 High St, 06-03 The Treasury, Singapore 179434; tel. 62259911; fax 63327435; e-mail mof_qsm@mof.gov.sg; internet www.mof.gov.sg.

Ministry of Foreign Affairs: MFA Bldg, Tanglin, off Napier Rd, Singapore 248163; tel. 63798000; fax 64747885; e-mail mfa@mfa.gov.sg; internet www.mfa.gov.sg.

Ministry of Health: 16 College Rd, College of Medicine Bldg, Singapore 169854; tel. 63259220; fax 62241677; e-mail moh_info@moh.gov.sg; internet www.moh.gov.sg.

Ministry of Home Affairs: New Phoenix Park, 28 Irrawaddy Rd, Singapore 329560; tel. 64787010; fax 62546250; e-mail mha_feedback@mha.gov.sg; internet www.mha.gov.sg.

Ministry of Law: 100 High St, 08-02 The Treasury, Singapore 179434; tel. 63328840; fax 63328842; e-mail contact@mlaw.gov.sg; internet www.mlaw.gov.sg.

Ministry of Manpower: 18 Havelock Rd, 07-01, Singapore 059764; tel. 64385122; fax 65344840; e-mail mom_hq@mom.gov.sg; internet www.mom.gov.sg.

Ministry of National Development: 5 Maxwell Rd, 21/22-00 Tower Blk, MND Complex, Singapore 069110; tel. 62221211; fax 63257254; e-mail mnd_hq@mnd.gov.sg; internet www.mnd.gov.sg.

Ministry of Social and Family Development: 512 Thomson Rd, MSF Bldg, Singapore 298136; tel. 63555000; fax 63536695; e-mail msf_email@msf.gov.sg; internet www.msf.gov.sg.

Ministry of Trade and Industry: 100 High St, 09-01 The Treasury, Singapore 179434; tel. 62259911; fax 63327260; e-mail mti_email@mti.gov.sg; internet www.mti.gov.sg.

Ministry of Transport: 460 Alexandra Rd, 39-00 PSA Bldg, Singapore 119963; tel. 62707988; fax 63757734; e-mail mot@mot.gov.sg; internet www.mot.gov.sg.

President and Legislature

PRESIDENT

Presidential Election, 27 August 2011

Candidate	Votes	% of votes
Tony Tan Keng Yam	744,397	35.19
Tan Cheng Bock	737,128	34.85
Tan Jee Say	529,732	25.04
Tan Kin Lian	103,931	4.91
Total	2,115,188	100.00*

* Adjusted for rounding.

PARLIAMENT

Parliament House

1 Parliament Place, Singapore 178880; tel. 63326666; fax 63325526; e-mail parl@parl.gov.sg; internet www.parliament.gov.sg.

Speaker: HALIMAH YACOB.

General Election, 7 May 2011

Party	Seats
People's Action Party	81*
Workers' Party	6
Total	87

* Five seats were uncontested.

Election Commission

Elections Department of Singapore (ELD): Prime Minister's Office, 11 Prinsep Link, Singapore 187949; tel. 62255353; fax 63323428; e-mail contact@eld.gov.sg; internet www.elections.gov.sg; govt body; Returning Officer NG WAI CHOONG.

Political Organizations

National Solidarity Party (NSP): 397 Jalan Besar, 02-01A, Singapore 209007; tel. 83823961; fax 63968645; e-mail nsp-cec@yahoogroups.com; internet www.nsp.sg; f. 1987; Pres. SEBASTIAN TEO; Sec.-Gen. HAZEL POA.

People's Action Party (PAP): Blk 57B, PCF Bldg, 01-1402 New Upper Changi Rd, Singapore 463057; tel. 62444600; fax 62430114; e-mail paphq@pap.org.sg; internet www.pap.org.sg; f. 1954; governing party since 1959; 18-mem. Cen. Exec. Cttee; Chair. KHAW BOON WAN; Sec.-Gen. LEE HSIEN LOONG.

Pertubuhan Kebangsaan Melayu Singapura (PKMS) (Singapore Malay National Organization): PKMS Bldg, 4th Floor, 218F Changi Rd, Singapore 419737; tel. 64470468; fax 63458724; e-mail info@pkms.org; internet www.pkms.org; f. 1950 as United Malay Nat. Org. (UMNO) of Malaysia; renamed UMNO Singapore in 1954; present name adopted 1967; seeks to advance the implementation of the special rights of Malays in Singapore, as stated in the Constitution; to safeguard and promote the advancement of Islam; and to encourage racial harmony and goodwill in Singapore; joined SDA in July 2001; Pres. ABU BIN MOHAMED; Sec.-Gen. ABDUL JAMAL BIN ABDUL RASHID JUSOF.

Reform Party: 18A Smith St, Singapore 058932; tel. 65349641; fax 65349640; e-mail enquiries@thereformparty.net; internet www.thereformparty.net; f. 2008; Chair. ANDY ZHU LAI CHENG; Sec.-Gen. KENNETH JEYARETNAM.

Singapore Democratic Alliance (SDA): Singapore; f. 2001 to contest 2001 general election, as coalition of PKMS, SPP, NSP and SJP; NSP left coalition in 2007; Chair. ABU MOHAMED; Sec.-Gen. DESMOND LIM BAK CHUAN.

Singapore Democratic Party (SDP): 1357A Serangoon Rd, Singapore 328240; tel. and fax 63981675; e-mail speakup@yoursdp.org; internet www.yoursdp.org; f. 1980; 12-mem. Cen. Cttee; Chair. MOHAMED JUFRIE MAHMOOD; Sec.-Gen. CHEE SOON JUAN.

Singapore Justice Party (SJP): Singapore; f. 1972; joined SDA in July 2001; Pres. A. R. SUIB; Sec.-Gen. AMINUDDIN BIN AMI.

Singapore People's Party (SPP): 22A Upper Weld Rd, Singapore 207379; tel. 68585771; fax 62970138; e-mail feedback@spp.org.sg; internet www.spp.org.sg; f. 1993; breakaway faction of SDP, espousing more moderate policies; joined SDA in July 2001; 12-mem. Cen. Exec. Cttee; Chair. LOH WOON LEE; Sec.-Gen. CHIAM SEE TONG.

Socialist Front: 24 Peck Seah St, 05-09-11 Nehsons Bldg, Singapore 079314; e-mail contact@socialistfront.org; internet www.socialistfront.org; f. 2010; encourages participation and ownership in politics; promotes equal opportunities for citizens; Chair. NG TECK SIONG; Sec.-Gen. CHIA TI LIK.

United Singapore Democrats (USD): Singapore; f. 2010 by fmr mems of SDP (q.v.); Pres. NARAYANASAMY GOGELAVANY; Sec. JASLYN GO.

Workers' Party: 216G Syed Alwi Rd 02-03, Singapore 207799; tel. 62984765; fax 64544404; e-mail webmaster@wp.sg; internet www.wp.org.sg; f. 1961; active as opposition party in Singapore since 1957; merged with Barisan Sosialis (Socialist Front) in 1988; seeks to establish a democratic socialist govt with a constitution guaranteeing fundamental citizens' rights; Chair. SYLVIA LIM SWEE LIAN; Sec.-Gen. LOW THIA KHIANG.

Other parties include the Alliance Party Singapura, the Democratic People's Party, the Democratic Progressive Party, the National Party of Singapore, the Partai Rakyat, the Parti Kesatuan Ra'ayat (United Democratic Party), the People's Front, the People's Republican Party, the Persatuan Melayu Singapura, the Singapore Chinese Party, the Singapore Indian Congress, the Singapore National Front, the United National Front, the United People's Front and the United People's Party.

Diplomatic Representation

EMBASSIES AND HIGH COMMISSIONS IN SINGAPORE

Angola: 9 Temasek Blvd, 44-03 Suntec Tower Two, Singapore 038989; tel. 63419360; fax 63419367; e-mail embangola@pacific.net.sg; Ambassador FIDELINO LOY DE JESUS FIGUEIREDO.

Australia: 25 Napier Rd, Singapore 258507; tel. 68364100; fax 67375481; e-mail enquiries-sg@dfat.gov.au; internet www.australia.org.sg; High Commissioner PHILIP VICTOR GREEN.

Bangladesh: 91 Bencoolen St, 06-01, Sunshine Plaza, Singapore 189652; tel. 62550075; fax 62551824; e-mail bdoot@singnet.com.sg; internet www.bangladesh.org.sg; High Commissioner MAHBUB UZ ZAMAN.

Belgium: 8 Shenton Way, 14-01, Singapore 068811; tel. 62207677; fax 62226976; e-mail Singapore@diplobel.fed.be; internet www.diplomatie.be/singapore; Ambassador ROLAND VAN REMOORTELE.

Brazil: 101 Thomson Rd, 10-05 United Sq., Singapore 307591; tel. 62566001; fax 62566619; e-mail cinbrem@brazil.org.sg; internet www.brazil.org.sg; Ambassador LUIS FERNANDO DE ANDRADE SERRA.

Brunei: 325 Tanglin Rd, Singapore 247955; tel. 67339055; fax 67375275; e-mail singapore.singapore@mfa.gov.bn; High Commissioner SAIFUL RIZAL PG HAJI RAZALI (acting).

Cambodia: 400 Orchard Rd, 10-03/04 Orchard Towers, Singapore 238875; tel. 63419785; fax 63419201; e-mail recamsingapore@gmail.com; internet www.recambodia.net; Ambassador SEREY SIN.

Canada: 1 George St 11-01, Singapore 049145; tel. 68545900; fax 68545930; e-mail spore@international.gc.ca; internet www.canadainternational.gc.ca/singapore-singapour; High Commissioner HEATHER A. GRANT.

Chile: 8 Temasek Blvd, 24-01 Suntec Tower 3, Singapore 038988; tel. 62238577; fax 62250677; e-mail contacto@chileabroad.gov.cl; internet chileabroad.gov.cl/republica-de-singapur; Ambassador Luis Fernando Danús Charpentier.

China, People's Republic: 150 Tanglin Rd, Singapore 247969; tel. 64180252; fax 64180250; e-mail chinaemb_sg@fmprc.gov.cn; internet www.chinaembassy.org.sg; Charge d'affaires a.i. Dai Bing.

Costa Rica: 896 Dunearn Rd, 03-02B Sime Darby Centre, Singapore 589472; tel. 64671355; fax 64678275; e-mail info@costaricaembassy-sg.net; internet www.costaricaembassy-sg.net; Ambassador Jairo Hernandez Milian.

Denmark: 101 Thomson Rd, 13-01/02 United Sq., Singapore 307591; tel. 63555010; fax 62533764; e-mail sinamb@um.dk; internet www.ambsingapore.um.dk; Ambassador Berit Basse.

Egypt: 8 Eu Tong Sen St, 25-82/85, The Central, Singapore 059818; tel. 62255991; fax 62258182; e-mail admin@egyptemb-sin.org; Ambassador Fatma Fathelbab Galal.

Finland: 101 Thomson Rd, 21-03 United Sq., Singapore 307591; tel. 62544042; fax 62534101; e-mail sanomat.sin@formin.fi; internet www.finland.org.sg; Ambassador Ari Heikkinen.

France: 101–103 Cluny Park Rd, Singapore 259595; tel. 68807800; fax 68807801; e-mail consulat@ambafrance-sg.org; internet www.ambafrance-sg.org; Ambassador Olivier Caron.

Germany: 12-00 Singapore Land Tower, 50 Raffles Pl., Singapore 048623; tel. 65336002; fax 65331132; e-mail consul@sing.diplo.de; internet www.singapur.diplo.de; Ambassador Angelika Viets.

Hungary: 250 North Bridge Rd, 29-01 Raffles City Tower, Singapore 179101; tel. 68830882; fax 68830177; e-mail mission.sin@kum.hu; internet www.mfa.gov.hu/kulkepviselet/SG; Ambassador Dr Csaba A. Faragó.

India: 31 Grange Rd, India House, Singapore 239702; tel. 67376777; fax 67326909; e-mail indiahc@pacific.net.sg; internet www.hcisingapore.com; High Commissioner Dr Tirumallai C. A. Raghavan.

Indonesia: 7 Chatsworth Rd, Singapore 249761; tel. 67377422; fax 67375037; e-mail info@indonesianembassy.sg; internet kemlu.go.id/singapore; Ambassador Andri Hadi.

Ireland: Ireland House, 541 Orchard Rd, 08-00 Liat Towers, Singapore 238811; tel. 62387616; fax 62387615; e-mail singaporeembassy@dfa.ie; internet www.embassyofireland.sg; Ambassador Joseph Hayes.

Israel: 24 Stevens Close, Singapore 257964; tel. 68349200; fax 68349299; e-mail press@singapore.mfa.gov.il; internet singapore.mfa.gov.il; Ambassador Amira Arnon.

Italy: 101 Thomson Rd, 27-02 United Sq., Singapore 307591; tel. 62506022; fax 62533301; e-mail ambasciata.singapore@esteri.it; internet www.ambsingapore.esteri.it; Ambassador Paolo Crudele.

Japan: 16 Nassim Rd, Singapore 258390; tel. 62358855; fax 67331039; e-mail eojsingfv@vsystem.com.sg; internet www.sg.emb-japan.go.jp; Ambassador Yoichi Suzuki.

Kazakhstan: 20 Raffles Pl., 14-06 Ocean Towers, Singapore 048620; tel. 62357150; fax 67358240; e-mail office@kazakhstan.org.sg; internet www.kazakhstan.org.sg; Ambassador Yerlan Baudarbek-Kozhatayev.

Korea, Democratic People's Republic: 7500 Beach Rd, 09-320 The Plaza, Singapore 199591; tel. 64403498; fax 63482026; e-mail embdprk@singnet.com.sg; Ambassador Jong Song Il.

Korea, Republic: 47 Scotts Rd, 08-00 Goldbell Towers, Singapore 228233; tel. 62561188; fax 62543191; e-mail info@koreaembassy.org.sg; internet sgp.mofat.go.kr; Ambassador Oh Joon.

Kuwait: c/o The Ritz-Carlton Millenia Singapore, 7 Raffles Ave, Suite 2109, Singapore 039799; tel. 68847401; fax 64345387; e-mail embassy@kuwait.org.sg; internet www.kuwait.org.sg; Ambassador Abd al-Aziz Ahmed S. al-Adwani.

Laos: 51 Newton Rd, 13-04/05 Goldhill Plaza, Singapore 308900; tel. 62506044; fax 62506014; e-mail laoembsg@singnet.com.sg; Ambassador Viengsavanh Sipraseuth.

Malaysia: 301 Jervois Rd, Singapore 249077; tel. 62350111; fax 67336135; e-mail mwspore@singnet.com.sg; internet www.kln.gov.my/perwakilan/singapore; High Commissioner Dato' Mohammed Hussin Nayan.

Maldives: 101 Thomson Rd, 30-01A United Sq., Singapore 307591; tel. 67209012; fax 67209014; e-mail info@maldiveshighcommission.sg; High Commissioner Mohamed Khaleel.

Mexico: 152 Beach Rd, 06-07 Gateway East Tower, Singapore 189721; tel. 62982678; fax 62933484; e-mail embamexsing@embamexsing.org.sg; internet portal.sre.gob.mx/singapur; Ambassador Alejandro Pescador Castañeda.

Mongolia: 600 North Bridge Rd, 24-08 Parkview Sq., Singapore 188778; tel. 63480745; fax 63481753; e-mail singapore@mfat.gov.mn; internet www.singapore.mfat.gov.mn; Ambassador Banzragchiin Delgermaa.

Myanmar: 15 St Martin's Dr., Singapore 257996; tel. 67350209; fax 67356236; e-mail ambassador@mesingapore.org.sg; internet www.mesingapore.org.sg; Ambassador Tin Oo Lwin.

Netherlands: 541 Orchard Rd, 13-01 Liat Towers, Singapore 238881; tel. 67371155; fax 67371940; e-mail sin@minbuza.nl; internet www.mfa.nl/sin; Ambassador Johannes W. Gunivortus Jansing.

New Zealand: 391 Orchard Rd, Tower A, 15-06/10 Ngee Ann City, Singapore 238873; tel. 62359966; fax 67339924; e-mail enquiries@nz-high-com.org.sg; internet www.nzembassy.com/singapore; High Commissioner Bernadette Cavanagh (designate).

Nigeria: 143 Cecil St, 15-01 GB Bldg, Singapore 069542; tel. 67321743; fax 67321742; e-mail nigerhighcommission@yahoo.com.sg; internet www.nigeriahcsinga.org.sg; High Commissioner Duru Rajis Benedicta Nonyelum.

Norway: 16 Raffles Quay, 44-01 Hong Leong Bldg, Singapore 048581; tel. 62207122; fax 62202191; e-mail emb.singapore@mfa.no; internet www.norway.org.sg; Ambassador Tormod Cappelen Endresen.

Pakistan: 1 Scotts Rd, 24-02/04 Shaw Centre, Singapore 228208; tel. 67376988; fax 67374096; e-mail secyhc@pakhicom.org.sg; internet www.parep.org.sg; High Commissioner Syed Hasan Javed.

Panama: 16 Raffles Quay, 41-06 Hong Leong Bldg, Singapore 048581; tel. 62218677; fax 62240892; e-mail general@panamaemb.org.sg; internet www.panamaemb.org.sg; Ambassador José Antonio Ruiz Blanco.

Peru: 390 Orchard Rd, 12-03 Palais Renaissance, Singapore 238871; tel. 67388595; fax 67388601; e-mail embperu@pacific.net.sg; internet www.embassyperu.org.sg; Ambassador Armando Raúl Patiño Alvistur.

Philippines: 20 Nassim Rd, Singapore 258395; tel. 67373977; fax 67339544; e-mail php@pacific.net.sg; internet www.philippine-embassy.org.sg; Ambassador Minda Cruz.

Poland: 435 Orchard Rd, 17-02/03 Wisma Atria, Singapore 238877; tel. 62359478; fax 62359479; e-mail secretary@pacific.net.sg; internet www.singapore.polemb.net; Ambassador Waldemar Dubaniowski.

Qatar: 8 Temasek Blvd, 41-02 Suntec Tower 3, Singapore 038988; tel. 65939900; fax 68365731; Ambassador Rashid bin Ali Hassan al-Khater.

Romania: 1 Claymore Dr., Singapore 229594; tel. 67355023; fax 67355021; e-mail comofrom@starhub.net.sg; Chargé d'affaires Alexandru Irimia.

Russia: 51 Nassim Rd, Singapore 258439; tel. 62351834; fax 67334780; e-mail mail@russia.org.sg; internet www.russia.org.sg; Ambassador Leonid Moiseev.

Rwanda: 8 Temasek Blvd, 14-03 Suntec Tower 3, Singapore 038988; tel. 68844621; fax 68844206; e-mail info@rwandaembassy.org.sg; internet www.rwandaembassy.org.sg; High Commissioner Jeanine Kambanda.

Saudi Arabia: 163 Penang Rd, 03-02/03 Winsland House 2, Singapore 238463; tel. 67345878; fax 67385291; e-mail enquiries@saudiembassy.org.sg; Ambassador Mansour Mohammad al-Mazmoumi.

South Africa: 331 North Bridge Rd, 15-01/06 Odeon Towers, Singapore 188720; tel. 63393319; fax 63396658; e-mail hom@southafricahc.org.sg; internet www.southafricahc.org.sg; High Commissioner Andries Francois Van Straten.

Spain: 7 Temasek Blvd, 39-00 Suntec City Tower 1, Singapore 038987; tel. 67259220; fax 63333025; e-mail emb.singapur@maec.es; internet www.maec.es/Subwebs/Embajadas/singapur; Ambassador Federico Palomera Guez.

Sri Lanka: 13-07/12 Goldhill Plaza, 51 Newton Rd, Singapore 308900; tel. 62544595; fax 62507201; e-mail slhcs@lanka.com.sg; internet www.lanka.com.sg; High Commissioner Ferial Ismail Ashraff.

Sweden: 111 Somerset Rd, 05-01 Singapore Power Bldg, Singapore 238164; tel. 64159720; fax 64159747; e-mail ambassaden.singapore@foreign.ministry.se; internet www.swedenabroad.com/singapore; Ambassador Bengt Ingemar Dolfe.

Switzerland: 1 Swiss Club Link, Singapore 288162; tel. 64685788; fax 64668245; e-mail sin.vertretung@eda.admin.ch; internet www.eda.admin.ch/singapore; Ambassador Thomas Kupfer.

Thailand: 370 Orchard Rd, Singapore 238870; tel. 67372158; fax 67320778; e-mail consular@thaiembassy.sg; internet www.thaiembassy.sg; Ambassador Marut Jitpatima.

Turkey: Shenton Way, 10-03 SGX Centre Tower 1, Singapore 068804; tel. 65333390; fax 65333360; e-mail turksin@signet.com.sg; internet singapur.be.mfa.gov.tr; Ambassador H. Taner Seben.

Ukraine: 50 Raffles Pl., 16-05 Singapore Land Tower, Singapore 048623; tel. 65356550; fax 65352116; e-mail emb_sg@mfa.gov.ua; internet www.mfa.gov.ua/singapore; Ambassador Pavlo Sultansky.

United Arab Emirates: 600 North Bridge Rd, 09-01 Parkview Sq., Singapore 188778; tel. 62388206; fax 62380081; e-mail emarat@ singnet.com.sg; internet www.uaeembassy-sg.com; Ambassador Mohammed Ahmed Hamil al-Qubaisi.

United Kingdom: 100 Tanglin Rd, Singapore 247919; tel. 64244200; fax 64244218; e-mail consular.singapore@fco.gov.uk; internet www.ukinsingapore.fco.gov.uk; High Commissioner Antony Phillipson.

USA: 27 Napier Rd, Singapore 258508; tel. 64769100; fax 64769340; e-mail singaporeusembassy@state.gov; internet singapore .usembassy.gov; Ambassador David Adelman.

Uzbekistan: 20 Kramat Lane, 04-01/02 United House, Singapore 228773; tel. 67343943; fax 67345849; e-mail info@uzbekistan.org.sg; internet www.uzbekistan.org.sg; Ambassador Alisher A. Kurmanov.

Venezuela: 3 Killiney Rd, 07-03 Winsland House 1, Singapore 239519; tel. 64911172; fax 62353167; e-mail embassy@embavenez .org.sg; Ambassador Alfredo Toro Hardy.

Viet Nam: 10 Leedon Park, Singapore 267887; tel. 64625938; fax 64625936; e-mail vnemb@singnet.com.sg; internet www .vietnamembassy-singapore.org; Ambassador Tran Hai Hau.

Judicial System

The judicial power of Singapore is vested in the Supreme Court and in the Subordinate Courts. The judiciary administers the law with complete independence from the executive and legislative branches of the Government; this independence is safeguarded by the Constitution. The Supreme Court consists of the High Court and the Court of Appeal. The Chief Justice is appointed by the President if the latter, acting at his discretion, concurs with the advice of the Prime Minister. The other judges of the Supreme Court are appointed in the same way, in consultation with the Chief Justice. Under a 1979 constitutional amendment, the position of judicial commissioner of the Supreme Court was created 'to facilitate the disposal of business in the Supreme Court'. A judicial commissioner has the powers and functions of a judge, and is appointed for such period as the President thinks fit.

The Subordinate Courts consist of District Courts and Magistrates' Courts. In addition, there are also specialized courts such as the Coroner's Court, Family Court, Juvenile Court, Mentions Court, Night Court, Sentencing Courts and Filter Courts. The Primary Dispute Resolution Centre and the Small Claims Tribunals are also managed by the Subordinate Courts. The Subordinate Courts have also established the Multi-Door Courthouse, which serves as a one-stop centre for the screening and channelling of any cases to the most appropriate forum for dispute resolution.

District Courts and Magistrates' Courts have original criminal and civil jurisdiction. District Courts try offences for which the maximum penalty does not exceed 10 years of imprisonment and in civil cases where the amount claimed does not exceed S \$250,000. Magistrates' Courts try offences for which the maximum term of imprisonment does not exceed three years. The jurisdiction of Magistrates' Courts in civil cases is limited to claims not exceeding S \$60,000. The Coroners' Court conducts inquests. The Small Claims Tribunal has jurisdiction over claims relating to a dispute arising from any contract for the sale of goods or the provision of services and any claim in tort in respect of damage caused to any property involving an amount that does not exceed S \$10,000. The Juvenile Court deals with offences committed by young persons aged under 16 years.

The High Court has unlimited original jurisdiction in criminal and civil cases. In its appellate jurisdiction it hears criminal and civil appeals from the District Courts and Magistrates' Courts. The Court of Appeal, which is the final appellate court, hears appeals against the decisions of the High Court in both criminal and civil matters. In criminal matters, the Court of Appeal hears appeals against decisions made by the High Court in the exercise of its original criminal jurisdiction. In civil matters, the Court of Appeal hears appeals against decisions made by the High Court in the exercise of both its original and appellate jurisdiction.

Supreme Court: 1 Supreme Court Lane, Singapore 178879; tel. 63360644; fax 63379450; e-mail supcourt_qsm@supcourt.gov.sg; internet www.supcourt.gov.sg; Chief Justice Sundaresh Menon.

Attorney-General's Chambers: 1 Upper Pickering St, Singapore 058288; tel. 63361411; fax 63325984; e-mail agc@agc.gov.sg; internet www.agc.gov.sg; Attorney-General Steven Chong.

Religion

According to the 2010 census, 57.4% of ethnic Chinese, who constituted 74% of the population, professed either Buddhism or Daoism (including followers of Confucius, Mencius and Lao Zi) and 20.1% of Chinese adhered to Christianity. Malays, who made up 13.3% of the population, were 98.7% Muslim. Among Indians, who constituted 9.2% of the population, 58.9% were Hindus, 21.7% Muslims, 12.8% Christians and 5.7% Sikhs, Jains or adherents of other faiths. There are small communities of Zoroastrians and Jews. Freedom of worship is guaranteed by the Constitution.

BAHÁ'Í FAITH

The Spiritual Assembly of the Bahá'ís of Singapore: 55 Cantonment Rd, Singapore 089754; tel. 62226200; fax 62229166; e-mail webmaster@bahai.org.sg; internet www.bahai.org.sg.

BUDDHISM

Buddhist Union: 28 Jalan Senyum, Singapore 418152; tel. 62419419; fax 64443280; e-mail thebu@singnet.com.sg.

Singapore Buddhist Federation: 59 Lorong 24A, Geylang, Singapore 398583; tel. 67444635; fax 67473618; e-mail buddhist@ singnet.com.sg; internet www.buddhist.org.sg; f. 1948; Pres. Kwang Sheng.

Singapore Buddhist Sangha Organization: 88 Bright Hill Drive, Singapore 579644.

CHRISTIANITY

National Council of Churches of Singapore: 1 Coleman St, B1-27 The Adelphi, Singapore 179803; tel. 63368177; fax 63368178; e-mail admin@nccs.org.sg; internet www.nccs.org.sg; f. 1948; Pres. Bishop Terry Kee; Gen. Sec. Lim K. Tham.

Singapore Council of Christian Churches (SCCC): Singapore; f. 1956.

The Anglican Communion

The Anglican diocese of Singapore (also including Indonesia, Laos, Thailand, Viet Nam and Cambodia) is part of the Province of the Anglican Church in South-East Asia.

Bishop of Singapore: The Rt Rev. Dr John Hiang Chea Chew, 01-01, St Andrew's Vill., 1 Francis Thomas Dr., Singapore 359340; tel. 62888944; fax 62885538; e-mail bpoffice@anglican.org.sg; internet www.anglican.org.sg.

Orthodox Churches

The Orthodox Syrian Church and the Mar Thoma Syrian Church are both active in Singapore.

The Roman Catholic Church

Singapore comprises a single archdiocese, directly responsible to the Holy See. In December 2007 there were an estimated 177,775 adherents in the country, representing 3.9% of the total population.

Archbishop of Singapore: Most Rev. Nicholas Chia, Archbishop's House, 31 Victoria St, Singapore 187997; tel. 63378818; fax 63334735; e-mail nc@catholic.org.sg; internet www.veritas.org.sg.

Other Christian Churches

Brethren Assemblies: Bethesda Hall (Ang Mo Kio), 601 Ang Mo Kio Ave 4, Singapore 569898; tel. 64587474; fax 64566771; e-mail bethesdahall@gmail.com; internet www.bethesdahall.com; f. 1864; Hon. Sec. Wong Tuck Keong.

Evangelical Fellowship of Singapore (EFOS): 06-03 Morning-star Centre, 12 New Industrial Rd, Singapore 536202; e-mail tonyyeo@gdop.sg; internet www.efosingapore.org; f. 1980; Chair. Dr Lawrence Chia.

Lutheran Church in Singapore: 28-30 Duke's Rd, Singapore 268912; tel. 64646337; fax 64646323; e-mail lutheran@lutheran .org.sg; internet www.lutheran.org.sg.

Methodist Church in Singapore: 70 Barker Rd, Singapore 309936; tel. 64784784; fax 64784794; e-mail mcs@methodist.org .sg; internet www.methodist.org.sg; f. 1885; 39,000 mems (July 2011); Leader Bishop Dr Robert Solomon.

Presbyterian Church: 3 Orchard Rd, cnr Penang Rd, Singapore 238825; tel. 63376681; fax 63391979; e-mail orpcenglish@orpc .org.sg; internet www.orpc.org.sg; f. 1856; services in English, Chinese (Mandarin), Indonesian and German; 2,000 mems; Moderator Rev. Graham Ng.

Singapore Baptist Convention: 1023 Upper Serangoon Rd, 04-01 Baptist Centre, Singapore 534761; tel. 62538004; fax

62538214; e-mail info@baptistconvention.org.sg; internet www
.baptistconvention.org.sg; f. 1974; Chair. Rev. EDWIN LAM; Exec. Dir
PETER TANG.

Other denominations active in Singapore include the Lutheran
Church and the Evangelical Lutheran Church.

HINDUISM

Hindu Advisory Board: c/o 397 Serangoon Rd, Singapore 218123;
tel. 62963469; fax 62929766; e-mail heb@pacific.net.sg; f. 1985;
Chair. R. BAJAWEE; Sec. S. RAMESH.

Hindu Endowments Board: 397 Serangoon Rd, Singapore
218123; tel. 62963469; fax 62929766; e-mail heb@pacific.net.sg;
internet www.heb.gov.sg; f. 1968; Chair. S. RAJENDRAN; Sec. P.
AVADIAR.

ISLAM

Majlis Ugama Islam Singapura (MUIS) (Islamic Religious Council of Singapore): Singapore Islamic Hub, 273 Braddell Rd, Singapore
579702; tel. 63591199; fax 62537572; e-mail info@muis.gov.sg;
internet www.muis.gov.sg; f. 1968; Pres. Haji MOHD ALAMI MUSA;
Sec. ABDUL RAZAK MARICAR.

Muslim Missionary Society Singapore (JAMIYAH): 31 Lorong,
12 Geylang Rd, Singapore 399006; tel. 67431211; fax 67450610;
e-mail info@jamiyah.org.sg; internet www.jamiyah.org.sg; Pres. Dr
MOHD HASBI ABU BAKAR; Sec.-Gen. KHALID HASSAN.

SIKHISM

Central Sikh Gurdwara Board (CSGB): c/o 2 Towner Rd, 03-01,
Singapore 327804; tel. 62993855; e-mail csgb@sikhs.org.sg; internet
www.sikhs.org.sg; Pres. KARPAL SINGH MEHLI.

The Press

DAILIES

English Language

The Business Times: 1000 Toa Payoh North, Podium Blk, Level 3,
Singapore 318994; tel. 63195318; fax 63198277; e-mail btocs@sph
.com.sg; internet www.businesstimes.com.sg; f. 1976; morning;
Editor ALVIN TAY; circ. 34,368.

The New Paper: 1000 Toa Payoh North, Annexe Blk, Level 6,
Singapore 318994; tel. 63196319; fax 63198266; e-mail tnp@sph.com
.sg; internet www.tnp.sg; f. 1988; afternoon tabloid; Editor DOMINIC
NATHAN; circ. 102,616.

The Straits Times: 1000 Toa Payoh North, Singapore 318994; tel.
63195397; fax 67320131; e-mail stonline@sph.com.sg; internet www
.straitstimes.com; f. 1845; morning; Editor-in-Chief PATRICK DANIEL;
circ. 359,989.

Today: Caldecott Broadcast Centre, Andrew Rd, Singapore 299939;
tel. 63333888; fax 65344217; e-mail news@newstoday.com.sg;
internet www.todayonline.com; f. 2000; merged with *Streats*, a rival
free morning tabloid, in 2004; Editor WALTER FERNANDEZ; circ.
584,000.

Chinese Language

Lianhe Wanbao: 1000 Toa Payoh North, Podium Blk, Level 4,
Singapore 318994; tel. 63196319; fax 63198133; e-mail wanbao@sph
.com.sg; f. 1983; evening; Editor CHUA CHIM KANG; circ. 110,000.

Lianhe Zaobao: 1000 Toa Payoh North, Podium Blk, Level 4,
Singapore 318994; tel. 63196319; fax 63198228; e-mail zaobao@
web1.asia1.com.sg; internet www.zaobao.com; f. 1923; Editor LIM
JIM KOON; circ. 169,420.

My Paper: 1000 Toa Payoh North, News Centre, Singapore 318994;
tel. 63192222; fax 63198115; e-mail mypaper@sph.com.sg; internet
www.mypaper.sg; f. 2006; free tabloid aimed at bilingual working
adults aged between 20 and 40 yrs; Editor APRIL PUNG KOON KING;
circ. 250,000.

Shin Min Daily News (S) Ltd: 1000 Toa Payoh North, Podium Blk,
Level 4, Singapore 318994; tel. 63196319; fax 63198166; e-mail
shinmin@sph.com.sg; f. 1967; evening; Editor PAN CHENG LUI; circ.
136,127.

Malay Language

Berita Harian: 1000 Toa Payoh North, Annexe Blk, Level 3,
Singapore 318994; tel. 63195137; fax 63198255; e-mail aadeska@
sph.com.sg; internet cyberita.asia1.com.sg; f. 1957; morning; Editor
MOHD GUNTOR SADALI; circ. 59,193.

Tamil Language

Tamil Murasu: SPH Media Centre, 82 Genting Lane 06-07, Singapore 349567; tel. 63196319; fax 63194001; e-mail murasu4@
cyberway.com.sg; internet www.tamilmurasu.com.sg; f. 1935; Editor
NIRMALA MURUGAIAN; circ. 13,766.

WEEKLIES

English Language

The Edge Singapore: 150 Cecil St 13-00, Singapore 069543; tel.
62328622; fax 62328620; e-mail theedgespore@bizedge.com; internet
www.theedgesingapore.com; business and investment; Editor BEN
PAUL; circ. 17,870.

The New Paper on Sunday: 1000 Toa Payoh North, Annexe Blk,
Level 6, Singapore 318994; tel. 63196319; fax 63198266; e-mail tnp@
sph.com.sg; internet www.tnp.sg; f. 1999; tabloid; Editor DOMINIC
NATHAN; circ. 125,107.

The Sunday Times: 1000 Toa Payoh North, Singapore 318994; tel.
63195397; fax 67320131; e-mail stonline@sph.com.sg; internet www
.straitstimes.com; f. 1931; Editor IGNATIUS LOW; circ. 372,809
(Singapore only).

Weekend Today: Caldecott Broadcast Centre, Andrew Rd, Singapore 299939; tel. 63333888; fax 65344217; e-mail today@mediacorp
.com.sg; internet www.todayonline.com; f. 2002; Editor P. N. BALJI;
circ. 150,000.

Chinese Language

Thumbs Up: 1000 Toa Payoh North, Annexe Blk, Level 5, Singapore
318994; tel. 63196319; fax 63198111; e-mail thumbsup@sph.com.sg;
f. 2000; newspaper aimed at primary school students; Editor LIM
SOON LAN; circ. 37,445.

Malay Language

Berita Minggu: 1000 Toa Payoh North, Annex Blk, Level 3,
Singapore 318994; tel. 63195665; fax 63198255; e-mail aadeska@
sph.com.sg; internet cyberita.asia1.com.sg; f. 1960; Sun.; Editor
ISMAIL PANTEK; circ. 65,608 (Singapore only).

SELECTED PERIODICALS

English Language

8 Days: 10 Ang Mo Kio St 65, 01-06/08 Techpoint, Singapore 569059;
tel. 62789822; fax 62724800; e-mail feedback@8daysonline.com;
internet www.8days.sg; f. 1990; weekly; Editor-in-Chief LAU KUAN
WEI; circ. 113,258.

Female: SPH Media Centre, 82 Genting Lane, Level 7, Singapore
349567; tel. 63196319; fax 63196345; e-mail magfemale@sph.com.sg;
internet www.femalemag.com.sg; f. 1974; monthly; circ. 60,000.

FHM Singapore: Caldecott Broadcast Centre, Andrew Rd, Singapore 299939; tel. 63333888; e-mail info@fhm.com.sg; internet www
.fhm.com.sg; Deputy Editor DENNIS YIN.

Her World: SPH Media Centre, 82 Genting Lane, Singapore 349567;
tel. 63196319; fax 63196345; e-mail magherworld@sph.com.sg;
internet www.herworldplus.com; f. 1960; monthly; women's; Editor
DENYSE YEO.

Her World Brides: SPH Media Centre, 82 Genting Lane, Singapore
349567; tel. 63196319; fax 63196345; e-mail maghwbrides@sph.com
.sg; internet www.hwbrides.com.sg; f. 1998; quarterly; circ. 13,193.

Home and Decor: SPH Media Centre, 82 Genting Lane, 5th Floor,
Singapore 349567; tel. 63196319; fax 63196345; e-mail hdecor@sph
.com.sg; internet www.homeanddecor.com.sg; f. 1987; 6 a year;
Editor SOPHIE KHO; circ. 27,000.

NSman: SAFRA National Service Association, 5200 Jalan Bukit
Merah, Singapore 159468; tel. 63779835; fax 63779898; e-mail hq@
safra.sg; internet www.safra.sg; f. 1972; est. as *Reservist*; renamed
1994; bi-monthly; publ. of SAFRA Nat. Service Asscn; Gen. Sec. TAN
KOK YAM; circ. 150,000.

Pioneer: 5 Depot Rd, 05-06 Defence Technology Tower B, Singapore
109681; tel. 63731114; fax 63731111; e-mail pioneer@starnet.gov.sg;
internet www.mindef.gov.sg/imindef/publications/cyberpioneer/
index.html; f. 1996; monthly; publication of the Singaporean Armed
Forces.

Republic of Singapore Government Gazette: Toppan Leefung
Pte Ltd, 1 Kim Seng Promenade, 18-01 Great World City East Tower,
Singapore 237994; tel. 68269600; fax 68203341; e-mail egazinfo@
toppanleefung.com; internet www.egazette.com.sg; weekdays.

SimplyHer: SPH Media Centre, 82 Genting Lane, Level 7, Singapore 349567; tel. 63196319; fax 63196345; e-mail magsimplyher@sph
.com.sg; internet www.simplyher.com.sg; f. 2004; monthly; women's;
Editor PENELOPE CHAN; circ. 21,000.

Singapore Medical Journal: Singapore Medical Asscn, Level 2,
Alumni Medical Centre, 2 College Rd, Singapore 169850; tel.

62231264; fax 62247827; e-mail smj@sma.org.sg; internet www.sma .org.sg/publications/smjcurrentissue.aspx; f. 1959; monthly; Editor Prof. TEO ENG KIONG; circ. 5,000.

Torque: SPH Media Centre, 82 Genting Lane, Level 7, Singapore 349567; tel. 63196319; fax 63196345; e-mail seowlka@sph.com.sg; internet www.torque.com.sg; f. 1990; monthly; automobile; Editor LEE NIAN TJOE.

Young Parents: SPH Media Centre, 82 Genting Lane, Level 7, Singapore 349567; tel. 63196319; fax 63196345; e-mail magyoungparents@sph.com.sg; internet www.youngparents.com .sg; f. 1987; monthly; family; Editor STEPHANIE YEO; circ. 20,000.

Chinese Language

Characters: 1 Kallang Sector, 04-04/05 Kolam Ayer Industrial Park, Singapore 349276; tel. 67458733; fax 67458213; f. 1987; monthly; television and entertainment; Editor SAM NG; circ. 45,000.

The Citizen: People's Association, 9 Stadium Link, Singapore 397750; tel. 63405138; fax 63468657; monthly; English, Chinese, Tamil and Malay; Man. Editor OOI HUI MEI.

Icon: SPH Media Centre, 82 Genting Lane, Level 7, Singapore 349567; tel. 63196319; fax 63196345; e-mail magicon@sph.com.sg; internet www.iconsingapore.com; f. 2005; monthly; Chinese language; lifestyle; Man. Editor ELSIE YAH.

i-weekly: Caldecott Broadcast Centre, Andriew Rd, Singapore 299939; tel. 63333888; fax 62549447; e-mail i-weekly@mediacorp .com.sg; f. 1981; weekly; lifestyle and entertainment; Editor-in-Chief JACKIE LIU; circ. 125,000.

NuYou: SPH Media Centre, 82 Genting Lane, Level 7, Singapore 349567; tel. 63196319; fax 63196345; internet www.nuyou.com.sg; f. 1976; monthly; Editor-in-Chief GRACE LEE.

Punters' Way: 4 Ubi View (off Ubi Rd 3), Pioneers and Leaders Centre, Singapore 408557; tel. 67458733; fax 67458321; e-mail pnlhldg@pnl-group.com; internet www.pnl-group.com; f. 1977; bi-weekly; English and Chinese; horse racing; Editor T. S. PHAN; circ. 90,000.

Racing Guide: 1 Scotts Rd, 26-03 Shaw Centre, Singapore 228208; tel. 67340111; e-mail inquiries@asiapacificpublishing.com; internet www.racingguide.com.sg; f. 1987; 2 a week; English and Chinese; sport; Editorial Consultant BENNY ORTEGA; Chinese Editor KUEK CHIEW TEONG; circ. 20,000.

Singapore Literature: Singapore Literature Society, 122B Sims Ave, Singapore 1438; quarterly; Pres. YAP KOON CHAN; Editor LUO-MING.

UW (U-Weekly): Focus Publishing Ltd,1000 Toa Payoh North, News Centre, Singapore 318994; tel. 63196319; fax 63198124; e-mail youmail@sph.com.sg; f. 2001 as You Weekly; renamed as above 2005; weekly; entertainment and lifestyle; circ. 80,000.

Young Generation: 1 New Industrial Rd, Times Centre, Singapore 536196; tel. 62139276; fax 62811327; e-mail kelenkoh@sg .marshallcavendish.com; internet www.marshallcavendish.com; monthly; children's; Asst Man. Editor SHIRLEY CHIA; circ. 100,000.

Malay Language

Manja: 10 Ang Mo Kio St 65, 01-06/08 Techpoint, Singapore 569059; tel. 64837118; fax 64812098; e-mail hello@manja.sg; f. 2000; monthly; entertainment and lifestyle; Editor RUSLINA AFFENDY.

NEWS AGENCIES

Foreign Bureaux

Various foreign bureaux operate in Singapore.

Publishers

ENGLISH LANGUAGE

Butterworths Asia: 3 Killiney Rd, 08-08 Winsland House 1, Singapore 239519; tel. 67331380; fax 67331175; e-mail help.sg@ lexisnexis.com; internet www.lexisnexis.com.sg/ butterworths-online; f. 1932; law texts and journals; Gen. Man. DEAN CORKERY.

Caldecott Publishing Pte Ltd: 10 Ang Mo Kio St 65, 01-06/08 Techpoint, Singapore 569059; tel. 64837118; fax 64837286; f. 1990; Editorial Dir MICHAEL CHIANG; Group Editor TAN LEE SUN.

FEP International Pte Ltd: 3A Phillips Ave, Singapore 546921; tel. 62814185; fax 67375561; f. 1960; textbooks, reference, children's and dictionaries; Gen. Man. RICHARD TOH.

Flame of the Forest Publishing Pte Ltd: Blk 5, Ang Mo Kio Industrial Park 2A, 07-22/23, AMK Tech II, Singapore 567760; tel. 64848887; fax 64842208; e-mail mail@flameoftheforest.com; internet www.flameoftheforest.com; f. 1989; Man. Dir ALEX CHACKO.

Graham Brash Pte Ltd: 45 Kian Teck Drive, Blk 1, Level 2, Singapore 628859; tel. 62624843; fax 62621519; e-mail evelyn@ grahambrash.com.sg; internet www.grahambrash.com.sg; f. 1947; general, academic, educational; English, Chinese and Malay; Publr and Man. Dir CHUAN I. CAMPBELL; Gen. Man. EVELYN LEE.

Institute of Southeast Asian Studies: 30 Heng Mui Keng Terrace, Pasir Panjang Rd, Singapore 119614; tel. 67780955; fax 67756259; e-mail pubsunit@iseas.edu.sg; internet www.iseas.edu .sg; f. 1968; scholarly works on contemporary South-East Asia and the Asia-Pacific region; Chair. Prof. WANG GUNGWU; Dir K. KESAVAPANY.

Intellectual Publishing Co: 113 Eunos Ave 3, 04-08 Gordon Industrial Bldg, Singapore 1440; tel. 67466025; fax 67489108; f. 1971; Man. POH BE LECK.

Marshall Cavendish International (Singapore) Pte Ltd: Times Centre, 1 New Industrial Rd, Singapore 536196; tel. 62139300; fax 62889254; e-mail timesales@sg.marshallcavendish.com; internet www.marshallcavendish.com/education; f. 1957; fmrly Times Media Pte Ltd; academic texts; Group Publr SHANE ARMSTRONG; Publr DURIYA AZIZ.

NUS Press (Pte) Ltd: National University of Singapore, 3 Arts Link, AS3-01/02, Singapore 117569; tel. 67761148; fax 67740652; e-mail nusbooks@nus.edu.sg; internet www.nus.edu.sg/nuspress; f. 1971; scholarly; Man. Dir PETER SCHOPPERT.

Pearson Education South Asia Pte Ltd: 23–25 First Lok Yang Rd, Jurong Town, Singapore 629733; tel. 63199388; fax 62651033; e-mail info@pearsoned.com.sg; internet www.pearsonlongman.com .sg; educational; Dir, Business Support, South Asia RASMIATI HARTANTO.

Stamford Media International Pte Ltd: 209 Kallang Bahru, Singapore 339344; tel. 62947227; fax 62944396; e-mail info@ stamford.com.sg; internet www.stamford.com.sg; f. 1963 as Stamford College Publrs; renamed Stamford Press Pte Ltd in 1983; present name adopted 2001; general, educational and journals; Man. LAWRENCE THOMAS.

Times Publishing Ltd: Times Centre, 1 New Industrial Rd, Singapore 536196; tel. 62139288; fax 62131186; e-mail tpl@tpl.com .sg; internet www.tpl.com.sg; f. 1978; political, social and cultural books, general works on Asia; Chair. LIM KIM SAN; CEO GOH SIK NGEE.

World Scientific Publishing Co Pte Ltd: 5 Toh Tuck Link, Singapore 596224; tel. 64665775; fax 64677667; e-mail wspc@wspc .com.sg; internet www.worldscientific.com; f. 1981; academic and research texts and science journals; Chair. and Editor-in-Chief Prof. K. K. PHUA; Man. Dir DOREEN LIU.

MALAY LANGUAGE

Malaysia Press Sdn Bhd (Pustaka Melayu): Singapore; tel. 62933454; fax 62911858; f. 1962; textbooks and educational; Man. Dir ABU TALIB BIN ALLY.

Pustaka Nasional Pte Ltd: 548 Changi Rd, Singapore 419931; tel. 67454321; fax 67452417; e-mail enquiry@pustaka.com.sg; internet www.pustaka.com.sg; f. 1963; Arabic, English, Malay and Islamic religious books and CD-ROMs; Dir SYED ALI SEMAIT.

CHINESE LANGUAGE

Shanghai Book Co (Pte) Ltd: 231 Bain St, 02-73 Bras Basah Complex, Singapore 180231; tel. 63360144; fax 63360490; e-mail shanghaibook@pacific.net.sg; f. 1925; educational and general; Man. Dir MA JI LIN.

Shing Lee Publishers Pte Ltd: 120 Hillview Ave, 05-06/07 Kewalram Hillview, Singapore 669594; tel. 67601388; fax 67623247; e-mail info@shinglee.com.sg; internet www.shinglee .com.sg; f. 1935; educational and general; Man. PEH SOH NGOH.

Union Book Co (Pte) Ltd: 231 Bain St, 03-01 Bras Basah Complex, Singapore 180231; tel. 63380696; fax 63386306; e-mail youlian@ singnet.com.sg; internet www.unionbook.com.sg; f. 1952; general and reference; Gen. Man. MARGARET XIAOMIN.

TAMIL LANGUAGE

EVS Enterprises: 16 Cuff Rd, Singapore 209727; tel. 62915334; fax 62952105; f. 1967; children's books, religion and general; Man. E. V. SINGHAN.

GOVERNMENT PUBLISHING HOUSE

Toppan Leefung Pte Ltd: 1 Kim Seng Promenade, 18-01 Great World City East Tower, Singapore 237994; tel. 68269600; fax 68203341; e-mail enquiries@toppanleefung.com; internet www .toppanleefung.com; f. 1973; fmrly SNP Corpn Ltd; present name adopted following acquisition by Toppan Printing Co Ltd in 2008; printers and publrs; Pres. and CEO YEO CHEE TONG.

PUBLISHERS' ORGANIZATIONS

National Book Development Council of Singapore (NBDCS): 50 Geylang East Ave 1, Singapore 389777; tel. 68488290; fax 67429466; e-mail info@bookcouncil.sg; internet www.bookcouncil .sg; f. 1969; independent non-profit org.; promotes reading, writing and publishing; offers professional training programmes; Chair. Prof. SERENE WEE.

Singapore Book Publishers' Association: 20 Maxwell Rd, Singapore 440086; tel. 64089712; fax 63993699; e-mail info@ singaporebookpublishers.sg; internet www.singaporebook publishers.sg; 75 mems; Pres. TRIENA ONG.

Broadcasting and Communications

TELECOMMUNICATIONS

Infocomm Development Authority of Singapore (IDA): 10 Pasir Panjang Rd, 10-01 Mapletree Business City, Singapore 117438; tel. 62110888; fax 62112222; e-mail info@ida.gov.sg; internet www.ida.gov.sg; f. 1999 as result of merger of Nat. Computer Bd and Telecommunication Authority of Singapore; the national policy maker; regulator of telecommunications and promoter of information and communication technologies in Singapore; CEO RONNIE TAY.

MobileOne (M1): 10 International Business Park, Singapore 609928; tel. 68951111; fax 66551977; e-mail ir@m1.com.sg; internet www.m1.com.sg; f. 1997; Chair. TEO SOON HOE; CEO KAREN KOOI.

Netrust Pte Ltd: 70 Bendemeer Rd, 05-03, Luzerne, Singapore 339940; tel. 62121388; fax 62121366; e-mail infoline@netrust.net; internet www.netrust.net; f. 1997; the only licensed Certification Authority (CA) in Singapore, jtly formed by Nat. Computer Bd and Network for Electronic Transfers; verifies the identity of parties doing business or communicating in cyberspace through the issuing of electronic identification certificates, in order to enable govt orgs and private enterprises to conduct electronic transactions in a secure manner; CEO FOO JONG AI.

OpenNet: 152 Beach Rd, 31-05/08, Singapore 189721; tel. 65634273; internet www.opennet.com.sg; f. 2008; jt venture between Axia NetMedia, Singapore Telecommunications, Singapore Press Holdings and Singapore Power Telecommunications; internet services provider; Chair. TAN GEE PAW; CEO MARK BLAKE.

Singapore Technologies Telemedia: 51 Cuppage Rd, 09-01 Starhub Centre, Singapore 229469; tel. 67238777; fax 67207266; e-mail contactus@sttelemedia.com; internet www.sttelemedia.com; Pres. STEPHEN MILLER.

Singapore Telecommunications Ltd (SingTel): 19-00 Comcentre, 31 Exeter Rd, Singapore 239732; tel. 68383388; fax 67331350; e-mail newsroom@singtel.com; internet info.singtel .com; f. 1992; postal and telecommunications service operator and holding co for a number of subsidiaries, serving both the corporate and consumer markets; 61.79%-owned by Temasek Holdings (Pvt) Ltd (a govt holding co), 38.21% transferred to the private sector; Chair. SIMON ISRAEL; Group CEO CHUA SOCK KOONG.

StarHub Pte Ltd: 67 Ubi Ave 1, 05-01 StarHub Green, Singapore 408942; tel. 68255000; fax 67215000; e-mail corpcomms@starhub .com; internet www.starhub.com; f. 2000; telecommunications and internet services provider; consortium includes Singapore Technologies Telemedia Pte Ltd, Singapore Power Ltd, Nippon Telegraph and Telephone Corpn (NTT) and British Telecom; CEO NEIL MONTEFIORE.

BROADCASTING

Broadcasting in Singapore was largely state-controlled until liberalization of the sector in the 1990s. A transition from analogue to digital Television was scheduled for completion between 2015 and 2020.

Regulatory Authority

Media Development Authority (MDA): 3 Fusionopolis Way, 16-22 Symbiosis, Singapore 138633; tel. 63773800; fax 65773888; internet www.mda.gov.sg; f. 1994; fmrly Singapore Broadcasting Authority; present name adopted 2003; licenses, regulates and promotes the devt of the media industry in Singapore; ensures the provision of an adequate range of media services to serve the interests of the general public, maintains fair and efficient market conduct and effective competition in the media industry, ensures the maintenance of a high standard of media services, regulates public service broadcasting; Chair. NIAM CHIANG MENG; CEO AUBECK KAM.

Radio

Far East Broadcasting Associates (FEBA Ltd): 30 Lorong Ampas, 07-01 Skywaves Industrial Bldg, Singapore 328783; tel.

62508577; fax 62508422; e-mail febadmin@febaltd.com; internet www.febaltd.com; f. 1960; Chair. GOH EWE KHENG; Exec. Dir LEE CHI KWAN (acting).

Media Corporation of Singapore: Caldecott Broadcast Centre, Andrew Rd, Singapore 299939; tel. 63333888; fax 62515628; e-mail tellmediacorp@mediacorp.com.sg; internet www.mediacorp.sg; f. 1994; est. as Singapore Int. Media (SIM), following corporatization of Singapore Broadcasting Corpn; 14 radio channels, broadcasting mainly in English and Chinese; 9 television channels, broadcasting in English, Chinese, Malaya and Tamil; Chair. TEO MING KAN; CEO SHAUN SEOW.

Radio Corpn of Singapore Pte Ltd (RCS): Caldecott Broadcast Centre, Radio Bldg, Andrew Rd, Singapore 299939; tel. 63597307; fax 63597500; e-mail tellmediacorp@mediacorp.com.sg; internet www.mediacorpradio.sg; f. 1936; subsidiary of MediaCorp; operates 13 domestic services—incl. in English (six), Mandarin (three), Malay (two) and Tamil (one)—and three international radio stations (manages Radio Singapore International (RSI)—services in English, Mandarin and Malay for three hours daily and service in Bahasa Indonesia for one hour daily); Man. Dir LEO GOH.

SAFRA Radio: Bukit Merah Central, POB 1315, Singapore 911599; tel. 63731924; fax 62783039; e-mail feedback@power98.com.sg; internet www.power98.com.sg; f. 1994; broadcasts in Mandarin and English.

SPH UnionWorks Pte Ltd: 1000 Toa Payoh North, News Centre, Podium Blk, Level 3, Singapore 318994; tel. 63191900; fax 63191099; e-mail margtan@sph.com.sg; internet www.sphuw.com.sg; f. 1991; fmrly Radio Heart and UnionWorks Pte Ltd; first private radio station; broadcasts in English and Mandarin; 3 channels covering news, music and entertainment; Chair. ZAINUL A. RASHEED.

Television

CNBC Asia Business News (S) Pte Ltd: 10 Anson Rd, 06-01 International Plaza, Singapore 079903; tel. 63230488; fax 62230020; e-mail contactus@cnbcasia.com; internet asia.cnbc.com; f. 1998; cable and satellite broadcaster of global business and financial news; US-controlled; broadcasts in English (24 hours daily) and Mandarin; Pres. and Man. Dir SATPAL BRAINCH.

Media Corporation of Singapore: see Radio.

SPH MediaWorks Ltd: 1000 Toa Payoh North, News Centre, Singapore 318994; tel. 63196319; fax 63198150; e-mail sphcorp@ sph.com.sg; internet www.sph.com.sg; f. 2000; subsidiary of Singapore Press Holdings Ltd (SPH); two channels—Channel U (Mandarin) and Channel i (English); also owns two radio stations; CEO ALAN CHAN HENG LOON.

Starhub CableVision Ltd: 51 Cuppage Rd, 01-02/03 Cuppage Centre, Singapore 229469; tel. 68255000; fax 67205000; internet www.starhub.com; f. 1992; fmrly Singapore CableVision Ltd; present name adopted 2002 following acquisition by Starhub Ltd; broadcasting and communications co, subscription television service; launched cable service in June 1995; offers 83 digital channels (March 2005); offers broadband access services; CEO NEIL MONTEFIORE.

Finance

(cap. = capital; res = reserves; dep. = deposits; m. = million; brs = branches; amounts in Singapore dollars)

BANKING

The Singapore monetary system is regulated by the Monetary Authority of Singapore (MAS) and the Ministry of Finance. The MAS performs all the functions of a central bank and also assumed responsibility for the issuing of currency following its merger with the Board of Commissioners of Currency in October 2002. In September 2012 there were 122 commercial banks (six local, 116 foreign) and 38 representative offices in Singapore. Of the foreign banks, 26 had full licences, 53 had wholesale licences and 37 had 'offshore' banking licences.

Government Financial Institution

Monetary Authority of Singapore (MAS): 10 Shenton Way, MAS Bldg, Singapore 079117; tel. 62255577; fax 62299229; e-mail webmaster@mas.gov.sg; internet www.mas.gov.sg; merged with Board of Commissioners of Currency Oct. 2002; cap. 17,000.0m., res 18,321.3m., dep. 139,498.4m. (March 2010); Chair. THARMAN SHANMUGARATNAM; Man. Dir RAVI MENON.

Domestic Full Commercial Banks

Bank of Singapore: 63 Market St, 22-00 Bank of Singapore Centre, Singapore 048942; tel. 65598000; fax 65598180; internet www .bankofsingapore.com; cap. US $596.3m., dep. US $5,742.2m. (Dec.

2010); subsidiary of Oversea-Chinese Banking Corpn Ltd; fmrly ING Asia Private Bank Ltd; CEO Renato de Guzman.

DBS Bank (Development Bank of Singapore Ltd): 12 Marina Blvd, Marina Bay Financial Centre Tower 3, Singapore 018982; tel. 68788888; fax 64451267; e-mail dbs@dbs.com; internet www.dbs.com/sg; f. 1968; merged with Post Office Savings Bank in 1998; 29% govt-owned; cap. 16,196m., res 2,718m., dep. 263,695m. (Dec. 2011); Chair. Peter Seah Lim Huat; CEO Piyush Gupta; 107 local brs, 9 overseas brs.

Far Eastern Bank Ltd: 80 Raffles Pl., UOB Plaza, Singapore 048624; tel. 62219055; fax 62242263; internet www.uobgroup.com; f. 1959; subsidiary of United Overseas Bank Ltd; cap. 100m., res 81.4m., dep. 797.1m. (Dec. 2011); Chair. Wee Cho Yaw; CEO Wee Ee Cheong; 3 brs.

Oversea-Chinese Banking Corpn Ltd (OCBC): 65 Chulia St, 09-00 OCBC Centre, Singapore 049513; tel. 65357222; fax 65337955; e-mail info@ocbc.com.sg; internet www.ocbc.com.sg; f. 1932; merged with Keppel TatLee Bank Ltd in 2001; cap. 9,157.5m., res 2,058.2m., dep. 185,302m. (Dec. 2011); Chair. Dr Cheong Choong Kong; CEO Samuel Tsien; 56 local brs, 52 overseas brs.

Singapore Island Bank: 65 Chulia St, 09-00 OCBC Centre, Singapore 049513; tel. and fax 65863200; f. 1954; subsidiary of Oversea-Chinese Banking Corpn Ltd; fmrly Bank of Singapore Ltd, name changed as above in Jan. 2010; Chair. David Philbrick Conner.

United Overseas Bank Ltd: 80 Raffles Pl., UOB Plaza, Singapore 048624; tel. 65339898; fax 65342334; internet www.uobgroup.com; f. 1935; merged with Overseas Union Bank Ltd in Jan. 2002 and with Industrial and Commercial Bank Ltd in Aug. 2002; cap. 5,576.5m., res 8,892m., dep. 189,210m. (Dec. 2011); Chair. Wee Cho Yaw; CEO Wee Ee Cheong; 61 local brs, 21 overseas brs.

Foreign Banks

Full Commercial Banks

Australia and New Zealand Banking Group Ltd (Australia): 50 Raffles Pl., 01-03 Singapore Land Tower, Singapore 048623; tel. 62692269; fax 66373450; internet www.anz.com/singapore; f. 1974; CEO Vishnu Shahaney.

Bangkok Bank Public Co Ltd (Thailand): 180 Cecil St, Bangkok Bank Bldg, Singapore 069546; tel. 64100400; fax 62255852; e-mail kanchana.kon@bangkokbank.com; internet www.bangkokbank.com; Sr Vice-Pres. and Gen. Man. Khun Kanchana Kongvananon.

Bank of America NA (USA): 9 50 Collyer Quay, 14-01 OUE Bayfront, Singapore 049321; tel. 66780000; fax 62393068; CEO Alan Koh.

Bank of China (People's Republic of China): 4 Battery Rd, Bank of China Bldg, Singapore 049908; tel. 65352411; fax 65343401; e-mail Service_SG@bank-of-china.com; internet www.bank-of-china.com; Gen. Man. Zhang Qingsong.

Bank of East Asia Ltd (BEA) (Hong Kong): 60 Robinson Rd, Bank of East Asia Bldg, Singapore 068892; tel. 66027702; fax 62251805; e-mail info@hkbea.com.sg; internet www.hkbea.com.sg; Gen. Man. Yap Gay Sin.

Bank of India (India): 01-01 to 03-01, Corporate Office Bldg, 138 Robinson Rd, Singapore 068906; tel. 62220011; fax 62271275; e-mail boi.singapore@bankofindia.co.in; internet www.boi.com.sg; Chief Exec. Pawan Kumar Bajaj.

PT Bank Negara Indonesia (Persero) Tbk (Indonesia): 39 Robinson Rd, 01-02 and 06-01/04 Robinson Point, Singapore 068911; tel. 62257755; fax 62254757; internet www.ptbni.com.sg; f. 1955; Gen. Man. Wahyu Purwandaka.

Bank of Tokyo-Mitsubishi UFJ Ltd (Japan): 9 Raffles Pl., 01-01 Republic Plaza, Singapore 048619; tel. 65383388; fax 65388083; internet www.bk.mufg.jp; Gen. Man. Yukiyasu Nishio.

BNP Paribas (France): 20 Collyer Quay, Tung Centre, Singapore 049319; tel. 62101288; fax 62243459; internet www.bnpparibas.com.sg; Regional Man. Jean-Pierre Bernard.

Citibank NA (USA): 8 Marine View, 21-00 Asia Sq. Tower 1, Singapore 018960; tel. 62255221; fax 66576882; internet www.citibank.com.sg; f. 1902; CEO Michael Zink.

HL Bank (Malaysia): 20 Collyer Quay, 01-02 Tung Centre, Singapore 049319; tel. 63498338; fax 65339340; internet www.hlb.com.my; Country Head Gan Hui Tin.

Hongkong and Shanghai Banking Corpn Ltd (Hong Kong): 14-01 HSBC Bldg, 21 Collyer Quay, Singapore 049320; tel. 4722669; fax 62250663; e-mail direct@hsbc.com.sg; internet www.hsbc.com.sg; f. 1877; CEO Alex Hungate.

ICICI Bank Ltd (India): 9 Raffles Pl., 50-01 Republic Plaza, Singapore 048619; tel. 67239288; fax 67239268; e-mail globalinvest@icicibank.com; internet www.icicibank.com.sg; Chief Exec. Bagawatiswar Krishna Iyer.

Indian Bank (India): 3 Raffles Pl., Bharat Bldg, Singapore 048617; tel. 65343511; fax 65331651; e-mail indbksg@pacific.net.sg; internet indianbank-singapore.com; f. 1941; CEO Veezhinathan Baskaran.

Indian Overseas Bank (India): 64 Cecil St, IOB Bldg, Singapore 049711; tel. 62251100; fax 62244490; e-mail iobrem@iob.com.sg; internet iobsingapore.com; f. 1941; Chief Exec. Kandasamy Sethu.

JP Morgan Chase Bank (USA): 168 Robinson Rd, 17-01 Capital Tower, Singapore 068912; tel. 68822888; fax 68821756; internet jpmorganchase.com; Country Man. Philip Lee Sooi Chuen.

Mizuho Corporate Bank Ltd (Japan): 168 Robinson Rd, 11-01 Capital Tower, Singapore 068912; tel. 64230330; fax 64230012; Gen. Man. Katsuyuki Mizuma.

RHB Bank Bhd (Malaysia): 5th Floor, 90 Cecil St, Singapore 069531; tel. 62253111; fax 622738056; e-mail contactus@rhbbank.com.sg; internet rhb.com.sg; f. 1961; Country Head Jason Wong; 7 brs.

Standard Chartered Bank (UK): 8 Marina Blvd, 27-01 Marina Bay Financial Centre Tower 1, Singapore 018981; tel. 65968888; fax 66348120; internet www.standardchartered.com.sg; f. 1859; Chief Exec. Ray Ferguson.

State Bank of India (India): 135 Cecil St, 01-00, Singapore 069536; tel. 62222033; fax 62253348; e-mail cecilstreet@sbising.com; internet www.sbising.com; CEO Anil Kishora.

Sumitomo Mitsui Banking Corpn (Japan) (SMBC): 3 Temasek Ave, 06-01 Centennial Tower, Singapore 039190; tel. 68820000; fax 68870220; internet www.smbc.co.jp; CEO Masayuki Shimura.

UCO Bank (India): 3 Raffles Pl., 01-01 Bharat Bldg, Singapore 048617; tel. 65325944; fax 65325044; e-mail general@ucobank.com.sg; internet www.ucobank.com.sg; f. 1951; Chief Exec. Kalpana; 2 brs.

Wholesale Banks

Agricultural Bank of China (People's Republic of China): 7 Temasek Blvd, 30-01/02/03, Suntec City Tower 1, Singapore 038987; tel. 65355255; fax 65387960; e-mail aboc@abchina.com.sg; Gen. Man. Fan Gang.

Bank of Communications (People's Republic of China): 50 Raffles Pl., 18-01 Singapore Land Tower, Singapore 048623; tel. 65320335; fax 65320339; Gen. Man. Niu Ke Rong.

Bank of Nova Scotia (Canada): 1 Raffles Quay, 20-01 North Tower, Singapore 048583; tel. 63058388; fax 65347830; Country Head Claude David Morin.

Barclays Bank PLC (UK): 1 Raffles Quay, Level 28, South Tower, Singapore 048583; tel. 63083000; fax 63083139; Man. Dir Ivan Ritossa.

China Construction Bank Corpn (People's Republic of China): 9 Raffles Pl., 33-01/02 Republic Plaza, Singapore 048619; tel. 65358133; fax 65356432; e-mail enquiry@ccb.com.sg; internet www.ccb.com.sg; Gen. Man. Jian Guo Yun.

Commerzbank AG (Germany): 8 Shenton Way, 42-01 Temasek Tower, Singapore 068811; tel. 63110000; fax 62253943; e-mail info@commerzbank.com.sg; internet www.commerzbank.com.sg; f. 1978; Man. Dirk Verlage.

Commonwealth Bank of Australia (Australia): 1 Temasek Ave, 17-01 Millenia Tower, Singapore 039192; tel. 63497000; fax 62245812; Gen. Man. Gregory Philip Williams.

Crédit Industriel et Commercial (France): 63 Market St, 15-01, Singapore 048942; tel. 65366008; fax 65367008; internet www.cic.com.sg; Gen. Man. Jean-Luc Anglada.

Crédit Suisse (Switzerland): 1 Raffles Link, 05-02, Singapore 039393; tel. 62126000; fax 62126200; e-mail ask.us@credit-suisse.com; internet www.credit-suisse.com/sg; CEO Jose Isidro N. Camacho.

Deutsche Bank AG (Germany): 1 Raffles Quay, 17-00 South Tower, Singapore 048583; tel. 64238001; fax 62259442; internet www.db.com/singapore; f. 1971; Gen. Man. Ronny Tan Chong Tee.

DnB NOR (Norway): 8 Shenton Way, 48-02 Temasek Tower, Singapore 068811; tel. 62206144; fax 62249743; e-mail dnbnor.singapore@dnbnor.no; internet www.dnbnor.no; Gen. Man. Erik Borgen.

First Commercial Bank (Taiwan): 77 Robinson Rd, 01-01, Singapore 068896; tel. 65930888; fax 62251905; e-mail fcbsin@singnet.com.sg; Gen. Man. Chiang Shang-Shing.

Habib Bank Ltd (Pakistan): 3 Phillip St, 01-03 Commerce Pt, Singapore 048693; tel. 64380055; fax 64380641; e-mail rizwan@hblsg.com; Gen. Man. Salman Ahmed Khan Malik.

HSBC Pvt Bank SA (Switzerland): 21 Collyer Quay, 18-01 HSBC Bldg, Singapore 049320; tel. 62248080; fax 62237146; CEO Amit Gupta.

Industrial and Commercial Bank of China (People's Republic of China): 6 Raffles Quay, 12-01 John Hancock Tower, Singapore

048580; tel. 65381066; fax 65381370; e-mail icbcsg@icbc.com.sg; Gen. Man. Xu Li.

ING Bank NV (Netherlands): 9 Raffles Pl., 19-02 Republic Plaza, Singapore 048619; tel. 65353688; fax 65338329; Gen. Man. KRISTA BAETENS.

Intesa Sanpaolo SpA (Italy): 6 Temasek Blvd, 42/04-05 Suntec Tower Four, Singapore 038986; tel. 63338270; fax 63338252; e-mail singapore.sg@intesasanpaolo.com; internet www.intesasanpaolo .com; Gen. Man. GIANFRANCO GIROMINI.

KBC Bank NV (Belgium): 30 Cecil St, 12-01/08 Prudential Tower, Singapore 049712; tel. 63952828; fax 63952929; e-mail reception@ kbc.com.sg; f. 1993; Gen. Man. THIERRY MEZERET.

Korea Exchange Bank (Republic of Korea): 30 Cecil St, 24-03/08 Prudential Tower, Singapore 049712; tel. 65361633; fax 65382522; e-mail kebspore@keb.co.kr; Gen. Man. JEONG OO YEOUNG.

Landesbank Baden-Württemberg (Germany): 25 International Business Park, 01-72 German Centre, Singapore 609916; tel. 65627722; fax 65627729; Man. CHRISTOPH WINNAT.

Mega International Commercial Bank Co Ltd (Taiwan): 80 Raffles Place, 23-20 UOB Plaza II, Singapore 048624; tel. 62277667; fax 62271858; Gen. Man. SHEU WEI DEI.

National Australia Bank Ltd (Australia): 5 Temasek Blvd, 15-01 Suntec Tower Five, Singapore 038985; tel. 64196875; fax 63380039; f. 1981; Gen. Man. VIVIEN KOH YOKE HAR.

National Bank of Kuwait SAK (Kuwait): 9 Raffles Place, 24-02 Republic Plaza, Singapore 048619; tel. 62225348; fax 62245438; f. 1984; Gen. Man. TAN KIM LAN.

Natexis Banques Populaires (France): 50 Raffles Place, 41-01, Singapore Land Tower, Singapore 048623; tel. 62241455; fax 62248651; Gen. Man. PIN CHUA.

Norddeutsche Landesbank Girozentrale (Germany): 6 Shenton Way, 16-00 DBS Bldg Tower Two, Singapore 068809; tel. 63231223; fax 63230223; e-mail nordlb.singapore@nordlb.com; internet www .nordlb.de; f. 1994; Gen. Man. OLAF-ALEXANDER WIEDEMANN.

Northern Trust Company (USA): 1 George St, 12-06, Singapore 049145; tel. 64376666; fax 64376609; e-mail LA16@ntrs.com; internet www.northerntrust.com; f. 1889; Gen. Man. WILLIAM MAK.

Rabobank International (Netherlands): 77 Robinson Rd, 08-00 SIA Bldg, Singapore 068896; tel. 65363363; fax 65363236; Man. MARCEL LEONARDUS MARIA VAN DOREMAELE.

Royal Bank of Scotland PLC (UK): 1 Raffles Quay, Level 26, South Tower, Singapore 048583; tel. 65188888; fax 65183108; Gen. Man. MADAN MENON.

Société Générale (France): 8 Marina Blvd, 07-01 Marina Bay Financial Centre Tower 1, Singapore 018981; tel. 62227122; fax 62252609; CEO MAURICE NHAN.

State Street Bank and Trust Co (USA): 168 Robinson Rd, 33-01 Capital Tower, Singapore 068912; tel. 68267100; fax 68267377; Br. Man. NICHOLAS WRIGHT.

UBS AG (Switzerland): 1 Raffles Quay, 50-01 North Tower, Singapore 048583; tel. 64958000; fax 64958188; e-mail rolf-w.gerber@wdr .com; CEO EDMUND KOH.

VTB Capital PLC (UK): 9 Battery Rd, 27-01 Straits Trading Bldg, Singapore 049910; tel. 62209422; fax 62250140; internet www .vtbcapital.com; fmrly Moscow Narodny Bank Ltd; CEO JUDY LIM YING LING.

Westpac Banking Corpn (Australia): 77 Robinson Rd, 19-00 SIA Bldg, Singapore 068896; tel. 65309898; fax 65326781; e-mail yhlee@ westpac.wm.au; Country Head YOGAVEL RASANAYAKAM.

'Offshore' Banks

Arab Bank PLC (Jordan): 80 Raffles Pl., 32-20 UOB Plaza 2, Singapore 048624; tel. 65330055; fax 65322150; e-mail abplc@ pacific.net.com.sg; Exec. Vice-Pres. KIM EUN-YOUNG.

PT Bank Mandiri (Persero) (Indonesia): 3 Anson Rd, 12-01/02 Springleaf Tower, Singapore 079909; tel. 62135688; fax 64383363; Gen. Man. PHILIP KOH JIT KIAN.

Bank of New York Mellon (USA): 1 Temasek Ave, 02-01 Millenia Tower, Singapore 039192; tel. 64320222; fax 63374302; formed through merger of Bank of New York with Mellon Financial Corpn in 2007; Man. Dir LEOW CHONG JIN.

Bank of Taiwan (Taiwan): 80 Raffles Pl., 28-20 UOB Plaza 2, Singapore 048624; tel. 65365536; fax 65368203; Gen. Man. PAN RONG-YAW.

Canadian Imperial Bank of Commerce (Canada): 16 Collyer Quay, 04-02 Hitachi Tower, Singapore 049318; tel. 65352323; fax 65357565; Br. Man. DEBORAH WONG SHIH HSIANG.

Chang Hwa Commercial Bank Ltd (China): 1 Finlayson Green, 08-00, Singapore 049246; tel. 65320820; fax 65320374; Gen. Man. CHEN BIN.

Hana Bank (Republic of Korea): 8 Cross St, 23-06 PWC Bldg, Singapore 048424; tel. 64384100; fax 64384200; Gen. Man. SEO JI SU.

Hang Seng Bank Ltd (Hong Kong): 21 Collyer Quay, 06-02 HSBC Bldg, Singapore 049320; tel. 65363118; fax 65363148; e-mail sgp@ hangseng.com; Country Man. YIU PAK CHOW.

HSH Nordbank AG (Germany): 3 Temasek Ave, 33–00 Centennial Tower, Singapore 039190; tel. 65509000; fax 65509003; e-mail info@ hsh-nordbank.com.sg; Gen. Man. and Regional Head RALF SCHMIDT.

Hua Nan Commercial Bank Ltd (Taiwan): 80 Robinson Rd, 14-03, Singapore 068898; tel. 63242566; fax 63242155; e-mail credit@hncb .com.sg; internet sg.hncb.com; Gen. Man. TSAI CHENG-CHIH.

Korea Development Bank (Republic of Korea): 8 Shenton Way, 07-01 Temasek Tower, Singapore 068811; tel. 62248188; fax 62256540; Gen. Man. PARK YONG SOO.

Krung Thai Bank Public Co Ltd (Thailand): 65 Chulia St, 32-05/08 OCBC Centre, Singapore 049513; tel. 65336691; fax 65330930; e-mail br.singapore@ktb.co.th; Gen. Man. NUANNAPHA WONGTH-AWATCHAI.

Land Bank of Taiwan: 80 Raffles Place, 34-01 UOB Plaza 1, Singapore 048624; tel. 63494555; fax 63494545; Gen. Man. CHAN YAO CHUAN.

Lloyds TSB Bank PLC (UK): 1 Temasek Ave, 18-01 Millenia Tower, Singapore 039192; tel. 65341191; fax 65322493; e-mail ims@lloydstsb.com.sg; internet www.lloydstsb.com.sg; Country Head BARRY LEA.

Mitsubishi UFJ Trust and Banking Corpn (Japan): 50 Raffles Pl., 42-01/06 Singapore Land Tower, Singapore 048623; tel. 62259155; fax 62241857; Gen. Man. MASARU MATSUO.

Nordea Bank Finland Plc (Finland): 3 Anson Rd, 22-01 Springleaf Tower, Singapore 079909; tel. 63176500; fax 63275616; e-mail singapore@nordea.com; Gen. Man. LARS KYVSGAARD.

Norinchukin Bank (Japan): 80 Raffles Pl., 53-01 UOB Plaza 1, Singapore 048624; tel. 65351011; fax 65352883; Gen. Man. YASUYUKI MATSUMOTO.

Philippine National Bank (Philippines): 304 Orchard Rd, 03-02/07 Lucky Plaza Shopping Centre, Singapore 238863; tel. 67374646; fax 67374224; e-mail singapore@pnb.com.ph; Gen. Man. CESAR C. SANTOS, Jr.

Raiffeisen Zentralbank Österreich Aktiengesellschaft (Austria): 1 Raffles Quay, 38-01 North Tower, Singapore 048583; tel. 63056000; fax 63056001; Gen. Man. STEFAN MANDI.

Royal Bank of Canada (Canada): 8 Marina View, 26-01 Asia Square Tower 1, Singapore 018960; tel. 65369206; fax 65322804; Gen. Man. RONNIE LIM.

Shinhan Bank (Republic of Korea): 1 George St, 15-03, Singapore 049145; tel. 65361144; fax 65331244; merged with Chohun Bank 2006; Gen. Man. JEONG JONG MIN.

Siam Commercial Bank Public Company Ltd (Thailand): 61 Robinson Rd, 10-03 Robinson Centre, Singapore 068893; tel. 65364338; fax 65364728; Gen. Man. BANDIT ROJANAVONGSE.

Skandinaviska Enskilda Banken AB Publ (Sweden): 50 Collyer Quay, 12-03 OUE Bayfront, Singapore 049321; tel. 62235644; fax 66343379; Gen. Man. BO INGEMAR CARLSSON.

Sumitomo Trust & Banking Co Ltd (Japan): 8 Shenton Way, 45-01 AXA Tower, Singapore 068811; tel. 62249055; fax 62242873; Gen. Man. TETSUYA YAMAWAKI.

Svenska Handelsbanken AB (publ) (Sweden): 65 Chulia St, 21-01/04 OCBC Centre, Singapore 049513; tel. 65323800; fax 65344909; Gen. Man. JAN BIRGER DJERF.

Toronto-Dominion (South East Asia) Ltd (Canada): 1 Temasek Ave, 15-02 Millenia Tower, Singapore 039192; tel. 64346000; fax 63369500; Man. Dir JAYANT JOBANPUTRA.

Union de Banques Arabes et Françaises (UBAF) (France): 7 Temasek Blvd, 07-04/05 Suntec Tower 1, Singapore 038987; tel. 63336188; fax 63336789; e-mail ubafsg@singnet.com.sg; Gen. Man. ERIC REINHART.

Woori Bank (Republic of Korea): 10 Marina Blvd, 13-05 Marina Bay Financial Centre Tower 2, Singapore 018983; tel. 64222000; fax 64222001; e-mail combksp@singnet.com.sg; Gen. Man. PARK MOO RYUNG.

Bankers' Association

The Association of Banks in Singapore: 10 Shenton Way, 12-08 MAS Bldg, Singapore 079117; tel. 62244300; fax 62241785; e-mail banks@abs.org.sg; internet www.abs.org.sg; f. 1973; Chair. PIYUSH GUPTA.

STOCK EXCHANGE

Singapore Exchange Ltd (SGX): 2 Shenton Way, 19-00 SGX Centre 1, Singapore 068804; tel. 62368888; fax 65356994; e-mail query@sgx.com; internet www.sgx.com; f. 1999; demutualized and integrated securities and derivatives exchange; Chair. CHEW CHOON SENG; CEO MAGNUS BÖCKER.

INSURANCE

The insurance industry is supervised by the Monetary Authority of Singapore (see Banking). In April 2012 there were 157 insurance companies, comprising 69 direct insurers (13 life insurance, 50 general insurance, six composite insurers), 29 reinsurers (three life reinsurers, 17 general reinsurers, nine composite reinsurers) and 59 captive insurers.

Domestic Companies

Life Insurance

Axa Life Insurance Singapore Pte Ltd: 8 Shenton Way, 27-02, Singapore 068811; tel. 68805500; fax 68805501; e-mail comsvc@axa .com.sg; internet www.axalife.com.sg; CEO GLENN JOHN WILLIAMS.

Friends Provident International Ltd (Singapore): 63 Market St, 06-05, Singapore 048942; tel. 63274019; fax 63274020; e-mail singapore.enquiries@fpiom.com; internet www.fpinternational.com; Prin. Officer CHRISTOPHER GAVIN GILL.

Great Eastern Life Assurance Co Ltd: 1 Pickering St, 13-01 Great Eastern Centre, Singapore 048659; tel. 62482000; fax 65322214; e-mail wecare@lifeisgreat.com.sg; internet www .lifeisgreat.com.sg; f. 1908; CEO TAN BENG LEE.

International Medical Insurers Pte Ltd: 585 North Bridge Rd, 13-00, Raffles Hospital, Singapore 188770; tel. 62982266; fax 63112396; e-mail enquiries@imi.sg; internet www.imi.sg; f. 1996; Prin. Officer VICTOR LYE.

Manulife (Singapore) Pte Ltd: 491B River Valley Rd, 07-00 Valley Pt, Singapore 248373; tel. 67371221; fax 62359158; e-mail service@ manulife.com; internet www.manulife.com.sg; acquired John Hancock Life Assurance Co Ltd in Dec. 2004; Pres. and CEO ANNETTE LOUISE KING.

Royal Scandia Life Assurance Ltd : Level 25, North Tower, 1 Raffles Quay, Singapore 048583; tel. 66225402; fax 66225400; internet www.royalskandia.com; Prin. Officer DAVID MACDONALD.

Swiss Life Private Placement (Singapore) Pte Ltd: 250 North Bridge Rd, 37-03/04 Raffles City Tower, Singapore 179101; tel. 65806680; fax 65806683; e-mail slpp@swisslife.com; internet www .sl-pp.com; f. 2008; Prin. Officer THOMAS VONRUETI.

Tokio Marine Life Insurance Singapore Ltd: 20 McCallum St, 07-01 Tokio Marine Centre, Singapore 069046; tel. 65926100; fax 62239120; internet www.tokiomarine-life.sg; CEO LANCE TAY.

Transamerica Life (Singapore) Ltd: 1 Finlayson Green, 13-00, Singapore 049246; tel. 62120620; fax 62120621; internet www .transamerica.com.sg; wholly owned subsidiary of Transamerica Occidental Life Insurance Co; Prin. Officer PETER MONKSFIELD.

Zurich International Life (Singapore) Ltd: 50 Raffles Pl., 29-05 Singapore Land Tower, Singapore 048623; tel. 68766750; fax 68766751; e-mail helppoint.singapore@zurich.com; internet www .zurich.com/international/singapore; Regional Dir NEAL PALMER ARMSTRONG.

General Insurance

Allianz Insurance Company of Singapore Pte Ltd: 3 Temasek Ave, 09-01 Centennial Tower, Singapore 039190; tel. 62972529; fax 62971956; e-mail askme@allianz.com.sg; internet www.allianz.com .sg; est. by merger between Allianz Insurance (Singapore) Pte Ltd and AGF Insurance (Singapore) Pte Ltd; CEO KEVIN M. H. LEONG.

Axa Insurance Singapore Pte Ltd: 8 Shenton Way, 27-01 AXA Tower, Singapore 068811; tel. 68804741; fax 68804740; e-mail customer.service@axa.com.sg; internet www.axa.com.sg; CEO CHUA KIM SOON.

China Taiping Insurance (Singapore) Pte Ltd: 105 Cecil St, 18-00 and 19-00 The Octagon, Singapore 069534; tel. 63896111; fax 62221033; internet www.sg.cntaiping.com; f. 1939; fmrly known as China Life Insurance Co Ltd; name changed as above in 2009; Gen. Man. LI WEIGUO.

Cosmic Insurance Corpn Ltd: 410 North Bridge Rd, 04-01 Cosmic Insurance Bldg, Singapore 188726; tel. 63387633; fax 63397805; e-mail query@cosmic.com.sg; internet www.cosmic.com.sg; f. 1971; Gen. Man. SWEE LEE CHUN.

ECICS Ltd: 7 Temasek Blvd, 10-03 Suntec City Tower 1, Singapore 038987; tel. 63374770; fax 63389267; e-mail principalofficer@ecics .com.sg; internet www.ecics.com.sg; CEO LUA TOO SWEE.

First Capital Insurance Ltd: 6 Raffles Quay 21-00, Singapore 048580; tel. 62222311; fax 62223547; e-mail enquiry@first-insurance .com.sg; internet www.first-insurance.com.sg; CEO RAMASWAMY ATHAPPAN.

India International Insurance Pte Ltd: 64 Cecil St, 04-00/05-00 IOB Bldg, Singapore 049711; tel. 63476100; fax 62244174; e-mail insure@iii.com.sg; internet www.iii.com.sg; f. 1987; all non-life insurance; CEO ISH KUMAR.

Liberty Insurance Pte Ltd: 5 Shenton Way, 03-00 UIC Bld, Singapore 068808; tel. 62218611; fax 62236434; e-mail feedback@ libertycitystate.com.sg; internet www.libertyinsurance.com.sg; division of Liberty Mutual Group (USA); fmrly Citystate Insurance Pte Ltd; Man. Dir MARTIN BRIDGER.

MSIG Insurance (Singapore) Pte Ltd: 4 Shenton Way, 21-01 SGX Centre 2, Singapore 068807; tel. 68277888; fax 68277800; internet www.msig.com.sg; f. 2010 following the merger of MSIG Insurance (Singapore) Pte Ltd and Mitsui Sumitomo Insurance Singapore; CEO PAUL FAULKNER.

QBE Insurance International Ltd Singapore: 60 Anson Rd, 11–01 Mapletree Anson, Singapore 079914; tel. 62246633; fax 65333270; e-mail info.sing@qbe.com; internet www.qbe.com.sg; Prin. Officer KENG KOON CHEE.

Royal & Sun Alliance Insurance (Singapore) Ltd: 77 Robinson Rd, 17-00 Robinson 77, Singapore 068896; tel. 64230888; fax 65339291; e-mail customer.service@sg.rsagroup.com; internet www.rsagroup.com.sg; Man. Dir and CEO MARK MITCHELL.

SHC Capital Ltd: 302 Orchard Rd, 09-01 Tong Bldg, Singapore 238862; tel. 68299199; fax 68299249; e-mail shccapital@shcsb.com .sg; internet www.shccapital.com.sg; f. 1956; fmrly The Nanyang Insurance Co Ltd; name changed as above following takeover in June 2004; Dir and Prin. Officer QUEK SUN HUI.

Singapore Aviation and General Insurance Co (Pte) Ltd: 25 Airline Rd, 06-A Airline House, Singapore 819829; tel. 65423333; fax 65450221; f. 1976; Man. GEORGE VARUGHESE.

Standard Steamship Owners' Protection and Indemnity Association (Asia) Ltd: 140 Cecil St, 15-00 PIL Bldg, Singapore 069540; tel. 65062896; fax 62211082; e-mail p&i.singapore@ctcplc .com; internet www.standard-club.com; Dir NICK SANSOM.

Tenet Insurance Co Ltd: 11 Collyer Quay, 09-00 The Arcade, Singapore 049317; tel. 62212211; fax 62213302; e-mail emailus@ tenetinsurance.com; internet www.tenetinsurance.com; CEO STELLA TAN YIAN HUA.

Tokio Marine Insurance Singapore Ltd: 20 McCallum St, 09-01 Tokio Marine Centre, Singapore 069046; tel. 62216111; fax 62240895; internet www.tokiomarine.com.sg; f. 1957 as The Tokio Marine and Fire Insurance Company (Singapore) Pte Ltd; name changed as above following merger with TM Asia Insurance Singapore Ltd in 2008; Prin. Officer CHER AH KOW.

United Overseas Insurance Ltd: 3 Anson Rd, 28-01 Springleaf Tower, Singapore 079909; tel. 62227733; fax 63273870; e-mail contactus@uoi.com.sg; internet www.uoi.com.sg; f. 1971; Man. Dir DAVID CHAN MUN WAI.

Zürich Insurance (Singapore) Pte Ltd: 50 Raffles Pl., 29-01 Singapore Land Tower, Singapore 048623; tel. 62362210; fax 65384184; Prin. Officer and Man. Dir CHAN TAT YOONG.

Composite Insurance

American International Assurance Co Ltd: 1 Robinson Rd, AIA Tower, Singapore 048542; tel. 62918000; fax 65385802; internet www.aia.com.sg; Prin. Officer TAN HAK LEH.

Aviva Ltd: 4 Shenton Way, 01-01 SGX Centre 2, Singapore 068807; tel. 68279929; fax 68277900; e-mail globalsolutions_sg@aviva-asia .com; internet www.aviva.com.sg; f. 2002; CEO SIMON NEWMAN.

HSBC Insurance (Singapore) Pte Ltd: 10 Eunos Rd 8, 11-01 Singapore Post Centre, Singapore 408600; tel. 62256111; fax 62212188; e-mail e-surance@hsbc.com.sg; internet www.insurance .hsbc.com.sg; Prin. Officer WALTER MARK DE OUDE.

NTUC Income Insurance Co-operative Ltd: 75 Bras Basah Rd, NTUC Income Centre, Singapore 189557; tel. 63363322; fax 63381500; e-mail inbox@income.wm.sg; internet www.income.com .sg; f. 1970; CEO TAN SUEE CHIEH; Gen. Man. ALOYSIUS TEO SENG LEE.

Overseas Assurance Corpn Ltd: 1 Pickering St, 01-01 Great Eastern Centre, Singapore 048659; tel. 62482000; fax 65322214; e-mail wecare@lifeisgreat.com.sg; internet www.lifeisgreat.com.sg; f. 1920; wholly owned subsidiary of Great Eastern Holdings; Chair. CHRISTOPHER WEI.

Prudential Assurance Co Singapore (Pte) Ltd: 30 Cecil St, 30-01 Prudential Tower, Singapore 049712; tel. 65358988; fax 65354043; e-mail customer.service@prudential.com.sg; internet www.prudential.com.sg; f. 1931; CEO KEVIN LEE HOLMGREN.

Associations

General Insurance Association of Singapore: 112 Robinson Rd, 05-03 HB Robinson, Singapore 068902; tel. 62218788; fax 62272051; e-mail feedback@gia.org.sg; internet www.gia.org.sg; f. 1965; Pres. DEREK TEO; Exec. Dir MARK LIM.

Life Insurance Association, Singapore: 79 Anson Rd, 11-05, Singapore 079906; tel. 64388900; fax 64386989; e-mail lia@lia.org.sg; internet www.lia.org.sg; f. 1967; Pres. ANNETTE KING.

Reinsurance Brokers' Association: 69 Amoy St, Singapore 069888; tel. 63723189; fax 62241091; e-mail secretariat@rbas.org .sg; internet www.rbas.org.sg; f. 1995; Chair. RICHARD AUSTEN.

Singapore Insurance Brokers' Association: 138 Cecil St, 15-00 Cecil Court, Singapore 069538; tel. 62227777; fax 62220022; e-mail siba@stcsamasmgt.com.sg; Pres. ANTHONY LIM; Vice-Pres. DAVID LUM.

Singapore Reinsurers' Association: 85 Amoy St, Singapore 069904; tel. 63247388; fax 62248910; e-mail secretariat@sraweb .org.sg; internet www.sraweb.org.sg; f. 1979; Chair. CHRISTOPHER HO SIOW SOONG.

Trade and Industry

Temasek Holdings Pte Ltd: 60B Orchard Rd, 06-18 Tower 2, The Atrium@ Orchard, Singapore 238891; tel. 68286828; fax 68211188; internet www.temasek.com.sg; f. 1974; 100% govt-owned; active shareholder and investor in banking and financial services, real estate, transport, infrastructure, telecommunications, media, bioscience and health care, education, consumer services, engineering and technology, energy and resources; revenue S $79,615m. (2008/09); Chair. S. DHANABALAN; Exec. Dir and CEO HO CHING.

GOVERNMENT AGENCIES

Housing and Development Board: 480 Lorong 6, Toa Payoh, Singapore 310480; tel. 64901111; fax 64901033; e-mail hdbmailbox@ hdb.gov.sg; internet www.hdb.gov.sg; f. 1960; public housing authority; Chair. JAMES KOH CHER SIANG; CEO Dr HEAN CHEONG-CHUA KOON.

Singapore Land Authority (SLA): 55 Newton Rd, 12-01 Revenue House, Singapore 307987; tel. 63239829; fax 63239937; e-mail SLA_enquiry@sla.gov.sg; internet www.sla.gov.sg; f. 2001; est. by merger of Land Office, Singapore Land Registry, Survey Dept and Land Systems Support Unit; responsible for management and devt of state land resources; Chair. CHALY MAH; CEO VINCENT HOONG SENG LEI.

Urban Redevelopment Authority (URA): 45 Maxwell Rd, URA Centre, Singapore 069118; tel. 62216666; fax 62275069; e-mail ura_email@ura.gov.sg; internet www.ura.gov.sg; f. 1974; est. to replace Urban Renewal Dept (f. 1967); statutory board; responsible for nat. planning; Chair. PETER HO; CEO NG LANG.

DEVELOPMENT ORGANIZATIONS

Agency for Science, Technology and Research (A*STAR): 1 Fusionopolis Way, 20-10 Connexis North Tower, Singapore 138632; tel. 68266111; fax 67771711; e-mail contact@a-star.edu.sg; internet www.a-star.edu.sg; f. 1991; fmrly National Science and Technology Board; statutory board; responsible for the devt of science and technology; Chair. LIM CHUAN POH; Man. Dir RAJ THAMPURAN.

Applied Research Corpn (ARC): Singapore; f. 1973; independent non-profit-making research and consultancy org. aiming to facilitate and enhance the use of technology and expertise from tertiary institutions to benefit industry and businesses.

Asian Infrastructure Fund (AIF): Singapore; f. 1994; promotes and directs investment into regional projects; Chair. MOEEN QURESHI.

Economic Development Board (EDB): 250 North Bridge Rd, 28-00 Raffles City Tower, Singapore 179101; tel. 68326832; fax 68326565; e-mail clientservices@edb.gov.sg; internet www.edb.gov .sg; f. 1961; statutory body for industrial planning, devt and promotion of investments in manufacturing, services and local business; Chair. LEO YIP SENG CHEONG; Man. Dir Dr BEH SWAN GIN.

Government of Singapore Investment Corpn Pte Ltd (GIC): 168 Robinson Rd, 37-01 Capital Tower, Singapore 068912; tel. 68898888; fax 68898722; e-mail contactgic@gic.com.sg; internet www.gic.com.sg; f. 1981; Chair. LEE HSIEN LOONG; Pres. LIM SIONG GUAN.

Infocomm Development Authority of Singapore (IDA): see under Telecommunications.

International Enterprise Singapore: 230 Victoria St, Level 10, Bugis Junction Office Tower, Singapore 188024; tel. 63376628; fax 63376898; e-mail enquiry@iesingapore.gov.sg; internet www .iesingapore.gov.sg; f. 1983; formed to develop and expand int. trade; fmrly Trade Development Board; statutory body; Chair. SUNNY VERGHESE; CEO CHONG LIT CHEONG.

JTC Corpn: The JTC Summit, 8 Jurong Town Hall Rd, Singapore 609434; tel. 65600056; fax 65655301; e-mail askjtc@jtc.gov.sg; internet www.jtc.gov.sg; f. 1968; statutory body responsible for planning, promoting and developing industrial space; Chair. CEDRIC FOO; CEO MANOHAR KHIATANI.

Standards, Productivity and Innovation Board Singapore (SPRING): 1 Fusionopolis Way, 01-02 South Tower, Solaris, Singapore 138628; tel. 62786666; fax 62786667; e-mail enterpriseone@ spring.gov.sg; internet www.spring.gov.sg; f. 1996 as Singapore Productivity and Standards Bd (PSB) following merger of Singapore Institute of Standards and Industrial Research and the Nat. Productivity Bd; present name adopted 2001; work-force devt, training, productivity and innovation promotion, standards devt, etc.; assistance for SMEs; Chair. PHILIP YEO; Chief Exec. PNG CHEONG BOON.

CHAMBERS OF COMMERCE

Singapore Business Federation (SBF): 10 Hoe Chiang Rd, 22-01 Keppel Towers, 089315 Singapore; tel. 68276828; fax 68276807; internet www.sbf.org.sg; f. 2002 following restructuring of Singapore Fed. of Chambers of Commerce and Industry; Chair. TONY CHEW LEONG CHEE; represents over 15,000 cos; constituent mems incl. the following:

Singapore Chinese Chamber of Commerce and Industry: 47 Hill St, 09-00 Singapore 179365; tel. 63378381; fax 63390605; e-mail corporate@sccci.org.sg; internet www.sccci.org.sg; f. 1906; Pres. TEO SIONG SENG; Sec.-Gen. LIM SAH SOON.

Singapore Indian Chamber of Commerce and Industry: 31 Stanley St, SICCI Bldg, Singapore 068740; tel. 62222855; fax 62231707; e-mail sicci@sicci.com; internet www.sicci.com; f. 1924; Chair. RANGARAJAN NARAYANAMOHAN; CEO HERNAIKH SINGH.

Singapore International Chamber of Commerce: 6 Raffles Quay, 10-01 John Hancock Tower, Singapore 048580; tel. 65000988; fax 62242785; e-mail general@sicc.com; internet www .sicc.com.sg; f. 1837; Chair. JENNIE CHUA.

Singapore Malay Chamber of Commerce and Industry (SMCCI): 15 Jalan Pinang, Singapore 199147; tel. 62979296; fax 63924527; e-mail inquiry@smcci.org.sg; internet www.smcci .org.sg; f. 1956; Pres. ABDUL ROHIM SARIP.

Singapore Manufacturers' Federation (SMa): 2 Bukit Merah Central, 03-00 SPRING Singapore Bldg, Singapore 159835; tel. 68263000; fax 68263008; e-mail hq@smafederation.org.sg; internet www.smafederation.org.sg; f. 1932 as Singapore Manufacturers' Asscn; renamed Singapore Confed. of Industries in 1996; name changed as above in 2002; Pres. GEORGE HUANG; Sec.-Gen. GWEE SENG KWONG.

INDUSTRIAL AND TRADE ASSOCIATIONS

Association of Singapore Marine Industries (ASMI): 30 Tuas Ave 10, 07-01 Freight Links E-Logistics Technopark, Singapore 639150; tel. 68633038; fax 68632881; e-mail admin@asmi.com; internet www.asmi.com; f. 1968; 12 hon. mems, 70 assoc. mems, 51 ordinary mems (Oct. 2003); Pres. WONG WENG SON.

Singapore Commodity Exchange (SICOM): 2 Shenton Way, 19-00 SGX Centre 1, Singapore 068804; tel. 62368888; fax 65366648; internet www.sicom.com.sg; f. 1968 as Rubber Asscn of Singapore; adopted present name in 1994; regulates, promotes, develops and supervises commodity futures trading in Singapore, including the establishment and dissemination of official prices for various grades and types of rubber; provides clearing facilities; endorses certificates of origin and licences for packers, shippers and mfrs; Chair. MAGNUS BOCKER; CEO JEREMY ANG PENG LEONG.

EMPLOYERS' ORGANIZATION

Singapore National Employers Federation (SNEF): 22-00 Keppel Towers, 10 Hoe Chiang Rd, Singapore 089315; tel. 68276827; fax 68276800; e-mail webmaster@snef.org.sg; internet www.sgemployers.com; f. 1948 as Fed. of Industrialists and Traders in Singapore; name changed to Singapore Employers Fed. in 1953; present name adopted in 1980 following merger with Nat. Employers Council; Pres. STEPHEN LEE CHING YEN.

UTILITIES

Electricity and Gas

Singapore Power Ltd: 111 Somerset Rd 10-01, Singapore 238164; tel. 68238888; fax 68238188; e-mail spservices@singaporepower.com .sg; internet www.singaporepower.com.sg; incorporated in 1995 to take over the piped gas and electricity utility operations of the Public Utilities Board (see Water), which now acts as a regulatory authority for the privately owned cos; 100% owned by government holding co, Temasek Holdings Pte Ltd; f. 1995; subsidiaries incl. PowerGrid, PowerGas, SP Services, Singapore Power International, Singapore District Cooling and SP Telecommunications; Chair. Tan Sri MOHAMED HASSAN MARICAN; Man. Dir PAUL ADAMS.

Water

Public Utilities Board: 40 Scotts Rd, 22-01 Environment Bldg, Singapore 228231; tel. 62358888; fax 62840363; e-mail pubone@singnet.com.sg; internet www.pub.gov.sg; f. 1963; statutory board responsible for water supply; manages Singapore's water system to optimize use of water resources; develops additional water sources; Chair. TAN GEE PAW; Chief Exec. CHEW MEN LEONG.

TRADE UNIONS

At the end of 2003 there were 68 employees' trade unions and associations, with 417,166 members, and three employer unions, with 2,052 members.

National Trades Union Congress (NTUC): NTUC Centre, 1 Marina Blvd 10-01, Singapore 018989; tel. 62138008; fax 63273740; e-mail membership@ntuc.org.sg; internet www.ntuc.org.sg; f. 1961; 60 affiliated unions, 6 affiliated assocs and approx. 540,000 mems (2009); Pres. DIANA CHIA SIEW FUI; Sec.-Gen. LIM SWEE SAY.

Transport

RAILWAYS

Singapore is linked to the Malaysian railway system via the Johor causeway. Branch lines provide a link to the industrial estate at Jurong. In February 2013 plans were announced for a high-speed rail link between Singapore and the Malaysian capital, Kuala Lumpur; this was due for completion in 2020.

The Mass Rapid Transit (MRT) system opened in 1990 and comprises the North–South, East–West and Circle lines. In 2011 the MRT system covered a total of 146.5 km, with 97 stations.

Singapore's first Light Rapid Transit (LRT) system, the Bukit Panjang LRT, opened in 1998. Construction of the 2.1-km Sentosa Express monorail system was completed in June 2006, and operations commenced in January 2007. In 2011 the LRT system covered 28.8 km, with 34 stations.

Land Transport Authority: 1 Hampshire Rd, Singapore 219428; tel. 63757100; fax 63757200; internet www.lta.gov.sg; f. 1995; planning, devt and man. of the land transport system; Chair. MICHAEL LIM CHOO SAN; Chief Exec. CHEW HOCK YONG.

SMRT Corpn Ltd: 251 North Bridge Rd, Singapore 179102; tel. 63311000; fax 63340247; e-mail corpcomms@smrt.com.sg; internet www.smrt.com.sg; f. 1987; operates the MRT and LRT rail systems, a fleet of more than 950 buses and more than 2,500 taxis (2010); Chair. KOH YONG GUAN; Pres. and CEO DESMOND KUEK BAK-CHYE.

ROADS

In 2011 Singapore had 3,411 km of roads, of which 161 km were motorway. A system of electronic road pricing, whereby vehicles are charged according to road use, is in operation. The 12-km Kallang–Paya Lebar expressway (with approximately 9 km of the expressway under ground) became fully operational in September 2008.

SHIPPING

Singapore is one of the world's busiest ports. The Port of Singapore Authority operates six cargo terminals: Tanjong Pagar Terminal, Keppel Terminal, Brani Terminal, Pasir Panjang Terminal (where the final two phases of construction were scheduled for completion in 2013), Sembawang Terminal and Jurong Port. In December 2012 the Singapore flag registered fleet comprised 4,656 vessels, with a total displacement of 64,549,400 grt.

Maritime and Port Authority of Singapore: 460 Alexandra Rd, 18-00 PSA Bldg, Singapore 119963; tel. 63751600; fax 62759247; e-mail shipping@mpa.gov.sg; internet www.mpa.gov.sg; f. 1996; regulatory body responsible for promotion and development of the port, overseeing all port and maritime matters in Singapore; Chair. LUCIEN WONG; Chief Exec. LAM YI YOUNG.

PSA International Pte Ltd: 460 Alexandra Rd, 38th Floor, PSA Bldg, Singapore 119963; tel. 62747111; fax 62744677; e-mail gca@psa.com.sg; internet www.internationalpsa.com; f. 1964; est. as Port of Singapore Authority; made a corporate entity in 1997 in preparation for privatization; present name adopted 2003; wholly owned by Temasek Holdings Pte Ltd; responsible for the provision and maintenance of port facilities and services; participates in 29 port projects in 17 countries in Asia, Europe and the Americas; Group Chair. SIEW WAH FOCK; Group CEO CHONG MENG TAN.

Major Shipping Companies

American President Lines Ltd (APL): 456 Alexandra Rd, 08-00 NOL Bldg, Singapore 119962; tel. 62789000; fax 62784900; e-mail erep_asia@apl.com; internet www.apl.com; container services to North and South Asia, the USA and the Middle East; Pres. KENNETH GLENN.

Glory Ship Management Private Ltd: 24 Raffles Pl., 17-01/02, Clifford Centre, Singapore 048621; tel. 65361986; fax 65361987; e-mail gene@gloryship.com.sg.

Guan Guan Shipping Pte Ltd: 2 Finlayson Green, 13-05 Asia Insurance Bldg, Singapore 049247; tel. 65343988; fax 62276776; e-mail golden@golden.com.sg; f. 1955; shipowners and agents; cargo services to East and West Malaysia, Indonesia, Pakistan, Sri Lanka, Bengal Bay ports, Persian (Arabian) Gulf ports, Hong Kong and China; Man. Dir RICHARD THIO.

IMC Shipping Co Pte Ltd: 5 Temasek Blvd, 37-01 Suntec City Tower, Singapore 038987; tel. 64119800; fax 63379715; e-mail corpcomms@imcpaa.com; internet www.imcshipping.com; Chair. FRANK TSAO WEN KING.

Maersk Singapore Pte Ltd: 200 Cantonment Rd, 10-100, Southpoint, Singapore 089763; tel. 63238323; fax 62247649; e-mail sinlinmng@maersk.com; f. 1929; operates under the brand name of Maersk Line; Head, Asia Pacific THOMAS KNUDSEN.

Neptune Orient Lines Ltd: 456 Alexandra Rd, 05-00 NOL Bldg, Singapore 119962; tel. 62789000; fax 62784900; e-mail nol_group_corp_comms@nol.com.sg; internet www.nol.com.sg; f. 1968; liner containerized services on the Far East/Europe, Far East/North America, Straits/Australia, South Asia/Europe and South-East Asia, Far East/Mediterranean routes; logistics services and terminals; Chair. SENG KWA CHONG; Group Pres. and CEO NG YAT CHUNG.

Ocean Tankers (Pte) Ltd: 37 Tuas Rd, Singapore 638503; tel. 68632202; fax 68639480; e-mail corporate@oceantankers.com.sg; internet www.oceantankers.com.sg; Dept Head DOUGLAS TAN.

Osprey Maritime Ltd: 8 Cross St, 24-02/03 PWC Bldg, Singapore 048424; tel. 62129722; fax 65570450; Sec. CHOO YVONNE.

Pacific International Lines (Pte) Ltd: 140 Cecil St, 03-00 PIL Bldg, POB 3206, Singapore 069540; tel. 62218133; fax 62273933; e-mail sherry.chua@sgp.pilship.com; internet www.pilship.com; shipowners, agents and managers; int. liner services; container services to South-East Asia; world-wide chartering, freight forwarding, etc.; Exec. Chair. Y. C. CHANG; Man. Dir S. S. TEO.

Syabas Tankers Pte Ltd: 10 Anson Rd, 34-10 International Plaza, Singapore 0207; tel. 62259522.

Tanker Pacific Management (Singapore) Private Ltd: 1 Temasek Ave, 38-01 Millenia Tower, Singapore; tel. 64335888; fax 63365311; internet www.tanker.com.sg; Chair. and CEO ALASTAIR McGREGOR.

CIVIL AVIATION

Singapore's international airport at Changi was opened in 1981. Construction of a terminal solely for the use of budget carriers was completed in 2006, and a third main terminal was opened in 2008, thereby increasing the airport's annual handling capacity to 70m. passengers. A fourth terminal was due to be opened in 2017, with a capacity of 16m. passengers a year. A second airport at Seletar operates as a base for charter and training flights.

Civil Aviation Authority of Singapore: Singapore Changi Airport, POB 1, Singapore 918141; tel. 65421122; fax 65421231; e-mail thennarasee_R@caas.gov.sg; internet www.caas.gov.sg; responsible for regulatory and advisory services, air services development, airport management and development, and airspace management and organization; Chair. LEE HSIEN YANG; Dir-Gen. YAP ONG HENG.

Jetstar Asia Airways: Singapore Changi Airport T1, POB 323, Singapore 918144; tel. 93470208; internet www.jetstar.com; f. 2004; 49% owned by Qantas (Australia); service to regional destinations; merged with ValuAir in 2005; continues to operate under the Jetstar name; CEO BARATHAN PASUPATHI.

Scoot: Singapore Changi Airport T1, Singapore 918144; tel. 31583388; e-mail info@flyscoot.com; internet www.flyscoot.com; f. 2011; low-cost long-haul subsidiary of Singapore Airlines; operates to 11 destinations in East Asia and Australia; CEO CAMPBELL WILSON.

SilkAir: 371 Beach Rd Unit, 17-08, Singapore 199597; tel. 62238888; fax 65426286; internet www.silkair.com; f. 1975; fmrly Tradewinds Private; wholly owned subsidiary of Singapore Airlines Ltd; began scheduled services in 1989; Chair. GOH CHOON PHONG; CEO LESLIE THING.

Singapore Airlines Ltd (SIA): Airline House, 25 Airline Rd, Singapore 819829; tel. 65415880; fax 65456083; e-mail investor_relations@singaporeair.com.sg; internet www.singaporeair.com; f. 1972; passenger services to over 90 destinations in about 40 countries; Chair. STEPHEN LEE CHING YEN; CEO GOH CHOON PHONG.

Tiger Airways: Singapore Changi Airport, POB 82, Singapore 918143; tel. 68222300; fax 68222310; internet www.tigerairways.com; f. 2003; 49% owned by Singapore Airlines, 24% owned by US co Indigo Partners, 11% owned by Temasek Holdings Pte Ltd;

services to 10 regional destinations; Chair. JOSEPH YUVARAJ PILLAY; CEO KOAY PENG YEN.

ValuAir: Singapore Changi Airport T1, POB 323, Singapore 918144; tel. 93470208; internet www.jetstar.com/vf/en/index.aspx; f. 2003; merged with Jetstar Asia in 2005; continues to operate under the ValuAir name; provides low-cost services between Singapore and Indonesia; CEO PAUL DAFF (acting).

Tourism

Singapore's tourist attractions include its blend of cultures and excellent shopping facilities. In 2005 the Government legalized gambling on the island, rescinding a 40-year ban and allowing for the construction of two major casino resorts, at Marina Bay and on Sentosa Island. The first hotels and the casino at the Sentosa resort opened in early 2010. A phased opening of the Marina Bay resort commenced in June 2010. The resorts were expected significantly to increase the number of visitors to Singapore. Foreign visitor arrivals rose from 13.2m. in 2011 to 14.4m. in 2012. Receipts from tourism (excluding passenger transport) totalled an estimated US \$17,990m. in 2011.

Singapore Tourism Board: Tourism Court, 1 Orchard Spring Lane, Singapore 247729; tel. 67366622; fax 67369423; e-mail feedback@stb.com.sg; internet www.stb.com.sg; f. 1964; Chair. CHEW CHOON SENG; Chief Exec. LIONEL YEO.

Defence

As assessed at November 2012, the total strength of the armed forces was 72,500 (including 39,000 conscripts): army 50,000 (35,000 conscripts), navy an estimated 9,000 (1,000 conscripts), air force 13,500 (3,000 conscripts). Military service lasts 24 months. Army reserves numbered an estimated 312,500. Paramilitary forces of an estimated 93,800 comprised the Singapore police force, Gurkha guard battalions and a civil defence force (numbering an estimated 81,800, including 3,200 conscripts). Singapore is a participant in the Five-

Power Defence Arrangements with Malaysia, Australia, New Zealand and the United Kingdom.

Defence Expenditure: Estimated at S \$12,300m. for 2012.

Chief of the Defence Forces: Maj.-Gen. NG CHEE MENG.

Chief of the Army: Maj.-Gen. RAVINDER SINGH.

Chief of the Air Force: Brig.-Gen HOO CHER MOU.

Chief of the Navy: Rear-Adm. NG CHEE PENG.

Education

From 2003 education in Singapore became compulsory for the first time at primary level, the six years of which are granted free to all children. Less able pupils are afforded an additional two years in which to complete primary education, under the New Primary Education System implemented in 1979.

In 2011 there were 174 primary institutions, at which 251,165 students were enrolled; and 154 secondary institutions, at which 189,735 students were enrolled. In the same year there were 15 mixed-level schools, at which 37,513 students were enrolled, and a further 13 pre-university institutions, at which 20,150 students were enrolled. Government operating expenditure on education in 2012 was estimated at S \$9,248m. (26.6% of total operating expenditure).

There were 13 tertiary institutions in 2011, including the National University of Singapore, the Nanyang Technological University, the Ngee Ann Polytechnic, the Singapore Polytechnic, the Nanyang Polytechnic and the Temasek Polytechnic. In 2011 total enrolment in the universities and colleges (not including SIM University, which opened in 2005) was 190,497. The Singapore Institute of Technology, which was to provide industry-orientated qualifications in partnership with several overseas universities, opened in 2010. The Institute of Technical Education provides and regulates vocational training. It conducts institutional training for school-leavers, offers part-time continuing education and training programmes and registers apprentices. It is also responsible for setting national skills standards, the conduct of public trade testing and certification of skills.

SLOVAKIA

Introductory Survey

LOCATION, CLIMATE, LANGUAGE, RELIGION, FLAG, CAPITAL

The Slovak Republic (formerly a constituent republic of the Czech and Slovak Federative Republic, or Czechoslovakia) is a land-locked state located in central Europe, bordered to the north by Poland, to the east by Ukraine, to the south by Hungary, to the west by Austria and to the north-west by the Czech Republic. The climate is typically continental, with cold, dry winters and hot, humid summers. Average temperatures in Bratislava range from $-0.7°C$ ($30.7°F$) in January to $21.1°C$ ($70.0°F$) in July. Average annual rainfall in the capital is 649 mm (26 ins). The official language is Slovak, although Hungarian, Czech and other languages are also spoken. The major religion is Christianity, the Latin-rite Catholic Church being the largest denomination, followed by the Evangelical Church of the Augsburg (Lutheran) Confession. The national flag (proportions 2 by 3) consists of three equal horizontal stripes, of white, blue and red; in the centre hoist there is a white-rimmed red shield containing a silver archiepiscopal (double-barred) cross surmounted on the central (and highest) of three blue hillocks. The capital is Bratislava.

CONTEMPORARY POLITICAL HISTORY

Historical Context

Slovaks and Czechs (who are closely related members of the western Slavic peoples) were first united in the ninth century AD, in the Great Moravian Empire, but were divided following the Empire's dissolution in 907. While the Slovaks came under Hungarian rule (which was to continue until the early 20th century), the Czechs established a kingdom that remained an important political force until the incorporation of the Czech Lands into the Habsburg Empire in the 16th and 17th centuries.

A movement of nationalist revival evolved in Slovakia in the late 18th and 19th centuries. During the First World War (1914–18) Slovaks joined with Czechs in campaigning for an independent state, which would be composed of the Czech Lands and Slovakia. The Republic of Czechoslovakia was established on 28 October 1918, as one of the successor states to the Austro-Hungarian Empire. The country's boundaries were defined by the Treaty of Trianon of 1920, under which a large Hungarian minority was incorporated into Slovakia. Czechoslovakia's first Constitution, promulgated in 1920, made no provision for a proper federal system, and Slovak proposals for self-government were rejected by the central authorities in the capital, Prague. There was also an ideological divide: while the majority of Slovaks were practising Catholics, the central Government in Prague was professedly anti-clerical.

In October 1938, following the Munich Agreement of 29 September (whereby the predominantly German-populated areas of Czechoslovakia were ceded to Germany), nationalists declared Slovak autonomy. On 14 March 1939, one day before Nazi armed forces occupied the Czech Lands, Germany agreed to the establishment of a separate Slovak state, under the pro-Nazi 'puppet' regime of Fr Jozef Tiso. Any opposition to the Tiso regime was harshly suppressed. In August 1944 an armed resistance (the Slovak National Uprising) against Tiso's regime was begun, but it was suppressed within two months.

Following the restoration of the Czechoslovak state in 1945, at the end of the Second World War, certain concessions were made to Slovak demands for autonomy, including the establishment of a regional legislature with restricted powers (the Slovenská národná rada—Slovak National Council) and an executive, both in Bratislava, the Slovak capital. However, communists (led by Gustav Husák) seized power in Slovakia in late 1947, and in the whole of the country in 1948. In May of that year a new Constitution was approved, which declared Czechoslovakia to be a 'people's democracy'. The communists' consolidation of power was completed in June with the election of the Czech Klement Gottwald, leader of the Communist Party of Czechoslovakia (CPCz) and Prime Minister since 1946, as President of Czechoslovakia.

In the first years of communist rule there was widespread repression. Expressions of Slovak nationalism were suppressed, and in 1954 Husák and other Slovaks were imprisoned on charges of separatism. The Constitution of 1960 restricted Slovak autonomy: the executive in Bratislava was dissolved, and legislative authority was removed from the Slovenská národná rada. In January 1968 Alexander Dubček (a Slovak, and hitherto leader of the Communist Party of Slovakia—CPS) was appointed First Secretary of the CPCz. The wide-ranging political and economic reforms introduced by Dubček and the new Government included plans for the creation of a federal system of two equal republics. Following the armed intervention of some 600,000 troops of the USSR and its allies in August, Dubček was replaced by Husák as First (subsequently General) Secretary of the CPCz, and there was a purge of party members, in particular reformists and associates of Dubček. Nevertheless, the federal system was realized in January 1969: separate Czech and Slovak Socialist Republics were established, each with its own government and legislature (Národná rada—National Council). Supreme legislative and executive power, meanwhile, were vested in the Federal Assembly and the Federal Government, respectively. However, renewed centralized rule, under Husák's leadership, left the new regional institutions largely powerless. In 1975 Husák was appointed President of Czechoslovakia. In 1987 he was replaced as General Secretary of the CPCz by Miloš Jakeš. The Government continued its repressive treatment of both the Catholic Church and the several dissident groups that had been established since the late 1970s (the most important being Charter 77). Nevertheless, the dissident movement was instrumental in organizing a series of anti-Government demonstrations, beginning in 1988, which were to culminate in the anti-communist revolution of late 1989.

Elections to the Federal Assembly and to the Czech and Slovak National Councils on 8–9 June 1990 were the first to be held freely since 1946. Of the Slovak organizations, Public Against Violence (PAV), which, with its Czech counterpart, Civic Forum, had been the principal force in effecting the end of communist rule, emerged with the largest representation at both federal and republican level. A coalition Slovak Government, dominated by PAV, was subsequently formed, with Vladimír Mečiar as Prime Minister.

The future of Czech-Slovak relations dominated political debate in the latter half of 1990, amid increasing support in Slovakia for greater decentralization. The Christian Democratic Movement (CDM), which formed part of the Slovak coalition Government, advocated greater Slovak autonomy within a common state; however, more radical parties—most notably the Slovak National Party (SNP), which held seats in both the federal and republican legislatures—favoured the complete secession of Slovakia. In March 1991 Mečiar was forced to resign as Slovak Prime Minister, following his support for full autonomy for Slovakia. Mečiar left PAV and formed the Movement for a Democratic Slovakia (MDS), being replaced as Prime Minister by Ján Carnogurský, the leader of the CDM.

Domestic Political Affairs

The Government of Vladimír Mečiar

Following elections to the federal and republican legislatures on 5–6 June 1992, the MDS was the largest Slovak party both in the Federal Assembly and the National Council. In the latter body the MDS won 74 of the 150 seats available, compared with the 18 obtained by the CDM and 15 by the SNP. The Party of the Democratic Left (PDL—the successor to the CPS) secured the second largest representation (29 seats). Mečiar was reinstated as Prime Minister, heading a new, MDS-dominated Slovak Government.

On 17 July 1992 the Slovenská národná rada approved a declaration of Slovak sovereignty, and later in the month Mečiar and his Czech counterpart, Václav Klaus, reached agreement on the necessary measures to permit the separation of the two republics. On 1 September a new Slovak Constitution was adopted by the Slovenská národná rada. In November the Federal Assembly finally approved at the third attempt (and by a margin of only three votes) legislation to permit the constitutional dissolution of Czechoslovakia, which was to take effect on 1 January 1993. During late 1992 the division of federal assets and liabilities, as well as the armed forces, between the Czech and Slovak Republics accelerated. The two republics signed a co-operation agreement, and subsequently established formal diplomatic relations. Recognition was rapidly accorded to the new countries by all those states that had maintained relations with Czechoslovakia, as well as by various international bodies.

Slovakia's MDS-dominated Government and legislature remained in place. In February 1993 the Národná rada Slovenskej republiky (National Council of the Slovak Republic, as the legislature was redesignated—Národná rada) elected Michal Kováč, Deputy Chairman of the MDS and former Chairman of Czechoslovakia's Federal Assembly, as President. Internal divisions in the MDS culminated in March with the dismissal of Milan Kňažko, the strongest critic of Mečiar within the party, from his post of Deputy Prime Minister and Minister of Foreign Affairs. Also in March the SNP leader, Ludovít Černák, resigned as Minister of the Economy, leaving the Government (with the exception of two independent ministers) composed exclusively of members of the MDS. However, as a result of several defections, the party (plus affiliates) lost its majority in the legislature. A new coalition Government, in which the SNP held several principal portfolios, was formed in November. In February 1994 six SNP deputies left the MDS to form what became the National Democratic Party—New Alternative (NDP—NA), led by Černák. In the same month the Minister of Foreign Affairs, Jozef Moravčík, and the Deputy Prime Minister, Roman Kováč, resigned from the Government, subsequently establishing the Democratic Union of Slovakia (DUS). In March the Národná rada approved a motion expressing no confidence in Mečiar's Government, prompting its resignation. A new, five-party, interim coalition was installed, led by Moravčík. Early legislative elections were scheduled for September.

The MDS was the leading party at elections to the Národná rada, held on 30 September and 1 October 1994, securing 35.0% of the votes cast and 61 seats in alliance with the Farmers' Party of Slovakia. An alliance of left-wing parties, led by the PDL, won 10.4% of the votes cast and 18 seats, followed by a coalition of Hungarian parties and the CDM (with 17 seats each). The remaining seats were taken by the DUS (15), the Association of Workers of Slovakia (AWS—13 seats) and the SNP (nine seats). Inter-party negotiations proved inconclusive, and Kováč requested that Mečiar form a Government. A coalition of the MDS, the SNP and the AWS was announced in December.

Following opposition demands for a referendum to be held on their proposals that the head of state be elected by direct popular vote, rather than chosen by the legislature, President Kováč scheduled a referendum for 23–24 May 1997. However, when the poll took place, the question on presidential elections was omitted from the ballot papers. The majority of voters consequently boycotted the referendum, and the rate of electoral participation (under 10%) rendered the vote invalid. The Minister of Foreign Affairs, Pavol Hamžík, resigned in protest at what he regarded as the Government's manipulation of the democratic process. In June several thousand people attended a rally to protest against the Government's intervention in the referendum. In February 1998, following a ruling by the Constitutional Court, Kováč announced that a new referendum would be held in April.

During January–March 1998 several attempts to elect a new President failed in the Národná rada, when candidates were unable to secure the required three-fifths' majority. The MDS had not contested the first rounds of voting, apparently confirming opposition fears that Mečiar was attempting to ensure that the presidency would remain vacant when Kováč left office, enabling him to assume a number of presidential powers. On 2 March Kováč's term expired, and certain presidential powers were transferred to the Government, in accordance with the Constitution. Mečiar immediately cancelled the referendum scheduled for April and announced the dismissal of some 28 of Slovakia's ambassadors abroad. He also granted an amnesty to various prisoners, and halted criminal proceedings relating to the May 1997 referendum. The Prime Minister's actions prompted a series of widely supported protest rallies organized by opposition parties, and were strongly criticized by the European Union (EU, see p. 281) and the USA.

In May 1998, in preparation for legislative elections scheduled for September, the Národná rada approved amendments to the electoral law, including a stipulation that political parties obtain at least 5% of the votes cast to secure parliamentary represen-

tation. Legislation was also approved that restricted pre-election campaigning to the state-run media. In June three ethnic Hungarian parties merged to create the Party of the Hungarian Coalition (PHC), and the SDC registered officially as a single party. In July the Národná rada adopted a constitutional amendment providing for the transfer of a number of presidential powers to the Chairman of the chamber, in the event of the presidency becoming vacant.

The Government of Mikuláš Dzurinda

The elections to the Národná rada were held on 25–26 September 1998, with the participation of 84.2% of the electorate. The MDS narrowly retained its position as the strongest party in the legislature, winning 43 seats (with 27.0% of the votes cast), but was unable to form a government, with its only possible ally, the SNP, holding 14 seats. The SDC obtained 42 seats (26.3% of the votes), the PDL 23 seats (14.7%), the PHC 15 seats and the Party of Civic Understanding (PCU—formed earlier that year) 13 seats. With a combined total of 93 seats, the SDC, the PDL, the PHC and the PCU agreed to form a new administration, and a new coalition Government, headed by Mikuláš Dzurinda, the leader of the SDC, was appointed at the end of October. Jozef Migaš of the PDL was elected Chairman of the Národná rada. The opposition's victory was welcomed both by Western institutions and by neighbouring countries. Dzurinda emphasized the new Government's intention to pursue early membership of the EU and the North Atlantic Treaty Organization (NATO, see p. 380), pledged to combat organized crime, and outlined measures to improve Slovakia's economic situation. In December the European Parliament adopted a resolution on Slovakia's application for membership of the EU, recommending that the European Commission consider initiating entry talks in 1999.

In January 1999 the Národná rada approved a constitutional amendment providing for the introduction of direct presidential elections. The ruling coalition nominated Rudolf Schuster, the Chairman of the PCU, as its presidential candidate. Nine candidates contested the first round of the presidential election, which was held on 15 May. Schuster (who was supported by Kováč) won 47.4% of the votes cast, and Mečiar obtained 37.2%. Schuster defeated Mečiar in a second round of voting on 29 May, with 57.2% of the votes cast, and was duly inaugurated as President on 15 June, having resigned the chairmanship of the PCU.

In September 1999 a large demonstration was staged in Bratislava to protest against declining living standards, resulting from austerity measures. In October Černák resigned as Minister of the Economy, and was succeeded by Lubomír Harach, the Chairman of the DUS. In February 2000 Dzurinda established a new party, the Slovak Democratic and Christian Union (SDCU), which was joined by several government ministers. Further SDC deputies subsequently resigned from the CDM and the DUS to join the SDCU. Following Dzurinda's election as SDCU Chairman at the party's opening congress in November, the SDC became effectively defunct.

Revisions to the Constitution, opposed by the MDS and the SNP, were adopted by a narrow majority in the legislature in February 2001. The amendments (which entered into effect on 1 July) facilitated the process of joining foreign alliances; strengthened the powers of the Constitutional Court; granted greater independence to the judiciary; and provided for public administration reform. In May Schuster replaced Pavol Hamzik, the Deputy Prime Minister for European Integration, who was held responsible for the suspension of EU payments in the previous month, following the misuse of funds. Also in May the Minister of the Interior tendered his resignation, following increasing criticism of an investigation into mismanagement under the Mečiar administration.

In July 2001 dissension increased between the government coalition parties over new legislation providing for the establishment of a higher level of regional self-administration. Following the adoption of the reforms, which provided for the creation of eight 'higher territorial units' (VÚCs), local government elections took place on 1 and 15 December. In a reflection of increasing popular support, MDS representatives secured 146 of the 401 seats in the regional councils and six of the eight gubernatorial posts. (However, voter participation in the second round was estimated at only 22% of the registered electorate.) In January 2002 the PDL demanded the resignation of the reformist Minister of Finance, Brigita Schmögnerová (a PDL member), after she allegedly withheld information regarding the privatization programme; threats by the PDL to withdraw from the coalition finally resulted in her replacement. Schmögnerová subsequently left the PDL and formed a new political party, the Social Democratic Alternative (SDA).

In July 2002 members of the MDS who had not been selected by the party to contest the forthcoming legislative elections established a new party, the Movement for Democracy. At the elections to the Národná rada on 20–21 September, the MDS received the highest proportion of the votes cast (19.5%), obtaining 36 mandates. The SDCU received 15.1% of the votes cast and 28 seats; a centre-right party, Direction, 13.5% and 25 seats; the PHC 11.2% and 20 seats; and the CDM 8.3% and 15 seats. The New Citizens' Alliance (NCA), established in 2001, won 8.0% of the votes and 15 seats, while the Slovak Communist Party (SCP) significantly increased its share, securing 6.3% and 11 seats. However, Mečiar proved unable to form a coalition government, and in late September Schuster invited Dzurinda to establish a new administration. A coalition agreement was signed in early October by four reformist, centre-right parties (the SDCU, the PHC, the CDM and the NCA), which together held 78 of the 150 seats in the Národná rada. On 16 October Schuster formally appointed a new coalition Government. The leader of the Democratic Party (DP), which had supported the SDCU in the elections, was also allocated a portfolio. Mikloš was retained in the administration as the new Minister of Finance. Local government elections took place on 6–7 December; mayoral offices were equally divided between the government coalition parties and the MDS.

In May 2003 a new party, the People's Union, was formed by disaffected members of the MDS. In the following month Mečiar was re-elected as Chairman of the MDS. At the same time, MDS members approved changing the party's name to the People's Party—Movement for a Democratic Slovakia (PP—MDS). Tensions emerged within the ruling coalition in July, after the Národná rada approved legislative amendments, proposed by the NCA, easing restrictions on abortion, which were strongly opposed by the CDM. In late July Schuster vetoed the legislation, fearing the collapse of the Government. In September the Deputy Prime Minister and Minister of the Economy, Robert Nemcsics, officially resigned his post, after losing the support of the NCA, following his criticism of Pavel Rusko, the party Chairman. Later that month Rusko was appointed as Deputy Prime Minister and Minister of the Economy. In October Juraj Liska was appointed as Minister of Defence, replacing Ivan Simko, who had been dismissed in September. A number of deputies subsequently left the SDCU to join Simko's newly formed Free Forum, rendering the ruling coalition a minority Government, with just 68 parliamentary seats.

Ivan Gašparovič elected President

In the first round of voting in the presidential election of 3 April 2004, Mečiar won 32.7% of the votes cast, followed by the Movement for Democracy leader (and former ally of Mečiar) Ivan Gašparovič, who won 22.3% of the votes. Eduard Kukan of the SDCU, the Minister of Foreign Affairs and the preferred candidate of Dzurinda's Government, took third place, with 22.1% of the votes, while Schuster, the incumbent, obtained just 7.4% of the votes. In the second round of voting, held on 17 April, Gašparovič was elected as President, receiving 59.9% of the votes cast; the rate of participation by the electorate in the second round was 43.5%. Gašparovič, who subsequently resigned from the leadership of the Movement for Democracy, was inaugurated on 15 June. Meanwhile, at Slovakia's first elections to the European Parliament in mid-June, the rate of participation by the electorate, at 17.0%, was the lowest recorded in any EU member state. The SDCU, the PP—MDS, Direction and the CDM each received three seats in the European Parliament, while the PHC obtained two.

In January 2005 a new party, Direction-Social Democracy, was formed by the merger of Direction, the Social Democratic Party of Slovakia, the SDA and the PDL. In August President Gašparovič dismissed Rusko from his post as Deputy Prime Minister and Minister of the Economy, after he was implicated in a loan scandal. Deputy Prime Minister and Minister of Finance Ivan Mikloš assumed the economy portfolio, in an acting capacity. Rusko, who remained leader of the NCA, subsequently urged Dzurinda to dismiss the Minister of Health, Rudolf Zajac (who had been nominated by the NCA, but was not a party member), and the Minister of Culture, František Tóth (an NCA member), both of whom had supported Rusko's removal, threatening to withdraw the NCA from the Government should Dzurinda refuse. Members of the NCA opposed to Rusko's leadership, including two party Vice-Chairmen, Lubomír Lintner and Jirko Malchárek, and Tóth, formed a splinter faction, led by

Lintner. At the beginning of September the SDCU, the CDM and the PHC agreed to expel the NCA from the ruling coalition; Zajac and Tóth were permitted to retain their posts. Lintner's group of deputies pledged its co-operation with the governing parties, and proposed Malchárek for the post of Minister of the Economy. On 11 September the NCA expelled nine members from the party, including Tóth and five Vice-Chairmen (among them Lintner and Malchárek). The following day the Government signed a co-operation agreement with Lintner's group of deputies. Opposition parties boycotted the Národná rada, but, after nine days, the Government narrowly managed to secure sufficient support to open a legislative session. In October Gašparovič appointed Malchárek as Deputy Prime Minister and Minister of the Economy.

In October 2005 DP leader Ľudovít Kaník resigned as Minister of Labour, Social Affairs and the Family. Kaník, who was replaced by Iveta Radičová, subsequently proposed a merger of the DP and the SDCU. In December a congress of the DP approved a draft agreement on the merger, which was confirmed in January 2006 at an extraordinary congress of the SDCU. The new political union was known as the SDCU-DP.

Meanwhile, on 26 November and 10 December 2005 an estimated 18% of the electorate took part in local government elections. Just 11% of the electorate voted in the second round, the lowest recorded rate of participation. Of the parties represented in the Národná rada, the CDM secured 87 of the 412 seats in the VUCs, Direction-Social Democracy took 70 and the SDCU won 64.

In January 2006 the Minister of Defence, Juraj Liška, tendered his resignation, after a military aircraft crashed on the Hungarian–Slovak border, killing some 42 people. Although the cause of the accident was unknown, the Government had been criticized for its decision to modernize Soviet-manufactured aircraft, rather than investing in new equipment. Liška was replaced by Martin Fedor. In February the CDM announced the withdrawal of its three ministers from the Government, following Dzurinda's refusal to submit for discussion a proposal to approve a treaty with the Holy See that would enable workers to refuse to perform duties on the basis of religious objections. The leader of the CDM subsequently resigned as Chairman of the Národná rada, and was replaced, in an acting capacity, by the PHC leader and Deputy Chairman of the legislature, Béla Bugár. As a result of the CDM's withdrawal, the ruling coalition controlled just 53 seats in the legislature, and three days later the Národná rada approved a proposal by Dzurinda for legislative elections, originally due to take place in September, to be held on 17 June. Gašparovič appointed Martin Pado of the SDCU-DP as Minister of the Interior, László Szigeti of the PHC as Minister of Education and Lucia Žitňanská, an independent, as Minister of Justice. In April 2006 Tóth was dismissed from his position as Minister of Culture, after being accused of misusing state funds; Rudolf Chmel, who had held the portfolio until May 2005, was subsequently reappointed to the post.

The Government of Robert Fico

In legislative elections held on 17 June 2006, 50 seats were won by Fico's Direction-Social Democracy, which secured 29.1% of the votes cast. The SDCU-DP obtained 18.4% of the votes (31 seats), while the SNP and the PHC both won 11.7% (20 seats). Fifteen seats were allocated to the PP—MDS, which attracted 8.8% of the ballot, while the CDM secured 14 seats, with 8.3%. The rate of participation in the elections was 54.7%. Three days later, Fico was invited by President Gašparovič to form a government. Fico's new administration, which was formed after a coalition agreement, predominantly comprised members of Direction-Social Democracy, with the SNP and the PP—MDS being allocated three and two cabinet posts, respectively. Neither Mečiar nor SNP Chairman Ján Slota were awarded cabinet positions. None the less, the Party of European Socialists, in protest at Direction-Social Democracy's involvement with the extreme right SNP, voted to suspend temporarily the party's membership. Fico was formally appointed Prime Minister on 4 July.

In August 2006, shortly after the installation of the new Government, extremist statements made by Slota on deportation and Slovakia's ethnic Hungarian population attracted domestic and international criticism. While the PHC appealed to prosecutors to take legal action against Slota, the SNP threatened to sue controversial PHC deputy Miklos Duray for describing it as a 'fascist' party. At the end of August the Chairman of the Parliamentary Assembly of the Council of Europe (see p. 260), Rane van der Linden, denounced manifestations of racial intolerance in Slovakia. On 7 September the Národná rada adopted a declaration against extremism and intolerance (112 deputies voted in favour of the motion, while 28 abstained).

By the end of 2006 Fico appeared to have consolidated his position; Direction-Social Democracy performed well at the municipal elections of 2 December (in which 47.7% of the electorate participated). In April a dispute erupted within the PHC when Duray accused outgoing Chairman Béla Bugár of co-operating with the communist-era secret police. (Bugár had been replaced as Chairman at the beginning of that month by Pál Csáky.)

In November 2007 the PP—MDS threatened to withdraw from the Government, in protest at Fico's dismissal of the Minister of Agriculture (a representative of that party), after evidence emerged of an illicit land sale agreement involving the Slovak State Land Fund. However, in December the Národná rada approved the budget for 2008, by 85 votes to 61, in a motion that was also regarded as expressing confidence in Fico's administration. In January 2008 the Minister of Defence, František Kašický, resigned, following allegations that his ministry had overpriced tenders for the maintenance of military barracks; he was succeed by Jaroslav Baška, also of Direction-Social Democracy. The formation of a new political party, the Conservative Democrats of Slovakia (CDS), was announced in March by four deputies who had recently defected from the CDM. In April President Gašparovič signed into law new regulations that were expected severely to restrict the activities of the print media; the new legislation, which entered into effect in June, had been drafted following government objections to press statements, and had attracted strong criticism from opposition parties and international organizations. Ján Kubiš resigned as Minister of Foreign Affairs in January 2009 to become Executive Secretary of the UN Economic Commission for Europe; he was succeeded by Miroslav Lajčák, hitherto High Representative of the International Community and EU Special Representative in Bosnia and Herzegovina.

Gašparovič re-elected President

Seven candidates contested the first round of voting in a presidential election held on 21 March 2009. Gašparovič, the incumbent, who was supported by the governing Direction-Social Democracy and the SNP, secured the largest share of the votes cast, with 46.7%, followed by Iveta Radičová, a Vice-Chairman of the SDCU-DP also supported by the PHC and the CDM, who won 38.1%. Gašparovič defeated Radičová in a second round of voting on 4 April, receiving 55.5% of the valid votes cast. The rate of participation by the electorate was 43.6% in the first round and 51.7% in the second round.

In April 2009 the Minister of Construction and Regional Development, Marian Janušek of the SNP, submitted his resignation, which had been requested by Fico after investigations by the Public Procurement Office and the Supreme Audit Office confirmed that Janušek's ministry had mishandled the tendering process for a €120m. contract that had been awarded to a consortium reported to have links to SNP Chairman Slota. In May Ján Chrbet was dismissed as Minister of the Environment, owing to controversy concerning his involvement in the sale of quotas for carbon dioxide emissions at unusually low cost; he was replaced by Viliam Turský (also of the SNP). In June the Deputy Prime Minister and Minister of Justice Stefan Harabin was elected Chairman of the Supreme Court and of the Judicial Council; Viera Petríková was appointed to his former government post. In August Turský was dismissed as Minister of the Environment, following his apparent mishandling of tendering for a contract. In response to the series of improprieties associated with activities of the ministry, the governing coalition agreed that responsibility for the Ministry of the Environment would be transferred from the SNP to Direction-Social Democracy; Jozef Medved was appointed as Minister of the Environment in October. In March 2010 President Gašparovič dismissed Stefanov as Minister of Construction and Regional Development, following an investigation into transactions related to a contract awarded by the ministry.

The 2010 elections and Government of Iveta Radičová

At elections to the Národná rada, which took place on 12 June 2010, Direction-Social Democracy obtained the greatest share of the votes cast (34.8%), securing 62 of the 150 legislative seats. The SDCU-DP was placed second, with 15.4% of the votes and 28 seats, followed by a liberal party formed in 2009, Freedom and Solidarity (FAS), with 12.1% and 22 seats, the CDM (8.5% and 15 seats), Bridge, founded in 2009 to promote inter-ethnic co-operation (8.1% and 14 seats), and the SNP (5.1% and nine

seats). The PHC and the PP—MDS, with less than 5% of the votes cast, both failed to secure legislative representation. Despite having obtained the highest number of seats, Direction-Social Democracy proved unable to form a coalition with a parliamentary majority, and President Gašparovič invited Radičová (who was the election leader of the SDCU-DP) to establish a coalition administration comprising the four centre-right parties in the Národná rada. On 8 July Fico and his Government resigned from office, and Radičová was appointed as Prime Minister (becoming the first woman to hold the post). On the same day Richard Sulík of Freedom and Solidarity was elected as the new parliamentary Chairman. A new Government, comprising a coalition of the SDCU-DP, the CDM, Bridge and FAS, was subsequently installed; principal appointments included Ján Figeľ as First Deputy Prime Minister, Minister of Transport, Post and Telecommunications, Daniel Lipšic as Minister of the Interior and Dzurinda as Minister of Foreign Affairs. On 10 August Radičová's Government secured a vote of confidence (with 79 votes in favour) in the Národná rada.

Following a successful public petition organized by FAS, a referendum on political reform took place on 18 September 2010; although a large majority of votes were cast in favour of the six proposals (which included a reduction in the number of parliamentary deputies from 150 to 100), only about 22.8% of the electorate participated in the poll, well below the 50% minimum required for its validation. The results of the municipal elections, which were conducted on 27 November, indicated a significant loss of support for Radičová's ruling coalition, following her announcement of austerity measures to reduce the budget deficit. From late 2010 trade unions organized a series of demonstrations, in protest at the Government's proposed austerity measures. In March 2011 planned amendments to the labour code attracted particular controversy and prompted further protests; despite opposition from both trade unions and employer associations, a revised labour code was approved by the Government in late April.

On 11 October 2011 FAS boycotted a parliamentary vote on Slovakia's endorsement of an expanded European Financial Stability Facility (EFSF—which had been established to support member countries of the eurozone suffering severe financial difficulties); the motion, effectively a vote of confidence in Radičová's administration, was consequently defeated in the Národná rada, causing the collapse of the coalition Government. After agreeing to a demand by Fico to schedule early elections for 10 March 2012, Radičová secured parliamentary approval of the EFSF, with the support of Direction-Social Democracy, in a second vote on 13 October 2011. Later that month President Gašparovič dismissed the Government, reappointing it in an interim capacity, while Radičová announced her intention to resign from the SDCU-DP, and from political life. Meanwhile, a new political party, Ordinary People and Independent Personalities (OPIP), led by Igor Matovič, a former member of FAS, was registered in October.

In November 2011 the Minister of Defence, Ľubomir Galko, was dismissed, after it emerged that the Military Defence Intelligence Department had been responsible for clandestinely recording the telephone conversations of three journalists employed by opposition newspaper *Pravda*, and of the director of television news station TA3. In December a file purportedly compiled by the Slovak Information Service from 2005–06 surveillance, which was published illicitly on the internet, provided details of a system of bribes paid to senior officials of Dzurinda's administration, notably by financial investment group Penta, in order to secure contracts. A series of nation-wide anti-corruption protests ensued in early 2012. In January five employees of the Military Defence Intelligence Department (including its former head) were charged with misuse of power.

Recent developments: early legislative elections

In the early elections to the Národná rada, held on 10 March 2012 (when a further anti-corruption protest was staged in Bratislava), Direction-Social Democracy obtained 83 seats, with 44.4% of the votes cast, hence winning an outright majority of seats; the CDM received 16 seats (with 8.8% of the votes), ahead of OPIP, with 16 seats (8.6%), and Bridge, with 13 seats (6.9%). Both the SDCU-DP and FAS experienced a substantial decline in support, each receiving 11 seats. On 3 April President Gašparovič appointed Fico as Prime Minister; a Government that principally comprised members of Direction-Social Democracy (becoming the first single-party administration since 1993) was installed on the following day. In addition to several long-standing Direction-Social Democracy politicians, the new Government included three non-party members, among them Laj-čák, who again became Minister of Foreign Affairs.

In accordance with pre-election pledges, in August 2012 the Government approved revisions to the labour code that strengthened the rights of employees (thereby reversing the amendments introduced by the previous administration); the measures, which were adopted in the Národná rada in October, were welcomed by the Confederation of Trade Unions. However, following continued austerity efforts by the Government, in September teachers staged a one-day strike (the largest since 2003), resulting in the closure of 80%–90% of the country's primary and secondary schools and 30% of universities, to demand a 10% increase in salaries. In November further strike action was staged, after the teachers unions' refused the government proposal of a 5% rise; this was suspended in early December to allow negotiations to proceed, although industrial unrest continued.

In January 2013 the parliamentary opposition parties proposed the impeachment of President Gašparovič on the grounds that he had violated the Constitution, after he refused to endorse the Národná rada's election, in June 2011, of Jozef Čentéš as Prosecutor-General (which had been upheld by the Constitutional Court). In March 2013, however, the motion for initiation of an impeachment process was rejected in the Národná rada, with the opposition of Direction-Social Democracy deputies. In April the SNP leadership announced that it had expelled Slota (who had been replaced as the party's Chairman by Andrej Danko the previous October), owing to discrepancies in financial management.

Roma Affairs

Although, according to the 2001 census, there were some 89,900 Roma in Slovakia, the community was unofficially estimated to number around 200,000. In January 2004 a report by the Council of Europe concluded that Slovakia's Roma were frequently victims of racial prejudice and were disadvantaged socially. In the following month proposed reductions in social welfare prompted violent protests by the Roma minority, and some 1,000 troops were deployed to control rioting. In July new legislation was introduced prohibiting discrimination on the grounds of ethnicity. In November 2006 the European Monitoring Centre on Racism and Xenophobia, based in Vienna, Austria, criticized Slovakia, along with the Czech Republic and Hungary, for segregating its Roma populations, particularly in the education sector, but also with regard to housing and the labour market. A report issued in February 2013 by the UN Committee on the Elimination of Racial Discrimination expressed concern at the continued segregation of Roma children in schools, a lack of adequate housing in Roma settlements, the forced sterilization of Roma women (following judgments by the European Court of Human Rights against Slovakia), and the need to implement anti-discrimination legislation.

Foreign Affairs

Regional relations

Slovakia's relations with Hungary have been strained by the issue of the large Hungarian minority (numbering some 520,500 at the 2001 census) resident in Slovakia, who are campaigning for cultural and educational autonomy. The two countries are also involved in a dispute over the Gabčíkovo-Nagymaros hydroelectric project, a scheme initiated by the Governments of Czechoslovakia and Hungary in 1977, which involved the construction of two dams and the diversion of the River Danube. Despite Hungary's decision in 1989 to abandon the project (following pressure by environmentalist groups), the Czechoslovak Government announced that it would proceed unilaterally with its part of the construction. In early 1993 Slovakia and Hungary agreed to forward the dispute to the International Court of Justice (ICJ) in The Hague, Netherlands, and to operate a temporary water-management scheme in the mean time. In March 1995, none the less, an historic bilateral Treaty of Friendship and Co-operation was signed by the Prime Ministers of Hungary and Slovakia. The Treaty, notably, guaranteed the rights of ethnic minorities in each republic, while confirming the existing state border. However, the language law approved by the Slovak legislature in November, declaring Slovak the only official language and thereby potentially restricting the use of minority languages, was criticized both by Hungarian residents of Slovakia and by the Hungarian Government as a violation of the Treaty. In August 1997 the Hungarian Prime Minister, Gyula Horn, and Mečiar agreed on the establishment of a joint commission to assess the implementation of the 1995 Treaty.

(The first meeting of the joint minorities commission was held in Budapest, Hungary, in February 1999.)

In September 1997 the ICJ pronounced its judgment on the Gabčíkovo-Nagymaros hydroelectric project, ruling that both countries had breached international law: Hungary was not justified in suspending work on the project, while the former Czechoslovakia should not have proceeded unilaterally. Both countries were to pay compensation for damages, and to negotiate regarding the realization of the original agreement. In July 1999 the Národná rada approved legislation that provided for the use of an ethnic minority language in towns where the minority accounted for at least 20% of the population. In May 2011 the Národná rada adopted an amendment to the legislation that reduced this to 15% (after the proportion had been determined by two population censuses); in June the legislature overturned a presidential veto of the amendment.

In December 1999 Hungary renounced any claim to a share of the hydroelectric energy produced by the Gabčíkovo-Nagymaros dam project, but requested an increase in the common flow of water along the Danube, for ecological reasons. In February 2001 Slovakia accepted that it had no legal means to compel Hungary to complete the project, but stated that it was to seek compensation. In December 2003 an intergovernmental commission was established to co-ordinate negotiations on the issue. Meanwhile, in January 2002 relations between Slovakia and Hungary had again become acrimonious, following Hungary's adoption of legislation that granted ethnic Hungarians resident in six neighbouring states, including Slovakia, education, employment and medical benefits. The Slovak Government protested that the new legislation violated Slovakia's sovereignty, and demanded that it be cancelled or amended. In March 2003 Hungary agreed to suspend the application of the law in Slovakia, and in December the Ministers of Foreign Affairs of Hungary and Slovakia signed an agreement on the issue. The provisions of the Hungarian 'status law' were effectively superseded by the accession of Hungary and Slovakia to the EU in May 2004 (see below). In February 2006 it was announced that Slovakia and Hungary had agreed to implement the 1997 ICJ ruling on the Gabčíkovo-Nagymaros hydroelectric project.

Tensions between Hungary and Slovakia were again apparent in August 2009, when the Slovak Ministry of Foreign Affairs prohibited the Hungarian President, László Sólyom, from entering Slovakia, despite EU regulations on freedom of movement between member states. Sólyom's visit (which was to have been in a private capacity, to unveil a statue to St István—Stephen, the first King of Hungary, in a predominantly ethnically Hungarian town in southern Slovakia, Komárno) was condemned by the Slovakian Government, on the grounds that it took place on 21 August, the anniversary of the 1968 invasion of Czechoslovakia by Warsaw Pact (including Hungarian) troops. The growth in support, in both Hungary and Slovakia, for extreme nationalist parties (Jobbik and the Slovak National Party, respectively) from the late 2000s was a further cause of tensions in relations. Legislation that took effect in Slovakia from 1 September 2009, placing restrictions on the use of languages other than Slovak, was a further source of controversy. In early September some 10,000 people, believed to be mainly ethnic Hungarians, attended a rally in the southern town of Dunajská Streda to demand that the legislation be amended. Concern was expressed that the legislation might criminalize the use of minority languages in private, as well as official, contexts. Slovakia and Hungary subsequently agreed that the Organization for Security and Co-operation in Europe (OSCE, see p. 397) would oversee the implementation of the law to ensure that it complied with international norms.

After elections in Hungary in April 2010 resulted in victory for centre-right party Fidesz, on 26 May the Hungarian parliament adopted legislation permitting ethnic Hungarians outside Hungary, including in Slovakia, to apply for Hungarian citizenship. This measure was described by Slovakian Prime Minister Fico as a threat to security; later on 26 May the Národná rada voted in favour of amending the country's citizenship law, providing for the removal of Slovak citizenship from those who applied for citizenship of a second state. The new Government of Prime Minister Iveta Radičová stated its intention to abrogate the Fico administration's law on dual citizenship (which had entered into effect on 17 July). In February 2011, however, the Národná rada voted in favour of amending, rather than abolishing, the law, which henceforth allowed citizens to hold dual nationality only if they met certain conditions. In August 2012 the Slovakian Ministry of Justice requested the extradition from Hungary of a 97-year-old former police commander of the pro-Nazi regime, László Csizsik-Csatáry, who in 1948 had been sentenced to death *in absentia* by a Czechoslovakian court for war crimes perpetrated against Jewish civilians in the town of Košice (now in eastern Slovakia). In March 2013 a court in Košice commuted the 1948 verdict against Csizsik-Csatáry (who remained under house arrest in Hungary) from the death penalty to life imprisonment. The Slovakian Supreme Court rejected a complaint by Csizsik-Csatáry against the verdict in April 2013.

Relations with neighbouring Austria were strained by the issue of the partially constructed, Soviet-designed nuclear power station at Mochovce (north-east of Bratislava), operated by Slovenské elektrárne (Slovak Electricity), the completion of which was opposed by the Austrian Government owing to safety concerns. An agreement on completion of the project was signed in April 1996, with Western European, Russian and Czech companies, according to which the first reactor would be commissioned by July 1998 and the second by March 1999. Tension increased in June 1998, when the first reactor was activated, despite a request from the Austrian Government that Slovakia delay the opening of the plant until an international team of inspectors, who had visited Mochovce in May, had submitted a final report on the plant's safety. In late 1999 the Slovak Government announced its decision to close two existing reactors at Jaslovské-Bohunice between 2006 and 2008, further antagonizing Austria, which had favoured closure by 2000. In May 2004, shortly after Slovakia's accession to the EU, tensions between the two countries heightened, following the Slovak Government's announcement that it intended to complete work on the Mochovce plant. Construction of Mochovce's two unfinished reactors by Slovenské elektrárne (majority owned by the Italian electricity group Enel since 2006) commenced in November 2008 and was scheduled to be completed during 2013, at an estimated cost of €2,800m.

In December 1999 Slovakia was formally invited to commence talks on accession to the EU; entry negotiations opened in February 2000. Following the return to power of a reformist coalition Government in October 2002, at an EU summit meeting held in Copenhagen, Denmark, in December, Slovakia was one of 10 nations invited to become a member in 2004. At a national referendum, which was conducted on 16–17 May 2003, 92.5% of votes were cast in favour of membership of the EU; some 52% of the electorate participated in the ballot. Slovakia's Treaty of Accession was formally ratified by the Národná rada on 1 July, and the country became a full member of the EU on 1 May 2004.

In December 2007 Slovakia, together with eight other EU member nations, implemented the Schengen Agreement on freedom of travel, effectively removing border controls between those states subject to the Agreement. In early 2008 the Slovak authorities announced a subsequent increase in the number of illegal immigrants detained. Following Kosovo's unilateral declaration of independence in February, Slovakia was among several EU member nations (including Spain, Romania and Cyprus) to refuse to recognize it as a sovereign state, although the Government offered it 'partnership'. The ratification of the EU's Lisbon Treaty, which was designed to reform the Union's institutions, was approved by the Národná rada in April and received presidential assent in May.

In May 2008 the European Commission approved Slovakia's planned accession to the eurozone on 1 January 2009. This decision was confirmed by EU finance ministers in July 2008, and Slovakia became the 16th member of the eurozone as scheduled. Following pressure from the European Commission, on 13 October 2011 Slovakia became the last member state of the eurozone to ratify an expanded European Financial Stability Facility (EFSF), which had been established to support member states suffering severe financial difficulties with the aim of preserving the stability of the currency; an initial parliamentary vote on the EFSF precipitated the collapse of Prime Minister Radičová's administration (see Domestic Political Affairs).

Other external relations

In February 1994 Slovakia joined NATO's 'Partnership for Peace' programme (see p. 383). At a NATO summit meeting in Prague at the end of November 2002, Slovakia (together with six other countries) was formally invited to join the Alliance, and it became a full member on 29 March 2004. In May Slovakia hosted a plenary session of the NATO Parliamentary Assembly, and in February 2005 it hosted a summit meeting between US President George W. Bush and Russian President Vladimir Putin. President Bush praised the deployment of 100 Slovak troops to Iraq to participate in the US-led military operations there.

However, in February 2007 Fico fulfilled one of his electoral promises by withdrawing his country's troops from Iraq. (This, in addition to controversial visits by the new premier to the People's Republic of China and Libya, was perceived as an effort by Fico to distance himself from the pro-US stance of his predecessor.) At early 2013, however, Slovakia contributed 236 troops to the NATO-led International Security Assistance Force (ISAF) mission deployed in Afghanistan, and in February the Ministry of Defence announced that a further 150 soldiers would be dispatched to the country to assist in training the Afghan security forces following the scheduled withdrawal of ISAF by the end of 2014.

CONSTITUTION AND GOVERNMENT

Supreme legislative power is vested in the Národná rada Slovenskej republiky (National Council of the Slovak Republic), the 150 members of which are elected for a term of four years by universal adult suffrage. The President of the Republic (Head of State) is directly elected by universal adult suffrage for a five-year term. The President, who is restricted to two consecutive terms of office, appoints the Prime Minister and, on the latter's recommendation, the other members of the Government (the supreme body of executive power). Judicial power is exercised by the Supreme Court, regional courts and district courts. For administrative purposes, Slovakia is divided into eight 'higher territorial units' (VÚCs), each with a regional council (together totalling 401 seats), and 79 electoral districts.

REGIONAL AND INTERNATIONAL CO-OPERATION

Slovakia is a member of the European Union (EU, see p. 281), the Council of Europe, the Organization for Security and Co-operation in Europe (OSCE, see p. 397), the Organisation for Economic Co-operation and Development (OECD, see p. 388) and the North Atlantic Treaty Organization (NATO, see p. 380).

Slovakia was admitted to the UN following independence in 1993 and, as a contracting party to the General Agreement on Tariffs and Trade, joined the World Trade Organization (WTO, see p. 444) on its establishment in 1995.

ECONOMIC AFFAIRS

In 2011, according to the World Bank, Slovakia's gross national income (GNI), measured at average 2009–11 prices, was US $87,411m., equivalent to $16,070 per head (or $22,230 per head on an international purchasing-power parity basis). During 2002–11, it was estimated, the population increased by an annual average of 0.1%, while gross domestic product (GDP) per head increased, in real terms, by an average of 4.6% per year. Overall GDP increased, in real terms, at an average annual rate of 4.8% in 2002–11; in 2011 GDP increased by 3.3%, measured at constant prices. In 2012 GDP increased by 2.0%, according to chain linked methodologies.

The agricultural sector (including hunting, forestry and fishing) contributed 3.6% of GDP and engaged 3.2% of the employed labour force in 2012. The principal crops are wheat, maize and sugar beet. Livestock-breeding is also important. According to the World Bank, during 2002–10 the GDP of the agricultural sector increased, in real terms, at an average annual rate of 2.9%. Agricultural GDP decreased by 5.4% in 2012, according to chain linked methodologies.

Industry (including mining, manufacturing, construction and power) contributed 35.9% of GDP, and engaged 37.5% of the employed labour force in 2012. The GDP of the industrial sector increased, in real terms, at an average annual rate of 6.3% during 2002–10, according to the World Bank; industrial GDP increased by 1.3% in 2010.

Mining and quarrying contributed 0.6% of GDP in 2010, and engaged 0.5% of the employed labour force in 2012. The principal minerals extracted include brown coal and lignite, copper, zinc, lead, iron ore and magnesite. There are also deposits of crude petroleum, natural gas and mercury, as well as materials used in construction (including limestone, gravel and brick loam).

The manufacturing sector contributed 22.1% of GDP in 2012, and engaged 24.5% of the employed labour force in the same year. According to the World Bank, the GDP of the manufacturing sector increased at an average annual rate of 7.9% in 2002–10; manufacturing GDP decreased by 21.3% in 2009, but increased by 2.2% in 2010.

The construction sector contributed 8.1% of GDP and engaged 10.3% of the employed labour force in 2012. According to chain linked methodologies, construction GDP increased by 4.8% in 2011, but decreased by 6.2% in 2012.

Energy is derived principally from nuclear power, which provided some 53.3% of electricity generated in 2010. In that year hydroelectric power accounted for 20.1% of electricity production, and coal for 15.2%. A nuclear power station at Jaslovské-Bohunice has been in operation since the early 1980s, although two reactors there were closed in 2006 and 2008. In mid-1998 the first block of a new nuclear power installation, at Mochovce, commenced operations; construction work on two unfinished reactors there was due to be completed during 2013. Mineral fuels and lubricants accounted for 14.5% of the value of total merchandise imports in 2011.

In 2012 the services sector contributed 60.4% of GDP, and engaged 59.2% of the employed labour force. During 2002–10, according to the World Bank, the GDP of the services sector decreased, in real terms, at an average annual rate of 4.5%; services GDP increased by 7.5% in 2010.

In 2011 Slovakia recorded a merchandise trade surplus of US $3,322.0m., and there was a surplus of some $12.4m. on the current account of the balance of payments. In 2011 the principal source of imports was Germany, which accounted for 16.4% of the total; other major suppliers were Russia, the Czech Republic, the Republic of Korea and the People's Republic of China. Germany was also the principal market for exports in that year (accounting for 20.4%); other important purchasers were the Czech Republic, Poland, Hungary, Austria and France. The main imports in 2011 were machinery and transport equipment (accounting for 40.4% of all imports), base metals, mineral products, plastic and rubber manufactures, and chemicals. The principal exports in that year were machinery and transport equipment (which accounted for 52.8% of all exports), base metals, plastic and rubber manufactures, and mineral products.

Slovakia's overall budgetary deficit was €3,106.9m. in 2012, equivalent to 4.3% of GDP. Slovakia's gross general government debt was €29,911m. in 2011, equivalent to 43.3% of GDP. At the end of 2006 Slovakia's total external debt was US $27,085m., of which $4,508m. was long-term public debt. In 2003 the cost of debt-servicing was equivalent to 13.8% of the value of exports of goods and services. The annual rate of inflation averaged 4.1% in 2002–12. Consumer prices increased by 3.6% in 2012. According to official figures, the average rate of unemployment was 13.9% in 2012.

Slovakia experienced more rapid economic growth than many other transition states of Central and South-Eastern Europe during the 1990s and 2000s. Foreign investment was further encouraged by the introduction of a 19% uniform rate of income tax, corporate tax and value-added tax in 2004. Although the Government subsequently adopted a more hesitant approach towards privatization, the requirements of the European Union (EU, see p. 281) exchange rate mechanism (ERM II), which Slovakia had entered in November 2005, effectively prevented any substantial redirection of economic policy. Slovakia adopted the euro on 1 January 2009. Despite the country's relatively strong recovery from the global economic crisis by 2011, in October the necessity of obtaining parliamentary approval for an expanded European Financial Stability Facility, which had been established to support those member states of the eurozone experiencing severe financial difficulties, precipitated the collapse of the Government. Following early legislative elections in March 2012, Robert Fico was appointed Prime Minister for a second time, after issuing pre-election pledges to reduce the budget deficit through targeted tax increases rather than stringent retrenchment measures. In October the Slovak Information Service identified corrupt public infrastructure tenders and the diversion of EU funds as having damaged the economy in the previous year. In December the legislature approved government proposals for the abolition of the 19% uniform income tax rate, an increase in the corporate tax rate to 23% and the imposition of a 25% maximum rate in income taxes for high earners. Opponents of the Government criticized both of these measures as deterrents to foreign investment, as well as the adoption, in October, of a revised labour code that reversed restrictions introduced by the previous administration. Amid a continuing debt crisis in the eurozone, in April 2013 the central bank forecast that Slovakia's estimated GDP growth of some 2.0% in 2012 would slow to about 0.9% in the following year, prompting concerns that a consequent fall in tax revenue would result in the Government failing to meet its commitment to reduce the budget deficit to below 3%, in accordance with EU criteria.

PUBLIC HOLIDAYS

2014: 1 January (Anniversary of the Slovak Republic), 6 January (Epiphany), 18 April (Good Friday), 21 April (Easter Monday), 1 May (Labour Day), 8 May (Anniversary of Liberation), 5 July (Day of the Slav Apostles, Cyril and Methodius), 29 August (National Day, Anniversary of the Slovak National Uprising), 1 September (Constitution Day), 15 September (Our Lady of Seven Sorrows), 1 November (All Saints' Day), 17 November (Day of Freedom and Democracy), 24–26 December (Christmas).

Statistical Survey

Source: Statistical Office of the Slovak Republic, Miletičova 3, 824 67 Bratislava; tel. (2) 5023-6340; fax (2) 5556-1361; e-mail agnesa.kralikova@statistics.sk; internet www.statistics.sk.

Area and Population

AREA, POPULATION AND DENSITY

Area (sq km)	49,033*
Population (census results)	
26 May 2001	5,379,455
21 May 2011	
Males	2,627,772
Females	2,769,264
Total	5,397,036
Density (per sq km) at 2011 census	110.1

* 18,932 sq miles.

POPULATION BY AGE AND SEX
(at 2011 census)

	Males	Females	Total
0–14	424,109	402,407	826,516
15–64	1,946,432	1,939,895	3,886,327
65 and over	256,507	426,366	682,873
Total*	2,627,772	2,769,264	5,397,036

* Including 1,320 persons (males 724, females 596) of unspecified age.

POPULATION BY ETHNIC GROUP
(at 2011 census)

	Number	%
Slovak	4,352,775	80.7
Hungarian	458,467	8.5
Gypsy (Roma)	105,738	2.0
Ruthenian, Ukrainian	40,912	0.8
Czech	33,635	0.6
German	4,690	0.1
Others (incl. undeclared)	400,819	7.4
Total	5,397,036	100.0

REGIONS
(population at 2011 census)

	Area (sq km)	Population	Density (per sq km)
Banská Bystrica . . .	9,455	660,563	69.9
Bratislava . . .	2,053	602,436	293.4
Košice	6,753	791,723	117.2
Nitra	6,343	689,867	108.8
Prešov	8,993	814,527	90.6
Trenčín	4,501	594,328	132.0
Trnava	4,148	554,741	133.7
Žilina	6,788	688,851	101.5
Total	49,034	5,397,036	110.1

Note: Each region is named after its principal city.

PRINCIPAL TOWNS
(population at 2011 census)

Bratislava (capital) .	411,228	Trnava . . .	66,358
Košice . . .	240,433	Martin . . .	57,428
Prešov . . .	91,782	Trenčín . . .	55,877
Žilina . . .	81,494	Poprad . . .	52,862
Banská Bystrica .	80,003	Prievidza . .	48,978
Nitra . . .	78,916	Zvolen . . .	43,318

BIRTHS, MARRIAGES AND DEATHS

	Registered live births Number	Rate (per 1,000)	Registered marriages Number	Rate (per 1,000)	Registered deaths Number	Rate (per 1,000)
2004 . .	53,747	10.0	27,885	5.2	51,852	9.6
2005 . .	54,430	10.1	26,149	4.9	53,475	9.9
2006 . .	53,904	10.0	25,939	4.8	53,301	9.9
2007 . .	54,424	10.1	27,437	5.1	53,856	10.0
2008 . .	57,360	10.6	28,293	5.2	53,164	9.8
2009 . .	61,217	11.3	26,356	4.9	52,913	9.8
2010 . .	60,410	11.1	25,415	4.7	53,445	9.8
2011 . .	60,813	11.3	25,621	4.7	51,903	9.6

Life expectancy (years at birth): 76.0 (males 72.3; females 79.8) in 2011 (Source: World Bank, World Development Indicators database).

ECONOMICALLY ACTIVE POPULATION
(labour force surveys, '000 persons)

	2010	2011	2012
Agriculture, hunting, forestry and fishing	75.0	71.7	75.4
Mining and quarrying	13.8	11.8	12.7
Manufacturing	530.0	568.0	570.3
Electricity, gas and water . . .	58.1	55.2	50.4
Construction	258.3	243.7	240.7
Wholesale and retail trade; repair of motor vehicles, motorcycles and personal and household goods	306.3	304.0	289.8
Hotels and restaurants . . .	103.5	100.7	97.2
Transport, storage and communications	201.3	211.0	218.1
Financial intermediation . . .	47.7	53.4	51.9
Real estate, renting and business services	148.6	150.3	149.6
Public administration and defence; compulsory social security . .	189.0	193.0	184.8
Education	165.0	164.2	157.4
Health and social work . . .	157.1	159.8	161.3

—*continued*	2010	2011	2012
Other community, social and personal service activities . .	58.0	56.8	63.2
Private households with employed persons	4.7	6.4	5.4
Extra-territorial organizations .	0.9	1.0	0.8
Sub-total	2,317.2	2,350.9	2,328.9
Activities not adequately defined .	0.3	0.5	0.1
Total	2,317.5	2,351.4	2,329.0
Unemployed	389.0	367.9	377.5
Total labour force . . .	2,706.5	2,719.3	2,706.5
Males	1,497.3	1,515.0	1,507.3
Females	1,209.2	1,204.4	1,199.3

Health and Welfare

KEY INDICATORS

Total fertility rate (children per woman, 2010)	1.3
Under-5 mortality rate (per 1,000 live births, 2010) . . .	8
HIV/AIDS (% of persons aged 15–49, 2009)	<0.1
Physicians (per 1,000 head, 2004)	3.1
Hospital beds (per 1,000 head, 2006)	6.8
Health expenditure (2009): US $ per head (PPP) . . .	2,084
Health expenditure (2009): % of GDP	9.1
Health expenditure (2009): public (% of total)	65.7
Total carbon dioxide emissions ('000 metric tons, 2008) . .	37,557.4
Carbon dioxide emissions per head (metric tons, 2008) . .	6.9
Human Development Index (2011): ranking	35
Human Development Index (2011): value	0.834

For sources and definitions, see explanatory note on p. vi.

Agriculture

PRINCIPAL CROPS
('000 metric tons)

	2009	2010	2011
Wheat	1,537.9	1,227.8	1,639.3
Barley	675.5	361.4	530.0
Maize	988.1	952.3	1,365.7
Rye	56.9	37.6	43.0
Oats	34.6	24.6	36.9
Triticale (wheat-rye hybrid) . .	33.9	24.8	33.4
Potatoes	216.1	125.9	217.3
Sugar beet	898.8	977.7	1,160.7
Peas, dry	11.7	15.0	14.7
Sunflower seed	187.2	150.3	200.9
Rapeseed	386.7	322.5	332.2
Cabbages and other brassicas .	50.2	46.7	56.8*
Tomatoes	51.9	36.5	6.6†
Chillies and peppers, green . .	26.2	23.6	25.2*
Cucumbers and gherkins . .	27.9	27.3	29.7*
Onions, dry	26.4	28.2	35.7*
Carrots and turnips . . .	35.7	34.9	42.0*
Apples	37.7	34.2	31.4
Grapes	42.1	21.1	49.0
Watermelons	4.5	2.8	1.8

* FAO estimate.
† Unofficial figure.

Aggregate production ('000 metric tons, may include official, semi-official or estimated data): Total cereals 3,332.8 in 2009, 2,632.2 in 2010, 3,654.6 in 2011; Total roots and tubers 216.1 in 2009, 125.9 in 2010, 217.3 in 2011; Total vegetables (incl. melons) 301.4 in 2009, 274.4 in 2010, 267.6 in 2011; Total fruits (excl. melons) 151.3 in 2009, 109.7 in 2010, 138.5 in 2011.

Source: FAO.

LIVESTOCK
('000 head, year ending 30 September)

	2009	2010	2011
Cattle	484	472	467
Pigs	749	741	687
Sheep	362	377	394
Goats	37	36	35
Horses	8	7	7
Chickens	10,879	13,249	12,664

Source: FAO.

LIVESTOCK PRODUCTS
('000 metric tons)

	2009	2010	2011
Cattle meat	17.7	15.6	13.2
Pig meat	88.4	84.1	70.6
Chicken meat	75.1	70.2	63.0
Cows' milk	957.3	918.0	928.3
Goats' milk*	7.8	7.7	7.5
Hen eggs	70.6	74.6	74.6*
Other poultry eggs*	5.0	5.3	5.3

* FAO estimate(s).

Source: FAO.

Forestry

ROUNDWOOD REMOVALS
('000 cubic metres, excl. bark)

	2009	2010	2011
Sawlogs, veneer logs and logs for sleepers	4,745	5,590	5,278
Pulpwood	3,721	3,469	3,254
Other industrial wood	36	31	38
Fuel wood	586	510	643
Total	9,087	9,599	9,213

Source: FAO.

SAWNWOOD PRODUCTION
('000 cubic metres, incl. railway sleepers)

	2009	2010	2011
Coniferous (softwood)	1,605	1,779	1,460
Broadleaved (hardwood)	649	797	744
Total	2,254	2,576	2,204

Source: FAO.

Fishing

(metric tons, live weight)

	2008	2009	2010
Capture	1,655	1,761	1,608
Common carp	1,178	1,241	1,159
Goldfish	63	71	51
Northern pike	54	51	52
Pike-perch	63	62	62
Breams	69	81	66
Aquaculture	1,071	823	687
Common carp	252	154	117
Rainbow trout	761	636	546
Total catch (incl. others)	2,726	2,584	2,295

Source: FAO.

Mining

('000 metric tons, unless otherwise indicated)

	2008	2009	2010
Coal (brown and lignite)	2,423	2,572	2,378
Crude petroleum*	21	21	21
Natural gas (million cu m)	111	110*	110*
Limestone and other calcareous stones for cement	4,992	5,099	4,952
Sands and gravel ('000 cubic m)*	9,300	8,500	8,500

* Estimated production.

Source: US Geological Survey.

Industry

SELECTED PRODUCTS
('000 metric tons unless otherwise indicated)

	2007	2008	2009
Wheat flour	315	369	282
Refined sugar	151	n.a.	n.a.
Beer ('000 hectolitres)	3,557	3,375	2,950
Wine ('000 hectolitres)	271	343	284
Distilled alcoholic beverages ('000 hectolitres)	138	178	160
Footwear with uppers of leather ('000 pairs)	12,869	8,519	6,369
Paints and enamels dissolved in an aqueous medium	16.4	15.2	19.9
Black-coal coke	1,817	1,644	1,631
Residual fuel oils	544	512	630
Gas-diesel (distillate fuel) oil	2,819	2,774	2,743
Cement	3,504	4,087	3,054
Pig-iron*	4,012	3,529	3,019
Crude steel*	5,089	4,478	3,747
Alumina*	160.5	163.0	149.6
Passenger motor cars ('000 units)	525	524	429
Electric energy	28,056	28,962	26,155

* Source: US Geological Survey.

Source: UN Industrial Commodity Statistics Database.

2010 ('000 metric tons): Cement 2,888; Pig-iron 3,649; Crude steel 4,580; Aluminium ingot (primary) 163.0 (Source: US Geological Survey).

Finance

CURRENCY AND EXCHANGE RATES

Monetary Units
100 cent = 1 euro (€).

Sterling, Dollar and Euro Equivalents (31 December 2012)
£1 sterling = 1.196 euros;
US $1 = 0.758 euros;
€10 = £8.36 = $13.19.

Average Exchange Rate (euros per US $)
2010   0.7550
2011   0.7194
2012   0.7779

Note: Slovakia adopted the euro on 1 January 2009, replacing the former national currency at a fixed exchange rate of €1 = 30.126 koruna.

GOVERNMENT FINANCE
(general government transactions, non-cash basis, € million)

Summary of Balances

	2009	2010
Revenue	21,199	21,551
Less Expense	26,514	26,642
Net operating balance	−5,315	−5,092
Less Net acquisition of non-financial assets	−294	−38
Net lending/borrowing	−5,022	−5,054

Revenue

	2009	2010
Taxes	9,955	10,084
Taxes on income, profits and capital gains .	3,322	3,315
Taxes on goods and services . .	6,377	6,502
Social contributions	7,993	8,183
Grants	595	736
Other revenue	2,657	2,548
Total	21,199	21,551

Expense/Outlays

Expense by economic type	2009	2010
Compensation of employees	4,867	4,864
Use of goods and services . . .	2,916	3,063
Compensation of fixed capital . . .	1,715	1,758
Interest	903	888
Subsidies	1,057	890
Grants	664	554
Social benefits	11,949	12,696
Other expense	2,443	1,930
Total	26,514	26,642

Outlays by functions of government*	2009	2010
General public services	3,685	2,827
Defence	800	741
Public order and safety	1,365	1,340
Economic affairs	3,615	3,697
Environmental protection	524	520
Housing and community amenities . . .	507	527
Health	4,715	5,166
Recreation, culture and religion . . .	713	854
Education	2,701	3,042
Social protection	7,769	8,080
Statistical discrepancy	−173	−190
Total	26,221	26,604

* Including net acquisition of non-financial assets.

Source: IMF, *Government Finance Statistics Yearbook*.

INTERNATIONAL RESERVES
(US $ million at 31 December)

	2009	2010	2011
Gold (Eurosystem valuation) . .	1,128	1,441	1,609
IMF special drawing rights . .	536	526	499
Foreign exchange	50	52	71
Total	1,714	2,019	2,179

Source: IMF, *International Financial Statistics*.

MONEY SUPPLY
(incl. shares, depository corporations, national residency criteria, € million at 31 December)

	2009	2010	2011
Currency issued	7,597	7,896	8,326
Demand deposits	16,707	18,371	18,173
Other deposits	17,480	17,444	19,838
Securities other than shares . .	3,530	3,456	3,529
Money market fund shares . .	1,757	1,739	377
Shares and other equity . . .	2,176	2,374	3,366
Other items (net)	−2,263	−1,958	−1,691
Total	46,988	49,323	51,919

Source: IMF, *International Financial Statistics*.

COST OF LIVING
(Consumer Price Index; base December 2000 = 100)

	2010	2011	2012
Foodstuffs and non-alcoholic beverages	124.9	132.5	138.1
Alcoholic beverages and tobacco .	173.6	180.0	187.0
Clothing and footwear	105.8	107.5	109.6
Housing, water, electricity, gas and other fuels	224.1	235.2	244.7
All items (incl. others) . . .	150.3	156.2	161.9

NATIONAL ACCOUNTS
(€ million at current prices)

Expenditure on the Gross Domestic Product

	2010	2011	2012
Final consumption expenditure .	51,162	52,133	53,515
Households	37,735	39,003	40,215
Non-profit institutions serving households	699	712	719
General government	12,727	12,418	12,581
Gross capital formation . .	14,862	16,539	14,841
Gross fixed capital formation .	13,851	15,957	15,392
Changes in inventories . . .	1,011	582	−552
Total domestic expenditure	66,024	68,671	68,356
Exports of goods and services . .	52,959	62,024	68,326
Less Imports of goods and services	53,113	61,587	64,774
Statistical discrepancy	—	—	−445
GDP in purchasers' values .	65,869	69,108	71,463

Gross Domestic Product by Economic Activity

	2010	2011	2012
Agriculture, hunting, forestry and fishing	1,686	2,146	2,376
Industry (incl. mining and utilities)	21,314	22,528	23,514
Manufacturing	12,243	13,163	14,477
Construction	5,466	5,698	5,311
Wholesale and retail trade; repair of motor vehicles; hotels and restaurants; transport and storage	13,035	13,202	13,785
Information and communication .	2,738	2,894	2,994
Financial intermediation . . .	2,161	2,368	2,422
Real estate, renting and business activities	8,574	8,950	9,495
Other services	10,381	10,442	10,823
Sub-total	59,888	62,530	65,409
Taxes, less subsidies, on products .	5,981	6,578	6,054
GDP in purchasers' values .	65,869	69,108	71,463

BALANCE OF PAYMENTS
(US $ million)

	2009	2010	2011
Exports of goods	55,488.5	64,635.4	78,397.8
Imports of goods	−54,142.0	−64,483.6	−75,075.8
Balance on goods	1,346.5	151.7	3,322.0
Exports of services	6,305.5	5,826.7	6,604.0
Imports of services	−8,006.6	−6,784.8	−7,080.3
Balance on goods and services	−354.6	−806.4	2,845.7
Primary income received	2,743.8	3,080.7	3,363.5
Primary income paid	−4,585.1	−4,739.1	−5,699.4
Balance on goods, services and primary income	−2,195.9	−2,464.8	509.8
Secondary income received	1,858.7	1,425.6	1,733.3
Secondary income paid	−2,823.9	−1,969.7	−2,230.6
Current balance	−3,161.1	−3,008.9	12.4
Capital account (net)	623.8	1,372.2	1,214.7
Direct investment assets	−2,047.1	−429.6	−2,060.4
Direct investment liabilities	1,605.2	663.7	3,658.3
Portfolio investment assets	−2,684.9	−3,393.3	−2,321.4
Portfolio investment liabilities	1,512.9	1,865.9	2,092.3
Financial derivatives and employee stock options (net)	354.1	−141.9	−46.1
Other investment assets	−3,857.5	−461.0	850.0
Other investment liabilities	9,849.0	1,252.4	1,816.9
Net errors and omissions	−2,365.8	2,317.2	−5,097.4
Reserves and related items	−171.3	36.7	119.2

Source: IMF, *International Financial Statistics*.

External Trade

PRINCIPAL COMMODITIES
(distribution by SITC, € million)

Imports f.o.b.	2009	2010	2011
Food and live animals	2,184.4	2,466.4	2,872.9
Crude materials (inedible) except fuels	1,008.0	1,776.7	1,973.9
Mineral fuels, lubricants, etc.	4,586.4	6,121.8	8,075.5
Petroleum, petroleum products, etc.	n.a.	3,248.6	4,592.2
Gas, natural and manufactured	n.a.	2,107.0	2,580.1
Chemicals and related products	3,689.7	4,022.3	4,890.8
Medicinal and pharmaceutical products	n.a.	1,314.7	1,532.7
Basic manufactures	5,824.6	7,198.0	8,536.7
Iron and steel	n.a.	1,831.3	2,204.1
Metal manufactures	n.a.	1,841.4	2,180.4
Machinery and transport equipment	16,443.4	20,260.5	22,525.8
General industrial machinery and equipment	n.a.	2,025.7	2,431.7
Telecommunication and sound-recording equipment	n.a.	5,680.8	5,079.7
Electrical machinery, apparatus and appliances	n.a.	4,040.1	4,747.8
Road vehicles	n.a.	5,225.9	6,218.1
Miscellaneous manufactured articles	4,435.3	4,971.7	6,077.9
Professional, scientific and controlling instruments	n.a.	1,114.0	1,508.5
Total (incl. others)	38,775.1	47,493.6	55,767.6

Exports f.o.b.	2009	2010	2011
Food and live animals	1,525.6	1,726.5	2,206.5
Mineral fuels, lubricants, etc.	1,823.5	2,330.0	3,596.2
Petroleum, petroleum products, etc.	n.a.	1,866.8	2,861.4
Chemicals and related products	1,777.3	2,253.7	2,806.6
Basic manufactures	7,419.4	9,206.2	10,681.5
Rubber manufactures	n.a.	1,037.4	1,354.8
Paper, paperboard and articles of paper pulp	n.a.	850.1	873.7
Iron and steel	n.a.	3,237.7	3,519.2
Metal manufactures	n.a.	1,684.9	2,011.5
Machinery and transport equipment	21,751.9	26,287.9	29,991.2
General industrial machinery and equipment	n.a.	2,281.6	2,956.7
Telecommunications and sound-recording equipment	n.a.	8,374.5	8,159.0
Electrical machinery, apparatus and appliances	n.a.	3,089.0	3,356.1
Road vehicles	n.a.	9,857.8	12,099.6
Miscellaneous manufactured articles	4,189.0	4,861.4	5,598.0
Total (incl. others)	39,721.2	48,272.1	56,783.2

2012 (preliminary figures): Total imports 59,223.8; Total exports 62,833.0.

PRINCIPAL TRADING PARTNERS
(€ million)

Imports f.o.b.	2009	2010	2011
Austria	1,006.1	1,193.0	1,331.8
Belgium	374.9	500.7	526.0
China, People's Republic	2,164.6	2,918.5	3,320.7
Czech Republic	4,318.8	4,862.6	5,661.4
France (incl. Monaco)	1,652.7	1,709.1	1,833.8
Germany	5,911.1	7,519.9	8,977.8
Hungary	1,851.2	2,049.3	2,238.0
Italy	1,439.9	1,588.6	1,842.2
Japan	496.2	820.8	842.6
Korea, Republic	2,618.6	3,788.1	4,183.2
Netherlands	416.1	490.6	592.2
Poland	1,434.2	1,937.9	2,212.6
Russia	3,466.9	4,658.9	6,183.2
Spain	434.6	480.6	610.5
Taiwan	565.2	673.7	843.7
Ukraine	250.7	445.5	607.8
United Kingdom	883.3	847.1	665.1
USA	436.4	433.3	512.0
Total (incl. others)	38,775.1	47,493.6	55,767.6

Exports f.o.b.	2009	2010	2011
Austria	2,349.9	3,270.9	3,982.4
Belgium	662.4	778.2	946.0
China, People's Republic	551.1	971.4	1,491.3
Czech Republic	5,277.2	6,612.2	8,181.2
France (incl. Monaco)	3,088.5	3,303.9	3,620.0
Germany	7,855.4	9,291.3	11,479.4
Hungary	2,737.4	3,209.5	4,058.2
Italy	2,379.5	2,670.1	2,815.2
Netherlands	1,171.5	1,405.3	1,366.9
Poland	2,788.2	3,526.8	4,134.5
Romania	669.0	840.5	1,095.2
Russia	1,413.7	1,921.4	2,070.5
Spain	945.8	1,242.8	1,201.0
Sweden	697.4	879.5	1,001.4
Switzerland (incl. Liechtenstein)	390.8	483.4	564.4
Turkey	683.9	839.6	767.6
United Kingdom	1,822.8	1,805.3	2,036.2
USA	426.3	728.8	896.6
Total (incl. others)	39,721.2	48,272.1	56,783.2

2012 (preliminary figures): Total imports 59,223.8; Total exports 62,833.0.

Transport

RAILWAYS

	2009	2010	2011
Railway transport:			
freight ('000 metric tons) . .	37,603	44,327	43,711
passengers ('000)	46,667	46,583	47,531
Public road transport:			
freight ('000 metric tons) . .	36,671	43,197	41,963
passengers ('000)	323,142	312,717	299,579
Waterway transport: freight ('000			
metric tons)	2,192	3,109	2,454

ROAD TRAFFIC
(motor vehicles in use at 31 December)

	2009	2010	2011
Passenger cars	1,589,044	1,669,065	1,749,271
Buses and coaches	9,400	9,350	9,074
Goods vehicles	246,667	252,866	256,869
Motorcycles	55,443	59,563	63,859

SHIPPING
Flag Registered Fleet
(at 31 December)

	2010	2011	2012
Number of vessels	20	10	5
Total displacement (grt) . . .	44,011	21,708	7,279

Source: Lloyd's List Intelligence (www.lloydslistintelligence.com).

CIVIL AVIATION
(traffic on scheduled services)

	2009	2010	2011
Passengers carried ('000) . . .	2,288	554	603
Freight carried (metric tons) . .	7	11	1

Tourism

FOREIGN TOURIST ARRIVALS
(visitors at accommodation facilities)

Country of origin	2009	2010	2011
Austria	50,065	51,678	58,983
Czech Republic	425,414	433,321	477,159
France	34,045	32,967	35,931
Germany	133,989	131,674	133,431
Hungary	56,111	51,324	59,000
Italy	50,982	54,439	51,957
Poland	164,712	161,851	172,001
United Kingdom	42,315	40,961	39,476
USA	20,815	22,051	26,482
Total (incl. others)	1,298,075	1,326,639	1,460,361

Tourism receipts (US $ million, excl. passenger transport): 2,336 in 2009; 2,233 in 2010; 2,429 in 2011 (provisional) (Source: World Tourism Organization).

Communications Media

	2009	2010	2011
Telephones ('000 main lines in use)	1,219.6	1,098.8	1,056.0
Mobile cellular telephones ('000			
subscribers)	5,497.7	5,925.0	5,983.1
Internet subscribers ('000) . .	674.1	731.3	779.6
Broadband subscribers ('000) . .	627.7	694.4	746.7
Newspapers: titles	11	482	585
Periodicals: titles	1,289	1,388	1,296

Personal computers: 3,140,000 (580.8 per 1,000 persons) in 2008.

Source: partly International Telecommunication Union.

Education

(2011 unless otherwise indicated)

	Institutions	Teachers	Students
Kindergarten	2,865	14,248	144,130
Primary (basic)	2,202	30,267	434,477
Secondary: grammar . . .	247	6,374	85,071
Secondary: specialized . . .	470	12,807	168,974
Secondary: vocational* . . .	181	2,589	51,882
Higher	35	14,864	138,742
Special schools	415	4,860	35,946

* 2007 data.

Pupil-teacher ratio (primary education, UNESCO estimate): 15.2 in 2009/10 (Source: UNESCO Institute for Statistics).

Directory

The Government

HEAD OF STATE

President of the Republic: IVAN GAŠPAROVIČ (elected 17 April 2004; inaugurated 15 June 2004; re-elected 4 April 2009; inaugurated 15 June 2009).

GOVERNMENT
(May 2013)

The Government is composed of members of Direction-Social Democracy (Smer-SD) and Independents.

Prime Minister: ROBERT FICO (Smer-SD).

Deputy Prime Minister, responsible for Investment: ĽUBOMÍR VÁŽNY (Smer-SD).

Deputy Prime Minister and Minister of the Interior: ROBERT KALIŇÁK (Smer-SD).

Deputy Prime Minister and Minister of Finance: PETER KAŽIMÍR (Smer-SD).

Deputy Prime Minister and Minister of Foreign and European Affairs: MIROSLAV LAJČÁK (Independent).

Minister of the Economy: TOMÁŠ MALATINSKÝ (Independent).

Minister of Transport, Construction and Regional Development: JÁN POČIATEK (Smer-SD).

Minister of Agriculture and Rural Development: ĽUBOMÍR JAHNÁTEK (Smer-SD).

Minister of Defence: MARTIN GLVÁČ (Smer-SD).

Minister of Justice: TOMÁŠ BOREC (Independent).

Minister of Labour, Social Affairs and the Family: JÁN RICHTER (Smer-SD).

Minister of the Environment: PETER ŽIGA (Smer-SD).

Minister of Education, Science, Research and Sport: DUŠAN ČAPLOVIČ (Smer-SD).

Minister of Culture: MAREK MAĎARIČ (Smer-SD).

Minister of Health: ZUZANA ZVOLENSKÁ (Smer-SD).

MINISTRIES

Office of the President: Hodžovo nám. 1, POB 128, 810 00 Bratislava; tel. (2) 5788-8173; fax (2) 5788-8105; e-mail informacie@prezident.sk; internet www.prezident.sk.

Office of the Government: nám. Slobody 1, 813 70 Bratislava; tel. (2) 5729-5111; fax (2) 5249-7595; e-mail urad@vlada.gov.sk; internet www.vlada.gov.sk.

Ministry of Agriculture and Rural Development: Dobrovičova 12, 812 66 Bratislava; tel. (2) 5926-6308; fax (2) 5296-3871; e-mail press@land.gov.sk; internet www.land.gov.sk.

Ministry of Culture: nám. SNP 33, 813 31 Bratislava; tel. (2) 2048-2111; fax (2) 2048-2174; e-mail info@culture.gov.sk; internet www.culture.gov.sk.

Ministry of Defence: Kutuzovova 8, 832 47 Bratislava; tel. 960-312-958; fax 960-312-642; e-mail press@mod.gov.sk; internet www.mosr.sk.

Ministry of the Economy: Mierová 19, 827 15 Bratislava; tel. (2) 4854-1072; fax (2) 4333-7827; e-mail info@economy.gov.sk; internet www.economy.gov.sk.

Ministry of Education, Science, Research and Sport: Stromová 1, 813 30 Bratislava; tel. (2) 5937-4315; fax (2) 5937-4333; e-mail info@minedu.sk; internet www.minedu.sk.

Ministry of the Environment: nám. Ľ. Štúra 1, 812 35 Bratislava; tel. (2) 5956-2284; fax (2) 5956-2481; e-mail info@enviro.gov.sk; internet www.minzp.sk.

Ministry of Finance: Štefanovičova 5, POB 82, 817 82 Bratislava; tel. (2) 5958-1111; fax (2) 5958-3048; e-mail podatelna@mfsr.sk; internet www.finance.gov.sk.

Ministry of Foreign and European Affairs: Hlboká cesta 2, 833 36 Bratislava; tel. (2) 5978-1111; fax (2) 5978-3333; e-mail info@mzv.sk; internet www.mzv.sk.

Ministry of Health: Limbová 2, POB 52, 837 52 Bratislava; tel. (2) 5937-3111; fax (2) 5477-7983; e-mail office@health.gov.sk; internet www.health.gov.sk.

Ministry of the Interior: Pribinova 2, 812 72 Bratislava; tel. (2) 5094-1111; fax (2) 5094-4397; internet www.minv.sk.

Ministry of Justice: Župné nám. 13, 813 11 Bratislava; tel. (2) 5935-3111; fax (2) 5935-3602; e-mail tlacove@justice.sk; internet www.justice.gov.sk.

Ministry of Labour, Social Affairs and the Family: Špitálska 4–6, 816 43 Bratislava; tel. (2) 2046-0000; fax (2) 5292-6136; e-mail okv@employment.gov.sk; internet www.employment.gov.sk.

Ministry of Transport, Construction and Regional Development: nám. Slobody 6, POB 100, 810 05 Bratislava; tel. (2) 5949-4111; fax (2) 5249-4794; e-mail info@mindop.sk; internet www.telecom.gov.sk.

President

Presidential Election, First Ballot, 21 March 2009

Candidates	Valid votes	%
Ivan Gašparovič	876,061	46.71
Iveta Radičová	713,735	38.05
František Mikloško	101,573	5.42
Zuzana Martináková	96,035	5.12
Milan Melník	45,985	2.45
Dagmara Bollová	21,378	1.14
Milan Sidor	20,862	1.11
Total	**1,875,629**	**100.00**

Second Ballot, 4 April 2009

Candidates	Valid votes	%
Ivan Gašparovič	1,234,787	55.53
Iveta Radičová	988,808	44.47
Total	**2,223,595**	**100.00**

Legislature

**Národná rada Slovenskej republiky
(National Council of the Slovak Republic)**

nám. Alexandra Dubčeka 1, 812 80 Bratislava; tel. (2) 5972-1111; fax (2) 5441-9529; e-mail info@nrsr.sk; internet www.nrsr.sk.

Chairman: PAVOL PAŠKA.

General Election, 10 March 2012

Party	Votes	% of votes	Seats
Direction-Social Democracy	1,134,280	44.42	83
Christian Democratic Movement	225,361	8.82	16
Ordinary People and Independent Personalities	218,537	8.56	16
Bridge	176,088	6.89	13
Slovak Democratic and Christian Union-Democratic Party	155,744	6.10	11
Freedom and Solidarity	150,266	5.88	11
Others	493,448	19.33	—
Total valid votes	**2,553,724**	**100.00**	**150**

Election Commission

Ústredná volebná komisia, Ministerstva vnútra (Central Elections Commission, Ministry of the Interior): Drieňova 22, 826 86 Bratislava; tel. (2) 4859-1111; fax (2) 4333-3175; e-mail ovr.svs@mvsr.vs.sk; Chair. TATIANA JANEČKOVÁ.

Political Organizations

99%—Civic Voice (99%–občiansky hlas): Bratislava; e-mail press@99percent.sk; internet www.99percent.sk; f. 2011; Leaders Dr ALENA DUŠATKOVÁ, PAVOL PAVLÍK, PETER VAČOK.

Bridge (Most/Híd): Trnavská cesta 37, 831 04 Bratislava; tel. (2) 4911-4555; fax (2) 4911-4500; e-mail office@most-hid.sk; internet www.most-hid.sk; f. 2009 by fmr mems of the Party of the Hungarian Coalition; promotes co-operation between all sections of society; Chair. BÉLA BUGÁR.

Christian Democratic Movement (CDM) (Kresťansko-demo-kratické hnutie—KDH): Bajkalská 25, 821 01 Bratislava; tel. (2) 5823-3431; fax (2) 5823-3434; e-mail sekretariat@kdh.sk; internet www.kdh.sk; f. 1990; conservative; supports Christian and family values; Chair. JÁN FIGEĽ.

Communist Party of Slovakia (CPS) (Komunistická strana Slovenska—KSS): Ústredný výbor, Hattalova 12A, 831 03 Bratislava; tel. (2) 4464-4101; fax (2) 4437-2540; e-mail sekr@kss.sk; internet www.kss.sk; f. 1992 following merger of two Marxist parties, the Union of Communists of Slovakia and the Communist Party of Slovakia—91; Pres. JOZEF HRDLIČKA.

Direction-Social Democracy (Smer-Sociálna demokracia—Smer-SD): Súmračná 25, 821 02 Bratislava; tel. and fax (2) 4342-6297; e-mail sekretariat.fico@strana-smer.sk; internet www.strana-smer.sk; f. 1999 as Direction (Smer); absorbed the Party of Civic Understanding in 2003; merged with the Social Democratic Party of Slovakia, the Social Democratic Alternative and the Party of the Democratic Left (unrelated to the party of the same name founded in 2005) in Jan. 2005, and name changed as above; absorbed the Left-wing Bloc in Dec. 2007; Chair. ROBERT FICO.

Free Speech Party—Nora Mojsejová (Strana Slobodné Slovo—Nory Mojsejovej—SSS—NM): Čermelská cesta 1411/88, 040 01 Košice; tel. (55) 633-5917; e-mail info-sssnm@inmail.sk; internet www.sss-nm.sk; f. 2001; fmrly known as Alliance of New Citizens (Aliancia nového občana); current name adopted 2011; Chair. NORA MOJSEJOVÁ.

Freedom and Solidarity (FAS) (Sloboda a Solidarita—SaS): Priemyselná 8, 821 09 Bratislava; fax (2) 5245-4089; e-mail sas@strana-sas.sk; internet www.strana-sas.sk; f. 2009; liberal; Chair. RICHARD SULÍK.

Green Party (Strana zelených): Sienkiewiczova 4, 811 09 Bratislava; tel. and fax (2) 5292-3231; e-mail sekretariat@stranazelenych.sk; f. 1989; regd 1991; supported Party of the Democratic Left in legislative elections of June 2010; Chair. PETER PILINSKÝ.

Ordinary People and Independent Personalities (OPIP) (Obyčajní Ľudia a nezávislé osobnosti—OĽaNO): Študentská 2, 917 01 Trnava; e-mail kontakt@obycajniludia.sk; internet www.obycajniludia.sk; f. 2011; conservative; Leader IGOR MATOVIČ.

Our Slovakia People's Party (Ľudová strana Naše Slovensko—LSNS): E. F. Scherera 4801/20, 921 01 Piešťany; internet www

.naseslovensko.org; f. 2000 as Party of Wine-Lovers; renamed People's Party of Social Solidarity in 2009; present name adopted in 2010; extreme nationalist; Chair MARIAN KOTLEBA.

Party of the Democratic Left (Strana demokratickej ľavice—SDL): Hurbanovo námestie 1, 811 06 Bratislava; tel. (2) 5464-2340; fax (2) 5464-2342; e-mail sdl@mojasdl.sk; internet www.mojasdl.sk; f. 2005; social democratic; Chair. JOZEF ĎURICA.

Party of the Hungarian Community (PHC) (Strana maďarskej komunity/Magyar Közösség Pártja): Cajakova 8, 811 05 Bratislava; tel. (2) 5249-5164; fax (2) 5249-5791; e-mail smk@smk.sk; internet www.mkp.sk; f. 1998 by merger of Coexistence (Spolužitie/Együttélés), the Hungarian Christian Democratic Movement and the Hungarian Civic Party; Chair. JÓZSEF BERÉNYI.

People's Party—Movement for a Democratic Slovakia (PP—MDS) (Ludová strana—Hnutie za Demokratické Slovensko—LS—HZDS): POB 49, Tomášikova 32A, 830 00 Bratislava; tel. (2) 4822-0309; fax (2) 4822-0329; e-mail predseda@hzds.sk; internet www.hzds.sk; f. 1991 as Movement for a Democratic Slovakia; present name adopted in 2003; Chair. VLADIMÍR MEČIAR.

Slovak Democratic and Christian Union-Democratic Party (SDCU-DP) (Slovenská demokratická a krestanská únia-Demokratická strana—SDKÚ-DS): Ružinovská 28, 827 35 Bratislava; tel. (2) 4341-4102; fax (2) 4341-4106; e-mail sdku@sdkuonline.sk; internet www.sdku-ds.sk; f. 2000 as the Slovak Democratic and Christian Union; name changed as above following merger with the Democratic Party in Jan. 2006; Chair. PAVOL FREŠO.

Slovak National Party (SNP) (Slovenská národná strana—SNS): Šafárikovo nám. 3, 814 99 Bratislava; tel. (2) 5292-4260; fax (2) 5296-6188; e-mail sns@sns.sk; internet www.sns.sk; f. 1990; extreme nationalist; against ethnic-Hungarian representation in govt; Chair. ANDREJ DANKO.

Diplomatic Representation

EMBASSIES IN SLOVAKIA

Albania: Podjavorinskej 4, 811 03 Bratislava; tel. (2) 6381-0048; fax (2) 5441-3525; e-mail agim.isaku@mfa.gov.al; Ambassador AGIM ISAKU.

Angola: Jelenia 4, 811 05 Bratislava 1; tel. (2) 5441-2164; fax (2) 5441-2182; e-mail embangola1@chello.sk; Ambassador ALBERTO CORREIA NETO.

Austria: Ventúrska 10, 811 01 Bratislava; tel. (2) 5930-1500; fax (2) 5443-2486; e-mail pressburg-ob@bmeia.gv.at; internet www.rakusko.eu; Ambassador JOSEF MARKUS WUKETICH.

Belarus: Jančova 5, 811 02 Bratislava; tel. (2) 6225-1052; fax (2) 6280-2026; e-mail slovakia@belembassy.org; Ambassador VLADIMIR SERPIKOV.

Belgium: Fraňa kráľa 5, 811 05 Bratislava; tel. (2) 5710-1211; fax (2) 5262-1111; e-mail ambabelbratis@stonline.sk; internet www.diplomatie.be/bratislava; Ambassador WALTER LION.

Brazil: Palisády 47, 811 06 Bratislava; tel. (2) 3218-1400; fax (2) 5441-8271; e-mail brasemb.bratislava@itamaraty.gov.br; internet bratislava.itamaraty.gov.br; Ambassador SUSAN KLEEBANK.

Bulgaria: Kuzmányho 1, 811 06 Bratislava 1; tel. (2) 5441-5308; fax (2) 5441-2404; e-mail bulharskoet@stonline.sk; internet www.bulgarianembassy.sk; Ambassador MARGARITA GANEVA.

China, People's Republic: Jančova 8B, 811 02 Bratislava; tel. and fax (2) 6280-4291; e-mail cinska.ambasada@gmail.com; internet sk.china-embassy.org; Ambassador PAN WEIFANG.

Croatia: Mišikova 21, 811 06 Bratislava; tel. (2) 5720-2091; fax (2) 5443-5365; e-mail vrhbrat@mvpei.hr; internet sk.mvp.hr; Ambassador JAKŠA MULJAČIĆ.

Cuba: Somolického 1A, 811 05 Bratislava; tel. (2) 3266-1440; fax (2) 5249-4200; e-mail embacuba@embacuba.sk; internet www.embacuba.sk; Ambassador LOIPA SÁNCHEZ LORENZO.

Cyprus: Michalská 12, 811 01 Bratislava; tel. (2) 3278-8111; fax (2) 3278-8122; e-mail office@cyembassy.sk; Ambassador MARIOS KOUNTOURIDES.

Czech Republic: POB 208, Hviezdoslavovo nám. 8, 810 00 Bratislava; tel. (2) 5920-3301; fax (2) 5920-3330; e-mail bratislava@embassy.mzv.cz; internet www.mzv.cz/bratislava; Ambassador JAROMÍR PLISEK.

Denmark: Panská 27, 816 06 Bratislava; tel. (2) 5930-0200; fax (2) 5443-3656; e-mail btsamb@um.dk; internet www.slovakiet.um.dk; Ambassador ANITA HUGAU.

Egypt: Holubyho 4, POB 322, 814 99 Bratislava 1; tel. (2) 5296-4462; fax (2) 5296-7791; e-mail embassy.bratislava@mfa.gov.eg; internet www.mfa.gov.eg/english/embassies/Egyptian_Embassy_Slovakia/Pages/default.aspx; Ambassador IHAB AHMAD TALAAT NASR.

Finland: Palisády 29, 811 06 Bratislava; tel. (2) 5980-5111; fax (2) 5980-5120; e-mail sanomat.brt@formin.fi; internet www.finlandembassy.sk; Chargé d'affaires a.i. HENNA KNUUTTILA.

France: Hlavné nám. 7, 812 83 Bratislava; tel. (2) 5934-7111; fax (2) 5934-7199; e-mail diplo@france.sk; internet www.france.sk; Ambassador JEAN-MARIE BRUNO.

Georgia: Michalská 9, 811 01 Bratislava 1; tel. (2) 5464-6484; fax (2) 5464-6486; e-mail bratislava.emb@mfa.gov.ge; internet www.slovakia.mfa.gov.ge; Ambassador ALEKSANDR NALBANDOV.

Germany: Hviezdoslavovo nám. 10, 813 03 Bratislava; tel. (2) 5920-4400; fax (2) 5441-9634; internet www.pressburg.diplo.de; Ambassador Dr AXEL HARTMANN.

Greece: Hlavné nám. 4, 811 01 Bratislava; tel. (2) 5443-4143; fax (2) 5443-4064; e-mail gremb.brt@mfa.gr; internet www.mfa.gr/bratislava; Ambassador NICOLAOS D. KANELLOS.

Holy See: Nekrasovova 17, 811 04 Bratislava; tel. (2) 5479-3528; fax (2) 5479-3529; e-mail nunziatura@nunziatura.sk; Apostolic Nuncio Most Rev. MARIO GIORDANA (Titular Archbishop of Minora).

Hungary: Nad Lomom 28, 811 02 Bratislava; tel. (2) 5920-5200; fax (2) 5443-5484; e-mail mission.pzs@kum.hu; internet www.mfa.gov.hu/emb/bratislava; Ambassador CSABA BALOGH.

India: Dunajská 4, 811 08 Bratislava; tel. (2) 5296-2915; fax (2) 5296-2921; e-mail eindia@slovanet.sk; internet www.indianembassy.sk; Ambassador RAJIV MISRA.

Indonesia: Brnianska 31, 81004 Bratislava; tel. (2) 5441-9886; fax (2) 5441-9890; e-mail indonesia@indonesia.sk; internet www.indonesia.sk; Ambassador DJUMANTORO PURWOKOPUTRO PURBO.

Iraq: Radvanská 15, 811 01 Bratislava; tel. (2) 5413-1466; fax (2) 5413-1464; e-mail embassy.iraq@gmail.com; Ambassador MATHIL DHAJIF MAJID AL-SABTI.

Ireland: Carlton Savoy Bldg, Mostavá 2, 811 02 Bratislava 1; tel. (2) 5930-9611; fax (2) 5443-0690; e-mail bratislava@dfa.ie; internet www.embassyofireland.sk; Ambassador BRIAN MCELDUFF.

Israel: Slávičie údolie 106, POB 6, 811 02 Bratislava; tel. (2) 6829-8550; fax (2) 6829-8555; e-mail cao-sec@bratislava.mfa.gov.il; internet bratislava.mfa.gov.il; Ambassador ALEXANDER BEN-ZVI.

Italy: Palisády 49, 811 06 Bratislava; tel. (2) 5980-0011; fax (2) 5441-3202; e-mail amb.bratislava@esteri.it; internet www.ambbratislava.esteri.it; Ambassador BRoberto MARTINI.

Japan: Hlavné nám. 2, 813 27 Bratislava 1; tel. (2) 5980-0100; fax (2) 5443-2771; e-mail info@bv.mofa.go.jp; internet www.sk.emb-japan.go.jp; Ambassador AKIRA TAKAMATSU.

Korea, Republic: Dunajská 4, 811 08 Bratislava; tel. (2) 3307-0711; fax (2) 3307-0730; e-mail admin2@rokembassy.sk; internet svk.mofat.go.kr; Ambassador SANG-HOON PARK.

Kuwait: Lodná 2, 811 02 Bratislava; tel. (2) 5998-0817; fax (2) 5998-0855; e-mail embassyofkuwait@kuw.sk; Ambassador BADER NASSER ALI AL-HOUTI.

Libya: Révova ul. 45, 811 02 Bratislava 1; tel. (2) 5441-0324; fax (2) 5441-0730; e-mail lpb@stonline.sk; Chargé d'affaires a.i. ABDULHAFID BENZEITUN.

Netherlands: Fraňa Kráľa 5, 811 05 Bratislava 1; tel. (2) 5262-5081; fax (2) 5249-1075; e-mail btl@minbuza.nl; internet www.holandskoweb.com; Ambassador DAPHNE BERGSMA.

Norway: Palisády 29, 811 06 Bratislava; tel. (2) 5910-0100; fax (2) 5910-0115; e-mail emb.bratislava@mfa.no; internet www.norway.sk; Chargé d'affaires a.i. HARALD HERMAN VAN REES ROTLER.

Poland: Hummelova 4, 814 91 Bratislava; tel. (2) 5949-0211; fax (2) 5441-3184; e-mail bratyslawa.amb.sekretariat@msz.gov.pl; internet www.bratyslawa.msz.gov.pl; Ambassador TOMASZ CHŁOŃ.

Portugal: Moskovská 10, 811 08 Bratislava 1; tel. (2) 5010-2211; fax (2) 5010-2222; e-mail embportbrat@stonline.sk; internet www.embport.sk; Ambassador JOAO LUÍS NIZA PINHEIRO.

Romania: Ticha 45A, 811 02 Bratislava; tel. (2) 2072-7147; fax (2) 2072-7547; e-mail embassy.ro@upcmail.sk; internet bratislava.mae.ro; Ambassador FLORIN VODIŢĂ.

Russia: Godrova 4, 811 06 Bratislava; tel. (2) 5441-4436; fax (2) 5443-4910; e-mail protocol@rusemb.sk; internet www.rusemb.sk; Ambassador PAVEL M. KUZNETSOV.

Serbia: Búdková 38, 811 04 Bratislava; tel. (2) 5443-1927; fax (2) 5443-1933; e-mail embassy.serbia@internet.sk; internet www.bratislava.mfa.gov.rs; Ambassador RADMILA HRUSTANOVIĆ.

Slovenia: Ventúrska 5, POB 37, 813 15 Bratislava 1; tel. (2) 5726-7700; fax (2) 5245-0009; e-mail vbs@gov.si; internet www.bratislava.embassy.si; Ambassador STANISLAV VIDOVIČ.

Spain: Prepoštská 10, 811 01 Bratislava; tel. (2) 5441-5724; fax (2) 5441-5717; e-mail emb.bratislava@maec.es; internet www.maec.es/Embajadas/bratislava; Ambassador FÉLIX VALDÉS.

Switzerland: Michalská 12, 811 01 Bratislava; tel. (2) 5930-1111; fax (2) 5930-1100; e-mail bts.vertretung@eda.admin.ch; internet www.eda.admin.ch/bratislava; Ambassador CHRISTIAN MARTIN FOTSCH.

Turkey: Holubyho 11, 811 03 Bratislava 1; tel. (2) 5441-5504; fax (2) 5441-3145; e-mail embassy.bratislava@mfa.gov.tr; internet bratislava.emb.mfa.gov.tr; Ambassador FATMA LEBIBE GÜLHAN ULUTEKIN.

Ukraine: Radvanská 35, 811 01 Bratislava; tel. (2) 5920-2810; fax (2) 5441-2651; e-mail ukremb@ukrembassy.sk; internet slovakia.mfa .gov.ua; Ambassador OLEH HAVAŠI.

United Kingdom: Panská 16, 811 01 Bratislava; tel. (2) 5998-2000; fax (2) 5998-2237; e-mail bebra@internet.sk; internet ukinslovakia .fco.gov.uk; Ambassador SUSANNAH MONTGOMERY.

USA: POB 309, 814 99 Bratislava; tel. (2) 5443-0861; fax (2) 5441-8861; e-mail consulbratislava@state.gov; internet slovakia .usembassy.gov; Ambassador THEODORE SEDGWICK.

Judicial System

The judicial system of Slovakia has three levels: district courts (45), regional courts (eight) and the Supreme Court. Regional courts serve as courts of appeal to the district courts, as well as serving as courts of first instance in some cases; the Supreme Court is the highest judicial authority in the country, operating as a court of cassation and appeal for Regional Courts. There is also a Constitutional Court to ensure compliance with the Constitution. In April 2002 an 18-member Judicial Council was elected, all of whom were lawyers, and nine of whom were judges. Three members are nominated by the President, three by the legislature, three by the Government, and eight are elected by the judges themselves. The final member is the Chairman of the Supreme Court. The Council proposes candidates for judgeships, decides on the assignment of judges, comments on the budget, and elects the Chief Justice of the Supreme Court.

Supreme Court of the Slovak Republic (Najvyšší súd Slovenskej republiky): Župné nám. 13, Bratislava 81 490; tel. (2) 3230-4100; fax (2) 5441-1535; e-mail president@nsud.sk; internet www.nssr.gov.sk; Chair. ŠTEFAN HARABIN.

Office of the Prosecutor-General: Štúrova ul. 2, 812 85 Bratislava; tel. (2) 2083-7505; fax (2) 5292-6596; e-mail gpsr@genpro.gov .sk; internet www.genpro.gov.sk; Prosecutor-General (vacant).

Judicial Council of the Slovak Republic (Súdna rada Slovenskej republiky): Župné nám. 13, Bratislava 81 422; tel. (2) 5935-3439; fax (2) 5935-3498; e-mail podatelna@sudnarada.gov.sk; internet www .sudnarada.gov.sk; f. 2002; Chair. ŠTEFAN HARABIN.

Constitutional Court of the Slovak Republic (Ústavný súd Slovenskej republiky): Hlavná 110, 042 65 Košice; tel. (55) 720-7211; fax (55) 622-7639; e-mail predsednicka@concourt.sk; internet www.concourt.sk; Chair. IVETTA MACEJKOVÁ.

Religion

The principal religion in Slovakia is Christianity, of which the largest denomination is Latin rite Catholicism. About 10% of the population profess no religious belief.

CHRISTIANITY

The Roman Catholic Church

Slovakia comprises four archdioceses (including one of the Slovak Byzantine rite) and five Latin rite dioceses, two Slovak Byzantine Rite eparchies, and a Military Ordinariate. There are an estimated 4m. adherents, equivalent to some 73.8% of the total population. Some 5.9% of the total population are adherents of the Byzantine rite.

Bishops' Conference: Kapitulská 11, POB 113, 81 499 Bratislava; tel. (2) 5920-6501; fax (2) 5920-6555; e-mail kbs@kbs.sk; internet www.kbs.sk; f. 1993; Pres. Most Rev. STANISLAV ZVOLENSKÝ (Latin Rite Archbishop of Bratislava).

Latin Rite

Archbishop of Bratislava: Most Rev. STANISLAV ZVOLENSKÝ, Špitálska 7, 814 92 Bratislava; tel. (2 5720-0611; internet www .abu-bratislava.sk.

Archbishop of Košice: Most Rev. ALOJZ TKÁČ, Hlavná 28, 041 83 Košice; tel. (55) 682-8111; fax (55) 622-1034; e-mail abukosice@kbs .sk; internet www.rimkat.sk.

Archbishop of Trnava: Most Rev. RÓBERT BEZÁK, Jána Hollého 10, POB 78, 919 66 Trnava; tel. (33) 591-2111; fax (33) 591-2280; e-mail abu@abu.sk; internet www.abu.sk.

Slovak Byzantine Rite

Archbishop of Prešov: Most Rev. JÁN BABJAK, Hlavná 1, POB 135, 081 35 Prešov; tel. (51) 773-4622; fax (51) 756-2625; e-mail mons .babjak@greckokat.sk; internet www.grkatpo.sk.

The Eastern Orthodox Church

Orthodox Church in the Czech Lands and Slovakia (Pravoslávna cirkev v českých krajinách a na Slovensku): Budovateľská 1, 080 01 Prešov; tel. (51) 773-2174; fax (51) 773-4045; e-mail dzugan@ orthodox.sk; internet www.orthodox.sk; divided into two eparchies in Slovakia: Prešov and Michalovce (the first of which is an archbishopric); and two eparchies in the Czech Republic: Prague and Olomouc-Brno (q.v.); Archbishop of Prešov Rev. JÁN.

Protestant Churches

Apostolic Church in Slovakia (Apoštolská cirkev na Slovensku): Sreznevského 2, 831 03 Bratislava; tel. and fax (2) 4425-0913; e-mail office@acsr.sk; internet www.acsr.sk; f. 1956; affiliated to international Assemblies of God; 6,000 mems; Pres. JÁN LACHO.

Baptist Union of Slovakia: Súľovská 2, 821 05 Bratislava; tel. and fax (2) 4342-1145; e-mail baptist@baptist.sk; internet www.baptist .sk; f. 1994; 1,973 mems (2005); Pres. Rev. JÁN SZŐLLŐS; Sec. Rev. TOMAS VALCHÁŘ.

Evangelical Church of the Augsburg (Lutheran) Confession in Slovakia (Evanjelická cirkev augsburského vyznania na Slovensku): Palisády 46, POB 289, 811 00 Bratislava; tel. and fax (2) 5443-2940; e-mail biskup@ecav.sk; internet www.ecav.sk; 321 parishes in 14 seniorates and two districts; 372,858 mems (2010); Bishop-Gen. MILOS KLÁTIK; Gen. Superintendent DELINGA PAVEL.

Reformed Christian Church of Slovakia: Synodal Office, Hlavné nám. 23, 979 01 Rimavská Sobota; tel. (47) 562-1936; fax (47) 563-3090; e-mail reformata@reformata.sk; internet www.reformata.sk; 109,735 mems and 325 parishes (2001); Bishop LÁSZLÓ FAZEKAS.

JUDAISM

Central Union of the Jewish Religious Communities in the Slovak Republic (Ústredný zväz židovských náboženských obcí v Slovenskej republike): Kozia ul. 21, 814 47 Bratislava; tel. (2) 5441-2167; fax (2) 5441-1106; e-mail uzzno@netax.sk; c. 3,000 mems; Exec. Chair. FERO ALEXANDER; Rabbi BARUCH MYERS.

The Press

In 2011 there were 585 newspapers and 1,296 periodicals published in Slovakia. The publications listed below are in Slovak, unless otherwise indicated.

PRINCIPAL DAILIES

Hospodárske noviny (Economic News): POB 35, Seberíniho 1, 820 07 Bratislava 27; tel. (2) 4823-8330; fax (2) 4823-8369; e-mail hn@hnx .sk; internet www.hnonline.sk; morning; Editor-in-Chief PETER VAVRO; circ. 17,232 (Oct. 2010).

Nový čas (New Time): Prievozská 14, Bratislava 821 09; tel. (2) 5822-7324; fax (2) 5822-7350; internet www.cas.sk; f. 1991; morning; Editor-in-Chief MARTIN PASTIEROVIČ; circ. 143,649 (Oct. 2010).

Pravda (Truth): Trnavská cesta 39A, 831 04 Bratislava; tel. (2) 4959-6111; fax (2) 4959-6281; e-mail pravda@pravda.sk; internet www .pravda.sk; f. 1920; independent; left-wing; Editor-in-Chief PAVOL MINARIK; circ. 52,392 (Oct. 2010).

Prešovský večerník (Prešov Evening Paper): Jarková 2, 080 01 Prešov; tel. (51) 772-4563; fax (51) 772-4163; e-mail presov@jantar .sk; internet www.vecernik.po.sk; f. 1990; Editor-in-Chief Dr ADRIENA ŠMIHULOVÁ; circ. 13,000.

Sme (We Are): Lazaretská 12, 811 08 Bratislava; tel. (2) 5923-3500; fax (2) 5923-3679; e-mail redakcia@sme.sk; internet www.sme.sk; f. 1993; merged with Práca (Labour) in Oct. 2002; Editor-in-Chief MATÚŠ KOSTOLNÝ; circ. 60,226 (Oct. 2010).

Smer magazín (Direction Magazine): Horná 37, 974 01 Banská Bystrica; tel. (48) 415-1582; e-mail hospodarka.bb@petitpress.sk; internet www.regionalnenoviny.sk/?sek=rn_sdm; f. 1948; independent; Editor-in-Chief ZITA SURÁKOVÁ.

Új szó (New Word): Lazaretská 12, 811 08 Bratislava; tel. (2) 5923-3421; fax (2) 5923-8321; e-mail redakcia@ujszo.com; internet www .ujszo.com; f. 1948; midday; in Hungarian; Editor-in-Chief MOLNÁR NORBERT; circ. 23,503 (Oct. 2010).

PRINCIPAL PERIODICALS

Avízo: Trnavská cesta 39A, 831 04 Bratislava; tel. (2) 4823-2139; e-mail obchod@avizo.sk; internet www.avizo.sk; 3 a week; advertising and information; Gen. Dir OTO LANC; circ. 50,000 (2008).

Eurotelevízia (Eurotelevision): Einsteinova 23, 851 04 Bratislava 5; tel. (2) 3333-5701; fax (2) 3333-5733; e-mail evargova@bauermedia .sk; weekly TV and radio guide; Editor-in-Chief Eva Vargová; circ. 88,911 (Oct. 2010).

Kamarát (Friend): Lotyšská 4, 821 04 Bratislava 214; tel. and fax (2) 4525-8777; e-mail kral@kamarat.eu; internet www.kamarat.eu; f. 1950; fortnightly; magazine for teenagers; Publr Bohumil Král; circ. 39,000 (Oct. 2010).

Katolícke noviny (Catholic News): Matúšova 22, POB 9, 810 01 Bratislava; tel. (2) 5930-6911; e-mail posta@katnoviny.sk; internet online.katnoviny.sk; f. 1849; weekly; Man. Editor Dr Ivan Šulík; circ. 78,161 (Oct. 2010).

Krásy Slovenska (Beauties of Slovakia): Ľublanská 2, 831 02 Bratislava; tel. (2) 5465-2055; fax (2) 5465-2056; e-mail info@ krasy-slovenska.sk; internet www.krasy-slovenska.sk; illustrated bi-monthly; Editor-in-Chief Zuzana Kollárová; circ. 10,000.

Línia: Pribišova 19A, 841 05 Bratislava; tel. (2) 6025-1123; fax (2) 6025-1130; monthly; lifestyle; Editor-in-Chief Ján Hanuška; circ. 25,000.

Romano nevo ľil/Rómsky nový list (The New Romany Journal): Jarková 4, 080 01 Prešov; tel. (51) 772-5283; fax (51) 773-3439; e-mail redakcia@rnl.sk; internet www.rnl.sk; f. 1991; in Romany, Slovak and English; publ. by the Association Jekhetane-Spolu (Together); Editor-in-Chief Roman Čonka; circ. 8,500.

Slovenka (Slovak Woman): Jaskový rad 5, 833 80 Bratislava; tel. (2) 5478-9652; fax (2) 5477-6118; e-mail slovenka@slovenka.sk; f. 1948; weekly; illustrated magazine; Editor-in-Chief Zuzana Krútka; circ. 41,697 (Oct. 2010).

Slovenské národné noviny (Slovak National News): Matica slovenská, Mudroňová 1, 036 52 Martin; tel. and fax (43) 413-4535; f. 1845; weekly; organ of Matica slovenská cultural organization; Editor-in-Chief Peter Mišák; circ. 7,000.

Trend: Tomášikova 23, 821 01 Bratislava 2; tel. (2) 2082-2222; fax (2) 2082-2223; e-mail redakcia@trend.sk; internet www.etrend.sk; f. 1991; weekly; for entrepreneurs; publ. by Trend Holding; Editor-in-Chief Pavol Suďa; circ. 13,866 (Oct. 2010).

Vasárnap (Sunday): Lazaretská 12, 811 08 Bratislava; tel. (2) 5923-3422; fax (2) 5923-3295; e-mail vasarnap@vasarnap.com; internet www.vasarnap.com; f. 1948; weekly; independent Hungarian-language magazine; Editor-in-Chief Liszka Györgyi; circ. 27,825 (Oct. 2010).

Život (Life): Prievozská 14, 821 09 Bratislava; tel. (2) 5822-7821; fax (2) 5822-7350; e-mail zivot@euroskop.ringier.sk; internet zivot.lesk .cas.sk; f. 1951; illustrated family weekly; Editor Andrej Šimončič; circ. 94,430 (Oct. 2010).

NEWS AGENCIES

Rómska tlačová agentúra (Roma Press Agency): Slovenskej jednoty 44, 040 01 Košice; tel. (55) 632-1372; e-mail rpa@mecem .sk; internet www.mecem.sk/rpa; reports on matters relating to the Roma minority, and aims to bring attention to issues affecting the community; Dir-Gen. Kristína Magdolenová.

SITA: POB 8, Mýtna 15, 810 05 Bratislava; tel. (2) 5249-2572; fax (2) 5249-3466; e-mail sita@sita.sk; internet www.sita.sk; f. 1997; independent; Chair. Ivan Sámel.

Tlačová agentúra Slovenskej republiky (TASR) (News Agency of the Slovak Republic): Pribinova 25, 811 09 Bratislava; tel. (2) 5921-0166; fax (2) 5296-3405; e-mail tasr@tasr.sk; internet www.tasr.sk; f. 1992; overseas bureaux in Belgium, Czech Republic, Hungary, Lebanon, Poland, Spain, United Kingdom and USA; Dir-Gen. Jaroslav Rezník.

PRESS ASSOCIATION

Slovenský syndikát novinárov (Slovak Syndicate of Journalists): Župné nám. 7, 815 68 Bratislava; tel. (2) 5443-5071; fax (2) 5443-2438; e-mail sekretariat@ssn.sk; internet www.ssn.sk; f. 1946; reorganized 1990; 2,500 mems (2012); Chair. Tamara Valková.

Publishers

Academic Electronic Press: Bajzova 7, 821 08 Bratislava; tel. and fax (2) 5556-4495; non-fiction.

Dajama: Ľublanská 2, 831 02 Bratislava; tel. and fax (2) 4463-1702; e-mail info@dajama.sk; internet www.dajama.sk; guide-books about Slovakia in Slovak, Hungarian, German, Polish, Russian and English.

Enigma: Javorová 4, 949 01 Nitra 1; tel. (87) 655-5551; e-mail enigma@enigma.sk; internet www.enigma.sk; f. 1991; textbooks, translations of children's books, illustrated books; Dir Vladimir Preloznik.

Epos, Ing. Miroslav Mračko: Pečnianska 27, 851 01 Bratislava 5; tel. and fax (2) 6241-2357; e-mail epos@epos.sk; internet www.epos .sk; f. 1990; economics, law, non-fiction.

Kalligram, s.r.o.: Staromestská 6D, POB 223, 810 00 Bratislava 1; tel. and fax (2) 5441-5028; e-mail szig@kalligram.sk; internet www .kalligram.sk; f. 1991; Slovak, Hungarian and Central European and world literature, literary criticism, philosophy, religion, history, social sciences, science; Dir László Szigeti.

Koloman Kertész Bagala (LCA Publishers Group): POB 99, 810 00 Bratislava 1; tel. (2) 5441-5366; fax (2) 5464-7393; e-mail lca@ lca.sk; internet www.lca.sk; f. 1991; fiction; Dir Koloman Kertész Bagala.

Matica slovenská: J. C. Hronského, 036 52 Martin; tel. (43) 413-2454; fax (43) 413-3188; e-mail msba@matica.sk; internet www .matica.sk; f. 1863; literary science, bibliography, biography and librarianship; Chair. Ing. Jozef Markuš.

Poradca podnikateľa, spol. s.r.o. (Entrepreneur's Adviser): Martina Rázusa 23A, 010 01 Žilina; tel. (41) 705-3777; fax (41) 705-3214; internet www.epi.sk; books and CD-ROMs providing economic and legal information; Dir Ján Brigant.

Príroda a.s. (Nature): Koceľova 17, Bratislava 821 08; tel. (2) 5556-6176; fax (2) 5557-3052; e-mail priroda@priroda.sk; internet www .priroda.sk; f. 1949; school textbooks, encyclopedias, reference books, etc. for children and young people; Chair. Ing. Emilia Jankovitsová.

Slovenské pedagogické nakladeteľstvo—Mladé letá, s.r.o. (Slovak Educational Publishing House—Young Years): Sasinkova 5, Bratislava 811 08; tel. (2) 5022-7312; fax (2) 5542-5758; e-mail spn@spn.sk; internet www.mladeleta.sk; f. 1920; pedagogical literature, educational, school texts, dictionaries; Exec. Man. Darina Torokova.

Slovenský spisovateľ a.s. (Slovak Writer): Vajnorská 128, 832 92 Bratislava 3; tel. (2) 4445-2707; fax (2) 4444-1239; e-mail slovenskyspisovatel@slovenskyspisovatel.sk; internet www .slovenskyspisovatel.sk; fiction, poetry; Dir Martin Chovanec.

Tatran: Michalská 9, 815 82 Bratislava; tel. (2) 5443-5849; fax (2) 5443-5777; f. 1949; fiction, art books, children's books, literary theory; Dir Dr Eva Mládeková.

Veda (Science): Dúbravská cesta 9, 842 34 Bratislava; tel. (2) 5477-4253; fax (2) 5477-2682; f. 1953; publishing house of the Slovak Academy of Sciences; scientific and popular scientific books and periodicals; Dir. Dr Milan Brnák.

PUBLISHERS' ASSOCIATION

Publishers' and Booksellers' Asscn of the Slovak Republic (Združenie vydavateľov a kníhkupcov Slovenskej republiky): Gregorovej 8, 821 03 Bratislava; tel. and fax (2) 4333-6700; e-mail alex .aust@post.sk; Pres. Dr Alex Aust.

Broadcasting and Communications

TELECOMMUNICATIONS

In 2010 there were 1m. active main fixed-connection telephone lines and 5.75m. mobile phone subscribers in Slovakia.

Orange Slovensko (Orange Slovakia): Metodova 8, 821 08 Bratislava; tel. (2) 5851-2345; internet www.orange.sk; f. 1997 as Globtel; present name adopted 2002; wholly owned by Orange (France); provides mobile cellular telecommunications and internet services; Dir-Gen. Pavol Lančarič.

Telefónica O2 Slovakia s.r.o.: Einsteinova 24, Bratislava 851 01; tel. (2) 6202-0100; fax (2) 6202-0444; internet www.o2.sk; f. 2007; subsidiary of Telefónica (Spain); mobile cellular telecommunications and internet services; Gen. Man. Ramiro Lafarga Brollo.

Telekom: Slovak Telekom, Karadžičova 10, 825 13 Bratislava; tel. (2) 4966-6777; fax (2) 5249-2492; e-mail emailcentrum@st.sk; internet www.telekom.sk; 51% owned by Deutsche Telekom (Germany), 34% govt-owned, 15% owned by the National Property Fund of the Slovak Republic; formerly Slovenské Telekomunikácie; name changed to Slovak Telecom in Jan. 2004; name changed to T-Com in March 2006; now known as Telekom; provides mobile cellular telecommunications and internet services; Pres., Chair. and Chief Exec. Miroslav Majoroš.

Regulatory Authority

Telecommunications Regulatory Authority of the Slovak Republic: Továrenská 7, POB 40, 828 55 Bratislava 24; tel. (2) 5788-1111; fax (2) 5293-2096; e-mail secretary@teleoff.gov.sk; internet www.teleoff.gov.sk; Pres. Ladislav Mikuš.

BROADCASTING

The publicly owned Rozhlas a televízia Slovenska, founded in 2011 by the merger of the former state TV and radio companies, is a major broadcaster.

Rozhlas a televízia Slovenska (RTVS) (Radio and Television of Slovenia): Mýtna 1, 817 55 Bratislava 15; f. 2011; two subsidiary cos: Slovenský rozhlas (see radio) and Slovenská televízia (q.v.); Chair. MIROSLAV KOLLÁR; Dir-Gen. MILOSLAVA ZEMKOVÁ.

Radio

The publicly owned Rozhlas a televízia Slovenska operates five radio stations through its Slovenský rozhlas subsidiary. In addition, there are 37 licensed commercial stations.

Slovenský rozhlas (Slovak Radio): Mýtna 1, POB 55, 817 55 Bratislava 15; tel. (2) 5727-3300; fax (2) 5249-8923; e-mail webmaster@rozhlas.sk; internet www.slovakradio.sk; f. 1926; Chair. IGOR GALLO; Dir VINCENT ŠTOFANÍK.

Television

Slovenská televízia (STV) (Slovak Television): Mýtna 1, POB 55, 817 55 Bratislava 15; tel. (2) 6542-3001; fax (2) 6542-2341; e-mail listydivakov@stv.sk; internet www.stv.sk; f. 1956; public broadcasting co; Chair. of Council MARTIN KÁKOŠ; Gen. Man. MILOSLAVA ZEMKOVÁ.

TA3: Gagarinova 12, POB 31, 820 15 Bratislava 215; tel. (2) 4820-3511; fax (2) 4820-3549; e-mail ta3@ta3.com; internet www.ta3.com; f. 2001; privately owned; Exec. Dir IGOR ČEKIRDA.

TV Joj: POB 33, 830 07 Bratislava 37; tel. (2) 5988-8111; fax (2) 5988-8112; e-mail joj@joj.sk; internet www.joj.sk; f. 2002; privately owned subsidiary of Nova TV (Czech Republic); Dir-Gen. VLADIMÍR ŽELEZNÝ; Dir MILAN KNAŽKO.

TV Markíza: Bratislavská 1A, POB 7, 843 56 Bratislava 48; tel. (2) 6827-4111; fax (2) 6595-6824; e-mail nazory@markiza.sk; internet tv.markiza.sk; f. 1996; first privately owned television channel; 80% owned by Central European Media Enterprises Ltd (USA); Dir-Gen. ZUZANA TAPÁKOVÁ.

Finance

(cap. = capital; res = reserves; dep. = deposits; m. = million; brs = branches; amounts in euros, unless otherwise indicated)

BANKING

Central Bank

National Bank of Slovakia (Národná banka Slovenska): Imricha Karvaša 1, 813 25 Bratislava; tel. (2) 5787-1111; fax (2) 5787-1100; e-mail info@nbs.sk; internet www.nbs.sk; f. 1993; res –106,331m. SKK, dep. 490,328m. SKK, total assets 437,114m. SKK (Dec. 2008); Gov. JOZEF MAKÚCH.

Commercial Banks

Československá obchodná banka, a.s.: Michalská 18, 815 63 Bratislava; tel. (2) 5966-8844; fax (2) 5441-4810; e-mail info@csob.sk; internet www.csob.sk; f. 1992; fmrly Istrobanka, a.s.; renamed as above after merger into Československá obchodná banka, a.s. in July 2009; 56.74% owned by Československá Obchodní banka, a.s., Prague, and 36.9% by KBC Bank NV, Brussels; cap. €248.0m., res €293.3m., dep. €3,889.8m. (Dec. 2011); Chair. DANIEL KOLLÁR; 11 brs.

OTP Banka Slovensko, a.s. (Investment and Development Bank): Štúrová 5, 813 54 Bratislava; tel. (2) 5979-1111; fax (2) 5296-3484; e-mail info@otpbanka.sk; internet www.otpbanka.sk; f. 1992; present name adopted 2002; 97.2% owned by OTP Bank (Hungary); cap. €78.5m., res €5.8m., dep. €1,033.3m. (Dec. 2012); Chair. of Bd PÉTER FORRAI; 71 brs.

Poštová banka, a.s. (Postal Bank): Prievozska 2B, 821 09 Bratislava; tel. (2) 5960-1122; fax (2) 5960-3344; e-mail info@pabk.sk; internet www.pabk.sk; f. 1993; cap. €232.7m., res €18.1m., dep. €2,765.6m. (Dec. 2011); Chair. and CEO MAREK TARDA; 41 brs.

Prima banka slovensko, a.s.: Hodžova 11, 010 11 Žilina; tel. (41) 511-1111; fax (41) 562-4129; e-mail info@dexia.sk; internet www.dexia.sk; f. 1993; present name adopted 2003; 84.4% owned by Dexia Kommunalkredit Bank AG (Austria); cap. €64.9m., res €126.2m., dep. €1,606.5m. (Dec. 2011); Chair. and CEO STEFAAN DEPAEPE; 80 brs.

Privatbanka, a.s.: Einsteinova 25, 851 01 Bratislava; tel. (2) 3226-6111; fax (2) 3226-6900; e-mail privatbanka@privatbanka.sk; internet www.privatbanka.sk; f. 1996; present name adopted 2005; cap. €25.1m., res €2.3m., dep. €509.3m. (Dec. 2011); Chair. and CEO ĽUBOŠ ŠEVČÍK.

Sberbank Slovensko, a.s.: Vysoká 9, POB 81, 810 00 Bratislava; tel. (2) 5965-1111; fax (2) 5965-1112; e-mail market@sberbank.sk;

internet www.sberbank.sk; f. 1991 as Ľudová banka; name changed as above in 2013; 99.39% owned by Sberbank Europe AG; cap. €33.2m., res €49.3m., dep. €1,293.3m. (Dec. 2011); Chair. SAMUEL VLČAN; 41 brs.

Tatra banka, a.s.: POB 42, Hodzovo nám. 3, 811 06 Bratislava; tel. (2) 5919-1000; fax (2) 5919-1110; e-mail tatrabanka@tatrabanka.sk; internet www.tatrabanka.sk; f. 1990; cap. €64.3m., res €303m., dep. €6,907.8m. (Dec. 2011); Chair. and Gen. Man. IGOR VIDA; 30 brs.

UniCredit Bank Slovakia, a.s.: Sancová 1A, 813 33 Bratislava; tel. (2) 4950-2112; fax (2) 5060-2287; internet www.unicreditbank.sk; f. 1990; present name adopted 2007; 99.0% owned by Bank Austria Creditanstalt AG (Austria); cap. €235.5m., res €15.6m., dep. €2,868.7m. (Dec. 2011); Chair. of Bd and CEO MIROSLAV STROKENDL; 10 brs, 83 sub-brs.

Všeobecná úverová banka, a.s. (General Credit Bank): Mlynské Nivy 1, POB 90, 829 90 Bratislava; tel. (2) 5055-1111; fax (2) 5556-6656; e-mail kontakt@vub.sk; internet www.vub.sk; f. 1990; 96.5% owned by Intesa Holding International SA (Luxembourg); cap. €430.8m., res €31.3m., dep. €7,516m. (Dec. 2011); Chair. and CEO IGNACIO JAQUOTOT; 249 brs.

Savings Banks

Prvá stavebná sporiteľňa, a.s.: Bajkalská 30, POB 48, 829 48 Bratislava; tel. (2) 5855-5855; fax (2) 5341-1131; internet www.pss.sk; f. 1992; cap. €66.5m., res €42.9m., dep. €1,909.2m. (Dec. 2011); Chair. IMRICH BÉREŠ.

Slovenská sporiteľňa, a.s. (Slovak Savings Bank): Tomášikova 48, 832 37 Bratislava; tel. (2) 5826-8111; fax (2) 5826-8670; e-mail info@slsp.sk; internet www.slsp.sk; f. 1842; 100% owned by Erste Bank (Austria); cap. €212m., res €85.3m., dep. €8,579.5m. (Dec. 2011); Chair. and CEO JAN ROLLO; 292 brs.

COMMODITY AND STOCK EXCHANGES

Bratislava Stock Exchange (Burza cenných papierov v Bratislave, a.s.): Vysoká 17, POB 151, 814 99 Bratislava 1; tel. (2) 4923-6111; fax (2) 4923-6103; e-mail info@bsse.sk; internet www.bsse.sk; f. 1991; Chair. VLADIMÍR KOCOUREK; Dir-Gen. MÁRIA HURAJOVÁ.

Commodity Exchange Bratislava (Komoditná burza Bratislava): Trnavská cesta 50A, 821 02 Bratislava; tel. (2) 5293-1010; fax (2) 5293-1007; e-mail sekretariat@kbb.sk; internet www.kbb.sk; f. 1992; Chair. ĽUDOVÍT SCHOLTZ.

INSURANCE

AEGON Životná poisťovňa, a.s.: Slávičie údolie 106, 811 02 Bratislava; tel. (2) 2066-8287; fax (2) 2066-8110; e-mail aegon@aegon.sk; internet www.aegon.sk; f. 2006; life, risk, retirement, mortgage loan; Chair. of Bd JANA GRUNTOVÁ.

Allianz—Slovak Insurance Co (Allianz—Slovenská poisťovňa, a.s.): Dostojevského rad 4, 815 74 Bratislava; tel. (2) 5963-1111; fax (2) 5963-2740; e-mail allianzsp@allianzsp.sk; internet www.allianzsp.sk; 84.5% owned by Allianz AG (Germany), 15% owned by European Bank for Reconstruction and Development; majority stake divested to Allianz AG (Germany) in 2002; name changed from Slovenská poisťovňa to Allianz—Slovenská poisťovňa in 2003; Chair. TORSTEN LEUE; 2,900 employees.

Amslico poisťovňa a.s.: Hviezdoslavovo nám. 20, 811 02 Bratislava; tel. (2) 5936-3225; fax (2) 5936-3255; e-mail amslico@amslico.sk; internet www.amslico.sk; f. 1995; life and accident; owned by MetLife (USA).

ERGO životná poisťovňa, a.s.: Lazaretská 12, 811 08 Bratislava; tel. (2) 3211-2020; fax (2) 3211-2099; e-mail info@ergo.sk; internet www.ergo.sk; life; Dir-Gen. PAVOL LÍM.

Generali Slovensko poisťovňa, a.s.: Plynárenská 7C, 824 79 Bratislava; tel. (2) 5827-6666; fax (2) 5827-6100; e-mail gsl@gsl.sk; internet www.generali.sk; f. 2008 by merger of Českej poistovne—Slovensko and Generali; life, pension and bank; Dir-Gen. ANTONÍN NEKVINDA.

ING Životná poisťovňa, a.s.: Trnavská cesta 50B, 821 02 Bratislava; tel. (2) 5931-3501; fax (2) 5931-3999; e-mail kontakt@ing.sk; internet www.ing.sk; f. 1996; subsidiary of ING Groep NV (Netherlands); life; CEO ALEXIS GEORGE.

Komunálna poisťovňa, a.s.: Štefánikova 8, 811 05 Bratislava; tel. (2) 4821-0544; fax (2) 4821-0570; e-mail info@kpas.sk; internet www.kpas.sk; f. 1994; subsidiary of Vienna Insurance Group (Austria); life and non-life; CEO and Chair. VLADIMIR BAKEŠ.

Kooperativa poisťovňa, a.s.: Štefanovičova 4, 816 23 Bratislava; tel. (2) 5729-9198; fax (2) 5249-5983; e-mail info@koop.sk; internet www.koop.sk; f. 1990; subsidiary of Vienna Insurance Group (Austria); personal, car, property and liability, and travel; CEO and Chair. JURAJ LELKES.

Trade and Industry

GOVERNMENT AGENCIES

National Property Fund of the Slovak Republic (Fond Národného Majetku Slovenskej Republiky): Drieňová 27, 821 01 Bratislava; tel. (2) 4827-1111; fax (2) 4827-1289; e-mail fnm@natfund.gov.sk; internet www.natfund.gov.sk; f. 1993; supervises the privatization process; Pres. PETER ŠIMKO.

SARIO—Slovak Investment and Trade Development Agency (SARIO—Slovenská agentúra pre rozvoj investícií a obchodu): Martinčekova 17, 821 01 Bratislava; tel. (2) 5826-0100; fax (2) 5826-0109; e-mail sario@sario.sk; internet www.sario.sk; f. 1991; CEO RÓBERT ŠIMONČIČ.

CHAMBERS OF COMMERCE

Slovak Chamber of Commerce and Industry (SOPK) (Slovenská obchodná a priemyselná komora): Gorkého 9, 816 03 Bratislava; tel. (2) 5443-3291; fax (2) 5413-1159; e-mail sopkurad@scci.sk; internet www.sopk.sk; f. 1992; Chair. Dr PETER MIHÓK.

Banská Bystrica Regional Chamber of the Slovak Chamber of Commerce and Industry (Banskobystrická Regionálna Komora SOPK): nám. Š. Moysesa 4, 974 01 Banská Bystrica; tel. (48) 412-5634; fax (48) 412-5636; e-mail sopkrbb@sopk.sk; internet bb.sopk.sk; Chair. MARÍNA SPIROVÁ.

Košice Regional Chamber of the Slovak Chamber of Commerce and Industry (Košická Regionálna Komora SOPK): Žižkova 6, 040 01 Košice; tel. (55) 622-0633; fax (55) 622-0045; e-mail sopkrkke@sopk.sk; internet ke.sopk.sk; Dir IVAN PEZLÁR.

Nitra Regional Chamber of the Slovak Chamber of Commerce and Industry (Nitrianska Regionálna Komora SOPK): Akademická 4, 949 01 Nitra; tel. (37) 653-5466; fax (37) 733-6739; e-mail sopkrknr@sopk.sk; internet nr.sopk.sk; Dir MIROSLAV MASARIK.

Prešov Regional Chamber of the Slovak Chamber of Commerce and Industry (Prešovská Regionálna Komora SOPK): Vajanského 10, POB 246, 080 01 Prešov 1; tel. (51) 773-2818; fax (51) 773-2413; e-mail sopkrkpo@sopk.sk; internet po.sopk.sk; Dir HELENA VIRČÍKOVÁ.

Trenčín Regional Chamber of the Slovak Chamber of Commerce and Industry (Trenčianska Regionálna Komora SOPK): ul. Jilemnického 2, 911 01 Trenčín; tel. (32) 652-3834; fax (32) 652-1023; e-mail sopkrktn@sopk.sk; internet tn.sopk.sk; Dir JÁN VÁCLAV.

Trnava Regional Chamber of the Slovak Chamber of Commerce and Industry (Trnavská Regionálna Komora SOPK): Trhová 2, 917 01 Trnava; tel. (33) 551-2588; fax (33) 551-2603; e-mail sopkrktt@sopk.sk; internet tt.sopk.sk; Dir EVA TOMÁNKOVÁ.

Žilina Regional Chamber of the Slovak Chamber of Commerce and Industry (Žilinská Regionálna Komora SOPK): ul. Halková 31, 010 01 Žilina; tel. (41) 723-5655; fax (41) 723-5653; e-mail sekrza@za.scci.sk; internet za.sopk.sk; Dir JÁN MIŠURA.

UTILITIES

Electricity

Slovenské elektrárne, a.s. (SE) (Slovak Electricity): Hraničná 12, 827 36 Bratislava 212; tel. (2) 5866-1111; fax (2) 5341-7525; e-mail info@hq.seas.sk; internet www.seas.sk; fmr state-owned utility; 66% share acquired by Enel (Italy) in April 2006; 34% owned by the National Property Fund; Chair. and Dir-Gen. PAOLO RUZZINI; Deputy Chair. MARCO ARCELLI.

Stredoslovenská energetika, a.s. (SSE) (Central Slovakia Energy): Republiky 5, 010 47 Žilina; tel. (41) 519-1111; fax (41) 519-2575; e-mail sse@sse.sk; internet www.sse.sk; 51% owned by the National Property Fund of the Slovak Republic, 49% by Éléctricité de France; regional electricity distributor; Chair. and Dir-Gen. PIERRE CHAZERAIN.

Východoslovenská energetika, a.s. (VSE) (East Slovakia Energy): Mlynská 31, 042 91 Košice; tel. (55) 610-2111; fax (55) 678-6516; e-mail info@vse.sk; internet www.vse.sk; 51% owned by the National Property Fund of the Slovak Republic, 49% by RWE Energie AG (Germany); regional electricity distributor; Chair. and CEO NORBERT SCHÜRMANN.

Západoslovenská energetika (ZSE) (West Slovakia Energy): Čulenova 6, 816 47 Bratislava; tel. (2) 5296-1741; fax (2) 5061-3901; e-mail kontakt@zse.sk; internet www.zse.sk; f. 1922; 51% owned by National Property Fund of the Slovak Republic, 40% by E.ON Energie AG (Germany) and 9% by the European Bank for Reconstruction and Development; regional electricity distributor; Chair. of Bd KONRAD KREUZER; Dir of Man. Bd Dr JÁN ORLOVSKÝ.

Gas

SPP—Slovenský Plynárenský Priemysel (Slovak Gas Co): Mlynské Nivy 44A, 825 11 Bratislava 26; tel. (2) 5869-1111; fax (2) 5869-2765; e-mail spp@spp.sk; internet www.spp.sk; 51% state-owned, 49% by consortium of cos incl. E.ON Ruhrgas (Germany) and GDF Suez (France); Chair. JEAN-JACQUES CIAZYNSKI.

TRADE UNION CONFEDERATION

Confederation of Trade Unions of the Slovak Republic (Konfederácia odborových zväzov Slovenskej republiky): Odborárské nám. 3, 815 70 Bratislava; tel. (2) 5557-6065; fax (2) 5023-9102; e-mail press@kozsr.sk; internet www.kozsr.sk; Pres. MIROSLAV GAZDIK; 347,760 mems (2007).

Transport

RAILWAYS

In 2011 the total length of railways in Slovakia was estimated at 3,624 km, of which 1,578 km were electrified.

Železnice Slovenskej republiky (Slovak State Railways): Klemensova 8, 813 61 Bratislava; tel. (2) 2029-1111; fax (2) 5296-2296; e-mail gr@zsr.sk; internet www.zsr.sk; f. 1993; became a joint-stock co with responsibility for management of rail infrastructure in 2001, when responsibility for operations was transferred to the newly established state-owned concern, Železničná spoločnosť a.s.; Chair. JURAJ MRAVČÁK; Dir-Gen. ŠTEFAN HLINKA.

Železničná spoločnosť Cargo Slovakia, a.s. (ZSSK Cargo): Drieňová 24, 820 09 Bratislava; e-mail infoservis@zscargo.sk; internet www.zscargo.sk; f. 2005, following division into two of the state railway company, Železničná spoločnosť, a.s.; operation of rail freight transport and freight-related commercial activities; state-owned; merger with ČD Cargo (Czech Republic) announced 2008; Chair. of Bd MATIEJ AUGUSTÍN.

Železničná spoločnosť Slovensko, a.s.: Železničná 1, 041 79 Košice; tel. (2) 2029-7362; fax (2) 5341-0128; e-mail info@slovakrail.sk; internet www.slovakrail.sk; f. 2005, following division into two of the state railway company, Železničná spoločnosť, a.s.; passenger transport; state-owned; Chair. and Dir-Gen. MILAN CHÚPEK.

Dopravný podnik Bratislava, a.s. (Bratislava Transport): Olejkárska 1, 814 52 Bratislava; tel. (2) 5950-1411; fax (2) 5950-1400; e-mail sekretariat.gr@dpb.sk; internet www.dpb.sk; tramway being upgraded to light-rail system; 11 routes with 154 stops; Dir-Gen. ROBERT KADNÁR.

ROADS

In 2010 the total length of the road system was estimated at 43,916 km, including 416 km of motorways.

Slovak Road Administration (Slovenská správa ciest): Miletičova 19, 826 19 Bratislava; tel. (2) 5025-5111; fax (2) 5556-7976; e-mail info@ssc.sk; internet www.ssc.sk; f. 1996; Dir-Gen. Ing. ROMAN ŽEMBERA.

INLAND WATERWAYS

The total length of navigable waterways in Slovakia (on the River Danube) is 172 km. The Danube provides a link with Germany, Austria, Hungary, Serbia, Bulgaria, Romania and the Black Sea. The main river ports are Bratislava and Komárno.

State Shipping Authority (Štátna plavebná správa): Prístavná 10, 821 09 Bratislava; tel. (2) 5556-6336; fax (2) 5556-6335; e-mail sekretariat@sps.sk; internet www.sps.sk; Dir Ing. JOZEF MORAVČÍK.

Slovak Shipping and Ports Co, a.s. (Slovenská plavba a prístavy, a.s.): Horárska 12, 815 24 Bratislava; tel. (2) 5827-1111; fax (2) 5827-1114; e-mail spap@spap.sk; internet www.spap.sk; Chair. of Bd JOZEF BLAŠKO; Gen. Man. JAROSLAV MICHALCO.

CIVIL AVIATION

There are five international airports in Slovakia: Bratislava (M. R. Štefánik Airport), Košice, Piešťany, Poprad and Sliač.

Air Slovakia: Pestovateľská ul. 2, 821 04 Bratislava; tel. (2) 4342-2744; fax (2) 4342-2742; e-mail airslovakia@airslovakia.sk; internet www.airslovakia.sk; f. 1993; scheduled passenger flights between Slovakia and Cyprus, India, Israel, Italy, Kuwait and the United Kingdom; charter and cargo services; Pres. HARJINDER SINGH SIDHU; Dir-Gen. MICHAEL HALPER.

Danube Wings (VIP Wings s. r. o.): POB 13, 820 02 Bratislava 22; tel. (2) 4363-8537; fax (2) 4363-8539; e-mail info@danubewings.eu; internet www.danubewings.eu; f. 2008; scheduled and charter passenger flights between Slovakia and various European destinations; Chair. PETER BENIK.

Tourism

Slovakia's tourist attractions include ski resorts in the High and Low Tatras and other mountain ranges, more than 20 spa resorts (with thermal and mineral springs), numerous castles and mansions, and historic towns, including Bratislava, Košice, Nitra, Bardejov, Kežmarok and Levoča. In 2011 some 1.5m. foreign tourists visited Slovakia. In that year revenue from tourism totalled US $2,429m., according to provisional figures.

Slovak Tourist Board: nám. L. Stura 1, POB 35, 974 05 Banská Bystrica; tel. (48) 413-6146; fax (48) 413-6149; e-mail sacr@sacr.sk; internet www.sacr.sk; Dir-Gen. Svetlana Gavorová.

Defence

As assessed at November 2012, the total active strength of Slovakia's armed forces was 15,850: army 6,250, air force 3,950, and some 5,650 centrally controlled personnel, logistical, and support staff. In December 2005 the army became fully professional. Slovakia became a full member of the North Atlantic Treaty Organization (NATO) on 29 March 2004.

Defence Expenditure: Budgeted at €736m. in 2013.

Chief of the General Staff: Maj.-Gen. Peter Vojtek.

Education

Education in Slovakia is provided free of charge at all levels in state-controlled and church-affiliated schools. Children between the ages of three and six may attend kindergarten (materská škola). Compulsory education begins at six years of age, when children enter basic school (základná škola), which takes nine years to complete (although the ninth year is optional). In 2011 some 434,477 pupils were enrolled at primary schools. In 2005 enrolment at primary schools included 92% of pupils in the relevant age-group, according to UNESCO estimates. There are three types of secondary school: the grammar school (gymnázium), of which there were 247 in 2011, which prepares students for higher education, the secondary specialized school (stredná odborná škola, 470 in 2011), and the secondary vocational school (stredné odborné učilište, 181 in 2011). In 2008/09 secondary enrolment was equivalent to 92% of children in the relevant age-group. In 2011 there were 35 institutions of higher education, with a total enrolment of 138,742 students. Some children with disabilities may receive instruction at special schools. There are also private schools (basic and secondary). Of total government expenditure in 2010, €3,042m. (11.4%) was allocated to education.

SLOVENIA

Introductory Survey

LOCATION, CLIMATE, LANGUAGE, RELIGION, FLAG, CAPITAL

The Republic of Slovenia is situated in south-central Europe. It is bounded by Austria to the north, Hungary to the north-east, Croatia to the south and east, and Italy to the west, and it has a short western coastline on the Adriatic Sea. The climate is Alpine in the mountainous areas, Mediterranean along the coast and continental in the interior. Average temperatures range from between 0°C (32°F) and 22°C (71.6°F) inland, and between 2°C (35.6°F) and 24°C (75.2°F) on the coast. Average annual rainfall ranges from 800 mm (31.5 ins) in the east to 3,000 mm (118.1 ins) in the north-west. The official language is Slovene, and, in ethnically mixed regions, also Hungarian and Italian. The majority religion in Slovenia is Roman Catholicism, although there are small communities of other Christian denominations and of Muslims. The national flag (proportions 2 by 3) consists of three horizontal stripes of white, blue and red, with a shield in the upper hoist depicting a white three-peaked mountain (Triglav), below which are two horizontal wavy blue lines and above which are three six-pointed yellow stars. The capital is Ljubljana.

CONTEMPORARY POLITICAL HISTORY

Historical Context

Following the collapse of the Austro-Hungarian Empire, the Kingdom of Serbs, Croats and Slovenes was proclaimed on 4 December 1918. (The territory of Slovenia was formally ceded by Austria by the Treaty of Saint-Germain in 1919.) In 1929 the name of the country was changed to Yugoslavia. Yugoslavia collapsed under German attack in 1941, and, during the Second World War (1939–45), Germany annexed lower Styria and Yugoslav Carinthia, while Italy annexed Istria and the territory around Ljubljana. (Following a continuing dispute with Italy over Istria, in 1954 Italy was awarded the city of Trieste, and Yugoslavia the remainder of the territory, giving Slovenia access to the sea.) Hungary occupied the plains along the Mura in north-eastern Slovenia.

The Slovene Liberation Front, formed in 1941, joined with the communist-led all-Yugoslav Partisan Army of Josip Broz (Tito), which was eventually recognized as an ally by the British and US Governments. Following the post-war proclamation of the Federal People's Republic of Yugoslavia (from 1963 the Socialist Federal Republic of Yugoslavia—SFRY), Slovenia became the most prosperous of the Yugoslav republics, but was increasingly suspicious of Serb domination. On 27 September 1989 the Slovene Assembly voted in favour of radical amendments to the Constitution of Slovenia, confirming Slovenia's sovereignty and its right to secede from the SFRY. The organization of multi-party elections was envisaged, and the establishment of opposition parties (the local League of Communists of Slovenia—LCS—having hitherto been the only legal party) was formally authorized. Slovenia was warned that the amendments contravened the Federal Constitution.

In January 1990 the Slovenian delegation withdrew from the 14th (Extraordinary) Congress of the League of Communists of Yugoslavia (LCY), following the rejection of their proposals to reform the federal party and to give greater autonomy to the respective Leagues of Communists of the republics. The LCY suffered a further reverse in February, when its Central Committee was unable to secure the quorum necessary to set a date for the reconvening of the Congress. A boycott by the entire Slovene contingent was supported by members of the Leagues of Communists of Croatia and Macedonia. The LCS suspended its links with the LCY, and changed its name to the Party of Democratic Reform (PDR). In that month Stefan Korošec of Slovenia was removed from the position of Secretary of the Presidium of the LCY Central Committee, in advance of the expiry of his mandate, and was replaced by a Serb. In March Slovenia was redesignated the Republic of Slovenia. Meanwhile, opposition parties had been formed, and in December 1989 six of the main parties formed a coalition, the Democratic Opposition of Slovenia (DEMOS). In multi-party elections, held in April 1990,

DEMOS won a majority in the republican parliament, and subsequently formed a Government under Lojze Peterle, the leader of the Slovenian Christian Democrats (SCD). However, the leader of the PDR, Milan Kučan, was elected President of the State Presidency, and the PDR remained the largest single party in the legislature.

On 2 July 1990 the Slovenian legislature declared the sovereignty of the republic. An amendment to the republican Constitution, resolving that republican laws should take precedence over federal laws, was approved by the legislature on 27 September. Slovenia also assumed control over the local territorial defence force, thereby bringing the republic into direct confrontation with the Serb-dominated federal army, which attempted to reassert its authority by seizing the headquarters of the republican force. Slovenian and Croatian proposals to reform the Yugoslav Federation were rejected, and Serbia imposed economic sanctions on imports from the secessionist states. None the less, in a referendum held in Slovenia on 23 December, some 89% of those who voted (about 94% of the electorate) endorsed Slovenian independence.

Relations between Slovenia and the SFRY deteriorated further in January 1991, when the Slovenian authorities refused to implement an order by the SFRY Presidency to disarm all paramilitary groups. In the same month Slovenia and Croatia signed friendship and military co-operation agreements. The Slovenian Government approved a programme for Slovenian dissociation from the SFRY in February, and following a Serbian-led crisis in the Federal State Presidency in March (see Serbia) became more resolved to withdraw from the federation. In May Slovenia declared its intention to secede before the end of June, and legislation was adopted that would enable eventual independence, including the establishment of a Slovenian army.

Domestic Political Affairs

Slovenia and Croatia declared their independence from the SFRY on 25 June 1991. In response, Serb-dominated federal troops were mobilized on 27 June. Sporadic fighting ensued, and, despite attempts by the European Community (EC—now European Union—EU, see p. 281) to arrange a cease-fire, there was an aerial bombardment of Brnik (Ljubljana) airport. On 7–8 July an EC-mediated cease-fire agreement (which included a three-month moratorium on dissociation) between Slovenia and the SFRY ended all hostilities in Slovenia. According to official figures, 79 people were killed in the fighting in Slovenia. On 8 October (following the expiry of the moratorium) Slovenia proclaimed its full independence, introduced its own currency, the tolar, and recalled all of its citizens serving in federal institutions. All federal army units had withdrawn from Slovenia by 26 October. A new Slovenian Constitution, providing for a bicameral legislature, was promulgated on 23 December. Slovenia was recognized by the EC in January 1992. The USA recognized the country in April, and withdrew sanctions against Slovenia (imposed on all states in the territory of the former SFRY in the previous year) in August. Slovenia was admitted to the UN in May.

Peterle's administration experienced increasing difficulties, as the struggle for independence became less of a unifying factor. In October 1991 the Slovenian Democratic Union, one of the larger and most influential DEMOS parties, split into two factions, both of which remained in the coalition. A liberal wing formed the Democratic Party (DP) under the Minister of Foreign Affairs, Dr Dmitrij Rupel, while the majority of the party's parliamentary delegates supported a more conservative programme and formed the National Democratic Party, led by the Minister of Justice and Administration, Dr Rajko Pirnat. DEMOS was dissolved in December. After the Government lost a parliamentary motion of no confidence in April 1992, Peterle resigned. He was replaced by Dr Janez Drnovšek, the leader of the Liberal Democratic Party (LDP) and a former President of the SFRY Presidency.

The 1992 parliamentary and presidential elections

Parliamentary and presidential elections took place on 6 December 1992. About 85% of the registered electorate participated in elections to the Državni zbor (National Assembly). Although the LDP returned the greatest number of deputies (22) to the 90-member body, it failed to secure a majority of seats. Among the groupings that obtained representation were the SCD, with a total of 15 seats, the United List (a four-party electoral alliance), with 14 seats, and the extreme nationalist Slovenian National Party (SNP), which won 12 seats. In the presidential election, Kučan (standing as an independent candidate) was re-elected to what had become, under the terms of the 1991 Constitution, a largely ceremonial post, obtaining 63.9% of the votes cast. His nearest rival, Ivan Bizjak of the SCD, secured 21.1% of the votes cast. Voting was held concurrently for the 22 directly elected members of the advisory Državni svet (National Council); its remaining 18 members were chosen by an electoral college shortly afterwards.

In January 1993 Drnovšek formed a coalition Government, comprising members of the LDP, the SCD, the United List (later renamed the United List of Social Democrats—ULSD), the Greens of Slovenia and the Social Democratic Party of Slovenia (SDPS). Peterle was appointed Minister of Foreign Affairs, and Bizjak Minister of Internal Affairs. In July the Minister of Defence, Janez Janša, was among several senior politicians implicated in a scandal involving the sale of armaments to Bosnian Muslims (Bosniaks), in contravention of the UN embargo on the transfer of military equipment between the former Yugoslav republics. Earlier in the year Janša (the President of the SDPS) had accused Kučan of protecting former officials of the communist regime. Janša was dismissed from the Government in March 1994, after a ministerial commission found that security forces under the command of the Ministry of Defence had ill-treated a former ministry employee. The SDPS withdrew from the Government, protesting that the coalition agreement had been breached, and also citing the change in the coalition's structure, following the merger of the LDP with three other organizations to form a new party, the Liberal Democracy of Slovenia (LDS). The LDS, led by Drnovšek, included the DP and the Greens of Slovenia—Eco-Social Party (comprising the parliamentary members of the Greens of Slovenia), and numbered 30 deputies in the Državni zbor. Drnovšek subsequently formed a new coalition Government with the SCD and the ULSD. However, Bizjak resigned as Minister of Internal Affairs in May, following allegations that security forces controlled by his ministry had been involved in criminal activities in Austria.

In September 1994 the appointment of an LDS member, Jožef Školjč, to the presidency of the Državni zbor prompted Peterle's resignation from the Government, in protest against the perceived dominance of LDS representatives. Although the SCD remained within the government coalition, Drnovšek refused to accede to the party's demand that Peterle's successor should also be a member of the SCD. In January 1995 an agreement was finally reached whereby Zoran Thaler of the LDS was appointed Minister of Foreign Affairs, and Janko Deželak of the SCD assumed the post of Minister of Economic Relations and Development (a portfolio hitherto held by the LDS).

The 1996 legislative elections

In January 1996 the ULSD withdrew from the governing coalition, following the Prime Minister's proposal to replace the ULSD Minister of Economic Affairs, Dr Maks Tajnikar. Tajnikar was subsequently replaced by an independent deputy, Metod Dragonja, and the three other positions left vacant by the ULSD's withdrawal were allocated to one member of the LDS and two of the SCD.

At the elections to the Državni zbor, which took place on 10 November 1996, the LDS returned 25 deputies to the chamber, and subsequently increased its overall strength to 45 seats, having secured the support of the ULSD, the Democratic Party of Pensioners of Slovenia (DeSUS), the SNP and the representatives of the Hungarian and Italian minorities. A newly formed opposition alliance, Slovenian Spring, comprising the Slovenian People's Party (SPP), the SCD and the SDPS, also held 45 seats in the Državni zbor. Consequently, Kučan's nomination of Drnovšek to the office of Prime Minister failed to obtain the requisite majority of more than one-half of the deputies. Eventually, an SCD deputy, after withdrawing from the party to become an independent deputy, agreed to support Drnovšek's candidacy, and in January 1997 Drnovšek was re-elected as Prime Minister. Following unsuccessful attempts by Drnovšek to form a new administration, in late February the SPP (which held 19 seats) finally agreed to join a coalition Government with the LDS and DeSUS, which was approved by 52 votes in the Državni zbor.

A presidential election took place on 23 November 1997. Kučan won a second term of office, with 55.6% of the votes cast. His nearest rival, the President of the Državni zbor, Janez Podobnik, secured 18.4% of the votes. Indirect elections to the Državni svet followed on 26 November.

The 2000 legislative elections

In January 2000 Boris Frlec resigned as Minister of Foreign Affairs, following criticism of his failure to resolve long-standing disputes between Slovenia and Croatia (see Regional Affairs). He was replaced in February by Dr Dmitrij Rupel. In March it was announced that the nine ministers belonging to the SPP were to resign from the Government, prior to a merger between the SPP and the SCD. Drnovšek was obliged to resign in April, after his proposed new government was rejected by the Državni zbor. The SPP and SCD duly merged, and formed a new alliance, Coalition Slovenia, with the SDPS. Following his nomination by Coalition Slovenia, Andrej Bajuk was endorsed as Prime Minister in early May. The Government, which was approved by the Državni zbor in June, notably included Peterle as Minister of Foreign Affairs and Janša as Minister of Defence.

In July 2000 the approval by 70 of the 90 deputies in the Državni zbor of constitutional amendments providing for the introduction of a system of proportional representation resulted in division within the reconstituted SPP. Bajuk (who had opposed the new legislation) resigned from the SPP, and in August became Chairman of the breakaway New Slovenia—Christian People's Party (NSi), which was joined by Peterle. Elections to the Državni zbor on 15 October were conducted under the new system, with 88 deputies elected on the basis of proportional representation, and the remaining two deputies elected as representatives of the Italian and Hungarian minority communities. The LDS secured 34 seats (an increase of nine seats compared with 1996), while the SDPS won 14 seats, the ULSD 11 seats, the SPP nine seats and the NSi eight seats. Drnovšek was re-elected to the premiership by the Državni zbor in early November, and a coalition agreement was reached by the LDS, the ULSD, the SPP and DeSUS. A new Government, which included several prominent members of Drnovšek's previous administrations, was endorsed by the legislature at the end of November.

The presidential election on 10 November 2002 was contested by nine candidates. (Kučan was prohibited, under the terms of the Constitution, from seeking election for a third term.) Drnovšek won the highest proportion of votes, with 44.4%, but failed to secure an outright majority; a second round between him and Barbara Brezigar, a state prosecutor, who was supported by the SDPS and the NSi (and had received 30.8% of the votes), was scheduled for 1 December. At this second ballot, Drnovšek was elected to the presidency, with 56.5% of the votes cast. Anton Rop, also a member of the LDS and hitherto Minister of Finance, was nominated to replace Drnovšek as Prime Minister, and on 19 December a new Government was approved by the Državni zbor. Drnovšek was inaugurated as President on 22 December. In September 2003 the SDPS was reconstituted as the Slovenian Democratic Party (SDP).

The 2004 legislative elections

In early 2004 the Državni zbor approved legislation providing for the restoration of citizenship to 18,000 nationals of former Yugoslav republics, who (resident in Slovenia at the time of its independence) had been removed from population records and lost their residency rights. However, at a referendum, which was conducted in April, following pressure from the SNP and right-wing parties, some 94% of the votes cast by 31% of the electorate rejected adoption of the new legislation. The SPP, the only party in the governing coalition to have supported the referendum, withdrew from the Government (which was subsequently reorganized). Following the accession of Slovenia to the EU on 1 May (see Regional Affairs), the first elections to the European Parliament took place on 13 June, in which about 28% of the electorate participated. The NSi, the SDP and the LDS each obtained two mandates, while the ULSD received one seat. In July Rop dismissed Rupel as Minister of Foreign Affairs, after he announced that he was transferring his support to the opposition SDP prior to forthcoming legislative elections.

At the legislative elections on 3 October 2004, the centre-right SDP secured 29.1% of the votes cast and 29 seats in the 90-member Državni zbor, defeating the ruling LDS (with 22.8% of the votes and 23 seats). Janša was appointed Prime Minister on 9 November. The SDP finally reached a coalition agreement with the SPP, the NSi and DeSUS, and a new Government was approved by 51 votes in the Državni zbor on 3 December. In April 2005 the ULSD was reconstituted as the Social Democrats (SD), under the continued leadership of Borut Pahor.

At a first round of voting in the presidential election of 21 October 2007, of the six candidates, Peterle, who contested the election as an independent with the support of the SDP, the SPP and the NSi, won 28.7% of the votes cast, while Danilo Türk, a former UN diplomat and an independent candidate supported by DeSUS and the SD, won 24.5% of the votes and Mitja Gaspari, another independent, obtained 24.1%. At a second round of voting, contested by Peterle and Türk on 11 November, Türk was elected President, with 68.0% of the votes cast. In mid-November the Government won a motion of confidence proposed by Janša. Türk was inaugurated on 22 December, upon the expiry of the mandate of Drnovšek (who died in early 2008).

Borut Pahor's Government

Prior to the elections to the Državni zbor conducted on 21 September 2008, a Finnish television broadcast implicated government members, including Prime Minister Janša, in the alleged receipt of unauthorized payments from a Finnish state-owned company, Patria, in association with a tender to supply military vehicles in 2006. In the event, the SD secured 29 seats in the chamber, with 30.5% of the votes cast, narrowly defeating Janša's SDP, which won 28 seats (29.3% of the votes); For Real—New Politics (Zares—a party established in 2007 by breakaway members of the LDS) received nine seats (9.4%), DeSUS seven seats (7.5%), the SNP five seats (5.4%), the SPP (allied with the Youth Party of Slovenia) five seats (5.2%) and the LDS five seats (5.2%). The rate of voter participation was 63.1%.

On 3 November 2008 Türk officially nominated the President of the SD, Borut Pahor, as Prime Minister; a coalition agreement was subsequently reached between the SD, Zares, DeSUS and the LDS, which together held 50 of the 90 seats in the legislature. Pahor's new Government was approved by the Državni zbor on 21 November; it contained seven independent members, including Samuel Zbogar (hitherto Slovenia's ambassador to the USA) as Minister of Foreign Affairs. A new post of Minister without Portfolio, responsible for Slovenes Abroad, was also created. In elections to the European Parliament, held on 7 June 2009, the SDP and the SD each obtained two seats, while the NSi, the LDS and Zares each secured one. The rate of participation by the electorate was 28.3%.

In January 2010 the President of DeSUS, Karl Erjavec, resigned from the post of Minister of the Environment and Physical Planning, after a ruling by the Court of Audit accused his ministry of financial mismanagement and inefficiency, and he lost an ensuing motion of confidence in the Državni svet. In July the Minister of the Economy, Matej Lahovnik, resigned from his post, three days after leaving Zares, apparently owing to disagreement with the Zares leader and Minister of Higher Education, Science and Technology, Gregor Golobič. In April 2011 a member of DeSUS, the Minister without Portfolio, responsible for Local Self-Government and Regional Policy, Dusa Trobec Bučan, resigned, citing a lack of trust from other government members. DeSUS subsequently announced its withdrawal from the ruling coalition; it was announced that the remaining party representative, the Minister of the Environment and Physical Planning, Roko Žarnić, as well as two independent ministers nominated by DeSUS, were to remain in their posts until after planned referendums had taken place in early June. (However, in May Žarnić resigned from DeSUS and retained his government post as an independent.)

Early legislative elections

Golobič's resignation from the Government at the beginning of June 2011 was followed by the resignations of the three remaining Zares ministers, after the party objected to Pahor's failure to reorganize the Government, after proposed legislation was rejected in three referendums. Consequently, the government coalition, comprising only the SD and the LDS, held only 34 of the 90 seats in the Državni zbor. In August LDS leader Katarina Kresal resigned as Minister of the Interior, after an anti-corruption commission cast suspicion on a property transaction made by her ministry. On 20 September the Government lost a motion of confidence in the Državni zbor, which was connected to a vote on required economic austerity measures (including the proposed increase in the retirement age that had been rejected at the referendum). Later that month Pahor announced that early legislative elections would take place on 4 December. In October several new political parties emerged, notably Positive Slovenia (PS), which was established by a wealthy businessman and

former mayor of Ljubljana, Zoran Janković, and the Civic List—Gregor Virant, led by a former minister.

At the elections to the Državni zbor on 4 December 2011, Janković's electoral grouping, Zoran Janković's List—Positive Slovenia, unexpectedly secured 28.5% of the votes cast and the highest representation of 28 seats, followed by Janša's SDP, with 26.2% of the votes and 26 seats, the SD, with only 10.5% and 10 seats, the Civic List—Gregor Virant, with 8.4% and eight seats, DeSUS, with 7.0% and six seats, the SPP, with 6.8% and six seats, and NSi, with 4.9% of the votes and four seats. In early January 2012 President Türk nominated Janković as Prime Minister, and a coalition agreement was reached between PS, the SD, the Civic List—Gregor Virant and DeSUS. Shortly before a scheduled parliamentary vote, however, the Civic List withdrew from the proposed coalition, citing differences with PS. Janković's nomination to the premiership was consequently rejected in the Državni zbor on 11 January. On 25 January Janša announced that he had negotiated a new coalition agreement between his SDP, DeSUS, the SPP, the Civic List—Gregor Virant and NSi, which together held 50 parliamentary seats. Although Türk objected to his candidacy owing to the outstanding charges of corruption against him, on 28 January Janša was proposed as the new Prime Minister by coalition deputies, and his nomination was approved by 51 votes to 39 in the Državni zbor. A coalition Government led by Janša was installed on 10 February. Janković (hitherto a parliamentary deputy) was re-elected as mayor of Ljubljana on 25 March. In September Janković and a number of other officials, including his son, were detained and interrogated over the misappropriation of funds during the construction of a sports complex in 2010; in January 2013 Janković was removed from the leadership of PS.

Recent developments: continuing government crisis

The first round of the presidential election on 11 November 2012 was contested by Türk, Pahor of the SD and Milan Zver of the SDP (who represented a coalition of the SDP and the NSi); Pahor secured the highest proportion of the votes cast, with 39.9%, while Türk received 35.9% of the votes and Zver 24.3%. The second round of voting, which took place on 2 December, was won by Pahor, with 67.4% of the votes. Pahor's victory, which was unexpected, given the results of pre-election opinion polls, was widely attributed to a low rate of participation by voters (48.4% in the first round and 42.4% in the second round), owing to public disaffection with economic austerity measures.

Meanwhile, trade unions organized a series of mass protests in major towns against alleged government corruption and the planned austerity measures, with violent clashes between demonstrators and police ensuing in early December 2012. Later that month the Constitutional Court rejected an initiative by opposition deputies and trade unions that referendums be organized on controversial banking management legislation that had been approved in the Državni zbor in October. However, in January 2013 the Civic List—Gregor Virant demanded that Janša resign, after an anti-corruption commission presented further allegations against him, relating to his purported failure fully to declare his private assets. Following the premier's refusal to resign, on 23 January the party withdrew its representatives (who had held the portfolios of finance, and justice and public administration, respectively) from the ruling coalition, thereby ending the Government's parliamentary majority. Meanwhile, public sector workers staged strike action, amid continued anti-Government protests, against planned retrenchment measures. Despite inter-party negotiations initiated by Janša, on 27 February a motion of no confidence in his minority Government was adopted in the Državni zbor, and Alenka Bratušek, the acting President of PS and a former Ministry of Finance official, was designated as the new premier. Bratušek's new coalition administration, comprising members of PS, the SD, the Civic List—Gregor Virant and DeSUS, was endorsed by the Državni zbor on 20 March.

Regional Affairs

Areas of disputed border territory with Croatia, most notably the maritime boundary in the Bay of Piran in Istria, undermined otherwise harmonious relations between the two countries following independence. In November 1993 Slovenian proposals to decommission the country's nuclear power plant at Krško (constructed by the former federal authorities to supply energy to both Slovenia and Croatia), prompted protests by Croatia, which was reliant on the installation for one-quarter of its energy requirements. In February 1995, following a dispute over the reorganization of local government boundaries in Slovenia, a

Slovenian-Croatian joint commission determined that the process of delineating the border should be pursued separately from other bilateral concerns. In March Slovenia and Croatia agreed to divide ownership of the Krško nuclear station equally between the two countries.

Following the election of a new Government in Croatia in early 2000, bilateral relations improved significantly. After negotiations between Drnovšek and the Croatian Prime Minister, Ivica Račan, an agreement on the outstanding issues of contention between Slovenia and Croatia, which was signed in July 2001, granted Slovenia access to the Adriatic Sea through the Bay of Piran, and provided for continued joint management of the Krško nuclear installation; four disputed border villages were to remain under Croatian sovereignty.

In August 2005 Croatia temporarily recalled its ambassador to Slovenia, in protest against the Slovenian Government's decision to declare a fishing zone in the disputed border region, and demanded that the issue be referred to international arbitration. Following the official opening of Croatia's accession negotiations with the EU earlier that month, Slovenia threatened to oppose Croatian membership over the issue. In January 2007 the dispute between Croatia and Slovenia over the joint maritime boundary was revived with a diplomatic protest by Slovenia that the Croatian Government had pre-empted a border demarcation by extending concessions for petroleum exploration in the disputed region. At the beginning of 2008 Croatia implemented legislation enforcing an environmental fishing zone in the Adriatic Sea, which it had declared in 2003; Slovenia, together with Italy, opposed the measure, claiming that it would result in significant financial damage for their fleets. Slovenia (which had assumed the EU's rotational presidency) indicated that the issue would impede Croatia's ongoing EU integration process. In March 2008, following continued pressure from the EU, Croatia agreed that implementation of the environmental fishing zone would be postponed until its anticipated accession to the Union. In October, however, the Slovenian Government demanded that Croatia withdraw documentation submitted as part of its EU membership negotiations, which was considered to predetermine the common maritime border that remained under dispute. At an intergovernmental conference in December, Croatia was prevented by a Slovenian veto from making progress in 11 EU negotiating chapters. The European Commission expressed concern at Slovenia's decision to impede the accession negotiations and urged both countries to resolve the issue through bilateral discussions.

In February 2009 the Državni zbor ratified the protocols for Croatia's accession to the North Atlantic Treaty Organization (NATO), which had been supported by Slovenia's governing coalition on the grounds that it would improve regional stability. Later in February, however, following an initiative by the SPP that a referendum be conducted on Croatia's prospective NATO membership, the Državni zbor adopted a declaration that Slovenia's national interests be protected during Croatia's NATO accession process and stating its territorial claim. Despite continued failure to resolve the border issue, Türk ratified Croatia's NATO accession protocol in March; Croatia was admitted as a member of the Alliance in April. Following discussions between new Croatian Prime Minister Jadranka Kosor and Pahor, it was finally agreed in September that Slovenia would end its obstruction of Croatia's EU membership negotiations, and that the border dispute would be resolved through international arbitration. On 4 November the Governments of Croatia and Slovenia signed an agreement allowing international arbitrators to delineate the joint border. In March 2010 the Slovenian Supreme Court ruled the agreement to be constitutional, and it was ratified by the legislature on 19 April. A legally binding referendum on the agreement took place in June, at which some 51.5% of the participating electorate voted in support of the initiative. In March 2013 the Slovenian and Croatian Governments signed a Memorandum of Understanding on a long-standing dispute over the reimbursement of Croatian depositors of Slovenia's former Ljubljanska Banka, under which Croatia was to suspend all associated legal proceedings and settlement was to be determined by international arbitration. Following resolution of the outstanding issue, the Državni zbor ratified Croatia's EU Treaty of Accession on 2 April.

Slovenia and Croatia are united in their opposition to movements for Istrian autonomy and to any revision to their detriment of the 1975 Treaty of Osimo, which had defined the borders between the SFRY and Italy, and had provided for the payment by the SFRY of compensation for Italian property transferred to Yugoslav sovereignty after 1947. In 1994 the Italian Government of Silvio Berlusconi stated that until the Slovenian authorities agreed to compensate Italian nationals who had fled after 1947 from territory now held by Slovenia, and whose property had been confiscated under communist rule, Italy would block Slovenia's EU integration efforts. Italy thus prevented scheduled negotiations on an association agreement between Slovenia and the EU until March 1995, when the new Italian Government of Lamberto Dini withdrew the veto. In May 1996 Slovenia and Italy agreed to a compromise solution, whereby Slovenia was to allow EU nationals to purchase property in Slovenia, on a reciprocal basis, within four years of the association agreement's ratification, and EU citizens who had previously permanently resided in Slovenia for a period of three years would be permitted to buy immediately. In June Slovenia finally signed an association agreement with the EU, and applied for full membership of the organization.

Formal accession negotiations with the EU commenced in November 1998. In December 2002, at a summit meeting in Copenhagen, Denmark, Slovenia was one of 10 nations officially invited to join the EU (with effect from 2004). Meanwhile, in November 2002 Slovenia was also invited to become a full member of NATO. A national referendum on the issue of joining both organizations was conducted on 23 March 2003; some 89.6% of voters endorsed membership of the EU, and 66.1% endorsed membership of NATO. On 29 March 2004 Slovenia was officially admitted to NATO. Slovenia's accession to the EU followed on 1 May. In June 2006 EU leaders, meeting in Brussels, Belgium, approved Slovenia's application to adopt the European common currency, the euro. Slovenia joined the eurozone as scheduled, on 1 January 2007. In December Slovenia implemented the EU's Schengen Agreement, which effectively removed border controls between those states subject to the Agreement. Ratification of the EU's Lisbon Treaty was approved by the Državni zbor in January 2008 and received presidential assent in the following month.

CONSTITUTION AND GOVERNMENT

The Constitution of the Republic of Slovenia was enacted on 23 December 1991. Under the terms of the Constitution, as subsequently modified, legislative power is vested in the 90-member Državni zbor (National Assembly). Of the 90 deputies, who serve a term of four years, 88 are elected on the basis of proportional representation; two members are representatives of the Hungarian and Italian minorities. The Državni svet (National Council), which is elected for five years, comprises 22 directly elected members and 18 members chosen by an electoral college to represent various social, economic, trading, political and local interest groups; the Council's role is mainly advisory, but it is empowered to veto decisions of the Državni zbor. The Prime Minister, who is elected by the Državni zbor, nominates the Government (subject to the approval of the legislature). The President of the Republic has largely ceremonial powers, and is directly elected for a maximum of two five-year terms. The judicial branch of government is independent. The Supreme Court is the highest court for civil and criminal cases in the republic. For administrative purposes, Slovenia is divided into 193 municipalities, 11 of which are designated as city municipalities.

REGIONAL AND INTERNATIONAL CO-OPERATION

Slovenia is a member of the European Bank for Reconstruction and Development (EBRD, see p. 276) and the Council of Europe (see p. 260). The country acceded to full membership of the European Union (EU, see p. 281) and the North Atlantic Treaty Organization (NATO, see p. 380) in 2004. Slovenia was invited to join the Organisation for Economic Co-operation and Development (OECD, see p. 388) in 2010.

Slovenia became a member of the UN in 1992, and joined the World Trade Organization (WTO, see p. 444) in 1995.

ECONOMIC AFFAIRS

In 2011, according to the World Bank, Slovenia's gross national income (GNI), measured at average 2009–11 prices, was US $48,452m., equivalent to $23,610 per head (or $26,960 per head on an international purchasing-power parity basis). During 2002–11, it was estimated, the population increased at an average annual rate of 0.3%, while gross domestic product (GDP) per head increased, in real terms, by an average of 1.9% per year. Overall GDP increased, in real terms, at an average annual rate of 1.8% in 2002–12, according to official figures. Real GDP increased by 0.6% in 2011, but decreased by 2.3% in 2012.

Agriculture (including hunting, forestry and fishing) contributed 2.6% of GDP in 2012, when it engaged 4.7% of the employed labour force. The principal crops are cereals (particularly maize and wheat), potatoes, sugar beet and fruits (especially grapes and apples). Slovenia's forests, which cover about one-half of the country, are an important natural resource. Agricultural GDP declined at an average rate of 1.3% per year during 2002–12. The GDP of the sector increased by 7.5% in 2011, but decreased by 5.8% in 2012.

Industry (including mining, manufacturing, construction and power) contributed 30.6% of GDP in 2012, when it engaged 31.8% of the employed labour force. Industrial GDP increased at an average rate of 1.4% per year in 2002–12. Sectoral GDP increased by 0.9% in 2011, but decreased by 2.6% in 2012.

Mining and quarrying contributed 0.5% of GDP in 2011 and engaged 0.3% of the employed labour force in 2012. The principal activity is coal-mining; lead and zinc are also extracted, together with relatively small amounts of natural gas, petroleum and salt. Slovenia also has small deposits of uranium. The GDP of the mining sector increased at an average rate of 3.5% per year in 2002–11. Mining GDP increased by 2.1% in 2011.

Manufacturing contributed 20.8% of GDP in 2012, and engaged 22.5% of the employed labour force in that year. Manufacturing GDP increased at an average rate of 1.9% per year in 2002–12. GDP in the manufacturing sector increased by 3.4% in 2011, but decreased by 0.9% in 2012.

Construction contributed 5.5% of GDP in 2012, when the sector engaged 6.7% of the employed labour force. The GDP of the sector decreased at an average rate of 1.5% per year in 2002–12. The sector contracted by 11.6% in 2012.

In 2010 nuclear power provided 34.8% of energy requirements, coal-fired electricity-generating stations provided 32.6%, and hydroelectric power stations provided 27.8%. Imports of fuel products comprised 16.9% of the value of merchandise imports in 2012.

The services sector contributed 66.8% of GDP in 2012, and engaged 63.5% of the employed labour force in that year. Tourism is a significant source of revenue; the number of tourist arrivals reached 2.2m. in 2012. The GDP of the services sector increased at an average rate of 2.4% per year in 2002–12. Services GDP grew by 0.4% in 2011, but declined by 1.8% in 2012.

In 2011 Slovenia recorded a visible merchandise trade deficit of US $1,187.2m., while there was a surplus of $4.3m. on the current account of the balance of payments. In 2012 Slovenia's principal sources of imports were Italy and Germany (accounting for 18.4% and 18.3% of the total, respectively); another major supplier was Austria. Germany was the principal market for exports (taking 21.3% of the total in that year); Italy, Austria, Croatia and France were also significant purchasers. The major imports in 2012 were machinery and transport equipment (particularly road vehicles and parts, and electrical machinery), basic manufactures (particularly iron and steel), mineral fuels, chemical products, miscellaneous manufactured articles, food and live animals, and crude materials. The principal exports in that year were machinery and transport equipment (particularly road vehicles and parts, and electrical machinery), basic manufactures (notably metal manufactures), chemicals (particularly pharmaceuticals) and miscellaneous manufactured articles.

According to preliminary figures, Slovenia's overall budgetary deficit for 2012 was €609.5m. Slovenia's general government gross debt was €16,954m. in 2011, equivalent to 46.9% of GDP. At the end of March 2013 total central government debt amounted to €16,733.4m. The annual rate of inflation averaged 3.0% in 2002–12. Consumer prices increased by 2.5% in 2012. The rate of unemployment was 13.0% in 2012.

Slovenia formally acceded to the European Union (EU, see p. 281) on 1 May 2004 and achieved entry into the exchange rate mechanism (ERM II) in June. Slovenia adopted the euro on 1 January 2007. Following a modest recovery in 2010 from the severe impact of the global economic crisis, a further downturn took place from 2011, owing to a deceleration in growth and worsening conditions in the eurozone. In September a parliamentary vote on economic austerity measures required under the country's eurozone obligations, including public sector wage reductions, a civil service recruitment 'freeze' and a proposed rise in the retirement age as part of planned reforms of the pensions system, precipitated the collapse of the Government. Later that month the legislature approved Slovenia's contribution to an enlarged European Financial Stability Facility (established to support member states of the eurozone suffering severe financial difficulties). Following early legislative elections, a new Government was established in February 2012, with a priority objective to stabilize public finances. Nevertheless, the economy contracted by 2.3% during 2012, and budget deficit and public debt levels again failed to meet eurozone criteria. In October the Government issued a 10-year, US $2,250m. sovereign bond. In the same month legislation regarded as crucial for financial stabilization, providing for the creation of a single institution to take over the unsustainable non-performing loans of state-owned banks, was adopted; however, its implementation was delayed, owing to a government crisis ensuing from corruption allegations against the premier in early 2013 (see Domestic Political Affairs). The essential public sector austerity measures (particularly a proposed 5% reduction in wages) also met with continued public and trade union opposition, and prompted widespread public sector strike action, in addition to anti-Government protests. Following the removal of the Government in a parliamentary motion of no confidence in February, a new coalition administration, which was installed on 20 March, pledged to continue efforts to stabilize the banking sector. In April, however, the European Commission emphasized that urgent action was essential for Slovenia to avert the need for international financial assistance. In early May the Government proceeded with a planned dollar bond issue, initially postponed after an international ratings agency, Moody's Investors Service, downgraded Slovenia's credit rating.

PUBLIC HOLIDAYS

2014: 1–2 January (New Year), 8 February (Prešeren Day, National Day of Culture), 18–21 April (Easter), 27 April (Resistance Day), 1–2 May (Labour Day), 25 June (National Statehood Day), 15 August (Assumption), 31 October (Reformation Day), 1 November (All Saints' Day), 25 December (Christmas Day), 26 December (Independence Day).

Statistical Survey

Source (unless otherwise indicated): Statistical Office of the Republic of Slovenia, 1000 Ljubljana, Vožarski pot 12; tel. (1) 2415104; fax (1) 2415344; e-mail info .stat@gov.si; internet www.stat.si.

Area and Population

AREA, POPULATION AND DENSITY

Area (sq km)	20,273*
Population (census results)	
31 March 2002	1,964,036
1 January 2011†	
Males	1,014,563
Females	1,035,626
Total	2,050,189
Population (official estimate at 1 January)†	
2012	2,055,496
Density (per sq km) at 1 January 2012	101.4

* 7,827 sq miles.

† As of 1 January 2011, Slovenia changed to a regular register-based system of census enumeration; estimates calculated on a *de jure* basis.

POPULATION BY AGE AND SEX
(official estimates at 1 January 2012)

	Males	Females	Total
0–14	151,314	142,835	294,149
15–64	727,951	688,396	1,416,347
65 and over	137,466	207,534	345,000
Total	1,016,731	1,038,765	2,055,496

POPULATION BY ETHNIC GROUP
(2002 census)

Ethnic group	Number	%
Slovenes	1,631,363	83.1
Serbs	38,964	2.0
Croats	35,642	1.8
Bosniaks	21,542	1.1
Muslims*	10,467	0.5
Others†	226,058	11.5
Total (incl. others)	1,964,036	100.0

* Including persons claiming Muslim ethnicity rather than religious adherence.

† Including unknown and not declared.

REGIONS
(official estimates at 1 January 2012)

	Area (sq km)	Population	Density (per sq km)
Pomurska	1,337	118,988	89.0
Podravska	2,170	323,534	149.1
Koroška	1,041	72,364	69.5
Savinjska	2,384	260,253	109.2
Zasavska	264	43,926	166.4
Spodnjeposavska . . .	885	70,164	79.3
Jugovzhodna Slovenija .	2,675	142,680	53.3
Osrednjeslovenska . .	2,555	536,484	210.0
Gorenjska	2,137	204,057	95.5
Notranjsko-kraška . .	1,456	52,387	36.0
Goriška	2,325	119,236	51.3
Obalno-kraška . . .	1,044	111,423	106.7
Total	20,273	2,055,496	101.4

PRINCIPAL TOWNS
(population at 1 January 2012, official estimates)

Ljubljana (capital) .	280,607	Celje		48,653
Maribor . . .	111,550	Novo mesto . .		36,371
Kranj	55,451	Nova Gorica . .		32,000
Koper (Capodistria) .	53,037			

BIRTHS, MARRIAGES AND DEATHS

	Registered live births		Registered marriages		Registered deaths	
	Number	Rate (per 1,000)	Number	Rate (per 1,000)	Number	Rate (per 1,000)
2004 . .	17,961	9.0	6,558	3.3	18,523	9.3
2005 . .	18,157	9.1	5,769	2.9	18,825	9.4
2006 . .	18,932	9.4	6,368	3.2	18,180	9.1
2007 . .	19,823	9.8	6,373	3.2	18,584	9.2
2008 . .	21,817	10.8	6,703	3.3	18,308	9.1
2009 . .	21,856	10.7	6,542	3.2	18,750	9.2
2010 . .	22,343	10.9	6,528	3.2	18,609	9.1
2011 . .	21,947	10.7	6,671	3.3	18,699	9.1

Life expectancy (years at birth): 80.0 (males 76.8; females 83.3) in 2011 (Source: World Bank, World Development Indicators database).

IMMIGRATION AND EMIGRATION

	2009	2010	2011
Long-term immigrants . . .	30,296	15,416	14,083
Long-term emigrants	18,788	15,937	12,024

ECONOMICALLY ACTIVE POPULATION
('000 persons aged 15 years and over, December)

	2010	2011	2012
Agriculture, hunting, forestry and fishing	33.1	37.9	37.4
Mining and quarrying	2.9	2.8	2.7
Manufacturing	184.1	185.1	178.4
Electricity, gas and water supply .	16.9	17.5	17.3
Construction	72.1	62.1	53.5
Wholesale and retail trade; repair of motor vehicles, motorcycles, and personal and household goods	109.4	109.2	106.4
Hotels and restaurants . . .	32.5	32.3	31.4
Transport, storage and communications	46.9	46.5	45.5
Information and communication .	22.6	22.7	23.0
Financial intermediation . . .	24.2	23.8	22.9
Real estate, renting and business activities	77.3	78.4	76.9
Public administration and defence; compulsory social security . .	51.5	51.2	49.6
Education	64.3	65.5	65.3
Health and social work . . .	53.3	54.8	55.3
Other social and personal services	27.4	27.2	26.9
Private households with employed persons	0.5	0.6	0.5
Total employed	819.0	817.3	792.9
Unemployed	110.0	112.8	118.1
Total labour force	929.0	930.1	911.0

Health and Welfare

KEY INDICATORS

Total fertility rate (children per woman, 2010) . . .	1.4
Under-5 mortality rate (per 1,000 live births, 2010) . . .	3.0
HIV/AIDS (% of persons aged 15–49, 2009)	<0.1
Physicians (per 1,000 head, 2005)	2.4
Hospital beds (per 1,000 head, 2006)	4.8
Health expenditure (2009): US $ per head (PPP)	2,551
Health expenditure (2009): % of GDP	9.3
Health expenditure (2009): public (% of total)	73.4
Access to water (% of total population, 2008)	99
Total carbon dioxide emissions ('000 metric tons, 2008) . .	17,157.9
Carbon dioxide emissions per head (metric tons, 2008) . .	8.5
Human Development Index (2011): ranking	21
Human Development Index (2011): value	0.8840

For sources and definitions, see explanatory note on p. vi.

Agriculture

PRINCIPAL CROPS
('000 metric tons)

	2009	2010	2011
Wheat	136.9	153.5	153.6
Barley	70.8	80.1	79.4
Maize	302.6	311.1	349.0
Oats	4.3	5.2	5.8
Triticale (wheat-rye hybrid) .	13.5	14.1	14.8
Potatoes	103.4	101.2	96.2
Cabbages and other brassicas .	30.4	21.2	21.8
Lettuce and chicory	15.3	9.9	15.7
Tomatoes	4.3	3.8	5.5
Chillies and peppers, green . .	4.6	3.4	3.7
Onions, dry	6.0	4.7	6.3
Apples	95.7	117.6	105.4
Pears	9.9	10.9	11.4
Peaches and nectarines . . .	10.0	8.0	8.6
Plums	4.1	6.9	4.9
Grapes	112.9	108.5	121.4

Aggregate production ('000 metric tons, may include official, semi-official or estimated data): Total cereals 535.6 in 2009, 571.8 in 2010, 611.0 in 2011; Total roots and tubers 139.8 in 2009, 125.1 in 2010, 107.7 in 2011; Total vegetables (incl. melons) 85.0 in 2009, 60.8 in 2010, 78.4 in 2011; Total fruits (excl. melons) 240.5 in 2009, 258.7 in 2010, 260.3 in 2011.

Source: FAO.

LIVESTOCK
('000 head)

	2009	2010	2011
Cattle	470	473	470
Pigs	432	415	396
Sheep	139	138	130
Goats	24	30	26
Horses	20*	20*	23
Chickens	2,393	2,945	2,529
Turkeys	145	94	69

* FAO estimate.

Source: FAO.

LIVESTOCK PRODUCTS
('000 metric tons)

	2009	2010	2011
Cattle meat	35.3	35.8	35.6
Pig meat	44.1	44.1	39.0
Sheep meat	1.7	1.6	1.5
Chicken meat	53.7	53.9	52.4
Turkey meat	6.3	6.8	5.4
Cows' milk	653.7	625.5	603.9
Hen eggs	21.5	21.6	21.4

Source: FAO.

Forestry

ROUNDWOOD REMOVALS
('000 cubic metres, excl. bark)

	2009	2010	2011
Sawlogs, veneer logs and logs for sleepers	1,514	1,452	1,582
Pulpwood	370	316	380
Other industrial wood	63	73	90
Fuel wood	983	1,104	1,336
Total	**2,930**	**2,945**	**3,388**

Source: FAO.

SAWNWOOD PRODUCTION
('000 cubic metres, incl. railway sleepers)

	2009	2010	2011
Coniferous (softwood)	449	625	610
Broadleaved (hardwood) . . .	76	135	93
Total	**525**	**760**	**703**

Source: FAO.

Fishing

(metric tons, live weight)

	2008	2009	2010
Capture	869	1,032	932
Common carp	89	72	69
European pilchard (sardine) .	306	429	403
European anchovy	184	210	144
Aquaculture	1,315	1,307*	778
Common carp	166	177	160
Rainbow trout	775	663	456
European seabass	50	65	42
Mediterranean mussel . . .	224	311	78
Total catch	**2,184**	**2,339***	**1,710**

* FAO estimate.

Source: FAO.

Mining

(metric tons unless otherwise indicated)

	2008	2009	2010
Brown coal ('000 metric tons) .	489	511	419
Lignite ('000 metric tons) . . .	4,032	3,918	4,011
Natural gas ('000 cu m) . . .	2,610	2,575	6,675
Crude petroleum (42-gallon barrels)	1,170	994	990*
Bentonite*	130	130	130
Silica sand	353,983	326,636	510,550
Sand and gravel, excl. glass sand ('000 metric tons)	19,171	15,720	16,000*
Pumice*	40,000	40,000	40,000
Salt*	2,000	2,000	2,000

* Estimate(s).

Source: US Geological Survey.

Industry

SELECTED PRODUCTS
('000 metric tons unless otherwise indicated)

	2009	2010	2011
Wine ('000 hectolitres) . .	258	227	249
Footwear (excl. rubber—'000 pairs)	3,269	3,216	2,909
Veneer sheets ('000 cu m) .	338	337	277
Plywood ('000 cu m)* . . .	103	100	81
Mechanical wood pulp* . .	164	43	43
Newsprint*	119	134	136†
Household and sanitary paper* .	41	37	48†
Wrapping and packaging paper and paperboard*	296	324	265
Cement‡§	1,000	1,000	n.a.
Crude steel ingots (incl. crude steel for casting)‖	430	606	648
Refined lead‡§	14.0	14.0	n.a.
Electric energy (million kWh) .	16,401	16,433	16,056

* Source: FAO.
† Unofficial figure.
‡ Estimated production.
§ Source: US Geological Survey.
‖ Source: International Iron and Steel Institute (Brussels, Belgium).

Finance

CURRENCY AND EXCHANGE RATES

Monetary Units
100 cent = 1 euro (€).

Sterling, Dollar and Euro Equivalents (31 December 2012)
£1 sterling = 1.196 euros;
US $1 = 0.758 euros;
€10 = £8.36 = $13.19.

Average Exchange Rate (euros per US $)
2010   0.7550
2011   0.7194
2012   0.7779

The tolar was introduced in October 1991, replacing (initially at par) the Yugoslav dinar. Slovenia participated in the common European currency, the euro, with effect from 1 January 2007; a fixed exchange rate of €1 = 239.640 tolars was in operation. The euro and the tolar circulated alongside each other until 14 January, after which time the euro (comprising 100 cent) became the sole legal tender.

BUDGET
(€ '000)*

Revenue	2010	2011	2012†
Tax revenue	12,848,422	13,209,222	13,117,635
Taxes on income and profits .	2,490,703	2,723,521	2,656,583
Taxes on property . . .	219,739	215,206	233,153
Social security contributions .	5,234,485	5,267,607	5,244,083
Domestic taxes on goods and services	4,780,711	4,856,170	4,876,009
Taxes on international trade and transactions	90,699	100,250	82,550
Other current revenue . .	923,048	828,664	909,664
Capital revenue and grants .	188,348	75,655	70,979
Transferred revenues . .	109,544	53,823	51,631
Receipts from EU budget . .	724,676	814,917	845,158
Total	**14,794,038**	**14,982,281**	**14,995,067**

Expenditure‡	2010	2011	2012†
Current expenditure (excl. transfers)	6,960,364	6,926,718	6,810,347
Interest payments . . .	488,159	526,688	647,951
Current transfers	7,628,532	7,818,907	7,684,731
Capital expenditure (excl. transfers)	1,310,584	1,023,512	912,281
Capital transfers	396,447	372,068	320,225
Payments to EU budget . .	396,785	405,136	390,301
Total	**16,692,711**	**16,546,341**	**16,117,886**

* Figures represent a consolidation of the accounts of the central Government (State Budget, Pension Fund and Health Insurance Fund) and local administrative authorities.
† Preliminary figures.
‡ Excluding net lending (€ '000): –164,529 in 2010; –696,499 in 2011; –513,288 in 2012 (preliminary).
Source: Ministry of Finance, Ljubljana.

INTERNATIONAL RESERVES
(US $ million at 31 December)

	2009	2010	2011
Gold (Eurosystem valuation) . .	113.71	144.32	160.60
IMF special drawing rights . .	310.61	305.20	320.32
Reserve position in IMF . . .	65.99	114.41	181.85
Foreign exchange	589.55	507.31	328.56
Total	**1,079.86**	**1,071.24**	**991.33**

Source: IMF, *International Financial Statistics*.

MONEY SUPPLY
(incl. shares, depository corporations, national residency criteria, € million at 31 December)

	2009	2010	2011
Currency issued	3,536	3,686	3,893
Demand deposits	7,375	8,375	8,495
Other deposits	12,416	12,156	12,564
Securities other than shares .	3,829	5,056	4,232
Money market fund shares . .	14	12	26
Shares and other equity . .	5,410	5,351	5,290
Other items (net)	–216	–50	815
Total	**32,363**	**34,587**	**35,316**

Source: IMF, *International Financial Statistics*.

COST OF LIVING
(Consumer Price Index for urban areas; base: 2000 = 100)

	2008	2009	2010
Food (incl. beverages) . . .	150.8	151.6	153.1
Fuel and light	171.6	172.9	194.3
Clothing (incl. footwear) . . .	120.0	119.3	117.0
Rent	210.7	209.6	206.7
All items (incl. others) . . .	**146.5**	**147.7**	**150.4**

2011: Food (incl. beverages) 159.9; All items (incl. others) 153.2.
2012: Food (incl. beverages) 166.5; All items (incl. others) 157.1.
Source: ILO.

NATIONAL ACCOUNTS
(€ million at current prices)

Expenditure on the Gross Domestic Product

	2010	2011	2012
Final consumption expenditure.	27,742.9	28,451.5	28,010.6
Households	20,111.7	20,675.4	20,452.2
Non-profit institutions serving households	262.4	242.8	238.3
General government . .	7,368.8	7,533.2	7,320.2
Gross capital formation . . .	7,501.3	7,280.8	6,046.7
Gross fixed capital formation .	7,168.9	6,694.1	6,156.8
Changes in inventories . .	330.7	584.9	−111.8
Acquisitions, less disposals, of valuables	1.8	1.8	1.7
Total domestic expenditure .	35,244.2	35,732.2	34,057.3
Exports of goods and services .	23,500.2	26,201.5	26,603.6
Less Imports of goods and services	23,137.3	25,761.8	25,194.6
GDP in purchasers' values .	35,607.0	36,171.8	35,466.3

Gross Domestic Product by Economic Activity

	2009	2010	2011
Agriculture, forestry and fishing .	729.2	763.1	832.8
Mining and quarrying . . .	140.1	133.9	143.3
Manufacturing	5,840.0	5,955.0	6,384.1
Electricity, gas and water supply .	1,131.4	1,153.7	1,189.8
Construction	2,464.8	2,016.6	1,888.7
Wholesale and retail trade; repair of motor vehicles, motorcycles and personal and household goods	3,932.0	3,850.3	3,876.7
Hotels and restaurants . .	702.0	690.4	719.2
Transport, storage and communications . . .	2,913.0	3,011.6	3,149.4
Financial intermediation . . .	1,581.6	1,730.1	1,661.7
Real estate, renting and business activities	5,367.9	5,344.3	5,250.8
Public administration and defence; compulsory social security . .	1,976.5	2,027.5	2,038.0
Education	1,752.7	1,808.0	1,839.0
Health and social work . .	1,631.8	1,644.7	1,670.1
Other community, social and personal services . .	836.3	829.8	829.1
Private households with employed persons	24.3	26.0	26.7
Gross value added at basic prices	31,023.5	30,985.2	31,499.4
Taxes on products	4,735.7	4,847.2	4,841.6
Less Subsidies	203.1	225.4	169.1
GDP in market prices . . .	35,556.1	35,607.0	36,171.8

2012: Agriculture, forestry and fishing 800.8; Industry 9,423.8 (Manufacturing 6,401.0; Construction 1,701.9); Trade, accommodation, transport 6,463.9; Information and communication 1,249.6; Financial and insurance activities 1,484.4; Real estate, renting and business activities 5,147.1; Public administration and defence, education and health 5,372.7; Other service activities 825.5; *Gross value added at basic prices* 30,767.8; Net taxes on products 4,698.5; *GDP in market prices* 35,466.4.

BALANCE OF PAYMENTS
(US $ million)

	2009	2010	2011
Exports of goods	22,974.9	24,886.9	29,569.9
Imports of goods	−23,441.2	−25,974.9	−30,757.2
Balance on goods . . .	−466.3	−1,087.9	−1,187.2
Exports of services . . .	5,871.8	5,900.5	6,544.5
Imports of services	−4,492.5	−4,438.6	−4,791.5
Balance on goods and services	912.9	374.0	565.8
Primary income received . .	933.4	758.3	1,276.9
Primary income paid . . .	−1,974.7	−1,543.2	−2,048.5
Balance on goods, services and primary income	−128.4	−411.0	−205.8
Secondary income received . .	1,353.0	1,603.1	1,906.1
Secondary income paid . .	−1,555.5	−1,462.2	−1,695.9
Current balance	−330.9	−270.1	4.3

—*continued*	2009	2010	2011
Capital account (net)	14.9	70.8	−138.6
Direct investment assets . . .	−552.7	−65.5	79.3
Direct investment liabilities . .	−349.3	633.3	818.0
Portfolio investment assets . .	26.0	−521.2	24.5
Portfolio investment liabilities .	6,414.2	3,164.8	2,445.3
Financial derivatives and employee stock options (net)	−0.8	−152.5	−187.4
Other investment assets . . .	−462.5	1,085.2	−2,033.5
Other investment liabilities . .	−4,748.2	−3,559.4	−1,743.7
Net errors and omissions . . .	65.2	−416.2	627.5
Reserves and related items .	76.0	−30.7	−104.3

Source: IMF, *International Financial Statistics*.

External Trade

PRINCIPAL COMMODITIES
(distribution by SITC, € million)

Imports c.i.f.	2010	2011	2012
Food and live animals . . .	1,296.4	1,492.2	1,493.2
Crude materials (inedible) except fuels	1,255.0	1,373.0	1,295.0
Mineral fuels, lubricants, etc. .	2,572.7	3,426.2	3,719.3
Petroleum, petroleum products, etc.	1,819.5	2,457.4	2,699.6
Chemicals and related products	2,748.4	3,027.9	3,165.8
Basic manufactures	3,853.7	4,298.1	4,047.9
Textile yarn, fabrics, etc. . . .	333.5	360.1	344.6
Iron and steel	899.1	1,055.0	939.5
Non-ferrous metals	750.2	814.9	745.9
Other metal manufactures . .	698.7	752.8	761.1
Machinery and transport equipment	6,039.3	6,345.9	5,969.3
Machinery specialized for particular industries . . .	364.9	428.7	433.3
General industrial machinery, equipment and parts . . .	773.8	852.0	866.3
Electrical machinery, apparatus, etc.	1,304.1	1,439.9	1,339.4
Road vehicles (incl. air-cushion vehicles) and parts (excl. tyres, engines and electrical parts) .	2,038.8	2,166.1	1,924.7
Miscellaneous manufactured articles	2,003.0	2,151.2	1,954.6
Clothing and accessories (excl. footwear)	439.7	473.5	409.8
Total (incl. others)	20,054.6	22,452.4	22,051.5

Exports f.o.b.	2010	2011	2012
Chemicals and related products	3,045.4	3,448.1	3,723.0
Medicinal and pharmaceutical products	1,687.0	1,907.1	2,087.6
Basic manufactures	4,058.8	4,790.0	4,602.7
Paper, paperboard and articles thereof	516.1	567.9	537.3
Textile yarn, fabrics, etc.	413.4	493.8	513.5
Iron and steel	641.4	828.4	785.0
Non-ferrous metals	569.5	666.5	628.4
Other metal manufactures	853.6	969.2	963.8
Machinery and transport equipment	7,128.5	7,617.6	7,453.4
General industrial machinery, equipment and parts	1,064.8	1,173.3	1,159.9
Electrical machinery, apparatus, etc.	2,007.5	2,174.8	2,115.8
Road vehicles (incl. air-cushion vehicles) and parts (excl. tyres, engines and electrical parts)	2,581.2	2,586.6	2,411.0
Miscellaneous manufactured articles	1,988.0	2,169.5	2,123.7
Furniture and parts; bedding mattresses, etc.	539.3	568.8	510.5
Clothing and accessories (excl. footwear)	215.3	210.2	189.1
Total (incl. others)	18,427.9	20,814.0	20,883.7

PRINCIPAL TRADING PARTNERS
(€ million)

Imports c.i.f.	2010	2011	2012
Austria	2,406.6	2,594.2	2,579.4
Belgium	430.2	442.2	436.9
Bosnia and Herzegovina	329.8	376.0	364.7
China, People's Republic	511.1	572.3	617.1
Croatia	785.0	913.7	942.5
Czech Republic	506.3	584.2	557.6
France	1,090.8	1,056.6	932.7
Germany	3,666.9	4,191.2	4,038.5
Hungary	804.9	950.2	997.6
Italy	3,541.4	3,997.7	4,052.3
Korea, Republic	184.2	205.6	283.1
Netherlands	657.3	728.4	674.6
Poland	418.1	469.5	475.9
Russia	303.6	399.3	378.9
Serbia	357.2	416.0	363.7
Slovakia	313.1	333.0	347.0
Spain	454.3	460.4	398.3
Switzerland	284.7	206.9	188.3
United Kingdom	263.9	358.5	303.0
USA	268.8	485.7	288.2
Total (incl. others)	20,054.6	22,452.4	22,051.5

Exports f.o.b.	2010	2011	2012
Austria	1,493.9	1,613.5	1,731.5
Belgium	209.5	241.0	231.4
Bosnia and Herzegovina	534.1	570.8	579.4
Croatia	1,237.1	1,403.6	1,343.3
Czech Republic	435.0	518.8	582.7
Denmark	163.8	200.3	213.3
France	1,479.1	1,406.7	1,158.7
Germany	3,616.3	4,389.5	4,455.6
Hungary	543.7	615.2	551.5
Italy	2,233.8	2,474.4	2,378.0
Netherlands	366.1	440.2	416.3
Poland	630.3	648.3	622.8
Romania	294.4	350.7	299.6
Russia	590.6	747.7	881.5

Exports f.o.b.—*continued*	2010	2011	2012
Serbia	593.2	616.7	643.5
Slovakia	266.2	310.0	368.9
Spain	229.3	238.9	212.0
Sweden	183.3	222.4	207.4
Switzerland	193.7	258.2	238.2
Turkey	197.1	218.2	204.6
Ukraine	171.6	201.2	219.7
United Kingdom	450.5	494.9	459.7
USA	286.5	323.1	335.3
Total (incl. others)	18,427.9	20,814.0	20,883.7

Transport

RAILWAYS
(traffic)

	2010	2011	2012
Passenger journeys ('000)	16,221	15,743	15,513
Passenger-km (million)	813	773	742
Freight carried ('000 metric tons)	16,233	17,024	15,828
Freight ton-km (million)	3,421	3,752	3,470

ROAD TRAFFIC
(registered motor vehicles at 31 December)

	2009	2010	2011
Motorcycles	46,185	48,686	49,887
Mopeds	42,243	42,322	42,296
Passenger cars	1,058,858	1,061,646	1,066,495
Buses	2,394	2,400	2,422
Lorries	68,122	68,320	68,635
Agricultural tractors	87,108	89,087	92,413
Total (incl. others)	1,366,561	1,375,556	1,386,890

SHIPPING

Flag Registered Fleet
(at 31 December)

	2010	2011	2012
Number of vessels	9	10	11
Total displacement (grt)	2,222	2,691	4,767

Source: Lloyd's List Intelligence (www.lloydslistintelligence.com).

International Sea-borne Freight Traffic
('000 metric tons)

	2006	2007	2008
Goods loaded	188	202	235
Goods unloaded	3,206	2,956	3,827

CIVIL AVIATION
(traffic)

	2010	2011	2012
Kilometres flown ('000)	22,884	22,113	18,779
Passengers carried ('000)	1,170	1,163	986
Passenger-km (million)	1,226	1,219	1,055
Freight carried (metric tons)	1,851	1,937	1,469
Freight ton-km ('000)	1,537	1,617	1,148

Tourism

FOREIGN TOURIST ARRIVALS*

Country of origin	2010	2011	2012
Austria	201,756	222,192	240,113
Belgium	35,209	45,312	48,817
Croatia	103,134	110,377	113,647
Czech Republic	53,205	58,817	63,077
France	62,104	67,019	67,619
Germany	194,386	218,894	238,352
Hungary	55,325	63,096	62,856
Italy	412,137	420,247	414,041
Japan	40,455	35,321	41,398
Netherlands	58,941	65,548	78,049
Poland	33,320	39,626	43,583
Russia	32,690	41,360	52,476
Serbia	76,156	80,995	78,207
United Kingdom	68,465	70,665	69,064
USA	41,566	45,796	51,754
Total (incl. others)	1,869,106	2,036,652	2,155,612

* Figures refer to arrivals at accommodation establishments.

Receipts from tourism (US $ million, excl. passenger transport): 2,516 in 2009; 2,566 in 2010; 2,708 in 2011 (provisional) (Source: World Tourism Organization).

Communications Media

	2009	2010	2011
Telephones ('000 main lines in use)	939.1	910.8	872.8
Mobile cellular telephones ('000 subscribers)	2,100.4	2,122.0	2,168.5
Television subscriptions ('000)	616	610	n.a.
Internet subscribers ('000)	465.3	487.1	499.3
Broadband subscribers ('000)	449.0	477.8	495.4
Daily newspapers	14	12	13
Non-daily newspapers	186	169	188
Other periodicals	1,458	1,540	1,665
Book production (titles published, including pamphlets)	6,139	5,621	5,991

Personal computers: 858,000 (425.1 per 1,000 persons) in 2007.

Source: partly International Telecommunication Union.

Education

(2010/11 unless otherwise indicated)

	Institutions	Teachers	Students		
			Males	Females	Total
Pre-primary*	922	10,198	42,116	39,105	81,221
Elementary†	485	18,544	83,034	77,849	160,883
Upper secondary†	240	10,8097	48,006	47,342	95,348
Higher education	49‡	5,898	35,959§	53,641§	89,600§

* 2011/12 figures.
† Including education of adults.
‡ 2006/07.
§ Excluding post-graduate students.

Pupil-teacher ratio (primary education, UNESCO estimate): 17.2 in 2008/09 (Source: UNESCO Institute for Statistics).

Adult literacy rate (UNESCO estimates): 99.7% (males 99.7%; females 99.7%) in 2010 (Source: UNESCO Institute for Statistics).

Directory

The Government

HEAD OF STATE

President: BORUT PAHOR (elected 2 November 2012; inaugurated 22 December 2012).

GOVERNMENT
(May 2013)

A coalition comprising Positive Slovenia (PS), the Social Democrats (SD), the Civic List—Gregor Virant and the Democratic Party of Pensioners of Slovenia (DeSUS)

Prime Minister: ALENKA BRATUŠEK (PS).

Deputy Prime Minister, Minister of Agriculture and the Environment: DEJAN ŽIDAN (SD).

Deputy Prime Minister, Minister of the Interior and Public Administration: Dr GREGOR VIRANT (Civic List—Gregor Virant).

Deputy Prime Minister, Minister of Foreign Affairs: KARL ERJAVEC (DeSUS).

Minister of Labour, the Family, Social Affairs and Equal Opportunities: Dr ANJA KOPAČ MRAK (SD).

Minister of Finance: Dr UROŠ ČUFER (Independent).

Minister of Economic Development and Technology: STANKO STEPIŠNIK (PS).

Minister of Education, Science and Sport: Dr JERNEJ PIKALO (SD).

Minister of Culture: Dr UROŠ GRILC (PS).

Minister of Defence: ROMAN JAKIČ (PS).

Minister of Justice: Dr SENKO PLIČANIČ (Civic List—Gregor Virant).

Minister of Infrastructure and Spatial Planning: SAMO OMERZEL (Independent).

Minister of Health: TOMAŽ GANTAR (DeSUS).

Minister without Portfolio, responsible for Slovenes Abroad: TINA KOMEL (PS).

MINISTRIES

Office of the President: 1000 Ljubljana, Erjavčeva 17; tel. (1) 4781222; fax (1) 4781357; e-mail gp.uprs@up-rs.si; internet www.up-rs.si.

Office of the Prime Minister: 1000 Ljubljana, Gregorčičeva 20; tel. (1) 4781000; fax (1) 4781721; e-mail gp.kpv@gov.si; internet www.vlada.si.

Government Office for Development and European Affairs: 1000 Ljubljana, Gregorčičeva 25–25A; tel. (1) 4782451; fax (1) 4782500; e-mail gp.svrez@gov.si; internet www.svrez.gov.si.

Government Office for Local Self-Government and Regional Policy: 1000 Ljubljana, Dunajska 58; tel. (1) 3201300; fax (1) 3201301; e-mail gp.svlr@gov.si; internet www.svlr.gov.si.

Government Office for Slovenes Abroad: 1000 Ljubljana, Komenskega 11; tel. (1) 2308000; fax (1) 2308017; e-mail urad .slovenci@gov.si; internet www.uszs.gov.si.

Ministry of Agriculture and the Environment: 1000 Ljubljana, Dunajska 22; tel. (1) 4789000; fax (1) 4789021; e-mail gp.mkgp@gov .si; internet www.mkgp.gov.si.

Ministry of Defence: 1000 Ljubljana, Vojkova cesta 55; tel. (1) 4712211; fax (1) 4712978; e-mail glavna.pisarna@mors.si; internet www.mors.si.

Ministry of Economic Development and Technology: 1000 Ljubljana, Kotnikova 5; tel. (1) 4003311; fax (1) 4001031; e-mail gp .mg@gov.si; internet www.mg.gov.si.

Ministry of Education, Science, Culture and Sport: 1000 Ljubljana, Masarykova 16; tel. (1) 4005200; fax (1) 4005321; e-mail gp.mss@gov.si; internet www.mss.gov.si.

Ministry of Finance: 1502 Ljubljana, Župančičeva 3; tel. (1) 3695200; fax (1) 3696659; e-mail gp.mf@gov.si; internet www.mf.gov.si.

Ministry of Foreign Affairs: 1001 Ljubljana, Prešernova 25; tel. (1) 4782000; fax (1) 4782340; e-mail info.mzz@gov.si; internet www.mzz.gov.si.

Ministry of Health: 1000 Ljubljana, Štefanova 5; tel. (1) 4786001; fax (1) 4786058; e-mail gp.mz@gov.si; internet www.mz.gov.si.

Minister of Infrastructure and Spatial Planning: 1535 Ljubljana, Langusova 4; tel. (1) 4788000; fax (1) 4788139; e-mail gp.mzip@gov.si; internet www.mzp.gov.si.

Ministry of Internal Affairs: 1501 Ljubljana, Štefanova 2; tel. (1) 4284000; fax (1) 2514330; e-mail gp.mnz@gov.si; internet www.mnz.gov.si.

Ministry of Justice: 1000 Ljubljana, Župančičeva 3; tel. (1) 3695200; fax (1) 3695783; e-mail gp.mpju@gov.si; internet www.arhiv.mp.gov.si.

Ministry of Labour, the Family, Social Affairs and Equal Opportunities: 1000 Ljubljana, Kotnikova 5; tel. (1) 3697700; fax (1) 3697832; e-mail gp.mddsz@gov.si; internet www.mddsz.gov.si.

President

Presidential Election, First Ballot, 11 November 2012

Candidate	Votes	% of votes
Borut Pahor (Social Democrats) . . .	326,006	39.87
Dr Danilo Türk (Independent)	293,429	35.88
Dr Milan Zver (Slovenian Democratic Party)	198,337	24.25
Total	817,772	100.00

Second Ballot, 2 December 2012

Candidate	Votes	% of votes
Borut Pahor (Social Democrats) . . .	478,859	67.37
Dr Danilo Türk (Independent)	231,971	32.63
Total	710,830	100.00

Legislature

The Slovenian legislature is bicameral, comprising the Državni zbor (National Assembly), the directly elected lower chamber, and the Državni svet (National Council), the indirectly elected upper chamber.

Državni zbor
(National Assembly)

1000 Ljubljana, Šubičeva 4; tel. (1) 4789400; fax (1) 4789845; e-mail gp@dz-rs.si; internet www.dz-rs.si.

President: JANKO VEBER.

General Election, 4 December 2011

Party	Votes	%	Seats
Zoran Janković's List—Positive Slovenia	314,273	28.51	28
Slovenian Democratic Party .	288,719	26.19	26
Social Democrats	115,952	10.52	10
Civic List—Gregor Virant . .	92,282	8.37	8
Democratic Party of Pensioners of Slovenia	76,853	6.97	6
Slovenian People's Party . .	75,311	6.83	6
New Slovenia—Christian People's Party	53,758	4.88	4
Others*	85,108	7.72	2
Total	1,102,256	100.00	90

* Two of the 90 seats in the Državni zbor are reserved for representatives of the Italian and Hungarian minorities.

Državni svet
(National Council)

1000 Ljubljana, Šubičeva 4; tel. (1) 4789802; fax (1) 4789851; e-mail gp@ds-rs.si; internet www.ds-rs.si.

There are 40 councillors in the Državni svet, who are indirectly elected for a five-year term by an electoral college.

President: MITJA BERVAR.

Election Commission

National Electoral Commission: 1000 Ljubljana, Slovenska 54; tel. (1) 4322002; fax (1) 4331269; e-mail gp.dvk@dvk-rs.si; internet www.dvk.gov.si; Pres. ANTON GAŠPER FRANTAR.

Political Organizations

Civic List (Državljanska lista): 1000 Ljubljana, Ukmarjeva 2; tel. (5) 1352467; e-mail info@d-l.si; internet www.d-l.si; f. 2011; contested 2011 legislative elections as Civic List—Gregor Virant; Leader Dr GREGOR VIRANT.

Democratic Party of Pensioners of Slovenia (DeSUS) (Demokratična stranka upokojencev Slovenije): 1000 Ljubljana, Kersnikova 6/VI; tel. (1) 4397350; fax (1) 4314113; e-mail info@desus.si; internet www.desus.si; Pres. KARL ERJAVEC.

For Real—Socially Liberal (Zares) (Zares—socialno liberalni): 1000 Ljubljana, Dunajska cesta 106; tel. (1) 2428750; fax (1) 2428753; e-mail info@zares.si; internet www.zares.si; f. 2007 as For Real—New Politics by fmr mems of Liberal Democracy of Slovenia; current name adopted in Oct. 2011; Pres. Dr PAVEL GANTAR.

Greens of Slovenia (Zeleni Slovenije): 10000 Ljubljana, Komenskega 11; tel. (2) 7781071; fax (2) 7878543; e-mail zeleni@zeleni.si; internet www.zeleni.si; f. 1989; in 1993 the party split into two factions, one retaining the original name, the other, more radical, wing adopting the title Greens of Slovenia—Eco-Social Party; Chair. Prof. VLADO CUŠ.

Liberal Democracy of Slovenia (LDS) (Liberalna demokracija Slovenije): 1000 Ljubljana, Dunajska cesta 5; tel. (1) 2000310; fax (1) 2000311; e-mail info@lds.si; internet www.lds.si; f. 1994 by a merger of the Liberal Democratic Party, the Greens of Slovenia—Eco-Social Party, the Democratic Party and the Socialist Party of Slovenia; Pres. IZTOK PODBREGAR; 18,000 mems.

New Slovenia—Christian People's Party (NSi) (Nova Slovenija—Krščanska ljudska stranka): 1000 Ljubljana, Cankarjeva 11; tel. (1) 2416650; fax (1) 2416670; e-mail tajnistvo@nsi.si; internet www.nsi.si; f. 2000 by mems of the Slovenian People's Party; Pres. LJUDMILA NOVAK.

Party of the Slovene People (Stranka Slovenskega Naroda—SSN): 2000 Maribor, Efenkova 10; tel. and fax (2) 6205025; e-mail ssn@ssn.si; internet www.ssn.si; nationalist; Pres. MIHA MAJC.

Positive Slovenia (PS) (Pozitivna Slovenija): 1000 Ljubljana, Dalmatinova 2; tel. (1) 3069915; e-mail info@pozitivnaslovenija.si; internet www.pozitivnaslovenija.si; f. 2011; contested 2011 legislative elections as Zoran Janković's List—Positive Slovenia; liberal conservative; Leader ALENKA BRATUŠEK.

Slovenian Democratic Party (SDP) (Slovenska Demokratska Stranka—SDS): 1000 Ljubljana, Trstenjakova 8; tel. (1) 4345450; fax (1) 4345452; e-mail tajnistvo@sds.si; internet www.sds.si; f. 1989 as Social Democratic Party of Slovenia; name changed in 2003; centre-right; Pres. JANEZ JANŠA; over 29,000 mems (2012).

Slovenian National Party (SNP) (Slovenska nacionalna stranka—SNS): 1000 Ljubljana, Tivolska 13; tel. (1) 2529020; fax (1) 2529022; e-mail info@sns.si; internet www.sns.si; f. 1991; nationalist; Pres. ZMAGO JELINČIČ PLEMENITI; 8,000 mems (2008).

Slovenian People's Party (SPP) (Slovenska ljudska stranka—SLS): 1000 Ljubljana, Beethovnova 4; tel. (1) 2418820; fax (1) 2511741; e-mail sls@sls.si; internet www.sls.si; f. 1989 as the Slovenian Farmers' Asscn; merged with the Slovenian Christian Democrats in April 2000; Pres. RADOVAN ŽERJAV.

Social Democrats (SD) (Socialni demokrati): 1000 Ljubljana, Levstikova 15; tel. (1) 2444100; fax (1) 2444111; e-mail info@socialnidemokrati.si; internet www.socialnidemokrati.si; f. 1993 as United List of Social Democrats; renamed 2005; Pres. IGOR LUKŠIČ; Gen. Sec. UROŠ JAUŠEVEC; 23,000 mems.

Diplomatic Representation

EMBASSIES IN SLOVENIA

Albania: 1000 Ljubljana, Zaloška cesta 69; tel. (1) 5473650; fax (1) 5473652; e-mail embassy.ljubljana@mfa.gov.al; Chargé d'affaires a.i. ARDIAN SIMONI.

Austria: 1000 Ljubljana, Prešernova cesta 23; tel. (1) 4790700; fax (1) 2521717; e-mail laibach-ob@bmaa.gv.at; internet www.bmeia.gv .at/laibach; Ambassador CLEMENS KOJA.

Azerbaijan: 1000 Ljubljana, ul. Bethovnova 4; tel. (1) 4252510; fax (1) 2566302; e-mail ljubljana@mission.mfa.gov.az; Chargé d'affaires a.i. AZER KHUDUYEV.

Belgium: 1000 Ljubljana, trg Republike 3/IX; tel. (1) 2006010; fax (1) 4266395; e-mail ljubljana@diplobel.fed.be; internet www.diplomatie .be/ljubljana; Ambassador PAUL JANSEN.

Bosnia and Herzegovina: 1000 Ljubljana, Kolarjeva 26; tel. (1) 2343250; fax (1) 2343261; e-mail ambasadabih@siol.net; Ambassador SLAVKO PULJIĆ.

Brazil: 1000 Ljubljana, Kongresni trg 3; tel. (1) 2442400; fax (1) 2442420; e-mail brasemb.liubliana@itamaraty.gov.br; Ambassador GILBERTO FONSECA GUIMARÃES DE MOURA.

Bulgaria: 1000 Ljubljana, Opekarska cesta 35; tel. (1) 2832899; fax (1) 2832825; e-mail bgembassysl@siol.net; internet www.mfa.bg/ embassies/slovenia; Ambassador FILIP BOKOV.

China, People's Republic: 1000 Ljubljana, Koblarjeva 3; tel. (1) 4202855; fax (1) 4202859; e-mail kitajsko.veleposlanistvo@siol.net; internet si.china-embassy.org; Ambassador ZHANG XIANYI.

Croatia: 1000 Ljubljana, Gruberjevo nabrežje 6; tel. (1) 4256220; fax (1) 4258106; e-mail vrhslo@mvep.hr; internet si.mvp.hr; Ambassador Dr SVJETLAN BERKOVIĆ.

Cyprus: 1000 Ljubljana, Komenskega 12; tel. (1) 2321542; fax (1) 2302002; e-mail embassy.cyprus@siol.net; Chargé d'affaires a.i. KYPROS GIORGALLIS.

Czech Republic: 1000 Ljubljana, Riharjeva 1; tel. (1) 4202450; fax (1) 2839259; e-mail ljubljana@embassy.mzv.cz; internet www.mzv .cz/ljubljana; Ambassador JARMILA REBICKOVA.

Denmark: 1000 Ljubljana, Tivolska 48, Eurocenter; tel. (1) 4380800; fax (1) 4317417; e-mail ljuamb@um.dk; internet slovenien.um.dk; Ambassador KARSTEN VAGN NIELSEN.

Egypt: 1000 Ljubljana, Opekarska cesta 18A; tel. (1) 4295420; fax (1) 2839122; e-mail embassy.ljubljana@mfa.gov.eg; Ambassador HEBA SEDHOM.

Finland: 1000 Ljubljana, Ajdovščina 4/8; tel. (1) 3002120; fax (1) 3002139; e-mail sanomat.lju@formin.fi; internet www.finland.si; Ambassador PEKKA METSO.

France: 1000 Ljubljana, Barjanska cesta 1; tel. (1) 4790400; fax (1) 4790410; e-mail contact@ambafrance-si.org; internet www .ambafrance-si.org; Ambassador PIERRE-FRANÇOIS MOURIER.

Georgia: 1000 Ljubljana, Cankarjeva cesta 7; tel. (8) 3826598; fax (8) 3826599; e-mail ljubljana.emb@mfa.gov.ge; Chargé d'affaires a.i. ALEKSANDR CHKUASELI.

Germany: 1000 Ljubljana, Prešernova cesta 27; tel. (1) 4790300; fax (1) 4250899; e-mail germanembassy-slovenia@siol.net; internet www.laibach.diplo.de; Ambassador WERNER BURKART.

Greece: 1000 Ljubljana, Trnovski pristan 14; tel. (1) 4201400; fax (1) 2811114; e-mail gremb.lju@mfa.gr; internet www.mfa.gr/ljubljana; Ambassador ATHANASIOS KALLIDOPOULOS.

Holy See: 1000 Ljubljana, Krekov trg 1; tel. (1) 4339204; fax (1) 4315130; e-mail apostolska.nunciatura@rkc.si; Apostolic Nuncio JULIUSZ JANUSZ (Titular Archbishop of Caprulae).

Hungary: 1210 Ljubljana-Šentvid, ul. Konrada Babnika 5; tel. (1) 5121882; fax (1) 5121878; e-mail mission.lju@mfa.gov.hu; internet www.mfa.gov.hu/kulkepviselet/SLO/hu; Ambassador ISTVÁN SZENT-IVÁNYI.

India: 1000 Ljubljana, Maurerjeva 29; tel. (1) 5133117; fax (1) 5133116; e-mail amb.ljubljana@mea.gov.in; internet www .indianembassy.si; Ambassador JAYAKAR JEROME.

Iran: 1000 Ljubljana, ul. Tolstojeva 8; tel. (1) 5897100; fax (1) 5897106; e-mail iranemb.lju@mfa.gov.ir; Ambassador MOHAMMAD RAHIM AGHAEIPOUR.

Ireland: 1000 Ljubljana, Palača kapitelj, Poljanski nasip 6; tel. (1) 3008970; fax (1) 2821096; e-mail ljubljanaembassy@dfa.ie; internet www.irishembassy.si; Ambassador KIERAN DOWLING.

Italy: 1000 Ljubljana, ul. Snežniška 8; tel. (1) 4262194; fax (1) 4253302; e-mail archivio.lubiana@esteri.it; internet www .amblubiana.esteri.it; Ambassador ROSSELLA FRANCHINI SHERIFIS.

Japan: 1000 Ljubljana, trg Republike 3/XI; tel. (1) 2008281; fax (1) 2511822; e-mail info@embjp.si; internet www.si.emb-japan.go.jp; Ambassador SHIGEMI JOMORI.

Kosovo: 1000 Ljubljana, Dvorec Sela, Zaloška cesta 69; tel. (1) 5415410; fax (1) 5415411; e-mail embassy.slovenia@ks-gov.net; Ambassador MIMOZA AHMETAJ.

Latvia: 1000 Ljubljana, ul. Tavčarjeva 10-7; tel. (1) 4341620; fax (1) 4341622; e-mail embassy.slovenia@mfa.gov.lv; Ambassador BAHTI-JORS HASANS.

Lithuania: 1000 Ljubljana, Emonska cesta 8; tel. (1) 2445600; fax (1) 2445603; e-mail amb.si@urm.lt; internet si.mfa.lt; Ambassador IZOLDA BRIČKOVSKIENĖ.

Macedonia, former Yugoslav republic: 1000 Ljubljana, Rožna dolina cesta IV/2; tel. (1) 4210021; fax (1) 4210023; e-mail makamb@ siol.net; Ambassador IGOR POPOV.

Montenegro: 1000 Ljubljana, Njegoševa cesta 14; tel. (1) 4395364; fax (1) 4395360; e-mail embamon-lj@t–2.net; Ambassador IVAN MILIĆ.

Netherlands: 1000 Ljubljana, Palača Kapitelj, Polijanski nasip 6; tel. (1) 4201460; fax (1) 4201470; e-mail lju@minbuza.nl; internet www.netherlands-embassy.si; Ambassador JOHANNES DOUMA.

Poland: 1000 Ljubljana, Bežigrad 10; tel. (1) 4364712; fax (1) 4362521; e-mail lublana.amb.sekretariat@msz.gov.pl; internet www.lublana.polemb.net; Ambassador CEZARY KRÓL.

Portugal: 1000 Ljubljana, trg Republike 3/10; tel. (1) 4790540; fax (1) 4790550; e-mail embportlju@siol.net; Chargé d'affaires MARIA LEONOR PENALVA ESTEVES.

Romania: 1000 Ljubljana, Smrekarjeva 33A; tel. (1) 5058294; fax (1) 5055432; e-mail embassy.of.romania@siol.net; internet ljubljana .mae.ro; Ambassador MARIUS COSMIN BOIANGIU.

Russia: 1000 Ljubljana, Tomšičeva 9; tel. (1) 4256875; fax (1) 4256878; e-mail ambrus.slo@siol.net; internet www.rus-slo.mid.ru; Ambassador DOKU ZAVGAYEV.

Serbia: 1000 Ljubljana, Slomškova 1; tel. (1) 4380110; fax (1) 4342688; e-mail ambasada@ambasadasrbije.si; internet www .ambasadasrbije.si; Ambassador ALEKSANDAR RADOVANOVIĆ.

Slovakia: 1000 Ljubljana, Bleiweisova cesta 4; tel. (1) 4255425; fax (1) 4210524; e-mail emb.ljubljana@mzv.sk; internet www.mzv.sk/ lublana; Ambassador Dr MARIANNA ORAVCOVÁ.

Spain: 1000 Ljubljana, Trnovski pristan 24; tel. (1) 4202330; fax (1) 4202333; e-mail emba.espa.eslovenia@siol.net; Ambassador ANUN-CIADA FERNÁNDEZ DE CÓRDOVA ALONSO-VIGUERA.

Switzerland: 1000 Ljubljana, trg Republike 3/VI; tel. (1) 2008640; fax (1) 2008669; e-mail lju.vertretung@eda.admin.ch; internet www .eda.admin.ch/ljubljana; Ambassador ROBERT REICH.

Turkey: 1000 Ljubljana, Livarska 4; tel. (1) 2364150; fax (1) 4365240; e-mail embassy.ljubljana@mfa.gov.tr; internet www .ljubljana.emb.mfa.gov.tr; Ambassador SERRA KALELI.

Ukraine: 1000 Ljubljana, Teslova 23; tel. (1) 4210604; fax (1) 4210603; e-mail emb_si@mfa.gov.ua; internet www.mfa.gov.ua/ slovenia; Ambassador MYKOLA KYRYCHENKO.

United Kingdom: 1000 Ljubljana, trg Republike 3/IV; tel. (1) 2003910; fax (1) 4250174; e-mail info@british-embassy.si; internet ukinslovenia.fco.gov.uk; Ambassador ANDREW PAGE.

USA: 1000 Ljubljana, Prešernova cesta 31; tel. (1) 2005500; fax (1) 2005555; e-mail usembassyljubljana@state.gov; internet slovenia .usembassy.gov; Ambassador JOSEPH A. MUSSOMELI.

Venezuela: 1000 Ljubljana, Emonska cesta 8; fax (1) 2006722; e-mail emba.venez.eslovenia@siol.net; Chargé d'affaires a.i. NÉSTOR ENRIQUE LÓPEZ MARTÍNEZ.

Judicial System

The Slovenian Constitution guarantees the independence of the judiciary.

The 44 district courts decide minor cases. The 11 regional courts act as courts of the first instance in all cases other than those for which the district courts have jurisdiction. Four regional courts act as courts of the second instance. There are, in addition, labour courts and social courts, which adjudicate in disputes over pensions, welfare allocations and other social benefits. A Higher Labour and Social Court has jurisdiction in the second instance. The Supreme Court is the highest authority for civil and criminal law. There is also a Constitutional Court, composed of nine judges, each elected for a single term of nine years.

Constitutional Court of the Republic of Slovenia (Ustavno sodišča Republike Slovenije): 1001 Ljubljana, Beethovnova 10; tel. (1) 4776400; fax (1) 2510451; e-mail info@us-rs.si; internet www .us-rs.si; Pres. Dr ERNEST PETRIČ.

Supreme Court of the Republic of Slovenia (Vrhovno Sodišče Republike Slovenije): 1000 Ljubljana, Tavčarjeva 9; tel. (1) 3664444; fax (1) 3664301; e-mail urad.vsrs@sodisce.si; internet www.sodisce .si; Pres. BRANKO MASLEŠA.

Office of the State Prosecutor-General: 1000 Ljubljana, trg Osvobodilne fronte 13; tel. (1) 4341936; fax (1) 4341945; e-mail dtrs@dt-rs.si; internet www.dt-rs.si; State Prosecutor-General Dr ZVONKO FIŠER.

Religion

Most of the population are Christian, predominantly adherents of the Roman Catholic Church. There are few Protestant Christians, despite the importance of a Calvinist sect (the Church of Carniola) to the development of Slovene literature in the 16th century. At the census of 2002 some 57.8% of the population described themselves as Roman Catholics, 10.1% as atheists, 2.4% as Muslims, 2.3% as Orthodox Christians and 0.8% as Protestants; 22.8% of all respondents did not answer the question requesting their religious allegiance.

CHRISTIANITY

The Roman Catholic Church

The Roman Catholic Church in Slovenia comprises two archdioceses and four dioceses. There are an estimated 1,592,644 adherents (equivalent to 78.8% of the total population).

Bishops' Conference: 1000 Ljubljana, p.p. 121/III, Ciril Metodov trg 4; tel. (1) 2342600; fax (1) 2314169; e-mail ssk@rkc.si; f. 1993; Pres. Most Rev. ALOJZIJ URAN (Archbishop of Ljubljana).

Archbishop of Ljubljana: Most Rev. ALOJZIJ URAN, 1001 Ljubljana, p.p. 1990, Ciril Metodov trg 4; tel. (1) 2342600; fax (1) 2314169; e-mail nadskofija.lubljana@rkc.si.

Archbishop of Maribor: Most Rev. MARJAN TURNŠEK, 2000 Maribor, Slomškov trg 19; tel. (2) 2290401; fax (2) 2523092; e-mail ordinariat@slomsek.net.

Protestant Church

Evangelical Lutheran Church of Slovenia: 9226 Moravske Toplice, 11 Levstikova; tel. (2) 5381323; fax (2) 5381324; e-mail evang.cerkev.si@siol.net; f. 1561; 20,000 mems; Chair. GEZA ERNIŠA.

ISLAM

Islamic Association in the Republic of Slovenia (Islamska Skupnost V Republiki Sloveniji): 1000 Ljubljana, Grabiovičeva 14; tel. (1) 2313625; fax (1) 2313626; internet www.islamska-skupnost.si; Dir NEVZET PORIĆ.

The Press

In 2011 there were 13 daily newspapers, 188 non-daily newspapers and 1,665 other periodicals published in Slovenia. The publications listed below are in Slovene, unless otherwise indicated.

PRINCIPAL DAILIES

Delo (Event): 1509 Ljubljana, Dunajska 5; tel. (1) 4737417; fax (1) 4737406; e-mail urednistvo@delo.si; internet www.delo.si; f. 1959; morning; Editor-in-Chief ROMANA DOBNIKAR-ŠERUGA; circ. 93,781.

Dnevnik (Daily): 1000 Ljubljana, Kopitarjeva 2; tel. (1) 3082300; fax (1) 3082329; e-mail info@dnevnik.si; internet www.dnevnik.si; f. 1951; evening; independent; Man. Dir BRANKO PAVLIN; Editor-in-Chief ZLATKO SETINC; circ. 63,000.

Slovenske novice (Slovene News): 1509 Ljubljana, Dunajska 5; tel. (1) 4737700; fax (1) 1737352; e-mail info@slovenskenovice.si; internet www.slovenskenovice.si; f. 1991; Editor-in-Chief BOJAN BUDJA; circ. 80,000.

Večer (Evening): 2504 Maribor, Svetozarevska 14; tel. (2) 2353500; fax (2) 2353368; internet www.vecer.si; f. 1945; evening; Dir UROŠ SKUHALA; Editor-in-Chief TOMAŽ RANC; circ. 70,000.

PERIODICALS

Avto magazin: 1000 Ljubljana, Vošnjakova 3; tel. (1) 3000700; fax (1) 3000713; e-mail avtomagazin@adriamedia.si; internet www.avto-magazin.si; f. 1967; fortnightly; cars, motorcycles and sports; Editor DUŠAN LUKIČ; circ. 16,000.

Delavska enotnost (Workers' Unity): 1000 Ljubljana, Dalmatinova 4; tel. (1) 4341200; fax (1) 2317298; e-mail delavska.enotnost@union-zsss.si; f. 1942; weekly, Thur. except in Aug.; trade union issues; Editor-in-Chief MOJCA MATOZ; circ. 16,000.

Dolenjski list: 8000 Novo mesto, ul. Germova 4/212; tel. (7) 3930500; fax (7) 3930540; e-mail info@dolenjskilist.si; internet www.dolenjskilist.si; f. 1950; weekly; general and local information; Editor-in-Chief JOŽICA DORNIŽ; circ. 24,000.

Družina: 1001 Ljubljana, trg Krekov 1; tel. (1) 1316202; fax (1) 3602800; e-mail druzina@druzina.si; internet www.druzina.si; f. 1952; Christian; Editor-in-Chief FRANCI PETRIČ; circ. 70,000.

Finance: 1538 Ljubljana, Dalmatinova 2; tel. (1) 3091540; fax (1) 3091545; e-mail finance@finance.si; internet www.finance.si; f. 1992; 2 a week; Editor-in-Chief PETER FRANKL; circ. 8,500.

Gea: 1536 Ljubljana, Slovenska 29; tel. (1) 2413230; fax (1) 1252836; e-mail gea@mkz-lj.si; f. 1990; monthly; popular science; Editor-in-Chief ANJA LESKOVAR; circ. 16,000.

Gorenjski glas (Voice of Gorenjska): 4000 Kranj, Bleiweisova cesta 4; tel. (4) 2014200; fax (4) 2014213; e-mail info@g-glas.si; internet www.gorenjskiglas.si; f. 1947; 2 a week; general and regional information; Editor-in-Chief MARIJA VOLČJAK; circ. 18,000 (2010).

Jana: 1509 Ljubljana, Dunajska 5; tel. (1) 4738201; fax (1) 4738220; e-mail jana@delo-revije.si; internet www.jana.si; f. 1972; weekly; women's interest; Editor-in-Chief MELITA BERZELAK; circ. 62,000.

Kaj: 62000 Maribor, Svetozarevska 14; tel. (2) 26951; fax (2) 227736; f. 1984; weekly; popular; Editor-in-Chief MILAN PREDAN; circ. 16,500.

Kmečki glas: 1000 Ljubljana, p.p. 47, Železna cesta 14; tel. (1) 4735350; fax (1) 4735377; e-mail info@czd-kmeckiglas.si; internet www.kmeckiglas.com; weekly; general and agricultural news; Dir PETER ZADEL; circ. 38,000.

Lipov list: 1000 Ljubljana, Miklosičeva 38/6; tel. (1) 4341670; fax (1) 4341680; e-mail info@turisticna-zveza.si; monthly; Editor-in-Chief RENATA PICEJ.

Mag: 1000 Ljubljana, Njegoševa 14; tel. (1) 319480; fax (1) 1329158; f. 1995; weekly; news and politics; Editor-in-Chief JANEZ MARKES.

Mladina: 1000 Ljubljana, Dunajska 51; tel. (1) 2306500; fax (1) 2306510; e-mail desk@mladina.si; internet www.mladina.si; f. 1942; weekly; news magazine; Editor-in-Chief GREGA REPOVŽ; circ. 30,000.

Moj mikro: 1000 Ljubljana, ul. Likozarjeva 5; tel. and fax (1) 4738261; e-mail mojmikro@mojmikro.si; internet www.mojmikro.si; monthly; personal computers; Editor-in-Chief MARJAN KODELJA.

Naš Čas (Our Time): 63320 Velenje, Foltova 10; tel. (3) 855450; fax (3) 851990; f. 1956; weekly; general and regional information; Editor-in-Chief STANE VOVK; circ. 6,250.

Nedeljski dnevnik (Weekly Record): 1000 Ljubljana, Kopitarieva 2; tel. (1) 3082100; fax (1) 3082329; e-mail zlatko.setinc@dnevnik.si; internet www.dnevnik.si/nedeljski_dnevnik; f. 1961; weekly; popular; Editor-in-Chief ZLATKO SETINC; circ. 145,000 (2006).

Nova Muska: 1000 Ljubljana, Cesta 27 Aprila 31; tel. (1) 1317039; e-mail revijamuska@gmail.com; internet www.novamuska.org; f. 2010; monthly; music; Editor-in-Chief Dr JOŽE VOGRINC.

Novi tednik (New Weekly): 3000 Celje, Prešernova 19; tel. (3) 4225100; fax (3) 5441032; e-mail tednik@nt-rc.si; internet www.novitednik.com; f. 1945; weekly; general and local information; Editor-in-Chief TATJANA CVIRN; circ. 16,980.

Obrtnik: 1000 Ljubljana, Celovška 71; tel. (1) 5830507; fax (1) 5054373; e-mail miran.jarec@ozs.si; internet www.ozs.si/obrtnik; f. 1971; monthly; small businesses; Editor-in-Chief MIRAN JAREC; circ. 60,000.

PIL: 1000 Ljubljana, Slovenska 29; tel. (1) 2413220; fax (1) 4252836; e-mail pil@mkz.si; internet www.pil-on.net; monthly; for children aged 9 to 12 years; Editor JANA ZIRKELBACH; circ. 21,000.

Podjetnik: 1000 Ljubljana, Celovška 71; tel. (1) 5830500; fax (1) 5054373; e-mail info@podjetnik.si; internet www.podjetnik.si; f. 1992; monthly; business and management; Editor-in-Chief PRIMOŽ KAUČIČ; circ. 8,500.

Primorske novice (News from the Primorska region): 6000 Koper, ul. Of. 12; tel. (5) 6648100; fax (5) 6648122; e-mail editors@primorske.si; internet www.primorske.si; f. 1947; daily; general and regional information; Editor-in-Chief SILVA KRIŽMAN; circ. 23,000.

Profit: 1000 Ljubljana, Dunajska 5; tel. (1) 4304310; fax (1) 2318940; e-mail profit.uredmistvo@sid.net; 2 a month; business; Editor-in-Chief JOŽE SIMČIČ.

Rodna gruda (Native Breast): 1000 Ljubljana, Cankarjeva 1/II, Združenje Slovenska izseljenska matica; tel. (1) 2410280; fax (1) 4251673; e-mail rodna.gruda@zdruzenje-sim.si; internet www.zdruzenje-sim.si; f. 1951; monthly; national issues and news; Editor-in-Chief VIDA POSINKOVIĆ; circ. 2,100.

Slovenian Business Report: 1000 Ljubljana, Sarhova 8; tel. and fax (1) 4305309; e-mail info@sbr.si; internet www.sbr.si; f. 1991; quarterly; in English; economic affairs; Editor-in-Chief ROBERT MULEJ; circ. 4,000 (2009).

Slovenija: 1000 Ljubljana, Cankarjeva 1/II; tel. (1) 2410280; fax (1) 4251673; e-mail sim@siol.net; f. 1987; quarterly; in English; news about Slovenia and Slovenes; Man. Editor (vacant); circ. 3,500.

Štajerski Tednik: 2250 Ptuj, Raičeva 14; tel. (2) 7493410; fax (2) 7493435; e-mail nabiralnik@radio-tednik.si; internet www.radio-tednik.si; f. 1948; weekly; politics, local information; Dir JOŽE BRAČIČ; circ. 12,000.

Stop: 1000 Ljubljana, Dunajska 5; tel. (1) 4738151; fax (1) 4738169; e-mail info@revijastop.si; internet www.revijastop.si; f. 1967; weekly; leisure, film, theatre, pop music, radio and television programmes; Editor-in-Chief MARTIN SENICA; circ. 44,600.

Tretji dan (The Third Day): 1000 Ljubljana, Jurčičev trg 2; tel. (1) 4268477; fax (1) 4268478; e-mail info@drustvo-skam.si; internet www.drustvo-skam.si/td; weekly; Christianity, culture, philosophy; Editor-in-Chief ALES MAVER.

Tribuna: 1000 Ljubljana, Kersnikova 4; tel. (1) 4380263; fax (1) 4380264; e-mail urednistvo@tribuna.si; internet www.tribuna.si; 3 a week; student newspaper; Dir ROMAN DIDOVIČ.

Vestnik Murska Sobota (Murska Sobota Herald): 9000 Murska Sobota, ul. Arhitekta Novaka 13; tel. (2) 5381710; fax (2) 5381711; e-mail vestnik@vestnik.si; internet www.p-inf.si; f. 1949; weekly; popular; Editor-in-Chief JANEZ VOTEK; circ. 20,000.

Zdravje (Health): 1509 Ljubljana, Dunajska 5; tel. (1) 4738136; fax (1) 4738253; e-mail zdravje@zdravje.si; internet www.zdravje.si; monthly; Editor-in-Chief MARTA KRPIĆ.

PRESS AGENCIES

Morel: 1000 Ljubljana, Reboljeva 13; tel. and fax 41511067; e-mail morel@siol.net; internet www.morel.si; f. 1992; Dir and Chief Editor EMIL LUKANČIĆ-MORI.

Slovenska Tiskovna Agencija (STA): 1000 Ljubljana, Tivolska cesta 50; tel. (1) 2410100; fax (1) 4342970; e-mail desk@sta.si; internet www.sta.si; f. 1991; Gen. Man. BOJAN VESELINOVIČ; Editor-in-Chief BARBARA ŠTRUKELJ.

Publishers

Cankarjeva Založba: 1000 Ljubljana, Kopitarjeva 2; tel. (1) 3603720; fax (1) 3603787; e-mail import.books@cankarjeva-z.si; internet www.cankarjeva-z.si; f. 1945; philosophy, science and popular science, dictionaries and reference books, Slovenian and translated literature, international co-productions; Dir-Gen. JOŽE KORINŠEK.

DZS d.d.: 1538 Ljubljana, Dalmatinova 2; tel. (1) 3069700; fax (1) 3069877; e-mail info@dzs.si; internet www.dzs.si; f. 1945; textbooks, manuals, world classics, natural sciences, art books, encyclopedias, dictionaries, educational CD-ROMs; Exec. Dir ADA DE COSTA PETAN.

Mladinska Knjiga Založba: 1000 Ljubljana, Slovenska 29; tel. (1) 2413288; fax (1) 4252294; e-mail intsales@mkz-lj.si; f. 1945; books for youth and children, incl. general, fiction, science, travel and school books, language courses, magazines and videos; Dir MILAN MATOS.

Slovenska Matica: 1000 Ljubljana, Kongresni trg 8; tel. and fax (1) 4224340; e-mail drago.jancar@siol.net; f. 1864; poetry, science, philosophy; Pres. Prof. Dr MILČEK KOMELJ.

Založba Lipa Koper: Koper; tel. (5) 6274883; fiction; Dir Prof. JOŽE A. HOČEVAR.

Založba Obzorja d.d. Maribor: 2000 Maribor, Partizanska 3–5; tel. (2) 2348102; fax (2) 2348135; e-mail info@zalozba-obzorja.si; internet www.zalozba-obzorja.si; f. 1950; popular science, general literature, periodicals, etc.; Man. Dir NEVENKA RICHTER PEČE.

Broadcasting and Communications

TELECOMMUNICATIONS

Slovenia's telecommunications market remains dominated by the majority state-owned Telekom Slovenije, although its market share has been declining as a result of increasing competition from other operators.

Si.mobil—Vodafone: 1000 Ljubljana, Šmartinska cesta 134B; tel. (1) 5440000; fax (1) 5440099; e-mail info@simobil.si; internet www.simobil.si; f. 1999; subsidiary of Mobilkom Austria; provides mobile and internet services; Chair. of Bd DEJAN TURK; 639,698 subscribers (Dec. 2011).

T-2: 1000 Ljubljana, Verovškova 64 A; tel. 59002257; fax 59000001; e-mail pr@t-2.net; internet www.t-2.net; f. 2004; mobile cellular telecommunications and internet services.

Telekom Slovenije: 1000 Ljubljana, Cigaletova 15; tel. (1) 2341000; fax (1) 2314736; e-mail info@telekom.si; internet www.telekom.si; f. 1949; 62.5% state-owned; mobile and internet services; Pres. RUDOLF SKOBE.

Mobitel: 1537 Ljubljana, Vilharjeva 23; tel. (1) 4722255; fax (1) 4722295; e-mail info@mobitel.si; internet www.mobitel.si; f. 1991; 100% owned by Telekom Slovenije; mobile cellular telecommunications and internet services; Chief Exec. ZORAN JANKO.

Tušmobil: 1231 Ljubljana, Brnčičeva 49; tel. (1) 6002020; fax (1) 6002021; e-mail info@tusmobil.si; internet www.tusmobil.si; f. 2006; mobile cellular telecommunications services; Dir GREGOR ŠTAMPO-HAR.

Regulatory Authority

Agency for Posts and Electronic Communications (Agencija za pošto in elektronske komunikacije Republike Slovenije—APEK): 1000 Ljubljana, Stegne 7; tel. (1) 5836300; fax (1) 5111101; e-mail info.box@apek.si; internet www.apek.si; Dir FRANC DOLENC.

BROADCASTING

Regulatory Authority

Slovenian Broadcasting Council (Svet za Radiodifuzijo—SRDF): 1000 Ljubljana, Stegne 7; tel. (1) 5836300; fax (1) 5111101; e-mail srdf.box@apek.si; internet www.srdf.si; f. 1994; seven mems; protects independence of radio and television programmes; supervises the activities of broadcasting and cable operators; Chair. Dr DEJAN JELOVAC.

Radio

In 2009 there were a total of 99 radio stations broadcasting in Slovenia, including three national channels of the state-owned Radiotelevizija Slovenija.

Radiotelevizija Slovenija (RTV Slo): 1550 Ljubljana, Kolodvorska 2; tel. (1) 4752111; fax (1) 4752150; e-mail webmaster@rtvslo.si; internet www.rtvslo.si; f. 1928; three radio programmes nationally; broadcasts in Slovene, Hungarian and Italian; Gen. Man. MARKO FILLI.

Radio Koper Capodistria: 6000 Koper, ul. OF 15; tel. (5) 6485483; fax (5) 6485488; e-mail radio.koper@rtvslo.si; internet www.rtvslo.si/rtvkc; f. 1949; Dir DRAGOMIR MIKELIĆ.

Radio Slovenia International: 2000 Maribor, Ilichova 33; tel. (2) 4299132; fax (2) 4299215; e-mail srecko.trglec@rtvslo.si; internet www.rtvslo.si; f. 2001; state-owned; broadcasts in Slovene, English and German 24 hours a day; Editor-in-Chief SREČKO TRGLEC.

Television

There are three publicly owned national television stations and 39 major commercial and two non-profit television stations operating in Slovenia. Analogue broadcasting ceased at the end of 2010.

Radiotelevizija Slovenija (RTV Slo): 1550 Ljubljana, Kolodvorska 2; tel. (1) 4752111; fax (1) 4752150; e-mail webmaster@rtvslo.si; internet www.rtvslo.si/html/radio-slo; f. 1957; three television programmes (TV1, TV2 and TV3) nationally; broadcasts in Slovene, Hungarian and Italian; Gen. Man. MARKO FILLI.

Kanal A: 1000 Ljubljana, Tivolska 50; tel. (1) 1334133; fax (1) 1334222; Pres. DOUGLAS FULTON.

Pop TV: 1000 Ljubljana, Kranjčeva 26; tel. (1) 1893200; fax (1) 1612222; Editor TOMAŽ PEROVIČ.

TV 3: PRVA TV d.o.o., 1000 Ljubljana, Vojkova 58; tel. (1) 2807800; fax (1) 2807840; e-mail info@tv3.si; internet www.tv3.si; f. 2006; Dir-Gen. GREGOR MEMEDOVIĆ.

Finance

BANKS

(cap. = capital; res = reserves; dep. = deposits; m. = million; amounts in euros, unless otherwise indicated; brs = branches)

In January 1999 new banking legislation allowed foreign banks to establish branches in Slovenia for the first time.

National Bank

Banka Slovenije (Bank of Slovenia): 1505 Ljubljana, Slovenska 35; tel. (1) 4719000; fax (1) 2515516; e-mail bsl@bsi.si; internet www.bsi.si; fmrly National Bank of Slovenia, as part of the Yugoslav banking system; assumed central bank functions in 1991; cap. and res 751.8m., dep. 1,408.3m. (Dec. 2008); Gov. Dr MARKO KRANJEC.

Selected Banks

Abanka Vipa d.d.: 1517 Ljubljana, Slovenska 58, POB 368; tel. (1) 4718100; fax (1) 4325165; e-mail info@abanka.si; internet www.abanka.si; f. 1955 as Ljubljana Branch of Yugoslav Bank for Foreign Trade; present name adopted 1989; cap. 30.0m., res 199.6m., dep. 2,632.4m. (Dec. 2011); Pres. ALES ZAJDELA; 32 brs.

Banka Celje d.d.: 3001 Celje, Vodnikova 2, POB 431; tel. (3) 4221000; fax (3) 4221100; e-mail info@banka-celje.si; internet www.banka-celje.si; cap. 16.9m., res 179.6m., dep. 1,598m. (Dec. 2011); Chair. of Bd DUŠAN DROFENIK.

Banka Koper d.d.: 6502 Koper, Pristaniška 14; tel. (5) 6661000; fax (5) 6662006; e-mail info@banka-koper.si; internet www.banka-koper.si; f. 1955; cap. 22.1m., res 234.6m., dep. 1,716.7m. (Dec. 2011); Pres. of Management Bd GIANCARLO MIRANDA; 14 brs.

Deželna banka Slovenije d.d.: 1000 Ljubljana, Kolodvorska 9; tel. (1) 4727100; fax (1) 4727405; e-mail info@dbs.si; internet www.dbs .si; f. 1990; present name adopted 2004; cap. 15.8m., res 53.1m., dep. 664.6m. (Dec. 2011); Pres. of Bd PETER VRISK; 10 brs.

Gorenjska Banka d.d. Kranj: 4000 Kranj, Bleiweisova cesta 1, POB 147; tel. (4) 2084000; fax (4) 2084491; e-mail info@gbkr.si; internet www.gbkr.si; f. 1955; cap. 13.8m., res 321.7m., dep. 1,301.9m. (Dec. 2011); CEO GORAZDA TRČEK; 6 brs.

Hypo Alpe-Adria-Bank d.d.: 1000 Ljubljana, Dunajska cesta 117; tel. (1) 5804000; fax (1) 5804001; e-mail hypo-bank@hypo.si; internet www.hypo-alpe-adria.si; f. 1999; cap. 174.0m., res 26.6m., dep. 1,434.4m. (Dec. 2011); Pres. ANTON ROMIH.

Nova Kreditna banka Maribor d.d. (Nova KBM): 2505 Maribor, Vita Kraigherja 4; tel. (2) 2292290; fax (2) 2524333; e-mail info@ nkbm.si; internet www.nkbm.si; f. 1955; present name adopted 1994; 51.1% state-owned; cap. 40.8m., res 439.9m., dep. 3,951.7m. (Dec. 2011); Pres. and CEO MATJAŽ KOVAČIČ; 90 brs and sub-brs.

Nova Ljubljanska banka d.d. (NLB): 1520 Ljubljana, trg Republike 2; tel. (1) 4763900; fax (1) 2522500; e-mail info@nlb.si; internet www.nlb.si; f. 1994; commercial, investment and savings bank; 55% state-owned, 25% owned by KBC Bank NV (Belgium); cap. 92.3m., res 852.8m., dep. 10,644.6m. (Dec. 2011); CEO JANKO MEDJA; 179 brs.

Probanka d.d.: 2000 Maribor, trg Leona Štuklja 12; tel. (2) 2520500; fax (2) 2526029; e-mail info@probanka.si; internet www.probanka.si; f. 1991; cap. 16.7m., res 82.3m., dep. 779.9m. (Dec. 2011); Pres. and Chair. ROMANA PAJENK.

Raiffeisen banka d.d.: 2000 Maribor, Zagrebška cesta 76; tel. (2) 2293100; fax (2) 2223502; e-mail info@raiffeisen.si; internet www .raiffeisen.si; f. 1992; present name adopted 2007; cap. 17.6m., res 62.1m., dep. 795.0m. (Dec. 2011); Chair. KLEMENS NOWOTNY; 14 brs.

SKB Banka d.d.: 1000 Ljubljana, Ajdovščina 4; tel. (1) 4715555; fax (1) 2314549; e-mail info@skb.si; internet www.skb.si; f. 1978; 99.6% owned by Société Générale (France); cap. 52.8m., res 115.5m., dep. 1,640.8m. (Dec. 2011); Pres. and Chief Exec. CVETKA SELŠEK; 60 brs.

UniCredit Banka Slovenija d.d.: 1000 Ljubljana, Smartinska 140; tel. (1) 5876600; fax (1) 5876684; e-mail info@unicreditgroup .si; internet www.unicreditgroup.si; f. 1991; fmrly Bank Austria Creditanstalt d.d. Ljubljana; name changed as above Sept. 2007; cap. 20.4m., res 79.4m., dep. 2,135.1m. (Dec. 2011); Chair. FRANCE ARHAR.

STOCK EXCHANGE

Ljubljana Stock Exchange (Ljubljanska Borza d.d.): 1000 Ljubljana, Slovenska 56; tel. (1) 4710211; fax (1) 4710213; e-mail info@ljse .si; internet www.ljse.si; f. 1989; operative 1990; owned by CEESEG AG; Pres. ANDREJ ŠKETA.

INSURANCE

Adriatic Slovenica Insurance Co: 6503 Koper, Ljubljanska cesta 3A; tel. (5) 6643100; fax (5) 6643109; e-mail info@adriatic-slovenica .si; internet www.adriatic-slovenica.si; f. 1990; CEO GABRIJEL ŠKOF.

Grawe Insurance Co d.d.: 2000 Maribor, Gregorčičeva 39; tel. (2) 2285500; fax (2) 2285526; e-mail grawe@grawe.si; internet www .grawe.si; Pres. BOŽO EMERŠIČ.

Maribor Insurance Co: 2507 Maribor, Cankarjeva 3; tel. (2) 2332100; fax (2) 2332530; e-mail info@zav-mb.si; internet www .zav-mb.si; Chair. DRAGO COTAR.

Merkur Insurance Co: 1000 Ljubljana, Dunajska 58; tel. (1) 3005450; fax (1) 4361092; e-mail info@merkur-zav.si; internet www.merkur-zav.si; f. 1992; CEO DENIS STROLIGO.

Sava Insurance Co (Sava Re) (Pozavarovalnica Sava d.d. Ljubljana): 1000 Ljubljana, Dunajska 56; tel. (1) 4750200; fax (1) 4750264; e-mail info@sava-re.si; internet www.sava-re.si; f. 1973; Chair. of Bd ZVONKO IVANUŠIČ.

Triglav Insurance Co (Zavarovalnica Triglav d.d.): 1000 Ljubljana, Miklošičeva 19; tel. (1) 4747200; fax (1) 4326302; e-mail info-triglav@triglav.si; internet www.triglav.si; f. 1900; CEO MATJAŽ RAKOVEC; Chair. of Supervisory Bd IGOR MIHAJLOVIĆ.

Trade and Industry

GOVERNMENT AGENCY

Agency of the Republic of Slovenia for Restructuring and Privatization (Agencija Republike Slovenije za Prestrukturiranje in Privatizacijo—ARSPIP): 1000 Ljubljana, Kotnikova 28; tel. (1) 1316030; fax (1) 1316011; e-mail webmaster@arspip.si; Dir MIRA PUC.

CHAMBERS OF COMMERCE

Chamber of Commerce and Industry of Slovenia (Gospodarska Zbornica Slovenije): 1504 Ljubljana, Dimičeva 13; tel. (1) 5898000;

fax (1) 5898100; e-mail info@gzs.si; internet www.gzs.si; f. 1852; Pres. SAMO HRIBAR MILIČ.

Chamber of Small Businesses of Slovenia: 1000 Ljubljana, Celovška 71; tel. (1) 4593241; fax (1) 4559270; Pres. MIHA GRAH; Sec. ANTON FILIPIČ; 50,000 mems.

UTILITIES

Electricity

Elektro-Slovenija d.o.o. (ELES): 1000 Ljubljana, Hajdrihova 2; tel. (1) 4743000; fax (1) 4742502; e-mail info@eles.si; internet www .eles.si; f. 1991; national electricity distributor; CEO MILAN JEVŠENAK.

Nuklearna Elektrarna Krško p.o. (NEK): 8270 Krško, Vrbina 12; tel. (7) 4802000; fax (7) 4921006; e-mail nek@nek.si; internet www .nek.si; f. 1974; 50% owned by GEN energija Ljubljana, 50% owned by Hrvatska Elektropriveda Zagreb (Croatia); production and distribution of electricity from nuclear power plant at Krško.

Gas

Geoplin d.o.o.: 1000 Ljubljana, Ljubljanska brigade 11; tel. (1) 5820600; fax (1) 5820601; e-mail info@geoplin.si; internet www .geoplin.si; f. 1975; national gas co; Gen. Man. ALOJZ STANA.

TRADE UNIONS

The Association of Independent Trade Unions of Slovenia: 1000 Ljubljana, Dalmatinova 4; tel. (1) 4317983; fax (1) 4318294; Pres. DUŠAN SEMOLIČ.

Independence—Confederation of New Trade Unions of Slovenia (Sindikat Ljubljanske regije KNSS—Neodvisnost): 1000 Ljubljana, Linhartova cesta 13; tel. (1) 3063951; fax (1) 4391815; e-mail neodvisnost.knss@siol.net; internet www.knss-neodvisnost .eu; f. 1990; Pres. DRAGO LOMBAR.

Transport

RAILWAYS

In 2011 the total length of railways was 1,209 km, of which 500 km were electrified.

Slovenske Železnice (SŽ) (Slovenian Railways): 1506 Ljubljana, Kolodvorska 11; tel. (1) 2914001; fax (1) 2914800; e-mail boris.zivec@ slo-zeleznice.si; internet www.slo-zeleznice.si; Dir-Gen. BORIS ŽIVEC.

ROADS

In 2010 the country had 43,916 km of roads, of which 416 km were motorways and expressways and 3,507 km were highways, main or national roads. An 84-km motorway links Ljubljana with the coastal region in the south-west.

Slovenian Roads Agency: 1000 Ljubljana, Tržaška cesta 19; tel. (1) 4788002; fax (1) 4788123; e-mail gp.drsc@gov.si; internet www.dc .gov.si; Dir GREGOR FICKO.

SHIPPING

Slovenia's principal international trading port, at Koper, handles some 3m. tons of freight annually.

Luka Koper d.d.: 6501 Koper, Vojkovo nabrežje 38; tel. (5) 6656100; fax (5) 6395020; e-mail portkoper@luka-kp.si; internet www.luka-kp .si; f. 1957; Pres. of Management Bd ROBERT CASAR.

Principal Shipping Company

Splošna Plovba: 6320 Portorož, Obala 55, POB 60; tel. (5) 6766000; fax (5) 6766130; e-mail plovba@5-plovba.si; transport of all types of cargo; regular liner service; Man. Dir ALDO KREJAČIČ.

CIVIL AVIATION

There are three international airports in Slovenia, at Brnik (Ljubljana), Maribor and Portorož.

Adria Airways: 4210 Brnik, Zgornji Brnik 130 H; tel. (4) 2559000; fax (4) 2594573; e-mail info@adria.si; internet www.adria.si; f. 1961; operates international scheduled services to destinations in Europe and the Middle East; Pres. MARK ANŽUR.

Tourism

Slovenia offers a variety of tourist attractions, including Mediterranean resorts to the west, the Julian Alps and the lakes of Bled and Bohinj to the north, and, in the south, the karst limestone regions, with more than 6,000 caves. The number of foreign tourist arrivals reached 2.2m. in 2012. Tourism receipts (excluding passenger transport) totalled US $2,708m. in 2011.

Slovenian Tourist Board: 1000 Ljubljana, Dunajska 156; tel. (1) 5891840; fax (1) 5891841; e-mail info@slovenia.info; internet www.slovenia.info; f. 1996; Gen. Man. DIMITRIJ PICIGA.

Defence

As assessed at November 2012, the active Slovenian armed forces numbered 7,600 (with 1,700 reserves). There was a paramilitary police force of 4,500 (plus 5,000 reserves). In September 2003 the Government announced the abolition of compulsory military service, prior to the country's official accession to the North Atlantic Treaty Organization (NATO) on 29 March 2004.

Defence Expenditure: Budgeted at 412m. tolars for 2011.

Chief of Staff of the Slovenian Army Supreme Headquarters: Brig. DOBRAN BOŽIČ.

Education

Primary education is free and compulsory for all children between the ages of six and 15 years. In ethnically mixed regions, two methods of schooling have been developed: bilingual or with instruction in the minority languages. Various types of secondary education, beginning at 15 and lasting between two and five years, are also available. In 2008/09 enrolment in primary education included 97% of children in the relevant age-group (males 98%; females 97%), while enrolment in secondary education included 92% of children in the appropriate age-group (males 91%; females 92%). Slovenia's four universities are situated in Ljubljana, Maribor, Koper (the University of Primorska) and Nova Gorica, with 60,284, 23,363, 6,490 and 725 students, respectively, in 2008/09; a further 7,266 students were enrolled in other higher education institutions in that year. In 2008 expenditure on education by all levels of government was equivalent to 6.2% of gross domestic product (GDP).

SOLOMON ISLANDS

Introductory Survey

LOCATION, CLIMATE, LANGUAGE, RELIGION, FLAG, CAPITAL

Solomon Islands is a scattered Melanesian archipelago in the south-western Pacific Ocean, east of Papua New Guinea. The country includes most of the Solomon Islands (those to the north-west being part of Papua New Guinea), Ontong Java Islands (Lord Howe Atoll), Rennell Island and the Santa Cruz Islands, about 500 km (300 miles) to the east. The climate is equatorial, with small seasonal variations, governed by the trade winds. In Honiara the average temperature is about 27°C (81°F) and the average annual rainfall about 2,160 mm (85 ins). The official language is standard English, although pidgin English is more widely used and understood. More than 80 different local languages exist, and no vernacular is common to the whole country. More than 95% of the inhabitants profess Christianity, and most of the remainder follow traditional beliefs. The national flag (proportions 1 by 2) comprises two triangles, one of blue (with its base at the hoist and its apex in the upper fly) and one of dark green (with its base in the fly and its apex in the lower hoist), separated by a narrow yellow diagonal stripe (from lower hoist to upper fly), with five white five-pointed stars (arranged to form a diagonal cross) in the upper hoist. The capital is Honiara, on the island of Guadalcanal.

CONTEMPORARY POLITICAL HISTORY

Historical Context

The northern Solomon Islands became a German protectorate in 1885 and the southern Solomons a British protectorate in 1893. Rennell Island and the Santa Cruz Islands were added to the British protectorate in 1898 and 1899. Germany ceded most of the northern Solomons and Ontong Java Islands to the United Kingdom between 1898 and 1900. The whole territory, known as the British Solomon Islands Protectorate, was placed under the jurisdiction of the Western Pacific High Commission (WPHC), with its headquarters in Fiji.

The Solomon Islands were invaded by Japan in 1942, but, after a fierce battle on Guadalcanal, most of the islands were recaptured by US forces in 1943. After the Second World War the protectorate's capital was transferred from Tulagi Island to Honiara. In January 1953 the headquarters of the WPHC also moved to Honiara. Meanwhile, elected local councils were established on most of the islands, and by 1966 almost the whole territory was covered by such councils.

Domestic Political Affairs

Under a new Constitution, introduced in October 1960, a Legislative Council and an Executive Council were established for the protectorate's central administration. Initially, all members of both bodies were appointed, but from 1964 the Legislative Council included elected members, and the elective element was gradually increased. Another Constitution, introduced in March 1970, established a single Governing Council of 17 elected members, three ex officio members and (until the end of 1971) up to six public service members. A new Governing Council of 24 directly elected members was formed in 1973, when a ministerial system was introduced.

A further new Constitution, adopted in April 1974, instituted a single Legislative Assembly, containing 24 members who chose a Chief Minister with the right to appoint his own Council of Ministers. A new office of Governor of the Protectorate was also created, to assume almost all of the functions previously exercised in the territory by the High Commissioner for the Western Pacific. Solomon Mamaloni, leader of the newly founded People's Progressive Party (PPP), was appointed the first Chief Minister in August 1974. The territory was officially renamed the Solomon Islands in June 1975, although it retained protectorate status. In January 1976 the Solomon Islands received internal self-government, with the Chief Minister presiding over the Council of Ministers in place of the Governor. In June elections were held for an enlarged Legislative Assembly, and in July the Assembly elected one of its new members, Peter Kenilorea, to the position of Chief Minister. Solomon Islands (as it was restyled, without the definite article) became an independent state, within the Commonwealth, on 7 July 1978, when a new Constitution came into effect. The Legislative Assembly became the National Parliament and designated Kenilorea the first Prime Minister. The main political issue confronting the new nation was the proposed decentralization of authority to the regions, support for which was particularly strong in the Western District, the most commercially developed part of the country.

The first general election since independence took place in August 1980. Independent candidates won more seats than any of the three parties. Parliament again elected Kenilorea Prime Minister by an overwhelming majority. In August 1981, however, Parliament approved a motion expressing no confidence in Kenilorea, and chose Mamaloni, who now led the People's Alliance Party (PAP) following the merger of the PPP with the Rural Alliance Party in 1979, to succeed him as Prime Minister.

After legislative elections in October 1984, Sir Peter Kenilorea (as he had become) was again elected as Prime Minister. The new Government consisted of a coalition of nine members of Kenilorea's Solomon Islands United Party (SIUPA), three members of the newly formed Solomone Ano Sagufenua (SAS) party and three independents. The five provincial ministries, established by Mamaloni, were abolished, in accordance with Kenilorea's declared policy of restoring to central government control some of the powers held by the provincial governments.

In October 1985 a new political party, which sought a resolution of ongoing land disputes, the Nationalist Front for Progress (NFP), was formed, under the leadership of Andrew Nori. The SAS subsequently withdrew from the coalition, and Kenilorea formed a new Cabinet, comprising nine members of the SIUPA, three of the NFP and three independents. Kenilorea resigned following the approval of a motion of no confidence (two others having previously been defeated); in December Ezekiel Alebua, the former Deputy Prime Minister, assumed the premiership.

A report published in 1988 by a specially commissioned constitutional review committee, chaired by Mamaloni, proposed that Solomon Islands become a federal republic within the Commonwealth, and that the President of the Republic be a native of the territory. In January 1989 the PAP announced that Solomon Islands would be declared a republic if the party won the general election in February. At the election the PAP won 11 of the 38 seats, while Alebua's United Party secured only four seats. In March Mamaloni was elected Prime Minister. His Cabinet included the former Governor-General of Solomon Islands, Sir Baddeley Devesi, and was the first since independence to comprise the members of a single party.

In October 1990 Mamaloni resigned as leader of the PAP, one week before Parliament was due to vote on another motion of no confidence in his premiership, declaring that he would remain as an independent Prime Minister. He dismissed five cabinet ministers, replacing them with four members of the opposition and a PAP backbencher. The Prime Minister defied persistent demands for his resignation by a majority of the members of Parliament. The remaining 10 PAP ministers were expelled from the party in February 1991, following their refusal to resign from their posts in the interests of party unity. Later in that year, as a result of continuing economic decline, the Solomon Islands Council of Trade Unions issued an ultimatum demanding Mamaloni's resignation.

At elections to the recently enlarged National Parliament in May 1993 the Group for National Unity and Reconciliation (GNUR), led by Mamaloni, won 21 of the 47 seats. However, a newly formed coalition of opposition parties and independents, the National Coalition Partners (NCP), was successful in electing an independent member, Francis Billy Hilly, to the premiership in June. Hilly defeated Mamaloni by a single vote.

In October 1994 a constitutional crisis arose, following attempts by the Governor-General, Moses (later Sir Moses) Pitakaka, to dismiss Hilly on the grounds that he no longer held a parliamentary majority. However, Hilly remained in office, with the support of a High Court ruling, and confusion intensified when Pitakaka appointed the opposition leader,

Mamaloni, to the position of Prime Minister. Hilly finally resigned at the end of October, and the post was declared vacant. In a parliamentary election to the premiership in November, Mamaloni defeated former Governor-General Devesi.

Controversy arose in mid-1996 over constituency payments by members of Parliament, and the reinstatement of the Constituency Development Fund, which entitled each member to US $66,000, and which had been widely used by members at the previous general election to secure re-election by purchasing gifts for voters. In September the regional trades union organization, the South Pacific and Oceanic Council of Trade Unions, cited the prevalence of corruption as the greatest obstacle to the islands' development. In February 1997 legislation to reform the provincial government system, which had been approved by Parliament but vehemently opposed by the larger provinces, was declared invalid by the High Court.

In May 1997 Mamaloni announced his intention to hold an early general election, following which he would resign as leader of the GNUR. Meanwhile, Alebua resigned from the leadership of the NCP, following accusations of misconduct, and was replaced by Edward Hunuehu. At the general election in August to a legislature that had recently been enlarged to 50 seats the GNUR won 24 seats and a new grouping, the Solomon Islands Alliance for Change Coalition (SIACC), secured the remainder. Bartholomew Ulufa'alu was elected Prime Minister, defeating the newly elected leader of the GNUR, Danny Philip, by 26 votes to 22. The new Government announced a programme of extensive structural reforms, including a rationalization of the public sector, a reduction in the number of ministerial portfolios (from 16 to 10), and measures to expand the private sector and to encourage greater participation of non-governmental organizations in the country's socio-economic development. Legislation proposing that a politician seeking to change party allegiance would automatically lose his or her seat and be subject to a by-election was similarly intended to increase political stability.

In April 1998 Job Dudley Tausinga, whose Coalition for National Advancement (CNA) constituted the largest group outside the Government, was appointed Leader of the Opposition. Numerous defections between the Government and opposition in 1998 created a climate of political instability, prompting the Government to reiterate its proposal to restrict the rights of elected members of Parliament to change party allegiance. In September Solomon Mamaloni was elected Leader of the Opposition. Mamaloni died in January 2000 and was succeeded by Manasseh Sogavare, under whose leadership the CNA subsequently reverted to its original name of the PPP.

Unrest and insecurity

From April 1998 violent unrest in Honiara was attributed to ethnic tensions, mainly between the inhabitants of Guadalcanal and Malaita provinces. One underlying cause of the disturbances was the alienation of land by the Government since independence. Title to some land thus expropriated had been returned to Guadalcanal, but this had not allayed a widespread feeling of resentment in the province at the financial burden imposed by hosting the country's capital. It was reported that a group styling itself the 'Guadalcanal Revolutionary Army' (GRA) had begun a campaign of militancy to force the Government to relocate the capital. In mid-1999 talks between the Premier of Guadalcanal Province, Alebua, and the Solomon Islands Prime Minister failed to alleviate inter-ethnic tensions. Riots broke out in Honiara, and some 80 Malaitan immigrants were evacuated following threats by armed GRA militants. The Guadalcanal Provincial Assembly subsequently declared that it had accepted an initial payment of SI $500,000 in compensation for accommodating the national capital. However, the Malaitans subsequently demanded that they too be given compensation, amounting to US $600,000, for damage to their property by the GRA militants.

A Commonwealth Special Envoy and a UN peace-keeping force arrived to assist in the negotiation of a peace agreement with the Isatabu Freedom Movement (IFM, formerly the GRA), led by Andrew Te'e. A number of peace agreements reached throughout 1999 quickly broke down, and a peace-monitoring group from Fiji and Vanuatu, jointly funded by Australia and New Zealand, arrived in Guadalcanal in October. In January 2000 a new guerrilla group emerged, the Malaita Eagle Force (MEF), and demanded US $40m. in compensation payments for loss of property incurred by Malaitans as a result of the conflict. Among their spokesmen was the former Minister for Finance, Andrew Nori.

Following further outbreaks of violence in the province in February 2000, the Governor-General issued a decree outlawing

membership of both the IFM and the MEF. Further clashes between the two rebel groups were reported in March, and riots took place in Honiara during which Malaitan immigrants stoned the headquarters of the Guadalcanal Provincial Government. In May the order that outlawed the groups was suspended. In early June members of the MEF, armed with weapons obtained in raids on police armouries, seized control of Honiara, placing Ulufa'alu under house arrest. The rebels demanded the immediate resignation of the Prime Minister, claiming that he, himself an ethnic Malaitan, had failed to compensate displaced Malaitans within the established deadline (allegedly set for that day) and also demanded the appointment of a new Commissioner of Police, the de facto head of national security. In renewed outbreaks of violence, up to 100 people were reportedly killed. The MEF, meanwhile, claimed to have gained control of the police force, 98% of the military-style weapons in the territory, broadcasting services and the telecommunications infrastructure. Ulufa'alu was released after four days, following an agreement that he would be subject to a motion of no confidence. In mid-June Ulufa'alu resigned, one day before the scheduled no-confidence vote, but remained as interim Prime Minister for a 14-day transitional period during which negotiations between the MEF, the IFM and a Commonwealth Special Envoy, Professor Ade Adefuye of Nigeria, were to take place. In a parliamentary vote at the end of June, Sogavare, hitherto Leader of the Opposition, was elected Prime Minister, defeating Rev. Leslie Boseto, the Minister for Lands and Housing, by 23 votes to 21. Sogavare declared that he would seek to establish peace without making significant changes to the policy of the previous Government. None the less, a new Ministry for National Unity, Reconciliation and Peace was established, and plans to create a Solomon Islands Defence Force and Ministry of Defence were announced. (Previously defence issues had fallen within the remit of the police service, which had become compromised because of reported MEF infiltration, and by allegations that about 75% of officers were ethnic Malaitans.)

New negotiations in August 2000 resulted in the declaration of a 90-day cease-fire between the IFM and the MEF, although intermittent violent disorder continued in Guadalcanal. In late August IFM dissidents kidnapped the brother of Deputy Prime Minister Allan Kemakeza, demanding that SI $6.5m. in compensation be paid to the displaced persons of Guadalcanal. Kemakeza was released unharmed after 10 days without the payment of a ransom. In September a breakaway group from the IFM, which had reverted to the former name of the GRA under the leadership of Harold Keke, held an airline pilot hostage with a demand for SI $2m.; he was released unharmed without the demands being acceded to, although Keke later claimed that the Government had paid him US $200,000.

The Townsville Peace Agreement and 2001 election

Following a further session of talks in Australia, the Townsville Peace Agreement was signed by the MEF, the IFM, the Solomon Islands Government and the Provincial Governments of Malaita and Guadalcanal on 15 October 2000. An amnesty for all those involved in crimes associated with the ethnic conflict was to be granted, subject to the surrender of all weaponry within 30 days. The agreement also envisaged the creation of an international peace-monitoring team (which was to work alongside a locally appointed Peace Monitoring Council), and the repatriation to their home villages of all MEF and IFM soldiers at the expense of the Solomon Islands Government. Infrastructure and services in the two provinces would be restored and developed. The two provinces would also be granted a greater degree of administrative autonomy. Malaita Province was to receive additional funding to reflect the demands placed on the region by the influx of 20,000 displaced persons from Guadalcanal.

The implementation of the peace process, overseen by monitors from Australia and New Zealand, was threatened in November 2000, when four people were killed in a shooting in Gizo, Western Province. Among the dead were two members of Papua New Guinea's secessionist Bougainville Revolutionary Army (BRA). Moreover, delays in the disarmament process involving the MEF and the IFM caused the deadline for the surrender of arms to be extended until 15 December. Following an announcement that the Guadalcanal Provincial Government headquarters (which had been occupied by members of the MEF since June) was to be rehabilitated as a symbol of national unity, arsonists believed to be linked with the MEF attacked the building. Despite a series of ceremonies in which members of the IFM and MEF surrendered arms, it was believed that at least 400 illegally held weapons remained in circulation at the end of

December. The legislation, granting immunity to those who had committed crimes during the conflict, which was approved in December, was criticized by the prominent human rights organization Amnesty International. The Guadalcanal Liberation Force (GLF), as the GRA had been restyled, led by Harold Keke, announced that it had not accepted the cease-fire.

In early 2001 further violence broke out between Guadalcanal militants and members of the Marau Eagle Force, a group from the eastern Marau region of Guadalcanal. A peace agreement between the group and the IFM was signed in February, although the Peace Monitoring Council observed that the infrastructure of the Marau region had been almost entirely destroyed since 1998 and that there was little immediate prospect of recovery. Continued violent incidents between the Marau Eagle Force, the GLF and government patrols led the International Peace Monitoring Team from Australia to state that the cease-fire arrangement reached under the Townsville Peace Agreement had been breached. In June 2001 the Premier of Guadalcanal, Alebua, was shot and seriously injured in an assassination attempt, apparently carried out on the orders of former leaders of the IFM. The failure of former militia groups to surrender their guns was the main obstacle to a lasting peace throughout 2001; officials estimated that there remained some 500 high-powered weapons in the community, in addition to handmade weapons. The Government declared an 'arms amnesty' in April 2002. Militants surrendered some 2,000 guns with impunity. Weapons disposal began in June, coinciding with the International Peace Monitoring Team's departure from the country.

Meanwhile, in the second half of 2000, Western, Choiseul, and Temutu provinces all declared themselves to be semi-autonomous states within Solomon Islands. Additionally, movements in Guadalcanal and Makira provinces demanding greater autonomy were reported to have gained strength. In November the Minister for Provincial Government and Rural Development, Nathaniel Waena, announced that legislation to amend the Constitution would be submitted in 2001, in order to institute a federal system of government. In March 2001 the Government announced that it would introduce legislation to extend the life of Parliament for a further year, to expire in August 2002, stating that elections scheduled for August 2001 should be postponed owing to the social and economic problems of the islands. This proposal attracted widespread opposition, including that of churches, trade unions, all provincial premiers, and the principal overseas aid donors to Solomon Islands. Sogavare subsequently withdrew the proposal, and it was announced that the elections would be held in December, funded wholly from overseas.

In October 2001 public services deteriorated as nation-wide power cuts resulted from the inability of the Solomon Islands Electricity Authority to pay for its supplies of diesel fuel. The Government announced the introduction of health charges in order to maintain medical services, and appealed to Australia and New Zealand for assistance in policing, as violent crime was becoming endemic. A storage container holding weapons relinquished under the Townsville Peace Agreement was broken into and, in November, the revelation that compensation totalling SI $17.4m. had been paid to former members of the MEF for alleged property damage precipitated a violent demonstration by protesters demanding similar recompense. The Prime Minister was prevented from leaving his office and the house of the Deputy Prime Minister was vandalized.

Accusations and rumours of bribery and intimidation were rife during the campaigning that preceded the general election of December 2001. The electoral grouping of the SIACC won 12 seats, the PAP secured nine and the PPP six, while 22 seats were won by independent candidates. In the absence of a clear SIACC leader, 11 elected members of the coalition convened with 11 elected independents to decide upon an acceptable premier. Sir Allan Kemakeza (as he had become), leader of the PAP and former Deputy Prime Minister, was subsequently declared Prime Minister. Despite having previously been accused of misappropriating state funds, the former Minister for Finance, Snyder Rini, was appointed Deputy Prime Minister and Minister for National Planning. However, the new Government was unable to improve the increasingly desperate political and economic situation on the islands. As the security situation deteriorated further, numerous international peace monitors began withdrawing from the islands. In March 2002 Kemakeza dismissed Michael Maina, the Minister for Finance, after the latter failed to consult the Cabinet prior to announcing a number of drastic budgetary measures, the most significant of which was

his decision to devalue the national currency by 25%. Maina was replaced by Laurie Chan, who revalued the currency in April.

There were reports of further disturbances on the western coast of Guadalcanal in June 2002 during which it was claimed that 11 Malaitans, who were part of a force attempting to capture the GLF leader, Harold Keke, had been killed. The country was further adversely affected by water and electricity shortages, and a series of strikes in mid-2002 by public sector workers protesting against the non-payment of their salaries. In August the Minister for Youth and Sports and Women's Affairs, Fr Augustine Geve, was assassinated; it was subsequently reported that Keke had claimed responsibility for the murder.

The National Peace Council

In October 2002 the Cabinet approved the establishment of the National Peace Council, an interim body, to replace the Peace Monitoring Council, the mandate of which expired on 15 October under the terms of the Townsville Peace Agreement. A permanent body was to be established after 16 January 2003. However, it was confirmed in the same month that more arms were in circulation in the country than when the peace agreement was signed in October 2000. The National Peace Council expressed a belief that many of the weapons surrendered under the arms amnesty of April 2002 had been removed for use by police officers in their campaign to capture Keke.

In December 2002 the Minister for Finance, Laurie Chan, resigned. The Government claimed that this action was in response to criticism of his recently approved budget. However, Radio New Zealand reported that his resignation was in protest against the Government's decision to pay unscheduled allowances to 'special constables' (former militants from the ethnic conflict who were allowed to join the police force as part of the peace agreement), who had demanded the payments with threats and violence.

The country's precarious peace process suffered a major reversal in February 2003 when a leading member of the National Peace Council, Sir Frederick Soaki, was assassinated. There was speculation that the killing might have been connected to his involvement in a 'demobilization' programme for 'special constables'. A report by Amnesty International in March claimed that the country's 'special constables' had tortured and killed numerous people along the southern coast of Guadalcanal in the operation against Harold Keke. In April three of Keke's close associates deserted him and reported that in recent weeks they had witnessed him committing nine murders, mostly, it was believed, of his own supporters whom he had suspected of collaborating with the police. In May it was reported that Keke had taken six missionaries hostage in southern Guadalcanal. In a separate incident on Malaita, in the same month, an Australian missionary was beheaded.

In June 2003 Kemakeza travelled to Australia to reiterate a request for direct foreign intervention in order to address the worsening law and order crisis in Solomon Islands. (Former Prime Minister Sogavare had made a similar appeal at the time of the signing of the Townsville Peace Agreement in October 2000, which had been rejected.) Later that month senior officials from Australia and New Zealand arrived in Solomon Islands to assess the possibility of mounting a regional intervention in the country, and the Pacific Islands Forum subsequently agreed to send a multinational intervention force. The proposed action was to constitute the largest armed intervention in the South Pacific region since the Second World War.

Meanwhile, reports of violence and intimidation by Keke and his rebel forces continued during June 2003. At least 23 people (including 11 members of a religious order) were taken hostage and several more were killed. An estimated 1,000 villagers fled their homes after Keke took control of a police post, thereby expanding the area under his control. The rebel leader also burned two villages where he believed that local people had informed the authorities of his activities. Furthermore, in the same month his militia forced some 1,200 people at gunpoint to stand along several stretches of beach in order to serve as a human shield and thereby prevent a planned police landing in the area. Atrocities continued in the following month when another settlement (of some 500 inhabitants) was burned on Keke's orders and a number of people (including several children) were beaten to death or beheaded.

Following further discussions in July 2003, the Australian Government stated its requirements for the intervention to proceed, which included unhindered access to the country's financial records and the appointment of up to 100 foreign nationals to senior positions in the islands' public service and government sectors. The economic component of the proposed intervention would also provide for the payment of Solomon Islands' domestic and foreign debts through increased aid from Australia and New Zealand. Displaced villagers (estimated to total 20,000 since ethnic violence intensified in 2000) were to receive a specific allocation of $A100,000 in aid from Australia. The Solomon Islands Government unanimously approved legislation to allow the deployment of the Australian-led force, the Regional Assistance Mission to Solomon Islands (RAMSI), and the Australian warship *HMAS Manoora* subsequently arrived in Honiara with 400 personnel, followed by a total of 2,225 troops and police from various other countries, including New Zealand, Papua New Guinea, Fiji, Tonga, Vanuatu and Samoa.

On 13 August 2003 Harold Keke surrendered and was arrested, along with 10 of his close associates; Keke handed over a large number of firearms and was taken away on *HMAS Manoora* for his own safety. By early September the regional forces announced that they had collected a total of 3,850 weapons since the start of a firearms amnesty a month earlier. Australia began to withdraw its troops in late October and by early December more than one-half of its personnel had left the islands.

The capture and arrest of members of various militia groups, including two individuals who had been signatories to the Townsville Peace Agreement, continued during late 2003. Police Superintendent Mannaseh Maelanga, who had served as the MEF's Supreme Commander, was arrested in November and sentenced to one year's imprisonment in March 2004. Andrew Te'e, former Supreme Commander of the IFM, was arrested and charged with the murder of three people. In March 2005 Keke and two of his associates were found guilty of the murder in 2002 of Augustine Geve (see The Townsville Peace Agreement and 2001 election) and sentenced to life imprisonment.

The Government was subject to considerable embarrassment in December 2003, when the Minister for Communications, Aviation and Meteorology, Daniel Fa'afunua, was arrested and charged with the assault of his wife and of a female police officer, with being drunk and disorderly, and with demanding money with menaces. He was found guilty in February 2004 and received a lengthy prison sentence. In September of that year the Minister for Agriculture and Livestock, Alex Bartlett, was arrested on charges relating to violent offences that had occurred during 2000, when he was involved in the leadership of the MEF.

In June 2004 Nathaniel Waena, the former Minister for National Unity, Reconciliation and Peace, was elected Governor-General, with 27 parliamentary votes.

In early 2005 the Minister for Provincial Government, Clement Rojumana, was arrested on 25 corruption charges and the Minister for Police, Michael Maina, was charged with theft. In April the former Minister for Finance, Francis Zama, was charged with official corruption over the alleged granting to himself of an exemption from the payment of goods tax during his period in office. Moreover, a police investigation in mid-2005 claimed that the Minister for Health, Benjamin Una, had been involved in two shooting incidents in 2004 that had targeted personnel from the regional intervention force, including the killing of an Australian officer; Una denied the allegations. In October 2005 the Minister for Fisheries and Marine Resources, Paul Maenu'u, was forced to resign following his vote at a meeting of the International Whaling Commission in favour of a reintroduction of commercial whaling, in defiance of the Government's stated position. In November Una submitted his resignation as Minister for Health, having been arrested and charged with stealing aid funds that had been donated for a development project in his parliamentary constituency. In November 2005 the Prime Minister became involved in controversy with regard to the allocation of loans from a Taiwanese bank. It was claimed that during his tenure of the post of Minister for National Unity and Reconciliation in 2001, Kemakeza had received compensation of US $121,000 for personal losses incurred during ethnic unrest. Following an audit, it was revealed that millions of dollars could not be accounted for and that the Cabinet had remained unaware of the situation.

The 2006 legislative elections and subsequent events
In the legislative elections held on 5 April 2006 around one-half of the incumbent members of Parliament lost their seats. It was believed that only 16 of the 50 incoming members had formally declared their party affiliation prior to the elections, confirming that electors tended to vote for individuals rather than for representatives of specific political parties. It was subsequently reported that independents occupied 29 seats and that the

recently formed Solomon Islands Party for Rural Advancement (SIPRA), led by Job Dudley Tausinga, held four seats, the National Party four seats, the PAP four seats and the Solomon Islands Democratic Party three seats, with the remainder being distributed among various other parties. Former Deputy Prime Minister Snyder Rini, the leader of the Independent Democratic Party (IDP—as the Association of Independent Members of Parliament had been renamed in 2004 on its registration as a political party), was elected Prime Minister with 27 parliamentary votes, while Job Dudley Tausinga won 23.

Rini's appointment as Prime Minister led to widespread protests. A group calling itself People's Power delivered a petition to the Governor-General demanding Rini's immediate resignation, claiming that he had been involved in corruption and bribery. It was variously alleged that Rini had accepted funding from the local Chinese business community and from both mainland Chinese and Taiwanese supporters who hoped to influence the electoral process. Rini was nevertheless sworn in on 20 April 2006. Public dissatisfaction culminated in two days of the most serious rioting witnessed in the country for many years. Much of the capital was left in ruins, and in particular many local Chinese businesses and homes were destroyed in arson attacks. It was reported that more than 300 Chinese citizens had been evacuated from Honiara to the People's Republic of China. In an attempt to restore law and order in the capital, Australia dispatched reinforcements of 110 soldiers and 70 police officers. Several opposition politicians were among those arrested in connection with the rioting. However, shortly before a parliamentary vote of no confidence was scheduled to take place, and after only eight days in the post, Rini announced his decision to resign as Prime Minister. On 4 May Manasseh Sogavare was elected to the premiership, securing 28 votes; Fred Fono, who had briefly served as Deputy Prime Minister in the interim Government, received 22 votes. The majority of Solomon Islanders appeared to welcome the appointment of Sogavare. Job Dudley Tausinga was appointed as Deputy Prime Minister, also assuming responsibility for the portfolio of forestry, environment and conservation.

Prime Minister Sogavare announced that the country's economic strategies were to be reorientated and that a new policy regarding the management of Taiwanese financial aid to Solomon Islands was to be formulated, to permit greater transparency. Francis Billy Hilly was dismissed from the post of Minister for Commerce, Industries and Employment in August 2006 following his alleged refusal to denounce a memorandum of understanding signed by his National Party with China. Sogavare effected a minor reorganization of the Cabinet in October, which included the replacement of Bartholomew Ulufa'alu as Minister for Finance and Treasury by Gordon Darcy Lilo. In December Tausinga resigned as Deputy Prime Minister, apparently over a dispute related to logging, and was replaced by Toswell Kaua.

In April 2007 a large earthquake in the South Pacific caused a tsunami that resulted in more than 50 fatalities in Solomon Islands and destroyed the homes of thousands in the Western and Choiseul provinces. Australia and Taiwan both supported emergency operations in the area. (In April 2011 a special report commissioned by the Office of the Auditor General revealed serious mismanagement of aid and relief supplies on the part of the local authorities.)

In May 2007 former Minister for Finance Francis Zama was convicted of official corruption (see The National Peace Council), receiving a 20-month prison sentence. Zama's sentence was subsequently suspended, and in October he was appointed Minister for Justice and Legal Affairs, before being transferred to the finance and treasury portfolio, and later to education and human resources. In November former Prime Minister Kemakeza was convicted of larceny, intimidation and demanding money with menaces, relating to a raid by members of the MEF on the local office of an Australian law firm in 2002.

In November 2007 13 members of Sogavare's Government resigned, including the Deputy Prime Minister, Toswell Kaua, and the Minister for Education and Human Resources Development, Derek Sikua. Sogavare's failure to attend an earlier meeting of the Pacific Islands Forum and his handling of the Moti affair (see Relations with Australia and the Pacific islands) were widely criticized. In December a no-confidence vote against Sogavare succeeded by a narrow margin; Sikua was elected to replace him as Prime Minister.

The premiership of Derek Sikua

Sikua's Cabinet included several ministers who had defected from the Sogavare Government, as well as Fred Fono as Deputy Prime Minister and William Haomae as Minister for Foreign Affairs. The Government announced its intention to reduce the number of political appointments in an attempt to curb government spending.

It was reported in June 2008 that the Government was promoting the federalization of Solomon Islands and was soon to introduce legislation to that effect. The dismissal of an appeal against the conviction of Sir Allan Kemakeza, Minister for Forestry and former Prime Minister, resulted in his departure from the Cabinet as well as from Parliament in September. In October the Prime Minister was acquitted of drink-driving charges brought against him in January. In June 2009 Frank Kabui, a former Attorney-General, was elected Governor-General, receiving 30 parliamentary votes.

In April 2009 the Government officially established the Solomon Islands Truth and Reconciliation Commission to investigate the causes of the violent conflict in Guadalcanal that occurred between 1997 and 2003. The Commission was composed of five members: its Chairman, Rev. Sam Ata, and two other Solomon Islands citizens; a former Vice-President of Fiji, Ratu Joni Madraiwiwi; and a Peruvian human rights activist. Amnesty International expressed concern that the establishment of the Commission might be detrimental to future court cases against alleged perpetrators of the violence, as any evidence brought before the Commission would thus become inadmissible in trials. Public hearings by the Commission commenced in Honiara in March 2010 (further hearings, in Malaita, took place in May), when victims of the ethnic conflict presented their testimonies. Also in March discussions between the political leaders of Guadalcanal and Malaita provinces began in Honiara, with the aim of achieving reconciliation and peaceful co-existence. In the same month the Australian-owned Gold Ridge gold mine, on Guadalcanal, which had been forced to close 10 years previously at the height of the period of ethnic violence, was formally reopened following a ceremony of reconciliation among local landowning communities. During 2010 a resettlement programme was launched, which was to involve the construction of around 300 new homes for the displaced landowners. In March 2011 the first gold bar from the mine was poured.

Meanwhile, in January 2010 a new political party, the Ownership, Unity and Responsibility (OUR) Party, was inaugurated, with Manasseh Sogavare, the Leader of the Opposition and former Prime Minister, as its President and Patterson Oti, a former Minister for Foreign Affairs, as its General Secretary. By March it was reported that 11 new parties had been formed to contest the forthcoming general election. Among these new groups was the Twelve Pillars to Peace and Prosperity (TP4), led by Delmah Nori, which was to represent the views of the country's women and to encourage the greater involvement of women in government. In April the six parties forming the incumbent governing coalition (known as the Coalition for National Unity and Rural Advancement—CNURA) announced that they would contest the election jointly. However, proposed legislation on the reform of the political party system, which aimed to increase stability (in particular by limiting the ability of members of the legislature to change their party allegiance), was defeated in Parliament; on the following day Sikua dismissed five ministers whom he accused of failing to support the reforms, and also removed several members of the legislature from the chairmanships of state-owned enterprises. Concern was expressed in some quarters over the donation of US $1.2m. to the Rural Constituency Development Fund presented to the outgoing members of Parliament by the Taiwanese Government, and over the significant pay rise that the legislators awarded themselves prior to their leaving office.

The 2010 election and premiership of Danny Philip

At least 19 parties contested the general election held on 4 August 2010. The poll was reported to have been conducted in a relatively orderly and peaceful manner. Of the 50 parliamentary seats, 19 were taken by independents, while the Solomon Islands Democratic Party secured 13 seats and Sogavare's OUR Party and the Reformed Democratic Party each took three seats. The IDP, led by former Prime Minister Rini, officially obtained only two seats in Parliament, but was believed to have the support of many independent legislators. Despite the recent formation of the TP4 party and the participation of 22 female candidates, no women were elected to the legislature. A number of prominent

politicians, including Deputy Prime Minister Fred Fono, the Minister for Finance and Treasury, Francis Billy Hilly, and the General Secretary of the OUR party, Patterson Oti, lost their seats at the election. Several weeks of difficult negotiations ensued as the various parties attempted to garner sufficient support to form a viable coalition government. On 25 August Danny Philip, the leader of the Reformed Democratic Party, was elected Prime Minister, defeating his only rival, Steve Abana of the Solomon Islands Democratic Party, by 26 parliamentary votes to 23 (there was one spoiled ballot). Philip appointed a new Government, entitled the National Coalition for Reform and Advancement (NCRA), which was composed of the IDP, SIPRA, the Reformed Democratic Party, the Rural and Urban Political Party, the Direct Development Party and independents. Among the members of the new Cabinet were two somewhat controversial appointees: Manasseh Maelanga, who became Deputy Prime Minister and Minister for Home Affairs, and Jimmy Lusibaea, who was appointed as Minister for Fisheries and Marine Resources. Both were former leaders of the now-defunct MEF and had served prison sentences for offences relating to the ethnic violence.

In September 2010 Sir Allan Kemakeza was elected as the new Speaker of the National Parliament. In the following month Prime Minister Philip announced that his Government intended to implement two wide-ranging reform programmes over the following four years: one covering constitutional reform (including proposed amendments to the electoral laws and the utilization of the country's valuable natural resources) and the other sector development reform (in an attempt to lessen the over-reliance of the economy on the logging industry). In November skirmishes were reported in the capital when the High Court sentenced cabinet minister Jimmy Lusibaea to 33 months in prison for his involvement in the ethnic violence a decade previously. Lusibaea's sentence (for unlawful wounding and for assaulting a police officer) resulted in the automatic loss of his parliamentary seat and of his cabinet position.

In January 2011 the opposition expressed outrage at Lusibaea's early release from prison, but the Government insisted that the former minister, who, because of the brevity of his time spent in prison, was now entitled to resume his parliamentary seat, had received no special treatment and that his release (less than two months after he had been sentenced) had been officially approved by the Correctional Services Parole Board. A few days later the opposition demanded the resignation of Prime Minister Philip following the defection of at least five cabinet ministers who claimed no longer to have confidence in Philip's leadership or in the Minister for Finance and Treasury, Gordon Darcy Lilo. In early February one of the defectors, Bodo Dettke, and another opposition member of Parliament escaped unharmed from a shooting incident in Honiara; the police were unable to determine whether the attack had been politically motivated. In the same week the Chairman of the Correctional Services Parole Board, Philip Tegevota, resigned from his post, claiming to have been informed that his life was under threat. The Government's position was considerably strengthened later in February by a number of reported defections by members of the opposition to the NCRA ranks. The opposition was further destabilized in March following the resignation of Steve Abana as Leader of the Opposition in response to an internecine power struggle; Abana was replaced by Derek Sikua.

In early April 2011 the Government's power was consolidated by the defection to its ranks of six more opposition members of Parliament, including Abana and the Leader of the Independent Group in Parliament, Clay Forau, and by the smooth passage of the budget. Later that month Philip carried out a cabinet reorganization, dismissing six ministers, four of whom had changed their party allegiance several times. The seven new appointees to the Cabinet included five members of Parliament who had recently crossed over from the opposition. However, Governor-General Kabui refused officially to approve the appointment of Lusibaea as Minister for Fisheries and Marine Resources, asserting that he was disqualified from holding a cabinet post according to the Constitution. Kabui claimed that, despite his early release from prison, the term of Lusibaea's original sentence remained the same, i.e. more than the maximum of six months' imprisonment allowed by the Constitution for individuals to be eligible to hold a government post (or sit in Parliament). In October the High Court endorsed Kabui's decision, ruling that Lusibaea's early release made no difference to the original sentence, and that he was therefore barred from taking up his seat in Parliament and from serving in the Government.

Recent developments: Lilo elected premier

On 9 November 2011 four cabinet ministers resigned, stating that they had lost confidence in Prime Minister Philip. Their action was thought to have related to allegations of abuse by Philip of the Rural Constituency Development Fund, some US $10m. of which had been provided by the Taiwanese Government. Gordon Darcy Lilo, who was believed to have released documents that detailed the misuse of the fund to the opposition, was dismissed as Minister for Finance and Treasury the following day. Having lost his parliamentary majority, Philip resigned on 11 November before the opposition could vote on a planned motion of no confidence in his leadership. However, serious disagreement within the opposition over the choice of candidates for the premiership ensued, leading one nominee, former Prime Minister Manasseh Sogavare, to rejoin the Government and two others to withdraw from the contest. In the parliamentary vote on 16 November Lilo received 29 votes, defeating Milner Tozaka and Sogavare, who each secured nine votes, and Samuel Manetoali, who received two. The election of Lilo led to a riot by more than 500 people in Honiara, most of whom were believed to be from Malaita and feared that funding to the island would be removed under the new Government. Lilo was sworn in as Prime Minister on 22 November and announced a Cabinet that was largely unchanged from the previous one (although Philip was not allocated a portfolio). Lilo stated that his Government would focus on improving prospects for the country's young people and would be open and transparent in its operations. He also urged Taiwan to exercise caution when making financial donations to the Government as these had contributed to political instability in the country.

A series of minor cabinet reorganizations in early 2012, together with continued allegations of corruption against members of Parliament, led to speculation concerning the stability of the Government. However, a motion of no confidence in Lilo's leadership was overwhelmingly defeated in October, when Derek Sikua, the opposition leader, and many opposition members were absent for the vote, apparently owing to fundamental disagreement on the matter within Sikua's parliamentary group. Speaker Sir Allan Kemakeza was strongly criticized by his predecessor, Sir Peter Kenilorea, for allowing the debate to proceed in the absence of Sikua, who had proposed the motion.

The persistent issue of corruption in Solomon Islands, which was emphasized by a number of trials of current and former members of Parliament during 2012—including charges of misconduct against former Prime Minister Danny Philip relating to the sale of government property to a political supporter—prompted an appeal by the Commissioner of Police, John Lansley, in late 2012 for the establishment of an independent commission against corruption. In November Solomon Islands joined the Anti-Corruption Initiative for Asia and the Pacific (administered by the Asian Development Bank, see p. 214), under which it would be required to implement a range of anti-corruption measures.

A state of disaster was declared in February 2013, when a tsunami struck the Santa Cruz Islands, killing at least 13 people and leaving some 1,000 homeless. The Australian Government pledged $A300,000 for the relief effort and New Zealand offered $NZ200,000 in assistance.

Environmental Concerns

The exploitation of Solomon Islands' timber resources provides a major source of foreign exchange, but has proved difficult to regulate. From 2004 the huge increase in the production of round logs in Solomon Islands led to considerable disquiet among community representatives, landowners and environmentalists. The total harvest of round logs in that year was estimated at more than 900,000 cu m, which was equivalent to five times the sustainable limit for timber production in the country. In November a petition of more than 1,000 signatures, containing endorsements from every province in Solomon Islands, urged the Government to approve legislation providing for the sustainable management of the forestry industry. However, the Government postponed consideration of the proposed legislation, and it was reported that logging rates had increased yet further in anticipation of its introduction. Although demand for timber exports declined in 2009, owing to the global recession, exploitation continued at an unsustainable rate, and in December a senior forestry official estimated that sources of timber for commercial logging would be exhausted within two or three years. A report

issued in April 2010 described numerous illegal practices perpetrated with impunity by logging companies, together with corruption, social problems and conflict among traditional landowning communities as a result of the companies' activities. With the aim of educating the Pacific nations about the importance of conserving their forests, the Secretariat of the Pacific Community designated 2011 as the International Year of the Forests.

The country's practice of capturing and exporting large numbers of live dolphins drew international criticism in 2003, when police mounted a large-scale security operation around Honiara Airport to prevent journalists from filming some 200 dolphins being loaded into a cargo aeroplane bound for Mexico. Several reports of harassment and violence against foreign journalists were received. It was believed that, owing to the high price commanded by the sale of the animals, senior Solomon Islands officials were likely to be involved. The trade in wild dolphins had been prohibited by most developed countries under the Convention on International Trade in Endangered Species of Wild Fauna and Flora (CITES). In December 2004 a consignment of dolphins was prevented from being exported after representatives from the fishing industry complained that the trade was harming the reputation of the islands' important tuna industry (widely perceived by Western countries to be 'dolphin-friendly'). The export of dolphins was subsequently banned when new legislation took effect in November 2005. In June 2007, however, the ban was removed, and in October of that year a consignment of 28 dolphins was sent to the United Arab Emirates, provoking criticism from environmentalists. In January 2010 it was reported that the Solomon Islands Government had approved the export of up to 100 dolphins per year, and in February 2011 Robert Satu, the Director of the Solomon Islands Marine Mammal Educational Centre and Exporters Ltd, claimed to have received orders from a number of European and Middle Eastern countries for the export of live dolphins.

In early 2013 a dispute with a US-based conservation group, Earth Island Institute, led to the slaughter of more than 1,000 dolphins by villagers in Malaita. The organization maintained that it had paid agreed compensation of SI $1.7m. to local representatives in exchange for the villagers' observation of a two-year ban on their annual hunt. However, the villagers claimed that they had not received the payments and began a large-scale slaughter of the animals in protest. The Government sent representatives to Malaita in an attempt to resolve the dispute.

In May 2009 Solomon Islands concluded an agreement with five other nations (Timor-Leste, Indonesia, Malaysia, Papua New Guinea and the Philippines) to protect the 'Coral Triangle', a huge area of biologically diverse coral reefs, which also contains spawning grounds vital for tuna fisheries. In March 2010 the National Parliament adopted legislation on establishing protected areas and conserving biodiversity in Solomon Islands' remaining areas of forest and elsewhere. Scientists meeting at the 12th International Coral Reef Symposium in Cairns, Australia, in July 2012 warned that at least 85% of reefs in the 'Coral Triangle' were seriously threatened by pollution, over-fishing and coastal development.

A report published in July 2012 on the international trade in wildlife claimed that Solomon Islands had become a hub for the illegal export of exotic wild birds. According to trade records, some 54,000 birds were exported between 2000 and 2010, including several species recognized to be critically endangered. Although traders claimed that the birds were bred in captivity, no breeding facilities were found in the islands. Conservationists urged an investigation by the authorities under CITES, to which Solomon Islands had become a signatory in 2007, and a suspension of the trade.

Regional Affairs

As a small Pacific island nation Solomon Islands is vulnerable to economic and environmental pressures, and depends on investment and aid from other countries, chiefly Australia, Japan and Taiwan, and from international sources.

Relations with Australia and the Pacific islands

Australia is Solomon Islands' most influential neighbour and a major source of economic assistance, as well as providing administrative, police and military personnel under RAMSI (see The National Peace Council). Relations between Solomon Islands and Australia became strained in 2006 over the extradition of Julian Moti, an Australian citizen who in September had been appointed as the Attorney-General of Solomon Islands. Moti, who was wanted by the Australian authorities on a charge of statutory rape (allegedly committed in Vanuatu several years previously), had been arrested in Papua New Guinea but contravened the conditions of his bail and gained refuge in the Solomon Islands' High Commission in Port Moresby, Papua New Guinea, in October. Shortly thereafter he was flown, reportedly on an aircraft of the Papua New Guinea Defence Force, to Solomon Islands, where he was arrested by police officers serving under RAMSI and charged with illegal immigration. Prime Minister Sogavare refused Australian extradition requests and claimed that Moti's detention was unlawful. Sogavare's threat to suspend the mandate for RAMSI and reappraise Australia's role in the mission attracted criticism from the parliamentary opposition, and fears were raised about the repercussions of the dispute on the security and stability of Solomon Islands, and on Australian aid. The rift deepened when RAMSI officers carried out a forcible search of Sogavare's office to obtain evidence relating to the Moti case while Sogavare was abroad. In December immigration charges against Moti were dismissed. However, RAMSI remained a point of contention: in February 2007 the Australian Minister for Foreign Affairs, in an open letter published in a Solomon Islands newspaper, appealed to the islanders to support the mission; in the same month the Solomon Islands Minister for Foreign Affairs, Patterson Oti, urged the formulation of an exit strategy for RAMSI. In July, having been suspended for several months, Moti was sworn in as Attorney-General, an act that was described by Australian Prime Minister John Howard as 'provocative and insensitive'. Sogavare, for his part, threatened to take Australia to the International Court of Justice, claiming that its pursuit of Moti was related to political interests. Australia applied for Moti's extradition, but this was refused in September.

Relations between the two countries improved following the replacement of Sogavare by Derek Sikua as Prime Minister, and the subsequent extradition of Moti to Australia in December 2007. (The case against Moti was finally heard in the Australian High Court in August 2011; in December Moti was granted a permanent stay of prosecution, and the court ruled that correct procedures had not been followed during the extradition process.)

In April 2009 Australia's Minister for Trade, Simon Crean, visited the Solomons to discuss trade and economic development issues, including a prospective free trade agreement, PACER Plus, between Australia and Pacific Island Forum members. In May Australian Prime Minister Kevin Rudd was reported to have expressed displeasure at the slow progress of projects in Solomon Islands financed by Australian aid. In August 2010 RAMSI admitted responsibility for the death of a local man in Honiara when it fired shots to disperse a crowd of rioters; the Solomon Islands police force subsequently launched an investigation into the death. In February 2011 a team of independent experts arrived in Honiara to review the partnership framework between RAMSI and the Solomon Islands Government and, following discussion between representatives of both sides, it was subsequently decided that the role of the organization would shift from one of providing security to one focused on development. This transition was scheduled to begin in mid-2013, when the military contingent of RAMSI was due to be withdrawn, while a police contingent would remain in Solomon Islands until 2017 to assist the national police force to strengthen its capacity. During an official visit to Australia in August 2012, Prime Minister Lilo held talks with his Australian counterpart, Julia Gillard, during which issues including RAMSI's transition and financial assistance under the Solomon Islands-Australia Partnership for Development were discussed.

In 1990 relations between Papua New Guinea and Solomon Islands deteriorated, following allegations by the latter that patrol boats from Papua New Guinea were interfering with the traditional crossing between Bougainville Island (Papua New Guinea) and the Shortland Islands. The Papua New Guinea Government accused Solomon Islands of harbouring members of the rebel BRA and of providing them with supplies. Despite the signing in that year of an agreement on joint border surveillance and arrangements to host peace negotiations between the BRA and the Papua New Guinea Government, relations worsened considerably in 1992 when Papua New Guinea forces carried out several unauthorized incursions into the Shortland Islands, in which a fuel depot was destroyed and two Solomon Islanders were killed. Alleging Australian involvement in the incursions, Prime Minister Mamaloni suspended surveillance flights by the Australian air force over the country's territory. Following the election of a new Solomon Islands Government in May 1993,

negotiations between the two countries resulted in an agreement to close the BRA office in Honiara. However, in 1996, as violence on Bougainville intensified, numerous incursions by Papua New Guinea defence forces into Solomon Islands' waters were reported, while the Papua New Guinea Government repeated accusations that Solomon Islands was harbouring BRA activists. Nevertheless, in June 1997 Papua New Guinea and Solomon Islands finally concluded a maritime border agreement. Concerns about the increase in weapons-trafficking from Bougainville to the Western Province led to renewed border discussions in 2003. A development agreement that included joint infrastructural development, technical assistance and information sharing was signed by the two Governments in March 2005. In January 2008 the new Solomon Islands Prime Minister, Derek Sikua, visited Papua New Guinea in an attempt to improve relations between the two countries, which, he maintained, had been damaged by the Moti affair. During a return visit in October 2009 by the Papua New Guinea Prime Minister, Sir Michael Somare, the two heads of government discussed investment promotion and protection, and the possibility of a double taxation treaty. In October 2011 Prime Minister Danny Philip and Papua New Guinea's new premier, Peter O'Neill, discussed proposals including the abolition of work permit requirements to increase labour mobility between the two countries and the removal of trade barrier duties; O'Neill also announced a commitment to provide Solomon Islands with financial assistance over the next five years. The last contingent of troops from Papua New Guinea serving under RAMSI left Solomon Islands in April 2013.

In March 1988 Solomon Islands signed an agreement with Vanuatu and Papua New Guinea to form the Melanesian Spearhead Group. The new group regarded as its principal aims the preservation of Melanesian cultural traditions and the attainment of independence by the French Overseas Territory of New Caledonia. In March 1990 the Melanesian Spearhead Group admitted the Front de Libération Nationale Kanak Socialiste (FLNKS—the main Kanak, or Melanesian, political group in New Caledonia). Furthermore, Fiji was admitted to the group in mid-1996, and in the following year Solomon Islands announced its commitment to further economic integration between the member countries. The members of the Melanesian Spearhead Group signed a constitution in March 2007. In February 2011 Prime Minister Philip announced proposals to develop a Pan Melanesian Economic Union to promote large-scale investment in the region.

In October 1995 Solomon Islands became a signatory to the Federated States of Micronesia Agreement on Regional Fisheries Access. In 1997 Solomon Islands and Vanuatu agreed to undertake negotiations on the maritime boundaries between the two countries in an attempt to clarify uncertainty regarding fishing rights.

Other regional relations

Diplomatic relations with Taiwan were established in 1983: Solomon Islands thus became one of the relatively few nations to accord diplomatic recognition to Taiwan, rather than to the People's Republic of China. A seven-member parliamentary delegation, including five cabinet ministers, travelled to Taiwan in September 2004 to discuss mutual co-operation and aid. In January 2005, during a visit to Solomon Islands as part of a tour of the Pacific islands, the Taiwanese President denied that his country was practising 'dollar diplomacy' (providing aid in exchange for diplomatic recognition). In May 2006 it was announced that Taiwan's first payment to the Rural Constituency Development Fund (RCDF) had been released. The payments proved controversial because they were made directly to members of the legislature for use in their respective constituencies, and were perceived as potentially open to abuse. During 2009 negotiations were undertaken on a free trade agreement between the two countries. In March 2010 the Taiwanese President, Ma Ying-jeou, paid an official visit to Solomon Islands, during which Sikua reiterated that his country supported Taiwan in its 'struggle for recognition'. Ma reportedly commented that misuse of Taiwanese aid was unacceptable, and Sikua subsequently stated that greater transparency would be required in accounting for RCDF expenditure.

Japan is a major provider of aid for Solomon Islands. The two countries' relations attracted international attention in mid-2005, when, following receipt of US $6.7m. from the Japanese Government for a major project to improve Honiara Airport, Solomon Islands voted with Japan in favour of the removal of a 20-year moratorium on commercial whaling at a meeting of the International Whaling Commission (thereby reneging on a recent commitment to abstain from the vote). In May 2009 Sikua expressed gratitude for Japanese assistance, especially in energy, infrastructure and fisheries, and reiterated his Government's support for Japan's application to become a permanent member of the UN Security Council.

CONSTITUTION AND GOVERNMENT

Under the 1978 Constitution, executive authority is vested in the British monarch, as head of state, and is exercisable by the monarch's representative, the Governor-General, who is appointed on the advice of Parliament and acts on the advice of the Cabinet. Legislative power is vested in the unicameral National Parliament, with 50 members elected by universal adult suffrage for four years (subject to dissolution) in single-member constituencies. The Cabinet is composed of the Prime Minister, elected by Parliament, and other ministers appointed by the Governor-General on the Prime Minister's recommendation. The Cabinet is responsible to Parliament. Judicial power is exercised by the High Court, magistrates' courts and local courts. Appeals from the High Court are heard by the Court of Appeal, the members of which are senior judges from Australia, New Zealand and Papua New Guinea. The country comprises four Districts, within which there are nine local government councils, elected by universal adult suffrage. The Constitution provides for further devolution of power to provincial authorities.

REGIONAL AND INTERNATIONAL CO-OPERATION

Solomon Islands is a member of the Pacific Community (see p. 422), the Pacific Islands Forum (see p. 426), the Asian Development Bank (see p. 214) and the UN's Economic and Social Commission for Asia and the Pacific (ESCAP, see p. 31), and is a signatory to the Lomé Conventions and the successor Cotonou Agreement (see p. 334) with the European Union. The country is also a member (with Fiji, Papua New Guinea and Vanuatu) of the Melanesian Spearhead Group, which provides for free trade among member countries

Solomon Islands joined the UN in 1978 and acceded to membership of the World Trade Organization (WTO, see p. 444) in 1996. The country is a member of the Commonwealth, and in early 2010 the Commonwealth Pacific Governance Facility was established in Honiara.

ECONOMIC AFFAIRS

In 2011, according to estimates by the World Bank, Solomon Islands' gross national income (GNI), measured at average 2009–11 prices, was US $615m., equivalent to $1,110 per head (or $2,360 on an international purchasing-power parity basis). During 2002–11, it was estimated, the population increased at an average annual rate of 2.8%, while gross domestic product (GDP) per head increased, in real terms, by an average of 3.4% per year. According to figures from the Asian Development Bank (ADB), overall GDP increased, in real terms, at an average annual rate of 6.6% in 2002–11. GDP increased by 10.6% in 2011 and by 5.5% in 2012.

Agriculture (including hunting, forestry and fishing) contributed 28.9% of GDP in 2011, according to UN estimates. In 2004 an estimated 28.7% of those working in the formal sector of the economy were involved in agriculture. In 2013, according to FAO, 66.5% of the labour force, including the informal sector, were projected to be engaged in agricultural activities. The principal cash crops have traditionally included coconuts, cocoa, rice and oil palm. Earnings from copra (which was for many years the country's main export) decreased from SI $45.6m. in 2006 to $36.8m. in 2007. The value of cocoa exports increased from SI $30.3m. in 2006 to $70.8m. in 2007. Meanwhile, the rehabilitation of the palm oil industry involved plans to replant thousands of hectares of former plantations and to clear other areas for new plantations. Spices are cultivated for export on a small scale. Tuna is important; fish accounted for 11.8% of export earnings in 2007. The forestry sector is the leading source of revenue, timber exports accounting for 65.2% of total export receipts in 2007. However, the dramatic increase in the production of timber from the early 1990s prompted several international organizations to express alarm at the rate of logging in the country (see Environmental Concerns). Output of timber exceeded 2m. cu m in 2011, in comparison with 536,000 cu m in 2000. The value of timber exports rose from SI $190.5m. in 2000 to $838.7m. in 2007. According to UN estimates, agricultural GDP expanded by an average of 5.8% per year during 2002–11, increasing by 11.8% in 2011.

Industry (including mining, manufacturing, construction and power) contributed 10.3% of GDP in 2011, according to UN estimates. The sector employed 6.4% of wage-earners in 2004. The mining sector's contribution to GDP is negligible. Gold has been the sole mineral export of significance. The other (mainly undeveloped) mineral resources include deposits of copper, lead, zinc, silver, cobalt, asbestos, phosphates, nickel and high-grade bauxite. In early 2013 the Solomon Islands Government was reportedly considering issuing a nickel mining licence to a Japanese mining company in the southern part of Choiseul province, after exploratory investigations identified significant deposits. According to UN estimates, industrial GDP increased at an average annual rate of 6.4% during 2002–11; the sector's GDP expanded by 48.5% in 2011.

According to UN estimates, manufacturing contributed 5.9% of GDP in 2011. The sector employed 15.6% of wage-earners in 1995. The most important branches are food-processing (notably fish-canning), coconut-based products, brewing, saw-milling, logging and handicrafts. According to UN estimates, the GDP of the manufacturing sector increased by an average of 2.9% per year during 2002–11, declining by 2.8% in 2010, but expanding by 4.3% in 2011.

Construction contributed 2.2% of GDP in 2011, according to UN estimates. The sector employed 2.7% of wage-earners in 2004. According to UN estimates, the GDP of the construction sector increased by an average of 2.4% per year during 2002–11; construction GDP increased by 10.4% in 2011.

Energy is derived principally from hydroelectric power, with solar energy being increasingly utilized. Mineral fuels accounted for 24.6% of total import costs in 2011. Several potential petroleum-producing areas in the islands have been identified. Coconut bio-fuel has been introduced in some areas. Electricity output totalled 74m. kWh in 2011.

Service industries contributed 60.8% of GDP in 2011, according to UN estimates, and engaged 64.9% of wage-earners in 2004. Earnings from the tourism sector reached US $73m. in 2011, compared with $13m. in 1998. Tourist arrivals increased from 13,748 in 2007 to 20,521 in 2010 and to a provisional 23,000 in 2011. According to UN estimates, during 2002–11 services GDP increased at an average annual rate of 6.1%, rising by 5.5% in 2011.

In 2010 there was a visible merchandise trade deficit of US $133.8m. and a deficit of $372.6m. on the current account of the balance of payments. In 2011 the principal sources of imports were Australia (which accounted for 27.0%), Singapore, the People's Republic of China, Malaysia and New Zealand, while the principal market for exports was China (51.2%), followed by Australia. The principal exports in 2011 were crude materials, food and live animals, and animal and vegetable oil. The principal imports were mineral fuels, machinery and transport equipment, food and live animals, basic manufactures, miscellaneous manufactured articles and chemical products.

An overall budgetary surplus of SI $353.2m., equivalent to 5.5% of GDP, was recorded in 2011. However, according to the ADB, a fiscal deficit equivalent to 1.9% of GDP followed in 2012. In 2012/13 aid from Australia was projected at $A222.7m., while financial assistance from New Zealand in 2011/12 was budgeted at $NZ40.0m. The European Union allocated some €16.5m. for assistance to Solomon Islands during 2008–13. In 2012, according to the ADB, the country's external debt totalled US $124m. The cost of debt-servicing was equivalent to 1.3% of the value of exports of goods and services in that year. The average annual rate of inflation in Honiara in 2002–11 was 8.3%. The rate of inflation in 2012 was estimated at 5.9% by the ADB. The extent of the islands' informal sector impedes an accurate assessment of the rate of unemployment; however, youth unemployment, particularly in urban areas, has remained at a high level.

The economy of Solomon Islands remains one of the least developed in the Pacific region. Progress has been impeded by inadequate infrastructure, while the country's major commodity exports are vulnerable to adverse weather conditions and to variations in prices on international markets. The regional intervention of 2003 (see Contemporary Political History) included an economic recovery programme involving increased assistance from Australia (totalling some $A1,000m. over 10 years). The islands' heavy dependence upon forestry, with logging being the prime constituent of both taxation and export revenues, has become a major economic, as well as environmental, concern. Despite some efforts by the Government to counter the detrimental impact of logging activities on the nation's forests, the industry continued to operate at an unsustainable rate. Growth in logging revenues was estimated at some 36% in both 2010 and 2011, but remained stagnant in 2012 as forestry resources dwindled. According to the ADB, depletion of the country's forests was expected to result in lower GDP growth of some 4% in 2013 and 2014, compared with rates of 5.5% and 10.6% recorded in 2012 and 2011, respectively. A significant increase in mining activity fuelled economic growth in 2012, with new licences issued to US and Japanese investors for exploration of gold, nickel and seabed deposits, and increased output from the Australian-owned Gold Ridge gold mine on Guadalcanal. Meanwhile, a major fisheries project, which was concluded between Solomon Islands and South Korea in mid-2011, was estimated to be worth some US $120m. and was expected to create 5,000 new jobs through a range of fisheries-related oper-

ations. Moreover, a new licensing policy introduced in 2012, under which fish caught in the islands' exclusive economic zone must be unloaded and processed in the country, was expected to lead to increased investment and employment in the tuna industry. In December 2012 the IMF approved a three-year arrangement for Solomon Islands, amounting to some US $1.59m., under its Extended Credit Facility.

PUBLIC HOLIDAYS

2014: 1 January (New Year's Day), 18–21 April (Easter), 9 June (Whit Monday), 13 June (Queen's Official Birthday), 7 July (Independence Day), 25–26 December (Christmas).

Statistical Survey

Source (unless otherwise indicated): National Statistics Office, Ministry of Finance and Treasury, POB G6, Honiara; tel. 27835; fax 23951; e-mail Stats_management@mof.gov.sb; internet www.spc.int/prism/country/sb/stats.

AREA AND POPULATION

Area: 27,556 sq km (10,639 sq miles).

Population: 409,042 (males 211,381, females 197,661) at census of 21–22 November 1999; 515,870 at census of 21–22 November 2009. *Mid-2013* (Secretariat of the Pacific Community estimate): 581,345 (males 300,797, females 280,548) (Source: Pacific Regional Information System).

Density (mid-2013): 21.1 per sq km.

Population by Age and Sex (Secretariat of the Pacific Community estimates at mid-2013): *0–14:* 226,708 (males 117,645, females 109,063); *15–64:* 335,260 (males 173,253, females 162,007); *65 and over:* 19,377 (males 9,899, females 9,478); *Total* 581,345 (males 300,797, females 280,548) (Source: Pacific Regional Information System).

Ethnic Groups (census of November 1986): Melanesians 268,536; Polynesians 10,661; Micronesians 3,929; Europeans 1,107; Chinese 379; Others 564.

Principal Towns (population at 1999 census): Honiara (capital) 49,107; Noro 3,482; Gizo 2,960 (Source: Thomas Brinkhoff, *City Population*—internet www.citypopulation.de). *Mid-2011* (incl. suburbs, UN estimate) Honiara 67,610 (Source: UN, *World Urbanization Prospects: The 2011 Revision*).

Births and Deaths (annual averages, 2005–10, UN estimates): Birth rate 33.3 per 1,000; Death rate 6.2 per 1,000 (Source: UN, *World Population Prospects: The 2010 Revision*).

Life Expectancy (years at birth): 67.9 (males 66.5; females 69.3) in 2011. Source: World Bank, World Development Indicators database.

Employment (excluding informal sector, 2004, estimates): Agriculture 6,342; Forestry 3,482; Fishing 5,114; Manufacturing (incl. mining and quarrying) 1,476; Electricity and water 469; Construction 1,397; Trade, restaurants and hotels 3,274; Transport, storage and communications 1,246; Finance, insurance, real estate and business services 806; Administration 6,758; Other community, social and personal service activities 21,757; *Total* 52,121. *2006* (excluding informal sector, estimate): Total employed 59,161. Source: IMF, *Solomon Islands: Tax summary and Statistical Appendix* (November 2008). *Mid-2013* ('000, estimates): Agriculture, etc. 163; Total labour force 245 (Source: FAO).

HEALTH AND WELFARE
Key Indicators

Total Fertility Rate (children per woman, 2010): 4.2.

Under-5 Mortality Rate (per 1,000 live births, 2010): 27.

Physicians (per 1,000 head, 2004): 0.2.

Hospital Beds (per 1,000 head, 2005): 1.5.

Health Expenditure (2009): US $ per head (PPP): 227.

Health Expenditure (2009): % of GDP: 8.7.

Health Expenditure (2009): public (% of total): 93.5.

Access to Water (% of persons, 2006): 70.

Access to Sanitation (% of persons, 2006): 32.

Total Carbon Dioxide Emissions ('000 metric tons, 2008): 198.0.

Carbon Dioxide Emissions Per Head (metric tons, 2008): 0.4.

Human Development Index (2011): ranking: 142.

Human Development Index (2011): value: 0.510.

For sources and definitions, see explanatory note on p. vi.

AGRICULTURE, ETC.

Principal Crops ('000 metric tons, 2011, FAO estimates, unless otherwise indicated): Coconuts 408 (unofficial figure); Oil palm fruit 220; Rice, paddy 4.6; Cocoa beans 5.2 (official figure); Sweet potatoes 91; Yams 43; Taro 41; Vegetables (incl. melons) 7.1; Fruits (excl. melons) 28.5.

Livestock ('000 head, year ending September 2011, FAO estimates): Cattle 14.5; Pigs 54; Chickens 235.

Livestock Products (metric tons, 2011, FAO estimates): Cattle meat 740; Pig meat 2,340; Chicken meat 288; Hen eggs 660; Cows' milk 1,495.

Forestry ('000 cu m, 2011): *Roundwood Removals* (excl. bark): Sawlogs and veneer logs 1,967 (FAO estimate); Fuel wood 129 (FAO estimate); Total 2,096. *Sawnwood Production:* 27 (FAO estimate, all broadleaved, incl. railway sleepers).

Fishing (metric tons, live weight, 2010): Skipjack tuna 245; Yellowfin tuna 3,197; Bigeye tuna 412; Total catch (incl. others): 35,180 (FAO estimate). Note: Figures exclude FAO estimates of capture data for trochus shells (18 metric tons) and of aquaculture data for aquatic plants (800 metric tons).

Source: FAO.

MINING

Production (kg, 2006): Gold 10. Source: US Geological Survey.

INDUSTRY

Production (metric tons, 2007, unless otherwise indicated): Copra 28,000; Coconut oil 741,000; Palm oil 22,000; Electric energy 74 million kWh (2011). Source: Asian Development Bank.

FINANCE

Currency and Exchange Rates: 100 cents = 1 Solomon Islands dollar (SI $). *Sterling, US Dollar and Euro Equivalents* (31 December 2012): £1 sterling = SI $11.510; US $1 = SI $7.29; €1 = SI $9.624; SI $100 = £8.69 = US $13.71 = €10.39. *Average Exchange Rate* (SI $ per US $): 8.0645 in 2010; 7.6413 in 2011; 7.3552 in 2012.

Budget (SI $ million, 2011): *Revenue:* Taxes 2,038.0; Non-tax revenue 194.9; Grants 395.4; Total 2,628.3. *Expenditure:* Total 2,275.1 (Current expenditure 1,841.6, Capital expenditure 433.4). Source: Asian Development Bank.

Official Development Assistance (US $ million, 2000): Bilateral 22.1; Multilateral 46.3; Total 68.4 (Grants 69.7, Loans –1.3). *2010:* Total 340. Source: UN, *Statistical Yearbook for Asia and the Pacific.*

International Reserves (excl. gold, US $ million at 31 December 2011): IMF special drawing rights 14.21; Reserve position in IMF 0.84; Foreign exchange 397.22; Total 412.27. Source: IMF, *International Financial Statistics.*

Money Supply (SI $ million at 31 December 2011): Currency outside depository corporations 481.16; Transferable deposits 1,391.68;

Other deposits 737.06; *Broad money* 2,609.90. Source: IMF, *International Financial Statistics*.

Cost of Living (Consumer Price Index for Honiara, average of quarterly figures; base: October–December 1992 = 100): 463.8 in 2009; 468.2 in 2010; 499.6 in 2011. Source: Asian Development Bank.

Gross Domestic Product (SI $ million at constant 2005 prices): 3,650.8 in 2009; 3,906.3 in 2010; 4,324.3 in 2011. Source: UN Statistics Division, National Accounts Main Aggregates Database.

Expenditure on the Gross Domestic Product (SI $ million at current prices, 2011): Government final consumption expenditure 1,956.1; Private final consumption expenditure 3,572.0; Changes in inventories 37.3; Gross fixed capital formation 1,305.3; *Total domestic expenditure* 6,870.7; Exports of goods and services 3,468.5; *Less* Imports of goods and services 4,483.5; Statistical discrepancy 548.8; *GDP in purchasers' values* 6,404.5. Source: UN Statistics Division, National Accounts Main Aggregates Database.

Gross Domestic Product by Economic Activity (SI $ million at current prices, 2011): Agriculture, hunting, forestry and fishing 1,838.4; Mining, manufacturing and utilities 519.1 (Manufacturing 378.0); Construction 137.2; Trade, restaurants and hotels 665.1; Transport, storage and communications 562.5; Other services 2,644.8; *Gross value added* 6,367.0; Net taxes on products 37.5 (obtained as residual); *GDP in market prices* 6,404.5. Source: UN Statistics Division, National Accounts Main Aggregates Database.

Balance of Payments (US $ million, 2010): Exports of goods 226.52; Imports of goods –360.33; *Balance on goods* –133.81; Exports of services 106.49; Imports of services –187.49; *Balance on goods and services* –214.81; Primary income received 17.50; Primary income paid –138.62; *Balance on goods, services and primary income* –335.93; Secondary income received 22.29; Secondary income paid –58.92; *Current balance* –372.56; Capital account (net) 49.78; Direct investment assets –2.29; Direct investment liabilities 237.90; Portfolio investment assets –2.65; Other investments assets –7.18; Other investment liabilities 34.82; Net errors and omissions –12.42; *Reserves and related items* –74.60. Source: IMF, *International Finance Statistics*.

EXTERNAL TRADE

Principal Commodities (SI $ '000, 2011): *Imports c.i.f.:* Food and live animals 625,970; Mineral fuels, etc. 888,629; Chemical products 336,501; Basic manufactures 524,598; Machinery and transport equipment 786,382; Miscellaneous manufactured articles 344,438; Total (incl. others) 3,607,213. *Exports f.o.b.:* Food and live animals 478,220; Crude materials, inedible, except fuels 1,680,675; Animal and vegetable oil 341,881; Basic manufactures 78,537; Total (incl. others) 3,115,157.

Principal Trading Partners (US $ million, 2011): *Imports:* Australia 141.4; China, People's Republic 33.7; Fiji 19.2; India 1.2; Indonesia 14.2; Japan 16.3; Malaysia 26.5; New Zealand 26.2; Papua New Guinea 18.6; Singapore 136.6; Total (incl. others) 523.3. *Exports:* Australia 73.2; China, People's Republic 316.7; Indonesia 9.7; Italy 21.6; Japan 5.6; Korea, Republic 11.4; Malaysia 5.8; Philippines 15.6; Spain 20.7; Thailand 27.1; Total (incl. others) 618.1.

Note: Data reflect the IMF's direction of trade methodology and, as a result, the totals may not be equal to those presented for trade in commodities.

Source: Asian Development Bank.

TRANSPORT

Road Traffic (motor vehicles in use at 30 June 1986): Passenger cars 1,350; Commercial vehicles 2,026.

Shipping: *Traffic* (international traffic, '000 metric tons, 1990): Goods loaded 278; Goods unloaded 349 (Source: UN, *Monthly Bulletin of Statistics*). *Flag Registered Fleet* (at 31 December 2012): Vessels 8; Total displacement (grt) 3,807 (Source: Lloyd's List Intelligence—www.lloydslistintelligence.com).

Civil Aviation (traffic on scheduled services, 2009): Kilometres flown 3 million; Passengers carried 94,000; Passenger-km 80 million; Total ton-km 8 million. Source: UN, *Statistical Yearbook. 2010* ('000): Passengers carried 143 (Source: World Bank, World Development Indicators database).

TOURISM

Visitor Arrivals by Country (2010): Australia 10,751; Japan 589; New Zealand 1,710; Papua New Guinea 1,361; United Kingdom 432; USA 862; Vanuatu 405; Total (incl. others) 20,521. *Total Tourist Arrivals* ('000): 23 in 2011 (provisional).

Tourism Receipts (US $ million, excl. passenger transport): 44 in 2009; 54 in 2010; 73 in 2011 (provisional).

Source: World Tourism Organization.

COMMUNICATIONS MEDIA

Telephones (2011): 8,400 main lines in use.

Mobile Cellular Telephones (2011): 274,900 subscribers.

Internet Users (2009): 10,000.

Broadband Subscribers (2011): 2,400.

Source: International Telecommunication Union.

EDUCATION

Pre-primary (2009/10): 22,720 pupils.

Primary: 523 schools (1993); 3,014 teachers (1999); 83,232 pupils (2006/07).

Secondary: 23 schools (1993); 1,337 teachers (2000); 27,332 pupils (2006/07).

Overseas Centres (1988): 405 students.

Source: UNESCO, *Statistical Yearbook*; UNESCO Institute for Statistics.

Adult Literacy Rate (estimate based on census data): 76.6% in 2003. Source: UN Development Programme, *Human Development Report*.

Directory

The Government

HEAD OF STATE

Queen: HM Queen ELIZABETH II.
Governor-General: FRANK OFAGIORO KABUI (sworn in 7 July 2009).

CABINET
(May 2013)

The Government is formed by the National Coalition for Reform and Advancement, which includes the Reformed Democratic Party, the Independent Democratic Party, the Solomon Islands Democratic Party, OUR Party, independents and others.

Prime Minister: GORDON DARCY LILO.

Deputy Prime Minister and Minister for Home Affairs: MANASSEH MAELANGA.

Minister for Foreign Affairs and External Trade: CLAY FORAU SOALAOI.

Minister for Finance and Treasury: RICK HOU.

Minister for Commerce, Industries, Labour and Immigration: ELIJAH DORO MUALA.

Minister for Development Planning and Aid Co-ordination: SNYDER RINI.

Minister for Agriculture and Livestock: CONNELLY SANDAKABATU.

Minister for Fisheries and Marine Resources: ALFRED GHIRO.

Minister for Forestry: DICKSON MUA.

Minister for Communication and Aviation: WALTER FOLOTALU.

Minister for Culture and Tourism: SAMUEL MANETOALI.

Minister for Education and Human Resources Development: DICKSON HA'AMORI.

Minister for Energy, Mines and Rural Electrification: MOSES GARU.

Minister for Environment, Conservation and Meteorology: JOHN MOFFAT FUGUI.

Minister for Health and Medical Services: CHARLES SIGOTO.

Minister for Infrastructure Development: SETH GUKUNA.

Minister for Justice and Legal Affairs: COMMINS ASTON MEWA.

Minister for Lands, Housing and Survey: JOSEPH ONIKA.

Minister for National Unity, Reconciliation and Peace: HYPOLITE TAREMAE.

Minister for Police, National Security and Correctional Services: DAVID TOME.

Minister for Provincial Government and Institutional Strengthening: SILAS TAUSINGA.

Minister for Public Service: BRADLEY TOVOSIA.

Minister for Women, Youth and Children's Affairs: PETER TOM.

Minister of Rural Development and Indigenous Affairs: LIONEL ALEX.

MINISTRIES

Office of the Prime Minister: POB G1, Honiara; tel. 21863; fax 28649; internet www.pmc.gov.sb.

Ministry of Agriculture and Livestock: POB G13, Honiara; tel. 27987; fax 28365; e-mail psagriculture@pmc.gov.sb.

Ministry of Commerce, Industries, Labour and Immigration: Honiara; tel. 28614; fax 25084; e-mail commerce@commerce.gov.sb; internet www.commerce.gov.sb.

Ministry of Communication and Aviation: Honiara; tel. 28049; fax 28054.

Ministry of Culture and Tourism: POB G26, Honiara; tel. 26848; fax 25084.

Ministry of Development Planning and Aid Co-ordination: Honiara; tel. 28608; fax 30163.

Ministry of Education and Human Resources Development: POB G28, Honiara; tel. 28643; fax 22042; e-mail pseducation@pmc.gov.sb.

Ministry of Energy, Mines and Rural Electrification: POB G37, Honiara; tel. 28609; fax 25811; e-mail psmines@pmc.gov.sb.

Ministry of Environment, Conservation and Meteorology: Honiara; tel. 28611; fax 28735; e-mail psforestry@pmc.gov.sb.

Ministry of Finance and Treasury: POB 26, Honiara; tel. 24102; fax 28619; e-mail psfinance@pmc.gov.sb.

Ministry of Fisheries and Marine Resources: POB G13, Honiara; tel. 39143; e-mail psfisheries@pmc.gov.sb.

Ministry of Foreign Affairs and External Trade: POB G10, Honiara; tel. 28612; fax 20351; e-mail psforeign@pmc.gov.sb.

Ministry of Forestry: POB G13, Honiara; tel. 28611; fax 28735.

Ministry of Health and Medical Services: POB 349, Honiara; tel. 20831; fax 20085; e-mail pshealth@pmc.gov.sb.

Ministry of Home Affairs: POB G11, Honiara; tel. 28602; fax 25591; e-mail psaffairs@pmc.gov.sb.

Ministry of Infrastructure Development: POB G30, Honiara; tel. 28605; fax 28705; e-mail kudu@mnpd.gov.sb.

Ministry of Justice and Legal Affairs: Honiara; tel. 21048; fax 28424; e-mail hclibrary@courts.gov.sb.

Ministry of Lands, Housing and Survey: POB G38, Honiara; tel. 22750; fax 27298; e-mail pslands@pmc.gov.sb.

Ministry of National Unity, Reconciliation and Peace: POB 1548, Honiara; tel. 28616.

Ministry of Police, National Security and Correctional Services: POB G1723, Honiara; tel. 28607; fax 28423; e-mail pspolice@pmc.gov.sb.

Ministry of Provincial Government and Institutional Strengthening: POB G35, Honiara; tel. 28606; fax 28708; e-mail psprovincial@pmc.gov.sb.

Ministry of Public Service: POB G1, Honiara; tel. 28617; fax 25559; e-mail pspublic@pmc.gov.sb.

Ministry of Rural Development and Indigenous Affairs: Honiara; tel. 25238; fax 22170.

Ministry of Women, Youth and Children's Affairs: Honiara; tel. 28602; fax 23547.

Legislature

National Parliament

POB G19, Honiara; tel. 28520; fax 24272; internet www.parliament.gov.sb.

Speaker: Sir ALLAN KEMAKEZA.

General Election, 4 August 2010

Party	Seats
Solomon Islands Democratic Party	13
Ownership, Unity and Responsibility (OUR) Party	3
Reformed Democratic Party	3
Independent Democratic Party	2
People's Alliance Party	2
Solomon Islands Party for Rural Advancement	2
People's Congress Party	1
People's Federation Party	1
Rural Development Party	1
Rural and Urban Political Party	1
Solomon Islands Liberal Party	1
Solomon Islands National Party	1
Independents	19
Total	50

Note: In many cases party affiliations were subject to review in the immediate aftermath of the election.

Election Commission

Electoral Commission: Ministry of Home Affairs, POB 1500, Honiara; tel. 21198; fax 26161; Chair. Sir ALLAN KEMAKEZA; Chief Electoral Officer POLYCARP HAUNUNU.

Political Organizations

Parties in the National Parliament can have a fluctuating membership and an influence disproportionate to their representation. There is a significant number of independents who are loosely associated in the amorphous, but often decisive, 'Independent Group'. The following parties represent the main groupings:

Autonomous Solomon Islanders Party: Honiara; f. 2010; advocates return of Solomon Islands' ownership to the people; Pres. ELIJAH OWA; Gen. Sec. NORBERT WATE.

Independent Democratic Party: c/o National Parliament, POB G19, Honiara; f. 2004; fmrly the Asscn of Independent Members of Parliament; Sec.-Gen. SNYDER RINI; Pres. Sir THOMAS CHAN.

Ownership, Unity and Responsibility (OUR) Party: c/o National Parliament, POB G19, Honiara; f. 2010; est. by opponents of Govt of Derek Sikua; Pres. MANASSEH SOGAVARE.

People's Alliance Party (PAP): Honiara; f. 1979; est. by merger of People's Progressive Party (f. 1973) and Rural Alliance Party (f. 1977); advocates establishment of a federal republic; Pres. JAMES MEKAB; Sec. EDWARD KINGMELE.

People's Congress Party: Honiara; f. 2010; advocates reform of the Rural Constituency Development Fund; Sec.-Gen. HENCE VAEKESA.

People's Federation Party: Honiara; f. 2010; aims to improve national infrastructure, education, health and medical services, and the stability of the political culture; Sec.-Gen. RUDDOLF DORAH.

Reformed Democratic Party: c/o National Parliament, POB G19, Honiara; f. 2010; Pres. DANNY PHILIP.

Rural and Urban Political Party (RUPP): Honiara; f. 2010; Pres. SAMUEL MANETOALI.

Solomon Islands Democratic Party: c/o National Parliament, POB G19, Honiara; campaigns for self-reliance and for ending of country's dependence on external aid; Leader STEVE WILLIAM ABANA; Gen. Sec. JOHN KENIAPISIA.

Solomon Islands Liberal Party (SILP): c/o National Parliament, POB G19, Honiara; f. 1976; est. as National Democratic Party (NADEPA); present name adopted in 1986; Leader DEREK SIKUA.

Solomon Islands National Party: c/o National Parliament, POB G19, Honiara; f. 1996; Leader FRANCIS BILLY HILLY.

Solomon Islands Party for Rural Advancement (SIPRA): Honiara; f. 2006; advocates the decentralization of powers and the recognition of community governance structures and traditional values; Pres. JOB DUDLEY TAUSINGA; Leader GORDON DARCY LILO.

Other parties that contested the 2010 election included the Direct Development Party (f. 2010 by Dick Ha'amori), New Nations Solomon Islands Party (f. 2010 by Belani Tekulu), People's Power Action Party (f. 2010 by Robert Wales Feratelia), Rural Congress People's Party (f. 2010 by Rev. Milton Talasasa), Rural Development Party, United Party (interim Pres. Joel Konofilia), Twelve Pillars to Peace and Prosperity Party (TP4, f. 2010 by Delmah Nori to represent the views of women).

Diplomatic Representation

EMBASSIES AND HIGH COMMISSIONS IN SOLOMON ISLANDS

Australia: Hibiscus Ave, POB 589, Honiara; tel. 21561; fax 23691; e-mail austhoniara.enquiries@dfat.gov.au; internet www .solomonislands.embassy.gov.au; High Commissioner MATTHEW ANDERSON.

Japan: Mendana Ave, POB 560, Honiara; tel. 22953; fax 21006; Chargé d'affaires AKIRA IWANADE.

New Zealand: Mendana Ave, POB 697, Honiara; tel. 21502; fax 22377; e-mail nzhicom@solomon.com.sb; High Commissioner MARK RAMSDEN.

Papua New Guinea: POB 1109, Honiara; tel. 20561; fax 20562; High Commissioner (vacant).

Taiwan (Republic of China): Panatina Plaza, POB 586, Honiara; tel. 38050; fax 38060; e-mail taiwanembassy04@gmail.com; internet www.taiwanembassy.org/sb; Ambassador WU YUAN-YEN.

United Kingdom: High Commissioner's Residence, Tanuli Ridge, POB 676, Honiara; tel. 21705; fax 21549; e-mail bhc@solomon.com .sb; internet ukinsolomonislands.fco.gov.uk; High Commissioner DOMINIC MEIKLEJOHN.

Judicial System

The High Court is a Superior Court of Record with unlimited original jurisdiction and powers (except over customary land) as prescribed by the Solomon Islands Constitution or by any law for the time being in force in Solomon Islands. The Judges of the High Court are the Chief Justice, resident in Solomon Islands and employed by its Government, and the Puisne Judges (of whom there are usually three). Appeals from this Court go to the Court of Appeal, the members of which are senior judges from Australia, New Zealand and Papua New Guinea. The Chief Justice and judges of the High Court are ex officio members of the Court of Appeal.

In addition there are Magistrates' Courts staffed by qualified and lay magistrates exercising limited jurisdiction in both civil and criminal matters. There are also Local Courts staffed by elders of the local communities, which have jurisdiction in the areas of established native custom, petty crime and local government by-laws. In 1975 Customary Land Appeal Courts were established to hear land appeal cases from Local Courts, which have exclusive original jurisdiction over customary land cases.

High Court and Court of Appeal: POB G21, Honiara; tel. 21632; fax 22702; Chief Justice of the High Court Sir ALBERT ROCKY PALMER; Pres. of the Court of Appeal Sir ROBIN AULD.

Office of the Attorney-General: Honiara; tel. 23886; fax 25498; e-mail siba@solomon.com.sb; Attorney-General BILLY TITIULU.

Religion

More than 95% of the population profess Christianity, and the remainder follow traditional beliefs. According to the census of 1976, about 34% of the population adhered to the Church of Melanesia (Anglican), 19% were Roman Catholics, 17% belonged to the South Seas Evangelical Church, 11% to the United Church (Methodist) and 10% were Seventh-day Adventists. Most denominations are affiliated to the Solomon Islands Christian Association. In many areas Christianity is practised alongside traditional beliefs, especially ancestor worship.

CHRISTIANITY

Solomon Islands Christian Association: POB 1335, Honiara; tel. 23350; fax 26150; e-mail essica@solomon.com.sb; f. 1967; 5 full mems, 7 assoc. mem. orgs; Chair. Most Rev. ADRIAN SMITH; Gen. Sec. EMMANUEL IYABORA.

The Anglican Communion

Anglicans in Solomon Islands are adherents of the Church of the Province of Melanesia, comprising eight dioceses: six in Solomon Islands (Central Melanesia, Malaita, Temotu, Ysabel, Hanuato'o and Central Solomons, which was established in May 1997) and two in Vanuatu (one of which also includes New Caledonia). The Archbishop is also Bishop of Central Melanesia and is based in Honiara. The Church had an estimated 180,000 members in 1988.

Archbishop of the Province of Melanesia: Rt Rev. DAVID VUNAGI, Archbishop's House, POB 19, Honiara; tel. 21137; fax 21098; e-mail dvunagi@comphq.org.sb.

General Secretary: GEORGE KIRIAU, Provincial Headquarters, POB 19, Honiara; tel. 21892; fax 21098; e-mail gkiriau@comphq.org.sb.

The Roman Catholic Church

For ecclesiastical purposes, Solomon Islands comprises one archdiocese and two dioceses. At 31 December 2007 there were an estimated 101,564 adherents in the country. The Bishops participate in the Bishops' Conference of Papua New Guinea and Solomon Islands (based in Papua New Guinea).

Archbishop of Honiara: Most Rev. ADRIAN THOMAS SMITH, Holy Cross, GPOB 237, Honiara; tel. 21943; fax 26426; e-mail chancery@ solomon.com.sb.

Other Christian Churches

Assembly of God: POB 928, Honiara; tel. and fax 25512; f. 1971; Gen. Supt Rev. JERIEL OTASUI.

Christian Fellowship Church: Paradise Village, Munda, Western Province; f. 1960; over 5,000 mems in 24 villages; runs 12 primary schools in Western Province; Rev. IKAN ROVE.

Seventh-day Adventist Mission: POB R145, Ranandi, Honiara; tel. 39267; fax 30653; e-mail sim@adventist.org.sb; internet www .adventist.org.sb; over 9,000 mems on Guadalcanal and over 6,800 on Malaita (Oct. 2000); Pres. WAYNE BOEHM; Sec. SAMUEL PANDA.

South Seas Evangelical Church: POB 16, Honiara; tel. 22388; fax 20302; Pres. ERIC TAKILA; Gen. Sec. CHARLES J. RAFEASI.

United Church in Solomon Islands: POB 82, Munda, Western Province; tel. 62125; fax 62143; e-mail ucsihq@solomon.com.sb; internet www.unitedchurchsi.com; a Methodist church; Moderator Rev. WILFRED KUREPITU; Gen. Sec. ISAAC VULA DAKEI.

BAHÁ'Í FAITH

National Spiritual Assembly: POB 245, Honiara; tel. 22475; fax 25368; e-mail secretary@bahai.org.sb.

ISLAM

Solomon Islands Muslim League: POB 219, Honiara; tel. 21773; fax 24243; Gen. Sec. Dr MUSTAPHA RAMO; 66 mems.

The Press

Agrikalsa Nius (Agriculture News): POB G13, Honiara; tel. 21211; fax 21955; f. 1986; monthly; Editor ALFRED MAESULIA; circ. 1,000.

Citizens' Press: Honiara; monthly.

Link: Solomon Islands Development Trust, POB 147, Honiara; tel. 21130; fax 21131; pidgin and English; 3 or 4 a year.

Solomon Nius: POB 718, Honiara; tel. 22031; fax 26401; monthly; Dept of Information publication; Editor-in-Chief THOMAS KIVO; monthly; circ. 2,000.

Solomon Star: POB 255, Honiara; tel. 22062; fax 25290; e-mail solstar@solomon.com.sb; internet www.solomonstarnews.com; f. 1982; daily; English; Man. Dir and Publr CATHERINE OFANI EREMAE; Editor EDNAL PALMER; circ. 7,000.

Solomon Times: POB 707, Honiara; tel. 23272; fax 39197; internet www.solomontimes.com; daily; online newspaper; Chief Editor and Man. Dir EDWARD KINGMELE.

Solomon Voice: POB 1235, Honiara; tel. 20116; fax 20090; f. 1992; weekly; circ. 10,000; Editor CAROL COLVILLE.

Broadcasting and Communications

TELECOMMUNICATIONS

Legislation adopted by Parliament in August 2009 ended the long-standing monopoly of the Solomon Telekom Company.

Bemobile: commenced operations in August 2010; provides mobile telephone services; 50% owned by Telikom PNG Pty Ltd; CEO MICHAEL AH KOY.

Telekom (Solomon Telekom Co Ltd): Mendana Ave, POB 148, Honiara; tel. 21576; fax 23110; e-mail info@ourtelekom.com.sb; internet www.telekom.com.sb; operates national and international telecommunications links and provides internet services; 64.74% owned by Solomon Islands National Provident Fund, 32.58% by Cable and Wireless plc, 2.68% by Investment Corpn of Solomon Islands; Chair. JOHN BEVERLEY; Chief Exec. LOYLEY NGIRA.

Regulatory Authority

Telecommunications Commission of the Solomon Islands (TCSI): POB 2180, Honiara; tel. 23855; fax 23860; internet www .tcsi.org.sb; f. 2010; Commr BERNARD HILL.

BROADCASTING

In December 2011 Media Niugini (a subsidiary of Fiji Television Ltd) was awarded a television licence to broadcast in Solomon Islands; at early 2013 the new service had yet to commence.

Radio

Solomon Islands Broadcasting Corporation: POB 654, Honiara; tel. 20051; fax 23159; e-mail sibcnews@solomon.com.sb; internet www.sibconline.com.sb; f. 1976; daily transmissions in English and pidgin; broadcasts total 112 hours per week through 4 radio stations; Chair. AUGUSTINE TANEKO; Gen. Man. CORNELIUS RATHAMANA; Editor WALTER NALANGU.

Finance

BANKING

(cap. = capital; res = reserves; brs = branches; amounts in Solomon Islands dollars)

Central Bank

Central Bank of Solomon Islands: POB 634, Honiara; tel. 21791; fax 23513; e-mail info@cbsi.com.sb; internet www.cbsi.com.sb; f. 1983; sole bank of issue; cap. 20m., res 350.6m. (Dec. 2010); Gov. DENTON RARAWA; Deputy Gov. GANE SIMBE.

Development Bank

Development Bank of Solomon Islands: POB 911, Honiara; tel. 21595; fax 23715; e-mail dbsi@welkam.solomon.com.sb; f. 1978; declared insolvent in Sept. 2004 and placed under the administration of the Central Bank of Solomon Islands; Chair. JOHN MICHAEL ASIPARA; Man. Dir LUKE LAYMAN ETA; 4 brs; 5 sub-brs.

Commercial Banks

Australia and New Zealand Banking Group Ltd (Australia): Mud Alley, POB 10, Honiara; tel. 21111; fax 26937; e-mail solomons@anz.com; internet www.anz.com/solomonislands; Gen. Man. BARRY SOWMAN; 4 brs.

Bank South Pacific Ltd (Papua New Guinea): Honiara; tel. 21874; fax 22612; e-mail mcorcoran@bsp.com.sb; internet www.bsp.com.sb; fmrly National Bank of Solomon Islands Ltd; became br. of Bank of South Pacific Ltd following acquisition in 2007; Gen. Man. MARK CORCORAN.

Westpac Banking Corporation (Australia): National Provident Fund Bldg, 721 Mendana Ave, Honiara; tel. 21222; fax 23419; e-mail westpacsolomons@westpac.com.au; internet www.westpac.com.sb; Man. GIAN TAVIANI.

INSURANCE

A number of British and Australian insurance companies maintain agencies in Solomon Islands.

Trade and Industry

GOVERNMENT AGENCY

Investment Corporation of Solomon Islands: POB 570, Honiara; tel. 22511; fax 21263; holding co through which the Govt retains equity stakes in a number of corpns; Chair. NAMSON TRAN.

DEVELOPMENT ORGANIZATION

Solomon Islands Development Trust (SIDT): POB 147, Honiara; tel. 23409; fax 21131; e-mail sidt@welkam.solomon.com.sb; f. 1982; development org.; Exec. Dir ABRAHAM BAENESIA.

CHAMBER OF COMMERCE

Solomon Islands Chamber of Commerce and Industry (SICCI): NPF Bldg, 2nd Floor, POB 650, Honiara; tel. 39542; fax 39544; e-mail sicci@solomon.com.sb; internet www.solomonchamber.com.sb; 69 member cos (July 2004); Chair. JAMES KIM; CEO CALVIN ZIRU.

INDUSTRIAL AND TRADE ASSOCIATIONS

Association of Mining and Exploration Companies: c/o POB G24, Honiara; f. 1988; Pres. NELSON GREG YOUNG.

Commodities Export Marketing Authority: POB 54, Honiara; tel. 22528; fax 21262; e-mail cema@solomon.com.sb; regulator of agricultural commodities such as coconut, cocoa, coffee, palm oil, spices and ngali nut products; agencies at Honiara, Noro and Yandina; Chair. (vacant); Gen. Man. PITAKIA MOSES PELOMO.

Livestock Development Authority: POB 525, Honiara; tel. 29649; fax 22214; f. 1977; privatized 1996; Man. Dir WARREN TUCKER.

Solomon Islands Forest Industries Association: POB 1617, Honiara; tel. 26026; fax 20267; Chair. and Sec. KAIPUA TOHI.

Solomon Islands Small Business Enterprise Centre: POB 972, Honiara; tel. 26650; fax 26653; e-mail manager.sbec@solomon.com.sb; Man. BEN NGINABULE.

EMPLOYERS' ORGANIZATIONS

Chinese Association: POB 1209, Honiara; tel. 22351; fax 23480; assen of business people from the ethnic Chinese community.

Federation of Solomon Islands Business: POB 320, Honiara; tel. 22902; fax 21477.

UTILITIES

Electricity

Solomon Islands Electricity Authority (SIEA): POB 6, Honiara; tel. 39422; fax 39472; e-mail mike@siea.com.sb; internet www.siea.com.sb; f. 1961; autonomous, govt-owned entity responsible for generation, transmission, distribution and sale of electrical energy; Chair. WALTON NAEZON; CEO MICHAEL NATION.

Water

Solomon Islands Water Authority (SIWA): POB 1407, Honiara; tel. 21395; fax 20723; f. 1994; Chair. (vacant); Gen. Man. DONALD MAKINI.

CO-OPERATIVE SOCIETIES

Central Co-operative Association (CCA): Honiara.

Salu Fishing Co-operative Association: POB 1041, Honiara; tel. 26550.

Solomon Islands Consumers Co-operative Society Ltd: Honiara; tel. 21798; fax 23640.

Western General Co-operative Association (WGCA): Gizo, Western Province.

TRADE UNIONS

There are 14 registered trade unions in Solomon Islands.

Solomon Islands Council of Trade Unions (SICTU): National Centre for Trade Unions, POB 271, Honiara; tel. 22566; fax 23171; f. 1986; Pres. DAVID P. TUHANUKU; Sec. TONY KAGOVAI.

.

Transport

ROADS

There are about 1,391 km of roads maintained by the central and provincial governments. In addition, there are 800 km of privately maintained roads mainly for plantation use. Honiara has a main road running about 65 km each side of it along the north coast of Guadalcanal, and Malaita has a 157 km road running north of Auki and around the northern end of the island to the Lau Lagoon, where canoe transport takes over; and one running south for 35 km to Masa. On Makira a road links Kira Kira and Kakoranga, a distance of 35 km.

SHIPPING

Regular shipping services (mainly cargo) exist between Solomon Islands and Australia, New Zealand, Hong Kong, Japan, Singapore, Taiwan and European ports. The four main ports are at Honiara, Yandina, Noro and Gizo.

Solomon Islands Ports Authority: POB 307, Honiara; tel. 22646; fax 23994; e-mail ports@solomon.com.sb; internet www.sipa.com.sb; f. 1956; responsible for the ports of Honiara and Noro; Gen. Man. WILLIAM BARILE.

Sullivans (SI) Ltd: POB 3, Honiara; tel. 21643; fax 23889; e-mail shipping@sullivans.com.sb; internet www.sullivans.com.sb; shipping agents, importers, wholesalers; CEO KEVIN CHANT.

Tradco Shipping Ltd: POB 114, Honiara; tel. 22588; fax 23887; e-mail tradco@solomon.com.sb; f. 1984; shipping agents; Man. Dir GERALD STENZEL.

CIVIL AVIATION

Two airports are open to international traffic and a further 25 serve internal flights. Air Niugini (Papua New Guinea) and Qantas (Australia) fly to Honiara International Airport (located 13 km from the capital).

Director of Civil Aviation: BEN KERE.

Solomon Airlines Limited: POB 23, Honiara; tel. 20031; fax 20232; e-mail it.man@flysolomons.com; internet www.flysolomons.com; f. 1968; govt-owned; international and domestic operator; scheduled services between Honiara and Port Moresby (Papua New Guinea), Nadi (Fiji), Brisbane (Australia) and Port Vila (Vanuatu); Chair. BILL TYSON; CEO RON SUMSUM.

Tourism

The development of the tourism sector is hindered by the relative inaccessibility of the islands and the inadequacy of tourist facilities. In 2011 tourism receipts were provisionally estimated at US $73m. Tourist arrivals rose from 20,521 in 2010 to a provisionally estimated 23,000 in 2011.

Solomon Islands Tourism Industry Association (SITIA): Honiara; tel. 26848; fax 26875; f. 2008; Pres. WILSON MAELAUA.

Solomon Islands Visitors Bureau: POB 321, Honiara; tel. 22442; fax 23986; e-mail info@sivb.com.sb; internet www.visitsolomons.com.sb; f. 1980; Gen. Man. MICHAEL TOKURU; Marketing Man. FREDA UNUSI.

Defence

In July 2003, as the security situation on Guadalcanal deteriorated, the Regional Assistance Mission to Solomon Islands (RAMSI), an Australian-led force comprising more than 2,500 troops and police from various countries in the region, arrived in Solomon Islands to restore law and order. Assisting the local security forces, some 160 RAMSI personnel remained in the country at early 2013. A phased withdrawal of the military contingent of RAMSI was scheduled to be completed at the end of June 2013, while the police contingent would remain in Solomon Islands until 2017 to assist the national police force to strengthen its capacity.

Commissioner of Police: JUANITA MATANGI (acting).

Education

About two-thirds of school-age children receive formal education, mainly in state schools. About 30% of the children who complete a primary school education receive secondary schooling, either in one of eight national secondary schools (at least one of which is run by the Government and the remainder by various churches) or in one of 12 provincial secondary schools, which are run by provincial assemblies. The provincial secondary schools provide curricula of a practical nature, with a bias towards agriculture, while the national secondary schools offer more academic courses.

In 1993 there were 523 primary schools and 23 secondary schools. In 2009/10 pre-primary pupils numbered 22,720. In 2006/07 primary pupils totalled 83,232 and secondary students numbered 27,332. In 2003 the Church of Melanesia announced plans to establish a new secondary school in each of the country's six dioceses. There are two teacher-training schools and a technical institute. According to the 1999 census, 57% of children aged between five and 14 years attended school. In 2009/10 the total enrolment at primary schools included 87% of children in the relevant age-group, while enrolment in secondary schools included 43% of children in the relevant age-group. The introduction of free basic education in 2009 was reported to have led to a substantial increase in primary enrolment. Scholarships are available for higher education at various universities overseas. In 2012 the University of the South Pacific completed the construction of a new campus in Solomon Islands. The Solomon Islands National University (formerly known as the Solomon Islands College of Higher Education) was established in early 2013.

SOMALIA

Introductory Survey

LOCATION, CLIMATE, LANGUAGE, RELIGION, FLAG, CAPITAL

The Somali Republic lies on the east coast of Africa, with Ethiopia to the north-west and Kenya to the west. There is a short frontier with Djibouti to the north-west. Somalia has a long coastline on the Indian Ocean and the Gulf of Aden, forming the 'Horn of Africa'. The climate is generally hot and dry, with an average annual temperature of 27°C (80°F). It is hotter in the interior and on the Gulf of Aden, but cooler on the Indian Ocean coast. Average annual rainfall is less than 430 mm (17 ins). The national language is Somali, but Arabic is also in official use. English and Italian are widely spoken. The state religion is Islam, and the majority of Somalis are Sunni Muslims. There is a small Christian community, mostly Roman Catholics. The national flag (proportions 2 by 3) is pale blue, with a large five-pointed white star in the centre. The capital is Mogadishu.

CONTEMPORARY POLITICAL HISTORY

Historical Context

Somalia was formed by a merger of two former colonial territories: British Somaliland, in the north, and its larger and more populous neighbour, Italian Somaliland. The United Kingdom established a protectorate in British Somaliland in 1886. Italian Somaliland originated in 1889, when Italy concluded agreements with two local rulers, who placed their territories under Italian protection. Italy's occupation of the region was subsequently extended along the coast and inland, and Italian control was completed in 1927. During the Second World War British Somaliland was conquered temporarily by Italian troops, but in 1941 it was recaptured by a British counter-offensive, which also forced the Italians to withdraw from Eritrea, Italian Somaliland and Ethiopia. A British military administration was then established in British and Italian Somaliland.

Under the provisions of the post-war peace treaty of February 1947, Italy renounced all rights to Italian Somaliland. In December 1950, however, the pre-war colony became the UN Trust Territory of Somalia, with Italy returning as the administering power for a 10-year transitional period, prior to independence. The territory's first general election on the basis of universal adult suffrage was held in March 1959, when 83 of the 90 seats in the Legislative Assembly were won by the Somali Youth League (SYL), a pro-Western party led by the Prime Minister, Seyyid Abdullah Issa.

British Somaliland reverted to civilian rule in 1948. The British colonial authorities prepared the territory for self-government, and the first general election took place in March 1959. Fresh elections, for a new legislative council, were held in February 1960, with all parties in favour of early independence and the unification of all Somali territories. Representatives of British Somaliland and the Trust Territory of Somalia met in April and agreed on a merger of the two territories in an independent republic. British Somaliland was granted independence on 26 June, and the merger received unanimous approval by the legislature on the following day.

Accordingly, the union of former British and Italian Somaliland took effect on 1 July 1960, when the independent Somali Republic was proclaimed. Dr Aden Abdullah Osman, hitherto President of the legislature of the southern territory, was elected to be the first President of the new Republic, and the legislatures of the two Somali regions merged to create a single National Assembly. The two dominant parties in former British Somaliland joined with the SYL to form a tripartite coalition Government. Dr Abd ar-Rashid Ali Shermarke of the SYL became Prime Minister. In June 1964 Shermarke resigned as Prime Minister and was replaced by Abd ar-Razak Hussein, who formed a Council of Ministers exclusively from members of the SYL. In June 1967, however, Shermarke was elected by the National Assembly to replace President Osman. He appointed a new Council of Ministers, led by Mohamed Ibrahim Egal, the former Prime Minister of British Somaliland.

On 15 October 1969 President Shermarke was assassinated. Six days later the army seized control in a coup on the eve of a planned presidential election. Power was assumed by the armed forces' Commander-in-Chief, Maj.-Gen. Mohamed Siad Barre, who proclaimed the Somali Democratic Republic. The 1960 Constitution was suspended, political parties were abolished and the National Assembly was dissolved. In October 1970 Siad Barre declared Somalia a socialist state and began a revolutionary programme of national unification and social and economic reform. In July 1976 power was transferred to the newly formed Somali Revolutionary Socialist Party (SRSP), with Siad Barre as Secretary-General.

A new Constitution came into force in September 1979. Elections were held in December for a new legislature, the People's Assembly, which, in January 1980, elected Siad Barre as President of the Republic. Constitutional amendments, approved by the Assembly in November 1984, effectively transferred all powers of government to the President. Despite continuing internal unrest, at elections to the Assembly, in December, a single list of SRSP candidates was reportedly endorsed by 99.9% of voters.

A presidential election, at which Siad Barre was the sole candidate, took place in December 1986, confirming his presidency for a further seven-year term by a reported 99.9% of votes cast. Although Lt-Gen. Mohamed Ali Samater was appointed to the newly created post of Prime Minister in February 1987, the President continued to dominate Somalia's political life.

Domestic Political Affairs

Anti-Government demonstrations in Mogadishu in July 1989, in protest against the arrest of several leading Muslim clerics, were violently suppressed by the armed forces, resulting in the deaths of more than 400 demonstrators. Two newly created opposition groups, the United Somali Congress (USC—composed of Hawiye clan intellectuals) and the National United Front of Somalia (allegedly dominated by disaffected army officers), were thought to have orchestrated the demonstrations. As Siad Barre's authority declined following insurgent fighting in the south, in July 1990 the Council of Ministers endorsed earlier proposals for the democratization of Somalia's political system. It was decided that, following a review by the People's Assembly, a new constitution would be submitted to a national referendum in October, and that multi-party legislative and local government elections would be held in February 1991. In August 1990 the USC, the Somali National Movement (SNM) and the Somali Patriotic Movement (SPM) agreed to co-ordinate their separate military campaigns to overthrow Siad Barre. In October the Government announced the immediate introduction of the new Constitution and a new electoral code. Siad Barre relinquished the post of Secretary-General of the SRSP, in accordance with the Constitution. Nevertheless, insurgent operations continued, and on 1 January 1991 the USC announced that it had captured most areas of Mogadishu and that it had besieged the home of Siad Barre. On 27 January Siad Barre was reported to have fled the capital with those forces remaining loyal to him, and the USC took power. It immediately invited all former opposition groups to participate in a national conference to discuss the democratization of Somalia. On 29 January the USC appointed Ali Mahdi Mohamed (a government minister in the 1960s) as acting President, and he, in turn, invited Umar Arteh Ghalib (a former foreign affairs minister) to form a government that would prepare the country for democracy. The provisional Government was approved by the President on 2 February.

By March 1991, however, Somalia was close to anarchy. Opposition movements rejected the USC's invitation to take part in a national conference, and the SNM was reported to have formed an 11-member administration and a legislature to govern the former territory of British Somaliland. In May the SNM announced its official support for the secession of that territory, and later that month the SNM Central Committee elected Abd ar-Rahman Ahmed Ali 'Tur' as President of the self-proclaimed 'Republic of Somaliland'. In June the Committee approved a 17-member government to administer the territory for a period of two years, after which free elections were to be held.

A conference of national reconciliation, convened in Djibouti in June 1991, was attended by representatives of the USC, the Somali Democratic Movement (SDM), the SPM and the Democratic Front for the Salvation of Somalia; it mandated delegates from the four organizations to travel to 'Somaliland' to persuade the SNM to abandon its declaration of independence. The SNM insisted, however, that the secession of 'Somaliland' from Somalia was irreversible. At a second reconciliation conference in July the four groups that had met in June were joined by the United Somali Front (USF) and the Somali Democratic Alliance. The leaders of the six groups signed a manifesto, which, *inter alia*, committed them to defeat the forces of Siad Barre (which had regrouped as the Somali National Front—SNF), to readopt the 1960 Constitution, which Siad Barre had suspended in 1969, and to implement a general cease-fire. The manifesto also confirmed Ali Mahdi in his position as Somalia's President for a period of two years pending free elections. Ali Mahdi was sworn in as President on 18 August 1991, and in September he reappointed Ghalib as Prime Minister; in October the latter announced the formation of an expanded Government, comprising 72 ministers and deputy ministers, in order to ensure equal representation for the six participating groups.

Meanwhile, in June 1991 a major rift had developed within the USC, and supporters of President Ali Mahdi clashed with those of the USC's military commander, Gen. Mohamed Farah Aidid, in Mogadishu. Aidid objected to Ali Mahdi's assumption of the presidency, since he had commanded the military campaign to overthrow Siad Barre. In October Aidid rejected the legitimacy of the Government appointed earlier that month, and in November his faction launched a major offensive on the President's positions in the capital. Following an appeal by Ali Mahdi for the UN to send a peace-keeping force to the country, a UN special envoy was dispatched to Mogadishu in January 1992. However, the envoy's attempts met with failure, and the mission was followed by an escalation in violence. In mid-January Aidid appointed his own, 21-member administration. By the end of March it was estimated that 14,000 people (mostly civilians) had been killed in the hostilities in Mogadishu.

International intervention

In January 1992 the UN imposed an embargo on the sale of armaments to Somalia. In the following month the UN, the Organization of African Unity (OAU, now the African Union—AU, see p. 191), the League of Arab States (the Arab League, see p. 372) and the Organization of Islamic Cooperation (OIC, see p. 413) issued a joint appeal for a cease-fire, stating that it was a prerequisite for the granting of humanitarian aid to Somalia. Representatives from the rival factions in Mogadishu subsequently agreed to the terms of a cease-fire accord devised by the international organizations. In March, in discussions with a joint mission of the UN, the OAU, the OIC and the Arab League in Mogadishu, Aidid agreed to the monitoring of the cease-fire by a foreign observer mission. In April the UN Security Council approved the establishment of a 'UN Operation in Somalia' (UNOSOM), comprising a 50-strong observer mission to monitor the cease-fire, while it also agreed, in principle, to dispatch forces to protect UN personnel. However, Aidid refused to consent to the deployment of foreign military personnel in Somalia.

In April 1992 Gen. Aidid's militias decisively repelled an advance by SNF forces, pursuing them to the south of the country. Siad Barre fled, with some 200 supporters, to Kenya. (Siad Barre was refused political asylum in Kenya, and in May he moved to Nigeria, where he died in January 1995.) In May Aidid's forces and those of the SPM, the SDM and the Southern Somali National Movement (SSNM), with which he had formed a military alliance known as the Somali Liberation Army (SLA), captured Kismayu, which had been held by the SNF. By June the SLA was in control of most of central and southern Somalia. In late June the UN secured agreement from the principal factions in Mogadishu for the deployment of the observer mission envisaged in the March cease-fire accord. In August Aidid agreed to the deployment of 500 UN troops mandated with escorting food aid from Mogadishu's port and airport to distribution points. Also in August the coalition of Gen. Aidid's faction of the USC with the SPM, the SDM and the SSNM was consolidated with the formation of the Somali National Alliance (SNA), of which Aidid was the leader. Meanwhile, Ali Mahdi strengthened ties with other armed groups hostile to Aidid, and forged links with Gen. Mohamed Siad Hersi 'Morgan' (who had led the SNF since the departure of his father-in-law, Siad Barre). In November, since the UN troops had still been prevented from securing delivery of food aid, the USA offered to lead a military operation in the

country, which was sanctioned by the Security Council in early December. Shortly afterwards an advance contingent of 1,800 US marines landed on the beaches of Mogadishu and took control of the port and airport. The US members of the Unified Task Force (UNITAF) were subsequently reinforced by troops from 21 other countries.

In January 1993 14 of Somalia's political organizations attended peace negotiations in Addis Abeba, Ethiopia, under the auspices of the UN, which resulted in agreements on an immediate cease-fire, disarmament under UN supervision and the holding of a conference of national reconciliation in March, at which an accord providing for the establishment of a Transitional National Council as the supreme authority in Somalia, with a mandate to hold elections within two years, was reached. The Council was to comprise 74 members: one from each of the 15 organizations represented at the conference, three from each of the 18 proposed administrative regions (inclusive of 'Somaliland') and five from Mogadishu.

Agreement on the future government of Somalia was reached hours after the UN Security Council approved the establishment of UNOSOM II, which was to take over responsibility for maintaining security from UNITAF by 1 May 1993. UNOSOM II was to be the UN's largest ever peace-keeping operation, comprising 28,000 military personnel and 2,800 civilian staff, and its first where peace-enforcement without consent from parties within the country was authorized. In May the USA transferred responsibility for international efforts in Somalia to UNOSOM II, the forces of which embarked on a series of armed initiatives, including air-strikes, against suspected strategic positions of the SNA. Despite the increased scale of UNOSOM operations, Aidid avoided injury or capture during June, prompting the Security Council to issue a formal warrant for his arrest. The violent deaths of three Italian UNOSOM soldiers in July provoked Italian media claims that the military emphasis of the mission, promoted by the USA in pursuit of Aidid, was threatening the security of UN personnel and jeopardizing diplomatic initiatives undertaken by the Italian Government. The situation was exacerbated by a US helicopter attack on a suspected pro-Aidid command centre, which resulted in the deaths of 50–100 Somalis, and the murder, in retaliation, of four foreign journalists by enraged Somali crowds.

Uncompromising media coverage of the deaths of three US soldiers in September 1993, and a violent exchange in the capital in October (which resulted in the deaths of some 300 Somalis, 18 US servicemen and the capture, by local militia, of a US helicopter pilot and a Nigerian soldier), prompted widespread public outrage in the USA. The US President, Bill Clinton, subsequently announced that all US troops were to be withdrawn by the end of March 1994, regardless of the outcome of attempts to negotiate a political settlement to the conflict by that date. Clinton's decision later in October 1993 to withdraw immediately the US special forces (which had been deployed to apprehend Aidid) prompted speculation that the release of the US pilot and the Nigerian soldier, secured in mid-October following discussions between representatives of the US Government and Aidid, had been achieved as part of an undisclosed bilateral agreement. Despite Aidid's declaration of a unilateral cease-fire prior to the talks, and subsequent indications of his willingness to enter into negotiations with the USA (in preference to the UN), fighting between pro-Aidid and pro-Mahdi factions escalated.

UN and US withdrawal

In February 1994, in the context of the imminent withdrawal of UNOSOM contingents from the USA and several other Western nations, the UN Security Council revised UNOSOM's mandate, reducing the troop strength of the mission to a maximum of 22,000. In November 1994 the UN Security Council extended UNOSOM's mandate by four months, to a final date of 31 March 1995. As the deadline for UNOSOM's departure approached, the competition for control of installations currently held by the UN, in particular the port and airport, became the focus of factional hostility. In November 1994 UN forces began to withdraw from positions outside Mogadishu in the first stages of UNOSOM's departure. 'Operation United Shield', to ensure the safe evacuation of the UN troops and civilian personnel, was organized and led by the USA. The USA stationed several thousand marines in warships off the Somali coast in December, and in early 1995 they were joined by a multinational force of naval and air force units in order to protect departing UN employees (some 136 members of UNOSOM had been killed since the beginning of the operation).

In late February 1995 1,800 US and 400 Italian marines landed on Mogadishu's beaches, and command of the remaining 2,400 UN troops and of the whole operation was passed from the UN to the US commander. The marines secured the port and airport, and evacuated the remaining UN soldiers. The departure of the last UN personnel on 2 March (almost one month ahead of schedule) was closely followed by that of the US and Italian marines themselves. Somali looters overran the airport, but armoured cars from Aidid's faction, reportedly accompanied by UN-trained police officers, took control of the area. Ali Mahdi's Abgal clansmen gained control of the eastern section of the airport, however, and fighting for control of the crucial sites continued.

Significant divisions within the SNA became more apparent in June 1995, following an attempt by disaffected members to replace Aidid with his former aide, Osman Hassan Ali 'Ato', as Chairman of the party. SNA members loyal to Aidid immediately rejected the legitimacy of the actions of the Ali 'Ato' faction and announced the expulsion of the faction from the SNA. In mid-June a conference of reconciliation, convened in southern Mogadishu by representatives of 15 pro-Aidid factions, elected Aidid President of the Republic of Somalia for a three-year term. However, Aidid's presidency and mandate to govern were immediately rejected in a joint statement issued by Ali Mahdi and Ali 'Ato'. In September Aidid's forces seized Baidoa.

Fighting between Gen. Aidid's supporters and those loyal to Ali 'Ato' intensified in early 1996. In July pro-Aidid factions clashed with supporters of Ali Mahdi in Mogadishu, resulting in some 90 fatalities. Aidid was wounded during the skirmishes, and on 1 August he died as a result of his injuries. On 4 August one of his sons, Hussein Mohamed Aidid (a former US marine and hitherto Aidid's chief of security), was appointed interim President by the SNA leadership council. Hussein Aidid (who was subsequently elected Chairman of the SNA) vowed to continue his father's struggle, and factional fighting quickly resumed.

In December 1996 representatives of some 26 Somali factions (notably excluding the SNA) held protracted talks in Sodere, Ethiopia, under the auspices of the Ethiopian Government and the Intergovernmental Authority on Development (IGAD). The conference culminated in January 1997 in the formation of a 41-member National Salvation Council (NSC), with an 11-member executive committee and a five-member joint chairmanship committee, to act as an interim government charged with drafting a transitional charter and holding a national reconciliation conference. Aidid condemned the establishment of the NSC and accused the Ethiopian authorities of interfering in Somali affairs.

In October 1999 IGAD delegates met in Addis Ababa to discuss a peace plan for Somalia proposed by President Ismaïl Omar Guelleh of Djibouti. In February 2000 IGAD member states endorsed Guelleh's plan, which envisaged the staging of a Somali national reconciliation conference in Djibouti in early May, to be attended by representatives of various sections of Somali society. Under the plan, they would elect a new national legislature, which would, in turn, elect a President. The President would choose a Prime Minister, subject to the approval of the legislature, who would head a transitional government for a period of no longer than two years, during which time a national constitution would be drafted and elections would be scheduled. The peace plan was unanimously endorsed by OAU foreign ministers in March, and also received the approval of the UN and the USA.

Formation of the Transitional National Assembly

The Somali national reconciliation conference opened in Arta, Djibouti, on 2 May 2000. By June the number of delegates attending had risen to around 900, although notably only one of the principal Somali faction leaders, Ali Mahdi, was present. In early July the conference produced a draft national charter, which envisaged the Somali Republic adopting a federal system of government, after a three-year interim period, comprising 18 regional administrations. Furthermore, it provided for the creation of the Somali Transitional National Assembly (TNA), to comprise 225 members, of whom 25 would be women. Each of the four major Somali clans (Dir, Hawiye, Darod and Rahanwin) was allocated 44 parliamentary seats, and an alliance of small clans was to receive 24 seats; the remaining 25 seats were reserved for women from the four major clans and the alliance of small clans, each of which would receive five seats. However, disagreements over the distribution of seats ensued, and in early August President Guelleh intervened, suggesting the appointment of a further 20 members to the Assembly, thus increasing the total

number to 245. Guelleh's proposal was accepted, and on 13 August the TNA held its inaugural session in Arta. On 26 August it was announced that Abdulkasim Salad Hasan, a member of the Hawiye clan, who had served in the Siad Barre administration, had been elected President of Somalia by the TNA. Hasan was sworn in as President on the following day at a ceremony in Arta. On 30 August President Hasan returned to Mogadishu, where he was greeted by tens of thousands of Somalis. On 8 October President Hasan appointed Ali Khalif Galaydh, a former Minister of Industry in the Siad Barre regime, to the post of Prime Minister; later that month Galaydh announced a 32-member Council of Ministers.

Relations between Somalia and Ethiopia deteriorated in January 2001, after Galaydh accused Ethiopia of providing arms to factions opposed to the Transitional National Government (TNG). Relations between the two countries were further strained in March, when the Ethiopian authorities allowed several Somali faction leaders to convene in Addis Ababa for a series of meetings, which resulted in the creation of the Somali Reconciliation and Restoration Council (SRRC), headed by Hussein Aidid.

In October 2001 a group of dissatisfied TNA members proposed a motion of no confidence in the TNG, citing the administration's lack of progress in the reconciliation process. Later that month 141 of the 174 TNA members participating voted to dismiss the Galaydh administration. In mid-November President Hasan appointed Col Hassan Abshir Farah, hitherto Minister of Water and Mineral Resources, as Prime Minister; the appointment of a new Council of Ministers was delayed until after the conclusion of further peace talks between the SRRC and members of the TNA. Although the talks were postponed until mid-December, they were attended by senior members of the SNA (again with the notable exception of Hussein Aidid) and representatives of several other Mogadishu faction leaders. On 24 December, in the Kenyan town of Nakura, Farah, on behalf of the TNA, and Mowlid Ma'aneh Mohamed, the Secretary-General of the SRRC, signed a peace agreement, which provided for the formation of an 'all-inclusive government' to ensure equitable power-sharing among all Somali clans and the establishment of a Kenya-based secretariat to oversee the implementation of the Somali peace process.

In mid-February 2002 Farah formed a new 31-member Council of Ministers, which notably included Dr Hussein Mohamed Usman Jimbir, a former senior member of the SRRC, as Minister of Education. However, several members of factions that had signed the Nakura peace agreement in December 2001 were reported to have refused to join the new Government. The reconciliation process in Somalia was further endangered in early April 2002, when the Rahanwin Resistance Army (RRA) announced that it had established a new autonomous region in south-western Somalia, based in Baidoa, to be known as the 'State of South-western Somalia'. The Chairman of the RRA, Mohamed Hasan Nur Shatigadud, was elected as 'President' of the new region for a four-year period.

Renewed reconciliation efforts

An IGAD-sponsored reconciliation conference opened in the Kenyan town of Eldoret in mid-October 2002, in the presence of representatives of regional governments. Following the conclusion of the first phase of the conference, the TNG and a number of Somali factions signed a temporary cease-fire and agreed to abide by the final outcome of the conference; to establish an all-inclusive federal system of government; to combat terrorism; and to enhance the safety of aid workers in the country. In early December the TNG and Mogadishu-based faction leaders Hussein Aidid, Mohammed Qanyare Afrah, Muse Sudi Yalahow and Ali 'Ato' signed a declaration committing themselves to ending violence in the Somali capital. (However, Yalahow and Qanyare subsequently withdrew from the conference.) In February 2003 the conference was moved to Nairobi, Kenya, and in the following month the TNG and the remaining faction leaders provisionally agreed on the formation of an administration for Mogadishu and further measures to bring peace to the capital.

In early July 2003 delegates at the Nairobi conference reached a provisional agreement, providing for the establishment of a transitional unicameral parliament, which would comprise 351 members selected by political leaders, and would remain in operation for four years. However, President Hasan rejected the agreement, which had been signed by Farah, stating that it would divide the country, and in August dissent between Hasan and Farah intensified. Later that month, just days before the expiry of the three-year mandate of the TNG, Hasan dismissed Farah and the Speaker of the TNA. Hasan insisted that the existing governing institutions would remain in place, despite the expiry of their mandate, until a new President, government and parliament had been installed. Dr Abdi Guled Mohamed, the Minister of Air and Land Transport, was appointed premier, in an acting capacity.

Despite the expiry of his mandate in August 2003, President Hasan appointed Mohamed Abdi Yusuf, hitherto Deputy Speaker of the TNA, as Prime Minister in early December. In January 2004 the TNA approved the appointment of a new 37-member TNG, which included three Deputy Prime Ministers. In the same month talks reconvened in Nairobi, with the aim of restoring the faltering peace process. Following a period of intense negotiations, during which Yalahow and the leaders of the Juba Valley Alliance (JVA), the RRA and the SNF rejoined the discussions, later that month representatives from more than 20 factions in attendance agreed to establish a new transitional parliament, comprising 275 members (rather than the 351 previously agreed), who would serve five-year terms. Agreement on a new Transitional Federal Charter (replacing the transitional national charter) was reached in Nairobi; it was approved by the TNA on 8 February and subsequently endorsed by a presidential decree.

In June 2004 an arbitration committee was formed in Nairobi to oversee the nomination of members to the new parliament by the major Somali clans; by mid-August the majority of the new members of the Transitional Federal Parliament (TFP) had been nominated and inauguration ceremonies commenced in Nairobi. On 15 September Sharif Hassan Sheikh Adan, a Mogadishu-based business executive, was elected Speaker of the TFP and later that month nominations were invited for the position of President. Following two rounds of voting in the TFP on 10 October, two presidential candidates remained: Col Abdullahi Yusuf Ahmed, the President of the autonomous region of 'Puntland' (see below), and Abdallah Ahmed Addow, a former Somali ambassador to the USA. At a third round of voting held later that day, Yussuf secured 189 of the 268 votes cast and was sworn in as President of Somalia at a ceremony in Nairobi on 14 October. In early November Yussuf appointed Ali Mohammed Ghedi, a member of the Hawiye clan and a former AU official, as Prime Minister.

The presidency of Abdullahi Yussuf Ahmed

Shortly after he had taken office, President Yussuf had appealed to the AU and the UN to approve the deployment of a peace-keeping force of up to 20,000 troops to assist with the relocation of the TFP and the Transitional Federal Government (TFG) to Mogadishu and to disarm militias in the Somali capital. However, ongoing violence in the city caused the plans to be stalled. In early January 2005 the AU stated its readiness 'in principle' to deploy a contingent of peace-keepers to Somalia. Despite further concerns over the security situation in the capital, plans for the relocation proceeded, and in early February a delegation of 30 members of the TFP arrived in Mogadishu, followed by a further 50 parliamentarians, led by Sheikh Adan, a few days later. As an AU mission arrived in Mogadishu in mid-February to assess the security situation, thousands of people staged protests against the proposed peace-keeping force and a bomb exploded in the capital, killing two people.

In mid-March 2005 IGAD defence ministers agreed to deploy a 10,000-strong peace-keeping force, the IGAD Peace Support Mission to Somalia (IGASOM), in the country from 30 April, to be replaced at an unspecified later date by an AU force. However, demonstrations were staged in Mogadishu opposing the deployment of peace-keeping troops from neighbouring countries, and members of the TFP were involved in a violent confrontation, following a vote to reject the planned deployment. In an attempt to allay fears in Somalia, the IGAD Council of Ministers proposed a compromise solution, in which a reduced IGASOM force of 6,800 would initially be deployed, comprised solely of Sudanese and Ugandan troops. In late March the Somali Government announced that it would temporarily relocate to Baidoa and Jowhar, 90 km north of Mogadishu, until violence in the capital subsided. However, heavy fighting in Baidoa later in March between supporters of Yussuf and militia opposed to the relocation of the TFG outside of Mogadishu resulted in at least 14 fatalities, and in late April the 80 parliamentarians situated in Mogadishu rejected appeals from the President and the UN-led Joint Co-ordination and Monitoring Committee to return to Nairobi, stating that a return to exile would jeopardize ongoing efforts to 'pacify' the capital.

At the end of April 2005 a bomb exploded in Mogadishu, killing 15 people and injuring at least 50 others, at a rally attended by Ghedi. In early May 100 members of the TFP opposed to Yussuf's relocation plans, including Sheikh Adan, boycotted a parliamentary vote in Nairobi, where supporters of the President approved the planned relocation to Baidoa and Jowhar and the deployment of the proposed peace-keeping force. Days later Qanyare Afrah, Yalahow and Ali 'Ato' undertook to combine their militias and withdraw them from Mogadishu, and a partial disarmament of their forces took place at a ceremony in the capital. Also in April, the AU approved plans to send 1,700 peace-keeping troops to Somalia but stated that the force would only arrive when its security could be guaranteed. In May 30 members of the TFP accompanied Sheikh Adan upon his return to Mogadishu, while a spokesman for the President announced that Jama had been removed from office. In June Ghedi and the remaining ministers and members of parliament left Nairobi and arrived in Jowhar, despite the opposition of local militia. A convoy carrying Ghedi on a visit to Mogadishu was attacked with grenades and a land mine in early November. Three people were killed in the apparent assassination attempt, although Ghedi was uninjured in the attack. Later that month 11 people were killed during fighting in Mogadishu, after the Union of Islamic Courts (UIC) of Mogadishu, which had established a court system in the capital based on *Shari'a* (Islamic) law, attempted to seize control of cinemas it had accused of encouraging immoral and criminal behaviour.

The rise of the Somali Supreme Islamic Courts Council

In early January 2006 Yussuf and Sheikh Adan signed an agreement for the TFP to meet in Somalia within 30 days, following further talks held in San'a, and in late January members of the group led by Sheikh Adan signalled their willingness to support a process of reconciliation. Despite the absence of Ali 'Ato', Yalahow and several other prominent ministers opposed to Yussuf, 205 parliamentarians assembled in Baidoa on 26 February as the TFP met for the first time since returning from Kenya. In late February a number of formerly opposed faction leaders, including Qanyare Afrah and Yalahow, formed a new political alliance—the Alliance for the Restoration of Peace and Counter-Terrorism (ARPCT)—which aimed to combat Islamist extremism in Somalia. Militia supported by the ARPCT were in conflict with forces loyal to the UIC in the south of Mogadishu, and at least 33 people were killed before a cease-fire was negotiated by Somali elders. However, some 140 people were killed and thousands fled the capital in late March as fighting resumed, and attempts by elders to renegotiate a cease-fire between the two factions continued. Unrest continued in the capital during early May with more than 80 people reported to have been killed in clashes between the two sides.

In early June 2006 the UIC claimed to have seized control of Mogadishu. Later that month, at a meeting convened by the Arab League in Khartoum, Sudan, the Government signed an agreement of mutual recognition with the UIC, in an attempt to avert a potential attack on Baidoa. Shortly after the agreement was signed, the UIC underwent a reorganization and was renamed the Somali Supreme Islamic Courts Council (SSICC). The US-led Contact Group on Somalia urged the Somali Government to enter into further dialogue with the SSICC to avoid more widespread conflict. In late July and early August some 40 ministers and assistant ministers resigned, citing their dissatisfaction with Prime Minister Ghedi's apparent unwillingness to negotiate with the SSICC. On 28 July the Minister of Constitutional and Federal Affairs, Abdallah Derow Isaq, was shot dead outside a mosque in Baidoa, and two days later Prime Minister Ghedi narrowly defeated a vote of no confidence in the TFP. However, President Yussuf dissolved the Council of Ministers on 7 August and instructed Ghedi to form a new administration, which he did later that month.

During late August 2006 SSICC forces took control of several towns to the north of Mogadishu, and continued to demand the withdrawal of all Ethiopian troops from Somalia, the presence of whom had repeatedly been denied by both the Somali and the Ethiopian Governments. Further peace talks took place in Khartoum on 4 September under the auspices of the Arab League, and the following day IGAD convened a meeting in Nairobi at which regional leaders resolved to deploy an international peace force to Somalia, despite continued opposition to the proposal from the SSICC. In mid-September President Yussuf narrowly escaped an assassination attempt outside the Parliament buildings. In exchanges of fire that followed the explosion 11 people were killed, including Yussuf's brother; the incident further increased tensions between the weakened

Government and the SSICC, although the latter denied any involvement.

Attempts to establish peace-keeping missions

Further peace talks were scheduled to take place in Khartoum in October 2006, but the SSICC refused to enter into discussions while the Ethiopian military remained in Somalia, and in early November negotiations were postponed. The SSICC issued a peace initiative to the Somali Government on 11 November; however, the Government rejected this and the following day violent conflict erupted, igniting fears that the situation could escalate into a regional war. Ethiopian reinforcements arrived in Baidoa, while SSICC troops were deployed to positions close to the Ethiopian border. In early December the Ethiopian Government reported attacks by insurgents who had crossed the border. At the same time, violence escalated in the area surrounding Baidoa as opposing troops sought to exert control over the seat of government. The UN Security Council hurriedly adopted a resolution (No. 1725) providing for peace-keeping missions from other African nations to enter Somalia in support of government forces. Meanwhile, the SSICC, although lacking military strength, was securing wider popular support. The SSICC claimed that the majority of the country, under Islamist control, remained peaceful and that international intervention was the cause of much of the conflict. Nevertheless, in mid-December the SSICC issued an ultimatum to the Ethiopian forces to leave Somalia within seven days or face a full-scale war. The Ethiopian Government (which only officially admitted to military involvement in Somalia in late December) rejected these demands, and civilians fled Baidoa and the surrounding areas as fighting broke out once more. During a meeting with the European Union (EU, see p. 281) Commissioner for Development and Humanitarian Aid on 20 December the SSICC declared that it would honour its commitment to attending peace talks in Sudan. However, Ethiopian troops advanced towards Mogadishu, forcing the SSICC to retreat. Pro-Government forces began to regain control over the capital and popular support for the SSICC reportedly waned.

On 1 January 2007, with the SSICC forces driven out of the Somali capital, Prime Minister Ghedi announced a three-day amnesty during which civilians were to surrender their weapons. The UN warned that the continued presence of Eritrean forces in Somalia remained a threat to the fragile peace, and as Ethiopia began to withdraw troops from Somalia there was increased pressure on the AU to establish a peace-keeping force in the region. Remaining pro-Government troops were subjected to guerrilla attacks in the weeks that followed, and the USA launched a series of air-strikes against Islamists who continued to pose a threat in southern areas of Somalia.

In January 2007 Sheikh Adan was dismissed as Speaker of the TFP, amid allegations that he supported the Islamist extremists and had failed to attend parliamentary meetings. Sheikh Adan Madobe was elected to replace Sheikh Adan on 31 January. Meanwhile, in mid-January 154 members of the TFP voted in favour of declaring martial law, to be imposed for a period of three months from 31 January.

At the end of January 2007 an AU summit convened in Addis Ababa, Ethiopia, concluded, having secured less than 4,000 troops of the 8,000 pledged to constitute a peace-keeping force. However, President Yussuf agreed to stage a national reconciliation conference with the aim of bringing an end to the conflict in the country and it was subsequently agreed that the reconciliation conference would be held in April. In February the UN Security Council adopted a resolution (No. 1744) authorizing the establishment of the AU Mission in Somalia (AMISOM), with an initial mandate of six months; it was envisaged that the force would replace the withdrawing Ethiopian troops and provide support to the TFG.

A tentative cease-fire was agreed on 22 March 2007 between elders of the Hawiye clan and Ethiopian military officials. However, it broke down almost immediately when government forces attacked Islamist militia in the southern region of the capital in an attempt to consolidate their control. Fighting continued into early April and by that time, according to the office of the UN High Commissioner for Refugees (UNHCR), some 47,000 people had fled Mogadishu and it was reported that around 1,500 people had been killed. The reconciliation talks were postponed until June.

Government institutions return to Mogadishu

On 12 March 2007 the TFP voted to relocate the TFG and the following day the office of the President moved from Baidoa to Mogadishu. Government ministers began preparations to transfer their offices to the capital, but progress was hindered by continuing violence in the city. The TFG announced in mid-March that additional security measures were to be implemented to quell the unrest, including deploying trained Ethiopian and AU troops to the worst affected areas. A UN agency reported that by late April more than 300,000 people—almost one-third of the city's population—had left Mogadishu, and in May Hawiye clan elders conceded defeat in the capital and the TFG urged the group to enter into negotiations over disarmament.

The reconciliation conference, which, amongst other issues, was to debate the holding of future elections and the resolution of clan divisions, finally began in July 2007. However, Islamists and Hawiye clan elders refused to attend the meeting, on the grounds that while Ethiopian troops remained in the country the conference would not provide a neutral base for discussions. The outcome of the seven-week conference was undermined by the absence of key parties, according to international observers. In late August AMISOM's mandate was extended for a further six months. An opposition conference was subsequently convened in September, attended by Sheikh Hassan Dahir Aweys, Chairman of the SSICC, who had been in hiding since being driven from Mogadishu by Ethiopian forces earlier that year. At the meeting, also attended by UN and EU observers, SSICC and opposition leaders formed a coalition, the Alliance for the Re-liberation of Somalia (ARS). The ARS aimed to remove the Ethiopian-backed Government and would be guided by a 191-member committee, headed by the former Speaker of the TFP, Sheikh Adan. A 10-member executive committee was elected, with Sheikh Sharif Sheikh Ahmed named as Chairman.

Meanwhile, relations between President Yussuf, a member of the Darod clan, and Prime Minister Ghedi of the Hawiye clan became increasingly strained in 2007. In October Prime Minister Ghedi tendered his resignation following further outbreaks of violence involving insurgents and Ethiopian troops. Nur Hassan Hussein, the Secretary-General of the Somali Red Crescent humanitarian organization and a Hawiye, was named as the new Prime Minister and sworn into office on 24 November. Prime Minister Hussein announced a new Council of Ministers in December. Shortly after their appointment, however, five ministers submitted their resignation, claiming that the composition of the new administration did not fully represent their clans. Having failed to gain approval for his first administration, Hussein formed a new TFG in mid-January 2008, which included Salim Aliow Ibrow as Minister of Justice and Religious Affairs and Acting Minister of Labour and Social Affairs, Aydid Abdullahi Ilka Hanaf as Minister of Education and Culture and Acting Minister of Health, and Muhammad Abdisalan Adan as Minister of Information, Youth Affairs and Sports; all three were also awarded the status of Deputy Prime Minister.

In late January 2008 AU security officials submitted a proposal for measures to establish lasting peace and security. The plan included increased efforts towards achieving reconciliation; ensuring a safe environment for humanitarian aid workers; and fostering greater co-operation from the international community in peace-keeping operations. Meanwhile, the UN was considering the deployment of a UN peace-keeping force to replace AMISOM, which by mid-April comprised only 2,450 troops and had largely been restricted to protecting transport facilities in Mogadishu and providing security for government officials. However, in February the UN Security Council authorized the extension of AMISOM's mandate until late August. In March the USA formally designated the militant Islamist group, al-Shabaab ('The Youth'), which had been established in 2007 by former members of the UIC, as a terrorist organization, claiming that it was linked to the al-Qa'ida (Base) network (see below).

Islamist insurgents seized the town of Adado, in the central region of Galgudud, in April 2008. In early May a leader of al-Shabaab, Aden Hashi Ayro, was killed in an air-strike launched by US forces on the town of Dhuusa Mareeb, which resulted in the deaths of at least seven other people. Later that month UN-sponsored peace talks between the TFG and the ARS commenced in Djibouti; however, Islamist leaders in Somalia, including hard-line elements of the ARS led by Aweys, reiterated their refusal to enter into negotiations until Ethiopian forces had been withdrawn from Somalia. Also in mid-May the UN Security Council approved the establishment of a joint planning unit and recommended the relocation of the UN Political Office for Somalia (UNPOS) from Nairobi to Mogadishu. UNPOS was to support the TFG in the development of a constitution and organization of a referendum and democratic elections in 2009.

Withdrawal of Ethiopian troops

In June 2008 an agreement was concluded by members of the TFG and a moderate faction of the ARS present in Djibouti, which included provisions for the withdrawal of Ethiopian troops from Somalia and the deployment of a UN peace-keeping force to replace them; it was also agreed that a cease-fire would be implemented within 30 days. (The agreement was officially signed in August.) Hard-line Islamists in Somalia, who had boycotted the talks, dismissed the agreement and in July the group split into two separate factions (the moderate 'Djibouti wing' and the more hard-line 'Asmara wing'). Despite the agreement, intense fighting continued between insurgents and government forces, with reports of clashes in Mogadishu that resulted in the deaths of at least 28 people. Furthermore, two policemen were killed when their vehicle was destroyed in a bomb attack in which three other people died, and in late June the SSICC claimed to have captured the cities of Hawdar, Wajid and Balad Weyn in central and south-west Somalia. In the following month the head of the UN Development Programme office in Mogadishu, Usman Ali Ahmad, was shot dead near his residence in the city, as part of a wider campaign by insurgents, in particular those affiliated to al-Shabaab, to target aid workers in the country.

The UN Security Council extended the mandate of AMISOM for a further six months in August 2008, while Ethiopian Prime Minister Meles Zenawi announced plans to begin the withdrawal of Ethiopian troops from Somalia. Nevertheless, violence continued in Mogadishu, while two Western journalists were kidnapped near the capital, and Islamists captured the southern port of Kismayu, after three days of intense fighting in which some 100 people were killed. (The journalists were released in November 2009.) Meanwhile, on 2 August 2008 it was reported that nine ministers and one deputy minister had resigned from the TFG, apparently in response to Hussein's dismissal of the Governor of the Banaadir region, Mohammed Umar Habeeb; Hussein subsequently appointed six new ministers to the TFG. In October the security situation in Mogadishu deteriorated further and there were also bombings in the capital of 'Somaliland' as well as co-ordinated suicide attacks against government buildings in 'Puntland'. None the less, a new peace treaty was signed between the TFG and the 'Djibouti wing' of the ARS, in which they agreed to implement an official cease-fire the following month. It was also revealed that Ethiopian troops would begin withdrawing from Somalia on 21 November; the Ethiopian Government subsequently announced that it would remove all of its forces by the end of the year. Meanwhile, al-Shabaab had taken control of large areas of central and southern Somalia, and with the imminent withdrawal of Ethiopian forces there were concerns that it would succeed in capturing Mogadishu.

In mid-December 2008 Yussuf announced that he had dismissed Prime Minister Hussein, following his attempts to establish a power-sharing administration with moderate Islamists. Hussein rejected this decision, insisting that only the TFP had the power to remove him, but, despite the TFP voting in favour of reinstating Hussein, the President later named Mohamed Mohamud Guled as the new Prime Minister. On 24 December Guled announced his resignation, stating that his appointment was causing dissension within the Government. President Yussuf, in turn, resigned on 29 December; he was replaced in an acting capacity by the Speaker of the TFP, Adan Madobe.

Sheikh Sharif Sheikh Ahmed becomes President

Amid the uncertainty that followed Yussuf's resignation in December 2008, the violence continued as insurgents shelled government forces and AMISOM positions in Mogadishu, while a number of Islamist groups began to fight among themselves. New groups, seeking to take advantage of the potential power vacuum created by the departure of Ethiopian troops, had formed in late December, including the Ahlu-Sunna Wal-Jama, which declared a *jihad* (holy war) against hard-line Islamist factions. On 16 January 2009 the UN Security Council adopted a resolution (No. 1863) expressing its intention to establish a peace-keeping force in Somalia to replace AMISOM and extending the mission's mandate for a further six months.

In late January 2009 Ethiopia completed the withdrawal of its forces. Shortly afterwards, al-Shabaab insurgents seized control of Baidoa, where the TFP had formerly been based. The TFP, which had been convened in Djibouti, agreed to increase its composition by 275 members to 550 deputies; 149 new members from the 'Djibouti wing' of the ARS were appointed to the TFP. On 30 January the TFP elected Sheikh Sharif Sheikh Ahmed, the

leader of the 'Djibouti wing' of the ARS, as President. Sheikh Ahmed defeated Gen. Maslah Mohamed Siyad (the son of Siad Barre) in a second round of voting by 293 votes to 126.

In February 2009 President Sheikh Ahmed appointed a new Prime Minister, Omar Abdirashid Ali Sharmarke (hitherto Somalia's ambassador-designate to the USA), and on 21 February Ali Sharmarke formed a new Council of Ministers. Former TFP Speaker Sheikh Adan was appointed Deputy Prime Minister and Minister of Finance, while Sheikh Abdulqadir Ali Umar, a senior member of the SSICC, became Minister of Internal Affairs. Nevertheless, fighting continued in Mogadishu, where at least 11 Burundian troops serving with the AMISOM peace-keeping force were reported to have been killed. On 10 March the TFG voted in favour of introducing *Shari'a* law, in an attempt to pacify al-Shabaab insurgents; however, the heavy fighting persisted, and later that month Osama bin Laden, the leader of the al-Qa'ida organization (see Other external relations), released an audio recording urging al-Shabaab to oust the administration of Sheikh Ahmed. In April at least eight people were killed following a mortar attack on the TFP building. (The legislative body had relocated to Mogadishu in March.)

Conflict in Mogadishu

By May 2009 al-Shabaab forces (reportedly supported by volunteer foreign combatants) had seized control of Jowhar and advanced to Mogadishu, prompting large numbers of civilians to flee from the capital. In late May the UN Security Council extended the mandate of AMISOM until the end of January 2010. Some 26 people, including the city's police commander, were killed in clashes between insurgents and government forces in Mogadishu in June 2009; al-Shabaab was also responsible for a suicide bomb attack in the town of Beledweyne, near the border with Ethiopia, which killed at least 30 people, including the Minister of National Security. On 22 June Sheikh Ahmed declared a state of emergency; nevertheless, heavy fighting, also involving AMISOM troops, continued in Mogadishu. In August Ali Sharmarke extensively reorganized the TFG; Abdallah Boss Ahmed, who originated from 'Somaliland', was appointed Minister of Defence, while Ali Jama Ahmed Jengeli became Minister of Foreign Affairs (having held the post under President Yussuf).

In September 2009 al-Shabaab threatened intensive attacks against Western targets, in reprisal for the killing of a prominent al-Qa'ida commander, Saleh Ali Saleh Nabhan, in a military operation by US special forces near the southern town of Baraawe. Two days later, some 15 AMISOM personnel were killed in a suicide bomb attack against AMISOM headquarters. Al-Shabaab secured control of Kismayu in October, following the collapse of its power-sharing agreement with Hizbul Islam (a major insurgent group which had emerged at the beginning of 2009). In early December some 22 people, including three ministers, were killed and 60 others injured in a suicide bomb attack at a graduation ceremony at a hotel in Mogadishu. Public indignation prompted the first ever demonstration against al-Shabaab in Mogadishu, which was organized by Ahlu-Sunna Wal-Jama. The TFG was subsequently reorganized.

Heavy fighting in Mogadishu continued in early 2010, causing the displacement of some 17,000 civilians during January, and further protests against al-Shabaab were staged. On 28 January the UN Security Council issued a resolution extending the mandate of AMISOM for a further year and requesting that the number of troops in the mission (then about 3,700) be increased to its total authorized strength of 8,000. Following negotiations, the TFG reached an agreement with Ahlu-Sunna Wal-Jama in February, whereby the milita group pledged to support efforts to suppress the al-Shabaab insurgency and was to be offered a number of government posts. (The power-sharing agreement was officially signed in Addis Ababa in mid-March.) Also in February al-Shabaab (which was reported to have divided into two factions) announced its alignment with al-Qa'ida.

In mid-May 2010 the TFP convened for the first time since December 2009, although during the session the parliament building came under attack from al-Shabaab and it was reported that at least 24 people had been killed. Nevertheless, proceedings continued and Adan Madobe claimed that a vote of no confidence in Prime Minister Ali Sharmarke had been approved by 280 of the deputies present. However, it was later stated that the motion had actually been taken on Adan Madobe's position and the following day he announced his resignation as Speaker. Ali Sharmarke maintained that he would remain in his post and that President Sheikh Ahmed, who had indicated that he had dissolved the Government, did not have the power to effect his dismissal. Sheikh Ahmed subsequently confirmed that Ali Sharmarke and his Government would remain in office. On 28 May Sheikh Adan was again elected Speaker of the TFP.

Al-Shabaab staged its first attack outside Somalia in July 2010, when bombs were detonated at two locations in Kampala, Uganda, killing 74 people. Al-Shabaab claimed responsibility for the bombings and stated that they were in retaliation for military action by AMISOM Ugandan troops in Mogadishu. On 24 August al-Shabaab, which had threatened to mount a large-scale offensive if the AU proceeded with plans to increase the military strength of AMISOM, attacked the Muna hotel in Mogadishu, killing at least 33 people, including six parliamentary deputies and several government officials; the perpetrators subsequently committed suicide after security forces surrounded the hotel. Later that month al-Shabaab forces fired mortars at the presidential palace, killing four Ugandan soldiers serving with AMISOM. In September numerous attacks by al-Shabaab in Mogadishu included a suicide bomb attack at the airport, in which at least 14 people were killed; Hizbul Islam claimed responsibility for a thwarted suicide attack attempt against the presidential palace.

In early September 2010 Sheikh Ahmed dismissed the Chief of Staff, Gen. Mohamed Gelle Kahiye, following allegations that the latter had sold weapons illegally. On 21 September, with a vote of confidence in him pending, Sharmarke announced his resignation, citing continuing differences with the President. On 14 October Sheikh Ahmed appointed a former diplomat, Mohamed Abdullahi Mohamed, as the new Prime Minister of the TFG. A new, 18-member Council of Ministers formed by Mohamed, in which only Minister of Finance and the Treasury Hussein Abdi Halane retained his post, was approved by the TFP on 27 November. On 22 December, amid continued fighting in Mogadishu, the UN Security Council adopted a resolution authorizing an extension of the existing AMISOM mandate until 30 September 2011 and an increase in the strength of the mission from 8,000 troops to a maximum of 12,000. On 3 February 2011 the TFP voted to extend its legislative mandate (which had been due to expire in August) for a further three years; the UN, the EU, the USA, and other donor states and international organizations expressed concern at the extension of the transitional period. In mid-February a demonstration at the presidential palace in Mogadishu, which had been organized by local authorities in support of peace, was violently dispersed by government troops, resulting in an exchange of gunfire in which three people were killed. (It was estimated that some 22,000 people had been killed in the capital since the concentration of hostilities there.) Sheikh Ahmed replaced all senior security officials in early March.

Meanwhile, in February 2011 government forces supported by AMISOM and ethnic militia launched an offensive in Mogadishu and subsequently succeeded in regaining control of strategic locations. Hostilities had also become concentrated at al-Shabaab bases near the borders with Ethiopia and Kenya, and between al-Shabaab and Ahlu-Sunna Wal-Jama forces in Gedo region, in south-western Somalia, while it was reported that Ethiopian troops were again assisting military action against al-Shabaab. In June an al-Shabaab commander who was also al-Qa'ida's leader in East Africa, Fazul Abdullah Mohammed, was killed by soldiers after failing to halt at a checkpoint near Mogadishu. Later that month several combatants, including two senior al-Shabaab militants, were injured in an attack by a US drone aircraft (the first to be staged in Somalia) on a vehicle near Kismayu.

Increasing regional involvement

In early June 2011 an agreement between Sheikh Ahmed and Sheikh Adan, who had threatened to force the President's resignation by scheduling elections prior to the expiry of the TFG's existing mandate in August, allowed the extension of the tenure of the TFG for a further year. In accordance with the agreement, Ahmed dismissed Abdullahi Mohamed from the office of Prime Minister, prompting protests by civilians and soldiers in Mogadishu. Ahmed's subsequent appointment of Abdiweli Mohamed Ali, hitherto a Deputy Prime Minister and Minister of Planning and International Co-operation, as Prime Minister was approved by the TFP on 28 June. In the same month al-Shabaab claimed responsibility for the assassination of the Minister of the Interior and National Security, Abdishakur Sheikh Hassan Farah, by a female suicide bomber at his residence in Mogadishu. Mohamed Ali formed a Government of completely new ministers, which was approved by the TFP on 23 July.

On 6 August 2011 al-Shabaab unexpectedly withdrew from Mogadishu, ceding most of the capital to government control; its leadership stated that the decision was due to a change in strategy (while the TFG claimed a military victory). At the end of September the UN Security Council adopted a resolution renewing the authorization of AMISOM for a further year. In early October al-Shabaab claimed responsibility for a suicide bomb explosion at an education ministry building in Mogadishu, in which some 100 people were killed, and threatened similar attacks. Later that month 12 members of AMISOM were killed during fighting to expel the final remaining al-Shabaab combatants from Mogadishu. Also in October, following a series of abductions of tourists and aid workers from Kenyan territory that were attributed to al-Shabaab, Kenyan troops were dispatched into southern Somalia where they staged concerted attacks against al-Shabaab bases. The Kenyan Government stated that its military action had been undertaken to prevent the conflict in Somalia from spreading into Kenyan territory, and also claimed that Western states had joined efforts to suppress al-Shabaab operations (after reports of attacks against insurgents by French and US forces). The TFG initially insisted that it opposed Kenya's military intervention; however, at the end of October the Governments of Somalia and Kenya appealed to other states to support them in the conflict against al-Shabaab. In November it was reported that Ethiopian troops were deployed in central regions. Following a request by the AU for a reinforcement of AMISOM (then comprising Ugandan and Burundian soldiers), in December the contingent was strengthened by forces from Djibouti. Later that month Médecins sans Frontières announced its withdrawal from the country, after two of its employees were killed in Mogadishu (and after al-Shabaab had expelled humanitarian aid workers from central and southern regions under its control in the previous month). Meanwhile, on 13 December more than one-half of parliamentary deputies removed Sheikh Adan from the post of Speaker by a vote of no confidence, accusing him of abuse of office after he failed to comply with their demands that he reconvene the TFP. Modobe Nunow Mohamed was elected as Interim Speaker. Supporters of Sheikh Adan, who had boycotted the vote, denounced the motion as illegitimate and fighting between the two factions erupted in the parliamentary chamber.

In early February 2012 it was announced that al-Shabaab had officially joined the al-Qa'ida network. In a resolution adopted on 22 February, the UN Security Council approved an increase in AMISOM troops from 12,000 to 17,731 (authorizing Kenyan troops deployed in the country to be redesignated as part of the mission), and strengthened its mandate to launch offensives against al-Shabaab. (The incorporation of 4,664 Kenyan personnel deployed in Somalia into AMISOM officially took place in July, reinforcing the mission to its authorized strength.) In March a mortar attack staged by al-Shabaab against the presidential palace in Mogadishu killed some six people at a nearby camp for internally displaced people. In early April a bomb attack was carried out at the capital's newly reopened national theatre, during a ceremony attended by Prime Minister Mohamed Ali; at least 10 people, including leading sports officials, were killed. During May government and AMISOM forces succeeded in regaining control of the al-Shabaab stronghold of Afgoye, some 30 km from the capital.

At the end of May 2012 an international conference on Somalia was organized by the Turkish Government, in İstanbul, Turkey; the delegates issued a communiqué which generally reiterated the objectives declared by an earlier conference, held in London, United Kingdom, in February, urging adherence to the transitional programme. In July a UN monitoring group on Somalia released a report warning that systemic corruption and dissension within the TFG could result in a resurgence of al-Shabaab. Consequently, on 25 July the UN Security Council approved a resolution affirming that the transitional period in Somalia would not be extended beyond 20 August.

Recent developments: presidential election and completion of the transitional process

In accordance with the transitional programme, an 825-member National Constituent Assembly, comprising representatives of the major Somali clans, was convened in Mogadishu in late July 2012. A Provisional Constitution, which had been drafted by the TFG in June, was overwhelmingly approved by the National Constituent Assembly on 1 August, with 621 delegates of 645 present voting in favour and 13 against (pending the adoption of a permanent constitution by national referendum). The

Provisional Constitution provided for a bicameral Federal Parliament (replacing the TFP), to comprise a 275-member House of the People and an Upper House, which was to elect a new President. A list of parliamentary members was approved by the National Constituent Assembly (although a number of deputies selected by the Constituent Assembly were rejected by a Technical Selection Committee in consultation with the UN), and a Federal Parliament was officially inaugurated for a four-year term on 20 August. The new members of the Federal Parliament included 30 women, significantly fewer than the proportion of 30% stipulated in the new Constitution. On 28 August Mohamed Osman Jawari, a former Minister of Labour of the Siad Barre period and Chairman of the committee that had drafted the new Constitution, was elected Speaker of the Federal Parliament.

Under the terms specified in the Provisional Constitution for presidential eligibility, candidates were required to be Muslim, over the age of 40 and without a criminal record. Among the most prominent of the 22 candidates who registered to contest the presidential poll were incumbent President Sheikh Ahmed, Prime Minister Abdiweli Mohamed Ali, former Speaker Sheikh Adan and former premier Abdullahi Mohamed. The election of the new President by the Federal Parliament took place on 10 September 2012, at the Police Academy in Mogadishu. Sheikh Ahmed narrowly won the first round, with 64 votes, followed by Hassan Sheikh Mohamud, with 60 votes, and Abdiweli Mohamed Ali, with 32 votes; no candidate therefore securing the necessary two-thirds of votes cast. Abdiweli and a fourth candidate withdrew from the election prior to the second poll. In the second round of voting, which took place on the same day, Hassan Sheikh Mohamud was elected by a substantial margin, receiving 190 votes, while Sheikh Ahmed took 79. Two days after the presidential election, al-Shabaab staged a suicide bomb attack at the Jazeera Hotel in Mogadishu, where Mohamud was holding a press conference; five people, including a member of AMISOM, were killed in the attack. Mohamud was formally inaugurated as President on 16 September, at a ceremony attended by many regional heads of state. On 6 October Mohamud appointed economist and businessman Abdi Farah Shirdon Saaid as the new Prime Minister; his appointment was unanimously endorsed by the Federal Parliament on 17 October. A new Council of Ministers formed by Shirdon (replacing the TFG) was approved by the Federal Parliament on 13 November. Shirdon's Government included two women, notably Fowsiyo Yusuf Haji Aden, who was appointed Deputy Prime Minister and Minister of Foreign Affairs.

Meanwhile, in October 2012 it was announced that a joint offensive by Somali government and Kenyan forces under the command of AMISOM had expelled al-Shabaab from Kismayu, the insurgents' sole remaining stronghold in the south. In early December government and AMISOM forces also regained control of Jowhar. Following a four-month extension in November, in January 2013 the UN Security Council renewed the mandate of AMISOM for a further six months. Also in January French forces launched an air attack against an al-Shabaab base at Bulo Marer, in an attempt to secure the release of a French agent who had been kidnapped in July 2009; al-Shabaab subsequently announced that the hostage had been killed. At the end of January at least six people were killed when a suicide bomb attack was perpetrated amongst a group of security officials outside the Office of the Prime Minister in Mogadishu. On 6 March the UN Security Council approved a relaxation of the armaments embargo that had been imposed on Somalia in 1992; the Somali Government was henceforth permitted to purchase light armaments (with prior notice of at least five days to the Security Council). In April 2013 at least 35 people (including nine assailants) were killed when al-Shabaab militants launched an offensive against the main court buildings in Mogadishu, which was suppressed by AMISOM troops, while two Turkish aid workers were killed in a car bomb attack near the airport on the same day.

The 'Republic of Somaliland'

In May 1993 Egal, who had been Somalia's Prime Minister in 1967–69, was elected as the new President of 'Somaliland'. In June Egal announced the composition of a 14-member council of ministers for 'Somaliland'. By late September a two-year transitional programme for reconstruction had been approved by a 47-member bicameral parliament (comprising a council of elders and a council of representatives). However, the OAU Secretary-General officially rejected the territory's independent status in October. Relations between the Egal administration and UN

officials improved in late 1993, following the assurances of the UN Secretary-General that the mission would not interfere in the region's affairs but would provide funding for reconstruction and the rehabilitation of the police force. Nevertheless, in August 1994 Egal expelled UN representatives from 'Somaliland', accusing them of interfering in internal affairs. This was apparently precipitated by talks between the new UN Special Representative to Somalia, James Victor Gbeho (appointed in July), and Ahmed Ali 'Tur', following the latter's disavowal of secession for 'Somaliland'. In October the rift between Egal and Ahmed Ali 'Tur' culminated in violent confrontations in Hargeysa between military units remaining loyal to Egal and those defecting to support Ahmed Ali 'Tur'. By December it was estimated that three-quarters of the population of Hargeysa had fled. Fighting spread to other parts of 'Somaliland', and in April 1995 government forces were in conflict with combatants from the Garhadji clan who had formed an alliance with Issa militia belonging to the anti-secessionist USF.

In August 1995 four sub-committees were established to draft a new constitution for 'Somaliland'. A provisional document was published in March 1996. Peace talks between the territory's warring factions were conducted in December 1995, and in May 1996 it was reported that rebel armed forces had surrendered their weapons at an official disarmament ceremony in Hargeysa. In February 1997, shortly after it was announced that the constitution had become effective for a three-year interim period, Egal was re-elected (by an electoral college) as President of 'Somaliland' for a five-year term.

At a referendum held in late May 2001, according to official results, 91.7% of the voters in 'Somaliland' approved a new constitution for the territory, which contained a clause confirming the self-declared state's independence. However, the outcome appeared unlikely to persuade the international community to grant recognition to 'Somaliland'. In mid-January 2002 Egal's term of office, which had been due to expire at the end of February, prior to scheduled presidential and parliamentary elections, was extended for one year by the council of elders. In early May, however, Egal died from complications following surgery in South Africa; the Vice-President, Dahir Riyale Kahin, was inaugurated as President of 'Somaliland'. Kahin appointed Ahmed Yusuf Yassin as Vice-President later that month, and in July Kahin announced that a presidential election would be held in January 2003. The election was delayed on a number of occasions, but finally proceeded on 14 April. According to results published by the 'Somaliland' Election Commission, Kahin defeated his nearest rival, Ahmad Muhammad Silanyo, by just 80 votes, securing 42.1% of votes cast. Silanyo immediately contested the result of the election and announced his intention to appeal against the outcome. However, in the following month the 'Somaliland' constitutional court confirmed the legitimacy of Kahin's victory, and he was sworn in as President on 16 May.

On 29 September 2005 candidates from three political parties contested the 82 seats in the House of Representatives. Kahin's Unity, Democracy and Independence Party (UDUB) emerged as the largest of the three parties with 33 seats; the Peace, Unity and Development Party (KULMIYE) won 28 seats and the Justice and Development Party (UCID) 21. At the official opening of parliament in November a disagreement over the election of a speaker developed into a physical confrontation between members of the Council. The role was eventually allocated to Abdirahman Mohamed Abdullahi of the UCID, and in mid-December the 'Somaliland' parliament held its first full session. In March 2009 it was announced that a presidential election, originally scheduled for August 2008 but postponed due to instability in the region, would instead be held in September 2009. In September opposition deputies in the House of Representatives introduced a motion accusing Kahin and members of his administration of 'corruption and constitutional violations' and demanding his impeachment. The election commission announced a further postponement of the presidential election, owing to the continuing unstable conditions and to allow the resolution of the technical issues related to voter registration. UDUB, KULMIYE and UCID agreed to a series of proposals drafted by the international sponsors of Somaliland's election process, whereby changes would be made to the electoral commission and the election date would be established by the commission, after consultation between all three political parties. In May 2010 it was announced that the election was to take place on 26 June. On that day Silanyo was decisively elected with 49.6% of votes cast, defeating Kahin, who received 33.2% of the votes. The new President was sworn in on 27 July. The elections were conducted without incident and were endorsed by international observers. Three countries were represented when Silanyo assumed office: Kenya, Djibouti and Ethiopia. In September the 'Somaliland' parliament voted to extend the mandates of both the upper chamber, the House of Elders, and the House of Representatives, and of appointed municipal and regional representatives, on the grounds that existing conditions did not permit the organization of further elections in the region. An increase in violent incidents was attributed to the emergence of a rebel movement with connections to the Islamist insurgents in southern and central Somalia, which opposed 'Somaliland's secession from Somalia.

From February 2012 a series of clashes were reported between 'Somaliland' forces and local militia in the northern Sool, Sanaag and Ayn regions, which had proclaimed the establishment of an independent state of 'Khatumo'. Somalian President Sheikh Ahmed's stated recognition of 'Khatumo' in March was contested by the authorities of 'Somaliland' and 'Puntland', which laid claim to the regions. In April Silanyo proposed the holding of peace negotiations with regional leaders (but not with a self-declared 'Khatumo' Government). The 'Khatumo' militia attacked 'Somaliland' forces near the northern town of Buhodle during August. However, in early September it was reported that the commander of the 'Khatumo' militia had defected and surrendered to the 'Somaliland' authorities. On 28 November local elections took place throughout 'Somaliland'; international observers reported that the conduct of the polls had been largely peaceful and democratic, although an opposition leader accused the authorities of electoral malpractice and two people were subsequently killed in clashes between police and opposition supporters in Hargeysa.

'Puntland'

In July 1998 Col Abdullahi Yussuf Ahmed announced the formation of 'Puntland', a new autonomous administration in north-eastern Somalia. In August Abdullahi Yussuf, as President of the new administration, appointed a Cabinet, which was subsequently approved by the recently inaugurated 69-member parliament (empowered to act as the legislature for a three-year transitional period, prior to the holding of regional elections). A charter for 'Puntland', released shortly afterwards, precluded 'Puntland' from seceding from Somalia, while it envisaged the adoption of a federal system of national government, with similar regional governments emerging around the country. Hussein Aidid declared his opposition to the administration, accusing the Ethiopian authorities of encouraging 'Puntland' to secede. In late June 2001 Yussuf's mandate was controversially extended for a further three years by the 'Puntland' parliament, at the behest of clan elders. The legality of the decision was challenged by several opposition figures, and the 'Puntland' High Court issued a decree, effective from 1 July, placing all security services and other government institutions under its supervision. The Chief Justice of 'Puntland', Yussuf Haji Nur, subsequently proclaimed himself President of the territory; senior clan elders confirmed Haji Nur as acting President until 31 August. However, Yussuf rejected this decision, and heavy fighting ensued between followers of Yussuf and Haji Nur. In late August a general congress, attended by representatives of all major 'Puntland' clans, opened in Garowe, the region's capital, to elect a new President and Vice-President, as well as members to a new 'Puntland' assembly, and in mid-November Jama Ali Jama and Ahmad Mahmud Gunle were sworn in as President and Vice-President, respectively. In April 2002 Yussuf and Ali Jama met for talks in Ethiopia, but no agreement was reached. Fighting continued in 'Puntland' during 2002 and early 2003, with numerous casualties reported on both sides. In May 2003 Yussuf sought to stabilize 'Puntland' by concluding a power-sharing agreement with opposition forces, under the terms of which opposition members were granted a number of ministerial portfolios. In July 2004, following a presidential decree which reduced the Government's term in office from two years to six months, Yussuf formed a new 15-member Government. In October Yussuf was elected President of Somalia (see above) and Mohamed Abdi Hashi succeeded him as President of 'Puntland' in an acting capacity. In early January 2005 Gen. Mohamud Muse Hersi 'Adde', a former Somali diplomat, secured the support of 35 members of the 'Puntland' parliament, thus defeating Hashi, who won 30 votes, and was elected President of 'Puntland'. Hassan Dahir Afqurac was elected Vice-President.

In late February 2006 an armed confrontation between security forces and a group loyal to the Minister for Planning, Abdirahman Farole, which had occupied the parliamentary building, resulted in at least three deaths. In early March parliament approved a new Cabinet, in which incumbent ministers retained their portfolios, with the exception of Farole, whom Hersi had dismissed following the siege. Meanwhile, in October 2005 it emerged that 'Puntland' had issued mineral and petroleum exploration rights to Range Resources of Australia in an agreement that included the regions of Sanaag and Sool, disputed by 'Puntland' and the neighbouring region of 'Somaliland', prompting vociferous criticism from the 'Somaliland' administration. From September 2004 troops from both regions had reportedly been engaged in heavy fighting near the border between the two self-declared states. In December 2007 Hersi effected a cabinet reorganization, which included the establishment of a new Ministry of Oil and Minerals. In January 2009 the parliament elected Farole as the new President of 'Puntland', with 49 of the 66 members voting for him. Farole named a new Cabinet. Following a process of constitutional review, which had begun under the previous administration, in June parliament officially approved a new constitution, which provided for the adoption of a multi-party system. In November Farole issued a decree appointing his son, Muhammad Abdirahman Farole, as presidential advisor for media services. In December the 'Puntland' parliament adopted a new state flag. In July 2010 a conference, organized by the Hawadle clan, to establish a local administration in Hiiraan, a central region with secessionist aspirations, took place in the Kenyan capital, Nairobi.

In September 2011 some 28 people were killed in clashes in the central town of Gaalkacyo between forces of the 'Puntland' Government and local militias linked to al-Shabaab. On 29 November politicians, civil society representatives and other local leaders signed an agreement with the aim of ending the conflict in Gaalkacyo. In February 2012 a local militant Islamist group led by Sheikh Mohamed Said Atam, which was opposed to the 'Puntland' administration, announced that it had joined al-Shabaab. It was reported that al-Shabaab forces, which had retreated from southern and central Somalia, had established new bases in 'Puntland' during that year.

Foreign Affairs

Regional relations

In April 1988 a decade of hostile relations between Somalia and Ethiopia, following the war in 1977–78 over the Ogaden area of Ethiopia (which is inhabited by ethnic Somalis), ended with a peace accord. It was agreed to re-establish diplomatic relations, to withdraw troops from border areas and to exchange prisoners of war. Following the overthrow of the Mengistu regime in May 1991, the new Government in Ethiopia declared itself neutral with regard to the factions fighting for control of Somalia. Ethiopia hosted peace conferences for the warring Somali factions in 1993, 1996 and 1997. The Egyptian, Kenyan and Libyan authorities also fostered peace initiatives for Somalia from the late 1990s.

Following the outbreak of the Eritrean–Ethiopian border conflict in mid-1998, rival Somali factions were the recipients of increasingly large consignments of weapons from the two warring countries, which sought to secure Somali allegiance to their causes. Growing concern about the activities of Eritrean-supported Somali militias prompted Ethiopia to launch cross-border raids into Somalia against warlords, and in June 1999 the RRA, assisted by Ethiopian troops, captured the town of Baidoa from Hussein Aidid's SNA. Aidid's continuing support of the Eritrean Government and Ethiopian insurgent groups led neutral observers to believe that the conflict was in danger of spreading elsewhere in the Horn of Africa. The Ethiopian Government claimed, however, that its actions were merely attempts to protect the border from attacks initiated by Somali-based rebel opposition groups. In September Ali 'Ato' and Aidid attended a meeting with the Ethiopian Minister of Foreign Affairs, Seyoum Mesfin, in Libya where an agreement was reached whereby Aidid would withdraw support for Ethiopian Oromo rebels in return for Ethiopian disengagement from Somalia. In November the SNA announced that it had disarmed several hundred Oromo Liberation Front (OLF) rebels living in Somalia, had closed down their offices and had asked the OLF leaders to leave the country. It was, however, reported that Ethiopian incursions into Somalia continued in the early 2000s.

In December 2004 a long-term ally of the Ethiopian authorities, Abdullahi Yussuf Ahmed, became President of Somalia (see Domestic Political Affairs). In mid-2006 the forces of the SSICC gained control of much of Somalia, including the capital; in July the SSICC declared a *jihad* on Ethiopia, which it accused of launching a military offensive against Islamist troops. The Ethiopian Government had repeatedly denied any military presence in Somalia, but in October the Ethiopian Prime Minister, Meles Zenawi, announced that his country was 'technically' at war with the Islamist forces. Ethiopian forces increasingly engaged in conflict in Somalia and by the end of that year had assisted government troops in regaining control of much of the country; violence continued, with militant Islamists refusing to participate in peace discussions unless Ethiopian troops withdrew. In November 2008 the Ethiopian Government announced the withdrawal of its troops from Somalia under a peace agreement, and the process was completed in January 2009. However, by early 2011 it was reported that (despite official denials by the Somalian and Ethiopian authorities) Ethiopian troops were again assisting military action against al-Shabaab. At the end of 2012 Ethiopian forces continued to be deployed in central regions of the country, and were reported to control the town of Baidoa.

Amid international concern at the intensifying anti-Government insurgency in 2009, it was widely believed that the Eritrean Government provided support to al-Shabaab and Hizbul Islam, and that senior officers of the Islamist groups had trained in Eritrean camps. In May the AU joined the regional Intergovernmental Authority on Development in urging the imposition of UN sanctions against Eritrea, in reprisal for its assistance of the Somali insurgents and undermining of the Somali peace process. (The Eritrean Government dismissed the accusations and suspended membership of the AU.) In December the UN Security Council adopted a resolution expressing concern at Eritrea's rejection of the 2008 peace accord in Somalia and imposing an armaments embargo against Eritrea, together with travel sanctions against its senior political and military officials. In July 2012 the UN monitoring group on Somalia and Eritrea released a report indicating that Eritrea's military and financial support for al-Shabaab had declined.

Despite the presence of AMISOM peace-keeping forces, which had restored government control in the capital by early 2012 (see above), continuing violence in southern and central Somalia resulted in large displacements. UNHCR estimated that at February 2013 the number of Somali refugees in neighbouring countries had risen to more than 1.0m., including 510,191 in Kenya, 231,327 in Ethiopia and 228,121 in Yemen (with 5,591 arrivals overall since January of that year). The number of internally displaced persons in Somalia (including 'Somaliland' and 'Puntland') totalled nearly 1.4m.

Other external relations

Following the suicide attacks on New York and Washington, DC, USA, on 11 September 2001, for which the US Administration held the al-Qa'ida organization of Osama bin Laden responsible, the USA froze the foreign assets of Somalia's al-Barakat bank, as it suspected that much of the estimated US $500m. remitted from Somalis abroad to the bank was being funnelled to terrorist organizations. Furthermore, al-Ittihad al-Islam was among 27 groups designated as foreign terrorist organizations in September by the US Government, which believed that al-Ittihad al-Islam had links to al-Qa'ida. In November the new Somali Prime Minister, Hassan Abshir Farah, denied that his Government had any links to al-Ittihad al-Islam or to al-Qa'ida and stated that he would not object to the deployment of US troops inside Somalia to monitor and detect alleged terrorist activities. US special forces raided a Mogadishu hospital in March 2003 and seized a suspected al-Qa'ida operative, who was believed to have been involved in the bombing of an Israeli-owned hotel in Mombasa, Kenya, in November 2002, which resulted in the deaths of 18 people. A report published by the UN in November 2003 stated that the al-Qa'ida cell that had launched the attack on the hotel had used Somalia as a base, and warned of the possibility of further acts of terrorism being plotted, after it discovered evidence of attempts by extremist groups to procure weapons in Mogadishu. In March 2006 US naval forces launched a missile attack on the southern town of Dobley, targeting a Kenyan national suspected of involvement with the bombings of the US embassies in Tanzania and Kenya in August 1998, and the November 2002 Mombasa attack.

Following a meeting with the new President, Hassan Sheikh Mohamud, in Washington, DC, in January 2013, US Secretary of State Hillary Clinton announced that the US Administration was to restore official diplomatic relations with the Government of Somalia (the country's links with the international community having been effectively suspended after 1991). In April 2013 US President Barack Obama approved the provision of military assistance to support the efforts of the Somalian Government in combating al-Shabaab operations.

By early 2008 increasingly frequent pirate attacks, particularly in the Gulf of Aden, prompted demands for an international response to the problem. The US and French Governments proposed amendments to international law that would allow naval forces to pursue pirates into Somalia's territorial waters, and arrest and prosecute them. On 2 June the UN Security Council adopted a resolution allowing any state or regional organization, in co-operation with the Somali Government, to enter Somalia's territorial waters in order to combat piracy. Nevertheless, the attacks became increasingly ambitious in scale. In January 2009 some 24 countries formed the Contact Group on Piracy off the Coast of Somalia under the aegis of the UN (which was subsequently expanded to 47 states and 10 international organizations). In November 2010 two British hostages, who had been kidnapped by Somali pirates in October 2009, were released following ransom payments by their relatives. Notable incidents in 2011 included the rescue by a Danish warship in April of 16 Pakistanis and two Iranians, who had been seized from several different vessels captured during 2010, from the custody of pirates off Somalia's coast. In August 2011 Somali pirates seized a tanker off Oman's Salalah port (the first hijacking of an anchored vessel in territorial waters). In September a Danish family and two crew members, who had been taken hostage by pirates in February, were released, following the payment of a ransom. Also in September pirates seized a British woman from a Kenyan coastal resort, after killing her husband; she was released in March 2012, following a ransom payment by her relatives. In a resolution adopted in October 2011, the UN Security Council condemned the increased violence employed by pirates, including the practice of hostage-taking, and proposed the establishment of specialized anti-piracy courts in Somalia and other states in the region. In January 2012 the International Maritime Bureau (IMB) reported that the number of attacks by Somali pirates had increased from 219 in 2010 to 237 in 2011, although the number of successful hijackings had fallen from 49 to 28. The IMB stated that pirate activities had, nevertheless, been restrained by the continued presence of international naval units patrolling the region. In March 2012 the EU extended the mandate of its anti-piracy operation until 2014, and expanded its remit to allow EU warships to attack land, as well as sea, targets. In January 2013 the IMB reported only 75 pirate attacks on ships in Somalia and the Gulf of Aden during 2012, while the number of Somali hijackings had been reduced to 14 in that year.

CONSTITUTION AND GOVERNMENT

On 1 August 2012 a new Provisional Constitution was adopted by the National Constituent Assembly, a body comprising 825 elders representing traditional Somali clans (pending the adoption of a permanent constitution by national referendum). The National Constituent Assembly selected the members of a new Federal Parliament later in August, which elected a new President on 10 September. Under the terms of the Provisional Constitution, there are two levels of government: the Federal Government level; and the Federal Member States level, which comprises the Federal Member State Government and the local governments. Until a region merges with another region (or other regions) to form a new Federal Member State, a region is directly administered by the Federal Government for a maximum period of two years. The Provisional Constitution provides for a directly elected Federal Parliament, comprising a 275-member House of the People and an Upper House of no more than 54 members representing the people of the Federal Member States; the two Houses have a mandate of four years from the day of the announcement of the election results. The Houses of the Federal Parliament elect the President for a term of four years. The President serves as Commander-in-Chief of the Armed Forces and appoints a Prime Minister, who forms a Council of Ministers.

REGIONAL AND INTERNATIONAL CO-OPERATION

Somalia is a member of the African Union (see p. 191) and the Islamic Development Bank (see p. 368).

Somalia became a member of the UN in 1960 and participates in the Group of 77 (G77) developing countries.

ECONOMIC AFFAIRS

In 2011, according to estimates by the UN, Somalia's gross national income (GNI) was US $1,024m., equivalent to $107 per head. In 2010 gross domestic product (GDP) was an estimated $1,067m., equivalent to $112 per head. During 2002–11, it was estimated, the population increased at an average annual rate of 2.3%, according to the World Bank. GDP grew, in real terms, at an average annual rate of 2.8% in 2002–11; growth of 2.6% was recorded in 2011.

According to UN estimates, agriculture (including forestry and fishing) contributed 60.2% of GDP in 2011. According to FAO estimates, 64.1% of the working population were employed in agriculture in mid-2013. Agriculture is based on the breeding of livestock, which accounted for 49% of GDP in 1989 and 38.4% of the total value of exports in 1988. Bananas have traditionally been the principal cash crop, accounting for 40.3% of export earnings in 1988. The GDP of the agricultural sector increased by an average of 2.4% per year in 2002–11; agricultural GDP grew by 2.6% in 2011. Total cereals production rose from an estimated 232,000 metric tons in 2010 to some 272,000 tons in 2011.

According to UN estimates, industry (including mining, manufacturing, construction and power) contributed 7.4% of GDP in 2011, and employed an estimated 12.0% of the working population in 2002. The combined GDP of the mining, manufacturing, construction and power sectors increased by an average of 3.6% per year in 2002–11; growth in 2011 was 2.6%.

Mining (including utilities) contributed 0.7% of GDP in 2011, according to the UN. Somalia's mineral resources include salt, limestone, gypsum, gold, silver, nickel, copper, zinc, lead, manganese, uranium and iron ore. Deposits of petroleum and natural gas have been discovered, but remain unexploited: US petroleum companies were granted exploration rights covering two-thirds of the country by Siad Barre, and were expected to start investigations once there was a durable peace. In February 2001 it was reported that the French petroleum company TotalFinaElf had signed an agreement with the transitional Somali Government to carry out oil exploration in the south of the country. The Canadian company Horn Petroleum Corporation began petroleum exploration in 'Puntland' in January 2012, carrying out the first drilling activity in the region for some 21 years. The Anglo-Turkish company Genel Energy, in co-operation with the British-based company Asante Oil, was due to start exploration for petroleum deposits in 'Somaliland' in the first half of 2013. The combined GDP of the mining and utilities sector increased by an average of 4.3% per year in 2002–11; growth in 2011 was 2.6%.

According to UN estimates, manufacturing contributed 2.5% of GDP in 2011. The most important sectors are food-processing, especially sugar-refining, the processing of hides and skins, and the refining of petroleum. Manufacturing GDP increased by an average of 3.9% per year in 2002–11; growth in 2011 was 2.6%.

According to UN estimates, construction contributed 4.2% of GDP in 2011. The GDP of the sector increased at an average annual rate of 3.4% in 2002–11; growth of 2.6% was recorded in 2011.

Energy is derived principally from oil-fired generators. Imports of fuel products comprised 14% of the value of merchandise imports in 1990.

The services sector contributed 32.5% of GDP in 2011, and engaged an estimated 21.1% of the employed labour force in 2002. Tourism accounted for some 9.3% of GDP in 1988, although since the outbreak of civil unrest there has been little tourist activity in Somalia. The GDP of the services sector increased at an average annual rate of 3.1% in 2002–11; growth of 2.6% was recorded in 2011.

In 1989 Somalia recorded a visible trade deficit of US $278.6m. and there was a deficit of $156.7m. on the current account of the balance of payments. The principal sources of imports in 2009 were the United Arab Emirates (providing 25.1% of the total), Kenya, Ethiopia and Brazil, according to the African Development Bank (AfDB). The principal exports in 1988 were livestock

and bananas. The principal imports were petroleum, fertilizers, foodstuffs and machinery. Livestock and bananas remained the principal exports in the 2000s, while vegetable products and refined sugar were the principal exports in 2009, according to the AfDB.

In 1988 Somalia recorded a budget deficit of 10,009.4m. Somali shillings. A provisional budget for 1991 was projected to balance at 268,283.2m. Somali shillings. Somalia's total external debt was US $2,942m. at the end of 2010, of which $1,990m. was long-term public debt. In 2000–03 the average annual rate of inflation was 10.2%. Consumer prices remained static from 2003 to 2007. The rate of unemployment was estimated at 47.4% in 2002.

Somalia's prolonged civil conflict, together with unreliable climatic conditions, have undermined the traditional agricultural base of the economy. In 2007 the China National Offshore Oil Corporation signed an agreement with the Somali Government that allowed Chinese exploration of any land with potential reserves of natural resources. However, ongoing conflict continued to prevent the development of an economic infrastructure. Meanwhile, a significant increase in piracy off the coast of Somalia from 2008 adversely affected trade (although it was subsequently reported that regional centres, particularly in 'Puntland', benefited from ransom payments). In late 2011 government forces regained control of the capital, Mogadishu, which had been occupied by Islamist insurgent group al-Shabaab. At an international aid conference on Somalia in February 2012, the creation of an international Stability Fund for government-controlled areas was announced and further substantial donor assistance was pledged. In July a UN report indicated that considerable corruption and mismanagement of public assets had taken place under the transitional authorities. The transitional programme was officially completed with the establishment of a Federal Parliament in August and the installation of a new President in September (see Domestic Political Affairs). In November a new Council of Ministers issued a request to the UN Security Council for assistance in recovering public assets and funds that were held abroad, after being frozen by foreign administrations in response to the overthrow of the Somali Government in 1991. Following the wider restoration of government control during 2012, there were indications of a resurgence in commercial activity across the country by the end of that year, including the commencement of petroleum exploration by a number of international companies, with businesses benefiting from the improved security situation. (However, al-Shabaab continued to hold many rural areas, and to stage numerous bomb attacks in Mogadishu.) In December the Federal Parliament approved a revised budget for 2013, which included provisions for an increase in salaries to government forces. The Government announced plans for the adoption of legislation to implement tax collection in all regions of the country, and for the introduction of a new Somali currency, which was being printed in Sudan. In January 2013 the US Administration officially restored relations with the Somali Government, thereby providing for its access to US development assistance to support the reconstruction process; discussions on the prospective cancellation of Somalia's debt arrears to international financial institutions were subsequently initiated.

PUBLIC HOLIDAYS

2014: 1 January (New Year's Day), 13 January* (Mouloud, birth of the Prophet), 1 May (Labour Day), 26 June (Independence Day), 1 July (Foundation of the Republic), 28 July* (Id al-Fitr, end of Ramadan), 4 October* (Id al-Adha, Feast of the Sacrifice), 2 November* (Ashoura).

* These holidays are dependent on the Islamic lunar calendar and may vary by one or two days from the dates given.

Statistical Survey

Sources (unless otherwise stated): Economic Research and Statistics Dept, Central Bank of Somalia, Mogadishu, and Central Statistical Dept, State Planning Commission, POB 1742, Mogadishu; tel. (1) 80385.

Area and Population

AREA, POPULATION AND DENSITY

Area (sq km)	637,657*
Population (census results)†	
7 February 1975	3,253,024
1986/1987 (provisional)	
Males	3,741,664
Females	3,372,767
Total	7,114,431
Population (UN estimates at mid-year)‡	
2011	9,556,872
2012	9,797,444
2013	10,052,842
Density (per sq km) at mid-2013	15.8

* 246,201 sq miles.
† Excluding adjustment for underenumeration.
‡ Source: UN, *World Population Prospects: The 2010 Revision.*

POPULATION BY AGE AND SEX
(UN estimates at mid-2013)

	Males	Females	Total
0–14	2,260,162	2,241,516	4,501,678
15–64	2,603,579	2,674,491	5,278,070
65 and over	123,580	149,514	273,094
Total	4,987,321	5,065,521	10,052,842

Source: UN, *World Population Prospects: The 2008 Revision.*

PRINCIPAL TOWNS
(estimated population in 1981)

Mogadishu (capital).	500,000	Berbera . . .	65,000
Hargeysa . .	70,000	Merca	60,000
Kismayu . . .	70,000		

Mid-2011 ('000, including suburbs, UN estimate): Mogadishu 1,554 (Source: UN, *World Urbanization Prospects: The 2011 Revision*).

BIRTHS AND DEATHS
(annual averages, UN estimates)

	1995–2000	2000–05	2005–10
Birth rate (per 1,000)	45.9	45.7	44.2
Death rate (per 1,000)	17.9	16.2	15.5

Source: UN, *World Population Prospects: The 2010 Revision.*

Life expectancy (years at birth): 51.2 (males 49.6; females 52.8) in 2011 (Source: World Bank, World Development Indicators database).

ECONOMICALLY ACTIVE POPULATION
(estimates, '000 persons, 1991)

	Males	Females	Total
Agriculture, etc.	1,157	1,118	2,275
Industry	290	46	336
Services	466	138	604
Total labour force	1,913	1,302	3,215

Source: UN Economic Commission for Africa, *African Statistical Yearbook.*

2002 (percentage distribution): Agriculture 66.9; Industry 12.0; Services 21.1 (Source: The World Bank and United Nations Development Programme, *Socio-Economic Survey 2002 Somalia*).

Mid-2013 (estimates in '000): Agriculture, etc. 2,605; Total labour force 4,062 (Source: FAO).

Health and Welfare

KEY INDICATORS

Total fertility rate (children per woman, 2010)	6.3
Under-5 mortality rate (per 1,000 live births, 2010) . .	180
HIV/AIDS (% of persons aged 15–49, 2009)	0.7
Physicians (per 1,000 head, 2006)	0.04
Hospital beds (per 1,000 head, 1997)	0.42
Health expenditure (2001): US $ per head (PPP) . . .	18
Health expenditure (2001): % of GDP	2.6
Health expenditure (2001): public (% of total)	44.6
Total carbon dioxide emissions ('000 metric tons, 2008) . .	649.1
Carbon dioxide emissions per head (metric tons, 2008) . .	0.1
Access to water (% of persons, 2010)	29
Access to sanitation (% of persons, 2010)	23

For sources and definitions, see explanatory note on p. vi.

Agriculture

PRINCIPAL CROPS
('000 metric tons, FAO estimates)

	2009	2010	2011
Rice, paddy	16.5	20.4	21.9
Maize	107	120	134
Sorghum	84	90	115
Sweet potatoes	7	9	8
Cassava (Manioc)	84	79	87
Sugar cane	230	230	230
Groundnuts, with shell	5	7	7
Sesame seed	64	76	81
Watermelons	9	11	10
Grapefruit and pomelos . . .	7	7	7
Bananas	42	44	38
Oranges	5	9	10
Lemons and limes	7	7	7
Dates	13	13	13

Aggregate production ('000 metric tons, may include official, semi-official or estimated data): Total cereals 209 in 2009, 232 in 2010, 272 in 2011; Total roots and tubers 91 in 2009, 88 in 2010, 95 in 2011; Total vegetables (incl. melons) 98 in 2009, 114 in 2010, 110 in 2011; Total fruits (excl. melons) 224 in 2009, 230 in 2010, 223 in 2011.

Source: FAO.

LIVESTOCK
('000 head, year ending September, FAO estimates)

	2009	2010	2011
Cattle	4,780	4,800	4,850
Sheep	11,760	12,000	12,250
Goats	11,400	11,500	11,500
Pigs	4	4	4
Asses	22	22	22
Camels	7,000	7,000	7,000
Chickens	3	3	3

Source: FAO.

LIVESTOCK PRODUCTS
('000 metric tons, FAO estimates)

	2009	2010	2011
Cows' milk	452	460	475
Goats' milk	395	501	501
Sheep's milk	466	590	590
Cattle meat	58	59	60
Sheep meat	43	44	44
Goat meat	38	38	39
Hen eggs	2	2	2

Source: FAO.

Forestry

ROUNDWOOD REMOVALS
('000 cubic metres, excl. bark, FAO estimates)

	2009	2010	2011
Sawlogs, veneer logs and logs for sleepers*	28	28	28
Other industrial wood	82	82	82
Fuel wood	13,093	13,501	13,957
Total	13,203	13,611	14,067

* Annual output assumed to be unchanged since 1975.

Source: FAO.

SAWNWOOD PRODUCTION
('000 cubic metres, incl. railway sleepers)

	1973	1974	1975
Total (all broadleaved)	15*	10	14

* FAO estimate.

1976–2011: Production assumed to be unchanged from 1975 (FAO estimates).

Source: FAO.

Fishing

('000 metric tons, live weight, FAO estimates)

	2004	2005	2006
Marine fishes	28.7	23.9	28.7
Total catch (incl. others)	30.0	25.0	30.0

2007–10: Figures assumed to be unchanged from 2006 (FAO estimates).

Source: FAO.

Mining

('000 metric tons, estimates)

	2002	2003	2004
Salt	1	1	1
Gypsum	2	2	2

Source: US Geological Survey.

Industry

SELECTED PRODUCTS
('000 metric tons unless otherwise indicated)

	1986	1987	1988
Sugar*	30.0	43.3	41.2
Canned meat (million tins)	1.0	—	—
Canned fish	0.1	—	—
Pasta and flour	15.6	4.3	—
Textiles (million yards)	5.5	3.0	6.3
Boxes and bags	15.0	12.0	5.0
Cigarettes and matches	0.3	0.2	0.1
Petroleum products	128	44	30

* Data from FAO.

Raw sugar ('000 metric tons): 20 in 2006–09 (Source: UN Industrial Commodity Statistics Database).

Electric energy (million kWh): 311 in 2007; 320 in 2008; 324 in 2009 (Source: UN Industrial Commodity Statistics Database).

Finance

CURRENCY AND EXCHANGE RATES

Monetary Units
100 cents = 1 Somali shilling (So. sh.).

Sterling, Dollar and Euro Equivalents (30 November 2012)
£1 sterling = 39,018.51 Somali shillings;
US $1 = 24,300.00 Somali shillings;
€1 = 31,555.98 Somali shillings;
100,000 Somali shillings = £2.56 = $4.12 = €3.17.

Average Exchange Rate (Somali shillings per US $)
1987   105.18
1988   170.45
1989   490.68

Note: A separate currency, the 'Somaliland shilling', was introduced in the 'Republic of Somaliland' in January 1995. The exchange rate was reported to be US $1 = 2,750 'Somaliland shillings' in March 2000.

CURRENT BUDGET
(million Somali shillings)

Revenue	1986	1987	1988
Total tax revenue	8,516.4	8,622.4	12,528.1
Taxes on income and profits	1,014.8	889.7	1,431.0
Income tax	380.5	538.8	914.8
Profit tax	634.3	350.9	516.2
Taxes on production, consumption and domestic transactions	1,410.4	1,274.2	2,336.4
Taxes on international transactions	6,091.2	6,458.5	8,760.6
Import duties	4,633.2	4,835.2	6,712.1
Total non-tax revenue	6,375.2	8,220.4	7,623.4
Fees and service charges	274.1	576.1	828.8
Income from government property	633.4	656.4	2,418.9
Other revenue	5,467.2	6,987.9	4,375.7
Total	14,891.6	16,842.8	20,151.5

Expenditure	1986	1987	1988
Total general services	11,997.7	19,636.7	24,213.6
Defence	2,615.9	3,145.0	8,093.9
Interior and police	605.0	560.7	715.4
Finance and central services	7,588.3	14,017.8	12,515.6
Foreign affairs	633.0	1,413.9	2,153.1
Justice and religious affairs	248.5	290.2	447.0
Presidency and general administration	93.0	148.0	217.4
Planning	189.0	24.9	24.3
National Assembly	25.0	36.2	46.9
Total economic services	1,927.6	554.1	600.3
Transportation	122.2	95.2	94.5
Posts and telecommunications	94.3	76.7	75.6
Public works	153.9	57.5	69.8

Expenditure—*continued*	1986	1987	1988
Agriculture	547.2	59.4	55.3
Livestock and forestry . . .	459.0	89.5	109.9
Mineral and water resources .	318.8	85.2	93.1
Industry and commerce . . .	131.0	45.1	43.9
Fisheries	101.2	45.5	58.2
Total social services	1,050.5	900.1	930.8
Education	501.6	403.0	478.1
Health	213.8	203.5	255.2
Information	111.5	135.0	145.8
Labour, sports and tourism .	139.6	49.3	51.7
Other	84.0	109.3	—
Total	14,975.8	21,091.0	25,744.7

1989 (estimates): Budget to balance at 32,429.0m. Somali shillings.

1990 (estimates): Budget to balance at 86,012.0m. Somali shillings.

1991 (estimates): Budget to balance at 268,283.2m. Somali shillings.

CENTRAL BANK RESERVES
(US $ million at 31 December)

	1987	1988	1989
Gold*	8.3	7.0	6.9
Foreign exchange	7.3	15.3	15.4
Total	15.6	22.3	22.3

* Valued at market-related prices.

Source: IMF, *International Financial Statistics*.

MONEY SUPPLY
(million Somali shillings at 31 December)

	1987	1988	1989
Currency outside banks . . .	12,327	21,033	70,789
Private sector deposits at central bank	1,771	1,555	5,067
Demand deposits at commercial banks	15,948	22,848	63,971
Total money	30,046	45,436	139,827

Source: IMF, *International Financial Statistics*.

COST OF LIVING
(Consumer Price Index; base: 2000 = 100)

	2001	2002	2003
All items	111.5	133.8	133.8

2004–06: Consumer prices assumed to be unchanged from 2003.

Source: African Development Bank.

NATIONAL ACCOUNTS
('000 million Somali shillings at current prices, estimates)

Expenditure on the Gross Domestic Product

	2009	2010	2011
Government final consumption expenditure	3,430	2,985	2,969
Private final consumption expenditure	28,569	24,839	24,725
Gross fixed capital formation . .	7,863	6,797	6,802
Changes in inventories . . .	22	18	19
Total domestic expenditure .	39,884	34,639	34,514
Exports of goods and services . .	120	104	104
Less Imports of goods and services	661	573	572
GDP at purchasers' values .	39,343	34,171	34,047

Gross Domestic Product by Economic Activity

	2009	2010	2011
Agriculture, hunting, forestry and fishing	20,802	18,075	18,001
Mining and quarrying	233	203	202
Manufacturing	859	746	743
Construction	1,451	1,261	1,256
Trade, restaurants and hotels .	3,671	3,190	3,177
Transport and communications .	3,234	2,821	2,810
Public administration and defence	4,311	3,740	3,724
Sub-total	34,560	30,036	29,914
Indirect taxes (net)*	4,782	4,135	4,133
GDP at purchasers' values .	39,343	34,171	34,047

* Figures obtained as residuals.

Source: UN, National Accounts Main Aggregates Database.

BALANCE OF PAYMENTS
(US $ million)

	1987	1988	1989
Exports of goods f.o.b.	94.0	58.4	67.7
Imports of goods f.o.b.	−358.5	−216.0	−346.3
Trade balance	−264.5	−157.6	−278.6
Imports of services	−127.7	−104.0	−122.0
Balance on goods and services	−392.2	−261.6	−400.6
Other income paid	−52.0	−60.6	−84.4
Balance on goods, services and income	−444.2	−322.2	−485.0
Current transfers received . .	343.3	223.7	331.2
Current transfers paid	−13.1	—	−2.9
Current balance	−114.0	−98.5	−156.7
Investment liabilities	−22.8	−105.5	−32.6
Net errors and omissions . . .	39.0	22.4	−0.8
Overall balance	−97.9	−181.7	−190.0

Source: IMF, *International Financial Statistics*.

External Trade

SELECTED COMMODITIES
(US $ million)

Imports c.i.f.	2007	2008	2009
Vegetables and vegetable products	69	95	173
Vegetables, fresh or chilled . .	0	49	124
Wheat or meslin flour	29	50	31
Refined sugar, solid	53	59	74
Foliage, branches, etc.	29	62	1
Total (incl. others)	920	1,180	1,021

Exports f.o.b.	2007	2008	2009
Livestock	66	55	127
Goats	44	28	48
Sheep	6	11	42
Cattle	16	16	37
Wood charcoal	20	27	16
Gold, waste and scrap	1	27	—

Note: No data were available for total exports (estimated at US $69m. in 2000).

Source: African Development Bank.

SELECTED TRADING PARTNERS
(US $ million)

Imports c.i.f.	2007	2008	2009
Brazil	19	9	58
Ethiopia	73	77	135
Kenya	124	187	145
United Arab Emirates	300	194	256
Total (incl. others)	920	1,180	1,021

Exports f.o.b.	2007	2008	2009
Nigeria	48	7	0
Oman	8	14	63
United Arab Emirates	41	63	81
Yemen	36	43	42

Note: No data were available for total exports (estimated at US $69m. in 2000).

Source: African Development Bank.

Transport

ROAD TRAFFIC
(estimates, motor vehicles in use)

	1994	1995	1996
Passenger cars	2,800	2,000	1,000
Commercial vehicles	7,400	7,300	6,400

Source: International Road Federation, *World Road Statistics*.

SHIPPING
Flag Registered Fleet
(at 31 December)

	2010	2011	2012
Number of vessels	12	12	12
Total displacement ('000 grt)	7.2	7.2	7.2

Source: Lloyd's List Intelligence (www.lloydslistintelligence.com).

International Sea-borne Freight Traffic
('000 metric tons)

	1989	1990	1991
Goods loaded	325	324	n.a.
Goods unloaded	1,252*	1,118	1,007*

* Estimate.

Source: UN Economic Commission for Africa, *African Statistical Yearbook*.

CIVIL AVIATION
(traffic on scheduled services)

	1989	1990	1991
Kilometres flown (million)	3	3	1
Passengers carried ('000)	89	88	46
Passenger-km (million)	248	255	131
Freight ton-km (million)	8	9	5

Source: UN, *Statistical Yearbook*.

Tourism

	1996	1997	1998
Tourist arrivals ('000)	10	10	10

Source: World Bank.

Communications Media

	2008	2009	2010
Telephones ('000 main lines in use)*	100	100	100
Mobile cellular telephones ('000 subscribers)	627	641	648
Internet users ('000)	102	106	n.a.

* Estimates.

2011: Mobile cellular telephones ('000 subscribers) 655.

Source: International Telecommunication Union.

Education

(1985, unless otherwise indicated)

	Institutions	Teachers	Pupils
Pre-primary	16	133	1,558
Primary	1,224	10,338	196,496
Secondary:			
general	n.a.	2,149	39,753
teacher training	n.a.	30*	613*
vocational	n.a.	637	5,933
Higher	n.a.	817†	15,672†

* Figure refers to 1984.
† Figure refers to 1986.

Source: UNESCO, *Statistical Yearbook*.

1990 (UN estimates): 377,000 primary-level pupils; 44,000 secondary-level pupils; 10,400 higher-level pupils.

1991: University teachers 549; University students 4,640.

2006/07 (UNESCO estimates): *Pupils:* Primary 457,132; Secondary 86,929 (General 86,929) *Teachers:* Primary 12,870; Secondary 4,504 (General 4,504 (Source: UNESCO Institute for Statistics).

Pupil-teacher ratio (primary education, UNESCO estimate): 35.5 in 2006/07 (Source: UNESCO Institute for Statistics).

Adult literacy rate (UNESCO estimates): 24.0% in 2002 (Source: UN Development Programme, *Human Development Report*).

Directory

The Government

HEAD OF STATE

President: HASSAN SHEIKH MOHAMUD (inaugurated 16 September 2012).

COUNCIL OF MINISTERS
(May 2013)

Prime Minister: ABDI FARAH SHIRDON SAAID.

Deputy Prime Minister and Minister of Foreign Affairs: FOWSIYO YUSUF HAJI ADEN.

Minister of Defence: ABDIHAKIM MOHAMED HAJI FIQI.

Minister of Justice, Religious Affairs and Endowment: ABDULLAHI ABYAN NUUR.

Minister of Information, Posts and Telecommunications: ABDULLAHI ALIMOGE HIRSI.

Minister of Public Works and Reconstruction: MUHAYADIN MOHAMED.

Minister of Mineral Resources, Water, Energy and Petroleum: ABDIRISAK OMAR MOHAMED.

Minister of Social Development: MARYAM KASSIM.

Minister of Trade and Industry: MOHAMUD AHMED HASSAN.

Minister of Finance and the Treasury: MOHAMUD HASSAN SULEIMAN.

Minister of the Interior and National Security: ABDIKARIM HUSEIN GULED.

In addition, there were five Ministers of State and 19 Deputy Ministers.

MINISTRIES

Office of the President: 1 Villa Baidao, 2525 Baydhabo; e-mail president@president.somaligov.net; internet www.president.somaligov.net.

Office of the Prime Minister: 1 Villa Somalia, 2525 Mogadishu; tel. (5) 543050; fax (5) 974242; e-mail primeminister@opm.somaligov.net; internet www.opm.somaligov.net.

Ministry of Agriculture and Livestock: 1 Villa Somalia, 2525 Mogadishu; internet www.moa.somaligov.net.

Ministry of Commerce and Industry: 1 Villa Somalia, 2525 Mogadishu; internet www.moin.somaligov.net.

Ministry of Constitutional and Federal Affairs: Mogadishu.

Ministry of Defence: Mogadishu; internet www.mod.somaligov.net.

Ministry of Education, Higher Education and Culture: Mogadishu.

Ministry of Finance and the Treasury: 1 Villa Somalia, 2525 Mogadishu; tel. (5) 404240; internet www.mof.somaligov.net.

Ministry of Fisheries, Marine Resources and the Environment: 1 Villa Somalia, 2525 Mogadishu; internet www.mminfisherysom.org.

Ministry of Foreign Affairs: 1 Villa Somalia, 2525 Mogadishu; tel. and fax (5) 424640; internet www.mfa.somaligov.net.

Ministry of Health and Human Services: 1 Villa Somalia, 2525 Mogadishu; tel. and fax (5) 424640; internet www.moh.somaligov.net.

Ministry of Information, Posts and Telecommunications: 1 Villa Somalia, 2525 Mogadishu; tel. and fax (5) 424640; internet www.moi.somaligov.net.

Ministry of the Interior and National Security: 1 Villa Somalia, 2525 Mogadishu; internet www.mois.somaligov.net.

Ministry of Justice, Religious Affairs and Endowment: Mogadishu.

Ministry of Land, Air and Sea Transport: Mogadishu.

Ministry of Minerals Resources, Water, Energy and Petroleum: Mogadishu.

Ministry of Planning and International Co-operation: 2525 Mogadishu.

Ministry of Public Works and Reconstruction: 1 Villa Somalia, 2525 Mogadishu; internet www.mopwh.somaligov.net.

Ministry of Women's Development and Family Welfare: 1 Villa Somalia, 2525 Mogadishu; internet www.mowfa.somaligov.net.

Ministry of Youth, Sports and Labour: 1 Villa Somalia, 2525 Mogadishu; internet www.moys.somaligov.net.

Legislature

FEDERAL PARLIAMENT

Speaker: MOHAMED OSMAN JAWARI.

The Federal Parliament of the Federal Republic of Somalia consists of the House of the People and the Upper House. The term of office of the Federal Parliament is four years from the day of the announcement of the election results. The members of the House of the People shall be elected by the citizens of the Federal Republic of Somalia in a direct, secret and free ballot. The number of ordinary members of the House of the People shall be 225. The House of the People is empowered to pass, amend or reject legislation tabled before it. The members of the Upper House shall be elected through a direct, secret and free ballot by the people of the Federal Member States, and their number shall be no more than 54 members based on the 18 regions that existed in Somalia before 1991. All Federal Member States should have an equal number of representatives in the Upper House. The Upper House represents the Federal Member States, and its legislative duties include: participation in the process of the amending the Constitution; and passing, amending, or rejecting the laws that are tabled before it.

Election Commission

The Provisional Constitution adopted on 1 August 2012 provided for the establishment of a National Independent Electoral Commission, within 60 days of the formation of the Council of Ministers. The Commission was to be responsible for the organization of all elections and was to be composed of no more than nine members.

Political Organizations

Alliance for the Re-liberation of Somalia (ARS): f. 2007; split into two factions in 2008; 'Djibouti wing' led by SHEIKH SHARIF SHEIKH AHMED signed a peace agreement with the TFG, while the 'Asmara wing' led by SHEIKH HASSAN DAHIR AWEYS remained in conflict with the Government.

Islamic Party (Hizb al-Islam): radical Islamist party; Chair. SHEIKH AHMAD QASIM.

Islamic Union Party (al-Ittihad al-Islam): aims to unite ethnic Somalis from Somalia, Ethiopia, Kenya and Djibouti in an Islamic state.

Juba Valley Alliance (JVA): f. 1999; alliance of militia and businessmen from the Habr Gedir and Marehan clans; Pres. BARE ADAN SHIRE.

National Democratic League: Beled Weyne; f. 2003; Chair. Dr ABDIRAHMAN ABDULLE ALI; Sec.-Gen. ABDIKARIM HUSAYN IDOW.

Peace and Development Party (PDP): Mogadishu; f. 2011; Chair. HASSAN SHEIKH MOHAMUD.

Rahanwin Resistance Army (RRA): guerrilla force active around Baidoa; Chair. HASAN MUHAMMAD NUR SHATIGADUD.

Al-Shabaab (The Youth): f. 2007 by former members of the Union of Islamic Courts; Leader IBRAHIM HAJI JAMA.

Somali Democratic Alliance (SDA): f. 1989; represents the Gadabursi ethnic grouping in the north-west; opposes the Isaaq-dominated SNM and its declaration of an independent 'Republic of Somaliland'; Leader MOHAMED FARAH ABDULLAH.

Somali Justice and Peace Party (Tayo Political Party): Maka, al-Mukarrama, Mogadishu; e-mail mqasim@tayoparty.org; internet tayoparty.org; f. 2012; Sec.-Gen. MOHAMED ABDULLAHI MOHAMED 'FARMAJO'.

Somali National Salvation Council: f. 2003; Chair. MUSE SUDI YALAHOW.

Somali Patriotic Movement (SPM): f. 1989 in southern Somalia; represents Ogadenis (of the Darod clan) in southern Somalia; this faction of the SPM has allied with the SNF in opposing the SNA; Chair. Gen. ADEN ABDULLAHI NOOR ('Gabio').

Somali Reconciliation and Restoration Council (SRRC): f. 2001 by faction leaders opposed to the establishment of the Hasan administration; aims to establish a rival national govt; Co-Chair. HUSSEIN MOHAMED AIDID, HILOWLE IMAN UMAR, ADEN ABDULLAHI NOOR, HASAN MOHAMED NUR, ABDULLAHI SHAYKH ISMA'IL; Sec.-Gen. MOWLID MA'ANEH MOHAMED.

Somali Revolutionary Socialist Party (SRSP): f. 1976 as the sole legal party; overthrown in Jan. 1991; conducts guerrilla operations in Gedo region, near border with Kenya; Sec.-Gen. (vacant); Asst Sec.-Gen. AHMED SULEIMAN ABDULLAH.

Somali Solidarity Party: Mogadishu; f. 1999; Chair. ABD AL-RAHMAN MUSA MOHAMED; Sec.-Gen. SA'ID ISA MOHAMED.

Southern Somali National Movement (SSNM): based on coast in southern Somalia; Chair. ABDI WARSEMEH ISAR.

Supreme Somali Islamic Courts Council: formerly the Union of Islamic Courts; seeks to create a Somali state under the guiding principles of *Shari'a* (Islamic) law; Chair. Sheikh HASSAN DAHIR AWEYS.

United Somali Congress (USC): f. 1989 in cen. Somalia; overthrew Siad Barre in Jan. 1991; party split in 1991, with this faction dominated by the Abgal sub-clan of the Hawiye clan, Somalia's largest ethnic group; Leader ABDULLAHI MA'ALIN; Sec.-Gen. MUSA NUR AMIN.

United Somali Congress—Somali National Alliance (USC—SNA): f. 1995 by dissident mems of the SNA's USC faction; represents the Habr Gedir sub-clan of the Hawiye; Leader OSMAN HASSAN ALI 'ATO'.

United Somali Congress—Somali Salvation Alliance (USC—SSA): Leader MUSE SUDI YALAHOW.

United Somali Party (USP): opposes the SNM's declaration of the independent 'Republic of Somaliland'; Leader MOHAMED ABDI HASHI.

Diplomatic Representation

EMBASSIES IN SOMALIA

Note: Following the overthrow of Siad Barre in January 1991, all foreign embassies in Somalia were closed and all diplomatic personnel left the country. Some embassies were reopened, including those of France, Sudan and the USA, following the arrival of the US-led Unified Task Force (UNITAF) in December 1992; however, nearly all foreign diplomats left Somalia in anticipation of the withdrawal of the UN peace-keeping force, UNOSOM, in early 1995. In December 2010 Djibouti reopened its embassy in Mogadishu, while Turkey reopened its embassy in September 2011. In early 2012 the United Kingdom also appointed its first ambassador to Somalia in 21 years, and in April 2013 the British embassy reopened. In early 2013 several other countries, including Italy, Egypt and the United Arab Emirates, announced that they to reopen their embassies in Mogadishu by the end of that year.

Djibouti: Mogadishu; Ambassador DAYIB DOUBAD ROBLEH.

Korea, Democratic People's Republic: Via Km 5, Mogadishu; Ambassador KIM RYONG SU.

Ethiopia: POB 368, Mogadishu; Ambassador ABDULAZIZ AHMED ADAM.

Libya: Via Medina, POB 125, Mogadishu; Ambassador SAID RABIC.

Pakistan: Via Afgoi, Km 5, POB 339, Mogadishu; tel. (1) 80856.

Sudan: Via al-Mukarah, POB 552, Mogadishu; Ambassador FADIL AL-JASULI MUSTAFA.

Turkey: Via Km 6, POB 2833, Mogadishu; tel. (1) 81975; reopened Sept. 2011; Ambassador CEMALETTIN KANI TORUN.

United Arab Emirates: Via Afgoi, Km 5, Mogadishu; tel. (1) 23178.

United Kingdom: Mogadishu; Ambassador MATT BAUGH.

Yemen: K4, Mogadishu; Ambassador AHMED HAMID ALI UMAR.

Judicial System

According to the draft Provisional Constitution adopted on 1 August 2012, the judiciary is independent of the legislative and executive branches of government. No law that is not compliant with the general principles of *Shari'a* (Islamic) law may be enacted. The national court structure shall be of three levels: the Constitutional Court; the Federal Government level courts; and the Federal Member State level courts. The highest court at the Federal Government level shall be the Federal High Court, whilst the highest court at the Federal Member State level shall be the Federal Member State High Court. If a case concerning the Federal Government is presented before a court, the court shall refer the case to a Federal Government level court. If a case concerning a constitutional matter is presented before a court, the court may refer the case to the Constitutional Court. Any court with judicial powers can decide on whether a matter brought before it is a constitutional matter or not, if this will not contradict the exclusive powers of the Constitutional Court. The Constitutional Court is the final authority in constitutional matters and is composed of five judges, including the Chief Judge and the Deputy Chief Judge.

Religion

ISLAM

Islam is the state religion. Most Somalis are Sunni Muslims.

Imam: Gen. MOHAMED ABSHIR.

CHRISTIANITY

The Roman Catholic Church

Somalia comprises a single diocese, directly responsible to the Holy See. The total number of Roman Catholics in Somalia is estimated at only around 100.

Apostolic Administrator of Mogadishu: Mgr Dr GIORGIO BERTIN, POB 273, Ahmed bin Idris, Mogadishu; tel. (1) 20184; e-mail evechcat@intnet.dj.

The Anglican Communion

Within the Episcopal Church in Jerusalem and the Middle East, the Bishop in Egypt has jurisdiction over Somalia.

The Press

The Country: POB 1178, Mogadishu; tel. (1) 21206; f. 1991; daily.

Dalka: POB 388, Mogadishu; tel. (1) 500533; e-mail dalka@somalinternet.com; internet www.dalka-online.com; f. 1967; current affairs; weekly.

Heegan Times (Vigilance): POB 1178, Mogadishu; tel. 6126369706 (mobile); e-mail abdiaziz.hassan@heegantimes.com; internet heegantimes.com; weekly; online newspaper; English; Editor ABDIAZIZ HASSAN.

Horseed: POB 1178, Mogadishu; tel. (1) 21206; e-mail horseednet@gmail.com; internet www.horseednet.com; weekly; in Somali and English.

Huuriya (Liberty): Hargeysa; daily.

Jamhuuriya (The Republic): Hargeysa; e-mail webmaster@jamhuuriya.info; internet www.jamhuuriya.info; independent; daily; Editor-in-Chief HASSAN SAÏD FAISAL ALI; circ. 2,500.

Al-Mujeehid: Hargeysa; weekly.

New Era: POB 1178, Mogadishu; tel. (1) 21206; quarterly; in English, Somali and Arabic.

Qaran Press (Maalinle Madaxbannaan): Mogadishu; tel. (1) 215305; financial information; daily; in Somali; Editor ABDULAHI AHMED ALI; circ. 2,000.

Riyaaq (Happiness): Bossasso.

Sahan (Pioneer): Bossasso; Editor MUHAMMAD DEEQ.

Somalia Times: POB 555, Mogadishu BN 03040; e-mail info@somalpost.com; internet www.somaliatimes.com; Somali; weekly; circ. 50,000.

NEWS AGENCIES

Horn of Africa News Agency: Mogadishu; e-mail info@hananews.org; f. 1990.

Somali National News Agency (SONNA): POB 1748, Mogadishu; tel. (1) 24058; Dir MUHAMMAD HASAN KAHIN.

Publishers

Government Printer: POB 1743, Mogadishu.

Somalia d'Oggi: Piazzale della Garesa, POB 315, Mogadishu; law, economics and reference.

Broadcasting and Communications

TELECOMMUNICATIONS

Following the collapse of the central Government in 1991 there was no authority in place to regulate the telecommunications sector. No licence was required to set up a telecommunications network or provide telephone services. However, in March 2012 the Government endorsed the National Communications Act, which provided for the establishment of a regulatory body for the broadcasting and communications sectors. In early 2012 there were three major telecommunications operators in the country.

Hormuud Telecom Somalia Inc.: Mogadishu; internet www.hortel.net; f. 2002; fixed-line and mobile cellular telecommunications operator.

NationLink Telecom: Mogadishu; internet www .nationlinktelecom.com; f. 1997; fixed-line and mobile cellular telecommunications operator; Pres. ABDIRIZAK IDO.

Somali Telecom (Olympic Telecommunications): Mogadishu.

Somaliland Telecommunications Corpn: Hargeysa; Dir MOHAMED ARWO.

Telcom Somaliland: Telcom Somaliland Bldg, Togdheer St, Hargeysa; tel. (2) 300161; fax (2) 300162; e-mail info@telcomsomaliland .com; internet www.telcomsomaliland.com; f. 2003; provides local, national long distance and int. telecommunications, mobile communications and data services.

BROADCASTING

In 2011 there were some 15 private radio stations operating in Mogadishu.

Radio

Holy Koran Radio: Mogadishu; f. 1996; religious broadcasts in Somali.

Radio Awdal: Boorama, 'Somaliland'; operated by the Gadabursi clan.

Radio Banaadir: Tahlil Warsame Bldg, 4 Maka al-Mukarama Rd, Mogadishu; tel. (5) 2960268; e-mail rbb@radiobanadir.com; internet www.radiobanadir.com; f. 2000; serves Mogadishu and its environs.

Radio Free Somalia: tel. (5) 630838; e-mail admin@ radiofreesomalia.com; internet www.radiofreesomalia.com; f. 1993; operates from Galacaio in north-eastern Somalia; relays humanitarian and educational programmes.

Radio Gaalkayco: operates from 'Puntland'.

Radio Hargeysa, the Voice of the 'Republic of Somaliland': POB 14, Hargeysa; tel. 155; e-mail radiohargeysa@yahoo.com; internet www.radiosomaliland.com/radiohargeisa.html; serves the northern region ('Somaliland'); broadcasts in Somali, and relays Somali and Amharic transmission from Radio Mogadishu; Dir of Radio IDRIS EGAL NUR.

Radio HornAfrik: Mogadishu; f. 1999; commercial independent station broadcasting music and programmes on social issues; Dir (vacant).

Radio Mogadishu, Voice of the Masses of the Somali Republic: southern Mogadishu; f. 1993 by supporters of Gen. Aidid after the facilities of the fmr state-controlled radio station, Radio Mogadishu (of which Gen. Aidid's faction took control in 1991), were destroyed by UNOSOM; broadcasts in Somali, Amharic, Arabic, English and Swahili; Chair. FARAH HASAN AYOBOQORE.

Radio Mogadishu, Voice of Somali Pacification: Mogadishu; f. 1995 by supporters of Osman Hassan Ali 'Ato'; broadcasts in Somali, English and Arabic; Dir-Gen. MUHAMMAD DIRIYEH ILMI.

Radio Mogadishu, Voice of the Somali Republic: Ministry of Information Bldg, nr Villa Somalia, 00252 Mogadishu; e-mail radiomogadishu@gmail.com; internet radiomuqdisho.net; f. 1951; state-owned.

Radio Shabelle: Mogadishu; tel. 7838775880 (mobile); e-mail ali .dahir@shabelle.net; internet www.shabelle.net; f. 2002; Chair. and CEO ABDIMAALIK YUSUF.

Radio Somaliland: internet www.radiosomaliland.com.

Voice of Peace: Galkayo; tel. 90795026 (mobile); e-mail codkanabadda@gmail.com; internet www.codkanabadda.com; f. 1993; aims to promote peace and reconstruction in Somalia; receives support from UNICEF and the AU.

Some radio receivers are used for public address purposes in small towns and villages.

Note: In January 2007 the Transitional Federal Government was granted emergency powers to proscribe four media companies in an attempt to restore order in Mogadishu. HornAfrik Media and Shabelle Media were believed to have ceased operations, although others condemned the ban and refused to close.

Television

A television service, financed by Kuwait and the United Arab Emirates, was inaugurated in 1983. Programmes in Somali and Arabic are broadcast for three hours daily, extended to four hours on Fridays and public holidays. Reception is limited to a 30-km radius of Mogadishu.

Somali National Television (SNTV): Mogadishu; re-launched 2011 after 20 years' hiatus; state-owned; broadcasts 24 hrs a day.

Somali Television Network (STN): Mogadishu; f. 1999; broadcasts 22 channels in Somali, English, French, Hindi, Gujarati, Bengali, Punjabi, Italian and Arabic; Man. Dir ABURAHMAN ROBLEY ULAYEREH.

Television HornAfrik: Mogadishu; f. 1999; broadcasts 6 channels in Somali and Arabic; CEO ALI IMAN SHARMARKEH.

Finance

(cap. = capital; res = reserves; m. = million; brs = branches; amounts in Somali shillings unless otherwise stated)

BANKING

Central Bank

Central Bank of Somalia: 1 Villa Somalia, Mogadishu; tel. (1) 657733; fax (1) 215026; internet www.somalbanca.org; Chair. ABDULLAHI JAMA ALI.

A central bank (with 10 branches) is also in operation in Hargeysa (in the self-proclaimed 'Republic of Somaliland').

Commercial Banks

Commercial Bank of Somalia: Via Primo Luglio, POB 203, Mogadishu; tel. (1) 22861; f. 1990 to succeed the Commercial and Savings Bank of Somalia; state-owned; cap. 1,000m. (May 1990); 33 brs.

Universal Bank of Somalia: Mogadishu; f. 2002; cap. US $10m.; Gen. Man. MAHAD ADAN BARKHADLE (acting).

Private Bank

Somali-Malaysian Commercial Bank: Mogadishu; f. 1997; cap. US $4m.

Development Bank

Somali Development Bank: Via Primo Luglio, POB 1079, Mogadishu; tel. (1) 21800; f. 1968; state-owned; cap. and res 2,612.7m. (Dec. 1988); Pres. MOHAMED MOHAMED NUR; 4 brs.

INSURANCE

State Insurance Co of Somalia: POB 992, Mogadishu; f. 1974; Gen. Man. ABDULLAHI GA'AL; brs throughout Somalia.

Trade and Industry

DEVELOPMENT ORGANIZATIONS

Agricultural Development Corpn: POB 930, Mogadishu; f. 1971 by merger of fmr agricultural and machinery agencies and grain marketing board; supplies farmers with equipment and materials and purchases growers' cereal and oil seed crops; Dir-Gen. MOHAMED FARAH ANSHUR.

Livestock Development Agency: POB 1759, Mogadishu; f. 1966; Dir-Gen. HASSAN WELI SHEIKH HUSSEN; brs throughout Somalia.

Somali Co-operative Movement: Mogadishu; Chair. HASSAN HAWADLE MADAR.

Somali Oil Refinery: POB 1241, Mogadishu; Chair. NUR AHMED DARAWISH.

Water Development Agency: POB 525, Mogadishu; Dir-Gen. KHALIF HAJI FARAH.

CHAMBER OF COMMERCE

Somali Chamber of Commerce and Industry (SCCI): Somali Chamber Bldg, nr Banadir Hotel, Shibis District, Mogadishu; tel. (1) 643081; fax (1) 221560; e-mail info@somalicci.com; f. 1970; Pres. IMAN ALI.

TRADE ASSOCIATION

National Agency of Foreign Trade: POB 602, Mogadishu; tel. (1) 120485; major foreign trade agency; state-owned; brs in Berbera and over 150 centres throughout Somalia; Dir-Gen. JAMA AW MUSE.

UTILITIES

Somali Energy Co (SECO): KM 5, Zobbe St, Wadajir District, Mogadishu; tel. 615589090 (mobile); internet somenergy.com; production and supply of electricity to Mogadishu using diesel generators; privately owned; Gen. Man. ABDURAZAK M. HALANE.

Water Development Agency: POB 525, Mogadishu; Dir-Gen. KHALIF HAJI FARAH.

Transport

RAILWAYS

There are no railways in Somalia.

ROADS

In 2000 there were an estimated 22,100 km of roads, of which some 11.8% were paved.

SHIPPING

Merca, Berbera, Bosaso, Mogadishu and Kismayu are the chief ports. It was reported that the port of Mogadishu, which had been largely closed since 1995, was reopened to commercial traffic in August 2006. There was a large increase in piracy off the coast of Somalia during the late 2000s.

Berbera Port Authority: Berbera; tel. (2) 740198; fax (2) 770224; e-mail bportadm@telesom.net; Gen. Man. ALI OMER MOHAMED.

Somali Ports Authority: POB 935, Mogadishu; tel. (1) 30081; Port Dir AHMED HAGI ALI ADANI.

Juba Enterprises Beder & Sons Ltd: POB 549, Mogadishu; privately owned.

Puntland Shipping Service: Bosaso.

Shosman Commercial Co Ltd: North-Eastern Bosaso; privately owned.

CIVIL AVIATION

There are international airports at Mogadishu, Hargeysa and Bosaso, as well as some 20 smaller airfields throughout the country.

Air Somalia: Mogadishu; f. 2001; operates internal passenger services and international services to destinations in Africa and the Middle East; Chair. ALI FARAH ABDULLEH.

Jubba Airways: POB 6200, 30th St, Mogadishu; tel. (1) 217000; fax (1) 227711; e-mail jubbaair@emirates.net.ae; internet www.jubba-airways.com; f. 1998; operates domestic flights and flights to destinations in Djibouti, Saudi Arabia, the United Arab Emirates and Yemen; Man. Dir ABDULLAHI WARSAME.

Defence

In November 2012 it was estimated that the armed forces of Somalia numbered around 3,200. The total armed forces of the self-proclaimed 'Republic of Somaliland' were estimated to number 15,000, while the armed forces of 'Puntland' were believed to number around 5,000–10,000. The authorized strength of the AU Mission in Somalia in early January 2013 was 17,709 troops (mostly from Burundi, Kenya and Uganda).

Chief of General Staff: Gen. DAHIR ADEN ELMI.

Air Force Commander: NUR ILMI ADAWE.

Navy Commander: Col MUSE SA'ID MOHAMED.

Army Commander: Gen. MUHAMMAD GHELLE KAHIYE.

Commander of Rapid Reaction Forces: Gen. ABDI'AZIZ ALI BARRE.

Education

Following the overthrow of Mohamed Siad Barre's Government in January 1991 and the ensuing internal disorder, Somalia's education system collapsed. In January 1993 a primary school was opened in the building of Somalia's only university, the Somali National University in Mogadishu (which had been closed in early 1991). A number of schools operating in the country were under the control of fundamentalist Islamist groups. According to a UNICEF survey, there were 1,172 primary schools operating in 2003/04, with a total enrolment of over 285,574 children representing a 19.9% gross enrolment ratio (data from Lower Jubba Region, El Waq district of Gedo Region and Jilib district of Middle Jubba Region were not collected). In 2006/07, according to UNESCO estimates, 457,132 children were enrolled at primary schools and 86,929 children at secondary schools.

SOUTH AFRICA

Introductory Survey

LOCATION, CLIMATE, LANGUAGE, RELIGION, FLAG, CAPITAL

The Republic of South Africa occupies the southern extremity of the African mainland. It is bordered by Namibia to the north-west, by Botswana and Zimbabwe to the north, by Mozambique to the north-east, and by Swaziland to the east. Lesotho is completely surrounded by South African territory. The climate is generally sub-tropical, but with considerable regional variations. Temperatures in Cape Town, on the south-west coast, vary from 7°C (45°F) to 26°C (79°F), with an annual average of about 17°C (63°F). Annual rainfall averages 510 mm (20 ins) at Cape Town, and 1,101 mm (43 ins) at Durban, on the east coast. The official languages are Sepedi, Sesotho, Setswana, siSwati, Tshivenda, Xitsonga, Afrikaans, English, isiNdebele, isiXhosa and isiZulu. About 79.4% of the population are black, 9.2% are white, 8.8% are Coloured (of mixed race), and 2.6% are Asian (mainly of Indian origin). Most of the inhabitants profess Christianity, although traditional African religions are still adhered to. There are also small minorities of Hindus (nearly all Asians) and Muslims (mainly Coloureds and Asians). The national flag (proportions 2 by 3) has a green 'Y' shape extending from the upper and lower hoist corners to the centre of the fly end, bordered in white on its outer edges, and in light orange on its inner edges near the hoist; the areas above and below the horizontal band of the 'Y' are red and blue, respectively, with a black triangle at the hoist. The administrative capital is Pretoria, the legislative capital is Cape Town, and the judicial capital is Bloemfontein.

CONTEMPORARY POLITICAL HISTORY

Historical Context

On 31 May 1910 four British dependencies were merged to form the Union of South Africa, a dominion under the British Crown. In 1931 the British Parliament recognized the Union as an independent country within the Commonwealth. From the establishment of South Africa until 1984, national administration was the exclusive preserve of the white population.

The National Party (NP), which acceded to power in 1948, introduced the doctrine of apartheid (in theory the separate, but equal, development of all racial groups, in practice leading to white, particularly Afrikaner, supremacy). The principal opposition to government policy during the 1950s took the form of a campaign of civil disobedience, led by the multiracial African National Congress of South Africa (ANC). In 1959 some members of the ANC formed the exclusively black Pan-Africanist Congress (PAC). In 1960 the ANC and the PAC protested against the 'pass laws' (which required blacks to be in possession of special documentation in designated white urban areas); at one demonstration, in Sharpeville, 67 blacks were killed by security forces, prompting international outrage, and further demonstrations within South Africa, as a result of which the ANC and the PAC were declared illegal. Both movements subsequently formed military wings, based outside South Africa, to conduct campaigns of sabotage. An influential leader of the ANC, Nelson Mandela, was detained in 1962 and sentenced to life imprisonment on a charge of sabotage in 1964, but remained a focus for opposition to apartheid.

On 31 May 1961, following a referendum among white voters in October 1960, South Africa became a republic, and left the Commonwealth. Dr Hendrik Verwoerd was Prime Minister from 1958 until his assassination in September 1966. He was succeeded by the former Minister of Justice, Balthazar Johannes (B. J.) Vorster.

As an integral part of the policy of apartheid, the territorial segregation of African ethnic groups was enforced, on the grounds that the Native Reserves (comprising only 13% of national territory) constituted the historic 'homelands' (Bantustans) of different African nations. In 1963 Transkei was accorded 'self-governing' status, with an Executive Council, headed by a Chief Minister, to be elected by a Legislative Assembly. Bophuthatswana (June 1972), Ciskei (August 1972), Lebowa (October 1972), Gazankulu (February 1973),

KwaZulu (April 1973), Qwaqwa (November 1974), KwaNdebele (October 1977), and KaNgwane (August 1984) were subsequently granted 'self-government'. Transkei was declared 'independent' in October 1976, Bophuthatswana in December 1977, Venda in September 1979 and Ciskei in December 1981. The population of the 'independent homelands' was not entitled to South African citizenship. The 'independent homelands' were not recognized by any government other than that of South Africa.

Domestic Political Affairs

The numerous discriminatory laws regulating the lives of the country's black, 'Coloured' (a term used to denote people of mixed race) and 'Indian' (Asian) populations, combined with stringent security legislation, led to the detention without trial of many of the Government's opponents, the banning of black political organizations outside the 'homelands', and the forced removal of hundreds of thousands of blacks in accordance with the provisions of the Group Areas Act of 1966 (which imposed residential segregation of the races) and the 'homelands' policy. In June 1976 violent riots occurred in Soweto (South-Western Townships), near Johannesburg, and rapidly spread to other black urban areas. Vorster used the executive's virtually limitless powers, conferred by the newly adopted Internal Security Act, to suppress riots and strikes. Several hundred people died in confrontations with the security forces, and many more were detained without trial. Allegations of human rights violations by security forces culminated in international indignation at the death in detention of a black community leader, Steve Biko, in September 1977. In 1978 black, Coloured and Indian activists founded the Azanian People's Organization (AZAPO).

In September 1978 Vorster resigned as Prime Minister, and was succeeded by Pieter Willem (P. W.) Botha, hitherto the Minister of Defence. In February 1981 a new, 60-member advisory body, the President's Council, comprising representatives of the white, Coloured and Indian population, was formed to consider constitutional reform. Its recommendations to include Coloureds and Indians (but not blacks) in a three-chamber Parliament, with a multiracial government (led by an executive President), exacerbated inter-party differences: the 'verligte' (liberal) wing of the NP, led by Botha, advocated the establishment of a confederation of South Africa and the 'homelands', with separate citizenships but a common South African nationality, and was strongly opposed by the 'verkrampte' (uncompromising) wing of the party.

Constitutional reforms were approved by the House of Assembly in September 1983, and by about 66% of voters in an all-white referendum in November. In the same month the Progressive Federal Party (PFP) decided to take part in the reformed system. However, six 'homeland' leaders, including Chief Mangosuthu Gatsha Buthelezi, the Chief Minister of KwaZulu (who had consistently opposed the 'homelands' policy), rejected the constitutional reforms on the grounds that blacks remained excluded from participation in the central Government. Despite a previous pledge by the Prime Minister to assess Coloured and Indian opinion on the reforms, elections to the Coloured and Indian chambers of the new Parliament, known as the House of Representatives and the House of Delegates, respectively, took place in August 1984, without prior referendums. As a result, the boycott that had been organized by the principal legal opposition movement, the United Democratic Front (UDF), was widely observed: about 18% of the eligible Coloured population voted in the elections to the House of Representatives, with the Coloured Labour Party (LP) winning 76 of the 80 directly elected seats, while only 16.6% of eligible Indian voters participated in the elections to the House of Delegates, with the National People's Party (NPP) winning 18 and the Solidarity Party 17 of the 40 directly elected seats. (The House of Assembly, as elected in 1981, remained in office.)

The new Constitution came into effect in September 1984. Under its terms, legislative power was vested in the State President and the tricameral Parliament, comprising the 178-member House of Assembly (for the representation of whites), the 85-member House of Representatives (for Coloureds) and the 45-member House of Delegates (for Indians). The post of Prime Minister was abolished and Botha was unanimously elected to the new office of State President (which combined the powers of Head of State and Prime Minister) by an electoral college, comprising members of all three parliamentary chambers. A President's Council, a new Cabinet and three Ministers' Councils (one for each population group) were subsequently established. The Cabinet comprised only two non-white members, the Chairmen of the Indian and Coloured Ministers' Councils, neither of whom was given a portfolio.

During 1985–86 a number of the laws on which apartheid was based were modified or repealed, prompting strong right-wing opposition. The Immorality Act (1927) and the Prohibition of Mixed Marriages Act (1949), which banned sexual relations and marriage between members of different races, were repealed in April 1985, and in the following month it was announced that the Prohibition of Political Interference Act (1967), prohibiting members of different racial groups from belonging to the same political party, was to be abrogated. In April 1986 the Government promulgated legislation that provided for the removal of a number of restrictions on the movement, residence and employment of blacks in white urban areas. On 1 July the 'pass laws' were officially repealed, with the introduction of uniform identity documents for all South African citizens. On the same day reforms concerning the structure of local and provincial government were implemented, and legislation granting blacks limited rights to own property in black urban areas entered into force. In the same month it was announced that citizens of the four 'independent homelands' who were residing and working permanently in South Africa were to regain South African citizenship; in effect, however, only a small proportion of the population of the 'homelands' was eligible. Following discussions, initiated by Buthelezi in April 1986, regarding the establishment of a joint authority for his 'homeland', KwaZulu, and the province of Natal, the Government agreed to the formation of an administrative body, the Joint Executive Authority (which was installed in November 1987).

The introduction of the new Constitution in September 1984 prompted severe rioting in the black townships. Factional clashes within the black community also occurred, notably between supporters of the ANC and of the Inkatha Movement, a Zulu organization led by Buthelezi. In July 1985 the Government declared a state of emergency in 36 districts; by March 1986 it was estimated that 757 people had been killed, and almost 8,000 arrested. In June of that year Botha declared a nation-wide state of emergency, on the grounds that national security was endangered by subversive elements. Press censorship subsequently became progressively stricter, and the powers of the security forces were extended. Opposition to the Government emerged from the influential Congress of South African Trade Unions (COSATU).

In January 1989 Botha withdrew from his official duties, owing to ill health; in February he resigned as leader of the NP, and was succeeded by Frederik Willem (F. W.) de Klerk, hitherto Minister of National Education. Despite almost unanimous demands from the party that he should share power with de Klerk before retiring at the next general election, Botha refused to allow his power as State President to be eroded, and in March he resumed his official duties. In April the PFP, the Independent Party (which had been formed by one of a number of 'verligte' defectors from the NP in 1988) and the National Democratic Movement (established by dissident PFP members in late 1987) merged to form the Democratic Party (DP).

The state of emergency was extended for a further 12 months in June 1989. In August Botha claimed that members of his Cabinet had omitted to inform him of a prospective visit by de Klerk to Zambia to meet with President Kenneth Kaunda (which he opposed, owing to Kaunda's support for the ANC). Following a confrontation with the Cabinet, Botha resigned as State President. Shortly afterwards de Klerk was appointed acting President.

Elections to the three Houses of Parliament took place in September 1989. The NP won 93 of the 166 elective seats in the House of Assembly, while the Conservative Party (CP) secured 39 seats, and the DP 33 seats. Less than 12% of the Coloured electorate voted in the general election to the House of Representatives, at which the LP won 69 of the 80 directly elective seats. Some 20% of the Indian electorate voted in the general election to the House of Delegates: the Solidarity Party secured 16 of the 40 directly elective seats, while the NPP won nine. In

mid-September, following his inauguration as State President, de Klerk stated that the implementation of constitutional reforms was his highest priority.

The release of Nelson Mandela

On 2 February 1990 de Klerk announced several radical reforms, including the legalization of the ANC, the PAC, the South African Communist Party (SACP), the UDF and more than 30 other banned political organizations. Mandela and a further 120 political prisoners were to be released unconditionally. In addition, most emergency regulations restricting the media were to be removed, as were repressive measures imposed on former political detainees; detention without trial was to be limited to a maximum of six months. De Klerk confirmed that the Government intended to initiate negotiations with the black opposition, with the aim of drafting a new democratic constitution. Leaders of the extreme right-wing parties reacted to de Klerk's reforms with threats of violence.

Mandela's release from prison, on 11 February 1990, received much international attention. In March he was elected Deputy President of the ANC. In spite of appeals by Mandela for reconciliation between rival factions within the black community, the continuing violence in Natal between supporters of the Inkatha Movement and mainly Xhosa-speaking supporters of the ANC intensified in March and April, and unrest erupted in several black townships. In May legislation was introduced that granted temporary immunity from prosecution to political exiles who had committed crimes, including leaders of the ANC. In July Buthelezi reconstituted the Inkatha Movement as the Inkatha Freedom Party (IFP), in order to participate in future constitutional negotiations. The following month the ANC and the Government reached an agreement whereby, in preparation for constitutional negotiations, the ANC was to suspend its guerrilla activities, and the Government was to release more than 3,000 political prisoners and to facilitate the return to South Africa of an estimated 40,000 exiles. However, the ANC subsequently continued to train recruits for its military wing (Umkhonto we Sizwe—MK) and to stockpile ammunition, thereby contravening the terms of its cease-fire and causing the Government to delay the release of political prisoners and the repatriation of exiles.

During August 1990 factional fighting between supporters of the IFP and of the ANC escalated in the black townships surrounding Johannesburg; more than 500 people were reported to have been killed by the end of that month. Nevertheless, in October the state of emergency was revoked in Natal. (It had been revoked in all other provinces in June.) Also that month the Separate Amenities Act of 1953 (which had imposed racial segregation with regard to public amenities) was repealed, prompting right-wing protests, particularly from the Afrikaner Weerstandsbeweging (AWB), a paramilitary organization that had been formed in 1973 under the leadership of Eugene Terre'Blanche. During October the NP opened its membership to all races.

In February 1991 de Klerk announced that he was to introduce draft legislation to repeal the principal remaining apartheid laws: the Land Acts of 1913 and 1936 (which stipulated that the black population was entitled to own only 13.6% of the land), the Group Areas Act, the Black Communities Act of 1984 (which enforced the separate status of black townships) and the Population Registration Act of 1950 (which decreed that all South Africans should be registered at birth according to race) were subsequently abolished. In the same month the Government agreed to assume joint administrative powers in Ciskei, following increasing pressure within the 'independent homeland' for its reincorporation into South Africa and for the resignation of its military ruler. In mid-February the Government and the ANC reached agreement on the release of political prisoners, the return of exiles and the curtailment of activities by the MK. However, increasing township violence continued to impede constitutional negotiations.

In July 1991, at a national congress of the ANC, Mandela was elected as its President and Cyril Ramaphosa, hitherto leader of the National Union of Mineworkers, was elected Secretary-General of the organization. A multi-party conference on South Africa's future, the Convention for a Democratic South Africa (CODESA), was convened in December. CODESA was attended by the Government and 18 political organizations, including the ANC, the NP, the DP, the LP, the NPP, New Solidarity (formerly the Solidarity Party) and representatives of the 'homelands' (including the IFP, which represented KwaZulu); the conference was boycotted by the PAC, AZAPO and the CP. The negotiating body's stated aim to create an undivided South Africa was rejected by the IFP, which favoured the concept of a South African federation of independent states, and by the Bophuthatswana administration, which demanded total independence from South Africa.

In mid-1992 the ANC announced that it was to organize a series of demonstrations in protest against 'homeland' leaders who wished their territories (Bophuthatswana, Ciskei, KwaZulu and Qwaqwa) to retain a strong measure of autonomy in the future South Africa. In September Ciskei security forces killed 28 ANC demonstrators, and injured about 200, prompting international outrage. The ANC accused the South African security forces (some of whose members had been seconded to Ciskei) of complicity in the incident. In mid-September de Klerk announced that measures to reduce the 'independence' of the 'homelands' would be implemented. In late 1992 the leaders of Bophuthatswana, Ciskei and KwaZulu formed a pressure group (the Concerned South Africans Group—COSAG) to campaign for a maximum degree of regional autonomy.

In March 1993 it was decided that CODESA was to be reconstituted, with the PAC, the IFP and the CP granted equal status with the other representatives, and in June 1993 legislation providing for the abolition of the President's Council was approved by Parliament. The IFP, CP and KwaZulu delegations subsequently withdrew from the negotiating forum, while the remaining representatives continued discussions on the precepts of a multiracial interim Constitution. The interim Constitution, promulgated in July, entrenched equal rights for citizens regardless of race, and vested executive power in a President and a Cabinet, which was to comprise representatives of the political parties that held a stipulated number of seats in the legislature. Legislative authority was vested in a bicameral Parliament, comprising a 400-member National Assembly (to be elected by proportional representation) and a Senate (with 10 members elected by each regional legislature). The National Assembly and Senate formed the Constitutional Assembly, which was to draft a new constitution, with adherence to the principles stipulated by the negotiating forum. Although the interim Constitution included provisions for the establishment of regional legislatures, it was rejected by COSAG (while the IFP, KwaZulu and CP delegations continued to boycott negotiations).

In early September 1993 the negotiating forum approved legislation providing for the establishment of a multiracial Transitional Executive Council (TEC), which was to rule in conjunction with the existing Government pending the elections, thereby allowing blacks to participate in central government for the first time. The TEC was to comprise representatives of the groups involved in the negotiating process; however, the IFP, the CP, the governments of Bophuthatswana, Ciskei and KwaZulu, and the PAC refused to participate. Later in September Parliament adopted legislation providing for the installation of the TEC, and the establishment of an Independent Electoral Commission (IEC), and an independent media commission and broadcasting authority.

In October 1993 the constituent members of COSAG, together with the Afrikaner Volksfront (AVF—an informal alliance of right-wing organizations), formed the Freedom Alliance (FA), with the stated objective of negotiating concessions regarding regional autonomy. The Bophuthatswana and Ciskei delegations subsequently withdrew from the negotiating forum. In November the negotiating forum repealed legislation providing for detention without trial. Later that month agreement was reached regarding the establishment of a new security force, which was to be under the control of both central and provincial government, and a reconstituted national defence force, which was to comprise members of the existing armed forces of South Africa and the 'independent homelands', and the military wings of political organizations.

Approval of the new Constitution

On 18 November 1993, following intensive discussions, 19 of the 21 delegations remaining in the negotiating forum approved the interim Constitution, which incorporated several amendments to the draft promulgated in July. A number of significant compromises between the Government and the ANC had been achieved: the Government abandoned its demand that cabinet decisions require a two-thirds' majority (thereby accepting that power-sharing would not be constitutionally entrenched), while the ANC agreed to a fixed five-year period for transition to majority rule. The President was to be elected by the National Assembly, and was to exercise executive power in consultation with at least two Deputy Presidents, who were to be nominated by parties with a minimum of 80 seats in the National Assembly

(equivalent to 20% of the national vote). A Constitutional Court was to be appointed by the President from a list of candidates nominated by an independent judicial commission. As a concession to the FA, the interim Constitution included a provision that entitled the legislatures of the nine redesignated provinces to draft their own constitutions, subject to the principles governing the national Constitution. Nevertheless, the FA, together with the PAC, rejected the interim Constitution.

In early December 1993 the negotiating forum reached agreement on the reincorporation of the four 'independent homelands' into South Africa on 27 April 1994, when the interim Constitution was to enter into force. On 1 January South African citizenship was to be restored to the population of the 'homelands', who would be entitled to vote in the elections. However, the governments of Bophuthatswana and Ciskei refused to recognize the decision. On 7 December 1993 the TEC commenced sessions, but was, as expected, boycotted by a number of delegations. In mid-December the IEC was established. On 22 December Parliament ratified the interim Constitution, thereby effecting its own dissolution as an organ of the apartheid regime.

In February 1994, in accordance with a decision by the TEC, de Klerk announced that the elections, which were to be monitored by international observers, would take place between 26 and 28 April. The IFP confirmed that it intended to boycott the elections, after the Zulu tribal monarch, King Goodwill Zwelithini (who was Buthelezi's nephew), rejected the interim Constitution and declared sovereignty over the territory traditionally owned by the Zulus. In mid-February Nelson Mandela announced a number of proposed amendments to the interim Constitution. The FA, however, rejected the concessions, on the grounds that the powers of regional government remained inadequate, and refused to attend discussions on the proposed amendments, which were, nevertheless, adopted by the negotiating forum. In early March, after the ANC and IFP agreed to accept international mediation regarding the issue of regional autonomy, Buthelezi announced that he was to register the IFP provisionally to contest the elections. The IFP, however, failed to present a list of candidates by the stipulated date, while Zwelithini continued to urge his followers to boycott the elections.

In March 1994 the President of Bophuthatswana, Lucas Mangope (a member of the FA), announced that the population of the 'homeland' would not participate in the elections. Following widespread protests in Bophuthatswana, Mangope fled from the capital, Mmabatho, after disaffected members of the security forces demanded that he allow participation in the elections and refused to take action against the demonstrators. At the apparent instigation of the AVF, some 5,000 armed right-wing extremists, principally members of the AWB, entered Bophuthatswana and occupied Mmabatho, with the aim of reinstating Mangope. Shortly afterwards the Government dispatched some 2,000 members of the armed forces to Bophuthatswana, which, together with disaffected local troops, regained control of the 'homeland'. The Government and the TEC formally deposed Mangope, whose removal signified the effective dissolution of the FA. Later in March members of the armed forces were deployed in Ciskei to maintain civil order, following the resignation of the 'homeland's' military ruler in response to a strike by reformist members of the security forces. (The TEC and the Government assumed joint responsibility for administration in Bophuthatswana and Ciskei pending the elections.)

In April 1994 an agreement was reached whereby the IFP was to participate in the elections, in exchange for guarantees that the institutions of the Zulu monarch and kingdom were to be recognized in the interim Constitution. Under the terms of a proposed draft constitution for KwaZulu/Natal (as Natal had been redesignated in February), the Zulu monarch was to be granted additional territorial powers and sovereignty with regard to traditional law and custom. However, the AVF announced that it would continue to boycott the elections. In April Terre'Blanche threatened that a campaign of recent bomb attacks would continue unless the Government acceded to demands for Afrikaner self-determination. Under the terms of an accord between the Government, the ANC and the Freedom Front (FF)—led by Gen. (retd) Constand Viljoen—earlier in April, the level of support for the FF in the elections was to be used to determine whether a separate Afrikaner state might be established in any region with the approval of the majority of the resident population.

On 27 April 1994 the interim Constitution came into force, with voting commencing on the previous day, as scheduled.

Although a number of reports of electoral malpractice emerged, the IEC declared that the elections had been free and fair. The promulgation of the official results was delayed, owing, in part, to disputed ballots in KwaZulu/Natal; following negotiations between the IFP and the ANC, it was agreed that the IFP would be allocated 50.3% of the vote in the province, thereby allowing it a majority of one seat in the regional legislature. On 2 May, after partial results indicated a substantial majority in favour of the ANC, de Klerk conceded defeat, prompting widespread jubilation. Shortly afterwards it was announced that the ANC had secured 62.7% of votes cast, while the NP had won 20.4%, the IFP 10.5% and the FF 2.2%. Consequently, the ANC narrowly failed to obtain a parliamentary majority of two-thirds, which, under the terms of the interim Constitution, would have allowed its members to draft and adopt the new constitution without consulting other parties. The NP, which secured a majority in the province of Northern Cape, received the stipulated percentage of the national vote entitling it to nominate a Deputy President. Mandela subsequently appointed a senior official of the ANC, Thabo Mbeki, as First Deputy President, while de Klerk was nominated as Second Deputy President.

The Mandela presidency

Mandela was officially elected as President by the National Assembly on 9 May 1994, and was inaugurated on the following day at a ceremony that was attended by a large number of international heads of state. A Cabinet of National Unity, comprising 18 representatives of the ANC, six of the NP and three of the IFP, was subsequently formed, with Buthelezi allocated the portfolio of home affairs. Later in May the provincial legislatures elected a 90-member Senate, comprising 60 representatives of the ANC, 17 of the NP, five of the IFP and FF, respectively, and three of the DP. The ANC thus held a slightly higher majority in the Constitutional Assembly than in the National Assembly, but failed, nevertheless, to obtain a two-thirds' majority. The Secretary-General of the ANC, Cyril Ramaphosa, was subsequently elected Chairman of the Constitutional Assembly.

The new Government adopted a Reconstruction and Development Programme (RDP), which comprised extensive measures for social and economic development. The Government also announced plans to establish a 'Truth and Reconciliation Commission' (TRC), composed of eminent citizens, which would investigate violations of human rights perpetrated under the apartheid regime; the TRC was to be empowered to grant indemnity to individuals who confessed to politically motivated crimes committed before 5 December 1993 (when the TEC was effectively installed). Although the FF had failed to obtain the level of support in the elections stipulated as a precondition to the consideration of its demands, the Government subsequently agreed to the establishment of a 'volkstaat council', in which Viljoen and other right-wing Afrikaners were to debate the issue of self-determination. Meanwhile, it was disclosed that de Klerk had authorized the transfer of state-owned land (comprising one-third of the territory of KwaZulu/Natal) to Zwelithini shortly before the elections. The ANC denied knowledge of the agreement.

In June 1994 it was announced that the new South African National Defence Force (SANDF) was to be constituted over a period of three years. In mid-June a cabinet committee decided that Zwelithini was to remain the statutory trustee of the territory in KwaZulu/Natal that had been transferred to his control prior to the elections. In September the Government officially ended the state of emergency in KwaZulu/Natal that had been imposed in March. In October the IFP majority in the provincial legislature of KwaZulu/Natal adopted legislation that provided for the establishment of an advisory council of Zulu chiefs, the House of Traditional Leaders, in which Zwelithini would be equal in status to other chiefs (including Buthelezi).

In November 1994 the Government adopted legislation that formally restored the rights of land ownership to members of the black population who had been dispossessed following the introduction of discriminatory legislation beginning in 1913; the Restitution of Land Rights Act provided for the establishment of a special commission and court to investigate and arbitrate claims.

In January 1995 the National Intelligence Service (NIS) was replaced with two new bodies, incorporating elements of the ANC's security department and agencies of the former 'homelands': the South African Secret Service, under the command of the former head of the NIS, was to control international intelligence, while the National Intelligence Agency (NIA), headed by a former ANC security official, was to be responsible for internal

intelligence. In the same month, amid reports of increasing political violence between ANC and IFP supporters in KwaZulu/Natal, Buthelezi was elected Chairman of the House of Traditional Leaders.

An 11-member Constitutional Court was installed in February 1995; the Court was to ensure that the executive, legislative and judicial organs of government adhered to the principles entrenched in the interim Constitution, and was to endorse a final constitutional text with respect to these principles. In the same month Mandela confirmed that he would not contest the elections in 1999.

At a party conference on constitutional policy in April 1995, the ANC rejected NP proposals that the principle of power-sharing be entrenched in the final constitution, thereby extending the tenure of the coalition Government. The conference also failed to accept IFP demands for international mediation on regional autonomy, and adopted constitutional proposals that provided for a Senate comprising members of provincial legislatures, which would be empowered to veto provincial legislation. Buthelezi subsequently suspended IFP participation in the Constitutional Assembly, and indicated that the IFP would not accept a constitution that had been drafted by the remaining parties in the Assembly. In late May Mandela consented to foreign mediation on constitutional discussions. In the same month the National Assembly approved draft legislation providing for the establishment of the TRC; only the FF deputies opposed the enactment of the legislation.

At the local elections, which took place in most parts of the country on 1 November 1995, the ANC secured 66.4% of the votes cast and the majority of the seats on the local councils, while the NP won 16.2% and the FF 4.0%. Elections in KwaZulu/Natal were postponed until March 1996, owing to continuing violence in the region. Voting took place in some parts of Western Cape, but not in the metropolitan area of Cape Town, nor in some rural areas of the province, as a result of delays in the demarcation of electoral boundaries. After further delays, the local elections in KwaZulu/Natal took place on 26 June, amid relative calm. The IFP won the largest share (44.5%) of the votes cast.

Meanwhile, in November 1995 Gen. Magnus Malan, the Minister of Defence in 1980–91, and a further 10 prominent officials in the former armed forces, were arrested on charges relating to the killing of 13 people in KwaMakutha (south of Durban) in 1987; they were accused of involvement in the establishment in 1985 of a military camp in Namibia where IFP commandos were trained to perpetrate attacks on prominent ANC supporters. Mandela was accused by members of the NP and FF of political bias in his refusal to grant temporary indemnity to the accused until their cases could be heard by the TRC, which was to commence sessions in April 1996. (In late November 1995 Archbishop Desmond Tutu was appointed as Chairman of the Commission.) Buthelezi was cited in the indictment as having in 1985 requested the assistance of the security forces in creating paramilitary units to combat the ANC.

The Truth and Reconciliation Commission

The trial of Gen. Malan and his 19 co-defendants began in Durban in early March 1996. (In May charges were abandoned against three of the former security force commanders, owing to insufficient evidence.) In mid-March the Government withdrew indemnity from prosecution that had been granted by de Klerk's Government to 73 ANC members, including Mbeki and Joe Modise. In April the TRC, comprising Archbishop Tutu and 16 other members drawn from all racial groups and a variety of professions, commenced hearings, which were to continue for up to two years. The Commission was empowered to grant judicial amnesties to perpetrators of human rights violations committed during the apartheid era, if it was satisfied that a full disclosure had been made and that the crime in question had been politically motivated (depending on the gravity of the crime). The TRC was also to advise on appropriate reparations to the victims (or to their families) of crimes committed.

On 8 May 1996 Parliament approved the final version of the Constitution, with the NP voting in favour, in spite of its reservations over some provisions. The IFP maintained its boycott of the Constitutional Assembly, while the 10 FF deputies abstained; only the two deputies of the African Christian Democratic Party (ACDP) voted against the adoption of the Constitution. The new Constitution incorporated an extensive Bill of Rights, and provided for the establishment of a commission to guarantee the rights of the white minority. A National Council of Provinces was to replace the existing Senate, and was designed to increase the influence of the provinces on the policy of the central Government (although falling short of the provincial powers demanded by the IFP). De Klerk subsequently announced that the NP was to withdraw from the Government of National Unity, attributing the decision to the diminishing influence of his party on government policy, the refusal of the ANC to include power-sharing arrangements in the new Constitution, and the necessity, in the interests of democracy, for an effective opposition. The NP later withdrew from all the Provincial Governments except for that of Western Cape (where it was in the majority). Mandela appointed members of his own party to the ministerial portfolios vacated by NP members and abolished the position of Second Deputy President.

In August 1996 de Klerk apologized before the TRC for the suffering that the apartheid policies of the NP had caused, but denied that any violations of human rights had been authorized during his time in government. Also in late August Eugene de Kock, a former commander of the notorious counter-insurgency 'hit squad', the Vlakplaas, was convicted of 89 charges relating to the activities of the unit, including six charges of murder. In September de Kock detailed to the Supreme Court his involvement in the apartheid regime's campaign against its opponents, claiming that de Klerk and Botha had both had full knowledge of these operations, which included assassinations.

In early September 1996 the Constitutional Court ruled that the new Constitution failed to adhere to the principles enshrined in the interim Constitution in a number of respects, notably with regard to the powers of the provinces, which the Court deemed insufficient. The Constitutional Assembly was to amend the document accordingly within a period of 90 days. The amended Constitution was approved by both chambers of Parliament on 11 October, with the ANC and the NP having negotiated a slight increase in the powers of the provinces. The new Constitution was promulgated by the President at a ceremony in Sharpeville on 10 December. The new Constitution entered into force on 4 February 1997. On 6 February the inaugural session of the new National Council of Provinces, which replaced the Senate as the second chamber of Parliament, was held.

Meanwhile, in October 1996 Gen. Malan and his co-defendants were acquitted of all charges in connection with the massacre in KwaMakutha. Although it was accepted that the killings had been committed by IFP supporters who had been trained by the former armed forces, the prosecution failed to prove that the attack had been authorized by military or political leaders. The judgment was regarded as a set-back for the TRC, with Gen. Malan urging former members of the armed forces not to seek amnesties from the TRC, but to submit to trial in the courts if charged (thus discouraging potential confessions to the Commission). Later in October the TRC proposed that the final date for indemnity be extended from 6 December 1993 to 10 May 1994. Shortly afterwards a former police commissioner submitted evidence to the TRC implicating Botha in an attack against the headquarters of the South African Council of Churches in 1988. Botha declared that he would not submit evidence to the Commission and denied involvement in any crimes for which he needed to apply for amnesty. Following discussions with Tutu, however, he agreed to co-operate with the TRC by means of correspondence.

On 13 December 1996 (the eve of the deadline for applications for amnesty from the TRC) Mandela announced that the final dates for the period in which crimes had been committed and the deadline for the receipt of amnesty applications were to be extended, to 10 May 1994 and 10 May 1997, respectively. The ANC confirmed that some 360 of its members, including three cabinet ministers, had applied for amnesty.

By the 10 May 1997 deadline nearly 8,000 amnesty applications had been received. In August de Klerk resigned from the leadership of the NP and retired from active politics; he was replaced by Marthinus van Schalkwyk. In December Mandela resigned from the presidency of the ANC, as anticipated, and was succeeded by Mbeki, who was elected unopposed. Jacob Zuma was elected Deputy President of the party.

In October 1998 the TRC commenced reparation payments to victims of human rights violations under the apartheid system and at the end of that month Tutu presented to Mandela the TRC's interim report detailing human rights violations committed in 1960–64, based on statements from some 21,000 victims of abuses and about 7,000 amnesty applicants. The report concluded that the apartheid system constituted a crime against humanity; it was alleged that, while the State was primarily accountable for violations of human rights, the ANC had also committed abuses in its legitimate struggle against apartheid

(notably in the MK's torture and execution of suspected dissidents in detention camps outside South Africa). Botha, as President of the State Security Council in 1978–89, was considered to be responsible for an increase in killings of government opponents and to have ordered the bomb attacks by state agents in the 1980s. Buthelezi was deemed accountable for human rights violations perpetrated by the IFP (which was responsible for the highest proportion of killings in 1990–94). The report also cited Viljoen and Terre'Blanche as being responsible for serious violations of human rights. It was stated that the South African business community had benefited from the apartheid system, and the introduction of a 'wealth tax' to assist in social reconstruction was proposed. The prosecution of those responsible for human rights violations who had not applied for amnesty, or who had been denied amnesty, was recommended. Buthelezi and Viljoen dismissed the findings of the report as reflecting pro-ANC bias in the TRC, and the former refuted the report's allegation that the IFP had colluded with the apartheid regime. In December 1998 Mandela confirmed that perpetrators of crimes committed under the apartheid regime would not be granted a general amnesty, which had been urged by the NP, IFP and some members of the ANC. Under TRC regulations, applicants would only be granted amnesty after submitting a full confession and evidence that the crime was politically motivated.

Mbeki replaces Mandela

More than 16m. voters participated in legislative elections, which took place peacefully, at national and provincial level, on 2 June 1999. The ANC secured 266 of the 400 seats in the National Assembly, with 66.4% of votes cast; the DP increased its representation in the Assembly from seven to 38 seats, while the IFP won 34, and the New National Party (NNP, as the NP had been reconstituted), which had lost much support to the DP, only 28 seats. The ANC subsequently formed a coalition with an Indian party, the Minority Front, thereby securing a two-thirds' majority in the National Assembly. The IFP reached a coalition agreement with the ANC in KwaZulu/Natal, where the IFP Premier retained his post. In Western Cape no party won a majority of seats in the provincial legislature, and, after intensive negotiations, the NPP and DP established a coalition Government to prevent the ANC, which had obtained the highest number of votes, from gaining power. On 16 June Mbeki was inaugurated as President, in a ceremony also marking the formal retirement of Mandela. The IFP joined the ANC in a further coalition Government, in which Buthelezi remained Minister of Home Affairs. Zuma became Deputy President.

In July 1999 the TRC released a report containing evidence from former members of the security forces that implicated Botha in the killing of eight anti-apartheid activists in 1988. (Botha died in October 2006.) In August the TRC granted amnesty to former NP Minister of Law and Order, Adriaan Vlok, the former Commissioner of Police, Gen. Johan van der Merwe, de Kock, and a further 14 members of the former security forces, in respect of ordering the bombing of the offices of the South African Council of Churches in 1988. In September the Minister of Justice announced that further cases were to be submitted to judges specially nominated by Mbeki. In October the trial of Wouter Basson, the head of the apartheid regime's chemical and biological armaments programme in 1982–92, on 64 charges (including responsibility for the killing of 200 members of the South West Africa People's Organization of Namibia—SWAPO), commenced at the High Court in Pretoria. He was acquitted of 15 charges in June 2001, and the remaining charges in April 2002. Later in October 1999 the TRC granted amnesty to nine former members of the security forces, including de Kock, who had provided evidence regarding the bombing of the ANC offices in London in 1982.

In January 2000 the National Assembly adopted extensive legislation prohibiting discrimination on any grounds and the use of racist terms in language. In June it was announced that the NNP and DP were to form a new coalition, the Democratic Alliance (DA), to contest the local government elections.

In September 2001 the South African Medical Research Council reported that HIV/AIDS was the largest single cause of death in South Africa, responsible for approximately 40% of adult deaths. Mbeki had attracted criticism in August 2001 after urging the Minister of Health to reduce the budget for HIV/AIDS treatment, citing mortality figures from 1995 (when the disease accounted for only 2.2% of deaths). In December the Ministry of Health lost a case brought by the Treatment Action Campaign (TAC), a group of AIDS activists, when the High Court in Pretoria ordered it to provide antiretroviral drugs to all pregnant women infected with HIV to reduce the chance of transmission to their children; the Government had argued that the drugs were toxic and excessively expensive to administer. (The Government lost its appeal against the ruling in April 2002.) In February 2002 Buthelezi, as Minister of Home Affairs, ordered the distribution of antiretroviral drugs in KwaZulu/Natal, in contravention of official government policy, and in March the High Court upheld the ruling that ordered state provision of antiretroviral drugs. In October the Government announced that it would investigate means of providing antiretroviral drugs through the public health system. Between 2008 and 2011 there was some success in combating HIV/AIDS in South Africa. The Government estimated that the mother-to-child transmission rate had fallen from about 8% in 2008 to just 3.5% in 2011. Moreover, in January 2013 an estimated 1.7m. South Africans were receiving antiretroviral treatment.

Meanwhile, in July 2001 the PAC drew attention to what it considered the Government's inadequate housing and land redistribution policies, by seizing land belonging to farmers and the Provincial Government in east Johannesburg. Within two weeks the Government had removed the estimated 7,000 squatters from the land, using armed police officers. COSATU and affiliated unions organized a two-day general strike in August in protest at the proposed privatization of public assets, which, it claimed, would result in large-scale redundancies. COSATU estimated that 4m. workers had participated in the strike, a figure that the Government described as exaggerated. In August Agri South Africa, an organization representing commercial farmers (mainly white) and 'emerging' black farmers, reported that there had been more than 6,000 attacks on South African farms since 1991, resulting in the deaths of more than 1,000 people. The South African Government declared land seizures illegal in August.

The leader of the NNP, van Schalkwyk, announced in October 2001 that the party was suspending its participation in the DA, following differences with the DP; the DP had dismissed the mayor of Cape Town, a prominent figure in the NNP, while the DP suspected the NNP of attempting to increase membership in an attempt to take overall control of the DA. Van Schalkwyk announced that the NNP would seek an accommodation with the ANC, as the IFP had done, retaining its independence, but holding positions in the Cabinet. In late November the ANC and NNP announced a power-sharing agreement in Western Cape (the only province not previously under ANC control).

A ruling by the Constitutional Court in late 2002, allowing national and provincial deputies to change parties without losing their seats, led to significant changes in the political landscape: in April 2003 the ANC secured a two-thirds' parliamentary majority when members of the United Democratic Movement and the NNP defected to the ruling party, while the FA and the Afrikaner Eenheidsbeweging lost all their seats. At provincial level, members of the IFP defected to the ANC in KwaZulu/Natal and assumed further positions in the Cabinet, although the premiership of the province remained under IFP control.

The TRC's final report was presented to Mbeki in March 2003. The Commission had granted amnesty to 1,200 people, but had rejected more than 5,000 applications. Tutu recommended that some US $240m. ($12,000 each) be paid to the 20,000 people identified as victims of apartheid, and urged companies that had benefited through their involvement with the apartheid regime to contribute to the reparations process. Publication of the final report had been delayed by a legal challenge brought by the IFP, which was heavily implicated in the perpetration of human rights violations. In April, having rejected the suggestion that a special tax be imposed on companies that had gained from apartheid, Mbeki announced that those designated victims by the TRC would receive single payments of just over $3,800 each.

In 2003 ambitious empowerment charters were created for the financial and mining sectors, which envisaged large increases in the number of non-white company executives and mine owners, respectively. In 1994 the Government had promised to transfer 30% of white-owned farms to non-whites over the next five years, but by 2004 only 2% had been transferred.

The 2004 elections

Elections to the National Assembly and the provincial legislatures took place concurrently on 14 April 2004. The ANC won 279 of the National Assembly's 400 seats, with 69.7% of the valid votes cast. The DA took 50 seats, with 12.4% of votes cast, and the IFP 28, with 7.0%. The ANC secured overall control of seven of the nine provincial assemblies; although it failed to win outright majorities in KwaZulu/Natal and Western Cape, the ANC

subsequently nominated premiers to head all nine provincial governments. The IEC declared the elections to have been free and fair. On 23 April members of the National Assembly voted unanimously to re-elect Mbeki to the presidency. President Mbeki announced the composition of a new Cabinet, which included most senior members of the previous administration: Zuma was reappointed Deputy President, while Mantombanza (Manto) Tshabalala-Msimang retained the health portfolio despite the slow progress regarding the provision of antiretroviral drugs to combat HIV/AIDS.

In August 2004 van Schalkwyk announced that the NNP was to merge with the ANC and that the NNP would be disbanded in September 2005. The NNP leader also stated his intention to join the ANC and urged all NNP members to do the same. Former President de Klerk subsequently announced his resignation from the NNP in protest at the decision. (The NNP officially ceased to exist at the end of February 2006.)

Meanwhile, in August 2003, the National Director of Public Prosecutions, Bulelani Ngcuka, had announced that Deputy President Zuma would not be prosecuted for alleged corruption in connection with an arms-procurement deal, despite an apparent recommendation from investigators that he be charged. This prompted accusations of government interference in the legal process and opposition demands for Zuma's resignation. Zuma repeatedly rejected the allegations against him; however, in early June 2005 his financial adviser, Schabir Shaik, was found guilty of corruption and fraud and sentenced to 15 years' imprisonment by the Durban High Court. The Court found evidence of a corrupt relationship between Shaik and Zuma, and that a series of payments made by Shaik on behalf of Zuma were intended to influence Zuma to benefit Shaik's business. Although Zuma did not give evidence, the trial revealed that Zuma had been party to a bid to solicit a bribe from a French defence company involved in the arms-procurement deal.

President Mbeki came under increasing pressure to dismiss Zuma and on 14 June 2005 he announced that the Deputy President would be 'released' from his duties. Zuma was replaced by Phumzile Mlambo-Ngcuka, hitherto the Minister of Energy and Mineral Affairs. In mid-September 2006 the High Court judge dismissed the case against Zuma, stating that he had suffered social prejudice as a result of the publicity the case had received. Zuma's supporters subsequently urged Mbeki, who was constitutionally prohibited from serving a third term, to reinstate him as Deputy President.

In November 2005 it was also reported that Zuma was under investigation for the alleged rape of a female family friend; he was charged with the offence in early December but strenuously denied the allegation and was acquitted in early May 2006. In a separate investigation into missing funds 16 current and former ministers were found guilty of theft and fraud in October 2006. As much as R 17m. had been stolen and parliamentary travel privileges had been abused.

In May 2007 Helen Zille, the Mayor of Cape Town, was elected leader of the DA, replacing Tony Leon who had led the party since its formation in 2000. Meanwhile, Zuma had secured the support of senior members of the SACP, and in September he received the endorsement of COSATU for his leadership campaign.

As the leadership contest gained momentum senior members of the ANC exerted pressure on both Mbeki and Zuma to withdraw their candidatures, claiming that their rivalry was causing a major rift within the party. Neither candidate was prepared to concede and in December 2007 ANC members elected Zuma to the party presidency after he secured 2,329 votes to Mbeki's 1,505; Kgalema Motlanthe was appointed ANC Deputy President. However, later that month the National Prosecuting Authority (NPA) indicted Zuma on charges of corruption and fraud. In April 2008 Mbeki agreed to include Motlanthe in the National Assembly.

Public frustration escalated in May 2008 amid worsening economic conditions; rising food and fuel prices placed greater strain on resources and in mid-May clashes broke out in several townships between local residents and foreigners. Some 20 people were killed in the fighting and several hundred more were injured, while aid workers in the area reported that as many as 30,000 people had been displaced by the violence.

Mbeki's power continued to decline and in July 2008 the ANC National Executive Committee (NEC) appointed Motlanthe to the newly created post of Minister in the Presidency, responsible for Government Business. In September the High Court dismissed the charges brought against Zuma, and ruled that there was evidence of political interference from high-ranking officials in the investigation. This caused the rift within the ANC to widen and it was subsequently announced that Mbeki had relinquished the presidency at the party's request, effective from 25 September. His resignation was followed by that of 11 cabinet ministers, including Mlambo-Ngcuka and Trevor A. Manuel, the long-serving Minister of Finance. A parliamentary vote elected Motlanthe as the new President with a clear majority and he was to remain in the post until the legislative elections in April 2009. Baleka Mbete, hitherto the Speaker of the National Assembly, was subsequently named Deputy President and Charles Nqakula was appointed Minister of Defence, while Manuel was reappointed Minister of Finance; Gwen Mahlangu-Nkabinde replaced Mbete as Speaker.

Divisions within the ANC deepened and in November 2008 a group of former ANC members and allies of Mbeki, led by Mosiuoa Lekota, formed a new political party, the Congress of the People (COPE). Members of COPE claimed that the party would provide a serious challenge to the ANC; its candidates won 12 seats in local by-elections in December.

As preparations for the general election began in early 2009, Zuma faced a further reverse when an appeal court overturned the earlier ruling that dismissed the corruption charges brought against him. However, in June the trial date was postponed indefinitely. In March Zuma approached the prosecutor's office with a deal offering to refrain from appointing only close ANC allies to high-profile positions, should he be elected in April, in return for all charges against him being dismissed. Meanwhile, Mlambo-Ngcuka announced that he had left the ANC to join COPE.

The Zuma administration

On 22 April 2009 elections duly took place to the National Assembly and to South Africa's nine provincial legislatures. Final results confirmed the overwhelming victory of the ANC, which, with 65.9% of total votes cast, won 264 of the National Assembly's 400 seats. The DA took 67 seats, with 16.7% of votes cast, and COPE secured 30 seats with 7.4%. The ANC also secured overall control of eight provincial assemblies. More than 77% of the registered electorate participated. As expected, Zuma was elected President by the National Assembly with 277 votes and was inaugurated on 9 May. The following day Zuma announced his new Government and the reorganization of a number of ministries: a National Planning Commission and a performance monitoring and evaluation competency were created within the presidency, to be led by Manuel and Collins Chabane, respectively; the Ministry of Minerals and Energy was divided into two separate ministries; and the Ministry for Education was separated into the Ministry of Basic Education and the Ministry of Higher Education. Appointments made to the enlarged administration included Motlanthe as Deputy President, Pravin Gordhan (the Commissioner of the South African Revenue Service) as Minister of Finance and Jeff Radebe as Minister of Justice and Constitutional Development; the hitherto Minister of Foreign Affairs, Nkosazana Dlamini-Zuma, was moved to the Ministry of Home Affairs. Also of note was the appointment of the leader of the Afrikaner nationalist Vryheidsfront Plus party, Dr Pieter Mulder, as Deputy Minister of Agriculture, Forestry and Fisheries.

COPE, which had failed to perform as strongly as expected in the national elections, was confronted with a number of organizational problems and growing dissatisfaction with Lekota's leadership. In July 2009 two senior party officials resigned, and in early May 2010 the party's Deputy President, Mbhazima Shilowa, formally stated his intention to challenge Lekota for the party presidency at COPE's national conference, which was scheduled to be held later that month. Lekota lost a vote of confidence in his leadership at the COPE conference in late May, leaving Shilowa as acting President of the party. In response, Lekota initiated a successful legal challenge against the vote and was reinstated as COPE President in June, although the deep divisions within the party remained.

In April 2010 Eugene Terre'Blanche, the AWB leader who was released from prison in 2004 after serving three years of a five-year sentence for attempted murder, was killed after a dispute over unpaid wages with two farm workers, both of whom were subsequently charged with his murder. In August 2012 one of the accused was found guilty of Terre'Blanche's murder and sentenced to life in prison; the other was given a suspended sentence for housebreaking. The judge ruled that the incident was not racially motivated.

New government proposals that had the potential to limit freedom of expression caused considerable controversy in mid-2010. Zuma argued that the Protection of Information Bill, which would impose harsh penalties for revealing (or attempting to reveal) classified information and which would allow the authorities to restrict a greater range of such information, was necessary to protect national security. He also claimed that the Media Appeals Tribunal, which could potentially have the authority to censor the media, would protect citizens from libellous allegations. However, critics condemned the proposals as damaging to press freedom and government transparency, designed solely to protect the political and business élites, and possibly unconstitutional. Nevertheless, in November 2011 the Protection of State Information Bill (as the legislation, which was commonly referred to as the 'Secrecy Bill', had been renamed) was passed in the National Assembly, although its passage was subject to amendments by the National Council of Provinces. Having been returned to the National Assembly for approval, in April 2013 that body voted to accept the amendments to the Bill by 189 votes to 74. Meanwhile, in July 2010 former National Commissioner of Police Jacob 'Jackie' Sello Selebi was convicted of accepting payments from a high-profile drugs trafficker, ostensibly in exchange for ignoring his criminal activities.

DA leader Zille announced in August 2010 that her party would merge with the Independent Democrats by 2014 in order to present the ANC with a stronger challenge in the legislative elections scheduled to be held in that year. Zille also declared that the DA would seek meetings with other parties to discuss the formation of a possible opposition coalition. Meanwhile, from mid-August 2010 public sector workers staged nation-wide strikes, reportedly involving over 1m. people, to demand increased salaries. Clashes occurred between strikers and the police, and soldiers were mobilized in some cases to deter further violence. The industrial action caused widespread disruption within the education sector, and the Government was forced to deploy military medics to hospitals to ensure that the provision of essential medical services was maintained. The strikes were ended in early September, after the Government offered a 7.5% pay raise and an R 800 housing allowance, which was accepted by the public sector unions in the following month. It was expected that the Government would have to arrange loans to pay for the wage increases, placing additional pressure on the country's already strained fiscal position.

In late October 2010 Zuma effected a cabinet reorganization. Seven ministers were removed from their posts, including those responsible for communications, labour, public enterprises and public works, although the major portfolios were unaltered. A number of new deputy ministerial positions were also created.

In January 2011 Zanele Magwaza-Msibi left the IFP to form the National Freedom Party (NFP) following the refusal of party veteran Mangosuthu Buthelezi to step down as the leader of the IFP. In local elections held on 18 May the ANC received 63.5% of votes cast (a slight decrease from 66% in 2006). The DA secured 22% of the votes, an increase of 6% compared with the party's performance in 2006. The IFP received just 3.9%, with the newly formed NFP and COPE obtaining 2.6% and 2.3%, respectively. Almost 58% of the electorate participated, representing the highest turn-out for local elections since 1994. The ANC was victorious in the major municipalities of Johannesburg, Pretoria, Durban, Bloemfontein and Port Elizabeth, while the DA won Cape Town and most other councils in the Western Cape province. There was an increase in the level of support for the DA in eight out of the nine provinces. In October the DA appointed its first black parliamentary leader in Lindiwe Mazibuko, who thus also became the first black politician in South Africa to lead an opposition party in parliament.

In September 2011 ANC Youth League President Julius Malema was found guilty of 'hate speech' for continuing publicly to sing the apartheid-era liberation song, the lyrics of which included the words 'shoot the white farmer'. A High Court ruled in favour of Afriforum, a group representing mostly white farmers. In November the ANC suspended Malema from the party for five years, pending the conclusion of the appeals process. He was found guilty of, *inter alia*, bringing the party into disrepute by calling for 'regime change' in Botswana. A number of other Youth League members, including spokesperson Floyd Shivambu (who was suspended from the ANC for three years), were convicted on similar charges. In March 2012 Malema lost his appeal against suspension from the ANC. He was subsequently relieved of his post as ANC Youth League President and, following reports that he had referred to President Zuma as a dictator, was prohibited from attending any ANC functions. In March 2013 Zuma disbanded the ANC

Youth League NEC and disbanded the Youth League's Limpopo provincial executive committee.

Meanwhile, in late 2011 the Government was criticized for delaying the granting of a visa to the Dalai Lama. He was scheduled to attend Desmond Tutu's birthday celebrations, but was forced to cancel his planned visit to South Africa after his visa application stalled. The Government's denial of a visa to the Buddhist leader for the second time in two years, appeared to some observers to suggest that the South African authorities were wary of offending the country's largest trading partner, the People's Republic of China.

In October 2011 President Zuma dismissed Minister of Co-operative Governance Sicelo Shiceka and Minister of Traditional Affairs and Public Works Gwen Mahlangu-Nkabinde from the Cabinet. The former was alleged to have used some R 10m. in state funds on private travel and luxury accommodation, while allegations of corruption were levelled against the latter for her role in the leasing of buildings for a new police headquarters at artificially inflated costs. Meanwhile, National Commissioner of the Police, Bheki Cele, was suspended with full pay for his reported role in the leasing scandal. President Zuma subsequently dismissed him in June 2012. He was replaced by Mangwashi Victoria 'Riah' Phiyega. Shiceka was replaced by Richard Baloyi, whose post of Public Service and Administration was assigned to Thembelani 'Thulas' Nxesi. Mahlangu-Nkabinde was replaced by Radhakrishna 'Roy' Padayachie, whose erstwhile role as Minister of Communications was assumed by his deputy, Dina Pule. However, in early May 2012 Padayachie died of a heart attack during an AU meeting in Addis Ababa, Ethiopia. He was replaced by Lindiwe Sisulu. Meanwhile, in December 2011 President Zuma suffered a setback when the Supreme Court of Appeal ruled that his appointment of Menzi Simelane as the National Director of Public Prosecutors in November 2009 was invalid. The DA had brought the case before the Court, claiming that, if appointed, Simelane would abuse his authority by protecting powerful allies from prosecution.

Recent developments: Marikana

In mid-July 2012 the Minister of Home Affairs, Nkosazana Dlamini-Zuma, was appointed Chairperson of the African Union (AU) Commission. She became the first South African and the first woman to hold the post. The former wife of President Zuma, Dlamini-Zuma defeated Gabonese incumbent Jean Ping after four rounds of voting. Grace Naledi Mandisa Pandor, hitherto Minister of Science and Technology, assumed the vacated home affairs portfolio in October 2012. In preparation for his re-election campaign as ANC president in December at Mangaung in the Free State, President Zuma effected a reorganization of his Cabinet in July of that year. Following Sisulu's assumption of the public service and administration portfolio, she was succeeded as Minister of Defence and Military Veterans by the erstwhile Minister of Correctional Services, Nosiviwe Mapisa-Nqakula. Sibusiso Ndebele left the transport ministry to take up the role of Minister of Correctional Services. He was replaced by Ben Martins.

Platinum miners working at Lonmin-operated Marikana near Rustenburg commenced industrial action on 10 August 2012. Some 3,000 rock drill operators working on the mine had been on strike for one week when, on August 16, clashes between striking miners and the police resulted in 34 workers being shot dead. Reports indicated that 10 people had already died prior to the shooting, including two policemen; the same reports suggested that miners' pay demands and rivalry between mining unions were the main causes of the violence. Following the commencement of industrial action on the mine, there had been clashes reported between miners from the National Union of Mineworkers (NUM) and its radical breakaway, the Association of Mineworkers and Construction Union (AMCU). Commentators suggested that many workers had lost faith with senior management of the NUM and other established unions, which they considered to be too close to the mining companies.

Meanwhile, Lonmin announced that one-third of its employees had returned to work by 22 August 2012. However, the mine at Marikana shut down operations when it became clear that striking miners were using intimidation tactics to dissuade their colleagues from returning: on 31 August just 5.7% of the 28,000 miners employed by Lonmin appeared for work. President Zuma subsequently appointed retired Supreme Court of Appeal Judge Ian Farlam to lead a commission of enquiry into the events at Marikana. During the proceedings in early 2013 National Police Commissioner Phiyega was criticized for allegedly being assisted

by the legal counsel of the South African Police Service during her testimony. As of March 2013 the enquiry was ongoing.

The events at Marikana were followed by further instances of illegal industrial action around the country, making the large-scale strikes the worst in the post-apartheid era. It was estimated that some 100,000 miners went on strike during August–September 2012. Anglo American Platinum suspended their operations in September before dismissing some 12,000 striking miners after they had failed to appear for disciplinary hearings. It was estimated that around R 700m. in revenue was lost over the course of the period before the company offered to re-hire the dismissed miners. However, in January 2013 miners at three Anglo American Platinum mines were dismissed after they went on strike in protest against the company's decision to remove around 14,000 jobs. The company claimed it would create a similar number of new jobs in order to make up for the losses. Meanwhile, Kumba Iron Ore halted operations at its Sishen mine in the Northern Cape in early October 2012 when 300 workers staged an unofficial strike. It was reported that 40 people were subsequently arrested. There was further violence at the Gold One mine near Johannesburg in early September: four people were wounded when police fired rubber bullets into a crowd that had gathered to protest against their dismissals in June. There was further industrial action at a number of Anglo Ashanti's operations; most of its 35,000-strong workforce went on strike, with the company suspending production on 26 September. Meanwhile, it was reported that President Zuma had on 20 September ordered military personnel to assist police in restoring calm to the mining sector. The following month unions and the Chamber of Mines—representing, *inter alia*, GoldFields and Harmony Gold—agreed a deal in which rock drill operators and other miners would reportedly receive wage increases of between 3% and 10.8%.

There were further violent demonstrations in the country in November 2012. Farmworkers in the wine-producing area of the Western Cape commenced industrial action over pay and poor working conditions. Protests began in De Doorns, where farmworkers were demanding wages of R 150 per day. (They currently earned between R 69 and R 75 per day.) Demonstrations spread to 15 other towns in the province, with strikers looting shops, blocking roads and setting fire to businesses. Some reports indicated that protesters had been brought into flashpoint areas by bus in order to destabilize the only province administered by the opposition party. Other reports indicated the police had fired rubber bullets at some protest gatherings. One man in Wolseley was reported to have died, while five others were wounded. Meanwhile, some residents of De Doorns alleged that they had been attacked by members of the local police, although they claimed not to be involved in the industrial action. Following negotiations between striking workers and the Government, the latter announced a raising of the minimum wage for farmworkers to R 105 per day. Many farmers had warned that they would not be able to afford the increase, and in early February some 2,000 farmworkers were issued with retrenchment notices.

The South African Police Service again came under intense media scrutiny in February 2013 when a video appeared online depicting a Mozambiquan taxi driver being tied to a police van and dragged through the streets near Johannesburg. He later died in police custody. Nine policemen were subsequently arrested and charged with his murder. In March they were denied bail.

At the ANC's Mangaung conference in December 2012 President Zuma retained the leadership of the party, despite a challenge from Motlanthe. Although Zuma had experienced a number of potentially damaging incidents (the massacre at Marikana; a scandal involving the non-delivery of essential textbooks to many schools in the province of Limpopo; and the alleged use of public funds to renovate his home in Nkandla, KwaZulu/Natal) the one-sided result was widely expected: Zuma received 2,986 out of a possible 3,977 delegate votes. Meanwhile, Cyril Ramaphosa was elected as the party's Deputy President, signalling a return to politics following a number of years in business. Gwede Mantashe remained in his post as ANC Secretary-General. During the conference, four men were arrested for allegedly plotting to bomb one of the plenary sessions. It was subsequently confirmed later that two of the men were senior members of the right-wing Federale Vryheid Party (Federal Freedom Party), which campaigns for the self-determination of South Africa's Afrikaner minority. In late February 2013 apartheid activist, academic and former Managing Director of the

World Bank Mamphela Ramphele announced the formation of new political party, Agang, to challenge the dominance of the ANC.

Foreign Affairs

Regional relations

South Africa became increasingly isolated politically in southern Africa after Zimbabwe (formerly Rhodesia) underwent the transition to independence in April 1980. In 1971 the International Court of Justice had declared South Africa's presence in Namibia to be illegal and the UN had, in 1973, recognized SWAPO as the 'authentic representative of the Namibian people'. Following the collapse of the semi-autonomous internal administration, South Africa resumed direct rule of Namibia in January 1983. In February 1984 South Africa and Angola agreed on a cease-fire along the Angola–Namibia border, and established a joint commission to monitor the withdrawal of South African troops from Angola. On 22 December 1988 Angola, Cuba and South Africa signed a formal treaty designating 1 April 1989 as the commencement date for the process leading to Namibian independence, as well as a treaty requiring all 50,000 Cuban troops to be withdrawn from Angola by July 1991. Elections were held in Namibia in November 1989, and independence for the former South African territory was achieved on 21 March 1990, under a SWAPO-controlled Government. South Africa relinquished the strategic port of Walvis Bay and 12 offshore islands in August 1993. They were officially transferred to Namibia in March 1994. In August 2001 the South African and Namibian foreign ministers met to discuss the issue of their joint border on the Orange river; Namibia claimed the border extended to the middle of the river, while South Africa claimed it lay on the northern bank, provoking differences over mineral and fishing rights.

In 1984 South Africa signed a mutual non-aggression pact with Mozambique (the Nkomati accord), which implied that South Africa would withdraw its covert support for the Resistência Nacional Moçambicana (Renamo), while Mozambique would prevent the ANC from using its territory as a base for attacks on South Africa. In May 1988 Mozambican and South African officials agreed to reactivate the Nkomati accord, and in September President Botha visited President Joaquim Chissano of Mozambique. In August 1994 South Africa, Mozambique and Swaziland signed a security co-operation accord, in an effort to combat the continuing illicit transport of armaments. In February 1997 South Africa appealed to the Government of Swaziland to release Swazi trade union leaders from detention. The Swazi Government protested at action mounted by COSATU in support of its Swazi counterparts, stating that it represented interference in the internal affairs of Swaziland. In April 2006 protests were staged by COSATU, the SACP and its Youth League, and the Swaziland Solidarity Network in support of Swaziland's campaign for democracy and human rights. Demonstrators attempted to blockade several crossing-points on the Swaziland border and more than 20 people were arrested.

In 1979 the Southern African Development Co-ordination Conference (SADCC) was established by southern African countries, to work towards a reduction of their economic dependence on South Africa. SADCC reformed in August 1992 as the Southern African Development Community (SADC, see p. 434), which aimed to achieve closer economic integration between its member states. South Africa was admitted to SADC in August 1994. In April 1997 members of the South African armed forces participated in military training exercises in Zimbabwe, as part of a nascent SADC regional peace-keeping force. In September 1998 about 600 South African and 200 Botswanan troops were dispatched to restore order in the Lesotho capital, Maseru, under the aegis of SADC, following a coup attempt by junior military officers. About 750 South African troops, together with some 350 Botswanan troops, remained in Lesotho to maintain civil order, before their withdrawal in May 2000.

In April 2000 Mbeki, together with the Presidents of Namibia and Mozambique, visited Zimbabwe to increase pressure on President Robert Mugabe to prevent the illegal occupation of white-owned farmland. Despite international condemnation of Mugabe and requests by a number of countries, most notably the United Kingdom, for more unequivocal criticism of President Mugabe's actions from South Africa, President Mbeki attempted to maintain 'constructive engagement' towards Zimbabwe. In March 2002, however, Mbeki was part of a Commonwealth troika (also comprising the President of Nigeria and the Prime Minister of Australia) that decided to suspend Zimbabwe from meetings of that organization for a period of one year. Mbeki had previously ignored pleas from Morgan Tsvangirai, the leader of the main opposition party in Zimbabwe, the Movement for Democratic Change, to impose sanctions on Zimbabwe prior to the presidential election held that month. In March 2003 the Secretary-General of the Commonwealth stated that the troika had concluded that Zimbabwe's suspension from the organization's meetings should remain in force for a further nine months. Zimbabwe withdrew from the Commonwealth in December 2003, shortly before the conclusion of the organization's Heads of Government meeting, at which the country's suspension had been extended indefinitely. Mbeki had criticized the decision to maintain the suspension, claiming that some Commonwealth members had failed to understand the question of land ownership in Zimbabwe. The Commonwealth appointed South Africa to a six-member advisory panel charged with monitoring the situation in Zimbabwe. Mbeki met separately with Mugabe and Tsvangirai in that month in an unsuccessful attempt to persuade them to form a coalition government. Mbeki continued to mediate between Mugabe and Tsvangirai prior to the Zimbabwean presidential and legislative elections held in March 2008, but, following the decision of the Zimbabwe Electoral Commission not to release the results of the presidential election, in April Mugabe boycotted an emergency SADC summit in Zambia called to discuss the situation in Zimbabwe. Mbeki travelled to Harare for talks with Mugabe, but the former's policy of 'quiet diplomacy' attracted criticism from a number of international observers, while Tsvangirai appealed for Mbeki to relinquish his role as mediator to Zambian President Levy Mwanawasa. Despite his resignation from the South African presidency, Mbeki continued to chair negotiations between Tsvangirai and Mugabe and in September the two sides concluded the Interparty Political Agreement (see Zimbabwe), which provided for a power-sharing arrangement. Further discussions, again with mediation by Mbeki, resulted in the installation of a new Council of Ministers in February 2009 and the appointment of Tsvangirai to the Zimbabwean premiership. Following his election in May 2009, South African President Jacob Zuma succeeded Mbeki as the Chairman of SADC and principal mediator in negotiations between the government parties in Zimbabwe. Zuma's approach to Zimbabwe during 2010 suggested that his predecessor's strategy of 'quiet diplomacy' would be maintained. Meanwhile, in September the Government announced that deportations of illegal Zimbabwean migrants, suspended since April 2009, would recommence from the end of 2010 (subsequently postponed until the end of September 2011) due to the improving situation in Zimbabwe. Human rights organizations and diaspora groups criticized the Government's decision to restart deportations in October 2011, arguing that conditions in Zimbabwe were still too unstable to justify the resumption of large-scale repatriations. It was reported that by the end of 2010 275,762 applications by undocumented Zimbabweans to normalize their status were received by the Home Affairs department, although this number was believed to represent only a fraction of the illegal Zimbabwean population in South Africa.

In November 1996 South Africa was criticized for its approval of a substantial sale of weapons to Rwanda, which was believed to be providing military support to rebels in eastern Zaire who were engaged in conflict with the Zairean army. In response to international pressure, the South African Government subsequently decided to suspend the sale of armaments to Rwanda. During 1996 South Africa supported efforts to achieve reconciliation in Angola and in early 1997 was involved in intensive diplomatic activity, along with other African countries, with the aim of negotiating an end to the civil war in Zaire. Following the assumption of power by Alliance des Forces Démocratiques pour la Libération du Congo-Zaïre, led by Laurent-Désiré Kabila, in May, South Africa became the first foreign government to recognize the new regime and pledged to assist in reconstruction efforts and in the holding of elections in the renamed Democratic Republic of the Congo (DRC). In October 2001 South African soldiers were dispatched to Burundi as part of a proposed 700-member peace-keeping mission, in an effort to enforce national security and to support the formation of a multi-ethnic transitional government. Mandela had been instrumental in negotiating a peace accord (signed in August 2000), whereby the Hutu and Tutsi ethnic groups, which had been engaged in civil conflict since 1993, were each to hold the presidency for 18 months during a three-year transitional period. Meanwhile, in March 2005 South Africa dispatched some 300 troops to Darfur, Sudan, to join an African Union (AU, see p. 191) mission to investigate and monitor events in the region. By early 2010

South Africa had 950 security personnel (including 781 soldiers) stationed in Darfur as part of the joint AU-UN hybrid peace-keeping operation in Darfur (UNAMID), which had been established in mid-2007.

In February 2007 South Africa signed a defence agreement with the Central African Republic (CAR) committing to the provision of military training and the donation of surplus military supplies. In late March 2013 13 South African soldiers died in clashes with rebel forces in the CAR, who deposed the President, François Bozizé Yangouvonda. Some reports suggested that the role of the South Africans in the region was to protect ANC business interests, including projects involving diamonds. In April President Zuma announced the withdrawal of all South African troops from the CAR.

In April 2008 South Africa signed a memorandum of understanding with the Republic of the Congo to develop co-operation between the two countries' military services, indicating that South Africa may be preparing to work more closely with other central African countries within the framework of the military organization established under the Communauté Economique des Etats de l'Afrique Centrale (see p. 460).

In June 2010 former head of the Rwandan armed forces Lt-Gen. Faustin Kayumba Nyamwasa, who had sought asylum in South Africa after being accused by the Rwandan authorities of orchestrating a series of deadly grenade attacks in the country earlier in the year (a charge he rejected), was shot outside his home in Johannesburg in an apparent assassination attempt. After fleeing to South Africa, Nyamwasa had become a prominent critic of Rwandan President Paul Kagame. Rwandans were reportedly among the suspects subsequently arrested by South African police, and the Ministry of International Relations and Co-operation later revealed that members of a foreign security service had been involved in the shooting. The Rwandan Government strenuously denied any complicity in the attack and expressed its discontent at the 'insinuations emanating from official circles in South Africa'. The incident strained bilateral relations, culminating in August in the South African Government's withdrawal of its ambassador to Rwanda 'for consultations'.

In October 2001 the New Partnership for Africa's Development (NEPAD) was launched, as part of a long-term strategy for socio-economic recovery in Africa, in accordance with a decision taken at the Organization of African Unity (OAU—now the AU) summit held in Lusaka, Zambia, in July. Mbeki formulated NEPAD's founding documents, in conjunction with the heads of state of Algeria, Egypt, Nigeria and Senegal, and South Africa was to host the Secretariat. In mid-2004 the AU agreed that the Pan-African Parliament (PAP) would be based in South Africa; the Government subsequently announced that the PAP would be housed in Midrand (between Johannesburg and Pretoria). The second session of the PAP—its first in South Africa—took place at temporary headquarters in Midrand in mid-September that year.

Other external relations

Following the implementation of political reforms in South Africa from February 1990, international sanctions imposed during the 1980s were reviewed. During 1991 South Africa was readmitted to international sporting competition, after many years of exclusion. In July the USA officially withdrew economic sanctions (which were, however, retained by a number of US states and cities). In October Commonwealth Heads of Government endorsed the withdrawal of cultural sanctions against South Africa; however, sanctions on finance, arms and trade and investment remained. Japan ended all its sanctions during that month. In 1992 the European Community (EC, now the European Union—EU, see p. 281) withdrew a number of sanctions against South Africa. In September 1993, following the adoption of legislation providing for the installation of a multiracial transitional administration (see above), the international community ended the remaining economic sanctions against South Africa. The UN Security Council ended its mandatory embargo on armaments, following the establishment of an interim Government of National Unity in May 1994; South Africa subsequently established diplomatic relations with more than 165 countries. South Africa was readmitted to the Commonwealth on 1 June, and joined the OAU later that month. The People's Republic of China refused to establish formal diplomatic links while South Africa maintained relations with Taiwan. In November 1996 President Mandela announced that South Africa's diplomatic relations with Taiwan were to be severed in favour of the People's Republic of China, with effect

from the end of 1997. In response, Taiwan withdrew its ambassador indefinitely and announced that the majority of its aid projects in South Africa would be suspended.

In March 1998, following four years of negotiations, the EU approved the terms for a comprehensive free-trade agreement with South Africa. The agreement provisionally came into force on 1 January 2000; a continuing dispute with the Governments of Italy, Spain, Portugal and Greece, which had refused to sign the accord on wines and spirits, was resolved after South Africa agreed to discontinue the use of traditional European names for alcoholic drinks within five years. In December 2000 a framework agreement was reached on a free-trade accord with the Southern Common Market (known as Mercosur—Mercado Común del Sur, comprising Argentina, Brazil, Paraguay and Uruguay). The Southern African Customs Union (SACU), consisting of South Africa and the smaller states of Botswana, Lesotho, Namibia and Swaziland, concluded a preferential trade agreement with Mercosur in December 2004. A revised version of this agreement was signed by representatives of Mercosur and SACU in December 2008 and April 2009, respectively.

CONSTITUTION AND GOVERNMENT

Under the terms of the Constitution, which was adopted on 8 May 1996 and entered into force on 4 February 1997, legislative power is vested in a bicameral Parliament, comprising a National Assembly and a National Council of Provinces (formerly the Senate). The National Assembly is elected by universal adult suffrage under a system of proportional representation and has between 350 and 400 members. The 90-member National Council of Provinces comprises six permanent delegates and four special delegates from each of the provincial legislatures (see below). The President, who is elected by the National Assembly from among its members, exercises executive power in consultation with the other members of the Cabinet. Any party that holds a minimum of 80 seats in the National Assembly (equivalent to 20% of the national vote) is entitled to nominate an Executive Deputy President. A Constitutional Court ensures that the executive, legislative and judicial organs of government adhere to the provisions of the Constitution.

Each of the nine provinces has a legislature, which is elected under a system of proportional representation. Each legislature is entitled to draft a constitution for the province, subject to the principles governing the national Constitution, and to elect a Premier, who heads an Executive Council. Parties that hold a minimum of 10% of seats in the provincial legislature are entitled to a proportional number of portfolios in the Executive Council.

REGIONAL AND INTERNATIONAL CO-OPERATION

South Africa is a member of the Southern African Customs Union (with Botswana, Lesotho, Namibia and Swaziland), of the Southern African Development Community (SADC, see p. 434) and of the African Union (see p. 191). The Secretariat of the New Partnership for Africa's Development (see p. 192) is located in South Africa.

South Africa was a founder member of the UN on its establishment in 1945. As a contracting party to the General Agreement on Tariffs and Trade, South Africa joined the World Trade Organization (WTO, see p. 444) on its establishment in 1995. South Africa participates in the G20 and in the Group of 77 (G77, see p. 461) developing countries. In recognition of South Africa's rising international prominence, in December 2010 the country joined the informal grouping of major developing nations known as BRIC (consisting of Brazil, Russia, India and China, and subsequently redesignated BRICS). South Africa began a two-year term as a non-permanent member of the UN Security Council on 1 January 2011.

ECONOMIC AFFAIRS

In 2011, according to estimates by the World Bank, South Africa's gross national income (GNI), measured at average 2009–11 prices, was US $352,038m., equivalent to $6,960 per head (or $10,790 per head on an international purchasing-power parity basis). During 2002–11, it was estimated, the population increased at an average annual rate of 1.2%, while gross domestic product (GDP) per head, in real terms, increased by 2.3%. Overall GDP increased, in real terms, at an average annual rate of 3.5% in 2002–11, according to official figures; overall GDP grew by 3.1% in 2011.

Agriculture (including forestry and fishing) contributed 2.5% of GDP in 2011. Some 4.9% of the employed labour force were engaged in the sector in 2012. Maize (also the principal subsistence crop), fruit and sugar are exported, and livestock-rearing is also important; wool is another significant export. The GDP of the agricultural sector increased by an average of 1.7% per year in 2002–11. Agricultural GDP increased by 0.4% in 2010, but decreased by 0.1% in 2011.

Industry (including mining, manufacturing, construction and power) contributed 29.2% of GDP in 2011, and engaged 23.6% of the employed labour force in 2012. Industrial GDP increased at an average annual rate of 2.3% in 2002–11. Industrial GDP grew by 2.4% in 2011.

Mining contributed 9.8% of GDP in 2011, and engaged 2.6% of the employed labour force in 2012. The People's Republic of China overtook South Africa as the world's leading producer of gold in 2007. Coal, platinum, iron ore, diamonds, chromium, manganese, vanadium, vermiculite, antimony, limestone, asbestos, fluorspar, uranium, copper, lead and zinc are also important mineral exports. There are reserves of petroleum, natural gas, sillimanite, titanium and zirconium. The GDP of the mining sector remained constant during 2002–11. Mining GDP increased by 0.3% in 2011.

Manufacturing contributed 12.8% of GDP in 2011, and engaged 12.7% of the employed labour force in 2012. The GDP of the manufacturing sector increased at an average annual rate of 2.4% in 2002–11. Manufacturing GDP increased by 3.6% in 2011.

The construction sector contributed 3.8% of GDP in 2011, and engaged 7.6% of the employed labour force in 2012. The GDP of the construction sector increased by an average of 7.9% per year in 2002–11; the sector's GDP increased by 0.5% in 2011.

Energy is derived principally from coal-based electricity (94.1% in 2009); this is supplemented by nuclear power and by hydroelectric power (5.2% and 0.6%, respectively). Exploitation of petroleum reserves in oilfields located 140 km south-west of the Southern Cape commenced in 1997. In 2001 substantial reserves of natural gas were discovered off the Western Cape. Imports of mineral fuels and lubricants comprised 19.6% of the value of total imports in 2010.

The services sector contributed 68.3% of GDP in 2011, and engaged 71.5% of the employed labour force in 2012. The real GDP of the services sector increased by an average of 4.3% per year in 2002–11. Services GDP increased by 3.8% in 2011.

In 2011 South Africa recorded a visible merchandise trade surplus of US $2,455m., although there was a deficit of $13,683m. on the current account of the balance of payments. In 2010 the principal source of imports for South Africa was the People's Republic of China (which provided 14.3% of the total); other major suppliers of imports were Germany, the USA and Japan. The principal market for exports in that year was also China (11.4%); other important purchasers were the USA, Japan, Germany and the United Kingdom. The principal exports in 2010 were basic manufactures (particularly platinum, iron and steel and diamonds), machinery and transport equipment, metalliferous ores and metal scrap, mineral fuels, chemical products and food and live animals. The principal imports were machinery and transport equipment (especially road vehicles), mineral fuels (particularly petroleum), chemical products, basic manufactures and miscellaneous manufactured articles.

In the financial year 2012/13 South Africa's estimated budget deficit was R 170,024.7m. South Africa's general government gross debt was R 1,151,499m. in 2011, equivalent to 38.9% of GDP. At the end of 2010 South Africa's total foreign debt was US $45,165m., of which $17,753m. was public and publicly guaranteed debt. In that year, the cost of servicing long-term public and publicly guaranteed debt and repayments to the IMF was equivalent to 4.9% of the value of exports of goods, services and income (excluding workers' remittances). The annual rate of inflation averaged 5.6% in 2002–12; consumer prices increased by 5.6% in 2012. According to official figures, 25.1% of the labour force were unemployed in 2012.

Following the removal of economic sanctions (imposed by the international community in protest against apartheid) in late 1993, and democratic elections in April 1994, foreign governments pledged considerable financial assistance to South Africa, and by 1999 financial market conditions had improved considerably, resulting in lower inflation, increased real GDP and greater investor confidence. Economic progress continued in the 2000s, but many problems remained, including widespread poverty, a high level of unemployment and the devastating social and economic impact of the HIV/AIDS epidemic. Several initiatives aimed at reducing social disparities had been introduced, such as the Broad-Based Black Economic Empowerment Act (instituted in 2004) to redistribute the nation's wealth among the black population. The country was negatively affected by the global economic slowdown from late 2008, with declining exports, dwindling production levels in the manufacturing and mining sectors, rising unemployment, and a resultant GDP contraction of 1.8% in 2009, although the construction industry was buoyed by the increase in resources allocated to infrastructure projects in advance of South Africa's hosting of the 2010 Fédération Internationale de Football Association World Cup. The economy returned to growth in 2010, and continued its recovery in 2011. However, the IMF forecast slowed growth in 2012 (of 2.6%) as a result of renewed crises in Europe, South Africa's main regional trading partner. (Average real GDP growth for sub-Saharan Africa was forecast at 5.5% for the same year.) Moreover, domestic problems, including strikes in the agriculture, mining and manufacturing sectors and inflationary pressures (due to a weakened rand), had a negative effect on consumption and economic growth. Labour unrest and high unemployment—particularly among the young—continued to threaten stability. Consequently, the Government's New Growth Plan and its National Development Plan both targeted labour-intensive growth. The Ministry of Finance estimated that industrial action in the gold and platinum mines in 2012 resulted in a loss to the economy of some R 10,000m. In August 2012, year-on-year mining output declined by 3.3%, with platinum group production 15.3% lower than one year earlier. Meanwhile, the country was downgraded by credit rating agencies in 2012 and was facing larger trade and budget deficits in the short term. Furthermore, South Africa continued to be vulnerable to external crises, particularly in Europe. However, growth prospects remained positive. Following subdued growth in 2012, the Finance Ministry projected rates of 3% and 4% in 2013 and 2014, respectively; while the budget deficit was forecast to fall to 3% of GDP by 2015/16.

PUBLIC HOLIDAYS

2014: 1 January (New Year's Day), 21 March (Human Rights Day), 18 April (Good Friday), 21 April (Family Day), 28 April (for Freedom Day), 1 May (Workers' Day), 16 June (Youth Day), 9 August (National Women's Day), 24 September (Heritage Day), 16 December (Day of Reconciliation), 25 December (Christmas Day), 26 December (Day of Goodwill).

Statistical Survey

Source (unless otherwise indicated): Statistics South Africa, Private Bag X44, Pretoria 0001; tel. (12) 3108911; fax (12) 3108500; e-mail info@statssa.pwv.gov.za; internet www.statssa.gov.za.

Area and Population

AREA, POPULATION AND DENSITY

Area (sq km)	1,220,813*
Population (census results)	
9 October 2001	44,819,778
9 October 2011	
Males	25,188,791
Females	26,581,769
Total	51,770,560
Population (UN estimates at mid-year)†	
2012	50,738,255
2013	50,981,076
Density (per sq km) at mid-2013	41.8

* 471,358 sq miles.
† Source: UN, *World Population Prospects: The 2010 Revision*; estimates not revised to take account of results of 2011 census.

POPULATION BY AGE AND SEX
('000 at 2011 census)

	Males	Females	Total
0–14	7,637.0	7,463.0	15,100.1
15–64	16,515.2	17,389.3	33,904.5
65 and over	1,036.6	1,729.4	2,766.0
Total	25,188.8	26,581.8	51,770.6

Note: Totals may not be equal to the sum of components, owing to rounding.

ETHNIC GROUPS
('000 at 2011 census)

	Number	% of total
Africans (Blacks)	41,000.9	79.2
Coloureds	4,615.4	8.9
Europeans (Whites)	4,586.8	8.9
Asians/Indians	1,286.9	2.5
Other	280.5	0.5
Total	51,770.6	100.0

Note: Totals may not be equal to the sum of components, owing to rounding.

PROVINCES
(population at 2011 census)

	Area (sq km)	Population ('000)	Density (per sq km)	Capital
Eastern Cape .	168,966	6,562.1	38.8	Bisho
Free State* . .	129,825	2,745.6	21.1	Bloemfontein
Gauteng† . . .	18,178	12,272.3	675.1	Johannesburg
KwaZulu/Natal .	94,361	10,267.3	108.8	Pietermaritzburg
Limpopo‡ . .	125,754	5,404.9	43.0	Pietersburg
Mpumalanga§ .	76,495	4,039.9	52.8	Nelspruit
Northern Cape .	372,889	1,145.9	3.1	Kimberley
North-West . .	104,882	3,510.0	33.5	Mmabatho
Western Cape .	129,462	5,822.7	45.0	Cape Town
Total	1,220,813	51,770.6	42.4	

* Formerly the Orange Free State.
† Formerly Pretoria-Witwatersrand-Vereeniging.
‡ Known as Northern Province (formerly Northern Transvaal) until February 2002.
§ Formerly Eastern Transvaal.

Note: Totals may not be equal to the sum of components, owing to rounding.

PRINCIPAL TOWNS
(metropolitan areas, population at 2001 census)

Johannesburg . .	3,225,812	Springs	80,776
Durban	3,090,122	Vanderbijlpark . .	80,201
Cape Town* . .	2,893,247	Vereeniging . .	73,288
Pretoria* . .	1,985,983	Uitenhage . .	71,668
Port Elizabeth . .	1,005,779	Rustenburg . .	67,201
Soweto . . .	858,649	Kimberley . . .	62,526
Tembisa . .	348,687	Brakpan . . .	62,115
Pietermaritzburg .	223,518	Witbank . . .	61,092
Botshabelo . .	175,820	Somerset West . .	60,609
Mdantsane . .	175,783	Klerksdorp . .	59,511
Boksburg . .	158,650	Midrand . .	44,566
East London . .	135,560	Newcastle . .	44,119
Bloemfontein* . .	111,698	Welkom . . .	34,158
Benoni . . .	94,341	Potchefstroom . .	26,725
Alberton . .	89,394	Carletonville . .	18,362
Krugersdorp . .	86,618	Westonaria . . .	8,440

* Pretoria is the administrative capital, Cape Town the legislative capital and Bloemfontein the judicial capital.

Mid-2011 (incl. suburbs, UN estimates): Cape Town 3,562,470; Pretoria 1,500,960; Bloemfontein 467,778 (Source: UN, *World Urbanization Prospects: The 2011 Revision*).

BIRTHS AND DEATHS
(annual averages, UN estimates)

	1995–2000	2000–05	2005–10
Birth rate (per 1,000)	25.1	24.0	21.9
Death rate (per 1,000)	10.4	13.9	15.2

Source: UN, *World Population Prospects: The 2010 Revision*.

Registered live births ('000): 1,255 in 2009; 1,295 in 2010; 1,202 in 2011.

Registered deaths: 603,094 in 2007; 592,073 in 2008; 572,673 in 2009.

Registered marriages: 171,989 in 2009; 170,826 in 2010; 167,264 in 2011.

Life expectancy (years at birth): 52.1 (males 51.4; females 52.8) in 2010 (Source: World Bank, World Development Indicators database).

IMMIGRATION AND EMIGRATION

	2001	2002	2003
Immigrants:			
Africa	1,419	2,472	4,961
Europe	1,714	1,847	2,567
Asia	1,289	1,738	2,328
Americas	213	244	354
Oceania	51	65	99
Total (incl. others and unspecified)	4,832	6,545	10,578
Emigrants:			
Africa	1,584	1,461	2,611
Europe	5,316	4,637	6,827
Asia	226	218	445
Americas	1,713	1,473	2,090
Oceania	2,912	2,523	3,248
Total (incl. others and unspecified)	12,260	10,890	16,165

Immigrants (2004): Africa 5,235; Europe 2,638; Asia 2,225; Americas 343; Total (incl. others) 10,714.

Note: Data are for documented migration only; emigrant figures are based on self-declaration.

ECONOMICALLY ACTIVE POPULATION

('000 persons aged 15 to 65 years, annual labour force survey)*

	2010	2011	2012
Agriculture, hunting, forestry and fishing	639	614	660
Mining and quarrying	305	312	350
Manufacturing	1,739	1,766	1,714
Electricity, gas and water . . .	90	86	98
Construction	1,060	1,054	1,026
Trade, restaurants and hotels .	2,927	2,995	2,977
Transport, storage and communications	774	762	806
Financing, insurance, real estate and business services . . .	1,656	1,711	1,773
Community, social and personal services	2,727	2,849	2,989
Private households	1,140	1,117	1,130
Total employed	**13,061**	**13,265**	**13,523**
Unemployed	4,332	4,397	4,541
Total labour force	**17,393**	**17,662**	**18,064**
Males	9,574	9,648	9,889
Females	7,819	8,015	8,175

* Figures have been assessed independently, so totals are not always equal to the sum of the component parts.

Health and Welfare

KEY INDICATORS

Total fertility rate (children per woman, 2010)	2.5
Under-5 mortality rate (per 1,000 live births, 2010) . .	57
HIV/AIDS (% of persons aged 15–49, 2009)	17.8
Physicians (per 1,000 head, 2004)	0.8
Hospital beds (per 1,000 head, 2005)	2.8
Health expenditure (2009): US $ per head (PPP)	930
Health expenditure (2009): % of GDP	9.2
Health expenditure (2009): public (% of total)	43.8
Access to water (% of persons, 2010)	91
Access to sanitation (% of persons, 2010)	79
Total carbon dioxide emissions ('000 metric tons, 2008) . .	435,878.0
Carbon dioxide emissions per head (metric tons, 2008) . .	8.9
Human Development Index (2011): ranking	123
Human Development Index (2011): value	0.619

For sources and definitions, see explanatory note on p. vi.

Agriculture

PRINCIPAL CROPS

('000 metric tons)

	2009	2010	2011
Wheat	1,958	1,430	2,005
Barley	216.0	194.0	312.0
Maize	12,050	12,815	10,360
Oats	37.0	34.0	57.0
Sorghum	276.5	196.5	155.0
Potatoes	1,866.6	2,090.2	2,195.4
Sweet potatoes	63.0	65.8	55.8
Sugar cane	18,655.1	16,015.6	16,800.0
Beans, dry	67.0	52.3	42.0
Soybeans (Soya beans) . . .	516.0	566.0	710.0
Groundnuts, with shell . .	99.5	88.0	64.3
Sunflower seed	801.0	490.0	860.0
Seed cotton	22.7	20.8	46.3
Cabbages and other brassicas .	136.0	150.8	150.9
Tomatoes	533.2	554.1	507.3
Pumpkins, squash and gourds .	158.3	172.0	177.9
Onions, dry	461.5	518.3	588.1
Carrots and turnips . . .	148.1	144.1	161.1
Maize, green*	352	402	403
Watermelons	72.2	139.2	78.0
Bananas	370.8	393.3	387.4
Oranges	1,369.5	1,414.6	1,496.2
Tangerines, mandarins, clementines and satsumas* .	145.0	141.2	148.6

—continued	2009	2010	2011
Lemons and limes	204.3	216.0	260.0
Grapefruit and pomelos . .	406.6	343.2	415.7
Apples	817.7	724.2	781.1
Pears	340.1	368.5	350.5
Apricots	46.6	44.3	57.4
Peaches and nectarines . .	159.3	164.2	155.6
Plums and sloes	61.6	61.0	63.5
Grapes	1,347.6	1,261.3	1,306.0
Mangoes, mangosteens and guavas	48.9	65.2	52.3
Avocados	76.7	83.2	75.2
Pineapples	123.0	94.3	108.6
Tobacco, unmanufactured . . .	9.6	12.3	15.0

* FAO estimates.

Aggregate production ('000 metric tons, may include official, semi-official or estimated data): Total cereals 14,576.7 in 2009, 14,699.3 in 2010, 12,918.6 in 2011; Total roots and tubers 1,929.7 in 2009, 2,156.0 in 2010, 2,251.2 in 2011; Total vegetables (incl. melons) 2,363.4 in 2009, 2,619.8 in 2010, 2,607.4 in 2011; Total fruits (excl. melons) 5,612.0 in 2009, 5,465.5 in 2010, 5,751.3 in 2011.

Source: FAO.

LIVESTOCK

('000 head, year ending September)

	2009	2010	2011
Cattle	13,761	13,731	13,688
Pigs	1,613	1,594	1,584
Sheep	24,989	24,501	24,303
Goats	6,358	6,275	6,165
Horses*	300	300	305
Asses*	151	152	153
Chickens*	163,000	180,000	190,000
Ducks*	375	380	385
Geese and guinea fowls* . .	137	137	138
Turkeys*	515	520	520

* FAO estimates.

Source: FAO.

LIVESTOCK PRODUCTS

('000 metric tons)

	2009	2010	2011
Cattle meat	771	848	829
Sheep meat	146.6	140.7	130.8
Goat meat*	36.3	35.5	34.6
Pig meat	313.0	312.0*	320.0*
Chicken meat	1,387.6	1,471.6	1,485.6
Cows' milk	3,104	3,233	3,256
Hen eggs	450	473	490
Wool, greasy	43	41	41

* FAO estimate(s).

Source: FAO.

Forestry

ROUNDWOOD REMOVALS

('000 cubic metres, excl. bark, unofficial figures unless otherwise indicated)

	2009	2010	2011
Sawlogs, veneer logs and logs for sleepers	4,374.8	3,963.9	4,179.1
Pulpwood	12,940.7	11,664.2	12,383.7
Other industrial wood . . .	1,572.1	1,360.5	1,389.5
Fuel wood*	12,000.0	12,000.0	12,000.0
Total	**30,887.6**	**28,988.6**	**29,952.3**

* FAO estimates.

Source: FAO.

SAWNWOOD PRODUCTION
('000 cubic metres, incl. railway sleepers, unofficial figures)

	2009	2010	2011
Coniferous (softwood)	1,753.3	1,583.7	1,451.8
Broadleaved (hardwood) . . .	122.3	296.8	115.0
Total	1,875.6	1,880.5	1,566.8

Source: FAO.

Fishing

('000 metric tons, live weight)

	2008	2009	2010
Capture*	644.7	512.3	623.9
Cape hakes (Stokvisse) . .	132.4	107.5	109.0
Southern African pilchard . .	91.0	94.4	112.4
Whitehead's round herring .	64.7	40.6	88.6
Southern African anchovy . .	265.8	174.5	217.0
Cape horse mackerel . . .	30.5	35.2	33.4
Aquaculture	3.6	3.4*	3.1*
Total catch*†	648.2	515.7	627.1

* FAO estimate(s).

† Excluding aquatic plants ('000 metric tons, FAO estimates): 1.8 in 2008; 1.9 in 2009; 2.0 in 2010.

Note: Figures exclude aquatic animals, recorded by number rather than weight. The number of Nile crocodiles captured was: 40,197 in 2008; 24,988 in 2009; 70,208 in 2010.

Source: FAO.

Mining

('000 metric tons unless otherwise indicated)

	2008	2009	2010
Hard coal	252,699	250,538	254,522
Crude petroleum ('000 barrels) .	1,976	1,070	1,358
Natural gas	1,812	1,048	963
Iron ore*	30,800	34,800	36,900
Copper ore (metric tons)* . .	108,700	107,600	102,600
Nickel ore (metric tons)* . .	31,675	34,605	39,960
Lead concentrates (metric tons)* .	46,440	49,149	50,625
Zinc ore (metric tons)* . . .	29,002	28,159	36,142
Manganese ore and concentrates (metallurgical and chemical)† .	6,806	4,579	7,172
Chromium ore†	9,682	7,561	10,871
Vanadium ore (metric tons)† . .	20,295	14,353	22,606
Zirconium concentrates (metric tons)‡	398,000	387,000	376,000
Antimony concentrates (metric tons)*	3,983	2,673‡	2,800‡
Cobalt ore (metric tons)‡* . .	400	400	400
Silver (kg)	75,199	77,780	79,315
Uranium oxide (metric tons) . .	654	629	682
Gold (kg)	212,571	197,628	188,701
Platinum-group metals (kg) . .	275,677	271,393	287,304
Kaolin	39.2	31.0	29.9
Magnesite—crude	83.9	47.6	48.0‡
Phosphate rock†	2,287	2,237	2,494
Fluorspar	299	140	140
Salt	429.9	408.4	394.5
Diamonds ('000 carats) . . .	12,895	6,113	8,868
Gypsum—crude	571.3	597.6	513.3
Mica (metric tons)	426	572	904
Talc (metric tons)	5,145	4,718	3,150
Pyrophyllite (metric tons) . .	80,704	114,889	122,511

* Figures refer to metal content of ores and concentrates.

† Gross weight.

‡ Estimated figure(s).

Source: US Geological Survey.

Industry

SELECTED PRODUCTS
('000 metric tons unless otherwise indicated)

	2007	2008	2009
Wheat flour*	2,242	2,237	2,260
Chemical wood pulp . . .	1,394	1,394	1,172
Newsprint	349	349	323
Motor spirit (petrol)	7,403	8,038	7,609
Kerosene	570	473	485
Jet fuel	1,711	1,962	1,868
Distillate fuel oils	7,482	10,157	9,455
Petroleum bitumen—asphalt . .	349	428	432
Cement (sales)†	15,316	14,869	13,000
Pig-iron†	5,358	5,350	4,376
Crude steel†	9,098	8,269	7,484
Refined copper—unwrought† . .	113.2	93.0	89.5
Electric energy (million kWh) .	263,479	258,291	249,557

* Twelve months ending September.

† Source: US Geological Survey.

2010: Cement (sales) 12,000 (estimate); Pig-iron 8,220; Crude steel 8,480; Refined copper—unwrought 81.1 (Source: US Geological Survey).

Source: mostly UN Industrial Commodity Statistics Database.

Electric energy (million kWh): 259,601 in 2010; 262,538 in 2011.

Finance

CURRENCY AND EXCHANGE RATES

Monetary Units
100 cents = 1 rand (R).

Sterling, Dollar and Euro Equivalents (31 December 2012)
£1 sterling = 13.41 rand;
US $1 = 8.50 rand;
€1 = 11.22 rand;
100 rand = £7.45 = $11.76 = €8.92.

Average Exchange Rate (rand per US $)
2010   7.3212
2011   7.2611
2012   8.2100

BUDGET
(million rand, year ending 31 March)

Revenue	2010/11	2011/12*	2012/13*
Tax revenue (gross)	674,183.1	738,734.8	826,401.1
Taxes on incomes and profits .	379,941.2	423,805.0	475,729.3
Individuals	226,925.0	249,700.0	285,969.7
Companies (including secondary tax)	150,079.9	171,500.0	186,888.6
Retirement funds	2.8	—	—
Other	2,933.6	2,605.0	2,871.0
Taxes on payroll and workforce.	8,652.3	10,100.0	11,131.2
Taxes on property	9,102.3	7,870.0	8,627.1
Domestic taxes on goods and services	249,490.4	264,649.8	294,554.2
Value-added tax	183,571.4	190,815.0	209,674.9
Excise duties	24,563.8	27,694.6	30,772.3
Levies on fuel	34,417.6	37,180.0	42,775.5
Air departure tax . . .	647.8	730.1	750.3
Other	1,293.3	1,800.0	1,979.7
Stamp duties and fees . . .	3.1	—	—
State Miscellaneous Revenue .	16.7	—	—
Taxes on international trade and transactions	26,977.1	32,310.0	36,359.3
Departmental revenue . . .	13,460.1	17,579.5	15,091.0
Sub-total	687,643.2	756,314.3	841,492.1
Less SACU payments† . . .	14,991.3	21,763.2	42,151.3
Other adjustments	−2,914.4	—	—
Total	669,737.5	734,551.0	799,340.8

Expenditure	2010/11	2011/12*	2012/13*
Central government administration	61,690.6	66,960.7	75,820.0
The Presidency	958.7	1,005.8	1,018.0
Parliament	1,198.9	1,249.7	1,333.3
Co-operative governance and traditional affairs . . .	41,821.4	46,177.3	54,715.6
Foreign affairs	4,417.2	5,153.4	5,116.6
Home affairs	6,521.7	5,850.8	5,296.3
Performance monitoring and evaluation	47.3	98.9	174.2
Public works	6,615.5	7,281.7	7,993.8
Women, children and people with disabilities . . .	109.9	143.1	172.2
Financial and administrative services	41,441.5	26,895.6	25,682.4
Government communication and information system . .	352.2	360.5	429.1
National treasury . . .	38,226.2	21,817.3	21,551.1
Public Enterprises . . .	540.0	353.3	1,249.1
Public services and administration	628.2	690.2	731.5
Statistics South Africa . .	1,694.9	3,674.3	1,721.6
Social services	154,308.7	176,635.5	193,271.6
Arts and culture	2,248.8	2,411.2	2,685.7
Education	32,430.3	41,929.2	47,844.0
Health	22,520.3	25,622.1	27,557.0
Labour	1,826.3	1,998.1	2,119.7
Social development . . .	94,031.0	103,858.9	112,216.8
Sport and Recreation South Africa	1,252.0	816.0	848.4
Justice and protection services .	109,484.2	120,820.7	130,987.2
Correctional services . .	14,698.8	16,203.1	17,732.2
Defence	30,442.4	34,349.1	37,493.0
Independent complaints directorate	128.4	153.5	197.0
Justice and constitutional development	10,684.9	11,564.5	13,079.6
Safety and security . . .	53,529.7	58,550.5	62,485.4
Economic services and infrastructure	88,667.8	111,320.5	117,868.8
Agriculture and forestry . .	3,850.7	4,964.4	5,798.8
Communications . . .	1,426.5	2,002.9	1,712.3
Economic development . .	400.7	567.6	672.7
Energy	5,505.4	6,098.8	6,805.9
Environmental affairs . .	3,279.5	4,201.6	4,512.2
Human settlements . . .	18,916.5	22,645.5	25,263.2
Mineral resources . . .	994.7	1,039.0	1,169.1
Rural development and land reform	7,122.9	8,136.7	8,877.6
Tourism	1,143.5	1,265.0	1,367.3
Science and technology . .	4,051.9	4,407.0	4,955.9
Trade and industry . . .	5,796.7	6,876.5	9,092.1
Transport	29,155.1	41,450.0	38,829.0
Water affairs	7,023.7	7,665.5	8,812.7
Sub-total	455,592.8	502,633.0	543,629.5
State debt costs	66,226.8	76,644.9	89,388.1
Provincial equitable share . .	265,139.4	291,735.5	309,057.4
Skills levy and seats . . .	8,379.3	9,148.7	9,606.1
Members' remuneration . . .	346.0	355.1	430.1
Judges' salaries	1,910.2	2,104.2	2,401.9
President and deputy-president salary	4.0	3.8	2.7
General fuel levy sharing with metros	7,542.4	8,573.1	9,039.7
Unallocated	—	—	30.0
Contingency reserve . . .	—	—	5,780.0
Total	805,141.0	891,198.7	969,365.5

* Estimates.

† Payments to Botswana, Lesotho, Namibia and Swaziland, in accordance with Southern African Customs Union agreements.

Source: National Treasury, Pretoria.

INTERNATIONAL RESERVES
(US $ million at 31 December)

	2009	2010	2011
Gold (national valuation) . . .	4,438	5,654	6,272
IMF special drawing rights . .	2,803	2,754	2,745
Reserve position in IMF . . .	2	2	3
Foreign exchange	32,432	35,419	39,847
Total	39,675	43,829	48,867

Source: IMF, *International Financial Statistics.*

MONEY SUPPLY
(million rand at 31 December)

	2009	2010	2011
Currency outside depository corporations	61,784	65,079	75,396
Transferable deposits	361,281	408,363	437,816
Other deposits	1,154,303	1,217,424	1,419,445
Securities other than shares . .	370,544	392,113	322,641
Broad money	1,947,911	2,082,980	2,255,298

Source: IMF, *International Financial Statistics.*

COST OF LIVING
(Consumer Price Index; base: 2000 = 100)

	2006	2007	2008
Food	147.8	163.1	190.0
Clothing	84.6	76.8	87.7
Housing	118.2	129.7	142.2
Electricity, gas and other fuels .	141.9	153.3	182.8
All items (incl. others) . . .	134.0	143.5	160.0

2009: Food 109.5; All items (incl. others) 171.4.

2010: Food 111.0; All items (incl. others) 178.7.

2011: Food 118.9; All items (incl. others) 187.7.

Source: ILO.

NATIONAL ACCOUNTS
(million rand at current prices, preliminary)

National Income and Product

	2009	2010	2011
Compensation of employees . .	1,081,640	1,211,556	1,330,315
Net operating surplus	736,427	810,761	874,877
Consumption of fixed capital . .	332,333	350,692	375,982
Gross domestic product (GDP) at factor cost	2,150,400	2,373,009	2,581,174
Taxes on production	278,015	309,298	362,558
Less Subsidies	22,014	22,941	26,193
GDP at market prices . . .	2,406,401	2,659,366	2,917,539
Primary incomes received from abroad	34,075	34,099	38,118
Less Primary incomes paid abroad	87,593	87,022	104,689
Gross national income at market prices	2,352,883	2,606,443	2,850,968
Current transfers received from abroad	10,334	9,089	11,287
Less Current transfers paid abroad	32,762	25,851	25,486
Gross national disposable income at market prices .	2,330,455	2,589,681	2,836,769

Expenditure on the Gross Domestic Product

	2009	2010	2011
Government final consumption expenditure	507,330	580,659	635,019
Private final consumption expenditure	1,460,746	1,584,264	1,743,989
Increase in stocks	−48,487	−2,641	15,562
Gross fixed capital formation	518,785	514,004	553,313
Residual item	−10,857	−11,647	−12,329
Total domestic expenditure	2,427,517	2,664,639	2,935,554
Exports of goods and services	657,192	727,721	854,343
Less Imports of goods and services	678,308	732,994	872,358
GDP at market prices	2,406,401	2,659,366	2,917,539
GDP at constant 2005 prices	1,786,897	1,842,052	1,905,736

Gross Domestic Product by Economic Activity

	2009	2010	2011
Agriculture, forestry and fishing	63,655	61,999	64,578
Mining and quarrying	196,521	221,731	256,651
Manufacturing	331,702	341,746	335,683
Electricity, gas and water	60,402	63,050	72,816
Construction (contractors)	86,522	91,899	100,454
Wholesale and retail trade, catering and accommodation	298,511	360,811	403,518
Transport, storage and communication	199,276	222,847	243,444
Finance, insurance, real estate and business services	464,831	509,822	557,955
Government services	342,725	391,892	431,289
Other community, social and personal services	134,174	141,467	154,991
Gross value added at basic prices	2,178,320	2,407,264	2,621,379
Taxes, less subsidies, on products	228,081	252,102	296,161
GDP at market prices	2,406,401	2,659,366	2,917,539

BALANCE OF PAYMENTS
(US $ million)

	2009	2010	2011
Exports of goods	66,542	85,700	102,858
Imports of goods	−65,975	−81,824	−100,403
Balance on goods	567	3,876	2,455
Exports of services	12,020	14,004	14,824
Imports of services	−14,841	−18,495	−19,703
Balance on goods and services	−2,254	−615	−2,425
Primary income received	3,988	4,651	5,304
Primary income paid	−10,377	−11,876	−14,590
Balance on goods, services and primary income	−8,643	−7,839	−11,711
Secondary income received	1,242	1,247	1,541
Secondary income paid	−3,926	−3,525	−3,513
Current balance	−11,327	−10,117	−13,683
Capital account (net)	26	31	33
Direct investment assets	−1,311	161	500
Direct investment liabilities	5,354	1,224	5,718
Portfolio investment assets	−1,746	−4,613	−6,308
Portfolio investment liabilities	13,368	14,386	6,678
Other investment assets	3,101	−3,215	−60
Other investment liabilities	−2,489	892	4,416
Net errors and omissions	−804	5,048	7,414
Reserves and related items	4,171	3,796	4,708

Source: IMF, *International Financial Statistics*.

External Trade

PRINCIPAL COMMODITIES
(distribution by SITC, US $ million)

Imports c.i.f.	2008	2009	2010
Food and live animals	3,184.8	2,873.1	3,171.8
Crude materials (inedible) except fuels	2,891.0	1,261.8	1,635.0
Mineral fuels, lubricants, etc.	19,555.0	13,663.3	15,722.5
Petroleum, petroleum products, etc.	18,512.8	12,949.0	14,769.4
Crude petroleum oils, etc.	14,957.2	10,294.4	11,199.5
Chemicals and related products	8,549.9	6,673.8	8,662.9
Basic manufactures	9,048.1	6,611.5	8,688.5
Non-metallic mineral manufactures	1,936.1	1,234.7	1,639.6
Machinery and transport equipment	30,670.0	22,201.3	28,400.4
Power generating machinery and equipment	2,627.8	1,762.0	2,128.7
Machinery specialized for particular industries	4,417.2	2,605.1	2,758.8
General industrial machinery, equipment and parts	4,271.9	3,341.7	3,795.9
Office machines and automatic data-processing equipment	3,020.8	2,452.4	3,223.4
Telecommunications and sound equipment	3,913.3	3,172.3	4,397.8
Other electrical machinery, apparatus, etc.	3,627.7	2,987.7	3,580.6
Road vehicles	6,161.2	4,339.8	6,856.0
Passenger motor vehicles (excl. buses)	2,749.7	2,335.8	4,067.2
Other transport equipment	2,038.2	1,107.8	1,219.7
Miscellaneous manufactured articles	6,468.1	5,729.1	7,122.3
Total (incl. others)	87,593.1	63,766.1	80,139.3

Exports f.o.b.	2008	2009	2010
Food and live animals	4,124.1	4,132.8	4,757.3
Vegetables and fruit	2,050.9	2,076.8	2,678.1
Beverages and tobacco	1,078.1	1,132.9	1,219.4
Crude materials (inedible) except fuels	10,624.6	8,448.0	13,078.6
Metalliferous ores and metal scrap	8,252.7	6,806.7	10,892.1
Mineral fuels, lubricants, etc.	7,120.3	6,022.7	7,197.7
Coal, lignite and peat	4,785.5	4,215.1	5,474.0
Petroleum, petroleum products, etc.	2,198.7	1,675.5	1,562.0
Chemicals and related products	5,723.7	4,100.2	5,077.5
Basic manufactures	26,946.0	17,535.4	24,584.1
Non-metallic mineral manufactures	2,647.1	1,588.8	2,298.8
Pearl, precious and semi-precious stones, unworked or worked	2,339.0	1,307.1	1,955.5
Diamonds (non-industrial), not mounted or set	2,282.5	1,300.8	1,944.4
Iron and steel	8,859.7	5,116.2	7,735.0
Pig-iron, etc.	5,954.6	2,912.7	4,976.8
Non-ferrous metals	12,578.3	8,614.0	11,973.2

Exports f.o.b.—*continued*	2008	2009	2010
Silver, platinum and other platinum group metals . .	9,817.6	6,769.7	9,394.9
Platinum group metals, unwrought, unworked or semi-manufactured . .	9,801.0	6,766.6	9,377.1
Aluminium	2,071.0	1,464.3	1,889.7
Aluminium and aluminium alloys, unwrought . . .	1,348.4	1,004.2	1,235.5
Machinery and transport equipment	16,229.1	10,786.6	13,450.8
General industrial machinery, equipment and parts . . .	4,078.9	2,489.2	3,211.0
Road vehicles	7,522.3	5,096.1	6,545.7
Passenger motor vehicles (excl. buses)	4,535.6	3,062.5	4,116.9
Miscellaneous manufactured articles	1,777.4	1,408.1	1,699.7
Total (incl. others)	73,965.5	53,863.9	71,484.3

Source: UN, *International Trade Statistics Yearbook.*

PRINCIPAL TRADING PARTNERS
(US $ million)*

Imports f.o.b.	2008	2009	2010
Angola	2,686.5	1,370.6	1,998.2
Argentina	1,003.2	858.2	919.4
Australia	1,630.4	1,083.0	1,312.7
Belgium	1,128.2	927.2	1,147.1
Brazil	1,661.1	1,242.2	1,353.8
China, People's Repub. . .	9,909.3	8,325.3	11,499.2
France (incl. Monaco) . . .	2,502.6	1,993.2	2,334.0
Germany	9,914.0	7,438.3	9,051.1
India	2,261.9	1,811.6	2,839.4
Iran	3,290.4	2,599.1	3,148.0
Ireland	857.5	n.a.	n.a.
Italy	2,133.8	1,608.2	2,008.4
Japan	4,882.6	3,093.7	4,245.3
Korea, Repub.	1,437.1	1,135.3	1,747.2
Malaysia	1,084.6	865.8	1,166.0
Netherlands	1,213.2	1,157.9	1,414.2
Nigeria	1,892.4	1,839.0	2,200.8
Saudi Arabia	5,523.0	3,204.1	3,243.5
Singapore	887.9	575.8	870.9
Spain	1,063.7	756.9	1,257.9
Sweden	1,614.7	1,104.3	1,403.7
Thailand	1,756.1	1,352.5	1,829.9
United Kingdom . . .	3,556.2	2,526.1	3,019.8
USA	7,038.0	4,949.4	5,837.6
Total (incl. others)	87,593.1	63,766.1	80,139.3

Exports f.o.b.	2008	2009	2010
Angola	897.8	682.0	700.1
Australia	1,494.4	725.8	952.0
Belgium	2,046.6	1,282.2	1,801.2
China, People's Repub. . .	4,309.8	5,670.1	8,132.4
Congo, Democratic Repub. .	1,125.2	573.8	865.8
France (incl. Monaco) . .	1,447.2	841.3	978.7
Germany	5,748.9	3,512.7	5,529.4
Hong Kong	645.1	963.4	966.5
India	2,279.5	2,067.7	2,980.6
Israel	841.4	575.5	718.0
Italy	1,595.2	1,080.6	1,425.3
Japan	8,119.6	4,096.1	6,425.0
Kenya	709.9	872.4	785.3
Korea, Repub.	1,506.7	900.8	1,713.3
Mozambique	1,609.0	1,606.6	1,893.9
Netherlands	3,463.6	2,036.6	2,284.6
Nigeria	955.0	678.1	622.8
Spain	1,876.6	1,088.5	1,102.9
Switzerland-Liechtenstein .	1,556.4	2,273.3	2,276.9
United Arab Emirates . .	769.9	610.4	850.7
United Kingdom . . .	4,905.9	3,002.1	3,703.5
USA	7,987.4	4,859.7	7,060.8
Zambia	1,965.4	1,416.0	1,750.9
Zimbabwe	1,689.0	1,608.0	2,156.1
Total (incl. others)	73,965.5	53,863.9	71,484.3

* Imports by country of origin; exports by country of destination.

Source: UN, *International Trade Statistics Yearbook.*

Transport

RAILWAYS
(traffic, preliminary)

	2010	2011	2012
Passengers ('000)	514,104	520,290	540,648
Total freight ('000 metric tons) .	184,688	197,560	209,416

ROAD TRAFFIC
(registered motor vehicles at 31 December)

	2007	2009*	2010
Passenger cars	5,160,844	5,411,093	5,596,343
Buses and coaches	316,540	328,158	333,324
Lorries and vans	2,125,784	2,267,896	2,325,824
Motorcycles and mopeds . . .	312,046	362,400	327,275

* Data for 2008 were not available.

Source: IRF, *World Road Statistics.*

SHIPPING

Flag Registered Fleet
(at 31 December)

	2010	2011	2012
Number of vessels	198	195	199
Total displacement ('000 grt) . .	206.6	177.8	191.4

Source: Lloyd's List Intelligence (www.lloydslistintelligence.com).

International Sea-borne Freight Traffic

	2003	2004	2005
Goods loaded (metric tons) . .	128,477,183	124,370,762	127,408,557
Goods unloaded (metric tons) . .	42,845,843	43,820,161	43,847,748
Containers loaded (TEU) . .	1,194,400	1,290,883	1,484,009
Containers unloaded (TEU) . .	1,220,167	1,341,888	1,530,227

Source: National Ports Authority of South Africa.

CIVIL AVIATION
(traffic on scheduled services)

	2007	2008	2009
Kilometres flown (million) . .	222	226	217
Passengers carried ('000) . . .	12,870	12,989	12,504
Passenger-km (million) . . .	29,893	28,953	26,926
Total ton-km (million)	3,690	3,386	3,108

Source: UN, *Statistical Yearbook.*

2010: Passengers carried ('000) 16,779 (Source: World Bank, World Development Indicators database).

Tourism

FOREIGN VISITOR ARRIVALS*

Country of origin	2008	2009	2010
Botswana	807,292	822,305	829,518
Germany	243,578	209,644	227,514
Lesotho	2,165,505	1,890,976	2,610,507
Mozambique	1,228,979	1,324,445	1,328,731
Namibia	222,817	212,098	226,541
Swaziland	1,090,056	1,057,957	1,037,165
United Kingdom . . .	493,415	482,779	490,071
USA	292,884	260,599	314,027
Zimbabwe	1,248,043	1,526,556	2,085,579
Total (incl. others and unspecified)	9,728,860	9,531,615	11,303,087

* Figures include same-day visitors (excursionists), but exclude arrivals of South African nationals resident abroad. Border crossings by contract workers are also excluded.

Total visitor arrivals: 8,339,000 in 2011 (provisional).

Tourism receipts (US $ million, excl. passenger transport): 7,543 in 2009; 9,070 in 2010; 9,547 in 2011 (provisional).

Source: World Tourism Organization.

Communications Media

	2009	2010	2011
Telephones ('000 main lines in use)	4,320	4,225	4,127
Mobile cellular telephones ('000 subscribers)	46,436	50,372	64,000
Internet users ('000)	4,420	n.a.	n.a.
Broadband subscribers ('000) . .	481	743	907

Personal computers: 3,966,000 (84.6 per 1,000 persons) in 2005.

Source: International Telecommunication Union.

Education

(2010)*

	Institutions	Teachers	Students
Primary	14,456	187,520	5,992,863
Secondary	6,231	142,181	3,821,763
Combined	4,425	67,281	2,025,105
Intermediate and middle . . .	738	21,127	420,368
ABET centres†‡§	2,395	15,657	297,900
ELSEN centres‖	423	8,781	104,633
Further education and training†§ .	49	6,255	420,475
ECD¶	4,313	12,504	279,476
Higher education†§	23	16,320	837,779

* Figures for public and independent institutions, unless otherwise indicated.
† Figures for 2009.
‡ Adult basic education and training.
§ Figures refer to public institutions only.
‖ Education for learners with special needs.
¶ Early childhood development.

Source: Department of Education.

Pupil-teacher ratio (primary education, UNESCO estimate): 30.7 in 2008/09 (Source: UNESCO Institute for Statistics).

Adult literacy rate (UNESCO estimates): 89.0% (males 89.9%; females 88.1%) in 2008 (Source: UNESCO Institute for Statistics).

Directory

The Government

HEAD OF STATE

President: JACOB ZUMA (inaugurated 9 May 2009).
Deputy President: KGALEMA MOTLANTHE.

THE CABINET
(May 2013)

Minister of Agriculture, Forestry and Fisheries: TINA JOEMAT-PETTERSSON.

Minister of Arts and Culture: PAUL MASHATILE.

Minister of Basic Education: MATSIE ANGIE MOTSHEKGA.

Minister of Communications: DINA PULE.

Minister of Co-operative Governance and Traditional Affairs: RICHARD BALOYI.

Minister of Correctional Services: JOEL SIBUSISO NDEBELE.

Minister of Defence and Military Veterans: NOSIVIWE NOLUTHANDO MAPISA-NQAKULA.

Minister of Economic Development: EBRAHIM PATEL.

Minister of Energy: ELIZABETH DIPUO PETERS.

Minister of Finance: PRAVIN JAMNADAS GORDHAN.

Minister of Health: Dr PAKISHE AARON MOTSOALEDI.

Minister of Higher Education and Training: Dr BONGINKOSI EMMANUEL 'BLADE' NZIMANDE.

Minister of Home Affairs: GRACE NALEDI MANDISA PANDOR.

Minister of Human Settlements: TOKYO MOSIMA GABRIEL SEXWALE.

Minister of International Relations and Co-operation: MAITE M. NKOANA-MASHABANE.

Minister of Justice and Constitutional Development: JEFFREY THAMSANQA RADEBE.

Minister of Labour: MILDRED OLIPHANT.

Minister of Mineral Resources: SUSAN SHABANGU.

Minister of Police: NATHI MTHETHWA.

Minister of Public Enterprises: MALUSI KNOWLEDGE NKANYEZI GIGABA.

Minister of Public Service and Administration: LINDIWE NONCEBA SISULU.

Minister of Public Works: THEMBELANI 'THULAS' NXESI.

Minister of Rural Development and Land Reform: GUGILE NKWINTI.

Minister of Science and Technology: DEREK ANDRE HANEKOM.

Minister of Social Development: BATHABILE OLIVE DLAMINI.

Minister of Sport and Recreation: FIKILE APRIL MBALULA.

Minister of State Security: SIYABONGA CYPRIAN CWELE.

Ministers in the Presidency: TREVOR ANDREW MANUEL (National Planning Commission), OHM COLLINS CHABANE (Performance Monitoring, Evaluation and Administration).

Minister of Tourism: MARTHINUS VAN SCHALKWYK.

Minister of Trade and Industry: Dr ROB DAVIES.

Minister of Transport: BEN MARTINS.

Minister of Water and Environmental Affairs: BOMO EDNA MOLEWA.

Minister of Women, Youth, Children and People with Disabilities: LULAMA XINGWANA.

In addition, there were 32 Deputy Ministers.

MINISTRIES

The Presidency: Union Bldgs, West Wing, Government Ave, Pretoria 0001; Private Bag X1000, Pretoria 0001; tel. (12) 3005200; fax (12) 3238246; e-mail president@po.gov.za; internet www.thepresidency.gov.za.

  Ministry in The Presidency: National Planning Commission: Union Bldgs, 2nd Floor, Government Ave, Pretoria 0001; Private Bag X1000, Pretoria 0001; tel. (12) 3005277; fax (12) 3238246; e-mail minister@po.gov.za; internet www .thepresidency.gov.za.

  Ministry in The Presidency: Performance Monitoring, Evaluation and Administration in The Presidency: Union Bldgs, 2nd Floor, Government Ave, Pretoria 0001; Private Bag X1000, Pretoria 0001; tel. (12) 3005331; fax (12) 3218870; e-mail samson@po.gov.za; internet www.thepresidency.gov.za.

Ministry of Agriculture, Forestry and Fisheries: Agriculture Bldg, 20 Beatrix St, Arcadia, Pretoria 0002; Private Bag X250, Pretoria 0001; tel. (12) 3197317; fax (12) 3197856; e-mail cco@nda .agric.za; internet www.doa.agric.za.

Ministry of Arts and Culture: 481 Church St, 10th Floor, cnr Church and Beatrix Sts, Kingsley Centre, Arcadia, Pretoria; Private Bag X899, Pretoria 0001; tel. (12) 4413709; fax (12) 4404485; e-mail sandile.memela@dac.gov.za; internet www.dac.gov.za.

Ministry of Basic Education: Sol Plaatje House, 123 Schoeman St, Pretoria 0002; Private Bag X603, Pretoria 0001; tel. (12) 3125501; fax (12) 3235989; internet www.education.gov.za.

Ministry of Communications: Nkululeko House, iParioli Office Park, 399 Duncan St, cnr Park St, Hatfield, Pretoria 0083; Private Bag X860, Pretoria 0001; tel. (12) 4278177; fax (12) 3626915; e-mail joe@doc.gov.za; internet www.doc.gov.za.

Ministry of Co-operative Governance and Traditional Affairs: 87 Hamilton St, Arcadia, Pretoria 0001; Private Bag X802, Pretoria 0001; tel. (12) 3340705; fax (12) 3264478; internet www.cogta.gov.za.

Ministry of Correctional Services: Poyntons Bldg, West Block, cnr Church and Schubart Sts, Pretoria 0002; Private Bag X853, Pretoria 0001; tel. (12) 3072000; fax (12) 3286149; e-mail communications@dcs.gov.za; internet www.dcs.gov.za.

Ministry of Defence and Military Veterans: Armscor Bldg, Block 5, Nossob St, Erasmusrand 0181; Private Bag X427, Pretoria 0001; tel. (12) 3556101; fax (12) 3470118; e-mail mil@mil.za; internet www .dod.mil.za.

Ministry of Economic Development: DTI Campus, 3rd Floor, Block A, 77 cnr Meintjies and Esselen Sts, Sunnyside, Pretoria; Private Bag X149, Pretoria 0001; tel. (12) 3941006; fax (86) 3940255.

Ministry of Energy: Mineralia Centre, 234 Visagie St, Pretoria 0002; Private Bag X59, Pretoria 0001; tel. (12) 3178000; fax (12) 3223416; internet www.dme.gov.za.

Ministry of Health: 226 Prinsloo St, Pretoria 0001; Private Bag X399, Pretoria 0001; tel. (12) 3120546; fax (12) 3255526; e-mail bhengu@health.gov.za; internet www.doh.gov.za.

Ministry of Higher Education and Training: Sol Plaatje House, 123 Schoeman St, Pretoria 0002; Private Bag X893, Pretoria 0001; tel. (12) 3125555; fax (12) 3235618; internet www.education.gov.za.

Ministry of Home Affairs: cnr Maggs and Petroleum Sts, Watloo, Pretoria; Private Bag X114, Pretoria 0001; tel. (12) 8108039; fax (12) 8107312; e-mail csc@dha.gov.za; internet www.home-affairs.gov.za.

Ministry of Human Settlements: Govan Mbeki House, 240 Walker St, Sunnyside, Pretoria 0002; Private Bag X644, Pretoria 0001; tel. (12) 4211310; fax (12) 3418513; e-mail mareldia@housing .gov.za; internet www.housing.gov.za.

Ministry of International Relations and Co-operation: Union Bldgs, East Wing, 1 Government Ave, Arcadia, Pretoria 0002; Private Bag X152, Pretoria 0001; tel. (12) 3511000; fax (12) 3291000; e-mail minister@foreign.gov.za; internet www.dfa.gov.za.

Ministry of Justice and Constitutional Development: Momentum Centre, 329 Pretorius St, cnr Pretorius and Prinsloo Sts, Pretoria 0001; Private Bag X276, Pretoria 0001; tel. (12) 313578217; fax (12) 3151749; e-mail znqayi@justice.gov.za; internet www.doj.gov.za.

Ministry of Labour: Laboria House, 215 Schoeman St, Pretoria 0002; Private Bag X117, Pretoria 0001; tel. (12) 3094000; fax (12) 3094030; e-mail page.boikanyo@labour.gov.za; internet www.labour .gov.za.

Ministry of Mineral Resources: Trevenna Campus, Bldg 2c, Meintje and Schoeman St, Sunnyside, Pretoria; Private Bag X59, Arcadia 0007, Pretoria; tel. (12) 4443000; fax (12) 3223416; e-mail enquiries@dmr.gov.za; internet www.dmr.gov.za.

Ministry of Police: Wachthuis, 7th Floor, 231 Pretorius St, Pretoria; Private Bag X463, Pretoria 0001; tel. (12) 3932810; fax (12) 3932812; e-mail bloemb@saps.org.za.

Ministry of Public Enterprises: Infotech Bldg, Suite 401, 1090 Arcadia St, Hatfield, Pretoria 0083; Private Bag X15, Hatfield 0028; tel. (12) 4311000; fax (86) 5012624; e-mail info@dpe.gov.za; internet www.dpe.gov.za.

Ministry of Public Service and Administration: Batho Pele House, 116 Proes St, Pretoria 0001; Private Bag X916, Pretoria 0001; tel. (12) 3361701; fax (12) 3267802; e-mail natasha@dpsa.gov.za; internet www.dpsa.gov.za.

Ministry of Public Works: AVN Bldg, 6th Floor, cnr Skinner and Andries Sts, Pretoria 0002; Private Bag X65, Pretoria 0001; tel. (12) 3105951; fax (12) 3105184; internet www.publicworks.gov.za.

Ministry of Rural Development and Land Reform: Old Bldg, 184 cnr Jacob Mare and Paul Kruger Sts, Pretoria; Private Bag X833, Pretoria 0001; tel. (12) 3128911; fax (12) 3236072; internet www .ruraldevelopment.gov.za.

Ministry of Science and Technology: DST Bldg (No. 53), Meiring Naude Rd, Brummeria 0001; Private Bag X894, Pretoria 0001; tel. (12) 8436300; fax (12) 3242687; e-mail nelvis.qekema@dst.gov.za; internet www.dst.gov.za.

Ministry of Social Development: HSRC Bldg, North Wing, 134 Pretorius St, Pretoria 0002; Private Bag X901, Pretoria 0001; tel. (12) 3127500; fax (12) 3122502; e-mail lakelak@dsd.gov.za; internet www .dsd.gov.za.

Ministry of Sport and Recreation: cnr Vermeulen and Queen Sts, 66 Queen St, Pretoria; Private Bag X896, Pretoria 0001; tel. (12) 3045000; fax (12) 3230795; e-mail stofile@srsa.gov.za; internet www .srsa.gov.za.

Ministry of State Security: Bogare Bldg, 2 Atterbury Rd, Menlyn, Pretoria; POB 1037, Menlyn 0077; tel. (12) 3670700; fax (12) 3670749; e-mail lornad@mweb.co.za; internet www.intelligence .gov.za.

Ministry of Tourism: Fedsure Forum Bldg, North Tower, 1st and 2nd Floors, 315 Pretorius St, cnr Pretorius and van der Walt Sts, Pretoria 0001; Private Bag X424, Pretoria 0001; tel. (12) 3103611; fax (12) 3220082; internet www.tourism.gov.za.

Ministry of Trade and Industry: 77 Meintjies St, Sunnyside, Pretoria 0002; Private Bag X84, Pretoria 0001; tel. (12) 3949500; fax (12) 3949501; e-mail contactus@thedti.gov.za; internet www.thedti .gov.za.

Ministry of Transport: Forum Bldg, 159 Struben St, Pretoria 0002; Private Bag X193, Pretoria 0001; tel. (12) 3093000; fax (12) 3283194; e-mail khozac@dot.gov.za; internet www.transport.gov.za.

Ministry of Water and Environmental Affairs: Sedibeng Bldg, 10th Floor, 185 Schoeman St, Pretoria 0002; Private Bag X313, Pretoria 0001; tel. (12) 3368733; fax (12) 3367817; e-mail pagel@dwaf .gov.za; internet www.dwaf.gov.za.

Ministry of Women, Youth, Children and People with Disabilities: Union Buildings, Room 290A, Government Ave, Pretoria; Private Bag X1000, Pretoria 0001; tel. (12) 3005575; e-mail tseleng@ po.gov.za.

National Treasury: 40 Church Sq., Pretoria 0002; Private Bag X115, Pretoria 0001; tel. (12) 3155372; fax (12) 3233262; e-mail dumisa.jele@treasury.gov.za; internet www.treasury.gov.za.

Legislature

PARLIAMENT

National Council of Provinces

Chairman: MNINWA JOHANNES MAHLANGU.

The National Council of Provinces (NCOP), which replaced the Senate under the new Constitution, was inaugurated on 6 February 1997. The NCOP comprises 90 members, with six permanent delegates and four special delegates from each of the nine provinces.

National Assembly

Speaker: MAX VUYISILE SISULU.

General Election, 22 April 2009

Party	Votes	% of votes	Seats
African National Congress . . .	11,650,748	65.90	264
Democratic Alliance	2,945,829	16.66	67
Congress of the People	1,311,027	7.42	30
Inkatha Freedom Party . . .	804,260	4.55	18
Independent Democrats . . .	162,915	0.92	4
United Democratic Movement . .	149,680	0.85	4
Vryheidsfront Plus	146,796	0.83	4
African Christian Democratic Party .	142,658	0.81	3
United Christian Democratic Party .	66,086	0.37	2
Pan-Africanist Congress of Azania .	48,530	0.27	1
Minority Front	43,474	0.25	1
Azanian People's Organization . .	38,245	0.22	1
African People's Convention . . .	35,867	0.20	1
Others	134,614	0.76	—
Total	**17,680,729**	**100.00**	**400**

Provincial Governments

(May 2012)

EASTERN CAPE

Premier: NOXOLO KIVIET (ANC).
Speaker of the Legislature: FIKILE XASA (ANC).

FREE STATE

Premier: ACE MAGASHULE (ANC).
Speaker of the Legislature: MOEKETSI SESELE (ANC).

GAUTENG

Premier: NOMVULA PAULA MOKONYANE (ANC).
Speaker of the Legislature: LINDIWE MASEKO (ANC).

KWAZULU/NATAL

Premier: Dr ZWELI LAWRENCE MKHIZE (ANC).
Speaker of the Legislature: NELISWA PEGGY NKONYENI (ANC).

LIMPOPO

Premier: CASSEL MATHALE (ANC).

Speaker of the Legislature: RUDOPH PHALA (ANC).

MPUMALANGA

Premier: DAVID D. MABUZA (ANC).

Speaker of the Legislature: JACKSON MTHEMBU (ANC).

NORTHERN CAPE

Premier: HAZEL JENKINS (ANC).

Speaker of the Legislature: GHOOLAM ACHARWARAY (ANC).

NORTH-WEST

Premier: THANDI MODISE (ANC).

Speaker of the Legislature: NONO DUMILE MALOY (ANC).

WESTERN CAPE

Premier: HELEN ZILLE (DA).

Speaker of the Legislature: SHAHID ESAU (DA).

Election Commission

Electoral Commission of South Africa (IEC): Election House, Riverside Office Park, 1303 Heuwel Ave, Centurion, Pretoria; tel. (12) 6225700; fax (12) 6225863; e-mail iec@elections.org.za; internet www.elections.org.za; f. 1996; Chair. PANSY TLAKULA.

Political Organizations

A total of 26 parties contested the elections to the National Assembly in April 2009, while 38 parties presented candidates in the concurrent provincial elections.

African Christian Democratic Party (ACDP): Stats Building, 1st Floor, 2 Fore St, POB 1677, Alberton; tel. (11) 8693941; fax (86) 6564411; e-mail office@acdp.org.za; internet www.acdp.org.za; f. 1993; Leader Rev. KENNETH MESHOE.

African National Congress of South Africa (ANC): 54 Sauer St, Johannesburg 2001; POB 61884, Marshalltown 2107; tel. (11) 3761000; fax (11) 3761100; e-mail nmtyelwa@anc.org.za; internet www.anc.org.za; f. 1912; in alliance with the South African Communist Party (SACP) and the Congress of South African Trade Unions (COSATU); governing party since April 1994; Pres. JACOB ZUMA; Deputy Pres. CYRIL RAMAPHOSA; Sec.-Gen. GWEDE MANTASHE.

African People's Convention (APC): Dr Neil Aggett House, 4th Floor, 90 President St, between Kruis and Small Sts, Johannesburg 2001; tel. (11) 4985535; fax (11) 4985938; e-mail mmazibuko@gpl.gov.za; internet www.theapc.org.za; f. 2008; Pres. THEMBA GODI; Sec.-Gen. PASEKA OA MOSHWADIBA.

Afrikaner Weerstandsbeweging (AWB) (Afrikaner Resistance Movement): POB 274, Ventersdorp 2710, Johannesburg; tel. (18) 2643669; fax (18) 2642516; e-mail awb@awb.co.za; internet www.awb.co.za; f. 1973; Afrikaner (Boer) nationalist group seeking self-determination for the Afrikaner people in South Africa; Leader STEYN VAN RONGE.

Al Jama-ah: The Business Hub, 1A Forest Pl., Pinelands, Cape Town 7405; tel. (21) 5314273; internet www.aljama.co.za; Muslim party; Leader MOGAMAD GANIEF EBRAHIM HENDRICKS.

Azanian People's Organization (AZAPO): 141 Commissioner St, Kine Centre, 19th Floor, Johannesburg 2001; POB 4230, Johannesburg 2000; tel. (11) 3316430; fax (11) 3316433; e-mail azapo@mail.ngo.za; internet www.azapo.org.za; f. 1978; to seek the establishment of a unitary, democratic, socialist republic; excludes white mems; Pres. JACOB DIKOBO; Nat. Chair. ZITHULELE NYANGANA ABSALOM CINDI.

Boerestaat Party (Boer State Party): POB 4995, Luipaardsvlei 1743; tel. (11) 7623841; fax (11) 7623842; e-mail info@boerestaatparty.co.za; internet www.boerestaatparty.co.za; f. 1988; seeks the reinstatement of the Boer Republics in a consolidated Boerestaat; Leader COEN VERMAAK.

Christian Democratic Alliance (CDA): Cape Town; tel. (21) 4033518; fax (21) 4033518; e-mail national.office@cda.org.za; f. 2008; Leader LOUIS MICHAEL GREEN; Sec.-Gen. KEVIN SOUTHGATE.

Congress of the People (COPE): Braampark, 1st Floor, Forum II, 33 Hoofd St, Braamfontein, Johannesburg 2000; tel. (11) 3396060; fax (11) 3396064; e-mail info@congressofthepeople.org.za; internet www.congressofthepeople.org.za; f. 2008 following split in the ANC; Pres. MOSIUOA LEKOTA.

Democratic Alliance (DA): POB 1475, Cape Town 8000; Theba Hosken House, 2nd Floor, cnr Breda and Mill Sts, Gardens, Cape Town; tel. (21) 4651431; fax (21) 4615559; e-mail info@da.org.za; internet www.da.org.za; f. 2000 by opposition parties, incl. the Democratic Party, the Federal Alliance and the New National Party (NNP), to contest that year's municipal elections; NNP withdrew in late 2001; Leader HELEN ZILLE; Chair. Dr WILMOT JAMES.

Herstigte Nasionale Party (HNP): 199 Neethling St, Eloffsdal, POB 1888, Pretoria 0001; tel. (12) 3358523; fax (12) 3358518; e-mail info@hnp.org.za; internet www.hnp.org.za; f. 1969 by fmr mems of the National Party; advocates 'Christian Nationalism'; Leader ANDRIES BREYTENBACH; Gen. Sec. LOUIS J. VAN DER SCHYFF.

Independent Democrats (ID): Rm 28, Marks Bldg, Parliament Plein St, POB 751, Cape Town 8000; tel. (21) 4038696; fax (21) 4032350; e-mail id@id.org.za; internet www.id.org.za; f. 2003; announced intention in 2010 to merge with the Democratic Alliance by the 2014 legislative elections; Pres. PATRICIA DE LILLE; Chair. MERVYN CIROTA.

Inkatha Freedom Party (IFP): 2 Durban Club Pl., Durban, 4000; POB 4432, Durban 4000; tel. (31) 3651300; fax (31) 3074964; e-mail ifpinfo@iafrica.com; internet www.ifp.org.za; f. 1975 as Inkatha National Cultural Liberation Movement with mainly Zulu support; reorg. in 1990 as a multiracial political party; Pres. Chief MANGOSUTHU GATSHA BUTHELEZI; breakaway faction entitled the National Freedom Party was established under the leadership of Zanele Magwaza-Msibi in Jan. 2011.

Minority Front: 330 Florence Nightingale Dr., Westcliff, Chatsworth; tel. (31) 4033360; fax (31) 4033354; e-mail mf@mf.org.za; internet www.mf.org.za; f. 1993; Indian support; Leader ROY BHOOLA.

National Democratic Convention (NADECO): 1615 Commercial City, 40 Commercial Rd, Durban 4001; tel. (31) 3042098; fax (31) 3042944; e-mail mbathah@nadeco.org; f. 2005; Pres. Rev. HAWU MBATHA; Chair. THEMBA MBUTHO.

Pan-Africanist Congress of Azania (PAC): 10th Floor, Renaissance House, 16–22 New St, Ghandi Sq., Johannesburg; POB 6010, Johannesburg 2000; tel. (11) 8389380; fax (11) 8389384; e-mail pacazania@telkomsa.net; internet www.panafricanperspective.com/pac/index.html; f. 1959; Pres. Dr MOTSOKO PHEKO; Nat. Exec. Sec. MFANELO SKWATSHA.

South African Communist Party (SACP): Cosatu House, 3rd Floor, 1 Leyds St, Braamfontein; POB 1027, Johannesburg 2000; tel. (11) 3393633; fax (11) 3396880; e-mail info@sacp.org.za; internet www.sacp.org.za; f. 1921; reorg. 1953; supports the ANC; Chair. SENZENI ZOKWANA; Gen. Sec. Dr BONGINKOSI EMMANUEL 'BLADE' NZIMANDE.

United Christian Democratic Party (UCDP): POB 3010, Mmabatho; tel. (18) 3815691; fax (18) 3817346; e-mail ucdpheadoff@ucdp.org.za; internet www.ucdp.org.za; f. 1972 as the Bophuthatswana Nat. Party; name changed to Bophuthatswana Dem. Party in 1974; present name adopted in 1991; multiracial; Pres. ISAAC SIPHO MFUNDISI; Sec.-Gen. J. B. S. MOLABI; Nat. Chair. IPUSENG CELIA DITSHETELO.

United Democratic Movement (UDM): Tomkor Bldg, 2nd Floor, cnr Vermeulen and Du Toit Sts, Pretoria; POB 26290, Arcadia 0007; tel. (12) 3210010; fax (12) 3210014; e-mail info@udm.org.za; internet www.udm.org.za; f. 1997; multiracial support; demands effective measures for enforcement of law and order; Pres. BANTU HOLOMISA; Sec.-Gen. BONGANI MSOMI.

Vryheidsfront Plus (Freedom Front Plus—VF Plus/FF Plus): Blok 8, Highveld Office Park, 11 Charles de Gaulle Cres., Highveld, Centurion Pretoria; POB 67391, Highveld, 0169; tel. (12) 6650564; fax (12) 6652420; e-mail info@vf.co.za; internet www.vryheidsfront.co.za; f. 1994 as Freedom Front; name changed after incorporating the Conservative Party and Afrikaner Eenheidsbeweging in Sept. 2003; right-wing electoral alliance; Leader Dr PIETER W. A. MULDER; Chair. PIETER GROENEWALD.

Diplomatic Representation

EMBASSIES AND HIGH COMMISSIONS IN SOUTH AFRICA

Algeria: 950 Arcadia St, Hatfield, Pretoria 0083; POB 57480, Arcadia 0007; tel. (12) 3425074; fax (12) 3426479; Ambassador MOHAMED LAMINE LAABAS.

Angola: 1030 Schoeman St, Hatfield, Pretoria 0083; POB 8685, Pretoria 0001; tel. (12) 3420049; fax (12) 3427039; Ambassador JOSEFINA PERPÉTUA P. D. PITRA DIAKITÉ.

Argentina: 200 Standard Plaza, 440 Hilda St, Hatfield, Pretoria 0083; POB 11125, Pretoria 0028; tel. (12) 4303524; fax (12) 4303521;

e-mail argembas@global.co.za; Ambassador CARLOS SERSALE DI CERISANO.

Australia: 292 Orient St, Arcadia, Pretoria 0083; Private Bag X150, Pretoria 0001; tel. (12) 4236000; fax (12) 3428442; e-mail pretoria.info@dfat.gov.au; internet www.southafrica.embassy.gov.au; High Commissioner GRAEME JOHN WILSON.

Austria: Momentum Office Park, 1109 Duncan St, Brooklyn, Pretoria 0181; POB 95572, Waterkloof 0145; tel. (12) 4529155; fax (12) 4601151; e-mail pretoria-ob@bmeia.gv.at; internet www.bmeia.gv.at/pretoria; Chargé d'affaires a.i. M. GARTNER.

Azerbaijan: 258 Jupiter St, Waterkloof Ridge 0181; POB 56014, Hatfield 0083; tel. 721412755 (mobile); fax 724429094 (mobile); Ambassador ELKHAN POLUKHOV.

Bangladesh: 410 Farenden St, Sunnyside, Pretoria 0002; tel. (12) 3432105; fax (12) 3435222; e-mail bangladeshpta@iburst.co.za; High Commissioner MUHAMMAD TOUHID HOSSAIN.

Belarus: 327 Hill St, Arcadia, Pretoria 0083; POB 4107, Pretoria 0001; tel. (12) 4307709; fax (12) 3426280; e-mail rsa@mfa.gov.by; internet www.rsa.mfa.gov.by; Ambassador ANDREI MOLCHAN.

Belgium: 625 Leyds St, Muckleneuk, Pretoria 0002; tel. (12) 4403201; fax (12) 4403216; e-mail pretoria@diplobel.fed.be; internet www.diplomatie.be/pretoria; Ambassador JOHAN MARICOU.

Benin: 900 Park St, cnr Orient and Park Sts, Arcadia, Pretoria 0083; POB 26484, Arcadia 0007; tel. (12) 3426978; fax (12) 3421823; e-mail embbenin@yebo.co.za; Ambassador CLAUDE RUBEN FASSINOU.

Botswana: 24 Amos St, Colbyn, Pretoria 0083; POB 57035, Arcadia 0007; tel. (12) 4309640; fax (12) 3421845; High Commissioner KENNY KINIOTIRO KAPINGA.

Brazil: Hillcrest Office Park, Woodpecker Pl., 1st Floor, 177 Dyer Rd, Hillcrest, Pretoria 0083; POB 3269, Pretoria 0001; tel. (12) 3665200; fax (12) 3665299; e-mail pretoria@brazilianembassy.org.za; internet www.brazilianembassy.org.za; Ambassador PEDRO LUIZ CARNEIRO DE MENDONÇA.

Bulgaria: 1071 Church St, Hatfield, Pretoria 0083; POB 29296, Arcadia 0007; tel. (12) 3423720; fax (12) 3423721; e-mail embulgsa@iafrica.com; internet www.mfa.bg/embassies/southafrica; Ambassador KATYA DELEVA.

Burundi: 20 Glyn St, Colbyn, Pretoria 0083; POB 12914, Hatfield 0028; tel. (12) 3424881; fax (12) 3424885; Ambassador ISAÏE NTIRIZOSHIRA.

Cameroon: 80 Marais St, Brooklyn, Pretoria 0181; POB 13790, Hatfield 0028; tel. (12) 4600587; fax (12) 4607942; e-mail hicocam@cameroon.co.za; High Commissioner ADRIEN KOUAMBO JOMAGUE.

Canada: 1103 Arcadia St, cnr Hilda St, Hatfield, Pretoria 0083; Private Bag X13, Hatfield 0028; tel. (12) 4223000; fax (12) 4223052; e-mail pret@international.gc.ca; internet www.dfait-maeci.gc.ca/southafrica/menu-en.asp; High Commissioner GASTON (GASTONE) BARBAN.

Chile: Delmondo Office Park, 169 Garsfontein Rd, Ashlea Gardens, Pretoria 0081; POB 2449, Brooklyn Sq. 0075; tel. (12) 4608090; fax (12) 4608093; e-mail chile@iafrica.com; internet www.embchile.co.za; Ambassador JOSE GABRIEL ZEPEDA ZEPEDA.

China, People's Republic: 965 Church St, Arcadia, Pretoria 0083; POB 95764, Waterkloof 0145; tel. (12) 4316500; fax (12) 3424244; e-mail reception@chinese-embassy.org.za; internet www.chinese-embassy.org.za; Ambassador ZHONG JIANHUA.

Colombia: Park Corner Bldg, 3rd Floor, 1105 Park St, Hatfield, Pretoria 0083; POB 12791, Hatfield 0028; tel. (12) 3420211; fax (12) 3420216; e-mail info@embassyofcolombia.co.za; Ambassador EDGAR JOSÉ PEREA-ARIAS.

Comoros: 817 Thomas St, cnr Church and Eastwood Sts, Arcadia, Pretoria 0083; tel. (12) 3439483; fax (12) 3420138; Ambassador AHMED MOHAMED THABIT.

Congo, Democratic Republic: 791 Schoeman St, Arcadia, Pretoria 0083; POB 28795, Sunnyside 0132; tel. (12) 3446475; fax (12) 3444054; e-mail rdcongo@lantic.net; Ambassador BENE M'POKO.

Congo, Republic: 960 Arcadia St, Arcadia, Pretoria 0083; POB 40427, Arcadia 0007; tel. (12) 3425508; fax (12) 3425510; Ambassador ROGER ISSOMBO.

Côte d'Ivoire: 795 Government Ave, Arcadia, Pretoria 0083; POB 13510, Hatfield 0028; tel. (12) 3426913; fax (12) 3426713; Ambassador AMOS DJADAN KOFFI.

Croatia: 1160 Church St, Colbyn, Pretoria 0083; POB 11335, Hatfield 0028; tel. (12) 3421206; fax (12) 3421819; internet za.mfa.hr; Ambassador IVAN PICUKARIĆ.

Cuba: 45 Mackenzie St, Brooklyn, Pretoria 0181; POB 11605, Hatfield 0028; tel. (12) 3462105; fax (12) 3462216; e-mail sudafri@iafrica.com; internet emba.cubaminrex.cu/sudafricaing; Ambassador CARLOS FERNÁNDEZ DE COSSÍO DOMÍNGUEZ.

Cyprus: cnr Church St and Hill St, Arcadia, Pretoria 0083; POB 14554, Hatfield 0028; tel. (12) 3425258; fax (12) 3425596; e-mail

pretoriahighcommission@mfa.gov.cy; High Commissioner ARGYROS ANTONIOU.

Czech Republic: 936 Pretorius St, Arcadia, Pretoria 0083; POB 13671, Hatfield 0028; tel. (12) 4312380; fax (12) 4302033; e-mail pretoria@embassymzv.cz; internet www.mzv.cz/pretoria; Ambassador MARTIN POHL.

Denmark: iParioli Office Park, Block B2, Ground Floor, 1166 Park St, Hatfield, Pretoria; POB 11439, Hatfield 0028; tel. (12) 4309340; fax (12) 3427620; e-mail pryamb@um.dk; internet www.ambpretoria.um.dk; Ambassador RENÉ DINESEN.

Dominican Republic: 276 Anderson St., Brooklyn, Pretoria 0181; tel. (12) 3602463; fax (12) 5679613; e-mail dominicanembassy@gmail.com; Ambassador RAÚL FERNANDO BARRIENTOS-LARA.

Ecuador: Suite 3, 36 Selati St, Selati Park, Alphen Park, Pretoria; tel. (12) 3461662; fax (12) 3467082; e-mail eecusudafrica@mmrree.gov.ec; Ambassador Dr JOSÉ VALENCIA.

Egypt: 270 Bourke St, Muckleneuk, Pretoria 0002; POB 30025, Sunnyside 0132; tel. (12) 3431590; fax (12) 3431082; e-mail egyptemb@global.co.za; Ambassador MOHAMED BADR ELDIN MOSTAFA ZAYED.

Equatorial Guinea: 48 Florence St, Colbyn, Pretoria; POB 12720, Hatfield 0028; tel. (12) 3429945; fax (12) 3427250; Ambassador F. EDU NGUA.

Eritrea: 1281 Cobham Rd, Queenswood, Pretoria 0186; POB 11371, Queenswood 0121; tel. (12) 3331302; fax (12) 3332330; Ambassador SALIH OMAR ABDU.

Ethiopia: 47 Charles St, Bailey's Muckleneuk, Brooklyn 0181; POB 11469, Hatfield 0028; tel. (12) 3463542; fax (12) 3463867; e-mail ethiopia@sentechsa.com; Ambassador Dr YESHIMEBRAT MERSHA.

Fiji: Pretoria; High Commissioner BEN SALACAKAU.

Finland: 628 Leyds St, Muckleneuk, Pretoria 0002; POB 443, Pretoria 0001; tel. (12) 3430275; fax (12) 3433095; e-mail sanomat.pre@formin.fi; internet www.finland.org.za; Ambassador PETRI SALO.

France: 250 Melk St, cnr Melk and Middle Sts, New Muckleneuk, Pretoria 0181; tel. (12) 4251600; fax (12) 4251689; e-mail france@ambafrance-rsa.org; internet www.ambafrance-rsa.org; Ambassador JACQUES LAPOUGE.

Gabon: 921 Schoeman St, Arcadia, Pretoria 0083; POB 9222, Pretoria 0001; tel. (12) 3424376; fax (12) 3424375; Ambassador SANNI AOUDOU AÏCHATOU.

Germany: 180 Blackwood St, Arcadia, Pretoria 0083; POB 2023, Pretoria 0001; tel. (12) 4278900; fax (12) 3433606; e-mail GermanEmbassyPretoria@gonet.co.za; internet www.pretoria.diplo.de; Ambassador HORST FREITAG.

Ghana: 1038 Arcadia St, Hatfield, Pretoria 0083; POB 12537, Hatfield 0028; tel. (12) 3425847; fax (12) 3425863; Chargé d'affaires a.i. S. J. K. PARKER-ALLOTEY.

Greece: Hadefields Office Park, 1st Floor, 1267 Church St, Block G, Hatfield, Pretoria 0001; tel. (12) 3427136; e-mail gremb.pre@mfa.gr; internet www.mfa.gr/pretoria; Ambassador SPYRIDON THEOCHAROPOULOS.

Guinea: 336 Orient St, Arcadia, Pretoria 0083; POB 13523, Hatfield 0028; tel. and fax (12) 3427348; e-mail embaguinea@iafrica.com; Ambassador GAOUSSOU TOURÉ.

Haiti: 808 George St, Arcadia, Pretoria 0007; POB 14362, Hatfield 0028; tel. (12) 4307560; fax (12) 3427042; Ambassador YOLETTE AZOR-CHARLES.

Holy See: Argo St, Waterkloof Ridge, Pretoria 0181; POB 95200, Waterkloof 0145; tel. (12) 3464235; fax (12) 3461494; e-mail nunziosa@iafrica.com; Apostolic Nuncio Most Rev. MARIO ROBERTO CASSARI (Titular Archbishop of Truentum).

Hungary: 959 Arcadia St, Hatfield, Pretoria 0083; POB 13843, Hatfield 0028; tel. (12) 4303030; fax (12) 4303029; e-mail mission.prt@mfa.gov.hu; internet www.mfa.gov.hu/emb/pretoria; Ambassador BELA LASZLO.

India: 852 Schoeman St, Arcadia, Pretoria 0083; POB 40216, Arcadia 0007; tel. (12) 3425392; fax (12) 3425310; e-mail polinf@hicomind.co.za; internet www.indiainsouthafrica.com; High Commissioner VIRENDRA GUPTA.

Indonesia: 949 Schoeman St, Arcadia, Pretoria 0082; POB 13155, Hatfield, Pretoria 0028; tel. (12) 3423350; fax (12) 3423369; e-mail fpanggabean@indonesia-pretoria.org.za; internet www.indonesia-pretoria.org.za; f. 1995; Ambassador SJAHRIL SABARUDDIN.

Iran: Block A2, Iparioli Office Park, 1166 Park St, Hatfield, Pretoria 0083; POB 12546, Hatfield 0028; tel. (12) 3425880; fax (12) 3421878; e-mail office@iranembassy.org.za; internet www.iranembassy.org.za; Ambassador MOHAMMAD FARAJI.

Iraq: 803 Duncan St, Brooklyn, Pretoria 0181; POB 11089, Hatfield 0028; tel. (12) 3622048; fax (12) 3622027; Ambassador Dr HISHAM ALI AKBAR IBRAHIM AL-ALAWI.

Ireland: Southern Life Plaza, 1st Floor, 1059 Schoeman St, cnr Festival and Schoeman Sts, Arcadia, Pretoria 0083; POB 4174, Arcadia 0001; tel. (12) 3425062; fax (12) 3424752; e-mail pretoria@dfa.ie; internet www.embassyireland.org.za; Ambassador BRENDAN MCMAHON.

Israel: 428 King's Hwy, Elizabeth Grove St, Lynnwood, Pretoria; Private Bag X50, Menlo Park 0102; tel. (12) 4703500; fax (12) 4703555; e-mail publicaffairs@pretoria.mfa.gov.il; internet pretoria.mfa.gov.il; Ambassador DOV SEGEV-STEINBERG.

Italy: 796 George Ave, Arcadia, Pretoria 0083; tel. (12) 4230001; fax (12) 4305547; e-mail segreteria.pretoria@esteri.it; internet www.ambpretoria.esteri.it; Ambassador ELIO MENZIONE.

Jamaica: 1119 Burnett St, Hatfield, Pretoria 0083; tel. (12) 3626667; fax (12) 3668510; e-mail jhcpretoria@telkomsa.net; High Commissioner NORMA TAYLOR-ROBERTS.

Japan: 259 Baines St, cnr Frans Oerder St, Groenkloof, Pretoria 0181; Private Bag X999, Pretoria 0001; tel. (12) 4521500; fax (12) 4603800; e-mail info@embjapan.org.za; internet www.japan.org.za; Ambassador TOSHIRO OZAWA.

Jordan: 252 Olivier St, Brooklyn, Pretoria 0075; POB 14730, Hatfield 0028; tel. (12) 3468615; fax (12) 3468611; e-mail embjordpta@telkomsa.net; Ambassador O. J. NADIF.

Kenya: 302 Brooks St, Menlo Park, Pretoria 0081; POB 35954, Menlo Park 0012; tel. (12) 3622249; fax (12) 3622252; e-mail info@kenya.org.za; internet www.kenya.org.za; High Commissioner THOMAS AMOLO.

Korea, Democratic People's Republic: 958 Waterpoort St, Faerie Glen, Pretoria; POB 1238, Garsfontein 0042; tel. (12) 9918661; fax (12) 9918662; e-mail dprkembassy@lantic.net; Ambassador JO YONG MAN.

Korea, Republic: Greenpark Estates, Bldg 3, 27 George Storrar Dr., Groenkloof, Pretoria 0081; POB 939, Groenkloof 0027; tel. (12) 4602508; fax (12) 4601158; e-mail embsa@mofat.go.kr; internet zaf.mofat.go.kr; Ambassador YOON LEE.

Kuwait: 890 Arcadia St, Arcadia, Pretoria 0083; Private Bag X920, Pretoria 0001; tel. (12) 3420877; fax (12) 3420876; e-mail safarku@global.co.za; Ambassador HASSAN BADER KAREEM AL-OQAB.

Lebanon: 788 Government St, Pretoria; POB 941, Groenkloof 0027; tel. (12) 4302130; fax (12) 4302238; e-mail embassyoflebanon@telkomsa.net; Ambassador MICHEL THOMAS KATRA.

Lesotho: 391 Anderson St, Menlo Park, Pretoria 0081; POB 55817, Arcadia 0007; tel. (12) 4607648; fax (12) 4607469; High Commissioner LINEO LYDIA KHECHANE-NTOANE.

Liberia: Suite 9 Section 7, Schoeman St Forum, 1157 Schoeman St, Hatfield, Pretoria; POB 14082, Hatfield, Pretoria; tel. (12) 3422734; fax (12) 3422737; e-mail libempta@pta.lia.net; Chargé d'affaires a.i. BEN SIE-TOE COLLINS.

Libya: 900 Church St, Arcadia, Pretoria 0083; POB 40388, Arcadia 0007; tel. (12) 3423902; fax (12) 3423904; e-mail libyasa@telkomsa.net; Ambassador (vacant).

Madagascar: 90B Tait St, Colbyn, Pretoria; POB 11722, Queenswood 0120; tel. (12) 3420983; fax (12) 3420995; e-mail consul@infodoor.co.za; Ambassador DENIS ANDRIAMANDROSO.

Malawi: 770 Government Ave, Arcadia, Pretoria 0083; POB 11172, Hatfield 0028; tel. and fax (12) 3421759; fax (12) 3420147; e-mail highcommalai@telkomsa.net; High Commissioner (vacant).

Malaysia: 1007 Schoeman St, Arcadia, Pretoria 0083; POB 11673, Hatfield 0028; tel. (12) 3425990; fax (12) 4307773; internet www.kln.gov.my/web/zaf_pretoria; High Commissioner M. KENNEDY JAWAN.

Mali: 876 Pretorius St, Arcadia 0083; POB 12978, Hatfield, Pretoria 0028; tel. (12) 3427464; fax (12) 3420670; Ambassador BALLADJI DIAKITE.

Mauritania: 146 Anderson St, Brooklyn, Pretoria; tel. (12) 3623578; fax (12) 3623304; e-mail rimambapretoria@webmail.co.za; Ambassador MOHAMED OULD HANNANI.

Mauritius: 1163 Pretorius St, Hatfield, Pretoria 0083; tel. (12) 3421283; fax (12) 3421286; e-mail mhcpta@mweb.co.za; High Commissioner MOHAMED ISMAEL DOSSA.

Mexico: 570 Ferhsen St, Parkdev Bldg, Ground Floor, Brooklyn Bridge, Pretoria 0181; POB 9077, Pretoria 0001; tel. (12) 4601004; fax (12) 4600973; e-mail info@embamexsud.org; internet www.embamexsud.org; Ambassador HÉCTOR HUMBERTO VALEZZI ZAFRA.

Morocco: 799 Schoeman St, cnr Farenden St, Arcadia, Pretoria 0083; POB 12382, Hatfield 0028; tel. (12) 3430230; fax (12) 3430613; e-mail sifmapre@mwebbiz.co.za; Chargé d'affaires DRISS ISBAYENE.

Mozambique: 529 Edmund St, Arcadia, Pretoria 0083; POB 40750, Arcadia 0007; tel. (12) 4010300; fax (12) 3266388; e-mail highcomm@embamoc.co.za; High Commissioner FERNANDO ANDRADE FAZENDA.

Myanmar: 201 Leyds St, Arcadia, Pretoria 0083; POB 12121, Queenswood 0121; tel. (12) 3412557; fax (12) 3412553; e-mail euompta@global.co.za; Ambassador HLAIMGN PHONE MYINT.

Namibia: 197 Blackwood St, Arcadia, Pretoria 0083; POB 29806, Sunnyside 0132; tel. (12) 4819100; fax (12) 3445998; e-mail secretary@namibia.org.za; High Commissioner MARTEN NENKETE KAPEWASHA.

Nepal: 453 Fehersen St, Baileys Muckleneuk, Pretoria; tel. (12) 346 2399; fax (12) 3460521; Ambassador ARUN PRASAD DHITAL.

Netherlands: 210 Queen Wilhelmina Ave, New Muckleneuk 0181, Pretoria; tel. (12) 4254500; fax (12) 4254511; e-mail pre@minbuza.nl; internet www.dutchembassy.co.za; Ambassador ANDRÉ HASPELS.

New Zealand: 125 Middel St, Muckleneuk, Pretoria 0181; Private Bag X25, Brooklyn Sq. 0075; tel. (12) 4359000; fax (12) 4359002; e-mail enquiries@nzhc.co.za; internet www.nzembassy.com/south-africa; High Commissioner RICHARD MANN.

Nigeria: 971 Schoeman St, Arcadia, Pretoria 0083; POB 27332, Sunnyside 0132; tel. (12) 3420805; fax (12) 3421668; High Commissioner Brig.-Gen. (retd) MOHAMMED BUBA MARWA.

Norway: Ozmik House, 165 Lynnwood Rd, Brooklyn 0181, Pretoria; POB 11612, Hatfield 0028; tel. (12) 3643700; fax (12) 3643799; e-mail emb.pretoria@mfa.no; internet www.norway.org.za; Ambassador KARI MAREN BJØRNSGAARD.

Oman: 42 Nicholson St, Muckleneuk, Pretoria 0081; POB 2650, Brooklyn 0075; tel. (12) 3460808; fax (12) 3461660; e-mail sult-oman@telkom.net; Ambassador KHALID BIN SULAIMAN BIN ABDUL RAHMAN BA'OMAR.

Pakistan: 312 Brooks St, Menlo Park, Pretoria 0181; POB 11803, Hatfield 0028; tel. (12) 3624072; fax (12) 3623967; e-mail pareppretoria@worldonline.co.za; High Commissioner ZAIGHAMUDDIN AZAM.

Panama: 229 Olivier St, Brooklyn, Pretoria; tel. (12) 4606677; fax (12) 3465474; e-mail panamaembassy@bodamail.co.za; Ambassador RODRIGO GUILLERMO CHIARI.

Paraguay: 189 Strelitzia Rd, Waterkloof Heights, Pretoria 0181; POB 95774, Waterkloof 0145; tel. (12) 3471047; fax (12) 3470403; e-mail embaparsudafrica@mre.gov.py; Ambassador JOSÉ MARTÍNEZ LEZCANO.

Peru: 200 Saint Patrick St, Muckleneuk Hill, Pretoria 0083; POB 907, Groenkloof 0027; tel. (12) 4401030; fax (12) 4401054; e-mail embaperu2@telkomsa.net; internet www.embassyofperu.co.za; Ambassador DAÚL MATUTE-MEJÍA.

Philippines: 54 Nicholson St, Muckleneuk, Pretoria 0181; POB 2562, Brooklyn Sq. 0075; tel. (12) 3460451; fax (12) 3460454; e-mail pretoriape@mweb.co.za; internet www.pretoriape.org; Ambassador CONSTANCIO R. VINGNO, Jr.

Poland: 14 Amos St, Colbyn, Pretoria 0083; POB 12277, Queenswood 0121; tel. (12) 4302631; fax (12) 4302608; e-mail amb.pol@pixie.co.za; internet www.pretoria.polemb.net; Ambassador MARCIN KUBIAK.

Portugal: 599 Leyds St, Muckleneuk, Pretoria 0002; POB 27102, Sunnyside 0132; tel. (12) 3412340; fax (12) 3413975; e-mail portemb@global.co.za; Ambassador GABRIELA SOARES DE ALBERGARIA.

Qatar: 355 Charles St, Waterkloof, Pretoria 0181; Private Bag X13, Brooklyn Sq. 0075; tel. (12) 4521700; fax (12) 3466732; e-mail qatar-emb@lantic.net; Ambassador Dr BASHIR ISSA AL-SHIRAWI.

Romania: 117 Charles St, Brooklyn, Pretoria 0181; POB 11295, Hatfield 0028; tel. (12) 4606941; fax (12) 4606947; e-mail pretoria@mae.ro; internet pretoria.mae.ro; Ambassador RADU GABRIEL SAFTA.

Russia: 316 Brooks St, Menlo Park, Pretoria 0081; POB 36034, Pretoria 0102; tel. (12) 3621337; fax (12) 3620116; e-mail ruspospr@mweb.co.za; internet www.russianembassy.org.za; Ambassador MIKHAIL PETRAKOV.

Rwanda: 983 Schoeman St, Arcadia, Pretoria; POB 55224, Arcadia 0007; tel. (12) 3426536; fax (12) 3427106; e-mail ambapretoria@minaffet.gov.rw; internet www.southafrica.embassy.gov.rw; Ambassador VINCENT KAREGA.

Saudi Arabia: 711 Duncan St, cnr Lunnon St, Hatfield, Pretoria 0083; POB 13930, Hatfield 0028; tel. (12) 3624230; fax (12) 3624239; Chargé d'affaires a.i. ABDULRAHMAN AL-NAJJAR.

Senegal: Charles Manor, 57 Charles St, Baileys Muckleneuk, Pretoria 0181; POB 2948, Brooklyn Sq. 0075; tel. (12) 4605263; fax (12) 3465550; e-mail ambassenepta@telkomsa.za; Ambassador CHEIKH NIANG.

Serbia: 163 Marais St, Brooklyn, Pretoria; POB 13026, Hatfield 0028; tel. (12) 4605626; fax (12) 4606003; e-mail ambas@srbembassy.org.za; internet www.srbembassy.org.za; Ambassador GORAN VUJIČIĆ.

Seychelles: Global House, 296 Glenwood Rd, Lynnwood Park, Pretoria 0081; POB 1548, Ferndale 2160, Randburg; High Commissioner CLAUDE MOREL.

Singapore: 980 Schoeman St, Arcadia, Pretoria 0083; POB 11809, Hatfield 0028; tel. (12) 4306035; fax (12) 3424425; e-mail sporehc@mweb.co.za; High Commissioner BERNARD WILLIAM BAKER.

Slovakia: 930 Arcadia St, Pretoria 0083; POB 12736, Hatfield 0028; tel. (12) 3422051; fax (12) 3423688; e-mail slovakemb@telkomsa.net; internet www.mfa.sk/zu; Ambassador LADISLAV STRAKA.

Somalia: Pretoria; Ambassador SAYID HASSAN SHARIF.

Spain: Lord Charles Bldg, 337 Brooklyn Rd, Menlo Park, Pretoria 0181; POB 35353, Pretoria 0001; tel. (12) 4600123; fax (12) 4602290; e-mail emb.pretoria@mae.es; internet www.maec.es/subwebs/Embajadas/Pretoria; Ambassador JUAN IGNACIO SELL SANZ.

Sri Lanka: 410 Alexander St, Brooklyn, Pretoria 0181; tel. (12) 4607690; fax (12) 4607702; e-mail srilanka@global.co.za; internet www.srilanka.co.za; High Commissioner DHARMASENA WIJESINGHE.

Sudan: 1203 Pretorius St, Hatfield, Pretoria 0083; POB 25513, Monument Park 0105; tel. (12) 3424538; fax (12) 3424539; internet www.sudani.co.za; Ambassador ALI YOUSIF AHMED.

Suriname: Suite No. 4, Groenkloof Forum Office Park, 57 George Storrar Drive, Groenkloof, 0181 Pretoria; POB 149, Pretoria; tel. (12) 3467627; fax (12) 3460802; e-mail embsur@lantic.net; Ambassador Dr WILFRIED RAMON ROSEVAL.

Swaziland: 715 Government Ave, Arcadia, Pretoria 0007; POB 14294, Hatfield 0028; tel. (12) 3441910; fax (12) 3430455; Ambassador SOLOMON MNUKWA DLAMINI.

Sweden: iParioli Bldg, 1166 Park St, Hatfield 0083; POB 13477, Hatfield 0028; tel. (12) 4266400; fax (12) 4266464; e-mail sweden@iafrica.com; internet www.swedenabroad.com/pretoria; Ambassador ANDERS HAGELBERG.

Switzerland: 225 Veale St, Parc Nouveau, New Muckleneuk, Pretoria 0181; POB 2508, Brooklyn Sq. 0075; tel. (12) 4520660; fax (12) 3466605; e-mail pre.vertretung@eda.admin.ch; internet www.eda.admin.ch/pretoria; Ambassador CHRISTIAN MEUWLY.

Syria: 963 Schoeman St, Arcadia, Pretoria 0083; POB 12830, Hatfield 0028; tel. (12) 3424701; fax (12) 3424702; e-mail syriaemb@telkomsa.net; Ambassador BASSAM DARWISH.

Tanzania: 822 George Ave, Arcadia, Pretoria 0007; POB 56572, Arcadia 0007; tel. (12) 3424393; fax (12) 4304383; e-mail thc@tanzania.org.za; internet www.tanzania.org.za; High Commissioner RADHIA NAIMA MTENGETI MSUYA.

Thailand: 428 cnr Hill and Pretorius Sts, Arcadia, Pretoria 0028; POB 12080, Hatfield 0083; tel. (12) 3424600; fax (12) 3424805; e-mail info@thaiembassy.co.za; internet www.thaiembassy.co.za; Ambassador N. BURANASIRI.

Trinidad and Tobago: 258 Lawley St, Waterkloof, 0181 Pretoria; POB 95872, Waterkloof, Pretoria 0145; tel. (12) 4609688; fax (12) 3467302; e-mail tthepretoria@telkomsa.net; High Commissioner HARRY PARTAP.

Tunisia: 850 Church St, Arcadia, Pretoria 0083; POB 56535, Arcadia 0007; tel. (12) 3426282; fax (12) 3426284; Ambassador MOHAMED FADHEL AYARI.

Turkey: 1067 Church St, Hatfield, Pretoria 0083; POB 56014, Arcadia 0007; tel. (12) 3426055; fax (12) 3426052; e-mail pretbe@global.co.za; internet www.turkishembassy.co.za; Ambassador AHMET VAKUR GÖKDERNIZLER.

Uganda: 882 Church St, Pretoria 0083; POB 12442, Hatfield 0083; tel. (12) 3426031; fax (12) 3426206; e-mail ugacomer@mweb.co.za; High Commissioner KWERONDA RUHEMBA.

Ukraine: 398 Marais St, Brooklyn, Pretoria 0181; POB 57291, Menlo Park 0102; tel. (12) 4601943; fax (12) 4601944; e-mail emb_za@mfa.gov.ua; Ambassador VALERY HREBENIUK.

United Arab Emirates: 992 Arcadia St, Arcadia, Pretoria 0083; POB 57090, Arcadia 0007; tel. (12) 3427736; fax (12) 3427738; e-mail uae@mweb.co.za; Ambassador HAMAD HAREB AL-HABSI.

United Kingdom: 255 Hill St, Arcadia, Pretoria 0002; tel. (12) 4217600; fax (12) 4217555; e-mail media.pretoria@fco.gov.uk; internet www.gov.uk/government/world/organisations/british-high-commission-pretoria; High Commissioner Dr NICOLA BREWER.

USA: 877 Pretorius St, Arcadia, Pretoria 0083; POB 9536, Pretoria 0001; tel. (12) 4314000; fax (12) 3422299; e-mail embassypretoria@state.gov; internet southafrica.usembassy.gov; Ambassador DONALD HENRY GIPS.

Uruguay: 301 MIB House, 3rd Floor, Hatfield Sq., 1119 Burnett St, Hatfield, Pretoria 0083; POB 14818, Pretoria 0028; tel. (12) 3626521; fax (12) 3626523; Ambassador LUIS BERMUDEZ ALVAREZ.

Venezuela: Hatfield Gables South Bldg, 1st Floor, Suite 4, 474 Hilda St, Pretoria 0083; POB 11821, Hatfield 0028; tel. (12) 3626593; fax (12) 3626591; e-mail embasudaf@icon.co.za; Ambassador ANTONIO MONTILLA-SALDIVIA.

Viet Nam: 87 Brooks St, Brooklyn, Pretoria 0181; POB 13692, Hatfield 0028; tel. (12) 3628119; fax (12) 3628115; e-mail embassy@vietnam.co.za; Ambassador MANH HUNG NGUYEN.

Yemen: 329 Main St, Waterkloof 0181; POB 13343, Hatfield 0028; tel. (12) 4250760; fax (12) 4250762; e-mail info@yemenembassy.org.za; internet www.yemenembassy.org.za; Chargé d'affaires MOHAMED JAMIL MUHARRAM.

Zambia: 570 Ziervogel St, Arcadia, Pretoria 0083; POB 12234, Hatfield 0028; tel. (12) 3261854; fax (12) 3262140; High Commissioner BIZWAYO NEWTON NKUNIKA.

Zimbabwe: Zimbabwe House, 798 Merton St, Arcadia, Pretoria 0083; POB 55140, Arcadia 0007; tel. (12) 3425125; fax (12) 3425126; e-mail zimpret@lantic.net; Ambassador PHELEKEZELA MPHOKO.

Judicial System

The common law of the Republic of South Africa is the Roman-Dutch law, the uncodified law of Holland as it was at the time of the secession of the Cape of Good Hope in 1806. The law of England is not recognized as authoritative, although the principles of English law have been introduced in relation to civil and criminal procedure, evidence and mercantile matters.

The Constitutional Court, situated in Johannesburg, consists of a Chief Justice, a Deputy Chief Justice and nine other justices. Its task is to ensure that the executive, legislative and judicial organs of government adhere to the provisions of the Constitution. It has the power to reverse legislation that has been adopted by Parliament. The Supreme Court of Appeal, situated in Bloemfontein, comprises a President, a Deputy President and a number of judges of appeal, and is the highest court in all but constitutional matters. There are also High Courts and Magistrates' Courts. A National Director of Public Prosecutions is the head of the prosecuting authority and is appointed by the President of the Republic. A Judicial Service Commission makes recommendations regarding the appointment of judges and advises central and provincial government on all matters relating to the judiciary.

Constitutional Court: cnr Queen and Sam Hancock/Hospital Sts, Constitution Hill, Braamfontein 2017; tel. (11) 3597400; fax (11) 4036524; e-mail cases@concourt.org.za; internet www.constitutionalcourt.org.za; f. 1995; Chief Justice MOGOENG MOGOENG.

Supreme Court of Appeal: cnr Elizabeth and President Brand Sts, Bloemfontein 9301; POB 258, Bloemfontein 9300; tel. (51) 4127437; fax (86) 6445991; e-mail astreet@justice.gov.za; internet www.supremecourtofappeal.gov.za; f. 1910; Pres. LEX MPATI.

Religion

Some 80% of the population profess the Christian faith. Other religions that are represented are Hinduism, Islam, Judaism and traditional African religions.

CHRISTIANITY

At mid-2000 there were an estimated 12.4m. Protestants and 18.7m. adherents of other forms of Christianity.

South African Council of Churches: POB 62098, Marshalltown 2107; tel. (11) 2417800; fax (11) 4921448; internet www.sacc.org.za; f. 1968; 26 mem. churches; Pres. Prof. TINYIKO MALULEKE; Gen. Sec. EDDIE MAKUE.

The Anglican Communion

Most Anglicans in South Africa are adherents of the Anglican Church of Southern Africa (formerly the Church of the Province of Southern Africa), comprising 25 dioceses (including Angola, Lesotho, Namibia, St Helena, Swaziland and two dioceses in Mozambique). The Church had an estimated 4.5m. communicant members at mid-2006. In November 2012 the Church consecrated the first ever woman bishop in Africa.

Archbishop of Cape Town and Metropolitan of the Province of Southern Africa: Most Rev. THABO CECIL MAKGOBA, 20 Bishopscourt Dr., Bishopscourt, Claremont, Cape Town 7700; tel. (21) 7612531; fax (21) 7614193; e-mail archbish@bishopscourt-cpsa.org.za; internet www.anglicanchurchsa.org.

The Dutch Reformed Church (Nederduitse Gereformeerde Kerk—NGK)

In 2005/06, including confirmed and baptized members, the Dutch Reformed Churches in South Africa consisted of: the Dutch Reformed Church, with 1,155,001 (mainly white) members; the Uniting Reformed Church, with 1,039,606 (mainly Coloured and black) members; the Reformed Church in Africa, with 1,708 Indian members; and the Dutch Reformed Church in Africa, with an estimated 150,000 (mainly black) members. All congregations were desegregated in 1986.

General Synod: POB 13528, Hatfield, Pretoria 0028; tel. (12) 3420092; fax (12) 3420370; e-mail algemenesinode@ngkerk.org.za; internet www.ngkerk.org.za; Moderator Prof. NELUS NIEMANDT; Gen. Sec. Dr KOBUS GERBER.

The Lutheran Churches

Lutheran Communion in Southern Africa (LUCSA): 24 Geldenhuys Rd, POB 7170, Bonaero Park 1619; tel. (11) 9731086; fax (11) 3951615; e-mail info@lucsa.org; internet www.lucsa.org; f. 1991; co-ordinating org. for the Lutheran churches in southern Africa, incl. Angola, Botswana, Malawi, Mozambique, Namibia, South Africa, Swaziland, Zambia and Zimbabwe; 1,618,720 mems (1999); Exec. Dir Bishop J. M. RAMASHAPA.

Evangelical Lutheran Church in Southern Africa (ELCSA): POB 7231, 1622 Bonaero Park; tel. (11) 977137; fax (86) 5026891; e-mail elcsaadmin@mweb.co.za; f. 1975 by merger of four non-white churches; seven dioceses, each headed by a bishop; Presiding Bishop Rt Rev. LOUIS SIBIYA; 615,000 mems (2011).

Evangelical Lutheran Church in Southern Africa (Cape Church): POB 3466, 7602 Matieland; tel. (21) 8869747; fax (21) 8869748; e-mail rohwernj@afrihost.co.za; Pres. Bishop NILS ROHWER; 4,298 mems (2011).

Evangelical Lutheran Church in Southern Africa (N-T): Church Council, 24 Geldenhuys Rd, Bonaero Park, Johannesburg; POB 7095, Bonaero Park 1622; tel. (11) 979 7137; fax (86) 5026891; e-mail bishop@elcsant.org.za; internet www.elcsant.org.za; f. 1981; Pres. Bishop HORST MUELLER; 9,855 mems (2011).

Free Evangelical Lutheran Synod in South Africa: POB 21559, Mayors Walk 3208; 15 Greenwood Rd, Boughton, Pietermaritzburg; tel. (33) 3443238; e-mail felsisamail@gmail.com; internet www .felsisa.org.za; Bishop of the Synodical Council Dr DIETER REINSTORF.

Lutheran Church in Southern Africa: POB 117, 1851 Meadowlands, Soweto; tel. (11) 9888227; fax (11) 9890762; e-mail tswaedi@gmail.com; Bishop DAVID P. TSWAEDI; 20,000 mems (2010).

Moravian Church in Southern Africa: 63 Albert Rd, POB 24111, Lansdowne 7779; tel. (21) 7614030; fax (21) 7614046; e-mail mcsa@iafrica.com; f. 1737; Pres. LENNOX MCBUSI; 50,000 mems (2010).

The Roman Catholic Church

Some 6% of the total population are Roman Catholics.

Southern African Catholic Bishops' Conference (SACBC) 399 Khanya House, Paul Kruger St, POB 941, Pretoria 0001; tel. (12) 3236458; fax (12) 3266218; e-mail sacbclib@wn.apc.org; internet www.sacbc.org.za.

f. 1947 mems representing South Africa, Botswana and Swaziland; Pres. JOSEPH BUTI TLHAGALE (Archbishop of Johannesburg); Sec.-Gen. Fr VINCENT BRENNAN.

Archbishop of Bloemfontein: JABULANI ADATUS NXUMALO, Archbishop's House, 7A Whites Rd, POB 362, Bloemfontein 9300; tel. (51) 4481658; fax (51) 4472420; e-mail bfnarch@mweb.co.za.

Archbishop of Cape Town: Most Rev. STEPHEN BRISLIN, Cathedral Place, 12 Bouquet St, Cape Town; POB 2910, Cape Town 8000; tel. (21) 4622417; fax (21) 4619330; e-mail info@catholic-ct.org.za; internet www.catholic-ct.co.za.

Archbishop of Durban: Cardinal WILFRID NAPIER, Archbishop's House, 154 Gordon Rd, Durban 4001; POB 47489, Greyville 4023; tel. (31) 3031417; fax (31) 3121848; e-mail vg@catholic-dbn.org.za.

Archbishop of Johannesburg: Most Rev. BUTI JOSEPH TLHAGALE, Archbishop's House, PMB X10, Doornfontein 2028; tel. (11) 4026400; fax (11) 4026406; e-mail catholic@icon.co.za.

Archbishop of Pretoria: Most Rev. WILLLIAM SLATTERY, Jolivet House, 140 Visagie St, Pretoria 0002; POB 8149, Pretoria 0001; tel. (12) 3265311; fax (12) 3253994; e-mail ptadiocese@absamail.co.za.

Other Christian Churches

In addition to the following Churches, there are a large number of Pentecostalist groups, and more than 4,000 independent African Churches.

African Gospel Church: POB 32312, 4060 Mobeni; tel. (31) 9074377; Moderator Rev. F. D. MKHIZE; Gen. Sec. O. MTOLO; 100,000 mems.

Afrikaanse Protestantse Kerk (Afrikaans Protestant Church): 109 Brooks St, Brooklyn, Pretoria 0028; POB 11488, Hatfield 0028; tel. (12) 3621390; fax (12) 3622023; internet www.apkerk.co.za; f. 1987 by fmr mems of the Dutch Reformed Church (Nederduitse Gereformeerde Kerk) in protest at the desegregation of church congregations; c. 33,623 mems.

Apostolic Faith Mission of South Africa: Bldg No. 14, Central Office Park, 257 Jean Ave, Centurion; POB 9450, Centurion 0046; tel. (12) 6440490; fax (12) 6440732; e-mail admin@afm-ags.org; internet www.afm-ags.org; f. 1908; Pres. Dr ISAK BURGER; Gen. Sec. Pastor M. G. MAHLABO; 1.4m. mems.

Assemblies of God: POB 4547, Tyger Valley 7536; tel. (21) 9144386; fax (21) 9144387; e-mail brian@assemblies.org.za; internet www .assemblies.org.za; f. 1915; Chair. Rev. HLETA OSBORN; Gen. Sec. Rev. ERNEST HLOPE; 500,000 mems.

Baptist Union of Southern Africa: Private Bag X45, Wilropark 1731; tel. (11) 7685980; fax (11) 7685983; e-mail secretary@ baptistunion.org.za; internet www.baptistunion.org.za; f. 1877; Pres. Rev. STUART OWEN CRANNA; Gen. Sec. Rev. ANGELO SCHEEPERS; 44,574 mems (2011).

Black Dutch Reformed Church: POB 137, Bergvlei 2012; Leader Rev. SAM BUTI; c. 1m. mems.

Church of England in South Africa (CESA): POB 2180, Clareinch 7740; tel. (21) 6717070; fax (86) 2739764; e-mail cameronb@cesa.org.za; internet www.cesa.org.za; Presiding Bishop Rt Rev. DESMOND INGLESBY; Gen Sec. Rev. BRIAN CAMERON; 207 churches.

Evangelical Presbyterian Church in South Africa: POB 31961, Braamfontein 2017; tel. (11) 3391044; fax (11) 4034144; e-mail secretary@epcsa.org.za; internet www.epcsa.org.za; f. 1875; Moderator Rev. H. DIXON MASANGU; Gen. Sec. Rev. Dr TITUS R. MOBBIE; 60,000 mems.

The Methodist Church of Southern Africa: 450A Che Guevara Rd, Glenwood, Durban; POB 50216, Musgrave 4062; tel. (31) 2024214; fax (31) 2017674; e-mail general@mco.org.za; internet www.methodist.org.za; f. 1883; Pres. Bishop Rev. ZIPHOZIHLE D. SIWA; Gen. Sec. Rev. VUYANI G. NYOBOLE; 800,000 mems.

Nederduitsch Hervormde Kerk van Afrika: POB 2368, Pretoria 0001; tel. (12) 3228885; fax (12) 3227909; e-mail elmar@nhk.co.za; internet www.nhk.co.za; f. 1652; Gen. Sec. F. J. LABUSCHAGNE; 123,534 mems.

Nederduitse Gereformeerde Kerk in Afrika: Portland Pl., 37 Jorissen St, 2017 Johannesburg; tel. (11) 4031027; 6 synods (incl. 1 in Swaziland); Moderator Rev. S. P. E. BUTI; Gen. Sec. W. RAATH; 350,370 mems.

Presbyterian Church of Africa: POB 72, Nyanga, Cape Town 7755; tel. (21) 3850687; e-mail faleni@absamail.co.za; internet www .presbyterianchurchofafrica.co.za; f. 1898; 8 presbyteries (incl. 1 in Malawi and 1 in Zimbabwe); Moderator Rev. G. M. MOKABO; 1,231,000 mems.

Reformed Church in South Africa (Die Gereformeerde Kerke): POB 20004, Noordbrug 2522, Potchefstroom; tel. (18) 2973986; fax (18) 2931042; e-mail direkteur@gksa.org.za; internet www.gksa.org .za; f. 1859; Prin. Officer Dr C. J. SMIT; 158,973 mems.

Seventh-day Adventist Church: POB 468, Bloemfontein 9300; tel. (51) 4478271; fax (51) 4488059; e-mail sau.president@adventist .org.za; internet www.adventist.org.za; Pres. Dr T. LETSELI; Sec. Pastor T. KUNENE; 126,175 mems.

United Congregational Church of Southern Africa: POB 96014, Brixton 2019; tel. and fax (11) 8379997; fax (11) 8372570; e-mail admin@uccsa.co.za; internet www.uccsa.co.za; f. 1967; Gen. Sec. Rev. Dr PRINCE DIBEELA; 500,000 mems in 450 churches.

Uniting Presbyterian Church in Southern Africa: 28 Rhodes Ave, Parktown 2193; POB 96188, Brixton 2019; tel. (11) 7273500; fax (11) 7273506; e-mail gensec@presbyterian.org.za; internet www .upcsa.org.za; f. 1999; Moderator Rt Rev. GEORGE MARCHINKOWSKI; Gen. Sec. Rev. Dr JERRY PILLAY; Clerk of the Assembly TOM COULTER; 130,000 mems.

Zion Christian Church: Zion City, Moria; f. 1910; South Africa's largest black religious group; Leader Bishop BARNABAS LEKGANYANE; c. 4m. mems.

ISLAM

In 2003 there were some 455 mosques and 408 Muslim colleges in South Africa.

United Ulama Council of South Africa (UUCSA): POB 4118, Cape Town 8000; tel. (21) 6965150; fax (21) 6968502; internet www .uucsa.net; f. 1994; Pres. ABDUL HAMIED GHABIER; Sec.-Gen. MOULANA YUSUF PATEL.

JUDAISM

According to the South African Jewish Board of Deputies, in 2006 there were about 80,000 Jews in South Africa, and around 200 organized Jewish communities.

African Jewish Congress: POB 87557, Houghton 2041; tel. (11) 6452556; fax (11) 4854325; e-mail moshe@beyachad.co.za; internet www.africanjewishcongress.com; f. 1994; co-ordinating body representing Jewish communities in sub-Saharan Africa; Pres. MERVYN SMITH; Spiritual Leader and Exec. Dir Rabbi MOSHE SILBERHAFT.

South African Jewish Board of Deputies: POB 87557, Houghton 2041; tel. (11) 6452500; fax (11) 6452559; e-mail sajbod@beyachad.co .za; internet www.jewishsa.co.za; f. 1903; the representative institution of South African Jewry; Chair. ZEV KRENGEL; Nat. Dir WENDY KAHN.

BAHÁ'Í FAITH

National Spiritual Assembly: 209 Bellairs Dr., North Riding 2169, POB 932, Banbury Cross 2164; tel. (11) 8013100; fax (11) 4620129; e-mail nsa.sec@bahai.org.za; internet www.bahai.org.za; f. 1956; Gen. Sec. KULLY ZIPHETHE; 11,000 mems resident in 320 localities.

The Press

Government Communication and Information System (GCIS): Midtown Bldg, cnr Vermeulen and Prinsloo Sts, Pretoria; Private Bag X745, Pretoria 0001; tel. (12) 3142911; fax (12) 3252030; e-mail information@gcis.gov.za; internet www.gcis.gov.za; govt agency; CEO PHUMLA WILLIAMS (acting).

South African Press Ombudsman: 7 St Davids's Park, 2nd Floor, St Davids Place, Parktown 2193; POB 47221, Parklands 2121, Johannesburg; tel. (11) 4843612; fax (11) 4843619; e-mail pressombudsman@ombudsman.org.za; internet www.presscouncil .org.za; Ombudsman JOE THLOLOE.

DAILIES

Eastern Cape

Die Burger (Oos-Kaap): 52 Cawood St, POB 525, Port Elizabeth 6001; tel. (41) 5036111; fax (41) 5036138; e-mail kontak@dieburger .com; internet www.dieburger.com; f. 1937; morning; Afrikaans; Publr ANDRE OLIVIER; circ. 23,849.

Daily Dispatch: 35 Caxton St, POB 131, East London 5200; tel. (43) 7022000; fax (43) 7435155; e-mail letters@dispatch.co.za; internet www.dispatch.co.za; f. 1872; publ. by Dispatch Media (Pty) Ltd; afternoon; also publ. *Weekend Dispatch* (Sat.); English; Editor BRENDAN BOYLE; circ. 33,338 (Mon.–Fri.), 27,927 (Sat.).

The Herald: Newspaper House, 19 Baakens St; POB 1117, Port Elizabeth 1; tel. (41) 5047238; fax (41) 5854966; e-mail heraldletters@avusa.co.za; internet www.theherald.co.za; f. 1845; fmrly *Eastern Province Herald*; publ. by Johnnic Publishing Ltd; morning; English; Editor HEATHER ROBERTSON; circ. 29,719 (Mon.–Fri.), 25,000 (Sat.).

Free State

Die Volksblad: 79 Voortrekker St, POB 267, Bloemfontein 9300; tel. (51) 4047600; fax (51) 4306949; e-mail nuus@volksblad.com; internet www.volksblad.com; f. 1904; publ. by Media 24; morning; Afrikaans; Editor JONATHAN CROWTHER; circ. 29,018 (Mon.–Fri.), 23,000 (Sat.).

Gauteng

Beeld: Media Park, Kingsway 69, Auckland Park, Johannesburg; POB 333, Auckland Park 2006; tel. (11) 7139000; fax (11) 7139960; e-mail nuus@beeld.com; internet www.beeld.com; f. 1974; publ. by Media 24; morning; weekly: *Kampus-Beeld*, student news and information, and *JIP* youth supplement; Afrikaans; Editor-in-Chief PEET KRUGER; Editor TIM DU PLESSIS; circ. 105,618 (Mon.–Fri.), 88,402 (Sat.).

Business Day: POB 1745, Saxonwold 2132; tel. (11) 2803000; fax (11) 2805505; internet www.bday.co.za; f. 1985; publ. by BDFM Publrs (Pty) Ltd; afternoon; English; financial; incl. *Wanted* arts and leisure magazine; Editor PETER BRUCE; circ. 40,451 (Mon.–Fri.).

The Citizen: POB 43069, Industria 2042; tel. (11) 2486000; fax (11) 2486213; e-mail info@citizen.co.za; internet www.citizen.co.za; f. 1976; publ. by Caxton Publrs & Printers Ltd; Mon.–Sat., morning; English; Editor M. WILLIAMS; circ. 76,183 (Mon.–Fri.), 57,935 (Sat.).

The Daily Sun: POB 121, Auckland Park 2006; tel. (11) 8776000; fax (11) 8776020; e-mail info@redink.co.za; internet www.dailysun.co .za; Editor MAZWI XABA.

The New Age: 52 Lechwe St, Corporate Park, Old Pretoria Rd, Midrand 1685; tel. (11) 5421222; fax (86) 7337000; e-mail info@ thenewage.co.za; internet www.thenewage.co.za; f. 2010; Editor MOEGSIEN WILLIAMS.

The Pretoria News: 216 Vermeulen St, Pretoria 0002; POB 439, Pretoria 0001; tel. (12) 3002000; fax (12) 3257300; e-mail pta .newsdesk@inl.co.za; internet www.iol.co.za/pretoria-news; f. 1898; publ. by Independent Newspapers Gauteng Ltd; afternoon; English; Editor VAL BOJÉ; circ. 28,690 (Mon.–Fri.), 17,406 (Sat.).

Sowetan: 4 Biermann Ave, Rosebank, Johannesburg 2196; POB 6663, Johannesburg 2000; tel. (11) 2803732; fax (11) 4748834; e-mail editor@sowetan.co.za; internet www.sowetanlive.co.za; f. 1981; publ. by New Africa Publs (NAP) Ltd; morning; English; Editor (vacant); circ. 4,122,825 (Mon.–Fri.).

The Star: 47 Sauer St, POB 1014, Johannesburg 2000; tel. (11) 6339111; fax (11) 8343918; e-mail starnews@star.co.za; internet www.iol.co.za/the-star; f. 1887; publ. by Independent Newspapers Gauteng Ltd; morning; English; also publ. *The Saturday Star*; Editor MOEGSIEN WILLIAMS; circ. 166,461 (Mon.–Fri.), 137,385 (Sat.).

KwaZulu/Natal

The Daily News: 18 Osborne St, Greyville 4001; POB 47549, Greyville 4023; tel. (31) 3082106; fax (31) 3082185; internet www .iol.co.za; f. 1878; Mon.–Fri., afternoon; English; Editor ALAN DUNN; circ. 33,011.

The Mercury: 18 Osborne St, Greyville 4001; POB 47397, Greyville 4023; tel. (31) 3082472; fax (31) 3082662; e-mail mercnews@inl.co.za; internet www.iol.co.za/mercury; f. 1852; publ. by Independent Newspapers KZN; morning; English; Editor PHILANI MGWABA; circ. 34,541 (Mon.–Fri.).

The Witness: 45 Willowton Rd, POB 362, Pietermaritzburg 3200; tel. (33) 3551111; fax (33) 3551122; e-mail angela.quintal@witness.co .za; internet www.witness.co.za; f. 1846; publ. by Natal Witness Printing and Publishing Co Ltd; Mon–Fri (morning); English; also publ. *Weekend Witness* (Sat); Editor ANGELA QUINTAL; circ. 23,700 (Mon.–Fri.), 29,000 (Sat.).

Northern Cape

Diamond Fields Advertiser: POB 610, cnr Bean and Villiers Sts, Kimberley 8300; tel. (53) 8326261; fax (53) 8328902; e-mail pbe@ independent.co.za; internet www.iol.co.za; publ. by Independent Newspapers Gauteng Ltd; morning; English; Editor KEVIN RITCHIE; circ. 8,948 (Mon.–Fri.).

North-West

Rustenburg Herald: 13 Coetzer St, POB 2043, Rustenburg 0299; tel. (14) 5928329; fax (14) 5921869; e-mail rustenburgweb@gmail .com; internet www.northwestnewspapers.co.za/herald; f. 1924; English and Afrikaans; Man. Editor WALDIE WOLSCHENK; circ. 20,368.

Western Cape

Die Burger: 40 Heerengracht, POB 692, Cape Town 8000; tel. (21) 4062222; fax (21) 4062913; e-mail kontak@dieburger.com; internet www.dieburger.com; f. 1915; publ. by Media 24; morning; Afrikaans; Editor BUN BOOYENS; circ. 104,102 (Mon.–Fri.), 117,092 (Sat.).

Cape Argus: 122 St George's St, POB 56, Cape Town 8000; tel. (21) 4884911; fax (21) 4884075; e-mail argusnews@ctn.independent.co .za; internet www.iol.co.za/capeargus; f. 1857; publ. by Independent Newspapers Cape Ltd; afternoon; English; also publ. *Weekend Argus*; Editor CHRIS WHITFIELD; circ. 73,230 (Mon.–Fri.), 103,953 (Sat. and Sun.).

Cape Times: Newspaper House, 122 St George's Mall, Cape Town 8001; POB 11, Cape Town 8000; tel. (21) 4884776; fax (21) 4884744; e-mail alide.dasnois@inl.co.za; internet www.iol.co.za/capetimes; f. 1876; publ. by Independent Newspapers Cape Ltd; morning; English; Dep. Editor ALIDE DASNOIS; circ. 49,526 (Mon.–Fri.).

WEEKLIES AND FORTNIGHTLIES

Eastern Cape

Weekend Post: 19 Baakens St, Private Bag X6071, Port Elizabeth 6000; tel. (41) 5047311; fax (41) 5854966; e-mail weekendpost .easterncape@gmail.com; internet theweekendpost.com; publ. by Johnnic Publishing Co Ltd; English; Editor JEREMY MCCABE; circ. 33,372 (Sat.).

Free State

Vista: POB 1027, Welkom 9460; tel. (57) 3571304; fax (57) 3532427; e-mail mwill@volksblad.com; internet www.media24.com/en/ newspapers/community-newspapers/central-newspapers/vista .html; f. 1971; weekly; English and Afrikaans; Editor MARTI WILL; circ. 38,000 (2005).

Gauteng

City Press: POB 3413, Johannesburg 2000; tel. (11) 7139002; fax (11) 7139977; e-mail news@citypress.co.za; internet www.citypress .co.za; f. 1983; publ. by RCP Media Bpk; weekly; English; Editor-in-Chief FERIAL HAFFEJEE; circ. 173,922 (Sun.).

Engineering News/Mining Weekly: POB 75316, Garden View 2047; tel. and fax (11) 6223744; fax (11) 6229350; e-mail newsdesk@ engineeringnews.co.za; internet www.miningweekly.com; f. 1981;

publ. by Creamer Media; weekly; Editor TERENCE CREAMER; circ. 20,000.

Financial Mail: Johncom Bldg, 4 Biermann Ave, Rosebank 2196; POB 1744, Saxenwold 2132; tel. (11) 2805808; fax (11) 2805800; e-mail fmmail@fm.co.za; internet www.fm.co.za; weekly; English; Editor BARNEY MTHOMBOTHI; circ. 33,000.

Mail and Guardian: POB 91667, Auckland Park 2006; tel. (11) 2507300; fax (11) 2507303; e-mail newsdesk@mg.co.za; internet www.mg.co.za; publ. by M&G Media (Pty) Ltd; weekly; English; CEO GOVIN REDDY; Editor NIC DAWES; circ. 40,162 (Fri.).

Noordwes Gazette: POB 515, Potchefstroom 2520; tel. (18) 2930750; e-mail potchherald@media24.com; weekly; English and Afrikaans; Editor H. STANDER; circ. 35,000.

Northern Review: 16 Grobler St, POB 45, Pietersburg 0700; tel. (152) 2959167; fax (152) 2915148; weekly; English and Afrikaans; Editor R. S. DE JAGER; circ. 10,300.

Potchefstroom and Ventersdorp Herald: POB 515, Potchefstroom 2520; tel. (18) 2930750; fax (18) 2930759; e-mail potchherald@media24.com; internet www.potchefstroomherald.co.za; f. 1908; Friday; English and Afrikaans; Editor H. STANDER; Man. Dir RASSIE VAN ZYL; circ. 8,000.

Rapport: POB 333, Auckland Park 2006; tel. (11) 7139628; fax (11) 7139977; e-mail briewe@rapport.co.za; internet www.rapport.co.za; publ. by RCP Media; weekly; Afrikaans; Sr Gen. Man. and Publr SAREL DU PLESSIS; Editor BOKKIE GERBER; circ. 322,731 (Sun.).

South African Jewish Report: POB 84650, Greenside 2034; tel. (11) 2741400; fax (11) 8864202; e-mail sharon@sajewishreport.co.za; internet www.sajewishreport.co.za; weekly; publ. by SA Jewish Report (Pty) Ltd; Editor GEOFF SIFRIN.

Springs Advertiser: 48, 5th Ave, POB 761, Springs 1560; tel. (11) 8124800; fax (11) 8124823; e-mail springseditorial@caxton.co.za; internet www.looklocal.co.za; f. 1916; English and Afrikaans; Editor LEANDI CAMERON; circ. 26,000.

Sunday Times: POB 1742, Saxonwold 2132; tel. (11) 2805155; fax (11) 2805111; e-mail feedback@avusa.co.za; internet www.timeslive.co.za/sundaytimes; f. 1906; weekly; English; also published in Zulu; Editor RAY HARTLEY; circ. 505,402 (Sun.).

Vaalweekblad: 27 Ekspa Bldg, D. F. Malan St, POB 351, Vanderbijlpark 1900; tel. (16) 817010; fax (16) 810604; e-mail rfichat@media24.com; internet www.vaalweekblad.com; weekly; Afrikaans and English; Editor RETHA FICHAT; circ. 16,000.

Die Vrye Afrikaan: POB 675, Durbanville 7551; tel. (12) 3268646; e-mail redakteur@vryeafrikaan.co.za; internet www.vryeafrikaan.co.za; f. 2004; weekly; Afrikaans; Editor JOHANN ROUSSOUW; circ. 13,000.

KwaZulu/Natal

Farmers' Weekly: 368 Jan Smuts Ave, Craighall, Johannesburg 2196; tel. (11) 8890836; fax (11) 8890862; e-mail farmersweekly@caxton.co.za; internet www.farmersweekly.co.za; f. 1911; weekly; agriculture and horticulture; Editor ALITA VAN DER WALT; circ. 17,000.

Ilanga: 19 Timeball Blvd, The Point, Durban 4001; POB 2159 Durban 4000; tel. (31) 3346700; fax (31) 3379785; e-mail peterc@ilanganews.co.za; internet www.ilanganews.co.za; f. 1903; publ. by Mandla Matla Publishing Co (Pty) Ltd; 2 a week; also publ. *Ilanga Lange Sonto* (Sun. circ. 87,000); Zulu; Editor SIPHO NGOBESE; circ. 107,000; circ. 100,000 (Mon. and Thur.).

Independent On Saturday: 18 Osborne St, Greyville 4001; POB 47397, Greyville 4023; tel. (31) 3082900; fax (31) 3082185; e-mail satmail@inl.co.za; internet www.iol.co.za/ios; f. 1878; publ. by Independent Newspapers KZN; English; Editor DEON DELPORT; circ. 56,216.

Ladysmith Gazette: 3 Keate St, POB 10019, Ladysmith 3370; tel. (36) 6376801; fax (36) 6372283; f. 1902; weekly; English, Afrikaans and Zulu; Editor DIANA PROCTER; circ. 7,000.

Post: 18 Osborne St, Greyville, Durban 4000; POB 47397, Greyville 4023; tel. (31) 3082400; fax (31) 3082427; e-mail post@inl.co.za; internet www.iol.co.za/thepost; f. 1955 as *Golden City Post*; publ. by Independent Newspapers KZN; weekly; English; focus on the Indian community; Editor AAKASH BRAMDEO; circ. 45,500 (Wed.).

Sunday Tribune: 18 Osborne St, POB 47549, Greyville 4023; tel. (31) 3082911; fax (31) 3082662; e-mail tribunenews@inl.co.za; internet www.iol.co.za/sunday-tribune; f. 1937; publ. by Independent Newspapers KZN; weekly; English; Editor ALAN DUNN; circ. 109,774 (Sun.).

Umafrika: Media House, 43 Imvubu Park Place, Riverhorse Valley, Business Estate, Durban 4017; tel. (31) 5337600; fax (31) 5337940; e-mail editor@umafrika.co.za; f. 1911; owned by Izimpoondo Communications; Friday; Zulu; Editor and Publisher FRASER MTSHALI; circ. 20,000.

Northern Cape

Die Gemsbok: POB 60, Upington 8800; tel. 27017; fax 24055; English and Afrikaans; Editor D. JONES; circ. 8,000.

Western Cape

Drum: Naspers Bldg, 7th Floor, 5 Protea Place, Sandown 2096; POB 653284, Benmore 2010; tel. (11) 3220885; fax (11) 3220891; e-mail khosi@drum.co.za; f. 1951; English and Zulu; Editor MAKHOSAZANA ZWANE SIGUQA; Publr NERISA COETZEE; circ. 79,895 (2006).

Eikestadnuus: 44 Alexander St, POB 28, Stellenbosch 7600; tel. (2231) 72840; fax (2231) 99538; e-mail eikestad@eikestadnuus.com; internet www.eikestadnuus.co.za; weekly; English and Afrikaans; Editor ELSABÉ RETIEF; circ. 7,000.

Fair Lady: POB 1802, Cape Town 8000; tel. (21) 4081278; fax (21) 4051042; e-mail flmag@fairlady.com; internet www.fairlady.com; fortnightly; English; Editor SUZY BROKENSHA; circ. 103,642.

Huisgenoot: 40 Heerengracht, POB 1802, Cape Town 8000; tel. (21) 4062115; fax (21) 4063316; e-mail hgnbrief@huisgenoot.com; internet www.huisgenoot.com; f. 1916; weekly; Afrikaans; Editor JULIA VILJOEN; circ. 355,487.

Move! Magazine: Media City, 10th Floor, 1 Heerengracht St, Foreshore, Cape Town 8001; tel. (21) 4461232; fax (21) 4461206; e-mail move@media24.com; f. 2005; weekly; English; Editor NOLUTHANDO GWEBA-PHILISANE.

The Southern Cross: POB 2372, Cape Town 8000; tel. (21) 4655007; fax (21) 4653850; e-mail editor@scross.co.za; internet www.scross.co.za; f. 1920; publ. by Catholic Newspapers and Publishing Co Ltd; weekly; English; Roman Catholic interest; Editor GÜNTHER SIMMERMACHER; circ. 11,000 (Wed.).

tvplus: Media City, 10th Floor, 1 Heerengracht St, Cape Town 8001; POB 7197, Roggebaai 8012; tel. (21) 4461222; fax (21) 4461206; e-mail tvplus@media24.com; internet www.tvplus.co.za; f. 2000; weekly; English and Afrikaans; Editor ANDRÉ NEVELING.

Tyger-Burger: Bloemhof Bldg, 112 Edward Rd, Bellville 7530; tel. (21) 9106500; e-mail mmeyer@tygerburger.co.za; internet www.tygerburger.co.za; weekly; Afrikaans and English; Editor MARITA MEYER.

Weekend Argus: 122 St George's Mall, POB 56, Cape Town 8000; tel. (21) 4884911; fax (21) 4884762; internet www.iol.co.za; f. 1857; Sat. and Sun.; English; Editor CHRIS WHITFIELD; circ. 108,294.

You Magazine: Naspers Bldg, 7th Floor, 40 Heerengracht St, Cape Town 8001; POB 7167, Roggebaai 8012; tel. (21) 4062116; fax (21) 4062937; e-mail letters@you.co.za; internet www.you.co.za; f. 1987; weekly; English; Editor LINDA PIETERSEN; circ. 222,845 (2004).

MONTHLIES
Free State

Wamba: POB 1097, Bloemfontein; publ. in seven vernacular languages; educational; Editor C. P. SENYATSI.

KwaZulu/Natal

Bona: POB 32083, Mobeni 4060; tel. (31) 422041; fax (31) 426068; f. 1956; English, Sotho, Xhosa and Zulu; Editor (vacant); circ. 256,631.

Living and Loving: CTP Caxton Magazines, 4th Floor, Caxton House, 368 Jan Smuts Ave, Craighall Park, Johannesburg; tel. (11) 8890621; fax (11) 8890668; e-mail livingandloving@caxton.co.za; internet www.livingandloving.co.za; f. 1970; publ. by Caxton Magazines; English; parenting magazine; Editor CLARE HUISAMEN; circ. 33,000.

Rooi Rose: POB 412982, Craighall 2024; tel. (11) 8890665; fax (11) 8890975; e-mail rooirose@caxton.co.za; internet www.rooirose.co.za; f. 1942; Afrikaans; women's interest; Editor MARTIE PANSEGROUW; circ. 122,296.

World Airnews: POB 35082, Northway 4065; tel. (31) 5641319; fax (31) 5637115; e-mail info@airnews.co.za; internet www.airnews.co.za; f. 1973; owned by TCE Publications; monthly; aviation news; Man. Editor TOM CHALMERS; circ. 11,634 (2012).

Your Family: POB 473016, Parklands 2121; tel. (11) 8890749; fax (11) 8890642; e-mail yourfamily@caxton.co.za; internet www.yourfamily.co.za; f. 1973; English; cooking, crafts, DIY; Editor JANINE COLLINS; circ. 164,115.

Western Cape

Car: Ramsay, Son & Parker (Pty) Ltd, Digital Publishing, 3 Howard Dr., Pinelands, Cape Town; POB 180, Howard Place 7450; tel. (21) 5303100; fax (21) 5322698; e-mail car@rsp.co.za; internet www.cartoday.com; English; Editor J. BENTLEY; circ. 99,411 (2008).

Femina: 21 St John's St, POB 3647, Cape Town 8000; tel. (21) 4646248; fax (21) 4612501; Editor ROBYNNE KAHN; circ. 68,591.

Reader's Digest (South African Edition): 5 Protea Pl., Protea Park, Sandown, Johannesburg 2146; POB 785266, Sandton 2146; tel. (11) 3220700; fax (11) 8839495; e-mail magazine.sa@readersdigest.com; internet www.readersdigest.co.za; f. 1948; English; Editor ANTHONY JOHNSON; circ. 62,399.

Sarie: POB 785266, Sandton 2146; tel. and fax (21) 4083090; fax (86) 5308712; e-mail mvanbre@sarie.com; internet www.media24.com/en/magazines/womens-interest/sarie.html; monthly; Afrikaans; women's interest; Editor MICHELLE VAN BREDA; circ. 137,970 (2004).

South African Medical Journal: MASA House, Central House, Private Bag X1, Pinelands 7430; tel. (21) 5306520; fax (21) 5314126; e-mail danjn@telkomsa.net; internet www.samj.org.za; f. 1884; publ. by the South African Medical Asscn; Editor-in-Chief DANIEL J. NCAYIYANA; circ. 20,000.

Die Voorligter: Private Bag, Tyger Valley 7536; tel. (21) 9177000; fax (21) 9141333; e-mail lig@cnw-inter.net; internet www.christene .co.za; f. 1937; journal of the Dutch Reformed Church of South Africa; Editor Dr F. M. GAUM; circ. 50,000.

Wineland Magazine: VinPro, POB 1411, Suider-Paarl 7624; tel. (21) 8634524; fax (21) 8634851; e-mail in@wineland.co.za; internet www.wineland.co.za; f. 1931; publ. by VinPro wine producers' org.; viticulture and the wine and spirit industry; incorporates *Wynboer* technical guide for wine producers; Editor CASSIE DU PLESSIS; circ. 7,000.

The Wisden Cricketer: POB 16368, Vlaeberg 8018; tel. (21) 4083813; e-mail aevlambi@touchline.co.za; internet www .wisdencricketer.co.za; f. 2005; Publr NIC WIDES; Editor ROB HOUWING.

Woman's Value: POB 1802, Cape Town 8000; tel. (21) 4062629; fax (21) 4062929; e-mail wvdited@womansvalue.com; internet www .women24.com; English; Editor and Publr TERENA LE ROUX; circ. 134,749.

PERIODICALS

Eastern Cape

African Journal of AIDS Research (AJAR): Centre for AIDS Development, Research and Evaluation, Institute of Social and Economic Research, 11th Floor, Braamfontein Centre, 23 Jorissen St, Braamfontein, Johannesburg 2001; tel. (11) 3392611; fax (11) 3392615; e-mail AJAR.editor@gmail.com; internet www.cadre.org .za; f. 2002; quarterly; Man. Editor KEVIN KELLY.

Gauteng

Africa Insight: Africa Institute of South Africa, POB 630, Pretoria 0001; tel. (12) 3049700; fax (12) 3213164; e-mail ngobenis@ai.org.za; internet www.ai.org.za; f. 1960; quarterly; journal of the Africa Institute of South Africa; Editor SOLANI NGOBENI; circ. 1,200.

Africanus: Unisa Press, POB 392, UNISA, 0003 Pretoria; tel. (12) 4292953; fax (12) 4293449; e-mail delpoa@unisa.ac.za; 2 a year; journal of the Centre for Development Studies, Unisa; African and Third World developmental issues; Editor LINDA CORNWELL.

Codicillus: Unisa Press, POB 392, UNISA, 0003 Pretoria; tel. (12) 4292953; fax (12) 4293449; e-mail delpoa@unisa.ac.za; 2 a year; journal of the School of Law at the Univ. of South Africa; South African and international law; Editor Prof. H. C. ROODT.

The ScienceScope: POB 395, Pretoria 0001; tel. (12) 8412911; fax (12) 3491153; e-mail callcentre@csir.co.za; internet www.csir.co.za; f. 1991 as *Technobrief*; quarterly; publ. by the South African Council for Scientific and Industrial Research; Editor THABO DITSELE; circ. 6,000.

South African Journal of Economics: 4.45 EBW Bldg, University of Pretoria, Pretoria 0002; POB 73354, Lynnwood Ridge 0040; tel. (12) 4203525; fax (12) 3625266; e-mail saje@up.ac.za; internet www .essa.org.za; f. 1933; quarterly; English and Afrikaans; journal of the Economic Soc. of South Africa; publ. by Blackwells; Editorial Sec. TITIA ANTONITES.

KwaZulu/Natal

South African Journal of Chemistry: POB 407, WITS 2050, Johannesburg; tel. (11) 7176741; fax (11) 7176779; e-mail sajc@saci .co.za; internet search.sabinet.co.za/sajchem; f. 1921; publ. by the South African Chemical Institute; digital; Co-ordinating Editor GRAHAM JACKSON.

North-West

Historia: c/o Dept of Historical and Heritage Studies, Faculty of Humanities, Humanities Bldg (Main Campus), University of Pretoria, Pretoria 0002; tel. (12) 4202323; fax (12) 4202656; e-mail wassermannj@ukzn.ac.za; f. 1956; 2 a year; journal of the Historical Asscn of South Africa; South African and African history; Coordinating Editor JOHAN WASSERMANN.

Western Cape

Economic Prospects: Bureau for Economic Research, Economics and Management Sciences Bldg, 7th Floor, Bosman St, Stellenbosch 7600; Private Bag 5050, Stellenbosch 7599; tel. (21) 8872810; fax (21) 8839225; e-mail hhman@sun.ac.za; internet www.ber.ac.za; quarterly; forecast of the South African economy for the coming 18–24 months; Man. Editor H. PIENAAR.

Ecquid Novi: c/o South African Journal for Journalism Research, POB 106, Stellenbosch 7599; tel. (21) 8082625; fax (21) 8083488; e-mail novi@sun.ac.za; internet www.sun.ac.za/ecquidnovi; f. 1980; 2 a year; focus on role of the media in southern Africa and Africa; Man. Editor ARNOLD S. DE BEER.

The Motorist: Highbury Monarch Pty, 8th Floor, Metlife Centre, 7 Coen Steytler Ave, Foreshore, 8001 Cape Town; tel. (21) 4160141; fax (21) 4187312; e-mail themotorist@monarchc.co.za; f. 1966; journal of the Automobile Asscn of SA; Editor FIONA ZERBST; circ. 131,584 (2000).

NEWS AGENCIES

East Cape News (ECN) Pty Ltd: POB 897, Grahamstown 6140; tel. (46) 6361050; e-mail editor@ecn.co.za; internet www.ecn.co.za; f. 1997; fmrly East Cape News Agencies; Dir MIKE LOEWE.

South African Press Association (SAPA): Cotswold House, Greenacres Office Park, cnr Victory and Rustenburg Rds, Victory Park; POB 7766, Johannesburg 2000; tel. (11) 7821600; fax (11) 7821587; e-mail comms@sapa.org.za; internet www.sapa.co.za; f. 1938; Man. WIM J. H. VAN GILS; Editor MARK A. VAN DER VELDEN; 40 mems.

PRESS ASSOCIATIONS

Foreign Correspondents' Association of South Africa: POB 1136, Auckland Park 2006; tel. and fax (11) 6467649; e-mail fca@ onwe.co.za; internet www.fcasa.co.za; represents 175 int. journalists; Chair. KIM NORGAARD; Sec. MARTINA SCHWIKOWSKI.

Newspaper Association of South Africa: Nedbank Gardens, 5th Floor, 33 Bath Ave, Rosebank 2196, Johannesburg; POB 47180, Parklands 2121; tel. (11) 7213200; fax (11) 7213254; e-mail na@ printmedia.org.za; internet www.printmedia.org.za; f. 1882; represents 42 national daily and weekly newspapers, and 178 community newspapers; Pres. PRAKASH DESAI.

Print and Media SA: Media Park, Ground Floor, 69 Kingsway Ave, Aucklandpark, Johannesburg; POB 47180, Parklands 2121; tel. (10) 2198600; fax (10) 2198621; e-mail info@pdmedia.org.za; internet www.pdmedia.org.za; f. 1995 following the restructuring of the Newspaper Press Union of Southern Africa; represents all aspects of the print media (newspapers and magazines); over 700 mems; CEO INGRID LOUW.

Publishers

Acorn Books: POB 4845, Randburg 2125; tel. (11) 8805768; fax (11) 8805768; e-mail acornbook@iafrica.com; f. 1985; Africana, general, natural history; Propr and Publr ELEANOR-MARY CADELL.

Jonathan Ball Publishers: 10–14 Watkins St, Denver Ext. 4, Johannesburg 2094; POB 33977, Jeppestown 2043; tel. (11) 6222900; fax (11) 6018183; e-mail orders@jonathanball.co.za; internet www .jonathanball.co.za; acquired by Via Afrika (Naspers Group) in 1992; fiction, reference, bibles, textbooks, general; imprints incl. AD Donker (literature), Delta (general fiction and non-fiction) and Sunbird; Man. Dir JONATHAN BALL.

Bible Society of South Africa: Bible House, 134 Edward St, POB 5500, Tyger Valley 7536; tel. (21) 9108777; fax (21) 9108799; e-mail biblia@biblesociety.co.za; internet www.biblesociety.co.za; f. 1820; bibles and religious material in 11 official languages; CEO Rev. G. S. KRITZINGER.

Brenthurst Press (Pty) Ltd: Federation Rd, POB 87184, Houghton 2041; tel. (11) 5445400; fax (11) 4861651; e-mail orders@brenthurst.co.za; internet www.brenthurst.org.za; f. 1974; Southern African history; Dir SALLY MACROBERTS.

Christelike Uitgewersmaatskappy (CUM): POB 1599, Vereeniging 1930; tel. (16) 4407000; fax (16) 4211748; e-mail orders@cabooks .co.za; internet www.cum.co.za; religious fiction and non-fiction.

Clever Books: POB 13816, Hatfield 0028; tel. (12) 3423263; fax (12) 4302376; e-mail info@cleverbooks.co.za; internet www.cleverbooks .co.za; f. 1981; subsidiary of Macmillan Publrs; Gen. Man. ELNA HARMSE.

Fisichem Publishers: 19 Hofmeyer St, Private Bag X3, Matieland 7602; tel. (21) 8870900; fax (21) 8839635; e-mail info@fisichem.co.za; internet fisichem.co.za; f. 1985; owned by FRJ Trust; science, maths and accounting study guides; Man. RETHA JORDAAN.

Flesch Publications: 11 Peninsula Rd, Zeekoevlei, Cape Town 7941; POB 31353, Grassy Park 7888; tel. (21) 7054317; fax (21) 7060766; e-mail sflesch@iafrica.com; f. 1954; biography, cookery, aviation; CEO STEPHEN FLESCH.

Fortress Books: POB 2475, Knysna 6570; tel. (44) 3826805; fax (44) 3826848; e-mail fortress@iafrica.com; internet www.uys.com/fortress; f. 1973; military history, biographies, financial; Man. Dir I. UYS.

Heinemann Publishers (Pty) Ltd: Heinemann House, Grayston Office Park, Bldg 3, 128 Peter Rd, Atholl Ext. 12, Sandton 2196; POB 781940, Sandown, Sandton 2146; tel. (11) 3228600; fax (11) 3228715; e-mail customerliaison@heinemann.co.za; internet www .heinemann.co.za; educational; incl. imprints Lexicon, Isando and Centaur; Man. Dir ORENNA KRUT.

Home Economics Publishers (Huishoudkunde Uitgewers): POB 7091, Stellenbosch 7599; tel. and fax (21) 8864722; e-mail mcv1@sun .ac.za; Man. M. C. VOSLOO.

HSRC Press: Human Sciences Research Council, Private Bag X9182, Cape Town 8000; tel. (21) 4668000; fax (21) 4610836; e-mail publishing@hsrc.ac.za; internet www.hsrcpress.ac.za; Chair. Prof. DAN NCAYIYANA.

Juta and Co Ltd: POB 14373, Lansdowne 7780, Cape Town; tel. (21) 6592300; fax (21) 6592360; e-mail cserv@juta.co.za; internet www .juta.co.za; f. 1853; academic and professional development, education, trade, law, electronics; imprints incl. UCT Press (scholarly and academic); CEO LYNNE DU TOIT.

LAPA Publishers (Lees Afrikaans Praat Afrikaans): 380 Bosman St, POB 123, Pretoria 0001; tel. (12) 4010700; fax (12) 3244460; f. 1996 as the publishing arm of the Afrikaans Language and Culture Asscn; present name adopted in 2000; Afrikaans; general fiction and non-fiction; CEO WIM DE WET.

Lemur Books (Pty) Ltd (The Galago Publishing (1999) (Pty) Ltd): POB 1645, Alberton 1450; tel. (11) 9072029; fax (11) 8690890; e-mail lemur@mweb.co.za; internet www.galago.co.za; f. 1980; military, political, history, hunting, general; Man. Dir F. STIFF.

LexisNexis Butterworths SA: 215 North Ridge Rd, Morningside, Durban 4001; POB 792, Durban 4000; tel. (31) 2683111; fax (31) 2683108; e-mail customercare@lexisnexis.co.za; internet www .lexisnexis.co.za; f. 1948 as Butterworths; adopted LexisNexis name in 2001; jtly owned by Reed Elsevier, USA, and Kagiso Media; law, tax, accountancy; Chair. W. ROGER JARDINE; CEO WILLIAM J. LAST.

Lux Verbi-BM: POB 5, Wellington 7654; tel. (21) 8648210; fax (21) 8648295; e-mail jmc@luxverbi-bm.co.za; internet www.luxverbi-bm .com; f. 1818 as the Dutch Reformed Church Publishing Co; merged with Bible Media in 1999; subsidiary of the Naspers Group; imprints incl. Hugenote, NG Kerk Uitgewers, Protea, and Waterkant; Christian media; Man. Dir H. S. SPIES; Editor-in-Chief W. BOTHA.

Maskew Miller Longman (Pty) Ltd: cnr Forest Dr. and Logan Way, Pinelands 7405; POB 396, Cape Town 8000; tel. (21) 5326000; fax (21) 5310716; e-mail customerservices@mml.co.za; internet www .mml.co.za; f. 1893 as Miller Maskew; merged with Longman in 1983; jtly owned by Pearson Education and Caxton Publrs and Printers Ltd; imprints incl. Kagiso Publishing (f. 1994; fmrly De Jager-HAUM) and Phumelela Books; educational and general; CEO JAPIE PIENAAR.

Methodist Publishing House: POB 13128, Woodstock, Cape Town 7915; tel. (21) 4483640; fax (21) 4483716; e-mail george@methbooks .co.za; f. 1894; Christian books and church supplies; Gen. Man. GEORGE VINE.

Nasou—Via Afrika: 40 Heerengracht, Cape Town 8001; POB 5197, Cape Town 8000; tel. (21) 4063005; fax (21) 4063086; e-mail CGillitt@ nasou.com; internet www.nasou-viaafrika.com; f. 1963; subsidiary of Via Afrika (Naspers Group); educational; imprints incl. Acacia, Action Publrs, Afritech, Afro, Atlas, Era, Juta, KZN Books, Gariep, Idem, Phoenix Education, Shortland and Y-Press Grade R-3; Man. Dir CLIVE GILLITT.

NB Publishers: Naspers Bldg, 12th Floor, 40 Heerengracht, Roggebai 8012; POB 879, Cape Town 8000; tel. (21) 4063033; fax (21) 4063812; e-mail nb@nb.co.za; internet www.nb.co.za; English, Afrikaans, Xhosa and Zulu; Human & Rousseau (f. 1959; general, children's and youth literature, cookery and self-help), Kwela (f. 1994; fiction), Pharos (dictionaries), Tafelberg (f. 1950; fiction and non-fiction, politics, children's and youth literature) and Best Books (educational texts); Head of Publishing C. T. BREYTENBACH.

Oxford University Press: POB 12119, N1 City, Cape Town 7463; tel. (21) 5962300; fax (21) 5961234; e-mail oxford.za@oup.com; internet www.oxford.co.za; f. 1914; Man. Dir LIEZE KOTZE.

Protea Book House: 1067 Burnett St, Hatfield, Pretoria; POB 35110, Menlo Park, 0102 Pretoria; tel. (12) 3623444; fax (12) 3625688; e-mail protea@intekom.co.za; internet www .proteaboekhuis.co.za; f. 1997; art and photography, Afrikaans fiction, South African history, spiritual, academic and general; Dir NICOL STASSEN.

Random House Struik (Pty) Ltd South Africa: POB 2002, Houghton 2041; tel. (11) 4843538; fax (11) 4846180; e-mail ruthc@ randomstruik.co.za; f. 1966; general fiction and non-fiction (lifestyle, nature, sport, politics, general reference, travel and heritage); Man. Dir S. E. CONNOLLY.

Shuter & Shooter Publishers (Pty) Ltd: 110CB Downes Rd, Pietermaritzburg; POB 13016, Cascades, Pietermaritzburg 3202; tel. (33) 8468700; fax (33) 8468701; e-mail sales@shuters.com; internet www.shuters.com; f. 1921; educational, general and African languages and trade books; Man. Dir PRIMI CHETTY.

University of KwaZulu-Natal Press (UKZN Press): Private Bag X01, Scottsville 3209; tel. (33) 2605226; fax (33) 2605801; e-mail books@ukzn.ac.za; internet www.ukznpress.co.za; academic and scholarly; Publr DEBRA PRIMO.

Van Schaik Publishers: 1064 Arcadia St, POB 12681, Hatfield 0028; tel. (12) 3422765; fax (12) 4303563; e-mail vanschaik@ vanschaiknet.com; internet www.vanschaiknet.com; f. 1915; acquired by Nasionale Pers, latterly Via Afrika-Naspers Group in 1986; English and Afrikaans; academic and scholarly; CEO LEANNE MARTINI.

Wits University Press: PO Wits, Johannesburg 2050; tel. (11) 4845910; e-mail Veronica.Klipp@wits.ac.za; internet witspress.co .za; f. 1922; general trade, non-fiction and scholarly; Publr VERONICA KLIPP.

PUBLISHERS' ASSOCIATION

Publishers' Association of South Africa (PASA): Suite 305, 2nd Floor, The Foundry, Prestwich St, Green Point, Cape Town 8005; tel. (21) 4252721; fax (21) 4213270; e-mail pasa@publishsa.co.za; internet www.publishsa.co.za; f. 1992; promotes and protects the rights and responsibilities of the independent publishing sector in South Africa; Exec Dir. DUDLEY H. SCHROEDER.

Broadcasting and Communications

REGULATORY AUTHORITY

Independent Communications Authority of South Africa (ICASA): Pinmill Farm, Blocks A, B, C and D, 164 Katherine St, Sandton 2146; Private Bag X10002, Marlboro 2063; tel. (11) 5663000; fax (11) 4441919; e-mail info@icasa.org.za; internet www.icasa.org .za; f. 2000 as successor to the Independent Broadcasting Authority (f. 1993) and South African Telecommunications Regulatory Authority (f. 1996); regulates telecommunications and broadcasting; Chair. Dr STEPHEN SIPHO MNCUBE; CEO THEMBA DLAMINI.

TELECOMMUNICATIONS

At the end of 2011 there were two providers of fixed-line telephone services and five providers of mobile telephone services in South Africa. In 2011 there were 4.1m. fixed-line subscribers and 64m. mobile subscribers.

Cell C (Pty) Ltd: 150 Rivonia Rd, Sandown 2196; Private Bag X36, Benmore 2010, Johannesburg; tel. (11) 3244000; fax (11) 3244009; e-mail customerservice@cellc.co.za; internet www.cellc.co.za; f. 2000; subsidiary of 3C Telecommunications (60% owned by Oger Telecom South Africa, 40% by CellSAf); mobile cellular telecommunications provider; Chair. SIMON DUFFY; CEO ALAN KNOTT-CRAIG.

Mobile Telephone Networks (Pty) Ltd (MTN): 3 Alice Lane, Ext. 38, PMB 9955, Sandton 2146; tel. (11) 3016000; fax (11) 3018448; internet www.mtn.co.za; f. 1994; mobile cellular telecommunications provider; operations in 21 countries in Africa and the Middle East; 11m. subscribers in South Africa (2006); Chair. MATAMELA CYRIL RAMAPHOSA; CEO SIFISO DABENGWA.

Neotel: 44 Old Pretoria Main Rd, Midrand, Johannesburg; PostNet Suite 612, Private Bag X29, Gallo Manor, Johannesburg, 2052; tel. (11) 5851000; fax (80) 0333636; e-mail info@neotel.co.za; internet www.neotel.co.za; Chair. SRINATH NARASIMHAN; Man. Dir and CEO SUNIL JOSHI.

Telkom SA Ltd: Telkom Towers North, 152 Proes St, Pretoria 0002; POB 925, Pretoria 0001; tel. (12) 3111007; fax (12) 3114031; e-mail letlapll@telkom.co.za; internet www.telkom.co.za; f. 1991; 38% govt-owned; ICT solutions service provider; Chair. LAZARUS ZIM; Group CEO NOMBULELO MOHOL.

Telkom Mobile: Telkom Towers North, 152 Proes St, Pretoria 0001; Private Bag X148, Centurion 0046; tel. 081180; internet www.8ta.com; f. 2010; operates under the brand name '8ta'; owned by Telkom SA Ltd; Man. Dir AMITH MAHARAJ.

Virgin Mobile South Africa (Pty) Ltd (VMSA): CitiGroup Bldg, 2nd Floor, 145 West St, Sandton, Johannesburg; POB 78331, Sandton 2146; tel. (11) 3244000; fax (11) 3244113; e-mail CustomerCare@ virginmobile.co.za; internet www.virginmobile.co.za; f. 2006; jt venture btwn Cell C and Virgin Mobile Telecoms Ltd, United

Kingdom; mobile cellular telecommunications provider; CEO STEVE BAILEY.

Vodacom Group (Pty) Ltd: Vodacom Corporate Park, 082 Vodacom Blvd, Vodavalley, Midrand 1685; tel. (11) 6535000; e-mail corporate.affairs@vodacom.co.za; internet www.vodacom.co.za; f. 1993; 50% owned by Telkom SA Ltd, 50% by Vodafone Group PLC, United Kingdom; subsidiaries in the DRC (f. 2002), Lesotho (f. 1996), Mozambique (f. 2003) and Tanzania (f. 1999); Chair. MTHANDAZO PETER MOYO; CEO PIETER UYS.

BROADCASTING

Radio

South African Broadcasting Corpn (SABC)—Radio: Private Bag X1, Auckland Park 2006, Johannesburg; tel. (11) 7149111; fax (11) 7149744; e-mail rpsales@sabc.co.za; internet www.sabc.co.za; f. 1936; comprises 15 public radio stations and three commercial radio stations broadcasting in 11 languages; Chair. Dr BEN NGUBANE; Group CEO LULAMA MOKHOBO.

Domestic Services

SAfm; Afrikaans Stereo; 5 FM; Radio 2000; Good Hope Stereo; Radio Kontrei; RPN Stereo; Jacaranda Stereo; Radio Algoa (www.algoafm.co.za; regional services); Radio Lotus (Indian service in English); Radio Metro (African service in English); Thobela FM; Ikwekwezi FM; Radio Sesotho; Setswana Stereo; Radio Swazi; Radio Tsonga; Radio Xhosa; Radio Zulu; Lesedi FM; Ligwalagwala FM; Motsweding FM; Phaphala FM; Radio Sonder Grense (Afrikaans); Tru FM; Ukhozi FM; Umhlobo Wenene FM; X-K FM.

External Services

567 CapeTalk: Suite 7D, Somerset Sq., Highfield Rd, Cape Town; Private Bag 567, Vlaeberg 8018; tel. (21) 4464700; fax (21) 4464800; e-mail 567webmaster@capetalk.co.za; internet www.capetalk.co.za; Man. COLLEEN LOUW.

Channel Africa Network: POB 91313, Auckland Park 2006; tel. (11) 7142255; fax (11) 7142072; e-mail molotod@sabc.co.za; internet www.channelafrica.org; f. 1966; external service of SABC; broadcasts 217 hours per week in English, French, Portuguese, Kiswahili, Chinyanja and Silozi; Gen. Man. DAVID MOLOTO.

Classic FM: Jorissen Place, 6th Floor, 66 Jorissen St, Braamfontein; POB 782, Auckland Park 2006; tel. (11) 4031027; fax (11) 4035451; e-mail info@classicfm.co.za; internet www.classicfm.co.za.

East Coast Radio: Durban; tel. (31) 5709495; fax (86) 6794951; e-mail news@ecr.co.za; internet www.ecr.co.za.

94.7 Highveld Stereo: Primedia Place, 5 Gwen Lane, cnr Gwen Lane and Fredman Dr., Sandown, Gauteng; POB 3438, Rivonia 2128; tel. (11) 5063947; fax (11) 5063393; e-mail comments@highveld.co.za; internet www.highveld.co.za.

Jacaranda 94.2: 1 Samrand Ave, Kosmosdal, POB 11961, Centurion 0046; tel. 800609942; e-mail enquiries@jacarandafm.com; internet www.jacarandafm.com.

Kaya FM 95.9: 1 Central Pl., 30 Jeppe St, Newtown, Johannesburg; POB 434, Newtown 2113; tel. (11) 6349500; fax (11) 6349574; e-mail pr@kayafm.co.za; internet www.kayafm.co.za; f. 1997.

Talk Radio 702: Primedia House, 2nd Floor, 5 Gwen Lane, Sandown, Sandton; POB 5572, Rivonia 2128; tel. (11) 5063702; e-mail 702webmaster@702.co.za; internet www.702.co.za.

YFM 99.2: Albury Rd, Dunkeld Cres., South West Blocks, Dunkeld West, Ext. 8, Sandton 2196; tel. (11) 2807070; fax (11) 2807556; e-mail webmaster@yfm.co.za; internet www.yworld.co.za; f. 1997; Man. Dir and CEO KANTHAN PILLAY.

Television

In February 2007 the Government announced that the country would begin digital terrestrial broadcasting in November 2008 and that the country's analogue signal would be switched off by December 2013.

e.tv: 5 Summit Rd, Hyde Park, Johannesburg 2196; Private Bag, X9944, Sandton 2146; tel. (11) 5379300; e-mail info@etv.co.za; internet www.etv.co.za; f. 1998; CEO MARCEL GOLDING.

Naspers: 40 Heerengracht, Cape Town 8001; tel. (21) 4062121; e-mail GKGreen@multichoice.co.za; internet www.naspers.co.za; provides subscription television through Multichoice, M-Net and SuperSport packages; Chair. TON VOSLOO; Chief Executive KOOS BEKKER.

South African Broadcasting Corpn (SABC)—Television: Private Bag X41, Auckland Park 2006; tel. (11) 7149111; fax (11) 7145055; e-mail enterpri@sabc.co.za; internet www.sabc.co.za; transmissions began in 1976; broadcasts television services in 11 languages over three channels; SABC1 broadcasts in English, isiZulu, isiXhosa, isiNdebele and siSwati; SABC2 broadcasts in English, Afrikaans, Sesotho, Setswana, Sepedi, Xitsonga and Tshivendi; SABC3 broadcasts documentaries, educational programmes and sport in English; Chair. Dr BEN NGUBANE; Group CEO LULAMA MOKHOBO.

Finance

(cap. = capital; auth. = authorized; res = reserves; dep. = deposits; m. = million; brs = branches; amounts in rand)

BANKING

In early 2011 the South African banking sector comprised 19 registered banks, two mutual banks, 13 local branches of foreign banks and 41 foreign banks with approved local representative offices. The five largest banks—Standard Bank, Nedbank, ABSA, FirstRand and Investec—controlled some 90% of total banking assets.

Central Bank

South African Reserve Bank: 370 Church St, POB 427, Pretoria 0002; tel. (12) 3133911; fax (12) 3133197; e-mail info@resbank.co.za; internet www.reservebank.co.za; f. 1921; cap. 2.0m., res 9,875.2m., dep. 181,196.5m. (March 2010); Gov. GILL MARCUS; Sen. Dep. Gov. X. P. GUMA; 7 brs.

Commercial Banks

ABSA Bank Ltd: ABSA Towers East, 3rd Floor, 170 Main St, Johannesburg 2001; POB 7735, Johannesburg 2000; tel. (11) 3504000; fax (11) 3504009; e-mail absa@absa.co.za; internet www.absa.co.za; subsidiary of Barclays Bank PLC; cap. 303m., res 17,675m., dep. 597,772m. (Dec. 2009); Chair. GARTH GRIFFIN; Group Chief Exec. MARIA RAMOS; 726 brs.

African Bank Ltd: 59 16th Rd, Private Bag X170, Midrand 1685; tel. (11) 2569000; fax (11) 2569217; e-mail ymistry@africanbank.co.za; internet www.africanbank.co.za; f. 1975; owned by African Bank Investments Ltd; cap. 121m., res 3,096m., dep. 16,794m. (Sept. 2009); CEO LEONIDAS KIRKINIS; 268 brs.

Albaraka Bank Ltd: 2 Kingsmead Blvd, Kingsmead Office Park, Stalwart Simelane St, Durban 4001; POB 4395, Durban 4000; tel. (31) 3649000; fax (31) 3649001; e-mail marketing@albaraka.co.za; internet www.albaraka.co.za; f. 1989; operates according to Islamic principles; cap. 150.0m., dep. 1,624.2m., total assets 1,870.7m. (Dec. 2008); Chair. ADNAN AHMED YOUSIF; CEO SHABIR CHOHAN.

Capitec Bank: 1 Quantum St, Techno Park, Stellenbosch 7600; tel. (21) 8095900; e-mail clientcare@capitecbank.co.za; internet www.capitecbank.co.za; f. 2001; Chair. MICHIEL SCHOLTZ DU PRÉ LE ROUX; CEO RIAAN STASSEN.

Bidvest Bank Ltd: Rennie House, 11th Floor, 19 Ameshoff St, Braamfontein 2001, Johannesburg; POB 185, Johannesburg 2000; tel. (11) 4073000; fax (11) 4073322; e-mail letstalk@bidvestbank.co.za; internet www.bidvestbank.co.za; f. 1850 as Rennies Bank Ltd; renamed as above in 2007; subsidiary of Bidvest Group Ltd; foreign exchange, trade finance and related activities; cap. 1.8m., res 603.1m., dep. 873.8m. (June 2009); Chair. J. L. PAMENSKY; Man. Dir A. C. SALOMON; over 60 brs.

FirstRand Bank Ltd: 4 First Place, 4th Floor, cnr Fredman Dr. and Rivonia Rd, Bank City, Sandton 2196; POB 786273, Sandton 2146; tel. (11) 2821808; fax (11) 2828088; e-mail information@firstrand.co.za; internet www.firstrand.co.za; f. 1971 as First National Bank of Southern Africa; merged with Rand Bank in 1998; cap. 4m., res 13,965m., dep. 496,512m. (June 2010); CEO SIZWE NXASANA; 600 brs.

GBS Mutual Bank: 18–20 Hill St, Grahamstown 6139; POB 114, Grahamstown 6140; tel. (46) 6227109; fax (46) 6228855; e-mail gbs@gbsbank.co.za; internet www.gbsbank.co.za; f. 1877; total assets 900m. (Dec. 2011); Chair. T. C. S. TAGG; CEO A. M. VORSTER; 4 brs.

Habib Overseas Bank Ltd: N77 Oriental Plaza, Fordsburg, Johannesburg 2092; POB 62369, Marshalltown, Johannesburg 2107; tel. (11) 8347441; fax (11) 8347446; e-mail habib@global.co.za; internet www.habiboverseas.co.za; f. 1992; cap. 20m., dep. 691m., total assets US $102m. (Dec. 2009); Chair. HABIB MOHAMED D. HABIB; 5 brs.

HBZ Bank Ltd: 135 Jan Hofmeyr Rd, Westville, Durban 3631; POB 1536, Wandsbeck 3631; tel. (31) 2674400; fax (31) 2671193; e-mail sazone@hbzbank.co.za; internet www.hbzbank.co.za; f. 1995; subsidiary of Habib Bank Ltd; cap. 10.0m., res 141.9m., dep. 1,746.1m. (Dec. 2009); Chair. MUHAMMAD HABIB; CEO ZAFAR ALAM KHAN; 6 brs.

Mercantile Bank Ltd: Mercantile Lisbon House, 142 West St, Sandown 2196; POB 782699, Sandton 2146; tel. (11) 3020300; fax (11) 3020700; internet www.mercantile.co.za; f. 1965; subsidiary of Mercantile Lisbon Bank Holdings; cap. 1,483.3m., res 74.2m., dep. 4,265.0m. (Dec. 2009); Chair. Dr JOAQUIM A. S. DE ANDRADE CAMPOS; CEO D. J. BROWN; 14 brs.

Nedbank Ltd: 135 Rivonia Rd, Sandown 2196, Johannesburg 2001; tel. (11) 2944444; fax (11) 2946540; e-mail Jackiek@nedbank.co.za;

internet www.nedbankgroup.co.za; f. 1988; name changed from Nedcor Bank Ltd in 2002; subsidiary of Nedbank Group Ltd; cap. 27m., res 24,856m., dep. 513,609m. (Dec. 2011); Chair. REUEL J. KHOZA; CEO MIKE BROWN; 472 brs.

South African Bank of Athens Ltd: Bank of Athens Bldg, 116 Marshall St, Johannesburg 2001; POB 7781, Johannesburg 2000; tel. (11) 6344300; fax (11) 8381001; e-mail info@bankofathens.co.za; internet www.bankofathens.co.za; f. 1947; 99.51% owned by National Bank of Greece; cap. 13.9m., res 166.5m., dep. 1,058.1m. (Dec. 2009); Chair. A. LEOPOULOS; CEO HECTOR ZARCA; 11 brs.

The Standard Bank of South Africa Ltd: Standard Bank Centre, 5 Simmonds St, Johannesburg 2001; POB 7725, Johannesburg 2000; tel. (11) 2994701; fax (11) 6364207; e-mail information@ standardbank.co.za; internet www.standardbank.co.za; f. 1862; cap. 60m., res 43,147m., dep. 696,805m. (Dec. 2009); Chair. DEREK E. COOPER; Jt CEOs SIM TSHABALALA, BEN KRUGER; 1,000 brs.

Ubank Ltd: Sanhill Park, 1 Eglin Rd, Sunninghill; Private Bag X101, Sunninghill 2157; tel. (11) 5185000; fax (86) 5457966; e-mail corpcomm@tebabank.co.za; internet www.tebabank.co.za; f. 2000; fmrly Teba Bank Ltd, name changed as above in 2010; specializes in microfinance and providing financial services to mining communities; total assets 2,639m. (Feb. 2008); Chair. AYANDA MJEKULA; CEO MARK WILLIAMS; 90 brs, 29 agencies.

Merchant Bank

Grindrod Bank Ltd: 1st Floor North, 20 Kingsmead Blvd, Kingsmead Office Park, Durban 4001; POB 3211, Durban 4001; tel. (31) 3336600; fax (31) 5710505; internet www.grindrodbank.co.za; f. 1994; present name adopted 2006; Man. Dir DAVID POLKINGHORNE.

Investment Banks

Cadiz Holdings: Fernwood House, 1st Floor, The Oval, 1 Oakdale Rd, Newlands 7700; POB 44547, Claremont 7735; tel. 6578300; fax 6578301; e-mail reception@cadiz.co.za; internet www.cadiz.co.za; f. 1993; 15% owned by Investec, 11% by Makana Financial Services; total assets 298.1m. (Dec. 2003); Chair. RAY CADIZ; CEO FRASER SHAW.

Investec Bank Ltd: 100 Grayston Dr., Sandown, Sandton 2196; POB 785700, Sandton 2146; tel. (11) 2867000; fax (11) 2867777; e-mail investorrelations@investec.com; internet www.investec.com; f. 1974; cap. 25,703m., res 18,837m., dep. 154,772m. (Mar. 2011); CEO STEPHEN KOSEFF; 6 brs.

Sasfin Bank Ltd: 29 Scott St, Waverley 2090; POB 95104, Grant Park 2051; tel. (11) 8097500; fax (11) 8872489; e-mail info@sasfin .com; internet www.sasfin.com; f. 1951; subsidiary of Sasfin Holdings Ltd; cap. 1.7m., res 383.5m., dep. 925.1m. (June 2009); Chair. NORMAN AXTEN; CEO ROLAND SASSOON.

Development Bank

Development Bank of Southern Africa (DBSA): 1258 Lever Rd, Headway Hill; POB 1234, Halfway House, Midrand 1685; tel. (11) 3133911; fax (11) 3133086; e-mail info@dbsa.org; internet www.dbsa .org; total assets 23,684.5m. (March 2004); f. 1983; Chair. JABU MOLEKETI; CEO PAUL BALOYI.

Bankers' Association

Banking Association South Africa: Sunnyside Office Park, Bldg D, 3rd Floor, 32 Princess of Wales Terrace, Parktown 2193; tel. (11) 6456700; fax (11) 6456800; e-mail webmaster@banking.org.za; internet www.banking.org.za; f. 1993; fmrly Banking Council of South Africa; name changed as above in 2005; 15,000 mems; Chair. STEPHEN KOSEFF; Man. Dir CASSIM COOVADIA.

STOCK EXCHANGE

JSE Ltd: One Exchange Sq., 2 Gwen Lane, Sandown, Sandton; Private Bag X991174, Sandton 2146; tel. (11) 5207000; fax (11) 5208584; e-mail info@jse.co.za; internet www.jse.co.za; f. 1887 as Johannesburg Stock Exchange; present name adopted in 2005; in late 1995 legislation was enacted providing for the deregulation of the Stock Exchange; automated trading commenced in June 1996; demutualized in July 2005 and became a listed co in June 2006; CEO NICKY NEWTON-KING.

INSURANCE

In 2010 South Africa was served by 100 short-term and 81 long-term insurers, and 13 reinsurance firms.

Allianz Insurance Ltd: 40 Ashford Rd, Parkwood, Johannesburg 2001; POB 62228, Marshalltown 2107; tel. (11) 4421111; fax (11) 4421125; e-mail baini@allianz.co.za; internet www.allianz.co.za; Chair. D. DU PREEZ; Man. Dir IAN BAIN.

Clientèle Life Assurance Co: Clientèle House, Morning View Office Park, cnr Rivonia and Alon Rds, Morningside, Johannesburg;

POB 1316, Rivonia 2128; tel. (11) 3203333; e-mail services@ clientelelife.com; internet www.clientelelife.com; f. 1997; subsidiary of Hollard Insurance Group; Chair. GAVIN ROUTLEDGE; Man. Dir BASIL WILLIAM REEKIE.

Credit Guarantee Insurance Corpn of Africa Ltd: 31 Dover St, POB 125, Randburg 2125; tel. (11) 8897000; fax (11) 8861027; e-mail info@cgic.co.za; internet www.creditguarantee.co.za; f. 1956; Chair. PETER TODD; Man. Dir MIKE C. TRUTER.

Discovery: 16 Fredman Dr., Sandton 2146; POB 784262, Sandton 2146; tel. (11) 5292888; fax (11) 5293590; e-mail worldinfo@discovery .co.za; internet www.discoveryworld.co.za; f. 1992; 64% owned by FirstRand; health and life assurance; Chair. MONTY HILKOWITZ; CEO ADRIAN GORE.

Liberty Life: Liberty Life Centre, 1 Ameshoff St, Braamfontein, Johannesburg 2001; POB 10499, Johannesburg 2000; tel. (11) 4083911; fax (11) 4082109; e-mail info@liberty.co.za; internet www .liberty.co.za; f. 1958; Chair. SAKI MACOZOMA; CEO BRUCE HEMPHILL.

Old Mutual (South African Mutual Life Assurance Society): Mutualpark, Jan Smuts Dr., POB 66, Cape Town 8001; tel. (21) 5099111; fax (21) 5094444; e-mail contact@oldmutual.com; internet www.oldmutual.com; f. 1845; Chair. MICHAEL J. LEVETT; CEO JAMES SUTCLIFFE.

Regent Insurance Co Ltd: 146 Boeing Rd East, Elma Park, POB 674, Edenvale 1609; tel. (11) 8795000; fax (11) 4539533; e-mail email@bob.co.za; internet www.regent.co.za; f. 1989; 100% owned by Imperial Holdings; Gen. Man. JONO SOAMES.

Santam Ltd: Santam Head Office, 1 Sportica Cres., Bellville 7530; POB 3881, Tyger Valley 7536; tel. (21) 9157000; fax (21) 9140700; e-mail info@santam.co.za; internet www.santam.co.za; f. 1918; Chair. D. K. SMITH; CEO IAN KIRK.

South African National Life Assurance Co Ltd (SANLAM): 2 Strand Rd, Bellville; POB 1, Sanlamhof 7532; tel. (21) 9479111; fax (21) 9479440; e-mail life@sanlam.co.za; internet www.sanlam.co.za; f. 1918; Chair. Dr J. VAN ZYL.

Zurich Insurance Co South Africa Ltd: 70 Fox St, Johannesburg 2001; tel. (11) 3709111; fax (11) 8368018; e-mail info@insurance.za .org; internet www.saeagle.co.za; fmrly South African Eagle Insurance Co Ltd; rebranded as above in 2007; Chair. M. C. SOUTH; CEO N. V. BEYERS.

Association

South African Insurance Association (SAIA): JCC House, 3rd Floor, 27 Owl St, Milpark; POB 30619, Braamfontein 2017; tel. (11) 7265381; fax (11) 7265351; e-mail adele@saia.co.za; internet www .saia.co.za; f. 1973; represents short-term insurers; Chair. RONNIE NAPIER; CEO BARRY SCOTT.

Trade and Industry

GOVERNMENT AGENCIES

National Empowerment Fund: West Block, 187 Rivonia Rd, Morningside 2057; POB 31, Melrose Arch, Melrose North 2076; tel. (11) 3058000; fax (11) 3058001; e-mail info@nefcorp.co.za; internet www.nefcorp.co.za; f. 1998; Chair. RONNIE NTULI; CEO PHILISIWE BUTHELEZI.

Small Enterprise Development Agency (SEDA): DTI Campus, Block G, 77 Meintjies St, Sunnyside, POB 56714, Pretoria; tel. (12) 4411000; e-mail info@seda.org.za; internet www.seda.org.za; f. 2004; CEO HLONELA NELISA LUPUWANA.

DEVELOPMENT ORGANIZATIONS

Business Partners Ltd: 37 West St, Houghton Estate, Johannesburg 2198; POB 7780, Johannesburg 2000; tel. (11) 7136600; fax (11) 7136650; e-mail enquiries@businesspartners.co.za; internet www .businesspartners.co.za; f. 1981 as Small Business Devt Corpn; invests in, and provides services to, small and medium-sized enterprises; Chair. THEO VAN WYK; Man. Dir NAZEEM MARTIN.

Independent Development Trust: Glenwood Office Park, cnr Oberon and Sprite Sts, Faerie Glen, Pretoria; POB 73000, Lynnwood Ridge 0043; tel. (12) 8452000; fax (12) 3480894; e-mail info@idt.org .za; internet www.idt.org.za; f. 1990; advances the national devt programme working with govt and communities in fields incl. poverty relief, infrastructure, empowerment, employment and capacity building; CEO THEMBI NWEDAMUSTWU.

Industrial Development Corpn of South Africa Ltd (IDC): 19 Fredman Dr., Sandown 2196; POB 784055, Sandton 2146; tel. (11) 2693000; fax (11) 2693116; e-mail callcentre@idc.co.za; internet www.idc.co.za; f. 1940; promotes entrepreneurship and competitiveness; total assets 90,421m. (March 2008); Chair. MONHLA HLAHLA; CEO M. G. QHENA.

Productivity SA: International Business Gateway, cnr New and Sixth Rds, Midrand; Private Bag 235, Midrand 1685; tel. (11) 8485300; fax (11) 8485555; e-mail info@productivitysa.co.za; internet www.productivitysa.co.za; f. 1968; Chair. ALWYN NEL; CEO Dr BONGANI COKA.

CHAMBERS OF COMMERCE

Cape Chamber of Commerce and Industry: Cape Chamber House, 19 Louis Gradner St, Foreshore, Cape Town 8001; tel. (21) 4024300; fax (21) 4024302; e-mail info@capechamber.co.za; internet www.capechamber.co.za; f. 1804; Pres. MICHAEL BAGRAIM; Exec. Dir VIOLA MANUEL; 3,000 mems.

Chamber of Commerce and Industry–Johannesburg: JCC House, 6th Floor, 27 Owl St, cnr Empire Rd, Milpark; Private Bag 34, Auckland Park 2006; tel. (11) 7265300; fax (11) 4822000; e-mail info@jcci.co.za; internet www.jcci.co.za; f. 1890; Pres. LAURENCE SAVILLE; CEO KEITH BREBNOR; 3,800 mems.

Durban Chamber of Commerce and Industry: Chamber House, 190 Stanger St, POB 1506, Durban 4000; tel. (31) 3351000; fax (31) 3321288; e-mail chamber@durbanchamber.co.za; internet www .durbanchamber.co.za; CEO ANDREW LAYMAN; 3,500 mems.

Gauteng North Chamber of Commerce and Industry (GNCCI): Tshwane Events Centre, Soutter St, Pretoria; POB 2164, Pretoria 0001; tel. (12) 3271487; fax (12) 3271490; internet www.gncci.co.za; f. 1929; fmrly Pretoria Business and Agricultural Centre; merged with Pretoria Sakekamer in 2004; Chair. BERT BADENHORST; CEO WIM DU PLESSIS; over 900 mems.

Mangaung Chamber of Commerce and Industry (MCCI): 104 Zastron St, Bloemfontein; POB 87, Bloemfontein 9301; tel. (51) 4473368; fax (51) 4475064; e-mail info@bcci.co.za; internet www .bcci.co.za; f. 2004; Pres. NANCY DE SOUSA; c. 550 mems (2010).

Nelson Mandela Bay Business Chamber: KPMG House, 200 Norvic Dr., Greenacres, Port Elizabeth 6045; POB 63866, Greenacres 6057; tel. (41) 3731122; fax (41) 3731142; e-mail info@ nmbbusinesschamber.co.za; internet nmbbusinesschamber.co.za; f. 1994; fmrly Port Elizabeth Regional Chamber of Commerce and Industry, present name adopted 2011; Pres. MANDIA MADWARA; CEO KEVIN HUSTLER; 840 mems.

Pietermaritzburg Chamber of Business (PCB): Chamber House, Royal Showgrounds, Chief Albert Luthuli Rd, Pietermaritzburg 3201; POB 11734, Dorpspruit, Pietermaritzburg 3206; tel. (33) 3452747; fax (33) 3944151; e-mail pcb@pcb.org.za; internet www.pcb .org.za; f. 2002 as successor to the Pietermaritzburg Chamber of Commerce and Industries (f. 1910); Pres. PARIS DLAMINI; CEO MELANIE VENESS; 750 mems.

South African Chamber of Commerce and Industry (SACCI): 24 Sturdee Ave, Rosebank, Johannesburg 2196; POB 213, Saxonwold 2132; tel. (11) 4463800; fax (11) 4463850; e-mail info@sacci.org.za; internet www.sacci.org.za; f. 1990 by merger of Asscn of Chambers of Commerce and Industry and South African Federated Chamber of Industries; fmrly known as South African Chamber of Business; Pres. Prof. ALWYN LOUW; CEO NEREN RAU.

Wesvaal Chamber of Business (WESCOB): POB 7167, Flamwood 2572; tel. (18) 4683750; fax (86) 6936365; e-mail chamber@gds .co.za; internet www.wesvaalchamber.co.za; f. 1898; Pres. BEN MOSALA; c. 200 mems.

INDUSTRIAL AND TRADE ORGANIZATIONS

Association of Cementitious Material Producers (ACMP): POB 168, Halfway House 1685; tel. (11) 2073037; fax (11) 3150315; e-mail naudek.acmp@mweb.co.za; internet www.acmp.co .za; f. 2002; Exec. Dir DHIRAJ B. K. RAMA.

Cape Wools: Wool House, 18 Grahamstown Rd, North End, Port Elizabeth 6001; POB 2191, Port Elizabeth 6056; tel. (41) 544301; fax (41) 546760; e-mail capewool@capewools.co.za; internet www .capewools.co.za; f. 1997; Section 21 service company; seven mems: three appointed by wool producer orgs, two by the Wool Textile Council, one by Wool Brokers and Traders and one by Labour; Chair. GEOFF KINGWILL; Gen. Man. ANDRÉ STRYDOM.

Chamber of Mines of South Africa: Chamber of Mines Bldg, 5 Hollard St, POB 61809, Marshalltown 2107; tel. (11) 4987100; fax (11) 8341884; e-mail webmaster@bullion.org.za; internet www .bullion.org.za; f. 1889; Pres. Dr XOLANI HUMPHREY MKHWANAZI; CEO BHEKI SIBIYA.

Clothing Trade Council (CloTrade): 35 Siemers Rd, 6th Floor, Doornfontein; POB 2303, Johannesburg 2000; tel. (11) 4020664; fax (11) 4020667; f. 2002; successor to the Clothing Fed. of South Africa; Pres. JACK KIPLING.

Grain Milling Federation: Embankment Park, 194 Kwikkie Cres., Centurion 0046; POB 7262, Centurion 0046; tel. (12) 6631660; fax (12) 6633109; e-mail gmf@grainmilling.org.za; internet www .grainmilling.org.za; f. 1944; Exec. Dir JANNIE DE VILLIERS.

Master Builders South Africa (MBSA): POB 1619, Halfway House, Midrand 1685; tel. (11) 2059000; fax (11) 3151644; e-mail info@mbsa.org.za; internet www.mbsa.org.za; f. 1904; fmrly known as Building Industries Fed. South Africa; Pres. DANIE HATTING; Exec. Dir ITUMELENG DLAMINI; 4,000 mems.

Master Diamond Cutters' Association of South Africa: Private Bag X1, Suite 105, Excom 2023; tel. (11) 3341930; fax (11) 3341933; e-mail info@masingita.co.za; f. 1928; Pres. MACDONALD TEMANE; 76 mems.

National Association of Automobile Manufacturers of South Africa: Nedbank Plaza, 1st Floor, cnr Church and Beatrix Sts, Pretoria 0002; POB 40611, Arcadia 0007; tel. (12) 3232980; fax (12) 3263232; e-mail naamsa@iafrica.com; internet www.naamsa.co.za; f. 1935; Dir N. M. W. VERMEULEN; 19 full mems and 23 assoc. mems.

National Chamber of Milling, Inc: POB 7262, Centurion 0046; tel. (12) 6631660; fax (12) 6633109; e-mail info@grainmilling.org.za; internet www.grainmilling.org.za; f. 1936; Exec. Dir JANNIE DE VILLIERS.

National Textile Manufacturers' Association: POB 81, New Germany 3620; tel. (31) 7104410; fax (31) 7056257; f. 1947; Sec. PETER MCGREGOR; 9 mems.

Plastics Federation of South Africa: 18 Gazelle Rd, Corporate Park South, Old Pretoria Rd, Midrand; Private Bag X68, Halfway House, Midrand 1685; tel. (11) 3144021; fax (11) 3143764; internet www.plasticsinfo.co.za; f. 1979; Exec. Dir DAVID HUGHES; 10 mems.

Printing Industries Federation of South Africa (PIFSA): Block D, The Braids, 113 Bowling Ave, Gallo Manor 2191; POB 1396, Gallo Manor 2052; tel. (11) 2871160; fax (11) 2871179; e-mail pifsa@pifsa .org; internet www.pifsa.org; f. 1916; CEO PATRICK LACY; c. 820 mems (representing 65% of printers in South Africa); four regional chambers.

Retail Motor Industry Organization (RMI): POB 2940, Randburg 2125; tel. (11) 8866300; fax (11) 7894525; e-mail rmi@rmi.org .za; internet www.rmi.org.za; f. 1908; affiliates throughout southern Africa; CEO JEFF OSBORNE; 7,400 mems.

South African Dairy Foundation: POB 72300, Lynnwood Ridge, Pretoria 0040; tel. (12) 3485345; fax (12) 3486284; e-mail dairy-foundation@pixie.co.za; f. 1980; Sec. S. L. VAN COLLER; 59 mems.

South African Federation of Civil Engineering Contractors (SAFCEC): 12 Skeen Blvd, POB 644, Bedfordview 2008; tel. (11) 4090900; fax (11) 4501715; e-mail admin@safcec.org.za; internet www.safcec.org.za; f. 1939; Exec. Dir H. P. LANGENHOVEN; 300 mems.

South African Fruit and Vegetable Canners' Association (Pty) Ltd (SAFVCA): Hoofstraat 258 Main St, POB 6175, Paarl 7620; tel. (21) 8711308; fax (21) 8725930; e-mail info@safvca.co.za; internet www.safvca.co.za; f. 1953; Gen. Man. JILL ATWOOD-PALM; 9 mems.

South African Inshore Fishing Industry Association (Pty) Ltd: POB 2066, Cape Town 8000; tel. (21) 4252727; e-mail safish@ new.co.za; f. 1953; Chair. W. A. LEWIS; Man. S. J. MALHERBE; 4 mems.

South African Paint Manufacturers' Association: POB 751605, Gardenview, Johannesburg 2047; tel. (11) 4552503; e-mail sapma@ sapma.org.za; internet www.sapma.org.za; Chair. TERRY ASHMORE; 100 mems.

South African Petroleum Industry Association (SAPIA): ABSA Centre, 14th Floor, Adderley St, Cape Town 8001; POB 7082, Roggebai 8012; tel. (21) 4198054; fax (21) 4198058; internet www.sapia.co.za; f. 1994; represents South Africa's six principal petroleum cos; Chair. JAMES SEUTLOADI; Dir AVHAPFANI TSHIFULARO.

South African Sugar Association (SASA): 170 Flanders Dr., POB 700, Mount Edgecombe 4300; tel. (31) 5087000; fax (31) 5087199; internet www.sugar.org.za; Exec. Dir M. K. TRIKAM.

Includes:

South African Sugar Millers' Association NPC (SASMA): POB 1000, Mt Edgecombe 4300; tel. (31) 5087300; fax (31) 5087310; e-mail sasmal@sasa.org.za; represents interests of sugar millers and refiners within the operations of SASA; Exec. Dir D. P. ROSSLER; 6 mem. cos.

Sugar Manufacturing and Refining Employers' Association (SMREA): POB 1000, Mount Edgecombe 4300; tel. (31) 5087300; fax (31) 5087310; e-mail sasmal@sasa.org.za; f. 1947; regulates relations between mems and their employees; participates in the Bargaining Council for the sugar manufacturing and refining industry; Chair. B. V. LANE; 6 mem. cos.

South African Wool Textile Council: POB 2201, North End, Port Elizabeth 6056; tel. (41) 4845252; fax (41) 4845629; Sec. BEATTY-ANNE STARKEY.

Steel and Engineering Industries Federation of South Africa (SEIFSA): 42 Anderson St, POB 1338, Johannesburg 2000; tel. (11) 2989400; fax (11) 2989500; e-mail info@seifsa.co.za; internet www

.seifsa.co.za; f. 1943; Exec. Dir BRIAN ANGUS; 38 affiliated trade asscns representing 2,350 mems.

VinPro (SA): POB 1411, Suider-Paarl 7624; tel. (21) 8073322; fax (21) 8632079; e-mail info@vinpro.co.za; internet www.vinpro.co.za; f. 1979; represents wine producers; Chair. ABRIE BOTHA; Exec. Dir JOS LE ROUX.

UTILITIES
Electricity

Electricity Supply Commission (ESKOM): POB 1091, Johannesburg 2000; tel. (11) 8008111; fax (11) 8004390; e-mail PAIA@eskom.co.za; internet www.eskom.co.za; f. 1923; state-controlled; Chair. ZOLA TSOTSI; CEO BRIAN DAMES.

Gas

SASOL Gas: POB 4211, Randburg 2125; tel. (11) 8897600; fax (11) 8897955; e-mail gascustomercare@sasol.com; internet www.sasol.com; f. 1964; Man. Dir HANS NAUDÉ.

Water

Umgeni Water: 310 Burger St, Pietermaritzburg 3201; POB 9, Pietermaritzburg 3200; tel. (331) 3411111; fax (331) 3411167; e-mail info@umgeni.co.za; internet www.umgeni.co.za; f. 1974; CEO MZIMKULU MSIWA.

Water Research Commission: Private Bag X03, Gezina 0031; tel. (12) 3300340; fax (12) 3312565; e-mail orders@wrc.org.za; internet www.wrc.org.za; Chair. Prof. J. B. ADAMS; CEO Dr RIVKA KFIR.

TRADE UNIONS

According to COSATU, some 40% of workers were unionized at March 2005. Under amendments to the Labour Relations Act (LRA), 1995, introduced in 2002, the Government sought to eliminate illegitimate trade unions and employers' organizations. The provisions of the LRA also stipulated that organizations that failed to provide annual audited financial accounts would be deregistered.

Trade Union Federations

Confederation of South African Workers' Unions (CONSAWU): 21 Adriana Cres., Gateway Industrial Park, Rooishuiskraal X25, Centurion; tel. (12) 6614265; fax (12) 6611793; e-mail consawu@mweb.co.za; internet www.consawu.co.za; f. 2003; Pres. MAGGIE MAKGOBA (acting); Gen. Sec. PIET DU PLOOY; 290,000 mems (2007).

Congress of South African Trade Unions (COSATU): COSATU House, 110 Jorissen St, cnr Simmonds, Braamfontein 2017; POB 1019, Johannesburg 2000; tel. (11) 3394911; fax (11) 3396940; e-mail patrick@cosatu.org.za; internet www.cosatu.org.za; f. 1985; 21 trade union affiliates representing c. 1.8m. paid-up mems; Pres. SDUMO DLAMINI; Gen. Sec. ZWELINZIMA VAVI.

Federation of Unions of South Africa (FEDUSA): Fedusa House, 10 Kingfisher St, Horizon Park, Roodepoort 1725; POB 7779, Westgate 1734; tel. (11) 2791800; fax (11) 2791821; e-mail dennis@fedusa.org.za; internet www.fedusa.org.za; f. 1997 by merger of the Fed. of South African Labour Unions and Fed. of Civil Servants; 22 mem. unions; politically non-aligned; Pres. KOOS BEZUIDENHOUT; Gen. Sec. DENNIS GEORGE; 500,000 mems (2012).

National Council of Trade Unions (NACTU): Metropolitan Life Centre, 4th Floor, 108 Fox St, Johannesburg; POB 10928, Johannesburg 2000; tel. (11) 8331040; fax (11) 8331032; e-mail info@nactu.org.za; internet www.nactu.org.za; f. 1986 by merger of the Council of Unions of South Africa and Azanian Confed. of Trade Unions; fed. of 22 African trade unions; aligned to the Pan-Africanist Congress of Azania party; Pres. JOSEPH MAQHEKENI; Gen. Sec. MANENE SAMELA; 310,000 mems (2007).

Transport

Most of South Africa's railway network, and the harbours and airways are administered by the state-owned Transnet Ltd. Private bus services are regulated to complement the railways.

Transnet Ltd: Carlton Centre, 150 Commissioner St, Johannesburg 2001; POB 72501, Parkview 2122; tel. (11) 3083000; fax (11) 3082638; e-mail unathi.mgobozi@transnet.net; internet www.transnet.net; CEO BRIAN MOLEFE.

RAILWAYS

With the exception of commuter services, the South African railways system is operated by Transnet Freight Rail Ltd (formerly Spoornet), the rail division of Transnet. The network comprised some 34,000 track-km in 2010, of which 16,946 km were electrified. Extensive rail links connect Transnet Freight Rail with the rail networks of neighbouring countries. In 2010 construction of the 80-km rapid

rail network Gautrain was under way in the province of Gauteng. The first phase of the system linking O. R. Tambo International Airport and Sandton was opened for commercial service in June 2010. The second phase linking Pretoria and Johannesburg was completed in August 2011 (with the exception of Johannesburg Park Station).

Transnet Freight Rail: Inyanda House, 21 Wellington Rd, Parktown 2193; Private Bag X47, Johannesburg 2000; tel. (11) 5449368; fax (11) 5449599; e-mail dan.motaung@transnet.net; internet www.spoornet.co.za; fmrly Spoornet; renamed as above in 2007; CEO SIYABONGA GAMA; 25,347 employees.

ROADS

In 2001 there were an estimated 364,131 km of classified roads, including 239 km of motorways. The S'hamba Sonke Programme, which aimed to repair and restore the secondary road network in the country, commenced in April 2011 and was scheduled for completion in 2014.

South African National Roads Agency Ltd (SANRAL): Ditsela Pl., 1204 Park St, cnr Duncan St, Hatfield, Pretoria; POB 415, Pretoria 0001; tel. (12) 4266000; fax (12) 3622116; e-mail info@nra.co.za; internet www.nra.co.za; f. 1998; responsible for design, construction, management and maintenance of 16,150 km of the national road network (2008); Chair. MADUKE LOT NDLOVU; CEO NAZIR ALLI.

SHIPPING

The principal harbours are at Richards Bay, Durban, Saldanha, Cape Town, Port Elizabeth, East London, Ngqura (Coega), and Mossel Bay. The deep-water port at Richards Bay has been extended and its facilities upgraded. Both Richards Bay and Saldanha Bay are major bulk-handling ports, while Saldanha Bay also has an important fishing fleet. More than 30 shipping lines serve South African ports. In December 2012 South Africa's flag registered fleet comprised 199 vessels, totalling 191,426 grt.

South African Maritime Safety Authority (SAMSA): 161 Lynnwood Rd, cnr Duncan St, Brooklyn, Pretoria 0181; POB 13186, Hatfield 0028; tel. (12) 3662600; fax (12) 3662601; e-mail services@samsa.org.za; internet www.samsa.org.za; f. 1998; advises the Govt on matters connected with sea transport to, from or between South Africa's ports, incl. safety at sea, and prevention of pollution by petroleum; Chair. Z. C. NGIDI; CEO TSIETSI MOKHELE.

Transnet National Ports Authority: POB 32696, Braamfontein 2017; tel. (11) 3519001; fax (11) 3519023; internet www.transnetnationalportsauthority.net; f. 2000; fmrly part of Portnet; subsidiary of Transnet; controls and manages the country's seven major seaports; CEO TAU MORWE.

Transnet Port Terminals: Kingsmead Office Park, cnr Stalwart and Stanger Sts, Durban 4001; tel. (31) 3088300; fax (31) 3088302; e-mail tptwebmaster@transnet.net; internet www.transnetportterminals.net; f. 2000 as South African Port Terminals, renamed as above in 2008; fmrly part of Portnet; subsidiary of Transnet; operates 13 container, bulk, breakbulk and car terminals at six of the country's major ports; CEO KARL SOCIKWA.

CIVIL AVIATION

Civil aviation is controlled by the Minister of Transport. The Chief Directorate: Civil Aviation Authority at the Department of Transport is responsible for licensing and control of domestic and international air services.

Airports Company South Africa (ACSA): 24 Johnson Rd, The Maples, Office Park-Bedfordview, Johannesburg; POB 75480, Gardenview 2047; tel. (11) 7231400; fax (11) 4539353; internet www.airports.co.za; f. 1993; owns and operates South Africa's 10 principal airports, of which four (at Johannesburg, Cape Town, Durban and Pilanesburg) are classified as international airports; Chair. BUSISIWE MABUZA; Man. Dir BONGANI MASEKO (acting).

Civil Aviation Authority (CAA): Ikhaya Lokundiza, Bldg 16, Treur Close, Waterfall Park, Bekker St, Midrand; Private Bag X73, Halfway House 1685; tel. (11) 5451000; fax (12) 5451465; e-mail mail@caa.co.za; internet www.caa.co.za; Chair. DESMOND GOLDING (acting); Dir ZAKHELE THWALA (acting).

Airlink Airline: No.3, Greenstone Hill Office Park, Emerald Blvd, Greenstone Hill, Modderfontein; POB 7529, Bonaero Park 1622; tel. (11) 4517300; fax (11) 4517367; e-mail info@flyairlink.com; internet www.saairlink.co.za; f. 1992; internal and external scheduled services and charters in Southern Africa; Man. Dirs RODGER FOSTER, BARRIE WEBB.

COMAIR Ltd: 1 Marignane Dr., Bonaero Park 1619; POB 7015, Bonaero Park 1622; tel. (11) 9210111; fax (11) 9733913; e-mail cr@comair.co.za; internet www.comair.co.za; f. 1946; scheduled domestic, regional and international services; Chair. D. NOVICK; Jt CEOs ERIK VENTER, GIDON NOVICK.

Interair South Africa: Finance House, 1st Floor, Ernest Oppenheimer Rd, Bruma Lake Office, Bruma, Johannesburg; Private Bag 8, OR Tambo Int. Airport, Johannesburg 1627; tel. (11) 6160636; fax (11) 6160930; e-mail info@interair.co.za; internet www.interair.co.za; Exec. Chair. DAVID P. TOKOPH.

Mango Airlines: POB 1273, Kempton Park 1627; tel. (11) 3591222; e-mail enquiries@flymango.com; internet www.flymango.com; CEO NICO BEZUIDENHOUT.

Safair (Pty) Ltd: Northern Perimeter Rd, Bonaero Park 1619; POB 938, Kempton Park 1620; tel. 9280000; fax 3951315; e-mail marketing@safair.co.za; internet www.safair.co.za; f. 1965; part of the ASL Aviation Group; aircraft leasing, engineering and maintenance services; Man. Dir DAVE ANDREW.

South African Airways (SAA): Airways Park, Jones Rd, Private Bag X13, Johannesburg 1627; tel. (11) 9782888; fax (11) 9789567; e-mail voyager@flysaa.com; internet www.flysaa.com; f. 1934; state-owned; internal passenger services linking all the principal towns; international services to Africa, Europe, North and South America and Asia; Chair DUDU MYENI (acting); CEO MONWABISI KALAWE.

South African Express Airways (SA Express): Tambo International Airport, Johannesburg; tel. (11) 9789905; fax (11) 9785578; e-mail reservations@flyexpress.aero; internet www.flyexpress.aero; f. 1994; CEO INATI NTSHANGA.

Tourism

Tourism is an important part of South Africa's economy. The chief attractions for visitors are the climate, scenery and wildlife reserves. In 2011 some 8.3m. tourists visited South Africa and receipts from tourism amounted to an estimated US $9,547m.

South African Tourism: Bojanala House, 90 Protea Rd, Chislehurston, Johannesburg 2196; Private Bag X10012, Sandton 2146; tel. (11) 8953000; fax (11) 8953001; internet www.southafrica.net; f. 1947; 11 overseas brs; CEO MOEKETSI MOSOLA.

Defence

As assessed at November 2012, the South African National Defence Force (SANDF) totalled about 62,100: army 37,150, navy 6,250, air force 10,650 and a medical corps numbering 8,050. There was also a reserve of 15,050 (army 12,250, navy 850, air 850, medical corps 1,100). The SANDF comprised members of the former South African armed forces, together with personnel from the former military wings of the ANC and the Pan-Africanist Congress, and the former 'homelands' militias. In 2012 a total of 2,043 South African troops were stationed abroad; of these, 31 were observers.

Defence Expenditure: Budgeted at R39,900m. in 2013.

Chief of the South African National Defence Force: Lt-Gen. GODFREY NHLANHLA NGWENYA.

Chief of the South African Air Force: Lt-Gen. CARLO GAGIANO.

Chief of the South African Army: Maj.-Gen. SOLLY ZACHARIA SHOKE.

Chief of the South African Navy: Vice-Adm. JOHANNES REFILOE MUDIMU.

Education

School attendance is compulsory for children of all population groups between the ages of seven and 16 years. From 1991 state schools were permitted to admit pupils of all races, and in 1995 the right to free state education for all was introduced. According to UNESCO estimates, in 2008/09 enrolment at primary schools included 85% of pupils in the relevant age-group (males 85%; females 85%), while enrolment at secondary schools was equivalent to 94% of pupils in the relevant age-group (males 92%; females 96%). In 2009 there were 23 higher education institutions, with a total of 837,779 students. Initial budget estimates for 2012/13 indicated the allocation of R47,844m. (4.9% of total expenditure) to education.

SOUTH SUDAN

Introductory Survey

LOCATION, CLIMATE, LANGUAGE, RELIGION, FLAG, CAPITAL

The Republic of South Sudan lies in north-eastern Africa. It is bordered by Sudan to the north, by Ethiopia to the east, by Kenya and Uganda to the south, by the Democratic Republic of the Congo to the south-west, and by the Central African Republic to the west. The climate is largely tropical, with most rainfall occurring between April and October. Temperatures vary with altitude and latitude. The annual average for the whole country is about 26°C (79°F). English is the official language, although Arabic is the lingua franca around Juba. Most South Sudanese are Christians. The national flag (proportions 2 by 3) has three equal horizontal stripes, of black, red and green, with two narrow white stripes bordering the central red band. At the hoist is a blue triangle containing a five-pointed yellow star. The capital is Juba. It was, however, announced in September 2011 that the capital was to be relocated to Ramciel in the centre of the country.

CONTEMPORARY POLITICAL HISTORY

Historical Context

Rebellion against the rule of authorities based in the north by the three southern provinces (Bahr El-Ghazal, Equatoria and Upper Nile) began in 1955, when arrangements for Sudan's forthcoming independence (which was formalized on 1 January 1956) failed to incorporate southern demands for federalism. Following 17 years of conflict, an agreement establishing the Southern Sudan Autonomous Region was finally reached between the Government of Col Gaafar Muhammad Nimeri and representatives of the South Sudan Liberation Movement in the Ethiopian capital, Addis Ababa, in March 1972. A High Executive Council for the Southern Region was established in April, and elections to the Regional People's Assembly for southern Sudan took place in November 1973.

During 1983 the political agreement between Nimeri's Government and the southern leaders disintegrated. In January former rebel army officers began a mutiny in Bor. In June President Nimeri announced the redivision of the south into three smaller regions, thereby abolishing the Southern Sudan Autonomous Region. Following increasing domestic pressure, in September Nimeri declared Sudan a state under *Shari'a* (Islamic) law, provoking further anger in the largely Christian and animist south. The north–south conflict continued to escalate, with the emergence in the south of the Sudan People's Liberation Movement (SPLM), whose armed forces, the Sudan People's Liberation Army (SPLA), rapidly gained military control over large areas of the provinces of Bahr El-Ghazal and Upper Nile.

Following a military coup in April 1985, the SPLM initially declared a cease-fire, but presented the new regime of Gen. Abdel-Rahman Swar al-Dahab with a series of demands concerning the southern region, and fighting resumed. The new Government subsequently announced that laws based on a 'Sudanese legal heritage' would replace those unacceptable to non-Muslims, who would be exempted from Islamic taxation and special penalties; however, the SPLM continued to insist on a total abrogation of Islamic law, while the National Islamic Front (NIF) demanded that the Islamic code be imposed throughout the country. After the NIF was excluded from a new Government formed in March 1989, peace negotiations between a government delegation and the SPLM, led by Col John Garang, commenced in Ethiopia in April. The negotiations culminated in an agreement to suspend Islamic laws, pending the proposed convening, in September, of a constitutional conference.

On 30 June 1989 Brig. (later Lt-Gen.) Omar Hassan Ahmad al-Bashir seized power in a further military coup and established a 15-member Revolutionary Command Council for National Salvation (RCC). By August the SPLM's terms for a negotiated settlement to the conflict included the immediate resignation of the RCC, prior to the establishment of an interim government, in which the SPLM would be represented. However, the new regime's proximity to the NIF had become apparent, and the negotiations collapsed over the issue of Islamic law. Hostilities

resumed later that year. The SPLM allied with banned political parties in the north to form an opposition grouping, known as the National Democratic Alliance (NDA). In February 1991 the RCC announced that a new penal code, based on *Shari'a* law, would take effect in March, but would not apply in the three southern states, pending the establishment there of elected assemblies to resolve the issue. The SPLM nevertheless regarded the application of Islamic law in the northern states as unacceptable, citing the large numbers of non-Muslims resident there.

In March 1994 delegations representing the Government and two principal rival factions of the SPLA participated in peace talks held in Nairobi, Kenya, under the auspices of the Inter-governmental Authority on Drought and Development (IGADD—superseded in 1996 by the Intergovernmental Authority on Development—IGAD, see p. 344), which in September 1993 had formed a committee on the Sudanese conflict comprising regional heads of state. All parties to the talks agreed to allow the free passage of relief supplies to southern Sudan.

In March 1995 Garang announced his intention to unite other insurgent groups against the Government, but he appeared unsuccessful in gaining the support of rival SPLA factions. Following presidential and legislative elections in March 1996, on 10 April a 'political charter for peace' was signed by the Government, the South Sudan Independence Movement (SSIM) and a breakaway faction, the SPLA-United, pledging to preserve Sudan's national unity and to take joint action to develop those areas of the country that had been affected by the civil war. In April 1997 a peace accord, covering major issues such as power-sharing and *Shari'a* law, and promising a referendum on southern secession after a four-year transition period, was signed by six rebel groups. Both the NDA and the SPLA, however, rejected the agreement. In August, in accordance with the terms of the agreement, the Southern States Co-ordination Council (SSCC) was established; Dr Riek Machar Teny-Dhurgon, the leader of the Southern Sudan Defence Force (SSDF), became its Chairman. At the beginning of September the SPLA-United declared a cease-fire, and its commander, Dr Lam Akol Ajawin, returned to Khartoum in the following month.

Domestic Political Affairs

In January 2002 discussions in Bürgenstock, Switzerland, under the aegis of the USA and Switzerland, resulted in agreement between the Sudanese Government and the SPLA to observe a six-month cease-fire, to be supervised by a joint military commission, in the central Nuba region in order to facilitate the delivery of vital aid supplies to the area. The cease-fire was extended for a further six months in July, and again, in late December. Meanwhile, in June a new round of IGAD-sponsored peace negotiations between the Government and the SPLM began in Machakos, Kenya. On 20 July delegations from the SPLM and the Government signed an accord, known as the Machakos Protocol, which provided for a six-year period of autonomy for the south, to be followed by an internationally monitored referendum on self-determination. The Protocol also stated that Sudan's Constitution would be rewritten to ensure that *Shari'a* law would not be applied to non-Muslim southerners. Nevertheless, negotiations between the Government and the SPLM were suspended in November, when no agreement could be reached on the number of government and civil service posts to be allocated to southerners and the distribution of petroleum revenues. The two sides did, however, agree to extend the cease-fire until the end of March 2003.

Negotiations resumed in Nairobi in January 2003, and the following month a memorandum of understanding was signed, under which the Government and the SPLM agreed to allow international observers to monitor the cease-fire. In April al-Bashir and Garang met for only the second time in 20 years and reaffirmed their commitment to the Machakos Protocol. In September the SPLA and the Sudanese Government agreed to extend their cease-fire for a further two months; shortly afterwards, the two sides signed a landmark security agreement, under which two separate armed forces were to be created, as well as a number of integrated units, comprising both government and SPLA troops. Both sides agreed to contribute 12,000 soldiers to a joint force, the Sudan Armed Forces (SAF), to be deployed in southern Sudan, and a further 6,000 soldiers from each side were to be dispatched to the disputed Nuba Mountains and Blue Nile provinces. Furthermore, 80% of the government forces in southern Sudan would be withdrawn to the north no later than two-and-a-half years after the signing of a Comprehensive Peace Agreement (CPA).

In early December 2003 SPLM delegates visited Khartoum for the first time since the escalation of the north–south conflict in 1983, prior to convening for further talks with the Government in Naivasha, Kenya. On 7 January 2004 the two sides signed an accord on revenue-sharing, which also provided for the establishment of two separate banking systems for the north and the south, as well as a new national currency on the signing of a final peace settlement. Further progress in the discussions in Kenya remained slow. On 26 May, however, the Government and the SPLM signed three protocols that removed the remaining obstacles to the conclusion of a comprehensive peace accord. Specifically, the protocols stated: that the SPLM and other southern groups would hold 30% of government seats in the north, while holding 70% of seats in the south; that the contested provinces of the Blue Nile and the Nuba Mountains would be governed by an administration in which 55% of the seats would be taken by government officials and 45% by the SPLM, while the petroleum-rich province of Abyei would be granted special status and be governed by the presidential office; and that Khartoum would remain under Islamic law, with certain protections for non-Muslims.

The Comprehensive Peace Agreement

The final round of the IGAD-sponsored talks began in Naivasha in June 2004, and on 31 December a permanent cease-fire was agreed by the Sudanese Government and the SPLM. On 9 January 2005 Garang and First Vice-President Ali Osman Muhammad Taha signed the CPA in Nairobi, in the presence of US Secretary of State Colin Powell, and representatives from the UN, the European Union (EU, see p. 281), the African Union (AU, see p. 191) and IGAD, thus formally bringing an end to more than 20 years of civil conflict between the SPLA and successive governments. Under the agreement, Garang was to assume the position of Sudanese Vice-President and would act as President of Southern Sudan during the six-year period of autonomy, after which a referendum on secession would be held. In mid-January the Government signed a peace accord with the NDA in the Egyptian capital, Cairo, which allowed the return of NDA leaders to Sudan and granted them the right to conduct their political activities in the country.

The UN appealed for the international community to assist with the reconstruction of southern Sudan's infrastructure, which had been extensively damaged during the civil conflict. On 25 January 2005 the UN announced that it had restored diplomatic ties with Sudan and would contribute some €50m. in aid, to be divided equally between the north and the south. In March the UN Security Council unanimously approved Resolution 1590, which provided for the establishment of the UN Mission in Sudan (UNMIS), comprising up to 10,000 peacekeeping troops and 715 civilian personnel, to be deployed in southern Sudan for an initial period of six months (which was subsequently renewed).

On 6 July 2005 the National Assembly ratified a new interim Constitution, and on 9 July Garang was appointed First Vice-President of Sudan, also becoming President of Southern Sudan. In mid-July government troops withdrew from Juba (the principal city of southern Sudan) and the surrounding area in accordance with the CPA, which stipulated that 17% of government troops were redeployed within six months of signing the agreement, and Garang named the SPLM deputy leader, Commdr (later Lt-Gen.) Salva Kiir Mayardit, as Vice-President of the new southern administration. On 1 August it was announced that Garang had been killed in a helicopter crash. Salva Kiir succeeded Garang as leader of the SPLA/SPLM, and was later appointed as First Vice-President of Sudan and President of Southern Sudan. In September agreement was reached on the formation of a new Government, in which 16 portfolios were awarded to members of the ruling National Congress Party (NCP), nine to the SPLM and four to members of smaller opposition parties. In January 2006 the National Assembly adopted controversial legislation prohibiting any member of the armed forces (excluding al-Bashir and Salva Kiir), the police, the security forces or the SPLA, and state officials from joining a political party; it also made provisions for

any party to be dissolved, or prevented from participating in elections, if it was believed to be undertaking activities that breached the CPA. Claiming that this contravened the Constitution, the NDA withdrew from the National Assembly.

Amidst ongoing peace talks on conflict in the Darfur region of western Sudan, in October 2007 the SPLM withdrew from the Government in protest against delays in implementing the CPA. Al-Bashir subsequently reorganized the Council of Ministers, naming SPLM members Deng Alor Kuol as Minister of Foreign Affairs and Mansur Khaled as Minister of Foreign Trade in an effort to appease the party's leadership. Salva Kiir also effected changes to the Government of Southern Sudan (GOSS). In December, after the SPLM formally rejoined the central Government, further SPLM ministers were appointed. Lam Akol, who had been demoted from the position of Minister of Foreign Affairs to Minister of Cabinet Affairs in the October reorganization, was dismissed from the cabinet and replaced by Pagan Amum of the SPLM. Akol had been accused by fellow SPLM members of developing close ties with the NCP. In May 2008 Lt-Gen. Nhial Deng Nhial was named GOSS Minister of SPLA Affairs, following the death of his predecessor, Dominic Dim Deng, in a plane crash.

Meanwhile, renewed violence in the ethnically divided Abyei region erupted in early 2008, with clashes between the SPLA and members of the Misseriya ethnic group (supported by the NCP). An interim administration was established in the Abyei region in August; Arop Moyak of the SPLM was named Chief Administrator, while Rahama Abuldrahman al-Nur of the NCP was appointed Deputy Chief Administrator. In July 2009, following a ruling by the PCA, a compromise agreement was reached regarding the boundaries of the Abyei region; however, significant issues of contention remained. With the terms of the CPA scheduled to come to an end in 2011, and a referendum on independence for the south to be held upon its expiry, discontent over the allocation of oil revenues and a dispute over the required proportion of votes required in order to approve secession again placed significant strain on relations between the NCP and the SPLM at national government level. The NCP demanded that 75% of the votes in favour of independence would be required at the referendum, while the SPLM insisted that a simple majority would suffice. However, in December 2009 the National Assembly approved legislation that required 60% of the electorate in southern Sudan to vote for the ballot to be deemed legitimate, but also stated that a simple majority of 51% would suffice in order to secure independence.

Referendum on secession

In February 2010 multi-party presidential and legislative elections, which were to include direct elections for the institutions of southern Sudan, were finally scheduled for April. On 11–15 April Salva Kiir was overwhelmingly elected as President of Southern Sudan, with about 93.0% of the votes cast in a poll that was contested by only one other candidate, Akol of the opposition Sudan People's Liberation Movement—Democratic Change (SPLM—DC). The SPLM secured 99 seats in the elections to the 450-member National Assembly, and 160 of the 170 seats in southern Sudan's Legislative Assembly. (Al-Bashir was concurrently re-elected to a further presidential term, with 68.2% of the votes cast.) On 21 May Salva Kiir was sworn in for a further presidential term. In June President Salva Kiir formed a new GOSS administration; notably, Deng Alor was appointed as the Southern Sudan Minister of Regional Co-operation, while the Secretary-General of the SPLM, Amum, became the Minister of Peace and CPA Implementation. Meanwhile, in May dissident troops led by Gen. George Athor, formerly a general in the southern Sudanese army, began to stage rebel attacks in protest against the outcome of legislative elections.

Despite concerns that the referendum on secession would be postponed, in October 2010 the Government announced a timetable for its organization, confirming that the poll was scheduled for 9 January 2011. Later in October 2010 NCP officials declared that a postponement of a parallel referendum in Abyei (which had also been stipulated under the CPA) was likely, after negotiations between the North and South Sudan authorities in Addis Ababa, Ethiopia failed to result in agreement over the composition of the region's electoral commission, the eligibility of voters and the demarcation of borders. The voter registration process commenced on 15 November as scheduled and was extended for an additional week, until 8 December. The NCP accused the SPLM of intimidating potential voters in Khartoum.

The referendum on the secession of southern Sudan was conducted on 9–15 January 2011. (The parallel referendum on secession for Abyei, where ethnic clashes continued, had been postponed as expected.) According to the final results of the referendum, which were announced on 7 February, about 98.8% of the population of southern Sudan had voted to secede from the north and officially form their own country. Some 97.6% of the electorate had participated in the poll (far higher than the 60% required to validate the results). On 16 February the GOSS approved the banner of the SPLM as the official flag for the new nation, and the SPLA as its official army. On the following day southern Sudanese political parties endorsed 'South Sudan' as the name of the new state, which was to be inaugurated on 9 July. In early February some 50 people were killed in southern Sudan in a mutiny over the redeployment of the northern and southern armies, which began in the southern town of Malakal.

In March 2011 the SPLM suspended negotiations with the NCP over a number of post-secession arrangements, accusing the northern Government of training and arming insurgent groups to destabilize southern Sudan. (At that time about 250,000 southerners had returned from northern Sudan.) Meanwhile, the SPLA clashed with rebel militia in the Unity and Upper Nile states, of which the two most prominent groups were led by Athor and Col Gatluak Gai, a former SPLM officer who had resigned from his post after accusing the SPLM of malpractice in the elections in southern Sudan.

In May 2011 the SAF occupied the town of Abyei, prompting the displacement of some 80,000 civilians, after an attack on one of its military convoys outside the town by the SPLA. Following AU-mediated negotiations, on 20 June representatives of the SPLM and the NCP signed an agreement providing for the demilitarization of Abyei and the deployment in the region of Ethiopian peace-keeping troops, under the auspices of the UN. Later in June the UN Security Council approved the establishment of the UN Interim Security Force for Abyei (UNISFA), which had a maximum authorized strength of 4,200 military personnel, for a renewable period of six months. Meanwhile, in early June a further conflict erupted between the SAF and the SPLA in Sudan's oil-producing Southern Kordofan State, where many communities supported the south, after the refusal of SPLA-allied forces to comply with an order by the northern authorities to disarm. In late June the AU mediated a preliminary agreement between the NCP and the SPLM over Southern Kordofan, involving pledges to disarm SPLA elements. On 8 July the UN Security Council adopted a resolution authorizing the establishment of the UN Mission in the Republic of South Sudan (UNMISS) for an initial period of one year. UNMISS, which was to comprise 7,000 military and 900 police personnel, received a mandate to support the southern authorities in peace consolidation and state-building.

Secession of the Republic of South Sudan

South Sudan's secession from Sudan officially took place on 9 July 2011, when Salva Kiir was inaugurated as President at a ceremony attended by UN Secretary-General Ban Ki-Moon and some 30 African heads of state, including al-Bashir. On the same day the Transitional Constitution of the Republic of South Sudan entered into effect, following its approval by the existing Legislative Assembly on 7 July. Under the Transitional Constitution, the Legislative Assembly was replaced by a bicameral National Legislature, comprising a Legislative Assembly and an upper Council of States. On 31 August the establishment of the first post-secession Government of South Sudan was approved by the National Legislature; Riek Machar was reappointed to the post of Vice-President.

Following negotiations on border demarcation from August 2011, the northern and southern authorities agreed later in September to establish 10 border points, and to form joint border monitoring teams. In October Lam Akol returned to South Sudan from Khartoum, pledging co-operation with the new Government. Later in October 2011 the SPLA clashed with a newly formed rebel group, the South Sudan Liberation Army (SSLA), led by former SPLA general Peter Gadet, at the town of Mayom in Unity State. In December Athor was killed in a clash with an SPLA border patrol in Morobo County, in Central Equatoria State.

Hostilities with Sudan

Amid increasing tensions at the border with Sudan, in November 2011 the South Sudanese Government claimed that the SAF had bombed a refugee camp in Unity State, killing at least 12 people. South Sudan was, meanwhile, accused by the Sudanese authorities of supporting a new armed grouping that aimed to overthrow al-Bashir's Government, the Sudan Revolutionary Front

(SRF), comprising the Sudan People's Liberation Army-North (the northern wing of the SPLA), and the Justice and Equality Movement and a further two movements from Darfur. At the end of December the SPLA claimed that 40 people had been killed in SAF air attacks in Raja County, in Western Bahr El-Ghazal State, appealing to the AU and to IGAD to intervene on its behalf. A non-aggression treaty was signed by the Governments of South Sudan and Sudan in Addis Ababa on 11 February 2012, after AU-mediated negotiations; nevertheless, mutual accusations of violations of the pact followed soon afterwards. Also in February South Sudan and Sudan established two framework agreements, according to which they were, respectively, to complete the demarcation of the joint border, excluding the disputed regions, within three months, and to allow their citizens to reside, work and own property on either side of the border, and travel between the two states. However, negotiations between al-Bashir and Salva Kiir to resolve a critical dispute over a transit fee imposed on petroleum exported by South Sudan, which had resulted in the suspension of petroleum production in January (see Economic Affairs), continued to prove unsuccessful. In March South Sudan claimed that Sudanese airplanes had bombed oil and water wells in its border territory, and later that month criticized al-Bashir's withdrawal from a planned summit meeting. In early April hostilities escalated further, when the SPLA seized the principal oil-producing region of Heglig in Southern Kordofan, after clashes with the SAF. The GOSS claimed that the occupation of Heglig, which was condemned by the AU as illegal, was in retaliation for continued air attacks by the SAF against South Sudan's territory; on 20 April, however, it announced that the SPLA troops had been withdrawn from the region, following international demands, including from the UN Security Council. On 2 May the UN Security Council adopted Resolution 2046 which ordered that the two sides cease hostilities within 48 hours and resume the AU-mediated negotiations within two weeks, threatening to impose sanctions for non-compliance.

Discussions between South Sudan and Sudan were accordingly convened under the aegis of the AU High-Level Implementation Panel (AUHIP) in Addis Ababa, but in early June 2012 failed to result in agreement on the establishment of a demilitarized border zone, after the Sudanese delegation rejected a demarcation map presented by the South Sudanese representatives. Although the UN-imposed cease-fire entered into effect, the South Sudanese authorities accused the SAF of continuing air attacks in border regions in subsequent months (and at the end of August the UN Security Council demanded that both sides immediately end violations of Resolution 2046). In July the UN Security Council renewed the mandate of UNMISS for a further year. Following continued AUHIP-mediated negotiations, on 27 September Salva Kiir and al-Bashir, meeting in Addis Ababa, signed nine co-operation agreements, which were ratified by the National Legislative Assembly on 16 October; these provided for, *inter alia*, the creation of a demilitarized border zone, the reopening of South Sudan's oil pipelines and the repatriation of large numbers of South Sudanese nationals who remained in refugee camps in Sudan. (No further progress was achieved in the dispute over Abyei's status, however, and the AU Peace and Security Council proposed that the issue be referred to a regional referendum in late 2013.)

In December 2012 four Russian members of UNMISS were killed, when their helicopter, on a reconnaissance mission in Jonglei State, was shot down by the SPLA; the UN Security Council condemned the incident, while the Russian Government demanded action against those responsible. Later that month the SAF launched further ground and air attacks in Bahr El-Ghazal State, prompting the South Sudanese Government to submit a formal complaint to the UN Security Council. Despite commitments issued by al-Bashir and Salva Kiir at a summit meeting, held under the aegis of the AUHIP in Addis Ababa on 5 January 2013, to the unconditional implementation of the co-operation agreements, tensions in the border regions subsequently rose, amid further SAF bombardments, particularly in Unity State. Later in January further discussions regarding the establishment of joint authorities in Abyei ended in failure, while Sudan accused the South Sudanese Government of continuing to support rebel groups in Blue Nile and Southern Kordofan. In the same month an increase in unrest in Jonglei State was reported, following massacres perpetrated by a rebel group led by David Yau Yau. Meanwhile, the Government, which dismissed rumours of a coup attempt, replaced some 30 senior army officers. In a report issued in February, human rights organization Amnesty International stated that South Sudanese security forces had, in December 2012, fired on protesters in the north-western town of Wau, killing 10 people, and that the authorities had subsequently increased the arbitrary arrest of opposition activists.

Recent developments: improved relations with Sudan

Following the resumption of the AU-mediated negotiations in Addis Ababa, on 8 March 2013 the South Sudanese and Sudanese Governments agreed to order their forces to withdraw from the border area by 14 March (thereby implementing the accord providing for establishment of a demilitarized border zone signed the previous September). Salva Kiir accordingly ordered withdrawal on 11 March; on the following day the two sides reached agreement on a timetable under which South Sudan would resume petroleum production within three weeks. It was subsequently reported that Sudanese forces had also commenced withdrawal from the border zone. The South Sudanese authorities officially recommenced the production of petroleum on 6 April, declaring the measure to be a gesture of reconciliation. Meanwhile, five UN personnel and seven civilians employed by UNMISS were killed in an attack by rebel forces in Jonglei State (following further hostilities in the region between the SPLA and Yau Yau's militia). On 12 April al-Bashir made his first visit to South Sudan since secession, when he announced his intention to normalize relations with South Sudan, and invited Salva Kiir to conduct further discussions in Khartoum. In mid-April Salva Kiir issued a decree cancelling a national reconciliation process that had been initiated by Vice-President Machar and removing some of his executive powers.

Foreign Affairs

Regional relations

Relations with South Sudan's neighbouring countries, with the exception of Sudan, in the immediate post-secession period were cordial. Kenyan President Mwai Kibaki, Ethiopian Prime Minister Meles Zenawi and Ugandan President Yoweri Museveni were amongst the heads of state to attend the independence celebrations in Juba on 9 July 2011. The new state was reliant on imports and skilled labour from Uganda and Kenya, in particular, and sought to increase economic ties prior to independence. South Sudan was officially admitted to the African Union (see p. 191) on 28 July, and acceded to the Intergovernmental Authority on Development (see p. 344) in November. Also in November South Sudan submitted an application to join the East African Community (EAC, see p. 460), which then comprised Kenya, Uganda, Rwanda, Tanzania and Burundi. However, in November 2012 a technical commission of the EAC recommended that South Sudan's admission be delayed until the country was able to meet a number of economic and institutional conditions.

Other external relations

Following South Sudan's official secession on 9 July 2011, the new state was formally admitted to the UN on 14 July. The UN Mission in the Republic of South Sudan, which was officially established on 8 July (see Domestic Political Affairs), comprised 5,484 military personnel at the end of February 2012. South Sudan's main international donor nation is the USA. The appointment of the first US ambassador to South Sudan, Susan Page, was confirmed in October 2011. In early 2012 it was reported that the US Administration of President Barack Obama had approved the provision of military assistance to South Sudan. In May the US Administration announced that it was to provide US $30m. to support an emergency relief operation being conducted by the UN World Food Programme. The British Government also announced that the United Kingdom would provide £90m. in bilateral aid during the first year of the new country's existence. In March the USA and other members of the international community expressed concern at the escalation in violence between South Sudan and Sudan, and urged a resumption in negotiations between the Presidents of the two states.

The People's Republic of China has also established a bilateral relationship with South Sudan, despite being a long-term ally of Sudan. China formally recognized South Sudan upon its independence, after having previously opened a consulate in Juba in September 2008. During 2012 Chinese enterprises that held petroleum concessions in South Sudan were adversely affected by an ongoing dispute with Sudan over transit fees (see Economic Affairs). In April President Salva Kiir made an official visit to the Chinese capital, Beijing; the Chinese Government subsequently denied reports that it had pledged to provide South Sudan with

US 8,000m. in development aid, but indicated that funding would be forthcoming if peace with Sudan was achieved. In January 2013 the Minister of Petroleum and Mining, Stephen Dhieu Dau, following an official visit to Tel Aviv, Israel, announced an agreement under which South Sudan would export oil to Israel.

CONSTITUTION AND GOVERNMENT

The Transitional Constitution of the Republic of South Sudan was approved by the South Sudan Legislative Assembly on 7 July 2011 and entered into force on 9 July 2011 at South Sudan's formal secession from Sudan. The President of the Republic of South Sudan is the Head of State and of Government, the Commander-in-Chief of the Sudan People's Liberation Army and the Supreme Commander of all the other regular forces. Legislative authority is vested in and exercised by the National Legislature, which consists of the 170-member National Legislative Assembly and the Council of States. The first National Legislative Assembly comprises former members of the South Sudan Legislative Assembly, and all South Sudanese who were members of the National Assembly of Sudan; the Council of States comprises the South Sudanese who were members of the Council of States of Sudan; and 20 representatives appointed by the President of South Sudan. The term of the National Legislature is five years. South Sudan is divided into 10 states, each of which has a State Government, consisting of a State Assembly and a State Executive.

REGIONAL AND INTERNATIONAL CO-OPERATION

South Sudan is a member of the African Union (see p. 191) and the Council of Arab Economic Unity (see p. 373).

South Sudan became a member of the UN in 2011.

ECONOMIC AFFAIRS

In 2010, according to official estimates, South Sudan's gross national income (GNI) was US $8,415m., equivalent to $984 per head. In that year, South Sudan's gross domestic product (GDP) was US $13,227m., equivalent to $1,546 per head.

South Sudan has huge agricultural potential: more than one-half of the total land area of 82m. ha is estimated to be suitable for agriculture. Among the principal crops are pineapples, cotton, groundnuts, sorghum, millet, wheat, cotton, sweet potatoes, mangoes, pawpaw, sugar cane, cassava and sesame. Natural forests and woodlands cover 29% of the total land area of South Sudan. Commercial exploitation is limited to teak, natural mahogany and gum Arabic.

South Sudan possesses significant oil reserves, particularly in the Unity, Upper Nile and Jonglei states, and the petroleum industry accounted for 98% of the semi-autonomous Government of Southern Sudan's revenues in 2010.

In 2012, according to official preliminary figures, South Sudan recorded an overall budget surplus of 107.2m. new Sudanese pounds. In 2008–12 the average annual rate of inflation was 22.7%. Consumer prices increased by an average of 1.2% in 2010, but by 47.3% in 2011, and by 45.0% in 2012.

In February 2011, after the secession of southern Sudan was approved in a referendum, an agreement was announced on the allocation of the proceeds of Sudan's petroleum reserves, principally located in southern Sudan: the newly established South Sudan was to assume control of about three-quarters of the country's current production, and pay the northern Government a transit fee for the use of a pipeline for petroleum exports. South Sudan's capital, Juba, had already emerged as a major distribution centre for the south of the country, and a trading centre with Uganda had been opened in the city. South Sudan's secession from Sudan officially took place on 9 July 2011; the state's new currency, the South Sudan pound, was introduced later that month. However, economic discord immediately began between the South Sudanese and Sudanese authorities, after the latter imposed a fee of about US $22.50 per barrel on petroleum transported through Sudan. In addition, frequent closures of the border with Sudan disrupted food trade, and contributed to a dramatic rise in food price inflation. The new South Sudanese Government planned to stimulate the agricultural and industrial sectors, in an effort to diversify from the country's dependence on petroleum (which was estimated to provide 98% of state revenue). In early 2012, however, the dispute over the petroleum transit fee escalated, and South Sudan suspended petroleum production at the end of January. The rate of inflation reached 80% in May, when relief organizations estimated that nearly one-half of the population were affected by food shortages. In

June the Government adopted an austerity budget for 2012/13, under which state expenditure was sharply reduced and taxes increased. According to the World Bank, consumer price inflation had been reduced to about 17% by the end of 2012. In April South Sudan was officially admitted to the IMF, which announced in August that the country was eligible for concessional lending. The IMF also co-ordinated a donor fund of $10m., which was to support a three-year capacity-building programme in South Sudan. In August a preliminary agreement was reached under which South Sudan would pay a transit fee of US $9.50 per barrel for the use of Sudan's pipeline infrastructure (although implementation of this and other co-operation accords was subsequently delayed). In March 2013 the South Sudanese Government announced that feasibility studies were to be undertaken into the construction of new pipelines connecting the country

with Kenya and Djibouti. Following progress in negotiations between Sudan and South Sudan in March (see Domestic Political Affairs), a border security agreement was finalized, and the subsequent resumption of petroleum production by the South Sudanese authorities on 6 April further improved prospects of an economic recovery. (However, protracted disputes over regional conflicts in both states remained unresolved.)

PUBLIC HOLIDAYS

2014: 9 January (Peace Agreement Day), 18–21 April (Easter), 1 May (Labour Day), 16 May (National Day), 9 July (Independence Day), 30 July (Martyrs' Day), 1 December (World Aids Day), 25 December (Christmas).

Statistical Survey

Source (unless otherwise stated): National Bureau of Statistics, Near South Sudan High Court, May Street, Juba; e-mail contact.ssnbs@gmail.com; internet www.ssnbs.org; Bank of South Sudan, Juba; tel. 249811820218; fax 249811820211; e-mail info@bankofsouthernsudan.org; internet www.bankofsouthernsudan.org.

Note: The Republic of South Sudan achieved independence from Sudan on 9 July 2011 following a referendum held in January at which voters overwhelmingly approved the secession of South Sudan. More detailed statistical information on pre-secession Sudan can be found in that country's chapter.

Area and Population

AREA, POPULATION AND DENSITY

Area (sq km)	644,329*
Population (census results)	
22 April 2008	
Males	4,287,300
Females	3,973,190
Total	8,260,490
Population (official projections at mid-year) . . .	
2010	9,415,421
2011	9,897,118
2012	10,386,101
Density (per sq km) at mid-2012	16.1

* 248,777 sq miles.

POPULATION BY AGE AND SEX
(population at 2008 census)

	Males	Females	Total
0–14	1,945,033	1,722,860	3,667,893
15–64	2,216,427	2,157,893	4,374,320
65 and over	125,840	92,437	218,277
Total	4,287,300	3,973,190	8,260,490

STATES
(population at 2008 census)

	Area (sq km)	Population	Density (per sq km)
Upper Nile	77,283	964,353	12.5
Jonglei	122,581	1,358,602	11.1
Unity	37,837	585,801	15.5
Warrap	45,567	972,928	21.4
Northern Bahr El-Ghazal . .	30,543	720,898	23.6
Western Bahr El-Ghazal . .	91,076	333,431	3.7
Lakes	43,595	695,730	16.0
Western Equatoria . . .	79,343	619,029	7.8
Central Equatoria . . .	43,033	1,103,557	25.6
Eastern Equatoria . . .	73,472	906,161	12.3
Total	644,329	8,260,490	12.8

PRINCIPAL TOWNS
(population at 2008 census)

Juba (capital) . .	368,436	Uror	178,519
Aweil East . .	309,921	Magwi	169,826
Gogrial West . .	243,921	Aweil West . .	166,217
Bor South . . .	221,106	Tonj North . . .	165,222
Luakpiny/Nasir .	210,002	Kapoeta East . .	163,997
Twic	204,905	Rumbek Centre .	153,550
Yei	201,443	Yambio	152,257
Kajo-Keji . . .	196,387	Wau	151,320

BIRTHS AND DEATHS
(official figures)

	2008	2009*	2010*
Births	338,453	347,136	355,099
Birth rate (per 1,000)	39.9	38.8	37.7
Deaths	87,673	89,050	90,262
Death rate (per 1,000)	10.4	10.0	9.6

* Projections.

Life expectancy (years at birth): 58.2 (males 56.9; females 59.5) in 2008.

Health and Welfare

KEY INDICATORS

Total fertility rate (children per woman, 2008)	5.5
Under-5 mortality rate (per 1,000 live births, 2010) . . .	105
Access to water (% of persons, 2010)	67
Access to sanitation (% of persons, 2010)	7

For sources and definitions, see explanatory note on p. vi.

Agriculture

Principal Crop (cereal production, '000 metric tons): 1,068 in 2008; 660 in 2009; 695 in 2010.

Livestock (cattle, '000 head): 10,860 in 2008; 11,735 in 2009; 11,814 in 2010.

Finance

CURRENCY AND EXCHANGE RATES Note: A new currency, the South Sudan pound was introduced, at par with the former new Sudanese pound (see the chapter on Sudan), in July 2011.

CENTRAL GOVERNMENT BUDGET
(million new Sudanese pounds)

Revenue				2009	2010	2011
Petroleum revenue	.	.	.	4,121.5	5,630.3	4,782.1
Non-petroleum revenue		.	.	118.3	126.6	107.0
Total	.	.	.	4,239.8	5,756.8	4,889.1

Expenditure				2009	2010	2011
Current expenditure		.	.	3,232.6	4,485.3	3,480.7
Wages and salaries		.	.	1,977.3	2,205.7	1,334.9
Operating	.	.	.	1,255.3	2,279.6	2,145.8
Capital expenditure		.	.	1,002.0	1,090.9	943.4
Total	.	.	.	4,234.7	5,576.1	4,424.1

2012/13 (million new Sudanese pounds, budget figures): *Revenue:* 6,771.4 (Petroleum reserves and borrowing 5,904.6, Non-petroleum revenue 866.7). *Expenditure:* 6,664.2 (Salaries 2,975.3, Operating expenditure 1,390.8, Capital expenditure 454.3, Transfers 1,816.3, Other expenditure 27.4).

MONEY SUPPLY
(million new Sudanese pounds at 31 December)

					2008	2009
Currency in circulation	.	.	.	.	963	4,254
Demand deposits	.	.	.	.	318	766
Total	.	.	.	.	1,281	5,020

COST OF LIVING
(Consumer Price Index; base: June 2011 = 100)

	2010	2011	2012
Food and non-alcoholic beverages .	69.6	106.8	153.8
Housing and fuels	80.3	101.0	141.6
Furnishings and household			
equipment	81.5	129.1	188.5
Transport	79.8	107.7	136.6
Recreation and culture . .	94.6	108.5	144.8
All items (incl. others) . . .	74.4	109.6	158.9

NATIONAL ACCOUNTS
(million new Sudanese pounds in current prices)

Expenditure on the Gross Domestic Product
(provisional estimates)

	2008	2009	2010
Government final consumption			
expenditure	4,644	3,978	5,674
Private final consumption			
expenditure	9,619	10,493	11,145
Gross capital formation . .	4,816	3,921	4,005
Total domestic expenditure .	19,079	18,392	20,824
Exports of goods and services . .	21,325	16,837	21,973
Less Imports of goods and services	11,898	10,284	12,310
GDP in purchasers' values .	28,505	24,946	30,488

Education

	2008	2009	2010
Permanent schools	6,794	9,884	n.a.
Teachers	25,972	26,575	26,658
Pupil-teacher ratio	50	52	53

Student enrolment: *Primary:* 1,284,252 (males 809,519, females 474,733) in 2007/08; 1,380,580 (males 871,804, females 508,776) in 2008/09; 1,401,874 (males 880,208, females 521,666) in 2009/10. *Secondary:* 44,027 (males 31,977, females 12,050) in 2008/09; 34,487 (males 24,498, females 9,989) in 2009/10.

Adult literacy rate (15 years and over): 27% in 2009.

Directory

The Government

HEAD OF STATE

President: Lt-Gen. SALVA KIIR MAYARDIT (took office on 11 August 2005 as President of the Government of Southern Sudan).

Vice-President: Dr RIEK MACHAR TENY-DHURGON.

COUNCIL OF MINISTERS
(May 2013)

Minister of Cabinet Affairs: DENG ALOR KUOL.

Minister of Defence and Veteran Affairs: Gen. JOHN KONG NYUON.

Minister of Foreign Affairs and International Co-operation: NHIAL DENG NHIAL.

Minister in the Office of the President: EMMANUEL LOWILLA.

Minister in the Office of the President, Responsible for National Security: Gen. OYAY AJAK.

Minister of Justice: JOHN LUYK JOK.

Minister of the Interior: Gen. ALISON MANANI MAGAYA.

Minister of Parliamentary Affairs: MICHAEL MAKUEI LUETH.

Minister of Finance and Economic Planning: KOSTI MANIBE NGAI.

Minister of Labour, Public Service and Human Resource Development: KWONG DANHIER GATLUAK (acting).

Minister of Health: Dr MICHAEL MILLY HUSSEIN.

Minister of Information and Broadcasting: Dr BARNABA MARIAL BENJAMIN.

Minister of Agriculture and Forestry: Dr BETTY ACHAN OGWARO.

Minister of Roads and Bridges: GIER CHUANG ALUONG.

Minister of Transport: AGNES PONI LOKUDU.

Minister of General Education and Instruction: USTAZ JOSEPH UKEL ABANGO.

Minister of Higher Education, Science and Technology: Dr PETER ADWOK NYABA.

Minister of Commerce, Industry and Investment: GARANG DIING AKUANG.

Minister of the Environment: ALFRED LADO GORE.

Minister of Housing and Physical Planning: JEMA NUNU KUMBA.

Minister of Telecommunications and Postal Services: MADUT BIAR YEL.

Minister of Petroleum and Mining: STEPHEN DHIEU DAU.

Minister of Electricity and Dams: DAVID DENG ATHORBEI.

Minister of Gender, Child and Social Welfare: AGNES KWAJE LAUBA.

SOUTH SUDAN

Directory

Minister of Humanitarian Affairs and Disaster Management: JOSEPH LUAL ACUIL.

Minister of Water Resources and Irrigation: PAUL MAYOM AKEC.

Minister of Wildlife Conservation and Tourism: GABRIEL CHANGSON.

Minister of Animal Resources and Fisheries: Dr MARTIN ELIA LOMURO.

Minister of Culture, Youth and Sports: Dr CIRINO HITENG OFUHO.

MINISTRIES

Office of the President: Juba.

Ministry of Agriculture and Forestry: Juba; tel. (+249) 917068933 (mobile); e-mail bedamachar@yahoo.com.

Ministry of Animal Resources and Fisheries: Juba; tel. (+249) 12221935; e-mail wimapa89@yahoo.co.uk.

Ministry of Cabinet Affairs: Juba.

Ministry of Commerce, Industry and Investment: POB 73, Juba; tel. (+249) 914113105 (mobile); e-mail kitoundo@hotmail.com; internet www.commerce-goss.org.

Ministry of Culture, Youth and Sports: Juba.

Ministry of Defence and Veteran Affairs: Juba; tel. (+249) 915485232 (mobile); e-mail kdeimkuol@yahoo.com; internet www.splamilitary.net.

Ministry of Electricity and Dams: Juba.

Ministry of the Environment: Juba.

Ministry of Finance and Economic Planning: Juba; tel. (+256) 477126466 (mobile).

Ministry of Foreign Affairs and International Co-operation: Juba.

Ministry of Gender, Child and Social Welfare: Juba; tel. (+249) 126925801; e-mail mgswragoss@gmail.com.

Ministry of General Education and Instruction: Juba; tel. (+249) 926168090 (mobile); e-mail datjoel@yahoo.com; internet www.moest.gov.sd.

Ministry of Health: Juba; tel. (+249) 917036278 (mobile); e-mail infomohgoss@gmail.com; internet www.mohgoss.com.

Ministry of Higher Education, Science and Technology: Juba.

Ministry of Housing and Physical Planning: Juba.

Ministry of Humanitarian Affairs and Disaster Management: Juba; tel. (+249) 912553790 (mobile); e-mail ajawinsenior@yahoo.com.

Ministry of Information and Broadcasting: Juba; tel. (+249) 922260000; e-mail musabiong@yahoo.ca.

Ministry of the Interior: Juba; tel. (+256) 477103368 (mobile); e-mail pmadol@yahoo.com.

Ministry of Justice: Juba.

Ministry of Labour, Public Service and Human Resource Development: Juba; tel. (+249) 917259719 (mobile).

Ministry of Parliamentary Affairs: Juba; tel. (+249) 912339369 (mobile); e-mail juliaduany@ymail.com.

Ministry of Petroleum and Mining: POB 376, Juba; tel. (+249) 918906406 (mobile); fax 249811829583 (mobile); e-mail megoss@ministryofenergygoss.net; internet www.ministryofenergygoss.net.

Ministry of Roads and Bridges: Juba; tel. (+249) 129187774; e-mail airroadwater@yahoo.com; internet www.mtr-goss.org.

Ministry of Telecommunications and Postal Services: POB 33 Juba; tel. 977102623 (mobile); fax 811820188; e-mail Juma.lugga@motps.goss.org; internet www.motps.goss.org/.

Ministry of Transport: Juba.

Ministry of Water Resources and Irrigation: Juba; tel. (+249) 126298074; e-mail alieroka@yahoo.co.uk; internet rwssp-mwrigoss.org.

Ministry of Wildlife Conservation and Tourism: Juba; tel. (+249) 955024191 (mobile); e-mail jameskenyi@yahoo.com.

STATE GOVERNORS
(May 2013)

Central Equatoria: Maj.-Gen. (retd) CLEMENT WANI KONGA (SPLM).

Eastern Equatoria: LOUIS LOBONG LOJORE (SPLM).

Jonglei: KUOL MANYANG JUUK (SPLM).

Lakes: MABOR ACHOL KUER (SPLM, acting).

Northern Bahr El-Ghazal: PAUL MALONG AWAN ANEI (SPLM).

Unity: Brig. TABAN DENG GAI (SPLM).

Upper Nile: SIMON KON PUOCH (SPLM).

Warrap: NYANDENG MALEK DELIECH (SPLM).

Western Bahr El-Ghazal: RIZIK HASSAN ZACHARIAH (SPLM).

Western Equatoria: Col BANGASI JOSEPH BAKOSORO (Ind.).

President and Legislature

PRESIDENT

Election, 11–15 April 2010

Candidate	Votes	% of votes
Lt-Gen. Salva Kiir Mayardit (Sudan People's Liberation Movement)	2,616,613	92.99
Dr Lam Akol Ajawin (Sudan People's Liberation Movement—Democratic Change)	197,217	7.01
Total	2,813,830	100.00

LEGISLATIVE ASSEMBLY

Speaker: JAMES WANI IQQA.

Election 11–15 April 2010

Party	Seats* A	B	C	Total
Sudan People's Liberation Movement	93	25	42	160
Independents	6	—	—	6
Sudan People's Liberation Movement—Democratic Change	2	—	1	3
National Congress Party	1	—	—	1
Total	102	25	43	170

* There are 170 members of the Legislative Assembly of whom 102 (A) are directly elected in single seat constituencies; 25 'party members' (B) are elected on the basis of proportional representation at the state level from separate and closed party lists; and a further 43 women members (C) are elected on the basis of proportional representation at the state level from separate and closed party lists.

Election Commission

National Elections Commission: Juba; Chair. Eng. ABEDNEGO AKOK KACUOL; Chief Electoral Officer MAC MAICA DENG.

Political Organizations

A Political Parties Council was established in 2013 to register and deregister political parties.

Sudan People's Liberation Movement (SPLM): Juba; e-mail info@splmtoday.com; internet www.splmtoday.com; Leader Lt-Gen. SALVA KIIR MAYARDIT; Sec.-Gen. PAGAN AMUM.

Sudan People's Liberation Movement—Democratic Change (SPLM—DC): Juba; f. 2009; Leader Dr LAM AKOL AJAWIN.

United Democratic Party: Juba; Leader TONG LUAL AYAT.

Diplomatic Representation

EMBASSIES IN SOUTH SUDAN

China, People's Republic: POB 249, Juba; tel. 912386010 (mobile); e-mail chinaemb_ss@mfa.gov.cn; internet ss.chineseembassy.org; Ambassador LI ZHIGUO.

Egypt: Iwzrat St, Plot No. J/119, Cinema Residential Area, Juba; Ambassador MOAYAD FATHALLAH MOHAMMED.

Eritrea: Juba; tel. 926228425 (mobile); fax 122488842; e-mail asengal@yahoo.com; Ambassador GIRMAI GEBREMARIAM.

Ethiopia: Hai Malakal, Juba; tel. 11845719; Ambassador TESFAMICHAEL TESTATSION.

France: EU Compound, Kololo Rd, Thomping, Juba; tel. 955999962 (mobile); fax 955587332 (mobile); internet soudandusud.ambafrance.org; Ambassador CHRISTIAN BADER.

Germany: EU Compound, Kololo Rd, Thomping, Juba; tel. 956008021 (mobile); Ambassador PETER FELTEN.

India: 522 Hai Matar, Juba; tel. (+249) 811822552; fax (+249) 811822236; e-mail cgjuba@indembsdn.com; Ambassador P. K. BAJAJ.

Kenya: POB 208, Juba; tel. (+249) 811823664; fax (+249) 811823666; e-mail keconju@yahoo.co.uk; Ambassador CLELAND LESHORE.

Nigeria: Juba; Ambassador DEDAN MADUGU.

Netherlands: European Union Compound, Kololo Rd, Juba; tel. 912117961 (mobile); e-mail jba@minbuza.nl; internet southsudan .nlembassy.org; Ambassador KEES VAN BAAR.

Norway: Hai Malakal, Juba; e-mail emb.juba@mfa.no; internet www.norway-south-sudan.org; Ambassador (vacant).

South Africa: House 873, South Block 3-K-3, Tongping Area, Juba; tel. 922000440 (mobile); e-mail juba@dirco.gov.za; Ambassador G. P. SETLHOKE.

Sudan: Juba; Ambassador Dr MUTRIF SIDDIQ.

Turkey: Block 3K South, Plots No. 880-881, Hai Matar, POB 252, Juba; tel. 955721817 (mobile); e-mail embassy.juba@mfa.gov.tr; internet juba.be.mfa.gov.tr; Ambassador AHMET ERGIN.

United Kingdom: EU Compound, Kololo Rd, Thomping, Juba; tel. 955584193 (mobile); e-mail ukinsouthsudan@dfid.gov.uk; internet www.gov.uk/government/world/organisations/ british-embassy-juba; Ambassador Dr ALASTAIR McPHAIL.

USA: Kololo Rd, Juba; e-mail usembassyjuba@state.gov; internet southsudan.usembassy.gov; Ambassador SUSAN DENISE PAGE.

Judicial System

The judicial system of South Sudan comprises a Supreme Court, composed of a President, a Deputy President and five justices; three Courts of Appeal, located in Malakal, Juba and Rumbek, each consisting of a President and two justices; 10 High Courts, one in each state, consisting of a President and one justice; county courts and other courts deemed necessary to be established; and town and rural courts. The President of the Supreme Court of South Sudan is the head of the judiciary and is answerable to the President of the Government of South Sudan for the administration of the judiciary. High Courts are the highest courts at the state level.

Supreme Court: Juba; Pres. CHAN REEC MADUT.

Courts of Appeal: Malakal: Pres. ALEU AKECHAK JOK; Juba: Pres. ACHOL MADING MAYEN; Rumbek: Pres. KUKUR LOPITA MARINO.

High Courts: Malakal: Pres. GEORGE ANGIER RING; Bor: Pres. MADUT SANTINO DENG; Bentiu: Pres. ATEM BIAI MAKUER; Juba: Pres. MALEK MATHIANG MALEK; Torit: Pres. GERI RIAMONDO LEGGE; Yambio: Pres. BOL BUL WANG; Rumbek: Pres. ALAKA MAKELELE NYAJOK; Kuajok: Pres. JAIRO AJANG KORNELIO; Wau: Pres. CHARLES UYO NYAWILO; Aweil: Pres. CHARLES ABYEI JOOK.

Religion

The majority of the South Sudanese population are Christians or animists.

CHRISTIANITY

Roman Catholic Church

The Roman Catholic Church in Sudan officially remained unified after the secession of South Sudan, although some bishops desired division of the church and the formation of two conferences. For ecclesiastical purposes, South Sudan comprises one archdiocese and six dioceses.

Archbishop of Juba: Most Rev. PAOLINO LUKUDU LORO, Catholic Church, POB 32, Juba; tel. (+249) 811820303; fax (+249) 811820755; e-mail archbishopofjuba@hotmail.com.

ISLAM

Council of Muslims: Juba; Chair. ATIR BIOR.

The Press

NEWSPAPERS

Al-Isteqlal: Juba; f. 2011; daily; Arabic; Man. Editor GAMAL DALMAN.

Al-Mussir: Juba; f. 2011; weekly; Arabic.

The Citizen: Hai Amarat, Airport Road, Juba; tel. (+249) 908760789 (mobile); e-mail thecitizen2006@yahoo.com; f. 2005; daily; Editor-in-Chief NHIAL BOL AKEN.

The Juba Monitor: Juba; f. 2011; Editor-in-Chief ALFRED TABAN.

The Juba Post: Juba; f. 2005; biweekly; Editor-in-Chief MICHAEL KOMA (acting).

The Southern Eye: Tong Ping, Airport Rd, POB 243, Juba; tel. 977100072 (mobile); e-mail southerneyegoss@yahoo.com; internet southerneyeonline.com.

NEWS AGENCY

News Agency of South Sudan: Juba.

Broadcasting and Communications

TELECOMMUNICATIONS

At the end of 2012 there were five mobile cellular telephone operators in South Sudan.

Gemtel Green Network (Gemtel): Yei Rd, Atlabara, Juba; internet www.gemtelgreen.com; CEO GHADAFI MOHAMED.

MTN South Sudan: Juba.

Sudatel South Sudan: Juba.

Vivacell: Juba.

Zain South Sudan: Juba; CEO JAMES M. HODGES.

BROADCASTING

Radio

Radio Miraya: Airport Rd, Juba; internet www.mirayafm.org; operated by the United Nations Mission in South Sudan (UNMISS) in partnership with Fondation Hirondelle.

South Sudan Radio: Juba; Dir-Gen. AROP BAGAT TINGLOTH.

Sudan Catholic Radio Network (SCRN): Juba; seven FM radio stations, at Juba, Malakal, Rumbek, Torit, Yei, Tonj and Nuba Mountains (2010)

Bakhita Radio: Juba; f. 2006; Catholic.

Television

South Sudan TV: Juba; Dir-Gen. AROP BAGAT TINGLOTH.

Finance

BANKING

Established in 2005 as a branch of the Bank of Sudan, the Bank of Southern Sudan operated as the central bank of South Sudan until 9 July 2011. After secession it was formally transformed into the Bank of South Sudan. On 18 July the Bank of South Sudan introduced a new currency, the South Sudan pound, which was to replace the Sudanese pound in South Sudan. In early 2012 there were 14 registered commercial banks in South Sudan.

Central Bank

Bank of South Sudan (BOSS): Juba; tel. (+249) 811821111 (mobile); fax (+249) 811820211 (mobile); e-mail info@ bankofsouthernsudan.org; internet www.bankofsouthernsudan .org; f. 2011 to replace the Bank of Southern Sudan; Gov. KORNELIO KORYOM MAYIIK.

Commercial Banks

Buffalo Commercial Bank: BCB Junction, Juba; e-mail info@ buffalocommercialbank.com; internet www.buffalocommercialbank .com; f. 2008; Chair. Dr LUAL ACUEK LUAL DENG; CEO BISWASH GAUCHAN.

Nile Commercial Bank Ltd: Juba; tel. +(256) 477101931 (mobile); f. 2003; Man. Dir AGGREY IDRI.

Trade and Industry

CHAMBER OF COMMERCE

South Sudan Chamber of Commerce, Industry and Agriculture (SSCCIA): adjacent to Summer Palace Hotel, Juba; tel. 955908673 (mobile); e-mail info@southsudanchamber-commerce .org; internet southsudanchamber-commerce.org; f. 2003; Chair. BENJAMIN BOL MELL; Sec.-Gen. SIMON AKUEI DENG.

Transport

RAILWAYS

South Sudan has 248 km of single track, narrow-gauge railway line from the Sudanese border to Wau terminus. The line, however, has not been operational since 1991. There are proposed extensions from Wau to Juba, the capital of South Sudan. There are also plans to link Juba with the Kenyan and Ugandan railway networks.

ROADS

The road network in South Sudan is underdeveloped. Most roads are unpaved and in poor condition, and they become impassable during the rainy season. A 192-km highway connecting Juba with Nimule, a town on the border with Uganda, was inaugurated in 2012.

South Sudan Road Authority: Juba; f. 2011.

CIVIL AVIATION

Juba Airport is the busiest and most developed international airport in South Sudan, with regular flights to Entebbe (Uganda), Nairobi (Kenya), Cairo (Egypt), Addis Ababa (Ethiopia) and Khartoum (Sudan). Other international airports include Malakal, with flights to Addis Ababa and Khartoum; Wau, with a weekly service to Khartoum; and Rumbek, also with weekly flights to Khartoum.

Feeder Airlines: Juba; f. 2007.

Southern Sudan Airlines: Shari El Mina, Juba; f. 2005.

Education

There are nine public universities and 16 private universities in South Sudan, although only five of the public universities were able to admit students in 2011. For the 2011/12 academic year, the four main public universities—Juba, Bahr El-Ghazal, Upper Nile and Rumbek—approved a total intake of 2,722 students, out of just over 4,500 applications, according to the Ministry of Higher Education, Science and Technology.

In October 2011 it was announced that English would become the language of instruction in South Sudanese schools by the end of the year.

SPAIN

Introductory Survey

LOCATION, CLIMATE, LANGUAGE, RELIGION, FLAG, CAPITAL

The Kingdom of Spain, in south-western Europe, forms more than four-fifths of the Iberian peninsula. The country also includes the Balearic Islands in the Mediterranean Sea, the Canary Islands in the Atlantic Ocean and a few small enclaves in North Africa. Mainland Spain is bounded to the north by Andorra and France and to the west by Portugal. To the east is the Mediterranean Sea, and Morocco lies 30 km to the south. The climate is less temperate than in most of Western Europe, with hot summers and, in the hilly interior, cold winters. The official national language is Spanish. Catalan, and its close relative Valencian, are widely spoken in the north-east, Basque in the north and Galician in the north-west; all have co-official status in their respective regions. The majority of the population are Roman Catholics, but the Constitution states that Spain has no official state religion. The national flag (proportions 2 by 3) carries three horizontal stripes, of red, yellow (one-half of the depth) and red. The state flag carries, in addition, the national coat of arms. The capital is Madrid.

CONTEMPORARY POLITICAL HISTORY

Historical Context

After winning the civil war of 1936–39, the Nationalist forces, led by Gen. Francisco Franco, established an authoritarian rule which restricted individual liberties and severely repressed challenges to its power. In 1942 Gen. Franco revived the traditional legislative assembly, the Cortes (Courts), with limited powers. After keeping Spain neutral in the Second World War, Franco announced in 1947 that the monarchy (abolished in 1931) would be restored after his death or retirement. In 1967, in the first elections since the civil war, a portion of the Cortes was directly elected under a limited franchise. In July 1969 Franco nominated Prince Juan Carlos de Borbón (grandson of the last reigning monarch, King Alfonso XIII) as his successor, and in June 1973 relinquished the post of President of the Government (Prime Minister) to Adm. Luis Carrero Blanco, who was killed in December. Responsibility for the assassination was claimed by Euskadi ta Askatasuna (ETA—Basque Homeland and Liberty), the Basque separatist organization. Carlos Arias Navarro became Prime Minister in January 1974.

Franco died in November 1975. He was succeeded as Head of State by King Juan Carlos, and in December a more liberal Council of Ministers was formed. In 1976 restrictions on political activity were lifted. In July Arias Navarro resigned at the King's request, and was replaced by Adolfo Suárez. The introduction of democratic government then proceeded rapidly, and an elected bicameral legislature was established. Most of the numerous de facto political parties were able to take part in the general elections for the Cortes, held in June 1977. An overall majority was won by the Unión de Centro Democrático (UCD), a coalition party headed by the Prime Minister. In December 1978 a new Constitution was endorsed by referendum and ratified by the King. It confirmed Spain as a parliamentary monarchy, with freedom for political parties, and guaranteed the right of Spain's 'nationalities and regions' to autonomy.

Domestic Political Affairs

A general election was held in March 1979, resulting in little change in the distribution of seats in the Cortes. The new Government was again headed by Suárez. Basque and Catalan autonomous parliaments were established in March 1980 and, in elections to both parliaments, the UCD was heavily defeated by the moderate regionalist parties. Confidence in Suárez diminished and in January 1981 he resigned. Leopoldo Calvo-Sotelo Bustelo, hitherto the Deputy Prime Minister, was named as his successor.

On 23 February 1981 a group of armed civil guards, led by Lt-Col Antonio Tejero Molina, stormed the Cortes, taking hostage all 350 deputies. The military commander of Valencia, Lt-Gen. Jaime Milans del Bosch, declared a state of emergency in that region and sent tanks on to the streets of the city of Valencia.

King Juan Carlos acted swiftly to secure the loyalty of other military commanders, and by the following morning, having declared his support for the Constitution in a televised address, had been able to persuade Milans del Bosch himself to stand down. Tejero surrendered, and the deputies were released unharmed. More than 30 military officers were subsequently brought to trial, and both Tejero and Milans del Bosch received lengthy prison sentences. (Milans del Bosch was released in 1990 and Tejero in 1996.)

Immediately after the attempted coup, Calvo-Sotelo was formally installed as Prime Minister and formed a new Council of Ministers, resisting pressure to establish a coalition government. The Prime Minister addressed various contentious issues during his term of office, including his decision to take Spain into the North Atlantic Treaty Organization (NATO, see p. 380). Following Calvo-Sotelo's replacement as UCD leader in July 1982, Suárez defected to found a rival party, the Centro Democrático y Social (CDS). Desertion from the UCD continued and in August, with the party no longer commanding a workable majority, an early general election was called. In October, shortly before the election, a right-wing plot to stage a pre-emptive military coup was uncovered. Four colonels were arrested (three of whom were subsequently sentenced to prison terms), and Milans was also implicated. The election in late October resulted in a decisive victory for the Partido Socialista Obrero Español (PSOE—Spanish Socialist Workers' Party), led by Felipe González, who formed a new Council of Ministers in December 1982.

Following large-scale demonstrations against Spain's membership of NATO, in March 1986 a long-awaited referendum on the question of Spain's continued membership of the alliance was held. Contrary to expectations, the Spanish people voted to remain within NATO, following Prime Minister González's reversal on the issue and an extensive campaign by the Government. In an early general election in June 1986 the PSOE was returned to power, defeating the Coalición Popular (CP), which incorporated the conservative Alianza Popular (AP), the Partido Demócrata Popular (subsequently Democracia Cristiana) and the Partido Liberal. A new Council of Ministers was appointed in July, again led by González. Following its defeat, the CP fell into disarray, and in December Manuel Fraga, the leader of the AP, resigned.

In January 1989 Fraga returned to the leadership of the AP, which was relaunched as the Partido Popular (PP) and which was subsequently joined by Democracia Cristiana and the Partido Liberal. The unity of the PSOE was undermined by the establishment of a dissident faction and by the defection to Izquierda Unida (IU—United Left, an alliance comprising the Partido Comunista de España and other left-wing parties) of 100 PSOE members. Nevertheless, at the general election, held eight months early, in October, the PSOE was returned to power on a provisional basis, pending investigations into allegations of polling irregularities. After several months of controversy, the PSOE's representation in the Congreso de los Diputados (Congress of Deputies) was reduced to 175 of the 350 seats, the PP holding 107 seats. The PSOE, however, was able to retain a majority by subsequently entering into a tactical alliance with the CDS, the Catalan nationalist Convergència i Unió (CiU) and the Euzko Alderdi Jeltzalea-Partido Nacionalista Vasco (EAJ-PNV—the Basque Nationalist Party).

At the general election in June 1993 the PSOE did not obtain an absolute majority in the Congreso de los Diputados, and negotiations with CiU and the EAJ-PNV failed to result in a coalition agreement. In July, therefore, González commenced his fourth term as Prime Minister, at the head of a minority administration. With the Spanish economy in recession González appealed for support for drastic measures to address the crisis. In November, however, thousands of protesters demonstrated against the Government's economic policies. Controversial labour legislation was approved by the Congreso in March 1994.

In 1994–95 the Government came under increasing pressure over suggestions that it had been involved in the establishment of the Grupos Antiterroristas de Liberación (GAL), a counter-terrorist grouping which had been formed in 1983 with the aim of combating ETA. It was alleged that members of the Ertzaintza (Basque Country police force) had given support to the organization, which was suspected of responsibility for the murders of 27 ETA members exiled in France. Investigations into the affair had begun in 1988, and in 1991 a senior police officer and an accomplice were convicted of organizing the groups of mercenaries. In December 1994, following further questioning of the pair and the reopening of the case, Julián Sancristóbal, a former director-general of state security in the Ministry of the Interior, was arrested on suspicion of financing and assisting GAL. The Prime Minister denied that the Government had been connected in any way with the so-called 'dirty war' of the 1980s against ETA. However, in February 1995 Baltasar Garzón, an investigating judge at the National Court, ordered the arrest of former Secretary of State for Security Rafael Vera on suspicion of involvement in the kidnapping in 1983 of Segundo Marey, a French business executive mistaken for an ETA member, and of misuse of public funds. Concluding that GAL had been established and financed by the Ministry of the Interior, Garzón indicted a total of 14 former officials, including Vera and Sancristóbal. Garzón's final report into the origins and financing of GAL implicated González along with the former Deputy Prime Minister and Minister of Defence, Narcís Serra, the Minister of the Interior during 1982–88, José Barrionuevo, and other PSOE officials.

In September 1995 Judge Eduardo Móner was appointed by the Supreme Court to examine the allegations against the Prime Minister and the other senior politicians; Sancristóbal, Vera and Barrionuevo were subsequently charged with misuse of public funds, while Barrionuevo was also charged with illegal detention and association with an armed group. However, Móner reported that he had found no evidence linking González to the activities of the death squads, while Serra was also exonerated. Móner concluded his inquiry into the abduction of Marey in April 1997, and in September the Supreme Court confirmed that 12 defendants were to stand trial. At the conclusion of the trial in July 1998, Barrionuevo, Vera and Sancristóbal were found guilty of kidnapping and misappropriation of public funds; each received a prison sentence of 10 years. The sentences of the other nine defendants ranged from two to nine years. A further trial began in September 2001, with González among some 100 witnesses called upon to testify. In January 2002 Barrionuevo was absolved of the charge of misappropriation of funds; however, Vera was sentenced to seven years' imprisonment and barred from holding public office for 18 years.

The Partido Popular in power

At an early general election in March 1996, the PP took 156 of the 350 seats in the Congreso de los Diputados, thus falling short of an outright majority. The PSOE, its reputation severely damaged by the ongoing investigation into the GAL affair, won 141 seats, while IU took 21 and CiU 16. The King invited José María Aznar, the President of the PP, to form a government. Having secured the support of CiU, of the five EAJ-PNV deputies and of the four representatives of Coalición Canaria (CC), the new Prime Minister's investiture finally took place in early May. (However, the EAJ-PNV abandoned its pact with the Government in 1997, before withdrawing its support entirely in 1999.)

One of the new administration's main priorities was the reduction of the budget deficit. Several aspects of the Government's policies, however, aroused intense opposition. In December 1996 civil servants took part in a 24-hour strike to protest against the Government's imposition of a pay freeze, while in February 1997 a two-week strike by truck drivers, in support of improved working conditions, caused severe disruption and led to the closure of the country's road borders. In early 1998 one miner died during violent protests in northern Spain, where the coal-miners of Asturias were demonstrating against proposed job losses (the Government having been obliged to plan decreases in coal output in order to comply with European Union (EU, see p. 281) directives regarding reductions in subsidies to state-owned industries).

The ruling party's strong performance at the legislative election of March 2000 was largely attributed to the Government's record of economic success (in particular its reduction of the unemployment rate). In the lower house the PP won 183 of the 350 seats, thus securing an absolute majority. The PSOE's representation was reduced to 125 seats, while IU, which had conducted a joint campaign with the PSOE, suffered a sharp decline in support, losing 13 of its 21 seats in the Congreso de los Diputados. Aznar was sworn in for a second term of office in April, having secured the support of CiU and CC. Joaquín

Almunia resigned as leader of the PSOE immediately after the election and was replaced by José Luis Rodríguez Zapatero, who excluded left-wingers from the new national executive committee, declaring his intention to modernize the party in order to form an effective opposition.

In June 2002 the leading trade unions organized the first general strike since 1988 in protest at changed to employment law, including the imposition of reforms to unemployment subsidies by decree. Revised legislation, which annulled the main provisions of the controversial decree, was approved by the Congreso de los Diputados in October.

In November 2002 the Aznar Government was faced with a serious crisis following the sinking of the Liberian-registered, Greek-owned oil tanker *Prestige* 240 km off the coast of Galicia. The vessel, whose hull had ruptured and was leaking oil, had been refused landfall and had been towed out to sea, where it split in two and sank six days later. An estimated 25,000 metric tons of the vessel's 77,000-ton capacity was believed to have been released into the sea, much of which soon reached the Galician coast, requiring the imposition of a prohibition of fishing in that area. Massive clean-up operations were launched, mostly by environmental groups and by the local population; a significant lack of aid from the Spanish military aroused widespread public discontent. Demonstrations were attended by some 150,000 people in Santiago de Compostela and by around 100,000 people in Vigo, at which protesters condemned the handling of the disaster by both the regional and national PP authorities and demanded the resignation of Aznar. A local commission launched by the regional Government of Galicia met with obstruction from the central Government, which also delayed the setting up of a national investigation. Meanwhile, the oil slicks spread to the Basque region, and also reached the coastlines of France and Portugal.

Amid the increasing likelihood of US-led military action in Iraq in early 2003, Aznar was one of eight European leaders to sign a declaration in January in support of US moves towards an ultimatum. Public opinion, however, already swayed against the PP by the Government's handling of the *Prestige* disaster, was, in general, strongly against military action, with 3m. people participating in anti-war demonstrations in February, and opinion polls suggesting that at least 80% of the population was against the launching of an armed conflict. A summit meeting hosted in the Azores, Portugal, in March led to a joint declaration by Aznar, the British Prime Minister, Tony Blair, and the US President, George W. Bush, condemning the regime of Saddam Hussein and expressing support for military action. The subsequent announcement by the USA of its intention to act, if need be, without international ratification received the PP Government's concerted support. In July, despite the level of popular feeling against the war (which had commenced on 20 March) and the dissent of all the opposition parties, the Government committed 1,300 troops to the peace-keeping force. Opinion polls reported that an estimated 90% of the Spanish population believed that the instigation of armed conflict in Iraq by the US-led coalition had been a mistake, and Zapatero, the leader of the PSOE, stated that if his party won the general election in March 2004, Spanish troops would be withdrawn from Iraq.

The Madrid bombings; the first Zapatero Government

On 11 March 2004, three days before the general election, 10 bombs exploded in four commuter trains in Madrid, killing 191 people and injuring more than 1,500. The Government immediately indicated that ETA was the principal suspect; however, Batasuna, ETA's political wing, was swift to condemn the attacks. Campaigning for the election was suspended, and three days of national mourning were declared. Suspicion as to who was responsible for the bombings increasingly came to rest on Islamist militants; in the days following the attacks, the authorities arrested three Moroccans, who were suspected of having links to the al-Qa'ida organization of the Saudi-born militant Islamist Osama bin Laden (who was killed by US forces in May 2011) and to the May 2003 suicide bombings in Casablanca, Morocco.

Opinion polls conducted before the attacks had widely predicted that the PP would win the general election with a reduced majority. However, the bombings became the central issue in the election, which took place as scheduled on 14 March 2004. The emergence of evidence suggesting that Islamists had perpetrated the attacks prompted criticism of the Government for its premature response in blaming ETA and its unwillingness to consider other possibilities. In the event, the PSOE secured an unexpected victory in the elections to the Congreso de los

Diputados, winning 164 seats, while the PP, led by the Deputy Prime Minister, Mariano Rajoy, won 148 seats. The PP retained its majority in the Senado (Senate), however, emerging with a total of 126 seats compared to the PSOE's 111. The election turn-out, at 77.2%, was nine percentage points higher than in 2000. On assuming office Zapatero announced that Spanish troops would be withdrawn from Iraq as quickly as possible; the withdrawal was completed by the end of May. Zapatero declined to form a coalition government, opting rather for the PSOE to make pacts with smaller parties in the two legislative chambers, effectively isolating the PP.

On 2 April 2004, meanwhile, a bomb of the same type discovered on the trains involved in the earlier Madrid attacks was defused on the railway line between Madrid and Seville (Sevilla). The following day seven men who were suspected of involvement in the bombings apparently blew themselves up, killing one police officer, during a police raid on an apartment in Leganés, a suburb of Madrid; Abdelmajid Farkhet, the man suspected of organizing the 11 March attacks, was among the dead. In May a parliamentary commission of inquiry into the train bombings was established. Former Prime Minister Aznar, questioned by the commission in November, maintained that ETA was linked to the Islamist militants suspected of carrying out the bomb attacks. Zapatero, who subsequently appeared before the commission, alleged that the PP administration had deleted all government computer records relating to the train bombings before leaving office. In March 2005 the preliminary findings of the commission, supported by all the parliamentary groups except the PP, were published. Recommendations included an increase in the implementation of security measures.

Despite opposition from leaders of the Roman Catholic church, legislation permitting marriage between couples of the same sex was adopted by the Senado in June 2005, following its approval by the Congreso de los Diputados in April. In November new defence legislation was passed that required any deployment of Spanish troops abroad to be approved by the Cortes. In February 2006 Spain's highest consultative body, the Council of State, voted to support the Government's proposed amendments to the Constitution, that included the alteration of the law of royal succession, removing the preference for a male heir, a restructuring of the Senado and an increase in the power of the Autonomous Communities in the upper house; also to be addressed was the contentious issue of whether the Autonomous Communities should be regarded as 'nations'.

During 2007 a principal topic of political debate concerned proposals, presented personally by Zapatero, to introduce a 'law on historic memory' that was intended to provide formal recognition to those who had lost their lives during and immediately before the civil war, and to those who had been the victims of political repression under the Franco regime. The draft legislation was criticized by the PP, which regarded the proposals as potentially socially divisive and unwarranted, and by human rights groups and the Catalan nationalist allies of the Government, the Esquerra Republicana de Catalunya (ERC), which considered the measures to be insufficiently rigorous. None the less, the Congreso de los Diputados approved the legislation in October. Public funds were to be provided to locate mass graves, and to identify, exhume and re-bury the dead. Trials on political charges conducted during the period of Franco's rule were to be declared illegitimate (sentences passed were not, however, to be repealed outright), while political rallies at Franco's place of burial were to be prohibited and public monuments to Franco and his regime were to be removed. In November 2008, following a request by surviving relatives and representatives of the victims, the investigating judge Baltasar Garzón launched a criminal investigation into the disappearance of tens of thousands of Spaniards during the civil war and Franco's dictatorship, and ordered the exhumation of several mass graves. Garzón claimed jurisdiction on the grounds that the crimes committed during this period constituted 'crimes against humanity' rather than political crimes, and were consequently not covered by an amnesty law of 1977 nor by any statute of limitations. However, the National Court ruled that Garzón did not have the authority to launch such an investigation and that any inquiries must be carried out by courts in the regions where the crimes were committed. It was also announced that some 500,000 descendants of those Spaniards who fled the country during the civil war and Franco's rule would be permitted to apply for Spanish citizenship.

Meanwhile, in February 2007 the trial began at the National Court in Madrid of 29 men suspected of involvement of the Madrid train bombings in March 2004—mostly Moroccan nationals, but including three Spanish citizens who had supplied the explosives. In October a total of 21 of the defendants were convicted of the attacks, while seven were acquitted, including an Egyptian citizen, Rabei Osman el-Sayed Ahmed, who had been accused of organizing the attacks. (Charges had been dropped against the remaining suspect, on grounds of lack of evidence.) Three defendants were sentenced to the equivalent of the maximum permissible prison term of 40 years, having been found guilty of murdering 191 people, procuring two involuntary abortions (as two of those killed in the attacks were pregnant women) and conspiring to cause the deaths of the 1,856 people injured in the attacks. In July 2008 four of the 21 convicts had their sentences overturned by the Supreme Court. A further principal suspect in the attacks, Hicham Ahmidan, was arrested in January 2008 in Morocco; in December he was sentenced to 10 years' imprisonment by a court in that country, having been convicted of providing logistical support to the bombers.

The second Zapatero Government

At the general election held on 9 March 2008, both the PSOE and PP increased their share of the votes cast, and their representation in the Congreso de los Diputados, to 43.6% and 169 seats, and to 40.1% and 154 seats, respectively. The IU and the ERC retained two and three seats, respectively, while CiU won 10 seats and the EAJ-PNV six. Four other parties, mostly representing regional interests, won seats in the chamber. As previously, no party controlled an overall majority of seats. The PP remained the largest faction in the Senado, with 98 of the directly elected seats, and a further 24 appointed seats. The PSOE obtained 79 directly elected seats, and held 14 appointees. Zapatero was confirmed as Prime Minister in April and the appointment of a new Government, including the formation of two new ministries—of Equality and of Science and Innovation—was announced later in the month. The new administration was notable for the fact that, excluding the premiership, women accounted for exactly one-half of the ministerial appointments.

Zapatero's new Government was faced with growing problems precipitated by the global economic slowdown. In the year to March 2009 unemployment in the country nearly doubled as some 2m. people lost their jobs and the construction industry collapsed. In response, the Government introduced stimulus plans during 2009 and an incentive aimed at unemployed immigrants in Spain, under the terms of which they could receive a lump sum of some €10,000 if they returned to their home countries and agreed not to return to Spain to seek work for at least three years.

The Government came into renewed conflict with the Roman Catholic Church and the conservative opposition in 2009 following the approval in May of planned reforms to the law on abortion. In October a demonstration, attended by more than 1m. people according to some reports, took place in Madrid in protest at the proposed measures, which would, *inter alia*, allow abortion on demand until the 14th week of pregnancy and allow girls over the age of 16 years to obtain an abortion without parental consent. (Existing legislation provided for abortion only in cases of rape, foetal malformation or potential danger to a woman's physical or mental health, although the latter provision was reported to be interpreted liberally in practice.) The draft legislation was approved by the Congreso de los Diputados in December and by the Senado in February 2010.

In April 2010 an investigating judge at the Supreme Court, Luciano Varela, ordered Garzón to stand trial on a charge of knowingly exceeding his judicial authority by investigating, in 2008, the disappearances that had occurred under Franco, despite being prohibited by the 1977 amnesty law. Varela's indictment was based on allegations brought by a little-known right-wing anti-corruption organization, Manos Limpias (Clean Hands), supported by Falange Española de las JONS, a successor grouping to the official political movement of the Franco regime. An estimated 60,000 people demonstrated in Madrid in support of Garzón (who denied all the allegations against him), while similar marches were held in other Spanish cities. In March Zapatero had publicly praised the investigating judge's actions in the fight against Basque terrorism, leading the opposition to criticize the Prime Minister for attempting to influence the Supreme Court's decision. In March 2011 Garzón filed a case at the European Court of Human Rights challenging his prosecution on the grounds that it violated Spain's obligations under the European Convention on Human Rights, in particular the obligation to protect judicial independence. In April another investigating judge at the Supreme Court, Alberto Jorge Barreiro, announced that Garzón would be tried on charges of perverting the course of justice for ordering recordings of conversations between imprisoned suspects and their lawyers while investigating a corruption scandal involving members of the PP in 2009. In February 2012 Garzón was found guilty of illegally ordering the recordings and received an 11-year ban from the legal profession. More significantly, however, was the ruling in the same month that cleared Garzón of all charges relating to his investigation of Franco-era human rights violations. The case had been regarded as politically motivated by Garzón's supporters, several thousand of whom had marched to show their support for him prior to the verdict.

Austerity measures and the election of Rajoy

The Government was subjected to renewed political pressure arising from the economic crisis in the first half of 2010, suffering a further decline in public approval as it attempted to address the country's acutely high public deficit. In May, amid fears that Spain would require financial assistance from the EU and the IMF to avoid defaulting on its sovereign debt (following a similar package of loans to Greece agreed earlier in the month), Zapatero announced the introduction of emergency legislation intended to reduce the deficit from 11.2% of gross domestic product (GDP) in 2009 to 6% in 2011. The proposed measures, which included a 5% reduction in public sector salaries, were approved in the Congreso de los Diputados by a margin of just one vote, indicating the fragility of parliamentary support for the PSOE administration. During 2010 the Government declared its intention to bring to a conclusion a long-running debate over the liberalization of labour market laws, which included a reduction in severance pay for workers on permanent contracts, the relaxation of conditions for dismissal, and measures intended to discourage the use of temporary contracts. The PP and the other centre-right parties did not support the reforms, which they claimed were insufficient, while the measures were opposed by the trade unions and the far-left parties. In September the trade unions organized a one-day general strike, the first since 2002 and the first against Zapatero's Government. Fears that the Government might be unable to complete its parliamentary term (which was due to expire in March 2012) were allayed in October 2010 when it concluded agreements with the EAJ-PNV and CC, thus ensuring a small majority in the Congreso de los Diputados and securing sufficient support for the 2011 budget. As part of the deal with the EAJ-PNV, the further devolution of powers from the central Government to the Basque regional administration (under the terms of the region's Statute of Autonomy) was agreed.

In April 2011 Zapatero sought to end speculation about his future leadership by announcing that he did not intend to seek a third term as Prime Minister. The PSOE suffered significant losses at the regional and local elections in May 2011, when the PP won control of 11 of the 13 regions in which voting took place. The PSOE lost elections in some areas, including Barcelona and the region of Castilla-La Mancha, that it had governed continuously for more than 30 years. The result was widely regarded as an expression of dissatisfaction with the Government's handling of the economic crisis. The poll was held amid protests, which began in Madrid in May and spread to many other Spanish cities, by groups of predominantly young people calling themselves 'los indignados' (the indignant ones). The protesters, who claimed to have no political affiliation, condemned the effects of the economic crisis, particularly youth unemployment and alleged political corruption, urging electors to cast blank votes. None the less, further austerity measures were approved during mid-2011, including an increase in the retirement age (from 65 to 67), increased electricity prices, the reintroduction of a so-called wealth tax and a constitutional amendment limiting the budget deficit to 0.4% of GDP from 2020. In July Alfredo Pérez Rubalcaba was named as the PSOE's prime ministerial candidate when the Government announced that in order to enable greater economic and political certainty an early general election would take place on 20 November. Opinion polls indicated that, even under a new leader, the PSOE was likely to suffer a heavy defeat by Rajoy's PP at the election.

At the election in November 2011 the PP, as widely predicted, won a convincing victory, with 44.6% of the votes cast and 186 seats in the Congreso de los Diputados. The PSOE secured just 28.7% of the votes and 110 seats in its worst result in 30 years. Of the 208 directly elected seats in the Senado the PP won 134 and the PSOE secured just 48. Mariano Rajoy was confirmed as Prime Minister and sworn in on 21 December; he subsequently appointed a 14-member cabinet, in which the former head of

international investment bank Lehman Brothers in Spain, Luis de Guindos Jurado, assumed the crucial economy portfolio. The new Government announced immediate reductions in public expenditure totalling €8,900m., together with plans to reform the banking system and to increase taxes on property and income.

Unresolved issues from Spain's recent history continued to feature in the social and political life of the country. A report published at the end of 2011 by a commission established under the Zapatero administration as part of the 'law on historic memory' made a series of recommendations concerning the memorial to the civil war and Franco's remains. These included the recommendation that Franco should not be buried at the memorial in the Valle de los Caídos (Valley of the Fallen), near Madrid, alongside some 34,000 victims of the war, as he had not been killed in the conflict, but had died of natural causes at an advanced age. It was suggested that the dictator's remains should be exhumed and handed over to his family. The previous Government had already passed legislation prohibiting public rallies at the site, which had become a focal point for gatherings by far-right groups. Moreover, in April 2012 a Spanish nun became the first person to appear in court in connection with the alleged theft of newborn babies, a practice believed to have been carried out on a wide scale during the Franco era, when babies were alleged to have been taken from parents thought to have left-wing sympathies and placed with those loyal to Franco.

Members of Spain's royal family were unusually the subject of criticism by many observers in early 2012, owing to a series of incidents which appeared to some to show them as detached from the majority of the Spanish people. In February King Juan Carlos' son-in-law, Iñaki Urdangarin, the Duke of Palma, appeared in court in connection with the misappropriation of public money by an organization under his management that arranged sporting and other events for regional governments. He was suspended from official royal engagements in December 2012 and in February 2013 was questioned at a legal inquest into the affair, although he was not formally charged; his wife, King Juan Carlos' daughter, Princess Cristina, was implicated, as she was a board member of the organization, and was to give evidence in the case in April. In April 2012 the King apologized to the Spanish people in a televised statement, following widespread criticism of his decision to travel to Botswana on a private elephant hunting trip. Many commentators expressed the view that such extravagant pursuits were insensitive at a time of economic crisis in Spain, in addition to being distasteful to many Spaniards. In July the conservation organization, WWF, announced the removal of the King from the role of Honorary President of the organization in Spain, following the receipt of a petition signed by some 80,000 WWF members demanding his removal.

Recent developments: the EU bail-out of the banking sector

Discontent with the impact of the ongoing austerity measures continued to prompt large-scale demonstrations and protest marches during early 2012, particularly by students and young people. In March the trade unions organized a one-day general strike to protest against the introduction of labour reforms approved in the previous year. Meanwhile, the proposed budget for 2012, announced in March (following an agreement by the Government to EU demands that the budget deficit in 2012 would not exceed 5.3% of GDP, relaxed from a target of 4.4%), included stringent government spending cuts and tax increases for companies and individuals. Following the revelation that Spain's public debt had reached 87% of GDP (compared with 69% in 2011), Rajoy announced a further package of measures in April, including additional reductions in health and education expenditure of some €10,000m. and new powers to intervene in the finances of the regions. Foreign minister José Manuel García-Margallo observed that Spain was undergoing 'a crisis of enormous proportions'. The country's credit rating was successively downgraded, further undermining investor confidence and sending 10-year bonds above the level regarded as sustainable. The collapse and subsequent nationalization of Spain's fourth largest bank, Bankia, led the Government in June to request emergency funding from the EU to recapitalize the banking sector. On 20 July eurozone finance ministers formally approved financial assistance of €100,000m. to be disbursed by the end of 2013, with an initial €30,000m. released by the end of that month. Under the terms of the loan Spain was required to restructure its banking sector, improving regulation and governance, and was given an additional year to meet its budget deficit target. However, the country's failure to meet its target for 2012, coupled with record unemployment of 26% (and 55% for 16–24 year olds) at the end of 2012, led to increasing speculation that the Government might seek a sovereign bail-out from the European Central Bank and IMF.

Demonstrations persisted throughout 2012 and into 2013 as ongoing and intensifying austerity measures continued to cause hardship for many Spaniards. In February 2013, during some of the largest protests of the crisis, demonstrators demanded changes to the stringent repossession laws that had resulted in more than 400,000 people losing their homes since 2008.

Meanwhile, allegations of corruption against several high-profile public figures, including senior members of the PP, fuelled popular discontent in early 2013. Most notable among these was the former treasurer of the PP, Luis Bárcenas, who was accused of operating a clandestine Swiss bank account containing some €22m. He denied the allegations.

The Autonomous Communities

Following the promulgation of the 1978 Constitution, Spain's historic regions were swift to take advantage of the new provisions for self-government. Autonomous regional parliaments were established in the Basque Country (País Vasco/Euskadi) and in Catalonia (Cataluña/Catalunya) in 1980. The parliaments of Galicia and Andalucía were established in October 1981 and May 1982, respectively, and the remaining 13 legislative assemblies of the Autonomous Communities (Comunidades Autónomas) were elected in May 1983.

In September 2005 the Catalan Parliament overwhelmingly approved the draft of a revised Statute of Autonomy, to replace the existing document which had been in force since 1979. The proposed statute provoked considerable controversy elsewhere in the country over its definition of Catalonia as a 'nation' and its provision for greater fiscal and judicial independence. In March 2006 the Congreso de los Diputados approved a revised version of the statute that significantly reduced the extent of financial independence that would be granted to Catalonia, despite the opposition of ERC, which favoured full independence, and the PP, which claimed that the statute violated the Constitution. The new Statute of Autonomy was approved by 73.2% of voters in a referendum held in Catalonia in June, and came into force in August. Meanwhile, in July the PP submitted an appeal to the Constitutional Court alleging that a number of the statute's articles were unconstitutional, in particular the definition of Catalonia as a 'nation', the privileged status afforded to the Catalan language and the provisions for judicial independence. In its ruling of July 2010 the Constitutional Court upheld the majority of the statute, although it declared unconstitutional or ordered the reinterpretation of some 41 articles; notably, it allowed the use of the term 'nation' to refer to the region's historical and cultural identity but ruled that it could have no constitutional meaning. On the following day more than 1m. people attended a demonstration in Barcelona in favour of Catalan autonomy and against the court's decision. At the election to the Catalan Parliament held in November, the outgoing coalition Government led by the Partit dels Socialistes de Catalunya (PSC—Socialist Party of Catalonia, allied to the PSOE) suffered a heavy defeat winning just 28 of the 135 seats. CiU increased its standing as the largest party in the legislature, taking 62 seats. Artur Mas, the leader of CiU, was subsequently inaugurated as President of the Generalitat (the regional administration) at the head of a minority CiU Government. The economic crisis led to increased tensions between the regional government and the administration in Madrid, particularly when appeals for a new fiscal pact allowing Catalonia greater control over taxation and expenditure in the region were rejected by Prime Minister Rajoy during 2012. As a relatively economically active region of Spain, Catalonia was required to contribute a disproportionate amount in taxation to the central Government, a situation that appeared likely to foster resentment and separatists sympathies. A pro-independence rally in Barcelona was attended by some 1.5m. people in September. Rajoy accused Mas of exploiting the country's economic situation to increase nationalist sentiment in Catalonia. In response, Mas called an early election, which took place in November. The CiU remained the largest party in the Catalan Parliament, although with reduced representation at 50 seats, while the separatist ERC more than doubled its parliamentary standing to 21 seats. However, an increase in the number of seats garnered by anti-independence parties appeared to provide evidence of increased polarization over the issue within Catalan society. The ERC

pledged to work with the new minority administration led by Mas, with the aim of holding a referendum on Catalan independence by 2014. The central Government warned that any such referendum would be illegal under the terms of the Constitution.

Several other autonomous communities, including Aragón, the Balearic Islands (Illes Balears), the Canary Islands (Canarias), Castilla-La Mancha and Galicia, began proceedings to reform their statutes of autonomy in 2005 and 2006. In April 2006 a new statute for the Valencia region entered into force, which, *inter alia*, defined Valencia as an 'historic nationality' (a term traditionally applied to Catalonia, the Basque Country and Galicia), made Valencian an official language and increased judicial and tax-raising independence. A new statute for Andalucía, which also defined the region as an 'historic nationality', took effect in March 2007, after being approved by 87% of the participating electorate in a referendum in February.

The conflict in the Basque region

The violent Basque separatist organization, ETA, founded in 1959 as a radical offshoot of the EAJ-PNV, came to increased prominence during the late 1960s. Having claimed its first victim, a civil guard, in 1968, the group achieved its most high-profile success in 1973 with the assassination of Adm. Carrero Blanco. Despite the establishment of the Basque Country Autonomous Community in 1979, ETA continued to demand a sovereign state comprising the three provinces of the Basque Country together with Navarre (Navarra—which was established as a separate Autonomous Community in 1982) and the historic Basque provinces of south-west France. In 1980 alone a total of 92 murders was attributed to the group. Despite bomb attacks in Bilbao in February 1983 and Madrid in July 1986, the central Government maintained its offer of social reintegration, instigated in mid-1984, to former ETA members.

The explosion in June 1987 of a bomb beneath a crowded Barcelona supermarket, which killed 21 and injured 45, was the most devastating attack committed by the organization, prompting Herri Batasuna (HB), ETA's political wing, to issue an unprecedented statement criticizing the attack. Co-operation with the authorities of France and Algeria (where numerous ETA members were discovered to be living) was strengthened, and in October the French police arrested 67 Basque suspects. In December five children were among the 12 killed in a bomb attack on the married quarters of a Civil Guard barracks in Zaragoza, which provoked a further public outcry and prompted the Government to break off negotiations with ETA. In January 1988, after protracted negotiations, six parties (all of those represented in the Basque Parliament except HB) signed the Ajuria Enea Pact, rejecting terrorism as a means of determining the region's future and in the following year ETA declared a unilateral truce in an effort to reopen negotiations with the Government. Subsequent discussions between representatives of the Government and of ETA quickly collapsed. A resolution declaring the right of the Basque people to self-determination was approved by the Basque Parliament in February 1990.

During the early and mid-1990s the authorities achieved considerable success in their counter-terrorist activities against ETA, particularly with increased co-operation from France. In July 1992 ETA's offer of a truce (to coincide with the forthcoming Olympic Games in Barcelona), in return for the reopening of dialogue, was rebuffed by the Government, which continued to insist upon the group's permanent renunciation of violence. Between then and February 1993 (when a major arsenal was discovered in France and ETA's operational head was captured) more than 500 ETA suspects were arrested. However, hopes of thereby terminating ETA's campaign of violence were ended in June by two car bomb explosions (one of which killed seven people) in Madrid.

Several senior ETA leaders were captured in late 1994 and in mid-1995, but attacks continued. In January 1995 Gregorio Ordóñez, a member of the Basque Parliament and the PP candidate for the mayoralty of San Sebastián at the forthcoming municipal elections, was shot dead. In April 1995 Aznar, leader of the opposition PP, narrowly survived a car-bomb attempt on his life in Madrid, which injured 19 others. In August the authorities announced that a plot to assassinate King Juan Carlos had been foiled. Successive murders of politicians in early 1996 provoked a public outcry.

In July 1996, following a brief truce, ETA renewed its bombing campaign, this time targeting the tourism industry. A resurgence of violence in 1997 culminated in the abduction in July of Miguel Angel Blanco, a PP councillor in the Basque town of

Ermua. ETA issued an ultimatum that prisoners belonging to the separatist organization be transferred to gaols in the Basque Country. Despite numerous appeals, including a message from the Pope, Blanco was duly shot upon the expiry of ETA's 48-hour deadline. His death provoked an unprecedented display of public outrage. In the largest demonstration since the attempted military coup of 1981, millions of Spaniards took to the streets, including Prime Minister Aznar, who led a protest march in Madrid. The Prime Minister vowed to intensify the Government's campaign against ETA, while urging (along with the moderate Basque parties) the isolation of HB.

In December 1997 the 23 members of the collective leadership of HB were each sentenced to seven years' imprisonment for collaborating with an armed group. In a significant development, for the first time the direct relationship between ETA and HB, which continued to claim to be independent of the terrorist organization, was recognized by the judiciary. The 23 members were released in July 1999, when their imprisonment was ruled unconstitutional. Meanwhile, in early 1998 a new HB leadership was elected, pledging to continue with the policies of its predecessors.

ETA declares a cease-fire

In September 1998, apparently attempting to pre-empt any ban on its activities and while still declining to renounce the use of violence, HB announced that it was to contest the forthcoming elections as Euskal Herritarrok (EH). In the same month both the PP and the opposition PSOE expressed reservations at the conclusion of an agreement (the Lizarra Pact) by the EAJ-PNV, Eusko Alkartasuna (EA), HB and IU on proposals for unconditional discussions with ETA. Nevertheless, following several months of secret talks between representatives of the EAJ-PNV and HB, on 16 September ETA declared an indefinite truce. In a conciliatory gesture, the Prime Minister indicated his willingness to transfer a number of ETA convicts to prisons in the Basque Country.

At the Basque elections in October 1998, the EAJ-PNV again received the greatest support, while the PP supplanted the Partido Socialista de Euskadi-Euskadiko Ezkerra (PSE-EE, affiliated to the PSOE) as the party with the second largest representation in the regional parliament. With the support of EH, an entirely nationalist coalition Government was established, with Juan José Ibarretxe of the EAJ-PNV as Lehendakari (President).

In July 1999, for the first time, EH joined other Basque parties in signing a declaration rejecting the use of violence. In September, as the first anniversary of the truce approached, it was revealed that a total of 180 ETA prisoners had been released within the last year. However, in November, on the eve of the opening in Paris of the trial of 13 ETA defendants, the terrorist organization announced the end of the 14-month cease-fire. Hours before the expiry of the truce on 3 December, the EAJ-PNV, along with other signatories to the Lizarra Pact, invited EH to sign a document demanding full sovereignty for the Basque Country and criticizing the policies of both the Spanish and French Governments. In January 2000 the organization exploded two car bombs in Madrid, one of which killed an army officer. In the following month a Basque socialist politician and his bodyguard were killed in a bomb attack in Vitoria, prompting Ibarretxe to sever all links with EH, which subsequently announced that it was withdrawing from the Basque Parliament.

During 2000 some 100 members or collaborators of ETA were detained following covert Civil Guard operations; six command units were dismantled; and 12 members of ETA were successfully extradited. However, street disturbances in Basque cities continued to escalate, and 23 people were killed in ETA attacks. At early elections to the Basque Parliament held in May 2001 the electoral coalition of the EAJ-PNV and EA, led by Ibarretxe, retained power. Following the election, HB, which had lost support, elected new members to its leadership and declared that henceforth it was to be known as Batasuna (Unity). In October Ibarretxe announced his intention to hold a referendum on self-determination for the Basque Country, should the Government in Madrid continue to reject dialogue and ETA continue its campaign of violence. However, Prime Minister Aznar condemned the proposal as unconstitutional.

Batasuna is outlawed

In May 2002 the trial of Batasuna spokesman Arnaldo Otegi for vocal support of ETA was dismissed by the Supreme Court, to the consternation of the Government. After a number of ETA actions

during the EU summit in Seville in June, however, the Senado approved measures to outlaw political parties deemed to support terrorist organizations. The legislation was widely seen as targeting Batasuna, and, indeed, in August a parliamentary vote outlawed the party. In March 2003, the Supreme Court officially outlawed Batasuna. In June 2009 the European Court of Human Rights rejected an appeal by Batasuna against the decision to ban it, ruling that the Spanish authorities' actions were justified.

In January 2003 the Cortes approved anti-terrorist legislation, extending the maximum sentence for terrorist activities from 30 to 40 years, and in February the Basque-language newspaper *Euskaldunon Egunkaria* was shut down on the grounds of its alleged links with ETA. Prior to regional and municipal elections in May, the central Government banned some 1,500 candidates from standing, on the grounds of their alleged links with ETA.

Immediately following the PSOE's victory in the general election in March 2004, ETA expressed a desire to begin a dialogue with the new Government; this was rejected, however, by the incoming administration of Prime Minister Zapatero. Following the establishment of a Franco-Spanish anti-terrorism police force, a series of arrests of suspected members of ETA took place in France and Spain, including the capture of the alleged leader of the organization, Mikel 'Antza' Albizu Iriarte. Subsequently, Batasuna announced that it was prepared to negotiate. However, in late 2004 and January 2005 ETA exploded a series of bombs around Spain, and in February a car bomb injured over 40 people at a conference centre in Madrid, which was due to be visited by the King and President Vicente Fox of Mexico.

Meanwhile, in September 2003 Ibarretxe presented to the regional legislature his plan for shared sovereignty over the Basque Country, which proposed the 'free association' of the Basque Country with Spain, the creation of a separate judiciary and education system and the right of the Basque Country to conduct international relations. The proposals—known as the 'Ibarretxe Plan'—were not widely supported in the region, and were strongly criticized by Madrid-based politicians and media on the grounds that it would be in breach of the Constitution. In December 2004 the Basque Parliament voted in favour of the Ibarretxe Plan, with the last-minute support of Sozialista Abertzaleak, the perceived successor to Batasuna in the Parliament. In February 2005 the Plan was overwhelmingly rejected by the Congreso de los Diputados, although Zapatero declared that he was prepared to enter into negotiations on the status of the Basque Country within Spain. The Basque regional elections in April were seen as a gauge of the popularity of the Ibarretxe Plan. Prior to the poll, Aukera Guztiak, a radical nationalist party, was banned on the grounds of being close to ETA. However, a legal but hitherto inactive party, Euskal Herrialdeetako Alderdi Komunista (EHAK, also known as the Partido Comunista de las Tierras Vascas—PCTV), subsequently declared that it would contest the election with the same electoral programme as Aukera Guztiak and Batasuna. In the event, Ibarretxe's EAJ-PNV and EA coalition won a reduced majority of 29 seats, while EHAK won nine seats.

Further cease-fire and negotiations

In May 2005 the Congreso de los Diputados approved government plans to open negotiations with ETA, should the group agree to disarm. In March of the following year the group declared a 'permanent cease-fire', the first time in its history that it had taken such a step. It was speculated that the cease-fire had been prompted by the arrest of many of the organization's leaders. Zapatero responded by stating that the Government intended to enter into peace talks with the group. Despite these advances, during late 2006 ETA issued a number of statements indicating that it was not prepared to abandon violence or relinquish its weapons until the Basque Country became fully independent. In December, less than two weeks after the Government held its first formal meeting with ETA officials, a car bomb exploded at Barajas airport in Madrid, killing two people. Although ETA claimed responsibility for the attack, it stated that its permanent cease-fire remained intact; none the less, Zapatero suspended talks in response to the bombing. (In May 2010 the National Court convicted three members of ETA of perpetrating the attack and sentenced them to lengthy prison terms.) In June 2007 ETA announced an immediate end to its cease-fire, accusing the Government of 'pursuing detentions, torture and persecution' of its members

In September 2007, in response to a request by Judge Baltasar Garzón, some 23 senior members of Batasuna were arrested during a clandestine meeting of the organization in Segura.

Batasuna described the arrests as a 'declaration of war' by the Spanish authorities; the EAJ-PNV was also critical of the arrests. In December two Spanish civil guards were shot by suspected members of ETA in Southern France; one of the officers was killed and the other left in a coma. In February 2008, in response to a further request by Garzón, the National Court announced a three-year suspension of the operations of EHAK and another radical nationalist party, Acción Nacionalista Vasca (ANV), and in September the two parties were definitively outlawed by the Supreme Court.

In June 2008 the Basque Parliament voted in favour of a referendum, on the Basque Country's future political status, which was scheduled for 25 October (the anniversary of the signing of the region's statute of autonomy in 1979). However, in September the Constitutional Court ruled that the planned referendum was unconstitutional since it did not have central government approval. On 25 October an estimated 20,000 protesters marched in six towns in the Basque Country demanding that a referendum on Basque self-determination take place.

Violence by ETA continued throughout 2008, including fatal attacks against a civil guard barracks in Legutiano in May and a military academy in Santoña in September, and the assassination of the owner of a construction company in December. Francisco Javier López Peña, the suspected political leader of ETA, was arrested in Bordeaux, France, in May after some 20 years in hiding. In July it was announced by the Spanish authorities that the most active ETA cell, the 'Vizcaya commando', had been dismantled with the arrest of nine people, including its suspected leader, Arkaitz Goikoetxea, and in November Miguel de Garikoitz Aspiazu Rubina (alias 'Txeroki'), the suspected military leader of ETA, was arrested in the French Pyrenees. (In July 2011 Aspiazu was sentenced to 377 years' imprisonment for his role in ETA's violent campaign.) In December 2008 the French authorities arrested Aspiazu Rubina's apparent successor as military leader, Aitzol Iriondo, and only four months later, in April 2009, Iriondo's successor, Jurdan Martitegi, was also arrested in France.

Non-nationalist Basque government elected

At elections to the Basque Parliament in March 2009 the EAJ-PNV won 30 of the 75 seats. The PSE-EE secured 25 seats, while the PP took 13; the nationalist parties Aralar and EA won four seats and one seat, respectively, while Ezker Batua-Berdeak (affiliated to IU) and the non-nationalist Unión Progreso y Democracia (UPyD) each took one seat. No party with links to ETA managed to circumvent the legal prohibitions and contest the elections, with the result that the new legislature was free of any connection with the violent separatist movement for the first time since 1980. In May, with the EAJ-PNV unable to achieve the required absolute majority of 38 seats, the PSE-EE's Patxi López was elected Lehendakari with the support of the PP and UPyD, becoming the Basque Government's first non-nationalist leader. The new Government set out as its priority the fight against ETA.

Attacks by ETA continued in 2009, despite the recent arrests among its leadership. In June a police inspector involved in anti-terrorism operations was killed in a suburb of Bilbao by a car bomb, and in July, coinciding with the 50th anniversary of ETA's foundation, two bomb attacks occurred within 48 hours against the Civil Guard in Burgos and on Mallorca; the first left more than 50 people injured, while the second caused the deaths of two officers. In October Otegi (who had been released from gaol in August 2008) and a number of other senior members of Batasuna were arrested on suspicion of attempting to resurrect the illegal party. Meanwhile, Aitor Elizarán Aguilar, believed to be López Peña's successor as political leader of ETA, was arrested in a joint operation between Spanish and French police in Carnac, north-west France. Evidence of ETA's increasing use of Portugal as a base for its operations emerged in February 2010, when Portuguese police discovered a cache of explosives in a house in Obidos. The suspected military leader of ETA, Ibon Gogeaskoetxea, became the fourth successive head of the organization to be detained in 15 months when he was arrested in Normandy, France, in February. Gogeaskoetxea's suspected successor as military leader of ETA, Mikel Kabikoitz Carrera Sarobe (alias 'Ata'), was arrested in May along with his deputy in Bayonne, France. Sarobe and two co-defendants were tried in France for the shooting in France in 2007 of two Spanish civil guards; in April 2013 Sarobe was sentenced to life imprisonment, one co-defendant, Saioa Sánchez Iturregui, was sentenced to 28 years, while a third was acquitted of murder charges but sentenced for other offences for a period of 15 years. Gogeaskoetxea's brother,

Eneko Gogeaskoetxea Arronategui, was arrested in Cambridge, United Kingdom, in July 2011 on suspicion of involvement in numerous terrorist incidents, including the attempted assassination of King Juan Carlos in October 1997 at the opening of the Guggenheim Museum in Bilbao. Gogeaskoetxea's appeal against extradition from the United Kingdom to Spain was defeated in mid-2012.

On 5 September 2010 ETA declared a cease-fire, stating in a communiqué that it had decided some months previously not to carry out armed attacks and that it was committed to achieving an independent Basque Country by democratic means. The Basque and Spanish Governments immediately declared the group's announcement insufficient, since it did not amount to a permanent or verifiable renunciation of violence. It was widely believed that ETA's truce was in response not only to the recent weakening of its military capability, but also to political pressure from within the Basque separatist movement. On 10 January 2011 ETA declared a 'permanent and general' cease-fire that would be 'verifiable by the international community'. However, the Government maintained that the declaration did not go far enough, demanding that the group renounce violence unconditionally and that it take steps towards disarmament and dissolution. In February a new radical nationalist party, to be called Sortu, that explicitly rejected violence (including that of ETA), and which intended to contest the municipal elections scheduled for 22 May, was established. The Government cautiously welcomed the new party's foundation, but stressed that the courts would decide if the new party could legally be registered. The case was subsequently referred to the Supreme Court, which in March ruled that Sortu was a successor to the illegal Batasuna and, as such, could not be registered as a legal political party, although seven of the court's 16 judges disagreed with the ruling. In April former members of Sortu formed a coalition called Bildu. Initially, this was also banned by the Supreme Court, but the ban was lifted in the Constitutional Court, permitting Bildu to contest the May 2011 regional and local elections, at which it won seven of the 50 seats in the Navarre legislative assembly.

Following a meeting in San Sebastián attended by high-profile international figures, including former UN secretary-general Kofi Annan and former Irish Prime Minister Bertie Ahern, to discuss the cease-fire, ETA announced a 'definitive cessation of armed activity' on 20 October 2011. The organization appealed to the Governments of Spain and France to commence a process of dialogue on the political future of the Basque Country. The announcement followed the decimation of ETA's leadership through a succession of arrests, a lack of popular support for the organization within the Basque region (some 64% of Basques 'totally rejected' ETA, according to a poll conducted in 2011) and appeals to end violence, including from imprisoned members of ETA. It was reported that a total of 829 people had been killed by ETA since the start of its violent campaign.

The arrests of senior members and ex-members of the organization, many of whom were living abroad, continued during 2012, with a total of 24 suspects detained between January and October. The capture of high profile ETA activists culminated in the arrest of Izaskun Lesaka, believed to be the organization's military commander, in France in October, prompting speculation that the group would be unable to continue. ETA's request for negotiations with the Government had been refused in May, with the administration demanding that the group disband entirely. However, at elections to the Basque Parliament in October support for those representing pro-independence parties increased significantly. Although EAJ-PNV remained the largest group in the legislature with 27 seats, a newly enlarged version of the left-wing, separatist coalition, Bildu, called Euskal Herria Bildu (EHB) and led by Laura Mintegi, which included EA and Aralar, secured 21 seats (compared with just five seats for its constituent parties in the previous election). Both the PSE-EE and the PP lost seats, securing 16 and 10, respectively. The success of the nationalists in the election was expected to lead to renewed demands for a referendum on independence.

Foreign Affairs

Regional relations

Spanish ratification of the Treaty on European Union (the Maastricht Treaty) was completed in November 1992. A national referendum on the EU Treaty establishing a Constitution for Europe took place in Spain on 20 February 2005, with 76.2% of the votes cast being in favour of ratifying the treaty. The turnout, however, was equivalent to only 42.3% of the electorate. Following the rejection of this treaty by voters in France and the

Netherlands later that year, in December 2007 a new, amended treaty was signed in Lisbon, Portugal, and Spain ratified the resultant Treaty of Lisbon by parliamentary approval in July 2008. In March 2012 Spain, along with all EU members except the Czech Republic and the United Kingdom, agreed to a 'fiscal compact', the Treaty on Stability, Co-ordination and Governance, according to which members agreed to adopt binding legislation on balancing their budgets.

Spain continues to claim sovereignty over the neighbouring British dependency of Gibraltar (q.v.). In 1997 the United Kingdom rejected Spanish initiatives entailing joint sovereignty for up to 100 years prior to an eventual transfer of power to Spain. In December Spanish proposals that, following a period of joint sovereignty, Gibraltar become an Autonomous Community were similarly rebuffed by the British Government. In April 2000 Spain and the United Kingdom signed an agreement relating to the administrative status of Gibraltar. The territory's identity cards would henceforth be accepted by Spain as valid for travel within the EU. Furthermore, the agreement permitted the implementation of numerous EU directives, long obstructed by Spain, which had refused to recognize the Government of Gibraltar as a 'competent authority' in EU affairs. The Minister of Foreign Affairs, Josep Piqué, and his British counterpart, Jack Straw, held discussions in October 2001, during which they agreed to work towards resolving the dispute by December 2002. The issue of the right of Gibraltarians to vote on any agreement reached by the two Governments continued to impede the progress of the discussions, with Piqué warning the British Government that Spain would not accept the results of such a referendum. In January 2002 it was reported that the Spanish Government had agreed to modify its demand for outright sovereignty over the territory and to reconsider the option of shared sovereignty with the United Kingdom. In May, however, Aznar announced that Spain would never withdraw its territorial claim to Gibraltar. Negotiations continued, although a stalemate emerged when Spain rejected the British conditions for joint sovereignty—that it be permanent, that the military base would remain under British control, and that all changes be approved by a referendum put to the people of Gibraltar. In a referendum organized by the local administration of Gibraltar in November, which was not, however, recognized by the Spanish or British Governments, the electorate voted overwhelmingly against joint sovereignty with Spain.

In December 2004 the first of what was to be an annual tripartite meeting between the United Kingdom, Spain and Gibraltar was held in the United Kingdom, and it was announced that henceforth decisions on the territory's future must be agreed by all three parties. In early 2006 Spain opposed the inclusion of references to the right to self-determination of Gibraltarians in a proposed new constitution for Gibraltar. However, in March Straw assured the Spanish Government that the draft constitution would not change the current international status of the territory, nor affect Spanish rights over Gibraltar under the Treaty of Utrecht, and that independence would therefore only be a future option for Gibraltar with Spain's consent. The Constitution was approved in a referendum in the territory in December. While relations between Spain and the United Kingdom improved from 2006, tensions still remained. In January 2009 several Spanish opposition parliamentarians accused a Gibraltarian development company of 'illegal incursion' into Spanish waters, after it proposed to erect platforms on the seabed. In March the Spanish Government made a formal complaint to the British authorities over a proposed visit to the territory by a member of the British royal family, describing it as 'an affront' to Spain. None the less, in July 2009 Spain's foreign minister, Miguel Angel Moratinos, became the first Spanish minister to visit Gibraltar when he attended the annual ministerial meeting of the tripartite Forum of Dialogue. Reports in mid-2012 that the Spanish Government had requested police patrols to escort Spanish fishing vessels into Gibraltarian waters prompted a swift reaction from the administration in Gibraltar that stated that United Kingdom naval warships might be required to intervene if further breaches of sovereignty occurred.

Relations with Morocco have been dominated by the issues of sovereignty of the Spanish exclaves of Ceuta and Melilla, illegal immigration and drugs-trafficking, and by disputes over fishing rights. By 2000 the problems of illegal immigration (not only via Spanish North Africa but increasingly via the Canary Islands) had become a major political issue. In May, during a visit to Morocco, the Spanish Prime Minister confirmed that the recently implemented immigration law, one of the most liberal

within the EU, which had encouraged more than 82,000 illegal migrants to apply for Spanish residency permits since the beginning of the year, was to be reformed. Protests against the reforms were staged in Spanish North Africa as well as in mainland Spain. Relations were severely strained in July 2002 following the occupation of a small uninhabited islet near Ceuta, the Isla de Perejil (Laila), by 12 Moroccan soldiers. Spain lodged a formal protest against this action on 12 July, but Morocco refused to withdraw its men, claiming that Perejil had been a part of Morocco since independence in 1956. Spanish soldiers reoccupied the island on 17 July, and a subsequent US-mediated agreement between Spain and Morocco left the island unoccupied. Issues over the sovereignty of Ceuta and Melilla continued to be problematic, however, with Morocco reasserting its claims over the exclaves before the UN. Diplomatic relations between the two countries were re-established in February 2003. However, a visit to the disputed territories by King Juan Carlos in November 2007 provoked protests by the Moroccan Government.

Other external relations

In 1988 Spain and the USA renewed their bilateral defence agreement, permitting the USA's continued use of bases in Spain. In mid-2003, despite widespread public opposition, Spain sent 1,300 peace-keeping troops to Iraq to join the US-led coalition forces, and in October of that year pledged €250m. to the reconstruction process in Iraq. Following the election of the PSOE Government in March 2004, however, the withdrawal of the Spanish troops was completed by the end of May. The hasty withdrawal of troops, together with Zapatero's expressed hostility towards the US Administration of George W. Bush, contributed to a sharp deterioration of relations with the USA. Tensions subsequently eased, and in October 2011 Spain agreed to host four US naval vessels equipped with anti-missile weaponry, as part of NATO's missile defence system.

In November 1992 Spain dispatched a substantial contingent of troops to Bosnia and Herzegovina, the first Spanish soldiers to serve in a UN peace-keeping operation. Continuing to assume a greater international role, Spain contributed troops to the multinational force deployed in Albania in April 1997, to the NATO offensive against Yugoslavia in April 1999 and committed 1,200 ground troops to the international peace-keeping force deployed in Kosovo in June 1999. Spain was one of five EU countries that refused to recognize Kosovo's unilateral declaration of independence from Serbia in 2008, and in March 2009 it was announced that the remaining 600 Spanish troops in Kosovo would be withdrawn. The withdrawal was completed in September. In early 2013 Spain was contributing to a number of international peace-keeping missions, including the United Nations Interim Force in Lebanon, in which some 700 Spanish troops were serving; this mission was expected to end on late 2014. Spain began the withdrawal of its 1,400 troops serving with the International Security Assistance Force in Afghanistan in March 2013. Spain also contributed five aircraft to the international mission to impose a no-fly zone over Libya that commenced in March 2011.

From 1998, under Spanish law, persons accused of crimes against humanity, no matter where they had taken place, could be tried in a Spanish court. In the late 1990s criminal proceedings continued in Spain against former Argentine and Chilean officials of the military dictatorships of Argentina (1976–83) and of Chile (1979–90), during which numerous Spanish citizens had been killed. In November 1998, following the arrest in the United Kingdom of Gen. Augusto Pinochet and the instigation by Judge Baltasar Garzón of extradition proceedings against the former Chilean President, Chile's ambassador to Madrid was recalled for consultations. In October 1999 a British judge ruled that the former Chilean President could be extradited to Spain to answer 35 charges of torture and conspiracy. In March 2000, however, Pinochet was permitted to return to Chile from the United Kingdom, where he had remained under house arrest, extradition proceedings having been abandoned on medical grounds. In April 2005, following an indictment by Garzón, Adolfo Scilingo, an Argentine former army officer, was given a prison sentence of 640 years (although, under Spanish law, he would serve a maximum of 30 years) for crimes against humanity during the military rule of 1976–83 in Argentina; Scilingo was the first person to be convicted in Spain according to the principle of universal jurisdiction. In November 2009 legislation took effect which limited the power of the courts to prosecute crimes against humanity to those cases in which there was a clear link to Spain, or in which the alleged perpetrator was present on Spanish territory.

Spain's relations with Argentina were severely strained in April 2012 when the Argentinian Government announced that it was to nationalize its principal oil company YPF and had seized the assets of Spanish oil company Repsol, which held a majority stake in the business. The decision was strongly condemned by the Spanish Government, which warned Argentina of diplomatic and commercial reprisals for its actions. Similarly, in the following month the Bolivian Government seized the assets of a subsidiary of the Spanish utility company, Red Eléctrica de España, which was operating much of Bolivia's electricity network. Relations with that country became severely strained when the Bolivian Government announced in February 2013 that it was to nationalize the airports of La Paz, Santa Cruz and Cochabamba, owned by Spanish company Sabsa, which had been contracted to manage them until 2025. The Spanish Government stated that it 'deeply deplored' the actions, which would cause it to reconsider its relations with Bolivia.

CONSTITUTION AND GOVERNMENT

Under the Constitution approved in 1978, Spain is an hereditary monarchy, with the King as Head of State. He appoints the President of the Government (Prime Minister) and, on the latter's recommendation, other members of the Council of Ministers. Legislation is initiated for discussion in the Cortes (national assembly) in Madrid, in the Parliaments of the Autonomous Communities, or by popular petition. The King's actions in state affairs must receive the prior approval of the Cortes, to which the Government is responsible. The Council of State is the supreme consultative organ of the Government.

Legislative power is vested in the Cortes Generales, comprising two chambers, elected by direct universal adult suffrage for four years (subject to dissolution). The Congreso de los Diputados (Congress of Deputies) has 350 members, elected by proportional representation, and the Senado (Senate) has 208 directly elected members, plus 51 regional representatives, elected by the autonomous parliaments. A party can gain representation only if it obtains at least 3% of the votes.

Regional self-government was established in the 1978 Constitution. In October 1979 the statutes of the first of 17 Autonomous Communities were approved by referendum. The first Legislative Assemblies (Basque and Catalan) were elected in March 1980. The Galician Legislative Assembly was elected in October 1981 and that of Andalucía in May 1982. The remaining 13 were constituted in May 1983, thus completing the process of devolution. The regions possess varying degrees of autonomy. Each Legislative Assembly is elected for four years.

Spain comprises 50 provinces, each with its own Council (Diputación Provincial). The system of Civil Governors was replaced (by royal decree) in April 1997: a government sub-delegate is appointed by each Autonomous Community's government delegate.

REGIONAL AND INTERNATIONAL CO-OPERATION

Spain is a member of the European Union (EU, see p. 281), the Council of Europe (see p. 260) and the Organization for Security and Co-operation in Europe (OSCE, see p. 397).

Spain was admitted to the UN in 1955; the headquarters of the World Tourism Organization (see p. 185) is in Madrid. As a contracting party to the General Agreement on Tariffs and Trade, Spain joined the World Trade Organization (WTO, see p. 444) on its establishment in 1995. Spain is also a member of the North Atlantic Treaty Organization (NATO, see p. 380) and the Organisation for Economic Co-operation and Development (OECD, see p. 388).

ECONOMIC AFFAIRS

In 2011, according to estimates by the World Bank, Spain's gross national income (GNI), measured at average 2009–11 prices, was US $1,432,813m., equivalent to $30,990 per head (or $31,660 per head on an international purchasing-power parity basis). During 2002–11, it was estimated, the population increased at an average annual rate of 1.3%, while gross domestic product (GDP) per head increased, in real terms, by an average of 0.4% per year. Overall GDP increased, in real terms, at an average annual rate of 1.7% in 2002–11; real GDP contracted by 0.1% in 2010, but increased by 0.7% in 2011.

Agriculture (including forestry and fishing) contributed 2.7% of GDP in 2012 and engaged 4.4% of the employed labour force in that year. The principal crops are barley, wheat, sugar beet, vegetables, citrus fruits, grapes and olives; wine and olive oil are important products. The fishing industry is significant. The Spanish fishing fleet is one of the largest in the world. Agricultural GDP decreased at an average annual rate of 0.2% in 2002–10, according to the World Bank; it declined by 8.2% in 2005, mainly owing to severe drought, but increased by 5.8% in 2006. The GDP of the sector increased by 1.0% in 2009, but decreased by 1.3% in 2010.

Industry (including mining, manufacturing, power and construction) contributed 26.0% of GDP in 2012, and engaged 20.7% of the employed labour force in that year. According to the World Bank, industrial GDP decreased at an average annual rate of 0.2% in 2002–10; it declined by 9.9% in 2009 and by 1.9% in 2010.

The mining and quarrying industry provided less than 1.0% of GDP in 2004 and engaged 0.2% of the employed labour force in 2012. The principal minerals produced include cement, industrial sand and gravel, aluminium, copper, gold, silver and zinc. Although coal is plentiful in Spain, the production costs are relatively high.

Manufacturing contributed an estimated 13.3% of GDP in 2012 and engaged 12.6% of the employed labour force in that year. Important industries include passenger cars, shipbuilding, chemicals, steel, textiles and footwear. Manufacturing GDP contracted at an average annual rate of 1.7% in 2002–09, according to the World Bank; GDP of the sector declined by 2.6% in 2008, and by 13.5% in 2009.

The construction sector contributed 9.1% of GDP and engaged 6.6% of the employed labour force in 2012.

Energy (comprising mining and power) contributed an estimated 3.6% of GDP in 2012, and employed 1.3% of the labour force in that year. Energy is derived principally from petroleum, most of which is imported. In 2010 imports of mineral fuels and lubricants accounted for 18.5% of total import costs (petroleum and petroleum products accounted for 14.4%). Natural gas became an increasingly important fuel source in the late 1990s. Some natural gas requirements are obtained from the Bay of Biscay, the remainder is imported by pipeline from Algeria. Nuclear energy provided 20.9% of total electricity production in 2010, while coal provided 8.8% and hydroelectric power 14.3%. Wind and solar power together accounted for 9.1% of the electricity supply in 2007.

In 2012, the services sector accounted for an estimated 71.3% of GDP, while it engaged 74.9% of the employed labour force. The tourism industry makes an important contribution to the Spanish economy. In 2011 the number of tourist arrivals was estimated at 57.7m. (23.7% from the United Kingdom), and receipts from tourism totalled €55,594m. in 2012. Remittances from emigrants are also significant; in 2007 remittances amounted to €5.3m. According to the World Bank, the GDP of the services sector increased at an average annual rate of 2.7% in 2002–10; services GDP decreased by 1.2% in 2009, but increased by 0.8% in 2010.

In 2011 Spain recorded a visible merchandise trade deficit of US $55,402m. and there was a deficit of $51,919m. on the current account of the balance of payments. In 2010 the principal sources of imports were Germany (11.7%), France, China and Italy. France was the main export market in that year (18.3%), followed by Germany, Portugal, Italy, and the United Kingdom. Other members of the European Union (EU, see p. 281) are also important trading partners. The principal imports in 2010 were machinery and transport equipment, mineral fuels and lubricants, chemical products, miscellaneous manufactured articles, basic manufactures, and food and live animals. The main exports were machinery and transport equipment, basic manufactures, chemicals and related products, and food and live animals (particularly fruit and vegetables).

In 2012 the budget deficit was €85,378.0m., equivalent to 8.1% of GDP. Spain's general government gross debt was €734,961.0m. in 2011, equivalent to 69.1% of GDP. The annual rate of inflation averaged 2.7% in 2002–11; consumer prices decreased by an average of 0.3% in 2009, but rose by 1.8% in 2010 and further increased by 3.2% in 2011. The unemployment rate was 25.0% in 2012.

Spain underwent an extended period of rapid expansion in the late 1990s and 2000s, driven by consumer demand based on the availability of inexpensive credit, a rapid rise in property prices and the expansion of the construction sector. GDP increased by an annual average of 3.7% in 1999–2007. The contraction of credit on the global financial markets from 2007 and subsequent downturn caused a collapse of the housing market and had a severe effect on the Spanish economy as a whole. GDP declined by 3.7% in 2009 and by 0.1% in 2010, when unemployment surpassed 20%. During 2008–09 the Government of José Luis

Rodríguez Zapatero implemented stimulus measures to support the economy, however, increased government spending caused a rapid deterioration of the fiscal balance, which went from a surplus of 2.3% in 2007 to a deficit of 11.1% of GDP in 2009, significantly above the EU's deficit limit of 3% of GDP. Harsh austerity measures were announced during 2010, partly in response to concern among international investors that Spain was at risk of defaulting on its sovereign debt. Concern remained over the potential cost to the economy and public finances of any further loss of confidence in Spain's indebted regional savings banks (cajas de ahorros), which were heavily exposed to the fall in property values; the Banco de España had been forced to intervene in the affairs of two regional banks in 2009 and 2010 in order to prevent their collapse. In the following year a further three banks were nationalized. The Government of Mariano Rajoy pledged to continue with the austerity programme, with the aim of meeting a budgetary deficit target of 5.3% (subsequently relaxed to 6.3%) of GDP for 2012; the deficit had amounted to 8.4% in 2011. In June 2012 the Government requested emergency EU funding to recapitalize its banking sector, which was threatened by an inability to secure credit and very low levels of investor confidence exacerbated by a succession of downgraded credit ratings and the collapse of another large bank. A loan package totalling €100,000m. was to be disbursed by the end of 2013. Under the terms of the agreement Spain was required to implement major reforms to its banking sector. The budget for 2013 contained further austerity measures, including spending reductions of €40,000m. and a new independent authority to monitor government finance. However, predictions that public debt would rise to 90.5% of GDP in 2013, that unemployment would increase further to some 27% (and to some 56% for 16–24 year-olds) and that the country would again exceed its budget deficit target for the year, led to intense speculation that the Government would seek a sovereign bail-out from the European Central Bank and IMF. According to official figures GDP increased by 0.7% in 2011, by 1.5% in 2012 but was predicted to decline by 1.5% in 2013.

PUBLIC HOLIDAYS

2014: 1 January (New Year's Day), 6 January (Epiphany)*, 17 April (Maundy Thursday)*, 18 April (Good Friday), 1 May (Labour Day), 15 August (Assumption), 12 October (National Day), 1 November (All Saints' Day), 6 December (Constitution Day), 8 December (Immaculate Conception), 25 December (Christmas Day).

In addition, various holidays are established by the Autonomous Communities and municipal authorities, giving an annual total of 14 public holidays.

* May not be observed in all Autonomous Communities.

Statistical Survey

Source (unless otherwise stated): Instituto Nacional de Estadística, Paseo de la Castellana 183, 28071 Madrid; tel. (91) 5839100; fax (91) 5839158; internet www .ine.es.

Area and Population

AREA, POPULATION AND DENSITY*

Area (sq km)	505,968†
Population (census results)	
1 November 2001	40,847,371
1 November 2011	
Males	23,104,303
Females	23,711,613
Total	46,815,916
Population (official estimate at 1 July)‡	
2012	46,163,116
Density (per sq km) at 1 July 2012	91.2

* Including the Spanish External Territories (Spanish North Africa—area 33 sq km), an integral part of Spain. Ceuta had a population of 77,329 on 1 July 2012, while Melilla's population was 77,839.
† 195,363 sq miles.
‡ Estimate not adjusted to take account of results of 2011 census.

POPULATION BY AGE AND SEX
('000 persons at 2011 census)

	Males	Females	Total
0–14	3,640.6	3,428.7	7,069.4
15–64	15,993.4	15,636.8	31,630.2
65 and over	3,470.3	4,646.1	8,116.4
Total	23,104.3	23,711.6	46,815.9

Note: Totals may not be equal to the sum of components, owing to rounding.

AUTONOMOUS COMMUNITIES AND CITIES
(population at 2011 census)*

	Area (sq km)	Population	Density (per sq km)	Capital
Autonomous Communities				
Andalucía (Andalusia) .	87,597	8,371,270	95.6	Sevilla (Seville)
Aragón	47,720	1,344,509	28.2	Zaragoza
Principado de Asturias .	10,602	1,075,183	101.4	Oviedo
Illes Balears (Balearic Is)	4,992	1,100,503	220.5	Palma de Mallorca
Canarias (Canary Is) .	7,447	2,082,655	279.7	Las Palmas de Gran Canaria/ Santa Cruz de Tenerife†
Cantabria	5,327	592,540	111.2	Santander
Castilla-La Mancha .	79,462	2,106,331	26.5	Toledo
Castilla y León . . .	94,227	2,540,188	27.0	Valladolid
Cataluña/Catalunya (Catalonia) . . .	32,091	7,519,843	234.3	Barcelona
Comunidad Valenciana/ Comunitat Valenciana . . .	23,254	5,009,931	215.4	Valencia
Extremadura . . .	41,635	1,104,498	26.5	Mérida
Galicia	29,575	2,772,928	93.8	Santiago de Compostela
Comunidad de Madrid .	8,028	6,421,874	800.0	Madrid
Región de Murcia . .	11,314	1,462,128	129.2	Murcia
Comunidad Foral de Navarra (Navarre) .	10,390	640,129	61.6	Pamplona
País Vasco/Euskadi (Basque Country) .	7,230	2,185,393	302.3	Vitoria-Gasteiz
La Rioja	5,045	321,173	63.7	Logroño
Autonomous Cities				
Ceuta	19	83,517	4,287.3	—
Melilla	13	81,323	6,064.4	—
Total	505,968	46,815,916	92.5	

* Including residents temporarily abroad.
† Joint capitals.

PRINCIPAL TOWNS*
(population at 2011 census)

Madrid (capital)	3,198,645	Vitoria-Gasteiz	240,753
Barcelona	1,611,013	Elche	227,417
Valencia	792,054	Oviedo	225,005
Sevilla (Seville)	698,042	Badalona	219,241
Zaragoza	678,115	Cartagena	215,757
Málaga	561,435	Terrassa	214,406
Murcia	437,667	Jerez de la Frontera	211,784
Palma de Mallorca	402,044	Sabadell	206,949
Las Palmas de Gran		Santa Cruz de	
Canaria	381,271	Tenerife	204,476
Bilbao	351,356	Móstoles	203,493
Alacant (Alicante)	329,325	Alcalá de Henares	200,505
Córdoba	328,326	Fuenlabrada	196,986
Valladolid	311,682	Pamplona	195,943
Vigo	295,623	Almería	189,680
Gijón	276,969	Leganés	185,758
Hospitalet de		Donostia-San	
Llobregat	256,509	Sebastián	185,512
A Coruña (La			
Coruña)	245,053	Burgos	178,864
Granada	241,003	Santander	178,095

*Population figures refer to *municipios*, each of which may contain some rural area as well as the urban centre.

BIRTHS, MARRIAGES AND DEATHS

	Registered live births		Registered marriages		Registered deaths	
	Number	Rate (per 1,000)	Number	Rate (per 1,000)	Number	Rate (per 1,000)
2004	454,591	10.7	216,149	5.1	371,934	8.7
2005	466,371	10.8	208,146	4.7	387,355	8.9
2006	482,957	11.0	203,453	4.6	371,478	8.4
2007	492,527	10.9	201,579	4.5	385,361	8.6
2008	519,779	11.2	194,022	4.3	386,324	8.4
2009	494,997	10.6	174,062	3.7	384,933	8.2
2010	486,575	10.3	167,247	3.6	382,047	8.1
2011	469,892	10.2	163,085	3.5	389,182	8.4

Life expectancy (years at birth): 81.6 (males 78.7; females 84.7) in 2010 (Source: World Bank, World Development Indicators database).

ECONOMICALLY ACTIVE POPULATION
('000 persons aged 16 years and over)

	2010	2011	2012
Agriculture, hunting, forestry and fishing	793.0	760.2	753.2
Mining and quarrying	44.8	41.2	36.6
Manufacturing	2,370.1	2,304.9	2,175.5
Electricity, gas and water supply	195.6	209.3	218.5
Construction	1,650.8	1,393.0	1,147.6
Wholesale and retail trade; repair of motor vehicles, motorcycles and personal and household goods	2,909.4	2,928.2	2,823.0
Hotels and restaurants	1,370.3	1,391.9	1,322.1
Transport, storage and communications	1,415.6	1,391.5	1,339.6
Financial intermediation	463.5	450.5	424.8
Real estate, renting and business activities	1,829.7	1,817.6	1,799.9
Public administration and defence; compulsory social security	1,406.3	1,412.9	1,307.7

—continued	2010	2011	2012
Education	1,181.6	1,177.3	1,172.7
Health and social work	1,364.6	1,426.7	1,380.1
Other community, social and personal service activities	711.7	698.6	716.1
Private households with employed persons	747.0	696.4	658.9
Extra-territorial organizations and bodies	2.7	4.6	5.2
Total employed	18,456.5	18,104.6	17,282.0
Total unemployed	4,632.4	4,999.0	5,769.0
Total labour force	23,088.9	23,103.6	23,051.0
Males	12,819.2	12,680.7	12,531.1
Females	10,269.7	10,422.9	10,519.9

Note: Totals may not be equal to the sum of components, owing to rounding.

Health and Welfare

KEY INDICATORS

Total fertility rate (children per woman, 2010)	1.5
Under-5 mortality rate (per 1,000 live births, 2010)	5
HIV/AIDS (% of persons aged 15–49, 2009)	0.4
Physicians (per 1,000 head, 2010)	4.0
Hospital beds (per 1,000 head, 2009)	3.2
Health expenditure (2009): US $ per head (PPP)	3,067
Health expenditure (2009): % of GDP	9.6
Health expenditure (2009): public (% of total)	73.6
Total carbon dioxide emissions ('000 metric tons, 2008)	329,285.6
Carbon dioxide emissions per head (metric tons, 2008)	7.2
Human Development Index (2011): ranking	23
Human Development Index (2011): value	0.878

For sources and definitions, see explanatory note on p. vi.

Agriculture

PRINCIPAL CROPS
('000 metric tons)

	2009	2010	2011
Wheat	4,724	5,611	6,900
Rice, paddy	899	926	930
Barley	7,349	8,157	8,328
Maize	3,492	3,179	3,856
Oats	906	1,018	1,351
Potatoes	2,460	2,278	2,361
Sugar beet	4,154	3,399	3,966
Olives	5,701	6,682	6,940
Sunflower seeds	870	887	1,084
Lettuce	875	809	868
Tomatoes	4,604	4,313	3,821
Chillies and peppers, green	1,012	872	898
Onions, dry	1,263	1,107	1,351
Oranges	2,618	3,120	2,825
Tangerines, mandarins, clementines and satsumas	2,026	1,708	1,584
Lemons and limes	620	724	700*
Apples	595	646	671
Pears	434	477	502
Peaches and nectarines	1,191	1,187	1,336
Grapes	5,573	6,107	6,100*
Watermelons	819	782	769
Cantaloupes and other melons	1,007	927	869

*FAO estimate.

Aggregate production ('000 metric tons, may include official, semi-official or estimated data): Total cereals 17,755 in 2009, 19,335 in 2010, 21,601 in 2011; Total roots and tubers 2,495 in 2009, 2,311 in 2010, 2,395 in 2011; Total vegetables (incl. melons) 13,457 in 2009, 12,680 in 2010, 12,409 in 2011; Total fruits (excl. melons) 14,497 in 2009, 15,456 in 2010, 15,452 in 2011.

Source: FAO.

LIVESTOCK
('000 head, year ending September)

	2009	2010	2011
Horses*	250	250	250
Asses*	142	142	142
Mules*	110	110	110
Cattle	6,082	6,075	5,923
Pigs	26,290	25,343	25,635
Sheep	19,718	18,552	17,003
Goats	2,265	2,934	2,693
Chickens*	138,000	138,000	138,000

* FAO estimates.

Source: FAO.

LIVESTOCK PRODUCTS
('000 metric tons)

	2009	2010	2011
Cattle meat	598	607	604
Sheep meat	124	131	131
Goat meat	9	11	11
Pig meat	3,291	3,369	3,469
Horse meat*	6	7	7
Rabbit meat*	70	66	67
Chicken meat	1,179	1,116	1,206
Cows' milk	6,251	6,357	6,522
Sheep's milk	507	585	550*
Goats' milk	515	602†	540*
Hen eggs	829	830*	830*
Honey	32	34*	34*
Wool, greasy	27	28*	28*

* FAO estimate(s).
† Unofficial figure.

Source: FAO.

Forestry

ROUNDWOOD REMOVALS
('000 cubic metres, excl. bark)

	2009	2010	2011
Sawlogs, veneer logs and logs for sleepers	3,332	3,455	2,615
Pulpwood	8,118	7,098	8,579
Other industrial wood	449	417	334
Fuel wood	2,080	5,120	5,120
Total	13,980	16,089	16,648

Source: FAO.

SAWNWOOD PRODUCTION
('000 cubic metres, incl. railway sleepers)

	2009	2010	2011
Coniferous (softwood)	1,757	1,477	1,706
Broadleaved (hardwood)	315	561	456
Total	2,072	2,038	2,162

Source: FAO.

Fishing

('000 metric tons, live weight)

	2008	2009	2010
Capture*	918.1	918.1	968.7
Blue whiting (Poutassou)	25.1	17.8	13.8
European pilchard (sardine)	56.5	44.3	46.5
Skipjack tuna	131.1	134.4	141.0
Yellowfin tuna	76.6	71.3	75.1
Jack and horse mackerels	44.7	44.4	40.8
Aquaculture	249.7	266.7	252.3
Blue mussel	180.3	198.5	189.1
Total catch*	1,167.8	1,184.8	1,221.0

* FAO estimates.

Note: Figures exclude Sardinia coral (metric tons): 5 in 2008–10.

Source: FAO.

Mining

('000 metric tons unless otherwise indicated)

	2008	2009	2010
Anthracite	7,238	7,700	7,200*
Crude petroleum ('000 barrels)	298	250	337
Natural gas (million cu m)*	330	330	330
Copper*†	10	10	10
Kaolin	356	300*	300*
Potash salts (crude)*	435	435	400
Sepiolite	708	770	770*
Dolomite*	15,000	15,000	15,000
Fluorspar‡	149	122	131*
Salt (unrefined)	4,141	7,400	7,500*
Gypsum (crude)	15,000*	11,500	11,500*

* Estimated production.
† Figures refer to the metal content of ores.
‡ Figures refer to total CaF_2 content (acid and metallurgical grades).

Source: US Geological Survey.

Industry

SELECTED PRODUCTS
('000 metric tons unless otherwise indicated)

	2007	2008	2009
Wheat flour	3,144	3,131	3,068
Vinegar	1,037	1,154	1,088
Distilled alcohol ('000 hl)	4,474	5,416	n.a.
Wine ('000 hl)	35,756	36,749	35,979
Beer ('000 hl)	33,502	32,555	33,649
Soft drinks ('000 hl)	58,880	59,070	59,182
Cigarettes (million units)	41,906	43,567	43,082
Washing powders and detergents	2,180.1	2,068.9	2,240.3
Aluminium (primary)*	408.0	408.0	408.0
Refined copper (primary)*†	255.0	255.0	255.0
Pig-iron*†	4,200	4,200	4,200
Cement (Portland)*	54,720	42,088	29,505
Motorcycles ('000)	154	133	121
Passenger cars ('000)	2,385.2	2,048.9	1,882.6
Electricity (million kWh)	305,052	313,758	293,847

* Data from the US Geological Survey.
† Estimated figures.

Source: mainly UN Industrial Commodity Statistics Database.

2010 ('000 metric tons unless otherwise indicated, estimates): Aluminium (primary) 408.0; Refined copper (primary) 255.0; Pig-iron 4,200; Cement (Hydraulic) 50,000 (Source: US Geological Survey).

Finance

CURRENCY AND EXCHANGE RATES

Monetary Units
100 cent = 1 euro (€).

Sterling and Dollar Equivalents (31 December 2012)
£1 sterling = 1.196 euros;
US $1 = 0.758 euros;
€10 = £8.36 = $13.19.

Average Exchange Rate (euros per US $)
2010   0.7550
2011   0.7194
2012   0.7779

Note: The national currency was formerly the peseta. From the introduction of the euro, with Spanish participation, on 1 January 1999, a fixed exchange rate of €1 = 166.386 pesetas was in operation. Euro notes and coins were introduced on 1 January 2002. The euro and local currency circulated alongside each other until 28 February, after which the euro became the sole legal tender.

BUDGET
(€ million)

Revenue	2011	2012	2013
Current operations	105,544	118,731	126,363
Direct taxation	55,239	54,846	66,181
Indirect taxation	36,142	21,095	40,734
Rates and other revenue	3,384	5,234	4,324
Current transfers	4,715	32,131	9,211
Estate taxes	6,063	5,426	5,913
Capital operations	476	502	661
Transfer of real investments	104	136	135
Capital transfers	372	366	527
Financial assets	13,370	10,093	1,520
Total	**119,390**	**129,326**	**128,545**

Expenditure*	2011	2012	2013
Current	132,406	139,958	150,895
Social security	8,092	8,868	15,537
Autonomous communities	16,098	22,862	20,346
Autonomous organs	17,810	15,072	12,035
Local corporations	13,544	14,921	15,762
Private companies	174	136	92
Foreign contributions	12,275	12,567	12,540
Families	2,970	2,596	2,319
Personnel	26,982	27,338	27,672
Purchase of goods and services	3,385	3,248	2,857
Interest	27,421	28,876	38,615
Contingency fund	2,472	2,367	2,595
Capital	15,178	10,305	11,597
Investment	5,817	5,281	3,903
Capital transfers	9,362	5,024	7,695
Financial assets	12,960	12,022	34,478
Financial liabilities	46,595	50,051	62,320
Total	**209,612**	**214,702**	**261,886**

* Calculated according to recognized obligations rather than payments made.

Source: Ministerio de Economía y Hacienda, Madrid.

INTERNATIONAL RESERVES
(US $ million at 31 December)

	2009	2010	2011
Gold (market prices)	9,996	12,768	14,256
IMF special drawing rights	4,639	4,517	4,090
Reserve position in IMF	780	1,323	2,911
Foreign exchange	12,787	13,306	25,842
Total	**28,202**	**31,914**	**47,099**

Source: IMF, *International Financial Statistics*.

MONEY SUPPLY
(incl. shares, depository corporations, national residency criteria, € '000 million at 31 December)

	2009	2010	2011
Currency issued	91.74	95.50	100.71
Banco de España	84.07	80.14	74.26
Demand deposits	523.15	510.21	500.66
Other deposits	1,144.59	1,177.71	1,107.42
Securities other than shares	439.88	432.89	434.51
Money market fund shares	13.44	8.13	8.01
Shares and other equity	285.11	300.46	388.58
Other items (net)	−130.62	−152.21	−239.49
Total	**2,367.28**	**2,372.69**	**2,300.39**

Source: IMF, *International Financial Statistics*.

COST OF LIVING
(Consumer Price Index; base: 2006 = 100)

	2009	2010	2011
Food (excl. alcoholic beverages and tobacco)	108.6	107.7	109.9
Alcohol and tobacco	121.1	134.3	148.0
Household expenses	106.8	107.4	108.6
Clothing (incl. footwear)	100.1	99.7	100.0
Rent	112.0	116.0	124.3
Transport	101.7	108.7	117.4
All items (incl. others)	**106.7**	**108.6**	**112.1**

NATIONAL ACCOUNTS
(€ million at current prices)

National Income and Product

	2009	2010	2011
Compensation of employees	519,955	506,791	508,620
Gross operating surplus and mixed income	450,788	451,868	464,198
Gross domestic product (GDP) at factor cost	**982,113**	**958,659**	**972,818**
Taxes, less subsidies, on production and imports	77,088	92,683	90,537
GDP in market prices	**1,047,831**	**1,051,342**	**1,063,355**
Primary incomes (net)	−34,184	−25,014	−21,455
Gross national income	**1,013,647**	**1,026,328**	**1,041,900**
Less Consumption of fixed capital	162,905	171,448	174,732
Net national income	**850,742**	**854,880**	**867,168**
Current transfers (net)	−10,760	−9,619	−9,471
Gross national disposable income	**839,982**	**845,261**	**857,697**

Expenditure on the Gross Domestic Product

	2010	2011	2012
Final consumption expenditure	828,626	842,733	834,090
Households	596,322	609,946	612,666
Non-profit institutions serving households	10,589	10,066	10,042
General government	221,715	222,721	211,382
Gross capital formation	244,987	229,054	206,414
Gross fixed capital formation	240,289	223,963	200,696
Changes in inventories	4,698	5,091	5,718
Total domestic expenditure	**1,073,613**	**1,071,787**	**1,040,504**
Exports of goods and services	283,936	321,819	338,014
Less Imports of goods and services	306,207	330,251	327,314
GDP in market prices	**1,051,342**	**1,063,355**	**1,051,204**

Gross Domestic Product by Economic Activity

	2010	2011	2012
Agriculture, hunting, forestry and fishing	25,454	24,383	26,019
Industry (excl. construction)*	155,191	165,051	163,331
Construction	114,776	98,546	87,719
Trade, transport and accommodation	231,581	242,066	246,135
Information and communications	37,980	42,280	41,258
Financial and insurance activities	43,092	40,650	41,949
Real estate activities	71,156	75,637	77,739
Professional activities	71,096	73,755	73,443
Public administration, health and education	177,394	178,184	170,467
Artistic, recreational and other service activities	33,872	35,759	36,345
Gross value added in basic prices	961,592	976,311	964,405
Import duties, value-added tax and other taxes, less subsidies on products	89,750	87,044	86,799
GDP in market prices	1,051,342	1,063,355	1,051,204

* Including mining, utilities and manufacturing.

BALANCE OF PAYMENTS
(US $ million)

	2009	2010	2011
Exports of goods	225,526	252,524	304,335
Imports of goods	−283,406	−316,027	−359,737
Balance on goods	−57,880	−63,503	−55,402
Exports of services	123,716	124,499	142,794
Imports of services	−88,978	−88,153	−94,747
Balance on goods and services	−23,142	−27,157	−7,356
Primary income received	63,206	61,039	58,971
Primary income paid	−98,891	−87,249	−95,282
Balance on goods, services and primary income	−58,827	−53,367	−43,667
Secondary income received	25,592	24,261	27,202
Secondary income paid	−36,540	−34,024	−35,454
Current balance	−69,775	−63,129	−51,919
Capital account (net)	5,869	8,350	7,628
Direct investment assets	−21,806	−43,034	−39,578
Direct investment liabilities	19,427	46,707	31,419
Portfolio investment assets	2,815	91,665	52,826
Portfolio investment liabilities	70,082	−46,668	−92,694
Financial derivatives and employee stock options (net)	−8,273	11,275	10
Other investment assets	−8,108	−22,923	−49,519
Other investment liabilities	23,809	21,406	160,730
Net errors and omissions	−8,070	−2,598	−5,288
Reserves and related items	5,970	1,050	13,616

Source: IMF, *International Financial Statistics*.

External Trade

PRINCIPAL COMMODITIES
(distribution by SITC, US $ million)

Imports c.i.f.	2008	2009	2010
Food and live animals	29,973.5	25,155.9	25,619.5
Fish, crustaceans and molluscs, and products thereof	7,149.5	5,885.2	6,420.2
Vegetables and fruit	4,938.3	4,123.2	4,253.5
Beverages and tobacco	4,705.0	4,047.2	4,059.8
Alcoholic beverages	2,180.6	1,713.5	1,783.5
Tobacco and tobacco manufactures	2,151.4	1,982.9	1,921.8
Mineral fuels and lubricants	81,328.4	47,358.5	58,231.6
Petroleum, petroleum products, etc.	60,547.9	34,415.2	45,296.6
Gas, natural and manufactured	16,947.1	10,781.6	11,163.2
Chemicals and related products	49,129.5	42,812.2	44,485.6
Organic chemicals	10,150.2	7,345.6	8,784.2
Medicinal and pharmaceutical products	15,273.9	16,977.4	15,163.0
Basic manufactures	51,213.3	31,961.3	35,192.8
Paper, paperboard and related products	5,421.4	4,299.7	4,361.0
Textile yarn, fabrics and articles thereof	5,203.5	3,848.9	4,135.3
Iron and steel	15,321.6	7,157.1	9,138.0
Non-ferrous metals	6,328.4	3,223.4	4,225.6
Manufactures of metal	9,175.4	6,501.7	6,168.8
Machinery and transport equipment	135,663.4	85,774.6	91,079.2
Telecommunications, sound recording and reproducing equipment	14,280.8	9,900.5	10,922.8
Electrical machinery, apparatus and appliances	25,082.3	13,166.7	15,150.8
Road vehicles	47,321.7	29,268.9	29,962.5
Passenger cars	22,187.4	12,921.7	11,608.9
Miscellaneous manufactured articles	45,787.7	37,285.1	39,551.7
Total (incl. others)	418,728.3	287,501.6	315,547.2

Exports f.o.b.	2008	2009	2010
Food and live animals	31,438.0	28,957.9	29,930.5
Vegetables and fruit	15,749.0	15,022.4	15,110.3
Tomatoes	1,252.5	1,138.8	1,085.5
Oranges, mandarins, clementines, etc.	3,102.8	2,979.8	2,923.3
Beverages and tobacco	4,127.0	3,768.6	3,726.1
Wine	2,963.6	2,723.1	2,576.7
Mineral fuels and lubricants	18,259.4	10,134.9	12,507.7
Animals and vegetable oils, fats and waxes	3,997.4	2,933.1	3,325.7
Olive oil	2,845.4	2,272.1	2,588.9
Chemicals and related products	34,918.4	30,045.3	35,457.6
Medicinal and pharmaceutical products	11,358.0	10,972.4	11,754.8
Basic manufactures	50,668.6	36,274.5	42,083.2
Ceramic products	3,528.0	2,572.9	2,533.1
Iron and steel	14,283.5	8,039.9	10,175.4
Machinery and transport equipment	99,616.9	78,608.3	83,165.2
Electrical machinery, apparatus and appliances	10,767.6	8,629.5	10,675.9
Road vehicles	53,665.1	40,654.1	42,982.2
Miscellaneous manufactured articles	24,020.3	21,547.3	21,741.9
Total (incl. others)	279,231.5	223,132.2	246,265.3

Source: UN, *International Trade Statistics Yearbook*.

2011 (€ million): Total imports 260,823.2; Total exports 214,485.5.

PRINCIPAL TRADING PARTNERS
(US $ million)

Imports c.i.f.	2008	2009	2010
Algeria	9,503.1	5,288.8	6,032.1
Austria	3,637.8	n.a.	n.a.
Belgium	10,524.4	7,720.7	7,933.4
Brazil	4,623.5	3,169.5	3,898.2
China, People's Republic . .	30,279.4	20,123.3	25,006.0
France (incl. Monaco) . .	46,502.5	33,672.5	33,872.1
Germany	58,377.6	38,615.7	37,029.7
Ireland	6,210.2	5,952.1	4,340.9
Italy	32,189.1	20,822.9	22,126.6
Japan	7,566.6	4,423.6	4,601.2
Korea, Republic . . .	3,974.5	2,540.8	2,186.2
Libya	4,640.8	2,993.1	4,443.2
Mexico	4,730.5	2,865.4	3,894.0
Morocco	4,171.3	3,289.1	3,637.7
Netherlands	15,908.0	12,857.6	14,179.0
Nigeria	6,934.2	3,895.9	5,754.4
Poland	3,949.3	3,417.1	4,034.4
Portugal	13,746.8	10,215.5	11,318.6
Russia	11,071.6	6,382.6	8,118.6
Saudi Arabia	6,209.8	3,383.1	4,691.3
Sweden	4,441.0	2,970.1	3,064.0
Switzerland-Liechtenstein .	4,262.6	3,731.2	3,576.3
United Kingdom . . .	19,245.9	13,818.0	14,298.0
USA	16,709.3	11,816.3	12,572.3
Total (incl. others) . . .	418,728.3	287,501.6	315,547.2

Exports f.o.b.	2008	2009	2010
Algeria	3,191.8	2,922.3	2,700.0
Austria	2,151.3	1,891.8	2,042.1
Belgium	8,353.1	6,135.6	6,921.5
China, People's Republic . .	3,176.7	2,771.7	3,510.0
France (incl. Monaco) . .	50,896.9	43,150.6	45,008.1
Germany	29,361.4	24,705.3	25,784.5
Greece	3,812.3	2,493.5	2,154.1
Italy	22,396.5	18,251.0	21,600.3
Mexico	4,141.4	3,446.8	3,719.7
Morocco	5,406.3	4,318.3	4,571.4
Netherlands	8,760.5	6,739.8	7,698.0
Poland	4,008.4	3,387.0	3,689.4
Portugal	24,672.3	20,526.6	21,973.5
Russia	4,186.3	2,057.0	2,644.3
Sweden	2,418.5	1,695.0	1,980.9
Switzerland-Liechtenstein .	3,693.5	3,720.8	4,544.4
Turkey	4,436.4	3,967.0	4,974.2
United Kingdom . . .	19,746.3	14,082.9	15,238.3
USA	11,134.3	7,963.4	8,665.4
Total (incl. others) . . .	279,231.5	223,132.2	246,265.3

Source: UN, *International Trade Statistics Yearbook*.

2011 (€ million): Total imports 260,823.2; Total exports 214,485.5.

Transport

RAILWAYS
(RENFE only)

	2008	2009	2010
Number of passengers ('000) . .	499,700	466,700	453,700
Passenger-km (million) . . .	22,074	21,699	20,978
Freight ('000 metric tons) . . .	22,012	16,563	16,064
Freight ton-km (million) . . .	9,737	6,973	7,471

ROAD TRAFFIC
('000 motor vehicles in use at 31 December)

	2008	2009	2010
Passenger cars	22,145.4	21,983.5	22,147.5
Buses	62.2	62.7	62.4
Lorries	5,192.2	5,136.2	5,104.0
Motorcycles	2,500.8	2,606.7	2,707.5
Tractors	213.4	206.7	199.5
Other vehicles	855.3	860.2	865.2

SHIPPING

Flag Registered Fleet
(at 31 December)

	2010	2011	2012
Number of vessels	1,200	1,190	1,186
Total displacement ('000 grt) . .	3,128.4	3,114.3	3,063.7

Source: Lloyd's List Intelligence (www.lloydslistintelligence.com).

International Sea-borne Freight Traffic

	2003	2004	2005
Goods loaded ('000 metric tons) .	68,227	74,576	81,066
Goods unloaded ('000 metric tons)	221,455	236,200	259,214

Source: partly Puertos del Estado, Ministerio de Fomento, Madrid.

CIVIL AVIATION
(domestic and international traffic on scheduled services)

	2009	2010	2011*
Passengers carried ('000) . . .	186,465	191,552	203,291
Goods carried (metric tons) . .	565,329	635,765	649,820

* Provisional figures.

Source: Dirección General de Aviación Civil, Ministerio de Fomento, Madrid.

Tourism

FOREIGN TOURIST ARRIVALS
(incl. Spaniards resident abroad)

Country of residence	2010	2011	2012*
Belgium	1,623,376	1,756,694	1,706,354
France	8,125,355	8,375,035	8,969,009
Germany	8,814,069	8,975,236	9,335,870
Ireland	1,177,253	1,284,167	1,189,523
Italy	3,490,354	3,764,819	3,571,660
Netherlands	2,276,392	2,771,903	2,548,656
Portugal	1,895,572	1,878,085	1,861,092
Switzerland	1,157,486	1,366,663	1,448,941
United Kingdom	12,440,240	13,615,386	13,653,864
Total (incl. others)	52,676,971	56,176,884	57,700,714

* Provisional figures.

Receipts from tourism (excl. excursionists, € million): 48,926 in 2010; 52,002 in 2011; 55,594 in 2012 (provisional)

Source: Instituto de Estudios Turísticos, Madrid.

Communications Media

	2009	2010	2011
Telephones ('000 main lines in use)	20,235.4	20,205.5	19,667.3
Mobile cellular telephones ('000 subscribers)	51,083.9	51,601.0	53,066.8
Internet subscribers ('000) . .	9,859.9	10,659.2	11,108.1
Broadband subscribers ('000) . .	9,706.7	10,534.5	11,048.5

Personal computers: 17,640,000 (393.1 per 1,000 persons) in 2007.

Source: International Telecommunication Union.

Education

(2010/11 unless otherwise indicated)

	Institutions	Teachers	Students
Pre-primary	22,545	351,674	1,872,829
Primary	13,880		2,754,986
Special education . .	1,546*	8,804†	31,043
Secondary: general . .	7,427	323,031	1,786,754
Secondary: vocational and university entrance .	12,241		1,254,789
Universities, etc. . . .	72‡	107,905§	1,445,392

* Referring to special schools and special education units, which are mainstream alternatives to special education.
† Referring to special school teachers in special education classrooms and mainstream alternatives to special education.
‡ 2005/06 figure.
§ 2007/08 figure.

Source: Ministerio de Educación y Ciencia, Madrid.

Pupil-teacher ratio (primary education, UNESCO estimate): 12.4 in 2009/10 (Source: UNESCO Institute for Statistics).

Adult literacy rate (UNESCO estimates): 97.7% (males 98.5%; females 97.0%) in 2010 (Source: UNESCO Institute for Statistics).

Directory

The Government

HEAD OF STATE

King of Spain: HM King JUAN CARLOS I (acceded to the throne 22 November 1975).

COUNCIL OF MINISTERS
(May 2013)

President of the Government (Prime Minister): MARIANO RAJOY.

Deputy Prime Minister, Minister of the Presidency and Government Spokesperson: MARÍA SORAYA SÁENZ DE SANTAMARÍA ANTÓN.

Minister of Foreign Affairs and Co-operation: JOSÉ MANUEL GARCÍA-MARGALLO.

Minister of Justice: ALBERTO RUÍZ GALLARDÓN.

Minister of Defence: PEDRO MORENÉS EULATE.

Minister of the Treasury and Public Administration: CRISTÓBAL MONTORO ROMERO.

Minister of Home Affairs: JORGE FERNÁNDEZ DÍAZ.

Minister of Public Works: ANA MARÍA PASTOR JULIÁN.

Minister of Education, Culture and Sports: JOSÉ IGNACIO WERT ORTEGA.

Minister of Employment and Social Security: MARÍA FÁTIMA BAÑEZ GARCÍA.

Minister of Industry, Energy and Tourism: JOSÉ MANUEL SORIA LÓPEZ.

Minister of Agriculture, Food and Environmental Affairs: MIGUEL ARIAS CAÑETE.

Minister of Economic Affairs and Competitiveness: LUIS JÁUREGUI DE GUINDOS JURADO.

Minister of Health, Social Services and Equality: ANA MATO ADROVER.

MINISTRIES

Office of the President of the Government: Complejo de la Moncloa, Avda de Puerta de Hierro s/n, 28071 Madrid; tel. (91) 3214000; fax (91) 3900429; e-mail secretariapresidente@presidencia.gob.es; internet www.la-moncloa.es.

Ministry of Agriculture, Food and Environmental Affairs: Paseo Infanta Isabel 1, 28071 Madrid; tel. (91) 3475368; fax (91) 3475412; e-mail informac@mapa.es; internet www.marm.es.

Ministry of Defence: Paseo de la Castellana 109, 28071 Madrid; tel. (91) 3955000; e-mail infodefensa@mde.es; internet www.mde.es.

Ministry of Economic Affairs and Competitiveness: Alcalá 9, Paseo de la Castellana 162, 28014 Madrid; tel. (90) 2218600; e-mail informacion.administrativa@meh.es; internet www.mineco.gob.es.

Ministry of Education, Culture and Sports: Alcalá 34, 28071 Madrid; tel. (91) 7018000; e-mail prensa@educacion.es; internet www.educacion.gob.es.

Ministry of Employment and Social Security: Agustín de Bethencourt 4, 28071 Madrid; tel. (91) 3630000; e-mail informacionmtin@meyss.es; internet www.empleo.gob.es.

Ministry of Foreign Affairs and Co-operation: Plaza de la Provincia 1, 28012 Madrid; tel. (91) 3799700; e-mail informaec@maec.es; internet www.exteriores.gob.es.

Ministry of Health, Social Services and Equality: Paseo del Prado 18–20, 28014 Madrid; tel. (901) 400100; fax (91) 5964480; e-mail oiac@msssi.es; internet www.msps.es.

Ministry of Home Affairs: Paseo de la Castellana 5, 28046 Madrid; tel. (91) 3192094; fax (91) 3085566; e-mail estafeta@mir.es; internet www.interior.gob.es.

Ministry of Industry, Energy and Tourism: Paseo de la Castellana 160, 28046 Madrid; tel. (902) 446006; fax (91) 4578066; e-mail info@mityc.es; internet www.minetur.gob.es.

Ministry of Justice: San Bernardo 45, 28071 Madrid; tel. (91) 3902000; fax (91) 3902244; e-mail prensa@mjusticia.es; internet www.mjusticia.gob.es.

Ministry of the Presidency: Complejo de la Moncloa, Avda de Puerta de Hierro s/n, 28071 Madrid; tel. (91) 3214000; e-mail sec@mpr.es; internet www.mpr.gob.es.

Ministry of Public Works: Paseo de la Castellana 67, 28071 Madrid; tel. (91) 5978171; fax (91) 5978503; e-mail fomento@fomento.es; internet www.fomento.es.

Ministry of the Treasury and Public Administration: Calle Alcalá 9, 28014 Madrid; tel. (91) 5958071; e-mail informacion.administrativa@minhap.es; internet www.minhap.gob.es.

COUNCIL OF STATE

The Council of State is the supreme consultative organ of the Government. It comprises eight permanent members, 11 ex officio members (including, *inter alia*, the Director of the Real Academia Española, the General Prosecutor, the General Chief of Staff of Defence and the Governor of the Banco de España) and up to 10 elective members appointed by the Government, as well as a President and a Secretary-General. In addition, former Prime Ministers may sit as ex officio members if they so choose.

Consejo de Estado: Mayor 79, 28013 Madrid; tel. (91) 5166262; fax (91) 5166244; e-mail tramitaciones@consejo-estado.es; internet www.consejo-estado.es.

President: JOSÉ MANUEL ROMAY BECCARÍA.

Legislature

LAS CORTES GENERALES

Congreso de los Diputados
(Congress of Deputies)

Carrera de Floridablanca s/n, 28071 Madrid; tel. (91) 3906000; fax (91) 4298707; e-mail informacion@congreso.es; internet www.congreso.es.

President: JESÚS MARÍA POSADA MORENO (PP).

First Vice-President: CELIA VILLALOBOS (PP).

General Election, 20 November 2011

	Votes	%	Seats
Partido Popular (PP)	10,830,693	44.62	186
Partido Socialista Obrero Español (PSOE)	6,973,880	28.73	110
Convergència i Unió (CiU)	1,014,263	4.17	16
Izquierda Unida—Los Verdes (IU-LV)	1,680,810	6.92	11
Amaiur	333,628	1.37	7
Unión Progreso y Democracia (UPyD)	1,140,242	4.69	5
Euzko Alderdi Jeltzalea-Partido Nacionalista Vasco (EAJ-PNV)	323,517	1.33	5
Esquerra Republicana de Catalunya (ERC)	256,393	1.05	3
Bloque Nacionalista Galego (BNG)	183,279	0.75	2
Coalición Canaria—Nueva Canarias (CC-NC-PNC)	143,550	0.59	2
Bloc—Iniciativa—Verds—Equo—Coalició Compromís (Compromís-Q)	125,150	0.51	1
Foro Asturias (FA)	99,173	0.40	1
Geroa Bai (G Bai)	42,411	0.17	1
Total (incl. others)	24,272,671	100.00	350

Senado
(Senate)

Plaza de la Marina Española 8, 28071 Madrid; tel. (91) 5381000; fax (91) 5381003; e-mail informacion@senado.es; internet www.senado.es.

President: PÍO GARCÍA-ESCUDERO MÁRQUEZ (PP).

First Vice-President: JUAN JOSÉ LUCAS GIMÉNEZ (PP).

The Senate comprises 266 members, 208 of whom are directly elected for a term of four years. The remaining 58 regional representatives are chosen by the assemblies of the autonomous regions and are renewed following legislative elections in those regions. At November 2011 the composition of the Senate by legislative grouping was as follows:

	Seats		
Grouping	Directly elected	Appointed	Total
Partido Popular (PP)	134	29	163
Partido Socialista Obrero Español (PSOE)	48	18	66
Convergència i Unió (CiU)	9	4	13
Entesa Catalana de Progrés*	7	3	10
Senadores Nacionalistas†	4	1	5
Others	6	3	9
Total	208	58	266

* An alliance of the Esquerra Republicana de Catalunya (ERC), the Esquerra Unida i Alternativa (EUiA), the Iniciativa per Catalunya Verds (ICV), and the Partit dels Socialistes de Catalunya (PSC-PSOE).

† Comprising the Euzko Alderdi Jeltzalea-Partido Nacionalista Vasco (EAJ-PNV).

Legislative Assemblies of the Autonomous Communities

(For full names of political parties, see Political Organizations)

ANDALUCÍA (ANDALUSIA)

President of the Government (Junta): JOSÉ ANTONIO GRIÑÁN MARTÍNEZ (PSOE).

President of the Parliament: MANUEL GRACIA NAVARRO (PSOE).

Election, 25 March 2012

	Seats
PP	50
PSOE	47
IU-LV-CA*	12
Total	109

* Izquierda Unida-Los Verdes-Convocatoria por Andalucía.

ARAGÓN

President of the Government: LUISA FERNANDA RUDI ÚBEDA (PP).

President of the Parliament (Cortes): JOSÉ ANGEL BIEL RIVERA (PSOE).

Election, 22 May 2011

	Seats
PP	30
PSOE	22
PAR	7
CHA	4
IU	4
Total	67

PRINCIPADO DE ASTURIAS

President: JAVIER FERNÁNDEZ FERNÁNDEZ (PSOE).

President of the Parliament (Junta General del Principado): PEDRO SANJURJO GONZÁLEZ (PSOE).

Election, 25 March 2012

	Seats
PSOE	16
FA*	13
PP	10
IU-IX	5
UPyD	1
Total	45

* Foro Asturias.

BALEARIC ISLANDS (SEE ILLES BALEARS)

BASQUE COUNTRY (SEE PAÍS VASCO)

CANARIAS (CANARY ISLANDS)

President of the Government: PAULINO RIVERO BAUTE (CC).

President of the Parliament: ANTONIO A. CASTRO CORDOBEZ (CC).

Election, 22 May 2011

	Seats
PP	21
CC	21
PSOE	15
NC	3
Total	60

CANTABRIA

President: IGNACIO DIEGO (PP).

President of the Parliament: JOSÉ ANTONIO CAGIGAS RODRÍGUEZ (PP).

Election, 22 May 2011

	Seats
PP	20
PRC	12
PSOE	7
Total	39

CASTILLA Y LEÓN (CASTILE AND LEON)

President of the Government (Junta): JUAN VICENTE HERRERA CAMPO (PP).

President of the Parliament (Cortes): MARÍA JOSEFA GARCÍA CIRAC (PP).

Election, 22 May 2011

	Seats
PP	53
PSOE	29
UPL	1
IUCyL*	1
Total	**84**

* Izquierda Unida Castilla y León.

CASTILLA-LA MANCHA (CASTILE-LA MANCHA)

President of the Government (Junta de Comunidades): MARÍA DOLORES DE COSPEDAL (PP).

President of the Parliament (Cortes): VICENTE TIRADO OCHOA (PP).

Election, 22 May 2011

	Seats
PP	25
PSOE	24
Total	**49**

CATALUÑA/CATALUNYA (CATALONIA)

President of the Government (Generalitat): ARTUR MAS I GAVARRÓ (CiU).

President of the Parliament: NÚRIA DE GISPERT I CATALÀ (CiU).

Election, 25 November 2012

	Seats
CiU	50
ERC-Cat Sí	21
PSC-PSOE	20
PP	19
ICV-EUiA*	13
C's	9
CUP	3
Total	**135**

* Coalition of Iniciativa per Catalunya Verds (ICV) and Esquerra Unida i Alternativa (EUiA).

COMUNIDAD VALENCIANA/COMUNITAT VALENCIANA (VALENCIA)

President of the Government (Generalitat): ALBERTO FABRA (PP).

President of the Parliament (Corts): JUAN COTINO (PP).

Election, 22 May 2011

	Seats
PP	55
PSOE	33
Compromís*	6
EUPV	5
Total	**99**

* A coalition of Bloc Nacionalista Valencià, Iniciativa del Poble Valencià (IdPV) and Els Verds Esquerra Ecologista del País Valencià (EV-EE).

EXTREMADURA

President of the Government (Junta): JOSÉ ANTONIO MONAGO (PP).

President of the Parliament (Asamblea): FERNANDO JESÚS MANZANO PEDRERA (PP).

Election, 22 May 2011

	Seats
PSOE	32
PP	30
IU-SIEX	3
Total	**65**

GALICIA

President of the Government (Xunta): ALBERTO NÚÑEZ FEIJÓO (PP).

President of the Parliament: PILAR ROJO NOGUERA (PP).

Election, 21 October 2012

	Seats
PP	41
PS de G-PSOE	18
AGE	9
BNG	7
Total	**75**

ILLES BALEARS (BALEARIC ISLANDS)

President of the Government: JOSÉ RAMÓN BAUZÁ (PP).

President of the Parliament: PERE ROTGER LLABRÉS (PP).

Election, 22 May 2011

	Seats
PP	35
PSOE	14
PSM-IV-ExM	4
PSOE-PACTE*	4
PSM-EN	1
GxF-PSOE	1
Total	**59**

* Pacte Progressista d'Eivissa.

MADRID

President: IGNACIO GONZÁLEZ GONZÁLEZ (PP) (acting).

President of the Parliament (Asamblea): JOSÉ IGNACIO ECHEVERRÍA (PP).

Election, 22 May 2011

	Seats
PP	72
PSOE	36
IU-LV	13
UPyD	8
Total	**129**

REGIÓN DE MURCIA

President of the Government: RAMÓN LUIS VALCÁRCEL SISO (PP).

President of the Parliament (Asamblea Regional): FRANCISCO CELDRÁN VIDAL (PP).

Election, 22 May 2011

	Seats
PP	33
PSOE	11
IU-VRM*	1
Total	**45**

* Izquierda Unida-Verdes de la Región de Murcia.

COMUNIDAD FORAL DE NAVARRA (NAVARRE)

President of the Government: YOLANDA BARCINA ANGULO (UPN).

President of the Parliament: ALBERTO CATALÁN HIGUERAS (UPN).

Election, 22 May 2011

	Seats
UPN	19
PSN-PSOE	9
Na-Bai	8
Bildu*	7
PP	4
IZQ-EZK	3
Total	**50**

* Coalition of Eusko Alkartasuna (EA) and Alternatiba.

PAÍS VASCO/EUSKADI (BASQUE COUNTRY)

Lehendakari (President): IÑIGO URKULLU RENTERÍA (EAJ-PNV).
President of the Parliament: BAKARTXO TEJERÍA OTERMIN (EAJ-PNV).
Election, 21 October 2012

	Seats
EAJ-PNV	27
EHB	21
PSE-EE/PSOE	16
PP	10
UPyD	1
Total	75

*Coalition of Eusko Alkartasuna, Aralar, Alternatiba, Sortu and independents of Ezker Abertzalea.

LA RIOJA

President of the Government: PEDRO MARÍA SANZ ALONSO (PP).
President of the Parliament: JOSÉ IGNACIO CENICEROS GONZÁLEZ (PP).
Election, 22 May 2011

	Seats
PP	20
PSOE	11
PR	2
Total	33

VALENCIA (SEE COMUNIDAD VALENCIANA)

Political Organizations

PRINCIPAL NATIONAL PARTIES

Izquierda Unida (IU) (United Left): Olimpo 35, 28043 Madrid; tel. (91) 7227500; fax (91) 3880405; e-mail info@izquierda-unida.es; internet www.izquierda-unida.es; f. 1986 as coalition of Partido Comunista de España and other left-wing parties; Co-ordinator-Gen. CAYO LARA MOYA.

Partido Comunista de España (PCE) (Communist Party of Spain): Olimpo 35, 28043 Madrid; tel. (91) 3004969; fax (91) 3004744; e-mail comitefederal@pce.es; internet www.pce.es; f. 1922; Euro-communist; absorbed Partido Comunista Obrero Español (PCOE) in 1986, and most of Partido Comunista de los Pueblos de España (PCPE) in Jan. 1989; Sec.-Gen. JOSÉ LUIS CENTELLA.

Partido Popular (PP) (People's Party): Génova 13, 28004 Madrid; tel. (91) 5577200; fax (91) 3122322; e-mail partidopopular@pp.es; internet www.pp.es; f. 1976 as Alianza Popular; adopted current name 1989; absorbed Democracia Cristiana (fmrly Partido Demócrata Popular) and Partido Liberal in early 1989; centre-right, Christian Democrat; 750,000 mems (2008); Pres. MARIANO RAJOY; Sec.-Gen. MARÍA DOLORES DE COSPEDAL GARCÍA.

Partido Socialista Obrero Español (PSOE) (Spanish Socialist Workers' Party): Ferraz 70, 28008 Madrid; tel. (91) 5820444; fax (91) 5820422; e-mail infopsoe@psoe.es; internet www.psoe.es; f. 1879; affiliated to the Socialist International; merged with the Partido Socialista Popular in 1978; joined by Partido de los Trabajadores de España-Unidad Comunista (PTE-UC) in 1991 and Partido de Nueva Izquierda (PDNI) in 2001; 551,469 mems (2006); Pres. JOSÉ ANTONIO GRIÑÁN; Sec.-Gen. ALFREDO PÉREZ RUBALCABA.

Unión Progreso y Democracia (UPyD): Cedaceros 11, 2°H, 28014 Madrid; tel. (91) 5982286; fax (91) 3896350; e-mail informacion@upyd.es; internet www.upyd.es; f. 2007; centrist; advocates constitutional and democratic reform; Spokesperson ROSA DÍEZ GONZÁLEZ.

Los Verdes (LV) (The Greens): C/Imagen n° 6, 4° B1, 41003 Sevilla; tel. (95) 4214756; fax (95) 4226888; e-mail losverdes@verdes.es; internet www.verdes.es; f. 1984; confederation of various regional environmentalist parties.

REGIONAL PARTIES

There are branches of the main national parties in most autonomous communities, some of which bear alternative or additional names. There are also numerous regional parties, including the following:

Andalucía
(Andalusia)

Partido Andalucista (PA): Rastro 8–10, 41004 Sevilla; tel. (95) 4502167; fax (95) 4212887; e-mail contacta@partidoandalucista.org;

internet www.partidoandalucista.org; f. 1971; Sec.-Gen. ANTONIO JESÚS RUIZ AGUILAR.

Aragón

Chunta Aragonesista (CHA): Conde de Aranda 14–16, 1°, 50003 Zaragoza; tel. (976) 284242; fax (976) 281311; e-mail sedenacional@chunta.com; internet www.chunta.com; f. 1986; left-wing; Pres. JOSÉ LUIS SORO DOMINGO; Sec.-Gen. JUAN MARTÍN.

Partido Aragonés (PAR): Coso 87, 50001 Zaragoza; tel. (976) 200616; e-mail sugerencias@partidoaragones.es; internet www.partidoaragones.es; f. 1977; fmrly Partido Aragonés Regionalista; centre-right; Pres. JOSÉ ANGEL BIEL; Sec.-Gen. ARTURO ALIAGA LÓPEZ.

Asturias

Foro Asturias (FA) (Asturias Forum): Pepe Cosmen 1, 33001 Oviedo; tel. (98) 5202745; fax (98) 5223554; e-mail sederegional@foroasturias.es; internet www.foroasturias.es; Pres. FRANCISCO ÁLVAREZ-CASCOS.

Unión Renovadora Asturiana (URAS): Menéndez Valdés 2, 1°, 33201 Gijón; tel. (98) 5353245; e-mail correo@uras.org; internet www.uras.es; f. 1999 following split in PP of Asturias; in 2004 formed coalition, Unión Asturianista, with Partíu Asturianista (PAS); Pres. JAVIER LÓPEZ ALONSO; Sec.-Gen. FERNANDO EXPÓSITO VENAYAS.

Canarias
(Canary Islands)

Agrupación Herreña Independiente (AHI): La Constitución 4, 38900 Valverde, El Hierro, Santa Cruz de Tenerife; tel. (922) 551134; fax (922) 551224; party of El Hierro island; Pres. DAVID CABRERA DE LEÓN; Sec.-Gen. BELÉN ALLENDE.

Coalición Canaria (CC): Buenos Aires 24, 35001 Las Palmas, Gran Canaria; tel. (928) 363142; e-mail lagomera@coalicioncanaria.org; internet www.coalicioncanaria.org; f. 1993 as coalition of Canary Islands parties incl. Agrupaciones Independientes de Canarias, Centro Canario Nacionalista, Iniciativa Canaria and Asamblea Majorera; united as a single party in 2005; Pres. PAULINO RIVERO BAUTE.

Nueva Canarias (NC): C/Venegas 1, Of. 2 y 4; tel. (928) 234234; fax (928) 230275; e-mail nc@nuevacanarias.org; internet nuevacanarias.org; f. 2005; Pres. ROMÁN RODRÍGUEZ RODRÍGUEZ.

Partido Nacionalista Canario (PNC): Bernabé Rodríguez 13, 38001 Santa Cruz de Tenerife; tel. and fax (922) 292475; e-mail partidonacionalistacanario@hotmail.com; internet www.pnc-canarias.eu; f. 1924; National Pres. JUAN MANUEL GARCÍA RAMOS; National Sec.-Gen. GUSTAVO DAVILA DE LEÓN.

Cantabria

Partido Regionalista de Cantabria (PRC): Amós de Escalante 2, 2°D, 39002 Santander; tel. (942) 229177; fax (942) 362337; e-mail prc@prc.es; internet www.prc.es; f. 1978; centre-right; Sec.-Gen. MIGUEL ÁNGEL REVILLA ROIZ.

Castilla y León
(Castile and Leon)

Unión del Pueblo Leonés (UPL): Avda República Argentina 13, 1°, 24004 León; tel. (987) 263309; fax (987) 204499; e-mail sede@upl.es; internet www.upl.es; f. 1986 as Unión Leonesista; advocates autonomy for León region; 4,000 mems; Pres. PEDRO ÁNGEL GALLEGO; Sec.-Gen. JAVIER CHAMORRO RODRÍGUEZ.

Cataluña/Catalunya
(Catalonia)

Candidatures d'Unitat Popular (CUP) (Popular Unity Candidatures): Plaça Gispert 4, 08240 Barcelona; internet www.cup.cat; f. 1986 as Assemblea Municipal de l'Esquerra Independentista; supports Catalan independence; Leader DAVID FERNÁNDEZ.

Ciutadans—Partit de la Ciutadania/Ciudadanos—Partido de la Ciudadanía (C's) (Citizens—Citizenship Party): Gran Vía 751A, 1°, 08013 Barcelona; tel. (93) 3429436; e-mail info@ciudadanos-cs.org; internet www.ciudadanos-cs.org; f. 2006; opposes Catalan nationalism; Pres. ALBERT RIVERA DÍAZ; Sec.-Gen. MATÍAS ALONSO RUIZ.

Convergència i Unió (CiU): Còrsega 331–333, 08037 Barcelona; tel. (93) 2363100; fax (93) 2363105; e-mail ciu@ciu.info; internet www.ciu.cat; f. 1978 as an electoral alliance; became confederation of parties in March 2001; Catalan nationalist, conservative; Sec.-Gen. JOSEP ANTONI DURANI LLEIDA; an alliance of the following two parties:

  Convergència Democràtica de Catalunya (CDC): Còrsega 331–333, 08037 Barcelona; tel. (93) 2363100; fax (93) 2363105; e-mail cdc@convergencia.org; internet www.convergencia.org; f. 1974; Catalan nationalist, centrist; Pres. JORDI PUJOL I SOLEY; Sec.-Gen. ORIOL PUJOL I FERRUSOLA.

Unió Democràtica de Catalunya (UDC): Napols 35–39, 08018 Barcelona; tel. (93) 2402200; fax (93) 2402201; e-mail info@unio .cat; internet www.unio.cat; f. 1931; Christian democrat; Pres. RAMON ESPADALER I PARCERISAS.

Esquerra Republicana de Catalunya (ERC) (Republican Left of Catalonia): Calàbria 166, 08015 Barcelona; tel. (93) 4536005; fax (93) 3237122; e-mail info@esquerra.org; internet www.esquerra.cat; f. 1931; advocates independence for Catalonia within European context, a just society and national solidarity of Catalan people; Pres. ORIOL JUNQUERAS I VIES; Sec.-Gen. MARTA ROVIRA I VERGÉS.

Esquerra Unida i Alternativa (EUiA): Doctor Aiguader 10–12, 08003 Barcelona; tel. (93) 3170034; fax (93) 3179251; e-mail euia@ euia.cat; internet www.euia.cat; federation of 5 communist and left-wing parties in Catalonia; republican; affiliated to Izquierda Unida; Co-ordinator-Gen. JOAN JOSEP NUET.

Iniciativa per Catalunya Verds (ICV): Passatge del Rellotge 3, 08002 Barcelona; tel. (93) 3010612; e-mail iniciativa@iniciativa.cat; internet www.iniciativa.cat; f. 1987 as Iniciativa per Catalunya, a federation of left-wing parties; adopted current name in 1998 following alliance with Els Verds (Confederació Ecologista de Catalunya); Pres. JOAN SAURA LAPORTA; Sec.-Gen. JOAN HERRERA TORRES.

Partit dels Socialistes de Catalunya (PSC-PSOE): Nicaragua 75–77, 08029 Barcelona; tel. (93) 4955400; fax (93) 4955435; e-mail info@socialistes.org; internet www.socialistes.cat; f. 1978 by merger of various Catalan parties of socialist ideology; allied to PSOE; Pres. ISIDRE MOLAS I BATLLORI; First Sec. PERE NAVARRO I MORERA.

Solidaritat Catalana per la Independència (SI): Avda Diagonal 339, 08037 Barcelona; tel. (93) 2703374; e-mail seunacional@ solidaritatcatalana.cat; internet www.solidaritatcatalana.cat; f. 2010; advocates independence for Catalonia; Pres. NÚRIA CADENES; Sec.-Gen. URIEL BERTRAN I ARRUÉ.

Comunidad Valenciana/Comunitat Valenciana
(Valencia)
(see also Cataluña)

Bloc Nacionalista Valencià: Sant Jacint 28, entresòl, 46008 Valencia; tel. (96) 3826606; fax (96) 3826276; e-mail bloc@bloc.ws; internet www.bloc.ws; f. 1998 as federation of Unitat del Poble Valencià (f. 1982), Partit Valencià Nacionalista (f. 1990) and Nacionalistes d'Alcoi (f. 1994); progressive Valencian nationalist party; Pres. JOSEP MARIA PAÑELLA ALCACER; Sec.-Gen. ENRIC XAVIER MORERA CATALÀ.

Esquerra Unida del País Valencià (EUPV): Borrull 25, 46008 Valencia; tel. (963) 841888; fax (963) 847678; e-mail eupv@eupv.org; internet www.eupv.org; left-wing; affiliated to Izquierda Unida; Co-ordinator MARGA SANZ.

Partido Socialista del País Valenciano (PSPV-PSOE) (Valencian Socialist Party): Palau de les Corts Valencianes, Plaza San Lorenzo 4, 46003 Valencia; e-mail info@socialistesvalencians.org; internet www.socialistesvalencians.org; affiliated to PSOE; Pres. TERESA SEMPERE; Sec.-Gen. XIMO PUIG I FERRER.

Extremadura

Socialistas Independientes de Extremadura (SIEX): Mérida; Leader JOSÉ ANTONIO JIMÉNEZ GARCÍA.

Galicia

Alternativa Galega de Esquerda (AGE): Santiago de Compostela; tel. (981) 551586; fax (981) 551587; e-mail prensa@ alternativagalega.com; internet alternativagalega.com; f. 2012 to contest the Galician regional elections; coalition of ANOVA-Nationalist Brotherhood, the Galician branches of United Left and Equo, and Galician Ecosocialist Space; Leaders XOSÉ MANUEL BEIRAS, YOLANDA DÍAZ.

Bloque Nacionalista Galego (BNG): Avda Rodríguez de Viguri 16, baixo, 15703 Santiago de Compostela; tel. (981) 555850; fax (981) 555851; e-mail sedenacional@bng-galiza.org; internet www .bng-galiza.org; f. 1982; Galician nationalist; Leader XAVIER VENCE DEZA.

Partido dos Socialistas de Galicia (PS de G-PSOE) (Galician Socialist Party): Rua do Pino 1–9, baixo, 15704 Santiago de Compostela; tel. (981) 552030; fax (981) 588708; e-mail ceng@psdeg-psoe.org; internet www.psdeg-psoe.org; Galician branch of the PSOE; Sec.-Gen. MANUEL (PACHI) VÁZQUEZ FERNANDEZ.

Illes Balears
(Balearic Islands)
(see also Cataluña)

Alternativa Esquerra Unida-Els Verds: Sindicat 74, 1r 2a, 07001 Palma de Mallorca; tel. (971) 724488; fax (971) 971711836; alliance of Esquerra Unida de les Illes Balears (affiliated to Izquierda Unida) and Els Verds de Mallorca; Spokespersons EBERHARD GROSSKE, MIQUEL ÀNGEL LLAUGER.

Eivissa pel Canvi (ExC) (Ibiza for Change): Avda d'Isidor Macabich 39, 1°, 07800 Eivissa; e-mail exc.grup@gmail.com; internet www .eivissapelcanvi.org; f. 2006; opposes municipal corruption.

Gent per Formentera (GxF): Palma de Mallorca; e-mail infogxf@ gmail.com; internet www.gentxformentera.org; f. 2007; contested the 2011 regional election in alliance with the Partido Socialista Obrero Español (PSOE).

IniciativaVerds (IV): Carrer General Riera 3, 07005 Palma de Mallorca; tel. and fax (971) 728241; e-mail info@iniciativaverds.org; internet www.iniciativaverds.org; f. 2010; Co-ordinator DAVID ABRIL.

PSM-Entesa Nacionalista (PSM-EN): Isidoro Antillón 9, baixos, 07006 Palma de Mallorca; tel. (971) 775252; fax (971) 774848; e-mail mallorca@psm-entesa.cat; internet www.psm-entesa.org; f. 1989 as Federació de l'Esquerra Nacionalista de les Illes Balears (FENIB); federation of PSM-Entesa Nacionalista de Mallorca (f. 1976 as Partit Socialista de les Illes, renamed Partit Socialista de Mallorca—PSM in 1977), PSM-Entesa Nacionalista de Menorca (f. 1977 as Partit Socialista de Menorca), Entesa Nacionalista i Ecologista d'Eivissa (f. 1989) and other groups; Socialist, Catalan nationalist, environmentalist; Sec.-Gen. GABRIEL BARCELÓ.

Populares de les Illes Balears: Palau Reial 10, 07001 Palma de Mallorca; tel. (971) 712348; fax (971) 727275; internet www .ppbalears.es; regional branch of Partido Popular (PP); Pres. JOSÉ RAMÓN BAUZÁ; Sec.-Gen. MIGUEL VIDAL.

Navarra
(Navarre)
(see also País Vasco)

Amaiur: Bilbao; e-mail web@ehbildu.net; internet ehbildu.net; f. 2011 by Basque left-wing nationalists; a coalition of Eusko Alkartasuna, Alternatiba and Aralar.

Aralar: Aduanaren txokoa 16–18, 31001 Pamplona; tel. (948) 206362; e-mail nafarroa@aralar.net; internet www.aralar.net; f. 2002 by fmr dissident mems of Euskal Herritarrok (subsequently Batasuna) opposed to that party's links with Euskadi ta Askatasuna (ETA); Basque separatist, left-wing; rejects violence; active throughout the Basque region; Co-ordinator-Gen. PATXI ZABALETA.

Bildu (Gather): Pamplona; e-mail nafarroa@bildu.info; internet www.bildu.info; f. 2011; coalition of Eusko Alkartasuna (EA) and Alternatiba; separatist; Leaders PELLO URIZAR, OSKAR MATUTE, BAKARTXO RUIZ.

Izquierda-Ezkerra (IZQ-EZK): Pamplona; internet www .izquierda-ezkerra.org; f. 2011; a coalition of Izquierda Unida de Navarra-Nafarroako Ezker Batua (IUN-NEB) and Batzarre.

Batzarre (Assembly): Navarrería 15, 1°C, 31001 Pamplona; tel. (948) 224757; fax (948) 210063; e-mail info@batzarre.org; internet www.batzarre.org; f. 1987; left-wing Basque nationalist party of Navarre.

Izquierda Unida de Navarra-Nafarroako Ezker Batua (IUN-NEB): Calle Mayor 20, 31001 Pamplona; tel. (948) 220405; fax (948) 212941; e-mail info@iun-neb.org; internet www.iun-neb.org; f. 1986; pursues social changes based on the principles of liberty, equality and solidarity; Co-ordinator-Gen. JOSÉ MIGUEL NUIN MORENO.

Geroa Bai (G Bai) (Yes to the Future): f. 2011 to contest the general elections; replaced the Nararroa Bai (Na Bai); coalition of Basque nationalist parties in Navarre: EAJ-PNV, Atarrabia Taldea and Asociación Zabaltzen; Leader UXUE BARKOS.

Partido Socialista de Navarra (PSN): Paseo de Sarasate 15, 2°, 31002 Pamplona; tel. (948) 225003; fax (948) 221534; e-mail info@ psn-psoe.org; internet www.psn-psoe.org; Navarrese branch of PSOE; Sec.-Gen. ROBERTO JIMÉNEZ ALLI.

Unión del Pueblo Navarro (UPN): Plaza Príncipe de Viana 1, 4°, 31002 Pamplona; tel. (948) 223402; fax (948) 210810; e-mail administrador@upn.org; internet www.upn.org; f. 1979; centre-right; opposes closer ties between Navarre and Basque Country; Pres. YOLANDA BARCINA; Sec.-Gen. OSCAR ARIZCUREN.

País Vasco/Euskadi
(Basque Country)

Amaiur: Bilbao; e-mail web@ehbildu.net; internet ehbildu.net; f. 2011 by Basque left-wing nationalists; a coalition of Eusko Alkartasuna, Alternatiba and Aralar.

Aralar: see Navarra above.

Euskal Herria Bildu (EHB): Bilbao; e-mail web@ehbildu.net; internet ehbildu.net/eu; f. 2012; a coalition of Eusko Alkartasuna, Aralar, Alternatiba, Sortu, and independents of Ezker Abertzalea; Leader LAURA MINTEGI.

Eusko Alkartasuna (EA) (Basque Solidarity): Camino de Portuetxe 23, 1°, 20018 San Sebastián; tel. (943) 020130; fax (943)

020131; e-mail gipuzkoa@euskoalkartasuna.org; internet www
.euskoalkartasuna.org; f. 1985 (as Eusko Abertzaleak—Basque
Nationalists) by dissident group of progressive EAJ-PNV mems;
Sec.-Gen. PELLO URIZAR KARETXE.

**Euzko Alderdi Jeltzalea-Partido Nacionalista Vasco (EAJ-
PNV):** Sabin Etxea, Ibáñez de Bilbao 16, 48001 Bilbao; tel. (94)
4039400; fax (94) 4039415; e-mail idazkaria.ebb@eaj-pnv.com;
internet www.eaj-pnv.com; f. 1895; Basque nationalist; seeks to
achieve autonomy through peaceful means; 32,000 mems; Pres.
IÑIGO URKULLU RENTERIA; Sec. BELÉN GREAVES BADILLO.

Ezker Batua-Berdeak (EB-B): Fernández del Campo 24, 48010
Bilbao; tel. (94) 4702100; fax (94) 4701012; internet www
.ezkerbatua-berdeak.org; f. 1986 as a coalition of left-wing, social
democratic and environmentalist parties; Co-ordinator-Gen. MIKEL
ARANA.

Partido Socialista de Euskadi-Euskadiko Ezkerra (PSE-EE)
(Basque Socialist Party-Basque Left): Alameda de Recalde 27, 4°,
48009 Bilbao; tel. (94) 4242142; fax (94) 4238904; e-mail prensa@
www.socialistasvascos.com; internet www.socialistasvascos.com;
f. 1993 by merger of PSE-PSOE (Basque branch of PSOE) and
Euskadiko Ezkerra; affiliated to PSOE; Pres. JESÚS EGUIGUREN; Sec.-
Gen. PATXI LÓPEZ ÁLVAREZ.

La Rioja

Partido Riojano (PR): Portales 17, 1°, 26001 Logroño; tel. (941)
238199; fax (941) 254396; e-mail partidoriojano@partidoriojano.es;
internet www.partidoriojano.es; f. 1982; Pres. MIGUEL GONZÁLEZ DE
LEGARRA; Sec.-Gen. JAVIER SÁENZ TORRE MERINO.

ILLEGAL ORGANIZATIONS

The principal illegal armed organization is the Basque separatist
Euskadi ta Askatasuna (ETA—Basque Homeland and Liberty,
f. 1959). The Political Parties Law of June 2002 facilitated the
banning of parties deemed to support violence or terrorism. The
legislation was employed against a number of parties in the Basque
Country, most notably Batasuna (f. 1978 as Herri Batasuna), a
radical separatist party led by Arnaldo Otegi Mondragón, which was
banned by the Supreme Court in March 2003 on account of its links to
ETA. Other parties deemed to be alternatives to Batasuna that have
been outlawed include Eusko Abertzale Ekintza/Acción Nacionalista
Vasca (EAE/ANV) and Euskal Herrialdeetako Alderdi Komunista/
Partido Comunista de las Tierras Vascas (EHAK/PCTV), both of
which were banned in September 2008. Sortu, which was founded in
February 2011 and publicly rejected violence, was nevertheless
banned in March as a successor party to Batasuna. Its members
subsequently joined in the formation of Bildu, which was initially
banned but later permitted to contest the regional and local elections
in May.

Election Commission

Junta Electoral Central: Congreso de los Diputados, Carretera de
San Jerónimo 36, 28071 Madrid; tel. (91) 3906367; fax (91) 4297778;
internet www.juntaelectoralcentral.es; independent; Pres. CARLOS
GRANADOS PÉREZ.

Diplomatic Representation

EMBASSIES IN SPAIN

Afghanistan: Calle de Nuria 16, 4°, 28034 Madrid; tel. (91) 7218581;
fax (91) 7216832; e-mail info@embassyafghanistanmadrid.com;
Ambassador MASSOD KHALILI.

Albania: María de Molina 64, 5°B, 28006 Madrid; tel. (91) 5612118;
fax (91) 5613775; e-mail embassy.madrid@mfa.gov.al; Ambassador
KASTRIOT ROBO.

Algeria: General Oraá 12, 28006 Madrid; tel. (91) 5629705; fax (91)
5629877; e-mail embargel@tsai.es; internet www.emb-argelia.es;
Ambassador MOHAMMED HANECHE.

Andorra: Alcalá 73, 28009 Madrid; tel. (91) 4317453; fax (91)
5776341; e-mail embajada@embajadaandorra.es; Ambassador
JAUME GAYTAN SANSA.

Angola: Lagasca 88, 2°A, 28001 Madrid; tel. (91) 4356166; fax (91)
4356430; e-mail gabembajador@embajadadeangola.com; internet
www.embajadadeangola.com; Ambassador VÍCTOR MANUEL RITA DA
FONSECA LIMA.

Argentina: Serrano 90, 7°, 28001 Madrid; tel. (91) 7710519; fax (91)
7710526; e-mail embajada@portalargentino.net; internet www
.portalargentino.net; Ambassador CARLOS ANTONIO BETTINI.

Armenia: Calle Mayor 81, 28013 Madrid; tel. and fax (91) 5422627;
fax (91) 5591806; e-mail armspainembassy@mfa.am; internet spain
.mfa.am; Chargé d'affaires a.i. KHOREN TERTERYAN.

Australia: Paseo de la Castellana 259D, Planta 24, Torre Espacio,
28046 Madrid; tel. (91) 3536600; fax (91) 3536692; e-mail madrid
.embassy@dfat.gov.au; internet www.spain.embassy.gov.au;
Ambassador JANE HARDY.

Austria: Paseo de la Castellana 91, 9°, 28046 Madrid; tel. (91)
5565315; fax (91) 5973579; e-mail madrid-ob@bmeia.gv.at;
internet www.bmeia.gv.at/madrid; Ambassador Dr RUDOLF LENNKH.

Azerbaijan: Ronda de la Avutarda 38, 28043 Madrid; tel. (91)
7596010; fax (91) 7597056; e-mail madrid@mission.mfa.gov.az;
internet www.azembassy.es; Ambassador ALTAI VASIFOGLU EFEN-
DIEV.

Bangladesh: Diego de León 69, 2°D, 28006 Madrid; tel. (91) 4019932;
fax (91) 4029564; Ambassador IKHTIAR MOMIN CHOWDHURY.

Belgium: Paseo de la Castellana 18, 6°, 28046 Madrid; tel. (91)
5776300; fax (91) 4318166; e-mail madrid@diplobel.fed.be; internet
www.diplomatie.be/madrid; Ambassador JAN DE BOCK.

Bolivia: Velázquez 26, 3°A, 28001 Madrid; tel. (91) 5780835; fax (91)
5773946; e-mail gestiones@embajadadebolivia.es; internet www
.embajadadebolivia.es; Ambassador MARÍA DEL CARMEN ALMENDRAS
CAMARGO.

Bosnia and Herzegovina: Lagasca 24, 2°, 28001 Madrid; tel. (91)
5750870; fax (91) 4355056; e-mail ambasada@ctv.es; Ambassador
JASNA KRIVOSIC PRPIC.

Brazil: Fernando el Santo 6, 28010 Madrid; tel. (91) 7004650; fax
(91) 7004660; e-mail brasemb.madrid@itamaraty.gov.br; internet
madri.itamaraty.gov.br; Ambassador PAULO CESAR DE OLIVEIRA
CAMPOS.

Bulgaria: Travesía de Santa María Magdalena 15, 28016 Madrid;
tel. (91) 3455761; fax (91) 3591201; e-mail embulmad@yahoo.es;
internet www.mfa.bg/embassies/spain; Ambassador KOSTADIN
TASHEV KODZHABASHEV.

Cameroon: Rosario Pino 3, 28020 Madrid; tel. (91) 5711160; fax (91)
5712504; e-mail ambcammadrid@telefonica.net; internet
ambacam-madrid.com; Chargé d'affaires a.i. THIMOTHÉE TABAPSSI.

Canada: Torre Espacio, Paseo de la Castellana 259D, 28046 Madrid;
tel. (91) 3828400; fax (91) 3828490; e-mail mdrid@international.gc
.ca; internet www.canadainternational.gc.ca/spain-espagne;
Ambassador JON ALLEN.

Chile: Lagasca 88, 6°, 28001 Madrid; tel. (91) 4319160; fax (91)
5775560; e-mail echile.espana@minrel.gov.cl; internet chileabroad
.gov.cl/espana; Ambassador SERGIO ROMERO PIZARRO.

China, People's Republic: Arturo Soria 113, 28043 Madrid; tel.
(91) 5194242; fax (91) 5192035; e-mail embajadachina@
embajadachina.es; internet www.embajadachina.es; Ambassador
ZHU BANGZAO.

Colombia: General Martínez Campos 48, 28010 Madrid; tel. (91)
7004770; fax (91) 3102869; e-mail emadrid@cancilleria.gov.co;
internet www.embajadaenespana.gov.co; Ambassador ORLANDO
SARDI DE LIMA.

Congo, Democratic Republic: Dr Fleming 44, 1°E/F/C, 28036
Madrid; tel. (91) 7332647; fax (91) 3231575; e-mail ambardc47@
yahoo.es; Ambassador (vacant).

Costa Rica: Paseo de la Castellana 178, 2° dcha, 28046 Madrid; tel.
(91) 3459622; fax (91) 3533709; e-mail embajada@embcr.org;
internet www.embajadadecostarica.es; Ambassador EKHART PETERS
SEEVERS.

Côte d'Ivoire: Serrano 154, 28006 Madrid; tel. (91) 5626916; fax (91)
5622193; internet www.ambaci.es; Ambassador PAUL ODETTE
N'GUESSAN AKISSI YAO YAO.

Croatia: Claudio Coello 78, 2°, 28001 Madrid; tel. (91) 5776881; fax
(91) 5776905; e-mail vrh.madrid@mvpei.hr; internet es.mvp.hr;
Ambassador NEVEN PELICARIC.

Cuba: Paseo de la Habana 194, 28036 Madrid; tel. (91) 3592500; fax
(91) 3596145; e-mail secreembajada@ecubamad.com; internet www
.cubadiplomatica.cu/espana; Ambassador ALEJANDRO GONZÁLEZ
GALIANO.

Cyprus: Paseo de la Castellana 45, 4°–5° izqda, 28046 Madrid; tel.
(91) 5783114; fax (91) 5782189; e-mail embajadachipre@telefonica
.net; internet www.mfa.gov.cy/embassymadrid; Ambassador ANT-
ONIS TOUMAZIS.

Czech Republic: Avda Pío XII 22–24, 28016 Madrid; tel. (91)
3531880; fax (91) 3531885; e-mail madrid@embassy.mzv.cz;
internet www.mfa.cz/madrid; Ambassador KAREL BERAN.

Denmark: Serrano 26, 7°, 28001 Madrid; tel. (91) 4318445; fax (91)
4319168; e-mail madamb@um.dk; internet www.ambmadrid.um.dk;
Ambassador LONE DENCKER WISBORG.

Dominican Republic: Paseo de la Castellana 30, 1° dcha, 28046
Madrid; tel. (91) 4315395; fax (91) 4358139; e-mail embajada@

embajadadominicana.es; internet www.embajadadominicana.es; Ambassador CÉSAR AUGUSTO MEDINA ABREU.

Ecuador: Velázquez 114, 2°, 28006 Madrid; tel. (91) 5627215; fax (91) 7450244; e-mail embajada@mecuador.es; Ambassador AMINTA BUENAÑO RUGEL.

Egypt: Velázquez 69, 28006 Madrid; tel. (91) 5776308; fax (91) 5781732; Ambassador AYMAN ABDULSAMIE OMAR ZAINELDINE.

El Salvador: Paseo de la Castellana 178, 1°D, 28046 Madrid; tel. (91) 5628002; fax (91) 5630584; e-mail esuarez@rree.gob.sv; Ambassador EDGARDO SUÁREZ MALLAGRAY.

Equatorial Guinea: Avda Pío XII 14, 28016 Madrid; tel. (91) 3532169; fax (91) 3532165; e-mail rge@embarege-madrid.com; Ambassador NARCISO NTUGU.

Estonia: Claudio Coello 91, 1°, 28006 Madrid; tel. (91) 4261671; fax (91) 4261672; e-mail embassy.madrid@mfa.ee; internet www.estemb.es; Ambassador TOOMAS KAHUR.

Finland: Paseo de la Castellana 15, 28046 Madrid; tel. (91) 3196172; fax (91) 3083901; e-mail sanomat.mad@formin.fi; internet www.finlandia.es; Ambassador MARKKU KEINÄNEN.

France: Salustiano Olózaga 9, 28001 Madrid; tel. (91) 4238900; fax (91) 4238908; internet www.ambafrance-es.org; Ambassador JÉRÔME BONNAFONT.

Gabon: Francisco Alcántara 3, 28002 Madrid; tel. (91) 4138211; fax (91) 4131153; e-mail emb-gabon-es@nemo.es; Ambassador SIMÓN WILFRID NTOUTOUME EMANE.

Georgia: Plaza de las Cortes 4, 5° dcha, 28014 Madrid; tel. (91) 4293329; fax (91) 4296883; e-mail embassymadrid@mfa.gov.ge; internet www.spain.mfa.gov.ge; Ambassador ZURAB POLOLIKASHVILI.

Germany: Fortuny 8, 28010 Madrid; tel. (91) 5579000; fax (91) 3102104; internet www.madrid.diplo.de; Ambassador REINHARD SILBERBERG.

Ghana: Capitán Haya 38, 10°A, 28020 Madrid; tel. (91) 5670390; fax (91) 5670393; e-mail mission@ghanaembassyspain.com; Ambassador FIDELIS WOENENYO YAO EKAR.

Greece: Avda Dr Arce 24, 28002 Madrid; tel. (91) 5644653; fax (91) 5644668; e-mail gremb.mad@mfa.gr; Ambassador FRANCISCOS VERROS.

Guatemala: Rafael Salgado 3, 10° dcha, 28036 Madrid; tel. (91) 3441722; fax (91) 4587894; e-mail informacion@embajadaguatemala.es; internet www.embajadaguatemala.es; Ambassador ANAMARÍA DIÉGUEZ ARÉVALO.

Haiti: Marques del Duero 3, 1°, 28001 Madrid; tel. (91) 5752624; fax (91) 4314600; e-mail embhaiti@ctv.es; Ambassador (vacant).

Holy See: Avda Pío XII 46, 28016 Madrid; tel. (91) 7668311; fax (91) 7667085; e-mail nunap@planalfa.es; Apostolic Nuncio Most Rev. RENZO FRATINI (Titular Archbishop of Botriana).

Honduras: Paseo de la Castellana 164, 2°B, 28046 Madrid; tel. (91) 3531806; fax (91) 3458193; e-mail info@embahonduras.es; internet www.embahonduras.es; Ambassador NORMAN GARCÍA PAZ.

Hungary: Fortuny 6, 4°, 28010 Madrid; tel. (91) 4137099; fax (91) 4134138; e-mail mission.mad@mfa.gov.hu; internet www.mfa.gov.hu/emb/madrid; Ambassador EDIT BUCSI-SZABÓ.

India: Avda Pío XII 30–32, 28016 Madrid; tel. (91) 3098870; fax (91) 3451112; e-mail amb@embassyindia.es; internet www.embajadaindia.com; Ambassador SUNIL LAL.

Indonesia: Agastia 65, 28043 Madrid; tel. (91) 4130294; fax (91) 4138994; e-mail kbri@embajadadeindonesia.es; internet www.embajadadeindonesia.es; Ambassador ADIYATWIDI ADIWOSO ASMADY.

Iran: Jerez 5, Villa El Altozano, Chamartín, 28016 Madrid; tel. (91) 3450112; fax (91) 3451190; Ambassador MORTEZA SAFFARI NATANZI.

Iraq: Carril del Conde 56, 28043 Madrid; tel. (91) 7590303; fax (91) 7218682; e-mail embajadairak@yahoo.es; Ambassador Dr ZIAD KHALED A. ALI.

Ireland: Paseo de la Castellana 46, 4°, 28046 Madrid; tel. (91) 4364093; fax (91) 4351677; e-mail madridembassy@dfa.ie; internet www.irlanda.es; Ambassador JUSTIN HARMAN.

Israel: Velázquez 150, 7°, 28002 Madrid; tel. (91) 7829500; fax (91) 7829555; e-mail embajada@embajada-israel.es; internet www.embajada-israel.es; Ambassador ALON BAR.

Italy: Lagasca 98, 28006 Madrid; tel. (91) 4233300; fax (91) 5757776; e-mail archivio.ambmadrid@esteri.it; internet www.ambmadrid.esteri.it; Ambassador PIETRO SEBASTIANI.

Japan: Serrano 109, 28006 Madrid; tel. (91) 5907600; fax (91) 5901321; internet www.es.emb-japan.go.jp; Ambassador SATORU SATOH.

Jordan: General Martínez Campos 41, 5°, 28010 Madrid; tel. (91) 3191100; fax (91) 3082536; e-mail jordania@telefonica.net; internet www.embjordaniaes.org; Ambassador GHASSAN MAJALI.

Kazakhstan: Sotillo 10, 28043 Madrid; tel. (91) 7216290; fax (91) 7219374; e-mail embajada@kazesp.org; internet www.kazesp.org; Ambassador BAKYT DYUSSENBAYEV.

Kenya: Jorge Juan 9, 3° dcha, 28001, Madrid; tel. (91) 7812000; fax (91) 5760854; e-mail info@kenyaembassyspain.es; internet www.kenyaembassyspain.es; Ambassador BRAMWEL KISUYA.

Korea, Republic: González Amigó 15, 28033 Madrid; tel. (91) 3532000; fax (91) 3532001; e-mail embspain.adm@mofat.go.kr; internet esp.mofat.go.kr; Ambassador OH DAE-SUNG.

Kuwait: Avda de Miraflores 61, 28035 Madrid; tel. (91) 3869666; fax (91) 3732388; Ambassador ADIL HAMAD M. AL-AYYAR.

Latvia: Alfonso XII 52, 1°, 28014 Madrid; tel. (91) 3691362; fax (91) 3690020; e-mail lespan@telefonica.net; Ambassador JANIS EICHMANIS.

Lebanon: Paseo de la Castellana 178, 2° izqda, 28046 Madrid; tel. (91) 3451368; fax (91) 3455631; e-mail leem-e@teleline.es; Ambassador (vacant).

Libya: Comandante Franco 32, 28016 Madrid; tel. (91) 5635753; fax (91) 5643986; e-mail secretaria@embajadadelibia.com; internet www.embajadadelibia.com; Ambassador MUHAMMAD ALFAQEEH SALEH.

Lithuania: Pisuerga 5, 28002 Madrid; tel. (91) 7022116; fax (91) 3104018; e-mail amb.es@urm.lt; internet es.mfa.lt; Ambassador AUDRA PLEPYTÉ-JARA.

Luxembourg: Claudio Coello 78, 1°, 28001 Madrid; tel. (91) 4359164; fax (91) 5774826; e-mail madrid.amb@mae.etat.lu; internet www.madrid.mae.lu/es; Ambassador JEAN A. WELTER.

Macedonia, former Yugoslav republic: Don Ramón de la Cruz 107, 2°B, 28006 Madrid; tel. (91) 5717298; fax (91) 5713481; e-mail emb.mkd.madrid@gmail.com; Ambassador (vacant).

Malaysia: Paseo de la Castellana 91, Edif. Centro 23, 10°, 28046 Madrid; tel. (91) 5550684; fax (91) 5555208; e-mail malmadrid@kin.gov.my; Ambassador Dato ILANKOVAN KOLANDAVELU.

Mali: Padilla 19, 5°D, 28006 Madrid; tel. (91) 7817212; fax (91) 4351516; e-mail info@embajadamali.es; Ambassador SEKOU GAOUSSOU CISSE.

Malta: Paseo de la Castellana 45, 6° dcha, 28046 Madrid; tel. (91) 3913061; fax (91) 3913066; e-mail maltaembassy.madrid@gov.mt; Ambassador TANYA VELLA.

Mauritania: Velázquez 90, 3°, 28006 Madrid; tel. (91) 5757006; fax (91) 4359531; e-mail ambarim@embajadamauritania.es; internet www.embajadamauritania.es; Ambassador MOHAMED M. OULD ABDELLAHI OULD BOYE.

Mexico: Carrera de San Jerónimo 46, 28014 Madrid; tel. (91) 3692814; fax (91) 4202292; e-mail embamex@embamex.es; internet www.embamex.es; Ambassador FRANCISCO JAVIER RAMÍREZ ACUÑA.

Moldova: Paseo de la Castellana 178, 5° dcha, 28046 Madrid; tel. (91) 8284530; fax (91) 8285366; e-mail madrid@mfa.md; internet www.spania.mfa.md; Ambassador VALERIU GHEORGHIU.

Monaco: Villanueva 12, 28001 Madrid; tel. (91) 5782048; fax (91) 4357132; e-mail emb.espana@gouv.mc; Ambassador PATRICK VAN KLAVEREN.

Morocco: Serrano 179, 28002 Madrid; tel. (91) 5631090; fax (91) 5617887; e-mail correo@embajada-marruecos.es; internet www.embajada-marruecos.es; Ambassador AHMED OULD SOUILEM.

Mozambique: Velázquez 109, 4° dcha, 28006 Madrid; tel. (91) 5776382; fax (91) 5776705; e-mail embamoc.madrid@hotmail.com; Ambassador FERNANDA E. MOISES LICHALE.

Netherlands: Paseo de la Castellana 259D, 28046 Madrid; tel. (91) 3537500; fax (91) 3537565; e-mail mad@minbuza.nl; internet www.mfa.nl/mad; Ambassador CORNELIS VAN RIJ.

New Zealand: Pinar 7, 3°, 28006 Madrid; tel. (91) 5230226; fax (91) 5230171; e-mail embnuevazelanda@telefonica.net; internet www.nzembassy.com/spain; Ambassador ROBERT MOORE-JONES.

Nicaragua: Paseo de la Castellana 127, 1°B, 28046 Madrid; tel. (91) 4171649; Ambassador AUGUSTO C. ZAMORA RODRÍGUEZ.

Nigeria: Segre 23, 28002 Madrid; tel. (91) 5630911; fax (91) 5636320; e-mail info@nigeriainspain.org; internet www.nigeriainspain.org; Ambassador BIANCA ODUMEGWU-OJUKWU.

Norway: Serrano 26, 5°, 28001 Madrid; tel. (91) 4363840; fax (91) 3190969; e-mail emb.madrid@mfa.no; internet www.noruega.es; Ambassador JOHAN CHRISTOPHER VIBE.

Oman: Cardenal Herrera Oria 138, 28034 Madrid; tel. (91) 7364445; fax (91) 7354536; e-mail oman.emb.madrid@gmail.com; Ambassador HILAL BIN MARHOON BIN SALIM AL-MAAMARY.

Pakistan: Pedro Valdivia 16, 28006 Madrid; tel. (91) 3458995; fax (91) 3458158; e-mail cancilleria@embajada-pakistan.org; internet www.embajada-pakistan.org; Ambassador RIZWAN-UL-HAQ MAHMOOD.

Panama: Claudio Coello 86, 1° dcha, 28006 Madrid; tel. (91) 5765001; fax (91) 5767161; Ambassador ROBERTO EDUARDO ARANGO.

Paraguay: Dr Fleming 3, 1°, 28036 Madrid; tel. (91) 4572456; fax (91) 4570924; e-mail embapar@arrakis.es; Ambassador (vacant).

Peru: Príncipe de Vergara 36, 5° dcha, 28001 Madrid; tel. (91) 4314242; fax (91) 5776861; e-mail lepru@embajadaperu.es; internet www.embajadaperu.es; Ambassador FRANCISCO EGUIGUREN.

Philippines: Eresma 2, 28002 Madrid; tel. (91) 7823830; fax (91) 4116606; e-mail madridpe@terra.es; internet www.philmadrid.com; Ambassador CARLOS C. SALINAS.

Poland: Guisando 23A, 28035 Madrid; tel. (91) 3736605; fax (91) 3736624; e-mail madryt.amb.sekretariat@msz.gov.pl; internet www .madryt.msz.gov.pl; Chargé d'affaires a.i. AGNIESZKA FRYDRYCHO-WICZ-TEKIELI.

Portugal: Pinar 1, 28006 Madrid; tel. (91) 7824960; fax (91) 7824972; e-mail madrid@mne.pt; internet www .embajadaportugal-madrid.org; Ambassador ALVARO JOSÉ DE MEN-DONÇA E MOURA.

Qatar: Paseo de la Castellana 15, 5°, 28046 Madrid; tel. (91) 3106926; fax (91) 3104851; Ambassador HAMAD BIN HAMAD AL-IBRAHIM AL-ATTIYYA.

Romania: Avda Alfonso XIII 157, 28016 Madrid; tel. (91) 3501881; fax (91) 3452917; e-mail secretariat@embajadaderumania.es; internet madrid.mae.ro; Ambassador ION VÎLCU.

Russia: Velázquez 155, 28002 Madrid; tel. (91) 4110807; fax (91) 5629712; e-mail embrues@infonegocio.com; internet www.spain.mid .ru; Ambassador YURIY P. KORCHAGIN.

San Marino: Padre de Jesús Ordóñez 18, 3°, 28002 Madrid; tel. (91) 5639000; fax (91) 5631931; e-mail embamadrid@sanmarino1.net; Ambassador EMANUELE RESTELLI PRANDONI DELLA FRATA (resident in San Marino).

Saudi Arabia: Dr Alvarez Sierra 3, 28033 Madrid; tel. (91) 3834300; fax (91) 3021145; e-mail info@arabiasaudi.org; internet www .arabiasaudi.org; Ambassador Prince MANSOUR KHALID AL-FARHAN AL-SAOUD.

Senegal: Moralzarzal 18, 28034 Madrid; tel. (91) 7451003; fax (91) 7451148; Ambassador MAMADOU DEME.

Serbia: Velázquez 3, 28001 Madrid; tel. (91) 5635045; fax (91) 5630440; e-mail office@embajada-serbia.es; internet www .embajada-serbia.es; Ambassador DANKO PROKIĆ.

Slovakia: Pinar 20, 28006 Madrid; tel. (91) 5903861; fax (91) 5903868; e-mail emb.madrid@mzv.sk; internet www.mzv.sk/ madrid; Ambassador JÁN ŠKODA.

Slovenia: Hermanos Bécquer 7, 2°, 28006 Madrid; tel. (91) 4116893; fax (91) 5646057; e-mail vma@gov.si; Ambassador ALJAZ GOSNAR.

South Africa: Claudio Coello 91,6°–7°, 28006 Madrid; tel. (91) 4363780; fax (91) 5777414; e-mail embassy@sudafrica.com; Ambassador FIKILE SYLVIA MAGUBANE.

Sudan: Paseo de la Castellana 115, 2° izqda, 28046 Madrid; tel. (91) 4174903; fax (91) 5972516; e-mail sudani49@hotmail.com; Ambassador AIDA ABDELMAGIED ELSHIEKH.

Sweden: Caracas 25, 28010 Madrid; tel. (91) 7022000; fax (91) 7022040; e-mail ambassaden.madrid@gov.se; internet www .swedenabroad.com/madrid; Ambassador CECILIA JULIN.

Switzerland: Núñez de Balboa 35A, Edif. Goya, 7°, 28001 Madrid; tel. (91) 4363960; fax (91) 4363980; e-mail vertretung@mad.rep .admin.ch; internet www.eda.admin.ch/madrid; Ambassador URS JOHANN ZISWILER.

Syria: Plaza Platerías Martínez 1, 1°, 28014 Madrid; tel. (91) 4203946; fax (91) 4202681; Ambassador (vacant).

Thailand: Joaquín Costa 29, 28002 Madrid; tel. (91) 5632903; fax (91) 5640033; e-mail madthai@temb.e.telefonica.net; internet www .thaiembassy.org/madrid; Ambassador KULKUMUT SINGHARA NA AYUDHAYA.

Tunisia: Avda Alfonso XIII 64–68, 28016 Madrid; tel. (91) 4473508; fax (91) 5938416; e-mail ambtnmad@terra.es; Ambassador EZZINE CHELAIFA.

Turkey: Rafael Calvo 18, 2°A y B, 28010 Madrid; tel. (91) (91) 3103904; fax (91) 3086602; e-mail info@tcmadridbe.org; Ambassador AYŞE SINIRLIOĞLU.

Ukraine: Ronda de la Abubilla 52, 28043 Madrid; tel. (91) 7489360; fax (91) 3887178; e-mail ucremb@ya.com; internet www.mfa.gov.ua/ spain; Ambassador SERHII POHORELTSEV.

United Arab Emirates: Hernández de Tejada 7, 28027 Madrid; tel. (91) 5701001; fax (91) 5715176; e-mail madrid@mofa.gov.ae; internet www.uae-embassy.ae/embassies/es; Ambassador Dr HASSA ABDUL-LAH AL-OTAIBA.

United Kingdom: Paseo de la Castellana 259D, Torre Espacio, 28046 Madrid; tel. (91) 7146300; fax (91) 7146301; internet ukinspain .fco.gov.uk; Ambassador GILES PAXMAN.

USA: Serrano 75, 28006 Madrid; tel. (91) 5872200; fax (91) 5872303; e-mail amemb@embusa.es; internet madrid.usembassy.gov; Ambassador ALAN D. SOLOMONT.

Uruguay: Paseo del Pintor Rosales 32, 1° D, 28008 Madrid; tel. (91) 7580475; fax (91) 5428177; e-mail urumatri@urumatri.com; Ambassador CARLOS BUSTILLO BONASSO.

Uzbekistan: Paseo de la Castellana 45, 4° dcha, 28046 Madrid; tel. (91) 3101639; fax (91) 3103123; Ambassador DILSHOD AKHATOV (resident in Berlin, Germany).

Venezuela: Capitán Haya 1, 13°, Edif. Eurocentro, 28020 Madrid; tel. (91) 5981200; fax (91) 5971583; Ambassador BERNARDO ALVAREZ HERRERA.

Viet Nam: Calle Segre 5, 28002 Madrid; tel. (91) 5102867; fax (91) 4157067; e-mail claudiomes@yahoo.com; internet www .vietnamembassy.es; Ambassador TRUONG TRIEU DUONG.

Yemen: Paseo de la Castellana 117, 8°D, 28046 Madrid; tel. (91) 4119950; fax (91) 5623865; e-mail secretaria@embajadayemen.es; internet www.embyemenesp.com; Ambassador MUSTAPHA AHMAD NOMAN.

Judicial System

Consejo General del Poder Judicial (CGPJ) (General Council of the Judiciary): Marqués de la Ensenada 8, 28071 Madrid; tel. (91) 7006100; fax (91) 7006358; e-mail webmaster@cgpj.es; internet www .poderjudicial.es; The highest governing body of the judiciary; comprises a President, and 20 members elected by the Cortes and appointed by the King for a five-year term (10 by the Congreso de los Diputados and 10 by the Senado); supervises the judicial system; independent of the Ministry of Justice; Pres. GONZALO MOLINER; Gen. Prosecutor CÁNDIDO CONDE-PUMPIDO.

CONSTITUTIONAL COURT

Tribunal Constitucional: Domenico Scarlatti 6, 28003 Madrid; tel. (91) 5508000; fax (91) 5444088; e-mail buzon@ tribunalconstitucional.es; internet www.tribunalconstitucional.es; Pres. PASCUAL SALA SÁNCHEZ.

SUPREME COURT

Tribunal Supremo: Palacio de Justicia, Plaza de la Villa de París s/ n, 28071 Madrid; tel. (91) 3971200; e-mail webmaster@cgpj.es; internet www.poderjudicial.es; composed of 5 courts: civil; criminal; litigation; company; and military, each with its president and its respective judges; Pres. GONZALO MOLINER.

HIGH COURTS

Audiencia Nacional (National Court): García Gutiérrez 1, 28004 Madrid; tel. (91) 3973381; fax (91) 3973306; internet www .audiencianacional.es; f. 1977; consists of 3 divisions: Penal, Social and Contencioso-Administrativo, each with its president and respective judges; attached to Second Court of Supreme Court; deals primarily with crimes associated with a modern industrial society, such as corruption, forgery, drugs-trafficking, as well as terrorism; Pres. ANGEL JUANES.

OTHER COURTS

The Higher Courts of Justice in the Autonomous Communities comprise civil, criminal, administrative and labour divisions, while Provincial Courts hear proceedings for prosecutions of offences by lengthy prison terms, and appeals against the rulings of lower courts. The lower courts are the Criminal, Administrative, Labour, Juvenile and Prison Supervisory Courts of First Instance and Trial Courts. In municipalities where there are no Courts of First Instance and Trial, there is a Magistrates' Court.

Religion

CHRISTIANITY

About 92.5% of Spain's inhabitants profess adherence to Roman Catholicism, and the country contains some 61,000 churches, with about 500 persons in each parish. The Roman Catholic organization Opus Dei, which seeks to integrate religious faith and professional work, plays an important role in Spanish society. There are some 30,000 Protestants in Spain.

The Roman Catholic Church

For ecclesiastical purposes, Spain (including Spanish North Africa) comprises 14 metropolitan archdioceses and 55 dioceses. At 31 December 2006 there were an estimated 40.8m. adherents, equivalent to 92.0% of the population.

Bishops' Conference

Conferencia Episcopal Española, Añastro 1, 28033 Madrid; tel. (91) 3439600; fax (91) 3439602; e-mail conferenciaepiscopal@planalfa.es; internet www.conferenciaepiscopal.es.

f. 1977; Pres. Cardinal ANTONIO MARÍA ROUCO VARELA (Archbishop of Madrid); Sec.-Gen. JUAN ANTONIO MARTÍNEZ CAMINO.

Archbishop of Barcelona: Cardinal LLUÍS MARTÍNEZ SISTACH.

Archbishop of Burgos: Most Rev. FRANCISCO GIL HELLÍN.

Archbishop of Granada: Most Rev. FRANCISCO JAVIER MARTÍNEZ FERNÁNDEZ.

Archbishop of Madrid: Cardinal ANTONIO MARÍA ROUCO VARELA.

Archbishop of Mérida-Badajoz: Most Rev. SANTIAGO GARCÍA ARACIL.

Archbishop of Oviedo: Most Rev. JESÚS SANZ MONTES.

Archbishop of Pamplona and Tudela: Most Rev. FRANCISCO PÉREZ GONZÁLEZ.

Archbishop of Santiago de Compostela: Most Rev. JULIÁN BARRIO BARRIO.

Archbishop of Sevilla: Most Rev. JUAN JOSÉ ASENJO PELEGRINA.

Archbishop of Tarragona: Most Rev. JAUME PUJOL BALCELLS.

Archbishop of Toledo: Most Rev. BRAULIO RODRÍGUEZ PLAZA.

Archbishop of Valencia: Most Rev. CARLOS OSORO SIERRA.

Archbishop of Valladolid: Most Rev. RICARDO BLÁZQUEZ PÉREZ.

Archbishop of Zaragoza: Most Rev. MANUEL UREÑA PASTOR.

Other Christian Churches

Iglesia Española Reformada Episcopal (IERE) (Spanish Reformed Episcopal Church): Beneficencia 18, 28004 Madrid; tel. (91) 4452560; fax (91) 5944572; e-mail eclesiae@arrakis.es; internet www.anglicanos.org; f. 1860; mem. of the Anglican Communion; 17 congregations (2004); Bishop Rt Rev. CARLOS LÓPEZ LOZANO.

Unión Evangélica Bautista Española (UEBE) (Baptist Evangelical Union of Spain): San Jacinto 26, 3°, 46008 Valencia; tel. (963) 591633; fax (963) 134581; e-mail secretaria@uebe.org; internet www.uebe.org; f. 1922; Pres. Rev. JUAN MARCOS VÁZQUEZ VARELA; Gen. Sec. Rev. MANUEL SARRIAS.

ISLAM

It is estimated that there are some 1m. Muslims in Spain, many of whom are Moroccan migrant workers.

Comisión Islámica de España: Anastasio Herrero 5, 28020 Madrid; tel. (91) 5714040; fax (91) 5708889; e-mail cie@teleline.es; umbrella org.; negotiates with Govt on Islamic affairs; Sec.-Gen. MANSUL ESCUDERO.

Federación Española de Entidades Religiosas Islámicas (FEERI): Calle Brescia 17, 28028 Madrid; f. 1989; 57 mem. groups; Pres. FÉLIX ANGEL HERRERO.

Unión de Comunidades Islámicas de España (UCIDE): Anastasio Herrero 5, Madrid 28020; tel. (91) 5714040; fax (91) 5708889; e-mail secretariogeneralcie@hotmail.com; Pres. RIAY TATARY BAKRY.

Comunidad Ahmadía del Islam en España: La Mezquita Basharat, 14630 Pedro Abad (Córdoba); tel. (957) 186203; fax (957) 186300; e-mail info@alislam.org; internet www.alislam.org; Pres. MUBARIK AHMAD KHAN.

JUDAISM

There are an estimated 48,000 Jews in Spain.

Federación de Comunidades Judías de España (Federation of Jewish Communities of Spain): Miguel Ángel 7, 1° c, 28010 Madrid; tel. (91) 7001208; fax (91) 3915717; e-mail fcje@fcje.org; internet www.fcje.org; 30 communities; Pres. ISAAC QUERUB CARO.

The Press

The most widely read newspapers are *ABC*, *El Mundo*, *El País* and *La Razón*, published in Madrid, and *La Vanguardia*, published in Barcelona. Important regional newspapers include *El Periódico de Catalunya* (Barcelona), *El Correo* (Bilbao) and *La Voz de Galicia* (A Coruña). Sporting dailies, notably *Marca* and *As*, enjoy very high circulation figures. Much of the Spanish media is owned by large corporations, of which the most prominent are Grupo PRISA (*El País*) and Vocento (*ABC* and various regional titles).

PRINCIPAL DAILIES

(arranged by province—circulation figures as at 2011 unless otherwise stated)

Albacete

La Tribuna de Albacete: Paseo de la Cuba 14, 02005 Albacete; tel. (967) 191000; fax (967) 211275; e-mail redaccion@latribunadealbacete.es; internet www.latribunadealbacete.es; Propr Promecaldi; Dir FRANCISCO JAVIER MARTÍNEZ GARCÍA; circ. 3,581.

Alicante

Información: Avda Dr Rico 17, Apdo 214, 03005 Alicante; tel. (96) 5989100; fax (96) 5989165; e-mail redaccion@epi.es; internet www.diarioinformacion.com; f. 1940; Propr Editorial Prensa Ibérica; Dir JUAN R. GIL; circ. 25,022.

Almería

La Voz de Almería: Avda Mediterráneo 159, 1°, Edif. Cadena Ser, 04007 Almería; tel. (950) 280036; fax (950) 256458; e-mail lavoz@lavozdealmeria.com; internet www.lavozdealmeria.com; morning; Dir PEDRO MANUEL DE LA CRUZ ALONSO; circ. 8,704.

Asturias

El Comercio: Diario El Comercio 1, 33207 Gijón; tel. (98) 5179800; fax (98) 5340955; e-mail digital.co@elcomerciodigital.com; internet www.elcomercio.es; f. 1878; Propr Vocento; Dir IÑIGO NORIEGA GÓMEZ; circ. 21,894.

La Nueva España: Calvo Sotelo 7, Edif. Sedes, 33007 Oviedo; tel. (98) 5279700; fax (98) 5279711; e-mail pam@lne.es; internet www.lne.es; f. 1937; Propr Editorial Prensa Ibérica; Dir MARIO BLASCO; circ. 54,890.

El Periódico—La Voz de Asturias: La Lila 6, bajo, 33006 Oviedo; tel. (98) 5101500; fax (98) 5101505; e-mail asturias@lavozdeasturias.com; internet www.lavozdeasturias.es; f. 1923; Propr Grupo Zeta; Dir JUAN CARLOS CUESTA; circ. 7,369.

Badajoz

Hoy—Diario de Extremadura: Carretera Madrid–Lisboa 22, 06008 Badajoz; tel. (924) 214300; fax (924) 229591; e-mail edigitales@hoy.es; internet www.hoy.es; f. 1933; Catholic; Badajoz and Cáceres editions; Propr Vocento; Dir Gen. MIGUEL ÁNGEL JARAÍZ; circ. 17,591.

Barcelona

Ara: Diputació 119, 08015 Barcelona; tel. (93) 2029595; fax (93) 4519264; e-mail web@ara.cat; internet www.ara.cat; f. 2010; Catalan; Dir CARLES CAPDEVILA; circ. 16,333.

Avui: Tàpies 2, 08001 Barcelona; tel. (93) 2276600; internet www.elpuntavui.cat; f. 1976; Catalan; Pres. JOAQUIM VIDAL; CEO JOAN VALL; circ. 28,591.

Mundo Deportivo: Avda Diagonal 577, 5°, 08036 Barcelona; tel. (93) 3444100; fax (93) 3444250; e-mail mdonline@mundodeportivo.com; internet www.mundodeportivo.com; f. 1906; sport; Propr Grupo Godó; Dir SANTI NOLLA ZAYAS; circ. 95,907.

El Periódico de Catalunya: Consell de Cent 400, 08009 Barcelona; tel. (93) 2655353; fax (93) 4846635; e-mail atencion.lector@elperiodico.com; internet www.elperiodico.com; daily; f. 1978; parallel edns in Spanish and Catalan; Propr Grupo Zeta; Dir ENRIC HERNÀNDEZ; circ. 177,830.

Sport: Consell de Cent 425–427, 08009 Barcelona; tel. (93) 2279400; fax (93) 2279405; e-mail redaccion@diariosport.com; internet www.sport.es; Propr Grupo Zeta; Dir JOAN VEHILS; circ. 91,753.

La Vanguardia: Avda Diagonal 477, 3°, 08036 Barcelona; tel. (93) 2704600; fax (93) 2704649; e-mail digital@lavanguardia.es; internet www.lavanguardia.com; f. 1881; Propr Grupo Godó; Dir JOSÉ ANTICH; circ. 190,033.

Burgos

Diario de Burgos: Avda Castilla y León 62–64, 09006 Burgos; tel. (947) 268375; fax (947) 277219; e-mail redaccion@diariodeburgos.es; internet www.diariodeburgos.es; f. 1891; Catholic; Propr Promecal; Dir RAUL BRIONGOS; circ. 11,598.

Cádiz

Diario de Cádiz: Edif. Fénix, Avda El Puerto 2, 11007 Cádiz; tel. (956) 297900; fax (956) 224883; e-mail nmartinez@diariodecadiz.com; internet www.diariodecadiz.es; f. 1867; Propr Grupo Joly; Dir RAFAEL NAVAS; circ. 21,839.

Diario de Jerez: Patricio Garvey s/n, 11402 Jerez Cádiz; tel. (956) 321411; fax (956) 349904; e-mail redaccion@diariodejerez.com;

internet www.diariodejerez.es; f. 1984; Propr Grupo Joly; Dir DAVID FERNÁNDEZ; circ. 6,578.

Cantabria

Alerta—el Diario de Cantabria: 1 de Mayo s/n, Barrio San Martín, 39011 Peñacastillo; tel. (942) 320033; fax (942) 322046; e-mail administracion@eldiarioalerta.com; internet www.eldiarioalerta .com; f. 1937; independent; Dir ISAÍAS DÍAZ TRUEBA; circ. 30,619.

El Diario Montañés: La Prensa s/n, 39012 Santander; tel. (942) 354000; fax (942) 341806; e-mail redaccion.dm@eldiariomontanes .es; internet www.eldiariomontanes.es; f. 1902; Propr Vocento; Dir MANUEL ANGEL CASTAÑEDA PÉREZ; circ. 31,442.

Castellón

El Periódico Mediterráneo: Carretera de Almassora s/n, 12005 Castellón; tel. (964) 349500; fax (964) 349505; e-mail epmediterraneo@elperiodico.com; internet www .elperiodicomediterraneo.com; f. 1938; Propr Grupo Zeta; Dir JOSÉ LUIS VALENCIA; circ. 9,558.

Ciudad Real

La Tribuna de Ciudad Real: Pedro Muñoz 3, 13005 Ciudad Real; tel. (926) 215301; fax (926) 215145; e-mail ciudadreal@ diariolatribuna.com; internet www.latribunadeciudadreal.es; Propr Promecal; Dir OSCAR GÁLVEZ MATÉ; circ. 3,435.

Córdoba

Córdoba: Ing. Juan de la Cierva 18 (Polígono Torrecilla), 14013 Córdoba; tel. (957) 420302; fax (957) 204648; e-mail cordoba1@ elperiodico.es; internet www.diariocordoba.com; f. 1941; Propr Grupo Zeta; Dir FRANCISCO LUIS CÓRDOBA BERJILLOS; circ. 11,139.

A Coruña

El Correo Gallego: Preguntoiro 29, 15704 Santiago de Compostela; tel. (981) 543700; fax (981) 543701; e-mail jsalgado@elcorreogallego .es; internet www.elcorreogallego.es; f. 1878; Propr Grupo Correo Gallego; Dir JOSÉ MANUEL REY NÓVOA; circ. 18,238.

Galicia Hoxe: Preguntoiro 29, 15704 Santiago de Compostela; tel. (981) 543700; fax (981) 543701; e-mail info@galicia-hoxe.com; internet www.galiciahoxe.com; f. 1994 as *O Correo Galego*; refounded under current name 2003; Galician; Propr Grupo Correo Gallego; Dir JOSÉ MANUEL REY NÓVOA.

El Ideal Gallego: Polígono de Pocomaco, C12, 15190 Mesoiro; tel. (981) 173040; e-mail elidealgallego@elidealgallego.com; internet www.elidealgallego.com; f. 1917; independent; Dir JUAN RAMÓN DÍAZ GARCÍA; circ. 15,500 (Sun. 20,000).

La Voz de Galicia: Avda de la Prensa 84–85, Polígono de Sabón, 15142 Arteixo; tel. (981) 180180; fax (981) 180410; e-mail webvoz@ lavoz.es; internet www.lavozdegalicia.es; f. 1882; Propr Grupo Voz; Dir XOSÉ LUIS VILELA CONDE; circ. 91,131.

Girona

El Punt: Santa Eugènia 42, 17005 Girona; tel. (972) 186400; fax (972) 186420; e-mail girona@elpunt.cat; internet www.elpuntavui .cat; f. 1979; Catalan; various regional edns; also publishes weekly edns covering Valencia and Perpignan (France); Pres. JOAQUIM VIDAL; circ. 24,134 (July 2008–June 2009).

Granada

Ideal: Huelva 2, Polígono de Asegra, 18210 Peligros; tel. (958) 809809; e-mail idealdigital@ideal.es; internet www.ideal.es; f. 1932; Propr Vocento; Dir EDUARDO PERALTA DE ANA; circ. 27,598; edns in Granada, Jaén and Almería.

Guipúzcoa

El Diario Vasco: Camino de Portuetxe 2, Barrio de Ibaeta, Apdo 201, 20018 San Sebastián; tel. (943) 410700; fax (943) 410814; e-mail contactanos@diariovasco.com; internet www.diariovasco.com; f. 1934; Propr Vocento; Dir JOSÉ GABRIEL MUJIKA; circ. 69,905.

Gara: Camino Portuetxe 23, 2°, 20018 San Sebastián; tel. (943) 316999; fax (943) 316998; internet www.gara.net; f. 1999; Basque and Spanish; left-wing Basque nationalist; independent; Dir IÑAKI SOTO.

Illes Balears

Diari de Balears: Paseo Mallorca, 9°A, 07011 Palma de Mallorca; tel. (971) 788300; fax (971) 455740; e-mail redaccio@ddbalears.cat; internet dbalears.cat; f. 1939 as *Baleares*; refounded as Catalan daily in 1996; Propr Grupo Serra; Dir MIQUEL SERRA MAGRANER.

Diario de Ibiza: Avda de la Paz, 07800 Ibiza; tel. (971) 190000; fax (971) 190322; e-mail diariodeibiza@epi.es; internet www .diariodeibiza.es; Propr Editorial Prensa Ibérica; Dir JOAN SERRA TUR; circ. 5,780.

Diario de Mallorca: Puerto Rico 15, Polígono de Levante, 07006 Palma de Mallorca; tel. (971) 170300; fax (971) 170301; e-mail secretaria.diariodemallorca@epi.es; internet www.diariodemallorca .es; f. 1953; Propr Editorial Prensa Ibérica; Dir PEDRO PABLO ALONSO; circ. 19,145.

Menorca, Diario Insular: Cap de Cavalleria 5, 07714 Mahón, Menorca; tel. (971) 351600; fax (971) 351983; e-mail redaccion@ menorca.info; internet www.menorca.info; f. 1941; Dir JOSEP BAGUR TORRES; circ. 4,832.

Última Hora: Paseo Mallorca 9A, 07011 Palma de Mallorca; tel. (971) 788300; fax (971) 454190; e-mail digital@ultimahora.es; internet ultimahora.es; f. 1893; Propr Grupo Serra; Dir PEDRO COMAS BARCELÓ; circ. 32,480.

León

Diario de León: Carretera León–Astorga, Km 4,5, 24010 León; tel. (987) 840300; fax (987) 840340; e-mail diariodeleon@diariodeleon.es; internet www.diariodeleon.es; Dir FERNANDO ALLER GONZÁLEZ; circ. 13,227.

Lleida (Lérida)

Segre: Carrer del Riu 6, Apdo 543, 25007 Lérida; tel. (973) 248000; fax (973) 246031; e-mail redaccio@segre.com; internet www.segre .com; f. 1982; Catalan and Spanish edns; independent; Dir JUAN CAL SÁNCHEZ; circ. 11,196.

Lugo

El Progreso: Rúa Ribadeo s/n, 27002 Lugo; tel. (982) 298100; fax (982) 298102; e-mail redaccion@galiciae.com; internet www .elprogreso.es; f. 1908; Dir LUIS RODRÍGUEZ GARCÍA; Pres. BLANCA GARCÍA MONTENEGRO; circ. 14,991.

Madrid

ABC: Juan Ignacio Luca de Tena 7, 28027 Madrid; tel. (91) 3399000; fax (91) 3203680; e-mail cartas@abc.es; internet www.abc.es; f. 1905; conservative, monarchist; various regional edns; Propr Vocento; Dir BIEITO RUBIDO RAMONDE; circ. 221,351.

As: Valentín Beato 44, 28037 Madrid; tel. (91) 3752500; fax (91) 3752558; e-mail diarioas@diarioas.es; internet www.as.com; f. 1967; sport; Propr Grupo PRISA; Dir ALFREDO RELAÑO ESTAPÉ; circ. 198,758.

Cinco Días: Miguel Yuste 42, 28037 Madrid; tel. (91) 5386100; fax (91) 3537991; e-mail redaccion@cinodias.com; internet www .cincodias.com; f. 1978; economic; Propr Grupo PRISA; Dir JORGE RIVERA; circ. 31,326.

El Economista: Condesa de Venadito 1, 3°, 28027 Madrid; tel. (91) 3246700; fax (91) 3246727; e-mail comunicacion@eleconomista.es; internet www.eleconomista.es; f. 2006; originally f. 1886 as weekly; daily; Pres. ALFONSO DE SALAS; Dir AMADOR G. AYORA; circ. 21,574.

Expansión: Paseo de la Castellana 66, 28046 Madrid; tel. (91) 3373220; fax (91) 3373266; e-mail expansion.com@expansion.com; internet www.expansion.com; economic; Propr Unidad Editorial, SA; Dir ANA I. PEREDA; circ. 37,495.

La Gaceta de los Negocios: Paseo de la Castellana 36–38, 28028 Madrid; tel. (902) 996611; fax (91) 4327733; e-mail info@ intereconomia.com; internet www.intereconomia.com; f. 1989; daily; business and finance; Pres. JULIO ARIZA IRIGOYEN; circ. 41,196.

Marca: Avda de San Luis 25–27, 28033 Madrid; tel. (902) 996111; e-mail cartasaldirector@unidadeditorial.es; internet www.marca .com; f. 1938 as weekly in San Sebastián, 1942 as daily in Madrid; sport; Propr Unidad Editorial, SA; Dir OSCAR CAMPILLO; circ. 244,456.

El Mundo (del Siglo Veintiuno): Pradillo 42, 28002 Madrid; tel. (91) 5864800; fax (91) 5864848; e-mail cartas.director@elmundo.es; internet www.elmundo.es; f. 1989; centre-right; various regional edns; Propr Unidad Editorial, SA; Dir FERNANDO BAETA; circ. 337,172.

El País: Miguel Yuste 40, 28037 Madrid; tel. (91) 3378200; fax (91) 3048766; e-mail redacciondigital@elpais.es; internet www.elpais .com; f. 1976; centre-left; regional edns in Andalusia, Basque Country, Catalonia, Galicia and Valencia; Propr Grupo PRISA; Pres. IGNACIO POLANCO MORENO; Dir JAVIER MORENO BARBER; circ. 365,117.

Qué!: Calle Juan Ignacio Luca de Tena 6, 28027 Madrid; tel. (91) 5726200; fax (91) 5710035; e-mail redaccion.madrid@que.es; internet www.que.es; f. 2005; free; 15 local edns; Propr Vocento; Dir RAFAEL MARTÍNEZ SIMANCAS; circ. 586,185.

La Razón: Josefa Valcárcel 42, 28027 Madrid; tel. (91) 3247000; fax (91) 3249451; e-mail sugerencias@larazon.es; internet www.larazon

.es; f. 1998; conservative; Pres. MAURICIO CASALS; Dir FRANCISCO MARHUENDA; circ. 103,789.

20 Minutos: Condesa de Venadito 1, Planta 2, 28027 Madrid; tel. (91) 7015600; fax (91) 7015660; e-mail grupo20minutos@20minutos.es; internet www.20minutos.es; f. 2000; free; 15 regional edns; Dir ARSENIO ESCOLAR; circ. 704,802.

Málaga

La Opinión de Málaga: Calle Granada 42, 29015 Málaga; tel. (95) 2126200; fax (95) 2126255; e-mail redaccion@opinionmalaga.com; internet www.laopiniondemalaga.es; f. 1999; Propr Editorial Prensa Ibérica; Dir JUAN DE MELLADO; circ. 5,692.

Sur: Avda Dr Marañón 48, 29009 Málaga; tel. (95) 2649600; fax (95) 2279508; e-mail redaccion@diariosur.es; internet www.diariosur.es; f. 1937; Propr Vocento; Dir MANUEL CASTILLO; circ. 47,564 (2010) (also publishes free English weekly, circ. 32,293).

Murcia

La Verdad: Camino Viejo de Monteagudo s/n, 30160 Murcia; tel. (968) 369100; fax (968) 369147; e-mail lectores@laverdad.es; internet www.laverdad.es; f. 1903; local edns published in Albacete and Alicante; propr Vocento; Dir JOSÉ MARÍA ESTEBAN IBÁÑEZ; circ. 30,561.

Navarra

Diario de Navarra: Carretera Zaragoza s/n, 31191 Cordovilla (Navarra); tel. (948) 236050; fax (948) 150484; e-mail redaccion@diariodenavarra.es; internet www.diariodenavarra.es; f. 1903; conservative; independent; Dir INÉS ARTAJO AYESA; circ. 44,924.

Diario de Noticias: Altzutzate 8, Polígono Areta, 31620 Huarte; tel. (948) 332533; fax (948) 332518; e-mail cad@noticiasdenavarra.com; internet www.noticiasdenavarra.com; f. 1994; independent; Dir JOSEBA SANTAMARÍA; circ. 16,185.

Ourense

La Región: Polígono Industrial de San Cibrao das Viñas C4, 32091 Ourense; tel. (988) 600102; e-mail info@laregion.es; internet www.laregion.es; f. 1910; independent; Pres. JOSÉ LUIS OUTEIRIÑO RODRÍGUEZ; Dir XOSÉ PASTORIZA MARTÍNEZ; circ. 10,906.

Las Palmas de Gran Canaria

Canarias 7: Profesor Lozano 7, Urbanización El Sebadal, 35008 Las Palmas; tel. (928) 301300; fax (928) 301333; e-mail redaccion@canarias7.es; internet www.canarias7.es; f. 1982; Dir FRANCISCO SUÁREZ ÁLAMO; circ. 16,357.

La Provincia—Diario de las Palmas: Alcalde Ramírez Bethencourt 8, 35003 Las Palmas; tel. (928) 479400; fax (928) 479401; e-mail laprovincia@epi.es; internet www.laprovincia.es; *La Provincia* f. 1911, *Diario de las Palmas* f. 1893; Propr Editorial Prensa Ibérica; Dir ANTONIO CACEREÑO IBÁÑEZ; circ. 21,856.

Pontevedra

Faro de Vigo: Factoría de Chapela, 36320 Redondela; tel. (986) 814600; fax (986) 814614; e-mail contenidos@farodevigomedia.es; internet www.farodevigo.es; f. 1853; Propr Editorial Prensa Ibérica; Dir JUAN CARLOS DA SILVA; circ. 36,816.

La Rioja

La Rioja: Vara del Rey 74, Apdo 28, 26002 Logroño; tel. (941) 279169; fax (941) 279147; e-mail redaccion@larioja.com; internet www.larioja.com; f. 1889; Propr Vocento; Man. Dir JAVIER GARCIA GALIANA; circ. 13,583.

Salamanca

La Gaceta Regional de Salamanca: Avda de los Cipreses 81, 37004 Salamanca; tel. (923) 125252; fax (923) 256155; e-mail info@lagacetadesalamanca.es; internet www.lagacetadesalamanca.es; f. 1920; independent; Dir JULIAN BALLESTEROS; circ. 13,467.

Santa Cruz de Tenerife

El Día: Avda de Buenos Aires 71, Apdo 97, 38005 Santa Cruz; tel. (922) 238300; fax (922) 214247; e-mail eldia@eldia.es; internet www.eldia.es; f. 1910; Dir JOSÉ E. RODRÍGUEZ RAMÍREZ; circ. 20,497.

Diario de Avisos: Salamanca 5, 38006 Santa Cruz; tel. (922) 272350; fax (922) 241039; e-mail redaccion@diariodeavisos.com; internet www.diariodeavisos.com; f. 1890; refounded 1976; Dir JUAN MANUEL PARDELLAS; circ. 8,805.

La Opinión de Tenerife: Plaza Santa Cruz de la Sierra 2, 38003 Santa Cruz; tel. (922) 471800; fax (922) 471801; e-mail tenerife@laopinion.es; internet www.laopinion.es; Propr Editorial Prensa Ibérica; Dir JOAQUÍN CATALÁN; circ. 5,426.

Sevilla
(Seville)

El Correo de Andalucía: Américo Vespucio 39, Isla de la Cartuja, 41092 Sevilla; tel. (95) 4488500; fax (95) 4460744; e-mail redaccion@correoandalucia.es; internet www.elcorreoweb.es; f. 1899; independent; Pres. JOSÉ RODRÍGUEZ DE LA BORBOLLA CAMOYÁN; Dir JUAN CARLOS BLANCO; circ. 10,254.

Diario de Sevilla: Rioja 14, 41001 Sevilla; tel. (95) 4506200; fax (95) 4506222; e-mail secretaria@diariodesevilla.es; internet www.diariodesevilla.es; f. 1999; Propr Grupo Joly; Dir JOSÉ ANTONIO CARRIZOSA; circ. 18,426.

Tarragona

Diari de Tarragona: Domènech Guansé 2, 43005 Tarragona; tel. (977) 299700; fax (977) 223013; e-mail tlopez@diaridetarragona.com; internet www.diaridetarragona.com; f. 1808; Spanish and Catalan; Dir JOSEP RAMON CORREAL; circ. 10,728.

Valencia

Levante—El Mercantil Valenciano (EMV): Traginers 7, 46014 Valencia; tel. (96) 3992200; fax (96) 3992308; e-mail levante-emv@epi.es; internet www.levante-emv.es; f. 1872; Propr Editorial Prensa Ibérica; Dir FERRAN BELDA; circ. 32,414.

Las Provincias: Polígono Industrial Vara de Quart, Gremis 1, 46014 Valencia; tel. (96) 3502211; fax (96) 3590188; e-mail redaccion@lasprovinciasdigital.es; internet www.lasprovincias.es; f. 1866; rightist; Propr Vocento; Dir JULIÁN QUIRÓS; circ. 29,648.

Valladolid

El Día de Valladolid: Edif. Promecal, Los Astros s/n, 47009 Valladolid; tel. (983) 325045; fax (983) 325047; e-mail redaccion@diavalladolid.es; internet www.eldiadevalladolid.com; f. 2003; Propr Promecal; Pres. ANTONIO MÉNDEZ POZO; circ. 4,876.

El Norte de Castilla: Vázquez de Menchaca 10 (Polígono de Argales), 47008 Valladolid; tel. (983) 412100; fax (983) 412111; e-mail redaccion.nc@nortecastilla.es; internet www.elnortedecastilla.es; f. 1854; Propr Vocento; Dir CARLOS F. AGANZO; circ. 29,679.

Vizcaya (Bizkaia)

El Correo: Pintor Losada 7, Apdo 205, 48004 Bilbao; tel. (94) 4870100; fax (94) 4870111; e-mail redaccion@elcorreo.com; internet www.elcorreo.com; f. 1910; edns in Vizcaya and Álava; Propr Vocento; Dir JUAN CARLOS MARTINEZ; circ. 97,313.

Deia: Camino de Capuchinos 6, 5°, 48004 Bilbao; tel. (94) 4599100; fax (94) 4599120; e-mail cartas@deia.com; internet www.deia.com; f. 1997; Basque nationalist, associated with the EAJ-PNV; publishes weekly satirical supplement, *Caduca Hoy*; Dir BINGEN ZUPIRIA; circ. 17,013.

Zaragoza

Heraldo de Aragón: Paseo de la Independencia 29, Apdo 175, 50001 Zaragoza; tel. (976) 765000; fax (976) 765001; e-mail redaccion@heraldo.es; internet www.heraldo.es; f. 1895; independent; also publishes edn in Huesca; Dir MIGUEL ITURBE MACH; circ. 44,354.

El Periódico de Aragón: Hernán Cortés 37, 50005 Zaragoza; tel. (976) 700400; fax (976) 700462; e-mail eparagon@elperiodico.com; internet www.elperiodicodearagon.com; f. 1990; Propr Grupo Zeta; Dir JAIME ARMENGOL; circ. 12,481.

SELECTED PERIODICALS

The Arts

Arquitectura y Diseño: RBA Revistas, SA, Pérez Galdós 36 bis, 08012 Barcelona; internet www.rba.es; monthly; architecture and design; Dir-Gen. ARIADNA HERNÁNDEZ; circ. 47,741 (June 2007).

Claves de Razón Práctica: Julián Camarillo 29B, 1°, 28004 Madrid; tel. (91) 5386104; fax (91) 5222291; e-mail claves@progresa.es; internet claves.progresa.es; f. 1990; monthly; books and culture; Dirs JAVIER PRADERA, FERNANDO SAVATER; circ. 4,500.

El Croquis: Avda de los Reyes Católicos 9, El Escorial, 28280 Madrid; tel. (91) 8969414; fax (91) 8969415; e-mail elcroquis@elcroquis.es; internet www.elcroquis.es; 6 a year; architecture, in Spanish and English; Dirs FERNANDO MÁRQUEZ CECILIA, RICHARD LEVENE; circ. 15,078 (2010).

Experimenta: Churruca 27, 4° ext. dcha, 28004 Madrid; tel. (91) 5214049; fax (91) 5213212; e-mail info@experimenta.es; internet www.experimenta.es; f. 1989; architecture and design; Dir PIERLUIGI CATTERMOLE FIORAVANTI.

Insula: Paseo de Recoletos 4, 2°, 28001; tel. and fax (91) 4233743; internet www.insula.es; f. 1946; monthly; literature and social sciences; Editor ARANTXA GÓMEZ SANCHO; circ. 6,000.

Letra Internacional: Monte Esquinza 30, 3° dcha, 28010 Madrid; tel. (91) 3104313; fax (91) 3194585; e-mail editorial@fpabloiglesias .es; internet www.fpabloiglesias.es; f. 1986; quarterly; culture; Dir SALVADOR CLOTAS I CIERCO.

El Magisterio Español: Jose Abascal 46, 4° dcha, 28003 Madrid; tel. (91) 5199131; fax (91) 4151124; e-mail jollero@magisnet.com; internet www.magisnet.com; f. 1866; Wed.; education; Dir JOSÉ MARÍA DE MOYA ANEGÓN; circ. 10,320 (2009).

Qué Leer: Passeig de Sant Gervasi 16–20, 08022 Barcelona; tel. (93) 2541250; fax (93) 2541263; e-mail queleer@hachette.es; internet www.que-leer.com; f. 1996; monthly; book news, etc.; Dir ANTONIO G. ITURBE; circ. 26,608.

Ritmo: Isabel Colbrand 10, Oficina 87, 28050 Madrid; tel. (91) 3588774; fax (91) 3588944; e-mail correo@ritmo.es; internet www .ritmo.es; monthly; classical music; Dir (vacant).

Current Affairs, History, Religion, etc.

Aceprensa: Núñez de Balboa 125, 6°, 28006 Madrid; tel. (91) 5158975; fax (91) 5631243; e-mail redaccion@aceprensa.com; internet www.aceprensa.com; f. 1973; weekly; news and features; Editorial Dir IGNACIO ARÉCHAGA DUQUE; circ. 4,000.

Boletín Oficial del Estado (BOE): Avda de Manoteras 54, 28050 Madrid; tel. (902) 365303; fax (91) 3841555; internet www.boe.es; f. 1936; successor of *Gaceta de Madrid*, f. 1661; daily except Sun.; laws, decrees, orders, etc.; Dir-Gen. JULIO SEAGE MARIÑO; circ. 60,000.

Cambio 16: Arroyo de Fontarrón 51, 28030 Madrid; tel. (91) 4201199; fax (91) 3601302; e-mail cambio16@cambio16.info; internet www.cambio16.info; f. 1972; weekly, Wed.; general; Dir MANUEL DOMÍNGUEZ MORENO.

El Ciervo: Calvet 56, 08021 Barcelona; tel. (93) 2005145; fax (93) 2011015; e-mail redaccion@elciervo.es; internet www.elciervo.es; f. 1951; monthly; politics and culture; Dir ROSARIO BOFILL; circ. 5,000.

Ciudad Nueva: José Picón 28, 28028 Madrid; tel. (91) 7259530; fax (91) 7130452; e-mail revista@ciudadnueva.com; internet www .ciudadnueva.com; f. 1964; monthly; Dir JAVIER RUBIO; circ. 7,000.

La Clave: Avda de Argón 336, 28022 Madrid; tel. (91) 8373131; fax (91) 8373136; e-mail redaccion@laclave.com; internet www.laclave .com; f. 2001; weekly; news magazine; Dir JOSÉ LUIS BALBIN; circ. 60,000.

Clío: Passeig San Gervasi 16–20, 08022 Barcelona; tel. (93) 2232136; fax (93) 4322907; e-mail clio@hachette.es; internet www.cliorevista .com; f. 2001; monthly; history; Dir JOSEP A. BORRELL; circ. 36,401.

Ecclesia: Alfonso XI 4, 28014 Madrid; tel. (91) 5315400; fax (91) 5225561; e-mail ecclesia@planalfa.es; f. 1941; weekly; religious information; Dir JESÚS DE LAS HERAS MUELA; Editor-in-Chief MIGUEL DE SANTIAGO; Propr Conferencia Episcopal Española; circ. 24,000.

Época: Paseo de la Castellana 36–38, 28046 Madrid; tel. (91) 5109100; fax (91) 5109149; weekly; Dir CARLOS DAVILA.

Historia 16: Rufino González 13, 1°, 28037 Madrid; tel. (91) 3271171; fax (91) 3271220; e-mail h16redaccion@telefonica.net; f. 1976; monthly; history; Dir MARÍA ALDAVE; circ. 25,000.

El Jueves: Avda Diagonal 468, 5°, 08006 Barcelona; tel. (93) 2922217; fax (93) 2375824; e-mail redaccion@eljueves.es; internet www.eljueves.es; f. 1977; weekly, Wed.; satirical; Dir MAYTE QUÍLES; circ. 105,029 (2010).

Mundo Cristiano: Paseo de la Castellana 210, 2°B, 28046 Madrid; tel. (91) 3507862; fax (91) 3590230; e-mail mundoc@palabra.es; internet www.palabra.es; f. 1963; monthly; Ediciones Palabra SA; Dir DARIO CHIMENO CANO; Editor-in-Chief JOSÉ M. NAVALPOTRO; circ. 25,000 (July 2012).

A Nosa Terra: Rúa Príncipe 22, 36202 Vigo; tel. (986) 222405; fax (986) 223101; e-mail info@anosaterra.com; internet www.anosaterra .com; f. 1907; weekly; Galician; Dir AFONSO EÍRÉ LÓPEZ.

Nueva Revista: Javier Ferrero 2, 28002 Madrid; tel. (91) 5199756; fax (91) 4151254; e-mail nuevarevista@tst.es; internet www .nuevarevista.net; f. 1990; 6 a year; politics, culture, art; Pres. ANTONIO FONTÁN PÉREZ.

Política—Revista Republicana: Ríos Rosas 10, 1° B, 28003 Madrid; tel. (902) 158935; fax (91) 4411165; e-mail ir@bitmailer .net; internet www.izquierdarepublicana.com; f. 1934; bi-monthly; organ of Izquierda Republicana; Dir ISABELO HERREROS.

Revista de Estudios Políticos: Plaza de la Marina Española 9, 28071 Madrid; tel. (91) 5401950; fax (91) 5419574; e-mail editer@cepc .es; internet www.cepc.es; f. 1941; quarterly; publishes research papers, original and unpublished, on the Theory of the Constitution, State Theory, Political Science, History and History of Political Thought; publ. by Centro de Estudios Políticos y Constitucionales; Dirs PEDRO DE VEGA, JUAN J. SOLOZÁBAL ECHAVARRÍA; circ. 1,000.

El Socialista: Gobelas 31, 28023 Madrid; tel. (91) 5820044; fax (91) 5820045; e-mail elsocialista@elsocialista.es; internet www .elsocialista.es; f. 1866; monthly; general information; Dir JOAQUÍN TAGAR; circ. 185,000.

El Temps: Octubre Centre de Cultura Contemporània, Sant Ferran 12, 46001 Valencia; tel. (96) 3535100; fax (96) 3534569; e-mail eltemps@eltemps.net; internet www.eltemps.net; f. 1984; weekly; general information; in Catalan; Dir JORDI FORTUNY I BATALLA; circ. 25,000.

Tiempo: O' Donnell 12, 3°, 28009 Madrid; tel. (91) 5863300; fax (91) 5863346; e-mail contacta.tiempo@zetadigital.es; internet www .tiempodehoy.com; weekly; Dir JESÚS RIVASÉS; circ. 43,408 (June 2007).

Treball: Passatge del Rellotge 3, 08002 Barcelona; tel. (93) 3010612; e-mail treball@iniciativa.cat; internet www.iniciativa.cat; f. 1991; 6 a year; organ of Iniciativa per Catalunya Verds; Dir DAVID CID; circ. 6,000.

Vida Nueva: Impresores 2, Urbanización Prado del Espino, 28660 Boadilla del Monte, Madrid; tel. (91) 4226255; fax (91) 4226118; e-mail director.vidanueva@ppc-editorial.com; internet www .vidanueva.es; f. 1958; weekly; society and religion; Dir JUAN RUBIO; circ. 20,000.

Finance

Actualidad Económica: Paseo de la Castellana 66, 4°, 28046 Madrid; tel. (91) 3370346; fax (91) 5628415; e-mail aeconomica@ recoletos.es; internet www.actualidad-economica.com; f. 1958; weekly, Mon.; Dir MIGUEL ÁNGEL BELLOSO; circ. 32,866 (June 2010).

Capital: Castellana 192, 11°, 28046 Madrid; tel. (91) 3832476; fax (91) 3832571; e-mail mmoreno@gyj.es; internet www.capital.es; f. 2000; monthly; business and economics; publ. by Grupo G+J; Dir JOSÉ LUIS GÓMEZ; circ. 35,088 (June 2010).

Dinero: Sepúlveda 7B, 28108 Madrid; tel. (91) 4327672; fax (91) 4327765; e-mail cgarcia@negocios.com; monthly; business and finance; Dir MIGUEL ORMAETXEA ARROYO; circ. 11,586 (June 2007).

El Empresario: Diego de León 50, 3°, 28006 Madrid; tel. (91) 4116161; fax (91) 5645269; e-mail cepyme@cepyme.es; internet www.cepyme.es; monthly; economics and business; circ. 15,000.

Información Comercial Española—Revista de Economía: Paseo de la Castellana 162, 5°, 28046 Madrid; tel. (91) 3493627; fax (91) 3493634; 8 a year; published by Ministry of the Economy and Competitiveness; Dir ANTONIO HERNÁNDEZ GARCÍA.

Mi Cartera de Inversión: José Abascal 56, 7°, 28003 Madrid; tel. (91) 4563320; fax (91) 4563328; e-mail sugerenciashoyinversion@ vocento.com; internet www.hoyinversion.com; Dir RAFAEL RUBIO GÓMEZ-CAMINERO; circ. 16,788 (Dec. 2006).

El Nuevo Lunes de la Economía y la Sociedad: Ferrocarril 37 duplicado, entreplanta, 28045 Madrid; tel. (91) 5160801; fax (91) 5160819; e-mail nuevolunes@elnuevolunes.com; internet www .elnuevolunes.es; weekly; Pres. JOSÉ GARCÍA ABAD.

Home, Fashion and General

Casa Diez: Avda Cardenal Herrera Oria 3, 28034 Madrid; tel. (91) 7287000; fax (91) 7289144; e-mail malvarez@hachette.es; internet www.casadiez.orange.es; monthly; home decoration; Dir MILAGROS ÁLVAREZ GORTARI; circ. 207,517 (June 2010).

Clara: Avda Diagonal 189, 08018 Barcelona; tel. (93) 4157374; fax (93) 2177378; f. 1992; monthly; Dir HORTÈNSIA GALÍ PÉREZ; circ. 196,948 (June 2010).

Cosmopolitan: Albasanz 15, Edif. A, 28037 Madrid; tel. (91) 4369820; fax (91) 4358701; e-mail cosmopolitanweb@cosmohispano .com; internet www.cosmohispano.com; f. 1990; monthly; Dir LALA HERRERO; circ. 222,419 (June 2010).

Diez Minutos: Santa Engracia 23, 28010 Madrid; tel. (91) 7287000; fax (91) 7289132; e-mail diezminutos@hachette.es; internet www .diezminutos.es; f. 1951; weekly; celebrity gossip; Dir CRISTINA ACEBAL; circ. 481,672 (June 2010).

Elle: Santa Engracia 23, 28010 Madrid; tel. (91) 7287000; fax (91) 7289306; e-mail elle@hachette.es; internet www.elle.es; f. 1986; monthly; Dir SUSANA MARTÍNEZ VIDAL; circ. 264,671 (June 2010).

Elle Deco: Santa Engracia 23, 28010 Madrid; tel. (91) 7287000; fax (91) 7289144; e-mail elledeco@hachette.es; internet www.elledeco .es; f. 1989; 5 a year; Dir MILAGROS ALVAREZ GORTARI.

GEO: Albasanz 15, Edif. A, 28037 Madrid; tel. (91) 4369862; fax (91) 4369781; e-mail mfuentes@gyj.es; internet www.mundo-geo.es; f. 1987; monthly; geography, nature, people, photo-journalism, travel, science, history, archeology, technology; Dir JULIÁN DUEÑAS; circ. 55,925 (June 2010).

GQ: Paseo de la Castellana 9–11, 2°, 28046 Madrid; tel. (91) 7004170; fax (91) 3199325; e-mail gq@condenast.es; internet www.revistagq .com; monthly; men's magazine; Dir DANIEL ENTRIALGO IBARRONDO; circ. 77,160 (July 2010).

¡Hola!: Miguel Angel 1, 3°, 28010 Madrid; tel. (91) 7021820; fax (91) 3197298; e-mail publinet@hola.com; internet www.hola.com; f. 1944; weekly; general illustrated; Dir EDUARDO SÁNCHEZ PÉREZ; circ. 540,902 (June 2007).

Interviú: O'Donnell 12, 5°, 28009 Madrid; tel. (91) 5863300; fax (91) 5863498; e-mail interviu@grupozeta.es; internet www.interviu.es; f. 1976; weekly; Dir TERESA VIEJO; circ. 115,487 (Sept. 2010).

Labores del Hogar: Avda Diagonal 189, 08018 Barcelona; tel. (93) 4157374; fax (93) 2177378; e-mail labores@hymsa.com; f. 1926; monthly; home textile crafts; Dir EULÀLIA UBACH; circ. 66,313 (June 2010).

Lecturas: Avda Diagonal 189, 08018 Barcelona; tel. (93) 4157374; fax (93) 2177378; e-mail lecturas@hymsa.com; internet www .lecturas.es; f. 1921; weekly, Fri.; Dir JAVIER DE MONTINI; circ. 342,129 (June 2010).

Mía: Albasanz 15, Edif. A, 28037 Madrid; tel. (91) 4369800; fax (91) 5752617; e-mail mia@gyj.es; internet www.miarevista.es; f. 1986; weekly; Dir KETTY RICO OLIVER; circ. 214,512 (June 2010).

Nuevo Estilo: Avda Cardenal Herrera Oria 3, 28034 Madrid; tel. (91) 7287000; fax (91) 7289338; e-mail nuevoestilo@hearst.es; internet www.nuevo-estilo.es; f. 1977; monthly; home decoration; Dir MARTA RIOPÉREZ; circ. 90,000 (June 2012).

Nuevo Vale: Gran Vía de Carlos III 124, 5°, 08034 Barcelona; tel. (93) 2061540; fax (93) 2805555; e-mail buzon@publicacionesheres .com; weekly; Dir ESTHER GIRALT; circ. 87,019 (June 2010).

Pronto: Gran Vía de Carlos III 124, 5°, 08034 Barcelona; tel. (93) 2061540; fax (93) 2805555; e-mail pronto@publicacionesheres.com; f. 1972; weekly; general information; Dir ANTONIO GÓMEZ ABAD; circ. 1,093,138 (June 2010).

Semana: Cuesta de San Vicente 28, 28008 Madrid; tel. (91) 5472300; fax (91) 5413642; e-mail redaccion@semana.es; internet www .semana.es; f. 1942; weekly; general, illustrated; Dir CHARO CARRACEDO ARMADA; circ. 281,814 (June 2010).

Ser Padres Hoy: Albasanz 15, Edif. A, 28037 Madrid; tel. (91) 4369800; fax (91) 5767881; e-mail publicidad@gyj.es; internet www .serpadres.es; f. 1974; monthly; for parents; Dir JAVIER J. GARCÍA GONZÁLEZ; circ. 37,462 (June 2008).

Súper Pop: Gran Vía Carlos III 124, 1°, 08034 Barcelona; tel. (93) 2521452; fax (93) 2521450; e-mail contenido@superpop.es; f. 1976; fortnightly; teenage magazine; Dir EVA MORENO; circ. 113,614 (June 2007).

Telva: Avda de San Luis 25, 28033 Madrid; tel. (91) 4435000; fax (91) 3373143; e-mail telva@telva.com; internet www.telva.com; f. 1963; beauty, fashion, weddings, interviews, cookery and fitness; monthly; Dir NIEVES FONTANA LÍBANO; circ. 253,136 (June 2010).

Vogue España: Paseo de la Castellana 9–11, 28046 Madrid; tel. (91) 7004170; fax (91) 7004199; e-mail vogue@condenast.es; internet www.vogue.es; f. 1988; monthly; Dir YOLANDA SACRISTÁN; circ. 188,445 (June 2010).

Woman: Bailén 84, 2°, 08009 Barcelona; tel. (93) 5863300; fax (93) 2324630; e-mail woman@grupozeta.es; internet www.woman.es; f. 1992; monthly; Dir EMPAR PRIETO; circ. 1,211,778 (June 2010).

Leisure Interests and Sport

Automóvil: Ancora 40, 28045 Madrid; tel. (91) 3470100; fax (91) 3470152; e-mail automovil@mpib.es; internet www .motorpress-iberica.es; monthly; motoring; Dir FERNANDO GÓMEZ BLANCO; circ. 114,286 (June 2010).

Autopista: Ancora 40, 28045 Madrid; tel. (91) 3470100; fax (91) 3470135; e-mail autopista@mpib.es; internet www .motorpress-iberica.es; weekly; motoring; Editor MARÍA WANDOSELL; circ. 43,000 (June 2010).

Cinemanía: Progresa (Grupo Prisa), Julián Camarillo 29B, 1°, 28037 Madrid; tel. (91) 5386104; fax (91) 5222291; e-mail cinemania@progresa.es; internet www.progresa.es; f. 1995; monthly; films; Dir CARLOS MARAÑÓN; circ. 55,220 (June 2010).

Coche Actual: Ancora 40, 28045 Madrid; tel. (91) 3470154; fax (91) 3470152; e-mail cocheactual@mpib.es; internet www .motorpress-iberica.es; weekly; cars; Dir ANTONIO RONCERO FERNÁNDEZ; circ. 46,837 (June 2010).

Don Balón: Avda Diagonal 435, 1°–2°, 08036 Barcelona; tel. (93) 2092000; fax (93) 2412358; e-mail info@donbalon.org; internet www .donbalon.com; f. 1975; weekly; sport; Editor-in-Chief ANTONIO CASALS; circ. 22,880 (June 2010).

Fotogramas: Santa Engracia 23, 28010 Madrid; tel. (91) 7287000; fax (91) 7289306; e-mail fotogramas@hachette.es; internet www

.fotogramas.es; f. 1946; monthly; cinema; Dir TONI ULLED NADAL; circ. 151,654 (June 2010).

Guía del Ocio—La Semana de Barcelona: Muntaner 492, bajos, 08022 Barcelona; tel. (93) 4185005; fax (93) 4173363; e-mail redaccion@guiadelociobcn.com; internet www.guiadelociobcn.com; f. 1977; weekly, Fri.; listings and reviews of events; Dir XAVIER MUNIESA CALDERÓ; circ. 50,000.

Guía del Ocio—La Semana de Madrid: Alcalá 106, 2°, 28009 Madrid; tel. (91) 4367500; fax (91) 4367501; e-mail guiadelocio@ guiadelociomad.com; internet www.guiadelocio.com; weekly, Fri.; listings and reviews of events; Dir-Gen. MARCOS DE MINONDO RUIZ-MORALES.

Motociclismo: Ancora 40, 28045 Madrid; tel. (91) 3470100; fax (91) 3470152; e-mail motociclismo@mpib.es; internet www.motociclismo .es; f. 1951; weekly; motorcycling; Dir and Editor AUGUSTO MORENO DE CARLOS; circ. 46,522 (June 2010).

Sport Life: Ancora 40, 28045 Madrid; tel. (91) 3470100; fax (91) 3470236; e-mail sportlife@mpib.es; internet www .motorpress-iberica.es; monthly; Editor FRANCISCO JESÚS CHICO; circ. 83,284 (June 2010).

Supertele: Avda Cardenal Herrera Oria 3, 28034 Madrid; tel. (91) 7287000; e-mail supertele@hearst.es; f. 1992; weekly; TV magazine; Dir PURIFICACIÓN BLANCO PAÍÑO; circ. 99,005 (June 2010).

Tele Digital: C/ Juan Bravo 3A, 28006 Madrid; tel. (91) 4451950; fax (91) 4450621; internet www.sateliteinfos.com; Dir JOSÉ DA CUNHA.

Tele Indiscreta: Avda Cardenal Herrera Oria 3, 28034 Madrid; tel. (91) 7287000; fax (91) 3581348; e-mail teleindiscreta@hachette.es; weekly; popular illustrated; TV programmes; Dir PURIFICACIÓN BLANCO PAÍÑO; circ. 31,852 (June 2007).

Telenovela: Avda Cardenal Herrera Oria 3, 28034 Madrid; tel. (91) 7287000; e-mail telenovela@hearst.es; f. 1993; TV series; Dir PURIFICACIÓN BLANCO PAÍÑO; circ. 74,579 (June 2010).

TP Teleprograma: Avda Cardenal Herrera Oria 3, 28034 Madrid; tel. (91) 7287000; fax (91) 7289129; e-mail tp@hearst.es; internet www.teleprograma.tv; f. 1966; weekly; TV, cinema and video; Dir PURIFICACIÓN BLANCO PAÍÑO; circ. 113,285 (June 2010).

Viajar: O'Donnell 12, 3°, 28009 Madrid; tel. (91) 5863300; fax (91) 5863411; e-mail mlopez.viajar@grupozeta.es; internet www .revistaviajar.es; f. 1978; monthly; travel; Dir MARIANO LÓPEZ; circ. 75,000.

Medicine, Science and Technology

Arbor: Vitruvio 8, 28006 Madrid; tel. (91) 5616651; fax (91) 5855326; e-mail director.arbor@csic.es; internet arbor.revistas.csic.es; f. 1944; monthly; science, thought and culture; publ. by Consejo Superior de Investigaciones Científicas (CSIC); Dir ALBERTO SÁNCHEZ ALVAREZ-INSUA.

Avión Revue: Apdo de Correos 6006, 46011 Valencia; e-mail director@avionrevue.com; internet www.es.avionrevue.com; f. 1982; monthly; aeroplanes; Exec. Dir JORGE PENALBA; circ. 21,307 (June 2010).

Computerworld: Fortuny 18, 5°, 28010 Madrid; tel. (91) 3496600; fax (91) 3196104; e-mail computerworld@idg.es; internet www.idg .es/computerworld; f. 1981; weekly; also available: *CIO, Comunicaciones World, Dealer World, iWorld, MacWorld, PC World Digital, PC World PRO*; Editor-in-Chief ESTHER MACÍAS; circ. 9,182 (March 2010).

El Ecologista: Marqués de Laganés 12, 28004 Madrid; tel. (91) 5312389; fax (91) 5312611; e-mail comunicacion@ ecologistasenaccion.org; internet www.ecologistasenaccion.org; f. 1979; quarterly; ecological issues; Dir JOSÉ LUIS GARCÍA CANO; circ. 13,000.

Gaceta Médica de Bilbao: Lersundi 9, Apdo 5073, 48009 Bilbao; tel. (94) 4233768; fax (94) 4232161; e-mail gacetamedica@telefonica .net; f. 1894; quarterly; official publication of the Academia de Ciencias Médicas de Bilbao/Bilboko Sendalarintz Jakindia; Dir Dr JUAN IGNACIO GOIRIA ORMAZABAL; circ. 5,000.

Investigación y Ciencia: Muntaner 339, Pral 1°, 08021 Barcelona; tel. (93) 4143344; fax (93) 4145413; e-mail precisa@ investigacionyciencia.es; internet www.investigacionyciencia.es; f. 1976; quarterly; Dir PILAR BRONCHAL GALLARDO; circ. 22,000 (Feb. 2013).

Mundo Científico: Pérez Galdós 36, 08012 Barcelona; tel. (93) 4157374; fax (93) 2177378; monthly; Dir JORGE ALCALDE.

Muy Interesante: Albasanz 15, 28037 Madrid; tel. (91) 4369800; fax (91) 5752617; e-mail publicidad@gyj.es; internet www .muyinteresante.es; f. 1981; monthly; history, medicine, nature, science; Dir JOSÉ PARDINA CANCER; circ. 295,342 (June 2010).

PC Actual: López de Hoyos 141, 1°, 28002 Madrid; tel. (91) 5106600; fax (91) 5194813; e-mail javier-perez@rba.es; internet www .pc-actual.com; monthly; Dir SUSANA HERRERO.

Tiempos Médicos: Editores Médicos, SA, Alsasua 16, 28023 Madrid; tel. (91) 3768140; fax (91) 3739907; e-mail edimsa@edimsa .es; internet www.edimsa.es; 10 a year; Dir Dr A. CHICHARRO PAPIRI; circ. 10,549 (Dec. 2009).

NEWS AGENCIES

Agencia EFE, SA: Espronceda 32, 28003 Madrid; tel. (91) 3467100; fax (91) 3467134; e-mail efe@efe.es; internet www.efe.es; f. 1939; national and international news; 140 bureaux and correspondents abroad; sports, features, radio and television, and photographic branches; Pres. ÁLEX GRIJELMO; Gen. Man. LOLA ÁLVAREZ.

Colpisa: José Abascal 56, 1°, 28003 Madrid; tel. (91) 4564600; fax (91) 4564701; f. 1972; Pres. JOSÉ MARÍA BERGARECHE; Dir ROGELIO RODRÍGUEZ.

Europa Press Noticias: Paseo de la Castellana 210, 3°, 28046 Madrid; tel. (91) 3592600; fax (91) 3503251; e-mail noticias@ europapress.es; internet www.europapress.es; Dir ANGEL EXPÓSITO MORA.

Iberia Press: Velázquez 46, 1°, 28001 Madrid; tel. and fax (91) 8155319; e-mail press-bulletin@jet.es; f. 1977; Dir JOSÉ RAMÓN ALONSO.

PRESS ASSOCIATIONS

National Organizations

Asociación de Corresponsales de Prensa Extranjera (ACPE): Monte Esquinza 41, 1°, 28010 Madrid; tel. (91) 3101433; fax (91) 3080950; e-mail acpe.corresponsales@wanadoo.es; internet www .acpe-corresponsales.com; f. 1923; foreign correspondents' asscn; Pres. SAID IDA HASSAN; Sec.-Gen. CARLOS MEZA; 150 mems.

Asociación de Editores de Diarios Españoles (AEDE): Orense 69, 2°, 28020 Madrid; tel. (91) 4251085; fax (91) 5796020; e-mail maribel@aede.es; internet www.aede.es; f. 1978; 33 mems, representing 95 daily newspapers (2008); Pres. PILAR DE YARZA.

Asociación de Revistas Culturales en España (ARCE): Hortaleza 75, 28004 Madrid; tel. (91) 3086066; fax (91) 3199267; e-mail info@arce.es; internet www.arce.es; f. 1983.

Federación de Asociaciones de Periodistas de España (FAPE): María de Molina 50, 2A planta, 28006 Madrid; tel. (91) 3605824; fax (91) 5230256; e-mail fape@fape.es; internet www.fape .es; f. 1922; Pres. ELSA GONZÁLEZ DÍAZ; Sec.-Gen. CARLOS SANZ ESTABLÉS; 48 mem. asscns.

Unión de Escritores y Periodistas Españoles: Madrid; f. 1978; journalists' asscn; Pres. ANTONIO ARIAS PIQUERAS; Sec.-Gen. ELOY S. CASTAÑARES; 4,000 mems.

Provincial Organizations

Barcelona

Centre Internacional de Premsa de Barcelona: Rambla de Catalunya 10, 1°, 08007 Barcelona; tel. (93) 4121111; fax (93) 3178386; e-mail cipb@periodistes.org; internet www.periodistes .org; f. 1988; facilities and services for journalists; Pres. XAVIER BATALLA GARCÍA; Dir MÓNICA VIÑAS.

Bilbao

Asociación de Periodistas de Bizkaia (Bizkaiko Kazetarien Elkartea): Dr Achucarro 10, 1°, 48011 Bilbao; tel. and fax (94) 4168748; e-mail asociacion@periodistasvascos.com; internet www .periodistasvascos.com; Pres. JOSÉ MANUEL ALONSO; Sec. BLANCA GARCÍA-EGOCHEAGA.

Madrid

Asociación de la Prensa de Madrid: Juan Bravo 6, 28006 Madrid; tel. (91) 5850010; fax (91) 5850050; e-mail apm@apmadrid.es; internet www.apmadrid.es; f. 1895; Pres. CARMEN DEL RIEGO DE LUCAS; Sec.-Gen. MARÍA JESÚS CHAO ÁLVAREZ DE SIERRA; 7,750 mems.

Centro de Prensa de Madrid: Claudio Coello 98, 28006 Madrid; tel. (91) 5850010; fax (91) 5850050; Sec.-Gen. JOSÉ MARÍA LORENTE TORIBIO.

Sevilla

Asociación de la Prensa de Sevilla: Plaza de San Francisco 9, 1°, 41004 Sevilla; tel. (95) 4500468; fax (95) 4225299; e-mail aps@ asociacionprensa.org; internet www.asociacionprensa.org; f. 1909; Pres. ANA MARÍA CARVAJAL LLORENS; Sec.-Gen. PILAR SURIÑACH MUÑOZ.

Zaragoza

Centro de Prensa de Zaragoza: Cinco de Marzo 9, 50004 Zaragoza; tel. (976) 223210; fax (976) 222963; e-mail aparagon@aparagon .es; internet www.aparagon.es/centrop.asp; Pres. RAMÓN J. BUETAS CORONAS; Sec. ROBERTO GARCÍA BERMEJO.

Publishers

Agencia Española de Cooperación Internacional para el Desarrollo: Avda Reyes Católicos 4, 28040 Madrid; tel. (91) 5838379; fax (91) 5838311; internet www.aecid.es; f. 1943; arts, law, history, economics for circulation in Latin America; Literary and Artistic Dir ANTONIO PAPELL.

Alianza Editorial: Juan Ignacio Luca de Tena 15, 28027 Madrid; tel. (91) 3938888; fax (91) 3207480; e-mail alianzaeditorial@ alianzaeditorial.es; internet www.alianzaeditorial.es; f. 1959; advanced textbooks, fiction, general non-fiction, reference, paperbacks; imprint of Grupo Anaya; Gen. Man. VALERIA CIOMPI.

Barcino Editorial: Carrer Acàcies 15, 08027 Barcelona; tel. and fax (93) 3495935; e-mail barcino@editorialbarcino.cat; internet www .editorialbarcino.com; f. 1924; Catalan classics, general; Dir CARLES DUARTE MONTSERRAT.

Carroggio, SA de Ediciones: Rambla Catalunya 38, 08001 Barcelona; tel. (93) 4949922; fax (93) 4949923; e-mail carroggio@carroggio .com; internet www.carroggio.es; f. 1911; art, literature, reference books, multimedia; Man. Dir SANTIAGO CARROGGIO GUERIM.

Columna Edicions: Peu de la Creu 4, 08001 Barcelona; tel. (93) 4437100; fax (93) 4417130; e-mail info@columnaedicions.cat; internet www.columnaedicions.cat; f. 1985; imprint of Grup 62; fiction and non-fiction in Catalan.

Durvan, SA de ediciones: Avda Manoteras 50, 28050 Madrid; tel. (91) 3842022; e-mail editorial@durvan.com; internet www.durvan .com; f. 1960; Sociedad Anónima de Promoción y Ediciones; Dir JAVIER PEREDA PRADO.

EDHASA (Editora y Distribuidora Hispano-Americana, SA): Avda Diagonal 519–521, 2°, 08029 Barcelona; tel. (93) 4949720; fax (93) 4194584; e-mail info@edhasa.es; internet www.edhasa.com; f. 1946; contemporary fiction, non-fiction, pocket books, historical fiction and non-fiction, crime, philosophy; Editorial Dir and Man. DANIEL FERNÁNDEZ.

Ediciones Cátedra: Juan Ignacio Luca de Tena 15, 28027 Madrid; tel. (91) 3938787; fax (91) 7412118; e-mail catedra@catedra.com; internet www.catedra.com; f. 1973; imprint of Grupo Anaya; literature, literary criticism, history, humanities, linguistics, arts, cinema, music, feminism; Pres. JOSÉ MANUEL GÓMEZ.

Ediciones Destino: Avda Diagonal 662–664, 08034 Barcelona; tel. (93) 4967001; fax (93) 4967002; e-mail edicionesdestino@edestino .es; internet www.edestino.es; f. 1942; imprint of Grupo Planeta; general fiction, history, art, children's books.

Ediciones Deusto: Avda Diagonal 662–664, 08034 Barcelona; tel. (94) 4356161; fax (94) 4356166; e-mail deustomail@ediciones-deusto .es; internet www.ediciones-deusto.es; f. 1960; imprint of Grupo Planeta; management and law.

Ediciones Encuentro: Ramírez de Arellano 17, 10°, 28043 Madrid; tel. (91) 5322607; fax (91) 5322346; e-mail encuentro@ ediciones-encuentro.es; internet www.ediciones-encuentro.es; f. 1978; theology, philosophy, art, history, biography, society, politics, literature.

Ediciones Mensajero, SAU: Sancho de Azpeitia 2, 48014 Bilbao; tel. (94) 4470358; fax (94) 4472630; e-mail mensajero@mensajero .com; internet www.mensajero.com; f. 1915; arts, biography, theology, psychology, pedagogy, social sciences and paperbacks; Editorial Dir JOSU LEGUINA ECHEBERRÍA.

Ediciones Morata, SL: Mejía Lequerica 12, 28004 Madrid; tel. (91) 4480926; fax (91) 4480925; e-mail morata@edmorata.es; internet www.edmorata.es; f. 1920; psychology, psychiatry, pedagogics, sociology; Dir FLORA MORATA.

Ediciones Obelisco: Pedro IV 78, 3° y 5°, 08005 Barcelona; tel. (93) 3098525; fax (93) 3098523; e-mail info@edicionesobelisco.com; internet www.edicionesobelisco.com; f. 1981; general fiction and non-fiction; Dir JULI PERADEJORDI.

Ediciones Omega: Plató 26, 08006 Barcelona; tel. (93) 2010599; fax (93) 2097362; e-mail omega@ediciones-omega.es; internet www .ediciones-omega.es; f. 1948; biology, field guides, geography, geology, agriculture, photography; Chair. ANTONIO PARICIO.

Ediciones Pirámide: Juan Ignacio Luca de Tena 15, 28027 Madrid; tel. (91) 3938989; fax (91) 7423661; e-mail piramide@anaya.es; internet www.edicionespiramide.es; f. 1973; scientific and technical books, business, economics, psychology; imprint of Grupo Anaya; Man. Dir MARIANO JOSÉ NORTE.

Ediciones Polígrafa: Balmes 54, 2°, 08007 Barcelona; tel. (93) 3968846; fax (93) 4672172; e-mail info@edicionespoligrafa.com; internet www.edicionespoligrafa.com; f. 1960; arts, leisure; Man. Dir JUAN DE MUGA DÒRIA; Editor-in-Chief FRANCISCO REI.

Ediciones Siruela: Almagro 25, 28010 Madrid; tel. (91) 3555720; fax (91) 3552201; e-mail atencionlector@siruela.com; internet www .siruela.com; f. 1982; history, literature, art, children's books, translations; Dir JACOBO FITZ-JAMES STUART.

Ediciones Universidad de Navarra, SA (EUNSA): Plaza de los Sauces 1 y 2, 31010 Barañain–Pamplona (Navarra); tel. (948) 256850; fax (948) 256854; e-mail info@eunsa.es; internet www .eunsa.es; f. 1967; architecture, natural sciences, law, history, social sciences, theology, philosophy, medical, engineering, journalism, education, economics and business administration, biology, literature, library science, paperbacks, etc.; Chair. GUIDO STEIN.

Edicións Xerais de Galicia: Doutor Marañón 12, 36211 Vigo; tel. (986) 214888; fax (986) 201366; e-mail xerais@xerais.es; internet www.xerais.es; f. 1979; imprint of Grupo Anaya; literature, education, history and reference books in Galician; Dir MANUEL BRAGADO RODRÍGUEZ.

Editorial Anagrama: Pedró de la Creu 58, 08034 Barcelona; tel. (93) 2037652; fax (93) 2037738; e-mail anagrama@anagrama-ed.es; internet www.anagrama-ed.es; f. 1969; fiction, essays, foreign literature in translation; Editor and Dir JORGE HERRALDE.

Editorial Bosch: Comte d'Urgell 51 bis, Apdo 928, 08011 Barcelona; tel. (93) 4521050; fax (93) 4521057; e-mail bosch@bosch.es; internet www.bosch.es; f. 1934; law, social sciences, classics; Man. ALBERT FERRÉ.

Editorial Castalia: Castelló 24, 1°, 28001 Madrid; tel. (91) 3195857; fax (91) 3102442; e-mail castalia@castalia.es; internet www.castalia .es; f. 1945; classics, literature; Pres. AMPARO SOLER GIMENO.

Editorial CEAC: Avda Diagonal 662–664, 08034 Barcelona; tel. (93) 4926956; e-mail info@ceacedit.com; internet www.editorialceac.com; f. 1947; imprint of Grupo Planeta; textbooks, education, leisure; Man. JAIME PINTANEL.

Editorial Desclée de Brouwer: Henao 6, 3° dcha, 48009 Bilbao; tel. (94) 4246843; fax (94) 4237594; e-mail info@edesclee.com; internet www.edesclee.com; f. 1945; general non-fiction in Spanish and Basque; Pres. JAVIER GOGEASCOECHEA.

Editorial Edaf: Jorge Juan 68, 1°, 28009 Madrid; tel. (91) 4358260; fax (91) 4315281; e-mail edaf@edaf.net; internet www.edaf.net; f. 1967; literature, dictionaries, occult, natural health, paperbacks; Dir-Gen. JOSÉ ANTONIO FOSSATI SEDDON.

Editorial Everest: Carretera León–Coruña, Km 5, Apdo 339, 24080 León; tel. (987) 844200; fax (987) 844202; e-mail info@everest.es; internet www.everest.es; f. 1957; general; Dir-Gen. JOSÉ ANTONIO LÓPEZ MARTÍNEZ.

Editorial Galaxia: Avda de Madrid 44, 36204 Vigo (Pontevedra); tel. (986) 432100; fax (986) 223205; e-mail galaxia@editorialgalaxia .es; internet www.editorialgalaxia.es; f. 1950; literary works, reviews, popular, children's, Galician literature; Dir VÍCTOR F. FREIXANES.

Editorial Gredos: Sánchez Pacheco 85, 28002 Madrid; tel. (91) 7444920; fax (91) 5192033; e-mail comercial@editorialgredos.com; internet www.editorialgredos.com; f. 1944; linguistics, philology, humanities, art, literature, dictionaries; Dir JOSÉ MANUEL MARTOS CARRASCO.

Editorial Gustavo Gili: Rosselló 87–89, 08029 Barcelona; tel. (93) 3228161; fax (93) 3229205; e-mail info@ggili.com; internet www.ggili .com; f. 1902; photography, art, architecture, design, fashion; Dirs GABRIEL GILI, MÓNICA GILI.

Editorial Hispano-Europea: Primer de Maig, 21, Pol. Ind. Gran Via Sud, 08908 L'Hospitalet de Llobregat (Barcelona); tel. (93) 2018500; fax (93) 4142635; e-mail hispanoeuropea@ hispanoeuropea.com; internet www.hispanoeuropea.com; f. 1954; technical, scientific, sport, pets and reference; Propr and Man. Dir JORGE J. PRAT ROSAL.

Editorial Juventud: Provença 101, 08029 Barcelona; tel. (93) 4441800; fax (93) 4398383; e-mail info@editorialjuventud.es; internet www.editorialjuventud.es; f. 1923; general fiction, biography, history, art, music, reference, dictionaries, travel books, children's books, paperbacks, in Catalan and Spanish; Dir LUIS ZENDRERA.

Editorial Marfil: San Eloy 17, 03804 Alcoy; tel. (96) 5523311; fax (96) 5523496; e-mail editorialmarfil@editorialmarfil.com; internet www.editorialmarfil.com; f. 1947; textbooks, psychology, pedagogy, university texts, literature; Man. RAFAEL LLORÉNS FIGUEROLA.

Editorial Nerea: Aldamar, 36 bajo, 20003 San Sebastián; tel. (943) 432227; fax (943) 433379; e-mail nerea@nerea.net; internet www .nerea.net; f. 1987; architecture, art, history, photography; Chair. MARTA CASARES.

Editorial Reus, SA: Preciados 23, 2°, 28013 Madrid; tel. (91) 5213619; fax (91) 5312408; e-mail reus@editorialreus.es; internet www.editorialreus.es; f. 1852; law; Pres. JESÚS M. PINTO VARELA.

Editorial Reverté: Loreto 13–15, Local B, 08029 Barcelona; tel. (93) 4193336; fax (93) 4195189; e-mail reverte@reverte.com; internet www.reverte.com; f. 1947; scientific and technical; Dir JAVIER REVERTÉ MASCÓ.

Editorial Seix Barral: Avda Diagonal 662–664, 7°, 08034 Barcelona; tel. (93) 4967003; fax (93) 4967004; e-mail editorial@seix-barral .es; internet www.seix-barral.es; f. 1911; literary fiction.

Editorial Tecnos: Juan Ignacio Luca de Tena 15, 28027 Madrid; tel. (91) 3938686; fax (91) 7426631; e-mail foro_tecnos@anaya.es; internet www.tecnos.es; f. 1947; law, social and political science, philosophy and economics; imprint of Grupo Anaya; Man. MANUEL GONZÁLEZ MORENO.

Editorial Teide: Viladomat 291, 08029 Barcelona; tel. (902) 233030; fax (93) 3212646; e-mail info@editorialteide.com; internet www .editorialteide.es; f. 1942; educational, scientific, technical and art; Man. Dir FEDERICO RAHOLA.

La Esfera de los Libros: Avda de Alfonso XIII 1, bajos, 28002 Madrid; tel. (91) 2960200; fax (91) 2960206; e-mail laesfera@ esferalibros.com; internet www.esferalibros.com; history, journalism, biography; Dir-Gen. JOSÉ MARÍA CALVÍN.

Espasa Libros: Avda Diagonal 662–664, 08034 Barcelona; tel. (91) 4230370; fax (91) 4233743; e-mail sugerencias@espasa.es; internet www.espasa.es; f. 1860; encyclopaedias, history, dictionaries, literature, biographies, paperbacks, etc.; CEO JESÚS BADENES.

Fondo de Cultura Económica de España, SL (FCE España): Librería Juan Rulfo México, Fernando el Católico 86, 28015 Madrid; tel. (91) 7632800; e-mail directora.general@ fondodeculturaeconomica.com; internet www .fondodeculturaeconomica.com; f. 1974; sciences, literature, children's books, history, academic; Dir JUAN GUILLERMO LÓPEZ.

Galaxia Gutenberg: Travessera de Gràcia 47–49, 08021 Barcelona; tel. (93) 3660100; fax (93) 3660104; e-mail galaxiagutenberg@circulo .es; internet www.galaxiagutenberg.com; f. 1995; literary fiction, poetry, economics.

Grup 62: Peu de la Creu 4, 08001 Barcelona; tel. (93) 4437100; fax (93) 4437130; e-mail correu@grup62.com; internet www.grup62 .com; f. 1962; 18 imprints publishing titles in Catalan and Spanish, including Art 62, Edicions 62, Editorial Empúries, Editorial Selecta, Ediciones Península, El Aleph Editores, Enciclopèdia Catalana, Luciérnaga, Nous Negocis, Planeta, Pòrtic i Mina, Proa, Salsa Books; Pres. J. M. MARTOS.

Grupo Anaya: Juan Ignacio Luca de Tena 15, 28027 Madrid; tel. (91) 3938800; fax (91) 7426631; e-mail administrador@anaya.es; internet www.anaya.es; f. 1959; imprints include Algaida, Alianza Editorial, Anaya, Barçanova, Clé Internacional, Del Prado, Ediciones Cátedra, Ediciones Pirámide, Edicións Xerais de Galicia, Editorial Tecnos, Eudema, Larousse and Oberon; reference, sciences, arts, literature, education; Pres. JOSÉ MANUEL GÓMEZ.

Grupo Edebé: Paseo San Juan Bosco 62, 08017 Barcelona; tel. (93) 2037408; fax (93) 2054670; e-mail informacion@edebe.net; internet www.edebe.com; f. 1888; imprints include Giltza, Rodeira, Marjal and Guadiel; children's and educational publications; Man. JOSÉ ALDUNATE JURÍO.

Grupo Editorial Bruño: Juan Ignacio Luca de Tena 15, 28027 Madrid; tel. (91) 7244800; fax (91) 3613133; e-mail informacion@ editorial-bruno.es; internet www.editorial-bruno.es; f. 1898; education, children's books.

Grupo Editorial Luis Vives: Xaudaró 25, 28034 Madrid; tel. (91) 3344883; fax (91) 3344882; e-mail dediciones@edelvivies.es; internet www.grupoeditorialluisvives.com; f. 1890; imprints include Edelvives, Baula (Catalan), Alhucema, Ibaizabal (Basque) and Tambre (Galician); children's books, textbooks, reference under the imprints.

Grupo Editorial Santillana: Torrelaguna 60, 28043 Madrid; tel. (91) 7449060; fax (91) 7449019; e-mail grupo@santillana.es; internet www.gruposantillana.com; f. 1960; part of Grupo PRISA; imprints include Aguilar, Alfarguara, Altea, Richmond Publishing and Taurus; Pres. EMILIANO MARTÍNEZ.

Grupo Océano: Milanesado 21–23, 08017 Barcelona; tel. (93) 2802020; fax (93) 2041073; e-mail info@oceano.com; internet www .oceano.com; f. 1950; imprints include Circe, Instituto Gallach de Librería y Ediciones and Oceano; general; Chair. JOSÉ LLUIS MONREAL.

Grupo Planeta: Avda Diagonal 662–664, 08034 Barcelona; tel. (93) 4928000; fax (93) 4928565; e-mail info@planeta.es; internet www .planeta.es; f. 1949; imprints include Ediciones Destino, Ediciones Deusto, Ediciones Minotauro, Ediciones Temas de Hoy, Editorial CEAC, Editorial Crítica, Editorial Planeta, Emcé Editores, GeoPlaneta, MR Ediciones, Timun Mas; Pres. JOSÉ MANUEL LARA BOSCH.

Herder Editorial, SA: Provença 388, 08025 Barcelona; tel. (93) 4762626; fax (93) 2073448; e-mail herder@herdereditorial.com; internet www.herdereditorial.com; f. 1944; literature, language, theology, sociology, psychology; Dir RAIMUND HERDER.

Iberoamericana de Libros y Ediciones, SL: Amor de Dios 1, 28014 Madrid; tel. (91) 4293522; fax (91) 4295397; e-mail info@ iberoamericanalibros.com; internet www.ibero-americana.net; f. 1996; owned by Vervuert Verlagsgesellschaft (Germany); academic books.

Larousse Editorial: Mallorca, 45, 3°, 08029 Barcelona; tel. (93) 2413505; fax (93) 2413511; e-mail larousse@larousse.es; internet www.larousse.es; f. 1912; encyclopaedias, dictionaries, atlases, linguistics.

Marcombo, SA de Boixareu Editores: Gran Vía de les Corts Catalanes 594, 08007 Barcelona; tel. (93) 3180079; fax (93) 3189339; e-mail info@marcombo.com; internet www.marcombo.com; f. 1945; reference, sciences, textbooks; Pres. and Man. Dir JOSEP M. BOIXAREU VILAPLANA.

Montagud Editores: Ausiàs March 25, 1°, 08010 Barcelona; tel. (93) 3182082; fax (93) 3025083; e-mail montagud@montagud.com; internet www.montagud.com; f. 1906; business; Chair. FRANCISCO ANTOJA GIRALT.

MR Ediciones, SA: Recoletos 4, 3°, 28001 Madrid; tel. (91) 4230314; fax (91) 4230306; e-mail info@mrediciones.es; internet www .edicionesmartinezroca.com; f. 1965; fmrly Ediciones Martínez Roca; fiction, New Age, spirituality, sport, 'how-to' books, psychology, psychiatry; Dir LAURA FALCÓ.

Narcea, SA de Ediciones: Avda Dr Federico Rubio y Galí 9, 28039 Madrid; tel. (91) 5546484; fax (91) 5546487; e-mail narcea@ narceaediciones.es; internet www.narceaediciones.es; f. 1968; humanities, pedagogy, psychology, spirituality, textbooks; Man. Dir MONICA B. GONZÁLEZ NAVARRO.

Nivola Libros y Ediciones, SL: Apartado de Correos 113, 28760 Tres Cantos (Madrid); tel. (902) 105185; fax (91) 8041482; e-mail contacto@nivola.com; internet www.nivola.com; science.

Plaza y Janés: Travessera de Gràcia 47–49, 08021 Barcelona; tel. (93) 3660300; fax (93) 2002219; internet www.plaza.es; f. 1959; fiction and non-fiction, reference; imprint of Random House Mondadori.

Random House Mondadori: Travessera de Gràcia 47–49, 08021 Barcelona; tel. (93) 3660300; fax (93) 3660449; e-mail gestionweb@ rhm.es; internet www.randomhousemondadori.es; f. 2001 as a joint venture between Random House (Germany and USA) and Mondadori (Italy); imprints include Areté, Beascoa, Debate, Electa, Grijalbo, Lumen, Montena, Plaza y Janés, Rosa dels Vents and Sudamericana; Gen. Man. NURIA CABUTÍ.

Siglo XXI de España, Editores: Sector Foresta 1, 28760 Tres Cantos (Madrid); tel. (91) 8061996; fax (91) 8044028; e-mail atencion .cliente@akal.com; internet www.sigloxxieditores.com; f. 1967; pocket collections, reference, history, social sciences; Pres. PABLO GARCÍA-ARENAL.

SM Grupo: Impresores 2, Urbanización Prado del Espino, 28660 Boadilla del Monte (Madrid); tel. (91) 4228800; fax (91) 5089927; e-mail clientes@grupo-sm.com; internet www.grupo-sm.com; f. 1940; textbooks, children's, reference, travel, literature; Pres. JUAN DE ISASA GONZÁLEZ UBIETA; Man. Dir JAVIER CORTÉS SORIANO.

Thomson Reuters Aranzadi: Camino de Galar 15, 31190 Cizur Menor (Navarra); tel. (902) 444144; fax (948) 297200; e-mail clientes@aranzadi.es; internet www.aranzadi.es; f. 1929; fmrly Editorial Aranzadi; law; Dir JUAN CARLOS FRANQUET CASAS.

Tusquets Editores: Cesare Cantú 8, 08023 Barcelona; tel. (93) 2530400; fax (93) 4176703; internet www.tusquets-editores.es; art, general fiction and non-fiction.

Vicens Vives: Polígono Industrial Pratense, 111, parcela 16, El Prat de Llobregat, 08820 Barcelona; tel. (93) 4782755; fax (93) 4783659; e-mail e@vicensvives.es; internet www.vicensvives.es; f. 1961; school and university, educational; Dir ROSARIO RAHOLA DE ESPONA.

PUBLISHERS' ASSOCIATIONS

Asociación de Editores de Madrid: Santiago Rusiñol 8, 28040 Madrid; tel. (91) 5544745; fax (91) 5532553; e-mail editoresmadrid@ editoresmadrid.org; internet www.editoresmadrid.org; f. 1977; Pres. JAVIER CORTÉS SORIANO; Sec.-Gen. AMALIA MARTÍN PEREDA.

Asociación de Editoriales Universitarias Españolas (AEUE): Plaza de las Cortes 2, 7°, 28014 Madrid; tel. (91) 3600698; fax (91) 3601201; e-mail secretariatecnica@une.es; Pres. MAGDA POLO PUJADAS; Sec. ISABEL TERROBA PASCUAL.

Associació d'Editors en Llengua Catalana (Association of Publishers in Catalan Language): València 279, 1°, 08009 Barcelona; tel. (93) 2155091; fax (93) 2155273; e-mail info@editorsencatala.org; internet www.catalanpublishers.org; f. 1978; Pres. MANUEL SANGLAS MUCHART; Sec.-Gen. SEGIMON BORRÁS.

Federación de Gremios de Editores de España (Federation of Publishers' Associations of Spain): Cea Bermúdez 44, 2° dcha, 28003 Madrid; tel. (91) 5345195; fax (91) 5352625; e-mail fgee@fge.es; internet www.federacioneditores.org; f. 1978; Pres. JAVIER CORTÉS SORIANO; Exec. Dir ANTONIO MARÍA ÁVILA.

Gremi d'Editors de Catalunya: València 279, 1°, 08009 Barcelona; tel. (93) 2155091; fax (93) 2155273; e-mail info@gremieditorscat .es; internet www.gremieditorscat.es; Pres. JOSEP M. PUIG DE LA BELLACASA; Sec.-Gen. SEGIMON BORRÀS.

Gremio de Editores de Euskadi/Euskadiko Editoreen Elkartea: Lehendakari Aguirre 11, 3°, 48014 Bilbao; tel. (94) 4764313; fax (94) 4761980; internet www.editores-euskadi.com; Pres. JAVIER GOGEASCOECHEA ARRIEN; Man. Dir ANDRÉS FERNÁNDEZ SECO.

Broadcasting and Communications

TELECOMMUNICATIONS

The telecommunications market was fully deregulated in December 1998.

BT España: Edif. Herre, Salvador de Madariaga 1, 28027 Madrid; tel. (91) 2708000; fax (91) 2708888; internet www.globalservices.bt .com; f. 1989; Dir-Gen. JACINTO CAVESTANY VALLEJO.

Euskaltel: Parque Tecnológico, Edif. 809, 48160 Derio (Vizcaya); tel. (94) 4011000; fax (94) 4011020; internet www.euskaltel.com; f. 1995; offers fixed-line and mobile cellular telecommunications, digital cable television, and broadband internet services in the Basque Country; Chair. ALBERTO GARCÍA ERAUZKIN.

Jazztel: Anabel Segura 11, Edif. C, 28108 Alcobendas, Madrid; tel. (91) 1839404; fax (91) 1839943; e-mail comunicacion@jazztel.com; internet www.jazztel.com; Pres. LEOPOLDO FERNÁNDEZ PUJALS.

ONO: Emisora 20, 28224 Pozuelo de Alarcón; tel. (902) 929000; e-mail investor.relations@ono.es; internet www.ono.es; f. 1998; broadband internet, telephone and television; owns Grupo Auna; Pres. JOSÉ MARÍA CASTELLANO; CEO ROSALÍA PORTELA.

Orange: Parque Empresarial La Finca, Paseo del Club Deportivo 1, Edif. 8, 28223 Pozuelo de Alarcón (Madrid); internet www.orange.es; f. 2006; owned by France Telecom España; fmrly Uni2 and Amena; CEO JEAN MARC VIGNOLLES.

Telefónica: Ronda de la Comunicación s/n, Edif. Central, 2A Planta, 28050 Madrid; tel. (91) 7406918; fax (91) 4828599; e-mail ir@ telefonica.es; internet www.telefonica.com; f. 1924; privatized in 1997; monopoly on telephone services removed in 1998; incl. mobile network Telefónica Móviles; provides services in 25 countries (2011); Chair. and CEO CÉSAR ALIERTA IZUEL.

Vodafone España: Avda Europa 1 (Central), Parque Empresarial La Moraleja, 28108 Alcobendas, Madrid; tel. (607) 133333; internet www.vodafone.es; f. 1998; fmrly Airtel; mobile services; Pres. and CEO FRANCISCO ROMÁN.

Xfera Moviles: Avda de la Vega 15, Alcobendas, 28108 Madrid; tel. (91) 1315200; e-mail prensa@yoigo.com; internet www.yoigo.com; f. 2006; 76.6% owned by TeliaSonera (Sweden); provides mobile cellular communications services under the brand name Yoigo; Dir-Gen. JOHAN ANDSJÖ.

Regulatory Authorities

Comisión del Mercado de las Telecomunicaciones (Telecommunications Market Commission—CMT): Carrer de Bolívia 56, 08018 Barcelona; tel. (93) 6036200; internet www.cmt.es; f. 1996; Pres. BERNARDO LORENZO ALMENDROS.

Secretaría de Estado de Telecommunicaciones y para la Sociedad de la Información: Ministerio de Industria, Energía y Turismo, Capitán Haya 41, 2°, 28071 Madrid; tel. (91) 3461583; fax (91) 3461520; e-mail planavanza@mityc.es; internet www .planavanza.es.

BROADCASTING

Corporación Radio Televisión Española (RTVE): Edif. Prado del Rey, 28223 Pozuelo de Alarcón, Madrid; tel. (91) 5817000; fax (91) 5815454; e-mail rtve.dircom@rtve.es; internet www.rtve.es; state-owned company; controls and co-ordinates radio and television; incorporates Televisión Española, Televisión Española Internacional, Televisión Española Temática, Radio Nacional de España, Instituto Oficial de Radio y Televisión and the Orquesta Sinfónica y Coro; formerly Ente Público Radio Televisión Española; renamed and reformed in 2007 to become independent of govt influence; Pres. MANUEL ESTEVE.

Independent Companies

Compañía de Radio y Televisión de Galicia (CRTVG): Bando-San Marcos, 15820 Santiago de Compostela (A Coruña); tel. (981) 540640; fax (981) 540619; e-mail dx@crtvg.es; internet www.crtvg.es; f. 1985; Galician-language station; Dir-Gen. ALFONSO SÁNCHEZ IZQUIERDO.

Corporació Catalana de Mitjans Audiovisuals (CCMA): Via Augusta, 252-260, 4A Planta, 08017 Barcelona; tel. (93) 4444800; fax (93) 4444824; e-mail comunicacio@ccma.cat; internet www.ccma.cat; f. 1983; Catalan—language station; 8 television channels, 4 radio stations and some internet sites; Pres. BRAULI DUART I LLINARES.

Euskal Irrati Telebista (EITB)/Radiotelevisión Vasca: Capuchinos de Basurto 2, 48013 Bilbao; tel. (94) 6563000; fax (94) 6563095; e-mail info@eitb.com; internet www.eitb.com; f. 1982; Basque station; 2 television channels, 2 international television channels and 5 radio stations; Dir-Gen. ALBERTO SURIO DE CARLOS.

Onda Regional de Murcia: Avda Libertad 6, 30009 Murcia; tel. (968) 200000; fax (968) 272665; e-mail info@orm.es; internet www.orm.es; f. 1990; Dir-Gen. JOAQUIN AZPARREN IRIGOYEN.

Ràdiotelevisió Valenciana (RTVV): Polígono Accés Ademús s/n, 46100 Burjassot (Valencia); tel. (96) 3183000; fax (96) 3183001; e-mail informacio.al.espectador@rtvv.es; internet www.rtvv.es; f. 1984; Dir-Gen. ROSA VIDAL MONFERRER.

Radio Televisión de Andalucía (RTVA): Sede Central RTVA, Pabellón de Canal Sur (Antigua Pabellón de Andalucía), José de Gálvez s/n, 41090 San Juan de Aznalfarache (Sevilla); tel. (95) 5054600; fax (95) 5054937; e-mail comunicacion@rtva.es; internet www.rtva.es; f. 1988; Dir-Gen. JOSÉ MARÍA GILLÉN MARISCAL.

Radio Televisión Madrid (RTVM): Paseo del Príncipe 3, 28223 Pozuelo de Alarcón (Madrid); tel. (91) 5128200; fax (91) 5128300; e-mail telemadrid@telemadrid.es; internet www.telemadrid.es; Dir-Gen. JOSÉ ANTONIO SÁNCHEZ.

Radiotelevisión Canaria (RTVC): Avda Bravo Murillo 5, Edif. Mapfre, 1°, 38003 Santa Cruz de Tenerife; tel. (922) 470600; fax (922) 273173; e-mail administracion@tvcanaria.tv; internet www.rtvc.es; f. 1997; broadcasts in the Canaries; Dir-Gen. GUILLERMO (WILLY) GARCÍA-MACHIÑENA GARCÍA-CHECA.

Radiotelevisión Castilla-La Mancha (RTVCM): Río Guadalmena 6, 45007 Toledo; tel. (925) 288600; fax (925) 287883; e-mail comunicacion@rtvcm.es; internet www.rtvcm.es; Dir-Gen. IGNACIO VILLA CALLEJA.

Federation

Federación de Asociaciones de Radio y Televisión de España: Evaristo San Miguel 8, 28008 Madrid; tel. (91) 5481222; fax (91) 5593630; e-mail rtvmadrid@telefonica.net; Pres. FEDERICO SÁNCHEZ AGUILAR.

RADIO

In March 1999 two digital radio licences were awarded for the frequencies MF-1 and MF-2. MF-1 was controlled by Cope, Intereconomía, Recoletos and *El Mundo*, while MF-2 was controlled by SER, Onda Rambla-Planeta, Onda Cero, Radio España, Onda Digital and Prensa Española. MF-1 began broadcasting in Madrid and Barcelona in July 2000.

In 2011 the Government announced its intention to convert all analogue radio broadcasts into the digital format under the Digitalization Plan for Terrestrial Broadcasting. In June 2011 a new law was introduced stipulating that Digital Audio Broadcast (DAB) must ensure a minimum coverage of 20% of the population, as against the 50% that had been in effect since 1999.

Radio Nacional de España (RNE): Casa de la Radio, Avda Radio Televisión 4, 28223 Pozuelo de Alarcón (Madrid); tel. (91) 3461000; fax (91) 5183240; e-mail secretario_general.rne@rtve.es; internet www.rne.es; broadcasts Radio 1, Radio Clásica, Radio 3, Radio 4, Radio 5 Todo Noticias; 17 regional stations; Dir-Gen. BENIGNO MORENO.

Radio Exterior de España (REE): Casa de la Radio, Avda Radio Televisión 4, 28223 Pozuelo de Alarcón (Madrid); tel. (91) 3461034; fax (91) 3461815; e-mail ree@rtve.es; internet www.radioexterior.es; overseas service of RNE; broadcasts in 6 languages; includes a world service in Spanish; Dir JUAN ROLDÁN.

Independent Stations

ABC Punto Radio: Juan Ignacio Luca de Tena 7, 28027 Madrid; tel. (91) 3399000; fax (91) 7417589; e-mail cartas@abc.es; internet www.abc.es/radio; f. 2005; Dir-Gen. ANA DELGADO GALÁN.

Cadena 100: Alfonso XI 4, 28014 Madrid; tel. (91) 5951244; fax (91) 5225454; e-mail contacto@cadena100.es; internet www.cadena100.es; Dir JAVIER LLANO ABRIL.

Cadena M80: Gran Vía 32, 7°, 28013 Madrid; tel. (91) 3477700; fax (91) 5228693; e-mail aalvarez@m80radio.com; internet www.m80radio.com; Dir RAMÓN REDONDO.

Cadena Dial: Gran Vía 32, 7°, 28013 Madrid; tel. (91) 3477740; fax (91) 5324769; e-mail direccion@cadenadial.com; internet www.cadenadial.com; Dir JUAN CARLOS CHAVES.

Cadena Ondacero RadioVoz Galicia: Avda de la Prensa, Arteixo, 15006 A Coruña; tel. (981) 180600; fax (981) 180477; internet www.radiovoz.es; f. 1994; Dir LOIS BLANCO PENAS.

Cadena de Ondas Populares Españolas/Radio Popular, SA (COPE): Alfonso XI 4, 28014 Madrid; tel. (91) 5951200; e-mail internet.usuarios@cope.es; internet www.cope.es; f. 1959; controlled by Roman Catholic Church; numerous medium-wave and FM stations; digital; Pres. and CEO FERNANDO GIMÉNEZ BARRIOCANAL.

Cadena Radiolé: Gran Vía 32, 7°, 28013 Madrid; tel. (91) 3477740; fax (91) 5324769; e-mail direccion@radiole.com; internet www.radiole.com; Dir MIGUEL ÁNGEL CORRAL SALAS.

Cadena TOP Radio España: Manuel Silvela 9, 28010 Madrid; tel. (91) 4475300; fax (91) 4477026; internet www.mmradio.com; Pres. JOSÉ ANTONIO SÁNCHEZ.

Catalunya Ràdio, SRG, SA: Avda Diagonal 614–616, 08021 Barcelona; tel. (93) 3069200; fax (93) 3069201; internet www.catradio.cat; f. 1983; run by Catalan autonomous govt; four channels: Catalunya Ràdio, Catalunya Música, Catalunya Informació, iCat; 6 internet channels; Dir RAMON MATEU.

COMRàdio: Travessera de les Corts 131–159, 08028 Barcelona; tel. (93) 5080600; fax (93) 5080810; e-mail comradio@comradio.com; internet www.comradio.com; Dir-Gen. RAFAEL DE RIBOT.

EITB Radio: Capuchinos de Basurto 4, 48013 Bilbao; tel. (946) 563000; fax (946) 563095; e-mail info@eitb.com; internet www.eitb.com; run by Basque autonomous govt; broadcasts on FM and MW as Euskadi Irratia, Radio Euskadi (Bilbao), Radio Vitoria (Vitoria-Gasteiz) and EITB Irratia; Dir ODILE KRUZETA.

Europa FM: Bueso Pineda 7, 28043 Madrid; tel. (902) 103262; fax (91) 4137175; e-mail europafm@europafm.es; internet europafm.com; Dir PATRICIO SÁNCHEZ.

Grupo Pevesa Comunicación, SL—Radio Ondas Riojanas: Santo Domingo 5, 26580 Arnedo; tel. (941) 383350; fax (941) 383383; e-mail radioarnedo@ondarioja.com; internet www.radioarnedo.com; f. 1990; Pres. PEDRO VEGA HERNÁNDEZ.

Los 40 Principales: Gran Vía 32, 28013 Madrid; tel. (91) 3470705; fax (91) 5317370; internet www.los40.com; Dir CARLOS MONTOYA.

Muinmo, SL: Castelló 36, 28001 Madrid; tel. (91) 3598079; fax (91) 3500704; Dir-Gen. MIGUEL ANGEL MONTERO QUEVEDO.

MUSICAM: Marie Curie 5–7, 28521 Rivas Vaciamadrid, Madrid; tel. (902) 522000; fax (91) 3591321; e-mail info@musicam.es; internet www.musicam.es; f. 1966; Dir-Gen. ISIDRO SÁNCHEZ-CRESPO.

Ona FM: Casp 6, 08010 Barcelona; tel. (93) 3441400; e-mail info@onafm.cat; internet www.ona-fm.cat.

Onda Cero Radio (OCR): Fuerteventura 12, San Sebastián de los Reyes, 28703 Madrid; tel. (91) 436400; fax (91) 436101; e-mail ondacero@ondacero.es; internet www.ondacero.es; owned by Telefónica; digital; Dir-Gen. FRANCISCO ESPINAR.

Radio Autonomía Madrid, SA: Paseo del Príncipe 3, Ciudad de la Imagen, 28223 Pozuelo de Alarcón, Madrid; tel. (91) 5128200; fax (91) 5128300; e-mail ondamadrid@ondamadrid.es; internet www.telemadrid.es; f. 1985; Dir MIGUEL PÉREZ-PLA DE VIU.

Ràdio Autonomia Valenciana, SA/Ràdio Nou: Avda Blasco Ibáñez 136, 46022 Valencia; tel. (96) 3183600; fax (96) 3183601; e-mail informacio.al.espectador@rtvv.es; internet www.radionou.com; Dir JAVIER GOMAR ALBERT.

Radio ECCA: Avda Escaleritas 64, 1°, 35011 Las Palmas de Gran Canaria; tel. (928) 257400; fax (928) 207395; e-mail info@radioecca.org; internet www.radioecca.org; f. 1965; adult education; Dir LUCAS LÓPEZ PÉREZ.

Radio Galega (RG): San Marcos, 15820 Santiago de Compostela; tel. (981) 540640; fax (981) 540919; e-mail dir.rg@crtvg.es; internet www.crtvg.es; f. 1985; run by Galician autonomous Govt; Man. Dir MARÍA DOMÍNGUEZ BASTIDA.

Radio Surco-Castilla La Mancha: Concordia 14, Bajo C, 13700 Tomelloso (Ciudad Real); tel. (926) 505959; fax (926) 505961; email r.surco@retemail.es; internet www.radiosurco.es; Dir FRANCISCO CASTELLANOS CUELLAR.

Sociedad Española de Radiodifusión (Cadena SER): Gran Vía 32, 28013 Madrid; tel. (91) 3470700; fax (91) 3470709; e-mail gprensa@unionradio.es; internet www.cadenaser.com; f. 1924; 235 regional stations; owned by Grupo PRISA; digital; Dir-Gen. RAÚL RODRÍGUEZ.

Radio Association

Asociación Española de Radiodifusión Comercial (AERC): Plaza Independencia 2, 4° dcha, 28001 Madrid; tel. (91) 4357072; fax (91) 4356196; e-mail aerc@aerc.es; groups nearly all commercial radio stations; Dir-Gen. ALFONSO RUIZ DE ASSIN.

TELEVISION

Analogue broadcasts ceased in April 2010.

Televisión Española (TVE): Edif. Prado del Rey, Avda. Radio Televisión 4, 28223 Pozuelo de Alarcón, Madrid; tel. (91) 3464000; fax (91) 3463055; e-mail consultas@rtve.es; internet www.tve.es; broadcasts on TVE-1 and La 2; production centres in Barcelona and Las Palmas de Gran Canaria and 15 regional centres; broadcasts to

Europe and the Americas on Canal Internacional; Dir SANTIAGO
GONZÁLEZ.

Independent Stations

Antena 3 Televisión: Avda de Isla Graciosa s/n, 28703 San
Sebastián de los Reyes, Madrid; tel. (91) 6230657; fax (91)
6230994; e-mail antena3tv@antena3tv.com; internet www.antena3
.com; f. 1989; owned by Grupo Planeta; Pres. JOSÉ MANUEL LARA
BOSCH.

Canal 9—Televisió Autonómica Valenciana (TVV): Polígon
Accés Ademús, 46100 Burjassot (Valencia); tel. (96) 3183000; fax
(96) 3183001; e-mail wmaster@rtvv.es; internet www.rtvv.es;
f. 1989; second channel commenced operations in 1997; Dir LUIS
REDONDO LÓPEZ.

Canal Sur Televisión: Carretera San Juan de Aznalfarache, Apdo
132, 41920 San Juan de Aznalfarache, Sevilla; tel. (95) 5054600; fax
(95) 5054740; e-mail comunicacion@rtva.es; internet www.canalsur
.es; f. 1989; regional station for Andalusia; Dir-Gen. JESÚS VIGORRA.

Euskal Telebista—ETB (TV Vasca): Capuchinos de Basurtu 2,
48013 Bilbao; tel. (94) 6563000; fax (94) 6563095; e-mail info@eitb
.com; internet www.eitb.com; f. 1982; 2 channels broadcasting to
Basque Country, 1 in Basque, 1 in Spanish; Dir PELLO SARASOLA
BARANDIARAN.

Popular TV: Alfonso XI 4, 28014 Madrid; tel. (902) 222728; e-mail
populartv@populartv.net; internet www.populartv.net; broadcasts
on a local and national level; Pres. and Dir-Gen. FERNANDO GIMÉNEZ
BARRIOCANAL.

La Sexta: Virgilio 2, Edif. 4, Ciudad de la Imagen, 28223 Pozuelo de
Alarcón (Madrid); tel. (91) 8382966; fax (91) 8382958; e-mail
comunicacion@lasexta.com; internet www.lasexta.com; f. 2006;
national terrestrial channel; Pres. EMILIO ARAGÓN; CEO JOSÉ MIGUEL
CONTRERAS.

Sogecable: Avda de los Artesanos 6, 28760 Tres Cantos (Madrid);
tel. (91) 7367000; fax (91) 7368995; e-mail prensa@sogecable.com;
internet www.sogecable.es; f. 1989; satellite and digital television,
internet services; operates Cuatro (national terrestrial channel),
Digital+ (digital provider), Canal Satélite Digital, CNN+, Compañía
Independiente de Televisión, Gestsport, Sogecine; owned by Grupo
PRISA; Pres. RODOLFO MARTÍN VILLA; CEO PEDRO GARCÍA GUILLÉN.

Grupo Telecinco: Federico Monpou 5B, 28049 Madrid; tel. (91)
3966300; fax (91) 3966478; e-mail telecinco@telecinco.es; internet
www.telecinco.es; f. 1990; private commercial national network; jtly
owned by Grupo Mediaset (Italy)and Grupo Correo de Comunicación,
Ice Finance (The Netherlands); Pres. ALEJANDRO ECHEVARRÍA.

Televisió de Catalunya (TV3): Carrer de la TV3 s/n, 08970 Sant
Joan Despi, Barcelona; tel. (93) 4999333; fax (93) 4730671; internet
www.tv3.cat; f. 1983; broadcasts in Catalan; Dir RAMON ROVIRA.

Televisión Autonomía Madrid, SA (Telemadrid): Paseo del
Príncipe 3, 28223 Pozuelo de Alarcón (Madrid); tel. (91) 5128200;
fax (91) 5128300; e-mail telemadrid@telemadrid.es; internet www
.telemadrid.es; commenced transmissions in 1989; controlled by
RTVM; cultural channel, laOtra, commenced transmission in March
2001; Dir-Gen. JOSÉ ANTÓNIO SÁNCHEZ.

Televisión de Galicia (TVG): Bando, San Marcos, 15820 Santiago
de Compostela; tel. (981) 540640; fax (981) 540719; e-mail info@crtvg
.es; internet www.crtvg.es; f. 1985; broadcasts in Galician; Dir-Gen.
ALFONSO SÁNCHEZ IZQUIERDO.

Other Satellite, Cable and Digital Television

Chello Multicanal: Calle de Saturno 1, Pozuelo de Alarcón, 28224
Madrid; tel. (91) 7141080; fax (91) 3516873; e-mail comunicacion@
chellomulticanal.com; internet chellomulticanal.es; f. 1996; cable;
operates 9 channels; Dir-Gen. EDUARDO ZULUETA.

Grupo Auna: Basauri 7 y 9, 28023 Madrid; internet www.ono.es;
part of ONO; telecommunications, internet and cable TV; operates
the cable telecommunications providers Aragón de Cable, Cable-
telca, Cable i Televisió de Catalunya, Madritel, Supercable de
Andalucía, Supercable Sevilla and Supercable Almería.

Hispasat: Gobelas 41, 2°, 28023 Madrid; tel. (91) 7102540; fax (91)
3729000; e-mail comunicacion@hispasat.es; internet www.hispasat
.com; f. 1989; satellite; Pres. ELENA PISONERO.

Telecable de Asturias: Parque Científico y Tecnológico de Gijón,
Carretera de Cabueñes, 33203 Gijón; tel. (984) 191000; fax (984)
191001; e-mail info@telecable.es; internet www.telecable.es; cable;
f. 1995; operator for Asturias; Pres. JUAN GARCIA CONDE; Dir-Gen.
ALEJANDRO MARTÍNEZ PEÓN.

Telefónica Servicios Audiovisuales: Calle Virgilio 2, Edif. 2, 2°,
28223 Pozuelo de Alarcón (Madrid); tel. (91) 5129510; internet www
.tsa.es; f. 1997; cable.

Veo TV: Avda San Luis 25, 28033 Madrid; internet www.veo.es;
f. 2001; digital; Dir EDUARDO SÁNCHEZ ILLANA.

Associations

**Asociación Nacional de Operadores de Telecomunicaciones y
Servicios de Internet (AOTEC):** San Crispín 30 Bajo, 02640
Almansa; tel. (902) 876788; e-mail aotec@aotec.es; internet www
.aotec.net; f. 2002; Pres. SERVANDO SÁNCHEZ CALERO.

Unión de Televisiones Comerciales Asociadas (UTECA):
Miguel Ángel 7, 1°B, 28010 Madrid; tel. (91) 3086746; fax (91)
3910049; e-mail uteca@uteca.com; internet www.uteca.com;
f. 1998; represents commercial television interests; Pres. ALEJANDRO
ECHEVARRÍA; Sec.-Gen. JORGE DEL CORRAL Y DÍEZ DEL CORRAL.

Finance

(cap. = capital, res = reserves, dep. = deposits, brs = branches,
m. = million, amounts in euros)

BANKING

Central Bank

Banco de España: Alcalá 48, 28014 Madrid; tel. (91) 3386063; fax
(91) 3385884; e-mail bde@bde.es; internet www.bde.es; f. 1782;
granted exclusive right of issue in 1874; nationalized 1962; granted a
degree of autonomy in 1994; cap. 1,000.0m., res 1,000.0m., dep.
68,080.6m. (Dec. 2009); Gov. LUIS MARÍA LINDE; 22 brs.

Principal Commercial and Development Banks

Banca March SA: Avda Alejandro Rosselló 8, 07002 Palma de
Mallorca; tel. (971) 779100; fax (971) 779187; e-mail divinter@
bancamarch.es; internet www.bancamarch.es; f. 1926; 100% owned
by the March family; cap. 29.2m., res 40.1m., dep. 8,464.5m. (Dec.
2011); Pres. JOSÉ CARLOS MARCH DELGADO; Man. Dir JOSÉ NIETO DE LA
CIERVA; 247 brs.

Banco Bilbao Vizcaya Argentaria (BBVA): Paseo de la Castellana 81, 28046 Madrid; tel. (91) 4876000; fax (91) 4876417; internet
www.bbva.es; f. 2000 by merger; cap. 2,403m., res 32,758m., dep.
314,238m. (Dec. 2011); Pres. JOSÉ IGNACIO GOIRIGOLZARRI TELLAECHE;
Chair. and Chief Exec. FRANCISCO GONZÁLEZ RODRÍGUEZ; 3,375 brs.

Banco Caixa Geral: Juan Ignacio Luca de Tena 1, 28027 Madrid;
tel. (91) 3099000; fax (91) 3209275; e-mail extranjero@bancaixageral
.es; internet www.bancocaixageral.es; f. 1969; present name adopted
2006; 99.8% owned by Caixa Geral de Depósitos (Portugal); cap.
518.8m., res −47.6m., dep. 6,467.1m. (Dec. 2011); Pres. RODOLFO
VASCO CASTRO GOMES MASCARENHAS LAVRADOR; Chief Exec. MANUEL
VÍCTOR LÓPEZ FIGUEROA; 210 brs.

Banco Cooperativo Español SA: Virgen de los Peligros 6, 28013
Madrid; tel. (91) 5956700; fax (91) 5956800; internet www.cajarural
.com; f. 1990; cap. 91m., res 74.8m., dep. 10,918.3m. (Dec. 2011);
Chair. JOSÉ LUIS GARCÍA PALACIOS; Gen. Man. JAVIER PETIT
ASUMENDI; 4,100 brs.

Banco Español de Crédito SA (Banesto): Gran Vía de Hortaleza
3, 28043 Madrid; tel. (91) 3383100; fax (91) 3381883; e-mail
uninternac@banesto.es; internet www.banesto.es; f. 1902; cap.
543.0m., res −161.5m., dep. 48,610.3m. (Dec. 2011); Chair. ANA
PATRICIA BOTÍN-SANZ DE SAUTUOLA Y O'SHEA; CEO JAVIER SAN FÉLIX;
1,952 brs.

Banco Gallego SA: Avda Linares Rivas 30, 15005 A Coruña; tel.
(981) 127950; fax (981) 126582; e-mail intervenciongeneral@
bancogallego.com; internet www.bancogallego.es; f. 1847; cap.
119.0m., res 22.6m., dep. 4,061.4m. (Dec. 2010); Pres. JUAN MANUEL
URGOITI LÓPEZ-OCAÑA; Gen. Man. JOSÉ LUIS LOSADA RODRÍGUEZ; 190
brs.

Banco Popular Español SA: Velázquez 34, 28001 Madrid; tel. (91)
5207000; fax (91) 5783274; internet www.bancopopular.es; f. 1926;
cap. 140.1m., res 933.6m., dep. 93,197.7m. (Dec. 2011); Pres. and
CEO ÁNGEL CARLOS RON GÜIMIL; 2,224 brs.

Banco Sabadell SA: POB 1, Plaza Sant Roc 20, Sabadell, 08201
Barcelona; tel. (93) 7289289; fax (93) 7270606; e-mail info@
bancsabadell.com; internet www.bancsabadell.com; f. 1881; cap.
177.9m., res 2,267.6m., dep. 63,619.3m. (Dec. 2011); Chair. JOSEP
OLIU; 1,339 brs.

Banco Santander SA: Plaza de Canalejas 1, 28014 Avda de
Cantabria s/n, 28660 Boadilla del Monte, Madrid; tel. (91)
2890000; internet www.santander.com; f. 1857; cap. 4,455m., res
66,608m., dep. 700,464m. (Dec. 2011); Chair. EMILIO BOTÍN-SANZ DE
SAUTUOLA Y GARCÍA DE LOS RÍOS; CEO JAVIER MARÍN ROMANO; 14,082
brs.

Banco de Valencia: Pintor Sorolla 2–4, 46002 Valencia; tel. (96)
3984500; fax (96) 3984570; internet www.bancodevalencia.es; f. 1900; cap.
122.1m., res 1,069.3m., dep. 17,933.6m. (Dec. 2011); Pres. JOSÉ LUIS
OLIVAS MARTÍNEZ; Gen. Man. DOMINGO PARRA SORIA; 452 brs.

Bankinter: Paseo de la Castellana 29, 28046 Madrid; tel. (91) 3397500; fax (91) 3397556; e-mail international@bankinter.es; internet www.bankinter.com; f. 1965 as Banco Intercontinental Español SA; name changed as above 1990; finances industrial and business dealings with medium- and long-term loans and investments; cap. 143.1m., res 1,062.1m., dep. 28,360.6m. (Dec. 2011); Chair. PEDRO GUERRERO; CEO MARÍA DOLORES DANCAUSA; 253 brs.

Barclays Bank SA: Plaza de Colón 1, 28046 Madrid; tel. (91) 3361000; fax (91) 3361134; internet www.barclays.es; f. 1974; name changed as above 1982; cap. 1,454.9m., res 912.2m., dep. 26,582.4m. (Dec. 2011); 99.7% owned by Barclays Bank PLC (United Kingdom); Chair. C. MARTÍNEZ DE CAMPOS; 600 brs.

Deutsche Bank SAE: Avda Diagonal 446, 08006 Barcelona; tel. (93) 3673788; fax (93) 3673311; internet www.deutsche-bank.es; f. 1950; present name adopted 1994; 99.7% owned by Deutsche Bank AG (Germany); cap. 88.8m., res 945.4m., dep. 14,441.5m. (Dec. 2011); Chair. (vacant); 250 brs.

Savings Banks

Bankia SA: Calle Pintor Sorolla, 8°, 46002 Valencia; e-mail accionista@bankia.com; internet www.bankia.com; f. 1983; name changed as above 2011; cap. 3,465.1m., res 10,888.1m., dep. 168,061.1m. (Dec. 2011); Chair. JOSÉ IGNACIO GOIRIGOLZARRI TELLAECHE; CEO FRANCISCO VERDÚ PONS; 3,107 brs.

CaixaBank: Avda Diagonal 621, 08028 Barcelona; tel. (93) 4092121; e-mail investors@caixabank.com; internet www.caixabank.com; f. 2011; 10th largest bank in Europe; cap. 3,840.1m., res 11,136.7m., dep. 140,069.6m. (Dec. 2011); Pres. ISIDRO FAINÉ CASAS; Chief Exec. JUAN MARÍA NIN; 6,500 brs.

Caja de Ahorros de Asturias (CAJASTUR): Plaza de la Escandalera 2, 33003 Oviedo; tel. (98) 5102222; fax (98) 5215649; e-mail extranjero@cajastur.es; internet www.cajastur.es; f. 1945; res 1,508.8m., dep. 13,477.5m., total assets 15,450.7m. (Dec. 2008); Pres. and CEO MANUEL MENÉNDEZ MENÉNDEZ; 343 brs.

Caja de Ahorros de la Inmaculada de Aragón (CAI): Paseo Independencia 10, 50004 Zaragoza; tel. (976) 718100; fax (976) 718377; e-mail info.corporativa@cai.es; internet www.cai.es; f. 1905; res 813.9m., dep. 10,361.5m., total assets 11,407.7m. (Dec. 2009); Pres. JUAN MARÍA PEMÁN GAVIN; 238 brs.

Caja de Ahorros y Monte de Piedad de las Baleares 'Sa Nostra': Ramón Llull 2, 07001 Palma de Mallorca; tel. (971) 171717; fax (971) 171797; e-mail sanostra@sanostra.es; internet www.sanostra.es; f. 1882; res 215.7m., dep. 11,082.9m., total assets 12,712.3m. (Dec. 2010); Chair. FERNANDO ALZAMORA CARBONELL; Gen. Man. PEDRO BATLE MAYO; 229 brs.

Caja de Ahorros y Monte de Piedad del Círculo Católico de Obreros de Burgos (CajaCírculo): Avda de los Reyes Católicos 1, 09005 Burgos; tel. (947) 288200; fax (947) 288210; internet www.cajacirculo.es; f. 1909; res 514.1m., dep. 4,575.5m., total assets 5,208m. (Dec. 2009); Chair. JOSÉ IGNACIO MIJANGOS LINAZA; Gen. Man. SANTIAGO RUIZ DIEZ; 176 brs.

Caja de Ahorros y Monte de Piedad de Zaragoza, Aragón y Rioja (IBERCAJA): Plaza del Paraíso 2, 50008 Zaragoza; tel. (976) 767676; fax (976) 214417; internet www.ibercaja.es; f. 1876; res 34.4m., dep. 24,615.4m., total assets 44,988.8m. (Dec. 2010); Chair. AMADO FRANCO LAHOZ; Gen. Man. JOSÉ LUIS AGUIRRE LOASO; 1,085 brs.

Caja de Ahorros de Murcia (Cajamurcia): Gran Vía Escultor Salzillo 23, 30005 Murcia; tel. (968) 361600; fax (968) 306160; internet www.cajamurcia.es; f. 1965; res 1,204.4m., dep. 20,439.7m., total assets 22,163.4m. (Dec. 2009); Pres. JUAN ROCA GUILLAMÓN; Gen. Man. CARLOS EGEA KRAUEL; 398 brs.

Caja España de Inversiones Salamanca y Soria Caja de Ahorros y Monte de Piedad: Ordoño II 17, 24001 León; tel. (987) 218683; fax (987) 218067; e-mail buzon@cajaespana.es; internet www.cajaespana.es; f. 2010 as a result of merger of Caja España with Caja Duero; Chair. SANTOS LLAMAS LLAMAS; Gen. Man. JOSÉ IGNACIO LAGARTOS RODRÍGUEZ.

Caja Laboral Popular Coop. de Crédito (Caja Laboral): Paseo José María Arizmendiarrieta s/n, 20500 Mondragón, Guipúzcoa; tel. (943) 719500; fax (943) 719778; e-mail cajalaboral.net@cajalaboral.es; internet www.cajalaboral.es; f. 1959; cap. 485.3m., res −211.4m., dep. 18,298.9m. (Dec. 2011); Pres. JUAN M. OTAEGUI MURUA; Gen. Man. ELIAS ATUCHA ARESTI; 401 brs.

CatalunyaCaixa (CX): Plaza Antonio Maura 6, 08003 Barcelona; tel. (93) 4845000; fax (93) 4845141; internet www.catalunyacaixa.com; f. 2010 as a result of merger of Caixa Catalunya, Caixa Tarragona and Caixa Manresa; cap. 2,449.4m., res −370m., dep. 46,657m. (Dec. 2010); Pres. NARCÍS SERRA; Gen. Man. JOSEP ADOLF TODÓ; 1,200 brs.

Confederación Española de Cajas de Ahorros (CECA): Alcalá 27, 28014 Madrid; tel. (91) 5965000; fax (91) 5965742; e-mail admin@ceca.es; internet www.ceca.es; f. 1928; national asscn of savings banks; in 2012 created Cecabank SA as a separate financial entity with the Confederación owing 89% of shares; cap. 30.1m., res 34.6m., dep. 11,704.3m. (Dec. 2010); Pres. ISIDRO FAINÉ.

Kutxabank: Gran Vía 30, 48009 Bilbao; internet www.kutxabank.es; f. 2012; Exec. Pres. MARIO FERNÁNDEZ PELAZ.

NCG Banco SA: Rúa Nueva 30, 15003 A Coruña; tel. (981) 188000; fax (981) 188001; internet www.novagalicia.es; f. 2010; banking business acquired by NCG Banco SA 2011; cap. 2,681.9m., res 47.2m., dep. 64,892.9m. (Dec. 2011); Pres. JOSE MARÍA CASTELLANO; Gen. Man. CÉSAR GONZÁLEZ BUENO.

Unicaja Banco: Avda Andalucía 10–12, 29007 Málaga; tel. (952) 138000; fax (952) 138130; e-mail info@personal.unicaja.es; internet www.unicaja.es; f. 1991; Pres. BRAULIO MEDEL CAMARÁ; Gen. Man. MANUEL AZUAGA MORENO; 935 brs.

Unnim Banc SAU (Unnim): Plaça Catalunya 9, 08002 Barcelona; tel. (902) 480808; e-mail info@unnim.cat; internet www.unnim.cat; f. 2010 by merger of 3 savings banks (Manlleu, Sabadell and Terrassa); 100% stake acquired by Banco Bilbao Vizcaya Argentaria (BBVA) in March 2012; res 494.8m., dep. 11,781.9m., total assets 12,380.5m. (Dec. 2008); Dir-Gen. JORDI MESTRE.

Banking Associations

Asociación Española de Banca (AEB): Velázquez 64–66, 28001 Madrid; tel. (91) 7891311; fax (91) 7891310; internet www.aebanca.es; f. 1977; Pres. MIGUEL MARTÍN; Sec.-Gen. PEDRO PABLO VILLASANTE.

Fondo de Garantía de Depósitos (FGD): José Ortega y Gasset 22, 28006 Madrid; tel. (91) 4316645; fax (91) 5755728; e-mail fogade@fgd.es; internet www.fgd.es; f. 1977; deposit guarantee fund; Pres. JOSÉ MARÍA VIÑALS IÑÍGUEZ.

STOCK EXCHANGES

Bolsas y Mercados Españoles (BME): Palacio de la Bolsa, Plaza de la Lealtad 1, 28014 Madrid; tel. (91) 7095000; fax (91) 5326816; e-mail accionista@bolsasymercados.es; internet www.bolsasymercados.es; integrates cos that manage securities market and financial system; Pres. ANTONIO J. ZOIDO MARTÍNEZ.

Bolsa de Barcelona: Paseo de Gracia 19, 08007 Barcelona; tel. (93) 4013555; fax (93) 4013650; e-mail informacion@borsabcn.es; internet www.borsabcn.es; f. 1915; Pres. JOAN HORTALÀ I ARAU.

Bolsa de Bilbao: José M. Olabarri 1, 48001 Bilbao; tel. (94) 4034400; fax (94) 4034430; e-mail bolsabilbao@bolsabilbao.es; internet www.bolsabilbao.es; f. 1890; CEO JOSÉ LUIS DAMBORENEA.

Bolsa de Madrid: Plaza de la Lealtad 1, 28014 Madrid; tel. (91) 5891161; fax (91) 5312290; e-mail internacional@bolsamadrid.es; internet www.bolsamadrid.es; f. 1831; 49 mems; Chair. and CEO ANTONIO ZOIDO MARTÍNEZ.

Bolsa de Valores de Valencia: Libreros 2 y 4, 46002 Valencia; tel. (96) 3870100; fax (96) 3870133; e-mail webmaster@bolsavalencia.es; internet www.bolsavalencia.es; f. 1980; Vice-Pres. and CEO MANUEL ESCÁMEZ SÁNCHEZ.

Regulatory Authority

Comisión Nacional del Mercado de Valores (CNMV): Miguel Ángel 11, 28010 Madrid; tel. (91) 5851500; fax (91) 3193373; internet www.cnmv.es; f. 1988; national securities and exchange commission; Pres. JULIO SEGURA SÁNCHEZ.

INSURANCE

Aegon Unión Aseguradora: Príncipe de Vergara 156, 28002 Madrid; tel. (90) 2108902; fax (91) 5639715; e-mail atencion.clv@aegon.es; internet www.aegon.es; f. 1980; owned by Aegon NV (The Netherlands); life, property, health and personal insurance and reinsurance; Chair. ALEJANDRO ROYO-VILLANOVA PAYÁ; CEO JESÚS QUINTANAL SAN EMETERIO.

Allianz, Compañía de Seguros y Reaseguros: Tarragona 109, 08014 Barcelona; tel. (90) 1272272; fax (91) 5578702; e-mail allianz_seguros@allianz.es; internet www.allianz.es; f. 1999; total premiums 2,292m. (2004); CEO IVÁN JOSÉ DE LA SOTA DUÑABEITIA; Pres. VICENTE TARDÍO BARUTEL.

Asistencia Sanitaria Interprovincial de Seguros (ASISA): Juan Ignacio Luca de Tena 10, 28027 Madrid; tel. (90) 2010010; e-mail asisa.informacion@asisa.es; internet www.asisa.es; f. 1971; Pres. Dr FRANCISCO IVORRA MIRALLES; CEO Dr ENRIQUE DE PORRES ORTIZ DE URBINA.

Axa: Camino Fuente de la Mora 1, 28050 Madrid; tel. (91) 3499345; fax (91) 8070075; e-mail fundacion@axa.es; internet www.axa.es; Pres. JEAN-LAURENT GRANIER; CEO JEAN-PAUL RIGNAULT.

BBVA Seguros: Alcalá 17, 28014 Madrid; tel. (91) 5379231; fax (91) 3747266; e-mail seguros@grupobbva.com; internet www.bbvaseguros.com.

Bilbao, Cía Anónima de Seguros y Reaseguros (Seguros Bilbao): Paseo del Puerto 20, 48992 Neguri-Getxo (Vizcaya); tel. (90) 2456645; fax (90) 2458745; internet www.segurosbilbao.com; f. 1918; gen. and life insurance, represented throughout Spain; part of Grupo Catalana Occidente; Pres. FRANCISCO JOSÉ ARREGUI; Man. Dir IÑAKI ALVARES.

Caja de Seguros Reunidos, Cía de Seguros y Reaseguros (Caser Seguros): Avda de Burgos 109, 28050 Madrid; tel. (90) 2011111; fax (91) 5955009; e-mail informacion@caser.es; internet www.caser.es; f. 1942; represented throughout Spain; total premiums 2,778m. (2010); Pres. AMADO FRANCO LAHOZ; Dir-Gen. IGNACIO EYRLES GARCÍA DE VINUESA.

Crédito y Caución (Compañía Española de Seguros y Reaseguros): Paseo de la Castellana 4, 28046 Madrid; tel. (91) 4326300; fax (91) 4326506; e-mail sac@creditoycaucion.es; internet www.creditoycaucion.es; f. 1929; total premiums 361m. (2005); Pres. JESÚS SERRA FARRÉ; CEO ISIDRO UNDA URZAIZ.

Generali España, Sociedad Anónima de Seguros y Reaseguros: Orense 2, 28020 Madrid; tel. (91) 3301400; fax (91) 5905790; e-mail info@generali.es; internet www.generali.es; total premiums 2,258.4m. (2011); Pres. CARLOS ZURITA DELGADO; CEO JAIME ANCHÚSTEGUI MELGAREJO.

Grupo Catalana Occidente: Avda Alcalde Barnils 63, 08174 Sant Cugat del Vallés (Barcelona); tel. (90) 2344000; fax (93) 5908257; e-mail analistas@catalanaoccidente.com; internet www.seguroscatalanaoccidente.com; insurance and reinsurance; Pres. JOSÉ MARÍA SERRA FARRÉ.

Mapfre (Mapfre Mutualidad de Seguros y Reaseguros): Sor Angela de la Cruz, 6, 28020 Madrid; tel. (90) 2140214; fax (91) 5508816; e-mail segviaje.masist@mapfre.com; internet www.mapfre.com; f. 1990; Pres. ANTONIO HUERTAS.

Mutua General de Seguros (MGS): Avda Diagonal 543, 08029 Barcelona; tel. (93) 4953232; fax (93) 3217284; e-mail sucbarcelonadiagonal@mgs.es; internet www.mgs.es; f. 1907; Pres. JOSÉ MARÍA SAMPIETRO VILLACAMPA.

Mutua Madrileña: Paseo de la Castellana 33, 28046 Madrid; tel. (902) 555550; fax (91) 3105223; internet www.mutua.es; f. 1930; Pres. IGNACIO GARRALDA RUÍZ DE VELASCO.

Ocaso, SA, Compañía de Seguros y Reaseguros: Princesa 23, 28008 Madrid; tel. (91) 5380100; fax (91) 5418509; e-mail ocaso@ocaso.es; internet www.ocaso.es; f. 1920; total premiums 513m., cap. 100m. (2002); 370 brs in Spain, 1 in United Kingdom, 1 in Puerto Rico; Pres. ISABEL CASTELO D'ORTEGA; Dir-Gen. D. ANTONIO DOMÍNGUEZ CUERDO.

Sanitas de Seguros: Ribera del Loira 52, 28042 Madrid; tel. 902 230220; fax (91) 5852516; e-mail iferrando@sanitas.es; internet www.sanitas.es; health; Pres. JUAN JOSÉ LÓPEZ-IBOR.

SantaLucía Seguros: Plaza de España 15, 28008 Madrid; tel. (91) 5419387; fax (91) 5410133; e-mail atencion@santalucia.es; internet www.santalucia.es; f. 1922; Pres. CARLOS J. ALVAREZ NAVARRO.

Vidacaixa: Juan Gris 20-26, 08014 Barcelona; tel. (93) 2278700; fax (93) 2989005; internet www.vidacaixa-segurcaixaadeslas.es; subsidiary of Grupo CaiFor; Pres. RICARDO FORNESA RIBÓ.

Zurich: Vía Augusta 192–200, 08021 Barcelona; tel. (93) 2099111; fax (93) 2014849; e-mail zurich.seleccion-es@zurich.com; internet www.zurich.es; f. 1884.

Regulatory Authority

Dirección General de Seguros y Fondos de Pensiones: Paseo de la Castellana 44, 28046 Madrid; tel. (91) 3397000; fax (91) 3397113; e-mail incidenciasdec@meh.es; internet www.dgsfp.meh.es; supervisory body; part of Ministry of the Economic Affairs and Competitiveness; Dir-Gen. MARIA FLAVIA RODRIGUEZ-PONGA SALAMANCA.

Insurance Association

Unión Española de Entidades Aseguradoras y Reaseguradoras (UNESPA): Núñez de Balboa 101, 28006 Madrid; tel. (91) 7451530; fax (91) 7451531; e-mail gabinete.prensa@unespa.es; internet www.unespa.es; f. 1977; Pres. PILAR GONZÁLEZ DE FRUTOS; Sec.-Gen. MIRENCHU DEL VALLE; c. 240 mem. cos.

Trade and Industry

GOVERNMENT AGENCIES

Comisión Nacional de la Competencia (CNC): Barquillo 5, 28004 Madrid; tel. (91) 5680510; fax (91) 5680590; e-mail informacion@cncompetencia.es; internet www.cncompetencia.es; f. 2007 by merger of the Servicio de Defensa de la Competencia and the Tribunal de Defensa de la Competencia; investigates anti-competitive practices and enforces competition law; Pres. JOAQUÍN GARCÍA BERNALDO DE QUIRÓS.

Instituto Español de Comercio Exterior (ICEX): Paseo de la Castellana 14–16, 28046 Madrid; tel. (91) 3496100; fax (91) 4316128; internet www.icex.es; f. 1982; institute for foreign trade; Pres. JAIME GARCÍA-LEGAZ PONCE.

Secretaría General de Comercio Exterior: Secretaría de Estado de Comercio y Turismo, Paseo de la Castellana 160, 28046 Madrid; tel. (902) 446006; fax (91) 4578066; part of Ministry of Industry, Energy and Tourism; Sec.-Gen. JAIME GARCÍA-LEGAZ PONCE.

DEVELOPMENT ORGANIZATIONS

Ade Gestión Sodical, SGECR: Jacinto Benavente 2, 3°, 47195 Valladolid; tel. (983) 343811; fax (983) 330702; e-mail sodical@sodical.es; internet www.sodical.es; f. 1982 as Sociedad para el Desarrollo Industrial de Castilla y León (SODICAL); promotes devt in Castile and León; Dir-Gen. MANUEL FERNÁNDEZ DÍEZ.

Consejería de Agricultura, Pesca y Medio Ambiente: Tabladilla s/n, 41071 Sevilla; tel. (95) 5032000; fax (95) 5032149; decides on policies related to agriculture, fishing, agri-food industry and rural development.

Instituto Galego de Promoción Económica (IGAPE): Complejo Administrativo Barrio de San Lázaro s/n, 15703 Santiago de Compostela (A Coruña); tel. (981) 541173; fax (981) 541114; e-mail igape@igape.es; internet www.igape.es; f. 1993; promotes devt in Galicia; overseas brs in People's Republic of China, Germany, Japan, Poland and USA; Dir-Gen. JAVIER AGUILERA.

Instituto Madrileño de Desarrollo (IMADE): José Abascal 57, 28003 Madrid; tel. (91) 3997400; e-mail informacion@imade.es; internet www.imade.es; f. 1984; public devt institution for Madrid region; Dir AURELIO GARCÍA DE SOLA Y ARRIAGA.

Sociedad de Desarrollo de Navarra (SODENA): Avda Carlos III el Noble 36, 1° dcha, 31003 Pamplona; tel. (848) 421942; fax (848) 421943; e-mail info@sodena.com; internet www.sodena.com; promotes devt in Navarra; Pres. LOURDES GOICOECHEA ZUBELZU.

Sociedad para el Desarrollo Económico de Canarias (Sodecan): Villalba Hervás 4, 6°, 38002 Santa Cruz de Tenerife; tel. (922) 298020; fax (922) 298131; e-mail info@sodecan.es; internet www.sodecan.es; promotes devt in the Canary Islands; Pres. JOSÉ MANUEL SORIA LÓPEZ.

Sociedad para el Desarrollo Industrial de Extremadura (Sodiex): Avda Ruta de la Plata 13, 10001 Cáceres; tel. (927) 224878; fax (927) 243304; e-mail sodiex@sodiex.es; internet www.sodiex.es; f. 1977; promotes industrial devt in Extremadura.

CHAMBERS OF COMMERCE

Cámara de Comercio Internacional (International Chamber of Commerce): Avda Diagonal 452–454, 08006 Barcelona; tel. (93) 4169300; fax (93) 4169301; e-mail iccspain@cambrabcn.es; internet www.iccspain.org; f. 1922; Pres. MIQUEL VALLS MASEDA; Sec.-Gen. JORDI SERRA SELLARÉS.

Confederación Española de Comercio (CEC): Castelló 82, 3°, 28006 Madrid; tel. (91) 5981050; fax (91) 5520967; e-mail secretaria@confespacomercio.es; internet www.confespacomercio.es; f. 1984; Pres. MANUEL GARCÍA-IZQUIERDO PARRALO; Sec.-Gen. JOSÉ GUERRERO HUESCA; 450,000 mems.

Consejo Superior de Cámaras Oficiales de Comercio, Industria y Navegación de España (High Council of Official Chambers of Commerce, Industry and Navigation of Spain): Ribera del Loira 12, 28042 Madrid; tel. (91) 5906900; fax (91) 5906913; e-mail info@cscamaras.es; internet www.camaras.org; f. 1922; Pres. MARCELO CASTRO-RIAL SCHULER; Dir-Gen. GONZALO ORTIZ AMOR; comprises 85 Chambers throughout Spain, incl. the following:

> **Cámara de Comercio de Bilbao/Bilboko Merkataritza Ganbera:** Alda Recalde 50, 48008 Bilbao; tel. (94) 4706500; fax (94) 4436171; e-mail atencionalclientes@camarabilbao.com; internet www.camarabilbao.com; Pres. JOSÉ ÁNGEL CORRES ABÁSOLO; Dir-Gen. MIKEL ARIETA.

> **Cámara Oficial de Comercio e Industria de Madrid:** Ribera del Loira 56–58, 28042 Madrid; tel. (91) 5383500; fax (91) 5383677; e-mail camara@camaramadrid.es; internet www.camaramadrid.es; f. 1887; Pres. ARTURO FERNÁNDEZ ÁLVAREZ; Dir-Gen. MIGUEL GARRIDO; 511,804 mems.

> **Cámara Oficial de Comercio, Industria y Navegación de Sevilla:** Plaza de la Contratación 8, 41004 Sevilla; tel. (902) 932320; fax (954) 225619; e-mail ccinsevilla@camaradesevilla.com; internet www.camaradesevilla.com; Pres. FRANCISCO LEÓN HERRERO; f. 1886.

> **Cámara Oficial de Comercio, Industria y Navegación de Valencia:** Jesús, 19, 46007 Valencia; tel. (96) 3103900; fax (96) 3531742; e-mail info@camaravalencia.com; internet www.camaravalencia.com; f. 1886.

Cambra de Comerç de Barcelona: Avda Diagonal 452–454, 08006 Barcelona; tel. (90) 2448448; fax (93) 4169301; e-mail cambra@cambrabcn.org; internet www.cambrabcn.es; f. 1886; Dir XAVIER CARBONELL I ROURA.

INDUSTRIAL AND TRADE ASSOCIATIONS

Agrupación de Fabricantes de Cemento de España (OFICEMEN): José Abascal 53, 28003 Madrid; tel. (91) 4411688; fax (91) 4423817; e-mail info@oficemen.com; internet www.oficemen.com; cement manufacturers; Pres. JUAN BÉJAR; Dir-Gen. ANICETO ZARAGOZA; 13 mem. cos.

Asociación de Comercio de Cereales y Oleaginosas de España (ACCOE): Dr Fleming 56, 3°D, 28036 Madrid; tel. (91) 3504305; fax (91) 3455009; e-mail info@accoe.org; internet www.accoe.org; f. 1977; cereal traders; Pres. MARCOS MARTÍNEZ.

Asociación de Criadores Exportadores de Sherry (ACES): Avda Alcalde Alvaro Domecq 6, 2°D, 11405 Jerez de la Frontera; tel. (956) 341046; fax (956) 346081; sherry exporters; Pres. FRANCISCO VALENCIA JAÉN.

Asociación de Empresas de Electrónica, Tecnologías de la Información, Telecomunicaciones de España y Contenidos Digitales (AMETIC): Príncipe de Vergara 74, 4°, 28006 Madrid; tel. (91) 5902300; e-mail ametic@ametic.es; internet www.ametic.es; f. 2010; electronic, information, digital content and telecommunication industries; Pres. JESÚS BANEGAS NÚÑEZ; Sec.-Gen. ESTEBAN EGEA SÁNCHEZ; c. 3,000 mem. cos.

Asociación Española de Exportadores de Electrónica e Informática (SECARTYS): Gran Vía de les Corts Catalanes 774, 4°, 08013 Barcelona; tel. (93) 1828800; fax (93) 4278561; e-mail secartys@secartys.org; internet www.secartys.org; f. 1968; electronics exporters; Pres. JOSEP ROF; Sec.-Gen. JULIO VIVERO; 1,200 mem. cos.

Asociación Española de Fabricantes de Automóviles y Camiones (ANFAC): Orense 34, Edif. Iberia Mart II, 9° 28020 Madrid; tel. (91) 3431343; fax (91) 3450377; e-mail prensa@anfac.com; internet www.anfac.es; f. 1977; car and lorry manufacturers; Pres. FRANCISCO JAVIER GARCÍA SANZ.

Asociación Española de Fabricantes de Equipos y Componentes para Automoción (SERNAUTO): Castelló 120, 28006 Madrid; tel. (91) 5621041; fax (91) 5618437; e-mail sernauto@sernauto.es; internet www.sernauto.es; f. 1967; asscn of manufacturers of equipment and components for automobile industry; Pres. JOSÉ MARÍA PUJOL ARTIGAS; Dir-Gen. JOSÉ ANTONIO JIMÉNEZ SACEDA.

Asociación Española de la Industria y Comercio Exportador de Aceite de Oliva (ASOLIVA): José Abascal 40, 2°, 28003 Madrid; tel. (91) 4468812; fax (91) 5931918; e-mail asoliva@asoliva.es; internet www.asoliva.es; f. 1928; olive oil exporters; Pres. JOSÉ PONT AMENOS.

Asociación Española de Productoras de Fibras Químicas (PROFIBRA): Via Laietana 46, 2°, 08003 Barcelona; tel. (93) 2682644; fax (93) 2682630; e-mail profibra@profibra.com; f. 1977; chemical fibre producers; Pres. RAFAEL ESPAÑOL NAVARRO; Sec.-Gen. GUILLERMO GRAELL DENIEL.

Asociación Industrial Textil de Proceso Algodonero (AITPA): Gran Vía de les Corts Catalanes 670, 08010 Barcelona; tel. (93) 3189200; fax (93) 3026235; e-mail aitpa@aitpa.es; internet www.aitpa.es; cotton textile industry; Pres. MANUEL DÍAZ.

Asociación Nacional Española de Fabricantes de Hormigón Preparado (ANEFHOP): Bretón de los Herreros 43, bajo, 28003 Madrid; tel. (91) 4416634; fax (91) 3993497; e-mail mgarcia@anefhop.com; internet www.anefhop.com; f. 1968; concrete manufacturers; Pres. SEBASTIAN ALEGRE ROSELLO; Dir-Gen. ANTONIO TOVAR TORRES.

Asociación Nacional de Fabricantes de Pastas Papeleras, Papel y Cartón (ASPAPEL): Avda de Baviera 15, 28028 Madrid; tel. (91) 5763003; fax (91) 5774710; e-mail aspapel@aspapel.es; internet www.aspapel.es; f. 1977; paper and cardboard manufacturers; Pres. IGNACIO DE COLMENARES; Dir-Gen. CARLOS REINOSO TORRES.

Comité de Gestión de Cítricos (CGC): Monjas de Santa Catalina 8, 4°, 46002 Valencia; tel. (96) 3521102; fax (96) 3510718; e-mail comite@citricos.org; internet www.citricos.org; citrus fruit exporters; Pres. JOSÉ MARTÍNEZ SERRANO.

Confederación Española de Organizaciones Empresariales del Metal (CONFEMETAL): Príncipe de Vergara 74, 5°, 28006 Madrid; tel. (91) 5625590; fax (91) 5635758; e-mail informacion@confemetal.es; internet www.confemetal.es; metal asscns; Pres. JAVIER FERRER DUFOL; Sec.-Gen. ANDRÉS SÁNCHEZ DE APELLÁNIZ.

Confederación Nacional de la Construcción (CNC): Diego de León 50, 2°, 28006 Madrid; tel. (91) 5624585; fax (91) 5615269; e-mail cnc@cnc.es; internet www.cnc.es; f. 1977; construction industry; Pres. JUAN FRANCISCO LAZCANO ACEDO.

Consejo Intertextil Español (CIE): Sant Quirze 30, 08201 Barcelona; tel. (93) 7451917; fax (93) 7480252; e-mail cinfo@consejointertextil.com; internet www.consejointertextil.com; textile industry; Pres. ALEJANDRO LAQUIDAIN; Sec.-Gen. SALVADOR MALUQUE; 7 mem. asscns.

Cooperativas Agro-alimentarias (Agri-food Co-operatives): Agustín de Bethencourt 17, 4°, 28003 Madrid; tel. (91) 5351035; fax (91) 5540047; e-mail cooperativas@agro-alimentarias.coop; internet www.agro-alimentarias.coop; fmrly Confederación de Cooperativas Agrarias de España; Pres. FERNANDO MARCÉN; Dir-Gen. EDUARDO BAAMONDE NOCHE.

Federación Empresarial de la Industria Química Española (FEIQUE): Hermosilla 31, 1°, 28001 Madrid; tel. (91) 4317964; fax (91) 5763381; e-mail info@feique.org; internet www.feique.org; chemical industry; Pres. LUIS SERRANO; Dir-Gen. FERNANDO GALBIS.

Federación Española de Asociaciones de Productores y Exportadores de Frutas, Hortalizas, Flores y Plantas Vivas (FEPEX): Miguel Angel 13, 4°A, 28010 Madrid; tel. (91) 3191050; fax (91) 3103812; e-mail fepex@fepex.es; internet www.fepex.es; f. 1987; fruit and vegetable producers and exporters; Pres. JORGE BROTONS; Dir JOSÉ MARÍA POZANCOS; 33 mem. asscns.

Federación Española de Industrias de la Alimentación y Bebidas (FIAB): Calle Velázquez 64, 3°, 28001 Madrid; tel. (91) 4117211; fax (91) 4117344; e-mail fiab@fiab.es; internet www.fiab.es; f. 1977; food and drink industries; Pres. JESÚS SERAFIN PÉREZ; Dir-Gen. HORACIO GONZALEZ ALEMAN; 50 mem. asscns.

Federación de Industrias del Calzado Español (FICE): Núñez de Balboa 116, 3°, 28006 Madrid; tel. (91) 5627003; fax (91) 5620094; e-mail info@fice.es; internet www.fice.es; f. 1977; footwear; Pres. RAFAEL CALVO RODRÍGUEZ; Sec.-Gen. JAVIER GARCÍA LILLO.

Fundación Cotec: Marqués de Salamanca 11, 2° izqda, 28006 Madrid; tel. (91) 4364774; fax (91) 4311239; internet www.cotec.es; f. 1990; promotes technological innovation and understanding; Pres. JUAN-MIGUEL VILLAR MIR; Dir JUAN MULET.

Sociedad Estatal de Participaciones Industriales (SEPI): Velázquez 134, 28006 Madrid; tel. (91) 3961000; fax (91) 5628789; e-mail informacion@sepi.es; internet www.sepi.es; f. 1996; asscn of state-owned cos; Pres. RAMÓN AGUIRRE; Sec.-Gen. ALFREDO PARRA GARCÍA-MOLINER; 36 mems.

Unión de Empresas Siderúrgicas (UNESID): Castelló 128, 3°, 28006 Madrid; tel. (91) 5624010; fax (91) 5626584; e-mail unesid@unesid.org; internet www.unesid.org; f. 1968; asscn of Spanish producers of steel; Chair. GONZALO URQUIJO; Dir-Gen. ANDRÉS BARCELÓ.

EMPLOYERS' ORGANIZATIONS

Círculo de Empresarios: Marqués de Villamagna 3, 10A Planta, 28001 Madrid; tel. (91) 5781472; fax (91) 5774871; e-mail asociacion@circulodeempresarios.org; internet www.circulodeempresarios.org; f. 1977; comprises CEOs of more than 200 major cos; Pres. MÓNICA DE ORIOL; Sec.-Gen. ANTONIO OPORTO DEL OLMO.

Confederación Empresarial de Madrid (CEIM) (Madrid Confederation of Employers and Industries): Diego de León 50, 1°, 28006 Madrid; tel. (91) 4115317; fax (91) 5627537; internet info@ceim.es; internet www.ceim.es; f. 1978; small, medium and large businesses; Pres. ARTURO FERNÁNDEZ ÁLVAREZ; Sec. SOL OLABARRI.

Confederación Empresarial Valenciana (CEV): Plaza Conde de Carlet 3, 46003 Valencia; tel. (96) 3155720; fax (96) 3923199; e-mail cev@cev.es; internet www.cev.es; f. 1977; Pres. JOSÉ VICENTE GONZÁLEZ PÉREZ; Sec.-Gen. ENRIQUE SOTO RIPOLL.

Confederación Empresarial Vasca/Euskal Entrepresarien Konfederakuntza (CONFEBASK): Gran Vía 45, 2°, 48011 Bilbao; tel. (94) 4021331; fax (94) 4021333; e-mail confebask@confebask.es; internet www.confebask.es; f. 1983; Pres. MIGUEL ÁNGEL LUJUA; Sec.-Gen. NURIA LÓPEZ DE GUEREÑU.

Confederación Española de Organizaciones Empresariales (CEOE) (Spanish Confederation of Employers' Organizations): Diego de León 50, 28006 Madrid; tel. (91) 5663400; fax (91) 5622562; e-mail ceoe@ceoe.es; internet www.ceoe.es; f. 1977; covers industry, agriculture, commerce and service sectors; comprises 210 orgs; Pres. JUAN ROSELL LASTORTRAS; Sec.-Gen. JOSÉ MARÍA LACASA ASO.

Confederación Española de la Pequeña y Mediana Empresa (CEPYME): Diego de León 50, 3°, 28006 Madrid; tel. (91) 4116161; fax (91) 5645269; e-mail contacto@cepyme.es; internet www.cepyme.es; small and medium businesses; Pres. JESÚS TERCIADO VALLS; Sec.-Gen. JOSÉ MANUEL VILAR MARTÍNEZ.

Fomento del Trabajo Nacional/Foment del Treball Nacional—Confederación Empresarial de Catalunya: Vía Laietana 32, 08003 Barcelona; tel. (93) 4841200; fax (93) 4841230; e-mail foment@foment.com; internet www.foment.com; f. 1771 as Real Compañía de Hilados de Algodón del Principado de Catalunya; devt

SPAIN

SPAIN

Directory

of national labour; Pres. JOAQUIM GAY DE MONTELLÀ; Sec.-Gen. JUAN PUJOL SEGARRA.

UTILITIES

Comisión Nacional de Energía (CNE): Alcalá 47, 28014 Madrid; tel. (91) 4329600; fax (91) 5776218; e-mail dri@cne.es; internet www.cne.es; f. 1999; part of Ministry of Industry, Energy and Tourism; regulates energy systems; Pres. ALBERTO LAFUENTE FÉLEZ.

Instituto para la Diversificación y Ahorro de la Energía (IDAE): Madera 8, 28004 Madrid; tel. (91) 4564900; fax (91) 5230414; e-mail comunicacion@idae.es; internet www.idae.es; f. 1974 as Centro de Estudios de la Energía; under control of General Secretariat of Energy (Ministry of Industry, Energy and Tourism); Dir-Gen. FIDEL PÉREZ MONTES.

Secretaría General de Energía: Paseo de la Castellana 160, 28046 Madrid; tel. (902) 446006; fax (91) 4587704; internet www.minetur.gob.es/energia; part of Ministry of Industry, Energy and Tourism; Sec.-Gen. FERNANDO MARTI SCHARFHAUSEN.

Electricity

Asociación Española de la Industria Eléctrica (UNESA): Paseo de la Castellana 141, 12°, 28046 Madrid; tel. (91) 5674800; fax (91) 5674987; e-mail info@unesa.es; internet www.unesa.es; f. 1944; groups principal electricity cos; Pres. EDUARDO MONTES; Sec.-Gen. PASCUAL SALA.

Operador del Mercado Ibérico de Energía—Polo Español (OMEL): Alfonso XI 6, 4° y 5°, 28014 Madrid; tel. (91) 6598900; fax (91) 5240396; e-mail info@omel.es; internet www.omel.es; f. 1997; Spanish branch of the Iberian Energy Market; Pres. PEDRO MEJÍA GÓMEZ.

Red Eléctrica de España (REE): Paseo del Conde de los Gaitanes 177, 28109 Madrid; tel. (91) 6508500; fax (91) 6504542; e-mail redelectrica@ree.es; internet www.ree.es; manages and operates the national grid; Pres. JOSÉ FOLGADO BLANCO.

Principal Electricity Companies

Endesa: Ribera del Loira 60, Campo de las Naciones, 28042 Madrid; tel. (91) 2131000; fax (91) 5638181; internet www.endesa.es; f. 1983; generator, distributor and vendor of electricity; also provides gas; 92% owned by Enel (Italy); Pres. BORJA PRADO EULATE; CEO ANDREA BRENTAN.

E.ON España: Medio 12, 39003 Santander; tel. (942) 246000; fax (942) 246034; e-mail informacion@eon.com; internet www.eon-espana.com; f. 2008 following the acquisition of Enel Viesgo; subsidiary of E.ON AG (Germany); generation, distribution and supply; also provides gas; CEO MIGUEL ANTOÑANZAS.

Gas Natural Fenosa: see Gas.

HC Energía: Plaza de la Gesta 2, 33007 Oviedo (Asturias); tel. (98) 5230300; e-mail hcenergia@hcenergia.com; internet www.hcenergia.com; f. 1919; fmrly Hidroeléctrica del Cantábrico; generation, distribution and supply; also provides gas; owned by Electricidade de Portugal; Pres. MANUEL MENÉNDEZ MENÉNDEZ.

Iberdrola: Plaza Euskadi 5, 48009 Bilbao; tel. (944) 151411; fax (944) 154579; e-mail informacion@iberdrola.com; internet www.iberdrola.com; generation, distribution and supply; supplies mainly hydroelectric power; also provides gas; Pres. JOSÉ IGNACIO SÁNCHEZ GALÁN.

Gas

Enagás: Paseo de los Olmos 19, 28005 Madrid; tel. (902) 443700; e-mail contacta@enagas.es; internet www.enagas.es; operates gas transportation network; f. 1972; Pres. ANTONI LLARDÉN CARRATLÁ.

Endesa: see Electricity.

Gas Natural Fenosa: Plaça del Gas 1, 08003 Barcelona; tel. (902) 199199; fax (93) 4029317; internet www.gasnatural.com; f. 1991 as Gas Natural; acquired Unión Fenosa (f. 1982) and adopted current name 2009; distributor of gas; generator, distributor and supplier of electricity; comprises regional distribution cos; Pres. SALVADOR GABARRÓ SERRA; CEO RAFAEL VILLASECA MARCO.

Naturgas Energía: Plaza Pío Baroja 3, 2°, 48001 Bilbao; tel. (94) 4035700; fax (94) 4249733; e-mail webnaturgas@naturgasenergia.com; internet www.naturgasenergia.com; f. 1982; 65.6% owned by HC Energía; distributor of gas and electricity; Pres. MANUEL MENÉNDEZ.

Water

Dirección General del Agua: Plaza de San Juan de la Cruz s/n, 28071 Madrid; tel. (91) 5976660; part of Ministry of the Agriculture, Food and Environmental Affairs; co-ordinates water policy and supervises water management; Dir-Gen. MARTA MOREN.

Grupo Agbar: Torre Agbar, Avda Diagonal 211, 08009 Barcelona; tel. (93) 3422000; fax (93) 3422662; e-mail comunicacion@agbar.es; internet www.agbar.es; treatment of water and waste liquid; provision of sanitation and certification services; Dir-Gen. ANGEL SIMÓN GRIMALDOS.

Grupo Aguas de Valencia: Gran Vía Marqués del Turia 19, 46005 Valencia; tel. (96) 3860600; e-mail aquas.valencia@aquasvalencia.es; internet www.aguasdevalencia.es; water and sewerage services; Pres. EUGENIO CALABUIG GIMENO.

TRADE UNIONS

Central Sindical Independiente y de Funcionarios (CSI-CSIF): Fernando el Santo 17, 28010 Madrid; tel. (91) 5674469; fax (91) 5987277; e-mail justicia@csi-csif.es; internet www.csi-csif.es; Pres. MIGUEL BORRA.

Confederación General de Trabajo (CGT) (General Confederation of Labour): Sagunto 15, 1°, 28010 Madrid; tel. (91) 4475769; fax (91) 4453132; e-mail sp-general@cgt.org.es; internet www.cgt.org.es; Sec.-Gen. JACINTO CEACERO CUBILLO.

Confederación Intersindical Galega (CIG): Rua Miguel Ferro Caaveiro 10, 3°, 15073 Santiago de Compostela; tel. (981) 564300; fax (981) 571082; e-mail secretarioxeral@galizacig.net; internet www.galizacig.com; Galician confederation; Sec.-Gen. XÉSUS E. SEIXO FERNÁNDEZ.

Confederación Nacional del Trabajo (CNT) (National Confederation of Labour): Historiador Domínguez Ortiz 7, 14002 Córdoba; tel. (957) 434897; fax (942) 940983; e-mail sp_cn@cnt.es; internet www.cnt.es; f. 1910; Sec.-Gen. ALFONSO ÁLVAREZ.

Confederación Sindical de Comisiones Obreras (CCOO) (Workers' Commissions): Fernández de la Hoz 12, 28010 Madrid; tel. (91) 7028000; fax (91) 3104804; e-mail ccoo@ccoo.es; internet www.ccoo.es; f. 1956; independent left-wing; Sec.-Gen. IGNACIO FERNÁNDEZ TOXO; 1,050,000 mems (2005).

Eusko Langilleen Alkartasuna/Solidaridad de Trabajadores Vascos (ELA—Euskal Sindikatua) (Basque Workers' Solidarity): Barrainkua 13, 48009 Bilbao; tel. (94) 4037700; fax (94) 4037777; e-mail naziorte@elasind.org; internet www.ela-sindikatua.org; f. 1911; legally recognized 1977; independent; Sec.-Gen. ADOLFO MUÑOZ SANZ; 109,318 mems.

Unión General de Trabajadores (UGT) (General Union of Workers): Hortaleza 88, 28004 Madrid; tel. (91) 5897100; fax (91) 5897603; e-mail info@cec.ugt.org; internet www.ugt.es; f. 1888; 8 affiliated federations; Sec.-Gen. CARLOS SILVA.

Unión Sindical Obrera (USO) (Workers' Trade Union): Príncipe de Vergara 13, 7°, 28001 Madrid; tel. (91) 5774113; fax (91) 5772959; e-mail uso@uso.es; internet www.uso.es; f. 1960; mem. of European Trade Union Confederation and the International Trade Union Confederation; Sec.-Gen. JULIO SALAZAR MORENO; 112,000 mems.

Transport

RAILWAYS

In 2011 the total rail network was 19,166 km, of which 8,738 km were electrified. Spain's high-speed rail network, Alta Velocidad Española (AVE), includes a route from Madrid to Barcelona, which was completed in 2008 and was extended as far as the French border by 2012, and a link from Madrid to Valencia, which was completed in late 2010. Construction of a high-speed line linking Madrid with the Portuguese capital, Lisbon, was cancelled by Portugal in 2012. In 2010 construction of another high-speed line connecting Madrid to Alicante was announced.

From January 2005 the state railway company, RENFE, was divided into an operating and a management division, and the goods transport sector was opened to competition. RENFE's monopoly on cross-border passenger transport ended in 2010.

Administrador de Infraestructuras Ferroviarias (Adif): Paseo del Rey 30, 28008 Madrid; tel. (91) 3008080; e-mail comunicacionweb@adif.es; internet www.adif.es; f. 2005; state-owned; fmrly part of state-owned railway co, Red Nacional de los Ferrocarriles Españoles (RENFE); manages railway infrastructure; Pres. GONZALO FERRE MOLTÓ; Sec.-Gen. MARÍA ROSA SANZ CEREZO.

RENFE Operadora: Avda Pío XII 110, 28036 Madrid; tel. (91) 3006600; fax (91) 3006177; e-mail comunicacion@renfe.es; internet www.renfe.com; f. 2005 following liberalization of railway sector; fmrly Red Nacional de los Ferrocarriles Españoles (RENFE); state-owned; Pres. JULIO GÓMEZ-POMAR RODRÍGUEZ; Sec.-Gen. JOSÉ L. MARROQUÍN MOCHALES.

Eusko Trenbideak—Ferrocarriles Vascos (ET/FV) (Eusko-Tren): Atxuri 6, 48006 Bilbao; tel. (94) 4019900; fax (94) 4019916; e-mail attcliente@euskotren.es; internet www.euskotren.es; f. 1982;

controlled by the Basque Govt; 188 km of 1,000 mm gauge; Dir-Gen. JOSÉ IGNACIO ASENSIO BAZTERRA.

Ferrocarriles de Vía Estrecha (Feve) (Narrow Gauge Railways): Plaza de los Ferroviarios, 33012 Oviedo; tel. (98) 5297656; fax (98) 5281708; e-mail info@feve.es; internet www.feve.es; f. 1965 by integration of private cos; state-owned; operates an extensive suburban and inter-urban network in northern Spain and the Murcia region; 1,194 km (2010) of which 321 km were electrified; Pres. ÁNGEL VILLALBA ÁLVAREZ; Dir-Gen. JUAN DIEZ LÓPEZ.

Ferrocarriles de la Generalitat de Catalunya (FGC): Pau Casals 24, 8°, 08021 Barcelona; tel. (93) 3663000; fax (93) 3663350; e-mail rrpp@fgc.cat; internet www.fgc.net; f. 1979; 290 km, of which 161 km are electrified; Pres. ENRIC TICÓ I BUXADÓS.

Ferrocarrils de la Generalitat de València (FGV): Partida de Xirivelleta, 46014 Valencia; tel. (96) 1924000; fax (96) 1924001; e-mail webmaster_fgv@gva.es; internet www.fgv.es; f. 1986; 249.6 km of track; also operates Valencia Metro, with 5 lines and 146.8 km of track, and Tram Alicante (102.8 km); Pres. ISABEL BONIG TRIGUEROS; Dir-Gen. MARISA GRACIA GIMÉNEZ.

Metro de Bilbao: Navarra 2, 48001 Bilbao; tel. (94) 4254025; fax (94) 4254039; e-mail info@metrobilbao.net; internet www.metrobilbao.net; f. 1993; 38.9 km; 2 lines and 38 stations; Pres. JOSÉ LUIS BILBAO.

Metro de Madrid: Cavanilles 58, 28007 Madrid; tel. (902) 444403; fax (91) 7212957; e-mail prensa@metromadrid.es; internet www.metromadrid.es; 284 km, 13 lines, 294 stations (2009), also light railway network (Metro Ligero) of 28 km, 3 lines, 38 stations; Pres. PABLO CAVERO MARTÍNEZ DE CAMPOS; Dir IGNACIO GONZÁLEZ VELAYOS.

Transports Metropolitans de Barcelona (TMB): Carrer 60, 21–23, Sector A, Polígono industrial Zona Franca, 08040 Barcelona; tel. (93) 2987000; fax (93) 2987300; e-mail tmb@tmb.net; internet www.tmb.net; 85.8 km, 6 lines, 104 stations (2008); Pres. JOAQUIM FORN.

ROADS

The total road network in 2010 was 667,064 km. In 2009 there were 14,021 km of motorway, 11,612 km of main roads and 139,833 km of secondary roads.

Dirección General de Carreteras: Paseo de la Castellana 67, 28071 Madrid; tel. (91) 5978014; fax (91) 5978535; e-mail jmpertierra@fomento.es; part of Ministry of Public Works; Dir-Gen. JOSE MARÍA PERTIERRA DE LA UZ.

SHIPPING

Spain has many ports. Among the most important are Algeciras, Barcelona, Valencia, Tarragona, Bilbao, Cartagena, Gijón, Huelva and Santa Cruz de Tenerife. The 1,186 ships of the flag registered fleet totalled 3.1m. grt at 31 December 2012, of which 12 were gas tankers and 51 were general cargo ships.

Asociación de Navieros Españoles (ANAVE): Dr Fleming 11, 1° dcha, 28036 Madrid; tel. (91) 4580040; fax (91) 4579780; e-mail info@anave.es; internet www.anave.es; f. 1951 as Oficemen; renamed in 1977; shipowners' asscn; Pres. ADOLFO UTOR MARTÍNEZ; Dir MANUEL CARLIER DE LAVALLE.

Dirección General de la Marina Mercante: Ruíz de Alarcón 1, 28071 Madrid; tel. (91) 5979020; fax (91) 5979120; part of Ministry of Public Works; Dir-Gen. RAFAEL RODRÍGUEZ VALERO.

Puertos del Estado (Spanish Ports Public Agency): Avda del Partenón 10, 28042 Madrid; tel. (91) 5245500; fax (91) 5245501; e-mail webmaster@puertos.es; internet www.puertos.es; f. 1992; Pres. JOSÉ LLORCA ORTEGA.

Principal Shipping Companies

Acciona Trasmediterránea: Complejo Albatros, Edif. D, 2°A, Calle Anabel Segura 11, 28018 Alcobendas, Madrid; tel. (91) 4238500; fax (91) 4238555; e-mail info@trasmediterranea.es; internet www.trasmediterranea.es; f. 1917; Spanish ports, Balearic and Canary Is and Spanish North African, Algerian and Moroccan ports; Pres. JORGE VEGA-PENICHET; Dir-Gen. ANTONIO GRÁVALO.

Agencia Marítima Española Evge: Avda Francesc Cambó 17, 08003 Barcelona; tel. (93) 3905800; fax (93) 2681750; e-mail evge@evgebcn.com; internet www.evgebcn.com; international shipping agents; Man. Dir RAMÓN OLIETE COSSIO.

Boluda Corporación Marítima: Paseo de Caro, s/n, 46024 Vanlencia; tel. (96) 3020200; fax (96) 3679372; e-mail valencia@boluda.com.es; internet www.boluda.com.es; international shipping, towing, salvage, tankers; Chair. VICENTE BOLUDA FOS.

Compañía de Remolcadores Ibaizabal: Muelle de Tomás Olabarri 4, 5°, 48930 Las Arenas (Vizcaya); tel. (94) 4645133; fax (94) 4645565; e-mail ibaizabal@ibaizabal.org; internet www.remolcadoresibaizabal.com; f. 1906; ocean-going, coastal, harbour, salvage; Pres. ALEJANDRO AZNAR SAINZ.

Empresa Naviera Elcano SA: José Abascal 2–4, 4°, 28003 Madrid; tel. (91) 5369800; fax (91) 4451324; e-mail elcanox@xelcano-sa.es; internet www.navieraelcano.com; f. 1942; Pres. JOSÉ SILVERA.

Ership: Lagasca 88, 28001 Madrid; tel. (91) 4263400; fax (91) 5750883; e-mail chart@ership.com; internet www.ership.com; fmrly TAC; CEO GONZALO ALVARGONZÁLEZ.

Naviera Pinillos: Capitán Haya 21, 28020 Madrid; tel. (91) 4183600; fax (91) 4183610; f. 1840; part of Boluda group; services between Canary Is and other Spanish ports; Pres. VICENTE BOLUDA; Dir ANGEL MATO.

Nenufar Shipping: Manuel Ferreo 13, 28036 Madrid; tel. (91) 3158393; fax (91) 3158384; e-mail nenufar@nenufar.com; f. 1983; part of Boluda group; services to Spanish ports, Canary Is, Italy, Portugal, the United Kingdom, Morocco and Mauritania.

Repsol Naviera Vizcaina: Juan de Aguriaguerra 35, 2°, 48009 Bilbao; tel. (94) 4251100; fax (94) 4251143; f. 1956; world-wide, but particularly Mediterranean, Near East and Persian (Arabian) Gulf to Spain and transatlantic trade.

CIVIL AVIATION

In 2011 there were more than 50 airports, almost all of which were equipped to receive international flights.

Dirección General de Aviación Civil: Paseo de la Castellana 67, 5A Planta, 28071 Madrid; tel. (91) 5975356; fax (91) 5975357; e-mail atencionciudadano@fomento.es; internet www.fomento.gob.es/mfom/lang_castellano/direcciones_generales/aviacion_civil; Dir-Gen. ÁNGEL LUIS ARIAS SERRANO.

Aeropuertos Españoles y Navegación Aérea (AENA): Arturo Soria 109, 2°, 28043 Madrid; tel. (91) 3211000; fax (91) 3213115; e-mail servicios-aeroportuarios@aena.es; internet www.aena.es; f. 1990; network of airports in Spain; Pres. JOSÉ MANUEL VARGAS GÓMEZ.

Principal Airlines

Air Europa Líneas Aéreas: Centro Empresarial Globalia, Apdo Correos-132, 07620 Llucmajor; tel. (971) 178190; fax (971) 178353; internet www.air-europa.com; f. 1986; charter and scheduled services to Canary and Balearic Is, North Africa, Central, Southern and Eastern Europe; also Mexico, Cuba and Dominican Republic; Pres. JUAN JOSÉ HIDALGO ACERA; Dir-Gen. MARÍA JOSÉ HIDALGO.

Binter Canarias: Aeropuerto de Gran Canaria, Parcela 9, del ZIMA Apdo 50, 35230 Gran Canaria; tel. (928) 579601; fax (928) 579603; e-mail info@bintercanarias.es; internet www.bintercanarias.com; f. 1989; scheduled services within Canary Islands and to Madeira (Portugal), Morocco, Western Sahara and Mauritania; subsidiary of Grupo Iberia; Pres. and CEO PEDRO AGUSTÍN DEL CASTILLO.

Iberia: Calle Velázquez 130, 28006 Madrid; tel. (91) 5878787; fax (91) 5874741; internet www.iberia.com; f. 1927; domestic and international passenger and freight services to 106 destinations in 43 countries; provides maintenance, handling in airport, IT system solutions; merged with British Airways PLC (United Kingdom) to form International Airlines Group in Jan. 2011; Chair. ANTONIO VÁZQUEZ ROMERO; CEO LUIS GALLEGO.

Iberia Express: 28080 Madrid; internet www.iberiaexpress.com; f. 2012; subsidiary of Grupo Iberia; operates short- and medium-haul, low-cost flights.

Vueling Airlines: Edif. Muntadas, Berguedà 1, Parque de Negocios Mas Blau, El Prat de Llobregat, 08820 Barcelona; tel. (93) 3787878; fax (93) 3787879; e-mail clients@vueling.com; internet www.vueling.com; f. 2004; low-cost airline; domestic and international flights; Pres. JOSEP PIQUÉ; CEO ALEX CRUZ.

Tourism

Spain's tourist attractions include its climate, beaches and historic cities. Tourism makes an important contribution to the country's economy. In 2012 some 57.7m. foreign tourists visited Spain (56.2m. in 2011). Receipts from tourism totalled an estimated €55,594m. in 2012.

Instituto de Turismo de España (Turespaña): José Lázaro Galdiano 6, 28036 Madrid; tel. (91) 3433500; e-mail infosmile@tourspain.es; internet www.tourspain.es; promotes tourism; offices in Spain and abroad; Pres. JOAN MESQUIDE FERRANDO; Dir-Gen. ANTONIO BERNABÉ GARCÍA.

Secretaría de Estado de Comercio y Turismo: Paseo de la Castellana 160, 28046 Madrid; fax (91) 4578066; internet www.comercio.es; Sec. PEDRO MEJÍA GÓMEZ.

Defence

Military service was compulsory in Spain until December 2002. Conscription was abolished in 2000, while the final stages of professionalization were completed in 2003. Legislation to permit the entry of women to all sections of the armed forces took effect in early 1989. As assessed at November 2012, the total strength of the armed forces was 135,500, comprising: army 70,800; navy 22,200 (including 5,300 marines); air force 21,200; and 21,300 in joint service. The paramilitary Guardia Civil (Civil Guard) numbered 79,950. Spain became a member of the North Atlantic Treaty Organization (NATO) in May 1982. In December 1997 Spain's full integration into the military structure of NATO (with effect from January 1999) was approved by the alliance. The US military presence in Spain totalled 1,483 at November 2011. In November 2004 the European Union (EU) ministers responsible for defence agreed to create a number of 'battlegroups' (each comprising about 1,500 men), which could be deployed at short notice to crisis areas around the world. The EU battlegroups, two of which were to be ready for deployment at any one time, following a rotational schedule, reached full operational capacity from 1 January 2007. Spain was the sole contributor to one battlegroup and led another with the participation of Germany, France and Portugal. Spain also participated in the Spanish-Italian Amphibious battlegroup, which was led by Italy.

Defence Budget: €11,800m. in 2012.

General Chief of Staff of Defence: Gen. FERNANDO GARCÍA SÁNCHEZ.

Chief of Staff of the Army: Gen. JAIME DOMÍNGUEZ BUJ.

Chief of Staff of the Navy: Adm. Gen. JAIME MUÑOZ-DELGADO.

Chief of Staff of the Air Force: Gen. FRANCISCO JAVIER GARCÍA ARNÁIZ.

Education

Responsibility for education is divided between the central Government and the Autonomous Communities. Education is compulsory, and available free of charge, from the ages of six to 16 years. Pre-primary education caters for children up to six years of age and comprises two three-year stages. Primary education begins at six years of age and also comprises two three-year cycles. Lower secondary education (*Educación Secundaria Obligatoria*) (ESO), which lasts for four years, is followed between the ages of 12 and 16 and culminates in the awarding of the *Graduado en ESO* certificate. Thereafter, students may take a vocational training course, lasting one or two years, or the two-year *Bachillerato* course, in preparation for university entrance; alternatively, they may follow a two-year specialist artistic or sports course. Private schools (which may be publicly funded), many of which are administered by the Roman Catholic Church, are responsible for the education of approximately one-third of Spanish children. In those Autonomous Communities in which a language other than Spanish is co-official (the Basque Country, the Balearic Islands, Catalonia, Galicia and Valencia), the teaching of the language of the Autonomous Community is compulsory at all levels, but the language of instruction varies according to location. In 2010/11 98% of children aged from three to five years were attending pre-primary institutions. In 2010/11 enrolment at primary schools included 100% of children in the relevant age-group, while enrolment at secondary schools in that year included 95% of children in the appropriate age-group.

Higher education includes university education, advanced vocational training, and advanced studies in the arts, plastic arts and design, and sport. In 2007 reforms to the university system were enacted with the aim of conforming to the Bologna Process, which sought to harmonize university systems within the European Higher Education Area. Under the reformed system, which was implemented during the 2010/11 academic year, there are three cycles within university education: Bachelor's (*Grado*), Master's (*Máster*) and Doctorate (*Doctor*). This replaced the previous three-cycle structure, which comprised the degrees of *Diplomatura*, *Licenciatura* and *Doctor*, complemented by degrees in engineering and architecture. Some 1.4m. students were attending university in 2010/11. There were 79 universities in that year, including the open university (Universidad Nacional de Educación a Distancia—UNED).

In 2010 general government expenditure on education amounted to €51,511m., equivalent to 4.9% of gross domestic product.

SPANISH EXTERNAL TERRITORIES

The Spanish External Territories comprise mainly Ceuta and Melilla, two enclaves within Moroccan territory on the north African coast. Attached to Melilla, for administrative purposes, are Peñón de Vélez de la Gomera, a small fort on the Mediterranean coast, and two groups of islands, Peñón de Alhucemas and the Chafarinas. Ceuta and Melilla are seen as integral parts of Spain by the Spanish Government and have the status of autonomous cities, although Morocco has put forward a claim to both. Sovereignty over the uninhabited island of Perejil (known as Laila to the Moroccans) is disputed between Spain and Morocco.

CEUTA

Introductory Survey

LOCATION, CLIMATE, LANGUAGE, RELIGION

Ceuta, one of the two main enclaves of Spanish North Africa, is situated on the north African coast opposite Gibraltar, the Strait here being about 25 km wide. The average temperature is 17°C. Spanish and Arabic are spoken. The majority of Europeans are Roman Catholic, most North Africans being Muslim. There are small Hindu and Jewish communities.

CONTEMPORARY POLITICAL HISTORY

The population of the enclave is mostly Spanish. The proportion of Arab residents, however, has increased, owing to the large number of immigrants from Morocco. Those born in the territory are Spanish citizens and subjects. An ancient port and walled city, Ceuta was retained by Spain upon Moroccan independence from France in 1956. Having developed as a military and administrative centre for the former Spanish Protectorate in Morocco, Ceuta now functions as a bunkering and fishing port. In 1974 the town became the seat of the Capitanía General de Africa. Two-thirds of Ceuta's land area are used exclusively for military purposes.

In November 1978 King Hassan of Morocco stated his country's claim to Ceuta and the other main Spanish enclave in North Africa, Melilla, a claim that was reiterated following the opening of the Spanish frontier with Gibraltar in early 1985. In October 1981 Spain declared before the UN that Ceuta and Melilla were integral parts of Spanish territory. Spain rejects any comparison between the two enclaves and Gibraltar. From 1984 there was increasing unease over Spanish North Africa's future, following rioting in Morocco in January and the signing of the treaty of union between Libya and Morocco in August. In July 1985 the joint Libyan-Moroccan assembly passed a resolution calling for the 'liberation' of Ceuta and Melilla.

Details of Ceuta and Melilla's new draft statutes, envisaging the establishment of two local assemblies, with jurisdiction over such matters as public works, agriculture, tourism, culture and internal trade, were approved by the central Government in December 1985. Unlike Spain's other regional assemblies, however, those of Ceuta and Melilla were not to be vested with legislative powers. After negotiations with representatives of the Muslim community, in May 1986 the central Government agreed to grant Spanish nationality to more than 2,400 Muslims resident in the enclaves. At the general election held in June, the ruling Partido Socialista Obrero Español (PSOE) was successful in Ceuta.

In February 1988 it was announced that, in accordance with regulations of the European Community (EC, now European Union—EU, see p. 281), to which Spain had acceded in 1986, Moroccan citizens would in due course require visas to enter Spain. Entry to Spanish North Africa, however, was to be exempt from the new ruling.

In March 1988, after several months of negotiations, the central Government and principal opposition parties in Madrid reached a broad consensus on draft autonomy statutes for Spanish North Africa. Morocco's Minister of Foreign Affairs formally presented his country's claim to Ceuta and Melilla to the UN General Assembly in October. At the Spanish general election held that month, the ruling PSOE retained its Ceuta seats, despite allegations by the opposition Partido Popular (PP) that many names on the electoral register were duplicated.

In April 1990 the Spanish Government presented the autonomy statutes for discussion in the territories. It was confirmed that the enclaves were to remain an integral part of Spain, and that they were to be granted self-government at municipal, rather than regional, level. The draft autonomy statutes of Ceuta and Melilla were submitted to the Congreso de los Diputados (Congress of Deputies) in Madrid for discussion in October 1991. In November thousands of demonstrators, many of whom had travelled from the enclaves, attended a protest march in Madrid (organized by the Governments of Ceuta and Melilla), in support of demands for full autonomy for the territories. In early 1992, however, the central Government confirmed that the assemblies of Ceuta and Melilla were not to be granted full legislative powers. At the general election of June 1993 the PSOE of Ceuta lost its one seat in the Congreso and its two seats in the Senado (Senate) to the PP.

The final statutes of autonomy were approved by the Spanish Government in September 1994. The statutes provided for 25-member local assemblies, with powers similar to those of the municipal councils of mainland Spain. Each assembly would elect from among its members a city president. The proposals for limited self-government were not well received in Ceuta where, in October, a general strike received widespread support. Following their approval by the Congreso de los Diputados in December, the autonomy statutes were ratified by the Senado in February 1995.

Elections for the new local assemblies were held in May 1995. In Ceuta the PP won nine of the 25 seats, Progreso y Futuro de Ceuta (PFC) six, the nationalist Ceuta Unida (CEU) four and the PSOE three. Basilio Fernández López of the PFC was re-elected Mayor/President, heading a coalition with CEU and the PSOE. Mustafa Mizziam Ammar, leader of the Partido Democrático y Social de Ceuta (PDSC), became the first Muslim candidate ever to be elected in the territory.

In February 1996 the Spanish and Moroccan Prime Ministers met in Rabat, Morocco, for their first summit meeting since December 1993. At the general election held in March 1996, the three PP delegates to the Cortes in Madrid were re-elected. In July Mayor/President Fernández López resigned after seven months at the head of a minority administration, and was replaced by Jesús Fortes Ramos of the PP.

In mid-1996 attention focused once again on the issue of illegal immigration from Africa. Both Ceuta and Melilla appealed to the EU for financial assistance to counter an increase in the number of migrants attempting to cross the border. Negotiations in Madrid in October between the Spanish Minister of the Interior and his Moroccan counterpart resulted in an agreement on the establishment of two joint commissions to address the specific problems of illegal immigration and drugs-trafficking. At further discussions in December, for the first time since the signing of a joint accord in 1992, Morocco agreed to the readmission of migrants held in the Spanish enclaves. In September the Secretary-General of the North Atlantic Treaty Organization (NATO) confirmed that Ceuta and Melilla would remain outside the Alliance's sphere of protection if Spain were to be fully integrated into NATO's military structure.

At the elections of June 1999 the most successful party was the Grupo Independiente Liberal (GIL), which secured 12 of the 25 seats in the Assembly. Antonio Sampietro Casarramona of the GIL replaced Jesús Fortes Ramos of the PP as Mayor/President in August, following the latter's removal from office by a motion of censure supported by a rebel PSOE deputy, Susana Bermúdez. The authorities subsequently announced that a judicial inquiry into the defection of Bermúdez was to be conducted. Both the PSOE and the PP accused the GIL of having bribed the deputy to transfer her allegiance. In March 2000 Sampietro and Bermúdez were charged with bribery. At the general election held on 12 March, Ceuta's three PP representatives in Madrid, one deputy and two senators, all secured re-election.

In early 1999 it was conceded that the security barrier along Ceuta's border with Morocco was proving inadequate. The EU-funded project had been initiated five years previously but remained unfinished. Between January and July alone a total of 21,411 migrants were apprehended on Ceuta's frontier and returned to Morocco. In November border security was reinforced by the army. Further improvements to the barrier were completed in February 2000. The implementation in that month of new legislation relating to immigrants' rights obliged the border post at Ceuta to provide legal assistance to those being denied entry to Spain by the police. In May it was revealed that during 1999 a total of 700,000 migrants had been refused admission to Spanish North Africa.

In January 2000 Prime Minister José María Aznar visited Ceuta and Melilla (although in his capacity as President of the PP, rather than President of the Government), describing the enclaves as constant parts of Spain's future. Morocco subsequently cancelled a scheduled official visit of the Spanish Minister of Foreign Affairs. In May Aznar declared that the controversial immigration law, which had taken effect in February, would need to be reviewed, as, since its entry into force, more than 82,000 immigrants had applied for Spanish residency permits. Large numbers of migrants continued to enter the two enclaves illegally throughout 2000, and further clashes between migrants and the security forces were reported. The immigration law reforms, which entered into force in January 2001, were intended to benefit those seeking asylum, but offered severe penalties to individuals who entered the enclaves illegally, and to traffickers and employers who assist them. Protests against the reforms were staged in Spanish North Africa, and mainland Spain.

In September 2000, following a ruling in the Spanish courts that Ceuta and Melilla could not be considered to be autonomous communities, the GIL proposed in the Ceuta Assembly that the enclave be granted greater autonomy. Discussions on the proposal, which proved highly emotive, led to disturbances within the Assembly. However, the motion was subsequently carried by a majority vote.

In January 2001 five Ceuta councillors resigned their posts and announced their departure from the GIL, thus depriving the party of its majority in the Assembly. Former PSOE deputy Bermúdez subsequently withdrew her support for the GIL, which had previously enabled the party to assume office. A motion of censure against Sampietro, proposed by the PP, the PSOE, the PDSC and one of the former GIL councillors, was carried in February, with the support of 17 of the 25 deputies, and Juan Jesús Vivas Lara of the PP was appointed Mayor/President. A new Council was subsequently announced, including the five 'rebel' councillors (now members of the Grupo Mixto).

Relations between Spain and Morocco were threatened again in July 2002, after the occupation of Perejil, a small islet near Ceuta, by 12 Moroccan soldiers. Spain made a formal protest to the Moroccan Government on 12 July, but Morocco refused to withdraw its men, claiming that Perejil (known as Laila to the Moroccans) had been a part of Morocco since independence in 1956. Four Spanish gunboats were dispatched to patrol the locality and Spanish soldiers reoccupied the island on 17 July. A subsequent US-mediated arrangement resulted in agreement by both countries to leave the islet unoccupied. However, in September Morocco reasserted its claims to Ceuta and Melilla at the UN. Later that month Morocco additionally accused Spain of violating its airspace and territorial waters more than 90 times since July, and cancelled a scheduled meeting with Spain in protest against the alleged landing of a Spanish military helicopter on Perejil; Spain denied the claim. In response to several border incidents and in an attempt to halt illegal immigration, Spain ordered the permanent closure of the border with Morocco at Benzu in October.

A bilateral immigration accord signed by Spain and Morocco in February 2003 proposed the repatriation to Morocco of 200 illegal immigrant minors from Ceuta and Melilla in March. In early 2003 measures to strengthen border security were increased. Moreover, a series of suicide bombings launched against Western targets in Casablanca in May, killing up to 45 people, resulted in a further tightening of border security. It was believed that one of the leaders of the militant Islamist group thought to be responsible for the attacks was a resident of Ceuta, and that others involved in the bombings had subsequently fled to mainland Spain via Ceuta. In June the Spanish Government's delegate in Ceuta initiated a request to the Ministry of Foreign Affairs in Madrid to withdraw citizenship from any dual-nationals in the enclave who were proven criminals, members of fundamentalist groups or pro-Moroccan. At the regional elections held in May 2003, the PP achieved an absolute majority in Ceuta for the first time, winning 19 of 25 seats, while the Unión Demócrata Ceutí (UDCE), which represented the Muslim population, secured three. Vivas remained as Mayor/President.

In September 2003 Aznar visited Morocco for bilateral discussions, although the issue of sovereignty over Spain's North African possessions was reportedly avoided. In 2003 it was estimated that around 3,000 migrants passed through Ceuta, and the enclave received more than 1,400 asylum requests, compared with 372 in 2002 and 82 in 2001. Official figures stated that 18% of the requests processed in 2003 were successful. In December 2003 Morocco and Spain made progress towards reaching an accord on the repatriation of illegal immigrant minors; however, a final agreement was not signed. Human rights groups criticized the two centres provided by the Spanish Government for migrants as inadequate.

At the March 2004 general election, the PP retained the deputy and senators elected by Ceuta. In September Vivas met with the newly elected Spanish Prime Minister, José Luis Rodríguez Zapatero, to discuss the possible change in status of Ceuta from Ciudad Autónoma (Autonomous City) to Comunidad Autónoma (Autonomous Community), in line with other areas of Spain. In November the central Government unveiled plans to build reception centres for immigrants on the mainland, to which illegal immigrants arrested in Ceuta and Melilla would be transported.

In 2005 potential immigrants continued to attempt to gain access to Europe through Ceuta and Melilla, with some attempting to scale the walls separating the enclaves from Morocco. In September five would-be immigrants were killed by security forces during an attempt by some 600 people to climb the wall into Ceuta. It was

announced at a Spanish-Moroccan summit held in late September in Seville, Spain, that security on both sides of the border would be increased following the attempts; however, increased attempts by migrants to enter the enclaves continued in early October, and more deaths resulted. Concern arose that immigrants captured by Moroccan security forces were being abandoned in Morocco's south-western desert. In October the Spanish Government authorized €3m. to improve facilities for immigrants in the enclaves. Heightened security reduced the number of attempts being made to climb the walls, but it appeared also that immigrants were looking for new (and potentially more dangerous) routes to Europe via the Canary Islands.

In early 2006 Zapatero made the first official visit by a Prime Minister to the enclaves in over 25 years. His visit was condemned by the Moroccan authorities as a provocation, despite the fact that relations between Spain and Morocco had been favourable during the first two years of Zapatero's administration.

In February 2007 the Spanish Government reached an agreement with the Governments of Ceuta and Melilla to abandon plans to change the cities' status to that of Autonomous Communities. In return, more powers would be devolved to the cities in the areas of employment and social services, and their budgets would be increased. At elections held in May, the PP retained its absolute majority in the Assembly, again winning 19 of the 25 seats; the UDCE, in alliance with the left-wing Izquierda Unida, secured four seats, while the PSOE won two. Vivas resumed office as Mayor/President. In October ongoing divisions within the local branch of the PSOE led to its dissolution, and the party's national leadership delegated a commission to assume temporary responsibility for PSOE activities in Ceuta. (The local branch of the PSOE resumed activities under a newly elected Secretary-General, José Antonio Carracao Meléndez, in December 2008.)

In early November 2007 a two-day visit to Ceuta and Melilla by King Juan Carlos, his first since acceding to the throne in 1975, was warmly welcomed by residents, but provoked considerable anger in Morocco. The Moroccan Government recalled its ambassador from Madrid ahead of the visit, which it deemed to be provocative. The Spanish Prime Minister sought to defuse tensions; Morocco's King Muhammad VI, however, noted that Spain risked jeopardizing bilateral relations, and urged Spain to engage in dialogue over the disputed enclaves. The Moroccan ambassador to Spain returned to Madrid in January 2008, following a visit to Rabat by the Spanish Minister of Foreign Affairs and Co-operation, Miguel Ángel Moratinos, who delivered a conciliatory letter from Prime Minister Zapatero to King Muhammad.

At the general election held in March 2008, the PP retained Ceuta's one seat in the Congreso de los Diputados and its two seats in the Senado. Efforts to strengthen border security were increased in late 2008, after the militant Islamist al-Qa'ida Organization in the Land of the Islamic Maghreb announced that it intended to intensify its campaign of violence against the governments of North Africa. (Previously confined largely to Algeria, the group had latterly staged several bomb attacks in neighbouring countries, and its leader, Abu Musab Abd al-Wadud, had reportedly stated his intention to expand its activities into Europe.)

At elections to the Assembly held on 22 May 2011, the PP retained the largest representation, with 18 seats. The 'Caballas' coalition—which comprised the UDCE and the Parti Socialista del Pueblo del Ceuta (PSPC)—won four seats, while the PSOE took the remaining three. A new Council of Government, under the continued leadership of Vivas, took office in mid-June.

At the general election held on 20 November 2011, the PP retained Ceuta's seat in the Congreso de los Diputados and both seats in the Senado. In January 2012 Francisco Antonio González Pérez, a former member of the Congreso for the enclave, assumed the role of Government Delegate in Ceuta. A minor reorganization of the Council was effected in March, in which the development and environment portfolio was divided, with responsibility for environmental affairs passing to the Councillor for Public Services and Communities. In late April Vivas announced a further reorganization, citing the need to adapt his administration to the changing economic circumstances in Spain. Most notably, Francisco Márquez de la Rubia assumed responsibility for a new Council of Planning and Relations with Governmental Organizations, and Guillermo Martínez Arcas became Councillor of Finance, the Economy and Human Resources.

CONSTITUTION AND GOVERNMENT

Following the adoption of statutes of autonomy and the establishment of local assemblies in 1995, Ceuta and Melilla remain integral parts of Spain, but have greater jurisdiction over matters such as public works, internal trade and tourism. Each enclave has its own Mayor/President. Ceuta, Melilla and the island dependencies are known as *plazas de soberanía*, fortified enclaves over which Spain has full sovereign rights. In both Ceuta and Melilla civil authority is vested in a Government Delegate (Delegado del Gobierno) directly responsible to the Ministry of Home Affairs in Madrid. This official is usually assisted by a government sub-delegate. There is also one delegate from each of the Ministries in Madrid.

ECONOMIC AFFAIRS

In 2011, according to official estimates, the gross domestic product (GDP) of Ceuta was equivalent to €19,952 per head, ranking 13th (in terms of GDP per head) in a list of the 19 Spanish autonomous regions. According to official estimates, total GDP was €1,529.1m. in 2011. The population of Ceuta increased by an annual average of 0.8% in 2002–12.

Agricultural activity in Ceuta is negligible, as is employment in the sector; according to official estimates, the sector contributed just 0.1% of GDP in 2011. The employment in the sector was negligible in 2012.

Industry is on a limited scale (although there is a local brewery), but the sector contributed 13.7% of GDP in 2011, while 8.0% of the employed population were engaged in the sector in 2012. Construction contributed 8.9% of GDP in 2011, and engaged 5.2% of the employed population in 2012.

Services contributed an estimated 86.2% of GDP in 2011, while some 92.0% of the employed population were engaged in the sector in 2012.

Most of the population's food is imported, with the exception of fish, which is obtained locally (sardines and anchovies are among the most significant catches). A large proportion of the tinned fish is sold outside Spain. More important to the economies of Ceuta and Melilla is the port activity; most of their exports take the form of fuel supplied—at very competitive rates—to ships. Most of the fuel comes from the Spanish refinery in Tenerife. Ceuta's port received a total of 13,023 ships in 2011. Most trade is conducted with other parts of Spain. In 2012 Ceuta's trade deficit was around €439m. In that year the principal source of imports (accounting for some 9.0% of the total value) was the People's Republic of China; other major suppliers were the Netherlands and Turkey. Switzerland was the principal market for exports. The principal imports in 2012 were mineral fuels and oils (accounting for more than 67.7% of the total value), and textiles and clothing. The principal exports in the same year were plastics. Tourism makes a significant contribution to the territory's economy. In 2012 there were 77,295 visitors to Ceuta (including 54,131 from Spain), attracted by duty-free goods. In 2011 there was a balanced budget, with revenue and expenditure both totalling €253.2m. The annual rate of inflation averaged 2.5% in 2002–12; the rate was 2.4% in 2012. According to official estimates, on average, some 38.6% of the labour force were unemployed in 2012.

Upon the accession in January 1986 of Spain to the European Community (EC, now European Union—EU, see p. 281), Ceuta was considered a Spanish city and therefore as European territory, and joined the organization as part of Spain. It retained its status as a free port. The statute of autonomy, adopted in early 1995, envisaged the continuation of the territory's fiscal benefits. Euro notes and coins became the sole legal tender on 28 February 2002.

Sustained Spanish economic growth in the 2000s and successive enlargements of the EU that took place during that decade limited Spain's access to EU aid, with the result that, although income in the enclave had not improved significantly, subsidies for Ceuta were progressively reduced from 2007, with a view to their eventual withdrawal. The city's consolidated budget for 2012 included current and capital transfers from the Spanish state of €69.4m. and €6.3m., respectively.

Statistical Survey

Sources (unless otherwise stated): Administración General del Estado, Beatriz de Silva 4, 51001 Ceuta; tel. (956) 512616; fax (956) 511893; Instituto Nacional de Estadística, Paseo de la Castellana 183, 28071 Madrid; tel. (91) 5839100; fax (91) 5839158; internet www.ine.es; *Memoria Socioeconómico y Laboral de 2004:* Consejo Económico y Social, Edif. La Tahoma, Esquina Salud Tejero y Dueñas, Ceuta; tel. (956) 519131; fax (956) 519146; e-mail ces-ceuta@ceuta.es.

AREA AND POPULATION

Area: 19.7 sq km (7.6 sq miles).

Population (census results): 71,505 at 1 November 2001; 83,517 at 1 November 2011 (males 42,765, females 40,752).

Density (at 2011 census): 4,239 per sq km.

Population by Age and Sex (official estimates at 1 July 2012): *0–14:* 15,486 (males 7,890, females 7,596); *15–64:* 52,402 (males 26,818, females 25,584); *65 and over:* 9,441 (males 4,110, females 5,331); *Total* 77,329 (males 38,817, females 38,512). Note: Estimates not adjusted to take account of results 2011 census.

Births, Marriages and Deaths (2011): Live births 1,138 (birth rate 14.8 per 1,000); Marriages 433 (marriage rate 5.6 per 1,000); Deaths 502 (death rate 6.6 per 1,000).

Life Expectancy (years at birth, 2011): 79.9 (males 77.2; females 82.8).

Immigration and Emigration (excl. Spanish territory, 2011): Immigrants 945; Emigrants 510.

Economically Active Population ('000 persons aged 16 years and over, 2012): Mining and utilities 0.4; Manufacturing 0.2; Construction 1.1; Trade, transport and accommodation 6.5; Finance, insurance, real estate and business services 1.9; Public administration, defence, education, health and social services 9.7; Other services 1.4; *Total employed* 21.2; Unemployed 13.3; *Total labour force* 34.5 (males 20.0, females 14.5).

AGRICULTURE, ETC.

Livestock (animals slaughtered, 2004): Sheep 1,025; Goats 108.

Fishing (metric tons, live weight of catch): 304.1 in 2002; 310.8 in 2003; 236.8 in 2004.

FINANCE

Currency and Exchange Rates: 100 cent = 1 euro (€). *Sterling and Dollar Equivalents* (31 December 2012): £1 sterling = 1.196 euros; US $1 = 0.758 euros; 10 euros = £8.00 = $12.40. *Average Exchange Rate* (euros per US $): 0.7550 in 2010; 0.7194 in 2011; 0.7779 in 2012. Note: The local currency was formerly the Spanish peseta. From the introduction of the euro, with Spanish participation, on 1 January 1999, a fixed exchange rate of €1 = 166.386 pesetas was in effect. Euro notes and coins were introduced on 1 January 2002. The euro and local currency circulated alongside each other until 28 February, after which the euro became the sole legal tender.

Budget (€ '000, 2011): *Revenue:* Current operations 209,376.8 (Direct taxation 8,543.9, Indirect taxation 122,765.0, Rates and other revenue 12,910.1, Current transfers 64,587.8, Property income 570.1); Capital operations 43,815.1 (Capital transfers 13,923.6, Transfers of real investments 16,358.5, Assets 1,633.0, Liabilities 11,900.0); Total 253,191.8. *Expenditure:* Current operations 197,310.6 (Wages and salaries 81,886.6, Goods and services 70,325.4, Financial 5,085.9, Current transfers 40,012.7); Capital operations 55,881.2 (Real investments 22,221.1, Capital transfers 19,876.6, Assets 1,667.0, Liabilities 12,116.5); Total 253,191.8.

Cost of Living (Consumer Price Index; base: 2006 = 100): All items 106.4 in 2009; 108.0 in 2010; 110.6 in 2011. *2012* (base: 2011 = 100): All items 102.1.

Gross Domestic Product (€ million at current prices, estimates): 1,509.3 in 2009; 1,526.2 in 2010; 1,529.1 in 2011.

Gross Domestic Product by Economic Activity (€ million at current prices, 2011, estimates): Agriculture and fishing 2.1; Manufacturing 32.5; Mining and energy 34.9; Construction 124.6; Services 1,209.7; *Sub-total* 1,403.9; Net taxes on products 125.2; *GDP at market prices* 1,529.1.

EXTERNAL TRADE

Principal Commodities (€ million, 2012): *Imports:* Milk and dairy products, eggs, honey, etc. 19.3; Mineral fuels and oils, and products thereof 297.4; Textile materials and clothing 20.4; Footwear 10.1; Machinery and equipment (incl. electrical), and parts thereof 6.6; Vehicles (excl. rail or tram), and parts thereof 4.3; Total (incl. others) 439.4. *Exports:* Total 0.3.

Principal Trading Partners (€ million, 2012): *Imports:* China, People's Republic 39.5; France 4.9; Germany 6.3; India 4.8; Indonesia 4.2; Netherlands 26.4; Switzerland 4.2; Turkey 25.4; USA 9.9; Viet Nam 6.6; Total (incl. others) 439.4. *Exports:* Switzerland 0.1; Total (incl. others) 0.3.

Source: Foreign Trade Database, Agencia Tributaria (Madrid).

TRANSPORT

Road Traffic (Ceuta and Melilla, 2009): Vehicles registered 5,085 (Passenger cars 3,435, Buses, etc. 7, Lorries and vans 737, Motorcycles 894, Tractors 2, Other 10).

Shipping (domestic and international, 2011): Vessels entered 13,023; Goods handled ('000 metric tons) 2,028; Passenger movements ('000) 1,812.

Civil Aviation (2011, provisional): Flights 5,004; Passengers carried ('000) 46; Goods transported 1 metric ton.

TOURISM

Visitor Arrivals (by country of residence, 2002): France 2,653; Germany 700; Italy 1,076; Portugal 1,062; Spain 41,593; United Kingdom 1,430; USA 2,939; Total (incl. others) 61,356. *2012:* Total 77,295 (Spain 54,131).

COMMUNICATIONS MEDIA

Telephones (main lines in use, 2004): 24,849.

EDUCATION

Pre-primary (2005/06): 24 schools; 149 teachers; 2,961 students. *2011/12:* 3,653 students.

Primary (2005/06): 22 schools; 411 teachers (excl. 42 engaged in both pre-primary and primary teaching); 5,948 students. *2011/12:* 6,626 students.

Secondary: First Cycle (2005/06): 16 schools (of which 6 schools also provided second-cycle education and 5 provided vocational education, see below); 209 teachers (excl. 34 engaged in both secondary and primary teaching and 234 engaged in more than one cycle of secondary); 3,874 students. *2011/12:* 3,984 students.

Secondary: Second Cycle (2005/06): 34 teachers; 1,298 students. *2011/12:* 1,531 students.

Secondary: Vocational (2005/06): 83 teachers; 970 students. *2011/12:* 1,504 students.

Source: Ministry of Education, Madrid.

Directory

Government

HEAD OF STATE

King of Spain: HM King JUAN CARLOS I (succeeded to the throne 22 November 1975).

Government Delegate in Ceuta: FRANCISCO ANTONIO GONZÁLEZ PÉREZ.

MEMBERS OF THE SPANISH PARLIAMENT

Deputy elected to the Congress in Madrid: FRANCISCO MÁRQUEZ DE LA RUBIA (PP).

Representatives to the Senate in Madrid: LUZ ELENA SANÍN NARANJO (PP), JOSÉ LUIS SASTRE ÁLVARO (PP).

COUNCIL OF GOVERNMENT
(May 2013)

The executive is formed by members of the Partido Popular (PP).

Mayor/President: JUAN JESÚS VIVAS LARA.

Councillor of the Presidency and Government and of Employment: YOLANDA BEL BLANCA.

Councillor of Planning and Relations with Governmental Organizations: FRANCISCO MÁRQUEZ DE LA RUBIA.

Councillor of Education, Culture and Women: MARÍA ISABEL DEU DEL OLMO.

Councillor of Social Affairs: RABEA MOHAMED TONSI.

Councillor of Finance, the Economy and Human Resources: GUILLERMO MARTÍNEZ ARCAS.

Councillor of Youth, Sport, Tourism and Festivals: PREMI MIRCHANDANI TAHILRAM.

Councillor of Health and Consumer Affairs: ABDELHAKIM ABDE-SELAM AL-LAL.

Councillor of Development: SUSANA ROMÁN BERNET.

Councillor of Environment, Public Services and Communities: GREGORIO GARCÍA CASTAÑEDA.

GOVERNMENT OFFICES

Delegación del Gobierno: Beatriz de Silva 4, 51001 Ceuta; tel. (956) 984400; fax (956) 513671; e-mail roberto@ceuta.map.es.

Office of the Mayor/President: Plaza de Africa s/n, Asamblea, 1°, 51001 Ceuta; tel. and fax (956) 528200; e-mail presidencia@ceuta.es; internet www.ceuta.es.

Council of Development: Plaza de Africa s/n, Asamblea, 3°, 51001 Ceuta; tel. and fax (956) 528240; e-mail fomento@ceuta.es.

Council of Education, Culture and Women: Plaza de Africa s/n, Asamblea, 2°, 51001 Ceuta; tel. and fax (956) 528153; e-mail educacion@ceuta.es.

Council of Employment: Edif. Ceuta Center, 1°, 51001 Ceuta; tel. and fax (956) 528386; e-mail economia@ceuta.es.

Council of Environment, Public Services and Communities: Plaza de Africa s/n, Asamblea, 3°, 51001 Ceuta; tel. and fax (956) 528164.

Council of Finance, the Economy and Human Resources: Edif. Ceuta Center, 51001 Ceuta; e-mail hacienda@ceuta.es.

Council of Health and Consumer Affairs: Carretera San Amaro 12, Ceuta; tel. (856) 200680; fax (856) 200723; e-mail sanidad@ceuta.es; internet www.ceuta.es/sanidad.

Council of Planning and Relations with Governmental Organizations: Plaza de Africa s/n, Asamblea, 3°, 51001 Ceuta.

Council of Social Affairs: Carretera San Amaro 12, Ceuta; tel. and fax (856) 200684; e-mail bsocial@ceuta.es.

Council of Youth, Sport, Tourism and Festivals: Avda de Africa s/n, Ceuta; tel. (956) 518844; fax (956) 510295.

Assembly

Election, 22 May 2011

	Seats
Partido Popular (PP)	18
Caballas*	4
Partido Socialista Obrero Español (PSOE)	3
Total	**25**

* Coalition of Unión Demócrata Ceutí (UDCE) and Parti Socialista del Pueblo de Ceuta (PSPC).

Election Commission

Junta Electoral de Zona y Provincial de Ceuta: Ceuta; Sec. FRANCISCO JAVIER IZQUIERDO CARBONERO.

Political Organizations

Izquierda Unida (IU): General Yagüe 4, 1°, 51001 Ceuta; tel. (956) 811941; e-mail izquierdaunidaceuta@hotmail.com; internet www.izquierda-unida.es; alliance of left-wing parties; Federal Coordinator CAYO LARA MOYA.

Partido Democrático y Social de Ceuta (PDSC): Bolivia 35, 51001 Ceuta; Muslim party; Leader MUSTAFA MIZZIAM AMMAR.

Partido Popular (PP): Teniente Arrabal 4, Edif. Ainara, Bajo, 51001 Ceuta; tel. (956) 518191; fax (956) 513218; e-mail ceuta@pp.es; internet popularesceuta.es; fmrly Alianza Popular; national-level, centre-right party; Pres. JUAN JESUS VIVAS LARA; Sec.-Gen. YOLANDA BEL BLANCA.

Partido Socialista Obrero Español (PSOE): Daóiz 1, 51001 Ceuta; tel. (956) 515553; e-mail psoeceuta@telefonica.net; internet www.ceuta.psoe.es; national-level, left-wing party; Pres. JUAN DIAZ TRIANO; Sec.-Gen. JOSÉ ANTONIO CARRACAO MELÉNDEZ.

Partido Socialista del Pueblo de Ceuta (PSPC): Echegarray 1, Local 1D, 51001 Ceuta; tel. and fax (956) 518869; e-mail pspc@pspc.info; internet www.pspc.es; f. 1986 by dissident members of PSOE and others; contested May 2011 elections as part of 'Caballas' coalition with Unión Demócrata Ceutí; Sec.-Gen. IVÁN CHAVES.

Unión Demócrata Ceutí (UDCE): Avda Teniente-Coronel Gautier 22, 2° dcha, Ceuta; Muslim party; contested May 2011 elections as part of 'Caballas' coalition with Partido Socialista del Pueblo de Ceuta; Leader MUHAMMAD ALÍ.

There are also various civic associations.

Judicial System

Tribunal Superior de Justicia de Andalucía, Ceuta y Melilla: Plaza Nueva, 10, Palacio de la Real Chancillería, 18071 Granada, Spain; tel. (958) 002600; fax (958) 002720; e-mail webmaster.ius@juntadeandalucia.es; internet www.juntadeandalucia.es; Pres. JOSÉ ANTONIO GRIÑÁN MARTÍNEZ.

Religion

CHRISTIANITY

The Roman Catholic Church

Bishop of Cádiz and Ceuta: ANTONIO CEBALLOS ATIENZA (resident in Cádiz), Vicar-Gen. FRANCISCO CORRERO TOCÓN, Obispado de Ceuta, Plaza de Nuestra Señora de Africa, 51001 Ceuta; tel. (956) 517732; fax (956) 513208; e-mail obispadoceuta@planalfa.es; internet www.obispadodecadizyceuta.org.

OTHER RELIGIONS

Ceuta has a large Muslim population (estimated at around 30,000), as well as Jewish and Hindu communities.

The Press

El Faro de Ceuta: Sargento Mena 8, 51001 Ceuta; tel. (956) 524035; fax (956) 524147; e-mail ceuta@grupofaro.es; internet www.elfaroceutamelilla.es; f. 1934; morning; Pres. RAFAEL MONTERO PALACIOS; Editors-in-Chief JOSÉ M. GALLARDO, TAMARA CRESPO; circ. 5,000.

El Pueblo de Ceuta: Independencia 11, 1°, 51001 Ceuta; tel. (956) 514367; fax (956) 517650; e-mail elpuebloredaccion@telefonica.net; internet www.elpueblodeceuta.es; f. 1995; daily; Dir and Editor-in-Chief SALVADOR VIVANCOS CANALES.

NEWS AGENCY

Agencia EFE: Milán Astray 1, 1°, Of. 8, 51001 Ceuta; tel. (956) 517550; fax (956) 516639; e-mail ceuta@agenciaefe.net; Correspondent RAFAEL PEÑA SOLER.

PRESS ASSOCIATION

Asociación de la Prensa: Beatriz de Silva 14, 1° E, 51001 Ceuta; tel. (956) 403713; fax (956) 528205; Pres. RAFAEL PEÑA SOLER.

Broadcasting

RADIO

Onda Cero Radio Ceuta: Delgado Serrano 1, 1° dcha, 51001 Ceuta; tel. (956) 200068; fax (956) 200179; internet www.ondacero.es; Dir RAFAEL ROMAGUERA MENA.

Radio Nacional de España: Real 90, 51001 Ceuta; tel. (956) 524688; fax (956) 519067; e-mail prensa@rtve.es; internet www.rtve.es; Dir EDUARDO SÁNCHEZ DORADO.

Radio Popular de Ceuta/COPE: Sargento Mena 8, 1°, 11701 Ceuta; tel. (956) 524200; fax (956) 524202; internet www.cope.es; Dir DANIEL OLIVA.

Radio Televisión Ceuta: Avda Alcalde Sánchez, Prado 3–5, Ceuta; tel. and fax (956) 524420; e-mail televidente@rtvce.es; internet www.rtvce.es; f. 2000; owned by Sociedad Española de Radiodifusión; commercial; Dir DANIEL OLIVA MARTÍN.

TELEVISION

Radio Televisión Ceuta: Real 90, Portón 4, 1° dcha, 51001 Ceuta; tel. (956) 511820; fax (956) 516820; internet www.rtvce.es; Dir MANUEL GONZÁLEZ BOLORINO.

Finance

BANKING

In 2007 there were nine banks operating in Ceuta, all of which were based in mainland Spain.

Banco Bilbao Vizcaya Argentaria (BBVA): Gonzalez de la Vega 8, 51001 Ceuta; tel. (956) 201238; fax (956) 510585; internet www.bbva.es; 4 brs.

Banco de España: Plaza de España 2, 51001 Ceuta; tel. (956) 513253; fax (956) 513108; internet www.bde.es.

Banco Español de Crédito (Banesto): Camoens 5, 51001 Ceuta; tel. (956) 524028; internet www.banesto.es.

Banco Popular Español: Paseo del Revellín 1, 51001 Ceuta; tel. (956) 515340; fax (956) 512970; internet www.bancopopular.es.

Banco Santander Central Hispano (BSCH): Paseo del Revellín 17–19, 51001 Ceuta; tel. (956) 511371; internet www.gruposantander.es; 2 brs.

Caja de Ahorros y Pensiones de Barcelona (La Caixa): Gran Vía s/n, 51001 Ceuta; tel. (956) 515886; fax (956) 513972; internet www.lacaixa.es; 4 brs.

Caja Duero: Sargento Coriat 5, 51001 Ceuta; tel. (956) 518040; fax (956) 517019; tel. www.cajaduero.es; 1 br.

Caja Madrid: Plaza de los Reyes s/n, 51001 Ceuta; tel. (956) 524016; fax (956) 524017; internet www.cajamadrid.es; 6 brs.

Montes de Piedad y Caja de Ahorros de Ronda, Cádiz, Almería, Málaga y Antequera (Unicaja): Paseo Revellín 21, 51001 Ceuta; tel. (956) 518340; fax (956) 519561; internet www.unicaja.es; 2 brs.

INSURANCE

MAPFRE: Paseo Marina Española 92, Edif. Patio Paramo, 51001 Ceuta; tel. (956) 519638; fax (956) 513916; e-mail balfaro@mapfre.com; internet www.mapfre.com; Commercial Man. BORJA ALFARO INFANTE; 3 offices.

Trade and Industry

Cámara Oficial de Comercio, Industria y Navegación: Dueñas 2, 51001 Ceuta; tel. (956) 509590; fax (956) 509589; e-mail camerceuta@camaras.org; internet www.camaraceuta.org; chamber of commerce; Pres. LUIS MORENO NARANJO; Sec.-Gen. MARÍA DEL ROSARIO ESPINOSA SUÁREZ.

Confederación de Empresarios de Ceuta: Paseo de las Palmeras, Edif. Corona 26–28, 51001 Ceuta; tel. (956) 200038; fax (956) 512010; e-mail info@confeceuta.es; internet www.confeceuta.es; employers' confed; Pres. RAFAEL MONTERO AVALOS; Sec.-Gen. ALEJANDRO RAMÍREZ HURTADO.

UTILITIES

Aguas de Ceuta Empresa Municipal, SA (ACEMSA): Solis 1, Edif. San Luis, Ceuta; tel. (956) 524619; e-mail aguasdeceuta@acemsa.es; internet www.acemsa.es; Pres. GUILLERMO MARTÍNEZ ARCAS; Dir-Gen. EMILIO CARREIRA RUIZ.

Empresa de Alumbrado Eléctrico de Ceuta SA: Beatriz de Silva 2, Ceuta; tel. (956) 511901; e-mail info@electricadeceuta.com; internet www.electricadeceuta.com; generates and transmits electricity; Rep. ALBERTO RAMÓN GAITÁN RODRÍGUEZ.

TRADE UNION

Comisiones Obreras de Ceuta: Alcalde Fructuoso Miaja 1, 51001 Ceuta; tel. (956) 516243; fax (956) 517991; e-mail ccoo.ce@ceuta.ccoo.es; internet www.ceuta.ccoo.es; 3,500 mems (2012); Sec.-Gen. JUAN LUIS ARÓSTEGUI RUIZ.

Transport

Much of the traffic between Spain and Morocco passes through Ceuta; there are ferry services to Algeciras, Melilla, Málaga and Almería. Plans for an airport are under consideration. Helicopter services to Málaga are provided by Helisureste. There were 37 km of paved roads in Ceuta in 2010. The Port of Ceuta is one of the most important in the Mediterranean. In 2011 2.0m. metric tons of goods, 1.8m. passengers and 13,023 ships passed through the port.

Port of Ceuta: Autoridad Portuaria de Ceuta, Muelle de España s/n, 51001 Ceuta; tel. (956) 527000; fax (956) 527001; e-mail apceuta@puertodeceuta.com; internet www.puertodeceuta.com; Pres. JOSÉ FRANCISCO TORRADO LÓPEZ.

Acciona Trasmediterránea: Muelle Cañorero Dato 6, 51001 Ceuta; tel. (956) 505390; fax (956) 504714; e-mail info@trasmediterranea.es; internet www.trasmediterranea.es; f. 1917; services between Algeciras and Ceuta.

Tourism

Visitors are attracted by the historical monuments, the Parque Marítimo and the museums, as well as by the Shrine of Our Lady of Africa. There were 77,295 visitors to Ceuta in 2012, of whom 54,131 were from mainland Spain.

Servicios Turísticos de Ceuta: Baluarte de los Mallorquines, Edrissis s/n, 51001 Ceuta; tel. (856) 200560; fax (856) 200565; e-mail turismo@ceuta.es; internet www.ceuta.es/turismo.

Defence

Military authority is vested in a commandant-general. The enclaves are attached to the military region of Sevilla. In August 2003 Spain had 8,100 troops deployed in Spanish North Africa, compared with 21,000 in mid-1987. Two-thirds of Ceuta's land area are used exclusively for military purposes.

Commandant-General: Gen. RAMÓN MARTÍN-AMBROSIO MERINO.

Education

The conventional Spanish facilities are available; however, there are also teachers of the Islamic religion in the city. Enrolment at primary schools in Ceuta totalled 6,626 in 2011/12, while the first cycle (from the ages of 12 to 16) of secondary education had an enrolment of 3,984 students; secondary schools enrolled some 1,531 students for the *bachillerato*, and 1,504 students were enrolled on vocational courses. In higher education, links with the University of Granada are maintained and there is a branch of the Spanish open university (Universidad Nacional de Educación a Distancia—UNED).

MELILLA

Introductory Survey

LOCATION, CLIMATE, LANGUAGE, RELIGION

Melilla is situated on a small peninsula jutting into the Mediterranean Sea. The average temperature is 17°C. Spanish and Arabic are spoken. The majority of Europeans are Roman Catholic, most North Africans being Muslim.

CONTEMPORARY POLITICAL HISTORY

The population of Melilla is mostly Spanish. The proportion of Arab residents, however, has greatly increased, owing to the large number of immigrants from Morocco. Those born in the territory are Spanish citizens and subjects. Melilla was the first Spanish town to rise against the Government of the Popular Front in July 1936, at the beginning of the Spanish Civil War. Like Ceuta, Melilla was retained by Spain when Morocco became independent in 1956. In addition to its function as a port, Melilla now serves as a military base, more than one-half of the enclave's land area being used solely for military purposes. In October 1978 King Hassan of Morocco attempted to link the question of the sovereignty of Melilla to that of the return of the British dependent territory of Gibraltar to Spain. (See the chapter on Ceuta for details on Morocco's relationship with Spain and the North African enclaves.)

After negotiations with representatives of the Muslim community, in early 1986 the central Government in Madrid agreed to grant Spanish nationality to more than 2,400 Muslims resident in Melilla and Ceuta. At that time only some 7,000 of the estimated 27,000-strong Muslim community in Melilla held Spanish nationality. In response to protests, particularly in Melilla, the central Government had given assurances that it would assist the full integration into Spanish society of Muslims in the enclaves. By mid-1986, however, the number of Muslims applying for Spanish nationality in Melilla had reached several thousand. As a result of delays in the processing of the applications, Aomar Muhammadi Dudú, the leader of the newly founded Muslim Partido de los Demócratas de Melilla (PDM), accused the Government of failing to fulfil its pledge to the Muslim residents.

At the general election of June 1986, the ruling Partido Socialista Obrero Español (PSOE) was defeated by the centre-right Coalición Popular (CP) in Melilla, the result indicating the strong opposition of the Spanish community to the Government's plan to integrate the Muslim population. Tight security surrounded the elections, and 'parallel elections', resulting in a vote of confidence in the PDM leader, were held by the Muslim community. Polling was accompanied by several days of unrest. Talks in Madrid between representatives of the main political parties in Melilla and the Ministry of the Interior resulted in concessions to the enclave. In September Dudú agreed to accept a senior post in the Ministry, with responsibility for relations with the Muslim communities of Spain. In November, however, Muslim leaders in Melilla announced that they wished to establish their own administration in the enclave, in view of the Madrid Government's failure to fulfil its promise of Spanish citizenship for Muslim residents. The Spanish Minister of the Interior reiterated assurances of the Government's commitment to integrating the Muslim community. Later in the month thousands of Muslims took part in a peaceful demonstration in support of Dudú, who had resigned his Madrid post after only two months in office. (He subsequently went into exile in Morocco and lost the support of Melilla's Muslim community.)

In February 1987 police reinforcements were dispatched from Spain, in response to a serious escalation of inter-racial tensions in Melilla. Numerous demonstrators were detained, and several prominent Muslims were charged with sedition and briefly held in custody. King Hassan reaffirmed his support for the Muslims of the Spanish enclaves.

In March 1988, after several months of negotiations, the central Government and main opposition parties in Madrid reached a broad consensus on draft autonomy statutes for the Spanish External Territories. (See the chapter on Ceuta for details of the statutes.)

The results of the October 1989 general election were declared invalid, following the discovery of serious irregularities. At the repeated ballot in March 1990, both seats in the Senado (Senate) and the one seat in the Congreso de los Diputados (Congress of Deputies) were won by the Partido Popular (PP), the latter result depriving the PSOE of an overall majority in the Madrid lower chamber. By 1990 almost all residents were in possession of an identity card.

At elections to the municipal council held in May 1991, the PP secured 12 of the 25 seats, and Ignacio Velázquez Rivera of the right-wing Partido Nacionalista de Melilla (PNM) was elected Mayor, replacing the previous PSOE incumbent. At the general election of June 1993 the PSOE candidate defeated the PP member in the Congreso de los Diputados; the PP also lost one of its two seats in the Senado.

The final statutes of autonomy for Ceuta and Melilla were approved by the Spanish Government in September 1994 (see the chapter on Ceuta). At elections for the new local assembly, held in May 1995, the level of participation was less than 62%. The PP won 14 of the 25 seats, the PSOE five seats, the Coalición por Melilla (CpM), a new Muslim grouping, four seats and the right-wing Unión del Pueblo Melillense (UPM) two seats. Ignacio Velázquez (PP/PNM) was returned to the position of Mayor/President.

At the general election held in March 1996, the PSOE lost its seat in the lower house to the PP, which also took both seats in the Senado. In the same month thousands of Muslims took part in a demonstration, organized by the CpM, to protest against their position on the margins of society.

In March 1997 a motion of censure against Velázquez resulted in the Mayor/President's defeat. The opposition then declared Enrique Palacios, who had earlier defected from the PP, to be Mayor/President, although the central Government continued to recognize Velázquez as the rightful incumbent. In May, for the first time, the Mayor/Presidents of both Ceuta and Melilla attended a conference of the autonomous regions' presidents, held in Madrid. Despite the attempted 'coup' in Melilla, the territory was represented by Velázquez. In November another defector from the PP, Abdelmalik Tahar, accused Velázquez and five associates of having subjected him to blackmail and threats, as a result of which he had relinquished his seat on the Council, thereby permitting the PP to replace him and to regain its majority. In December Tahar, who was now under police protection, declared to the investigating judge that he had been offered 50m. pesetas (of which he had received 3m.) and a monthly sum of 200,000 pesetas. Following a judicial ruling leading to the successful revival of the motion of censure against Velázquez in February 1998, Palacios took office as Mayor/President of Melilla, accusing his predecessor of serious financial mismanagement. A new motion of censure, presented by the PP, urging that (despite the bribery charges against him) Velázquez be restored to office, was deemed to be illegal and therefore rejected in a decree issued by Palacios, who also ordered the temporary closure of the assembly. In July Palacios accused the PP of having employed public funds, amounting to more than 200m. pesetas, to secure the votes of some 2,500 Muslims at the 1995 local elections. The allegations were denied by the PP.

During 1997 there was increased concern regarding the numbers of illegal immigrants. In June police reinforcements were drafted into Melilla, following renewed disturbances in which one immigrant died. More than 100 illegal immigrants were immediately returned to Morocco as part of a special security operation, and on the same day a total of 873 Moroccans were denied entry to Melilla. (More than 10,000 Moroccans continued to cross the border each day, to work in the enclave.) In August the Spanish General Prosecutor demanded emergency measures to address the immigration crisis, having urged the Ministry of the Interior in June to find an immediate solution. In the same month various non-governmental organizations condemned the rudimentary conditions in which more than 900 illegal immigrants, mainly from sub-Saharan Africa and Algeria, were being held in Melilla. In December the Spanish Government announced that 1,206 sub-Saharan Africans were to be transferred from Ceuta and Melilla to the mainland.

At the June 1999 local elections the Grupo Independiente Liberal (GIL), recently founded by Jesús Gil, the controversial Mayor of Marbella, secured seven of the 25 seats in the assembly of Melilla. In

July the two newly elected PSOE councillors defied a central directive to vote with the five PP delegates (in order to obstruct the accession of the GIL to the city presidency), and instead gave their support to Mustafa Aberchán Hamed of the CpM, which had won five seats. Aberchán was thus elected to replace Palacios as Mayor/President of Melilla. In mid-July Aberchán and the GIL agreed to form a minority Government. The two rebel PSOE councillors subsequently relinquished their seats. In October, following a disagreement between the CpM and the GIL, Aberchán reached a broad agreement with members of the PP and UPM, enabling him to remain in office. In November the Melilla branch of the GIL announced that henceforth it was to operate independently of the mainland party, and concluded a new agreement with Aberchán to renew its participation in the Melilla Government. As a result, the socialist councillors withdrew from the administration.

In December 1999 Aberchán announced the composition of a new coalition Government, the post of First Vice-President being allocated to Crispín Lozano, the local leader of the GIL, while Palacios of the newly founded Partido Independiente de Melilla (PIM) became Second Vice-President. In the same month Ignacio Velázquez, the former PP Mayor/President, was barred from public office for six years, having been found guilty of neglecting his duty during his tenure of office. The conviction was in respect of an incident in 1992 when Velázquez had convened a session of the Council, which was scheduled to vote on a motion of censure against him, in full knowledge of the fact that at least one member was due to be in Madrid that day, thus rendering any vote invalid. However, he was acquitted of charges of misappropriation of public funds. In May 2000, following the defection to the opposition of two GIL deputies and one UPM representative, Aberchán declared that, despite the Government's loss of its majority, he would not resign. Later in the month the national leadership of the PP and the PSOE met in Madrid in an attempt to negotiate a solution to the political crisis in Melilla. The two parties agreed that, if Aberchán's Government was removed from office, they would form a coalition government in partnership with the UPM, whose leader, Juan José Imbroda Ortiz, would be nominated Mayor/President. In July the remaining five GIL members left the Government and joined the opposition. The opposition subsequently introduced a motion of censure against Aberchán, who subsequently announced that the CpM was to withdraw from the legislature. In mid-July some 2,000 Muslim citizens of Melilla demonstrated in support of Aberchán. At the same time Palacios suspended the motion of censure by decree, reportedly without having consulted Aberchán. (Palacios was subsequently barred from public office for seven years, having been found guilty of perversion of the course of justice.) The opposition later successfully overturned the decree in the courts, and the vote on the motion of censure against Aberchán was therefore able to proceed. The motion was adopted in September, with the support of 16 of the 25 deputies, and Imbroda was elected as Mayor/President. In late 2000 four members of the GIL announced their departure from the party. In January 2002 Velázquez resigned as Councillor of the Presidency, after the Supreme Court upheld his 1999 conviction.

At the regional elections held in May 2003, a coalition of the PP and the UPM won 15 seats, with the CpM taking seven. The incumbent Mayor/President, Imbroda, remained in power. At the general election held on 14 March 2004, meanwhile, the PP retained Melilla's seats in the Congreso de los Diputados and the Senado. In September Imbroda met the recently elected Spanish Prime Minister, José Luis Rodríguez Zapatero, to discuss the possibility that Melilla would become a Comunidad Autónoma (Autonomous Community), a move that would give legislative powers to the government of the territory. The plan was, however, abandoned in February 2007, owing to disagreement over the content of the proposed statute of autonomy; instead, the Spanish Government agreed to devolve more powers to Ceuta and Melilla in the areas of education and social services.

In May 2004, meanwhile, the Government of Melilla announced plans to improve security along the border with Morocco. In August, however, in the first mass entry for three years, some 450 people attempted to enter Melilla illegally by climbing the security fence; as many as 40 people were believed to have succeeded in entering the territory. During August–October 2005 increasing numbers of would-be migrants attempted to scale the security barriers separating Melilla from Morocco. It was subsequently announced that one barrier would be doubled in height (to 6 m), and that border security would be increased. Meanwhile, the Spanish Government announced funding of €17m. for security in Melilla.

At the local election held in May 2007, the PP (which had by then absorbed its coalition partner, the UPM) obtained 15 seats in the Assembly, the same number as previously, thereby retaining its overall majority; the CpM and the PSOE each won five seats. The inauguration of the Assembly was delayed until early July owing to an appeal against the election result by the CpM, which alleged that the PP had engaged in acts of electoral fraud. The appeal was rejected by the Supreme Court of Justice of Andalusia, which ruled that the evidence presented by the CpM was not sufficient. Imbroda was subsequently re-elected as Mayor/President. A two-day visit to Melilla and Ceuta by King Juan Carlos and Queen Sofía in early November was strongly condemned by the Moroccan authorities; several thousand Moroccans, including politicians and trade union representatives, took part in a demonstration at the border with Melilla to protest against the King's presence.

At the March 2008 general election the PP retained Melilla's one seat in the Congreso de los Diputados, although only by a narrow margin, as well as its two seats in the Senado. At the regional PP congress held in late October Imbroda was appointed to succeed Arturo Esteban Albert as local President of the PP.

Two suspected Islamist militants were detained in Melilla at the beginning of April 2008, in accordance with international arrest warrants issued by the Moroccan Government in connection with their alleged involvement in terrorist activities, including a series of suicide bombings against Western targets in Casablanca in May 2003, in which 45 people died.

Attempts by illegal migrants to cross the border between Melilla and Morocco increased in October 2008, after heavy flooding damaged the recently fortified fence separating the two territories. Although additional security forces were deployed to patrol the damaged areas, it was reported that in one incident almost one-half of a group of some 60 sub-Saharan Africans succeeded in entering Melilla; 17 others were reportedly arrested. In the weeks that followed, further attempts were made to breach the fence: more than 150 people were reported to have tried to enter Melilla during November; and a number of people were injured in clashes with Moroccan and Spanish security forces (including several members of the security forces).

At the May 2011 local elections the PP won 15 seats, the same number as it had held in the previous two Assemblies. CpM took six seats, while the PSOE's representation declined to just two. The Partido Populares en Libertad (PPL), which had been established in March by former PP Mayor/President Ignacio Velázquez, also won two seats. A new Council of Government, under Imbroda, took office in mid-July. At the general election held in November, the PP retained both Melilla's seat in the Congreso de los Diputados and its two seats in the Senado. Abdelmalik el-Barkani Abdelkader was sworn in as Government Delegate to Melilla in January 2012, becoming the first Muslim to hold that post. In January 2013 the district court began an investigation into accusations that funds totalling €70,000 from the Council of Culture and Festivals intended for the production of a book discussing the history of Judaism in Melilla had been diverted to a Jewish religious school in the USA. The Councillor, Simi Chocrón Chocrón, denied any wrongdoing.

CONSTITUTION AND GOVERNMENT

See the chapter on Ceuta.

ECONOMIC AFFAIRS

In 2011, according to official estimates, the gross domestic product (GDP) of Melilla was equivalent to €18,069 per head, ranking 17th (in terms of GDP per head) in a list of the 19 Spanish autonomous regions. In 2011, according to official estimates, GDP totalled €1,356.4m. The population of Melilla increased by an annual average of 1.6% in 2002–12.

Agricultural activity in Melilla is negligible, as is employment in that sector; according to official estimates, the sector contributed just 0.1% of GDP in 2011. Employment in the sector was negligible in 2012.

Although industry is on a limited scale, the sector contributed 14.8% of GDP in 2011, while 10.4% of the employed population were engaged in the sector in 2012. Construction contributed 9.6% of GDP in 2011, and engaged 8.3% of the employed population in 2012.

Services contributed an estimated 85.1% of GDP in 2011. Some 89.6% of the employed population were engaged in the sector in 2012.

Most of the population's food is imported, with the exception of fish, which is obtained locally (sardines and anchovies are among the most significant catches). A large proportion of the tinned fish is sold outside Spain. Apart from the ferries from Málaga and Almería in mainland Spain, Melilla's port is not busy—a total of 1,357 vessels entered in 2011—and its exports are correspondingly low. Most trade is conducted with other parts of Spain. In 2012 Melilla recorded a trade deficit of almost €192m. In that year the principal source of imports (accounting for more than 27.4% of the total value) was the People's Republic of China; other major suppliers were the USA, Viet Nam, Canada, Thailand and India. Morocco was the principal market for exports, taking more than 68.8% of the total value. The principal imports in 2012 were fruits and vegetables (some 22.9% of the total value), coffee, tea, maté and spices, textiles and clothing, and cereals. The principal exports in the same year were man-made filaments and plastic, rubber and their articles. Tourism makes a significant contribution to the territory's economy. In 2012 visitor arrivals numbered 49,778 (incl. 36,697 from Spain). In 2011 there was a balanced budget, with revenue and expenditure both totalling €233.0m. The annual rate of inflation averaged 2.8% in 2002–12; the rate was 2.3% in 2012. On average, some 28.6% of the labour force were unemployed in 2012.

Upon the accession in January 1986 of Spain to the European Community (EC, now European Union—EU, see p. 281), Melilla was considered a Spanish city and European territory, and joined the organization as part of Spain. It retained its status as a free port. The statute of autonomy, adopted in early 1995, envisaged the continuation of the territory's fiscal benefits. Euro notes and coins became the sole legal tender on 28 February 2002.

In June 1994 the EU announced substantial regional aid: between 1995 and 1999 Melilla was to receive a total of ECU 45m., of which ECU 18m. was to be in the form of direct aid. However, successive enlargements of the EU and sustained Spanish economic growth during the 2000s limited Spain's access to EU aid, with the result that, although income in the enclave had not improved significantly, subsidies for Melilla were progressively reduced from 2007, with a view to their eventual withdrawal. The city's consolidated budget for 2012 included current and capital transfers from the Spanish state of €109.2m. and €11.6m., respectively. In May 2009 it was reported that the Spanish Government was considering increasing existing tax concessions to the aviation industry in some non-peninsular regions of Spain, including Melilla, as part of a new initiative to stimulate economic growth.

THE PEÑÓN DE VÉLEZ DE LA GOMERA, PEÑÓN DE ALHUCEMAS AND CHAFARINAS ISLANDS

These rocky islets, situated, respectively, just west and east of al-Hocima (Alhucemas) and east of Melilla off the north coast of Morocco, are administered with Melilla. The three Chafarinas Islands lie about 3.5 km off Ras el-Ma (Cabo de Agua). The Peñón de Alhucemas is situated about 300 m from the coast. The Peñón de Vélez de la Gomera is situated about 80 km further west, lying 85 m from the Moroccan shore, to which it is joined by a narrow strip of sand. A small military base is maintained on the Peñón de Vélez, while a military garrison of fewer than 100 men is stationed on the Peñón de Alhucemas, and a garrison of about 100 Spanish soldiers is maintained on the Isla del Congreso, the most westerly of the Chafarinas Islands. A supply ship calls at the various islands every two weeks. Prospective visitors must obtain the necessary military permit in Ceuta or Melilla.

Statistical Survey

Source (unless otherwise stated): Instituto Nacional de Estadística, Paseo de la Castellana 183, 28071 Madrid; tel. (91) 5839100; fax (91) 5839158; internet www.ine.es.

AREA AND POPULATION

Area: 12.5 sq km (4.8 sq miles).

Population (census results): 66,411 at 1 November 2001; 81,323 at 1 November 2011 (males 42,067, females 39,256).

Density (at 2011 census): 6,506 per sq km.

Population by Age and Sex (official estimates at 1 July 2012): *0–14:* 17,337 (males 8,856, females 8,481); *15–64:* 51,986 (males 26,906, females 25,080); *65 and over:* 8,516 (males 3,586, females 4,930); *Total* 77,839 (males 39,347, females 38,492). Note: Estimates not adjusted to take account of results of 2011 census.

Births, Marriages and Deaths (2011): Live births 1,401 (birth rate 18.7 per 1,000); Marriages 324 (marriage rate 4.3 per 1,000); Deaths 475 (death rate 6.3 per 1,000).

Life Expectancy (years at birth, 2011): 80.4 (males 77.4; females 83.6).

Immigration and Emigration (excl. Spanish territory, 2011): Immigrants 1,270; Emigrants 784.

Economically Active Population ('000 persons aged 16 years and over, 2012): Mining and utilities 0.3; Manufacturing 0.2; Construction 1.9; Trade, transport and accommodation 5.6; Information and communication 0.1; Finance, insurance, real estate and business services 2.7; Public administration, defence, education, health and social services 10.2; Other services 2.0; *Total employed* 23.0; *Unemployed* 9.2; *Total labour force* 32.2 (males 19.3, females 12.9).

FINANCE

Currency and Exchange Rates: 100 cent = 1 euro (€). *Sterling and Dollar Equivalents* (31 December 2012): £1 sterling = 1.196 euros; US $1 = 0.758 euros; 10 euros = £8.36 = $13.19. *Average*

Exchange Rate (euros per US $): 0.7550 in 2010; 0.7194 in 2011; 0.7779 in 2012. Note: The local currency was formerly the Spanish peseta. From the introduction of the euro, with Spanish participation, on 1 January 1999, a fixed exchange rate of €1 = 166.386 pesetas was in effect. Euro notes and coins were introduced on 1 January 2002. The euro and local currency circulated alongside each other until 28 February, after which the euro became the sole legal tender.

Budget (€ '000, 2011): *Revenue:* Current operations 193,459.2 (Direct taxation 10,942.5, Indirect taxation 70,046.0, Rates and other revenue 13,870.6, Current transfers 98,350.1, Property income 250.0); Capital operations 39,514.0 (Capital transfers 15,147.5, Transfers of real investments 1,000.0, Assets 459.7, Liabilities 22,906.8); Total 232,973.2. *Expenditure:* Current operations 192,969.2 (Wages and salaries 67,705.3, Goods and services 91,023.3, Financial 3,081.0, Current transfers 31,159.5); Capital operations 40,004.0 (Real investments 23,618.1, Capital transfers 2,780.0, Assets 459.7, Liabilities 13,146.2); Total 232,973.2.

Cost of Living (Consumer Price Index, annual averages; base: 2006 = 100): All items 106.8 in 2009; 109.1 in 2010; 111.6 in 2011. *2012* (base: 2011 = 100): All items 101.7.

Gross Domestic Product (€ million at current prices, estimates): 1,348.4 in 2009; 1,360.0 in 2010; 1,356.4 in 2011.

Gross Domestic Product by Economic Activity (€ million at current prices, 2011, estimates): Agriculture and fishing 1.4; Manufacturing 19.6; Mining and energy 45.6; Construction 119.1; Services 1,059.7; *Sub-total* 1,245.4; Net taxes on products 111.0; *GDP at market prices* 1,356.4.

EXTERNAL TRADE

Principal Commodities (€ million, 2012): *Imports:* Fruits and vegetables 44.2; Coffee, tea, maté and spices 27.2; Cereals 15.0; Textile materials and clothing 21.1; Footwear 3.7; Vehicles (excl. rail or tram), and parts thereof 3.9; Total (incl. others) 193.3. *Exports:* Man-made filaments 0.4; Plastic, rubber and their articles 0.4; Total (incl. others) 1.6.

Principal Trading Partners (€ million, 2012): *Imports:* Brazil 6.3; Canada 15.8; China, People's Republic 52.9; France 2.2; Germany 8.7; India 12.4; Indonesia 2.2; Iran 2.6; Morocco 2.0; Netherlands 8.7; Thailand 13.8; USA 33.4; Viet Nam 17.0; Total (incl. others) 193.3. *Exports:* Morocco 1.1; Total (incl. others) 1.6.

Source: Foreign Trade Database, Agencia Tributaria (Madrid).

TRANSPORT

Road Traffic (Ceuta and Melilla, 2009): Vehicles registered 5,085 (Passenger cars 3,435, Buses, etc. 7, Lorries and vans 737, Motorcycles 894, Tractors 2, Other 10).

Shipping (domestic and international, 2011): Vessels entered 1,357; Goods handled ('000 metric tons) 864; Passenger movements ('000) 642.

Civil Aviation (2011, provisional): Flights 8,648; Passengers transported ('000) 281; Goods transported 266 metric tons.

TOURISM

Visitor Arrivals (by country of residence, 2002): France 476; Germany 432; Italy 331; Netherlands 425; Spain 23,648; Total (incl. others) 31,812. *2012:* Total 49,778 (Spain 36,697).

EDUCATION

Pre-primary (2005/06): 20 schools; 159 teachers, 3,237 students. *2011/12:* 4,283 students.

Primary (2005/06): 15 schools; 422 teachers (excl. 20 engaged in both pre-primary and primary teaching); 5,996 students. *2011/12:* 6,636 students.

Secondary: First Cycle (2005/06): 9 schools (of which 4 schools also provided second-cycle education and 5 provided vocational education); 255 teachers (excl. 10 engaged in both primary and secondary teaching, and 198 engaged in more than one secondary cycle, and excl. 33 specialists); 3,923 students. *2011/12:* 4,372 students.

Secondary: Second Cycle (2005/06): 53 teachers; 1,339 students. *2011/12:* 1,616 students.

Secondary: Vocational (2005/06): 65 teachers; 703 students. *2011/12:* 1,330 students.

Source: Ministry of Education, Madrid.

Directory

Government

HEAD OF STATE

King of Spain: HM King JUAN CARLOS I (succeeded to the throne 22 November 1975).

Government Delegate in Melilla: ABDELMALIK EL-BARKANI ABDELKADER.

MEMBERS OF THE SPANISH PARLIAMENT

Deputy elected to the Congress in Madrid: ANTONIO GUTIÉRREZ MOLINA (PP).

Representatives to the Senate in Madrid: MARÍA DEL CARMEN DUEÑAS MARTÍNEZ (PP), JUAN JOSÉ IMBRODA ORTIZ (PP).

COUNCIL OF GOVERNMENT
(May 2013)

The executive is formed by members of the Partido Popular (PP).

Mayor/President of Melilla: JUAN JOSÉ IMBRODA ORTIZ.

First Vice-President and Councillor of Development, Youth and Sports: MIGUEL MARÍN COBOS.

Second Vice-President and Councillor of Economy and Finance: DANIEL CONESA MÍNGUEZ.

Councillor of Public Administration: CATALINA MURIEL GARCÍA.

Councillor of Social Welfare and Health: MARÍA ANTONIA GARBÍN ESPIGARES.

Councillor of Culture and Festivals: SIMI CHOCRÓN CHOCRÓN.

Councillor of Education and Social Groups: ANTONIO MIRANDA MONTILLA.

Councillor of the Environment: JOSÉ ÁNGEL PÉREZ CALABUIG.

Councillor of Presidency and Citizenship: ESTHER DONOSO GARCÍA-SACRISTÁN.

Councillor of Civic Security: FRANCISCO JAVIER CALDERÓN CARRILLO.

Deputy Councillor to the President: FRANCISCO JAVIER GONZÁLEZ GARCÍA.

GOVERNMENT OFFICES

Delegación del Gobierno: Avda de la Marina Española 3, 52001 Melilla; tel. (95) 2675840; fax (95) 2672657; e-mail puri@melilla.map.es.

Office of the Mayor/President: Palacio de la Asamblea, Plaza de España, 52001 Melilla; tel. (95) 2699100; fax (95) 2679230; e-mail presidencia@melilla.es; internet www.melilla.es.

Council of Civic Security: Jefatura Policía Local, General Astilleros 25, Melilla; tel. (95) 2698111; fax (95) 2698121; e-mail policialocal@melilla.es.

Council of Culture and Festivals: Palacio de la Asamblea, Plaza de España, 52001 Melilla; tel. (95) 2699193; fax (95) 2699158; e-mail consejeriacultura@melilla.es.

Council of Development, Youth and Sports: Antiguo Edif. Mantelete, Duque de Ahumada s/n, 52071 Melilla; tel. (95) 2699223; fax (95) 2699224; e-mail consejeriafomento@melilla.es.

Council of the Economy and Finance: Justo Sancho Miñano 2, 52801 Melilla; tel. (95) 2676241; fax (95) 2676242; e-mail consejeriaeconomia@melilla.es.

Council of Education and Social Groups: Querol 7, 52001 Melilla; tel. (95) 2699214; fax (95) 2699279; e-mail educacion@melilla.es.

Council of the Environment: Palacio de la Asamblea, Plaza de España, 52001 Melilla; tel. (95) 2699134; fax (95) 2699161; e-mail consejeriamedioambiente@melilla.es.

Council of the Presidency and Citizenship: Palacio de la Asamblea, Plaza de España, 52001 Melilla; tel. (95) 2699207; fax (95) 2699137; e-mail consejeriapresidencia@melilla.es.

Council of Public Administration: Palacio de la Asamblea, Plaza de España, 52001 Melilla; tel. (95) 2699102; fax (95) 2699103; e-mail cap@melilla.es.

Council of Social Welfare and Health: Carlos Ramírez de Arellano 10, Melilla; tel. (95) 2699301; fax (95) 2699302; e-mail consejeriabienstarsocial@melilla.es.

Assembly

Election, 22 May 2011

	Seats
Partido Popular (PP)	15
Coalición por Melilla (CpM)	6
Partido Socialista Obrero Español (PSOE)	2
Partido Populares en Libertad (PPL)	2
Total	**25**

Election Commission

Junta Electoral de Zona y Provincial de Melilla: Melilla; Sec. RUPERTO MANUEL GARCÍA HERNÁNDEZ.

Political Organizations

Coalición por Melilla (CpM): Ejército Español 21, 1° dcha, 52001 Melilla; tel. (95) 2969188; fax (95) 2699247; internet www.coalicionpormelilla.com; f. 1995 by merger of Partido del Trabajo y Progreso de Melilla and Partido Hispano Bereber; majority of members are from the Muslim community; mem. of left-wing Izquierda Unida coalition; Pres. MUSTAFA HAMED MO ABERCHÁN; Sec.-Gen. HASSAN MOHATAR.

Partido Popular (PP): Roberto Cano 2, 1° izqda, POB 384, 52001 Melilla; tel. (95) 2681095; fax (95) 2684477; e-mail melilla@pp.es; internet www.ppmelilla.es; national-level, centre-right party; absorbed the Unión del Pueblo Melillense in 2007; Pres. JUAN JOSÉ IMBRODA ORTIZ; Sec.-Gen. MARÍA DEL CARMEN DUEÑAS MARTÍNEZ.

Partido Populares en Libertad (PPL): Calle Carlos V, 21, Local 1, 52006 Melilla; tel. (95) 2694007; fax (95) 2694627; e-mail popularesenlibertad@gmail.com; internet www.popularesenlibertad.es; f. 2011; centrist, liberal party formed to contest elections of May 2011; Pres. IGNACIO VELÁZQUEZ RIVERA; Sec.-Gen. ALBERTO WEIL GONZÁLEZ.

Partido Socialista de Melilla-Partido Socialista Obrero Español (PSME-PSOE): Doctor García Martínez 3, 52006 Melilla; tel. (95) 2677807; fax (95) 2679857; e-mail infopsoe@psoe.es; internet www.psoe.es; national-level, left-wing party; Pres. ANDRÉS VISIEDO SEGURA; Sec.-Gen. DIONISIO MUÑOZ PÉREZ.

There are also various civic associations in Melilla.

Religion

As in Ceuta, most Europeans are Roman Catholics. The registered Muslim community numbered 20,800 in 1990. The Jewish community numbered 1,300. There is also a Hindu community.

ISLAM

Comisión Islámica de Melilla (CIM): García Cabrelles 13, Melilla; Sec.-Gen. DRIS MUHAMMAD.

CHRISTIANITY

The Roman Catholic Church

Melilla is part of the Spanish diocese of Málaga.

The Press

El Faro de Melilla: Castelar 5, 1°, Melilla; tel. (95) 2690029; fax (95) 2683992; e-mail melilla@grupofaro.es; internet www.elfaroceutamelilla.es; Pres. RAFAEL MONTERO PALACIOS; Editor-in-Chief ANGELA M. PERAZZI.

Melilla Hoy: Polígono Industrial SEPES, La Espiga, Naves A-1/A-2, 52006 Melilla; tel. (95) 2690000; fax (95) 2675725; e-mail redaccion@melillahoy.es; internet www.melillahoy.es; f. 1985; Pres. ENRIQUE BOHÓRQUEZ LÓPEZ-DÓRIGA; Editor-in-Chief MUSTAFA HAMED; circ. 2,000.

Sur: Músico Granados 2, 52001 Melilla; tel. (95) 2691283; fax (95) 2673674; e-mail surmelilla@rusadirmedia.com; internet www.diariosur.es; local edn of Málaga daily; Perm. Rep. AVELINO GUTIÉRREZ PÉREZ.

El Telegrama de Melilla: Polígono La Espiga, Nave A-8, 52006 Melilla; tel. (95) 2691443; fax (95) 2691469; e-mail telegramademelilla@yahoo.es; internet www.eltelegrama.com; Dir JUAN CARLOS HEREDIA.

NEWS AGENCY

Agencia EFE: Teniente Aguilar de Mera 1, Edificio Monumental, 1º, Local 9, 52001 Melilla; tel. (95) 2685235; fax (95) 2680043; e-mail melilla@efe.es; Correspondent NOELIA RAMOS.

PRESS ASSOCIATION

Asociación de la Prensa: Apdo de Correos 574, 29880 Melilla; e-mail correo@apmelilla.com; Pres. FRANCISCO JAVIER CALDERÓN GALLARDO.

Broadcasting

RADIO

Cadena Dial Melilla: Muelle Ribera 18B, 52005 Melilla; tel. (95) 2682328; fax (95) 2681573; e-mail radiomelilla@unionradio.es; internet www.cadenadial.com; Rep. ROCÍO GONZÁLEZ JUSTO.

Onda Cero Radio Melilla: Músico Granados 2, 52004 Melilla; tel. (95) 2691283; e-mail ondaceromelilla@ondaceromelilla.net; internet www.ondaceromelilla.net; Dir JOSÉ JESÚS NAVAJAS TROBAT.

Radio Melilla: Muelle Ribera s/n, 52005 Melilla; tel. (95) 2681708; fax (95) 2681573; e-mail radiomelilla@unionradio.es; internet www.cadenaser.com; owned by Sociedad Española de Radiodifusión; commercial; Dir ANTONIA RAMOS PELÁEZ.

Radio Nacional de España (RNE): Duque de Ahumada 5, 52001 Melilla; tel. (95) 2681907; fax (95) 2683108; internet www.rtve.es; state-controlled; Rep. MONTSERRAT COBOS RUANO.

TELEVISION

A fibre optic cable linking Melilla with Almería was laid in 1990. From March 1991 Melilla residents were able to receive three private TV channels from mainland Spain: Antena 3, Canal+ and Tele 5.

Antena 3: Edif. Melilla, Urbanización Rusadir, 29805 Melilla; tel. (95) 2688840; internet www.antena3.com.

Finance

BANKING

There were seven banks operating in Melilla in 2007, all of which were based in mainland Spain.

Banco Bilbao Vizcaya Argentaria (BBVA): Teniente Aguilar De Mera 3 52001 Melilla; tel. (952) 686076; fax (952) 685249; internet www.bbva.es; 5 brs.

Banco de España: Plaza de España 3, 52001 Melilla; tel. (95) 2683940; fax (95) 2683942; internet www.bde.es.

Banco Español de Crédito (Banesto): Avda Juan Carlos I 12, 52001 Melilla; tel. (95) 2684348; fax (95) 2683645; internet www.banesto.es; 2 brs.

Banco Popular Español: Avda Juan Carlos I 14, 52001 Melilla; tel. (95) 2684847; fax (95) 2676844; internet www.bancopopular.es.

Banco Santander Central Hispano (BSCH): Ejército Español 1, 52001 Melilla; tel. (95) 2681422; internet www.gruposantander.es; 3 brs.

Caja de Ahorros y Pensiones de Barcelona (La Caixa): Avda Juan Carlos I 28, 52001 Melilla; tel. (95) 2685760; fax (95) 2960276; internet www.lacaixa.es; 2 brs.

Montes de Piedad y Caja de Ahorros de Ronda, Cádiz, Almería, Málaga y Antequera (Unicaja): Ejército Español 9, 52001 Melilla; tel. (952) 682595; fax (952) 683684; internet www.unicaja.es; 4 brs.

INSURANCE

MAPFRE: Avda Democracia 9, 52004 Melilla; tel. (95) 2673189; fax (95) 2674977; e-mail maberna@mapfre.com; internet www.mapfre.com; Commercial Man. BERNABE ESCOZ; 2 offices.

Trade and Industry

Cámara Oficial de Comercio, Industria y Navegación: Cervantes 7, 52001 Melilla; tel. (95) 2684840; fax (95) 2683119; e-mail info@camaramelilla.es; internet www.camaramelilla.es; f. 1906; chamber of commerce; Pres. MARGARITA LÓPEZ ALMENDÁRIZ; Vice-Pres. HAMED MAANAN BENAISA BOUJI.

Confederación de Empresarios de Melilla (CEME-CEOE): Plaza 1 de Mayo, bajo dcha, 52003 Melilla; tel. (95) 2673696; fax (95) 2676175; e-mail ceme@cemelilla.org; internet www.cemelilla.org; f. 1979; employers' confed; Pres. MARGARITA LÓPEZ ALMENDÁRIZ; Sec.-Gen. JERÓNIMO PÉREZ HERNÁNDEZ.

UTILITIES

The Spanish electricity company Endesa operates an oil-fired power station in Melilla. In 2007 a new 12.6-MW generator was installed, increasing capacity by 22%.

TRADE UNION

Confederación Sindical de Comisiones Obreras (CCOO): Calle Primero de Mayo, 1º, 52001 Melilla; tel. (95) 2676535; fax (95) 2672571; e-mail orga.melilla@melilla.ccoo.es; internet www.melilla.ccoo.es; Sec.-Gen. CARIDAD NAVARRO RINCÓN.

Transport

There is a daily ferry service to Málaga and a service to Almería. Melilla airport, situated 4 km from the town, is served by daily flights to various destinations on the Spanish mainland, operated by Iberia Regional/Air Nostrum. There were 26 km of paved roads in Melilla in 2010. The Port of Melilla handled 864,282 metric tons of goods and 642,017 passengers in 2011; 1,357 ships passed through the port in that year.

Port of Melilla: Autoridad Portuaria de Melilla, Avda de la Marina Española 4, 52001 Melilla; tel. (95) 2673600; fax (95) 2674838; e-mail informatica@puertodemelilla.es; internet www.puertomelilla.es; Pres. ARTURO ESTEBAN; Dir JOSÉ LUIS ALMAZÁN.

Acciona Trasmediterránea: Avda General Marina 1, 52001 Melilla; tel. (95) 2681635; fax (95) 2682685; e-mail correom@trasmediterranea.es; internet www.trasmediterranea.es; operates ferry service between Melilla and Almería and Málaga, in mainland Spain.

Tourism

There is much of historic interest to the visitor, while Melilla is also celebrated for its modernist architecture. Several new hotels, including a luxury development, were constructed in the 1990s. In 2012 tourist arrivals numbered 49,778 (including 36,697 visitors from mainland Spain).

Oficina Provincial de Turismo: Pintor Fortuny 21, 52004 Melilla; tel. (95) 2976151; fax (95) 2976153; e-mail info@melillaturismo.com; internet www.melillaturismo.com.

Defence

(See Ceuta.) More than one-half of Melilla's land area is used solely for military purposes.

Commandant-General: Gen. ÁLVARO DE LA PEÑA CUESTA.

Education

In addition to the conventional Spanish facilities, the Moroccan Government finances a school for Muslim children in Melilla, the languages of instruction being Arabic and Spanish. Total enrolment at the primary level in Melilla was recorded at 6,636 in 2011/12, while secondary schools had an enrolment of 4,372 for the first cycle of secondary education (between the ages of 12 and 16); 1,616 students were enrolled for the *bachillerato* and 1,330 students enrolled on vocational courses. The Spanish open university (Universidad Nacional de Educación a Distancia—UNED) maintains a branch in Melilla.

SRI LANKA

Introductory Survey

LOCATION, CLIMATE, LANGUAGE, RELIGION, FLAG, CAPITAL

The Democratic Socialist Republic of Sri Lanka lies in southern Asia. It comprises one large island and several much smaller ones, situated in the Indian Ocean, about 80 km (50 miles) east of the southern tip of India. The climate is tropical, with an annual average temperature of about 27°C (81°F) in Colombo. There is very little seasonal variation in temperature: the monthly average in Colombo ranges from 25°C (77°F) to 28°C (82°F). The south-western part of the island receives rain from both the south-west and the north-east monsoons: average annual rainfall in Colombo is 2,365 mm (93 ins). Sinhala and Tamil are the two official languages, the former being spoken by more than 70% of the population. Tamil was made a recognized national language in 1978 and became the country's second official language in 1988. According to the 2001 census, in 18 out of 25 districts 76.7% of the population were Buddhist, 8.5% were Muslim, 7.9% were Hindu and 6.1% were Roman Catholic. The census results did not cover the Tamil-dominated (and therefore mainly Hindu) northern and eastern districts. The national flag (proportions 1 by 2) consists mainly of a dark crimson rectangular panel, with a yellow border, in the fly. In the centre of the panel is a gold lion, carrying a sword, while in each corner (also in gold) there is a leaf of the bo (bodhi) tree, which is sacred to Buddhists. At the hoist are two vertical stripes, also edged in yellow, to represent Sri Lanka's minorities: one of green (for Muslims) and one of orange (for Tamils). The commercial capital is Colombo. In 1982 the ancient capital of Sri Jayawardenepura (Kotte) became the administrative capital.

CONTEMPORARY POLITICAL HISTORY

Historical Context

Sri Lanka, known as Ceylon until 1972, gained its independence from the United Kingdom in February 1948. From then until 1956 the country was ruled by the United National Party (UNP), which was concerned to protect the rights of the Tamils, Hindu members of an ethnic minority (closely linked with the inhabitants of the southern Indian state of Tamil Nadu), who are concentrated in the north (and, to a lesser extent, in the east) of the main island. The socialist Sri Lanka Freedom Party (SLFP), formed in 1951 by Solomon Bandaranaike, emphasized the national heritage, winning the support of groups that advocated the recognition of Sinhala as the official language and the establishment of Buddhism as the predominant religion. The SLFP won the 1956 elections decisively and remained in power, except for a three-month interruption in 1960, until 1965, having formed a coalition Government with the Lanka Sama Samaja Party (LSSP), a Trotskyist group, in 1964. Following the assassination of Solomon Bandaranaike in 1959, his widow, Sirimavo Bandaranaike, assumed the leadership of the SLFP. At the 1970 elections the SLFP became the leading partner of a United Front coalition Government with the LSSP and the Communist Party of Sri Lanka (CPSL). In 1971 the United Front Government suppressed an uprising led by the left-wing Janatha Vimukthi Peramuna (JVP—People's Liberation Front). A state of emergency was declared, and the party was banned.

Domestic Political Affairs

In 1976 the main Tamil party, the Federal Party, and other Tamil groups formed the Tamil United Liberation Front (TULF), demanding a separate Tamil state ('Eelam') in the northern and eastern parts of the country. In December of that year the communists supported strikes in the transport sector, which were initiated by the UNP and the LSSP (the latter had been expelled from the governing coalition in 1975). The strikes ended in January 1977, and in February Sirimavo Bandaranaike prorogued the National State Assembly until May. Several members of the SLFP resigned, and seven members of the CPSL left the coalition Government, forming an independent group within the opposition. In February the state of emergency, which had been imposed in 1971, was lifted and the JVP was legalized again.

Sri Lanka under Junius Richard Jayewardene (1977–88)

A general election was held in July 1977, accompanied by widespread violence. The UNP won the election, with an overwhelming majority, and the party's leader, Junius Richard Jayewardene, became Prime Minister. In August riots broke out between the Sinhalese majority and the Tamil minority. The TULF, which had become the main opposition party, increased its demands for an independent Tamil state. A constitutional amendment approved in October provided for the establishment of a presidential system of government, and in February 1978 Jayewardene became the country's first executive President.

Continued violence and pressure from the Tamils during 1978 led the Government to make some concessions, such as the recognition of the Tamil language (not as an official language, but under the new status of 'national language'), in the new Constitution of the Democratic Socialist Republic of Sri Lanka, which came into force in September. In view of this, the Ceylon Workers' Congress (CWC) joined the Government, but the TULF remained undecided, mainly for fear of reprisals by Tamil extremists. Further violence prompted the declaration of a state of emergency in July 1979 in the northern district of Jaffna, where the Tamils were in a majority. At the same time, stringent anti-terrorist legislation was passed in Parliament (as the National State Assembly had been renamed in 1978), and a presidential commission was established to study the Tamil issue.

In August 1980 the TULF agreed to the establishment of district development councils, providing for a wide measure of regional autonomy. Elections to these, held in June 1981, were boycotted by the SLFP, the LSSP and the CPSL, and the UNP won control of 18 of the 24 councils. Subsequent communal disturbances between Sinhalese and Tamils led to the imposition of a state of emergency in the north for five days in June, and throughout the country from August 1981 to January 1982. Tamil legislators proposed a motion of no confidence in the Government and subsequently boycotted Parliament until November 1981, when a peace initiative to ease ethnic tension was proposed by the Government.

Meanwhile, in October 1980 former Prime Minister Sirimavo Bandaranaike was found guilty of having abused her position by a special presidential commission, which deprived her of all civic rights and effectively prevented her from standing in the next elections.

In August 1982 Parliament approved an amendment to the 1978 Constitution that enabled President Jayewardene to call a presidential election before his term of office expired, i.e. after four years instead of six. Sri Lanka's first presidential election was held in October 1982, and Jayewardene was returned to office with 53% of the votes cast.

Following this success, the President announced, with the approval of Parliament and the Supreme Court, that, instead of a general election, a referendum would be held to decide whether to prolong the life of Parliament for a further six years after the session ended in July 1983. A state of emergency was in force between October 1982 and January 1983, and all opposition newspapers were closed by the Government. Sirimavo Bandaranaike was allowed to campaign in the referendum, which took place in December 1982. On a 71% turn-out, the proposal to prolong Parliament until 1989 was approved by some 55% (3.1m.), with the dissenting minority of 2.6m. being concentrated mainly in and around Jaffna.

A state of emergency was declared in May 1983 to combat mounting terrorism, and in June Tamil militant activity led to army reprisals and the worst outbreak of violence for many years, with more than 400 deaths and particularly severe rioting in Jaffna and Colombo. A curfew and press censorship were imposed, and three left-wing parties (including the JVP) were banned. In July the 16 TULF legislators resigned in protest at the extension of Parliament, as approved by the referendum. In August Parliament passed a 'no-separation' amendment to the Constitution, depriving those espousing Tamil separatism of their civic rights. An All-Party Conference (APC), which began in

January 1984 with the informal mediation of India and comprising representatives of the Buddhist, Christian and Muslim faiths as well as political leaders from the Sinhalese and Tamil communities, was abandoned in December, with the various parties having failed to reach agreement on the crucial question of the extent of regional autonomy.

An escalation in violence in the northern part of the island in November and December 1984 led to the proclamation of another state of emergency. There were widespread accusations of gross military indiscipline, along with condemnation of government-sponsored settlement of Sinhalese in Tamil areas in the eastern province. A restricted zone was established between Mannar and Mullaitivu, to prevent contact with the Indian state of Tamil Nadu, where many of the Tamil militants were reportedly based.

In February 1986 there was a resurgence of violence in the northern and eastern provinces. In May a series of explosions in Colombo was widely believed to have been carried out by Tamil extremists. The Government intensified its campaign against the insurgents by increasing defence expenditure and by launching an offensive against the militant Tamils in the Jaffna peninsula. This offensive made little headway, but the government cause was helped by internecine fighting between two of the principal Tamil militant groups, the Tamil Eelam Liberation Organization (TELO) and the Liberation Tigers of Tamil Eelam (LTTE—also known as the Tamil Tigers), the latter of which, over the year, emerged as the dominant Tamil separatist group under the leadership of Velupillai Prabhakaran. In May Tamil militants renewed their attacks on Sinhalese villagers who had been settled by the Government in Tamil-dominated areas in the eastern province.

In January 1987 all the powers previously vested in the Prime Minister, Ranasinghe Premadasa, as Minister of Emergency Civil Administration were transferred to a new Ministry of National Security, directly supervised by the President. In February the Government launched an offensive against the insurgents in the Batticaloa district of the eastern province. The situation worsened in April, when the LTTE, having rejected an offer of a cease-fire by the Sri Lankan Government, carried out a series of outrages against the civilian population, including a bomb explosion in Colombo's main bus station, which killed more than 100 people. In response, the Government attempted to regain control of the Jaffna peninsula, the stronghold of the LTTE. During the resultant struggle between the LTTE and government forces, India demonstrated its support for the Tamils by violating Sri Lankan airspace to drop food and medical supplies in Jaffna.

In July 1987 President Jayewardene and the Indian Prime Minister, Rajiv Gandhi, signed an accord that attempted to settle the country's ethnic crisis. The main points included: the provision of an Indian Peace-Keeping Force (IPKF) to oversee its proper implementation; a complete cessation of hostilities; and the surrender of all weapons held by the Tamil militants; the amalgamation of the northern and eastern provinces into one administrative unit, with an elected provincial council (together with the creation of provincial councils in the seven other provinces); the holding of a referendum in the eastern province to determine whether the mixed population of Tamils, Sinhalese and Muslims supported an official merger with the northern province into a single Tamil-dominated north-eastern province; a general amnesty for all Tamil militants; the repatriation of some 130,000 Tamil refugees from India to Sri Lanka; the prevention of the use of Indian territory by Tamil militants for military or propaganda purposes; and the provision that Tamil and English should have equal status with Sinhala as official languages. The accord encountered widespread disapproval among the Sinhalese population and from the SLFP, which claimed that it granted too much power to the Tamil minority.

In July and August 1987 more than 7,000 Indian troops were dispatched to Sri Lanka. However, implementation of the peace accord was impeded by bitter internecine fighting among the Tamil militias (involving the LTTE in particular), which necessitated direct intervention by the IPKF. By October the surrender of arms by the LTTE had virtually ceased; the group resumed its terrorist attacks on Sinhalese citizens, and declared itself to be firmly opposed to the peace accord. In response, the IPKF launched an offensive against the LTTE stronghold in the Jaffna peninsula, forcing LTTE militants to establish a new base in the Batticaloa district of the eastern province. In November 1987, despite strong opposition from the SLFP (which vehemently opposed the proposed merger of the northern and eastern prov-

inces), Parliament adopted the legislation establishing provincial councils.

Another major threat to the successful implementation of the peace accord was the re-emergence in 1987 of the outlawed JVP, which claimed that the accord conceded too much power to the Tamils. The JVP was widely believed to have been responsible for an assassination attempt on President Jayewardene in August, in which one legislator was killed and several cabinet ministers were seriously wounded, and to have murdered more than 200 UNP supporters by February 1988, including the Chairman of the UNP, Harsha Abeywardene, and the leader of the left-wing Sri Lanka Mahajana Pakshaya (SLMP—Sri Lanka People's Party), Vijaya Kumaratunga, who supported the accord.

Elections to seven of the new provincial councils were held in April and June 1988 (in defiance of the JVP's threats and violence); elections in the northern and eastern provinces were postponed indefinitely. The UNP won a majority and effective control in all seven, while the SLFP boycotted the elections, in protest at the continuing presence in Sri Lanka of the IPKF (which now numbered about 50,000). In September President Jayewardene officially authorized the merger of the northern and eastern provinces into a single north-eastern province, prior to provincial council elections there. In response, the JVP organized a series of strikes and violent demonstrations, and was widely believed to have been responsible for the subsequent murder of the Minister of Rehabilitation and Reconstruction. Despite boycotts and threats by both the JVP and the LTTE, elections to the new north-eastern provincial council took place in November, resulting in victory for the moderate and pro-accord Tamil groups, the Eelam People's Revolutionary Liberation Front (EPRLF) and the Eelam National Democratic Liberation Front (ENDLF), as well as the Sri Lanka Muslim Congress (SLMC); the UNP won only one seat. In early December Parliament unanimously approved a constitution amendment bill to make Tamil one of the country's two official languages (with Sinhala), thus fulfilling one of the major commitments envisaged in the peace accord. On 19 December the presidential election took place, in circumstances of unprecedented disruption, and was boycotted by the LTTE and the JVP. None the less, about 55% of the total electorate was estimated to have voted. Prime Minister Ranasinghe Premadasa (the UNP's candidate) won by a narrow margin, with 50.4% of the total votes, while SLFP leader Sirimavo Bandaranaike (whose civil rights had been restored in January 1986) received 44.9%.

The UNP retains power under President Ranasinghe Premadasa (1989–93)

In January 1989 Premadasa was sworn in as Sri Lanka's new President, and an interim Cabinet was appointed. In the same month the Government repealed the state of emergency, which had been in force since May 1983, and abolished the Ministry of National Security. Concurrently, however, special security measures were invoked in an attempt to curb the escalating violence. Shortly after his inauguration, Premadasa offered to confer with the extremists and invited all groups to take part in the electoral process. The JVP and the LTTE, however, intensified their campaigns of violence in protest at the forthcoming general election. Meanwhile, the moderate, pro-accord Tamil groups, the EPRLF, the ENDLF and the TELO, formed a loose election alliance, under the leadership of the TULF. In the election, which was held on 15 February and which was, again, marred by widespread violence, the UNP won 125 of the 225 contested seats. The new system of proportional representation, which was introduced at this election, was especially advantageous to the SLFP, which became the major opposition force in Parliament, with 67 seats. A few days later President Premadasa installed a new Cabinet, and in March he appointed the Minister of Finance, Dingiri Banda Wijetunga, as the country's new Prime Minister.

In May 1989 the Sri Lankan Government demanded a full withdrawal of Indian troops by the end of July. Rajiv Gandhi responded that a condition of the IPKF's withdrawal was the security of the Tamils and the devolution of real power to the elected local government in the north-eastern province. In protest against the IPKF's continued presence, the JVP organized a series of demonstrations and strikes, precipitating the reimposition of a state of emergency in June. In September the Governments of Sri Lanka and India agreed that the IPKF would declare an immediate unilateral cease-fire and India would make 'all efforts' to withdraw its remaining 45,000 troops from Sri Lanka by the end of the year; in turn, the Sri Lankan Government pledged immediately to establish a peace committee for the north-eastern province in an attempt to reconcile the various Tamil groups and to incorporate members of the LTTE into the peaceful administration of the province.

The JVP suffered a serious set-back in November 1989 when its leader, Rohana Wijeweera, and his principal deputy were shot dead by the security forces. By the end of January 1990 the Sri Lankan security forces had effectively destroyed the JVP as a political force, killing all but one member of its political bureau and most leaders at district level, and thus substantially transforming the country's political scene. It was estimated, however, that the number of civilians killed in the lengthy struggle between the JVP and the Government might have been as high as 25,000–50,000.

Following months of peace talks with the Government, the political wing of the LTTE was recognized as a political party by the commissioner of elections in December 1989. The LTTE leaders then proclaimed that the newly recognized party would take part in the democratic process (it demanded immediate fresh elections in the north-eastern province) under the name of the People's Front of the Liberation Tigers.

In early March 1990 the EPRLF-dominated north-eastern provincial council, under the leadership of Annamalai Varadharajah Perumal, renamed itself the 'National Assembly of the Free and Sovereign Democratic Republic of Eelam' and gave the central Government a one-year ultimatum to fulfil a charter of demands. Two weeks later, however, Perumal was reported to have fled to southern India. The last remaining IPKF troops left Sri Lanka on 24 March, after a postponement of the deadline. In the following month the Government eased emergency regulations (including the ban on political rallies) in an effort to restore a degree of normality to the country after years of violence. At the same time, Sri Lanka's security forces, encouraged by the relative lull in violence, halted all military operations against the now much-weakened JVP and the Tamil militant groups. A fragile peace was maintained until June, when the LTTE abandoned their negotiations with the Government and renewed hostilities with surprise attacks on military and police installations in the north and north-east. Consequently, the Sri Lankan security forces were compelled to launch a counter-offensive. In mid-June the Government dissolved the north-eastern provincial council (despite protests by the EPRLF), and the holding of fresh elections in the province was postponed indefinitely pending the LTTE's agreement to participate in them (as earlier promised). In August the LTTE intensified their campaign of violence in the eastern province against the Muslim population, which retaliated with counter-attacks. At the end of August the Government launched a major offensive against the Tamil strongholds in the Jaffna peninsula.

It was widely suspected that the LTTE were responsible for the assassination in March 1991 of the Minister of Plantation Industries and Minister of State for Defence, Ranjan Wijeratne (who had been in charge of both the government forces' successful campaign against the JVP, several years earlier, and the ongoing offensive against the LTTE), and for the bomb attack on a military building in Colombo in June. More significantly, for its regional implications, the LTTE were believed to have been responsible for the assassination of the former Indian Prime Minister, Rajiv Gandhi, near Madras (now Chennai), the state capital of Tamil Nadu, in May. In early 1992 the Indian Government proscribed the LTTE and banned their activities on Indian territory.

An impeachment motion filed against the President by the opposition, with the support of a number of UNP parliamentary members, was rejected in October 1992 by the Speaker of Parliament on the grounds that some of the signatures on the resolution, which listed 24 instances of alleged abuse of power, were invalid. Dissident UNP parliamentary members, including two former cabinet members, Lalith Athulathmudali and Gamini Dissanayake, formed the Democratic United National Front (DUNF) in December.

The security forces suffered a serious reversal in August 1992, when 10 senior officers, including the northern military commander and the Jaffna peninsula commander, were killed in a landmine explosion near Jaffna. Tension between the Muslim and Tamil populations in the north-eastern district of Polonnaruwa drastically increased following the massacre of more than 170 Muslim villagers by suspected LTTE guerrillas in October. In the next month the LTTE were also widely believed to have been responsible for the murder of the naval commander Vice-Admiral Clancy Fernando in Colombo.

The assassination of Premadasa and the assumption of power by Dingiri Banda Wijetunga (1993–94)

In April 1993 the DUNF accused Premadasa's Government of having been responsible for the assassination of the party's leader, Lalith Athulathmudali. Premadasa accused the LTTE of the murder, a charge the militant group denied. The country was thrown into greater political turmoil on 1 May, when President Premadasa was assassinated in a bomb explosion in Colombo. The LTTE were officially blamed for the murder, although, again, they strenuously denied any involvement. A few days later Parliament unanimously elected the incumbent Prime Minister, Dingiri Banda Wijetunga, to serve the remaining presidential term (expiring in December 1994), and the erstwhile Minister of Industries, Science and Technology, Ranil Wickremasinghe, was appointed to replace him in the premiership. In provincial elections held in May 1993 the UNP won control of four of the seven councils, with 47% of the votes—the first time since 1977 that its percentage of the ballot had fallen below 50%. No polling was carried out in the area covered by the now defunct north-eastern province (the province was officially declared invalid by the Supreme Court in October 2006).

Despite continuing violence between the Sri Lankan forces and the LTTE, provincial elections were held in the eastern province and in the northern town of Vavuniya in March 1994; the UNP secured the greatest number of seats, while independent Tamil groups also performed well. The LTTE and the TULF boycotted the poll. The ruling party suffered its first major electoral reverse for 17 years at the end of the month, however, when a new opposition grouping known as the People's Alliance (PA) won a clear majority in elections to the southern provincial council. The PA, of which the main constituents were the SLFP and the traditional Marxist left, was headed by Chandrika Bandaranaike Kumaratunga (the widow of the assassinated SLMP leader Vijaya Kumaratunga and daughter of former Prime Minister Sirimavo Bandaranaike).

The SLFP returns to power under Chandrika Kumaratunga (1994–2001)

In June 1994, in an apparent attempt to catch the opposition by surprise, the President dissolved Parliament and announced that early legislative elections were to be held on 16 August, ahead of the presidential election. Wijetunga's ploy failed, however: the PA obtained 105 seats with 48.9% of the votes, thus bringing an end to the 17-year parliamentary rule of the UNP, which received 94 seats (44%). On 18 August Chandrika Kumaratunga was appointed Prime Minister, the PA having secured the support of the SLMC, the TULF, the Democratic People's Liberation Front and a small, regional independent group. A new SLFP-dominated Cabinet was appointed on the following day. In line with her electoral pledge to abolish the executive presidency and to establish a parliamentary system in its place, the Prime Minister removed the finance portfolio from the President and assumed responsibility for it herself. The Prime Minister's mother, Sirimavo Bandaranaike, was appointed as Minister without Portfolio.

As a gesture of goodwill, the new Government partially lifted the economic blockade on LTTE-occupied territory, and unconditional peace talks between the two sides commenced in October 1994. The Prime Minister also assumed the newly created role of Minister of Ethnic Affairs and National Integration, thus illustrating her determination to seek a solution to the civil strife. However, following the assassination of Gamini Dissanayake, the leader of the opposition and the UNP's candidate for the forthcoming presidential poll, by a suspected LTTE suicide bomber in Colombo in October 1994, the Government declared a state of emergency and suspended the ongoing peace talks with the LTTE (of which Dissanayake had been an outspoken critic). More than 50 other people, including the General Secretary of the UNP, Gamini Wijesekara, and the leader of the SLMP, Ossie Abeyagoonasekera, were also killed in the explosion. Dissanayake's widow, Srima Dissanayake, was chosen by the UNP to replace him as the party's presidential candidate. The state of emergency was revoked on 7 November (with the exception of the troubled areas in the north and east) to facilitate the fair and proper conduct of the presidential election, which was held on 9 November and which was won by Kumaratunga, the PA's candidate, with 62.3% of the votes; Srima Dissanayake obtained 35.9% of the ballot. The Government viewed the victory as a clear mandate for the peace process initiated earlier that year. Sirimavo Bandaranaike was subsequently appointed Prime Minister for the third time. The new President pledged to abolish the executive presidency before mid-July 1995, on the grounds that she believed that the post vested too much power in one individual, and promised to initiate a programme of social, economic and constitutional change.

Following the failure of peace talks with the LTTE in early 1995, in July the Government launched another major offensive in the Jaffna peninsula. The recapture of Jaffna city in December led to a resurgence in terrorist activity; in January 1996 more than 100 people were killed in a suicide bomb attack on the Central Bank in Colombo. The President extended the state of emergency to cover the whole country in April. Although the army had gained control of the entire Jaffna peninsula by May, the LTTE continued to inflict heavy military and civilian casualties. In October Prabhakaran and nine other militants were charged with more than 700 criminal acts of terrorism, the first time that the Government had taken legal action against the LTTE leader. Fierce fighting between the Tamil militants and government troops continued into 1997, both in the north and east of the country.

The Government achieved an overwhelming success in local elections in March 1997 (voting did not take place in the troubled northern and eastern provinces). In May government forces launched a fresh military offensive against the LTTE, with the aim of gaining control of a vital land route to the Jaffna peninsula (the operation, which cost the lives of more than 3,000 government troops, was cancelled in December 1998). In October 1997 18 people were killed when a bomb exploded at a Colombo hotel. It was widely believed that the LTTE had deliberately targeted foreigners following the US Administration's decision a few days earlier to place the organization on its official list of international terrorist groups. In January 1998 the suspected LTTE suicide bombing of Sri Lanka's most sacred Buddhist temple, the Dalada Maligawa ('Temple of the Tooth') in Kandy, prompted the Government to formally outlaw the LTTE. Meanwhile, the UNP rejected the Government's proposal to devolve wide-ranging powers to regional councils—including a Tamil-administered area—favouring the concept of power-sharing at the centre. At the end of January, polls were conducted in Jaffna for the first time in 15 years; the largest number of seats was won by the Eelam People's Democratic Party (EPDP), but the turn-out was a mere 28%, owing to LTTE threats to disrupt the voting. The newly elected mayor of Jaffna was assassinated in a suspected LTTE attack in May, and his successor was also killed, allegedly by the LTTE, in September. Both were members of the moderate TULF.

At elections to seven provincial councils held during January–May 1999, the PA emerged as the leading party. One noteworthy feature of the polls was the resurgence of the JVP as a credible political force. In July the TULF Vice-President, Neelan Tiruchelvam, a leading peace campaigner and human rights activist, was assassinated by a suspected LTTE suicide bomber in Colombo. Meanwhile, in March 1999 the army launched another offensive against the LTTE in the northern province to reduce the area under the effective control of the Tamil guerrillas; however, LTTE victories in the north-eastern Wanni region in November reversed more than two years of territorial gains by the military and led to reports of large-scale desertions and mutiny in the army ranks.

A few days before an early presidential election, which was held on 21 December 1999 (almost one year ahead of schedule), Kumaratunga survived an assassination attempt by a suspected LTTE suicide bomber in Colombo; the explosion killed more than 20 people, while the President sustained wounds to her right eye. The election, which was contested by 13 candidates and attracted a 73% turn-out of the electorate, was marred by widespread allegations of vote-rigging, intimidation and violence. Kumaratunga was returned to power by a narrow majority, winning 51% of the total votes, while her main rival, Ranil Wickremasinghe of the UNP, secured 43%.

In early 2000 the Government confirmed that, at Kumaratunga's request, the Norwegian Government had agreed to play an intermediary role in any peace negotiations with the LTTE. However, heavy fighting continued between the army and the LTTE in the north. In April the LTTE announced that they had captured the large military base at Elephant Pass at the strategic entrance point to the peninsula. In response to the escalating military crisis, the Government imposed draconian security measures, banning all activities perceived as a threat to national security and giving extensive powers to the armed forces and police, and renewed press censorship. In June the Minister of Industrial Development, Clement V. Gunaratna, and more than

20 others were killed by a suspected LTTE suicide bomber in Colombo.

At the end of June 2000 President Kumaratunga and Wickremasinghe began discussions on the draft of a new constitution designed to resolve the ethnic conflict, which recommended converting the country into a de facto federal state through the establishment of eight semi-autonomous regional councils. However, the Tamil parliamentary parties rejected the proposals as providing inadequate autonomy to the Tamil regions of the country. Senior Buddhist monks also opposed the reforms, owing to fears that devolution would threaten the Sinhalese-dominated population and prominence of Buddhism in Sri Lanka. In July the UNP withdrew its support for the reforms, forestalling a successful parliamentary vote on the issue. On 10 August Sirimavo Bandaranaike announced her resignation as Prime Minister, owing to ill health (she died later that year). She was replaced by Ratnasiri Wickremanayake, the erstwhile Minister of Public Administration, Home Affairs and Plantation Industries. In September the Minister of Shipping and Shipping Development, Mohammad H. M. Ashraff, and the President of the SLMC, along with 14 others, were killed in a helicopter crash in Kegalle district; the aircraft was widely believed to have been shot down by LTTE guerrillas.

The parliamentary elections of 10 October 2000 were marred by allegations of electoral malpractice and by systematic violence and intimidation. Nevertheless, the elections attracted a turn-out of 75% of the electorate. Neither the PA nor the UNP won an absolute majority (taking 107 and 89 of the 225 parliamentary seats, respectively), but, having gained the support of the EPDP and National Unity Alliance (NUA—primarily a constituent of the SLMC), the PA was able to form a new, expanded coalition under the premiership of Wickremanayake.

In June 2001, following the dismissal of the leader of the SLMC, Abdul Rauff Hakeem, from his position as Minister of Internal and International Trade, Commerce, Muslim Religious Affairs and Shipping Development, several members of the SLMC withdrew their support for the ruling PA, thereby reducing the coalition Government to a minority in Parliament. Immediately afterwards, opposition parties challenged the Government with a no-confidence motion. In order to prevent the motion from being debated in Parliament, on 10 July the President suspended the legislature until 7 September, and announced that a referendum on a new constitution would take place on 21 August. The UNP-led opposition organized a series of demonstrations against the President's decision to prorogue Parliament. The President also faced opposition within the Cabinet itself, particularly with regard to the referendum. As a result, Kumaratunga announced in August that the referendum would be postponed until October.

Meanwhile, efforts by Norwegian emissaries to bolster the peace process from late 2000 met with little progress. In July 2001 President Kumaratunga circumvented Parliament and reimposed a state of emergency under anti-terrorist regulations. In July an LTTE assault on the country's only international airport, hitherto renowned for its impenetrable security, adversely affected the tourist industry (and thus the economy), and raised questions about the air force and the airport's defence system.

In an attempt to resolve the political crisis, the Prime Minister and senior cabinet members attempted to form a coalition government. The UNP rejected the initiative, but in early September 2001 the JVP formally agreed to support the minority Government for one year (but not to join the administration), in return for a set of conditions. The President had already granted the JVP two of its demands by cancelling the referendum and reconvening Parliament. In addition, the President agreed to suspend negotiations with the LTTE for one year and to postpone the privatization programme. In accordance with further JVP demands, in mid-September the size of the Cabinet was halved to 22 members. However, three senior cabinet members resigned, refusing to participate in an administration supported by the left-wing party. On 10 October 13 members of the PA, including several ministers, defected to the opposition, thereby reducing the coalition once again to a minority. In order to forestall defeat in a vote of no confidence due to take place the following day, President Kumaratunga dissolved Parliament.

The UNP holds parliamentary power under an SLFP President (2001–04)

The general election on 5 December 2001, one of the most violent in Sri Lanka's history, was also marred by incidents of vote-rigging and other electoral malpractices. Some tens of thousands of Tamils were prevented from leaving LTTE-controlled areas to cast their vote. Nevertheless, 72% of the electorate voted. The UNP won 109 of the 225 seats (with 45.6% of the vote) and the PA received 77 seats (37.2%). The JVP secured 16 seats (9.1%) and the Tamil National Alliance (TNA—a Tamil opposition alliance, comprising the TULF, TELO, EPRLF and All Ceylon Tamil Congress, formed prior to the election) won 15 seats (3.9%). The UNP leader, Ranil Wickremasinghe, formed the United National Front (UNF) with the SLMC to ensure a majority of 114 seats in Parliament, and on 9 December he was sworn in as Prime Minister. For the first time since 1984, the Prime Minister and the President were from two opposing parties. The President was at first reluctant to relinquish her defence and finance portfolios, which she eventually gave up in return for full control over the élite Presidential Security Division that was deployed for her personal protection. After lengthy negotiations, a new coalition Government, including, significantly, representatives of the TNA and 12 members of the former PA administration, was sworn in on 12 December.

The UNP's electoral victory was largely attributed to the party's eagerness to resume negotiations with the LTTE. On 19 December 2001 the LTTE announced a unilateral one-month cease-fire from 25 December, and on 21 December the Government responded with the declaration of a reciprocal cease-fire as a 'gesture of goodwill'. The Prime Minister also announced that the free movement of food, medicine and other non-military supplies into the Tamil-controlled areas would be allowed (a concession refused, hitherto, by the President); economic sanctions were later also reduced. At the end of January both sides extended the cease-fire by one month. On 22 February 2002 the Government and LTTE signed an agreement on an internationally monitored indefinite cease-fire to take effect on the following day; the Norwegian-led Sri Lanka Monitoring Mission (SLMM) was subsequently established.

In March 2002 Prime Minister Wickremasinghe visited Jaffna, the first premier to do so since 1982. In early April the Government lifted a six-year ban on domestic flights and allowed commercial airlines to resume flights to Jaffna. A week later the A9 highway was opened for the first time in 12 years, linking the Jaffna peninsula with the rest of the country. On 10 April LTTE leader Prabhakaran addressed an international press conference for the first time in more than 10 years. He demanded the lifting of the ban on the LTTE as a prerequisite to negotiations and declared his commitment to peace and full support of the cease-fire. A few days later he signed a pact with the SLMC, allowing the largest Muslim party in Sri Lanka to participate in proposed negotiations with the Government. It was also agreed that nearly 100,000 Muslims expelled from the north by the LTTE about 10 years ago would be permitted to return to their homes. In May a Tamil-owned trawler, reported to have been illegally importing weapons, was destroyed by the Sri Lankan navy in an exchange of gunfire off the coast of the eastern Batticaloa district—the first major violation of the cease-fire to have occurred. The LTTE accused the army of attacking a civilian fishing boat in an effort to undermine the cease-fire.

The official ban on the LTTE was lifted in May 2002 and the first round of official peace talks between the Government and the LTTE for more than seven years, held in September in Thailand, proved successful: the two sides agreed to collaborate on security and reconstruction, the clearing of landmines and the resettling of 800,000 internally displaced people to high-security zones. On the final day of negotiations Anton Balasingham, the LTTE's chief negotiator, unexpectedly renounced the LTTE's long-standing demand for independence, instead agreeing to consider regional autonomy and self-government.

Despite cease-fire violations and the *in absentia* sentencing of Prabhakaran to 200 years' imprisonment for a 1996 bombing in Colombo, the second round of peace negotiations, in October, concluded in a breakthrough, with both sides agreeing to create a subcommittee to examine a political solution to the conflict. Balasingham announced that the LTTE were willing to participate in the democratic process, would allow other political parties to operate in the areas under their control and would cease the recruitment of child soldiers. The LTTE also abandoned their demand for an interim government in the north-east. Sinhalese nationalists dismissed this progress as an LTTE attempt to win publicity and international favour. Nevertheless, Prabhakaran confirmed in his annual address that the LTTE were prepared to accept regional autonomy rather than an independent state—warning that violence would resume if negotiations collapsed

In December 2002, at the third round of peace talks, held in Norway, the two sides agreed on 'internal self-determination' based on a federal system of government within a united Sri Lanka. Balasingham and Prof. G. L. Peiris—the Sri Lankan Minister of Constitutional Affairs and the Government's chief negotiator—described the developments as unprecedented and historic. However, in order to achieve the two-thirds' majority required in Parliament to pass a constitutional amendment, the Government needed to secure the support of the President. In mid-December a close adviser of the President stated that the PA would not support a political solution unless the LTTE disarmed, but at the fourth round of negotiations, held in Thailand in January 2003, Balasingham refused to disarm the Tamil forces prior to a political settlement. Instead, the talks concluded with an agreement to accelerate the rate of return and resettlement of up to 250,000 displaced people. Meanwhile, despite Tamil promises to halt the forced recruitment of children, the SLMM reported that the LTTE had enlisted hundreds of child soldiers since the instigation of the cease-fire. The fifth round of negotiations, held in Germany in February, focused on human rights issues; it was agreed that the UN Children's Fund (UNICEF) would monitor a joint programme to rehabilitate child soldiers.

With tensions rising in the 'cohabitation Government', the sixth round of negotiations, held in Japan in March, ended without agreement, amid reports of renewed violence in Sri Lanka. In April the LTTE announced its temporary withdrawal from the peace negotiations because it had been excluded from an aid conference on Sri Lanka's reconstruction, held in the USA (the LTTE was still banned in that country). The LTTE also criticized the continued presence of government troops in many Tamil-controlled areas in a clear violation of the cease-fire, and the way in which the Government was carrying out rehabilitation and relief measures. Although the LTTE expressed its intention to uphold the cease-fire, the President placed the security forces on high alert. Increased discord was evident with the assassination of a senior EPRLF leader in June, which was blamed on the LTTE, and the sinking of an LTTE oil tanker during a confrontation with a Sri Lankan navy patrol. In late June the LTTE organized a demonstration, attended by some 150,000 protesters, to demand the return of thousands of homes on the Jaffna peninsula occupied by the Sri Lankan army as high-security zones since the 1980s. Controversy later intensified over the LTTE's refusal to dismantle a camp in the north-east; the military and opposition accused the LTTE of establishing several new camps since the beginning of the cease-fire.

On 4 November 2003 the country was plunged into a constitutional crisis when President Kumaratunga took advantage of the Prime Minister's absence abroad and suspended the legislature for a period of two weeks, dismissed the Minister of Interior and Christian Affairs, the Minister of Defence and of Transport, Highways and Aviation, and the Minister of Mass Communication, assuming these portfolios herself, and deployed troops to key positions in the capital in the stated interest of preserving national security. The President claimed that Wickremasinghe, who returned from the USA on 7 November, had made too many concessions to the LTTE during peace negotiations. The Prime Minister rejected the offer to form a government of national unity, but agreed to appoint a committee to establish new power-sharing arrangements by mid-December. In the mean time, the Norwegian peace negotiators announced that they would withdraw from the peace process until it was clarified who held power and authority in Sri Lanka.

In January 2004 the crisis worsened when President Kumaratunga declared that she had held an undisclosed inauguration ceremony in 2000 to give herself another year in office, thereby extending her term to December 2006. Analysts debated whether the action was constitutional. Later in January 2004 the SLFP and the JVP formed the United People's Freedom Alliance (UPFA). The UPFA was joined by four other left-wing parties, which had been members of the erstwhile PA, in early February. On 7 February Kumaratunga dissolved Parliament and called a general election for 2 April, almost four years ahead of schedule. Both the Cabinet and the LTTE condemned the decision, amid fears that the election would further undermine the peace process.

In March 2004 a rift within the LTTE appeared after a senior Tamil eastern regional commander declared his independence from the rest of the group. Vinayagamoorthy Muralitharan (commonly known as Col Karuna) withdrew his 6,000 fighters from the 15,000-strong LTTE in a dispute with the northern-based LTTE leader, Prabhakaran. Karuna, who accused northern Tamil groups of ignoring and discriminating against eastern groups, stated that he would not recognize the cease-fire agreement between the Government and Prabhakaran, and instead demanded a separate truce agreement with the Sri Lankan administration. In late March the LTTE vowed to remove Karuna from Sri Lanka and in early April fighting between the two Tamil factions broke out around the eastern town of Batticaloa. Four days later it was reported that Karuna had fled from his base and gone into hiding, that his forces had dispersed and that the LTTE had assumed full control of the eastern areas.

The UPFA gains control of Parliament

At the general election on 2 April 2004, the UPFA won 105 of the 225 seats, having taken 45.6% of the votes cast; Wickremasinghe's UNP retained 82 seats (with 37.8% of the votes), while the TNA won 22 seats (with 7.0%). In an unexpected development, the Buddhist Jathika Hela Urumaya (JHU—National Heritage Party) secured nine seats. The LTTE, which had openly supported the TNA during the election campaign, interpreted the latter's relative success as recognition of the LTTE as 'the sole representative' of the Tamil population. Turn-out was reportedly 75% of eligible voters and the poll concluded peacefully, but there were claims of voter intimidation and electoral malpractice, particularly in the north and east of the country. Mahinda Rajapaksa, a senior member of the SLFP, was sworn in as Prime Minister on 6 April and a few days later a new Cabinet was inaugurated. In September the UPFA Government achieved a legislative majority with the additional support of the CWC. In the following month three members of the opposition SLMC defected to the UPFA, further strengthening the Government.

Meanwhile, the cease-fire between the LTTE and the Government came under increasing pressure from June 2004 onwards. Upon accusations from the LTTE, the Sri Lankan armed forces eventually admitted that they had helped Col Karuna to escape, while insisting that the plan had been carried out without the Government's knowledge. Fears that the cease-fire was close to collapse were heightened by a suicide bombing at a police station in Colombo in July (the LTTE denied involvement), and the assassination of an EPDP politician in Ampara district later that month. In the mean time, clashes continued to occur between the LTTE and members of the breakaway Karuna faction.

Political events were overshadowed by a devastating tsunami caused by a massive earthquake in the Indian Ocean on 26 December 2004. More than 31,000 Sri Lankans were killed in the disaster, which also left thousands homeless and without livelihoods. The tourism industry was badly affected by the catastrophe, with many hotels and resorts being damaged or destroyed. It was initially hoped that the scale of the disaster would serve to ease tensions between the Government and the LTTE, particularly as the Tamil areas of the island were among those worst hit. However, conflicts soon surfaced over the distribution of aid; the LTTE claimed that the Government was restricting the flow of international aid into Tamil-controlled areas and demanded that it be delivered directly to them. In June 2005 the Government finally signed an agreement—entitled the Post-Tsunami Operational Management Structure (P-TOMS)— that would allow the LTTE to participate in the distribution of aid for the reconstruction effort. The agreement had only been reached following the withdrawal from the ruling coalition of the JVP, which had remained staunchly opposed to any deal with the LTTE. The JVP's exit left the Government with a minority in the legislature, although the opposition UNP had assured the Government of its support for the aid-sharing mechanism. In the following month, however, in response to a petition from the JVP and the JHU, the Supreme Court suspended the implementation of the P-TOMS, ruling that several of its clauses were illegal. Meanwhile, increasing tensions between the LTTE and government forces, complicated by the former's ongoing clashes with the rebel Karuna faction, led to an upsurge in violence. At the end of May the chief of military intelligence in Colombo, Maj. Nizam Muthalif, had become the most senior official to have been assassinated by the LTTE since the signing of the cease-fire in February 2002.

In August 2005 the peace process between the Government and the LTTE was further jeopardized when the Minister of Foreign Affairs, Lakshman Kadirgamar, was assassinated by unidentified gunmen at his home in Colombo. Although they denied involvement, the LTTE were held responsible for the attack. In the aftermath of the murder, President Kumaratunga declared a state of emergency, granting the security forces broad powers of detention. Amid widespread fears that the cease-fire would collapse, both sides announced their commitment to its

maintenance, and the LTTE promised to meet with the Government to review the truce agreement; however, the two sides were unable to agree on a location for talks. In September the European Union (EU, see p. 281) issued a statement banning LTTE delegations from visiting any of its member states. Sporadic violence continued throughout the following months.

Mahinda Rajapaksa assumes the presidency; the four-year cease-fire collapses

Despite President Kumaratunga claiming that the holding of an undisclosed inauguration ceremony in 2000 (see above) had extended her second term until December 2006, in August 2005 the Supreme Court ruled that the election should be staged by 22 November 2005, as stipulated under the terms of the Constitution. The election was held on 17 November and the SLFP's candidate, Rajapaksa, emerged victorious with 50.3% of the vote, narrowly defeating the UNP's candidate, Wickremasinghe, who polled 48.4%. The election was notable for the low turn-out among the country's Tamil population, particularly in the LTTE-controlled northern and eastern areas; there was widespread evidence that, despite their assurances, the LTTE had prevented people from voting. Rajapaksa subsequently nominated the incumbent Minister of Agriculture, Public Security, Law and Order and of Buddha Sasana, Ratnasiri Wickremanayake, as Prime Minister. In the new Cabinet, announced shortly afterwards, neither the JVP nor the JHU were awarded any portfolios.

There was an escalation in violence from December 2005: at least 60 people died over the course of the month as a result of various attacks believed to have been co-ordinated by the LTTE. In February 2006 negotiators representing the LTTE and the Government convened in Geneva, Switzerland, issuing a joint statement committing both sides to upholding the cease-fire, which appeared in imminent danger of collapse. The LTTE agreed to attempt to prevent further attacks on the security forces, while the Government pledged to try to disarm the Karuna faction of the LTTE, which was believed to have been acting on behalf of the armed forces against its erstwhile comrades. However, in April the LTTE stated that it would not attend the second round of talks scheduled to be held in Geneva that month, alleging that government forces had carried out attacks on Tamil civilians and that the Sri Lankan navy had prevented the LTTE commanders in the east of the country from meeting the LTTE political leaders in the north. In late April a suicide bombing at the army headquarters in Colombo killed at least 11 people and seriously injured the Chief of Staff of the Army, Lt-Gen. Sarath Fonseka. In response, the Government ordered a number of air-strikes on alleged LTTE bases near Trincomalee, which, according to the LTTE, caused widespread displacement of local people. As the violence continued, the SLMM acknowledged that a 'low intensity war' was taking place. At the end of the month the EU classified the LTTE as a terrorist organization, which entailed a suspension of LTTE fund-raising in EU member states, a freeze on the organization's assets and a ban on travel to the EU. The LTTE responded by demanding the withdrawal of EU members of the SLMM, resulting in the departure of Danish, Finnish and Swedish monitors in July and August.

Amid escalating violence the LTTE withdrew from peace talks planned for June 2006. A new front in the conflict opened up over access to the Maavil-Aru waterway, which became the scene of a number of air and ground offensives in July. The violence spread to the town of Muttur, north of the waterway, forcing thousands of inhabitants, many of them Muslims, to flee in August. Clashes between LTTE fighters and army troops continued in the north and east of the country, with rising death tolls of civilians, rebels and government forces. At the end of September the SLMM estimated that the resumption of hostilities had resulted in the displacement of some 200,000 people. In October, following a suicide bombing near Habarana that killed approximately 100 naval officers, it was feared that relatively unaffected areas of the country would be drawn into the conflict when the LTTE attacked a naval base in the southern town of Galle. Little progress was made at peace talks held in Geneva at the end of October, although both sides agreed to uphold the terms of the cease-fire agreement. In November it was reported that an army attack on a Tamil refugee camp in LTTE-held territory had resulted in at least 65 civilian fatalities. At the end of November Prabhakaran declared the cease-fire to be 'defunct' and blamed the Government for failing to find a solution. In early December the Government amended existing laws to extend the powers of security officials and support anti-terrorist operations. Anton Balasingham, the chief LTTE negotiator, died in mid-December.

Meanwhile, at the end of June 2006 Rajapaksa was elected unopposed to replace Kumaratunga as President of the SLFP. In January 2007 more than 20 dissident politicians from opposition parties (including the UNP and the SLMC) joined the Government, thus giving it a parliamentary majority. In June two former SLFP ministers founded a new political party, the Sri Lanka Freedom Party—Mahajana Wing (SLFP—M), in reaction to the 'path of extremism' that they believed the SLFP to be taking. In December the SLMC withdrew its support for the governing coalition, and the party's leader, Abdul Rauff Hakeem, resigned from his position as Minister of Posts and Telecommunication.

As fighting continued in the north and east of the country, in mid-2007 it was estimated that the resumption of hostilities had resulted in approximately 5,000 fatalities since 2005. There were frequent reports of human rights violations on both sides. In June 2007 hundreds of Tamils were apparently forced to leave Colombo by the police, and accounts of abductions and disappearances were commonplace. The LTTE, in turn, was criticized for its alleged recruitment of children, forced recruitment and abduction of adults, and political killings. The UN High Commissioner for Human Rights also expressed concern over the conduct of Col Karuna's troops. However, the Government declined the Commissioner's offer to establish an office in the country. In July the army claimed that its operations in the eastern province had resulted in a decisive victory over the LTTE and had led to its recapture of the region. The front line shifted as fighting intensified in the north of the country. S. P. Thamilselvan, the head of the LTTE's political wing and a leading member of its negotiating team, was killed in an aerial bombardment by the military in October. In early January 2008 D. M. Dassanayake, the Minister of Nation Building, was killed in a bomb attack. The Government formally withdrew from the cease-fire agreement on 16 January. As a result, the SLMM announced the end of its activities in Sri Lanka. Also in January, Col Karuna, who had been apprehended while attempting to enter the United Kingdom using a counterfeit passport in late 2007, was sentenced to nine months' imprisonment by a British court on charges of identity fraud. Speculation had arisen over the links between Karuna's faction and the Sri Lankan Government, and the role that this alleged alliance had played in the Government wresting control of the eastern province from the LTTE. In July 2008 the British authorities deported Karuna from the United Kingdom. In March 2009, having left his faction's political front, the Tamil Makkal Viduthalai Pulikal, and joined the SLFP, Karuna (using his civilian name, Vinayagamoorthy Muralitharan) was appointed as Minister of National Integration and Reconciliation (a non-cabinet post). Meanwhile, in April 2008 the Minister of Highways and Road Development, Jeyaraj Fernandopulle, (together with at least 14 other people) was killed in a suspected LTTE suicide bombing carried out near Colombo.

Defeat of the LTTE and the end of the civil war

In the latter half of 2008 the Sri Lankan army made considerable advances against the LTTE, which, nevertheless, put up fierce resistance and increasingly resorted to terrorist attacks across the country. Both sides suffered heavy casualties, although, owing to stringent media restrictions, exact numbers were impossible to confirm. In January 2009 the rebels lost control of their de facto capital, Kilinochchi, and later that month their last remaining stronghold, Mullaitivu, fell to the advancing government troops. By April the LTTE were cornered in a small stretch of coastal territory in the north-east of the country. Despite the Government having established a designated 5 sq km 'no-fire' zone for the thousands of civilians fleeing from the violence, thousands of (mainly Tamil) civilians were reported to have been killed by both sides in the conflict. The LTTE and the army both denied any responsibility for civilian deaths, and the latter claimed to have stopped using heavy artillery (although the evidence of intensive shelling suggested otherwise) while alleging that the retreating LTTE was using the civilian population as a human shield. With more than 200,000 refugees living in makeshift accommodation, and medical and food provisions in short supply, there were growing demands from the international community (including the US Administration and the UN) for an immediate cease-fire to allow the safe evacuation of the 50,000 civilians trapped in the conflict zone. However, the government forces, in their determination to rout the LTTE, refused to halt their bombardment, while the rebels, for their part, continued to attempt to prevent the refugees from leaving the conflict zone.

On 17 May 2009 the Government reported that all the civilians remaining in the war zone had been freed and claimed to have defeated the last remnants of the rebel forces (who were holding out in a small area on the coast), thereby bringing the 26-year civil conflict that had claimed at least 70,000 lives to its conclusion. The LTTE were reported to have finally laid down their arms and released a statement declaring that their struggle had 'reached its bitter end'. On the following day Prabhakaran, together with several other senior LTTE officials, was reported to have been killed while attempting to escape the advancing army; the LTTE leader's death was subsequently confirmed following DNA testing. Amid scenes of jubilation on the streets of Colombo, President Rajapaksa formally announced the army's victory over the LTTE on 19 May and declared the following day as a public holiday. In an attempt to allay the concerns of the Tamil population, Rajapaksa pledged immediately to address the political issues arising from the conflict's conclusion by negotiating some form of power-sharing agreement with the Tamils in the north and east of the island.

However, the army's victory created a further humanitarian problem: the displacement of approximately 290,000 non-combatant Tamils who had been driven into refugee camps around Mullaitivu and other locations in the northern province. In May 2009 the UN Human Rights Council (UNHRC) convened a special emergency session on Sri Lanka at the request of 17, mostly European, countries seeking to secure approval of a proposed resolution condemning the Sri Lankan Government for its alleged disregard for civilian life during the civil war's final stages. However, the proposed resolution was rejected; instead, a resolution tabled by the Sri Lankan Government itself, commending its handling of the war and, in particular, its commitment to human rights, was approved by a vote of 29 to 12. Among those who voted in support of the Sri Lankan Government were the two main Asian regional powers, China and India. During the year many aid and human rights agencies expressed concern over the poor conditions suffered by the 'internally displaced persons' (IDPs) in the overcrowded internment camps ('welfare villages'). The Government claimed that the process of resettlement had been delayed by the need for the authorities to identify any disguised LTTE fighters or cadres among the IDPs, but in October the reported threat of EU trading sanctions accelerated the pace. In December the Government finally gave permission for the remaining 130,000 IDPs to leave the camps if they so wished (although it was expected that many of them would remain in the camps indefinitely since either their villages had been destroyed or the journey would be too perilous given the number of unexploded landmines and ordnance).

Rajapaksa consolidates his power following the defeat of the LTTE

In October 2009, following local elections, the UPFA took control of the provincial council of the southern province, and within days it was announced that legislative and presidential elections would be held by April 2010. Although parliamentary elections were due, Rajapaksa's presidential term was not scheduled to expire until November 2011; the President's decision to call an early election appeared to reflect the Government's confidence in its popularity and strength in the aftermath of the defeat of the LTTE.

In the mean time, there were reports of growing friction between the Government and the army commander who had masterminded the defeat of the LTTE, Gen. Sarath Fonseka. In July Fonseka was moved to the largely ceremonial post of Chief of Defence Staff. In November Fonseka resigned from this position and announced his intention to contest the forthcoming presidential election as the candidate of the recently formed New Democratic Front. He claimed that President Rajapaksa had become increasingly corrupt and dictatorial and that he had done little to promote national reconciliation since the demise of the LTTE. The TNA (the long-standing spokesbody of the LTTE) pledged its support for Fonseka in the presidential poll. In the election, which was held on 26 January 2010 with a turn-out of 74.5%, President Rajapaksa was returned to power for a second term, securing 57.9% of the votes cast, while Fonseka obtained 40.2%. In early February the Supreme Court ruled that Rajapaksa could begin his new term in November rather than immediately, thus effectively giving him almost an extra year in power. In mid-February Fonseka, who had vowed to contest the presidential election results, was arrested on charges of conspiring to overthrow the Government while he was in command of the army; violent clashes between thousands of government supporters and opposition activists ensued in Colombo. Fonseka further angered the Government when he quoted allegations that high-ranking military officials, including Defence Secretary Gotabhaya Rajapaksa, the President's brother, had ordered army officers to shoot and kill surrendering LTTE troops in the closing days of the conflict. In March Fonseka appeared before a court martial in Colombo on charges of engaging in politics while serving in the armed forces and of violating military procurement procedures; the court martial was subsequently adjourned.

The ruling UPFA secured an overwhelming victory in the general election held on 8 April 2010, winning 144 of the 225 parliamentary seats; the UNP (which contested the election on its own and not at the head of the UNF) won 60 seats, the Ilankai Tamil Arasu Katchi (a constituent party of the TNA) 14 seats and the newly formed Democratic National Alliance (DNA, led by Fonseka) seven seats (one of which was secured by Fonseka himself). President Rajapaksa appointed the veteran statesman and incumbent Minister of Plantation Industries, D. M. Jayaratne, as Prime Minister on 21 April and a new, substantially reduced Cabinet was sworn in two days later. The President was accused of nepotism by some observers following the appointment of his older brother, Chamal Rajapaksa, as Speaker of Parliament (two other brothers—Gotabhaya and Basil Rajapaksa—also held senior government posts) and the securing of a parliamentary seat by his son, Namal Rajapaksa. In early May the Government announced the partial relaxation of emergency regulations that had been in place since 2006.

In mid-May 2010 the Government announced plans for the establishment of a Lessons Learnt and Reconciliation Commission (LLRC), which was to investigate the reasons behind the collapse of the 2002 cease-fire agreement, promote national unity and determine compensation for the numerous victims of the civil conflict. However, the LLRC's mandate would not cover investigations into allegations of the violation of humanitarian law by government forces and the LTTE during the final stages of the war, and there was considerable scepticism internationally about its credibility. In the same month a study undertaken by the International Crisis Group (an independent non-governmental organization based in Brussels, Belgium) was published, which claimed that the Sri Lankan army and the LTTE were responsible for the deaths of thousands more civilians than previously estimated and that there was strong evidence that the government forces had deliberately targeted hospitals and humanitarian operations during their final onslaught against the Tamil militants. The report estimated that as many as 75,000 civilians, who were known to have been alive in the 'no-fire' zone in February 2009, remained unaccounted for. In June 2010 the UN Secretary-General, Ban Ki-Moon, appointed a special three-member panel of experts to advise him on appropriate courses of action regarding alleged war crimes perpetrated by both sides in the final months of the civil war. The UN estimated that around 7,000 civilians were killed in the last five months of the conflict (and a total of approximately 100,000 during the course of the entire 26-year conflict). The Sri Lankan Government insisted that the establishment of the UN human rights advisory panel, which was headed by a former Attorney-General of Indonesia, Marzuki Darusman, was unnecessary and that it would not be allowed to enter the country; the panel's members were denied visas on the grounds that their investigation violated Sri Lankan sovereignty. In July the Minister of Construction, Engineering Services, Housing and Common Amenities, Wimal Weerawansa, led a demonstration of hundreds of protesters who laid siege to the UN's office compound in Colombo in protest at the controversial advisory panel. The UN responded to the protests by temporarily recalling its envoy to Sri Lanka and by closing its compound in Colombo.

In August 2010 Fonseka was found guilty by a court martial of having engaged in politics while on active military service and was sentenced to a dishonourable discharge and divested of all military ranks and privileges. In September a second court martial sentenced Fonseka to 30 months' imprisonment for the violation of military tender procedures. The former general was stripped of his parliamentary seat and was immediately transferred to a high-security prison in Colombo.

In September 2010 Rajapaksa's hold on power was considerably strengthened by Parliament's approval of a constitutional reforms bill (the Eighteenth Amendment Bill) that included provisions allowing an individual to hold the presidency for an unlimited number of terms (previously limited to two terms) and the bestowal on the President of final authority over appointments to the judiciary, police, electoral commission and the civil service (the latter measure effectively rescinding the Seventeenth Amendment Bill of 2001, which curbed presidential power by depoliticizing important state appointments). The bill's introduction had instigated a boycott by the UNP and large demonstrations in Colombo.

On 19 November 2010 President Rajapaksa was formally sworn in for his second term in office in a ceremony that was boycotted by the main opposition parties. A few days later the President appointed a new, considerably enlarged Cabinet; the majority of senior ministers, including Prime Minister Jayaratne, retained their portfolios. Abdul Rauff Hakeem, the leader of the SLMC, which had recently left the ranks of the opposition to join the UPFA, was appointed as Minister of Justice. Despite its stated wish to seek reconciliation for all parties in the aftermath of the civil war, the Government risked heightening ethnic tension in December when it abandoned the Tamil language version of the national anthem.

Political events were temporarily overshadowed in December 2010–January 2011 by devastating monsoon floods that affected more than 1.2m. people in Sri Lanka and destroyed vast areas of agricultural crops (mostly in the eastern province). In mid-January 2011 the first round of negotiations were held between representatives of the Government and the TNA with a view to brokering a mutually agreeable political solution to the ongoing dispute over plans for the devolution of central authority to the Tamils in the north and east of the country.

In April 2011 the UN panel of experts submitted its report on alleged human rights violations (thenceforth widely referred to as the Darusman report) to the UN Secretary-General and to the Sri Lankan Government. The report concluded that as many as 40,000 civilians were killed during the final weeks of the civil conflict and deemed that allegations against both the Sri Lankan army and the LTTE of widespread human rights abuses that could potentially amount to war crimes were 'credible'. Government forces were alleged to have engaged in widespread shelling within the supposedly safe 'no-fire' zones, including attacks on hospitals and humanitarian facilities, in which thousands of civilians were estimated to have been killed, as well as to have blocked food and medicine supplies to those trapped within conflict zones, while Tamil militants were alleged to have used civilians as human shields and shot at or otherwise killed those attempting to escape from areas caught up in the violence. The report appealed for a full and independent international investigation. The Sri Lankan Government maintained that government forces had not wittingly been responsible for any civilian deaths during the final phase of the civil conflict in 2009. To express its outrage at the panel's allegations, the UPFA staged a mass rally (headed by Rajapaksa) in Colombo in May 2011.

Further allegations emerged with the broadcast of a documentary by the British television station Channel 4 in June 2011 that included video footage, first broadcast in August 2009, purporting to depict members of the Sri Lankan army summarily executing blindfolded and bound Tamil prisoners; the footage also showed the bodies of female Tamil militants who appeared to have been sexually assaulted. The Sri Lankan Government insisted that the documentary was grossly biased, included fabricated footage, was based largely on testimony from LTTE cadres and was a deliberate attempt by supporters of the Tamil militants to taint the country's international reputation. (However, during a subsequent UN investigation, independent experts determined that both the video and accompanying audio footage were authentic and had not been manipulated.) In August the Sri Lankan Government released a documentary video entitled 'Lies Agreed Upon', to address what it described as the false claims made by the Channel 4 film.

Meanwhile, local elections held in three stages in 2011 were marred by violence and allegations of electoral malpractice. The UPFA won an overwhelming mandate at local elections held in March, securing power in 205 of the 234 bodies where polling took place. However, ongoing ethnic divisions were revealed in July, when the TNA gained control of 20 councils located in Tamil-dominated areas in the northern and eastern regions, despite the UPFA's expensive electoral campaign. The Government was keen to emphasize that the successful staging of elections in those areas represented a successful return to order and democracy after decades of violence in the region. Although the UPFA fared better in the October local elections, securing control of 21 of the 23 contested councils, the ruling coalition significantly lost control of Colombo Municipal Council, which was won by the UNP, largely owing to the latter's greater popularity among the city's sizeable Muslim and Tamil populations.

In September 2011 the state of emergency was rescinded, owing to the lack of 'terrorist activities' since the end of the civil conflict in May 2009. However, Rajapaksa swiftly issued a new proclamation providing for the deployment of the armed forces and the police in order to maintain public order throughout the country, and the Attorney-General subsequently announced that no prisoners detained under the emergency regulations were to be released, prompting claims that the revocation of the state of emergency was merely a ploy intended to appease the international community. Meanwhile, in July it was announced that 2,924 former Tamil militants remained in detention within rehabilitation centres in Sri Lanka; 7,969 were reported to have been released, having already completed the rehabilitation process, which included vocational training and adult education programmes. Approximately 160 former Tamil cadres were detained pending court hearings for crimes that they were alleged to have committed during the 26-year conflict.

In August 2011, following the failure of the Government and the TNA to reach agreement on the scope and structure of the proposed devolved authority in the northern and eastern provinces, the Government announced plans to appoint a parliamentary select committee as a forum for broad-based discussions and to formulate solutions to the ongoing stalemate. In the same month the Ministry of Defence released a report into the final stages of the civil conflict, in which the Government conceded for the first time that the Sri Lankan army had been responsible for civilian deaths, although it insisted that such deaths had been unavoidable given the intensity of the fighting and the 'ruthless' nature of the LTTE. The report was widely dismissed by rights groups. In September the Sri Lankan Government strongly condemned the decision by UN Secretary-General Ban Ki-Moon to submit the Darusman report to UNHRC, maintaining that the report had no official status.

The LLRC's final report on the Sri Lankan civil conflict was presented to Parliament in November 2011. Although the report included criticism of certain government policies—including the 'overly centralized and militarized' manner in which the authorities were governing the northern province and the continued repression by the authorities of media freedoms—it concluded that the government forces had adopted a strategy 'in which the protection of the civilian population was given the highest priority'. However, the report did state that security forces might have been implicated in specific instances of civilian deaths and that these should be investigated. None the less, the LLRC's findings were dismissed or deemed inadequate by a wide array of international human rights groups and foreign governments, who emphasized the Commission's limited mandate, its lack of neutrality and its failure to provide accountability for alleged human rights abuses. The Sri Lankan army announced in February 2012 that it had appointed a five-member fact-finding court of inquiry to examine the LLRC report, as well as the Channel 4 documentary (see above); the authorities denied that the development was a response to external pressures.

Meanwhile, in November 2011 Fonseka was sentenced to a further three years' imprisonment on charges of 'spreading disaffection', having been found to have supported allegations that Gotabhaya Rajapaksa, in his capacity as Defence Secretary, had sanctioned the killing of LTTE leaders as they tried to surrender in May 2009. Fonseka, who still faced a number of additional charges, including that of harbouring army deserters, denounced the verdict as politically motivated. At the beginning of January 2012 it was announced that Fonseka had become a member of the UNP, which in December 2011 had initiated a public campaign to secure his release, launching a petition that it planned to submit to the UN Secretary-General upon the collection of 1m. signatures. UNP leader Wickremasinghe asserted that the Government's treatment of Fonseka contravened Sri Lanka's obligations as a signatory to the International Covenant on Civil and Political Rights. Fonseka was released in May 2012, but banned from political office for seven years. Attempts by the former military commander to register a new political organization, the Democratic Party, with the Election Commission were unsuccessful in 2012, and in February 2013 he filed a complaint regarding the delay. As leader of the Democratic Party, he did, however, hold a rally in Colombo in October 2012, during which he reiterated his criticism of the Government.

Recent developments: human rights allegations and international pressure

A resolution adopted by UNHRC in March 2012 called for action on the part of the Sri Lankan Government on allegations of human rights' violations in the final stages of the civil war and recommended that the Government follow the recommendations of the LLRC report. Significantly, India voted in favour of the resolution (which had been tabled by the USA), while China and Russia opposed it. The Sri Lankan permanent mission to the UN dismissed the resolution as the result of 'strategic alliances and domestic political issues in other countries', but in July the Cabinet approved a 'national action plan' to implement the LLRC's recommendations, dividing its approach into four areas: national policy; the final stages of the war; human rights; and resettlement and development. According to the Government, 60% of the short- and medium-term recommendations had already been put into practice. Nevertheless, major issues remained unresolved, including the continuing military presence in the north (which Rajapaksa steadfastly defended), and the long delay to promised elections in the northern province. In September the US Assistant Secretary of State, Robert Blake, attended talks with Rajapaksa and expressed concern over these matters; Rajapaksa was said to have pledged to hold the northern provincial election by December 2013, but for Blake the postponement, along with the slow pace of the national action plan and the lack of any progress in negotiations between the Government and the TNA, were disappointing. A UN internal report released in November 2012 blamed the UN Security Council, UNHRC and other UN bodies for failures in the final months of the civil war, including the withdrawal of UN staff from areas of fighting. International dissatisfaction with the Government's efforts to address the outstanding post-conflict issues was evident in March 2013, when the USA sponsored a further resolution at UNHRC, encouraging the Sri Lankan authorities to launch a fully independent investigation into the human rights allegations. The resolution, which also noted the inadequacy of the Sri Lankan national action plan and expressed concern at increasing reports of extrajudicial killings and of intimidation of non-governmental organizations (NGOs) and journalists, was adopted by 25 countries (including India) voting in favour, 13 voting against and eight abstentions.

Concerns over government constraints on media freedom were highlighted in July 2012 when new rules governing the registration of news websites were introduced. In September the outspoken editor of the *Sunday Leader*, which was known for publishing articles critical of the Government, was dismissed after the newspaper was bought by a business executive with links to Rajapaksa. The abduction of journalists and activists in the country was also reported, with numerous complaints submitted to the UN Working Group on Disappearances. In the 2013 World Press Freedom Index compiled by the international NGO Reporters without Borders, Sri Lanka ranked 162nd out of 179 countries—lower than all of its South Asian neighbours. Meanwhile, the Government closed down most of the country's state universities in August 2012, following a two-month strike by academics, which the Minister of Higher Education, S. B. Dissanayake, claimed was an attempt to foment a 'political crisis'; the universities were reopened in September. In November confrontations between Jaffna University students and security forces as the former commemorated LTTE deaths on its so-called 'Martyrs' Day' erupted into violence. Also in November, a riot at the Welikada prison in Colombo resulted in the deaths of 27 prisoners, prompting criticism from the UNP over the brutality of the security forces.

Provincial council elections were held in the North Central, Sabaragamuwa and Eastern provinces in September 2012; in the first two, the ruling UPFA retained power with an actual gain in seats. In the Eastern province, where the SLMC had opted to contest the election independently of the UPFA, the latter won the largest number of seats but failed to secure a majority, while the TNA became the second-largest party. Following negotiations, the SLMC agreed to form a governing coalition with the UPFA.

In January 2013 the impeachment of the Chief Justice of the Supreme Court, Shirani Bandaranaike, sparked outrage and led to large protests by the legal community and the opposition. Bandaranaike faced allegations of corruption, but claimed the charges were politically motivated; she was dismissed by a parliamentary vote despite a Supreme Court ruling that the move was unlawful. Mohan Peiris, a former attorney-general who was said to be pro-Rajapaksa, was swiftly appointed to replace Bandaranaike.

Foreign Affairs

Regional relations

While officially adhering to a policy of non-alignment, Sri Lanka has long fostered close diplomatic and economic relations with its large neighbour India. Following its direct intervention in 1987–90 in the Sri Lankan civil conflict, when an Indian peace-keeping force was dispatched to the island to oversee the implementation of a peace accord between the Sri Lankan Government and the Tamil militants, India subsequently resisted further demands that it become directly involved again. Since the defeat of the LTTE in 2009 India has played a major role in the resettlement and rehabilitation of thousands of displaced Tamil civilians and in the reconstruction of the war-ravaged north-east of Sri Lanka. In 2010 India opened two new consulates in Sri Lanka, one in the southern city of Hambantota and the other in Jaffna, and announced further investment in Sri Lanka (notably in the energy sector). During an official visit to India by President Mahinda Rajapaksa in June of that year an agreement was signed regarding the possibility of Sri Lanka supplying India with electricity (following the commissioning of new coal and thermal power plants) through an undersea power line. Bilateral relations came under pressure in January 2011 as a result of the alleged shooting of two Indian fishermen in separate incidents by the Sri Lankan navy. Nevertheless, the reopening in June of a ferry service across the Palk Strait, linking Colombo with the southern Indian port of Tuticorin, was hailed as a reflection of burgeoning bilateral ties. (Ferry services between the two countries had been suspended in the 1980s as a result of the Sri Lankan conflict.)

Bilateral tensions re-emerged following India's decision to vote in support of a US-sponsored resolution, adopted by UNHRC in March 2012, urging the Sri Lankan Government to investigate allegations of human rights violations levelled against both the Sri Lankan Government and the Tamil militants in the final stages of the civil conflict; this prompted an angry response from members of the Sri Lankan Cabinet, who contended that India's stance was in direct contravention of the long-standing policy among South Asian Association for Regional Cooperation (SAARC) countries of supporting fellow member states in the event of an international issue arising. Analysts surmised that the Indian Government was, at least in part, responding to pressure from the Tamil Nadu-based Dravida Munnetra Kazhagam (DMK) party, a vital partner in India's governing coalition, which reportedly threatened to withdraw its support if the Government failed to support the resolution. Visits by President Rajapaksa to India in September 2012 and February 2013 were marred by protests against the Sri Lankan administration's treatment of Tamils. India's support for a further US-sponsored UNHRC resolution on Sri Lanka in March 2013 (see Other external relations) was believed to be closely linked to the withdrawal of the DMK from India's coalition Government a few days before the vote. None the less, bilateral trade was reported to have increased by more than 60% during 2011, reaching a record high of US $5,000m.

As relations between Sri Lanka and the West came under pressure over the former's human rights record (in August 2010 the EU temporarily suspended Sri Lanka's preferential access to EU markets under the Generalised System of Preferences known as GSP Plus), Sri Lanka looked increasingly towards its Asian neighbours to foster closer ties. In recent years relations with the People's Republic of China have strengthened considerably. China has invested heavily in Sri Lanka, especially in the areas of energy and infrastructure development; the large international port at Hambantota (which opened for transhipment in June 2012) and the Mattala Rajapaksa International Airport, serving Hambantota (which was inaugurated in March 2013), both of which involve extensive Chinese funding, are of particular note. In June 2010 Chinese Vice-Premier Zhang Dejiang visited Colombo for talks with President Rajapaksa, during which the two leaders signed six agreements on co-operation in industry and technology. In June 2011 the Sri Lankan Government announced a memorandum of understanding with the China Development Bank under the terms of which the Chinese bank agreed to provide US $1,500m. in financial assistance for infrastructure development in Sri Lanka, including road, bridge, water supply and power projects, during the next three years. President Rajapaksa completed a state visit to China in August, whereupon he met with Chinese President Hu

Jintao and Premier Wen Jiabao; the Chinese authorities stated their support for Sri Lanka's attempts to promote national reconciliation without external interference, and pledged to expand bilateral trade, investment and tourism co-operation. The Chairman of the Standing Committee of China's National People's Congress, Wu Bangguo, visited Sri Lanka in September 2012, signing agreements in areas including infrastructure, telecommunications and port development.

Pakistan, which provided the Sri Lankan Government with large amounts of advanced military equipment during the civil war, has also promoted the development of closer ties with Sri Lanka, particularly with regard to the expansion of bilateral trade (which totalled an estimated US $500m. in 2010). Moreover, Pakistan voted against UNHRC resolutions in 2009 and 2013 that called on Sri Lanka to take greater accountability for alleged human rights violations during the civil war. In April 2011 President Rajapaksa paid a three-day official visit to Bangladesh, in the course of which the two countries signed five memorandums of understanding on a number of subjects, including export promotion, education and agricultural research.

Other external relations

Sri Lanka has enjoyed generally cordial relations with the USA, which has been a significant source of financial assistance, providing in excess of US $2,000m. in aid since Sri Lanka acceded to independence in 1948. The USA has also provided training to the Sri Lankan authorities in the field of counter-terrorism. In its *Country Reports on Terrorism 2010*, published in August 2011, the US Department of State commended the Sri Lankan authorities' demonstrable commitment to counter-terrorism efforts and measures to combat money-laundering during the course of 2010. However, US criticism of Sri Lanka's perceived poor record on human rights has engendered intermittent bilateral tensions, and led to the suspension in late 2010 of the GSP arrangement under which Sri Lanka was granted preferential access to US markets (the GSP was reauthorized in October 2011—retroactively, with effect from January 2011). In December 2010 WikiLeaks, an organization publishing leaked private and classified content, released a series of diplomatic cables from the US embassy in Sri Lanka in which the US ambassador was reported to have given credence to allegations of war crimes against President Rajapaksa and his brother, Gotabhaya Rajapaksa. Following the publication in December 2011 of the LLRC's report into the conflict between the Sri Lankan Government and the LTTE (see Domestic Political Affairs), the US Department of State expressed concern that the commission had failed comprehensively to address allegations of serious human rights violations levelled against both sides in the conflict. In response, the Sri Lankan Government criticized the US Government for singling it out while failing to condemn other countries that had proven much more reticent in dealing with similar post-conflict situations. Relations were further strained following the adoption in mid-March 2012 by UNHRC of a US-sponsored resolution that urged the Sri Lankan Government 'to fulfil its relevant legal obligations and commitment to initiate credible and independent actions to ensure justice, equity, accountability and reconciliation for all Sri Lankans' and 'to address alleged violations of international law' (see Domestic Political Affairs). The resolution was approved by 24 votes to 15, with eight abstentions; Canada and India were among those to support the resolution, while those who voted against the motion included China and Russia. The Sri Lankan Government contested that the resolution constituted unwarranted interference in Sri Lanka's internal affairs. None the less, US pressure on Sri Lanka over human rights concerns continued with the adoption of a further US-sponsored resolution on Sri Lanka in March 2013. The resolution, which encouraged Sri Lanka to facilitate an independent investigation into allegations of humanitarian violations during the civil war, was again supported by India.

An announcement in April 2013 confirming that the next biennial Commonwealth Heads of Government Meeting would be held in Colombo in November attracted criticism from some Commonwealth member states and NGOs. Canada's Minister of Foreign Affairs, John Baird, indicated that his Government was considering a boycott of the meeting, on the grounds of Sri Lanka's 'appalling' human rights record, while the United Kingdom-based NGO Amnesty International published a report at the end of April in which it highlighted growing harassment and violent suppression by the Sri Lankan Government of its critics and opponents.

CONSTITUTION AND GOVERNMENT

The Constitution of Sri Lanka was approved by the National State Assembly (renamed Parliament) on 17 August 1978, and promulgated on 7 September 1978.

A presidential form of government was adopted in October 1977 and confirmed in the Constitution of September 1978. The Constitution provides for a unicameral Parliament as the supreme legislative body, its members being elected by a system of modified proportional representation. Executive powers are vested in the President, who is head of state. The President is directly elected for a term of six years and is not accountable to Parliament. The President has the power to appoint or dismiss the Prime Minister and members of the Cabinet; may assume any portfolio; and is empowered to dismiss Parliament. In 1982 the Constitution was amended, allowing the President to call a presidential election before his/her first term of office was completed. In 1983 the Constitution was further amended to include a 'no-separation' clause, making any division of Sri Lanka illegal, and any advocates of separatism liable to lose their civic rights. In 2010 a constitutional amendment abolished the stipulation restricting the President to two terms of office.

Sri Lanka comprises nine provinces and 25 administrative districts, each with an appointed Governor and elected Development Council. A network of 68 Pradeshiya Sabhas (district councils) was inaugurated throughout the country in 1988.

REGIONAL AND INTERNATIONAL CO-OPERATION

Sri Lanka is a member of the Asian Development Bank (ADB, see p. 214) and a founder member of both the South Asian Association for Regional Cooperation (SAARC, see p. 430) and the Colombo Plan (see p. 460), which seek to improve regional co-operation, particularly in economic and social development.

Having joined the UN in 1955, Sri Lanka is a member of the Economic and Social Commission for Asia and the Pacific (ESCAP, see p. 31). Sri Lanka is also member of The Commonwealth (see p. 244). As a contracting party to the General Agreement on Tariffs and Trade (GATT), Sri Lanka joined the World Trade Organization (WTO, see p. 444) on its establishment in 1995.

ECONOMIC AFFAIRS

In 2011, according to estimates by the World Bank, Sri Lanka's gross national income (GNI), measured at average 2009–11 prices, was US $53,832m., equivalent to $2,580 per head (or $5,560 per head on an international purchasing-power parity basis). During 2002–11, it was estimated, the population increased at an average annual rate of 1.1%, while gross domestic product (GDP) per head grew, in real terms, by an average of 5.3% per year. Overall GDP increased, in real terms, at an average annual rate of 6.4% in 2002–12; real GDP rose by 8.2% in 2011 and by 6.4% in 2012.

In 2012 agriculture (including hunting, forestry and fishing) contributed an estimated 11.1% of GDP, while 33.8% of the employed labour force (excluding inhabitants of the northern and eastern provinces) were engaged in the sector in 2011. The principal cash crops are tea (which accounted for an estimated 14.1% of total export earnings in 2011), rubber and coconuts. In 2010 Sri Lanka was the world's largest tea exporter, accounting for around 25% of global exports. Rice production is also important. Cattle, buffaloes, goats and poultry are the principal livestock. During 2002–12 agricultural GDP increased at an average annual rate of 3.8%; agricultural GDP expanded by 5.8% in 2012.

Industry (including mining and quarrying, manufacturing, construction and power) contributed an estimated 31.5% of GDP in 2012 and engaged 25.5% of the employed labour force (excluding inhabitants of the northern and eastern provinces) in 2011. During 2002–12 industrial GDP increased at an average annual rate of 7.3%; industrial GDP rose by 10.3% in 2012.

Mining and quarrying contributed an estimated 2.0% of GDP in 2012, and, according to the Asian Development Bank (ADB), engaged 1.8% of the employed labour force in 2001. Diamonds are the major mineral export (accounting for an estimated 5.2% of total export earnings in 2010). Another commercially important mineral in Sri Lanka is graphite, and there are also deposits of iron ore, monazite, uranium, ilmenite sands, limestone and clay.

Manufacturing contributed an estimated 17.9% of GDP in 2012 and engaged 18.4% of the employed labour force (excluding inhabitants of the northern and eastern provinces) in 2011. The principal branches of manufacturing include wearing apparel (excluding footwear), textiles, food products, and also petroleum and coal products. The garment industry is Sri Lanka's largest earner of foreign exchange, with sales of garments and textiles providing an estimated 39.7% of total export earnings in 2011. During 2002–12 manufacturing GDP increased by an average of 5.6% per year; the GDP of the manufacturing sector rose by 7.9% in 2011 and by 5.2% in 2012.

Construction contributed an estimated 9.4% of GDP in 2012. During 2002–12 construction GDP increased at an average annual rate of 9.4%; the sector grew by 14.2% in 2011 and by 21.6% in 2012.

Energy is derived principally from petroleum, which accounted for 60.3% of electricity production in 2009. In the same year hydroelectric power accounted for 39.5% of electricity produced. The country's first coal-fired electricity plant, the 300 MW Norochcholai facility at Puttalam, in the north-west of the country, was inaugurated in 2011; the plant was expected to alter significantly the structure of the energy sector. Imports of petroleum comprised 23.7% of the value of total imports in 2011.

The services sector, which is dominated by tourism, contributed an estimated 57.5% of GDP in 2012 and engaged 40.7% of the employed labour force (excluding inhabitants of the northern and eastern provinces) in 2011. During 2002–12 services GDP increased at an average annual rate of 6.6%; the sector's GDP grew by 8.6% in 2011 and 4.6% in 2012.

In 2011 Sri Lanka recorded a visible merchandise trade deficit of US $7,683m. and there was a deficit of $4,675m. on the current account of the balance of payments. In 2011 the principal source of imports (26.0%) was India followed by the People's Republic of China, Singapore, Iran and Japan. The USA was the principal market for exports (20.1%) and other major trading partners were the United Kingdom, India, Italy and Germany. The principal exports in 2011 were textiles and garments, and agricultural products (principally tea). The principal imports were petroleum, machinery and transport equipment, and textiles.

According to the ADB, the budgetary deficit for 2011 was estimated at Rs 450,181m. Sri Lanka's total external debt was US $20,452m. at the end of 2010, of which $16,449 was public and publicly guaranteed debt. In that year, the cost of servicing long-term public and publicly guaranteed debt and repayments to the IMF was equivalent to 13.0% of the value of exports of goods, services and income (excluding workers' remittances). During 2002–2012 the average annual rate of inflation was 7.3%; according to the ILO, the rate was 7.5% in 2012. According to official figures, 4.0% of the labour force were unemployed in 2011.

Despite a strong recovery from the devastating effects of the tsunami in late 2004, the persistent fiscal deficit remained a considerable obstacle to Sri Lanka's development in 2005–10. The Government increasingly relied on external creditors to finance this deficit, thus contributing to escalating levels of public debt and higher rates of inflation. Following the resolution of the conflict between the Government and the Tamil militants in May 2009 (see Contemporary Political History), the subsequent rehabilitation and reconstruction programmes (many of which were funded by China) provided a significant boost to the economy, and helped to attract greater levels of domestic and foreign investment. In December 2009 the main highway to the Jaffna peninsula was reopened for the first time in 25 years, thus facilitating the economic integration and recovery of the northern and eastern areas of the island that were previously controlled by the insurgents. In September 2012 the Jaffna peninsula was reconnected to the national electricity grid, its electricity supply having been disrupted by the LTTE in 1987. The tourism sector performed particularly well from 2010, reaching a record high of 1,005,605 arrivals in 2012. Following a substantial decrease in late 2011 and early 2012, the rate of consumer price growth again accelerated, with the rate of inflation reaching 9.8% by January 2013. Foreign direct investment was estimated by the Board of Investment to have reached US $1,200m. in 2012, with a target of $1,500m. set for 2013. However, the ongoing global economic slowdown, coupled with a severe drought, contributed to a decrease in GDP growth, from 8.2% in 2011 to 6.4% in 2012. Extensive infrastructural development, together with effective reform of the tax system and an increase in the level of private sector investment, have been identified as crucial conditions for achieving long-term, sustainable economic growth in Sri Lanka. A new Country Partnership Strategy for the period 2012–16, concluded between the ADB and the Sri Lankan Government in October 2011, was to focus on reducing regional disparities, catalysing private sector participation in development, and removing human resources constraints. In May 2012 the World Bank approved a $314m. grant to Sri Lanka for primary and secondary education and the urban development of Colombo.

PUBLIC HOLIDAYS

2014: 14 January (Tamil Thai Pongal Day), 13 January (Milad un-Nabi, Birth of the Prophet), 4 February (Independence Day), 27 February (Maha Shivaratri), 13 April (Sinhala and Tamil New Year's Eve), 14 April (Sinhala and Tamil New Year's Day), 18 April (Good Friday), 1 May (May Day), 28 July (Id al-Fitr,

Ramazan Festival Day), 4 October (Id al-Adha, Hadji Festival Day), 23 October (Diwali—Festival of Lights), 25 December (Christmas Day).

Note: A number of Hindu, Muslim and Buddhist holidays depend on lunar sightings. There is a holiday every lunar month on the day of the full moon. The day following Vesak Full Moon Poya Day (celebrating the birth of Buddha) is an important public holiday, which usually occurs in May in the Gregorian calendar.

Statistical Survey

Source (unless otherwise stated): Department of Census and Statistics, 15/12 Maitland Crescent, POB 563, Colombo 7; tel. (11) 2682176; fax (11) 2697594; e-mail dcensus@lanka.ccom.lk; internet www.statistics.gov.lk.

Area and Population

AREA, POPULATION AND DENSITY

Area (sq km)	65,525*
Population (census results)	
17 July 2001†	16,864,544
20 March 2012	
Males	9,832,401
Females	10,431,322
Total	20,263,723
Density (per sq km) at 2012 census	309.3

* 25,299 sq miles. This figure includes inland water (3,189 sq km).

† Figures refer to 18 out of 25 districts where enumeration was carried out completely. Enumeration was only partially conducted in Mannar, Vavuniya, Batticaloa and Trincomalee districts, owing to security concerns; data from these districts brought the total enumerated population to approximately 17,560,000. The census was not conducted in the districts of Jaffna, Mullaitivu and Kilinochchi, also owing to security concerns. The total estimated population for the entire country at July 2001 was 18,732,255.

POPULATION BY AGE AND SEX
('000, official estimates at mid-2011)

	Males	Females	Total
0–14	2,786	2,702	5,488
15–64	6,960	7,105	14,065
65 and over	611	705	1,316
Total	**10,357**	**10,512**	**20,869**

ETHNIC GROUPS
(census results)

	1981	2001*	2012
Sinhalese	10,979,561	13,810,664	15,173,820
Sri Lankan Tamil . . .	1,886,872	736,484	2,270,924
Indian Tamil	818,656	855,888	842,323
Sri Lankan Moors . . .	1,046,926	1,349,845	1,869,820
Others	114,735	111,663	106,836
Total	**14,846,750**	**16,864,544**	**20,263,723**

* Provisional; figures refer to 18 out of 25 districts where full enumeration was possible.

DISTRICTS
(population at 2012 census)

	Area (sq km, excl. inland water)*	Population	Density (persons per sq km)
Ampara	4,222	648,057	153
Anuradhapura . . .	6,664	856,232	128
Badulla	2,827	811,758	287
Batticaloa	2,610	525,142	201
Colombo	676	2,309,809	3,417
Galle	1,617	1,058,771	655
Gampaha	1,341	2,294,641	1,711
Hambantota . . .	2,496	596,617	239
Jaffna	929	583,378	628
Kalutara	1,576	1,217,260	772
Kandy	1,917	1,369,899	715
Kegalle	1,685	836,603	497
Kilinochchi . . .	1,205	112,875	94
Kurunegala . . .	4,624	1,610,299	348
Mannar	1,880	99,051	53
Matale	1,952	482,229	247
Matara	1,270	809,344	637
Moneragala . . .	5,508	448,142	81
Mullaitivu . . .	2,415	91,947	38
Nuwara Eliya . . .	1,706	706,588	414
Polonnaruwa . . .	3,077	403,335	131
Puttalam	2,882	759,776	264
Ratnapura . . .	3,236	1,082,277	334
Trincomalee . . .	2,529	378,182	150
Vavuniya	1,861	171,511	92
Total	**62,705**	**20,263,723**	**323**

* As at 1988; revised total land area is 62,336 sq km.

PRINCIPAL TOWNS
(provisional, population at 2001 census)

Colombo (Kolamba)* .	642,020	Sri Jayawardenepura (Kotte)†	115,826
Dehiwala-Mount Lavinia . . .	209,787	Kandy (Maha Nuwara)	110,049
Moratuwa	177,190	Kalmunai (Galmune) .	94,457
Jaffna (Yapanaya) .	145,600‡	Galle (Galla) . . .	90,934
Negombo (Migamuwa)	121,933		

* Commercial capital.

† Administrative capital.

‡ Estimated population at mid-1997 (Source: Provincial Councils, Department of Elections).

Source: Thomas Brinkhoff, *City Population* (internet www.citypopulation.de).

Mid-2011 (incl. suburbs, UN estimates): Colombo (Kolamba) 693,470; Sri Jayawardenepura (Kotte) 125,515 (Source: UN, *World Urbanization Prospects: The 2011 Revision*).

BIRTHS, MARRIAGES AND DEATHS
(year of registration, provisional)

	Registered live births		Registered marriages	Registered deaths	
	Number	Rate (per 1,000)	Number	Number	Rate (per 1,000)
2004	360,220	18.5	191,985	112,568	5.8
2005	370,424	18.8	194,352	129,822	6.6
2006	371,264	18.7	197,458	115,424	5.8
2007	380,069	19.0	195,193	116,883	5.8
2008	373,575	18.5	198,578*	123,814	6.1
2009*	376,843	18.4	194,970	120,085	5.9
2010*	364,565	17.7	n.a.	128,603	6.2
2011*	363,415	17.4	n.a.	123,261	5.9

* Provisional.

Life expectancy (years at birth): 74.7 (males 77.1; females 77.9) in 2010 (Source: World Bank, World Development Indicators database).

ECONOMICALLY ACTIVE POPULATION
('000 persons aged 10 years and over, excluding northern and eastern provinces)

	2009	2010	2011
Agriculture, hunting, forestry and fishing	2,318.6	2,353.6	2,445.3
Manufacturing	1,301.3	1,270.3	1,327.6
Mining and quarrying . . .			
Electricity, gas and water . .	521.4	506.8	513.8
Construction			
Wholesale and retail trade, repair of motor vehicles, motorcycles and personal household goods . . .	913.4	985.9	987.8
Restaurants and hotels . . .	133.2	139.0	134.1
Transport, storage and communications	419.6	462.7	461.7
Financing, insurance, real estate and business services . .	221.0	256.0	269.1
Public administration and defence	487.4	490.7	506.9
Education	300.1	269.3	281.7
Health and social work . . .	128.5	105.0	122.0
Other community, social and personal services . . .	104.6	120.8	106.4
Private households with employed persons	96.1	83.8	76.7
Sub-total	6,945.2	7,043.9	7,233.1
Activities not adequately defined	194.3	191.7	196.6
Total employed	7,139.5	7,235.6	7,429.8
Unemployed	432.9	374.7	307.9
Total labour force . . .	7,527.4	7,610.3	7,737.7

Health and Welfare

KEY INDICATORS

Total fertility rate (children per woman, 2010) . . .	2.3
Under-5 mortality rate (per 1,000 live births, 2010) . . .	17
HIV/AIDS (% of persons aged 15–49, 2009)	<0.1
Physicians (per 1,000 head, 2006)	0.5
Hospital beds (per 1,000 head, 2004)	3.1
Health expenditure (2009): US $ per head (PPP) . . .	149
Health expenditure (2009): % of GDP	3.2
Health expenditure (2009): public (% of total)	46.2
Access to water (% of persons, 2010)	91
Access to sanitation (% of persons, 2010)	92
Total carbon dioxide emissions ('000 metric tons, 2008) . .	11,763.7
Carbon dioxide emissions per head (metric tons, 2008) . .	0.6
Human Development Index (2011): ranking	97
Human Development Index (2011): value	0.691

For sources and definitions, see explanatory note on p. vi.

Agriculture

PRINCIPAL CROPS
('000 metric tons)

	2009	2010	2011
Rice, paddy	3,652	4,301	3,875
Maize	130	162	138
Potatoes	62	52	59
Sweet potatoes	47	46	47
Cassava (Manioc)	278	283	293
Sugar cane	920	915	729
Beans, dry	9	12	11
Cow peas, dry	13	12	10
Coconuts	2,168	1,762	1,523*
Cabbages	63	63	71
Tomatoes	74	75	76
Pumpkins, squash and gourds .	117	119	128
Cucumbers and gherkins . . .	32	34	32
Aubergines (Eggplants) . . .	106	107	117
Chillies and peppers, green . .	46	49	44
Onions, dry	128	121	118
Beans, green	41	43	40
Carrots and turnips	36	34	38
Plantains	512	572	605
Lemons and limes	4	5	6
Guavas, mangoes and mangosteens	82	87	88
Pineapples	50	53	53
Coffee, green	5	5	5
Tea	290	331	328
Pepper	25	27	26
Cinnamon	15	16	16
Natural rubber	136	153	158

* Unofficial figure.

Aggregate production ('000 metric tons, may include official, semi-official or estimated data): Total cereals 3,788 in 2009, 4,470 in 2010, 4,018 in 2011; Total roots and tubers 387 in 2009, 381 in 2010, 399 in 2011; Total vegetables (incl. melons) 732 in 2009, 733 in 2010, 759 in 2011; Total fruits (excl. melons) 710 in 2009, 786 in 2010, 824 in 2011.

Source: FAO.

LIVESTOCK
('000 head, year ending September)

	2009	2010	2011
Buffaloes	372	423	405
Cattle	1,137	1,170	1,192
Sheep	8	8	8
Goats	377	373	373
Pigs	81	84	82
Chickens	13,615	14,018	14,199

Source: FAO.

LIVESTOCK PRODUCTS
('000 metric tons)

	2009	2010	2011
Cattle meat	22.9	28.5	28.7*
Buffalo meat*	4.4	5.0	4.7
Goat meat	1.3	1.4	1.4*
Pig meat	1.6	1.4	1.4*
Chicken meat	99.3	102.3	103.0*
Cows' milk	155.5	162.1	171.8
Buffaloes' milk	41.6	47.0	46.3
Goats' milk*	5.2	5.7	5.7
Hen eggs	64.8	64.7	67.3

* FAO estimate(s).

Source: FAO.

Forestry

ROUNDWOOD REMOVALS
('000 cubic metres, excl. bark, FAO estimates)

	2009	2010	2011
Sawlogs, veneer logs and logs for sleepers	34	34	34
Other industrial wood	577	577	577
Fuel wood	5,283	5,212	5,136
Total	5,894	5,823	5,747

Source: FAO.

SAWNWOOD PRODUCTION
('000 cubic metres, incl. railway sleepers)

	1999*	2000	2001
Coniferous (softwood)	—	—	30
Broadleaved (hardwood) . . .	5	29	31
Total	5	29	61

* FAO estimates.

2002–11: Production assumed to be unchanged from 2001 (FAO estimates).
Source: FAO.

Fishing

('000 metric tons, live weight)

	2008	2009	2010
Capture	327.6	355.7	436.4
Tilapias	25.2	26.3	28.3
Demersal percomorphs . . .	12.7	16.0	20.2
Clupeoids	66.9	71.6	74.3
Skipjack tuna	78.9	82.1	99.8
Carangids	11.2	13.0	17.2
Mackerels	18.3	19.4	24.9
Sharks, rays, skates, etc. . .	3.9	4.3	6.8
Aquaculture	7.5	7.5	8.1
Total catch	335.0	363.3	444.4

Source: FAO.

Mining

('000 metric tons unless otherwise indicated)

	2009	2010	2011
Natural graphite (metric tons) .	3,171	3,437	3,500
Salt—unrefined	11	10	11
Kaolin	10	8	8
Phosphate rock (gross weight) .	36	48	48

Sources: US Geological Survey.

Industry

SELECTED PRODUCTS
('000 metric tons unless otherwise indicated)

	2007	2008	2009
Raw sugar	75	75	41
Cigarettes (million units) . . .	4,719	n.a.	n.a.
Jet fuel	171	154	195
Motor gasoline—petrol . . .	163	164	179
Kerosene	97	111	83
Distillate fuel oil	445	451	485
Residual fuel oil	810	768	817
Cement*	1,700	1,800	1,900
Plywood ('000 cu m)† . . .	14	6	6
Electric energy (million kWh) .	9,814	9,901	9,882

* Estimates.
† FAO estimates.

2010: Cement ('000 metric tons) 2,000 (estimate); Plywood ('000 cu m) 6 (FAO estimate); Electric energy (million kWh) 10,714 (estimate).

2011: Cement ('000 metric tons) 2,200 (estimate); Plywood ('000 cu m) 6 (FAO estimate); Electric energy (million kWh) 11,521 (estimate).

Sources: US Geological Survey; Asian Development Bank, *Key Indicators of Developing Asian and Pacific Countries*; FAO; UN, *Industrial Commodity Statistics Yearbook* and Database.

Finance

CURRENCY AND EXCHANGE RATES

Monetary Units
100 cents = 1 Sri Lanka rupee (R).

Sterling, Dollar and Euro Equivalents (31 December 2012)
£1 sterling = Rs 200.532;
US $1 = Rs 127.080;
€1 = Rs 167.669;
1,000 Sri Lanka rupees = £4.99 = $7.87 = €5.96.

Average Exchange Rate (rupees per US $)
2010   113.064
2011   110.565
2012   127.619

BUDGET
(Rs million)

Revenue	2011	2012*	2013†
Taxation	812,647	896,599	1,131,090
Taxes on income and profits .	157,309	177,303	221,984
Taxes on domestic goods and services	461,483	492,423	619,083
Value-added tax	215,420	223,961	283,342
Excise duty (ordinance) . .	55,286	60,971	70,189
Excise duty (special provisions)	130,692	140,566	177,032
Taxes on international trade .	187,778	221,556	278,797
Import duties	76,010	76,830	97,353
Licence taxes and other . .	6,078	5,317	11,227
Non-tax revenue	145,688	158,702	152,409
Capital revenue	15,392	16,970	16,696
Other	130,296	141,732	135,713
Foreign grants	15,962	20,000	20,000
Total	974,297	1,075,301	1,303,500

Expenditure by category			2011	2012*	2013†
Recurrent expenditure	.	.	1,020,169	1,081,117	1,289,900
Personal emoluments	.	.	251,124	263,706	290,956
Salaries and wages	.	.	136,795	140,852	143,662
General public services	.	.	33,954	34,637	34,968
Transfers	.	.	303,836	328,912	370,512
Retirement benefits	.	.	100,277	111,385	129,458
Provincial councils	.	.	94,645	96,026	102,865
Interest payments	.	.	353,009	370,030	444,835
Other purposes	.	.	35	2,557	46,081
Capital expenditure	.	.	398,546	538,883	530,100
Public debt repayments	.	.	542,337	570,000	747,000
Domestic	.	.	470,075	420,000	634,000
Foreign	.	.	72,262	150,000	113,000
Total expenditure	.	.	**1,961,053**	**2,190,000**	**2,567,000**

Expenditure by institution			2011	2012*	2013†
Special spending units	.	.	12,016	12,776	13,572
Ministries	.	.	1,949,036	2,177,224	2,553,428
Finance and planning	.	.	922,441	975,232	1,288,072
Defence	.	.	241,560	243,400	289,503
Health	.	.	63,354	73,713	93,522
Public administration and home affairs	.	.	125,865	140,185	157,385
Local government and provincial councils	.	.	122,384	132,257	132,790
Total expenditure	.	.	**1,961,053**	**2,190,000**	**2,567,000**

* Revised budget estimates.
† Budget estimates.

Source: Ministry of Finance and Planning, Colombo.

INTERNATIONAL RESERVES
(excluding gold, US $ million at 31 December)

	2009	2010	2011
IMF special drawing rights .	20	2	4
Reserve position in IMF .	75	74	73
Foreign exchange .	4,521	6,634	6,170
Total .	**4,616**	**6,710**	**6,248**

Source: IMF, *International Financial Statistics.*

MONEY SUPPLY
(Rs million at 31 December)

	2009	2010	2011
Currency outside banks .	181,840	216,549	242,871
Demand deposits at commercial banks	154,849	190,637	195,835
Total money (incl. others) .	**339,036**	**410,275**	**440,505**

Source: IMF, *International Financial Statistics.*

COST OF LIVING
(Consumer Price Index for Colombo; base: 2002 = 100)

	2010	2011	2012
Food (incl. beverages) .	234.2	255.9	268.0
Clothing (excl. footwear) .	176.6	n.a.	n.a.
Rent .	230.8	n.a.	n.a.
All items (incl. others) .	**219.1**	**234.4**	**252.0**

Source: ILO.

NATIONAL ACCOUNTS
(Rs million at current prices)

Expenditure on the Gross Domestic Product

	2009	2010	2011*
Government final consumption expenditure	851,549	872,610	967,702
Private final consumption expenditure	3,116,221	3,651,578	4,568,393
Gross capital formation .	1,181,449	1,545,500	1,958,833
Total domestic expenditure	5,149,219	6,069,688	7,494,928
Exports of goods and services	1,031,289	1,254,021	1,508,565
Less Imports of goods and services	1,345,216	1,719,605	2,460,830
GDP at market prices .	**4,835,293**	**5,604,104**	**6,542,663**
GDP at factor cost, at constant 2002 prices	2,449,214	2,645,542	2,863,854

* Provisional.

Gross Domestic Product by Economic Activity

	2010	2011*	2012*
Agriculture, hunting, forestry and fishing	717,910	791,155	837,883
Mining and quarrying .	89,226	112,342	152,113
Manufacturing	1,009,003	1,191,579	1,354,897
Construction	423,414	511,220	712,272
Electricity, gas and water .	127,625	141,474	168,377
Transport, storage and communications	709,400	818,386	988,688
Wholesale and retail trade .	1,096,961	1,357,662	1,519,995
Hotels and restaurants .	33,213	44,254	57,943
Finance and real estate .	597,540	709,316	841,369
Ownership of dwellings .	171,871	189,269	212,129
Public administration .	500,547	532,455	570,973
Private services .	127,393	143,551	165,736
GDP at market prices .	**5,604,104**	**6,542,663**	**7,582,376**

* Provisional.

BALANCE OF PAYMENTS
(US $ million)

	2009	2010	2011
Exports of goods .	7,085	8,626	10,559
Imports of goods .	−9,186	−12,106	−18,242
Balance on goods .	**−2,101**	**−3,480**	**−7,683**
Exports of services .	1,892	2,474	3,084
Imports of services .	−2,523	−3,113	−4,012
Balance on goods and services	**−2,732**	**−4,119**	**−8,611**
Primary income received .	122	323	467
Primary income paid .	−609	−940	1,114
Balance on goods, services and primary income	**−3,219**	**−4,735**	**−9,258**
Secondary income received .	3,330	4,116	5,145
Secondary income paid .	−403	−508	−562
Current balance .	**−292**	**−1,128**	**−4,675**
Capital account (net) .	233	164	164
Direct investment assets .	−20	−43	−60
Direct investment liabilities .	404	478	956
Portfolio investment assets .	−47	172	−469
Portfolio investment liabilities .	−382	−1,049	−623
Other investment assets .	−435	249	183
Other investment liabilities .	−625	−760	−296
Net errors and omissions .	−140	−866	−656
Reserves and related items .	**−1,304**	**−2,782**	**−5,476**

Source: IMF, *International Financial Statistics.*

External Trade

PRINCIPAL COMMODITIES
(Rs million)

Imports c.i.f.	2009	2010	2011*
Consumer goods	179,722	279,762	404,037
Sugar	25,045	41,077	47,091
Other consumer goods	72,567	130,194	230,760
Intermediate goods	707,655	910,010	1,357,505
Petroleum	251,006	343,809	530,389
Textiles	175,681	204,542	256,592
Investment goods	240,284	311,496	473,974
Machinery and transport equipment	164,657	218,214	354,594
Total (incl. others)	1,172,618	1,519,737	2,241,488

Exports f.o.b.	2009	2010	2011*
Agricultural products	210,092	260,632	279,466
Tea	136,194	162,793	164,869
Petroleum products	15,447	29,761	61,170
Textiles and garments	374,645	379,185	463,509
Total (incl. others)	813,911	974,387	1,167,588

* Provisional.

Source: Central Bank of Sri Lanka, Colombo.

PRINCIPAL TRADING PARTNERS
(US $ million)

Imports c.i.f.	2009	2010	2011
China, People's Republic	1,726.6	2,194.5	3,288.5
Hong Kong	343.5	377.2	444.9
India	1,906.2	3,645.3	5,379.6
Indonesia	270.9	327.6	n.a.
Iran	772.8	1,012.4	1,285.8
Japan	224.6	704.5	1,036.6
Malaysia	369.9	511.6	671.4
Singapore	836.6	1,319.0	1,466.1
Thailand	359.6	441.7	529.6
United Arab Emirates	305.1	399.6	507.5
USA	252.5	n.a.	n.a.
Total (incl. others)	10,871.1	15,495.1	20,703.8

Exports f.o.b.	2009	2010	2011
Belgium	349.0	371.3	441.3
France	150.7	136.7	146.8
Germany	389.9	413.7	496.5
India	298.2	472.4	625.1
Italy	405.2	436.8	501.1
Japan	166.7	200.2	244.2
Russia	239.8	280.5	353.6
United Arab Emirates	247.6	284.8	327.5
United Kingdom	946.8	884.4	919.3
USA	1,515.9	1,664.7	1,985.2
Total (incl. others)	7,309.0	8,405.5	9,873.1

Note: Data reflect the IMF's direction of trade methodology and, as a result, the totals may not be equal to those presented for trade in commodities.

Source: Asian Development Bank.

Transport

RAILWAYS

	2009	2010	2011
Passengers (million)	101.8	101.5	46.0
Freight carried ('000 metric tons)*	1,641	2,702	1,934

* Excluding livestock.

ROAD TRAFFIC
(motor vehicles in use)

	2009	2010	2011
Passenger cars	387,210	410,282	468,168
Buses and coaches	81,789	84,280	88,528
Lorries and vans	482,363	505,920	554,256
Motorcycles and mopeds	2,339,916	2,630,375	3,022,132
Total (incl. others)	3,291,278	3,954,311	4,479,732

SHIPPING

Flag Registered Fleet
(at 31 December)

	2010	2011	2012
Number of vessels	76	78	81
Total displacement ('000 grt)	186.5	182.3	176.4

Source: Lloyd's List Intelligence (www.lloydslistintelligence.com).

International Sea-borne Shipping
(freight traffic, '000 metric tons, Colombo, Trincomalee and Galle only)

	2009	2010	2011*
Goods loaded	19,494	24,655	25,610
Goods unloaded	29,283	36,585	39,443

* Provisional.

Source: Central Bank of Sri Lanka, Colombo.

CIVIL AVIATION
(traffic on scheduled services)

	2009	2010	2011*
Kilometres flown (million)	38	40	53
Passengers carried ('000)	2,435	2,808	3,261
Passenger-km (million)	7,851	9,400	10,677
Total ton-km (million)	976	1,473	1,632

* Provisional.

Source: Central Bank of Sri Lanka, Colombo.

Tourism

FOREIGN TOURIST ARRIVALS*

Country of residence	2008	2009	2010
Australia	19,145	23,249	33,512
Belgium	2,394	2,613	5,371
Canada	9,745	10,785	21,231
France	10,703	16,205	31,119
Germany	30,154	29,664	45,981
India	88,628	83,650	125,112
Italy	9,137	7,214	11,512
Japan	10,578	10,931	14,998
Maldives	31,458	31,890	35,401
Netherlands	13,180	11,297	17,628
Pakistan	7,702	7,388	9,001
Switzerland	5,261	6,247	9,514
United Kingdom	80,214	81,682	105,938
USA	13,458	14,259	19,321
Total (incl. others)	438,475	447,890	654,476

* Excluding Sri Lanka nationals residing abroad.

Total foreign tourist arrivals ('000): 654 in 2010; 856 in 2011 (provisional).

Tourism receipts (US $ million, excl. passenger transport): 576 in 2010; 830 in 2011 (provisional).

Sources: World Tourism Organization.

Communications Media

	2009	2010	2011
Telephones ('000 main lines in use)	3,436.0	3,578.5	3,608.4
Mobile cellular telephones ('000 subscribers)	16,305.4	17,359.3	18,319.4
Internet subscribers ('000)	249.8	298.1	n.a.
Broadband subscribers ('000) . .	169.6	228.3	359.0

Source: International Telecommunication Union.

Education

(1995)

	Institutions	Teachers	Students
Primary	9,657	70,537	1,962,498
Secondary	5,771*	103,572	2,314,054
Universities and equivalent . .	n.a.	2,344	40,035
Distance learning	n.a.	206	20,601

* 1992 figure.

1996: Primary: 9,554 institutions, 66,339 teachers, 1,843,848 students.

1997: Primary: 60,832 teachers, 1,807,751 students; Secondary: 2,313,511 students.

1998: Primary: 1,798,162 students.

2011 (all levels, provisional): *Schools:* Total 10,545 (state 9,732, private 97, Pirivena monastic colleges 716). *Teachers:* Total 228,556 (state 216,281, private 5,788, Pirivena monastic colleges 6,487). *Pupils:* Total 4,156,173 (state 3,973,901, private 119,627, Pirivena monastic colleges 62,645).

Higher education (2011): 15 institutions, 5,064 teachers (including temporary staff), 115,012 students.

Source: Ministry of Education, Colombo.

Pupil-teacher ratio (primary education, UNESCO estimate): 23.9 in 2009/10 (Source: UNESCO Institute for Statistics).

Adult literacy rate (UNESCO estimates): 91.2% (males 92.6%; females 90.0%) in 2010 (Source: UNESCO Institute for Statistics).

Directory

The Government

HEAD OF STATE

President: MAHINDA RAJAPAKSA (sworn in 19 November 2005; re-elected 26 January 2010; sworn in for a second term 19 November 2010).

THE CABINET
(May 2013)

The Cabinet is formed by the United People's Freedom Alliance.

Prime Minister and Minister of Buddha Sasana and Religious Affairs: D. M. JAYARATNE.

Minister of Defence and Urban Development, of Finance and Planning, and of Ports and Highways: MAHINDA RAJAPAKSA.

Senior Minister and Minister of Good Governance and Infrastructure: RATHNASIRI WICKRAMANAYAKA.

Senior Minister and Minister of Human Resources: D. E. W. GUNASEKERA.

Senior Minister and Minister of Rural Affairs: ATHAUDA SENEVIRATNE.

Senior Minister and Minister of Food Security: P. DAYARATNE.

Senior Minister and Minister of Urban Affairs: A. H. M. FOWZIE.

Senior Minister and Minister of Social Welfare: MILROY FERNANDO.

Senior Minister and Minister of Consumer Welfare: S. B. NAVINNE.

Senior Minister and Minister of National Resources: PIYASENA GAMAGE.

Senior Minister and Minister of Scientific Affairs: Prof. TISSA VITHARANA.

Senior Minister and Minister of International Monetary Co-operation: SARATH AMUNUGAMA.

Minister of Irrigation and Water Resources Management: NIMAL SIRIPALA DE SILVA.

Minister of Health: MAITHRIPALA SIRISENA.

Minister of Petroleum Industries: ANURA PRIYADARSHANA YAPA.

Minister of Livestock and Rural Community Development: ARUMUGAM THONDAMAN.

Minister of Water Supply and Drainage: DINESH C. R. GUNAWARDENA.

Minister of Traditional Industries and Small Enterprise Development: DOUGLAS DEVANANDA.

Minister of Local Government and Provincial Councils: A. L. M. ATHAULLAH.

Minister of Industry and Commerce: RISHAD BATHIYUTHEEN.

Minister of Power and Energy: PAVITHRA WANNIARACHCHI.

Minister of Construction, Engineering Services, Housing and Common Amenities: WIMAL WEERAWANSA.

Minister of Justice: ABDUL RAUFF HAKEEM.

Minister of Economic Development: BASIL RAJAPAKSA.

Minister of National Languages and Social Integration: VASUDEVA NANAYAKKARA.

Minister of Higher Education: S. B. DISSANAYAKE.

Minister of External Affairs: Prof. G. L. PEIRIS.

Minister of Public Administration and Home Affairs: W. D. J. SENEVIRATNE.

Minister of Parliamentary Affairs: SUMEDHA JAYASENA.

Minister of Postal Services: JEEWAN KUMARANATUNGA.

Minister of Technology, Research and Atomic Energy: CHAMPIKA RANAWAKA.

Minister of Environment and Renewable Energy: SUSIL PREMAJAYANTHA.

Minister of Child Development and Women's Affairs: TISSA KARALIYADDE.

Minister of Labour and Labour Relations: GAMINI LOKUGE.

Minister of Education: BANDULA GUNAWARDENA.

Minister of Plantation Industries: MAHINDA SAMARASINGHE.

Minister of Fisheries and Aquatic Resources Development: RAJITHA SENARATNE.

Minister of Land and Land Development: JANAKA BANDARA TENNEKOON.

Minister of Social Services: FELIX PERERA.

Minister of Private Transport Services: C. B. RATHNAYAKE.

Minister of Agriculture: MAHINDA YAPA ABEYWARDENA.

Minister of Mass Media and Information: KEHELIYA RAMBUKWELLA.

Minister of Transport: KUMARA WELGAMA.

Minister of Youth Affairs and Skills Development: DULLAS ALAHAPERUMA.

Minister of Co-operatives and Internal Trade: JOHNSTON FERNANDO.

Minister of Rehabilitation and Prison Reforms: CHANDRASIRI GAJADEERA.

Minister of Indigenous Medicine: SALINDA DISSANAYAKE.

Minister of Minor Export Crop Promotion: REGINALD COORAY.

Minister of Foreign Employment Promotion and Welfare: DILAN PERERA.

Minister of Coconut Development and Janatha Estate Development: JAGATH PUSHPAKUMARA.

Minister of Culture and the Arts: T. B. EKANAYAKE.

Minister of Disaster Management: MAHINDA AMARAWEERA.

Minister of Wildlife Resources Conservation: GAMINI VIJITH VIJAYAMUNI SOYSA.

Minister of Resettlement: GUNARATNE WEERAKOON.

Minister of Public Relations and Public Affairs: MERVIN SILVA.

Minister of Sports: MAHINDANANDA ALUTHGAMAGE.

Minister of State Resources and Enterprise Development: DAYASRITHA TISSERA.

Minister of Telecommunications and Information Technology: RANJITH SIYAMBALAPITIYA.

Minister of National Heritage: JAGATH BALASURIYA.

Minister of Productivity Promotion: BASIR SEGUDAWOOD.

Minister of Public Management Reforms: NAVIN DISSANAYAKE.

Minister of Civil Aviation: PRIYANKARA JAYARATNA.

Minister of Investment Promotion: LAKSHMAN YAPA ABEYWARDENA.

Minister of Education Services: DUMINDA DISSANAYAKE.

Minister of Sugar Industry Development: LAKSHMAN SENEVIRATNE.

Minister of Botanical Gardens and Public Recreation: JAYARATNE HERATH.

MINISTRIES

President's Secretariat: Republic Sq., Colombo 1; tel. (11) 2324801; fax (11) 2331246; e-mail priu@presidentsoffice.lk; internet www.president.gov.lk.

Prime Minister's Office: 58 Sir Ernest de Silva Mawatha, Colombo 7; tel. (11) 2575317; fax (11) 2575454; e-mail slpm@pmoffice.gov.lk; internet www.pmoffice.gov.lk.

Ministry of Agriculture: 'Govijana Mandiraya', 80/5 Rajamalwatta Rd, Battaramulla, Colombo; tel. (11) 2869553; fax (11) 2868910; e-mail ituagrimin@gmail.com; internet www.agrimin.gov .lk.

Ministry of Buddha Sasana and Religious Affairs: 135 Dharmapala Mawatha, Colombo 7; tel. (11) 2307674; fax (11) 2307405; e-mail religiousaffairs@religiousaffairs.gov.lk.

Ministry of Child Development and Women's Affairs: 175A Nawala Rd, Nugegoda, Colombo; tel. (11)2827028; fax (11)2827023; e-mail secycdwe@sltnet.lk; internet www .childwomenmin.gov.lk.

Ministry of Civil Aviation: 51E 2nd Floor, Bristol Bldg, York St, Colombo 1; tel. (11) 2431657; fax (11) 2433357; e-mail civimyad@ sltnet.lk; internet www.aviationmin.gov.lk.

Ministry of Coconut Development and Janatha Estate Development: 8th Floor, Sethsiripaya 2nd Stage, Baththaramulla, Colombo 1; tel. (11) 2187078; fax (11) 2187078; e-mail mcdjedplanning@gmail.com; internet www.cdjedmin.gov.lk.

Ministry of Construction, Engineering Services, Housing and Common Amenities: 'Sethsiripaya', 2nd Floor, Sri Jayawardanpura Kotte, Battaramulla, Colombo; tel. (11) 2882412; fax (11) 2867952; e-mail info@houseconmin.gov.lk; internet houseconmin .gov.lk.

Ministry of Co-operatives and Internal Trade: 'Rakshana Mandiraya', 7th Floor, 21 Vauxhall St, Colombo 2; tel. (11) 2300345; fax (11) 2447669; e-mail secretary@trade.gov.lk; internet www.trade.gov.lk.

Ministry of Culture and the Arts: 'Sethsiripaya', 8th Floor, Battaramulla, Colombo; tel. (11) 2885970; fax (11) 2879280; e-mail addlsecadmin@cultural.gov.lk; internet www.cultural.gov.lk.

Ministry of Defence and Urban Development: 15/5 Baladaksha Mawatha, POB 572, Colombo 3; tel. (11) 2430860; fax (11) 2446300; e-mail webinfo@defence.lk; internet www.defence.lk.

Ministry of Disaster Management: 2 Wijerama Mawatha, Colombo 7; tel. (11) 2665185; fax (11) 2665098; e-mail sameerajayarathna@yahoo.com; internet www.disastermin.gov.lk.

Ministry of Economic Development: 464A TB Jaya Mawatha, Colombo 10; tel. (11)2681973; fax (11) 2673692; e-mail edmediaunit@ gmail.com; internet www.med.gov.lk.

Ministry of Education: 'Isurupaya', Battaramulla, Colombo; tel. (11) 2784811; fax (11) 2787578; e-mail secretary.education@moe.gov .lk; internet www.moe.gov.lk.

Ministry of Environment and Renewable Energy: 82 Sampath Paya, Rajamalwatte Rd, Battaramulla, Colombo; tel. (11) 2877290; fax (11) 2877292; e-mail promotion@menr.lk; internet www .environmentmin.gov.lk.

Ministry of External Affairs: Republic Bldg, Colombo 1; tel. (11) 2437633; fax (11) 2472488; e-mail publicity@mea.gov.lk; internet www.mea.gov.lk.

Ministry of Finance and Planning: Galle Face Secretariat, Colombo 1; tel. (11) 2484500; fax (11) 2449823; e-mail info@mo .treasury.gov.lk; internet www.treasury.gov.lk.

Ministry of Fisheries and Aquatic Resources Development: New Secretariat, Maligawatta, Colombo 10; tel. (11) 2446183; fax (11) 2541184; e-mail secretary@fisheries.gov.lk; internet www .fisheries.gov.lk.

Ministry of Foreign Employment Promotion and Welfare: 12th Floor, Central Bank Bldg, Janadhipathi Mawatha, Colombo 1; tel. (11) 2477971; fax (11) 2477950; e-mail secyces@gmail.com; internet www.foreignemploymin.gov.lk.

Ministry of Health: 'Suwasiripaya', 385 Wimalawansha Himi Mawatha, Colombo 10; tel. (11) 2694033; fax (11) 2692694; e-mail postmaster@health.gov.lk; internet www.health.gov.lk.

Ministry of Higher Education: 18 Ward Place, Colombo 7; tel. (11) 2694486; fax (11) 2697239; e-mail info@mohe.gov.lk; internet www .mohe.gov.lk.

Ministry of Indigenous Medicine: Old Kottawa Rd, Nawinna, Maharagama, Colombo; tel. (11) 2850093; fax (11) 5651966; e-mail ita@ayurveda.gov.lk; internet www.indigenousmedimini.gov.lk.

Ministry of Industry and Commerce: 73/1 Galle Rd, Colombo 3; tel. (11) 2392149; fax (11) 2449402; e-mail secretarymid@gmail.com; internet www.industry.gov.lk.

Ministry of Irrigation and Water Resources Management: 11 Jawatta Rd, Colombo 5; tel. (11) 2676844; fax (11) 2676846; e-mail secretary@irrigationmin.gov.lk; internet www.irrigationmin.gov.lk.

Ministry of Justice: Superior Courts Complex Bldg, Colombo 12; tel. (11) 2449959; fax (11) 2445447; e-mail secretary@justiceministry .gov.lk; internet www.justiceministry.gov.lk.

Ministry of Labour and Labour Relations: Labour Secretariat, 2nd Floor, Narahenpita, Colombo 5; tel. (11) 2368164; fax (11) 2582938; e-mail slmol@slt.lk; internet www.labourmin.gov.lk.

Ministry of Land and Land Development: 'Mihikatha Medura', 1200/06 Ave, Battaramulla, Colombo; tel. (11) 2797500; fax (11) 2887442; e-mail seclme@sltnet.lk; internet www.landmin.gov.lk.

Ministry of Livestock and Rural Community Development: 45 St Michael's Rd, POB 562, Colombo 3; tel. (11) 2441849; fax (11) 2328117; e-mail secretary@livestock.gov.lk; internet www.livestock .gov.lk.

Ministry of Local Government and Provincial Councils: 330 Union Place, Colombo 2; tel. (11) 2305326; fax (11) 2329725; e-mail info@pclg.gov.lk; internet www.pclg.gov.lk.

Ministry of Mass Media and Information: 163 Kirulappona Mawatha, Polhengoda, Colombo 5; tel. (11) 2513467; fax (11) 2513458; e-mail secretary@media.gov.lk; internet www.media.gov .lk.

Ministry of Minor Export Crop Promotion: 'Govijana Mandiraya', 80/5 Rajamalwatta Ave, Battaramulla, Colombo; tel. (11) 2886505; fax (11) 2863548; e-mail info@mcropmin.lk; internet mcropmin.lk.

Ministry of National Heritage: 'Sethsiripaya', 8th Floor, Battaramulla, Colombo 3; tel. (11) 2872027; fax (11) 2872327; e-mail secretary@heritagemin.gov.lk; internet www.heritagemin.gov.lk.

Ministry of National Languages and Social Integration: 40 Buthgamuwa Rd, Rajagiriya; tel. (11) 2883926; fax (11) 2883929; e-mail info@lanintegration.gov.lk; internet lanintegmin.gov.lk.

Ministry of Parliamentary Affairs: 464B Pannipitiya Rd, Pelewatta, Battaramulla, Colombo; tel. (11) 2786966; fax (11) 2786968; e-mail webmaster@parliament.lk; internet www.minparliament .gov.lk.

Ministry of Petroleum Industries: 80 Sir Ernest de Silva Mawatha, Colombo 7; tel. (11) 2370115; fax (11) 2564362; e-mail pisec@sltnet.lk; internet www.petroleummin.gov.lk.

Ministry of Plantation Industries: 55/75 Vauxhall Lane, Colombo 2; tel. (11) 2445397; fax (11) 2438031; e-mail secypi@ sltnet.lk; internet www.plantationindustries.gov.lk.

Ministry of Ports and Highways: 9th Floor, Sethsiripaya, Battaramulla; tel. (11) 2887462; fax (11) 2862705; e-mail sec@mohsl.gov.lk; internet www.mohsl.gov.lk.

Ministry of Postal Services: 310 D. R. Wijewardene Mawatha, Colombo 10; tel. (11) 2422591; fax (11) 2323465; e-mail gen@telepost.gov.lk; internet www.telepost.gov.lk.

Ministry of Power and Energy: 72 Coomaraswamy Mw, Colombo 7; tel. (11) 2574922; fax (11) 2574743; e-mail info@powerministry.asia; internet www.power.lk.

Ministry of Private Transport Services: 241 Park Rd, Colombo 5; tel. (11) 2807282; fax (11) 2807280; e-mail cbr@cbratnayake.org.

Ministry of Productivity Promotion: 318 High Level Rd, Colombo 6; tel. (11) 2856415; fax (11) 2856412; e-mail info@productivitymon.gov.lk; internet www.productivitymin.gov.lk.

Ministry of Public Administration and Home Affairs: Independence Sq., Colombo 7; tel. (11) 2695738; fax (11) 2695279; e-mail secretary@pubad.gov.lk; internet www.pubad.gov.lk.

Ministry of Public Management Reforms: 29/2 D. P. Wijesinghe Mawatha, Pellawatte, Battaramulla; tel. (11) 2187152; fax (11) 2187153; e-mail secmpmr@sltnet.lk; internet www.reformsmin.gov.lk.

Ministry of Public Relations and Public Affairs: 302 Galle Rd, Colombo 4; tel. (11) 2592674; fax (11) 2593773; e-mail minprpa@gmail.com.

Ministry of Rehabilitation and Prison Reforms: 35A Dr N. M. Perera Mawatha, Colombo 8; tel. (11) 2697912; fax (11) 2697910; e-mail secretary@reprimin.gov.lk; internet www.reprimin.gov.lk.

Ministry of Resettlement: 146 Galle Rd, Colombo 3; tel. (11) 2395513; fax (11) 2395517; e-mail secretary@resettlementmin.gov.lk; internet www.resettlementmin.gov.lk.

Ministry of Social Services: 'Sethsiripaya', 5th Floor, Battaramulla, Colombo; tel. (11) 2877124; fax (11) 2877381; e-mail msssec@sltnet.lk; internet www.socialwelfare.gov.lk.

Ministry of Sports: 100/7 Independent Ave, Colombo 7; tel. (11) 2674718; fax (11) 2689161; e-mail secretary@sportsmin.gov.lk; internet www.sportsmin.gov.lk.

Ministry of State Resources and Enterprise Development: 561/3 Elvitigala Mawatha, Colombo 5; tel. (11) 2368358; fax (11) 2368145; e-mail secpemd@sltnet.lk; internet www.sredmin.gov.lk.

Ministry of Technology, Research and Atomic Energy: 408 Galle Rd, POB 1571, Colombo 3; tel. and fax (11) 2374700; e-mail mstsasad@sltnet.lk; internet www.motr.gov.lk.

Ministry of Telecommunications and Information Technology: 79/1, 5th Lane, Colombo 3; tel. (11) 2577777; fax (11) 2301712; e-mail info@ictmin.gov.lk; internet www.ictmin.gov.lk.

Ministry of Traditional Industries and Small Enterprise Development: 780 Maradana Rd, Colombo 10; tel. (11) 2669269; fax (11) 2669281; e-mail info@tisedmin.gov.lk; internet www.tisedmin.gov.lk.

Ministry of Transport: 1 D. R. Wijewardene Mawatha, POB 588, Colombo 10; tel. (11) 2687105; fax (11) 2684930; e-mail mintrans@sltnet.lk; internet www.transport.gov.lk.

Ministry of Water Supply and Drainage: 'Lakdiya Medura', 35 New Parliament Rd, Battaramulla, Colombo; tel. (11) 2177240; fax (11) 2177242; e-mail info@watermin.gov.lk; internet www.mwsd.gov.lk.

Ministry of Youth Affairs and Skills Development: 'Nipunatha Piyasa', 354/2 Elvitigala Mawatha, Colombo 5; tel. (11) 2597677; fax (11) 2597804; e-mail info@youthskillsmin.gov.lk; internet www.youthskillsmin.gov.lk.

President and Legislature

PRESIDENT

Presidential Election, 26 January 2010

Candidate	Valid votes	% of votes
Mahinda Rajapaksa (SLFP) . . .	6,015,934	57.88
Gen. Sarath Fonseka (New Democratic Front)	4,173,185	40.15
Total (incl. others)*	10,393,613	100.00

* In addition to the two main candidates, there were 20 other candidates, none of whom won more than 0.4% of valid votes.

PARLIAMENT

Speaker: CHAMAL RAJAPAKSA.
Deputy Speaker: CHANDIMA WEERAKKODY.

General Election, 8 April 2010

Party/Alliance	Votes	% of votes	Seats
United People's Freedom Alliance . .	4,846,388	60.33	144
United National Party	2,357,057	29.34	60
Democratic National Alliance . .	441,251	5.49	7
Ilankai Tamil Arasu Katchi . .	233,190	2.90	14
Others	155,831	1.94	—
Total	8,033,717	100.00	225

Election Commission

Department of Elections: Elections Secretariat, Sarana Mawatha, Rajagiriya, Jayawardenapura 10107; tel. (11) 2868441; fax (11) 2868426; e-mail election@slt.lk; internet www.slelections.gov.lk; f. 1947; govt dept; Commr of Elections MAHINDA DESHAPRIYA.

Political Organizations

Akhila Ilankai Tamil United Front (AITUK): 5 Boundary Rd, Jinnanagar, Trincomalee, Colombo; tel. (11) 2581182; e-mail secretary@tamilunitedfront.com; internet www.tamilunitedfront.com; f. 2006; Tamil; advocates federal solution to ethnic conflict; Gen. Sec. Dr K. VIGNESWARAN.

All Ceylon Tamil Congress (ACTC): 15 Queen's Rd, Colpetty. Colombo 3; tel. (11) 2581677; fax (11) 2586254; f. 1944; aims to secure Tamil self-determination; fmr mem of Tamil National Alliance (TNA) in 2001; left TNA in 2010 to establish Tamil National People's Front; Leader GAJENDRAKUMAR PONNAMBALAM; Pres. EDWARD ANANDARAJAH.

Ceylon Workers' Congress (CWC): 'Savumia Bhavan', 72 Ananda Coomarasamy Mawatha, POB 1294, Colombo 7; tel. (11) 2574528; fax (11) 2301355; e-mail cwconline@sltnet.lk; f. 1939 as Ceylon Indian Congress; name changed as above in 1950; political wing of CWC trade union; represents the interests of workers in the mercantile and local government sectors and of workers on tea, rubber and coconut plantations; mem. of United People's Freedom Alliance; Pres. and Gen. Sec. ARUMUGAN THONDAMAN.

Communist Party of Sri Lanka (CPSL): 91 Dr N. M. Perera Mawatha, Colombo 8; tel. (11) 2695328; fax (11) 2691610; e-mail compartysl@gmail.com; f. 1943; seeks broadening of democratic rights and processes, political solution to ethnic problem, defence of social welfare and presses for social justice; supports national sovereignty, territorial integrity and national unity of the country; mem. of United People's Freedom Alliance; Chair. RAJA COLLURE; Gen. Sec. D. E. W. GUNASEKERA.

Democratic National Alliance (DNA): Royal Ave, Colombo; alliance est. to contest the parliamentary elections of 2010; led by the JVP; Leader Gen. SARATH FONSEKA; Sec.-Gen. VIJITHE HERATH.

Democratic People's Front: 72 Bankshall St, Colombo 11; tel. (11) 2473511; fax (11) 2435961; has operated as a national political party since Sept. 1988; mem. of the United National Front; Leader MANO GANESHAN; Dep. Leader and Gen. Sec. NALLIAH KUMARAGURUPARAN.

Democratic United National Front (DUNF): 60 1st Lane, Rawathawatte, Moratuwa; tel. and fax (11) 3164278; fax (11) 2645566; e-mail dissana@gmail.com; f. 1991 by dissident group of UNP politicians; 500,000 mems; Leader ARIYAWANSA DISSANAYAKE; Pres. D. M. G. EKANAYAKE.

Desha Vimukthi Janatha Pakshaya (National Liberation People's Party): 152/1, 1/2 Baddagana HS, Duwa Rd, Baddagana; tel. (11) 2338812; has operated as a national political party since Sept. 1988; leftist; Sec. P. M. PODIAPPUHAMY.

Eelam People's Democratic Party (EPDP): 121 Park Rd, Colombo 5; tel. (11) 2551015; fax (11) 2585255; e-mail epdp@sltnet.lk; internet www.epdpnews.com; Tamil; advocates devolution of powers to the provinces within a united Sri Lanka, and the merger of the North and East Provinces into a single administrative unit; mem. of United People's Freedom Alliance; Sec.-Gen. DOUGLAS DEVANANDA.

Eelam People's Revolutionary Liberation Front (EPRLF): 6 1st St, Point Pedro Rd, Jaffna; tel. (11) 2685826; e-mail editor_eprlf_net@yahoo.com; internet www.eprlf.net; Tamil rights group; mem. of Tamil National Alliance; the party split into two factions, one led by ANNAMALAI VARADHARAJAH PERUMAL, known as the Varadharajah faction, and the other by SURESH K. PREMACHANDRAN, known as the Premachandran faction.

Eksath Lanka Podujana Pakshaya: 100/16 Via Kurunduwatte Rd, Nawala, Rajagiriya; tel. (11) 2867069; Sec. SUNIL W. JINASENA.

Ilankai Tamil Arasu Katchi (ITAK): 30 Martin Rd, Jaffna; tel. (21) 2223576; Tamil; main constituent of the Tamil National Alliance; Leader RAJAVAROTHIAM SAMPANTHAN; Gen. Sec. MAVAI SENATHIRAJAH.

Janatha Vimukthi Peramuna (JVP) (People's Liberation Front): 464/20 Pannipitiya Rd, Pelawatte, Battaramulla, Colombo; tel. (11) 2785612; fax (11) 2786050; e-mail jvplanka@sltnet.lk; internet www .jvpsrilanka.com; f. 1965; banned following a coup attempt in 1971, regained legal status in 1977, banned again in 1983, but regained legal status in 1994; founder mem. of UPFA in 2004, but withdrew from alliance in 2005; contested 2010 elections as mem. of DNA; Marxist; Sinhalese support; Leader SOMAWANSA AMARASINGHE; Gen. Sec. TILVIN SILVA.

Jathika Hela Urumaya (JHU) (National Heritage Party): 1047/3A Denzil Kobbekaduwa Mawatha, Pannipitiya Rd, Pelawatte, Battaramulla, Colombo; tel. (11) 2882585; fax (11) 2866125; e-mail jhu2004@gmail.com; f. 2004; Buddhist; Sinhalese nationalist; mem. of United People's Freedom Alliance; Sec. Dr OMALPE SOBHITHA THERO.

Jathika Nidahas Peramuna (JNP) (National Freedom Front): 21/1 Asoka Mawatha, Battaramulla, Colombo; tel. (11) 3071340; fax (11) 2882176; e-mail info@nffsrilanka.com; internet www.jnpsrilanka .com; f. 2008 as a breakaway faction of the JVP; mem. of United People's Freedom Alliance; Chair. WIMAL WEERAWANSA; Gen. Sec. PRIYANJITH WITHARANA.

Lanka Sama Samaja Party (LSSP) (Lanka Equal Society Party): 457 Dr Colvin R. de Silva Mawatha, Colombo 2; tel. (11) 2676770; f. 1935; Trotskyist; mem. of United People's Freedom Alliance; Gen. Sec. WIMALASIRI DE MEL.

Liberal Party: 88/1 Rosmead Place, Colombo 7; tel. (11) 2691589; fax (11) 2699772; e-mail libparty@sri.lanka.net; internet www .liberalparty-srilanka.org; f. 1987; Sec.-Gen. KAMAL NISSANKA; Pres. SWARNA AMARATUNGA.

Mahajana Eksath Peramuna (MEP) (People's United Front): 351A 2nd Floor, Pannipitiya Rd, Thalawathugoda, Colombo; tel. and fax (11) 2796899; f. 1956; Sinhalese and Buddhist support; leftwing; advocates economic self-reliance; mem. of United People's Freedom Alliance; Pres. DINESH C. R. GUNAWARDENA; Sec. D. M. KARUNATHILAKA DISSANAYAKE.

Nava Sama Samaja Party (NSSP) (New Equal Society Party): Left Front, 17 Barracks Lane, Colombo 2; tel. (11) 2430621; fax (11) 2305963; e-mail nssp.lk@gmail.com; internet www.nssp.info; f. 1977; Trotskyist; Gen. Sec. LINUS JAYATILAKE; Presidium Member Dr VICKRAMABAHU KARUNARATHNE.

New Democratic Front: Colombo; f. 2009 as breakaway faction of Democratic United National Front; fielded Gen. Sarath Fonseka as candidate in 2010 presidential election; Leader ARIYAWANSA DISSANAYAKE; Sec. SHAMILA PERERA.

New Democratic Party (NDP): S47, 3rd Floor, C. C. S. M. Complex, Colombo 11; tel. (71) 4302909; fax (11) 2473757; e-mail info@ ndpsl.org; internet www.ndpsl.org; f. 1978 as the Sri Lanka Communist Party; adopted current name in 1991; upholds Marxist-Leninist-Mao Zedong philosophy in anti-imperialist campaigning for social justice; publs monthly party newsletter *Puthiya Poomi*; Gen. Sec. S. K. SENTHIVEL.

Sri Lanka Freedom Party (SLFP): 307 T. B. Jayah Mawatha, Colombo 10; tel. (11) 2694677; fax (11) 2689288; e-mail slfp@ srilankafreedomparty.org; f. 1951; democratic socialist; advocates a non-aligned foreign policy, industrial development in both the state sector and the private sector, rapid modernization in education and in the economy, and safeguards for minorities; main constituent of the United People's Freedom Alliance; Chair. MAHINDA RAJAPAKSA; Gen. Sec. MAITHRIPALA SIRISENA.

Sri Lanka Mahajana Pakshaya (SLMP) (Sri Lanka People's Party): 196 Kolonnawa Rd, Wellampitiya; f. 1984 by fmr mems of the SLFP; social democrats; mem. of United People's Freedom Alliance; Leader SARATH KONGAHAGE; Gen. Sec. PREMASIRI PERERA.

Sri Lanka Muslim Congress (SLMC): Dharussalam, 53 Vauxhall Lane, Colombo 2; tel. (74) 717720; fax (74) 717722; e-mail info@slmc .org.uk; internet www.slmc.org; fmr mem. of United National Front; transferred its support to the UPFA Govt from early 2011; Leader RAUFF HAKEEM; Sec.-Gen. M. T. HASSEN ALI.

Tamil Eelam Liberation Organization (TELO): 14 Vairawa Kovil Rd, 10th Lane, Vairawapuliankullam, Vavuniya; tel. (24) 2222977; fax (24) 2224457; e-mail contact@telo.org; internet telo .org; f. 1969 as a militant group; supports 1987 Indo-Sri Lankan peace accord; has operated as a national political party since 1988; mem. of Tamil National Alliance; Pres. SELVAM ADAIKALANTHAN.

Tamil Makkal Viduthalai Pulikal (TMVP) (Tamil People's Liberation Tigers—Karuna Group): 39 Kavinton Rd, Batticaloa; e-mail info@tmvponline.com; internet tmvponline.com; f. 2004; political and paramilitary group, fmrly of LTTE; joint asscn with the Eelam National Democratic Liberation Front (India); Leader SIVANESATHURAI CHANDRAKANTHAN ('PILLAYAN'); Gen. Sec. A. KAILESVARARAJAH.

Tamil National Alliance (TNA): 3rd Floor, Parliamentary Complex, Sri Jeyawardanapura Kotte, Colombo; tel. (11) 2778470; fax (11) 2778470; e-mail enquiries@tamilalliance.net; internet www .tnainfo.com; f. 2001; alliance of Tamil parties, incl. ITAK and TELO; Leader RAJAVAROTHIAM SAMPANTHAN.

Tamil National People's Front: 43 3rd Cross St, Jaffna; f. 2010 as breakaway faction of the Tamil National Alliance; main constituent is the All Ceylon Tamil Congress party; espouses Tamil self-determination; Gen. Sec. SELVARAJA KAJENDRAN.

Tamil United Liberation Front (TULF): 5/3A Wijayaba Mawatha, Kalubowila, Dehiwala, Colombo; tel. (11) 2552372; e-mail tulfsl@yahoo.com; internet tamilunitedliberationfront.org; f. 1972 by several Tamil parties, incl. All Ceylon Tamil Congress; fmr mem. of Tamil National Alliance; contested 2010 general election independently; Pres. VEERASINGHAM ANANDASANGAREE.

United National Front (UNF): Colombo; f. 2001; revived 2009 to contest 2010 legislative election; political coalition led by the United National Party; fmr mems incl. Ceylon Workers' Congress and Sri Lanka Muslim Congress; Leader RANIL WICKREMASINGHE.

United National Party (UNP): 'Sirikotha', 400 Kotte Rd, Pitakotte, Colombo; tel. (11) 2865375; fax (11) 2865374; e-mail info@unp.lk; internet www.unp.lk; f. 1946; leading mem. of the United National Front; advocates a market economy, economic liberalization and non-aligned foreign policy; Leader RANIL WICKREMASINGHE; Chair. RUKMAN SENANAYAKE; Gen. Sec. TISSA ATTANAYAKE.

United People's Freedom Alliance (UPFA): 301, T. B. Jaya Mawatha, Colombo 10; tel. (60) 2700259; fax (11) 2674363; e-mail slfpmedia@gmail.com; internet www.sandanaya.lk; f. 2004; left wing coalition incl. communists and Trotskyists; Leader MAHINDA RAJAPAKSA; Gen. Sec. SUSIL PREMAJAYANTHA.

Upcountry People's Front: 56, Rosita Housing Scheme, Kotagala; tel. (52) 2258227; represents interests of workers (mainly of Indian Tamil origin) on tea plantations; Chair. P. CHANDRASEKARAN.

Tamil separatist groups also include the Liberation Tigers of Tamil Eelam (LTTE; Leader SELVARASA PATHMANATHAN), the Tamil Eelam Liberation Front (TELF; Gen. Sec. M. K. EELAVENTHAN), the People's Liberation Organization of Tamil Eelam (PLOTE; Leader DHARMALINGAM SIDDHARTHAN; Vice-Pres. KARUVAI A. SRIKANTHASAMI), the People's Revolutionary Action Group, the Ellalan Force and the Tamil People's Protection Party.

Diplomatic Representation

EMBASSIES AND HIGH COMMISSIONS IN SRI LANKA

Australia: 21 Gregory's Rd, Colombo 7; tel. (11) 2463200; fax (11) 2686453; e-mail austcom@sltnet.lk; internet www.srilanka.embassy .gov.au; High Commissioner ROBYN MUDIE.

Bangladesh: 5 Ward Pl., Colombo 7; tel. (11) 2695744; fax (11) 2695556; e-mail bdootlanka@sltnet.lk; High Commissioner MD SUFIUR RAHMAN.

Canada: 33A 5th Lane, Colpetty, Colombo 3; tel. (11) 5226232; fax (11) 5226296; e-mail clmbo@international.gc.ca; internet www .canadainternational.gc.ca/sri_lanka; High Commissioner SHELLEY WHITING.

China, People's Republic: 381/A Bauddhaloka Mawatha, Colombo 7; tel. (11) 2694491; fax (11) 2693799; e-mail chinaemb_lk@mfa.gov .cn; internet lk.china-embassy.org; Ambassador WU JIANGHAO.

Cuba: 27 Anderson Rd, Colombo 5; tel. (11) 2501583; fax (11) 2504381; e-mail cubaembalk@sltnet.lk; internet www .cubadiplomatica.cu/srilanka/EN/Home.aspx; Chargé d'affaires a.i INDIRA LÓPEZ ARGÜELLES.

Egypt: 39 Dr Lester James Peries Mawatha, Colombo 5; tel. (11) 2508752; fax (11) 2585292; e-mail egyptemb@sltnet.lk; Ambassador FAWZI MUHAMMAD EL-SAID GOHAR.

France: 89 Rosmead Pl., POB 880, Colombo 7; tel. (11) 2639400; fax (11) 2639402; e-mail contact@ambafrance-lk.org; internet www .ambafrance-lk.org; Ambassador CHRISTINE ROBICHON.

Germany: 40 Alfred House Ave, POB 658, Colombo 3; tel. (11) 2580431; fax (11) 2580440; e-mail info@colombo.diplo.de; internet www.colombo.diplo.de; Ambassador JÜRGEN MORHARD.

Holy See: 220 Bauddhaloka Mawatha, Colombo 7 (Apostolic Nunciature); tel. (11) 2582554; fax (11) 2580906; e-mail nuntius@sltnet .lk; Apostolic Nuncio Most Rev. Dr JOSEPH SPITERI (Titular Archbishop of Serta).

India: 36–38 Galle Rd, Colombo 3; tel. (11) 2421605; fax (11) 2446403; e-mail hc.colombo@mea.gov.in; internet www.hcicolombo .org; High Commissioner Y. K. SINHA (designate).

Indonesia: 400/50 Sarana Rd, off Bauddhaloka Mawatha, Colombo 7; tel. (11) 2674337; fax (11) 2678668; e-mail indocol@indonesia-colombo.lk; internet indonesia-colombo.lk; Ambassador HARIMAWAN SUYITNO.

Iran: 5 Independence Ave, Colombo 7; tel. (11) 2681018; fax (11) 2681017; e-mail iranemb@cga.lk; Ambassador MOHAMMAD NABI HASSANI POUR.

Iraq: 19 Barnes Pl., POB 79, Colombo 7; tel. (11) 2698600; fax (11) 230030; e-mail colemb@mofaml.gov.iq; Ambassador KAHTAAN TAHA KHALAF.

Italy: 55 Jawatta Rd, Colombo 5; tel. (11) 2588388; fax (11) 2596344; e-mail ambasciata.colombo@esteri.it; internet www.ambcolombo.esteri.it; Ambassador FABRIZIO PIO ARPEA.

Japan: 20 Gregory's Rd, Colombo 7; tel. (11) 2693831; fax (11) 2698629; e-mail cultujpn@co.mofa.go.jp; internet www.lk.emb-japan.go.jp; Ambassador NOBUHITHO HOBO.

Korea, Democratic People's Republic: Colombo; Ambassador RIM HOE SONG.

Korea, Republic: 98 Dharmapala Mawatha, Colombo 7; tel. (11) 2699036; fax (11) 2696699; e-mail korembsl@mofat.go.kr; internet lka.mofat.go.kr; Ambassador CHOI JONG-MOON.

Kuwait: 292 Bauddhaloka Mawatha, Colombo 7; tel. (11) 2597958; fax (11) 2597954; e-mail contact@kuwaitembassy.net; internet www.kuwaitembassy.net; Ambassador YAQOUB AL-ATEEQI.

Libya: 120 Horton Pl., POB 155, Colombo 7; tel. (11) 2697300; fax (11) 5338881; Ambassador HAFIM M. A. MAHFOM.

Malaysia: 33 Bagatalle Rd, Colombo 3; tel. (11) 7557711; fax (11) 7557714; e-mail malcolombo@kln.gov.my; internet www.kln.gov.my/perwakilan/colombo; High Commissioner AZMI ZAINUDIN.

Maldives: 25 Melbourne Ave, Colombo 4; tel. (11) 2587827; fax (11) 2581200; e-mail info@maldiveshighcom.lk; internet www.maldiveshighcom.lk; High Commissioner HUSSAIN SHIHAB.

Myanmar: 4A Rosmead Ave, Rosmead Pl., Colombo 7; tel. (11) 2696440; fax (11) 2682052; e-mail mmembcmb@sltnet.lk; Ambassador U MYO LWIN.

Nepal: 153 Kynsey Rd, Colombo 8; tel. (11) 2689657; fax (11) 2689655; e-mail colombo@mofa.gov.np; Ambassador SUSHIL CHANDRA AMATYA.

Netherlands: 25 Torrington Ave, Colombo 7; tel. (11) 2510200; fax (11) 2502855; e-mail col@minbuza.nl; internet srilanka.nlembassy.org; Ambassador LUDOVICUS W. M. PIET.

Norway: 49 Bullers Lane, Colombo 7; tel. (11) 5608700; fax (11) 5608799; e-mail emb.colombo@mfa.no; internet www.norway.lk; Ambassador CRETE LOCHEN.

Pakistan: 53/6 Gregory's Rd, Colombo 7; tel. (11) 2696301; fax (11) 2695780; e-mail parepcolombo@sltnet.lk; internet www.pakistanhc.lk; High Commissioner Maj. Gen. QASIM QURESHI.

Qatar: 11 Rajakeeya Mawatha, Old Race Course Ave, Colombo 7; tel. (11) 2690440; fax (11) 2690443; e-mail qatarembcmb@sltnet.lk; Ambassador (vacant).

Romania: 25/1 Horton Pl., Colombo 7; tel. (11) 2673331; fax (11) 2673332; e-mail romania@sltnet.lk; internet colombo.mae.ro; Chargé d'affaires a.i. VICTOR CHIUJDEA.

Russia: 62 Sir Ernest de Silva Mawatha, Colombo 7; tel. (11) 2573555; fax (11) 2574957; e-mail rusemb@itmin.net; internet www.sri-lanka.mid.ru; Ambassador ALEKSANDR A. KARCHAVA.

Saudi Arabia: 39 Sir Ernest de Silva Mawatha, Colombo 7; tel. (11) 2682087; fax (11) 2682088; e-mail lkemb@mofa.gov.sa; internet embassies.mofa.gov.sa/sites/srilanka; Ambassador ABDULAZIZ BIN AL-JEMAZ.

South Africa: 114 Rosmead Pl., Colombo 7; tel. (11) 2689926; fax (11) 2688670; e-mail colombo.admin@dirco.gov.za; High Commissioner GEOFFREY QUINTON DOIDGE.

Switzerland: 63 Gregory's Rd, POB 342, Colombo 7; tel. (11) 2695117; fax (11) 2695176; e-mail col.vertretung@eda.admin.ch; internet www.eda.admin.ch/colombo; Ambassador THOMAS LITSCHER.

Thailand: Greenlanka Towers, 9th Floor, 46/46 Nawam Mawatha, Colombo 2; tel. (11) 2302500; fax (11) 2304511; e-mail thaicmb@sltnet.lk; internet www.thaiembassy.org/colombo; Ambassador POLDEJ WORACHAT.

United Arab Emirates: 44 Sir Ernest de Silva Mawatha, Colombo 7; tel. (11) 2565052; fax (11) 2564104; e-mail uaecmb@yahoo.com; Ambassador ABDUL FATTAH KAZIM AL-MULLA.

United Kingdom: 389 Bauddhaloka Mawatha, Colombo 7; tel. (11) 5390639; fax (11) 5390694; e-mail colombo.general@fco.gov.uk; internet ukinsrilanka.fco.gov.uk; High Commissioner JOHN JAMES RANKIN.

USA: 210 Galle Rd, Colombo 3; tel. (11) 2498500; fax (11) 2437345; e-mail commercialcolombo@state.gov; internet srilanka.usembassy.gov; Ambassador MICHELE JEANNE SISON.

Judicial System

The judicial system consists of the Supreme Court, the Court of Appeal, the High Court, District Courts, Magistrates' Courts and Primary Courts. The last four are Courts of the First Instance and appeals lie from them to the Court of Appeal and from there, on questions of law or by special leave, to the Supreme Court. The High Court deals with all criminal cases and the District Courts with civil cases. There are Labour Tribunals to decide labour disputes.

The Judicial Service Commission comprises the Chief Justice and two judges of the Supreme Court, nominated by the President. All judges of the Courts of First Instance (except High Court Judges) and the staff of all courts are appointed and controlled by the Judicial Service Commission. The Supreme Court consists of the Chief Justice and not fewer than six and not more than 10 other judges. The Court of Appeal consists of the President and not fewer than six and not more than 11 other judges.

Supreme Court: Superior Court Complex, Hultsdorf, Colombo 12; tel. (1) 2435446; internet www.supremecourt.lk; Chief Justice MOHAN PEIRIS.

Court of Appeal: Superior Courts Complex, Colombo 12; tel. (11) 2433466; internet courtofappeal.lk; Pres. S. SRISKANDARAJAH; Registrar SANATH KUMARA PINNADUWA.

Attorney-General's Department: Colombo 12; tel. (11) 2320848; fax (11) 2436421; e-mail administration@attorneygeneral.gov.lk; internet www.attorneygeneral.gov.lk; Attorney-General PALITHA FERNANDO.

Religion

According to the 2001 census, the distribution of the population by religion in 18 out of 25 districts was: Buddhist 76.7%, Muslim 8.5%, Hindu 7.9%, Roman Catholics 6.1% and other Christians 0.8%. The census results did not cover the Tamil-dominated northern and eastern districts, where a higher proportion of Hindus could be expected.

BUDDHISM

Theravada Buddhism is the predominant sect. There are an estimated 53,000 Buddhist *bhikkhus* (monks), living in about 6,000 temples.

All Ceylon Buddhist Congress: 380 Bauddhaloka Mawatha, Colombo 7; tel. (11) 2691695; e-mail info@acbc.lk; internet www.acbc.lk; f. 1919; Pres. JAGATH SUMATHIPALA; Jt Secs SUNIL SARATH, RANJITH EKANAYAKE.

Sri Lanka Regional Centre of the World Fellowship of Buddhists: 380 Bauddhaloka Mawatha, Colombo 7; tel. (11) 2681886; fax (11) 2833362; e-mail palikann@sltnet.lk; Pres. Dr MALINI DIAS; Sec. JAYANTHA WEERAKOON.

HINDUISM

The majority of the Tamil population are Hindus. According to the 2001 census the Hindu population in 18 out of 25 districts was 1,329,020.

CHRISTIANITY

National Christian Council of Sri Lanka: 368/6 Bauddhaloka Mawatha, Colombo 7; tel. (11) 2671723; fax (11) 2671721; e-mail sec@nccsl.org; internet www.nccsl.org; f. 1945; 15 mem. bodies; Gen. Sec. Rev. WILLIAM P. EBENEZER JOSEPH.

The Anglican Communion

The Church of Ceylon (Sri Lanka) comprises two Anglican dioceses. In 1985 there were about 78,000 adherents.

Bishop of Colombo: Rt Rev. DHILORAJ RANJITH CANAGASABEY, Bishop's House, 358/2 Bauddhaloka Mawatha, Colombo 7; tel. (11) 2684810; fax (11) 2684811; e-mail bishop@eureka.lk; diocese f. 1845.

Bishop of Kurunegala: Rt Rev. GREGORY SHANTHA KUMARA FRANCIS, Bishop's House, Kandy Rd, Kurunegala; tel. (37) 22191; fax (37) 26806; e-mail bishopkg@sltnet.lk; diocese f. 1950.

The Roman Catholic Church

For ecclesiastical purposes, Sri Lanka comprises one archdiocese and 10 dioceses. At 31 December 2009 there were an estimated 1,359,788 adherents in the country.

Catholic Bishops' Conference in Sri Lanka: 19 Balcombe Pl., Cotta Rd, Borella, Colombo 8; tel. (11) 2697062; fax (11) 2699619; e-mail conferencesl@sltnet.lk; f. 1975; Pres. Most Rev. JOSEPH VIANNEY FERNANDO (Bishop of Kandy); Sec.-Gen. Rt Rev. Dr NORBERT M. ANDRADI.

Archbishop of Colombo: Cardinal ALBERT MALCOLM RANJITH, St Mary's Church, No. 66, Lauries Rd, Bambalapitiya, Colombo 4; tel. (11) 2588745; fax (11) 2692009; e-mail sunilde@sltnet.lk; internet www.archdioceseofcolombo.com.

The Church of South India

The Church comprises 21 dioceses, including one, Jaffna, in Sri Lanka. The diocese of Jaffna, with an estimated 18,500 adherents in 1997, was formerly part of the South India United Church (a union of churches of the Congregational and Presbyterian/Reformed traditions), which merged with the Methodist Church in South India and the four southern dioceses of the (Anglican) Church of India to form the Church of South India in 1947.

Bishop in Jaffna: Rt Rev. Dr DANIEL S. THIAGARAJAH, Bishop's House, Vaddukoddai; tel. (21) 3210855; e-mail bishopthiagarajah@gmail.com; internet csijaffnadiocese.com.

Other Christian Churches

Christian Reformed Church: General Consistory Office, 363 Galle Rd, Colombo 6; tel. (11) 2360861; fax (11) 2582469; e-mail crcsl1642@gmail.com; internet www.crcsl.org; f. 1642; Pres. of Gen. Consistory Rev. CHARLES N. JANSZ.

Lanka Lutheran Church: Lutheran Centre, 53 Mount Mary Rd, Nuwara Eliya; e-mail govindan.nadraja@yahoo.com; Pres. Rev. GOVINDAN NADARAJA.

Methodist Church: Methodist Headquarters, 252 Galle Rd, Colombo 3; tel. (11) 2575707; fax (11) 2436090; e-mail methhq@sltnet.lk; internet methodistsrilanka.org; 35,000 mems (2012); Pres. of Conference Rev. Dr ALBERT W. JEBANESAN; Sec. of Conference Rev. JACOB KATHIRESAPILLAI.

Other denominations active in the country include the Sri Lanka Baptist Sangamaya.

BAHÁ'Í FAITH

Spiritual Assembly: Bahá'í National Centre, 65 Havelock Rd, Colombo 5; tel. and fax (11) 2587360; e-mail nsasrilanka@sltnet.lk.

The Press

NEWSPAPERS

Newspapers are published in Sinhala, Tamil and English. There are five main newspaper publishing groups:

Associated Newspapers of Ceylon Ltd: Lake House, 35 D. R. Wijewardene Mawatha, POB 248, Colombo 10; tel. (11) 2429429; fax (11) 2429329; e-mail webmanager@lakehouse.lk; internet www.lakehouse.lk; f. 1926; nationalized 1973; publr of *Daily News*, *Evening Observer*, *Thinakaran*, *Lak Janatha* and *Dinamina* (dailies); three Sunday papers: *Sunday Observer*, *Silumina* and *Thinakaran Vaara Manjari*; and 11 periodicals; Chair. BANDULA PADMAKUMARA; Gen. Man. ABHAYA AMARADASA.

Express Newspapers (Ceylon) Ltd: 185 Grandpass Rd, POB 160, Colombo 14; tel. (11) 5322735; fax (11) 2327827; e-mail onlinenews@virakesari.lk; internet www.virakesari.lk; f. 1930; publr of *Virakesari Daily*, *Mithran Varamalar*, *Metro News* and *Virakesari Weekly* (Sunday); Chair. HARI SELVANATHAN; Man. Dir KUMAR NADESAN.

Leader Publications (Pvt) Ltd: 24 Katukurunduwatte Rd, Ratmalana; tel. (11) 4977220; fax (11) 4641942; e-mail editor@thesundayleader.lk; internet www.thesundayleader.lk; f. 1994; publr of *The Sunday Leader* and *Irida Peramuna*; Chair. LAL WICKREMATUNGE.

Upali Newspapers Ltd: 223 Bloemendhal Rd, POB 133, Colombo 13; tel. (11) 2497500; fax (11) 2497543; e-mail prabath@unl.upali.lk; f. 1981; publr of *The Island*, *Divaina* (dailies), two Sunday papers, *Sunday Island* and *Sunday Divaina*, four weeklies, *Vidusara*, *Navaliya*, *Bindu* and *The Island International* (for sale abroad only), and one bi-weekly, *Vathmana–News Magazine*; English and Sinhala; Editor-in-Chief PRABATH SAHABANDU; Man. Dir NIMAL WELGAMA.

Wijeya Newspapers Ltd: 8 Hunupitiya Cross Rd, Colombo 2; tel. (11) 2314714; fax (11) 2449504; e-mail pradeep@admin.wnl.lk; internet www.wijeyanewspapers.lk; f. 1979; publr of *Daily Mirror*, *The Sunday Times*, *Lankadeepa*, *Irida Lankadeepa* and *Sirikatha*; Sinhala and English; Chair. RANJIT SUJIVA WIJEWARDENE.

Dailies

Budusarana: Lake House, 35 D. R. Wijewardene Mawatha, POB 248, Colombo 10; tel. (11) 2429598; fax (11) 2449069; e-mail budusarana@lakehouse.lk; internet www.lakehouse.lk/budusarana; Editor N. S. PERERA.

Daily Mirror: 8 Hunupitiya Cross Rd, Colombo 2; tel. (11) 2479479; fax (11) 5530811; e-mail dmnews@dailymirror.wnl.lk; internet www.dailymirror.lk; f. 1996; English and Sinhala; Editor CHAMPIKA LIYANAARACHCHI; circ. 30,000.

Daily News: 35 D. R. Wijewardene Mawatha, POB 1217, Colombo 10; tel. (11) 2421181; fax (11) 2343694; e-mail editor@dailynews.lk; internet www.dailynews.lk; f. 1918; morning; English; Editor JAYATHILLEKE DE SILVA; circ. 88,000.

Dinamina: Lake House, 35 D. R. Wijewardene Mawatha, POB 248, Colombo 10; tel. (11) 2429241; fax 2429250; e-mail editor@dinamina.lk; internet www.dinamina.lk; f. 1909; morning; Sinhala; Editor MAHINDA ABEYSUNDARA; circ. 140,000.

Divaina: 223 Bloemendhal Rd, POB 133, Colombo 13; tel. (11) 4609000; fax (11) 2344253; e-mail divaina@unl.upali.lk; internet www.divaina.com; f. 1982; morning and Sunday; Chief Editor MERRILL PERERA.

The Island: 223 Bloemendhal Rd, POB 133, Colombo 13; tel. (11) 2497500; fax (11) 2448185; e-mail prabath@unl.upali.lk; internet www.island.lk; f. 1981; English; Editor PRABATH SAHABANDU; circ. 80,000.

Lakbima: 445/1 Sirimavo Bandaranayake Mawatha, Colombo 14; tel. (11) 2343407; fax (11) 2449593; e-mail daily@labkima.lk; internet www.lakbima.lk; publ. by Sumathi Newspapers Pvt Ltd; Chief Editor RAJPAL ABEYNAYAKE.

Lankadeepa: 8 Hunupitiya Cross Rd, Colombo 2; tel. (11) 2479200; fax (11) 2314651; e-mail siri@wijeya.lk; internet www.lankadeepa.lk; f. 1986; Sinhala and English; Editor SIRI RANASINGHE; circ. 160,000.

Thinakaran: Lake House, 35 D. R. Wijewardene Mawatha, POB 248, Colombo 10; tel. (11) 2429271; fax (11) 2429270; e-mail editor.tkn@lakehouse.lk; internet www.thinakaran.lk; f. 1932; morning; Tamil; Editor K. V. SIVASUPRAMANIAM; circ. daily 14,000.

Thinakkural: 68 Ellie House Rd, Colombo 15; tel. (11) 2522555; fax (11) 2540691; e-mail thinakkural@yahoo.com; internet www.thinakkural.com; Tamil; also publ. from Jaffna; daily, incl. Sunday; Chief Editor V. THANABALASINGHAM.

Uthayan: 359 Kasthuriyar Rd, Jaffna; tel. (21) 5672222; fax (21) 2220549; e-mail admin@uthayan.com; internet www.uthayan.com; f. 1985; Tamil; publ. by New Uthayan Publications Pvt Ltd; Man. Dir E. SARAVANAPAVAN; Chief Editor M. V. KAANAMYLNATHAN; circ. 22,000.

Valampurii: 3, 2nd Lane, Brown Rd, Jaffna; tel. (21) 2227829; fax (21) 2223378; e-mail editor@valampurii.com; internet www.valampurii.com; f. 1999; Tamil; Chief Editor N. VIJAYASUNTHARAM; circ. 10,000.

Virakesari Daily: 185 Grandpass Rd, POB 160, Colombo 14; tel. (11) 5322750; fax (11) 2448205; e-mail onlinenews@virakesari.lk; internet www.virakesari.lk; f. 1931; morning; Tamil; Man. Dir KUMAR NADESAN; Chief Editor R. PRABAGAN; circ. 60,000.

Sunday Newspapers

Irida Lankadeepa: 8 Hunupitiya Cross Rd, Colombo 2; tel. (11) 2347248; fax (11) 2314886; e-mail ariyad@wijeya.lk; internet www.lankadeepa.lk; Sinhala; Chief Editor ARIYANANDA DOBAGAHAWATTA.

Janasathiya: 47 Jayantha Weerasekara Mawatha, Colombo 10; f. 1965; Sinhala; publ. by Suriya Publishers Ltd; Editor SARATH NAWANA; circ. 50,000.

Mithran Varamalar: 185 Grandpass Rd, POB 160, Colombo 14; tel. (11) 2323841; fax (11) 4614374; e-mail kesari22@virasekari.lk; internet www.virakesari.lk; f. 1969; Tamil; Man. Dir KUMAR NADESAN; Chief Editor V. THEVARAJ; circ. 29,000.

The Nation: 742 Maradana Rd, Colombo 10; tel. (11) 4708888; fax (11) 4708800; e-mail editor@nation.lk; internet www.nation.lk; publ. by Rivira Media Corpn Ltd; Chief Editor GAMINI ABEYWARDANE; circ. 132,376 (2010).

Silumina: Lake House, 35 D. R. Wijewardene Mawatha, POB 248, Colombo 10; tel. (11) 2429351; fax (11) 2429260; e-mail editor@silumina.lk; internet www.silumina.lk; f. 1930; Sinhala; Editor KARUNADASA SOORIYARACHCHI; circ. 264,000.

Sunday Island: 223 Bloemendhal Rd, POB 133, Colombo 13; tel. (11) 2421599; fax (11) 2448185; e-mail manik@unl.upali.lk; f. 1981; English; Editor MANIK DE SILVA; circ. 40,000.

Sunday Lakbima: 445/1 Sirimavo Bandaranayake Mawatha, Colombo 14; tel. (11) 4619312; fax (11) 4617902; e-mail news@lakbima.lk; internet www.lakbimanews.lk; Chief Editor SUNDARA NIHATHAMANI DE MEL.

The Sunday Leader: 24 Katukurunduwatte Rd, Ratmalana; tel. (11) 4977220; fax (75) 7247222; e-mail editor@thesundayleader.lk; internet www.thesundayleader.lk; English; Editor SHAKUNTALA PERERA.

Sunday Observer: Lake House, 35 D. R. Wijewardene Mawatha, POB 248, Colombo 10; tel. (11) 2429231; fax (11) 2429230; e-mail editor@sundayobserver.lk; internet www.sundayobserver.lk; f. 1923; English; Editor DINESH WEERAWANSA; circ. 125,000.

The Sunday Times: 8 Hunupitiya Cross Rd, Colombo 2; tel. (11) 2326247; fax (11) 2423922; e-mail editor@sundaytimes.wnl.lk; internet www.sundaytimes.lk; f. 1986; English and Sinhala; Editor SINGHA RATNATUNGA; circ. 116,000.

Thinakaran Vaara Manjari: Lake House, 35 D. R. Wijewardene Mawatha, POB 248, Colombo 10; tel. (11) 2221181; internet www.thinakaran.lk/vaaramanjari; f. 1948; Tamil; Editor R. SRIKANTHAN; circ. 35,000.

Virakesari Weekly: 185 Grandpass Rd, POB 160, Colombo 14; tel. (11) 5322760; fax (11) 4614374; e-mail onlinenews@virakesari.lk; internet www.virakesari.lk; f. 1931; Tamil and English; Man. Dir KUMAR NADESAN; Chief Editor V. THEVARAJ; circ. 110,000.

PERIODICALS
(weekly unless otherwise stated)

Business Lanka: Trade Information Service, Sri Lanka Export Development Board, Level 7, 42 Navam Mawatha, POB 1872, Colombo 2; tel. (11) 2300705; fax (11) 2305211; e-mail edb@tradenetsl.lk; f. 1981; quarterly; information for visiting business executives, etc.; Editor (vacant).

Business Today: 2 Temple Lane, Colombo 3; tel. (11) 2597991; fax (11) 2597990; e-mail info@btoptions.com; internet www.businesstoday.lk; monthly; business; publ. by BT Options.

Ceylon Medical Journal: 6 Wijerama Mawatha, Colombo 7; tel. (11) 2693324; fax (11) 2698802; e-mail office@cmj.slma.lk; internet www.sljol.info/index.php/CMJ; f. 1887; quarterly; Editors Prof. H. JANAKA DE SILVA, Dr A. ABEYGUNASEKERA.

The Economic Times: 130/C/8 Jothikarama Mawatha, Kalalgoda, Pannipitiya; tel. (11) 2796134; fax (11) 4305787; f. 1970; Editor THIMSY FAHIM.

Gnanarthapradeepaya: Colombo Catholic Press, 2 Gnanarthapradeepaya Mawatha, Borella, Colombo 8; tel. (11) 2695984; fax (11) 2692586; e-mail info@colombocatholicpress.lk; internet www.colombocatholicpress.lk; f. 1866; Sinhala; Roman Catholic; Chief Editor Rev. Fr CYRIL GAMINI FERNANDO; Exec. Dir Rev. Fr ROHAN DE ALWIS; circ. 45,000.

Irudina: Lithira Publications (Pvt) Ltd, 24 Katukurunduwatte Rd, Ratmalana, Colombo; tel. and fax (11) 7247222; f. 2004; Sinhala; Editor MOHAN LAL PIYADASA.

Lanka Monthly Digest (LMD): LMD House, 4 Greenlands Ave, Colombo 5; tel. (11) 2599600; fax (11) 2599444; e-mail editorial@lmd.lk; internet lmd.lk; f. 1994; monthly; business; Editor-in-Chief HIRAN HEWAVISENTI.

Mihira: Lake House, 35 D. R. Wijewardene Mawatha, POB 248, Colombo 10; tel. (11) 2429583; fax (11) 2429329; f. 1964; Sinhala children's magazine; Editor AJITH DHARMASIRI; circ. 145,000.

Morning Star: 17 Francis Rd, Colombo 6; tel. (60) 2150795; fax (11) 2505805; e-mail editor@csijaffnadiocese.com; internet csijaffnadiocese.com; f. 1841; English and Tamil; monthly newsletter; publ. by the Jaffna diocese of the Church of South India.

Nava Yugaya: Lake House, 35 D. R. Wijewardene Mawatha, POB 248, Colombo 10; tel. (11) 2429521; fax (11) 2429329; e-mail dissbhanu@yahoo.com; f. 1956; literary; fortnightly; Sinhala; Editor INDIKA KUDAHETTY; circ. 57,000.

Navaliya: 223 Bloemendhal Rd, Colombo 13; tel. (11) 2331688; fax (11) 2344252; e-mail upalit@unl.upali.lk; internet www.navaliya.com; Sinhala; women's interest; Editor WASANTHA SRIYAKANYHI; circ. 86,000.

Navamani: 156 Hospital Rd, Kalubowila, Dehiwala, Colombo; tel. (11) 4204766; fax (11) 4204765; e-mail navamani@wow.lk; f. 1996; Man. Dir M. D. M. RIZVI; Chief Editor N. M. AMEEN.

Ravaya: 83 Piliyandala Rd, Maharagama, Colombo; tel. (11) 2851672; e-mail ravaya@gmail.com; internet www.ravaya.lk; Sinhala; Editor VICTOR IVAN.

Sarasaviya: Lake House, 35 D. R. Wijewardene Mawatha, POB 248, Colombo 10; tel. (11) 2429586; e-mail sarasaviya@lakehouse.lk; internet www.sarasaviya.lk; f. 1963; Sinhala; films; Chief Editor ARUNA GUNARATNE; circ. 56,000.

Sinhala Bauddhaya: Maha Bodhi Mandira, 130 Rev. Hikkaduwe Sri Sumangala Nahimi Mawatha, Colombo 10; e-mail mahabodhi@asia.com; f. 1906; publ. by The Maha Bodhi Society of Ceylon; Hon. Sec. KIRTHI KALAHE; circ. 25,000.

Sirikatha: 8 Hunupitiya Cross Rd, Colombo 2; tel. (11) 2479200; fax (11) 2314651; e-mail sirikatha@wijeya.lk; Sinhala women's magazine; Chief Editor SIRI RANASINGHE.

Sri Lanka Government Gazette: Government Press, POB 507, Colombo; tel. (11) 2691460; fax (11) 2698653; e-mail online.govtpres@gmail.com; internet www.documents.gov.lk; f. 1802; Sinhala and Tamil; official govt bulletin; circ. 54,000.

Subasetha: Lake House, 35 D. R. Wijewardene Mawatha, POB 248, Colombo 10; tel. (11) 2429429; f. 1967; Sinhala; astrology, the occult and indigenous medicine; Editor Capt. K. CHANDRA SRI KULARATNE; circ. 100,000.

Tharuni: Lake House, 35 D. R. Wijewardene Mawatha, POB 248, Colombo 10; tel. (11) 2429591; fax (11) 2449069; e-mail editor@tharunee.lk; f. 1969; Sinhala; women's journal; Editor ANTON SAMSON; circ. 95,000.

Vidusara: 223 Bloemendhal Rd, Colombo 13; tel. (11) 2331687; fax (11) 2344252; e-mail rajendra@unl.upali.lk; internet www.vidusara.com; Sinhala; Chief Editor RAJENDRA KULASINGHE; circ. 103,992.

NEWS AGENCIES

Lankapuvath (National News Agency of Sri Lanka): 166/3/1, Havelock Rd, Colombo 05; tel. (11) 2585927; fax (11) 2585930; e-mail office@lankapuvath.net; internet www.lankapuvath.lk; f. 1978; Man. THILAK SIRIMANNE.

TamilNet: e-mail tamilnet@tamilnet.com; internet www.tamilnet.com; f. 1997; reports on Tamil affairs.

PRESS ASSOCIATIONS

Foreign Correspondents' Association of Sri Lanka: 27th Floor, East Tower, World Trade Centre, Colombo 1; tel. (11) 2346166; fax (11) 2357909; Pres. BRYSON HULL.

Press Complaints Commission of Sri Lanka: 96 Kirula Rd, Colombo 5; tel. (11) 5353635; fax (11) 5335500; e-mail info@pccsl.lk; internet www.pccsl.lk; f. 2003; independent asscn; receives complaints on editorial content and seeks to resolve disputes via conciliation and arbitration; Chair. SAM WIJESINHA.

Sri Lanka Press Association: Media House, 17A, 2/1, Stanley Tillakaratne Mawatha, Nugegoda, Colombo; tel. (11) 2775606; fax (11) 2816516; Pres. B. H. S. JAYAWARDHANA; Sec.-Gen. MUDITHA KARIYAKARAWANA.

Publishers

Buddhist Cultural Centre: 125 Anderson Rd, Nedimala, Dehiwala, Colombo; tel. (11) 2734256; fax (11) 2736737; e-mail info@buddhistcc.com; internet www.buddhistcc.net; f. 1992; Dir Ven. KIRAMA WIMALAJOTHI THERO.

Buddhist Publication Society: 54 Sangaraja Mawatha, POB 61, Kandy; tel. (81) 2237283; fax (81) 2238901; e-mail bps@sltnet.lk; internet www.bps.lk; f. 1958; philosophy, religion and theology; Pres. Prof. P. D. PREMASIRI; Editor BHIKKU NYANATUSITA.

Colombo Catholic Press: 2 Gnanarthapradeepaya Mawatha, Borella, Colombo 8; tel. (11) 2695984; fax (11) 2692586; e-mail colombocatholicpress.lk; internet www.colombocatholicpress.lk; f. 1865; religious; publrs of *Lama Pradeepaya*, *The Messenger*, *Gnanarthapradeepaya*, *The Weekly*; Exec. Dir Rev. Fr ROHAN DE ALWIS.

Dayawansa Jayakody and Co: 86–112 Ven. S. Mahinda Himi Mawatha, Maradana, Colombo 10; tel. (11) 2695773; fax (11) 2696653; e-mail dayawansa@dayawansajayakody.com; internet dayawansajayakody.com; publishes novels in Sinhala and books on Buddhism; Man. Dir DAYAWANSA JAYAKODY.

Godage International Publishers: 661 P. D. S. Kularathna Mawatha, Maradana Rd, Colombo 10; tel. (11) 2686925; fax (11) 2674187; e-mail info@godage.com; internet www.godage.com; f. 1959; sciences, fiction, religion, etc.; Chair. SIRISUMANA GODAGE.

M. D. Gunasena and Co Ltd: 217 Olcott Mawatha, POB 246, Colombo 11; tel. (11) 2323981; fax (11) 2323336; e-mail publishingmgr@mdgunasena.com; internet www.mdgunasena.com; f. 1913; educational and general; Chair M. D. PERCY GUNASENA; Man. Dir M. D. ANANDA GUNASENA.

International Book House Publishers: 1 Kumaran Ratnam Rd, Colombo 2; tel. (11) 2330743; fax (11) 2330742; e-mail newpet@sltnet.lk; internet www.bookhouse-lk.com; school text books in English; Founder NEWTON PEIRIS.

Lake House Printers and Publishers Ltd: 41 W. A. D. Ramanayake Mawatha, POB 1458, Colombo 2; tel. (11) 2433271; fax (11) 2449504; e-mail wnl@wijeya.lk; f. 1965; Chair. R. S. WIJEWARDENE; Sec. D. P. ANURA NISHANTHA KUMARA.

National Institute of Education: POB 21, High Level Rd, Maharagama, Colombo; tel. (11) 7601601; fax (11) 7601800; e-mail info@nie.lk; internet www.nie.lk; f. 1986; educational literature; Dir Gen. W. M. ABEYRATNE BANDARA.

Pradeepa Publishers: 34/34 Lawyers' Office Complex, Colombo 12; tel. and fax (11) 2435074; e-mail kjayathie@slt.lk; academic and fictional; Propr K. JAYATILAKE.

Sathara Publishers: 122 Awissawella Rd, Maharagama, Colombo; tel. (11) 2850981; fax (11) 2846256; e-mail sathara@sathara.com; internet www.sathara.com; f. 1979; primary school curricula and children's education; Man. Dir CHANDRASOMA PERERA.

K. V. G. de Silva and Sons (Colombo) Ltd: Shop No. 5, Liberty Plaza, Colombo 3; tel. (11) 7455646; fax (11) 7555543; f. 1898; art, philosophy, scientific, technical, academic, 'Ceyloniana', fiction; Man. FREDERICK JAYARATNAM.

PUBLISHERS' ASSOCIATIONS

Sri Lanka Association of Publishers: 112 S. Mahinda Himi Mawatha, Maradana, Colombo 10; tel. (11) 2695773; fax (11) 2696653; e-mail dayawansa@dayawansajayakody.com; f. 1972; Pres. DAYAWANSA JAYAKODY; Sec.-Gen. DHARMADASA PANDITHARATNA.

Sri Lanka Book Publishers' Association: 53 Maligakanda Rd, Colombo 10; tel. (11) 2696821; e-mail bookpub@sltnet.lk; internet www.bookpublishers.lk; f. 1984; 155 mems; Pres. RANJITH SAMARANAYAKE; Gen. Sec. UPALI WANIGASURIYA.

Broadcasting and Communications

TELECOMMUNICATIONS

Telecommunications Regulatory Commission of Sri Lanka: 276 Elvitigala Mawatha, Manning Town, Colombo 8; tel. (11) 2689345; fax (11) 2689341; e-mail dgtsl@trc.gov.lk; internet www.trc.gov.lk; f. 1996; Chair. LALITH WEERATHUNGA; Dir-Gen. V. P. K. ANUSHA PALPITA.

Bharti Airtel Lanka: 598 Elvitigala Mawatha, Colombo 5; tel. and fax 755755755 (mobile); e-mail 555@airtel.lk; internet www.airtel.lk; f. 2009; subsidiary of Bharti Airtel (India); digital mobile services; CEO AMALI NANAYAKKARA; 1m. subscribers.

Dialog Telekom PLC: 475 Union Pl., Colombo 2; tel. (11) 7678678; fax (11) 2678692; e-mail dialog@dialog.lk; internet www.dialog.lk; operates Dialog GSM, Sri Lanka's largest mobile telephone network; Chair. DATUK AZZAT KAMALUDIN; Chief Exec. Dr SHRIDHIR SARIPUTTA HANSA WIJAYASURIYA.

Etisalat Sri Lanka: Mukthar Plaza,78 Grandpass Rd, Colombo 14; tel. 722123123 (mobile); fax 722541100 (mobile); e-mail customercare@int.etisalat.lk; internet www.etisalat.lk; f. 2010; following takeover of Tigo Sri Lanka by Etisalat (UAE); CEO DUMINDRA RATNAYAKA.

Hutchison Telecommunications Lanka (Pvt) Ltd: 234 Galle Rd, Bambalapitiya, Colombo 4; e-mail cs@hutchison.lk; internet www.hutch.lk; f. 2004; subsidiary of Hutchison Telecommunications Int. Ltd; CEO THIRUKUMAR NADARASA.

Lanka Communication Services (Pvt) Ltd: 65c Dharmapala Mawatha, Colombo 7; tel. (11) 2437545; fax (11) 2537547; e-mail webmaster@lankacom.net; internet www.lankacom.net; f. 1991; subsidiary of Singapore Telecom International; Man. Dir ROHITH UDALAGAMA.

Sri Lanka Telecom Ltd: Telecom Headquarters, 7th Floor, Lotus Rd, POB 503, Colombo 1; tel. (11) 2329711; fax (11) 2440000; e-mail pr@slt.lk; internet www.slt.lk; 45.0% owned by Global Telecommunication Holdings N. V. (Netherlands), 49.5% by Govt of Sri Lanka and the remainder by employees; Chair. NIMAL WELGAMA; Chief Exec. GREG YOUNG.

Mobitel (Pvt) Ltd: 108 W. A. D. Ramanayake Mawatha, Colombo 2; tel. 712755777 (mobile); fax (11) 2330396; e-mail info@mobitel.lk; internet www.mobitel.lk; acquired by Sri Lanka Telecom Ltd in 2002; mobile telecommunications services; CEO SUREN AMERASEKERA.

RADIO

Sri Lanka Broadcasting Corpn: Independence Sq., POB 574, Colombo 7; tel. (11) 2697491; fax (11) 2691568; e-mail dg@slbc.lk; internet www.slbc.lk; f. 1967; under Ministry of Mass Media and Information; controls all broadcasting in Sri Lanka; operates 7 nat. channels as well as several regional and community services; domestic broadcasts in Sinhala, Tamil and English; foreign service also in Tamil, English, Sinhala, Hindi, Kannada, Malayalam, Nepali and Telugu; Chair. HUDSON SAMARASINGHE; Dir-Gen. SAMANTHA WELIWERIYA.

Asura FM: 52, 5th Lane, Colombo 3; tel. (11) 2575000; fax (11) 2301082; e-mail asura@tnlradio.com; broadcasts 24 hrs daily in Sinhala; Gen. Man. CHANDANA THILAKARATNA.

Colombo Communications (Pvt) Ltd: 686 Galle Rd, Colombo 3; tel. (11) 5577777; fax (11) 2505796; e-mail info@efm.lk; internet www.efm.lk; commercial station; three channels broadcast 24 hrs daily in English, Sinhala and Tamil.

Lite FM: 52, 5th Lane, Colombo 3; tel. (11) 7777555; fax (11) 2301082; e-mail litefm@tnlradio.com; internet www.litefm.me; f. 1999; commercial station; broadcasts 24 hrs daily in English; Chair. NIRAJ WICKREMESINGHE.

MBC Networks (Pvt) Ltd: 7 Braybrooke Pl., Colombo 2; tel. (11) 5340111; fax (11) 5340116; e-mail info@maharaja.lk; internet www.capitalmaharaja.com; commercial station comprising four channels; broadcasts 24 hrs daily in English, Sinhala and Tamil; Dir SHANTHI BHAGIRATHAN.

TNL Radio Network Pvt Ltd: 52, 5th Lane, Colombo 3; tel. (11) 7777555; fax (11) 2301082; e-mail info@tnlradio.com; internet www.rhythmfm.me; f. 1993; commercial station; broadcasts 24 hrs daily in English; CEO and Chair. NIRAJ WICKREMESINGHE.

Trans World Radio: Orchid Pl., off Swarnadisi Pl., Koswatte, Nawala, Colombo; tel. (5) 559321; fax (11) 2877750; e-mail rkoch@twr.org; internet www.twr.org; f. 1978; international Christian evangelical station; broadcasts 2–3 hrs every morning and 6.5 hrs each evening to Indian subcontinent; Dir (Finance/Admin) ROGER KOCH; Eng. P. VELMURUGAN.

TELEVISION

Sri Lanka Rupavahini Corpn (SLRC): Independence Sq., POB 2204, Colombo 7; tel. (11) 2501050; fax (11) 2580929; e-mail dg@rupavahini.lk; internet www.rupavahini.lk; f. 1982; studio at Colombo; transmitting stations at nine locations; broadcasts 18 hrs daily on Channel I, 15 hrs daily on Channel II; Chair. MOHAN SAMARANAYAKE.

Independent Television Network (ITN): Wickremasinghepura, Battaramulla; tel. (11) 2774424; fax (11) 2774591; e-mail itnch@slt.lk; internet www.itn.lk; broadcasts about 18 hrs daily; operates Lakhanda Radio (24 hrs; daily); Chair. ROSMAND SENARATHNA; Gen. Man. W. P. A. M. WIJESINGHE.

MTV Channel (Pvt) Ltd: 36 Araliya Uyana, Depanama, Pannipitiya; tel. (11) 5340111; fax (11) 2851373; e-mail info@media.maharaja.lk; internet www.capitalmaharaja.com; f. 1992; broadcasts on three channels in English, Sinhala and Tamil; Group Dir MANO WICKRAMANAYAKE.

Swarnavahini: 676 Galle Rd, Colombo 3; tel. (11) 2503818; fax (11) 2503788; e-mail admin@swarnavahini.lk; internet www.swarnavahini.lk; f. 1997; owned by EAP Network (Pvt) Ltd; Chair. SOMA EDIRISINGHE; Man. Dir JEEVAKA EDIRISINGHE.

Telshan Network (Pvt) Ltd (TNL): 9D Tower Bldg, 25 Station Rd, Colombo 4; tel. (11) 2706124; fax (11) 2706125; e-mail tnltvr@slt.lk; Chair. and Man. Dir SHANTILAL NILKANT WICKREMESINGHE.

Finance

(cap. = capital; res = reserves; dep. = deposits; m. = million; brs = branches; amounts in Sri Lanka rupees)

BANKING

Central Bank

Central Bank of Sri Lanka: 30 Janadhipathi Mawatha, POB 590, Colombo 1; tel. (11) 2477000; fax (11) 2346304; e-mail cbslgen@cbsl.lk; internet www.cbsl.gov.lk; f. 1950; sole bank of issue; cap. 25,000m., dep. 220,361m. (Dec. 2009), res 125,978.2m. (Dec 2008); Gov. and Chair. of the Monetary Board AJITH NIVARD CABRAAL; Dep. Govs K. G. D. D. DHEERASINGHE, P. D. J. FERNANDO; 5 brs.

Commercial Banks

Bank of Ceylon: 4 Bank of Ceylon Mawatha, POB 241, Colombo 1; tel. (11) 2446811; fax (11) 2320864; e-mail boc@boc.lk; internet www.boc.lk; f. 1939; 100% state-owned; cap. 5,000m., res 11,117m., dep. 597,138.38m. (Dec. 2011); Chair. MOHAMED RAZIK ZAROOK; Gen. Man. D. M. GUNASEKARA; 315 brs in Sri Lanka, 3 brs abroad.

Commercial Bank of Ceylon PLC: Commercial House, 21 Bristol St, POB 856, Colombo 1; tel. (11) 2430416; fax (11) 2449889; e-mail e-mail@combank.net; internet www.combank.net; f. 1969; 29.77% owned by DFCC Bank, 29.91% by govt corpns and 40.32% by public; cap. 18,008.8m., res 30,786.8m., dep. 390,568.7 (Dec. 2012); Chair. DINESH WEERAKKODY; Man. Dir RAVI DIAS; 168 brs.

Hatton National Bank PLC: 479 T. B. Jayah Mawatha, POB 837, Colombo 10; tel. (11) 2664664; fax (11) 2446523; e-mail moreinfo@hnb.net; internet www.hnb.net; f. 1970; as Hatton National Bank

Ltd; name changed to above in 2007; 11% owned by individuals, 89% by institutions; cap. 11,451m., res 23,960.9m., dep. 283,712m. (Dec. 2011); Chair. Dr RANEE JAYAMAHA; Man. Dir and CEO RAJENDRA THEAGARAJAH; 187 brs.

Nations Trust Bank PLC: 242 Union Pl., Colombo 2; tel. (11) 4313131; fax (11) 2307854; e-mail info@nationstrust.com; internet www.nationstrust.com; f. 1999 as Nations Trust Bank Ltd; privately owned; acquired Mercantile Leasing Ltd by merger to form Nations Leasing business; name changed as above in 2008; cap. 5,101m., res 949.6m., dep. 87,069.3m. (Dec. 2012); Chair. J. R. F. PEIRIS; CEO SALIYA RAJAKARUNA.

Pan Asia Banking Corpn PLC: 450 Galle Rd, Colombo 3; tel. (11) 2565556; fax (11) 2565558; e-mail pabc@pabcbank.com; internet www.pabcbank.com; f. 1995; 100% privately owned (87.6% owned by local shareholders, 12.4% by foreign shareholders); cap. 1,548.9m., res 511.8m., dep. 47,911m. (Dec. 2012); Chair. W. D. N. H. PERERA; CEO CLAUDE PEIRIS; 41 brs.

People's Bank: 75 Sir Chittampalam A. Gardiner Mawatha, POB 728, Colombo 2; tel. (11) 2327841; fax (11) 2433127; e-mail info@peoplesbank.lk; internet www.peoplesbank.lk; f. 1961; 92% owned by Govt, 8% by co-operatives; subsidiaries incl. People's Leasing Co Ltd and People's Merchant Finance PLC; cap. 49.9m., res 15,031m., dep. 466,182.7m. (Dec. 2010); Chair. (vacant); Gen. Man. N. VASANTHA KUMAR; 325 brs.

Sampath Bank PLC: Sampath Centre Bldg, 110 Sir James Peiris Mawatha, POB 997, Colombo 2; tel. (11) 2303050; fax (11) 2303085; e-mail info@sampath.lk; internet www.sampath.lk; f. 1987 as Investment and Credit Bank Limited; name changed as above in 2008; cap. 3,564m., res 20,996.6m., dep. 244,161m. (Dec. 2011); Chair. DHAMMIKA PERERA; Man. Dir ARAVINDA PERERA; 131 brs.

Seylan Bank PLC: Ceylinco Seylan Towers, 90 Galle Rd, POB 400, Colombo 3; tel. (11) 2456789; fax (11) 2456456; e-mail info@seylan.lk; internet www.eseylan.com; f. 1988 as Seylan Bank Ltd; cap. 9,388m., res 3,937m., dep. 149,300m. (Dec. 2012); Chair. MOHAN PIERIS; Exec. Dir R. NADARAJAH; 116 brs.

Union Bank of Colombo PLC: 15A Alfred Pl., Colombo 3; tel. (11) 2370870; fax (11) 4525576; e-mail info@unionb.com; internet www.unionb.com; f. 1995; cap. 4,979.8m., res 91., dep. 19,598.8m. (Dec. 2011); Chair. AJITA DE ZOYSA; CEO and Dir ANIL AMARASURIYA; 30 brs.

Development Banks

DFCC Bank: 73/5 Galle Rd, POB 1397, Colombo 3; tel. (11) 2442442; fax (11) 2440376; e-mail info@dfccbank.com; internet www.dfccbank.com; f. 1956 as Development Finance Corpn of Ceylon; name changed as above 1997; provides long- and medium-term credit, investment banking and consultancy services; cap. 2,650.9m., res 17,329.9m., dep. 45,120m. (March 2012); Chair. J. M. S. BRITO; CEO A. N. FONSEKA; 19 brs.

National Development Bank PLC: DHPL Bldg, 42 Nawam Mawatha, POB 1825, Colombo 2; tel. (11) 2448448; fax (11) 2314642; e-mail contact@ndbbank.com; internet www.ndbbank.com; f. 1979 by an Act of Parliament as National Development Bank of Sri Lanka; subsequently privatized and name changed as above in June 2008; provides long-term finance for projects, equity financing and merchant banking services; cap. 863.9m., res 7,608m., dep. 107,393m. (Dec. 2012); Chair. HEMAKA AMARASURIYA; CEO RUSSELL DE MEL; 48 brs.

State Mortgage and Investment Bank: 269 Galle Rd, Colombo 3; tel. (11) 2573561; fax (11) 2573346; e-mail agmit@smib.lk; internet www.smib.lk; f. 1979; following the merger of the Ceylon State Mortgage Bank and the Agricultural and Industrial Credit Corpn of Ceylon; Chair. JAGATH WELLAWATTE; 14 brs.

Merchant Banks

Merchant Bank of Sri Lanka PLC: Bank of Ceylon Merchant Tower, 28 St Michael's Rd, POB 1987, Colombo 3; tel. (11) 4711711; fax (11) 4711743; e-mail mbslbank@mbslbank.com; internet www.mbslbank.com; f. 1982; 53.8% owned by Bank of Ceylon; public ltd liability co; Chair. M. R. SHAH; CEO LAKSHMAN KALUARACHCHI (acting); 11 brs.

People's Merchant Finance PLC: 21 Navam Mawatha, Colombo 2; tel. (11) 2300191; fax (11) 2300190; e-mail info@pmb.lk; internet peoplesmerchant.lk; f. 1984 as a subsidiary of People's Bank; Chair. P. A. AJITH PANDITHARATNE; Man. Dir and CEO ANURA WICKREMA-SINGHE; 10 brs.

Savings Bank

National Savings Bank: No. 255, Savings House, Galle Rd, Colombo 3; tel. (11) 2573008; fax (11) 2573178; e-mail nsbgen@nsb.lk; internet www.nsb.lk; govt owned; cap. 3,200m., res 19,378.9m., dep. 411,012.7m. (Dec. 2011); Chair. SUNIL S. SIRISENA; CEO and Gen. Man. H. M. HENNAYAKE BANDARA; 219 brs.

Financial Association

The Finance Houses' Association of Sri Lanka: No. 16, 2/2 42nd Lane, Welawatta, Colombo 6; tel. (11) 2362669; fax (11) 2362668; e-mail finass@sltnet.lk; internet www.fhalanka.lk; f. 1958; represents the finance cos registered and licensed by the Central Bank of Sri Lanka; Chair. RAVANA WIJEYERATNE.

STOCK EXCHANGES

Securities and Exchange Commission of Sri Lanka: East Tower, 28th and 29th Floors, World Trade Centre, Echelon Sq., Colombo 1; tel. (11) 2439144; fax (11) 2439149; e-mail mail@sec.gov.lk; internet www.sec.gov.lk; f. 1987; Dir-Gen. D. B. P. HAREENDRA DISSABANDARA (acting); Chair. (vacant).

Colombo Stock Exchange: 04-01, West Block, World Trade Centre, Echelon Sq., Colombo 1; tel. (11) 2356456; fax (11) 2445279; e-mail info@cse.lk; internet www.cse.lk; f. 1896; stock market; 28 mem. firms and 234 listed cos; Chair. KRISHAN BALENDRA; CEO SUREKHA SELLAHEWA.

INSURANCE

Aviva NDB Insurance: Eagle House, 75 Kumaran Ratnam Rd, Colombo 2; tel. (11) 2310310; fax (11) 2447620; e-mail info@avivandb.com; internet www.avivandb.com; f. 1988 as CTC Eagle Insurance Co Ltd; renamed as above in 2010; general and life insurance; mem. of Aviva International Holdings Ltd; Chair. T. R. RAMACHANDRAN; Man. Dir SHAH ROUF.

Ceylinco Insurance LC: Ceylinco House, 4th Floor, 69 Janadhipathi Mawatha, Colombo 1; tel. (11) 4702702; fax (11) 2485769; e-mail ceylincoinsurance@ceyins.lk; internet www.ceylinco-insurance.com; f. 1987; general and life insurance; Chair. J. G. PERERA; Man. Dir and CEO A. R. GUNAWARDENA.

Hayleys PLC: Hayley Bldg, 400 Deans Rd, Colombo 10; tel. (11) 2696331; fax (11) 2699299; e-mail info@cauhayleys.com; internet www.hayleys.com; f. 1952; Chair. A. M. PANDITHAGE.

National Insurance Corpn Ltd: 47 Muttiah Rd, POB 2202, Colombo 2; tel. (11) 2445738; fax (11) 2445733; e-mail nicopl@slt.lk; general; Chair. T. M. S. NANAYAKKARA; Sec. A. C. J. DE ALWIS.

Sri Lanka Insurance Corpn Ltd: 'Rakshana Mandiraya', 21 Vauxhall St, POB 1337, Colombo 2; tel. (11) 2357357; fax (11) 2447742; e-mail email@srilankainsurance.com; internet www.srilankainsurance.com; f. 1961; privatized in 2003; all classes of insurance; Chair. R. A. JAYATISSA; CEO and Man. Dir MOHAN DE ALWIS.

Union Assurance Ltd: Union Assurance Centre, 20 St Michael's Rd, Colombo 3; tel. (11) 2428428; fax (11) 2343065; e-mail unionassurance@ualink.lk; internet www.ualink.lk; f. 1987; general and life insurance; CEO DIRK PEREIRA.

Insurance Association

Insurance Association of Sri Lanka (IASL): 143 A. Vajira Rd, Colombo 5; tel. (11) 5635582; e-mail info@iasl.lk; internet www.iasl.lk; f. 1989; 16 mem. cos; Pres. RAMAL JASINGHE.

Trade and Industry

GOVERNMENT AGENCIES

Board of Investment of Sri Lanka: World Trade Centre, West Tower, 26th Floor, Echelon Sq., Colombo 1; tel. (11) 2427060; fax (11) 2422407; e-mail info@boi.lk; internet www.investsrilanka.com; f. 1978 as the Greater Colombo Economic Commission; promotes foreign direct investment and administers the eight Export Processing Zones at Katunayake, Biyagama, Koggala, Mirigama, Malwatta, Horana, Mawathagama and Polgahawela; also administers industrial township at Watupitiwala and industrial parks at Seetawaka and Kandy; Chair. and Dir-Gen. M. M. C. FERDINANDO (acting).

Sri Lanka Gem and Jewellery Exchange: World Trade Centre, East Low Blk, Levels 4 and 5, Echelon Sq., Colombo 1; tel. 777536674 (mobile); e-mail gemautho@sltnet.lk; internet www.srilankagemautho.com; f. 1990; testing and certification of gems, trading booths; Dir-Gen. RAVI SAMARANAYAKE.

National Gem and Jewellery Authority: 25 Galle Face Terrace, Colombo 3; tel. (11) 2390645; fax (11) 2320758; e-mail gemautho@slnet.lk; internet www.srilankagemautho.com; f. 1971 as State Gem Corpn; Chair. PRASAD GALHENA; Dir-Gen. W. H. M. N. BANDARA.

Trade Information Service: Sri Lanka Export Development Board, Level 7, 42 Navam Mawatha, POB 1872, Colombo 2; tel. (11) 2300723; fax (11) 2300676; e-mail tisinfo@edb.tradenetsl.lk; internet www.srilankabusiness.com; f. 1981 to collect and disseminate commercial information and to provide advisory services to trade circles; Chair. and Chief Exec. JANAKA RATNAYAKE; Dir-Gen. SUJATHA WEERAKOON.

DEVELOPMENT ORGANIZATIONS

Coconut Development Authority: 54 Nawala Rd, Narahenpita, POB 1572, Colombo 5; tel. (11) 2502502; fax (11) 2508729; e-mail dgcda@sltnet.lk; internet www.cda.lk; f. 1972; state body; promotes the coconut industry through financial assistance for mfrs of coconut products, market information, consultancy services and quality assurance; Chair. SUGATH HANDUNGE.

Industrial Development Board of Ceylon (IDB): 615 Galle Rd, Katubedda, POB 09, Moratuwa; tel. (11) 2605323; fax (11) 2607002; e-mail info@idb.gov.lk; internet www.idb.gov.lk; f. 1969; under Ministry of Traditional Industries and Small Enterprise Development; promotes industrial development through provincial network; Chair. UDAYASRI KARIYAWASAM.

Information and Communication Technology Association of Sri Lanka (ICTA): 160/24 Kirimandala Mawatha, Colombo 5; tel. (11) 2369100; fax (11) 2369091; e-mail info@icta.lk; internet www.icta.lk; f. 2003; responsible for development of information communication technology in Sri Lanka; govt-owned; Chair. Prof. P. W. EPASINGHE.

Sri Lanka Export Development Board: Trade Information Service, Level 7, 42 Navam Mawatha, Colombo 2; tel. (11) 2300705; fax (11) 2300715; e-mail edb@tradenetsl.lk; internet www.srilankabusiness.com; f. 1979; Chair. and Chief Exec. JANAKA RATNAYAKE; Dir-Gen. SUJATHA WEERAKOON.

CHAMBERS OF COMMERCE

Federation of Chambers of Commerce and Industry of Sri Lanka: 53 Vauxhall Lane, 3rd Floor, Colombo 2; tel. (11) 2304253; fax (11) 2304255; e-mail info@fccisl.lk; internet www.fccisl.lk; f. 1973; a central org. of 53 chambers of commerce and industry and trade asscns representing 15,000 cos throughout Sri Lanka; Pres. KUMAR MALLIMARATCHI; Sec.-Gen. THUSITHA TENNAKOON.

Ceylon Chamber of Commerce: 50 Navam Mawatha, POB 274, Colombo 2; tel. (11) 2421745; fax (11) 2449352; e-mail info@chamber.lk; internet www.chamber.lk; f. 1839; 500 mems; Chair. SUSANTHA RATNAYAKE; Sec.-Gen. and CEO HARIN MALWATTE.

Ceylon National Chamber of Industries (CNCI): Galle Face Court 2, Apt No. 20, 1st Floor, POB 1775, Colombo 3; tel. (11) 2452181; fax (11) 2331443; e-mail info@cnci.biz; internet www.cnci.biz; f. 1960; 325 mems; Chair. PREETHI JAYAWARDENA; Sec.-Gen. and CEO KUMARA KANDALAMA.

International Chamber of Commerce Sri Lanka: 5th Floor, 53 Vauxhall St, POB 1733, Colombo 2; tel. (11) 2307825; fax (11) 2307841; e-mail iccsl@sltnet.lk; internet www.iccsrilanka.com; f. 1955; Chair. TISSA JAYAWEERA.

National Chamber of Commerce of Sri Lanka (NCCSL): NCCSL Bldg, 450 D. R. Wijewardene Mawatha, POB 1375, Colombo 10; tel. (11) 2689600; fax (11) 2689596; e-mail sg@nccsl.lk; internet www.nccsl.lk; f. 1948; Pres. ASOKA HETTIGODA; Sec.-Gen. E. M. WIJETILLEKE.

INDUSTRIAL AND TRADE ASSOCIATIONS

Association of Computer Training Organizations: 51 Sir Marcus Fernando Mawatha, Colombo 7; tel. (11) 2665261; fax (11) 4713821; e-mail actos@infotel.lk; internet www.actos.lk; f. 1991; 29 mems; Pres. KITHSIRI MANCHANAYAKE.

Ceylon Coir Fibre Exporters' Association: c/o Volanka Ltd, 193 Minuwangoda Rd, Kotugoda; tel. (11) 2232476; fax (11) 2232477; e-mail com@volanka.com; internet www.volanka.com; Chair. INDRAJITH PIYASENA.

Ceylon Planters' Society: 40/1 Sri Dhammadara Mawatha, Ratmalana; tel. (11) 2715656; fax (11) 2716758; e-mail planterssociety@yahoo.com; f. 1936; 500 mems (plantation mans); Pres. NISALA JAYAWARDANA; Sec. N. NIHAL PERERA.

Coconut Products Traders' Association: c/o Ceylon Chamber of Commerce, 50 Navam Mawatha, POB 274, Colombo 2; tel. (11) 2421745; fax (11) 2449352; e-mail info@chamber.lk; internet www.chamber.lk; f. 1925; Chair. THARAKA DADAGAMUWA; Sec. E. P. A. COORAY.

Colombo Rubber Traders' Association (CRTA): c/o Ceylon Chamber of Commerce, 50 Navam Mawatha, POB 274, Colombo 2; tel. (11) 5588881; fax (11) 2449352; e-mail info@chamber.lk; internet www.chamber.lk; f. 1918; Chair. M. RAHEEM; Gen. Sec. DAVID JANSZE.

Colombo Tea Traders' Association: c/o Ceylon Chamber of Commerce, 50 Navam Mawatha, POB 274, Colombo 2; tel. (11) 5588801; fax (11) 2449352; e-mail info@chamber.lk; internet www.chamber.lk; f. 1894; 203 mems; Chair. JAYANTHA KERAGALA.

Exporters Association of Sri Lanka (EASL): 50 Nawam Mawatha, Colombo 2; tel. (11) 2421745; fax (11) 2437477; e-mail irangika@chamber.lk; internet www.exporterssrilanka.net; f. 1997; Chair. DAWN AUSTIN.

Fabric Apparel Accessory Manufacturers' Association (FAAMA): 8 Arunachalum Ave, Colombo 7; tel. (11) 2303782; fax (11) 4710687; e-mail info@faama.lk; internet www.faama.lk; f. 2003; Chair. BEAUNO FERNANDO; 59 mems.

Joint Apparel Association Forum (JAAF): 8 Arunachalam Ave, Horton Pl., Colombo 7; tel. (11) 4528494; fax (11) 2698827; e-mail info@jaafsl.com; internet www.jaafsl.com; f. 2002; co-ordinates and develops apparel industry; Chair. A. SUKUMARIN; Sec.-Gen. M. P. T. COORAY.

Sea Food Exporters' Association: c/o Tropic Frozen Foods Ltd, 16/1 Thammita Rd, Negombo; tel. (31) 2222959; fax (31) 2233348; Pres. ROSHAN FERNANDO.

Software Exporters' Association: 65 Walukarama Rd, Colombo 3; tel. (11) 4721194; fax (11) 4721198; e-mail mano@eurocenter.lk; f. 1999; 52 mems; Chair. MANO SEKARAM.

Sri Lanka Apparel Exporters' Association: 45 Rosmead Pl., Colombo 7; tel. (11) 2675050; fax (11) 2683118; e-mail sl-apparel@sltnet.lk; internet www.srilanka-apparel.com; f. 1982; Chair. ROHAN ABAYAKOON; Sec. HEMAMALI SIRISENA.

Sri Lanka Association of Manufacturers and Exporters of Rubber Products (SLAMERP): Associated Motorways Ltd, Nagoda, Kalutara; tel. (34) 2227066; fax (34) 2226476; e-mail slamerp@panlanka.net; f. 1984; Chair. ANANDA CALDERA; Pres. ANANDA CALDERA.

Sri Lanka Association of Printers (SLAP): 290 D. R. Wijewardene Mawatha, Colombo 10; tel. (11) 2472315; fax (11) 2386716; e-mail slap@srilankaprint.com; internet www.srilankaprint.com; f. 1956; 390 mems; publs quarterly magazine *Printceylon*; Pres. SANJEEV MOHAN; Sec. V. KUMARAN.

Sri Lanka Chamber of Garment Exporters (SLCGE): 108A-1 Maya Ave, Colombo 6; tel. (11) 2504379; fax (11) 4517585; f. 1992; Pres. JAYASIRI SILVA; Gen. Sec. J. J. SOURJAH; 78 mems.

Sri Lanka Chamber of the Pharmaceutical Industry: 15 Tichbourne Passage, Colombo 10; tel. (11) 2231560; fax (11) 2671877; e-mail aperera@sol.lk; internet www.slcpi.org; f. 1999; 31 mems; Pres. VISH GOVINDASAMY; Sec. SUDARSHANA JAYATILLEKE.

Sri Lanka Fruit and Vegetables Producers, Processors and Exporters' Association: c/o Consolidated Business Systems, 27A Papiliya Rd, Nugegoda, Colombo; tel. (11) 2332330; fax (11) 2332331; e-mail info@lankafruit.org; internet www.lankafruit.org; f. 1981; 35 mems; Chair. S. GNANASKANDAN.

Sri Lanka Gem and Jewellery Association (SLGJA): Subud Home, 2nd Floor, 38 Frankfort Pl., Colombo 4; tel. (11) 2597226; fax (11) 2597250; e-mail info@slgja.org; internet www.slgja.org; f. 2003, following merger of Sri Lanka Gem Traders' Asscn, Sri Lanka Jewellery Manufacturing Exporters' Asscn, Sri Lanka Lapidarists' and Exporters' Asscn and Sri Lanka Jewellers' and Gem Merchants' Fed.; 297 mems; Chair. DESHABANDU M. MACKY HASIM; Sec. ZIQUFI ISMAIL.

Sri Lanka Shippers' Council (SLSC): c/o Ceylon Chamber of Commerce, 50 Nawam Mawatha, POB 274, Colombo 2; tel. (11) 2421745; fax (11) 2449352; e-mail slsc@chamber.lk; internet www.shipperscouncil.lk; f. 1966; Chair. DINESH DE SILVA; Sec. MANORI DISSANAYAKA.

Sri Lanka Tea Board: 574 Galle Rd, POB 1750, Colombo 3; tel. (11) 2587814; fax (11) 2589132; e-mail teaboard@pureceylontea.com; internet www.pureceylontea.com; f. 1976 for development of tea industry through quality control and promotion in Sri Lanka and in world markets; regulatory and administrative body for the tea industry; Chair. JANAKI KURUPPU; Dir-Gen. H. D. HEMARATNE.

EMPLOYERS' ORGANIZATION

Employers' Federation of Ceylon: 385 J3 Old Kotte Rd, Rajagiriya, Colombo; tel. (11) 2867966; fax (11) 2867942; e-mail efc@empfed.lk; internet www.employers.lk; f. 1929; mem. of International Organization of Employers and Confederation of Asia Pacific Employers; 510 mems; Chair. J. M. S. BRITO; Dir-Gen. R. L. P. PEIRIS.

UTILITIES

Electricity

Ceylon Electricity Board: 50 Sir Chittampalam A. Gardiner Mawatha, POB 540, Colombo 2; tel. (11) 324472; fax (11) 2323935; e-mail admin@ceb.lk; internet www.ceb.lk; f. 1969; Chair. W. ABEYWICKREME; Gen. Man. NIMAL WICKREMASURIYA.

Water

National Water Supply and Drainage Board (NWSDB): Galle Rd, Ratmalana, Colombo; tel. (11) 2635990; fax (11) 2636449; e-mail gm@waterboard.lk; internet www.waterboard.lk; f. 1975; govt corpn; Chair. KARUNASENA HETTIARACHCHI; Gen. Man. K. L. L. PREMANATH.

CO-OPERATIVES

In 2000 there were an estimated 11,793 co-operative societies in Sri Lanka, with membership totalling 17,235,000.

National Co-operative Council of Sri Lanka (NCCSL): 455 Galle Rd, POB 1469, Colombo 03; tel. (11) 2585496; fax (11) 2587062; e-mail slncc@sltnet.lk; internet www.slncc.lk; f. 1955; Gen.-Sec. Dr SUNIL SILVA.

The top co-operatives in Sri Lanka include:

Mahiyangana Multi-Purpose Co-operative: Mahiyangana; tel. and fax (55) 2257226; f. 1971; food and agriculture; Chair. P. M. C. BANDARA.

Morawakkorale Tea Producers' Co-operative Society: Deniyaya Rd, Kotapola; tel. (41) 2271259; e-mail info@mkteacoop .com; internet mkteacoop.com; f. 1953; 3,800 mems (2008); Chair. UPALI SHANTHA ABYWICKRAMA; Gen. Man. W. W. LEENAS PRIYASHANTHA.

TRADE UNIONS

In 2009 there were more than 1,650 trade unions registered in Sri Lanka and 19 trade union federations. Many of the trade unions have political affiliations.

All Ceylon Federation of Free Trade Unions (ACFFTU): 94-1/6 York Bldg, York St, Colombo 1; tel. (11) 2431847; fax (11) 2470874; e-mail nwc@itmin.com; 10 affiliated unions; 84,000 mems; Pres. MARCELL C. RAJAHMONEY; Sec.-Gen. ANTON LODWICK.

All Ceylon Trade Union Federation (ACTUF): 198/19 Panchikawatte Rd, Colombo 10; tel. (11) 2595566; fax (11) 5358783; e-mail editor@unions.lk; internet www.unions.lk; f. 1941; Pres. K. D. LAL KANTHA.

Ceylon Federation of Labour (CFL): 457 Union Pl., Colombo 2; tel. (11) 2694273; fax (11) 2686188; e-mail ceylonfederationoflabour@ yahoo.com; f. 1957; 16 affiliated unions; 155,969 mems; Pres. T. M. R. RASSEEDIN; Pres. S. SIRIWARDENA.

Ceylon Workers' Congress (CWC): 'Savumia Bhavan', 72 Ananda Coomarasamy Mawatha, POB 1294, Colombo 7; tel. (11) 2301359; fax (11) 2301355; e-mail cwconline@sltnet.lk; f. 1939; political entity; represents mainly plantation workers of recent Indian origin; 50 district offices and seven regional offices; 250,000 mems; Pres. ARUMUGAN THONDAMAN.

Democratic Workers' Congress (DWC): 70 Bankshall St, POB 1009, Colombo 11; tel. (11) 2423746; fax (11) 2435961; f. 1939; 201,382 mems (1994); Pres. MANO GANESHAN; Gen. Sec. R. KITNAN.

Jathika Sevaka Sangamaya (JSS) (National Employees' Union): 416 Kotte Rd, Pitakotte, Colombo; tel. (11) 2865436; fax (11) 2865438; e-mail jathika.ss@gmail.com; f. 1959; 357,000 mems; represents over 70% of unionized manual and clerical workers of Sri Lanka; Pres. Dr JAYALATH JAYAWARDENA; Gen. Sec. SIRINAL DE MEL.

Lanka Jathika Estate Workers' Union (LJEWU): 60 Bandaranayakepura, Sri Jayawardenepura Mawatha, Welikada, POB 1918, Rajagiriya; tel. (11) 2865138; fax (11) 2862262; e-mail ljewusl@gmail .com; f. 1958; 13 affiliated unions; Pres. RAVINDRA SAMARAWEERA; Gen. Sec. K. VELAYUDAM.

National Trade Union Federation: 60 Bandaranayakepura Mawatha, Welikada, Rajagiriya; tel. (11) 2885599; fax (11) 2862262; e-mail ntufsl@gmail.com.

National Workers' Congress: 1/6 York Bldg, 94 York St, Colombo 1; tel. (11) 2431847; fax (11) 2470874; e-mail nwc@itmin.net; internet www.slnwc.org; f. 1947; Pres. M. C. RAJAHMONEY; Sec.-Gen. and Treas. A. LODWICK.

Public Services National Trade Union Federation (PSNTUF): Colombo; internet www.psntuf.lk; f. 1973; 48 affiliated unions; 25,000 mems; Pres. JOSEPH M. PERERA; Gen. Sec. J. M. L. R. JAYASUNDARA.

Sri Lanka Nidahas Sewaka Sangamaya (Sri Lanka Free Workers' Union): 301 T. B. Jayah Mawatha, POB 1241, Colombo 10; tel. and fax (11) 2694074; f. 1960; 834 br. unions; 88,000 mems; Pres. ALAVI MOWLANA; Gen. Sec. LESLIE DEVENDRA.

Trade Union Confederation: Colombo; f. 2008; 40 affiliated unions; Pres. K. S. WEERASEKERA; Sec. ANTON MARCUS.

United Federation of Labour: 17 Barrack Lane, Colombo 2; tel. (11) 2324053; Pres. LINUS JAYATILLAKE.

Transport

RAILWAYS

In 2010 the total length of the Sri Lankan railways network was 1,362 km. In that year the network transported 101.5m. passengers and 2.7m. tons of freight. In 2010 a 10-year railway development strategy was introduced by the Government. In the same year plans were finalized for the reconstruction, with funding from Indian sources, of two northern sections of the rail network that had been destroyed during Sri Lanka's civil war: Medawachchiya to Thalaimannar on the North-Western Line and Omanthai to Kankasanthurai on the Northern Line (scheduled for completion by September 2013 and the end of 2014, respectively). In 2012 Sri Lanka and the People's Republic of China concluded an agreement concerning the construction of an electrified line connecting Veyangoda and Kalutara South, serving Colombo and surrounding districts.

Sri Lanka Railways Authority (SLRA): Colombo; f. 2003; responsible for running of nat. railway network; Gen. Man. T. LALITHASIRI GUNARUWAH.

Sri Lanka Railways (SLR): Olcott Mawatha, POB 335, Colombo 10; tel. (11) 2431177; fax (11) 2446490; e-mail gmr-slr@sltnet.lk; internet www.railway.gov.lk; f. 1864; under Ministry of Transport; operates 1,447 track-km; 10 railway lines across the country and 164 stations, with 134 sub-stations (2008); Gen. Man. B. A. P. ARIYARATNE.

ROADS

In 2011 there were an estimated 116,113 km of roads in Sri Lanka, of which 2,900 km were highways, 1,706 km provincial roads and 35,755 km rural roads. About 90% of all freight and passenger transport in Sri Lanka is conveyed by road. Delayed construction of a four-lane 126-km Southern Expressway, extending from Colombo to Matara and jointly funded by the Asian Development Bank and the Japanese Bank for International Co-operation, was scheduled to be completed by 2013; the Kottawa–Galle section was opened in November 2011. Other significant road projects scheduled for completion in 2013 included the Colombo–Katunayake Expressway and the Colombo Outer Circular Highway. Plans to extend the Southern Expressway from Matara to Hambantota to improve the connectivity between the western and southern parts of the country were also under consideration.

Department of Motor Traffic: 341 Elvitigala Mawatha, POB 533, Colombo 5; tel. (11) 2694331; fax (11) 2694338; e-mail comm@dmt .gov.lk; internet www.dmt.gov.lk; Commr BADULLAGE WIJAYARATNE.

National Transport Commission (NTC): 241 Park Rd, Colombo 5; tel. (11) 2595555; fax (11) 2503969; e-mail info@ntc.gov.lk; internet www.ntc.gov.lk; advisory and supervisory body for national passenger bus services; Dir G. A. S. GANEPOLA.

Sri Lanka Transport Board: 200 Kirula Rd, Narahenpita, POB 1435, Colombo 5; tel. (11) 2581120; fax (11) 2368921; e-mail chairmanctb@sltnet.lk; f. 1958; nationalized organization responsible for road passenger transport services consisting of a central transport board, 11 Cluster Bus Cos and one regional transport board; fleet of 4,077 buses (2006); Chair. TUDER CAYARATNE; Sec. D. P. W. DE LIVERA.

SHIPPING

Colombo is one of the most important ports in Asia and is situated at the junction of the main trade routes. The other main ports of Sri Lanka are Hambantota, Trincomalee, Galle and Jaffna. Trincomalee is the main port for handling tea exports. The construction of a major new Chinese-funded industrial port at Hambantota (the Magama Ruhunupura Mahinda Rajapaksa Port) commenced in 2008. The first phase was inaugurated in November 2010. Plans for the construction of a new South Container Terminal at Colombo were finalized in late 2011; the first phase of the project, which was to be implemented by a joint Chinese-Sri Lankan venture, was scheduled for completion in mid-2014. A passenger ferry service linking Colombo with the Indian state of Tamil Nadu, which had been inactive for almost 30 years due to the civil conflict in Sri Lanka, recommenced in mid-2011. At December 2012 Sri Lanka's flag registered fleet had a total of 81 ships, including 13 general cargoes, 5 bulk carriers and 1 fishing tanker, with a total displacement of 176,385 grt.

Ceylon Association of Ships' Agents (CASA): 56 Ward Pl., Colombo 7; tel. (11) 2696227; fax (11) 2698648; e-mail casa@sltnet .lk; internet www.casa.lk; f. 1944; primarily a consultative organization; represents mems in dealings with govt authorities; 110 mems; Chair. NIMAL RANCHIGODA; Sec.-Gen. DHAMMIKA WALGAMPAYA.

Sri Lanka Ports Authority: 19 Chaithya Rd, POB 595, Colombo 1; tel. (11) 2421201; fax (11) 2440651; e-mail info@slpa.lk; internet www.slpa.lk; f. 1979; responsible for all cargo handling operations and harbour development and maintenance in the ports of Colombo,

Galle, Kankasanthurai, Trincomalee, Oluvil, Point Pedro and Hambantota; Chair. PRIYATH BANDU WICKRAMA; Man. Dir Capt. NIHAL KEPPETIPOLA.

Shipping Companies

Ceylon Ocean Lines Ltd: 'Sayuru Sevana', 46/12 Nawam Mawatha, Colombo 2; tel. (11) 2434928; fax (11) 2439245; e-mail oceanlines@col.lk; f. 1956; shipping agents, freight forwarders, charterers, container freight station operators and bunkers; Dirs Capt. L. P. WEINMAN, Capt. A. V. RAJENDRA.

Ceylon Shipping Corpn Ltd: MICH Bldg, 27 Bristol St, Colombo 1; tel. (11) 2328772; fax (11) 2449486; e-mail cscl@cscl.lk; internet www .cscl.lk; f. 1971 as a govt corpn; became govt-owned limited liability co in 1992; operates fully containerized service to Europe, the Far East, the Mediterranean, USA and Canada (East Coast); Chair. PRASAD GALHENA.

Ceylon Shipping Lines Ltd: 450 D. R. Wijewardene Mawatha, POB 891, Colombo 10; tel. (11) 2689500; fax (11) 2689510; e-mail cslmgmt@sltnet.lk; internet www.ceylonshippinglines.com; f. 1954; shipping agents, travel agents, terminal operators; Chair. ARMYNE WIRASINHA; Man. Dir D. P. C. LAWRENCE.

Colombo Dockyard Ltd: Port of Colombo, Graving Docks, POB 906, Colombo 15; tel. (11) 2429000; fax (11) 2446441; e-mail coldock@ cdl.lk; internet www.cdl.lk; f. 1974; 51% owned by Onomichi Dockyard Co Ltd, Japan, and 49% by Sri Lankan public and government institutions; four dry-docks, seven repair berths (1,200 m), repair of ships up to 125,000 dwt, and builders of steel/ aluminium vessels of up to 3,000 dwt; Chair. AKIHIKO NAKAUCHI; Man. Dir and CEO M. P. B. YAPA.

Mercantile Shipping Co Ltd: 441 K. Cyril C. Perera Mawatha, Colombo 13; tel. (11) 2331792; fax (11) 2331799; e-mail info@mscl.lk; internet www.mscl.lk; f. 1981; Man. Dir THOMAS KRIWAT.

Sri Lanka Shipping Co Ltd: 46/5 Robert Sennayake Bldg, Navam Mawatha, POB 1125, Colombo 2; tel. (11) 2336853; fax (11) 2437479; e-mail lankaship@slsc.lk; internet www.srilankashipping.com; f. 1956; Chair. Capt. LESTER POEL WEINMAN.

INLAND WATERWAYS

There are more than 160 km of canals open for traffic.

CIVIL AVIATION

There are airports at Batticaloa, Colombo (Bandaranaike for external flights and Ratmalana for internal), Gal Oya, Palali, Jaffna and Trincomalee. A second international airport, Mattala Rajapaksa International (near Hambantota), was inaugurated in March 2013.

Civil Aviation Authority of Sri Lanka: Supreme Bldg, 64 Galle Rd, Colombo 3; tel. (11) 2433213; fax (11) 2440231; e-mail info@caa .lk; internet www.caa.lk; f. 2002; Chair. W. D. R. M. J. GOONETILEKE; CEO and Dir-Gen. Civil Aviation H. M. C. NIMALSIRI.

Deccan Aviation (Lanka) Pvt Ltd: 385, Galle Rd, Colombo 03; f. 2004; only co. authorized to operate both helicopters and fixed wing aircraft in the country.

Expo Aviation Pvt Ltd: tel. (11) 2576941; fax (11) 2576943; e-mail expoair@expoavi.com; internet www.expoavi.com; f. 1997; private carrier of int. cargo in Sri Lanka; Man. Dir SHAFIK KASSIM.

Helitours: Air Headquarters, POB 594, Colombo 2; tel. (11) 2342577; fax (11) 2343969; e-mail ops1@slaf.gov.lk; commercial wing of Sri Lankan Air Force; charter services to domestic destinations; Dir Wing-Commdr DAYAL WIJERATNE.

Mihin Lanka: No. 61, W. A. D. Ramanayake Mawatha, Colombo 2; tel. (11) 7800300; fax (11) 7800304; e-mail info@mihinlanka.com; internet www.mihinlanka.com; f. 2007; govt-owned; int. services to India, the Maldives, United Arab Emirates, Thailand and Singapore; Chair. KAPLIA CHANDRASENA.

SriLankan Airlines Ltd: Airline Centre, Bandaranaike International Airport, Katunayake, Colombo; tel. (11) 97335555; fax (11) 97335122; e-mail ulweb@srilankan.aero; internet www .srilankan.lk; f. 1979 as Air Lanka Ltd, name changed as above in 1999; int. services to Europe, the Middle East, South Asia and the Far East; Chair. NISHANTA WICKREMASINGHE; CEO KAPILA CHANDRASENA.

Tourism

As a stopping place for luxury cruises and by virtue of the spectacle of its Buddhist festivals, ancient monuments and natural scenery, Sri Lanka is one of Asia's most important tourist centres.

Sri Lanka's tourism industry was adversely affected by the intercommunal violence in 1983–2009. However, following the end of the civil war in May 2009, the tourism sector recovered strongly; according to figures from the Sri Lanka Tourism Development Authority, tourist arrivals grew by 46.1% in 2010, compared with the previous year, to 654,476, before increasing by a further 30.8%, to 855,975, in 2011. In 2010 India and the United Kingdom were the most important sources of tourist arrivals, providing 19.4% and 16.1% of total arrivals, respectively. Receipts from tourism (not including passenger transport) increased from US $349.3m. in 2009 to an estimated $830m. in 2011.

Sri Lanka Convention Bureau (SLCB): Hotel School Bldg, 4th Floor, 78 Galle Rd, Colombo 03; tel. (11) 4865050; fax (11) 2472985; e-mail slcb@sltnet.lk; internet www.visitsrilanka.net; f. 2005 as one of several entities replacing the Sri Lanka Tourism Board; aims to promote Sri Lanka as a prime destination for meetings, incentives, conferences and exhibitions (MICE) tourism; Chair. Dr NALAKA GODAHEWA; Gen. Man. VIPULA WANIGASEKARA.

Sri Lanka Tourism Development Authority (SLTDA): 80 Galle Rd, Colombo 3; tel. (11) 2437059; fax (11) 2440001; e-mail info@sltda .gov.lk; internet www.sltda.gov.lk; f. 2005 as one of several entities replacing the Sri Lanka Tourism Board; Chair. NALAKA GODAHEWA; Dir-Gen. S. KALAISELVAM.

Sri Lanka Tourism Promotion Bureau (SLTPB): 80 Galle Rd, Colombo 3; tel. (11) 2426900; fax (11) 2440001; e-mail info@srilanka .travel; internet www.srilanka.travel; f. 2005 as one of several entities replacing the Sri Lanka Tourism Board; Chair. NALAKA GODAHEWA; Man. Dir RUMY JAUFFER.

Defence

As assessed at November 2011, the total strength of the active armed forces was some 160,900 (including recalled reservists): army 117,900, navy 15,000, air force 28,000; the reserve forces numbered 5,500. There were also paramilitary forces of an estimated 62,200 (including an estimated 15,000 National Guard, 13,000 Home Guard and a 3,000-strong anti-guerrilla Special Task Force). Military service is voluntary.

Defence Budget: Estimated at Rs 243,400m. for 2012 (equivalent to 11.1% of total expenditure).

Chief of Defence Staff: Air Chief Marshal W. D. R. M. J. GOONETILEKE.

Commander of the Army: Lt.-Gen. JAGATH JAYASURIYA.

Commander of the Air Force: Air Vice Marshal HARSHA ABEYWICKREMA.

Commander of the Navy: Vice-Adm. JAYANATH COLOMBAGE.

Education

The formulation of educational policy is the responsibility of the Ministry of Education and the Ministry of Higher Education. The administration and management of the school system is divided into 15 regions. Government expenditure on education was estimated at Rs 99,043m. in 2011, representing 9.8% of total recurrent expenditure.

Since 1945 education has been available free of charge. In 2011, according to provisional estimates, about 4.15m. pupils attended schools, and teachers numbered about 228,556. The total number of schools (including denominational schools and Pirivenas, which are attended by Buddhist clergy and lay students) was estimated at 10,545 in that year.

School attendance is officially compulsory for 11 years between five and 15 years of age. Schools are streamed according to the language medium used, either Sinhala or Tamil. Improving the standard of English, which is a compulsory second language, is one of the policy priorities of the Government. In 1960 almost all denominational schools were brought under state control.

ELEMENTARY AND SECONDARY EDUCATION

Elementary education lasts five years from the ages of five to 10. Secondary schooling, beginning at 10 years of age, lasts for up to eight years, comprising a first cycle of six years and a second of two years. A new system of public examinations, the National Certificate of General Education (NCGE), came into effect in 1975 to replace the British examination system. It places emphasis on practical subjects such as mathematics, science, health and physical education, social studies and pre-vocational studies. The Higher National Certificate of Education (HNCE) is more employment-orientated. Enrolment at primary schools in 2009/10 included an estimated 94% of children in the relevant age-group. Secondary enrolment was equivalent to an estimated 87% of children in the relevant age-group in 2003/04.

SUDAN

Introductory Survey

LOCATION, CLIMATE, LANGUAGE, RELIGION, FLAG, CAPITAL

The Republic of Sudan lies in north-eastern Africa. It is bordered by Egypt to the north, by the Red Sea, Eritrea and Ethiopia to the east, by the Central African Republic, Chad and Libya to the west, and by South Sudan to the south. The climate shows a marked transition from the desert of the north to the rainy equatorial south. Temperatures vary with altitude and latitude. The annual average for the whole country is about 21°C (70°F). Arabic is the official language, although other languages are spoken and English is widely understood. Most northern Sudanese are Muslims, while in the south most of the inhabitants are animists or Christians. The national flag (proportions 1 by 2) has three equal horizontal stripes, of red, white and black, with a green triangle at the hoist. The capital is Khartoum.

CONTEMPORARY POLITICAL HISTORY

Historical Context

The Sudan (as the country was known before 1975) achieved independence as a parliamentary republic on 1 January 1956. In May 1969 power was seized by a group of officers, led by Col Gaafar Muhammad Nimeri. All existing political institutions and organizations were abolished, and the 'Democratic Republic of the Sudan' was proclaimed, with supreme authority held by a Revolutionary Command Council (RCC). In October 1971 a referendum confirmed Nimeri's nomination as President. A new Government was formed, the RCC was dissolved, and the Sudanese Socialist Union (SSU) was recognized as the only political party.

The Nimeri Government was challenged by violence in the three southern provinces (Bahr El-Ghazal, Equatoria and Upper Nile), where the population is predominantly Christian and animist. Rebellion against rule from the north had first broken out in 1955, and fighting continued until March 1972, when an agreement allowing the three provinces a degree of autonomy was concluded between the Government and representatives of the South Sudan Liberation Movement. Sudan's permanent Constitution was endorsed in April 1973. Elections to the Regional People's Assembly for southern Sudan took place in November 1973, followed by elections to the National People's Assembly in April 1974.

In April 1983 President Nimeri was re-elected for a third six-year term. Following a resurgence of rebel activity in the south, in June 1983 Nimeri redivided the south into three smaller regions, thereby revoking the arrangements of the 1972 agreement. In September 1983 Nimeri announced the imposition of strict Islamic law (the *Shari'a*), further aggravating north–south tensions, and in April 1984 he proclaimed a state of emergency. In May Nimeri replaced his Council of Ministers with a 64-member Presidential Council, in accordance with the 'Shoura' (consultation) principle of *Shari'a* law. In July, however, the National People's Assembly rejected his proposed constitutional amendments to make Sudan a formal Islamic state. In October Nimeri ended the state of emergency. After the emergence of the Sudan People's Liberation Movement (SPLM) in the south, its armed forces, the Sudan People's Liberation Army (SPLA), rapidly made military advances.

Domestic Political Affairs

On 6 April 1985, while Nimeri was visiting the USA, he was deposed in a bloodless military coup. The country's new leader, Gen. Abdel-Rahman Swar al-Dahab (who had recently been made Minister of Defence and Commander-in-Chief of the army by Nimeri), appointed a Transitional Military Council (TMC) to govern the country, but he pledged a return to civilian rule after a one-year transitional period. The SSU and the National People's Assembly were dissolved, and hundreds of Nimeri's officials were arrested; Nimeri went into exile in Cairo, Egypt. A transitional Constitution was introduced in October that allowed new political groupings to emerge in preparation for a general election, and in December the name of the country was officially changed to 'the Republic of Sudan'.

In a general election in April 1986 the Umma Party (UP), led by Sadiq al-Mahdi, won 99 of the 264 seats in the new National Assembly, followed by the Democratic Unionist Party (DUP), with 63 seats. A coalition Government was formed by the UP and DUP, with four portfolios in the Council of Ministers allocated to southern parties. Al-Mahdi became Prime Minister and Minister of Defence, and a six-member Supreme Council assumed the functions of Head of State. With these appointments, the TMC was dissolved, signifying a return to civilian rule.

In February 1989 Dr Hassan al-Turabi, the leader of the National Islamic Front (NIF), was appointed Deputy Prime Minister. Although a peace agreement concluded by the DUP and the SPLM in November had been widely endorsed, the NIF opposed its provision for the suspension of Islamic laws as a prelude to the negotiation of a peace settlement. The NIF was consequently excluded from a new Government formed in March. Peace negotiations between a government delegation and the SPLM, which commenced in Ethiopia in April, resulted in an agreement to suspend Islamic laws, pending the proposed convening, in September, of a constitutional conference.

Al-Bashir seizes power

On 30 June 1989 a bloodless coup, led by Brig. (later Lt-Gen.) Omar Hassan Ahmad al-Bashir, removed al-Mahdi's Government. Al-Bashir formed a 15-member Revolutionary Command Council for National Salvation (RCC), which declared its primary aim to be the resolution of the southern conflict. Al-Bashir, who became Head of State, Chairman of the RCC, Prime Minister and Minister of Defence, and Commander-in-Chief of the armed forces, abolished the Constitution, the National Assembly and all political parties and trade unions. In July Lt-Gen. al-Bashir offered amnesty to political opponents of the Government; however, subsequent negotiations with the SPLM collapsed immediately over the issue of Islamic law, and hostilities resumed later that year. Meanwhile, the SPLM allied with banned political parties in the north (including the UP and the DUP) to form an opposition grouping, known as the National Democratic Alliance (NDA).

In February 1991 the RCC enacted a decree instituting a new, federal system of government. Sudan was divided into nine states, each of which had its own governor, deputy governor and cabinet of ministers, and assumed responsibility for local administration and the collection of some taxes. In the same month it was announced that a new penal code, based on *Shari'a* law, would take effect in March, but would not apply in the three southern states, pending the establishment there of elected assemblies to resolve the issue. In February 1992 al-Bashir appointed all 300 members of a new transitional National Assembly, which included the entire RCC, all government ministers and the governors of Sudan's nine states. The Assembly was accorded legislative authority, with the power to examine all decrees issued by the RCC, and responsibility for preparing the country for parliamentary elections. In October 1993 al-Bashir announced political reforms in preparation for presidential and legislative elections in 1994 and 1995, respectively. The RCC was dissolved after it had appointed al-Bashir as President and as head of a new civilian Government. In February 1994 Sudan was redivided into 26 states instead of the nine that had formed the basis of administration since 1991. The executive and legislative powers of each state government were to be expanded, and southern states were to be exempted from *Shari'a* law.

In March 1995 the leader of the main faction of the SPLA, Col John Garang, announced a new northern offensive in collaboration with other rebels. Later that month, following mediation by former US President Jimmy Carter, the Government offered rebel groups an amnesty if they surrendered their weapons, and declared a cease-fire for a period of two months, which was extended in May. However, it was reported that the army continued to conduct military operations in the south.

The 1996 elections

Legislative and presidential elections took place in March 1996. Some 5.5m. of Sudan's 10m. eligible voters were reported to have participated in the election of 275 deputies to a new, 400-seat

National Assembly. The remaining 125 deputies had been appointed at a national conference in January. Representatives of opposition groups and parties alleged that electoral malpractice had been widespread. In the presidential election al-Bashir obtained 75.7% of the total votes cast, and formally commenced a five-year term of office on 1 April. On the same day al-Turabi was unanimously elected President of the National Assembly.

On 10 April 1996 a 'political charter for peace' was signed by the Government, the South Sudan Independence Movement (SSIM) and the splinter group SPLA-United, pledging to preserve Sudan's national unity and to take joint action to develop those areas of the country that had been affected by the civil war. The charter also provided for the holding of a referendum as 'a means of realizing the aspirations of southern citizens' and affirmed that Islamic law would be the basis of future legislation. The formation of a new military and Islamist Cabinet was announced on 21 April. In April 1997 a peace accord, covering major issues such as power-sharing and *Shari'a* law, and promising a referendum on southern secession after a four-year transition period, was signed by six rebel groups, but was rejected by the NDA and the SPLA.

In March 1998 al-Bashir announced a government reorganization in which a number of former rebel leaders were appointed to the Cabinet, including the former commander of SPLA-United, Dr Lam Akol Ajawin, as Minister of Transport. In April a new Constitution was approved by the National Assembly and endorsed by 96.7% of voters in a referendum held between 1 and 20 May. New legislation approved in November provided for the establishment of an independent election commission and of a Constitutional Court, and for the legalization of political associations. Registration of political parties began in January 1999. In May former President Nimeri returned to Sudan after 14 years in exile in Egypt. His return was welcomed by the Government, although opposition parties demanded his prosecution for crimes he had allegedly committed while President.

In November 1999 Djibouti hosted a summit meeting of the Intergovernmental Authority on Development (IGAD, see p. 344), (which in September 1993 had formed a committee on the Sudanese conflict comprising the Heads of State of Kenya, Ethiopia, Uganda and Eritrea), to discuss issues related to development and stability in the region. While in Djibouti, President al-Bashir met the UP leader, al-Mahdi, following which the Sudanese Government and the UP signed a declaration of principles, envisaging a federal system of government and the holding of a referendum within four years to allow southerners to choose between the division of the country or unity with decentralized powers. The agreement was welcomed by many parties; however, it was criticized by the NDA, and later rejected by Garang.

During 1999 there were increasing reports of rivalry between al-Bashir and al-Turabi, particularly following the proposal of a bill in the National Assembly that sought to remove the President's power to appoint and dismiss state governors. Consideration of the draft legislation was repeatedly delayed, but a vote was scheduled to be held in mid-December in which the National Assembly was widely expected to approve it. However, on 12 December al-Bashir dissolved the National Assembly and imposed a state of emergency, claiming that he had taken these measures in order to end the 'duality' in the administration. An emergency order suspended some articles of the Constitution, although provincial councils and governors were to continue working. Al-Turabi accused al-Bashir of having carried out a coup, although a legal challenge, mounted against the measures, was later rejected by the Constitutional Court.

In March 2000 the Government extended the state of emergency until the end of the year, and approved a law allowing the formation of political parties (superseding the 1998 law), although this was rejected by the opposition, as it still incorporated provisions to suspend the activities of any party. In the same month the UP announced its decision to suspend its membership of the NDA during a meeting in Asmara, Eritrea. In April 2000 it was reported that a presidential election was planned for October; the ruling National Congress Party (NCP) had nominated al-Bashir as its candidate in October 1999. However, most opposition parties, including the UP, indicated that they would not participate in any elections until the convening of a national conference to discuss the problems in Sudan. In June 2000 al-Turabi announced the formation of a new political party, the Popular National Congress (PNC).

Al-Bashir re-elected

Presidential and legislative elections were held concurrently over a 10-day period in mid-December 2000, although they were boycotted by the main opposition parties. Al-Bashir was re-elected President, with 86.5% of the votes cast, comfortably defeating his nearest rival, former President Nimeri, who obtained 9.6% of the vote. Voting did not take place in the three southern states. The NCP secured 355 seats in the new 360-member National Assembly; the remaining five seats were won by small opposition parties. On 3 January 2001 al-Bashir extended the state of emergency for a further year.

On 21 February 2001 al-Turabi was arrested at his home in Khartoum, after it was announced that the PNC and the SPLM had signed a memorandum of understanding in Switzerland urging the Sudanese people to participate in 'peaceful popular resistance' against the al-Bashir regime. In March al-Turabi and several other members of the PNC's leadership council were reported to have been charged with criminal conspiracy, undermining the constitutional order, waging war on the state and calling for violent opposition to public authority. (In May al-Turabi was released from prison and placed under house arrest.) Meanwhile, the day after al-Turabi's arrest, al-Bashir implemented a major reorganization of the Cabinet and replaced many of the country's state governors. Although the new Cabinet was dominated by NCP members, al-Bashir incorporated four members of two minor opposition parties into the Government.

In July 2001 it was reported that the Sudanese Government and the NDA had both provisionally accepted a renewed Libyan-Egyptian peace initiative, which provided for an immediate cease-fire, the establishment of a transitional government and a number of constitutional reforms. Later that month the leadership council of the NCP approved the Libyan-Egyptian plan. However, al-Bashir maintained that he would not support any proposals that involved the separation of state and religion or the partition of the country, thus endangering the success of the initiative, as the NDA concurrently reiterated its demand for the right of the southern states to be granted self-determination. In December the state of emergency was again extended for a further 12 months.

In January 2002 talks convened under the aegis of the USA and Switzerland in Bürgenstock, Switzerland, resulted in an agreement between the Sudanese Government and the SPLA to observe a six-month cease-fire, to be supervised by a joint military commission, in the central Nuba region in order to facilitate the delivery of vital aid supplies to the area. However, the following month the USA announced that it had suspended discussions with the Sudanese Government, after two separate incidents earlier that month in which Sudanese air force planes had bombed civilians collecting food supplies in the Bahr El-Ghazal province. The Sudanese Minister of External Relations subsequently issued an apology for the attack and in March the USA brokered an agreement between the SPLA and the Sudanese Government, which aimed to guarantee the protection of civilians from military attacks. The cease-fire was extended for a further six months in July, and again, in December. In August al-Bashir renewed the detention order that had been placed on al-Turabi the previous year for a further 12 months, and in September al-Turabi was transferred to prison. In December 2003 the state of emergency was once again extended for a further 12 months.

Towards the Comprehensive Peace Agreement

Meanwhile, in June 2002 a new round of IGAD-sponsored peace talks between the Government and the SPLM began in Machakos, Kenya. A major breakthrough in the conflict was achieved on 20 July, when delegations from the SPLM and the Government signed an accord, known as the Machakos Protocol, which provided for a six-year period of autonomy for the south, to be followed by an internationally monitored referendum on self-determination. The Protocol also stated that Sudan's Constitution would be rewritten to ensure that *Shari'a* law would not be applied to non-Muslim southerners.

Negotiations resumed in Nairobi, Kenya, in January 2003, and the following month the Government and the SPLM agreed to allow international observers to monitor the cease-fire (which had been extended). In April al-Bashir and Garang met for only the second time in 20 years and reaffirmed their commitment to the Machakos Protocol and pledged to facilitate unrestricted delivery of humanitarian assistance to those in the south of the country. In September the SPLA and the Sudanese Government agreed to extend their cease-fire for a further two months, and days later the two sides signed a landmark security agreement, under which two separate armed forces were to be created, as well as a number of integrated units, comprising both government and SPLA troops. Both sides agreed to contribute 12,000 soldiers to a joint force, the Sudan Armed Forces (SAF), to be deployed in southern Sudan, and a further 6,000 soldiers from each side were to be dispatched to the disputed Nuba Mountains and Blue Nile provinces. Furthermore, 80% of the government forces in southern Sudan would be withdrawn to the north no later than two-and-a-half years after the signing of a Comprehensive Peace Agreement (CPA). It was also agreed that both sides' forces would be reduced at a later, unspecified date and that they would be placed under the command of a joint defence board composed of SPLM and government officials. In October al-Turabi was released from detention, and all restrictions on the PNC's activities were lifted.

After further talks between the Government and the SPLM were convened in Naivasha, Kenya, on 7 January 2004 the two sides signed an accord on revenue-sharing, which also provided for the establishment of two separate banking systems for the north and the south, as well as a new national currency on the signing of a final peace settlement. On 26 May the Government and the SPLM signed three protocols, which removed the remaining obstacles to the conclusion of a CPA. Specifically, the protocols stated that the SPLM and other southern groups would hold 30% of government seats in the north, while holding 70% of seats in the south; that the contested regions of the Blue Nile and the Nuba Mountains would be governed by an administration in which 55% of the seats would be taken by government officials and 45% by the SPLM, while the petroleum-rich region of Abyei would be granted special status and be governed by the presidential office; and that Khartoum would remain under Islamic law with certain protections for non-Muslims.

The final round of the IGAD-sponsored talks proceeded in Naivasha in October 2004, following protracted delays, and on 31 December a permanent cease-fire was agreed by the Sudanese Government and the SPLM. On 9 January 2005 Garang and First Vice-President Ali Osman Muhammad Taha signed the CPA in Nairobi in the presence of representatives from the UN, the European Union (EU, see p. 281), the African Union (AU, see p. 191) and IGAD, thus formally bringing an end to more than 20 years of civil conflict between the SPLA and successive governments. Under the agreement, Garang was to assume the position of Sudanese Vice-President and would act as President of Southern Sudan during the six-year period of autonomy, after which a referendum on secession would be held. Meanwhile, in mid-January the Government signed a peace accord with the NDA in Cairo, which allowed for the return of NDA leaders to Sudan and granted them the right to conduct their political activities in the country. On 25 January the UN announced that it had restored diplomatic ties with Sudan and would contribute some €50m. in aid, to be divided equally between the north and the south. In March the UN Security Council unanimously approved Resolution 1590, which provided for the establishment of the UN Mission in Sudan (UNMIS), comprising up to 10,000 peace-keeping troops and 715 civilian personnel, to be deployed in southern Sudan for an initial period of six months (which was subsequently renewed).

In June 2005 al-Bashir announced the release of 'all political detainees', among them al-Turabi. Earlier that month the President had lifted the ban prohibiting all political activity by the PNC. On 6 July the National Assembly ratified the new interim Constitution, and on 9 July Garang was appointed as First Vice-President of the new Government, replacing Taha who took the role of Vice-President, and as President of Southern Sudan. On 1 August it was announced that Garang had been killed in a helicopter crash; the SPLM deputy leader, Commdr (later Lt-Gen.) Salva Kiir Mayardit, succeeded him as leader of the SPLA/SPLM, and was later appointed as First Vice-President of Sudan and President of Southern Sudan. During August differences regarding wealth-sharing and the allocation of the energy portfolio continued to obstruct the formation of a government of national unity. However, in late September an agreement was reached and the list of government ministers was announced, in which 16 portfolios (including those of defence, interior, finance and energy and mining) were awarded to members of the NCP, nine to the SPLM and four to members of smaller opposition parties. In January 2006 the National Assembly adopted controversial legislation prohibiting any member of the armed forces (excluding al-Bashir and Salva Kiir), the police, the security forces or the SPLA, judges,

diplomats and high-ranking civil servants from joining a political party; it also made provisions for any party to be dissolved, or prevented from participating in elections, if it was believed to be undertaking activities that breached the CPA. Claiming that this contravened the Constitution, the NDA withdrew from the National Assembly.

The Darfur conflict

Meanwhile, in February 2003 a new area of conflict emerged in the Darfur region of western Sudan. The Sudan Liberation Movement (SLM) announced the commencement of an armed campaign to end Darfur's political and economic marginalization and to combat the Government's 'ethnic cleansing' activities in the region. The SLM, which was reported to have some 1,500 troops and received support from Eritrea, subsequently attacked the provincial capital, al-Fasher. In an attempt to suppress the revolt the Sudanese authorities armed pro-Government ethnic Arab militias, known as the *Janjaweed*, who systematically razed entire villages to the ground and carried out indiscriminate killings. In April the Sudanese authorities refused offers of talks with the rebels, dismissed senior security officials in the region, and deployed additional forces to Darfur to retake most of the territory that had been lost to the SLM. In December aid agencies maintained that the Sudanese Government was preventing food and medical supplies from reaching the Darfur region, and in January 2004 Sudanese planes reportedly bombed a number of villages in the border area, after the rebels claimed to have killed some 700 government troops. At the end of March indirect peace talks between the Government, the SLM and the Justice and Equality Movement (JEM), attended by international observers, commenced, and on 8 April a 45-day humanitarian cease-fire was signed by representatives of the three parties. By early June it was estimated that as a result of continued violence in Darfur more than 30,000 people had been killed and a further 1m. people had been displaced.

Following a visit from UN Secretary-General Kofi Annan to refugee camps in Darfur in late June 2004 and the threat of the imposition of UN sanctions on the *Janjaweed*, in early July the Sudanese authorities committed to a series of actions, including the more aggressive use of the security forces to deal with the militia, the easing of travel restrictions for aid workers and deployment of AU troops in Darfur. AU-sponsored peace talks between the Sudanese Government and the rebels began in Addis Ababa, Ethiopia, in mid-July, but swiftly collapsed. In late July the US House of Representatives approved a resolution declaring the human rights abuses in Darfur a 'genocide' and on 30 July the UN Security Council adopted a resolution urging the Sudanese Government to end the conflict in Darfur, to facilitate the delivery of humanitarian aid, and to grant AU peace monitors access to the region. The resolution was rejected by the Sudanese Government and the armed forces spokesman, Gen. Muhammad Bashir Suleiman, described it as a 'declaration of war'.

In September 2004 the UN Security Council approved a second resolution, stating that it would consider imposing sanctions affecting Sudan's petroleum industry should it fail to take steps to disarm the *Janjaweed* and protect civilians from further attacks. The UN was also to establish a commission to investigate claims that the human rights abuses in Darfur amounted to genocide, while the AU planned to increase the size of its monitoring force in the region (the African Union Mission in Sudan—AMIS) from 350 to some 3,500. In October the British Prime Minister, Tony Blair, visited Sudan to conduct talks with President al-Bashir in an attempt to resolve the Darfur conflict. A five-point peace plan, proposed by Blair, was accepted by the Sudanese Government, which thereby agreed to allow an increase in the number of AU troops in the country; to commit to a cessation of hostilities in Darfur within three months; to negotiate a comprehensive agreement to the ongoing conflict in southern Sudan by the end of 2004; and to assist with the distribution of humanitarian aid.

In November 2004, following talks in Abuja, Nigeria, the Government agreed to establish a 'no-fly' zone over the Darfur region (the rebels had accused government forces of using aircraft to support *Janjaweed* attacks). In December AU cease-fire monitors reported that they had witnessed large quantities of arms and ammunition being delivered to government forces in Darfur. Continued *Janjaweed* attacks were reported and in February 2005 a UN commission of inquiry revealed that although serious crimes against humanity had taken place, these did not amount to genocide. It did, however, identify 51 suspected war criminals and recommended that they be tried by the International Criminal Court (ICC, see p. 349), which was to undertake preparatory analysis of the situation prior to deciding whether to commence a full investigation into allegations of war crimes committed in Darfur. Al-Bashir pledged not to send any Sudanese nationals abroad for trial, but the Minister of External Relations, Dr Mustafa Osman Ismail, subsequently offered to hold any future ICC trial in Sudan. In late April the AU confirmed that additional peace-keeping troops would arrive in Darfur by the end of September, increasing the number of AMIS troops to 7,731.

In May 2005 the SLM and the JEM agreed to maintain a cease-fire and to engage in further talks with the Government. In June the ICC commenced an investigation into allegations that the Sudanese Government and the *Janjaweed* had committed crimes against humanity in the Darfur region. Also in that month the Government established a court at which 162 people accused of committing crimes against humanity in the Darfur region were to be tried, and referred to the institution as 'an alternative' to the ICC. In October four AU peace-keepers were killed in southern Darfur and concerns over escalating violence prompted the UN to withdraw all non-essential staff from Darfur. The human rights organization Human Rights Watch (HRW) released a report in December, which accused al-Bashir, Taha and several other senior government officials of involvement in crimes against humanity committed in Darfur. The report also appealed for them to be investigated by the ICC and added to a UN list of suspects eligible for sanctions. ICC investigators were subsequently refused permission by the Government to visit Darfur to gather evidence of alleged crimes against humanity.

Proposed UN intervention in Darfur

In January 2006 Annan urged the USA and European countries to contribute logistical support and troops for a planned UN peace-keeping mission in Darfur; Sudan declared its vehement opposition to the proposal. In late January the SLM and the JEM announced the formation of the Alliance of Revolutionary Forces in West Sudan, in a move intended to strengthen the rebels' position in AU-mediated negotiations, which had resumed in Abuja. In early March the AU voted to extend the mandate of AMIS until September, when a UN force was expected to assume peace-keeping duties. However, Arab League heads of state, meeting in Khartoum later in March, agreed to provide funds for the AU force to remain and voted to support Sudanese opposition to the deployment of non-African peace-keeping troops. In late April the UN Security Council approved a resolution, imposing sanctions on four individuals suspected of involvement in crimes committed in the Darfur region: Maj.-Gen. Gaafar Muhammad el-Hassan, Commander of the Western Military Region for the Sudanese Air Force; the Commander of the SLA, Adam Yacub Shant; the Field Commander of the rebel National Movement for Reform and Development, Gabril Abdulkareem Badri; and Sheikh Musa Hilal of the *Janjaweed* militia. All four were banned from travelling outside of Sudan and any assets they held abroad were to be 'frozen'.

Meanwhile, following continued peace negotiations in Abuja, in late April 2006 the Government agreed to accept an agreement proposed by AU mediators. A deadline of 30 April was subsequently extended, and officials from the USA and United Kingdom arrived in Abuja to aid the negotiations. In early May an SLM faction led by Minni Minawi announced that it had accepted the proposals, despite reservations regarding certain conditions, and the Darfur Peace Agreement (DPA) was signed on 5 May, although it was rejected by the JEM and an SLM faction led by Abd al-Wahid Muhammad al-Nur. The measures stipulated in the document included, *inter alia*, a Government undertaking to disarm completely the *Janjaweed* by mid-October; the establishment of buffer zones around refugee camps and access routes for humanitarian aid organizations; the integration of rebel forces into the Sudanese armed forces and police; and the allocation of eight seats in the National Assembly to Minawi's group.

In July 2006, at an AU Summit in Banjul, The Gambia, the UN Secretary-General announced that President al-Bashir had refused to allow UN troops to be deployed in succession to AMIS, which was scheduled to withdraw from Darfur at the end of September. Minawi repeatedly appealed for UN forces to be sent to the region, and threatened to withdraw from the peace agreement. Also in July the two signatories of the DPA, the Government and Minawi's faction of the SLM, launched violent attacks on the rebel groups who had rejected the peace agreement. New factions had begun to emerge to challenge Minawi's increasing power in the north of Darfur, joining forces to form the National Redemption Front (NRF). Fighting subsequently spread from northern Darfur towards the west of the region.

On 31 August 2006 the UN Security Council adopted a resolution, which provided for some 17,300 additional military personnel and 3,300 civilian police to be dispatched to Sudan to support UNMIS, and for its mandate to be extended to assume the responsibilities of AMIS in Darfur. Violence in the region had escalated during that month and the UN, the AU and humanitarian agencies alleged that Minawi's troops had joined Government forces and the *Janjaweed* militia in fighting the rebel groups. The Sudanese Government continued to refuse to allow UN forces into Darfur and reinforcements were deployed to the region; AU forces remaining in the area reported that Government troops had bombed rebel-held villages, threatening the delivery of aid supplies. In response the AU increased the number of peace-keeping personnel and stated that AMIS would remain in Darfur until the end of the year.

On 27 September 2006 President al-Bashir issued a decree establishing an interim authority in Darfur, in accordance with the terms of the DPA. The authority was to be headed by Minawi, in his capacity as senior assistant to the President, a position to which he was appointed following the signing of the CPA. In October the Government issued a statement that a plan had been devised to fulfil the commitments of the DPA, including the disarmament of the Arab militia group. The plan was submitted to the AU and was to be implemented over a two-month period, extending the original deadline for disarming the militia group by two months. The following month Minawi alleged that the Government was rearming and mobilizing the *Janjaweed* and appealed for the international community to act swiftly to find a resolution to the conflict.

In November 2006 discussions took place in Addis Ababa on measures to reinforce AMIS, and proposals were made for a joint AU-UN force, with a greater role to be assumed by the UN troops. Meanwhile, the AU again agreed to extend the mandate of AMIS, to mid-2007. Following continued pressure from the UN Security Council, in late December 2006 al-Bashir accepted the proposed establishment of a joint AU-UN mission in Darfur; however, it was stipulated that the AU was to remain in command of the hybrid force. A three-part UN plan was initiated: the first phase included reinforcing the much-weakened AU force with UN troops and supplies, to be followed by further support packages. By 31 December the AU had secured a tentative cease-fire agreement from rebel groups in northern Darfur.

Breakdown of the Darfur cease-fire

Peace efforts were undermined on 1 January 2007, when insurgent-held positions were bombed in violation of the cease-fire. Al-Bashir subsequently admitted that government troops had bombed rebel forces, but claimed that this did not breach the cease-fire agreement since they were defending themselves from rebel attacks. The Government subsequently agreed to measures to restore peace, including a 60-day cease-fire and an AU-UN-sponsored peace summit, to be held in Ethiopia later that month. In January the ICC dispatched a team of officials to Khartoum to investigate crimes committed during the conflict in Darfur and in February the ICC indicted the former Minister of State for the Interior, Ahmad Muhammad Harun, and the leader of the *Janjaweed* militia, Ali Muhammad Ali Abd al-Rahman, on multiple charges of war crimes and crimes against humanity. The following month the Sudanese authorities announced that they had suspended all co-operation with the ICC. In May that body issued arrest warrants for Harun and al-Rahman. Meanwhile, in February al-Bashir appointed two members of rebel factions to executive positions in the Council of Ministers and in the Darfur administration.

Following general acceptance that the DPA signed in May 2006 had broken down, rebel factions agreed upon a need to collaborate in order to challenge the power of the ruling NCP. By the end of December an alliance had formed, uniting many of the rebel groups that had refused to sign the DPA, styled the Non-Signatory Factions (NSF). A conference of NSF and remaining NRF commanders, due to be held in early 2007 to renegotiate the terms of the failed peace agreement, was delayed as government forces carried out a series of bomb attacks in the area where the conference was to take place. Despite further clashes, the conference eventually commenced in February.

As the conflict in western Sudan continued, the people of eastern Sudan, including the Rashaida and the Beja communities, expressed their increasing resentment towards the Government. The eastern regions had been severely affected by drought and famine and, encouraged by the success of the SPLA

in forcing negotiations with the Government, some of the Beja launched an armed struggle, supported by NDA and SPLA forces. The Beja Congress, which emerged during the 1960s, was joined during the 1990s by the Rashaida Free Lions group, and in 2005 the two groups merged to form the Eastern Front (EF). Although their forces were much smaller than those rebel groups fighting in Darfur, they occupied strategic points and launched attacks on essential road and rail routes. Military offensives by government forces failed to prevent the EF from launching more attacks on eastern Sudan's transport and economic infrastructure and in 2006 the Government agreed to negotiate with the group. In June 2006 talks were held in Asmara, presided over by the Eritrean authorities, and on 19 June the Government and the EF signed an agreement on a set of principles for developing a peace agreement; a cease-fire was also implemented, to be monitored by Eritrean military officials. Peace talks resumed in July and, after lengthy negotiations, a power-sharing agreement was signed on 9 October. The following day the positions of presidential assistant and presidential adviser were assigned to members of the rebel group, along with other positions in the Government at both national and regional level. The peace deal was ratified by the Sudanese authorities on 18 October, ending several years of conflict between the Government and the EF.

In June 2007, following further discussions in Addis Ababa, the Government of Sudan agreed to accept a joint AU-UN peace-keeping force, comprising up to 20,000 troops. However, shortly after issuing a statement accepting the deployment of peace-keeping personnel, the Government began to delay the process, questioning the command structure of the operation. Nevertheless, the following month the UN Security Council adopted Resolution 1769 establishing UNAMID, the UN-AU hybrid operation in Darfur, with an initial mandate of 12 months. Further disagreements threatened to disrupt the process when, in August, the AU announced that UNAMID peace-keeping forces would comprise only African personnel, safeguarding the AU's lead role in Sudan. UNAMID assumed peace-keeping operations on 31 December but was severely under-resourced, with less than one-half of the pledged 20,000 troops deployed. In February 2008 a legal framework was agreed, which would allow UNAMID peace-keepers to move freely within the country without fear of attacks by government forces. In July the UN Security Council extended UNAMID's mandate until July 2009.

Renewed hostilities in Darfur

In September 2007 the UN Secretary-General, Ban Ki-Moon, announced that a further round of peace talks on Darfur was to be convened in the following month, in Tripoli, Libya. The Government later agreed to comply with the terms of a cease-fire agreement, to be enforced during the peace negotiations. Talks commenced in Tripoli on 27 October; however, in response to continued attacks by government forces, many rebel groups refused to participate. The Tripoli talks were further hindered by the collapse of the coalition Government in Khartoum earlier that month, following the SPLM's withdrawal in protest against delays in implementing the CPA. In an effort to appease the SPLM leadership, al-Bashir announced a government reorganization, which included the appointment of SPLM members as Minister of Foreign Affairs and Minister of Foreign Trade. In December further SPLM members were appointed to the Council of Ministers, after the movement formally rejoined the central Government.

Reports emerged in September 2008 that government forces had launched a renewed campaign of violence in eastern Darfur, attacking rebel strongholds in an attempt to secure access to oil reserves and transport routes to Chad. Al-Bashir announced a unilateral cease-fire in November, including the disarmament of pro-Government militia, on the condition that sufficient measures for monitoring the situation were implemented. However, rebel leaders demanded that the *Janjaweed* be disarmed before they would consider relinquishing their own weapons. Reinforcements from Pakistan and Ethiopia were deployed to Darfur in December to assist the peace-keeping operation, increasing the number of UNAMID troops to some 12,737. (Following the renewal of its mandate in August, UNAMID's personnel had been increased to 16,852 by February 2010.)

Meanwhile, renewed violence in the ethnically divided Abyei region broke out in early 2008 after a period of relative calm. Clashes between the SPLA and members of the Misseriya ethnic group (supported by the NCP) threatened to exacerbate the situation in Darfur and undermine progress towards holding presidential and legislative elections planned for July 2009. Nevertheless, a national census commenced in April 2008 in an attempt to ensure the general election could take place, although rebel groups opposed the census. It was also agreed that the dispute over Abyei's status should be referred to the Permanent Court of Arbitration (PCA) in The Hague, Netherlands. An interim administration was established in the Abyei region in August; Arop Moyak of the SPLM was named Chief Administrator, while the NCP's Rahama Abuldrahman al-Nur was appointed Deputy Chief Administrator.

In July 2009, following a ruling by the PCA, a compromise agreement was reached regarding the boundary lines of the Abyei region. The border to the north, as established in 2005, would remain, while new demarcations in the east and west would return the Heglig oilfields and the oil pipeline infrastructure to government control. Although both parties appeared to accept the ruling, tensions nevertheless remained as discussions on the composition of the Abyei electorate continued to be disputed and violent clashes between the north and the south intensified. Further contention arose over the proportion of votes required to approve southern Sudan's secession at the referendum due to be held upon the expiry of the CPA in 2011; in December 2009 the National Assembly approved legislation that required 60% of the electorate in southern Sudan to vote for the ballot to be deemed legitimate, but also stated that a simple majority of 51% would suffice in order to secure independence.

Having been suspended in June 2009, peace talks on Darfur resumed in August in an attempt to reconcile the rebel factions. However, the negotiations were not attended by the SPLM. A UN report published in November claimed that armed factions in Darfur continued to use excessive force in breach of the UN arms embargo, infringe human rights and impede the peace process. Following months of faltering negotiations, some progress was achieved in February 2010 when, with mediation from Chadian authorities, the Sudanese Government signed a framework agreement with the JEM, providing for a cease-fire and the possibility of further peace negotiations. Al-Bashir, who approved the release from prison of 57 members of the JEM involved in an attack on Khartoum in mid-2008, claimed that the agreement had resolved the conflict in Darfur.

Multi-party elections

In March 2009 an international arrest warrant for al-Bashir was formally issued, following evidence presented in July 2008 by the Chief Prosecutor of the ICC, Luis Moreno Ocampo, in respect of war crimes committed in Darfur from March 2003. The Sudanese Government, which strongly rejected the decision, retaliated by expelling a number of international aid agencies that had been operating in the country, and a demonstration in support of al-Bashir was staged in Khartoum. The indictment, the first to be brought by the ICC against an incumbent Head of State, was welcomed by the US Administration and international human rights groups, but notably opposed by the AU and the Arab League. In February 2010 judges at the ICC ruled that an appeal could be heard that, if successful, would result in charges of genocide being added to the seven counts of crimes against humanity and war crimes, with which al-Bashir had already been charged.

Having initially been scheduled to take place in July 2009, and then in February 2010, it was announced that, following a further postponement (after a number of political parties threatened to boycott the ballot amid demands for changes to legislation on civil liberties and freedom of speech), the first democratic, multi-party elections to take place in Sudan for 24 years would be held in April 2010. In addition to national presidential and legislative polls, the President of Southern Sudan and provincial governors were also to be elected. In January Salva Kiir confirmed that he would not seek the national presidency and that Yasir Saeed Arman would contest that office on behalf of the SPLM. Later that month al-Bashir announced that the NCP would not present a candidate in the poll to elect the President of Southern Sudan, and in the period immediately preceding the elections a number of opposition parties announced their withdrawal from the various electoral contests.

Voting in the elections commenced on 11 April 2010; however, the initial three-day voting period was extended by two days, after technical issues and delays in delivering ballot papers in a number of regions. On 26 April the National Elections Commission (NEC) announced the results of the presidential election, according to which al-Bashir secured 68.2% of the votes cast; Arman took 21.7%, despite having withdrawn from the poll at the end of March, citing concerns over potential irregularities in

the conduct of the ballot. (The Umma National Party—UNP, as the UP had been restyled—had also withdrawn from the presidential election.) Salva Kiir was overwhelmingly elected as President of Southern Sudan, with about 93.0% of votes cast. At the concurrent legislative elections, the NCP secured a total of 312 of the 450 seats in the National Assembly, according to provisional results, while the SPLM won 99 seats (with the UNP boycotting the elections). Several opposition parties denounced the election results as fraudulent, and alleged that widespread malpractice had been perpetrated. Observer missions dispatched by the EU and the US Carter Center declared that the elections had failed to meet international standards; the Carter Center subsequently issued a report criticizing the conduct of the voting, and urging the NEC to review the results. The NEC decided that polls were to be repeated in 17 national constituencies, which took place in early June, increasing the NCP's representation to 323 seats. On 24 May the new National Assembly held its first session and re-elected Ahmad Ibrahim al-Tahir of the NCP as its Speaker. Al-Bashir was inaugurated for a further five-year term on 27 May (at a ceremony that was boycotted by many Arab and African Heads of State). Meanwhile, Gen. George Athor, formerly a general in the Southern Sudanese army, and a small contingent of troops under his command began to stage rebel attacks in protest against the outcome of legislative elections. Following a declaration of dissatisfaction with the conduct of the elections, the JEM suspended its participation in peace negotiations and escalated military operations in Darfur.

In June 2010 al-Bashir announced a new 35-member coalition Government, which included nine members of the SPLM (two more than required under the terms of the CPA); Salva Kiir retained the office of First Vice-President and Taha of Vice-President. Lual Achwel Deng of the SPLM, who had served as Minister of Foreign Affairs in the previous Government, was appointed as Minister of Petroleum (a decision that was designed to placate southern suspicions following the alleged siphoning of petroleum revenues under the previous Government, and to assist discussions on a post-secession revenue-sharing agreement).

On 12 July 2010 the ICC issued a second arrest warrant for President al-Bashir, on three counts of genocide committed in the Darfur region. (However, the AU instructed member states not to arrest al-Bashir and he continued to make official regional visits.) At the end of July the UN Security Council extended the mandate of UNAMID for a further year. In October the Government announced a timetable for the referendum on secession, confirming that it was scheduled for 9 January 2011; however, NCP officials declared that a postponement of a parallel referendum in Abyei (which had also been stipulated under the CPA) was likely, after negotiations between the northern and southern authorities failed to result in agreement over the composition of the region's electoral commission, the eligibility of voters and the demarcation of borders.

Secession of South Sudan

The referendum on the secession of southern Sudan was conducted on 9–15 January 2011; according to the final results, which were announced on 7 February, about 98.8% of the population of southern Sudan had voted to secede from the north, with a participation rate of some 97.6% of the electorate. (The parallel referendum on secession for Abyei had been postponed as expected.) The new state of South Sudan was to be officially established on 9 July. Meanwhile, in February it was announced that al-Bashir would not seek re-election in 2015. Nevertheless, in early March 2011 reports emerged that security forces had violently suppressed an opposition demonstration against al-Bashir's Government in Khartoum.

In March 2011 two new states were established in the region of Darfur (increasing the total number to five states). On 24 April the NEC announced plans to conduct a referendum in Darfur, in accordance with the DPA, to determine the permanent administrative status of the region; however, the JEM and other rebel groups rejected the legitimacy of a referendum, insisting that the issue be resolved through further negotiations. On 31 May the Doha Document for Peace in Darfur (DDPD) was adopted at an All Darfur Stakeholders Conference, which was convened in Doha, Qatar, under the aegis of the UN, the AU and the Arab League; the DDPD was to provide the framework for the future peace process in Darfur. (On 14 July the Sudanese Government and the Darfur rebel Liberation and Justice Movement signed an agreement pledging commitment to the DDPD.)

Meanwhile, in early May 2011 SAF troops occupied the town of Abyei, prompting the displacement of some 80,000 civilians; the Government announced that the military action was in response to a nearby attack on one of its convoys by the SPLA (after both sides were reported to have deployed forces in the territory earlier that year). The UN Security Council subsequently demanded that the SAF end its occupation of Abyei, which was in violation of the CPA. Later in May Luka Biong of the SPLM resigned as Minister of Cabinet Affairs, in protest at alleged war crimes perpetrated by the SAF in Abyei. Following AU-mediated negotiations, on 20 June representatives of the SPLM and the NCP signed an agreement providing for the demilitarization of Abyei and the deployment in the region of Ethiopian peace-keeping troops, under the auspices of the UN. Later in June the UN Security Council approved the establishment of the UN Interim Security Force for Abyei (UNISFA), which had a maximum authorized strength of 4,200 military personnel, for a renewable period of six months. Meanwhile, in early June the SAF engaged in hostilities with the SPLA in Southern Kordofan State, causing more than 70,000 people to flee, after the refusal of SPLA-allied forces to comply with an order by the northern authorities to disarm. Human rights violations committed by the SAF against local civilians sympathetic to the south, particularly members of the Nuba ethnic group, were reported. In late June the AU mediated a framework agreement between the NCP and the SPLM over Southern Kordofan, under which cease-fire talks were to be initiated and the SPLA forces disarmed; however, al-Bashir subsequently withdrew commitment to the agreement and SAF operations continued in Southern Kordofan.

The secession of South Sudan officially took place on 9 July 2011; al-Bashir attended the inauguration ceremonies and Sudan immediately extended recognition to the new state. However, a number of post-secession issues remained unresolved, including the demarcation of borders and citizenship rights; on the following day the Sudanese Government's announcement that southerners would be obliged to leave employment in the north prompted further tensions. UNMIS was succeeded by the UN Mission in the Republic of South Sudan, which was officially established by the UN Security Council on 8 July for an initial period of one year. Later in July the UN Security Council extended the mandate of UNAMID for a further year. At the end of August Sudan submitted a formal complaint to the UN Security Council, accusing South Sudan of encouraging instability and supporting rebel activity in Southern Kordofan.

In September 2011 al-Bashir reorganized the Council of Ministers, following the departure of all the SPLM representatives from the Government on 9 July; Taha again became First Vice-President, and, in accordance with the DDPD, was succeeded as Vice-President by a Darfur representative, Al-Haj Adam Yousef. The registration of 17 political parties was suspended, after their southern leaders and predominantly southern members lost Sudanese nationality. In the same month al-Bashir declared a state of emergency in central Blue Nile State, after the SAF clashed with SPLM-allied forces in the region, and removed the Governor of the state, Lt-Gen. Malik Agar, who was also the leader of the northern branch of the SPLM (the SPLM-N). The SPLM-N was subsequently banned and a number of its members were arrested. In October three members of UNAMID were killed in an attack by southern rebels in Darfur. On 10 December a new Government of national unity was established, with the appointment of further Darfur representatives to ministerial posts. Later that month the leader of the JEM, Khalil Ibrahim, was killed in an air attack by the SAF in Northern Kordofan. On 27 December the Government established the new Darfur Regional Authority, which was to implement the DDPD.

Hostilities with South Sudan

Following a number of air attacks by the SAF in South Sudanese border territory, in November 2011 the South Sudanese Government claimed that the SAF had bombed a refugee camp in Unity State, killing at least 12 people. South Sudan was, meanwhile, accused by the Sudanese authorities of supporting a new armed grouping that aimed to overthrow al-Bashir's Government, the Sudan Revolutionary Front (SRF), comprising the Sudan People's Liberation Army-North (the northern wing of the SPLA), the JEM, and a further two movements from Darfur. In December the UN Security Council extended the mandate of UNIFSA, and reiterated demands that the Governments of Sudan and South Sudan withdraw from Abyei. A non-aggression treaty was signed by the Governments of South Sudan and

Sudan in Addis Ababa on 11 February 2012, after AU-mediated negotiations; nevertheless, mutual accusations of violations of the pact followed soon afterwards. Later that month the SRF claimed military successes against the SAF, including the capture of a Sudanese army garrison in Southern Kordofan.

On 1 March 2012 the ICC issued an arrest warrant against the Minister of Defence, Abd al-Rahim Mohamed Hussein, in connection with war crimes perpetrated in the Darfur region between August 2003 and March 2004. Meanwhile, the continuing conflict increased popular opposition to al-Bashir's Government, and violent protests were staged in Khartoum in early March 2012. Amid increasing tensions with South Sudan, later that month al-Bashir withdrew from a planned summit meeting in the South Sudanese capital, Juba, on outstanding post-secession issues, including a draft citizenship law that was to allow the repatriation of large numbers of South Sudanese who had remained in Sudan. In early April hostilities escalated further, when the SPLA seized the principal petroleum-producing region of Heglig in Southern Kordofan, after clashes with the SAF, claiming that the occupation was in retaliation for continued air attacks by the SAF against South Sudan's territory. Addressing a rally of his supporters in Khartoum later in April, al-Bashir declared his intention to overthrow the SPLM Government of South Sudan. Several days later, the South Sudanese Government announced that it had withdrawn its troops from the Heglig region, following criticism from the UN Security Council and the AU; it was reported that principal petroleum installations had been severely damaged. The SAF nevertheless launched further bombardments against targets in Unity State. On 2 May the UN Security Council adopted a resolution demanding that the two sides cease hostilities within 48 hours and resume the AU-mediated dialogue within two weeks, threatening to impose sanctions for non-compliance. Negotiations between Sudanese and South Sudanese government delegations, under the aegis of the AU High-Level Implementation Panel (AUHIP), were accordingly convened in Addis Ababa in late May.

Anti-Government protests and negotiations with South Sudan

In June 2012 protests at economic conditions in Khartoum escalated when al-Bashir announced a number of austerity measures, including the removal of fuel subsidies, and tax increases. Large-scale anti-Government demonstrations were staged in Khartoum and other major towns; security forces violently dispersed anti-Government protesters, many of whom were arrested and, it was reported, tortured in detention. As part of his retrenchment efforts, al-Bashir dismissed nine presidential advisers and several junior ministers, and in early July effected a government reorganization in which the number of ministries was reduced.

Despite the UN-imposed cease-fire, in early July 2012 Southern Kordofan officials who were travelling in the territory were attacked and killed by members of the SPLA. On 14 July al-Bashir met his South Sudanese counterpart, Salva Kiir, on the occasion of an AU summit meeting in Addis Ababa, when both heads of state issued positive statements regarding the ongoing negotiations. At the end of July the UN Security Council extended the mandate of UNAMID for a further year. Following pressure from US Secretary of State Hillary Clinton, in early August it was announced that the AU-mediated discussions had resulted in agreement on the transit fees to be paid to the Sudanese Government for the use of its petroleum pipelines (which had been a major issue of contention since the secession of South Sudan—see Economic Affairs). (Sudan also sought substantial compensation from the international community for the loss of petroleum revenue after secession.) On 19 August some 32 government, military and security officials, including the incumbent Minister of Religious Affairs and Awqaf, who had been travelling to Southern Kordofan, were killed when their plane crashed in a mountainous area.

On 27 September 2012 al-Bashir and Salva Kiir, meeting in Addis Ababa under the aegis of the AUHIP, signed nine co-operation agreements, which provided, *inter alia*, for the creation of a demilitarized zone along the border, the reopening of South Sudan's petroleum pipelines and the repatriation of South Sudanese nationals remaining in the country. (However, the disputes over Abyei and border demarcation remained unresolved.) The National Assembly ratified the nine agreements with South Sudan on 17 October. In the same month it was reported that SPLM-N forces had bombarded the capital of

Southern Kordofan, Kadugli, killing at least six people, while four members of UNAMID were killed in Darfur. Following continued negotiations, in December Sudanese and South Sudanese delegations agreed to begin the immediate establishment of the demilitarized zone. At a summit meeting, held in Addis Ababa in early January 2013, al-Bashir and Salva Kiir affirmed commitment to the unconditional implementation of the co-operation agreements. Nevertheless, later in January further discussions regarding the establishment of joint authorities in Abyei ended in failure, while Sudan accused the South Sudanese Government of failing to fulfil terms regarding security arrangements and the withdrawal of its troops from the disputed areas, and of continuing to support rebel groups in Blue Nile State and Southern Kordofan. It was reported in February that some 60 people had been killed in clashes between rival ethnic communities over control of a gold mine in northern Darfur, while hostilities erupted between the SAF and the SRF in the south of Darfur.

Meanwhile, in November 2012 the Sudanese authorities announced that 13 suspects, including former senior members of the security forces, had been arrested in connection with a conspiracy to stage a coup. (In April 2013 nine military officers received prison sentences of between two and five years for involvement in the coup attempt.) In December 2012 opposition activists were prevented by police from delivering a petition critical of the Government to the state Human Rights Commission. Furthermore, several opposition leaders were arrested by the Sudanese authorities in January 2013, after a coalition of opposition parties known as the National Consensus Forces, the SRF and other groups signed a 'New Dawn Charter' in the Ugandan capital, Kampala, under which they agreed to co-operate in efforts to overthrow al-Bashir's Government. It was subsequently reported that the Sudanese Government had threatened to prohibit the activities of opposition parties unless they rejected the Charter.

Recent developments: improved relations with South Sudan

Following the resumption of the AU-mediated dialogue in Addis Ababa, on 8 March 2013 the Sudanese and South Sudanese Governments agreed to order their forces to withdraw from the border area by 14 March (thereby implementing the agreement on the establishment of a demilitarized zone that had been signed the previous September). After Salva Kiir accordingly ordered withdrawal, on 12 March the two sides reached agreement on a timetable under which South Sudan would resume petroleum production within three weeks. It was subsequently reported that Sudanese forces had also commenced withdrawal from the border zone. Later in March First Vice-President Taha publicly invited rebel groups to participate in the drafting of a new constitution. Amid the easing of tensions with South Sudan, at the beginning of April al-Bashir announced that all political prisoners would be released and pledged the Government's commitment to dialogue with all opposition groups. Seven political prisoners were released shortly afterwards. The South Sudanese authorities officially recommenced the delivery of petroleum on 6 April, after which, on 12 April, al-Bashir made his first visit to South Sudan since its secession; he announced in Juba that Sudan's relations with South Sudan would be normalized, and invited Salva Kiir to visit Khartoum for further discussions. In mid-April the SPLM-N claimed to have seized control of a strategic military base in Southern Kordofan, about 18 km east of Kadugli; later that month the Sudanese Government agreed to enter into AU-mediated peace negotiations with the movement.

Refugees

In addition to civil war and economic crisis, Sudan has experienced drought and famine, and the problem has been compounded by a very large number of refugees in the southern provinces, mainly from Ethiopia and Chad. By late 2004, as a result of the Darfur conflict, it was estimated by the office of the UN High Commissioner for Refugees (UNHCR) that some 1.6m. people were displaced within Darfur and that some 200,000 people had fled to neighbouring Chad. In early 2010 it was believed that almost 2.7m. people were classified as internally displaced in the Darfur region alone. Following a referendum overwhelmingly in favour of the secession of South Sudan in January 2011, an estimated 350,000 southerners returned from the north during that year; however, owing to delays in the finalization of citizenship agreements, large numbers of people of South Sudanese origin remained in Sudan subsequent to South

Sudan's independence in July. According to UNHCR estimates, at the end of 2012 the number of internally displaced persons in Sudan totalled 2.3m., and there were some 140,000 refugees (principally from Eritrea).

Foreign Affairs

Regional relations

In January 2006, at the sixth AU summit, which took place in Khartoum, the emergence of President al-Bashir as the leading candidate for the chairmanship of the organization provoked widespread criticism from the international community and was opposed by a number of AU member states. Following two days of negotiations, it was agreed that the President of the Republic of the Congo, Gen. Denis Sassou-Nguesso, would assume the chairmanship in 2006, to be succeeded by al-Bashir in 2007. Faced with unanimous opposition, in January 2007 al-Bashir withdrew his candidacy and the President of Ghana, John Kufuor, assumed the role of Chairman. In June 2011 Sudan applied to join the East African Community (EAC, see p. 460), comprising Kenya, Uganda, Rwanda, Tanzania and Burundi, pre-empting the application of the new state of South Sudan after its secession on 9 July; however, in November Sudan's application for membership of the EAC was rejected by Uganda and Tanzania, which cited concerns at the democratic practices of al-Bashir's Government.

Concerns increased in late 2005 that the ongoing conflict in Darfur (see Domestic Political Affairs) could spread into neighbouring Chad. In December Chadian rebels based in Darfur attacked the border town of Adre and the Chadian Government declared 'a state of belligerence' with Sudan, which it held ultimately responsible for the assault. In February 2006 the two countries held talks in Libya aimed at preventing further escalation in the dispute and agreement was reached to restore diplomatic relations and to prevent rebels from using territory to launch cross-border raids. However, in March Chadian President Idriss Deby Itno publicly questioned Sudan's commitment to the accord following a series of attacks on villages in Chad by the *Janjaweed*, allegedly with Sudanese assistance. In April Deby expelled the Sudanese ambassador to Chad and ordered the closure of the land border between the two countries following an attack on the Chadian capital, N'Djamena, by rebel forces. In August, at a meeting convened in N'Djamena, the two countries agreed to restore diplomatic relations and reopen border crossings. By November it had become apparent that the conflict in Darfur had spread into the Central African Republic (CAR). In the north of that country, groups of rebel fighters had begun to join together, forming allegiances with Chadian factions and providing a route to Chad for the Sudanese rebels. In February 2007 a summit was held under the auspices of French President Jacques Chirac, during which the CAR, Chad and Sudan agreed that they would cease support for rebel fighters in any of the three countries. In early May, following mediation by Saudi Arabia's King Abdallah, Presidents al-Bashir and Deby agreed to co-operate with the AU and the UN in their attempts to stabilize the Chad–Sudan border. Both countries approved the formation of a joint border force, and pledged to cease training and funding rebel groups and to stop all cross-border attacks. Further peace negotiations were initiated by President Abdoulaye Wade of Senegal, and in March 2008, at a meeting in Dakar, Senegal, attended by regional leaders and EU and UN representatives, Chad and Sudan signed a non-aggression agreement renewing their commitment to restoring peace. Nevertheless, violence in the region continued; in May Sudan accused Chadian rebels of involvement in an attack on Sudan's largest city, Omdurman, and severed diplomatic relations with Chad. In June military leaders from Chad and Sudan met in Senegal to discuss mechanisms for ensuring security in the border region, including the deployment of troops at strategic positions along the border; diplomatic ties were later restored.

Talks between delegates from Libya, Sudan and Eritrea were held in Tripoli in March 2010 to discuss means of increasing security in the region. Meanwhile, in January Chadian and Sudanese authorities signed an agreement on the normalization of relations between the two countries, including a pledge to establish a joint force to be deployed later that year along the common border in an attempt to foster greater security and to assist in efforts to resolve the Darfur situation. In February President al-Bashir announced that an official visit to Khartoum by Deby Itno had put a 'definitive end' to the troubled relations between Sudan and Chad. The decision of the Chadian authorities to deny entry to JEM leader Khalil Ibrahim and his entou-

rage at N'Djamena international airport in May was considered to demonstrate Deby's commitment to the new agreement. In January 2012 al-Bashir made an official visit to Libya to establish relations with the new Libyan administration, following the overthrow of Libyan leader Col Muammar al-Qaddafi the previous year.

In September 1995 Ethiopia accused Sudan of harbouring terrorists implicated in the attempted assassination of Egyptian President Hosni Mubarak in June and, in response, announced the closure of some Sudanese diplomatic facilities in the country and of non-governmental organizations connected with Sudan. In April 1996 Sudan claimed that Ethiopian government forces had collaborated with the SPLA in attacks on two towns in southeastern Sudan, while in June Ethiopia accused Sudan of attempting to destabilize the region. In January 1997 relations deteriorated further when, following alleged attacks on Sudan, President al-Bashir declared a *jihad* (holy war) against Ethiopia and ordered a general mobilization. Ethiopia, however, denied any involvement in the attacks and tensions between the two states eased during 2008. One of the suspects in the attempted assassination of Mubarak was extradited from Sudan in 1999 (see below), and in November, on his return from a visit to Ethiopia, al-Bashir stated that relations with that country were fully normalized. The common border was reopened in early 2000, and in March the Sudanese and Ethiopian Governments signed a number of agreements, which provided for increased co-operation in political, cultural, commercial and transport sectors. Further agreements regarding border security were signed in the following month. A seven-year dispute over border demarcation appeared to have been resolved in June 2008 when an accord was concluded, under which Ethiopia returned small pockets of land to the al-Qadaref region. However, Ethiopians complained that the Ethiopian Government had failed to consult its citizens on the matter and that the agreement granted Sudanese nationals the right to occupy certain areas of holy or historic importance. The chair of the joint border committee declared he would repeal the decision, although the Sudanese Government insisted that progress on the issue had been made. In November 2009 Ethiopia deployed a 200-strong air force unit to Darfur, in support of the 1,600 ground troops already stationed in the region.

Sudan's relations with Eritrea deteriorated after 1991; in December 1994 Eritrea severed diplomatic relations with Sudan, also sponsoring meetings of the principal groups opposed to the Sudanese regime, which it accused of lending support to the insurgent Eritrean *jihad*. In April 1997 Sudan protested to the UN over alleged Eritrean involvement in attacks on Sudanese territory. The border was closed in June, and again in February 1998, as a result of the violence; further attacks were reported in the border area by both Eritrea and Sudan throughout 1998. Following talks held in November 1998, an accord was signed by the Presidents of Sudan and Eritrea in May 2009, in which they agreed to restore diplomatic relations, to refrain from hostile propaganda and to establish joint committees, both to implement the terms of the accord and to study any further issues that might arise between the two countries. A further agreement was signed in Asmara in January 2000, providing for the immediate reopening of the two countries' borders and the resumption of flights between their airports. However, relations between the two countries deteriorated in July, when the Sudanese Government accused Eritrea of assisting the NDA with a planned offensive in eastern Sudan. In October Eritrean President Issaias Afewerki visited Khartoum, where he held talks with al-Bashir, during which both sides expressed their desire for a fresh beginning to their bilateral relations and agreed to take measures to settle differences between the two countries in a peaceful manner. In July 2001 Eritrea and Sudan signed an agreement on border security, which aimed to eradicate smuggling and illegal infiltration. Nevertheless, in October 2002 the Sudanese authorities closed the common border, claiming that Eritrea had been involved in an NDA offensive in eastern Sudan. Following a meeting with the Yemeni President, Ali Abdullah Saleh, and the Ethiopian Prime Minister, Meles Zenawi, in December 2003, President al-Bashir accused Eritrea of arming and training rebels in the Darfur region of Sudan and maintained that Eritrea was a destabilizing force in the region. Following further strains, at a meeting in Khartoum in October 2005 the Sudanese and Eritrean Ministers of Foreign Affairs signed an agreement to work towards the normalization of relations between Sudan and Eritrea. In June 2006 President Afewerki met al-Bashir in Khartoum, and later that month the two countries agreed to restore diplomatic relations to ambassadorial level. Following Eritrean mediation, the Sudanese Government and the rebel Eastern Front signed a peace agreement in Asmara in October (see above). In June 2008 the Sudanese authorities banned all activity of Eritrean opposition groups that had been operating from Sudan, demonstrating a marked improvement in relations between the two countries. Al-Bashir visited Asmara in March 2009, when he reiterated his commitment to the June 2008 agreement.

Sudan and Uganda have accused each other of supporting groups opposed to their respective regimes, and in 1995 Uganda broke off diplomatic relations with Sudan. A further deterioration in relations in December brought the two countries close to full-scale hostilities. In 1996 Sudan and Uganda agreed to restore diplomatic relations, provided that each side undertook to cease its support for rebel factions operating from the other's territory, and to participate in an international committee to monitor the agreement. Relations between Sudan and Uganda improved during 1999, and in December, following a meeting in Nairobi, mediated by Jimmy Carter, the two countries signed an accord in which they agreed to restore diplomatic relations and to end support to each other's rebel groups; shortly afterwards it was announced that eight leaders of the Lord's Resistance Army (LRA) were to be relocated from Sudan to a country of their choice in accordance with the agreement. In February 2000, however, Uganda expressed its dissatisfaction with Sudan's implementation of the accord and appealed for Sudan to disarm the LRA and to disband all LRA camps within Sudan. Sudan reaffirmed its commitment to the agreement and in June 2001 the two countries exchanged diplomats. In August the Ugandan embassy in Khartoum reopened and a chargé d'affaires was appointed. In March 2002 the two countries signed an agreement whereby Sudan temporarily authorized Ugandan troops to pursue LRA rebels within Sudan, and later that month the Ugandan Government announced that its troops had captured all four main bases in Sudan belonging to the LRA. In November the Sudanese authorities agreed to extend permission for Ugandan troops to remain on its territory for as long as Uganda deemed necessary. Meanwhile, the two countries upgraded relations to ambassadorial level. Following the secession of South Sudan in July 2011 (see above), Sudan no longer had a common border with Uganda. However, in April 2012 the Sudanese Government condemned alleged statements by the Ugandan Chief of Defence Forces that Uganda would dispatch troops to assist South Sudan in the event of a full-scale attack against it by the Sudanese army, and that Sudan was again providing support to the LRA.

In 1992 previously cordial relations with Egypt deteriorated sharply, following the announcement that Sudan had awarded a Canadian company a concession to explore for petroleum in the disputed Halaib border area. In August the Sudanese Government sought international arbitration on the Halaib issue, claiming that Egypt had been settling families in the area in an effort to bring it under Egyptian control. In January 1993 Sudan complained to the UN Security Council that Egyptian troops had infringed Sudan's territorial integrity. In March Egypt announced the construction of a new road link to Halaib. Sudan retaliated by appropriating the Khartoum campus of the University of Cairo. In June Sudan announced that it was closing two Egyptian consulates in Sudan and two of its own consulates in Egypt. In June 1995 relations suffered a further serious setback after the attempted assassination of President Mubarak of Egypt on his arrival in Addis Ababa to attend the annual conference of the Organization of African Unity (OAU, now African Union). The Egyptian Government immediately accused Sudan of complicity in the attack, and the OAU made the same allegation in September. In January 1996 the UN Security Council condemned Sudan's role in the attempted assassination and adopted Resolution 1044 seeking the extradition of three individuals implicated in the attack. Tensions between Sudan and Egypt improved in 1997, and in December talks were held between President al-Bashir and senior Egyptian officials. In May a joint Sudanese-Egyptian technical committee met in Khartoum to finalize details for the return of several institutions in Sudan to Egyptian control. Both sides agreed that the institutions should be returned, although differences remained over the time period for this operation. In October Sudan and Egypt agreed on a plan to hasten the normalization of relations. In July 1999 it was announced that Sudan had extradited one of the three suspects implicated in the attempted assassination of Mubarak. In December the two countries agreed to normalize their relations and to resolve their dispute over the Halaib issue

amicably. In March 2000 it was announced that the University of Cairo in Khartoum was to be reopened, and later that month Egypt appointed an ambassador to Sudan for the first time since the assassination attempt on Mubarak. In September the Sudanese and Egyptian ministers responsible for foreign affairs held the first session of the Egyptian-Sudanese Commission for 10 years, at which the two countries expressed their commitment to further bilateral economic development. In May 2003 Mubarak visited Khartoum for the first time since the attempted assassination. In March 2011 al-Bashir became the first Arab leader to visit Egypt after the resignation of Mubarak in February; the new Egyptian authorities, which planned that the country join the ICC, issued assurances that they would support Sudan's case with regard to the arrest warrant issued by the Court against al-Bashir.

Other external relations

The USA has frequently expressed concern about the Sudanese Government's links with Iran, and in 1997 imposed economic sanctions against Sudan, owing to its alleged continued support for terrorism. In August 1998 the USA launched a missile attack on what it claimed was a chemical weapons factory in Khartoum. Immediately after the attack, however, the Sudanese Government denied these claims and stated that it was, in fact, a private pharmaceuticals plant. Sudan recalled its ambassador to the USA and refused permission for US aircraft to use its airspace; its requests for a UN inquiry into the attack were unanimously refused by the Security Council, despite backing from the League of Arab States (see p. 372) and the Organization of the Islamic Conference—now Organization of Islamic Cooperation (see p. 413). By early 1999 it had become evident that the US intelligence on which the attack had been based was fundamentally flawed, and Sudan requested compensation for the damage caused by the bomb attack. In April the USA announced its decision to ease sanctions on the export of food and medicine to Sudan, and at the end of May Sudan fulfilled one of the conditions set by the USA for a review of the sanctions regime by signing a treaty banning chemical weapons. In November, however, the USA enacted controversial legislation allowing food aid to be delivered direct to the Sudanese rebels. An improvement in relations was evident in March 2000 following a visit to Sudan by a US diplomat to discuss the possibility of reopening the US embassy in Khartoum; in mid-April the embassy was duly reopened. However, relations once again deteriorated in December, when Sudan lodged an official complaint with the UN after the US Assistant Secretary of State, Susan Rice, visited rebel-held areas of southern Sudan in November, without the permission of the Sudanese Government.

Following the September 2001 suicide attacks on New York and Washington, DC, USA, Sudan agreed to assist the US Administration of President George W. Bush with its search for terrorist suspects, and by late September the Sudanese authorities had arrested some 30 individuals resident in Sudan who were suspected of having links to Osama bin Laden, a Saudi-born Islamist activist, and the al-Qa'ida (Base) organization, which the USA held responsible for the attacks. Nevertheless, US sanctions remained in place, and Sudan continued to be listed by the US Department of State as a sponsor of terrorism. Furthermore, two Sudanese banks were among numerous institutions under US investigation as possible sources of financial support for bin Laden. In October 2002 Bush approved legislation that allowed the USA to impose further sanctions, including the suspension of multilateral loans, on the Sudanese Government, should it fail to negotiate with the southern rebels or interfere with humanitarian efforts in the south of the country. The USA also froze the financial assets of 12 Sudanese companies, including the National Broadcasting Corporation. Under the Sudan Peace Act, conditions in Sudan would be evaluated every six months, although the law also made provision for the expenditure of US $100m. a year by the USA until 2005 in areas of Sudan not under the Sudanese Government's control. In October 2003 the US Agency for International Development pledged a further $40m. to finance initiatives to assist Sudan to recover from the civil war. However, the additional aid was conditional on the implementation of a CPA. The conflict in Darfur resulted in the deterioration of relations between Sudan and the USA and in September 2004 the US Administration accused the Sudanese Government of committing genocide. In October 2006 President Bush approved the Darfur Peace and Accountability Act of 2006, which provided for the imposition of sanctions against those responsible for genocide, war crimes, and crimes against humanity, and supported humanitarian efforts and measures to secure peace in the region of Darfur. He also issued an executive order freezing the assets and property of the Sudanese Government and prohibiting financial transactions with that body. The USA threatened to impose economic sanctions on state-controlled companies in Sudan in April 2007 unless the Government agreed to co-operate in restoring peace to the Darfur region. The following month President Bush implemented measures to exclude Sudanese companies from the US financial system. Following his election to the US presidency in November 2008, Barack Obama announced a new US strategy on Sudan, pledging to engage the Sudanese authorities in meaningful dialogue, with a focus on ending the conflict in Darfur, ensuring the implementation of the CPA with a view to securing peace in the region and continuing to address the threat of terrorism. After the organization of a referendum on secession for southern Sudan in January 2011, the US Administration announced that it would begin to normalize relations with Sudan. However, in November 2012 Obama again renewed the US sanctions in force against Sudan, acknowledging partial resolutions in the disputes with South Sudan, but citing continued conflict in Darfur and Southern Kordofan as an impediment to the restoration of normal bilateral relations.

In September 2012 the US, German and British embassies in Khartoum were attacked by Muslim protesters, who were repelled by security forces, after a film ridiculing the Prophet Muhammad that had been produced in California, USA, and released on the internet provoked international outrage. (The particular targeting of the German embassy was believed to have been provoked by an anti-Islam demonstration by members of a nationalist group, some of whom carried caricatures of the Prophet Muhammad, in the German capital, Berlin, in August.) The Sudanese Minister of Foreign Affairs had also formally condemned the film to the US and German ambassadors.

In October 2012 the Sudanese Government accused Israel of responsibility for an air attack against a reportedly Iranian-owned armaments factory in Khartoum, in which two people were killed.

CONSTITUTION AND GOVERNMENT

In early July 2005 the National Assembly approved an interim Constitution as part of the CPA, which had been signed in January between the Sudanese Government and the Sudan People's Liberation Movement (SPLM). The interim Constitution provided for the establishment of a Government of National Unity, representation in which was to be divided between northerners and southerners, with the former holding 70% of the posts and the latter 30%. Following a transitional period, presidential and legislative elections took place in April 2010, in accordance with the CPA. The President is directly elected for a five-year term, and appoints the Government. The National Assembly comprises 450 members, of whom 270 are directly elected in single seat constituencies, 68 are elected on the basis of proportional representation from party lists, and a further 112 women representatives are elected on the basis of proportional representation.

In accordance with the terms of the CPA, a referendum on the secession of southern Sudan was conducted in January 2011; 98.8% of the population (with a participation rate of 97.6% of the electorate) voted to secede from the north and officially form their own country. On 9 July 2011 the Republic of South Sudan declared independence from Sudan.

Sudan is divided into 17 states. A governor is responsible for each state, assisted by five state ministers.

REGIONAL AND INTERNATIONAL CO-OPERATION

Sudan is a member of the African Union (see p. 191) and the Council of Arab Economic Unity (see p. 373). In 1997 Sudan's membership of both the Arab Fund for Economic and Social Development (AFESD, see p. 205) and the Arab Monetary Fund (see p. 206) was suspended. Membership of the AFESD was restored in April 2000.

Sudan became a member of the UN in 1956, and participates in the Group of 77 (G77, see p. 461) developing countries.

ECONOMIC AFFAIRS

In 2010, according to estimates by the World Bank, Sudan's gross national income (GNI), measured at average 2008–10 prices, was US $56,656m., equivalent to $1,300 per head (or $2,020 on an international purchasing-power parity basis). During 2002–11, it was estimated, the population increased at an average annual rate of 2.0%, while gross domestic product (GDP) per head grew,

in real terms, by an average of 2.6% per year. Overall GDP increased, in real terms, at an average annual rate of 5.1% in 2002–11; growth in 2010 was 4.5%, however, GDP declined by 4.9% in 2011.

Agriculture (including forestry and fishing) contributed an estimated 27.2% of GDP in 2011, according to the World Bank. According to FAO, the sector employed an estimated 49.6% of the labour force in mid-2012. The principal cash crop is sesame seed (including oil cake), which accounted for 1.6% of total export earnings in 2009. The principal subsistence crops are sorghum, millet and wheat. The GDP of the agricultural sector increased by an average of 2.7% per year in 2002–11, according to the World Bank; agricultural GDP grew by 4.3% in 2011.

Industry (including mining, manufacturing, construction and power) contributed an estimated 39.8% of GDP in 2011, according to the World Bank, and employed 7.9% of the labour force in 1983. In 2002–11 industrial GDP increased at an average annual rate of 11.0%, according to the World Bank; industrial GDP grew by 9.4% in 2011.

Mining accounted for an estimated 15.3% of GDP in 2009, according to the African Development Bank (AfDB). Only 0.1% of the labour force was employed in the mining sector in 1983; however, this figure had risen considerably by the late 2000s. Sudan has reserves of petroleum, chromite, gypsum, gold, iron ore and wollastonite. Sudan began to develop its petroleum reserves in the mid-1990s; proven reserves totalled 6,700m. barrels at the end of 2011, sufficient to sustain production at current levels for about more than 40 years. In 2007 Sudan was the sixth largest producer of petroleum in Africa, and in 2009 petroleum and petroleum products accounted for 78.8% of total export earnings. However, following the secession of South Sudan (where the majority of petroleum extraction takes place), revenue from the sector was expected substantially to decline. According to the AfDB, the GDP of the mining sector increased by 10.5% in 2009.

Manufacturing contributed an estimated 6.7% of GDP in 2011, according to the World Bank. The most important branch of the sector is food-processing, especially sugar-refining, while the textile industry, cement production and petroleum-refining are also significant. Some 4.6% of the labour force were employed in manufacturing in 1983. According to the World Bank, in 2002–11 manufacturing GDP increased at an average annual rate of 5.5%; sectoral GDP grew by 8.0% in 2011.

The construction sector contributed an estimated 4.2% of GDP in 2009, according to the AfDB; it engaged some 2.3% of the employed labour force in 1983. According to the AfDB, the GDP of the sector increased by 8.5% in 2009.

Energy is derived from petroleum (which contributed 52.2% of total output in 2009) and hydroelectric power (47.8%). Sudan is a net exporter of fuels, with imports of refined petroleum products comprising an estimated 4.0% of the total value of imports in 2009.

Services contributed an estimated 33.0% of GDP in 2011, according to the World Bank, and employed 18.8% of the labour force in 1983. During 2002–11, according to the World Bank, the GDP of the services sector increased at an average annual rate of 11.0%; the GDP of the sector declined by 7.3% in 2010, before increasing by 52.0% in 2011.

In 2010 Sudan recorded a visible merchandise trade surplus of US $2,564.9m. and there was a surplus of $156.8m. on the current account of the balance of payments. In 2009 the principal sources of imports were the People's Republic of China (accounting for 16.6% of the total), Japan, Saudi Arabia, the United Arab Emirates (UAE) and India. In 2009 the principal market for Sudanese exports was also the People's Republic of China (taking 65.3% of the total); the UAE and Canada were other major purchasers. The principal exports in 2009 were mineral products (notably petroleum and petroleum products, and gold). The principal imports in 2009 were machinery and transport equipment, iron and steel, food and live animals, and chemicals and related products.

In 2011, according to preliminary figures from the IMF, Sudan recorded an overall budget deficit of 2,263m. new Sudanese pounds. Sudan's general government gross debt was 126,479m. new Sudanese pounds in 2011, equivalent to 74.1% of GDP. At the end of 2010 Sudan's total external debt was US $21,846m., of which $14,444m. was public and publicly guaranteed debt. In that year the cost of servicing long-term public and publicly guaranteed debt and repayments to the IMF was equivalent to 4.2% of the value of exports of goods, services and income (excluding workers' remittances). In 2002–11 the average annual rate of inflation was 10.4%. Consumer prices increased by an average of 13.0% in 2010 and by 18.0% in 2011.

Sudan's formidable economic problems have been compounded by civil conflict. Sudan began exporting petroleum in late 1999 and further discoveries of petroleum in 2001 led to a vast increase in export revenues; however, much of these earnings were used by the Government to fund the war against the rebels in the south of the country. Following the signing of the Comprehensive Peace Agreement in January 2005, levels of foreign investment increased, although the donor community remained concerned by the ongoing conflict and humanitarian crisis in the Darfur region. Following the secession of South Sudan in July 2011, Sudan's loss of the greater part of former state revenue from petroleum resulted in a widening budget deficit and a sharp devaluation in its currency. The Government of President Omar Hassan Ahmad al-Bashir (which had issued a new currency) consequently announced the adoption of a three-year emergency austerity programme. In early 2012 a dispute over the petroleum transit fee to be paid by South Sudan escalated, and the South Sudanese Government suspended the delivery of petroleum. In April the occupation of Sudan's principal oil-producing region of Heglig by South Sudanese forces precipitated a crisis; although the troops were withdrawn after a few days, the damage to Sudan's petroleum infrastructure and disruption to output resulted in further economic strains. In June al-Bashir adopted a number of further austerity measures, including the removal of subsidies and comprehensive tax increases, under a revised budget, provoking large-scale anti-Government protests (popular opposition to the Government continued in subsequent months). The Sudanese authorities also announced plans to assist trade with the rehabilitation of the road and rail networks. According to IMF projections, in 2012 real GDP contracted by about 11% and the average inflation rate reached nearly 29%. Two new oilfields, which entered into operation in December, were anticipated to generate additional revenue of US $300m. in the following year. A provisional arrangement for oil-revenue sharing with South Sudan was reached in August, and nine co-operation agreements were signed in September. Following progress in negotiations between Sudan and South Sudan in March 2013 (see Domestic Political Affairs), the South Sudanese Government resumed the delivery of petroleum on 6 April; it was envisaged that full production would be restored by the end of May, raising hopes of a rapid economic recovery. At an international conference hosted by Qatar in April, donor nations pledged some $3,600m. towards the development and reconstruction of Darfur. In the same month, however, IMF officials indicated that Sudan was unlikely to qualify for substantial relief on its accumulated external debt arrears.

PUBLIC HOLIDAYS

2014: 1 January (Independence Day), 13 January* (Mouloud, Birth of the Prophet), 6 April (Uprising Day, anniversary of 1985 coup), 6 May (Sham al-Nassim, Coptic Easter Monday), 30 June (Revolution Day), 28 July* (Id al-Fitr, end of Ramadan), 4 October* (Id al-Adha, Feast of the Sacrifice), 24 October* (Muharram, Islamic New Year), 25 December (Christmas).

* The dates of Islamic holidays are determined by sightings of the moon, and may be slightly different from those given above.

Statistical Survey

Source (unless otherwise stated): Department of Statistics, Ministry of Finance and National Economy, POB 735, Khartoum; tel. (183) 777563; fax (183) 775630; e-mail info@mof-sudan.net; internet www.mof-sudan.net; Central Bureau of Statistics, POB 700, Khartoum; tel. (183) 777255; fax (183) 771860; e-mail info@cbs .gov.sd; internet www.cbs.gov.sd.

Note: The Republic of South Sudan achieved independence from Sudan on 9 July 2011 following a referendum held in January at which voters overwhelmingly approved the secession of South Sudan. Unless otherwise indicated, data in this survey refer to pre-secession Sudan. For detailed statistical information on South Sudan, see separate chapter on that country.

Area and Population

AREA, POPULATION AND DENSITY

Area (sq km)	2,505,813*
Population (census results)†	
1 February 1993	24,940,683
22 April 2008	
Males	20,073,977
Females	19,080,513
Total	39,154,490
Population (official projections at mid-year)	
2011	33,975,593
2012	35,055,538
2013	36,163,778
Density (per sq km) at mid-2013	14.4

* 967,500 sq miles; includes South Sudan (see Note).
† Excluding adjustments for underenumeration, estimated to have been 6.7% in 1993.

Note: Data for South Sudan published by the Republic of South Sudan's National Bureau of Statistics (NBS) in 2011 indicated a residual post-secession total area of 1,861,484 sq km (718,724 sq miles) for Sudan. Of the total enumerated population of 39,154,490 at the time of the 2008 census, according to NBS estimates, 30,894,000 were estimated to be resident in areas not part of the secession state of South Sudan.

POPULATION BY AGE AND SEX
(population at 2008 census)

	Males	Females	Total
0–14	8,718,975	7,964,829	16,683,804
15–64	10,606,796	10,538,986	21,145,782
65 and over	748,206	576,698	1,324,904
Total	**20,073,977**	**19,080,513**	**39,154,490**

PROVINCES
(1983 census, provisional)*

	Area (sq miles)	Population	Density (per sq mile)
Northern	134,736	433,391	3.2
Nile	49,205	649,633	13.2
Kassala	44,109	1,512,335	34.3
Red Sea	84,977	695,874	8.2
Blue Nile	24,009	1,056,313	44.0
Gezira	13,546	2,023,094	149.3
White Nile	16,161	933,136	57.7
Northern Kordofan . . .	85,744	1,805,769	21.1
Southern Kordofan . . .	61,188	1,287,525	21.0
Northern Darfur . . .	133,754	1,327,947	9.9
Southern Darfur . . .	62,801	1,765,752	28.1
Khartoum	10,883	1,802,299	165.6
Eastern Equatoria . . .	46,073	1,047,125	22.7
Western Equatoria . . .	30,422	359,056	11.8
Bahr El-Ghazal . . .	52,000	1,492,597	28.7
Al-Buhayrat	25,625	772,913	30.2
Sobat	45,266	802,354	17.7
Jonglei	47,003	797,251	17.0
Total	**967,500**	**20,564,364**	**21.3**

* In 1991 a federal system of government was inaugurated, whereby Sudan was divided into nine states, which were sub-divided into 66 provinces and 281 local government areas. A constitutional decree, issued in February 1994, redivided the country into 26 states.

PRINCIPAL TOWNS
(population at 1993 census)

Omdurman	1,271,403	Nyala		227,183
Khartoum (capital)	947,483	El-Gezira		211,362
Khartoum North	700,887	Gedaref		191,164
Port Sudan	308,195	Kosti		173,599
Kassala	234,622	El-Fasher		141,884
El-Obeid	229,425	Juba		114,980

Source: UN, *Demographic Yearbook*.

Mid-2011 ('000, including suburbs, UN estimate): Khartoum 4,632,310 (Source: UN, *World Urbanization Prospects: The 2011 Revision*).

BIRTHS AND DEATHS
(annual averages, UN estimates)

	1995–2000	2000–05	2005–10
Birth rate (per 1,000)	38.6	36.5	33.8
Death rate (per 1,000)	12.0	10.3	9.4

Source: UN, *World Population Prospects: The 2010 Revision*.

Life expectancy (years at birth, WHO estimates): 61.1 (males 59.4; females 62.9) in 2010 (Source: World Bank, World Development Indicators database).

ECONOMICALLY ACTIVE POPULATION*
(persons aged 10 years and over, 1983 census, provisional)

	Males	Females	Total
Agriculture, hunting, forestry and fishing	2,638,294	1,390,411	4,028,705
Mining and quarrying	5,861	673	6,534
Manufacturing	205,247	61,446	266,693
Electricity, gas and water	42,110	1,618	43,728
Construction	130,977	8,305	139,282
Trade, restaurants and hotels	268,382	25,720	294,102
Transport, storage and communications	209,776	5,698	215,474
Financing, insurance, real estate and business services	17,414	3,160	20,574
Community, social and personal services	451,193	99,216	550,409
Activities not adequately defined	142,691	42,030	184,721
Unemployed persons not previously employed	387,615	205,144	592,759
Total	**4,499,560**	**1,843,421**	**6,342,981**

* Excluding nomads, homeless persons and members of institutional households.

Mid-2012 (estimates in '000): Agriculture, etc. 7,336; Total 14,800 (Source: FAO).

Health and Welfare

KEY INDICATORS

Total fertility rate (children per woman, 2010)	4.4
Under-5 mortality rate (per 1,000 live births, 2010)	103
HIV/AIDS (% of persons aged 15–49, 2007)	1.4
Physicians (per 1,000 head, 2008)	0.3
Hospital beds (per 1,000 head, 2009)	0.7
Health expenditure (2009): US $ per head (PPP)	159
Health expenditure (2009): % of GDP	7.3
Health expenditure (2009): public (% of total)	27.5
Access to water (% of persons, 2010)	58
Access to sanitation (% of persons, 2010)	26
Total carbon dioxide emissions ('000 metric tons, 2008)	14,051.9
Carbon dioxide emissions per head (metric tons, 2008)	0.3
Human Development Index (2011): ranking	169
Human Development Index (2011): value	0.408

For sources and definitions, see explanatory note on p. vi.

Agriculture

PRINCIPAL CROPS
('000 metric tons)

	2008	2009	2010
Wheat	587	642	403
Rice, paddy	30	23	23
Maize	62	66	35
Millet	721	630	471
Sorghum	3,869	4,192	2,630
Potatoes	284	301	315
Cassava (Manioc)*	10	11	14
Yams*	148	154	193
Sugar cane	7,453	7,527	7,527
Beans, dry	17	12	16*
Broad beans, horse beans, dry	140	113	152
Groundnuts, with shell	716	942	763
Sunflower seed	100	247	200†
Sesame seed	350	318	248
Melonseed*	52	69	52
Seed cotton	107	169	136*
Tomatoes	453	480	504
Pumpkins, squash and gourds*	84	73	79
Aubergines (Eggplants)	235	75	77
Onions, dry*	73	63	68
Garlic	38	25	27
Canteloupes (incl. other melons)*	22	23	24
Watermelons*	107	128	112
Dates	339	422	431
Oranges*	19	21	21
Lemons and limes*	67	80	71
Grapefruits and pomelos*	63	66	54
Guavas, mangoes and mangosteens*	183	186	192
Bananas*	84	89	85

* FAO estimate(s).
† Unofficial figure.

Aggregate production ('000 metric tons, may include official, semi-official or estimated data): Total cereals 5,269 in 2008, 5,552 in 2009, 3,562 in 2010; Total roots and tubers 590 in 2008, 682 in 2009, 785 in 2010; Total vegetables (incl. melons) 2,204 in 2008, 1,905 in 2009, 2,021 in 2010; Total fruits (excl. melons) 1,201 in 2008, 1,374 in 2009, 1,421 in 2010.

Note: Data for 2011 were not available.

Source: FAO.

LIVESTOCK
('000 head, year ending September)

	2008	2009	2010*
Horses*	26	26	26
Asses*	751	751	751
Cattle	41,400	41,563	41,727
Camels	4,400	4,521	4,645
Sheep	51,100	51,555	52,014
Goats	43,100	43,270	43,441
Chickens	41,502	42,400*	43,000

* FAO estimate(s).

Note: Data for 2011 were not available.

Source: FAO.

LIVESTOCK PRODUCTS
('000 metric tons)

	2008	2009	2010*
Cattle meat	1,369	1,442	1,505
Sheep meat	332	335	349
Goat meat	148	150	160
Chicken meat	27	29	29
Cows' milk	5,329	5,366	5,555
Sheep's milk	503	508	452
Goats' milk	1,474	1,493	1,602
Hen eggs*	54	55	56
Wool, greasy*	53	55	55

* FAO estimates.

Note: Data for 2011 were not available.

Source: FAO.

Forestry

ROUNDWOOD REMOVALS
('000 cubic metres, FAO estimates)

	2008	2009	2010
Sawlogs, veneer logs and logs for sleepers	123	123	123
Other industrial wood	2,050	2,050	2,050
Fuel wood	18,326	18,547	18,776
Total	20,499	20,720	20,949

2011: Production assumed to be unchanged from 2010 (FAO estimates).

Source: FAO.

Gum arabic ('000 metric tons, year ending 30 June): 18 in 1996/97; 18 in 1997/98; 28 in 1998/99 (Source: IMF, *Sudan: Statistical Appendix*—July 2000).

Fishing

('000 metric tons, live weight)

	2007	2008*	2009
Capture	65.5*	68.6	71.7
Nile tilapia	22.9	31.9	40.9
Other freshwater fishes	36.9	31.0	25.1
Marine fishes	5.7	5.6	5.6
Aquaculture	2.0*	2.0	2.2*
Total catch	67.5*	70.6	73.9*

* FAO estimate(s).

2010: Catch assumed to be unchanged from 2009 (FAO estimates).

Source: FAO.

Mining

('000 metric tons, unless otherwise stated)

	2008	2009	2010
Crude petroleum ('000 barrels)	168,898	173,453	168,656
Salt (unrefined)	10.6	35.8	141.8
Chromite	27.1	14.1	56.8
Gold ore (kilograms)*	7,508	14,914	26,317

* Figures refer to the metal content of ores.

Source: US Geological Survey.

Industry

PETROLEUM PRODUCTS
(metric tons)

	2008	2009	2010
Motor spirit (petrol)	9,244	9,488	10,593
Naphtha	219	207	180
Jet fuels	836	981	1,059
Kerosene	251	240	196
Gas-diesel (distillate fuel) oils	13,903	19,115	17,489
Residual fuel oils	4,534	2,108	1,732

Source: US Geological Survey.

SELECTED OTHER PRODUCTS
('000 metric tons)

	2006	2007	2008
Wheat flour	1,200	1,245	1,360
Raw sugar	767	743	652
Cement	227	327	340

2002 ('000 metric tons): Refined sugar 674; Vegetable oils 63.

Source: UN Industrial Commodity Statistics Database.

Electric energy (million kWh): 5,021.0 in 2007; 5,506.0 in 2008; 6,372 in 2009.

Finance

CURRENCY AND EXCHANGE RATES

Monetary Units
100 piastres = 1 new Sudanese pound (SDG).

Sterling, Dollar and Euro Equivalents (30 November 2012)
£1 sterling = 7.080 new Sudanese pounds;
US $1 = 4.409 new Sudanese pounds;
€1 = 5.726 new Sudanese pounds;
10 new Sudanese pounds = £1.41 = $2.27 = €1.75.

Average Exchange Rate (new Sudanese pounds per US $)
2009   2.3015
2010   2.3060
2011   2.6666

Note: On 1 March 1999 the Sudanese pound (£S) was replaced by the Sudanese dinar (SDD), equivalent to £S10. The pound was withdrawn from circulation on 31 July 1999. A new Sudanese pound (SDG), equivalent to 100 dinars (and 1,000 old pounds) was introduced on 10 January 2007. The new currency was to circulate along with previous currencies (the old pound had continued to circulate in some regions) for a transitional period, but became the sole legal tender on 1 July 2007.

CENTRAL GOVERNMENT BUDGET
(million new Sudanese pounds)

Revenue*	2010	2011†	2012‡
Tax revenue	10,008	11,426	13,091
Petroleum revenue	16,880	17,519	6,612
Sales to refineries	4,569	6,500	6,447
Export revenues	12,311	11,019	166
Other non-petroleum non-tax revenue	925	1,627	2,286
Total	27,814	30,572	21,989

Expenditure	2010	2011†	2012‡
Current expenditure	25,437	31,115	29,049
Wages	7,516	9,763	11,149
Goods and services	2,417	2,603	2,251
Interest	1,669	2,210	2,243
Subsidies	1,367	4,880	5,459
Fuel	1,276	4,822	4,866
Transfers	11,655	11,037	6,779
To South	5,867	4,820	0
To North	5,755	6,187	6,671
Other current expenditure	814	623	1,168
Capital expenditure	3,900	3,032	2,512
Total	29,337	34,147	31,561

* Excluding grants totalling (million new Sudanese pounds): 976 in 2010; 1,312 in 2011 (preliminary); 2,599 in 2012 (projection).
† Preliminary.
‡ Projections.

Source: IMF, *Sudan: Staff Report for the 2012 Article IV Consultation* (November 2012).

INTERNATIONAL RESERVES
(US $ million at 31 December)

	2008	2009	2010
IMF special drawing rights . .	—	197.2	193.5
Foreign exchange	1,399.0	897.0	842.8
Total	1,399.0	1,094.2	1,036.2

2011: IMF special drawing rights 192.5.

2012: IMF special drawing rights 192.6.

Source: IMF, *International Financial Statistics.*

MONEY SUPPLY
(million Sudanese dinars at 31 December)

	2009	2010	2011
Currency outside depository corporations	8,066	10,068	12,850
Transferable deposits	9,595	11,593	13,719
Other deposits	10,624	13,800	15,248
Broad money	28,285	35,461	41,817

Source: IMF, *International Financial Statistics.*

COST OF LIVING
(Consumer Price Index for middle income group; base: 2007 = 100)

	2009	2010	2011
Food and beverages	133.1	153.8	185.2
Clothing and footwear . . .	118.3	130.0	152.6
Housing	128.1	140.8	156.3
Household operations . . .	116.4	126.1	151.9
Health care	118.1	124.1	149.1
Transport	107.7	110.3	126.6
Entertainment	109.5	116.7	126.7
Education	119.2	156.5	196.6
All items (incl. others) . .	127.2	143.7	169.6

NATIONAL ACCOUNTS
(million new Sudanese pounds at current prices)

Expenditure on the Gross Domestic Product

	2007	2008	2009
Government final consumption expenditure	9,635	10,811	12,107
Private final consumption expenditure	85,780	92,073	100,447
Changes in inventories . . .	7,373	5,852	3,038
Gross fixed capital formation . .	16,170	18,645	26,808
Total domestic expenditure .	118,958	127,381	142,400
Exports of goods and services . .	18,665	25,401	19,120
Less Imports of goods and services	23,607	25,035	25,859
GDP in purchasers' values .	114,018	127,747	135,659

Gross Domestic Product by Economic Activity

	2007	2008	2009
Agriculture, hunting, forestry and fishing	32,985	37,481	44,970
Mining and quarrying . . .	17,824	20,064	9,931
Manufacturing	8,782	9,726	11,508
Electricity, gas and water . .	1,981	2,242	2,513
Construction	4,651	5,239	6,171
Wholesale and retail trade, restaurants and hotels . .	16,728	18,376	19,706
Transport and communications .	13,781	15,046	17,076
Finance, insurance, real estate and business services	7,809	8,961	10,399
Government services . . .	5,944	6,681	7,482
Other services	2,255	2,503	2,729
Sub-total	112,740	126,319	132,485
Less Imputed bank service charge.	1,095	1,126	1,244
Indirect taxes (net)	2,373	2,553	4,418
GDP in purchasers' values .	114,018	127,747	135 659

Source: African Development Bank.

BALANCE OF PAYMENTS
(US $ million)

	2008	2009	2010
Exports of goods f.o.b.	11,670.5	8,257.1	11,404.3
Imports of goods f.o.b.	−8,229.4	−8,528.0	−8,839.4
Trade balance	3,441.1	−270.9	2,564.9
Exports of services	492.8	392.0	253.8
Imports of services	−2,619.5	−1,907.1	−2,321.4
Balance on goods and services	1,314.4	−1,786.0	497.3
Other income received . . .	43.4	36.7	137.9
Other income paid	−3,056.5	−2,261.4	−2,609.5
Balance on goods, services and income	−1,698.6	−4,010.7	−1,974.4
Current transfers received . .	4,023.6	2,973.8	3,360.0
Current transfers paid	−3,638.6	−1,961.5	−1,228.8
Current balance	−1,313.6	−2,998.4	156.8
Direct investment abroad . . .	−89.2	—	—
Direct investment from abroad .	2,600.5	1,816.2	2,063.7
Portfolio investment assets . .	−33.4	20.0	−14.3
Portfolio investment liabilities .	−0.1	−0.5	21.4
Other investment assets . .	−866.5	−860.2	−2,785.7
Other investment liabilities . .	−101.6	2,250.3	1,365.1
Net errors and omissions . .	−125.4	−737.1	−859.9
Overall balance	70.8	−509.6	−52.9

Source: IMF, *International Financial Statistics.*

External Trade

PRINCIPAL COMMODITIES
(US $ million)

Imports c.i.f.	2007	2008	2009
Food and live animals . . .	465.4	1,152.5	1,191.7
Cereals and cereal preparations .	205.2	569.5	537.4
Unmilled durum wheat . . .	161.2	493.1	386.9
Mineral fuels, lubricants, etc. .	32.3	14.3	346.9
Refined petroleum products . .	32.2	13.8	346.7
Chemicals and related products	1,027.8	395.5	920.6
Medicinal and pharmaceutical products	814.7	216.6	284.6
Basic manufactures	1,017.1	1,352.1	1,807.3
Textiles and textile products (excl. clothing)	152.9	125.3	243.8
Cement	91.5	129.1	109.7
Iron and steel	211.5	768.0	620.3
Machinery and transport equipment	6,264.3	8,774.5	3,254.6
Power generating machinery and equipment	649.7	252.8	317.0
Machinery specialized for particular industries . . .	1,110.5	393.3	520.1
Miscellaneous industrial machinery	260.5	249.6	298.7
Telecommunication and recording equipment	1,310.8	221.1	205.2
Road vehicles	1,043.9	953.9	1,223.2
Passenger vehicles (excl. buses).	301.3	401.9	405.0
Lorries and special purpose vehicles	495.6	327.0	567.9
Miscellaneous manufactured articles	898.1	652.1	817.5
Total (incl. others)	9,853.6	16,416.7	8,589.9

Exports f.o.b.		2006	2008*	2009
Food and live animals . . .		150.8	126.1	298.4
Live animals		109.9	71.5	249.7
Sheep and goats		106.5	50.0	224.2
Sheep		103.2	49.4	220.4
Crude materials (inedible)				
except fuels		291.2	370.8	281.1
Oil seeds and oleaginous fruit .		147.5	173.6	153.8
Sesame seeds		143.7	167.9	147.5
Cotton		71.1	58.3	40.2
Mineral fuels, lubricants, etc. .		4,796.1	8,935.4	7,151.8
Petroleum and petroleum products		4,791.7	8,934.0	7,151.8
Machinery and transport				
equipment		58.3	33.0	46.3
Other commodities and				
transactions		174.2	3.2	1,279.5
Non-monetary gold, unwrought .		148.2	—	1,278.5
Total (incl. others)		5,478.7	9,500.9	9,079.5

* Data for 2007 were not available.

Source: UN, *International Trade Statistics Yearbook.*

PRINCIPAL TRADING PARTNERS
(US $ million)

Imports c.i.f.		2007	2008	2009
Australia		116.0	287.9	278.3
Canada		136.7	257.0	92.7
China, People's Repub. . . .		1,614.0	1,295.6	1,426.7
Egypt		357.2	422.8	410.3
France (incl. Monaco) . . .		258.3	147.4	113.3
Germany		481.9	119.7	328.4
India		276.6	579.4	548.5
Indonesia		196.0	17.0	46.6
Italy		192.7	124.7	248.5
Japan		744.7	632.1	817.1
Jordan		268.3	126.2	86.2
Kenya		36.8	254.5	63.7
Korea, Repub.		265.3	174.2	205.4
Malaysia		22.1	43.6	52.9
Netherlands		218.9	63.7	90.6
Russia		30.5	738.8	97.3
Saudi Arabia		1,429.6	4,096.6	650.4
Sweden		476.7	64.6	99.1
Switzerland (incl. Liechtenstein) .		57.3	16.3	n.a.
Turkey		65.2	80.9	381.0
Ukraine		31.2	621.9	83.3
United Arab Emirates . . .		714.2	499.3	634.0
United Kingdom		564.0	1,075.4	192.0
USA		59.1	43.0	288.3
Total (incl. others)		9,853.6	16,416.7	8,589.9

Exports f.o.b.		2006	2008*	2009
Canada		66.8	0.1	802.1
China, People's Repub. . . .		4,324.3	7,553.5	5,932.2
Egypt		68.6	130.8	93.5
France (incl. Monaco) . . .		15.2	22.8	35.1
Germany		21.3	17.6	9.7
India		22.2	72.6	164.6
Indonesia		5.1	119.1	143.3
Japan		299.0	690.9	213.1
Korea, Repub.		6.5	55.6	7.9
Malaysia		—	107.8	40.6
Saudi Arabia		154.7	114.7	254.4
Singapore		12.2	70.9	94.5
United Arab Emirates . . .		280.5	221.4	951.1
United Kingdom		50.8	7.5	24.0
Yemen		1.2	170.1	24.4
Total (incl. others)		5,478.7	9,500.9	9,079.5

* Data for 2007 were not available.

Source: UN, *International Trade Statistics Yearbook.*

Transport

RAILWAY TRAFFIC

		2007	2008	2009
Passengers carried ('000) . . .		51	91	87
Passenger-km (million) . . .		50	67	62
Freight carried ('000 metric tons) .		1,091	1,033	907
Freight ton-km (million) . . .		781	919	800

ROAD TRAFFIC
('000 motor vehicles in use)

		2000	2001	2002
Passenger cars		46.0	46.4	47.3
Commercial vehicles . . .		60.5	61.8	62.5

Source: UN, *Statistical Yearbook.*

2007 ('000 vehicles in use): Passenger cars 768; Buses and motor coaches 12; Vans and lorries 300; Motorcycles and mopeds 36 (Source: IRF, *World Road Statistics*).

SHIPPING
Flag Registered Fleet
(at 31 December)

		2010	2011	2012
Number of vessels		11	11	11
Total displacement (grt) . . .		23,031	23,031	23,031

Source: Lloyd's List Intelligence (www.lloydslistintelligence.com).

International Sea-borne Freight Traffic
(estimates, '000 metric tons)

		1991	1992	1993
Goods loaded		1,290	1,387	1,543
Goods unloaded		3,800	4,200	4,300

Source: UN Economic Commission for Africa, *African Statistical Yearbook.*

CIVIL AVIATION
(traffic on scheduled services)

		2007	2008	2009
Kilometres flown (million) . .		9	9	9
Passengers carried ('000) . .		598	618	607
Passenger-km (million) . . .		1,132	1,154	1,111
Total ton-km (million) . . .		146	148	140

Source: UN, *Statistical Yearbook.*

2010: Passengers carried 601,668 (Source: World Bank, World Development Indicators database).

Tourism

	2009	2010	2011*
Foreign visitor arrivals . . .	420,000	495,000	536,000
Tourism receipts (US $ million, excl. passenger transport) . .	299	94	n.a.

* Provisional.

Source: World Tourism Organization.

Communications Media

	2009	2010	2011
Telephones ('000 main lines in use)	370.4	545.0	483.6
Mobile cellular telephones ('000 subscribers)	15,340	18,093	25,056
Internet subscribers ('000 subscribers)	n.a.	27	32
Broadband subscribers ('000) . .	n.a.	13.5	17.4

Source: International Telecommunication Union.

Education

(2008/09 unless otherwise stated)

	Institutions*	Teachers	Students		Total
			Males	Females	
Pre-primary .	5,984	20,738	316,792	315,443	632,235
Primary . .	11,982	123,633	2,539,712	2,204,756	4,744,468
Secondary .	3,512	82,665	992,446	845,010	1,837,456
Universities, etc. . . .	n.a.	4,486†	n.a.	n.a.	200,538†

* Figures refer to 1998.
† Estimates for 2000.

Source: UNESCO Institute for Statistics.

Pupil-teacher ratio (primary education, UNESCO estimate): 38.4 in 2008/09 (Source: UNESCO Institute for Statistics).

Adult literacy rate (UNESCO estimates): 71.1% (males 80.1%; females 62.0%) in 2010 (Source: UNESCO Institute for Statistics).

Directory

The Government

HEAD OF STATE

President: Lt-Gen. OMAR HASSAN AHMAD AL-BASHIR (took power as Chairman of the Revolutionary Command Council for National Salvation (RCC) on 30 June 1989; appointed President by the RCC on 16 October 1993; elected President in March 1996; re-elected in December 2000 and in April 2010).

First Vice-President: ALI OSMAN MUHAMMAD TAHA.

Vice-President: AL-HAJ ADAM YOUSEF.

COUNCIL OF MINISTERS
(May 2013)

Prime Minister: Lt-Gen. OMAR HASSAN AHMAD AL-BASHIR.

Minister of Presidential Affairs: Maj.-Gen. BAKRI HASSAN SALEH.

Minister of Cabinet Affairs: AHMED SAAD OMAR KHADR.

Minister of Defence: Maj.-Gen. Eng. ABD AL-RAHIM MOHAMED HUSSEIN.

Minister of the Interior: IBRAHIM MAHMOUD HAMED.

Minister of Foreign Affairs: ALI AHMED KARTI.

Minister of Justice: MOHAMED BUSHARA DOUSA.

Minister of Finance and National Economy: ALI MAHMOOD ABD AL-RASOOL.

Minister of Human Resources Development and Labour: ISHRAGA SAYED MAHMOUD.

Minister of Agriculture and Irrigation: ABD AL-HALIM ISMAIL AL-MUTAAFI.

Minister of Industry: ABDUL-WAHAB MOHAMMED OSMAN.

Minister of Guidance and Endowments: ALFATIH TAJ ELSIR ABDULLAH.

Minister of Culture and Information: Dr AHMED BILAL OSMAN.

Minister of Petroleum: AWAD AHMED AL-JAZ.

Minister of Higher Education and Scientific Research: Dr KHAMES KAJO KUNDAH.

Minister of Public Education: SU'AD ABDEL RAZIQ MOHAMMED SAEED.

Minister of Water Resources and Electricity: OSAMA ABDALLA MOHAMED AL-HASSAN.

Minister of Minerals: KAMAL ABD AL-LATIF ABDUL-RAHIM.

Minister of Sciences and Communications: Dr ESHA BASHERI MOHAMED.

Minister of Health: BAHAR IDRIS ABU GARDAH.

Minister of Welfare and Social Security: MASHAIR MOHAMED AL-AMIN.

Minister of Youth and Sports: SEDDIQ MOHAMED TOUM HAMED ELNAIR.

Minister of Transport, Roads and Bridges: Dr AHMED BABIKER NAHAR.

Minister of Antiquities, Tourism and Wildlife: MOHAMMED ABDUL KAREEM AL-HADD.

Minister of the Environment, Forestry and Urban Development: Dr HASSAN ABDEL QADER HILAL.

Minister of Animal and Fishery Resources and Pastures: Dr FAISAL HASSAN IBRAHIM.

Minister of Commerce: OSMAN OMER AL-SHARIF.

Minister of Investment: MUSTAFA OSMAN ISMAIL.

Minister of Federal Government: HASBOU MOHAMED ABDULLAH.

In addition, there are 34 State Ministers.

MINISTRIES

Office of the President: Khartoum; internet www.presidency.gov.sd.

Ministry of Agriculture and Irrigation: POB 285, al-Gamaa Ave, Khartoum; tel. (183) 780951; e-mail moafcc@sudanmail.net.

Ministry of Animal and Fishery Resources and Pastures: Khartoum; internet www.marf.gov.sd.

Ministry of Antiquities, Tourism and Wildlife: POB 2424, Khartoum; tel. (183) 471329; fax (183) 471437; e-mail admin@sudan-tourism.com; internet www.sudan-tourism.gov.sd.

Ministry of Cabinet Affairs: POB 931, Khartoum; tel. (183) 784205; fax (183) 771331; e-mail info@sudan.gov.sd; internet www.sudan.gov.sd/en.

Ministry of Commerce: Khartoum.

Ministry of Culture and Information: Khartoum.

Ministry of Defence: POB 371, Khartoum; tel. (183) 774910.

Ministry of the Environment, Forestry and Urban Development: POB 300, Khartoum; tel. (183) 462604.

Ministry of Federal Government: Khartoum.

Ministry of Finance and National Economy: POB 735, Khartoum; tel. (183) 777563; fax (183) 775630; e-mail info@mof-sudan.net; internet www.mof.gov.sd.

Ministry of Foreign Affairs: POB 873, Khartoum; tel. (183) 773101; fax (183) 772941; e-mail ministry@mfa.gov.sd; internet mfa.gov.sd.

Ministry of Guidance and Endowments: Khartoum.

Ministry of Health: POB 303, Khartoum; tel. (183) 773000; e-mail inhsd@sudanet.net; internet www.fmoh.gov.sd.

Ministry of Higher Education and Scientific Research: POB 2081, Khartoum; tel. (183) 779312; fax (183) 783394; e-mail srp@mohe.gov.sd; internet mohe.gov.sd.

Ministry of Human Resources Development and Labour: Khartoum.

Ministry of Industry: POB 2184, Khartoum; tel. (183) 777830.

Ministry of the Interior: POB 2793, Khartoum; tel. (183) 776554.

Ministry of Investment: Khartoum.

Ministry of Justice: POB 302, al-Nil Ave, Khartoum; tel. (183) 774842; fax (183) 771479; e-mail moj@moj.gov.sd; internet www.moj .gov.sd.

Ministry of Minerals: POB 2087, Khartoum; tel. (183) 775595; fax (183) 775428.

Ministry of Petroleum: Khartoum.

Ministry of Presidential Affairs: Khartoum.

Ministry of Public Education: Khartoum; tel. (183) 772808; e-mail moe-sd@moe-sd.com.

Ministry of Sciences and Communications: Khartoum.

Ministry of Transport, Roads and Bridges: Khartoum.

Ministry of Water Resources and Electricity: POB 878, Khartoum; tel. 912549751 (mobile); e-mail oehamad@hotmail.com.

Ministry of Welfare and Social Security: University Ave, POB 12661, Khartoum; tel. 83776101 (mobile); fax 83777633 (mobile); e-mail info@welfare.gov.sd; internet www.welfare.gov.sd.

Ministry of Youth and Sports: Khartoum.

STATE GOVERNORS
(May 2013)

Blue Nile: HUSSEIN YASSIN HAMAD.

Central Darfur: YOUSEF TIBIN MUSA ADAM.

East Darfur: ABDUL HAMID MUSA KASHA.

Gadarif: ALDAW MOHAMED EL-MAHI (NCP).

Gezira: Dr AL-ZUBEIR BASHIR TAHA (NCP).

Kassala: MOHAMMED YUSUF ADAM BESHIR (NCP).

Khartoum: Dr ABD AL-RAHMAN AL-KHIDIR (NCP).

Northern: IBRAHIM AL-KHEDR (acting).

North Darfur: OSMAN MUHAMMAD YUSUF KIBIR (NCP).

North Kordofan: MOATASIM MIRGHANI ZAKI EL-DIN (NCP).

Red Sea: MOHMED TAHEIR AILA (NCP).

River Nile: AL-HADI ABDULLAH MOHAMMED AL-AWWAD (NCP).

Sennar: AHMED ABBAS MOHAMED SAAD AL-THOAM.

South Darfur: HAMAD ISMAIL HAMAD ABU KAREEM (NCP).

South Kordofan: AHMED HAROUN (NCP).

West Darfur: GALO KOMA ATIM (SLJM).

White Nile: YUSUF AHMED EL-SHANBALY.

President and Legislature

PRESIDENT
Election, 11–15 April 2010

Candidate	Votes	% of votes
Omar Hassan Ahmad al-Bashir (National Congress Party)	6,901,694	68.24
Yasir Saeed Arman (Sudan People's Liberation Movement)	2,193,826	21.69
Abdullah Deng Nhial Ayom (Popular Congress Party)	396,139	3.92
Hatim as-Sir Ali Sikunji (Democratic Unionist Party)	195,668	1.93
Others	426,983	4.22
Total	**10,114,310**	**100.00**

MAJLIS WATANI
(National Assembly)

Speaker: AHMAD IBRAHIM AL-TAHIR.

Deputy Speakers: ANGELO BEDA, ABDALLAH AL-HARDELLO.

Election, 11–15 April 2010, provisional results

Party	Seats*			
	A	B	C	Total
National Congress Party . . .	180	50	82	312
Sudan People's Liberation Movement	56	17	26	99
Popular Congress Party . . .	—	1	3	4
United Democratic Party . . .	4	—	—	4
Independents	3	—	—	3
Umma Federal Party . . .	2	—	1	3
Sudan People's Liberation Movement—Democratic Change.	2	—	—	2
Umma Reform and Renewal Party	2	—	—	2
Democratic Unionist Party—Original	1	—	—	1
Muslim Brotherhood	1	—	—	1
Umma National Party . . .	1	—	—	1
Total	**252†**	**68**	**112**	**432†**

* There are 450 members of the Majlis Watani of which 270 (A) are directly elected in single seat constituencies; 68 'party members' (B) are elected on the basis of proportional representation at the state level from separate and closed party lists; and a further 112 women members (C) are elected on the basis of proportional representation at the state level from separate and closed party lists.

† Voting in 16 constituencies was postponed, the result in one seat was not released and one seat was declared vacant. Following by-elections held in June 2010 the NCP increased its representation to 323 seats, while the Democratic Unionist Party—Original secured an additional seat. Two seats were taken by minor parties, while four seats remained vacant.

Election Commission

National Elections Commission (NEC): Khartoum; tel. (183) 520282; e-mail info@nec.org.sd; internet www.nec.org.sd; Abd Alla MAULANA AHMED ABD ALLA.

Political Organizations

The right to political association, subject to compliance with the law, was guaranteed in the Constitution approved by referendum in June 1998. (All political organizations had been banned following the military coup of 30 June 1989.) The registration of parties began in January 1999. The following parties are among the most active:

Communist Party of Sudan (CPS): Khartoum; e-mail cpsudan@ gmail.com; internet www.midan.net; f. 1946; Gen. Sec. MOHAMED IBRAHIM NUGUD MUNAWAR.

Democratic Unionist Party (DUP): Khartoum; Leader MUHAMMAD OSMAN AL-MIRGHANI.

Islamic Ummah Party: Khartoum; Chair. WALI AL-DIN AL-HADI AL-MAHDI.

Moderate Trend Party: Khartoum; Leader MAHMUD JIHA.

Muslim Brotherhood: Khartoum; Islamist fundamentalist; Leader Dr HABIR NUR AL-DIN.

National Congress Party (NCP): Khartoum; successor to National Islamic Front; Pres. Lt-Gen. OMAR HASSAN AHMAD AL-BASHIR; Sec.-Gen. Prof. IBRAHIM AHMAD UMAR.

National Democratic Party: Khartoum; f. 2002 following merger of the Union of Nationalistic Forces, the Communist Party and the National Solidarity Party.

New National Democratic Party: Leader MUNEER SHEIKH EL-DIN JALAB.

Nile Valley Conference: Khartoum; Founder Lt-Gen. (retd) UMAR ZARUQ.

Popular Congress Party (PCP): Khartoum; f. 2000; Founder HASSAN AL-TURABI.

Sudan Green Party: Khartoum; Founder Prof. ZAKARAIA BASHIR IMAM.

Sudan National Alliance (SNA): f. 1994; Leader ABDEL AZIZ KHALID.

Sudanese National Party (SNP): Khartoum; Leader HASAN AL-MAHI.

Sudanese Socialist Democratic Union (SSDU): Leader FATIMA AHMED ABDEL MAHMOUD MOHAMED.

Umma National Party (UNP): internet www.umma.org; f. 1945; Mahdist party based on the Koran and Islamic traditions; Chair. Dr UMAR NUR AL-DA'IM; Leader SADIQ AL-MAHDI.

Umma Reform and Renewal Party: Khartoum; f. 2002; Leader MUBARAK AL-FADIL.

Union of Sudan African Parties (USAP): f. 1987; Chair. JOSEPH OKELLO; Sec.-Gen. Prof. AJANG BIOR.

United Democratic Party.

United Democratic Salvation Front (UDSF): Khartoum; political wing of the Sudan People's Defence Force; Chair. Dr GABRIEL CHANGSON CHANG.

In 2003 two rebel groups, the **Sudan Liberation Movement (SLM)** (Leader MINNI ARKUA MINAWI) and the **Justice and Equality Movement (JEM)**, (Leader GIBRIL IBRAHIM) began an armed rebellion in the Darfur region of western Sudan.

At a meeting convened in Asmara, Eritrea, in 2006 the **National Redemption Front (NRF)** was formed by the leader of the JEM, Dr KHALIL IBRAHIM MOHAMED, his counterpart, AHMAD DREIGE of the SFDA, and KHAMIS ABDALLA ABAKAR, the former Deputy Chairman of Abd al-Wahid Muhammad al-Nur's faction of the SLM, and leader of the **Group of 19 (G-19)**. The G-19 emerged as the principal faction of the NRF, originally formed as a group of commanders who defected from al-Nur's faction during the Abuja, Nigeria, negotiations. In December 2006 a group of Arab rebels, opposed to the Sudanese army and the *Janjaweed*, formed an alliance called the **Popular Forces Troops (PFT)**.

Diplomatic Representation

EMBASSIES IN SUDAN

Afghanistan: Madinatol Riyadh, Shareol Moshtal Sq. 10, House No. 81, Khartoum; tel. (183) 221852; fax (183) 222059; e-mail afembsudan@hotmail.com; Chargé d'affaires a.i. KHALILURRAHMAN HANANI.

Algeria: Blvd El-Mechtel Eriad, POB 80, Khartoum; tel. (183) 234773; fax (183) 224190; Ambassador MUHAMMAD YARKI.

Brazil: Kamel Magzob St, House No. 110, Block 21, al-Amarat, POB 8255, Riyadh, 12217 Khartoum; tel. (183) 217079; fax (183) 217049; e-mail ambassador@brasilemb-sd.org; Ambassador ANTONIO CARLOS DO NASCIMENTO PEDRO.

Bulgaria: St 31, House No. 9, Block 10, al-Amarat, POB 1690, 11111 Khartoum; tel. (183) 560106; fax (183) 560107; e-mail bgembsdn@yahoo.co.uk; Chargé d'affaires a.i. SVILEN BOZHANOV.

Chad: St 57, al-Amarat, Khartoum; tel. (183) 471612; Ambassador ALI AHAMAT AKHABACHE.

China, People's Republic: POB 1425, Khartoum; tel. (183) 272730; fax (183) 271138; e-mail ssddssgg@yahoo.com.cn; Ambassador LUO XIAOGUANG.

Congo, Democratic Republic: St 13, Block 12 CE, New Extension, 23, POB 4195, Khartoum; tel. (183) 471125; Chargé d'affaires a.i. BAWAN MUZURI.

Egypt: University St, POB 1126, Khartoum; tel. (183) 777646; fax (183) 778741; e-mail sphinx-egysud@yahoo.com; Ambassador ABDUL-GHAFFAR AL-DEEB.

Eritrea: St 39, House No. 26, POB 1618, Khartoum 2; tel. (183) 483834; fax (183) 483835; e-mail erena@sudanet.net; Ambassador Gen. ISSA AHMED ISSA.

Ethiopia: Plot No. 4, Block 384BC, POB 844, Khartoum; tel. (183) 471379; fax (183) 471141; e-mail eekrt@hotmail.com; Ambassador ATO ALI ABDO.

France: al-Amarat, St 13, Plot No. 11, Block 12, POB 377, 11111 Khartoum; tel. (183) 471082; fax (183) 465928; e-mail cad.khartoum-amba@diplomatie.gouv.fr; internet www.ambafrance-sd.org; Ambassador PATRICK NICOLOSO.

Germany: 53 Baladia St, Block No. 8D, Plot 2, POB 970, Khartoum; tel. (183) 777990; fax (183) 777622; e-mail reg1@khar.auswaertiges-amt.de; internet www.khartum.diplo.de; Ambassador ROLF WELBERTS.

Holy See: Kafouri Belgravia, POB 623, Khartoum (Apostolic Nunciature); tel. (183) 330037; fax (183) 330692; e-mail kanuap@yahoo.it; Apostolic Nuncio Most Rev. LEO BOCCARDI (Titular Archbishop of Bitetto).

India: Plot No. 2, Al Amarat St 01, Block 12DH, Eastern Extension, POB 707, Khartoum II; tel. (183) 574001; fax (183) 574050; e-mail ambassador@indembsdn.com; internet www.indembsdn.com; Ambassador SANJAY KUMAR VERMA.

Indonesia: St 60, 84, Block 12, ar-Riyadh, POB 13374, Khartoum; tel. (183) 225106; fax (183) 225528; e-mail kbri_khartoum@sudanmail.com; Ambassador Dr M. A. SUJATMIKO.

Iran: Sq. 15, House No. 4, Mogran, POB 10229, Khartoum; tel. (183) 781490; fax (183) 778668; e-mail iransud@yahoo.com; Ambassador JAVAD TORKABADY.

Iraq: Sharia ash-Shareef al-Hindi, POB 1969, Khartoum; tel. (183) 271867; fax (183) 271855; e-mail krtemb@iraqmofamail.net; Ambassador Dr SALEH HUSSEIN ALI.

Italy: St 39, Block 61, POB 793, Khartoum; tel. (183) 471615; fax (183) 471217; e-mail ambasciata.khartoum@esteri.it; internet www.ambkhartoum.esteri.it; Ambassador ARMANDO BARUCCO.

Japan: St 43, House No. 67, POB 1649, Khartoum; tel. (183) 471601; fax (183) 471600; internet www.sdn.emb-japan.go.jp; Ambassador RYOICHI HORIE.

Jordan: St 33, House No. 13, POB 1379, Khartoum; tel. (183) 483125; fax (183) 471038; Ambassador MUNTHER QUBAAH.

Kenya: Plot No. 516, Block 1 West Giraif, POB 8242, Khartoum; tel. (155) 772800; fax (155) 772802; e-mail kenemb@yahoo.com; Ambassador (vacant).

Korea, Republic: St 1, House No. 2, New Extension, POB 2414, Khartoum; tel. (183) 451136; fax (183) 452822; e-mail ssudan@mofat.go.kr; Ambassador DONG EOK KIM.

Kuwait: Africa Ave, near the Tennis Club, POB 1457, Khartoum; tel. (183) 781525; Ambassador MUNTHIR BADR SALMAN.

Lebanon: St 5, Al-Amarat, Khartoum; tel. (183) 461320; fax (113) 461246; e-mail amliban@hotmail.com; Ambassador SHARBEL STEPHAN.

Libya: 50 Africa Rd, POB 2091, Khartoum; Secretary of People's Bureau (vacant).

Malaysia: St 3, Block 2, al-Amarat, POB 11668, Khartoum; tel. (183) 482763; fax (183) 482762; e-mail malkhtoum@kln.gov.my; internet www.kln.gov.my/web/sdn_khartoum/home; Ambassador Dato' MOHD ASHRI MUDA.

Morocco: St 19, 32, New Extension, POB 2042, Khartoum; tel. (183) 473068; fax (183) 471053; e-mail sifmasoud@sudan.mail.net; Ambassador MUHAMMAD MAA EL-AININE.

Netherlands: St 47, House No. 76, POB 391, Khartoum; tel. (183) 480315; fax (183) 472653; e-mail kha@minbuza.nl; internet sudan.nlambassade.org; Ambassador SUSAN T. BLANKHART.

Nigeria: St 17, Sharia al-Mek Nimr, POB 1538, Khartoum; tel. (183) 779120; fax (183) 771491; e-mail nigeriankhartoum@yahoo.com; Ambassador HALLIRU SODANGI-SHUAIB.

Norway: St 49, House No. 63, POB 13096, Khartoum; tel. (183) 578336; fax (183) 577180; e-mail emb.khartoum@mfa.no; internet www.norway-sudan.org; Ambassador SVEIN SEVJE.

Oman: St 1, New Extension, POB 2839, Khartoum; tel. (183) 471606; fax (183) 471017; Ambassador ABDULLAH BIN-RASHID BIN-ALI AL-MEDELWI.

Pakistan: Dr Mehmood Sharif St, House No. 78, Block 25, POB 1178, Khartoum; tel. (183) 265599; fax (183) 273777; e-mail embkhartoum@yahoo.com; Ambassador MUHAMMAD ALAM BROHI.

Qatar: Elmanshia Block 92H, POB 223, Khartoum; tel. (183) 261113; fax (183) 261116; e-mail qatarembkht@yahoo.com; Ambassador ALI HASSAN ABDULLAH AL-HAMADI.

Romania: Kassala Rd, Plot No. 172–173, Kafouri Area, POB 1494, Khartoum North; tel. (185) 338114; fax (185) 341497; e-mail ambro_khartoum@hotmail.com; Chargé d'affaires a.i. Dr DRAGOS SERBANESCU.

Russia: A10 St, B1, New Extension, POB 1161, Khartoum; tel. (183) 471042; fax (183) 471239; e-mail rfsudan@hotmail.com; Ambassador ENVARBIK M. FAZELIYANOV.

Rwanda: Al-Manshia, Block 28G, St 57, House No. 4, Block 10. POB 243, Khartoum; tel. (183) 278842; fax (183) 155174663; e-mail rwaembassy@gmail.com; internet www.sudan.embassy.gov.rw; Chargé d'affaires Maj. JOSEPH RUTABANA.

Saudi Arabia: St 11, New Extension, Khartoum; tel. (183) 741938; Ambassador MOHAMMED IBN ABAS AL-KALABI.

Somalia: St 23–25, New Extension, POB 1857, Khartoum; tel. (183) 744800; Ambassador Prof. MAHDI ABUKAR.

South Africa: St 11, House No. 16, Block B9, al-Amarat, POB 12137, Khartoum; tel. (183) 585301; fax (183) 585082; e-mail khartoum@foreign.gov.za; Ambassador GRAHAM MAITLAND.

South Sudan: Khartoum; Ambassador MAYAN DUT WOL.

Switzerland: St 15, House No. 7, Amarat, POB 1707, Khartoum; tel. (183) 471010; fax (183) 472804; e-mail kha.vertretung@eda.admin.ch; internet www.eda.admin.ch/khartoum; Ambassador LOUIS-JOSÉ TOURON.

Syria: St 3, New Extension, POB 1139, Khartoum; tel. (183) 471152; fax (183) 471066; Ambassador HABIB ALI ABBAS.

Tunisia: St 15, 35, al-Amarat, Khartoum; tel. (183) 487947; fax (183) 487950; e-mail at_khartoum@yahoo.fr; Ambassador ELOUALID DOUDECH.

Turkey: Baladia St, House No. 21, Block 8H, POB 771, Khartoum; tel. (183) 794215; fax (183) 794218; e-mail hartumbe@gmail.com; Ambassador (vacant).

Uganda: POB 2676, Khartoum; tel. (183) 158571; fax (183) 797868; e-mail ugembkht@hotmail.com; Ambassador BETTY AKECH.

United Arab Emirates: St 3, New Extension, POB 1225, Khartoum; tel. (183) 744476; e-mail uaembassy@sudanmail.net; Ambassador HASSAN AHMED SULIEMAN AL-SHIHI.

United Kingdom: St 10, off Baladia St, POB 801, Khartoum; tel. (183) 777105; fax (183) 776457; e-mail media.khartoum@fco.gov.uk; internet ukinsudan.fco.gov.uk; Ambassador Dr PETER TIBBER.

USA: Kilo 10, Soba, off Wad Medani Highway, POB 699, Khartoum; tel. 1-870-2-2000; fax 1-870-2-2012; internet sudan.usembassy.gov; Chargé d'affaires JOSEPH D. STAFFORD, III.

Yemen: St 11, New Extension, POB 1010, Khartoum; tel. (183) 743918; Ambassador SALAH AL-ANSI.

Judicial System

In September 1983 President Nimeri replaced all existing laws with Islamic (*Shari'a*) law. However, following the coup in April 1985, the *Shari'a* courts were abolished, and it was announced that the previous system of criminal courts was to be revived. In 1987 a new legal code, based on a 'Sudanese legal heritage', was introduced. Islamic law was reintroduced in March 1991, but was not applied in the southern states of Equatoria, Bahr al-Ghazal and Upper Nile.

The Supreme Court is the highest court of justice in the country. There are also Courts of Appeal, district courts, urban and rural courts and various other courts.

Supreme Court: Khartoum; Chief Justice GALAL EL-DIN MUHAMMAD OSMAN.

Religion

The majority of the population of post-secession Sudan are Muslims.

ISLAM

Islam is the state religion. Sudanese Islam has a strong Sufi element, and is estimated to have more than 15m. adherents.

CHRISTIANITY

Sudan Council of Churches: Inter-Church House, St 35, New Extension, POB 469, Khartoum; tel. (183) 742859; e-mail Ramadan.chan@gmail.com; f. 1967; 12 mem. churches; Chair. Fr ANTHONIO; Gen. Sec. ABDALLA ALI.

Roman Catholic Church

Latin Rite

Sudan comprises two archdioceses and seven dioceses. The Roman Catholic Church officially remained undivided following the secession of South Sudan.

Sudan Catholic Bishops' Conference

General Secretariat, POB 6011, Khartoum; tel. (183) 225075. f. 1971; Pres. Mgr RUDOLF DENG MAJAK (Bishop of Wau); Sec.-Gen. JOHN DINGI MARTIN.

Archbishop of Khartoum: Cardinal GABRIEL ZUBEIR WAKO, Catholic Church, POB 49, Khartoum; tel. (183) 782174; fax (183) 783518; e-mail taban_roko@yahoo.com.uk.

Maronite Rite

Maronite Church in Sudan: POB 244, Khartoum; Rev. Fr YOUSEPH NEAMA.

Melkite Rite

Patriarchal Vicariate of Egypt and Sudan: Greek Melkite Catholic Patriarchate, 16 Sharia Daher, 11271 Cairo, Egypt; tel. (2) 5905790; fax (2) 5935398; e-mail grecmelkitecath_egy@hotmail.com; General Patriarchal Vicar in Egypt and Sudan Mgr (JOSEPH) JULES ZEREY (Titular Archbishop of Damietta); Patriarchal Vicar in Sudan Mgr Exarkhos GEORGE BANNA; POB 766, Khartoum; tel. (183) 777910.

Syrian Rite

Syrian Church in Sudan: Under the jurisdiction of the Patriarch of Antioch; Protosyncellus Rt Rev. JOSEPH-CLÉMENT HANNOUCHE (Bishop of Cairo).

Orthodox Churches

Coptic Orthodox Church

Metropolitan of Khartoum, Southern Sudan and Uganda: Rt Rev. ANBA DANIAL, POB 4, Khartoum; tel. (183) 770646; fax (183) 785646; e-mail metaous@email-sudan.net.

Bishop of Atbara, Omdurman and Northern Sudan: Rt Rev. ANBA SARABAMON, POB 628, Omdurman; tel. (183) 550423; fax (183) 556973.

Greek Orthodox Church

Metropolitan of Nubia: POB 47, Khartoum; tel. (183) 772973; Archbishop DIONYSSIOS HADZIVASSILIOU.

The Ethiopian Orthodox Church is also active.

The Anglican Communion

Anglicans are adherents of the (Episcopal) Church of the Province of the Sudan. The Province, with 24 dioceses and about 1m. adherents, was established in 1976.

Archbishop in Sudan and Bishop of Juba: Most Rev. DANIEL DENG BUL YAK, ECS Liaison Office, POB 604, Khartoum; tel. (11) 485720; fax (11) 485717; e-mail ecsprovince@hotmail.com; internet www.sudan.anglican.org.

Other Christian Churches

Evangelical Church: POB 57, Khartoum; c. 1,500 mems; administers schools, literature centre and training centre; Chair. Rev. RADI ELIAS.

The Lutheran Church of Sudan: Omdurman Elarda-Markh Studo, POB 12354, Omdurman Khartoum; tel. 912972828 (mobile); e-mail rev_yousifkh@hotmail.com; Bishop AKILLA YOUSIF ELTAHIR; 10,650 mems (2010).

Presbyterian Church: POB 40, Malakal; autonomous since 1956; 67,000 mems (1985); Gen. Sec. Rev. THOMAS MALUIT.

The Africa Inland Church, the Sudan Interior Church and the Sudanese Church of Christ are also active.

The Press

Following the secession of South Sudan, the licences of six newspapers, partially or wholly owned by South Sudanese nationals, were revoked by the Sudanese National Council for Press and Publications, citing a law that bars foreigners from owning newspapers. The list includes: Ajras Al-Hurriya, Khartoum Monitor, Juba Post, Sudan Tribune, Advocate and The Democrat.

DAILIES

Abbar al-Youm: Khartoum; tel. (183) 779396; daily; Editor AHMED AL-BALAL AL-TAYEB.

Al-Anbaa: Khartoum; tel. (183) 466523; f. 1998; Editor-in-Chief NAJIB ADAM QAMAR AL-DIN.

Al-Nasr: Khartoum; tel. (183) 772494; Editor Col YOUNIS MAHMOUD.

Al-Rai al-Akhar: Khartoum; tel. (183) 777934; daily; Editor MOHI AL-DIN TITTAWI.

Al-Rai al-Amm: Khartoum; tel. (183) 778182; fax (183) 772176; e-mail info@rayaam.net; internet www.rayaam.net; daily; Editor SALAH MUHAMMAD IBRAHIM.

Al-Wan: Khartoum; tel. (183) 775036; e-mail alwaan@cybergates.net; daily; independent; pro-Govt; Editor HOUSSEN KHOGALI.

Sudan Mirror: POB 59163, 00200 Nairobi, Kenya; tel. and fax (20) 3876439; e-mail daneiffe@gmail.com; internet www.sudanmirror.co.ke; f. 2003; Dir DANIEL EIFFE.

Sudan Standard: Ministry of Culture and Information, Khartoum; daily; English.

PERIODICALS

Al-Guwwat al-Musallaha (The Armed Forces): Khartoum; f. 1969; publs a weekly newspaper and monthly magazine for the armed forces; Editor-in-Chief Maj. MAHMOUD GALANDER; circ. 7,500.

New Horizon: POB 2651, Khartoum; tel. (183) 777913; f. 1976; publ. by the Sudan House for Printing and Publishing; weekly; English; political and economic affairs, devt, home and international news; Editor AL-SIR HASSAN FADL; circ. 7,000.

Sudanow: POB 2651, Khartoum; tel. (183) 777913; f. 1976; publ. by the Sudan House for Printing and Publishing; monthly; English; political and economic affairs, arts, social affairs and diversions; publ. online only since 2010; Editor-in-Chief MOHAMED OSMAN ADAM; circ. 10,000.

NEWS AGENCIES

Sudan News Agency (SUNA): Sharia al-Gamhouria, POB 1506, Khartoum; tel. (183) 775770; e-mail suna@sudanet.net; internet www.suna-sd.net; Dir-Gen. Awad Jadain Mohi-Eddin.

Sudanese Press Agency: Khartoum; f. 1985; owned by journalists.

PRESS ASSOCIATION

Sudanese Media Center (SMC): 21 October St, Khartoum East, Khartoum; tel. (183) 787604; fax (183) 787605; e-mail info@smc.sd; internet smc.sd.

Publishers

Ahmad Abd al-Rahman al-Tikeine: POB 299, Port Sudan.

Al-Ayyam Press Co Ltd: Aboulela Bldg, POB 363, United Nations Sq., Khartoum; f. 1953; general fiction and non-fiction, arts, poetry, reference, newspapers, magazines; Man. Dir Beshir Muhammad Said.

Al-Sahafa Publishing and Printing House: POB 1228, Khartoum; f. 1961; newspapers, pamphlets, fiction and govt publs.

Al-Salam Co Ltd: POB 944, Khartoum.

Claudios S. Fellas: POB 641, Khartoum.

Khartoum University Press: POB 321, Khartoum; tel. (183) 776653; f. 1964; academic, general and educational in Arabic and English; Man. Dir Ali El-Mak.

GOVERNMENT PUBLISHING HOUSE

El-Asma Printing Press: POB 38, Khartoum.

Broadcasting and Communications

TELECOMMUNICATIONS

In 2011 Sudan Telecom provided both fixed-line telephone services and mobile telephone services. In addition, there was one other fixed-line operator and two other mobile operators in the country.

Canar Telecommunication (Canartel): Al-Qibla Centre, Block 37, cnr Al-Sahafa and Madani Rds, POB 8182, Khartoum; tel. (15) 5550000; fax (15) 5550055; e-mail support@canar.sd; internet www.canar.sd; f. 2005; operates fixed-line telephone and internet services; CEO Ali Ahmed Yarouf.

MTN-Sudan: Manchiya East 60th Ave, Block 64, District 1, POB 34611111, Khartoum; tel. (92) 1111111; e-mail customercare@mtn.sd; internet www.mtn.sd; f. 2005; mobile cellular telephone provider; CEO Hassan Jaber; 1.4m. subscribers (2007).

Sudan Telecom Co (SUDATEL): Sudatel Tower, POB 11155, Khartoum; tel. (183) 797400; fax (183) 782322; e-mail info@sudatel.net; internet www.sudatel.sd; f. 1993; Chair. Abdelaziz Osman; CEO Imad Addin Hussein Ahmed.

Zain: Khartoum; tel. 91230000 (mobile); e-mail info@sd.zain.com; internet www.sd.zain.com; f. 1997 as MobiTel; name changed as above in 2007; provides mobile cellular telephone services; Man. Dir Elfatih M. Erwa.

Regulatory Authority

National Telecommunication Corpn: NTC Tower, Buri, North to Manshya Bridge, POB 2869, Khartoum; tel. (183) 484489; fax 0187171140; e-mail customer@ntc.gov.sd; internet www.ntc.gov.sd; Dir-Gen. Dr Izzeldin Kamil Amin.

BROADCASTING

Radio

Sudan Radio: POB 572, Omdurman; tel. (187) 559315; fax (187) 560566; e-mail info@sudanradio.info; internet www.sudanradio.info; f. 1940; state-controlled service broadcasting daily in Arabic, English, French and Swahili; Dir-Gen. Mutasim Fadul Usud.

Sudan Radio Service (SRS): Umeme Plaza, Old Naivasha Rd, off Ngong Rd, Dagoretti, POB 4392, 00100 Nairobi, Kenya; tel. (20) 2346218; fax (20) 2346216; e-mail srs@sudanradio.org; internet www.sudanradio.org; f. 2003; by the Education Development Center with support from the United States Agency for International Development; broadcasts in 10 languages including Dinka, Bari, Nuer, Zande, Shilluk, Arabic, Juba-Arabic and English; Chief of Party Charles Northrip.

Voice of Sudan: e-mail informationsec@ndasudan.org; active since 1995; run by the National Democratic Alliance; Arabic and English.

Television

Sudan Television: POB 1094, Omdurman; tel. (15) 550022; internet www.sudantv.net; f. 1962; state-controlled; 60 hours of programmes per week; Dir-Gen. Mohammed Hatem Suleiman.

Finance

(cap. = capital; res = reserves; dep. = deposits; m. = million; brs = branches; amounts in new Sudanese pounds, unless otherwise indicated)

BANKING

All domestic banks are controlled by the Bank of Sudan. Foreign banks were permitted to resume operations in 1976. In December 1985 the Government banned the establishment of any further banks. It was announced in December 1990 that Sudan's banking system was to be reorganized to comply with Islamic principles. In May 2000 the Bank of Sudan issued new policy guidelines under which Sudan's banks were to merge into six banking groups to improve their financial strength and international competitiveness; plans for implementing this merger were ongoing in 2010. In 2009 there were a total of 38 banks in Sudan. Following the secession of South Sudan, a new currency, also called the pound, was introduced in Sudan on 24 July 2011.

Central Bank

Bank of Sudan: Gamhoria St, POB 313, Khartoum; tel. (183) 782246; fax (183) 787226; e-mail sudanbank@sudanmail.net; internet www.bankofsudan.org; f. 1960; bank of issue; cap. and res 274.2m., dep. 8,695.2m. (Dec. 2009); Gov. Mohammad Khair al-Zubair; 13 brs.

Commercial Banks

Al-Baraka Bank: Baraka Tower, Zubeir Pasha St, POB 3583, Khartoum; tel. (183) 785810; fax (183) 778948; e-mail khairy@albarakasudan.com; internet www.albaraka.com.sd; f. 1984; 87.8% owned by Al-Baraka Banking Group (Bahrain); investment and export promotion; cap. SDD 3,353.6m., res SDD 4,042.7m., dep. SDD 37,220.2m. (Dec. 2006); Chair. Osman Ahmed Suliman; Gen. Man. Abdallah Khairy Hamid; 24 brs.

Al-Shamal Islamic Bank: Al-Shamal Islamic Tower, al-Sayid Abd al-Rahman St, POB 10036, 11111 Khartoum; tel. (183) 779078; fax (183) 772661; e-mail info@alshamalbank.com; internet www.alshamalbank.com; f. 1990; total assets SDD 18,258.0m. (Dec. 2003); Pres. Gafaar Osman Fagir; Gen. Man. Abdelmoneim Hassan Sayed; 17 brs.

Bank of Khartoum: Intersection Gamhouria St and El-Gaser St, POB 1008, Khartoum; tel. 156660000; fax (183) 781120; e-mail info@bok.sd; internet www.bok-sd.com; f. 1913; 60% owned by Dubai Islamic Bank PJSC (United Arab Emirates); absorbed National Export/Import Bank and Unity Bank in 1993; cap. 92.9m., dep. 2,818.2m. (Dec. 2009); Chair. Dr Khalid M. Ali Al Kamda; Gen. Man. Fadi Salim Al-Faqih; 118 brs.

Blue Nile Mashreg Bank: Barlaman St, POB 984, Khartoum; tel. (183) 776092; fax (183) 782562; e-mail info@bluemashreg.com; internet www.bluemashreg.com; f. 1983; cap. 112.2m., res 173.5m., dep. 618.6m. (Dec. 2011); Chair. Muhammad Ismail Mohammad; Gen. Man. Isam Osman Mahgoub.

Farmers Commercial Bank: POB 11984, Al-Qasr Ave, Khartoum; tel. (183) 774960; fax (183) 773687; e-mail mozarea@alnlilin.com; internet www.fcbsudan.com; f. 1960 as Sudan Commercial Bank; name changed as above in 1999 following merger with Farmers Bank for Investment and Rural Development; cap. 69.7m., res 13.5m., dep. 377.1m. (Dec. 2009); Chair. al-Tayb Elobeid Badr; Pres. Suliman Hashim Mohamed Toum; 28 brs.

National Bank of Sudan: Kronfli Bldg, Zubeir Pasha St, POB 1183, Khartoum; tel. (183) 778153; fax (183) 779545; e-mail contactus@nbs.com.sd; internet www.nbs.com.sd; f. 1982; 70% owned by Bank Audi SAL, Lebanon; cap. 150.0m., res 39.3m., dep. 164.9m. (Dec. 2009); Chair. Dr Imad Itani; 13 brs in Sudan, 2 abroad.

Omdurman National Bank: Al-Qaser Ave, POB 11522, Khartoum; tel. (183) 770400; fax (183) 777263; e-mail info@omd-bank.com; internet www.omd-bank.com; f. 1993; cap. 523.3m., res 116.9m., dep. 5,597.0m. (Dec. 2009); Gen. Man. Abdel Rahman Hassan Abdel Rahman; 17 brs; 852 employees.

Sudanese French Bank: Plot No. 6, Block A, Al-Qasr St, POB 2775, Khartoum; tel. (183) 771730; fax (183) 790391; e-mail info@sfbank.net; internet www.sfbank.net; f. 1978 as Sudanese Investment Bank; name changed as above in 1993; cap. 100.1m., res 34.0m., dep. 896.2m. (Dec. 2009); Chair. Osman Salman Mohamed Nour; Gen. Man. Massad Mohammed Ahmed Abdul Karim; 20 brs.

Tadamon Islamic Bank: Baladia St, POB 3154, Khartoum; tel. (183) 771505; fax (183) 773840; e-mail info@tadamonbank-sd.com; internet www.tadamonbank-sd.com; f. 1981; cap. 101.6m., res 2,134.1m., dep. 23,216.9m. (Dec. 2012); Chair. Dr HASSAN OSMAN SAKOTA; Gen. Man. ABBAS ABDALLA ABBAS; 20 brs.

Foreign Banks

Byblos Bank Africa Ltd: 21 al-Amarat St, POB 8121, Khartoum; tel. (183) 566444; fax (183) 566454; e-mail Byblosbankafrica@byblosbank.com; internet www.byblosbank.com.lb; 65% owned by Byblos Bank SAL (Lebanon); f. 2003; cap. 93.3m., res 43.8m., dep. 394.2m. (Dec. 2009); Chair. Dr FRANÇOIS S. BASSIL; Gen. Man. NADIM GHANTOUS.

Faisal Islamic Bank (Sudan) (Saudi Arabia): Faih'a Bldg, Ali al-Latif St, POB 2415, Khartoum; tel. (183) 777920; fax (183) 780193; e-mail fibsudan@fibsudan.com; internet www.fibsudan.com; f. 1977; cap. 110.0m., res 10.4m., dep. 1,800.0m. (Dec. 2009); Chair. Prince MUHAMMAD AL-FAISAL AL-SA'UD; Gen. Man. ALI OMAR IBRAHIM FARAH; 30 brs.

Saudi Sudanese Bank: Baladia St, POB 1773, Khartoum; tel. (183) 780307; fax (183) 781836; e-mail saudi-sud@saudisb.sd; internet www.saudisb.sd; f. 1986; cap. 60.0m., res –49.8m., dep. 372.8m. (Dec. 2009); Chair. FAWZI IBRAHIM MAHMOUD WASSFI; Gen. Man. ABDUL ALIM MOHAMMED ALI (acting); 13 brs.

Sudanese Egyptian Bank (SEB): Ingaz Rd, Elsafia, Khartoum; tel. (183) 745583; fax (183) 745580; e-mail msiralkhatim@sebank.sd; internet www.sebank.sd; f. 2005; total assets 422.6m. (Dec. 2008); Man. Dir AMR BAHAA; 5 brs.

Development Banks

Agricultural Bank of Sudan: Ghoumhoria Ave, POB 1263, Khartoum; tel. (183) 777432; fax (183) 778296; e-mail agribank@yahoo.com; f. 1957; cap. SDD 5,200.0m., res SDD 3,609.4m., dep. SDD 18,864.9m. (Dec. 2003); provides finance for agricultural projects; Pres. AL-SAYID GAFFAR MUHAMMAD AL-HASSAN; Gen. Man. AL-SAYID AL-KINDI MUHAMMAD OSMAN; 40 brs.

Islamic Co-operative Development Bank (ISCOB): Et-Tanmha Tower, Kolyat Eltib St, POB 62, Khartoum; tel. (183) 777789; fax (183) 777715; e-mail info@iscob.com; internet www.iscob.com; f. 1983; cap. and res SDD 3,821.0m., total assets SDD 28,250.4m. (Dec. 2003); Chair. El-Haj ATTA EL-MANAN IDRIS; 6 brs.

El-Nilein Bank: United Nations Sq., POB 1722, Khartoum; tel. (183) 771984; fax (183) 785811; e-mail info@nidbg.com; internet www.nidbg.com; f. 1993 by merger of En-Nilein Bank and Industrial Bank of Sudan; name changed as above in 2007; 99% owned by Bank of Sudan; provides tech. and financial assistance for private sector industrial projects and acquires shares in industrial enterprises; cap. SDD 3,282.6m., res SDD –861.4m., dep. SDD 54,046.9m. (Dec. 2005); Man. Dir MOHAMED ABBAS AGAB; 37 brs.

NIMA Development and Investment Bank: Hashim Hago Bldg, As-Suk al-Arabi, POB 665, Khartoum; tel. (183) 779496; fax (183) 781854; f. 1982 as National Devt Bank; name changed as above 1998; 90% owned by NIMA Groupe, 10% private shareholders; finances or co-finances economic and social devt projects; Dir-Gen. SALIM AS-SAFI HUGIR; 6 brs.

Real Estates Commercial Bank: Baladia St, POB 309, Khartoum; tel. (183) 777917; fax (183) 779465; f. 1967; mortgage bank financing private sector urban housing devt; Chair. Eng. MUHAMMAD ALI EL-AMIN; 6 brs.

STOCK EXCHANGE

Sudanese Stock Exchange: Al-Baraka Tower, 5th Floor, POB 10835, Khartoum; tel. (183) 776235; fax (183) 776134; f. 1995; Chair. HAMZA MUHAMMAD JENAWI; 27 mems.

INSURANCE

African Insurance Co (Sudan) Ltd: New Abu Ella Bldg, Parliament Ave, Khartoum; tel. (183) 173402; fax (183) 177988; f. 1977; fire, accident, marine and motor; Gen. Man. AL-NOMAN AL-SANUSI.

Blue Nile Insurance Co (Sudan) Ltd: Al-Qasr Ave, Blue Nile Insurance Bldg, POB 2215, Khartoum; tel. (183) 170580; fax (183) 172405; internet www.blue-nile-insurance.com; f. 1965; Gen. Man. MUHAMMAD AL-AMIN MIRGHANI.

Foja International Insurance Co Ltd: POB 879, Khartoum; tel. (183) 784470; fax (183) 783248; fire, accident, marine, motor and animal; Gen. Man. MAMOON IBRAHIM ABD ALLA.

General Insurance Co (Sudan) Ltd: El-Mek Nimr St, POB 1555, Khartoum; tel. (183) 780616; fax (183) 772122; f. 1961; Gen. Man. AL-SAMAWL AL-SAYED HAFIZ.

Islamic Insurance Co Ltd: Al-Faiha Commercial Bldg, Ali Abdullatif St, POB 2776, Khartoum; tel. (183) 772656; fax (183) 778959;

e-mail islamicins@sudanmail.net; internet www.islamicinsur.com; f. 1979; all classes; CEO Dr KAMAL JADKAREEM.

Khartoum Insurance Co Ltd: Al-Taminat Bldg, Al-Jamhouriya St, POB 737, Khartoum; tel. (183) 778647; f. 1953; Chair. MUDAWI M. AHMAD; Gen. Dir YOUSIF KHAIRY.

Juba Insurance Co Ltd: Al-Baladiya St, Sayen Osnam Al-Amin Bldg, 2nd Floor, POB 10043, Khartoum; tel. (183) 783245; fax (183) 781617; Gen. Man. ABDUL AAL AL-DAWI.

Middle East Insurance Co Ltd: Al-Qasr St, Kuronfuli Bldg, 1st Floor, POB 3070, Khartoum; tel. (183) 772202; fax (183) 779266; f. 1981; fire, marine, motor and general liability; Chair. AHMAD I. MALIK; Gen. Dir ALI MUHAMMAD AHMED EL-FADL.

Sudanese Insurance and Reinsurance Co Ltd: Al-Gamhouria Ave, Nasr Sq., Abd Al-Rahman Makawi Bldg, 3rd Floor, POB 2332, Khartoum; tel. (183) 777796; fax (183) 771820; e-mail info@sudinreco.com; internet www.sudinreco.com; f. 1967; Gen. Man. HASSAN EL-SAYED MUHAMMAD ALI.

United Insurance Co (Sudan) Ltd: United Insurance Tower, 9th and 10th Floors, Parliament St, POB 318, Khartoum; tel. (183) 776630; fax (183) 770783; e-mail info@unitedinsurance.ws; internet www.unitedinsurance.ws; f. 1968; Chair. HASHIM EL-BERIER; Gen. Man. MOHAMAD ABDIN BABIKER.

Trade and Industry

GOVERNMENT AGENCIES

Agricultural Research Corpn (ARC): POB 126, Wadi Medani; tel. (51) 1842226; fax (51) 1843213; e-mail arcdg@sudanmail.net; internet www.arcsudan.sd; f. 1967; Dir-Gen. ADIL OMER SALIH ABDEL RAHIM (acting).

Animal Production Public Corpn: POB 624, Khartoum; tel. (183) 778555; Gen. Man. Dr FOUAD RAMADAN HAMID.

Gum Arabic Co Ltd: POB 857, Khartoum; tel. (183) 462111; fax (183) 467923; e-mail info@gac-arabicgum.com; internet www.gac-arabicgum.com; f. 1969; Chair. ABD EL-HAMID MUSA KASHA; Gen. Man. HASSAN SAAD AHMED.

Industrial Production Corpn: POB 1034, Khartoum; tel. (183) 771278; f. 1976; Dir-Gen. OSMAN TAMMAM.

Cement and Building Materials Sector Co-ordination Office: POB 2241, Khartoum; tel. (183) 774269; Dir T. M. KHOGALI.

Food Industries Corpn: POB 2341, Khartoum; tel. (183) 775463; Dir MUHAMMAD AL-GHALI SULIMAN.

Leather Industries Corpn: POB 1639, Khartoum; tel. (183) 778187; f. 1986; Man. Dir IBRAHIM SALIH ALI.

Oil Corpn: POB 64, Khartoum North; tel. (183) 332044; Gen. Man. BUKHARI MAHMOUD BUKHARI.

Spinning and Weaving General Co Ltd: POB 765, Khartoum; tel. (183) 774306; f. 1975; Dir MUHAMMAD SALIH MUHAMMAD ABDALLAH.

Sudan Tea Co Ltd: POB 1219, Khartoum; tel. (183) 781261.

Sudanese Mining Corpn: POB 1034, Khartoum; tel. (183) 770840; f. 1975; Dir IBRAHIM MUDAWI BABIKER.

Sugar and Distilling Industry Corpn: POB 511, Khartoum; tel. (183) 778417; Man. MIRGHANI AHMAD BABIKER.

Mechanized Farming Corpn: POB 2482, Khartoum; Man. Dir AWAD AL-KARIM AL-YASS.

National Cotton and Trade Co Ltd: POB 1552, Khartoum; tel. (183) 80040; f. 1970; Chair. ABD EL-ATI A. MEKKI; Man. Dir ABD AL-RAHMAN A. MONIEM; Gen. Man. ZUBAIR MUHAMMAD AL-BASHIR.

Port Sudan Cotton Trade Co Ltd: POB 590, Port Sudan; POB 590, Khartoum; Gen. Man. SAÏD MUHAMMAD ADAM.

Public Agricultural Production Corpn: POB 538, Khartoum; Chair. and Man. Dir ABDALLAH BAYOUMO; Sec. SAAD AL-DIN MUHAMMAD ALI.

Public Corpn for Building and Construction: POB 2110, Khartoum; tel. (183) 774544; Dir NAIM AL-DIN.

Public Corpn for Irrigation and Excavation: POB 619, Khartoum; tel. (183) 780167; Gen. Sec. OSMAN AL-NUR.

Public Corpn for Oil Products and Pipelines: POB 1704, Khartoum; tel. (183) 778290; Gen. Man. ABD AL-RAHMAN SULIMAN.

Rahad Corpn: POB 2523, Khartoum; tel. (183) 775175; financed by the World Bank, Kuwait and the USA; Man. Dir HASSAN SAAD ABDALLA.

State Trading Corpn: POB 211, Khartoum; tel. (183) 778555; Chair. E. R. M. TOM.

Automobile Corpn: POB 221, Khartoum; tel. (183) 778555; importer of vehicles and spare parts; Gen. Man. DAFALLA AHMAD SIDDIQ.

Captrade Engineering and Automobile Services Co Ltd: POB 97, Khartoum; tel. (183) 789265; fax (183) 775544; e-mail cap1@sudanmail.net; f. 1925; importers and distributors of engineering and automobile equipment; Gen. Man. Essam Mohd el-Hassan Kambal.

Gezira Trade and Services Co: POB 17, Port Sudan; tel. (311) 825109; fax (311) 822029; e-mail gtsportsudan@hotmail.com; f. 1980; importer of agricultural machinery, spare parts, electrical and office equipment, foodstuffs, clothes and footwear; exporter of oilseeds, grains, hides and skins and livestock; provides shipping insurance and warehousing services; agents for Lloyds and P & I Club; Chair. Nasr el-Din M. Omer.

Khartoum Commercial and Shipping Co: POB 221, Khartoum; tel. (183) 778555; f. 1982; import, export and shipping services, insurance and manufacturing; Gen. Man. Idris M. Salih.

Silos and Storage Corpn: POB 1183, Khartoum; stores and handles agricultural products; Gen. Man. Ahmad al-Taieb Harhoof.

Sudan Cotton Co Ltd: POB 1672, Khartoum; tel. (183) 775755; fax (183) 770703; e-mail sccl@sudanmail.net; internet www .sudan-cotton.com; f. 1970; exports and markets cotton; Chair. Abbas Abd al-Bagi Hammad; Dir-Gen. Dr Abdin Muhammad Ali.

Sudan Gezira Board: POB 884, HQ Barakat Wadi Medani, Gezira Province; tel. 2412; Sales Office, POB 884, Khartoum; tel. (183) 740145; f. 1950; responsible for Sudan's main cotton-producing area; the Gezira scheme is a partnership between the Govt, the tenants and the Board. The Govt provides the land and is responsible for irrigation. Tenants pay a land and water charge and receive the work proceeds. The Board provides agricultural services at cost, technical supervision and execution of govt agricultural policies relating to the scheme. Tenants pay a percentage of their proceeds to the Social Development Fund. The total potential cultivable area of the Gezira scheme is c. 850,000 ha and the total area under systematic irrigation is c. 730,000 ha. In addition to cotton, groundnuts, sorghum, wheat, rice, pulses and vegetables are grown for the benefit of tenant farmers; Man. Dir Prof. Fathi Muhammad Khalifa.

Sudan Oilseeds Co Ltd: Parliament Ave, POB 167, Khartoum; tel. (183) 780120; f. 1974; 58% state-owned; exporter of oilseeds (groundnuts, sesame seeds and castor beans); importer of foodstuffs and other goods; Chair. Sadiq Karar al-Tayeb; Gen. Man. Kamal Abd al-Halim.

Sudan Petroleum Corpn Ltd (Sudapet): POB 2649, Khartoum; tel. (183) 776684; fax (183) 778979; e-mail secretarygeneral@spc.sd; internet www.spc.sd; f. 1998; Chair. Dr Awad Ahmed al-Jazz; Sec.-Gen. Dr Omer Mohamed Kheir.

DEVELOPMENT CORPORATIONS

Sudan Development Corpn (SDC): 21 al-Amarat, POB 710, Khartoum; tel. (183) 472151; fax (183) 472148; f. 1974 to promote and co-finance devt projects with special emphasis on projects in the agricultural, agri-business and industrial sectors; cap. p.u. US $200m.; Man. Dir Abdel Wahab Ahmed Hamza.

Sudan Rural Development Co Ltd (SRDC): POB 2190, Khartoum; tel. (183) 773855; fax (183) 773235; e-mail srdfc@hotmail .com; f. 1980; SDC has 27% shareholding; cap. p.u. US $20m.; Gen. Man. El-Awad Abdalla H. Hijazi.

Sudan Rural Development Finance Co (SRDFC): POB 2190, Khartoum; tel. (183) 773855; fax (183) 773235; f. 1980; Gen. Man. Omran Muhammad Ali.

CHAMBERS OF COMMERCE

Union of Sudanese Chambers of Commerce: POB 81, Khartoum; tel. (183) 772346; fax (183) 780748; e-mail chamber@ sudanchamber.org; f. 1908; Pres. al-Tayeb Ahmed Osman; Sec.-Gen. Ibrahim Muhammad Osman.

INDUSTRIAL ASSOCIATION

Sudanese Chambers of Industries Association: Africa St, POB 2565, Khartoum; tel. (183) 471716; fax (183) 471720; e-mail info@ sudanindustries.org; internet www.sudanindustry.org; f. 1974; Chair. Nour Eldin Saeed al-Said; Sec.-Gen. Dr El Fatih Abbas.

UTILITIES

Public Electricity and Water Corpn: POB 1380, Khartoum; tel. (183) 81021; Dir Dr Yasin al-Haj Abdin.

CO-OPERATIVE SOCIETIES

There are about 600 co-operative societies, of which 570 are officially registered.

Central Co-operative Union: POB 2492, Khartoum; tel. (183) 780624; largest co-operative union operating in 15 provinces.

TRADE UNIONS

Federations

Sudan Workers Trade Unions Federation (SWTUF): POB 2258, Khartoum; tel. (183) 777463; includes 42 trade unions representing c. 1.75m. public service and private sector workers; affiliated to the Int. Confed. of Arab Trade Unions and the Org. of African Trade Union Unity; Pres. Ibrahim Ghanour; Gen. Sec. Yousuf Abu Shama Hamed.

Sudanese Federation of Employees and Professionals Trade Unions: POB 2398, Khartoum; tel. (183) 773818; f. 1975; includes 54 trade unions representing 250,000 mems; Pres. Ibrahim Awadallah; Sec.-Gen. Kamal al-Din Muhammad Abdallah.

Transport

RAILWAYS

The total length of railway in operation in 2002 was 5,978 route-km. The main line runs from Wadi Halfa, on the Egyptian border, to al-Obeid, via Khartoum. Lines from Atbara and Sinnar connect with Port Sudan. There are lines from Sinnar to Damazin on the Blue Nile (227 km) and from Aradeiba to Nyala in the south-western province of Darfur (689 km), with a 446-km branch line from Babanousa to Wau in Bahr al-Ghazal province. The latter was reopened in 2010, having ceased operations during the civil war. In 2009 plans were announced for the construction of a 10,000-km transcontinental railway project linking Port Sudan with Dakar, Senegal.

Sudan Railways Corpn (SRC): Sudan Railways Corpn Bldg, al-Tabia St, POB 1812, Khartoum; tel. (183) 774009; fax (183) 770652; internet www.sudanrailways.gov.sd; f. 1875; Chair. Mohammed Ahmed; Gen. Man. Hamza Mohamed Osman.

ROADS

Roads in Sudan, other than town roads, are only cleared tracks and often impassable immediately after rain. Over 48,000 km of tracks are classed as 'motorable'; there were 3,160 km of main roads and 739 km of secondary roads in 1985. A 484-km highway links Khartoum, Haiya and Port Sudan.

National Transport Corpn: POB 723, Khartoum; Gen. Man. Mohi al-Din Hassan Muhammad Nur.

Public Corpn for Roads and Bridges: POB 756, Khartoum; tel. (183) 770794; f. 1976; Chair. Abd al-Rahman Haboud; Dir-Gen. Abdou Muhammad Abdou.

INLAND WATERWAYS

The total length of navigable waterways served by passenger and freight services is 4,068 km, of which approximately 1,723 km is open all year. From the Egyptian border to Wadi Halfa and Khartoum navigation is limited by cataracts to short stretches, but the White Nile from Khartoum to Juba, in South Sudan, is almost always navigable.

River Navigation Corpn: Khartoum; f. 1970; jtly owned by Govts of Egypt and Sudan; operates services between Aswan and Wadi Halfa.

River Transport Corpn (RTC): POB 284, Khartoum North; operates 2,500 route-km of steamers on the Nile; Chair. Ali Amir Taha.

SHIPPING

Port Sudan, on the Red Sea, 784 km from Khartoum, and Suakin are the only commercial seaports. In December 2012 Sudan's flag registered fleet comprised 11 vessels, totalling 23,031 grt.

Axis Trading Co Ltd: POB 1574, Khartoum; tel. (183) 775875; f. 1967; Chair. Hassan A. M. Suliman.

Red Sea Shipping and Services Co: POB 308, Khartoum; tel. (183) 580885; fax (183) 5119090; e-mail redseaco@redsea-sd.com; internet www.redsea-sd.com; Gen. Man. Awad Hag Ali Hamed.

Sea Ports Corpn: Port Sudan; tel. (311) 822061; fax (311) 822258; e-mail info@sudanports.gov.sd; internet sudanports.gov.sd; f. 1906; Gen. Man. Jalal Eldin Shilia.

Sea Pride Enterprise: POB 76, Port Sudan; tel. (311) 820583; fax (311) 825220; e-mail info@spesudan.com; internet www.spesudan .com; f. 1932; fmrly Sea Prince Enterprise; Man. Dir Alnasser Sidki.

Sudan Shipping Line Ltd: POB 426, Port Sudan; tel. 2655; POB 1731, Khartoum; tel. (183) 780017; f. 1960; 10 vessels totalling 54,277 dwt operating between the Red Sea and western Mediterranean, northern Europe and United Kingdom; Chair. Ismail Bakheit; Gen. Man. Salah al-Din Omer al-Aziz.

United African Shipping Co: POB 339, Khartoum; tel. (183) 780967; Gen. Man. Muhammad Taha al-Gindi.

CIVIL AVIATION

In June 2005 the Government announced that preliminary construction work had been completed for a new international airport at a site 40 km south-west of Khartoum. The airport was expected to open in 2012. In 2010 there were 17 airports in Sudan, of which seven were international airports.

Civil Aviation Authority: Sharia Sayed Abd al-Rahman, POB 430, Khartoum; tel. (183) 787757; fax (183) 779715; e-mail info@caa.gov.sd; internet www.caa-sudan.net; f. 1936; Dir-Gen. ABOU BAKR GAAFAR AHMAD.

Azza Transport: Mak Nimir St, POB 11586, Khartoum; tel. (183) 783761; fax (183) 770408; e-mail info@azzatransport.com; internet www.azzatransport.com; f. 1993; charter and dedicated freight services to Africa and the Middle East; Man. Dir Dr GIBRIL I. MOHAMED.

Badr Airlines: Arkaweet Block 65, Bldg No. 393, POB 6899, Khartoum; tel. 249912327000 (mobile); fax 249155144662 (mobile); e-mail badr@badrairlines.com; internet www.badrairlines.com; operates cargo and passenger air services for humanitarian aid.

Sudan Airways Co Ltd: Sudan Airways Complex, 161 Obeid Khatim St, Riadh Block No. 10, POB 253, Khartoum; tel. (183) 243738; fax (183) 115951; e-mail gm@sudanair.com; internet www.sudanair.com; f. 1947; internal flights and international services to Africa, the Middle East and Europe; Man. Dir ALOBIED FADLULMULA ALI.

Trans Arabian Air Transport (TAAT): POB 1461, Africa St, Khartoum; tel. (183) 451568; fax (183) 451544; e-mail ftaats@sudanmail.net; f. 1983; dedicated freight services to Africa, Europe and Middle East; Man. Dir Capt. EL-FATI ABDIN.

United Arabian Airlines: POB 3687, Office No. 3, Elekhwa Bldg, Atbara St, Khartoum; tel. (183) 773025; fax (183) 784402; e-mail krthq@uaa.com; f. 1995; charter and dedicated freight services to Africa and the Middle East; Man. Dir M. KORDOFANI.

Tourism

Although tourism in Sudan remains relatively undeveloped, the eastern Red Sea coast and Nile tributaries offer opportunities for water sports. Other attractions include ancient Egyptian remains and the Al-Dinder National Tourist Park, a game reserve established in 1935. In 1991 Sudan's first Marine National Park opened on Sanganeb atoll. There was an estimated total of 536,000 foreign visitor arrivals in Sudan in 2011. Receipts from tourism in 2010 were US $94m.

Public Corpn of Tourism and Hotels: POB 7104, Khartoum; tel. (183) 781764; f. 1977; Dir-Gen. Maj.-Gen. EL-KHATIM MUHAMMAD FADL.

Defence

As assessed at November 2012, the armed forces comprised: army an estimated 240,000; navy an estimated 1,300; air force 3,000. A paramilitary Popular Defence Force included 17,500 active members and 85,000 reserves. Military service is compulsory for males aged 18–30 years and lasts for two years.

Defence Expenditure: Budgeted at an estimated US $1,160m. for 2011.

Chief of Staff of the Air Forces and the Air Defence Forces: Gen. MOHYDEEN AHMED ABDALLA.

Chief of Staff of the Ground Forces: Gen. MUSTAFA OSMAN OBEID.

Chief of Staff of the Marine Forces: Gen. MOHAMED FADL.

Education

The Government provides free primary education from the ages of six to 13 years. Secondary education begins at 14 years of age and lasts for up to three years. According to UNESCO estimates, enrolment at primary schools in 2008/09 was equivalent to 73% of children in the relevant age-group (boys 76%; girls 69%), while in that year enrolment at secondary schools was equivalent to 39% of children in the relevant age-group (boys 41%; girls 36%). There are 26 public universities in Sudan.

SURINAME

Introductory Survey

LOCATION, CLIMATE, LANGUAGE, RELIGION, FLAG, CAPITAL

The Republic of Suriname lies on the north-east coast of South America. It is bordered by Guyana to the west, by French Guiana to the east, and by Brazil to the south. The climate is sub-tropical, with fairly heavy rainfall and average temperatures of between 21°C (70°F) and 30°C (86°F). Average annual rainfall varies from 3,720 mm (146 ins) in the north to 804 mm (32 ins) in the south. The official language is Dutch. The other main languages are Hindustani and Javanese. The majority of the people can speak the native language Sranang Tongo, a Creole language known as Negro English or taki-taki, while Chinese, English, French and Spanish are also used. The principal religions are Christianity (professed by about 48% of the population), Hinduism (24%) and Islam (16%). The national flag (proportions 2 by 3) has five horizontal stripes: a broad central band of red (with a five-pointed yellow star in the centre), edged with white, between bands of green. The capital is Paramaribo.

CONTEMPORARY POLITICAL HISTORY

Historical Context

Settlers from England landed in Suriname in the 1630s, and the territory was alternately a British and a Dutch colony until it was eventually awarded to the Netherlands by the Treaty of Vienna in 1815. The colony's economy depended on large sugar plantations, for which labour was provided by slaves of African origin. Following the abolition of slavery in 1863, immigration of labourers from India and the then Dutch East Indies was encouraged, and many of them settled permanently in Suriname. This history explains the country's current ethnic diversity: there are small communities of the original Amerindian population (mainly in the interior) and of ethnic Chinese and Europeans; a Creole population, largely of African descent, constitutes about one-third of the population, as do the Asian-descended 'East' Indians (known locally as Hindustanis); the Indonesian-descended 'Javanese' form about 15% of the population, and another Creole group, the 'boschnegers' or Bush Negroes, forms a further 10% (the Bush Negroes are the Dutch-speaking descendants of escaped slaves, long-established in the rainforest as a tribalized society of four clans). Under a Charter signed in 1954, Suriname (also known as Dutch Guiana) became an equal partner in the Kingdom of the Netherlands and gained full autonomy in domestic affairs.

Domestic Political Affairs

The Hindustani-dominated Government, in power since 1969 and led by Dr Jules Sedney, resigned in February 1973. General elections in November were won by an alliance of parties, the Nationale Partij Kambinatie (NPK), which favoured complete independence from the Netherlands, and in December Henck Arron, leader of the Nationale Partij Suriname (NPS—a predominantly Creole party), became Prime Minister. Suriname became independent on 25 November 1975. Dr Johan Ferrier, hitherto the Governor of Suriname, became the new republic's first President. Some 40,000 Surinamese emigrated to the Netherlands after independence, leaving Suriname with a severely underskilled work-force. Border disputes with French Guiana and Guyana also ensued. The 1977 general election resulted in a clear majority for the NPK, and Arron continued as Prime Minister.

Military rule

The Arron administration was overthrown in February 1980 by a group of soldiers, who formed a military council, the Nationale Militaire Raad (NMR). President Ferrier refused to agree to the retention of supreme power by the NMR, and appointed a civilian administration led by Dr Henk Chin-A-Sen, a former leader of the Partij Nationalistische Republiek. In August the Army Chief of Staff, NMR member Sgt-Maj. (later Lt-Col) Désiré (Desi) Bouterse (subsequently Commander-in-Chief of the armed forces), led a coup. Ferrier was replaced by Chin-A-Sen; the legislature was dissolved, and a state of emergency declared. A Hindustani-inspired counter-coup, led by Sgt-Maj. Wilfred

Hawker, failed in March 1981. In September the President announced details of a draft Constitution, which sought to limit the army to a supervisory role in government. The army responded with the formation of the Revolutionary People's Front, a comprehensive political alliance headed by Bouterse and two other members of the NMR, Maj. Roy Horb and Lt (later Commdr) Iwan Graanoogst, together with three leaders of workers' and students' organizations. In February 1982 the NMR, led by Bouterse, seized power from Chin-A-Sen and his civilian Government. The Vice-President of the Supreme Court, L. Fred Ramdat Misier, was appointed interim President. Hawker was executed after attempting a further coup in March.

A state of siege was declared, and martial law was imposed, as a result of the attempted coup of March 1982. In order to prevent the Netherlands from suspending its aid, a 12-member Cabinet of Ministers with a civilian majority was appointed, and a moderate economist, Henry Neyhorst, became Prime Minister, although Bouterse remained effectively in control. Failure to effect promised social and economic changes lost Bouterse the support of left-wing groups and trade unions, which supported the business community in demanding a return to constitutional rule. In October the arrest of Cyriel Daal, the leader of Suriname's principal trade union (De Moederbond), prompted strikes and demonstrations. In order to avert a general strike, Bouterse agreed to arrange for the election of a constituent assembly to draft a new constitution by March 1983 (to be followed by the establishment of an elected government), but he later reneged on this commitment. In December 1982 members of the armed forces burned down several buildings used by the opposition. During the ensuing disturbances, 15 prominent citizens, including Daal, were killed, in what became known as the 'December Murders'. The Government resigned, the Netherlands and the USA halted all aid, and the country was placed under rule by decree; an interim, military-dominated Government was appointed. An attempted coup in January 1983, the sixth since February 1980, resulted in the dismissal of two-thirds of the officers of the armed forces and the death of Maj. Horb. In February 1983 Dr Errol Alibux, a former Minister of Social Affairs, was appointed Prime Minister. He formed a new Cabinet of Ministers, composed of members of two left-wing parties, the Progressieve Arbeiders en Landbouwers Unie (PALU) and the Revolutionaire Volkspartij. The new Government immediately ended the restrictions imposed in December 1982.

The restoration of civilian rule

In January 1984, after a series of widely observed strikes in support of demands for the restoration of civilian rule and the organization of free elections, Bouterse dismissed the Cabinet of Ministers. Agreement was reached with the strike organizers, following the withdrawal of proposals to increase taxation rates. An interim Government, with Wim Udenhout, a former adviser to Bouterse, as Prime Minister, was created in February to formulate a timetable for the gradual restoration of constitutional rule. Nominees of the trade unions and business sector were also included in the new Government. Bouterse hoped to consolidate his position by securing a political base through his Standvaste (the 25 February Movement). In December 1984 plans for a nominated National Assembly (comprising representatives of Standvaste, the trade unions and the business community) were announced. However, the Dutch Government, deemed the changes insufficient to merit the resumption of aid. None the less, the National Assembly was inaugurated in January 1985 and a new Cabinet of Ministers was formed by Udenhout.

The tripartite administration collapsed in April 1985, after the withdrawal of three of the four trade union nominees. A reconstituted Cabinet, formed in June, contained new members with links to traditional political parties. In November the ban on political parties was revoked, and in the same month, former NPS Prime Minister Henck Arron, together with Jaggernath Lachmon of the Hindustani-based Vooruitstrevende Hervormings Partij (VHP) and Willy Soemita of the Kaum Tani Persatuan Indonesia (KTPI), accepted an invitation to join the NMR, renamed the Topberaad (Supreme Council). In July 1986 Bouterse appointed a new Cabinet of Ministers, including representatives from industry, business, political parties, trade unions and Standvaste. Pretaap Radhakishun, a business executive and member of the VHP, was appointed Prime Minister. The Cabinet drafted a new Constitution, which was approved by a national referendum in 1987.

From July 1986 anti-Government guerrillas began a series of attacks on military posts on the eastern border of the country. The guerrillas were led by Ronnie Brunswijk (a former presidential bodyguard). Mainly Bush Negroes, they claimed that government resettlement policies threatened the autonomy of their tribal society, as guaranteed by treaties, signed in 1760, with the former Dutch authorities. By November most of the eastern district of Marowijne was under guerrilla control, and the rebels had also occupied the area near the international airport, south of Paramaribo. Rebel attacks on the mining town of Moengo forced the closure of the country's principal bauxite mines. At the beginning of December a state of emergency was declared in eastern and southern Suriname, and a curfew was imposed. Reports that some 200 civilians had been massacred by government troops in the search for guerrillas led to protests by the Netherlands and US Governments.

In February 1987 five members of the Cabinet of Ministers, including Radhakishun, resigned. Jules Wijdenbosch, hitherto the Minister of Internal Affairs and a member of Standvaste, was appointed Prime Minister. The entire Cabinet resigned at the end of March, and a new Cabinet, led by Wijdenbosch, was appointed by Bouterse in April.

The Front voor Demokratie en Ontwikkeling (FDO—Front for Democracy and Development), an alliance of the NPS, the VHP and the KTPI, won a decisive victory in elections to the 51-seat National Assembly in November 1987. In January 1988 the National Assembly unanimously elected Ramsewak Shankar (a former Minister of Agriculture) as President of the Republic, and Henck Arron was elected Vice-President and thus (in accordance with the new Constitution) Prime Minister. In December 1987 Bouterse was appointed leader of a five-member Military Council, established under the new Constitution to 'guarantee a peaceful transition' to democracy. In July 1988 the Netherlands agreed to resume some aid to Suriname. However, relations remained tense, largely owing to the Dutch administration's mistrust of the intentions of the Surinamese army.

In July 1989 representatives of the Government and the Surinamese Liberation Army (SLA), meeting in French Guiana, signed an agreement at Kourou, which provided for a general amnesty for those involved in the recent conflicts, the ending of the state of emergency, the incorporation of many guerrillas into a special police unit for the interior of the country, and significant investment in the interior. The armed forces declared their opposition to the Accord, but took no direct action against continuing negotiations. However, at the end of August there was a further outbreak of guerrilla activity, in the west of the country, by an Amerindian group critical of some of the provisions of the Accord. The group, known as the Tucayana Amazonica, principally opposed the involvement of the SLA in the proposed police force. It also requested the restoration of the Bureau for Amerindian Affairs. Several of the group's demands were similar to those of the army command, and there were allegations that Tucayana were being armed and encouraged by the military, exploiting the traditional antipathy between the Amerindians and many of the Bush Negroes. In October, however, the Tucayana spokesmen joined elected representatives of the Amerindian communities (the Commission of Eight) to meet representatives of the National Assembly, who stated that the Government was prepared to supplement, but not rescind, the Kourou Accord.

Also in October 1989 Tucayana received the support of another new insurgent group, the Mandela Bush Negro Liberation Movement (BBM), which declared itself to be dissatisfied with the Kourou Accord. The BBM was formed by members of the most westerly (and, hitherto, least involved in the civil war) of the Bush Negro clans, the Matauriërs. In the same month, however, Brunswijk's SLA secured the support of another new insurgent group, the Union for Liberation and Democracy (UBD), which occupied the mining town of Moengo. The UBD declared its support for the Accord.

Bouterse resigned as Commander-in-Chief of the armed forces in December 1990. Suspicions that Bouterse's resignation might portend a military coup were realized two days later, when the acting Commander-in-Chief of the armed forces, Graanoogst,

seized power. The coup was immediately condemned by the Dutch Government, which suspended development aid to Suriname. Johan Kraag (honorary chairman of the NPS) was appointed provisional President on 29 December, and promptly invited Bouterse to resume command of the armed forces, thus substantiating speculation that Kraag was merely acting on behalf of Bouterse. A transitional Government (led by Jules Wijdenbosch) was sworn in in January 1991. In March Brunswijk and Bouterse (who had continued negotiations intermittently since 1989) signed a peace accord in the rebel stronghold of Drietabbetje. In April four rebel groups, the SLA, Tucayana, the BBM and Angula (or 'Defiance', led by Carlos Maassi), signed a further agreement with the Government, promising to respect the law and not to obstruct the conduct of free elections.

The election of Venetiaan

Elections, monitored by a delegation from the Organization of American States (OAS, see p. 404), were held in May 1991. Despite the fact that the Nieuw Front (NF), an electoral alliance comprising the members of the former FDO and the Surinaamse Partij van de Arbeid, failed to secure the two-thirds' majority in the Assembly necessary to elect its presidential candidate, Runaldo R. Venetiaan, automatically, the group refused to consider the formation of a coalition government. In July the Chairman of the Assembly, Jaggernath Lachman, convened the Verenigde Volksvergadering (United People's Assembly), a body comprising the members of the National Assembly and representatives of the municipal and district councils, in order to elect a President. Venetiaan was elected with an overwhelming 79% of the votes. One of Venetiaan's first acts as President was to announce the reduction of the armed forces by two-thirds and a reduction in the defence budget of 50%. These measures were introduced as part of a government programme of 'socialization' of the armed forces. In addition, amendments to the Constitution, approved in March 1992, included measures to curb the political influence of the military: the Military Council, established under the 1987 Constitution, was abolished.

In August 1992 a peace agreement was signed by the Government and the SLA and the Tucayana; the BBM also supported the agreement. Under its terms, the amnesty law of the Kourou Accord, covering all civil conflicts since 1985 and amended to include insurgent groups formed since the ratification of the Kourou Accord, was to be implemented. All weapons were to be surrendered to the Government, under OAS supervision. Following disarmament, members of all the groups would be eligible for recruitment into a special police force for the interior of the country. In addition, the Government gave assurances that the interior would receive priority in its programmes for economic development and social welfare.

In November 1992 Bouterse resigned as Commander-in-Chief of the armed forces, prompting public concern that the move might once again signal a coup. Venetiaan's appointment of Col (retd) Arthy Gorré as Bouterse's successor resulted in a confrontation between the Government and senior military officers in April 1993. Graanoogst, who had occupied the position of Commander-in-Chief on an interim basis, refused to concede the post to Gorré. He was supported by his fellow members of the military high command and by Bouterse, who, despite his resignation, remained effectively in control of the armed forces. Gorré's appointment was endorsed by a majority in the National Assembly in May, despite veiled threats of a military coup and an attack on the national television station, which had allegedly been instigated by Bouterse. All four members of the military high command subsequently acceded to a request by the National Assembly for their resignations. Three of them, including Graanoogst, later accepted posts as advisers to the Government, thus assuaging fears of an escalation of the conflict. Indications that the Netherlands might intervene to assist the Government were also considered influential in averting further military defiance of civilian rule.

The election of Wijdenbosch

At a general election conducted in May 1996 no single party secured a legislative majority. Venetiaan rejected an offer from Bouterse to form a coalition government. Neither Venetiaan nor former Prime Minister Jules Wijdenbosch, the candidate of the Nationale Democratische Partij (NDP—National Democratic Party, as the Standvaste had been reconstituted), were able to command the two-thirds' majority in the National Assembly necessary to secure the presidency, and responsibility for choosing the president consequently passed to the Verenigde Volksvergadering, which elected Wijdenbosch. The KTPI and a dissident faction of the VHP, the Basispartij voor Vernieuwing en Democratie (BVD), subsequently left the NF alliance, joining an NDP-led coalition. The new coalition Government, appointed in September, comprised members of the NDP, KTPI, BVD and the Hernieuwde Progressieve Partij (HPP).

The Government recalled its ambassador to the Netherlands in August 1997, following the Dutch Government's decision to seek an international arrest warrant for Bouterse on charges of illegal drugs-trafficking. Talks between the Governments of Suriname and the Netherlands were conducted in New York, USA, in 1998. Bouterse's continued membership of the Council of State remained a serious source of dissatisfaction for the Netherlands' delegation. In March 1999 the Dutch authorities began legal proceedings against Bouterse *in absentia*, on charges of corruption and drugs-trafficking. Similar proceedings were initiated in the Netherlands against the guerrilla leader Ronnie Brunswijk (who was found guilty on charges of drugs-trafficking in April, and sentenced to eight years' imprisonment) and the President of the Central Bank of Suriname, Henk Goedschalk, who was accused of deliberate financial mismanagement. Despite the Suriname Government's refusal to accede to Dutch demands for the extradition of Bouterse, in April President Wijdenbosch dismissed Bouterse from the Council of State. In July Bouterse was convicted and sentenced, *in absentia*, to 16 years in prison (later reduced to 11 years) and fined US $2.3m. The Attorney-General of the Netherlands filed further charges (this time for torture resulting in death relating to the 1982 December Murders) against Bouterse in January 2000.

Dissatisfaction with the Government's management of the economy increased in 1998 and 1999. In June 1998 widespread industrial action brought chaos to the country for several days. Following another national strike, which brought the country to a virtual standstill, the entire Cabinet resigned in May 1999. A vote of no confidence in the President in June fell short of the two-thirds' majority needed to force him from office and Wijdenbosch refused to resign. Instead he called for early elections, prior to which, in an apparent attempt to distance himself from Bouterse, Wijdenbosch left the NDP and formed a new electoral coalition, Democratisch Nationaal Platform 2000 (DNP 2000).

The re-election of Venetiaan

Voting proceeded on 25 May 2000, when Venetiaan's NF (an electoral alliance comprising the NPS, the Pertajah Luhur, the Surinaamse Partij van de Arbeid, and the VHP) secured a majority of seats. Having narrowly failed to secure the two-thirds' majority to appoint a new President directly, the NF entered into coalition negotiations with the smaller parties. As a result, Venetiaan was elected to the presidency for the second time. In October the Dutch Government agreed to resume aid to Suriname, which had been suspended since 1998.

In November 2000 the Suriname Court of Justice ruled that Bouterse must stand trial in Suriname in connection with the December Murders. In the following year the Dutch High Court ruled that Bouterse could not be prosecuted in the Netherlands under the UN's Convention on Torture, as the legislation had not been ratified in that country until 1989, seven years after the atrocities took place. In June 2002 the Dutch Government dispatched forensic specialists to assist Surinamese police officers investigating the December Murders and the exhumation of the remains of the 15 murder victims was ordered. As a result of a four-year investigation, a military court indicted Bouterse and 25 other suspects for the 1982 December Murders in December 2004. Bouterse publicly apologized to the families of the 15 victims in 2007, although he denied direct involvement in their deaths, and advocated an amnesty for the suspects. In February 2009 proceedings began against Bouterse and 23 other suspects in the December Murders. In 2005 the OAS's Inter-American Court of Human Rights instructed the Government to investigate a massacre that occurred in the village of Moiwana in 1986, during Bouterse's presidency, and to pay compensation to the 130 survivors. President Venetiaan formally apologized for the massacre at a ceremony in Moengo in 2006.

In March 2005 the NDP formally nominated Bouterse as its candidate in the indirect presidential election that was to follow the legislative ballot in May. The USA reacted to the NDP's nomination by threatening to sever diplomatic links with Suriname in the event of Bouterse being re-elected President. The NDP accused the USA of political interference and lodged a formal complaint with the Caribbean Community and Common Market (CARICOM, see p. 231) and the OAS. At the election the NF retained its position as the largest party in the National Assembly, although it lost its majority and the NDP increased its representation. Bouterse and former guerrilla leader Ronnie Brunswijk were both elected to the legislature.

Following the election the NF entered into negotiations with smaller parties in order to garner the two-thirds' parliamentary majority needed to re-elect Venetiaan to the presidency. As a result, on 13 July 2005 Venetiaan was nominated by a coalition of the NF, the Democratisch Alternatief 1991 (DA '91, comprising former members of the FDO) and the A-Combinatie (a coalition that included the Algemene Bevrijdings- en Ontwikkeling Partij—General Liberation and Development Party—led by Brunswijk). In an unexpected move, two days later the NDP presidential candidate Bouterse withdrew from the contest, nominating his former running mate, Rabin Parmessar, in his stead. However, neither Venetiaan nor Parmessar secured the requisite two-thirds' majority during the two rounds of voting. Responsibility for electing the new head of state once again passed to the 891-member Verenigde Volksvergadering, which opted for Venetiaan.

In an attempt to reduce the cost of imported petroleum, in July 2005 the Government signed the PetroCaribe energy accord with Venezuela, thereby gaining access to favourable energy concessions and the option of preferential terms should the price of petroleum exceed US $40 per barrel. However, the steep increases in the retail cost of petroleum products, and consequently of transportation, led to civil unrest in 2005–08.

The Government of Bouterse

A total of 20 parties, mostly grouped into coalitions, contested the general election on 25 May 2010. With 40.2% of the votes cast, the Megacombinatie (an alliance headed by Bouterse that included the NDP, Nieuw Suriname, PALU and the KTPI) became the largest grouping within the National Assembly after gaining control of 23 of the 51 legislative seats. The NF secured 14 seats, while Brunswijk's A-Combinatie and the Volksalliantie (a coalition of four Javanese parties) won seven and six seats, respectively. The rate of participation by the electorate was high, at 73.2%. OAS and CARICOM observation missions declared the election fair and peaceful. After securing the support of the A-Combinatie and the Volksalliantie, Bouterse was elected President by the National Assembly in mid-July, winning the votes of 36 of the 51 deputies (and thus exceeding the necessary two-thirds' parliamentary majority). Bouterse's inauguration ceremony was not attended by any foreign leaders, an indication of the international community's reluctance to engage with a President with a dictatorial past, a drugs-trafficking conviction and connections to the December Murders. Bouterse's election to the presidency meant that, in theory, he would be able to pardon himself if he were found guilty of involvement in the murders.

Six A-Combinatie members received positions in Bouterse's Cabinet of Ministers, including Martin Misiedjan, who was appointed Minister of Justice and the Police. The Volksalliantie was allocated three government posts, with Soewarto Moestadja becoming the new Minister of Home Affairs. The remaining eight ministries were assigned to members of the Megacombinatie; most notably, Wonnie Boedhoe became Minister of Finance, Winston Lackin received the foreign affairs portfolio and Lamuré Latour was given responsibility for defence. Robert Ameerali, an independent, was awarded the position of Vice-President. In June 2011 Wonnie Bledhoe resigned as Minister of Finance. It was reported that she was increasingly at odds with President Bouterse over fiscal policy, favouring spending cuts to ministerial budgets, while Bouterse advocated increased public spending. She was replaced by Adeline Wijnerman.

In early 2012 Minister of Defence Lamuré Latour announced that the Government would honour President Bouterse's promise to reintroduce military conscription. However, the plan still required comment from the Ministry of Justice and Police, and would have to be approved by both the State Council and Legislature before becoming law.

Recent developments: amnesty law

Human rights organizations and the international community reacted with concern to plans, introduced by NDP legislators to the National Assembly in March 2012, to revise a 1989 amnesty law. The proposed legislation would, if approved, provide immunity to those who committed crimes in the 'defence of the state' during the military dictatorship of the 1980s. This would include those currently on trial for the 1982 December Murders. The Dutch Government urged the legislature to abandon the proposals, and to allow investigation of alleged human rights abuses to continue; however, the law was approved on 4 April. In response, the Netherlands immediately recalled its ambassador from the country and, a week later, announced a suspension of aid to Suriname. Several thousand people protested in Paramaribo at the change in the law. The UN High Commissioner for Refugees was said to be 'disturbed' by the amendment, and expressed the concern that it would deny victims' families the right to justice and reparation. In early May the trial of Bouterse was adjourned until a constitutional court could rule on whether the amnesty law covered the murder charges. By early 2013 the constitutional court had yet to be established.

Bouterse's parliamentary majority was reduced from 36 to 30 seats in mid-2012 when four members of the A-Combinatie left the Government because of internal disagreements, and the two members of Nieuw Suriname were dismissed from the coalition following their failure to support the budget earlier in the year. Moreover, a total of five ministers were dismissed when Bouterse carried out a major cabinet reorganization in May.

Foreign Affairs

Suriname has a territorial dispute with Guyana over an estimated 15,000 sq km (6,000 sq miles) of land in the Corentije region, and another with French Guiana over land to the east of the Litani river. In 1990 France and Suriname agreed terms providing for the repatriation of an estimated 10,000 Surinamese refugees from French Guiana. In 2002 the Suriname Government protested to the French authorities concerning the alleged compulsory repatriation of refugees. Relations with France deteriorated in 2007 when the French Government designated a 2m. ha region along the disputed border with French Guiana as a national park. Under its new protected status, the traditional hunting and fishing practices of the indigenous Surinamese communities were strictly prohibited in the park. The Organization of Indigenous People in Suriname protested against the restrictions to the French Government.

In 1995 Guyana and Suriname reached agreement on the establishment of a joint commission in order to seek a resolution of the countries' territorial dispute. In 1998 Guyana granted the Canadian-based company CGX Energy Inc a concession to explore for petroleum and gas along the continental margin off Guyana, part of which lay within the disputed maritime area. In 2000 Suriname formally claimed that Guyana had violated its territorial integrity, and invited Guyana to begin negotiations regarding the maritime boundary. CGX was forced to remove the drilling platform. In 2001 the two countries issued a declaration of their Governments' commitment to peace and co-operation and in the following year revived the Guyana–Suriname Bilateral Co-operation Council, agreeing to investigate the possibility of a joint exploration for petroleum in the disputed territory. However, relations again became strained in 2003 when the Surinamese Government decreed that maps of the country circulated by diplomatic missions in Paramaribo must include the disputed territory. Guyana lodged a formal protest and sent a naval detachment to patrol the Corentiyne river. Guyana referred the maritime boundary dispute to arbitration at the UN's International Tribunal for the Law of the Sea, in Hamburg, Germany. In 2007 the Tribunal ruled in favour of Guyana, granting sovereignty over 33,152 sq km (12,800 sq miles) of coastal waters; Suriname was awarded 17,891 sq km (6,900 sq miles).

In September 2010 President Bouterse held talks with his Guyanese counterpart, Bharrat Jagdeo. The two leaders agreed to put aside any unresolved border issues and concentrate instead upon enhancing bilateral co-operation in areas of mutual interest such as trade and security. Relations continued to improve in late 2010 following further amicable discussions, during which plans to build a bridge across the Corentyne river were revived. In February 2012 the two countries agreed jointly to request funding for construction work from the Inter-American Development Bank (IDB, see p. 341). However, in mid-2011 Bouterse announced that Suriname would not renounce its claim to the New River Triangle (known to Surinamese as Tigri), located in southern Guyana. In addition to potential petroleum reserves, the area has also yielded gold deposits in recent years. Relations between the two countries were strained in 2012 owing to a boom in small-scale gold mining in the disputed area, which led to large quantities of the commodity being smuggled from Guyana into Suriname where royalties were considerably lower. The violence and environmental damage associated with the practice provoked accusations of criminality and led to increased tensions in the region.

Violent clashes between local residents and Brazilian mineworkers in the Surinamese town of Albina in late 2009 highlighted the issue of ethnic tensions connected with the presence of large numbers of migrant workers in Suriname. Following negotiations with Brazil, in December 2010 a bilateral immigration accord was concluded to monitor the flow of peoples across their shared border.

In 2002 the Surinamese and Dutch Ministers of Foreign Affairs approved the establishment of a Returned Emigration Committee to oversee the voluntary repatriation of Surinamese with Dutch nationality, without the loss of social benefits. In 2004 customs officials in Suriname and the Netherlands reached an agreement to share information in an attempt to reduce tax evasion on imports from the Netherlands. The Dutch authorities expressed dissatisfaction at Bouterse's election as President in 2010 and declared that he would only be permitted entry into the Netherlands if he were arriving to commence his prison sentence for drugs-trafficking (Bouterse, *in absentia*, had been found guilty of this crime by a Dutch court in 1999). The Netherlands also announced that engagement with the new Surinamese administration would not progress beyond the 'functional necessities', while the provision of Dutch finance and training for the Surinamese police force was cancelled. Changes to a 1989 amnesty law (see above), approved by Bouterse's Government in April 2012, prompted the Dutch Government to recall its ambassador in Paramaribo and to suspend aid to Suriname.

Deteriorating relations with the Netherlands prompted the Government of Bouterse to seek to establish and deepen diplomatic links with other countries. During 2012 Suriname opened embassies in France and South Africa, and was expected to establish similar missions in Germany and Equatorial Guinea in 2013. Meanwhile, official visits to China in late 2012 and to Turkey in early 2013 aimed to secure international finance for a range of infrastructural projects in Suriname and to attract investment in the country's mining, agricultural, timber and tourist industries.

CONSTITUTION AND GOVERNMENT

Under the 1987 Constitution, legislative power is held by the National Assembly, with 51 members, elected by universal adult suffrage for a five-year term. The Assembly elects the President and the Vice-President of the Republic. Executive power is vested in the President, who appoints the Cabinet of Ministers, led by the Vice-President, who is also the Prime Minister. The Cabinet is responsible to the National Assembly. A Council of State, comprising civilians and members of the armed forces, advises the President and the Cabinet of Ministers on policy, and has power of veto over legislation approved by the Assembly. Suriname comprises 10 administrative districts.

REGIONAL AND INTERNATIONAL CO-OPERATION

In February 1995 Suriname was granted full membership of the Caribbean Community and Common Market (CARICOM, see p. 231). It was also one of the six founder members of CARICOM's Caribbean Single Market and Economy (CSME), established on 1 January 2006. The CSME was intended to enshrine the free movement of goods, services and labour throughout the CARICOM region, although persistent delays in implementation meant that the CSME was not expected to be fully operational until 2015. Suriname is a member of the Organization of American States (see p. 404), the Association of Caribbean States (see p. 459), the IDB (see p. 341), and the Community of Latin American and Caribbean States (see p. 475), which was formally inaugurated in December 2011. In early 2013 Argentina and Brazil announced that they would endorse Suriname's incorporation into the Southern Common Market (Mercado Común del Sur—Mercosur) as an associate member. The country joined the UN in December 1975. As a contracting party to the General Agreement on Tariffs and Trade, Suriname joined the World Trade Organization (see p. 444) on its establishment in 1995. The country is also a member of the Group of 77 (see p. 461) organization of developing states.

ECONOMIC AFFAIRS

In 2010, according to estimates by the World Bank, Suriname's gross national income (GNI), measured at average 2008–10 prices, was US \$4,006m., equivalent to \$7,640 per head (or \$7,710 per head on an international purchasing-power parity basis). During 2002–11, it was estimated, the population increased at an average annual rate of 1.1%, while gross domestic product (GDP) per head increased, in real terms, by an average of 3.8% per year in 2002–10. According to the UN estimates, overall GDP increased, in real terms, at an average annual rate of 5.0% in 2002–11; growth totalled 4.5% in 2011.

Agriculture (including hunting, forestry and fishing) contributed 10.5% of GDP (excluding the informal sector) in 2011, according to the UN, and the sector engaged 8.0% of the employed population at the 2004 census. The principal crop is rice, which supplies domestic demand and provided 1.9% of export earnings in 2010. Bananas are cultivated for export, together with sugar cane, plantains and citrus fruits, while Suriname also produces coconuts, maize and vegetables. Livestock is being developed, as are the extensive timber reserves (more than 80% of Suriname's total land area is covered by forest). Commercial fishing is important (exports of shrimp and fish providing an estimated 7.3% of total export revenue in 2007). According to the UN estimates, agricultural GDP increased by 3.4% per year in 2002–11; the sector grew by 0.5% in 2010, but fell by 2.0% in 2011.

Industry (including mining, manufacturing, public utilities and construction) contributed 39.3% of GDP (excluding the informal sector) in 2011, according to the UN, and the sector engaged some 22.9% of the employed labour force at the 2004 census. The principal activity is the bauxite industry, which dominates both the mining and manufacturing sectors. According to the UN estimates, industrial GDP increased by an annual average of 5.4% in 2002–11; the sector increased by 7.1% in 2011.

Mining, quarrying and utilities contributed 9.9% of GDP in 2011, according to the UN, and the sector engaged 5.9% of the employed labour force at the 2004 census. The principal product is bauxite (used in the manufacture of aluminium), of which Suriname is one of the world's leading producers (providing an estimated 3.2m. metric tons in 2011). Gold was also a significant contributor to the economy. Annual gold production rose significantly in the 2000s, and stood at 21,000 kg in 2011. In 2011 gold contributed some 37.1% of total export revenue. Construction of a gold refinery, the first in the Caribbean, was announced in early 2013; operations were expected to begin in 2014. The state petroleum concern, Staatsolie Maatschappij Suriname, intended to expand capacity at its refinery from some 7,000 barrels per day (b/d) to 16,000 b/d by 2013. Some 40% of production is for export, but much is used domestically in the bauxite industry. Unproven reserves are also thought to exist in the Saramacca district. Petroleum production stood at 5.84m. barrels in 2011. Staatsolie invited bids to explore four offshore blocks in early 2013. Suriname also has extensive deposits of iron ore and reserves of manganese, copper, nickel, platinum and kaolin. According to UN estimates, the GDP of the sector increased by an average of 6.7% per year in 2002–11; the sector grew by 7.5% in 2011.

Manufacturing contributed 24.0% of GDP (excluding the informal sector) in 2011, according to the UN, and the sector engaged an estimated 7.0% of the employed labour force at the 2004 census. Bauxite refining and smelting is the principal industry (alumina accounted for an estimated 47.5% of export revenue in 2007), but there are also important food-processing industries and manufacturers of cigarettes, beverages and chemical products. According to the UN, manufacturing GDP increased by an estimated average of 4.5% per year in 2002–11; the sector contracted by 8.6% in 2011.

The construction sector contributed 5.5% of GDP (excluding the informal sector) in 2011, according to the UN, and the sector engaged an estimated 9.0% of the employed labour force at the 2004 census. According to UN estimates, construction GDP increased by an estimated average of 7.0% per year in 2002–11; the sector expanded by 14.1% in 2010, but remained constant in 2011.

Energy is derived principally from hydroelectricity and hydrocarbon fuels, which are mainly imported; in 2011 mineral fuels and lubricants accounted for 25.7% of total merchandise imports. The country has considerable potential for the further development of hydroelectric power. In 2009 Suriname produced 1,618m. kWh of electricity, derived mostly from hydroelectric power.

The services sector contributed 50.3% of GDP (excluding the informal sector) in 2011, according to the UN, and the sector engaged an estimated 64.3% of the employed labour force at the 2004 census. According to UN estimates, the GDP of the services sector increased by an average of 6.4% per year in 2002–11; sectoral growth was 3.9% in 2011.

In 2011 Suriname recorded a visible trade surplus of US $787.6m., and there was a surplus of $251.1m. on the current account of the balance of payments. The principal source of imports in 2011 was the USA (providing 26.7% of total imports); other significant suppliers in that year were Trinidad and Tobago, the Netherlands and the People's Republic of China. The principal markets for exports in the same year were the United Arab Emirates (some 26.1% of the value of total exports), Canada, the USA, Belgium, Switzerland and Guyana. The principal imports in 2011 were machinery and mechanical appliances, chemical and related products, and prepared foodstuffs, beverages and tobacco. The principal exports (excluding re-exports) in that year were mineral fuels and lubricants, and machinery and mechanical appliances.

In 2007 there was an estimated budgetary surplus of 195.5m. Surinamese dollars (equivalent to around 3.0% of GDP, excluding the contributions of the informal sector). Suriname's general government gross debt was 2,870m. Surinamese dollars in 2011, equivalent to 19.1% of GDP. At the end of 2007 the total external public debt stood at an estimated US $161.1m. According to the ILO, the annual rate of inflation averaged 10.8% in 2002–11. According to official data, consumer prices increased by 5.0% in 2012. According to official sources, the rate of unemployment was 9.5% in 2004. The informal sector contributed around 14.3% of GDP in 2006.

Economic activity is relatively diversified in range, with the dominant sector being the bauxite/alumina industry. Agriculture is also important, particularly the production of rice and bananas, but the sector remains relatively undeveloped. The mining of gold, mostly on a small scale (and much of it illegal), has become an increasingly important industry, with exports of the commodity estimated to total US $914m. in 2011. Plans to open a gold refinery in 2014 were expected further to boost revenues. Following the global economic downturn a recovery in demand and prices for the country's key mineral commodities in 2010 led to an increase in export revenues. However, rising food prices and higher negotiated public sector salaries resulted in increased levels of inflation, which, exacerbated by a 20% devaluation of the Surinamese dollar against the US dollar, rose to an estimated 17.7% in 2011. By early 2013 the rate had slowed to an estimated 3.5%. An IMF-endorsed reform agenda launched in late 2010 included plans to privatize 12 state-owned companies by 2015 and to set up a Sovereign Wealth Fund, which would contain revenues generated from the country's mining industries. In January 2012 an interim fund was created, with initial capital of some US $20m. In December 2011 the Inter-American Development Bank granted Suriname a loan of $40m. to help develop the country's financial sector and in December 2012 approved an additional loan of $40m. to help complete a project to improve a strategic route between Paramaribo and French Guiana. The loan formed part of a 20-year, $70m. aid programme. According to the IMF, real GDP was estimated to have grown by 4.0% in 2012 and was forecast to increase by a further 6.0% in 2013.

PUBLIC HOLIDAYS

2014: 1 January (New Year's Day), 31 January (Chinese New Year), 25 February (Day of the Revolution), 27 March* (Phagwa), 18–21 April (Easter), 1 May (Labour Day), 1 July (Emancipation Day), 28 July (Id al-Fitr, end of Ramadan), 4 October (Id al-Adha, Feast of the Sacrifice), 23 October (Diwali), 25 November (Republic Day), 25–26 December (Christmas).

* Exact date dependent upon sightings of the moon.

Statistical Survey

Sources (unless otherwise stated): Algemeen Bureau voor de Statistiek, Kromme Elleboogstraat 10, POB 244, Paramaribo; tel. 473927; fax 425004; e-mail info@statistics-suriname.org; internet www.statistics-suriname.org; Ministry of Trade and Industry, Havenlaan 3, POB 9354, Paramaribo; tel. 402080; fax 402602.

AREA AND POPULATION

Area: 163,820 sq km (63,251 sq miles).

Population: 492,829 at census of 2 August 2004; 534,189 at census of 13 August 2012. *Mid-2013* (estimate): 538,883 (Source: UN, *World Population Prospects: The 2010 Revision*).

Density (at mid-2013): 3.3 per sq km.

Population by Age and Sex (UN estimates at mid-2013): *0–14:* 146,811 (males 75,157, females 71,654); *15–64:* 356,022 (males 179,532, females 176,490); *65 and over:* 36,050 (males 15,377, females 20,673); *Total* 538,883 (males 270,066, females 268,817) (Source: UN, *World Population Prospects: The 2010 Revision*).

Ethnic Groups (1980 census, percentage): Creole 34.70; Hindustani 33.49; Javanese 16.33; Bush Negro 9.55; Amerindian 3.10; Chinese 1.55; European 0.44; Others 0.84.

Administrative Districts (population at census of 13 August 2012): Paramaribo 236,065; Wanica 117,584; Nickerie 34,241; Coronie 3,153; Saramacca 17,251; Commewijne 31,087; Marowijne 18,114; Para 23,874; Brokopondo 14,662; Sipaliwini 38,158; *Total* 534,189.

Principal Towns (census of 2 August 2004): Paramaribo (capital) 205,000; Lelydorp 15,600; Nieuw Nickerie 11,100. Source: Thomas Brinkoff, *City Population* (internet www.citypopulation.de).

Births, Marriages and Deaths (2009 unless otherwise indicated): Registered live births 9,792 (birth rate 18.7 per 1,000); Marriages (2007) 2,161 (4.2 per 1,000); Registered deaths 3,293 (death rate 6.3 per 1,000). *2010:* Birth rate 18.3 per 1,000; Death rate 7.2 per 1,000. *2011:* Birth rate 18.0 per 1,000; Death rate 7.2 per 1,000. Sources: UN, *Demographic Yearbook*; Pan American Health Organization.

Life Expectancy (years at birth): 70.7 (males 67.5; females 74.0) in 2011. Source: Pan American Health Organization.

Economically Active Population (persons aged 15–64 years, census of 2004): Agriculture, hunting, forestry and fishing 12,593; Mining and quarrying 9,308; Manufacturing 10,971; Utilities 1,659; Construction 14,031; Trade 25,012; Hotels, restaurants and bars 4,833; Transport, storage and communication 8,711; Financial intermediation 2,723; Real estate, renting and business activities 6,350; Public administration and defence 27,995; Education 8,355; Health and social work 6,797; Other community, social and personal service activities 9,911; *Sub-total* 149,249; Unknown 7,456; *Total employed* 156,705 (males 101,919, females 54,768, unknown 18); Unemployed 16,425; *Total labour force* 173,130.

HEALTH AND WELFARE

Key Indicators

Total Fertility Rate (children per woman, 2011): 2.3.

Under-5 Mortality Rate (per 1,000 live births, 2011): 27.7.

HIV/AIDS (% of persons aged 15–49, 2009): 1.0.

Physicians (per 1,000 head, 2008): 0.9.

Hospital Beds (per 1,000 head, 2009): 2.6.

Health Expenditure (2009): US $ per head (PPP): 567.

Health Expenditure (2009): % of GDP: 7.5.

Health Expenditure (2009): public (% of total): 51.0.

Access to Water (% of persons, 2010): 92.

Access to Sanitation (% of persons, 2010): 83.

Total Carbon Dioxide Emissions ('000 metric tons, 2008): 2,438.6.

Carbon Dioxide Emissions Per Head (metric tons, 2008): 4.7.

Human Development Index (2011): ranking: 104.

Human Development Index (2011): value: 0.680.

Source: partly Pan American Health Organization; for other sources and definitions, see explanatory note on p. vi.

AGRICULTURE, ETC.

Principal Crops ('000 metric tons, 2011): Rice, paddy 235; Roots and tubers 4; Sugar cane 120 (FAO estimate); Coconuts 4; Vegetables 15; Bananas 85; Plantains 12; Oranges 15; Other citrus fruit 2.

Livestock ('000 head, 2011): Cattle 55; Sheep 8; Goats 6; Pigs 34; Chickens 6,900.

Livestock Products ('000 metric tons, 2011): Cattle meat 2; Pig meat 2 (FAO estimate); Chicken meat 10; Cows' milk 7; Hen eggs 1 (FAO estimate).

Forestry ('000 cu metres, 2011, FAO estimates): *Roundwood Removals:* Sawlogs, veneer logs and logs for sleepers 360; Other industrial wood 5; Fuel wood 48; Total 413. *Sawnwood Production:* Total (incl. railway sleepers) 113.

Fishing ('000 metric tons, 2010): Capture 34.4 (Marine fishes 25.7; Penaeus shrimps 0.5; Atlantic seabob 7.6); Aquaculture 0.1; *Total catch* 34.5.

Source: FAO.

MINING

Selected Products (2011): Crude petroleum ('000 barrels) 5,840; Bauxite 3,236 ('000 metric tons); Gold (Au content, kg) 21,000 (estimate). Sources: US Geological Survey.

INDUSTRY

Selected Products ('000 metric tons, 2009, unless otherwise indicated): Gold-bearing ores 16,500 (kg); Gravel and crushed stone 85 (2002); Distillate fuel oil 42; Residual fuel oils 347; Cement 65 (2004); Alumina 1,536; Beer of barley 30 (2011, FAO estimate); Coconut oil 0.40 (2011, FAO estimate); Palm oil 0.23 (2011, FAO estimate); Cigarettes 483 (million, 1996); Plywood 3 (2011, '000 cubic metres); Electricity 1,618 (million kWh). Sources: mainly UN Industrial Commodity Statistics Database and FAO.

FINANCE

Currency and Exchange Rates: 100 cents = 1 Surinamese dollar. *Sterling, Dollar and Euro Equivalents* (31 December 2012): £1 sterling = 5.207 Surinamese dollars; US $1 = 3.300 Surinamese dollars; €1 = 4.354 Surinamese dollars; 100 Surinamese dollars = £19.20 = US $30.30 = €22.97. *Average Exchange Rate* (Surinamese dollars per US $): 2.745 in 2010; 3.268 in 2011; 3.300 in 2012. *Note:* Between 1971 and 1993 the official market rate was US $1 = Surinamese 1.785 guilders. A new free market rate was introduced in June 1993, and a unified, market-determined rate took effect in July 1994. A mid-point rate of US $1 = 401.0 guilders was in effect between September 1996 and January 1999. A new currency, the Surinamese dollar, was introduced on 1 January 2004, and was equivalent to 1,000 old guilders.

Budget (million Surinamese dollars, 2007, estimates): *Revenue:* Direct taxation 778.8; Indirect taxation 804.0 (Domestic taxes on goods and services 368.8, Taxes on international trade 430.9, Other taxes (incl. bauxite levy) 4.3); Non-tax revenue 319.7; Total 1,902.5 (excl. grants 99.5). *Expenditure:* Wages and salaries 678.4; Subsidies and transfers 217.0; Goods and services 590.1; Interest payments 94.5; Capital 225.4; Total 1,805.4 (excl. net lending 1.1). Source: IMF, *Suriname: Statistical Appendix* (August 2008).

International Reserves (US $ million at 31 December 2011): Gold (national valuation) 106.87; IMF special drawing rights 123.77; Reserve position in IMF 9.40; Foreign exchange 807.71; Total 1,047.75. Source: IMF, *International Financial Statistics*.

Money Supply ('000 Surinamese dollars at 31 December 2011): Currency outside depository corporations 685,074; Transferable deposits 2,838,076; Other deposits 3,055,615; Securities other than shares 107,955; *Broad money* 6,686,721. Source: IMF, *International Financial Statistics*.

Cost of Living (Consumer Price Index for Paramaribo area; base: April–June 2009 = 100): 108.3 in 2010; 127.5 in 2011; 133.9 in 2012.

Gross Domestic Product (million Surinamese dollars at constant 2005 prices): 7,144.6 in 2009; 7,437.5 in 2010; 7,772.5 in 2011. Source: UN National Accounts Main Aggregates Database.

Expenditure on the Gross Domestic Product (million Surinamese dollars at current prices, 2011): Government final consumption expenditure 1,878.5; Private final consumption expenditure 5,314.5; Gross capital formation 6,064.3; Changes in inventories −215.5; *Total domestic expenditure* 13,041.8; Exports of goods and non-factor services 9,053.6; *Less* Imports of goods and non-factor services 6,484.2; Statistical discrepancy −544.3; *GDP in purchasers' values* 15,066.9. Source: UN National Accounts Main Aggregates Database.

Gross Domestic Product by Economic Activity (million Surinamese dollars at current prices, 2011): Agriculture, hunting, forestry and fishing 1,458.6; Mining, quarrying and utilities 1,377.9; Manufacturing 3,343.0; Construction 761.2; Wholesale, retail trade, hotels and restaurants 3,239.4; Transport, storage and communications 923.3; Other services 2,852.4; *Sub-total* 13,955.9; Net of indirect taxes 1,111.0 (obtained as residual); *GDP in purchasers' values* 15,066.9. Source: UN National Accounts Main Aggregates Database.

Balance of Payments (US $ million, 2011): Exports of goods 2,466.7; Imports of goods –1,679.1; *Balance on goods* 787.6; Exports of services 200.8; Imports of services –562.5; *Balance on goods and services* 425.9; Primary income received 16.2; Primary income paid –278.3; *Balance on goods, services and primary income* 163.8; Secondary income received 159.4; Secondary income paid –72.1; *Current balance* 251.1; Capital account (net) 35.0; Direct investment assets –72.4; Direct investment liabilities 145.3; Portfolio investment assets 5.5; Other investment assets –483.2; Other investment liabilities 319.9; Net errors and omissions –77.1; *Reserves and related items* 124.1. Source: IMF, *International Financial Statistics*.

EXTERNAL TRADE

Principal Commodities (distribution by HS, US $ million, 2011): *Imports c.i.f.:* Prepared foodstuff, beverages and tobacco 137.8; Mineral fuels, lubricants, etc. 420.9; Chemicals 200.5; Plastic, rubber and their article 87.0; Iron and steel, base metals and their articles 113.3; Machinery and mechanical appliances 298.7; Transport and transport equipment 113.3; Total (incl. others) 1,637.8. *Exports f.o.b.:* Vegetable products 37.6; Prepared foodstuff, beverages and tobacco 48.7; Mineral fuels, lubricants, etc. 221.0; Machinery and mechanical appliances 50.1; Total (incl. others) 2,466.9. Source: Trade Map-Trade Competitiveness Map, International Trade Centre, www.intracen.org/marketanalysis.

Principal Trading Partners (US $ million, 2011): *Imports c.i.f.:* Antigua and Barbuda 19.6; Brazil 52.9; China, People's Republic 106.6; Colombia 22.2; Dominican Republic 17.3; Japan 42.0; Netherlands Antilles 17.5; Netherlands 262.5; Panama 21.4; Trinidad and Tobago 416.1; USA 437.1; Total (incl. others) 1,637.8. *Exports f.o.b.:* Barbados 97.8; Belgium 250.7; Canada 458.2; France (incl. Monaco) 37.8; Guyana 137.5; Jamaica 40.5; Netherlands 37.9; Norway 85.0; Switzerland-Liechtenstein 231.1; Trinidad and Tobago 58.6; United Arab Emirates 643.0; USA 276.2; Total (incl. others) 2,466.9. Source: Trade Map-Trade Competitiveness Map, International Trade Centre, www.intracen.org/marketanalysis.

TRANSPORT

Road Traffic (registered motor vehicles, 2010): Passenger cars 119,270; Buses and coaches 3,022; Lorries and vans 30,117; Motorcycles and mopeds 45,013 (Source: IRF, *World Road Statistics*).

Shipping: *International Sea-borne Freight Traffic* (estimates, '000 metric tons, 2001): Goods loaded 2,306; Goods unloaded 1,212. *Flag Registered Fleet* (at 31 December 2012): Number of vessels 9; Total displacement 4,737 grt (Source: (Lloyd's List Intelligence—www.lloydslistintelligence.com).

Civil Aviation (traffic on scheduled services, 2009): Kilometres flown (million) 6; Passengers carried ('000) 303; Passenger-km (million) 1,749; Total ton-km (million) 212. Source: UN, *Statistical Yearbook*.

TOURISM

Tourist Arrivals (number of non-resident arrivals at national borders, '000): 150.7 in 2009; 204.0 in 2010; 220.0 in 2011 (provisional).

Tourism Receipts (US $ million, incl. passenger transport, unless otherwise indicated): 83 in 2008; 70 in 2009; 61 in 2010 (excl. passenger transport).

Source: World Tourism Organization.

COMMUNICATIONS MEDIA

Telephones (2011): 84,000 main lines in use.

Mobile Cellular Telephones (2011): 947,000 subscribers.

Personal Computers: 20,000 (40.0 per 1,000 persons) in 2005.

Internet Subscribers (2011, preliminary): 24,200.

Broadband Subscribers (2011, preliminary): 24,200.

Source: International Telecommunication Union.

EDUCATION

Pre-primary (2008/09): 503 teachers; 17,695 pupils.

Primary (2008/09 unless otherwise stated, incl. special education): 308 schools (2001/02); 4,620 teachers; 71,074 pupils.

Secondary (2008/09 unless otherwise stated, incl. teacher-training): 141 schools (2001/02); 3,549 teachers; 47,221 pupils.

University (2001/02): 1 institution; 350 teachers; 3,250 students.

Other Higher (2001/02): 3 institutions; 200 teachers; 1,936 students.

Pupil-teacher Ratio (primary education, UNESCO estimate): 15.4 in 2008/09.

Adult Literacy Rate (UNESCO estimates): 94.7% (males 95.4%; females 94.0%) in 2010.

Source: mainly UNESCO Institute for Statistics.

Directory

The Government

HEAD OF STATE

President: DESIRÉ (DESI) DELANO BOUTERSE (took office 12 August 2010).

Council of State: Chair. DESIRÉ (DESI) DELANO BOUTERSE (President of the Republic); 14 mems; 10 to represent the political parties in the National Assembly, one for the National Army, two for the trade unions and one for employers.

CABINET OF MINISTERS
(May 2013)

The Government is formed by members of the Megacombinatie (MC), A-Combinatie (AC) and Volksalliantie (VA) alliances.

Vice-President: ROBERT AMEERALI (Ind.).

Minister of Foreign Affairs: WINSTON LACKIN (MC).

Minister of Finance: ADELIEN WIJNERMAN (MC).

Minister of Defence: LAMURÉ LATOUR (MC).

Minister of Home Affairs: SOEWARTO MOESTADJA (VA).

Minister of Sport and Youth Affairs: ISMANTO ADNA (MC).

Minister of Agriculture, Animal Husbandry and Fisheries: HENDRIK SETROWIDJOJO (VA).

Minister of Transport, Communications and Tourism: VALISI PINAS (AC).

Minister of Public Works: RAMON ABRAHAMS (MC).

Minister of Social Affairs and Housing: ALICE AMAFO (AC).

Minister of Trade and Industry: RAYMOND SAPOEN (VA).

Minister of Regional Development: STANLEY BETTERSON (AC).

Minister of Education and Community Development: SHIRLEY SITALDIEN (MC).

Minister of Health: MICHAEL BLOKLAND (MC).

Minister of Labour, Technological Development and the Environment: MICHAEL MISKIN (MC).

Minister of Natural Resources: JIM HOK (MC).

Minister of Physical Planning, Land and Forestry Management: GINMADRO KROMOSOETO (MC).

Minister of Justice and the Police: EDWARD BELFORT (AC).

MINISTRIES

Office of the President: Kleine Combéweg 2–4, Centrum, Paramaribo; tel. 472841; fax 475266; e-mail secretariaat@president.gov.sr; internet www.kabinet.sr.org.

Office of the Vice-President: Dr Sophie Redmondstraat 118, Frank Essed Gebouw, Paramaribo; tel. 474805; fax 472917; e-mail kabinet@vicepresident.gov.sr; internet www.gov.sr/sr/kabinet-van-de-vice-president.aspx.

Ministry of Agriculture, Animal Husbandry and Fisheries: Letitia Vriesdelaan 8–10, Paramaribo; tel. 479112; fax 470301; e-mail minlvvv@sr.net; internet www.gov.sr/sr/ministerie-van-lvv.aspx.

Ministry of Defence: Kwattaweg 29, Paramaribo; tel. 471511; fax 420055; e-mail defensie@sr.net; internet www.gov.sr/sr/ministerie-van-defensie.aspx.

Ministry of Education and Community Development: Dr Samuel Kafiluddistraat 117–123, Paramaribo; tel. 498383; fax 495083; e-mail minond@sr.net; internet www.gov.sr/sr/ministerie-van-onderwijs-en-volksontwikkeling.aspx.

Ministry of Finance: Tamarindelaan 3, Paramaribo; tel. 472610; fax 476314; e-mail secmin@finance.gov.sr; internet www.gov.sr/sr/ministerie-van-financiën.aspx.

Ministry of Foreign Affairs: Henck Aaronstraat 8, Paramaribo; tel. 471209; fax 410411; e-mail sec.minister@foreignaffairs.gov.sr; internet www.gov.sr/sr/ministerie-van-buza/contact.aspx.

Ministry of Health: Henck Arronstraat 64, POB 201, Paramaribo; tel. 474941; fax 410702; e-mail vogez@sr.net; internet www.gov.sr/sr/ministerie-van-volksgezondheid.aspx.

Ministry of Home Affairs: Wilhelminastraat 3, Paramaribo; tel. 473141; fax 421170; e-mail minbiza@sr.net; internet www.gov.sr/sr/ministerie-van-biza.aspx.

Ministry of Justice and the Police: Henck Arronstraat 1, Paramaribo; tel. 427197; fax 412109; e-mail min.jus-pol@sr.net; internet www.gov.sr/sr/ministerie-van-juspol.aspx.

Ministry of Labour, Technological Development and the Environment: Wageswegstraat 22, POB 911, Paramaribo; tel. 475241; fax 410465; e-mail voorlichting@atm.sr.org; internet www.atm.sr.org.

Ministry of Natural Resources: Dr J. C. de Mirandastraat 13–15, Paramaribo; tel. 474666; fax 472911; e-mail minnh@sr.net; internet www.gov.sr/sr/ministerie-van-nh.aspx.

Ministry of Physical Planning, Land and Forestry Management: Cornelis Jongbawstraat 10–12, Paramaribo; tel. 470700; fax 470876; e-mail mpjong@datsunsuriname.com; internet www.gov.sr/sr/ministerie-van-rgb.aspx.

Ministry of Public Works: Verlengde Jagernath Lachmonstraat 167, Paramaribo; tel. 490666; fax 464901; e-mail voorlichting@publicworks.gov.sr; internet www.gov.sr/sr/ministerie-van-openbare-werken.aspx.

Ministry of Regional Development: Van Rooseveltkade 2, Paramaribo; tel. 471574; fax 424517; e-mail regon@sr.net; internet www.gov.sr/sr/ministerie-van-ro.aspx.

Ministry of Social Affairs and Housing: Waterkant 30, Paramaribo; tel. 472340; fax 470516; e-mail soza@sr.net; internet www.gov.sr/sr/ministerie-van-sozavo.aspx.

Ministry of Sport and Youth Affairs: Directorate of Sports, Dr Samuel Kaffiludistraat 117, Paramaribo; tel. 499021; fax 498662; Directorate of Youth Affairs, Prince Hendrikstraat 11, Paramaribo; tel. 473411; fax 477827; e-mail dir-jeugdzaken@sr.netinternet www.gov.sr/sr/ministerie-van-sport-en-jeugdzaken.aspx.

Ministry of Trade and Industry: Havenlaan 3, POB 9354, Paramaribo; tel. 402080; fax 402602; e-mail hi.voorlichting@minhi.gov.sr; internet www.gov.sr/sr/ministerie-van-hi.aspx.

Ministry of Transport, Communications and Tourism: Prins Hendrikstraat 26–28, Paramaribo; tel. 420905; fax 420100; e-mail secretariaatdirecteur@tct.gov.sr; internet www.tct.gov.sr.

Legislature

NATIONAL ASSEMBLY

Chairman: JENNIFER GEERLINGS-SIMONS.

General Election, 25 May 2010

Party	% of votes cast	Seats
Megacombinatie (MC)*	40.22	23
Nieuw Front (NF)†	31.65	14
A-Combinatie (AC)‡	4.70	7
Volksalliantie§	12.98	6
Partij voor Demokratie en Ontwikkeling in Eenheid (DOE)	5.09	1
Basispartij voor Vernieuwing en Democratie/ Politieke Vleugel van de FAL (BVD/PVF)	5.07	—
Other parties	0.29	—
Total	**100.00**	**51**

* An alliance of the Kerukunan Tulodo Pranatan Inggil (KTPI), the Nationale Democratische Partij (NDP), the Nieuw Suriname (NS) and the Progressieve Arbeiders en Landbouwers Unie (PALU).

† An alliance of the Nationale Partij Suriname (NPS), the Surinaamse Partij van de Arbeid (SPA) and the Vooruitstrevende Hervormings Partij (VHP).

‡ Including candidates of the Algemene Bevrijdings- en Ontwikkelingspartij (ABOP) and the Broederschap en Eenheid in Politiek (BEP).

§ An alliance of the Democraten van de 21, Pertijajah Luhur (PL), the Progressieve Surinaamse Volkspartij (PSV) and the Unie van Progressieve Surinamers (UPS).

Election Commission

Centraal Hoofdstembureau (CHS) (Central Polling Authority): Wilhelminastraat 3, Paramaribo; tel. 410362; independent; Chair. LOTHAR BOKSTEEN.

Political Organizations

A-Combinatie (AC): Paramaribo; alliance including:

Algemene Bevrijdings- en Ontwikkelingspartij (ABOP) (General Liberation and Development Party): Jaguarstraat 15, Paramaribo; e-mail webmaster@abop-suriname.net; internet www.abop-suriname.net; f. 1990; Pres. RONNIE BRUNSWIJK; Sec. C. ADA.

Seeka: Paramaribo; Chair. PAUL ABENA.

Basispartij voor Vernieuwing en Democratie (BVD) (Base Party for Renewal and Democracy): Hoogestraat 28–30, Paramaribo; tel. 422231; e-mail info@bvdsuriname.org; contested the 2010 election in coalition with the Politiek Vleugel van de FAL (PVF); new faction *De Nieuwe Leeuw (DNL)* created after split in 2012 led by *Dharm Mungra*; Chair. DILIPKOEMAR SARDJOE; Sec. ANUSHKA GOPALRAJ.

Broederschap en Eenheid in Politiek (BEP): Theodorusstraat 55, Land van Dijk, Paramaribo; tel. 402509; fax 422996; e-mail info@bep.sr; internet beppartij.org; f. 1957 as Maroon Party Suriname (MPS); name changed as above in 1987; contested the 2010 elections as part of the A-Combinatie alliance; left the alliance in 2012; Chair. CAPRINO ALLENDY; Sec. WENSLEY MISIEDJAN.

Megacombinatie (MC) (Mega Combination): Paramaribo; Leader DESIRÉ (DESI) DELANO BOUTERSE; alliance formed to contest the 2010 election, comprising:

Kerukunan Tulodo Pranatan Ingit (KTPI) (Party for National Unity and Solidarity): Bonistraat 64, Geyersvlijt, Paramaribo; tel. 456116; f. 1949 as the Kaum Tani Persatuan Indonesia; largely Indonesian; Leader WILLY SOEMITA; Sec. ROBBY DRAGMAN.

Nationale Democratische Partij (NDP) (National Democratic Party): Dr H. D. Benjaminstraat 38, Paramaribo; tel. 432174; e-mail ndpsur@sr.net; internet www.ndp.sr; f. 1987 by Standvaste (the 25 February Movt); army-supported; Chair. DESIRÉ (DESI) DELANO BOUTERSE; Sec. DENNIS MENZO.

Progressieve Arbeiders en Landbouwers Unie (PALU) (Progressive Workers' and Farmers' Union): Dr S. Kafiluddistraat 27, Paramaribo; tel. 400115; e-mail palu.suriname@gmail.com; internet www.palu-suriname.org; f. 1977; socialist party; Chair. JIM K. HOK; Vice-Chair. HENK R. RAMNANDANLAL.

Nationale Unie (NU): Postbus 5193, Paramaribo; tel. 499675; fax 499678; e-mail info@nationaleunie.net; internet www.nationaleunie.net; f. 1991; Leader MAHIN JANKIE; Sec.-Gen. SOENIEL DEWKALI.

Naya Kadam (New Step): Naarstraat 5, Paramaribo; tel. 482014; fax 481012; e-mail itsvof@sr.net; Chair. INDRA DJWALAPERSAD; Sec. WALDO RAMDIHAL.

Nieuw Front (NF) (New Front): Paramaribo; f. 1987 as Front voor Demokratie en Ontwikkeling (FDO—Front for Democracy and Devt); name changed as above in 1991; Pres. RUNALDO R. VENETIAAN; an alliance comprising:

Democratisch Alternatief 1991 (DA '91) (Democratic Alternative 1991): Gladiolenstraat 17, POB 91, Paramaribo; tel. 432342; fax 493121; e-mail info@da91.sr; f. 1991 as the Alternatief Forum (AF); social democratic; Chair. WINSTON JESSURUN; Sec. WILFRIED MEYER.

Nationale Partij Suriname (NPS) (Suriname National Party): Grun Dyari, Johan Adolf Pengelstraat 77, Paramaribo; tel. 477302; fax 475796; e-mail nps@sr.net; internet www.nps.sr; f. 1946; predominantly Creole; Pres. RUNALDO VENETIAAN; Sec. S. OEMRAWSINGH.

Surinaamse Partij van de Arbeid (SPA) (Suriname Labour Party): Rust en Vredestraat 64, Paramaribo; tel. 425912; fax 420394; f. 1987; affiliated with C-47 trade union; social democratic party; joined NF in 1991; Chair. GUNO CASTELEN; Sec.-Gen. ROY ADEMA.

Vooruitstrevende Hervormings Partij (VHP) (Progressive Reform Party): De Olifant, Jagernath Lachmonstraat, Paramaribo; tel. 494497; fax 434158; e-mail Info@vhp.sr; internet www.vhp.sr; f. 1949 as Verenigde Hindostaanse Partij; name changed as above in 1973; leading left-wing party; predominantly Indian; Leader CHANDRIKAPERSAD SANTOKHI; Sec. GANESHKOEMAR KANDHAI.

Nieuw Suriname (NS) (New Suriname): Paramaribo; f. 2003; Pres. JOHN NASIBDAR; Sec. SAFIEK JAHANGIER.

Partij voor Demokratie en Ontwikkeling in Eenheid (DOE) (Party for Democracy and Development in Unity): Prinsenstraat 47, Hoek Waaldijkstraat, Paramaribo; tel. 491701; e-mail info@doepartij .org; internet www.doepartij.org; f. 1999; Chair. CARL BREEVELD; Sec. PAUL BRANDON.

Pendawa Lima: Bonistraat 115, Geyersvlij, Paramaribo; tel. 551802; f. 1977; predominantly Indonesian; Chair. RAYMOND SAPOEN; Sec. RANDY KROMODIHARDJO.

Permanente Voorspoed Republiek Suriname (PVRS) (Lasting Prosperity Party of Suriname): Engelslootstraat 8, Projectsloot, Paramaribo; tel. 493928; e-mail info@nieuwpvrs.com; internet www.nieuwpvrs.com; Chair. CHAS MIJNALS.

Politieke Vleugel van de FAL (PVF): Keizerstraat 150, Paramaribo; f. 1995; political wing of farmers' org. Federatie van Agrariërs en Landarbeiders; contested the 2010 election in coalition with the Basispartij voor Vernieuwing en Democratie (BVD); Chair. SOEDESCHAND JAIRAM; Sec. RADJOE BIKHARIE.

Volksalliantie (People's Alliance): Paramaribo; alliance formed to contest the 2010 election; Leader PAUL SALAM SOMOHARDJO; comprising:

Democraten van de 21 (D21) (Democrats of the 21st Century): Goudstraat 22, Paramaribo; f. 1996; Chair. SOEWARTO MOESTADJA; Sec. KANIMAN PASIRAN.

Pertjajah Luhur (PL) (Full Confidence Party): Hoek Gemenlandsweg-Daniel Coutinhostraat, Paramaribo; tel. 401087; fax 420394; internet www.pertijajahluhur.org; f. 1998; left Nieuw Front alliance in 2010; Pres. PAUL SALAM SOMOHARDJO.

Progressieve Surinaamse Volkspartij (PSV) (Suriname Progressive People's Party): Keizerstraat 122, Paramaribo; tel. 472979; f. 1947; resumed political activities 1987; Christian democratic party; Chair. JOHN COURTAR.

Unie van Progressieve Surinamers (UPS): Keizerstraat 122, Paramaribo; tel. 472979; f. 2004; Chair. HENRI ORI.

Diplomatic Representation

EMBASSIES IN SURINAME

Brazil: Maratakkastraat 2, Zorg en Hoop, POB 925, Paramaribo; tel. 400200; fax 400205; e-mail brasemb.paramaribo@itamaraty.gov.br; internet paramaribo.itamaraty.gov.br; Ambassador MARCELO BAUMBACH.

China, People's Republic: Anton Dragtenweg 131, POB 3042, Paramaribo; tel. 451570; fax 452540; e-mail chinaemb_sr@mfa.gov .cn; internet sr.china-embassy.org; Ambassador YANG ZIGANG.

Cuba: Brokopondolaan 4, Paramaribo; tel. 434917; fax 432626; e-mail embajadacubasuriname@gmail.com; internet www .cubadiplomatica.cu/suriname; Ambassador JULIO ARMANDO SOLÍS FERREIRO.

France: Henck Arronstraat 5–7, POB 2648, Paramaribo; tel. 476455; fax 471208; e-mail ambafrance.paramaribo@diplomatie .gouv.fr; internet www.ambafrance-sr.org; Ambassador JOEL GODEAU.

Guyana: Gravenstraat 82, POB 785, Paramaribo; tel. 477895; fax 472679; e-mail guyembassy@sr.net; Ambassador KEITH GEORGE.

India: Dr Sophie Redmondstraat 221, POB 1329, Paramaribo; tel. 498344; fax 491106; e-mail india@sr.net; internet www .indembassysuriname.com; Ambassador M. SUBASHINI (designate).

Indonesia: Van Brussellaan 3, Uitvlugt, POB 157, Paramaribo; tel. 431230; fax 498234; e-mail indonemb@sr.net; internet paramaribo .kemlu.go.id; Ambassador NUR SYAHRIR RAHARDJO.

Netherlands: Van Roseveltkade 5, POB 1877, Paramaribo; tel. 477211; fax 477792; e-mail prm@minbuza.nl; internet www .nederlandseambassade.sr; Chargé d'affaires a.i. ROBERT PETRI.

USA: Dr Sophie Redmondstraat 129, POB 1821, Paramaribo; tel. 472900; fax 425690; e-mail embuscen@sr.net; internet suriname .usembassy.gov; Ambassador JAY NICHOLAS ANANIA.

Venezuela: Henck Arronstraat 23–25, POB 3001, Paramaribo; tel. 475401; fax 475602; e-mail embve.srprm@mppre.gob.ve; internet suriname.embajada.gob.ve; Chargé d'affaires a.i. THAIS ROMERO FERRER.

Judicial System

The administration of justice is entrusted to a Court of Justice, the six members of which are nominated for life, and three Cantonal Courts. Suriname recognizes the Caribbean Court of Justice (CCJ) on matters of original jurisdiction pertaining to international trade. The CCJ was inaugurated in Trinidad and Tobago in April 2005.

President of the Court of Justice: CYNTHIA VALSTEIN-MONTNOR.
Attorney-General: SUBHAS PUNWASI.

Religion

CHRISTIANITY

According to the 2004 census, Christians represent approximately 48% of the population.

Committee of Christian Churches: Paramaribo; tel. 476306; Chair. Rev. WILHELMUS DE BEKKER (Bishop of Paramaribo).

The Roman Catholic Church

For ecclesiastical purposes, Suriname comprises the single diocese of Paramaribo, suffragan to the archdiocese of Port of Spain (Trinidad and Tobago). The Bishop participates in the Antilles Episcopal Conference (currently based in Port of Spain, Trinidad and Tobago). Some 25% of the population are Roman Catholics.

Bishop of Paramaribo: WILHELMUS ADRIANUS JOSEPHUS MARIA DE BEKKER, Bisschopshuis, Henck Arronstraat 12, POB 1230, Paramaribo; tel. 425918; fax 471602; e-mail cabisdom@sr.net.

The Anglican Communion

Within the Church in the Province of the West Indies, Suriname forms part of the diocese of Guyana. The Episcopal Church is also represented.

Anglican Church: St Bridget's, Hoogestraat 44, Paramaribo.

Protestant Churches

Evangelisch Lutherse Kerk in Suriname: Waterkant 102, POB 585, Paramaribo; tel. and fax 425503; e-mail elks@sr.net; f. 1741; Pres. MARY-AN MOLGO; 4,000 mems.

Moravian Church in Suriname (Evangelische Broeder Gemeente): Maagdenstraat 50, POB 1811, Paramaribo; tel. 473073; fax 475794; e-mail ebgs@sr.net; f. 1735; Praeses MAARTEN MINGOEN; 40,000 mems (2004).

Adherents to the Moravian Church constitute some 15% of the population. Also represented are the Christian Reformed Church, the Dutch Reformed Church, the Baptist Church, the Evangelical Methodist Church, Pentecostal Missions, the Seventh-day Adventists and the Wesleyan Methodist Congregation.

HINDUISM

According to the 2004 census, around 24% of the population are Hindus.

Arya Dewaker: Johan Adolf Pengelstraat 210, Paramaribo; tel. 400706; e-mail aryadewaker@sr.net; members preach the Vedic Dharma; disciples of Maha Rishi Swami Dayanand Sarswati, the founder of the Arya Samaj in India; f. 1929; Chair. INDERDATH TILAKDHARIE.

Sanatan Dharm: Koningstraat 31–33, POB 760, Paramaribo; tel. 404190; f. 1930; Pres. Dr R. M. NANNAN PANDAY; over 150,000 mems.

ISLAM

Some 16% of the population are Muslims, according to the 2004 census.

Federatie Islamitische Gemeenten in Suriname: Paramaribo; Indonesian Islamic org.; Chair. K. KAAIMAN.

Stichting der Islamitische Gemeenten Suriname: Verlengde Mahonielaan 39, Paramaribo; Indonesian Islamic org.

Surinaamse Islamitische Organisatie (SIO): Watermolenstraat 10, POB 278, Paramaribo; tel. 475220; fax 472075; e-mail ijamaludin@hotmail.com; f. 1978; Pres. Dr I. JAMALUDIN; Sec. Dr K. M. MOENNE; 6 brs.

Surinaamse Moeslim Associatie: Kankantriestraat 55–57, Paramaribo; Javanese Islamic org.

JUDAISM

The Dutch Jewish Congregation and the Dutch Portuguese-Jewish Congregation are represented in Suriname.

Jewish Community: The Synagogue Neve Shalom, Keizerstraat, POB 1834, Paramaribo; tel. 400236; fax 402380; e-mail rene-fernandes@cq-link.sr; internet www.ujcl.org; f. 1854; mem. of Union of Jewish Congregations of Latin America and the Caribbean (UJCL); Officiant JACQUES VAN NIEL; 300 mems (2005).

The Press

DAILIES

Dagblad Suriname: Zwartenhovenbrugstraat 154, POB 975, Paramaribo; tel. 426336; fax 471718; e-mail general@dbsuriname.com; internet www.dbsuriname.com; f. 2002; Dir FARIED PIERKHAN; Editor LAL MAHOMED JAMES.

De Ware Tijd: Malebatrumstraat 9, POB 1200, Paramaribo; tel. 472823; fax 411169; e-mail m.helstone@dwt.net; internet www.dwtonline.com; f. 1957; morning; Dutch; independent/liberal; Asst Dir FABIENNE SPONG; Editor-in-Chief MEREDITH HELSTONE.

De West: Dr J. C. de Mirandastraat 2–6, POB 176, Paramaribo; tel. 473327; fax 470322; f. 1909; midday; Dutch; liberal; Editor GEORGE D. C. FINDLAY; circ. 15,000–18,000.

PERIODICAL

Kerkbode: Burenstraat 17–19, POB 219, Paramaribo; tel. 473079; fax 475635; e-mail stadje@sr.net; f. 1906; weekly; religious; CEO CONSTAN LANDVREUGD; circ. 1,200.

Publishers

Afaka International NV: Residastraat 23, Paramaribo; tel. and fax 530640; e-mail info@afaka.biz; internet www.afaka.net; f. 1996; Dir GERRIT BARRON.

IMWO, Universiteit van Suriname: Universiteitscomplex, Leysweg 86, POB 9212, Paramaribo; tel. 462003; fax 439100; e-mail imwo@sr.net; internet www.uvs.edu; f. 1987; Dir Dr EDGAR AKRUM.

Okopipi Publ. (Publishing Services Suriname): Van Idsingastraat 133, Paramaribo; tel. 472746; e-mail pssmoniz@sr.net; fmrly I. Krishnadath.

Papaya Media Counseling: Hendrikstraat 2, POB 8304, Paramaribo; tel. and fax 432041; e-mail roy_bhikharie@sr.net; f. 2002; Man. Dir ROY BHIKHARIE.

Stichting Wetenschappelijke Informatie (Foundation for Information and Development): Prins Hendrikstraat 38, Paramaribo; tel. 475232; fax 422195; e-mail swin@sr.net; internet www.swi77.org; f. 1977; Chair. JACK MENKE.

VACO, NV: Domineestraat 26, POB 1841, Paramaribo; tel. 472545; fax 410563; f. 1952; Dir EDUARD HOGENBOOM.

Broadcasting and Communications

TELECOMMUNICATIONS

Digicel Suriname: Henck Arronstraat 27–29, POB 1848, Paramaribo; tel. 462626; fax 475502; e-mail customer.caresuriname@digicelgroup.com; internet www.digicelsuriname.com; mobile operating licence granted in 2006; operations commenced Dec. 2007; Chair. DENIS O'BRIEN; CEO (Suriname) HANS LUTE.

Telesur (Telecommunication Corporation Suriname): Heiligenweg 14, POB 1839, Paramaribo; tel. 473944; fax 421919; internet www.telesur.sr; liberalization of the telecommunications sector ended Telesur's monopoly in 2007; supervisory function of Telesur assumed by Telecommunications Authority Suriname; Chair. ADOLFINA CAIRO; Man. Dir DIRK CURRIE.

Uniqa (IntelSur/UTS): Bonistraat 114, Paramaribo; tel. 459802; fax 459801; e-mail info@uniqa.sr; internet www.uniqa.sr; jt venture between UTS, NV and Intelsur, NV; mobile operating licence granted in 2006, formalized in 2007; CEO RUSSEL BERNADINA.

Regulatory Authority

Telecommunications Authority Suriname (TAS): Lalla Rookhweg 228, POB 3013, Paramaribo; tel. 532523; fax 497411; e-mail dsecretariaat@tas.sr; internet www.tas.sr; f. 2007; Dir G. GADDEN-AMELO (acting).

BROADCASTING

Radio

ABC Radio (Ampie's Broadcasting Corporation): Maystraat 57, Paramaribo; tel. 464609; fax 464680; e-mail info@abcsuriname.com; internet www.abcsuriname.com; f. 1975; re-opened in 1993; commercial; Dutch and some local languages; Man. JOHNNY KAMPERVEEN.

Radika Radio & TV: Indira Gandhiweg 165, Paramaribo; tel. 482800; fax 482910; e-mail radika@sr.net; internet www.radikartv.com; f. 1962; re-opened in 1989; Dutch and Hindi; Dir ROSHNI RADHAKISHUN.

Radio Apintie: Verlengde Gemenelandsweg 37, POB 595, Paramaribo; tel. 400500; fax 400684; e-mail apintie@sr.net; internet www.apintie.sr; f. 1958; commercial; Dutch and some local languages; Dir CHARLES VERVUURT.

Radio Bersama: Bonnistraat 115, Paramaribo; tel. 551802; fax 551803; internet www.radio-bersama.com; f. 1997; Gen. Man. AJOEB MOENTARI.

Radio Boskopu: Roseveltkade 1, Paramaribo; tel. 410300; govt-owned; Sranang Tongo and Dutch; Head LEO VAN VARSSEVELD.

Radio Nickerie (RANI): Waterloostraat 3, Nieuw Nickerie; tel. 231462; commercial; Hindi and Dutch.

Radio Paramaribo (Rapar): Verlengde Jagernath Lachmonstraat 34, POB 975, Paramaribo; tel. 499995; fax 493121; e-mail rapar@sr.net; f. 1957; commercial; Dutch and some local languages; Dir FARIED PIERKHAN.

Radio Sangeet Mala: Indira Gandhiweg 40, Paramaribo; tel. 485893; e-mail info@sgmsuriname.com; internet www.sgmsuriname.com; f. 1998; Dutch and Hindi; Dirs RADJEN SOEKHRADJ, SOEDESH RAMSARAN.

Radio SRS (Stichting Radio Omroep Suriname): Jacques van Eerstraat 20, POB 271, Paramaribo; tel. 498115; fax 498116; e-mail adm@radiosrs.com; internet www.radiosrs.com; f. 1965; commercial; govt-owned; Dutch and some local languages; Dir ROSELINE A. DAAN.

Radio & Televisie Garuda: Goudstraat 14–16, Paramaribo; tel. 456869; f. 2001; Dir TOMMY RADJI.

Radio Ten: Stadionlaan 3, POB 110, Paramaribo; tel. 410881; fax 422294; e-mail info@radio10.sr; internet www.radio10.sr; Dir WERNER DUTTENHOFER.

Television

ABC Televisie (Ampie's Broadcasting Corporation): Maystraat 57, Paramaribo; tel. 464555; fax 464680; e-mail info@abcsuriname.com; internet www.abcsuriname.com; f. 1975, re-opened 1993; Channel 4.

Algemene Televisie Verzorging (ATV): van het Hogerhuysstraat 58–60; tel. 404611; fax 402660; e-mail info@atv.sr; internet www.atv.sr; f. 1985; govt-owned; commercial; Dutch, English, Portuguese, Spanish and some local languages; Channel 12; Man. GUNO COOMAN.

Radio & Televisie Garuda: see Radio section.

Radika Radio & TV: see Radio section; Hindi entertainment TV channel.

STVS (Surinaamse Televisie Stichting): Letitia Vriesdelaan 5, POB 535, Paramaribo; tel. 473032; fax 477216; e-mail info@stvs.sr; internet www.stvs.sr; f. 1965; govt-owned; commercial; local languages, Dutch and English; Channels 6, 8, 11 and 13; Dir SHURLY LACKIN.

Finance

(cap. = capital; res = reserves; dep. = deposits; m. = million; brs = branches; amounts in Surinamese dollars)

BANKING

Central Bank

Centrale Bank van Suriname: Waterkant 20, POB 1801, Paramaribo; tel. 473741; fax 476444; e-mail info@cbvs.sr; internet www.cbvs.sr; f. 1957; cap.and res. 210.7m., dep. 858.2m. (Dec. 2009); Gov. GILMORE HOEFDRAAD; Exec. Dir O. EZECHIËLS.

Commercial Banks

Finabank NV: Dr Sophie Redmondstraat 59–61, Paramaribo; tel. 472266; fax 422672; e-mail finabank@sr.net; internet www.finabanknv.com; f. 1991; cap. 1m., res. 10.1m., dep. 275.4m. (Dec. 2011); Chair. JULES A. TJIN WONG JOE; CEO EBLEIN FRANGIE.

Handels-Krediet- en Industriebank (Hakrinbank NV): Dr Sophie Redmondstraat 11–13, POB 1813, Paramaribo; tel. 477722; fax 472066; e-mail hakrindp@sr.net; internet www.hakrinbank.com; f. 1936; cap. 0.1m., res 85.6m., dep. 592.1m. (Dec. 2011); Pres. and Chair. A. K. R. SHYAMNARAIN; CEO J. D. BOUSAID; 7 brs.

Landbouwbank NV: FHR Lim A Postraat 34, POB 929, Paramaribo; tel. 475945; fax 411965; e-mail lbbank@sr.net; f. 1972; govt-owned; agricultural bank; Chair. D. FERRIER; Pres. D. HINDORI; 5 brs.

RBC Royal Bank (Suriname) NV: Kerkplein 1, Paramaribo; tel. 471555; fax 411325; e-mail tt-info@rbc.com; internet www.rbtt.com/sr/personal; fmrly Amsterdam Rotterdam Bank NV; present name adopted in 2012; CEO, Caribbean SURESH SOOKOO.

Stichting Surinaamse Volkscredietbank (VCB): Waterkant 104, POB 1804, Paramaribo; tel. 472616; fax 473257; e-mail info@vcbbank.sr; internet www.vcbbank.sr; f. 1949; Man. Dir P. CLENEM; 3 brs.

Surichange Bank NV: Dr Sophie Redmondstraat 71, Paramaribo; tel. 471151; fax 474554; e-mail info@surichange.sr; internet www .scbbank.sr; cap. 4.5m., res. 8.2m., dep. 200.3m. (Dec. 2011); Exec. Dirs STANLEY MATHURA, RAJINDREKOEMAR MERHAI.

De Surinaamsche Bank NV: Henck Arronstraat 26–30, POB 1806, Paramaribo; tel. 471100; fax 411750; e-mail info@dsbbank.sr; internet www.dsbbank.sr; f. 1865; cap. 0.9m., res 143.6m., dep. 2,201m. (Dec. 2011); Chair. S. SMIT; CEO SIGMUND L. J. PROEVE; 8 brs.

INSURANCE

Assuria NV: Grote Combeweg 37, POB 1501, Paramaribo; tel. 477955; fax 472390; e-mail assurialeven@assuria.sr; internet www .assuria.sr; f. 1961; life and indemnity insurance; Man. Dir Dr S. SMIT.

Assuria Schadeverzekering NV: Henck Arronstraat 5–7, POB 1030, Paramaribo; tel. 473400; fax 476669; e-mail customer.service@ assuria.sr; internet www.assuria.sr; Chair. J. J. HEALY; Man. Dir Dr S. SMIT.

Fatum Levensverzekering NV: Noorderkerkstraat 5–7, Paramaribo; tel. 471541; fax 410067; e-mail fatum@sr.net; internet www.fatum-suriname.com; Chair. C. A. CALOR; Exec. Dir N. W. LALBIHARIE.

Parsasco NV: Henck Arronstraat 119, Paramaribo; tel. 421212; fax 421325; e-mail parsasco@sr.net; internet www.parsasco.com; f. 1995; Man. Dir AMAR RANDJITSING.

Self Reliance: Heerenstraat 48–50 en Henck Arronstraat 69–71, Paramaribo; tel. 472582; fax 475588; e-mail self-reliance@sr.net; internet www.self-reliance.sr; f. 1980; general and life insurance; Pres. MAURICE L. ROEMER.

Trade and Industry

DEVELOPMENT ORGANIZATIONS

Stichting Planbureau Suriname (National Planning Office of Suriname): Dr Sophie Redmondstraat 118, POB 172, Paramaribo; tel. 447408; fax 475001; e-mail dirsps@sr.net; internet www .planbureau.net; f. 1951; responsible for regional and socio-economic long- and short-term planning; Man. Dir LILIAN J. M. MONSELS-THOMPSON.

Suriname Business Development Centre (SBC): Hofstraat 1, 4th Floor, Paramaribo; tel. 471521; fax 471579; e-mail info@sbc.sr; internet www.sbc.sr; f. 2008; devt of private sector industries; Gen. Man. GILBERT VAN DIJK.

CHAMBERS OF COMMERCE

Kamer van Koophandel en Fabrieken (Chamber of Commerce and Industry): Dr J. C. de Mirandastraat 10, POB 149, Paramaribo; tel. 530311; fax 437971; e-mail chamber@sr.net; internet www .surinamechamber.com; f. 1910; Pres. ROBERT AMEERALI; 16,109 mems.

Surinaams–Nederlandse Kamer voor Handel en Industrie (Suriname–Netherlands Chamber of Commerce and Industry): Jagernath Lachmonstraat 158, Paramaribo; tel. and fax 476909; e-mail nedcar@xs4all.nl; internet nederlandscaribischekamer.com; f. 1976; Sec.-Gen. RONALD SCHERMEL; Dir LEON FERRIER.

INDUSTRIAL AND TRADE ASSOCIATIONS

Associatie van Surinaamse Fabrikanten (ASFA) (Suriname Manufacturers' Asscn): Jaggernath Lachmonstraat 187, POB 3046, Paramaribo; tel. 434014; fax 439798; e-mail info@asfasuriname.com; internet www.asfasuriname.com; f. 1980; Chair. RAHID DOEKHIE; 317 mems.

Vereniging Surinaams Bedrijfsleven (Suriname Trade and Industry Association): Prins Hendrikstraat 18, POB 111, Paramaribo; tel. 475286; fax 475287; e-mail info@vsbstia.org; internet www .vsbstia.org; f. 1950; Pres. FERDINAND WELZIJN; 245 mems.

UTILITIES

Electricity

NV Energie Bedrijven Suriname (EBS): Noorderkerkstraat 2–14, POB 1825, Paramaribo; tel. 471045; fax 474866; e-mail g.lau@ nvebs.com; internet www.nvebs.com; f. 1932 as Nederlands-Indische Gas Maatschappij; present name adopted in 1968; electricity and gas distribution; owns and operates Electricity Co of Paramaribo (EPAR) and Ogane Paramaribo (OPAR); Dir GERARD LAU.

Staatsolie Maatschappij Suriname NV: Dr Ir H. S. Adhinstraat 21, POB 4069, Paramaribo; tel. 499649; fax 491105; e-mail mailstaatsolie@staatsolie.com; internet www.staatsolie.com; f. 1980; state petroleum exploration and exploitation co; electricity and steam generation and supplies; aims to produce 16,000 barrels per

day of Saramacca Crude oil by 2013; Man. Dir MARC C. H. WAALDIJK; 810 employees (2011).

Paradise Oil Company: Dr Ir H. S. Adhinstraat 21, POB 4069, Paramaribo; tel. and fax 499649; e-mail poc@staatsolie.com; internet www.paradise-oil.com; f. 2005; 100% owned by Staatsolie Maatschappij Suriname NV; oil exploration co; Operations Man. PATRICK BRUNINGS.

Water

NV Surinaamsche Waterleiding Maatschappij (SWM): Henck Arronstraat 9–11, POB 1818, Paramaribo; tel. 471414; fax 476343; e-mail swmsecretariaat@swm.sr; internet www.swm.sr; f. 1932; govt-owned; Dir SVEN SJAUW KOEN FA; 578 employees (2012).

TRADE UNIONS

Council of the Surinamese Federation of Trade Unions (RAVAKSUR) (Raad van Vakcentrales Suriname): f. 1987; Pres. ROBBY BERENSTEIN; includes:

Algemeen Verbond van Vakverenigingen in Suriname 'De Moederbond' (AVVS) (General Confederation of Trade Unions): Verlengde Jagernath Lachmonstraat 134, POB 2951, Paramaribo; tel. 465118; fax 463116; e-mail avvsmoederbond51@hotmail.com; right-wing; Pres. ERROLL G. SNIJDERS; Gen. Sec. ALESSANDRO SPRONG; 15,000 mems.

Progressive Trade Union Federation (C-47): Johan Adolf Penegelstraat 230, Paramaribo; tel. 401120; fax 401149; e-mail c47@sr.net; Pres. ROBBY BERENSTEIN; Gen. Sec. CLAUDETTE ETNEL.

Transport

RAILWAYS

There are no public railways operating in Suriname.

ROADS

In 2003 Suriname had an estimated 4,304 km (2,674 miles) of roads, of which 26.3% were paved. The principal east–west road, 390 km in length, links Albina, on the eastern border, with Nieuw Nickerie, in the west. A government plan to modernize the Martin Luther King Highway into a four-lane, south-bound highway was expected to begin in mid-2013. The US $250m. project was funded by the China Investment Bank.

SHIPPING

Suriname is served by many shipping companies and has about 1,500 km (930 miles) of navigable rivers and canals. There are two ferry services linking Suriname with Guyana, across the Corantijn river, and with French Guiana, across the Marowijne river. In 2012 Suriname and Guyana asked the Inter-American Development Bank to fund a feasibility study looking into the construction of a bridge across the Corentyne river.

Continental Shipping Agencies NV (CSA): Abattoirstraat 8, Paramaribo; tel. 401801; fax 401805; e-mail nfo@csasr.com; internet www.csa.sr; f. 1988; shipping agents and stevedores; Man. DINO IROKARSO.

Maritieme Autoriteit Suriname (Maritime Authority Suriname): Cornelis Jongbawstraat 2, POB 888, Paramaribo; tel. 476733; fax 472940; e-mail info@mas.sr; internet www.mas.sr; fmrly Dienst voor de Scheepvaart; govt authority supervising and controlling shipping in Surinamese waters; Dir and Harbour Master M. AMAFO.

Scheepvaart Maatschappij Suriname NV (SMS) (Suriname Shipping Line Ltd): Waterkant 44, POB 1824, Paramaribo; tel. 472447; fax 474814; e-mail surinam_line@sr.net; f. 1936; state-owned; passenger services in the interior; Dir. J. ROZENHOUT.

Suriname Coast Traders NV: Flocislaan 4, Duisburglaan, POB 9216, Paramaribo; tel. 463040; fax 463831; internet www .pasonsgroup.com; f. 1981; subsidiary of Pasons Group.

NV VSH Verenigde Surinaamse Holdingmij (United Suriname Shipping Company): van 't Hogerhuysstraat 9–11, POB 1860, Paramaribo; tel. 402558; fax 403515; e-mail info@vshunited.com; internet www.vshunited.com/shipping.html; shipping agents and freight carriers; operates NV VSH Scheepvaartmij, NV VSH Transportmij and NV Uniblue Shipping; Man. Dirs JAMES J. HEALY, Jr, PATRICK HEALY.

CIVIL AVIATION

The main airport is Johan Adolf Pengel International Airport, 45 km from Paramaribo. Domestic flights operate from Zorg-en-Hoop Airport, located in a suburb of Paramaribo. There are some 35 airstrips throughout the country.

Blue Wing Airlines (BWA): Doekhieweg 3, Zorg-en-Hoop Airport, POB 13007, Paramaribo; tel. 434393; fax 433909; e-mail sales@

bluewingairlines.com; internet www.bluewingairlines.com; f. 2002; privately owned; chartered and scheduled flights; services the domestic and Caribbean region; Chair. F. PENGEL; Gen. Man. A. JHAUW.

Civil Aviation Department of Suriname (CAD): Paramaribo; e-mail cad.dca@tct.gov.sr; internet www.cadsur.sr; govt. regulatory authority; Dir STANLEY BETTERSON (acting).

Gum Air NV: Doekhieweg 3, Zorg-en-Hoop Airfield, Paramaribo; tel. 498760; fax 491740; e-mail info@gumair.com; internet www.gumair.com; f. 1974; privately owned; unscheduled domestic and regional flights; Man. DEAN GUMMELS.

Surinaamse Luchtvaart Maatschappij NV (SLM) (Suriname Airways): Mr Jagernath Lachmonstraat 136, POB 2029, Paramaribo; tel. 465700; fax 491213; e-mail publicrelations@slm.firm.sr; internet www.flyslm.com; f. 1962; services to Amsterdam (Netherlands) and to destinations in North America, South America and the Caribbean; Vice-Pres. CLYDE CAIRO.

Tourism

Tourist attractions include the varied cultural activities, a number of historical sites and an unspoiled interior with many species of plants, birds and animals. There are 13 nature reserves and one nature park. There were an estimated 220,000 stop-over arrivals in 2011, of which the majority came from the Netherlands. In 2010 tourism receipts totalled US $61m.

Suriname Tourism Foundation: Dr J. F. Nassylaan 2, POB 656, Paramaribo; tel. 424878; fax 477786; e-mail sharida.sewnath@suriname-tourism.org; internet www.suriname-tourism.org; f. 1996; Exec. Dir KAREL DAWSON (acting).

Defence

The army numbered an estimated 1,840 men and women, as assessed at November 2012. There was an army of 1,400, a navy of 240 and an air force of some 200.

Defence Budget: an estimated 134m. Surinamese dollars in 2010.

Commander of the Army: Col HEDWICH GILAARD.

Education

Education is compulsory for children between the ages of seven and 12. Primary education lasts for six years, and is followed by a further seven years of secondary education, comprising a junior secondary cycle of four years followed by a senior cycle of three years. All education in government and denominational schools is provided free of charge. In 2008/09 enrolment in primary education included 91% of children in the relevant age-group, while enrolment in secondary education included 50% of children in the relevant age-group. Higher education is provided by three technical and vocational schools and by the University of Suriname at Paramaribo. In 2003 the Inter-American Development Bank (IDB) approved a US $12.5m. loan to fund the reform of the basic education system into a single 10-year cycle. It was hoped that the funds would result in a 10% increase in the number of pupils who finished sixth grade and a 20% reduction in drop-out and repetition rates. In 2012 the IDB approved a further grant of $13.7m. towards a second Basic Education Improvement Program for developing the curriculum framework and improving learning outcomes in the junior secondary grades.

SWAZILAND

Introductory Survey

LOCATION, CLIMATE, LANGUAGE, RELIGION, FLAG, CAPITAL

The Kingdom of Swaziland is a land-locked country in southern Africa, bordered by South Africa to the north, west, south and south-east, and by Mozambique to the east. The average annual temperature is about 16°C (61°F) on the Highveld, and about 22°C (72°F) in the sub-humid Lowveld, while annual rainfall ranges from 1,000 mm (40 ins) to 2,280 mm (90 ins) on the Highveld, and from 500 mm (20 ins) to 890 mm (35 ins) in the Lowveld. English and siSwati are the official languages. About 60% of the population profess Christianity, while most of the remainder adhere to traditional beliefs. The national flag (proportions 2 by 3) is blue, with a yellow-edged horizontal crimson stripe (one-half of the depth) in the centre. On this stripe is a black and white Swazi shield, superimposed on two spears and a staff, all lying horizontally. The capital is Mbabane.

CONTEMPORARY POLITICAL HISTORY

Historical Context

Swaziland, which was previously under the joint rule of the United Kingdom and the South African (Transvaal) Republic, became a British protectorate in 1903, and one of the High Commission Territories in 1907, the others being the colony of Basutoland (now the Kingdom of Lesotho) and the protectorate of Bechuanaland (now the Republic of Botswana). The British Act of Parliament that established the Union of South Africa in 1910 also provided for the inclusion in South Africa of the three High Commission Territories, subject to consultation with the local inhabitants.

Swaziland's first Constitution, which was introduced by the British Government, entered into force in January 1964. The Paramount Chief (iNgwenyama—the Lion), King Sobhuza II, subsequently established a traditionalist political party, the Imbokodvo National Movement (INM), which secured all of the seats in the new Legislative Council at elections in June of that year. A new Constitution, which was promulgated in 1966 and came into effect in April 1967, provided for the introduction of internal self-government pending the attainment of full independence by the end of 1969. Executive power was vested in King Sobhuza as the hereditary monarch and constitutional Head of State. The Legislative Council was dissolved in March 1967, and elections to the new bicameral Parliament took place in April. The INM secured all 24 elective seats in the House of Assembly, although the Ngwane National Liberatory Congress (NNLC) received 20% of the votes cast. In May King Sobhuza formed Swaziland's first Cabinet, appointing the leader of the INM, Prince Makhosini Dlamini, as Prime Minister. On 6 September 1968 Swaziland was granted full independence within the Commonwealth, and a new Constitution (based on the existing Constitution) was adopted.

In April 1973, in accordance with a parliamentary resolution, King Sobhuza repealed the Constitution, imposed a state of emergency under which all political activity was suspended, introduced legislation providing for detention without trial for a period of 60 days, and announced the formation of a national army. A new Constitution, promulgated on 13 October 1978, confirmed the King's control of executive and legislative decisions. The functions of the bicameral parliament, comprising a House of Assembly and a Senate, were confined to debating government proposals and advising the King. The existing 40 traditional local councils (Tinkhundla—singular: Inkhundla) were each to nominate two members to an 80-member electoral college, which was, in turn, to elect 40 deputies to the House of Assembly. Members of the House of Assembly were to select 10 members of the Senate, while the King was to nominate a further 10 members to each chamber. All political parties (including the INM) were prohibited. Legislative elections took place later that year, and the parliament was inaugurated in January 1979. In June 1982 the Swaziland National Council, an advisory body on matters of Swazi tradition, comprising members of the royal family, was redesignated as the Supreme Council of State (Liqoqo).

Domestic Political Affairs

King Sobhuza died in August 1982. In accordance with Swazi tradition, the powers of Head of State devolved upon the Queen Mother (Ndlovukazi—Great She Elephant) Dzeliwe, who was authorized to act as Regent until King Sobhuza's designated successor, Prince Makhosetive (born in 1968), attained the age of 21. Shortly afterwards Queen Regent Dzeliwe appointed the Liqoqo, which was to advise her in all affairs of State. Competition to secure supreme executive power subsequently emerged between the Prime Minister, Prince Mabandla N. F. Dlamini, and several prominent members, led by Prince Mfanasibili Dlamini, of the Liqoqo. In March 1983 Prince Mabandla was replaced as Prime Minister by a traditionalist, Prince Bhekimpi Dlamini. In August, under the powers of the 'Authorized Person' (an important hereditary post, held by Prince Sozisa Dlamini, the Chairman of the Liqoqo), Queen Regent Dzeliwe was deposed, apparently as a result of her reluctance to dismiss Prince Mabandla. Following an attempt by Queen Regent Dzeliwe to appeal against her deposition, Prince Mfanasibili and his followers obtained an official declaration that the High Court had no jurisdiction in matters concerning Swazi custom and tradition. Widespread opposition to the deposition of Queen Regent Dzeliwe was suppressed, and in September Queen Ntombi, the mother of Prince Makhosetive, was officially invested as Regent. In November elections to the Libandla took place, and a new Cabinet was appointed, in which only Prince Bhekimpi and the Minister of Foreign Affairs, Richard Dlamini, were retained.

In October 1985, following protests by prominent members of the royal family at the Liqoqo's monopoly of power, Queen Regent Ntombi dismissed Prince Mfanasibili. It was subsequently announced that the Liqoqo was to be reconstituted in its former capacity as an advisory body on matters pertaining to traditional law and custom. In December all those convicted of conspiracy in late 1984 were pardoned and released. In January 1986 it was announced that Prince Makhosetive was to be crowned in April, three years earlier than expected, in order to end the competition for power among vying royal factions.

Prince Makhosetive was crowned on 25 April 1986, and assumed the title of King Mswati III. In May King Mswati dissolved the Liqoqo, thereby consolidating his power. In July the King reorganized the Cabinet, and in October he appointed a former senior member of the security forces, Sotsha Dlamini, as Prime Minister. In May 1987 12 prominent officials, including Prince Bhekimpi and Prince Mfanasibili, were charged with sedition and treason, in connection with the removal from power of Queen Regent Dzeliwe in 1983. In November King Mswati established a special tribunal to preside over all cases involving alleged offences against the King or the Queen Regent; defendants appearing before the tribunal were not to be granted the right to legal representation or appeal. In March 1988 10 of those accused of involvement in the deposition of Queen Regent Dzeliwe were convicted of treason by the special tribunal, and received custodial sentences; two defendants were acquitted.

In November 1987 elections to the legislature took place, one year earlier than scheduled. In July 1989 King Mswati dismissed Sotsha Dlamini for alleged disobedience, replacing him with Obed Dlamini, a former leader of the Swaziland Federation of Trade Unions (SFTU).

In early 1990 the People's United Democratic Movement (PUDEMO), which had been established in 1983, distributed tracts questioning the legitimacy of the monarchy in its existing form and demanding constitutional reform. Security forces subsequently arrested a number of suspected members of PUDEMO, who were variously charged with treason, sedition or conspiring to form a political party. All the defendants were acquitted of the principal charges, although five were convicted of illegally attending a political gathering (the sentences of two of the five were annulled on appeal in October 1991). In an attempt to advance its objectives through legal bodies, PUDEMO subsequently established a number of affiliated organizations, including the Human Rights Association of Swaziland (HUMARAS)

SWAZILAND

Introductory Survey

and the Swaziland Youth Congress (SWAYOCO), but these were not accorded official recognition.

In September and October 1991 a committee, termed Vusela (Greetings), conducted a series of public forums throughout the country to elicit popular opinion on political reforms. Widespread demands for the abolition of the existing electoral system were reported, while there was substantial criticism of the composition of the Vusela committee itself. In February 1992 PUDEMO declared itself a legal opposition party (in contravention of the prohibition on political associations), rejected King Mswati's efforts to institute political reform, and demanded a constitutional referendum. Two further opposition movements, the Swaziland United Front (SUF) and the Swaziland National Front (SWANAFRO), subsequently re-emerged. In February King Mswati appointed a second committee (Vusela 2), which was to present recommendations for consideration by the King, based on the conclusions of the first committee.

In October 1992 King Mswati approved several proposals submitted by Vusela 2. The House of Assembly (redesignated the National Assembly) was to be expanded to 65 deputies (of whom 55 were to be directly elected by secret ballot from candidates nominated by the Tinkhundla, and 10 appointed by the King), and the Senate to 30 members (10 selected by the National Assembly and 20 appointed by the King); in addition, the legislation providing for detention without trial was to be abrogated, and a new constitution, incorporating the amendments, enshrining an hereditary monarchy and confirming the fundamental rights of the individual and the independence of the judiciary, was to be drafted. However, opposition groups protested at the committee's failure to recommend the immediate restoration of a multi-party political system: the issue was to be postponed until the forthcoming elections, in order to determine the extent of public support. PUDEMO announced its opposition to the electoral reforms, and demanded that the Government organize a national convention to determine the country's constitutional future. King Mswati subsequently dissolved parliament, and announced that he was to rule by decree, with the assistance of the Council of Ministers (as the Cabinet had been restyled), pending the adoption of a new constitution and the holding of parliamentary elections. Later in October King Mswati announced that elections to the National Assembly would take place in the first half of 1993. At a series of public meetings doubts were expressed as to the viability of the reformed electoral system; in early 1993, in response to public concern, it was announced that legislation preventing the heads of the Tinkhundla from exerting undue influence in the nomination of candidates had been introduced.

The 1993 elections

The first round of elections to the expanded National Assembly took place on 25 September 1993. The second round of parliamentary elections, on 11 October, was contested by the three candidates in each Inkhundla who had obtained the highest number of votes in the first poll; the majority of members of the former Council of Ministers (which had been dissolved in late September), including Obed Dlamini, failed to secure seats in the Assembly. Later in October King Mswati nominated a further 10 deputies to the National Assembly, which elected 10 of its members to the Senate; King Mswati subsequently appointed the remaining 20 senators, among them Obed Dlamini and Prince Bhekimpi. In November the former Minister of Works and Construction, Prince Jameson Mbilini Dlamini, considered a traditionalist, was appointed Prime Minister, and a new Council of Ministers was formed.

In February 1994 it was announced that King Mswati was to appoint a 15-member commission, comprising representatives of organs of State and non-governmental organizations, to draft a new constitution, and a national policy council, which was to prepare a manifesto of the Swazi people. Elections to the Tinkhundla (which had been postponed from March) finally took place, although a high rate of abstention by voters was reported. (The heads of the Tinkhundla had previously been appointed by the King.)

In January 1996 PUDEMO announced a campaign of protests and civil disobedience, owing to the Government's failure to respond to demands for the installation of a multi-party system and for the adoption of a constitution restricting the monarch to a largely ceremonial role. Security forces intervened to suppress demonstrations by SFTU members, and violent clashes ensued, in which three people were reported to have been killed. King Mswati accused the trade unions of attempting to overthrow the monarchy, and threatened to order his traditional warriors to

suppress the strike. The SFTU subsequently suspended strike action to allow negotiations to proceed with the Government. In May 1996 King Mswati indicated that a 'People's Parliament', comprising a series of consultative meetings between citizens and government leaders, had been initiated to solicit public opinion regarding constitutional reform. At the same time King Mswati dismissed Prince Mbilini as Prime Minister, and announced that he would appoint his successor in consultation with the Swaziland National Council.

In late July 1996, following an emergency meeting (attended by the Heads of State of Mozambique, Botswana, Zimbabwe and South Africa) to discuss Swaziland's political situation, King Mswati appointed a Constitutional Review Commission, comprising chiefs, political activists and trade unionists, to collate submissions from the Swazi people and subsequently draft proposals for a new constitution. (The Commission received substantial funds from international donors.) At the same time, Dr Barnabas Sibusiso Dlamini, an IMF Executive Director and former Minister of Finance, was appointed Prime Minister.

In January 1997 the SFTU claimed that there had been no response to its demands for democratic reform, and resolved to begin indefinite strike action from February. Meanwhile, the PUDEMO President, Mario Masuku, withdrew from the Constitutional Review Commission. The strike, pronounced illegal by the Government, proceeded, and was apparently observed by approximately one-half of the labour force. On the ninth day of industrial action six strikers were seriously injured in violent clashes with the security forces. The SFTU leaders declined the Government's offer to release them on condition that they end the strike; their trial was dismissed in February, owing to lack of evidence. At the beginning of March the Congress of South African Trade Unions (COSATU), which had asserted its support for the SFTU throughout the strike, initiated a one-day blockade of the Swazi border. The SFTU decided to suspend the strike shortly afterwards, as the Government had agreed to commence negotiations, but resolved to continue industrial action on the first two days of each month until its 27 demands had been met.

In August 1998 King Mswati dissolved the National Assembly, in preparation for elections scheduled for October. Opposition groups urged voters to boycott the polls, in the absence of the immediate legalization of political parties. Some 350 candidates were nominated by the Tinkhundla to contest the 55 elective seats in the Assembly. Voting took place on 16 and 24 October; turn-out was reportedly low. A new Cabinet, with Sibusiso Dlamini as Prime Minister, was appointed in mid-November, and a new Senate and Swaziland National Council were formed.

A judicial crisis developed in late 2002 when, with reference to decrees issued by the King in connection with the evictions of some 200 people from their homes in October 2000, the six South African judges of the Swaziland Court of Appeal resigned in protest at the Government's refusal to accept two rulings that the King had no power to overrule the National Assembly. The judges of the High Court subsequently announced that they would refuse to sit or set dates for hearings, and a strike by members of the legal profession ensued. In April 2003 a report by the International Bar Association attributed the judicial crisis to the lack of clearly defined roles for the executive, legislature and judiciary. In May the Government withdrew a statement in which it had accused the judges of being under external influence. In mid-September 2004 the Government reversed its position on the rulings which had provoked the crisis. Hearings were scheduled to resume at the Court of Appeal in November on condition that those evicted were allowed to return to their villages.

Meanwhile, in June 2001 King Mswati provoked international criticism by promulgating a decree that, it was claimed, effectively amounted to the declaration of a state of emergency; the legislation ensured that no person or body, including the courts, had the authority to challenge the King, prevented newspapers from challenging publishing bans, allowed the King to appoint judges and traditional chiefs personally, and made ridiculing or impersonating the King a criminal offence. Opposition groups in Swaziland condemned the decree as reinforcing tyrannical rule, and criticized the international community's lack of interest in the country's political situation. The King revoked the decree in July, in response to international diplomatic pressure, notably a threat by the USA to impose economic sanctions. However, at the same time the King issued a new decree that retained certain sections of the original decree, including a provision allowing the detention of Swazi citizens without the option of bail for some offences.

Constitutional review

In August 2001 the Constitutional Review Commission submitted its report, which recommended that the King's powers be extended and political parties remain outlawed, but stated that the introduction of a bill of rights that was not in conflict with Swazi laws and customs was a possibility. In February 2002 a 15-member committee, appointed by the King, began drafting a new constitution; PUDEMO criticized the Government for allegedly manipulating the Commission's report and selecting members of the drafting committee who were sympathetic to government policy. In May Prince David, the King's brother, and Chairman of the constitution-drafting committee, announced a new draft constitution, which, *inter alia*, envisaged the retention of the Tinkhundla system for forthcoming elections to the National Assembly.

King Mswati introduced the Internal Security Bill in June 2002, intended to suppress political dissent. It provided variously for fines and prison sentences for those found guilty of carrying or wearing banners or flags of banned political formations, or of participating in mass strikes or boycotts. Training abroad to commit acts of insurgency in Swaziland would be punishable by up to 20 years' imprisonment. The bill was severely criticized by the SFTU, PUDEMO and various foreign governments, which considered it to be inconsistent with the bill of rights and the proposed constitutional reform.

In May 2003 King Mswati announced the dissolution of the National Assembly. Pending elections to a new Assembly, scheduled for October, a council, styled the King's Order-in-Council, was charged with debating and enacting legislation in collaboration with the King. The elections to the National Assembly, duly held in October, were reportedly marked by a very low turn-out, many voters having apparently heeded an appeal by pro-democracy groups for a boycott of the polls. Although several members of proscribed political organizations stood as independent candidates, a Commonwealth monitoring team subsequently declared that the elections had been largely meaningless, in view of the lack of basic democratic freedoms that prevailed in Swaziland. In November the King appointed Themba Dlamini, a former incumbent on various parastatal bodies and a close associate of the royal family, as the new Prime Minister. At the same time, the King accepted a new draft constitution that, observers noted, safeguarded many of the monarchy's existing prerogatives. Among the provisions of the proposed new basic law was that the King should remain the head of the executive and retain responsibility for appointing the Prime Minister. He would, furthermore, retain a power of veto over any bill that received parliamentary approval. However, the draft Constitution did propose the removal of the King's power to rule by decree and provided for the replacement of the Court of Appeal by a new Supreme Court as Swaziland's highest judicial body.

In January 2005 the SFTU commenced a two-day general strike in protest at the proposed constitutional reform, which it maintained entrenched the power of the monarchy. The new Constitution was finally approved by a joint sitting of the Senate and the National Assembly in early June. It was ratified by King Mswati on 26 July and came into effect on 7 February 2006. The Constitution was viewed as being socially progressive, according greater rights to women—legally recognized as adults for the first time—and guaranteeing the right to primary education, but politically conservative: executive power was concentrated in the King and the Tinkhundla remained as the basis of the parliamentary system; the King would also continue to appoint the Prime Minister and the Cabinet, Chiefs and High Court judges and could dissolve the legislature. A bill of rights guaranteed freedom of assembly and speech; however, these rights could be suspended by the King if he considered it to be in the public interest. Furthermore, while there existed provision for the judiciary to interpret the Constitution, ultimate authority was vested with the King. There also remained considerable ambiguity regarding the legality of political parties, although the Constitution stated that the 'people of Swaziland have a right to be heard through and represented by their own freely chosen representatives in the government of the country'. Later in February the King effected a reorganization of the Cabinet.

The 2008 elections

In February 2008 six opposition parties announced that they would boycott forthcoming legislative elections, which were scheduled for September, and demanded the introduction of a system of multi-party democracy. A spokesman for PUDEMO stated that it was important to 'deny the state legitimacy' by refusing to take part. In April the Deputy President of that party, Gabriel Mkhumane, was shot dead in South Africa, where he had lived in exile for 24 years. The following month the Elections and Boundaries Commission announced that voter registration had begun for the elections, although political parties were still effectively proscribed. In June the King dissolved the House of Assembly (as the lower legislative body had been redesignated in the 2006 Constitution), and on 19 September the elections proceeded as scheduled, despite demonstrations by pro-democracy activists. The SFTU organized a march in Mbabane, and a further demonstration was planned on the border with South Africa; however, this was suppressed by the security forces and a number of activists were arrested. In the same month an extravagant ceremony was held to celebrate the King's 40th birthday and the 40th anniversary of Swaziland's independence.

Following the announcement of the election results there were reports that two men had been killed, and a third injured, when a bomb exploded on a road close to the King's Lozitha palace, east of Mbabane: it was believed that the men were planning to detonate the bomb near the royal palace but that it exploded prematurely. A South African national, was taken into custody and charged with treason. He was subsequently found guilty in August 2012 and sentenced to 85 years in prison the following month, though it was reported that he would only serve 25 years of his sentence. Meanwhile, in October 2008 the King reappointed Sibusiso Dlamini as Prime Minister, and a new Council of Ministers was subsequently formed.

In November 2008 Masuku, was arrested and charged under new anti-terrorism laws in connection with the attempted bomb attack on the royal palace. In the same month Prime Minister Dlamini formally listed four opposition organizations (PUDEMO, the Swaziland Liberation Army, the Swaziland Solidarity Network—SSN—and SWAYOCO) as terrorist groups. The Attorney-General, Majahenkhaba Dlamini, also warned journalists that reports in which they criticized the Government could lead to their arrest under the Suppression of Terrorism Act 2008. In February 2009 SWAYOCO Secretary-General Thabile Zwane was arrested for alleged terrorist activities, while in September Masuku was eventually acquitted and released from prison following a court ruling.

In early May 2010 a PUDEMO supporter, Sipho Jele, was arrested at a trade union rally, reportedly for wearing a T-shirt displaying that party's emblem; he was later found hanged in his gaol cell. The police declared his death a suicide, but this explanation was dismissed by his family and by Masuku (although the results of a subsequent investigation corroborated the suicide theory). Properties belonging to Masuku and other opposition leaders were searched by police in June, and up to 16 SWAYOCO members were arrested in the same month for their alleged involvement in a series of recent bomb attacks against police, judicial and political targets.

The Minister of Justice and Constitutional Affairs, Ndumiso Mamba, resigned in August 2010. The SSN claimed that Mamba had been forced to step down after it was discovered that he had been involved in a relationship with King Mswati's 12th wife. Prime Minister Dlamini appointed the Minister of Home Affairs, Chief Mgwagwa Gamedze, as acting justice minister.

In early September 2010 the major trade unions staged demonstrations in Manzini, attended by several hundred people, to demand democracy and greater rights for workers. Violent clashes between demonstrators and the security forces were reported, and SWAYOCO leader Wandile Dludlu was detained and allegedly assaulted by police officers after joining the march. Masuku and approximately 50 other opposition activists were arrested the day before the protest action commenced; Masuku, along with most of the other detainees, was swiftly released, but he was prevented by the police from participating in the demonstrations, while several COSATU members who had intended to join the protests were deported to South Africa. Further protests took place in March and April 2011 against proposed reductions to the size of the civil service and wage freezes.

Meanwhile, the Senate in February 2011 ruled that the discounted sale of state-owned land to six cabinet members (the Prime Minister, the Deputy Prime Minister, and the ministers responsible for home affairs, economic planning, natural resources, and agriculture), which had been authorized by Minister of Housing and Urban Development Lindiwe Dlamini in 2009, was unconstitutional and demanded that the land be returned to the state. The Constitution stipulated that only Land Management Boards had the authority to sell crown land, which was to be subject to public auction, a process that Lindiwe Dlamini had dismissed as 'time consuming'.

Recent developments: financial crisis

Thousands of people took part in protest marches in Mbabane in March 2011 in response to the Government's planned austerity measures, which included significant reductions in social spending. Teachers, students and numerous others expressed their displeasure at the state budget—approved the previous month—which would result in the losses of some 7,000 jobs and a freeze on public sector workers' pay for three years. The protests came amid increasing concerns of a fiscal crisis in the country, following a decline of 60% in revenues from the Southern African Customs Union (SACU). Furthermore, on 12 April—the anniversary of the decree banning political parties—a new round of pro-democracy protests began. Demonstrators were dispersed by riot police using water cannons, tear gas and rubber bullets, and some 100 people were arrested. COSATU indicated that it had sent some of its members to attend in an act of solidarity with protesters. Concurrent protests were also held in South Africa. Demonstrations continued into the following day, during which two prominent political leaders were detained by security forces on suspicion of making an explosive device, a claim they denied.

It was reported in early June 2011 that King Mswati had cancelled a celebration to mark 25 years in power in response to the protests earlier in the year and amid concerns that the country was bankrupt. Moreover, in September a number of civic groups attempted to deliver a petition to King Mswati demanding the reversal of the ban on opposition parties and that the fiscal crisis be resolved. However, they were prevented from handing over the petition by the police. In August it was announced that South Africa would provide a loan of US $350m. to ensure that the Swazi Government was able to purchase stocks of antiretroviral drugs (ARVs) and keep schools open. However, it subsequently emerged that while the South Africa Reserve Bank had approved the release of the loan in three tranches to the Central Bank of Swaziland, it had placed conditions on the loan (namely, the promotion of human rights and commitment to democratic reforms), which King Mswati and his advisors had refused to accept. In the meantime, the Government announced that funds were not available to pay the quarterly elderly grant to more than 40,000 beneficiaries. Nonetheless, the Swazi Government had been able to secure loans to cover the salaries of public sector workers, although it was reluctant to reveal the origin of the funding and what conditions had been attached to the lending. Analysts speculated that the Government may have offered its shares in a number of financial institutions as collateral to secure the credit, which amounted to some $170m.

Meanwhile, in October 2011 Prime Minister Dlamini announced a significantly reorganized Cabinet, replacing, *inter alia*, the ministers responsible for justice and constitutional affairs; information, communication and technology; foreign affairs; and labour and social security

Further strikes took place in July 2012 during which Swazi police fired rubber bullets to disperse crowds. Reports indicated that eight people were injured and 13 arrested during the industrial action in Mbabane. Meanwhile some 500 public sector workers—including nurses and teachers—began demonstrating in late June over meagre wage increases amidst ongoing reports of King Mswati's profligacy. About 1,000 students subsequently joined the demonstrations in solidarity with their teachers. They were allegedly beaten and fired on with water cannons by police. After the Government refused to negotiate increased wage demands, other unions joined the strike, including the Swaziland Transport and Allied Workers Union. Teachers were subsequently instructed to return to work by a court order. However, it was reported in early August that 110 teachers had been dismissed for failing to do so.

In late August 2012 the Government announced that the deadline for registering for local elections had been extended after only 27,000 voters signed up to vote, compared with the 350,000 eligible voters who had participated in parliamentary elections in 2008. Commentators blamed the low turn-out in part on PUDEMO and the Trade Union Congress of Swaziland, both of which remained proscribed in early 2013. The two organizations continued to urge the Swazi population not to legitimize the elections by participating in them. Following a parliamentary vote of no confidence in Prime Minister Dlamini in August 2012, King Mswati failed to remove him and the Cabinet. In accordance with the Constitution, King Mswati would have been required to endorse the parliamentary resolution for the

Government to step down. Dissatisfaction with the premier stemmed from an abrupt decision he had taken to cease the operations of the Swaziland Post and Telecommunications Corporation—the country's sole telephone operator—after a court ruled that it had violated a joint venture agreement with MTN Swaziland. It was widely speculated that both Mswati and Prime Minister Dlamini were shareholders in MTN, the South African-based telecommunications group.

HIV/AIDS

Swaziland has been severely affected by the HIV/AIDS pandemic. It has the highest prevalence of HIV/AIDS and one of the lowest life expectancies in the world. The Government has been criticized for its reluctance to confront the problem directly; proposed measures have included sterilizing or branding those infected with HIV, and in an attempt to prevent the spread of the disease, in September 2001 the Government ordered women aged 18 years or younger to remain celibate and avoid shaking hands with men for a period of five years. However, in recent years the Government has had a degree of success: Swaziland is on target to provide 90% of pregnant women living with HIV/AIDS with ARVs. In 2009 88% of pregnant women living with HIV/AIDS had access to ARVs, according to UNICEF. Overall ARV coverage was at around 83% in 2011, just over the WHO's universal coverage threshold of 80%. Nevertheless, around one-quarter of the adult population (aged between 15 and 49 years) is infected with HIV; while a recent survey of pregnant women between the ages of 25 and 29 had indicated a prevalence rate of 56.3%. Prompted by research that indicated that circumcision dramatically reduced HIV transmission rates, the Government initiated a US $15m. circumcision programme in early 2011, with funding provided by the USA. During the fiscal crisis in the country in late 2011 and early 2012 the country was experiencing difficulties in funding its HIV/AIDS programmes. Moreover, Round 11 of the Global Fund to Fight HIV, TB and Malaria was cancelled because of a lack of donors. The funding was crucial for increasing numbers of nurses, and analysts expressed serious concern that the country's financial problems, combined with the withdrawal of funding, could reverse recent gains in the fight against HIV/AIDS.

Foreign Affairs

During the apartheid era Swaziland pursued a policy of dialogue and co-operation with South Africa. In 1982 the two countries signed a secret non-aggression pact; several members of the African National Congress of South Africa (ANC), which had increasingly used Swaziland as a base for guerrilla attacks into South Africa, were subsequently arrested and expelled from Swaziland. The signing, in March 1984, of the Nkomati accord between South Africa and Mozambique (which banned both countries from harbouring dissidents) led many ANC members to flee from Mozambique to neighbouring Swaziland. Following the murder, in 1984, of the deputy chief of the Swazi security police, the Government initiated a campaign to arrest all ANC fugitives remaining in the country (the ANC denied involvement in the killing). In 1986 leading Swazi politicians expressed opposition to the imposition of economic sanctions against South Africa, owing to the dependence of Swaziland's own economy on that country. Following the legalization of the ANC in 1990, the Swazi Prime Minister, Obed Dlamini, pledged to conduct an inquiry (which, however, he failed to initiate) into state operations against ANC members. Formal diplomatic relations were established in 1993. From the late 1990s prominent South African organizations, including the ANC and COSATU, expressed support for the SFTU's demands for political reform, prompting the Swazi Government to complain of interference in its domestic affairs. In April 1995 the South African Government announced that it had rejected a long-standing claim by Swaziland to a region in the Mpumalanga province (formerly Eastern Transvaal). However, King Mswati declared in a letter to South African President Thabo Mbeki in early 2001 that he had not abandoned his intention to reincorporate parts of Mpumalanga and KwaZulu/Natal provinces into Swaziland. In 2003 the Chairperson of the Swaziland Border Adjustment Committee, Prince Khuzulwandle, criticized Mbeki for declining to discuss realignments of the border. In February 2010 the Swaziland Democracy Campaign was launched by domestic and South African organizations with a view to creating global momentum for democracy in Swaziland.

Following the ratification of the October 1992 peace accord in Mozambique (q.v.), an agreement signed by the Governments of

Swaziland and Mozambique and the office of the UN High Commissioner for Refugees in August 1993 provided for the repatriation of some 24,000 Mozambican nationals from Swaziland. In December the number of Swazi troops deployed at the border with Mozambique was increased, following clashes between Swazi and Mozambican forces in the region. In 1994 discussions took place between Swazi and Mozambican officials to seek mutually satisfactory arrangements for the joint patrol of the border, and in 1995 it was announced that the Mhlumeni border post, closed since the 1970s, would reopen as the second official transit point between the two countries. In September 1997, during the first visit to Swaziland made by a Mozambican Prime Minister, a bilateral extradition agreement was signed, with the aim of reducing cross-border crime. In December 1999 the Swazi authorities expelled some 500 Mozambican citizens who had been declared illegal immigrants.

CONSTITUTION AND GOVERNMENT

The Constitution of 7 February 2006 vests supreme executive power in the hereditary King, who is the Head of State, and provides for a bicameral legislature, comprising a House of Assembly and a Senate. The functions of the legislature are confined to debating government proposals and advising the King. Executive power is exercised through the Cabinet, which is appointed by the King.

The Parliament of Swaziland consists of the Senate, comprising not more than 31 members (of whom 20 are appointed by the King—at least eight of these are women—and 10 elected by the House of Assembly, one-half of these being women) and the House of Assembly, which comprises not more than 76 members. Of these, 60 are directly elected from candidates nominated by traditional local councils, known as Tinkhundla, and 10 are appointed by the King, one-half of whom are women. Additionally one woman is selected from each of the four regions of Swaziland and the Attorney-General is also an ex officio member.

The King appoints the Prime Minister and the Cabinet and has the power to dissolve the bicameral legislature. The Swazi National Council (Sibaya) constitutes the highest policy and advisory council of the nation and functions as the annual general meeting of the nation. A Council of Chiefs, composed of 12 chiefs drawn from the four regions of Swaziland advises the King on customary issues and any matter relating to chieftancy.

REGIONAL AND INTERNATIONAL CO-OPERATION

Swaziland is a member of the Common Market for Eastern and Southern Africa (see p. 241), of the Southern African Development Community (SADC, see p. 434) and of the Southern African Customs Union (SACU), which also includes Botswana, Lesotho, Namibia and South Africa.

Swaziland became a member of the UN in 1968. As a contracting party to the General Agreement on Tariffs and Trade, Swaziland joined the World Trade Organization (WTO, see p. 444) on its establishment in 1995. Swaziland participates in the Group of 77 (G77, see p. 461) developing countries.

ECONOMIC AFFAIRS

In 2011, according to estimates by the World Bank, Swaziland's gross national income (GNI), measured at average 2009–11 prices, was US \$3,520m., equivalent to \$3,300 per head (or \$5,970 per head on an international purchasing-power parity basis). During 2002–11, it was estimated, the population increased at an average annual rate of 0.6%, while gross domestic product (GDP) per head increased, in real terms, by an average of 1.8% per year. Overall GDP increased, in real terms, at an average annual rate of 2.4% in 2002–11; growth in 2011 was 1.3%.

Agriculture (including forestry) contributed 7.2% of GDP in 2011, according to African Development Bank (AfDB) estimates. About 26.9% of the labour force was employed in the agricultural sector in mid-2013 (including subsistence farming), according to FAO. The principal cash crops are sugar cane (sugar accounted for 14.1% of domestic export earnings in 2007), cotton, citrus fruits, pineapples and maize. Tobacco and rice are also cultivated. Livestock-rearing is traditionally important. Commercial forestry (which employs a significant proportion of the population) provides wood for the manufacture of pulp. During 2002–11, according to the World Bank, agricultural GDP increased by an average of 1.2% per year. Agricultural GDP increased by 6.8% in 2010, but decreased by 1.9% in 2011.

According to AfDB estimates, industry (including mining, manufacturing, construction and power) contributed 46.2% of GDP in 2011, and engaged 28.8% of those in paid employment in June 2005. During 2002–11, according to the World Bank, industrial GDP increased at an average annual rate of 1.3%. Industrial GDP increased by 7.6% in 2010, but decreased by 1.9% in 2011.

Mining contributed 0.3% of GDP in 2011, according to AfDB estimates, and engaged 1.3% of those in paid employment in June 2005. Swaziland has extensive reserves of coal, much of which is exported. Asbestos is also an important mineral export. In addition, Swaziland has reserves of tin, kaolin, talc, iron ore, pyrophyllite and silica. During 2000–04, according to the IMF, mining GDP declined by an average of 5.0% per year. Mining GDP increased by 9.0% in 2011, according to AfDB estimates.

Construction contributed 2.2% of GDP in 2011, according to AfDB estimates, and in June 2005 engaged 21.2% of those in paid employment. According to AfDB estimates, the GDP of the construction sector declined by 2.6% in 2011

Manufacturing contributed 42.5% of GDP in 2011, according to AfDB estimates, and in June 2005 engaged 5.4% of those in paid employment. During 2002–11 manufacturing GDP increased at an annual average rate of 1.3%. Manufacturing GDP increased by 7.4% in 2010, but decreased by 1.9% in 2011.

Swaziland imports most of its energy requirements from South Africa. The Swazi Government aimed to increase domestic energy output to cover approximately 50% of the country's needs, following the construction of a hydroelectric power station on the Maguga Dam, which began operations in 2002. However, in 2005 80.7% of total electrical energy generated and imported was obtained from South Africa and Mozambique, compared with 77.1% in 2002. Mineral fuels and lubricants accounted for an estimated 14.1% of imports in 2007.

The services sector contributed 46.5% of GDP in 2011, according to World Bank estimates. The sector engaged 50.3% of those in paid employment in June 2005. According to the World Bank, the GDP of the services sector increased by an average of 3.7% per year in 2002–11. Services GDP decreased by 3.4% in 2010, but increased by 6.2% in 2011.

In 2010, according to the IMF, Swaziland recorded a visible merchandise trade deficit of US \$148.6m., while there was a deficit of \$388.6m. on the current account of the balance of payments. In 2007 the principal source of imports was South Africa (81.3%), which was also the principal market for exports (79.8%); Italy was also an important export market. The principal imports in 2007 were machinery and transport equipment, food and live animals, and mineral fuels and lubricants; the principal exports in 2007 were chemicals and chemical products, and food and live animals.

In the financial year ending 31 March 2012 there was an estimated overall budgetary deficit of E1,471m. Swaziland's general government gross debt was E4,383m. in 2010, equivalent to 15.9% of GDP. Swaziland's external debt totalled US \$616m. at the end of 2010, of which \$385m. was public and publicly guaranteed debt. In 2009, the cost of servicing long-term public and publicly guaranteed debt and repayments to the IMF was equivalent to 2.1% of the value of exports of goods, services and income (excluding workers' remittances). In 2000–09 annual inflation averaged 7.6%. According to AfDB estimates, consumer prices increased by an average of 7.9% in 2011.

Swaziland's economy is vulnerable to fluctuations in international prices for some major exports, including sugar, as well as to the effects of unfavourable weather conditions. In addition, prevailing economic conditions in neighbouring South Africa have a pronounced impact on the Swazi economy: although Swaziland may determine the exchange rate of its currency, the lilangeni, this has remained at par with the South African rand. Moreover, the economy is almost wholly dependent on South Africa, which provides some 75% of government revenues through the Southern African Customs Union (SACU). Food security also remains a concern with the country heavily dependent on maize imports. In early 2010 the Government announced that it was to implement a plan of subsidies to improve nutrition. (In 2009 around 20% of the population were malnourished.) Meanwhile, the securing of much-needed foreign investment in Swaziland remained dependent on a satisfactory political settlement. The US had imposed economic sanctions on Swaziland, restricting financial assistance, but in September 2009 these were lifted and assistance resumed after the Swazi Government approved new legislation prohibiting the smuggling and trafficking of people in the country. The global financial crisis had a severe impact upon Swaziland's economy during 2009, with the resulting decline in trade leading to a reduction in activity in the manufacturing sector and a drastic contraction in vital revenues from SACU. SACU receipts continued to decline in 2010 and 2011 as a result of restructuring of tariffs, prompting a liquidity crisis in the country that resulted in Swaziland facing the prospect of being unable to pay its public sector wage bill (one of the largest in sub-Saharan Africa) and social grants for the elderly; the Swazi Government also raised concerns that it would be unable to restock its supply of antiretroviral medication (see Recent Developments and HIV/AIDS). In August 2012 unfavourable weather conditions and overgrazing were blamed for the death of some 10,000 cattle in the country. Following the IMF's withdrawal of funding from the country in mid-2012, in February 2013 it concluded its latest consultation with Swaziland, noting that higher revenues from SACU had improved the fiscal situation in the country (SACU transfers doubled in 2012/13), which enabled the Government to repay a central bank advance. The IMF also noted improved revenue collection, aided by the introduction of a value-added tax in April 2012, and supported the Ministry of Finance's proposed Public Finance Management bill. However, IMF authorities recommended improving competitiveness and the business climate; and suggested that more targeted spending (primarily on education, poverty alleviation and health care), and significant reductions to public sector wages, was required in order to improve economic growth: the IMF estimated that the economy had contracted by some 1.5% in 2012, and projected no growth in GDP for 2013.

PUBLIC HOLIDAYS

2014: 1 January (New Year's Day), 18–21 April (Easter), 19 April (Birthday of King Mswati), 25 April (National Flag Day), 1 May (Workers' Day), 29 May (Ascension Day), 22 July (Birthday of the late King Sobhuza), 6 September (Somhlolo—Independence—Day), 24 October (UN Day), 25–26 December (Christmas and Boxing Day).

The Incwala and Umhlanga Ceremonies are held in December or January, and August or September (respectively), but the exact dates are variable each year.

Statistical Survey

Source (unless otherwise stated): Central Statistical Office, POB 456, Mbabane; internet www.gov.sz/home.asp?pid=75.

Area and Population

AREA, POPULATION AND DENSITY

Area (sq km)	17,363*
Population (census results)†	
11–12 May 1997	929,718
11 May 2007 (provisional)‡§	
Males	460,498
Females	493,026
Total	953,524
Population (UN estimates at mid-year)‖	
2011	1,203,331
2012	1,220,406
2013	1,237,166
Density (per sq km) at mid-2013	71.3

* 6,704 sq miles.
† Excluding absentee workers.
‡ Source: UN, *Population and Vital Statistics Report.*
§ Population data are *de jure*, although the totals were the subject of some dispute on publication; in early 2009 the Ministry of Economic Planning and Development published the State of Swaziland Population Report, which contained a revised population estimate of 1,018,449 for 2007.
‖ Source: UN, *World Population Prospects: The 2010 Revision.*

POPULATION BY AGE AND SEX
(UN estimates at mid-2013)

	Males	Females	Total
0–14	230,890	227,682	458,572
15–64	360,732	374,334	735,066
65 and over . . .	18,562	24,966	43,528
Total	**610,184**	**626,982**	**1,237,166**

Source: UN, *World Population Prospects: The 2010 Revision.*

ETHNIC GROUPS
(census of August 1986)

Swazi	661,646
Other Africans . . .	14,468
European	1,825
Asiatic	228
Other non-Africans . .	412
Mixed	2,403
Unknown	77
Total	**681,059**

REGIONS
(population at census of May 2007, provisional figures)

	Area (sq km)	Population	Density (per sq km)
Hhohho . . .	3,569	263,761	73.9
Manzini . . .	5,945	293,260	49.3
Shiselweni . .	4,070	202,686	49.8
Lebombo . . .	3,779	193,817	51.3
Total . . .	**17,363**	**953,524**	**54.9**

Source: UN, *2010 World Population and Housing Census Programme.*

PRINCIPAL TOWNS
(population at census of May 1997)

Mbabane (capital) .	57,992	Manzini . . .	25,571

Mid-2011 (incl. suburbs, UN estimate): Mbabane 65,536 (Source: UN, *World Urbanization Prospects: The 2011 Revision*).

BIRTHS AND DEATHS
(annual averages, UN estimates)

	1995–2000	2000–05	2005–10
Birth rate (per 1,000)	34.1	31.8	30.1
Death rate (per 1,000)	11.9	15.7	14.9

Source: UN, *World Population Prospects: The 2010 Revision.*

Life expectancy (years at birth): 48.7 (males 49.1; females 48.2) in 2011 (Source: World Bank, World Development Indicators database).

EMPLOYMENT
(persons in paid employment at June)

	2003	2004	2005
Agriculture, hunting, forestry and fishing	21,491	20,804	19,955
Mining and quarrying	1,153	1,407	1,283
Manufacturing	19,485	19,874	20,272
Electricity, gas and water	1,418	1,389	859
Construction	4,824	5,293	5,115
Distribution	9,021	9,988	11,454
Transportation	2,491	2,265	3,007
Finance	6,422	5,202	6,430
Social services	26,758	27,247	27,228
Total employed	**93,063**	**93,469**	**95,603**

Source: IMF, *Kingdom of Swaziland: Selected Issues and Statistical Appendix* (March 2008).

Mid-2013 (estimates in '000): Agriculture, etc. 136; Total labour force 506 (Source: FAO).

Health and Welfare

KEY INDICATORS

Total fertility rate (children per woman, 2010)	3.4
Under-5 mortality rate (per 1,000 live births, 2010)	78
HIV/AIDS (% of persons aged 15–49, 2009)	25.9
Physicians (per 1,000 head, 2004)	0.16
Hospital beds (per 1,000 head, 2006)	2.1
Health expenditure (2009): US $ per head (PPP)	336
Health expenditure (2009): % of GDP	6.7
Health expenditure (2009): public (% of total)	66.5
Access to water (% of persons, 2010)	71
Access to sanitation (% of persons, 2010)	57
Total carbon dioxide emissions ('000 metric tons, 2008)	1,092.8
Carbon dioxide emissions per head (metric tons, 2008)	1.1
Human Development Index (2011): ranking	140
Human Development Index (2011): value	0.522

For sources and definitions, see explanatory note on p. vi.

Agriculture

PRINCIPAL CROPS
('000 metric tons, FAO estimates)

	2009	2010	2011
Maize	57.0	68.0	54.9
Potatoes	7.1	7.2	7.3
Sweet potatoes	2.5	2.6	2.2
Sugar cane	5,000	5,000	5,000
Groundnuts, with shell	3.6	3.7	2.7
Tomatoes	4.4	4.8	4.8
Oranges	36.0	42.5	43.0
Grapefruit and pomelos	36.0	37.0	37.3
Pineapples	25.0	26.5	30.5

Aggregate production ('000 metric tons, may include official, semi-official or estimated data): Total cereals 57.9 in 2009, 68.9 in 2010, 55.9 in 2011; Total roots and tubers 63.6 in 2009, 64.8 in 2010, 66.9 in 2011; Total vegetables (incl. melons) 11.9 in 2009, 12.5 in 2010, 12.6 in 2011; Total fruits (excl. melons) 111.2 in 2009, 120.7 in 2010, 126.0 in 2011.

Source: FAO.

LIVESTOCK
('000 head, year ending September, FAO estimates)

	2009	2010	2011
Horses	1.5	1.5	1.5
Asses	14.8	14.8	14.8
Cattle	585	620	625
Pigs	30	32	34
Sheep	28	35	35
Goats	276	275	270
Chickens	3,200	3,500	3,600

Source: FAO.

LIVESTOCK PRODUCTS
('000 metric tons, FAO estimates)

	2009	2010	2011
Cattle meat	15.4	15.9	16.5
Goat meat	1.9	1.8	1.8
Pig meat	1.8	1.9	1.9
Chicken meat	4.9	5.4	5.5
Cows' milk	42.0	42.3	42.5

Source: FAO.

Forestry

ROUNDWOOD REMOVALS
('000 cubic metres, excl. bark, FAO estimates)

	2009	2010	2011
Sawlogs, veneer logs and logs for sleepers	260	260	260
Other industrial wood	70	70	70
Fuel wood	1,045	1,063	1,078
Total	**1,375**	**1,393**	**1,408**

Source: FAO.

SAWNWOOD PRODUCTION
('000 cubic metres, incl. railway sleepers, FAO estimates)

	1995	1996	1997
Total (all coniferous)	90	100	102

1998–2011: Production assumed to be unchanged from 1997 (FAO estimates).

Source: FAO.

Fishing

(metric tons, live weight)

	1999	2000*	2001*
Capture	70*	70	70
Aquaculture	61	69	72
Common carp	18	20	20
Mozambique tilapia	20	25	25
Redbreast tilapia	12	13	15
North African catfish	5	6	6
Red claw crayfish	6	5	6
Total catch	**131***	**139**	**142**

* FAO estimate(s).

2002–08 (metric tons, live weight, FAO estimate): Capture 70.

2009–10 (metric tons, live weight, FAO estimates): Capture 70; Aquaculture 73; Total catch 143.

Source: FAO.

Mining

(metric tons, unless otherwise indicated)

	2009	2010	2011
Coal	129,647	145,903	121,050
Ferrovanadium	500	500*	500*
Quarrystone ('000 cu m)	202	305	206

* Estimated production.

Source: US Geological Survey.

Industry

SELECTED PRODUCTS

	2007	2008	2009
Raw sugar ('000 metric tons)	631	664	628
Electrical energy (million kWh)	454	432	517

Source: UN Industrial Commodity Statistics Database.

Wood pulp ('000 metric tons, FAO estimates): 102.0 in 2009; 150.0 in 2010; 150 in 2011 (Source: FAO).

Finance

CURRENCY AND EXCHANGE RATES

Monetary Units
100 cents = 1 lilangeni (plural: emalangeni).

Sterling, Dollar and Euro Equivalents (31 December 2012)
£1 sterling = 13.415 emalangeni;
US $1 = 8.501 emalangeni;
€1 = 11.216 emalangeni;
100 emalangeni= £7.45 = $11.76 = €8.92.

Average Exchange Rate (emalangeni per US $)
2010   7.321
2011   7.261
2012   8.210

Note: The lilangeni is at par with the South African rand.

BUDGET
(million emalangeni, year ending 31 March)

Revenue*	2005/06	2006/07	2007/08
Tax revenue	5,189.5	7,682.8	7,564.9
Taxes on net income and profits.	1,267.4	1,534.3	1,644.4
Companies	472.5	560.9	522.1
Individuals	761.7	892.4	1,058.4
Non-resident dividends and interest	33.3	81.0	63.9
Taxes on property	13.3	10.3	18.1
Taxes on goods, services and international trade	3,894.4	6,102.2	5,886.0
Receipts from Southern African Customs Union	3,101.1	5,321.8	4,989.9
Levies on sugar exports	21.1	33.1	32.1
Hotel and gaming taxes	7.8	9.6	13.5
Sales tax	734.9	620.1	725.0
Licences and other taxes	29.4	27.2	30.3
Other taxes	14.4	36.0	16.4
Other current revenue	137.3	172.0	713.5
Property income	53.4	89.6	596.6
Fees, fines and non-industrial sales	83.9	82.3	116.9
Total	5,326.8	7,854.8	8,278.4

Expenditure†	2005/06	2006/07	2007/08
Current expenditure	4,416.3	4,681.3	5,217.3
Wages and salaries	2,443.0	2,588.7	2,750.2
Other purchases of goods and services	995.8	1,202.8	1,343.0
Interest payments	194.4	163.4	211.3
Domestic	31.6	35.3	84.9
Foreign	162.9	128.1	126.4
Subsidies and other current transfers	783.1	726.4	912.8
Capital expenditure	1,409.7	1,436.6	1,732.7
Health	47.8	48.5	69.8
Education	18.9	42.6	82.2
Agriculture	171.6	321.4	587.7
Transport and communications	387.0	632.3	745.6
Other	784.4	391.9	247.4
Total	5,826.0	6,117.9	6,950.0

* Excluding grants received (million emalangeni): 172.2 in 2005/06; 165.6 in 2006/07; 62.8 in 2007/08.
† Excluding net lending (million emalangeni): −68.3 in 2005/06; −55.2 in 2006/07; 43.0 in 2007/08.

Source: IMF, *Kingdom of Swaziland: Selected Issues and Statistical Appendix* (October 2008).

2009/10 (million emalangeni, year ending 31 March): Total revenue (incl. grants) 9,225; Total expenditure (incl. net lending) 9,225 (Source: IMF, *Kingdom of Swaziland: Staff Report for the 2011 Article IV Consultation*—February 2012).

2010/11 (million emalangeni, year ending 31 March, preliminary): Total revenue (incl. grants) 6,944; Total expenditure (incl. net lending) 8,220 (Source: IMF, *Kingdom of Swaziland: Staff Report for the 2011 Article IV Consultation*—February 2012).

2011/12 (million emalangeni, year ending 31 March, projections): Total revenue (incl. grants) 7,212; Total expenditure (incl. net lending) 8,683 (Source: IMF, *Kingdom of Swaziland: Staff Report for the 2011 Article IV Consultation*—February 2012).

INTERNATIONAL RESERVES
(excl. gold, US $ million at 31 December)

	2009	2010	2011
IMF special drawing rights	69.62	68.39	68.18
Reserve position in IMF	10.29	10.11	10.07
Foreign exchange	878.96	677.85	522.25
Total	958.87	756.35	600.51

Source: IMF, *International Financial Statistics*.

MONEY SUPPLY
(million emalangeni at 31 December)

	2009	2010	2011
Currency outside depository corporations	327.63	349.35	357.01
Transferable deposits	2,009.35	2,189.70	2,524.99
Other deposits	5,376.24	5,783.69	5,896.41
Broad money	7,713.23	8,322.74	8,778.41

Source: IMF, *International Financial Statistics*.

COST OF LIVING
(Consumer Price Index; base: 2000 = 100, unless otherwise indicated)

	2006	2007	2008
Food	194.1	228.3	271.5
Clothing	114.6	113.9	116.0
Housing*	101.3	102.5	113.0
All items (incl. others)	147.3	159.2	179.8

* Base 2005 = 100.

2009 (Consumer Price Index; base: 2000 = 100): All items 193.2.

Source: ILO.

Cost of Living (Consumer Price Index; base: 2000 = 100): All items 199.9 in 2010; 215.6 in 2011 (Source: African Development Bank).

NATIONAL ACCOUNTS
(million emalangeni at current prices)

Expenditure on the Gross Domestic Product

	2009	2010*	2011*
Government final consumption expenditure	3,663	4,021	4,413
Private final consumption expenditure	23,622	24,226	25,140
Gross capital formation	2,757	2,758	2,759
Total domestic expenditure	30,042	31,005	32,312
Exports of goods and services	14,875	15,190	14,875
Less Imports of goods and services	18,129	19,217	19,162
GDP at purchasers' values	26,788	26,978	28,025

Gross Domestic Product by Economic Activity

	2009	2010*	2011*
Agriculture, forestry and fishing	1,588	1,630	1,679
Mining	57	73	80
Manufacturing	8,519	9,371	9,840
Electricity, gas and water	188	269	284
Construction	535	519	503
Wholesale and retail trade; restaurants and hotels	2,107	2,166	2,243
Finance, insurance and real estate	1,275	1,507	1,622
Transport and communications	1,446	1,549	1,671
Public administration and defence	3,263	4,258	4,809
Other services	852	389	438
Sub-total	19,830	21,731	23,169
Indirect taxes	7,389	5,721	5,387
Less Imputed bank service charge	431	474	530
GDP at purchasers' values	26,788	26,978	28,025

* Provisional figures.

Source: African Development Bank.

BALANCE OF PAYMENTS
(US $ million)

	2008	2009	2010
Exports of goods	1,489.2	1,564.9	1,805.3
Imports of goods	−1,529.3	−1,696.1	−1,953.9
Balance on goods	−40.1	−131.2	−148.6
Exports of services	255.1	210.5	257.5
Imports of services	−650.9	−562.9	−670.9
Balance on goods and services	−435.9	−483.5	−562.0
Primary income received	298.0	290.8	212.5
Primary income paid	−303.2	−413.4	−438.6
Balance on goods, services and primary income	−441.1	−606.2	−788.1
Secondary income received	417.7	404.9	482.6
Secondary income paid	−208.0	−213.8	−83.1
Current balance	−231.4	−415.1	−388.6
Capital account (net)	−8.8	−4.0	14.4
Direct investment assets	7.9	−7.0	−3.9
Direct investment liabilities	105.7	65.7	135.7
Portfolio investment assets	−75.5	122.8	49.7
Portfolio investment liabilities	43.9	−6.6	4.7
Other investment assets	190.1	249.7	−161.6
Other investment liabilities	176.0	48.4	63.3
Net errors and omissions	12.0	−55.0	55.5
Reserves and related items	219.9	−1.1	−230.9

Source: IMF, *International Financial Statistics*.

External Trade

PRINCIPAL COMMODITIES
(US $ million)

Imports c.i.f.	2005	2006	2007
Food and live animals	230.1	158.8	222.2
Beverages and tobacco	29.9	20.6	26.1
Crude materials (inedible)	26.9	21.2	25.8
Minerals, fuels and lubricants	194.0	180.4	178.5
Chemicals and chemical products	324.4	158.5	166.8
Basic manufactures	323.7	250.5	243.4
Machinery and transport equipment	308.8	279.9	240.6
Miscellaneous manufactures	180.1	134.3	146.8
Total (incl. others)	1,656.1	1,242.4	1,270.1

Exports f.o.b. (incl. re-exports)	2005	2006	2007
Food and live animals	230.5	366.0	230.2
Beverages and tobacco	10.0	16.4	4.8
Crude materials (inedible)	114.3	134.6	85.2
Minerals, fuels and lubricants	8.4	15.1	14.0
Chemicals and chemical products	598.1	638.8	600.9
Basic manufactures	31.1	36.3	31.8
Machinery and transport equipment	57.6	52.7	44.8
Miscellaneous manufactures	222.6	199.0	99.2
Total (incl. others)	1,277.8	1,462.8	1,113.3

Source: UN, *International Trade Statistics Yearbook*.

Total imports (million emalangeni): 10,624 in 2008; 15,094 in 2009; 14,315 in 2010 (Source: African Development Bank).

Total exports (million emalangeni): 12,959 in 2008; 14,067 in 2009; 13,217 in 2010 (Source: African Development Bank).

PRINCIPAL TRADING PARTNERS
(US $ million)

Imports c.i.f.	2005	2006	2007
China, People's Repub.	65.9	24.6	50.8
Germany	1.2	25.4	0.9
Hong Kong	11.8	19.8	2.2
India	0.4	10.7	16.2
Japan	5.8	26.1	30.1
Mozambique	57.3	11.3	17.0
South Africa	1,339.3	995.2	1,033.2
United Kingdom	32.6	8.5	8.5
USA	11.5	10.1	17.4
Zimbabwe	15.8	13.2	4.9
Total (incl. others)	1,656.1	1,242.4	1,270.1

Exports f.o.b.	2005	2006	2007
Australia	441.5	2.3	2.2
Botswana	6.6	13.1	3.3
Italy	0.1	0.4	153.5
Lesotho	8.0	25.6	1.3
Mozambique	96.6	247.4	20.2
Namibia	8.3	11.5	31.1
New Zealand	0.4	22.9	0.9
South Africa	478.8	446.1	888.5
Uganda	0.0	246.7	0.0
United Kingdom	128.4	4.6	1.3
USA	56.2	48.9	1.1
Zimbabwe	0.6	369.0	0.0
Total (incl. others)	1,277.8	1,462.8	1,113.3

Source: UN, *International Trade Statistics Yearbook*.

Total imports (million emalangeni): 10,624 in 2008; 15,094 in 2009; 14,315 in 2010 (Source: African Development Bank).

Total exports (million emalangeni): 12,959 in 2008; 14,067 in 2009; 13,217 in 2010 (Source: African Development Bank).

Transport

RAILWAYS
(traffic)

	2002	2003	2004
Net total ton-km (million) . . .	728	726	710

Source: UN, *Statistical Yearbook*.

ROAD TRAFFIC
(motor vehicles in use at 31 December 2007)

Passenger cars	52,223
Buses and coaches	8,124
Lorries and vans	41,778
Motorcycles and mopeds	3,482

Source: IRF, *World Road Statistics*.

CIVIL AVIATION
(traffic on scheduled services)

	1998	1999	2000
Kilometres flown (million) . .	1	1	2
Passengers carried ('000) . .	41	12	90
Passenger-km (million) . .	43	13	68
Total ton-km (million) . . .	4	1	6

Source: UN, *Statistical Yearbook*.

Tourism

TOURIST ARRIVALS
(at hotels)

Country of residence	2008	2009	2010
Australia	2,197	2,423	1,717
Mozambique	12,177	9,613	15,326
South Africa	147,639	167,520	227,986
United Kingdom	9,300	13,351	10,780
Total (incl. others)	323,538	334,391	338,032

Tourism receipts (US $ million, excl. passenger transport): 36 in 2008; 40 in 2009; 51 in 2010.

Source: World Tourism Organization.

Communications Media

	2009	2010	2011
Telephones ('000 main lines in use)	45.2	53.0	75.8
Mobile cellular telephones ('000 subscribers)	664.4	725.8	766.5
Internet subscribers ('000) . .	22.0	4.2	4.7
Broadband subscribers ('000) . .	1.5	1.6	2.8

Source: International Telecommunication Union.

Education

(2009/10 unless otherwise indicated)

	Institutions	Teachers	Students
Pre-primary	n.a.	1,924	20,755
Primary	541*	7,462	241,237
Secondary	182*	4,883	88,787
University†	1‡	462§	5,692§

* Figure for 2001/02.
† Figures exclude vocational, technical and teacher-training colleges. In 2000 there were 1,822 students enrolled at these institutions, which numbered 10 in 2003.
‡ Figure for 2000.
§ Figure for 2005/06.

Source: UNESCO Institute for Statistics.

Pupil-teacher ratio (primary education, UNESCO estimate): 32.3 in 2009/10 (Source: UNESCO Institute for Statistics).

Adult literacy rate (UNESCO estimates): 86.8% (males 88.1%; females 87.4%) in 2010 (Source: UNESCO Institute for Statistics).

Directory

The Government

HEAD OF STATE

King: HM King MSWATI III (succeeded to the throne 25 April 1986).

COUNCIL OF MINISTERS
(May 2013)

Prime Minister: BARNABAS SIBUSISO DLAMINI.

Deputy Prime Minister: THEMBA MASUKU.

Minister of Economic Planning and Development: Prince HLANGUSEMPHI.

Minister of Finance: MAJOZI SITHOLE.

Minister of Foreign Affairs and International Co-operation: MTITI FAKUDZE.

Minister of Public Works and Transport: NTUTHUKO DLAMINI.

Minister of Health: BENEDICT XABA.

Minister of Commerce, Industry and Trade: JABULILE MASHWAMA.

Minister of Housing and Urban Development: Pastor LINDIWE DLAMINI.

Minister of Education and Training: WILSON M. NTJANGASE.

Minister of Agriculture: CLEMENT DLAMINI.

Minister of Tourism and Environmental Affairs: MDUDUZI DLAMINI.

Minister of Labour and Social Security: LUTFO DLAMINI.

Minister of Natural Resources and Energy: Princess TSANDZILE.

Minister of Sports, Culture and Youth Affairs: HLOBSILE NDLOVU.

Minister of Information, Communication and Technology: WINNIE MAGAGULA.

Minister of Home Affairs: PRINCE GCOKOMA.

Minister of Public Service: PATRICK MAGWEBETANE MAMBA.

Minister of Justice and Constitutional Affairs: Chief MGWAGWA GAMEDZE.

Minister of Tinkhundla Administration and Development: ROGERS MAMBA.

MINISTRIES

Office of the Prime Minister: Cabinet Offices, Hospital Hill, POB 395, Swazi Plaza, Mbabane; tel. 24042251; fax 24043943; internet www.gov.sz.

Office of the Deputy Prime Minister: Gwamile St, POB A33, Swazi Plaza, H101, Mbabane; tel. 24042723; fax 24044073.

Ministry of Agriculture: Hospital Hill, opposite Fire and Emergency Services, POB 162, H100, Mbabane; tel. 24042731; fax 24044730; e-mail ps@agriculture.gov.sz.

Ministry of Commerce, Industry and Trade: Interministerial Bldg, Block 8, 1st Floor, Mhlambanyatsi Rd, POB 451, Mbabane; tel. 24043201; fax 24044711; e-mail mcit@gov.sz.

Ministry of Economic Planning and Development: Finance Bldg, 4th and 5th Floors, Lusutfu Rd, POB 602, Mbabane; tel. 24043765; fax 24042157; e-mail ps@planning.gov.sz.

Ministry of Education and Training: Hospital Rd, POB 39, Mbabane; tel. 24042491; fax 24043880; e-mail ps_education@gov.sz.

Ministry of Finance: Mhlambanyatsi Rd, POB 443, Mbabane; tel. 24048148; fax 24043187; e-mail ps@finance.gov.sz.

Ministry of Foreign Affairs and International Co-operation: Interministerial Bldg, Block 8, Level 3, Mhlambanyatsi Rd, POB 518, Mbabane; tel. 24042661; fax 24042669; e-mail psforeignaffairs@realnet.co.sz.

Ministry of Health: POB 5, Mbabane; tel. 24042431; fax 24047420; e-mail infohealth@gov.sz.

Ministry of Home Affairs: Home Affairs and Justice Bldg, 1st Floor, Mhlambanyatsi Usuthu Link Rd, POB 432, Mbabane; tel. 24042941; fax 24044303.

Ministry of Housing and Urban Development: Income Tax Bldg, 5th Floor, Mhlambanyatsi Rd, POB 1832, Mbabane; tel. 24046049; fax 24044085; e-mail ps_housing@gov.sz.

Ministry of Information, Communication and Technology: Interministerial Complex, Block 8, 3rd Floor, Mhlambanyatsi Rd, POB 642, Mbabane; tel. 24054000; fax 24041898; e-mail ps_mict@gov.sz.

Ministry of Justice and Constitutional Affairs: Ministry of Justice Bldg, 5th Floor, cnr Mhlambanyatsi and Usuthu Link Rds, POB 924, Mbabane; tel. 24046010; fax 24043533; e-mail ps@justice.gov.sz.

Ministry of Labour and Social Security: Interministerial Office Block, Mhlambanyatsi Rd, POB 198, Mbabane; tel. 24041971; fax 24041966; e-mail deptlab@realnet.sz.

Ministry of Natural Resources and Energy: Income Tax Bldg, 4th Floor, Mhlambanyatsi Rd, POB 57, Mbabane; tel. 24046244; fax 24044851; e-mail nergyswa@realnet.co.sz.

Ministry of Public Service: Finance Bldg, 2nd and 3rd Floors, Mhlambanyatsi Rd, POB 170, Mbabane; tel. 24043521; fax 24045379; e-mail ps_mops@gov.sz.

Ministry of Public Works and Transport: Mhlambanyatsi Rd, POB 58, Mbabane; tel. 24099000; fax 24042364; e-mail nkanmbulep@gov.sz.

Ministry of Sports, Culture and Youth Affairs: Swazi Bank Bldg, 4th Floor, Gwamile St, POB 4843, Mbabane; tel. 24045053.

Ministry of Tinkhundla Administration and Development: Post and Telecom Bldg, Ground, 1st and 2nd Floors, Sheffield Rd, POB 2701, Mbabane; tel. 24041244; fax 24041012.

Ministry of Tourism and Environmental Affairs: Income Tax Bldg, 2nd Floor, Mhlambanyatsi Rd, POB 2652, Mbabane; tel. 24046162; fax 24045415; e-mail ps_tourism@gov.sz.

Legislature

SENATE

The Senate comprises not more than 31 members, of whom 20 are appointed by the King—at least eight of these are women—and 10 elected by the House of Assembly, one-half of whom are women.

President: GELANE ZWANE.

HOUSE OF ASSEMBLY

The House of Assembly comprises not more than 76 members. Of these, not more than 60 are directly elected from candidates nominated by traditional local councils, known as Tinkhundla, and not more than 10 are appointed by the King, one-half of whom are women. Additionally, one woman is selected from each of the four regions of Swaziland and the Attorney-General is also an ex officio member. The most recent elections to the House of Assembly took place on 19 September 2008.

Speaker: PRINCE GUDUZA.

Election Commission

Elections and Boundaries Commission: POB 4842, Mbabane; tel. 24162813; fax 24161970; five mems; Chair. Chief GIJA DLAMINI.

Political Organizations

Party political activity was banned by royal proclamation in April 1973, and formally prohibited under the 1978 Constitution. Since 1991, following indications that the Constitution was to be revised, a number of political associations have re-emerged. Following the introduction of the new Constitution in February 2006, the legal status of party political activity remained unclear.

African United Democratic Party (AUDP): f. 2006; advocates full democratization of Swaziland; Pres. STANLEY MAUNDZISA; Sec.-Gen. SIBUSISO DLAMINI.

Imbokodvo National Movement (INM): f. 1964 by King Sobhuza II; traditionalist movement, which also advocates policies of devt and the elimination of illiteracy; Leader (vacant).

Ngwane National Liberatory Congress (NNLC): Ilanga Centre, Martin St, Manzini; tel. 25053935; f. 1962 by fmr mems of the SPP; advocates democratic freedoms and universal suffrage, and seeks abolition of the Tinkhundla electoral system; Pres. OBED DLAMINI; Sec.-Gen. DUMISA DLAMINI.

People's United Democratic Movement (PUDEMO): POB 4588, Manzini; tel. and fax 25054181; internet pudemo.org; f. 1983; seeks constitutional limitation of the powers of the monarchy; affiliated orgs include the Human Rights Asscn of Swaziland and the Swaziland Youth Congress (SWAYOCO—Pres. ALEX LANGWENYA; Sec.-Gen. KENNETH KUNENE); Pres. MARIO BONGANI MASUKU; Sec. SIKHUMBUZO PHAKATHI.

Swaziland National Front (SWANAFRO): Mbabane; Pres. ELMOND SHONGWE; Sec.-Gen. GLENROSE DLAMINI.

Diplomatic Representation

EMBASSIES IN SWAZILAND

Mozambique: Princess Dr., POB 1212, Mbabane; tel. 24041296; fax 24048482; e-mail moz.high@swazi.net; Ambassador JUQUEIRO JOAO GRACA MANHIQHUE.

South Africa: New Mall, 2nd Floor, Dr Sishayi Rd, POB 2507, Mbabane; tel. 24044651; fax 24044335; e-mail sahc@africaonline.co.sz; High Commissioner Dr REDDY JAN MABUSE MAMPANE.

Taiwan (Republic of China): Makhosikhosi St, Mbabane; tel. 24044739; fax 24046688; e-mail rocembassy@africaonline.co.sz; Ambassador TSAI MING-YAW.

USA: Central Bank Bldg, 7th Floor, Mahlokohla St, Mbabane Pl., POB 199, Mbabane; tel. 24046441; fax 24045959; e-mail USEmbassyMbabane@state.gov; internet swaziland.usembassy.gov; Ambassador MAKILA JAMES.

Judicial System

Following the introduction of the new Constitution, the Swaziland Superior Court of Judicature comprised the Supreme Court and the High Court, which replaced the existing Court of Appeal and the High Court. The Supreme Court is headed by the Chief Justice and consists of not fewer than four other Justices of the Supreme Court, and is the final Court of Appeal. The High Court consists of the Chief Justice and not fewer than four Justices of the High Court, and has unlimited original jurisdiction in civil and criminal matters.

Chief Justice of the High Court: MICHAEL MATHEALIRA RAMOLI-BELI.

Attorney-General: MAJAHENKHABA DLAMINI.

Religion

About 60% of the adult Swazi population profess Christianity. Under the new Constitution, which came into effect on 7 February 2006, Christianity ceased to be recognized as the country's official religion. There was a growing Muslim population, reported to number some 10,000 adherents. Most of the remainder of the population hold traditional beliefs.

CHRISTIANITY

At mid-2000 there were an estimated 153,000 Protestants and 466,000 adherents professing other forms of Christianity.

Council of Swaziland Churches: Mandlenkosi Ecumenical House, 142 Esser St, Manzini; POB 1095, Manzini; tel. 25053697; fax 25055841; e-mail c.o.c@africaonline.co.sz; f. 1976; Chair. Bishop ABSALOM MNISI; Gen. Sec. GIDEON C. M. DLAMINI; 9 mem. churches incl. Roman Catholic, Anglican, Kukhany'okusha Zion Church and Lutheran.

League of African Churches: POB 230, Lobamba; asscn of 48 independent churches; Chair. SAMSON HLATJWAKO.

Swaziland Conference of Churches: 175 Ngwane St, POB 1157, Manzini; tel. and fax 25055253; e-mail scc@africaonline.co.sz; internet www.swazilandcc.org; f. 1929; Pres. Rev. JOHANNES V. MAZIBUKO; Gen. Sec. Rev. S. F. DLAMINI.

The Anglican Communion

Swaziland comprises a single diocese within the Church of the Province of Southern Africa. The Metropolitan of the Province is the Archbishop of Cape Town, South Africa. The Church had some 40,000 members at mid-2000.

Bishop of Swaziland: Rt Rev. ELLINAH WAMUKOYA, Bishop's House, Muir St, POB 118, Mbabane; tel. 24043624; fax 24046759; e-mail anglicanchurch@africaonline.co.sz.

The Roman Catholic Church

The Roman Catholic Church was established in Swaziland in 1913. For ecclesiastical purposes, Swaziland comprises the single diocese of Manzini, suffragan to the archdiocese of Pretoria, South Africa. Some 6% of the total population are adherents of the Roman Catholic Church. The Bishop participates in the Southern African Catholic Bishops' Conference (based in Pretoria, South Africa).

Bishop of Manzini: Rt Rev. LOUIS NCAMISO NDLOVU, Bishop's House, Sandlane St, POB 19, Manzini; tel. 25056900; fax 25056762; e-mail bishop@africaonline.co.sz.

Other Christian Churches

Church of the Nazarene: POB 832, Manzini; tel. 25054732; f. 1910; 7,649 adherents (1994).

The Evangelical Lutheran Church in Southern Africa: POB 117, Mbabane; tel. 24043411; fax 24041847; f. 1902; Bishop JEREMIAH BHEKI MAGAGULA; 2,800 adherents in Swaziland (1994).

Mennonite Central Committee: POB 329, Mbabane; tel. 24042805; fax 24044732; f. 1971; Co-ordinator HLOB'SILE NXUMALO.

The Methodist Church in Southern Africa: POB 42, Mbabane; tel. 26321975; e-mail brianj@bcmc.co.za; internet www.methodist.org.za; f. 1880; Bishop BRIAN C. JENNINGS; 2,578 adherents (1992).

United Christian Church of Africa: POB 1345, Nhlangano; tel. 22022648; f. 1944; Pres. Rev. WELLINGTON B. MKHALIPHI; Founder and Gen. Sec. Dr J. J. NQUKU.

The National Baptist Church, the Christian Apostolic Holy Spirit Church in Zion and the Religious Society of Friends (Quakers) are also active.

BAHÁ'Í FAITH

National Spiritual Assembly: POB 298, Mbabane; tel. 25052689; f. 1960; mems resident in 153 localities.

ISLAM

Ezulwini Islamic Institute: Al Islam Dawah Movement of Swaziland, POB 133, Ezulwini.

The Press

PRINCIPAL NEWSPAPERS

The Swazi News: Sheffield Rd, POB 156, Mbabane; tel. 24041550; fax 24042438; e-mail swazinews@times.co.sz; internet www.times.co.sz; f. 1983; weekly; English; owned by *The Times of Swaziland*; Editor PHEPHISA KHOZA; circ. 28,000.

Swazi Observer: Observer House, 3 West St, POB A385, Swazi Plaza, Mbabane; tel. 24049600; fax 24045503; e-mail info@observer.org.sz; internet www.observer.org.sz; f. 1981; owned by Tibiyo Taka Ngwane; Mon.–Sat.; *Weekend Observer* (Sun.); CEO S. MYZO MAGAGULA; Editor-in-Chief (vacant).

The Times of Swaziland: Sheffield Rd, POB 156, Mbabane; tel. 24042211; fax 24042438; e-mail editor@times.co.sz; internet www.times.co.sz; f. 1897; Mon.–Fri., Sun.; also monthly edn; English; other publs incl. *What's Happening* (tourist interest); Man. Editor MBOGANI MBINGO; circ. 18,000.

PRINCIPAL PERIODICALS

The Nation: Mbabane House, 3rd Floor, Mahlokohla St, POB 4547, Mbabane; tel. and fax 24046611; e-mail thenation@realnet.co.sz; f. 1997; monthly; independent news magazine; Editor BHEKI MAKHUBU.

Swaziview: Mbabane; tel. 24042716; monthly magazine; general interest; circ. 3,500.

UNISWA Research Journal of Agriculture, Science and Technology: Private Bag 4, Kwaluseni; tel. 25274418; fax 25274428; e-mail research@uniswa.sz; internet www.uniswa.sz; 2 a year; publ. of the Faculties of Agriculture, Health Sciences and Science of the Univ. of Swaziland; Chair. Prof. E. M. OSSOM.

Publishers

GBS Printing and Publishing (Pty) Ltd: POB 1384, Mbabane; tel. 25052779.

Longman Swaziland (Pty) Ltd: POB 2207, Manzini; tel. 25053891.

Macmillan Boleswa Publishers (Pty) Ltd: POB 1235, Manzini; tel. 25184533; fax 25185247; e-mail macmillan@africaonline.co.sz; f. 1978; textbooks and general; CEO DUSANKA STOJAKOVIC.

Swaziland Printing & Publishing Co Ltd: POB 28, Mbabane; tel. 24042716; fax 24042710.

Whydah Media Publishers Ltd: Mbabane; tel. 24042716; f. 1978.

Broadcasting and Communications

TELECOMMUNICATIONS

MTN Swaziland: Karl Grant St, POB 5050, H100 Mbabane; tel. 24060000; fax 24046215; e-mail feedback@mtn.co.sz; internet www.mtn.co.sz; f. 1998; jt venture between MTN Group, South Africa, and Swaziland Posts and Telecommunications Corpn; operates mobile cellular telephone network; 213,000 subscribers (2005); Chair. DAVID DLAMINI; CEO AMBROSE DLAMINI.

Swaziland Posts and Telecommunications Corpn (SPTC): Phutfumani Bldg, Mahlokohla St, POB 125, H100 Mbabane; tel. 24052000; fax 24052001; e-mail info@sptc.co.sz; internet www.sptc.co.sz; f. 1983; Acting Man. Dir AMON DLAMINI.

BROADCASTING

Radio

Swaziland Broadcasting and Information Service (SBIS): POB 338, Mbabane; tel. 24042763; fax 24046953; e-mail sbisnews@africaonline.co.sz; f. 1966; broadcasts in English and siSwati; Dir BHEKI GAMA (acting).

Swaziland Commercial Radio (Pty) Ltd: POB 1586, Alberton 1450, South Africa; tel. (11) 24344333; fax (11) 24344777; privately owned commercial service; broadcasts to Southern Africa in English and Portuguese; music and religious programmes; Man. Dir A. DE ANDRADE.

Trans World Radio: POB 64, Manzini; tel. 25052781; fax 25055333; internet www.twr.org; f. 1974; religious broadcasts from five transmitters in 30 languages to Southern, Central and Eastern Africa and to the Far East.

Television

Swaziland Television Authority (Swazi TV): Hospital Hill, POB A146, Swazi Plaza, Mbabane; tel. 24043036; fax 24042093; e-mail info@swazitv.co.sz; internet www.swazitv.co.sz; f. 1978; state-owned; broadcasts seven hours daily in English; CEO BONGANI AUSTIN DLAMINI.

Finance

(cap. = capital; res = reserves; dep. = deposits; m. = million; brs = branches; amounts in emalangeni)

BANKING

In 2010 there were four commercial banks in Swaziland.

Central Bank

Central Bank of Swaziland: Mahlokohla St, POB 546, Mbabane; tel. 24082000; fax 24040013; e-mail info@centralbank.org.sz; internet www.centralbank.org.sz; f. 1974; bank of issue; cap. 21.8m., res 31.4m., dep. 1,388.7m. (March 2006); Gov. MARTIN G. DLAMINI; Dep. Gov. S. G. MDLULI.

Commercial Banks

First National Bank of Swaziland Ltd: Sales House Bldg, 2nd Floor, POB 261, Swazi Plaza, Mbabane; tel. 25184637; fax 24044735; e-mail hnsibande@fnb.co.za; internet www.fnbswaziland.co.sz; f. 1988; fmrly Meridien Bank Swaziland Ltd; wholly owned by FirstRand Bank Holdings Ltd, Johannesburg; cap. and res 61.5m., dep. 484.5m. (June 2002); Chair. Dr D. M. J. VON WISSEL; Man. Dir DAVE WRIGHT; 7 brs.

Nedbank (Swaziland) Ltd: cnr Plaza-Dr Sishayi St and Bypass Rd, POB 68, Mbabane; tel. 24081000; fax 24044060; e-mail info@nedbank.co.sz; internet www.nedbank.co.sz; f. 1974; fmrly Standard Chartered Bank Swaziland Ltd; 23.1% state-owned; cap. 11.9m., res 134.6m., dep. 1,006.2m. (Dec. 2007); Chair. MABILI DLAMINI; Man. Dir FIKILE NKOSI; 6 brs and 1 agency.

Development Banks

Standard Bank Swaziland Ltd: Standard House, 1st Floor, Swazi Plaza, POB A294, Mbabane; tel. 24046587; fax 24045899; e-mail standardbankswaziland@iafricaonline.co.sz; internet www.standardbank.co.sz; f. 1988; fmrly Stanbic Bank Swaziland, present name adopted 1997; merged with Barclays Bank of Swaziland in Jan. 1998; 25% state-owned; cap. 14.6m., res 89.3m., dep. 1,454.3m. (Dec. 2005); Chair. R. J. ROSSOUW (acting); Man. Dir TINEYI MAWOCHA; 10 brs, 1 agency.

Swaziland Development and Savings Bank (SwaziBank—Libhange LeSive): Engungwini Bldg, Gwamile St, POB 336, Mbabane; tel. 24042551; fax 24041214; e-mail swazibank@swazibank.sz; internet www.swazibank.co.sz; f. 1965; state-owned; taken over by central bank in 1995; under independent management since 2000; cap. and res 143.0m., total assets 557.9m. (March 2002); Acting Chair. NOAH M. NKAMBULE; Man. Dir STANLEY M.N. MATSEBULA; 8 brs.

Financial Institution

Swaziland National Provident Fund: POB 1857, Manzini; tel. 25082000; fax 25082001; internet www.snpf.co.sz; f. 1974; provides benefits for employed persons on retirement from regular employment or in the event of becoming incapacitated; employers are required by law to pay a contribution for every eligible staff member; total assets 290m. (June 1996); Chair. MDUDUZI GINA; CEO Prince LONKHOKHELA DLAMINI.

STOCK EXCHANGE

Swaziland Stock Exchange: Capital Markets Development Unit, Infumbe Bldg, 1st Floor, Warner St, POB 546, Mbabane; tel. 24082164; fax 24049493; e-mail info@ssx.org.sz; internet www.ssx.org.sz; f. 1990 as Swaziland Stock Market (SSM); state-owned; Chair. MARTIN G. DLAMINI.

INSURANCE

Between 1974 and 1999 the state-controlled Swaziland Royal Insurance Corpn (SRIC) operated as the country's sole authorized insurance company, although cover in a number of areas not served by SRIC was available from several specialized insurers. In 1999 it was proposed that legislation would be enacted to end SRIC's monopoly and provide for the company's transfer to private sector ownership. The legislation was adopted as the Insurance Act in 2005.

Insurance Companies

Metropolitan Life Swaziland: Mbabane; tel. 24090282; e-mail info@metropolitan.co.sz; internet www.metropolitan.co.sz; f. 2008; Chair. STANLEY MATSEBULA; Man. Dir MUZI DLAMINI.

Swaziland Royal Insurance Corpn (SRIC): SRIC House, Somhlolo Rd, Gilfillan St, POB 917, H100 Mbabane; tel. 24043231; fax 24046415; e-mail sric@sric.sz; internet www.sric.sz; f. 1974; 41% state-owned, 59% owned by Munich-Reinsurance Co of Africa Ltd, Mutual and Federal, INBA Holdings, Public Service Provident Fund, Zurich Insurance Company and SA Mutual Life Assurance; Chair. KENNETH MBULI; Gen. Man. ZOMBODZE R. MAGAGULA.

Insurance Association

Insurance Brokers' Association of Swaziland (IBAS): POB 222, Mbabane H100; tel. 24043226; fax 24046412; e-mail mzamo_dlamini@aon.co.sz; f. 1983; Chair. MZAMO ELLIOT DLAMINI; 4 mems.

Trade and Industry

GOVERNMENT AGENCIES

Small Enterprise Development Co (SEDCO): POB A186, Swazi Plaza, Mbabane; tel. 24042811; fax 24040723; e-mail business@sedco.co.sz; internet www.sedco.biz; f. 1970; devt agency; supplies workshop space, training and expertise for 165 local entrepreneurs at eight sites throughout the country; Chair. PHOLILE DLAMINI; CEO DORRINGTON MATIWANE.

Swaziland Investment Promotion Authority (SIPA): Nkhotfotjeni Bldg, 1st Floor, cnr Msakato and Dzeliwe Sts, POB 4194, Mbabane; tel. 24040472; fax 24043374; e-mail info@sipa.org.sz;

internet www.sipa.org.sz; f. 1998; Chair. NICK JACKSON; CEO PHUMELELE DLAMINI (acting).

DEVELOPMENT ORGANIZATIONS

National Industrial Development Corpn of Swaziland (NIDCS): POB 866, Mbabane; tel. 24043391; fax 24045619; f. 1971; state-owned; administered by Swaziland Industrial Devt Co; Admin. Dir P. K. THAMM.

Swaziland Coalition of Concerned Civic Organisations (SCCCO): Smithco Industrial Centre, Mswati III Ave, 11th St, Matsapha; POB 4173, Mbabane; tel. and fax 25187688; e-mail webmaster@swazicoalition.org.sz; internet www.swazicoalition.org.sz; f. 2003; promotes constitutional democracy, poverty alleviation, fiscal discipline, economic stability, competitive regional and international trade, social justice, and the rule of law; Sec.-Gen. MUSA HLOPE; 9 mems incl.:

Coordinating Assembly of Non-Governmental Organisations (CANGO): POB A67, Swazi Plaza, Mbabane; tel. 24044721; fax 24045532; e-mail director@cango.org.sz; internet www.cango.org.sz; f. 1983; Exec. Dir EMMANUEL NDLANGAMANDLA; over 70 mem. orgs.

Federation of Swaziland Employers and Chamber of Commerce (FSECC): Emafini Business Center, Malagwane Hill, POB 72, Mbabane; tel. 24040768; fax 24090051; e-mail fsecc@business-swaziland.com; internet www.business-swaziland.com; f. 2003 by merger of Fed. of Swaziland Employers (f. 1964) and Swaziland Chamber of Commerce (f. 1916); CEO ZODWA MABUZA; c. 500 mems (2005).

Swaziland Industrial Development Co (SIDC): Dhlan'Ubeka House, 5th Floor, cnr Mdada and Lalufadlana Sts, POB 866, Mbabane; tel. 24044010; fax 24045619; e-mail info@sidc.co.sz; internet www.sidc.co.sz; f. 1986; 35% state-owned; finances private sector projects and promotes local and foreign investment; cap. E24.1m., total assets E577m. (June 2010); Chair. TIMOTHY M. J. ZWANE; CEO Dr VINCENT MZWANDILE MHLANGA.

Swaki (Pty) Ltd: Liqhaga Bldg, 4th Floor, Nkoseluhlaza St, POB 1839, Manzini; tel. 25052693; fax 25052001; e-mail info@swaki.co.sz; jtly owned by SIDC and Kirsh Holdings; comprises a number of cos involved in manufacturing, services and the production and distribution of food.

Swaziland Solidarity Network (SSN): c/o COSATU House, 3rd Floor, 1–5 Leyds St, Braamfontein, South Africa; POB 1027, Johannesburg 2000, South Africa; tel. (11) 23393621; fax (11) 23394244; e-mail ssnnetwork@gmail.org.za; internet www.swazisolidarity.org; f. 1997; umbrella org. promoting democracy; incorporates mems from Swaziland and abroad incl. PUDEMO, SWAYOCO, and the Swaziland Democratic Alliance (f. 1999); also incl. the African National Congress of South Africa, South African Communist Party and Congress of South African Trade Unions.

Tibiyo Taka Ngwane (Bowels of the Swazi Nation): POB 181, Kwaluseni, Manzini; tel. 25184306; fax 25184399; internet www.tibiyo.com; f. 1968; national devt agency, with investment interests in all sectors of the economy; participates in domestic and foreign jt investment ventures; total assets: E604m. (1999); Chair. Prince LOGCOGCO MANGALISO; Man. Dir ABSALOM THEMBA DLAMINI.

CHAMBERS OF COMMERCE

Sibakho Chamber of Commerce: POB 2016, Manzini; tel. and fax 25057347.

Swaziland Chamber of Commerce and Industry: see Fed. of Swaziland Employers and Chamber of Commerce.

INDUSTRIAL AND TRADE ASSOCIATIONS

National Agricultural Marketing Board: POB 4261, Manzini; tel. 25055314; fax 25054072; internet www.namboard.co.sz; Chair. Dr MICAH B. MASUKU; CEO PHUMELELA SHONGWE.

National Maize Corpn (NMC): 11th St Matsapha Indstrial Sites; tel. 25187432; fax 25184461; e-mail info@nmc.co.sz; internet www.nmc.co.sz; f. 1985; Chair. NATHI GUMEDZE; Acting CEO SIFISO NXUMALO.

Swaziland Citrus Board: Sokhamila Bldg, cnr Dzeliwe and Mdada Sts, POB 343, Mbabane H100; tel. 24044266; fax 24043548; e-mail citrus@realnet.co.sz; f. 1969; Chair. P. S. NODDEBOE.

Swaziland Cotton Board: POB 220, Manzini; tel. and fax 25052775; e-mail dlaminiaa@gov.sz; f. 1967; CEO TOM JELE.

Swaziland Dairy Board: Enguleni Bldg, 3rd Floor, 287 Mahleka St, POB 2975, Manzini; tel. 25058262; fax 25058260; e-mail ceo-swazidairy@africaonline.co.sz; internet swazidairy.org; f. 1971; Gen. Man. N. T. GUMEDE.

Swaziland Sugar Association: 4th Floor, cnr Dzeliwe and Msakato Sts, POB 445, Mbabane; tel. 24042646; fax 24045005; e-mail info@ssa.co.sz; internet www.ssa.co.sz; CEO Dr MICHAEL MATSE-BULA.

EMPLOYERS' ORGANIZATIONS

Building Contractors' Association of Swaziland: POB 518, Mbabane; tel. 24040071; fax 24044258; e-mail soconswad@realnet.co.sz.

Swaziland Association of Architects, Engineers and Surveyors: POB A387, Swazi Plaza, Mbabane; tel. 24042227.

Swaziland Institute of Personnel and Training Managers: c/o UNISWA, Private Bag, Kwaluseni; tel. 25184011; fax 25185276.

UTILITIES

Electricity

Swaziland Electricity Company: POB 258, Mbabane; tel. 24094000; fax 24042335; e-mail sifiso.dhlamini@sec.co.sz; internet www.sec.co.sz; statutory body; f. 1963; Chair. S'THOFENI GININDZA; Man. Dir BANELE NYAMANE (acting).

Water

Swaziland Water Services Corpn: Emtfonjeni Bldg, Below Gables Shopping Complex, Ezulwini, MR103, POB 20, Mbabane H100; tel. 24163621; fax 24163617; e-mail headoffice@swsc.co.sz; internet www.swsc.co.sz; state authority; Chair. ESAU N. ZWANE; CEO PETER N. BHEMBE.

TRADE UNIONS

Swaziland Amalgamated Trade Unions (SATU): POB 7138, Manzini; tel. 25059544; fax 25052684; f. 2003 by merger of five industrial unions; Sec.-Gen. FRANK NKULULEKO MNCINA; 3,500 mems (2005).

Trade Union Congress Of Swaziland (TUCOSWA): POB 1158, Manzini; tel. 25059514; fax 25059515; e-mail sftu1@swazi.net; f. 2011 following merger of the Swaziland Federation of Labour and the Swaziland Federation of Trade Unions; subsequently joined by the Swaziland National Association of Teachers; deregistered by the Govt in April 2012; Acting Sec.-Gen. MDUDUZI GINA; Pres. BARNES DLAMINI.

Transport

Buses are the principal means of transport for many Swazis. Bus services are provided by private operators; these are required to obtain annual permits for each route from the Road Transportation Board, which also regulates fares.

RAILWAYS

The rail network, which totalled 301 km in 2011, provides a major transport link for imports and exports. Railway lines connect with the dry port at Matsapha, the South African ports of Richards Bay and Durban in the south, the South African town of Komatipoort in the north and the Mozambican port of Maputo in the east. Goods traffic is mainly in wood pulp, sugar, molasses, coal, citrus fruit and canned fruit. In January 2012 Transnet of South Africa announced plans to route a new railway through Swaziland to connect with Richards Bay and a number of ports in Mozambique.

Swaziland Railways: Swaziland Railway Bldg, cnr Johnston and Walker Sts, POB 475, Mbabane; tel. 24047211; fax 24047210; internet www.swazirail.co.sz; f. 1962; Chair. B. A. G. FITZPATRICK; CEO GIDEON J. MAHLALELA.

ROADS

In 2002 there were an estimated 3,594 km of roads, including 1,465 km of main roads and 2,129 km of secondary roads. About 30% of the road network was paved in that year. The rehabilitation of about 700 km of main roads and 600 km of district gravel-surfaced roads began in 1985, financed by World Bank and US loans totalling some E18m. In 1991 work commenced on the reconstruction of Swaziland's main road artery, connecting Mbabane to Manzini, via Matsapha, and in 2001 the Government announced the construction of two main roads in the north of the country, financed by Japanese loans.

Roads Department: Ministry of Public Works and Transport, POB 58, Mbabane; tel. 24042321; fax 24045825; e-mail tshabalalatr@gov.sz; Chief Roads Engineer TREVOR M. TSHABALALA.

SHIPPING

Royal Swazi National Shipping Corpn Ltd: POB 1915, Manzini; tel. 25053788; fax 25053820; f. 1980 to succeed Royal Swaziland Maritime Co; 76% owned by Tibiyo Taka Ngwane; owns no ships, acting only as a freight agent; Gen. Man. M. S. DLAMINI.

CIVIL AVIATION

Swaziland's only airport is at Matsapha, near Manzini, about 40 km from Mbabane. In mid-1997 the Government initiated a three-year programme to upgrade the airport. In early 2003 construction began of an international airport at Sikhupe, in eastern Swaziland. In March 2006 Swaziland Airlink was one of 92 airlines banned from landing at European Union airports owing to safety concerns.

Swaziland Airlink: POB 2042, Matsapha; tel. 25186155; fax 25186148; e-mail info@flyairlink.com; internet www.flyswaziland.com; f. 1999; fmrly Royal Swazi Nat. Airways Corpn; jt venture between SA Airlink, South Africa (40%) and the Govt of Swaziland; scheduled passenger services from Manzini to Johannesburg, South Africa; Chair. SIBUSISO MOTSA.

Tourism

Swaziland's attractions for tourists include game reserves (at Malolotja, Hawane, Mlawula and Mantenga) and magnificent mountain scenery. In 2010 tourist arrivals at hotels totalled 338,032; receipts from tourism amounted to US $51m. in that year.

Hotel and Tourism Association of Swaziland: Oribi Court, 1st Floor, Gwamile St, POB 462, Mbabane; tel. 24042218; fax 24044516; e-mail aliand@realnet.co.sz; internet www.visitswazi.com/tourismassoc; f. 1979.

Swaziland National Trust Commission (SNTC): POB 100, Lobamba; tel. 24161516; fax 24161875; e-mail director@sntc.org.sz; e-mail curator@sntc.org.sz (museums and monuments); internet www.sntc.org.sz; f. 1972; parastatal org. responsible for conservation of nature and cultural heritage (national parks, museums and monuments); CEO T. DLAMINI.

Swaziland Tourism Authority (STA): POB A1030, Swazi Plaza, Mbabane H101; tel. 24049693; fax 24049683; e-mail www.thekingdomofswaziland.com; internet www.welcometoswaziland.com; f. 2001; CEO ERIC SIPHO MASEKO.

Defence

The Umbutfo Swaziland Defence Force was created in 1973. Compulsory military service of two years was introduced in 1983.

Defence Expenditure: Budgeted at E168m. for 2001/02.

Commander of the Umbutfo Swaziland Defence Force: Maj.-Gen. STANLEY S. DLAMINI.

Deputy Commander of the Umbutfo Swaziland Defence Force: Brig.-Gen. PATRICK V. MOTSA.

Education

Education is not compulsory in Swaziland. Primary education begins at six years of age and lasts for seven years. Secondary education begins at 13 years of age and lasts for up to five years, comprising a first cycle of three years and a second of two years. According to UNESCO estimates, in 2009/10 86% of children in the relevant age-group (males 86%; females 85%) were enrolled at primary schools, while in that year secondary enrolment included 33% of children in the appropriate age-group (males 29%; females 37%). In 2005/06 5,692 students were enrolled at the University of Swaziland, which has campuses at Luyengo and Kwaluseni. However, the university closed in mid-2011 as a result of a lack of funding. There are also a number of other institutions of higher education: in 2000 there were 1,822 students enrolled at 10 vocational, technical and teacher-training colleges. In 2008 1.18% of total government expenditure was allocated to education.

SWEDEN

Introductory Survey

LOCATION, CLIMATE, LANGUAGE, RELIGION, FLAG, CAPITAL

The Kingdom of Sweden lies in north-western Europe, occupying about two-thirds of the Scandinavian peninsula. It is bordered by Finland to the north-east, and by Norway to the north-west and west. About 15% of Sweden's area lies north of the Arctic Circle. The Baltic Sea and the Gulf of Bothnia are to the east, the Skagerrak and Kattegat channels to the south-west. The country is relatively flat and is characterized by thousands of inland lakes and small coastal islands. There is a mountain range, the Kjolen mountains, in the north-west. Winters are cold and summers mild. In Stockholm the mean summer temperature is 18°C (64°F) and the mean winter temperature −3°C (27°F). The national language is Swedish, but there are Finnish and Lapp (Sámi) minorities (the latter numbering between 17,000 and 20,000), retaining their own languages. A majority of the inhabitants profess Christianity, and about 71% are adherents of the Evangelical Lutheran Church of Sweden. The national flag (proportions 5 by 8) is light blue with a yellow cross, the upright of the cross being to the left of centre. The capital is Stockholm.

CONTEMPORARY POLITICAL HISTORY

Historical Context

Sweden has been a constitutional monarchy, traditionally neutral, since the early 19th century. During this time the country has not participated in any war or entered any military alliance. Norway, formerly united with Sweden, became independent in 1905. Sweden adopted parliamentary government in 1917, and universal adult suffrage was introduced in 1921. From 1932 until 1976, except for a short break in 1936, Sweden was governed by the Socialdemokratiska Arbetareparti (SAP—Swedish Social Democratic Party), either alone or as the senior partner in coalitions (1936–45 and 1951–57). During those 44 years the country had only three Prime Ministers, all Social Democrats. Since the Second World War Sweden has become an active member of many international organizations, including the UN (to which it has given military support), the Council of Europe (see p. 260) and, from 1995, the European Community (EC, now European Union—EU, see p. 281).

Domestic Political Affairs

Olof Palme succeeded Dr Tage Erlander as Prime Minister and leader of the SAP in October 1969. After a general election in September 1970, Palme formed a minority Government. Under a constitutional reform, the Riksdag (Parliament) was reconstituted from January 1971, its two chambers being replaced by a unicameral assembly. King Gustaf VI Adolf, who had reigned since 1950, died in September 1973 and was succeeded by his grandson, Carl XVI Gustaf. A revised Constitution, effective from January 1975, ended the monarch's prerogative to appoint the Prime Minister: the Speaker of the Riksdag was to have this responsibility in future.

At the September 1976 election, dissatisfaction with high rates of taxation, necessary to maintain the advanced social welfare system that Sweden had developed, brought about the defeat of the SAP. Thorbjörn Fälldin, leader of the Centerpartiet (CP—Centre Party), formed a centre-right coalition in October. The CP's desire to abandon Sweden's nuclear power programme caused serious controversy in June 1978, when an independent commission recommended its continuation. This view was endorsed by the Folkpartiet (FP—Liberals) and Moderata Samlingspartiet (MS—Moderates), whose rejection of a proposal by Fälldin to submit the nuclear issue to a national referendum precipitated the Government's resignation in October 1978. The FP formed a minority Government, led by Ola Ullsten. Following a general election in September 1979, Fälldin returned as Prime Minister of a coalition comprising members of the CP, the MS and the FP, with an overall parliamentary majority of only one seat. A referendum on the future of nuclear power was held in March 1980, at which a narrow majority of the electorate approved a limited programme of nuclear reactor development,

to be progressively eliminated by 2010 and replaced by alternative energy resources.

During 1980 the Government's economic policies came under attack, mainly because of the rising rate of inflation, and there was severe industrial unrest. The MS, who disagreed with proposed tax reforms, left the coalition in May 1981. At the next general election, held in September 1982, the SAP was returned to power, securing 166 of the 349 seats in the Riksdag, but gaining an overall majority over the three non-socialist parties. In October Palme formed a minority Government, following an undertaking by the Vänsterpartiet—Kommunisterna (VpK—Left Party—Communists), which held 20 seats, to support the SAP. Palme's Government was returned to power in September 1985, with the backing of the VpK. The SAP and the VpK together won 178 seats, while the three main non-socialist parties took 171 seats. The FP increased its share of seats in the legislature from 21 to 51.

In February 1986 Palme was murdered by an unknown assailant in Stockholm. The Deputy Prime Minister, Ingvar Carlsson, took office as Prime Minister the following month. In mid-1989 Christer Pettersson, a man with a history of mental illness and violent crime, was convicted of Palme's murder amid some controversy, only to be acquitted on appeal in October. In May 1998 the Supreme Court ruled that there was insufficient new evidence to conduct a retrial.

At the general election in September 1988 the SAP remained in power with the continued support of the VpK. The MS remained the second largest party in the Riksdag. In February 1990 the VpK (subsequently restyled the Vänsterpartiet—VP—Left Party) and the Miljöpartiet de Gröna (MP—Green Party) refused to endorse the Government's proposed austerity measures. Carlsson resigned, but, having secured support for a more moderate set of proposals, he formed another minority Government. During 1990 the Swedish economy entered into recession, and in December the Riksdag approved further austerity measures.

The MS-led Government of Carl Bildt

The popularity of the SAP continued to decline, and in the general election of September 1991 the party did not win enough seats to form a government, although, with 138 seats, it remained the largest party in the Riksdag. The MS increased their representation to 80 seats, while the Kristdemokratiska Samhällspartiet (KdS—Christian Democrats) and a recently formed right-wing party, Ny demokrati (ND—New Democracy), won 26 and 25 seats respectively, at the expense of the FP and the CP. In early October Carl Bildt, the leader of the MS (the largest non-socialist party in the legislature), formed a minority Government comprising members of four non-socialist parties—the MS, the CP, the FP and the KdS. The coalition was obliged to rely on the ND for support in securing approval for legislation. The new Government began to accelerate the deregulation of the economy already undertaken by its predecessor.

Although the Government's austerity measures succeeded in reducing inflation, the high level of the budgetary deficit was a cause of concern in 1992. In September speculation on the international currency markets caused a rapid outflow of capital, and in November a fresh outflow of capital, following the SAP's refusal to approve reductions in public expenditure, forced the Government to allow the krona to 'float' in relation to other currencies, thereby effectively devaluing it by some 10%. In March 1993 the Government was defeated in the Riksdag when the ND refused to support budgetary proposals, but later in the same month the Government won a parliamentary vote of confidence (the ND abstained from voting).

SAP-led minority Governments: 1994–2002

At the general election in September 1994 the SAP increased its representation to 161 seats. The VP won 22 seats and the environmentalist MP 18. Although the MS maintained the level of support they had gained at the previous election, the other parties in the incumbent coalition Government fared badly. Bildt resigned as Prime Minister, and in October 1994 Carlsson formed a minority SAP Government. The election results appeared to indicate a trend of increased support for parties opposed to Sweden's joining the EU (as the EC had become). Despite opposition to EU membership within the SAP, Carlsson declared that a major objective of his Government would be to secure a popular mandate for Sweden to join the EU. Following approval by national referendum in November, Sweden became a member of the EU on 1 January 1995.

In March 1996 Carlsson relinquished his dual posts as Prime Minister and leader of the SAP, in order to retire from political life. Göran Persson, hitherto Minister of Finance, was elected unopposed as Prime Minister and leader of the SAP. In November an independent study group, which had been commissioned by the Government to consider Sweden's proposed participation in Economic and Monetary Union (EMU, see p. 318), recommended that Sweden should not join EMU until the country's unemployment rate had been significantly reduced. Although the central bank advocated membership of EMU from its inception in 1999, in June 1997 the Government announced that Sweden would not be participating in the first stage of EMU, citing a lack of public support for the project. In October it was also announced that Sweden had no intention of participating in the European Exchange Rate Mechanism (ERM).

At the general election held in September 1998 the SAP maintained its position as the largest party in the Riksdag (winning 131 seats), despite a substantial reduction in its representation. This was the SAP's worst electoral performance for some 70 years, and the party required the support of the VP and the MP to remain in government. The MS retained the position of second largest party in the Riksdag, obtaining 82 seats. At about 81%, the participation rate at the election was the lowest for some 50 years. Post-electoral analysis identified the SAP's pursuit of financial regularity at the perceived expense of socialist policies as the probable cause of its poor performance. In early October the new Government presented its statement of policy, which envisaged a more active role in Europe for Sweden, and measures intended to achieve sustainable economic growth and a reduction in unemployment. Following the announcement of former premier Bildt's retirement from party politics, in August 1999 Bo Lundgren was elected to succeed him as leader of the MS.

In late 1999 it was reported that public spending on defence equipment was to be reduced drastically. Additionally, proposed reform of the national defence system was likely to result in the loss of some 10,000 military and civilian jobs. Earlier in the year the military high command had indicated that the Government's programme of defence rationalization would lead to an eventual halving of the strength of the armed forces, in terms of both personnel and equipment, prompting speculation that Sweden might be about to reconsider its neutral status with regard to regional security. In November 2000 Persson announced proposals to that effect. He asserted that neutrality was no longer relevant after the end of the Cold War, and that it did not cover all aspects of Sweden's security policy, such as disarmament, the non-proliferation of nuclear weapons and stability in Europe. However, Persson did not propose to join the North Atlantic Treaty Organization (NATO, see p. 380), contending that it was essential for the stability of northern Europe that Sweden remain non-aligned.

SAP-led minority Government: 2002–06

At the general election held on 15 September 2002 the SAP maintained its position as the largest party in the Riksdag, winning 144 of the 349 seats. Persson formed a minority SAP Government with the parliamentary backing of the MP and the VP. In return for their support, the MP and the VP required the Government to espouse some of their policies, including a reduction of 6,000m. kronor in defence expenditure over five years and a moratorium on cod-fishing in the Baltic Sea from 1 January 2003, with compensation for the fishing industry.

In March 2000 a national congress of the SAP had endorsed future EMU entry as official party policy, despite a significant degree of internal opposition. Following the 2002 general election, Persson announced that a referendum would be held on the adoption of the euro in September 2003. The SAP remained divided on the issue; the MS and other centre-right parties supported entry into EMU. The campaign for the adoption of the euro was supported by the national media and the business community, whereas opposition to the new currency was focused in the trade unions, the MP and the VP. Opponents of EMU feared that membership would force Sweden to reduce public spending so as not to breach the 3% budget deficit limit imposed by the EU's Stability and Growth Pact. In September, four days

prior to the referendum on entry into EMU, the Minister for Foreign Affairs, Anna Lindh, one of the Government's most effective campaigners for the adoption of the euro, was stabbed in central Stockholm; she died of her injuries the following day. Sympathy for Lindh, however, did not prevent voters from rejecting the adoption of the euro. The result of the referendum was 42.0% in favour of entry to EMU, 55.9% against and 2.1% blank votes. Only in Stockholm did the proposal to adopt the euro receive a majority of the votes cast. A Swede of Serbian origin, who had a history of mental illness and claimed there was no political motive for the attack, was convicted of Lindh's murder and sentenced to life imprisonment in March 2004.

With the prospect of the enlargement of the EU from 15 to 25 countries on 1 May 2004, concerns arose that the Swedish welfare system would be unduly burdened by an influx of workers from the new member states. In April, however, the Riksdag rejected government-proposed legislation providing for welfare and labour restrictions on migrant workers from the 10 accession countries for at least two years, meaning that Sweden was one of the few EU countries without any such restrictions.

The perceived failure of the main political parties adequately to address the strong current of scepticism concerning the EU, as expressed in Sweden's rejection of the euro, led to the formation, in February 2004, of a new political grouping, the Junilistan (June List), which opposed further integration with the EU, but did not advocate withdrawal. The grouping stressed that it was not itself a political party, and went as far as appending its candidates' usual party affiliation to their names on the ballots for the forthcoming elections to the European Parliament. This strategy proved successful, allowing the June List to draw support from across the political spectrum. At the elections, held on 13 June, the June List won three of Sweden's 19 seats in the European Parliament. The SAP, by contrast, obtained five seats, while the MS won four. The VP and FP each took two seats, and the CP, MP and the Kristdemokraterna (Kd, as the KdS had been renamed) one apiece. Despite expectations that the June List's success in the European elections might increase pressure on the Government to hold a national referendum on the ratification of the EU constitutional treaty, which had been approved by the Council of the EU in June 2004, the Government chose to present the treaty for approval (or otherwise) in the Riksdag. However, following the rejection of the treaty at national referendums in France and the Netherlands in mid-2005, Sweden was one of several member states to delay the ratification process indefinitely. The Treaty of Lisbon, which replaced the constitutional treaty, was ratified by the Riksdag in November 2008, finally entering into force in December 2009.

In March 2006 Laila Freivalds resigned as Minister for Foreign Affairs, following criticism of her ministry's involvement in forcing the temporary closure, in February, of the website of *SD-Kuriren*—the newspaper of the far-right Sverigedemokraterna (SD, Sweden Democrats)—which had asked readers to submit cartoons of the Prophet Muhammad. Freivalds had already come under pressure to resign in December 2005 after an independent commission held her partly responsible for the Government's slow response to the tsunamis in South-East Asia on 26 December 2004 (which killed more than 500 Swedes). Jan Eliasson, the President of the UN General Assembly, was appointed as the new Minister for Foreign Affairs; he held both positions until the expiry of his UN term in September 2006.

Reinfeldt's MS-led Government

At the general election held on 17 September 2006, the centre-right Alliance for Sweden, comprising the MS, the FP, the CP and the Kd, emerged as the largest group in the Riksdag, the four parties together winning 178 seats. Of those, the MS, led by Fredrik Reinfeldt, secured 97 seats (compared with 55 seats in the 2002 elections), the CP 29, the FP 28 and the Kd 24. The four main non-socialist parties had presented a joint programme for government, which included plans to reduce welfare dependency and increase the labour supply by means of tax cuts for the lower paid and reductions in the levels of unemployment benefit, to reduce the role of the State in the economy through the privatization of state-owned companies and to introduce private sector competition in health care and education. In contrast to its partners in the Alliance, the FP suffered a significant decline in support, recording a loss of 20 seats compared with the 2002 election. The revelation of a scandal regarding a group of FP activists, who had gained illegal access to the computer network of the SAP during the election campaign and distributed information they had obtained to fellow activists in the FP, was considered to have been a decisive factor in the party's poor electoral performance. The SAP, despite remaining the largest party in the Riksdag (with 130 seats), recorded its worst electoral result since 1914. Persson immediately resigned as Prime Minister and announced that he would relinquish the leadership of the SAP in March 2007. As the leader of the largest party in the Alliance, Reinfeldt assumed the role of Prime Minister.

Reinfeldt's appointments to the new coalition Government in October 2006 included Maud Olofsson, of the CP, as Deputy Prime Minister and Minister for Enterprise and Energy, and former Prime Minister Bildt as Minister for Foreign Affairs. The appointment of Nyamko Sabuni, a former refugee from Zaire (now the Democratic Republic of the Congo), as Minister for Integration and Gender Equality in the new Cabinet was controversial, with Muslim groups organizing a petition calling for her resignation, in response to her outspoken views on integration. Shortly after assuming office, the Minister for Culture, Cecilia Stegö Chilò, and the Minister for Foreign Trade, Maria Borelius, both of the MS, were forced to resign, following allegations of irregularities in their personal finances. Lena Adelsohn Liljeroth and Sten Tolgfors, also both of the MS, assumed responsibility for the culture and foreign trade portfolios, respectively.

Mona Sahlin was elected to succeed Persson as party leader at an SAP party conference in March 2007. In April, at the trial of six people on charges relating to the illegal accessing of SAP computer data by FP activists, three of the defendants were convicted and received substantial fines, while three members of the FP were acquitted. In that month Lars Leijonborg, the Minister for Education and Research, whose leadership of the FP had been the subject of criticism for several months, announced that he would resign as party leader following the party conference, scheduled for September. He was replaced as leader of the FP by Jan Björklund.

A Swedish artist, Lars Vilks, provoked anger among Muslim communities in August 2007, when he depicted the head of the Prophet Muhammad on a dog's body. The decision by the Swedish newspaper *Nerikes Allehanda* to print the caricature resulted in formal protests by Egypt, Iran and Pakistan. In September Reinfeldt met with diplomats from a number of Muslim countries in an effort to defuse the tension. He apologized for any offence the image might have caused, but defended the right of Swedish citizens to freedom of expression. Vilks was subsequently placed under police protection. In March 2010 seven people were arrested in Ireland and charged with plotting to murder Vilks; several Swedish newspapers then reprinted the caricature, in solidarity with the artist, provoking further protests. In July a Swedish court sentenced two men who had attacked the artist's home in May to two and three years' imprisonment, respectively, having convicted them of attempted arson.

A minor government reorganization took place in September 2007. Sten Tolgfors, the Minister for Foreign Trade, was appointed Minister for Defence, following Mikael Odenberg's decision to resign from the post over government proposals to reduce the annual defence budget by up to 4,000m. kronor by 2010. Ewa Björling succeeded Tolgfors as the Minister for Foreign Trade.

Six people were arrested in Sweden and Norway in February 2008, on suspicion of financing militant organizations and planning terrorist acts. Three of the suspects, who were reported to be Swedish citizens, were apprehended in Stockholm. In June the Riksdag narrowly approved a controversial bill allowing for all cross-border e-mails and telephone calls to be monitored for reasons of national security. The law took effect from 1 January 2009 and was strongly criticized by many commentators as an attack on civil liberties.

The country's opposition parties in December 2008 announced plans to form a coalition government if they were to win sufficient votes in the general election, scheduled for September 2010. The SAP, MP and VP stated that they would campaign as separate parties but would present a joint economic policy prior to the election. This followed previous attempts to form a coalition, which had been frustrated by the VP's reluctance to accept certain areas of the SAP-MP agreement, particularly in relation to economic policy.

In February 2009, despite divisions between the four governing parties on the issue, Reinfeldt announced the reversal of the decision to phase out the country's remaining nuclear power stations, as part of a new programme to combat global warming and increase energy security. Although the phased decommissioning of nuclear plants had been ratified in a referendum in 1980, by 2009 only two of the country's 12 nuclear reactors had been closed. Reinfeldt claimed that as the referendum result had not specified the means by which nuclear power would be replaced, the Government should not be bound by it. The new programme, which envisaged the replacement of the 10 ageing reactors with new models, also aimed to ensure that the country would use 50% renewable energy by 2020, reduce greenhouse gas emissions by 40% and become carbon neutral by 2050. The Government's proposals, which specified that the replacement reactors could only be constructed at existing sites and would not be permitted to exceed 10 in number, were narrowly approved by the Riksdag in June 2010.

At elections to the European Parliament, held in early June 2009, the SAP won five of the 18 allocated seats, the MS four, the FP three and the MP two, while the VP, the CP and the Kd won one seat apiece, as did the Pirate Party, which had been formed in 2006 to campaign against laws that made the sharing of internet files a criminal offence. Birgitta Ohlsson, of the FP, took office as Minister for EU Affairs in February 2010, succeeding Cecilia Malmström, who had been appointed to the European Commission.

Recent developments: Reinfeldt's second term in office

At a general election held on 19 September 2010, the four parties of the governing centre-right Alliance won a total of 173 of the 349 seats in the Riksdag, just two seats short of a majority, with the MS securing 107 seats, the FP 24, the CP 23 and the Kd 19. The MS was the only party in the coalition to increase its representation (from 97 seats in the 2006 election). The Red-Green alliance, comprising the SAP, the MP and the VP, together took 156 seats, 15 fewer than their combined total in 2006. Although the SAP narrowly retained its position as the largest single party, it suffered a further loss of support, its strength declining from 130 seats to 112, while the MP, hitherto the smallest parliamentary party, became the third largest as a result of the election, increasing its representation to 25 seats. The far-right SD, which advocated a drastic reduction in immigration, entered the Riksdag for the first time, winning 20 seats and effectively depriving the MS-led Alliance of its majority. A turn-out of 84.6% was recorded.

In early October 2010 Prime Minister Reinfeldt announced the formation of a minority Government, in which many of the ministerial posts remained unchanged. With the FP having supplanted the CP as the second largest party in the coalition, Jan Björklund, the FP's leader and Minister for Education, became Deputy Prime Minister, replacing Olofsson, who remained Minister for Enterprise and Energy. New appointees included Erik Ullenhag, of the FP, as Minister for Integration and Deputy Minister for Employment, and Peter Norman, of the MS, as Minister for Financial Markets. Reinfeldt had ruled out any co-operation with the SD, the electoral success of which had prompted the organization of several rallies in protest against the party's policies, hoping instead to gain the support of the MP and the SAP in securing approval for legislation. In November Mona Sahlin announced her intention to resign as leader of the SAP; Håkan Juholt was elected as her replacement at a party congress held in March 2011.

A number of constitutional amendments were adopted by the Riksdag in November 2010, receiving the support of all parliamentary parties except the SD, and took effect in January 2011. The reforms notably enshrined Sweden's membership of the EU in the Constitution, reduced the threshold for independent candidates to be elected to the Riksdag from 8% of the votes cast to 5%, and required the conduct of a parliamentary confidence vote in the Prime Minister within two weeks of a general election.

Sweden experienced its first suicide bombing in December 2010, when an Iraqi-born Swede, Taimour Abdulwahab al-Abdaly, detonated a car bomb in central Stockholm before killing himself when a second device exploded; two passers-by were injured in the second explosion. Shortly before the incident the Swedish security service and a news agency had received messages threatening attacks on Swedes in retribution for the deployment of Swedish forces in Afghanistan and also referring to the caricature of the Prophet Muhammad by Lars Vilks. In March 2011 a man was arrested in Glasgow, Scotland, in connection with the bombing; he was sentenced to seven years' imprisonment in August 2012, having been convicted by the High Court in Glasgow of providing funding for the bombing. Meanwhile, in September 2011 al-Abdaly's widow was arrested in Luton, England, and charged with aiding her late husband in preparing the attack. The issue of the threat posed by Islamist terrorism in Sweden came to the fore again in that month when four Muslim men, reportedly of Somali and Iraqi origin, were arrested in Gothenburg on suspicion of plotting to perpetrate a terrorist attack on an exhibition centre in the city. There were reports that Vilks had planned to attend an arts event at the centre (on the day that the alleged terrorists were believed to have intended to carry out their attack), but, in the end, did not. One of the detainees was released a few days later, while the other three were charged with conspiring to murder Vilks. However, in January 2012 all three were acquitted of planning to murder Vilks on the grounds of insufficient evidence, although they were convicted of violating legislation on weapons (having been carrying knives when arrested). This verdict was upheld by an appeals court in September.

The minority Government suffered a reverse in March 2011 in its plans to proceed with the privatization of a range of state-owned companies, when the opposition parties united in the Riksdag to approve legislation aimed at preventing the planned divestment of government stakes in four companies: the power utility, Vattenfall; the telecommunications company, Telia-Sonera; the postal service, Posten; and SBAB Bank.

The SAP, the MP, the CP and the VP all selected new party leaders in 2011–12. Notably, having succeeded Sahlin as SAP leader in March 2011, Juholt resigned from the post in January 2012, following a sharp decline in public support, amid some controversy provoked by media revelations regarding the amount he had claimed in parliamentary allowances in recent years; he was replaced by trade union leader Stefan Löfven. The popularity of the largest party in the Riksdag recovered swiftly under Löfven's leadership, with opinion polls indicating that the SAP's share of voter support increased by some nine percentage points between January and March 2012, to exceed that of the MP for the first time in seven months. The SAP retained the highest share of support throughout the following year, while support for the coalition Government reportedly reached a five-year low in March 2013, with the CP and the Kd failing to achieve the 4% threshold required for parliamentary representation.

In late March 2012, meanwhile, the Minister for Defence, Sten Tolgfors, resigned from his post following intense criticism from various sources over the Government's controversial plans to help the Saudi authorities construct an advanced weapons plant in Saudi Arabia. Prime Minister Reinfeldt confirmed that in 2005 the Swedish Government had signed an initial military co-operation agreement (renewed in 2010) with Saudi Arabia regarding the so-called Project Simoom. The Swedish Defence Research Agency (Totalförsvarets forskningsinstitut—FOI) had led the project between 2007 and 2009, but, owing to the perceived sensitive nature of the situation and the potential legal obstacles, had subsequently transferred responsibility for the plant to a private company, Swedish Security Technology and Innovation (SSTI), which had then been given an export permit to buy weapons equipment. It was alleged, however, that the SSTI had been specially created by the FOI to act as a cover to conceal the Swedish military's continuing involvement in Project Simoom. Although Sweden has no ban on exports to Saudi Arabia, the secretive nature of the Swedish authorities' involvement in the matter and the apparent attempt at a cover-up caused particular consternation. The MP demanded an independent investigation into the arms deal and asserted that Sweden should not support the 'dictatorship' in Saudi Arabia. Karin Enström assumed responsibility for the defence portfolio.

Nyamko Sabuni of the FP resigned as Minister for Gender Equality and Deputy Minister for Education in January 2013, citing her decision not to contest the general election scheduled to take place on 14 September 2014 and a consequent desire to allow her successor sufficient time in the post prior to the polls. She was replaced by party colleague Maria Arnholm, who had hitherto served as Sabuni's state secretary.

Foreign Affairs

Sweden's tradition of neutrality has prevented it from joining NATO, but it is an active member of many international organizations, both in Europe and world-wide, and is a significant donor of development assistance.

Regional relations

Sweden attaches considerable importance to co-operation with its Nordic and Baltic neighbours. It was a founder member of the Nordic Council (in 1952), the Nordic Council of Ministers (in 1962), and of the Council of the Baltic Sea States (established in 1992 and including the former Soviet Baltic republics).

In March 1991 the Swedish and Danish Governments agreed to construct a 16-km combined bridge and tunnel for road and rail traffic, across the Öresund strait, between Malmö and Copenhagen (to be known as the Öresund Link). The plan aroused opposition in Sweden, on the grounds that the link might hinder the flow of water into the Baltic Sea, as well as increasing pollution by emissions from vehicles. In May 1994 a Swedish marine commission concluded that plans for the link did not provide sufficient guarantees to protect the flow of water into the Baltic. In the following month, however, the Swedish Government approved construction plans, and the link was opened in July 2000.

In November 2009 the Swedish Government gave its approval for the construction within its territorial waters of Nord Stream, a twin pipeline (comprising Line 1 and Line 2) beneath the Baltic Sea, to carry natural gas from Russia to Germany. The Government declared itself satisfied with commitments by the construction consortium to safeguard fisheries, shipping and the environment. Line 1 began operating in November 2011, followed by Line 2 in October 2012.

Within the wider European context, Sweden was a founder member of the Council of Europe in 1949, and of the European Free Trade Association (EFTA, see p. 461) in 1960. It also belongs to the Organization for Security and Co-operation in Europe (see p. 397) (founded in 1995 as a permanent organ of the Conference on Security and Co-operation in Europe, first held in 1973). Prior to Sweden's membership of the EU, trade with EU countries was conducted by means of a free trade area, the European Economic Area (EEA), created in 1994 under the aegis of EFTA. Negotiations on admission to the EU began in February 1993, when the Bildt Government declared that the country's tradition of neutrality would not prevent Sweden from participating fully in the common foreign and security policy of the EU. The negotiations were concluded in March 1994. Sweden obtained safeguards for its traditional policy of freedom of official information, and for its strict environmental standards, and won concessions on the maintenance of subsidies for agriculture in remote areas. A national referendum on membership was held on 13 November, producing a 52.2% majority in favour of joining the EU. The Riksdag formally ratified membership in December, and Sweden's accession to the EU took effect from 1 January 1995 (whereupon Sweden withdrew from EFTA). It was widely held that concern about the possible effects on the domestic economy of remaining outside the EU, together with fears regarding Sweden's ability to influence international affairs, such as the maintenance of effective environmental controls, had been major factors in the outcome of the referendum. Following the vote, the Carlsson Government reiterated that Sweden would retain its non-aligned policy within the EU, although it successfully applied for observer status within Western European Union (WEU) with effect from 1995. Sweden remained outside European Monetary Union (EMU) following the electorate's rejection in 2003 of proposals to join EMU (see Domestic Political Affairs). From the beginning of 2008 Swedish forces formed part of the Nordic Battlegroup, under the EU's rotating schedule of forces on standby for deployment to areas of crisis.

In May 2011 the Danish Government unilaterally announced that it was planning to reintroduce customs controls on its frontiers with Sweden and Germany in an attempt to combat cross-border crime and illegal immigration. The re-imposition of border controls in early July was criticized by the European Commission, which claimed that the Danish deployment of customs officials could constitute a violation of the EU's Schengen Agreement on open borders.

Other external relations

Although not a member of NATO, Sweden co-operated with the alliance in its Partnership for Peace programme from 1994 onwards, and in the Euro-Atlantic Partnership Council (established in 1997), and has participated in NATO-led peace-keeping operations in the Balkan region and Afghanistan.

The Swedish Government expressed its opposition to the US-led military operation against the regime of Saddam Hussein in Iraq from early 2003. However, Sweden contributed funds towards the reconstruction of Iraq, in addition to humanitarian aid.

Sweden's relations with Turkey were strained in March 2010, following the adoption by the Riksdag of a resolution recognizing as 'genocide' the killing of some 1.5m. Armenians under the Ottoman Empire during 1915–23. The Turkish ambassador was withdrawn from Sweden in response, but returned to the country at the end of the month, after Swedish Prime Minister Reinfeldt distanced his Government from the legislature's decision.

Tensions between Sweden and Belarus arose in July 2012, when a Swedish advertising agency flew a light aircraft into Belarusian airspace and dropped hundreds of teddy bears bearing messages supporting freedom of speech. In early August Belarus expelled the Swedish ambassador for meeting Belarusian opposition groups, claiming that he had sought to 'destroy' rather than strengthen bilateral relations, and withdrew its own envoy from Stockholm. In response, the Swedish Minister for Foreign Affairs, Carl Bildt, declared that Sweden would not allow a new Belarusian ambassador to assume his post, and that a further two Belarusian diplomats had been ordered to leave the country. The incident also resulted in the dismissals in Belarus of several senior defence officials and of the country's Minister of Foreign Affairs.

In 2012 Sweden was the world's second largest donor of development assistance in proportion to its gross national income (GNI)—closely following Luxembourg—providing 0.99% of its GNI, or some US $5,240m.

Attempts by the Swedish authorities to prosecute Julian Assange, the Australian founder of the website WikiLeaks, an organization publishing leaked private and classified content, for sexual offences allegedly committed during a visit to Sweden in August 2010, attracted considerable international media attention. In February 2011 a British court ruled that Assange should be extradited from the United Kingdom to Sweden, but Assange appealed against the decision, denying the allegations against him, which he claimed were politically motivated. In November the British High Court rejected Assange's appeal and upheld the extradition ruling, as did the Supreme Court in May 2012. Following the Supreme Court's rejection in June of an application by Assange for it to reconsider its decision, Assange took refuge in the Ecuadorean embassy in the British capital, London, and applied for political asylum, which he was granted in August. The Swedish Government reacted angrily to Ecuadorean suggestions that Assange would not receive fair treatment under its judicial system, summoning Ecuador's ambassador for an explanation. Assange remained in the embassy in March 2013, with the British Government refusing to grant him safe passage out of the United Kingdom. He maintained that his action was motivated by a fear that Sweden would ultimately extradite him to the USA on charges related to the activities of WikiLeaks.

CONSTITUTION AND GOVERNMENT

The Swedish Constitution is based on four fundamental laws and the Riksdag Act of 1974. The four fundamental laws are the Instrument of Government (originally dating from 6 June 1809), the Act of Succession (1810), the Freedom of the Press Act (1949) and the Fundamental Law on Freedom of Expression (1992). A new Instrument of Government came into force in 1975. Further constitutional amendments took effect in 2011. Sweden is a constitutional monarchy. The hereditary monarch is head of state, but has very limited formal prerogatives. Executive power rests with the Cabinet (Regeringen), which is responsible to the legislature (Riksdag). The unicameral Riksdag was introduced in January 1971. It has 349 members, elected by universal adult suffrage for four years, on the basis of proportional representation. The Prime Minister is nominated by the Speaker of the Riksdag and later confirmed in office by the whole House. The country is divided into 21 counties (Län) and 288 municipal districts (Kommun). Both counties and municipalities have popularly elected councils.

REGIONAL AND INTERNATIONAL CO-OPERATION

Sweden is a founding member of the Nordic Council (see p. 477) and the Nordic Council of Ministers (see p. 477). Sweden is a member of the European Union (EU, see p. 281), although it does not use the single currency, the euro. It is a founding member of both the Council of Europe (see p. 260) and the Council of the Baltic Sea States (see p. 258), which is based in Stockholm. It participates in the Organization for Security and Co-operation in Europe (OSCE, see p. 397) and the Arctic Council (see p. 459).

Sweden joined the UN in 1946. As a contracting party to the General Agreement on Tariffs and Trade, Norway joined the World Trade Organization (WTO, see p. 444) on its establishment in 1995. Although not a member of NATO, Sweden has participated in NATO's Partnership for Peace programme since 1994. It is a member of the Organisation for Economic Co-operation and Development (OECD, see p. 388).

ECONOMIC AFFAIRS

In 2011, according to estimates by the World Bank, Sweden's gross national income (GNI), measured at average 2009–11 prices, was US $503,188m., equivalent to $53,230 per head (or $42,200 on an international purchasing-power parity basis). During 2002–11, it was estimated, the population grew at an average annual rate of 0.6%, while gross domestic product (GDP) per head increased, in real terms, by an average of 1.7% per year. According to official figures, Sweden's overall GDP increased, in real terms, by an average of 2.2% per year in 2002–12; GDP grew by 3.7% in 2011 but only by 0.8% in 2012.

Agriculture (including hunting, forestry and fishing) contributed 1.6% of GDP in 2012 and employed 2.0% of the working population in 2011. The main agricultural products are dairy produce, meat, cereals and potatoes, primarily for domestic consumption. In 2012 forestry products (wood, pulp and paper) accounted for 3.5% of total merchandise exports. Agricultural GDP increased by an average of 1.5% per year during 2002–12; it grew by 2.0% in 2012.

Industry (including mining, manufacturing, construction and power) provided 25.8% of GDP in 2012 and employed 20.0% of the working population in 2011. According to Statistics Sweden, industrial GDP increased by an average of 2.5% per year in 2002–12; sectoral GDP grew by 6.5% in 2011, but declined by 2.0% in 2012.

Mining contributed 0.9% of GDP in 2012 and employed 0.2% of the working population in 2008. The principal product is iron ore, but there are also reserves of uranium, copper, lead and zinc. The GDP of the mining and quarrying sector declined, in real terms, by an average of 2.8% per year in 2002–12, according to Statistics Sweden; it increased by 6.5% in 2011, but declined by 3.6% in 2012.

Manufacturing contributed 15.7% of GDP in 2012 and employed 6.2% of the working population in 2011. Sweden's principal manufactures were paper and paper products, motor vehicles, chemicals, basic iron and steel, television and radio transmitters and other communications apparatus and general purpose machinery. Manufacturing GDP increased, in real terms, by an average of 2.8% per year in 2002–12, according to Statistics Sweden; it grew by 6.6% in 2011, but declined by 4.0% in 2012.

Construction contributed 5.8% of GDP in 2012 and employed 6.7% of the working population in 2011. Construction GDP increased by an average of 1.7% a year in 2002–12; it increased by 9.3% in 2011 and by 2.8% in 2012.

Energy is derived principally from hydroelectric power and nuclear power, which provided 44.7% and 25.0% of electricity generated in 2010, respectively, according to official figures. Conventional thermal power contributed 24.8% of electricity and wind power 5.5%. In February 2009, despite a resolution to phase out nuclear power that was approved in a referendum in 1980, the Swedish Government announced proposals to replace the 10 remaining nuclear reactors in Sweden as they became obsolete. The decision reflected ambitious targets for climate change and the desire for energy security. The legislation phasing out nuclear power was repealed in June 2010. Imports of petroleum and petroleum products accounted for 14.8% of total imports in 2012.

The services sector contributed 72.6% of GDP in 2012 and engaged 78.0% of the employed population in 2011. The GDP of the services sector increased, in real terms, at an average annual rate of 2.2% during 2002–12, according to Statistics Sweden; it grew by 1.5% in 2012.

In 2011 Sweden recorded a visible merchandise trade surplus of US $12,970m., and there was a surplus of $35,220m. on the current account of the balance of payments. The European Union (EU, see p. 281) dominates Swedish trade: in 2012 it provided 67.8% of imports and took 56.9% of exports. The European Free Trade Association (EFTA, see p. 461) is also an important trading partner. In 2012 the principal single source of imports was Germany (contributing 17.3% of total imports); other major suppliers were Norway, Denmark, the Netherlands, the United Kingdom, Russia and Finland. Norway was the principal market for exports in that year (accounting for 10.3% of total exports); other major purchasers were Germany, the United Kingdom, the USA, Denmark, Finland and the Netherlands. The principal exports in 2012 were machinery and transport equipment, basic manufactured goods, chemicals and related products, mineral fuels and lubricants, miscellaneous manufactured articles, and crude materials. The principal imports in that year were machinery and transport equipment, mineral fuels and lubricants, basic and other manufactures, chemicals and related products, and food and live animals.

In 2012 there was a budget deficit of 18,183m. kronor, equivalent to 0.5% of GDP. In 2011 Sweden's general government gross debt was 1,341,110m. kronor, equivalent to 37.9% of GDP. The annual rate of inflation averaged 1.4% in 2002–12; consumer prices increased by 0.9% in 2012. The unemployment rate averaged 7.5% in 2012.

Sweden is a small open economy, which is more diversified than is usual for a country of its size, with important sectors such as engineering, high technology, domestic aviation, nuclear power, automotive manufacturing, armaments and telecommunications. High levels of taxation in the country have traditionally financed a generous social welfare system. However, this has also proved an obstacle to entrepreneurship and to the attraction and retention of skilled labour from abroad. From 2006 the centre-right coalition Government attempted to reduce welfare dependency and increase the labour supply, by lowering income taxes for low- and medium-income groups and curtailing unemployment benefits. However, the economic programme encountered significant difficulties as the global financial crisis adversely affected the economy, with GDP contracting by 0.6% in 2008. In October 2008 the Riksdag approved the establishment of a stability fund to guarantee banks' medium-term loans and provide emergency support to financial institutions. In an attempt to mitigate the effects of the financial crisis, the central bank reduced its key interest rate, the repo rate, to a record low of 0.25% in July 2009. Despite these expansionary policies, GDP contracted by 5.0% in 2009, while the rate of unemployment rose. However, the economy recovered strongly in 2010: GDP expanded by 6.6%, comfortably outperforming other Western European economies. In response to this rapid growth, from July 2010 the central bank gradually increased the repo rate, to 2% by July 2011. The debt crisis in 2011 in the countries of the eurozone

had a dampening effect on the Swedish economy—notably through a marked decrease in exports—and more moderate GDP growth, of 3.7%, was recorded in that year. The central bank reduced the repo rate in four stages between December 2011 and December 2012, to 1%, citing a continued slowdown in growth and low inflationary pressures. Amid weak public demand and investment, GDP growth decelerated further in 2012, to 0.8%, as the economy of the eurozone continued to struggle. The unemployment rate remained high, at 8.5% overall in February 2013, with youth unemployment, at 26.4%, of particular concern, while the strength of the krona presented a challenge to exporters. GDP growth of 1.2% was forecast for 2013. That year's budget contained stimulus measures worth some 23,000m. kronor, including increased investment in infrastructure, research and development and initiatives to boost youth employment, as well as a reduction in the corporate tax rate from 26.3% to 22%.

PUBLIC HOLIDAYS*

2014: 1 January (New Year's Day), 6 January (Epiphany), 18 April (Good Friday), 20 April (Easter), 21 April (Easter Monday), 1 May (May Day), 29 May (Ascension Day), 6 June (National Day), 9 June (Whit Sunday), 21 June (Midsummer Holiday), 1 November (All Saints' Day), 25 December (Christmas), 26 December (Boxing Day).

* The eve of a holiday is as important or more so than the holiday itself. Most Swedes have the day off work, including those working in the civil service, banks, public transport, hospitals, shops and the media. Others have at least a half-day. This applies especially to Midsummer's Eve, All Saints' Day Eve and Christmas Eve. The eve of May Day is sometimes called Valborg Eve or St Walpurgis. When a holiday falls on a Thursday many Swedes have the following Friday off in addition. When a holiday falls on a Saturday or Sunday it is not taken on the following Monday.

Statistical Survey

Sources (unless otherwise stated): Statistics Sweden, Klostergatan 23, 701 89 Örebro; tel. (19) 17-60-00; fax (19) 17-70-80; e-mail information@scb.se; internet www.scb.se.

Area and Population

AREA, POPULATION AND DENSITY

Area (sq km)	
Land	410,335
Inland waters	39,960
Total	450,295*
Population (census results)†	
1 November 1985	8,360,178
1 November 1990	
Males	4,242,351
Females	4,345,002
Total	8,587,353
Population (at 31 December)†	
2010	9,415,570
2011	9,482,855
2012	9,555,893
Density (per sq km) at 31 December 2012	23.3‡

* 173,859 sq miles.

† Population is *de jure*; from 2005 a new continuous register-based system of population count was adopted in place of traditional methods of census enumeration.

‡ Density refers to land area only.

POPULATION BY AGE AND SEX
(at 31 December 2012)

	Males	Females	Total
0–14	827,996	783,863	1,611,859
15–64	3,107,551	3,008,200	6,115,751
65 and over	830,358	997,925	1,828,283
Total	4,765,905	4,789,988	9,555,893

COUNTIES
(population at 31 December 2012)

	Land area (sq km)*	Population	Density (per sq km)
Stockholms län	6,519.3	2,127,006	326.3
Uppsala län	7,036.7	341,977	48.6
Södermanlands län . . .	6,103.1	274,723	45.0
Östergötlands län	10,604.6	433,784	40.9
Jönköpings län	10,495.4	339,116	32.3
Kronobergs län	8,467.3	185,887	22.0
Kalmar län	11,219.1	233,548	20.8
Gotlands län	3,151.4	57,241	18.2
Blekinge län	2,946.7	152,315	51.7
Skåne län	11,035.4	1,263,088	114.5
Hallands län	5,461.6	304,116	55.7
Västra Götalands län . . .	23,956.1	1,600,447	66.8
Värmlands län	17,591.3	273,080	15.5
Örebro län	8,546.3	283,113	33.1
Västmanlands län . . .	6,317.9	256,224	40.6
Dalarnus län	28,195.6	276,555	9.8
Gävleborgs län	18,200.1	276,637	15.2
Västernorrlands län . . .	21,684.5	241,981	11.2
Jämtlands län	49,343.1	126,201	2.6
Västerbottens län . . .	55,189.7	260,217	4.7
Norrbottens län	98,249.0	248,637	2.5
Total†	410,335.4	9,555,893	23.3

* According to new estimates for land area.

† Including area of 21.2 sq km outside of existing county boundaries.

PRINCIPAL TOWNS
(municipalities at 31 December 2012)*

Stockholm (capital) .	881,235	Norrköping . . .	132,124
Göteborg			
(Gothenburg) .	526,089	Helsingborg . .	132,011
Malmö	307,758	Jönköping . . .	129,478
Uppsala . . .	202,625	Umeå	117,294
Linköping . . .	148,521	Lund	112,950
Västerås . . .	140,499	Borås	104,867
Örebro	138,952		

* According to the administrative subdivisions of 1 January 2006.

BIRTHS, MARRIAGES AND DEATHS

	Registered live births		Registered marriages		Registered deaths	
	Number	Rate (per 1,000)	Number	Rate (per 1,000)	Number	Rate (per 1,000)
2005 . .	101,346	11.2	44,381	4.9	91,710	10.1
2006 . .	105,913	11.6	45,551	5.0	91,177	10.0
2007 . .	107,421	11.7	47,898	5.2	91,729	10.0
2008 . .	109,301	11.8	50,332	5.4	91,449	9.9
2009 . .	111,801	12.0	48,033	5.1	90,080	9.6
2010 . .	115,641	12.3	50,730	5.4	90,487	9.6
2011 . .	111,770	11.8	47,564	5.0	89,938	9.5
2012 . .	113,177	11.8	50,616	5.3	91,938	9.6

Life expectancy (years at birth): 81.5 (males 79.5; females 83.5) in 2010 (Source: World Bank, World Development Indicators database).

IMMIGRATION AND EMIGRATION

	2010	2011	2012
Immigrants	98,801	96,467	103,059
Emigrants	48,853	51,179	51,747

ECONOMICALLY ACTIVE POPULATION
('000 persons aged 16 to 64 years)

	2009	2010	2011
Agriculture, forestry and fishing .	98	96	93
Mining, quarrying and utilities .	323	322	326
Manufacturing	288	280	286
Construction	294	305	312
Wholesale and retail trade, repair of motor vehicles, motorcycles and personal and household goods	551	560	567
Hotels and restaurants . . .	144	153	144
Transport, storage and communications	420	423	434
Financial intermediation and business activities	703	709	737
Public administration and defence, compulsory social security, extra-territorial organizations and bodies	267	274	280
Education	480	494	504
Health and social work . .	702	700	723
Other community, social and personal service activities, private households with employed persons	223	225	223
Sub-total	4,493	4,541	4,629
Activities not adequately defined .	7	6	13
Total employed	4,499	4,546	4,642
Unemployed	408	416	378
Total labour force	4,907	4,962	5,020
Males	2,581	2,625	2,643
Females	2,326	2,337	2,376

Health and Welfare

KEY INDICATORS

Total fertility rate (children per woman, 2010)	1.9
Under-5 mortality rate (per 1,000 live births, 2010) . . .	3
HIV/AIDS (% of persons aged 15–49, 2009)	0.1
Physicians (per 1,000 head, 2008)	3.8
Hospital beds (per 1,000 head, 2009)	2.8
Health expenditure (2009): US $ per head (PPP)	3,722
Health expenditure (2009): % of GDP	10.0
Health expenditure (2009): public (% of total)	81.5
Total carbon dioxide emissions ('000 metric tons, 2008) . .	49,049.8
Carbon dioxide emissions per head (metric tons, 2008) . .	5.3
Human Development Index (2011): ranking	10
Human Development Index (2011): value	0.904

For sources and definitions, see explanatory note on p. vi.

Agriculture

PRINCIPAL CROPS
('000 metric tons; holdings of more than 2 ha of arable land)

	2009	2010	2011
Wheat	2,277.9	2,143.0	2,253.1
Rye	218.4	123.4	131.6
Barley	1,680.9	1,228.1	1,389.5
Oats	744.2	563.4	698.1
Triticale (wheat-rye hybrid) . .	252.7	164.9	111.7
Potatoes	857.9	815.6	878.4
Rapeseed	298.4	278.6	266.6
Sugar beet	2,405.8	1,973.7	2,493.2

Aggregate production ('000 metric tons, may include official, semi-official or estimated data): Total cereals 5,241.9 in 2009, 4,291.5 in 2010, 4,651.0 in 2011; Total roots and tubers 857.9 in 2009, 815.6 in 2010, 878.4 in 2011; Total vegetables (incl. melons) 342.5 in 2009, 298.7 in 2010, 331.5 in 2011; Total fruits (excl. melons) 39.8 in 2009, 42.6 in 2010; 41.8 in 2011.

Source: FAO.

LIVESTOCK
('000 head, year ending September; holdings of more than 2 ha of arable land, or with large numbers of livestock)

	2009	2010	2011
Cattle	1,538.3	1,536.7	1,511.9
Sheep	540.5	564.9	622.7
Pigs	1,528.7	1,519.9	1,482.6
Horses*	95.0	96.0	97.0
Chickens	7,159	7,708	8,204
Turkeys†	112	116	134

* FAO estimates.
† Unofficial figures.

Source: FAO.

LIVESTOCK PRODUCTS
('000 metric tons)

	2009	2010	2011
Cattle meat	135.2	133.5	133.5
Horse meat	1.0	1.0	1.0
Sheep meat	5.1	5.0	5.1
Pig meat	260.7	263.5	256.1
Chicken meat	105.2	112.0	111.5
Game meat	17.9	17.9	18.0*
Cows' milk	2,974.0	2,902.1	2,890.0
Hen eggs	105.0	111.0	116.0

* FAO estimate.

Source: FAO.

Forestry

ROUNDWOOD REMOVALS
('000 cubic metres; rounded figures)

	2009	2010	2011
Sawlogs, veneer logs and logs for sleepers	30,100	35,100	34,500
Pulpwood	28,600	30,700	31,203
Fuel wood	5,900	5,900	5,900
Other industrial wood	500	500	500
Total	65,100	72,200	72,103

Source: FAO.

SAWNWOOD PRODUCTION
('000 cubic metres, incl. railway sleepers; rounded figures)

	2009	2010	2011
Coniferous (softwood)	16,100	16,650	16,700
Broadleaved (hardwood)	100	100	100
Total	16,200	16,750	16,800

Source: FAO.

Fishing

('000 metric tons, live weight)

	2008	2009	2010
Capture	231.3	203.4	212.0
Atlantic cod	12.6	13.2	12.4
Sandeels (Sandlances)	12.5	12.7	32.7
Atlantic herring	94.7	76.2	71.1
European sprat	95.6	81.8	82.6
Atlantic mackerel	3.7	7.3	3.4
Aquaculture	7.6	8.5	10.6
Total catch	238.9	212.0	222.7

Note: Figures exclude aquatic mammals, recorded by number rather than by weight. The number of harbour porpoises caught was: 1 in 2008; 1 in 2009; nil in 2010.

Source: FAO.

Mining

('000 metric tons unless otherwise indicated)

	2008	2009	2010
Iron ore	16,628*	12,233*	16,750
Copper ore	57.7	55.4	76.5*
Gold (kg)	4,900	5,600	6,300*
Silver (metric tons)	293.1	288.6	302.1
Zinc ore	188.0	192.5	198.7
Lead ore	65.1*	69.3	67.7

* Estimate.

Note: Figures relate to the metal content of ores.

Source: US Geological Survey.

Industry

SELECTED PRODUCTS
('000 metric tons unless otherwise indicated)

	2008	2009	2010
Pig-iron and sponge-iron*	3,583	3,800†	3,800†
Crude steel*	5,196	2,805	4,844
Aluminium*†‡	113.5	99.7	103.5
Copper (refined)*†‡	252.8	230.8	235.0
Lead (refined)*†‡	99.4	97.0	96.0
Mechanical wood pulp§	3,570	3,322	3,551
Chemical wood pulp§	8,237	7,679	7,886
Newsprint§	2,560	2,198	2,258‖
Printing and writing paper§	3,264	3,012	3,255
Other paper and paperboard§	5,839	5,722	5,897
Cement (hydraulic)*†	2,500	2,600	2,600
Dwellings completed (number)	32,021	22,900	19,500
Electricity (million kWh)¶	150,036	136,717	n.a.

* Source: US Geological Survey.
† Estimate(s).
‡ Primary and secondary metals.
§ Source: FAO.
‖ Unofficial figure.
¶ Source: UN Industrial Commodity Statistics Database.

2011: Dwellings completed (number) 20,064; Mechanical wood pulp 3,558; Chemical wood pulp 7,810; Newsprint 2,120; Printing and writing paper 3,347; Other paper and paperboard 5,831.

Finance

CURRENCY AND EXCHANGE RATES

Monetary Units
100 öre = 1 Swedish krona (plural: kronor).

Sterling, Dollar and Euro Equivalents (31 December 2012)
£1 sterling = 10.264 kronor;
US $1 = 6.505 kronor;
€1 = 8.582 kronor;
100 Swedish kronor = £9.74 = $15.37 = €11.65.

Average Exchange Rate (kronor per US $)
2010   7.2075
2011   6.4935
2012   6.7750

STATE BUDGET
(million kronor)

Revenue	2010	2011	2012*
Tax revenue	713,966	769,094	740,612
Other current revenue	41,783	55,333	49,810
Capital revenue	167	23,124	70
Loan repayment	1,687	1,452	1,344
Computed revenue	8,940	11,086	9,776
Contributions from the European Union	12,978	12,328	11,403
Total	779,521	872,417	813,015

Expenditure	2010	2011	2012*
Justice	35,486	37,164	38,132
Defence	45,665	44,153	45,165
Health	56,015	56,538	58,848
Social insurance for the sick and disabled	99,933	95,800	95,033
Social insurance for the elderly .	41,473	41,590	41,300
Social insurance for families and children	70,177	71,994	75,608
Social insurance for the unemployed	5,192	4,968	7,714
Employment	68,556	63,285	67,284
Education and university research	53,234	53,685	53,821
Community planning and housing	1,559	1,110	977
Communications	39,784	38,710	43,560
Agriculture, forestry and fisheries	17,447	16,372	17,254
General grants to municipalities .	75,691	88,023	85,138
Interest on central government debt	23,361	34,491	27,603
Contributions to the European Union	30,407	30,596	30,875
Total (incl. others)	780,573	804,616	831,198

* Forecasts.

INTERNATIONAL RESERVES
(US $ million at 31 December)

	2009	2010	2011
Gold	4,431	5,735	6,324
IMF special drawing rights . .	3,591	3,522	3,382
Reserve position in IMF . . .	725	1,123	1,736
Foreign exchange	38,543	37,919	38,907
Total	47,290	48,299	50,349

Source: IMF, *International Financial Statistics*.

MONEY SUPPLY
(million kronor at 31 December)*

	2009	2010	2011
Currency outside depository corporations	100,070	96,390	92,100
Transferable deposits . . .	1,361,060	1,464,830	1,485,930
Other deposits	441,900	500,270	607,430
Securities other than shares . .	1,196,460	773,790	846,770
Broad money	3,099,490	2,835,290	3,032,230

* Totals may not be equal to the sum of components, as figures are rounded to the nearest 10m. kronor.

Source: IMF, *International Financial Statistics*.

COST OF LIVING
(Consumer Price Index; base: 1980 = 100)

	2010	2011	2012
Food and non-alcoholic beverages .	273.2	276.7	280.8
Alcoholic beverages and tobacco .	428.3	432.7	452.5
Clothing and footwear . . .	174.2	176.9	175.3
Housing, water, electricity and fuels	355.7	386.7	392.1
Furniture and household goods .	224.3	222.6	221.6
Health	793.9	807.4	830.3
Transport	404.9	417.4	425.7
Communication	165.0	161.8	158.9
Recreation and culture . . .	182.0	179.7	175.8
Restaurants and hotels . . .	470.6	483.6	485.9
Miscellaneous goods and services .	349.5	353.0	362.0
All items	302.5	311.4	314.2

NATIONAL ACCOUNTS
(million kronor at current prices)

National Income and Product

	2010	2011	2012
Compensation of employees .	1,775,649	1,837,425	1,904,412
Net operating surplus . . .			
Net mixed income . . . . }	573,852	615,526	580,771
Domestic factor incomes .	2,349,501	2,452,951	2,485,183
Consumption of fixed capital .	446,482	454,799	470,036
Gross domestic product (GDP) at factor cost . .	2,795,983	2,907,750	2,955,219
Taxes on production and imports	602,183	655,345	666,050
Less Subsidies	60,635	63,181	65,930
GDP in market prices . .	3,337,531	3,499,914	3,555,339
Primary incomes received from abroad (net)	75,036	90,645	82,914
Gross national income .	3,412,567	3,590,559	3,638,253
Less Consumption of fixed capital	446,482	454,799	470,036
Net national income . . .	2,966,085	3,135,760	3,168,217
Other current transfers from abroad (net)	−50,328	−51,202	−51,281
Net national disposable income	2,915,757	3,084,558	3,116,936

Expenditure on the Gross Domestic Product

	2010	2011	2012
Final consumption expenditure .	2,506,673	2,596,614	2,675,503
Households	1,566,476	1,620,266	1,664,261
Non-profit institutions serving households	50,574	52,620	54,637
General government . . .	889,623	923,728	956,605
Gross capital formation . .	624,493	685,996	660,916
Gross fixed capital formation .	601,691	644,479	669,905
Changes in inventories . .	22,802	41,517	−8,989
Total domestic expenditure .	3,131,166	3,282,610	3,336,419
Exports of goods and services . .	1,651,448	1,748,823	1,733,210
Less Imports of goods and services	1,445,083	1,531,519	1,514,290
GDP in market prices . . .	3,337,531	3,499,914	3,555,339
GDP at constant 2011 prices .	3,374,821	3,499,914	3,529,555

Gross Domestic Product by Economic Activity

	2010	2011	2012
Agriculture, forestry and fishing .	50,029	54,298	50,899
Mining and quarrying . . .	28,022	30,766	28,282
Manufacturing	494,175	515,314	491,502
Electricity, gas and water . .	109,812	106,503	105,547
Construction	152,049	171,275	180,826
Wholesale and retail trade . .	338,805	357,596	359,619
Hotels and restaurants . .	40,666	42,814	45,455
Transport, storage and communications	296,767	317,868	325,458
Financial intermediation . .	117,505	118,287	129,787
Real estate and business services*	517,747	558,992	576,755
Government services . . .	578,707	598,089	620,957
Education, health and social services	103,303	110,280	119,293
Other community, social and personal services	44,135	46,688	47,883
Non-profit institutes serving households	42,304	43,869	45,756
Sub-total	2,914,026	3,072,639	3,128,019
Taxes on products	441,018	446,210	448,743
Less Subsidies on products . .	17,513	18,935	21,423
GDP in market prices . . .	3,337,531	3,499,914	3,555,339

* Including imputed rents of owner-occupied dwellings.

Note: Financial intermediation services indirectly measured data are distributed to production sectors.

BALANCE OF PAYMENTS
(US $ million)

	2009	2010	2011
Exports of goods	132,240	160,124	188,782
Imports of goods	-120,275	-148,979	-175,813
Balance on goods	11,965	11,145	12,970
Exports of services	59,355	63,319	74,688
Imports of services	-44,558	-47,461	-53,874
Balance on goods and services	26,762	27,004	33,785
Primary income received	47,090	55,652	64,618
Primary income paid	-39,815	-46,777	-55,872
Balance on goods, services and primary income	34,037	35,878	42,531
Secondary income received	4,854	5,255	6,494
Secondary income paid	-10,200	-11,460	-13,805
Current balance	28,691	29,673	35,220
Capital account (net)	286	-116	303
Direct investment assets	-25,363	-17,800	-20,220
Direct investment liabilities	8,946	-2,232	7,889
Portfolio investment assets	-18,245	-19,059	-11,385
Portfolio investment liabilities	82,045	40,260	37,717
Financial derivatives and employee stock options (net)	-2,324	4,187	-3,148
Other investment assets	13,893	-30,702	-60,910
Other investment liabilities	-50,848	-11,065	7,862
Net errors and omissions	-21,922	5,777	7,545
Reserves and related items	15,159	-1,078	872

Source: IMF, *International Financial Statistics*.

OFFICIAL ASSISTANCE TO DEVELOPING COUNTRIES
(million kronor)

	2009	2010	2011
Bilateral assistance	22,997	20,951	20,951
Multilateral assistance	11,747	11,655	12,728
Total	34,744	32,606	33,679

External Trade

PRINCIPAL COMMODITIES
(distribution by SITC, million kronor)

Imports c.i.f.	2010	2011	2012
Food and live animals	80,849	83,716	87,030
Crude materials (inedible) except fuels	35,405	38,163	35,554
Mineral fuels, lubricants, etc.	143,245	162,365	178,089
Petroleum, petroleum products, etc.	119,032	139,951	162,422
Chemicals and related products	121,090	127,982	124,407
Medical and pharmaceutical preparations	29,842	29,311	30,729
Basic manufactures	151,963	164,835	147,080
Iron and steel	43,250	50,436	39,790
Machinery and transport equipment	397,363	425,708	388,087
General industrial machinery, equipment and parts	51,048	56,474	51,024
Office machinery and data-processing equipment	37,294	36,287	36,711
Telecommunications and sound equipment	56,208	66,253	64,239

Imports c.i.f.—*continued*	2010	2011	2012
Other electrical machinery, apparatus, etc.	85,713	81,562	66,121
Road vehicles and parts*	103,078	111,177	97,420
Miscellaneous manufactured articles	125,316	129,582	125,438
Other miscellaneous manufactured articles	42,923	42,729	40,901
Total (incl. others)	1,069,445	1,147,901	1,100,994

Exports f.o.b.	2010	2011	2012
Food and live animals	45,285	45,940	48,222
Crude materials (inedible) except fuels	77,017	80,392	77,722
Mineral fuels, lubricants, etc.	85,683	96,774	117,502
Petroleum, petroleum products, etc.	77,395	86,355	104,626
Chemicals and related products	137,894	130,737	130,972
Medical and pharmaceutical preparations	66,546	57,801	57,490
Basic manufactures	223,228	236,937	220,592
Paper, paperboard and manufactures	77,811	78,786	75,859
Iron and steel	59,965	68,353	57,115
Machinery and transport equipment	448,587	500,863	450,445
Power-generating machinery and equipment	41,911	52,094	49,541
Machinery specialized for particular industries	44,998	51,699	53,394
General industrial machinery, equipment and parts	73,626	78,220	75,252
Telecommunications and sound equipment	85,064	85,038	61,017
Other electrical machinery, apparatus, etc.	61,405	63,311	61,560
Road vehicles and parts*	107,342	132,411	116,132
Miscellaneous manufactured articles	106,627	106,136	106,240
Other miscellaneous manufactured articles	42,874	41,082	40,610
Total (incl. others)	1,138,167	1,212,271	1,169,252

* Data on parts exclude tyres, engines and electrical parts.

PRINCIPAL TRADING PARTNERS
(million kronor)

Imports c.i.f.	2010	2011	2012
Austria	11,553	13,175	11,662
Belgium	41,486	44,489	41,051
China, People's Republic	43,301	44,411	44,786
Czech Republic	12,902	14,315	13,498
Denmark	89,033	93,935	93,217
Estonia	12,179	20,042	15,354
Finland	56,486	61,245	55,861
France	49,073	51,857	45,787
Germany	193,202	209,963	190,555
Ireland	13,976	20,144	18,891
Italy	31,444	33,610	31,475
Japan	15,015	14,578	12,662
Korea, Republic	15,488	8,376	9,431
Netherlands	69,511	70,853	72,327
Norway	97,479	97,406	100,689
Poland	31,216	32,452	31,517
Russia	50,304	53,120	58,032
Spain	13,110	14,885	13,741
United Kingdom	60,255	68,176	72,169
USA	34,289	35,045	35,652
Total (incl. others)	1,069,445	1,147,901	1,100,994

Exports f.o.b.	2010	2011	2012
Australia	15,078	16,662	14,824
Belgium	46,052	54,363	55,384
Brazil	10,793	13,372	11,788
China, People's Republic	35,527	39,915	37,766
Denmark	74,742	74,962	74,622
Finland	70,350	73,993	74,463
France	55,481	55,412	53,368
Germany	113,024	119,816	114,580
India	13,149	13,482	11,320
Italy	32,759	30,016	26,219
Japan	14,302	15,219	17,076
Netherlands	56,008	59,514	61,260
Norway	113,367	114,854	120,457
Poland	29,104	31,590	30,268
Russia	20,781	27,614	23,679
Spain	22,396	21,904	18,360
Turkey	13,405	16,531	13,417
United Kingdom	83,856	84,623	90,066
USA	83,425	76,808	74,998
Total (incl. others)	1,138,167	1,212,271	1,169,252

Transport

RAILWAYS
(traffic)

	2009	2010	2011
Passengers (million)	179	180	188
Passenger-km (million)	11,321	11,219	11,434
Freight (million metric tons)	56	68	68
Freight ton-km (million)	20,389	23,464	22,705

ROAD TRAFFIC
('000 motor vehicles in use at 31 December)

	2009	2010	2011
Passenger cars	4,301	4,335	4,401
Buses and coaches	13	14	14
Lorries and vans	515	526	548
Motorcycles	303	304	305

SHIPPING
Flag Registered Fleet
(at 31 December)

	2010	2011	2012
Number of vessels	530	501	477
Total displacement ('000 grt)	3,738.6	3,411.7	3,011.7

Source: Lloyd's List Intelligence (www.lloydslistintelligence.com).

International Sea-borne Freight Traffic

	2009	2010	2011
Vessels entered ('000 grt)	114,181	120,332	118,797
Vessels cleared ('000 grt)	114,257	118,581	119,014
Goods loaded ('000 metric tons)	66,624	70,624	69,058
Goods unloaded ('000 metric tons)	74,569	84,372	83,662

CIVIL AVIATION
(traffic on scheduled services)*

	2007	2008	2009
Kilometres flown (million)	40	20	92
Passengers carried ('000)	2,573	585	8,036
Passenger-km (million)	5,128	4,180	8,933
Total ton-km (million)	739	645	1,012

* Including an apportionment (3/7) of the international services of Scandinavian Airlines System (SAS), operated jointly with Denmark and Norway.

Source: UN, *Statistical Yearbook*.

2010 ('000): Passengers carried 363 (Source: World Bank, World Development Indicators database).

Tourism

VISITORS BY ORIGIN
(nights in all types of tourist accommodation)

	2008	2009	2010
Denmark	1,348,399	1,620,559	1,538,968
Finland	475,634	521,606	527,349
France	270,828	281,848	297,748
Germany	2,690,148	2,619,562	2,598,505
Italy	262,240	315,110	296,578
Japan	100,991	93,433	95,764
Netherlands	750,975	704,576	685,834
Norway	3,084,018	3,332,729	3,176,610
Russia	206,394	192,284	225,015
United Kingdom	648,227	599,826	602,307
USA	393,153	355,604	409,781
Total (incl. others)	12,495,002	12,872,513	12,802,832

Tourism receipts (US $ million, excl. passenger transport): 11,080 in 2010; 13,886 in 2011 (provisional).

Source: World Tourism Organization.

Communications Media

	2009	2010	2011
Telephones ('000 main lines in use)	5,140	4,924	4,600
Mobile cellular telephones ('000 subscribers)	10,440	10,885	11,194
Internet subscribers ('000)	3,281.7	3,231.1	n.a.
Broadband subscribers ('000)	2,942	2,987	2,999
Daily newspapers:			
titles	171	169	170
average net circulation ('000 copies)	3,605	3,470	3,060
Weekly newspapers and periodicals:			
titles	427	415	401
average net circulation ('000 copies)	22,328	21,818	21 322
Book production	19,829	21,631	14,957

Source: mainly International Telecommunication Union.

Education

(2011/12 unless otherwise indicated)

	Institutions	Teachers*	Students
Primary: grades 1–6 / Secondary: grades 7–9	4,616	96,023	888,658
Integrated upper secondary schools	1,196	40,099	480,645
Higher education	64†	20,000‡	397,679§
People's colleges	147‖	n.a.	100,760¶
Municipal adult education	327	4,916	198,172

* Full-time and part-time teachers and teachers on leave.
† 2007/08.
‡ 1994/95.
§ 2003/04.
‖ 1996/97.
¶ 2008/09.

Pupil-teacher ratio (primary education, UNESCO estimate): 9.5 in 2009/10 (Source: UNESCO Institute for Statistics).

Directory

The Government

HEAD OF STATE

Monarch: HM King CARL XVI GUSTAF (succeeded to the throne 15 September 1973).

THE CABINET
(May 2013)

A coalition of the parties comprising Alliansen (The Alliance): the Moderata Samlingspartiet (MS), the Centerpartiet (CP), the Folkpartiet Liberalerna (FP) and the Kristdemokraterna (Kd).

Prime Minister: FREDRIK REINFELDT (MS).

Deputy Prime Minister and Minister for Education and Research: JAN BJÖRKLUND (FP).

Minister for Health and Social Affairs: GÖRAN HÄGGLUND (Kd).

Minister for Finance: ANDERS BORG (MS).

Minister for Employment: HILLEVI ENGSTRÖM (MS).

Minister for Information Technology and Energy: ANNA-KARIN HATT (CP).

Minister for Enterprise: ANNIE LÖÖF (CP).

Minister for Defence: KARIN ENSTRÖM (MS).

Minister for Justice: BEATRICE ASK (MS).

Minister for Culture and Sport: LENA ADELSOHN LILJEROTH (MS).

Minister for EU Affairs: BIRGITTA OHLSSON (FP).

Minister for the Environment: LENA EK (CP).

Minister for Foreign Affairs: CARL BILDT (MS).

Minister for Gender Equality and Deputy Minister for Education: MARIA ARNHOLM (FP).

Minister for Infrastructure: CATHARINA ELMSÄTER-SVÄRD (MS).

Minister for Children and the Elderly: MARIA LARSSON (Kd).

Minister for Integration: ERIK ULLENHAG (FP).

Minister for Financial Markets: PETER NORMAN (MS).

Minister for Rural Affairs: ESKIL ERLANDSSON (CP).

Minister for Public Administration and Housing: STEFAN ATTEFALL (Kd).

Minister for Trade: EWA BJÖRLING (MS).

Minister for Migration and Asylum Policy: TOBIAS BILLSTRÖM (MS).

Minister for International Development Co-operation: GUNILLA CARLSSON (MS).

Minister for Social Security: ULF KRISTERSSON (MS).

MINISTRIES

Prime Minister's Office: Rosenbad 4, 103 33 Stockholm; tel. (8) 405-10-00; fax (8) 723-11-71; e-mail sb.registrator@regeringskansliet.se; internet www.regeringen.se.

Ministry of Culture: Drottninggt. 16, 103 33 Stockholm; tel. (8) 405-10-00; fax (8) 21-68-13; e-mail registrator@culture.ministry.se; internet www.regeringen.se/sb/d/8339.

Ministry of Defence: Jakobsgt. 9, 103 33 Stockholm; tel. (8) 405-10-00; fax (8) 723-11-89; e-mail registrator@defence.ministry.se; internet www.regeringen.se/sb/d/495.

Ministry of Education and Research: Drottninggt. 16, 103 33 Stockholm; tel. (8) 405-10-00; fax (8) 723-11-92; e-mail registrator@education.ministry.se; internet www.regeringen.se/sb/d/1454.

Ministry of Employment: Mäster Samuelsgt. 70, 103 33 Stockholm; tel. (8) 405-10-00; fax (8) 411-36-16; e-mail registrator@employment.ministry.se; internet www.regeringen.se/sb/d/8270.

Ministry of Enterprise, Energy and Communications: Mäster Samuelsgt. 70, 103 33 Stockholm; tel. (8) 405-10-00; fax (8) 411-36-16; e-mail registrator@enterprise.ministry.se; internet www.regeringen.se/sb/d/1470.

Ministry of the Environment: Tegelbacken 2, 103 33 Stockholm; tel. (8) 405-10-00; fax (8) 24-16-29; e-mail registrator@environment.ministry.se; internet www.regeringen.se/sb/d/1471.

Ministry of Finance: Jakobsgt. 24, 103 33 Stockholm; tel. (8) 405-10-00; fax (8) 21-73-86; e-mail registrator@finance.ministry.se; internet www.regeringen.se/sb/d/1468.

Ministry for Foreign Affairs: Gustav Adolfs torg 1, 103 39 Stockholm; tel. (8) 405-10-00; fax (8) 723-11-76; e-mail foreign.registrator@gov.se; internet www.regeringen.se/sb/d/1475.

Ministry of Health and Social Affairs: Fredsgt. 8, 103 33 Stockholm; tel. (8) 405-10-00; fax (8) 723-11-91; e-mail registrator@gov.se; internet www.regeringen.se/sb/d/1474.

Ministry of Justice: Rosenbad 4, 103 33 Stockholm; tel. (8) 405-10-00; fax (8) 20-27-34; e-mail registrator@justice.ministry.se; internet www.regeringen.se/sb/d/584.

Ministry of Rural Affairs: Fredsgt. 8, 103 33 Stockholm; tel. (8) 405-10-00; fax (8) 20-64-96; e-mail registrator@agriculture.ministry.se; internet www.regeringen.se/sb/d/1473.

Legislature

SVERIGES RIKSDAG

100 12 Stockholm; tel. (8) 786-40-00; e-mail riksdagsinformation@riksdagen.se; internet www.riksdagen.se.

Speaker: PER WESTERBERG.

General Election, 19 September 2010

Party	Votes	% of votes	Seats
Sveriges Socialdemokratiska Arbetareparti (SAP)*	1,827,497	30.66	112
Moderata Samlingspartiet (MS)†	1,791,766	30.06	107
Miljöpartiet de Gröna (MP)*	437,435	7.34	25
Folkpartiet Liberalerna (FP)†	420,524	7.06	24
Centerpartiet (CP)†	390,804	6.56	23
Sverigedemokraterna (SD)	339,610	5.70	20
Vänsterpartiet (VP)*	334,053	5.60	19
Kristdemokraterna (Kd)†	333,696	5.60	19
Others	85,023	1.43	—
Total	5,960,408	100.00	349

* Contested the election as part of De rödgröna (The Red-Greens).
† Contested the election as part of Alliansen (The Alliance).

Election Commission

Valmyndigheten (Election Authority): Fleminggt. 14, POB 12191, 102 25 Stockholm; tel. (8) 635-69-00; fax (8) 635-69-20; e-mail valet@val.se; internet www.val.se; independent; Chair. HANS-ERIC HOLMQVIST.

Political Organizations

Centerpartiet (CP) (Centre Party): Stora Nygt. 4, POB 2200, 103 15 Stockholm; tel. (8) 617-38-00; fax (8) 617-38-10; e-mail info@centerpartiet.se; internet www.centerpartiet.se; f. 1910 as an agrarian party; aims at social, environmental and progressive development and decentralization; Leader ANNIE LÖÖF; 68,000 mems.

Feministiskt initiativ (Fi) (Feminist Initiative): POB 498, 101 29 Stockholm; tel. (0) 706-100-190; e-mail info@feministisktinitiativ.se; internet www.feministisktinitiativ.se; f. 2005; Principal Speakers STINA SVENSSON, SISSELA NORDLING BLANCO.

Folkpartiet Liberalerna (FP) (Liberal Party): Stora Nygt. 2A, POB 2253, 103 16 Stockholm; tel. (8) 410-242-00; fax (8) 509-116-60; e-mail info@folkpartiet.se; internet www.folkpartiet.se; f. 1902; advocates market-orientated economy and social welfare system; Leader JAN BJÖRKLUND.

Junilistan (June List): Vasagt. 40, 111 20 Stockholm; tel. and fax (8) 23-01-11; fax (8) 23-02-11; e-mail info@junilistan.se; internet www.junilistan.se; f. 2004 to contest elections to the European Parliament; opposes further powers for EU; Pres BIRGITTA SWEDENBORG.

Kristdemokraterna (Kd) (Christian Democratic Party): Munkbron 1, POB 2373, 103 18 Stockholm; tel. (8) 723-25-00; fax (8) 723-25-10; e-mail info@kristdemokraterna.se; internet www.kristdemokraterna.se; f. 1964 as Kristdemokratiska Samhällspartiet (KdS); promotes emphasis on Christian values in political life; Leader GÖRAN HÄGGLUND; 21,600 mems.

Miljöpartiet de Gröna (MP) (Green Party): International Secretary, Swedish Parliament, 100 12 Stockholm; tel. (8) 786-57-86; fax (8) 786-53-75; e-mail international@mp.se; internet www.mp.se; f. 1981; Principal Speakers GUSTAF FRIDOLIN, ÅSA ROMSON; c. 9,400 mems.

Moderata Samlingspartiet (MS) (Moderate Party): Stora Nygt. 30, POB 2080, 103 12 Stockholm; tel. (8) 676-80-00; fax (8) 21-61-23; e-mail info@moderat.se; internet www.moderat.se; f. 1904; advocates liberal-conservative policies and market-orientated economy; Chair. FREDRIK REINFELDT; Sec.-Gen. KENT PERSSON; 100,000 mems.

Piratpartiet (Pirate Party): POB 307, 101 26 Stockholm; tel. (8) 720-04-00; e-mail info@piratpartiet.se; internet www.piratpartiet.se; f. 2006; advocates the citizen's right to complete and exclusive control of information pertaining to his or her private life and the abolition of copyright on all material for non-commercial use; Chair. ANNA TROBERG.

Sverigedemokraterna (SD) (Sweden Democrats): POB 200 85, 104 60 Stockholm; tel. (8) 50-00-00-50; fax (8) 643-92-60; e-mail info@sverigedemokraterna.se; internet www.sverigedemokraterna.se; f. 1988; nationalist, anti-immigration; Leader JIMMIE ÅKESSON; 9,000 mems.

Sveriges Socialdemokratiska Arbetareparti (SAP) (Swedish Social Democratic Party): Sveavägen 68, 105 60 Stockholm; tel. (8) 700-26-00; fax (8) 20-42-57; e-mail info@socialdemokraterna.se; internet www.socialdemokraterna.se; f. 1889; egalitarian; Leader STEFAN LÖFVEN; Sec.-Gen. CARIN JÄMTIN; 100,000 mems.

Vänsterpartiet (VP) (Left Party): Kungsgt. 84, POB 12 660, 112 93 Stockholm; tel. (8) 654-08-20; fax (8) 653-23-85; e-mail vansterpartiet@riksdagen.se; internet www.vansterpartiet.se; f. 1917 as Left Social Democratic Party of Sweden; renamed Communist Party 1921; renamed Left Party—Communists 1967; renamed Left Party 1990; policies based on the principles of Marxism, feminism and other theories; Chair. JONAS SJÖSTEDT.

Diplomatic Representation

EMBASSIES IN SWEDEN

Albania: Capellavägen 7, 181 32 Lidingö; tel. (8) 731-09-20; fax (8) 767-65-57; e-mail embassy.stockholm@mfa.gov.al; Ambassador RUHI HADO.

Algeria: Danderydsgt. 3–5, POB 26027, 100 41 Stockholm; tel. (8) 679-91-30; fax (8) 611-49-57; e-mail embassy.algeria@telia.com; internet www.embalgeria.se; Ambassador FATAH MAHRAZ.

Angola: Skeppsbron 8, POB 3199, 103 64 Stockholm; tel. (8) 24-28-90; fax (8) 34-31-27; e-mail info@angolaemb.se; internet www.angolaemb.se; Ambassador BRITO ANTÓNIO SÓZINHO.

Argentina: Narvavägen 32, 3rd Floor, Apartment 3, POB 14039 104 40 Stockholm; tel. (8) 663-19-65; fax (8) 661-00-09; e-mail cancilleria@argemb.se; Chargé d'affaires a.i. LAURA RAMIREZ BARRIOS.

Australia: Klarabergsviadukten 63, 8th Floor, POB 824, 101 36 Stockholm; tel. (8) 613-29-00; fax (8) 613-29-82; e-mail reception@austemb.se; internet www.sweden.embassy.gov.au; Ambassador GERALD BRUCE THOMSON.

Austria: Kommendörsgt. 35, 5th Floor, 114 58 Stockholm; tel. (8) 665-17-70; fax (8) 662-69-28; e-mail stockholm-ob@bmeia.gv.at; internet www.aussenministerium.at/stockholm; Ambassador Dr ULRIKE TILLY.

Azerbaijan: Karlavägen 60, 114 49 Stockholm; tel. (8) 411-24-55; fax (8) 411-24-58; e-mail azerembassy@gmail.com; internet www.azembassy.se; Ambassador RAFAEL IBRAHIMOV.

Bangladesh: Anderstorpsvägen 12, 1st Floor, 171 54 Solna; tel. (8) 730-58-50-52; fax (8) 730-58-70; e-mail banijya@bangladeshembassy.se; Ambassador A. F. M. GOUSAL AZAM SARKER.

Belgium: Kungsbroplan 2, 2nd Floor, POB 1040, 101 38 Stockholm; tel. (8) 534-802-00; fax (8) 534-802-07; e-mail stockholm@diplobel.fed.be; internet www.diplomatie.be/stockholm; Chargé d'affaires a.i. MURIELLE MARCHAND.

Bolivia: Stjärnvägen 2A, 7th Floor, 181 34 Lidingö; tel. (8) 731-58-30; fax (8) 767-63-11; e-mail embolivia-estocolmo@telia.com; Ambassador MILTON RENÉ SOTO SANTIESTEBAN.

Bosnia and Herzegovina: Birger Jarlsgt. 55, POB 7102, 103 87 Stockholm; tel. (8) 440-05-40; fax (8) 24-98-30; e-mail amb.bih.sto@telia.com; Ambassador JADRANKA KALMETA.

Botswana: Tyrgt. 11, POB 26024, 100 41 Stockholm; tel. (8) 545-258-80; fax (8) 723-00-87; e-mail botstock@gov.bw; Ambassador LAMECK NTHEKELA.

Brazil: Odengt. 3, 114 24 Stockholm; tel. (8) 545-163-00; fax (8) 545-163-14; e-mail stockholm@brazilianembassy.se; internet estocolmo.itamaraty.gov.br; Ambassador LEDA LÚCIA MARTINS CAMARGO.

Bulgaria: Karlavägen 29, 114 31 Stockholm; tel. (8) 723-09-38; fax (8) 21-45-03; e-mail bg.embassy@telia.com; internet www.bulgarien.se; Ambassador SVETLAN CHRISTOV STOEV.

Canada: Klarabergsgt. 23, 6th Floor, POB 16129, 103 23 Stockholm; tel. (8) 453-30-00; fax (8) 453-30-16; e-mail stkhm@international.gc.ca; internet www.canadainternational.gc.ca/sweden-suede; Ambassador KENNETH MACARTNEY.

Chile: Mäster Samuelsgt. 1, 2nd Floor, 111 44 Stockholm; tel. (8) 679-82-80; fax (8) 679-85-40; e-mail echilese@embassyofchile.se; internet www.embassyofchile.se; Ambassador HORACIO DEL VALLE IRARRÁZAVAL.

China, People's Republic: Lidovägen 8, 115 25 Stockholm; tel. (8) 579-364-37; fax (8) 579-364-54; e-mail protocol@chinaembassy.se; internet www.chinaembassy.se; Ambassador LAN LIJUN.

Colombia: Östermalmsgt. 46, 3rd Floor, POB 5627, 114 86 Stockholm; tel. (8) 21-43-20; fax (8) 21-84-90; e-mail embcol@telia.com; Ambassador VICTORIANA MEJIA MARULANDA.

Congo, Democratic Republic: Stjärnvägen 2, 7th Floor, POB 1171, 181 23 Lidingö; tel. (8) 765-83-80; fax (8) 765-85-91; e-mail missionrdchbstockholm22@gmail.com; Chargé d'affaires a.i. HENRI MBAYAHE NDUNGO.

Congo, Republic: Dalagt. 32, 1st Floor, 113 24 Stockholm; tel. (8) 300-59-0; e-mail ambacosuede@hotmail.fr; Ambassador ANDRÉ HOMBESSA.

Croatia: Engelbrektsplan 2, 3rd Floor, 144 34 Stockholm; tel. (8) 440-52-80; fax (8) 678-83-20; e-mail croemb.stockholm@mvp.hr; Ambassador VLADIMIR MATEK.

Cuba: Sturevägen 9, 182 73 Stocksund; tel. (8) 545-83-277; fax (8) 545-83-270; e-mail info@kuba.se; Ambassador FRANCISCO ROBERTO FLORENTINO GRAUPERA.

Cyprus: Birger Jarlsgt. 37, 4th Floor, POB 7649, 103 94 Stockholm; tel. (8) 24-50-08; fax (8) 24-45-18; e-mail stockholmembassy@mfa.gov.cy; internet www.mfa.gov.cy/embassystockholm; Ambassador GEORGE CHACALLI.

Czech Republic: POB 26156, 100 41 Stockholm; Villagt. 21, 114 32 Stockholm; tel. (8) 440-42-10; fax (8) 440-42-11; e-mail stockholm@embassy.mzv.cz; internet www.mzv.cz/stockholm; Ambassador JANA HYNKOVÁ.

Denmark: Jakobs Torg 1, POB 16119, 103 23 Stockholm; tel. (8) 406-75-00; fax (8) 791-72-20; e-mail stoamb@um.dk; internet sverige.um.dk; Ambassador KIRSTEN MALLING BIERING.

Dominican Republic: Kungsholmsgt. 10, 5th Floor, 112 27 Stockholm; tel. (8) 667-46-11; fax (8) 667-51-05; e-mail stockholm@domemb.se; Ambassador MARINA ISABEL CÁCERES DE ESTÉVEZ.

Ecuador: Västra Trädgårdsgt. 11A, 1st Floor, 111 53 Stockholm; tel. (8) 679-60-43; fax (8) 611-55-93; e-mail mecuador.suecia@embecu.se; internet www.embecu.se; Ambassador MARIO ANÍBAL GUERRERO.

Egypt: Strandvägen 35, POB 14230, 104 40 Stockholm; tel. (8) 459-98-60; fax (8) 661-26-64; e-mail embassyofegypt@telia.com; Ambassador MUHAMMAD OSAMA TAHA EL-MAGDOUB.

El Salvador: Herserudsvägen 5A, 5th Floor, 181 34 Lidingö; tel. (8) 765-86-21; fax (8) 731-72-42; e-mail embassy@elsalvador.se; internet www.elsalvador.se; Ambassador MARTIN ALBERTO RIVERA GÓMEZ.

Eritrea: Stjärnvägen 2B, 4th Floor, POB 1164, 181 23 Lidingö; tel. (8) 441-71-70; fax (8) 446-73-40; e-mail info@eritrean-embassy.se; internet www.eritrean-embassy.se; Chargé d'affaires a.i. YONAS MANNA BAIRU.

Estonia: Tyrgt. 3/3A, POB 26076, 100 41 Stockholm; tel. (8) 545-122-80; fax (8) 545-122-98; e-mail info@estemb.se; internet www.estemb.se; Ambassador JAAK JÕERÜÜT.

Finland: Gärdesgt. 11, POB 24285, 104 51 Stockholm; tel. (8) 676-67-00; fax (8) 20-74-97; e-mail info@finland.se; internet www.finland.se; Ambassador HARRY GUSTAF HELENIUS.

France: Kommendörsgt. 13, POB 5135, 102 43 Stockholm; tel. (8) 459-53-00; fax (8) 459-53-41; e-mail info@ambafrance-se.org; internet www.ambafrance-se.org; Ambassador JEAN-PIERRE LACROIX.

Georgia: Karlavägen 60, 2nd Floor, 114 49 Stockholm; tel. (8) 678-02-60; fax (8) 678-02-64; e-mail geoemb.sweden@telia.com; internet www.sweden.mfa.gov.ge; Ambassador KONSTANTIN KAVTARADZE.

Germany: Skarpögt. 9, POB 27832, 115 27 Stockholm; tel. (8) 670-15-00; fax (8) 670-15-72; e-mail info@stockholm.diplo.de; internet www.stockholm.diplo.de; Ambassador HARALD KINDERMANN.

Greece: Kommendörsgt. 16, 102 04 Stockholm; tel. (8) 545-660-10; fax (8) 660-54-70; e-mail info.stockholm@mfa.gr; internet www.mfa.gr/stockholm; Ambassador ALIKI HADJI.

Guatemala: Scheelegt. 8, 1st Floor, 112 23 Stockholm; tel. (8) 660-52-29; fax (8) 660-42-29; e-mail embassy@guatemala.se; internet www.guatemala.se; Ambassador JORGE RICARDO PUTZEYS URIGÜEN.

Holy See: Svalnäsvägen 10, 182 63 Djursholm; tel. (8) 446-51-10; fax (8) 622-51-10; e-mail nunciature@telia.com; Apostolic Nuncio Most Rev. HENRYK JÓZEF NOWACKI (Titular Archbishop of Blera).

Hungary: Dag Hammarskjölds Väg 10, POB 24125, 104 51 Stockholm; tel. (8) 661-67-62; fax (8) 660-29-59; e-mail mission.sto@mfa.gov.hu; internet www.mfa.gov.hu/emb/stockholm; Ambassador GÁBOR SZENTIVÁNYI.

Iceland: Kommendörsgt. 35, 114 58 Stockholm; tel. (8) 442-83-00; fax (8) 660-74-23; e-mail icemb.stock@utn.strj.is; internet www.iceland.org/se; Ambassador GUNNAR GUNNARSSON.

India: Adolf Fredriks Kyrkogt. 12, POB 1340, 111 83 Stockholm; tel. (8) 10-70-08; fax (8) 24-85-05; e-mail political@indianembassy.se; internet www.indianembassy.se; Ambassador BANASHRI BOSE HARRISON.

Indonesia: Kungsbroplan 1, 4th Floor, 112 27 Stockholm; tel. (8) 545-55-880; fax (8) 650-87-50; e-mail kbri@indonesiskaambassaden.se; internet www.indonesiskaambassaden.se; Ambassador DEWA MADE JUNIARTA SASTRAWAN.

Iran: Västra Yttringe Gård, Elfviksvägen, POB 6031, 181 06 Lidingö; tel. (8) 636-36-77; fax (8) 636-36-13; internet www.iran.se; Ambassador HAMID REZA SHAKERI NIASAR.

Iraq: Baldersgt. 6A, POB 26031, 100 41 Stockholm; tel. (8) 411-44-43; fax (8) 796-83-66; e-mail ambassador.office@iraqembassy.se; internet www.iraqembassy.se; Ambassador Dr HUSSAIN MAHDI ABID AL-AMERI.

Ireland: Hovslagargt. 5, POB 10326, 100 55 Stockholm; tel. (8) 545-040-40; fax (8) 660-13-53; e-mail stockholmembassy@dfa.ie; internet www.embassyofireland.se; Ambassador JAMES JOSEPH CARROLL.

Israel: Strandvägen 58, POB 14006, 104 40 Stockholm; tel. (8) 528-065-00; fax (8) 528-065-55; e-mail info@stockholm.mfa.gov.il; internet stockholm.mfa.gov.il; Ambassador ISAAC BACHMAN.

Italy: Oakhill, Djurgården, Djurgårdsvagen 174, 115 21 Stockholm; tel. (8) 545-671-00; fax (8) 660-05-05; e-mail info.stockholm@esteri.it; internet www.ambstoccolma.esteri.it; Ambassador ELENA BASILE.

Japan: Gärdesgt. 10, 115 27 Stockholm; tel. (8) 579-353-00; fax (8) 661-88-20; e-mail protocol@japansamb.se; internet www.se.emb-japan.go.jp; Ambassador YOSHIKI WATANABE.

Kenya: Birger Jarlsgt. 37, 2nd Floor, POB 7694, 103 95 Stockholm; tel. (8) 21-83-04; fax (8) 20-92-61; e-mail kenya.embassy@telia.com; Ambassador Dr JOSEPH SANG.

Korea, Democratic People's Republic: Norra Kungsvägen 39, 181 31 Lidingö; tel. (8) 767-38-36; fax (8) 767-38-35; e-mail koryo@telia.com; Ambassador PAK KWANG CHOL.

Korea, Republic: Laboratoriegt. 10, POB 27237, 102 53 Stockholm; tel. (8) 545-894-00; fax (8) 660-28-18; e-mail koremb.sweden@mofat.go.kr; internet swe.mofat.go.kr; Ambassador EOM SEOCK-JEONG.

Kosovo: Birger Jarlsgt. 33, 1st Floor, POB 3643, 111 45 Stockholm; tel. (8) 614-68-60; fax (8) 678-30-02; e-mail embassy.sweden@rks-gov.net; internet www.ambasada-ks.net/se; Ambassador LULZIM PECI.

Kuwait: Adolf Fredriks Kyrkogt. 13, POB 7279, 103 89 Stockholm; tel. (8) 450-99-80; fax (8) 450-99-55; e-mail kuwaitambassad@telia.com; Ambassador ALI I. AL-NIKHAILAN.

Laos: Badstrandsvägen 11, POB 35006, 112 65 Stockholm; tel. (8) 618-20-10; fax (8) 618-20-01; e-mail info@laoembassy.se; internet www.laosembassystockholm.egnaverk.se; Chargé d'affaires a.i. KOBKEO LUANGKHOT.

Latvia: Odengt. 5, POB 19167, 104 32 Stockholm; tel. (8) 700-63-00; fax (8) 14-01-51; e-mail embassy.sweden@mfa.gov.lv; internet www.stockholm.mfa.gov.lv; Ambassador MAIJA MANIKA.

Lebanon: Kommendörsgt. 35, POB 5360, 102 49 Stockholm; tel. (8) 665-19-65; fax (8) 662-68-24; internet www.lebanonembassy.se; Chargé d'affaires a.i. HADI JABER.

Libya: Valhallavägen 74, POB 10133, 100 55 Stockholm; tel. (8) 14-34-35; fax (8) 10-43-80; e-mail libyanembassy2012@hotmail.com; Chargé d'affaires a.i. Dr SIHAM SHAHEEN.

Lithuania: Grevgt. 5, 114 53 Stockholm; tel. (8) 667-54-55; fax (8) 667-54-56; e-mail amb.se@urm.lt; internet www.litemb.se; Ambassador EITVYDAS BAJARŪNAS.

Macedonia, former Yugoslav republic: Riddargt. 35, POB 10128, 100 55 Stockholm; tel. (8) 661-18-30; fax (8) 661-03-25; e-mail stockholm@mfa.gov.mk; Ambassador KIRE ILIOSKI.

Malaysia: Karlavägen 37, POB 26053, 100 41 Stockholm; tel. (8) 440-84-00; fax (8) 791-87-60; e-mail mwstholm@algohotellet.se; Ambassador Dato' BADRUDIN RAHMAN.

Mexico: Grevgt. 3, 114 53 Stockholm; tel. (8) 663-51-70; fax (8) 663-24-20; e-mail suecia.embamex@telia.com; internet www.sre.gob.mx/suecia; Ambassador JORGE LOMÓNACO.

Moldova: Engelbrektsgt. 10, 114 32 Stockholm; tel. (8) 411-40-64; fax (8) 411-40-74; e-mail stockholm@moldovaembassy.se; internet www.suedia.mfa.md; Ambassador EMIL DRUC.

Mongolia: Svärdvägen 25B, 182 33 Danderyd; tel. (8) 753-11-35; fax (8) 753-11-38; e-mail stockholm@mfat.gov.mn; internet stockholm.mfat.gov.mn; Ambassador BALDAN ENKHMANDAKH.

Morocco: Kungsholmstorg 16, 112 21 Stockholm; tel. (8) 545-511-30; fax (8) 545-511-39; e-mail morocco@telia.com; Ambassador YAHDIH BOUCHAAB.

Mozambique: Sturegt. 46, 4th Floor, POB 5801, 102 48 Stockholm; tel. (8) 666-03-50; fax (8) 663-67-29; e-mail info@embassymozambique.se; internet www.embassymozambique.se; Ambassador FRANCES VICTÓRIA VELHO RODRIGUES.

Namibia: Luntmakargt. 86–88, POB 19151, 104 32 Stockholm; tel. (8) 442-98-00; fax (8) 612-66-55; e-mail info@embassyofnamibia.se; internet www.embassyofnamibia.se; Ambassador DANIEL RUDOLPH SMITH.

Netherlands: Götgt. 16A, POB 15048, 104 65 Stockholm; tel. (8) 556-933-00; fax (8) 556-933-11; e-mail sto@minbuza.nl; internet www.nlemb.se; Ambassador PHILIP DE HEER.

Nicaragua: Sandhamnsgt. 40, 6th Floor, 115 28 Stockholm; tel. (8) 667-18-57; fax (8) 662-41-60; e-mail embajada.nicaragua@telia.se; Chargé d'affaires a.i. FRANCISCO RAMÓN CHAVARRIA.

Nigeria: Tyrgt. 8, POB 628, 101 32 Stockholm; tel. (8) 24-63-90; fax (8) 24-63-98; e-mail info@nigerianembassysweden.se; internet nigerianembassysweden.se; Ambassador BENEDICT ONOCHIE AMOBI.

Norway: Skarpögt. 4, POB 27829, 115 93 Stockholm; tel. (8) 587-236-00; fax (8) 587-236-99; e-mail emb.stockholm@mfa.no; internet www.norge.se; Ambassador ANNE K. LUND.

Pakistan: Karlavägen 65, 1st Floor, 114 49 Stockholm; POB 5872, 102 40 Stockholm; tel. (8) 20-33-00; fax (8) 24-92-33; e-mail info@pakistanembassy.se; internet www.pakistanembassy.se; Ambassador SAJJAD KAMRAN.

Panama: Östermalmsgt. 59, POB 55547, 102 04 Stockholm; tel. (8) 662-65-35; fax (8) 662-89-91; e-mail contacto@embassyofpanama.se; Ambassador RICARDO QUINTERO NASSAR.

Paraguay: Stureplan 4C, 114 35 Stockholm; tel. (8) 463-32-07; fax (8) 463-10-10; e-mail jose_gorostiagap@hotmail.com; Ambassador (vacant).

Peru: Kommendörsgt. 35 NB, 114 58 Stockholm; tel. (8) 440-87-40; fax (8) 20-55-92; e-mail info@peruembassy.se; internet www.peruembassy.se; Chargé d'affaires a.i. LOURDES HILBCK DE ARROSPIDE.

Poland: Karlavägen 35, 114 31 Stockholm; tel. (8) 505-750-00; fax (8) 505-750-86; e-mail sztokholm.amb.info@msz.gov.pl; internet www.sztokholm.polemb.net; Ambassador ADAM HALACINSKI.

Portugal: Narvavägen 32, 2nd Floor, POB 10194, 100 55 Stockholm; tel. (8) 545-670-60; fax (8) 662-53-29; e-mail portugal@embassyofportugal.se; internet www.embassyportugal.se; Ambassador MANUEL MARCELO MONTEIRO CURTO.

Romania: Östermalmsgt. 36, POB 26043, 100 41 Stockholm; tel. (8) 10-86-03; fax (8) 10-28-52; e-mail simona.tentea@mae.ro; internet www.stockholm.mae.ro; Ambassador RADUTA DANA MATACHE.

Russia: Gjörwellsgt. 31, 112 60 Stockholm; tel. (8) 13-04-41; fax (8) 618-27-03; e-mail rusembassy@telia.com; internet www.ryssland.se; Ambassador IGOR NEVEROV.

Rwanda: Dalvägen 2, 3rd Floor, 169 27 Solna; tel. (8) 500-019-70; fax (8) 500-019-73; e-mail ambastockholm@minaffet.gov.rw; internet sweden.embassy.gov.rw; Ambassador VENETIA SEBUDANDI.

Saudi Arabia: Sköldungagt. 5, POB 26073, 100 41 Stockholm; tel. (8) 23-88-00; fax (8) 796-99-56; e-mail saudi.ambassador@telia.com; Ambassador Dr ABD AL-RAHMAN GDAIA.

Serbia: Valhallavägen 70, POB 26209, 100 41 Stockholm; tel. (8) 21-84-36; fax (8) 21-84-95; e-mail serbiaemb@telia.com; Ambassador Dr DUŠAN CRNOGORČEVIĆ.

Slovakia: Arsenalsgt. 2, 3rd Floor, POB 7183, 103 88 Stockholm; tel. (8) 545-039-60; fax (8) 545-039-69; e-mail emb.stockholm@mzv.sk; internet www.mzv.sk/stockholm; Ambassador Dr JAROSLAV AUXT.

South Africa: Fleminggt. 20, 4th Floor, 112 26 Stockholm; tel. (8) 24-39-50; fax (8) 660-71-36; e-mail saemb.swe@telia.com; internet www.southafrica.se; Ambassador MANDISA DONA MARASHA.

Spain: Djurgårdsvägen 21, POB 10295, 100 55 Stockholm; tel. (8) 522-808-00; fax (8) 663-30-34; e-mail emb.estocolmo@maec.es; internet www.maec.es/embajadas/estocolmo; Ambassador FRANCISCO JAVIER JIMÉNEZ-UGARTE HERNÁNDEZ.

Sri Lanka: Strandvägen 39, 1st Floor, POB 24055, 104 50 Stockholm; tel. (8) 663-65-23; fax (8) 660-00-89; e-mail slembassy@comhem.se; internet www.slembassy.se; Ambassador OSHADHI ALAHAPPERUMA.

Sudan: Stockholmsvägen 33, 181 33 Lidingö; tel. (8) 611-77-80; fax (8) 611-77-82; e-mail sudanembassy@telia.com; Ambassador ABU BAKR HUSSEIN.

Switzerland: Valhallavägen 64, POB 26143, 100 41 Stockholm; tel. (8) 676-79-00; fax (8) 21-15-04; e-mail sto.vertretung@eda.admin.ch; internet www.eda.admin.ch/stockholm; Ambassador YVANA ENZLER.

Syria: Vendevägen 90, 5th Floor, POB 4, 182 11 Danderyd; tel. (8) 622-18-70; fax (8) 660-88-05; e-mail info@syrianembassy.se; internet www.syrianembassy.se; Chargé d'affaires a.i. HANADI KABOUR.

Tanzania: Näsby Allé 6, 183 55 Täby; tel. (8) 732-24-30; fax (8) 732-24-32; e-mail mailbox@tanemb.se; internet www.tanemb.se; Ambassador MUHAMMED MWINYI MZALE.

Thailand: Floragt. 3, POB 26220, 100 40 Stockholm; tel. (8) 588-04-25-0; fax (8) 791-73-51; e-mail info@thaiembassy.se; internet www.thaiembassy.se; Ambassador SOMCHAI CHARANASOMBOON.

Tunisia: Narvavägen 32, 1st Floor, POB 24030, 104 50 Stockholm; tel. (8) 545-855-20; fax (8) 662-19-75; e-mail at.stockholm@swipnet.se; Chargé d'affaires OMRANI CHARGUI.

Turkey: Dag Hammarskjölds Väg 20, POB 24105, 104 51 Stockholm; tel. (8) 23-08-40; fax (8) 663-55-14; e-mail embassy.stockholm@mfa.gov.tr; internet www.stokholm.be.mfa.gov.tr; Ambassador ZERGÜN KORUTÜRK.

Ukraine: Stjärnvägen 2A, 181 34 Lidingö; tel. (8) 522-28-400; fax (8) 522-28-411; e-mail emb_se@mfa.gov.ua; internet www.mfa.gov.ua/sweden; Ambassador Dr VALERII STEPANOV.

United Arab Emirates: Torsgt. 2, 5th Floor, POB 164, 101 23 Stockholm; tel. (8) 411-12-44; fax (8) 411-12-45; e-mail stockholm@mofa.gov.ae; internet www.uaeembassy.se; Ambassador Sheikha NAJLA MOHAMED SALEM AL-QASSIMI.

United Kingdom: Skarpögt. 6–8, POB 27819, 115 93 Stockholm; tel. (8) 671-30-00; fax (8) 671-31-04; e-mail stockholm@fco.gov.uk; internet ukinsweden.fco.gov.uk/en; Ambassador PAUL JOHNSTON.

USA: Dag Hammarskjölds Väg 31, 115 89 Stockholm; tel. (8) 783-53-00; fax (8) 661-19-64; e-mail stockholmirc@state.gov; internet stockholm.usembassy.gov; Ambassador MARK F. BRZEZINSKI.

Uruguay: Kommendörsgt. 35, 114 58 Stockholm; tel. (8) 660-31-96; fax (8) 665-31-66; e-mail urustoc@uruemb.se; Ambassador Dr ZULMA GUELMAN GUIGOU.

Venezuela: Engelbrektsgt. 35B, POB 26012, 100 41 Stockholm; tel. (8) 411-09-96; fax (8) 21-31-00; e-mail venezuela.embassy@telia.com; internet venezuelasambassad.com; Chargé d'affaires a.i. ZULIMA ROJAS MAVARES.

Viet Nam: Örby Slottsvägen 26, 125 71 Älvsjö; tel. (8) 556-210-70; fax (8) 556-210-80; e-mail info@vietnamemb.se; internet www.vietnamemb.se; Ambassador NGUYEN DUC HOA.

Zambia: Gårdsvägen 18, 3rd Floor, POB 3056, 169 03 Solna; tel. (8) 679-90-40; fax (8) 679-68-50; e-mail info@zambiaembassy.se; internet www.zambiaembassy.se; Ambassador EDITH MUTALE.

Zimbabwe: Herserudsvägen 5A, 7th Floor, 181 34 Lidingö; POB 3253, 103 65 Stockholm; tel. (8) 765-53-80; fax (8) 21-91-32; e-mail mbuya@stockholm.mail.telia.com; internet www.zimembassy.se; Ambassador STEPHEN CLETUS CHIKETA.

Judicial System

The judiciary and the executive are separate, although judges are appointed by the Government. A judge can be removed by an authority other than a court, but may, in such an event, request a judicial trial of the decision.

To supervise the courts in administrative matters, there is a central authority, *Domstolsverket*, in Jönköping. This authority has no control over the judicial process, in which the court is independent even of the legislature and Government.

There are state officers who exercise control over the judiciary as well as the administrative authorities. The *Justitiekansler* (Chancellor of Justice or Attorney-General) and the four *Justitieombudsmän* supervise the courts and the general administration including the armed forces. The *Justitiekansler* performs his or her functions on behalf of the Government. The *Justitieombudsmän* are appointed by and act on behalf of the legislature.

Attorney-General (Justitiekansler): ANNA SKARHED.

SUPREME COURT

Högsta domstolen (Supreme Court in Stockholm): POB 2066, 103 12 Stockholm; Riddarhustorget 8, 111 28 Stockholm; tel. (8) 561-666-00; fax (8) 561-666-86; e-mail hogsta.domstolen@dom.se; internet www.hogstadomstolen.se; the Supreme Court in Stockholm, consisting of a minimum of 14 members, is the Court of Highest Instance. The Court works in three chambers, each of which is duly constituted of five members. Certain cases are decided by full session of the Court. There are also special divisions with three members (or, in simple cases, one member) which decide whether the Court is to consider a case; Chair. of the Supreme Court MARIANNE LUNDIUS.

APPELLATE COURTS

The Court of Appeal, the Court of Second Instance, consists of a president, judges of appeal and associate judges of appeal. The work is apportioned between various divisions, each of which has five or six members. In criminal cases the bench consists of three professional judges and two lay assessors; in petty and civil cases there are three professional judges only. There are six Courts of Appeal (*hovrätter*).

President of the Court of Appeal (Stockholm): FREDRIK WERSÄLL.

President of the Court of Appeal (Jönköping): STEN ANDERSSON.

President of the Court of Appeal (Malmö): LENNART SVENSÄTER.

President of the Court of Appeal (Göteborg): PER HALL.

President of the Court of Appeal (Sundsvall): STEN BURMAN.

President of the Court of Appeal (Umeå): MARGARETA BERGSTRÖM.

DISTRICT COURTS

The District Court acts as a Court of First Instance in both civil and criminal cases. In 2012 there were 48 District Courts (*tingsrätter*). In criminal cases the court is composed of a presiding professional judge and three or, in serious cases, five lay assessors; in petty cases the court consists of the professional judge only. In civil cases the court is ordinarily composed of three professional judges; however, preparatory sessions are conducted by one professional judge. In family law cases, the court is composed of a professional judge and three lay assessors. The lay assessors are elected for a period of four years (during which they are on duty for about 10 days a year). They act as members of the bench and should consequently be distinguished from the jurors of other countries. In certain types of case technical experts may sit alongside the judges.

ADMINISTRATIVE COURTS

In each of the 23 administrative districts of the country there is a County Administrative Court (*länsrätt*). This court handles appeal cases concerning the assessment of social security and welfare. The bench ordinarily consists of a professional judge and three lay assessors, although in simple cases a professional judge may preside alone.

Appeals against decisions by the County Administrative Courts may be made to Administrative Courts of Appeal (*kammarrätter*) consisting of a president, judges of appeal and associate judges of appeal. The courts work in divisions, each of which normally has six members. The bench consists of at least three and not more than four judges. In certain cases there are, however, three professional judges and two lay assessors. There are four Administrative Courts of Appeal.

The Supreme Administrative Court of Sweden (*Regeringsrätten*) in Stockholm, consisting of 19 members, is the Court of Highest Instance in Administrative cases. The composition of the court is governed by rules very similar to those that apply to the Supreme Court.

Chairman of the Supreme Administrative Court: MATS MELIN.

President of the Administrative Court of Appeal (Stockholm): THOMAS ROLÉN.

President of the Administrative Court of Appeal (Göteborg): MARGARETA ÅBERG.

President of the Administrative Court of Appeal (Sundsvall): BERTIL EKHOLM.

President of the Administrative Court of Appeal (Jönköping): PETER ROSÉN.

SPECIAL COURTS

Special courts exist for certain categories of cases, such as real estate courts (*fastighetsdomstolar*).

OMBUDSMEN

The post of *Justitieombudsman* was created in 1800 to supervise the manner in which judges, government officials and other civil servants observe the laws, and to prosecute those who act illegally, misuse their position or neglect their duties. The Ombudsman is allowed access to all documents and information and has the right to be present at the considerations of the courts and other authorities. Government ministers in Sweden are not subject to supervision by the Ombudsman. The term of office is four years.

Ombudsmen: ELISABET FURA, HANS-GUNNAR AXBERGER, LILIAN WIKLUND, LARS LINDSTRÖM.

Religion

CHRISTIANITY

About 71.3% of the population were members of the Svenska kyrkan (Church of Sweden) in 2009. Since the constitutional link between the Church and the state was severed in 2000 a significant number of people have left the Church each year.

Sveriges Kristna Råd (Christian Council of Sweden): Ekumeniska Centret, Starrbäcksgt. 11, 172 99 Sundbyberg; tel. (8) 453-68-00; fax (8) 453-68-29; e-mail info@skr.org; internet www.skr.org; f. 1993; 27 mem. churches; Gen. Sec. KARIN WIBORN.

Church of Sweden

Svenska kyrkan

Kyrkokansliet, Sysslomansgt. 4, 751 70 Uppsala; tel. (18) 16-95-00; fax (18) 16-96-40; e-mail info@svenskakyrkan.se; internet www .svenskakyrkan.se.

Evangelical Lutheran; 13 dioceses, 2,225 parishes, 3,500 active clergy (including missionaries in the mission fields); the Archbishop of Uppsala is head of the Church.

Archbishop of Uppsala: Most Rev. ANDERS WEJRYD, 751 70 Uppsala; tel. (18) 16-95-00.

Evangeliska Fosterlands-Stiftelsen (Swedish Evangelical Mission): Prästgatan 11, POB 23001, 750 23 Uppsala; tel. (18) 430-25-00; e-mail efs@efs.nu; internet www.efs.nu; f. 1856; an independent mission org. within the Church of Sweden; 17,994 mems; Chair. RAY RAWALL; Mission Dir ANDERS SJÖBERG.

Other Protestant Churches

Eesti Evangeeliumi Luteri Usu Kirik (Estonian Evangelical Lutheran Church): POB 450 74, 104 30 Stockholm 45; tel. (8) 20-69-78; e-mail ingo.jaagu@bredband.net; 12,000 mems; Dean INGO TIIT JAAGU; Gen. Sec. IVAR NIPPAK.

Metodistkyrkan i Sverige (United Methodist Church): Danska vägen 20, 412 66 Göteborg; tel. (31) 733-78-40; e-mail info@ metodistkyrkan.se; internet www.metodistkyrkan.se; f. 1868; 3,565 mems; Bishop CHRISTIAN ALSTED; Pres. of Conference Board ANDERS SVENSSON.

Sjundedags Adventistsamfundet (Seventh-day Adventists): Olof Palmes Gt. 25, POB 536, 101 30 Stockholm; tel. (8) 545-297-70; fax (8) 20-48-68; e-mail info@adventist.se; internet www.adventist.se; f. 1880; 2,800 mems; Pres. BOBBY SJÖLANDER; Sec. DANIEL HAILEMAR-IAM.

Svenska Baptistsamfundet (Baptist Union of Sweden): POB 14038, 167 14 Bromma; tel. (8) 564-827-00; fax (8) 564-827-27; e-mail info@baptist.se; internet www.baptist.se; f. 1848; 207 churches, 17,411 mems (Dec. 2010); mem. European Baptist Fed., Baptist World Alliance and Christian Council of Sweden (Sveriges Kristna Råd); Pres. Rev. SÖREN CARLSVÄRD; Gen. Sec. LENNART GUSTAFSON.

Svenska Missionskyrkan (Mission Covenant Church of Sweden): POB 6302, 113 81 Stockholm; tel. (8) 580-031-00; e-mail info@ gemensamframtid.se; internet www.missionskyrkan.se; f. 1878; 133,400 mems; Pres. GÖRAN ZETTERGREN; Chair. of Board ULF HÅLLMARKER.

The Roman Catholic Church

For ecclesiastical purposes, Sweden comprises the single diocese of Stockholm, directly responsible to the Holy See. At 31 December 2006 there were 140,000 adherents in the country, representing 1.5% of the total population.

Scandinavian Bishops' Conference

POB 135, 421 22 Västra Frölunda; tel. (31) 709-57-15; fax (31) 49-21-70; e-mail nbk@bishopsoffice.org.

f. 1960; new statutes approved 2000; covers Sweden, Norway, Denmark, Finland and Iceland; Pres. Rt Rev. ANDERS ARBORELIUS; Sec.-Gen. Rt Rev. GEORG MÜLLER.

Bishop of Stockholm: Rt Rev. ANDERS ARBORELIUS, Götgt. 68, POB 4114, 102 62 Stockholm; tel. (8) 462-66-00; fax (8) 462-94-25; e-mail info@katolskakyrkan.se; internet www.katolskakyrkan.se.

Other Denominations

Other Christian Churches include the Pentecostal Movement (with an estimated 90,000 mems in 2004), the Orthodox Churches of the Greeks, Romanians, Russians, Serbians and Finnish (together numbering about 100,000 mems in 2004), the Church of Jesus Christ of Latter-day Saints (Mormons—9,000 mems in 2004), the Swedish Alliance Missionary Society (12,895 mems in 1997), the Jehovah's Witnesses (23,000 mems in 2004) and the Salvation Army (25,531 mems in 1997).

ISLAM

In 2004 there were approximately 300,000 to 350,000 Muslims in Sweden, of whom around 100,000 were believed to be religiously active.

Islamiska Radet i Sverige (IRIS) (Islamic Council of Sweden): POB 3053, 14503 Norsborg; tel. (8) 531-707-95; fax (8) 531-706-65; f. 1986.

Islamiska Kulturcenterunionen i Sverige (IKUS) (Union of the Islamic Cultural Centres in Sweden): POB 3053, 145 03 Norsborg; tel. (8) 531-707-95; fax (8) 531-706-65; f. 1984.

Sveriges Muslimska Förbund (SMUF): Stockholms Moske, Kapellgränd 10, 116 25 Stockholm; tel. (8) 509-109-00; f. 1981; Chair. MAHMOUD ALDEBE; 70,000 mems.

Sveriges Muslimska Råd (SMR) (Muslim Council of Sweden): Stockholms Moske, Kapellgränd 10, 116 25 Stockholm; tel. and fax (8) 509-109-00; e-mail info@sverigesmuslimskarad.se; internet www .sverigesmuslimskarad.se; f. 1990; members include the Sveriges Muslimska Förbund; Chair. HELENA BENAOUDA.

JUDAISM

In 2004 the total number of Jews living in Sweden was estimated to be approximately 18,500–20,000; however, the Jewish community estimated 10,000 active, or practising, members. There are Orthodox, Conservative and Reform Jewish synagogues. The largest Jewish community is in Stockholm.

Judiska Församlingen i Stockholm (Jewish Community in Stockholm): Wahrendorffsgt. 3B, POB 7427, 103 91 Stockholm; tel. (8) 587-858-00; fax (8) 587-858-58; e-mail info@jfst.se; internet www .jfst.se; f. 1775; c. 4,400 mems; Exec. Dir THOMAS BAB.

OTHER RELIGIONS

In 2004 there were approximately 3,000–4,000 Buddhists and a similar number of Hindus in Sweden.

The Press

Press freedom in Sweden dates from a law of 1766. The 1949 Freedom of the Press Act, a fundamental law embodying the whole of the press legislation in the Constitution, guarantees the press's right to print and disseminate ideas; protects those supplying information by forbidding editors to disclose sources under any circumstances; authorizes all public documents to be publicly available, official secrets being the only exception; and contains provision for defamation. Press offences are to be referred to common law, and all cases against the press must be heard by jury.

In 1916 the Press Council was founded by press organizations to monitor ethical matters within the press. Lacking judicial status, it has powers to rehabilitate persons wronged by the press who refuse to apply to courts of law. Its judgments are widely published and highly respected.

In 1969 the office of Press Ombudsman was established to supervise adherence to ethical standards. Public complaints shall be directed to the Press Ombudsman, who is also entitled to act on his own initiative. He may dismiss a complaint if unfounded, or if the newspaper agrees to publish a retraction or rectification acceptable to the complainant. When he finds that the grievance is of a more serious nature, he will file a complaint with the Press Council, which will then publish a statement acquitting or criticizing the newspaper. The findings of the Council are published in the newspaper concerned.

The dominating influence of the few major dailies is largely confined to Stockholm, the provinces having a strong press of their own. The major dailies are: *Dagens Nyheter, Expressen, Svenska Dagbladet, Dagens Industri* (all Stockholm), *Göteborgs-Posten* (Gothenburg), *Sydsvenskan* (Malmö). In 2010 there were 169 daily newspapers with a combined circulation of 3.5m.

The two principal magazine publishers in Sweden are the Bonnier group (also a large book publisher and the majority shareholder in the newspapers *Dagens Nyheter, Expressen* and *Sydsvenskan*) and the Aller company. Four other companies produce most of the remainder of Sweden's magazine circulation. The most popular weekly periodicals include the family magazines *Året Runt, Hemmets Veckotidning, Allers* and *Hemmets Journal*, and the home and household magazine *ICA Kuriren*.

PRINCIPAL NEWSPAPERS

Newspapers with a circulation exceeding 15,000 are listed below.

Ängelholm

Nordvästra Skånes Tidningar: 262 32 Ängelholm; tel. (431) 84-000; fax (431) 84-194; e-mail angelholm@hd.se; f. 1847; daily; Editor MICHAEL HANSSON.

Borås

Borås Tidning: 501 85 Borås; tel. (33) 700-07-00; fax (33) 10-14-36; e-mail kundtjanst@bt.se; internet www.bt.se; f. 1826; morning; Editor STEFAN EKLUND; circ. 50,000 (2011).

Eksjö

Smålands-Tidningen: POB 261, 575 23 Eksjö; tel. (381) 63-85-00; fax (381) 12-215; e-mail eksjored@smt.se; internet www.smalandstidningen.se; f. 1899; morning; independent; Editor MATS OTTOSSON.

Eskilstuna

Eskilstuna-Kuriren Strengnäs Tidning: POB 120, 631 02 Eskilstuna; tel. (16) 15-60-00; fax (16) 51-63-04; e-mail redaktion@ekuriren.se; internet www.ekuriren.se; f. 1890; morning; Editor PEO WÄRRING; circ. 30,300 (2010).

Falkenberg

Hallands Nyheter: 311 81 Falkenberg; tel. (10) 471-52-55; fax (10) 471-52-89; e-mail redaktionen@hn.se; internet www.hn.se; f. 1905; morning; Editor ANDERS SVENSSON; circ. 28,100 (2011).

Falun

Dala-Demokraten: POB 825, Stigaregat. 17, 791 29 Falun; tel. (23) 47-500; fax (23) 20-668; e-mail nyhetschef.falun@daladem.se; internet www.dalademokraten.se; f. 1917; morning; Editor GÖRAN GREIDER; circ. 16,100 (2011).

Falu-Kuriren: POB 265, 791 26 Falun; tel. (23) 93-600; fax (23) 12-073; e-mail fk.red@dt.se; internet www.dt.se; f. 1894; part of *Dalarnas Tidningar*; morning; Editor JENNY ANDREASSON; circ. 57,100 (2011).

Gävle

Arbetarbladet: POB 287, 801 06 Gävle; tel. (26) 15-93-00; fax (26) 18-52-70; e-mail redaktionen@arbetarbladet.se; internet www.arbetarbladet.se; f. 1902; morning; Editor SVEN JOHANSSON; circ. 21,600 (2011).

Gefle Dagblad: POB 367, 801 05 Gävle; tel. (26) 15-95-00; fax (26) 15-97-00; e-mail gefle.dagblad@gd.se; internet www.gd.se; f. 1895; morning; Editor MARIA BRANDEN; circ. 25,100 (2011).

Göteborg
(Gothenburg)

Göteborgs-Posten: Polhemsplatsen 5, 405 02 Göteborg; tel. (31) 62-40-00; fax (31) 62-45-85; e-mail jonathan.falck@gp.se; internet www.gp.se; f. 1858; part of the Stampen Group; morning; Editor-in-Chief JONATHAN FALCK; circ. 216,300 (2011).

Halmstad

Hallandsposten: 301 81 Halmstad; tel. (35) 14-75-00; fax (35) 14-76-88; e-mail redaktionen@hallandsposten.se; internet www.hallandsposten.se; f. 1850; morning; Editor VIVEKA HEDBJÖRK; circ. 30,000 (2011).

Hässleholm

Norra Skåne: Väpnaregatan 6, 281 50 Hässleholm; tel. (451) 74-50-00; fax (451) 74-50-32; e-mail mimmi.karlsson-bernfalk@skd.se; internet www.nsk.se; f. 1899; morning; Editor MIMMI KARLSSON-BERNFALK; circ. 17,500 (2011).

Helsingborg

Helsingborgs Dagblad: Vasatorpsvägen 1, 251 83 Helsingborg; tel. (42) 489-90-00; e-mail redaktionen@hd.se; internet www.hd.se; f. 1867; morning; independent; Editor-in-Chief LARS JOHANSSON; circ. 74,800 (2011).

SD-Kuriren: POB 130 45, 250 13 Helsingborg; tel. (73) 62-60-661; fax (455) 151-33; e-mail redaktion@sdkuriren.se; f. 1988; Editor-in-Chief RICHARD JOMSHOF; circ. 30,000 (2006).

Jönköping

Jönköpings-Posten/Smålands Allehanda: 551 80 Jönköping; tel. (36) 30-40-50; fax (36) 12-61-11; e-mail mats.ottosson@jonkopingsposten.se; internet www.jonkopingsposten.se; f. 1865; morning; independent; Editor MATS OTTOSSON; circ. 24,400 (2011).

Kalmar

Barometern med Oskarshamns-Tidningen: 391 88 Kalmar; tel. (480) 59-100; fax (480) 59-131; internet www.barometern.se; f. 1841; morning; Editor GUNILLA SAX; circ. 42,100 (2011).

Karlskrona

Blekinge Läns Tidning: 371 89 Karlskrona; tel. (455) 77-000; fax (455) 82-170; e-mail kerstin.armann@blt.se; internet www.blt.se; f. 1869; morning; Editor-in-Chief KERSTIN ÅRMANN; circ. 33,900 (2011).

Karlstad

Nya Wermlands-Tidningen: POB 28, 651 02 Karlstad; tel. (54) 19-90-00; fax (54) 19-96-00; e-mail redaktion@nwt.se; internet www.nwt.se; f. 1836; morning; Editor STAFFAN ANDER; circ. 51,900 (2011).

Värmlands Folkblad: POB 67, 651 03 Karlstad; tel. (54) 17-55-40; fax (54) 17-55-99; e-mail redaktion@vf.se; internet www.vf.se; f. 1918; morning; Editor PETER FRANKE; circ. 17,800 (2011).

Kristianstad

Kristianstadsbladet: 291 84 Kristianstad; tel. (44) 18-55-00; fax (44) 12-62-76; e-mail kundservice@kristianstadsbladet.se; internet www.kristianstadsbladet.se; f. 1856; morning; Editor JÖRGEN SVENSSON; circ. 25,700 (2011).

Lidköping

Nya Lidköpings-Tidningen: 531 81 Lidköping; tel. (510) 89-700; fax (510) 89-730; e-mail redaktion@nlt.se; internet www.nlt.se; f. 1903; morning; 3 a week; Editor ANDERS HÖRLING; circ. 25,200 (2011).

Linköping

Östgöta Correspondenten: 581 89 Linköping; tel. (13) 28-00-00; fax (13) 28-03-24; e-mail nyhet@corren.se; internet www.corren.se; f. 1838; morning; Editor CHARLOTTA FRIBORG; circ. 51,600 (2011).

Luleå

Norrbottens-Kuriren: 971 81 Luleå; tel. (920) 26-29-00; fax (920) 26-29-53; e-mail redaktionen@kuriren.com; internet www.kuriren.nu; f. 1861; morning; Editor MATS EHNBOM; circ. 19,100 (2011).

Norrländska Socialdemokraten: 971 83 Luleå; tel. (920) 23-60-00; fax (920) 23-60-39; e-mail redaktion@nsd.se; internet www.nsd.se; f. 1919; morning; Editor ANDERS INGVARSSON; circ. 32,300 (2011).

Malmö

Kvällsposten: 205 26 Malmö; tel. (40) 602-01-00; fax (40) 18-90-90; e-mail redaktionen@kvp.se; internet www.kvp.se; f. 1990; edition of *Expressen*; evening; Editor LARS MOHLIN.

Skånska Dagbladet: Östergt. 11, POB 165, 201 21 Malmö; tel. (40) 660-55-00; fax (40) 97-47-70; e-mail webbred@skd.se; internet www.skanskan.se; f. 1888; morning; Editor JAN A. JOHANSSON; circ. 29,500 (2011).

Sydsvenskan: 205 05 Malmö; tel. (40) 28-12-00; fax (40) 93-54-75; e-mail nyhetsred@sydsvenskan.se; internet sydsvenskan.se; f. 1848; morning; Editor DANIEL SANDSTRÖM; circ. 111,000 (2011).

Norrköping

Norrköpings Tidningar: 601 83 Norrköping; tel. (11) 20-01-66; fax (11) 20-01-40; e-mail redaktionen@nt.se; internet www.nt.se; f. 1758; morning; Editor ANDERS NILSSON; circ. 40,600 (2011).

Nyköping

Södermanlands Nyheter: 611 79 Nyköping; tel. (155) 76-700; fax (155) 26-88-01; e-mail redaktionen@sn.se; internet www.sn.se; f. 1893; morning; Editor GÖRAN CARSTORP; circ. 24,400 (2011).

Örebro

Nerikes Allehanda: 701 92 Örebro; tel. (19) 15-50-00; fax (19) 12-03-83; e-mail redaktionen@na.se; internet www.na.se; f. 1843; morning; Editor KATARINA EKSPONG; circ. 54,700 (2011).

Örnsköldsvik

Örnsköldsviks Allehanda: POB 110, 891 23 Örnsköldsvik; tel. (660) 29-50-00; fax (660) 15-064; e-mail jimmie.naslund@allehanda.se; internet allehanda.se; f. 1843; morning; Editor JIMMIE NÄSLUND; circ. 16,200 (2011).

Östersund

Östersunds-Posten: POB 720, 831 28 Östersund; tel. (63) 16-16-00; fax (63) 16-16-55; e-mail redaktion@op.se; internet www.op.se; f. 1877; morning; Editor HANS LINDEBERG; circ. 23,400 (2011).

Piteå

Piteå-Tidningen: POB 193, 941 24 Piteå; tel. (911) 64-500; fax (911) 64-640; e-mail redaktionen@pitea-tidningen.se; internet www.pitea-tidningen.se; f. 1915; morning; Editor MATTI LILJA; circ. 15,100 (2011).

Directory

Skara

Skaraborgs Läns Tidning: POB 214, 532 23 Skara; tel. (511) 13-010; fax (511) 18-815; e-mail red.sklt@vgt.se; internet www .skaraborgslanstidning.se; f. 1884; morning; Editor HANS OLOFSSON.

Skellefteå

Norran: POB 58, 931 21 Skellefteå; tel. (910) 57-808; fax (910) 57-875; e-mail redaktion@norran.se; internet www.norran.se; f. 1910; previously *Norra Västerbotten*; morning; 6 a week; Editor LARS ANDERSSON; circ. 23,800 (2011).

Skövde

Skaraborgs Allehanda: POB 407, 541 28 Skövde; tel. (500) 46-75-00; fax (500) 48-05-82; e-mail redaktion@sla.se; internet www.sla.se; f. 1884; morning; Editor NICLAS LINDSTRAND; circ. 23,500 (2011).

Stockholm

Aftonbladet: 105 18 Stockholm; tel. (8) 725-20-00; fax (8) 600-01-70; e-mail redaktion@aftonbladet.se; internet www.aftonbladet.se; f. 1830; evening; Editor-in-Chief JAN HELIN.

Dagen: 105 36 Stockholm; tel. (8) 619-24-00; fax (8) 619-60-51; e-mail daniel.grahn@dagen.se; internet www.dagen.se; f. 1945; morning; 4 a week; Editor DANIEL GRAHN; circ. 16,600 (2011).

Dagens Industri: 113 90 Stockholm; tel. (8) 736-50-00; fax (8) 736-52-20; e-mail pren@di.se; internet www.di.se; f. 1976; 6 a week; business news; Editor PETER FELLMAN; circ. 103,100 (2011).

Dagens Nyheter: 105 15 Stockholm; tel. (8) 738-10-00; fax (8) 738-21-80; e-mail gunilla.herlitz@dn.se; internet www.dn.se; f. 1864; morning; independent; Editor-in-Chief and CEO GUNILLA HERLITZ; circ. 292,100 (2011).

Expressen: Gjörwellsgt. 30, 105 16 Stockholm; tel. (8) 738-30-00; fax (8) 738-33-40; e-mail redaktion@expressen.se; internet www .expressen.se; f. 1945; evening; Editor THOMAS MATTSSON; circ. 262,300 (2011).

Svenska Dagbladet: 105 17 Stockholm; tel. (8) 13-50-00; fax (8) 13-56-80; e-mail svd@svd.se; internet www.svd.se; f. 1884; morning; Editor-in-Chief LENA K. SAMUELSSON; circ. 186,000 (2011).

Sundsvall

Sundsvalls Tidning: 851 72 Sundsvall; tel. (60) 19-70-00; fax (60) 15-44-33; e-mail tips@st.nu; internet www.st.nu; f. 1841; morning; Editor MATS ÅMVALL; circ. 28,800 (2011).

Trollhättan

TTELA: POB 54, 461 22 Trollhättan; tel. (520) 42-26-00; fax (520) 49-43-19; e-mail redaktionen@ttela.se; internet www.ttela.se; f. 2004; through the merger of *Trollhättans Tidning* and *Elfsborgs Läns Allehanda*; Stampen Group; morning; 5 a week; Editor MORGAN AHLBERG; circ. 26,100 (2011).

Uddevalla

Bohusläningen: 451 83 Uddevalla; tel. (522) 99-000; fax (522) 51-18-88; e-mail redaktionen@bohuslaningen.se; internet www .bohuslaningen.se; f. 1878; morning; Editor INGALILL SUNDHAGE; circ. 28,700 (2011).

Umeå

Västerbottens-Kuriren: 901 70 Umeå; tel. (90) 17-60-00; e-mail redaktion@vk.se; internet www.vk.se; f. 1900; morning; Editor INGVAR NÄSLUND; circ. 33,500 (2011).

Uppsala

Upsala Nya Tidning: Danmarksgt. 28, POB 36, 751 03 Uppsala; tel. (18) 478-00-00; fax (18) 12-95-07; e-mail kristina.lernevall@unt.se; internet www.unt.se; f. 1890; morning; Editor-in-Chief HANNA STJÄRNE; circ. 48,400 (2011).

Värnamo

Värnamo Nyheter: 331 84 Värnamo; tel. (370) 30-06-00; fax (370) 499-15; e-mail redaktion@varnamonyheter.se; internet www .varnamonyheter.se; f. 1917; morning; independent; Editor LARS ALKNER; circ. 18,100 (2011).

Västerås

Vestmanlands Läns Tidning (VLT): POB 3, 721 03 Västerås; tel. (21) 19-90-00; fax (21) 19-90-60; e-mail nyheter@vlt.se; internet www .vlt.se; f. 1831; morning; Editor MÅRTEN ENBERG; circ. 37,000 (2011).

Växjö

Smålandsposten: 351 70 Växjö; tel. (470) 77-05-00; fax (470) 209-49; e-mail nyheter@smp.se; internet www.smp.se; f. 1866; morning; Editor MAGNUS KARLSSON; circ. 36,300 (2011).

Ystad

Ystads Allehanda: 271 81 Ystad; tel. (411) 55-78-00; e-mail nyheter@ystadsallehanda.se; internet www.ystadsallehanda.se; f. 1873; morning; Editor JÖRGEN SVENSSON; circ. 21,500 (2011).

POPULAR PERIODICALS

Allas Veckotidning: Allers Förlag, 205 35 Malmö; tel. (40) 38-59-00; fax (40) 38-59-64; e-mail allas@aller.se; internet www.allas.se; f. 1931; owned by Aller Media; weekly; family; Editor-in-Chief GUNILLA HÅKANSSON; circ. 117,700.

Allers: Aller Media AB, Landskronavägen 23, 251 85 Helsingborg; tel. (42) 17-35-00; fax (42) 17-35-68; e-mail redaktionen@allers.se; f. 1877; weekly; family; Editor-in-Chief LOTTA HYLANDER; circ. 213,800.

Allt om Mat: Sveavägen 53, 105 44 Stockholm; tel. (8) 736-53-00; fax (8) 34-00-88; e-mail red@aom.bonnier.se; internet www.alltommat .se; f. 1970; 18 a year; food specialities; Editor-in-Chief MONA JOHANSSON; circ. 125,800.

Antik och Auktion: Landskronavägen 23, 251 85 Helsingborg; tel. (42) 12-35-00; fax (42) 17-37-40; e-mail carin.stentorp@aller.se; internet www.antikochauktion.se; f. 1978; monthly; antiques; Editor CARIN STENTORP; circ. 57,900.

Året Runt: 105 44 Stockholm; tel. (8) 736-52-00; fax (8) 30-49-00; f. 1946; weekly; family; Editor LILLIAN EHRENHOLM-DAUN; circ. 243,500.

Bilsport: POB 529, 371 23 Karlskrona; tel. (455) 33-53-25; fax (455) 186-60; e-mail bilsport@fabas.se; internet www.bilsport.se; f. 1962; fortnightly; motor-sport, cars; Editor-in-Chief FREDRIK SJÖQVIST; circ. 67,300.

Damernas Värld: Sveavägen 53, 105 44 Stockholm; tel. (8) 736-53-00; fax (8) 24-46-46; e-mail martina.bonnier@dv.bonnier.se; internet www.damernasvarld.se; f. 1940; monthly; women's interest; Editor MARTINA BONNIER; circ. 118,800.

Elle: POB 27700, 115 91 Stockholm; Humlegårdsgatan 6, 114 46 Stockholm; tel. (8) 457-80-00; fax (8) 457-80-80; e-mail ellered@ hachette.se; internet www.elle.se; f. 1988; monthly; women's interest; Editor HERMINE COYET OHLÉN; circ. 81,900.

Femina Månadens Magasin: Landskronavägen 23, 251 85 Helsingborg; tel. (42) 17-35-00; fax (42) 17-36-82; e-mail femina@aller.se; e-mail femina.se; f. 1981; monthly; women's interest; Editor ULRIKA NORBERG; circ. 118,000.

Frida: Hammarby Kaj 18, 120 30 Stockholm; tel. (8) 587-481-00; fax (8) 587-481-07; e-mail frida@frida.forlag.se; internet www.frida.se; f. 1981; fortnightly; for teenage girls; Editor-in-Chief CAMILLA LORD; circ. 67,000.

Hänt Extra: POB 27704, 115 91 Stockholm; tel. (8) 679-46-00; fax (8) 679-46-77; f. 1986; weekly; family; Editor-in-Chief BENGT GUSTAVSSON; circ. 129,500 (2010).

Hänt i Veckan: POB 27704, 115 91 Stockholm; tel. (8) 679-46-00; fax (8) 679-46-33; f. 1964; weekly; family; Editor-in-Chief STEN HEDMAN; circ. 132,300.

Hemmets Journal: Egmont Tidskrifter AB, 205 07 Malmö; tel. (40) 38-52-00; fax (40) 38-53-98; e-mail red.hj@egmont.se; internet www .hemmetsjournal.se; f. 1920; weekly; family; Editor-in-Chief HÅKAN STRÖM; circ. 202,100 (2010).

Hemmets Veckotidning: Allers Förlag AB, 205 35 Malmö; tel. (40) 38-59-00; fax (40) 38-59-14; f. 1929; weekly; family; Editor ULLA COCKE; circ. 215,300.

Hus & Hem: ICA Förlaget AB, POB 6630, 113 84 Stockholm; tel. (8) 728-23-00; fax (8) 34-56-37; e-mail kundtjanst.husohem@formapg .se; internet www.husohem.se; 12 a year; for house owners; Editor ANNA LILJEBERG; circ. 86,500 (2010).

ICA Kuriren: Hälsingegt. 49, POB 6630, 113 84 Stockholm; tel. (8) 728-23-00; fax (8) 728-23-50; e-mail red.kuriren@forlaget.ica.se; internet www.icakuriren.se; f. 1942; weekly; home and household; Editor ANN DAHL; circ. 158,100 (2010).

Kalle Anka & Co: 205 08 Malmö; tel. (40) 693-94-00; fax (40) 693-94-95; e-mail webeditor@egmont.se; internet www.kalleanka.se; f. 1948; weekly; comic; Editor TORD JÖNSSON; circ. 65,300 (2010).

Kvällsstunden: Tidningshuset Kvällsstunden AB, Klockartorpsgt. 14, POB 1080, 721 27 Västerås; tel. (21) 19-04-00; fax (21) 13-62-62; e-mail info@tidningshuset.com; internet www.tidningshuset.com; weekly; family magazine; Editor ÅKE LINDBERG; circ. 45,800 (2010).

Må Bra: Tysta Gt. 12, POB 27780, 115 93 Stockholm; tel. (8) 679-46-00; fax (8) 667-34-39; e-mail liselotte.stalberg@mabra.aller.se;

internet mabra.com; f. 1978; monthly; health and nutrition; Editor-in-Chief LISELOTTE STÅLBERG; circ. 85,700 (2010).

Privata Affärer: Sveavägen 53, 105 44 Stockholm; tel. (8) 736-53-00; fax (8) 31-25-60; e-mail pren@privataaffarer.se; internet www.privataaffarer.se; f. 1978; monthly; personal money management; Editor-in-Chief PER HAMMARLUND; circ. 59,500 (2010).

Röster i Radio/TV: POB 27704, 115 91 Stockholm; tel. (8) 679-46-00; fax (8) 679-46-33; f. 1934; weekly; family magazine and programme guide to radio and television; Editor-in-Chief EDGAR ANTONSSON; circ. 140,000.

Sköna hem: Sveavägen 53, 105 44 Stockholm; tel. (8) 736-53-00; fax (8) 33-74-11; e-mail skonahem@skh.bonnier.se; internet www.skonahem.com; f. 1979 (*Sköna hem*), 1956 (*Allt i Hemmet*), merged 1992; monthly; interior decoration; Editor-in-Chief CLAES BLOM; circ. 93,400 (2010).

Svensk Damtidning: Humlegårdsgt. 6, POB 27710, 115 91 Stockholm; tel. (8) 679-46-00; fax (8) 679-47-50; e-mail svenskdam@aller.se; internet svenskdam.se; f. 1980; weekly; women's interest; Editor-in-Chief KARIN LENMOR; circ. 149,600 (2010).

Tara: Kungsgt. 34, 105 44 Stockholm; tel. (8) 736-52-00; e-mail red@tara.bonnier.se; internet www.tara.se; fitness, nutrition, fashion, relationships; Editor-in-Chief ANN FREDLUND.

Teknikens Värld: Rådmansgt. 49, 105 44 Stockholm; tel. (8) 736-53-00; fax (8) 736-00-11; e-mail ventilen@tv.bonnier.se; internet www.teknikensvarld.se; f. 1948; fortnightly; motoring; Editor-in-Chief DANIEL FRODIN; circ. 43,400 (2010).

Vecko-Revyn: Kungsgt. 34, 105 44 Stockholm; tel. (8) 736-52-00; fax (8) 24-16-02; e-mail ebba@veckorevyn.com; internet veckorevyn.net; f. 1935; weekly; young women's interest; Editor EBBA VON SYDOW; circ. 43,200 (2010).

Vi Bilägare: Ynglingagt. 12, POB 23800, 104 35 Stockholm; tel. (8) 736-12-00; fax (8) 736-12-49; e-mail redaktionen@vibilagare.se; internet www.vibilagare.se; f. 1930; fortnightly; auto and travel; Editor NILS-ERIC FRENDIN; circ. 118,400 (2010).

Vi Föräldrar: Sveavägen 53, 105 44 Stockholm; tel. (8) 736-53-00; e-mail red@vf.bonnier.se; internet www.viforaldrar.se; f. 1968; 13 a year; parents' magazine; Editor-in-Chief LOUISE BRATT TIDMARSH; circ. 42,200 (2011).

SPECIALIST PERIODICALS

Aktuellt i Politiken: Sveavägen 68, 105 60 Stockholm; tel. (8) 700-26-00; fax (8) 11-65-42; weekly; social, political and cultural affairs; organ of Swedish Social Democratic Party; Editor FREDRIK KORNE-BÄCK; circ. 55,000.

Allt om Jakt & Vapen: POB 3263, 103 65 Stockholm; tel. (8) 30-16-30; fax (8) 28-59-74; e-mail jaktochvapen@pressdata.se; internet www.jaktovapen.com; 11 a year; hunting; Editor ERIK WALLIN; circ. 41,500.

Arbetsledaren: POB 12069, 102 22 Stockholm; tel. (8) 652-01-20; fax (8) 653-99-68; f. 1908; 10 a year; journal for foremen and supervisors; Editor INGRID ASKEBERG; circ. 87,400.

Barn: 107 88 Stockholm; tel. (8) 698-90-00; fax (8) 698-90-14; e-mail barn@rb.se; internet www.rb.se/barn; owned by Rädda Barnen (Save the Children Sweden); 6 a year; children's rights; Editor-in-Chief SOFIE ARNÖ; circ. 115,700 (2011).

Båtliv: POB 8097, 371 38 Karlskrona; tel. (445) 297-80; fax (455) 36-97-99; e-mail info@batliv.se; internet www.batliv.se; 5 a year; for boat owners and boat club members; Editor LARS-ÅKE REDÉEN; circ. 147,100 (2010).

Byggnadsarbetaren: Hagagt. 2, 106 32 Stockholm; tel. (8) 728-48-00; fax (8) 728-49-80; e-mail redaktionen@byggnadsarbetaren.se; internet www.byggnadsarbetaren.se; f. 1949; 15 a year; construction; Editor KENNETH PETTERSON; circ. 114,900 (2010).

Dina Pengar: Konsument Göteborg, POB 11364, 404 28 Göteborg; tel. (8) 573-650-60; fax (8) 573-651-00; e-mail dise@di.se; internet www.di.se; 9 a year; finance; Editor LINUS PAULSSON; circ. 83,000.

Du&jobbet: Långholmsgt. 34, POB 17550, 118 91 Stockholm; tel. (8) 442-46-00; fax (8) 442-46-08; e-mail redaktionen@duochjobbet.se; internet www.duochjobbet.se; f. 1912; monthly; working environment, health, management; Editor-in-Chief EVA BERLIN; circ. 15,400 (2010).

Handelsnytt: POB 1146, 111 81 Stockholm; tel. (8) 412-68-00; fax (8) 21-43-33; e-mail handelsnytt@handels.se; internet www.handelsnytt.se; f. 1906; 11 a year; organ of the Union of Commercial Employees; Editor ANNA FILIPSSON; circ. 147,900 (2010).

Hundsport: POB 20136, 161 02 Bromma; tel. (8) 80-85-65; fax (8) 80-85-95; monthly; for dog owners; Editor TORSTEN WIDHOLM; circ. 99,700 (2010).

Jaktmarker och Fiskevatten: Västra Torggt. 18, 652 24 Karlstad; tel. (54) 10-03-70; fax (54) 10-09-83; 11 a year; hunting and fishing; circ. 48,100.

Kommunalarbetaren: Hagagt. 2, POB 19034, 104 32 Stockholm; tel. (8) 728-28-00; fax (8) 30-61-42; e-mail kommunalarbetaren@kommunal.se; internet www.ka.se; 22 a year; organ of the Union of Municipal Workers; Editor LIV BECKSTRÖM; circ. 535,500 (2010).

Kyrkans Tidning: Kungsholmstorg 5, POB 22543, 104 22 Stockholm; tel. (8) 462-28-00; fax (8) 644-76-86; e-mail redaktionen@kyrkanstidning.se; internet www.kyrkanstidning.se; f. 1982; weekly; organ of the Church of Sweden; Man. Dir THOMAS GRAHL; Editor ANDERS AHLBERG; circ. 35,700 (2010).

LAND-Familjetidningen: Gävlegt. 22, 113 92 Stockholm; tel. (8) 588-365-10; fax (8) 588-369-59; e-mail land@lrfmedia.lrf.se; internet www.tidningenland.com; f. 1971; weekly; organ of the farmers' asscn; circ. 234,000 (2006).

LAND Lantbruk: Gävlegt. 22, 113 92 Stockholm; tel. (8) 787-51-00; fax (8) 787-55-02; e-mail internetredaktionen@lantbruk.com; internet www.lantbruk.com; f. 1971; weekly; organ of the farmers' asscn; agriculture, forestry; Editor OLLE ERIKSSON; circ. 118,700.

Lärarförbundet: Segelbåtsvägen 15, POB 12229, 102 26 Stockholm; tel. (8) 737-65-00; fax (8) 656-94-15; e-mail sten.svensson@lararforbundet.se; internet www.lararforbundet.se; 22 a year; for teachers; Editor-in-Chief STEN SVENSSON; circ. 225,000.

Metallarbetaren: Olof Palmesgt. 11, 105 52 Stockholm; tel. (8) 10-68-30; fax (8) 11-13-02; f. 1888; weekly; organ of Swedish Metal Workers' Union; Editor PER AHLSTRÖM; circ. 415,400.

Motor: POB 23142, 104 35 Stockholm; tel. (8) 690-38-00; fax (8) 690-38-22; monthly; cars and motoring; circ. 117,300 (2010).

Motorföraren: Heliosgt. 11, 120 30 Stockholm; tel. (8) 555-765-55; fax (8) 555-765-95; e-mail info@mhf.se; internet www.mhf.se; f. 1927; 8 a year; motoring and tourism; Editor ARNE WINERDAL; circ. 31,400 (2010).

Ny Teknik: Mäster Samuelsgt. 56, 106 12 Stockholm; tel. (8) 796-66-00; fax (8) 613-30-28; e-mail redaktion@nyteknik.se; internet www.nyteknik.se; f. 1967; weekly; technical publication owned by the 2 largest engineering societies of Sweden; Editor-in-Chief JAN HUSS; circ. 155,500 (2010).

PRO-Pensionären: POB 3274, 103 65 Stockholm; tel. (8) 701-67-00; fax (8) 20-33-58; e-mail info@pro.se; internet www.pro.se; f. 1942; 10 a year; magazine for pensioners; Editor BETTAN ANDERSSON; circ. 303,200 (2010).

SEKO-magasinet: Barnhusgt. 10, POB 1102, 111 81 Stockholm; tel. (8) 791-41-00; fax (8) 21-16-94; f. 1955; 11 a year; organ of the National Union of Services and Communications Employees; Editor-in-Chief JESPER BENGTSSON; circ. 154,700.

SIA-Skogsindustriarbetaren: Olof Palmesgt. 31, POB 1138, 111 81 Stockholm; tel. (8) 470-83-00; fax (8) 20-79-04; e-mail sia@skogstrafacket.org; monthly; forestry; circ. 69,100.

SIF-Tidningen: SIF-huset, Olof Palmesgt. 17, 105 32 Stockholm; tel. (8) 508-970-00; fax (8) 508-970-12; e-mail bjorn.oijer@sif.se; 19 a year; organ of the Union of Clerical and Technical Employees; Editor-in-Chief BJORN OIJER; circ. 331,800.

Skog & Såg: Sag i Syd, POB 37, 551 12 Jönköping; tel. (36) 34-30-00; fax (36) 12-86-10; f. 1966; 4 a year; sawmills and forestry; Editor SVEN MAGNUSSON; circ. 73,800 (2010).

SKTF-Tidningen: POB 7825, 103 97 Stockholm; tel. (8) 789-63-00; fax (8) 789-64-79; e-mail sktftidningen@sktf.se; internet www.sktftidningen.se; 20 a year; organ of the Union of Municipal Employees; Editor KENT KÄLLQVIST; circ. 159,200 (2010).

Sunt Förnuft: 114 95 Stockholm; tel. (8) 613-17-00; fax (8) 21-38-58; 8 a year; taxpayers' magazine; circ. 65,200 (2010).

Svensk Bokhandel (Journal of the Swedish Book Trade): Birkagt. 16C, POB 6888, 113 86 Stockholm; tel. (8) 545-417-70; fax (8) 545-417-75; e-mail redaktion@svb.se; internet www.svb.se; co-publ. by Swedish Publrs' Asscn and Swedish Booksellers' Asscn, for booksellers, publishers, antiquarians and librarians; Editor LASSE WINKLER; circ. 3,300 (2010).

Svensk Golf: POB 84, 182 11 Danderyd; tel. (8) 622-15-00; fax (8) 755-84-39; e-mail info@golf.se; internet www.golf.se; f. 1946; 10 a year; golf; Editor TOBIAS BERGMAN; circ. 315,000 (2010).

Svensk Jakt: Öster Malma, 611 91 Nyköping; tel. (155) 24-62-90; fax (155) 24-62-95; e-mail redaktionen@svenskjakt.se; internet www.jagareforbundet.se/svenskjakt; f. 1862; 11 a year; for hunters and dog breeders; circ. 141,900 (2010).

Sveriges Natur: Åsögt. 115, POB 4625, 116 91 Stockholm; tel. (8) 702-65-00; fax (8) 702-27-02; e-mail sveriges.natur@snf.se; f. 1909; 5 a year; organ of Swedish Society for Nature Conservation; Editor CARL-AXEL FALL; circ. 112,000 (2010).

Tidningen C: POB 2200, 103 15 Stockholm; tel. (8) 617-38-30; fax (8) 617-38-10; e-mail c.redaktionen@centrepartiet.se; f. 1929; 4 a year; organ of the Centre Party; Editor SUSANNE SIGNAHL; circ. 68,000.

Transportarbetaren: POB 714, 101 33 Stockholm; tel. (8) 723-77-00; fax (8) 723-00-76; 11 a year; organ of the Swedish Transport Workers' Union; Editor JAN LINDKVIST; circ. 63,400 (2010).

Turist: 101 20 Stockholm; tel. (8) 463-21-00; 6 a year; tourism and travel; Editor MONIKA TROZELL; circ. 160,700 (2010).

NEWS AGENCIES

Svenska Nyhetsbyrån (Swedish Conservative Press Agency): POB 3553, 103 69 Stockholm; tel. (8) 14-07-50; fax (8) 10-10-48; e-mail red@snb.se; internet www.snb.se; Pres. FREDRIK HAAGE; Editor-in-Chief and Dir PER SELSTAM.

Svensk-Internationella Pressbyrån AB (SIP) (Swedish-International Press Bureau): Stymansgt. 4, 114 54 Stockholm; tel. (8) 528-088-10; fax (8) 528-088-30; e-mail ld@publicitet.com; internet www.publicitet.se; f. 1927; Editor-in-Chief CHRISTER LIEDHOLM.

Tidningarnas Telegrambyrå (TT) (Swedish News Agency): Katarinavägen 15, 105 12 Stockholm; tel. (8) 692-26-00; fax (8) 692-28-55; e-mail redaktionen@tt.se; internet www.tt.se; f. 1921; co-operative news agency, working in conjunction with Reuters, AFP and other agencies; Chair. RAOUL GRÜNTHAL; Gen. Man. and Editor-in-Chief THOMAS PETERSSOHN.

PRESS ASSOCIATIONS

Pre Cent (Centre Party's Press Agency): POB 2033, 103 11 Stockholm; tel. (8) 786-48-84; fax (8) 24-30-04; e-mail red@precent.se; f. 1987; Editor-in-Chief JIMMY DOMINIUS; 33 mems.

Svenska Journalistförbundet (Swedish Union of Journalists): POB 1116, 111 81 Stockholm; tel. (8) 613-75-00; fax (8) 21-26-80; e-mail kansliet@sjf.se; internet www.sjf.se; f. 1901; Pres. JONAS NORDLING; 17,500 mems.

Svenska Tidningsutgivareföreningen (Swedish Newspaper Publishers' Asscn): Kungsholmstorg 5, POB 22500, 104 22 Stockholm; tel. (8) 692-46-00; fax (8) 692-46-38; e-mail info@tu.se; internet www.tu.se; f. 1898; Man. Dir PÄR FAGERSTRÖM; 200 mems.

Sveriges Tidskrifter (Swedish Magazine Publishers' Asscn): Vasagt. 50, 111 20 Stockholm; tel. (8) 545-298-90; fax (8) 14-98-65; e-mail info@sverigestidskrifter.se; internet www.sverigestidskrifter.se; f. 1931; Man. Dir KERSTIN NELD.

Sveriges Vänsterpressförening (Liberal Press Asscn): 901 70 Umeå; tel. (90) 15-10-00; fax (90) 77-46-47; f. 1905; Pres. OLOF KLEBERG; Sec. MATS OLOFSSON; c. 130 mems.

Publishers

Alfabeta Bokförlag AB: Bondegt. 21, POB 4284, 102 66 Stockholm; tel. (8) 714-36-30; fax (8) 643-24-31; e-mail info@alfamedia.se; internet www.alfamedia.se; fiction, psychology, biography, cinema, art, music, travel guides, children's books; Man. Dir DAG HERNRIED.

Bokförlaget Arena: Fersens väg 9, 211 42 Malmö; tel. (40) 10-92-55; fax (40) 10-92-51; e-mail info@arenabok.se; internet www.arenabok.se; f. 1920; non-fiction; Publr JOHANNA EKBERG.

Bokförlaget Atlantis AB: Sturegt. 24, 114 36 Stockholm; tel. (8) 545-660-70; fax (8) 545-660-71; e-mail info@atlantisbok.se; internet www.atlantisbok.se; f. 1977; fiction, non-fiction, art; imprint: Signum; Man. Dir PETER LUTHERSSON.

Berghs Förlag AB: Observatoriegt. 10, POB 45084, 104 30 Stockholm; tel. (8) 31-65-59; fax (8) 32-77-45; e-mail info@berghsforlag.se; internet www.berghsforlag.se; f. 1954; non-fiction for adults and children, picture books and fiction for children, craft books, popular science, New Age literature; Publr LENA ANDERSSON.

Bonnier Carlsen Bokförlag AB: Sveavägen 56, POB 3159, 103 63 Stockholm; tel. (8) 696-89-30; fax (8) 696-89-31; e-mail info@carlsen.bonnier.se; internet www.bonniercarlsen.se; picture books, juvenile books, non-fiction, board books, comics; Man. Dir ANNA BORNÉ MINBERGER.

Bonnierförlagen AB: Sveavägen 56, POB 3159, 103 63 Stockholm; tel. (8) 696-80-00; fax (8) 696-80-46; e-mail info@bok.bonnier.se; internet www.bok.bonnier.se; f. 1837; fiction, non-fiction, encyclopaedias, reference books, quality paperbacks; includes Albert Bonniers Förlag AB, Bonnier Utbildning AB, Bokförlaget Forum AB, Wahlström & Widstrand, Autumn Publishing, Bonnier Audio, Bonnier Carlsen, Bokförlaget Rebus, Bokförlaget Max Ström, Reseförlaget; Chair. JACOB DALBORG.

Bokförlaget Bra Böcker: Ångbåtsbron 1, POB 892, 201 80 Malmö; tel. (40) 665-46-00; internet www.bbb.se; f. 1965; fiction, biography, books in translation; Man. Dir ERIK JOHANSSON.

Brombergs Bokförlag AB: Hantverkargt. 26, POB 12886, 112 98 Stockholm; tel. (8) 562-620-80; fax (8) 562-620-85; e-mail info@brombergs.se; internet www.brombergs.se; literary fiction, non-fiction; Man. Dir DOROTEA BROMBERG.

Brutus Östlings Bokförlag Symposion: Rönneholm 604, 240 36 Stehag; tel. (413) 606-90; fax (413) 109-48; e-mail order@symposion.se; internet www.symposion.se; poetry, drama, non-fiction.

Carlsson Bokförlag AB: Stora Nygt. 31, 111 27 Stockholm; tel. (8) 657-95-00; fax (8) 796-84-57; e-mail info@carlssonbokforlag.se; internet www.carlssonbokforlag.se; art, photography, ethnology, history, politics; Man. Dir TRYGVE CARLSSON.

Bokförlaget DN: POB 703 21, 107 23 Stockholm; tel. (8) 696-87-90; fax (8) 696-83-67; e-mail marknad@forum.se; internet www.bokforlagetdn.se; publishing division of *Dagens Nyheter* newspaper; Publr and Pres. ALBERT BONNDER.

Bokförlaget T. Fischer & Co: Svartmangt. 18, POB 2036, 103 11 Stockholm; tel. (8) 643-38-46; fax (8) 643-38-98; e-mail bokforlaget@fischer-co.se; internet www.fischer-co.se; non-fiction; owned by Lind & Co.

Forma Publishing Group: Port-Anders-Gt., T3, 721 85 Västerås; tel. (21) 19-40-00; fax (21) 19-41-36; e-mail patrik.widlund@formapg.se; internet www.formapg.se; f. 1945 as ICA Förlaget AB; present name adopted 2004; non-fiction, cookery, handicrafts, gardening, natural history, popular psychology, health, domestic animals, sports; magazine publisher; Chair. CLAES-GÖRAN SYLVÉN; Man. Dir PATRIK WIDLUND.

Forum Publishers: Sveavägen 56, POB 3159, 103 63 Stockholm; tel. (8) 696-84-40; fax (8) 696-83-47; e-mail brittinger.nordstrand@forum.se; internet www.forum.se; f. 1944; general fiction, non-fiction; Man. Dir MAGNUS NYTELL.

Gehrmans Musikförlag AB: POB 42026, 126 12 Stockholm; Västberga allé 5, 126 30 Hägersten; tel. (8) 610-06-00; fax (8) 610-06-27; e-mail info@gehrmans.se; internet www.gehrmans.se; f. 1893; orchestral and choral music; general music publishing; Pres. JOE LINDSTRÖM; CEO GUNNAR HELGESSON.

Hermods AB: Warfvinges väg 33, 112 51 Stockholm; tel. (8) 410-251-00; e-mail keith.fransson@hermods.se; internet www.liberhermods.se; f. 1993; further and higher education; Man. Dir KEITH FRANSSON.

Informationsförlaget: Sveavägen 61, POB 6884, 113 86 Stockholm; tel. (8) 545-560-50; fax (8) 31-39-03; e-mail red@informationsforlaget.se; internet www.informationsforlaget.se; f. 1979; publishers of books for cos and orgs on demand; reference, encyclopaedias, gastronomy, illustrated books; Man. Dir ULF HEIMDAHL.

Liber AB: 113 98 Stockholm; tel. (8) 690-90-00; fax (8) 690-93-36; e-mail export@liber.se; internet www.liber.se; general and educational publishing; owned by Bridgepoint Capital Ltd (London, UK); Man. Dir JERKER NILSSON.

J. A. Lindblads Bokförlags AB: Warfvingesväg 30, POB 30195, 104 25 Stockholm; tel. (8) 618-78-98; e-mail bertil.wahlstrom@lindblads.se; fiction, non-fiction, juvenile, paperbacks; Man. Dir BERTIL WAHLSTRÖM.

Abraham Lundquist AB Musikförlag: POB 93, 182 11 Danderyd; tel. (8) 732-92-35; fax (8) 732-92-38; e-mail info@abrahamlundquist.se; internet www.abrahamlundquist.se; f. 1838; music.

Bokförlaget Natur och Kultur: Karlavägen 31, POB 27323, 102 54 Stockholm; tel. (8) 453-86-00; fax (8) 453-87-90; e-mail info@nok.se; internet www.nok.se; f. 1922; textbooks, general literature, fiction; Man. Dir GUNN JOHANSSON.

Norstedts Förlagsgrupp: Tryckerigt. 4, POB 2052, 103 12 Stockholm; tel. (8) 769-87-00; fax (8) 769-88-64; e-mail anna.ivarsson@norstedts.se; internet www.norstedts.se; subsidiaries: Norstedts Förlag, Norstedts Akademiska Förlag, Rabénförlagen; Man. Dir PETER WILCKE.

Norstedts Förlag AB: Tryckerigt. 4, POB 2052, 103 12 Stockholm; tel. (8) 769-88-50; fax (8) 769-88-64; e-mail info@norstedts.se; internet www.norstedts.se; f. 1823; fiction, non-fiction; imprints: Norstedts, Prisma, Nautiska, Norstedts Pocket and Norstedts Audio; part of Norstedts Förlagsgrupp; Man. Dir PETER WILCKE.

Norstedts Juridik AB: 106 47 Stockholm; tel. (8) 598-191-00; fax (8) 598-191-91; e-mail kundservice@nj.se; internet www.nj.se; f. 1837; owned by Wolters Kluwer NV (Netherlands); fmrly C. E. Fritzes AB; CEO OLOV SUNDSTRÖM.

Bokförlaget Opal AB: Tegelbergsvägen 31, POB 20113, 161 02 Bromma; tel. (8) 28-21-79; fax (8) 29-66-23; e-mail opal@opal.se; internet www.opal.se; f. 1973; Man. Dir BENGT CHRISTELL.

Ordfront Förlag AB: Bellmansgt. 30, POB 17506, 118 91 Stockholm; tel. (8) 462-44-00; fax (8) 462-44-90; e-mail info@ordfront.se; internet www.ordfront.se; fiction, history, politics; Man. Dir JAN-ERIK PETTERSSON.

Prisma Bokförlaget: Tryckerigt. 4, POB 2052, 103 12 Stockholm; tel. (8) 769-87-00; fax (8) 769-89-13; e-mail info@prismabok.se; internet www.prismabok.se; f. 1963; imprint of Norstedts Bokförlag AB; Dir VIVECA EKELUND.

Rabén & Sjögren: Tryckerigt. 4, POB 2052, 103 12 Stockholm; tel. (8) 744-22-00; internet www.rabensjogren.se; children's books; Man. Dir ANN SKÖLD NILSSON.

Rabénförlagen: Tryckerigt. 4, POB 2052, 103 12 Stockholm; tel. (8) 769-88-00; fax (8) 769-88-13; e-mail info@raben.se; internet www.raben.se; f. 1942; general, juvenile; imprints: Rabén & Sjögren, Gammafon, Tiden, Eriksson & Lindgren; part of Norstedts Förlagsgrupp; Dir ERIK LIEDBERG.

Bokförlaget Semic: Esplanaden 3B, POB 1243, 172 25 Sundbyberg; tel. (8) 799-30-50; fax (8) 799-30-64; e-mail info@semic.se; internet www.semic.se; handbooks, calendars, comic magazines, juvenile; Pres. RICKARD EKSTRÖM.

Stenströms Bokförlag AB: Linnégt. 98, POB 24086, 104 50 Stockholm; tel. (8) 663-76-01; fax (8) 663-22-01; f. 1983; Man. Dir BENGT STENSTRÖM.

Reseförlaget: Sveavägen 56, POB 3159, 103 63 Stockholm; tel. (8) 696-80-00; fax (8) 696-80-46; e-mail info@reseforlaget.se; internet www.reseforlaget.se; f. 1990 as Streiffert Förlag AB; acquired by Bonnierförlagen AB and adopted current name 2006; travel guides.

Bokförlaget Semic: Esplanaden 3B, POB 1243, 172 25 Sundbyberg; tel. (8) 799-30-50; fax (8) 799-30-64; e-mail info@semic.se; internet www.semic.se; handbooks, calendars, comic magazines, juvenile; Pres. RICKARD EKSTRÖM.

Stenströms Bokförlag AB: Linnégt. 98, POB 24086, 104 50 Stockholm; tel. (8) 663-76-01; fax (8) 663-22-01; f. 1983; Man. Dir BENGT STENSTRÖM.

Timbro Förlag/SFN: Kungsgt. 60, POB 3037, 103 61 Stockholm; tel. (8) 587-898-00; fax (8) 667-00-37; e-mail info@timbro.se; internet www.timbro.se; economics, political science; Man. Dir MARKUS UVELL.

Verbum Förlag AB: St Paulsgt. 2, POB 15169, 104 65 Stockholm; tel. (8) 743-65-00; fax (8) 641-45-85; e-mail info.forlag@verbum.se; internet www.verbum.se; f. 1911; theology, fiction, juvenile, music; imprints: Verbum and Nordia; Man. Dir CLAES-GÖRAN GUNNARSSON.

Wahlström & Widstrand: Sveavägen 58, POB 3159, 103 63 Stockholm; tel. (8) 696-84-80; fax (8) 696-83-80; e-mail info@wwd.se; internet www.wwd.se; f. 1884; fiction, non-fiction, biography, history, science, paperbacks; owned by Bonnierförlagen AB; Man. Dir KERSTIN ANGELIN.

PUBLISHERS' ASSOCIATIONS

Föreningen Svenska Läromedel (Swedish Asscn of Educational Publishers): Vegagt. 14, 113 29 Stockholm; tel. (8) 588-314-00; fax (8) 736-19-44; e-mail info@svenskalaromedel.se; internet svenskalaromedel.se; f. 1973; Chair. JERKER NILSSON; Dir RICKARD VINDE; 11 mems.

Svenska Förläggareföreningen (Swedish Publishers' Asscn): Drottninggt. 97, 113 60 Stockholm; tel. (8) 736-19-40; fax (8) 736-19-44; e-mail info@forlaggare.se; internet www.forlaggare.se; f. 1843; Chair. EVA BONNIER; Man. Dir KRISTINA AHLINDER; 60 mems.

Broadcasting and Communications

TELECOMMUNICATIONS

Hi3G Access AB: Lindhagensgt. 98, POB 30213, 104 25 Stockholm; tel. (7) 633-333-33; fax (7) 633-372-00; e-mail info@tre.se; internet www.tre.se; f. 2003; mobile communications; 60% shares owned by Hutchison Whampoa Ltd (Hong Kong), 40% owned by Investor AB (Sweden); CEO PEDER RAMEL.

Tele 2 AB: Skeppsbron 18, POB 2094, 103 13 Stockholm; tel. (85) 562-000-60; fax (85) 562-000-40; e-mail press.relations@tele2.com; internet www.tele2.com; f. 1993; Pres. and CEO MATS GRANRYD.

Telefonaktiebolaget LM Ericsson: Torshamngt. 23, 164 83 Stockholm; tel. (8) 719-00-00; fax (8) 719-19-76; e-mail investor.relations.se@ericsson.com; internet www.ericsson.com; parent co of the Ericsson group; mobile and fixed network provider; represented in 140 countries; Chair. LEIF JOHANSSON; CEO CARL-HANS VESTBERG.

Telenor Sverige AB: Campus Gräsvik 12, 371 80 Karlskrona; tel. (4) 553-310-00; fax (4) 553-312-22; internet www.telenor.se; fmrly Vodafone Sverige AB; provides mobile cellular communications under brand name Djuice, as well as broadband internet access and digital television services; acquired by Telenor AS (Norway) in 2005; Man. Dir LARS-ÅKE NORLING.

TeliaSonera AB: Stureplan 8, 106 63 Stockholm; tel. (8) 504-550-00; fax (8) 504-550-01; e-mail teliasonera@teliasonera.se; internet www.teliasonera.se; f. by merger of Telia AB (Sweden) with Sonera Ltd (Finland); 37.3% owned by Govt of Sweden, 13.7% by Govt of Finland; Chair. MARIE EHRLING; Pres. and CEO PER-ARNE BLOMQUIST (acting).

Teracom AB: POB 30150, 104 25 Stockholm; tel. (8) 555-420-00; fax (8) 555-420-01; e-mail webmaster@teracom.se; internet www.teracom.se; provides digital television and radio services, fixed-line telephony and broadband internet access; CEO STEPHAN GUIANCE; Pres. CRISTER FRITZSON.

Regulatory Authority

Post- och Telestyrelsen (PTS) (Post and Telecom Authority): Valhallavägen 117, POB 5398, 102 49 Stockholm; tel. (8) 678-55-00; fax (8) 678-55-05; e-mail info@pts.se; internet www.pts.se; Dir-Gen. GÖRAN MARBY.

BROADCASTING

Until the end of 1992 public service radio and television were organized within the state broadcasting corporation, Sveriges Radio AB, a public service organization financed by licence fees; this operated two national television channels and three national radio channels, together with 24 local radio stations. On 1 January 1993 the state corporation was replaced by three companies, Sveriges Radio AB, Sveriges Television AB, and Sveriges Utbildningsradio AB, responsible for radio, television, and educational radio and television, respectively. The operations of these companies are regulated by law and by agreements with the Government. From 1 January 1994 the three companies came into the ownership of three foundations.

Radio

There are four public service radio channels, as well as neighbourhood radio stations and private local radio stations (financed by advertising).

IBRA Radio AB: Gustavslundsvägen 18, 167 15 Stockholm; tel. (8) 608-96-80; fax (8) 608-96-50; e-mail info@ibra.se; internet www.ibra.se; f. 1955; non-commercial private Christian co broadcasting to all continents; Dir PONTUS FRIDOLFSSON.

Sveriges Radio AB (SR): Oxenstiernsgt. 20, 105 10 Stockholm; tel. (8) 784-50-00; fax (8) 784-15-00; e-mail lyssnarservice@sverigesradio.se; internet sverigesradio.se; f. 1993; independent co responsible for national radio broadcasting; CEO MATS SVEGFORS.

Sveriges Utbildningsradio AB: Oxenstiernsgt. 34, 105 10 Stockholm; tel. (8) 784-40-00; fax (8) 784-43-91; e-mail kundtjanst@ur.se; internet www.ur.se; f. 1978; public service co responsible for educational broadcasting on radio and television; Man. Dir ERIK FICHTELIUS.

Television

There are two public service television channels (SVT 1 and SVT 2). The broadcasts are financed by licence fees. In 1991 the Government awarded the licence for a third terrestrial nation-wide television channel to TV 4 (which is financed by advertising). Television channels transmitted by satellite and cable, and directed at the Swedish audience, include: TV 3, Kanal 5, TV 6, Kanal 9, Z-TV, and the film channels TV 1000, FilmMax, Filmnet Plus and Filmnet Movie.

Kanal 5: Rådmansgt. 42, 114 99 Stockholm; tel. (8) 520-555-55; fax (8) 612-05-95; e-mail info@kanal5.se; internet www.kanal5.se; commercial satellite channel; owned by ProSiebenSat1 (Germany); Dir-Gen. JONAS SJÖGREN.

Sveriges Television AB (SVT): Oxenstiernsgt. 26-34, 105 10 Stockholm; tel. (8) 784-00-00; fax (8) 784-15-00; e-mail eva.hamilton@svt.se; internet www.svt.se; f. 1956; independent; operates 7 channels: SVT1, SVT2, SVT24, SVT Barnkanalen, Kunskapskanalen, SVT Europa and SVT HD; CEO EVA HAMILTON.

Sveriges Utbildningsradio AB: see Radio.

TV 3: Stockholm; tel. (8) 562-023-00; fax (8) 562-023-30; e-mail info@tv3.se; internet www.tv3.se; commercial satellite channel.

TV 4: Tegeluddsvägen 3, 115 79 Stockholm; tel. (8) 459-40-00; fax (8) 459-44-44; internet www.tv4.se; commercial terrestrial channel; CEO CASTEN ALMQVIST.

Finance

(cap. = capital; res = reserves; dep. = deposits; m. = million; brs = branches; amounts in kronor unless otherwise stated)

SUPERVISORY BODY

Finansinspektionen (Financial Supervisory Authority): Brunnsgt. 3, POB 7821, 103 97 Stockholm; tel. (8) 787-80-00; fax (8) 24-13-35; e-mail finansinspektionen@fi.se; internet www.fi.se; f. 1991 by merger of Bankinspektionen (Bank Inspection Board, f. 1907) and Försäkringsinspektionen (Private Insurance Supervisory Service, f. 1904), for the supervision of commercial and savings banks, financial companies, insurance companies, insurance brokers, friendly societies, mortgage institutions, securities firms and unit trusts, the stock exchange and clearing functions, the securities registry centre and the information registry centre; Chair. BENGT WESTERBERG; Dir-Gen. MARTIN ANDERSSON.

BANKING

In 2012 there were 119 banks in Sweden, comprising 37 commercial banks, 31 foreign banks, 49 savings banks and two co-operative banks.

Central Bank

Sveriges Riksbank: Brunkebergstorg 11, 103 37 Stockholm; tel. (8) 787-00-00; fax (8) 21-05-31; e-mail registratorn@riksbank.se; internet www.riksbank.se; f. 1668; bank of issue; led by an executive board of 6 members (including a Governor), appointed by a General Council of 11 members, all of whom are, in turn, appointed by the Riksdag; cap. 1,000m., res 63,025m., dep. 455,999m. (Dec. 2009); Chair., Gen. Council JOHAN GERNANDT; Gov. STEFAN INGVES; 2 brs.

Commercial Banks

Danske Bank: Norrmalmstorg 1, POB 7523, 103 92 Stockholm; tel. (8) 524-800-00; e-mail danskebank@danskebank.com; internet www .danskebank.se; f. 1837 as Östgöta Enskilda Bank; subsidiary of Den Danske Bank (Denmark); Chair. PETER STRAARUP; Pres. and CEO ULF LUNDAHL; 30 brs.

DNB Sweden: Kungsgatan 18, 111 35 Stockholm; tel. (8) 473-41-00; e-mail info@cim.se; internet www.dnbnor.se; f. 1995; subsidiary of financial services group DnB NOR (Norway); Head PETER H. CARLSSON; 3 brs.

Länsförsäkringar Bank: Tegeluddsvägen 21, 115 97 Stockholm; tel. (8) 562-834-00; internet www.lansforsakringar.se; f. 1996; cap. 954.9m., res 5,893.3m., dep. 84,238.1m. (Dec. 2012); Chair. CHRISTER VILLARD; CEO HANS BENNDORF; 125 brs.

Nordea Bank AB: Smålandsgt. 17, 105 71 Stockholm; tel. (8) 614-70-00; fax (8) 20-08-46; internet www.nordea.com; f. 1974 as Post- och Kreditbanken; present name adopted 2001; part of Nordea Group; 19.9% owned by Swedish Govt; cap. €4,050m., res €1,156m., dep. €294,638m. (Dec. 2012); Chair. HANS DALBORG; Pres. and CEO CHRISTIAN CLAUSEN; 252 brs in Sweden.

SBAB Bank: Löjtnantsgatan 21, 102 54 Stockholm; tel. 771453000 (mobile); fax (8) 614-38-60; e-mail kundcenter@sbab.se; internet www.sbab.se; f. 1985; part of the SBAB group comprising the parent company SBAB Bank AB (publ) and 2 subsidiaries, namely Swedish Covered Bonds (publ) and Frispar Mortgage Group; Chair ARNE LILJEDAHL; CEO EVA CEDERBALK; 4 brs.

SkandiaBanken: Kungsgatan 28, 106 55 Stockholm; tel. (8) 788-30-50; internet www.skandiabanken.se; f. 1994; CEO ØYVIND THOMASSEN.

Skandinaviska Enskilda Banken AB (SEB): Kungsträdgårdsgt. 8, 106 40 Stockholm; tel. (8) 771-62-10-00; fax (8) 763-83-89; internet www.seb.se; f. 1972; cap. 21,942m., res –2,552m., dep. 1,329,584m. (Dec. 2012); Chair. MARCUS WALLENBERG; Pres. and Group CEO ANNIKA FALKENGREN; 160 brs.

Sparbanken Öresund: Iceberg St, 3 Malmö; tel. (40) 608-10-00; fax (40) 608-10-50; internet www.sparbankenoresund.se; f. 2010; by the merger of Hellenic Aerospace Industry SA and Savings Bank Gripen; res 2,671.9m., dep. 24,204.44m., total assets 29,260.9m. (Dec. 2011); Chair. LARS ANDERSSON; CEO LARS-ERIK SKJUTARE; 34 brs.

Svenska Handelsbanken AB: Kungsträdgårdsgt. 2, 106 70 Stockholm; tel. (8) 701-10-00; fax (8) 701-24-37; e-mail info@ handelsbanken.se; internet www.handelsbanken.se; f. 1871 as A. B. Stockholms Handelsbank; present name adopted 1956; cap. 2,943m., res 2,662m., dep. 1,104,273m. (Dec. 2012); Chair. HANS LARSSON; Pres. and CEO PÄR BOMAN; 459 brs in Sweden.

Swedbank AB: Brunkebergstorg 8, 105 34 Stockholm; tel. (8) 585-900-00; fax (8) 796-80-92; internet www.swedbank.se; f. 1997 by merger of Föreningsbanken and Sparbanken Sverige; present name adopted 2006; cap. 24,904m., res 32,914m., dep. 786,525m. (Dec. 2012); Chair. LARS IDERMARK; Pres. and CEO MICHAEL WOLF; 470 brs in Sweden.

Banking Organization

Svenska Bankföreningen (Swedish Bankers' Asscn): Regeringsgt. 38, POB 7603, 103 94 Stockholm; tel. (8) 453-44-00; fax (8) 796-93-95; e-mail info@bankforeningen.se; internet www .bankforeningen.se; f. 1880; Pres. JAN LIDÉN; Man. Dir PÄR BOMAN; 29 mems.

STOCK EXCHANGE

NASDAQ OMX Nordic Exchange Stockholm: Tullvaktsvägen 15, 105 78 Stockholm; tel. (8) 405-60-00; fax (8) 405-60-01; internet www.nasdaqomx.com; f. 1863 under govt charter; automated trading system introduced by 1990; Stockholmsbörsen merged with OMX AB in 1998; acquired by NASDAQ Stock Market, Inc (USA) in 2008; part of OMX Nordic Exchange with the Copenhagen (Denmark), Helsinki (Finland) and Reykjavík (Iceland) exchanges; Group CEO ROBERT GREIFELD.

INSURANCE

The assets of Swedish insurance companies totalled 2,988,000m. kronor at the end of 2011.

Principal Insurance Companies

ERV: Löfströms allé 6A, POB 1, 172 13 Sundbyberg; tel. 770456900; fax (8) 20-14-84; e-mail info@erv.se; internet www.erv.se; f. 1920; subsidiary of the European International Holding A/S since 1995; name changed from Europeiska in 2012; all branches of life insurance; Man. Dir JOHANNES VON HÜLSEN.

Folksam: Bohusgt. 14, 106 60 Stockholm; tel. (8) 771-950-950; fax (8) 702-99-22; e-mail kundservice@folksam.se; internet www.folksam .se; f. 1908; all branches of life and non-life insurance; Pres. and CEO ANDERS SUNDSTRÖM.

If Skadeförsäkring: Barks väg 15, Solna, 106 80 Stockholm; tel. 771430000; internet www.if.se; f. 1999; by merger of Svenska Skandias and Norska Storebrands; fully owned by Sampo PLC since 2004; all branches of life insurance; Chair KARI STADIGH; Pres. and CEO TORBJÖRN MAGNUSSON.

Länsförsäkringar: Tegeluddsvägen 21, 115 97 Stockholm; tel. (8) 562-834-00; e-mail info@sth.lansforsakringar.se; internet www .lansforsakringar.se; f. 1985; as Länsförsäkringar Liv; all branches of life and non-life insurance; CEO HANS BENNDORF; Chair. CHRISTER VILLARD.

Moderna Försäkringar: POB 7830, 103 98 Stockholm; tel. (8) 684-12-000; internet www.modernaforsakringar.se; f. 1916; acquired by Tryg in 2009; all branches of non-life insurance; Country Man. PER FORNANDER.

Skandia Insurance Co Ltd: Lindhagensgatan 86, 106 55 Stockholm; tel. (8) 788-10-00; fax (8) 788-30-80; e-mail adm@skandia.se; internet www.skandia.se; f. 1855; owned by Skandia Liv; all branches of life insurance; Chair. ANNA-CARIN SÖDERBLOM AGIUS; CEO ANN-CHARLOTTE STJERNA.

SveLand Försäkringar: POB 82, 351 03 Växjö; tel. 771388300; e-mail foretag@svelandsak.se; internet www.svelandsak.se; f. 1911; all branches of life and non-life insurance; Chair. KARL GUSTAV; CEO ANDERS STRAND.

Trygg-Hansa: Flemminggt. 18, 106 26 Stockholm; tel. (8) 243-10-00; internet www.trygghansa.se; f. 1828; all branches of life and non-life insurance; owned by Codan Forsikring A/S (Denmark); Chair. DAVID WEYMOUTH; CEO MIKE HOLLIDAY-WILLIAMS.

Zurich: Linnégatan 5, POB 5069, 102 42 Stockholm; tel. (8) 579-330-00; fax (8) 579-330-01; e-mail zurich@zurich.se; internet www.zurich .com/nordic; all branches of non-life insurance; Chair. MANFRED GENTZ; CEO MARTIN SENN.

Insurance Associations

Konsumenternas försäkringsbyrå (Swedish Consumers' Insurance Bureau): Karlavägen 108, POB 24215, 104 51 Stockholm; tel. (8) 22-58-00; fax (8) 24-88-91; e-mail angela.olsson@konsumenternas .se; internet www.bankforsakring.konsumenternas.se; f. 1979; provides free advice to consumers on various insurance matters; principles are the Konsumentverket (Swedish Consumer Agency), the Finansinpektionen (Financial Supervisory Authority) and the Sveriges Försäkringsförbund (Swedish Insurance Fed.); Chair. GUNNAR OLSSON.

Svensk Försäkring (Swedish Insurance): Karlavägen 108, POB 24043, 104 50 Stockholm; tel. (8) 522-785-00; e-mail info@ insurancesweden.se; internet www.svenskforsakring.se; f. 1937; as Svenska Försäkringsbolags Riksförbund; name changed as above 2011; Chair. STEN DUNÉR; CEO CHRISTINA LINDENIUS.

Svenska Försäkringsföreningen (Swedish Insurance Society): Karlavägen 108, 6th Floor, POB 24213, 104 51 Stockholm; tel. (8) 522-789-00; fax (8) 522-789-95; e-mail info@forsakringsforeningen .se; internet www.forsakringsforeningen.se; f. 1875; promotes sound development of the Swedish insurance business; Chair. HANS G. SVENSSON; Sec. SARA RÅSMAR.

Trade and Industry

GOVERNMENT AGENCIES

Arbetsförmedlingen (Public Employment Service): Hälsingegt. 38, 113 99 Stockholm; tel. (771) 60-00-00; fax (8) 508-801-99; e-mail registrator@arbetsformedlingen.se; internet www .arbetsformedlingen.se; f. 2008 to replace Arbetsmarknadsverket and Arbetsmarknadsstyrelsen; central agency, responsible for administration of Sweden's labour market; main aims: to match those seeking employment to suitable vacancies; to encourage those outside the labour market to seek employment; and to maintain a high level of employment within the labour market; managed by a board appointed by Govt; Chair. CHRISTINA JOHANSSON (acting); Dir-Gen. ANGELES BERMUDEZ-SVANKVIST.

Exportrådet (Swedish Trade Council): World Trade Center, Klarabergsviadukten 70, POB 240, 101 24 Stockholm; tel. (8) 588-660-00; fax (8) 588-661-90; e-mail info@swedishtrade.se; internet www .swedishtrade.se; f. 1972; Chair. BO DANKIS; Man. Dir ULF BERG.

Tillväxtverket (Swedish Agency for Economic and Regional Growth): Götgt. 74, POB 4044, 102 61 Stockholm; tel. (8) 681-91-00; fax (8) 19-68-26; e-mail tillvaxtverket@tillvaxtverket.se; internet www.tillvaxtverket.se; Dir-Gen. BIRGITTA BÖHLIN (acting).

CHAMBERS OF COMMERCE

Handelskammaren Jönköpings Län: Elmiavägen 11, 554 54 Jönköping; tel. (36) 30-14-30; fax (36) 12-95-79; e-mail info@ jonkoping.cci.se; internet www.jonkoping.cci.se; f. 1975; Pres. JOHAN SVEDBERG; Man. Dir JONAS EKEROTH; 400 mems.

Handelskammaren Mälardalen: Rudbecksgatan 7, POB 8044, 700 08 Örebro; tel. (19) 689-35-00; e-mail info@ handelskammarenmalardalen.se; internet www .handelskammarenmalardalen.se; f. 1907; Pres. CHRISTER HENE-BÄCK; Man. Dir CHRISTINA HEDBERG.

Handelskammaren Mittsverige (Mid-Sweden Chamber of Commerce): Kyrkogt. 26, 852 32 Sundsvall; tel. (60) 17-18-80; fax (60) 61-86-40; e-mail info@midchamber.se; internet www.midchamber.se; f. 1913; Chair. FRANZ BERGSTRAND; Man. Dir DICK JANSSON; 350 mems.

Handelskammaren Värmland: Södra Kyrkogt. 6, 652 24 Karlstad; tel. (54) 22-14-80; fax (54) 22-14-90; e-mail info@ handelskammarenvarmland.se; internet www .handelskammarenvarmland.se; f. 1912; Chair. ANDERS BJÖRN; CEO ANNALENA HULTMAN; 1,200 mems.

Mellansvenska Handelskammaren: POB 296, 801 04 Gävle; tel. (26) 66-20-80; fax (26) 66-20-99; e-mail chamber@mhk.cci.se; internet www.mhk.cci.se; f. 1907; Pres. and CEO PER-OLOF HANSÉRS; Chair. ÅKE AXELSON; 465 mems.

Norrbottens Handelskammare: Kyrkogt. 13, 972 32 Luleå; tel. (920) 45-56-60; fax (920) 45-56-66; e-mail info@ norrbottenshandelskammare.se; internet www.north.cci.se; f. 1904; Chair. THOMAS LEJON; Man. Dir ANDREAS LIND.

Östsvenska Handelskammaren: Nya Rådstugugt. 3, 602 24 Norrköping; tel. (11) 28-50-30; fax (11) 13-77-19; e-mail info@east .cci.se; internet www.ostsvenskahandelskammaren.se; f. 1913; covers Östergötland, Södermanland and Gotland; c. 600 mem. cos; Chair. BENGT ASSARSSON; Man. Dir JOHANNA PALMÉR.

Stockholms Handelskammare: Malmskillnadsgt. 46, POB 16050, 103 21 Stockholm; tel. (8) 555-100-00; fax (8) 566-316-00; e-mail info@ chamber.se; internet www.chamber.se; f. 1902; Pres. PEJE EMILSSON; CEO MARIA RANKKA; 2,400 mems.

Sydsvenska Industri- och Handelskammaren: Skeppsbron 2, 211 20 Malmö; tel. (40) 690-24-00; fax (40) 690-24-90; e-mail info@ handelskammaren.com; internet www.handelskammaren.com; f. 1905; Pres. NICOLAS HASSBJER; CEO STEPHAN MÜCHLER; 2,800 mems.

Västsvenska Handelskammaren: Mässans Gt. 18, POB 5253, 402 25 Göteborg; tel. (31) 83-59-00; fax (31) 83-59-36; e-mail info@ handelskammaren.net; internet www.handelskammaren.net; f. 1661; Chair. FINN JOHNSSON; Man. Dir JOHAN TROUVÉ; c. 2,600 mems.

INDUSTRIAL AND TRADE ASSOCIATIONS

Svenskt Näringsliv (Confederation of Swedish Enterprise): Storgt. 19, 114 82 Stockholm; tel. (8) 553-430-00; fax (8) 553-430-99; internet www.svensktnaringsliv.se; f. 2001 by merger of Sveriges Industriförbund (f. 1910) and Svenska Arbetsgivareföreningen (f. 1902); central org. representing Swedish business and industry; Pres. KENNETH BENGTSSON; Dir-Gen. URBAN BÄCKSTRÖM; consists of 49 mem. asscns, representing c. 60,000 cos.

Företagarna (Federation of Private Enterprises): Regeringsgt. 52, 106 67 Stockholm; tel. (8) 406-17-00; fax (8) 24-55-26; e-mail info@ foretagarna.se; internet www.foretagarna.se; f. 1991; Chair. JENS SPENDRUP; Man. Dir ELISABETH THAND RINGQVIST; 55,000 mems.

Grafiska Företagens Förbund (Graphic Companies' Federation): Storgt. 19, 3rd Floor, POB 55525, 102 04 Stockholm; tel. (8) 762-68-00; fax (8) 611-08-28; e-mail info@grafiska.se; internet www.grafiska .se; Chair. GÖRAN GUSTAFSSON; 540 mem. cos.

Jernkontoret (Steel Producers' Asscn): Kungsträdgårdsgt. 10, POB 1721, 111 87 Stockholm; tel. (8) 679-17-00; fax (8) 611-20-89; e-mail office@jernkontoret.se; internet www.jernkontoret.se; f. 1747; Chair. MARTIN LINDQVIST; Man. Dir BO-ERIK PERS.

Lantbrukarnas Riksförbund (LRF) (Federation of Swedish Farmers): Franzéngt. 6, 105 33 Stockholm; tel. (0) 771-573-573; e-mail info@lrf.se; internet www.lrf.se; Chair. HELENA JONSSON; Man. Dir ANDERS KÄLLSTRÖM; 171,000 mems.

Plast- & Kemiföretagen (Swedish Plastics and Chemicals Asscn): Storgt. 19, POB 55915, 102 16 Stockholm; tel. (8) 783-86-00; fax (8) 663-63-23; e-mail info@plastkemiforetagen.se; internet www .plastkemiforetagen.se; f. 2003 by merger of the Asscn of Swedish Chemical Industries and the Plastics and Chemicals Fed.; Pres. JAN SVÄRD; Man. Dir MAGNUS HUSS; c. 230 mems.

Skogsindustrierna (Swedish Forest Industries' Federation): POB 55525, 102 04 Stockholm; tel. (8) 762-72-60; fax (8) 611-71-22; e-mail info@forestindustries.se; internet www.forestindustries.se; Chair. ULF LARSSON; Dir-Gen. MARIE S. ARWIDSON.

SveMin (Föreningen för gruvor, mineral- och metallproducenter i Sverige) (Swedish Asscn of Mines, Mineral and Metal Producers): Kungsträdgårdsgt. 10, POB 1721, 111 87 Stockholm; tel. (8) 762-67-55; fax (8) 678-02-10; e-mail info@industriarbetsgivarna.se; internet www.svemin.se; f. 2004; Pres. LENNART EVRELL; Man. Dir PER AHL; 40 mem. cos.

Svensk Handel (Swedish Federation of Trade): Regeringsgt. 60, 103 29 Stockholm; tel. (10) 471-85-00; fax (10) 471-86-65; e-mail info@ svenskhandel.se; internet www.svenskhandel.se; f. 1883; Chair. CHRISTIAN W. JANSSON; Man. Dir DAG KLACKENBERG; 13,000 mems.

Svensk Industriförening (SINF) (Swedish Industry Asscn): Klara Norra Kyrkogt. 31, POB 22307, 104 22 Stockholm; tel. (8) 440-11-70; fax (8) 440-11-71; e-mail info@sinf.se; internet www.sinf .se; f. 1941; Man. Dir ANDERS EKDAHL; 1,500 mems.

TEKO (Textile and Clothing Industries' Asscn): Storgt. 5, POB 5510, 114 85 Stockholm; tel. (8) 762-68-80; fax (8) 762-68-87; e-mail teko@ teko.se; internet www.teko.se; f. 1907; Chair. SVEN GATENHEIM; Man. Dirs OLA TOFTEGAARD; 206 mems.

EMPLOYERS' ORGANIZATIONS

Almega: Sturegat. 11, POB 55545, 102 04 Stockholm; tel. (8) 762-69-00; fax (8) 762-69-48; internet www.almega.se; f. 1921; 7 mem. asscns: Swedish IT and Telecom Industries, Almega Samhall Employers' Asscn, Almega Service Asscns, Almega Service Employers' Asscn, Media and Information Employers' Asscn, Asscn of Private Care Providers, Swedish Asscn of Staff Agencies; Chair. HÅKAN BRYNGELSON; Dir-Gen. JONAS MILTON; 10,000 mems.

Byggnadsämnesförbundet (Building Material Manufacturers Employers): Kungsträdgårdsgt. 10, POB 1721, 111 87 Stockholm; tel. (8) 762-65-35; fax (8) 611-62-64; e-mail info@baf.se; internet www .baf.se; f. 1902; Chair. LARS-ERIK EDGARSSON; Man. Dir ARNE SEHLSTRÖM; c. 180 mem. cos.

Elektriska Installatörsorganisationen (EIO) (Swedish Electrical Contractors' Association): Rosenlundsgt. 40, POB 17537, 118 91 Stockholm; tel. (8) 762-75-00; fax (8) 668-86-17; e-mail info@eio.se; internet www.eio.se; f. 1906; Chair. THOMAS CARLSSON; Man. Dir JAN SIEZING; 2,600 mems. cos.

Entreprenörföretagen (EPF): Årstaängsvägen 19C, POB 47235, 100 74 Stockholm; tel. (8) 762-75-85; fax (8) 616-00-72; e-mail info@ entreprenorforetagen.se; internet www.entreprenorforetagen.se; a joint initiative owned 50% each by Mekaniska Verkstädernas Riksförbund (MVR) and Plåtslageriernas Riksförbund (PLR); Chair. PER ANDERSSON; Man. Dir THOMAS DAHLBERG.

Försäkringsbranschens Arbetsgivareorganisation (Insurance Employers): Karlavägen 108, 6th Floor, POB 24168, 104 51 Stockholm; tel. (8) 522-786-00; fax (8) 522-786-70; e-mail info@fao.se; internet www.fao.se; Chair. STEN DUNÉR; Man. Dir CHRISTINA LINDENIUS; 160 mem. cos.

Livsmedelsföretagen (Li) (Food Industry): Storgt. 19, POB 55680, 102 15 Stockholm; tel. (8) 762-65-00; fax (8) 762-65-12; e-mail info@li .se; internet www.li.se; f. 2001 by merger of Livsmedelsbranschens Arbetsgivareförbund and Livsmedelsindustrierna; Chair. GÖRAN HOLM; Man. Dir MARIE SÖDERQVIST; c. 850 mems.

Maskinentreprenörerna (Earth-moving Contractors): Storgt. 19, POB 1609, 111 86 Stockholm; tel. (8) 762-70-65; fax (8) 611-85-41; e-mail info@me.se; internet www.me.se; Chair. HÅKAN NORÉN; Man. Dir HAMPE MOBÄRG; c. 3,700 mems. cos.

Stål och Metall Arbetsgivareförbundet (Steel and Metal Industry Employers): Kungsträdgårdsgt. 10, POB 1721, 111 87 Stockholm; tel. (8) 762-67-55; fax (8) 678-02-10; e-mail info@ industriarbetsgivarna.se; internet www.stalometall.se; f. 1906; Pres. PETER GOSSAS; Man. Dir PER AHL; 200 mems with 40,000 employees.

SVEMEK (Welding Engineering): POB 1721, 111 87 Stockholm; tel. (8) 762-67-35; fax (8) 611-62-64; e-mail info@metallgruppen.se; internet www.svemek.se; fmrly Svets Mekaniska Arbetsgivareförbundet; Pres. PER LINDE; Man. Dir PER AHL; 400 mems with 5,000 employees.

Sveriges Bagare & Konditorer AB (Swedish Bakers and Confectioners): Storgt. 19, POB 55680, 102 15 Stockholm; tel. (8) 762-67-90; e-mail martin@bageri.se; internet www.bageri.se; f. 1900; Chair. STEFAN FRITZDORF; Man. Dir MARTIN LUNDELL; 500 mems.

Sveriges Byggindustrier (Swedish Construction Federation): Storgat. 19, POB 5054, 102 42 Stockholm; tel. (8) 698-58-00; fax (8) 698-59-00; e-mail info@bygg.org; internet www.bygg.org; Chair. THOMAS CARLSSON; Man. Dir OLA MÅNSSON; c. 3,200 mem. cos.

Teknikföretagen (Asscn of Swedish Engineering Industries): Storgt. 5, POB 5510, 114 85 Stockholm; tel. (8) 782-08-00; fax (8) 782-09-00; e-mail info@teknikforetagen.se; internet www.teknikforetagen.se; f. 1896 as VI Sveriges Verkstadsindustrier; Pres. MATS ELFSBERG; Man. Dir ÅKE SVENSSON; 3,500 mem. cos.

TransportGruppen (Transport Industry): Storgt. 19, POB 5384, 102 49 Stockholm; tel. (8) 762-71-00; fax (8) 611-46-99; e-mail info@transportgruppen.se; internet www.transportgruppen.se; 8 mem. asscns: Swedish Road Transport Employers' Asscn, Swedish Bus and Coach Employers' Asscn, Swedish Air Transport Industry Employers' Asscn, Swedish Motor Trade Employers' Asscn, Employers' Asscn of the Swedish Petroleum Industry, Swedish Shipowners Employers' Asscn, Asscn Ports of Sweden, Swedish International Freight Asscn; Chair. BJÖRN N. ALVENGRIP; Man. Dir PETER JEPPSSON.

Trä- och Möbelföretagen (Wood Products Companies): Storgt. 19, POB 55525, 102 04 Stockholm; tel. (8) 762-72-50; fax (8) 762-72-24; e-mail info@tmf.se; internet www.tmf.se; Chair. ULF ADOLFSSON; Man. Dir LEIF G. GUSTAFSSON; 750 mem. cos.

VVS Företagen (Heating, Plumbing, Refrigeration and Insulation Employers): Arstaängsvägen 19c, POB 47160, 100 74 Stockholm; tel. (8) 762-73-00; fax (8) 669-41-19; e-mail info@vvsforetagen.se; internet www.vvsforetagen.se; f. 1918; Chair. ANDERS MATTSSON; Man. Dir ROINE KRISTIANSON; c. 1,450 mems.

UTILITIES

Regulatory Authority

Energimyndigheten (Swedish Energy Agency): Kungsgt. 43, POB 310, 631 04 Eskilstuna; tel. (16) 544-20-00; fax (16) 544-20-99; e-mail registrator@energimyndigheten.se; internet www.energimyndigheten.se; f. 1998; monitors and advises electricity and natural gas cos, also undertakes research into renewable energy; Dir-Gen. ERIK BRANDSMA.

Electricity and Gas

E.ON Sverige AB: Carl Gustafs väg 1, 205 09 Malmö; tel. (40) 25-50-00; e-mail info@eon.se; internet www.eon.se; f. 2000; fmrly Sydkraft AB; part of E.ON Group (Germany); generation, distribution and supply of electricity and natural gas; Pres. and CEO JONAS ABRAHAMSSON.

Fortum AB: Hangövägen 19, 115 77 Stockholm; tel. (8) 671-70-00; fax (8) 671-77-77; e-mail res.koncernkommunikationsverige@fortum.com; internet www.fortum.com; f. 1998 by merger of Imatran Voima and Neste Oyj (both Finland); mem. of Fortum Corpn (Finland), international energy co with core businesses in gas, power and heat; electricity production, distribution and supply; Chair. SARI BALDAUF; Pres. and CEO TAPIO KUULA.

Göteborg Energi AB: POB 53, 401 20 Gothenberg; tel. (31) 62-60-00; fax (31) 15-25-01; internet www.goteborgenergi.se; distribution of electricity and natural gas; co-owns electricity supplier Plusenergi with Vattenfall; Chair. KIA ANDREASSON; Man. Dir LOTTA BRÄNDSTRÖM.

Lunds Energi AB: Råbyvägen 37, POB 25, 221 00 Lund; tel. (46) 35-60-00; fax (46) 18-92-62; e-mail kundservice@lundsenergi.se; internet www.lundsenergi.se; f. 1907; distribution and supply of electricity and natural gas; subsidiaries incl.: Billinge Energi AB, Kraftringen Service AB, KREAB Energi AB, Nynäshamn Energi; Chair. LARS LEONARDSSON; CEO SYLVIA MICHEL.

Öresundskraft AB: Västra Sandgt. 4, POB 642, 251 06 Helsingborg; tel. (42) 490-30-00; fax (42) 490-30-60; e-mail info@oresundskraft.se; internet www.oresundskraft.se; f. 1859; distribution and supply of electricity and natural gas; Chair. PETER KNUTSSON; Man. Dir ANDERS ÖSTLUND.

Umeå Energi AB: Storgt. 34, POB 224, 901 05 Umeå; tel. (90) 16-00-00; fax (90) 16-00-10; e-mail umea.energi@umeaenergi.se; internet www.umeaenergi.se; production, distribution and supply of electricity; Man. Dir KURT ÅSTRÖM.

Vattenfall AB: 169 92 Stockholm; tel. (8) 739-50-00; fax (8) 739-51-29; e-mail info@vattenfall.se; internet www.vattenfall.se; f. 1909; became limited liability co in 1992; state-owned; power generation and distribution; co-owns electricity supplier Plusenergi with Göteborg Energi AB; some 90 directly or indirectly owned operational subsidiaries; interests in Denmark, Finland, Germany and Poland; Chair. LARS G. NORDSTRÖM; Pres. and CEO ØYSTEIN LØSETH.

Water

Responsibility for water supply lies with the municipalities. Since the 1990s many municipalities have formed limited companies under public ownership to manage water supply, such as the supplier for the capital (Stockholm Vatten AB). Several municipalities have contracted private companies to manage water supply.

TRADE UNIONS

Principal Federations

Landsorganisationen i Sverige (LO) (Swedish Trade Union Confederation): Barnhusgt. 18, 105 53 Stockholm; tel. (8) 796-25-00; fax (8) 796-28-00; e-mail mailbox@lo.se; internet www.lo.se; f. 1898; affiliated to ITUC; Pres. KARL-PETTER THORWALDSSON; 14 affiliated unions, with a total membership of 1.7m. (October 2009).

Sveriges Akademikers Centralorganisation (SACO) (Swedish Confederation of Professional Asscns): Lilla Nygt. 14, POB 2206, 103 15 Stockholm; tel. (8) 613-48-00; fax (8) 24-77-01; e-mail kansli@saco.se; internet www.saco.se; f. 1947; affiliated to ITUC and ETUC; Chair. GÖRAN ARRIUS; 22 affiliated unions and professional orgs, 636,000 mems.

Tjänstemännens Centralorganisation (TCO) (Confederation of Professional Employees): Linnégt. 14, 114 94 Stockholm; tel. (8) 782-91-00; fax (8) 663-75-20; e-mail info@tco.se; internet www.tco.se; f. 1944; affiliated to ITUC, European Trade Union Confed. and Council of Nordic Trade Unions; Chair. EVA NORDMARK; 15 affiliated unions with total membership of 1.2m.

Transport

TRANSPORT AUTHORITY

Swedish Transport Administration (Trafikverket): Röda vägen 1, 781 70 Borlänge; tel. (771) 92-19-21; fax (10) 124-07-85; e-mail trafikverket@trafikverket.se; internet www.trafikverket.se; f. 2010; state-owned agency for long-term transport infrastructure planning and maintenance; Dir-Gen. GUNNAR MALM.

RAILWAYS

In 2010 there were 11,633 km of standard- and narrow-gauge railways, of which 7,632 km of track was electrified. A new railway line extending 190 km, connecting Nyland and Umeå on the north-eastern coast of Sweden, entered into service in August 2010. A 6-km commuter line in Stockholm connecting Tomteboda and Stockholm South was expected to be completed by 2017.

Green Cargo: POB 39, 171 11 Solna; tel. (10) 455-71-11; fax (10) 455-71-13; e-mail info@greencargo.com; internet www.greencargo.com; f. 2001; nat. and int. railway logistics company; state-owned, under the Ministry of Finance; Chair. LENNART PIHL.

SJ AB (Statens Järnvägar): 105 50 Stockholm; tel. (10) 751-60-00; fax (10) 751-54-24; e-mail foretag@sj.se; internet www.sj.se; f. 1856; state-owned; runs passenger traffic on all state-owned railway track; Chair. JAN SUNDLING; CEO CRISTER FRITZSON.

ROADS

The road network totalled 578,274 km in 2010. In 2010 motorways accounted for 1,927 km of roads, 13,507 km were main or national roads and 83,031 km secondary or regional roads. In 2000 a road-rail link between Malmö and Copenhagen (Denmark), across the 16-km Öresund strait, was opened. Construction of the 21-km Förbifart Stockholm bypass, including 18 km of tunnels, was expected to begin in 2013.

SHIPPING

The principal ports in terms of cargo handled are Göteborg (Gothenberg), Brofjorden, Trelleborg, Luleå and Malmö. Stockholm is also an important port. At 31 December 2012 the Swedish flag registered fleet numbered 477 vessels, with a combined displacement of 3.0m. grt.

Principal Shipping Companies

Broström Ship Management AB: Industrivägen 7, POB 39, 471 21 Skärhamn; tel. (304) 67-67-00; fax (304) 67-11-10; e-mail info@brostrom.se; internet www.brostrom.se; 97.3% owned by Maersk Product Tankers AB; management co, operating specialized tanker services; Man. Dir ROBERT UGGLA.

Broström Tankers AB: Mölndalsvägen 24, 403 30 Göteborg; tel. (31) 61-60-00; fax (31) 61-60-12; e-mail gotbroinfo@brostrom.com; internet www.brostrom.se; f. 1990; specializes in transporting petroleum products, in north-west Europe and world-wide; Man. Dir TORE ANGERVALL.

Rederi AB Transatlantic: POB 8809, 402 71 Göteborg; tel. (31) 763-23-00; fax (31) 763-23-70; e-mail info@rabt.se; internet www.rabt.se; f. 2005 by merger of B&N Nordsjöfrakt AB (f. 1972) and Gorthon Lines AB (f. 1915); freight shipping, forwarding, storage, agency, ice-breaking; CEO HENNING E. JENSEN.

Stena AB: Masthuggskajen, 405 19 Göteborg; tel. (31) 85-50-00; fax (31) 12-06-51; e-mail info@stenaline.com; internet www.stena.com; f. 1939; parent co of Stena Line, Stena Bulk, Stena RoRo, Stena Drilling, Concordia Maritime and Northern Marine Management; CEO DAN STEN OLSSON.

Wallenius Lines AB: Swedenborgsgt. 19, POB 17086, 104 62 Stockholm; tel. (8) 772-05-00; fax (8) 640-68-54; e-mail info@walleniuslines.com; internet www.walleniuslines.com; f. 1934; car and truck carriers; Pres. ANDERS BOMAN.

Associations

Föreningen Sveriges Sjöfart och Sjöförsvar (Swedish Maritime League): Kastellet, Kastellholmen, 111 49 Stockholm; tel. (8) 611-74-81; fax (8) 611-74-76; e-mail fsss@algonet.se; f. 1983 by merger of Swedish General Shipping Asscn and Swedish Navy League; Pres. CLAES TORNBERG; Gen. Sec. STEN GÖTHBERG; 2,000 mems.

Sveriges Redareförening (Swedish Shipowners' Asscn): Södra Hamngt. 53, POB 330, 401 25 Göteborg; tel. (31) 62-95-25; fax (31) 15-23-13; e-mail srf@sweship.se; internet www.sweship.se; f. 1906; Pres. LARS HØGLAND; Man. Dir HÅKAN FRIDBERG.

CIVIL AVIATION

In 2010 there were a total of 249 airports. The main international airport is at Arlanda, 42 km from Stockholm. Gothenburg (Göteborg) and Malmö are also served by international airports. There are regular flights between the main cities in Sweden. Many domestic flights operate from Bromma (Stockholm's city airport).

NextJet: Frösundaviks Allé 15, 169 70 Solna; tel. (771) 90-00-90; e-mail info@nextjet.se; internet www.nextjet.se; f. 2002; operates 18 domestic flights and 2 international flights; CEO MAGNUS IVARSSON.

Swedavia AB: Stockholm-Arlanda Airport, 190 45 Stockholm; tel. (10) 109-00-00; fax (10) 109-05-00; e-mail info@swedavia.se; internet swedavia.se; f. 2010; responsible for commercial airport operation of the fmr Swedish Civil Aviation Authority; state-owned; owns 11 airports, including Åre Östersund, Stockholm-Arlanda, Luleå and Malmö; Chair. INGEMAR SKOGÖ.

Scandinavian Airlines System (SAS): Frösundaviks Allé 1, Solna, 195 87 Stockholm; tel. (8) 797-00-00; fax (8) 797-15-15; internet www.sas.se; f. 1946; the national carrier of Denmark, Norway and Sweden. It is a consortium owned two-sevenths by SAS Danmark A/S, two-sevenths by SAS Norge ASA and three-sevenths by SAS Sverige AB. Each parent org. is a limited co owned 50% by Govt and 50% by private shareholders. The SAS group includes the consortium and the subsidiaries in which the consortium has a majority or otherwise controlling interest; the Board consists of two members from each of the parent cos and the chairmanship rotates among the three national chairmen on an annual basis. SAS absorbed Linjeflyg AB (domestic passenger, newspaper and postal services in Sweden) in 1993; strategic alliance with Lufthansa (Germany) formed in 1995; Chair. FRITZ H. SCHUR; Pres. and CEO RICKARD GUSTAFSON.

West Atlantic: POB 5433, 402 29 Göteborg; tel. (31) 703-04-50; fax (31) 703-04-55; e-mail info@westatlantic.eu; internet www.westatlantic.eu; f. 2008 following merger of West Air Sweden and Atlantic Airlines (United Kingdom); Pres. GUSTAF THUREBORN.

Tourism

Sweden offers a variety of landscape, from the mountains of the 'Midnight Sun', north of the Arctic Circle, to the white sandy beaches of the south. There are many lakes, waterfalls and forests, and Stockholm is famed for its beautiful situation and modern architecture. Most tourists come from the other Scandinavian countries, Germany and the United Kingdom. In 2010 tourism arrivals totalled 12.8m., while in 2011 receipts were estimated at US $13,886m.

Svenska Turistföreningen (Swedish Touring Club): POB 17251, 104 62 Stockholm; tel. (8) 463-21-00; fax (8) 678-19-58; e-mail info@stfturist.se; internet www.stfturist.se; f. 1885; 300,000 mems; owns and operates mountain hotels and youth hostels; co-ordinates nature and cultural activities in local clubs; Pres. TORGNY HÅSTAD; Sec.-Gen. YVONNE ARENTOFT.

Turistdelegationen: Götgt. 74, POB 4044, 102 61 Stockholm; tel. (8) 681-90-00; e-mail nutek@nutek.se; internet www.tillvaxtverket.se/turistnaringen; f. 1995; Swedish Tourist Authority became part of Nutek, the Swedish Agency for Economic and Regional Growth, in January 2006; state-owned; promotes enterprise and entrepreneurship in the tourist industry in Sweden and produces and disseminates tourism information; Dir DENNIS BEDEROFF.

Defence

As assessed at November 2012, Sweden maintained total armed forces of 20,400. The army consisted of 5,550 men; the navy 3,000 men; and the air force 3,300 men. There were also 8,550 staff. In addition, there were voluntary auxiliary organizations with a total of 22,000 members. Compulsory military service was abolished from July 2010. In November 2004 the European Union (EU) ministers responsible for defence agreed to create a number of 'battlegroups' (each comprising about 1,500 men), which could be deployed at short notice to crisis areas around the world. The EU battlegroups, two of which were to be ready for deployment at any one time, following a rotational schedule, reached full operational capacity from 1 January 2007. Sweden contributed 2,300 troops to the Nordic battlegroup of 2,800 troops, with smaller contingents from Finland, Norway, Ireland and Estonia, and was also committed to being the sole contributor to a Swedish battlegroup. In November 2012 Denmark, Finland, Iceland, Norway and Sweden agreed to operate military transport aircraft jointly.

Defence Expenditure: Budgeted at 40,600m. kronor in 2013.

Supreme Commander of the Swedish Armed Forces: Gen. SVERKER GÖRANSON.

Education

The Swedish National Agency for Education, *Skolverket*, is the main central authority responsible for education at pre-school, comprehensive, upper secondary and municipal adult levels. Non-compulsory pre-primary education is provided by the municipalities to children between one and five years of age. Basic education, which is compulsory, extends for nine years, starting at the age of six or seven years, and is received at the comprehensive school (*grundskola*). At the end of this period a pupil may enter the integrated upper secondary school (*gymnasieskola*). Courses at upper secondary schools last three years, and are organized into 17 nationally defined study programmes of which 14 are vocational. All publicly funded schools follow a national curriculum. However, most schools are operated by municipal authorities, which have some autonomy over the profile of each school. In addition, parents have the right to send their children to independent schools, which are publicly funded and must share the same objectives as municipally run schools, but may differ in character and methods. Enrolment at pre-primary level included 95% of children in the relevant age-group in 2010/11. Enrolment at primary schools in 2010/11 included 99% of children in the relevant age-group, while the comparable ratio for secondary enrolment in that year was 94%.

Higher education is administered by the Swedish National Agency for Higher Education, *Högskoleverket*.There were 64 higher education institutions in Sweden in 2007/08, consisting of universities and university colleges as well as independent colleges. Slightly more than 30% of young people in Sweden proceed to higher education within five years of completing their upper secondary schooling.

The budget for 2012 forecast an allocation of 53,821m. kronor (6.5% of total expenditure) for education and academic research.

SWITZERLAND

Introductory Survey

LOCATION, CLIMATE, LANGUAGE, RELIGION, FLAG, CAPITAL

The Swiss Confederation lies in central Europe, bounded to the north by Germany, to the east by Austria and Liechtenstein, to the south by Italy and to the west by France. The climate is generally temperate, but varies considerably with altitude and aspect. In Zürich the average temperature ranges from −1°C (30°F) in winter to 16°C (61°F) in summer. There are four national languages: German, French, Italian and Romansh (Rumantsch), spoken by 72.5%, 21.0%, 4.3% and 0.6% of resident Swiss nationals, respectively, in 2000. Other languages are spoken by the remaining 1.6% of the population. Including resident aliens, the linguistic proportions in 2000 were: German 63.7%, French 20.4%, Italian 6.5%, Romansh 0.5% and other languages 9.0%. Most Swiss citizens profess Christianity: in 2000 42.7% were Protestants and 41.2% Roman Catholics. In 2010 the religious adherence of the population was 28% Protestant and 38.6% Roman Catholic. The federal flag, which is square, consists of a white upright cross in the centre of a red ground. The capital is Bern (Berne).

CONTEMPORARY POLITICAL HISTORY

Historical Context

Switzerland, whose foundation is traditionally dated to 1291, has occupied its present area since its borders were fixed by treaty in 1815. At the same time, it was internationally recognized as a neutral country. Despite the strategic importance of Switzerland, its 'permanent neutrality' has never since been violated. The country has not entered any military alliances, and it avoided participation in both World Wars. The federal system of government dates back to 1848. Executive authority is exercised on a collegial basis by the Federal Council (cabinet), with a President who serves, for only one year at a time, as 'the first among equals'. Owing to the restricted powers of the Federal Council, initiatives and referendums form the core of the political process. Switzerland is a confederation of 26 cantons. In 1979 the mainly French-speaking region of Jura seceded from the predominantly German-speaking canton of Bern, becoming the first new canton to be established since 1815.

Despite the fact that Switzerland has long been the headquarters of many international organizations, the country did not join the UN until 2002, owing to concerns that it would conflict with the country's traditional neutrality. Switzerland was a founder member of the European Free Trade Association (EFTA, see p. 461) in 1960 and joined the Council of Europe (see p. 260) in 1963.

Domestic Political Affairs

The enfranchisement of women in federal elections was approved at a referendum in February 1971. However, the cantons of Appenzell Ausserrhoden and Appenzell Innerrhoden introduced female suffrage only in 1989 and 1990, respectively. In October 1984 the Federal Assembly elected Switzerland's first female cabinet minister, Dr Elisabeth Kopp of the Radical Democratic Party, who became Head of the Federal Department of Justice and Police. In December 1988 the Assembly elected Kopp to be Vice-President of the Swiss Confederation for 1989. In the same month, however, she announced her resignation from the cabinet, following allegations that she had violated regulations concerning official secrecy, although she was acquitted by the Federal Supreme Court in February 1990.

The commission that had investigated the allegations against Kopp during 1989 subsequently revealed that the office of the Federal Public Prosecutor held about 900,000 secret files on some 200,000 Swiss citizens and foreigners. In March 1990 riots ensued when around 30,000 people demonstrated in Bern in protest against the existence of such files. The Government subsequently announced that it would commission a report on the activities of the security services. Published in June 1993, the report found that security service observation had been largely restricted to left-wing groups since 1945 and that security service personnel had at times behaved in an unprofessional manner.

In November 1989 64.4% of voters in a referendum rejected a proposal to abolish the armed forces by 2000. Following the referendum, which had been instigated by the Group for Switzerland Without an Army (an alliance of socialist, pacifist, youth and ecological organizations), the Federal Military (Defence) Department established a working party to examine proposals for reforms in the armed forces; consequently, the strength of the armed forces was considerably reduced during the early 1990s.

Meanwhile, in 1986 the Government introduced legislation that aimed to restrict the number of refugees who were to be granted political asylum in Switzerland. However, the new legislation was criticized by socialist, religious and humanitarian groups, and in April 1987 a national referendum on the issue was held. Of the 41.8% of the electorate who voted at the referendum, a substantial majority was in favour of the new restrictions. In March 1994, in an attempt to control increasing drugs-related crime (following allegations that immigrants trading in illicit drugs were exploiting the asylum laws to avoid extradition), the Government approved legislation restricting the rights of asylum seekers and immigrants, which included provisions for their arrest and detention without trial for failure to possess the requisite identification documents; further stringent measures against foreigners suspected of trafficking in illegal drugs were approved by national referendum in December.

The rise of the Swiss People's Party

The elections to the National Council and the Council of States (which together constitute the Federal Assembly) held in October 1999 were characterized by the strong performance of the Swiss People's Party, which, in terms of votes gained, became the country's largest party. In the National Council the Swiss People's Party overtook both the Radical Democratic Party and the Christian Democratic People's Party to become the second largest party after the Social Democratic Party. Seats in the National Council are allotted in proportion to votes gained. However, the complex, 'cantonal' nature of the electoral system ensured ultimate victory for the Social Democratic Party. In the Council of States, the Swiss People's Party obtained seven seats, thereby becoming the third largest party (after the Radical Democrats and the Christian Democrats).

In the early years of the 21st century the stability of the 'grand coalition' that had governed Switzerland since 1959 was increasingly threatened by the growing influence of the Swiss People's Party. Under the so-called 'magic formula' traditionally used to determine the distribution of government seats among the coalition partners, the Social Democratic Party, the Radical Democratic Party and the Christian Democratic People's Party each received two seats and the Swiss People's Party received only one. However, at the general election in October 2003 the Swiss People's Party received the greatest share of the votes cast and thus for the first time became the largest party in the National Council, with 55 seats. The party demanded a second seat on the Federal Council to reflect this (to be taken by Christoph Blocher), and threatened to withdraw from the coalition, effectively ending the era of consensus politics, if its demand was not met. Traditionally, Swiss ministers were reappointed at each election, and kept their seats until such time as they resigned. However, when the Federal Assembly elected the Federal Council in December, Blocher contested the seat held by Ruth Metzler of the Christian Democratic People's Party, and, after three ballots, won with a majority of just five votes. This was the first ministerial deselection for 130 years, and the first time the composition of the governing coalition had been changed in 44 years. When the new Federal Council took office on 1 January 2004, Blocher became Head of the Federal Department of Justice and Police, which carried with it responsibility not only for policy on immigration and asylum but also for negotiating with the European Union (EU, see p. 281) on Swiss membership of the Schengen Agreement (which binds signatories to the abolition of border controls) and the Dublin Convention on Asylum (relating to common formal arrangements on asylum).

In June 2004 the National Council approved a two-tier immigration policy whereby priority was to be given to EU and EFTA nationals, with immigration otherwise restricted to only highly skilled workers in the agricultural, construction, health and tourism sectors. At a national referendum held in September, a government plan to ease citizenship procedures for Swiss-born second-generation immigrants was opposed by 56.8% of those who participated, while a plan to grant automatic citizenship to third-generation immigrants was rejected by 51.6%. At a national referendum in September 2006, 67.8% of the valid votes cast were in favour of a proposal, supported by the Swiss People's Party, further to curtail the rights of asylum seekers and foreign migrants to Switzerland. Under the proposals, refugees would be required to present valid identification documents to the authorities within two days of their arrival in Switzerland and the issuance of work permits to non-skilled individuals from non-EU and non-EFTA countries would effectively be ended.

Events following the 2007 general election
Campaigning for the general election in October 2007 was characterized by the increased polarization of the electorate. In September controversy arose following accusations of racism against the Swiss People's Party, arising from the party's use of images deemed to be xenophobic in its campaign posters. In early October violent clashes took place in the capital, Bern, between police and left-wing activists who had attempted to disrupt a rally held by the Swiss People's Party. At the election on 21 October the Swiss People's Party strengthened its position as the largest party, winning 62 seats in the National Council. The Social Democratic Party secured 43 seats, while the Radical Democratic Party and the Christian Democratic People's Party won 31 seats apiece. The Green Party increased its representation, winning 20 seats.

Opposition to the Swiss People's Party centred increasingly on Blocher. Many Federal Assembly members opposed Blocher's re-election to the Federal Council, in particular the Green Party, which announced its intention to propose its own candidate. However, prior to the vote, which took place in December 2007, the Green Party withdrew its candidate in order to support a moderate member of the Swiss People's Party, Eveline Widmer-Schlumpf, who eventually defeated Blocher. In defiance of the party leadership, Widmer-Schlumpf announced that she would accept a role in the Federal Council. The Swiss People's Party subsequently withdrew its support for the Government.

Following Blocher's deselection, both Widmer-Schlumpf and the Head of the Federal Department of Defence, Civil Protection and Sports, Samuel Schmid, were excluded from the party's parliamentary group, on the grounds that their moderate views conflicted with those of the majority of the party's supporters. In March 2008 the party leadership initiated measures to expel Widmer-Schlumpf. When the executive of the Graubünden cantonal organization—of which Widmer-Schlumpf was a leading figure—refused to revoke her membership of the party, it was replaced by a committee of more right-wing members. The attempt by the Swiss People's Party to impose discipline upon its regional organizations prompted the secession, in June, of executives in other traditionally moderate cantonal sections, notably Bern, where dissident members formed a new party, the Conservative Democratic Party. The former Swiss People's Party executives in Glarus and Graubünden subsequently formed parties under the same name in their respective cantons. The new parties immediately gained representation in the Federal Council, as Widmer-Schlumpf and Schmid were among the leading members. The Conservative Democratic Party was formally inaugurated as a national party in November 2008 when Hans Grunder was elected as party President.

In November 2008 Schmid announced his intention to resign from the Federal Council. (He had been subject to media criticism since mid-2008, following an incident at a military training camp in which six soldiers died, which was compounded by the resignation of the head of the armed forces, following allegations of personal misconduct.) At the election for Schmid's successor in December, the list of candidates included three members of the Swiss People's Party, notably Blocher and the head of the Zürich cantonal organization, Ueli Maurer; Maurer was elected to the role and confirmed his commitment to bipartisan government. The Radical Democratic Party and the Liberal Party of Switzerland merged as FDP.The Liberals in January 2009 under the leadership of Fulvio Pelli, the former leader of the Radical Democratic Party.

In early 2009 the Swiss Government was subject to intense pressure from several countries, including France, Germany and the USA, over its continued reluctance to implement changes to the country's laws on banking secrecy. In February the Federal Council appointed a committee of financial and legal experts to recommend measures designed to uphold banking secrecy. In March, however, the cabinet approved proposals to relax the legislation to permit the sharing of information on accounts held in Swiss banks with investigators in cases where allegations of tax evasion could be proven. Nevertheless, the Government insisted that it continued to endorse the principle of banking secrecy and that the reform would affect a very small number of cases. In April the Organisation for Economic Co-operation Development (OECD, see p. 388) notably included Switzerland in a so-called 'grey' list of states that had adopted OECD standards on exchanging tax information but had not yet adequately implemented them. Switzerland secured its removal from this list in September after signing a 12th bilateral agreement on the exchange of tax information. Meanwhile, in August, in the most significant case of its kind to date, an agreement was reached whereby Switzerland's largest bank, UBS, was to accede within 12 months to a US request for information concerning 4,450 accounts held by US citizens who were suspected of tax evasion. After the Federal Administrative Court ruled in January 2010 that the release of confidential banking data to US investigators was illegal, the Swiss Government was forced to seek parliamentary approval of the agreement, which was narrowly secured in June.

In a referendum held in November 2009, 57.5% of voters approved an initiative proposed by the Swiss People's Party to ban the construction of minarets in Switzerland. The party had once again been subject to accusations of racism in its campaign for the ban, which it maintained was intended to halt what it claimed was the increasing Islamization of the country and to uphold Swiss democratic values. (It was reported, however, that of the approximately 200 mosques in Switzerland just four had a minaret, and that, in practice, planning consent for new minarets was rarely granted.) The Government—which, together with the other principal political parties, had opposed the initiative—announced that it would abide by the decision of the electorate, but declared that freedom of religion in Switzerland was not compromised by the new legislation and that it would seek to ease tensions with Muslim countries and organizations engendered by the referendum.

Moritz Leuenberger, the Head of the Federal Department of the Environment, Transport, Communications and Energy, announced his resignation from the Federal Council in July 2010, as did Hans-Rudolf Merz, the Head of the Federal Department of Finance, in August. Critics of Merz had accused him of weakening banking secrecy and of being slow to respond to the dispute with the US authorities over allegations of tax evasion by US clients of UBS. Simonetta Sommaruga, of the Social Democratic Party, and Johann Schneider-Ammann, of FDP.The Liberals, were elected to the Federal Council in September, replacing party colleagues Leuenberger and Merz, respectively. Sommaruga's election produced a female majority in the cabinet for the first time. A reorganization of the Federal Council was announced a few days later and took effect at the beginning of November. Schneider-Ammann became Head of the Federal Department of Economic Affairs and Sommaruga Head of the Federal Department of Justice and Police, while their predecessors in these posts, Doris Leuthard and Widmer-Schlumpf, assumed responsibility for the Federal Department of the Environment, Transport, Communications and Energy and the Federal Department of Finance, respectively. In December Micheline Calmy-Rey, the Head of the Federal Department of Foreign Affairs, was elected President of the Confederation for 2011.

An initiative proposed by the Swiss People's Party on the mandatory deportation of foreigners convicted of serious crimes (ranging from murder to social security fraud) was approved by 52.3% of voters in a referendum in November 2010. A less extreme counter-proposal submitted by the Federal Assembly, amid concerns that automatic expulsion would violate Switzerland's commitments under international law, was rejected by 52.6% of voters.

In May 2011 proposals to prohibit assisted suicide and to impose restrictions on foreign nationals travelling to Switzerland in order to seek an assisted suicide were put to the electorate in Zürich in a referendum. The proposals, which had been presented by the conservative Federal Democratic Union and supported by some Christian groups were rejected by 85% and 78% of voters, respectively.

Amid increasing public hostility to nuclear power in the aftermath of the Fukushima nuclear disaster in Japan in early 2011, the Government announced in May of that year that all four of Switzerland's nuclear power plants (which together incorporated five reactors) would be closed at the end of their operative lives, between 2019 and 2035, and not replaced with new nuclear facilities. The decision followed a series of protests by anti-nuclear campaigners, including a march in mid-May by some 20,000 people to the Beznau nuclear plant, near the northern town of Döttingen.

The issue of banking secrecy again came to the fore in 2011 when the Swiss authorities signed agreements with Germany and the United Kingdom in August to tax the undeclared assets held in Swiss banks by their respective citizens. Under the historically significant agreements, Germany was to receive a payment of at least 2,000m. Swiss francs and the United Kingdom 500m. Swiss francs to settle past tax liabilities on undeclared accounts. Income and capital gains taxes were then to be levied on such accounts from 2013. An amended agreement was signed with Germany in April 2012 after the upper house of the German parliament (the Bundesrat) demanded the imposition of stricter conditions on tax evaders. However, in November the Bundesrat acted against the wishes of the German Government by refusing to ratify the agreement.

The 2011 general election

At the general election of 23 October 2011 the ruling Swiss People's Party remained the largest political grouping in the National Council, despite experiencing a decline in support for the first time in some 20 years. The party lost eight seats to secure a total of 54. The Social Democratic Party increased its representation by three seats to win a total of 46. The Radical Democratic Party and the Christian Democratic People's Party secured 30 and 28 seats, respectively, while the Green Party and Green Liberal Party won 15 and 12 seats, respectively.

On 14 December 2011 the Federal Assembly elected the Head of the Federal Department of Finance, Eveline Widmer-Schlumpf, as President of the Confederation for 2012 by 174 votes to 65. Ueli Maurer, the Head of the Federal Department of Defence, Civil Protection and Sports, was elected Vice-President, while Alain Berset of the Social Democratic Party and Didier Burkhalter of the Radical Democratic Party were assigned the home affairs and foreign affairs portfolios, respectively. On 5 December 2012 the Federal Assembly elected incumbent Vice-President Maurer as President of the Confederation for 2013 by 148 votes to 54. Burkhalter was elected to succeed him as Vice-President.

Amid growing concern over the widening economic divide in the country, in a referendum held in early March 2013 nearly 68% of those who participated approved an initiative to impose stringent controls over corporate salaries.

'Nazi Gold'

In September 1995 the Swiss Bankers' Association (SBA) announced the introduction of measures that would enable relatives to trace and recover the assets deposited in Swiss bank accounts by victims of the Nazi massacre of Jews in the Second World War. To assist in this process an accord was signed in May 1996 by the SBA and the World Jewish Congress establishing an Independent Committee of Eminent Persons (ICEP), which was to be responsible for auditing all dormant Swiss bank accounts. In September documents were released from British and US archives, claiming that gold valued at several thousand million dollars, at current prices, had been deposited in Swiss banks during the Second World War. Much of it was suspected to have belonged to Jews killed during the Holocaust. The Swiss Federal Assembly subsequently approved legislation ordering banks to release all records that might pertain to dealings with the Nazi regime in Germany or its victims; in December the Federal Government appointed an international commission to conduct a historical investigation of Switzerland's role as a financial centre during the Second World War.

In March 1998 senior US public finance officials placed Swiss banks under increasing pressure to agree to a swift 'global settlement' of the issue of Holocaust victims' accounts, involving the establishment of a victims' fund and a timetable for payment. In August UBS and Crédit Suisse agreed to pay US $1,250m. to the World Jewish Congress as compensation for the role of Swiss financial institutions in retaining dormant Jewish assets, handling gold deposited by the Nazis and lending money during the Second World War to German companies that had utilized

Jewish slave labour. In return, all threats of boycotts and legal action against Swiss concerns were withdrawn.

In December 1999 the ICEP reported that its audit of all dormant Swiss bank accounts had shown that some 54,000 of these might have belonged to Jews murdered during the Holocaust (the figure was subsequently reduced to 36,000). The Committee recommended that details of 25,000 of the accounts should be publicized in order to alert survivors of the Holocaust or their heirs to their existence. The Committee did not attempt to value the funds held in the accounts, but stated that the total would probably not exceed the US $1,250m. already committed by UBS and Crédit Suisse to the World Jewish Congress. The international historical commission (appointed in December 1996) concluded in its report that, by closing its border to an estimated 24,500 fugitive Jews from 1942, Switzerland bore partial responsibility for their deaths at the hands of the Nazis. Following the release of the commission's report, the Government formally apologized for Switzerland's role in the Second World War. Further details emerged in August 2001, which indicated that several of Switzerland's largest companies had ignored reports of Nazi atrocities and had continued to trade with Germany during the Second World War. In December another report indicated that Switzerland had harboured substantial amounts of Nazi funds and assets, even concealing entire German companies during the Second World War, and had provided a refuge for several prominent Nazi war criminals following the end of hostilities.

The proposed settlement of US $1,250m. to end the threat of litigation by Holocaust survivors against Swiss banks was approved by a judge in the USA in July 2000. Four Swiss insurers added a further $50m. in response to claims that the insurance policies of Holocaust survivors had not been honoured. Swiss companies that had used forced labour during the Second World War were also required to contribute. In February 2001 Swiss banks published lists of dormant bank accounts, thought to be linked to the Holocaust, to be claimed by the account holders or their heirs.

Foreign Affairs

Regional relations

Switzerland began to emerge from its traditional isolation in the early 1990s. This was largely due to economic pressures resulting from the world recession and the further integration of the European Community (EC). In May 1992 the Federal Council announced that it was to apply for membership of the EC. In a referendum in December, however, the Swiss electorate voted against ratification of an agreement to create a free trade zone encompassing both EC and EFTA member states. (The European Economic Area was established, without Switzerland, in January 1994.) Despite this setback, the Government declared its intention to continue to pursue its application for membership of the EC. During 1993 Switzerland confined itself to seeking bilateral negotiations with the EC (which became the EU in that year) on issues of particular national interest. Agreement was reached in December 1996 to phase out Swiss work permits for citizens of EU member states over a period of six years. By February 2000 the Government had negotiated seven bilateral free trade agreements with the EU, including the gradual elimination of immigration controls between Switzerland and the EU over a period of 12 years, which were approved in a referendum in May. In a referendum in March of the following year 77% of voters rejected a motion to begin 'fast-track' accession negotiations with the EU. The Government insisted that the vote did not represent a rejection of the EU, but rather reflected the desire to move towards accession at a slower pace, and that its plans for eventual membership of the EU remained unchanged.

In December 2004 the Federal Assembly approved a second set of bilateral agreements with the EU, under which Switzerland was to introduce (incrementally between 1 July 2005 and 2011) a withholding tax of 35% on the income of EU citizens' savings held in Swiss banks, with banking secrecy to be retained. The agreements also provided for co-operation against customs fraud and for Switzerland's associate membership of the Schengen Agreement and Dublin Convention, as well as for the extension of the first set of bilateral agreements to the 10 states that had acceded to full membership of the EU earlier in the year. At a referendum in June 2005 54.6% of participating voters supported Switzerland's adherence to the Schengen/Dublin accords, which were duly implemented in December 2008. The extension of existing bilateral agreements to the new EU member states was approved by 56.0% of voters at a referendum in September 2005. During

2010 the Swiss Government came under increasing pressure from the EU to reform its institutional relations with the Union. However, although the President of the Confederation, Doris Leuthard, acknowledged in August that changes might be desirable, she insisted that the Government would not agree to the automatic adoption of EU rules, as advocated by the Union, and would instead seek the negotiation of a third set of bilateral agreements. The EU, meanwhile, insisted that the 'institutional issue', as it had become known, must be resolved before any further bilateral agreements with Switzerland could be undertaken.

The Swiss Government's decision, in April 2012, to re-impose immigration quotas on workers from the eight central and eastern European countries that joined the EU in 2004 (limits that had only been lifted about one year earlier), invoking a 'safeguard clause' in its agreement with the EU on freedom of movement, prompted stern criticism from the Union. The EU claimed that the agreement did not allow for differentiation between EU citizens. In April 2013 the EU was further angered by Switzerland's extension of the limit on immigration to cover 17 other EU member states (immigration from the Union's newest members, Bulgaria and Romania, was curbed separately, and more severely); the new limit was to be imposed in May for a period of one year. The Swiss Government had come under increasing pressure to limit immigration from both the Swiss People's Party and the Green Liberal Party, which both claimed that immigration had reached unsustainable levels.

Other external relations

In June 1993 the Federal Assembly approved legislation that sought permission for Swiss forces to be included in future UN peace-keeping operations. However, at a referendum on the issue, which took place in June 1994, 57.3% of voters rejected the proposal. Switzerland did, however, subsequently join the Partnership for Peace programme of the North Atlantic Treaty Organization (NATO, see p. 380) in 1996. Furthermore, Swiss peace-keepers have participated in EU operations in Bosnia and Herzegovina, and Swiss truce-verifiers have worked in Kosovo under the Organization for Security and Co-operation in Europe (OSCE, see p. 397). In November 2000 a referendum proposing to reduce the military budget by one-third was rejected by 62.4% of voters. A further proposal to abolish the armed forces was rejected by 78.1% of voters in a referendum in December 2001.

Until 2002, although Switzerland maintained a permanent observer at the UN and had joined the organization's non-political specialized agencies, it was not a full member of the UN. (At a referendum in 1986 some 75.7% of voters had rejected full UN membership.) In September 2001 the Federal Assembly approved proposals for Switzerland to join the UN and these were narrowly adopted at a referendum in March 2002. Switzerland was formally admitted as a member of the UN in September.

In the late 1990s a series of high-profile money-laundering cases threatened to damage Switzerland's reputation as a stable financial centre. Most notably, these included the freezing of assets and accounts linked to Gen. Sani Abacha and Slobodan Milošević, the former leaders of Nigeria and Yugoslavia, respectively, and the former head of the Peruvian secret service, Vladimiro Montesinos. Suspect funds found in Swiss bank accounts were linked to missing IMF aid paid to Russia and also to the former leader of the Philippines, Ferdinand Marcos. The total value of suspect funds under investigation in Switzerland increased from 333m. Swiss francs in 1999 (representing 160 cases) to 1,543m. Swiss francs (representing 370 cases) in 2000. In August 2003 Switzerland declared itself willing to co-operate with Nigeria's efforts to recover funds stolen and deposited in Switzerland by Abacha. By 2006 the Swiss Government announced that it had returned all of the funds, thought to total $700m., to the Nigerian Government. Appeals from the Abacha family for ownership of the money had been rejected.

In 2006 the Federal Supreme Court ruled that indefinite freezes imposed by the Government on privately held assets in Swiss banks were unconstitutional. Non-governmental organizations expressed fears that the ruling could lead to the release of further assets whose provenance was suspected to be illegal, including an estimated 7.7m. Swiss francs believed to have been deposited by former President Mobutu Sese Seko of Zaire (now the Democratic Republic of the Congo). In April 2009 the Swiss Federal Prosecutor ruled that, owing to the statute of limitations, assets believed to have been deposited by former President Mobutu should be returned to his family upon the expiry of the order freezing those funds at the end of April. An appeal to the Federal Criminal Court by a private individual against the

decision to release the funds was rejected in July, and Mobutu's assets were duly released. In 2011 the Government froze assets held in Switzerland by several current or former heads of state: the President of Côte d'Ivoire, Laurent Gbagbo, who was refusing to concede defeat following a presidential election in that country; the former Presidents of Tunisia and Egypt, Zine al-Abidine Ben Ali and Hosni Mubarak, who had both left office following popular uprisings; and Col Muammar al-Qaddafi, the leader of Libya, where opposition protests had been violently suppressed. New legislation, designed to facilitate the freezing, confiscation and restitution of suspect funds deposited in Swiss banks by heads of state, had come into effect in February. The law, which was aimed particularly at resolving cases in which the country of origin of the assets was unable to conduct a criminal procedure that met the requirements of Swiss legislation on international mutual assistance, allowed the authorities to act without having received a formal request from the state in question and removed the statute of limitations on the return of illegally acquired assets. It also stipulated that restored funds should be used to benefit the people of the country of origin. In May 2011 the Swiss Government also initiated legal proceedings to return assets (believed to total some US $5.7m.) of the former Haitian President Jean-Claude Duvalier, which had been frozen since 1986, to the Government of Haiti.

Relations between Switzerland and the USA, although traditionally very cordial, have in recent years been marred by the issue of tax evasion. In January 2013 it was announced that Switzerland's oldest private bank, Wegelin & Co, was to close after admitting at a trial held in the USA (the first of its kind) that it had helped more than 100 of its US clients to avoid paying taxes. Thirteen other Swiss banks, including Crédit Suisse, were under investigation by US authorities in that year.

CONSTITUTION AND GOVERNMENT

The Swiss Confederation, composed of 26 cantons, has a republican federal Constitution. Originally promulgated in 1848, it was wholly revised in 1874 and again in 2000. Legislative power is held by the bicameral Federal Assembly: the Council of States, with 46 members, elected for three to four years, representing the cantons (of which 20 send two members each and six, known as 'half-cantons', are represented by one member each); and the National Council, with 200 members directly elected by universal adult suffrage for four years, on the basis of proportional representation. Executive power is held by the Federal Council, which has seven members elected for four years by a joint session of the Federal Assembly. The Assembly also elects one of the Federal Councillors to be President of the Confederation (head of state) for one year at a time.

National policy is the prerogative of the Federal Government, but considerable power is vested in the cantons. Under the Constitution, the autonomous cantons hold all powers not specifically delegated to the federal authorities. The Swiss citizen shares three distinct allegiances—communal, cantonal and national. Direct participation is very important in communal government, and all adult Swiss residents may take part in the communal assemblies or referendums, which decide upon local affairs. Each canton has its own written constitution, government and legislative assembly. The referendum, which can be on a communal, cantonal or national scale, further ensures the possibility of direct public participation in decision-making.

REGIONAL AND INTERNATIONAL CO-OPERATION

Switzerland was a founder member of the European Free Trade Association (EFTA, see p. 461), and is a member of the Council of Europe (see p. 260). Switzerland has signed a number of bilateral free trade agreements with the European Union (EU, see p. 281), and is a signatory to the EU's Schengen Agreement on border controls and the Dublin Convention on Asylum. It is also a member of the Organization for Security and Co-operation in Europe (OSCE, see p. 397).

Switzerland joined the UN in 2002 following a referendum, although many of the UN's institutions had been located in Geneva since 1946. It joined the World Trade Organization (WTO, see p. 444) in 1995, and was a founder member of the Organisation for Economic Co-operation and Development (OECD, see p. 388). Switzerland participates in the Partnership for Peace programme of the North Atlantic Treaty Organization (NATO, see p. 380).

ECONOMIC AFFAIRS

In 2011, according to estimates by the World Bank, Switzerland's gross national income (GNI), measured at average 2009–11 prices, was US $603,917m., equivalent to $76,380 per head (or $52,320 per head on an international purchasing-power parity basis). During 2002–11, it was estimated, the population grew by an average of 0.9% per year, while gross domestic product (GDP) per head increased, in real terms, at an average annual rate of 1.0%. Overall GDP increased, in real terms, by an average of 1.9% per year in 2002–11; real GDP expanded by 2.1% in 2011.

Agriculture (including forestry and fishing) contributed an estimated 0.8% of GDP in 2011, according to provisional figures. The sector engaged 3.7% of the employed labour force in 2011. The principal cash crops are sugar beet, potatoes and wheat. Dairy products, notably cheese, are also important. At a national referendum held in November 2005, 55.7% of voters approved a five-year ban on the use of genetically modified crops. In March 2010 the moratorium was extended until November 2013. According to UN figures, agricultural GDP increased at an average annual rate of 0.5% in 2002–11; it contracted by 3.0% in 2010, but grew by 5.5% in 2011.

Industry (including mining and quarrying, manufacturing, power and construction) contributed an estimated 26.2% of GDP in 2011, according to provisional figures. The sector engaged 22.4% of the employed labour force in 2011. According to UN figures, in 2002–11 industrial GDP increased by an average of 1.9% per year; sectoral GDP rose by 3.0% in 2011.

Switzerland is not richly endowed with mineral deposits, and only rock salt and building materials are mined or quarried in significant quantities. In 2011 a mere 0.1% of the working population were employed in mining and quarrying. The sector contributed an estimated 0.1% of GDP in 2011.

The manufacturing sector contributed an estimated 18.4% of GDP and engaged 14.4% of the employed labour force in 2011. The most important branches are precision engineering (in particular clocks and watches, which provided 7.0% of export revenue in 2012), heavy engineering, machine-building, textiles, chocolate, chemicals and pharmaceuticals.

The construction sector contributed an estimated 5.6% of GDP in 2011, according to provisional figures. The sector engaged 7.0% of the employed labour force in 2011.

Of total electricity output in 2009, 54.2% was provided by hydroelectric power and 40.1% by nuclear power (from five reactors with a total generating capacity of 3,077 MW). Imports of mineral fuels comprised 7.5% of the value of total imports in 2010 (including imports to Liechtenstein). Switzerland is a net exporter of electricity. Following damage to a nuclear power station in Japan after a severe earthquake in March 2011, in May of that year the Government announced that all four of Switzerland's nuclear power plants would be closed at the end of their operative lives and would not be replaced with new nuclear facilities.

The services sector contributed an estimated 73.0% of GDP in 2011, according to provisional figures. The sector engaged 74.0% of the employed labour force in 2011. Switzerland plays an important role as a centre of international finance, and Swiss markets account for a significant share of international financial transactions. The insurance sector is also highly developed, and Swiss companies are represented throughout the world. Switzerland draws considerable revenue from tourism; according to provisional figures, receipts from tourism totalled 15,577m. Swiss francs in 2011. According to UN figures, during 2002–11 services GDP increased by an average of 2.0% per year; GDP of the sector rose by 1.5% in 2011.

In 2011 Switzerland recorded a visible merchandise trade surplus of US $25,191m. and there was a surplus of $35,900m. on the current account of the balance of payments. The European Union (EU, see p. 281) accounted for the majority of Switzerland's trade, providing 76.1% of the country's imports and taking 55.5% of exports in 2012. In 2012 the principal source of imports was Germany (providing 30.6% of the total), followed by Italy,

France, the People's Republic of China and the USA. Germany was also the principal market for exports (accounting for 19.9% of the total), followed by the USA, Italy and France. The principal exports in 2012 were chemicals, machinery, clocks and watches, precision instruments and metals. The main imports in that year were chemicals, machinery, precision instruments and motor vehicles.

According to official estimates, Switzerland recorded a consolidated budgetary surplus of 2,466m. Swiss francs in 2013. Switzerland's general government gross debt was 275.899m. Swiss francs in 2010, equivalent to 48.0% of GDP. The annual rate of inflation averaged 0.7% in 2003–12; consumer prices increased by 0.3% in 2011, but decreased by 0.7% in 2012. The annual rate of unemployment averaged 3.4% in 2012. Of all the major European countries, Switzerland has the highest percentage of foreign workers (27.6% of the working population in 2012).

Switzerland is a prosperous country, despite its small size, with a high level of income per head. Its economic success, built around financial services and a modern industrial sector, is in large part due to a highly educated labour force and a flexible labour market. Although Switzerland is not a member of the EU, it is nevertheless largely dependent on the eurozone for economic growth and enjoys privileged access to the EU's internal market through numerous bilateral agreements. During 2004–08 Switzerland enjoyed continued growth in real GDP; however, the prominence of the financial services sector left the Swiss economy vulnerable to the effects of the global financial crisis from 2008. In October 2008 the Swiss National Bank (SNB) provided 6,000m. Swiss francs of additional capital to the country's largest bank, UBS, which subsequently revealed losses of some 20,000m. Swiss francs for the year. The Government introduced three sets of stimulus measures in November 2008, and March and June 2009, with a total value of nearly 3,000m. Swiss francs. A fall in demand, concomitant with a strong currency, precipitated a steep decline in the value of exports from late 2008, while a decrease in consumer spending prompted the SNB to reduce interest rates, in an attempt to offset the risk of deflation. Real GDP contracted by 1.9% in 2009, but increased by an estimated 2.6% in 2010. Interest rates remained extremely low throughout 2010, while the SNB intervened in the foreign exchange market in the first half of the year in an attempt to curb the appreciation of the Swiss franc against the euro, as a surge in inflows of capital reflected concerns regarding sovereign debt in the eurozone. However, the Swiss currency strengthened further, adversely affecting exports and tourism revenue towards the end of the year. By mid-2011 the Swiss franc had almost reached parity with the euro and in September the SNB intervened to cap its value at 1.20 against the euro (a ceiling which was still in place at April 2013). The announcement led to an immediate decline in the value of the currency of some 9%, which was expected to have a positive impact on most areas of the economy. The adverse effects of the strong appreciation of the Swiss currency on exports in 2011 contributed to a moderation in GDP growth to 2.1% in that year. During 2012 the economy remained relatively stable and robust, despite the ongoing fiscal crisis in the eurozone and the weak export market in that region, and there was a notable growth in employment and domestic demand (the latter being fuelled by persistently low interest rates). However, GDP slowed further to 1.4% in 2012, at which level it was projected to remain in 2013. In spite of the SNB's continuing policy of currency intervention, consumer prices fell by 0.7% in 2012.

PUBLIC HOLIDAYS

2014: 1 January (New Year's Day), 18 April (Good Friday)*, 21 April (Easter Monday)*, 29 May (Ascension Day), 20 May (Whit Monday)*, 1 August (National Day), 25 December (Christmas Day), 26 December (St Stephen's Day)*.

In addition, various cantonal and local holidays are observed.

* Observation varies by canton.

Statistical Survey

Source (unless otherwise stated): Federal Statistical Office, Information Service, 10 Espace de l'Europe, 2010 Neuchâtel; tel. 327136011; fax 327136012; e-mail info@bfs.admin.ch; internet www.bfs.admin.ch.

Area and Population

AREA, POPULATION AND DENSITY

Area (sq km)	41,284*
Population (enumerated census result)	
5 December 2000	7,288,010
Population (register-based annual census at 31 December)†	
2010	7,870,134
2011	
Males	3,922,253
Females	4,032,409
Total	7,954,662
Density (per sq km) at 31 December 2011	192.7

* 15,940 sq miles.

† Figures refer to permanent resident population.

POPULATION BY AGE AND SEX
(official estimates at 31 December 2011)

	Males	Females	Total
0–14	613,414	581,235	1,194,649
15–64	2,718,741	2,676,120	5,394,861
65 and over	590,098	775,054	1,365,152
Total	3,922,253	4,032,409	7,954,662

LANGUAGES
(Swiss nationals, %)

	1980	1990	2000
German	73.5	73.4	72.5
French	20.1	20.5	21.0
Italian	4.5	4.1	4.3
Romansh	0.9	0.7	0.6
Others	1.0	1.3	1.6

REGIONS AND CANTONS

Region/Canton	Area (sq km)*	Population (2011)† Total ('000)	Per sq km	Capital (with population, 2000‡)
Région lémanique	8,718.7	1,503.4	172.4	—
Genève . . .	282.4	460.5	1,630.7	Genève (177,964)
Valais . . .	5,224.4	317.0	60.7	Sion (27,171)
Vaud . . .	3,211.9	725.9	226.0	Lausanne (124,914)
Espace Mittelland	10,062.0	1,770.4	175.9	—
Bern . . .	5,959.3	985.0	165.3	Bern (128,634)
Fribourg . .	1,670.6	284.7	170.4	Fribourg (35,547)
Jura . . .	838.5	70.5	84.1	Delémont (11,353)
Neuchâtel . .	802.9	173.2	215.7	Neuchâtel (32,914)
Solothurn . .	790.7	257.0	325.0	Solothurn (15,489)
Nordwestschweiz .	1,958.2	1,080.0	551.5	—
Aargau . . .	1,403.6	618.3	440.5	Aarau (15,470)
Basel-Stadt .	37.0	186.3	5,035.1	Basel (166,558)
Basel-Landschaft	517.6	275.4	532.1	Liestal (12,930)
Zürich . . .	1,728.9	1392.4	805.4	Zürich (363,273)
Ostschweiz . .	11,521.1	1,113.9	96.7	—
Appenzell Ausserrhoden	242.8	53.3	219.5	Herisau (15,882)
Appenzell Innerrhoden .	172.5	15.7	91.0	Appenzell (5,447)
Glarus . . .	685.1	39.2	57.2	Glarus (5,556)
Graubünden .	7,105.5	193.4	27.2	Chur (32,989)
St Gallen . .	2,025.7	483.2	238.5	St Gallen (72,626)
Schaffhausen .	298.5	77.1	258.3	Schaffhausen (33,628)

Region/Canton—*continued*	Area (sq km)*	Population (2011)† Total ('000)	Per sq km	Capital (with population, 2000‡)
Thurgau . .	991.0	252.0	254.3	Frauenfeld (21,954)
Zentralschweiz	4,483.6	757.6	169.0	—
Luzern . . .	1,493.5	382.0	255.8	Luzern (59,496)
Nidwalden . .	275.9	41.3	149.7	Stans (6,983)
Obwalden . .	490.6	35.9	73.2	Sarnen (9,145)
Schwyz . . .	908.2	147.9	162.8	Schwyz (13,802)
Uri	1,076.7	35.4	32.9	Altdorf (8,541)
Zug	238.7	115.1	482.2	Zug (22,973)
Ticino	2,812.2	336.9	119.8	Bellinzona (16,463)
Total	41,284.2	7,954.7	192.7	—

* Figures exclude lakes larger than 5 sq km (total area 1,289.5 sq km). Also excluded are special territories (total area 7.2 sq km).

† Estimated permanent resident population at 31 December.

‡ Census figures.

PRINCIPAL TOWNS
(estimated population at 1 January 2011)

Zürich (Zurich) . .	376,990	Biel (Bienne) . .	51,635
Genève (Genf or Geneva) . . .	188,234	Thun (Thoune) . .	42,764
Basel (Bâle) . . .	164,516	Köniz . . .	38,936
Lausanne . . .	129,383	La Chaux-de-Fonds	37,843
Bern (Berne, capital)	125,681	Fribourg (Freiburg) .	35,680
Winterthur (Winterthour) .	103,075	Schaffhausen (Schaffhouse) .	35,121
Luzern (Lucerne) .	78,093	Chur (Coire) . .	33,984
St Gallen (Saint-Gall)	73,505	Neuchâtel (Neuenburg) . .	33,412

BIRTHS, MARRIAGES AND DEATHS

	Registered live births Number	Rate (per 1,000)	Registered marriages Number	Rate (per 1,000)	Registered deaths Number	Rate (per 1,000)
2005 . .	72,903	9.8	40,139	5.4	61,124	8.2
2006 . .	73,371	9.8	39,817	5.3	60,283	8.1
2007 . .	74,494	9.8	40,330	5.3	61,089	8.0
2008 . .	76,691	10.0	41,534	5.4	61,233	8.0
2009 . .	78,286	10.1	41,918	5.4	62,476	8.0
2010 . .	80,290	10.4	43,257	5.5	62,649	8.0
2011 . .	80,808	10.2	42,083	5.3	62,091	7.8
2012* . .	81,500	n.a.	42,500	n.a.	64,000	n.a.

* Provisional figures rounded to the nearest 100 persons.

Life expectancy (years at birth): 82.2 (males 80.1; females 84.5) in 2010 (Source: World Bank, World Development Indicators database).

ECONOMICALLY ACTIVE POPULATION*
(quarterly averages, April–June, '000 persons aged 15 years and over)

	2009	2010	2011
Agriculture, hunting, forestry and fishing	152	154	173
Mining and quarrying	5	5	5
Manufacturing	691	669	680
Electricity, gas and water supply	39	40	42
Construction	313	320	329
Wholesale and retail trade; repair of motor vehicles, motorcycles and personal and household goods	679	688	699
Hotels and restaurants	251	256	252
Transport, storage and communications	373	373	386
Financial intermediation	252	253	258
Real estate, renting and business activities	559	570	582
Public administration and defence; compulsory social security	177	188	197
Education	298	299	297
Health and social work	541	556	584
Other community, social and personal service activities	169	173	171
Private households with employed persons	72	51	65
Total employed	4,572	4,594	4,719
Unemployed	183	190	163
Total labour force	4,755	4,784	4,882
Males	2,589	2,621	2,683
Females	2,166	2,163	2,199

* Refers to workers who are employed for at least one hour per week, and includes foreign workers ('000): 1,242 in 2009; 1,255 in 2010; 1,317 in 2011.

2012: Total employed 4,759; Unemployed 170; Total labour force 4,929.

Note: Totals may not be equal to the sum of components, owing to rounding.

Health and Welfare

KEY INDICATORS

Total fertility rate (children per woman, 2010)	1.5
Under-5 mortality rate (per 1,000 live births, 2010)	5
HIV/AIDS (% of persons aged 15–49, 2009)	0.4
Physicians (per 1,000 head, 2009)	4.1
Hospital beds (per 1,000 head, 2009)	5.2
Health expenditure (2009): US $ per head (PPP)	5,105
Health expenditure (2009): % of GDP	11.4
Health expenditure (2009): public (% of total)	59.7
Total carbon dioxide emissions ('000 metric tons, 2008)	40,392.0
Carbon dioxide emissions per head (metric tons, 2008)	5.3
Human Development Index (2011): ranking	11
Human Development Index (2011): value	0.903

For sources and definitions, see explanatory note on p. vi.

Agriculture

PRINCIPAL CROPS
('000 metric tons)

	2009	2010	2011
Wheat	549.9	524.0	553.2
Barley	198.1	174.1	183.4
Maize	174.0	143.5	151.3
Rye	15.9	13.7	12.7
Oats	10.5	8.9	8.7
Triticale (wheat-rye hybrid)	56.3	58.3	62.0
Potatoes	521.5	420.8	512.0
Sugar beet	1,719.7	1,302.1	1,828.2
Rapeseed	67.0	67.9	74.0
Cabbages and other brassicas	35.7	37.4	44.5
Lettuce and chicory	69.9	68.4	75.7
Tomatoes	38.4	40.1	41.9
Onions and shallots, green	37.4	31.7	43.4
Carrots and turnips	69.5	61.2	75.7
Apples	251.1	201.0	360.9
Pears	67.8	39.6	54.7
Grapes	141.0	130.6	128.9

Aggregate production ('000 metric tons, may include official, semi-official or estimated data): Total cereals 1,006 in 2009, 924 in 2010, 973 in 2011; Total roots and tubers 522 in 2009, 421 in 2010, 512 in 2011; Total vegetables (incl. melons) 381.4 in 2009, 364.4 in 2010, 425.1 in 2011; Total fruits (excl. melons) 506 in 2009, 406 in 2010, 591 in 2011.

Source: FAO.

LIVESTOCK
('000 head, year ending September)

	2009	2010	2011
Cattle	1,597.5	1,591.2	1,577.4
Horses	60.2	62.1	57.2
Asses	18.4	19.4	19.0
Pigs	1,557.2	1,589.0	1,578.9
Sheep	431.9	434.1	424.0
Goats	85.1	87.0	86.2
Chickens	8,741	8,944	9,391

Source: FAO.

LIVESTOCK PRODUCTS
('000 metric tons)

	2009	2010	2011
Cattle meat	141.6	142.9	143.9
Sheep meat	5.4	5.5	5.4
Pig meat	237.8	249.5	249.0
Chicken meat	63.8	67.3	71.3
Cows' milk	4,068.5	4,079.4	4,118.6
Goats' milk	21.5	22.0	22.4
Hen eggs	43.5	45.3	45.6

Source: FAO.

Forestry

ROUNDWOOD REMOVALS
('000 cubic metres, excluding bark)

	2009	2010	2011
Sawlogs, veneer logs and logs for sleepers	2,846	2,944	2,822
Pulpwood	425	478	484
Other industrial wood	16	17	16
Fuel wood	1,415	1,499	1,539
Total	4,702	4,938	4,861

Source: FAO.

SAWNWOOD PRODUCTION
('000 cubic metres, including railway sleepers)

	2009	2010	2011
Coniferous (softwood)	1,413	1,397	1,251
Broadleaved (hardwood) . . .	68	59	63
Total	1,481	1,456	1,314

Source: FAO.

Fishing

(metric tons, live weight)

	2008	2009	2010
Capture	1,582	1,687	1,653
Roach	176	170	149
European perch	292	342	285
Whitefishes	956	1,020	1,056
Aquaculture	1,214	1,244	1,256
Rainbow trout	1,110	1,140	1,100
Total catch	2,796	2,931	2,909

Source: FAO.

Industry

SELECTED PRODUCTS
('000 metric tons unless otherwise indicated)

	2007	2008	2009
Cement*†	4,000	4,000	4,000
Cigarettes (million)	54,348	n.a.	n.a.
Aluminium (unwrought, primary)*†	25,000	n.a.	n.a.
Flour (wheat)	368	368	373
Chocolate and chocolate products .	181.3	n.a.	n.a.
Motor spirit (petrol, '000 barrels)† .	10,880	11,534	12,045
Distillate fuel oils ('000 barrels)† .	16,203	17,301	17,739
Residual fuel oil ('000 barrels)† .	3,909	3,833	2,482
Electric energy (million kWh)‡ .	67,926	68,939	68,453

* Estimated production.
† Source: US Geological Survey.
‡ Including Liechtenstein.

Source (unless otherwise indicated): UN Industrial Commodity Statistics Database.

2010 ('000 barrels, unless otherwise indicated, estimated production): Cement ('000 metric tons) 4,000; Motor spirit (petrol) 12,000; Distillate fuel oils 18,000; Residual fuel oil 2,500 (Source: US Geological Survey).

2011 ('000 barrels, unless otherwise indicated, estimated production): Cement ('000 metric tons) 4,000; Motor spirit (petrol) 12,000; Distillate fuel oils 18,000; Residual fuel oil 2,500 (Source: US Geological Survey).

Finance

CURRENCY AND EXCHANGE RATES

Monetary Units
  100 Rappen (centimes) = 1 Schweizer Franken (franc suisse) or Swiss franc.

Sterling, Dollar and Euro Equivalents (31 December 2012)
  £1 sterling = 1.446 francs;
  US $1 = 0.917 francs;
  €1 = 1.209 francs;
  100 Swiss francs = £69.137 = $109.10 = €82.69.

Average Exchange Rates (Swiss francs per US $)
  2010 1.0429
  2011 0.8880
  2012 0.9377

GENERAL BUDGET
('000 million Swiss francs)

Revenue*	2008	2009	2010
Tax revenue	122,573	121,128	122,366
Taxes on income, profits and capital gains	74,948	74,320	73,767
Taxes on international trade and transactions	6,239	6,216	6,213
Taxes on goods and services .	29,562	28,841	30,522
Taxes on property	11,824	11,750	11,864
Social contributions	37,133	38,142	38,286
Grants	130	163	157
Other revenue	27,987	27,291	27,810
Total	187,823	186,723	188,620

Expenditure by government function	2008	2009	2010
General public services . . .	26,226	23,458	24,225
Public order and safety . . .	8,463	8,755	9,035
Defence	4,987	5,000	4,777
Economic affairs	20,392	22,860	22,895
Education	29,226	29,420	29,884
Culture and leisure activities . .	4,755	4,827	4,991
Health	10,600	11,240	11,294
Social protection	67,563	72,699	74,611
Housing and community amenities	1,139	1,099	1,173
Environment	4,220	4,563	4,694
Total	177,570	183,920	187,581

* Not including parish taxes.

2011 (million Swiss francs, estimates): Total revenue 198,250; Total expenditure 196,769 (Source: Swiss National Bank).

2012 (million Swiss francs, estimates): Total revenue 198,618; Total expenditure 194,860 (Source: Swiss National Bank).

2013 (million Swiss francs, estimates): Total revenue 202,207; Total expenditure 199,741 (Source: Swiss National Bank).

INTERNATIONAL RESERVES
(US $ million at 31 December)

	2009	2010	2011
Gold (national valuation) . . .	37,055	46,816	52,482
IMF special drawing rights . .	5,391	4,993	4,927
Reserve position in IMF . . .	1,194	1,141	3,341
Foreign exchange	91,614	217,347	271,122
Total	135,254	270,297	331,872

Source: IMF, *International Financial Statistics.*

MONEY SUPPLY
('000 million Swiss francs at 31 December)

	2009	2010	2011
Currency outside banks . . .	49.97	51.50	55.73
Demand deposits at deposit money banks	311.77	335.85	379.93
Total money	361.73	387.35	435.66

Source: IMF, *International Financial Statistics.*

COST OF LIVING
(Consumer Price Index; annual averages; base: December 2010 = 100)

	2010	2011	2012
Foodstuffs	101.6	98.3	97.4
Alcoholic beverages and tobacco	99.4	101.0	102.1
Clothing and footwear	93.2	94.5	88.9
Housing and energy	99.3	101.7	102.5
Household equipment, etc.	100.1	98.8	97.0
Health	100.4	100.2	99.9
Transport	99.4	100.5	98.3
Communication	100.0	100.1	99.4
Education	98.9	100.3	102.0
Recreation and culture	100.5	97.2	94.5
Restaurants and hotels	100.1	101.6	102.2
Other goods and services	100.2	100.4	100.5
All items	99.7	100.0	99.3

NATIONAL ACCOUNTS
(million Swiss francs at current prices)

National Income and Product

	2009	2010	2011*
Compensation of employees	337,539	337,279	350,083
Operating surplus	96,280	115,011	112,802
Domestic factor incomes	433,818	452,290	462,885
Consumption of fixed capital	103,048	103,338	104,972
Gross domestic product (GDP) at factor cost	536,866	555,628	567,856
Indirect taxes	35,677	37,445	38,563
Less Subsidies	18,171	18,759	19,635
GDP in purchasers' values	554,372	574,314	586,784
Factor income received from abroad	99,644	120,795	101,227
Less Factor income paid abroad	87,181	86,798	86,302
Gross national product	566,835	608,311	601,709
Less Consumption of fixed capital	103,048	103,338	104,972
National income in market prices	463,788	504,973	496,737

* Provisional figures.

Expenditure on the Gross Domestic Product

	2009	2010	2011*
Final consumption expenditure	386,189	395,320	401,830
Households and non-profit institutions serving households	324,146	332,066	336,595
General government	62,042	63,254	65,236
Gross capital formation	106,950	114,581	121,777
Gross fixed capital formation	110,409	115,016	119,726
Changes in inventories	−5,357	124	2,195
Acquisitions, less disposals, of valuables	1,898	−559	−144
Total domestic expenditure	493,139	509,902	523,607
Exports of goods and services	279,221	296,963	300,448
Less Imports of goods and services	217,988	232,551	237,271
GDP in market prices	554,372	574,314	586,784

* Provisional figures.

Gross Domestic Product by Economic Activity

	2009	2010	2011*
Agriculture, hunting, forestry and fishing	4,512	4,336	4,308
Mining and quarrying	835	893	807
Manufacturing	95,497	100,183	102,016
Electricity, gas and water supply	11,866	11,456	11,450
Construction	27,651	29,509	31,072
Wholesale and retail trade; repair of motor vehicles and motorcycles	84,262	91,688	91,634
Hotels and restaurants	11,482	11,666	11,479
Transportation, storage and communications	42,673	44,873	46,804
Financial intermediation	61,487	59,846	60,520
Real estate, renting and business activities	48,692	49,271	51,215
Public administration	54,366	55,662	57,181
Education	2,853	2,736	2,785
Health and social work	32,994	33,916	35,007
Other community, social and personal service activities	8,925	8,865	8,642
Private households with employed persons	36,319	38,110	40,018
Sub-total	524,415	543,009	554,940
Taxes on products	32,864	34,210	34,920
Less Subsidies on products	2,908	2,906	3,075
GDP in market prices	554,372	574,314	586,784

* Provisional figures.

BALANCE OF PAYMENTS
(US $ million)

	2009	2010	2011
Exports of goods	219,355	277,432	345,615
Imports of goods	−204,830	−246,037	−320,424
Balance on goods	14,525	31,394	25,191
Exports of services	63,244	64,675	74,297
Imports of services	−38,321	−41,496	−51,655
Balance on goods and services	39,448	54,573	47,833
Primary income received	91,620	117,770	103,880
Primary income paid	−82,911	−86,730	−102,715
Balance on goods, services and primary income	48,157	85,613	48,998
Secondary income received	26,387	24,905	31,296
Secondary income paid	−38,425	−37,056	−44,394
Current balance	36,120	73,462	35,900
Capital account (net)	−3,477	−4,436	−1,605
Direct investment assets	−44,904	−67,832	−45,078
Direct investment liabilities	47,659	21,662	10,077
Portfolio investment assets	−35,481	7,882	4,329
Portfolio investment liabilities	7,019	22,193	−23,909
Financial derivatives and employee stock options (net)	1937	1,154	5,080
Other investment assets	119,229	32,158	−10,015
Other investment liabilities	−49,415	13,576	83,243
Net errors and omissions	−30,550	25,565	−3,356
Reserves and related items	48,137	125,382	54,666

Source: IMF, *International Financial Statistics*.

External Trade

Note: Swiss customs territory includes the Principality of Liechtenstein, the German enclave of Büssingen and the Italian commune of Campione, but excludes the free zone of the Samnaun Valley.

PRINCIPAL COMMODITIES
(million Swiss francs)

Imports c.i.f.	2010	2011	2012
Machinery, equipment and electronics	31,438	30,680	29,408
Precision instruments, watches and jewellery	18,620	18,088	18,710
Chemicals	37,787	37,435	39,362
Textiles, clothing and footwear	8,956	8,880	8,716
Motor vehicles	16,581	16,838	17,073
Total (incl. others)	173,991	174,388	176,517

Exports f.o.b.	2010	2011	2012
Machinery, equipment and electronics	36,435	36,889	33,352
Chemicals	75,909	74,647	78,988
Metals	12,738	13,034	12,011
Watches	16,167	19,304	21,418
Precision instruments	14,395	14,068	14,121
Textiles, clothing and footwear	3,386	3,249	3,115
Total (incl. others)	193,480	197,907	200,902

PRINCIPAL TRADING PARTNERS
(million Swiss francs)*

Imports c.i.f.	2010	2011	2012
Austria	7,860.4	7,903.5	7,664.6
Belgium	4,682.6	4,790.8	4,303.8
China, People's Republic	6,071.6	6,287.5	10,258.6
France	15,218.7	15,436.0	14,937.8
Germany	57,266.6	58,490.7	54,074.6
Ireland	5,853.8	5,880.5	6,755.5
Italy	18,366.6	18,972.9	18,283.8
Japan	3,239.4	465.4	3,670.8
Netherlands	8,271.7	7,997.6	6,306.3
Spain	4,141.3	4,135.2	5,004.4
United Kingdom	6,234.0	5,712.9	7,664.6
USA	8,154.0	7,824.7	9,160.0
Total (incl. others)	173,990.9	174,387.9	176,517.0

Exports f.o.b.	2010	2011	2012
Australia	2,169.2	2,348.4	2,472.7
Austria	6,115.0	5,986.8	5,772.6
Belgium	3,638.2	3,994.7	4,684.9
Brazil	2,314.7	2,228.0	2,350.9
Canada	2,743.0	2,751.5	3,000.0
China, People's Republic	7,079.2	8,448.8	7,416.6
France	15,144.1	14,394.4	14,356.9
Germany	37,780.0	39,872.6	39,914.8
Hong Kong	5,297.5	6,316.0	6,969.4
India	2,547.5	2,932.6	2,636.2
Italy	15,546.9	15,802.5	14,633.5
Japan	6,426.4	6,405.9	6,861.6
Korea, Republic	2,236.5	2,313.0	2,403.1
Netherlands	5,741.0	5,130.6	5,144.6
Singapore	2,879.8	3,119.2	3,559.5
Spain	6,345.7	5,775.1	5,446.5
Turkey	2,109.0	2,144.3	1,835.6
United Kingdom	9,077.6	8,255.9	5,772.6
USA	19,478.3	19,994.8	22,297.0
Total (incl. others)	193,479.8	197,907.0	200,902.2

* Imports by country of production; exports by country of consumption.

Transport

RAILWAY TRAFFIC

	2009	2010	2011*
Passengers carried (million)†	431	446	n.a.
Passenger-km (million)	18,571	19,177	19,471
Freight carried (million metric tons)	61.8	64.0	n.a.
Freight ton-km (million)	10,565	11,074	11,526

* Provisional.
† Excluding multi-leg journeys.

ROAD TRAFFIC
(motor vehicles in use at 30 September)

	2010	2011	2012
Passenger cars	4,075,825	4,163,003	4,254,725
Buses and coaches	52,751	55,422	61,435
Goods vehicles	335,200	348,553	361,926
Agricultural vehicles	186,485	187,130	188,358
Other industrial vehicles	58,492	60,324	62,219
Motorcycles	651,202	665,870	679,822

INLAND WATERWAYS
(freight traffic at port of Basel, '000 metric tons)

	1996	1997	1998
Goods loaded	876.9	837.5	688.4
Goods unloaded	6,283.4	7,002.4	7,420.3

Source: Federal Department of Transport.

SHIPPING

Flag Registered Fleet
(at 31 December)

	2010	2011	2012
Number of vessels	64	67	69
Total displacement ('000 grt)	724.7	762.6	798.4

Source: Lloyd's List Intelligence (www.lloydslistintelligence.com).

CIVIL AVIATION
(traffic on scheduled services)

	2007	2008	2009
Kilometres flown (million)	181	220	216
Passengers carried ('000)	12,157	14,353	14,701
Passenger-km (million)	25,150	30,268	29,560
Total ton-km (million)	3,660	4,225	4,023

Source: UN, *Statistical Yearbook*.

Passengers carried ('000): 21,477 in 2010 (Source: World Bank, World Development Indicators database).

Tourism

FOREIGN TOURIST ARRIVALS
(at hotels and similar establishments)

Country of residence	2008	2009	2010
Austria	189,159	187,528	195,190
Belgium	246,741	241,830	240,784
France	670,663	685,842	700,578
Germany	2,344,337	2,294,411	2,237,941
Italy	552,953	546,564	520,542
Japan	277,657	275,505	297,562
Netherlands	412,559	396,953	383,039
Spain	215,365	212,622	221,311
United Kingdom	825,719	691,409	732,050
USA	651,876	609,878	680,216
Total (incl. others)	8,608,337	8,293,918	8,628,284

Tourism receipts (million Swiss francs): 15,377 in 2009; 15,550 in 2010; 15,577 in 2011 (provisional).

Source: mainly World Tourism Organization.

Communications Media

	2009	2010	2011
Telephones ('000 main lines in use)	4,644.2	4,378.0	4,612.8
Mobile cellular telephones ('000 subscribers)	9,322.6	9,527.0*	10,122.1*
Internet subscribers ('000)	2,847.2	2,993.5	3,150.3
Broadband subscribers ('000)	2,739.1	2,908.1*	3,077.9*
Books published (titles)	11,105	10,568	10,972

* Provisional figure.

Source: mainly International Telecommunication Union.

Education

(2010/11 unless otherwise indicated)

	Institutions*	Teachers	Students
Pre-primary	5,006	14,226†	148,573
Compulsory primary‡	} 6,141	{ 44,117†	} 769,314§
Compulsory secondary‡		36,780†	
Upper secondary	893	28,247†	
General	n.a.	11,287†	} 351,296
Vocational	n.a.	16,960	
Higher	382	101,169	258,623
Vocational	n.a.	n.a.	52,094
Universities of applied sciences	n.a.	45,422‖	75,035
Universities	n.a.	55,747‖	131,494

* 2004.
† May include double-counted data.
‡ Excluding schools with special curriculums.
§ 2009/10.
‖ Including teaching assistants and administrative and technical personnel.

Pupil-teacher ratio (primary education, UNESCO estimate): 12.6 in 2007/08 (Source: UNESCO Institute for Statistics).

Directory

The Government

FEDERAL COUNCIL
(May 2013)

President of the Swiss Confederation for 2013 and Head of the Federal Department of Defence, Civil Protection and Sports: UELI MAURER (Swiss People's Party).

Vice-President of the Swiss Confederation for 2013 and Head of the Federal Department of Foreign Affairs: DIDIER BURKHALTER (FDP.The Liberals).

Head of the Federal Department of Economic Affairs, Education and Research: JOHANN N. SCHNEIDER-AMMANN (FDP.The Liberals).

Head of the Federal Department of Finance: EVELINE WIDMER-SCHLUMPF (Conservative Democratic Party).

Head of the Federal Department of Home Affairs: ALAIN BERSET (Social Democratic Party).

Head of the Federal Department of Justice and Police: SIMONETTA SOMMARUGA (Social Democratic Party).

Head of the Federal Department of the Environment, Transport, Energy and Communications: DORIS LEUTHARD (Christian Democratic People's Party).

Chancellor of the Swiss Confederation: CORINA CASANOVA (Christian Democratic People's Party).

FEDERAL DEPARTMENTS

Federal Chancellery: Bundeshaus West, 3003 Bern; tel. 313222111; fax 313223706; e-mail info@bk.admin.ch; internet www.bk.admin.ch.

Federal Department of Defence, Civil Protection and Sports: Schwanengasse 2, 3003 Bern; tel. 313222111; fax 313245104; e-mail postmaster.vbs@gs-vbs.admin.ch; internet www.vbs.admin.ch.

Federal Department of Economic Affairs, Education and Research: Schwanengasse 2, 3003 Bern; tel. 313222007; fax 313222194; e-mail info@gs-wbf.admin.ch; internet www.wbf.admin.ch.

Federal Department of the Environment, Transport, Energy and Communications: Bundeshaus Nord, Kochergasse 10, 3003 Bern; tel. 313225511; fax 313242692; e-mail info@gs-uvek.admin.ch; internet www.uvek.admin.ch.

Federal Department of Finance: Bernerhof, Bundesgasse 3, 3003 Bern; tel. 313222111; fax 313226187; e-mail info@gs-efd.admin.ch; internet www.efd.admin.ch.

Federal Department of Foreign Affairs: Bundeshaus West, 3003 Bern; tel. 313222111; fax 313249047; e-mail info@eda.admin.ch; internet www.eda.admin.ch.

Federal Department of Home Affairs: Inselgasse 1, 3003 Bern; tel. 313228041; fax 313227901; e-mail info@gs-edi.admin.ch; internet www.edi.admin.ch.

Federal Department of Justice and Police: Bundeshaus West, 3003 Bern; tel. 313222111; fax 313227832; e-mail info@gs-ejpd.admin.ch; internet www.ejpd.admin.ch.

Legislature

BUNDESVERSAMMLUNG/ASSEMBLÉE FÉDÉRALE
(Federal Assembly)

Nationalrat/Conseil National
(National Council)

Parlamentsgebäude, 3003 Bern; tel. 313228790; e-mail information@pd.admin.ch.

President: MAYA GRAF (2012/13).

General Election, 23 October 2011

	Seats
Swiss People's Party	54
Social Democratic Party	46
FDP.The Liberals	30
Christian Democratic People's Party	28
Green Party of Switzerland	15
Green Liberal Party of Switzerland	12
Conservative Democratic Party	9
Evangelical People's Party	2
Ticino League	2
Christian Social Party	1
Geneva Citizens' Movement	1
Total	**200**

Ständerat/Conseil des Etats
(Council of States)

Parlamentsgebäude, 3003 Bern; tel. 313228790; e-mail information@pd.admin.ch.

President: FILLIPPO LOMBARDI (2012/13).

Elections, 2011

	Seats
Christian Democratic People's Party	13
FDP.The Liberals	11
Social Democratic Party	11
Swiss People's Party	5
Green Party of Switzerland	2
Green Liberal Party of Switzerland	2
Conservative Democratic Party	1
Others	1
Total	**46**

Note: Members are elected by canton; method and period of election differs from canton to canton

Political Organizations

Alternative Liste (AL) (Alternative List): Postfach 1005, 8026 Zürich; tel. 442421945; fax 442421960; e-mail sekretariat@al-zh.ch; internet al-zh.ch; f. 2007; cantonal orgs Zürich, Schaffhausen and Aargau.

Bürgerlich-Demokratische Partei (BDP) (Conservative Democratic Party): Postfach 119, 3000 Bern 6; tel. 313521482; fax 313521471; e-mail mail@bdp.info; internet www.bdp.info; f. Nov. 2008 by fmr mems of Swiss People's Party (q.v.); cantonal orgs in Aargau, Basel-Landschaft, Basel-Stadt, Bern, Fribourg, Glarus, Graubünden, Luzern, Neuchâtel, St Gallen, Schwyz, Solothurn, Thurgau, Valais, Vaud and Zürich; Pres. MARTIN LANDOLT.

Christlichdemokratische Volkspartei der Schweiz/Parti démocrate-chrétien suisse (CVP) (Christian Democratic People's Party): Klaraweg 6, Postfach 5835, 3001 Bern; tel. 313573333; fax 313522430; e-mail info@cvp.ch; internet www.cvp.ch; f. 1912; advocates a Christian outlook on world affairs, federalism and Christian social reform by means of professional asscns; non-sectarian; Pres. CHRISTOPHE DARBELLAY; Gen. Sec. BÉATRICE WERTLI; Leader of Parliamentary Group URS SCHWALLER.

Christlichsoziale Partei/Parti chrétien-social (CSP) (Christian Social Party): Eichenstr. 79, 3184 Wünnewil; tel. 264963074; e-mail info@csp-pcs.ch; internet www.csp-pcs.ch; f. 1997; Pres. MARIUS ACHERMANN; Sec. MARLIES SCHAFER-JUNGO.

Eidgenössisch-Demokratische Union/Union Démocratique Fédérale (EDU) (Federal Democratic Union): Postfach, 3601 Thun; tel. 332223637; fax 332223744; e-mail info@edu-schweiz.ch; internet www.edu-schweiz.ch; conservative Christian principles; Pres. HANS MOSER.

Evangelische Volkspartei der Schweiz/Parti évangélique suisse (EVP) (Evangelical People's Party): Nägelisgasse 9, Postfach 294, 3000 Bern 7; tel. 313517171; fax 313517102; e-mail info@evppev.ch; internet www.evppev.ch; f. 1919; Pres. HEINER STUDER; Gen. Sec. JOEL BLUNIER.

FDP.Die Liberalen/PLR.Les Libéraux-Radicaux (FDP.The Liberals): Neuengasse 20, Postfach 6136, 3001 Bern; tel. 313203535; fax 313203500; e-mail info@fdp.ch; internet www.fdp.ch; f. 2009 by merger of the Radical Democratic Party (Freisinnig-Demokratische Partei der Schweiz/Parti radical-démocratique suisse—FDP) and the Liberal Party of Switzerland (Liberale Partei der Schweiz/Parti liberal suisse); predecessor org. led the movement that gave rise to the Federative State and the Constitution of 1848;

promotes a strong Fed. Govt, while respecting the legitimate rights of the cantons and all the minorities; liberal democratic principles; Pres. PHILIPP MÜLLER; Leader of Parliamentary Group GABI HUBER; Gen. Sec. STEFAN BRUPBACHER.

Freiheits-Partei der Schweiz/Die Auto-Partei (Freedom Party of Switzerland/The Automobile Party): Eigasse 13, Postfach 332, 4622 Egerkingen; tel. 623983838; fax 623984848; e-mail auto-partei@bluewin.ch; internet www.freiheits-partei.ch; f. 1985 to support motorists' rights; subsequently campaigned for restricted immigration; Pres. JÜRG SCHERRER.

Grüne Partei der Schweiz/Les Verts—Parti écologiste suisse (GPS) (Green Party of Switzerland): Waisenhauspl. 21, 3011 Bern; tel. 313126660; fax 313126662; e-mail gruene@gruene.ch; internet www.gruene.ch; f. 1983; Co-Pres ADÈLE THORENS, REGULA RYTZ; Gen. Sec. MIRIAM BEHRENS.

Grünliberale Partei Schweiz (GLP) (Green Liberal Party of Switzerland): Postfach 367, 3000 Bern 7; tel. 313230530; e-mail schweiz@grunliberale.ch; internet www.grunliberale.ch; f. 2004; Pres. MARTIN BÄUMLE; Gen. Sec. SANDRA GURTNER-OESCH.

Lega dei Ticinesi (Ticino League): Via Monte Boglia 3, CP 2311, 6904 Lugano; tel. 919731048; fax 919731040; internet www.legaticinesi.ch; f. 1991; 1,500 mems; Pres. (vacant); Sec. MAURO MALANDRA.

Liberal-Demokratische Partei Basel-Stadt (Die Liberalen) (Liberal-Democratic Party Basel-City): Postfach, 4010 Basel; tel. 612721236; fax 612721743; e-mail info@ldp.ch; internet www.ldp.ch; Pres. PATRICIA VON FALKENSTEIN.

Mouvement Citoyens Genevois (MCG) (Geneva Citizens' Movement): CP 340, 1211 Geneva 17; tel. 228497333; fax 223214507; e-mail info@mcge.ch; internet www.mcge.ch; f. 2005; Pres. ROGER GOLAY.

Partei der Arbeit der Schweiz/Parti suisse du travail (Parti ouvrier et populaire) (Workers' Party): Postfach 533, 3000 Bern 22; tel. 442417722; e-mail secretariat@pst.ch; internet www.pst.ch; f. 1944; Pres. NORBERTO CRIVELLI.

Schweizer Demokraten/Démocrates suisses (SD) (Swiss Democrats): Postfach 8116, 3001 Bern; tel. 319742010; fax 319742011; e-mail schweizer-demokraten@bluewin.ch; internet www.schweizer-demokraten.ch; f. 1961 as Nationale Aktion gegen die Überfremdung von Volk und Heimat/Action nationale; present name adopted 1990; 6,000 mems; main objectives are preservation of the country's political independence and of individual freedom, protection of the environment, and restriction of immigration; Pres. RUDOLF KELLER; Gen. Sec. ADRIAN PULVER.

Schweizerische Volkspartei/Union démocratique du centre (SVP) (Swiss People's Party): Brückfeldstr. 18, Postfach 8252, 3001 Bern 26; tel. 313005858; fax 313005859; e-mail gs@svp.ch; internet www.svp.ch; f. 1971; Pres. TONI BRUNNER; Gen. Sec. MARTIN BALTISSER.

Sozialdemokratische Partei der Schweiz/Parti socialiste suisse (SP) (Social Democratic Party): Spitalgasse 34, 3001 Bern; tel. 313296969; fax 313296970; e-mail sekretariat@sp-ps.ch; internet www.sp-ps.ch; f. 1888; bases its policy on democratic socialism; mem. of Socialist International and assoc. mem. of Party of European Socialists; c. 33,000 mems; Pres. CHRISTIAN LEVRAT; Co-Gen. Secs FLAVIA WASSERFALLEN, LEYLA GÜL.

Jungsozialistinnen (JUSO) (Young Socialists): Spitalgasse 34, Postfach, 3001 Bern; tel. 313296999; fax 313296970; e-mail info@juso.ch; internet www.juso.ch; f. 1906; affiliated to Social Democratic Party; Gen. Sec. KRISTINA SCHÜPBACH.

Partito Socialista, sezione ticinese del PSS (Socialist Party): piazza Governo 4, 6500 Bellinzona; tel. 918259462; fax 918259601; e-mail segreteria@ps-ticino.ch; internet www.ps-ticino.ch; f. 1992; fmrly the Partito Socialista Unitario; Leader PELIN KANDEMIR BORDOLI.

Diplomatic Representation

EMBASSIES IN SWITZERLAND

Afghanistan: 623 ave de France, 1202 Geneva; tel. 227311616; fax 227314510; e-mail mission.afghanistan@bluewin.ch; internet www.mission-afghanistan.ch; Ambassador NANGUYALAI TARZI.

Albania: Pourtalèsstr. 45A, 3074 Muri bei Bern; tel. 319526010; fax 319526012; e-mail emalb.ch@bluewin.ch; Ambassador MEHMET ELEZAJ.

Algeria: Willadingweg 74, 3000 Bern 15; tel. 313501050; fax 313501059; e-mail ambalg.berne@bluewin.ch; internet www.ambassade-algerie.ch; Ambassador EL-HAOUÉS RIACHE.

Angola: Thunstr. 73, 3006 Bern; tel. 313518585; fax 313518586; e-mail berna@ambassadeangola.ch; internet www.ambassadeangola.ch; Ambassador OSVALDO DOS SANTOS VARELA.

Argentina: Jungfraustr. 1, 3005 Bern; tel. 313564343; fax 313564340; internet www.suiza.embajada-argentina.gov.ar; Ambassador ANTONIO GUSTAVO TROMBETTA.

Armenia: 28 ave du Mail, 1205 Geneva; tel. 223201100; fax 223206148; e-mail mission.armenia@bluewin.ch; internet www .switzerland.mfa.am; Ambassador CHARLES AZNAVOUR.

Austria: Kirchenfeldstr. 77–79, 3005 Bern; tel. 313565252; fax 313515664; e-mail bern-ob@bmeia.gv.at; internet www .aussenministerium.at/bern; Ambassador JÜRGEN MEINDL.

Azerbaijan: Kramburgstr. 10, 3006 Bern; tel. 313505040; fax 313505041; e-mail bern@mission.mfa.gov.az; internet www .azembassy.ch; Ambassador AKRAM ZEYNALLI.

Bangladesh: 65 rue de Lausanne, 1202 Geneva; tel. 229068020; fax 227384616; e-mail mission.bangladesh@ties.itu.int; Ambassador ABDUL HANNAN.

Belarus: Quartierweg 6, CP 438, 3074 Muri bei Bern; tel. 319527914; fax 319527616; e-mail swiss@belembassy.org; internet switzerland.mfa.gov.by; Chargé d'affaires a.i. LEONID SHINKEVICH.

Belgium: Jubiläumsstr. 41, Postfach 150, 3000 Bern; tel. 313500150; fax 313500165; e-mail bern@diplobel.fed.be; internet www.diplomatie.be/bern; Ambassador JAN LUYKX.

Benin: 28 chemin du Petit-Saconnex, 1209 Geneva; tel. 229068460; fax 229068461; e-mail info@missionbenin.ch; Ambassador SÉRAPHIN LISSASSI.

Bhutan: 17–19 chemin du Champ-d'Anier, 1209 Geneva; tel. 227990890; fax 227990899; e-mail mission.bhutan@ties.itu.int; Ambassador DAW PENJO.

Bosnia and Herzegovina: Thorackerstr. 3, 3074 Muri bei Bern; tel. 313511052; fax 313511079; e-mail emb-ch-brn@vtxmail.ch; Ambassador BORO BRONZA.

Botswana: 80 rue de Lausanne, 5ème étage, 1202 Geneva; tel. 229061060; fax 229061061; e-mail botgen@bluewin.ch; Ambassador MOTHUSI BRUCE RABASHA PALAI.

Brazil: Monbijoustr. 68, 3007 Bern; tel. 313718515; fax 313710525; e-mail brasemb.berna@itamaraty.gov.br; internet berna.itamaraty .gov.br; Ambassador IGOR KIPMAN.

Bulgaria: Bernastr. 2–4, 3005 Bern; tel. 313511455; fax 313510064; e-mail bulembassy@bluewin.ch; internet www.mfa.bg/embassies/ switzerland; Ambassador MEGLENA IVANOVA PLUGTSCHIEVA-ALEXANDROVA.

Burkina Faso: 51 ave Blanc, 1202 Geneva; tel. 227346330; fax 227346331; e-mail info@ambaburkinafaso-ch.org; internet www .ambaburkinafaso-ch.org; Ambassador PROSPER VOKOUMA.

Burundi: 44 rue de Lausanne, 1201 Geneva; tel. 227327705; fax 227327734; e-mail mission.burundi@bluewin.ch; Ambassador PIERRE CLAVER NDAYIRAGIJE.

Cambodia: 3 chemin de Taverney, CP 213, 1218 Le Grand-Saconnex; tel. 227887773; fax 227887774; e-mail cambodge@ bluewin.ch; internet www.cambodiaembassy.ch; Ambassador SUN SUON.

Cameroon: Brunnadernrain 29, 3006 Bern; tel. 313524737; fax 313524736; e-mail info@ambacamberne.ch; internet www .ambacamberne.ch; Ambassador LÉONARD HENRI BINDZI.

Canada: Kirchenfeldstr. 88, 3005 Bern; POB 234, 3006 Bern; tel. 313573200; fax 313573210; e-mail bern@international.gc.ca; internet www.canadainternational.gc.ca/switzerland-suisse; Ambassador ROBERTA SANTI.

Cape Verde: 47 ave Blanc, 1202 Geneva; tel. (22) 7313336; fax 227313540; e-mail cap.vert@bluewin.ch; Ambassador JOSÉ LUIS MONTEIRO.

Central African Republic: 9 chemin de Taverney, 1218 Le Grand-Saconnex; tel. 227888883; fax 227888885; e-mail ambacage@yahoo .fr; Ambassador LÉOPOLD SAMBA.

Chile: Eigerpl. 5, 12th Floor, 3007 Bern; tel. 313700050; fax 313700055; e-mail embajada@embachile.ch; internet chileabroad .gov.cl/suiza; Chargé d'affaires a.i. JULIO MÉNDEZ OLAVE.

China, People's Republic: Kalcheggweg 10, 3006 Bern; tel. 313527333; fax 313514573; e-mail china-embassy@bluewin.ch; internet www.china-embassy.ch; Chargé d'affaires a.i. YANG XIAORONG.

Colombia: Dufourstr. 47, 3005 Bern; tel. 313501400; fax 313501405; e-mail eberna@cancilleria.gov.co; internet www.emcol.ch; Ambassador BEATRIZ LONDONO SOTO.

Congo, Democratic Republic: Sulgenheimweg 21, CP 5261, 3001 Bern; tel. 313713538; fax 313727466; e-mail rdcambassy@bluewin .ch; Chargé d'affaires a.i. SÉBASTIEN MUTOMB MUJING.

Congo, Republic: 8 rue Chabray, 1201 Geneva; tel. 227318821; fax 227318817; e-mail missioncongo@bluewin.ch; Ambassador LUC-JOSEPH OKIO.

Costa Rica: Marktgasse 51, 3011 Berne; tel. 313727887; fax 313727834; e-mail costa.rica@bluewin.ch; Ambassador ISABEL MONTERO DE LA CÁMARA.

Côte d'Ivoire: Thormannstr. 51, CP 170, 3005 Bern; tel. 313508080; fax 313508081; e-mail acibe-sp1@acibe.org; internet www.acibe.org; Ambassador KOUADIO ADJOUMANI.

Croatia: Thunstr. 45, 3005 Bern; tel. 313520275; fax 313520373; e-mail vrhbern@mvep.hr; Ambassador ALEKSANDAR HEINA.

Cuba: Gesellschaftsstr. 8, CP 5275, 3012 Bern; tel. 313022111; fax 313029830; e-mail embacuba.berna@bluewin.ch; internet www .cubadiplomatica.cu/suiza; Ambassador MARIA DEL PILAR FERNANDEZ OTERO.

Czech Republic: Muristr. 53, CP 537, 3000 Bern 31; tel. 313504070; fax 313504098; e-mail bern@embassy.mzv.cz; internet www.mfa.cz/ bern; Ambassador Dr BORIS LAZAR.

Denmark: Thunstr. 95, 3006 Bern 31; tel. 313505454; fax 313505464; e-mail brnamb@um.dk; internet www.ambbern.um.dk; Ambassador HANS KLINGENBERG.

Dominican Republic: Weltpoststr. 4, CP 22, 3000 Bern 15; tel. 313511585; fax 313511587; e-mail embaj.rep-dom@sunrise.ch; Ambassador TERESITA MIGDALIA TORRES GARCÍA.

Ecuador: Kramgasse 54, 3011 Bern; tel. 313516254; fax 313512771; e-mail embecusuiza@bluewin.ch; internet www .embajadadelecuadorenberna.ch; Ambassador RAFAEL ALFONSO PAREDES PROAÑO.

Egypt: Elfenauweg 61, 3006 Bern; tel. 313528012; fax 313520625; Ambassador SAHER TAWFIK HAMZA.

Eritrea: 9 rue de Vermont, CP 85, 1211 Geneva; tel. 227404940; fax 227404949; e-mail eritrean.embassy@bluewin.ch; Chargé d'affaires a.i. ATO BEREKET WOLDEYOHANNES.

Ethiopia: 56 rue de Moillebeau, CP 338, 1211 Geneva 19; tel. 229197010; fax 229197029; e-mail mission.ethiopia@ties.itu.int; internet www.ethiopianmission.ch; Ambassador MINELIK ALEMU GETAHUN.

Finland: Weltpoststr. 4, Postfach 11, 3015 Bern 15; tel. 313504100; fax 313504107; e-mail sanomat.brn@formin.fi; internet www .finlandia.ch; Ambassador ALPO RUSI.

France: Schosshaldenstr. 46, 3006 Bern; tel. 313592111; fax 313592191; e-mail presse@ambafrance-ch.org; internet www .ambafrance-ch.org; Ambassador MICHEL DUCLOS.

Georgia: Mottastr. 3, 3005 Bern; tel. 313515855; fax 313515862; e-mail geoembassy.bern@bluewin.ch; internet www.switzerland .mfa.gov.ge; Ambassador IRAKLI KURASHVILI.

Germany: Willadingweg 83, Postfach 250, 3000 Bern 15; tel. 313594111; fax 313594444; e-mail info@bern.diplo.de; internet www.bern.diplo.de; Ambassador KLAUS-PETER GOTTWALD.

Ghana: Belpstr. 11, Postfach, 3001 Bern; tel. 313817852; fax 313814941; e-mail ghanaemb@tcnet.ch; internet www .ghanaembassy.ch; Ambassador SAMMIE PESKY EDDICO.

Greece: Weltpostr. 4, 3015 Bern; tel. 313561414; fax 313681272; e-mail gremb.brn@mfa.gr; Ambassador JOHN MOURIKIS.

Holy See: Thunstr. 60, CP 259, 3006 Bern (Apostolic Nunciature); tel. 313526040; fax 313525064; e-mail nunziaturach@yahoo.com; Apostolic Nuncio Most Rev. DIEGO CAUSERO (Titular Archbishop of Gradum).

Hungary: Muristr. 31, CP 216, 3000 Bern 15; tel. 313528572; fax 313512001; e-mail brn.missions@mfa.gov.hu; internet www.mfa.gov .hu/emb/bern; Ambassador ISTVAN NAGY.

India: Kirchenfeldstr. 28, 3005 Bern; tel. 313501130; fax 313511557; e-mail india@indembassybern.ch; internet www.indembassybern .ch; Ambassador CHITRA NARAYANAN.

Indonesia: Elfenauweg 51, Postfach 270, 3000 Bern; tel. 313520983; fax 313516765; e-mail info@indonesia-bern.org; internet www .indonesia-bern.org; Ambassador DJOKO SUSILO.

Iran: Thunstr. 68, CP 227, 3006 Bern 6; tel. 313510801; fax 313515652; e-mail secretariat@iranembassy.ch; internet www .iranembassy.ch; Ambassador ALIREZA SALARI SHARIFABAD.

Iraq: Elfenstr. 6, 3006 Bern; tel. 313514043; fax 313518312; e-mail bernemb@iraqmofamail.net; internet www.irakembassy.ch; Ambassador PIROT AHMED IBRAHIM IBRAHIM.

Ireland: Kirchenfeldstr. 68, Postfach 262, 3005 Bern; tel. 313521442; fax 313511455; e-mail berne@dfa.ie; internet www .embassyofireland.ch; Ambassador MARTIN BURKE.

Israel: Alpenstr. 32, 3000 Bern 6; tel. 313563500; fax 313563556; e-mail press@bern.mfa.gov.il; internet bern.mfa.gov.il; Ambassador YIGAL CASPI.

Italy: Elfenstr. 14, 3000 Bern 16; tel. 313500777; fax 313500711; e-mail ambasciata.berna@esteri.it; internet www.ambberna.esteri .it; Ambassador CARLA ZUPPETTI.

Jamaica: 23 ave de France, 1202 Geneva; tel. 229080760; fax 227384420; e-mail info@jamaicamission.ch; Ambassador WAYNE MCCOOK.

Japan: Engestr. 53, 3000 Bern 9; tel. 313002222; fax 313002255; e-mail eojs@bluewin.ch; internet www.ch.emb-japan.go.jp; Ambassador RYUHEI MAEDA.

Jordan: Thorackerstr. 3, 3074 Muri bei Bern; tel. 313840404; fax 313840405; e-mail info@jordanembassy.ch; Ambassador NABIL SALEEM MASARWEH.

Kazakhstan: Melchenbühlweg 79, 3006 Bern; tel. 313517969; fax 313517975; e-mail kasachische.botschaft@freesurf.ch; internet www .kazakhstan-bern.ch; Ambassador MUKHTAR TILEUBERDI.

Korea, Democratic People's Republic: Pourtalèsstr. 43, 3074 Muri bei Bern; tel. 319516621; fax 319515704; e-mail dprk.embassy@ bluewin.ch; Ambassador SO SE-PYONG.

Korea, Republic: Kalcheggweg 38, 3006 Bern 15; tel. 313562444; fax 313562450; e-mail swiss@mofat.go.kr; internet che-berne.mofat .go.kr; Ambassador BAE YOUNG-HAN.

Kosovo: Amthausgasse 3, 3011 Bern; tel. 313100690; fax 313100691; e-mail embassy.switzerland@ks-gov.net; Ambassador NAIM MALAJ.

Kuwait: Brunadernrain 19, CP 458, 3006 Bern; tel. 313567000; fax 313567001; e-mail info@kuwaitembassy.ch; internet www .kuwaitembassy.ch; Ambassador Dr SUHAIL KHALIL YOUSEF SHUHAI-BER.

Kyrgyzstan: 4–6 rue du Lac, 1ère étage, 1207 Geneva; tel. 227079220; fax 227079221; e-mail kyrgyzmission@bluewin.ch; internet www.kyrgyzmission.net; Ambassador GULNARA T. ISKA-KOVA.

Laos: 14 bis route de Colovrex, 1218 Le Grand-Saconnex; tel. 227982441; fax 227982440; e-mail laomission_geneva@bluewin.ch; Ambassador YONG CHANTHALANGSY.

Lebanon: Thunstr. 10, 3074 Muri bei Bern; tel. 319506565; fax 319506566; e-mail ambalibch@hotmail.com; internet ambassadeliban.ch; Chargé d'affaires a.i. ASSAF DOUMIT.

Lesotho: 45–47 rue de Lausanne, 2ème étage, 1201 Geneva; tel. 229061050; fax 229000525; e-mail mission.lesotho@ties.itu.int; Chargé d'affaires a.i. ALPHONCE LEFEU RAMONE.

Libya: Tavelweg 2, 3006 Bern 31; tel. 313500122; fax 313511325; e-mail libya_bern@bluewin.ch; Ambassador SLIMAN BOUCHUIGUIR.

Liechtenstein: Willadingweg 65, Postfach, 3000 Bern 15; tel. 313576411; fax 313576415; e-mail info@bbrn.llv.li; internet www .bern.liechtenstein.li; Ambassador Dr DORIS FRICK-BURKARD.

Lithuania: Kramgasse 12, 3011 Bern; tel. 313525291; fax 313525292; e-mail amb.ch@urm.lt; internet ch.mfa.lt; Ambassador JONAS RUDALEVIČIUS.

Luxembourg: Kramgasse 45, Postfach 619, 3000 Bern 8; tel. 313114732; fax 313110019; e-mail berne.am@mae.etat.lu; internet berne.mae.lu/ge; Ambassador JEAN HENRI FALTZ.

Macedonia, former Yugoslav republic: Kirchenfeldstr. 30, 3005 Bern; tel. 313520002; fax 313520037; e-mail bern@mfa.gov.mk; Chargé d'affaires a.i. EKREM EBIBI.

Madagascar: 32 ave de Riant-Parc, 1209 Geneva; tel. 227401650; fax 227401616; e-mail ambamadsuisse@bluewin.ch; internet www .madagascar-diplomatie.ch; Ambassador ALBERT CAMILLE VITA.

Malaysia: Jungfraustr. 1, 3005 Bern; tel. 313504700; fax 313504702; e-mail malberne@kln.gov.my; Ambassador HO MAY YONG.

Mali: 20 route de Pré-Bois, 1215 Geneva 15 Aéroport; tel. 227100960; fax 227100696; e-mail malisuisse@yahoo.fr; Ambassador SIDIKI LAMINE SOW.

Mexico: Weltpoststr. 20, 3015 Bern; tel. 313574747; fax 313574749; e-mail embamex1@swissonline.ch; internet www.sre.gob.mx/suiza; Chargé d'affaires a.i. JOSÉ ROBLES AGUILAR.

Moldova: 28 chemin du Petit-Saconnex, 1209 Geneva; tel. 227339103; fax 227339104; e-mail geneva@mfa.md; Ambassador VICTOR MORARU.

Monaco: Gryphenhübeliweg 7, 3006 Bern; tel. 313562858; fax 313562855; e-mail ambassademonaco@bluewin.ch; Ambassador CAROLE HENRIETTE JEANNE LANTERI.

Montenegro: 147 rue de Lausanne, 7ème étage, 1202 Geneva; tel. 227326680; fax 227326682; e-mail missionofmontenegro@bluewin .ch; Ambassador LJUBISA PEROVIĆ.

Morocco: Helvetiastr. 42, 3005 Bern; tel. 313510362; fax 313510364; e-mail sifamaberne2@bluewin.ch; internet www .amb-maroc.ch; Chargé d'affaires a.i. MUHAMMAD BALBACHA.

Nepal: 81 rue de la Servette, 1202 Geneva; tel. 227332600; fax 227332722; e-mail mission.nepal@bluewin.ch; internet www .nepalmissiongeneva.org; Ambassador SHANKER DAS BAIRAGI.

Netherlands: Seftigenstr. 7, 3007 Bern; tel. 313508700; fax 313508710; e-mail ben@minbuza.nl; internet www.nlembassy.ch; Ambassador Dr ENGELBERTUS TWAALFHOVEN.

Nigeria: Zieglerstr. 45, Postfach 574, 3007 Bern; tel. 313842600; fax 313842626; e-mail info@nigerianbern.org; internet www .nigerianbern.org; Ambassador AKUABATA FIDELIA NJEZE.

Norway: Bubenbergpl. 10, Postfach 5264, 3011 Bern; tel. 313105555; fax 313105550; e-mail emb.bern@mfa.no; internet www.amb-norwegen.ch; Ambassador ROLF TROLLE ANDERSEN.

Pakistan: Bernastr. 47, 3005 Bern; tel. 313501790; fax 313501799; e-mail parepberne@bluewin.ch; Ambassador MUHAMMAD SALEEM.

Paraguay: Kramgasse 58, Postfach 523, 3000 Bern 8; tel. 313123222; fax 313123432; e-mail embapar@embapar.ch; Ambassador RODOLFO LUIS GONZÁLEZ GARABELLI.

Peru: Thunstr. 36, 3005 Bern; tel. 313518555; fax 313518570; e-mail info@embaperu.ch; internet www.embaperu.ch; Ambassador JUAN CARLOS GAMARRA.

Philippines: Kirchenfeldstr. 73–75, 3005 Bern; tel. 313501717; fax 313522602; e-mail info@philembassyberne.ch; internet www .philembassyberne.ch; Ambassador LESLIE BAJA.

Poland: Elfenstr. 20A, 3006 Bern 15; tel. 313580202; fax 313580216; e-mail berno.amb.sekretariat@msz.gov.pl; internet berno.msz.gov .pl; Ambassador JAROSŁAW STARZYK.

Portugal: Weltpoststr. 20, 3015 Bern; tel. 313528668; fax 313514432; e-mail embassy.portugal@scber.dgaccp.pt; Ambassador JOÃO NUGENT RAMOS PINTO.

Romania: Kirchenfeldstr. 78, 3005 Bern; tel. 313523522; fax 313526455; e-mail ambasada@roamb.ch; internet berna.mae.ro; Ambassador ANCA ELENA OPRIŞ.

Russia: Brunnadernrain 37, 3006 Bern; tel. 313520566; fax 313525595; e-mail rusbotschaft@bluewin.ch; internet www .switzerland.mid.ru; Ambassador ALEKSANDR GOLOVIN.

Rwanda: 37–39 rue de Vermont, 4ème étage, 1202 Geneva; tel. 229191000; fax 229191001; e-mail ambageneve@minaffet.gov.rw; internet switzerland.embassy.gov.rw; Ambassador SOLINE NYIRAHA-BIMANA.

Saudi Arabia: Kirchenfeldstr. 64, 3005 Bern; tel. 313521555; fax 313514581; e-mail chemb@mofa.gov.sa; Ambassador HAZEM M. S. KARAKOTLY.

Serbia: Seminarstr. 5, 3006 Bern; tel. 313524996; fax 313514474; e-mail info@ambasadasrbije.ch; internet www.ambasadasrbije.ch; Ambassador MILAN PROTIĆ.

Slovakia: Thunstr. 63, 3074 Muri bei Bern; tel. 313563930; fax 313563933; e-mail emb.bern@mzv.sk; Ambassador JAN FOLTIN.

Slovenia: Schwanengasse 9, 3011 Bern; tel. 313109000; fax 313124414; e-mail vbe@gov.si; internet bern.embassy.si; Ambassador BOJAN GROBOVŠEK.

South Africa: Alpenstr. 29, Postfach, 3000 Bern 6; tel. 313501313; fax 313513944; e-mail bern.admin@dirco.gov.za; internet www .southafrica.ch; Ambassador GEORGE HENRY JOHANNES.

South Sudan: 23 ave de France, 1202 Geneva; tel. 229194040; fax 229194059; e-mail mission.rss.geneva@hotmail.com; Chargé d'affaires a.i. RIEK PUOK RIEK.

Spain: Kalcheggweg 24, Postfach 99, 3000 Bern 15; tel. 313505252; fax 313505255; e-mail emb.berna@maec.es; internet www.maec.es/ embajadas/berna; Ambassador MIGUEL ANGEL DE FRUTOS GÓMEZ.

Sudan: 51–53 ave Blanc, 3ème étage, 1202 Geneva; tel. 227312663; fax 227161970; e-mail mission.sudan@bluewin.ch; internet www .sudanembassy-mission.ch; Ambassador JOHN OMER ABD AL-RAHMAN MOHAMED ABD ALLA DHIRAR.

Sweden: Bundesgasse 26, Postfach, 3011 Bern; tel. 313287000; fax 313287001; e-mail ambassaden.bern@foreign.ministry.se; internet www.swedenabroad.com/bern; Ambassador PER THÖRESSON.

Thailand: Kirchstr. 56, 3097 Liebefeld-Bern; tel. 319703030; fax 319703035; e-mail thai.bern@bluewin.ch; internet thaiembassybern .org; Ambassador CHALERMPO THANCHITT.

Timor-Leste: 7 rue Pestalozzi, 1202 Geneva; tel. 227883562; fax 227883564; e-mail info@timor-lestemission.ch; Chargé d'affaires a.i. SEBASTIANA BARROS.

Tunisia: Kirchenfeldstr. 63, 3005 Bern; tel. 313528226; fax 313510445; e-mail at.berne@bluewin.ch; Ambassador TARAK BEN HAMIDA.

Turkey: Lombachweg 33, 3006 Bern 15; tel. 313597070; fax 313528819; e-mail botschaft.bern@mfa.gov.tr; internet www.bern .emb.mfa.gov.tr; Ambassador TANJU SÜMER.

Turkmenistan: 23 ave de France, 1202 Geneva; tel. 227491000; fax 227491001; e-mail office@turkmenistanmission.ch; Ambassador ESEN AYDOGDYEV.

Uganda: 6 bis rue Antoine Carteret, 1202 Geneva; tel. 223398810; fax 223407030; e-mail chancery@ugandamission.ch; internet www

.ugandamission.ch; Chargé d'affaires a.i. Rossette Nyirinkindi Katungye.

Ukraine: Feldeggweg 5, 3005 Bern; tel. 313522316; fax 313516416; e-mail emb_ch@mfa.gov.ua; internet www.mfa.gov.ua/switzerland; Ambassador Ihor Dir.

United Arab Emirates: Thunstr. 160, 3074 Muri bei Bern; tel. 313121710; fax 313118092; e-mail bern@mofa.gov.ae; Ambassador Mohammed Atiq al-Rumaithi.

United Kingdom: Thunstr. 50, 3000 Bern 15; tel. 313597700; fax 313597701; e-mail info.berne@fco.gsi.gov.uk; internet ukinswitzerland.fco.gov.uk; Ambassador Sarah Gillett.

USA: Sulgeneckstr. 19, 3007 Bern; tel. 313577011; fax 313577320; e-mail bernacs@state.gov; internet bern.usembassy.gov; Ambassador Donald Sternoff Beyer, Jr.

Uruguay: Kramgasse 63, 3011 Bern; tel. 313122226; fax 313112747; e-mail uruhelve@bluewin.ch; Ambassador Luis Ricardo Nario Fagúndez.

Venezuela: Schwarzenburgstr. 73, CP 1059, 3000 Bern 23; tel. 313505757; fax 313716469; e-mail embajada@embavenez-suiza.ch; internet www.embavenez-suiza.ch; Ambassador César Osvelio Méndez González.

Viet Nam: Schlösslistr. 26, 3008 Bern; tel. 313887872; fax 313887879; e-mail vietsuisse@bluewin.ch; internet www.vietnam-embassy.ch; Ambassador Nguyen The Phiet.

Judicial System

Switzerland has had a common Civil Code since 1912, but the Penal Code was only unified in 1942. Under the Code, capital punishment was abolished by the few cantons that still retained it. Minor cases are decided by a single judge, more complex cases by a panel of judges, while cases of murder and other serious crimes are decided by a public jury.

The individual cantons continue to elect and maintain their own magistracy, and retain certain variations in procedure. The canton of Zürich, for example, has justices of the peace (Friedensrichter—normally one for each commune), District Courts (Bezirksgerichte), Labour Courts (Arbeitsgerichte), Courts for Tenancy Matters, an Appeal Court (Obergericht) with various specialized benches, a Cassation Court (Kassationsgericht), and, for the more important cases under penal law, a Jury Court (Geschworenengericht).

At the federal level, the Federal Supreme Court has, in principle, jurisdiction over judicial matters. From 1997 a revision of the federal judicial system was undertaken that saw the establishment of two new judicial bodies of first instance, in order to alleviate the burden on the Federal Supreme Court. These were the Federal Criminal Court (from April 2004) and the Federal Administrative Court (from January 2007). Most disputes relating to the application of federal administrative law are first judged by the Federal Administrative Court. Also in January 2007 the competences of the Federal Insurance Court were assumed by the Federal Supreme Court. There are also military courts at the federal level.

FEDERAL SUPREME COURT

Schweizerisches Bundesgericht—Tribunal fédéral: Schweizerhofquai 6, 6004 Luzern; 29 ave du Tribunal fédéral, 1000 Lausanne 14; tel. 213189111; e-mail direktion@bger.ch; internet www.bger.ch; composed of 38 judges elected for a six-year term by the Federal Assembly; according to the Constitution any citizen eligible for election to the National Council can theoretically be elected Justice to the Court, but in practice only lawyers are considered for this office; all of the official Swiss languages must be represented in the Court; the President of the Federal Supreme Court is elected by the Federal Assembly for a two-year term, with a possibility of one re-election, from among the senior judges of the Court; the Court is divided into seven permanent branches or chambers, each of which has jurisdiction over cases pertaining to a specific subject, namely: (a) two 'Public', i.e. Constitutional and Administrative Law Divisions, each being composed of six judges; (b) two Civil or Private Law Divisions of five and six judges in each, which serve mainly as Courts of Appeal in civil matters; (c) two Socio-Legal Divisions, each consisting of five judges; (d) the Criminal Law Division, the so-called Court of Cassation, which is composed of five judges and which hears mainly appeals in criminal law matters; there are also four non-permanent divisions hearing exclusively cases that involve certain crimes against the Confederation, certain forms of terrorism, and other offences related to treason; Pres. Lorenz Meyer; Vice-Pres. Gilbert Kolly.

FEDERAL CRIMINAL COURT

Bundesstrafgericht—Tribunal pénal fédéral: CP 2720, 6501 Bellinzona; Viale Stefano Franscini 3, 6500 Bellinzona; tel.

918226262; fax 918226242; e-mail info@bstger.admin.ch; internet www.bstger.ch; composed of 18 judges elected by the Federal Assembly; court of first instance for criminal cases assigned to federal jurisdiction; in particular, may adjudicate offences such as crimes and misdemeanours against the Confederation's interests, offences committed using explosives, economic crime, organized crime or money-laundering beyond the internal or external borders of Switzerland; Pres. Andreas J. Keller; Vice-Pres. Daniel Kipfer Fasciati.

FEDERAL ADMINISTRATIVE COURT

Bundesverwaltungsgericht—Tribunal administratif fédéral: Kreuzackerstr. 12,9023 St Gallen; tel. 587052626; fax 587052980; internet www.bvger.ch; f. 2007; composed of 75 judges elected by the Federal Assembly for a renewable period of six years; court of first instance for cases arising from administrative decisions at the federal level; appeals in some cases relating to civil and public law matters may be heard in the Federal Supreme Court; Pres. Markus Metz; Vice-Pres. Michael Beusch.

Religion

In 2010 the religious adherence of the population was as follows: Roman Catholic 38.6%, Protestant 28.0%, other denominations 13.3% and those without religion some 20.1%.

CHRISTIANITY

The Roman Catholic Church

For ecclesiastical purposes, Switzerland comprises six dioceses and two territorial abbacies. All of the dioceses and abbacies are directly responsible to the Holy See. In 2010 there were some 2,513,850 adherents (some 38.6% of the population).

Bishops' Conference

Secrétariat de la Conférence des Evêques Suisses, CP 278, 1701 Fribourg; tel. 265101515; fax 265101516; e-mail secretariat@conferencedeseveques.ch; internet www.bischoefe.ch.

f. 1863; Pres. Rt Rev. Norbert Brunner (Bishop of Sion); Sec.-Gen. Erwin Tanner.

Bishop of Basel: Dr Felix Gmür, Bischöfliches Ordinariat, Baselstr. 58, Postfach 216, 4501 Solothurn; tel. 326255825; fax 326255845; e-mail generalvikariat@bistum-basel.ch; internet www.bistum-basel.ch.

Bishop of Chur: Rt Rev. Vitus Huonder, Bischöfliches Ordinariat, Hof 19, 7000 Chur; tel. 812586000; fax 812586001; e-mail ordinariat@bistum-chur.ch; internet www.bistum-chur.ch.

Bishop of Lausanne, Geneva and Fribourg: Rt Rev. Charles Morerod, 86 rue de Lausanne, CP 512, 1701 Fribourg; tel. 263474850; fax 263474851; internet www.diocese-lgf.ch.

Bishop of Lugano: Rt Rev. Pier Giacomo Grampa, CP 5382, 6901 Lugano; tel. 919138989; fax 919138990; e-mail segretaria.vescovo@catt.ch; internet www.diocesilugano.ch.

Bishop of Sankt Gallen: Rt Rev. Markus Büchel, Bischöfliches Ordinariat, Klosterhof 6b, Postfach 263, 9001 St Gallen; tel. 712273340; fax 712273341; e-mail kanzlei@bistum-stgallen.ch; internet www.bistum-stgallen.ch.

Bishop of Sion: Rt Rev. Norbert Brunner, 12 rue de la Tour, CP 2124, 1950 Sion 2; tel. 273291818; fax 273291836; e-mail diocese.sion@cath-vs.ch; internet www.cath-vs.ch.

Protestant Churches

Federation of Swiss Protestant Churches (Schweizerischer Evangelischer Kirchenbund—Fédération des Eglises protestantes de Suisse): Sulgenauweg 26, Postfach, 3000 Bern 23; tel. 313702525; fax 313702580; e-mail info@sek.ch; internet www.sek-feps.ch; f. 1920; comprises the reformed cantonal churches of Aargau, Appenzell (incl. Appenzell Ausserrhoden and Appenzell Innerrhoden), Basel-Landschaft, Basel-Stadt, Bern-Jura-Solothurn, Fribourg, Geneva, Glarus, Graubünden, Luzern, Neuchâtel, Nidwalden, Obwalden, St Gallen, Schaffhausen, Schwyz, Solothurn, Thurgau, Ticino, Uri, Valais, Vaud, Zug, Zürich, the Free Evangelical Church of Geneva and the United Methodist Church; the exec. organ is the Council of the Federation (Rat des Schweizerischen Evangelischen Kirchenbundes—Conseil de la Fédération); Pres. Rev. Dr Gottfried Locher.

The Old Catholic Church

Christkatholische Kirche der Schweiz (Old Catholic Church of Switzerland): Willadingweg 39, 3006 Bern; tel. 313513530; fax 313725004; e-mail bischof@christkath.ch; internet www.christkath.ch; f. 1875; c. 14,000 mems; Pres., Synodical Council Manuela Petraglio; Bishop Dr Harald Rein.

ISLAM

According to the 2000 census there were 310,807 Muslims recorded in Switzerland, making Islam the second largest religion in the country. In 2010 some 4.5% of the population was Muslim. There are two major mosques, one in Zürich and one in Geneva, and approximately 200 Islamic centres located throughout the country.

Federation of Islamic Organizations in Switzerland (Föderation Islamischer Dachorganisationen in der Schweiz—Fédération d'Organisations Islamiques de Suisse): Bahnstr. 80, 8105 Regensdorf; tel. 85331418; e-mail info@fids.ch; internet www.fids.ch; f. 2006; 13 mem. orgs; Pres. Dr HISHAM ABU MAIZAR.

Föderation Islamischer Gemeinschaften in der Schweiz: Hohlstrasse 615A, 8050 Zürich; tel. 443013151; f. 1978.

JUDAISM

According to the 2000 census there were 17,900 Jews in Switzerland. in 2010 some 0.2% of the population was Jewish.

Schweizerischer Israelitischer Gemeindebund—Fédération suisse des communautés israélites: Gotthardstr. 65, Postfach 2105, 8027 Zürich; tel. 433050777; fax 433050766; e-mail info@swissjews.ch; internet www.swissjews.ch; f. 1904; Pres. Dr HERBERT WINTER; Gen. Sec. JONATHAN KREUTNER.

The Press

Freedom of the press in Switzerland is guaranteed by Article 17 of the amended 1999 Constitution, and the only formal restrictions on the press are the legal restraints concerned with abuses of this freedom.

Switzerland's federal constitutional structure and the coexistence of diverse languages and religions have tended to produce a decentralized press, fragmented into numerous local papers, often with very low circulations. The majority of newspapers are regional, even such high circulation ones as *Berner Zeitung*, *Tages-Anzeiger* and national dailies such as *Neue Zürcher Zeitung*. About 67% of newspapers are printed in German, 27% in French, 4% in Italian and less than 1% in Romansh. In 2008 there were a total of 203 newspapers, with an average circulation of 2.2m. Some 100,000 copies of French, German, Italian and Spanish newspapers are imported daily.

PRINCIPAL DAILIES

Baden

Aargauer Zeitung: Neumattstr. 1, 5000 Aarau; tel. 582005858; fax 582005859; e-mail redaktion@azmedien.ch; internet www.aargauerzeitung.ch; f. 1996 by merger of *Aargauer Tagblatt* and *Badener Tagblatt*; Editor-in-Chief CHRISTIAN DORER; circ. 93,862 (2011).

Basel/Bâle

Basler Zeitung: Hochbergerstr. 15, 4002 Basel; tel. 616391111; fax 616311582; e-mail redaktion@baz.ch; internet www.baz.ch; f. 1976; liberal; Editor-in-Chief MARKUS SOMM; circ. 77,619 (2011).

Bellinzona

laRegione Ticino: Via Ghiringhelli 9, 6500 Bellinzona; tel. 918211121; fax 918211122; e-mail info@laregione.ch; internet www.laregione.ch; f. 1992; Italian; Editor GIACOMO SALVIONI; circ. 32,379 (2011).

Bern/Berne

Berner Zeitung: Dammweg 9, 3001 Bern; tel. 3133003111; fax 313313686; e-mail redaktion@bernerzeitung.ch; internet www.bzonline.ch; f. 1844; independent; Editor-in-Chief MICHAEL HUG; circ. 174,162 (2011).

Der Bund: Bubenbergpl. 8, 3001 Bern; tel. 313851111; fax 313851112; e-mail redaktion@derbund.ch; internet www.derbund.ch; f. 1850; liberal; Editor-in-Chief ARTUR K. VOGEL; circ. 50,231 (2011).

Biel/Bienne

Bieler Tagblatt: Robert-Walser-Pl. 7, Postfach 624, 2502 Biel; tel. 323219111; fax 323219119; e-mail btredaktion@bielertagblatt.ch; internet www.bielertagblatt.ch; independent; Editor-in-Chief BERNHARD RENTSCH; circ. 24,471 (2011).

Brig

Walliser Bote: Furkastr. 21, 3900 Brig; tel. 279229988; fax 279229989; e-mail info@walliserbote.ch; internet www.walliserbote.ch; Catholic; Editor-in-Chief THOMAS RIEDER; circ. 24,046 (2011).

La Chaux-de-Fonds

L'impartial: 14 rue Neuve, 2300 La Chaux-de-Fonds; tel. 329102000; fax 329102009; e-mail redaction@limpartial.ch; internet www.limpartial.ch; f. 1880; independent; Editor-in-Chief NICOLAS WILLEMIN; circ. 13,043 (2011).

Chur/Coire

Bündner Tagblatt: Comercialstr. 22, 7007 Chur; tel. 812555000; fax 812555123; e-mail redaktion-bt@suedostschweiz.ch; internet www.suedostschweiz.ch/medien/bt; f. 1852; independent; Editor-in-Chief CHRISTIAN BUXHOFER.

Die Südostschweiz: Comercialstr. 22, 7007 Chur; tel. 812255050; fax 812255102; e-mail zentralredaktion@suedostschweiz.ch; internet www.suedostschweiz.ch; publ. regional editions for Gaster und See and Glarus; independent; Publr Südostschweiz Presse AG; Editor-in-Chief DAVID SIEBER; circ. 122,723 (2011).

Delémont

Le Quotidien Jurassien: 6 route de Courroux, 2800 Delémont; tel. 324211818; fax 324211890; e-mail lqj@lqj.ch; internet www.lqj.ch; f. 1993; independent; Editor-in-Chief RÉMY CHÉTELAT; circ. 18,848 (2011).

Dielsdorf

Zürcher Unterländer: Schulstr. 12, Postfach, 8157 Dielsdorf; tel. 18548282; fax 18530690; e-mail redaktion@zuonline.ch; internet www.zuonline.ch; Editor-in-Chief BENJAMIN GEIGER; circ. 20,297 (2011).

Frauenfeld

Thurgauer Zeitung: Promenadenstr. 16, 8501 Frauenfeld; tel. 527235757; fax 527235707; e-mail redaktion@thurgauerzeitung.ch; internet www.thurgauerzeitung.ch; f. 1798; independent; Publrs Huber & Co AG; Editor-in-Chief DAVID ANGST; circ. 39,643 (2011).

Freiburg/Fribourg

La Liberté: 42 blvd de Pérolles, 1705 Fribourg; tel. 264264411; fax 264264444; e-mail redaction@laliberte.ch; internet www.laliberte.ch; Editor-in-Chief LOUIS RUFFIEUX; circ. 39,086 (2011).

Genève
(Geneva)

Le Temps: 3 pl. de Cornavin, CP 2570, 1211 Geneva 2; tel. 228885858; fax 228885859; e-mail info@letemps.ch; internet www.letemps.ch; f. 1998; Editor-in-Chief PIERRE VEYA; circ. 42,433 (2011).

Tribune de Genève: 11 rue des Rois, CP 5115, 1211 Geneva 11; tel. 223224000; fax 227810107; e-mail remplace@edipresse.ch; internet www.tdg.ch; f. 1879; independent; morning; Editor-in-Chief PIERRE RUETSCHI; circ. 51,487 (2011).

Herisau

Appenzeller Zeitung: Kasernenstr. 64, 9100 Herisau; tel. 713546474; fax 713546475; e-mail redaktion@appon.ch; internet www.appenzellerzeitung.ch; radical democratic; f. 1828; Publrs Appenzeller Medienhaus Schläpfer AG; Editor-in-Chief MONIKA EGLI; circ. 13,555 (2011).

Lausanne

Le Matin: 33 ave de la Gare, 1001 Lausanne; tel. 213494949; fax 21494929; internet www.lematin.ch; f. 1862; independent; Editor-in-Chief PETER ROTHENBÜHLER; circ. 57,107 (2011).

24 heures: 33 ave de la Gare, 1001 Lausanne; tel. 213494444; fax 213494419; internet www.24heures.ch; f. 1762; independent; Editor-in-Chief THIERRY MAYER; circ. 75,796 (2011).

Lugano

Corriere del Ticino: Via Industria, CP 620, 6933 Muzzano; tel. 919603131; fax 919603370; e-mail cdt@cdt.ch; internet www.cdt.ch; f. 1891; independent; Dir GIANCARLO DILLENA; circ. 36,274 (2011).

Giornale del Popolo: Via San Gottardo 50, 6900 Lugano; tel. 919223800; fax 919223805; e-mail redazione@gdp.ch; internet www.gdp.ch; f. 1926; independent; Editor-in-Chief GREGORIO SCHIRA; circ. 16,343 (2011).

Luzern/Lucerne

Neue Luzerner Zeitung: Maihofstr. 76, 6006 Lucerne; tel. 414295151; fax 414295181; e-mail redaktion@luzernerzeitung.ch; internet www.luzernerzeitung.ch; f. 1996; Editor-in-Chief THOMAS BORNHAUSER; circ. 121,371 (2011).

Neuchâtel/Neuenburg

L'Express: 39 rue de la Pierre-à-Mazel, 2000 Neuchâtel; tel. 327235300; fax 327235209; e-mail redaction@lexpress.ch; internet www.lexpress.ch; f. 1738; independent; Editor-in-Chief NICOLAS WILLEMIN; circ. 20,628 (2011).

Sankt Gallen/Saint-Gall

St Galler Tagblatt: Fürstenlandstr. 122, 9001 St Gallen; tel. 712727711; fax 712727476; e-mail zentralredaktion@tagblatt.ch; internet www.tagblatt.ch; f. 1839; liberal; Editor-in-Chief PHILIPP LANDMARK; circ. 118,420 (2011).

Schaffhausen/Schaffhouse

Schaffhauser Nachrichten: Vordergasse 58, 8201 Schaffhausen; tel. 526333111; fax 526333401; e-mail redaktion@shn.ch; internet www.shn.ch; f. 1861; liberal; Editor-in-Chief NORBERT NEININGER; circ. 22,228 (2011).

Sion

Le Nouvelliste: 13 rue de l'Industrie, 1950 Sion; tel. 273297511; fax 273297578; e-mail redaction@nouvelliste.ch; internet www.lenouvelliste.ch; Catholic; Editor-in-Chief JEAN-FRANÇOIS FOURNIER; circ. 41,129 (2011).

Stäfa

Zürichsee-Zeitung: Seestr. 86, 8712 Stäfa; tel. 19285555; fax 19285550; e-mail redaktion.staefa@zsz.ch; internet www.zsz.ch; f. 1845; radical democratic; Editor-in-Chief BENJAMIN GEIGER; circ. 38,853 (2011).

Thun/Thoune

Berner Oberländer: Bahnhofstr. 20, 3800 Interlaken; tel. 338288040; fax 338288049; e-mail redaktion@berneroberlaender.ch; internet www.berneroberlaender.ch; f. 1898; independent; Berner Oberland Medien AG; Editor-in-Chief BRUNO STÜDLE; circ. 25,798 (2011).

Thuner Tagblatt: Rampenstr. 1, 3602 Thun; tel. 332251515; fax 332251505; e-mail redaktion-tt@bom.ch; internet www.thunertagblatt.ch; independent; publ. by Berner Oberland Medien AG; Editor-in-Chief STEFAN GEISSBÜHLER; circ. 22,456 (2011).

Wetzikon

Zürcher Oberländer: Rapperswilerstr. 1, 8620 Wetzikon; tel. 19333333; fax 19323232; e-mail redaktion@zol.ch; internet www.zo-medien.ch; f. 1852; liberal; Editor-in-Chief CHRISTOPH VOLLENWEIDER; circ. 33,663 (2011).

Winterthur/Winterthour

Der Landbote: Garnmarkt 1–10, Postfach, 8401 Winterthur; tel. 522669901; fax 522669911; e-mail redaktion@landbote.ch; internet www.landbote.ch; f. 1836; independent; morning; Editor-in-Chief COLETTE GRADWOHL; circ. 32,205 (2011).

Zofingen

Zofinger Tagblatt: Henzmannstr. 20, 4800 Zofingen; tel. 627459393; fax 627459419; e-mail ztredaktion@ztonline.ch; internet www.zofingertagblatt.ch; f. 1873; liberal; Editor BEAT KIRCHHOFER; circ. 12,629 (2011).

Zürich

Blick: Dufourstr. 23, 8008 Zürich; tel. 442596262; fax 442596665; e-mail redaktion@blick.ch; internet www.blick.ch; independent; Editor-in-Chief RALPH GROSSE-BLEY; circ. 208,360 (2011).

Neue Zürcher Zeitung: Falkenstr. 11, Postfach, 8021 Zürich; tel. 442581111; fax 442521329; e-mail redaktion@nzz.ch; internet www.nzz.ch; f. 1780; independent liberal; Editor-in-Chief MARKUS SPILLMANN; circ. 129,627 (2012).

Tages-Anzeiger: Werdstr. 21, 8021 Zürich; tel. 442484411; fax 442484471; e-mail redaktion@tages-anzeiger.ch; internet www.tagesanzeiger.ch; f. 1893; independent; Editors-in-Chief MARKUS EISENHUT, RES STREHLE; circ. 195,618 (2011).

20 Minuten: Werdstr. 21, Postfach, 8021 Zürich; tel. 442486820; fax 442486821; e-mail redaktion@20minuten.ch; internet www.20min.ch; f. 1999; distributed free of charge; 6 regional editions: Bern/Basel, Geneva, Luzern, Région, St Gallen and Zürich; Editor-in-Chief MARCO BOSELLI; circ. 496,205 (2011).

PERIODICALS AND JOURNALS

Allgemeine Schweizerische Militärzeitschrift: Brunnenstr. 7, 8604 Volketswil; tel. 449084560; fax 449084540; e-mail redaktion@ asmz.ch; internet www.asmz.ch; f. 1834; 11 a year; Editor-in-Chief ROLAND BECK; circ. 21,000.

Die Alpen: Monbijoustr. 61, Postfach, 3000 Bern 23; tel. 313701885; fax 313701890; e-mail alpen@sac-cas.ch; internet www.sac-cas.ch; monthly; publ. by Schweizer Alpen-Club SAC; circ. 105,159.

Auto & Lifestyle (ACS Clubmagazin): Wasserwerkgasse 39, 3000 Bern 13; tel. 313283111; fax 313110310; e-mail acszv@acs.ch; internet www.acs.ch; publ. by the Automobile Club of Switzerland; 10 a year; circ. 63,200.

Automobil Revue: Dammweg 9, 3001 Bern; tel. 582181320; fax 582181321; e-mail office@automobilrevue.ch; internet www.automobilrevue.ch; f. 1906; weekly publ. in German and French (*Revue automobile*); Editor OLAF KUHLMANN; circ. 67,412.

Beobachter: Förrlibuckstr. 70, 8021 Zürich; tel. 434445252; fax 434445353; e-mail redaktion@beobachter.ch; internet www.beobachter.ch; f. 1927; 2 a month; circ. 306,531.

Bilanz: Förrlibuckstr. 70, 8021 Zürich; tel. 434445520; fax 434445521; e-mail redaktion@bilanz.ch; internet www.bilanz.ch; f. 1977; review of business in Switzerland; circ. 57,548.

Courrier neuchâtelois: 2013 Colombier; tel. 328417250; fax 328411521; weekly; Editor RENÉ GESSLER; circ. 88,087.

Du—Zeitschrift für Kultur: Du Verlags AG, Holbeinstr. 8, 8008 Zürich; tel. 432434600; fax 432434611; f. 1941; monthly art review; Editor ANDREAS KLÄUI; circ. 31,915.

Echo Magazine: 12 rue de Meyrin, CP 80, 1211 Geneva 7; tel. 225930303; fax 225930319; e-mail abo.echo.magazine@saripress.ch; internet www.echomagazine.ch; f. 1929; weekly; Editor-in-Chief PATRICE FAVRE; circ. 22,000.

L'Eco dello Sport: via San Gottardo 25, 6500 Bellinzona; tel. 918262710; fax 91575750; circ. 44,000.

Finanz und Wirtschaft: Verlag Finanz und Wirtschaft AG, Hallwylstr. 71, Postfach, 8021 Zürich; tel. 442983535; fax 442983500; e-mail verlag@fuw.ch; internet www.fuw.ch; f. 1928; 2 a week; finance, economics, investments, companies, markets, market data; circ. 29,517 (2011).

Freisinn: Postfach 6136, 3001 Bern; tel. 313203535; fax 313203500; e-mail zila@fdp.ch; internet www.fdp.ch; f. 1979; monthly; politics; Editor-in-Chief NICO ZILA; circ. 71,160.

GlücksPost: Dufourstr. 49, 8008 Zürich; tel. 442596912; fax 442596930; e-mail glueckspost@ringier.ch; internet www.glueckspost.ch; women's interest; f. 1977; weekly; Editor-in-Chief BÉATRICE ZOLLINGER; circ. 148,737.

Handelszeitung: Seestr. 37, 8027 Zürich; tel. 442883555; fax 442883575; e-mail redaktion@handelszeitung.ch; internet www.handelszeitung.ch; f. 1862; financial, commercial and industrial weekly; Publr JÖRG TOBUSCHAT; Editor-in-Chief BEAT BALZLI; circ. 33,044.

L'Hebdo: Pont Bessières 3, POB 6682, 1002 Lausanne; tel. 213317600; fax 213317601; e-mail courrier.hebdo@ringier.ch; internet www.hebdo.ch; f. 1981; weekly; news magazine; Editor-in-Chief ALAIN JEANNET; circ. 48,451 (2007).

L'Illustré: Pont Bessières 3, POB 6505, 1002 Lausanne; tel. 213317500; fax 213317501; e-mail illustre@ringier.ch; internet www.illustre.ch; f. 1921; weekly; Chief Editor MICHEL JEANNERET; circ. 97,974.

Museum Helveticum: Steinentorstr. 13, 4010 Basel; tel. 612789565; fax 612789566; e-mail verlag@schwabe.ch; internet www.schwabe.ch; f. 1944; publ. by Schwabe AG; 2 a year; Swiss journal for classical philology, ancient history and classical archaeology; Editors Prof. M. GUGGISBERG, Prof. S. REBENICH, Prof. THOMAS SCHMIDT, Prof. H. HARICH-SCHWARZBAUER.

Music Scene: Neuenhoferstr. 101, 5401 Baden; tel. 562032272; fax 562032299; e-mail info@music-scene.ch; internet www.music-scene.ch; f. 1924; young people's fortnightly; circ. 50,000.

Nebelspalter: Bahnhofstr. 17, 9326 Horn; tel. 718468876; fax 718468879; e-mail verlag@nebelspalter.ch; internet www.nebelspalter.ch; f. 1875; publ. by Engeli & Partner Verlag; 10 a year; satirical; Editor-in-Chief MARCO RATSCHILLER; circ. 12,600.

Revue militaire suisse: 3 ave de Florimont, 1006 Lausanne; tel. 213114817; fax 213119709; e-mail info@jcrc.ch; internet www.revuemilitairesuisse.ch; f. 1856; 8 a year; Editor-in-Chief Lt Col ALEXANDRE VAUTRAVERS.

Revue suisse de zoologie: Muséum d'Histoire Naturelle, CP 6434, 1211 Geneva 6; tel. 224186300; fax 224186301; e-mail danielle.decrouez@mhn.ville-ge.ch; f. 1893; quarterly; Dir DANIELLE DECROUEZ.

Schweizer Archiv für Neurologie und Psychiatrie (Archives Suisses de Neurologie et de Psychiatrie): EMH Schweizerischer Ärzteverlag AG, Farnsburgerstr. 8, 4132 Muttenz; tel. 614678555; fax 614678556; e-mail sanp@emh.ch; internet www.sanp.ch; f. 1917; 8 a year; Publr Dr NATALIE MARTY.

Schweizer Familie: Werdstr. 21, Postfach, 8021 Zürich; tel. 442486106; fax 444248096; e-mail redaktion@schweizerfamilie.ch; internet www.schweizerfamilie.ch; f. 1893; weekly; Editor-in-Chief DANIEL DUNKEL; Man. Dir JOSEF BURCH; circ. 205,529.

Schweizer Illustrierte: Dufourstr. 23, 8008 Zürich; tel. 442596363; fax 442620442; e-mail info@schweizer-illustrierte.ch; internet www.schweizer-illustrierte.ch; f. 1911; illustrated weekly; Chief Editor NIK NIETHAMMER; circ. 232,519.

Schweizer Monat: Vogelsangstr. 52, 8006 Zürich; tel. 443612606; fax 443637005; e-mail info@schweizermonat.ch; internet www .schweizermonat.ch; f. 1921; political, economic and cultural monthly; Editor-in-Chief RENÉ SCHEU; circ. 5,000.

Schweizerisches Handelsamtsblatt (Feuille officielle suisse du commerce): POB 1025, 3000 Bern; tel. 313240992; fax 313240961; e-mail info@sogc.ch; internet www.shab.ch; f. 1883; commercial daily; publ. by State Secretariat for Economic Affairs (SECO); Editor-in-Chief MARKUS TANNER; circ. 10,000.

Snowactive: Strike Media Schweiz AG, Gösgerstr. 15, POB 170, 5012 Schönenwerd; tel. 628582820; fax 628582829; e-mail j.weibel@snowactive.ch; internet www.snowactive.ch; f. 1968; 7 a year; German and French/Italian editions; Editor JOSEPH WEIBEL; circ. 85,000.

Swiss Engineering (STZ): Technoparkstr. 1, 8005 Zürich; tel. 444451991; e-mail kontakt@sprachwerk.ch; internet www .swissengineering-stz.ch; 10 a year; technical journal in German; Editor-in-Chief CHRISTA ROSATZIN-STROBEL; circ. 20,000.

Swiss Journal of Psychology/Schweizerische Zeitschrift für Psychologie/Revue suisse de psychologie: Länggassstr. 76, Postfach, 3000 Bern 9; tel. 313004500; fax 313004593; e-mail verlag@hanshuber.com; internet www.verlag-hanshuber.com; f. 1942; quarterly; in German, French and English; Editor-in-Chief Prof. Dr FRED MAST.

Swiss Medical Weekly: EMH Swiss Medical Publrs Ltd, Steinentorstr. 13, 4010 Basel; tel. 614678555; fax 614678556; e-mail red@smw.ch; internet www.smw.ch; f. 1871; fortnightly; Man. Editor Dr NATALIE MARTY.

TCS-Zürich: Geissbüelstr. 24–26, 8604 Volketswil; tel. 442868636; fax 442868607; official organ of the Zürich Touring Club; monthly; Chief Editor RETO CAVEGN; circ. 200,000.

Tele: Förrlibuckstrasse 70, Postfach, 8021 Zürich; tel. 434445950; fax 434445999; e-mail telesekr@ringier.ch; internet www.tele.ch; f. 1967; television, cinema and multimedia; weekly; Editor GION STECHER; circ. 214,214.

Touring: Maulbeerstr. 10, 3001 Bern; tel. 313805000; fax 313805006; f. 1935; fortnightly; German, French and Italian editions; Chief Editor STEFAN SENN; circ. 1,306,000.

TV 8: 3 Pont Bessières, 1005 Lausanne; tel. 213317000; fax 213317001; e-mail tv8@ringier.ch; weekly; circ. 83,119 (2007).

Vox Romanica: Centre de dialectologie, Université de Neuchâtel, 6 ave DuPeyrou, 2000 Neuchâtel; tel. 327181720; fax 327181721; e-mail andres.kristol@unine.ch; internet www.unine.ch/dialectologie/vox/vox.html; f. 1936; annual review of Romance linguistics and medieval literature; publ. by Collegium Romanicum (Swiss Association of Romanists); Editors Prof. Dr RITA FRANCESCHINI, Prof. ANDRES KRISTOL.

Weltwoche: Förrlibuckstr. 70, 8021 Zürich; tel. 434445700; fax 434445669; e-mail redaktion@weltwoche.ch; internet www .weltwoche.ch; f. 1933; weekly; independent; Editor-in-Chief ROGER KÖPPEL; circ. 92,337.

Werk, Bauen + Wohnen: Talstr. 39, 8001 Zürich; tel. 442181430; fax 442181434; e-mail info@wbw.ch; internet www .werkbauenundwohnen.ch; f. 1914; monthly; architecture; Publishing Man. REGULA HAFFNER; circ. 8,000.

NEWS AGENCY

Schweizerische Depeschenagentur AG/Agence Télegraphique Suisse SA (SDA/ATS) (Swiss News Agency): Länggassstr. 7, 3001 Bern; tel. 313093333; fax 313093030; e-mail sekretariat.reda@sda.ch; internet www.sda.ch; f. 1894; agency for political and general news; Chair., Management Bd MARKUS SCHWAB; Chief Editor BERNARD MAISSEN.

PRESS ASSOCIATIONS

Impressum—Die Schweizer Journalistinnen/Les journalistes suisses/I giornalisti svizzeri: Grand'Places 14A, 1701 Fribourg; tel. 263471500; fax 263471509; e-mail info@impressum.ch; internet www.impressum.ch; Pres ANTOINE GESSLER, STEFAN ROHRBACH.

Médias Suisses: 1 ave de Florimont, 1006 Lausanne; tel. 213434090; fax 213434099; e-mail admin@pressesuisse.ch; internet www.pressesuisse.ch; f. 1921 as Union Romande des éditeurs de journaux et de périodiques; present name adopted 2011; 54 mems and 6 assoc. mems; Pres. VALÉRIE BOAGNO.

Verband Schweizer Presse: Konradstr. 14, Postfach 1202, 8021 Zürich; tel. 3186464; fax 3186462; e-mail contact@schweizerpresse .ch; internet www.schweizerpresse.ch; f. 1899; Pres. HANSPETER LEBRUMENT; c. 150 mems.

Publishers

FRENCH-LANGUAGE PUBLISHING HOUSES

Academic Press Fribourg: 42 blvd de Pérolles, CP 176, 1705 Fribourg; tel. 264264311; fax 264264300; e-mail info@paulusedition .ch; internet www.paulusedition.ch; Dir MAURICE GREDER.

Editions l'Age d'Homme SA: 10 rue de Genève, Postfach 5076, 1002 Lausanne 9; tel. 213120095; fax 213208440; e-mail info@agedhomme.com; internet www.lagedhomme.com; f. 1966; fiction, biography, music, art, social sciences, science fiction, literary criticism; Man. Dir VLADIMIR DIMITRIJEVIC.

Editions de l'Aire SA: 15 rue de l'Union, CP 57, 1800 Vevey; tel. 219236836; fax 219236823; e-mail editionaire@bluewin.ch; internet www.editions-aire.ch; f. 1978; literature, history, philosophy, religion; Man. MICHEL MORET.

La Bibliothèque des Arts: 55 ave de Rumine, 1005 Lausanne; tel. 213123667; fax 213123615; e-mail webmaster@bibliotheque-des-arts.com; internet www.bibliotheque-des-arts .com; f. 1954; art, culture; Dir OLIVIER DAULTE.

Librairie Droz SA: 11 rue Firmin-Massot, POB 389, 1211 Geneva 12; tel. 223466666; fax 223472391; e-mail droz@droz.org; internet www.droz.org; f. 1924; history, medieval literature, French literature, linguistics, social sciences, economics, archaeology; Dir MAX ENGAMMARE.

Edipresse Publications SA: 33 ave de la Gare, 1001 Lausanne; tel. 213494545; fax 213494540; e-mail epsa.info@edipresse.ch; internet www.edipresse.com; f. 1988; newspapers, magazines; Pres. PIERRE LAMUNIÈRE.

Editions d'En Bas: 30 rue des Côtes-de-Montbenon, 1003 Lausanne; tel. 213233918; fax 213123240; e-mail enbas@bluewin.ch; internet www.enbas.ch; f. 1976; literature, politics, history, sociology, memoirs, travel, poetry, photography; Dir JEAN RICHARD.

Françoise Gonin Editions d'Art: 1 chemin du Grand-Praz 1, 1012 Lausanne-Chailly; tel. and fax 217285948; e-mail ogonin@freesurf .ch; internet www.gonin.org/editions; f. 1926; art books.

Editions du Grand-Pont: 2 pl. Bel-Air, 1003 Lausanne; tel. 213124466; fax 213113222; f. 1971; general, art books and literature; Dir JEAN-PIERRE LAUBSCHER.

Editions du Griffon: 17 Faubourg du Lac, 2000 Neuchâtel; tel. 327252204; f. 1944; science, arts.

Editions Ides et Calendes: Évole 19, 2000 Neuchâtel; tel. 327253861; fax 327255880; e-mail info@idesetcalendes.com; internet www.idesetcalendes.com; f. 1941; art, photography, literature; Dir ALAIN BOURET.

Institut de Hautes Etudes Internationales et du Développement: 20 rue Rothschild, CP 136, 1211 Geneva 21; tel. 229085700; fax 229065947; e-mail webmaster@graduateinstitute.ch; internet graduateinstitute.ch; f. 1927; educational, development; Dir PHILIPPE BURRIN.

La Joie de Lire SA: 5 chemin Neuf, 1207 Geneva; tel. 228073399; fax 228073392; e-mail info@lajoiedelire.ch; internet www .lajoiedelire.ch; f. 1987; juvenile; Dir FRANCINE BOUCHET.

Editions Labor & Fides SA: 1 rue Beauregard, 1204 Geneva; tel. 223113290; fax 227813051; e-mail g.montmollin@laboretfides.com; internet www.laboretfides.com; f. 1924; theological and religious publs; Dir GABRIEL DE MONTMOLLIN.

Loisirs et Pédagogie SA (LEP): en Budron B4A, 1052 Le Mont-sur-Lausanne; tel. 216512570; fax 216535751; e-mail contact@editionslep.ch; internet www.editionslep.ch; f. 1980; Dir PHILIPPE BURDEL.

Médecine et Hygiène: 46 chemin de la Mousse, 1225 Chêne-Bourg; tel. 227029311; fax 227029355; e-mail admin@medhyg.ch; internet www.medhyg.ch; f. 1943; medicine, psychology, general science, university textbooks; Man. Dir BERTRAND KIEFER.

Editions Mondo SA: 12 Entre Deux Villes, CP 720, 1800 Vevey; tel. 219241450; fax 219245048; e-mail info@mondo.ch; internet www .mondo.ch; Dir ARSLAN ALAMIR.

Olizane: 11 rue des Vieux-Grenadiers, 1205 Geneva; tel. 223285252; fax 223285796; e-mail guides@olizane.ch; internet www.olizane.ch; f. 1981; travel, tourism, orientalism, photography; Dir MATTHIAS HUBER.

Editions Payot Lausanne: Nadir SA, 18 ave de la Gare, CP 529, 1001 Lausanne; tel. 213290264; fax 213290266; f. 1875; technical, textbooks, medicine, law, popular science, art books, tourism, history, music, general non-fiction, academic publs; Dir JACQUES SCHERRER.

Presses Polytechniques et Universitaires Romandes: EPFL, RLC, CP 119, 1015 Lausanne-Ecublens; tel. 216932130; fax 216934027; e-mail ppur@epfl.ch; internet www.ppur.org; f. 1980; technical and scientific; also publishes in English as EPFL Press; Man. Dir OLIVIER BABEL.

Slatkine Reprints: 5 rue des Chaudronniers, CP 3625, 1211 Geneva 3; tel. 227762551; fax 227763527; e-mail slatkine@slatkine.com; internet www.slatkine.com; Dir M. E. SLATKINE.

Editions du Tricorne: 14 rue Lissignol, 1201 Geneva; tel. 227388366; e-mail tricorne@tricorne.org; internet www.tricorne.org; f. 1976; philosophy, human sciences, art, religion, psychology, mathematics; Dir SERGE KAPLUN.

Editions Zoé: 11 rue des Moraines, 1227 Carouge-Geneva; tel. 223093606; fax 223093603; e-mail info@editionszoe.ch; internet www.editionszoe.ch; literature, criticism, fiction, essays, theatre, art, music, cookery; Dir CAROLINE COUTAU.

GERMAN-LANGUAGE PUBLISHING HOUSES

Arche Literatur Verlag AG: Heinrichstr. 249, 8005 Zürich; tel. 447605171; fax 447602068; internet www.arche-verlag.com; f. 1944; literature; Dir NIKOLAUS HANSEN.

Benteli Verlags AG: Steinackerstr. 8, 8583 Sulgen; tel. 716449131; fax 716449139; e-mail info@benteli.ch; internet www.benteli.ch; f. 1898; fine arts, photography, non-fiction, philology; Dir TILL SCHAAP.

Birkhäuser Verlag AG: Viaduktstr. 42, Postfach 133, 4010 Basel; tel. 615689800; fax 612050799; e-mail info@birkhauser.ch; internet www.birkhauser.ch; books and journals; mathematics, biology, architecture, design; Man. Dir SVEN FUND.

Carl-Huter-Verlag GmbH: Ohm-Str. 14, 8050 Zürich; tel. 443117471; fax 443117485; e-mail verlag@carl-huter.ch; internet www.carl-huter.ch; physiognomy and nature; Dirs FRITZ AERNI, ELISABETH AERNI.

Cosmos Verlag AG: Kräyigenweg 2, 3074 Muri bei Bern; tel. 319506464; fax 319506460; e-mail info@cosmosverlag.ch; internet www.cosmosverlag.ch; f. 1923; fiction, literature, local history, reference, children's, tax management; Dir RETO M. AEBERLI.

Diogenes Verlag AG: Sprecherstr. 8, 8032 Zürich; tel. 442548511; fax 442528407; e-mail info@diogenes.ch; internet www.diogenes.ch; f. 1952; belles-lettres, fiction, graphic arts, children's; Publrs PHILIPP KEEL, RUDOLF C. BETTSCHART.

Europa Verlag AG: Scheuchzersrasse 50, 8006 Zürich; tel. 443622023; fax 443622025; e-mail mail@europaverlag.ch; internet www.europa-verlag.ch; f. 1933; politics, philosophy, history, biography, sociology, fiction; Dir LARS SCHULTZE-KOSSACK.

Hallwag Kümmerly+Frey AG: Grubenstr. 109, 3322 Schönbühl; tel. 318503131; fax 318503100; e-mail info@swisstravelcenter.ch; internet www.swisstravelcenter.ch; f. 1912; maps and guides, road maps, atlases, travel guides; CEO PETER NIEDERHAUSER.

H. E. P. Verlag AG: Brunngasse 36, Postfach, 3000 Bern 7; tel. 313102929; fax 313183135; e-mail info@hep-verlag.ch; internet www.hep-verlag.ch; imprints Baufachverlag and Ott Verlag; educational and training material; Dir PETER EGGER.

S. Karger AG: Allschwilerstr. 10, Postfach, 4009 Basel; tel. 613061111; fax 613061234; e-mail karger@karger.ch; internet www.karger.com; f. 1890 in Berlin, 1937 in Basel; international medical journals, books on medicine, chemistry, psychology; Pres. Dr THOMAS KARGER; CEO GABRIELLA KARGER, RALPH WEIL.

Peter Lang AG: Moosstr. 1, Postfach 350, 2542 Pieterlen; tel. 323761717; fax 323761727; e-mail info@peterlang.com; internet www.peterlang.com; f. 1977; humanities, social sciences, German language and literature, Romance literatures and languages, linguistics, music, art, theatre, ethnology; CEO TONY ALBALÁ.

Müller Rüschlikon Verlags AG: Gewerbestr. 10, 6330 Cham; tel. 417417755; fax 417417115; e-mail info@bucheli-verlag.ch; f. 1936; non-fiction; Dir HEINZ JANSEN.

Nagel & Kimche AG, Verlag: Neptunstr. 20, 8032 Zürich; tel. 443666680; fax 443666688; e-mail info@nagel-kimche.ch; internet www.nagel-kimche.ch; f. 1983; belles-lettres, juvenile; Dir Dr DIRK VAIHINGER.

Neptun Verlag AG: Erlenstr. 2, 8280 Kreuzlingen; tel. 716779655; fax 716779650; e-mail neptun@bluewin.ch; internet www.neptun.ch; f. 1946; travel books, children's, contemporary history; Dir H. BERCHTOLD-MÜHLEMANN.

Neue Zürcher Zeitung, Buchverlag: Postfach, 8021 Zürich; tel. 442581505; fax 442581399; e-mail buch.verlag@nzz.ch; internet www.nzz-libro.ch; Man. HANS-PETER THÜR.

Verlag Niggli AG: Steinackerstr. 8, Postfach 135, 8583 Sulgen; tel. 716449111; fax 716449190; e-mail info@niggli.ch; internet www.niggli.ch; f. 1950; art, architecture, design, typography; Gen. Man. Dr J. CHRISTOPH BÜRKLE.

Orell Füssli Verlag: Dietzingerstr. 3, Postfach, 8036 Zürich; tel. 444667711; fax 444667412; e-mail info@ofv.ch; internet www.ofv.ch; f. 1519; management, history, law, schoolbooks, trade directories.

Verlag Pro Juventute/Atlantis Kinderbücher: Thurgauerstr. 39, 8050 Zürich; tel. 442567777; fax 442567778; e-mail info@projuventute.ch; internet www.projuventute.ch; social sciences, children's, families; Man. URS GYSLING.

Friedrich Reinhardt Verlag: Missionsstr. 36, Postfach 393, 4012 Basel; tel. 612646450; fax 612646488; e-mail verlag@reinhardt.ch; internet www.reinhardt.ch; f. 1900; belles-lettres, theology, periodicals; Dir ALFRED RÜDISÜHLI.

Rex-Verlag: Arsenalstr. 24, 6011 Kreins; tel. 414194719; fax 414194711; e-mail info@rex-verlag.ch; internet www.rex-verlag.ch; f. 1931; theology, pedagogics, fiction, juvenile; Dir MARKUS KAPPELER.

Ringier AG: Dufourstr. 23, 8008 Zürich; tel. 442596111; fax 442598635; e-mail info@ringier.ch; internet www.ringier.ch; f. 1831; newspapers, magazines, online services, television, print; CEO MARC WALDER.

Sauerländer Verlage AG: Industriestr. 1, 5000 Aarau; tel. 628368686; fax 628368695; e-mail verlag@sauerlaender.ch; internet www.sauerlaender.ch; f. 1807; juvenile, school books, textbooks, history, chemistry, periodicals (professional, trade, science); Man. Dir FRANK THALHOFER.

Schulthess Juristische Medien AG: Zwinglipl. 2, Postfach, 8022 Zürich; tel. 442002929; fax 442002998; e-mail buch@schulthess.com; internet www.schulthess.com; f. 1791; legal, social sciences, university textbooks; Man. Dir ANDREAS HOHNHEISER.

Schwabe AG: Steinentorstr. 13, 4010 Basel; tel. 612789565; fax 612789566; e-mail verlag@schwabe.ch; internet www.schwabe.ch; f. 1488; medicine, art, history, philosophy; Dir DAVID MARC HOFFMANN.

Stämpfli Verlag AG: Wölflistr. 1, Postfach 8326, 3001 Bern; tel. 313006311; fax 313006688; e-mail verlag@staempfli.com; internet www.staempfliverlag.com; f. 1799; law, economics, history, art; Man. Dir Dr RUDOLF STÄMPFLI.

Tobler Verlag AG: Quellenstr. 4E, 9402 Mörschwil; tel. 718452010; fax 718452091; e-mail info@klv.ch; internet www.tobler-verlag.ch; f. 1995; part of Kaufmännischer Lehrmittelverlag AG since 2011; Dir SASCHA GLOOR.

TVZ Theologischer Verlag Zürich AG: Badenerstr. 73, Postfach, 8026 Zürich; tel. 442993355; fax 442993358; e-mail tvz@ref.ch; internet www.tvz-verlag.ch; f. 1934; religion, theology; Dir MARI-ANNE STAUFFACHER.

Ch. Walter Verlag AG: Dorfstr. 81/87, Postfach 121, 8706 Meilen; tel. 449233177; e-mail info@walter-verlag.ch; internet www.walter-verlag.ch; f. 1992; children's books, history, literature; Pres. Dr CHLAUS WALTER.

Wepf & Co AG Verlag: Eisengasse 5, 4001 Basel; tel. 612698515; fax 612630244; e-mail wepf@dial.eunet.ch; internet www.wepf.ch; f. 1755; architecture, engineering, ethnology, geography, geology, mineralogy; Dir H. HERRMANN.

PUBLISHERS' ASSOCIATIONS

Association Suisse des Editeurs de Langue Française: 2 ave Agassiz, CP 1215, 1001 Lausanne; tel. 213197111; fax 213197910; e-mail aself@centrepatronal.ch; f. 1975; asscn of French-speaking publrs; Pres. FRANCINE BOUCHET; Vice-Pres. OLIVIER BABEL; Sec.-Gen. FRANÇOIS PERRET; 75 mems.

Schweizer Buchhändler- und Verleger-Verband (SBVV): Alderstr. 40, Postfach, 8034 Zürich; tel. 444213600; fax 444213618; e-mail sbvv@swissbooks.ch; internet www.swissbooks.ch; f. 1849; asscn of German-speaking Swiss booksellers and publrs; Central Pres. MARIANNE SAX; Dir DANI LANDOLF; 516 mem. and affiliated firms.

Broadcasting and Communications

TELECOMMUNICATIONS

Cablecom GmbH: Zollstr. 42, 8021 Zürich; tel. 2779111; internet www.cablecom.ch; f. 1994; offers cable television, broadband internet access and fixed-line and mobile cellular telecommunications; owned by Liberty Global, Inc. (USA); Man. Dir ERIC TVETER.

In & Phone SA: 33 rue de Lausanne, 1800 Vevey; tel. 219221941; fax 219221940; e-mail info@inphone.ch; internet www.inphone.ch; f. 2003; mobile communications; owned by Unify Group Holding; Gen. Man. OLIVIER LEUENBERGER.

Orange Communications SA: Hardturmstr. 161, 8005 Zürich; tel. 212161010; fax 212161515; internet www.orange.ch; f. 1999; mobile cellular communications and broadband internet access; owned by Orange SA (France); Chair. THOMAS SIEBER; CEO JOHAN ANDSJÖ; 1.6m. subscribers (Dec. 2011).

Sunrise Communications AG: Binzmühlestr. 130, Postfach, 8050 Zürich; tel. 587777777; fax 587777778; internet www.sunrise.ch; f. 1997; mobile cellular and fixed-line telecommunications and internet access; owned by TDC A/S (Denmark); CEO OLIVER STEIL; 3m. subscribers (Dec. 2011).

Swisscom AG: Alte Tiefenaustr. 6, 3048 Worblaufen; tel. 313421111; fax 313422549; e-mail swisscom@swisscom.com; internet www.swisscom.com; fmrly Swiss Telecom PTT; 56.9% owned by Federal Govt; Chair. HANSUELI LOOSLI; CEO CARSTEN SCHLOTER.

Tele2 Schweiz: Postfach 171, 8833 Samstagern; tel. 842242420; fax 842242422; internet www.tele2.ch; f. 1998; broadband internet access, fixed-line and mobile cellular telecommunications; CEO MATS TILLY.

BROADCASTING

The Swiss Broadcasting Corporation (SBC) is a private non-profit-making company, which fulfils a public duty on the basis of a licence granted to it by the Federal Government. The SBC uses the electrical and radio-electrical installations of Swisscom AG for public broadcasting of radio and television programmes. Swisscom is responsible for all technical aspects of transmission. Some 75.1% of the receiver licence fee is allocated to the SBC, while Swisscom takes 24.2% and the remainder is distributed among local radio and television stations.

SRG SSR idée suisse (Swiss Broadcasting Co—SBC; Schweizerische Radio- und Fernsehgesellschaft; Société suisse de radiodiffusion et télévision): Giacomettistr. 1, 3000 Bern 31; tel. 313509111; fax 313509256; e-mail info@srgssrideesuisse.ch; internet www.srgssrideesuisse.ch; f. 1931; Pres. RAYMOND LORETAN; Dir-Gen. ROGER DE WECK; SRG SSR idée suisse is composed of the following regional companies:

Radio-Télévision suisse romande (RTSR): 40 ave du Temple, CP 78, 1010 Lausanne; tel. 582366975; fax 213181976; e-mail info@rtsr.ch; internet www.rtsr.ch; Pres. JEAN-FRANÇOIS ROTH.

Radiotelevisiun Svizra Rumantscha (RTR): Via da Masans 2, 7002 Chur; tel. 812557575; fax 812557500; internet www.rtr.ch; Pres. DURI BEZZOLA.

Società cooperativa per la radiotelevisione Svizzera di lingua italiana (CORSI): Segreteria CORSI, via Canevascini 7, 6903 Lugano; tel. 918036017; fax 918036337; e-mail info@corsi-rsi.ch; internet www.corsi-rsi.ch; Pres. CLAUDIO GENERALI.

SRG Idée suisse DEUTSCHSCHWEIZ (Radio- und Fernsehgesellschaft DRS): Fernsehstr. 1–4, Postfach, 8052 Zürich; tel. 443056611; fax 443056710; e-mail info@srgdeutschschweiz.ch; internet www.srgdeutschschweiz.ch; formerly Radio- und Fernsehgesellschaft der Deutschen und der Rätoromanischen Schweiz (RDRS); Pres. VIKTOR BAUMELER.

Radio

Digital audio broadcasting (DAB) began in 1999 in Bern, Biel, Interlaken and Solothurn and had expanded to cover most of the German-speaking cantons, the Italian-speaking canton of Ticino, Geneva and Lausanne by 2007. DAB programmes were received by more than 90% of the population at the end of 2012.

Radio Rumantsch (RR): Via da Masans 2, 7002 Chur; tel. 812557575; fax 812557500; e-mail contact@rtr.ch; internet www.rtr.ch; operated by Radio e Televisiun Rumantscha (RTR); 24-hour programming in Romansh; Dir ERWIN ARDÜSER.

Radio Télévision Suisse (RTS): 40 ave du Temple, CP 78, 1010 Lausanne; tel. 213181111; fax 216523719; internet www.rts.ch; offers 4 stations: **La 1ère** news and background reports, stories, entertainment and music; **Espace 2** classical and contemporary music, jazz and folk, with features on the arts, history and society, radio plays and concert broadcasts; **Couleur 3** youth station playing rock and pop, with current affairs features; **Option Musique** music station with news bulletins, traffic reports and weather forecasts; Dir GILLES MARCHAND; Dir of Programmes GILLES PACHE; Dir of Information JEAN-JACQUES ROTH.

Radiotelevisione svizzera di lingua italiana (RSI): CP, 6903 Lugano; tel. 918035111; fax 918035355; e-mail info@rsi.ch; internet www.rsi.ch; operates 3 Italian-language stations: **Rete Uno** current affairs and reportage, also general entertainment programmes and public service broadcasts; **Rete Due** educational and general interest programmes, music and news; **Rete Tre** rock and pop music.

Schweizer Radio und Fernsehen (SRF): Fernsehstr. 1–4, Postfach, 8052 Zürich; tel. 443661111; fax 443055088; e-mail srf@srf.ch; internet www.srf.ch; f. 2011 by the merger of Schweizer Radio DRS

and Schweizer Fernsehen; SRF offers radio programme for the German part of Switzerland with 3 main studios in Zürich, Basel and Bern from which it operates 6 radio stations: **DRS 1** current affairs, traffic and weather reports and entertainment, 6 regional news magazines report regularly from around Switzerland; **DRS 2** classical music, jazz, culture, science, economics, politics and philosophy; **DRS 3** pop music and information, specializes in live concert broadcasts; **DRS 4 News** non-stop news; **DRS Musikwelle** traditional music of all genres, with news and DRS 1 programmes; **DRS Virus** youth and multimedia; Dir RUDOLF MATTER.

Swiss Satellite Radio (SsatR): Novarastr. 2, Postfach, 4002 Basel; tel. 613653831; fax 613653839; 3 Swiss Satellite Radio music channels, broadcast via the internet, cable and satellite; **Radio Swiss Pop** music-only service; **Radio Swiss Classic** classical music service with minimal presentation; **Radio Swiss Jazz** music service playing jazz, blues and soul; Dir SHENJA ERISMANN.

There are also 48 local and regional radio stations active in Switzerland.

Television

A complete television programme service for each linguistic region and regular broadcasts in Romansh are provided on the first (VHF) channel. The second and third (UHF) channels are used in each linguistic region for transmitting programmes of the other two linguistic regions. Limited direct advertising is allowed.

The transition from analogue to digital television broadcasting was completed in 2008.

Radio Télévision Suisse (RTS): see Radio; offers 2 channels: **TSR1** news on society, culture and entertainment; **TSR2** sports, documentaries, cultural programmes.

Schweizer Fernsehen (SF): see Radio; operates **SF1**, **SF zwei** and a third channel, **SF info**, which repeats current affairs programmes from **SF1**, **SF zwei** and **Presse TV** in hourly and half-hourly blocks.

Radiotelevisione svizzera di lingua italiana (RSI): see Radio; 2 Italian-language channels: **La 1** full-service channel aimed at a broad audience; **La 2** complementary channel with sport and children's programmes; Dir of TV DINO BALESTRA.

Televisiun Rumantscha (TvR): Via da Masans 2, 7002 Chur; tel. 812557575; fax 812557500; e-mail contact@rtr.ch; internet www.rtr.ch; operated by Radio e Televisiun Rumantscha (RTR); provides programming in Romansh (*Telesguard* and *Cuntrasts*) which is broadcast on SF1; Dir MARIANO TSCHUOR.

There are also 83 local and regional television stations, 18 of which have high transmission activity.

Finance

(cap. = capital; res = reserves; dep. = deposits; m. = million; brs = branches; all values are in Swiss francs)

REGULATORY AUTHORITY

Eidgenössische Finanzmarktaufsicht (FINMA) (Swiss Financial Market Supervisory Authority): Schwanengasse 2, 3003 Bern; tel. 313279100; fax 313279101; e-mail info@finma.ch; internet www.finma.ch; f. 2009 by merger of the Federal Office of Private Insurance, the Swiss Federal Banking Commission and the Anti-Money Laundering Control Authority; supervises banks, insurance cos, stock exchanges, securities dealers and other financial intermediaries; Chair. Prof. ANNE HÉRITIER LACHAT; CEO Dr PATRICK RAAFLAUB.

BANKING

Switzerland's banks have a long-standing reputation as a secure repository for foreign capital. The Swiss Banking Law of 1934 declared it a penal offence for a bank to provide information about its clients without their explicit authorization, unless a court had ordered otherwise. When foreign authorities wish to investigate Swiss accounts, criminal charges must have been made in a foreign court and accepted as valid by Switzerland. The system of numbered accounts has also shielded depositors' shares from investigation. However, the abuse of bank secrecy by organized crime led Switzerland and the USA to sign a treaty in May 1973, whereby banking secrecy rules may be waived in the case of common-law crime (although not for non-criminal tax evasion and anti-trust law infringements). Further amendments to banking secrecy legislation were introduced in 1990 and 1998.

In June 1977 the Swiss banks agreed a code of practice which required the introduction of stricter controls over the handling of foreign funds. The opening of numbered accounts was subjected to closer scrutiny and the practice of actively encouraging the flow of foreign money into the country was checked. The agreement was modified in 1982. In 1987, following the withdrawal from the agreement of the Swiss National Bank, the code was adapted by the Swiss

Bankers' Association into rules of professional conduct; further modifications to the code were introduced in 1992. In 1978, in view of the steady increase in Swiss banks' international business, the Federal Banking Commission was given greater supervisory powers. Banks were required for the first time to submit consolidated balance sheets to the Commission and new consolidation requirements forced banks to raise capital to between 6% and 8% of total liabilities. The capital requirement is now one of the highest in the world.

On 1 January 2009 the Federal Banking Commission merged with two other federal bodies to form the Swiss Financial Market Supervisory Authority (FINMA), which assumed responsibility for regulating the entire financial services sector.

In 2011 there were 312 banks operating in Switzerland. The 24 cantonal banks are mostly financed and controlled by the cantons, and their activities are co-ordinated by the Association of Swiss Cantonal Banks. In 2011 they had 702 branches in Switzerland and in 2010 they controlled more than one-third of Switzerland's savings deposits.

Central Bank

Schweizerische Nationalbank/Banque nationale suisse (Swiss National Bank): Börsenstr. 15, Postfach 2800, 8022 Zürich; tel. 446313111; fax 446313911; e-mail snb@snb.ch; internet www .snb.ch; f. 1907; conducts the country's monetary policy as an independent central bank; obliged by the Constitution and statute to act in accordance with the interests of the country as a whole; primary goal is to ensure price stability, while taking due account of economic developments; Dept I handles international affairs, economic affairs, legal and administrative affairs, human resources and communications; Dept II handles cash, finance and controlling, financial stability and oversight, and security; Dept III handles financial markets, asset management, risk management, banking operations and information technology; cap. 25m., res 22,872m., dep. 76,019m. (Dec. 2007); Chair., Governing Bd THOMAS JORDAN.

Canton Banks

There are 24 cantonal banks, of which the following are the largest:

Aargauische Kantonalbank: Bahnhofstr. 58, Postfach, 5001 Aarau; tel. 628357777; fax 628357778; e-mail akb@akb.ch; internet www.akb.ch; f. 1913; cap. 200m., res 950.8m., dep. 15,552.7m. (Dec. 2011); Pres. ARTHUR ZELLER; CEO RUDOLF DELLENBACH; 28 brs.

Banca dello Stato del Cantone Ticino: Viale H. Guisan 5, 6501 Bellinzona; tel. 918037111; fax 918037170; internet www.bancastato .ch; f. 1915; cap. 110m., res 365.4m., dep. 5,993.4m. (Dec. 2011); Chair. Dott. FULVIO PELLI; Pres., Exec. Bd DONATO BARBUSCIA; 3 brs.

Banque Cantonale de Fribourg: 1 blvd de Pérolles, 1701 Fribourg; tel. 848223223; fax 263507709; e-mail info@bcf.ch; internet www.bcf.ch; f. 1892 as Banque de l'Etat de Fribourg; present name adopted 1996; cap. 70m., res 1,139m., dep. 10,464.1m. (Dec. 2009); Chair. GILBERT MONNERON; CEO ALBERT MICHEL; 26 brs.

Banque Cantonale de Genève: 17 quai de l'Ile, CP 2251, 1211 Geneva; tel. 582112100; fax 582112199; e-mail info@bcge.ch; internet www.bcge.ch; f. 1994; cap. 360m., res 337m., dep. 12,061.7m. (Dec. 2011); Chair. JEAN-PIERRE ROTH; CEO BLAISE GOETSCHIN; 24 brs.

Banque Cantonale du Jura: 10 rue de la Chaumont, CP 278, 2900 Porrentruy; tel. 324651301; fax 324651495; e-mail bcj@bcj.ch; internet www.bcj.ch; f. 1979; cap. 42m., res 144m., dep. 1,680.2m. (Dec. 2011); Chair. Dr PAUL-ANDRÉ SANGLARD; Gen. Man. BERTRAND VALLEY; 12 brs.

Banque Cantonale du Valais: 8 pl. des Cèdres, CP 133, 1951 Sion; tel. 848765765; fax 273246666; e-mail info@bcvs.ch; internet www .bcvs.ch; f. 1917; cap. 150m., res 658.4m., dep. 9,166.8m. (Dec. 2011); Chair. KARIN PERRAUDIN; CEO JEAN-DANIEL PAPILLOUD; 6 brs.

Banque Cantonale Neuchâteloise: 4 pl. Pury, 2001 Neuchâtel; tel. 327236111; fax 327236236; e-mail info@bcn.ch; internet www .bcn.ch; f. 1883; cap. 100m., res 451.8m., dep. 5,914.9m. (Dec. 2011); Pres. JEAN-PIERRE GHELFI; Gen. Man. JEAN-NOËL DUC; 1 br.

Banque Cantonale Vaudoise: 14 pl. St François, CP 300, 1003 Lausanne; tel. 212121000; fax 212121596; e-mail info@bcv.ch; internet www.bcv.ch; f. 1845; cap. 86m., res 1,056m., dep. 28,152m. (Dec. 2011); Chair. OLIVIER STEIMER; CEO PASCAL KIENER; 66 brs.

Basellandschaftliche Kantonalbank: Rheinstr. 7, 4410 Liestal; tel. 619259494; fax 619259674; e-mail info@blkb.ch; internet www .blkb.ch; f. 1864; cap. 217m., res 1,300.4m., dep. 13,944m. (Dec. 2011); Pres. ELISABETH SCHIRMER; CEO Dr BEAT OBERLIN; 8 brs.

Basler Kantonalbank: Spiegelgasse 2, 4002 Basel; tel. 612662555; fax 612662915; e-mail bkb@bkb.ch; internet www.bkb.ch; f. 1899; cap. 254.2m., res 56.3m., dep. 26,624.8m. (Dec. 2011); Chair. Dr ANDREAS C. ALBRECHT; CEO HANS-RUDOLF MATTER; 19 brs.

BEKB/BCBE (Berner Kantonalbank/Banque Cantonale Bernoise): Bundespl. 8, Postfach, 3001 Bern; tel. 316661111; fax 316666040; e-mail bekb@bekb.ch; internet www.bekb.ch; f. 1834 as Banque Cantonale de Berne; present name adopted 1991; cap. 186.4m., res 1,681.1m., dep. 20,529m. (Dec. 2011); Pres. Dr JÜRG RIEBEN; CEO HANSPETER RÜFENACHT; 79 brs.

Graubündner Kantonalbank: Postfach, 7002 Chur; tel. 812569111; fax 812599588; e-mail info@gkb.ch; internet www.gkb .ch; f. 1870; cap. 250m., res 1,299.9m., dep. 14,330.1m. (Dec. 2012); Pres. Dr HANS HATZ; CEO ALOIS VINZENS; 8 brs.

Luzerner Kantonalbank: Pilatusstr. 12, 6002 Lucerne; tel. 844822811; fax 412062090; e-mail info@lukb.ch; internet www .lukb.ch; f. 1850; cap. 357m., res 628.4m., dep. 18,691.7m. (Dec. 2011); Chair. MARK BACHMANN; CEO BERNARD KOBLER; 26 brs.

Schwyzer Kantonalbank (SKZB): Bahnhofstr. 3, Postfach 263, 6431 Schwyz; tel. 588002020; fax 588002021; e-mail kundenzentrum@szkb.ch; internet www.szkb.ch; f. 1889 as Kantonalbank Schwyz, present name adopted 1997; cap. 50m., res 1,245.5m., dep. 9,420m. (Dec. 2012); Pres. ALOIS CAMENZIND; CEO Dr PETER HILFIKER; 27 brs.

St Galler Kantonalbank: St Leonhardstr. 25, Postfach 2063, 9001 St Gallen; tel. 712313131; fax 712313232; e-mail info@sgkb.ch; internet www.sgkb.ch; f. 1868; cap. 390.1m., res 33.5m., dep. 19,210.1m. (Dec. 2011); Chair. Dr FRANZ-PETER OESCH; Pres., Exec. Bd ROLAND LEDERGERBER; 36 brs.

Thurgauer Kantonalbank: Bankpl. 1, Postfach 160, 8570 Weinfelden; tel. 848111444; fax 848111445; e-mail info@tkb.ch; internet www.tkb.ch; f. 1871; cap. 400m., res 1,184.5m., dep. 11,008.1m. (Dec. 2011); Chair. RENÉ BOCK; CEO PETER HINDER; 30 brs.

Urner Kantonalbank: Bahnhofstr. 1, 6460 Altdorf; tel. 418756000; fax 418756313; e-mail info@urkb.ch; internet www.urkb.ch; f. 1915; cap. 30m., res 193m., dep. 1,815.4m. (Dec. 2011); Pres. Dr HANSRUEDI STADLER; CEO URS TRAXEL; 9 brs.

Zuger Kantonalbank: Baarerstr. 37, 6301 Zug; tel. 417091111; fax 417091555; e-mail service@zugerkb.ch; internet www.zugerkb.ch; f. 1892; cap. 144.1m., res 933.5m., dep. 8,019.4m. (Dec. 2012); Chair. and Pres. BRUNO BONATI; Gen. Man. PASCAL NIQUILLE; 10 brs.

Zürcher Kantonalbank: Bahnhofstr. 9, 8010 Zürich; tel. 442939393; fax 442923802; e-mail info@zkb.ch; internet www.zkb .ch; f. 1870; cap. 1,925m., dep. 97,896m. (Dec. 2011); Chair. Dr JÖRG MÜLLER-GANZ; CEO MARTIN SCHOLL; 82 brs.

Commercial Banks (Selected List)

Baloise Bank SoBa: Amthauspl. 4, Postfach 262, 4502 Solothurn; tel. 582853591; fax 582850333; e-mail bank@baloise.ch; internet www.baloise.ch; f. 1994; subsidiary of Bâloise-Gruppe; cap. 50m., res 154m., dep. 4,552.8m. (Dec. 2011); Group Chair. ANDREAS BURCKHARDT; Group CEO MARTIN STROBEL.

Bank Julius Baer & Co Ltd: Bahnhofstr. 36, 8010 Zürich; tel. 588881111; fax 588881122; internet www.juliusbaer.com; f. 1890; cap. 575m., res 2,732.4m., dep. 44,394.9m. (Dec. 2011); Chair. DANIEL J. SAUTER; CEO BORIS COLLARDI; 16 brs.

Banque Thaler SA: 3 rue Pierre-Fatio, Postfach 3335, 1211 Geneva 3; tel. 227070909; fax 227070910; e-mail info@banquethaler.ch; internet www.banquethaler.ch; f. 1982 as KBC Bank (Suisse) SA; present name adopted 2000; cap. 20m., res 9.8m., dep. 201.6m. (Dec. 2011); Pres. ROBERT CUYPERS; Gen. Man. DIRK EELBODE.

BNP Paribas (Suisse) SA: 2 pl. de Hollande, 1211 Geneva; tel. 582122111; fax 582122222; internet www.bnpparibas.ch; f. 1961 as United Overseas Bank SA; present name adopted 2001; cap. 320.3m., res 138.3m., dep. 28,492.4m. (Dec. 2011); Chair. MICHEL PÉBEREAU; CEO PASCAL BORIS; 5 brs.

BSI SA: Via Franscini 8, 6900 Lugano; tel. 588093111; fax 588093678; e-mail info@bsibank.com; internet www.bsibank.com; f. 1873 as Banca della Svizzera italiana; present name adopted 1998; absorbed Banca del Gottardo in 2008; cap. 1,840m., res 313.8m., dep. 26,654.1m. (Dec. 2011); Chair. Dr GIORGIO GHIRINGHELLI; CEO Dr ALFREDO GYSI; 10 brs.

Coutts & Co Ltd: Stauffacherstr. 1, 8022 Zürich; tel. 432455111; fax 432455396; e-mail info@coutts.com; internet www.coutts.com; fmrly RBS Coutts Bank Ltd; current name adopted 2011; cap. 110m., res 238.9m., dep. 16,452.3m. (Dec. 2011); Chair. DAVID DOUGLAS-HOME, Earl of Home; 5 brs.

Crédit Suisse Group: Paradepl. 8, Postfach 100, 8070 Zürich; tel. 442121616; fax 443332587; internet www.credit-suisse.ch; f. 1856; acquired Clariden Leu AG in Apr. 2012; cap. 4,400m., res 12,232m., dep. 339,183m. (Dec. 2011); Pres. URS ROHNER; Group CEO BRADY W. DOUGAN; 290 brs.

Migros Bank AG: Seidengasse 12, 8021 Zürich; tel. 442298111; fax 442298715; internet www.migrosbank.ch; f. 1958; cap. 700m., res 1,191.1m., dep. 28,475.8m. (Dec. 2012); Chair. HERBERT BOLLIGER; Pres., Exec. Bd Dr HARALD NEDWED; 44 brs.

Neue Aargauer Bank: Bahnhofstr. 49, 5001 Aarau; tel. 628388080; fax 628388280; e-mail webmaster@nab.ch; internet www.nab.ch; f. 1989; 98.6% owned by Crédit Suisse Group; cap. 134.1m., res 918.8m., dep. 14,945.7m. (Dec. 2011); Pres. Josef Meier; CEO Peter Bühlmann; 33 brs.

Raiffeisen Schweiz Genossenschaft/Raiffeisen Switzerland Cooperative: Raffeisenpl., 9001 St Gallen; tel. 712258888; fax 712258887; e-mail info@raiffeisen.ch; internet www.raiffeisen.ch; f. 1902; cap. 598.9m., dep. 115,215.7m. (Dec. 2011); Chair., Bd of Dirs Franz Marty; Chair., Exec. Bd Dr Pierin Vincenz; 367 associated banks.

Swissquote Bank: 33 chemin de la Créteaux, CP 391, 1196 Gland; tel. 229999898; fax 229999412; e-mail info@swissquote.ch; internet www.swissquote.ch; f. 2000; cap. 25m., res 9m., dep. 1,675m. (Dec. 2010); Chair. Mario Fontana; CEO Marc Bürki.

UBS AG: Bahnhofstr. 45, 8021 Zürich; tel. 442341111; fax 442399111; e-mail info@ubs.com; internet www.ubs.com; f. 1998 by merger of Union Bank of Switzerland (f. 1912) and Swiss Bank Corpn (f. 1872); cap. 383m., res 29,460m., dep. 443,987m. (Dec. 2011); Chair. Axel A. Weber; Group CEO Sergio P. Ermotti; 357 brs.

Union Bancaire Privée: 96–98 rue du Rhône, CP 1320, 1211 Geneva 1; tel. 588192111; fax 588192200; e-mail ubp@ubp.com; internet www.ubpbank.com; f. 1990 by merger of TDB American Express Bank (f. 1956) and Compagnie de Banque et d'Investissements (f. 1969); cap. 300m., res 550m., dep. 15,557.5m. (Dec. 2011); Chair. Edgar de Picciotto; CEO Guy de Picciotto; 6 brs.

Valiant Bank: Bundespl. 4, 3001 Bern; tel. 313209111; fax 313209112; internet www.valiant.ch; f. 2001 by merger of Spar- und Leihkasse in Bern, Gewerbekasse in Bern, bank in Langnau, BB Bank Belp and Ersparnikasse Murten; cap. 153.8m., res 1,410.8m., dep. 17,650m. (Dec. 2011); Chair. Jürg Bucher; CEO Michael Hobmeier; 88 brs.

Private Banks

Switzerland's private banking sector is the largest, in terms of assets, in the world. In 2009 there were 14 privately owned banks in Switzerland, of which the following are among the most important:

Banque Privée Edmond de Rothschild SA: 18 rue de Hesse, 1204 Geneva; tel. 588189111; fax 588189121; e-mail contact@bper.ch; internet www.lcf-rothschild.ch; f. 1924; cap. 45m., res 267.9m., dep. 11,996.3m. (Dec. 2011); Chair. Baron Benjamin de Rothschild; CEO Christophe de Backer; 2 brs.

EFG Bank: Bahnhofstr. 16, Postfach 2255, 8022 Zürich; tel. 442261717; fax 442261729; e-mail enquiries_ch@efgbank.com; internet www.efgbank.com; f. 1997 as EFG Private Bank SA; present name adopted 2005; cap. 162.4m., res 244.1m., dep. 14,545.7m. (Dec. 2010); Chair. Jean-Pierre Cuoni; CEO Alain Diriberry.

HSBC Private Bank (Suisse) SA: 2 quai Général Guisan, CP 3580, 1211 Geneva 3; tel. 587055555; fax 587055151; internet www.hsbcprivatebank.com; f. 1988 as Republic National Bank New York (Suisse) SA; present name adopted 2004; cap. 708.5m., res 1,607.1m., dep. 60,655.3m. (Dec. 2011); Chair. Stuart Gulliver; CEO Alexandre Zeller; 3 brs.

Hyposwiss Private Bank AG: Stauffacherstr. 41, Postfach 3180, 8021 Zürich; tel. 442143111; fax 442115223; e-mail info@hyposwiss.ch; internet www.hyposwiss.ch; f. 1889 as Schweizerische Hypothekenbank; present name adopted 2002; cap. 26m., res 86.2m., dep. 1,900.6m. (Dec. 2011); Chair. Roland Ledergerber; CEO Siegfried R. Peyer.

Lombard Odier & Cie: 11 rue de la Corraterie, Postfach 5215, 1211 Geneva 11; tel. 227092111; fax 227092911; e-mail contact@lombardodier.com; internet www.lombardodier.com; f. 2002 by merger of Lombard Odier & Cie (f. 1796) and Darier Hentsch & Cie (f. 1991); name changed from Lombard Odier Darier Hentsch in 2012; Partners Thierry Lombard, Patrick Odier, Bernard Droux, Anne-Marie de Weck, Christophe Hentsch, Hubert Keller, Frédéric Rochat, Arthur Caye.

Pictet & Cie: 60 route des Acacias, 1211 Geneva 73; tel. 583232323; fax 583232324; e-mail info@pictet.com; internet www.pictet.com; f. 1805; Sr Partner Ivan Pictet; Partners Claude Demole, Jacques de Saussure, Nicolas Pictet, Philippe Bertherat, Jean-François Demole, Renaud de Planta, Rémy Best.

Central Co-operative Credit Institution

Bank Coop AG: Aeschenpl. 3, 4002 Basel; tel. 612862121; fax 612714595; e-mail info@bankcoop.ch; internet www.bankcoop.ch; f. 1927 as Co-operative Central Bank; present name adopted 2001; 56.3% stake owned by Basler Kantonalbank; cap. 337.5m., res 82.3m., dep. 10,396.7m. (Dec. 2011); Chair. Dr Ralph Lewin; Pres., Exec. Bd Andreas Wäspi; 33 brs.

Bankers' Organizations

Association of Foreign Banks in Switzerland: Usteristr. 23, Postfach 1211, 8021 Zürich; tel. 442244070; fax 442210029; e-mail info@foreignbanks.ch; internet www.foreignbanks.ch; f. 1972; 141 mems (Dec. 2011); Chair. Dr Alfredo Gysi; Sec.-Gen. Dr Martin Maurer.

Schweizerische Bankiervereinigung/Association Suisse des Banquiers (Swiss Bankers' Asscn): Aeschenpl. 7, Postfach 4182, 4002 Basel; tel. 612959393; fax 612725382; e-mail office@sba.ch; internet www.swissbanking.org; f. 1912; 363 institutional mems and 16,000 individual mems; Chair. Patrick Odier; CEO Dr Urs P. Roth.

Verband Schweizerischer Kantonalbanken/Union des Banques Cantonales Suisses (Asscn of Swiss Cantonal Banks): Wallstr. 8, 4002 Basel; tel. 612066666; fax 612066667; e-mail vskb@vskb.ch; internet www.kantonalbank.ch; f. 1907; perm. office est. 1971; Chair. Paul Nyffeler.

STOCK EXCHANGES

BX Berne eXchange (Berner Börsenverein): Aarbergergasse 36, 3011 Bern; tel. 313294040; fax 313115309; e-mail office@berne-x.com; internet www.berne-x.com; f. 1884; 9 mems, 6 assoc. mems; CEO Luca Schenk.

SIX Swiss Exchange: Selnaustr. 30, 8021 Zürich; tel. 588542091; fax 588543091; e-mail six@six.com; internet www.six-swiss-exchange.com; f. 1873; 51 mems; Pres. Prof. Dr Peter Gomez; Group CEO Dr Urs Rüegsegger.

INSURANCE

In early 2013 there were 219 insurance and reinsurance companies under the supervision of FINMA.

Allianz Suisse: Bleicherweg 19, Postfach, 8022 Zürich; tel. 583587111; fax 583584042; e-mail contact@allianz-suisse.ch; internet www.allianz-suisse.ch; subsidiaries: Allianz Suisse Versicherungen, Allianz Suisse Leben, Allianz Suisse Personal Financial Services; Chair. Prof. Ulrich Zimmerli; CEO Dr Manfred Knof.

AXA Winterthur: Gen. Guisan-Str. 40, Postfach 357, 8401 Winterthur; tel. 522189595; fax 522136620; e-mail info.ch@axa-winterthur.ch; internet www.axa-winterthur.ch; f. 1875; fmrly Winterthur Schweizerische Versicherungs-Gesellschaft; both life and non-life; owned by AXA Group (France); Pres. Jacques de Vaucleroy; CEO Philippe Egger.

Basler Versicherungen: Aeschengraben 21, Postfach 2275, 4002 Basel; tel. 582852828; fax 582859073; e-mail insurance@baloise.ch; internet www.baloise.ch; f. 1864; all classes; part of Bâloise-Gruppe; CEO Michael Müller.

Generali (Schweiz) Holding AG: Soodmattenstr. 10, 8134 Adliswil; tel. 584724040; fax 584724425; e-mail info@generali.ch; internet www.generali.ch; life and non-life; part of Generali Group (Italy); CEO Alfred Leu.

Helvetia Versicherungen: St Alban-Anlage 26, 4002 Basel; tel. 582801000; fax 582801001; internet www.helvetia.ch; f. 1861; owned by Helvetia Holding; life, fire, burglary, accident liability, motor; Chair. Dr Erich Walser; CEO, Switzerland Philipp Gmür.

Schweizerische Mobiliar Versicherungsgesellschaft (Die Mobiliar): Bundesgasse 35, 3001 Bern; tel. 313896111; fax 313896852; e-mail diemobiliar@mobi.ch; internet www.mobi.ch; f. 1826; accident, sickness, fire and damage by the elements, theft, valuables, damage by water, glass breakage, machines, construction work, interruption of business, epidemics, warranty, guarantee, third-party liability, motor vehicles, travel, transport; CEO Markus Hongler.

Schweizerische National-Versicherungs-Gesellschaft (Nationale Suisse): Steinengraben 41, 4003 Basel; tel. 612752111; fax 612752656; e-mail info@nationalesuisse.ch; internet www.nationalesuisse.ch; f. 1883; CEO Hans Künzle.

Swiss Life: 40 quai General Guisan, POB 2831, 8022 Zürich; tel. 432843311; fax 432846311; e-mail info.com@swisslife.ch; internet www.swisslife.com; f. 1857; specializes in international employee benefit and pension plans; brs in France, Germany, Liechtenstein, Luxembourg and Singapore; Group CEO Bruno Pfister.

Swiss Re (Schweizerische Rückversicherungs-Gesellschaft) (Swiss Reinsurance Co): Mythenquai 50/60, 8022 Zürich; tel. 432852121; fax 432852999; e-mail contact@swissre.com; internet www.swissre.com; f. 1863; world-wide reinsurance; Chair. Walter Kielholz; CEO Michel M. Liès.

Vaudoise Assurances: pl. de Milan, POB 120, 1001 Lausanne; tel. 216188000; fax 216188181; internet www.vaudoise.ch; f. 1895; subsidiaries: Vaudoise Générale (non-life), Vaudoise Vie (life); Pres. Paul-André Sanglard; Dir-Gen. Philippe Hebeisen.

Zürich Versicherungs-Gesellschaft: Mythenquai 2, 8002 Zürich; tel. 446282828; fax 446292929; e-mail contact@zurich.ch; internet www.zurich.ch; f. 1872; part of Zurich Financial Services group; life and non-life; CEO (life) YVONNE LANG KETTERER; CEO (non-life) JOACHIM MASUR.

Insurance Organization

Schweizerischer Versicherungsverband—Association suisse d'assurances (SVV—ASA) (Swiss Insurance Asscn): C. F. Meyer-Str. 14, Postfach 4288, 8022 Zürich; tel. 442082828; fax 442082800; e-mail info@svv.ch; internet www.svv.ch; f. 1901; Pres. URS BERGER; Dir LUCIUS DÜRR; 71 mems.

Trade and Industry

GOVERNMENT AGENCY

Osec Business Network Switzerland: Stampfenbachstr. 85, Postfach 2407, 8021 Zürich; tel. 443655151; fax 443655221; e-mail info@osec.ch; internet www.osec.ch; f. 1927; offices in Lausanne and Lugano; promotes trade; Pres. RUTH METZLER-ARNOLD; CEO DANIEL KÜNG.

PRINCIPAL CHAMBERS OF COMMERCE

Aargauische Industrie- und Handelskammer (AIHK): Entfelderstr. 11, 5001 Aarau; tel. 628371818; fax 628371819; e-mail info@aihk.ch; internet www.aihk.ch; f. 1874; Pres. DANIEL KNECHT.

Camera di commercio, dell'industria, dell'artigianato e dei servizi del Cantone Ticino (Cc-Ti): Corso Elvezia 16, 6900 Lugano; tel. 919115111; fax 919115112; e-mail info@cc-ti.ch; internet www.cciati.ch; f. 1917; Pres. FRANCO AMBROSETTI; Dir LUCA ALBERTONI; 800 mems.

Chambre de commerce Fribourg (CCF): 37 route du Jura, CP 304, 1701 Fribourg; tel. 263471220; fax 263471239; e-mail info@ccfribourg.ch; internet www.ccfribourg.ch; f. 1917; Pres. RENÉ JENNY.

Chambre de commerce et d'industrie du Jura: 23 rue de l'Avenir, CP 274, 2800 Delémont 1; tel. 324214545; fax 324214540; e-mail ccjura@cci.ch; internet www.ccij.ch; Pres. RÉMY LAURENT; Dir JEAN-FRÉDÉRIC GERBER; 400 mems.

Chambre de commerce, d'industrie et des services de Genève (CCIG): 4 blvd du Théâtre, 1211 Geneva 11; tel. 228199111; fax 228199100; e-mail ccig@ccig.ch; internet www.ccig.ch; f. 1865; Pres. JEAN-BERNARD RONDEAU; Dir JACQUES JEANNERAT; 1,700 mems.

Chambre neuchâteloise du commerce et de l'industrie: 4 rue de la Serre, 2001 Neuchâtel; tel. 327272410; fax 327272428; e-mail cnci@cnci.ch; internet www.cnci.ch; Pres. FRÉDÉRIC GEISSBUHLER; Dir PIERRE HILTPOLD; 780 mem. cos.

Chambre valaisanne de commerce et d'industrie: 6 rue Pré-Fleuri, CP 288, 1951 Sion; tel. 273273535; fax 273273536; e-mail info@cci-valais.ch; internet www.cci-valais.ch; Pres. BERNARD BRUTTIN; Dir VINCENT RIESEN; 356 mem. cos.

Chambre vaudoise du commerce et de l'industrie (CVCI): 47 ave d'Ouchy, CP 315, 1001 Lausanne; tel. 216133535; fax 216133505; e-mail cvci@cvci.ch; internet www.cvci.ch; f. 1898; Pres. BERNARD RÜEGER; Dir CLAUDINE AMSTEIN; 2,900 mems.

Glarner Handelskammer: Postgasse 27, 8750 Glarus; tel. 556406121; fax 556406122; e-mail glhk@althauslegal.ch; internet www.glhk.ch; Pres. PETER RUFIBACH; Sec. DANIEL ALTHAUS; 185 mems.

Handels- und Industrieverein des Kantons Bern (Berner Handelskammer): Kramgasse 2, Postfach 5464, 3001 Bern; tel. 313888787; fax 313888788; e-mail info@bern-cci.ch; internet www.bern-cci.ch; Pres. BERNHARD LUDWIG; 3600 mems.

Handelskammer und Arbeitgeberverband Graubünden: Hinterm Bach 40, 7000 Chur; tel. 812543800; fax 812543809; e-mail info@hkgr.ch; internet www.hkgr.ch; Pres. LUDWIG LOCHER.

Handelskammer und Arbeitgebervereinigung Winterthur (HAW): Neumarkt 15, 8401 Winterthur; tel. 522130763; fax 522089934; e-mail office@haw.ch; internet www.haw.ch; f. 1992; Pres. THOMAS ANWANDER; Dir CHRISTIAN MODL.

Handelskammer beider Basel: Aeschenvorstadt 67, Postfach, 4010 Basel; tel. 612706060; fax 612706005; e-mail info@hkbb.ch; internet www.hkbb.ch; f. 1997 by merger of Basler Handelskammer (f. 1876) and Verband der Industriellen Baselland (f. 1919); Pres. THOMAS STAEHELIN; 800 mem. cos.

Industrie- und Handelskammer St Gallen-Appenzell: Gallusstr. 16, Postfach, 9001 St Gallen; tel. 712241010; fax 712241060; e-mail info@ihk.ch; internet www.ihk.ch; f. 1466; Pres. PETER SPENGER; Dir Dr KURT WEIGELT; 1,500 mems.

Industrie- und Handelskammer Thurgau: Schmidstr. 9, Postfach 396, 8570 Weinfelden; tel. 716221919; fax 716226257; e-mail info@ihk-thurgau.ch; internet www.ihk-thurgau.ch; f. 1870; Pres. CHRISTIAN NEUWEILER; Dir PETER MAAG; 620 mems.

Solothurner Handelskammer: Grabackerstr. 6, Postfach 1554, 4502 Solothurn; tel. 326262424; fax 326262426; e-mail info@sohk.ch; internet www.sohk.ch; f. 1874; Pres. HANS KUHN; Dir ROLAND FÜRST; 500 mems.

Zentralschweizerische Handelskammer: Kapellpl. 2, Postfach 2941, 6002 Lucerne; tel. 414106865; fax 414105288; e-mail info@hkz.ch; internet www.hkz.ch; f. 1889; Pres. HANS WICKI; Dir FELIX HOWALD; 600 mems.

Zürcher Handelskammer: Selnaustr. 32, Postfach 3058, 8022 Zürich; tel. 442174050; fax 442174051; e-mail direktion@zurichcci.ch; internet www.zurichcci.ch; f. 1873; represents businesses in Zürich, Schaffhausen and Zug cantons; Pres. PETER QUADRI; CEO Dr REGINE SAUTER; 1,800 mems.

INDUSTRIAL AND TRADE ASSOCIATIONS

Associazione Industrie Ticinesi: Corso Elvezia 16, CP 5130, 6901 Lugano; tel. 919118484; fax 919234636; e-mail info@aiti.ch; internet www.aiti.ch; f. 1962; Pres. DANIELE LOTTI; Dir STEFANO MODENINI; 200 mems.

Chocosuisse—Verband Schweizerischer Schokoladefabrikanten: Münzgraben 6, 3000 Bern 7; tel. 313100990; fax 313100999; e-mail info@chocosuisse.ch; internet www.chocosuisse.ch; f. 1901; asscn of chocolate mfrs; Pres. WALTER ANDERAU; Dir Dr FRANZ SCHMID; 18 mems, 2 assoc. mems.

Economiesuisse (Swiss Business Federation): Hegibachstr. 47, Postfach 1072, 8032 Zürich; tel. 444213535; fax 444213434; e-mail info@economiesuisse.ch; internet www.economiesuisse.ch; f. 1870; as Schweizerischer Handels- und Industrie-Verein; present name adopted 2000; Pres. Dr RUDOLF WEHRLI; Exec. Dir Dr PASCAL GENTINETTA; 163 mems.

Electrosuisse: Luppmenstr. 1, 8320 Fehraltorf; tel. 449561111; fax 449561112; e-mail info@electrosuisse.ch; internet www.electrosuisse.ch; f. 1889 as Swiss Electrotechnical Association; electronics; Chair. WILLY R. GEHRER; Man. Dir MARKUS BURGER; 1,880 mem. cos.

Fédération de l'Industrie Horlogère Suisse (FH): 6 rue d'Argent, 2502 Bienne; tel. 323280828; fax 323280880; internet www.fhs.ch; f. 1982 by merger of Swiss Chamber of Watchmaking and Swiss Watchmaking Fed.; watch industry; Pres. JEAN-DANIEL PASCHE; 500 mems.

Föderation der Schweizerischen Nahrungsmittel-Industrien: Thunstr. 82, 3000 Bern 6; Münzgraben 6, 3000 Bern 7; tel. 313562121; fax 313510065; e-mail info@thunstrasse82.ch; internet www.fial.ch; foodstuffs; Pres. ROLF SCHWEIGER; 199 mems.

Schweizerischer Baumeisterverband (SBV): Weinbergstr. 49, Postfach, 8042 Zürich; tel. 442588111; fax 442588335; e-mail verband@baumeister.ch; internet www.baumeister.ch; f. 1897; building contractors; Pres. WERNER MESSMER; Dir DANIEL LEHMANN; 3,500 mems.

Schweizerischer Gewerbeverband (SGV) (Swiss Union of Small and Medium Enterprises): Schwarztorstr. 26, 3001 Bern; tel. 313801414; fax 313801415; e-mail info@sgv-usam.ch; internet www.sgv-usam.ch; f. 1879; Pres. JEAN-FRANÇOIS RIME; Dir HANS-ULRICH BIGLER; 280 mems.

Schweizerischer Verband für visuelle Kommunikation (Viscom): Speichergasse 35, Postfach 678, 3000 Bern 7; tel. 582255500; fax 582255510; e-mail info@viscom.ch; internet www.viscom.ch; f. 1869; printing industry; Pres. PETER EDELMANN; Dir THOMAS GSPONER; 750 mem. cos.

scienceindustries: Nordstr. 15, Postfach, 8021 Zürich; tel. 443681711; fax 443681770; e-mail info@scienceindustries.ch; internet www.scienceindustries.ch; f. 1882; branch asscn of the chemical, pharmaceutical and biotechnology industry; Pres. CHRISTOPH MÄDER; Dir-Gen. Dr BEAT MOSER; c. 250 mems.

Swiss Cigarette: Monbijoustr. 14, CP 5236, 3001 Bern; tel. 313909918; fax 313909903; e-mail office@swiss-cigarette.ch; internet www.swiss-cigarette.ch; f. 1933; formerly Communauté de l'industrie suisse de la cigarette; cigarette mfrs; Dir CHANTAL AEBY PÜRRO; 3 mem. cos.

Swiss Retail Federation: Marktgasse 50, 3000 Bern 7; tel. 313124040; fax 313124041; e-mail info@swiss-retail.ch; internet www.swiss-retail.ch; formerly Verband der Schweizerischen Waren- und Kaufhäuser; Pres. BRUNO FRICK; 35 mem. cos.

Swiss Textile Federation: Beethovenstr. 20, Postfach 2900, 8022 Zürich; tel. 442897979; fax 442897980; e-mail zuerich@swisstextiles.ch; internet www.swisstextiles.ch; f. 1874; textiles and fashion; Pres. ANDREAS SALLMANN; Dir PETER FLÜCKIGER; 200 mems.

Verband Schweizerischer Kreditbanken und Finanzierungsinstitute (VSKF): Uraniastr. 12, POB 3228, 8021 Zürich; tel. 442504340; fax 442504349; e-mail office@gigersimmen.ch; internet www.vskf.org; f. 1945; asscn of credit banks and finance institutes; Pres. HEINZ HOFER; Sec. Dr ROBERT SIMMEN; 12 mems.

Verband Schweizerische Ziegelindustrie: Elfenstr. 19, 3006 Bern; tel. 313565757; e-mail mail@domoterra.ch; internet www .domoterra.ch; f. 1874; heavy clay; Sec.-Gen. Dr PETER R. BURK-HALTER; 11 mem. cos.

EMPLOYERS' ORGANIZATIONS
Central Organizations

Schweizerischer Arbeitgeberverband (Confed. of Swiss Employers): Hegibachstr. 47, Postfach, 8032 Zürich; tel. 444211717; fax 444211718; e-mail verband@arbeitgeber.ch; internet www.arbeitgeber.ch; f. 1908; Pres. VALENTIN VOGT; Dir THOMAS DAUM; 80 mems.

Schweizerischer Bauernverband (Union Suisse des Paysans, Lega svizzera dei contadini, Swiss Farmers' Union): Laurstr. 10, 5200 Brugg; tel. 564625111; fax 564415348; internet www.sbv-usp .ch; f. 1897; Pres. HANSJÖRG WALTER; Dir JACQUES BOURGEOIS.

Principal Regional Organizations

Arbeitgeberverband Basel: Aeschenvorstadt 71, Postfach 4010 Basel; tel. 612059600; fax 612059609; e-mail info@arbeitgeberbasel .ch; internet www.arbeitgeberbasel.ch; f. 2007 by merger of Basler Volkswirtschaftsbund and Arbeitgeber-Verband Basel; Pres. MARC R. JAQUET; Dir BARBARA GUTZWILLER-HOLLIGER; 2,200 mems.

Fédération des entreprises romandes: 98 rue de Saint-Jean, CP 5278, 1211 Geneva 11; tel. 227153111; fax 227380434; e-mail info@ fer-sr.ch; internet www.fer-sr.ch; f. 1947; Pres. NICOLAS BRUNSCHWIG; Sec.-Gen. BLAISE MATTHEY.

Industrie- und Handelskammer Zentralschweiz (IHZ): Kapellpl. 2, Postfach 2941, 6002 Lucerne; tel. 414106889; fax 414105288; e-mail info@hkz.ch; internet www.liv-luzern.ch; f. 1889; Pres. HANS WICKI; Dir FELIX HOWALD; 600 mems.

Union des associations patronales genevoises (UAPG): 98 rue de Saint-Jean, 1211 Geneva 11; tel. 227153445; fax 227380434; e-mail uapg@uapg.ch; internet www.uapg.ch; f. 1912; union of employers' asscns in Geneva; Pres. JEAN-LUC FAVRE.

Union des industriels valaisans: 6 rue de Lausanne, 1950 Sion; tel. 273232992; e-mail info@uiv.ch; internet www.uiv.ch; f. 1955; Pres. GRÉGOIRE ITEN.

Verband der Arbeitgeber Region Bern (VAB): Effingerstr. 1, Postfach 6916, 3001 Bern; tel. 313902581; fax 313902582; e-mail info@berner-arbeitgeber.ch; internet www.berner-arbeitgeber.ch; f. 1919; employers' asscn for the Bern region; Pres. ENRICO CASANOVAS; Dir Dr CLAUDE THOMANN.

Vereinigung Zürcherischer Arbeitgeberorganisationen: Selnaustr. 30, 8021 Zürich; tel. 442012875; fax 442012877; e-mail dieter .sigrist@swx.com; f. 1947; asscn of Zürich employers' orgs; Pres. THOMAS ISLER; Sec. DIETER SIGRIST.

Sectional Organizations

Arbeitgeberverband Schweizerischer Papier-Industrieller: Bergstr. 110, 8032 Zürich; tel. 442669920; fax 442669949; e-mail zpk@zpk.ch; internet www.zpk.ch; paper mfrs; Pres. FRANK R. RUEPP; Dir MAX FRITZ; 11 mems.

Convention Patronale de l'Industrie Horlogère Suisse: 65 ave Léopold-Robert, 2301 La Chaux-de-Fonds; tel. 329100383; fax 329100384; e-mail info@cpih.ch; internet www.cpih.ch; f. 1937; watch mfrs; Pres. ELISABETH ZÖLCH; Gen. Sec. FRANÇOIS MATILE; 6 mems.

Swissmem (Swiss Mechanical and Electrical Engineering Industries): Pfingstweidstr. 102, Postfach, 8037 Zürich; tel. 443844111; e-mail info@swissmem.ch; internet www.swissmem.ch; f. 1905; Pres. HANS HESS; Dir PETER DIETRICH; c. 1000 mems.

UTILITIES
Electricity

Verband Schweizerischer Elektrizitätsunternehmen: Hintere Bahnhofstr. 10, Postfach, 5001 Aarau; tel. 628252525; fax 628252526; e-mail info@strom.ch; internet www.strom.ch; electricity producers' asscn; f. 1895; Pres. KURT ROHRBACH; Dir MICHAEL FRANK; 385 mems, 56 assoc. mems.

Gas

Verband der Schweizerischen Gasindustrie: Grütlistr. 44, Postfach, 8027 Zürich; tel. 442883131; fax 442021834; e-mail vsg@ erdgas.ch; internet www.erdgas.ch; f. 1928; Pres. Dr HAJO LEUTEN-EGGER; Dir DANIELA DECURTINS; 80 mems.

Water

The cantons are responsible for the supply of water, but delegate to the municipalities and communes. As a result Switzerland has some 3,000 water companies. Water is usually supplied by a public company or co-operative, such as the municipal water suppliers for Basel, Winterthur and Zürich (Industrielle Werke Basel, Stadtwerk Winterthur, Wasserversorgung Zürich).

TRADE UNIONS
National Federations

Schweizerischer Gewerkschaftsbund (SGB) (Swiss Fed. of Trade Unions): Monbijoustr. 61, 3000 Bern 23; tel. 313770101; fax 313770102; e-mail info@sgb.ch; internet www.sgb.ch; f. 1880; main trade union org.; 16 affiliated unions; affiliated to ITUC; Pres. PAUL RECHSTEINER; c. 380,000 mems.

Travail.Suisse: Hopfenweg 21, Postfach 5775, 3001 Bern; tel. 313702111; fax 313702109; e-mail info@travailsuisse.ch; internet www.travailsuisse.ch; f. 2002 by merger of Confédération des Syndicats Chrétiens de Suisse and Fédération des Sociétés Suisses d'Employés; 12 affiliated unions; Pres. MARTIN FLÜGEL; 168,352 mems (Jan. 2008).

Transport
RAILWAYS

Switzerland has an extensive rail network with an average track density of 122 km per 1,000 square km. In 2010 the total length of railway track stood at 3,137 km, all of which were electrified. In order to improve and expand the existing infrastructure, the Swiss Federal Office of Transport, Bundesamt für Verkehr (BAV), launched a project entitled Rail 2030 in 2011. The 35-km Lötschberg Base Tunnel was opened to traffic in 2008, shortening travel time between Germany and the Italian city of Milan by about one hour. Excavation of a further 57-km rail tunnel, the Gotthard Base Tunnel, was completed in 2010; the tunnel was scheduled to become operational in 2017 and was expected to reduce journey times between Zürich and Milan by one-and-a-half hours.

Schweizerische Bundesbahnen (SBB) (Chemins de fer fédéraux suisses): Hochschulstr. 6, 3000 Bern 65; tel. 512201111; e-mail railinfo@sbb.ch; internet www.sbb.ch; f. 1902; 3,034 km in 2007 (of which 1,707 km were multiple track); Chair. ULRICH GYGI; CEO ANDREAS MEYER.

Small private companies control private railways in Switzerland, chiefly along short mountain routes, with a total length of around 2,032 km. The following are among the principal private railways:

BLS AG: Genfergasse 11, Postfach, 3001 Bern; tel. 583272727; fax 583272910; e-mail info@bls.ch; internet www.bls.ch; f. 1906 as Berner Alpenbahn-Gesellschaft Bern–Lötschberg–Simplon (BLS); present co f. 2006 by merger; 900 km; network includes the 34.6 km Lötschberg Base Tunnel; regional passenger services; cargo services on Lötschberg–Simplon route; direct car-train connection from Bern to the Valais and Italy; boat services on Lakes Thun and Brienz; commuter rail services in Bern area; Chair. RUDOLF STÄMPFLI; CEO BERNARD GUILLELMON.

Centovalli Railway: Via Franzoni 1, CP 146, 6601 Locarno; tel. 917560400; fax 917560499; e-mail fart@centovalli.ch; internet www .centovalli.ch; f. 1923; 19 km of track in Switzerland; owned by Ferrovie Autolinee Regionali Ticinesi SA; Locarno–Camedo-Domodossola (Italy); Dir MAURO CARONNO.

Matterhorn Gotthard Bahn AG: Bahnhofpl. 7, 3900 Brig; tel. 848642442; fax 279277779; e-mail info@mgbahn.ch; internet www .mgbahn.ch; f. 2003 by merger of BVZ Zermatt-Bahn AG and Furka Oberalp Bahn AG; 25% state-owned, 75% owned by BVZ Holding AG; Zermatt–Brig–Disentis and Andermatt–Göschenen; 144 km; Chair. DANIEL LAUBER; Dir HANS-RUDOLF MOOSER.

Matterhorn Gotthard Bahn Infrastruktur AG: Bahnhofpl. 7, 3900 Brig; tel. 279277777; fax 279277779; e-mail info@mgbahn.ch; internet www.mgbahn.ch; 100% state-owned; responsible for track, overhead catenary equipment, operating control centres, station bldgs and workshops; Pres. ROLF ESCHER.

Matterhorn Gotthard Bahn Verkehrs AG: Bahnhofpl. 7, 3900 Brig; tel. 279277777; fax 279277779; e-mail info@mgbahn.ch; internet www.mgbahn.ch; 75% owned by BVZ Holding AG, 25% state-owned; controls all railway operations, incl. rolling stock, depots and related maintenance; Pres. DANIEL LAUBER.

Montreux-Oberland Bernois: CP 1426, 1820 Montreux; tel. 219898181; fax 219898100; e-mail info@goldenpass.ch; internet www.goldenpass.ch; f. 1899; 75 km; Montreux–Château d'Oex–Gstaad–Zweisimmen–Lenk im Simmental; operates tour services incl. GoldenPass Panoramic, GoldenPass Classic, Belle Epoque, Rochers-de-Naye, Les Pléiades and the Chocolate Train; operates funicular railways on Vevey–Chardonne–Mont-Pèlerin and Les Avants–Sonloup routes; Dir W. VON SIEBENTHAL.

Rhätische Bahn AG (Rhaetian Railway): Bahnhofstr. 25, 7002 Chur; tel. 812886100; fax 81886101; internet www.rhb.ch; f. 1889;

384 km; the most extensive of the privately run railways; Chair. STEFAN ENGLER.

Südostbahn AG: Bahnhofpl. 1A, 9001 St Gallen; tel. 712282323; fax 712282333; e-mail info@sob.ch; internet www.sob.ch; f. 1889; f. 2001 by merger of Schweizerische Südostbahn and Bodensee–Toggen-burg-Bahn; 35.8% owned by Federal Govt; 147 km; Pres. WILLI HAAG.

ROADS

In 2010 Switzerland had 71,456 km of roads, of which 18,050 km were national roads and highways while 1,790 km were motorways. The 17-km road tunnel through the Saint Gotthard Pass, a European road link of paramount importance, was opened in 1980.

Swiss Federal Roads Office (Bundesamt für Strassen/Office fédéral des routes): Mühlestr. 2, Ittigen, 3003 Bern; tel. 313229411; fax 313232303; e-mail info@astra.admin.ch; internet www.astra.admin .ch; f. 1998; federal authority responsible for road infrastructure and private road transport; Dir RUDOLF DIETERLE.

INLAND WATERWAYS

The Rhine river provides the only inland waterway from Basel to the North Sea. Inland navigation legislation is the responsibility of the Confederation, but sovereignty over the waterways rests with the cantons. This means, in practice, that the Confederation limits its activities to the supervision of the licensed shipping companies (passenger ships and the related infrastructure, such as landing stages) and pilots; the cantons supervise pleasure-boat navigation (sports boats, i.e. sail and motor boats, etc.) and the non-licensed passenger vessels and goods shipping on the lakes and rivers.

SHIPPING

Although Switzerland is landlocked, the Rhine river is navigable by sea-going vessels as far as Basel; in addition, Swiss-registered merchant ships operate on the world's oceans. At 31 December 2012 Switzerland's flag registered fleet comprised 69 vessels, with an aggregate displacement of some 798,375 grt. The principal shipping companies in Switzerland are:

ABCmaritime: 1 rue Perdtemps, 1260 Nyon; tel. 223657100; fax 223657111; e-mail info@abcmaritime.ch; internet www.abcmaritime .ch; f. 1982; ship management; CEO DANIEL WOLF.

Agility Logistics AG: Sankt Jakobs-Str. 220, 4002 Basel; tel. 613165151; fax 613135557; e-mail switzerland@agilitylogistics .com; internet www.agilitylogistics.com; fmrly Natural AG; shipping management and freight forwarder; Man. Dir, Area West PATRICK JAEGER.

Keller Shipping Ltd: Holbeinstr. 68, Postfach 3479, 4002 Basel; tel. 612818686; fax 612818679; e-mail info@lloydsagency.ch; internet www.lloydsagency.ch; agency of Lloyds of London (United Kingdom) in Switzerland and Liechtenstein; Pres. A. R. KELLER.

Mediterranean Shipping Co SA: 12–14 Chemin Rieu, 1208 Geneva; tel. 227038888; fax 227038787; e-mail info@mscgva.ch; internet www.mscgva.ch; f. 1970; operates 458 container vessels (April 2013); CEO G. APONTE.

Reederei Zürich AG: Postfach, 8032 Zürich; tel. 442571040; fax 442571045; e-mail chartering@reedereizurich.com; internet www .reedereizurich.com; ship management.

Suisse-Atlantique, Société de Navigation Maritime SA: 7 ave des Baumettes, CP 48, 1020 Renens 1; tel. 216372201; fax 216372202; internet www.suisat.com; world-wide tramping services; Pres. E. ANDRE; Dir P. GRUAZ.

CIVIL AVIATION

In 2010 there were a total of 65 airports. Switzerland's principal airports are situated at Zürich and Geneva. A major airport at Basel-Mulhouse-Freiburg (EuroAirport) serves northern Switzerland, but is situated across the border in France.

Darwin Airline: Via Campagna, Centro Nord Sud, Stabile 2, 6934 Bioggio; tel. 916124500; fax 916124517; e-mail info@darwinairline .com; internet www.darwinairline.com; f. 2003; low-cost airline; flights from 4 Swiss airports to destinations in Italy and Spain; took over the operations of Baboo Airlines in 2011; Pres. EMILIO MARTINENGHI; CEO MAURIZIO MERLO.

Edelweiss Air: Operations Center, Postfach, 8058 Zürich-Flug-hafen; tel. 438165060; fax 438165061; e-mail office@flyedelweiss .com; internet www.edelweissair.ch; f. 1995; operates charter flights to destinations world-wide; subsidiary of Lufthansa; CEO KARL KISTLER.

Helvetic Airways AG: Postfach 250, 8058 Zürich-Flughafen; tel. 442708500; e-mail info@helvetic.com; internet www.helvetic.com;

f. 2003; charter flights and scheduled services to destinations in Italy and Germany; Chair. LEONARDO DE LUCA; CEO BRUNO JANS.

Swiss (Swiss International Air Lines): Postfach, 4002 Basel; tel. 615820000; fax 615823333; e-mail communications@swiss.com; internet www.swiss.com; f. 1979 as Crossair, took over operations from Swissair and adopted current name in 2002; national carrier operating routes to 74 destinations in 38 countries; subsidiary of Deutsche Lufthansa AG (Germany); CEO HARRY HOHMEISTER.

Tourism

Switzerland's principal attractions are the lakes and lake resorts and the mountains. Walking, mountaineering and winter sports are among the chief pastimes. Foreign tourist arrivals at hotels and similar establishments totalled 8.6m. in 2010. Receipts from tourism totalled 15,550m. Swiss francs in 2010 and a provisional 15,577m. Swiss francs in 2011.

Switzerland Tourism: Tödistr. 7, 8027 Zürich; tel. 442881111; fax 442881205; e-mail info@myswitzerland.com; internet www .myswitzerland.com; f. 1917; Dir JÜRG SCHMID.

Defence

National defence is based on compulsory military service for all able-bodied male citizens; women may serve voluntarily. Switzerland maintains no standing army except for a small permanent personnel of commissioned and non-commissioned officers primarily concerned with training. Military service consists of 18 weeks' compulsory recruit training at the age of 19–20 years, followed by seven three-week 'refresher' training courses between the ages of 20 and 30 years. Each soldier keeps his equipment in his own home, and receives compulsory marksmanship training between periods of service. As assessed at November 2012, the total strength of the armed forces, when mobilized, was 180,200, comprising an active force of 23,100 and reserves of 157,100 (army 107,900; air force 24,050; command support organization 16,150; and logistics organization 9,000). In addition, there was a civil defence force numbering 76,000 reservists. The Confederation belongs to no international defence organizations, and the strategy of the army and air force is defensive. In December 1996 Switzerland signed the Partnership for Peace framework document of the North Atlantic Treaty Organization (NATO). It was emphasized, however, that this in no way compromised the country's 'permanent neutrality', and that Switzerland had no intention of joining NATO itself.

Defence Expenditure: Budgeted at 4,690m. Swiss francs for 2013.

Chief of the General Staff: Maj.-Gen. ANDRÉ BLATTMANN.

Education

Pre-primary education in Switzerland is largely financed by the 26 cantons; pupils may undertake one or two years of kindergarten education. Primary and secondary education are also controlled by the cantons, thus there are 26 different systems in operation. Responsibility for higher education is shared between the cantons and the Federal Government. Education is compulsory for children between the ages of seven and 16 years. The duration of primary education, which commences at the age of six or seven, is nine years. The duration and system of secondary education depends on individual cantonal policy. Some 20% of 17-year-olds continue their studies at a higher secondary school (*Gymnasium/collège*), and a leaving certificate (*Matura/maturité*) from one of these is a prerequisite for entry to academic higher education. About 70% proceed to vocational training (trade and technical) for a period of three to four years. There are 10 cantonal universities, two Federal Institutes of Technology (of university standing) and one Academic Institute (a teacher training college of university standing), as well as nine universities of applied sciences. Numerous private schools exist, as well as one private university of applied sciences; many foreign children receive part of their education in Switzerland. In 2010/11 enrolment at pre-primary level included 76% of children in the relevant age-group; enrolment at primary and secondary levels included 94% and 83% of children in the relevant age-group, respectively. In 2010/11 the number of students enrolled at Swiss universities stood at 131,494. In 2010 general government expenditure on education amounted to 32,700m. Swiss francs (17.3% of total expenditure).

SYRIA

Introductory Survey

LOCATION, CLIMATE, LANGUAGE, RELIGION, FLAG, CAPITAL

The Syrian Arab Republic lies in western Asia, with Turkey to the north, Iraq to the east and Jordan to the south. Lebanon and Israel are to the south-west. Syria has a coastline on the eastern shore of the Mediterranean Sea. Much of the country is mountainous and semi-desert. The coastal climate is one of hot summers and mild winters. The inland plateau and plains are dry but cold in winter. Average temperatures in Dimashq (Damascus) range from 2°C to 12°C (36°F to 54°F) in January and from 18°C to 37°C (64°F to 99°F) in August. The national language is Arabic, with Kurdish a minority language. According to the UN Relief and Works Agency for Palestine Refugees in the Near East (UNRWA), at January 2013 there were 499,189 Palestinian refugees registered in Syria. More than 80% of the population are Muslims (mostly Sunnis), but there is a substantial Christian minority of various sects. The national flag (proportions 2 by 3) has three equal horizontal stripes, of red, white and black, with two five-pointed, green stars in the centre of the white stripe. The capital is Damascus.

CONTEMPORARY POLITICAL HISTORY

Historical Context

Syria was formerly part of Turkey's Ottoman Empire. Turkish forces were defeated in the First World War (1914–18), and Syria was occupied in 1920 by France, in accordance with a League of Nations mandate. Syrian nationalists proclaimed an independent republic in September 1941. French powers were transferred in January 1944, and full independence was achieved on 17 April 1946. In December 1949 Syria came under a military dictatorship, led by Brig. Adib Shishekly. He was elected President in July 1953, but was overthrown by another army coup in February 1954.

In February 1958 Syria merged with Egypt to form the United Arab Republic (UAR). In September 1961, following a military coup in Damascus, Syria seceded and formed the independent Syrian Arab Republic. In 1963 Maj.-Gen. Amin al-Hafiz formed a Government in which members of the Arab Socialist Renaissance (Baath) Party were predominant. In February 1966 the army deposed the Government of President al-Hafiz, replacing him with Dr Nur el-Din al-Atasi. However, in November 1970, after a bloodless coup, the military (moderate) wing of the Baath Party seized power, led by Lt-Gen. Hafiz al-Assad, who was elected President in March 1971. In March 1972 the National Progressive Front (NPF), a grouping of the five main political parties (including the Baath Party), was formed under President Assad's leadership.

Domestic Political Affairs

Syria's regional influence under President Hafiz al-Assad

Increasing border tension between Syria and Israel was a major influence leading to the Six-Day War of June 1967, when Israeli forces attacked their Arab neighbours in reprisal for the closure of the Strait of Tiran by the UAR (Egypt). Israel's territorial gains included the Golan Heights region of Syria, which remains under Israeli occupation. An uneasy truce lasted until October 1973, when Egyptian and Syrian forces launched simultaneous attacks on Israeli-held territory. There was fierce fighting in the Golan Heights until a cease-fire was agreed after 18 days. In May 1974 the US Secretary of State, Henry Kissinger, secured an agreement for the disengagement of forces. However, Israel formally annexed the Golan Heights in December 1981.

Syria disapproved of the second interim Egyptian-Israeli Disengagement Agreement, signed in September 1975, but agreed to acknowledge it as a *fait accompli* in return for Egypt's acceptance of Syria's role in Lebanon. Syria had progressively intervened in the Lebanese civil war during 1976, finally providing the bulk of the 30,000-strong Arab Deterrent Force (ADF). Syria condemned the Egyptian President, Anwar Sadat, for Egypt's peace initiative with Israel in late 1977, the Camp David agreements signed in September 1978 and subsequent Egyptian-Israeli peace treaty.

From 1977 Assad blamed the outlawed Muslim Brotherhood, a conservative Islamist group, for a number of assassinations of Alawites, the minority Shi'a Islamic sect to which the President belonged. He ordered the brutal suppression of a Brotherhood uprising in Hamah (Hama) in February 1982. From November 1983, after Assad suffered a heart attack, rivals to the succession—including his brother, Col Rifaat al-Assad—vied for pre-eminence. In March 1984 three Vice-Presidents (including Rifaat) were appointed in order to distribute power equally among the President's potential successors. Assad was also able to rely on the army's continued support.

The ADF, based in northern Lebanon, was unable to act when Israel invaded southern Lebanon in June 1982 and surrounded Beirut, trapping Syrian troops and fighters of the Palestine Liberation Organization (PLO). The Syrian and Palestinian forces in Beirut were evacuated in August, under the supervision of a multinational peace-keeping force, and some 50,000 Syrian troops, deployed in the Beqa'a valley and northern Lebanon, opposed 25,000 Israelis in the south of the country, even though the ADF's mandate had expired. Syria rejected the May 1983 Israel-Lebanon peace agreement, refusing to withdraw its forces from Lebanon and continuing to supply the militias of the Lebanese Druze and Shi'ite factions in their fight against the Lebanese Government and the Christian Phalangists. From May 1983 Syria supported a revolt against Yasser Arafat and the leadership of Fatah (the Palestine National Liberation Movement), and by November Syrian and rebel PLO forces had cornered Arafat, the PLO Chairman, in the Lebanese port of Tarabulus (Tripoli). Arafat and some 4,000 of his supporters were eventually evacuated, under UN protection, in December.

In March 1984 President Amin Gemayel of Lebanon, under Syrian influence, abrogated the May 1983 agreement with Israel. In April 1984 President Assad approved Gemayel's plans for a Lebanese government of national unity, giving equal representation to Muslims and Christians. In September Syria arranged a truce to end fighting in Tripoli between the pro-Syrian Arab Democratic Party and the Sunni Tawhid Islami (Islamic Unification Movement). The Lebanese army entered the city in late 1984, under the terms of a Syrian-backed extended security plan, to assert the authority of the Lebanese Government. Syria also authorized Lebanon's participation in talks with Israel to co-ordinate the departure of Israeli forces from southern Lebanon. After the final stage of the Israeli withdrawal in June 1985, several hundred Israeli troops and advisers remained in Lebanon to assist the Israeli-backed 'South Lebanon Army' in policing a narrow buffer zone along the Lebanese side of the international border. Syria removed 10,000–12,000 troops from the Beqa'a valley in July, leaving some 25,000 in position.

President Assad was re-elected for a third seven-year term of office in February 1985, and his administration involved itself in seeking to resolve Lebanon's sectarian unrest. Through its proxy, Amal, Syria sought to prevent Yasser Arafat from re-establishing a power base in Beirut, and around 650 people died in the fighting before a cease-fire was agreed in Damascus in June. In December the three main Lebanese militias—the Druze, Amal and Lebanese Forces (LF) Christian militia—met in Damascus to sign a Syrian-brokered accord outlining a settlement of the civil war. However, the Shi'ite Hezbollah and Sunni Murabitoun militias were not party to the accord and President Gemayel refused to endorse it. In June 1986 Syria brokered another cease-fire in the Palestinian refugee camps around Beirut (where fighting between Palestinian guerrillas and Shi'ite Amal militiamen had escalated); this proved to be the first stage in a Syrian-sponsored peace plan for Muslim west Beirut. The co-operation of the Amal, Druze and Sunni militias was dependent upon the deployment of uniformed Syrian troops in Beirut for the first time since 1982. However, the plan was strongly opposed in Christian east Beirut and was not extended to the predominantly Shi'ite southern suburbs, where most of the city's Palestinian refugees lived. By early 1987 heavy fighting had resumed in west Beirut between Amal forces and an alliance of Druze, Murabitoun and Communist Party militias. Syrian troops (soon numbering some 7,500) succeeded in enforcing a cease-fire in the central and northern areas of this district.

At a general election held in February 1986 the Baath Party and other members of the NPF obtained 151 of the 195 seats in the People's Assembly. The Communist Party separately won nine seats, and independents 35. In November 1987 Mahmoud al-Zoubi, the Speaker of the Assembly, was appointed Prime Minister. In May 1988 Syria's interest in the Lebanese presidential election, scheduled to be held in August, prompted intense fighting between Amal and Hezbollah in Beirut's southern suburbs. Overt Syrian support for the candidacy of Sulayman Franjiya (President of Lebanon during 1970–76), and later for Mikhail al-Daher (after the first postponement of the election), aroused the opposition of Lebanese Christian leaders, who objected to candidates imposed by foreign powers. Consequently, Syria refused to recognize the interim military administration appointed by President Gemayel shortly before his term of office expired. From March 1989 Christian forces, commanded by Gen. Michel Aoun (head of the interim Lebanese Government), attempted to expel Syrian forces from Lebanon, thereby provoking one of the most violent confrontations of the civil war.

In October 1989, under the auspices of the League of Arab States (the Arab League, see p. 372), the Lebanese National Assembly endorsed a charter of national reconciliation (the Ta'if agreement—see the chapter on Lebanon). The Lebanese authorities stipulated that the Syrian army should assist in the implementation of two security plans incorporated in the accord, which also included the constitutional amendments that Syria had long sought to effect in Lebanon. In May 1991 Syria and Lebanon signed a treaty of 'fraternity, co-operation and co-ordination'. Israel, fearing the formal transformation of Lebanon into a Syrian protectorate, deployed armed forces inside the buffer zone in southern Lebanon. This further diminished any likelihood of Israel complying with UN Security Council Resolution 425 of March 1978, which demanded the withdrawal of Israeli forces from southern Lebanon. Syria was the only Arab state that refused to recognize the independent Palestinian state (proclaimed by the Palestine National Council in November 1988), viewing it as a potential challenge to Syrian interests in Lebanon. Meanwhile, Syria persistently denied claims, principally by the USA, that it was sponsoring international terrorism, and refused to restrict the activities of Palestinian groups on its territory. Following a series of bomb attacks in Europe in 1985–86, in November 1986 members of the European Community (EC, now European Union—EU, see p. 281), excluding Greece, imposed limited diplomatic and economic sanctions against Syria, as did the USA and Canada. However, the EC (with the exception of the United Kingdom) ended its ban on ministerial contacts with Syria in July 1987; financial aid was resumed in September, although a ban on the sale of weapons to Syria remained in force.

Domestic affairs following Lebanon's civil war

At elections to the People's Assembly (now expanded to 250 seats) in May 1990, the Baath Party won 134 seats and other parties 32, while 84 seats were reserved for independent candidates. In December 1991 it was announced that 2,864 political prisoners were to be released. Assad also indicated in March 1992 that new political parties might in future be established, but he rejected the implementation of foreign democratic frameworks as unsuited to the country's level of economic development. In January 1994 Basel al-Assad, President Assad's eldest son and presumed successor, was killed in a road accident; the President's second son, Bashar, was reportedly instructed to assume the role of his late brother in order to avoid a power struggle.

The Baath Party and its NPF allies reinforced their dominance of Syrian affairs at elections to the People's Assembly in August 1994, winning 167 of the 250 seats. In November 1995—the 25th anniversary of President Assad's seizure of power—some 1,200 political prisoners, including members of the banned Muslim Brotherhood, were released, while a number of the Brotherhood's leaders were allowed to return from exile. During 1996 there were reports of several explosions in Damascus; in December 11 people died in a bomb attack in central Damascus, for which the Islamic Movement for Change claimed responsibility. In February 1998 Assad unexpectedly dismissed his brother Rifaat as Vice-President, and in July appointed new chiefs of both the Syrian army and the intelligence service, prompting speculation that he was seeking to extend the political influence of his presumed successor, Bashar.

Elections to the People's Assembly were held in November and December 1998, at which the NPF, led by the Baath Party, again won 167 of the 250 seats. In February 1999 a national referendum ratified the incoming Assembly's decision to nominate President Assad for a fifth term of office. In the previous month Bashar al-Assad had been promoted to the rank of army colonel and reportedly granted new powers over important domestic matters. In June the Syrian authorities were said to be undertaking an 'unprecedented' campaign, led by Bashar, to counter corruption in public office. Details emerged in September of large-scale arrests by security forces in Damascus and the port city of Latakia against supporters and relatives of Rifaat al-Assad. Subsequent closures of Rifaat's interests provoked violent clashes between his supporters and the security forces, in which, according to independent sources, hundreds of people were killed or injured.

Having accepted the resignation of Mahmoud al-Zoubi and his administration in March 2000, President Assad named Muhammad Mustafa Mero, formerly governor of Halab (Aleppo), as Prime Minister. A radically altered cabinet was subsequently inaugurated, with a programme to accelerate social and economic reforms, tackle corruption and resume peace negotiations with Israel. However, in May al-Zoubi was expelled from the Baath Party for alleged 'irregularities and abuses' during his period in office and his assets seized. With al-Zoubi expected to stand trial on corruption charges, later that month it was announced that he had committed suicide.

Bashar al-Assad's succession to the presidency

President Assad died on 10 June 2000. Shortly after his death the People's Assembly amended the Constitution, lowering the minimum age required of a President from 40 to 34 years, thus enabling Bashar al-Assad to assume the presidency. Bashar was also nominated as Commander-in-Chief of the Armed Forces and his military rank upgraded to that of Lieutenant-General. Following approval of Bashar's nomination for the presidency by the People's Assembly in late June, a national referendum on the succession was scheduled for July; the First Vice-President, Abd al-Halim Khaddam, assumed the role of acting President. In mid-June Bashar was elected Secretary-General of the Baath Party. However, Rifaat al-Assad claimed that the assumed succession by his nephew was unconstitutional, leading the Syrian authorities to issue a warrant for his arrest should he attempt to enter the country from exile to challenge for the presidency. At the referendum held on 10 July, Bashar al-Assad (the sole presidential candidate) received the endorsement of a reported 97.3% of voters. He subsequently emphasized as priorities for his administration economic reform, the elimination of official corruption and the conclusion of a peace treaty with Israel.

In July 2000 President Assad released a significant number of political prisoners, the majority of whom were communists and members of the Muslim Brotherhood. Nevertheless, in January 2001 at least 1,000 intellectuals, among them a prominent businessman and deputy, Riad Seif, urged the Syrian regime to approve political reforms. They demanded an end to the state of emergency (in force since 1963), the holding of free elections, a free press, the further release of political detainees and an end to discrimination against women. Meanwhile, following a decision by the Baath Party in November 2000 to permit the other members of the NPF to issue their own newspapers, in early 2001 the first non-state-controlled newspaper for several decades was published by the Communist Party. Syria's first privately owned newspaper for almost 40 years was also issued from February, while legislation relating to private broadcasting was relaxed in January 2002.

An independent deputy, Mamoun al-Homsi, was detained in August 2001 after starting a hunger strike in protest against official corruption and the Government's failure to end martial law. In September Riad Seif, who had held an 'illegal' discussion forum on political reform, was arrested. Following trial proceedings against al-Homsi and Seif, they were both convicted of illegally attempting to change the Constitution and given five-year custodial terms in March and April 2002, respectively. President Assad effected an extensive reorganization of the Government under Prime Minister Mero in December 2001. Maj.-Gen. Ali Hammoud, formerly head of the intelligence service, was named as Minister of the Interior, while 'pro-reform' ministers were reportedly appointed to strategic economic portfolios.

Meanwhile, there was increasing agitation in Lebanon for a cessation of Syrian influence on Lebanese political affairs after the inauguration of the new Syrian President and the Israeli withdrawal from southern Lebanon. In July 2000 Maronite Christian leaders in Lebanon requested that President Assad release all Lebanese political prisoners held in Syria, and in August a coalition of Christian political parties urged Lebanese voters to boycott the forthcoming parliamentary elections, on the grounds that Syria would predetermine the outcome of the poll. At the Lebanese elections, former premier Rafiq Hariri resoundingly defeated the Syrian-sponsored Government of Selim al-Hoss. Syrian officials reacted angrily when the Lebanese Druze leader and traditional ally of Syria, Walid Joumblatt, demanded a 're-evaluation' of Syria's role in Lebanon. In December 46 Lebanese prisoners (many of whom were Christians detained by Syrian troops during the civil war) were released from Syrian detention.

In June 2001 Syria withdrew some 6,000–10,000 of its armed forces from predominantly Christian districts of east and south Beirut, and from Mount Lebanon; some of the troops were redeployed in the Beqa'a valley. However, Syria retained a number of military bases in strategic areas of the Lebanese capital. Redeployments of Syrian troops from central Lebanon took place in April 2002, and from northern Lebanon in February 2003. The new Lebanese Government formed under Hariri in April was widely considered to be the most pro-Syrian administration in Lebanon for more than a decade.

Developments following the 2003 legislative elections

At elections to the People's Assembly held in March 2003, the NPF—led by the ruling Baath Party—again won 167 of the 250 seats, with the remaining 83 going to independents. Opposition parties boycotted the election on the grounds that it was undemocratic. In July President Bashar al-Assad was reported to have adopted a decree effectively ending the Baath Party's monopoly on government, military and public sector positions. In September Prime Minister Mero resigned, along with his cabinet, apparently as a result of his failure to accelerate the process of political reform. Muhammad Naji al-Otari, the Speaker of the People's Assembly, was appointed as Prime Minister, and his first administration was announced at the end of the month. In May 2004 the Chief of Staff of the Armed Forces, Hassan al-Turkmani, was named as Minister of Defence and Deputy Commander-in-Chief of the Armed Forces; his former post was assumed by Gen. Ali Habib Mahmoud.

Issues of civil rights came to the fore in early 2004. In February a prominent lawyer and human rights activist, Haitham Maleh, was prevented from travelling to the United Arab Emirates (UAE); the Syrian Human Rights Association claimed that Maleh was being punished for having criticized the ongoing state of emergency in a speech he made in Germany two months earlier. At the same time the Lebanese newspaper *An-Nahar* published a petition signed by 1,500 Syrian intellectuals, democratic activists and lawyers urging the Government to instigate radical reforms, including the lifting of the state of emergency and the release of political prisoners.

There was a widespread outbreak of violent, predominantly Kurdish, protest in March 2004. The unrest started in the north-eastern town of Al-Qamishli, close to the border with Turkey, when fighting at a football match escalated into large-scale anti-Government protests and fighting between the Arab majority and Kurdish minority. A number of deaths were reported, and hundreds of Kurds were detained by the authorities in connection with the clashes. The Government accused Kurdish political groups of deliberately inciting the riots, which quickly spread to the town of Al-Hasakah. In October Assad announced a significant reorganization of the Council of Ministers. Prominent appointees included Maj.-Gen. Ghazi Kanaan, a former head of Syrian military intelligence in Lebanon, who assumed the interior portfolio from Hammoud, and Mahdi Dakhlallah, a well-known journalist, who was appointed Minister of Information.

Demonstrating Syria's continued influence on Lebanese political affairs, Prime Minister Hariri, following meetings with Syrian officials, withdrew his objection to the extension, in August 2004, of Lebanese President Emile Lahoud's mandate by three years. However, international pressure on Syria increased following the adoption in September of UN Security Council Resolution 1559, which, without referring to Syria explicitly, demanded that Lebanon's sovereignty be respected and that all foreign forces leave the country. The Syrian army subsequently redeployed about 3,000 special forces from positions south of Beirut, and further troops were withdrawn in December from the northern town of Batrun and from Beirut's southern suburbs and airport to the Beqa'a valley. However, the

new Lebanese Government installed under Prime Minister Omar Karami in November was regarded as being even more favourable than its predecessor to continued Syrian influence in Lebanese affairs.

Former Lebanese Prime Minister Rafiq Hariri was killed in a car bombing in Beirut on 14 February 2005. Although President Assad condemned the attack, the USA, without accusing Syria of any involvement, withdrew its ambassador to Damascus for consultations, and later demanded the complete withdrawal of Syrian troops from Lebanon and a thorough and transparent investigation into the incident. Mass protests against Syria's political and military influence in Lebanon followed, and in late February US President George W. Bush demanded that Syria: withdraw all troops and security service personnel from Lebanon; stop using its territory to support militant groups; support free and fair elections in Lebanon; and adhere to UN Security Council Resolution 1559. The UN Secretary-General, Kofi Annan, urged Syria to withdraw its troops from Lebanon by April. Meanwhile, Syria and Iran agreed to form a 'united front' against foreign threats to their states.

In early March 2005 Presidents Assad and Lahoud agreed to the withdrawal of Syrian troops to the Beqa'a valley by the end of the month; Syria later promised to withdraw all troops before Lebanon's general election in May, and to provide the UN with a timetable for the withdrawal. Syria reportedly withdrew 4,000–6,000 of its troops from Lebanon in mid-March, removing Syrian soldiers and intelligence agents from their barracks and offices around Tripoli and Beirut; 8,000–10,000 troops reportedly remained in the Beqa'a valley. A UN report released in late March blamed Syria for allowing political tension in Lebanon to mount before the murder of Hariri; it also criticized Lebanon's initial attempts to investigate the incident. In early April the UN Security Council approved Resolution 1595, which established an International Independent Investigation Commission (UNIIIC) to investigate Hariri's murder. The German prosecutor Detlev Mehlis was appointed to head the commission. Later in April Syria declared that it had withdrawn all of its troops and security forces from Lebanon; this appeared to be confirmed following a UN inspection carried out in early May. President Assad and Prime Minister al-Otari met the new Lebanese premier, Fouad Siniora, in Syria in August, when the two states reportedly agreed to improve relations based on mutual respect. Various prominent Lebanese figures opposed to Syrian influence in Lebanon were killed or injured in bomb attacks during mid- to late 2005, including George Hawi, the former Secretary-General of the Parti communiste libanais, who was killed in a car bombing in Beirut in June.

At the 10th national congress of the Baath Party in June 2005, President Assad was re-elected as Secretary-General. Vice-President and member of the party leadership Abd al-Halim Khaddam reportedly asked to be relieved of his duties, citing a wish to allow more young people to be represented in the party and state leadership. The political committee of the Baath Party endorsed proposals to relax laws relating to the state of emergency, and to produce legislation allowing the formation of independent parties and increased freedom of the press. However, although the Syrian leadership responded to anti-Government unrest from March 2011 by abolishing martial law in April, and by amending the Constitution in February 2012 to allow for the latter two reforms, by this time the country was embroiled in a bitter civil conflict (see Recent developments).

In December 2005 Khaddam, who was now living in exile in Paris, France, held an interview with the Dubai (UAE)-based satellite television station *Al Arabiya* in which he accused Assad of having personally threatened Rafiq Hariri prior to his assassination. Khaddam subsequently declared that, in his view, Assad had ordered Hariri's killing, although he awaited the final decision of the investigating commission. He declared that the current Syrian regime could not be reformed, and appealed to opposition groups in Syria to co-operate to defeat it. In January 2006 the Baath Party announced that it had formally expelled Khaddam, accusing him of treachery against the party, his country and the Arab nation for his accusations against the Syrian President. The Government also froze Khaddam's assets, and in April a military court formally charged the former Vice-President with a series of offences, including inciting a foreign attack on Syrian soil and plotting to seize political and civil power.

The UN investigation into the assassination of Rafiq Hariri

Reports emerged in June 2005 that Syrian intelligence agents might not, in fact, have completely withdrawn from Lebanon. Meanwhile, UNIIIC began its inquiry into Rafiq Hariri's assassination in mid-June, with a three-month mandate. In August UNIIIC arrested three former Lebanese security officials with close ties to Syria, who had tendered their resignations in April, for questioning regarding the assassination. A fourth security chief subsequently handed himself in to the organization. A former, pro-Syrian parliamentary deputy was also detained. In mid-October, shortly before UNIIIC issued its first report on the investigation, the official Syrian Arab News Agency announced the death, by suicide, of the Minister of the Interior, Maj.-Gen. Ghazi Kanaan; a formal investigation subsequently confirmed the cause of death. Shortly before his apparent suicide, Kanaan had issued a statement to a Lebanese radio station defending Syria's role in Lebanon and announcing that he had been questioned by UNIIIC, but had not given any evidence against Syria. Some analysts noted that Kanaan, a potential alternative to the Syrian President who had opposed the decision to extend Lebanese President Lahoud's tenure in 2004, had been seen as a threat to Assad.

According to its first report, issued in October 2005, UNIIIC had found evidence that Lebanese and Syrian intelligence and security services were directly involved in the assassination of Rafiq Hariri. Moreover, the report reasoned, the act was too complex and too well planned to have taken place without the approval of senior Syrian security officials and their Lebanese counterparts. UNIIIC expressed its extreme concern at the lack of co-operation by the Syrian authorities. Lebanon and Syria both criticized the investigation's findings as politically motivated, and Syria announced that it had established a special judicial commission to deal with all matters relating to UNIIIC's mission. The UN commission was granted an extension to its mandate to mid-December. At the end of October 2005 the UN Security Council adopted Resolution 1636, which was sponsored by the USA, France and the United Kingdom. The resolution established measures against suspects in the assassination—including prohibitions on travel and asset freezes—and urged Syria to detain persons identified by the inquiry as suspects in the crime, threatening unspecified 'further action' should Syria not comply by 15 December. Meanwhile, in late October the UN Special Envoy, Terje Rød-Larsen, published his report on compliance with UN Security Council Resolution 1559, in which he commended Syria's withdrawal of its troops from Lebanon, but criticized Lebanon for not fulfilling the resolution's demands.

In his second report to the UN Security Council, issued in December 2005, Mehlis noted that Syria had presented five officials suspected of involvement in the murder of Hariri to UNIIIC for interrogation in Vienna, Austria. However, the report again accused Syria of reluctance to co-operate with the investigating body. UNIIIC had found further evidence of the involvement of the Lebanese and Syrian intelligence and security services in the assassination, and Mehlis identified 19 suspects, six of whom were Syrian (of which five were those currently under interrogation in Vienna). Mehlis resigned as head of UNIIIC shortly afterwards, and was replaced by Serge Brammertz. In January 2006, following former Vice-President Khaddam's allegations against President Assad, UNIIIC investigators declared that they wished to question Assad and the Minister of Foreign Affairs, Farouk al-Shara'. However, the Minister of Information, Mahdi Dakhlallah, declared that Syria would not permit UNIIIC to interview the President. Al-Shara' announced in March that he had reached an agreement with Brammertz that Syria would co-operate fully with the UNIIIC investigation provided that the country's 'sovereignty and dignity' was maintained.

President Assad effected a comprehensive reorganization of the Council of Ministers in February 2006. Al-Shara' was appointed as Vice-President to replace Khaddam, and given additional responsibility for Foreign Affairs and Information; he was succeeded as Minister of Foreign Affairs by Walid Mouallem. Brig.-Gen. Bassam Abd al-Majid was accorded the interior portfolio, which had been vacant since Kanaan's death in October 2005. In March 2006 Dr Najah al-Attar was also named as a Vice-President. In May 274 Lebanese and Syrian intellectuals and activists signed the Beirut-Damascus Declaration, a petition urging the Syrian Government to reassess its policy on Lebanon, to respect the sovereign independence of that country and to establish normal diplomatic relations. Many of the Declaration's

signatories were subsequently arrested, and in early 2007 five prominent activists were convicted on charges of disseminating false information and damaging national morale; they were sentenced to terms of imprisonment of between three and 10 years.

Meanwhile, the third and fourth UNIIIC reports on the assassination of Hariri were published in March and June 2006, respectively. Recent Syrian co-operation was described as 'generally satisfactory', and the investigators claimed to have made considerable progress with regard to their understanding of the circumstances surrounding the crime. However, the report acknowledged that more thorough investigation was required into alleged links between Hariri's murder and 14 other attacks against anti-Syrian figures in Lebanon since October 2004. In mid-June 2006 UNIIIC's mandate was extended for another year. The fifth UNIIIC report was released by Brammertz in September, and again expressed overall satisfaction with the level of Syrian co-operation. (For details of the sixth to 11th UNIIC reports and subsequent extensions of the commission's mandate, see the chapter on Lebanon.)

In November 2006 the Syrian authorities were forced to deny accusations—including by Rafik Hariri's son, Saad—that they had orchestrated the assassination in Beirut of Pierre Gemayel, the Lebanese Minister of Industry, a well-known opponent of Syrian influence in Lebanon. During 2007 the Syrian leadership continued to oppose demands by the international community, including the US Administration, that an international tribunal be established in order to try suspects in Hariri's murder. In response to the adoption by the UN Security Council, in May, of Resolution 1757, establishing a special tribunal for this purpose, Syria asserted that the tribunal represented a violation of Lebanese sovereignty, and that it would refuse to hand over any Syrian suspects to the new body.

Domestic unrest following the 2007 elections

In January 2007, in preparation for legislative elections scheduled to take place in April, President Assad approved amendments to electoral legislation, including the introduction of stricter regulations on the financing of campaigns. Ten days before the polls the Government announced that the number of seats reserved for the NPF would be increased from 167 to 170 (out of 250), thus reducing the quota for independent candidates to just 80. At the elections to the People's Assembly on 22–23 April, voter turn-out was officially reported at 56.1% of the registered electorate; however, opponents of the Government claimed that the true rate of participation was, at most, 10%–20%. On 26 April the Minister of the Interior announced that the NPF had in fact secured 172 seats; the number of independents thus fell to 78. The opposition, which had boycotted the polls, called upon the international community to acknowledge the illegitimacy of the newly installed legislature. Moreover, human rights groups and even government-controlled newspapers denounced the elections as undemocratic. In the following month the legislature unanimously approved the Baath Party's nomination of Bashar al-Assad for a second term as President. At a national referendum held on 27 May, Assad was endorsed for another seven-year term of office by a reported 97.6% of votes.

A coalition of political activists and members of banned political organizations had, in October 2005, issued a document entitled the Damascus Declaration for Democratic National Change, which urged the peaceful establishment of a democratic state, built on moderate Islamic principles, with a new constitution to guarantee liberty and human rights for all. The Declaration also appealed for a democratic solution to the issue of Kurdish nationalism. In December 2007 168 signatories convened to reaffirm the Declaration's message and to elect a National Council; Fida' al-Hourani, daughter of Akram al-Hourani, a founder of the Baath Party, was elected President. In subsequent weeks up to 40 members of the movement were detained, and legal proceedings against 12 dissidents were initiated in July 2008 on charges including spreading false information and weakening national morale. The accused, who had pleaded not guilty to all charges, were convicted in October and accorded sentences of some two years' imprisonment.

In February 2008 Imad Mughniyeh, a senior member of Hezbollah, was killed in a car bombing in Damascus. Hezbollah claimed that the attack had been carried out by Israeli secret service operatives, an allegation that was denied by Israel. The fact that no findings were released following a Syrian investigation into the incident prompted widespread speculation concerning the possible involvement of Syrian or other Arab nationals in the bombing. Brig.-Gen. Muhammad Suleiman, an adviser and close ally of President Assad, was shot dead near the port city of Tartous in August. Suleiman had allegedly acted as a liaison with Hezbollah, as well as with the International Atomic Energy Agency (IAEA—which was investigating Syria's alleged nuclear facility, see The Israeli-Syrian track of the Middle East peace process). In September a car bomb, detonated close to both a security forces' base and an important Shi'a shrine, on the outskirts of Damascus, killed 17 people. In November Syrian state television broadcast what it claimed were the confessions of 11 militants responsible for the bombing, which was the deadliest attack on Syrian territory for more than 20 years. The militants, as well as a 12th operative who had carried out the suicide attack, were described as being members of Fatah al-Islam, a Sunni Islamist group active in Lebanon's Palestinian refugee camps. The confessions also contained the allegation that the group had been funded by Saad Hariri's Future Movement. The Future Movement strongly denied this allegation, and countered with the claim that Fatah al-Islam was, in fact, funded by the Syrian intelligence authorities. Unsubstantiated reports in December suggested that the leader of Fatah al-Islam, Shaker al-Abassi, had been either captured or killed by security forces in Syria.

A protracted political crisis in Lebanon, during which pro-Syrian factions, including Hezbollah, obstructed a new presidential election (the tenure of President Lahoud having ended in November 2007), threatened to escalate into civil war in that country during 2008. Syria was swift to deny claims by many Western governments that it was preventing the presidential vote from taking place, and that it was seeking to bring about the collapse of Lebanon's Western-backed Government by providing military assistance to Hezbollah and its allies. However, following the signing of the Qatari-brokered Doha Agreement in May 2008, which led to the formation of a national unity administration and the election of Michel Suleiman as President, renewed rapprochement between Syria and Lebanon became possible. In fact, Syria's support for the agreement was regarded as providing the catalyst for a marked improvement in its international standing generally.

A landmark agreement was reached between Lebanon and Syria in July 2008, when the two countries declared that they were to enter into diplomatic relations and open embassies in one another's capitals for the first time. During a two-day state visit to Syria by President Suleiman in August, it was announced that the work of a committee to demarcate the Lebanese–Syrian border would be resumed. The countries also agreed jointly to investigate the issue of persons missing since Lebanon's civil war and to review existing bilateral agreements. President Assad issued a decree formally establishing diplomatic relations with Lebanon in October. In an unexpected development, Gen. Michel Aoun, leader of the Christian opposition in Lebanon and a former adversary of Syria, was a guest of Assad in December. By late March 2009 both countries had opened their respective embassies and approved their ambassadors' nominations. The Special Tribunal for Lebanon (STL), established to try those suspected of involvement in the assassination of Rafiq Hariri, had begun operating earlier that month in Leidschendam, Netherlands. One of the main suspects in the case, Zuhair al-Siddiq, a former officer in the Syrian intelligence service, was reportedly arrested in Dubai in April.

Continuing criticism of Syria's human rights record

President Assad announced a significant reorganization of the Council of Ministers in April 2009. Notable changes included the appointment of Gen. Saeed Muhammad Sammour, a senior military intelligence officer, as Minister of the Interior, and the appointment of Ahmad Hammoud Younis, a judge, as the new Minister of Justice. In a further reorganization in June, Lt-Gen. Hassan al-Turkmani, hitherto Minister of Defence, was appointed Assistant Vice-President with the rank of Minister. Turkmani's former post was accorded to Gen. Ali Habib Mahmoud, who was replaced as Chief of Staff of the Armed Forces by Gen. Dawoud bin Abdullah Rajiha.

In October 2009 Syria attracted international criticism following the arrest of the prominent human rights campaigner Haitham Maleh, on charges of spreading false information that would undermine national morale. In an interview with a United Kingdom-based Arabic television channel shortly before his arrest, Maleh, a former judge, had condemned the arbitrary and undemocratic exercise of power by the Government and security forces. He was given a three-year prison term in July 2010, having been convicted by a military court in Damascus. In

June of that year another lawyer and leading human rights activist, Muhammad al-Hassani, had been found guilty of a similar offence and sentenced to a prison term of the same duration; al-Hassani was detained in July 2009 after having accused the Syrian authorities of conducting 'unfair trials' of political prisoners. In March 2010 a petition seeking early release for 12 signatories to the Damascus Declaration, imprisoned in October 2008, was rejected by the Court of Appeals.

The new Lebanese Prime Minister, Saad Hariri, made a landmark visit to Damascus to meet President Assad in December 2009. Hariri's March 14 Alliance had secured victory in the Lebanese national elections in June and formed a national unity Government in November. The Lebanese Prime Minister, who had blamed Syria for the assassination of his father in 2005, declared that his visit represented the beginning of a 'new phase' in relations between the two countries. Furthermore, in what was regarded by observers as an indication of waning anti-Syrian sentiment among the supporters of the March 14 Alliance, in March 2010 Walid Joumblatt, leader of the Parti socialiste progressiste, also travelled to Damascus for talks with Assad. In September Hariri stated that he had been mistaken in accusing Syria of involvement in his father's murder.

In July 2010, in response to evidence that increasing numbers of Syrian women were choosing to wear the *niqab* (veil), the Government ordered all universities and colleges to ban female students from wearing the veil on their campuses. The new policy apparently demonstrated the secular regime's determination to prevent the rise in Islamist fundamentalism seen elsewhere in the region from taking hold in Syria. It was also reported that about 1,000 primary school teachers who continued to wear the *niqab* had been transferred to administrative posts. A report published by Human Rights Watch at this time asserted that Syria's poor record on individual freedoms and human rights had essentially remained unchanged since President Assad assumed the role from his father in July 2000. The organization castigated the Syrian authorities for practices such as the: repression of any form of dissent by members of the opposition, Kurdish journalists and human rights activists; continued use of emergency legislation; mistreatment and torture of prisoners; lack of accountability in state institutions; and heavy media censorship.

Anti-Government unrest leads to civil conflict

Syria was initially little affected by the mass popular protests that took place in many Arab countries from early 2011. However, on 15 March protests began in the southern city of Dar'a, initially against the arrest and reported torture of a group of children who had been writing anti-regime graffiti (as popularized during the uprisings in Egypt and Tunisia). Demonstrations, with demands including the release of political prisoners and an end to corruption, continued in Dar'a and nearby towns over the following days, and were suppressed by security forces; a number of protesters were reported to have been shot dead, including 15 during the funeral of some earlier victims. On 25 March protests erupted in towns across Syria; army troops were subsequently deployed to Dar'a and to Latakia, where some 12 people were killed after the offices of the Baath Party were set on fire by protesters. The Government attributed the deaths in Latakia to sectarian strife (the town and its surroundings are divided between Sunni and Alawite communities), and declared that it intended to meet one of the demonstrators' principal demands, the lifting of the state of emergency. On 29 March President Assad accepted the resignation of the Council of Ministers led by al-Otari, apparently in an effort to appease the protesters, and on the following day he addressed the People's Assembly. However, although Assad declared the need for reform and ordered an inquiry into the recent deaths, he failed to announce an immediate end to the state of emergency, and denounced 'foreign conspirators' (implying Israelis in particular) as the cause of the ongoing unrest.

Protests, by this time increasingly demanding the fall of Assad's regime and the introduction of democracy, continued in early April 2011, notably in Dar'a, the western city of Homs, and the town of Douma, north-east of Damascus; these were again violently repressed. On 3 April Assad appointed Dr Adel Safar, hitherto Minister of Agriculture and Agrarian Reform, to form a new administration. In further efforts to appease forces hostile to the Government, which reportedly included Muslim clerics, in the following days the ban on the wearing of the *niqab* by teachers was rescinded, while some 200,000 stateless Kurds were granted Syrian citizenship. However, the protests continued to spread, taking hold in Banias, on the Mediterranean coast, where troops were deployed. On 14 April it was announced that Safar's new Council of Ministers included Maj.-Gen. Muhammad Ibrahim al-Shaar as the new Minister of the Interior. However, the ministers responsible for defence and foreign affairs both retained their posts, the latter assuming additional responsibility for the expatriates' portfolio following the merger of two ministries. The new Council was sworn in by President Assad on 16 April. Meanwhile, on 15 April large-scale protests took place in Damascus for the first time. The lifting of the state of emergency and abolition of the Supreme State Security Court were officially announced on 19 April, and the laws ratified two days later; however, legislation restricting the right to demonstrate was introduced simultaneously. Anti-Government protests continued to escalate across the country and, amid violent repression by the army and security forces, tanks were sent into Dar'a on 25 April. A number of army officers reportedly refused to open fire on demonstrators, and there were unconfirmed reports that some were subsequently killed by forces loyal to President Assad. As many prominent human rights campaigners and political activists were arrested by security forces, Riad Seif was detained in Damascus in early May. The army also sent tanks into Homs, Hama, Banias and parts of Damascus, and there were reports—despite the absence of foreign journalists, who were prevented from entering Syria to access these cities—of live ammunition being used against unarmed civilians. Large numbers of Syrians began to flee the violence, seeking refuge in neighbouring countries, in particular Jordan, Lebanon, Turkey and Iraq.

During the first week of May 2011 some tanks withdrew from Dar'a, as Syrian officials declared that their military operation to defeat 'terrorists' there had been successful. However, they refused permission for a UN humanitarian mission to enter the city, and denied reports by human rights groups that a mass grave had been discovered in Dar'a in mid-May. In the second week of May the authorities sought to quell the rebellion by blocking opposition activists' access to phone and internet connections. Despite the Government's announcement, on 13 May, that it was willing to enter into a 'national dialogue', the military intensified its actions against alleged anti-Government rebels in Homs in mid-May, with heavy shelling and gunfire reported in the city's Bab Amr district. Meanwhile, the UN published a report on human rights in Syria, which outlined what it described as the 'arbitrary detentions, summary executions' and 'torture' used by the regime to end the unrest. There was widespread anger in late May, when reports emerged of the death in police detention in Dar'a of a 13-year-old boy, who had apparently been tortured and then shot. According to the Local Co-ordination Committees (LCC), a network of opposition activists that was organizing and monitoring the protests, at least 25 children had been killed since the start of the uprising. However, by early June Amnesty International claimed to have evidence that 77 children had been killed thus far.

President Assad announced an amnesty for political prisoners, including members of the Muslim Brotherhood, on 31 May 2011, although the announcement was not taken seriously by activists. In early June the United Kingdom, France, Germany and Portugal drafted a UN Security Council resolution that demanded, *inter alia*, the withdrawal of Syrian forces from urban centres and the implementation of key political reforms. However, Russia and the People's Republic of China failed to attend the talks intended to discuss the measure. On 15 June a report published by the Office of the UN High Commissioner for Human Rights suggested that the security forces had 'perpetrated acts of torture and other cruel and inhuman treatment' against detained protesters, and cited 'grave concern' at the deterioration of human rights. In the first week of June, as the Syrian military attempted to crush what it termed an uprising by 'armed gangs' in Jisr al-Shughour, in the north-west of the country close to the Turkish border, Syrian government officials reported that 120 security personnel had been killed. It was estimated later that month that at least 11,000 refugees had arrived in Turkey as a result of the military offensive. Following large-scale demonstrations against Assad's rule in Hama, the security forces responded at the end of July with a heavy military assault on the city (causing an estimated 100 fatalities on 31 July alone), as well as in Homs and Deir el-Zor. On 1 July significant anti-Government protests were held in Aleppo, where (as in Damascus) the President retained considerable support. During 16–17 July sectarian clashes were reported in Homs between Alawite supporters of the regime and anti-Assad Sunnis, in response to the discovery of the bodies of three supporters of the President.

After President Assad had, in a speech on 20 June 2011, again appealed for a 'national dialogue' on political reform to take place, on 10 July a two-day National Dialogue Commission was inaugurated by the Vice-President, responsible for Foreign Affairs and Information, Farouk al-Shara'. However, the talks were boycotted by many opposition groups, who asserted that Syria's leadership was not genuinely seeking to engage with them. Several meetings between the diverse, often youthful, rebel groups and exiled opposition activists were held in Turkey between the end of May and August 2011, but they were prevented from establishing a united front against the Syrian establishment by their vastly different political stances and aspirations, as well as the lack of an obvious leader. Although a 31-member consultative council—to represent dissidents abroad—was formed in Antalya on 3 June 2011, urging Assad to step down and allow al-Shara' to assume power, it was not until 15 September that the broad-based, 140-member Syrian National Council (SNC) was established in Istanbul, Turkey. The SNC, which was formally inaugurated as a 'government-in-exile' on 2 October, included dissidents—among them grassroots activists, Islamists and Kurds—based in both Syria and abroad, and declared as its aim the establishment of a 'pluralist and democratic state'.

On 11 July 2011 pro-Government activists attacked the US and French embassies in Damascus, in protest against the recent visit by the respective ambassadors to Hama in support of pro-democracy protesters there. On 25 July the Council of Ministers approved draft legislation governing political parties, which, it stated, would end the Baath Party's monopoly on forming such organizations. On 3 August, largely in response to the regime's intense military bombardment of Hama, the UN Security Council finally approved a non-binding statement condemning 'widespread violations of human rights and the use of force against civilians by the Syrian authorities', and urging 'an immediate end to all violence'; however, the move was not supported by Lebanon. As President Assad intensified military action against anti-Government protesters in several cities, including Dar'a, Deir el-Zor and Hama, on 9 August Gen. Dawoud bin Abdullah Rajiha, hitherto Chief of Staff of the Armed Forces, was appointed Minister of Defence, in place of Gen. Ali Habib Mahmoud; officials cited poor health as the reason for Mahmoud's replacement. Gen. Fahd Jassem al-Freij was named as the new army Chief of Staff a day later. On 18 August US President Barack Obama, along with French President Nicolas Sarkozy, German Federal Chancellor Angela Merkel and British Prime Minister David Cameron, urged President Assad to relinquish office. It was subsequently reported that some senior officials of Syria's political and military establishment had chosen to defect to the opposition in protest against the killings and other extreme acts of violence being perpetrated by government forces against peaceful demonstrators. For example, the former Attorney-General of Hama, Adnan Muhammad al-Bakkour, accused the regime of having killed 72 prisoners on 31 July and then buried them in a mass grave.

Although the opposition movement remained largely peaceful, in August 2011 a group of army defectors formed the so-called Free Syrian Army (FSA), led by a former air force colonel, Riad al-Assad, and based their headquarters in Turkey. By the end of September the FSA was reported to be engaged in heavy fighting with government troops in Rastan, close to Homs. On 16 November the FSA staged its first major military assault, targeting an army base close to Damascus; in subsequent months the FSA proceeded to attack a number of strategic targets in the capital and elsewhere. Meanwhile, in mid-August 2011 UNRWA reported that more than 5,000 Palestinians residing at a refugee camp in Latakia had been forced to leave, after the camp was attacked by tank- and gunfire; thousands more people subsequently fled Latakia as government forces reportedly used gunboats to shell parts of the city. On 21 August President Assad made a defiant speech to the nation, declaring that he would not resign and that his military was winning its campaign against the anti-Government rebels. At the same time, officials from the UN's Office for the Co-ordination of Humanitarian Affairs arrived in Syria to examine the humanitarian situation in urban areas that had been besieged by government forces.

On 4 October 2011 the adoption of a draft UN Security Council resolution, co-sponsored by France, the United Kingdom, Germany and Portugal, which had strongly condemned the military action being taken against civilians by the Syrian regime and threatened to impose sanctions, was opposed by China and Russia. (See Foreign Affairs for further details concerning international sanctions imposed against Syria.) Nevertheless, there was evidence in late 2011 that Russia's attitude towards President Assad's administration was hardening. On 7 October Russian President Dmitrii Medvedev urged the Syrian leader either to introduce reforms or cede power.

Meanwhile, in late October 2011, in his latest report concerning implementation of UN Security Council Resolution 1559, UN Secretary-General Ban Ki-Moon urged the Syrian Government to halt the military incursions being carried out in parts of northern Lebanon close to the Syrian border and in disputed territory. Ban warned that the incursions risked escalating the Syrian conflict, and urged both sides to reach agreement on the delineation of their border. It was reported in October that Syrian forces had placed landmines along the border in an effort to prevent weapons from being smuggled from Lebanon into Syria for use by opposition forces. Hezbollah was forced to deny that it was providing military support to the Assad regime, its traditional ally, although Western governments persisted with claims of Hezbollah's direct involvement in the conflict during 2012 and early 2013. Meanwhile, following an intensification of the Government's crackdown on dissent, particularly in Homs, by early March 2012 it was estimated that more than 7,000 Syrians had been displaced to Lebanon since April 2011; this number had increased significantly by early 2013 (see Recent developments).

After some eight months of anti-Government protests, on 2 November 2011 the Arab League in Cairo, Egypt, secured Syrian consideration of a plan for a political resolution of the conflict. The agreement required the Syrian Government to: withdraw all troops from residential areas; allow independent monitors into those areas to assess the situation; free all political prisoners detained since March; and begin talks in the Egyptian capital with Syrian opposition groups on political reform. Meeting in emergency session on 12 November, Arab League ministers responsible for foreign affairs threatened the Syrian regime with expulsion from the League and the imposition of punitive sanctions if it did not comply with the terms of the peace initiative by 19 November. Lebanon joined Yemen in voting against the decision, while Iraq abstained. The Syrian Government failed to adhere to several extensions to the deadline by which it was to implement the terms of the peace plan, and thus it was formally suspended from the League on 16 November. Several foreign embassies in Damascus, including those of Saudi Arabia, Qatar and Turkey, were subsequently attacked by pro-Government demonstrators. On 27 November the Arab League also imposed a series of economic sanctions on the Syrian regime, which included an end to funding on development projects, asset freezes, and a ban on transactions with the Central Bank of Syria and the Commercial Bank of Syria. On the following day the UN's Human Rights Council published a report in which it expressed 'grave concern' that Syrian security forces had committed crimes against humanity during their recent military offensives. On 19 December the Syrian leadership agreed to allow an independent monitoring mission composed of Arab League states to be sent to the country in order to observe its adherence to the terms of the 2 November plan; the first group of monitors arrived in Syria, with a one-month mandate, on 26 December. However, the effectiveness of the mission was immediately questioned as the Government appeared routinely to withdraw its troops from urban centres before the observers entered, and then intensify its military operations after their departure. The Arab League monitors were withdrawn from Syria on 28 January 2012, in response to the deteriorating security situation.

The violence had thus continued unabated despite the presence of Arab League monitors. By mid-December 2011 the UN put the death toll at some 5,000, and this figure had risen to more than 9,000 by the end of March 2012 (the first anniversary of the start of the uprising). During 19–20 December 2011 up to 140 people were reported to have died as a result of conflict in Idleb province, with many of the deaths being caused by fighting between government forces and the FSA; however, large numbers of civilians were also the victims of the shelling of residential areas or sniper fire. Two suicide car bombs exploded close to security buildings in Damascus on 23 December; up to 44 people died in the blasts, which Syrian officials attributed to al-Qa'ida militants; opposition groups, however, accused government forces of having carried out the attacks for propaganda purposes. At the end of December the Syrian authorities were accused of

having failed to abide by their pledge to release 700 detainees as part of the Arab League-sponsored peace plan. Meanwhile, the UN Human Rights Commissioner, Navi Pillay, assessed in that month that the conflict in Syria between pro-regime forces and anti-Government rebels had escalated into a civil war.

Recent developments: Constitution amended and legislative elections held amid worsening civil conflict

While continuing his military campaign against those opposed to his rule, on 15 February 2012 President Assad launched his proposals for the reform of Syria's political system. Amendments to the Constitution included: the establishment of a multi-party system, removing reference to the dominant role of the Baath Party; and the introduction of a two-term limit for the presidency, effective from the expiry of Assad's current term in 2014. Amid a widespread boycott by opposition groups, a referendum on the proposed constitutional amendments took place on 26 February 2012. According to official figures, 89.4% of those participating in the poll had voted in favour of the new Constitution. Turn-out was officially recorded at 57.4%, although the validity of the results was questioned by opponents of Assad's regime. The Constitution entered into effect on 27 February. Despite the ongoing conflict, elections to the People's Assembly—originally postponed from May 2011—were scheduled to take place in May; however, opposition parties again declared that they would boycott the polls. On 8 March 2012 Abdo Hossam el-Din, a Deputy Minister of Petroleum and Mineral Resources, apparently announced his resignation from the Assad Government, declaring his support for the opposition.

Meanwhile, there was considerable international anger on 4 February 2012, when China and Russia again vetoed the approval of a draft UN Security Council resolution condemning the Syrian regime for its actions against its own people. Their failure to endorse the draft resolution was followed by an intensification of the Government's military campaign. Cities such as Homs came under renewed bombardment, resulting in many fatalities, as government forces battled to secure control of the city from rebel forces; there were widespread claims that the former had carried out massacres of civilians.

In March 2012 members of the UN Security Council approved the terms of a non-binding plan to end the conflict, which had been formulated by the UN-Arab League Joint Special Envoy, Kofi Annan. The plan—which required both sides to end the violence, Syrian forces to withdraw tanks and heavy weaponry from populated areas, as well as permitting a two-hour daily cease-fire to allow humanitarian aid to reach the required areas, political reform, prisoner releases and free movement for journalists—was eventually endorsed by Russia and China. After an initial meeting was convened in Tunisia in late February 2012, on 31 March–1 April 70 countries were represented at what was termed a Friends of the Syrian People conference, held in Istanbul. At the summit delegates agreed to recognize the SNC as the 'legitimate representative' of the Syrian people, and pledged their support to the UN-Arab League peace plan. On 2 April Annan declared that President Assad had agreed to withdraw his troops from residential areas by the stated deadline of 10 April, although on 3 April Syrian armed forces again targeted opposition strongholds such as Dar'a and Hama. The deadline was subsequently extended to 12 April, and the cease-fire took effect on this date. Both the Government and opposition agreed to refrain from violence, but to act in self-defence if they were targeted by the other side. On 14 April the Security Council authorized the deployment to Syria of an advance group of 30 UN observers in order to monitor implementation by all parties of the cease-fire and peace plan. On 21 April the Council agreed to establish a UN Supervision Mission in Syria, comprising an expanded group of 300 unarmed military observers. However, on 25 April Annan described the continuing violence as 'unacceptable', laying particular blame on the Syrian regime for its failure to end its military assault on heavily populated areas. Events in May (see below) effectively signalled an end to the cease-fire and the failure of international efforts to ensure that both sides in the conflict fulfilled the requirements of the UN-Arab League peace plan.

Despite the ongoing violence and a significant opposition boycott, elections to the People's Assembly were held as scheduled on 7 May 2012. President Assad hailed the polls as being the country's first multi-party legislative elections. The NPF secured 184 of the 250 seats, of which 162 seats went to Assad's Baath Party. Independents won 59 seats, while the remaining seven seats were allocated to various smaller parties. Voter turn-out was officially recorded as some 51.3%. However, opposition groups denounced the elections as being undemocratic, and listed a series of irregularities which they claimed had affected the results. On 10 May at least 55 people were killed in a double car bombing in Damascus, which the Syrian Government stated had been carried out by 'foreign-backed terrorists'. Responsibility for the bombings—thought to have targeted a military intelligence building—was subsequently claimed by the al-Nusra Front, a militant Sunni Islamist group affiliated with al-Qa'ida. (Al-Nusra was designated as a 'foreign terrorist organization' by the US Administration in early December 2012, and the FSA and other Syrian opposition forces emphasized that they did not adhere to the militant group's Islamist principles.) Subsequent bombings in the capital resulted in claims by the Assad leadership that the opposition, working in tandem with al-Qa'ida militants, had carried out the attacks, and counter-claims by rebel groups that the regime had planned them to enable it to intensify its military campaign. It had become increasingly clear by mid-2012 that there was a strong sectarian element to the conflict. On 25 May 2012 a reported 108 civilians, including 49 children, were the victims of an apparent massacre by a pro-Government militia in predominantly Sunni villages around Houla, to the north-west of Homs; the Assad regime denied that it had been responsible for the deaths. The crime provoked outrage among the international community and an apparent determination on the part of Syrian opposition forces to intensify efforts to remove President Assad from power.

On 6 June 2012 President Assad invited Riyad Farid Hijab, who had replaced Safar as Minister of Agriculture and Agrarian Reform in mid-April 2011 (when the latter unveiled his first Council of Ministers) to become Prime Minister. Hijab's list of ministers was announced on 23 June 2012, and the new Government—in which the most senior ministers retained their posts—was inaugurated on 26 June. Although the new cabinet line-up was promoted by government officials as containing two former opposition politicians, claims that it represented a 'national unity' administration were dismissed by anti-Assad campaigners.

The Deputy Prime Minister and Minister of Defence, Gen. Dawoud Rajiha, was killed on 18 July 2012, when a bomb exploded at the headquarters of the national security service in Damascus. It was subsequently confirmed that Assistant Vice-President Gen. Hassan al-Turkmani and Rajiha's deputy, Assef Shawkat—the brother-in-law of President Assad—had also died in the explosion. The Minister of the Interior, Lt-Gen. Muhammad Ibrahim al-Shaar, was reported to have been among those injured. On 20 July Gen. Hassan Bakhtiar, head of the security service, reportedly died of injuries sustained in the bombing. Both the FSA and a militant Islamist group, Liwa al-Islam, claimed to have carried out the attack. Later on 18 July President Assad appointed the erstwhile Chief of Staff of the Armed Forces, Gen. Fahd al-Freij, to succeed Rajiha as Minister of Defence; he was sworn into office on 19 July. Lt-Gen. Ali Abdullah Ayyub was named as Syria's new army Chief of Staff on 22 July. During that month the heavy bombardment by government forces inflicted on other urban districts appeared to be focused on Damascus and Aleppo, where fierce clashes between the opposing sides were also reported. Meanwhile, on 19 July Russia and China vetoed a UN Security Council resolution intended to extend the sanctions already in place against the Syrian regime.

On 6 August 2012 President Assad's recently appointed premier, Riyad Hijab, unexpectedly announced his defection to opposition forces. Omar Ibrahim Ghalawanji was appointed as acting Prime Minister on the same day. However, on 9 August Assad named Dr Wael Hader al-Halqi, hitherto Minister of Health, as Prime Minister; he was sworn into office two days later. Ghalawanji returned to his previous role of Deputy Prime Minister for Services Affairs and Minister of Local Administration. On 16 August, in response to Hijab's defection, Assad announced a minor reorganization of the Council of Ministers. Saad Abd al-Salam al-Nayef assumed responsibility for the health portfolio, while Najim Hamad al-Ahmad and Adnan Abdo al-Sukhni became Minister of Justice and Minister of Industry, respectively.

The UN Supervision Mission in Syria was terminated on 19 August 2012, only four months after its establishment, following an acknowledgement by the UN Security Council that there had been no reduction in the levels of violence and that the mission was therefore no longer able to fulfil its mandate. A political liaison office was to be established to retain a UN presence in the country. On 30 August Lakhdar Brahimi

(Algerian Minister of Foreign Affairs in 1991–93) assumed the role of UN-Arab League Joint Special Representative, succeeding former UN Secretary-General Kofi Annan, who had resigned at the beginning of that month. As the number of fatalities caused by the civil conflict increased at a rapid rate, by mid-September the UN estimated that more than 20,000 people had been killed since the start of the anti-Government uprising in March 2011. On 3 October 2012 four suicide car bomb attacks in the centre of Aleppo resulted in the deaths of at least 33 people; the al-Nusra Front claimed to have carried out the attacks, which targeted government and security officials.

President Assad issued a decree reorganizing the Council of Ministers on 9 February 2013. Most notably, Ismael Ismael was nominated as Minister of Finance and Suleiman al-Abbas as Minister of Petroleum and Mineral Resources. The responsibilities of the former Ministry of Labour and Social Affairs were divided: Hassan Hijazi became Minister of Labour, and Kinda al-Shammat Minister of Social Affairs. On 18 March, at a meeting held in Istanbul, the opposition National Coalition for Syrian Revolutionary and Opposition Forces elected Ghassan Hitto as its interim Prime Minister; Hitto was to take charge of a 'government' that would administer areas over which the rebel forces had seized control from government forces. The President of the National Coalition, Ahmad Moaz al-Khatib, resigned from the organization on 24 March, reportedly citing his opposition to Hitto's appointment and his frustration concerning the failure of foreign governments actively to support the Syrian opposition. It was also reported that the FSA did not support Hitto's appointment. Nevertheless, despite his resignation announcement, al-Khatib did represent Syria at the opening session of the Arab League summit meeting held in Doha, Qatar, on 26 March. Arab governments attending the summit endorsed the right of member states to provide military backing to the FSA. It was announced on 22 April that the Vice-President of the National Coalition, George Sabra, would lead the group on an interim basis pending an election scheduled for May.

By early March 2013 the UN estimated that more than 70,000 people had been killed since the start of the Syrian uprising in March 2011. At least 1m. Syrians had sought refuge in neighbouring states, and many thousands more had been displaced to other parts of the country as a result of the violence. In mid-August 2012 the Syrian Arab Red Crescent assessed that the number of internally displaced persons exceeded 1.5m. At the beginning of April 2013 the United Kingdom-based Syrian Observatory for Human Rights reported that March had seen the highest fatality count since the start of the unrest. At least 6,000 people, including up to 300 children, died in that month alone. The group assessed the overall number of fatalities at close to 120,000, although it could only confirm 62,554 deaths (including some 4,390 children). Moreover, there were fears of an impending humanitarian disaster as Syria's health service was close to collapse, many people were without adequate food or sanitation, and power supplies were permanently disrupted. A significant rise in the number of kidnapping cases had also been reported in recent months. There was evidence of significant destruction of many buildings in urban areas, following months of heavy bombardment by troops loyal to President Assad and fighting between pro-regime forces and those of the opposition. The ancient city of Aleppo, listed by UNESCO as a World Heritage Site, had suffered serious damage in the escalating violence, while several important cultural artefacts had been looted from national museums.

International concerns regarding the likelihood of the Syrian conflict spreading to neighbouring countries intensified in mid-March 2013, following reports that Syrian military aircraft had fired four rockets over the border into northern Lebanon, near the town of Arsal in the Beqa'a valley. The air-strike followed warnings by the Assad leadership that it would target anti-Government fighters who had sought refuge across the border. Both the US and French Governments condemned the rocket attack as representing a grave violation of Lebanese sovereignty and a dangerous escalation of the conflict. At the same time, the number of Syrian refugees entering Lebanon increased at a rapid rate: according to estimates by UNHCR, by early May 2013 there were 455,415 Syrian refugees in Lebanon. The UN refugee agency also assessed that there were 448,370 Syrian refugees resident in Jordan, 322,845 in Turkey, 143,177 in Iraq and 62,032 in Egypt.

During late March and April 2013 spokespeople for the regime and opposition both claimed that the other side had used chemical weapons to further their military aims. The verification of such allegations was extremely difficult, owing to the deteriorating security situation within Syria; however, the UN's International Commission of Inquiry on Syria—established in August 2011 to examine human rights abuses being perpetrated in the country—was undertaking an investigation into the claims in early May 2013 (see also Foreign Affairs). A member of the Commission, Carla del Ponte, subsequently claimed in an interview that evidence indicated that rebel forces had used sarin gas; however, those claims were dismissed by the US Administration and strongly denied by the FSA. In late April 2013 the LCC claimed that government forces had committed a further massacre, having gained control of the previously rebel-held town of Jdaidet al-Fadl, south-west of Damascus; according to the LCC, hundreds of civilians had died in the military operation, although government sources maintained that all of those killed had been 'terrorists'. On 29 April Prime Minister al-Halqi survived an assassination attempt in Damascus; nine people were reported to have died in the bombing, which targeted al-Halqi's motorcade; two of the victims were bodyguards of the premier. No group claimed responsibility in the immediate aftermath of the bomb attack.

The Israeli-Syrian track of the Middle East peace process

In July 1991, following US mediation, President Hafiz al-Assad agreed for the first time to participate in direct negotiations with Israel at a regional peace conference, for which the terms of reference would be a comprehensive settlement based on UN Security Council Resolutions 242 (of 1967) and 338 (1973). In August 1991 the Israeli Cabinet formally agreed to attend a peace conference on terms proposed by the USA and the USSR. An initial, 'symbolic' session of the conference was held in Madrid, Spain, in October, and attended by Israeli, Syrian, Egyptian, Lebanese and Palestinian-Jordanian delegations. Syria's principal aim was to recover the Golan Heights, occupied by Israel since 1967. However, it emphasized that it was not prepared to achieve national goals at the expense of a comprehensive Middle East peace settlement. Syria regarded the Declaration of Principles on Palestinian Self-Rule in the Occupied Territories—the basis of a peace settlement signed by Israel and the PLO in September 1993—as deeply flawed. Furthermore, President Assad viewed the secret negotiations between Israel and the PLO prior to the agreement as having undermined the united Arab position in the peace process, and Syria gave no indication that it would cease to support those Damascus-based Palestinian factions which actively opposed the accord.

President Assad met US President Bill Clinton in Geneva, Switzerland, in January 1994—his first such meeting with a US leader since 1977—in an attempt to give fresh impetus to the Syrian track of the peace process. In June 1994 Syria reacted warily to the signing by Jordan and Israel of 'sub-agendas' for future bilateral discussions, and continued to adhere to the principle of a united Arab approach to negotiation with Israel. In September Israel published details of a plan for the partial withdrawal of its armed forces from the Golan Heights; Syria rejected the proposals, although President Assad continued to affirm his willingness to achieve peace with Israel. Clinton held talks with Assad in Damascus in October—the first visit by a US President to Syria for some 20 years. However, it was not until March 1995 that bilateral negotiations finally resumed.

In May 1995 Israel and Syria concluded a 'framework understanding on security arrangements', in order to facilitate the participation in the discussions of the two countries' military Chiefs of Staff. Israel stated publicly that it had proposed a four-year timetable for the withdrawal of its armed forces from the Golan Heights, but that Syria had insisted on one of 18 months. Negotiations became deadlocked once again, and the situation was aggravated by political turmoil in Israel following the assassination of the Prime Minister, Itzhak Rabin, in November. The acting Israeli Prime Minister, Shimon Peres, indicated that no further discussions would take place until after the Israeli general election in May 1996, owing to Syria's refusal to condemn the violence in Israel and to take firmer action against terrorism generally. Following the election to the Israeli premiership of Likud leader Binyamin Netanyahu, an emergency Arab League summit meeting, held in Cairo in June, urged the new right-wing Government in Israel not to abandon the principle of negotiating 'land-for-peace', and demanded the removal of all Israeli settlements in the Golan Heights and their return to Syria. Netanyahu rejected the 'land-for-peace' policies of his Labour predecessor and also insisted that continued Israeli sovereignty over the

Golan Heights must be the basis of any peace settlement with Syria.

In early 1997 the Israeli Knesset (parliament) approved a preliminary reading of proposed legislation stipulating that the return of land to Syria would require the approval of at least two-thirds of deputies. In March 1998 Syria accused Israel of attempting to sabotage its relationship with Lebanon after the Israeli Prime Minister offered to withdraw from southern Lebanon in exchange for a security arrangement before reaching a formal agreement with Syria regarding the Golan Heights. Both Syria and Lebanon reiterated that any withdrawal must be unconditional, in compliance with UN Security Council Resolution 425. Syria was sceptical regarding the likely success of the US-brokered Wye Memorandum, signed in October by Israel and the Palestinian (National) Authority (PA), towards achieving a lasting peace in the Middle East, and President Assad again demanded a resumption of 'land-for-peace' negotiations.

Syria welcomed the success of Ehud Barak and his Labour-led One Israel coalition in the Israeli elections of May 1999. At the inauguration of the new Israeli Cabinet in early July, Barak promised to negotiate a bilateral peace with Syria, based on UN Security Council Resolutions 242 and 338, thus apparently signalling to the Assad regime his intention to return most of the occupied Golan Heights to Syria in exchange for peace and normalized relations. In mid-July, prior to a meeting in Washington, DC, between Barak and President Clinton, Syria was reported to have warned dissidents of Damascus-based Palestinian organizations to cease their military operations against Israel, and to have interrupted the supply of Iranian weapons to Hezbollah guerrillas in southern Lebanon. Moreover, in late July Syria reported a 'cease-fire' with Israel, although mutual disagreements remained, most notably over the point at which previous negotiations had been suspended.

In early December 1999, following mediation by Clinton, Israel and Syria agreed to resume negotiations from the point at which they had stalled in 1996. The first round of discussions between the Syrian Minister of Foreign Affairs, Farouk al-Shara', and the Israeli premier, Ehud Barak, was opened by the US President in mid-December 1999 in Washington, DC. Later that month the two sides were reported to have agreed an informal 'cease-fire' to limit the conflict in Lebanon. A second round of talks between al-Shara' and Barak proceeded in early January 2000 in Shepherdstown, West Virginia, USA. Syria and Israel had agreed meanwhile on the establishment of committees to discuss simultaneously the issues of borders, security, normalization of relations, and water-sharing. However, in mid-January the peace talks were postponed indefinitely. Syria declared that it required a 'written' commitment from Israel to withdraw from the Golan Heights prior to a resumption of talks, while Israel demanded the personal involvement of President Assad in the negotiating process, and that Syria take action to restrain Hezbollah in southern Lebanon. In March the Israeli Cabinet voted unanimously to withdraw its forces from Lebanon by July, even in the absence of a peace settlement with Syria. Meanwhile, the Knesset voted to change the majority required in the event of an Israeli withdrawal from the Golan from 50% of participating voters to 50% of the registered electorate.

In May 2000, prior to the planned Israeli withdrawal from southern Lebanon, it was reported that Saudi Arabia and Egypt had pledged military support to Syria in the event of Israeli aggression. The accelerated withdrawal of Israeli armed forces from southern Lebanon was completed on 24 May, several weeks ahead of the original Israeli deadline. Following the death, in June, of President Assad, and the succession of his second son, Bashar al-Assad, in July, the Israeli-Syrian track of the Middle East peace process remained stalled. The escalation of the Palestinian al-Aqsa *intifada* from September further strained Syria's relations with Israel, and, as tensions increased throughout the Middle East, Israel accused Syria of involvement in the abduction of Israeli military personnel by Hezbollah in the disputed Shebaa Farms area of southern Lebanon. (Shebaa Farms was designated by the UN as being part of Syria, and thus subject to the Syrian track of the peace process.)

Following the election of Likud leader Ariel Sharon to the Israeli premiership in February 2001, President Assad reiterated Syria's position that negotiations would only be resumed upon a full Israeli withdrawal from the Golan Heights. Tensions between the two sides increased in April following an attack by Israeli forces on a Syrian radar station in eastern Lebanon, in which at least one Syrian soldier died. In January 2003 another Syrian soldier was killed during a rare exchange of gunfire between Israeli and Syrian forces in the Golan Heights. In November 2004 Assad announced that he was willing to resume peace talks with Israel unconditionally (although it was unclear whether the Syrian President intended for negotiations to resume from where they had collapsed in 2000); however, Israel demanded that Syria first close the headquarters of the Islamic Resistance Movement (Hamas) and Islamic Jihad, and Assad rejected Israel's setting of conditions as unacceptable.

In April 2003 US President George W. Bush handed to the Israeli and Palestinian leaderships the so-called 'roadmap' peace plan, which had been drawn up by the Quartet group (comprising the USA, the UN, Russia and the EU). The plan envisaged an end to the Arab–Israeli conflict, including a fully negotiated settlement between Israel and Syria, and the creation of a sovereign Palestinian state by 2005–06 (see the chapter on Israel). Syria emphasized that the roadmap must run in tandem with the Syrian track of negotiations on the Golan Heights issue; however, in May 2003 President Assad reportedly agreed to accept it unconditionally. An offer from Syria to resume peace talks with Israel in July was firmly rejected by Israeli Prime Minister Ariel Sharon as 'insincere'. In October Israeli forces launched an air attack against an alleged Palestinian militant training camp inside Syria. Israel claimed that the camp at Ain Saheb near Damascus was being used by Hamas and Islamic Jihad, and that the attack was in retaliation for a suicide bomb attack in Haifa, Israel, in which 19 Israelis were killed. In January 2004 Assad rejected Israeli offers to resume peace negotiations, describing them as a 'media manoeuvre'.

In December 2006 Israeli Prime Minister Ehud Olmert also rejected an appeal from President Assad for a resumption of formal peace negotiations with Syria. Olmert accused Assad of merely trying to solicit international approval at a time when Syria was under intense scrutiny for its alleged complicity in the assassinations in Lebanon of Rafiq Hariri and Pierre Gemayel. In January 2007 a former Israeli diplomat claimed that Israel and Syria had in fact conducted secret negotiations concerning a possible peace deal between September 2004 and July 2006, in which month the outbreak of the conflict between Israel and Hezbollah (see the chapters on Israel and Lebanon) had abruptly brought the proceedings to a close. The diplomat's claims were strongly denied by the Syrian Government; however, in March 2007 President Assad was reported to have acknowledged that secret talks had taken place between 'non-official' channels.

Amid reports that Olmert had established a ministerial committee to examine Israel's military preparedness for a potential conflict with Syria, in June 2007 the Israeli premier apparently declared that he was ready to engage in direct negotiations with the Syrian regime, without preconditions. The Israeli media commented that Olmert had relayed to Syria, through Turkish and German officials, the proposal that Israel withdraw from the Golan Heights in exchange for Syria's undertaking to 'gradually dissolve' its links with Iran and militant organizations in Lebanon and the Palestinian territories. However, tensions between Israel and Syria worsened in September, after Israel carried out an air-strike on a military installation at al-Kibar, 'deep within' Syrian territory. In October President Assad stated that the Israeli strike had hit a military building that was under construction, and denied media reports speculating that it might have been a concealed nuclear reactor. In April 2008 US intelligence officials reportedly presented evidence that the target of the Israeli air-strike was in fact a nuclear facility that was being constructed with assistance from the Democratic People's Republic of Korea (North Korea); the Syrian authorities again strongly rejected the claims. An investigation of the site by the IAEA in June found that the remains of the original building had been razed and buried under the concrete foundations of a new construction. The IAEA investigators stated in November that traces of uranium had been discovered, although the source of the material remained uncertain. The Syrian authorities refused to grant the agency additional access to al-Kibar, or to other sites, stating that the source of the uranium was Israeli missiles used in the bombing of the installation. In a report issued in February 2009, the IAEA contended there was a 'low probability' that Israeli munitions were the source of the radioactive material, and described Syria's co-operation with their investigation as unsatisfactory. During 2010 the IAEA again criticized the Syrian authorities for failing to co-operate with its investigations into the exact purpose of the al-Kibar facility and three other apparently related military sites. In May 2011 the Agency described al-Kibar as 'very likely' to have been a nuclear reactor, and it referred Syria to the UN Security Council in June.

Meanwhile, in May 2008 Turkey's Minister of Foreign Affairs, Ali Babacan, confirmed that indirect talks aimed at achieving a comprehensive peace agreement between Israel and Syria were to begin in Istanbul. Four rounds of Turkish-mediated talks were held between May and August. However, a fifth round of talks, scheduled for September, was postponed due to the political uncertainty in Israel following the resignation of Prime Minister Olmert (see the chapter on Israel). Following Israel's military offensive against Hamas targets in the Gaza Strip, launched in December 2008 (see the chapters on Israel and the Palestinian Territories), President Assad formally suspended the talks with Israel. Following the Israeli general election of February 2009, a new coalition Government was sworn in under the leadership of the Likud leader, Binyamin Netanyahu; during the campaign Netanyahu had declared his outright opposition to the surrender of the Golan Heights as part of any peace agreement with Syria.

After President Assad had accused Israel of pushing the region towards war, in February 2010 Israel's new Minister of Foreign Affairs, Avigdor Lieberman, issued a controversial statement demanding that Syria relinquish all territorial claims over the Golan Heights and asserting that any act of aggression by Syria towards Israel would result in the removal of Assad from power. Israel held a series of military exercises in that month that reportedly simulated a major assault on Syrian territory. In April Israeli President Shimon Peres publicly accused Syria of delivering long-range Scud missiles and providing relevant training to Hezbollah militants in Lebanon; the allegations were denied by Syria, Hezbollah and the Lebanese Prime Minister, Saad Hariri. Although Assad expressed his willingness to resume Turkish-mediated peace talks with Israel, the Syrian leadership was strongly critical of Israel's military raid on a Turkish ship attempting to break the Israeli blockade of Gaza at the end of May, which resulted in the deaths of nine pro-Palestinian Turkish activists. Moreover, the likelihood of a breakthrough appeared more remote when, in November, the Knesset approved legislation stating that any withdrawal from the Golan Heights would require the prior endorsement of Israeli voters in a national referendum.

On 15 May 2011, the anniversary of the establishment of the State of Israel in 1948, a group of mainly Palestinian protesters attempted to cross the border from Syria into the Golan Heights as part of a wider protest by Palestinians in Lebanon, Egypt, Jordan and the Palestinian territories. The strong response of Israeli armed forces resulted in the deaths of a reported four protesters. However, Israeli officials alleged that the demonstration had been organized by the Syrian regime in order to divert attention from its military crackdown against its own opposition movement. A similar claim was made on 5 June, when another group of protesters trying to breach the border into the Golan Heights was reportedly killed by Israeli troops. Although it was estimated that 12 demonstrators had died, the exact circumstances of the deaths were disputed by the two sides. During 2011–12, despite the long-standing hostility between Israel and Syria, the Israeli Government was extremely anxious about the possible repercussions for Israel's security in the event that the Assad regime was overthrown and replaced by a more militant, Islamist-led government. Amid a rapid deterioration in Syria's security situation as the civil conflict intensified, in July 2012 the Israeli Ministry of Defence issued a firm warning that it would take military action in the event that militant organizations such as Hezbollah took advantage of a potential power vacuum in Syria to build up supplies of chemical weapons. Israel did carry out a series of air-strikes against what appeared to be military facilities around Damascus in early May 2013, stating that its intention was to disrupt shipments of sophisticated Iranian-made weapons to Hezbollah.

Foreign Affairs

Relations with the USA

The Syrian Government condemned the suicide attacks carried out in New York and Washington, DC, on 11 September 2001. However, Syria was openly critical of the military campaign initiated by the US Administration of George W. Bush—as part of its international 'war on terror'—against targets in Afghanistan linked to the Taliban regime and to the militant Islamist al-Qa'ida network that was held principally responsible for the attacks. In October the British Prime Minister, Tony Blair, undertook an official visit to Syria to garner Arab support for the US-led campaign in Afghanistan, and asked the Syrian leadership to end its support for militant groups such as Hezbollah and the Popular Front for the Liberation of Palestine.

However, President Bashar al-Assad condemned the West's bombing of Afghan civilians and stated that organizations engaged in fighting the Israeli occupation were 'legitimate'. In December 2002 Assad became the first Syrian leader to visit the United Kingdom, where he expressed his opposition to a likely US-led military campaign to bring about 'regime change' in Iraq, and rejected Blair's demand to curb militant Palestinian groups operating in Syria.

The Syrian leadership referred to the campaign launched by the US-led coalition forces in March 2003 to oust the Iraqi regime of Saddam Hussain as an 'illegal invasion'. Moreover, Syrians were angered in late March when a bus close to the border with Iraq was hit by a stray US missile, killing five Syrian civilians. Syria strongly denied claims by the Bush Administration that it was providing military equipment to Iraq during the conflict. The USA alleged that Syria had assisted leading members of the Iraqi Baath Party to flee the country after the collapse of Saddam Hussain's regime in April, and that Iraqi weapons of mass destruction might have been smuggled across the border into Syria. However, President Bush subsequently acknowledged that Syria had sealed its border with Iraq. Nevertheless, US officials from the Department of the Treasury estimated that US $3,000m. of Iraqi money was being held by Syrian-controlled banks in Damascus and Lebanon, in contravention of a UN resolution requiring all Iraqi funds held abroad to be handed over to the US-controlled Iraqi Fund for Development. In December President Bush signed the Syria Accountability Act, which allowed the USA to impose a range of sanctions on Syria unless the country met a series of conditions—including ending its support for terrorist groups. The sanctions were eventually put in place on 11 May 2004; they included a ban on all US exports to Syria other than food or medicine, and a halt to flights between the two countries.

In March 2007 Syria appealed for a 'serious dialogue' with the USA on a wide range of concerns pertaining to the Middle East. In the following month Nancy Pelosi, Speaker of the US House of Representatives, became the most senior US official to visit Syria since 2003. Pelosi's unauthorized visit drew strong criticism from President Bush, who, angered by the challenge to his Administration's policy of isolation towards the Syrian Government, accused her of usurping executive powers and of sending 'mixed signals' to a 'state sponsor of terrorism'. Syria's ambassador to the USA, Imad Moustapha, described Pelosi's overture as a 'positive step', but one that offered little likelihood of a change in US policy. However, in May 2007 the US Secretary of State, Condoleezza Rice, held talks with Syria's Minister of Foreign Affairs, Walid Mouallem, on the sidelines of a major summit meeting held in Egypt, intended to address the situation in Iraq. The sideline negotiations represented the first official high-level talks between the two countries since the murder of Rafiq Hariri in Lebanon. Rice reportedly urged the Syrian leadership to take action to prevent foreign fighters from crossing into Iraq from Syria in order to participate in the anti-US insurgency.

Syria agreed to send a low-level delegation to the international peace meeting held under US auspices in Annapolis, Maryland, USA, in November 2007, with the aim of relaunching the Middle East peace process. However, in February 2008 President Bush approved an expanded range of sanctions against the Syrian regime, which he accused of destabilizing both Iraq and Lebanon. The new sanctions included a freeze on the assets of prominent Syrian officials or businessmen deemed to have benefited from corrupt practices. In March the US Administration also announced that maritime vessels docking in US ports that had previously visited Syrian ports would henceforth be placed on a Port Security Advisory List, amid US concerns regarding Syrian links with international terrorist networks. In May the Bush Administration imposed a further embargo on certain exports to Syria, following allegations by US intelligence agencies that there existed a covert nuclear co-operation between Syria and North Korea.

Bilateral tensions increased in late October 2008, when four US military helicopters, flying from Iraq, carried out a covert raid some 10 km inside Syrian territory, targeting a building under construction in the Abu Kamal district. Official Syrian sources claimed that eight civilians, among them children, had been killed. This account was disputed by an unnamed US intelligence source, which asserted that the operation had successfully targeted a prominent associate of al-Qa'ida, Abu Gha-diya, who was allegedly responsible for smuggling foreign militants and weapons across the Syrian border into Iraq, and

that all those killed were militants. Mouallem described the operation as a 'criminal and terrorist act'.

Following the inauguration of Barack Obama as US President in January 2009, there was renewed optimism concerning US-Syrian relations. In the opening weeks of his presidency Obama announced his intention to pursue a pragmatic and reconciliatory foreign policy approach in the Middle East. During late January and February three separate US congressional delegations visited Damascus for talks with President Assad on improving bilateral relations. The process of dialogue grew in significance when Jeffrey Feltman, Acting Assistant Secretary of the Bureau of Near Eastern Affairs at the US Department of State, along with Daniel Shapiro, a senior White House official who had been involved in drafting the Syria Accountability Act in 2003, held talks in Damascus with Mouallem. However, neither side denied that there remained significant obstacles to a full normalization of relations—notably Syria's support for Hamas and Hezbollah, and its relationship with Iran, on the one hand; and the USA's continued policy of diplomatic and economic sanctions against Syria, and support for Israel, on the other.

Although in May 2009 the US Administration renewed its programme of sanctions against Syria, in June diplomatic relations advanced to a higher level, following the visit to Damascus of George Mitchell, the US special envoy to the Middle East, for discussions with President Assad on US efforts to relaunch the stalled Middle East peace process. Mitchell asserted that Syria could play a crucial role in efforts to secure a comprehensive peace settlement. In February 2010 Robert Ford was formally nominated as US ambassador to Syria, the post having been vacant since the withdrawal of the former envoy in 2005, in protest against Syria's alleged involvement in the assassination of Rafiq Hariri. Immediately following the nomination, the US Under Secretary of State for Political Affairs, William Burns, visited Damascus for talks with Assad on strengthening bilateral relations. However, despite Ford's appointment being approved by the US Senate Foreign Relations Committee in April 2010, the Senate subsequently failed to ratify it (owing to the concerns of many US senators regarding the return of an ambassador to Syria), leading President Obama to appoint Ford directly during a congressional recess in December.

The US sanctions programme was extended for a further year on 3 May 2010, since the Obama Administration assessed that Syria remained an 'extraordinary threat' to US national security and foreign policy with its 'continuing support for terrorist organizations and pursuit of weapons of mass destruction'. President Obama did acknowledge, however, that the Syrian Government had taken measures to prevent foreign insurgents from crossing its border into Iraq. Furthermore, after the USA removed its objections to Syria joining the World Trade Organization, the country was granted observer status on 4 May. However, prospects of an improvement in relations were ended following the Syrian authorities' response to anti-Government protests from March 2011. In April President Obama denounced the violent repression of demonstrators by Syrian security forces, and on 18 May he signed an Executive Order implementing targeted sanctions against Assad and six prominent Syrian officials (including al-Shara', Prime Minister Safar, and the Ministers of Defence and the Interior). Following an attack on the US embassy in Damascus by militant supporters of President Assad in early July, the US Secretary of State, Hillary Clinton, declared that his presidency had 'lost legitimacy'. On 10 August the Obama Administration imposed further sanctions on the Syrian banking sector, and on 18 August it froze all Syrian government assets and imposed a trade embargo prohibiting all hydrocarbon imports. On 30 August the sanctions were extended to target Minister of Foreign Affairs Mouallem. The USA withdrew its ambassador, Robert Ford, from Damascus in late October, amid concerns for his safety after the envoy had strongly criticized the actions of the Syrian Government, and had met with several opposition leaders.

After the violence in Syria had intensified during 2012 and the worsening civil conflict had resulted in an immense loss of life, in early May 2013 the recently appointed US Secretary of Defense, Chuck Hagel, admitted that the Obama Administration was reconsidering its previous refusal to provide arms to any of Syria's opposition forces. This stance had been adopted during the latter part of 2012, amid fears that Islamist militant groups might obtain US-supplied weaponry, and due to a widespread uncertainty concerning the democratic intentions of the Syrian opposition's emerging leadership. The USA's apparent change of position came following claims made by US, British and other countries' intelligence agencies in late April 2013 that the Assad regime might have used small quantities of chemical weapons against civilians in its struggle to hold onto power. Nevertheless, there were subsequent suggestions that it might, in fact, have been rebel forces who had used the banned weapons.

Regional relations

A diplomatic crisis developed between Syria and the Palestinian (National) Authority (PA) in August 1999, after the Syrian Deputy Prime Minister and Minister of Defence, Maj.-Gen. Mustafa Tlass, insulted and publicly accused Yasser Arafat of having 'sold Jerusalem and the Arab nation' in peace agreements concluded with Israel since 1993. The PA demanded that Tlass resign, and Fatah reportedly issued a death warrant against the minister. Arafat attended the funeral of President Hafiz al-Assad, and in mid-2000 the PA renewed its demand that Syria free all remaining Palestinian prisoners from its gaols; seven Palestinians were released into Lebanese custody in December. Amid Syrian efforts to support the Palestinians in their escalating conflict with the Israelis, and following talks between Bashar al-Assad and Arafat during the Arab League summit meeting in Jordan in March 2001, the two leaders declared that they had achieved a reconciliation. In December 2004 PLO leader Mahmud Abbas made the first official Palestinian visit to Damascus since 1996; President Assad emphasized Syria's support for the Palestinian people and their struggle for national unity.

By January 2013 there were 499,189 Palestinian refugees registered in Syria. After administration of the Palestinian territories had effectively been divided between the West Bank (governed by Fatah) and the Gaza Strip (by Hamas) since June 2007 (see the chapter on the Palestinian Territories), the Syrian Government retained close ties with Hamas, as part of an informal alliance that also included Iran and Lebanon's Hezbollah movement. However, the Hamas leadership formally declared in February 2012 that it was ending co-operation with the Assad regime and that it was backing opposition forces seeking his removal from power. Palestinian officials reported in December 2011 that Hamas was taking steps to close its offices in Syria and return many of its leaders to Gaza. There was speculation later that month regarding the Hamas leadership's possible relocation to either Jordan, Qatar or Tunisia; however, Hamas officials denied that any such decision had been taken.

In October 1998 the Jordanian Government demanded 'immediate answers' from Syria concerning a list of 239 Jordanians allegedly missing in Syria, and a further 190 who it claimed were being held in Syrian prisons. The Syrian authorities maintained that most of those listed were in fact members of Palestinian organizations linked with Jordan and had violated Syrian laws. In February 1999 President Assad unexpectedly attended the funeral of King Hussein of Jordan, and reportedly held a private meeting with the new monarch, King Abdullah, whose succession Syria had welcomed. Syria agreed to supply Jordan with water during a drought in 1999 (as it did in 2000), and both sides agreed to hold future discussions regarding the Jordanian prisoners in Syria. The joint Syrian-Jordanian Higher Committee met in August in Amman under the chairmanship of both countries' premiers—the first time in almost a decade that a senior Syrian delegation had visited Jordan's capital. Meanwhile, the Syrian Government stated that many of the Jordanian prisoners held in Syria had been released under a general amnesty granted in July 2000 and that the 'very few' who remained in Syrian gaols were non-political detainees. Following the death of President Assad in June of that year, King Abdullah visited Damascus in July for talks with Syria's new President, Bashar al-Assad. It was reported in November that Syria had upgraded its diplomatic representation in Jordan to ambassadorial level. The joint Wahdah Dam project on Jordan's River Yarmuk was completed in September 2006, aiming to provide Jordan with water and Syria with electricity. Relations with Jordan have been complicated by the military crackdown being carried out by Syrian government forces against anti-Government protesters since March 2011, and by the large influx of Syrian refugees into the country (see Domestic Political Affairs). Despite his fears for Jordan's stability should the Syrian regime be ousted, in November King Abdullah issued a public demand that President Assad step down.

Relations between Syria and Iraq had been strained since the early 1970s due to a rivalry between the respective factions of the Baath Party in Damascus and Baghdad. Notably, Syria supported Iran in its war with Iraq in 1980–88. Although an extraordinary summit meeting of the Arab League in November 1987 produced a unanimous statement expressing solidarity with Iraq and condemning Iran for prolonging the war and for its occupation of Arab territory, Syria announced subsequently that a reconciliation with Iraq had not taken place, and that Syrian relations with Iran remained fundamentally unchanged. Syria also used its veto to prevent the adoption of an Iraqi proposal to readmit Egypt to the Arab League, but it could not prevent the inclusion in the final communiqué of a clause permitting individual member nations to re-establish diplomatic relations with Egypt. However, Egypt's recognition of the newly proclaimed Palestinian state in November 1988 led ultimately to the restoration of diplomatic relations with Syria in December 1989.

Syria endorsed Egypt's efforts to co-ordinate an Arab response to Iraq's invasion of Kuwait in August 1990, and agreed to send troops to Saudi Arabia as part of a pan-Arab deterrent force, supporting the US-led effort to deter an Iraqi invasion of Saudi Arabia. Indications that Syria's participation in the multinational force was transforming its relations with the West were confirmed in November when diplomatic ties were restored with the United Kingdom. Iraq's overwhelming military defeat by the US-led multinational force in February 1991 strengthened Syria's position with regard to virtually all its major regional concerns. In March, after a regional security summit in Damascus between Egyptian and Syrian officials and representatives of the Cooperation Council for the Arab States of the Gulf (Gulf Cooperation Council—GCC, see p. 255), the formation of an Arab peace-keeping force, comprising mainly Egyptian and Syrian troops, was announced. However, in May Egypt declared its intention to withdraw its forces from the Gulf region within three months. Syria's decision to ally itself, in opposition to Iraq, with the Western powers and the 'moderate' Arab states led the USA to realize that it could no longer exclude Syria from any role in the resolution of the Arab–Israeli conflict. A shift in Syria's relations with the USSR, a major source of military assistance but whose programmes of political liberalization President Assad had recently criticized, provided another reason for its realignment with the West.

After Iraq's defeat in 1991, Syria became a centre for elements of the Iraqi opposition. However, it remained committed to the territorial integrity of Iraq, fearing that disintegration might encourage minorities within Syria (particularly the Kurds) to pursue their own autonomy. Three crossing points on the Syria–Iraq border were reopened in June 1997 to facilitate bilateral trade, and in September 1998 Iraq, Iran and Syria agreed to establish a joint forum for foreign policy co-ordination (particularly with regard to the USA). In the same month Syria and Iraq reopened commercial centres in one another's capitals, and in April 1999 a series of mutual agreements were signed, as part of the process of normalizing relations.

In August 2000 a rail link between Aleppo and the Iraqi capital was reopened after an interval of some 20 years, and in December the Syrian authorities reportedly removed all restrictions on Iraqi citizens travelling to Syria. In November, furthermore, Iraq was reported to have begun transporting crude petroleum to Syria via a pipeline not used since the early 1980s; it was subsequently alleged that Syria was in violation of UN sanctions regarding the supply of petroleum from Iraq. In August 2001 the Syrian Prime Minister, leading a ministerial and commercial delegation, became the most senior Syrian official to visit Iraq for two decades. Syria was particularly concerned (as was Turkey) by the potential ascendance of Iraqi Kurdish groups should the incumbent regime in Baghdad be overthrown. There were reports in mid-2002 that Syria (having been elected as a nonpermanent member of the UN Security Council for 2002–03) was involved in mediation efforts between Iraq and Kuwait. Despite its unexpected support for UN Security Council Resolution 1441, approved in November, which imposed strict terms according to which Iraq must disarm or else face probable military action, Syria expressed its firm opposition to the US-led military campaign against the Iraqi regime, which began in March 2003 (see the chapter on Iraq).

Three years after the overthrow of Saddam Hussein's regime in Iraq, in November 2006 Syria and Iraq announced that had restored full diplomatic relations and agreed to co-operate on a number of security issues. It was hoped that the renewal of diplomatic ties, ending a hiatus of more than 20 years, would facilitate the policing of the shared border, across which a large number of militants were still reported to be entering Iraq. In February 2007 a spokesman for the Iraqi Government claimed that 50% of those who had committed suicide bomb attacks in Iraq had entered the country from Syria, although this was staunchly denied by the Syrian Government. Meanwhile, new regulations requiring Iraqi citizens to obtain a visa before entering Syria were introduced in October.

A series of bomb attacks targeting government buildings in Baghdad in August 2009 led to a renewed diplomatic crisis between Iraq and Syria. The Iraqi authorities claimed to have evidence that the attacks had been directed and financed by two former Iraqi Baath Party officials living in exile in Syria, and responded by withdrawing their ambassador from Syria and demanding the extradition of the alleged conspirators. The Syrian authorities rejected Iraq's allegations and recalled their own ambassador from Baghdad. None the less, in September the Iraqi and Syrian ministers responsible for foreign affairs entered into talks, mediated by Turkey, aimed at resolving the dispute. As was the case with Iraq's other neighbours, Syria played a role in the protracted negotiations towards forming a new Iraqi national unity government following the legislative elections of March 2010. It was agreed in October to return ambassadors to Baghdad and Damascus, marking an end to the diplomatic crisis that had begun in mid-2009.

The office of UNHCR estimated the number of displaced Iraqis in Syria at some 1m. people in January 2011. As the situation in Syria became increasingly violent following the uprising against President Assad's rule from early 2011, some Iraqi refugees chose to return home; one official estimate put the number of those returning to Iraq between March 2011 and March 2012 at 17,000. However, many of Iraq's refugees were either unwilling or unable to leave Syria. Meanwhile, there was a significant flow of Syrian refugees to Iraq as the conflict in Syria worsened (see Domestic Political Affairs). The apparently 'neutral' position adopted by the Iraqi Government under Prime Minister Nuri al-Maliki towards the Syrian uprising and subsequent civil conflict was strongly criticized by other Arab governments who favoured giving military assistance to the anti-Government opposition in Syria. Western governments also alleged, in March 2013, that Iran was being allowed to use Iraqi airspace to supply sophisticated weaponry to the Assad regime and its ally, Hezbollah. Meanwhile, in one of the most high-profile defections from the Syrian regime, in July 2012 Nawef al-Fares, the ambassador to Iraq, left his Baghdad post to seek refuge in Qatar, reportedly announcing that he would be joining the Syrian opposition.

Allegations about Syria's involvement in the assassination of Rafiq Hariri in February 2005, and its role in Lebanon generally, led to increasing international and regional isolation, which, in turn, increased the strategic importance of Syria's ties with Iran. In August President Assad visited the recently elected Iranian President, Mahmoud Ahmadinejad, in Tehran, and the two leaders announced their solidarity in the face of common foreign threats. Despite the widely held opinion that Syria's growing rapprochement with the USA from early 2009 would necessitate a weakening of relations with Iran, President Assad continued to promote close ties with the Iranian Government during 2010. In late February, following the nomination of a new US ambassador to Syria, President Ahmadinejad travelled to Damascus for consultations on regional affairs with Assad. The summit was seen as a symbolic response to a statement by US Secretary of State Hillary Clinton that the USA was urging Syria to distance itself from Iran and cancel its support for militant groups in Lebanon, the Palestinian territories and Iraq. In a further gesture of defiance, President Assad also hosted an official banquet attended by Ahmadinejad and the Secretary-General of Hezbollah, Sheikh Hasan Nasrallah.

Owing to Iran's close relationship with Syria and its military and financial support for the Assad regime, during the early months of the uprising against his rule from March 2011, the Iranian leadership denounced the protest movement. However, as the crackdown by government forces intensified, by September President Ahmadinejad was urging the Syrian President to end the violence and to begin talks with representatives of the Syrian opposition. Nevertheless, as the uprising had developed into a civil conflict by the early part of 2012, the Iranian Government continued to offer support to its Syrian counterpart. In early 2013 many Western governments expressed grave concerns regarding the extent of Iranian military support for President Assad's forces and the Iranian-made weaponry that was being smuggled to Hezbollah militants believed to be fighting alongside Syrian government forces in their campaign to crush the rebellion.

A summit meeting of Arab League member states, held in Damascus in March 2008, was boycotted (among others) by Egypt's President Hosni Mubarak and Saudi Arabia's King Abdullah, both of whom blamed Syria and Iran for contributing to the crisis in Lebanon through their support for the Hezbollah-led opposition. When Saudi Arabia had transferred its ambassador in Damascus to Qatar in February, it declined to appoint a new ambassador to Syria. The conflicting interests of Saudi Arabia and Syria in the region were highlighted again by their divergent responses to Israel's military offensive in Gaza, launched in December 2008. President Assad attended an emergency Arab League meeting in Doha in January 2009, convened by Qatar with the stated aim of formulating a unified Arab response to the crisis in Gaza. However, the Doha summit was boycotted by several nations, notably Egypt and Saudi Arabia, and did not achieve the quorum of 15 participating states required to grant the meeting official status. Shortly afterwards, however, during the Arab Economic, Social and Development Summit in Kuwait, Assad attended a private meeting hosted by the Saudi King and also attended by the leaders of Qatar, Egypt and Kuwait, which was heralded as achieving significant progress towards greater Arab unity.

The appointment, in July 2009, of a new Saudi ambassador to Syria confirmed the positive trend in bilateral relations. In October King Abdullah, accompanied by a senior ministerial delegation, completed his first official visit to Syria since acceding to the throne in 2005; discussions included plans to promote Saudi investment in Syrian infrastructure projects. King Abdullah and President Assad issued a concluding statement confirming their joint support for: the establishment of a government of national unity in Lebanon; joint Arab measures in support of the Palestinian cause; and the safeguarding of stability and national unity in Yemen. The Saudi and Syrian leaders held a tripartite summit meeting with the Lebanese President, Michel Suleiman, in Beirut in July, in an effort to persuade Lebanon's competing Sunni and Shi'ite political factions from once again resorting to violence. The meeting was convened amid growing tensions in Lebanon over reports that an indictment by the STL (the UN-sponsored tribunal investigating the murder of former premier Rafiq Hariri) was imminent, and that members of (the Shi'ite) Hezbollah were likely to be named. However, in mid-January 2011, with the first indictments due to be issued later that month, the Lebanese 'national unity' Government collapsed, following the resignations of Hezbollah and allied ministers. The previous day the Saudi and Syrian Governments had apparently failed to achieve a compromise agreement for Lebanon, with some sources claiming that the USA had intervened to prevent a political deal from enabling Hezbollah to avoid censure by the STL. It was not until mid-June that a new Lebanese Government, dominated by Hezbollah and its allies, was formed. The first indictment relating to the Hariri case was confirmed in late June, and it was subsequently revealed that the targets of the arrest warrants were four Hezbollah operatives, including a brother-in-law of Imad Mughniyeh, who were suspected of having carried out the assassination. (For further developments concerning the STL, see the chapter on Lebanon.)

Apparently fearful of the consequences for its own stability should the Syrian uprising succeed, the Saudi leadership initially backed President Assad as far as his tough stance towards pro-democracy demonstrations was concerned. However, in early August 2011—by which time the death toll arising from the Government's military crackdown against opposition activists had reached at least 2,000—King Abdullah launched a strong condemnation of the regime's actions, urging the Syrian President to 'stop the killing machine'. The Saudi ambassador to Damascus was recalled soon afterwards, and the country's embassy was formally closed (along with those of other GCC member states) in March 2012; the Gulf states also demanded that Syrian ambassadors leave their capitals. Meanwhile, in March Syria's Minister of Information, Dr Adnan Mahmoud, accused the Saudi and Qatari Governments of providing military assistance to what he termed the 'armed terrorist gangs' engaged in fighting President Assad's forces. The opposition FSA did receive military backing from these two largely Sunni Gulf countries from early 2012.

Relations between Syria and Turkey became increasingly strained in the 1990s, owing to disagreements over the sharing of water from the Euphrates river. No permanent agreement on this resource has been concluded, and both Syria and Iraq are concerned that new dams in Turkey will reduce their share of water from the Euphrates. Syria's relations with Turkey deteriorated sharply in April 1996, after it was revealed that Turkey and Israel had concluded a military co-operation agreement earlier in the year. In October 1998 Turkey threatened to invade Syria if its demands for an end to alleged Syrian support for the separatist Kurdistan Workers' Party (Partiya Karkeren Kurdistan—PKK) were not met. The Turkish authorities also demanded the extradition of the PKK leader, Abdullah Öcalan (whom they alleged to be directing PKK operations from Damascus), and insisted that Syria renounce its historic claim on the Turkish province of Hatay. Turkey's aggressive stance was viewed by Syria as evidence of a Turkish-Israeli military and political alliance, and as a result both Syria and Turkey ordered troops to be deployed along their joint border. Diplomatic efforts to defuse the crisis by Egypt, Iran and the UN, and Syrian assurances that Öcalan was not residing in Syria, allowed a degree of normalization in bilateral relations. In late October Syrian and Turkish representatives signed an agreement whereby the PKK was to be banned from entering Syrian territory, while the organization's active bases in Syria and Lebanon's Beqa'a valley were to be closed.

In September 2000 Syria and Turkey signed a co-operation agreement relating to countering terrorism and organized crime, and in June 2002 they signed two military co-operation accords. In December 2003 bilateral relations were further strengthened by Syria's decision to hand over 22 suspects sought by the Turkish authorities in connection with four fatal suicide bombings in İstanbul in November. In January 2004 President Assad made the first ever visit by a Syrian head of state to Turkey. Syria's initiative to improve bilateral relations was attributed to Turkey's membership of the North Atlantic Treaty Organization, and hence its relatively close relationship with the USA, as well as shared concerns about a possible 'ripple-effect' of increased Kurdish autonomy in northern Iraq following the removal of Saddam Hussain's regime in early 2003. In January 2007 an agreement between the Syrian and Turkish Governments to create a bilateral free trade zone took effect. A Joint Technical Committee on water resources, involving Syria, Turkey and Iraq, was reconvened in May, after some 15 years of inactivity, and by early 2010 various joint initiatives aimed at resolving disagreements over water resources were under discussion; these included a proposed joint Turkish-Syrian dam on the Orontes river at the border between Syria and Turkey. The so-called 'friendship dam' construction project commenced in February 2011.

Meanwhile, political and economic relations with Turkey continued to progress in 2008, with Turkey adopting the role of mediator for indirect Syrian-Israeli peace talks and several new trade and investment agreements being signed in December. At a bilateral summit convened in İstanbul in September 2009, discussions between President Assad and Turkish Prime Minister Recep Tayyip Erdoğan included the development of a joint response to the stalled Middle East peace process. An accord establishing a High-Level Strategic Co-operation Council and an agreement on the removal of reciprocal visa requirements were also signed by the respective Ministers of Foreign Affairs. Following the Council's inaugural meeting in Damascus in December, more than 50 co-operation agreements were signed concerning fields including security, economy and trade, water, energy, education, the environment and transport. In May 2010 Assad participated in a tripartite summit in Turkey with the Turkish and Qatari leaders, and pledged his support for Turkey's efforts to mediate in the international dispute concerning Iran's nuclear programme (see the chapter on Iran). A second meeting of the Strategic Co-operation Council was held in the Turkish capital, Ankara, in December, at which a further 11 co-operation accords were signed.

Having initially taken a cautious stance over Syria's response to the anti-Government protests that had erupted in March 2011, in September the Turkish Government reportedly ended official contact with the Syrian regime. Turkey had permitted Syrian opposition groups to hold several meetings in Antalya and İstanbul between May and August. In late November, after an incident during which a convoy of Turkish pilgrims came under attack by Syrian armed forces, the Turkish President, Abdullah Gül, who had close ties with President Assad, affirmed his view that a change of Syrian leadership had become inevitable. On 30 November the Erdoğan Government announced that Turkey (Syria's largest trading partner) was suspending all bilateral trade with Syria in protest against the continuing violence being waged by government forces; the sanctions also included a freeze on official assets and a ban on financial transactions with the Central Bank of Syria. In June 2012 a Turkish fighter jet was shot down by Syrian air forces in waters close to Latakia, in what the Turkish Government claimed to be international airspace.

Athough Syrian officials insisted that the jet was in Syrian airspace, the incident provoked Turkish armed forces to move a consignment of ground-to-air missiles and other military equipment to the border region. However, despite the rapid deterioration in Turkish–Syrian diplomatic relations from the latter part of 2011, it was reported by the Turkish Minister of Forestry and Water Works, Veysel Eroğlu, in July 2012 that the 'friendship dam' project had not been abandoned.

Other external relations

In February 2005 Russia confirmed its intention to sell missiles to Syria; however, although the weapons could reportedly be used against targets in Israel, Russian President Vladimir Putin asserted that they would only be used for defensive purposes. In 2009 work commenced on the development of an extensive Russian naval facility at the Syrian port of Tartous, which would be protected by Russian cruise missiles. An official visit by Russia's President Dmitrii Medvedev to Syria in May 2010—the first by a Russian head of state since 1917—was seen as demonstrating the growing importance of Russia in the Middle East region, particularly as the US Administration, having just renewed sanctions against the Syrian regime, was still widely perceived among Arab states as being pro-Israeli. The talks reportedly focused on how to achieve a comprehensive regional peace settlement and on increased bilateral co-operation in the fields of defence and energy, including a possible collaboration on the construction of a Syrian nuclear power plant. A formal agreement finalizing Syria's purchase of Russian fighter planes, anti-tank missiles and air defence systems was signed a few days after Medvedev's visit. Following the Syrian leadership's violent response to the widespread pro-democracy demonstrations from March 2011, Russia (together with China) was extremely reluctant to join the other members of the UN Security Council in adopting a resolution condemning the military action. However, amid worsening violence, Russia finally agreed to support a UN-Arab League peace plan for Syria in March 2012.

Syria's relations with France became increasingly strained following the killing of Rafiq Hariri in February 2005. French President Jacques Chirac, a friend and supporter of Hariri, accused Syria of involvement in the assassination, and Chirac's successor, Nicolas Sarkozy, announced in December 2007 that his Government would cease all diplomatic contacts with Syria until the regime demonstrated that it was committed to enabling the Lebanese National Assembly to elect a successor to President Lahoud. However, after the signing of the Doha Agreement in May 2008 there was a rapid rapprochement between Syria and France. In July President Assad attended a summit in Paris on President Sarkozy's new Union for the Mediterranean initiative, and in the following month the French Minister of Foreign Affairs, Bernard Kouchner, launched what he termed a 'new era of relations' with his Syrian counterpart. During an official visit to Syria by Sarkozy in September, a quadripartite summit was held by the leaders of France, Syria, Turkey and Qatar; foremost on the agenda were the ongoing Turkish-mediated indirect talks between Syria and Israel. In August 2010 President Sarkozy announced that Jean-Claude Cousseran, formerly France's ambassador in both Syria and Egypt, was to act as a mediator between Syria and Israel in order to facilitate the resumption of bilateral discussions. In June 2011, amid a rapid escalation of the Syrian regime's brutal crackdown on political dissent, the French Minister of State and Minister of Foreign Affairs, Alain Juppé, was the first Western leader to declare that President Assad should leave office. In November 2012 France was also the first Western government officially to recognize the newly established Syrian National Coalition for Opposition and Revolutionary Forces as the 'sole legitimate representative of the Syrian people and as future government of a democratic Syria'.

The EU had resumed a formal dialogue with Syria in March 2007, and in October 2008 negotiations recommenced on an EU association agreement, which had stalled after the assassination of Rafiq Hariri in 2005. However, although a draft co-operation agreement was signed in December, with ratification of an association agreement anticipated by mid-2009, the subsequent decision by the Dutch Government to attach a clause allowing for a suspension of the agreement should Syria commit human rights violations led to ratification being postponed until late October. In mid-October 2009 the Syrian Government indicated that it was not yet ready to conclude the agreement and postponed indefinitely a decision on ratification. In addition to the human rights issue, Syria was believed to have concerns about exposing the beleaguered agricultural sector, weakened by several years of severe drought, to increased international competition.

In response to the Syrian leadership's military actions against the rebellion that began in March 2011, the EU tightened its sanctions in place against the regime on 9 May: restrictions were placed on 13 Syrian officials—including the Minister of the Interior, Maj.-Gen. Muhammad Ibrahim al-Shaar, and close relatives of President Assad—and an arms embargo was introduced. On 23 May Assad and his Vice-President, responsible for Foreign Affairs and Information, Farouk al-Shara', both appeared on a list of 10 senior officials on whom EU restrictions were also imposed. Moreover, EU officials declared that the Union was ending discussions on the association agreement for an indefinite period. Further sanctions were imposed on 24 June, this time targeting Syrian establishment figures who were deemed to be involved in the crackdown on anti-Government rebels. On 2 September the EU prohibited imports of Syrian petroleum and extended the list of individuals whose assets were frozen; further measures on 24 September included a ban on foreign companies investing in Syria's oil industry. On 27 February 2012 the EU froze the assets of the Central Bank and other Syrian government officials, as well as introducing an embargo on trade in precious metals and diamonds.

As the persistent bombardment of residential districts by Syrian government forces led to a dramatic rise in the number of deaths being recorded, it was apparent by late 2012 that two EU member states, the United Kingdom and France, were considering a change to their previous position not to provide weapons to Syrian opposition forces in order to facilitate a military victory over the Assad regime. An EU-wide embargo on such weapons sales ended on 30 November, but was subsequently extended until 1 March 2013 and then further, to 1 June. A majority of EU states remained firmly opposed to an agreement to commence arms sales to Syrian rebel groups, fearing that they would be used by Islamist militants to seek to create an Islamic state in Syria and to harm Western interests, as well as leading to increased military assistance for the Assad regime and Hezbollah from countries such as Iran and Russia.

CONSTITUTION AND GOVERNMENT

A new and permanent Constitution was endorsed in a national referendum held on 26 February 2012. Legislative power is vested in the unicameral People's Assembly, with 250 members elected by universal adult suffrage to serve a four-year term. Executive power is vested in the President, elected by direct popular vote for a seven-year term. Effective from the end of the current presidential term in 2014, the President will be limited to serve only two consecutive terms of office. The President governs with the assistance of an appointed Council of Ministers, led by the Prime Minister. Syria has 14 administrative districts (*mohafazat*).

REGIONAL AND INTERNATIONAL CO-OPERATION

Syria is a member of the Organization of Arab Petroleum Exporting Countries (OAPEC, see p. 410). Its membership of the League of Arab States (the Arab League, see p. 372) was suspended in November 2011, in protest against the regime's harsh crackdown on anti-Government protests (see Contemporary Political History). Syria joined the UN on its establishment in October 1945. In May 2010 the World Trade Organization (WTO, see p. 444) agreed to commence accession negotiations with Syria; however, the discussions stalled in 2011, as a result of the political unrest and subsequent civil conflict. The country also participates in the Organization of Islamic Cooperation (OIC, see p. 413).

ECONOMIC AFFAIRS

In 2010, according to estimates by the World Bank, Syria's gross national income (GNI), measured at average 2008–10 prices, was US $56,255m., equivalent to $2,750 per head (or $5,090 per head on an international purchasing-power parity basis). During 2002–11, it was estimated, the population increased at an average annual rate of 2.3%, while gross domestic product (GDP) per head increased, in real terms, by an average of 2.3% per year during 2002–10. Overall GDP increased, in real terms, at an average annual rate of 4.7% in 2002–10; growth was 3.4% in 2010, according to provisional official figures.

Agriculture (including forestry and fishing) contributed an estimated 19.5% of GDP in 2010, and engaged 13.2% of the employed labour force (excluding foreign workers) in 2011. The principal cash crops are cotton (which accounted for about 2.4%

of export earnings in 2003), and fruit and vegetables. According to official estimates, agricultural GDP increased at an average annual rate of 0.7% in 2000–10; the sector's GDP increased by 12.8% in 2009, but declined by an estimated 9.6% in 2010.

Industry (comprising mining, manufacturing, construction and utilities) provided an estimated 31.5% of GDP in 2010, and engaged 31.4% of the employed labour force (excluding foreign workers) in 2011. The GDP of the industrial sector increased at an average annual rate of 2.9% during 2000–10, according to preliminary official figures; industrial GDP increased by 7.8% in 2010.

Mining contributed an estimated 19.7% of GDP in 2003, and employed 0.9% of the working population (excluding foreign workers) in 2011. Crude petroleum is the major mineral export, accounting for 58.5% of total export earnings in 2003, and phosphates are also exported. Syria also has reserves of natural gas and iron ore. At the end of 2011 Syria had proven oil reserves of 2,500m. barrels, and estimated average oil production was 332,000 barrels per day (b/d), having declined from 596,000 b/d in 1995. Syria was estimated to have 285,000m. cu m of proven natural gas reserves at the end of 2011, in which year production of natural gas reached an estimated daily average of 8,320m. cu m.

Manufacturing contributed an estimated 7.3% of GDP in 2004, and employed 14.2% of the working population in 2011. Along with mining, the sector contributed an estimated 27.7% of GDP in 2010, and employed 15.1% of the working population in 2011. The principal branches of manufacturing, measured by gross value of output, are: food products, beverages and tobacco; chemicals, petroleum, coal, rubber and plastic products; textiles, clothing, leather products and footwear; metal products, machinery, transport equipment and appliances; and non-metallic mineral products. According to official estimates, the GDP of the manufacturing sector (which includes mining and quarrying) increased by an average of 2.5% per year during 2000–10; mining and manufacturing GDP increased by 8.5% in 2010.

Construction contributed an estimated 3.8% of GDP in 2010, and employed 15.4% of the working population in that year. According to official estimates, the GDP of the sector increased by an average of 6.3% per year during 2000–10; construction GDP increased by 4.0% in 2010.

Energy is derived principally from petroleum (providing 50.0% of total electricity production in 2009), and also natural gas (45.7%) and hydroelectric power (4.3%). Imports of mineral fuels and lubricants comprised 19.7% of the value of total imports in 2010. Serious power shortages have occurred across Syria since the start of the recent conflict, due to damage caused to power plants by fighting between pro- and anti-Government forces or through acts of sabotage, a significant decline in the provision of fuel to such plants, and the postponement of several government projects involving the construction of new electricity-generating facilities.

Services accounted for an estimated 49.0% of GDP in 2010, and engaged 55.3% of the employed labour force (excluding foreign workers) in 2011. According to official estimates, the GDP of the services sector increased at an average rate of 2.0% per year in 2000–10; growth of the sector was 0.6% in 2010.

In 2010 Syria recorded a visible merchandise trade deficit of US $3,603m., and there was a deficit of $367m. on the current account of the balance of payments. In 2010 the principal source of imports (9.5%) was Turkey; other important suppliers were the People's Republic of China, Italy and Russia. Italy was the primary market for exports in that year (12.4%); other major purchasers were Germany and Turkey. The principal exports in 2010 were mineral fuels and lubricants, food and live animals, basic manufactures, and chemicals and related products, while the principal imports were machinery and transport equipment, mineral fuels and lubricants, basic manufacturers, food and live animals, and chemicals.

According to preliminary figures from the IMF, a budget deficit of £S133,400m. was recorded in 2009 and an increased deficit of £S122,200m. was projected for 2010. Syria's general government gross debt was £S791,198m. in 2009, equivalent to 31.4% of GDP. At the end of 2009 Syria's total external debt was US $5,236m., of which $4,480m. was long-term public debt. In that year, the cost of servicing long-term public and publicly guaranteed debt and repayments to the IMF was equivalent to 3.4% of the value of exports of goods, services and income (excluding workers' remittances). Annual inflation averaged 6.9% in 2002–10. Consumer prices increased by 4.4% in 2010, compared with an increase of

2.8% in 2009. According to official figures, 14.9% of the labour force were unemployed in 2011.

Since President Bashar al-Assad had assumed office in 2000, the Syrian Government had followed a programme of gradual economic liberalization. The reduction of the economy's dependence on revenue from petroleum was a priority since Syria had become a net importer of petroleum; oil industry sources estimated in 2011 that Syria's reserves would be exhausted by 2031. The Development Plan for 2011–15 focused on improving living standards, creating job opportunities, encouraging investment and stimulating GDP growth. Other planned reforms included the introduction of a value-added tax (VAT) in 2011, and the phasing out of petroleum price subsidies. In late 2010 the Government projected growth of more than 5.5% over the next five years, and planned to attract at least US $55,000m. in foreign direct investment during this period. However, the country's descent into civil conflict between pro- and anti-Government forces during 2011–12 led to a dramatic decline in foreign investment and a collapse in Syria's important tourism industry, as well as completely disrupting the wider economy and causing a humanitarian disaster. As the crisis worsened, the authorities were forced to abandon their economic liberalization programme. In an initial, unsuccessful effort to appease protesters, the Government reintroduced fuel and food subsidies, postponed the introduction of VAT, and announced wage increases for public sector employees. Moreover, the increasingly restrictive sanctions being imposed against the Assad Government by, *inter alia*, the USA, the European Union, the League of Arab States (Arab League) and Turkey (Syria's largest trading partner) had a profound effect on the Syrian economy, particularly when the sanctions began to target oil exports. According to the Institute of International Finance (IIF), the country's GDP was estimated to have contracted by 6% in 2011 and by 20% in 2012. By April 2012 economic activity was virtually at a standstill, and the value of the Syrian pound declined by around 72% between December 2010 and March 2013. High inflation was also seriously affecting both consumers and businesses, essential services were disrupted, refugees were continuing to flee Syria at an alarming rate, and, with the apparent failure of international efforts to stem the violence, there was little prospect of a rapid reversal of the downward trend in economic growth.

PUBLIC HOLIDAYS

2014: 1 January (New Year's Day), 13 January* (Mouloud/Yum al-Nabi, Birth of Muhammad), 8 March (Revolution Day), 21 March (Mother's Day), 17 April (Independence Day), 18–21 April (Greek Orthodox Easter), 1 May (Labour Day), 6 May (Martyrs' Day), 26 May* (Leilat al-Meiraj, Ascension of Muhammad), 28 July* (Id al-Fitr, end of Ramadan), 4 October* (Id al-Adha, Feast of the Sacrifice), 6 October (Anniversary of October War), 24 October* (Muharram, Islamic New Year), 25 December (Christmas Day),

* These holidays are dependent on the Islamic lunar calendar and may vary by one or two days from the dates given.

Statistical Survey

Sources (unless otherwise stated): Central Bureau of Statistics, rue Abd al-Malek bin Marwah, Malki Quarter, Damascus; tel. (11) 3335830; fax (11) 3322292; e-mail infocbs@cbssyr.org; internet www.cbssyr.org; Central Bank of Syria, place du 17 avril, Damascus; tel. (11) 2216802; fax (11) 2248329; e-mail info@bcs.gov.sy; internet www.banquecentrale.gov.sy.

Area and Population

AREA, POPULATION AND DENSITY

Area (sq km)	
Land	184,050
Inland water	1,130
Total	185,180*
Population (census results)	
3 September 1994	13,782,315
22 September 2004	
Males	9,196,878
Females	8,723,966
Total	17,920,844
Population (official estimate at 1 January)	
2009	23,027,000
2010	23,695,000
2011	24,504,000
Density (per sq km) at 1 January 2011	132.3

* 71,498 sq miles; including the Israeli-occupied Golan region (1,154 sq km).

Note: According to the United Nations Relief and Works Agency for Palestine Refugees in the Near East (UNRWA), there were 486,946 Palestinian refugees in Syria at 31 December 2011.

POPULATION BY AGE AND SEX
('000 persons at 2004 census)

	Males	Females	Total
0–14	3,637	3,434	7,071
15–64	5,213	5,046	10,259
65 and over	311	280	591
Total	**9,161**	**8,760**	**17,921**

GOVERNORATES
(official estimates at 1 January 2011)

	Area (sq km)	Population ('000)	Density (per sq km)
Dar'a	3,730	1,126	301.9
Deir el-Zor	33,060	1,692	51.2
Dimashq (Damascus, capital) . .	—	1,780	—
Halab (Aleppo)	18,500	5,927	320.4
Hamah (Hama)	10,160	2,113	208.0
Al-Hasakah	23,330	1,604	68.8
Hims (Homs)	40,940	2,147	52.4
Idleb	6,100	2,072	34.0
Al-Ladhiqiyah (Latakia) . . .	2,300	1,229	534.3
Quneitra	1,860	489	262.9
Al-Raqqah (Rakka)	19,620	1,008	51.3
Rif Dimashq (Rural Damascus) .	18,140*	1,877	103.5
Al-Suweida	5,550	486	87.6
Tartous	1,890	954	504.8
Total	**185,180**	**24,504**	**132.3**

* Includes area for Dimashq (Damascus, capital).

BIRTHS, MARRIAGES AND DEATHS

(excl. nomad population and Palestinian refugees, estimates)

	Registered live births			
	Number	Rate (per 1,000)	Registered marriages	Registered deaths
1997 . .	496,140	32.9	128,146	53,366
1998 . .	505,008	32.4	130,835	57,893
1999 . .	503,473	31.3	136,157	56,564
2000 . .	505,484	31.0	139,843	57,759
2001 . .	524,212	31.4	153,842	60,814
2002 . .	471,970	27.6	174,449	53,252
2003 . .	492,639	28.1	n.a.	53,778
2004 . .	491,476	n.a.	178,166	57,855

2007: Live births 727,439; Marriages 237,592; Deaths 76,064.

2009: Live births 670,793; Deaths 76,650.

Source: UN, *Demographic Yearbook*.

Life expectancy (years at birth): 75.7 (males 74.2; females 77.3) in 2010 (Source: World Bank, World Development Indicators database).

ECONOMICALLY ACTIVE POPULATION

(labour force sample survey, persons aged 15 years and over, 2011)*

	Males	Females	Total
Agriculture, hunting, forestry and fishing . .	579,191	75,696	654,887
Mining and quarrying	39,933	3,851	43,784
Manufacturing	657,319	45,017	702,336
Electricity, gas and water . . .	42,268	5,002	47,270
Construction	757,739	4,594	762,333
Wholesale and retail trade . .	795,327	27,673	823,000
Restaurants and hotels . . .	60,979	2,340	63,319
Transport, storage and communications	310,625	13,241	323,866
Financing, insurance, real estate .	124,794	18,886	143,680
Public administration and defence .	560,426	83,167	643,593
Community, social and personal services	405,133	336,039	741,172
Total employed	4,333,734	615,506	4,949,240
Unemployed	503,622	362,663	866,285
Total labour force	4,837,356	978,169	5,815,525

* Figures refer to Syrians only, excluding armed forces.

Health and Welfare

KEY INDICATORS

Total fertility rate (children per woman, 2010)	2.9
Under-5 mortality rate (per 1,000 live births, 2010) . . .	16
HIV/AIDS (% of persons aged 15–49, 2003)	<0.1
Physicians (per 1,000 head, 2008)	1.5
Hospital beds (per 1,000 head, 2010)	1.5
Health expenditure (2009): US $ per head (PPP)	182
Health expenditure (2009): % of GDP	3.5
Health expenditure (2009): public (% of total)	46.0
Access to water (% of persons, 2010)	90
Access to sanitation (% of persons, 2010)	95
Total carbon dioxide emissions ('000 metric tons, 2008) .	71,598.2
Carbon dioxide emissions per head (metric tons, 2008) . .	3.6
Human Development Index (2011): ranking	119
Human Development Index (2011): value	0.632

For sources and definitions, see explanatory note on p. vi.

Agriculture

PRINCIPAL CROPS

('000 metric tons)

	2009	2010	2011
Wheat	3,701.8	3,083.1	3,858.3
Barley	845.7	679.8	666.8
Maize	183.3	133.1	298.4
Potatoes	705.6	673.2	715.3
Sugar beet	732.7	1,493.0	1,805.2
Chick-peas	57.4	42.9	50.1
Lentils	102.5	77.3	112.5
Almonds	97.0	73.1	130.3
Olives	885.9	960.4	1,095.0
Cabbages and other brassicas .	44.4	44.7	42.3
Lettuce and chicory . . .	52.2	62.4	61.8
Tomatoes	1,165.6	1,156.4	1,155.0
Cauliflowers	35.9	36.8	36.9
Pumpkins, squash and gourds .	121.8	120.9	122.3
Cucumbers and gherkins . .	132.9	155.0	154.4
Aubergines (Eggplants) . .	147.0	149.1	141.7
Chillies and peppers, green .	48.4	76.9	59.0
Onions and shallots, green . .	74.9	51.8	69.4
Onions, dry	81.7	109.6	84.9
Oranges	689.8	668.9	734.0
Lemons and limes . . .	140.6	142.2	161.6
Apples	361.0	393.1	308.8
Apricots	98.9	62.0	75.9
Sweet cherries	56.9	58.1	62.2
Peaches and nectarines . .	62.6	48.8	54.4
Grapes	358.0	325.7	338.0
Watermelons	749.7	538.7	670.6
Cantaloupes and other melons .	106.5	75.9	99.3
Figs	53.7	41.0	42.9
Cotton lint	224.3	165.4	151.3
Cotton seed	423.8	307.1	436.6

Aggregate production ('000 metric tons, may include official, semi-official or estimated data): Total cereals 4,739 in 2009, 3,901 in 2010, 4,829 in 2011; Total roots and tubers 706 in 2009, 673 in 2010, 715 in 2011; Total oilcrops 276 in 2009, 273 in 2010, 319 in 2011; Total vegetables (incl. melons) 3,089 in 2009, 2,983 in 2010, 3,207 in 2011; Total fruits (excl. melons) 2,253 in 2009, 2,152 in 2010, 2,217 in 2011.

Source: FAO.

LIVESTOCK

('000 head, year ending September)

	2009	2010	2011
Horses	14.7	14.0	15.0
Asses	92.7	109.0	97.0
Cattle	1,084.5	1,010.0	1,158.0
Camels	32.5	50.0	55.0
Sheep	18,336.0	15,511.0	18,071.0
Goats	1,508.0	2,057.0	2,294.0
Chickens	24,490	25,401	26,203

Source: FAO.

LIVESTOCK PRODUCTS

('000 metric tons)

	2009	2010	2011
Cattle meat	63.0	61.6	70.9
Sheep meat	189.5	153.2	172.4
Chicken meat	182.2	189.7	179.0
Cows' milk	1,600.3	1,453.0	1,701.8
Sheep's milk	706.0	644.3	705.6
Goats' milk	97.0	139.0	145.0
Hen eggs	162.4	163.3	171.9
Wool, greasy	21.9	18.7	21.1

Source: FAO.

Forestry

ROUNDWOOD REMOVALS
('000 cubic metres, excl. bark, FAO estimates)

	2008	2009	2010
Sawlogs, veneer logs and logs for sleepers	16	16	16
Other industrial wood	24	24	24
Fuel wood	26	27	28
Total	**66**	**67**	**68**

2011: Production assumed to be unchanged from 2010 (FAO estimates).

Sawnwood production ('000 cubic metres): *1980*: Coniferous (softwood) 6.6; Broadleaved (hardwood) 2.4; Total 9.0. *1981–2011*: Production as in 1980 (FAO estimates).

Source: FAO.

Fishing

(metric tons, live weight)

	2008	2009	2010
Capture	6,996	6,607	6,635
Freshwater fishes	3,784	3,500	3,679
Aquaculture	8,595	8,697	8,610
Common carp	3,696	3,739	3,862
Tilapias	3,874	3,914	3,163
Total catch	**15,591**	**15,304**	**15,245**

Source: FAO.

Mining

('000 metric tons unless otherwise indicated)

	2008	2009	2010
Phosphate rock	3,221	2,466	3,765
Salt (unrefined)	89	78	81
Gypsum	573	403	540
Natural gas (million cu m) . .	5,311	5,572	7,652
Crude petroleum	19,841	19,937	19,141

2011: Crude petroleum ('000 metric tons) 16,516; Natural gas (million cu m) 8,320.

Sources: US Geological Survey; BP, *Statistical Review of World Energy*.

Industry

SELECTED PRODUCTS
('000 metric tons unless otherwise indicated)

	2008	2009	2010
Plywood (cu m)*	7.8	7.8	7.8
Paper and paperboard* . . .	75	75	75
Cement (hydraulic)	5,646	5,176	6,000
Olive oil (virgin)	156.3	168.2	177.4†
Soybean oil	60.1*	91.3†	91.4†
Cottonseed oil†	48.5	46.7	43.8
Motor spirit (petrol, '000 barrels) .	11,339	11,589	12,958
Distillate fuel oils ('000 barrels) .	27,863	29,689	29,346
Residual fuel oils ('000 barrels) .	29,142	27,415	33,653

* FAO estimate(s).
† Unofficial figure(s).

2011 (estimates unless otherwise indicated): Plywood (cu m) 7.8; Paper and paperboard 75; Soybean oil 55.9 (unofficial figure); Cottonseed oil 41.6 (unofficial figure).

Sources: FAO; US Geological Survey.

Electric energy (million kWh): 41,170 in 2008; 43,406 in 2009; 46,590 in 2010.

Finance

CURRENCY AND EXCHANGE RATES

Monetary Units
100 piastres = 1 Syrian pound (£S).

Sterling, Dollar and Euro Equivalents (31 December 2012)
£1 sterling = £S17.713;
US $1 = £S11.225;
€1 = £S14.810;
£S1,000 = £56.456 sterling = $89.09 = €67.52.

Exchange Rate: Between April 1976 and December 1987 the official mid-point rate was fixed at US $1 = £S3.925. On 1 January 1988 a new rate of $1 = £S11.225 was introduced. In addition to the official exchange rate, there is a promotion rate (applicable to most travel and tourism transactions) and a flexible rate.

BUDGET
(£S '000 million)

Revenue	2005	2006	2007
Oil-related proceeds	106.2	127.0	99.6
Non-oil tax revenue	160.3	196.3	221.4
Income and profits	59.3	65.0	74.2
International trade	30.7	32.9	33.4
Excises	4.5	6.6	9.1
Other	65.8	91.9	104.7
Non-oil non-tax revenue . . .	89.9	111.5	137.5
Total	**356.3**	**434.9**	**458.6**

Expenditure	2005	2006	2007
Current expenditure	277.0	317.2	325.7
Wages and salaries . . .	157.0	207.0	223.2
Goods and services . . .	21.5	22.5	24.3
Interest payments	29.0	29.5	30.0
Subsidies and transfers . . .	69.5	51.2	41.6
Development expenditure . . .	154.4	176.5	194.8
Social	60.3	65.7	68.8
Agriculture	15.5	17.9	22.5
Extractive industries . . .	8.1	11.6	16.7
Manufacturing industries . .	8.4	9.4	7.7
Utilities	34.6	39.9	39.3
Construction	0.4	0.9	0.7
Trade	1.8	3.9	2.6
Transport and communications .	21.3	24.8	31.2
Finance	2.4	3.3	4.4
Other	1.5	0.2	1.0
Total	**431.4**	**493.7**	**520.5**

2011 (£S '000 million, estimates): Total revenue 835.0; Total expenditure 835.0.

Source: Ministry of Finance, Damascus.

2008 (£S '000 million, preliminary): *Revenue:* Oil-related proceeds 131.4; Non-oil tax revenue 258.0; Non-oil non-tax revenue 101.5; Total 491.2. *Expenditure:* Current expenditure 388.3; Development expenditure 173.1; Total 561.3 (Source: IMF, see below).

2009 (£S '000 million, projections): *Revenue:* Oil-related proceeds 111.2; Non-oil tax revenue 296.2; Non-oil non-tax revenue 125.3; Total 533.0. *Expenditure:* Current expenditure 415.8; Development expenditure 250.6; Total 666.4 (Source: IMF, see below).

2010 (£S '000 million, projections): *Revenue:* Oil-related proceeds 148.8; Non-oil tax revenue 319.2; Non-oil non-tax revenue 124.0; Total 592.4. *Expenditure:* Current expenditure 451.0; Development expenditure 263.6; Total 714.6 (Source (2008–10): IMF, *Syrian Arab Republic: 2009 Article IV Consultation—Staff Report; and Public Information Notice*—March 2010).

INTERNATIONAL RESERVES
(excluding foreign exchange, US $ million at 31 December)

	2008	2009	2010
Gold (national valuation) . . .	38	38	54
IMF special drawing rights . .	56	438	430
Total	**94**	**476**	**484**

2011: IMF special drawing rights 429.

Source: IMF, *International Financial Statistics*.

MONEY SUPPLY
(£S million at 31 December)

	2008	2009	2010
Currency outside depository corporations	468,820	480,952	540,246
Transferable deposits	469,456	507,088	610,145
Other deposits	717,811	810,695	890,649
Broad money	1,656,087	1,798,734	2,041,040

Source: IMF, *International Financial Statistics.*

COST OF LIVING
(Consumer Price Index; base: 2000 = 100)

	2008	2009	2010
Food and beverages	181.8	182.2	190.8
Electricity, gas and other fuels (incl. water)	173.4	228.6	249.4
Clothing and footwear	139.0	134.9	141.9
Rent	182.7	177.2	176.8
All items (incl. others)	161.4	165.9	173.2

Source: ILO.

NATIONAL ACCOUNTS
(£S million at current prices)

Expenditure on the Gross Domestic Product

	2008	2009	2010*
Government final consumption expenditure	274,879	301,815	346,055
Private final consumption expenditure	1,390,933	1,508,579	1,691,479
Gross fixed capital formation	408,725	451,605	579,911
Changes in stocks	351,583	304,709	165,163
Total domestic expenditure	2,426,120	2,566,708	2,782,608
Exports of goods and services	919,542	732,502	911,773
Less Imports of goods and services	897,602	778,505	902,606
GDP in market prices	2,448,060	2,520,705	2,791,775
GDP at constant 2000 prices	1,341,516	1,420,832	1,469,703

* Provisional.

Gross Domestic Product by Economic Activity

	2008	2009	2010*
Agriculture, hunting, forestry and fishing	456,746	570,177	547,475
Mining and quarrying			
Manufacturing	787,430	635,310	778,312
Electricity, gas and water			
Construction	78,174	78,590	106,003
Wholesale and retail trade	513,092	582,617	620,710
Transport and communications	225,157	237,677	265,548
Finance and insurance	128,380	123,513	142,979
Government services	224,304	244,004	278,517
Other community, social and personal services	53,621	61,664	68,615
Non-profit private services	1,002	1,152	1,268
Sub-total	2,467,906	2,534,704	2,809,427
Import duties	33,112	37,118	41,448
Less Imputed bank service charges	52,958	51,117	59,100
GDP in market prices	2,448,060	2,520,705	2,791,775

* Provisional.

BALANCE OF PAYMENTS
(US $ million)

	2008	2009	2010
Exports of goods	15,334	10,883	12,273
Imports of goods	−16,107	−13,933	−15,876
Balance on goods	−773	−3,049	−3,603
Exports of services	4,415	4,798	7,333
Imports of services	−3,171	−2,734	−3,533
Balance on goods and services	471	−985	197
Primary income received	540	344	313
Primary income paid	−1,689	−1,451	−1,827
Balance on goods, services and primary income	−678	−2,092	−1,317
Secondary income received	1,335	1,247	1,450
Secondary income paid	−185	−185	−500
Current balance	472	−1,030	−367
Capital account (net)	73	210	287
Direct investment from abroad	1,466	2,570	1,469
Portfolio investment assets	−55	−241	−193
Other investment assets	−631	−626	61
Other investment liabilities	−42	212	−85
Net errors and omissions	−1,232	−747	905
Reserves and related items	50	348	2,076

Source: IMF, *International Financial Statistics.*

External Trade

PRINCIPAL COMMODITIES
(distribution by SITC major group, £S million)

Imports	2008	2009	2010
Food and live animals	96,531	122,366	130,513
Beverages and tobacco	3,829	10,697	17,754
Crude materials, inedible, except fuels	36,603	44,173	37,633
Mineral fuels and lubricants	265,332	91,544	159,610
Animal and vegetable oils and fats	7,034	10,097	8,356
Chemicals and related products	102,839	98,915	105,918
Basic manufactures	217,264	204,515	138,633
Machinery and transport equipment	98,469	119,882	167,211
Total (incl. others)	839,419	714,216	812,209

Exports	2008	2009	2010
Food and live animals	87,576	107,950	99,526
Beverages and tobacco	53,583	9,996	5,301
Crude materials, inedible, except fuels	26,462	13,500	20,089
Mineral fuels and lubricants	261,275	169,577	261,933
Animal and vegetable oils and fats	7,629	4,465	4,317
Chemicals and related products	35,198	31,796	32,518
Basic manufactures	118,927	54,888	64,851
Machinery and transport equipment	31,575	18,216	11,288
Total (incl. others)	707,798	488,330	569,064

PRINCIPAL TRADING PARTNERS
(£S million)

Imports c.i.f.	2008	2009	2010
China, People's Republic	91,500	60,621	71,497
Egypt	28,701	40,522	34,245
France	9,351	10,475	16,169
Germany	17,414	21,055	34,161
India	17,223	15,317	19,483
Italy	39,164	25,786	59,786
Japan	9,545	8,815	10,656
Lebanon	7,885	7,221	8,456
Netherlands	11,253	6,356	11,809
Romania	5,641	9,537	8,018
Russia	108,790	42,879	51,283
Saudi Arabia	31,030	28,908	37,357
Spain	11,724	8,724	8,446
Turkey	23,064	54,269	77,332
United Arab Emirates	15,043	9,559	10,477
USA	16,390	21,740	26,442
Total (incl. others)	839,419	714,216	812,209

Exports f.o.b.	2008	2009	2010
Egypt	34,011	16,927	17,972
France	47,434	31,474	22,426
Germany	75,984	44,409	68,315
Italy	55,147	27,537	70,308
Jordan	21,006	16,182	18,774
Lebanon	62,179	16,292	20,176
Netherlands	9,593	11,205	18,369
Russia	667	586	15,411
Saudi Arabia	48,019	27,418	25,095
Spain	19,860	15,907	10,848
Turkey	29,593	14,707	29,100
United Arab Emirates	8,799	8,101	4,174
USA	16,373	10,459	18,479
Total (incl. others)	707,798	488,330	569,064

Transport

RAILWAYS
(traffic)

	2008	2009	2010
Passengers carried ('000)	3,369	3,676	3,587
Passenger-km ('000)	1,120,146	1,224,098	1,195,100
Freight ('000 metric tons)	9,307	8,842	8,578
Freight ton-km (million)	2,370	2,263	2,196

ROAD TRAFFIC
(motor vehicles in use)

	2008	2009	2010
Passenger cars	551,858	637,604	741,260
Buses	6,201	6,611	7,486
Lorries, trucks, etc.	552,841	623,359	683,906
Motorcycles	205,518	242,090	380,852

SHIPPING
Flag Registered Fleet
(at 31 December)

	2010	2011	2012
Number of vessels	100	76	70
Total displacement ('000 grt)	255.6	144.7	99.1

Source: Lloyd's List Intelligence (www.lloydslistintelligence.com).

International Sea-borne Traffic

	1996	1997	1998
Vessels entered ('000 net regd tons)	2,901*	2,640	2,622
Cargo unloaded ('000 metric tons)	4,560	4,788	5,112
Cargo loaded ('000 metric tons)	1,788	2,412	2,136

* Excluding Banias.

Vessels entered ('000 net registered tons): 2,928 in 1999; 2,798 in 2000; 2,827 in 2001.

Source: mainly UN, *Monthly Bulletin of Statistics* and *Statistical Yearbook*.

CIVIL AVIATION
(traffic on scheduled services)

	2007	2008	2009
Kilometres flown (million)	23	26	26
Passengers carried ('000)	1,272	1,359	1,343
Passenger-km (million)	2,333	2,519	2,507
Total ton-km (million)	221	250	246

Source: UN, *Statistical Yearbook*.

2010 ('000): Passengers carried 1,018 (Source: World Bank, World Development Indicators database).

Tourism

FOREIGN VISITOR ARRIVALS
(incl. excursionists)*

Country of nationality	2008	2009	2010
Iran	361,605	455,012	891,807
Iraq	889,463	894,477	1,006,434
Jordan	1,044,564	1,062,990	1,949,551
Kuwait	126,977	146,724	134,255
Lebanon	1,587,115	1,815,003	2,291,802
Saudi Arabia	403,140	476,346	484,087
Turkey	562,832	733,132	1,459,580
Total (incl. others)	6,950,852	7,720,795	10,969,682

* Figures exclude Syrian nationals resident abroad.

Total tourist arrivals ('000): 5,070 in 2011 (provisional).

Tourism receipts (US $ million, excl. passenger transport): 3,757 in 2009; 6,190 in 2010.

Source: World Tourism Organization.

Communications Media

	2009	2010	2011
Telephones ('000 main lines in use)	3,871	4,069	4,345
Mobile cellular telephones ('000 in use)	10,022	11,799	13,117
Internet subscribers ('000) . .	851	986	n.a.
Broadband subscribers ('000) . .	34.7	69.8	121.3

Source: International Telecommunication Union.

Education

(2009/10 unless otherwise indicated)

	Institutions*	Teachers	Pupils/Students		
			Males	Females	Total
Pre-primary . .	1,431	7,591	78,468	70,642	149,110
Primary . . .	n.a.	132,099†	1,265,470	1,163,980	2,429,450
Secondary: general . .	1,140	162,758†	1,338,083	1,287,299	2,625,382
Secondary: vocational . .	595	18,439‡	63,915	42,528	106,443
Higher* . . .	5	8,084	141,310	138,304	279,614

* Excluding private universities; data for 2006/07.
† 2007/08.
‡ 2008/09.
Source: mainly UNESCO Institute for Statistics.

Pupil-teacher ratio (primary education, UNESCO estimate): 17.8 in 2007/08 (Source: UNESCO Institute for Statistics).

Adult literacy rate (UNESCO estimates): 83.4% (males 89.9%; females 76.9%) in 2010 (Source: UNESCO Institute for Statistics).

Directory

The Government

HEAD OF STATE

President: Lt-Gen. BASHAR AL-ASSAD (assumed office 17 July 2000).
Vice-President, responsible for Foreign Affairs and Information: FAROUK AL-SHARA'.
Vice-President: Dr NAJAH AL-ATTAR.

COUNCIL OF MINISTERS
(May 2013)

Prime Minister: Dr WAEL NADER AL-HALQI.
Deputy Prime Minister and Minister of Foreign Affairs and Expatriates: WALID MOUALLEM.
Deputy Prime Minister for Economic Affairs and Minister of Internal Trade and Consumer Protection: Dr QADRI JAMIL.
Deputy Prime Minister for Services Affairs and Minister of Local Administration: OMAR IBRAHIM GHALAWANJI.
Minister of Defence: Lt-Gen. FAHD JASSEM AL-FREIJ.
Minister of Communications and Technology: Dr IMAD ABD AL-GHANI SABOUNI.
Minister of Awqaf (Religious Endowments): Dr MUHAMMAD ABD AL-SATTAR AL-SAYYID.
Minister of Presidential Affairs: MANSOUR AZZAM.
Minister of Justice: NAJIM HAMID AL-AHMAD.
Minister of the Interior: Lt-Gen. MUHAMMAD IBRAHIM AL-SHAAR.
Minister of Finance: Dr ISMAEL ISMAEL.
Minister of Health: SAAD ABD AL-SALAM AL-NAYEF.
Minister of Tourism: HALA MUHAMMAD NASSER.
Minister of Electricity: IMAD MUHAMMAD DEEB KHAMIS.
Minister of Water Resources: BASSAM HANNA.
Minister of Agriculture and Agrarian Reform: AHMAD AL-QADRI.
Minister of Higher Education: Dr MUHAMMAD YAHYA MOALLA.
Minister of Education: Dr HAZWAN AL-WAZZ.
Minister of Economy and Foreign Trade: Dr MUHAMMAD ZAFER MIHBEK.
Minister of Industry: Dr ADNAN ABDO AL-SUKHNI.
Minister of Transport: Dr MAHMOUD IBRAHIM SAID.
Minister of Housing and Urban Development: HUSSEIN FARZAT.
Minister of Public Works: HUSSEIN ARNOUS.
Minister of Petroleum and Mineral Resources: SULEIMAN AL-ABBAS.
Minister of Culture: Dr LUBANAH MSHAWEH.

Minister of Labour: Dr HASSAN HIJAZI.
Minister of Social Affairs: Dr KINDA AL-SHAMMAT.
Minister of Information: OMRAN AHED AL-ZOUBI.
Minister of State for National Reconciliation Affairs: Dr ALI HAIDAR.
Minister of State for Environmental Affairs: Dr NAZIRA FARAH SARKIS.
Ministers of State: HUSSEIN MAHMOUD FARZAT, JOSEPH JURJI SUWAID, MUHAMMAD TURKI AL-SAYYED, NAJM EDDIN KHREIIT, ABDULLAH KHALIL HUSSEIN, JAMAL SHAABAN SHAHIN.

MINISTRIES

Office of the President: Damascus.
Office of the Prime Minister: rue Chahbandar, Damascus; tel. (11) 2226000; fax (11) 2237842.
Ministry of Agriculture and Agrarian Reform: rue Jabri, place Hedjaz, Baramkeh, Damascus; tel. (11) 2213613; fax (11) 2244078; e-mail info@moaar.gov.sy; internet www.syrian-agriculture.org.
Ministry of Awqaf (Religious Endowments): place al-Misat, Damascus; tel. (11) 4470005; fax (11) 4470006; e-mail admin@syrianawkkaf.org; internet www.syrianawkkaf.org.
Ministry of Communications and Technology: rue Abed, Damascus; tel. (11) 2221133; fax (11) 2323273; e-mail info@moct.gov.sy; internet www.moct.gov.sy.
Ministry of Culture: rue George Haddad, Rawda, Damascus; tel. (11) 3331556; fax (11) 3342606; e-mail info@moc.gov.sy; internet www.moc.gov.sy.
Ministry of Defence: place Omayad, Damascus; tel. (11) 7770700; fax (11) 2237842.
Ministry of Economy and Foreign Trade: rue Maysaloun, Damascus; tel. (11) 2324680; fax (11) 2225695; e-mail econ-min@net.sy; internet www.syrecon.org.
Ministry of Education: rue Shahbander, al-Masraa, Damascus; tel. (11) 3313206; fax (11) 4420435; e-mail info@syrianeducation.org.sy; internet www.syrianeducation.org.sy.
Ministry of Electricity: BP 4900, rue al-Kouatly, Damascus; tel. (11) 5810730; fax (11) 5811689; e-mail pmoe@net.sy; internet moe.gov.sy.
Ministry of Finance: BP 13136, rue Jule Jammal, Damascus; tel. (11) 2211300; fax (11) 2224701; e-mail mof@net.sy; internet www.syrianfinance.org.
Ministry of Foreign Affairs and Expatriates: Island 20, Dummar, Damascus; tel. (11) 2181000; fax (11) 2146252; e-mail info@mofaex.gov.sy; internet www.mofaex.gov.sy.
Ministry of Health: rue Majlis al-Sha'ab, Damascus; tel. (11) 3311020; fax (11) 3311114; e-mail info@moh.gov.sy; internet www.moh.gov.sy.

Ministry of Higher Education: BP 9251, place Mezzeh Gamarik, Damascus; tel. (11) 2119865; fax (11) 2128919; e-mail mhe@mhe.gov.sy; internet www.mhe.gov.sy.

Ministry of Housing and Urban Development: place Yousuf al-Azmeh, al-Salheyeh, Damascus; tel. (11) 2211494; fax (11) 2259400; e-mail diwan@mohc.gov.sy; internet www.mhc.gov.sy.

Ministry of Industry: BP 12835, rue Maysaloun, Damascus; tel. (11) 3720959; fax (11) 2231096; e-mail industry-min@mail.sy; internet www.moid.gov.sy.

Ministry of Information: Immeuble Dar al-Baath, Autostrade Mezzeh, Damascus; tel. and fax (11) 6664681; e-mail info@moi.gov.sy; internet www.moi.gov.sy.

Ministry of the Interior: rue al-Bahsah, al-Marjeh, Damascus; tel. (11) 2219400; fax (11) 2324835; e-mail admin@civilaffair-moi.gov.sy; internet www.syriamoi.gov.sy.

Ministry of Internal Trade and Consumer Protection: Damascus.

Ministry of Justice: rue al-Nasr, Damascus; tel. (11) 2214105; fax (11) 2246250.

Ministry of Labour: place Yousuf al-Azmeh, al-Salheyeh, Damascus; tel. (11) 2325387; fax (11) 2255143.

Ministry of Local Administration: rue 17 Nissan, Damascus; tel. (11) 2145700; fax (11) 2145731; e-mail info@mla-sy.org; internet mla-sy.org.

Ministry of Petroleum and Mineral Resources: BP 40, al-Adawi, Insha'at, Damascus; tel. (11) 4451624; fax (11) 4463942; e-mail mopmr-central@mail.sy.

Ministry of Public Works: Damascus.

Ministry of Social Affairs: Damascus.

Ministry of State for Environmental Affairs: BP 3773, Damascus; tel. (11) 2138682; fax (11) 2320885; e-mail env-min@net.sy; internet www.gcea.gov.sy.

Ministry of State for National Reconciliation Affairs: Damascus.

Ministry of Tourism: BP 6642, rue Barada, Damascus; tel. (11) 2210122; fax (11) 2242636; e-mail info@syriatourism.org; internet www.syriatourism.org.

Ministry of Transport: BP 33999, rue al-Jala'a, Damascus; tel. (11) 3316840; fax (11) 3323317; e-mail min-trans@net.sy; internet www.mot.gov.sy.

Ministry of Water Resources: Damascus.

Legislature

Majlis al-Sha'ab
(People's Assembly)

People's Council, Damascus; tel. (11) 2226127; fax (11) 3712532; e-mail info@parliament.sy; internet www.parliament.gov.sy.

Speaker: MUHAMMAD JIHAD AL-LAHAM.

Election, 7 May 2012

Party	Seats
National Progressive Front*	184
Others	7
Independents	59
Total	**250**

* The National Progressive Front (NPF) reportedly comprised 10 political parties, headed by the Baath Arab Socialist Party, which accounted for 162 of the 184 seats won by the NPF.

Political Organizations

The **National Progressive Front (NPF—Al-Jabha al-Wataniyah al-Taqadumiyah)**, headed by the late President Hafiz al-Assad, was formed in March 1972 as a coalition of five political parties. At the time of the legislative elections in May 2012, the NPF consisted of 10 parties:

Arab Democratic Unionist Party (Hizb al-Ittihad al-'Arabi al-Dimuqrati): f. 1981, following split from the Arab Socialist Union; considers the concerns of the Arab world in general as secondary to those of Syria itself in the pursuit of pan-Arab goals; Chair. GHASSAN AHMAD OSMAN.

Arab Socialist Movement (Harakat al-Ishtiraki al-'Arabi): Damascus; f. 1963, following split from Arab Socialist Union; contested the 2007 election to the People's Assembly as two factions (see also National Vow Movement); Leader AHMAD AL-AHMAD.

Arab Socialist Union (al-Ittihad al-Ishtiraki al-'Arabi): Damascus; f. 1973, following the separation of the Syrian branch from the international Arab Socialist Union; Nasserite; supportive of the policies of the Baath Arab Socialist Party; Leader SAFWAN AL-QUDSI.

Baath Arab Socialist Party (al-Hizb al-Ba'th al-'Arabi al-Ishtiraki): National Command, BP 9389, Autostrade Mezzeh, Damascus; tel. (11) 6622142; fax (11) 6622099; e-mail baath@baath-party.org; internet www.baath-party.org; Arab nationalist socialist party; f. 1947, as a result of merger between the Arab Revival (Baath) Movement (f. 1940) and the Arab Socialist Party (f. 1940); in power since 1963; supports creation of a unified Arab socialist society; approx. 1m. mems in Syria; brs in most Arab countries; Pres. Lt-Gen. BASHAR AL-ASSAD.

Democratic Socialist Unionist Party (al-Hizb al-Wahdawi al-Ishtiraki al-Dimuqrati): f. 1974, following split from the Arab Socialist Union; Chair. FADLALLAH NASR AL-DIN.

National Vow Movement (Harakat al-'ahd al-Watani): a break-away party from the Arab Socialist Union; a faction of the Arab Socialist Movement; awarded three seats in 2007 election to the People's Assembly; Leader GHASSAN ABD AL-AZIZ OSMAN.

Socialist Unionists (Al-Wahdawiyyun al-Ishtirakiyyun): e-mail alwahdawinet@hotmail.com; internet www.alwahdawi.net; f. 1961, through split from the Baath Arab Socialist Party following that organization's acceptance of Syria's decision to secede from the United Arab Republic; Nasserite; aims for Arab unity, particularly a new union with Egypt; produces weekly periodical *Al-Wehdawi*; Chair. FAYEZ ISMAIL.

Syrian Arab Socialist Union Party: Damascus; tel. (11) 239305; Nasserite; Sec.-Gen. SAFWAN KOUDSI.

Syrian Communist Party (Bakdash) (al-Hizb al-Shuyu'i al-Suri): BP 7837, Damascus; tel. (11) 4455048; fax (11) 4446390; e-mail info@syriancp.org; internet www.syriancp.org; f. 1924 by Fouad Shamal in Lebanon and Khalid Bakdash (died 1995); until 1943 part of joint Communist Party of Syria and Lebanon; party split into two factions under separate leaders, Bakdash and Faisal (q.v.), in 1986; Marxist-Leninist; publishes fortnightly periodical *Sawt al-Shaab*; Sec.-Gen. AMMAR BAKDASH.

Syrian Communist Party (Faisal) (al-Hizb al-Shuyu'i al-Suri): Damascus; f. 1986, following split of Syrian Communist Party into two factions under separate leaders, Faisal and Bakdash (q.v.); aims to end domination of Baath Arab Socialist Party and the advantages given to mems of that party at all levels; advocates the lifting of the state of emergency and the release of all political prisoners; publishes weekly periodical *An-Nour*; Sec.-Gen. YOUSUF RASHID FAISAL.

Syrian Social Nationalist Party (Centralist Wing) (al-Hizb al-Suri al-Qawmi al-Ijtima'i): e-mail administrator@ssnp.com; internet www.ssnp.com; f. 1932 in Beirut, Lebanon; fmrly mem. of NPF, but withdrew prior to 2012 legislative elections; also known as Parti populaire syrien; seeks creation of a 'Greater Syrian' state, incl. Syria, Lebanon, Jordan, the Palestinian territories, Iraq, Kuwait, Cyprus and parts of Egypt, Iran and Turkey; advocates separation of church and state, the redistribution of wealth, and a strong military; supports Syrian involvement in Lebanese affairs; has brs worldwide, and approx. 90,000 mems in Syria; Pres. ALI HAIDAR.

There are numerous opposition parties, within Syria or in exile, which are forced to operate on a clandestine basis. Formed in 1980, the **National Democratic Rally** (NDR—Tajammu' al-Watani al-Dimuqrati) is an alliance of banned, secularist opposition parties, several of which are opposition wings of parties that joined the ruling NPF.

A current member of the NDR, the **Syrian Democratic People's Party** (al-Hizb al-Sha'ab al-Suri al-Dimuqrati—leader ABULLAH HOSHA) was founded in 1973 as the Syrian Communist Party (Political Bureau), following the decision by founder Riad at-Turk to split from that party after its leader, Khalid Bakdash, decided to allow the organization to join the NPF. The party adopted its current name in 2005. The party publishes an online newsletter (www.arraee.com).

There is also a **Marxist-Leninist Communist Action Party**, which regards itself as independent of all Arab regimes.

An illegal Syrian-based organization, the **Islamic Movement for Change (IMC)**, claimed responsibility for a bomb attack in Damascus in December 1996.

Diplomatic Representation

EMBASSIES IN SYRIA

In February 2012 both Switzerland and the USA closed their embassies in Damascus, citing concerns regarding the safety of diplomatic staff, amid ongoing use of violence by the Syrian armed forces to quell protests against the rule of President Bashar al-Assad. Meanwhile, Libya and Tunisia were ordered to close their embassies in Damascus by the Syrian Government, following the expulsion of

Syria's representatives to those countries. By mid-2012 several other countries, including Belgium, Canada, Finland, France, Germany, Greece, Italy, Japan, the Netherlands, Norway, Spain, Turkey and the United Kingdom, as well as the member states of the Cooperation Council for the Arab States of the Gulf (Gulf Cooperation Council), had also closed their respective embassies, and by early 2013 the operations of most diplomatic missions in Syria had been significantly reduced owing to the escalating civil conflict.

Algeria: Immeuble Noss, Raouda, Damascus; tel. (11) 3331446; fax (11) 3334698; Ambassador SALEH BOUSHEH.

Argentina: BP 116, Damascus; tel. (11) 3334167; fax (11) 3327326; e-mail easir@net.sy; Ambassador ROBERTO AHUAD.

Armenia: 2 Saad Ben Abi Uakksi, Bldg 2, West Mezze, Damascus; tel. (11) 6133617; fax (11) 6133618; e-mail armsyriaembassy@mfa.am; Ambassador ARSHAK POLADIAN.

Austria: BP 5634, Immeuble Mohamed Naim al-Deker, 1 rue Farabi, Mezzeh Est, Damascus; tel. (11) 61380100; fax (11) 6116734; e-mail damaskus-ob@bmeia.gv.at; Ambassador MARIA KUNZ.

Belarus: BP 16239, 27 rue Qurtaja, Mezzeh Est, Damascus; tel. (11) 6118097; fax (11) 6631143; e-mail syria@mfa.gov.by; internet syria.mfa.gov.by; Ambassador ALEG YERMALOVICH.

Brazil: BP 2219, 39 rue al-Farabi, Mezzeh Est, Damascus; tel. (11) 6124551; fax (11) 6124553; e-mail braemsyr@net.sy; Ambassador EDGAR ANTONIO CASIANO.

Bulgaria: BP 2732, 8 rue Pakistan, place Arnous, Damascus; tel. (11) 3318445; fax (11) 4419854; e-mail bul_emb@abv.bg; internet www.mfa.bg/bg/62/; Ambassador DIMITAR MIHAILOV.

Chile: BP 3561, 6 rue Ziad bin Abi Soufian, Rawda, Damascus; tel. (11) 3338443; fax (11) 3331563; e-mail embachile.siria@gmail.com; internet chileabroad.gov.cl/siria; Ambassador PATRICIO EDUARDO DAMM VAN DER VALK.

China, People's Republic: BP 2455, 83 rue Ata Ayoubi, Damascus; tel. (11) 3339594; fax (11) 3338067; e-mail chinaemb_sy@mfa.gov.cn; internet sy.chineseembassy.org; Ambassador ZHANG XUN.

Cuba: Immeuble Istouani and Charbati, 40 rue al-Rachid, Damascus; tel. (11) 3339624; fax (11) 3333802; e-mail embacubasy@net.sy; Ambassador FERNANDO PÉREZ MAZA.

Cyprus: BP 9269, 278G rue Malek bin Rabia, Mezzeh Ouest, Damascus; tel. (11) 6130812; fax (11) 6130814; e-mail cyembdam@scs-net.org; Ambassador ANTONIS GRIVAS.

Czech Republic: BP 2249, place Abou al-Ala'a al-Maari, Damascus; tel. (11) 3331383; fax (11) 3338268; e-mail damascus@embassy.mzv.cz; internet www.mzv.cz/damascus; Ambassador EVA FILIPI.

Denmark: BP 2244, Fatmeh Idriss 6, rue al-Ghazzawi, Mezzeh Ouest, Damascus; tel. (11) 61909000; fax (11) 61909033; e-mail damamb@um.dk; internet www.ambdamaskus.um.dk; Ambassador CHRISTINA MARKUS LASSEN.

Egypt: BP 12443, rue al-Gala'a, Abou Roumaneh, Damascus; tel. (11) 3330756; fax (11) 33500911; e-mail egypt@tvcabo.co.mz; Ambassador SHAWKI ISMAIL ALI SOLIMAN.

Eritrea: BP 12846, Autostrade al-Mazen West, 82 rue Akram Mosque, Damascus; tel. (11) 6112357; fax (11) 6112358; Chargé d'affaires a.i. HUMMED MOHAMED SAEED KULU.

Holy See: BP 2271, 14 rue Masr, Damascus (Apostolic Nunciature); tel. (11) 3332601; fax (11) 3327550; e-mail noncesy@mail.sy; Apostolic Nuncio Most Rev. MARIO ZENARI (Titular Archbishop of Iulium Carnicum).

Hungary: BP 2607, 12 rue al-Salam, Mezzeh Est, Damascus; tel. (11) 6110787; fax (11) 6117917; e-mail mission.dam@mfa.gov.hu; internet www.mfa.gov.hu/kulkepviselet/sy; Ambassador JÁNOS BUDAI.

India: BP 685, 3455 rue ibn al-Haitham, Abou Roumaneh, Damascus; tel. (11) 3347351; fax (11) 3347912; e-mail damascus@mea.gov.in; internet www.indianembassysyria.com; Ambassador (vacant).

Indonesia: BP 3530, Immeuble 26, Bloc 270A, 132 rue al-Madina al-Munawar, Mezzeh Est, Damascus; tel. (11) 6119630; fax (11) 6119632; e-mail kbridams@net.sy; Ambassador ASSAYID WAHIB.

Iran: BP 2691, Autostrade Mezzeh, nr al-Razi Hospital, Damascus; tel. (11) 6117675; fax (11) 6110997; e-mail iran-dam@net.sy; Ambassador MUHAMMAD REZA RAOUF SHEIBANI.

Iraq: Damascus; tel. (11) 3341290; fax (11) 3341291; e-mail dmkemb@iraqmofamail.net; Ambassador Dr ALA'A HUSSAIN AL-JAWADI.

Jordan: rue Abou Roumaneh, Damascus; tel. (11) 3334642; fax (11) 3336741; internet www.jordanembassydemascus.gov.jo; Ambassador OMAR AL-AMED.

Korea, Democratic People's Republic: rue Fares al-Khouri-Jisr Tora, Damascus; Ambassador CHOE SU HON.

Lebanon: Abou Roumaneh, Damascus; Ambassador MICHEL EL-KHOURY.

Malaysia: Immeuble 117, Mezzeh Est Villas, Damascus; tel. (11) 6122811; fax (11) 6122814; e-mail malsyria@kln.gov.my; Ambassador MAT DRIS BIN Haji YAACOB.

Mauritania: ave al-Jala'a, rue Karameh, Damascus; tel. (11) 3339317; fax (11) 3330552; Ambassador AAL OULD AHMADO.

Morocco: 35 rue Abu Bakr al-Karkhi Villas, Mezzeh Est, Damascus; tel. (11) 6110451; fax (11) 6117885; e-mail sifmar@scs-net.org; Ambassador MUHAMMAD LAKHSASSI.

Pakistan: BP 9284, rue al-Farabi, Mezzeh Est, Damascus; tel. (11) 6132694; fax (11) 6132662; e-mail parepdam@scs-net.org; Ambassador WAHEED AHMAD.

Panama: Bldg 10, Office 4, rue al-Bizm, Malki St, Damascus; tel. (11) 3739001; fax (11) 3738801; e-mail consuladodepanamadamasco@gmail.com; Chargé d'affaires HAISAM CHEHABI.

Philippines: BP 36849, 56 rue Hamzeh bin al-Mutaleb, Mezzeh, Damascus; tel. (11) 6132626; fax (11) 6110152; e-mail info@ambaphilsyria.com; Chargé d'affaires a.i. NESTOR N. PADALHIN.

Poland: BP 501, rue Baha Eddin Aita, Abou Roumaneh, Damascus; tel. (11) 3333010; fax (11) 3315318; e-mail damaszek.amb.sekretariat@msz.gov.pl; internet www.damaszek.polemb.net; Ambassador MICHAŁ MURKOCIŃSKI.

Romania: BP 4454, 8 rue Ibrahim Hanano, Damascus; tel. (11) 3327572; fax (11) 3327571; e-mail damascamb@gmail.com; internet damasc.mae.ro; Ambassador DANUT FLORIN SANDOVICI.

Russia: BP 3153, rue Umar bin al-Khattab, al-Dawi, Damascus; tel. (11) 4423155; fax (11) 4423182; e-mail rusemb@scs-net.org; Ambassador AZAMAT KULMUKHAMETOV.

Serbia: BP 739, 18 rue al-Jala'a, Abou Roumaneh, Damascus; tel. (11) 3336222; fax (11) 3333690; e-mail ambasada@srbija-damask.org; internet www.srbija-damask.org; Ambassador JOVAN VUJASINOVIĆ.

Slovakia: BP 33115, 158 rue al-Shafi, Mezzeh Est, Damascus; tel. (11) 6132114; fax (11) 6132598; e-mail emb.damascus@mzv.sk; internet www.damascus.mfa.sk; Ambassador IVAN SURKOS.

Somalia: 7 rue Abu Bakr al-Karkhi Villas, Mezzeh Est, Damascus; tel. and fax (11) 6111220; e-mail webmaster@somaligov.net; internet www.syria.somaligov.net; Ambassador ABD AL-RAHMAN NUR MUHAMMAD DINAARI.

South Africa: BP 9141, rue al-Ghazaoui, 7 Jadet Kouraish, Mezzeh Ouest, Damascus; tel. (11) 61351520; fax (11) 6111714; e-mail admin.damascus@foreign.gov.za; Ambassador SHAUN EDWARD BYNEVELDT.

Sudan: BP 3940, Immeuble al-Kassar Assadi, Damascus; tel. (11) 6112901; fax (11) 6112904; e-mail sud-emb@net.sy; Ambassador ABD AL-RAHMAN DIRAR.

Sweden: BP 4266, Immeuble du Patriarcat Catholique, rue Chakib Arslan, Abou Roumaneh, Damascus; tel. (11) 33400700; fax (11) 3327749; e-mail ambassaden.damaskus@foreign.ministry.se; internet www.swedenabroad.com/damascus; Ambassador NIKLAS KEBBON.

Turkmenistan: Miset, 4097 Ruki el-Din, 2e étage, Damascus; tel. (11) 2241834; fax (11) 3320905.

Ukraine: BP 33944, 14 rue al-Salam, Mezzeh Est, Damascus; tel. (11) 6113016; fax (11) 6121355; e-mail emb_sy@mfa.gov.ua; internet www.mfa.gov.ua/syria; Chargé d'affaires a.i. YEVHEN ZHUPEYEV.

Venezuela: BP 2403, Immeuble al-Tabbah, 5 rue Lisaneddin bin al-Khateb, place Rauda, Damascus; tel. (11) 6124835; fax (11) 6124833; e-mail embavenez@tarassul.sy; internet www.embavensiria.com; Ambassador IMAD SAAB.

Yemen: Abou Roumaneh, Charkassieh, Damascus; Ambassador (vacant).

Judicial System

The Courts of Law in Syria are principally divided into two juridical court systems: Courts of General Jurisdiction and Administrative Courts. Since 1973 the Supreme Constitutional Court has been established as the paramount body of the Syrian judicial structure.

The Supreme Constitutional Court: Damascus; tel. (11) 3331902; This is the highest court in Syria. It has specific jurisdiction over: (i) judicial review of the constitutionality of laws and legislative decrees; (ii) investigation of charges relating to the legality of the election of members of the Majlis al-Sha'ab (People's Assembly); (iii) trial of infractions committed by the President of the Republic in the exercise of his functions; (iv) resolution of positive and negative jurisdictional conflicts and determination of the competent court between the different juridical court systems, as well as other bodies exercising judicial competence. The Supreme Constitutional Court is composed of a Chief Justice and six Justices. They are appointed by decree of the President of the Republic for a renewable period of four years; Chief Justice ADNAN ZUREIQ.

Courts of General Jurisdiction: The Courts of General Jurisdiction in Syria are divided into six categories: (i) The Court of Cassation; (ii) The Courts of Appeal; (iii) The Tribunals of First Instance; (iv) The Tribunals of Peace; (v) The Personal Status Courts; (vi) The Courts for Minors. Each of the above categories (except the Personal Status Courts) is divided into Civil, Penal and Criminal Chambers; (i) The Court of Cassation: This is the highest court of general jurisdiction. Final judgments rendered by Courts of Appeal in penal and civil litigations may be petitioned to the Court of Cassation by the Defendant or the Public Prosecutor in penal and criminal litigations, and by any of the parties in interest in civil litigations, on grounds of defective application or interpretation of the law as stated in the challenged judgment, on grounds of irregularity of form or procedure, or violation of due process, and on grounds of defective reasoning of judgment rendered. The Court of Cassation is composed of a President, seven Vice-Presidents and 31 other Justices (Councillors); (ii) The Courts of Appeal: Each court has geographical jurisdiction over one governorate (*mohafazat*). Each court is divided into Penal and Civil Chambers. There are Criminal Chambers, which try felonies only. The Civil Chambers hear appeals filed against judgments rendered by the Tribunals of First Instance and the Tribunals of Peace. Each Court of Appeal is composed of a President and sufficient numbers of Vice-Presidents (Presidents of Chambers) and Superior Judges (Councillors). There are 54 Courts of Appeal; (iii) The Tribunals of First Instance: In each governorate there are one or more Tribunals of First Instance, each of which is divided into several Chambers for penal and civil litigations. Each Chamber is composed of one judge. There are 72 Tribunals of First Instance; (iv) The Tribunals of Peace: In the administrative centre of each governorate, and in each district, there are one or more Tribunals of Peace, which have jurisdiction over minor civil and penal litigations. There are 227 Tribunals of Peace; (v) Personal Status Courts: These courts deal with marriage, divorce, etc. For Muslims, each court consists of one judge, the 'Qadi Shari'i'. For Druzes, there is one court consisting of one judge, the 'Qadi Mazhabi'. For non-Muslim communities, there are courts for Roman Catholics, Orthodox believers, Protestants and Jews; (vi) Courts for Minors: The constitution, officers, sessions, jurisdiction and competence of these courts are determined by a special law.

Public Prosecution: Public prosecution is headed by the Attorney-General, assisted by a number of Senior Deputy and Deputy Attorneys-General, and a sufficient number of chief prosecutors, prosecutors and assistant prosecutors. Public prosecution is represented at all levels of the Courts of General Jurisdiction in all criminal and penal litigations and also in certain civil litigations as required by the law. Public prosecution controls and supervises enforcement of penal judgments.

Administrative Courts System: The Administrative Courts have jurisdiction over litigations involving the state or any of its governmental agencies. The Administrative Courts system is divided into two courts: the Administrative Courts and the Judicial Administrative Courts, of which the paramount body is the High Administrative Court.

Military Courts: The Military Courts deal with criminal litigations against military personnel of all ranks and penal litigations against officers only. There are two military courts: one in Damascus, the other in Aleppo. Each court is composed of three military judges. There are other military courts, consisting of one judge, in every governorate, which deal with penal litigations against military personnel below the rank of officer. The different military judgments can be petitioned to the Court of Cassation.

Religion

The majority of Syrians follow a form of Islamic Sunni orthodoxy. There are also a considerable number of religious minorities: Shi'a Muslims; Isma'ili Muslims; the Isma'ili of the Salamiya district, whose spiritual head is the Aga Khan; a large number of Druzes, the Nusairis or Alawites of the Jebel Ansariyeh (a schism of the Shi'ite branch of Islam, to which about 11% of the population, including President Assad, belong) and the Yezidis of the Jebel Sinjar; and a minority of Christians.

The Constitution states only that 'Islam shall be the religion of the head of the state'. The original draft of the 1973 Constitution made no reference to Islam at all, and this clause was inserted only as a compromise after public protest. The Syrian Constitution is thus unique among the constitutions of Arab states (excluding Lebanon) with a clear Muslim majority in not enshrining Islam as the religion of the state itself.

ISLAM

Grand Mufti: Sheikh AHMAD BADER EL-DIN HASSOUN, BP 7410, Damascus; tel. (11) 2688601; fax (11) 2637650; e-mail info@drhassoun.com; internet www.drhassoun.com.

CHRISTIANITY

Orthodox Churches

Greek Orthodox Patriarchate of Antioch and all the East: BP 9, Damascus; tel. (11) 5424400; fax (11) 5424404; e-mail info@antiochpat.org; internet www.antiochpat.org; Patriarch of Antioch and all the East His Beatitude JOHN X; has jurisdiction over Syria, Lebanon, Iran and Iraq.

Syrian Orthodox Patriarchate of Antioch and all the East: BP 22260, Bab Touma, Damascus; tel. (11) 54498989; e-mail patriarch-z-iwas@scs-net.org; Patriarch of Antioch and all the East His Holiness IGNATIUS ZAKKA I IWAS; the Syrian Orthodox Church includes one Catholicose (of India), 37 Metropolitans and one Bishop, and has an estimated 4m. adherents throughout the world.

The Armenian Apostolic Church is also represented in Syria.

The Roman Catholic Church

Armenian Rite

Patriarchal Exarchate of Syria: Exarchat Patriarcal Arménien Catholique, BP 22281, Bab Touma, Damascus; tel. (11) 5413820; fax (11) 5419431; e-mail damazmcath@hotmail.com; f. 1985; represents the Patriarch of Cilicia (resident in Beirut, Lebanon); 4,500 adherents (31 Dec. 2011); Exarch Patriarchal Bishop JOSEPH ARNAOUTIAN.

Archdiocese of Aleppo: Archevêché Arménien Catholique, BP 97, 33 al-Tilal, Aleppo; tel. (21) 2123946; fax (21) 2116637; e-mail armen.cath@mail.sy; 17,500 adherents (31 Dec. 2007); Archbishop BOUTROS MARAYATI.

Diocese of Kamichlié: Evêché Arménien Catholique, BP 17, al-Qamishli; tel. (53) 424211; fax (53) 422711; e-mail armen.cath@mail.sy; 5,400 adherents (2012); Archbishop BOUTROS MARAYATI.

Chaldean Rite

Diocese of Aleppo: Evêché Chaldéen Catholique, BP 4643, 1 rue Patriarche Elias IV Mouawwad, Soulémaniyé, Aleppo; tel. (21) 4441660; fax (21) 4600800; e-mail audoa@scs-net.org; 15,000 adherents (31 Dec. 2007); Bishop ANTOINE AUDO.

Latin Rite

Apostolic Vicariate of Aleppo: BP 327, 19 rue al-Fourat, Aleppo; tel. (21) 2682399; fax (21) 2689413; e-mail vicariatlatin@mail.sy; f. 1762; 12,000 adherents (31 Dec. 2008); Vicar Apostolic GIUSEPPE NAZZARO (Titular Bishop of Forma).

Maronite Rite

Archdiocese of Aleppo: Archevêché Maronite, BP 203, 57 rue Fares el-Khoury, Aleppo; tel. and fax (21) 2118048; e-mail maronite@scs-net.org; 4,000 adherents (31 Dec. 2007); Archbishop YOUSUF ANIS ABI-AAD.

Archdiocese of Damascus: Archevêché Maronite, BP 2179, 6 rue al-Deir, Bab Touma, Damascus; tel. (11) 5412888; fax (11) 5436002; e-mail mgrsamirnassar@gmail.com; f. 1527; 14,000 adherents (31 Dec. 2007); Archbishop SAMIR NASSAR.

Diocese of Latakia: Evêché Maronite, BP 161, rue Hamrat, Tartous; tel. (43) 223433; fax (43) 322939; 33,000 adherents (31 Dec. 2007); Bishop YOUSUF MASSOUD MASSOUD.

Melkite Rite

Melkite Greek Catholic Patriarchate of Antioch: Patriarcat Grec-Melkite Catholique, BP 22249, 12 ave al-Zeitoun, Bab Charki, Damascus; tel. (11) 5441030; fax (11) 5417900; e-mail pat.melk@scs-net.org; internet www.pgc-lb.org; or BP 70071, Antélias, Lebanon; tel. (4) 413111; fax (4) 418113; f. 1724; jurisdiction over 1.5m. Melkites throughout the world (incl. 234,000 in Syria); Patriarch of Antioch and all the East, of Alexandria and of Jerusalem His Beatitude GREGORIOS III LAHAM; the Melkite Church includes the patriarchal sees of Damascus, Cairo and Jerusalem and four other archdioceses in Syria; seven archdioceses in Lebanon; one in Jordan; one in Israel; and seven eparchies (in the USA, Brazil, Canada, Australia, Venezuela, Argentina and Mexico).

Archdiocese of Aleppo: Archevêché Grec-Catholique, BP 146, 9 place Farhat, Aleppo; tel. (21) 2119307; fax (21) 2119308; e-mail gr.melkcath@mail.sy; 17,000 adherents (31 Dec. 2007); Archbishop JEAN-CLÉMENT JEANBART.

Archdiocese of Busra and Hauran: Archevêché Grec-Catholique, Khabab, Hauran; tel. (15) 855012; e-mail derbosra@hotmail.com;

27,000 adherents (31 Dec. 2007); Archbishop BOULOS NASSIF BORKHOCHE.

Archdiocese of Homs: Archevêché Grec-Catholique, BP 1525, rue el-Mo'tazila, Boustan al-Diwan, Homs; tel. (31) 2482587; fax (31) 2464587; e-mail isidore_battikha@yahoo.fr; 30,000 adherents (31 Dec. 2007); Archbishop (vacant).

Archdiocese of Latakia: Archevêché Grec-Catholique, BP 151, rue al-Moutannabi, Latakia; tel. (41) 460777; fax (41) 476002; e-mail saouafnicolas@yahoo.fr; 10,000 adherents (31 Dec. 2007); Archbishop NICOLAS SAWAF.

Syrian Rite

Archdiocese of Aleppo: Archevêché Syrien Catholique, place Mère Teresa de Calcutta, Azizié, Aleppo; tel. (21) 2126750; fax (21) 2126752; e-mail a_chahda@hotmail.com; 8,000 adherents (31 Dec. 2007); Archbishop DENYS ANTOINE CHAHDA.

Archdiocese of Damascus: Archevêché Syrien Catholique, BP 2129, 157 rue Al-Mustaqeem, Bab Charki, Damascus; tel. and fax (11) 5445343; e-mail psamirm@cyberia.met.lb; 14,000 adherents (31 Dec. 2007); Archbishop GRÉGOIRE ELIAS TABÉ.

Archdiocese of Hassaké-Nisibi: Archevêché Syrien Catholique, BP 6, Hassaké; tel. (52) 320812; e-mail b.hindo@hotmail.com; 35,000 adherents (31 Dec. 2007); Archbishop JACQUES BEHNAN HINDO.

Archdiocese of Homs: Archevêché Syrien Catholique, BP 303, rue Hamidieh, Homs; tel. (31) 221575; fax (21) 224350; 10,000 adherents (31 Dec. 2007); Archbishop THÉOPHILE GEORGES KASSAB.

The Anglican Communion

Within the Episcopal Church in Jerusalem and the Middle East, Syria forms part of the diocese of Jerusalem (see the chapter on Israel).

Other Christian Groups

Protestants in Syria are largely adherents of either the National Evangelical Synod of Syria and Lebanon or the Union of Armenian Evangelical Churches in the Near East (for details of both organizations, see the chapter on Lebanon).

The Press

Since the Baath Arab Socialist Party came to power, the structure of the press has been modified according to socialist patterns. Most publications are issued by political, religious or professional associations (such as trade unions), and several are published by government ministries. However, two privately owned daily newspapers have been launched in recent years. Anyone wishing to establish a new paper or periodical must apply for a licence.

The major dailies are *Al-Baath* (the organ of the party), *Tishreen*, *Al-Thawra* and the *Syria Times*, all published in Damascus.

PRINCIPAL DAILIES

Al-Baath (Renaissance): BP 9389, Autostrade Mezzeh, Damascus; tel. (11) 6622142; fax (11) 6622099; e-mail baath@baath-party.org; internet www.albaath.news.sy; f. 1946; morning; Arabic; organ of the Baath Arab Socialist Party; Editor ILYAS MURAD; circ. 45,000.

Baladna: BP 2000, al-Huda Bldg, al-Eskandaria St, Damascus; tel. (11) 6122515; fax (11) 6122514; e-mail info@ug.com.sy; internet www.baladnaonline.net; Arabic; privately owned; publ. by United Group for Publishing, Advertising and Marketing; Chief Editor SAMIR AL-SHIBANI.

Champress: Immeuble Arnos, place Arnos, Damascus; tel. (11) 44681199; fax (11) 44681190; e-mail mail@champress.com; internet www.champress.com; privately owned; political; online only; Arabic; Dir ALI JAMALO.

Al-Fida' (Redemption): Hama; Al-Wahda Foundation for Press, Printing and Publishing, BP 2448, Dawar Kafr Soussat, Damascus; tel. (11) 225219; fax (11) 2216851; e-mail fedaa@thawra.com; internet fedaa.alwehda.gov.sy; morning; Arabic; political; Editor A. AULWANI; circ. 4,000.

Al-Furat: Al-Wahda Foundation for Press, Printing and Publishing, BP 2448, Dawar Kafr Soussat, Damascus; tel. (51) 224494; fax (51) 218418; e-mail furat@thawra.com; internet furat.alwehda.gov.sy; Editor ADNAN OWAID.

Al-Horubat: Homs; Al-Wahda Foundation for Press, Printing and Publishing, BP 2448, Dawar Kafr Soussat, Damascus; tel. (11) 225219; fax (11) 2216851; e-mail ouroba@thawra.com; internet ouroba.alwehda.gov.sy; morning; Arabic; political; circ. 5,000.

Al-Jamahir (The People): Aleppo; Al-Wahda Foundation for Press, Printing and Publishing, BP 2448, Dawar Kafr Soussat, Damascus;

tel. (21) 214309; fax (21) 214308; e-mail jamahir@thawra.com; internet jamahir.alwehda.gov.sy; Arabic; political; Chief Editor MORTADA BAKACH; circ. 10,000.

Syria Times: BP 5452, Medan, Damascus; tel. (11) 2247359; fax (11) 2231374; e-mail syriatimes@teshreen.com; internet syriatimes.tishreen.info; English; publ. by Tishreen Foundation for Press and Publishing; Editor FOUAD MARDOUD; circ. 15,000.

Al-Thawra (Revolution): Al-Wahda Foundation for Press, Printing and Publishing, BP 2448, Dawar Kafr Soussat, Damascus; tel. (11) 2210850; fax (11) 2216851; e-mail admin@thawra.com; internet thawra.alwehda.gov.sy; f. 1963; morning; Arabic; political; Editor ASAAD ABBOUD; circ. 40,000.

Tishreen (October): BP 5452, Medan, Damascus; tel. (11) 2131100; fax (11) 2246860; e-mail tnp@mail.sy; internet www.tishreen.info; Arabic; publ. by Tishreen Foundation for Press and Publishing; Chief Editor KHALAF AL-JARAAD; circ. 50,000.

Al-Wahda (Unity): Latakia; Al-Wahda Foundation for Press, Printing and Publishing, BP 2448, Dawar Kafr Soussat, Damascus; tel. (11) 225219; fax (11) 2216851; e-mail wehda@thawra.com; internet wehda.alwehda.gov.sy; Arabic; political.

Al-Watan: Duty Free Zone, Damascus; tel. (11) 2137400; fax (11) 2139928; internet www.alwatan.sy; f. 2006; Arabic; political; privately owned; Chief Editor WADDAH ABED RABBO.

WEEKLIES AND FORTNIGHTLIES

Abyad wa Aswad (White and Black): 8 rue Hekmat Alasale, Almastaba 4, Muhajirin; tel. (11) 3739968; fax (11) 3739949; e-mail a-and-a@scs-net.org; internet www.awaonline.net; f. 2002; weekly; Arabic; political; privately owned; Editor AYMAN AL-DAQUQ.

Al-Iqtisadiya: rue Abd al-Munim Riyad 13, Damascus; tel. (11) 3737344; fax (11) 3737348; e-mail info@iqtissadiya.com; internet www.iqtissadiya.com; f. 2001; weekly; Arabic; economic; privately owned; Editor WADDAH ABD AL-RABBO.

Kantsasar: BP 133, Aleppo; tel. and fax (21) 2246753; e-mail kantsasar@excite.com; internet www.periotem.com; weekly; publ. by Armenian Prelacy of Aleppo; Editor MARY MERDKHANIAN.

Kassioun: BP 35033, Damascus; tel. (11) 3346681; fax (11) 3346681; e-mail general@kassioun.org; internet www.kassioun.org; weekly; publ. by the Syrian Communist Party (Bakdash).

Kifah al-Oummal al-Ishtiraki (The Socialist Workers' Struggle): Fédération Générale des Syndicats des Ouvriers, rue Qanawat, Damascus; weekly; Arabic; labour; publ. by Gen. Fed. of Labour Unions; Editor SAEED AL-HAMAMI.

Al-Maukef al-Riadi (Sport Stance): Al-Wahda Foundation for Press, Printing and Publishing, BP 2448, Dawar Kafr Soussat, Damascus; tel. (11) 225219; e-mail riadi@thawra.com; internet riadi.alwehda.gov.sy; weekly; Arabic; sports; circ. 50,000.

An-Nour (Light): BP 7394 Damascus; tel. (11) 3324914; fax (11) 3342571; e-mail annour@mail.sy; internet www.an-nour.com; f. 2001; weekly; Arabic; political and cultural; organ of the Syrian Communist Party (Faisal); Editor-in-Chief YAQUB GARRO.

Sawt al-Shaab (Voice of the People): Damascus; f. 1937, but publ. suspended in 1939, 1941, 1947 and 1958; relaunched in 2001; fortnightly; Arabic; organ of the Syrian Communist Party (Bakdash).

OTHER PERIODICALS

Al-Arabieh (The Arab Lady): Syrian Women's Asscn, BP 3207, Damascus; tel. (11) 3313275; fax (11) 3311078; monthly; Editor MAJEDA KUTEIT.

Al-Fikr al-Askari (The Military Idea): BP 4259, blvd Palestine, Damascus; fax (11) 2125280; f. 1950; 6 a year; Arabic; official military review publ. by the Political Administration Dept.

Al-Ghad (Tomorrow): Association of Red Cross and Crescent, BP 6095, rue Maysat, Damascus; tel. (11) 2242552; fax (11) 7777040; monthly; environmental health; Editor K. ABED-RABOU.

Al-Irshad al-Zirai (Agricultural Information): Ministry of Agriculture and Agrarian Reform, rue Jabri, Damascus; tel. (11) 2213613; fax (11) 2216627; 6 a year; Arabic; agriculture.

Jaysh al-Sha'ab (The People's Army): Ministry of Defence, BP 3320, blvd Palestine, Damascus; fax (11) 2125280; f. 1946; monthly; Arabic; army magazine; publ. by the Political Dept of the Syrian Army.

Al-Kalima (The Word): Al-Kalima Association, Aleppo; monthly; Arabic; religious; Publr and Editor FATHALLA SAKAL.

Al-Kanoun (The Law): Ministry of Justice, rue an-Nasr, Damascus; tel. (11) 2214105; fax (11) 2246250; monthly; Arabic; juridical.

Layalina: Damascus; tel. (11) 6122515; fax (11) 6122514; e-mail info@layalinamag.com; internet layalina.sy.pressera.com; monthly; Arabic; social and lifestyle; publ. by United Group for Publishing, Advertising and Marketing; Chair. MAJD SULEIMAN.

Al-Maaloumatieh (Information): National Information Centre, BP 11323, Damascus; tel. (11) 2127551; fax (11) 2127648; e-mail nice@

net.sy; f. 1994; quarterly; computer magazine; Editor ABD AL-MAJID AL-RIFAI; circ. 10,000.

Al-Ma'arifa (Knowledge): Ministry of Culture, rue al-Rouda, Damascus; tel. (11) 3336963; f. 1962; monthly; Arabic; literary; Editor ABD AL-KARIM NASIF; circ. 7,500.

Al-Majalla al-Batriarquia (The Magazine of the Patriarchate): Syrian Orthodox Patriarchate, BP 914, Damascus; tel. (11) 4447036; f. 1962; monthly; Arabic; religious; Editor SAMIR ABDOH; circ. 15,000.

Al-Majalla al-Tibbiya al-Arabiyya (Arab Medical Magazine): rue al-Jala'a, Damascus; tel. (11) 3331890; e-mail kfkallas@net.sy; internet www.arabmedmag.com; monthly; Arabic and English; publ. by Arab Medical Comm; Dir KHALID KALLAS; Editor Dr AL-LOUJAMI MAZEN.

Majallat Majma' al-Lughat al-Arabiyya bi-Dimashq (Magazine of the Arab Language Academy of Damascus): Arab Academy of Damascus, BP 327, Damascus; tel. (11) 3713145; fax (11) 3733363; e-mail mla@net.sy; f. 1921; quarterly; Arabic; Islamic culture and Arabic literature, Arabic scientific and cultural terminology; Chief Editor Dr SHAKER FAHAM; circ. 1,600.

Al-Mouallem al-Arabi (The Arab Teacher): National Union of Teachers, BP 2842-3034, Damascus; tel. (11) 225219; f. 1948; monthly; Arabic; educational and cultural.

Al-Mouhandis al-Arabi (The Arab Engineer): Order of Syrian Engineers and Architects, BP 2336, Immeuble Dar al-Mouhandisen, place Azme, Damascus; tel. (11) 2214916; fax (11) 2216948; e-mail lbosea@net.sy; f. 1961; 4 a year; Arabic; scientific and cultural; Dir Eng. M. FAYEZ MAHFOUZ; Chief Editor Dr Eng. AHMAD AL-GHAFARI; circ. 50,000.

Al-Munadel (The Militant): c/o BP 11512, Damascus; fax (11) 2126935; f. 1965; monthly; Arabic; magazine of Baath Arab Socialist Party; Dir Dr FAWWAZ SAYYAGH; circ. 100,000.

Al-Nashra al-Iktissad (Economic Bulletin): Damascus Chamber of Commerce; tel. (11) 2218339; fax (11) 2225874; e-mail dcc@dcc-sy.com; f. 1922; quarterly; finance and investment; Editor GHASSAN KALLA; circ. 3,000.

Al-Sinaa (Industry): Damascus Chamber of Commerce, BP 1305, rue Mou'awiah, Harika, Damacus; tel. (11) 2222205; fax (11) 2245981; e-mail dcc@dcc-sy.com; monthly; commerce, industry and management; Editor Y. HINDI.

Souriya al-Arabiyya (Arab Syria): Ministry of Information, Immeuble Dar al-Baath, Autostrade Mezzeh, Damascus; tel. (11) 6622141; fax (11) 6617665; monthly; publicity; in four languages.

Syria Today: Baramkeh, Free Zone, Damascus; tel. (11) 88270310; fax (11) 2137343; e-mail mail@syria-today.com; internet www.syria-today.com; monthly; English; economic and social development; Chair. LOUMA TARABINE; Man. Editor FRANCESCA DE CHÂTEL.

Al-Tamaddon al-Islami (Islamic Civilization Society): Darwichiyah, Damascus; tel. (11) 2240562; fax (11) 3733563; e-mail isltmddn@hotmail.com; f. 1932; monthly; Arabic; religious; published by Al-Tamaddon al-Islami Asscn; Pres. of Asscn AHMAD MOUAZ AL-KHATIB.

Al-Yakza (The Awakening): Al-Yakza Association, BP 6677, rue Sisi, Aleppo; f. 1935; monthly; Arabic; literary social review of charitable institution; Dir HUSNI ABD AL-MASSIH; circ. 12,000.

Al-Zira'a (Agriculture): Ministry of Agriculture and Agrarian Reform, rue Jabri, Damascus; tel. (11) 2213613; fax (11) 2244023; f. 1985; monthly; Arabic; agriculture; circ. 12,000.

NEWS AGENCY

Syrian Arab News Agency (SANA): BP 2661, Baramka, Damascus; tel. (11) 2129702; fax (11) 2228265; e-mail public-relation@sana.sy; internet www.sana.sy; f. 1966; supplies bulletins on Syrian news to foreign news agencies; 16 offices abroad; 16 foreign correspondents; Dir-Gen. AHMAD DAWA.

Publishers

Arab Advertising Organization: BP 2842-3034, 28 rue Moutanabbi, Damascus; tel. (11) 2225219; fax (11) 2220754; e-mail sy-adv@net.sy; internet www.elan-sy.com; f. 1963; exclusive govt establishment responsible for advertising; publishes *Directory of Commerce and Industry*, *Damascus International Fair Guide*, *Daily Bulletin of Official Tenders*; Dir-Gen. MONA F. FABAH.

Damascus University Press: Baramkeh, Damascus; tel. (11) 2119890; fax (11) 2235779; e-mail noubough@gmail.com; internet www.damascusuniversity.edu.sy; f. 1923; medicine, engineering, social sciences, law, agriculture, arts, etc.; Dir NOUBOUGH YASSIN.

Dar al-Awael: BP 10181, Damascus; tel. (11) 44676270; fax (11) 44676273; e-mail alawael@scs-net.org; internet www.daralawael.com; f. 1999; academic publr; Dir-Gen. ISMAIL ABDULLAH.

Dar al-Fikr: BP 962, Damascus; tel. (11) 2211166; fax (11) 2239716; e-mail fikr@fikr.net; internet www.fikr.com; f. 1957; Islamic studies, academic and gen. non-fiction; Dir-Gen. MUHAMMAD ADNAN SALIM.

Institut Français du Proche-Orient: BP 344, Damascus; tel. (11) 3330214; fax (11) 3327887; e-mail secretariat@ifporient.org; internet www.ifporient.org; f. 1922; sociology, anthropology, Islamic studies, archaeology, history, language and literature, arts, philosophy, geography, religion; publs include *Syria* (bi-annual journal), *Bulletin d'Etudes Orientales* (annual journal), *Bibliotheque Archeologique et Historique* (series), *Publications de l'Instituit Français de Damas* (series); Dir FRANÇOIS BURGAT.

OFA-Business Consulting Center—Documents Service: BP 3550, 3 place Chahbandar, Damascus; tel. (11) 3318237; fax (11) 4426021; e-mail ofa1@net.sy; internet www.ofa-bcc.com; f. 1964; numerous periodicals, monographs and surveys on political and economic affairs; Dir-Gen. SAMIR A. DARWICH; has one affiliated br., OFA-Business Consulting Centre (foreign co representation and services).

The Political Administration Press: BP 3320, blvd Palestine, Damascus; fax (11) 2125280; publishes *Al-Fikr al-Askari* (six a year) and *Jaysh al-Sha'ab* (monthly).

Syrian Documentation Papers: BP 2712, Damascus; f. 1968; publishers of *Bibliography of the Middle East* (annual), *General Directory of the Press and Periodicals in the Arab World* (annual), and numerous publications on political, economic, literary and social affairs, as well as legislative texts concerning Syria and the Arab world; Dir-Gen. LOUIS FARÈS.

Tishreen Foundation for Press and Publishing: BP 5452, Medan, Damascus; tel. (11) 2131100; fax (11) 2246860; publishes *Syria Times* and *Tishreen* (dailies).

United Group for Publishing, Advertising and Marketing: Immeuble al-Huda, rue al-Eskandaria, Mazzeh, Damascus; tel. (11) 6122515; fax (11) 6122514; e-mail info@ug.com.sy; internet www.ug.com.sy; publs *Baladna* newspaper, *Layalina* magazine, *What's On* magazine; Chair. MAJD SULEIMAN.

Al-Wahda Foundation for Press, Printing and Publishing (Institut al-Ouedha pour l'impression, édition et distribution): BP 2448, Dawar Kafr Soussat, Damascus; tel. (11) 225219; internet www.alwehda.gov.sy; publs *Al-Fida'*, *Al-Horubat*, *Al-Jamahir*, *Al-Thawra* and *Al-Wahda* (dailies), *Al-Maukef al-Riadi* (weekly) and other commercial publs; Dir-Gen. FAHD DIYAB.

Broadcasting and Communications

TELECOMMUNICATIONS

Syrian Telecommunications Establishment (STE—Syrian Telecom): BP 11774, Autostrade Mezzeh, Damascus; tel. (11) 2240000; fax (11) 6110000; e-mail ste-gm@net.sy; internet www.ste.gov.sy; f. 1975; Gen. Dir Dr NAZEM BAHSAS.

MTN Syria: BP 34474, Immeuble al-Mohandis al-Arabi, Autostrade Mezzeh, Damascus; fax (11) 6666094; e-mail customercare@mtn.com.sy; internet www.mtn.com.sy; f. 2001 as Spacetel Syria; name changed to Areeba Syria in 2004; present name adopted in 2007 following the acquisition of a 75% stake by MTN Group (South Africa); provider of mobile telephone services; Chair. JAMAL RAMADAN; CEO ISMAIL JAROUDI.

Syriatel: Immeuble STE, 6e étage, rue Thawra, Damascus; tel. (11) 932190000 (mobile); fax (11) 3341917; e-mail info@syriatel.com.sy; internet syriatel.sy; f. 2000; provider of mobile telephone services; Chair. RAMI MAKHLOUF; CEO NADER KALAI; 3.5m. subscribers (2007).

BROADCASTING

Radio

General Organization of Radio and Television (ORTAS—Organisme de la Radio-Télévision Arabe Syrienne): place Omayyad, Damascus; tel. (11) 720700; fax (11) 2234930; e-mail contact@rtv.gov.sy; internet www.rtv.gov.sy; radio broadcasts started in 1945, television broadcasts in 1960; radio directorate consists of four departments: Radi, Shaab, Shabab FM, and a multilingual news service; television directorate operates one satellite and two terrestrial channels, broadcasting in Arabic, English and French; Dir-Gen. FAYEZ AL-SAYEGH; Dirs NAIF HAMMOUD (Radio), Dr FOUAD SHERBAJI (Television).

Syriana FM Radio: Damascus; f. 2012.

Television

General Organization of Radio and Television: see Radio.

Addounia TV: Damascus; tel. (11) 4472630; fax (11) 4472632; e-mail info@addounia.tv; internet www.addounia.tv; privately owned news channel; awarded broadcasting licence mid-2007; began broadcasting Oct. 2008; Gen. Man. FOUAD AL-SHARBAJI.

Talaqi TV: Damascus; f. 2012; Head MAHER AL-KHOULI.

Finance

(cap. = capital; res = reserves; dep. = deposits; m.= million;
brs = branches; amounts in £S unless otherwise indicated)

BANKING

Central Bank

Central Bank of Syria (Banque Centrale de Syrie): place du 17 avril, Damascus; tel. (11) 2212642; fax (11) 2248329; e-mail info@bcs .gov.sy; internet www.banquecentrale.gov.sy; f. 1956; cap. and res 5,027m., dep. 620,946m. (Dec. 2008); Gov. Dr ADIB MAYALEH; 12 brs.

Other Banks

Agricultural Co-operative Bank: BP 4325, rue al-Tajehiz, Damascus; tel. and fax (11) 2213462; e-mail syrianagrobank@gmail .com; internet www.agrobank.org; f. 1888; cap. 10,000m., res 671m., dep. 12,000m. (Dec. 2001); Chair. Dr ABD AL-RAZZAQ KASSEM; 106 brs.

Arab Bank Syria SA (ABS): BP 38, rue al-Mahdi bin Barakeh, Abou Roumaneh, Damascus; tel. (11) 3348125; fax (11) 3349844; e-mail ali.zatar@arabbank-syria.com; internet www.arabbank-syria .com; f. 2005; jt venture between Syrian investors (51%) and Arab Bank (Jordan—49%); private commercial bank; cap. 3,180m., res 303m., dep. 36,905m. (Dec. 2010); Chair. Dr KHALID WASSIF AL-WAZANI; Gen. Man. MUHAMMAD AL-HASSAN; 9 brs.

Bank Audi Syria SA: BP 6228, Damascus; e-mail contactus.syria@ banqueaudi.com; internet www.banqueaudi.com/basy/syria.html; f. 2005; 47% owned by Audi Saradar Group (Lebanon), 26% by Syrian investors, 2% by a Saudi investor; remaining 25% oversubscribed in an initial public offering in Aug. 2005; private commercial bank; cap. 5,000m., res 171m., dep. 68,114m. (Dec. 2009); Chair. GEORGES ACHI; CEO BASSEL S. HAMWI; 19 brs.

Bank of Syria and Overseas: BP 3103, Harika-Bab Barid, Lawyers' Syndicate Bldg, nr Chamber of Commerce, Damascus; tel. (11) 2460560; fax (11) 2460555; e-mail bsomail@bso.com.sy; internet www.bso.com.sy; f. 2004; jt venture between Banque du Liban et d'Outre Mer (BLOM, Lebanon—39%), the World Bank's Int. Finance Corpn (10%) and Syrian investors (51%); private commercial bank; cap. 4,000m., res 1,087m., dep. 62,132m. (Dec. 2011); Chair. Dr RATEB AL-SHALLAH; CEO AMR AZHARI; 11 brs.

Banque BEMO Saudi Fransi SA (BBSF): 39 rue Ayyar, Salhiah, Damascus; tel. (11) 2317778; fax (11) 2318778; e-mail bbsf@mail.sy; internet www.bbsfbank.com; f. 2004; jt venture between Syrian investors (51%), Banque Saudi Fransi (Saudi Arabia—27%) and Banque Européenne pour le Moyen-Orient (Lebanon—22%); private commercial bank; cap. 3,705m., res 789m., dep. 107,435m. (Dec. 2010); Chair. RIAD OBEGI; CEO NABIL HCHAIME; 22 brs.

Byblos Bank Syria: BP 5424, al-Chaalan, rue Amine Loutfi Hafez, Damascus; tel. (11) 3348240; fax (11) 3348205; e-mail byblosbanksyria@byblosbank.com; internet www.byblosbank.com .lb/aboutbbkgroup/bbk_sa/board/index.shtml; f. 2005; 41.5% owned by Byblos Bank SAL (Lebanon), 51% by Syrian investors and 7.5% by the Org. of Petroleum Exporting Countries' Fund for Int. Devt; private commercial bank; cap. 4,000m., res 224m., dep. 37,432m. (Dec. 2010); Chair. and Gen. Man. Dr FRANÇOIS S. BASSIL; 9 brs.

CHAM Bank: BP 33979, place al-Najmeh, Damascus; tel. (11) 3348720; fax (11) 3348731; e-mail info@chambank.com; internet www.chambank.com; f. 2006; jt venture between Dar Investment Co (Kuwait—12.5%), Commercial Bank of Kuwait (10%), Islamic Devt Bank (Kuwait—9%) and several Syrian and other Gulf investors; cap. 4,981m., res −87m., dep. 11,895m., (Dec. 2010); private commercial bank run on Islamic principles; Chair. ALI YOUSEF AL-AWADHI.

Commercial Bank of Syria (Banque Commerciale de Syrie): BP 933, place Yousuf al-Azmeh, Damascus; tel. (11) 2218890; fax (11) 2216975; e-mail cbos@mail.sy; internet www.cbs-bank.com; f. 1967; govt-owned bank; cap. US $1,616m., res $699m., dep. $13,237m. (Dec. 2009); Chair. Dr ISAM RUDWAN KHOORI; Gen. Man. AHMAD MUHAMMAD DIAB; 84 brs.

Industrial Bank: BP 7578, Immeuble Dar al-Mohandessin, rue Maysaloon, Damascus; tel. and fax (11) 2222222; e-mail info@ industrialbank.gov.sy; internet www.industrialbank.gov.sy; f. 1959; nationalized bank providing finance for industry; cap. 257m., total assets 8,131m. (Dec. 2001); Gen. Man. ANIS AL-MARAWI; 17 brs.

International Bank for Trade and Finance: place Hejazz, Damascus; tel. (11) 2460500; fax (11) 2460505; e-mail info@ibtf .com; internet www.ibtf.com.sy; f. 2004; 49% owned by Housing Bank for Trade and Finance (Jordan), 51% by Syrian investors; cap. 5,000m., res 849m., dep. 68,844m. (Dec. 2010); private commercial bank; Chair. Dr MICHAEL MARTO; CEO SULTAN AL-ZU'BI; 30 brs.

Popular Credit Bank: BP 2841, 6e étage, Immeuble Dar al-Mohandessin, rue Maysaloon, Damascus; tel. (11) 2227604; fax (11) 2211291; f. 1967; govt-owned bank; provides loans to the services sector and is sole authorized issuer of savings certificates; Pres. and Gen. Man. MUHAMMAD HASSAN AL-HOUJJEIRI; 50 brs.

Real Estate Bank: BP 2337, place Yousuf al-Azmeh, Damascus; tel. (11) 2218602; fax (11) 2233107; e-mail realestate@realestate-sy.com; internet www.reb.sy; f. 1966; govt-owned bank; provides loans and grants for housing, schools, hospitals and hotel construction; cap. 10,000m., res 7,650m., dep. 197,487m. (Dec. 2010); Chair. MUHAMMAD SALEH KENG; Gen. Man. Dr MULHAM DIBO; 21 brs.

Syria International Islamic Bank: BP 35494, Damascus; tel. (11) 2241135; fax (11) 2241132; e-mail info@siib.sy; internet www.siib.sy; f. 2006; 49% Qatari-owned (incl. Qatar Int. Islamic Bank—30%); private commercial bank run on Islamic principles; cap. 5,461m., res 242m., dep. 70,427m. (Dec. 2010); Chair. YOUSUF AHMAD AL-NAAMA; CEO ABD AL-QADER AL-DUWAIK; 14 brs.

Syrian Lebanese Commercial Bank SAL (SLCB): c/o Commercial Bank of Syria, BP 933, Immeuble G.M., 6e étage, place Yousuf Azmeh, Damascus; tel. (11) 2225206; fax (11) 2243224; e-mail hamra@slcbk.com; internet www.slcb.com.lb; f. 1974; 84.2% owned by Commercial Bank of Syria, 10% by Banque du Crédit Populaire SAL, 5% by Syrian Insurance Co; head office in Beirut, Lebanon; brs in Damascus and Aleppo; cap. 125,000m., res 26,331m., dep. 516,142m. (Dec. 2009); Chair. ANTOINE FRANJIEH; 2 brs.

STOCK EXCHANGE

Six companies were listed on the Damascus Securities Exchange when it opened for trading in March 2009.

Damascus Securities Exchange: BP 6564, Damascus; tel. (11) 5190000; fax (11) 5190099; e-mail info@dse.sy; internet www.dse.sy; f. 2009; 18 listed cos (Sept. 2010); Chair. Dr RATEB AL-SHALLAH.

Supervisory Body

Syrian Commission on Financial Markets and Securities: BP 31845, Damascus; tel. (11) 3310487; fax (11) 3310722; e-mail info@ scfms.sy; internet www.scfms.sy; f. 2005; Chair. MUHAMMAD AL-IMADY.

INSURANCE

A legislative decree, issued in 2005, allowed for the establishment of privately owned insurance companies.

Arabia Insurance Co—Syria (AICS): rue al-Alam, Damascus; tel. (11) 6627745; fax (11) 6627750; e-mail arabia-insurance@arabiasyria .com; f. 2006; Asst Gen. Man. ROGER COTON.

General Social Security Organization: BP 2684, rue Port Said, Damascus; tel. (11) 2316932; fax (11) 2323115; e-mail taminat@gov .sy; internet www.taminat.gov.sy; Dir-Gen. KHALAF AL-ABDULLAH.

Syria International Insurance (Arobe Syria): BP 33015, Immeuble Malki 18, rue Zuheir Ben Abi Sulma, Rawda, Damascus; fax (11) 3348144; e-mail info@aropesyria.com; internet www.aropesyria .com; f. 2006; owned by Arope Insurance (Lebanon); all classes of insurance; Chair. AMR AZHARI.

Syrian General Organization for Insurance (Syrian Insurance Co): BP 2279, 29 rue Ayyar, Damascus; tel. (11) 2218430; fax (11) 2220494; e-mail syrinsur@syrian-insurance.com; internet www .syrian-insurance.com; f. 1953; auth. cap. 1,000m.; nationalized co; operates throughout Syria; Chair. ADEL AL-KADAMANI; Dir-Gen. SULAYMAN AL-HASSAN.

Syrian Kuwaiti Insurance Co: BP 5778, Immeuble 4, King Abd al-Aziz Al Sa'ud St, Abou Roumaneh, Damascus; tel. (11) 3328060; fax (11) 3328061; e-mail info@skicins.com; internet www.skicins.com; f. 2006; owned by Gulf Insurance Co of Kuwait; cap. 850m.; all classes of insurance; Chair. KHALID SAUD AL-HASSAN.

Trust Syria Insurance Co: BP 30578, Immeuble Trust, rue Murshid Khatir, Damascus; tel. (11) 4472650; fax (11) 4472652; e-mail mail@trustsyria.com; internet www.trustsyria.com; f. 2006; all classes of insurance; CEO TAHER BIN TALEB KAMAL AL-HERAKI.

United Insurance Co: BP 4419, Damascus; tel. (11) 3341933; fax (11) 3341934; e-mail info@uic.com.sy; internet www.uic.com.sy; awarded Syria's first-ever private insurance co licence in 2006; Gen. Man. MUHAMMAD AL-SABI.

Supervisory Body

Syrian Insurance Supervisory Commission (SISC): BP 5648, 5e étage, Immeuble Insurance, rue 29 mai, Damascus; fax (11) 2226224; e-mail sisc.sy@mail.sy; internet www.sisc.sy; f. 2004; Gen. Man. EYAD ZAHRA.

Trade and Industry

STATE ENTERPRISES

Syrian industry is almost entirely under state control. There are national organizations responsible to the appropriate ministry for the operation of all sectors of industry, of which the following are examples:

Cotton Marketing Organization: BP 729, rue Bab al-Faraj, Aleppo; tel. (21) 2238486; fax (21) 2218617; e-mail cmo-aleppo@mail.sy; internet www.cmo.gov.sy; f. 1965; governmental authority for purchase of seed cotton, ginning and sales of cotton lint; Pres. and Dir-Gen. Dr AHMAD SOUHAD GEBBARA.

General Company for Phosphate and Mines (GECOPHAM): BP 288, Homs; tel. (31) 2751122; fax (31) 2751123; e-mail gecopham@net.sy; internet www.gecopham.com; f. 1970; production and export of phosphate rock; Gen. Dir Eng. FARHAN AL-MOHSEN.

General Organization for Engineering Industries: BP 3120, Damascus; tel. (11) 2121834; fax (11) 2116201; e-mail g.o.eng.ind@net.sy; internet www.handasieh.org; 13 subsidiary cos.

General Organization for the Exploitation and Development of the Euphrates Basin (GOEDEB): Rakka; Dir-Gen. Dr Eng. AHMAD SOUHAD GEBBARA.

General Organization for Food Industry (GOFI): BP 105, rue al-Fardous, Damascus; tel. (11) 2457008; fax (11) 2457021; e-mail foodindustry@mail.sy; internet www.syriafoods.net; f. 1975; food-processing and marketing; Chair. and Gen. Dir KHALIL JAWAD.

General Organization for the Textile Industries: BP 620, rue al-Fardoss, Bawabet al-Salhieh, Damascus; tel. (11) 2216200; fax (11) 2216201; e-mail syr-textile@mail.syr; internet textile.org.sy; f. 1975; control and planning of the textile industry and supervision of textile manufacture; 27 subsidiary cos; Dir-Gen. Dr JAMAL AL-OMAR.

Syrian Petroleum Company (SPC): BP 2849, Damascus; tel. (11) 3137935; fax (11) 3137979; e-mail spccom1@scs-net.org; internet www.spc-sy.com; f. 1958; state agency; holds the oil and gas concession for all Syria; exploits the Al-Suweida, Karatchouk, Rumelan and Jbeisseh oilfields; also organizes exploration, production and marketing of oil and gas nationally; Chair. and Man. Dir Dr Eng. OMAR AL-HAMAD.

> **Al-Furat Petroleum Company:** BP 7660, Damascus; tel. (11) 6183333; fax (11) 6184444; e-mail afpc@afpc.net.sy; internet www.afpc-sy.com; f. 1985; 50% owned by SPC and 50% by a foreign consortium of Syria Shell Petroleum Devt B.V. and Deminex Syria GmbH; exploits oilfields in the Euphrates river area; Chair. SAID HUNEDI; Gen. Man. OLE MYKLESTAD.

DEVELOPMENT ORGANIZATIONS

State Planning Commission: Rukeneddin, Damascus; tel. (11) 5161015; fax (11) 5161010; e-mail info@planning.gov.sy; internet www.planning.gov.sy; Head AMER HOSNI LUTFI.

Syrian Consulting Bureau for Development and Investment: BP 12574, Bldg 1, 2nd Floor, cnr Zuheir Ben Abi Sulma St and ibn al-Khateeb St, Rawda, Damascus; tel. (11) 3345757; fax (11) 3340711; e-mail scb@scbdi.com; internet www.scbdi.com; f. 1991; independent; Man. Dir NABIL SUKKAR.

CHAMBERS OF COMMERCE AND INDUSTRY

Federation of Syrian Chambers of Commerce: BP 5909, rue Mousa Ben Nousair, Damascus; tel. (11) 3337344; fax (11) 3331127; e-mail syr-trade@mail.sy; internet www.fedcommsyr.org; f. 1975; Pres. GHASSAN AL-QALLA'A; Sec.-Gen. BASSAM GHRAWI.

Aleppo Chamber of Commerce: BP 1261, Aleppo; tel. (21) 2238236; fax (21) 2213493; e-mail alepchmb@mail.sy; internet www.aleppochamber.org; f. 1885; Pres. Dr HASSAN ZEIDO; Gen. Sec. MUHAMMAD MANSOUR.

Aleppo Chamber of Industry: BP 1859, rue al-Moutanabbi, Aleppo; tel. (21) 3620601; fax (21) 3620040; e-mail info@aleppo-coi.org; internet www.aleppo-coi.org; f. 1935; Pres. SALEH AL-MALLAH; Gen. Man. MUHAMMAD GHREWATI; 7,705 mems.

Damascus Chamber of Commerce: BP 1040, rue Mou'awiah, Damascus; tel. (11) 2245475; fax (11) 2225874; e-mail dcc@net.sy; internet www.dcc-sy.com; f. 1890; Pres. MUHAMMAD GHASSAN AL-QALLAA; Gen. Sec. BASSAM GHRAOUI; 11,500 mems.

Damascus Chamber of Industry: BP 1305, rue Harika Mou'a-wiah, Damascus; tel. (11) 2215042; fax (11) 2245981; e-mail dci@mail.sy; internet www.dci-syria.org; Pres. Eng. IMAD GHRIWATI; Sec. Eng. AYIMEN MAOULAWI.

Hama Chamber of Commerce: BP 147, rue al-Kouatly, Hama; tel. (33) 2525203; fax (33) 2517701; e-mail hamacham@scs-net.org; internet hama-chamber.org; f. 1934; Pres. HAMZEH KASSAB BASHI; Man. Dir ABD AL-RAZZAK AL-HAIT.

Homs Chamber of Commerce: BP 440, rue Abou al-Of, Homs; tel. (31) 2471000; fax (31) 2464247; e-mail hcc@homschamber.org.sy; internet www.homschamber.org.sy; f. 1928; Pres. Eng. M. ADEL TAYYARA; Gen. Man. M. FARES AL-HUSSAMY.

Latakia Chamber of Commerce and Industry: 8 rue Attar, Latakia; tel. (41) 479531; fax (41) 478526; e-mail lattakia@chamberlattakia.com; internet www.chamberlattakia.com; Pres. KAMAL ISMAIL AL-ASSAD.

Tartous Chamber of Commerce and Industry: POB 403, Tartous; tel. (43) 329852; fax (43) 329728; e-mail info@tcci-sy.com; internet tcci-sy.net; Pres. WAHIB KAMEL MERI; Gen. Man. MANAH ASSAF.

EMPLOYERS' ORGANIZATIONS

Fédération de Damas: Damascus; f. 1949.

Fédération Générale à Damas: Damascus; f. 1951; Dir TALAT TAGLUBI.

Fédération des Patrons et Industriels à Lattaquié: Latakia; f. 1953.

UTILITIES

Electricity

Public Establishment for Electricity Generation and Transmission (PEEGT): BP 3386, 17 rue Nessan, Damascus; tel. (11) 2229654; fax (11) 2229062; e-mail peegt@net.sy; f. 1965; present name adopted 1994; state-owned; operates 11 power stations through subsidiary cos; Dir-Gen. Dr AHMAD AL-ALI; Gen. Man. HISHAM MASIAJ.

Gas

Syrian Gas Company: BP 4499, Homs; tel. (31) 2451925; fax (31) 2451933; e-mail info@sgc.gov.sy; internet www.sgc.gov.sy; f. 2003; state-owned; responsible for production, processing and distribution of gas supplies; Dir-Gen. ALI ABBAS.

Water

The Ministry of Housing and Urban Development is responsible for planning and regulation in the Syrian water sector; it oversees the operations of 14 regional water establishments that manage the provision of drinking water and sewerage facilities. The Ministry of Water Resources is responsible for the management of water resources and the provision of irrigation water. An Integrated Water Resource Management Project, co-ordinated by the State Planning Commission, was initiated in 2006 with the aim of modernizing and integrating the various authorities responsible for the sector (see www.water.co.sy).

TRADE UNION

General Federation of Labour Unions (Ittihad Naqabat al-'Ummal al-'Am fi Suriya): BP 2351, rue Qanawat, Damascus; f. 1948; Chair. MUHAMMAD SHAABAN AZZOUZ; Sec. MAHMOUD FAHURI.

Transport

RAILWAYS

In 2010 the total length of Syrian railways was 2,139 route-km. A new railway line linking Aleppo with Mersin in southern Turkey began operating in March 2009. Another new line connecting Aleppo with Gaziantep, also in southern Turkey, was inaugurated in December; services commenced in late 2010. Meanwhile, by 2011 plans were under way for a mixed underground/elevated metro system in Damascus. Construction work on the Green Line, consisting of a 16.5-km line and 17 stations, was initially scheduled to commence in 2012, with completion anticipated by 2016. However, the project was thought to have been halted by the country's descent into civil conflict.

General Establishment of Syrian Railways: Ministry of Transport, BP 182, Aleppo; tel. (21) 2294690; fax (21) 2225697; e-mail cfs-syria@net.sy; internet www.cfssyria.org; f. 1897; Dir-Gen. GEORGE MAKABARI.

General Organization of the Hedjaz-Syrian Railway: BP 2978, rue Hedjaz, Damascus; tel. (11) 3331625; e-mail generaldirector@hijazerail.com; internet hijazerail.com; f. 1908; the Hedjaz Railway has 347 km of track (gauge 1,050 mm) in Syria; services operate between Damascus and Amman, Jordan, on a branch line of about 24 km from Damascus to Katana, and there is a further line of 64 km from Damascus to Serghaya; Dir-Gen. MAHMOUD SAQBANI.

ROADS

Arterial roads run across the country linking the north to the south and the Mediterranean to the eastern frontier. In 2010 Syria's total road network was 69,873 km, of which 45,345 km were asphalted. In mid-2009 the Government announced plans for the construction of two major new motorways: a north–south highway linking Bab al-Hawha, near the Turkish border, with Nasib, on the border with Jordan; and an east–west highway linking the Mediterranean port of Tartous with the Iraqi border.

Public Establishment for Road Communications: BP 34203, Damascus; tel. (11) 2458411; fax (11) 2452682; e-mail director-g@perc.gov.sy; internet www.perc.gov.sy; f. 2003; Dir-Gen. Dr YOUSEF AL-HAMOUD.

SHIPPING

Latakia is Syria's principal port; it has a 972-m quay with draughts ranging from 11.8 m–13.3 m. A concession to manage and operate the container terminal at Latakia was awarded to a consortium led by the French CMA CGM Group in March 2009. Latakia handled 8.9m. tons of cargo in 2010. The other major ports are at Banias and Tartous. Tartous handled 15.4m. tons of cargo in 2010.

At 31 December 2013 Syria's flag registered fleet totalled 70 vessels, with an aggregate displacement of 99,074 grt, of which one was a bulk carrier and 45 were general cargo ships.

Regulatory and Port Authorities

General Directorate of Syrian Ports: BP 505, Algazaer St, Latakia; tel. (41) 479041; fax (41) 475805; e-mail gdp-itm@syrianport.com; internet www.syrianports.com; Dir-Gen. Rear-Adm. GHAZI HAMDAN.

Latakia Port Authority: BP 220, rue Baghdad, Latakia; tel. (41) 476452; fax (41) 475760; e-mail info@lattakiaport.gov.sy; internet www.lattakiaport.gov.sy; Gen. Man. SULEIMAN A. BALOUCH.

Syrian General Authorities for Maritime Transport (SYRIA-MAR): BP 314, place Zat al-Sawary, Latakia; tel. (41) 370681; fax (41) 371013; internet syriamar.net.

Tartous Port Authority: BP 86, Tartous; tel. (43) 225150; fax (43) 315602; e-mail ta-pco@mail.sy; internet www.tartousport.com; Gen. Man. ZAKI E. NAJIB.

Principal Shipping Companies

Ismail, A. M., Shipping Agency Ltd: BP 74, rue al-Mina, Tartous; tel. (43) 221987; fax (43) 318949; operates 8 general cargo vessels; Man. Dir MAHMOUD ISMAIL.

Muhieddine Shipping Co: BP 1099, rue al-Chourinish, Tartous; tel. (43) 323090; fax (43) 317139; e-mail info@muhieddineshipping.net; internet www.muhieddineshipping.net; operates 7 general cargo ships.

Riamar Shipping Co Ltd: BP 284, Immeuble Tarwin, rue du Port, Tartous; tel. (43) 314999; fax (43) 212616; e-mail aksabra@riamar.org; operates 6 general cargo vessels; Chair. and Man. Dir ABD AL-KADER SABRA.

Al-Sham Shipping Co: BP 33436, Damascus; tel. (11) 3311960; fax (11) 3311961; e-mail al-sham@al-sham.com; internet www.al-sham.com; f. 1994; operates 2 general cargo vessels; Chair. MUHAMMAD A. HAYKAL.

Syro-Jordanian Shipping Co: BP 148, rue Port Said, Latakia; tel. (41) 471635; fax (41) 470250; e-mail syjomar@net.sy; f. 1976; operates 2 general cargo ships; Chair. OSMAN LEBBADY; Tech. Man. M. CHOUMAN.

Tartous International Container Terminal JSC: BP 870, Tartous; tel. (43) 328882; fax (43) 328831; e-mail info@ictsi.sy; internet www.ictsi-sy.com; f. 2006; owned by Int. Container Terminal Services, Inc; awarded 10-year concession to operate a container terminal at Tartous; CEO and Gen. Man. ROMEO A. SALVADOR.

CIVIL AVIATION

There are international airports at Damascus and Aleppo. Syrianair also operates domestic flights from airports in al-Qamishli and Deir el-Zor. Extensive renovation work at Deir el-Zor was completed in 2008. Damascus International Airport handled 4.2m. passengers in 2010, while Aleppo handled 0.6m. passengers in the same year.

Syrian Civil Aviation Authority (SCAA): BP 6257, place Nejmeh, Damascus; tel. (11) 3331306; fax (11) 2232201; internet www.scaasy.com; Dir-Gen. Dr WAFIK HASAN.

Cham Wings Airlines: rue al-Fardous, Damascus; tel. (11) 2244086; fax (11) 2454506; e-mail info@chamwings.com; internet www.chamwings.com; f. 2007; first private int. airline in Syria; flights from Damascus serving seven destinations in the Middle East and Europe; Chair. ISSAM SHAMMOUT.

Syrian Arab Airlines (Syrianair): BP 417, Social Insurance Bldg, 5th Floor, Youssef al-Azmeh Sq., Damascus; tel. (11) 2220700; fax (11) 224923; e-mail syr-air@syriatel.net; internet www.syriaair.com; f. 1946; refounded 1961 to succeed Syrian Airways, after revocation of merger with Misrair (Egypt); domestic passenger and cargo services

(from Damascus, Aleppo, Latakia and Deir el-Zor) and routes to Europe, the Middle East, North Africa and the Far East; Chair. and Man. Dir NACHAAT NUMIR; Dir-Gen. GHAYDA ABD AL-LATIF.

Syrian Pearl Airlines: BP 31219, Damascus; tel. (11) 5010; fax (11) 3349557; e-mail info@flysyrianpearl.com; internet www.flysyrianpearl.com; f. 2008; commenced operations May 2009; 69% owned by CHAM Holding, 25% by Syrian Arab Airlines and 6% by Kuwaiti investors; domestic flights, and services to Sharm el-Sheikh (Egypt), Jeddah (Saudi Arabia) and İstanbul (Turkey); flights suspended in June 2009; Chair. Dr ABD AL-RAHMAN AL-ATTAR; CEO FINN THAULOW.

Tourism

Syria's tourist attractions include a pleasant Mediterranean coastline, the mountains, town bazaars, and the antiquities of Damascus, Aleppo and Palmyra, as well as hundreds of deserted ancient villages in the north-west of the country. According to provisional figures, an estimated 5.1m. tourists visited Syria in 2011; tourism receipts totalled US $6,190m. in 2010.

Ministry of Tourism: BP 6642, rue Barada, Damascus; tel. (11) 2210122; fax (11) 2242636; e-mail min-tourism@mail.sy; internet www.syriatourism.org; f. 1972; Counsellor to the Minister SAWSAN JOUZY; Dir of Tourism Promotion and Marketing NIDAL MACHFEJ.

Middle East Tourism: BP 201, Malki St, Shawki ave, Damascus; tel. (11) 3325655; fax (11) 3326266; e-mail daadouche@net.sy; internet www.daadouche.com; f. 1952; Pres. MAHER DAADOUCHE; 7 brs.

Syrian Arab Co for Hotels and Tourism (SACHA): BP 5549, Mezzeh, Damascus; tel. (11) 2223286; fax (11) 2219415; f. 1977; Chair. DIRAR JUMA'A; Gen. Man. ELIAS ABOUTARA.

Defence

Commander-in-Chief of the Armed Forces: Lt-Gen. BASHAR AL-ASSAD.

Minister of Defence and Deputy Commander-in-Chief of the Armed Forces: Lt-Gen. FAHD JASSEM AL-FREIJ.

Chief of Staff of the Armed Forces: Lt-Gen. ALI ABDULLAH AYYUB.

Air Force Commander: Maj.-Gen. JAMIL HASSAN.

Republican Guard Commander: Gen. MAHER AL-ASSAD.

Defence Budget (2012): est. £S243,000m.

Military Service: 30 months.

Total Armed Forces (as assessed at November 2012): 178,000 (army 110,000—including conscripts; air defence command—an army command—36,000; navy 5,000; air force 27,000); reserves 314,000 (army 280,000; air force 10,000; air defence 20,000; navy 4,000).

Education

Primary education, which begins at six years of age and lasts for six years, is officially compulsory. In 2008/09 primary enrolment included 93% of children in the relevant age-group. In 2009/10 an estimated 2,429,450 pupils were enrolled in primary education (males 1,265,470; females 1,163,980). Secondary education, beginning at 12 years of age, lasts for a further six years, comprising two cycles of three years each. In 2009/10 enrolment at secondary schools included 67% of children in the appropriate age-group. An estimated 2,625,382 pupils (males 1,338,083; females 1,287,299) were enrolled in secondary education (excluding vocational courses) in 2009/10.

There are agricultural and technical schools for vocational training, and by 2006/07 there were eight private universities and numerous private schools. In that year there were 250,000 students at state universities, 6,000 at private institutions and a further 2,500 at the Syrian Virtual University (which offers degree courses via the internet). In 2012 there were six government universities and eight private universities. The main language of instruction in schools is Arabic, but English and French are widely taught as second languages. The combined budgetary expenditure of the Ministries of Education and of Higher Education in 2008 was an estimated S£63,286m. (equivalent to some 10.5% of total government spending).

The UN Relief and Works Agency for Palestine Refugees in the Near East (UNRWA) provides education for Palestinian refugees in Syria. During the academic year 2010/11 UNRWA operated 118 schools in Syria, with a total enrolment of 66,014 pupils.

TAIWAN

Introductory Survey

LOCATION, CLIMATE, LANGUAGE, RELIGION, FLAG, CAPITAL

The Republic of China has, since 1949, been confined mainly to the province of Taiwan (comprising one large island and several much smaller ones), which lies off the south-east coast of the Chinese mainland. The territory under the Republic's effective jurisdiction consists of the island of Taiwan (also known as Formosa) and nearby islands, including the Penghu (Pescadores) group, together with a few other islands which lie just off the mainland and form part of the province of Fujian (Fukien), west of Taiwan. The largest of these is Kinmen (Jinmen), also known as Quemoy, which, with three smaller islands, is about 10 km from the port of Xiamen (Amoy), while five other islands under Taiwan's control, chiefly Matsu (Mazu), lie further north, near Fuzhou. Taiwan itself is separated from the mainland by the Taiwan (Formosa) Strait, which is about 130 km (80 miles) wide at its narrowest point. The island's climate is one of rainy summers and mild winters. Average temperatures are about 15°C (59°F) in the winter and 26°C (79°F) in the summer. The average annual rainfall is 2,580 mm (102 in). The official language is Northern Chinese (Mandarin), but Taiwanese, a dialect based on the language of Fujian Province, is widely spoken. The predominant religions are Buddhism and Daoism (Taoism), but there are also adherents of I-kuan Tao, Christianity and Islam. The philosophy of Confucianism has a large following. The national flag (proportions 2 by 3) is red, with a dark blue rectangular canton, containing a white sun, in the upper hoist. The capital is Taipei.

CONTEMPORARY POLITICAL HISTORY

Historical Context

China ceded Taiwan to Japan in 1895. The island remained under Japanese rule until the end of the Second World War in 1945, when it was returned to Chinese control, becoming a province of the Republic of China, then ruled by the Kuomintang (KMT, Nationalist Party). The leader of the KMT was Gen. Chiang Kai-shek, President of the Republic since 1928. The KMT Government's forces were defeated in 1949 by the Communist revolution in China. President Chiang and many of his supporters withdrew from the Chinese mainland to Taiwan, where they established a KMT regime in succession to their previous all-China administration. This regime continued to assert that it was the rightful Chinese Government, in opposition to the People's Republic of China, proclaimed by the victorious Communists in 1949. The Nationalists successfully resisted attacks by their Communist rivals, and declared that they intended to recover control of mainland China.

Although its effective control was limited to Taiwan, the KMT regime continued to be dominated by politicians who had formerly been in power on the mainland. Unable to replenish their mainland representation, the National Assembly (last elected fully in 1947) and other legislative organs extended their terms of office indefinitely, although fewer than one-half of the original members were alive on Taiwan by the 1980s. The political domination of the island by immigrants from the mainland caused some resentment among native Taiwanese, and led to demands for increased democratization and for the recognition of Taiwan as a state independent of China. The KMT consistently rejected demands for independence, restating the party's long-standing policy of seeking political reunification, although under KMT terms, with the mainland.

The KMT regime continued to represent China at the UN (and as a permanent member of the UN Security Council) until October 1971, when it was replaced by the People's Republic. After 1971 a number of countries severed diplomatic relations with Taiwan and recognized the People's Republic. Nationalist China was subsequently expelled from several other international organizations. In November 1991, however, as 'Chinese Taipei', Taiwan joined the Asia-Pacific Economic Cooperation (APEC, see p. 208) forum. In September 1992, under the name of the 'Separate Customs Territory of Taiwan, Penghu, Kinmen and Matsu', Taiwan was granted observer status at the General

Agreement on Tariffs and Trade (GATT) and was finally approved for membership of the successor body in September 2001: on 1 January 2002 Taiwan formally became a member of the World Trade Organization (WTO, see p. 444). In June 1995 Taiwan offered to make a donation of US $1,000m., to be used for the establishment of an international development fund, if the island were permitted to rejoin the UN. In February 2004 it was announced that Taiwan would become a member of the Commission for the Conservation and Management of Highly Migratory Fish Stocks in the Western and Central Pacific Ocean (responsible for implementing the 1995 UN Fish Stocks Agreement). Following its admission to the WTO, therefore, this represented the second recognition of Taiwan by an international organization.

In September 2006, for the 14th consecutive year, the General Committee of the UN General Assembly rejected a proposal urging Taiwan's participation in the UN. The Taiwanese leadership pledged to continue the island's campaign to gain re-entry, stating that henceforth it would make its application under the name of Taiwan, rather than the 'Republic of China'. In September 2007, however, the island's membership application, as Taiwan, was again rejected. In September 2008 a further proposal enjoining Taiwan's entry to the UN was turned down. The issue was submitted to Taiwanese voters in two referendums held in March 2008, but the results were declared invalid owing to the low level of voter participation (see Domestic Political Affairs). As Taiwan began to consider the adoption of a different approach to the issue of UN representation, the island was expected to focus henceforth on securing representation in selected UN specialized agencies. In September 2009 the Ministry of Foreign Affairs confirmed that it was renouncing its immediate quest for a seat at the UN. This change of strategy was confirmed in August 2010. In May 2003, meanwhile, the People's Republic of China strongly opposed a US proposal that Taiwan be permitted to participate in the World Health Organization (WHO). The People's Republic reiterated its view in May 2008, when for the 12th time the World Health Assembly (the WHO governing body) rejected a proposal, supported by The Gambia and by the Pacific nation of Palau, that Taiwan be granted observer status in WHO. In April 2009 China abandoned its objections to Taiwan's attendance as an observer, under the name of 'Chinese Taipei', at the World Health Assembly. In May 2011, however, the Taiwanese President claimed that China had exerted pressure on WHO to refer to Taiwan as a Chinese province in its documentation.

Domestic Political Affairs

In December 1972 legislative elections were held, for the first time in 24 years, to fill 53 seats in the National Assembly. The new members, elected for a fixed term of six years, joined 1,376 surviving 'life-term' members of the Assembly. President Chiang Kai-shek remained in office until his death in April 1975. He was succeeded as leader of the ruling KMT by his son, Gen. Chiang Ching-kuo, who had hitherto been Premier. Dr Yen Chia-kan, Vice-President since 1966, became the new President. In 1978 President Yen retired and was succeeded by Gen. Chiang. At elections for 71 seats in the Legislative Yuan in December 1983, the KMT won an overwhelming victory, confirming its dominance over the independent 'Tangwai' (non-party) candidates. In March 1984 President Chiang was re-elected for a second six-year term, and Lee Teng-hui, a former mayor of Taipei and a native Taiwanese, became Vice-President. President Chiang died in January 1988 and was succeeded by Lee Teng-hui.

In September 1986 135 leading opposition politicians formed the Democratic Progressive Party (DPP), in defiance of the KMT's ban on the formation of new political parties. Partial elections to the National Assembly and the Legislative Yuan were held in December. The KMT achieved a decisive victory, but the DPP received about one-quarter of the total votes, and more than doubled the non-KMT representation. In February 1987 the KMT began to implement a programme of political reform. Martial law (which had remained in force since 1949) was replaced by the National Security Law in July 1987: political parties other than the KMT were permitted, and civilians were removed from the jurisdiction of military courts. In April, in a reorganization of the Executive Yuan (cabinet), seven major posts were allocated to reformist members of the KMT. In November the second annual Congress of the DPP approved a resolution declaring that Taiwanese citizens had the right to advocate independence. In January 1988, however, two opposition activists were imprisoned on charges of sedition.

In February 1988 a plan to restructure the legislative bodies was approved by the Central Standing Committee of the KMT. Voluntary resignations were to be sought from 'life-term' members of the Legislative Yuan and National Assembly, and seats were no longer to be reserved for representatives of mainland constituencies. Following a decision to hold free elections for two-thirds of the members of the KMT's Central Committee, numerous new members were elected at the party congress in July, and the proportion of native Taiwanese increased sharply. In January 1989 three legislative measures were enacted: a revision of regulations concerning the registration of political parties; a retirement plan for those members of the three legislative assemblies who had been elected by mainland constituencies in 1947; and a new law to give greater autonomy to the Taiwan Provincial Government (which retained responsibility for the general administration of the island, with the exception of the cities of Taipei and Kaohsiung) and the Provincial Assembly. In the following month the KMT became the first political party to register under the new legislation. Despite its objections to the size of the retirement pensions being offered and the terms of the Civic Organizations Law (under which political parties were obliged to reject communism and any notion of official political independence for Taiwan), the DPP applied for official registration in April.

Partial elections to the Legislative Yuan and the Taiwan Provincial Assembly were held in December 1989. A total of 101 seats in the Legislative Yuan were contested, with the KMT obtaining 72 seats and the DPP winning 21, thus securing the prerogative to propose legislation in the Legislative Yuan. In February 1990 the opening of the National Assembly's 35-day plenary session, convened every six years to elect the country's President, was disrupted by DPP members' violent action in a protest against the continuing domination of the Assembly by elderly KMT politicians, who had been elected on the Chinese mainland prior to 1949 and who had never been obliged to seek re-election. Many people were injured in the ensuing clashes between riot police and demonstrators. In March 1990 DPP members were barred from the National Assembly for refusing to swear allegiance to the 'Republic of China', attempting instead to substitute 'Taiwan' upon taking the oath. Various amendments to the Temporary Provisions, which for more than 40 years had permitted the effective suspension of the Constitution, were approved by the National Assembly in mid-March. Revisions included measures to strengthen the position of the mainland-elected KMT members, who were granted new powers to initiate and veto legislation, and also an amendment to permit the National Assembly to meet annually. The revisions were opposed not only by the DPP but also by more moderate members of the KMT, and led to a large protest rally in Taipei, demanding the abolition of the National Assembly and the holding of direct presidential elections. Nevertheless, President Lee was duly re-elected, unopposed, by the National Assembly for a six-year term, two rival KMT candidates having withdrawn.

The National Affairs Conference (NAC) convened in June 1990 to discuss proposals for reform. A Constitutional Reform Planning Group was subsequently established. The NAC reached consensus on the issue of direct presidential elections, which would permit the citizens of Taiwan, rather than the members of the National Assembly, to select the head of state. Meanwhile, the Council of Grand Justices had ruled that elderly members of the National Assembly and of the Legislative Yuan should step down by the end of 1991. The National Unification Council (NUC), chaired by President Lee, was formed in October 1990. In the same month the Mainland Affairs Council, comprising heads of government departments and led by the Vice-Premier of the Executive Yuan, was founded. In December President Lee announced that Taiwan would formally end the state of war with the mainland; the declaration of emergency was to be rescinded by May 1991. Plans were announced for gradual constitutional reform. Meanwhile, in early December 1990 Huang Hwa, the leader of a faction of the DPP and independence activist, had received a 10-year prison sentence upon being found guilty of 'preparing to commit sedition'.

In April 1991 the National Assembly was convened, the session again being marred by violent clashes between KMT and DPP members. The DPP subsequently boycotted the session, arguing that a completely new constitution should be introduced and that elderly KMT delegates, who did not represent Taiwan constituencies, should not have the right to make amendments to the existing Constitution. Some 20,000 demonstrators attended a DPP-organized protest march. Nevertheless, the National Assembly duly approved the constitutional amendments, and at midnight on 30 April the 'period of mobilization for the suppression of the Communist rebellion' and the Temporary Provisions were formally terminated. The existence, but not the legitimacy, of the Government of the People's Republic was officially acknowledged by President Lee. Furthermore, Taiwan remained committed to its 'one China' policy. In May 1991 widespread protests following the arrest of four advocates of independence for Taiwan led to the abolition of the Statute of Punishment for Sedition. The law had been adopted in 1949 and had been frequently employed by the KMT to suppress political dissent.

A senior UN official visited the island in August 1991, the first trip by such a representative since Taiwan's withdrawal from the organization in 1971. Large-scale rallies to demand the holding of a referendum on the issue of Taiwan's readmission to the UN as an independent state took place in September and October 1991, resulting in clashes between demonstrators and the security forces.

In August 1991 the opposition DPP officially announced its alternative draft constitution for 'Taiwan', rather than for the 'Republic of China', thus acknowledging the de facto position regarding sovereignty. In September, after being reinstated in the Legislative Yuan, Huang Hsin-chieh, the Chairman of the DPP, relinquished his seat in the legislature and urged other senior deputies to do likewise. Huang had been deprived of his seat and imprisoned in 1980, following his conviction on charges of sedition. At the party congress in October 1991, Huang was replaced as DPP Chairman by Hsu Hsin-liang. The DPP congress adopted a resolution henceforth to advocate the establishment of 'the Republic of Taiwan'.

Elections to the new 405-member National Assembly, which was to be responsible for amending the Constitution, took place in December 1991. The 225 seats open to direct election were widely contested. The campaign was dominated by the issue of independence. However, the DPP suffered a humiliating defeat. The KMT secured a total of 318 seats (179 of which were won by direct election), while the DPP obtained 75 seats (41 by direct election). All elderly mainland-elected delegates were obliged to relinquish their seats. In February 1992 20,000 demonstrators protested against the sedition laws and demanded a referendum on the issue of independence.

In March 1992, at a plenary session of the KMT Central Committee, it was agreed to reduce the President's term of office from six to four years. However, the important question of arrangements for future presidential elections remained unresolved. In April street demonstrations were organized by the DPP to support demands for direct presidential elections. In May the National Assembly adopted eight amendments to the Constitution, one of which empowered the President to appoint members of the Control Yuan.

Taiwan's first full elections since the establishment of Nationalist rule in 1949 were held in December 1992. The KMT retained 102 of the 161 seats in the Legislative Yuan. However, the DPP garnered 31% of the votes and more than doubled its representation in the legislature, winning 50 seats. Following this setback, the Premier and the KMT Secretary-General resigned. In February 1993 Lien Chan, hitherto Governor of Taiwan Province, became the island's first Premier of Taiwanese descent.

In May 1993 about 30 conservative rebels resigned from the KMT, and formed the New Alliance Nationalist Party. Furthermore, in June the Government was defeated in the Legislative Yuan, when a group of KMT deputies voted with the opposition to approve legislation on financial disclosure requirements for elected and appointed public officials. The unity of the KMT was further undermined in August, when six dissident legislators belonging to the New Kuomintang Alliance, which had registered as a political group in March, announced their decision to leave the ruling party in order to establish the New Party (NP). Nevertheless, at the KMT congress in August Lee Teng-hui was re-elected Chairman of the party. A new 31-member Central Standing Committee and 210-member Central Committee, comprising mainly Lee's supporters, were selected. In a conciliatory gesture by the KMT Chairman, four vice-chairmanships were created, the new positions being filled by representatives of different factions of the party.

In September 1993, following a series of bribery scandals, the Executive Yuan approved measures to combat corruption. In the same month a KMT member of the Legislative Yuan was sentenced to 14 years' imprisonment for bribery of voters during the 1992 election campaign; other similar convictions followed. At local government elections held in November 1993, although its share of the votes declined, the KMT secured 15 of the 23 posts at stake. The DPP, which accused the KMT of malpractice, won only six posts, despite receiving a substantial proportion of the votes; it retained control of Taipei County. Following allegations of extensive bribery at further local polls in early 1994 (at which the DPP and independent candidates made strong gains), the Ministry of Justice intensified its campaign against corruption. Proposals for constitutional amendments to permit the direct election in 1996 of the Taiwanese President by popular vote (rather than by electoral college) and to limit the powers of the Premier were approved by the National Assembly in July 1994.

At gubernatorial and mayoral elections in December 1994 the DPP took control of the Taipei mayoralty, in the first such direct polls for 30 years, while the KMT succeeded in retaining the provincial governorship of Taiwan, in the first ever popular election for the post, and the mayoralty of Kaohsiung. The NP established itself as a major political force, its candidate for the mayoralty of Taipei having received more votes than the KMT incumbent.

Elections to the Legislative Yuan were held in December 1995. A major campaign issue was that of corruption. The KMT's strength declined to 84 of the 164 seats, the party faring particularly badly in Taipei. The DPP increased its representation to 53 seats. The NP, which favoured reconciliation with the mainland, secured 21 seats. In mid-March 1996 a DPP demonstration on the streets of Taipei, in support of demands for Taiwan's independence, was attended by 50,000 protesters. At Taiwan's first direct presidential election, held on 23 March, the incumbent President Lee received 54.0% of the votes cast, thus securing his re-election for a four-year term. At the concurrent elections for the National Assembly, the KMT took 183 of the 334 seats. The DPP won 99 seats and the NP 46 seats. The Chairman of the DPP, Shih Ming-teh, resigned and Hsu Hsin-liang, who had stood down in November 1993, returned to the post.

In June 1996 the President's announcement of the composition of the new Executive Yuan aroused much controversy. Although several members retained their previous portfolios, the President (apparently under pressure from within the KMT) demoted the popular Ministers of Justice and of Transportation and Communications, both of whom had exposed malpractice and initiated campaigns against corruption. Other changes included the replacement of the Minister of Foreign Affairs by John Chang, the grandson of Chiang Kai-shek. However, the most controversial nomination was the reappointment as Premier of Lien Chan, despite his recent election as the island's Vice-President. Opposition members of the Legislative Yuan, along with a number of KMT deputies, demanded that the President submit the membership of the Executive Yuan to the legislature for approval.

In December 1996 the multi-party National Development Conference (NDC), established to review the island's political system, held its inaugural meeting. The convention approved KMT proposals to abolish the Legislative Yuan's right to confirm the President's choice of Premier, to permit the legislature to introduce motions of no confidence in the Premier and to empower the President to dismiss the legislature. The Provincial Governor, (James) Soong Chu-yu, subsequently tendered his resignation in protest against the NDC's recommendations that elections for the provincial governorship and assembly be abolished, as the first stage of the dissolution of the system of provincial administration. An historical legacy duplicating many of the functions of central and local government, the Provincial Government had remained responsible for the entire island, with the exception of the cities of Taipei and Kaohsiung. In January 1997 President Lee refused to accept the Governor's resignation, but the affair drew attention to the uneasy relationship between the island's President and its Governor.

In May 1997 more than 50,000 demonstrators, protesting against the increase in violent crime, demanded the resignation of President Lee. Three members of the Executive Yuan subsequently resigned. The appointment of Yeh Chin-feng as Minister

of the Interior (the first woman to oversee Taiwan's police force) did little to appease the public, which remained highly suspicious of the alleged connections between senior politicians and the perpetrators of organized crime. Thousands of protesters again took to the streets of Taipei, renewing their challenge to President Lee's leadership and demanding the immediate resignation of Premier Lien Chan. In June a 'Say No to China' rally attracted as many as 70,000 supporters.

In July 1997 the National Assembly approved the various constitutional reforms proposed by the NDC in December 1996, including the suspension of the Provincial Government (which was finally abolished in December 1998.), the empowerment of the President of Taiwan to appoint the Premier without the Legislative Yuan's confirmation, the authorization of the legislature to hold a binding vote of no confidence in the Executive Yuan, and the bestowal on the President of the right to dissolve the Legislative Yuan.

In August 1997 Vincent Siew, former Chairman of the Council for Economic Planning and Development and also of the Mainland Affairs Council, replaced Lien Chan as Premier (the latter retained the post of Vice-President), and John Chang was appointed Vice-Premier. In the same month President Lee was re-elected unopposed as Chairman of the ruling KMT. In elections at mayoral and magistrate levels, held in November, the DPP, which had campaigned on a platform of more open government, secured 12 of the 23 constituency posts contested, while the KMT won only eight posts. More than 70% of Taiwan's population was thus to come under DPP administration. The Secretary-General of the KMT resigned and was replaced by John Chang. A major reorganization of the party followed.

At local elections held in January 1998, the KMT won an overwhelming majority of the seats contested, while the DPP, in a reversal of fortune, performed badly. In April the Minister of Justice tendered, and then subsequently withdrew, his resignation, claiming that lawmakers with connections to organized crime were exerting pressure on the Government to dismiss him. However, in July he was forced to resign, following his mishandling of an alleged scandal concerning the acting head of the Investigation Bureau.

In June 1998 Lin Yi-hsiung won a convincing victory in the first ever direct election for the leadership of the DPP. At local elections that month, the KMT suffered a setback, winning fewer than 50% of the seats contested. Independent candidates performed well. In August 17 new members were elected to the KMT Central Standing Committee, the 16 others being appointed by President Lee.

Elections to the newly expanded 225-member Legislative Yuan took place in December 1998. The KMT secured 125 seats, the DPP 72 seats and the pro-unification NP 11 seats. The New Nation Alliance, a breakaway group from the DPP (formed in September), won only one seat. In the simultaneous election to select the mayor of Taipei, the KMT candidate, Ma Ying-jeou, a popular former Minister of Justice, defeated the DPP incumbent, Chen Shui-bian. However, Frank Hsieh, the DPP candidate, won the office of mayor of Kaohsiung. The KMT retained control of both city councils.

Chiou I-jen resigned as Secretary-General of the DPP in December 1998 and was replaced by Yu Shyi-kun. Later in that month Chao Shu-po, a Minister without Portfolio, was appointed Governor of Taiwan Province, replacing the elected incumbent, James Soong, as part of the plans to dismantle the provincial government, agreed in 1997. In March 1999 an unprecedented vote of no confidence in the leadership of Premier Vincent Siew was defeated in the Legislative Yuan. The motion was presented by the opposition following Siew's decision to reduce the tax on share transactions, apparently as a result of pressure from President Lee. In September the National Assembly approved a controversial constitutional amendment, which, *inter alia*, extended the terms of the deputies from May 2000 to June 2002. Election to the Assembly was henceforth to be on the basis of party proportional representation. Shortly afterwards, the KMT leadership expelled the Speaker of the National Assembly, Su Nan-cheng, from the party on the grounds that he had violated its policy on the tenure extension, thereby also removing him from his parliamentary seat and the post of Speaker. In March 2000, however, the Council of Grand Justices of the Judicial Yuan ruled the National Assembly's action to be unconstitutional. The DPP and the KMT then reached an agreement on the abolition of the National Assembly and the cancellation of elections scheduled for early May. In April the National Assembly convened, and approved a series of constitutional amendments, which effectively deprived the body of most of its powers, and reduced it to an ad hoc institution. The powers to initiate constitutional amendments, to impeach the President or Vice-President and to approve the appointment of senior officials were transferred to the Legislative Yuan. The National Assembly was to retain the functions of ratifying constitutional amendments and impeachment proceedings, in which case 300 delegates, appointed by political parties according to a system of proportional representation, would convene for a session of a maximum duration of one month.

In November 1999 it was announced that a presidential election was to be held in March 2000. Five candidates registered: Lien Chan (with Vincent Siew as candidate for Vice-President) was the KMT nominee, while Chen Shui-bian, a former mayor of Taipei, was to stand for the DPP (with the feminist Annette Lu as vice-presidential candidate), and Li Ao was to represent the NP; the former DPP Chairman, Hsu Hsin-liang, qualified as an independent candidate, as did James Soong, who, along with a number of his supporters, was consequently expelled from the KMT, his prospects being jeopardized by charges of embezzlement. In January 2000 Lien Chan proposed that the KMT's extensive business holdings be placed in trust and that the party terminate its direct role in the management of the numerous companies in which it owned shares. The KMT adopted the proposal shortly afterwards. In a reflection of the tense political situation between Taiwan and China, Chen Shui-bian of the DPP modified the party's stance and pledged not to declare formal independence for the island unless Chinese forces attacked.

The administration of President Chen

The presidential election of 18 March 2000 was won by Chen Shui-bian, who obtained 39.3% of the votes cast. James Soong, his closest rival, received 36.8% of the votes. Lien Chan of the KMT secured only 23.1% of the votes. The remaining candidates obtained less than 1%. (Upon his inauguration in May, Chen thus became Taiwan's first non-KMT President since 1945.) Violence erupted as disappointed KMT supporters besieged the party's headquarters, attributing the KMT's defeat to the leadership's expulsion of James Soong and the resultant division of the party. Lee Teng-hui subsequently resigned from the chairmanship of the party and was replaced by Lien Chan. However, as the KMT continued to dominate the Legislative Yuan, the party did not entirely relinquish its influence, and in April 2000 it gave permission for Tang Fei, a KMT member and hitherto Minister of National Defense, to serve as Premier, although he was to be suspended from party activities while in the post. Following protracted negotiations, the membership of the new Executive Yuan, which incorporated 11 DPP members and 13 KMT members, was approved in early May. The incoming Government largely lacked ministerial experience. Furthermore, the absence of a legislative majority for the DPP impeded the passage of legislation. In July Frank Hsieh replaced Lin Yi-hsiung as Chairman of the DPP.

In October 2000 Tang Fei resigned as Premier, ostensibly owing to ill health. It was suggested that his departure from the post was due to the Government's failure to agree upon the fate of Taiwan's fourth nuclear power plant, the DPP being opposed to the project. Vice-Premier Chang Chun-hsiung was appointed Premier, and a minor reorganization of the Executive Yuan was effected (including the appointment of Yen Ching-chang as Minister of Finance). In the same month the Minister of Economic Affairs, Lin Hsin-yi, was expelled from the KMT for 'seriously opposing KMT policies and impairing the people's interests' after he had demonstrated his support for the cancellation of the nuclear power project. Chang Chun-hsiung announced that the Executive Yuan had decided to halt construction of the plant for financial reasons. The outraged KMT rejected the Government's right to cancel a project previously approved by the legislature. Together with the NP and the People First Party (PFP—founded by James Soong immediately after the election), the KMT began collecting legislators' signatures for the recall (censure) of Chen Shui-bian. Despite Chen's subsequent apology, the Legislative Yuan approved revised legislation on the process for presidential impeachment. The business community issued an unprecedented public message that economic recovery should take priority over political differences, but in December some 10,000 protesters in Taipei demanded that Chen resign. In November the Government requested a constitutional interpretation of the issue from the Council of Grand Justices, which in January 2001 ruled that the Government should have sought the legislature's approval before terminating the project. The Government therefore

decided to resume construction of the nuclear plant. In March a minor government reorganization included the appointment of Hu Ching-piao, hitherto a Minister without Portfolio, as Chairman of the Atomic Energy Council, replacing Hsia Der-yu.

In July 2001 the KMT issued a radical policy document arguing that Taiwan's best option in terms of its relations with China was to form a 'confederation' with the mainland. However, the KMT's Central Standing Committee refrained from adopting the proposal, reflecting the party's uncertainty over mainland policy. In August the Taiwan Solidarity Union (TSU) was formally established with the support of erstwhile President Lee Teng-hui. Led by the former Minister of the Interior, Huang Chu-wen, and consisting of breakaway members of the KMT and DPP, the party hoped to secure for President Chen a majority in the forthcoming legislative elections. Lee was expelled from the KMT in September.

At the elections held on 1 December 2001 the DPP emerged as the biggest single party in the new legislature, having won 87 of the 225 seats. The KMT secured 68 seats, thereby losing its dominance of the Legislative Yuan for the first time in its history. The PFP came third, winning 46 seats, while the newly formed TSU came fourth, with 13 seats. The NP won only one seat, while independents took nine seats. The level of voter participation was registered as 66.2%.

In January 2002 President Chen reorganized the Executive Yuan, appointing his Secretary-General, Yu Shyi-kun, as Premier. Other notable appointments included Chen Shih-meng, hitherto Deputy Governor of the Central Bank, as the Secretary-General to the President, replacing Yu. Lin Hsin-i, the erstwhile Minister of Economic Affairs, was appointed Vice-Premier and Chairman of the Council for Economic Planning and Development. Eugene Chien was appointed as Minister of Foreign Affairs, and Lee Yung-san became Minister of Finance. The new administration incorporated several members of the KMT, including Gen. Tang Yao-ming, hitherto Chief of the General Staff, who was appointed as Minister of National Defense; Tang was the first native-born Taiwanese to hold the newly augmented defence post in a military dominated by mainlanders.

At elections for provincial city and town councils, held in January 2002, the KMT won the largest number of seats. In February an alliance of the KMT and PFP ('pan-blue' camp) successfully blocked the candidate of the DPP-TSU ('pan-green' camp) for the post of Vice-President of the Legislative Yuan, electing Chiang Ping-kun of the KMT to that position. At the same time, the incumbent President of the legislature, Wang Jin-pyng of the KMT, was re-elected to his post. The KMT-PFP alliance immediately challenged the new Government by attempting to force it to accept revisions to local budget allocations, which had been hastily approved by the outgoing Legislative Yuan, but the alliance failed to secure the majority necessary in the new legislature. However, an early setback for the DPP administration occurred in March 2002 when the Minister of Economic Affairs, Christine Tsung, resigned, citing a hostile political environment. She was replaced by her deputy, Lin Yi-fu.

A major scandal emerged in March 2002 when it was reported that the Government of former President Lee Teng-hui had, in co-operation with the island's intelligence service (National Security Bureau—NSB), clandestinely established an unauthorized fund of US $100m. in order to finance covert operations on the mainland and to further Taiwanese interests among influential lobby groups abroad. It was widely believed that the source of the 'leaks' was a former NSB colonel who had embezzled US $5.5m. and then fled the island.

In April 2002 the Executive Yuan approved plans to abolish the posts of Speaker and Deputy Speaker of the National Assembly, and replace them with that of a chairman of the session. In May the Government revealed proposals to reform the electoral system, which would reduce the number of seats in the Legislative Yuan from 225 to 150 and extend the term of legislators from three to four years. Some 90 seats would be filled from single-seat constituencies (thereby eliminating the need for candidates from the same party to compete against each other, as in the existing multi-seat constituencies), with the remaining seats divided proportionally among parties that received more than 5% of the total vote. Also in May, KMT Chairman Lien Chan announced that his party would form an official alliance with the PFP in order to strengthen opposition to the ruling DPP. In the same month thousands of people demonstrated in favour of changing Taiwan's official name from the 'Republic of China' to 'Taiwan'.

In June 2002 Premier Yu Shyi-kun appointed Liu Shyh-fang as the first female Secretary-General of the Executive Yuan, replacing Lee Ying-yuan, who was standing as the DPP's candidate in elections for the mayoralty of Taipei in December. In July President Chen Shui-bian formally assumed the chairmanship of the DPP. In September the Executive Yuan approved drafts of the new Political Party Law, which would ban political parties from operating or investing in profit-making enterprises, and allow the Government to investigate and confiscate assets unlawfully obtained by political parties. Although ostensibly aimed at creating greater political fairness and financial openness, the draft legislation was viewed as being directed at the KMT; during its decades of rule, the KMT had amassed a vast commercial fortune, estimated at NT $53,750m. by 2001. As a result, the party would be obliged to sell many of its assets.

A new political dispute emerged in late September 2002 over planned reforms of the debt-ridden agricultural and fishermen's credit co-operatives. The Government sought to reduce the activities of these local financial bodies, which had traditionally been used as a source of funds and influence for local KMT politicians. However, opposition to the reforms was so intense that by late November President Chen was forced to suspend the plans. At the same time, more than 120,000 farmers and fishermen marched through Taipei to protest against the reforms, in what was the largest demonstration on the island since Chen took office. Premier Yu Shyi-kun offered to resign, but was retained by Chen, who instead accepted the resignations of the Minister of Finance, Lee Yung-san, and the Chairman of the Council of Agriculture, Fan Chen-tsung. They were replaced by Lin Chuan and Lee Chin-lung, respectively. The departure of the respected Lee Yung-san, and the appointment of the third finance minister in as many years, raised concerns about political stability.

Elections for the mayoralties of Taipei and Kaohsiung took place in December 2002. In Taipei the incumbent mayor, Ma Ying-jeou of the KMT, defeated his DPP rival, Lee Ying-yuan, winning 64.1% of the votes cast. He thus immediately emerged as a potential presidential candidate. Ma's popularity complicated efforts by the KMT and PFP to select one of their respective party chairmen, Lien Chan or James Soong, as the joint presidential candidate of the 'pan-blue' camp. In Kaohsiung the incumbent mayor, Frank Hsieh of the DPP, narrowly defeated his KMT rival, Huang Chun-ying, by 50.0% to 46.8% of the votes cast.

In February 2003 President Chen appointed Chiou I-jen, hitherto Secretary-General of the National Security Council, as Secretary-General to the President, while Kang Ning-hsiang, the erstwhile Vice-Minister of National Defense, succeeded Chiou in his former position. Following criticism of his handling of the outbreak of Severe Acute Respiratory Syndrome (SARS), the Minister of Health, Twu Shiing-jer, resigned in May 2003. By June the virus had killed more than 80 people on the island.

The issue of Taiwan's very identity came to the fore once again in September 2003, when as many as 150,000 independence activists, led by former President Lee Teng-hui, rallied in Taipei to demand that the island's name be formally changed from the 'Republic of China' to 'Taiwan'. The continued use of the former had remained the source of much international confusion, and it was believed that the adoption of 'Taiwan' would facilitate wider diplomatic recognition. A rival rally, attended mainly by veterans of the civil war and their descendants (who continued to favour eventual reunification with the mainland), attracted several thousand supporters. Also in September, President Chen proposed the drafting of a new constitution for Taiwan.

In November 2003 Taiwan's legislature approved a new law to allow referendums to be held on the island, prompting strong criticism from China (see Cross-Strait Relations). The approval of the legislation followed President Chen's formal declaration of his intention to stand for re-election in the 2004 presidential election. In December 2003 President Chen announced plans to hold a referendum on the issue of China's deployment of missiles against Taiwan, to coincide with the forthcoming presidential poll. Also in December, President Chen confirmed that Vice-President Annette Lu, a vocal supporter of Taiwanese independence, would also stand for re-election. Opposition presidential candidate Lien Chan and vice-presidential candidate James Soong, of the KMT and of the allied PFP, respectively, as well as the popular mayor of Taipei, Ma Ying-jeou of the KMT, expressed strong opposition to the proposed referendum. In February 2004 demonstrations involving more than 70,000 people took place in southern Taiwan in support of the referendum. At the end of February, in Taiwan's largest ever demonstration, an estimated 1.5m. people formed a 500-km 'human chain', linking hands across the island to protest against China's deployment of missiles. Meanwhile, the wording of the referendum question had been modified to ask voters whether, in the event of China's refusal to withdraw its missiles, they would favour a strengthening of Taiwan's defence system.

President Chen's re-election and subsequent events

In a dramatic development on the day prior to the presidential election, both President Chen and Vice-President Lu were injured in a shooting incident while campaigning in Tainan. (The alleged assailant, Chen Yi-hsiung, was an unemployed man who was reported to have committed suicide shortly afterwards; however, doubts with regard to these events were subsequently raised—see below). Neither Chen nor Lu was seriously hurt in the apparent assassination attempt, and the poll proceeded as planned on 20 March 2004. President Chen was re-elected by a narrow margin of 29,518 votes, equivalent to only 0.2% of valid votes, with 337,297 ballot papers being declared invalid. A turnout of 80.3% of the electorate was recorded. However, in the concurrent referendum on the issue of Taiwan's response to the deployment of mainland missiles, the majority of citizens declined to vote on President Chen's proposals, indicating widespread division within Taiwan on the issue of the island's relationship with China. President Chen's re-election was immediately challenged by opposition candidate Lien Chan, who claimed that there had been electoral irregularities and demanded a recount of the votes. Supporters of Lien rioted in Taipei and other cities.

In April 2004 the Minister of the Interior, Yu Cheng-hsien, resigned, citing the failure to prevent the shooting of President Chen as the reason for his departure. In the same month the Minister of Foreign Affairs, Eugene Chien, stood down from his post in connection with the departure of the head of the American Institute in Taiwan (see Foreign Affairs). A recount of votes cast in the presidential election was completed on 19 May. It was estimated that 38,000 ballots were controversial, and that, of these, 23,000 were votes for Chen. Nevertheless, President Chen was inaugurated for a second term on 20 May, and on the same day he announced appointments to the new Executive Yuan, including the retention of Yu Shyi-kun as Premier. In July remarks by Vice-President Annette Lu suggesting a resettlement of Taiwan's aboriginal communities to South America caused widespread offence among the island's indigenous population. In the same month a new political party, the pro-independence Formosa Party, was inaugurated. In August the Legislative Yuan approved a bill on constitutional changes, including plans for a reduction in the number of legislators and for reform of the electoral system. Also in August, there was controversy surrounding the establishment of an independent committee to investigate the shooting of President Chen, with the President of the Judicial Yuan claiming that the investigatory powers being given to this body were unconstitutional. In September protests took place in Taipei against the special budget of NT $610,800m. for the purchase of US weapons, which had been approved by the Executive Yuan in June.

In the elections for the Legislative Yuan in December 2004 the 'pan-green' alliance of the DPP and the TSU secured 101 seats, whereas the 'pan-blue' alliance, comprising the KMT, the PFP and the NP, won 114 seats. The resulting opposition majority in the legislature was expected to hinder President Chen's plans for constitutional changes. Chen resigned as DPP Chairman after the elections, taking responsibility for the party's failure to secure a larger number of seats. Meanwhile, disputes over the legitimacy of President Chen's victory in March continued, with a High Court rejecting two opposition attempts, in November and December respectively, to nullify the presidential election result.

In January 2005 the Executive Yuan approved a draft amendment to the 2003 referendum law (see above), requiring any changes to Taiwan's boundaries to be approved by the population. Later in January Premier Yu Shyi-kun and all members of the Executive Yuan resigned prior to the first meeting of the new Legislative Yuan. President Chen subsequently appointed Frank Hsieh, mayor of Kaohsiung and a leading member of the DPP, as Premier. Most outgoing ministers were reappointed to their former posts. Also in January, Secretary-General Su Tseng-chang was appointed Chairman of the DPP, replacing Chen; former Premier Yu Shyi-kun was subsequently appointed Secretary-General in his place. In February Premier Hsieh appointed Wu Rong-i as Vice-Premier and Minister of the Consumer Protection Commission.

In March 2005 a large rally, attended by President Chen, took place in Taipei in protest against the approval of anti-secession legislation by China's National People's Congress (NPC). On 14 May elections were held for an ad hoc National Assembly, which was to convene in order to ratify or reject the constitutional amendments approved by the Legislative Yuan in August 2004. The DPP secured 127 of the Assembly's 300 seats, while the KMT won 117 seats. When the Assembly came to vote in June 2005, 248 members were in favour of the amendments, 23 more than the two-thirds' majority required for ratification. The amendments to the Constitution were thus passed into law. They included a reduction in the number of seats in the Legislative Yuan (from 225 to 113), reforms to the electoral system, the transfer of the power to impeach the President and Vice-President from the National Assembly to the Judicial Yuan, and the ratification of all future constitutional amendment proposals by popular referendum (requiring the approval of 50% of eligible voters, following endorsement by 75% of the Legislative Yuan). These reforms were due to come into effect before the next legislative elections, scheduled for 2007. Meanwhile, in June and again in September 2005 the Supreme Court rejected the appeals of the 'pan-blue' alliance to have the results of the presidential election declared invalid. In July Ma Ying-jeou, the mayor of Taipei, was chosen as Chairman of the KMT, in the party's first leadership election, defeating Wang Jin-pyng, President of the Legislative Yuan. In August the Supreme Prosecutor's Office announced that it was closing its investigation into the shooting of President Chen and Vice-President Lu in the previous year.

The mid-term elections for city mayors and county magistrates held in December 2005 resulted in significant gains for the KMT, which took 14 of the 23 contested constituencies, while the DPP won in only six. The KMT also outperformed the DPP in elections for county councillors, township governors and magistrates. Su Tseng-chang resigned from the post of Chairman of the DPP, and Yu Shyi-kun, the former Premier and latterly Secretary-General to the President, was subsequently elected as his replacement.

In January 2006 Frank Hsieh resigned as Premier, citing the failure of the legislature to approve his proposed budget for that year as the main reason for his departure, while also hinting at policy disagreements with President Chen; in his farewell speech Hsieh warned Chen that the policy of a separate sovereign identity for Taiwan was not supported by the majority of the population. The DPP's recent poor electoral performance was also regarded by some as a contributory factor in his resignation, as was a scandal over allegations of corruption and exploitation surrounding the construction of the metro system in the city of Kaohsiung, where hundreds of Thai construction workers had reportedly rioted in August 2005 in protest against their poor living and working conditions. President Chen appointed Su Tseng-chang to replace Hsieh; the new appointee thereby became Chen's fifth Premier since the President's accession to power in 2000. The new Executive Yuan was sworn in on 25 January 2006. Among 14 new appointments, Tsai Ing-wen became Vice-Premier and Minister of the Consumer Protection Commission, Lee Yi-yang was appointed Minister of the Interior, Huang Chih-fang was the new Minister of Foreign Affairs, and Joseph J. C. Lyu took the post of Minister of Finance.

President Chen's reiteration in January 2006 of his commitment to the ratification by referendum of a new constitution by 2008, his proposed abolition of the NUC and his declaration that he intended to reapply for membership of the UN under the name of 'Taiwan' (see above) drew strong criticism from the opposition. Joseph Wu, Minister of the Mainland Affairs Council, noted that the NUC had not in fact convened since 1999 and was so poorly funded as to be effectively useless. In February 2006 the DPP administration announced its intention to change Taiwan's official name, its flag, its national anthem and the definition of its territory. In April the special defence budget proposed in June 2004 was opposed for the 50th time by the 'pan-blue' alliance in the Legislative Yuan.

In May 2006 President Chen's authority was greatly undermined by the detention of his son-in-law, Chao Chien-ming, on charges of insider dealing involving the purchase in 2005 of shares in the Taiwan Development Corporation. Chao relinquished his membership of the DPP in an attempt to protect the party's image. (Subsequently indicted, along with his father and three others, Chao was sentenced to six years' imprisonment in December.) Although Chen had apologized to the nation for his family's involvement in the affair, the PFP instigated a campaign to remove the President from office.

Also in May 2006, former DPP legislator Shen Fu-hsiung confirmed an allegation that in the 1990s, during his campaign for the mayoralty of Taipei, President Chen had received no fewer than six political donations from the fugitive tycoon Chen You-hao. (Chen You-hao, the former head of the Tuntex group, had fled Taiwan in 2002 when the conglomerate was in financial difficulties; he was subsequently accused of embezzling funds from the group.) Shen also claimed that he had accompanied Chen You-hao on a visit to the President's wife, Wu Shu-jen (also a former legislator), to whom the tycoon had given nearly US $200,000, an accusation that Wu had previously denied. Two days later the 'pan-blue' alliance submitted a recall motion to the legislature, in the hope of removing President Chen.

On 1 June 2006, under intense political pressure, President Chen ceded much of his authority to Premier Su Tseng-chang. Henceforth the President would no longer have the power to dictate policy or to appoint members of the Executive Yuan, but would remain in charge of foreign and defence policy and would oversee relations with the People's Republic. The President also announced that he would play no further active role within the DPP. However, opposition politicians continued to demand Chen's resignation and protest rallies were held in an effort to increase pressure on the President to stand down. In a live televised speech Chen defended his administration and denied the allegations that had been made against his family. The motion of recall was voted upon in late June: despite gaining some support from the KMT (90 votes, including that of Wang Jin-pyng, the President of the Legislative Yuan, who was supposed to remain neutral), the 'pan-blue' alliance received just 119 votes, thus falling short of the number of votes (two-thirds of currently occupied seats) required to submit the motion to a national referendum.

At the end of June 2006 it was announced that Ho Chih-chin, an academic, would succeed Joseph J. C. Lyu as Minister of Finance. Lyu, who had come under criticism for his handling of negotiations over the management of Mega Financial Holding (a major provider of financial services), retained a position within the Executive Yuan, as Minister without Portfolio. In early July party factions within the DPP unanimously approved the candidacy of former Premier Frank Hsieh in the forthcoming Taipei mayoral election.

The increasing unpopularity of President Chen

Controversy surrounding President Chen continued. In July 2006 prosecutors questioned Wu Shu-jen in relation to allegations that the President's wife and her doctor, Huang Fang-yen, had acted on behalf of businessmen who wished to acquire the Sogo department store, and that in return Wu had accepted gift vouchers worth about US $185,000. Other allegations claimed that forged receipts to the value of around US $600,000 had been submitted for reimbursement under the special allowances budget of the Office of the President, and that taxpayers' money had been improperly used by the President to pay the wages of a housekeeper. DPP legislators in turn accused KMT Chairman Ma Ying-jeou of remitting a proportion of his official allowance as mayor of Taipei into his personal account for private use, and reported their suspicions to the National Audit Office. Meanwhile, Premier Su Tseng-chang appeared to be consolidating his position within the DPP after the Conference on Sustaining Taiwan's Economic Development, held in late July 2006, during which he gained the support of local business groups and trade unions. At the DPP convention, also held in July, the party voted by a small majority to dissolve its factions in an attempt to promote unity.

In August 2006 the Executive Yuan underwent a further reorganization when the Minister of Economic Affairs, Hwang In-san, who had resigned on the grounds of ill health, was replaced by his deputy, Chen Ruey-long. Also in August, the Minister of Transportation and Communications, Kuo Yao-chi, proffered her resignation, in order to take responsibility for a scandal that had arisen from the controversial awarding of a contract for an electronic motorway toll collection system. She was replaced by Tsai Duei. Prosecutors began to question President Chen over the alleged misuse of public funds. Meanwhile, the President continued to antagonize the KMT (and mainland China) by reiterating that he intended to draft a new constitution and that Taiwan should apply to join the UN as an observer under the name of 'Taiwan'. In early August the PFP announced that it would begin an attempt to impeach Chen. Shih Ming-teh, a former DPP chairman, subsequently announced the formation of a 'one million people' mass movement to remove the President from office. Within days Shih's campaign had attracted more than 1m. supporters, each of whom donated NT $100 to demonstrate their commitment to the cause. Shih vowed that he and his supporters would stage a round-the-clock protest outside the presidential office in the following month and that they would not disperse until the President resigned. Neither the KMT nor the PFP was prepared officially to participate in the campaign, instead encouraging party members to attend the rallies.

In September 2006 at least 100,000 demonstrators took to the streets of Taipei, wearing red to signify their anger at Chen's alleged corruption. The PFP again attempted to initiate a recall motion against the President, and in late September the Legislative Yuan voted by 106 to 82 to refer the motion for review by a parliamentary committee prior to a full debate in the Legislative Yuan in October. By mid-October the momentum against the President had increased, with demonstrations and violent skirmishes disrupting the official National Day celebrations. None the less, the next recall motion against Chen again failed when the opposition secured only 116 votes, still short of the requisite two-thirds' majority. Later in October the opposition once more blocked a controversial arms bill involving multi-million dollar weapons purchases from the USA.

In early November 2006 prosecutors declared that they had sufficient evidence to charge Chen with misuse of public funds and that they were prevented from doing so only by his presidential immunity. However, no such immunity protected his wife, Wu Shu-jen, who was indicted along with three former presidential aides on charges of forgery and corruption. According to the prosecutors, Wu and the three senior aides had misappropriated NT $14.8m. from the 'state affairs fund'. While the prosecutors accepted Chen's explanation that in two of the six cases being investigated the funds had been used for covert diplomatic missions, they concluded that the use of such assets in four other cases could not be verified. Opposition members immediately demanded Chen's resignation and urged the DPP to join them in approving a motion of recall against the President, who attributed the apparent irregularities in the use of the state affairs fund to poorly defined regulations. Meanwhile, thousands of protesters once more took to the streets of Taipei, again demanding the President's resignation. The demonstration was not officially supported by the PFP and the KMT; the latter warned that the President could be impeached only by formal legal proceedings. The opposition then initiated a third recall motion against the President. Furthermore, disagreements began to emerge within the ranks of the DPP, when two members resigned from the Legislative Yuan in order to demonstrate dissatisfaction with their party's handling of the scandal.

When the crucial recall vote was held in late November 2006, the DPP again rallied to support its leader, boycotting the vote and thus preventing the motion from obtaining the requisite two-thirds' majority. Moreover, at mayoral elections held in Taipei and Kaohsiung in December the DPP performed better than anticipated. Although the DPP candidate in Taipei, Frank Hsieh, lost to his KMT rival, Hau Long-bin, Hsieh nevertheless garnered 40.9% of the votes, an increase of 5.0% in comparison with the mayoral election of 2002. In Kaohsiung the DPP candidate, Chen Chu, won by a narrow margin to become the island's first female mayor.

Party differences were temporarily, and somewhat unexpectedly, put aside in late December 2006 when the KMT voted with the Government to place the long-delayed arms procurement bill (see above) on the legislative agenda. The proposed legislation, which the KMT had previously boycotted along with the PFP, would provide for the purchase of US weapons from the annual budget of the Ministry of National Defense, rather than from a special budget (as previously planned). The bill was finally approved by the Legislative Yuan in June 2007.

In January 2007 the KMT and PFP formalized a party alliance, undertaking to present a single candidate in each district in the forthcoming legislative elections. In March Lee Jye, the Minister of National Defense, was expelled from the KMT as a result of a dispute regarding a government order to remove statues of Chiang Kai-shek from military premises, a decision with which Lee had complied. Ma Ying-jeou had resigned from the chairmanship of the KMT in February following the filing of a lawsuit by DPP legislators accusing him of forgery and of the embezzlement of NT $11.2m. during his tenure of the mayoralty of Taipei. Ma denied the allegations and reiterated his intention to stand as a presidential candidate in 2008. Although he was replaced as KMT Chairman in April by Wu Poh-hsiung, in May the party confirmed Ma's candidacy for the presidency of Taiwan,

and in August 2007 he was acquitted of all charges. Meanwhile, in May 2007, following his defeat by former Premier Frank Hsieh in the contest for the nomination of the DPP presidential candidate, Su Tseng-chang resigned as Premier. President Chen appointed Chang Chun-hsiung, who had served as Premier in 2000–02, to replace Su. Premier Chang Chun-hsiung subsequently effected a government reorganization, although many of the incumbent members of the Executive Yuan were retained; notable exceptions included Tsai Ing-wen, who was succeeded by Chiou I-jen as Vice-Premier and Minister of the Consumer Protection Commission, and Lee Jye, who was replaced by Lee Tien-yu in the position of Minister of National Defense.

In September 2007 several prominent members of the DPP, including Chairman Yu Shyi-kun, Vice-President Annette Lu and former Minister of Foreign Affairs (Mark) Chen Tan-sun, were indicted on charges of corruption and forgery. Yu Shyi-kun, who resigned from the DPP chairmanship with immediate effect, was charged with the misuse of funds, which he claimed had been spent on public, rather than private, affairs. Meanwhile, similar charges against the DPP's presidential candidate, Frank Hsieh, and his vice-presidential candidate, Su Tseng-chang, were abandoned. President Chen reassumed the position of DPP Chairman in October. In September the DPP had adopted a resolution affirming Taiwan's separate identity and appealing for a new constitution and a referendum on the issue of sovereignty; the name of Taiwan, it was stated, should enter into common usage without necessarily abolishing the official designation of the 'Republic of China'. The DPP continued its campaign against the commemoration of Chiang Kai-shek, cancelling two public holidays honouring the former President in August, and removing Chiang's name from a memorial hall in Taipei in December.

The return to power of the KMT

Legislative elections held on 12 January 2008 resulted in a resounding victory for the KMT, which secured 81 seats (out of a reduced total of 113 seats in accordance with the constitutional amendments of 2005); the DPP, with only 27 seats, was thus defeated by a considerable margin. The Non-Partisan Solidarity Union (NPSU) won three seats and the KMT's alliance partner, the PFP, only one. Turn-out was extremely low in comparison with previous elections, at approximately 58%. Wang Jin-pyng was subsequently re-elected President of the Legislative Yuan. Voters were also presented with two proposals at referendums, both of which were rejected: the first proposed measure was the seizure of state assets allegedly appropriated by the KMT during and after its assumption of power in 1945; the second, submitted by the KMT, entailed additional anti-corruption measures. The election results were widely regarded as an indication of public opposition to the DPP's forceful stance on sovereignty and Taiwan's status, as well as of the fear of jeopardizing relations with the mainland and of alienating the island's strategic allies. Following the DPP's defeat, Chen resigned as the party's Chairman and was replaced by Frank Hsieh. Premier Chang Chunhsiung and the other members of the Executive Yuan submitted their resignations, but President Chen refused to accept these, citing a need for stability. In February, however, the Premier accepted the resignation of Lee Tien-yu from the post of Minister of National Defense, owing to criticism of the latter's role in the establishment of a weapons company. In March the Minister of Finance, Ho Chih-chin, resigned, following his involvement in a scuffle at the offices of the DPP's presidential candidate, Frank Hsieh. Meanwhile, the election pledges of presidential candidate Ma Ying-jeou included an undertaking to pursue neither unification nor independence.

On 22 March 2008 Ma Ying-jeou of the KMT was elected the island's President, having received almost 58.5% of the votes cast, thus defeating Frank Hsieh, who subsequently announced that he would resign as Chairman of the DPP. At 76.3%, the level of participation by voters in the presidential election was high. However, the results of two concurrent referendums on the issue of the island's application for membership of the UN were declared invalid: although the number of votes in favour of each proposal exceeded 50% of the ballots cast, the total number of votes exercised failed to reach the requisite threshold of 50% of the registered electorate. The first proposal, which sought approval for the island's application under the name of Taiwan, was supported by the DPP; the KMT urged that this referendum be boycotted. The second referendum, initiated by the KMT, asked voters if they supported an application to return to the UN as 'the Republic of China' or alternatively as Taiwan or under any other suitable designation. Liu Chao-shiuan, a former Vice-Premier and hitherto President of Soochow University, was subsequently nominated as the island's Premier by the President-elect. In early May, just weeks before the swearing-in of the new Government, Vice-Premier Chiou I-jen and Minister of Foreign Affairs Huang Chih-fang submitted their resignations as a result of a funding controversy: it was alleged that an attempt in 2006 to persuade Papua New Guinea to transfer diplomatic recognition from China to Taiwan, using almost US $30m. in aid, had failed, and that one of the intermediaries had absconded with the money. As the scandal widened, President Chen denied his involvement in the affair; however, he and several others were subsequently prosecuted and brought to trial (see below). It was feared that the scandal had damaged Taiwan's reputation by drawing international attention to the practice of so-called 'chequebook diplomacy'.

Ma Ying-jeou was sworn in as President on 20 May 2008. Significant appointments to the Executive Yuan, led by incoming Premier Liu Chao-shiuan and incorporating many who had served as ministers in the previous KMT administration, included that of Li Sush-der as Minister of Finance and Francisco H. L. Ou as Minister of Foreign Affairs. The new cabinet also included a record 11 women, notably Wang Ching-feng as Minister of Justice. Almost immediately, his presidential immunity having been removed upon his departure from office, it emerged that a corruption inquiry involving former President Chen had been instigated; in August, amid further allegations of financial impropriety, Chen left the DPP. Meanwhile, in May Tsai Ing-wen, a former Vice-Premier, was elected Chairwoman of the DPP, replacing Frank Hsieh.

In the latter part of 2008, as the island's economy began to weaken, large anti-Government protests were held. In October an estimated 600,000 Taiwanese attended a rally in Taipei, organized by the opposition DPP, to protest against the President's handling of the economy and his policy of wider engagement with mainland China. The visit of a senior mainland official, Chen Yunlin (see Cross-Strait Relations), in November provoked violent clashes in Taipei.

During 2008 public concern about the issue of corruption continued. Former Vice-Premier Chiou I-jen was arrested on charges of embezzlement in October; the senior DPP member was accused of having misappropriated diplomatic funds totalling US $500,000 in 2004. Former President Chen Shui-bian was formally indicted in December 2008 on charges of forgery, corruption, embezzlement and money-laundering. Chen's wife, son, daughter-in-law and 10 former colleagues were indicted on similar charges. In February 2009 Wu Shu-jen, the former President's wife, pleaded guilty to charges of money-laundering and forgery, but she continued to deny charges of embezzlement. Her son, Chen Chih-chung, and other defendants also pleaded guilty to money-laundering charges. The trial of former President Chen, who had been an outspoken critic of the KMT Government, opened in March 2009, amid suggestions that it was politically motivated and related to his support for the independence of Taiwan. In September Chen was sentenced to life imprisonment upon his conviction by the Taipei District Court on various charges of corruption related to his misuse between 2000 and 2008 of public funds totalling the equivalent of US $15m. The former President's wife, who earlier in September had been found guilty of perjury, also received a life sentence. In addition, Chen Chih-chung and the former President's daughter-in-law were found guilty of money-laundering. Later in September prosecutors issued a series of new indictments against the former President and four others, including former Vice-Premier Chiou I-jen, alleging that funds allocated to the advancement of diplomatic relations had been embezzled, but in June 2010 Chen was acquitted on the charge of misappropriating diplomatic funds. However, the pursuit of various other charges against the former President, which included the abetting of his subordinates to give false testimony, continued (see below).

Following the publication in November 2009 of the findings of a new investigation into the apparent attempt to assassinate Chen in 2004, fresh suspicions about the pre-election incident were raised. The KMT, which had ordered the new inquiry following its return to office, continued to maintain that the former President had fabricated the incident in order to attract the sympathy of voters.

In May 2009, meanwhile, as the first anniversary of President Ma Ying-jeou's assumption of office approached, thousands of protesters again demonstrated on the streets of Taipei and elsewhere against the Government's policy of greater engagement with the mainland. Tsai Ing-wen, Chairwoman of the opposition DPP, claimed that Taiwanese sovereignty was being

seriously compromised and stated that the DPP would seek the holding of a referendum on the issue of Ma's plans for a free trade agreement with China.

In August 2009 Taiwan was devastated by Typhoon Morakot. More than 600 people were killed in the resultant mudslides and flooding. The Government was subsequently criticized for the perceived shortcomings in its response to the disaster. On 7 September Premier Liu Chao-shiuan unexpectedly announced that President Ma Ying-jeou had accepted his resignation, submitted in mid-August in order to take responsibility for the failings in the Government's handling of the aftermath of the typhoon. Liu was replaced by Wu Den-yih, hitherto the Secretary-General of the ruling KMT. Chu Li-luan was appointed as Vice-Premier. In a major reorganization of the Executive Yuan, veteran diplomat Timothy Yang replaced Francisco Ou as Minister of Foreign Affairs. Other appointments included that of Jiang Yi-huah as Minister of the Interior and Kao Hua-chu as Minister of National Defense.

In July 2009 President Ma Ying-jeou was elected unopposed by party members as Chairman of the KMT, to replace Wu Poh-hsiung in October. As Chairman of the ruling party, therefore, Ma would be in a position to exercise greater control over the legislature, particularly with regard to the approval of appointments. On a party-to-party basis, Ma would also be able to exert more influence over Taiwan's relations with mainland China.

At local elections held in December 2009 the DPP won a much larger percentage of votes than that secured at previous local polls. A significant factor in the decline in support for the KMT was thought to be President Ma's focus on closer relations with mainland China, which many believed would ultimately jeopardize the island's sovereignty and lead to job losses. Shortly after the polls, King Pu-tsung replaced Chan Chun-po as Secretary-General of the KMT. Furthermore, having returned to the post only eight months previously, Wu Nai-jen resigned as Secretary-General of the DPP on the grounds of ill health; he was replaced by Su Jia-chyuan. Amid increasing fears about Taiwan's growing economic dependency on China, later in December an estimated 30,000 Taiwanese joined a march through the city of Taichung to protest against another visit by the senior mainland official Chen Yunlin to attend negotiations on a bilateral trade agreement. The KMT suffered further reverses at by-elections in early 2010, when it lost six of seven seats contested to the DPP. Although the latter's representation in the Legislative Yuan was increased to 33 seats, the KMT nevertheless retained a large majority. In June the KMT fared better than the DPP at local elections in 17 counties and cities.

Wang Ching-feng, the Minister of Justice, unexpectedly resigned in March 2010, owing to her opposition to the removal of the five-year moratorium on the implementation of the death penalty. A former human rights activist, Wang had refused to approve the enforcement of the penalty on 44 prisoners who awaited execution, her stance being at variance with that of the Government. She was replaced by Tseng Yung-fu. Other new appointments to the Executive Yuan included that of Emile Chi-jen Sheng, who assumed the post of Minister of the Council for Cultural Affairs.

There were violent scenes in the Legislative Yuan in April 2010, when opponents clashed during a debate on the issue of the opening of Taiwanese institutes of higher education to students from mainland China. In May, in order to pursue his election campaign for a mayoralty, Vice-Premier Eric Chu resigned from the Executive Yuan. He was replaced by Sean Chen, hitherto the Chairman of the Financial Supervisory Commission, who also assumed his predecessor's responsibility for the Consumer Protection Commission. Chen Yu-chang was appointed to chair the Financial Supervisory Commission, and Christina Liu became Minister of the Council for Economic Planning and Development, succeeding Tsai Hsun-hsiung.

In late June 2010 tens of thousands of demonstrators, including former President Lee Teng-hui, rallied in Taipei to protest against the Government's proposals for a new trade agreement with China. The opposition DPP and TSU maintained that the proposed Economic Co-operation Framework Agreement (ECFA) would not only jeopardize Taiwanese manufacturing industries, by permitting a substantial increase in imports of inexpensive products from the mainland, but also undermine the island's separate political identity; however, the parties' demands for the holding of a referendum on the issue of the ECFA were repeatedly rejected. In the following month several members of the Legislative Yuan were injured and the Premier was prevented from delivering his speech when the opposition disrupted the introduction of the law into the chamber. The President of the Legislative Yuan then ruled that the bill should proceed directly to its second reading, thereby circumventing the committee stage. In response to this omission of the process of detailed examination, the DPP declared that it would boycott forthcoming parliamentary proceedings.

Further corruption scandals

In July 2010 the President of the Judicial Yuan, Lai In-jaw, and the body's Vice-President resigned in response to the arrest of three high court judges and one prosecutor in connection with a new corruption scandal. It was alleged that the senior judges had collectively accepted bribes, totalling as much as NT $1m., in exchange for the acquittal of a former KMT legislator and county magistrate on charges of financial impropriety related to the development of a science park. In the same month, responding to public concern about the involvement of senior functionaries in such cases, President Ma announced the establishment of a new agency to combat official corruption. The agency, which was to form part of the Ministry of Justice, was to comprise four departments, one of which was to be responsible for government ethics. A human rights commission, headed by Vice-President Vincent Siew, was established in December. In September, meanwhile, eight incumbent and former members of the Legislative Yuan received prison sentences of between seven and 10 years, following their conviction on charges of bribery. Six of the defendants had been acquitted in a previous trial. In the following month the new President of the Judicial Yuan, Rai Hau-min, expressed his determination to eradicate corruption. In November a total of 13 officials were indicted in connection with the judicial corruption case. In January 2011 the Commander of the Air Force, Gen. Lei Yu-chi, was removed from his post, following the revelation that he had enlisted air force personnel to serve at lavish celebrations for the wedding of his son. Lei was replaced by Gen. Yen Ming. In March impeachment proceedings began against the three high court judges and the prosecutor arrested on charges of bribery.

Former President Chen's appeal against his conviction was rejected by the High Court in June 2010. However, on the basis that the sum involved was less than previously stated, his sentence was reduced from life imprisonment to 20 years, as was that of his wife. In November, in the Taipei District Court, Chen was acquitted of bribery charges relating to the approval of bank mergers and to money-laundering activities. Wu Shu-jen and other family members, along with several others, were also acquitted on related charges. In the same month, however, the Supreme Court upheld Chen's conviction in connection with two other bribery cases. In December the High Court ruled that the former President serve a maximum combined sentence of 17 years and six months. In February 2011, having recently received an additional sentence upon her conviction of further charges of bribery, the frail Wu Shu-jen was deemed unfit to remain in prison and released from detention. In October the High Court reversed the Taipei District Court's decision to acquit Chen in the previous November, and sentenced him to a further 18 years' imprisonment, while Wu received a further 11-year sentence. Also in October 2011 a hearing began in the Taipei District Court concerning illegal transactions allegedly conducted by former President Lee Teng-hui while in office.

In the mayoral elections of November 2010, regarded as a major test for President Ma, the KMT won three important mayoralties, including that of Taipei, while the opposition DPP took the southern cities of Kaohsiung and Tainan. The KMT was also successful in elections for local speaker and vice-speaker posts in December, when the DPP won only that of Tainan. Also in December, having been persuaded to return to the position in May, Wu Nai-jen confirmed his retirement as Secretary-General of the DPP. Su Jia-chyuan agreed to resume the post. The DPP was encouraged by its resounding success at by-elections to fill two vacant seats in the Legislative Yuan, held in Kaohsiung and Tainan in March 2011.

Recent developments: the 2012 elections

In January 2011 King Pu-tsung resigned as Secretary-General of the KMT, in order to lead President Ma Ying-jeou's campaign for re-election in 2012; King was replaced by Liao Liao-yi. At the beginning of February a minor reorganization of the Executive Yuan included the appointment of Chiu Wen-ta as Minister of the Department of Health, in place of Yaung Chi-liang who had resigned in early January. At the end of April President Ma was nominated unopposed as the KMT's candidate for the presidential election to be held in January 2012, and in June 2011 he

announced that he had selected the Premier, Wu Den-yih, as his candidate for the vice-presidency (Wu was to retain the post of Premier in the interim). Meanwhile, in April Tsai Ing-wen became Taiwan's first female presidential candidate when she defeated former Premier Su Tseng-chang to secure the nomination of the DPP. After the unsuccessful Su declined an offer of candidacy for the island's vice-presidency, in September Tsai selected Su Jia-chyuan, the DPP's Secretary-General, as her electoral partner. Also in September James Soong, the Chairman of the PFP, announced his candidacy for the presidential election: it was speculated that, as when he unsuccessfully contested the presidential election in March 2000, Soong might attract votes that would otherwise have gone to the KMT and thus bring about that party's defeat. Meanwhile, the establishment of the Taiwanese National Party (TNP) was announced in July 2011, with the aim of promoting Taiwanese identity. The objectives of the TNP included the holding of a referendum on the issue of self-determination for Taiwan. Huang Hua, erstwhile adviser to former President Chen, was appointed Chairman of the new party, which endorsed the candidacy of the DPP's Tsai Ing-wen in the contest for the Taiwanese presidency.

The latter part of 2011 was dominated by the forthcoming legislative and presidential elections. (In a departure from tradition, the two elections were to be held simultaneously, on 14 January 2012.) Ma was supported by major business interests, but his popularity was perceived as having declined as a result of the difficulties affecting Taiwan's economy (which was technically in recession in the second half of 2011, although this was largely due to external factors). Ma's policy of economic engagement with China had greatly improved relations with the mainland, but had aroused suspicions among some Taiwanese that Ma favoured reunification with the People's Republic, especially after he declared, in October 2011, that a formal peace agreement between the two sides could be signed within 10 years (subject to approval in Taiwan by referendum). In November the Minister for the Council of Cultural Affairs, Emile Sheng, resigned in response to accusations of extravagance in the celebrations staged in October for the centenary of the overthrow of the imperial dynasty. The DPP presidential candidate, Tsai, campaigned to win the support of agricultural and urban workers, affected by rising prices and unemployment, but her opponents claimed that the DPP's advocacy of Taiwanese independence would endanger the country's economic and political stability. In the event, Ma was successful in the presidential election, winning a second term of office with 51.6% of the votes cast; Tsai secured 45.6% and Soong 2.8%. In the concurrent legislative elections, the KMT won 64 of the 113 seats in the Legislative Yuan, while the DPP took 40 seats; of the other parties in the KMT's 'pan-blue' coalition, the PFP won three seats and the NPSU two, while in the 'pan-green' coalition the DPP's ally, the TSU, won three. Voter participation was reportedly over 74%. Tsai immediately announced her resignation from the chair of the DPP: her successor, former Premier Su Tseng-chang, was elected in late May 2012.

At the beginning of February 2012, meanwhile, the appointment of a new Executive Yuan was announced. Sean Chen, the former Vice-Premier, was appointed Premier (to succeed the newly elected Vice-President, Wu Den-yih), and about one-third of the 47 cabinet posts were reallocated: new appointments included that of Jiang Yi-huah (hitherto Minister of the Interior) as Vice-Premier and Minister of Justice, Lee Hong-yuan (hitherto Minister of the Public Construction Commission) as Minister of the Interior, and Christina Liu (hitherto Minister of the Council for Economic Planning and Development) as Minister of Finance. Also in early February Lin Join-sane (hitherto Secretary-General of the Executive Yuan) replaced Liao Liao-yi as KMT Secretary-General. President Ma declared that the new Government's priorities would include countering the effects of the eurozone debt crisis on Taiwan's economy, introducing taxation reform, resolving the ongoing dispute over US beef imports (see Relations with the USA), and maintaining peaceful cross-Strait relations. Proposals for taxation reform were intended to address widespread concern over increasing disparities in income, but legislative proposals submitted in April on the introduction of a capital gains tax on securities and futures investments proved controversial, with opponents declaring that such a measure would deter investors and harm the economy.

Following Ma Ying-jeou's inauguration for a second term as President in May 2012, Sean Chen was reappointed Premier and the composition of the Executive Yuan remained largely unchanged. Later in May, however, the Minister of Finance,

Christina Liu, resigned after criticizing amendments suggested by KMT members to the proposed capital gains tax, which in her view made the tax unfairly favourable to large corporate investors. She was replaced by her deputy, Chang Sheng-ford. The capital gains tax was approved by the legislature in July (taking effect on 1 January 2013). The Government's removal of a subsidy on petrol in April 2012 led to an increase in prices, particularly in the cost of food, and electricity prices were also raised, an especially unpopular policy since wages had hardly increased, in real terms, for several years; a further widely expressed grievance was the high cost of housing, largely owing to property speculation, which had made it impossible for many Taiwanese to buy their own homes. In June Lin Yi-shih, the Secretary-General of the Executive Yuan, resigned after allegations that he had accepted bribes, which he later admitted: he was replaced by his deputy, Steven Chen. In September the DPP proposed a motion of no confidence in Sean Chen's administration, citing the Government's lack of success in improving the national economy, but the motion was defeated in the legislature. In the same month Ma announced ministerial and party changes: David Y. L. Lin (hitherto Taiwan's representative to the European Union) was appointed Minister of Foreign Affairs, and Wang Yu-chi (President Ma's national security adviser) became Minister of the Mainland Affairs Council. Tseng Yung-chuan (hitherto Secretary-General to the President) was appointed Secretary-General of the KMT, replacing Lin Join-sane, who became Chairman of the Straits Exchange Foundation (see Cross-Strait Relations). Later in September the Minister of the Council of Labor Affairs, Wang Ju-hsian, resigned in protest against the Government's decision to make an increase in the minimum wage conditional on an improvement in economic growth; she was replaced by Pan Shih-wei.

In early February 2013 Sean Chen resigned as Premier, because of ill health, and was succeeded by the Vice-Premier, Jiang Yi-huah. Several ministerial posts connected with the economy were reallocated: the Ministry of Economic Affairs was assigned to Chang Chia-juch (the Chairman of China Airlines and previously a deputy minister in the same department), and the new Minister of the Council for Economic Planning and Development was Kuan Chung-ming (hitherto a Minister without Portfolio). The new Vice-Premier was Mao Chi-kuo, hitherto Minister of Transportation and Communications, a post now assumed by Yeh Kuang-shih, the former deputy minister. Chen Wei-zen, the deputy mayor of Taipei, became Secretary-General of the Executive Yuan, replacing Steven Chen, who remained in the Government as a Minister without Portfolio. In March President Ma declared his intention to renew his candidacy for the chair of the KMT, despite a recent scandal in which a senior KMT official, closely associated with him, had been accused of accepting bribes. During the early months of 2013 there was controversy over the country's fourth nuclear power plant, under construction in New Taipei City: although the Government argued that the country's future electricity supply would not be adequate without the new plant, many felt that construction should be halted, owing to fears concerning nuclear safety, and demanded a national referendum on the matter. The Government also attracted criticism for its proposals for pension reform, involving higher contributions and lower payments, which were intended to counteract the demands imposed on pension funds by the increasing number of older people.

Cross-Strait Relations

The Government of Taiwan repeatedly rejected offers from the People's Republic to hold discussions on the reunification of China. In 1984, following the agreement between the People's Republic of China and the United Kingdom that China would regain sovereignty over the British colony of Hong Kong in 1997, mainland Chinese leaders urged Taiwan to accept similar proposals for reunification on the basis of 'one country—two systems'. In May 1986 the Government was forced to make direct contact with the Chinese Government for the first time, over the issue of a Taiwanese pilot who had defected to the mainland. In October 1987 the Government announced the repeal of the 38-year ban on visits to the mainland by Taiwanese citizens: only visits by civil servants and military personnel were still prohibited, and this ban was relaxed in November 1998. However, reconciliation initiatives were abruptly halted after the violent suppression of the pro-democracy movement in Beijing, China, in June 1989. In May 1990 a proposal by the President of Taiwan to open direct dialogue on a government-to-government basis with the People's Republic was rejected by China, which continued to maintain that it would negotiate only on a party-to-party basis with the KMT.

In February 1991 the recently formed NUC, under the chairmanship of the President of Taiwan, put forward radical new proposals, whereby Taiwan and the People's Republic of China might recognize each other as separate political entities. In April a delegation from the Straits Exchange Foundation (SEF), established in late 1990 to deal with bilateral issues, travelled to Beijing for discussions, the first such delegation ever to visit the People's Republic. Also in April, Taiwanese President Lee Teng-hui announced the end of the state of war with the People's Republic, and 10 amendments to the Constitution were promulgated. In September the island's President asserted that Taiwan was a de facto sovereign and autonomous country. In November both Taiwan (as 'Chinese Taipei') and the People's Republic became members of the regional forum APEC, meetings of which subsequently provided opportunities for senior politicians and officials from both sides to meet indirectly. In December the non-governmental Association for Relations across the Taiwan Straits (ARATS) was established in Beijing.

In July 1992 President Lee urged the establishment of 'one country, one good system'. Statutes to permit the further expansion of economic and political links with the People's Republic were adopted by the Legislative Yuan. Delegates from the SEF and ARATS met in Hong Kong in October for discussions. However, the Chairman of the Mainland Affairs Council insisted that the People's Republic renounce the use of military force prior to any dialogue on the reunification question.

In 1993 divisions between Taiwan's business sector and political groupings (the former advocating much closer links with the People's Republic, the latter urging greater caution) became evident. In April discussions between the Chairmen of the SEF and of the ARATS resulted in the establishment of a formal structure for negotiations on economic and social issues. In August 1994 the two sides reached tentative agreement on several issues, including procedures for the settlement of cross-Strait fishing disputes. In late November a further round of SEF-ARATS talks took place in Nanjing, at which agreement in principle on the procedure for the repatriation of aircraft hijackers and illegal immigrants from Taiwan to the mainland was confirmed. It was announced in March 1995 that the SEF board of directors would henceforth include government officials, while meetings of the Mainland Affairs Council would be attended by officials of the SEF. In the same month the Mainland Affairs Council approved a resolution providing for the relaxation of restrictions on visits by mainland officials and civilians.

In April 1995 President Lee proposed a 'six-point' programme for cross-Strait relations, the objectives of which included unification in accordance with the reality of separate rules and increased trade relations. However, a meeting between the SEF Chairman, Koo Chen-fu, and his mainland counterpart, Wang Daohan, was postponed by the ARATS, in protest at President Lee's recent visit to the USA. In July and August, furthermore, the People's Republic unexpectedly conducted guided missile and artillery-firing tests off the northern coast of Taiwan. In January 1996 the Taiwanese Premier again urged the early resumption of cross-Strait dialogue, but in March the People's Republic began a new series of missile tests. Live artillery exercises continued in the Taiwan Strait until after the island's presidential election, arousing international concern.

In November 1996 the Mainland Affairs Council announced that the permanent stationing of mainland media representatives in Taiwan was to be permitted. Despite repeated SEF requests, the ARATS continued to assert that Taiwan's pursuit of its 'two Chinas' policy (a reference to President Lee's attempts to raise the diplomatic profile of the island) prevented the resumption of cross-Strait discussions. In January 1997, however, shipping representatives of Taiwan and of the People's Republic reached a preliminary consensus on the establishment of direct sea links. Limited services resumed in April, thus ending a ban of 48 years. In July, upon the reversion to Chinese sovereignty of the British colony of Hong Kong, President Lee firmly rejected the concept of 'one country, two systems' and any parallel with Taiwan.

In March 1997 a six-day visit to Taiwan by the Dalai Lama, the first to the island by the exiled spiritual leader of Tibet, was strongly condemned by the People's Republic of China, which denounced a meeting between President Lee and the Buddhist leader as a 'collusion of splittists'. The Dalai Lama's subsequent visits to Taiwan were similarly criticized by China.

The declaration by an ARATS official in January 1998 that Taiwan did not need to recognize the Government of the People's Republic as the central Government as a precondition for dialogue was regarded as a significant concession on the part of the mainland authorities. However, Taiwan continued to insist that China abandon its demand that talks be conducted under its 'one China' principle. In October Koo Chen-fu, the SEF Chairman, travelled to the People's Republic for meetings with his ARATS counterpart, Wang Daohan, thus resuming the dialogue that had been suspended since 1995. Koo's meeting with Chinese President Jiang Zemin represented the highest level of bilateral contact since 1949. Koo also had discussions with other senior officials. A four-point agreement was reached, allowing for increased bilateral communications. In April 1999 President Lee reaffirmed that the People's Republic should recognize Taiwan as being of equal status, that cross-Strait negotiations should concentrate on practical issues and that reunification could take place only if the mainland were to become a democracy. In August the ARATS suspended contacts with the SEF, following President Lee's insistence on the 'two-state theory' (see below).

Meanwhile, China was becoming increasingly demonstrative in its opposition to Taiwan's inclusion in the US-led Theater Missile Defense (TMD) anti-missile system. Ballistic missiles were deployed in mainland coastal regions opposite Taiwan. In July 1999 the People's Republic announced that it had developed a neutron bomb, after declaring itself ready for war should Taiwan attempt to gain independence. This declaration was prompted by a radio interview given by President Lee, during which he asserted that relations with the People's Republic were 'state-to-state'. Chinese military exercises were conducted in the Taiwan Strait later that month, and in August the USA reaffirmed its readiness to defend Taiwan. Also in August, the ruling KMT incorporated the 'two-state theory' into the party resolution. In September, following a severe earthquake in Taiwan that killed or injured several thousand people, China was among the many countries to offer emergency assistance to the island; however, Taiwan accused the People's Republic of contravening humanitarian principles by trying to force other countries to seek its approval before offering help.

In February 2000 the People's Republic threatened to attack Taiwan if it indefinitely postponed reunification talks. In April the Vice-President-elect, Annette Lu, was denounced by the Chinese media after she made 'separatist' remarks, televised in Hong Kong, declaring that Taiwan was only a 'remote relative and close neighbour' of China. In October China published a policy document on its national defence, which confirmed that the People's Republic would use force to prevent Taiwanese secession. In November, however, Wu Poh-hsiung, the Vice-Chairman of the KMT, travelled to Beijing and met unofficially with Chinese Vice-Premier Qian Qichen. Wu was the most senior KMT official to visit mainland China for more than 50 years. Also in November, Taiwan announced that journalists from the People's Republic were to be granted permission to stay in Taiwan for periods of up to one month. In December plans were announced for direct trade, transport and postal links between the islands of Kinmen and Matsu and the mainland, albeit subject to rigorous security checks. Economic links continued to develop, with many Taiwanese companies investing on the mainland. In August 2001 President Chen endorsed a plan to expand commercial links with the People's Republic, a reversal of the previous Government's policy of limiting trade with the mainland.

In October 2001 Taiwan boycotted the APEC summit meeting in Shanghai, China, following China's refusal to allow Taiwan's chosen delegate, former Vice-President Li Yuan-tsu, to attend, on the grounds that he was not an 'economic' official. Despite this, the opposition DPP deleted from its charter a vow to achieve the island's formal independence, since it was already a de facto separate entity. In January 2002 the Government announced a list of more than 2,000 items that were to be legally importable from the mainland. In March China announced that, for the first time, two Taiwanese banks would be permitted to open offices on the mainland. Taiwan would allow mainland banks to establish offices on the island. The Taiwanese Government also eased restrictions on the island's companies investing in computer-chip manufacturing on the mainland, although controls would remain on the number of plants established and type of chips produced, mainly owing to security concerns.

In July 2002 the Taiwanese Ministry of National Defense warned in a biannual report that China's military spending was accelerating rapidly and that it would possess 600 short-range missiles targeted at the island by 2005. President Chen further antagonized the mainland in August 2002 by supporting demands for a referendum to determine the island's future. Taiwan then cancelled planned military exercises as a gesture of good faith, but Chen's comments delayed the introduction of direct transport links. At the end of July the Government announced that Chinese products could be advertised on the island and that Chinese employees of Taiwanese or foreign companies would be allowed to work in Taiwan. However, bilateral relations remained volatile, and in September President Chen described China's threats against the island as a form of 'terrorism'. China accused Taiwan of allowing the banned Falun Gong sect to use the island as a base for disrupting Chinese television and satellite broadcasts.

During 2002 Taiwan and China acquired advanced weaponry from the USA and Russia, respectively. In January 2003 President Chen stated that Taiwan was a sovereign state, and would never accept a Hong Kong-style solution nor federate with the mainland. Vice-President Lu described China as being of a 'terrorist nature', referring to its missile build-up across the Taiwan Strait. In late January, none the less, the first Taiwanese airliner in more than 50 years flew to mainland China, via Hong Kong, and landed in Shanghai, one of 16 charter operations organized by the Taiwanese carrier China Airlines. In February the Minister of National Defense stated that Taiwan would not reduce weapons purchases from the USA in return for the dismantling of Chinese missiles targeting the island. His remarks followed Chinese President Jiang Zemin's offer of such an arrangement, made to US President George W. Bush in October 2002.

An outbreak on the mainland of a pneumonia-like virus—SARS (see The administration of President Chen)—spread to Taiwan in early 2003. Taiwan accused the Chinese authorities of concealing the seriousness of the outbreak. In August the island's authorities arrested two Taiwanese citizens and a Taiwanese American on charges of spying for China. Military exercises simulating an attack on Taiwan by China were conducted in September. Taiwan's announcement in the same month that it was to issue new passports for its citizens, which for the first time would have 'Taiwan' printed on the front (ostensibly to distinguish Taiwanese passports more clearly from mainland documents), heightened cross-Strait tensions, as did mass protests in Taipei demanding that the name 'Taiwan' be used officially by government agencies and private companies. In October the island's legislature approved a framework for the regulation of travel and business links between Taiwan and the mainland.

In November 2003 the Taiwanese legislature approved a bill allowing referendums to take place on the island. Although the legislation in its final version prohibited a vote on Taiwan's sovereignty except in the event of an external attack, China feared that the new law might lead to the holding of a vote on Taiwan's independence. In December the issue of Taiwan dominated a visit by Chinese Premier Wen Jiabao to Washington, DC, with Wen seeking assurance from the USA that it would not support moves towards Taiwanese independence. President Chen defended plans to hold a referendum in March 2004 on the subject of a proposed request to China that it remove hundreds of missiles aimed at the island. In January Chen stated that the referendum might include 'counter-proposals' such as direct transport links between Taiwan and China if the latter were to withdraw its missiles. In February Chen also stated that he would not declare Taiwanese independence, were he to win the forthcoming presidential election, although his attitude to relations with the Chinese mainland, for example in rejecting the 'one country, two systems' model advocated by China, was regarded by some as tantamount to stating that independence already existed.

The Chinese Government did not attempt directly to influence the presidential election held in March 2004, resulting in a narrow victory for Chen. However, following widespread controversy and protests over the election result, the Chinese Government stated that it would not tolerate social instability in Taiwan. In the event, President Chen's referendum, held concurrently with the presidential election, did not produce a valid result. Anti-secession legislation, drafted with the intention of preventing Taiwan from declaring independence, was approved by the NPC in Beijing in March 2005.

In January 2005 direct commercial flights between Taipei and the Chinese mainland were permitted for the first time over the

Lunar New Year period. In April, in the first such visit since 1949, the Chairman of the opposition KMT, Lien Chan, embarked upon an official visit to the mainland, where he and Chinese President Hu Jintao agreed to remain opposed to Taiwanese independence. Following Chan's visit, in May 2005 the Government of the People's Republic offered Taiwan a pair of giant pandas, along with a series of concessions that included the easing of restrictions for mainland Chinese tourists visiting Taiwan. In June the Chinese Government announced that regulations restricting employment by Chinese companies of residents of Taiwan (and Hong Kong and Macao) were to be relaxed. The approval of a series of constitutional amendments by the Taiwanese National Assembly in June enabled future constitutional changes, including any declaration of independence, to be endorsed by referendum.

In a New Year speech on 1 January 2006 President Chen reiterated his commitment to achieving a new constitution, ratified by referendum, by 2008, with the implication that this would enshrine Taiwan's independence and sovereignty. This objective was repeated by Chen on the occasion of the Chinese Lunar New Year, when he also proposed the abolition of the NUC, along with the guidelines for unification proposed by the council and accepted by the Executive Yuan in 1991. Furthermore, Chen stated his intention of reapplying for membership of the UN under the name of 'Taiwan', instead of the 'Republic of China'. In March 2006 tens of thousands of protesters participated in a rally in Taipei to protest against the perceived threat of domination by the People's Republic. In April former KMT Chairman Lien Chan made a further controversial trip to Beijing to meet with President Hu Jintao, who urged the restoration of bilateral talks at the highest level. In June it was announced that up to 168 charter passenger flights would operate between the island and the mainland at four important annual holiday periods, and that cargo and humanitarian flights would be licensed on an individual basis. (One month later the first non-stop cargo charter flight was made from Taiwan to Shanghai.) At a Conference on Sustaining Taiwan's Economic Development, held in July, it was decided that investment limits might be relaxed for some Taiwanese companies operating on the mainland. In August the Mainland Affairs Council established the Taiwan Strait Tourism and Travel Association, in response to China's foundation earlier in the month of the Cross-Strait Tourism Exchange Association.

By mid-2006 official Chinese statistics showed that 70,256 Taiwanese companies had invested on the mainland (excluding companies that had invested via third territories, such as Hong Kong). This investment was estimated to have reached a total of US $50,800m., despite measures introduced by the Taiwanese Government in May to ensure stricter supervision. As concerns persisted that many of the island's business people were contravening existing Taiwanese investment regulations, the Government remained under heavy pressure from the business community, which was becoming increasingly frustrated at the inability of Taiwanese companies to deal more directly with China. In September the Mainland Affairs Council announced that it was to raise the limit on the number of Chinese visitors attending business meetings in Taiwan from 30 to 50. By the end of the year, furthermore, tourists from the mainland would be able to visit Taiwan without first passing through a third location. In November a spokesman from the mainland's Taiwan Affairs Office urged the island to reduce its control over cross-Strait tourism.

In a defence document published in December 2006, however, China described Taiwan as a 'major threat'. In March 2007 the Taiwanese President's confirmation that he wished the island to pursue independence, draft a new constitution and change its official designation from the 'Republic of China' to 'Taiwan' prompted the mainland Chinese Minister of Foreign Affairs to denounce such statements as 'criminal'. On the same day Chinese Premier Wen Jiabao expressed a willingness to open a dialogue with Taiwan on condition that the island recognized the 'one China' principle. In February Taiwan declined to confirm reports that it had test-fired a missile that had a range of 1,000 km (and was therefore capable of reaching Shanghai). Taiwan's National Day celebrations in October featured a military parade, the first of its kind since the early 1990s, apparently in response to the perceived threat of military action from the mainland. Also in October 2007, at the 17th Congress of the Chinese Communist Party (CCP) convened in Beijing, President Hu Jintao reaffirmed Premier Wen's position, stressing the need for a dialogue to attain 'peaceful reunification'.

Relations with the People's Republic improved considerably following the election of the KMT candidate, Ma Ying-jeou, as President of Taiwan in March 2008. Ma, who was born in Hong Kong, emphasized the importance of economic and transport links with China and distanced himself from his predecessor's policies, but maintained that a peace treaty could not be agreed while an estimated 1,000 Chinese missiles were directed at Taiwan. A meeting between the Taiwanese Vice-President-elect, Vincent Siew, and President Hu Jintao, at the Boao Forum for Asia in April, was described as the most senior-level encounter ever to take place between Taiwan and China. In May the Chairman of the KMT, Wu Poh-hsiung, attended an historic meeting with President Hu in China, and formal talks between representatives of the two sides recommenced, following a long hiatus, in June. As a result of these SEF-ARATS negotiations, the two parties agreed to establish offices on each other's territory; to initiate 36 (and eventually 96) regular direct charter flights between China and Taiwan every weekend; and to allow entry to a total of 3,000 tourists per day in each direction. President Ma proposed that bilateral agreements should expand into areas such as taxation and investment, through a process of 'economic normalization'. From late June, banks began offering the conversion of Chinese yuan into New Taiwan dollars.

Emergency aid was swiftly mobilized by Taiwanese charity organizations and religious groups to support the victims of a major earthquake in Sichuan Province in May 2008, in the first such cross-Strait relief operation ever mounted. At the end of May the Taiwanese Government announced that it planned to allocate a total of US $67m. in emergency relief funds, while private Taiwanese donations had exceeded US $80m.

In November 2008 Chiang Pin-kung, Chairman of the SEF, and Chen Yunlin, President of the ARATS, signed a series of agreements in Taipei. Chen was the most senior mainland Chinese official to travel to Taiwan since 1949, although his five-day visit was opposed by demonstrators. The agreements included the expansion of bilateral transport links, permitting the establishment of daily direct flights, shipping and postal services between Taiwan and mainland China. The two sides also agreed, in view of concerns with regard to the safety of Chinese products, to co-operate in the area of food safety. In December 2008 the first regular direct flights and cargo shipping services began. No longer required to operate via an intermediary point such as Hong Kong, about 100 regular passenger flights a week, serving eight cities in Taiwan and more than 20 on the mainland, were envisaged.

Following the return to power of the KMT, negotiations resumed with regard to China's offer of two giant pandas, traditionally the most esteemed diplomatic gift. The offer had been declined in 2006 on the grounds that Taiwan lacked the requisite facilities for panda care. In December 2008, following the preparation of a special enclosure at Taipei Zoo, two pandas (whose names together signified 'Reunion') were flown to the island. The Taiwanese Government's acceptance of this highly symbolic gift was criticized by the opposition DPP.

As bilateral relations continued to improve, in December 2008 the Taiwanese Government announced that the restrictions hitherto imposed on mainland spouses, notably with regard to issues such as the right to work and the processing of applications for permanent residency on the island, were to be relaxed. At the end of December President Hu Jintao urged the adoption of a more pragmatic approach to the issue of Taiwan. He also indicated some support for Taiwan's ongoing efforts to attain membership of various international organizations. At the annual session of the NPC convened in Beijing in March 2009, Premier Wen Jiabao stated his willingness to negotiate with Taiwan on political and military issues, reiterating that any discussions would be based on the 'one China' principle. In response, the Taiwanese Government expressed its preference to focus on economic matters.

In April 2009 Chiang Pin-kung of the SEF and Chen Yunlin of the ARATS signed agreements to permit further cross-Strait investment. The two sides pledged to 'realize the normalization of cross-strait economic ties'. Also in April agreement was reached on several important issues, including the combating of crime, judicial assistance and financial co-operation. A substantial expansion of cross-Strait air transport was also agreed, providing for the addition of six new airport destinations in mainland China and an increase in the number of weekly flights from 108 to 270. By May 2009, one year after President Ma Ying-jeou's assumption of office, a total of nine bilateral agreements on economic co-operation had been signed. Furthermore, in an unprecedented bilateral exchange in late July, President Hu Jintao sent a message of congratulation to President Ma following the latter's election as Chairman of Taiwan's ruling KMT.

The Dalai Lama's five-day visit to Taiwan in late August 2009, following a severe typhoon earlier in the month, provoked condemnation from the mainland. Having stressed the humanitarian nature of his visit, the spiritual leader of Tibet offered comfort to the victims of the disaster. However, mindful of the importance of the island's economic relations with the People's Republic, President Ma declined to meet the Dalai Lama.

In a report issued in October 2009, the Taiwanese Ministry of National Defense warned that its efforts to improve relations with the Chinese military continued to be impeded by the mainland's confrontational stance. The report urged the withdrawal of missiles aimed at the island (the number of which was estimated by Taiwanese officials to have risen to 1,500) and suggested the establishment of a 'hotline' between Taipei and Beijing. The document also drew attention to the increasing frequency of military exercises being conducted on the mainland. President Ma, meanwhile, remained in favour of a formal peace accord with the mainland. In January 2010 China strongly condemned an agreement between Taiwan and the USA on the provision of defence equipment (see Relations with the USA).

Despite military tensions, bilateral economic relations continued to expand. In November 2009 Taiwan and China signed a memorandum of understanding that provided for better access to financial services. Negotiations with regard to the conclusion of a free trade pact continued to progress. During four days of discussions held in Taiwan in December Chiang Pin-kung of the SEF and his mainland counterpart concluded a series of economic agreements.

In June 2010 Taiwan and China reached consensus on the details of an historic Economic Co-operation Framework Agreement (ECFA). This major accord provided for the eventual removal of many trade tariffs and permitted wider access to the two respective markets. However, there was much domestic opposition to the agreement in Taiwan, and the passage of the requisite legislation was seriously disrupted. None the less, the legislation was finally approved in August, and the ECFA took effect in the following month. Under the ECFA a Cross-Strait Economic Co-operation Committee (CSECC) was to conduct negotiations on trade and investment matters, meeting every six months within the existing SEF-ARATS framework: the CSECC was formally inaugurated in January 2011.

In May 2010, meanwhile, the first semi-official Taiwanese presence in mainland China was established, when a representative office of the Taiwan Strait Tourism Association, headed by a senior government official, was inaugurated. In the same month the mainland Cross-Strait Tourism Association opened an office in Taipei. In July the KMT and the CCP reached agreement on the expansion of co-operation between the two ruling parties in the areas of culture, education, sports and economic development. In September Cai Wu, the mainland Minister of Culture, undertook an official visit to Taiwan, only the second official of cabinet rank to visit the island. In February 2011 Chen Yunlin visited Taiwan at the head of a delegation of more than 50 business people and government officials: his itinerary incorporated major enterprises in southern Taiwan. His visit prompted protests by pro-independence activists in Kaohsiung. Nevertheless, bilateral agreement was reached on permitting larger numbers of mainland tourists to visit Taiwan on an individual basis. In April, amid much domestic controversy, the Taiwanese authorities accepted the first applications from mainland students wishing to further their higher education on the island. Following his conviction on charges of espionage, bribery and extortion, at the end of April an intelligence officer at the Taiwanese Ministry of National Defense, Col Lo Chi-cheng, was sentenced to life imprisonment. Col Lo had apparently collaborated with a Taiwanese businessman based on the mainland to gather intelligence for the People's Republic of China. In July a general of the Taiwanese army, Lo Hsien-che, was also sentenced to life imprisonment, having been found guilty of supplying classified data to mainland Chinese agents in exchange for bribes during 2002–05, while serving as a military attaché in Thailand. In May 2011, meanwhile, following his attendance at a bilateral forum in the Chinese city of Chengdu, Wu Poh-hsiung, honorary Chairman of the KMT, was received in Beijing by President Hu Jintao. In the same month, however, following the revelation by an opposition legislator that China had apparently exerted pressure on WHO to refer to Taiwan as a province of China in its documentation, the Taiwanese President

issued a strong protest to China. The Chinese Government condemned a new agreement announced by the US Government in September on the provision of defence equipment for Taiwan (see Relations with the USA). In November, at a meeting of the CSECC, the two sides signed an accord on nuclear safety.

In January 2012 the official Beijing media welcomed the re-election of Ma Ying-jeou to the Taiwanese presidency as offering 'new chances for the peaceful development of cross-Strait relations'. During the election campaign Ma had advocated maintaining the 'status quo of no unification, no independence and no use of force', but he also suggested the consideration of a formal peace treaty with the People's Republic, subject to approval by referendum in Taiwan. In August senior officials of the SEF and the ARATS concluded agreements on investment protection (including a formal mechanism for arbitration in disputes) and on customs co-operation between Taiwan and the mainland; negotiations on trade in services were described as being next on the CSECC agenda. In September the veteran SEF Chairman, Chiang Pin-kung, announced his retirement, and Lin Join-sane replaced him as the principal negotiator with the People's Republic; Chiang's ARATS counterpart, Chen Yunlin, was also expected to retire in the near future. In April 2013 the recently inaugurated Chinese President, Xi Jinping, met Vincent Siew (the former Taiwanese Vice-President) at the annual Boao Forum conference, and declared his resolve to maintain the peaceful development of cross-Strait relations, particularly through economic co-operation. Later in April, however, Taiwan undertook a military exercise, supervised by President Ma, simulating an attack by mainland forces on a Taiwanese island (the first such exercise to use live ammunition since 2008); Ma, while emphasizing that cross-Strait relations were more peaceful than they had been for 60 years, reiterated Taiwan's determination to protect itself in view of the increasing military strength of the People's Republic.

Foreign Affairs

Taiwan's foreign policy has been characterized by competition with the People's Republic for influence and diplomatic recognition. From 2008, however, President Ma placed emphasis on 'viable diplomacy', aiming to redirect resources more effectively towards providing humanitarian aid, cultural exchanges and business opportunities. In 2012 Taiwan had full diplomatic relations with only 23 countries, of which 12 were Central American and Caribbean states, four were in Africa, and six were Pacific island nations; in Europe only the Holy See maintained diplomatic relations with Taiwan. Despite the relative lack of formal recognition in the international community, Taiwan maintained representative offices in 57 countries in 2012, and its commercial relations with many nations continued to flourish.

Relations with the USA

In January 1979 Taiwan suffered a serious setback when the USA recognized the People's Republic of China. Diplomatic relations with Taiwan were therefore severed, and the USA terminated the 1954 mutual security treaty with Taiwan. However, commercial links were maintained, and Taiwan's purchase of armaments from the USA (under the 1979 Taiwan Relations Act, whereby the USA undertook to provide Taiwan with defensive weapons) subsequently remained a controversial issue. In August 1982 a joint Sino-US communiqué was published, in which the USA pledged to reduce gradually its sale of armaments to Taiwan. In September 1992 President George Bush announced the sale of up to 150 F-16 fighter aircraft to Taiwan. In September 1994 the USA announced a modification of its policy towards Taiwan, henceforth permitting senior-level bilateral meetings to be held in US government offices. A bilateral Trade and Investment Framework Agreement (TIFA) was signed in that month. In June 1995 President Lee was permitted to make a four-day unofficial visit to the USA, where he met members of the US Congress, following which China recalled its ambassador from Washington.

In March 1996, as China began a new series of missile tests off the Taiwanese coast (see Cross-Strait Relations), the USA stationed two naval convoys in waters east of the island. In early 1997 the first of the *Patriot* anti-missile air defence systems, purchased from the USA under an arrangement made in 1993, were reported to have been deployed on the island. The first of the F-16 aircraft were delivered to Taiwan in April 1997. However, in mid-1998 a statement by US President Bill Clinton affirming that the USA would not support Taiwan's membership of the UN was sharply criticized by the Taiwanese Government.

In January 1999 the People's Republic was antagonized by Taiwan's proposed inclusion in the US-led TMD system (see Cross-Strait Relations). In August the USA reaffirmed its commitment to defend Taiwan against Chinese military action. In October Taiwan welcomed the adoption, albeit in modified form, of the Taiwan Security Enhancement Act, establishing direct military links, by the International Relations Committee of the US House of Representatives, despite opposition from the Clinton Administration. The House of Representatives overwhelmingly approved the Act in February 2000. In April, however, the US Senate postponed consideration of the Act at the behest of the Taiwanese President-elect, Chen Shui-bian, in order not to antagonize China during the sensitive period preceding his inauguration. In the same month the US Government announced that it had decided to defer the sale of four naval destroyers to Taiwan. In October China condemned a resolution approved by the US Congress that supported Taiwan's participation in the UN and other international organizations.

The election of George W. Bush to the US presidency in late 2000 was widely expected to boost US-Taiwan relations at the expense of the USA's relations with the mainland. In April 2001 the USA agreed to sell Taiwan military equipment and armaments worth a total of US $4,000m., and President Bush declared that the USA would do whatever was necessary to defend Taiwan, in the event of an invasion by mainland forces. President Chen Shui-bian visited the USA in May, when he met business leaders and members of the US Congress. Chen's visit was followed by that of his predecessor, Lee Teng-hui, in June, as well as by a group of Taiwanese military and intelligence officials on an exchange programme, the first such exchange since 1979. In August 2001 two US Navy aircraft carrier battle groups conducted a one-day exercise in the South China Sea, coinciding with Chinese military exercises in the Taiwan Strait. In December the US House of Representatives approved the 2002 Defense Authorization Act, which included weapons sales to Taiwan.

In March 2002 the Minister of National Defense, Gen. (retd) Tang Yao-ming, visited the USA to attend a private three-day defence and security conference in Florida, where he met the US Deputy Secretary of Defense, Paul Wolfowitz, and Assistant Secretary of State James Kelly. Tang was the first incumbent official to make a non-transit visit to the USA since 1979. Meanwhile, the scandal in late March 2002 concerning former President Lee Teng-hui's co-operation with the island's intelligence services in secretly establishing an unauthorized fund (see Domestic Political Affairs) embarrassed Taiwan and several US lobbying groups, which had received sums of this money.

In September 2002 the US Congress approved the Foreign Relations Authorization Act, Fiscal Year 2003, which for the first time allowed staff of the US Department of State and other government agencies to work at the American Institute in Taiwan (the unofficial US mission to the island). Previously, US officials were required to embark upon sabbatical leave before serving at the institute. US military officers would also be allowed to work there, albeit not in uniform. Furthermore, the bill recognized Taiwan as a major non-North Atlantic Treaty Organization ally of the USA. In August 2003 plans for Taiwan's purchase of four naval destroyers from the USA were finalized. Taiwan also made an advance payment towards the acquisition of eight new diesel submarines from the USA. In November President Chen made a visit to New York, in the course of which he was permitted to make a public speech.

In April 2004 Therese Shaheen, head of the American Institute in Taiwan, resigned after reportedly having misrepresented US policy on Taiwanese independence. Her departure prompted the resignation of the Taiwanese Minister of Foreign Affairs. In June the Executive Yuan approved a special defence budget for the purchase of weapons from the USA, which had been agreed in April 2001 (see above). Following public opposition in Taiwan to the special defence budget, the USA warned that there would be serious implications if the armaments purchase were not approved by the Taiwanese legislature. However, in late 2005 the opposition parties in the Legislative Yuan continued to obstruct the special defence budget, despite significant reductions in the overall scale of the proposed purchase. In January 2006 the US Government described as 'inflammatory' President Chen's proposals for the abolition of the NUC and the reunification guidelines established by it (see Cross-Strait Relations). The US Department of State emphasized that it supported the maintenance of the status quo in cross-Strait relations, within the overall framework of a 'one China' policy.

During 2006 the USA continued to press Taiwan to purchase its weapons, with US officials expressing 'grave concern' over Taiwan's defence capabilities. As President Chen became increasingly embroiled in various scandals, the director of the American Institute in Taiwan, Stephen Young, entered the fray to state that the USA wished Chen to remain in power for the sake of the stability of the island. In February 2007 the US Department of Defense announced the sale of more than 450 missiles to the island. In May, furthermore, Young reiterated his appeal to the Taiwanese legislature to grant approval to the outstanding defence budget that would permit the purchase of weaponry from the USA (aspects of the sale were expected to proceed following the legislature's approval of an amended budget in June).

The USA continued to exert pressure on Taiwan to abandon its efforts to join the UN under the proposed name of Taiwan, and criticized the proposal to conduct a referendum on the issue of UN membership concurrently with the 2008 Taiwanese presidential election, urging the Government to respect the status quo. The referendums were duly conducted in March 2008 (although the required turn-out of 50% was not achieved—see Domestic Political Affairs). The Taiwanese President-elect, Ma Ying-jeou, maintained that he would work to improve relations with the USA. Meanwhile, Taiwan's purchase of various types of US defence equipment, which had been approved by the Taiwan legislature in 2007, made little progress until October 2008, when the Bush Administration confirmed its intention to sell a substantial amount of weaponry, although the agreement excluded the advanced F-16 fighter aircraft and diesel submarines requested by Taiwan.

No immediate change in US policy towards Taiwan followed Barack Obama's inauguration as US President in January 2009, although the lack of any reference to the Taiwan Relations Act in a joint statement issued by Presidents Hu Jintao and Barack Obama during the latter's visit to China in November aroused much concern on the island. The USA remained Taiwan's leading supplier of weaponry, and in January 2010 the Obama Administration's decision to proceed with the sale of defence equipment to the value of US $6,400m., which included 60 helicopters, was welcomed by Taiwan. However, the announcement provoked an unusually strong reaction from the Chinese Government, which temporarily severed military contacts. In September 2011 the US Government announced that it had undertaken to modernize Taiwan's fleet of F-16 fighter aircraft (acquired in 1992), at a cost of US $5,850m., although it had not agreed to the Taiwanese request, originally made in 2007, for the supply of new aircraft. The Chinese Government again condemned the announcement, stating that it 'gravely violated' previous agreements between the People's Republic and the USA.

In January 2011 a ban on imports of US beef was imposed by Taiwan, owing to fears that residual amounts of a cattle-feed additive, ractopamine, could affect human health. Previous intermittent bans had been imposed from 2003 onwards as a precaution against infection by bovine spongiform encephalopathy (BSE or 'mad cow disease'), and largely as a result of these bans trade negotiations under the TIFA had been in abeyance since 2007. There was considerable public controversy in Taiwan when, in March 2012, the Government announced a 'conditional' resumption of US beef imports containing residues at what were deemed to be safe levels. President Ma pointed out that, particularly in view of the recent conclusion of a free trade agreement between the USA and the Republic of Korea, it was essential for Taiwan's economy that normal trade relations with the USA should be resumed and developed under the TIFA. In July the Taiwan legislature voted to remove the ban on US beef imports, following which the Government asked the USA to resume the TIFA negotiations; these recommenced in March 2013.

Regional relations
Taiwan severed diplomatic relations with Japan in 1972, following the latter's rapprochement with China; however, bilateral relations continued informally through the Association of East Asian Relations in Taiwan and the equivalent Interchange Association in Japan. Mainland displeasure was incurred in February 1993 when the Taiwanese Minister of Foreign Affairs paid a visit to Japan. In September 1994 pressure from China resulted in the withdrawal of President Lee's invitation to attend the forthcoming Asian Games in Hiroshima, Japan. Instead, the Taiwanese Vice-Premier was permitted to visit Japan. Similarly, in July 1995 Japan announced that the Taiwanese Vice-Premier would not be permitted to attend a meeting of APEC members to

be held in Osaka, Japan, in November. Instead, President Lee was represented by Koo Chen-fu, the SEF Chairman. Taiwan's relations with Japan were also strained by the issue of adequate compensation for the thousands of Asian (mostly Korean) women used by Japanese troops for sexual purposes during the Second World War. In October 1996 Taiwan rejected a Japanese offer of nominal compensation for such Taiwanese women.

Taiwan's relations with Japan were also affected by a dispute relating to a group of uninhabited islets in the East China Sea: known as the Tiaoyutai (Diaoyu Dao) in Chinese, or Senkaku in Japanese, the islands are claimed by Taiwan, China and Japan. In July 1996, following the construction of a lighthouse on one of the islands by a Japanese right-wing group, the Taiwanese Ministry of Foreign Affairs lodged a strong protest over Japan's decision to incorporate the islands within its 200-mile (370-km) exclusive economic zone. Further tensions related to the issue of Taiwanese fishing rights within the disputed waters. In October 1997 it was reported that Japanese patrol boats were forcibly intercepting Taiwanese fishing vessels. In November 1999, however, the Governor of the Japanese capital, Tokyo, paid an official visit to Taiwan. In March 2002 it was revealed that Japanese politicians, including former Prime Minister Ryutaro Hashimoto, had received money from an unauthorized fund established by former President Lee Teng-hui in order to procure influence in Japan. However, the incident did not damage commercial relations. In September 2003 the second Taiwan-Japan Forum opened in Tokyo, at which issues of mutual concern were discussed. In February 2005, as part of a revised strategic understanding with the USA, Japan identified Taiwan's security as a 'common strategic objective' for the first time. In June 2007 a visit by former President Lee to the Yasukuni Shrine, a controversial war memorial in Japan, further antagonized the mainland.

The dispute over the sovereignty of the Tiaoyutai (Diaoyu/ Senkaku) Islands, and disagreements over fishing rights, continued, with Taiwanese fishermen repeatedly complaining of harassment by Japanese patrol boats. In June 2005 an armed naval frigate, carrying the Taiwanese Minister of National Defense, the President of the Legislative Yuan and 15 legislators, was dispatched to the region, reportedly in response to these complaints of harassment. Subsequent negotiations between Taiwan and Japan over fishing rights, the 15th round of talks on the issue since 1996, concluded without agreement in July 2005. In September the Taiwanese President's Secretary-General, Yu Shyi-kun, attended a forum on relations between Taiwan and Japan in Tokyo, thus becoming the most senior Taiwanese official to visit Japan since the withdrawal of diplomatic recognition in 1972. In June 2008, following an accident involving a Taiwanese boat and a vessel of the Japanese coastguard off the Tiaoyutai Islands, Taiwanese protesters entered the islands' territorial waters, accompanied by the Taiwanese coastguard. The newly elected President, Ma Ying-jeou, reiterated Taiwan's sovereignty over the islands shortly afterwards.

In July 2009, in a major concession to expatriate Taiwanese, the Japanese legislature approved a revision of immigration law to permit Taiwanese resident in Japan henceforth to declare Taiwan, rather than China, as their nation of citizenship when submitting an application for residence in Japan. Like its predecessor, the incoming administration of the Democratic Party of Japan, elected in August, did not support Taiwanese independence and opposed the use of force by the People's Republic against the island. With the inauguration of a new air link, in October 2010 Shinzo Abe, the former Japanese Prime Minister, flew to Taiwan, where he had discussions with President Ma. In April 2011 the Taiwanese Government formally protested against Japan's renewal of its claim over the Tiaoyutai (Diaoyu/Senkaku) Islands. In September a bilateral agreement was signed on the promotion, protection and liberalization of investment, and in November an 'open skies' agreement removed restrictions on air traffic between Taiwan and Japan.

During 2012 the dispute between Japan and the People's Republic of China concerning the Tiaoyutai (Diaoyu/Senkaku) Islands became more vociferous, and Taiwan, in turn, reasserted its claim. In July the Japanese Government officially protested after Japanese coastguard vessels intercepted Taiwanese activists sailing near the islands. In August President Ma, while reasserting Taiwan's sovereignty over the islands, proposed an 'East China Sea Peace Initiative', urging a three-way discussion on the possibility of jointly developing the resources of the archipelago and its surrounding waters. In September Taiwan lodged a formal protest, describing as 'extremely unfriendly' the Japanese Government's recent purchase of three of the islands from a private owner; in that month there was a further confrontation between Japanese coastguard patrols and a fleet of more than 50 boats carrying Taiwanese protesters, accompanied by the Taiwanese coastguard. In April 2013, however, Taiwan and Japan concluded an agreement on fishing rights in the East China Sea, including the waters around the disputed islands.

Despite the lack of formal diplomatic links and repeated obstruction from mainland China, Taiwan continued its attempts to develop good relations with the countries of South-East Asia. In March 1989 President Lee undertook a state visit to Singapore, the first official visit overseas by a Taiwanese head of state for 12 years. (In October 1990, however, Singapore established diplomatic relations with the People's Republic of China.) In February 1994 President Lee embarked upon an eight-day tour of the Philippines, Indonesia and Thailand, all three of which maintained diplomatic relations with the People's Republic of China. Although the tour was described as informal, President Lee had meetings with the three countries' heads of state, leading to protests from China. In September 1996 the Taiwanese Minister of Foreign Affairs was obliged to curtail an ostensibly private visit to the Indonesian capital, Jakarta (where he was reported to have had discussions with his Indonesian counterpart), following objections from China. The Malaysian and Singaporean Prime Ministers met their Taiwanese counterpart in Taiwan in November 1997. In January 1998 the Taiwanese Premier, Vincent Siew, met senior officials during a visit to the Philippines and Singapore, and in February he held negotiations in Taiwan with the Malaysian Deputy Prime Minister and Minister of Finance, paying a reciprocal visit to Malaysia in April. China was highly critical of these visits, accusing Taiwan of seeking to gain political advantage from the regional economic crisis through its offers of financial support. Vice-President Lu also visited Indonesia in August 2002 and met several cabinet ministers. While in Indonesia, Lu discussed possible liquefied natural gas projects, investment and migrant labour. In December, however, President Chen was forced to cancel a trip to Indonesia after that country came under heavy pressure from China.

Relations with the Philippines were tested in February 2011 when, despite Taiwan's request that they be repatriated to their homeland, 14 Taiwanese citizens suspected of fraud were deported to China by the Philippine authorities, along with 10 mainland Chinese alleged to be their accomplices. Taiwan recalled its representative from the Philippines and demanded a formal apology for the incident. A presidential envoy was dispatched to Taipei by the Philippine Government in an attempt to restore good relations.

The question of the sovereignty of the Spratly Islands, situated in the South China Sea and to which five countries as well as Taiwan laid claim, remained unresolved. Believed to possess petroleum and gas resources, in addition to encompassing rich fishing areas, the grouping comprises more than 100 small islands and reefs. A contingent of Taiwanese marines has been maintained on Taiping Island, the largest of the disputed islands, located some 1,574 km south-west of Taiwan. A satellite telecommunications link between Taiping and Kaohsiung was inaugurated in October 1995. In December 1998 the Legislative Yuan approved the first legal definition of Taiwan's sea borders. The Spratly Islands were claimed, as were the disputed Tiaoyutai (Diaoyu/Senkaku) Islands (see above), within the 12- and 24-nautical mile zones. In November 2002, in Phnom Penh, Cambodia, members of the Association of Southeast Asian Nations (ASEAN, see p. 218) signed a 'declaration on the conduct of parties in the South China Sea', which aimed to avoid conflict in the area. Under this agreement, which was similar to one drafted in late 1999 but not implemented, claimants would practise self-restraint in the event of potentially hostile action (such as inhabiting the islands), effect confidence-building measures and give advance notice of military exercises in the region. However, the agreement did not include the Paracel Islands (also in the South China Sea and claimed by China, Taiwan and Viet Nam). In February 2008 President Chen Shui-bian visited Taiwanese forces stationed on Taiping, where he inaugurated a new airstrip and proposed a 'Spratly Initiative', urging claimant countries to disregard the issue of sovereignty and to co-operate in the protection of the islands' environment and resources. The Philippines and Viet Nam had been particularly critical of the construction of the airstrip. In April 2011, in response to China's agreement with Viet Nam to co-operate in the area (which prompted an official complaint to the UN from the Philippines),

Taiwan announced that it was to reinforce its coastguard deployment in the area of the Spratly Islands.

In 2012 a total of six Pacific nations, namely Kiribati, the Marshall Islands, Nauru, Palau, Solomon Islands and Tuvalu, recognized Taiwan, which was increasingly vying with China for influence in the region. Taiwan maintained several embassies in the Pacific Islands and provided considerable financial support to these nations. In January 2005 President Chen undertook an official visit to Palau, thus becoming the first Taiwanese President to visit the Pacific nation. He also travelled to Solomon Islands and to the US territory of Guam. In May Chen became the first head of any foreign state to visit the Marshall Islands in an official capacity, as part of a diplomatic tour of Pacific nations, during which the Taiwanese President also became the first foreign head of state to visit Kiribati and Tuvalu. However, he controversially altered his published itinerary to visit Fiji, a country that maintained diplomatic relations with the People's Republic of China. Also in May 2005, diplomatic relations with Nauru, which had been terminated in July 2002 after the country established relations with China, were re-established.

As competition with China for diplomatic support in the Pacific region continued, in May 2008 two senior members of the Taiwanese Government, Vice-Premier Chiou I-jen and the Minister of Foreign Affairs, Huang Chih-fang, were forced to resign (see The return to power of the KMT) over a funding scandal involving an alleged attempt to influence the allegiance of Papua New Guinea, a country with which Taiwan had briefly succeeded in establishing diplomatic relations in 1999. During 2009 President Ma held discussions with the heads of government of Palau, Tuvalu and Solomon Islands during their respective state visits to Taiwan. In March 2010 President Ma embarked upon his first official visit to all six diplomatic allies in the Pacific. The Prime Minister of Tuvalu, Apisai Ielemia, undertook an official visit to Taiwan in April. In June the various bilateral projects were also among the topics discussed with their Taiwanese counterpart during the respective visits to Taipei of Kiribati President Anote Tong and Marshallese President Jurelang Zedkaia.

Other external relations

Taiwan's relations with Africa have been similarly governed by competition with China for influence. In January 1997 the Taiwanese Minister of Foreign Affairs embarked upon a tour of seven African nations, including South Africa, in an attempt to consolidate relations. In January 1998, however, South Africa transferred diplomatic recognition from Taiwan to China. In February the Minister of Foreign Affairs visited eight African countries, and in April it was announced that Taiwan's overseas aid budget was to be substantially increased, in an attempt to retain diplomatic support. In August 2000 the new Taiwanese President, Chen Shui-bian, embarked upon a tour of diplomatic allies in West Africa, and in July 2002 he visited Senegal, São Tomé and Príncipe, Malawi and Swaziland. In subsequent years Taiwan suffered several diplomatic reverses in Africa, when diplomatic recognition was transferred to the People's Republic of China by Liberia in October 2003, Senegal in October 2005, and Chad in August 2006. The Taiwanese Minister of Foreign Affairs visited several other African states in 2007, and in September Taiwan hosted the first Taiwan-Africa Summit, which was attended by its five African allies. In January 2008, however, it was announced that Malawi had severed diplomatic relations with Taiwan. President Yahya Jammeh of The Gambia undertook his eighth state visit to Taiwan in April 2009. In July 2010 President Ma received King Mswati III of Swaziland. In April 2012 Ma undertook an African tour, visiting Burkina Faso, The Gambia and Swaziland, where various assistance agreements were concluded.

Similar trends characterized Taiwan's relations with the countries of Central America and the Caribbean. In July 1997, following the Bahamas' establishment of diplomatic relations with the People's Republic of China, the Taiwanese Minister of Foreign Affairs undertook an extensive tour of the countries of Central America and the Caribbean, in an effort to maintain their support. In September President Lee also toured Central America, the six nations of the region having become the core of Taiwan's remaining diplomatic allies. In August 2000 the new Taiwanese President, Chen Shui-bian, embarked upon a tour of diplomatic allies in Central America. As Taiwan continued to seek diplomatic recognition in return for aid and investment, in May 2001 President Chen began a tour of five Latin American nations: El Salvador, Guatemala, Panama, Paraguay and Honduras. In March 2004 Dominica withdrew its diplomatic recog-

nition of Taiwan, as did Grenada in January 2005. Saint Lucia restored recognition in May 2007, but Costa Rica terminated diplomatic links in June. Following his assumption of office in the previous year, in mid-2009 President Ma Ying-jeou undertook official visits to Belize, Guatemala, El Salvador, Panama and Nicaragua. In January 2010 President Ma visited Honduras and the Dominican Republic.

In the 1990s relations with Europe were dominated by the issue of purchases of French defence equipment. In January 1993 official confirmation of Taiwan's purchase of 60 *Mirage* fighter aircraft from France provoked a strong protest from China. Taiwan suffered a reverse in January 1994 when (following pressure from the People's Republic) France recognized Taiwan as an integral part of Chinese territory and agreed not to sell weapons to the island. In March 1995, however, it was reported that Taiwan was to purchase anti-aircraft missiles from a French company; the sale was subsequently confirmed. In 1996 the first delivery of *Mirage* aircraft to Taiwan from France took place. It was confirmed that, as agreed in 1991, France would proceed with the sales of six frigates to Taiwan; delivery of these was completed in March 1998. There were tensions in Taiwan's relations with France in early 2004, after President Jacques Chirac expressed his support for China's opposition to a proposed referendum in Taiwan (see Domestic Political Affairs) during a visit by Chinese President Hu Jintao to Paris. Two visits by Taiwanese ministers to France were subsequently cancelled, and joint military exercises between the French and mainland Chinese navies were held in March off Taiwan's northern coast. In May 2010, ruling that the payment of commission to intermediaries involved in the sale of the six French frigates to the island in the 1990s had been a breach of the terms of the contract, an international court of arbitration ordered France and the company concerned to pay the sum of €630m. to Taiwan in compensation.

In January 1997 the Taiwanese Vice-President was received by the Pope during a visit to the Holy See, the only European state that continued to recognize Taiwan. A visit to Europe in October by Vice-President Lien Chan was curtailed when pressure from China forced the Spanish Government to withdraw an invitation. In November 2001 Wu Shu-jen, wife of President Chen, travelled to Strasbourg, France, to accept the 'Prize for Freedom' awarded to her husband by Liberal International, a world grouping of liberal parties. Chen himself had been refused a visa by the European Union (EU). In March 2003 President Chen was again refused a visa by the EU, and was thus unable to travel to Belgium to address members of the European Parliament in Brussels. In early 2010 Taiwan's proposed purchase from the European Aeronautic Defence and Space Company, a corporation based in the Netherlands, of three helicopters attracted some controversy. Although the aircraft were ostensibly being acquired for civilian purposes, observers noted that the Taiwanese air force, rather than the police or coastguard, was to receive the helicopters.

Despite the lack of official diplomatic relations, Taiwan has close links with the EU through the European Chamber of Commerce Taipei, which represents European business interests in Taiwan. In 2011 Taiwan was the EU's fourth largest trading partner in Asia. Taiwan's exports were, however, adversely affected by the ongoing economic difficulties of heavily indebted members of the eurozone.

CONSTITUTION AND GOVERNMENT

Under the provisions of the amended 1947 Constitution, the head of state is the President, who is elected by popular vote for a four-year term. There are five Yuans (governing bodies), the highest legislative organ being the Legislative Yuan, to which the Executive Yuan (the Cabinet) is responsible. Since the elections of January 2008, the Legislative Yuan has comprised 113 members; 73 chosen by direct election and most of the remainder appointed from separate lists of candidates on the basis of proportional representation. The Legislative Yuan serves a four-year term. There are also Control, Judicial and Examination Yuans. Their respective functions are: to investigate the work of the executive; to interpret the Constitution and national laws; and to supervise examinations for entry into public office. In 2000 the role of the National Assembly was revised. The powers to initiate constitutional amendments, to impeach the President or Vice-President, and to approve the appointment of senior officials were transferred to the Legislative Yuan. The National Assembly retained the functions of ratifying constitutional amendments and responsibility for impeachment proceedings, in which case 300 delegates appointed by political parties according to a system of proportional representation were to convene for a session of a maximum duration of one month. In 1997 the National Assembly approved a series of constitutional amendments, in the first stage of the dissolution of the long-standing provincial apparatus. The Fukien (Fujian) Provincial Government has remained responsible for the administration of various islands, including Kinmen (Quemoy) and Matsu.

REGIONAL AND INTERNATIONAL CO-OPERATION

Taiwan, under the name of 'Chinese Taipei', is a member of the Asian Development Bank (ADB, see p. 214) and of Asia-Pacific Economic Cooperation (APEC, see p. 208).

The Republic of China was removed from the UN in 1971. In 1992 Taiwan was granted observer status at the General Agreement on Tariffs and Trade (GATT) as the 'Separate Customs Territory of Taiwan, Penghu, Kinmen and Matsu (Chinese Taipei)'; it became a full member of the successor World Trade Organization (WTO, see p. 444) in 2002.

ECONOMIC AFFAIRS

In 2012, according to provisional official figures, Taiwan's gross national income (GNI), at current prices, totalled US $489,366m., equivalent to US $21,035 per head. During 2002–12, it was estimated, the population increased at an average annual rate of 0.3%, while in real terms, on the basis of figures in US dollars, gross domestic product (GDP) per head grew at an average annual rate of 4.3% over the same period. In terms of New Taiwan dollars, overall GDP increased at an average annual rate of 3.9% in 2002–12. GDP expanded by 1.3% in 2012.

Agriculture (including hunting, forestry and fishing) contributed 1.9% of GDP and engaged 5.0% of the employed labour force in 2012. The principal crops are vegetables, rice, sugar cane and pineapples. Agricultural GDP decreased at an average annual rate of 0.1%, in real terms, during 2002–12. Agricultural GDP rose by 7.2% in 2011, but declined by 5.8% in 2012.

Industry (comprising mining, manufacturing, construction and utilities) engaged 36.2% of the employed labour force in 2012, when it provided 29.9% of GDP. Industrial GDP increased, in real terms, at an average rate of 6.5% per year in 2002–12. Industrial GDP expanded by 0.9% in 2012.

Mining contributed 0.3% of GDP in 2012, employing a negligible percentage of the labour force. Marble, sulphur and dolomite are the principal minerals extracted. The GDP of the mining sector decreased, in real terms, at an average rate of 1.7% per year in 2002–12. Mining GDP increased by 10.4% in 2012.

Manufacturing contributed 25.0% of GDP and engaged 27.4% of the employed labour force in 2012. The most important branches, measured by gross value of output, are electronics (particularly personal computers), plastic goods, synthetic yarns and the motor vehicle industry. The sector's GDP grew at an average annual rate of 7.4%, in real terms, in 2002–12. Manufacturing GDP increased by 1.0% in 2012.

Construction contributed 2.9% of GDP and engaged 7.8% of the employed labour force in 2012. The sector's GDP grew at an average annual rate of 0.6%, in real terms, in 2002–12. The GDP of the construction sector decreased by 1.0% in 2012.

In 2011 45.4% of Taiwan's energy supply was derived from imported petroleum and 8.1% from nuclear power. Imports of crude petroleum accounted for 13.2% of total import expenditure in 2012. Taiwan has substantial reserves of natural gas.

The services sector contributed 68.2% of GDP in 2012, when it engaged 58.8% of the employed labour force. The number of foreign visitors in 2011 was reported to have increased to almost 6.1m. (of whom nearly 3.6m. were tourists), rising to more than 7.3m. in 2012. Overseas Chinese visitors and travellers from Japan and accounted for the majority of arrivals. Tourism receipts reached US $11,065m. in 2011. In 2002–12 the GDP of the services sector increased, in real terms, at an average annual rate of 3.0%. The GDP of the services sector expanded by 1.0% in 2012.

In 2012 Taiwan recorded a visible merchandise trade surplus of US $30,735m. and there was a surplus of US $49,550m. on the current account of the balance of payments. In 2012 the principal sources of imports were Japan (providing 17.6% of total imports), the People's Republic of China, the USA, the Republic of Korea and Saudi Arabia. The principal markets for exports in that year were the People's Republic of China (accounting for 26.8% of total exports), Hong Kong, the USA, Singapore and Japan. Trade with the People's Republic of China (mainly via Hong Kong) has expanded rapidly in recent years. The value of exports to mainland China increased from US $4,391.5m. in 2000 to US $80,729.2m. in 2012. Taiwan's principal imports in 2012 were machinery, mechanical appliances and electrical equipment, crude petroleum, and chemical and allied products. The principal exports in that year were machinery, mechanical appliances and electrical equipment (especially electronic products), base metals, plastics, mineral products and chemicals.

A budget deficit of NT $306,646m., equivalent to 2.2% of GDP, was recorded in 2011. According to the Asian Development Bank, Taiwan's external debt amounted to US $124,325m. in 2012, in which year the cost of debt-servicing was equivalent to 1.6% of the value of exports of goods and services. The annual rate of inflation averaged 1.2% during the period 2002–11. Consumer prices rose by 1.9% in 2012. The rate of unemployment averaged 4.2% of the labour force in 2012.

Owing to its heavy dependence on external trade, Taiwan was badly affected by the global recession of 2008/09. Foreign direct investment declined, and in late 2008 the Government began to implement fiscal stimulus measures, which included tax concessions for new investment by companies and support for low-income families. Historically, the island has held consistently large reserves of foreign exchange, which in March 2013 stood at US $401,890m., among the largest in the world. In 2010 increasing demand for residential property, arising largely from speculative activity, prompted the authorities to restrict lending for the purposes of purchasing a second home. The central bank's interest rate was raised to reach 1.875% in September 2011, at which level it remained in early 2013. Despite intermittent political tensions, economic links with the People's Republic of China have become increasingly significant, with the value of Taiwan's exports to the mainland rising from less than 8% of total exports in 2002 to around 27% in 2012; Taiwanese investment on the mainland also grew substantially. The Economic Co-operation Framework Agreement, concluded with mainland China in 2010, was expected to enhance bilateral trade exchanges, through the reduction of tariffs on hundreds of items, and promote investment in Taiwan. The first tariff reductions were implemented in January 2011, and during 2011–12 restrictions on mainland investors were reduced. In August 2012 the two sides signed an agreement on investment protection, providing formal means of settling any disputes. Taiwanese exports were adversely affected in 2011–12 by the debt crisis in the eurozone, one of its principal markets, and by the slow progress of economic recovery in the USA, although domestic demand was maintained, with support from the growing number of tourists from mainland China (more than 2.2m. in 2012, an increase of some 49% over the previous year). Although unemployment averaged just over 4.2% in 2012, labour shortages were reported in some sectors. Following the exceptional economic growth of 10.8% achieved in 2010, the Government reported a more modest growth rate of 4.1% in 2011, declining to 1.3% in 2012; it predicted growth of some 3.6% in 2013, anticipating an increase in export revenue, particularly that derived from electronic products. In September 2012 the Government announced measures to stimulate the economy, including support for the development of new export markets, the encouragement of industrial innovation and diversification of businesses, the promotion of tourism, and the attraction of investment from mainland China and elsewhere, while also urging Taiwanese businesses based overseas to invest in Taiwan.

PUBLIC HOLIDAYS

2014: 1 January (Founding of the Republic/New Year), 30 January–3 February (Chinese New Year), 28 February (Peace Memorial Day), 4 April (Children's Day), 5 April (Ching Ming/Tomb Sweeping Day), 2 June (Dragon Boat Festival), 3 September (Armed Forces Day), 8 September (for Mid-Autumn Moon Festival), 10 October (Double Tenth Day, anniversary of 1911 revolution).

Statistical Survey

Source (unless otherwise stated): Directorate-General of Budget, Accounting and Statistics (DGBAS), 1, Section 1, Jhongsiao East Rd, Taipei 10058; tel. (2) 23803542; fax (2) 23803547; e-mail sicbs@dgbas.gov.tw; internet www.dgbas.gov.tw.

Area and Population

AREA, POPULATION AND DENSITY

Area (sq km)	36,193*
Population (census results)	
16 December 2000	22,300,929
26 December 2010 (preliminary)	
Males	11,489,285
Females	11,634,581
Total	23,123,866
Population (official estimates at 31 December)	
2011	23,224,912
2012	23,315,822
Density (per sq km) at 31 December 2012	644.2

* 13,974 sq miles.

POPULATION BY AGE AND SEX
(official estimates at 31 December 2011)

	Males	Females	Total
0–14	1,827,145	1,674,645	3,501,790
15–64	8,619,981	8,574,892	17,194,873
65 and over	1,198,548	1,329,701	2,528,249
Total	11,645,674	11,579,238	23,224,912

PRINCIPAL TOWNS
(population at 2010 census, preliminary)

Taipei (capital) . .	2,655,570	Jhongli	403,047
Kaohsiung . . .	1,515,335	Sanchong . . .	394,106
Taichung . . .	1,147,925	Keelung . . .	381,891
Tainan . . .	787,224	Fongshan . . .	376,420
Banciao . . .	597,279	Sindian . . .	302,629
Hsinchu . . .	476,237	Chiayi . . .	264,876
Jhunghe . . .	427,225	Tucheng . . .	253,283
Taoyuan . . .	419,821	Yonghe . . .	236,744
Sinjhuang . . .	406,150	Jhanghua . . .	226,476

BIRTHS, MARRIAGES AND DEATHS
(registered)

	Live births		Marriages		Deaths	
	Number	Rate (per 1,000)	Number	Rate (per 1,000)	Number	Rate (per 1,000)
2005 . .	205,854	9.06	141,140	6.21	139,398	6.13
2006 . .	204,459	8.96	142,669	6.25	135,839	5.95
2007 . .	204,414	8.92	135,041	5.89	141,111	6.16
2008 . .	198,733	8.64	154,866	6.73	143,624	6.25
2009 . .	191,310	8.29	117,099	5.07	143,582	6.22
2010 . .	166,886	7.21	138,819	6.00	145,772	6.30
2011 . .	196,627	8.48	165,327	7.13	152,915	6.59
2012 . .	229,481	9.86	143,384	6.16	154,251	6.63

Life expectancy (years at birth, 2011, provisional): 79.1 (males 76.0; females 82.7).

ECONOMICALLY ACTIVE POPULATION
(annual averages, '000 persons aged 15 years and over)*

	2010	2011	2012
Agriculture, forestry and fishing .	550	542	544
Mining and quarrying	4	4	4
Manufacturing	2,861	2,949	2,975
Construction	797	831	845
Electricity and gas supply . . .	29	29	29
Water supply and remediation services	78	79	82
Services	6,174	6,275	6,381
Trade	1,747	1,763	1,800
Hotels and restaurants . . .	727	728	750
Transport and storage . . .	404	411	414
Information and communication	208	218	228
Finance and insurance . . .	428	428	426
Education	619	629	630
Public administration, defence and compulsory social security	389	388	384
Total employed	10,493	10,709	10,860
Unemployed	577	491	481
Total labour force	11,070	11,200	11,341
Males	6,242	6,304	6,369
Females	4,828	4,896	4,972

* Excluding members of the armed forces and persons in institutional households.

Health and Welfare

KEY INDICATORS

Total fertility rate (children per woman, 2011)	1.1
Under-5 mortality rate (per 1,000 live births, 2006)	6.06
HIV/AIDS (% of persons aged 15–49, 2006)	0.03
Physicians (per 1,000 head, 2008)	1.83
Hospital beds (per 1,000 head, 2011)	69.1
Health expenditure (2009): NT $ per head	37,224
Health expenditure (2009): % of GDP	6.9
Health expenditure (2005): public (% of total)	62.90
Human Development Index (2004): value	0.925

For definitions, see explanatory note on p. vi.

Note: Data are mainly from Directorate-General of Budget, Accounting and Statistics (DGBAS).

Agriculture

PRINCIPAL CROPS
('000 metric tons)

	2009	2010	2011
Rice, paddy	1,578.2	1,451.0	1,666.3
Sweet potatoes	229.0	209.2	205.9
Sorghum	0.7	4.4	3.4
Tea	16.8	17.5	17.3
Tobacco	1.9	1.9	1.7
Groundnuts	56.9	65.0	68.2
Sugar cane	613.2	665.4	654.0
Bananas	172.6	287.9	305.7
Pineapples	434.8	420.2	401.4

LIVESTOCK
('000 head at 31 December)

	2008	2009	2010
Cattle	134.0	133.7	140.0
Buffaloes	3.6	3.9	3.8
Pigs	6,427.6	6,130.0	6,186.0
Goats	229.5	206.4	204.9
Chickens	100,298	100,770	98,988
Ducks	9,177	9,319	9,474
Geese	1,990	2,001	2,136
Turkeys	147	132	131

LIVESTOCK PRODUCTS

	2009	2010	2011
Beef (metric tons)	6,099	6,343	6,169
Pig meat ('000 metric tons)	857.2	845.5	864.8
Sheep and goat meat (metric tons)	3,000	2,694	2,438
Chickens ('000 head)*	329,151	334,761	n.a.
Ducks ('000 head)*	29,246	30,301	n.a.
Geese ('000 head)*	4,593	4,700	n.a.
Turkeys ('000 head)*	230	216	n.a.
Cow's milk (metric tons)	321,781	336,036	350,894
Duck eggs ('000)	442,355	483,822	469,955
Hen eggs ('000)	6,431,571	6,728,450	6,680,044

* Figures refer to numbers slaughtered.

Forestry

ROUNDWOOD REMOVALS
('000 cubic metres)

	2009	2010	2011
Industrial wood	25.2	19.1	23.3
Fuel wood	2.6	0.3	0.7
Mill wood	0.1	0.0	0.2
Total	27.9	19.5	24.2

Fishing

('000 metric tons, live weight)

	2008	2009	2010
Tilapias	81.0	67.3	74.9
Japanese eel	21.0	19.0	19.4
Milkfish	46.9	40.8	35.7
Pacific saury	139.5	104.2	165.7
Skipjack tuna	168.9	179.0	171.1
Albacore	37.6	37.3	50.5
Yellowfin tuna	71.3	50.7	67.4
Bigeye tuna	53.8	60.7	49.7
Chub mackerel	56.0	70.2	62.2
Sharks, rays, skates, etc.	39.8	33.0	32.5
Pacific cupped oyster	34.4	27.2	36.1
Common squids	5.0	4.6	5.8
Argentine shortfin squid	240.3	68.8	59.8
Sailfish	24.2	22.3	24.7
Total catch (incl. others)	1,339.3	1,087.8	1,167.1

Mining

(metric tons unless otherwise indicated)

	2004	2005	2006
Crude petroleum ('000 litres)	44,562	32,389	23,565
Natural gas ('000 cu m)	706,991	486,646	411,524
Sulphur*	222,760	267,790	245,789
Marble (raw material)*	22,970,546	24,069,551	25,492,633
Dolomite*	114,598	173,986	61,224

* Preliminary figures.

Crude petroleum ('000 litres): 15,996 in 2009; 14,229 in 2010; 11,344 in 2011.

Natural gas ('000 cu m): 311,701 in 2009; 263,291 in 2010; 293,476 in 2011.

Industry

SELECTED PRODUCTS
('000 metric tons unless otherwise indicated)

	2009	2010	2011
Carbonated beverages ('000 litres)	310,554	297,099	310,101
Alcoholic beverages—excl. beer ('000 hectolitres)	625.5	825.7	1,007.6
Paperboard	2,775.3	2,850.4	2,931.1
Spun yarn	153.4	161.9	144.4
Cement	15,918.5	16,301.0	16,852.0
Steel ingots	15,566.4	20,498.1	22,878.5
Sewing machines ('000 units)	1,118.4	1,374.2	1,357.6
Electric fans ('000 units)	4,853.2	6,680.4	5,775.7
Portable personal computers ('000 units)	378.7	333.1	3,292.6
Mobile phones ('000 units)	15,983.5	n.a.	n.a.
LCD displays ('000 units)	943.7	1,171.6	1,192.9
Integrated circuits (million units)	4,756.1	7,407.8	7,867.9
Electronic condensers (million units)	166,372	199,886	176,624
Global positioning systems	20,661	21,157	20,931
Telephone sets ('000 units)	469.6	461.8	450.7
Passenger motor cars ('000 units)	178.3	233.8	270.6
Trucks, buses and commercial vans ('000 units)	46.9	67.4	70.6
Bicycles ('000 units)	4,778.9	5,276.4	4,677.1
Electric energy (million kWh)	217,485	233,109	238,661

2012: Carbonated beverages ('000 litres) 292,400; Paperboard 3,073.6; Cement 15,807.6; Steel ingots 21,803.3; Personal computers ('000 units) 740.9; Electronic condensers (million units) 165,243; Global positioning systems 18,581; Electric energy (million kWh) 237,289.

Finance

CURRENCY AND EXCHANGE RATES

Monetary Units
100 cents = 1 New Taiwan dollar (NT $).

Sterling, US Dollar and Euro Equivalents (31 December 2012)
£1 sterling = NT $45.977;
US $1 = NT $29.136;
€1 = NT $38.442;
NT $1,000 = £21.75 = US $34.32 = €26.01.

Average Exchange Rate (NT $ per US $)
2010   31.647
2011   29.469
2012   29.616

GENERAL GOVERNMENT BUDGET
(NT $ million, year ending 31 December)

Revenue	2009	2010	2011
Current revenue	2,041,412	2,062,022	2,238,964
Taxes	1,483,518	1,565,847	1,703,989
Income tax	640,967	590,387	710,191
Business tax	223,503	268,214	283,884
Fees	92,008	96,458	96,250
Fines and indemnities . .	41,402	43,021	41,675
Public enterprise and utilities surplus	330,928	286,479	293,954
Public properties profits . .	14,110	16,085	14,279
Donations, etc.	8,657	12,204	9,333
Other	70,789	41,928	79,484
Capital revenue	72,232	53,532	67,151
Total	2,113,644	2,115,554	2,306,115

Expenditure	2009	2010	2011
General administration . . .	357,412	368,420	375,991
National defence	297,746	286,929	288,969
Education, science and culture .	581,535	554,254	588,652
Economic development . . .	601,896	517,039	473,520
Agriculture	162,784	191,955	170,978
Industry	38,155	36,691	27,856
Transport and communication .	250,679	228,049	232,408
Other	150,278	60,345	42,278
Social welfare	388,562	415,356	446,949
Social insurance	189,263	203,082	225,305
Social relief	24,143	30,835	31,172
Benefit service	136,716	138,619	147,756
Employment service . . .	2,742	4,784	5,317
Medical care	35,698	38,037	37,400
Community development and environmental protection .	91,639	89,388	88,784
Community development . .	18,953	12,047	8,772
Environmental protection . .	72,686	77,341	80,012
Pensions and survivors' benefits .	205,291	201,002	213,039
Obligations	129,484	119,615	121,125
Miscellaneous	17,333	14,801	15,733
Total	2,670,898	2,566,804	2,612,761
Current	2,008,372	1,911,511	2,020,149
Capital	662,526	655,293	592,612

Note: Totals may not be equal to the sum of components, owing to rounding.

INTERNATIONAL RESERVES
(US $ million at 31 December)

	2010	2011	2012
Gold (national valuation) . . .	5,202	5,043	5,283
Foreign exchange	382,005	385,547	403,169
Total	387,207	390,590	408,452

MONEY SUPPLY
(NT $ '000 million at 31 December)

	2010	2011	2012
Currency outside banks . . .	995.9	1,107.3	1,203.2
Demand deposits at deposit money banks	10,461.3	10,722.9	11,215.0
Total money	11,457.1	11,830.2	12,418.2

COST OF LIVING
(Consumer Price Index; base: 2006 = 100)

	2009	2010	2011
Food	111.2	111.8	114.4
Clothing	104.8	107.3	110.8
Housing	102.1	102.6	103.4
Transport and communications .	99.9	102.7	104.2
Medicines and medical care . .	106.8	107.5	109.5
Education and entertainment . .	100.1	100.1	100.6
All items (incl. others) . . .	104.5	105.5	107.0

NATIONAL ACCOUNTS
(NT $ million in current prices)

National Income and Product

	2010	2011	2012
Domestic factor incomes . .	10,816,862	10,801,207	11,108,977
Consumption of fixed capital . .	2,004,347	2,090,867	2,144,980
Gross domestic product (GDP) at factor cost	12,821,209	12,892,074	13,253,957
Indirect taxes, *less* subsidies . .	730,890	782,272	782,917
GDP in purchasers' values .	13,552,099	13,674,346	14,036,874
Net factor income from abroad .	429,639	388,372	452,333
Gross national product (GNP) .	13,981,738	14,062,718	14,489,207
Less Consumption of fixed capital .	2,004,347	2,090,867	2,144,980
Statistical discrepancy . . .	100,451	165,711	−129,682
National income in market prices	12,077,842	12,137,562	12,214,545
Other current transfers from abroad (net)	−85,762	−108,770	−70,690
National disposable income .	11,992,080	12,028,792	12,143,855

Expenditure on the Gross Domestic Product

	2010	2011	2012
Government final consumption expenditure	1,642,101	1,698,360	1,738,303
Private final consumption expenditure	7,924,534	8,234,626	8,464,359
Gross capital formation . . .	3,035,232	2,836,456	2,787,151
Total domestic expenditure .	12,601,867	12,769,442	12,989,813
Exports of goods and services . .	10,001,116	10,400,169	10,339,015
Less Imports of goods and services	9,050,884	9,495,265	9,291,954
GDP in purchasers' values .	13,552,099	13,674,346	14,036,874
GDP at constant 2006 prices .	14,215,069	14,792,928	14,978,940

Gross Domestic Product by Economic Activity

	2010	2011	2012
Agriculture, hunting, forestry and fishing	224,501	250,604	260,377
Mining and quarrying . . .	65,357	31,125	45,418
Manufacturing	3,536,574	3,474,749	3,374,028
Construction	383,943	394,823	396,447
Electricity, gas and water . . .	245,808	218,006	212,789
Transport, storage and communications	927,882	904,274	920,995
Trade, restaurants and hotels . .	2,775,076	2,908,825	2,919,841
Finance, insurance and real estate*	2,033,794	2,088,031	2,112,458
Public administration, defence, health and social work . .	1,491,562	1,527,079	1,568,584
Education	626,532	638,960	654,332
Other services	939,732	976,676	1,023,868
Sub-total	13,250,761	13,413,152	13,489,137
Value added tax	249,680	264,154	260,540
Import duties	152,109	162,751	157,515
Statistical discrepancy	−100,451	−165,711	129,682
GDP in purchasers' values .	13,552,099	13,674,346	14,036,874

*Including imputed rents of owner-occupied dwellings.

BALANCE OF PAYMENTS
(US $ million)

	2010	2011	2012
Exports of goods f.o.b.	273,823	307,030	299,756
Imports of goods f.o.b.	−247,310	−279,182	−269,021
Trade balance	26,513	27,848	30,735
Exports of services	40,357	45,920	49,046
Imports of services	−37,864	−42,026	−42,909
Balance on goods and services	29,006	31,742	36,872
Other income received . . .	23,265	24,832	25,861
Other income paid	−9,688	−11,654	−10,584
Balance on goods, services and income	42,583	44,920	52,149
Current transfers received . .	5,251	5,547	5,446
Current transfers paid	−7,961	−9,238	−8,045

—*continued*			2010	2011	2012
Current balance	. . . .	.	39,873	41,230	49,550
Capital account (net)	. . .	.	−116	−119	−100
Direct investment abroad	. .	.	−11,574	−12,766	−13,031
Direct investment from abroad	.	.	2,492	−1,957	3,205
Portfolio investment assets	.	.	−33,487	−19,503	−45,361
Portfolio investment liabilities	.	.	12,823	−16,188	2,914
Financial derivatives assets	.	.	4,497	5,777	4,526
Financial derivatives liabilities	.	.	−3,920	−4,739	−4,198
Other investment assets	. .	.	12,317	−7,988	5,771
Other investment liabilities	.	.	16,494	25,318	14,671
Net errors and omissions	. .	.	775	−2,826	−2,463
Overall balance	. . . .	.	40,173	6,239	15,484

External Trade

PRINCIPAL COMMODITIES
(US $ million)

Imports c.i.f.		2010	2011	2012
Mineral products	. . . .	55,326.2	68,166.9	74,204.0
Crude petroleum	. . . .	25,676.9	30,320.2	35,661.0
Products of chemical or allied				
industries	. . . .	29,339.1	34,026.8	30,061.6
Organic chemicals	. .	10,675.1	13,598.2	11,728.9
Base metals and articles thereof	.	24,352.5	27,033.2	23,155.9
Iron and steel products	. .	12,433.6	14,340.8	12,326.1
Other metal products	. .	11,918.8	12,692.4	10,829.6
Machinery and mechanical				
appliances; electrical equipment;				
sound and television apparatus .		86,522.7	89,043.6	81,304.9
Electronic products	. . .	42,719.2	44,502.6	40,762.2
Machinery	. . . .	26,325.0	24,633.4	21,299.9
Vehicles, aircraft, vessels and				
associated transport equipment .		6,132.8	7,139.2	7,638.3
Optical, photographic,				
cinematographic, measuring,				
precision and medical apparatus;				
clocks and watches; musical				
instruments	. . . .	10,857.9	11,266.2	10,602.2
Total (incl. others)	. . . .	251,236.2	281,437.2	270,726.5

Exports f.o.b.		2010	2011	2012
Mineral products	. . . .	14,846.4	17,921.3	22,068.4
Chemicals	. . . . .	19,227.4	22,463.3	20,792.2
Plastics, rubber and articles thereof		22,254.7	25,199.8	24,192.5
Plastics and articles thereof		19,652.1	21,942.7	21,069.4
Textiles and textile articles	. .	11,301.5	12,715.5	11,821.4
Fibre and yarn	. . .	8,493.8	9,653.8	8,954.0
Base metals and articles thereof	.	25,884.4	30,177.8	28,094.6
Iron and steel	. . . .	16,376.9	19,292.1	17,711.3
Other metal products	. .	9,507.3	10,886.2	10,383.3
Machinery and mechanical				
appliances; electrical equipment;				
sound and television apparatus .		131,276.9	144,308.1	138,781.0
Electronic products	. . .	77,306.1	83,909.1	83,306.9
Machinery	. . . .	16,725.4	20,469.7	20,093.9
Electrical machinery products .		11,282.1	9,453.6	9,628.8
Information and communication				
products	. . . .	14,095.4	19,808.4	15,479.2
Vehicles, aircraft, vessels and				
associated transport equipment .		9,333.2	10,301.7	11,082.3
Optical, photographic,				
cinematographic, measuring,				
precision and medical apparatus;				
clocks and watches; musical				
instruments	. . . .	23,623.6	23,904.7	23,349.4
Total (incl. others)	. . . .	274,600.8	308,257.4	301,110.7

PRINCIPAL TRADING PARTNERS
(US $ million)

Imports c.i.f.		2010	2011	2012
Angola	. . . . .	2,878.1	5,658.8	5,003.3
Australia	. . . . .	8,921.4	10,907.3	9,312.7
China, People's Republic	. . .	35,946.0	43,596.5	40,910.0
France	. . . . .	2,250.2	2,725.9	2,960.0
Germany	. . . . .	8,264.1	9,427.6	7,755.2
India	. . . . .	2,837.5	3,136.5	2,623.7
Indonesia	. . . . .	6,020.2	7,428.2	7,339.0
Iran	. . . . .	2,714.4	2,491.8	1,465.2
Iraq	. . . . .	1,928.9	954.3	2,612.8
Japan	. . . . .	51,917.4	52,199.7	47,583.4
Korea, Republic	. . .	16,058.8	17,860.3	15,075.4
Kuwait	. . . . .	6,124.8	7,695.8	8,620.1
Malaysia	. . . . .	7,695.0	8,601.5	7,886.7
Netherlands	. . . . .	3,199.9	2,936.0	3,624.7
Russia	. . . . .	2,335.8	2,357.2	3,135.1
Saudi Arabia	. . . . .	11,859.2	13,846.6	14,807.6
Singapore	. . . . .	7,636.1	7,953.1	8,105.8
Thailand	. . . . .	3,829.0	4,393.5	3,696.3
United Arab Emirates	. . .	3,511.6	4,280.2	4,638.5
USA	. . . . .	25,379.4	25,758.8	23,605.0
Total (incl. others)	. . . .	251,236.4	281,437.5	270,727.2

Exports f.o.b.		2010	2011	2012
Australia	. . . . .	3,132.1	3,652.6	3,653.3
China, People's Republic	. . .	76,935.1	83,960.0	80,729.2
Germany	. . . . .	6,511.6	6,868.9	5,644.8
Hong Kong*	. . . .	37,807.1	40,084.5	37,936.9
India	. . . . .	3,628.4	4,427.4	3,384.5
Indonesia	. . . . .	4,509.6	4,836.6	5,190.1
Italy	. . . . .	2,447.2	2,459.0	1,833.1
Japan	. . . . .	18,006.0	18,228.1	18,876.6
Korea, Republic	. . .	10,681.6	12,378.2	11,845.3
Malaysia	. . . . .	5,947.9	6,891.7	6,560.4
Netherlands	. . . . .	5,261.1	4,578.9	4,413.7
Philippines	. . . . .	5,982.0	6,964.3	8,876.6
Singapore	. . . . .	12,096.4	16,879.8	20,090.8
Thailand	. . . . .	5,288.5	6,139.6	6,566.3
United Kingdom	. . .	3,621.4	4,619.6	5,064.7
USA	. . . . .	31,466.0	36,364.3	32,980.5
Viet Nam	. . . . .	7,533.5	9,026.5	8,432.2
Total (incl. others)	. . . .	274,600.5	308,257.3	301,111.2

* The majority of Taiwan's exports to Hong Kong are re-exported.

Transport

RAILWAYS
(traffic)

		2010	2011	2012
Passengers ('000)	. . . .	778,779	864,491	925,243
Passenger-km ('000)	. . .	20,930,785	22,825,848	24,207,701
Freight ('000 metric tons)	. .	15,106	14,451	13,905
Freight ton-km ('000)	. . .	872,520	853,362	833,102

ROAD TRAFFIC
(motor vehicles in use at 31 December)

		2010	2011	2012
Passenger cars	. . . . .	5,803,413	5,960,088	6,091,324
Buses and coaches	. . .	29,030	29,991	31,098
Goods vehicles	. . . . .	993,550	1,012,953	1,019,484
Motorcycles and scooters	. .	14,844,932	15,173,602	15,139,628

SHIPPING

Flag Registered Fleet
(at 31 December)

	2010	2011	2012
Number of vessels	297	306	312
Total displacement ('000 grt) . .	2,595.3	2,691.8	2,933.4

Source: Lloyd's List Intelligence (www.lloydslistintelligence.com).

International sea-borne freight traffic

	2009	2010	2011
Vessels entered ('000 grt) . . .	525,502	559,768	592,117
Vessels cleared ('000 grt) . . .	515,483	548,691	572,716
Goods loaded ('000 metric tons) .	45,750	49,257	47,347
Goods unloaded ('000 metric tons).	157,039	168,826	167,340

CIVIL AVIATION
(traffic on scheduled services)

	2010	2011	2012
Passengers carried ('000) . . .	37,469	39,577	43,547
Freight carried ('000 metric tons) .	1,200.6	1,144.5	1,138.2

Tourism

TOURIST ARRIVALS BY COUNTRY OF ORIGIN

	2009	2010	2011
Australia	56,697	61,831	59,623
Canada	59,490	64,074	67,049
Germany	39,372	42,280	44,506
Hong Kong and Macao . . .	84,685	93,662	97,222
Indonesia	106,272	123,409	155,881
Japan	998,973	1,078,459	1,292,999
Korea, Republic	164,152	213,863	239,740
Malaysia	166,354	285,038	307,301
Philippines	73,182	84,464	98,740
Singapore	194,129	241,008	299,238
Thailand	77,344	91,657	101,695
United Kingdom	44,619	44,242	43,278
USA	365,266	391,440	408,054
Total (incl. others)	2,770,082	3,235,477	3,588,727

Note: Figures exclude arrivals of Overseas Chinese (i.e. those bearing Taiwan passports) resident abroad (especially Hong Kong and Macao): 2,331,800 in 2010; 2,498,757 in 2011; 3,479,835 in 2012.

Total visitor arrivals: 5,567,277 in 2010; 6,087,484 in 2011; 7,311,470 in 2012.

Tourism receipts (US $ million): 6,816 in 2009; 8,719 in 2010; 11,065 in 2011.

Communications Media

	2010	2011	2012
Book production (titles) . . .	43,208	42,566	n.a.
Newspapers (titles)	193	207	209
Magazines	1,078	1,121	1,183
Telephone subscribers ('000) . .	12,696	12,679	12,411
Mobile telephones ('000 in use) .	27,840	28,862	29,449
Internet subscribers ('000) . .	5,888	6,092	6,988
Broadband subscribers ('000)* . .	5,312	5,516	n.a.

* Source: International Telecommunication Union.

Television receivers (2006): 152.3 colour television receivers per 100 households; 79.9 cable television receivers per 100 households.

Education

(2011/12 unless otherwise indicated)

	Schools	Full-time teachers	Students
Pre-school*	3,154	16,904	182,049
Primary	2,657	97,533	1,373,375
Secondary (incl. vocational) . .	1,235	106,206	1,617,003
Higher	162	50,158	1,355,290
Special	27	1,827	6,885
Supplementary*	834	1,488	240,392

* 2008/09.

Pupil-teacher ratio (primary education, official estimate): 14.1 in 2011/12.

Adult literacy rate (official estimate): 93.0% (males 96.3%; females 89.5%) in 2008.

Directory

Note: the issue of the implementation of a uniform system of romanization of Taiwanese names has remained unresolved; the central Government favours the use of a system of Pinyin similar to that employed in mainland China but with certain differences (Tongyong), while local authorities in Taiwan remain divided between usage of the standard mainland Pinyin system (Hanyu) and a form of the traditional Wade-Giles system.

The Government

HEAD OF STATE

President: MA YING-JEOU (elected 22 March 2008; inaugurated 20 May 2008; re-elected 14 January 2012; inaugurated 20 May 2012).

Vice-President: WU DEN-YIH.

Secretary-General: TIMOTHY YANG CHIN-TIEN.

EXECUTIVE YUAN
(May 2013)

The Government is formed by the Kuomintang.

Premier: JIANG YI-HUAH.

Vice-Premier: MAO CHI-KUO.

Secretary-General: CHEN WEI-ZEN.

Ministers without Portfolio: HUANG KUANG-NAN, LIN JUNQ-TZER, CHANG SAN-CHENG, YANG CHIU-HSING, SCHIVE CHI, STEVEN S. K. CHEN.

Minister of the Interior: LEE HONG-YUAN.

Minister of Foreign Affairs: DAVID Y. L. LIN.

Minister of National Defense: KAO HUA-CHU.

Minister of Finance: CHANG SHENG-FORD.

Minister of Education: CHIANG WEI-LING.

Minister of Justice: TSENG YUNG-FU.

Minister of Economic Affairs: CHANG CHIA-JUCH.

Minister of Transportation and Communications: YEH KUANG-SHIH.

Minister of Culture: LUNG YING-TAI.

Minister of the Mongolian and Tibetan Affairs Commission: LUO YING-SHAY.

Minister of the Overseas Compatriot Affairs Commission: WU YING-YIH.

Governor of the Central Bank: PERNG FAI-NAN.

Minister of the Directorate-General of Budget, Accounting and Statistics: SHIH SU-MEI.

Minister of the Directorate-General of Personnel Administration: HUANG FU-YUAN.

Minister of the Department of Health: CHIU WEN-TA.

Minister of the Environmental Protection Administration: STEPHEN SHU-HUNG SHEN.

Director of the National Palace Museum: FUNG MING-CHU.

Minister of the Mainland Affairs Council: WANG YU-CHI.

Minister of the Council for Economic Planning and Development: KUAN CHUNG-MING.

Minister of the Public Construction Commission: CHERN JENN-CHUAN.

Minister of the Veterans' Affairs Commission: TSENG JING-LING.

Minister of the National Youth Commission: CHEN YI-CHEN.

Minister of the Atomic Energy Council: TSAI CHUEN-HORNG.

Minister of the National Science Council: CYPRUS C. Y. CHU.

Minister of the Research, Development and Evaluation Commission: SUNG YU-HSIEH.

Minister of the Council of Agriculture: CHEN BAO-JI.

Minister of the Council of Labor Affairs: PAN SHIH-WEI.

Chairperson of the Fair Trade Commission: WU SHIOW-MING.

Minister of the Sports Affairs Council: TAI HSIA-LING.

Minister of the Council of Indigenous Peoples: SUN TA-CHUAN.

Minister of the Coast Guard Administration: WANG GINN-WANG.

Minister of the Council for Hakka Affairs: HUANG YU-CHENG.

Chairperson of the Central Election Commission: CHANG PO-YA.

Minister of the Financial Supervisory Commission: CHEN YUH-CHANG.

Chairperson of the National Communications Commission: HOWARD S. H. SHYR.

MINISTRIES, COMMISSIONS, ETC.

Office of the President: 122 Chungking South Rd, Zhongzheng District, Taipei 10048; tel. (2) 23113731; fax (2) 23311604; e-mail public@mail.oop.gov.tw; internet www.president.gov.tw.

Ministry of Culture: 30-1 Beiping East Rd, Zhongzheng District, Taipei 10049; tel. (2) 23434000; internet www.moc.gov.tw.

Ministry of Economic Affairs: 15 Foo Chou St, Taipei 10015; tel. (2) 23212200; fax (2) 23919398; e-mail minister@moea.gov.tw; internet www.moea.gov.tw.

Ministry of Education: 5 Chung Shan South Rd, Zhongzheng District, Taipei 10051; tel. (2) 77366666; fax (2) 23976978; internet www.moe.gov.tw.

Ministry of Finance: 2 Ai Kuo West Rd, Taipei 10066; tel. (2) 23228000; fax (2) 23568774; e-mail mof@mail.mof.gov.tu; internet www.mof.gov.tw.

Ministry of Foreign Affairs: 2 Kaitakeland Blvd, Taipei 10048; tel. (2) 23482999; fax (2) 23805678; e-mail eyes@mofa.gov.tw; internet www.mofa.gov.tw.

Ministry of the Interior: 5–9/F, 5 Syujhou Rd, Taipei 10017; tel. (2) 23565005; fax (2) 23566201; e-mail service@minister.moi.gov.tw; internet www.moi.gov.tw.

Ministry of Justice: 130 Chungking South Rd, Sec. 1, Taipei 10048; tel. (2) 21910189; fax (2) 23896274; internet www.moj.gov.tw.

Ministry of National Defense: 2/F, 164 Bo Ai Rd, Taipei 10048; tel. (2) 23116117; fax (2) 23144221; internet www.mnd.gov.tw.

Ministry of Transportation and Communications: 50 Ren Ai Rd, Sec. 1, Zhongzheng District, Taipei 10048; tel. (2) 23492900; fax (2) 23492491; e-mail motceyes@motc.gov.tw; internet www.motc.gov.tw.

Mongolian and Tibetan Affairs Commission: 4/F, 5 Hsu Chou Rd, Sec. 1, Taipei 10055; tel. (2) 23514280; fax (2) 23416186; e-mail mtacserv@mtac.gov.tw; internet www.mtac.gov.tw.

Overseas Compatriot Affairs Commission: 15–17/F, 5 Hsu Chou Rd, Taipei 10055; tel. (2) 23272600; fax (2) 23566323; e-mail ocacinfo@mail.ocac.gov.tw; internet www.ocac.gov.tw.

Directorate-General of Budget, Accounting and Statistics: 1 Chung Hsiao East Rd, Sec. 1, Taipei 10058; tel. (2) 33566500; fax (2) 23825267; e-mail sicbs@dgbas.gov.tw; internet www.dgbas.gov.tw.

Directorate-General of Personnel Administration: 10/F, 2-2 Chinan Rd, Taipei 10051; tel. (2) 23979298; fax (2) 23975505; internet www.dgpa.gov.tw.

Council of Indigenous Peoples: 172 Chungking North Rd, Datong District, Taipei 10357; tel. (2) 25571600; fax (2) 23454323; e-mail minister@apc.gov.tw; internet www.apc.gov.tw.

Council of Agriculture: see under Trade and Industry—Government Agencies.

Atomic Energy Council (AEC): 2–8/F, 80 Cheng Kung Rd, Sec. 1, Yonghe City, Taipei County 23452; tel. (2) 82317250; fax (2) 82317284; e-mail public@aec.gov.tw; internet www.aec.gov.tw.

Consumer Protection Commission: 12 Jihe Rd, Taipei 11166; tel. (2) 28863200; fax (2) 28866646; e-mail tcpc@ms1.hinet.net; internet www.cpc.gov.tw.

Council for Economic Planning and Development: 3 Baocing Rd, Zhongzheng District, Taipei 10020; tel. (2) 23165300; fax (2) 23700415; internet www.cepd.gov.tw.

Council for Hakka Affairs: 8/F, 3 Songren Rd, Taipei 11010; tel. (2) 87894567; fax (2) 87894620; e-mail src@mail.hakka.gov.tw; internet www.hakka.gov.tw.

Environmental Protection Administration: 83 Chung Hua Rd, Sec. 1, Taipei 10042; tel. (2) 23117722; fax (2) 23115486; e-mail umail@epa.gov.tw; internet www.epa.gov.tw.

Public Construction Commission: 9/F, 3 Songren Rd, Taipei 11010; tel. (2) 87897500; fax (2) 87897800; e-mail secr@mail.pcc.gov.tw; internet www.pcc.gov.tw.

Fair Trade Commission: 12–14/F, 2-2 Chi Nan Rd, Sec. 2, Taipei 10051; tel. (2) 23517588; fax (2) 23974997; e-mail ftcpub@ftc.gov.tw; internet www.ftc.gov.tw.

Department of Health: 36 Ta Cheng St, Datong District, Taipei 10341; tel. (2) 85906666; fax (2) 25502052; internet www.doh.gov.tw.

Council of Labor Affairs: 9/F, 83 Yangping North Rd, Sec. 2, Taipei 10346; tel. (2) 85902866; fax (2) 85902960; internet www.cla.gov.tw.

Mainland Affairs Council: 15/F, 2-2 Chi Nan Rd, Sec. 1, Taipei 10051; tel. (2) 23975589; fax (2) 23975300; e-mail macst@mac.gov.tw; internet www.mac.gov.tw.

National Science Council: 17–22/F, 106 Ho Ping East Rd, Sec. 2, Taipei 10622; tel. (2) 27377992; fax (2) 27377566; e-mail nsc@nsc.gov.tw; internet www.nsc.gov.tw.

National Youth Commission: 14/F, 5 Hsu Chou Rd, Taipei 10055; tel. (2) 23566232; fax (2) 23566307; e-mail nycn@nyc.gov.tw; internet www.nyc.gov.tw.

Research, Development and Evaluation Commission: 6/F, 2-2 Chi Nan Rd, Sec. 1, Taipei 10051; tel. (2) 23419066; fax (2) 23969990; e-mail service@rdec.gov.tw; internet www.rdec.gov.tw.

Sports Affairs Council: 20 Zhu Lun St, Taipei 10481; tel. (2) 87711800; fax (2) 27523600; internet www.sac.gov.tw.

Veterans' Affairs Commission: 222 Chung Hsiao East Rd, Sec. 5, Xinyi District, Taipei 11025; tel. (2) 27571750; fax (2) 27230170; e-mail eyes@mail.vac.gov.tw; internet www.vac.gov.tw.

Financial Supervisory Commission: 18/F, 7 Hsien Ming Blvd, Sec. 2, Panchiao City, Taipei County 22041; tel. (2) 89680899; fax (2) 89681215; e-mail fscey@fscey.gov.tw; internet www.fscey.gov.tw.

Coast Guard Administration: 296 Singlong Rd, Taipei 11698; tel. (2) 22399201; fax (2) 22399258; e-mail master@cga.gov.tw; internet www.cga.gov.tw.

President and Legislature

PRESIDENT

Election, 14 January 2012

Candidates*	Votes	% of votes
Ma Ying-jeou (Kuomintang—KMT) . .	6,891,139	51.60
Tsai Ing-wen (Democratic Progressive Party—DPP)	6,093,578	45.63
James Soong (People First Party—PFP) .	369,588	2.77
Total	13,354,305†	100.00

* The vice-presidential candidates were Wu Den-yih of the KMT, Su Jia-chyuan of the DPP and Lin Ruey-shiung of the PFP.

† Not including invalid or spoiled ballot papers.

LI-FA YUAN
(Legislative Yuan)

President: WANG JIN-PYNG.

Election, 14 January 2012

Party	Seats
Kuomintang (KMT)	64
Democratic Progressive Party (DPP)	40
Taiwan Solidarity Union (TSU)	3
People First Party (PFP)	3
Non-Partisan Solidarity Union (NPSU) . . .	2
Independents	1
Total	**113**

Election Commission

Central Election Commission: 10/F, 5 Hsu Chou Rd, Taipei 10055; tel. (2) 23565484; fax (2) 23976898; e-mail cec13@cec.gov.tw; internet www.cec.gov.tw; f. 1980; Chair. and 11–19 commrs nominated by Premier and approved by the President; Chair. is also a member of the Exec. Yuan; Chair. CHANG PO-YA.

Political Organizations

At August 2006 a total of 109 parties were registered with the Ministry of the Interior.

Democratic Progressive Party (DPP): 10/F, 30 Beiping East Rd, Taipei 10051; tel. (2) 23929989; fax (2) 23930342; e-mail foreign@dpp.org.tw; internet www.dpp.org.tw; f. 1986; advocates 'self-determination' for the people of Taiwan and UN membership; supports establishment of independent Taiwan following plebiscite; 530,975 mems (2004); Chair. SU TSENG-CHANG; Sec.-Gen. LIN HSI-YAO.

Green Party Taiwan: 5/F, 13 Chung Hsiao East Rd, Zhongzheng District, Taipei 10049; tel. (2) 23920508; fax (2) 23920512; e-mail contact@greenparty.org.tw; internet www.greenparty.org.tw; f. 1996; est. by breakaway faction of DPP.

Jiann Gwo Party (Taiwan Independence Party—TAIP): 9/F, 15-8 Nanjing East Rd, Sec. 5, Taipei 10564; tel. (2) 22800879; f. 1996; est. by dissident mems of DPP; Chair. HUANG CHIEN-MING; Sec.-Gen. LI SHENG-HSIUNG.

Kuomintang (KMT) (Nationalist Party of China): 232–234 Bade Rd, Sec. 2, Taipei 10492; tel. (2) 87711234; fax (2) 23434561; internet www.kmt.org.tw; f. 1894; aims to supplant communist rule in mainland China; supports democratic, constitutional govt, and advocates the unification of China; aims to promote market economy and equitable distribution of wealth; 1.1m. mems; Chair. MA YING-JEOU; Sec.-Gen. TSENG YUNG-CHUAN.

New Party (NP): 4/F, 65 Guangfu South Rd, Taipei 10563; tel. (2) 27562222; fax (2) 27565750; e-mail webmaster@mail.np.org.tw; internet www.np.org.tw; f. 1993 by dissident KMT legislators (hitherto mems of New Kuomintang Alliance faction); merged with China Social Democratic Party in late 1993; advocates co-operation with the KMT and DPP in negotiations with the People's Republic, maintenance of security in the Taiwan Straits, modernization of the island's defence systems, measures to combat govt corruption, support of small and medium-sized businesses and establishment of a universal social security system; 80,000 mems; Chair. YOK MU-MING.

Non-Partisan Solidarity Union: 3/F, 5–1 Zhenjiang St, Taipei 10051; tel. (2) 23585066; f. 2004; Chair. LIN PIN-KUAN.

People First Party (PFP): 2/F, 63 Chang-an East Rd, Sec. 1, Taipei 10455; tel. (2) 25068556; internet www.pfp.org.tw; f. 2000; advocates the unification of China; seeks economic and cultural interaction between Taiwan and the mainland; Chair. JAMES C. Y. SOONG; Sec.-Gen. CHIN CHIN-SHENG.

Taiwan Solidarity Union (TSU): 7/F, Shaoxing North Rd, Zhongzheng District, Taipei; tel. (2) 23940230; fax (2) 23946616; e-mail service@tsu.org.tw; internet www.tsu.org.tw; f. 2001; est. by breakaway faction of KMT; Chair. HUANG HUN-KUI; Sec.-Gen. LIN CHIH-CHIA.

Taiwanese National Party (TNP): Taipei; f. 2011; advocates self-determination for Taiwan and the holding of a referendum on the issue; Chair. HUANG HUA.

Young China Party (YCP): 12/F, 2 Sinsheng South Rd, Sec. 3, Taipei 10660; tel. (2) 23626715; f. 1923; aims to recover sovereignty over mainland China, safeguard the Constitution and democracy, and foster understanding between Taiwan and the non-communist world; Chair. JEAN JYI-YUAN.

Diplomatic Representation

EMBASSIES IN TAIWAN (REPUBLIC OF CHINA)

Belize: 11/F, 9 Lane 62, Tien Mou West Rd, Taipei 11156; tel. (2) 28760894; fax (2) 28760896; e-mail embelroc@ms41.hinet.net; Chargé d'affaires CHERIE NISBET.

Burkina Faso: 6/F, 9-1 Lane 62, Tien Mou West Rd, Taipei 11157; tel. (2) 28733096; fax (2) 28733071; e-mail abftap94@ms17.hinet.net; internet www.ambaburkinataipei.org.tw; Ambassador JACQUES Y. SAWADOGO.

Dominican Republic: 6/F, 9 Lane 62, Tien Mou West Rd, Taipei 11156; tel. (2) 28751357; fax (2) 28752661; e-mail domtaipei@hotmail.com; Ambassador RAFAELA ALBURQUERQUE DE GONZÁLEZ.

El Salvador: 2/F, 9 Lane 62, Tien Mou West Rd, Taipei 11157; tel. (2) 28763606; fax (2) 28763514; e-mail embasal.taipei@msa.hinet.net; Ambassador MARTA CHANG DE TSIEN.

The Gambia: 9/F, 9-1 Lane 62, Tien Mou West Rd, Taipei 11156; tel. (2) 28753911; fax (2) 28752775; e-mail gm.roc@msa.hinet.net; Ambassador Alhaji EBRIMA N. H. JARJOU.

Guatemala: 3/F, 9-1 Lane 62, Tien Mou West Rd, Taipei 11156; tel. (2) 28756952; fax (2) 28740699; e-mail embchina@minrex.gob.gt; Ambassador ARTURO DUARTE ORTIZ.

Haiti: 8/F, 9-1 Lane 62, Tien Mou West Rd, Taipei 11156; tel. (2) 28766718; fax (2) 28766719; e-mail haiti@ms26.hinet.net; Chargé d'affaires a.i. RACHEL COUPAUD.

Holy See: 87 Ai Kuo East Rd, Taipei 10642 (Apostolic Nunciature); tel. (2) 23216847; fax (2) 23911926; e-mail nuntius.taipei@gmail.com; Chargé d'affaires Mgr PAUL RUSSELL.

Honduras: 9/F, 9 Lane 62, Tien Mou West Rd, Taipei 11156; tel. (2) 28755507; fax (2) 28755726; e-mail honduras@ms9.hinet.net; Ambassador MARIO ALBERTO FORTÍN MIDENCE.

Marshall Islands: 4/F, 9-1 Lane 62, Tien Mou West Rd, Taipei 11157; tel. (2) 28734884; fax (2) 28734904; e-mail rmiemb.tpe@msa.hinet.net; Ambassador PHILIP K. KABUA.

Nauru: 11/F, 9-1 Lane 62, Tien Mou West Rd, Taipei 11156; tel. (2) 28761950; fax (2) 28761930; Ambassador LUDWIG D. KEKE.

Nicaragua: 3/F, Lane 62, Tien Mou West Rd, Taipei 11156; tel. (2) 28749034; fax (2) 28749080; e-mail icaza@ms13.hinet.net; Ambassador WILLIAM M. TAPIA.

Palau: 5/F, 9 Lane 62, Tien Mou West Rd, Taipei 11156; tel. (2) 28765415; fax (2) 28760436; e-mail palau.embassy@msa.hinet.net; Ambassador PETER R. ADELBAI.

Panama: 6/F, 111 Sung Kiang Rd, Taipei 10486; tel. (2) 25099189; fax (2) 25099801; Ambassador LUIS CUCALÓN D'ANELLO.

Paraguay: 7/F, 9-1 Lane 62, Tien Mou West Rd, Taipei 11156; tel. (2) 28736310; fax (2) 28736312; e-mail embapartaiwan@embapartwroc.com.tw; internet www.embapartwroc.com.tw; Charge d'affaires a.i. CARLOS JOSÉ FLEITAS RODRÍGUEZ.

Saint Christopher and Nevis: 5/F, 9-1 Lane 62, Tien Mou West Rd, Taipei 11157; tel. (2) 28733252; fax (2) 28733246; e-mail embskn.tw@msa.hinet.net; Ambassador JASMINE HUGGINS.

São Tomé and Príncipe: 10/F, 9-1 Lane 62, Tien Mou West Rd, Taipei 11156; tel. (2) 28766824; fax (2) 28766984; e-mail stptw@ms69.hinet.net; Chargé d'affaires a.i. AMÉRICO AFONSO LIMA VIEGAS.

Solomon Islands: 7/F, 9-1 Lane 62, Tien Mou West Rd, Taipei 11156; tel. (2) 28731168; fax (2) 28735224; e-mail embassy@solomons.org.tw; internet www.solomons.org.tw; Ambassador LAURIE CHAN.

Swaziland: 10/F, 9 Lane 62, Tien Mou West Rd, Taipei 11156; tel. (2) 28725934; fax (2) 28726511; e-mail swazitpi@ms41.hinet.net; Ambassador NJABULISO GWEBU.

Judicial System

Judicial Yuan: 124 Chungking South Rd, Sec. 1, Taipei 10048; tel. (2) 23618577; fax (2) 23898923; e-mail judicial@mail.judicial.gov.tw; internet www.judicial.gov.tw; highest judicial organ; interprets the Constitution and national laws and ordinances; supervises the lower courts; Pres. RAI HAU-MIN.

Supreme Court: 6 Chang Sha St, Sec. 1, Taipei 10048; tel. (2) 23141160; fax (2) 23114246; e-mail tpsemail@mail.judicial.gov.tw; internet tps.judicial.gov.tw; court of third and final instance for civil and criminal cases; Pres. WU CHII-PIN.

High Court: 124 Chungking South Rd, Sec. 1, Taipei 10048; tel. (2) 23713261; internet tph.judicial.gov.tw; court of second instance for appeals of civil and criminal cases; four branch courts: Taichung, Tainan, Kaohsiung and Hualien; Pres. CHANG SHING-SHYONG.

District Courts: courts of first instance in civil, criminal and non-contentious cases.

Supreme Administrative Court: 1 Lane 126, Chungking South Rd, Sec. 1, Taipei 10048; tel. (2) 23113691; fax (2) 23111791; e-mail jessie@judicial.gov.tw; internet tpa.judicial.gov.tw; court of final resort in appeals against rulings of the High Administrative Courts and of the Intellectual Property Court; Pres. CHANG DENG-KE.

High Administrative Courts: courts of first instance in cases brought against govt agencies; three courts based in Taipei, Taichung and Kaohsiung.

Intellectual Property Court: 3/F, 7 Citizen Rd Banciao, Sec. 2, Taipei; tel. (2) 22726696; e-mail ipc@mail.judicial.gov.tw; Pres. KAO HSIOW-JEN.

Commission on Disciplinary Sanctions Against Functionaries: 3/F, 124 Chungking South Rd, Sec. 1, Taipei 10048; tel. (2) 23119375; fax (2) 23826255; decides on disciplinary measures against public functionaries impeached by the Control Yuan; Chair. LIN KUO-HSIEN.

Religion

According to the Ministry of the Interior, in 2004 35% of the population were adherents of Buddhism, 33% of Daoism (Taoism), 3.5% of I-kuan Tao and 2.6% of Christianity.

BUDDHISM

Buddhist Association of Taiwan: Mahayana and Theravada schools; 1,613 group mems and more than 5.4m. adherents; Leader Ven. CHIN-HSIN.

CHRISTIANITY

The Roman Catholic Church

Taiwan comprises one archdiocese, six dioceses and one apostolic administrative area. In December 2007, according to official figures, there were 299,130 adherents.

Bishops' Conference: Chinese Regional Bishops' Conference, 39 An Ju St, Taan District, Taipei 10672; tel. (2) 27328603; fax (2) 27326602; e-mail bishconf@catholic.org.tw; internet www.catholic .org.tw; f. 1967; Pres. Most Rev. JOHN HUNG SHAN-CHUAN (Archbishop of Taipei).

Archbishop of Taipei: Most Rev. JOHN HUNG SHAN-CHUAN, Archbishop's House, 94 Loli Rd, Taipei 10668; tel. (2) 27371311; fax (2) 27373710.

The Anglican Communion

Anglicans in Taiwan are adherents of the Protestant Episcopal Church. In 2004 the Church had 1,000 members.

Bishop of Taiwan: Rt Rev. DAVID JUNG-HSIN LAI, 7 Lane 105, Hangchow South Rd, Sec. 1, Taipei 10044; tel. (2) 23411265; fax (2) 23962014; e-mail skhtpe@ms12.hinet.net.

Lutheran Church

Taiwan Lutheran Church: 15 Hang Chow S. Rd, Sec. 2, Taipei 10641; tel. (2) 23519317; fax (2) 23913993; e-mail tlc@mail .twlutheran.org.tw; internet www.twlutheran.org.tw; 12,295 mems; Pastor CHEN ZHIHONG.

Presbyterian Church

Tai-oan Ki-tok Tiu-Lo Kau-Hoe (Presbyterian Church in Taiwan): No. 3, Lane 269, Roosevelt Rd, Sec. 3, Taipei 10647; tel. (2) 23625282; fax (2) 23628096; e-mail pct@mail.pct.org.tw; internet www.pct.org.tw; f. 1865; 224,679 mems (2000); Gen. Sec. Rev. CHANG TE-CHIEN.

DAOISM (TAOISM)

In 2004 there were about 7.6m. adherents. Temples numbered 18,274, and clergy totalled 33,850.

I-KUAN TAO

Introduced to Taiwan in the 1950s, this 'Religion of One Unity' is a modern, syncretic religion, drawn mainly from Confucian, Buddhist and Daoist principles and incorporating ancestor worship. In 2004 there were 3,260 temples. Adherents totalled 810,000.

ISLAM

Leader MOHAMMED NI GUO-AN; 58,000 adherents in 2004.

The Press

In 2011 the number of registered newspapers stood at 2,210. The majority of newspapers are privately owned.

PRINCIPAL DAILIES

Taipei

Apple Daily News: 38, 141 Lane, Xinyi Rd, Taipei 11494; tel. (2) 66013456; fax (2) 66018866; e-mail enquiry@appledaily.com.tw; internet tw.nextmedia.com; jt venture between Hong Kong-based Next Media and several Singapore cos.

The China Post: 8 Fu Shun St, Taipei 10452; tel. (2) 25969971; fax (2) 25957962; e-mail info@mail.chinapost.com.tw; internet www .chinapost.com.tw; f. 1952; morning; English; Publr and Editor JACK HUANG; readership 400,000.

China Times: 132 Da Li St, Taipei 10801; tel. (2) 23087111; fax (2) 23048138; internet www.chinatimes.com; f. 1950; morning; Chinese; Chair. TSAI YAN-MING; Editor-in-Chief WANG MEI-YU; circ. 1.2m.

Commercial Times: 132 Da Li St, Taipei; tel. (2) 66320008; fax (2) 23069456; e-mail service@ctee.com.tw; internet ctee.com.tw; f. 1978; morning; Chinese; Publr PENG CHWEI-MING; Editor-in-Chief SIMON CHENG; circ. 300,000.

Economic Daily News: 369 Datong Rd, Xizhi, Sec. 1, Taipei 22161; tel. (2) 86925588; fax (2) 86925851; internet co.udn.com; f. 1967; morning; Chinese; publ. by United Daily News Group; Chair. ANN WANG.

Liberty Times: 399 Rueiguang Rd, Neihu District, Taipei 11492; tel. (2) 26562828; fax (2) 26561034; e-mail newstips@libertytimes .com.tw; internet www.libertytimes.com.tw; f. 1980; Publr WU A-MING; Editor-in-Chief ROGER CHEN; circ. 682,000 (2009).

Mandarin Daily News: 2 Foo Chou St, Taipei 10078; tel. (2) 23921133; fax (2) 23410203; e-mail feedback@mdnkids.com; internet www.mdnkids.com; f. 1948; children's newspaper; morning; Publr LIN LIANG.

Taipei Times: 14/F, 399 Ruiguang Rd, Neihu District, Taipei 11492; tel. (2) 26561000; fax (2) 26561099; e-mail letters@taipeitimes.com; internet www.taipeitimes.com; f. 1999; English; circ. 700,000 (2007).

Taiwan News: 8/F, 88 Xin Yi Rd, Sec. 2, Taipei 10641; tel. (2) 23517666; fax (2) 23515330; e-mail taiwannewseditor@gmail.com; internet www.etaiwannews.com; f. 1949; English; Pres. JACK WONG; Publr LUIS KO.

United Daily News: 369 Datong Rd, Xizhi, Sec. 1, Taipei 22161; tel. (2) 86925588; fax (2) 86925851; e-mail service@udndata.com; internet udn.com; f. 1951; morning; CEO DUNCAN WANG; Editor-in-Chief SUNNY YOU; circ. 1.2m.

Provincial

China Daily News (Southern Edn): 57 Hsi Hwa St, Tainan 70449; tel. (6) 2202691; fax (6) 2201804; f. 1946; morning; Publr C. S. LIU; circ. 670,000.

The Commons Daily: Kaohsiung; tel. (7) 2692121; fax (7) 2692685; e-mail commons911@gmail.com; internet www.thecommonsdaily .tw; f. 1950; fmrly Min Chung Daily News; morning; Executive-in-Chief WANG CHIN-HSIUNG; circ. 148,000.

Keng Sheng Daily News: 36 Wuchuan St, Hualien 97048; tel. (38) 340131; fax (38) 341406; e-mail kengshen@ms6.hinet.net; internet www.ksnews.com.tw; f. 1947; morning; Publr HSIEH LEADER; circ. 50,000.

Taiwan Hsin Wen Daily News: 3 Woo Fu I Rd, Kaohsiung 80252; tel. (7) 2226666; f. 1949; morning; Publr CHANG REI-TE.

Taiwan Times: 32 Kaonan Rd, Renwu Township, Kaohsiung 81453; tel. (7) 3428666; fax (7) 3102828; internet www.twtimes.com.tw; f. 1978; Publr WANG YUH-FA.

SELECTED PERIODICALS

Artist Magazine: 6/F, 147 Chung Ching South Rd, Sec. 1, Taipei 10048; tel. (2) 23866715; fax (2) 23317096; e-mail artvenue@seed.net .tw; f. 1975; monthly; Publr HO CHENG KUANG; circ. 37,600.

Better Life Monthly: 11 Lane 199, Hsin-yih Rd, Sec. 4, Taipei 10685; tel. (2) 27549488; fax (2) 27001516; e-mail bettlife@ms14 .hinet.net; f. 1987; Publr JACK S. LIN.

Brain: 12/F, 100 Nanking East Rd, Sec. 2, Taipei 10457; tel. (2) 27132644; fax (2) 25621578; e-mail askbrain@brain.com.tw; internet www.brain.com.tw; f. 1977; media industry; monthly; Publr JOHNSON WU.

Business Next: e-mail service@bxnext.com.tw; internet www .bxnext.com.tw; f. 1999; bi-weekly; circ. 160,000.

Business Weekly: 12/F, 141, Sec. 2, Minsheng East Rd, Taipei 10483; tel. (2) 25056789; fax (2) 27364620; e-mail mailbox@bwnet .com.tw; internet www.businessweekly.com.tw; f. 1987; Publr JIN WEI-TSUN.

Car Magazine: 1/F, 3 Lane 3, Tung Shan St, Taipei 10014; tel. (2) 23218168; fax (2) 23935614; e-mail carguide@ms13.hinet.net; f. 1982; monthly; Publr H. K. LIN; Editor-in-Chief LIN TA-WEI; circ. 85,000.

China Times Weekly: 5/F, 25 Min Chuan East Rd, Sec. 6, Taipei 11494; tel. (2) 27936000; fax (2) 87918589; internet www.chinatimes .com; f. 1978; weekly; Chinese; Publr CHANG KUO-LI.

Commonwealth Monthly: 11/F, 139, Sec. 2, Nanking East Rd, Taipei 10553; tel. (2) 26620332; fax (2) 25082941; e-mail cwadmin@ cw.com.tw; internet www.cw.com.tw; f. 1981; monthly; business; Pres. CHARLES H. C. KAO; Publr and Editor DIANE YING; circ. 110,000.

CompoTech Asia: Room 3B, 7 Xinyi Rd, Sec. 5, Taipei; tel. (2) 27201789; fax (2) 27201628; e-mail carol_liao@compotechasia.com; internet www.compotech.com.tw; f. 1999; monthly; computing; Editor-in-Chief CAROL LIAO.

Cosmopolitan: 5/F, 8 Lane 181, Jiou-Tzung Rd, Taipei 11494; tel. (2) 28797890; fax (2) 287978990; e-mail hwaker@ms13.hinet.net; f. 1992; monthly; Publr MINCHUN CHANG.

Crown Magazine: 50 Alley 120, Tun Hua North Rd, Sec. 4, Taipei; tel. (2) 27168888; fax (2) 25148285; internet www.crown.com.tw; f. 1954; monthly; literature and arts; Publr PING HSIN TAO; Editor CHEN LIH-HWA; circ. 76,000.

Defense Technology Monthly: 6/F, 6 Nanking East Rd, Sec. 5, Taipei 10564; tel. (2) 27669628; fax (2) 27666092; e-mail service@dtm .com.tw; internet www.dtmonline.com; f. 1894; Publr J. D. BIH.

Elle Taiwan: 5/F, 9 Lane 130, Minsheng East Rd, Sec. 3, Taipei 10596; tel. (2) 67706168; fax (2) 87706170; e-mail newmedia@hft.com .tw; internet www.elle.com.tw; f. 1991; monthly; women's magazine; Publr JEAN DE WITT; Editors-in-Chief CINDY HU, DORIS LEE; circ. 50,000.

Evergreen Monthly: 11/F, 2 Pa Teh Rd, Sec. 3, Taipei 10558; tel. (2) 25782321; fax (2) 25786838; f. 1983; health care knowledge; Publr LIANG GUANG-MING; circ. 50,000.

Excellence Magazine: 3/F, 15 Lane 2, Chien Kuo North Rd, Sec. 2, Taipei 10487; tel. (2) 25093578; fax (2) 25173607; f. 1984; monthly; business; Man. LIN HSIN-JYH; Editor-in-Chief LIU JEN; circ. 70,000.

Families Monthly: 11/F, 2 Pa Teh Rd, Sec. 3, Taipei 10558; tel. (2) 25785078; fax (2) 25786838; f. 1976; family life; Editor-in-Chief THELMA KU; circ. 155,000.

Foresight Investment Weekly: 7/F, 52 Nanking East Rd, Sec. 1, Taipei 10450; tel. (2) 25512561; fax (2) 25119596; f. 1980; weekly; Dir and Publr SUN WUN-SIUNG; Editor-in-Chief WU WEN-SHIN; circ. 55,000.

Global Views Monthly: 2/F, 1 Lane 93, Sungkiang Rd, Taipei 10455; tel. (2) 25173688; fax (2) 25082941; e-mail gvm@cgvm.com.tw; internet www.gvm.com.tw; f. 1986; Editor-in-Chief TIAO MING-FANG.

Gourmet World: 3/F, 53 Jen-Ai Rd, Sec. 1, Taipei 10052; tel. (2) 23972215; fax (2) 23412184; f. 1992; Publr HSU TANG-JEN.

Harvest Farm Magazine: 14 Wenchow St, Taipei 10648; tel. (2) 23628148; fax (2) 23636724; e-mail h3628148@ms15.hinet.net; internet www.harvest.org.tw; f. 1951; every 2 weeks; CEO LIN SHUE-CHENG; Editor-in-Chief YU SHU-LIEN.

Issues and Studies: A Social Science Quarterly on China, Taiwan and East Asian Affairs: Institute of International Relations, National Chengchi University, 64 Wan Shou Rd, Taipei 11666; tel. (2) 82377377; fax (2) 82377231; e-mail issues@nccu.edu.tw; internet iir.nccu.edu.tw/english_web/e_per.htm; f. 1965; quarterly; English; contemporary Chinese studies and East Asian affairs; Editor YEN CHEN-SHEN.

The Journalist: 16/F, 218 Tun Hua South Rd, Sec. 2, Taipei 10669; tel. (2) 23779977; fax (2) 23775850; f. 1987; weekly; Publr WANG SHIN-CHING.

Ladies Magazine: 11/F, 3, 187 Shin Yi Rd, Sec. 4, Taipei 10681; tel. (2) 27026908; fax (2) 27014090; f. 1978; monthly; Publr CHENG CHIN-SHAN; Editor-in-Chief THERESA LEE; circ. 60,000.

Madame Figaro Taiwan: e-mail service@heritage.com.tw; internet www.figaro.tw; f. 2001; fashion; published by Stone Media.

Management Magazine: 14/F, 248 Nan Jing East Rd, Sec. 3, Taipei County 22103; tel. (2) 86471828; fax (2) 86471466; e-mail frankhung@mail.chinamgt.com; internet www.harment.com; f. 1973; monthly; Chinese; Publr and Editor FRANK L. HUNG; Pres. KATHY T. KUO; circ. 65,000.

Money Monthly: 10/F, 289 Chung Hsiao East Rd, Taipei 10696; tel. (2) 25149822; fax (2) 27154657; f. 1986; monthly; personal financial management; Publr PATRICK SUN; Man. Editor JENNIE SHUE; circ. 55,000.

National Geographic/The Earth: 4/F, 319, Sec. 4, Bade Rd, Taipei 10565; tel. (2) 27485988; fax (2) 27480188.

National Palace Museum Monthly of Chinese Art: 221, Sec. 2, Jishan Rd, Taipei 11143; tel. (2) 28821230; fax (2) 28821507; e-mail wyc@npm.gov.tw; f. 1983; monthly in Chinese; Publr CHOU KUNG-SHIN; circ. 3,500.

Nong Nong Magazine: 11/F, 141, Sec. 2, Minsheng East Rd, Taipei 10483; tel. (2) 2502689; fax (2) 25051989; e-mail group@nongnong .com.tw; f. 1984; monthly; women's interest; Publr ANTHONY TSAI; Editor VIVIAN LIN; circ. 70,000.

PC Home: 4/F, 141, Sec. 2, Minsheng East Rd, Taipei 10483; tel. (2) 25000888; fax (2) 25001920; internet www.pchome.com.tw; f. 1996; monthly; Chair. HUNG-TZE JANG; CEO ARTHUR LEE.

PC Office: 11/F, 8 Tun Hua North Rd, Taipei 10547; tel. (2) 25007779; fax (2) 25007903; internet www.pcoffice.com.tw; f. 1997; monthly; Publr HUNG-TZE JANG.

Reader's Digest (Chinese Edn): 2/F, 2 Minsheng East Rd, Sec. 5, Taipei 10572; tel. (2) 82531198; fax (2) 82531211; internet www .readersdigest.com.tw; monthly; Editor-in-Chief VICTOR FUNG.

Studio Classroom: 10 Lane 62, Ta-Chih St, Taipei 10462; tel. (2) 25338082; fax (2) 25326406; internet www.studioclassroom.com; f. 1962; monthly; English teaching magazine; Publr DORIS BROUGHAM.

Taiwan Journal: 2 Tientsin St, Taipei 10051; tel. (2) 23970180; fax (2) 23568233; e-mail tj@mail.gio.gov.tw; internet taiwanjournal.nat .gov.tw; f. 1964; fmrly Free China Journal; weekly; English; news review; Publr VANESSA YEA-PING SHIH; Editor-in-Chief SUSAN YU; circ. 30,000.

Taiwan Panorama: 5/F, 54 Chung Hsiao East Rd, Sec. 1, Taipei 10049; tel. (2) 23922256; fax (2) 23970655; e-mail service@mail .taiwan-panorama.com; internet www.sinorama.com.tw; f. 1976; fmrly *Sinorama*; monthly; bilingual cultural magazine, with edns in Chinese with Japanese or English; Publr PASUYA WEN-CHIH YAO; Editor-in-Chief LAURA LEE; circ. 70,000.

Taiwan Review: 2 Tientsin St, Taipei 100; tel. (2) 23516419; fax (2) 23510829; e-mail tr@mail.gio.gov.tw; internet taiwanreview.nat.gov .tw; f. 1951; fmrly *Taipei Review*, renamed as above March 2003; monthly; English; illustrated; Publr SU JIN-PIN; Editor-in-Chief CHANG HUI-JHEN.

Time Express: B1/F, 205-1 Beisin Rd, Sec. 3, Sinolian City, Taipei County 23143; tel. (2) 89131717; fax (2) 89132332; e-mail timeex@ccw .com.tw; f. 1973; monthly; Publr RICHARD C. C. HUANG.

Unitas: 10/F, 180 Keelung Rd, Sec. 1, Taipei 11006; tel. (2) 27666759; fax (2) 27567914; e-mail unitas@udngroup.com.tw; monthly; Chinese; literary journal; Publr CHANG PAO-CHING; Editor-in-Chief HSU HUI-CHIH.

Vi Vi Magazine: 7/F, 550 Chung Hsiao East Rd, Sec. 5, Taipei 11081; tel. (2) 27275336; fax (2) 27592031; f. 1984; monthly; women's interest; Pres. TSENG CHING-TANG; circ. 60,000.

Vogue/GQ Conde Nast Interculture: 15/F, 51, Sec. 2, Keelung Rd, Sinyi District, Taipei 11082; tel. (2) 27328899; fax (2) 27390504; e-mail vogueeditor@mail.condenast.com.tw; internet www.vogue .com.tw; f. 1996; monthly; Publr BENTHAM LIU.

Wealth Magazine: 7/F, 52 Nanking East Rd, Sec. 1, Taipei 10444; tel. (2) 25512561; fax (2) 25236933; internet www.wealth.com.tw; f. 1974; monthly; finance; Pres. HSIEH CHIN-HO; Editor PHILIP CHEN; circ. 75,000.

Win Win Weekly: 7/F, 52 Nanking East Rd, Taipei 10444; tel. (2) 25816196; fax (2) 25119596; f. 1996; Publr HSIEH CHIN-HO.

Youth Juvenile Monthly: 3/F, 66-1 Chung Cheng South Rd, Sec. 1, Taipei 10045; tel. (2) 23112836; fax (2) 23115368; e-mail customer@ youth.com.tw; internet www.youth.com.tw; f. 1965; Publr LEE CHUNG-GUAI.

NEWS AGENCY

Central News Agency (CNA): 209 Sung Chiang Rd, Taipei 10485; tel. (2) 25058379; fax (2) 25023805; e-mail cnamark@mail.cna.com .tw; internet www.cna.com.tw; f. 1924; news service in Chinese, English and Spanish; feature and photographic services; 25 domestic and 32 overseas bureaux; Pres. SU TZEN-PING; Chair. LIU CHIH-TSUNG.

Publishers

There were 14,016 registered publishing corporations in Taiwan in 2011. In that year a total of 42,566 titles were published.

Art Book Co: 1/F, 18 Lane 283, Roosevelt Rd, Sec. 3, Taipei 10647; tel. (2) 23620578; fax (2) 23623594; e-mail artbook@ms43.hinet.net; Publr HO KUNG-SHANG.

Cheng Wen Publishing Co: 3/F, 277 Roosevelt Rd, Sec. 3, Taipei 10647; tel. (2) 23628032; fax (2) 23660806; e-mail book@chengwen .com.tw; internet www.chengwen.com.tw; f. 1965; Publr LARRY C. HUANG.

Children's Publication Co Ltd: 7F-1, 314 Neihu Rd, Sec. 1, Taipei 11444; tel. (2) 87972799; fax (2) 87972700; e-mail nell-012@012book .com.tw; internet www.012book.com.tw; f. 1994.

China Times Publishing Co: 5/F, 240 Hoping West Rd, Sec. 3, Taipei 10803; tel. (2) 23047103; fax (2) 23049302; e-mail jess@

readingtimes.com.tw; internet www.readingtimes.com.tw; f. 1975; Pres. MO CHAO-PING.

Chinese Culture University Press: 55 Hua Kang Rd, Yangming-shan, Taipei 11114; tel. (2) 28610511, ext. 17503; fax (2) 28617164; e-mail euca@staff.pccu.edu.tw; internet www2.pccu.edu.tw/cuca/ad3.htm; Publr LEE FU-CHEN.

Cite Publishing Ltd: 2/F, 141 Minsheng East Rd, Sec. 2, Taipei 10482; tel. (2) 25007088; fax (2) 25007579; e-mail regina@hmg.com.tw; internet www.cite.com.tw; f. 1996.

The Commercial Press Ltd: 37 Chungking South Rd, Sec. 1, Taipei 10046; tel. (2) 23713712; fax (2) 23752201; e-mail ecptw@cptw.com.tw; internet www.cptw.com.tw; f. 1897; Chair. SHI JIAMING; Sr Chief Editor JONATHAN LEE.

Commonwealth Publishing Co: 2/F, 1 Lane 93, Sung Chiang Rd, Taipei; tel. (2) 25173688; fax (2) 25173685; e-mail cwpc@cwgv.com.tw; internet www.bookzone.com.tw; f. 1982.

Crown Publishing Group: 50 Lane 120, Tun Hua North Rd, Taipei 10547; tel. (2) 27168888; fax (2) 27133422; e-mail edit3@crown.com.tw; internet www.crown.com.tw; f. 1954; Publr PHILIP PING.

The Eastern Publishing Co Ltd: 4/F, 121 Chungking South Rd, Sec. 1, Taipei 100; tel. (2) 23114514; fax (2) 23317402; e-mail lola@1945.com.tw; f. 1945; Publr CHENG SI-MING.

Elite Publishing Co: 1/F, 33-1 Lane 113, Hsiamen St, Taipei 10048; tel. (2) 23654036; fax (2) 23657047; e-mail elite113@ms12.hinet.net; internet www.elitebooks.com.tw; f. 1975; Publr KO CHING-HWA.

Far East Book Co: 66 Chungking South Rd, Sec. 1, Taipei 10045; tel. (2) 23118740; fax (2) 23114184; e-mail service@mail.fareast.com.tw; internet eng.fareast.com.tw; art, education, history, physics, mathematics, law, literature, dictionaries, textbooks, language tapes, Chinese-English dictionaries; Publr GEORGE C. L. PU.

Global Group Holding Ltd: 3/F, 88 Zhou Zi Rd, Neihu District, Taipei; tel. (2) 27992788; fax (2) 27990909; e-mail readers@gobooks.com.tw; internet www.gobooks.com.tw; Publr CHU PAO-LOUNG; Dir KELLY CHU.

Hsin Yi Foundation: 75 Chungking South Rd, Sec. 2, Taipei 10015; tel. (2) 23913384; fax (2) 23965015; e-mail arni@hsin-yi.org.tw; internet www.hsin-yi.org.tw; f. 1971; children's education and devt; Exec. Dir CHANG SING-JU.

Kwang Hwa Publishing Co: 13/F, 15-1 Hangzhou South Rd, Taipei 10050; tel. (2) 23922256; fax (2) 23970655; e-mail service@mail.taiwan-panorama.com; internet www.sinorama.com.tw; Publr CHENG WEN-TSANG.

Li-Ming Cultural Enterprise Co: 1/F, 49 Chungking South Rd, Sec. 1, Taipei 10045; tel. (2) 23314046; fax (2) 23817230; e-mail king@mail.limingco.com.tw; internet www.limingco.com.tw; f. 1971; Pres. SHEN FANG-SHIN.

Linking Publishing Co Ltd: 561, Sec. 1, Chung Hsiao East Rd, Taipei 10055; tel. (2) 27683708; fax (2) 27567668; e-mail bookcs@udngroup.com; internet www.linkingbooks.com.tw; Publr LIU KUO-JUEI.

Locus Publishing Co: 11/F, 25 Nanking East Rd, Sec. 4, Taipei 10550; tel. (2) 87123898; fax (2) 25453927; e-mail locus@locuspublishing.com; internet www.locuspublishing.com; f. 1996.

San Min Book Co Ltd: 386 Fusing North Rd, Taipei 10476; tel. (2) 25006600; fax (2) 25064000; e-mail editor@sanmin.com.tw; internet www.sanmin.com.tw; f. 1953; literature, history, philosophy, social sciences, dictionaries, art, politics, law; Publr LIU CHEN-CHIANG.

Ta Chien Publishing Co Ltd: 19 Hsinheheng Rd, Tainan 70248; tel. (6) 2917489; fax (6) 2921618; e-mail tcpublish@hotmail.com; internet www.tachien.com.tw.

Tung Hua Book Co Ltd: 105 Emei St, Taipei 10844; tel. (2) 23114027; fax (2) 23116615; e-mail service@bookcake.com.tw; internet www.bookcake.com.tw; f. 1965; Publr CHARLES CHOH.

The World Book Co: 6/F, 99 Chungking South Rd, Sec. 1, Taipei 10045; tel. (2) 23113834; fax (2) 23317963; e-mail wbc.ltd@msa.hinet.com; internet www.worldbook.com.tw; f. 1921; literature, textbooks; Chair. YEN FENG-CHANG; Publr YEN ANGELA CHU.

Youth Cultural Enterprise Co Ltd: 3/F, 66-1 Chungking South Rd, Sec. 1, Taipei 10045; tel. (2) 23112836; fax (2) 23115368; e-mail customer@youth.com.tw; internet www.youth.com.tw; f. 1958; Publr LEE CHUNG-KUEI.

Yuan Liou Publishing Co Ltd: 6/F, 81, Sec. 2, Nanchang Rd, Taipei 10084; tel. (2) 23926899; fax (2) 23926658; e-mail ylib@ylib.com; internet www.ylib.com; f. 1975; fiction, non-fiction, children's; Publr WANG JUNG-WEN.

Broadcasting and Communications

REGULATORY AUTHORITY

National Communications Commission: 50 Ren-Ai Rd, Sec. 1, Taipei 10052; tel. (2) 33437377; fax (2) 23433994; e-mail po2@ncc.gov.tw; internet www.ncc.gov.tw; f. 2006; telecommunications and broadcasting regulatory authority; Chair. HOWARD S. H. SHYR.

TELECOMMUNICATIONS

Chunghwa Telecommunications Co Ltd: 21 Hsinyi Rd, Sec. 1, Taipei 10048; tel. (2) 23445488; fax (2) 33938188; e-mail chtir@cht.com.tw; internet www.cht.com.tw; f. 1996; previously state-controlled co, privatization completed in 2005; Chair. and CEO LEE YEN-SUNG.

Far EasTone Telecom: 468 Ruei Guang Rd, Neihu District, Taipei 11492; tel. (2) 77235000; e-mail ir@fareastone.com.tw; internet www.fareastone.com.tw; mobile telephone services; Pres. YVONNE LI.

Taiwan Mobile Co Ltd: 18/F, 172–1, Ji-Lung Rd, Sec. 2, Taipei 106; tel. (2) 66363159; fax (2) 66368669; e-mail ir@taiwanmobile.com; internet www.taiwanmobile.com; f. 1998; est. as Pacific Cellular Corpn; merged with Taiwan Tele-Shop in 2005; mobile telephone and internet services; Chair. RICHARD TSAI; Pres. CLIFF LAI; Co-Pres. VIVIEN HSU.

BROADCASTING

There is considerable press freedom in Taiwan. A switch from analogue to digital television was initiated in May 2012 and was scheduled for full completion in 2014.

Radio

In June 2010 there were 172 radio broadcasting corporations in operation.

Broadcasting Corpn of China (BCC): 10/F, 375 Sung Chiang Rd, Taipei 10482; tel. (2) 25019688; fax (2) 25018545; internet www.bcc.com.tw; f. 1928; domestic (5 networks and 1 channel) services; 9 local stations, 131 transmitters; Chair. JAW SHAO-KONG.

Central Broadcasting System (CBS): 55 Pei An Rd, Tachih, Taipei 10464; tel. (2) 28856168; fax (2) 28862382; e-mail rti@rti.org.tw; internet www.cbs.org.tw; f. 1928; national broadcasting system of Taiwan; broadcasts internationally in 13 languages via medium and short wave under the call sign Radio Taiwan International (RTI); Chair. CHANG YUNG-KYUNG.

Cheng Sheng Broadcasting Corpn Ltd: 7/F, 66-1 Chungking South Rd, Sec. 1, Taipei 10045; tel. (2) 23617231; fax (2) 23712715; e-mail csbc_server@csbc.com.tw; internet www.csbc.com.tw; f. 1950; 6 stations, 3 relay stations; Chair. GUO RONG-CHANG; Pres. LI YUNG-GUIE.

International Community Radio Taipei (ICRT): 19–5F, 107 Jhongshan Rd, Sec. 1, Sinjhuang, Taipei 24250; tel. (2) 85227766; fax (2) 85227077; internet www.icrt.com.tw; f. 1979; predominantly English-language broadcaster.

Kiss Radio: 34/F, 6 Min Chuan 2 Rd, Kaohsiung 80658; tel. (7) 3365888; fax (7) 3380999; e-mail helena@kiss.com.tw; internet www.kiss.com.tw; Pres. HELENA YUAN.

M-radio Broadcasting Corpn: 8/F, 1-18 Taichung Kang Rd, Sec. 2, Taichung City 40751; tel. (4) 23235656; fax (4) 23231199; e-mail jason@mradio.com.tw; internet www.mradio.com.tw.

UFO Broadcasting Co Ltd: 25/F, 102 Roosevelt Rd, Sec. 2, Taipei 10084; tel. (2) 23636600; fax (2) 23688833; internet www.ufo.net.tw; f. 1996; Pres. CHANG HSIAO-YEN.

Voice of Taipei Broadcasting Co Ltd: 10/F, B Rm, 15-1 Han Chou South Rd, Sec. 1, Taipei 10050; tel. (2) 23957255; fax (2) 23947855; internet www.vot.com.tw; Pres. NITA ING.

Television

China Television Co (CTV): 118 Chung Yang Rd, Nan Kang District, Taipei 11523; tel. (2) 27838308; fax (2) 27896530; e-mail prog@mail.chinatv.com.tw; internet www.ctv.com.tw; f. 1969; owned by Chinatimes Group; Pres. LI TAI-LIN.

Chinese Television System (CTS): 100 Kuang Fu South Rd, Taipei 10694; tel. (2) 27756789; fax (2) 27775414; e-mail cts-service@cts.com.tw; internet www.cts.com.tw; f. 1971; Chair. LOUIS CHEN; Pres. LI YUAN.

Formosa Television Co (FTV): 14/F, 30 Pa Teh Rd, Sec. 3, Taipei 10551; tel. (2) 25786686; fax (2) 25798715; e-mail service@ftv.com.tw; internet www.ftv.com.tw; f. 1997; Chair. TIEN TZAI-TING; Pres. CHEN KANG-HSING.

Public Television Service Foundation (PTS): 50 Lane 75, Sec. 3, Kang Ning Rd, Neihu, Taipei 11460; tel. (2) 26338037; fax (2) 26301895; e-mail pub@mail.pts.org.tw; internet www.pts.org.tw;

some services merged with Chinese Television System July 2006; Chair. YALY CHAO; Gen. Man. KUANG HSIANG-HSIA.

Taiwan Broadcasting System (TBS): tel. (2) 26332000; fax (2) 26338124; e-mail prg50044@mail.pts.org.tw; internet www.tbs.org .tw; f. 2006; est. following the merger of CTS and PTS, and six other channels; Chair. Dr LOUIS CHEN.

Taiwan Television Enterprise (TTV): 10 Pa Teh Rd, Sec. 3, Taipei 10502; tel. (2) 27758888; fax (2) 27758957; internet www.ttv.com.tw; f. 1962; Pres. and Chair. HUANG SONG.

Finance

(cap. = capital; res = reserves; dep. = deposits; m. = million;
brs = branches; amounts in New Taiwan dollars, unless otherwise
stated)

REGULATORY AUTHORITY

Financial Supervisory Commission: 18/F, 7 Xianmin Blvd, Sec. 2, Banqiao District, Taipei 22041; tel. (2) 89680899; fax (2) 89691215; internet www.fsc.gov.tw; supervises banking, securities and insurance sectors; Chair. CHEN YUH-CHANG.

BANKING

In February 2013 there were 68 banks operating in Taiwan.

Central Bank

Central Bank of the Republic of China (Taiwan): 2 Roosevelt Rd, Sec. 1, Taipei 10066; tel. (2) 23936161; fax (2) 23571974; e-mail adminrol@mail.cbc.gov.tw; internet www.cbc.gov.tw; f. 1928; fmrly Central Bank of China; name changed as above in 2007; bank of issue; cap. and res 1,223,386m., dep. 9,515,944m. (Dec. 2009); Gov. PERNG FAI-NAN.

Domestic Banks

Bank of Taiwan: 120 Chungking South Rd, Sec. 1, Taipei 10007; tel. (2) 23493456; fax (2) 23315840; e-mail botservice@mail.bot.com.tw; internet www.bot.com.tw; f. 1946; subsidiary of govt-owned Taiwan Financial Holdings Co Ltd (f. 2008 by merger of Bank of Taiwan, Land Bank of Taiwan and Export-Import Bank of China); cap. 70,000m., res 170,105.3m., dep. 3,426,937m. (Dec. 2011); Chair. LIU TENG-CHENG; Pres. CHANG MING-DAW; 162 domestic brs, 6 overseas brs.

Export-Import Bank of the Republic of China (Eximbank): 8/ F, 3 Nan Hai Rd, Taipei 10066; tel. (2) 23210511; fax (2) 23940630; e-mail eximbank@eximbank.com.tw; internet www.eximbank.com .tw; f. 1979; merged with Bank of Taiwan and Land Bank of Taiwan in Jan. 2008 to form Taiwan Financial Holding Co, but withdrew from parent co in June; cap. 12,000m., res 6,430m., dep. 28,826.4m. (Dec. 2011); Chair. YEN SHIH; Pres. CHU RUEEN-FONG; 3 brs.

Land Bank of Taiwan Co Ltd: 46 Kuan Chien Rd, Taipei 10047; tel. (2) 23483456; fax (2) 23757023; e-mail lbot@landbank.com.tw; internet www.landbank.com.tw; f. 1946; subsidiary of govt-owned Taiwan Financial Holdings Co Ltd (f. 2008 by merger between Land Bank of Taiwan, Bank of Taiwan and Export-Import Bank of China); cap. 50,000m., res 42,687.6m., dep. 2,067,405m. (Dec. 2011); Chair. WANG YAO-SHING; Pres. SU LER-MING; 148 domestic brs, 6 overseas brs.

Taiwan Co-operative Bank: 77 Kuan Chien Rd, Taipei 10047; tel. (2) 23118811; fax (2) 23885075; e-mail ib02@tcb-bank.com.tw; internet www.tcb-bank.com.tw; f. 1946; acts as central bank for co-operatives, and as major agricultural credit institution; merged with Farmers' Bank of China in May 2006; cap. 60,855m., res 42,141.4m., dep. 2,338,024m. (Dec. 2011); Chair. SHEN LING-LONG; Pres. TSAI CHIU-JUNG; 294 brs.

Commercial Banks

Bank of Kaohsiung: 168 Po Ai 2nd Rd, Zuoying Qu, Kaohsiung 81357; tel. (7) 5570535; fax (7) 5590549; e-mail service@mail.bok.com .tw; internet www.bok.com.tw; f. 1982; cap. 7,069.4m., res 3,700.6m., dep. 205,377.6m. (Dec. 2011); Chair. TSAI HSIAN-CHUNG; Pres. WU CHU-HUNG; 33 brs.

Bank of Panhsin: 2/F, 18 Cheng Tu St, Ban Chiau City, Taipei County 220; tel. (2) 29629170; fax (2) 29572011; e-mail 0473@bop .com.tw; internet www.bop.com.tw; f. 1997; cap. 9,558m., res −29m., dep. 140,791m. (Dec. 2010); Chair. LIU PING-HUI; Pres. CHEN AN-HSIUNG; 48 brs.

Bank SinoPac Co Ltd: 6/F, 306 Sec. 2, Bade Rd, Jhongshan District, Taipei 10492; tel. (2) 81618000; fax (2) 87720639; internet www.banksinopac.com.tw; f. 1992; cap. 52,574.4m., res 15,506m., dep. 1,006,054.2m. (Dec. 2011); Chair. CHIU CHENG-HSIUNG; Pres. and CEO TINA CHIANG; 133 brs, including 4 overseas.

Cathay United Bank: 1/F, 7 Sungren Rd, Taipei, 110; tel. (2) 87226666; fax (2) 87898789; e-mail webservice@cathaybk.com.tw;

internet www.cathaybk.com.tw; f. 1974; merged with United World Chinese Commercial Bank in 2003; cap. 52,277m., res 23,936m., dep. 1,371,688.4m. (Dec. 2010); Chair. GREGORY K. H. WANG; Pres. TSU PEI-CHEN; 140 domestic brs, 2 overseas brs.

Chang Hwa Commercial Bank Ltd: 57 Chung Shan North Rd, Sec. 2, Taipei 10412; tel. (2) 25362951; fax (2) 25114735; e-mail fi@chb .com.tw; internet www.chb.com.tw; f. 1905; cap. 67,683.2m., res 18,850.4m., dep. 1,275,022m. (June 2012); Chair. JULIUS CHEN; Pres. DANIEL TARNG; 184 brs, 7 overseas.

China Development Industrial Bank: 125 Nanjing East Rd, Sec. 5, Taipei 10504; tel. (2) 27532201; fax (2) 27532203; internet www .cdibank.com; f. 1959; cap. 77,604m., res 38,371m., dep. 75,008m. (Dec. 2011); Chair. CHEN MU-TSAI; Pres. PAUL YANG; 3 brs.

Chinatrust Commercial Bank: 3 SongShou Rd, Xinyi District, Taipei 11051; tel. (2) 27222002; fax (2) 27251499; internet www .chinatrust.com.tw; f. 1966; cap. 75,371.3m., res 40,979m., dep. 1,510,891.5m. (Dec. 2011); 100% owned by Chinatrust Financial Holding Co; Chair. JEFFREY KOO; Pres. JAMES CHEN; 142 brs.

Cosmos Bank: 5–10/F, 39 Tun Hua South Rd, Sec. 2, Taipei 10681; tel. (2) 27011777; fax (2) 27849848; e-mail ibd@cosmosbank.com.tw; internet www.cosmosbank.com.tw; f. 1992; cap. 16,234m., res 12,982.6m., dep. 112,817.6m. (Dec. 2010); Chair. and Pres. PAUL PO; 66 brs.

Cota Commercial Bank: 59, Shih Fu Rd, Taichung 40045; tel. (4) 22245161; fax (4) 22275237; internet www.cotabank.com.tw; f. 1999; cap. 4,180.4m., res 900.6m., dep. 106,758m. (Dec. 2010); Chair. LIAO CHUN-TSE; Pres. CHANG CHIN-TING; 18 brs.

DBS Taiwan: 15/F, 32 Songren Rd, Xinyi District, Taipei 11073; tel. (2) 66129888; fax (2) 66129285; internet www.dbs.com/tw; f. 2008; Chair JEANETTE WONG; Gen. Man. JERRY CHEN.

E. Sun Commercial Bank: 13/F, 117 Minsheng East Rd, Sec. 3, Taipei 10546; tel. (2) 21751313; fax (2) 87128613; e-mail tonycheng-06795@email.esunbank.com.tw; internet www .esunbank.com.tw; f. 1992; cap. 43,725m., res 15,708m., dep. 1,189,752m. (Sept. 2012); Chair. GARY TSENG; Pres. JOSEPH N. C. HUANG; 132 domestic brs, 4 overseas brs.

Entie Commercial Bank: 2/F, 156 Minsheng East Rd, Sec. 3, Taipei 10596; tel. (2) 27189999; fax (2) 27187843; internet www .entiebank.com.tw; f. 1993; cap. 16,796.7m., res 1,987.1m., dep. 302,972.6m. (Dec. 2011); Chair. MARK ZOLTAN CHIBA; Pres. and CEO JESSE DING; 53 brs.

Far Eastern International Bank: 27/F, 207 Tun Hua South Rd, Sec. 2, Taipei 10602; tel. (2) 23786868; fax (2) 23779000; e-mail secretarial@feib.com.tw; internet www.feib.com.tw; f. 1992; cap. 20,071.4m., res 540.8m., dep. 348,828.25m. (Dec. 2010); Chair. HOU CHING-ING; Pres. ELI HONG; 36 brs.

First Commercial Bank: 30 Chungking S Rd, Sec. 1, Taipei 10005; tel. (2) 23481111; fax (2) 23610036; e-mail fcb@mail.firstbank.com .tw; internet www.firstbank.com.tw; f. 1899; cap. 58,700m., res 46,103m., dep. 1,609,661m. (Dec. 2011); Chair. TSAI CHING-NAIN; Pres. CHIANG JIN-DER; 187 domestic brs, 15 overseas brs.

Hua Nan Commercial Bank: 38 Chungking S Rd, Sec. 1, Taipei 10006; tel. (2) 23713111; fax (2) 23316741; e-mail service@ms.hncb .com.tw; internet www.hncb.com.tw; f. 1919; cap. 47,671m., res 37,761.5m., dep. 1,630,071.6m. (Dec. 2011); Chair. LIN MING-CHEN; Pres. WANG JIUNN-CHIH; 183 brs, 6 overseas.

Hwatai Bank: 246 Chang An E Rd, Sec. 2, Taipei 10492; tel. (2) 27525252; fax (2) 27812492; e-mail callcenter@hwataibank.com.tw; internet www.hwataibank.com.tw; f. 1999; cap. 6,543.2m., res 385m., dep. 112,070.5m. (Dec. 2011); Chair. M. H. LIN; Pres. THOMAS C. W. LEE; 30 brs.

Industrial Bank of Taiwan: 99 Tiding Blvd, Sec. 2, Taipei; tel. (2) 87527000; fax (2) 27985337; internet www.ibt.com.tw; cap. 23,905m., res 1,629.2m., dep. 127,664m. (Dec. 2011); Chair. KENNETH C. M. LO; Pres. YANG JIN-YU.

Jih Sun International Bank: 85 Nanjing E Rd, Sec. 2, Taipei 10407; tel. (2) 25615888; fax (2) 25217698; e-mail planning@jsun .com; internet www.jihsunbank.com.tw; f. 1992 as Baodao Commercial Bank, assumed present name in Dec. 2001; cap. 13,195.5m., res 11.8m., dep. 186,170.3m. (Dec. 2010); Chair. EDWARD CHEN; Pres. DOLLY YANG; 34 brs.

King's Town Bank: 506 His Men Rd, Sec. 1, Tainan 70051; tel. (6) 2139171; fax (6) 2136885; e-mail president@mail.ktb.com.tw; internet www.ktb.com.tw; fmrly Tainan Business Bank; name changed as above in April 2006; cap. 10,512.3m., res 378.2m., dep. 134,923m. (Dec. 2010); Chair. DAI CHENG-ZHI; Pres. J. C. SU.

Mega International Commercial Bank Co Ltd (Megabank): 100 Chi Lin Rd, Sec. 2, Jhongshan District, Taipei 10424; tel. (2) 25633156; fax (2) 25632614; e-mail service@megabank.com.tw; internet www.megabank.com.tw; f. 2006; est. from merger of International Commercial Bank of China and Chiao Tung Bank; cap. 68,000m., res 79,978.2m., dep. 1,875,933.2m. (Dec. 2011); Chair.

McKinney Y. T. Tsai; Pres. Shiu Kuang-si; 66 domestic brs, 17 overseas brs.

Shanghai Commercial and Savings Bank: 2 Min Chuan East Rd, Sec. 1, Taipei 10452; tel. (2) 25523111; fax (2) 25318501; e-mail service@scsb.com.tw; internet www.scsb.com.tw; f. 1915; cap. 35,388.4m., res 37,435.6m., dep. 1,031,234m. (Dec. 2011); Chair. H. C. Yung; Pres. Y. P. Chen; 61 brs.

Standard Chartered Bank (Taiwan) Ltd: 4/F, 168 Dun Hua North Rd, Songshan, Taipei 10548; tel. (2) 66027743; fax (2) 66027711; internet www.standardchartered.com.tw; f. 1948; fmrly Hsinchu International Bank; acquired by Standard Chartered Bank in Oct. 2006; cap. 29,105.7m., res 7,757m., dep. 620,677m. (Dec. 2011); Pres. and CEO Ajay Kanwal; 86 brs.

Sunny Bank: 88 Shih Pai Rd, Sec. 1, Taipei 11271; tel. (2) 28208166; fax (2) 28233414; internet www.esunnybank.com.tw; f. 1997; absorbed Kao Shin Bank in Nov. 2005; cap. 12,750m., res 154m., dep. 226,665m. (Dec. 2011); Chair. Lin Peng-lang; Pres. Ding Wei-hao; 96 brs.

Ta Chong Bank Ltd: 2/F, 2 Xinyi Rd, Sec. 5, Xinyi District, Taipei 11049; tel. (2) 87869888; fax (2) 87869800; e-mail service@tcbank.com.tw; internet www.tcbank.com.tw; f. 1992; cap. 21,834.6m., res 2,430m., dep. 384,517.1m. (Dec. 2011); Chair. Chen Chien-ping; Pres. Justin Tsai; 52 brs.

Taichung Commercial Bank: 87 Min Chuan Rd, Taichung 40341; tel. (4) 22236021; fax (4) 22240748; e-mail service@ms2.tcbbank.com.tw; internet www.tcbbank.com.tw; f. 1953; cap. 22,338.5m., res 1,666.6m., dep. 335,679m. (Dec. 2011); Chair. Soo Jin-fong; Pres. Lee Chun-sheng; 79 brs.

Taipei Fubon Commercial Bank Co Ltd: 169 Renai Rd, Sec. 4, Taipei 106; tel. (2) 27716999; fax (2) 66069398; internet www.fubon.com; f. 1969; fmrly City Bank of Taipei; acquired by Fubon Financial Holding in 2002; present name adopted following merger of Taipei Bank and Fubon Commercial Bank in 2005; cap. 51,093m., res 31,941.5m., dep. 1,190,104m. (Dec. 2011); Chair. Daniel M. Tsai; Pres. Jerry Harn; 126 brs, 5 overseas.

Taishin International Bank: 44 Zhong Shan North Rd, Sec. 2, Taipei 104; tel. (2) 25683988; fax (2) 25230539; e-mail pr@taishinbank.com.tw; internet www.taishinbank.com.tw; f. 1992; absorbed Dah An Commercial Bank in Feb. 2002; cap. 49,157.5m., res 6,065.6m., dep. 793,005.6m. (Dec. 2011); Chair. Thomas T. L. Wu; Pres. Larry Chung; 24 brs.

Taiwan Business Bank: 30 Tacheng St, Taipei 103; tel. (2) 25597171; fax (2) 25507942; e-mail tbb@mail.tbb.com.tw; internet www.tbb.com.tw; f. 1915; reassumed present name 1976; cap. 42,098.2m., res 1,784m., dep. 1,094,369.5m. (Dec. 2011); Chair. Liao Tsan-chang; Pres. Huang Tien-chang; 128 brs.

Taiwan Shin Kong Commercial Bank: 26–28/F, 66 Chung Hsiao West Rd, Sec. 1, Taipei 100; tel. (2) 23895858; fax (2) 23120164; e-mail service@mail.skbank.com.tw; internet www.skbank.com.tw; f. 2000; cap. 20,512.7m., res 2,481.2m., dep. 483,048.1m. (Dec. 2011); Chair. Patrick C. J. Liang; Gen. Man. Lai Jin-yuan; 28 brs.

Union Bank of Taiwan: 2/F, 109 Minsheng East Rd, Sec. 3, Taipei 10544; tel. (2) 27180001; fax (2) 27137515; e-mail 014_0199@email.ubot.com.tw; internet www.ubot.com.tw; f. 1992; cap. 19,485m., res –567.1m., dep. 299,893.2m. (Dec. 2010); Chair. Lee Shiang-chang; Pres. Jeff Lin; 76 brs.

Yuanta Commercial Bank Co Ltd: 66 Tun Hua S Rd, Sec. 1, Taipei 100557; tel. (2) 21736699; fax (2) 27725303; e-mail service@yuanta.com; internet www.yuantabank.com.tw; f. 1992; fmrly Fuhwa Commercial Bank, name changed as above in 2007; cap. 25,108.1m., res 3,291.4m., dep. 443,097.7m. (Dec. 2011); Pres. Chin Chia-lin; 88 brs.

There are also a number of Medium Business Banks throughout the country.

Community Financial System

The community financial institutions include both credit co-operatives and credit departments of farmers' and fishermen's associations. These local financial institutions focus upon providing savings and loan services for the community. In February 2013 there were 24 credit co-operatives in Taiwan.

Foreign Banks

In February 2013 a total of 30 foreign banks had branches in Taipei.

STOCK EXCHANGE

Under new regulations introduced in 2003, foreign investors were divided into two categories: foreign institutional investors (FINIs) and foreign individual investors (FIDIs). While FIDIs were subject to a US $5m. investment quota, FINIs could benefit from an investment quota with no upper limit. However, some industries continued to impose investment 'ceilings' for foreign investors.

Taiwan Stock Exchange Corpn: 3/F, No. 7, Sec. 5, Xinyi Rd, Taipei 11049; tel. (2) 81013101; fax (2) 81013066; internet www.tse.com.tw; f. 1961; Chair. Schive Chi; Pres. Samuel Hsu.

Supervisory Body

Securities and Futures Bureau: 85 Hsin Sheng South Rd, Sec. 1, Da-an District, Taipei 106; tel. (2) 87735100; fax (2) 87734143; e-mail sfbmail@sfb.gov.tw; internet www.sfb.gov.tw; Dir-Gen. Lee Chi-hsien.

INSURANCE

AIG General Insurance: 16/F, 200 Kee-Lung Rd, Sec. 1, Taipei 110; tel. (2) 37251827; fax (2) 87884338; e-mail aiggeneral@aig.com; internet www.aiggeneral.com.tw.

Allianz President General Insurance Co Ltd: 8/F, 178 Ming Chuan East Rd, Sec. 3, Taipei; tel. (2) 27155888; fax (2) 27176616; e-mail azpl@ms2.seeder.net; internet www.allianz.com.tw; f. 1995; Chair. Bruce Bowers.

Bank Taiwan Life Insurance Co Ltd: 6/F, 69 Tun Hua South Rd, Sec. 2, Taipei 10682; tel. (2) 27849151; fax (2) 27052214; internet www.twfhclife.com.tw; f. 1941; life insurance; Dir Zhang Guoqin; Gen. Man. Fu Deng-hsieh.

Cathay Life Insurance Co Ltd: 296 Jen Ai Rd, Sec. 4, Taipei 10650; tel. (2) 27551399; fax (2) 27082166; e-mail service@cathaylife.com.tw; internet www.cathaylife.com.tw; f. 1962; Chair. Tsai Hong-tu; Pres. T. K. Huang.

Central Reinsurance Corpn: 12/F, 53 Nanking East Rd, Sec. 2, Taipei 104; tel. (2) 25115211; fax (2) 25629683; e-mail centralre@centralre.com; internet www.crc.com.tw; f. 1968; Chair. Yang Cheng-tui; Pres. C. T. Juang.

China Life Insurance Co Ltd: 5/F, 122 Tun Hua North Rd, Taipei; tel. (2) 27196678; fax (2) 27125966; e-mail services@chinalife.com.tw; internet www.chinalife.com.tw; f. 1963; Chair. Chang Ching-wang; Gen. Man. Alan Wang.

Chung Kuo Insurance Co Ltd: 58 Wucheng St, Sec. 1, Taipei 104; tel. (2) 23812727; fax (2) 23814878; e-mail ckibest@mail.cki.com.tw; internet www.cki.com.tw; f. 1931; Chair. Leon Shen; Pres. C. Y. Liu.

Far Glory Life Insurance Co Ltd: 18/F, 200 Keelung Rd, Sec. 1, Taipei 110; tel. (2) 27583099; fax (2) 23451635; internet www.fglife.com.tw; f. 1993; Chair. T. S. Chao; Pres. C. S. Tu.

The First Insurance Co Ltd: 54 Chung Hsiao East Rd, Sec. 1, Taipei 100; tel. (2) 23913271; fax (2) 23412864; internet www.firstins.com.tw; f. 1962; Chair. Cheng Hang-lee; Pres. James Lai.

Fubon Insurance Co Ltd: 237 Chien Kuo South Rd, Sec. 1, Da-an District, Taipei 10657; tel. (2) 27067890; fax (2) 27042915; internet www.fubon.com; f. 1961; Chair. Dan Canming.

Fubon Life Insurance Co Ltd: 14/F, 108 Tun Hua South Rd, Sec. 1, Taipei 105; tel. (2) 87716699; fax (2) 88098889; internet www.fubon.com; f. 1993; Gen. Man. Cheng Peng-yuan.

Global Life Insurance Co Ltd: 9/F, 50 Chung Hsiao West Rd, Sec. 1, Taipei 10041; tel. (2) 23883399; fax (2) 23887676; e-mail services@globallife.com.tw; internet www.globallife.com.tw; f. 1993; Chair. John Tseng; Pres. Lai Yi-ming.

Hontai Life Insurance Co Ltd: 4/F, 156 Minsheng East Rd, Sec. 3, Taipei; tel. (2) 27166888; fax (2) 27166812; e-mail service@hontai.com.tw; internet www.hontai.com.tw; f. 1994; fmrly Hung Fu Life Insurance Co; Chair. David Jou.

Kuo Hua Life Insurance Co Ltd: 277 Song-Ren Rd, Xinyi District, Taipei; tel. (2) 21765166; fax (2) 55519707; internet www.khltw.com; f. 1963; Chair. M. S. Hsia; Pres. Ching Jiang-chen.

Mercuries Life Insurance Co Ltd: 6/F, Lane 150, Hsin-Yi North Rd, Sec. 2, Taipei 110; tel. (2) 23455511; fax (2) 23456616; e-mail mmli@mail.mli.com.tw; internet www.mli.com.tw; f. 1993; Chair. Henry Chen; Pres. Lu Chung-shin.

MSIG Mingtai Insurance Co Ltd: 1 Jen Ai Rd, Sec. 4, Taipei; tel. (2) 27725678; fax (2) 27726666; internet www.msig-mingtai.com.tw; f. 1961; Chair. Larry P. C. Lin; Pres. H. T. Chen.

Nan Shan Life Insurance Co Ltd: 168 Zhuangjing Rd, Xinyi District, Taipei 11049; tel. (2) 87588888; fax (2) 87867087; internet www.nanshanlife.com.tw; f. 1963; Chair. Edmund Tse; Pres. Frank Chan.

Prudential Life Assurance Co Ltd: 10/F, 161 Nanking East Rd, Sec. 5, Taipei; tel. (2) 27678866; fax (2) 27679299; internet www.pcalife.com.tw; f. 1962; Chair. Stephen D. Jin.

Shin Kong Life Insurance Co Ltd: 37/F, 66 Chung Hsiao West Rd, Sec. 1, Taipei 100; tel. (2) 23895858; fax (2) 23758688; internet www.skl.com.tw; f. 1963; Chair. Eugene T. C. Wu; Pres. Po Tseng-pan.

Shinkong Insurance Co Ltd: 15 Chien Kuo North Rd, Sec. 2, Taipei 104; tel. (2) 25075335; fax (2) 25071645; internet www.skinsurance.com.tw; f. 1963; Chair. Anthony T. S. Wu; Pres. Jun Yu-zhan.

Singfor Life Insurance Co Ltd: 8/F, 6 Chung Hsiao West Rd, Sec. 1, Taipei; tel. (2) 23817172; fax (2) 23917176; e-mail sc_lin@singforlife.com.tw; internet www.singforlife.com.tw; f. 1993; Chair. DENG WEN-CONG; Gen. Man. WEN YEN-CHEN.

South China Insurance Co Ltd: 5/F, 560 Chung Hsiao East Rd, Sec. 4, Xinyi District, Taipei 11071; tel. and fax (2) 27588418; fax (2) 27611069; e-mail ecover@south-china.com.tw; internet www.south-china.com.tw; f. 1963; Chair. JACK E. S. TAI; Pres. KEVIN TU.

Taian Insurance Co Ltd: 59 Kwantsien Rd, Taipei; tel. (2) 23819678; fax (2) 23315332; e-mail eservice@mail.taian.com.tw; internet www.taian.com.tw; f. 1961; Chair. C. H. CHEN; Gen. Man. PATRICK S. LEE.

Taiwan Fire and Marine Insurance Co Ltd: 8–9/F, 49 Kuan Chien Rd, Jungjeng Chiu, Taipei 100; tel. (2) 23821666; fax (2) 23882555; e-mail info@tfmi.com.tw; internet www.tfmi.com.tw; f. 1946; Chair. STEVE LEE; Pres. CHARLES SUNG.

Taiwan Life Insurance Co Ltd: 16–19/F, 17 Hsu Chang St, Taipei; tel. (2) 23116411; fax (2) 23759714; e-mail service1@twlife.com.tw; internet www.twlife.com.tw; f. 1947; Chair. CHU PING-YU; Pres. LIN CHENG-TAO.

Tokio Marine Newa Insurance Co Ltd: 7–12/F, 130 Nanking East Rd, Sec. 3, Taipei 104; tel. (2) 87707777; fax (2) 87891190; internet www.tmnewa.com.tw; f. 1999; Chair. HUANG WEN-CHENG; Pres. CHEN REN-TZE.

Union Insurance Co Ltd: 4/F, 219 Chung Hsiao East Rd, Sec. 4, Taipei; tel. (2) 27765567; fax (2) 27737199; internet www.unionins.com.tw; f. 1963; Chair. S. H. CHIN; Gen. Man. FRANK S. WANG.

Zurich Insurance Taiwan Ltd: 9–12/F, 56 Tun Hua North Rd, Taipei 10551; tel. (2) 27752888; fax (2) 27416004; e-mail webmail.twz@zurich.com; internet www.zurich.com.tw; f. 1961; CEO DANIEL RAYMOND.

Trade and Industry

GOVERNMENT AGENCIES

Bureau of Foreign Trade (Ministry of Economic Affairs): 1 Houkow St, Taipei 10066; tel. (2) 23510271; fax (2) 23517080; e-mail boft@trade.gov.tw; internet www.trade.gov.tw; Dir-Gen. CHANG CHUN-FU.

Council of Agriculture (COA): 37 Nan Hai Rd, Taipei 10014; tel. (2) 23812991; fax (2) 23719233; e-mail coa@mail.coa.gov.tw; internet www.coa.gov.tw; f. 1984; govt agency directly under the Executive Yuan, with ministerial status; a policy-making body in charge of national agriculture, forestry, fisheries, the animal industry and food administration; promotes technology and provides external assistance; Chair. CHEN BAO-JI.

Department of Investment Services (Ministry of Economic Affairs): 8/F, 71 Guancian Rd, Taipei 10047; tel. (2) 23892111; fax (2) 23820497; e-mail generaldois@moea.gov.tw; internet www.dois.moea.gov.tw; f. 1959 to assist investment and planning; Dir-Gen. LING CHIA-YUH.

Industrial Development Bureau (Ministry of Economic Affairs): 41-3 Hsin Yi Rd, Sec. 3, Taipei 10651; tel. (2) 27541255; fax (2) 27030160; e-mail service@moeaidb.gov.tw; internet www.moeaidb.gov.tw; Dir-Gen. DUH TYZZ-JIUN.

CHAMBERS OF COMMERCE

General Chamber of Commerce of the Republic of China: 6/F, 390 Fu Hsing South Rd, Sec. 1, Taipei 10665; tel. (2) 27012671; fax (2) 27555493; e-mail service@roccoc.org.tw; internet www.roccoc.org.tw; f. 1946; 86 group mems, incl. 43 nat. feds of trade asscns, 18 nat. commercial asscns, 22 district export asscns and district chambers of commerce; Chair. CHANG PEN-TSAO; Sec.-Gen. PETER LEE.

Taiwan Chamber of Commerce: 13/F, 168 Sung Chiang Rd, Taipei; tel. (2) 25365455; fax (2) 25211980; e-mail tcoc@tcoc.org.tw; internet www.tcoc.org.tw; f. 1946; 113 mems, comprising 93 provincial trade asscns and 20 local chambers of commerce; Chair. CHANG JONG-WEI.

INDUSTRIAL AND TRADE ASSOCIATIONS

China Productivity Center: 2/F, 79 Hsin Tai 5 Rd, Sec. 1, Hsichih, Taipei County 22101; tel. (2) 26982989; fax (2) 26982976; internet www.cpc.org.tw; f. 1956; management, technology, training, etc.; Pres. CHEN MING-CHANG.

Chinese National Association of Industry and Commerce: 13/F, 390 Fu Hsing South Rd, Sec. 1, Taipei; tel. (2) 27070111; fax (2) 27070977; e-mail service@cnaic.org; internet www.cnaic.org; f. 1975; private, independent, non-profit organization comprising major commercial and industrial firms, financial institutions, business asscns, industrialists and business people; Chair. KENNETH C. M. LO.

Chinese National Federation of Industries (CNFI): 12/F, 390 Fu Hsing South Rd, Sec. 1, Taipei 10665; tel. (2) 27033500; fax (2) 27058317; e-mail cnfi@cnfi.org.tw; internet www.cnfi.org.tw; f. 1948; 152 mem. asscns; Chair. PRESTON W. CHEN; Sec.-Gen. TSAI LIEN-SHENG.

Taiwan External Trade Development Council: 5–7/F, 333 Keelung Rd, Sec. 1, Taipei 11003; tel. (2) 27255200; fax (2) 27576652; e-mail taitra@taitra.org.tw; internet www.taitra.org.tw; trade promotion body; Chair. WANG CHIH-KANG; Pres. and CEO CHAO YUEN-CHUAN.

Taiwan Handicraft Promotion Centre: 1 Hsu Chou Rd, Taipei 10055; tel. (2) 23933655; fax (2) 23937330; e-mail thpc@handicraft.org.tw; internet www.handicraft.org.tw; f. 1957; Pres. J. H. LIN.

Taiwan Robot Industry Asscn (Robotics Association Taiwan): Taichung; tel. (4) 23581866; fax (4) 23581566; e-mail service@roboat.org.tw; internet www.roboat.org.tw; f. 2007; industry promotion body; Chair. ZHOU YONG-CHOI.

Taiwan Transportation Vehicle Manufacturers Asscn (TTVMA): 9/F, 390, Sec. 1, Fushing South Rd, Da-an District, Taipei 10656; tel. (2) 27051101; fax (2) 27066440; internet www.ttvma.org.tw; f. 1948; 600 mems; Chair. CHEN KUO-RONG.

UTILITIES

Electricity

Taiwan Power Co (Taipower): 242 Roosevelt Rd, Sec. 3, Taipei 10016; tel. (2) 23651234; fax (2) 23650037; e-mail service@taipower.com.tw; internet www.taipower.com.tw; f. 1946; electricity generation; Chair. HWANG JUNG-CHIOU; Pres. HAN SHEN-LEE.

Gas

The Great Taipei Gas Corpn: 5/F, Lane 11, 35 Kwang Fu North Rd, Taipei 10577; tel. (2) 27684999; fax (2) 27630480; e-mail k2@taipeigas.com.tw; internet www.taipeigas.com.tw; supply of gas and gas equipment; Chair. LI FENG-YAO.

Hsin Kao Gas Co Ltd: 56 Ta-Yi St, Yen Cheng, Kaohsiung; tel. (7) 5315701; fax (7) 5312932; internet www.hkgas.com.tw; Chair. CHEN TIEN-MIAO; Gen. Man. CHEN CHIEN-TONG.

Shin Shin Natural Gas Co Ltd: 100 Yungho Rd, Sec. 1, Yungho, Taipei; tel. (2) 29217811; fax (2) 29282829; e-mail ssngas11@ms67.hinet.net; internet www.shinshingas.com.tw; f. 1971; supplies natural gas to non-industrial users; Chair. CHEN HO-CHIA; Gen. Man. LI QINGGUO.

Water

Taiwan Water Corpn: 2-1 Shuangshih Rd, Sec. 2, Taichung 40425; tel. (4) 2224191; fax (4) 2224201; e-mail chairman@mail.water.gov.tw; internet www.water.gov.tw; f. 1974; supplies water throughout Taiwan Province and Kaohsiung City; Chair. JUAN KANG-MENG; Pres. CHEN FU-TIEN.

TRADE UNIONS

Chinese Federation of Labour: 4/F, 177 Roosevelt Rd, Sec. 3, Taipei 10647; tel. (2) 23660111; fax (2) 23696111; e-mail cfl.labor@msa.hinet.net; internet www.cfl.org.tw; f. 1948; comprises 53 feds of unions representing more than 1m. workers; Pres. CHIEH CHEN.

Transport

RAILWAYS

Taiwan Railway Administration (TRA): 3 Peiping West Rd, Taipei 10041; tel. (2) 23815226; fax (2) 23831367; internet www.railway.gov.tw; f. 1891; public utility under the Ministry of Transportation and Communications; operates both the west line and east line systems, with a route length of 1,101.5 km; Dir-Gen. FRANK FAN.

Taipei Rapid Transit Corpn (TRTC): 7 Lane 48, Zhong Shan North Rd, Sec. 2, Taipei 10448; tel. (2) 25363001; fax (2) 25239284; e-mail email@mail.trtc.com.tw; internet www.trtc.com.tw; f. 1994; 90.5 km (incl. 10.5 km medium-capacity rail) open, with further lines under construction; also operates the Maokong Gondola cable car system; Chair. YANG HSI-AN; Pres. Dr TAN GWA-GUANG.

Taiwan High Speed Rail Corpn (THSRC): 3/F, 100 Hsin Yi Rd, Taipei 110; tel. (2) 40666600; fax (2) 66268866; internet www.thsrc.com.tw; f. 1996; operates 345-km high-speed rail link between Taipei and Kaohsiung; Chair. and CEO OU CHIN-DER.

An Airport Rail service linking Taipei with Taiwan Taoyuan International Airport is under construction by the Ministry of

Transportation and Communications; following several delays, the system was not expected to commence operating until October 2014 at the earliest.

ROADS

There were 40,901 km of roads in 2011 (including 15,716 km of highways). The Sun Yat-sen Freeway, linking Taipei, Keelung and Kaohsiung, was completed in 1978. Construction of a 505-km Second Freeway, which extends to Pingtung, in southern Taiwan, was completed in 2004. The Nantou branch, from the Wufeng system interchange of the Second Freeway to Puli in central Taiwan, with a length of 38 km, was completed in 2008. The 31-km Taipei–Ilan freeway and its 24.1-km extension, from Toucheng to Suao, were completed in 2005.

Directorate-General of Highways: 70 Chung Hsiao West Rd, Sec. 1, Taipei 10041; tel. (2) 23113456; fax (2) 23111644; e-mail dghmail@thb.gov.tw; internet www.thb.gov.tw; Dir-Gen. WU MEN-FENG.

Kuo-Kuang Motor Transport Co Ltd: 4/F, 17 Hsu Chang St, Taipei 10047; tel. (2) 23810731; fax (2) 23810268; internet www.kingbus.com.tw; f. 2001; operates national bus service; Chair. LEE HONG-SEN.

Taiwan Area National Expressway Engineering Bureau: 1 Lane 1, Hoping East Rd, Sec. 3, Taipei 10669; tel. (2) 27078808; fax (2) 27017818; e-mail neebeyes@taneeb.gov.tw; internet www.taneeb.gov.tw; f. 1990; responsible for planning, design, construction and maintenance of provincial and county highways; Dir-Gen. BANE L. B. CHJOU.

Taiwan Area National Freeway Bureau: 70 Banshanya, Liming Village, Taishan Township, Taipei County 24303; tel. (2) 29096141; fax (2) 29093218; e-mail tanfb1@freeway.gov.tw; internet www.freeway.gov.tw; f. 1970; Dir-Gen. TSENG DAR-JEN.

SHIPPING

Taiwan has seven international ports: Anping, Kaohsiung, Keelung, Taichung, Hualien, Suao and Taipei. In December 2012 the flag registered fleet comprised 312 vessels, with a total displacement of 2,933,439 grt. Some of the main shipping companies are as follows:

Evergreen International Storage & Transport Corpn: 899 Ching Kuo Rd, Taoyuan 3305; tel. (3) 3252060; fax (3) 3252059; e-mail mgt@evergreen-eitc.com.tw; internet www.evergreen-eitc.com.tw; Chair. YE JIONG-CHAO.

Evergreen Marine Corpn (Taiwan) Ltd: Evergreen Bldg, 166 Minsheng East Rd, Sec. 2, Taipei 10423; tel. (2) 25057766; fax (2) 25058159; e-mail mgt@evergreen-marine.com; internet www.evergreen-marine.com; f. 1968; world-wide container liner services; Chair. ZONGJIN WANG; Pres. WANG LONG-SHUNG.

Taiwan Navigation Co Ltd: 2–6/F, 29 Chi Nan Rd, Sec. 2, Taipei 10054; tel. (2) 23927177; fax (2) 23936578; e-mail tnctpe@taiwanline.com.tw; internet www.taiwanline.com.tw; Chair. ZHANG YI-YUAN; Pres. WU SHENG-QING.

U-Ming Marine Transport Corpn: 29/F, Taipei Metro Tower, 207 Tun Hua South Rd, Sec. 2, Taipei 10602; tel. (2) 27338000; fax (2) 27359900; e-mail uming@metro.feg.com.tw; internet www.uming.com.tw; world-wide transportation services; Chair. TSAI HSIUNG-CHAN; Pres. C. K. ONG.

Wan Hai Lines Ltd: 10/F, 136 Sung Chiang Rd, Taipei 10485; tel. (2) 25677961; fax (2) 25216000; e-mail serv@wanhai.com.tw; internet www.wanhai.com.tw; f. 1965; regional container liner services; Chair. C. H. CHEN; Pres. P. T. CHEN.

Yang Ming Marine Transport Corpn (Yang Ming Line): 271 Ming De 1st Rd, Keelung 20646; tel. (2) 24559988; fax (2) 24559958; e-mail tara@yml.com.tw; internet www.yml.com.tw; f. 1972; world-wide container liner services, bulk carrier and supertanker services; Chair. and CEO FRANK LU; Pres. ROBERT HO.

CIVIL AVIATION

There are two international airports: Taiwan Taoyuan International Airport (formerly known as Chiang Kai-shek) near Taipei, which opened in 1979, a second passenger terminal and expansion of freight facilities being completed in 2000; and Kaohsiung International Airport, which also offers domestic services. The construction of a third terminal at Taiwan Taoyuan International Airport was due to begin in 2014, with an expected completion date of 2018. There are 16 domestic airports, three of which offer international charter services.

Civil Aeronautics Administration: 340 Tun Hua North Rd, Taipei 10548; tel. (2) 23496000; fax (2) 23496277; e-mail gencaa@mail.caa.gov.tw; internet www.caa.gov.tw; Dir-Gen. CHI SHEN.

China Airlines Ltd (CAL): 131 Nanjing East Rd, Sec. 3, Taipei 10410; tel. (2) 27151212; fax (2) 25146004; e-mail ju-reng_chen@email.china-airlines.com; internet www.china-airlines.com; f. 1959; international services to destinations in the Far East, Europe, the Middle East, the USA and Australia; Chair. PHILIP HSING-HSIUNG WEI; Pres. SUN HUANG-HSIANG.

EVA Airways (EVA): Eva Air Bldg, 376 Hsin-nan Rd, Sec. 1, Luchu Township, Taoyuan County 33801; tel. (3) 3515151; fax (3) 3510023; e-mail prd@evaair.com; internet www.evaair.com; f. 1989; subsidiary of Evergreen Group; commenced flights in 1991; services to destinations in Asia, the Middle East, Europe, North America, Australia and New Zealand; Chair. LIN BOU-SHIU; Pres. JENG KUNG-YEUN.

Mandarin Airlines (MDA): 13/F, 134 Minsheng East Rd, Sec. 3, Taipei 10596; tel. (2) 27171188; fax (2) 27170716; e-mail mandarin@mandarin-airlines.com; internet www.mandarin-airlines.com; f. 1991; subsidiary of CAL; merged with Formosa Airlines 1999; domestic and regional services; Chair. HARRIS WANG.

TransAsia Airways (TNA): 9/F, 139 Chengchou Rd, Taipei 10341; tel. (2) 87125656; fax (2) 87128086; e-mail tna@tna.com.tw; internet www.tna.com.tw; f. 1951; fmrly Foshing Airlines; domestic and international services; Chair. LIN MING-SHENG; Gen. Man. CHEN JIA.

UNI Airways Corpn (UIA): 9/F, 100 Chang An East Rd, Sec. 2, Taipei 10491; tel. (2) 25135533; fax (2) 25133202; e-mail communication@uniair.com.tw; internet www.uniair.com.tw; f. 1989; fmrly Makung Airlines; merged with Great China Airlines and Taiwan Airlines 1998; domestic flights and international services (to Bali, Indonesia; Seoul, South Korea; Bangkok, Thailand; and Hanoi, Viet Nam); Chair. SU HOMNG-YIH; Pres. PETER CHEN.

Tourism

The attractions of Taiwan include the island's scenery and cultural heritage. In 2012 visitor arrivals (including Overseas Chinese) rose by 20.1% to reach 7.3m. Revenue from tourism in 2011 totalled US $11,065m. The relaxation of official restrictions on the numbers of mainland Chinese visitors has led to a substantial increase in arrivals from the People's Republic.

Tourism Bureau, Ministry of Transportation and Communications: 9/F, 290 Chung Hsiao East Rd, Sec. 4, Taipei 10694; tel. (2) 23491500; fax (2) 27717036; e-mail tbroc@tbroc.gov.tw; internet taiwan.net.tw; f. 1972; Dir-Gen. DAVID HSIEH.

Taiwan Visitors' Association: 5/F, 9 Min Chuan East Rd, Sec. 2, Taipei 10470; tel. (2) 25943261; fax (2) 25943265; internet www.tva.org.tw; f. 1956; promotes domestic and international tourism; Chair. CHOU CHING-SHYONG.

Defence

As assessed at November 2012, the armed forces totalled an estimated 290,000: army 200,000, navy 45,000 (including 15,000 marines), and air force 45,000. Paramilitary forces totalled 17,000. Reserves numbered 1,657,000. Military service is for 12 months.

Defence Expenditure: Budgeted at NT $317,300m. for 2012.

Chief of the General Staff: Gen. YEN MING.

Commander of the Army: Gen. LEE HSIANG-CHOU.

Commander of the Navy: Adm. TUNG HSIANG-LUNG.

Commander of the Air Force: Gen. LIU JEN-WU.

Education

Pre-school education is optional, although in 2008/09 a total of 182,049 children were attending kindergarten. In 2011/12 1,373,375 pupils attended primary school, and a total of 1,617,003 pupils were enrolled in secondary (including vocational) education. There are three types of secondary school: junior high, senior high and senior vocational. The net enrolment ratio for children between the ages of six and 14 was 100.2% in 2008. In 2011/12 there were 162 universities, junior colleges and independent colleges. Most of these offer postgraduate facilities. A total of 1,355,290 students were enrolled in higher education in 2011/12. General government expenditure on education, science and culture in 2011 amounted to NT $588,652m., equivalent to 22.5% of total spending (current and capital).

TAJIKISTAN

Introductory Survey

LOCATION, CLIMATE, LANGUAGE, RELIGION, FLAG, CAPITAL

The Republic of Tajikistan is situated in the south-east of Central Asia. To the north and west it borders Uzbekistan, to the north-east Kyrgyzstan, to the east the People's Republic of China and to the south Afghanistan. The climate varies considerably according to altitude. The average temperature in January in Khujand (lowland) is −0.9°C (30.4°F); in July the average is 27.4°C (81.3°F). In the southern lowlands the temperature variation is somewhat more extreme. Rainfall is low in the valleys, in the range of 150–250 mm (6–10 ins) per year. In mountain areas winter temperatures can fall below −45°C (−51°F); the average January temperature in Murgab, in the mountains of south-east Kuhistoni Badakhshon, is −19.6°C (−3.3°F). Levels of rainfall are very low in mountain regions, seldom exceeding 60–80 mm (2–3 ins) per year. The official language is Tajik, a Persian language; the Constitution grants Russian the status of a language of inter-ethnic communication, and all ethnic groups are guaranteed the right to use their native languages freely. The major religion is Islam. Most Tajiks and ethnic Uzbek residents follow the Sunni tradition, but the Pamiris are mostly Isma'ilis, a Shi'ite sect. The national flag (proportions 1 by 2) consists of three horizontal stripes from top to bottom of red, white and green, with a stylized gold crown surmounted by seven gold stars arranged in a semicircle in the centre of the white stripe. The capital is Dushanbe.

CONTEMPORARY POLITICAL HISTORY

Historical Context

In 1918 northern Tajikistan (which had been part of the Russian Empire since the 19th century) was conquered by the Bolsheviks, and the territory was incorporated into the Turkestan Autonomous Soviet Socialist Republic (ASSR). However, Dushanbe and the other southern regions of Tajikistan (subject to the Emirate of Bukhara) did not come under the control of the Bolsheviks until 1921. Opposition to Soviet rule was led by the *basmachis* (local guerrilla fighters) and foreign interventionists. In 1924 the Tajik ASSR was established as a part of the Uzbek Soviet Socialist Republic (SSR), and in January 1925 the south-east of Tajikistan was designated a Special Pamir Region (later renamed the Kuhistoni Badakhshon—Gornyi Badakhshan Autonomous Viloyat) within the Tajik ASSR. On 16 October 1929 the Tajik ASSR became a full Union Republic of the USSR and was slightly enlarged by the addition of the Khujand district from the Uzbek SSR. Soviet rule brought economic and social benefits to Tajikistan, but living standards remained low, and cattle-breeding, the main occupation in the uplands, was severely disrupted by collectivization. During the 1930s almost all Tajiks in the republican Government were replaced by Russians.

During the 1970s increased Islamic influence was reported, as was violence towards non-indigenous nationalities. In 1978 there were reports of an anti-Russian riot, involving some 13,000 people, and after 1979 there were arrests of activists opposed to Soviet intervention in Afghanistan. The first manifestation of the reformist policies of Mikhail Gorbachev, who came to power as Soviet leader in 1985, was a campaign against corruption. Rahmon Nabiyev, First Secretary of the Communist Party of Tajikistan (CPT) since 1982, was replaced in late 1985 by Qahhor Makhkamov. Censorship was relaxed, and greater freedom of expression encouraged greater interest in Tajik and Persian culture; in 1989 Tajik became the state language. In February 1990, following reports that Armenian refugees from the conflict in Nagornyi Karabakh (see Azerbaijan) were to be settled in the capital, Dushanbe, a protest rally degenerated into violence. A state of emergency was declared, and troops suppressed further demonstrations; 22 people were reported to have been killed and 565 injured.

Domestic Political Affairs

In 1990 two nascent opposition parties, Rebirth (Rastokhez), which had been involved in the February demonstrations, and the Democratic Party of Tajikistan (DPT), were refused official registration, while the Islamic Rebirth Party of Tajikistan (IRPT) was denied permission to hold a founding congress. Opposition politicians were barred from contesting the elections to the republic's Supreme Soviet (Supreme Council), held in March; 94% of the deputies elected were members of the CPT. None the less, in an apparent concession, the Supreme Soviet adopted a declaration of sovereignty on 25 August. In November Makhkamov was elected to the new post of executive President of the Republic by the Supreme Soviet; his only opponent was Nabiyev.

The Tajikistani Government displayed enthusiasm for a new Union Treaty (effectively providing for the continuation of the USSR), and 90.2% of eligible voters in the republic were reported to have voted for the preservation of the USSR in a referendum held in March 1991. Makhkamov failed to oppose the abortive coup staged by conservative communists in the Soviet and Russian capital, Moscow, in August; on 31 August he resigned as President, following demonstrations which continued throughout much of September. On 9 September, after declarations of independence by Uzbekistan and Kyrgyzstan, the Tajikistani Supreme Soviet voted to proclaim an independent Republic of Tajikistan. Kadriddin Aslonov, the Chairman of the Supreme Council and acting President, banned the CPT and nationalized its assets. In response, the communist majority in the Supreme Council demanded Aslonov's resignation, declared a state of emergency in the republic and rescinded the prohibition of the CPT. Aslonov resigned, and was replaced by Nabiyev, who was rapidly obliged to make substantial concessions to the opposition. In early October the Supreme Council revoked the state of emergency, suspended the CPT and legalized the IRPT. Shortly afterwards Nabiyev resigned as acting President, in advance of the presidential election.

Seven candidates contested the direct presidential election, which took place on 24 November 1991. Nabiyev won 57% of the votes cast, compared with 30% for the principal opposition candidate, Davlat Khudonazarov. Nabiyev took office in December. In late December Tajikistan signed the declaration establishing the Commonwealth of Independent States (CIS, see p. 251), the successor body to the USSR. In January 1992 a new Prime Minister, Akbar Mirzoyev, was appointed.

Civil war

Anti-Government demonstrations began in Dushanbe in March 1992, initially prompted by Nabiyev's dismissal of Mamadayez Navzhuvanov as Minister of Internal Affairs. Protests against his dismissal were led by the group Lale Badakhshon, which advocated greater autonomy for the Pamiri peoples of the southern Kuhistoni Badakhshon region. It was joined by Rebirth, the IRPT and the DPT. Protesters demanding the resignation of Nabiyev and the Government remained encamped in the centre of Dushanbe for nearly two months; in response, the Government organized rival demonstrations, bringing supporters to the capital from the southern region of Kulob (Kulyab) and from Leninobod (later Khujand), in the north—historic areas of support for the CPT. In April members of the newly formed national guard loyal to Nabiyev opened fire on demonstrators, killing at least eight people. The National Security Committee (NSC—the successor to the Soviet Committee for State Security—KGB) allegedly distributed weapons to pro-communist supporters in May, and the ensuing violent clashes escalated into civil war. Fighting in Dushanbe ended after Nabiyev negotiated a truce with opposition leaders and formed a new 'Government of National Reconciliation' led by Mirzoyev, in which eight of the 24 ministers were members of opposition parties. However, violent clashes erupted in Kulob Viloyat (region) between pro-communist forces, who opposed the President's compromise with the opposition, and an informal alliance of Islamist and pro-democracy groups. In late May the conflict spread into Qurghonteppa Viloyat, where a Kulobi militia, the Tajik People's Front (TPF), led by Sangak Safarov, attempted to suppress the local rebel forces. The TPF alleged that their opponents were receiving weapons and assistance from Islamist groups in Afghanistan, and there were reports that Gulbuddin Hekmatyar, the leader of the Afghan *mujahidin* group Hizb-i Islami (Islamic Party), had established training camps in Afghanistan for Tajikistani fighters.

Several members of the DPT and Lale Badakhshon were killed by Kulobi militia forces in Qurghonteppa in August 1992. A violent conflict ensued between local members of the opposition and Kulobis, in which several hundred people were reportedly killed. At the end of August demonstrators entered the presidential palace in Dushanbe and took 30 officials hostage. In September Nabiyev was seized by opposition forces at Dushanbe airport, and was forced to resign. Akbarsho Iskandarov, the Chairman of the Supreme Council, temporarily assumed the responsibilities of head of state. Mirzoyev also resigned, and Abdumalik Abdullojonov, a communist from Leninobod Viloyat (later Sughd Viloyat), was appointed acting Prime Minister. Iskandarov's administration, however, had little influence outside Dushanbe; much of the south of the country was under the control of the TPF, and some leaders of Leninobod Viloyat threatened to secede from Tajikistan if there was any attempt to introduce an Islamic state. In October the opposition alliance's control of Dushanbe was threatened when forces led by Safarali Kenjayev, a supporter of Nabiyev and a former Chairman of the Supreme Soviet, entered the city and attempted to seize power. Although Kenjayev briefly proclaimed himself head of state, his troops were forced to retreat, despite effectively enforcing an economic blockade of the capital for the following two months.

In November 1992 Iskandarov and the Government resigned. The legislature abolished the office of President, and Emomali Rahmonov, a collective-farm chairman from Kulob Viloyat, was appointed Chairman of the Supreme Council (Head of State). The legislature appointed a new Government, retaining Abdullojonov as Prime Minister. All opposition representatives lost their portfolios, and the majority of the new ministers were Kulobis or supporters of Nabiyev. The Supreme Council also voted to combine Qurghonteppa and Kulob Viloyats into one unit, Khatlon Viloyat, in an attempt to secure control of the south of the country by pro-communist forces. In December forces loyal to the new Government captured Dushanbe, hitherto under the control of the Islamist-dominated Popular Democratic Army (PDA).

Between December 1992 and January 1993 some 60,000 Tajikistanis fled to Afghanistan, after reprisals were undertaken against supporters of the PDA. Among those who fled was the influential *qazi* (Islamic judge) of Tajikistan, Akbar Turajonzoda, a senior member of the IRPT, whom the new Government accused of seeking to establish an Islamist state. In February he was replaced as spiritual leader of Tajikistan's Muslims by Fatkhullo Sharifzoda, who was given the title of *mufti*.

In February 1993 insurgents in the central region of Garm attempted to declare an 'autonomous Islamic republic', but the Government had secured control of most of the country by March. The Government estimated that 30,000 people had been killed during the civil war, while other sources claimed that as many as 100,000 people had died. Although the civil war effectively ended in early 1993, the continued insurgency by Islamist-dominated forces, notably from across the Afghan border, continued to destabilize the country. In June the Supreme Court formally proscribed the IRPT, Lale Badakhshon, Rebirth and the DPT, leaving the CPT as the only legal party. Two new parties established later in the year—the Party of Economic Freedom and the People's Democratic Party of Tajikistan (PDPT)—were founded or sponsored by members of the Government or its associates.

Abdujalil Samadov succeeded Abdullojonov as premier in December 1993, after the latter resigned. From the end of 1993 Rahmonov, who secured for his own office responsibility for the powerful Ministries of Defence and Internal Affairs, as well as for the NSC, began to show signs of compromise. In April negotiations between Rahmonov and opposition members began in Moscow, under the auspices of the UN and in the presence of representatives from Iran, Pakistan, Russia and the USA. However, from March border incursions from Afghanistan intensified, resulting in clashes with the CIS troops stationed on the frontier, and there was renewed insurgency in Kuhistoni Badakhshon. The continuing conflict along the Tajikistani–Afghan border was interpreted by some observers as being partly a battle for control of drugs-smuggling routes: since securing independence Tajikistan had become a major conduit for illicit drugs (chiefly opium) from Pakistan, Iran and Afghanistan to Russia and Europe.

Emomali Rahmonov (Rahmon) elected President

In August 1994 the forthcoming presidential election was postponed, to allow time for opposition candidates to be included in the poll. The implementation of a temporary cease-fire was deferred until October, after rebel forces launched a large-scale offensive in the eastern Tavildara region, which was successfully repelled. In December the UN Security Council authorized the deployment of a Mission of Observers in Tajikistan (UNMOT). When the election was conducted on 6 November, the only two candidates were Rahmonov and Abdullojonov. Some 85% of eligible voters were reported to have participated in the election, which was won by Rahmonov, with some 58% of the votes cast. In a concurrent referendum, some 90% of voters approved a new Constitution. In December Jamshed Karimov was appointed as Chairman of the Council of Ministers.

In February 1995 renewed peace talks, conducted in Almatı, Kazakhstan, proved largely fruitless. In the same month Abdullojonov's newly formed Party of Popular Unity and Accord (PPUA) announced that it would not contest the forthcoming elections to the new Majlisi Oli (Supreme Assembly), after Abdullojonov's candidature was disallowed. The Organization for Security and Co-operation in Europe (OSCE, see p. 397) refused to send observers to the elections, expressing dissatisfaction with the electoral law. Despite the opposition boycott, legislative elections took place on 26 February, with the participation of an estimated 84% of the electorate. In some 40% of constituencies there was only one candidate, and most of those elected were reported to be state officials loyal to the President.

In March 1995 the opposition announced a unilateral, 50-day extension of the cease-fire, but later that month there were further attacks on border posts along the Afghan frontier. In early April there was a serious escalation of the conflict, when 34 border guards and 170 rebel troops were reportedly killed. Nevertheless, the cease-fire was subsequently extended for a further three months, from May, when an exchange of prisoners was also agreed. In August, after Rahmonov met the leader of the IRPT, Sayed Abdullo Nuri, and other opposition leaders for talks in Tehran, Iran, the cease-fire was extended for six months. However, conflict continued in the south of the country and on the border with Afghanistan. In September clashes in Qurghonteppa between two military units, both formerly loyal to the Government, were reported to have resulted in 300 deaths before government forces regained control of the town. The opposition withdrew from peace negotiations, convened under UN auspices, in Aşgabat, Turkmenistan, in November, after the Government refused to agree to the formation of a transitional national reconciliation council to govern the country alongside Rahmonov.

In January 1996 Sharifzoda was killed by gunmen. At the end of January opposition forces began a major offensive in Tavildara, and military commanders of the government troops initiated rebellions and obtained control of Qurghonteppa and the western town of Tursunzoda. The commanders who led the rebellions (both ethnic Uzbeks) demanded changes to the Government, including the removal of several Kulobi ministers. In early February troops loyal to Makhmoud Khudoberdiyev (who had led the uprising in Qurghonteppa) approached Dushanbe, but retreated when they encountered government forces. Following negotiations, Rahmonov agreed to the commanders' demands, including the replacement of Karimov as premier with Yakhyo Azimov.

Despite the announcement of an indefinite extension of the cease-fire, fighting intensified in March–May 1996 near Tavildara, resulting in the capture of the town itself by opposition forces. Talks resumed in Aşgabat in July. A cease-fire was brokered in Tavildara, and agreement was reached on the conduct of further peace negotiations and on a gradual exchange of prisoners of war. However, large-scale hostilities resumed and opposition forces regained control of Tavildara in mid-August; meanwhile, government and rebel troops fought for command of the strategic central regions. A further cease-fire agreement was reached, but was almost immediately violated as fierce fighting continued around Garm. Later that month Rahmonov and Nuri, meeting in Moscow, agreed to form a National Reconciliation Council (NRC), to be headed by a representative of what had come to be known as the United Tajik Opposition (UTO), which was to have extensive executive powers. A general amnesty was agreed, as were terms for an exchange of prisoners and the repatriation of refugees.

Negotiations were held in Tehran in January 1997 to determine the structure and composition of the NRC, and at further

UN-mediated peace talks held in Mashhad, Iran, in February, it was agreed that the NRC was to comprise 26 seats divided equally between the Government and the UTO. Negotiations on the reintegration of opposition forces into Tajikistan's military structures, the exchange of prisoners and the legalization of opposition parties were held in Moscow and Tehran throughout March and April. In April Rahmonov was wounded in an assassination attempt (condemned by the UTO) in Khujand. A General Agreement on Peace and National Accord in Tajikistan, signed by Rahmonov and Nuri in Moscow on 27 June 1997, formally ended the five-year civil conflict. In July Nuri was elected Chairman of the NRC, at its inaugural session; an amnesty to allow UTO fighters to return to Tajikistan were agreed.

The National Reconciliation Council

Some 200 UTO fighters were deployed in Dushanbe to guard members of the NRC, sessions of which formally commenced in mid-September. In October at least 14 servicemen were killed following an attack on the barracks of the presidential guard, attributed to Makhmoud Khudoberdiyev. By mid-November some 10,000 Tajikistani refugees had been repatriated from Afghanistan. Meanwhile, negotiations were held between Nuri and Rahmonov to determine the allocation of portfolios in the new government (under the terms of the peace agreement, the UTO was to receive one-third of posts in both the central and regional administrations). Following the return of Turajonzoda, the deputy leader of the UTO, from Iran in February 1998, he was appointed First Deputy Chairman, with responsibility for relations with CIS countries.

In March 1998 several people, including the brother of the former Prime Minister, Abdullojonov, were sentenced to death for their part in the attempt to assassinate Rahmonov in April 1997. An upsurge in fighting between government and opposition forces, in the vicinity of Dushanbe, resulted in many civilian deaths. In April 1998 Rahmonov, who had joined the PDPT in March, was elected Chairman of the party. In May a cease-fire was agreed, following renewed fighting between government and opposition forces near Dushanbe. In August Rahmonov confirmed the appointment of several UTO members to government posts. However, other opposition appointments were rejected by the President, bringing the number of UTO members in the Government to 11, rather than the 14 agreed under the terms of the peace accord. In September the trial of four associates of Khudoberdiyev, accused of attempting to overthrow the Government in August 1997, began in Dushanbe. Also in September 1998 a senior opposition figure, Otakhon Latifi, was assassinated in the capital.

In October 1998 an operation by government forces against two rebel factions in Dushanbe resulted in 13 deaths and the detention of six rebels. Heavy fighting was reported around Khujand in November, in the most extensive outbreak of violence since the 1997 peace agreement, in which Khudoberdiyev's forces seized police and security headquarters and a nearby airport. Khudoberdiyev's forces were defeated after five days of fighting, in which as many as 300 people were killed. After President Rahmonov accused Abdullojonov of having instigated the rebellion, criminal proceedings were initiated against the former premier (who had fled into exile in the USA), as well as against Khudoberdiyev and two other prominent figures. In mid-November the Majlisi Oli endorsed the appointment of several UTO members to the Council of Ministers, including Davlat Usmon as Minister of the Economy and Foreign Economic Relations. In December 1998 Nuri announced that the UTO would disband its armed forces in early 1999. In March 1999 the re-registration of political parties was effected by the Ministry of Justice: of the eight parties previously registered, only five received new licences. Criminal charges against leading opposition party members, including Nuri and Turajonzoda, were abandoned. At the end of the month the Supreme Court sentenced seven supporters of Khudoberdiyev to 10–14 years' imprisonment, following their conviction on charges of involvement in the attack on government forces in October 1997.

The Majlisi Oli adopted a resolution in May 1999 providing for a general amnesty to be granted to the estimated 5,500 registered opposition fighters. Later in the month the UTO leadership withdrew from the NRC, expressing discontent that several of its demands, including further UTO appointments to government posts (so that it held the agreed share of one-third of all government positions) had not been met. In June 1999 Rahmonov and Nuri signed an agreement outlining a timetable for the implementation of the remaining provisions of the peace agreement,

while an additional four UTO members were appointed to government posts. In July Rahmonov appointed another five UTO representatives to government positions, and also announced that 21 of the 69 local government posts were to be offered to opposition members. In August the UTO leadership announced that the integration of its fighters into the regular armed forces had been completed. Rahmonov subsequently lifted a ban on opposition parties and their media 6that had been imposed in 1993.

At a referendum held on 26 September 1999, some 72% of the votes cast by an estimated 92% of the electorate approved amendments to the Constitution, proposed by President Rahmonov, including the formation of a bicameral legislature, the extension of the presidential term from five to seven years and the legalization of religiously based political parties (including the IRPT). It was reported in October that Turajonzoda had been expelled from both the UTO and its largest constituent party, the IRPT, after a policy disagreement.

Constitutional amendments of 1999 and 2003

In the presidential election, held on 6 November 1999, Rahmonov received some 97.0% of the total votes cast, according to official sources, defeating his only opponent, Usmon. The rate of participation by the electorate was reported to be almost 99%. The opposition demanded that the election (to which the OSCE had refused to send monitors) be declared invalid. Following Rahmonov's inauguration as President on 16 November, the Government tendered its resignation, although ministers remained in office until the formation of a new Government in late December. Oqil Oqilov was appointed Chairman of the Council of Ministers (Prime Minister).

In December 1999 the legislature approved the reconstitution of the Majlisi Oli on a bicameral basis. Six political parties were registered to participate in forthcoming elections to the two chambers. In the elections to the Majlisi Namoyandagon (Assembly of Representatives), the lower chamber of the Majlisi Oli, held on 27 February 2000, Rahmonov's PDPT with its allies secured 45 of the 63 seats, having reportedly won 64.5% of the votes cast. The CPT won around 20.6% of the votes (13 seats), while the IRPT secured about 7.5% (two seats). According to official sources, some 93% of eligible voters participated in the election. The OSCE and opposition parties stated that electoral malpractice had been widespread, and several opposition parties were barred from competing. A second round of voting took place in 11 constituencies on 12 March 2000. On 23 March indirect elections to the Majlisi Milliy (National Assembly), the legislative upper chamber, were held. Regional deputies elected 25 members of the chamber, and the eight remaining members were presidential appointees. At the end of the month the NRC was dissolved. On 1 June UNMOT was succeeded by the UN Tajikistan Office of Peace-building (UNTOP).

In June 2001 some 36 rebels linked with the former UTO field commander, Rahmon Sanginov, were killed by state security forces near Dushanbe. In August Sanginov was himself killed by security forces. In September the Minister of Culture, Press and Information, Abdurakhim Rakhimov, was assassinated. It was reported in December that 10 men had been sentenced to between eight and 25 years' imprisonment on charges of treason, terrorism and sedition, related to the November 1998 insurrection in Khujand. In March 2002 two men were sentenced to death, and a further six received terms of imprisonment of between two and 25 years, having been found guilty of belonging to an armed grouping loyal to Khudoberdiyev.

In January 2003 President Rahmonov carried out a major governmental reorganization. On 22 June some 96% of the electorate were reported to have participated in a referendum on proposed amendments to the Constitution, which were approved by 93% of the votes cast, according to official figures. Consequently, Rahmonov would also be permitted to stand for two further seven-year terms of office upon the expiry of his existing mandate in 2006. Among the other amendments approved was the abolition of a system of categorization under which registered political parties were compulsorily defined as being religious, democratic or atheistic in character.

A Deputy Chairman of the IRPT, Shamsiddin Shamsiddinov, was arrested in May 2003, and in October he became the first person to be tried on charges relating to the period of civil conflict. Following a closed trial, in January 2004 Shamsiddinov was sentenced to 16 years' imprisonment. Meanwhile, in October 2003 the former commander of the interior ministry rapid-reaction forces, Maj. Shodi Alimadov, was sentenced to eight years in prison, after being convicted on charges of corruption, extortion and abuse of office. In December and in January 2004 Rahmonov effected a number of high-level government changes. In September 20 members of the proscribed transnational militant Islamist group Hizb-ut-Tahrir al-Islami (Party of Islamic Liberation—Hizb-ut-Tahrir) were sentenced to prison terms ranging from six months to 15 years, as part of a long-term campaign against the group in Tajikistan. (According to the Office of the Prosecutor-General, between 2000 and July 2005 209 people in the country were convicted of membership of Hizb-ut-Tahrir.)

Rahmonov undertook a further reorganization of the Government in January–February 2005. Meanwhile, in January the Chairman of the DPT, Mahmadruzi Iskandarov, was denied permission to register as a candidate in the parliamentary elections scheduled for 27 February, owing to the existence of outstanding criminal charges against him; Iskandarov had been arrested in Moscow in December 2004, accused of corruption and involvement in an attack on government buildings. Sulton Kuvvatov, the leader of the Union and Development Party (which had been denied registration in March 2004), was also detained and refused permission to register as a candidate in the elections, having been accused of insulting the President and of inciting ethnic hatred. In January 2006, following the completion of an investigation into the two bomb attacks against buildings of the Ministry of Emergency Situations and Civil Defence, the Minister of Internal Affairs, Khomiddin Sharipov, announced that a number of members of the proscribed militant Islamist group, the Islamic Movement of Uzbekistan (IMU), had been imprisoned.

The 2005 legislative elections

Six political parties participated in the elections to the Majlisi Namoyandagon held on 27 February and 13 March 2005. Rahmonov's PDPT secured 52 of the 63 seats in the chamber, having won 74% of the votes cast nation-wide on the basis of party lists. The CPT won four seats, and the IRPT secured two seats. It was reported that 92.6% of the electorate participated in the poll. Both the OSCE and opposition parties claimed that electoral malpractice was widespread. Several members of the IRPT and other opposition parties received prison sentences after they were found guilty of charges of hooliganism, defamation and embezzlement. The first session of the new Majlisi Namoyandagon was held on 17 March 2005. Indirect elections to the Majlisi Milliy took place on 24 March, and the eight members of the chamber nominated by the President were announced one day later.

In April 2005 it was reported that a former Minister of the Interior, Yakub Salimov, had been sentenced to 15 years' imprisonment for treason. Meanwhile, in early April the Russian authorities released Iskandarov, after refusing a request by Tajikistan for his extradition. However, Iskandarov was arrested in Dushanbe later that month; he claimed to have been kidnapped in Russia. After the Russian and Tajikistani authorities failed to clarify the details of Iskandarov's transfer to Tajikistan, the DPT announced in May its temporary withdrawal from the Public Council (a body established in 1994 by Rahmonov to bring together representatives of social and cultural organizations with those of the officially registered political parties. The IRPT and CPT subsequently also announced their withdrawal from the Public Council, in protest at the conduct of the elections. In June the deputy leader of the Union and Development Party was sentenced to almost six years' imprisonment, having been found guilty of provoking ethnic discord and insulting President Rahmonov. In October the Supreme Court sentenced Iskandarov to 23 years' imprisonment, after he was found guilty on charges of terrorism, embezzlement and the illegal possession of weapons. In March 2006 the European Union (EU, see p. 281) released a statement in which it expressed concern at the unclear circumstances surrounding Iskandarov's transfer from Russia to Tajikistan, and at his reported mistreatment prior to his trial.

There was considerable concern regarding the freedom of the media in 2005. The authorities reportedly prevented several independent newspapers and printing houses from publishing, and in April a privately owned television station was closed. Meanwhile, in November 2005 two new political parties were registered: the Party of Economic Reforms (PER) and the Agrarian Party of Tajikistan (APT). Rehmatullo Zoyirov, the Chairman of the Social Democratic Party of Tajikistan (SDPT), asserted that the organizations were instruments of the Government. In August 2006 the former commander of the presidential guard, Lt-Gen. Ghaffor Mirzoyev, was sentenced to life

imprisonment, following his conviction in a closed trial on charges of terrorism and of conspiring to overthrow the Government. Following the death of Nuri, in September Muhiddin Kabiri was elected as his successor as Chairman of the IRPT.

A presidential election, held on 6 November 2006, was contested by five candidates; Rahmonov was re-elected to office, with 79.3% of the votes cast, while Olimjon Boboyev of the PER, with 6.2% of votes cast, was the second-placed candidate. The OSCE declared that the elections failed to meet democratic standards. A new Council of Ministers was approved by the Majlisi Oli on 16 December; some 10 ministries and government agencies were either dissolved or merged with other ministries and agencies. Prominent new ministers included Hamrokhon Zaripov, former ambassador to the USA, as Minister of Foreign Affairs, and Mahmadnazar Solehov as Minister of Internal Affairs. New appointments were also made to the chairmanships of the Constitutional Court and the Supreme Court. In January 2007 the Procurator-General announced that 10 extremist opposition and Islamist organizations had been banned. In February the DPT was refused registration by the Ministry of Justice.

In March 2007 President Rahmonov declared that he henceforth wished to be known as Emomali Rahmon, on the grounds that it was more authentically Tajik. Minister of Foreign Affairs Zaripov made a similar declaration in April, stating that he wished to be known as Hamrokhon Zarifi, and parents were encouraged to follow these examples when naming their children. Other presidential decrees introduced a new dress-code in schools (reinforcing a prohibition on girls and women wearing headscarves that had been introduced in 2005), and the abolition of numerous Soviet-era holidays. In July the mandate of UNTOP was officially concluded. In November it was reported that the central government office complex in Dushanbe had been damaged by a bomb explosion, as a result of which one civilian was killed; the perpetrators of the attack remained unknown. In April 2008 the authorities ordered the closure of an independent radio station, Radio Imruz, which was perceived as unusually critical of the authorities. In September the Tajikistani authorities announced the institution of criminal proceedings against a prominent opposition journalist and leader of the Vatandor (Patriot) Movement, Dodojon Atovullo, on charges of anti-state activities and public defamation of the President; Atovullo, who had been exiled in Russia since 1992, was reported to have fled to Germany following the issuing of an extradition request to Russia from Tajikistan.

In March 2009 the State Committee for Television and Radio Broadcasting suspended operations of a Russian state television channel, RTR-Planeta (the only terrestrial broadcaster of Russian-language programming operating in Tajikistan), on the grounds that it had accrued debt equivalent to some US $130,000, and announced that a new broadcasting contract would be negotiated; the decision followed a visit by President Rahmon to Moscow in February and a significant increase in anti-Russian sentiment in the Tajikistani media.

Resurgence of Islamist militancy

In May 2009 military and police units carried out large-scale military operations in the eastern Rasht Valley region. Although official sources stated that the mobilization was associated with an annual anti-narcotics operation, other reports suggested that the operation had been intended to locate an Islamist leader, Mullo Abdullo (Abdullo Rahimov), who had recently returned to Tajikistan from Afghanistan, having reportedly been in the company of numerous militants. The authorities subsequently stated that Abdullo had proclaimed a *jihad* (Islamic holy war) against the Tajikistani state, and that several of his associates had been arrested.

In July 2009 Lt-Gen. Mirzo Ziyoev (also known as Mirzo Jaga), a former UTO commander who had subsequently served as Minister of Emergency Situations, and who continued to be regarded as an influential leader of the Islamic opposition, was killed in a gun-fight in the Tavildara district. Official reports (which were contested by other sources) attributed his killing to armed militants associated with the IMU, and stated that Ziyoev, having been captured with the militants, had subsequently agreed to reveal the locations of the rebels' arms caches to the authorities, and was negotiating their surrender. Nemat Azizov, an insurgent leader who was alleged to have led the group of militants who killed Ziyoev, was killed in Tavildara later in July. In early August it was reported that 11 IMU fighters had been captured and a further 20 detained in Tavildara. Later that month four Tajikistani citizens extradited from Afghanistan were sentenced to between eight and 15 years' imprisonment, having been found guilty of engaging in terrorist activities in Afghanistan and Pakistan as members of the transnational militant Islamist al-Qa'ida organization.

In October 2009 an independent newspaper, *Paykon*, was found guilty of libel and fined US $40,000, after it published an open letter to the President from several businessmen that accused the state standards body, Tajikstandart, of corruption. In January 2010 the Ministry of Agriculture brought charges of libel against another independent newspaper, *Millat*, in connection with the publication of an article that had documented apparent corruption and misappropriation of funds in the ministry. In February three senior judges, including two who were members of the Supreme Court, filed a lawsuit urging the closure of three independent newspapers, *Asia Plus*, *Farazh* and *Ozodagon*. The judges alleged that the newspapers had defamed them in the coverage of a controversial trial, in which 31 people were imprisoned on charges of gangsterism, tax evasion and the misappropriation of funds.

Elections to the Majlisi Namoyandagon were held on 28 February 2010; voting was repeated in one constituency on 14 March, when municipal elections were also conducted. The PDPT obtained 55 of the 63 legislative seats, having obtained around 72% of the votes cast to seats awarded on the basis of party lists and some 39 of the 41 seats elected in single-mandate constituencies. The IRPT, CPT, the APT and the PER each obtained two seats. Shukurjon Zuhurov, the hitherto Minister of Labour and Social Welfare, was elected as the new President of the Majlisi Namoyandagon. Maxmadamin Maxmadaminov, previously the Chairman of the state savings bank, Amonatbonk, assumed Zuhurov's former ministerial position. Meanwhile, the son of President Rahmon, Rustami Emomali, was elected to a position on Dushanbe City Council (the President's daughter, Ozoda Rahmonova, having been appointed as Deputy Minister of Foreign Affairs in September 2009). Indirect elections for a new Majlisi Milliy were held on 25 March, and the nomination of eight members by the President followed on 29 March. The chamber convened on 23 April, when Mahmadsaid Ubaidulloyev (who was also the Mayor of Dushanbe) was re-elected for a second term as its President.

In August 2010 the Supreme Court convicted 46 people (including nationals of Afghanistan, Russia and Uzbekistan) on charges that included terrorism, planning to stage a coup, and drugs-trafficking. Many of those convicted had been arrested in association with the armed rebellion in Tavildara in July 2009. Additionally, among those sentenced was Abdurasoul Mirzoyev (the brother of Ghaffor Mirzoyev), who, having been extradited from the United Arab Emirates in January 2010, was sentenced to 30 years' imprisonment for involvement in the coup attempt for which his brother had been imprisoned in 2006. Later in August 2010, however, 25 prisoners, including Abdurasoul Mirzoyev together with others who had been recently convicted, and several prominent militant Islamists, escaped from a prison in Dushanbe, killing several prison guards. Several days later President Rahmon replaced the head of the State Committee for National Security, and other senior security officials were dismissed. In early September a suicide bomber detonated a car bomb outside a police station in Khujand, injuring at least 25 people in what was believed to be the first suicide attack in Tajikistan. The authorities accused Abdullo of having organized the attack, and also accused militants from Afghanistan, Pakistan and the Russian territory of Chechnya of involvement. (In December 2011 some 53 people were convicted of involvement in the Khujand suicide bombing, 43 of whom, according to the authorities, were members of the IMU.) In September 2010 Islamist militants staged an ambush of soldiers near Tavildara, resulting in the deaths of at least 23 government troops. In early October militants of the IMU claimed responsibility for shooting down a Tajikistani military helicopter near Rasht (as a result of which 25 soldiers were killed), although official reports attributed the incident to a collision with a power line.

Amid increasing concern that Tajikistani students were being exposed to radical Islamist ideology while studying at universities or Islamic religious institutes abroad (notably in Iran, Pakistan and several Arab states), in November 2010 President Rahmon called for students studying abroad to return to Tajikistan, and announced that the Government would operate a stricter system of control and registration of students studying abroad. The Tajikistani authorities also entered into negotiations with the Governments of Egypt, Iran, Pakistan, Saudi Arabia and Yemen on the repatriation of Tajikistani students.

In January 2011 Tajikistani government troops killed a militant Islamist leader, Aloviddin Davlatov (Ali Bedak) in an operation in the Rasht district. The authorities accused Bedak of involvement in the ambush of soldiers in the previous September and also described him as a commander of al-Qa'ida. In April Abdullo was among around 15 militants killed during another major security operation in Rasht. In November the Supreme Court imposed terms of imprisonment on 28 people on charges of supporting terrorist activities, in connection with the violence in Rasht. The father of Davlatov and seven other defendants were sentenced to life imprisonment. In April 2011 the trial, *in camera*, of nine of those men who had escaped from prison in August 2010 commenced at the Supreme Court, along with that of two accomplices. In May 2011 four of the accused were sentenced to life imprisonment, and three others received custodial sentences of 30 years; a fifth defendant was sentenced to life imprisonment in December. By that time, following further security operations in July and September, 17 of the fugitives had been recaptured, while the remaining eight had been killed.

Reported human rights violations

Controversy was raised, both domestically and internationally, by legislation, which had been proposed by President Rahmon in December 2010, prohibiting those aged under 18 years from visiting any kind of religious institution. Despite continued criticism, the bill was approved by both legislative chambers and was signed into law by President Rahmon in August 2011. In the same month, it was announced that the fee payable for Tajikistani citizens who wished to perform *Hajj* (the annual pilgrimage of Muslims to Mecca, Saudi Arabia) was to increase, and in October new compulsory uniforms were introduced for Tajikistani pilgrims to Mecca, bearing the national flag. Contention had also arisen from the enforced closure of a number of Islamic schools and mosques, including a mosque in Dushanbe closely associated with the IRPT, and the dismissal of numerous imams and their replacement by government appointees.

Press freedom and the police treatment of prisoners remained prominent matters of international concern during 2011. In February Hikmatulloh Saifullohzoda, the IRPT's press secretary and editor of the newspaper, *Najot* (Salvation), was hospitalized, after he was violently assaulted outside his home. In March a drugs-trafficking suspect, Safarali Sangov, died after he sustained injuries while in custody. The trial of two police officers in connection with his death commenced in June. (In October 2012, however, legal proceedings against them on charges of negligence were abandoned.) Also in June 2011 another man arrested in relation to narcotics charges, Ismoil Bachjanov, died in police custody. Later that month Urinboy Usmonov, a reporter for the British Broadcasting Corporation (BBC) who was known for reporting critically on government policies, was detained on suspicion of affiliation with Hizb-ut-Tahrir. Usmonov was released on bail in July, and sentenced in October to three years in prison—a sentence that was subsequently commuted under amnesty—for failing to report to the authorities the members of Hizb-ut-Tahrir whom he had interviewed. (Four members of Hizb-ut-Tahrir who were tried with Usmonov were sentenced to between 20 and 22 years' imprisonment.) In August Xurshed Atovulloh, the editor of the *Farazh* newspaper, was beaten by unknown assailants. In October journalist Mahmadyusuf Ismoilov, who had been held in detention since November 2010, was cleared of charges of extortion but convicted of libel, insult and inciting hatred, resulting in the imposition of a fine of over US $7,000 and a three-year ban from reporting. In January 2012 the journalist Dodojon Atovulloyev, leader of the opposition Vatandor (Patriot) movement and editor of the newspaper *Charogi Ruz* (Light of Day), was attacked in Moscow. A suspect of Tajikistani citizenship was detained, but subsequently released. Meanwhile, in August 2011 the Majlisi Namoyandagon approved an amnesty for 4,000 prisoners, prior to the 20th anniversary of Tajikistan's independence in September.

In January 2012 Rahmon effected a major reorganization of the Government. Notably, Ramazon Rahimov became Minister of Internal Affairs, replacing Abdurahim Kahharov, while Rustam Mengliyev assumed the justice portfolio in place of Bakhtiyor Khudoyorov, who became head of the Presidential Administration. Matlubhon Davlatov was appointed First Deputy Prime Minister, replacing Asadullo Ghulomov. Later in January, several senior anti-narcotics officials, including the head of the anti-narcotics department in Farhor district and the head of the anti-narcotics division at the Ministry of Internal Affairs, were arrested on suspicion of involvement in the smuggling of narcotics from Afghanistan. In February a court in Sughd Viloyat sentenced seven people to between three and five years' imprisonment for membership of the banned Islamist Jamoat-i Tabligh organization. In March the Tajikistani Government blocked internet access to a number of news media and social networking sites (including Facebook), following the publication of an article critical of President Rahmon on the news website *zvezda.ru*.

Recent developments: violence in Kuhistoni Badakhshon

On 21 July 2012 the assassination, in Kuhistoni Badakhshon, of Maj.-Gen. Abdullo Nazarov, the head of the regional branch of the State Committee for National Security, precipitated a major military operation in the territory. Around 70 people were killed in clashes before the chief suspect, Tolib Ayombekov, a deputy commander of a border force unit who had formerly been allied to the opposition, surrendered to the authorities on 12 August. An appeal by the spiritual leader of the Isma'ili people resident in the territory, the Aga Khan, was believed to have been an instrumental factor in quelling the rebellion. However, the fatal shooting of another rebel leader, Imomnazar Imomnazarov, later in August, was followed by renewed protests in the regional capital, Khorugh, where police officers opened fire on a crowd attempting to storm a government building. Following further negotiations, it was agreed that government forces would begin to withdraw from the territory on 24 August. President Rahmon visited Khorugh in September, after an open letter was sent to him by residents, who complained of repressive treatment by local officials.

In November 2012 it was announced that the Dushanbe mayoral office had taken legal action against Kabiri (who had been re-elected as Chairman of the IRPT in September 2011) to demand that he apologize for criticizing the environmental record of municipal officials in the previous month. Later in November the Tajikistani authorities again prevented internet access to the social networking website Facebook, claiming that users had received financial incentives to post derogatory comments about President Rahmon and other prominent officials on the site; at that time access had not been restored to the websites of Russian state-owned news agency RIA Novosti and Russian-language television channel Rossiya 24, which had been blocked in March. In December access to some 130 domestic and foreign websites was suspended by the authorities; some sources suggested that measures to suppress dissent were in preparation for the campaign preceding the presidential election in November 2013.

In February 2013 former premier Abdullojonov, who had been charged by the Tajikistani authorities with a number of crimes, including organization of the assassination attempt against Rahmon in April 1997 and involvement in the insurrection in November 1998, was arrested in Ukraine. Tajikistan formally requested Abdullojonov's extradition; however, the Ukrainian Office of the Prosecutor-General announced in April 2013 that he had been released and would not be extradited. Meanwhile, the disappearance, in March, of a lawyer and Uzbek community leader, Salim Shamsiddinov, who had been assaulted the previous May, prompted concerns that he had been abducted by the authorities in connection with his participation in an activist group demanding changes to the country's presidential electoral legislation, and his public support for the anticipated candidacy of SDPT leader Zoyirov.

Foreign Affairs

Regional relations

After the dissolution of the USSR, Russian troops remained in Tajikistan and openly assisted pro-communist troops in quelling the opposition forces after the communist victory in Dushanbe in December 1992. In 1993 Russia and the Central Asian states (excluding Turkmenistan) signed an agreement establishing a CIS peace-keeping force to police the Tajikistani border with Afghanistan. In October 2004 Russia officially opened a military base in Tajikistan and took formal control of the Nurek space-monitoring centre; in return, Russia agreed to cancel US \$242m. of Tajikistan's \$300m. debt to Russia. Russian troops withdrew from the Tajikistani-Afghan border in 2005. In February 2009 President Rahmon (as he had become) held talks with Russian President Dmitrii Medvedev in Moscow, although relations between the two countries were reported to be strained owing to Russian sympathy for the opposition expressed by the Uzbekistani authorities to the construction of a hydroelectric plant at

Roghun, in central Tajikistan. In October 2012 Presidents Rahmon and Putin (the latter having returned to the Russian presidency earlier in the year), meeting in Dushanbe, signed an agreement under which Russia's military-fbasing rights in Tajikistan, due to expire at the beginning of 2014, would be extended until 2042, while Russia was to assist in the modernization of Tajikistan's armed forces. Other bilateral agreements, providing for Russian investment in hydroelectric power projects in Tajikistan, were signed, while the Russian Government gave assurances that the visa regime for migrant Tajikistani workers in Russia would be eased. (However, despite reported pressure, the Tajikistani Government failed to issue pledges to join the Russian-led customs union—see below.)

During the civil conflict in Tajikistan, the leadership of Uzbekistan provided military and political support to the Rahmonov administration. In April 2000 Tajikistan was strongly criticized by Uzbekistan and Kyrgyzstan for having failed to expel the leader of a group of Islamist rebels opposed to the Uzbekistani authorities, who had allegedly established a permanent base in Tajikistan, and who subsequently pursued armed incursions into those two countries. The Uzbekistani authorities, which had begun to lay landmines along their country's border with Tajikistan from mid-2000, in an effort to prevent further cross-border incursions, officially informed Tajikistan of this only in May 2001. However, bilateral relations improved with a meeting between President Rahmonov and Uzbekistani President Islam Karimov in Tashkent, Uzbekistan, in December. Tajikistani–Uzbekistani relations deteriorated sharply following the suspension in January 2009 of Turkmenistan's electricity exports to Tajikistan, resulting from the continued failure to agree a transit rate. Tajikistan accused the Uzbekistani state utility company, Uzbekenergo, of interrupting deliveries of Turkmenistani electricity, and threatened, in response, to restrict the amount of water flowing downstream to Uzbekistan. An additional matter of contention was the construction of a hydroelectric plant at Roghun, in central Tajikistan, which was opposed by Uzbekistan, owing to concerns regarding the potential impact of the project on its own water supplies and status as a major regional energy supplier. However, in February Karimov unexpectedly announced that Uzbekistan was prepared to reconsider its opposition to the project, provided that international auditors verified its viability. Electricity supplies from Turkmenistan were subsequently resumed.

Relations with Uzbekistan again deteriorated from late 2009, as rail traffic from Uzbekistan into Tajikistan was repeatedly disrupted. Moreover, in early 2010 a series of protests against pollution allegedly being produced at the Tajikistani state-owned Talco aluminium plant in Tursunzoda, western Tajikistan, was organized in various cities across Uzbekistan, seemingly with official endorsement. Following a meeting between the two Presidents, in May several freight trains were permitted to enter Tajikistan. The blockading of railway traffic continued intermittently, and in January 2011 a senior official of the Tajikistani state railway company announced that the blockade had resulted in the country experiencing losses amounting to an estimated US \$20m. In March Uzbekistan significantly increased transit tariffs for goods travelling to Tajikistan by rail. (These tariffs were again raised in January 2012.) Rail traffic between the countries was further disrupted in November 2011, when an explosion at a bridge disabled the cross-border railway line. The Uzbekistani authorities described the explosion as a terrorist attack; however, speculation arose that the incident had been deliberately orchestrated by Uzbekistan's authorities in order to disrupt rail traffic to Tajikistan. In early 2013 plans announced by Uzbekistan for the construction of a new railway that bypassed Tajikistan prompted concerns that the Tajikistani Government would ultimately be deprived of international transit fees.

Tajikistan had begun to develop relations outside the USSR before its dissolution in 1991, notably with Iran, with which the Tajiks have strong ethnic and linguistic ties, although the effective collapse of central authority in Tajikistan in 1992 severely hindered the further development of foreign relations. In July 1995 President Rahmonov visited Tehran, where a number of agreements on cultural and economic co-operation were signed. Further agreements, including defence accords, were signed in 1996 and 1998. In April 2002 Tajikistan and Iran signed nine protocols on co-operation in economic, political and social affairs. In April 2005 the two countries signed a memorandum of understanding on enhanced co-operation in defence matters, and for the provision by Iran of equipment and training to Tajikistani military personnel. In September 2011 Iranian President Mahmoud Ahmadinejad visited Dushanbe. In that month Iranian troops marched in the celebrations to mark the 20th anniversary of Tajikistan's independence.

Relations with Afghanistan in the early 1990s were strained by the apparent inability of the Afghan Government to prevent *mujahidin* fighters and consignments of weapons from crossing the frontier into Tajikistan. The widespread victory of the militant Islamist Taliban forces in Afghanistan in 1995 threatened to destabilize further the fragile situation in Tajikistan. As fighting escalated in Afghanistan in September 2000, the Tajikistani Government closed its border with that country. In December 2004 Russia began to transfer military control of the Pamir stretch of the Tajikistani–Afghan border to Tajikistan. The transfer was completed in September 2005. In October the Majlisi Namoyandagon ratified a bilateral security agreement with Afghanistan on co-operation in countering terrorism, extremism and transnational organized crime. Meanwhile, the Tajikistani President visited Afghanistan for the first time in April 2005, meeting President Hamid Karzai. In August 2007 the Presidents of Tajikistan and Afghanistan inaugurated a 680m-long bridge (funded principally by the USA) across the river Pyanzh, at the border between the two countries. Rahmon visited Afghanistan again in October 2010, when he and Karzai signed several co-operation agreements, and it was announced that the two countries would intensify efforts to combat terrorism.

In the mid-1990s Tajikistan sought to develop relations with other Asian states, in particular the People's Republic of China. In April 1996 Tajikistan signed (together with Russia, Kazakhstan and Kyrgyzstan) a wide-ranging border agreement with China. This was supplemented by a further border accord, signed in August 1999. In January 2002 Tajikistan signed a further treaty with China, resolving contentious issues regarding the two countries' joint border, and in May a border agreement was signed by the two countries, in accordance with which Tajikistan conceded 1,000 sq km of disputed territory to China. The Tajikistani legislature did not, however, ratify this agreement until January 2011. Members of the Shanghai Co-operation Organization (SCO, see p. 478), comprising China, Kazakhstan, Kyrgyzstan, Russia, Tajikistan and Uzbekistan, signed the Shanghai Convention on Combating Terrorism, Separatism and Extremism in mid-2001. In October of that year the SCO agreed to establish an anti-terrorism centre. In 2010 an SCO summit was held in Dushanbe, on which occasion the Chinese Prime Minister, Wen Jiabou, signed seven documents of bilateral co-operation with Tajikistan.

In May 2001 the signatory countries of the Collective Security Treaty (Armenia, Belarus, Kazakhstan, Kyrgyzstan, Russia and Tajikistan) formed a Rapid Reaction Force to combat Islamist militancy in Central Asia. In March 2002 the Central Asian Economic Community, which Tajikistan joined in March 1998, was superseded by the Central Asian Co-operation Organization (CACO). In April 2003 the signatories of the Collective Security Treaty inaugurated a successor organization, the Collective Security Treaty Organization (CSTO). In April 1998 Tajikistan joined a customs union, already comprising Russia, Belarus, Kazakhstan and Kyrgyzstan. In October 2000 a new economic body, the Eurasian Economic Community (EURASEC, see p. 461), was established to supersede the customs union, and this organization merged with CACO in January 2006. In October 2007, meeting in Dushanbe, EURASEC leaders approved the legal basis for the establishment of a new customs union that was initially to comprise Belarus, Kazakhstan and Russia. Doubts were voiced domestically about the economic benefits of membership for Tajikistan, and the Government subsequently demonstrated reluctance to join the union. In October 2011, however, Tajikistan and seven other member states of the CIS signed a free trade agreement.

Other external relations

Following the suicide attacks on the USA of 11 September 2001 by the militant Islamist al-Qa'ida organization, US specialists were granted entry to Tajikistan, initially to oversee the distribution of humanitarian aid to Afghanistan. The Government declared its support for the aerial bombardment of Taliban and al-Qa'ida targets in Afghanistan, which commenced on 7 October, and in November it was confirmed that Tajikistan had permitted US troops and forces of the North Atlantic Treaty Organization (NATO, see p. 380) to utilize three of its airbases. In January 2002 it was announced that US restrictions on the transfer of defence equipment to Tajikistan, imposed in 1993,

had been lifted. In February 2002 Tajikistan joined NATO's 'Partnership for Peace' programme of military co-operation. In October 2004 the Secretary-General of NATO, Jaap de Hoop Scheffer, signed a bilateral transit agreement with Rahmonov in support of NATO's International Security Assistance Force in Afghanistan. The first official visit to Tajikistan by a high-level NATO delegation took place in April 2009, when the Government agreed to permit the country to serve as a transit route for non-military supplies to forces operating in Afghanistan and pledged further assistance in stabilization and reconstruction efforts in that country. In October 2012 a new US ambassador to Tajikistan declared that bilateral relations would not be affected by a new agreement extending Russian military basing rights in the country. US Assistant Secretary of State Robert Blake visited Dushanbe in February 2013, when, discussing the impending withdrawal of the NATO-led International Security Assistance Force in Afghanistan, he stated that Tajikistan would not be used as a transit country for US troops, although it was reported that the country remained an option for the transit of US and British military equipment.

CONSTITUTION AND GOVERNMENT

Under the Constitution of 1994 (as amended in 1999 and 2003), Tajikistan has a presidential system of government. The President is Head of State and Chairman of the Government. The President appoints a Prime Minister to head the Government (Council of Ministers). Legislative power is vested in the 63-member lower chamber, the Majlisi Namoyandagon (Assembly of Representatives), and the upper chamber, the Majlisi Milliy (National Assembly), which has a minimum of 33 members. Judicial power is exercised by the Constitutional Court, the Supreme Court, the Supreme Economic Court, the Military Court, the Court of Kuhistoni Badakhshon Autonomous Viloyat, and courts of viloyats, the city of Dushanbe, towns and districts. For administrative purposes, the country is divided into two viloyats (regions or oblasts) and the nominally autonomous viloyat of Kuhistoni Badakhshon. These regions are further subdivided into districts and towns. The city of Dushanbe has a separate status. Three cities and 10 districts of central and eastern Tajikistan are not incorporated into any of the viloyats, and are known as the Districts of Republican Subordination.

REGIONAL AND INTERNATIONAL CO-OPERATION

Tajikistan is a member of the Commonwealth of Independent States (CIS, see p. 251), the Eurasian Economic Community (EURASEC, see p. 461), the Shanghai Cooperation Organization (SCO, see p. 478), the Economic Cooperation Organization (ECO, see p. 274) and the Organization of Islamic Cooperation (see p. 413).

Tajikistan joined the UN in 1992. The country became a member of the World Trade Organization (WTO, see p. 444) in March 2013.

ECONOMIC AFFAIRS

In 2011, according to estimates by the World Bank, Tajikistan's gross national income (GNI), measured at average 2009–11 prices, was US $6,078m., equivalent to $870 per head (or $2,310 per head on an international purchasing-power parity basis). During 2002–11, it was estimated, the population increased by an annual average of 1.2%, while gross domestic product (GDP) per head increased by an annual average of 6.7%, in real terms. Overall GDP increased, in real terms, by an average of 8.0% per year during 2002–11. According to the Asian Development Bank (ADB, see p. 214), GDP increased by 7.4% in 2011.

Agriculture contributed 27.0% of GDP, according to the ADB, and engaged 70.2% of the employed labour force in 2011. According to IMF estimates, the rural population accounted for some 72.4% of the total in 2000–03. Only 7% of Tajikistan's land is arable, the remainder being largely mountainous. The principal crop is grain, followed in importance by cotton, vegetables and fruit. Approximately 95% of the country's arable land is irrigated. Although in mid-1998 legislation was passed to establish a centre to aid farm privatization, agricultural reform has proceeded slowly. The IMF estimated that 51% of Tajikistan's arable land was privately owned at the end of 2001. According to the World Bank, during 2002–11 agricultural GDP increased, in real terms, at an annual average rate of 6.3%. Real agricultural GDP increased by 4.9% in 2011.

Industry (comprising manufacturing, mining, utilities and construction) contributed 22.4% of GDP, according to the

ADB, and engaged 6.1% of the employed labour force in 2011. There is little heavy industry, except for mineral extraction, aluminium production and power generation. Light industry concentrates on food-processing, textiles and carpet-making. According to the World Bank, industrial GDP increased, in real terms, by an average annual rate of 8.5% in 2002–11. Sectoral GDP increased by 6.1% in 2011.

Mining contributed 1.7% of GDP, according to the ADB, and engaged 0.9% of the employed labour force in 2011. Tajikistan has considerable mineral deposits, including gold, antimony, silver, aluminium, iron, lead, mercury and tin. There are deposits of coal, as well as reserves of petroleum and natural gas. Mineral extraction is hampered by the mountainous terrain.

Manufacturing contributed 10.0% of GDP, according to the ADB, and engaged 2.4% of the employed labour force in 2011. The GDP of the manufacturing sector increased, in real terms, at an annual average rate of 7.2% in 2002–11, according to the World Bank. Real manufacturing GDP increased by 5.0% in 2011.

Construction contributed 8.3% of GDP, according to the ADB, and engaged 2.1% of the employed labour force. According to the ADB, construction GDP increased, in real terms, by an average annual rate of 49.7% in 2002–11. Sectoral GDP increased by 48.4% in 2010, but decreased by 7.3% in 2011.

Although imports of natural gas and petroleum products comprised 15.5% of the value of merchandise imports in 2011, Tajikistan is believed to have sufficient unexploited reserves of petroleum and natural gas to meet its requirements, while Tajikistan is one of the largest producers of hydroelectric power world-wide. In 2009 hydroelectricity accounted for 98.0% of energy production. In January 2005 Tajikistan signed a protocol with Russia and Iran on the construction of two hydroelectric power plants, Sangtuda-1 and Sangtuda-2. In March an agreement was signed with Pakistan on the construction of a 700-km transmission line to transport electricity to Pakistan, from 2009. Sangtuda-1 was officially launched in July 2009, while Sangtuda-2 was inaugurated in late 2011, and was scheduled to begin operating at full capacity in 2013. The completion of Sangtuda-1 was fully funded by Russia, and Iran provided significant funding for the construction of the Sangtuda-2 plant, ownership of which was to be secured by Tajikistan in 2018. Tajikistan imports some 90% of its gas requirements, principally from Uzbekistan.

The services sector contributed 50.6% of GDP, according to the ADB, and engaged 23.7% of the employed labour force in 2011. According to the World Bank, the GDP of the services sector increased, in real terms, by an annual average of 6.6% in 2002–11; real services GDP increased by 4.8% in 2011.

In 2011, according to the IMF, Tajikistan recorded a visible merchandise trade deficit of US $3,572.0m., and there was a deficit of $787.0m. on the current account of the balance of payments. In 2011 the principal source of imports was the People's Republic of China (accounting for 45.7% of the total); other important suppliers were Russia and Kazakhstan. Turkey was the principal market for exports in that year (accounting for 30.2% of the total); Russia, Iran, China, Afghanistan and Italy were also significant purchasers. The principal exports in 2011 were aluminium and cotton fibre; the principal imports were alumina and petroleum products.

The state budget for 2011 provided for an overall deficit of 2,007.1m. somoni. Tajikistan's general government gross debt was 10,664m. somoni in 2011, equivalent to 35.5% of GDP. Tajikistan's total external debt was US $2,955m. at the end of 2010, of which $1,806m. was public and publicly guaranteed debt. According to the ADB, in 2011 Tajikistan's total external debt was US $2,041m. In 2010, the cost of servicing long-term public and publicly guaranteed debt and repayments to the IMF was equivalent to 12.3% of the value of exports of goods, services and income (excluding workers' remittances). According to the ADB, the rate of inflation was 8.5% in 2012. The official rate of unemployment was 2.3% in 2011.

The poorest of the republics of the former USSR, Tajikistan's economy improved significantly after the civil war of 1992–97, and substantially reduced its external debt in 2000–07. Cotton production declined during 2007–09, and areas previously designated for cotton were appropriated for food crops. In April 2009 the IMF approved a three-year arrangement to extend some US $120m. (subsequently increased to $161.9m.) under a Poverty Reduction and Growth Facility. The National Bank estimated that remittances from abroad accounted for some 45% of GDP in 2011. International trade was affected by blockades of rail transport at the border with Uzbekistan from 2009, and by increases in Uzbekistani transit tariffs from 2011 (see Regional relations). The Tajikistani Government undertook a number of transport infrastructure projects that were designed to assist trade with a US $50.5m. loan from the Export and Import Bank of China (of the People's Republic of China). Frequent critical shortages of energy became particularly severe in late 2011: the habitual rationing of electricity supplies was expanded in that year. It was anticipated that the eventual completion of the Sangtuda-2 hydropower plant, and of the Roghun plant, would provide a source of export earnings as well as to improve Tajikistan's energy security. However In May 2012 the World Bank ordered construction on the Roghun hydroelectric project to be suspended, pending an ecological impact study, while the first unit of the Sangtuda-2 hydropower plant was officially inaugurated in September 2011, and the plant was expected to reach full operational capacity in 2013. Meanwhile, in October 2011, the country signed a free trade agreement with seven other members of the Commonwealth of Independent States (see p. 251) (although its implementation was delayed pending ratification by all signatory states). The IMF estimated GDP growth of 7.5% for 2012. In December 2012 the World Trade Organization (WTO, see p. 444) approved Tajikistan's membership application, the Government having committed to the fulfilment of pre-accession criteria, including the standardization of import tariffs, and membership entered into effect in March 2013. It was anticipated that Tajikistan's membership of the organization would bring substantial benefits, including a reduction in the price of domestic goods, and increased foreign investment.

PUBLIC HOLIDAYS

2014: 1 January (New Year's Day), 8 March (International Women's Day), 21–24 March (Navrus, Spring Holiday), 1 May (International Labour Day), 9 May (Victory Day), 27 June (National Accord Day), 28 July* (Id-al-Fitr, end of Ramadan), 9 September (Independence Day), 4 October* (Id-al-Adha, Feast of the Sacrifice), 6 November (Constitution Day).

*These holidays are dependent on the Islamic lunar calendar and may vary by one or two days from the dates given.

Statistical Survey

Source (unless otherwise indicated): State Committee for Statistics, 734001 Dushanbe, Kuchai Boxtar 17; tel. (372) 23-25-53; fax (372) 21-43-75; e-mail stat@ tojikiston.com; internet www.stat.tj.

Area and Population

AREA, POPULATION AND DENSITY

Area (sq km)	143,100*
Population (census results)	
20 January 2000	6,127,493
21 September 2010 (preliminary)	
Males	3,813,000
Females	3,752,000
Total	7,565,000
Population (estimates at 1 January)†	
2011	7,616,400
2012	7,800,500
Density (per sq km) at 1 January 2012	54.5

* 55,251 sq miles.
† Figures rounded to nearest 100 persons.

POPULATION BY AGE AND SEX
(UN estimates at mid-2013)

	Males	Females	Total
0–14	1,311,754	1,255,891	2,567,645
15–64	2,111,370	2,264,786	4,376,156
65 and over	100,970	138,761	239,731
Total	3,524,094	3,659,438	7,183,532

Note: Estimates not adjusted to take account of the results of the 2010 census.

Source: UN, *World Population Prospects: The 2010 Revision*.

POPULATION BY ETHNIC GROUP
(2000 census)

	Number ('000 persons)	%
Tajik	4,898.4	79.9
Uzbek	936.7	15.3
Russian	68.2	1.1
Kyrgyz	65.5	1.1
Others	158.7	2.6
Total	6,127.5	100.0

ADMINISTRATIVE DIVISIONS
(population at 2010 census, preliminary)

	Area (sq km)	Population	Density (per sq km)	Capital city
Viloyats				
Khatlon	24,800	2,676,000	107.9	Qurgonteppa
Sughd	25,400	2,237,000	88.1	Khujand
Autonomous Viloyat				
Kuhistoni				
Badakhshon . .	64,200	206,000	3.2	Khorugh
Capital City				
Dushanbe . . .	100	724,000	7,240.0	—
Districts of				
Republican				
Subordination * .	28,600	1,722,000	60.2	—
Total	143,100	7,565,000	52.9	

* The Districts of Republican Subordination comprise three cities (Hisor, Roghun and Vahdat) and 10 raions or districts (Fayzobod, Jirgatul, Nurobod, Rasht, Rudaki, Shahrinav, Tojikobod, Tavildara, Tursunzoda and Varzob) in central and eastern Tajikistan, where there is no higher tier of local government.

PRINCIPAL TOWNS
(population at 2010 census, preliminary)

Dushanbe (capital) .	724,000	Tursunzoda . . .	47,000
Khujand . .	162,000	Kanibodom . . .	46,000
Kulob . . .	95,000	Isfara . . .	43,000
Qurgonteppa . .	75,000	Panjakent . . .	43,000
Istaravshan* . .	55,000	Kofarnihon . . .	40,000

* Formerly Uroteppa (Ura-Tyube).

Mid-2011 (incl. suburbs, UN estimate): Dushanbe 738,883 (Source: UN, *World Urbanization Prospects: The 2011 Revision*).

BIRTHS, MARRIAGES AND DEATHS*

	Registered live births		Registered marriages		Registered deaths	
	Number	Rate (per 1,000)	Number	Rate (per 1,000)	Number	Rate (per 1,000)
2004 . .	179,600	26.8	47,320	7.1	29,700	4.4
2005 . .	180,800	26.4	52,352	7.6	31,500	4.6
2006 . .	186,500	26.7	57,278	8.2	32,000	4.6
2007 . .	200,000	28.0	97,713	13.7	33,700	4.7
2008 . .	203,300	27.9	106,388	14.6	32,000	4.4
2009 . .	199,800	26.8	100,678	13.5	32,300	4.3
2010 . .	222,400	29.4	100,759	13.3	33,300	4.4
2011 . .	224,200	29.1	94,646	13.1	33,800	4.4

* Figures for registered births and deaths are rounded to the nearest 100.

Life expectancy (years at birth): 67.5 (males 64.4; females 70.8) in 2011 (Source: World Bank, World Development Indicators database).

IMMIGRATION AND EMIGRATION

	2009	2010	2011
Immigrants	25,563	29,637	32,619
Emigrants	37,231	36,134	38,867

ECONOMICALLY ACTIVE POPULATION
(annual averages, '000 persons)

	2008	2009	2010
Activities of the material sphere .	1,800	1,829	1,831
Agriculture*	1,447	1,468	1,471
Industry†	104	104	94
Construction	65	65	72
Trade and catering‡ . . .	113	125	136
Transport and communications .	61	58	58
Activities of the non-material			
sphere	368	390	402
Housing and municipal services	50	55	57
Health care, social security,			
physical culture and sports .	75	81	81
Education, culture and arts .	183	180	193
Science, research and			
development	5	5	5
Government and finance . .	35	35	45
Other non-material . . .	6	6	21
Total employed	2,168	2,219	2,233
Unemployed	49	45	47
Total labour force	2,217	2,264	2,280

* Including forestry.
† Comprising manufacturing (except printing and publishing), mining and quarrying, electricity, gas, water, logging and fishing.
‡ Including material and technical supply.

2011 (annual averages, '000 persons): Agriculture, forestry and fishing 1,578; Mining and quarrying 20; Manufacturing 53; Electricity, gas and water supply 18; Construction 47; Trade and repair of motor vehicles 78; Hotels and restaurants 6; Transport, storage and communication 49; Financial intermediation 16; Real estate, renting and business activities 13; Public administration 36; Education 189; Science and scientific services 84; Other public, social and personal services 60; Extra-territorial organizations and bodies 2; *Total employed* 2,249; Unemployed 54; *Total labour force* 2,303.

Health and Welfare

KEY INDICATORS

Total fertility rate (children per woman, 2010)	3.3
Under-5 mortality rate (per 1,000 live births, 2010) . . .	63
HIV/AIDS (% of persons aged 15–49, 2009)	0.2
Physicians (per 1,000 head, 2009)	2.1
Hospital beds (per 1,000 head, 2009)	5.2
Health expenditure (2009): US $ per head (PPP) . . .	123
Health expenditure (2009): % of GDP	5.9
Health expenditure (2009): public (% of total)	24.9
Access to water (% of persons, 2010)	64
Access to sanitation (% of persons, 2010)	94
Total carbon dioxide emissions ('000 metric tons, 2008) . .	3,146.3
Carbon dioxide emissions per head (metric tons, 2008) . .	0.5
Human Development Index (2011): ranking	127
Human Development Index (2011): value	0.607

For sources and definitions, see explanatory note on p. vi.

Agriculture

PRINCIPAL CROPS
('000 metric tons)

	2009	2010	2011
Wheat	1,089	1,033	727
Rice, paddy	63	77	77
Barley	102	116	74
Maize	143	151	155
Potatoes	691	760	863
Cabbages and other brassicas*	68	74	80
Tomatoes	372	289	304
Onions, dry	269	302	343
Carrots and turnips . . .	207	214	234
Watermelons	425	482	423
Apples*	148	157	183
Apricots*	20	21	25
Peaches and nectarines* . . .	19	20	23
Grapes	139	124	155
Seed cotton	296	311	416
Tobacco, unmanufactured . .	0.2	0.4	0.7

* Unofficial figures.

Aggregate production ('000 metric tons, may include official, semi-official or estimated data): Total cereals 1,400 in 2009, 1,383 in 2010, 1,035 in 2011; Total roots and tubers 691 in 2009, 760 in 2010, 863 in 2011; Total vegetables (incl. melons) 1,468 in 2009, 1,612 in 2010, 1,657 in 2011; Total fruits (excl. melons) 353 in 2009, 350 in 2010, 418 in 2011.

Source: FAO.

LIVESTOCK
('000 head at 1 January)

	2009	2010	2011
Horses	76	76	77
Asses	174	180	178
Cattle	1,830	1,897	2,015
Camels	56	45	46
Sheep	2,617	2,729	2,894
Goats	1,583	1,666	1,724
Chickens	3,939	4,403	4,655

Source: FAO.

LIVESTOCK PRODUCTS
('000 metric tons)

	2009	2010	2011
Cattle meat	26.0	28.6	29.3
Sheep meat	36.8	39.2	42.1
Chicken meat	4.4	1.1	2.2
Cows' milk*	574	602	634
Goats' milk*	55.7	58.8	62.0
Hen eggs*	10.6	13.1	14.3
Wool, greasy	5.4	5.8	6.0

* Unofficial figures.

Source: FAO.

Forestry

ROUNDWOOD REMOVALS
('000 cubic metres, excluding bark)

	2005*	2006†	2007†
Total (all fuel wood)	90	90	90

* Unofficial estimate.
† FAO estimate.

2008–11: Figures assumed to be unchanged from 2007 (FAO estimates).

Source: FAO.

Fishing

(metric tons, live weight)

	2008	2009	2010
Capture*	150	150	160
Freshwater bream*	5	5	n.a.
Common carp*	25	20	20
Silver carp*	35	40	50
Wels (Som) catfish*	5	5	n.a.
Pike-perch*	10	10	10
Aquaculture	26	255	517
Common carp	12	35	57
Grass carp (White amur) . .	3	54	41
Silver carp	7	144	168
Total catch*	176	405	677

* FAO estimates.

Source: FAO.

Mining

(metric tons unless otherwise indicated)

	2008	2009	2010
Coal	198,500	176,100	199,700
Crude petroleum	25,900	26,200	27,000
Natural gas (million cu m) . .	16.1	19.2	22.8
Lead concentrate*†	800	800	800
Antimony ore*†	2,000	2,000	2,000
Mercury*†	30	30	30
Silver (kilograms)*†	3,110	3,110	3,110
Gold (kilograms)†	1,672	1,361	2,049
Gypsum (crude)	8,500*	26,400	14,600*

* Estimated production.
† Figures refer to the metal content of ores and concentrates.

Source: US Geological Survey.

Industry

SELECTED PRODUCTS
('000 metric tons unless otherwise indicated)

	2009	2010	2011
Meat (incl. offal)	25.0	27.1	27.7
Animal butter (metric tons) . .	18.5	20.9	16.5
Vegetable oil	13.1	14.1	15.1
Cottonseed oil (refined)* . . .	13	14	15
Wine (metric tons)* . . .	28	22	18
Woollen garments ('000 units) .	4	n.a.	n.a.
Woven cotton fabrics (million sq metres)	36.5	25.6	21.4
Cotton fibre	92	95	103
Rugs and carpets (million sq metres)	0.5	0.6	0.7
Stockings, etc (million pairs) . .	5.7	5.7	6.1
Leather footwear ('000 pairs) . .	30.8	34.8	65.9
Aluminium, unwrought‡ . . .	359.4	348.9	n.a.
Clay building bricks (million units)	49.8	70.9	57.2
Slate (million sheets)	2.8	0.3	0.6
Cement	195.0	288.2	299.0
Electric energy (million kWh)†	16,117	16,410	16,219

* Source: FAO.
† Source: Asian Development Bank.
‡ Source: US Geological Survey.

Finance

CURRENCY AND EXCHANGE RATES

Monetary Units
100 diram = 1 somoni.

Sterling, Dollar and Euro Equivalents (31 December 2012)
£1 sterling = 7.518 somoni;
US $1 = 4.764 somoni;
€1 = 6.286 somoni;
100 somoni = £13.30 = $20.99 = €15.91.

Average Exchange Rate (somoni per US $)
2010   4.3790
2011   4.6102
2012   4.7377

Note: The Tajikistani rouble was introduced in May 1995, replacing the Russian (formerly Soviet) rouble at the rate of 1 Tajikistani rouble = 100 Russian roubles. A new currency, the somoni (equivalent to 1,000 Tajikistani roubles), was introduced in October 2000.

BUDGET
(million somoni)*

Revenue†	2009	2010	2011
Tax revenue	3,659.1	4,443.9	5,892.2
Income and profit tax . .	610.2	778.7	985.5
Social duties	494.7	567.3	782.7
Property taxes	142.4	151.2	171.3
Internal taxes on goods and services	1,915.3	2,364.0	3,196.8
International trade and operations tax	165.6	168.4	189.3
Non-tax revenue	210.9	329.1	501.2
Income from property and enterprise activities . .	40.7	47.0	130.2
Administrative fees and levies .	35.4	37.8	39.5
Total	3,869.9	4,773.0	6,393.3

Expenditure	2009	2010	2011
General government administration	376.6	384.3	691.8
Education	845.4	990.0	1,443.1
Health	287.9	354.9	564.0
Social security and welfare . .	713.5	860.2	1,129.7
Housing and communal services .	324.7	377.4	686.8
Sporting, cultural and religious associations	177.5	297.3	376.2
Energy and fuel sector . . .	562.6	691.9	1,138.8
Agriculture, forestry, fisheries and hunting	88.8	92.6	300.3
Natural resources, mining and construction	24.0	49.3	82.5
Transport and communications .	94.9	109.6	1,045.8
Total (incl. others)	5,687.3	6,712.6	8,562.0

* Figures refer to the consolidated operations of the State Budget, comprising the budgets of the central (republican) Government and local authorities, and the Social Security Fund.
† Excluding grants received (million somoni): 317.6 in 2009; 175.0 in 2010; 161.6 in 2011.

INTERNATIONAL RESERVES
(US $ million at 31 December)

	2009	2010	2011
Gold (national valuation) . . .	81.6	79.2	243.1
IMF special drawing rights . .	109.5	107.5	107.1
Foreign exchange	65.0	216.7	182.2
Total	256.1	403.4	532.4

Source: IMF, *International Financial Statistics*.

MONEY SUPPLY
(million somoni at 31 December)

	2006	2007	2008
Currency outside banks . . .	823.7	1,029.9	1,444.7
Demand deposits	146.2	1,174.0	816.3
Total money (incl. others) . .	971.5	2,226.6	2,263.5

Source: IMF, *International Financial Statistics*.

COST OF LIVING
(Consumer Price Index; base: previous year = 100)

	2009	2010	2011
Food	102.3	113.4	110.3
Non-food	106.7	105.5	107.2
All items	105.0	109.8	109.3

Source: Asian Development Bank.

NATIONAL ACCOUNTS
(million somoni at current prices)

Expenditure on the Gross Domestic Product

	2008	2009	2010
Government final consumption expenditure	1,652.7	2,570.8	2,798.5
Private final consumption expenditure	15,503.8	17,809.4	20,927.7
Changes in inventories . . .	352.5	−298.8	−158.9
Gross fixed capital formation . .	4,341.4	5,423.9	6,050.6
Total domestic expenditure .	21,850.3	25,505.3	29,617.9
Exports of goods and services . .	5,782.4	5,048.0	6,620.7
Less Imports of goods and services	14,004.9	12,686.7	14,577.7
Statistical discrepancy* . . .	4,079.0	2,761.9	3,046.4
GDP in purchasers' values .	17,706.9	20,628.5	24,707.1

2011: GDP in purchasers' values 30,069.3.

Gross Domestic Product by Economic Activity

	2009	2010	2011
Agriculture	3,827.0	4,839.3	7,153.5
Mining, manufacturing and electricity, gas and water . .	2,957.4	3,642.8	3,729.7
Construction	2,098.4	2,528.2	2,208.4
Trade	4,340.0	5,000.0	4,731.7
Transport and communications .	2,264.9	2,758.0	4,288.3
Financial intermediation . .	438.7	513.6	73.9
Public administration . . .	619.3	646.1	1,146.8
Other services	2,040.1	2,223.1	3,182.6
Sub-total	18,585.8	22,151.1	26,514.9
Less Financial intermediation services indirectly measured .	243.8	225.7	—
Gross value added in basic prices	18,342.0	21,925.4	26,514.9
Indirect taxes, less subsidies . .	2,286.5	2,781.7	3,554.4
GDP in purchasers' values .	20,628.5	24,707.1	30,069.3

* Referring to the difference between the expenditure and production approaches.

Source: Asian Development Bank.

BALANCE OF PAYMENTS
(US $ million)

	2009	2010	2011
Exports of goods	1,038.5	459.1	592.9
Imports of goods	−2,770.8	−3,320.6	−4,164.9
Balance on goods	−1,732.3	−2,861.4	−3,572.0
Exports of services	179.8	333.8	564.5
Imports of services	−291.3	−528.2	−670.8
Balance on goods and services	−1,844.0	−3,055.8	−3,678.3
Primary income received . . .	7.2	14.4	21.8
Primary income paid	−78.5	−93.1	−80.3
Balance on goods, services and primary income	−1,915.2	−3,134.5	−3,736.8
Secondary income received . .	1,861.8	2,420.7	3,171.4
Secondary income paid . . .	−126.9	−180.7	−221.6
Current balance	−180.3	−894.4	−787.0
Capital account (net) . . .	120.4	68.5	49.9
Direct investment (net) . . .	15.8	−14.7	11.1
Portfolio investment (net) . . .	0.1	6.5	0.1
Other investment assets . . .	177.7	352.8	403.7
Other investment liabilities . .	−49.9	337.8	314.7
Net errors and omissions . . .	31.1	243.5	116.9
Reserves and related items .	114.9	99.9	109.5

Source: IMF, *International Financial Statistics*.

External Trade

PRINCIPAL COMMODITIES
(US $ million, excl. alumina and aluminium)

Imports c.i.f.*	2009	2010	2011
Beverages (incl. alcoholic) . .	10	12	16
Tobacco and tobacco products .	2	3	4
Animal and vegetable fats and oil .	49	73	88
Flour	117	98	131
Tea, coffee and spices . . .	3	4	5
Wheat	79	82	116
Sugar and confectionery . . .	52	62	87
Fertilizers	19	7	9
Natural gas	52	42	48
Petroleum products	323	438	450
Electricity	76	13	1
Total (incl. others)	2,570	2,657	3,206

Exports f.o.b.†	2009	2010	2011
Fruits and vegetables	51	54	45
Cotton fibre	100	201	197
Electricity	63	4	4
Total (incl. others)	1,010	1,195	1,257

* These figures do not include separate data for imports of alumina, one of Tajikistan's principal import goods. The most recent data available were for 2001, when imports of alumina accounted for US $184m. of $688m. in total imports (c.i.f.).

† These figures do not include separate data for exports of aluminium, Tajikistan's principal export item. The most recent data available were for 2001, when exports of aluminium accounted for US $397m. of $909m. in total exports (f.o.b.).

PRINCIPAL TRADING PARTNERS
(US $ million)

Imports	2009	2010	2011
China, People's Rep.	266.5	238.2	2,196.7
Iran	78.8	141.6	179.9
Kazakhstan	278.9	292.7	327.8
Russia	795.2	856.5	785.5
Turkey	58.9	60.0	190.0
Turkmenistan	63.4	83.5	93.5
Ukraine	115.1	188.7	161.4
United Arab Emirates . . .	73.1	61.0	77.5
USA	71.2	94.9	196.0
Uzbekistan	125.9	71.8	80.4
Total (incl. others)	2,505.5	2,655.5	4,802.2

Exports	2009	2010	2011
Afghanistan	26.9	52.2	58.5
China, People's Rep.	405.4	447.0	65.4
Iran	48.7	59.6	68.5
Italy	15.1	17.9	50.3
Latvia	7.4	20.8	0.1
Netherlands	30.5	0.1	0.8
Russia	102.8	101.8	81.1
Switzerland	23.3	29.2	—
Turkey	152.1	377.0	294.8
Uzbekistan	71.5	8.6	9.7
Total (incl. others)	1,009.6	1,194.7	975.0

Note: Data reflect the IMF's direction of trade methodology and, as a result, the totals may not be equal to those presented for trade in commodities.

Source: Asian Development Bank.

Transport

RAILWAYS

	2009	2010	2011
Passengers (million journeys) .	0.7	0.6	0.6
Freight carried ('000 metric tons) .	14,546.0	10,445.6	9,256.7

CIVIL AVIATION
(traffic on scheduled services)

	2009	2010	2011
Passengers carried ('000) . . .	700	800	800
Passenger-km (million) . . .	1,645	1,915	2,148
Freight carried ('000 metric tons) .	2.2	2.2	2.6
Freight ton-km (million) . . .	5.6	5.3	6.4

Communications Media

	2009	2010	2011
Telephones ('000 main lines in use)	290.0	367.7	380.0
Mobile cellular telephones ('000 subscribers)	4,900.0	5,940.8	6,324.0
Internet users ('000)	700.0	n.a.	n.a.
Broadband subscribers ('000) . .	4.4	4.7	5.0

Source: International Telecommunication Union.

Education

(2011/12)

	Institutions*	Students ('000)		
		Males	Females	Total
Pre-primary . . .	94	36.7	31.2	67.9
Primary	532	n.a.	n.a.	1,702.2
Secondary:	3,291			
Lower	683	n.a.	n.a.	164.3
General	2,557	n.a.	n.a.	85.9
Vocational . . .	51	17.7	22.4	40.1
Professional/Technical	67	18.9	5.0	23.9
Higher (incl. universities) . .	33	109.4	42.8	152.2

* Figures exclude 11 schools for pupils with mental or physical disabilities and 8 evening schools.

Teachers: Pre-primary 6,615 (1996/97); Primary *and* Secondary—Lower, General and Vocational 94,200 (2011/12); Professional/Technical n.a.; Higher (incl. universities) 6,100 (2001/02).

Pupil-teacher ratio (primary education, UNESCO estimate): 25.2 in 2009/10 (Source: UNESCO Institute for Statistics).

Adult literacy rate (UNESCO estimates): 99.7% (males 99.8%; females 99.6%) in 2010 (Source: UNESCO Institute for Statistics)

Directory

The Government

HEAD OF STATE

President: EMOMALI RAHMON (elected by popular vote 6 November 1994; re-elected 6 November 1999 and 6 November 2006).

COUNCIL OF MINISTERS
(May 2013)

Chairman of the Government: EMOMALI RAHMON.

Prime Minister: OQIL OQILOV.

First Deputy Prime Minister: MATLUBHON DAVLATOV.

Deputy Prime Minister: RUQIYA QURBONOVA.

Deputy Prime Minister: MURODALI ALIMARDON.

Minister of Justice: RUSTAM MENGLIYEV.

Minister of Agriculture: QOSIM QOSIMOV.

Minister of Internal Affairs: RAMAZON RAHIMOV.

Minister of Foreign Affairs: HAMROKHON ZARIFI.

Minister of Education: NURUDDIN SAIDOV.

Minister of Land Reclamation and Water Resources: RAHMAT BOBOKALONOV.

Minister of Labour and Social Welfare: MAXMADAMIN MAXMADA-MINOV.

Minister of Finance: SAFARALI NAJMIDDINOV.

Minister of Defence: Maj.-Gen. SHERALI XAYRULLOYEV.

Minister of Transport: NIZOM HAKIMOV.

Minister of Economic Development and Trade: SHARIF RAHIM-ZODA.

Minister of Health: NUSRATULLO SALIMOV.

Minister of Culture: MIRZOSHOHRUH ASRORI.

Minister of Energy and Industry: SHERALI GUL.

Note: The Chairmen of the State Committees for National Security, Statistics, and Investment and the Management of State Property are also members of the Council of Ministers.

MINISTRIES

Office of the President: 734023 Dushanbe, Xiyoboni Rudaki 80; tel. and fax (372) 21-25-20; e-mail mail@president.tj; internet www.president.tj.

Secretariat of the Prime Minister: 734023 Dushanbe, Xiyoboni Rudaki 80; tel. (372) 21-18-71; fax (372) 21-51-10.

Ministry of Agriculture: 734025 Dushanbe, Xiyoboni Rudaki 44; tel. (372) 21-15-96; fax (372) 21-57-94.

Ministry of Culture: 734025 Dushanbe, Xiyoboni Rudaki 34; tel. (372) 21-03-05; fax (372) 21-53-07.

Ministry of Defence: 734025 Dushanbe, Kuchai Bokhtar 59; tel. (372) 21-69-83; fax (372) 21-32-47.

Ministry of Economic Development and Trade: 734002 Dushanbe, Kuchai Bokhtar 37; tel. (372) 27-34-34; fax (372) 21-04-04; e-mail info@medt.tj; internet www.medt.tj.

Ministry of Education: 734024 Dushanbe, Kuchai Nosirmuhammad 13A; tel. (372) 21-46-05; fax (372) 21-70-41; e-mail malumot@netrt.org.

Ministry of Energy and Industry: 734012 Dushanbe, Xiyoboni Rudaki 22; tel. (372) 221-82-81; fax (372) 221-52-59; e-mail minprom@netrt.org; internet www.minenergoprom.tj.

Ministry of Finance: 734025 Dushanbe, Xiyoboni Rajabov 3; tel. (372) 21-14-17; fax (372) 21-33-29; e-mail min_fin@tojikiston.com; internet www.minfin.tj.

Ministry of Foreign Affairs: 734051 Dushanbe, Xiyoboni Rudaki 42; tel. (372) 21-18-08; fax (372) 21-02-59; e-mail info@mfa.tj; internet mfa.tj.

Ministry of Health: 734025 Dushanbe, Kuchai Shevchenko 69; tel. (372) 21-12-48; e-mail info@health.tj; internet www.health.tj.

Ministry of Internal Affairs: 734025 Dushanbe, Kuchai Texron 29; tel. (372) 21-17-40; fax (372) 21-18-97; internet mvd.tj.

Ministry of Justice: 734025 Dushanbe, Xiyoboni Rudaki 25; tel. (372) 21-00-82; fax (372) 21-80-66.

Ministry of Labour and Social Welfare: 734026 Dushanbe, Kuchai Navoi 5/2; tel. (372) 36-22-45; fax (372) 35-18-18; internet tj.labour.tj.

Ministry of Land Reclamation and Water Resources: 734001 Dushanbe, Xiyoboni Shamsi 5/1; tel. (372) 35-55-89; e-mail info@mwr.tj; internet www.mwr.tj.

Ministry of Transport: 734042 Dushanbe, Kuchai Aini 14; tel. (372) 21-17-13; fax (372) 221-20-03; e-mail snr@mintrans.tj; internet www.mintrans.tj.

President

Presidential Election, 6 November 2006*

Candidates	%
Emomali Rahmonov† (People's Democratic Party of Tajikistan)	79.3
Olimjon Boboyev (Party of Economic Reforms) . .	6.2
Amirkul Karakulov (Agrarian Party of Tajikistan)	5.3
Ismoil Talbakov (Communist Party of Tajikistan) . .	5.1
Abdukhalim Ghafforov (Socialist Party of Tajikistan) .	2.8
Total‡	100.0

* Provisional results.
† Known as Emomali Rahmon from 2007.
‡ Including invalid votes, equivalent to 1.3% of the total.

Legislature

Constitutional amendments approved by a referendum in September 1999 provided for the establishment of a bicameral legislative body, the Majlisi Oli (Supreme Assembly), comprising a 63-member lower chamber, the Majlisi Namoyandagon (Assembly of Representatives), and an upper chamber, the Majlisi Milliy (National Assembly), which has a minimum of 33 members.

Majlisi Milliy
(National Assembly)

734051 Dushanbe, Xiyoboni Rudaki 42; tel. (372) 23-19-33; fax (372) 21-51-10; e-mail mejparl@parliament.tojikiston.com; internet www .majlisimilli.tj.

President: MAHMADSAID UBAIDULLOYEV.

The Majlisi Milliy has a minimum of 33 members, of whom 25 (five from each of the five administrative regions of Tajikistan) are indirectly elected for a term of five years by regional deputies. Eight members of the chamber, who also serve for a term of five years, are appointed by the President of the Republic. All former Presidents of Tajikistan are also entitled to a seat in the Majlisi Milliy. Elections to the Majlisi Milliy were held on 25 March 2010 and the eight presidential nominees were announced on 29 March. The chamber convened on 23 April.

Majlisi Namoyandagon
(Assembly of Representatives)

734051 Dushanbe, Xiyoboni Rudaki 42; tel. (372) 21-23-66; fax (372) 21-92-81; e-mail mejparl@parliament.tojikiston.com; internet parlament.tj.

President: SHUKURJON ZUHUROV.
Elections, 28 February and 14 March 2010

Parties	%*	Seats A†	B†	Total
People's Democratic Party of Tajikistan	72	16	39	55
Islamic Rebirth Party of Tajikistan .	8	2	—	2
Communist Party of Tajikistan . .	7	2	—	2
Agrarian Party of Tajikistan . . .	5	1	1	2
Party of Economic Reforms . .	5	1	1	2
Others	3	—	—	—
Total	100	22	41	63

* Percentage refers to the share of the vote cast for seats awarded on the basis of party lists.
† Of the 63 seats in the Majlisi Namoyandagon, 22 (A) are awarded according to proportional representation on the basis of party lists, and 41 (B) are elected in single-mandate constituencies.

Election Commission

Central Commission for Elections and Referenda: 734051 Dushanbe, Xiyoboni Rudaki 42; tel. (372) 21-13-75; comprises Chair., Sec. and 13 mems, elected by the Majlisi Namoyandagon at the proposal of the President of the Republic; Chair. SHERMUHAMAD SHOHIYON.

Political Organizations

In September 2006 there were eight registered, and several unregistered, parties in Tajikistan.

Agrarian Party of Tajikistan (APT) (Agrarnaya partiya Tadzhikistana): 734000 Dushanbe; f. 2005; supports creation of a civil society and aims to protect the interests of the agricultural sector and its workers; Chair. AMIRQUL QARAQULOV; 1,300 mems (Jan. 2005).

Communist Party of Tajikistan (CPT) (Kommunisticheskaya partiya Tadzhikistana): 734002 Dushanbe, Kuchai F. Niyazi 37; tel. (372) 23-29-53; f. 1924; sole registered party until 1991; Chair. SHODI D. SHABDOLOV; Sec. of Central Cttee TUNGUN B. QARIMOV; 60,000 mems (Jan. 2005).

Democratic Party of Tajikistan (DPT) (Xizbi demokrati Tochikiston): 734000 Dushanbe, Kuchai Pushkin 64; tel. (372) 21-77-87; f. 1990; banned in 1993; permitted to re-register 1996 and 1999; secular nationalist and pro-Western; Chair. SAIDJAFAR ISMONOV (Chair. of Vatan—Fatherland faction registered by the Ministry of Justice in Sept. 2006); Chair. (of unregistered faction) MAHMADRUZI ISKANDAROV; c. 4,500 mems (Jan. 2005).

Islamic Rebirth Party of Tajikistan (IRPT): 734000 Dushanbe, pos. Kalinina, Kuchai Tukhagul 55; tel. (372) 27-25-30; fax (372) 27-53-93; f. 1990 by split from the All-Union Islamic Renaissance Party of the USSR; leadership fmrly based in Tehran, Iran; registered in 1991; banned 1993–99; Chair. MUHIDDIN KABIRI; 20,000 mems (Jan. 2005).

Justice (Adolatkoh): 734000 Dushanbe, Kuchai S. Nosirov 41; tel. (372) 24-90-55; f. 1996; campaigns for the establishment of social justice and construction of a state based on the rule of law; registration revoked 2001; Leader ABDURAHMON KARIMOV.

Party of Economic Reforms (PER) (Partiya ekonomicheskikh reform): 734000 Dushanbe; f. 2005; supports establishment of a market economy on the basis of democratic principles; aims to reduce poverty, undertake privatization and increase foreign investment; Chair. OLIMJON BOBOYEV; c. 1,000 mems (2005).

Party of Popular Unity and Accord (PPUA): 734000 Dushanbe; f. 1994; represents interests of northern Tajikistan; banned 1998; Leader ABDUMALIK ABDULLOJONOV.

People's Democratic Party of Tajikistan (PDPT) (Xizbi Xalkii Demokratii Tochikiston): 734000 Dushanbe, Xiyoboni Rudaki 107; tel. (372) 221-05-45; fax (372) 21-25-36; e-mail admin@hhdt.tj; internet www.tribun.tj; f. 1994; campaigns for a united and secular state; Chair. EMOMALI SH. RAHMON; First Dep. Chair. SAFAR SAFAROV; 100,000 mems (2008).

Social Democratic Party of Tajikistan (SDPT/KhSDT): 734000 Dushanbe, Xiyoboni Rudaki 81/49; tel. (372) 23-47-40; f. 1998; registered 2003; fmrly Justice and Progress of Tajikistan; Chair. RAHMATULLO H. ZOYIROV; 5,000 mems (Dec. 2004).

Socialist Party of Tajikistan (SPT): 734000 Dushanbe, Xiyoboni Rudaki 137; tel. (372) 34-77-11 (officially registered faction led by A. Gafforov); tel. (372) 27-39-59 (unregistered faction led by M. Narziyev); f. 1996; split into two factions in 2003, only one of which was registered by the Ministry of Justice; Chairmen ABDUKHALIM GAFFOROV (Chair. of faction registered by the Ministry of Justice), MIRKHUSEYN NARZIYEV (Chair. of unregistered faction); 15,000 mems (2003).

Union and Development Party (Xizb-i Ittihod va Taraqqiyot—Taraqqiyot): 734000 Dushanbe; f. 2000; unregistered; fmrly a faction of the Democratic Party of Tajikistan (q.v.); Chair. SULTON KUVVATOV; 3,000 mems (2001).

Unity Party (Hizb-i-Vahdat): 734000 Dushanbe, Xiyoboni Rudaki 4; tel. (372) 27-73-74; f. 2001; unregistered; Leader HIKMATULLO SAIDOV.

The transnational militant Islamist **Hizb-ut-Tahrir al-Islami** (Party of Islamic Liberation—Hizb-ut-Tahrir) was believed to be operative in Tajikistan. As in neighbouring states, the organization was banned in Tajikistan, and a number of people have received gaol sentences for their alleged membership of the group, despite its stated intention of using only peaceful means to pursue its goals, notably the restoration of a caliphate.

Diplomatic Representation

EMBASSIES IN TAJIKISTAN

Afghanistan: 734000 Dushanbe, Kuchai Pushkin 34; tel. (372) 21-67-35; fax (372) 51-00-96; e-mail afghanemintj@yahoo.com; Ambassador SAYED MUHAMMAD KHAIRKHA.

Azerbaijan: 734000 Dushanbe, Kuchai Farhor 1; tel. (372) 27-11-90; fax (372) 27-66-51; e-mail dushanbe@mission.mfa.gov.az; internet www.azembassy.tj; Ambassador ABBASALI HÄSÄNOV.

China, People's Republic: 734002 Dushanbe, Xiyoboni Rudaki 143; tel. (372) 24-20-07; fax (372) 51-00-24; internet tj .chineseembassy.org; Ambassador FAN XIANRONG.

France: 734025 Dushanbe, Kuchai Rakhimi 17; tel. (372) 21-78-55; fax (372) 51-00-82; e-mail ambassade.douchanbe@diplomatie.gouv .fr; internet ambafrance-tj.org; Ambassador DIDIER LEROY.

Germany: 734064 Dushanbe, Kuchai Somoni 59/1; tel. (372) 377-30-00; fax (372) 377-30-81; e-mail info@duschanbe.diplo.de; internet www.duschanbe.diplo.de; Ambassador DORIS HERTRAMPF.

India: 734025 Dushanbe, Kuchai Buxoro 45; tel. (372) 21-71-72; fax (372) 51-00-45; e-mail info.dushanbe@mea.gov.in; internet www .indianembassy.tj; Ambassador ASITH KUMAR BHATTACHARJEE.

Iran: 734000 Dushanbe, Kuchai Boxtar 18; tel. (372) 21-00-74; fax (372) 51-00-89; e-mail iranembassy.tj@gmail.com; internet www .iranembassytj.com; Ambassador ALI ASGHAR SHEARDOOST.

Japan: 734000 Dushanbe, Kuchai X. Nazarov 80A; tel. (372) 21-39-70; fax (372) 901-50-30; e-mail embjpn@embjpn.tojikiston.com; Ambassador HIROYUKI IMAHASHI.

Kazakhstan: 734000 Dushanbe, Kuchai Xuseinzoda 31/1; tel. (37) 21-89-40; fax (37) 251-01-08; Ambassador AGYBAY D. SMAGULOV.

Korea, Republic: 734000 Dushanbe, Kuchai Ghani Abdullo 61; tel. (44) 600-21-14; fax (37) 221-24-23; e-mail tajik@mofa.go.kr; internet tjk.mofat.go.kr; Ambassador YEON JEONG-KU.

Kyrgyzstan: 734000 Dushanbe, Kuchai Said-Nusur 56A; tel. and fax (37) 224-26-11; e-mail kg@kgembassy.tj; internet www .kgembassy.tj; Ambassador URMAT SARALAYEV.

Pakistan: 734000 Dushanbe, Kuchai Azizbekov 20A; tel. (372) 27-62-55; fax (372) 21-17-29; e-mail parepdushanbe_taj@yahoo.com; Ambassador AMJAD HUSSAIN B. SIAL.

Russia: 734026 Dushanbe, Kuchai Abu Ali ibni Sino 29/31; tel. (372) 35-70-65; fax (372) 35-88-06; e-mail rusemb_dushanbe@rambler.ru; internet www.rusemb.tj; Ambassador YURII F. POPOV.

Saudi Arabia: Dushanbe; Ambassador Dr BANDAR BIN MOHAMMED JAMEEL.

Turkey: 734019 Dushanbe, Xiyoboni Rudaki 17/2; tel. (372) 21-00-36; fax (372) 21-14-81; e-mail embassy.dushanbe@mfa.gov.tr; internet dushanbe.emb.mfa.gov.tr; Ambassador MEHMET MUNIS DIRIK.

Turkmenistan: 734000 Dushanbe, Kuchai Chexov 22; tel. and fax (372) 21-68-84; e-mail embturkm@tjinter.com; Ambassador CHYNAR RUSTEMOVA.

United Kingdom: 734002 Dushanbe, Kuchai M. Tursunzoda 65; tel. (372) 24-22-21; fax (372) 27-17-26; e-mail dushanbe.reception@ fco.gov.uk; internet ukintajikistan.fco.gov.uk; Ambassador ROBIN JEREMY ORD-SMITH.

USA: 734019 Dushanbe, Xiyoboni I. Somoni 109A; tel. (372) 29-20-00; fax (372) 29-20-50; e-mail usembassydushanbe@state.gov; internet dushanbe.usembassy.gov; Ambassador SUSAN ELLIOTT.

Uzbekistan: 734003 Dushanbe, Ozodi Zanon 9; tel. (372)24-90-77; fax (372) 24-47-21; e-mail ruzintaj@rambler.ru; Ambassador SHOQOSIM I. SHOISLOMOV.

Judicial System

Chairman of the Constitutional Court: M.A. MAHMUDOV, 734025 Dushanbe, Kuchai Boxtar 48; tel. (372) 21-61-96; fax (372) 21-29-28; e-mail constcourt.tj@mail.ru; internet www.constcourt.tj.

Chairman of the Supreme Court: NASRATULLO ABDULLOYEV, 734018 Dushanbe, Xiyoboni N. Karabayev 1; tel. (372) 33-48-21; fax (372) 33-93-69.

Chairman of the Supreme Economic Court: AMIRKHOJA GOIBNAZAROV, 734000 Dushanbe, Kuchai F. Niyazi 37; tel. (372) 21-15-58.

Prosecutor-General: SHERHON SALIMZODA, 734000 Dushanbe, Kuchai Abu Ali ibni Sino 126; tel. (372) 35-19-72.

Religion

ISLAM

The majority of Tajiks are adherents of Islam and are mainly Sunnis (Hanafi school). Many of the Pamiri peoples, however, are Isma'ilis (followers of the Aga Khan), a Shi'ite sect. Under the Soviet regime the Muslims of Tajikistan were subject to the Muslim Board of Central Asia and a muftiate, both of which were based in Tashkent, Uzbekistan. The senior Muslim cleric in Tajikistan was the *qazi* (supreme judge). In 1992 the incumbent *qazi* fled to Afghanistan, and in 1993 the Government appointed an independent *mufti* (expert in Islamic law). The Tajikistani Government, however, abolished the post of *mufti* in 1996, following the murder of the incumbent, and

established a Council of Islamic Scholars (or *ulema*), as the highest Islamic religious authority in the country.

Council of Islamic Scholars (Ulema): 734000 Dushanbe; Chair. QARI AMANULLOH NEMATZADE.

CHRISTIANITY

Most of the minority Christian population is Slav, the main denomination being the Russian Orthodox Church. There are some Protestant and other groups.

Roman Catholic Church

The Church is represented in Tajikistan by a Mission, established in September 1997. There were 314 adherents at 31 December 2007.

Superior: Rev. CARLOS AVILA, 734006 Dushanbe, Xiyoboni Titova 21/10; tel. (372) 26-75-17; fax (372) 26-76-63; e-mail carlosavila@ive .org; internet www.catholic.tj.

The Russian Orthodox Church (Moscow Patriarchate)

The Church in Tajikistan comes under the jurisdiction of the Eparchy of Tashkent and Central Asia, based in Uzbekistan and headed by the Metropolitan of Tashkent and Central Asia, VIKENTII (MORAR).

JUDAISM

In the late 2000s there were an estimated 350 Jews in Dushanbe. In 2008 the only synagogue remaining in Tajikistan was demolished by order of the Government, which planned to construct state buildings on its site. A new synagogue was opened elsewhere in Dushanbe in May 2009.

Leader of the Religious Society of Jews of Tajikistan: Rabbi MIHAIL ABURAHMANOV, 734001 Dushanbe, Kuchai N. Xikmata 26; tel. (372) 21-76-58.

The Press

In 2000 there were four national newspapers. In 1996 two daily newspapers and 73 non-daily newspapers and 11 periodicals were published in Tajikistan, although by 2010 both the daily newspapers had ceased publication.

PRINCIPAL NEWSPAPERS

Biznes i Politika (Business and Politics): 734025 Dushanbe, Kuchai M. Tursunzoda 30; tel. (372) 23-52-50; e-mail b_p@rambler .ru; f. 1992; weekly; in Russian; Editor-in-Chief U. RAHMON; circ. 10,000.

Charxi Gardun (Wheel of Fortune): 734016 Dushanbe, Xiyoboni S. Sherozi 16; tel. (372) 33-56-72; e-mail info@gazeta.tj; internet www .gazeta.tj; f. 1996; weekly; in Tajik; general; Editor-in-Chief AKBARALI SATTOROV; circ. 6,000 (2009).

Daijest Press (Press Digest): 734016 Dushanbe, Xiyoboni S. Sherozi 16; tel. (372) 238-53-47; e-mail gazeta@tojikiston.com; f. 1994; weekly; in Russian; overview of world press, incl. economics, popular culture; Editor-in-Chief AKBARALI SATTOROV; circ. 9,750 (2011).

Farazh: Dushanbe; weekly; Chief Editor XURSHED ATOVULLOH.

Ittixod (Unity): 734000 Dushanbe, Xiyoboni Rudaki 137; tel. (372) 34-77-11; organ of the Socialist Party of Tajikistan (q.v.).

Jumhuriyat (Republic): 734018 Dushanbe, Xiyoboni S. Sherozi 16; tel. (372) 33-08-11; e-mail jumhuriyat@tojikiston.com; f. 1925; 3 a week; organ of the Govt and presidential administration; in Tajik; Editor-in-Chief KAMOL ABDURAHIMOV; circ. 8,000.

Kurer Tadzhikistana (Tajikistan Courier): 734018 Dushanbe, Xiyoboni S. Sherozi 16; tel. (372) 33-08-15; e-mail ttemirov@td.silk .org; weekly; independent; in Russian; Editor KH. YUSIPOV; circ. 40,000.

Millat (Nation): 734000 Dushanbe, Xiyoboni S. Sherozi 16/8; tel. (378) 81-11-97; e-mail millat@mail.ru; internet www.millat.tj; f. 2005; in Tajik; independent; Editor ADOLAT UMAROVOI.

Minbari Xalk (People's Tribune): 734018 Dushanbe, Xiyoboni S. Sherozi 16; tel. (372) 33-79-07; fax (372) 33-72-10; organ of the People's Democratic Party of Tajikistan (q.v.); Editor MANSUR SAIFIDDINOV; circ. 20,000.

Najot (Salvation): 734000 Dushanbe, Kuchai Toktogul 55; tel. (372) 31-47-38; weekly; organ of the Islamic Rebirth Party of Tajikistan (q.v.); Editor-in-Chief HIKMATULLOH SAIFULLOHZODA.

Oila: 734018 Dushanbe, Xiyoboni S. Sherozi 16; tel. (372) 33-32-51; f. 2000; weekly; independent; Editor-in-Chief FIRUZA SATTORI.

Ozodagon (The Independent): Dushanbe; weekly; Editor ZAFAR SUFIEV.

Paykon (Arrowhead): 734000 Dushanbe; internet paikon
.wordpress.com; weekly newspaper; Editor-in-Chief JUMABOY TOLI-
BOV.

Sadoi Mardum (The Voice of the People): 734018 Dushanbe,
Xiyoboni S. Sherozi 16; tel. (372) 33-89-22; e-mail sadoimardum@
yandex.ru; f. 1991; 3 a week; organ of the legislature; in Tajik; Chief
Editor JUMAHON NABOTOV; circ. 8,000.

Tojikiston (Tajikistan): 734018 Dushanbe, Xiyoboni S. Sherozi 16;
tel. (372) 34-94-11; f. 1938; weekly; social and political; in Tajik;
Editor-in-Chief SHARIF HAMDAMOV; circ. (annual) 9,000.

Tribun.tj: 731000 Dushanbe, Xiyoboni Rudaki 107; tel. (372) 21-05-
45; fax (372) 24-27-59; e-mail tribun.tj@mail.ru; internet www
.tribun.tj; f. 2005; daily; online only; in Russian; organ of the People's
Democratic Party of Tajikistan.

Vechernii Dushanbe (Dunshanbe Evening News): 734018 Dushanbe, Xiyoboni S. Sherozi 16; tel. (372) 33-08-15; fax (372) 33-30-25;
f. 1968; weekly; social and political; in Russian; Editor-in-Chief
AKBARALI SATTAROV.

Xalk ovozi (Voice of the People): 734018 Dushanbe, Xiyoboni S.
Sherozi 18; tel. (372) 33-05-04; f. 1929; 3 a week; organ of the
President; in Uzbek; Editor I. MUKHSINOV; circ. 8,600.

Zindagi (Life): 734000 Dushanbe; f. 2004; weekly; in Tajik; independent; politics; Editor-in-Chief KHURSHED ATOVULLO.

PRINCIPAL PERIODICALS

Monthly, unless otherwise indicated.

Adab: 734025 Dushanbe, Kuchai Chexov 13; tel. (372) 23-49-36;
organ of the Ministry of Education; in Tajik; Editor SH. SHOKIRZODA;
circ. (annual) 24,000.

Avitsenna: 734018 Dushanbe, Xiyoboni S. Sherozi 16; tel. (372) 34-
34-44; e-mail gazeta@tojikiston.com; weekly; in Russian; medicine;
Editor-in-Chief AKBARALI SATTAROV.

Djashma (Spring): 734018 Dushanbe, Xiyoboni S. Sherozi 16; tel.
(372) 33-08-48; f. 1986; journal of the Ministry of Culture; for
children; Editor KAMOL NASRULLO; circ. (annual) 10,000.

Ilm va khayot (Science and Life): 734025 Dushanbe, Xiyoboni
Rudaki 34; tel. (372) 27-48-61; f. 1989; organ of the Academy of
Sciences; popular science; Editor T. BOIBOBO; circ. (annual) 12,000.

Istikbol: 734018 Dushanbe, Xiyoboni S. Sherozi 16; tel. (372) 33-14-
52; f. 1952; organ of the Ministry of Culture; in Tajik; Chief Editor L.
KENJAYEVA; circ. (annual) 10,000.

Marifat: 734024 Dushanbe, Kuchai Aini 45; tel. (372) 23-42-84;
organ of the Ministry of Education; in Tajik; Editor O. BOZOROV; circ.
(annual) 40,000.

Pamir: 734001 Dushanbe, Kuchai I. Somoni 8; tel. (372) 24-56-56;
f. 1949; journal of the Union of Writers of Tajikistan; fiction; in
Russian; Editor-in-Chief BORIS PSHENICHNYI.

Sadoi shark (Voice of the East): 734001 Dushanbe, Kuchai I.
Somoni 8; tel. (372) 24-56-79; f. 1927; journal of the Union of Writers
of Tajikistan; fiction; in Tajik; Editor URUN KUKHZOD; circ. 1,600.

NEWS AGENCIES

Asia-Plus TV-Radio Company: 734002 Dushanbe, Kuchai Boxtar
35/1, 8th Floor; tel. (372) 21-72-20; fax (372) 21-78-63; e-mail agency@
asiaplus.tj; internet www.news.tj; f. 2002; independent; reports in
Tajik and Russian; Gen. Dir UMED BABAKHANOV.

Avesta News Agency: 734025 Dushanbe, Xiyoboni Sherozi 16A; tel.
(372) 27-10-84; e-mail info@avesta.tj; internet www.avesta.tj;
f. 2004; Dir ZAFAR ABDULLAYEV.

Khovar (East): 737025 Dushanbe, Xiyoboni Rudaki 40; tel. (372) 21-
21-37; fax (372) 23-23-83; e-mail maktub@khovar.tj; internet www
.khovar.tj; f. 1925; govt information agency; Dir SADRIDDIN SHAM-
SIDDINOV.

Varorud: 735700 Sughd Viloyat, Khujand, Kuchai Ferdovsi 123; tel.
and fax (3422) 4-09-33; e-mail varorud@varorud.org; f. 2000; independent; Dir ILHOM JAMOLOV.

PRESS ASSOCIATION

Internews Network—Tajikistan: 734025 Dushanbe, Kuchai Ak.
Rajabov 7/1/4; tel. (372) 21-99-33; fax (372) 21-99-34; e-mail
reception@inewstj.org; internet www.internews.tj; f. 1995; non-
governmental org.; provides support and funding to media organizations, and in the training of journalists; Country Dir CHARLES
RICE.

Publishers

Adib (Writer): 734018 Dushanbe, Xiyoboni Karabaev 17A; tel. (372)
33-84-35; fax (372) 33-19-73; e-mail karimov-adib@mail.ru; state-

owned; publishes in Tajik and Russian; fiction, incl. poetry, and non-
fiction, incl. books on Tajikistani and Central Asian culture.

Donish (Knowledge): 734000 Dushanbe, Xiyoboni Akademiya Nauk
33; state-owned; Russian and Tajik; non-fiction, incl. geography,
literature, history and art; associated with the Academy of Sciences.

Irfon (Light of Knowledge) Publishing House: 734018 Dushanbe, Kuchai N. Karabayev 17; tel. (372) 233-39-06; e-mail
irfon_company@mail.ru; f. 1925; politics, social sciences, economics,
agriculture, medicine and technology; Dir JURA SHARIFOV; Editor-in-
Chief ABDURAHMON OLIMOV.

**Maorif va Farxang (Education and Culture) Publishing
House:** 734018 Dushanbe, Kuchai N. Karabayev 17; tel. and fax
(372) 33-93-97; e-mail najmidin@netrt.org; f. 1958; educational,
academic; Gen. Dir NAJMIDDIN ZAYNIDDINOV.

**Sarredaksiyai Ilmii Entsiklopediyai Millii Tajik (Tajik
National Scientific Encyclopaedia) Publishing House:**
731000 Dushanbe, Kuchai Aini 126; tel. (372) 25-81-55; e-mail
encyclopedia@yahoo.com; f. 1969; Editor-in-Chief A. QURBONOV.

Sharki Ozod Publishing House: 734018 Dushanbe, Xiyoboni S.
Sherozi 16; tel. (372) 34-94-11; state-owned; Dir MANZURHON DODO-
HONOV.

Surushan Publishing House: 734025 Dushanbe, Xiyoboni Rudaki
37; tel. and fax (372) 21-54-62; e-mail surushan@net.org; f. 1997;
literary fiction, educational; Dir NURIDDIN ZAYNIDDINOV.

Broadcasting and Communications

TELECOMMUNICATIONS

Tajikistan's telecommunications infrastructure is the least
developed of all the eastern European and central Asian countries.
By 2010 over 90% of the country's fixed-line network had been
converted from analogue to digital. At that time there were
367,700 fixed telephone lines in use, and 5.9m. subscriptions to
mobile telephone services.

Babilon-Mobil (Babilon-M): 734012 Dushanbe, Kuchai Dehlavi 4;
tel. (44) 600-10-10; fax (44) 600-20-20; e-mail info@babilon-m.tj;
internet www.babilon-m.com; f. 2002; mobile cellular telecommunications and internet services.

Beeline TJ: Dushanbe; tel. (372) 29-06-11; e-mail pr@beeline.tj;
internet www.beeline.tj; f. 2006; fmrly Tacom; 60% owned by
VympelKom-Bilain (Russia); mobile cellular telecommunications
services; Dir SERGEY MIRONOV.

Indigo Somonkom (Tcell): 735700 Sughd Viloyat, Khujand, 50 let
SSSR 2; tel. (3422) 6-07-50; internet www.somoncom.com; f. 2000;
majority share owned by TeliaSonera (Sweden); provides mobile
cellular telecommunications in northern regions, particularly Sughd
Viloyat; Chair. of Bd of Dirs MAMAJON HAMIDOV; 130,000 subscribers
(2006).

Indigo Tajikistan (Tcell): 734000 Dushanbe, Kuchai M. Tursunzoda 23; tel. (372) 23-21-21; fax (372) 23-21-23; e-mail corporate@tcell
.tj; internet www.indigo.tj; f. 2001; majority share owned by
TeliaSonera (Sweden); mobile cellular telecommunications in central and southern regions of Tajikistan; Dir-Gen. MANSUR KHAMIDOV.

Megafon Tajikistan: 734043 Dushanbe, Kuchai Huvaidulloev 73/
2; tel. (372) 21-42-24; e-mail ttmobile@mlt.tj; internet www.megafon
.tj; f. 2001; fmrly TT Mobile, and then MLT (Mobile Lines of
Tajikistan); mobile cellular telecommunications and internet services.

Tajiktelecom: 734025 Dushanbe, Kuchai Jerjinski 2A; tel. (372) 21-
31-78; fax (372) 23-21-19; e-mail ttelecom@rs.tj; internet www
.tajiktelecom.tj; f. 1996; national telecommunications operator; Dir-
Gen. MUZAFAR H. HIMATOV (acting).

BROADCASTING

Tajikistan has about 30 radio and television stations, most of which
are privately owned. In addition to several state-run radio and
television stations, including two nation-wide channels and the
recently established 24-hour news channel, Jahonnamo, there are
18 independent radio and television stations, mostly in Dushanbe
and the northern Sughd province. There are two independent TV
stations in the heavily populated southern Khatlon province: Mavji
Ozod and Independent TV.

Regulatory Authority

State Committee for Television and Radio Broadcasting:
734000 Dushanbe; Chair. ASADULLO K. RAKHMONOV.

Radio

State TV-Radio Broadcasting Co of Tajikistan: 734025 Dushanbe, Kuchai Chapayev 31; tel. (372) 27-75-27; fax (372) 21-34-95; e-mail soro@ctvrtj.td.silk.org; Chair. ABDODZHABBOR RAKHMONOV.

Asia-Plus: 734018 Dushanbe, Xiyoboni Saadi Sherozi 16, 13th Floor; tel. and fax (44) 600-71-07; e-mail radio@asiaplus.tj; internet www.asiaplusradio.tj; f. 2002; radio and television station; broadcasts 24 hours a day in Russian and Tajik; Exec. Dir ZEBO TADJIBAEVA.

Tajik Radio: 734025 Dushanbe, Kuchai Chapayev 31; tel. (372) 27-65-69; broadcasts in Russian, Tajik and Uzbek.

Tiroz: 735716 Sughd Viloyat, Khujand, Mikroraion 27, Kuchai Tiroz 9; tel. (3422) 5-32-94; fax (3422) 5-66-89; e-mail radio@tiroz.org; internet www.tiroz.org; f. 2001; broadcasts music and entertainment and other programming on FM to much of Sughd Viloyat; Dir KHURSHED ULMASOV.

Television

State TV-Radio Broadcasting Co of Tajikistan: 734025 Dushanbe, Kuchai Chapayev 31; tel. (372) 27-75-27; fax (372) 21-34-95; e-mail soro@ctvrtj.td.silk.org; Chair. ABDODZHABBOR RAKHMONOV.

Poitaxt: 734013 Dushanbe, Kuchai Azizbekov 20; tel. (372) 23-26-29; independent; Dir RAKHMON OSTONOV.

Tajik Television (TTV): 734013 Dushanbe, Kuchai Behzod 7; tel. (372) 22-43-57.

TV Safina: 734000 Dushanbe, Kuchai Buxoro 43; tel. (372) 27-80-29; fax (372) 27-79-05; e-mail info@safina.tj; internet www.safina.tj; f. 2005; state-owned national TV channel; Dir LUTFULLO DAVLATOV.

Finance

(cap. = capital; res = reserves; dep. = deposits; brs = branches; m. = million; amounts in somoni, unless otherwise stated)

BANKING

Central Bank

National Bank of the Republic of Tajikistan (Bonki Millii Tochikiston): 734003 Dushanbe, Xiyoboni Rudaki 107A; tel. (44) 600-32-27; fax (44) 600-32-35; e-mail info@nbt.tj; internet www.nbt.tj; f. 1991; cap. 0.8m., res 25.4m., dep. 604.8m. (Oct. 2003); Chair. ABDUDJABOR SHIRINOV.

State Savings Bank

Amonatbonk: 734018 Dushanbe, Kuchai Loxuti 24; tel. (372) 21-70-81; fax (372) 27-38-43; e-mail info@amonatbonk.tj; internet www.amonatbonk.tj; f. 1991; fmrly br. of USSR Sberbank; licensed by presidential decree and not subject to the same controls as the commercial and trading banks; Chair. of Bd GULNORA HASANOVA; 58 brs, 480 sub-brs.

Other Banks

In June 2005 President Rahmonov announced the removal of all restrictions on the activities of foreign banks in Tajikistan. There were reported to be 16 commercial banks in operation in Tajikistan in early 2005, including the following:

Agroinvestbank: 734018 Dushanbe, Xiyoboni S. Sherozi 21; tel. (372) 233-21-14; fax (372) 236-51-66; e-mail info@agroinvestbank.tj; internet www.agroinvestbank.tj; f. 1992; fmrly Agroprombank; open jt-stock co; cap. 182.3m., res 85.7m., dep.1,471.3m. (Dec. 2011); Chair. NIYOZMUROD M. SAIDMURODOV; 61 brs.

Orienbank: 734001 Dushanbe, Xiyoboni Rudaki 95/1; tel. (372) 21-05-68; fax (372) 21-18-77; e-mail info@orienbank.com; internet www.orienbank.com; f. 1922; cap. 277.8m., res 4.4m., dep. 1,014.5m. (Dec. 2011); commercial bank; Chair. of Bd HASAN ASADULLOZODA; Chair. of Bank Council SHERMALIK MALIKOV; 32 brs.

Tajbank: 734064 Dushanbe, Kuchai I. Somoni 59/1; tel. (372) 27-46-54; f. 1992.

Tajprombank (Tajik Joint-Stock Bank for Reconstruction and Development): 734025 Dushanbe, Rudaki 22; tel. (372) 21-27-20; fax (372) 21-25-85; e-mail tpb@tjinter.com; internet www.tajprombank.com; cap. US $1m., res $3m., dep. $4m.; Chair. DZHAMSHED ZIYAYEV; 8 brs.

Tojik Sodiot Bonk (Bank for Foreign Economic Affairs of the Republic of Tajikistan): 734012 Dushanbe, Kuchai X. Dexlavi 4; tel. (372) 21-59-52; fax (372) 21-47-38; e-mail sham@sodirotbonk.com; f. 1990 as a br. of USSR Vneshekonombank; renamed as Tojiksodirotbonk in 1999, and as above in 2009; Chair. I. L. LALBEKOV; 10 brs.

COMMODITY EXCHANGE

Tajik Republican Commodity Exchange 'Navruz': 734001 Dushanbe, Kuchai Orjonikidze 37; tel. (372) 23-48-74; fax (372) 27-03-91; f. 1991; Chair. SULEYMAN CHULEBAYEV.

INSURANCE

Muin Insurance Co: 734025 Dushanbe, Kuchai Sh. Rustaveli 16/1; tel. (372) 21-32-80; fax (372) 21-72-09; e-mail info@muin.tj; internet www.muin.tj; f. 1992; Dir-Gen. SHARIFJON ISHAKOV.

Orien Insurance: 734001 Dushanbe, Xiyoboni Rudaki 100; tel. (44) 600-30-71; fax (372) 21-12-30; e-mail info@orieninsurance.tj; internet www.orieninsurance.tj; f. 2004; life and non-life; Dir ISKANDAR KH. SHARIPOV.

Tojiksurguta State Insurance Co: 734025 Dushanbe, Kuchai Chexov 4A; tel. (372) 21-75-07.

Trud Insurance Co: 734000 Dushanbe, Kuchai Bekzod 70; tel. (372) 27-24-24; fax (372) 21-72-21; e-mail info@trud.tj; internet www.trud.tj; f. 2004; life and non-life.

Trade and Industry

CHAMBER OF COMMERCE

Chamber of Commerce and Industry of the Republic of Tajikistan: 734012 Dushanbe, Kuchai Valamatzade 21; tel. (372) 21-52-84; fax (372) 21-14-80; e-mail chamber@tpp.tj; internet www.tpp.tj; f. 1960; brs in Khujant, Qurghonteppa, Khorugh, and Chamber of Services in Dushanbe; Chair. SHARIF S. SAIDOV.

INDUSTRIAL ASSOCIATION

Tajikvneshtorg (Tajik External Trade) Industrial Asscn: 734035 Dushanbe, Xiyoboni Rudaki 25, POB 48; tel. (372) 23-29-03; fax (372) 22-81-20; f. 1988; co-ordinates trade with foreign countries in a wide range of goods; Pres. ABDURAKHMON MUKHTASHOV.

EMPLOYERS' ORGANIZATION

National Asscn of Small and Medium-sized Businesses of Tajikistan: 734000 Dushanbe, Kuchai Bofanda 9; tel. (372) 27-79-78; fax (372) 21-17-26; f. 1993 with govt support; independent org.; Chair. MATLJUBA ULJABAEVA.

UTILITIES

Electricity

Barqi Tojik (Tajik Electricity): 734000 Dushanbe, Kuchai I. Somoni 64; tel. (372) 35-86-68; fax (372) 35-86-92; Gen. Dir SANAT RAKHIMOV.

Pamir Energy Co (PamirEnergy): 736100 Kuhistoni Badakhshon, Khorugh; tel. (352) 22-33-83; fax (352) 22-25-19; e-mail daler.jumaev@pamirenergy.com; f. 2002; jt venture between Governments of Tajikistan and Switzerland, the Aga Khan Fund for Economic Development, the International Finance Corpn and the International Development Association to provide electricity to Kuhistoni Badakhshon; Gen. Dir DALER JUMAYEV.

Gas

Dushanbegaz: 734000 Dushanbe; tel. (372) 27-89-28; supplies gas to Dushanbe City.

Sughdgaz: 735700 Sughd Viloyat, Khujand, 20 Kvartal; tel. (3422) 2-53-95; fax (3422) 4-35-16; supplies gas to Sughd Viloyat.

Tojikgaz: 734012 Dushanbe, Xiyoboni Rudaki 6; tel. (372) 21-66-68; fax (372) 21-28-16; state-controlled gas utility co.

TRADE UNIONS

Federation of Trade Unions: 734012 Dushanbe, Xiyoboni Rudaki 20; tel. (372) 23-17-79; fax (372) 23-25-06; f. 1926; present name adopted 1992; Chair. MURODALI S. SALIKHOV; 1.3m. mems.

Transport

RAILWAYS

There are few railways in Tajikistan. Lines link the major centres of the country with the railway network of Uzbekistan, connecting Khujand to the Farg‘ona (Fergana) valley lines, and the cotton-growing centre of Qurghonteppa to Termiz. A new line, between the town of Isfara, in Sughd Viloyat, and Xavast, in Uzbekistan, was opened in 1995, and in 1997 a passenger route between Dushanbe and Volgograd, Russia, was inaugurated. The first section of a new line between Qurghonteppa and Kulob, in the south-west of Tajikistan, was inaugurated in 1998. In October 2002 a route from Kulob to

Astrakhan, Russia, was opened. In 2010 the total length of the rail network in use was 620.7 km.

Tajik Railways: 734012 Dushanbe, M. Nazarshoeva 35; tel. (372) 21-60-59; fax (372) 21-83-34; e-mail tajrwv@rs.tj; state-owned; Dir AMONULLO HUKUMATULLO.

ROADS

In mid-2002 Tajikistan's road network totalled an estimated 30,000 km, including 13,747 km of highways. The principal highway links the northern city of Khujand, across the Anzob Pass (3,372 m), with the capital, Dushanbe, continuing to Khorugh (Kuhistoni Badakhshon), before wending through the Pamir Mountains, to the east and north, to Osh, Kyrgyzstan, across the Akbaytal Pass (4,655 m). This arterial route exhibits problems common to much of the country's land transport: winter weather is likely to cause the road to be closed by snow for up to eight months of the year. In 2000 Tajikistan and the Asian Development Bank signed a memorandum of understanding for the rehabilitation of the road linking Dushanbe to the south-western cities of Qurghonteppa and Kulob. In the same year a road linking eastern Tajikistan with the People's Republic of China was completed, giving Tajikistan access to the Karakorum highway, which connects China and Pakistan.

CIVIL AVIATION

The main international airport is at Dushanbe, and there is also a major airport at Khujand. The country is linked to cities in Russia and other former Soviet republics, and to a growing number of destinations in Europe and Asia.

Somon Air: 734012 Dushanbe, Kuchai Titova 40; tel. (44) 640-40-40; fax (44) 640-12-34; e-mail info@somonair.com; internet www.somonair.com; f. 2008; operates 18 routes; also serves as the official carrier of the President of the Republic of Tajikistan; CEO ALISHER RUSTAMOV; 180 employees (2011).

TajikAir: 734006 Dushanbe, Kuchai Titova 32/1; tel. (372) 21-32-83; fax (372) 21-86-85; e-mail isakov.m@tajikairlines.com; internet www.tajikair.tj; f. 1924; state-owned; operates flights to 20 international destinations; Dir MUZAFAR ISHAKOV.

Tourism

There was little tourism in Tajikistan even before the 1992–97 civil war. There is some spectacular mountain scenery, hitherto mainly visited by climbers, and, particularly in the Farg'ona (Fergana) valley, in the north of the country, there are sites of historical interest, notably the city of Khujand.

State Committee for Youth, Sports and Tourism: 734000 Dushanbe; f. 2006.

Defence

A Tajikistani Ministry of Defence was established in September 1992; in December it was announced that Tajikistan's national armed forces were to be formed on the basis of the Tajik People's Front and other paramilitary units supporting the Government. Integration of United Tajik Opposition force members into the Tajikistani armed forces took place from 1998. Military service lasts for 24 months. As assessed at November 2012, the armed forces numbered 8,800, comprising an army of 7,300 and an air force of 1,500. There were also 7,500 paramilitary troops, comprising members of the National Guard and of forces answerable to the Ministry of Internal Affairs. Tajikistan became a member of the North Atlantic Treaty Organization's 'Partnership for Peace' programme of military co-operation in February 2002.

Defence Expenditure: Budgeted at 923m. somoni in 2013.

Chief of General Staff: Lt-Gen. RAMIL NODIROV.

Commander of the Air Force: RAXMONALI D. SAFARALIYEV.

Education

Education is officially compulsory for nine years, to be undertaken between seven and 17 years of age. Primary education begins at seven years of age and lasts for four years. Secondary education, beginning at the age of 11, lasts for as much as seven years, comprising a first cycle of five years and a second of two years. In 2009/10 total enrolment at primary schools included 97% of children in the relevant age-group (males 99%; females 95%). In that year total enrolment at secondary schools included 85% of children in the relevant age-group (males 90%; females 80%).

The majority of pupils receive their education in Tajik. Following the adoption of Tajik as the state language, greater emphasis was placed in the curriculum on Tajik language and literature, including classical Persian literature. However, in 2003 President Emomali Rahmonov announced that the compulsory teaching of Russian was to be reintroduced to schools from September of that year.

In 2011/12 there were 152,200 students enrolled at 33 institutes of higher education. In 2000 the Presidents of Kazakhstan, Kyrgyzstan and Tajikistan co-signed a charter of foundation for a new University of Central Asia, which was to be established in Khorugh (in Kuhistoni Badakhshon Autonomous Viloyat) and administered by the Aga Khan Development Network, based in Geneva, Switzerland. Budgetary expenditure on education by all levels of government was 1,443.1m. somoni (16.9% of total government budgetary expenditure) in 2011.

TANZANIA

Introductory Survey

LOCATION, CLIMATE, LANGUAGE, RELIGION, FLAG, CAPITAL

The United Republic of Tanzania consists of Tanganyika, on the African mainland, and the nearby islands of Zanzibar and Pemba. Tanganyika lies on the east coast of Africa, bordered by Uganda and Kenya to the north, by Rwanda, Burundi and the Democratic Republic of the Congo (formerly Zaire) to the west, and by Zambia, Malawi and Mozambique to the south. Zanzibar and Pemba are in the Indian Ocean, about 40 km (25 miles) off the coast of Tanganyika, north of Dar es Salaam. The climate varies with altitude, ranging from tropical in Zanzibar and on the coast and plains to semi-temperate in the highlands. The official languages are Swahili and English and there are numerous tribal languages. There are Muslim, Christian and Hindu communities. Many Africans follow traditional beliefs. The national flag (proportions 2 by 3) comprises two triangles, one of green (with its base at the hoist and its apex in the upper fly) and the other of blue (with its base in the fly and its apex at the lower hoist), separated by a broad, yellow-edged black diagonal stripe, from the lower hoist to the upper fly. The administrative capital is Dodoma, although most government offices remain in Dar es Salaam, the commercial capital.

CONTEMPORARY POLITICAL HISTORY

Historical Context

Tanganyika became a German colony in 1884, and was later incorporated into German East Africa, which also included present-day Rwanda and Burundi. In 1918, at the end of the First World War, Tanganyika was placed under a League of Nations mandate, with the United Kingdom as the administering power. In 1946 Tanganyika became a UN Trust Territory, still under British rule. At a general election in September 1960 the Tanganyika African National Union (TANU) won 70 of the 71 seats in the National Assembly, and the party's leader, Dr Julius Nyerere, became Chief Minister. Internal self-government was achieved in May 1961, when Nyerere became Prime Minister. Tanganyika became independent, within the Commonwealth, on 9 December 1961, but Nyerere resigned as Prime Minister in January 1962, in order to devote himself to the direction of TANU. He was succeeded as premier by Rashidi Kawawa. On 9 December 1962, following elections in November, Tanganyika became a republic, with Nyerere as the country's first President. Kawawa became Vice-President. Zanzibar (including the island of Pemba), a British protectorate since 1890, became an independent sultanate in December 1963. Following an armed uprising by the Afro-Shirazi Party (ASP) in January 1964, the Sultan was deposed and a republic proclaimed. The new Government signed an Act of Union with Tanganyika in April, thus creating the United Republic. The union was named Tanzania in October, and a new Constitution was introduced in July 1965, which provided for a one-party state (although, until 1977, TANU and the ASP remained the respective official parties of mainland Tanzania and Zanzibar, and co-operated in affairs of state). Nyerere was elected President of the United Republic in September 1965, and was subsequently re-elected in 1970, 1975 and 1980.

Despite its incorporation into Tanzania, Zanzibar retained a separate administration, which suppressed all opposition. A separate Constitution for Zanzibar was adopted in October 1979, providing for a popularly elected President and a House of Representatives elected by delegates of the ruling party. The first elections to the 40-member Zanzibar House of Representatives were held in January 1980. Aboud Jumbe won an overwhelming majority at Zanzibar's first presidential election, held in October; however, mounting dissatisfaction among Zanzibaris concerning the union with Tanganyika culminated in the resignation, in January 1984, of Jumbe and three of his ministers. In April Ali Hassan Mwinyi, a former Zanzibari Minister of Natural Resources and Tourism, was elected unopposed as President of Zanzibar, winning 87.5% of the votes cast. A new Constitution for Zanzibar came into force in January 1985, providing for the House of Representatives to be directly elected by universal adult suffrage.

Meanwhile, in February 1977 TANU and the ASP were amalgamated to form Chama Cha Mapinduzi (CCM), the Revolutionary Party of Tanzania. In April the National Assembly approved a permanent Constitution for Tanzania; this provided for the election to the National Assembly of representatives from Zanzibar, in addition to those from the Tanzanian mainland. Major changes to the Constitution were approved by the National Assembly in October 1984, limiting the President's powers and increasing those of the National Assembly.

Domestic Political Affairs

President Nyerere retired in November 1985, and was succeeded by Mwinyi, who, as the sole candidate, had won 96% of the votes cast at a presidential election in October. Elections to the National Assembly were held on the same day, while at presidential and legislative elections in Zanzibar, also held in October, Idris Abdul Wakil (formerly Speaker of the Zanzibar House of Representatives) was elected President of Zanzibar to replace Mwinyi. Nyerere remained Chairman of the CCM until August 1990 when he resigned and Mwinyi was appointed in his place.

In early 1988 tension began to increase in Zanzibar, reflecting underlying rivalries between the inhabitants of the main island and those of the smaller island of Pemba, and between supporters and opponents of unity with Tanganyika. In January Wakil suspended the islands' Government, the Supreme Revolutionary Council, and assumed control of the armed forces from the office of his main rival, Chief Minister Seif Sharrif Hamad, following earlier claims by Wakil that a group of dissidents, including members of the Council, had been plotting the overthrow of his administration. Hamad was replaced later that month by Dr Omar Ali Juma and in May Hamad and six other officials were expelled from the CCM for allegedly opposing the party's aims and endangering Tanzanian unity.

In October 1990 concurrent parliamentary and presidential elections were held in Zanzibar. Wakil did not stand for re-election; the sole presidential candidate, Dr Salmin Amour, was elected as Wakil's successor by 97.7% of the votes cast. Amour subsequently reappointed Juma as Chief Minister of Zanzibar. At the end of October national parliamentary and presidential elections took place. Mwinyi, the sole candidate in the presidential election, was re-elected for a second term, taking 95.5% of the votes cast.

In February 1992 proposed constitutional amendments, which would establish a multi-party political system, were ratified by a special congress of the CCM, which stipulated that, in order to protect national unity, all new political organizations should command support in both Zanzibar and mainland Tanzania, and should be free of tribal, religious and racial bias. In May the Constitutions of both the United Republic and Zanzibar were amended to enshrine a multi-party system. Several political organizations were officially registered from mid-1992.

In October 1995 multi-party legislative elections were held for the first time, concurrently with presidential elections, both in Zanzibar and mainland Tanzania. At elections on 22 October the CCM secured 26 of the 50 elective seats in the Zanzibari House of Representatives, while the Civic United Front (CUF) took 24 seats. Amour was re-elected President of the islands by 50.2% of the votes cast, only narrowly defeating Hamad, who represented the CUF. Amour appointed a new ruling council, with Dr Mohamed Gharib Bilali, formerly a government official, as Chief Minister. The CUF contested the election results, accusing the Zanzibari authorities of electoral malpractice and refusing to recognize the legitimacy of the new Amour administration. The Tanzanian national elections, on 29 October, were followed by further opposition allegations of electoral fraud. Administrative inefficiency led to the cancellation of the election results in seven constituencies in Dar es Salaam; these polls were repeated in mid-November. The opposition parties, alleging that the CCM was manipulating the voting process, refused to re-run, withdrew their candidates from the presidential election, and unsuccessfully petitioned the High Court to declare all results null and void. The Government proceeded to publish the results, whereby the CCM won 186 of the 232 elective seats in the National Assembly, the CUF 24, the National Convention for Construction and Reform (NCCR—Mageuzi) 16, and Chama Cha Demokrasia na Maendeleo (Chadema) and the United Democratic Party (UDP) three seats each. Benjamin Mkapa, hitherto Minister of Science, Technology and Higher Education, was deemed to have been elected President, winning 61.8% of the votes cast. The former Minister of Home Affairs, Augustine Mrema, took 27.8% of the votes. President Mkapa was inaugurated in late November; Juma (hitherto Chief Minister of Zanzibar) was appointed Vice-President. Shortly afterwards Mkapa announced a new Cabinet, with Frederick Sumaye (formerly Minister of Agriculture) as Prime Minister.

In accordance with his pre-election pledges, Mkapa appointed a special presidential commission, which in December 1996 issued a report asserting that corruption was widespread in the public sector. In September a parliamentary select committee investigating bribery allegations against the Minister of Finance, Simon Mbilinyi, had published a report recommending that he be made accountable for having illegally granted tax exemptions. Mbilinyi subsequently resigned. In October Mrema unexpectedly won a parliamentary by-election in a Dar es Salaam constituency for NCCR—Mageuzi, of which he had become Chairman following his dismissal from Government in 1995; although his campaign had focused on financial impropriety in government, Mrema had recently been accused of having presented false evidence to the parliamentary select committee on corruption in order to undermine the Government's credibility.

In August 1998 a car bomb exploded outside the US embassy in Dar es Salaam (concurrently with a similar attack at the US mission in Nairobi, Kenya); 11 people were killed in Dar es Salaam and some 75 were injured. The attacks were believed to have been co-ordinated by radical international Islamist terrorists led by a Saudi-born dissident, Osama bin Laden, and the USA retaliated by launching air-strikes against targets in Afghanistan and Sudan. Four men were convicted of involvement in the bombings by a court in New York, USA, in May 2001 and were later sentenced to life imprisonment.

In April 1999 Mrema and his faction of NCCR—Mageuzi defected to the Tanzania Labour Party (TLP). Mrema initially assumed the chairmanship of the TLP, but in May he was banned by the High Court from holding any official post in that party. There was speculation that the death in October of former President Nyerere might give rise to increased pressure for a restructuring of the United Republic of Tanzania. This was, to some extent, reinforced by the release in December of the report of a committee charged with assessing public opinion on constitutional reform. While it found that some 96.3% of Zanzibaris and 84.8% of mainland Tanzanians favoured a 'two-tier' government for the United Republic, the committee itself recommended the establishment of a 'three-tier' system. In so doing it was adjudged by President Mkapa to have exceeded its mandate. In February 2000 the National Assembly approved draft legislation to amend the Constitution in accordance with popular opinion as reported by the committee, whereby the President was henceforth to be elected by a majority vote.

At a presidential election held on 29 October 2000 Mkapa was re-elected as President, securing 71.7% of votes cast; Prof. Ibrahim Lipumba, the Chairman of the CUF, won 16.3% of the votes cast, Augustine Mrema 7.8% and John Cheyo 4.2%. The participation rate was 84%. In the following month the CUF and Chadema agreed to form a five-year alliance and field joint candidates for the presidential elections in both the United Republic of Tanzania and in Zanzibar. It was agreed that if either candidate (both from the CUF) won, the respective prime minister would be drawn from Chadema. Candidates from the TLP and NCCR—Mageuzi failed to secure the minimum 200 referees and thus were not allowed to stand for election. At legislative elections, held concurrently, the CCM secured 244 seats in the National Assembly. The largest opposition group to obtain representation was the CUF, with 15 seats; the three other opposition parties (Chadema, the TLP and the UDP) won four, three and two seats, respectively. The polls were declared by international observers to have been freely and fairly conducted. In November Mkapa appointed a new Cabinet, reappointing Frederick Sumaye as Prime Minister.

Tensions on Zanzibar

Presidential and legislative elections, which were also held in Zanzibar and Pemba on 29 October 2000, were marred by

widespread accusations of electoral fraud. Voting in 16 of the islands' 50 constituencies was annulled owing to a lack of ballot papers and voter registration lists. The Zanzibar Electoral Commission (ZEC) announced that new polls would be held in the 16 constituencies (all areas where the CUF enjoyed strong support), and that counting for the presidential elections for both Zanzibar and the United Republic would be delayed until the new results were received. Opposition parties and Commonwealth electoral observers demanded a full re-run of the elections, but this was rejected by the ZEC. Following a week of confusion and violent clashes between the police and opposition supporters, the repeated polls were held on 5 November. Accusations of electoral fraud persisted, and the participation rate was reported to be low. Following the poll, the CCM claimed that it had won 67% of the votes cast (thereby winning 34 seats in the House of Representatives). The CUF refused to recognize the results of the ballot. Despite the concerns of the opposition parties and international observers, the ZEC proclaimed Amani Abeid Karume of the CCM as President of Zanzibar. The CUF refused to recognize Karume as President and demanded that a repeat election be held within four months.

In April 2001 supporters of 12 opposition parties gathered peacefully in Dar es Salaam to demand that the Government hold fresh elections in Zanzibar, draft a new Constitution for the United Republic and establish independent electoral commissions. A similar demonstration was staged in Zanzibar later that month. President Karume, however, continued to reject the opposition's demands. In May 11 members of the Zanzibar House of Representatives and five members of the National Assembly were dismissed from their respective legislatures for having boycotted three successive sittings as part of the CUF's ongoing refusal to recognize the 2000 election results. The Attorney-General rejected subsequent demands from the CUF for their reinstatement. By-elections were held on 15 May 2003, at which the CUF won every seat it contested (amounting to 15 in the National Assembly and 11 in the Zanzibar House of Representatives). CUF candidates were disqualified from contesting six seats in the House of Representatives; these were won by CCM candidates.

In June 2001 it emerged that, following the violence of the 2000 elections, the CCM and the CUF had been holding a series of secret negotiations intended to resolve the political impasse in Zanzibar. The negotiations concluded with the signing of a *muafaka* (peace accord) between the two parties in Zanzibar in October 2001. Shortly afterwards the State withdrew all legal cases related to the post-election demonstrations. In accordance with the CCM-CUF accord, amendments to the Zanzibari Constitution were approved by the House of Representatives in April 2002. The amendments provided for the restructuring of the electoral commission to include opposition representatives (duly appointed in October 2002), the creation of a permanent voters' register and the removal of legislation requiring a person to live in a particular area for five consecutive years in order to qualify as a voter. Also included were the introduction of the right to appeal against High Court decisions and the appointment of a separate director of public prosecutions for Zanzibar.

In late 2003 and early 2004 political tension in Zanzibar intensified ahead of the elections due in late 2005. In November 2003 the CUF Chairman, Lipumba, threatened to obtain a court injunction blocking the 2005 elections unless the register of voters was completed in time, and in April 2004 the leader of the Democratic Party stated his intention to sue the National Electoral Commission (NEC) and the ZEC unless both bodies were reformed to include members of parties other than the CCM and the CUF. Opposition supporters were also concerned that the Government's efforts to encourage mainlanders who had been living in Zanzibar for more than 10 years to register for Zanzibari citizenship (thus making them eligible to vote in Zanzibar) constituted an attempt to manipulate voter registration in favour of the CCM. The Government, in contrast, deplored the circulation of leaflets throughout Zanzibar urging mainlanders to leave and alleged intimidation of mainlanders.

In early 2004 Islamism appeared to be exerting an increasing influence on politics in Zanzibar. Moderate Zanzibari Muslim leaders expressed concern about rising extremism, and in March the island's Mufti, Sheikh Harith bin Kalef, denounced a radical Islamic group, the Zanzibar Union for Awakening and Islamic Forums Community (known as Uamsho), as a political organization that used religion to disguise its efforts to destabilize Zanzibar. A series of bomb attacks followed, targeting Zanzibari power stations, schools, and other government and private property. In late March two bombs exploded in Stone Town, outside the residences of the Mufti and the Minister of Communications and Transport, Zubeir Ali Maulid. A number of Uamsho leaders were subsequently arrested in connection with the bombings.

The 2005 elections

In August 2004, amid growing tension in Zanzibar, the CUF petitioned the UN to dispatch observers to monitor the 2005 elections. The CUF complained that a permanent voters' register had yet to be established, and that the reformed ZEC still lacked a director. Moreover, the Joint Presidential Supervisory Commission (JPSC), established to implement the 2001 *muafaka*, was under investigation following allegations of embezzlement, which had prompted international donors to suspend funding of the Commission.

In February 2005 Lipumba declared his candidacy for the presidential election, at which he would represent the CUF. The CCM elected Jakaya Mrisho Kikwete as its presidential candidate at its national party congress in May. (Under the terms of the Constitution, Mkapa was prohibited from standing for re-election to the presidency.) There were sporadic outbreaks of civil unrest on Zanzibar during the voter registration period, where new legislation requiring voters to have lived in their constituencies for at least three years resulted in some 32,000 potential voters being disqualified. Hamad, the CUF's presidential candidate in Zanzibar, had initially been barred from registering (which would have disqualified him from standing in the election) but appealed successfully against the decision.

Following the death of a candidate, it was announced in October 2005 that the elections on the mainland would be delayed until December. The elections in Zanzibar proceeded as scheduled on 30 October 2005, when Karume was elected President, securing 53.2% of the valid votes cast; Hamad received 46.1% and the four other candidates who contested the presidential election received negligible support. In the legislative elections, the CCM won 31 seats in the House of Representatives, and the CUF 18. The ZEC declared the poll to have been free and fair, while observers from the Commonwealth generally agreed, but recommended investigations into violent incidents and irregularities in voting in Stone Town. The CUF accused the authorities of electoral malpractice and announced an indefinite parliamentary boycott. Karume was sworn in as President of Zanzibar on 2 November.

On mainland Tanzania the delayed presidential and legislative elections were held concurrently on 14 December 2005. Turn-out was officially recorded at 72% and voting proceeded without notable incident. Kikwete was elected President with 80.3% of the votes cast, while Lipumba received 11.7%. The CCM won 207 seats in the National Assembly, the CUF 18, Chadema five and the TLP and UDP one seat each. The CCM received a further 59 of the 75 seats reserved for women (of the remainder, the CUF received 10 and Chadema six) and six of the 10 seats reserved for presidential nominees (four remained vacant). Of the five representatives sent from the Zanzibari legislature, three were from the CCM and two from the CUF. The Attorney-General was also a CCM member. Thus, the CCM's final strength in the National Assembly totalled 276 seats and the CUF's 30; Chadema secured 11 seats and the TLP and UDP one each. At his inauguration, on 21 December, Kikwete stated that his main priority as President would be to resolve the tensions on Zanzibar. On 4 January 2006 Kikwete announced his new Cabinet, appointing Edward Lowassa, hitherto the Minister of Water, Livestock and Development, as Prime Minister. In late June Kikwete assumed the chairmanship of the CCM.

The Kikwete administration

In October 2006 Kikwete effected a reshuffle in which 10 cabinet ministers were reassigned to new portfolios. Further changes to the Cabinet were implemented in early January 2007, following the death of Juma Akukweti, the Minister of State in the Prime Minister's Office, responsible for Parliamentary Affairs; Dr Batilda Burian was named as his replacement. Bernard Kamillius Membe also assumed the foreign affairs and international co-operation portfolio, after the incumbent, Dr Asha Rose Migiro, was appointed as Deputy Secretary-General of the UN.

In January 2008 President Kikwete dismissed the Governor of the central bank, Daudi Balali, after an external audit revealed that some US \$116m. worth of fraudulent payments had been made from the bank's External Payment Arrears account during the 2005/06 financial year. Balali was replaced by his hitherto deputy, Prof. Beno Ndulu, and some 20 bank employees and a

number of prominent businessmen were arrested in connection with the case. In February 2008 Prime Minister Lowassa tendered his resignation in response to the findings of a parliamentary investigation into his administration's awarding of a power-generation contract in 2006; the Minister of Energy and Minerals and the Minister of East African Co-operation also resigned as a result of their alleged involvement. Lowassa denied any wrong-doing and no criminal charges were brought against him. President Kikwete named Mizengo Pinda, hitherto Minister of State in the Prime Minister's Office, as Lowassa's successor. Pinda subsequently named a new Cabinet, which included Membe as Minister of Foreign Affairs and International Co-operation. In April Andrew Chenge resigned as Minister of Infrastructure Development, following reports that he was being investigated in relation to corruption inquiries against the British arms manufacturer, BAE Systems. He was replaced the following month by Dr Shukuru Kawambwa, hitherto Minister of Communication, Science and Technology; that portfolio was assumed by Prof. Peter Msolla.

Meanwhile, at a meeting of representatives from the ruling CCM and the CUF in Zanzibar in February 2008, a proposed power-sharing accord between the two parties was discussed. However, the CCM rejected the proposal in March, claiming that the issue of power-sharing should be decided at a referendum. In early April the CUF staged demonstrations in opposition to the proposed referendum, in an attempt to exert pressure on the CCM to accept the power-sharing agreement.

In October 2008 a peaceful demonstration was held in Dar es Salaam by albino Tanzanians, in response to an increasing number of murders and mutilations committed against people with albinism over the previous year. President Kikwete announced that there would be a campaign to end these killings, which were carried out by people who believed that the body parts of albinos could be used for ritual medicine and witchcraft. Although government statistics indicated that there were only 8,000 albinos in the country, the Albino Society of Tanzania claimed that the number of albinos totalled more than 150,000; several thousand were believed to be living in hiding. In January 2009 the Government revoked the licences of traditional healers and in March Kikwete ordered a national campaign to identify perpetrators of the murders. In September the high court in the north-western Shinyanga district sentenced three men to death, after finding them guilty of the killing of an albino boy in December 2008 (the first conviction for the murder of an albino). At that time it was reported that at least 46 murders of albinos had been committed since 2007, and that 173 people had been arrested on suspicion of killing albino people or trading in their body parts. In November 2009 a further four people were sentenced to death in northern Tanzania for killing an albino man and selling his body parts.

Meanwhile, in April 2009 at least 11 people were killed and several hundred injured in an explosion at a munitions dump at the Mbagala military base, on the outskirts of Dar es Salaam. Demands by the NCCR—Mageuzi for the resignation of the President and the Minister of Defence and National Service were rejected, although an official inquiry into the incident was launched.

In August 2009 the European Union and the USA expressed concerns over shortcomings in the process of voter registration in Zanzibar, which had begun in July in preparation for elections in October 2010. The CUF had accused the authorities of preventing its supporters from registering as voters, while protests and clashes between CUF members and security personnel had been reported, particularly on the island of Pemba. In November 2009 the CUF ended its ongoing boycott of the Zanzibar House of Representatives, prior to the forthcoming elections. It was subsequently announced that CCM and CUF politicians had reached agreement on submitting proposals to allow the formation of a government of national unity at a referendum in Zanzibar. A referendum on the matter was duly held on 31 July: 66.4% of those who voted (some 71.9% of the registered electorate) supported the adoption of constitutional amendments permitting rival parties to form coalition governments.

Presidential and legislative elections were conducted in Tanzania and Zanzibar on 31 October 2010, as scheduled. President Kikwete was decisively re-elected, with 62.8% of votes cast, according to official results, while his closest challenger, Willibrod Peter Slaa of Chadema, received 27.1% of the votes. Slaa claimed that the authorities had perpetrated malpractice in some voting districts; however, the Commonwealth Observer Group endorsed the conduct of the elections. In Zanzibar the incumbent Vice-President of Tanzania, Dr Ali Mohammed Shein of the CCM, was elected President by a narrow margin of 50.1% of votes cast, defeating the CUF candidate, Maalim Seif Sharif Hamad, who took 49.1% of the votes. In the legislative elections in Tanzania, the CCM won 251 of the total 335 seats in the National Assembly, while Chadema obtained 45 seats and the CUF 33 seats. The CCM also secured the highest representation in the Zanzibar House of Representatives, with 28 of the 50 elective seats, the CUF taking the remaining 22 seats. On 3 November Shein was inaugurated as President of Zanzibar. On 6 November Kikwete was sworn in for a second term; Dr Mohamed Gharib Bilal became Vice-President of Tanzania, replacing Shein. When the National Assembly was convened on 12 November, Anne Makinda of the CCM was elected as Speaker, becoming the first woman to assume the post. For the first time, an albino (a CUF candidate) was elected as a deputy of the National Assembly. On 23 November Kikwete formed a new Government, again under the premiership of Pinda and in which most senior members of the previous administration retained their posts. In February 2011 it was reported that at least 17 people had been killed and more than 100 injured following a number of explosions at the Gongola Mboto army base in Dar es Salaam; the incident again increased concerns over the safety of armaments depots in the capital.

In early 2012 the country's Auditor-General issued a 2010/11 report on financial management in the Government, which implicated eight incumbent cabinet ministers and a number of other state officials in the alleged misappropriation of public funds; among those accused of misconduct were the Minister of Finance and Economic Affairs, Mustafa Mkuro, the Minister of Energy and Minerals, William Ngeleje, and the Minister of Industry, Trade and Marketing, Cyril Cham. Following opposition demands for the resignation of the ministers concerned, in April deputies initiated a parliamentary petition to propose a motion of no confidence in Prime Minister Pinda, which received the support of Chadema and the CUF. Later in April, however, the CCM Central Committee announced that it had given its assent to a decision by President Kikwete, reached in consultation with Pinda, that several government ministers be removed following the corruption allegations against them, and endorsed a planned reorganization of the Cabinet. In early May Kikwete accordingly reorganized the Government, replacing Cham, Ngeleje and Mkuro, along with the ministers responsible for tourism, health and transport. New cabinet members notably included William Mgimwa, who was appointed Minister of Finance and Economic Affairs.

Recent developments: Muslim protests

In September 2012 the killing of a television reporter during the police suppression of an unauthorized Chadema rally in Iringa region prompted domestic condemnation. The arrest and disappearance of prominent Muslim clerics provoked rioting in Dar es Salaam and major towns in Zanzibar in October. The head of the Uamsho group (which demanded Zanzibar's secession), Sheikh Ponda Issa Ponda, was subsequently arrested on a number of charges, including incitement to violence. Police dispersed ensuing protests by Muslims demanding his release. Sheikh Ponda was formally charged (together with 49 followers) and was refused bail in mid-November. Meanwhile, on 14 November Kikwete was re-elected Chairman of the CCM, at a party congress in Dodoma. In February 2013 a Roman Catholic priest was killed by unidentified Islamist militants in Zanzibar, following previous attacks against leaders of the island's Christian community. In March a building under construction in central Dar es Salaam collapsed, killing a total of 34 people; Kikwete ordered the local authorities to take action against those responsible. In April a court verdict against Sheikh Ponda and the 49 other defendants was postponed until early May.

Foreign Affairs

Tanzania's relations with Uganda and Kenya were strained throughout the 1970s, particularly after the dissolution of the East African Community (EAC, see p. 460) in 1977. The Tanzania–Kenya border, closed since 1977, was reopened in November 1983, following an agreement on the distribution of the EAC's assets and liabilities. In the following month Tanzania and Kenya agreed to establish full diplomatic relations. The two countries reached agreement on a trade treaty and on the establishment of a joint co-operation commission in 1986. Tanzania pledged its support for the Government of Yoweri Museveni, which took power in Uganda in January of that year, and in November Tanzania began to send military advisers to assist in

the training of Ugandan government troops. In November 1994, meeting in Arusha, the Presidents of Tanzania, Kenya and Uganda established a commission for co-operation; in March 1996 they met again in Nairobi, Kenya, to inaugurate formally the Secretariat of the Permanent Tripartite Commission for East African Co-operation, which aimed to revive the EAC. A treaty for the re-establishment of the EAC, providing for the creation of a free trade area (with the eventual introduction of a single currency), and for the establishment of a regional legislative assembly and court, was formally ratified by the Tanzanian, Kenyan and Ugandan Heads of State in November 1999. The new East African Council of Ministers held its first meeting in Tanzania in January 2001. Talks on integrating the economies of the three EAC members followed, and in March 2004 Mkapa, Museveni, and President Mwai Kibaki of Kenya signed a protocol on the creation of a customs union, eliminating most duties on goods within the EAC, which came into force on 1 January 2005. The EAC was expanded to include Rwanda and Burundi in 2007. In November 2009 the Heads of State of Tanzania, Kenya, Uganda, Rwanda and Burundi signed a common market protocol, allowing the free movement of goods, services, people and capital within the EAC; the protocol entered into force in July 2010.

In April 1994, following the assassination of the Rwandan President, Juvénal Habyarimana, hundreds of thousands of Rwandans fled to Tanzania to escape the atrocities being perpetrated in their homeland. In March 1995 Tanzania banned the admission of further refugees from both Rwanda and Burundi (where violent unrest had erupted in late 1994). The International Criminal Tribunal for Rwanda, authorized by the UN to charge and try Rwandan nationals accused of direct involvement in the genocide perpetrated in that country during 1994, was inaugurated in June 1995 in Arusha. After the Tutsi-led military coup, which took place in Burundi in July 1996 (following the failure of peace talks mediated by former President Nyerere), the Mkapa administration imposed economic sanctions against the new regime of President Pierre Buyoya, in co-operation with other regional governments. Relations between Tanzania and Burundi remained strained, owing both to the presence of Burundian rebels in northern Tanzania, which the Buyoya regime accused the Mkapa administration of supporting, and to the increasing numbers of Burundians seeking refuge in Tanzania throughout 1996 and 1997. Talks between the Buyoya Government and opposition politicians, once again mediated by Nyerere, were convened in Arusha in 1998 and early 1999. The regional economic sanctions that were imposed against Burundi in 1996 were suspended in January 1999. In July 2002, following a meeting between President Mkapa and the Burundian Vice-President, Domitien Ndayizeye, the two countries stated that they were to normalize their relations.

In February 2000 the Tanzanian Government announced that nine refugee camps in the west of the country had become saturated, after instability in Burundi and the Democratic Republic of the Congo (DRC—formerly Zaire) had led to heavy influxes of refugees. In May 2001 the United Nations High Commissioner for Refugees (UNHCR) and the Governments of Tanzania and Burundi signed an agreement to establish a tripartite commission for the voluntary repatriation of Burundian refugees in Tanzania. In August 2003 Burundi and Tanzania agreed to open additional border crossings to facilitate the return of refugees. Following the signature of a peace accord in Burundi in August 2004, the UNHCR-assisted repatriation of refugees increased. In early 2008 the Tanzanian Government announced an initiative (commended by UNHCR), under which the remaining Burundian refugees would be permitted to remain in the country and apply for Tanzanian citizenship or be repatriated. By October 2009 some 53,500 long-term Burundian refugees had been repatriated under the UNHCR programme since March 2008, following the restoration of peace in Burundi. In April 2010 the Government announced that it had granted Tanzanian citizenship to some 162,000 Burundian refugees. At the end of 2012, in accordance with a decision of the tripartite commission, the Mtabila refugee camp in south-western Tanzania was closed and its inhabitants, reported to number about 38,000, repatriated to Burundi, after their refugee status was removed (and the Tanzanian Government ended the offer of citizenship). Following an increase in conflict in the DRC, however, some 63,000 refugees from that country remained in Tanzania, according to UNHCR estimates.

Tanzania's relations with Malawi became severely strained in late 2012, following the revival of a long-standing dispute over sovereignty of Lake Malawi (Lake Nyasa in Tanzania); the Tanzanian Government contested Malawi's ownership under an 1890 accord, and opposed planned Malawian oil exploration projects in the lake (which was believed to hold significant petroleum and gas resources). In October the Government of Malawi suspended scheduled negotiations and expelled the Tanzanian ambassador, after the Tanzanian authorities presented a map that claimed sovereignty over one-half of the lake. In November, however, it was announced that the two states had agreed to international mediation. The African Union (AU) subsequently mandated a high-level team to mediate the dispute, although in April 2013 Malawi announced that it had decided to refer the issue to the International Court of Justice.

In January 2009 it was reported that the Tanzanian Government had pledged to contribute troops to reinforce the joint UN–AU (UNAMID) peace-keeping mission in the Darfur region of western Sudan. In August the Government dispatched 275 military personnel to Darfur; a further 600 Tanzanian troops were deployed in Darfur from February 2010. In February 2009 Chinese President Hu Jintao pledged US $22m. in aid to Tanzania during an official visit to the country. Shortly after he assumed the Chinese presidency, Xi Jinping visited Tanzania at the beginning of a regional tour in March 2013, when he signed 16 trade agreements, including for rehabilitation of the country's hospitals and ports.

CONSTITUTION AND GOVERNMENT

Under the provisions of the 1977 Constitution, with subsequent amendments, legislative power is held by the unicameral National Assembly, whose members serve for a term of five years. There is constitutional provision for both directly elected members (chosen by universal suffrage) and nominated members (including five members elected by and from the Zanzibar House of Representatives). The number of directly elected members exceeds the number of nominated members. The Electoral Commission may review and, if necessary, increase the number of constituencies before every general election. Executive power lies with the President, elected by popular vote for five years. The President must be at least 40 years of age and his mandate is limited to a maximum of two five-year terms. The President appoints a Vice-President, to assist him in carrying out his functions, and presides over the Cabinet, which is composed of a Prime Minister and other ministers who are appointed from among the members of the National Assembly. In May 1992 the United Republic's Constitution was amended to legalize a multi-party political system.

Zanzibar has its own administration for internal affairs, and the amended Zanzibar Constitution, which came into force in January 1985, provides for the President, elected by universal adult suffrage, to hold office for a maximum of two five-year terms, and for the House of Representatives, of 45–55 members, to be directly elected by universal adult suffrage. The President of Zanzibar appoints the Chief Minister, and the two co-operate in choosing the other members of the Supreme Revolutionary Council, which has a maximum of 20 members.

REGIONAL AND INTERNATIONAL CO-OPERATION

Tanzania is a member of the African Union (AU, see p. 191) and of the Southern African Development Community (see p. 434). Tanzania is a founder member (with Kenya and Uganda) of the restored East African Community (EAC, see p. 460).

Tanzania became a member of the UN in 1964. As a contracting party to the General Agreement on Tariffs and Trade, Tanzania joined the World Trade Organization (WTO, see p. 444) on its establishment in 1995. Tanzania participates in the Group of 77 (G77, see p. 461) developing countries.

ECONOMIC AFFAIRS

In 2011, according to estimates by the World Bank, mainland Tanzania's gross national income (GNI), measured at average 2009–11 prices, was US $24,2916m., equivalent to $540 per head (or $1,510 per head on an international purchasing-power parity basis). During 2002–11, it was estimated, the population of the country as a whole increased at an average annual rate of 2.9%, while gross domestic product (GDP) per head grew, in real terms, by an average of 4.0% per year. According to official figures, overall GDP increased, in real terms, at an average annual rate of 7.0% in 2002–11; growth was 6.4% in 2011.

Agriculture (including hunting, forestry and fishing) contributed an estimated 27.3% of Tanzania's GDP in 2011, according to provisional official figures, and employed some 74.6% of the engaged labour force (including Zanzibar) in 2006. According to FAO estimates, the sector engaged 74.4% of the total labour force in mid-2013. The principal cash crops are coffee (which provided 4.8% of export revenues in 2010), cotton, cashew nuts and cloves (Zanzibar's most important export, cultivated on the island of Pemba—they provided 0.2% of export revenues in 2010). Tobacco farming has increased steadily in recent years, and by 2007 Tanzania had become the third largest producer in Africa, according to official sources. In 2010 exports of tobacco accounted for 3.5% of export revenue. Other cash crops include tea, sisal, pyrethrum, coconuts, sugar and cardamom. Exports of cut flowers (grown in the vicinity of Kilimanjaro Airport and freighted to Europe) commenced in the mid-1990s. Seaweed production is an important activity in Zanzibar. Farmers have been encouraged to produce essential food crops, most importantly cassava and maize. Cattle-rearing is also significant. A large proportion of agricultural output is produced by subsistence farmers. The predominance of illegal logging activities remains a concern, and timber exports have consequently been subject to intermittent bans, owing to the threat of deforestation and lost revenues through unofficial foreign sales. Tanzania's agricultural GDP increased at an average annual rate of 4.1% during 2002–11, according to official figures. Agricultural GDP grew by 3.4% in 2011.

According to provisional figures, industry (including mining, manufacturing, construction and power) contributed an estimated 24.8% of Tanzania's GDP in 2011; the sector employed 5.0% of the United Republic's working population in 2006. During 2002–11 industrial GDP increased by an average of 9.0% per year; growth in 2011 was 6.9%.

Mining provided an estimated 3.6% of Tanzania's GDP in 2011. The sector employed 0.6% of the working population on both Zanzibar and mainland Tanganyika in 2006. Gold, diamonds, other gemstones (including rubies and sapphires), salt, phosphates, coal, gypsum, tin, kaolin, limestone and graphite are mined, and plans are under way to exploit the country's large offshore reserves of natural gas. Other mineral deposits include nickel, silver, cobalt, copper, soda ash, iron ore and uranium. Petroleum was discovered on Tanzania's coastal belt in the 1960s, but was only recently being considered seriously by companies searching for sources of petroleum outside the Middle East. According to official figures, the GDP of the mining sector increased by an average of 9.1% per year in 2002–11; it grew by 2.2% in 2011.

Manufacturing contributed 10.1% of Tanzania's GDP in 2011, according to provisional figures. The sector employed 3.1% of the working population on Zanzibar and mainland Tanganyika in 2006. The most important manufacturing activities are food-processing, textile production, cigarette production and brewing. Pulp and paper, fertilizers, cement, clothing, footwear, tyres, batteries, pharmaceuticals, paint, bricks and tiles and electrical goods are also produced, while other activities include oil-refining, metal-working, vehicle assembly and engineering. Tanzania's manufacturing GDP increased at an average annual rate of 8.8% in 2002–11; the sector grew by 7.8% in 2011.

According to provisional official figures, construction contributed an estimated 8.7% of Tanzania's GDP in 2011. The sector employed 1.2% of the United Republic's working population in 2006. The GDP of the construction sector increased by an average of 10.3% per year in 2002–11; growth in the sector in 2011 was 9.0%.

Energy is derived principally from hydroelectric power, which supplied 60.2% of Tanzania's electricity in 2009; however, dependence upon this source means that the electricity supply remains vulnerable to drought conditions. The contribution of petroleum to the national grid increased from 1.5% of total supply in 2004 to 38.2% in 2005. In September 2008 a 70-MW gas-fired power plant on Songo Songo Island became operational. Another plant, with a projected capacity of 45 MW, was completed in Tegeta in 2009. Natural gas had not previously been used to generate electricity in any significant quantity in Tanzania. Imports of petroleum and petroleum products accounted for 27.4% of the total value of imports in 2010.

The services sector contributed an estimated 47.9% of Tanzania's GDP in 2011, according to provisional official figures. The sector employed 20.3% of the United Republic's working population in 2006. Tourism is an important potential growth sector: tourism receipts were approximately US $1,457m. in 2011. According to official figures, the GDP of the services sector increased by an average of 7.9% per year in 2002–11. Growth in the sector was 7.9% in 2011.

In 2011 Tanzania recorded a visible merchandise trade deficit of US $4,729.8m. and there was a deficit of $4,561.1m. on the current account of the balance of payments. In 2010 the principal sources of imports were India (providing 11.2% of total imports), the People's Republic of China, South Africa, the United Arab Emirates, Japan, Switzerland and Singapore. The main markets for exports in that year were Switzerland and Liechtenstein (which, together, purchased 17.5% of total exports), China, South Africa, Kenya, India and Japan. The principal exports in 2010 were crude materials (inedible, except fuels), gold (non-monetary, unwrought or semi-manufactured), food and live animals, and basic manufactures. The principal imports were machinery and transport equipment (largely road vehicles), mineral fuels, lubricants, etc., basic manufactures, chemicals and related products, and food and live animals.

A budgetary deficit of 19,689,000m. shillings was envisaged for the financial year ending 30 June 2012. Tanzania's general government gross debt was 13,790,168m. shillings in 2010, equivalent to 42.7% of GDP. At the end of 2010 Tanzania's external debt totalled US $8,664m., of which $5,572m. was public and publicly guaranteed debt. In that year, the cost of servicing long-term public and publicly guaranteed debt and repayments to the IMF was equivalent to 3.0% of the value of exports of goods, services and income (excluding workers' remittances). The annual rate of inflation for Tanganyika averaged 7.8% in 2002–11; consumer prices there increased by 5.4% in 2010 and by 12.7% in 2011. The annual rate of inflation for Zanzibar averaged 6.4% in 2000–05; consumer prices on the islands increased by 9.8% in 2005.

Although Tanzania had by the mid-2000s become one of Africa's better-performing economies, it remained encumbered by a high level of external debt and dependence on foreign aid. (Tanzania has qualified for debt relief under the IMF's initiative for heavily indebted poor countries.) Following his election in 2005, President Jakaya Kikwete stated that he would continue the free-market policies of his predecessor, and GDP growth subsequently increased. In June 2010 the IMF approved a new three-year Policy Support Instrument (PSI) for Tanzania. Following the establishment of an East African Community (EAC, see p. 460) customs union in 2005, a common market protocol allowing the free movement of goods, services, people and capital between Tanzania and the four other EAC member states entered into force in July 2010. In August 2011 the Government adopted an emergency power plan in response to widespread drought-related power shortages, which, however, was subsequently criticized as having not been fully implemented; in January 2012 electricity tariffs were raised by 40% in order to cover the higher generating costs. Meanwhile, in September 2011 China's Sichuan Hongda Group signed a US $3,000m. joint-venture agreement with the Tanzanian Government (regarded as the largest single investment agreement in East Africa) for the development of a coal-mining project in the Mchuchuma region and an iron-ore project in Liganga, in the south of the country. In July 2012 the IMF extended a precautionary 18-month arrangement totalling $224.9m., under its stand-by credit facility. Following its fifth review of economic performance under the PSI-supported programme, in January 2013 the IMF commended the continued progress made by the Tanzanian authorities in the implementation of fiscal adjustment measures; GDP growth of about 7% was projected for 2013, while inflation was expected to return to single digits in that year. In February the Government announced that it was to draw $114.2m. made available under the credit arrangement. (Growth in the Zanzibar economy, meanwhile, remained strong, at 6%–7% in 2012, based on agriculture, particularly the clove industry, and tourism.) Following vast offshore discoveries of natural gas in late 2012 and early 2013, total gas reserves of an estimated 40,000,000m. cu ft were anticipated to double by early 2015, and ultimately to transform Tanzania's economy; the Government announced that it intended to strengthen regulations prior to issuing exploration permits later in 2013. In April 2013 the Government granted the first licence for uranium-mining, although non-governmental organizations expressed concerns about the lack of regulatory framework.

PUBLIC HOLIDAYS

2014: 1 January (New Year's Day), 12 January (Zanzibar Revolution Day), 13 January* (Maulid, Birth of the Prophet), 5 February (Chama Cha Mapinduzi Day), 18–21 April (Easter), 26 April (Union Day), 1 May (International Labour Day), 7 July (Saba Saba, Industry's Day), 28 July* (Id El Fitr, end of Ramadan), 8 August (Peasants' Day), 26 August (Sultan's Birthday)†, 4 October* (Id El Haji, Feast of the Sacrifice), 24 October* (Muharram, New Year), 29 October (Naming Day), 9 December (Independence Day), 25–26 December (Christmas).

* These holidays are dependent on the Islamic lunar calendar and may vary by one or two days from the dates given.

† Zanzibar only.

Statistical Survey

Sources (unless otherwise stated): Economic and Research Policy Dept, Bank of Tanzania, POB 2939, Dar es Salaam; tel. (22) 2110946; fax (22) 2113325; e-mail info@hq.bot-tz.org; internet www.bot-tz.org; National Bureau of Statistics, POB 796, Dar es Salaam; tel. (22) 2122722; fax (22) 2130852; e-mail dg@nbs.go.tz; internet www.nbs.go.tz.

Area and Population

AREA, POPULATION AND DENSITY

Area (sq km)	945,087*
Population (census results)	
25 August 2002	34,443,603
26 August 2012 (preliminary)	
Males	21,869,990
Females	23,058,933
Total	44,928,923†
Density (per sq km) at 2012 census	47.5

* 364,900 sq miles. Of this total, Tanganyika (mainland) is 942,626 sq km (363,950 sq miles), and Zanzibar 2,461 sq km (950 sq miles).

† Tanganyika (mainland) 43,625,354, Zanzibar 1,303,569.

POPULATION BY AGE AND SEX
(UN estimates at mid-2013)

	Males	Females	Total
0–14	11,127,839	10,954,102	22,081,941
15–64	12,745,303	12,751,315	25,496,618
65 and over	702,128	872,315	1,574,443
Total	**24,575,270**	**24,577,732**	**49,153,002**

Source: UN, *World Population Prospects: The 2010 Revision.*

REGIONS
(at 2012 census, preliminary)

	Area (sq km)*	Population	Density (per sq km)
Arusha	36,486	1,694,310	46.4
Dar es Salaam . . .	1,393	4,364,541	3,133.2
Dodoma	41,311	2,083,588	50.4
Geita†	n.a.	1,739,530	n.a.
Iringa†	56,864‡	941,238	16.6
Kagera†	28,388‡	2,458,023	86.6
Katavi†	n.a.	564,604	n.a.
Kigoma	37,037	2,127,930	57.5
Kilimanjaro	13,309	1,640,087	123.2
Lindi	66,046	864,652	13.1
Njombe†	n.a.	702,097	n.a.
Manyara	45,820	1,425,131	31.1
Mara	19,566	1,743,830	89.1
Mbeya	60,350	2,707,410	44.9
Morogoro	70,799	2,218,492	31.3
Mtwara	16,707	1,270,854	76.1
Mwanza†	19,592‡	2,772,509	141.5
Pwani	32,407	1,098,668	33.9
North Pemba§ . . .	574	211,732	368.9
North Unguja§ . . .	470	187,455	398.8
Rukwa†	68,635‡	1,004,539	14.6
Ruvuma	63,498	1,376,891	21.7
Shinyanga†	50,781‡	1,534,808	30.2
Simiyu†	n.a.	1,584,157	n.a.
Singida	49,341	1,370,637	27.8
South Pemba§ . . .	332	195,116	587.7
South Unguja§ . . .	854	115,588	135.3
Urban West§	230	593,678	2,581.2
Tabora	76,151	2,291,623	30.1
Tanga	26,808	2,045,205	76.3
Total	**883,749**	**44,928,923**	**50.8**

* Land area only, excluding inland water.
† Four new regions were created in March 2012: Geita was formed from territory previously included in Kagera, Mwanza and Shinyanga regions, Katavi was formed from territory previously included in Rukwa region, Njombe was formed from territory previously included in Iringa region, and Simiyu was formed from territory previously included in Mwanza and Shinyanga regions; land area data for the new regional configuration were not available.
‡ Land area prior to regional reorganization in March 2012.
§ Part of the autonomous territory of Zanzibar.

PRINCIPAL TOWNS
(estimated population at mid-1988)

Dar es Salaam*	.	1,360,850	Mbeya	152,844
Mwanza . . .		223,013	Arusha . . .	134,708
Dodoma (capital)*	.	203,833	Morogoro . . .	117,760
Tanga . . .		187,455	Shinyanga . . .	100,724
Zanzibar . . .		157,634		

* Although Dodoma is officially the administrative capital, Dar es Salaam is still considered the commercial capital, and many government offices remain there.

Source: UN, *Demographic Yearbook*.

Mid-2011 (incl. suburbs, UN estimate): Dodoma (capital) 226,139 (Source: UN, *World Urbanization Prospects: The 2011 Revision*).

BIRTHS AND DEATHS
(annual averages, UN estimates)

	1995–2000	2000–05	2005–10
Birth rate (per 1,000)	41.7	41.7	41.6
Death rate (per 1,000)	14.8	13.5	11.5

Source: UN, *World Population Prospects: The 2010 Revision*.

Life expectancy (years at birth): 58.2 (males 57.2; females 59.1) in 2011 (Source: World Bank, World Development Indicators database).

ECONOMICALLY ACTIVE POPULATION
(labour force survey, '000 persons aged 15 years and over, 2006)

	Males	Females	Total
Agriculture, hunting and forestry .	6,064.8	7,120.3	13,185.1
Fishing	184.6	25.0	209.6
Mining and quarrying . . .	90.8	14.1	104.9
Manufacturing	332.9	232.2	565.1
Electricity, gas and water supply .	13.5	3.5	17.0
Construction	204.8	6.7	211.5
Wholesale and retail trade and restaurants and hotels . . .	907.7	665.0	1,572.7
Hotel and restaurants . . .	98.5	279.0	377.5
Transport, storage and communications	245.0	13.1	258.1
Financial intermediation . . .	11.3	6.2	17.5
Real estate, renting and business activities	69.0	13.0	82.0
Public administration and defence; compulsory social security . .	157.4	27.3	184.7
Education	126.9	98.7	225.6
Health and social work . . .	46.1	59.1	105.2
Community, social and personal services	88.3	38.2	126.5
Households with employed persons	138.2	563.3	701.5
Total employed	**8,779.8**	**9,164.7**	**17,944.6**
Unemployed	274.3	602.7	877.0
Total labour force	**9,054.2**	**9,767.4**	**18,821.5**

Source: ILO.

2011 (labour force survey, persons aged 15 years and over): Total employed 19,783,648; Unemployed 2,368,672; Total labour force 22,152,320.

Mid-2013 (estimates in '000): Agriculture, etc. 18,309; Total labour force 24,625 (Source: FAO).

Health and Welfare

KEY INDICATORS

Total fertility rate (children per woman, 2010) . . .	5.5
Under-5 mortality rate (per 1,000 live births, 2010) . . .	76
HIV/AIDS (% of persons aged 15–49, 2009)	5.6
Physicians (per 1,000 head, 2004)	0.02
Hospital beds (per 1,000 head, 2010)	7.0
Health expenditure (2009): US $ per head (PPP)	73
Health expenditure (2009): % of GDP	5.5
Health expenditure (2009): public (% of total)	66.1
Access to water (% of persons, 2010)	53
Access to sanitation (% of persons, 2010)	10
Total carbon dioxide emissions ('000 metric tons, 2008) . .	6,464.9
Carbon dioxide emissions per head (metric tons, 2008) . .	0.2
Human Development Index (2011): ranking	152
Human Development Index (2011): value	0.466

For sources and definitions, see explanatory note on p. vi.

Agriculture

PRINCIPAL CROPS
('000 metric tons)

	2009	2010	2011
Wheat	82.4	62.4	112.7
Rice, paddy	1,334.8	2,650.1	2,248.3
Maize	3,326.2	4,733.1	4,340.8
Millet	312.4	350.9	235.0*
Sorghum	709.3	798.5	806.6
Potatoes	861.0	1,472.6	1,555.5
Sweet potatoes	1,417.4	2,424.2	3,573.3
Cassava (Manioc)	5,916.4	4,547.9	4,646.5
Sugar cane*	2,370.0	2,400.0	2,500.0
Beans, dry	773.7	867.5	675.9
Cashew nuts, with shell . .	79.1	74.2	75.0*
Groundnuts, with shell . .	348.0	465.3	651.4
Coconuts*	577.1	570.0	550.0
Oil palm fruit*	65.0	69.5	71.0

—*continued*	2009	2010	2011
Seed cotton*	267.0	305.0	315.0
Tomatoes*	203.9	235.0	250.0
Onions, dry* . . .	29.6	53.0	69.1
Bananas	3,006.4	3,155.7	3,143.8
Plantains*	518.0	660.0	728.9
Guavas, mangoes and			
mangosteens . . .	320.0	325.0*	330.0*
Pineapples*	47.6	40.0	45.7
Coffee, green . . .	62.4	40.0	60.6
Tea	34.2	33.2	32.0
Cloves*	8.3	8.3	6.8
Tobacco, unmanufactured . .	58.7	60.9	130.0

* FAO estimate(s).

Aggregate production ('000 metric tons, may include official, semi-official or estimated data): Total cereals 5,807.3 in 2009, 8,636.7 in 2010, 7,779.3 in 2011; Total roots and tubers 8,205.8 in 2009, 8,456.1 in 2010, 9,786.8 in 2011; Total vegetables (incl. melons) 1,750.5 in 2009, 1,913.3 in 2010, 2,182.0 in 2011; Total fruits (excl. melons) 4,158.8 in 2009, 4,494.5 in 2010, 4,557.4 in 2011.

Source: FAO.

LIVESTOCK
('000 head, year ending September)

	2009	2010	2011
Asses*	182	182	182
Cattle	19,100	19,246	21,300
Pigs*	490	495	500
Sheep*	4,150	4,200	4,300
Goats*	13,600	13,600	15,200
Chickens*	33,000	33,500	34,000

* FAO estimates.

Source: FAO.

LIVESTOCK PRODUCTS
('000 metric tons)

	2009	2010	2011
Cattle meat* . . .	290.0	291.6	308.0
Sheep meat* . . .	11.9	12.1	12.3
Goat meat* . . .	32.4	32.5	34.8
Pig meat* . . .	13.9	14.0	14.1
Chicken meat* . . .	53.3	55.0	55.5
Cows' milk . . .	1,604.1	1,650.0*	1,650.0*
Goats' milk . . .	106.1	108.0	108.0
Hen eggs* . . .	31.2	32.5	32.5
Honey*	33.4	34.1	34.1

* FAO estimate(s).

Source: FAO.

Forestry

ROUNDWOOD REMOVALS
('000 cubic metres, excluding bark, FAO estimates)

	2009	2010	2011
Sawlogs, veneer logs and logs for			
sleepers . . .	317	317	317
Pulpwood	153	153	153
Other industrial wood . .	1,844	1,844	1,844
Fuel wood	22,588	22,836	23,069
Total	24,902	25,150	25,383

Source: FAO.

SAWNWOOD PRODUCTION
('000 cubic metres, including railway sleepers, FAO estimates)

	1992	1993	1994
Coniferous (softwood) . . .	26	21	13
Broadleaved (hardwood) . .	22	18	11
Total	48	39	24

1995–2011: Production assumed to be unchanged from 1994 (FAO estimates).

Source: FAO.

Fishing
('000 metric tons, live weight)

	2008	2009	2010
Capture	326.8	316.2	342.5
Tilapias	35.6	38.7	44.7
Nile perch . . .	94.2	101.1	97.2
Dagaas	13.0	10.3	15.2
Other freshwater fishes . .	133.3	108.2	119.7
Sardinellas . . .	11.8	14.3	8.0
Aquaculture	0.2*	0.2*	0.5
Total catch	327.0*	316.4*	342.9

* FAO estimate.

Note: Figures exclude aquatic plants ('000 metric tons): 5.3 (FAO estimate) (capture 0.3, aquaculture 5.0) in 2008; 5.8 (FAO estimate) (capture 0.3, aquaculture 5.5) in 2009; 7.3 (FAO estimate) (capture 0.3, aquaculture 7.0) in 2010. Also excluded are crocodiles, recorded by number rather than by weight. The number of Nile crocodiles caught was: 1,784 in 2008; 790 in 2009; 1,796 in 2010.

Source: FAO.

Mining
('000 metric tons, unless otherwise indicated)

	2008	2009	2010
Coal (bituminous) . . .	15.2	—	—
Diamonds ('000 carats)* . .	237.7	181.9	80.5
Gold (refined, kilograms) . .	36,434.0	39,112.0	39,448.0
Salt	25.9	28.4	24.3
Gypsum and anhydrite . .	55.7	8.1	18.6
Limestone, crushed . .	1,281.8	1,370.9	928.5
Pozzolanic materials . .	260.4	171.9	45.2
Sand†	8,500.0	8,500.0	8,500.0

* Estimated at 85% gem-quality and 15% industrial-quality stones. Excluding smuggled artisanal production.
† Estimates.

Source: US Geological Survey.

Industry

SELECTED PRODUCTS
(Tanganyika, '000 metric tons, unless otherwise indicated)

	2007	2008	2009*
Refined sugar . . .	285.6	287.1	292.3
Cigarettes (million) . .	5,821	6,101	5,831
Beer (million litres) . .	318	294	289
Textiles (million sq m) . .	169	80	84
Cement	1,632	1,756	1,941
Rolled steel . . .	38	68	83
Iron sheets . . .	36	32	51
Sisal ropes . . .	7.0	7.8	7.9
Paints ('000 litres) . .	17,451	24,857	25,781

* Provisional figures.

Selected Products for Zanzibar ('000 metric tons, 2008, unless otherwise indicated): Beverages (million litres) 9.4; Animal feeds (metric tons) 0.2; Coconut oil (metric tons) 77; Bread ('000 loaves, 2007) 77; Copra cake (metric tons, 2007) 49.

Electric energy (Tanganyika and Zanzibar, kWh million): 4,175 in 2007; 4,414 in 2008; 4,628 in 2009 (Source: UN Industrial Commodity Statistics Database).

Finance

CURRENCY AND EXCHANGE RATES

Monetary Units
100 cents = 1 Tanzanian shilling.

Sterling, Dollar and Euro Equivalents (31 December 2012)
£1 sterling = 2,480.02 Tanzanian shillings;
US $1 = 1,571.62 Tanzanian shillings;
€1 = 2,073.60 Tanzanian shillings;
10,000 Tanzanian shillings = £4.03 = $6.36 = €4.82.

Average Exchange Rate (Tanzanian shillings per US $)
2009	1,320.31
2010	1,409.27
2011	1,572.12

BUDGET
('000 million shillings, year ending 30 June)*

Revenue†	2010/11	2011/12‡	2012/13§
Tax revenue	5,296	6,480	8,070
Import duties	449	498	648
Value-added tax	1,531	1,975	2,457
Excises	1,052	1,029	1,384
Income tax	1,660	2,247	2,732
Other taxes	604	732	849
Non-tax revenue	443	741	1,007
Total	5,739	7,221	9,077

Expenditure	2010/11	2011/2012‡	2012/13§
Recurrent expenditure	6,690	6,990	9,060
Wages	2,346	2,722	3,147
Interest	353	436	660
Goods, services and transfers	3,991	3,831	5,252
Development expenditure and net lending	2,749	3,775	4,533
Local	985	1,872	2,214
Foreign	1,764	1,902	2,319
Total	9,439	10,765	13,592

* Figures refer to the Tanzania Government, excluding the revenue and expenditure of the separate Zanzibar Government.
† Excluding grants received ('000 million shillings): 1,627 in 2010/11; 1,855 in 2011/12 (preliminary figure); 1,861 in 2012/13 (projection).
‡ Preliminary figures.
§ Projections.
Source: IMF, *United Republic of Tanzania: Fifth Review Under the Policy Support Instrument, First Review Under the Standby Credit Facility, and Requests for a Waiver of Nonobservance of a Performance and Assessment Criterion, Rephasing of the Standby Credit Facility Arrangement and Modification of Performance and Assessment Criteria—Staff Report; Press Release on the Executive Board Discussion; and Statement by the Executive Director for Tanzania* (January 2013).

INTERNATIONAL RESERVES
(excl. gold, US $ million at 31 December)

	2009	2010	2011
IMF special drawing rights	248.8	243.8	240.7
Reserve position in IMF	15.7	15.4	15.4
Foreign exchange	3,205.9	3,645.4	3,470.1
Total	3,470.4	3,904.6	3,726.2

Source: IMF, *International Financial Statistics*.

MONEY SUPPLY
('000 million shillings at 31 December)

	2009	2010	2011
Currency outside depository corporations	1,566.75	1,897.13	2,235.83
Transferable deposits	3,288.92	4,400.03	5,565.55
Other deposits	3,924.47	4,715.50	5,219.94
Broad money	8,780.14	11,012.66	13,021.32

Source: IMF, *International Financial Statistics*.

COST OF LIVING
(Consumer Price Index)

Tanganyika
(base: 2000 = 100)

	2007	2008	2009
Food (incl. beverages)	152.9	172.2	202.4
Fuel, light and water	170.5	188.7	185.6
Clothing (incl. footwear)	120.9	122.6	130.3
Rent	136.0	139.3	156.7
All items (incl. others)	146.2	161.2	180.8

All items: 190.7 in 2010; 216.4 in 2011.

Source: ILO.

Zanzibar
(base: 2001 = 100)

	2002	2003
Food (incl. beverages)	106.9	116.7
Fuel, light and water	100.0	106.0
Clothing (incl. footwear)	106.7	128.3
Rent	104.9	118.0
All items (incl. others)	105.2	114.7

2004: Food (incl. beverages) 128.6; All items (incl. others) 124.0.
2005: Food (incl. beverages) 143.7; All items (incl. others) 136.1.
Source: ILO.

NATIONAL ACCOUNTS
('000 million shillings at current prices)

Expenditure on the Gross Domestic Product

	2009	2010	2011*
Government final consumption expenditure	4,926.8	5,208.2	6,145.7
Private final consumption expenditure	18,476.8	20,209.4	24,815.7
Changes in inventories	152.3	164.8	228.0
Gross fixed capital formation	8,021.0	10,177.7	13,534.1
Total domestic expenditure	31,576.9	35,760.1	44,723.5
Exports of goods and services	6,553.2	8,988.3	11,656.8
Less Imports of goods and services	9,917.3	12,455.0	18,847.2
GDP in purchasers' values	28,212.6	32,293.5	37,533.0

Gross Domestic Product by Economic Activity

	2009	2010	2011*
Agriculture, hunting, forestry and fishing	7,344.9	8,241.8	9,429.2
Mining and quarrying	941.1	1,072.8	1,255.2
Manufacturing	2,434.8	2,899.1	3,482.1
Electricity, gas and water	584.0	684.8	810.7
Construction	2,233.9	2,569.0	2,990.3
Wholesale and retail trade, hotels and restaurants	3,976.9	4,663.6	5,454.1
Transport and communications	2,005.9	2,338.3	2,807.4
Financial intermediation	477.5	567.8	666.2
Real estate, renting and business activities	2,532.8	2,848.9	3,233.2
Public administration and defence	2,282.8	2,579.5	2,985.6
Education	392.5	455.3	519.8
Health and social work	455.0	532.3	627.5
Other community, social and personal service activities	176.8	202.4	232.1
Sub-total	25,838.9	29,655.7	34,493.3
Less Imputed bank service charge	328.5	358.0	432.3
Indirect taxes, less subsidies	2,702.4	2,995.8	3,471.9
GDP in purchasers' values	28,212.6	32,293.5	37,533.0

* Provisional.

BALANCE OF PAYMENTS
(US $ million)

	2009	2010	2011
Exports of goods	3,298.1	4,324.3	5,097.7
Imports of goods	−5,834.1	−7,165.5	−9,827.5
Balance on goods	−2,536.1	−2,841.2	−4,729.8
Exports of services	1,854.6	2,045.7	2,362.5
Imports of services	−1,709.1	−1,852.4	−2,165.3
Balance on goods and services	−2,390.5	−2,647.9	−4,532.6
Primary income received . .	161.1	160.1	184.2
Primary income paid . . .	−458.9	−487.0	−544.5
Balance on goods, services and primary income	−2,688.3	−2,974.8	−4,892.9
Secondary income received . .	301.3	332.1	424.5
Secondary income paid . . .	−68.4	−79.0	−92.7
Current balance	−2,455.4	−2,721.7	−4,561.1
Capital account (net) . . .	446.6	536.4	638.3
Direct investment liabilities . .	952.6	1,022.8	1,095.4
Portfolio investment assets . .	0.4	0.1	0.7
Portfolio investment liabilities .	3.0	3.2	3.4
Other investment assets . . .	−251.2	−205.8	−32.2
Other investment liabilities . .	1,391.2	1,389.6	1,735.4
Net errors and omissions . .	−373.6	−473.7	350.4
Reserves and related items .	−286.4	−449.2	−769.8

Source: IMF, *International Financial Statistics*.

External Trade

PRINCIPAL COMMODITIES
(US $ million)

Imports c.i.f.	2008	2009	2010
Food and live animals . .	366.7	402.2	539.0
Cereals and cereal preparations .	258.4	281.0	376.2
Wheat and meslin, unmilled .	182.0	209.3	291.9
Mineral fuels, lubricants, etc. .	2,381.0	1,478.2	2,211.5
Petroleum, petroleum products, etc.	2,359.0	1,467.1	2,196.3
Petroleum products, refined .	2,337.7	1,430.2	2,152.9
Animal and vegetable oils, fats and waxes	223.1	130.8	212.0
Fixed vegetable oils and fats . .	195.0	120.9	203.5
Palm oil	175.5	106.1	173.3
Chemicals and related products	938.2	783.1	1,049.1
Medicinal and pharmaceutical products	145.3	111.0	160.7
Plastics in primary forms . .	237.6	218.8	351.2
Basic manufactures	1,244.2	1,014.2	1,149.9
Iron and steel	399.9	323.5	347.2
Other metal manufactures . .	255.5	210.7	228.4
Machinery and transport equipment	2,488.6	2,295.9	2,381.0
Power generating machinery and equipment	170.2	111.2	102.8
Rotating electric plant, and parts thereof	98.3	47.8	59.6
Machinery specialized for particular industries . . .	503.2	477.7	472.0

Imports c.i.f.—*continued*	2008	2009	2010
General industrial machinery, equipment and parts . . .	264.7	285.4	272.8
Telecommunications, sound recording and reproducing equipment	306.2	220.1	176.0
Telecommunication equipment, parts and accessories . . .	286.4	200.5	151.0
Other electrical machinery, apparatus and appliances, and parts	206.5	286.0	249.7
Road vehicles	742.4	755.1	868.7
Passenger motor vehicles, excl. buses	222.5	239.2	300.6
Lorries and special purpose motor vehicles	254.0	243.8	246.3
Vehicles for the transportation of goods or materials . .	237.9	218.4	221.2
Miscellaneous manufactured articles	312.7	294.9	327.5
Total (incl. others)	8,087.7	6,530.8	8,012.9

Exports f.o.b.	2008	2009	2010
Food and live animals . . .	597.2	571.4	686.9
Fish, crustaceans, molluscs and preparations thereof . . .	140.6	127.8	141.5
Fish, fresh, chilled or frozen .	119.3	106.8	121.4
Fish fillets, fresh or chilled .	61.3	48.7	44.1
Fish fillets, frozen	55.0	55.8	71.5
Cereals and cereal preparations .	63.4	22.8	79.9
Vegetables and fruit	157.8	159.4	229.4
Fruit and nuts, fresh, dried .	78.7	64.2	99.0
Cashew nuts, fresh or dried .	69.4	90.2	125.1
Coffee, tea, cocoa, spices, and manufactures thereof . . .	188.9	227.0	193.7
Coffee and coffee substitutes .	105.9	117.4	118.7
Coffee, not roasted; coffee husks and skins	100.0	111.2	102.3
Spices	14.7	21.2	8.7
Cloves	14.3	18.0	8.5
Beverages and tobacco . . .	189.8	106.7	152.5
Tobacco and tobacco manufactures	180.6	97.9	141.2
Tobacco, wholly or partly stripped	171.6	90.0	111.9
Crude materials, inedible, except fuels	643.1	811.7	1,268.2
Textile fibres (not wool tops) and their wastes (not in yarn) . .	138.9	125.3	99.7
Raw cotton, excl. linters, not carded or combed . . .	80.9	89.0	72.4
Metalliferous ores and metal scrap	364.3	507.8	971.5
Ores and concentrates of precious metals	349.5	497.7	461.5
Basic manufactures	362.5	259.3	351.9
Non-metallic mineral manufactures	101.6	63.5	79.5
Pearl, precious and semi-precious stones, unworked or worked .	73.5	40.3	37.4
Diamonds cut or otherwise worked, but not mounted or set	20.1	18.4	8.6
Gold, non-monetary, unwrought or semi-manufactured	759.4	818.6	966.1
Total (incl. others)	3,121.1	2,982.4	4,050.5

Source: UN, *International Trade Statistics Yearbook*.

2010/11 (US $ million, year ending 30 June, estimates): Imports f.o.b. 8,012; Exports f.o.b. 4,896 (Source: IMF (see below)).

2011/12 (US $ million, year ending 30 June, estimates): Imports f.o.b. 10,617; Exports f.o.b. 5,584 (Source: IMF, *United Republic of Tanzania: Fifth Review Under the Policy Support Instrument, First Review Under the Standby Credit Facility, and Requests for a Waiver of Nonobservance of a Performance and Assessment Criterion, Rephasing of the Standby Credit Facility Arrangement and Modification of Performance and Assessment Criteria—Staff Report; Press Release on the Executive Board Discussion; and Statement by the Executive Director for Tanzania*—January 2013).

PRINCIPAL TRADING PARTNERS
(US $ million)

Imports c.i.f.	2008	2009	2010
Australia	102.8	125.7	161.0
Belgium	142.5	109.7	132.3
China, People's Repub.	721.3	692.1	876.5
France	162.1	112.2	129.0
Germany	220.7	226.8	183.8
India	865.7	772.9	895.0
Indonesia	94.9	109.3	112.5
Italy	95.6	99.6	96.4
Japan	366.8	422.1	568.1
Kenya	430.7	304.5	275.3
Korea, Repub.	86.9	75.6	128.6
Malaysia	163.0	67.8	106.9
Netherlands	213.0	123.3	143.9
Russian Federation	74.3	65.0	101.6
Saudi Arabia	263.4	164.7	199.1
Singapore	441.9	192.0	444.4
South Africa	829.4	686.6	771.7
Sweden	152.0	84.1	61.3
Switzerland-Liechtenstein	139.8	134.6	562.6
Thailand	76.8	71.3	80.4
Turkey	79.6	76.5	59.6
United Arab Emirates	978.9	631.6	672.2
United Kingdom	175.6	183.2	207.9
USA	224.9	141.0	155.9
Total (incl. others)	8,087.7	6,530.8	8,012.9

Exports f.o.b.	2008	2009	2010
Belgium	50.4	81.5	95.8
Burundi	20.6	24.6	56.1
China, People's Repub.	270.4	387.3	656.7
Comoros	50.8	2.3	42.8
Congo, Democratic Repub.	144.6	85.5	156.1
Germany	67.1	57.9	139.3
Hong Kong	13.9	87.4	13.2
India	173.0	187.8	226.5
Italy	67.6	55.0	67.8
Japan	147.8	178.4	217.5
Kenya	252.7	192.9	324.9
Malawi	49.6	25.6	46.3
Mozambique	34.0	22.1	18.5
Netherlands	163.2	182.4	93.3
Rwanda	22.5	15.8	116.8
Saudi Arabia	16.4	31.9	n.a.
South Africa	265.5	187.9	433.7
Switzerland-Liechtenstein	630.0	584.7	710.4
Uganda	59.8	51.7	60.2
United Arab Emirates	68.1	91.4	58.8
United Kingdom	83.9	32.8	34.3
USA	56.8	47.9	48.8
Viet Nam	22.5	29.5	42.5
Zambia	47.1	46.6	60.3
Total (incl. others)	3,121.1	2,982.4	4,050.5

Source: UN, *International Trade Statistics Yearbook*.

Transport

RAILWAYS

	2008	2009	2010
Passengers ('000)	459	443	290
Freight ('000 metric tons)	505	453	256

Source: National Bureau of Statistics, *Tanzania in Figures 2010*.

ROAD TRAFFIC
(estimates, '000 motor vehicles in use)

	1994	1995	1996
Passenger cars	28.0	26.0	23.8
Buses and coaches	78.0	81.0	86.0
Lorries and vans	27.2	27.7	29.7
Road tractors	6.7	6.7	6.6

2007: Passenger cars 171,821; Buses and coaches 27,200; Lorries and vans 103,611; Motorcycles and mopeds 77,371.

Source: IRF, *World Road Statistics*.

SHIPPING

Flag Registered fleet
(at 31 December)

	2010	2011	2012
Number of vessels	155	215	303
Displacement ('000 grt)	383.6	532.1	5,645.3

Source: Lloyd's List Intelligence (www.lloydslistintelligence.com).

International sea-borne traffic
(port of Dar es Salaam only)

	2007	2008	2009
Vessels docked	3,038	518	2,169
Cargo ('000 metric tons)	7,426	7,167	8,103
Passengers ('000)	714	310	141

2010: Cargo ('000 metric tons) 8,814.

CIVIL AVIATION
(traffic on scheduled services)

	2007	2008	2009
Kilometres flown (million)	6	4	12
Passengers carried ('000)	251	203	684
Passenger-km (million)	252	152	395
Total ton-km (million)	24	15	36

Source: UN, *Statistical Yearbook*.

2010: Passengers carried ('000) 749 (Source: World Bank, World Development Indicators database).

Tourism

FOREIGN VISITOR ARRIVALS
(by country of origin)

	2008	2009	2010
Burundi	11,721	14,581	17,440
Canada	16,482	14,642	14,819
France	19,598	20,127	15,650
Germany	27,100	25,508	25,246
India	17,530	17,002	19,101
Italy	49,950	47,804	59,603
Kenya	184,269	177,929	193,474
Malawi	21,459	19,851	22,233
Netherlands	16,945	16,507	14,598
Rwanda	14,394	14,331	14,754
South Africa	28,721	25,586	29,823
Uganda	31,682	32,826	31,869
United Kingdom	58,245	53,753	48,587
USA	66,953	47,943	49,215
Zambia	37,682	26,999	34,983
Total (incl. others)	770,469	714,367	782,699

Tourism receipts (US $ million, excl. passenger transport) 1,160 in 2009; 1,254 in 2010; 1,457 in 2011 (provisional).

Source: World Tourism Organization.

Communications Media

	2009	2010	2011
Telephones ('000 main lines in use)	172.9	174.5	161.1
Mobile cellular telephones ('000 subscribers)	17,469.5	20,983.9	25,666.5
Internet subscribers ('000) . .	397.5	487.3	n.a.
Broadband subscribers ('000) . .	2.8	3.2	3.5

Source: International Telecommunication Union.

Education

(2010 unless otherwise indicated)

	Institutions	Teachers	Students
Primary (state) . . .	15,265	159,081	2,265,000
Primary (private) . .	551	6,775	39,818
Secondary (state) . .	3,397	30,252	708,941
Secondary (private) . . .	869	10,265	128,715
Higher (state)*	46†	n.a.	35,718
Higher (private)‡ . . .	64†	n.a.	5,275

* Comprising 34 teacher training colleges, 8 full universities and 4 university colleges.

† 2009 figure.

‡ Comprising 43 teacher training colleges, 11 full universities and 10 university colleges.

Pupil-teacher ratio (primary education, UNESCO estimate): 50.8 in 2009/10 (Source: UNESCO Institute for Statistics).

Adult literacy rate (UNESCO estimates): 73.2% (males 79.0%; females 67.5%) in 2010 (Source: UNESCO Institute for Statistics).

Directory

The Government

HEAD OF STATE

President: Lt-Col (retd) JAKAYA MRISHO KIKWETE (took office 21 December 2005; re-elected 31 October 2010).

Vice-President: Dr MOHAMED GHARIB BILAL.

CABINET
(May 2013)

President and Commander-in-Chief of the Armed Forces: Lt-Col (retd) JAKAYA MRISHO KIKWETE.

Prime Minister: MIZENGO KAYANZA PETER PINDA.

Ministers of State in the President's Office: STEPHEN MASATU WASSIRA (Social Relations and Co-ordination), GEORGE MKUCHIKA (Good Governance), CELINA OMPESHI KOMBANI (Public Service Management), MARK JAMES MWANDOSYA (Without Portfolio).

Ministers of State in the Vice-President's Office: SAMIA H. SULUHU (Union Affairs), Dr TEREZYA LUOGA HOVISA (Environment).

Ministers of State in the Prime Minister's Office: HAWA ABDULRAHMAN GHASIA (Regional Administration and Local Governments), WILLIAM LUKUVI (Policy, Co-ordination and Parliamentary Affairs), Dr MARY MICHAEL NAGU (Investment and Empowerment).

Minister of Foreign Affairs and International Co-operation: BERNARD KAMILLIUS MEMBE.

Minister of East African Co-operation: SAMWEL JOHN SITTA.

Minister of Finance and Economic Affairs: Dr WILLIAM MGIMWA.

Minister of Industry, Trade and Marketing: Dr ABDALLAH O. KIGODA.

Minister of Agriculture, Food Security and Co-operatives: Eng. CHRISTOPHER CHIZA.

Minister of Natural Resources and Tourism: KHAMIS SUED KAGASHEKI.

Minister of Water and Irrigation: Prof. JUMANNE ABDALLAH MAGHEMBE.

Minister of Energy and Minerals: Prof. SOSPETER MUHONGO.

Minister of Works: Dr JOHN POMBE JOSEPH MAGUFULI.

Minister of Transport: Dr HARRISON MWAKYEMBE.

Minister of Communication, Science and Technology: Prof. MAKAME MNYAA MBARAWA.

Minister of Health and Social Welfare: Dr HUSSEIN ALI MWINYI.

Minister of Education and Vocational Training: Dr SHUKURU JUMANNE KAWAMBWA.

Minister of Labour and Employment: GAUDENSIA MUGOSI KABAKA.

Minister of Lands, Housing and Human Settlements Development: Prof. ANNA TIBAIJUKA.

Minister of Information, Youth, Culture and Sports: Dr FENELLA E. MUKANGARA.

Minister of Defence and National Service: SHAMSI VUAI NAHODHA.

Minister of Home Affairs: Dr EMMANUEL JOHN NCHIMBI.

Minister of Justice and Constitutional Affairs: MATHIAS MEINRAD CHIKAWE.

Minister of Community Development, Gender and Children: SOPHIA MNYAMBI SIMBA.

Minister of Livestock and Fisheries Development: Dr DAVID MATHAYO DAVID.

There were also 25 deputy ministers.

MINISTRIES

Office of the President: State House, POB 2483, Dar es Salaam; tel. (22) 2116538; fax (22) 2113425; e-mail permsec@estabs.go.tz; internet www.tanzania.go.tz.

Office of the Vice-President: POB 5380, Dar es Salaam; tel. (22) 2113857; fax (22) 2113856; e-mail makamu@twiga.com; internet www.tanzania.go.tz.

Office of the Prime Minister: POB 3021, Dar es Salaam; tel. (22) 2111249; fax (22) 2117266; e-mail ps@pmo.go.tz; internet www.pmo.go.tz.

Ministry of Agriculture, Food Security and Co-operatives: Kilimo I Building, Temeke, POB 9192, Dar es Salaam; tel. (22) 2862480; fax (22) 2865951; e-mail psk@kilimo.go.tz; internet www.kilimo.go.tz.

Ministry of Communication, Science and Technology: Plot 1168/19, Jamhuri St, POB 2645, Dar es Salaam; tel. (22) 2111254; fax (22) 2112533; e-mail mst@mst.go.tz; internet www.mst.go.tz.

Ministry of Community Development, Gender and Children: Kivukoni Front, POB 3448, Dar es Salaam; tel. (22) 2111459; fax (22) 2110933; e-mail info_wic@uccmail.co.tz; internet www.mcdcg.go.tz.

Ministry of Defence and National Service: POB 9544, Dar es Salaam; tel. (22) 2117153; fax (22) 2116719; internet www.modans.go.tz.

Ministry of East African Co-operation: NSSF Water Front Bldg, 5th Floor, POB 9280, Dar es Salaam; tel. (22) 2126660; fax (22) 2120488; e-mail ps@meac.go.tz; internet www.meac.go.tz.

Ministry of Education and Vocational Training: POB 9121, Dar es Salaam; tel. (22) 2120403; fax (22) 2113271; e-mail psmoevt@moe.go.tz; internet www.moe.go.tz.

Ministry of Energy and Minerals: POB 2000, Dar es Salaam; tel. (22) 2112793; fax (22) 2121606; e-mail info@mem.go.tz; internet www.mem.go.tz.

Ministry of Finance and Economic Affairs: POB 9111, Dar es Salaam; tel. (22) 2111174; fax (22) 2110326; internet www.mof.go.tz.

Ministry of Foreign Affairs and International Co-operation: Kivukoni Front, POB 9000, Dar es Salaam; tel. (22) 2111906; fax (22) 2116600; e-mail nje@foreign.go.tz; internet www.foreign.go.tz.

Ministry of Health and Social Welfare: 36/37 Samore Ave, POB 9083, Dar es Salaam; tel. (22) 2120261; fax (22) 2139951; e-mail moh@moh.go.tz; internet www.moh.gov.tz.

Ministry of Home Affairs: POB 9223, Dar es Salaam; tel. and fax (22) 2119050; e-mail permsec@moha.go.tz; internet www.moha.go.tz.

Ministry of Industry, Trade and Marketing: POB 9503, Dar es Salaam; tel. (22) 2127898; fax (22) 2125832; e-mail tnwinfo@plancom.go.tz; internet www.mitm.go.tz.

Ministry of Information, Youth, Culture and Sports: Dar es Salaam; internet www.hum.go.tz.

Ministry of Infrastructure Development: Pamba Rd, Tancot House, POB 9144, Dar es Salaam; tel. (22) 2137650; fax (22) 2112751; e-mail permsec@infrastructure.go.tz; internet www.infrastructure.go.tz.

Ministry of Justice and Constitutional Affairs: POB 70069, Dar es Salaam; tel. 2137833; fax (22) 2137831; e-mail katibumkuu@sheria.go.tz; internet www.sheria.go.tz.

Ministry of Labour and Employment: POB 1422, Dar es Salaam; tel. (22) 2120419; fax (22) 2113082; e-mail permsec@kazi.go.tz; internet www.kazi.go.tz.

Ministry of Lands, Housing and Human Settlements Development: Kivukoni Front, Ardhi House, POB 9132, Dar es Salaam; tel. (22) 2121241; fax (22) 2124576; internet www.ardhi.go.tz.

Ministry of Livestock and Fisheries Development: POB 9152, Dar es Salaam; tel. (22) 2861910; fax (22) 2861908; internet www.mifugo.go.tz.

Ministry of Natural Resources and Tourism: POB 9372, Dar es Salaam; tel. (22) 2111061; fax (22) 2110600; e-mail nature.tourism@mnrt.org; internet www.mnrt.org.

Ministry of Transport: Tancot House, cnr Sokoine Dr. and Pamba Rd, POB 9144, Dar es Salaam; tel. (22) 2137650; fax (22) 2112751; e-mail permsec@mot.go.tz; internet www.mot.go.tz.

Ministry of Water and Irrigation: POB 9153, Dar es Salaam; tel. (22) 2452036; fax (22) 2452037; e-mail dppmaj@raha.com; internet www.maji.go.tz.

Ministry of Works: Holland House, Garden Ave, POB 9423, Dar es Salaam; tel. (22) 2111553; fax (22) 2113335; internet www.mow.go.tz.

ZANZIBAR GOVERNMENT OF NATIONAL UNITY
(May 2013)

The Government is formed by members of Chama Cha Mapinduzi (CCM) and the Civic United Front (CUF).

President: Dr ALI MOHAMMED SHEIN (CCM).

First Vice-President: MAALIM SEIF SHARIF HAMAD (CUF).

Second Vice-President: SEIF ALI IDDI (CCM).

Minister of State in the President's Office and Chairman of the Revolutionary Council: Dr MWINYIHAJI MAKAME (CCM).

Minister of State in the President's Office, in charge of Finance, the Economy and Development Planning: OMAR YUSSUF MZEE (CCM).

Minister of State in the President's Office, in charge of Public Service and Good Governance: HAJI OMAR KHERI (CCM).

Minister of State in the Vice-President's Office: FATMA ABDUL-HABIB FEREJI (CUF).

Minister of State in the Second Vice-President's Office: MOHAMMED ABOUD MOHAMMED (CCM).

Minister of Constitutional Affairs and Justice: ABOUBAKAR KHAMIS BAKARY (CUF).

Minister of Infrastructure and Communications: RASHID SEIF SULEIMAN (CUF).

Minister of Education and Vocational Training: RAMADHAN ABDULLA SHAABAN (CCM).

Minister of Health: JUMA DUNI HAJI (CUF).

Minister of Social Welfare, Women Development and Children: ZAINAB OMAR MOHAMMED (CCM).

Minister of Lands, Housing, Water and Energy: ALI JUMA SHAMHUNA (CCM).

Minister of Agriculture and Natural Resources: MANSOOR YUSSUF HIMID (CCM).

Minister of Trade, Industry and Marketing: NASSOR AHMED MAZRUI (CUF).

Minister of Livestock and Fisheries: SAID ALI MBAROUK (CUF).

Minister of Labour, Economic Empowerment and Co-operatives: HAROUN ALI SULEIMAN (CCM).

Members of the Revolutionary Council and Ministers without Portfolio: SULEIMAN OTHMAN NYANGA (CCM), HAJI FAKI SHAALI (CUF), MACHANO OTHMAN SAID (CCM).

There were also six deputy ministers.

MINISTRIES

Office of the President: POB 776, Zanzibar; tel. (24) 2230814; fax (24) 2233722.

Office of the Chief Minister: POB 239, Zanzibar; tel. (24) 2311126; fax (24) 233788.

Ministry of Agriculture and Natural Resources: Zanzibar; tel. (24) 232662.

Ministry of Communication and Transport: POB 266, Zanzibar; tel. (24) 2232841.

Ministry of Constitutional Affairs and Justice: Zanzibar.

Ministry of Education and Vocational Training: POB 394, Zanzibar; tel. (24) 232827.

Ministry of Finance and Economic Affairs: Vuga St, POB 1154, Zanzibar; tel. (24) 2231169; fax (24) 2230546; e-mail info@mofeaznz.org; internet www.mofeaznz.org.

Ministry of Health: Zanzibar.

Ministry of Information, Culture and Sport: POB 236, Zanzibar; tel. (24) 232640.

Ministry of Infrastructure and Communications: Zanzibar.

Ministry of Labour, Economic Empowerment and Co-operatives: Zanzibar.

Ministry of Lands, Housing, Water and Energy: Zanzibar.

Ministry of Livestock and Fisheries: Zanzibar.

Minister of Social Welfare, Women Development and Children: POB 884, Zanzibar; tel. (24) 30808.

Ministry of Trade, Industry and Marketing: POB 772, Zanzibar; tel. (24) 232321.

President and Legislature

PRESIDENT

Election, 31 October 2010

Candidate	Votes	% of votes
Lt-Col (retd) Jakaya Mrisho Kikwete (CCM)	5,276,827	62.83
Dr Willibrod Peter Slaa (Chadema) .	2,271,941	27.05
Prof. Ibrahim Haruna Lipumba (CUF) .	695,667	8.28
Peter Mziray Kuga (APPT-Maendeleo) .	96,933	1.15
Hasim Spunda Rungwe (NCCR—Mageuzi)	26,388	0.31
Muttamwega Bhatt Mgaywa (TLP) . .	17,482	0.21
Yahmi Nassoro Dovutwa (UPDP) . . .	13,176	0.16
Total	**8,398,414***	**100.00**

* According to results released by the National Election Commission of Tanzania, the total number of valid votes cast was 8,398,394. In addition there were 227,889 spoilt ballots.

NATIONAL ASSEMBLY

Speaker: ANNE MAKINDA.

Election, 31 October 2010

Party	Seats*
Chama Cha Mapinduzi (CCM)	251
Chama Cha Demokrasia na Maendeleo (Chadema) .	45
Civic United Front (CUF)	33
National Convention for Construction and Reform (NCCR—Mageuzi)	4
Tanzania Labour Party (TLP)	1
United Democratic Party (UDP)	1
Total	**335†**

* In addition to the 239 elective seats and 103 special seats, 10 seats are reserved for presidential nominees and five for members of the Zanzibar House of Representatives; the Attorney-General is also an ex officio member of the National Assembly.

† Voting in seven constituencies was postponed until 14 November 2010. At elections held on that date the CUF and the CCM each secured three seats, while Chadema took one seat.

ZANZIBAR PRESIDENT
Election, 31 October 2010

Candidate	Votes	% of votes
Dr Ali Mohammed Shein	179,809	50.11
Maalim Seif Sharif Hamad . . .	176,338	49.14
Kassim Ali Bakari	803	0.22
Haji Khamis Haji	525	0.15
Juma Ali Khatib	497	0.14
Said Soud Said	480	0.13
Haji Ambar Khamis	363	0.10
Total	358,815	100.00

ZANZIBAR HOUSE OF REPRESENTATIVES
Speaker: PANDU AMEIR KIFICHO.
Election, 31 October 2010

Party	Seats*
Chama Cha Mapinduzi (CCM)	28
Civic United Front (CUF)	22
Total	50

*In addition to the 50 elective seats, 10 seats are reserved for presidential nominees, 20 for women (on a party basis in proportion to the number of elective seats gained) and one for the Attorney-General.

Election Commissions

National Election Commission of Tanzania (NEC): Posta House, POB 10923, Ghana/Ohio St, 6th and 7th Floor, Dar es Salaam; tel. (22) 2114963; fax (22) 2116740; e-mail info@nec.go.tz; internet www.nec.go.tz; f. 1993; Chair. LEWIS M. MAKAME; Dir of Elections R. R. KIRAVU.

Zanzibar Electoral Commission (ZEC): POB 1001, Zanzibar; tel. (24) 2231489; fax (24) 2233828; e-mail election@zec.go.tz; internet www.zec.go.tz; f. 2007; Chair. KHATIB MWINYI CHANDE.

Political Organizations

At 2010 there were 18 registered parties in Tanzania.

African Progressive Party of Tanzania (APPT-Maendeleo): House No. 294, Wibu St, Kinondoni, POB 31932, Dar es Salaam; tel. 754300302 (mobile); f. 2003; Leader PETER MZIRAY KUGA; Sec.-Gen. AHMED HAMAD.

Chama Cha Amani na Demokrasia Tanzania (CHADETA): House No. 41, Sadan St Ilala, POB 15809, Dar es Salaam; tel. 744889453 (mobile); granted temporary registration in 2003.

Chama Cha Demokrasia na Maendeleo (Chadema—Party for Democracy and Progress): House No. 170 Ufipa St, POB 31191, Dar es Salaam; tel. (22) 2668866; e-mail info@chadema.or.tz; internet www.chadema.or.tz; supports democracy and social development; Chair. FREEMAN MBOWE; Sec.-Gen. WILLIBROD PETER SLAA.

Chama Cha Haki na Usitawi (Chausta—Party for Justice and Development): Drive Inn Oysterbay, POB 5450, Dar es Salaam; tel. 754990228 (mobile); e-mail chausta@yahoo.com; f. 1998; officially regd 2001; Chair. JAMES MAPALALA.

Chama Cha Kijamii (CCJ): Kinondoni, Dar es Salaam; f. 2010; Chair. CONSTANTINE AKITANDA; Sec.-Gen. RENATUS MUHABHI.

Chama Cha Mapinduzi (CCM) (Revolutionary Party of Tanzania): Kuu St, POB 50, Dodoma; tel. 2180575; e-mail katibumkuu@ccmtz.org; internet www.ccmtz.org; f. 1977 by merger of the mainland-based Tanganyika African National Union (TANU) with the Afro-Shirazi Party, which operated on Zanzibar and Pemba; sole legal party 1977–92; socialist orientation; Chair. JAKAYA MRISHO KIKWETE; Vice-Chair. PIUS MSEKWA, AMANI A. KARUME; Sec.-Gen. YUSUF MAKAMBA.

Civic United Front (CUF): Mtendeni St at Malindi, POB 3637, Zanzibar; tel. and fax (24) 2237446; e-mail headquarters@cuftz.org; internet www.cuftz.org; f. 1992 by merger of Zanzibar opposition party Kamahuru and the mainland-based Chama Cha Wananchi; commands substantial support in Zanzibar and Pemba, for which it demands increased autonomy; Chair. Prof. IBRAHIM HARUNA LIPUMBA; Sec.-Gen. SEIF SHARIF HAMAD.

Democratic Party (DP): Ilala Mchikichini, POB 63102, Dar es Salaam; tel. 713430516 (mobile); e-mail dp_watanganyika@yahoo.com; f. 2002; Chair. Rev. CHRISTOPHER MTIKILA.

Demokrasia Makini (MAKINI): Mbezi Beach Makonde, nr Nguruko Int. School, POB 75636, Dar es Salaam; tel. 754295670 (mobile); officially regd 2001; Sec.-Gen. DOMINICK LYAMCHAI.

Forum for Restoration of Democracy (FORD): 13 Kibambawe St, Kariakoo, POB 15587, Dar es Salaam; tel. 741292271 (mobile); f. 2002; Chair. RAMADHANI MZEE; Sec.-Gen. EMMANUEL PATUKA.

Movement for Democratic Alternative (MDA): Zanzibar; seeks to review the terms of the 1964 union of Zanzibar with mainland Tanzania; supports democratic institutions and opposes detention without trial and press censorship.

National Convention for Construction and Reform (NCCR—Mageuzi): Plot No. 2 Kilosa St, Ilala, POB 72444, Dar es Salaam; tel. (22) 2111484; f. 1992; Chair. JAMES F. MBATIA; Sec.-Gen. SAMWELI A. RUHUZA.

National League for Democracy (NLD): Plot No. D/73 Sinza, POB 352, Dar es Salaam; tel. 714259442 (mobile); fax (22) 2462180; f. 1993; Chair. EMMANUEL J. E. MAKAIDI; Sec.-Gen. FERUZI MSAMBICHAKA.

National Reconstruction Alliance (NRA): Bububu St, Tandika Kilimahewa, POB 100125, Dar es Salaam; tel. 754496724 (mobile); f. 1993; Chair. RASHID MTUTA; Sec.-Gen. MARSHEED H. HEMED.

Tanzania Democratic Alliance Party (TADEA): Buguruni Malapa, POB 482, Dar es Salaam; tel. (22) 2865244; f. 1993; Pres. JOHN D. LIFA-CHIPAKA; Sec.-Gen. JUMA ALI KHATIB.

Tanzania Labour Party (TLP): Argentina Manzese, POB 7273, Dar es Salaam; tel. (22) 2443237; f. 1993; Chair. AUGUSTINE MREMA; Sec.-Gen. JOHN KOMBA.

Tanzania People's Party (TPP): Mbezi Juu, Kawe, POB 60847, Dar es Salaam; removed from register of political parties 2002; Chair. ALEC H. CHE-MPONDA; Sec.-Gen. GRAVEL LIMO.

United Democratic Party (UDP): Plot No. 34, Block 28, Ilemela St, Mwananyamala, Kinondoni, POB 5918, Dar es Salaam; tel. 784613723 (mobile); f. 1994; Chair. JOHN MOMOSE CHEYO.

Union for Multi-Party Democracy (UMD): House No. 84, Plot No. 630, Block No. 5, Kagera St. Magomeni, POB 2985, Dar es Salaam; tel. 744478153 (mobile); f. 1993; Chair. SALUM S. ALLI; Sec.-Gen. ALI MSHANGAMA ABDALLAH.

United People's Democratic Party (UPDP): 46 Kagera St, POB 11746, Dar es Salaam; tel. 754753075 (mobile); e-mail opodsm@yahoo.com; f. 1993; Chair. YAHMI NASSORO DOVUTWA; Sec.-Gen. HAMAD MOHAMED IBRAHIM.

Diplomatic Representation

EMBASSIES AND HIGH COMMISSIONS IN TANZANIA

Algeria: 34 Ali Hassan Mwinyi Rd, POB 2963, Dar es Salaam; tel. (22) 2117619; fax (22) 2117620; e-mail algemb@twiga.com; Ambassador ABDELMOUN'AAM AHRIZ.

Angola: Plot 78, Lugalo Rd, POB 20793, Dar es Salaam; tel. (22) 2117674; fax (22) 2132349; Ambassador AMBRÓSIO LUKOKI.

Belgium: 5 Ocean Rd, POB 9210, Dar es Salaam; tel. (22) 2112688; fax (22) 2117621; e-mail daressalaam@diplobel.fed.be; internet www.diplomatie.be/dar-es-salaam; Ambassador KOENRAAD ADAM.

Burundi: Plot 1007, Lugalo Rd, POB 2752, Upanga, Dar es Salaam; Ambassador (vacant).

Canada: 38 Mirambo St, Garden Ave, POB 1022, Dar es Salaam; tel. (22) 2163300; fax (22) 2116897; e-mail dslam@international.gc.ca; internet www.canadainternational.gc.ca/tanzania-tanzanie; High Commissioner ALEXANDRE LÉVÊQUE.

China, People's Republic: 2 Kajificheni Close at Toure Dr., POB 1649, Dar es Salaam; tel. (22) 2668063; fax (22) 2666353; e-mail chinaemb_tan@mfa.gov.cn; internet tz.chineseembassy.org; Ambassador LV YOUQING.

Congo, Democratic Republic: 438 Malik Rd, POB 975, Upanga, Dar es Salaam; tel. (22) 2150282; fax (22) 2153341; Ambassador JUMA-ALFANI MPANGO.

Cuba: Plot 313, Lugalo Rd, POB 9282, Upanga, Dar es Salaam; tel. (22) 2115928; fax (22) 2132338; e-mail embajada@sasamail.co.tz; internet www.cubadiplomatica.cu/tanzania; Ambassador ERNESTO GÓMEZ DÍAZ.

Denmark: Ghana Ave, POB 9171, Dar es Salaam; tel. (22) 2165200; fax (22) 2116433; e-mail daramb@um.dk; internet www.ambdaressalaam.um.dk; Ambassador JOHNNY FLENTOE.

Egypt: 24 Garden Ave, POB 1668, Dar es Salaam; tel. (22) 2117622; fax (22) 2112543; e-mail egypt.emb.tz@Cats-net.com; Ambassador WAEL ADEL ABDEL AZEEM NASR.

Finland: cnr Mirambo St and Garden Ave, POB 2455, Dar es Salaam; tel. (22) 2196565; fax (22) 2196573; e-mail sanomat.dar@formin.fi; internet www.finland.or.tz; Ambassador SINIKKA ANTILA.

France: Ali Hassan Mwinyi Rd, POB 2349, Dar es Salaam; tel. (22) 2198800; fax (22) 2198815; e-mail contact@ambafrance-tz.org; internet www.ambafrance-tz.org; Ambassador MARCEL ESCURE.

Germany: Umoja House, Mirambo St/Garden Ave, 2nd Floor, POB 9541, Dar es Salaam; tel. (22) 2117409; fax (22) 2112944; e-mail info@daressalam.diplo.de; internet www.daressalam.diplo.de; Ambassador KLAUS-PETER BRANDES.

Holy See: Oyster Bay, Plot 146, Haile Selassie Rd, POB 480, Dar es Salaam (Apostolic Nunciature); tel. (22) 2666422; fax (22) 2668059; e-mail nunzio@cats-net.com; Apostolic Nuncio Most Rev. FRANCISCO MONTECILLO PADILLA (Titular Archbishop of Nebbio).

Indonesia: 299 Ali Hassan Mwinyi Rd, POB 572, Dar es Salaam; tel. (22) 2119119; fax (22) 2115849; e-mail kbridsm@raha.com; Ambassador ZAKARIA ANDHAR.

Ireland: 353 Toure Dr., POB 9612, Oyster Bay, Dar es Salaam; tel. (22) 2602355; fax (22) 2602362; e-mail embassydaresalaam@dfa.ie; internet www.embassyofireland.or.tz; Ambassador FIONNUALA GIL-SENAN.

Italy: Plot 316, Lugalo Rd, Upanga, POB 2106, Dar es Salaam; tel. (22) 2115935; fax (22) 2115938; e-mail segr.dar@esteri.it; internet www.ambdaressalaam.esteri.it; Ambassador PIERLUIGI VELARDI.

Japan: 1018 Ali Hassan Mwinyi Rd, POB 2577, Dar es Salaam; tel. (22) 2115827; fax (22) 2115830; e-mail embassyofjapan_tz@dr.mofa.go.jp; internet www.tz.emb-japan.go.jp; Ambassador MASAKI OKADA.

Kenya: Plot 1858, Oysterbay, Kinondoni, POB 5231, Dar es Salaam; tel. (22) 2668285; fax (22) 2668213; e-mail info@kenyahighcomtz.org; internet www.kenyahighcomtz.org; High Commissioner MUTINDA MUTISO.

Korea, Democratic People's Republic: Plot 5, Ursino Estate, Kawawa Rd, Msasani, POB 2690, Dar es Salaam; tel. (22) 2775395; fax (22) 2700838; Ambassador SOON CHUN LEE.

Korea, Republic: Plot 97, Msese Rd, Kingsway, Kinondoni, POB 1154, Dar es Salaam; tel. (22) 2668788; fax (22) 2667509; e-mail embassy-tz@mofat.go.kr; internet tza.mofat.go.kr; Ambassador CHUNG IL.

Libya: 386 Mtitu St, POB 9413, Dar es Salaam; tel. (22) 2150188; fax (22) 2150068; Secretary of People's Bureau Dr AHMED IBRAHIM EL-ASHHAB.

Malawi: Plot 38, Ali Hassan Mwinyi Rd, POB 7616, Dar es Salaam; tel. (22) 2666284; fax (22) 2668161; e-mail mhc@africaonline.co.tz; High Commissioner FLOSSIE CHIDYAONGA.

Mozambique: 25 Garden Ave, POB 9370, Dar es Salaam; tel. and fax (22) 2124673; fax (22) 2116502; e-mail embamoc.tanzania@minec.gov.mz; High Commissioner (vacant).

Netherlands: Umoja House, 4th Floor, Garden Ave, POB 9534, Dar es Salaam; tel. (22) 2110000; fax (22) 2110044; e-mail dar@minbuza.nl; internet tanzania.nlembassy.org; Ambassador Dr KUINDERT ADRIAAN KOEKKOEK.

Nigeria: 83 Haile Selassie Rd, POB 9214, Oyster Bay, Dar es Salaam; tel. (22) 2666000; fax (22) 2668947; e-mail nhc-dsm@raha.com; High Commissioner ISHAYA MAJAMBU.

Norway: 160/50 Mirambo St, POB 2646, Dar es Salaam; tel. (22) 2163100; fax (22) 2163199; e-mail emb.daressalaam@mfa.no; internet www.norway.go.tz; Ambassador INGUNN KLEPSVIK.

Russia: Plot No. 73, Ali Hassan Mwinyi Rd, POB 1905, Dar es Salaam; tel. (22) 2666005; fax (22) 2666818; e-mail embruss@bol.co.tz; internet www.tanzania.mid.ru; Ambassador LEONID SAFANOV.

Rwanda: Plot 32, Ali Hassan Mwinyi Rd, POB 2918, Dar es Salaam; tel. (22) 2701394; fax (22) 2701381; e-mail ambadsm@minaffet.gov.rw; internet www.tanzania.embassy.gov.rw; High Commissioner BENJAMIN RUGANGAZ.

South Africa: Plot 1338/1339, Mwaya Rd, Msaski, POB 10723, Dar es Salaam; tel. (22) 2601800; fax (22) 2600684; e-mail ntombelal@foreign.gov.za; High Commissioner T. H. CHILIZA.

Spain: 99B Kinondoni Rd, POB 842, Dar es Salaam; tel. (22) 2666936; fax (22) 2666938; e-mail embesptz@mail.mae.es; Ambassador LUIS MANUEL CUESTA CIVIS.

Sudan: 'Albaraka', 64 Ali Hassan Mwinyi Rd, POB 2266, Dar es Salaam; tel. (22) 2117641; fax (22) 2115811; e-mail sudan.emb.dar@raha.com; Ambassador Dr YASSIR MOHAMED ALI.

Sweden: Mirambo St and Garden Ave, POB 9274, Dar es Salaam; tel. (22) 2196500; fax (22) 2196503; e-mail ambassaden.dar-es-salaam@foreign.ministry.se; internet www.swedenabroad.se/daressalaam; Ambassador LENNARTH HJELMÅKER.

Switzerland: 79 Kinondoni Rd/Mafinga St, POB 2454, Dar es Salaam; tel. (22) 2666008; fax (22) 2666736; e-mail dar.vertretung@eda.admin.ch; internet www.eda.admin.ch/daressalaam; Ambassador OLIVIER CHAVE.

Syria: 276 Alykhan Rd, Upanga East, POB 2442, Dar es Salaam; tel. (22) 2117656; fax (22) 2115860.

Uganda: Extelcom Bldg, 7th Floor, Samora Ave, POB 6237, Dar es Salaam; tel. (22) 2116754; fax (22) 2112974; e-mail ugadar@intafrica.com; High Commissioner (vacant).

United Arab Emirates: 2415 Kaunda Drive House, Dar es Salaam; tel. (22) 2669999; fax (22) 2669996; e-mail uaeembassy@bol.co.tz; Ambassador MALALLAH MUBARAK SUWAID AL-AMIRI.

United Kingdom: Umoja House, Garden Ave, POB 9200, Dar es Salaam; tel. (22) 2290000; fax (22) 2110102; e-mail bhc.dar@fco.gov.uk; internet ukintanzania.fco.gov.uk; High Commissioner DIANNA PATRICIA MELROSE.

USA: 686 Old Bagamoyo Rd, Msasani, POB 9123, Dar es Salaam; tel. (22) 2294000; fax (22) 2294970; e-mail embassyd@state.gov; internet tanzania.usembassy.gov; Ambassador ALFONSO E. LENHARDT.

Yemen: 353 United Nations Rd, POB 349, Dar es Salaam; tel. (22) 2117650; fax (22) 2115924; Chargé d'affaires a.i. MOHAMED ABDULLA ALMAS.

Zambia: 5–6 Ohio St/Sokoine Dr. Junction, POB 2525, Dar es Salaam; tel. and fax (22) 2112977; e-mail zhcd@raha.com; Deputy High Commissioner ELIZABETH PHIRI.

Zimbabwe: 2097 East Upanga, off Ali Hassan Mwinyi Rd, POB 20762, Dar es Salaam; tel. (22) 2116789; fax (22) 2112913; e-mail zimdares@cats-net.com; Ambassador EDZAI CHIMONYO.

Judicial System

The judicial system of Tanzania is composed of a Court of Appeal, a High Court, Magistrates' and District Courts, and Primary Courts. The Court of Appeal is the highest court of the country (including Zanzibar) and hears appeals from the lower courts. The High Court comprises 15 zones, with three specialized divisions—Commercial Division, Land Division and Labour Division. There are 22 Resident Magistrates' Courts and 109 District Courts, in addition to 1,105 Primary Courts. There are also several specialized quasi-judicial tribunals, including the District Land and Housing Tribunal, the Tax Tribunal and the Tax Appeals Tribunal. Zanzibar has a separate judicial system headed by the Chief Justice of Zanzibar, comprising a High Court, Regional Magistrates' Courts, District Magistrates' Courts and Primary Courts. There is also a Labour Court, Juvenile Courts and Kadhis' Courts (with exclusive jurisdiction over matters of Islamic law) in Zanzibar.

Court of Appeal: Dar es Salaam; internet www.judiciary.go.tz; f. 1979; consists of the Chief Justice and 14 Justices of Appeal; Chief Justice MOHAMED CHANDE OTHMAN.

High Court: Dar es Salaam; internet www.judiciary.go.tz; Principal Judge FAKIHI A. R. JUNDU.

High Court of Zanzibar: Kaunda Rd, near Victoria Gardens, Stone Town, Zanzibar; Chief Justice of Zanzibar ABDULHAKIM AMEIR ISSA.

District Courts: situated in each district and presided over by either a Resident Magistrate or District Magistrate; limited jurisdiction, with a right of appeal to the High Court.

Primary Courts: established in every district and presided over by Primary Court Magistrates; limited jurisdiction, with a right of appeal to the District Courts and then to the High Court.

Permanent Commission of Enquiry: POB 2643, Dar es Salaam; tel. (22) 2113690; fax (22) 2111533; Chair. and Official Ombudsman Prof. JOSEPH F. MBWILIZA; Sec. A. P. GUVETTE.

Attorney-General: FREDERICK WEREMA.

Attorney-General of Zanzibar: OTHMAN MASOUD.

Director of Public Prosecutions: ELIEZER FELESHI.

Director of Public Prosecutions of Zanzibar: IBRAHIM MZEE IBRAHIM.

People's Courts were established in Zanzibar in 1970. Magistrates are elected by the people and have two assistants each. Under the Zanzibar Constitution, which came into force in January 1985, defence lawyers and the right of appeal, abolished in 1970, were reintroduced.

Religion

Religious surveys were eliminated from all government census reports after 1967. However, religious leaders and sociologists generally believe that the country's population is 30%–40% Christian and 30%–40% Muslim, with the remainder consisting of practitioners of other faiths, traditional indigenous religions and atheists. Foreign missionaries operate in the country, including Roman Catholics, Lutherans, Baptists, Seventh-day Adventists, Mormons, Anglicans and Muslims.

ISLAM

The Muslim population is most heavily concentrated on the Zanzibar archipelago and in the coastal areas of the mainland. There are also large Muslim minorities in inland urban areas. Some 99% of the population of Zanzibar is estimated to be Muslim. Between 80% and 90% of the country's Muslim population is Sunni; the remainder consists of several Shi'a groups, mostly of Asian descent. A large proportion of the Asian community is Isma'ili.

Ismalia Provincial Church: POB 460, Dar es Salaam.

National Muslim Council of Tanzania: POB 21422, Dar es Salaam; tel. (22) 234934; f. 1969; supervises Islamic affairs on the mainland only; Chair. Sheikh HEMED BIN JUMA BIN HEMED; Exec. Sec. Alhaj MUHAMMAD MTULIA.

Supreme Muslim Council: Zanzibar; f. 1991; supervises Islamic affairs in Zanzibar; Mufti Sheikh HARITH BIN KALEF.

Wakf and Trust Commission: POB 4092, Zanzibar; f. 1980; Islamic affairs; Exec. Sec. YUSUF ABDULRAHMAN MUHAMMAD.

CHRISTIANITY

The Christian population is composed of Roman Catholics, Protestants, Pentecostals, Seventh-day Adventists, members of the Church of Jesus Christ of Latter-day Saints (Mormons) and Jehovah's Witnesses.

Jumuiya ya Kikristo Tanzania (Christian Council of Tanzania): Church House, POB 1454, Dodoma; tel. (26) 2324445; fax (26) 2324352; f. 1934; Chair. Rt Rev. PETER KITULA (Bishop of the African Inland Church); Gen. Sec. Rev. Dr LEONARD AMOS MTAITA.

The Anglican Communion

Anglicans are adherents of the Church of the Province of Tanzania, comprising 16 dioceses.

Archbishop of the Province of Tanzania and Bishop of Dar es Salaam: Most Rev. Dr VALENTINO MOKIWA, POB 1028, Iringa; fax (26) 2702479; e-mail ruaha@maf.or.tz.

Provincial Secretary: Rev. CANON DICKSON CHILONGANI, POB 899, Dodoma; tel. (26) 2321437; fax (26) 2324265; e-mail cpt@maf.org.

Greek Orthodox

Archbishop of East Africa: NICADEMUS OF IRINOUPOULIS (resident in Nairobi, Kenya); jurisdiction covers Kenya, Uganda and Tanzania.

Lutheran

Evangelical Lutheran Church in Tanzania: POB 3033, Boma Rd, Arusha; tel. (27) 2508856; fax (27) 2508858; e-mail elcthq@elct.or.tz; internet www.elct.or.tz; Presiding Bishop ALEX G. MALASUSA; Exec. Sec. AMANI MWENEGOHA; 5.6m. mems (2010).

The Roman Catholic Church

Tanzania comprises five archdioceses and 29 dioceses. Roman Catholics constitute an estimated 28% of the total population.

Tanzania Episcopal Conference

Catholic Secretariat, Mandela Rd, POB 2133, Dar es Salaam; tel. (22) 2851075; fax (22) 2851133; e-mail info@tec.co.tz; internet www.tec.or.tz.

f. 1980; Pres. Mgr JUDE THADDAEUS RUWA'ICHI (Bishop of Dodoma); Sec. Gen. Fr ANTHONY MAKUNDE.

Archbishop of Arusha: Most Rev. JOSAPHAT LOUIS LEBULU, Archbishop's House, POB 3044, Arusha; tel. (27) 2544361; fax (27) 2548004; e-mail angelo.arusha@habari.co.tz.

Archbishop of Dar es Salaam: Cardinal POLYCARP PENGO, Archbishop's House, POB 167, Dar es Salaam; tel. (22) 2113223; fax (22) 2125751; e-mail nyumba@cats-net.com.

Archbishop of Mwanza: Most Rev. JUDE THADAEUS RUWA'ICHI, Archbishop's House, POB 1421, Mwanza; tel. and fax (28) 2501029; e-mail archmwz@mwanza-online.com.

Archbishop of Songea: Most Rev. NORBERT WENDELIN MTEGA, Archbishop's House, POB 152, Songea; tel. (25) 2602004; fax (25) 2602593; e-mail songea-archdiocese@yahoo.com.

Archbishop of Tabora: PAUL R. RUZOKA, Archbishop's House, Private Bag, PO Tabora; tel. (26) 2605608; fax (26) 2604000; e-mail archbishops-office@yahoo.co.uk.

Other Christian Churches

Baptist Mission of Tanzania: POB 9414, Dar es Salaam; tel. (22) 2170130; fax (22) 2170127; f. 1956; Admin. FRANK PEVEY.

Christian Missions in Many Lands (Tanzania): German Branch, POB 34, Tunduru, Ruvuma Region; f. 1957; Gen. Sec. THOMAS MÜHLING.

Moravian Church in Tanzania: POB 747, Mbeya; tel. (25) 2503626; fax (25) 2502155; e-mail mct@moravian.or.tz; internet www.moravian.or.tz; 113,656 mems; Chair. Bishop A. CHEYO; Gen. Sec. Rev. CONRAD NGUVUMALI.

Pentecostal Church: POB 34, Kahama.

Presbyterian Church: POB 2510, Dar es Salaam; tel. (22) 229075.

BAHÁ'Í FAITH

National Spiritual Assembly: POB 585, Dar es Salaam; tel. and fax (22) 2152766; e-mail bahaitz@cats-net.com; internet www.bahai.org; f. 1950; mems resident in 3,000 localities.

OTHER RELIGIONS

Many people follow traditional beliefs. There are also some Hindu communities.

The Press

NEWSPAPERS

Daily

The Citizen: Plot No. 34/35, Mandela Rd, POB 19754, Dar es Salaam; tel. 788455234 (mobile); internet www.thecitizen.co.tz; f. 2004; Man. Editor BAKARI MACHUMU.

Daily News: POB 9033, Dar es Salaam; tel. (22) 2110595; fax (22) 2112881; e-mail newsdesk@dailynews-tsn.com; internet www.dailynews.co.tz; f. 1972; govt-owned; Man. Editor SETHI KAMUHANDA; circ. 50,000.

The Guardian: POB 31042, Dar es Salaam; tel. (22) 275250; fax (22) 273583; e-mail guardian@ipp.co.tz; internet www.ippmedia.com; f. 1994; English and Swahili; Man. Dir KIONDO MSHANA; Man. Editor PASCAL SHIJA.

Kipanga: POB 199, Zanzibar; Swahili; publ. by Information and Broadcasting Services.

Majira: POB 71439, Dar es Salaam; tel. (22) 238901; fax (22) 231104; independent; Swahili; Editor THEOPHIL MAKUNGA; circ. 15,000.

Mwananchi: Plot No. 34/35, Mandela Rd, POB 19754, Dar es Salaam; internet www.mwananchi.co.tz; f. 2000; Swahili; Man. Editor DENNIS MSACKY.

Uhuru: POB 9221, Dar es Salaam; tel. (22) 2182224; fax (22) 2185065; f. 1961; official publ. of CCM; Swahili; Man. Editor SAIDI NGUBA; circ. 100,000.

Weekly

Business Times: POB 71439, Dar es Salaam; tel. (22) 238901; fax (22) 231104; e-mail majira@bcsmedia.com; independent; English; Editor ALLI MWAMBOLA; circ. 15,000.

The Express: POB 20588, Dar es Salaam; tel. (22) 2180058; fax (22) 2182665; e-mail express@raha.com; internet www.theexpress.com; independent; English; Editor FAYAZ BHOJANI; circ. 20,000.

Gazette of the United Republic: POB 9142, Dar es Salaam; tel. (22) 231817; official announcements; Editor H. HAJI; circ. 6,000.

Government Gazette: POB 261, Zanzibar; f. 1964; official announcements.

Kasheshe: POB 31042, Dar es Salaam; Swahili; Editor VENANCE MLAY.

Kiongozi (The Leader): POB 9400, Dar es Salaam; tel. (22) 2851075; fax (22) 2851133; e-mail kiongozinews@yahoo.com; f. 1950; owned by Catholic Publishers Ltd; weekly; Swahili; Roman Catholic; Dir JOSEPH MATUMAINI; circ. 33,500.

Mfanyakazi (The Worker): POB 15359, Dar es Salaam; tel. (22) 226111; Swahili; trade union publ; Editor NDUGU MTAWA; circ. 100,000.

Mwanaspoti: POB 19754, Dar es Salaam; tel. (22) 2150312; fax (22) 2180183; e-mail mwanaspoti@mwanaspoti.co.tz; internet www.mwanaspoti.co.tz.

Mzalendo: POB 9221, Dar es Salaam; tel. (22) 2182224; fax (22) 2185065; e-mail uhuru@udsm.ac.tz; f. 1972; publ. by CCM; Swahili; Man. Editor SAIDI NGABA; circ. 115,000.

Nipashe Jumapili: POB 31042, Dar es Salaam; Swahili.

Sunday News: POB 9033, Dar es Salaam; tel. (22) 2116072; fax (22) 2112881; f. 1954; govt-owned; Man. Editor SETHI KAMUCHANDA; circ. 50,000.

Sunday Observer: POB 31042, Dar es Salaam; e-mail guardian@ipp.co.tz; Man. Dir VUMI URASA; Man. Editor PETER MSUNGU.

PERIODICALS

The African Review: POB 35042, Dar es Salaam; tel. (22) 2410130; e-mail mubakar@udsm.ac.tz; 2 a year; journal of African politics, development and international affairs; publ. by the Dept of Political Science, Univ. of Dar es Salaam; Chief Editor Dr MOHAMMED BAKARI; circ. 1,000.

Eastern African Law Review: POB 35093, Dar es Salaam; tel. (22) 243254; f. 1967; 2 a year; Chief Editor N. N. N. NDITI; circ. 1,000.

Elimu Haina Mwisho: POB 1986, Mwanza; monthly; circ. 45,000.

Habari za Washirika: POB 2567, Dar es Salaam; tel. (22) 223346; monthly; publ. by Co-operative Union of Tanzania; Editor H. V. N. CHIBULUNJE; circ. 40,000.

Jenga: POB 2669, Dar es Salaam; tel. (22) 2112893; fax (22) 2113618; journal of the National Development Corpn; circ. 2,000.

Kweupe: POB 222, Zanzibar; weekly; Swahili; publ. by Information and Broadcasting Services.

Mlezi (The Educator): POB 41, Peramiho; f. 1970; every 2 months; Editor Fr DOMINIC WEIS; circ. 8,000.

Mwenge (Firebrand): POB 1, Peramiho; f. 1937; monthly; Editor JOHN P. MBONDE; circ. 10,000.

Nchi Yetu (Our Country): POB 9142, Dar es Salaam; tel. (22) 2110200; f. 1964; govt publ; monthly; Swahili; circ. 50,000.

Nuru: POB 1893, Zanzibar; f. 1992; bi-monthly; official publ. of Zanzibar Govt; circ. 8,000.

Safina: POB 21422, Dar es Salaam; tel. (22) 234934; publ. by National Muslim Council of Tanzania; Editor YASSIN SADIK; circ. 10,000.

Tantravel: POB 2485, Dar es Salaam; tel. (22) 2111244; fax (22) 2116420; e-mail safari@ud.co.tz; internet www .tanzaniatouristboard.com; f. 1987; quarterly; publ. by Tanzania Tourist Board; Editor GERVAS TATAH MLOLA.

Tanzania Adventist Press: POB 635, Morogoro; tel. and fax (23) 2604374; e-mail reuben.kingamkono@gmail.com; quarterly; Seventh-day Adventist; Editor REUBEN KINGAMKONO; circ. 100,000.

Tanzania Trade Currents: POB 5402, Dar es Salaam; tel. (22) 2850238; fax (22) 2850539; e-mail info@tantrade.or.tz; bi-monthly; publ. by Tanzania Trade Development Authority; circ. 2,000.

Uhuru na Amani: POB 3033, Arusha; tel. (57) 8855; fax (57) 8858; quarterly; Swahili; publ. by Evangelical Lutheran Church in Tanzania; Editor ELIZABETH LOBULU; circ. 15,000.

Ukulima wa Kisasa (Modern Farming): Farmers' Education and Publicity Unit, POB 2308, Dar es Salaam; tel. (22) 2116496; fax (22) 2122923; e-mail fepu@hotmail.co.uk; internet www.kilimo.go.tz; f. 1955; bi-monthly; Swahili; publ. by Ministry of Agriculture, Food Security and Co-operatives; Editor LUCAS NYANGI; circ. 15,000.

Ushirika Wetu: POB 2567, Dar es Salaam; tel. (22) 2184081; e-mail ushirika@covision2000.com; monthly; publ. by Tanzania Federation of Co-operatives; Editor SIMON J. KERARYO; circ. 40,000.

NEWS AGENCY

Press Services Tanzania (PST) Ltd: POB 31042, Dar es Salaam; tel. and fax (22) 2119195.

Publishers

Central Tanganyika Press: POB 1129, Dodoma; tel. (26) 2390015; fax (26) 2324565; e-mail ctp@anglican.or.tz; internet www.anglican .or.tz/ctp.htm; f. 1954; religious; Man. PETER MANG'ATI MAKASSI.

DUP (1996) Ltd: POB 7028, Dar es Salaam; tel. and fax (22) 2410137; e-mail director@dup.udsm.ac.tz; f. 1979; educational, academic and cultural texts in Swahili and English; Dir Dr N. G. MWITTA.

Eastern Africa Publications Ltd: POB 1002 Arusha; tel. (57) 3176; f. 1979; general and school textbooks; Gen. Man. ABDULLAH SAIWAAD.

Inland Publishers: POB 125, Mwanza; tel. (68) 40064; general non-fiction, religion, in Kiswahili and English; Dir Rev. S. M. MAGESA.

Oxford University Press: Maktaba Rd, POB 5299, Dar es Salaam; tel. (22) 229209; f. 1969; literature, literary criticism, essays, poetry; Man. SALIM SHAABAN SALIM.

Tanzania Publishing House: 47 Samora Machel Ave, POB 2138, Dar es Salaam; tel. (22) 2137402; e-mail tphhouse@yahoo.com; f. 1966; educational and general books in Swahili and English; Gen. Man. PRIMUS ISIDOR KARUGENDO.

GOVERNMENT PUBLISHING HOUSE

Government Printer: Office of the Prime Minister, POB 3021, Dar es Salaam; tel. (22) 2860900; fax (22) 2866955; e-mail gptz@pmo.go .tz; Dir KASSIAN C. CHIBOGOYO.

Broadcasting and Communications

REGULATORY AUTHORITY

Tanzania Communications Regulatory Authority (TCRA): Mawasiliano Towers, Plot 2005/5/1, Block C, Sam Nujoma Rd, POB 474, Dar es Salaam; tel. (22) 2199760; fax (22) 2412009; e-mail dg@tcra.go.tz; internet www.tcra.go.tz; f. 1993; licenses postal and telecommunications service operators; manages radio spectrum; acts as ombudsman; Chair. BUXTON CHIPETA; Dir-Gen. Prof. JOHN S. NKOMA.

TELECOMMUNICATIONS

In 2011 there were seven providers of telecommunications services in Tanzania. In December of that year there were 25.7m. subscribers to mobile telephone services and 161,063 subscribers to fixed-line telephone services.

Airtel Tanzania: Airtel House, cnr Ali Hassan Mwinyi and Kawawa Rds, Dar es Salaam; tel. 784103001 (mobile); e-mail info.africa@ airtel.com; internet africa.airtel.com/tanzania; f. 2001; fmrly Zain Tanzania, present name adopted 2010; Man. Dir SAM ELANGALLOOR.

Benson Informatics Ltd (BOL): A. H. Mwinyi Rd, Plot No 37, POB 78914, Dar es Salaam; tel. (22) 2666670; fax (22) 2666471; e-mail boldar@bol.co.tz; internet www.bolmobile.co.tz; f. 2000; internet and mobile services provider; CEO NIZAR ABDOU.

MIC Tanzania (Mobitel) Ltd: Lugoda St, POB 2929, Dar es Salaam; tel. 713800800 (mobile); fax (22) 2120474; e-mail mobitel@mobitel.co.tz; internet www.tigo.co.tz; operates mobile cellular telecommunications services through Mobitel network; brand name Tigo; 100% owned by Millicom International Cellular (Luxembourg); Man. Dir MARCELO ALEMAN.

Sasatel: Dar es Salaam; tel. 614200200 (mobile); fax 614200201 (mobile); e-mail customercare@sasatel.co.tz; internet www.sasatel .co.tz; mobile cellular telephone operator.

Tanzania Telecommunications Co Ltd (TTCL): Extelcoms House, Samora Ave, POB 9070, Dar es Salaam; tel. (22) 2142000; fax (22) 2113232; e-mail ttcl@ttcl.co.tz; internet www.ttcl.co.tz; 35% sold to consortium of Detecon (Germany) and Mobile Systems International (Netherlands) in Feb. 2001; operates fixed-line and CDMA network; CEO SAID AMIR SAID.

Vodacom (Tanzania) Ltd: PPF Towers, 14th Floor, Garden Ave/ Ohio St, POB 2369, Dar es Salaam; tel. 754705000 (mobile); fax 754704014 (mobile); e-mail feedback@vodacom.co.tz; internet www .vodacom.co.tz; mobile cellular telephone operator; Man. Dir RENE MEZA.

Zanzibar Telecom (Zantel): POB 3459, Zanzibar; tel. (24) 2234823; fax (24) 2234850; e-mail customerservices@zantel.co.tz; internet www.zantel.co.tz; f. 1999; mobile cellular telephone operator for Zanzibar; 18% state-owned, 65% owned by Emirates Telecommunications Corpn (ETISALAT, UAE) and 17% owned by Meeco International; Chair. ESSA AL-HADDAD; CEO ALI BIN JARSH.

BROADCASTING

In 2006 there were 47 radio stations and 29 radio stations licensed to operate in Tanzania.

Radio

Clouds FM: POB 31513, Dar es Salaam; Gen. Man. RUGE MUTAHABA.

Parapanda Radio Tanzania: POB 9191, Dar es Salaam; tel. (22) 2860760; e-mail radiotanzania@raha.com; state-run FM station.

Radio 5 Arusha: POB 11843, Arusha; tel. (27) 8052; fax (27) 4201; e-mail impala@cybernet.co.tz.

Radio FM Zenj 96.8: Zanzibar; f. 2005; owned by Zanzibar Media Corpn; broadcasts to 60% of Zanzibar, to be extended to all of Zanzibar and mainland coast from southern Tanzania to Kenya; Gen. Man. AUSTIN MAKANI.

Radio Kwizera: POB 154, N'Gara; tel. and fax (28) 2226079; e-mail rkngara@jrstz.co.tz; internet www.radiokwizera.org; f. 1995; station's objective is to educate, entertain and inform refugee and local communities, with the aim of bringing about peace and reconciliation; Dir DAMAS S. J. MISSANGA.

Radio One: Mikocheni Light Industrial Area, POB 4374, Dar es Salaam; tel. (22) 275914; fax (22) 2775915; e-mail info@itv.co.tz; internet www.ippmedia.com; wholly owned by IPP Ltd; Man. Dir JOYCE MHAVILLE.

Radio Tanzania Zanzibar: state-owned.

Radio Tumaini (Hope): 1 Bridge St, POB 9916, Dar es Salaam; tel. (22) 2117307; fax (22) 2112594; e-mail tumaini@cats-net.com; internet radiotumaini.tripod.com; broadcasts in Swahili within Dar es Salaam; operated by the Roman Catholic Church; broadcasts on religious, social and economic issues; Dir ESTHER CHILAMBO.

Sauti Ya Tanzania Zanzibar (The Voice of Tanzania Zanzibar): POB 1178, Zanzibar; f. 1951; state-owned; broadcasts in Swahili on three wavelengths; Dir SULEIMAN JUMA.

Tanzania Broadcasting Corporation (TBC): Broadcasting House, Nyerere Rd, POB 9191, Dar es Salaam; tel. (22) 2860760; fax (22) 2865577; e-mail info@tbcorp.org; internet www.tbcorp.org; f. 2008; incorporates Radio Tanzania Dar es Salaam and the national TV network, Televisheni ya Taifa; Dir-Gen. DUNSTAN TIDO MHANDO.

> **Radio Tanzania Dar es Salaam (RTD):** POB 9191, Dar es Salaam; tel. (22) 2860760; fax (22) 2865577; e-mail info@tbcorp .org; internet www.tbcorp.org; f. 1951; state-owned; subsidiary of TBC; domestic services in Swahili; external services in English; Gen. Man. EDDA SANGA.

Television

The process of switching from analogue to digital television was completed, as scheduled, on 31 December 2012.

Dar es Salaam Television (DTV): POB 21122, Dar es Salaam; tel. (22) 2116341; fax (22) 2113112; e-mail franco.dtv@raha.com; f. 1994; Man. Dir FRANCO TRAMONTANO.

Independent Television (ITV): Mikocheni Light Industrial Area, POB 4374, Dar es Salaam; tel. (22) 2775914; fax (22) 2775915; e-mail itv@ipp.co.tz; internet www.ippmedia.com; f. 1994; wholly owned by IPP Ltd; 65% of programmes are locally produced and in Kiswahili; Man. Dir JOYCE MHAVILLE.

Star TV: Post Rd, POB 1732, Mwanza; tel. (28) 2503262; fax (28) 2500713; e-mail marketing@startvtz.com; internet www.startvtz .com; f. 2000.

Tanzania Broadcasting Corporation (TBC): see Radio

> **Televisheni ya Taifa (TVT):** POB 31519, Dar es Salaam; tel. (22) 2700011; fax (22) 2773078; e-mail info@tbcorp.org; internet www .tbc.go.tz; f. 2000; state-owned; subsidiary of TBC since 2008; Gen. Man. CLEMENT MSHANA.

Television Zanzibar: Karume House, POB 314, Zanzibar; tel. and fax (24) 22315951; e-mail karumehouse@tvz.co.tz; internet www.tvz .co.tz; f. 1973; Dir OMAR O. CHANDE.

Finance

(cap. = capital; res = reserves; dep. = deposits; m. = million; brs = branches; amounts in Tanzanian shillings, unless otherwise indicated)

BANKING

In 2010 there were 41 banking institutions in Tanzania: 29 commercial banks, seven regional unit banks and five other financial institutions. Of these, four were fully owned by the Government and the rest were privately owned.

Central Bank

Bank of Tanzania (Benki Kuu Ya Tanzania): 10 Mirambo St, POB 2939, Dar es Salaam; tel. (22) 2110946; fax (22) 2113325; e-mail info@ hq.bot-tz.org; internet www.bot-tz.org; f. 1966; bank of issue; cap. 10,000m., res 639,286m., dep. 1,854,572m. (June 2009); Gov. and Chair. Prof. BENNO NDULU; 4 brs.

Principal Banks

Akiba Commercial Bank Ltd: TDFL Bldg, Upanga Rd, POB 669, Dar es Salaam; tel. (22) 2118340; fax (22) 2114173; e-mail akiba@ cats-net.com; internet www.acb-bank.com; f. 1997; cap. 8,170.7m., res 4,049.5m., dep. 59,796.2m. (Dec. 2009); Chair. Dr IDRIS RASHIDI; Man. Dir JOHN LWANDE.

Azania Bank Ltd: Mawasiliano Towers, 3rd Floor, Plot No. 2005/5/ 1/2, Block C, Sinza, Sam Nujoma Rd, POB 32089, Dar es Salaam; tel. (22) 2412025; fax (22) 2412028; e-mail info@azaniabank.co.tz; internet www.azaniabank.co.tz; 55% owned by National Social Security Fund, 31% owned by Parastatal Pension Fund, 9% owned by East African Development Bank, 5% owned by individuals; cap. 10,867.6m., res 918,4m., dep. 120,854.0m (Dec. 2009); Chair. WILLIAM E. ERIO; CEO CHARLES SINGILI; 14 brs.

BancABC (Tanzania) Ltd: Barclays House, 1st Floor, Ohio St, POB 31, Dar es Salaam; tel. (22) 2119303; fax (22) 2112402; e-mail abct@africanbankingcorp.com; internet www.africanbankingcorp .com; wholly owned by African Banking Corpn Holdings Ltd; cap. 5,404m. (Dec. 2003); Man. Dir ISRAEL CHASOSA.

Bank M (Tanzania) Ltd: POB 96, 8 Ocean Rd, Dar es Salaam; tel. (22) 2127825; fax (22) 2127824; e-mail ganpath.pillai@bankm.co.tz; internet www.bankm.co.tz; f. 2007; 19.82% owned by Negus Holdings, 17.65% by Equity & Allied Ltd; cap. 10,502.5m., dep. 97,457.6m. (Dec. 2009); Chair. NIMROD MKONO; CEO SANJEEV KUMAR; 4 brs.

Barclays Bank (Tanzania) Ltd: Barclays House, Ohio St, POB 5137, Dar es Salaam; tel. (22) 2136970; fax (22) 2129750; e-mail kihara.maina@barclays.com; internet www.barclays.com/africa/ tanzania; 99.9% owned by Barclays PLC (United Kingdom), 0.1% owned by Ebbgate Holdings Ltd; cap. 18,750m. (Dec. 2003); Man. Dir CHRISTOPHER KIHARA MAINA.

BOA Bank (Tanzania) Ltd: NDC Development House, cnr Kivukoni Front and Ohio St, POB 3054, Dar es Salaam; tel. (22) 2111229; fax (22) 2113740; e-mail eab@eurafricanbank-tz.com; internet www .boatanzania.com; f. 1994 as Eurafrican Bank (Tanzania) Ltd, name changed as above in 2007; 36.68% owned by Bank of Africa Kenya Ltd, 25.01% by Aureos Capital East Africa LLC, 25.01% by Belgian Investment Co; total assets 89,486m. (Dec. 2007); Chair. FULGENCE M. KAZAURA; Man. Dir KOBBY ANDAH.

Citibank Tanzania Ltd: Ali Hassan Mwinyi Rd, POB 71625, Dar es Salaam; tel. (22) 2117575; fax (22) 2113910; 99.98% owned by Citibank Overseas Investment Corpn; Chair. EMEKA EMUWA; CEO JAMAL ALI HUSSEIN.

CRDB Bank: Azikiwe St, POB 268, Dar es Salaam; tel. (22) 2117442; fax (22) 2116714; e-mail crdb@crdbbank.com; internet www .crdbbank.com; f. as Co-operative and Rural Development Bank in 1947, transferred to private ownership and current name adopted 1996; 30% owned by DANIDA Investment; cap. 54,413.3m., res 153,209.5m., dep. 1,625,227.7m. (Dec. 2009); Chair MARTIN J. MMARI; Man. Dir Dr CHARLES S. KIMEI; 56 brs.

Dar es Salaam Community Bank Ltd (DCB): Arnautoglu Bldg, Bibi Titi Mohamed St, POB 19798, Dar es Salaam; tel. (22) 2180253; fax (22) 2180239; e-mail dcb@africaonline.co.tz; f. 2001; cap. 1,796m. (Dec. 2003); Chair. PAUL MILVANGE RUPIA; Man. Dir EDMUND PANCRAS MKWAWA.

Diamond Trust Bank Tanzania Ltd: POB 115, 9th Floor, Harbour View Towers, Dar es Salaam; tel. (22) 2114891; fax (22) 2124244; internet www.dtbafrica.com; f. 1946 as Diamond Jubilee Investment Trust; converted to bank and adopted current name in 1996; 55% owned by Diamond Trust Bank Kenya Ltd, 23% owned by Aga Khan Fund for Economic Development SA (Switzerland); cap. 1,550.6m., res 5,452.9m., dep. 176,827.4m. (Dec. 2009); Chair. ABDUL SAMJI; CEO VIJU CHERIAN.

EXIM Bank (Tanzania) Ltd: NIC Investment House, Samora Ave, POB 1431, Dar es Salaam; tel. (22) 2113091; fax (22) 2119737; e-mail marketing@eximbank-tz.com; internet www.eximbank-tz.com; cap. 12,900m., res 15,452m., dep. 462,039m. (Dec. 2009); Chair. YOGESH MANEK; Man. Dir S. M. J. MWAMBENJA.

FBME Bank Ltd: Samora Ave, POB 8298, Dar es Salaam; tel. (22) 2126000; fax (22) 2126006; e-mail headoffice@fbme.com; internet www.fbme.com; f. 1982; cap. US $43.2m., res US $5.9m., dep. US $1,562.8m. (Dec. 2009); Chair. AYOUB-FARID M. SAAB, FADI M. SAAB; Gen. Man. (Tanzania) JOHN LISTER; 5 brs.

Habib African Bank Ltd: Indira Gandhi/Zanaki St, POB 70086, Dar es Salaam; tel. (22) 2111107; fax (22) 2111014; e-mail hasanrizvi@habibafricanbank.co.tz; f. 1998; cap. 7,475m., dep. 65,236m. (Dec. 2009); Chair. HABIB MOHAMMED D. HABIB; Man. Dir SYED HASAN RIZVI; 2 brs.

I & M Tanzania Ltd Bank Ltd: Jivan Hirji Bldg, Indira Gandhi/ Mosque St, POB 1509, Dar es Salaam; tel. (22) 2110212; fax (22) 2118750; e-mail cfunionbank@raha.com; internet www.imbank .com; f. 2002 by merger of Furaha Finance Ltd and Crown Finance & Leasing Ltd; present name adopted 2010; cap. 4m. (Dec. 2006); Chair. SARIT S. RAJA SHAH; CEO SUBRAMANIAN GOPALAN.

International Bank of Malaysia (Tanzania) Ltd: Upanga/ Kisutu St, POB 9363, Dar es Salaam; tel. (22) 2110518; fax (22) 2110196; e-mail ibm@afsat.com; Chair. JOSEPHINE PREMLA SIVARETNAM; CEO M. RAHMAT.

International Commercial Bank (Tanzania) Ltd: 1st Floor, Jamhuri St/Morogoro Rd, POB 9362, Dar es Salaam; tel. (22) 2134989; fax (22) 2134286; e-mail enquiry@icbank-tz.com; f. 1998; CEO L. K. GANAPATHIRAMANI; 5 brs.

Kenya Commercial Bank (Tanzania) Ltd: National Audit House, Samora/Ohio St, POB 804, Dar es Salaam; tel. (22) 2115386; fax (22) 2115391; internet www.kcb.co.ke; cap. 6,000m. (Dec. 2003); Chair. PETER MUTHOKA; Man. Dir Dr EDMUND BERNARD MNDOLWA.

Mufindi Community Bank: POB 147, Mafinga; tel. and fax (26) 2772165; e-mail mucoba@africaonline.co.tz; cap. 100m. (Dec. 2003); Chair. ATTILIO MOHELE; Gen. Man. DANY MPOGOLE.

Mwanga Community Bank: Mwanga Township, POB 333, Mwanga, Kilimanjaro; tel. and fax (27) 2754235; Man. Dir CHRIS HALIBUT.

National Microfinance Bank Ltd (NMB): Samora Ave, POB 9213, Dar es Salaam; tel. (22) 2124048; fax (22) 2110077; e-mail ceo@nmbtz.com; internet www.nmbtz.com; f. 1997 following disbandment of the National Bank of Commerce; 51% state-owned, 49% owned by a consortium led by Rabobank Group; Chair. MISHECK NGATUNGA; CEO MARK H. WIESSING; 140 brs.

NBC Ltd (National Bank of Commerce Ltd): NBC House, Sokoine Drive, POB 1863, Dar es Salaam; tel. (22) 2112082; fax (22) 2112887; e-mail nbcltd@nbctz.com; internet www.nbctz.com; f. 1997; 55% owned by ABSA Group Ltd (South Africa), 30% by Govt and 15% by International Finance Corpn; cap. 10,000m., res 154,446m., dep. 1,051,393m. (Dec. 2009); Man. Dir LAWRENCE MAFURU; 56 brs.

NIC Bank Tanzania Ltd: Mezannine Floor, Harbour View Towers, Mission St/Samora Ave, POB 20268, Dar es Salaam; tel. (22) 2118625; fax (22) 2116733; e-mail james.muchiri@nic-bank.com; internet www.nic-bank.com; name changed as above in 2010; 51% owned by National Industrial Credit Bank Ltd (Kenya); Chair. ABDULSULTAN HASHAM JAMAL; Man. Dir JAMES MUCHIRI; 4 brs.

People's Bank of Zanzibar Ltd (PBZ): POB 1173, Stone Town, Zanzibar; tel. (24) 2231119; fax (24) 2231121; e-mail pbzltd@zanlik .com; f. 1966; controlled by Zanzibar Govt; cap. 5,000.0m., res 10,785.2m., dep. 99,480.4m. (Dec. 2009); Chair. ABDUL RAHMAN M. JUMBE; Man. Dirs J. M. AMOUR, N. S. NASSOR; 3 brs.

Stanbic Bank Tanzania Ltd: Sukari House, cnr AH Mwinyi/ Kinondoni Rd, POB 72647, Dar es Salaam; tel. (22) 2666430; fax (22) 2666301; e-mail tanzaniainfo@stanbic.com; internet www .stanbic.co.tz; f. 1993; wholly owned by Standard Africa Holdings Ltd; cap. 2,000m., res 871m., dep. 230,804m. (Dec. 2005); Chair ARNOLD B. S. KILEWO; Man. Dir BASHIR AWALE; 10 brs.

Standard Chartered Bank Tanzania Ltd: International House, 1st Floor, cnr Shaaban Robert St and Garden Ave, POB 9011, Dar es Salaam; tel. (22) 2122125; fax (22) 2113770; f. 1992; wholly owned by Standard Chartered Holdings (Africa) BV, Netherlands; cap. 15,032.0m., res 2,525.9m., dep. 713,527.3m. (Dec. 2009); Man. Dir JEREMY AWORI; 7 brs.

Tanzania Development Finance Co Ltd (TDFL): TDFL Bldg, Plot 1008, cnr Upanga Rd and Ohio St, POB 2478, Dar es Salaam; tel. (22) 2116417; fax (22) 2116418; e-mail mail@tdfl.co.tz; f. 1962; owned by Govt (32%), govt agencies of the Netherlands and Germany (5% and 26%, respectively), the Commonwealth Development Corpn (26%) and the European Investment Bank (11%); cap. 3,303m. (Dec. 2001); Chair. H. K. SENKORO; CEO J. McGUFFOG.

Tanzania Investment Bank (TIB): Bldg No. 3, Mlimani City Office Park, Sam Nujoma Rd, POB 9373, Dar es Salaam; tel. (22) 2411101; fax (22) 2411095; e-mail md@tib.co.tz; internet www.tib.co .tz; f. 1970; 99% govt-owned; cap. 7,641m., res 2,823m., dep. 45,746m. (Dec. 2005); Man. Dir PETER E. M. NONI.

Tanzania Postal Bank (TPB): Extelecoms Annex Bldg, Samora Ave, POB 9300, Dar es Salaam; tel. (22) 2112358; fax (22) 2114815; e-mail md@postalbank.co.tz; internet www.postalbank.co.tz; f. 1991; state-owned; cap. 1,041m. (Dec. 2003); Chair. Prof. LETICIA RUTA-SHOBYA; Man. Dir and CEO ALPHONSE R. KIHWELE; 4 brs and 113 agencies.

United Bank for Africa Tanzania Ltd: 30C/30D Nyerere Rd, POB 80514, Dar es Salaam; tel. (22) 2863452; fax (22) 2863454; e-mail uba@cats-net.com; Chair. N. N. KITOMARI; Man. Dir AYOBOLA ABIOLA.

BANKING ASSOCIATION

Tanzania Bankers Association: 4th Floor, Sukari House, Ohio/ Sokoine Dr., POB 70925, Dar es Salaam; tel. (22) 2127764; fax (22) 2124492; e-mail info@tanzaniabankers.org; internet www .tanzaniabankers.org; f. 1995; Chair. BEN CHRISTIAANSE; Exec. Dir PASCAL L. KAMUZORA.

STOCK EXCHANGE

Dar es Salaam Stock Exchange: Twigga Bldg, 4th Floor, Samora Ave, POB 70081, Dar es Salaam; tel. (22) 2135779; fax (22) 2133849; e-mail info@darstockexchange.com; internet www.dse.co.tz; f. 1998; Chair. PETER MACHUNDE; Chief Exec. Dr HAMISI S. KIBOLA.

INSURANCE

In 2010 there were 23 licensed insurance companies in Tanzania, of which two were fully owned by the Government.

African Life Assurance Co Ltd: International House, POB 79651, Dar es Salaam; tel. (22) 2122914; fax (22) 2122917; e-mail charlesw@ aflife.co.tz; Chair. CHARLES WASHOMA.

Alliance Insurance Corpn Ltd: 7th Floor, Exim Tower, POB 9942, Dar es Salaam; tel. (22) 2139100; fax (22) 2139098; e-mail admin@ alliancetz.com; internet www.alliancetz.com; Chair. SHAFFIN JAMAL; Man. Dir K. V. A. KRISHNAN.

Jubilee Insurance Co of Tanzania Ltd (JICT): 4th Floor, Amani Plaza, Ohio St, POB 20524, Dar es Salaam; e-mail jictz@ jubileetanzania.com; internet www.jubileetanzania.com; 40% owned by Jubilee Insurance Kenya, 24% by local investors, 15% by the IFC, 15% by the Aga Khan Fund for Economic Devt, 6% by others; cap. US $2m; Prin. Officer S. RAVI.

National Insurance Corporation of Tanzania Ltd (NIC): POB 9264, Dar es Salaam; tel. (22) 2113823; fax (22) 2113403; e-mail info-nic@nictanzania.com; internet www.nictanzania.co.tz; f. 1963; state-owned; all classes of insurance; Chair. Prof. J. L. KANYWANYI; Man. Dir OCTAVIAN W. TEMU; 30 brs.

Niko Insurance (Tanzania) Ltd: PPF House, 8th Floor, Morogoro Rd/Samora Ave, POB 21228, Dar es Salaam; tel. (22) 2120188; fax (22) 2120193; e-mail info@nikoinsurance.co.tz; internet www .nikoinsurance.co.tz; f. 1998; subsidiary of NICO Holdings Ltd (based in Malawi); Gen. Man. MANFRED Z. SIBANDE.

REGULATORY AUTHORITY

Tanzania Insurance Regulatory Authority (TIRA): Block 33, Plot No. 85/2115, Mtendeni St, POB 9892, Dar es Salaam; tel. (22) 2132537; fax (22) 2132539; e-mail coi@tira.go.tz; internet www.tira .go.tz; f. 2009; Chair. Prof. G. M. FIMBO; Commr of Insurance I. L. KAMUZORA.

Trade and Industry

GOVERNMENT AGENCIES

Parastatal Sector Reform Commission (PSRC): Sukari House, POB 9252, Dar es Salaam; tel. (22) 2115482; fax (22) 2113065; e-mail masalla@raha.com.

Tanzania Investment Centre (TIC): Shaaban Robert St, POB 938, Dar es Salaam; tel. (22) 2116328; fax (22) 2118253; e-mail information@tic.co.tz; internet www.tic.co.tz; f. 1997; promotes and facilitates investment in Tanzania; Chair. E. MTANGO; Exec. Dir RAYMOND MBILINYI (acting).

Tanzania Trade Development Authority (TanTrade): Mwl J. K. Nyerere Fair Grounds, Kilwa Rd, POB 5402, Dar es Salaam; tel. (22) 2850238; fax (22) 2850239; internet www.tantrade .or.tz; f. 2009 to replace the Board of Internal Trade and the Board of External Trade; aims to develop and promote internal and external trade; Chair. SALUM SHAMTE; Dir-Gen. RAMADHAN H. KHALFAN.

CHAMBERS OF COMMERCE

Dar es Salaam Chamber of Commerce: Kelvin House, Samora Machel Ave, POB 41, Dar es Salaam; tel. (754) 270438; fax (22) 2112754; e-mail dcc1919@yahoo.com; f. 1919; Exec. Dir BERNARD MSEKWA.

Tanzania Chamber of Commerce, Industry and Agriculture (TCCIA): 21 Ghana Ave, POB 9713, Dar es Salaam; tel. (22) 2119436; fax (22) 2119437; e-mail info@tccia.com; internet www .tccia.com; f. 1988; Pres. ALOYS MWAMANGA; Exec. Dir DANIEL MACHEMBA (acting).

Zanzibar Chamber of Commerce: POB 1407, Zanzibar; tel. (24) 2233083; fax (24) 2233349.

DEVELOPMENT CORPORATIONS

Capital Development Authority: POB 1, Dodoma; tel. (26) 2324053; fax (26) 2322650; e-mail cda@pmo.com.tz; f. 1973 to develop the new capital city of Dodoma; govt-controlled; Dir-Gen. M. L. KITILLA.

Economic Development Commission: POB 9242, Dar es Salaam; tel. (22) 2112681; f. 1962 to plan national economic development; state-controlled.

National Development Corporation: Kivukoni Front, Ohio St, POB 2669, Dar es Salaam; tel. (22) 2112893; fax (22) 2113618; e-mail epztz@ndctz.com; f. 1965; state-owned; cap. Ts. 30.0m.; promotes progress and expansion in production and investment; Man. Dir GIDEON NASSARI.

Small Industries Development Organization (SIDO): Mfaume/ Fire Rd, Upanga, POB 2476, Dar es Salaam; tel. (22) 2151947; fax (22) 2152070; e-mail dg@sido.go.tz; internet www.sido.go.tz; f. 1973; parastatal; promotes and assists development of small-scale enterprises in public, co-operative and private sectors, aims to increase the involvement of women in small businesses; Chair. JAPHET S. MLAGALA; Dir-Gen. MIKE LAISOR.

Sugar Development Corporation: Dar es Salaam; tel. (22) 2112969; fax (22) 230598; Gen. Man. GEORGE G. MBATI.

Tanzania Petroleum Development Corporation (TPDC): POB 2774, Dar es Salaam; tel. (22) 2181407; fax (22) 2180047; internet www.tpdc-tz.com; f. 1969; state-owned; oversees petroleum exploration and undertakes autonomous exploration, imports crude petroleum and distributes refined products; Man. Dir YONA S. M. KILLAGANE.

There is also a development corporation for textiles.

INDUSTRIAL AND TRADE ASSOCIATIONS

Cashewnut Board of Tanzania (CBT): POB 533, Mtwara; tel. (23) 2333303; fax (23) 2333536; e-mail info@cashewnut-tz.org; internet www.cashewnut-tz.org; govt-owned; regulates the marketing, processing and export of cashews; Chair. ANNA M. ABDALLAH; Dir-Gen. A. BENO MHAGAMA.

Confederation of Tanzania Industries (CTI): NIC Investment House, 9th Floor, Samora Ave, POB 71783, Dar es Salaam; tel. (22) 2114954; fax (22) 2115414; e-mail cti@cti.co.tz; internet www.cti.co .tz; f. 1991; Chair. FELIX MOSHA; Exec. Dir CHRISTINE KILINDU.

National Coconut Development Programme: POB 6226, Dar es Salaam; tel. (22) 2700552; fax (22) 275549; e-mail mari@mari.or.tz; f. 1979 to revive coconut industry; processing and marketing via research and devt in disease and pest control, agronomy and farming systems, breeding and post-harvest technology; based at Mikocheni Agricultural Research Inst; Dir Dr ALOIS K. KULLAYA.

Sugar Board of Tanzania: Sukari House, 6th Floor, cnr Ohio St and Sokoine Dr., Dar es Salaam; tel. (22) 2111523; fax (22) 2130598; internet www.sbt.go.tz; f. 2001; Dir-Gen. MATHEW M. KOMBE.

Tanzania Coffee Board (TCB): Kahawa House, POB 732, Moshi; tel. (27) 2752324; fax (27) 2752026; e-mail info@coffeeboard.or.tz; internet www.coffeeboard.or.tz; Chair. EVA HAWA SINARE; Dir-Gen. ADOLPH KUMBURU.

Tanzania Cotton Board: Pamba House, Garden Ave, POB 9161, Dar es Salaam; tel. (22) 2122564; fax (22) 2112894; e-mail info@ cotton.co.tz; internet www.cotton.or.tz; f. 1984; regulates, develops and promotes the Tanzanian cotton industry; Chair. Dr FESTUS BULUGU LIMBU; Dir-Gen. MARCO MTUNGA.

Tanzania Exporters' Association: NIC Investment House, 6th Floor, Wing A, Samora Ave, POB 1175, Dar es Salaam; tel. and fax (22) 2125438; e-mail tanexa.exporters@yahoo.com; f. 1994; Exec. Dir MTEMI LAWRENCE NALUYAGA.

Tanzania Horticultural Association (TAHA): Kanisa Rd, House No. 49, POB 16520, Arusha; tel. and fax (27) 2544568; e-mail info@ tanzaniahorticulture.com; internet www.tanzaniahorticulture.com; f. 2004; Chair. COLMAN M. NGALO; Exec. Dir JACQUELINE MKINDI.

Tanzania Pyrethrum Board: POB 149, Iringa; f. 1960; Chair. Brig. LUHANGA; CEO P. B. G. HANGAYA.

Tanzania Sisal Board: POB 277, Tanga; tel. and fax (27) 2645060; e-mail tansisal@tsbtz.org; internet www.tsbtz.org; f. 1997; Chair. Prof. JOSEPH SEMBOJA; Dir-Gen. HAMISI MAPINDA.

Tanzania Tobacco Board: POB 227, Mazimbu Rd, Morogoro; tel. (23) 2603364; fax (23) 2604401; Chair. V. KAWAWA; Dir-Gen. FRANK S. URIO.

Tanzania Wood Industry Corporation: POB 9160, Dar es Salaam; Gen. Man. E. M. MNZAVA.

Tea Association of Tanzania: POB 2177, Dar es Salaam; tel. (22) 2122033; e-mail trit@twiga.com; f. 1989; Chair. Dr NORMAN C. KELLY; Exec. Dir DAVID E. A. MGWASSA.

Tea Board of Tanzania: TETEX House, 1st Floor, Pamba Rd, POB 2663, Dar es Salaam; tel. and fax (22) 2114400; e-mail info@ teaboardtz.org; internet teaboardtz.org; Chair. ANNE S. MAKINDA; Dir-Gen. Eng. MATHIAS ASSENGA BENEDICT.

Zanzibar State Trading Corporation: POB 26, Zanzibar; internet www.zstczanzibar.com; govt-controlled since 1964; sole exporter of cloves, clove stem oil, chillies, copra, copra cake, lime oil and lime juice; Dir SULEIMAN JONGO.

UTILITIES

Regulatory Authority

Energy and Water Utilities Regulatory Authority (EWURA): 6th Floor, Harbour View Towers, Samora Ave, POB 72175, Dar es Salaam; tel. (22) 2123850; fax (22) 2123180; e-mail info@ewura.go.tz; internet www.ewura.go.tz; f. 2001; technical and economic regulation of the electricity, petroleum, natural gas and water sectors; Chair. SIMON F. SAYORE; Dir-Gen. HARUNA MASEBU.

Electricity

Tanzania Electric Supply Co Ltd (TANESCO): POB 9024, Dar es Salaam; tel. (22) 2451130; fax (22) 2113836; e-mail info@tanesco .com; internet www.tanesco.co.tz; state-owned; placed under private management in May 2002; privatization pending; Chair. Gen. ROBERT MBOMA; Man. Dir WILLIAM MHANDO.

Gas

Enertan Corpn Ltd: POB 3746, Dar es Salaam.

Songas Ltd: cnr Nelson Mandela and Morogoro Rds, POB 6342, Dar es Salaam; tel. (22) 2452160; fax (22) 2452161; internet www.songas .com; f. 1998; Gen. Man. JIM MCCARDLE.

Water

Dar es Salaam Water and Sewerage Authority: Dawasco House, 2453/188 Sokoine Dr., POB 5340, Dar es Salaam; tel. (22) 2110931; e-mail info@dawasco.com; internet www.dawasco.com; privatization pending.

National Urban Water Authority: POB 5340, Dar es Salaam; tel. (22) 2667505.

Dar es Salaam Water and Sewerage Corporation (DAWASCO): POB 5340, Dar es Salaam; tel. and fax (22) 2110931; internet www.dawasco.com; sole provider of water supply and sewerage services in Dar es Salaam and parts of the coastal region; CEO ALEX KAAYA.

CO-OPERATIVES

There are some 1,670 primary marketing societies under the aegis of about 20 regional co-operative unions. The Co-operative Union of Tanzania is the national organization to which all unions belong.

Tanzania Federation of Co-operatives Ltd: Ushirika Bldg, 9th Floor, Lumumba St, POB 2567, Dar es Salaam; tel. (22) 2184084; fax (22) 2184081; e-mail ushirika@ushirika.co.tz; internet www .ushirika.coop; f. 1962; Exec. Sec. WILLIGIS O. MBOGORO; 700,000 mems.

Department of Co-operative Societies: POB 1287, Zanzibar; f. 1952; promotes formation and development of co-operative societies in Zanzibar.

Principal Societies

Kagera Co-operative Union Ltd: POB 5, Bukoba; tel. (28) 2220229; fax (28) 2221168; e-mail kcu@africaonline.co.tz; internet www.kcu-tz.com; 74 affiliated societies; 75,000 mems.

Kilimanjaro Native Co-operative Union (1984) Ltd: POB 3032, Moshi; tel. (27) 2752785; fax (27) 2754204; e-mail kncu@kilinet.co.tz; f. 1984; represents smallholder farmers and coffee producers; 68 regd co-operative societies; Gen. Man. TOBIA MASAKI.

Nyanza Co-operative Union Ltd: POB 9, Mwanza.

TRADE UNIONS

Trade Union Congress of Tanzania (TUCTA): Dar es Salaam; f. 2000; Pres. OMARY AYOUB JUMA; Sec.-Gen. NICHOLAS MGAYA.

Zanzibar Trade Union Congress (ZATUC): Zanzibar; f. 2002; Sec.-Gen. MAKAME LAUNI MAKAME.

Transport

RAILWAYS

In 2010 2,707 km of 1,000-mm-gauge railway track were operated by Reli Assets Holding Co Ltd, which develops, promotes and manages rail infrastructure assets. Construction of a new US $4,700m. railway line linking Tanga with Musoma on Lake Victoria was scheduled to commence in 2014. The 1,067-mm-gauge Tazara railway line linking Dar es Salaam with New Kapiri Mposhi, Zambia, has a total length of 1,860 km, of which 969 km are within Tanzania. In 2007 the Tanzania Railways Corpn was privatized under a 25-year lease agreement with the Indian company RITES, and renamed Tanzania Railways Ltd (TRL). However, in 2010 the lease was terminated due to disagreements between the two parties and the Tanzanian Government resumed its control over TRL.

Tanzania Railways Ltd (TRL): POB 468, Dar es Salaam; tel. and fax (22) 2110599; e-mail ccm_shamte@trctz.com; internet www.trctz .com; f. 1977 after dissolution of East African Railways; operates 2,600 km of lines within Tanzania; Chair. J. K. CHANDE; Dir-Gen. LINFORD MBOMA.

Tanzania-Zambia Railway Authority (Tazara): Nyerere Rd, POB 2834, Dar es Salaam; tel. and fax (22) 2862033; e-mail mdhq@tazarasite.com; internet www.tazarasite.com; jtly owned and administered by the Tanzanian and Zambian Govts; operates a 1,860-km railway link between Dar es Salaam and New Kapiri Mposhi, Zambia, of which 975 km are within Tanzania; Man. Dir AKASHAMBATWA MBIKUSITA-LEWANIKA; Regional Man. (Tanzania) ABDALLAH SHEKIMWERI.

ROADS

In 2009 Tanzania had an estimated 90,807 km of classified roads, of which some 14.9% were paved. A 1,930-km main road links Zambia and Tanzania, and there is a road link with Rwanda.

The island of Zanzibar has 619 km of roads, of which 442 km are bituminized, and Pemba has 363 km, of which 130 km are bituminized.

Tanzania National Roads Agency (TANROADS): Airtel House, 3rd Floor, Ali Hassan Mwinyi/Kawawa Rd Junction, POB 11364, Dar es Salaam; tel. (22) 2926001; fax (22) 2926011; e-mail tanroadshq@tanroads.org; internet www.tanroads.org; f. 2000; responsible for the maintenance and development of the trunk and regional road network; Chair. ABEL MWAISUMO; Chief Exec. P. A. L. MFUGALE.

INLAND WATERWAYS

Steamers connect with Kenya, Uganda, the Democratic Republic of the Congo, Burundi, Zambia and Malawi. A rail ferry service operates on Lake Victoria between Mwanza and Port Bell.

SHIPPING

Tanzania's major harbours are at Dar es Salaam (eight deep-water berths for general cargo, three berths for container ships, eight anchorages, lighter wharf, one oil jetty for small oil tankers up to 36,000 gross tons, offshore mooring for oil supertankers up to 100,000 tons, one 30,000-ton automated grain terminal) and Mtwara (two deep-water berths). There are also ports at Tanga (seven anchorages and lighterage quay), Bagamoyo, Zanzibar and Pemba. At 31 December 2012 the flag registered fleet numbered 303 vessels, totalling 5,645,253 grt, of which 125 were general cargo ships and 53 tankers.

Tanzania Ports Authority (TPA): POB 9184, Dar es Salaam; tel. (22) 2116258; fax (22) 2113432; e-mail dp@tanzaniaports.com; internet www.tanzaniaports.com; f. 2005 to replace the Tanzania Harbours Authority, in preparation for privatization; Chair. RAPHAEL MOLLEL; Dir-Gen. EPHRAIM MGAWE.

Chinese-Tanzanian Joint Shipping Co: 31 Kisutu Rd, POB 696, Dar es Salaam; tel. (22) 2113389; fax (22) 2113388; e-mail admin@sinotaship.com; f. 1967; services to People's Republic of China, South-East Asia, Eastern and Southern Africa, Red Sea and Mediterranean ports.

National Shipping Agencies Co Ltd (NASACO): POB 9082, Dar es Salaam; f. 1973; state-owned shipping co; Man. Dir D. R. M. LWIMBO.

Shipping Management Services (SHMASE): POB 5480, Dar es Salaam; tel. (22) 2123796; fax (22) 2123352; e-mail infor@shmase.com; internet www.shmase.com; Man. Dir HASHIM MASHELLE.

Tanzania Coastal Shipping Line Ltd: POB 9461, Dar es Salaam; tel. (22) 237034; fax (22) 2116436; regular services to Tanzanian coastal ports; occasional special services to Zanzibar and Pemba; also tramp charter services to Kenya, Mozambique, the Persian (Arabian) Gulf, Indian Ocean islands and the Middle East; Gen. Man. RICHARD D. NZOWA.

CIVIL AVIATION

There are more than 100 airports and landing strips in Tanzania. The major international airport is at Dar es Salaam, 13 km from the city centre, and there are also international airports at Kilimanjaro, Mwanza and Zanzibar.

Tanzania Civil Aviation Authority (TCAA): IPS Bldg, cnr Samora Machel Ave and Azikiwe St, POB 2819, Dar es Salaam; tel. (22) 2198100; fax (22) 2844304; e-mail tcaa@tcaa.go.tz; internet www.tcaa.go.tz; f. 2003; replaced Directorate of Civil Aviation (f. 1977); ensures aviation safety and security, provides air navigation services; Dir-Gen. FADHILI MANONGI.

Air Zanzibar: POB 1784, Zanzibar; f. 1990; operates scheduled and charter services between Zanzibar and destinations in Tanzania, Kenya and Uganda.

New ACS Ltd: Peugeot House, 36 Upanga Rd, POB 21236, Dar es Salaam; fax (22) 237017; operates domestic and regional services; Dir MOHSIN RAHEMTULLAH.

Precision Air Services Ltd: Along Nyerere/Pugu Rd, POB 70770, Dar es Salaam; tel. (22) 2860701; fax (22) 2860725; e-mail info@precisionairtz.com; internet www.precisionairtz.com; f. 1993; operates scheduled and charter domestic and regional services; Man. Dir and CEO ALFONSE KIOKO.

Tanzanair: Julius Nyerere Int. Airport, POB 364, Dar es Salaam; tel. (22) 2843131; fax (22) 2844600; e-mail info@tanzanair.com; internet www.tanzanair.com; f. 1969; operates domestic and regional charter services, offers full engineering and maintenance services for general aviation aircraft; agent for sales of Cessna aircraft; Man. Dir JOHN SAMARAS.

Tourism

Mount Kilimanjaro is a major tourist attraction. Tanzania has set aside about one-quarter of its land area for 12 national parks, 17 game reserves, 50 controlled game areas and a conservation area. Other attractions for tourists include beaches and coral reefs along the Indian Ocean coast, and the island of Zanzibar. Visitor arrivals totalled 782,699 in 2010, and in the following year revenue from tourism was an estimated US $1,457m. (excluding passenger transport).

Tanzania Tourist Board: IPS Bldg, 3rd Floor, POB 2485, Dar es Salaam; tel. (22) 2111244; fax (22) 2116420; e-mail safari@ud.co.tz; internet www.tanzaniatouristboard.com; f. 1993; state-owned; supervises the development and promotion of tourism; Man. Dir PETER J. MWENGUO.

Tanzania Wildlife Co Ltd: POB 1144, Arusha; tel. 787787459 (mobile); e-mail info@tanzaniawildlifecompany.com; internet www.tanzaniawildlifecompany.com; f. 1974; organizes hunting, photographic, horseback and adventure safaris; Man. Dir LEON LAMPRECHT.

Zanzibar Tourist Corporation: POB 216, Zanzibar; tel. (24) 2238630; fax (24) 2233417; e-mail ztc@zanzinet.com; internet www.zanzibartouristcorporation.net; f. 1985; operates tours and hotel services; Gen. Man. SABAAH SALEH ALI.

Defence

As assessed at November 2012, the total armed forces numbered 27,000, of whom an estimated 23,000 were in the army, 1,000 in the navy and 3,000 in the air force. Paramilitary forces comprised a 1,400-strong Police Field Force and an 80,000-strong reservist Citizens' Militia. In 2012 a total of 1,081 Tanzanian troops were stationed abroad, of whom 29 were observers.

Defence Expenditure: Budgeted at 531,000m. shillings in 2013.

Commander-in-Chief of the Armed Forces: President JAKAYA MRISHO KIKWETE.

Chief of Defence Forces: Gen. DAVIS MWAMUNYANGE.

Education

In 2004/05 enrolment at pre-primary level was 23% (23% of both boys and girls). Education at primary level is officially compulsory and is provided free of charge. In secondary schools a government-stipulated fee is paid. Villages and districts are encouraged to construct their own schools with government assistance. Almost all primary schools are government-owned. Primary education begins at seven years of age and lasts for seven years. In 2009/10 enrolment at primary level included 92% of pupils in the appropriate age-group (91% of boys; 92% of girls). Secondary education, beginning at the age of 14, lasts for a further six years, comprising a first cycle of four years and a second of two years. Secondary enrolment in 2008/09 was equivalent to 27% of children in the appropriate age-group (males 31%; females 24%), according to UNESCO estimates. Enrolment at tertiary level included just 1% of those in the relevant age-group in 2004/05 (males 2%; females 1%). There are 10 universities, including one on Zanzibar. Tanzania also has a number of vocational training centres and technical colleges. The 2010 budget allocated 18.3% of total government expenditure for education.

THAILAND

Introductory Survey

LOCATION, CLIMATE, LANGUAGE, RELIGION, FLAG, CAPITAL

The Kingdom of Thailand lies in South-East Asia. It is bordered to the west and north by Myanmar (Burma), to the north-east by Laos and to the south-east by Cambodia. Thailand extends southward, along the isthmus of Kra, to the Malay Peninsula, where it borders Malaysia. The isthmus, shared with Myanmar, gives Thailand a short coastline on the Indian Ocean, and the country also has a long Pacific coastline on the Gulf of Thailand. The climate is tropical and humid, with an annual average temperature of 29°C (85°F). There are three main seasons: hot, rainy and cool. Temperatures in Bangkok are generally between 20°C (68°F) and 35°C (95°F). The national language is Thai. There are small minorities of Chinese, Malays and indigenous hill peoples. The predominant religion is Buddhism, mainly of the Hinayana (Theravada) form. About 4% of the population, predominantly Malays, are Muslims, and there is also a Christian minority, mainly in Bangkok and the north. The national flag (proportions 2 by 3) has five horizontal stripes, of red, white, blue, white and red, the central blue stripe being twice as wide as each of the others. The capital is Bangkok.

CONTEMPORARY POLITICAL HISTORY

Historical Context

Formerly known as Siam, Thailand took its present name in 1939. Under the leadership of Marshal Phibul Songkhram, Thailand entered the Second World War (1939–45) as an ally of Japan. Phibul was deposed in 1944, but returned to power in 1947 after a military coup. His influence declined during the 1950s, and in 1957 he was overthrown in a bloodless coup, led by Field Marshal Sarit Thanarat. Elections took place, but in 1958 martial law was declared and all political parties were dissolved. Sarit died in 1963 and was succeeded as Prime Minister by Gen. (later Field Marshal) Thanom Kittikachorn, who had served as Deputy Prime Minister since 1959. Thanom continued the combination of military authoritarianism and economic development instituted by his predecessor. A Constitution was introduced in 1968, and elections to a National Assembly took place in 1969, but in November 1971, following an increase in communist insurgency and internal political unrest, Thanom annulled the Constitution, dissolved the National Assembly and imposed martial law.

Domestic Political Affairs

During 1972 there were frequent student demonstrations against the military regime, and in October 1973 the Government was forced to resign, after the army refused to use force to disperse student protesters and King Bhumibol withdrew his support for the administration. An interim Government was formed under Dr Sanya Dharmasakti, the President of the Privy Council. In October 1974 a new Constitution, legalizing political parties, was promulgated, and in January 1975 elections were held to the new House of Representatives. A coalition Government was formed in February by Seni Pramoj, the leader of the Democrat Party (DP), but it was defeated by a vote of no confidence in the following month.

A new right-wing coalition Government, headed by the leader of the Social Action Party (SAP), Kukrit Pramoj (brother of Seni), was unable to maintain its unity, and Kukrit resigned in January 1976. After a further general election in April, a four-party coalition Government was formed, with Seni as Prime Minister. However, following the violent suppression of student demonstrations in October, during which the security forces killed hundreds of protesters, the Seni Government was dissolved, and a right-wing military junta, the National Administrative Reform Council (NARC), seized power. Martial law was declared, the Constitution was annulled, political parties were banned and strict press censorship was imposed. A new Constitution was promulgated, and a new Cabinet was announced, with Thanin Kraivixien, a Supreme Court judge, as Prime Minister.

Under the Thanin Government there was considerable repression of students and political activists. In October 1977 the Government was overthrown in a bloodless coup by a Revolutionary Council (later known as the National Policy Council) of military leaders, most of whom had been members of the NARC. The 1976 Constitution was abrogated, and the Secretary-General of the National Policy Council (who was also the Supreme Commander of the Armed Forces), Gen. Kriangsak Chomanan, became Prime Minister. Many detainees were released, censorship was partially relaxed and the King nominated a National Assembly on the advice of the National Policy Council. In December 1978 the National Assembly approved a new Constitution, and elections to a new House of Representatives were held in April 1979. However, members of the Senate were all nominated by the Prime Minister, and were almost all military officers. Kriangsak remained Prime Minister and formed a new Cabinet, after which the National Policy Council was dissolved. When Kriangsak resigned in March 1980, he was replaced by Gen. Prem Tinsulanonda, the Commander-in-Chief of the Army and the Minister of Defence. A new coalition Government, composed largely of centre-right politicians acceptable to the armed forces, was formed.

Prem's administration survived an abortive coup attempt in April 1981. In December Prem effected a ministerial reorganization, reincorporating members of the SAP (who had been excluded from the Government in March), in order to repulse a challenge from the new National Democracy Party (NDP), established by Kriangsak. In April 1983 no single party won an overall majority in legislative elections, and a coalition Government was formed by the SAP, Prachakorn Thai, the DP and the NDP, despite Chart Thai (Thai Nation) having won the largest number of seats. Prem was reappointed to the premiership.

In September 1985 an attempted coup by a group of military officers in Bangkok was quickly suppressed by troops loyal to the Government, but at least five people were killed during the fighting. The leader of the revolt, Col Manoon Roopkachorn (who had also led the coup attempt in 1981), fled the country, and 40 others, including Kriangsak, were put on trial in October, accused of inciting sedition and rebellion. Gen. Arthit Kamlang-ek, the Supreme Commander of the Armed Forces and Commander-in-Chief of the Army (who was believed to have been sympathetic to the aims of the coup leaders), was replaced in his posts by Gen. Chavalit Yongchaiyudh, hitherto the army Chief of Staff.

In September 1985 and January 1986 there were extensive government changes, including the replacement of all members of the SAP, following the resignation of Kukrit as the party's leader. In May 1986, after a parliamentary defeat for the Government over proposed vehicle taxation, the House of Representatives was dissolved. At elections for an enlarged legislature in July, the DP won 100 of the 347 seats (compared with 56 of the 324 seats at the previous elections). A coalition Government was formed, including members of the DP, Chart Thai, the SAP, Rassadorn and seven independent ministers. Prem remained Prime Minister.

In April 1988 the rejection by dissident members of the DP of proposed legislation on copyright prompted 16 DP ministers to resign from the Government for failing to maintain party unity. The King dissolved the House of Representatives, at Prem's request, and new elections were held in July. Internal disputes weakened support for the DP (25 dissidents had resigned in May), and Chart Thai won the largest number of seats (87). Gen. Chatichai Choonhavan, the leader of Chart Thai, was appointed Prime Minister in August, after Prem declined an invitation to remain in the post. A new Cabinet was formed, comprising members of Chart Thai, the DP, the SAP, Rassadorn, the United Democratic Party and the Muan Chon party. In April 1989 Ruam Thai, the Community Action Party, the Prachachon Party and the Progressive Party merged to form an opposition grouping called Ekkaparb (Solidarity). Nine members of the Prachachon Party subsequently defected to Chart Thai, giving the ruling coalition control of 229 of the 357 seats in the legislature.

In March 1990 Chavalit resigned as acting Supreme Commander of the Armed Forces; he also stood down as Commander-in-Chief of the Army, in which post he was succeeded by Gen.

Suchinda Kraprayoon, hitherto his deputy. In July, despite growing criticism of Chatichai's administration, following a number of corruption scandals and labour unrest, the House of Representatives overwhelmingly rejected an opposition motion of no confidence in the Government. In August, however, Chatichai reorganized the Cabinet, incorporating Puangchon Chao Thai in the ruling coalition, and reducing the influence of the SAP, following the implication of many of its members in allegations of corruption.

In November 1990 Chatichai demoted the leader of the Muan Chon party, Chalerm Yoobamrung, an outspoken critic of the armed forces, from his position as Minister to the Prime Minister's Office. The leadership of the armed forces had demanded Chalerm's dismissal, threatening unspecified intervention if government changes did not take place. In early December Chatichai resigned as Prime Minister; he was reappointed on the next day and subsequently formed a coalition Government comprising Chart Thai, Rassadorn, Puangchon Chao Thai and former opposition parties Prachakorn Thai and Ekkaparb, which provided him with reduced—although still majority—support (227 of the 357 seats) in the House of Representatives.

On 23 February 1991 Chatichai's Government was ousted in a bloodless military coup. Gen. Sunthorn Kongsompong, the Supreme Commander of the Armed Forces, assumed administrative power as the Chairman of the newly created National Peace-keeping Council (NPC). The NPC was actually dominated by the effective head of the armed forces, Gen. Suchinda, who was appointed as one of four Deputy Chairmen of the Council. The coup leaders cited government corruption and abuse of power to justify their action; however, the coup was also widely believed to have been organized in response to the recent erosion of military influence.

Under the NPC, the Constitution was abrogated, the House of Representatives, the Senate and the Cabinet were dissolved, and martial law was imposed. The NPC won unprecedented royal approval, and in March 1991 an interim Constitution was published. Anand Panyarachun, a business executive and former diplomat, was appointed acting Prime Minister pending fresh elections. Anand selected a primarily civilian interim Cabinet, composed mainly of respected technocrats and former ministers. Chatichai and Arthit, who had been arrested at the time of the coup, were released after two weeks. The NPC appointed a 292-member National Legislative Assembly, which included 149 serving or former military personnel, as well as many civilians known to have links to the armed forces.

In May 1991 martial law was repealed in most areas, and political activity was permitted to resume. The New Aspiration Party (NAP—formed in October 1990 by Chavalit) gathered support as the traditional parties were in disarray, largely owing to investigations of corruption by the newly created Assets Examination Committee. In June 1991 the Commander-in-Chief of the Air Force, Air Chief Marshal Kaset Rojananin, sponsored the creation of a new party, Samakkhi Tham, led by Narong Wongwan, a former leader of Ekkaparb. In August Suchinda assumed, in addition to the post of Commander-in-Chief of the Army, the role of Supreme Commander of the Armed Forces.

A new Constitution was approved by the National Legislative Assembly in December 1991. However, opposition parties, including the NAP and Palang Dharma (led by the popular and influential Governor of Bangkok, Maj.-Gen. Chamlong Srimuang), voiced concerns over certain provisional clauses (which were to remain in effect for four years), under which the NPC was to appoint the Prime Minister and the 270-member Senate, and regarding the Senate's right to vote jointly with the elected House of Representatives on motions of no confidence, thus enabling the Senate potentially to dismiss a government with the support of only 46 elected representatives.

A general election took place on 22 March 1992, in which 59.2% of the electorate voted. Samakkhi Tham and Chart Thai won 79 and 74 seats, respectively, of the 360 seats in the House of Representatives, while the NAP secured 72 seats and Palang Dharma took 41 seats (32 of which were in Bangkok). On the day of the election the NPC appointed the 270 members of the Senate, 154 of whom were officers of the armed forces or police. In late March it was announced that Narong Wongwan would lead a coalition government comprising his own party (Samakkhi Tham), Chart Thai, Prachakorn Thai, the SAP and Rassadorn. However, US allegations of Narong's involvement in illicit drugs-trafficking led to the nomination being rescinded. In early April Suchinda was named as Prime Minister; his accession to the premiership prompted an immediate popular protest by more than 50,000 demonstrators against the appointment of an unelected Prime Minister. Later in April Suchinda appointed eight other unelected members to a new Cabinet, retaining several technocrats from Anand's interim Government.

Constitutional reform and other developments

In early May 1992 Chamlong announced, at a rally attended by 100,000 demonstrators, that he would fast until death unless Suchinda resigned. The demonstrations continued uninterrupted for one week until the government parties agreed to amend the Constitution to prevent an unelected Prime Minister (including the incumbent Suchinda) from taking office, and to limit the power of the unelected Senate. However, violent demonstrations erupted in Bangkok when it appeared that the Government might renege on its commitments. The Government declared a state of emergency in Bangkok and neighbouring provinces. Chamlong was arrested and more than 3,000 people were detained by security forces in an attempt to suppress the riots, which continued for several days. Following unprecedented intervention by King Bhumibol, Suchinda ordered the release of Chamlong, announced a general amnesty for those involved in the protests and pledged to introduce amendments to the Constitution. Suchinda resigned on 24 May, after failing to retain the support of the five coalition parties.

On 10 June 1992 the National Assembly (comprising the Senate and the House of Representatives) approved constitutional amendments, whereby the Prime Minister was required to be a member of the House of Representatives, the authority of the Senate was restricted and the President of the House of Representatives was to be the President of the National Assembly. Contrary to expectations, the King named Anand as Prime Minister. Anand appointed a politically neutral, unelected Cabinet, and dissolved the National Assembly in preparation for a general election. At the end of June the four parties that had opposed the military Government (the DP, the NAP, Palang Dharma and Ekkaparb) formed an electoral alliance, the National Democratic Front. In July Chatichai declined the leadership of Chart Thai and formed a new party, Chart Pattana, which quickly gained widespread support. During mid-1992 Anand introduced measures to curb the political power of the armed forces, reduce military control of state enterprises, and remove the authority of the armed forces to intervene in situations of social unrest. In August Air Chief Marshal Kaset and the Commander-in-Chief of the Army, Issarapong Noonpakdi, were dismissed from their positions and demoted to inactive posts. The new Commander-in-Chief of the Army, Gen. Wimol Wongwanit, pledged that the army would not interfere in politics under his command.

Some 62.1% of the electorate voted in a general election on 13 September 1992. 'Vote-buying' and violence persisted, especially in the north-eastern region. The DP won the largest number of seats, taking 79 of the 360 seats in the House of Representatives, while Chart Thai and Chart Pattana secured 77 and 60 seats, respectively. The DP was able to form a coalition with its allies, the NAP, Palang Dharma and Ekkaparb, and thus command 185 of the 360 seats. Despite its participation in the previous administration, the SAP (with 22 seats) was also subsequently invited to join the Government. On 23 September Chuan Leekpai, the leader of the DP, was formally approved as Prime Minister. Chuan declared his intention to eradicate corruption, to decentralize government, to enhance rural development and to reduce the powers of the Senate.

Following its announcement in September 1993 that it was to merge with four opposition parties, including Chart Pattana, under the leadership of Chatichai, the SAP was expelled from the Government and replaced by the Seritham Party. In September 1994 Chamlong resumed the leadership of Palang Dharma in party elections, and subsequently persuaded the party executive committee to approve the replacement of the party's 11 cabinet members. Chamlong's nominations for cabinet membership included Thaksin Shinawatra, a prominent business executive, as Minister of Foreign Affairs. Despite some opposition to the selection of unelected candidates, the appointments were confirmed in October, when Chamlong was named a Deputy Prime Minister.

In December 1994 the NAP withdrew from the ruling coalition over a constitutional amendment providing for the future election of local government representatives. The NAP voted against the Government to protect the vested interests of incumbent local administrators who would control many votes at the next election. In order to secure a parliamentary majority, Chuan was obliged to include Chatichai's Chart Pattana in the governing coalition, although this severely compromised the Government's claims to represent honesty and reform.

In January 1995 Chuan finally obtained the approval of the National Assembly for amendments to the Constitution to expand the country's democratic base. The reforms included a reduction in the size of the appointed Senate to two-thirds of that of the elective House of Representatives, the lowering of the eligible voting age from 20 years to 18, equality for women, the establishment of an administrative court, the introduction of parliamentary ombudsmen and the prohibition of senators and members of the Government from holding monopolistic concessions with government or state bodies. This last amendment necessitated the resignation of Thaksin as Minister of Foreign Affairs, owing to his extensive business interests.

In May 1995, dissatisfied with the Government's response to revelations that a land reform programme had been used to benefit wealthy landowners, the opposition tabled a motion of no confidence in the Government. (The scandal had already prompted the resignation of the Minister of Agriculture and Co-operatives in December 1994.) Following an announcement by Chamlong that Palang Dharma would not support the governing coalition in the no-confidence vote, Chuan dissolved the House of Representatives on 19 May 1995. Chamlong resigned as leader of Palang Dharma later that month and was replaced by Thaksin, who had relinquished majority control of his company.

At elections to an enlarged 391-seat House of Representatives, which took place on 2 July 1995 and attracted a turn-out of 62.0% of the electorate, Chart Thai won the largest number of seats (92), followed by the DP (86) and the NAP (57). Support for these parties was based on provincial patronage politics, and allegations of 'vote-buying' were widespread. The leader of Chart Thai, Banharn Silpa-archa, formed a coalition Government comprising Chart Thai, the NAP, Palang Dharma, the SAP, Prachakorn Thai, Muan Chon and later Nam Thai (a business-orientated party established in 1994 by Amnuay Viravan, a former cabinet minister). Banharn appointed all the leaders of the coalition parties (except for the Muan Chon party) as Deputy Prime Ministers. The composition of Banharn's Cabinet was widely criticized, owing to the predominance of professional politicians (who were often subject to allegations of corruption and 'vote-buying').

In March 1996 Banharn announced the composition of the new Senate, the first to be appointed by a democratically elected Prime Minister. In contrast to the previous Senate, only 39 active military officers were named as senators; other appointees included academics and business executives. Palang Dharma withdrew from the ruling coalition in August, following a cabinet dispute over alleged bribery in the awarding of bank licences, thereby reducing the Government's legislative majority by 23 seats. In September Banharn was able to secure the support of his coalition partners in a scheduled motion of no confidence in his administration only by undertaking to resign from the premiership. However, the inability of the coalition partners to agree on the appointment of a new Prime Minister led to the dissolution of the House of Representatives on 27 September.

In the general election on 17 November 1996, which was marred by violence and alleged extensive irregularities, the NAP won 125 of the 393 seats, while the DP secured 123 seats. The majority of NAP seats were gained through provincial patronage politics, while the more politically aware electorate of Bangkok returned the DP to 29 of the city's 37 seats. Chavalit, the leader of the NAP, was appointed Prime Minister, heading a coalition that incorporated Chart Pattana, the SAP, Prachakorn Thai, Muan Chon and the Seritham Party. The ruling coalition thus held 221 seats in the House of Representatives. Most major cabinet posts were assigned to members of Chart Pattana and the NAP. Thaksin resigned as leader of Palang Dharma following the party's failure to win more than one seat in the House of Representatives.

The Government's indecisive handling of the economy contributed to a financial crisis in mid-1997, which prompted an increase in popular protests. The Government introduced measures in June to constrain media attacks on the authorities and to limit mass protests. Successive cabinet reorganizations in August and October failed to restore public or investor confidence in the Government, and the Thai currency continued to depreciate. Chavalit's subsequent announcement that he would resign from the premiership on 6 November, following the adoption of important electoral and financial legislation, led to a slight recovery of the Thai baht. On 9 November Chuan, who maintained his reputation for integrity, assumed the premiership, following the formation of a coalition comprising Chuan's DP, Chart Thai, the SAP, Ekkaparb, the Seritham Party, Palang Dharma and the Thai Party (as well as 12 of the 18 Prachakorn Thai deputies), which commanded the support of 210 of the 393 seats in the House of Representatives. The transfer of power to Chuan, under the terms of the new Constitution (see below), without the intervention of the armed forces or resort to a non-elected leader, received widespread approval and represented significant democratic progress. The new Cabinet included Tarrin Nimmanhaeminda as Minister of Finance (a post that he had occupied in Chuan's previous administration). However, the baht continued to depreciate, causing intermittent social unrest.

Meanwhile, a new Constitution was approved on 27 September 1997, and was promulgated on 11 October. The new charter provided for, *inter alia*, a directly elected Senate; an expanded House of Representatives comprising 400 deputies from single-member constituencies and 100 deputies elected by proportional representation; the resignation of cabinet ministers from the legislature; the establishment of a minimum educational requirement for members of the National Assembly; the formation of an Election Commission to supervise elections (in place of the Ministry of the Interior); the centralization of vote-counting; compulsory voting; and the guarantee of press freedom. In July 1998 a new political party, Thai Rak Thai, was established by former Deputy Prime Minister Thaksin.

Although Thailand's economy appeared to have stabilized by August 1998, the Government was beset by allegations of corruption. In October Chuan reorganized his Government, bringing the Chart Pattana party into the ruling coalition and thereby increasing to 257 the number of seats held by the coalition in the House of Representatives. Five new ministers were appointed to the Cabinet, including the Secretary-General of Chart Pattana, Suwat Liptapanlop, who was assigned the industry portfolio.

In July 1999 the SAP withdrew from the governing coalition, following disputes within the party concerning the allocation of ministerial positions, prompting a reorganization of the Cabinet. In August a report on the state-owned Krung Thai Bank, exposing dubious loan policies and other irregularities, led to allegations of corruption being made against Minister of Finance Tarrin, whose brother, Sirin Nimmanhaeminda, had been the President of Krung Thai Bank until his resignation in January. The controversy surrounding the bank constituted the main focus of a no-confidence motion filed by the opposition against the Government in December, in which the ruling coalition was accused of mismanagement of the economy and of condoning corruption. Although the Government survived the censure debate, the proceedings exposed divisions within the governing coalition (particularly between the DP and Chart Thai).

On 4 March 2000 elections to the new 200-member Senate were contested by more than 1,500 candidates. The level of voter participation was reported at 70%, with voting being compulsory for the first time. Later in the month the Election Commission disqualified 78 of the 200 winning candidates (including the wives of two cabinet ministers) owing to allegations of electoral fraud. Further allegations of malpractice necessitated four subsequent rounds of polling in April–July. However, on 1 August Thailand's first-ever democratically elected Senate was formally inaugurated. Meanwhile, in March the Deputy Prime Minister and Minister of the Interior, Maj.-Gen. (retd) Sanan Kajornprasart, resigned from the Government (and was replaced by Banyat Bantadtan), amid allegations made by the National Counter Corruption Commission (NCCC) that he had falsified his assets declaration statement (recently required of all cabinet ministers). Sanan was convicted of corruption by the Constitutional Court in August.

The premiership of Thaksin Shinawatra

In November 2000 it was announced that elections to the House of Representatives would be held in January 2001. One notable feature of Thai Rak Thai's electoral campaign was its targeting of rural votes by pledging grants of 1m. baht for each of Thailand's 70,000 villages and offering a debt relief scheme for farmers. At the legislative elections held on 6 January Thai Rak Thai won 248 of the 500 seats in the House of Representatives. However, many domestic and international observers declared that, despite the vigilance of the Election Commission, the elections had been the most corrupt ever held in Thailand. In late January re-polling was held in more than 60 constituencies where the Election Commission had found evidence of malpractice. In February all but five of those appointed to the Cabinet by the new Prime Minister, Thaksin, were members of Thai Rak Thai, with which the Seritham Party had merged since the elections, thus affording Thai Rak Thai an unprecedented absolute majority in the House of Representatives. With the support of its coalition partners, the NAP and Chart Thai, the incoming Thai Rak Thai administration controlled 339 of the 500 seats in the House.

On 30 June 2001 by-elections were held in seven constituencies to fill seats in the House of Representatives vacated by members disqualified for breaches of campaign rules after the January elections. However, the polls were again marred by allegations of corruption. Meanwhile, in April two bombs exploded in southern Thailand, killing a child and injuring 42 people. The involvement of a militant Islamist separatist organization, the Patani United Liberation Organization (PULO), was suspected. The PULO belonged to Bersatu, an umbrella organization of three separatist movements, which, the Government claimed, was seeking to establish a Muslim state in southern Thailand.

In August 2001 the Constitutional Court acquitted Prime Minister Thaksin, by a narrow margin, of corruption charges pertaining to the concealment of financial assets. In October the Government introduced a plan to provide low-cost health care for the nation's poorest people, thus implementing one of Thaksin's election pledges. Doubts remained, however, over the quality of the service provided.

Having voted to merge with its coalition partner, Thai Rak Thai, in January 2002, the NAP was legally dissolved in March. Also in March the Government was further strengthened when Chart Pattana joined the ruling coalition; Suwat Liptapanlop, Secretary-General of Chart Pattana, was allocated a ministerial position shortly thereafter. Meanwhile, by-elections were held in 14 constituencies where the January 2001 general election results had been invalidated owing to electoral fraud and corruption. Thai Rak Thai lost five seats as a result, but retained its commanding majority in the National Assembly. Shortly afterwards six police officers died after suspected members of a militant Islamist separatist organization attacked security outposts—two in Pattani province and one in Yala province. Two bombs later exploded in Yala province, coinciding with a tour of the region by the Minister of the Interior. The explosions were attributed to the Gerakan (or Guragan) Mujahideen Islam Pattani, a constituent group of Bersatu thought to be linked to the international terrorist network al-Qa'ida.

In October 2002 Thaksin implemented an extensive cabinet reorganization, including the replacement of Chavalit Yongchaiyudh as Minister of Defence by Thammarak Isarangura and the creation of six new ministries. A further redistribution of cabinet portfolios took place in February 2003, in which, *inter alia*, the Minister of Finance, Somkid Jatusripitak, and the Minister of Justice, Purachai Piumsombun, were both appointed Deputy Prime Ministers.

Meanwhile, the Government announced the commencement of an intensive anti-drugs campaign. As the campaign progressed, the large number of suspected drug dealers being killed prompted criticism from both local and international human rights groups, which claimed that the Thai authorities were operating an illegal 'shoot to kill' policy and effectively condoning extra-judicial violence. The Government rejected a request from the Office of the UN High Commissioner for Human Rights (OHCHR, see p. 45) that it be permitted to send a representative to the country to investigate the killings. In March Thaksin acknowledged that mistakes had been made during the campaign, but denied that the police had been responsible for any extra-judicial killings. Later in that month Thaksin ordered that the campaign should henceforth be concentrated upon provinces along the border with Myanmar, where the majority of drugs-smuggling activity was believed to take place. By mid-April 2003, according to a police statement, some 2,275 people had been killed during the campaign, of whom the police admitted to shooting 51 dead for reasons of self-defence. At the end of April Thaksin claimed that the campaign had eradicated about 90% of the country's drugs problem. Meanwhile, two attacks on army bases in the south of the country were attributed to the PULO. In May, following the success of the anti-drugs offensive, Thaksin announced the commencement of a 'war on dark influences' intended to eradicate criminal networks operating in the country. In October a 60-day government campaign was launched with the aim of ridding Thailand of 'social evils' such as drug addiction, poverty and organized crime.

In April 2003 the DP elected Banyat Bantadtan as its new leader, following the retirement of Chuan Leekpai. In May five cabinet ministers evaded censure, following the tabling of an opposition no-confidence motion accusing them of corruption. In the following month three men were arrested on suspicion of being members of the regional terrorist organization Jemaah Islamiah (JI); they later confessed to having plotted to attack embassies and tourist destinations in the country. A further suspect was arrested in July. In the following month, in response to the perceived terrorist threat to Thailand, the Cabinet approved two anti-terrorism laws by decree, circumventing the legislature owing to the reported gravity of the threat. Shortly afterwards, the alleged former operational head of JI, the Indonesian citizen Riduan Isamuddin, also known as Hambali, was apprehended in Thailand; he was later taken into custody by the USA. In September the four suspected members of JI arrested earlier in the year were officially charged with membership of the organization and with plotting terrorist attacks in Thailand; their trial began in November. (They were acquitted of the charges against them in June 2005.) Meanwhile, Chart Pattana was removed from the Government in November 2003 upon the ousting from the Cabinet of Deputy Prime Minister Korn Dabbaransi and Minister of Labour and Social Welfare Suwat Liptapanlop.

Escalating violence in the southern provinces

In January 2004 an outbreak of violence in the south of the country, which resulted in the deaths of several members of the security forces and included arson attacks on a number of schools, prompted the Government to declare martial law in the predominantly Muslim provinces of Pattani, Yala and Narathiwat, on the border with Malaysia. The Government suspected that the violence had been perpetrated by Gerakan Mujahideen Islam Pattani, although possible involvement by militants affiliated to JI was not discounted. Two suspects arrested in January were believed to be members of Bersatu. The unrest continued, resulting in the temporary closure of approximately 1,000 schools in the area. Meanwhile, the Government responded by arresting local Islamic leaders and conducting army raids on *madrasahs* (Islamic religious schools), angering many members of the local Muslim population.

In March 2004 a further cabinet reorganization was implemented, in which, *inter alia*, the incumbent Ministers of Defence, Finance and the Interior were replaced. The ministerial changes were widely interpreted as a response to the deterioration in the security situation in the south of the country, together with a decline in the performance of the Stock Exchange of Thailand and public protests at the Government's planned privatization of the Electricity Generating Authority of Thailand. In the same month, following further arson attacks in the south, which destroyed some 36 government buildings, Prime Minister Thaksin dismissed the national police chief and the army commander for the southern region. Later in March a bomb explosion in Sungai Kolok, in Narathiwat province, which injured 29 people, including 10 Malaysian tourists, prompted the Government to suspend a US $300m. development aid programme intended for Narathiwat, Pattani and Yala. In April more than 100 suspected Islamist militants carried out a series of raids on police and army bases in the south of the country. The security forces suppressed the attacks, killing 108 of the insurgents; five security officials also died in the fighting. The UN, human rights groups and some Muslim leaders questioned the level of force (including the deployment of grenades) used by the security forces to quash the attacks. Further attacks were reported in May and June.

At the end of June 2004 Chart Pattana rejoined the Government when Suwat Liptapanlop was appointed as a Deputy Prime Minister, in what was regarded as an attempt by Thaksin to consolidate support ahead of the legislative elections due to be held in early 2005. A number of deputies from Chart Thai and the DP subsequently defected to Thai Rak Thai, and in August 2004 Chart Pattana merged into Thaksin's party. Meanwhile, several former senior members of the DP established a new party, Mahachon. In early August, in its first report since its establishment in 2001, the National Human Rights Commission claimed that human rights violations had increased under Thaksin's administration, notably during the anti-drugs campaign in 2003, and accused the Government of becoming increasingly authoritarian. Thaksin rejected the report's criticisms, and declared a second anti-drugs offensive in October 2004, which was to last for one year.

More than 300 suspected insurgents had surrendered to the authorities by mid-July 2004 in response to a government campaign. Nevertheless, violent attacks and minor bomb explosions continued to occur in the southern provinces, with killings of public officials, police officers, Buddhist monks and civilians regularly reported. At the end of August Thaksin visited Narathiwat, Pattani and Yala provinces, one day after a bomb had exploded at a market in Sukhirin, in Narathiwat, killing one person and injuring 31 others. The Government conceded that it had failed to control the violence in the south, and pledged to develop new strategies to quell the unrest.

In October 2004 Thaksin effected a cabinet reorganization, including the replacement of the Ministers of Defence and of Agriculture and Co-operatives, in an apparent response to the ongoing crisis in the south and an outbreak of avian influenza ('bird flu'). In late October troops fired tear gas to disperse more than 2,000 Muslim protesters who were demonstrating in Tak Bai, in Narathiwat province, against the detention of six suspected militants. Seven of the protesters were killed in the ensuing clashes and 78 of the 1,300 demonstrators who were arrested later died, many from suffocation, as they were transported in overcrowded trucks to an army barracks. Amid increasing international concern, Thaksin ordered an independent inquiry into the deaths. Most of those detained in connection with the protests were subsequently released. A few days later two people were killed in a bomb attack in Sungai Kolok. The deteriorating security situation in the south prompted rare interventions from the monarchy. King Bhumibol urged the Government to use more restraint, and Queen Sirikit appealed for an end to the violence. In the first two weeks of November around 30 Buddhists were killed in apparent revenge attacks attributed to the PULO, which had earlier vowed to retaliate in response to the deaths in Tak Bai. Later in that month an alleged leader of Bersatu was killed in a gunfight with the security forces in Panare, in Pattani province.

In December 2004 four Islamic teachers, who were suspected of being leaders of the separatist group Barisan Revolusi Nasional (part of Bersatu), were charged with terrorism and treason. Meanwhile, the inquiry into the incident at Tak Bai in October concluded that the deaths had not been caused deliberately, but that the dispersal of the crowd and the transport of the prisoners had been mishandled and that senior officials had been negligent; three army commanders were subsequently transferred to inactive posts. The Cabinet later approved compensation worth more than 30m. baht for families of the dead and those injured.

The west coast of Thailand, in particular the province of Phang Nga, was severely affected by a series of tsunamis caused by a massive earthquake in the Indian Ocean on 26 December 2004. More than 5,300 people, including at least 1,700 foreigners from some 36 countries, were killed, and a further 2,900 were reported missing.

In legislative elections held on 6 February 2005 Thai Rak Thai secured a large majority with 377 of the 500 seats in the House of Representatives; the DP took 96 seats, Chart Thai 25 and Mahachon two. The rate of voter participation was reported at 72%. Thai Rak Thai's success, which enabled it to form a single-party government (the first in Thailand's history), was widely attributed to Thaksin's prompt response to the devastation caused by the tsunamis in December and the strong performance of the economy under his premiership. However, as in previous election campaigns, there were numerous allegations of electoral malpractice. The election results prompted the immediate resignation of Banyat Bantadtan as leader of the DP; Abhisit Vejjajiva was elected as his replacement in March. Prime Minister Thaksin began an unprecedented second consecutive term in office in March, following his formal re-election to the premiership by the House of Representatives.

The violence in southern Thailand continued unabated and by early March 2005 more than 690 people had died since January 2004. In February 2005 the Government approved the formation of a new 12,000-strong army regiment to be stationed in the south. The troops were to focus on development work, as well as on improving security, but local Islamic leaders warned that an increased military presence in the region (where Thai Rak Thai had failed to secure a single seat in the recent elections) would only heighten disillusionment with the Government. As a three-day visit to the south by Thaksin in mid-February came to an end, a car bomb in Sungai Kolok killed six people and injured more than 40.

In March 2005 Thaksin appointed former premier Anand Panyarachun to chair a 48-member National Reconciliation Commission (NRC), which was charged with restoring peace in the south, and announced his intention to reduce the number of troops deployed in the region. In April two people were killed

and more than 60 injured in three bomb explosions in the southern province of Songkhla, the first major attacks to occur outside the provinces of Narathiwat, Pattani and Yala. In November Thaksin extended martial law, already in force in the three southernmost provinces, to encompass the districts of Chana and Thepha in Songkhla province. The state of emergency was subsequently renewed on numerous occasions and remained in place at mid-2013.

The ousting of Thaksin and imposition of military rule

In January 2006, in the largest corporate take-over in Thailand's history, Prime Minister Thaksin's family sold its 49.6% holding stake in national telecommunications firm Shin Corporation Public Co Ltd (Shin Corp) to Singapore's state investment wing, Temasek Holdings, at a price of 70,000m. baht (US $1,900m.). The transaction took place on the same day on which a new law raising the limit on foreign ownership in telecommunication firms from 25% to 49% took effect. The sale provoked outrage within Thailand, with many people angered by the massive tax-free gains made by the Shinawatra family; there were demands for the Prime Minister to donate to the State the 26,000m. baht that had been waived in tax. Considerable suspicion was also aroused by the fact that Thaksin's son and daughter had purchased shares in Shin Corp from Ample Vision (an investment company established by the Prime Minister in the British Virgin Islands) at a cost of one baht per share and yet had been able to sell them, just three days later, at a price of 49.25 baht per share. Furthermore, there was widespread concern about the sale of a telecommunications firm to a foreign company on account of the potential threat to national security.

In February 2006 the Minister of Culture, Uraiwan Thienthong, tendered her resignation from the Cabinet, citing 'the decline in political morality' as the reason for her decision. Later in that month, and without prior warning, Prime Minister Thaksin announced that the House of Representatives was being dissolved in preparation for early elections; it was subsequently declared that the polls were to be held in April. However, the three main opposition parties—DP, Chart Thai and Mahachon—all announced that they were to boycott the elections, which they argued had been called to divert attention from the Shin Corp scandal. In an attempt to defuse the political tension, Thaksin offered to include the three parties within a national coalition government, regardless of whether or not they participated in the elections; however, the offer was rejected. Thaksin also declared his intention to resign if Thai Rak Thai failed to secure more than 50% of the votes cast. Prior to the elections, demonstrators demanded the removal from power of the Prime Minister at numerous protest rallies in the capital, which were organized by the People's Alliance for Democracy (PAD)—a loose coalition of anti-Thaksin groups and individuals, popularly known as the 'Yellow Shirts', which had been established in 2005 by Sondhi Limthongkul, the founder of the Manager Media Group. The political tension was accompanied by a further intensification of violence in the southern regions. Hundreds of schools in Yala were closed temporarily following the killing of three Buddhist teachers, allegedly by Muslim militants. In March the Prime Minister's son, Phantongtae Shinawatra, was adjudged to have been guilty of securities violations relating to the sale of Shin Corp, and was fined 5.98m. baht (US $153,000), by the Securities and Exchange Commission (SEC).

In the legislative elections held on 2 April 2006 Thai Rak Thai secured victory (as expected), winning approximately 57% of votes cast. Turn-out was estimated at 64.8% of the electorate. However, 33.1% of those who voted selected the 'no vote' option on ballot papers. Owing to the boycott of the polls by the three main opposition parties, the House of Representatives was unable to convene by the end of the month as a significant number of seats remained vacant, despite the holding of several by-elections. Shortly after the elections Thaksin announced that he would not seek to return to the premiership on a permanent basis and appointed the Deputy Prime Minister, Gen. Chidchai Wannasathit, to the role in an acting capacity. In May the Constitutional Court annulled the election results, declaring them invalid as the polls had been organized too quickly following the dissolution of the House of Representatives. The Election Commission subsequently announced that new legislative elections would take place in October. At the end of May Thaksin announced that he was returning to the post of interim Prime Minister.

In June 2006 a team of prosecutors from the Office of the Attorney-General urged the disbandment of various parties, including Thai Rak Thai and the DP—the former was accused of funding minor opposition parties to field candidates in constituencies in which it would have been unlikely to achieve the 20% of the vote required to secure election in uncontested seats, while the latter was alleged to have instigated a boycott of the poll. In July the Chairman of the Election Commission and two commissioners were found guilty of election law contravention and sentenced to four years' imprisonment by the Criminal Court. Meanwhile, militants carried out a series of co-ordinated bomb attacks in June and August across the three southernmost provinces, in which at least six people were killed and around 50 others were injured.

On 19 September 2006, while Thaksin was out of the country, the Government was ousted from power in a bloodless military coup led by the Commander-in-Chief of the Army, Gen. Sonthi Boonyaratglin. Gen. Sonthi, acting as part of the so-called Council for Democratic Reform, imposed martial law and suspended the Constitution, the Government and the legislature. Within a week the Council had initiated an investigation into allegations of corruption within the Thaksin Government. At the beginning of October, following the signing of an interim Constitution by King Bhumibol, Gen. (retd) Surayud Chulanont was sworn in as Prime Minister by the military leadership, which had been renamed the Council for National Security and retained significant powers over the Government and the Constitution. Fresh elections were projected for 2007, upon the drafting and approval of a new constitution. The Governor of the Bank of Thailand, Pridiyathorn Devakula, and the Chairman of Bangkok Bank, Kosit Panpiemras, were appointed Deputy Prime Ministers in the Cabinet that was subsequently announced, taking additional charge of the finance and industry portfolios, respectively. A National Legislative Assembly, comprising the Council's appointees, was approved by the King and convened in mid-October 2006. In November martial law was rescinded in approximately 40 provinces (although this did not take effect until January 2007). Meanwhile, Thaksin, who had remained overseas since the coup, announced his resignation from Thai Rak Thai in October 2006, following a large number of departures from the party, which were said to have been prompted by the military leadership's assertion that those associated with political organizations guilty of electoral malpractice would be punished. In November Thaksin's son and daughter were ordered to pay tax on their share of the proceeds of the Shin Corp sale.

Hopes of a resolution to the ongoing insurgency in the south were raised by Gen. Sonthi's announcement in October 2006 that the military leadership was willing to engage in dialogue with certain groups. In the following month Prime Minister Surayud formally apologized for the deaths of the Muslim protesters in Tak Bai in 2004 (see Escalating violence in the southern provinces), and it was later announced that charges against a number of demonstrators would be rescinded. Nevertheless, the violence continued into 2007: by March it was estimated that the conflict in the south had caused more than 2,100 fatalities, of which more than 400 had occurred since the coup. In December 2006 a series of eight bomb explosions in Bangkok killed three people; it was implied by some sources that associates of Thaksin were responsible, a claim that he subsequently denied. In January 2007 the Government suspended Thaksin's diplomatic passport and requested a media ban on his lawyer's statements. Surayud later affirmed that Thaksin would be permitted to return to Thailand on the condition that he did not engage in political activity. Doubts were expressed in February about the stability of the Government after the Deputy Prime Minister and Minister of Finance, Pridiyathorn Devakula, resigned, citing internal discord among other reasons. The interim Government's economic policies, which were based on a principle of 'self-sufficiency' advocated by the King and had thus far included measures to restrict the movement of foreign capital and foreign ownership of Thai companies, had been widely criticized and had damaged investor confidence. Chalongphob Sussangkarn succeeded Pridiyathorn as Minister of Finance, while the Minister of Social Development and Human Security, Paiboon Wattanasiritham, was promoted to the concurrent position of Deputy Prime Minister. In March Thaksin's wife, Pojaman Shinawatra, was charged with tax evasion in relation to a 1997 share transaction of the company that later became known as Shin Corp. Meanwhile, Gen. Sonthi was reported to have requested the enforcement of emergency rule to address the alleged threat of instability posed by regular anti-coup demonstrations in Bangkok. Surayud denied the request and announced that elections

would be held in December 2007, following a constitutional referendum, which was to be conducted by September.

In May 2007 the Constitutional Tribunal (which had replaced the Constitutional Court under the interim Constitution) found Thai Rak Thai guilty of violating electoral legislation prior to the April 2006 polls, but acquitted the DP of all charges of malpractice. The Tribunal ordered the dissolution of Thai Rak Thai and a ban on 111 party members, including Thaksin, from participating in politics for five years. In June 2007 the Assets Examination Committee froze bank accounts held by Thaksin (some jointly with Pojaman) containing a total of 52,900m. baht; the Committee later ordered additional assets to be frozen as investigations continued into Thaksin, who remained in self-imposed exile. A week later corruption charges were filed against Thaksin and Pojaman in relation to the latter's purchase in 2003 of a plot of land in Bangkok from a state agency for a sum allegedly far lower than its true value. Thaksin was also accused of concealing assets. Meanwhile, in early June 2007 the ban on activities by political organizations was removed to allow parties to begin campaigning for the forthcoming legislative elections.

A new draft charter, designed to curb the powers of the Prime Minister, was endorsed by 57.8% of those voting in a referendum on 19 August 2007, and, after receiving royal assent, the new Constitution took effect on 24 August. (More detailed voting results indicated the country's deep political divisions, with the charter rejected by nearly 63% of voters in the rural north-east, a stronghold of the dissolved Thai Rak Thai, but approved by some 88% of voters in the south.) The new Constitution, which was dismissed by its critics as being 'anti-Thaksin' and less democratic than the 1997 charter, provided for, *inter alia*, the restriction of the Prime Minister, who was to be barred from owning large stakes in private companies, to two four-year terms; the transformation of the Senate from a fully elected body of 200 senators to one in which 74 of its 150 senators would be selected by a seven-member committee of judges and other senior state officials (such as the President of the Constitutional Court and the Chairperson of the Election Commission), with the remainder directly elected in each province; a reduction in the number of deputies in the House of Representatives from 500 to 480 (400 to be elected on a multi-member constituency basis and 80 on a proportional representation basis); and an amnesty for those involved in the coup of September 2006. Meanwhile, in July 2007 a demonstration against military rule by several thousand people in Bangkok ended in violence, as protesters clashed with police officers after staging a rally outside the house of former Prime Minister Prem Tinsulanonda, now a senior royal adviser, who they claimed had been involved in co-ordinating the coup. Nine alleged leaders of the demonstration, reported to be either allies of Thaksin or pro-democracy activists, were subsequently arrested and charged with illegal assembly and inciting violence.

In late July 2007 the National Legislative Assembly adopted legislation prohibiting new political parties from using the same names, logos or acronyms as parties dissolved by the Constitutional Tribunal for a period of five years. Many former Thai Rak Thai deputies joined the little-known People's Power Party (PPP), while others participated in the formation of new parties, such as Puea Pandin and Ruam Jai Thai (the latter subsequently merging with Chart Pattana); Samak Sundaravej, a right-wing political veteran and former Governor of Bangkok, was elected leader of the PPP in August. In mid-August the Supreme Court issued arrest warrants for Thaksin and Pojaman after they failed to answer a summons to appear before the Court to answer the corruption charges relating to the land purchase in 2003. Further arrest warrants were issued for the couple by a criminal court in Bangkok in September 2007 in connection with a police inquiry into alleged violations of stock-trading legislation.

Gen. Sonthi was appointed Deputy Prime Minister in charge of Security in October 2007, having retired as Commander-in-Chief of the Army and resigned as Chairman of the Council for National Security, prompting speculation that he intended to remain in political office beyond the elections scheduled for December. Sonthi's appointment was part of a wider cabinet reorganization necessitated by the recent resignations of five ministers who were under investigation by the NCCC for allegedly breaching a 5% limit on ministerial shareholdings in private companies. Prime Minister Surayud and the Deputy Prime Minister and Minister of Industry, Kosit Panpiemras, assumed additional responsibility for the portfolios of the interior and of information and communications technology, respectively. Later in October the Cabinet ordered martial law to be revoked in 221 districts, but maintained in 179 districts in 31 provinces.

The restoration of civilian rule

During the week preceding the December 2007 legislative elections, amid protests outside the parliament building by students and civil society activists, the National Legislative Assembly adopted many new pieces of legislation, most notably a controversial act giving the Internal Security Operations Command, an agency comprising military and civilian representatives, wide-ranging powers to counter perceived threats to national security. These enhanced powers, which were strongly criticized by human rights groups, included the ability to order curfews, detain suspects without trial, restrict freedom of movement and override the authority of government officials.

Some 74.5% of registered voters participated in the legislative elections, which took place, as scheduled, on 23 December 2007. Polls were repeated in the following month in a number of constituencies where the Election Commission had annulled results owing to 'vote-buying' and other irregularities. The PPP emerged as the largest party in the House of Representatives, securing 233 of the 480 seats, while the DP won 164, Chart Thai 34, Puea Pandin 24, Matchimathipataya 11, Ruam Jai Thai Chart Pattana nine and Pracharaj five. Essentially the successor to Thai Rak Thai, the PPP achieved greatest success in the north and north-east of the country, and its victory was regarded as a rejection of the 2006 coup and the outgoing military leadership. None the less, its failure to secure an outright majority of seats forced the PPP to negotiate with other parties to establish a coalition administration.

In January 2008 the PPP leader, Samak Sundaravej, announced the formation of a six-party coalition controlling 316 of the 480 seats in the House of Representatives, leaving the DP as the sole opposition party in the legislature. The new House of Representatives was convened two days later, subsequently electing Samak as Prime Minister and Yongyuth Tiyapairat, the deputy leader of the PPP, as Speaker. Meanwhile, the Council for National Security was disbanded. Many strategic posts in the new Government, which took office in early February, were allocated to personal allies of Thaksin. Samak assumed personal responsibility for the defence portfolio, while Surapong Suebwonglee, the Secretary-General of the PPP, was appointed Deputy Prime Minister and Minister of Finance. Noppadon Pattama, Thaksin's legal adviser, and Chalerm Yoobamrung, another close associate of the deposed Prime Minister, became Minister of Foreign Affairs and Minister of the Interior, respectively. Later in that month the Government announced plans to resume several populist policies initiated by Thaksin and to commence a new anti-drugs campaign, similar to those conducted under the former Prime Minister (which had resulted in some 2,500 deaths). Amendments to the Constitution were also envisaged. Thaksin returned to Thailand in late February after 17 months in exile, insisting that he had retired from active politics. He was immediately taken to hear the corruption charges against him and was granted bail. In mid-March he pleaded not guilty before the Supreme Court to using his influence to assist his wife with her land purchase in 2003. Thaksin's wife, Pojaman, had already returned in January 2008, when she was also granted bail and denied the charges against her. Elections to fill 76 of the 150 seats in the Senate were held on 2 March, the other 74 members having been appointed in the previous month by the selection committee. Electoral turn-out was estimated at 55.9%. The appointed senators, who were exceptionally to serve a three-year term (in accordance with transitional measures included in the 2007 Constitution), were considered to be closer to the outgoing military leadership, while many of the elected senators (who would serve the standard six years) were reported to be allies of Thaksin. Prasobsuk Boondech, an appointed senator and former Chief Justice of the Court of Appeals, was elected Speaker of the Senate in mid-March.

Despite the restoration of civilian rule, political uncertainty persisted in early 2008. In February the Election Commission voted in favour of disqualifying Speaker Yongyuth from office, concluding that he had bribed local officials in exchange for votes during the general election campaign, and referred the case to the Supreme Court; Yongyuth stood down as Speaker pending the Court's verdict. In April the Election Commission recommended the dissolution of Chart Thai and Matchimathipataya on the grounds of electoral fraud allegedly committed by senior party officials; the case was referred to the Constitutional Court. Meanwhile, the DP accused the coalition Government of self-interest in its plans to revise the Constitution, particularly its

desire to amend the article allowing for an entire party to be held responsible for the wrongdoing of a single party executive. Martial law was rescinded in April in all areas of the country except for the southern provinces of Narathiwat, Yala, Pattani and part of Songkhla.

Political tensions rose in May 2008, as the PAD, which had led the campaign against Thaksin in 2006, resumed its anti-Government demonstrations in Bangkok, protesting against the plans for constitutional reform. The Minister in the Prime Minister's Office, Chakrapob Penkair, a close ally of Thaksin, was forced to resign from the Cabinet in late May, after it emerged that he was to be charged under *lèse-majesté* legislation (prohibiting criticism of the monarch) in connection with a speech that he gave in August 2007. Notwithstanding Samak's decision to refer the issue of constitutional change to a parliamentary committee, daily demonstrations continued, albeit on a smaller scale than those of 2006, amid speculation regarding the possibility of another military coup. The Government also provoked criticism by endorsing an application made by the Cambodian Government to UNESCO (see p. 158) seeking World Heritage status for Preah Vihear, an 11th-century temple in an area of disputed sovereignty on the Thai–Cambodian border (see Foreign Affairs). None the less, in June 2008 DP-proposed motions of no confidence in Samak and seven of his ministers were easily defeated in the House of Representatives, owing to the ruling coalition's strong majority. However, the controversy over Preah Vihear persisted, leading to the resignation of the Minister of Foreign Affairs, Noppadon, in July, after the Constitutional Court ruled that he had violated the Constitution by signing an agreement supporting Cambodia's (recently successful) bid without securing legislative approval; Tej Bunnag, hitherto adviser to the Office of His Majesty's Principal Private Secretary, was appointed as Noppadon's replacement. Meanwhile, earlier in July the Supreme Court found Yongyuth guilty of electoral fraud, banning him from participating in politics for five years.

In July 2008 Pojaman and her brother were convicted of failing to pay tax of 546m. baht on a Shin Corp share transaction in 1997 and sentenced to three years' imprisonment; Pojaman's secretary received a two-year sentence. All three were released on bail, pending an appeal. In August the Supreme Court issued an arrest warrant for Thaksin and Pojaman, who had absconded to the United Kingdom shortly before they were due to appear before the Court on charges related to Pojaman's 2003 purchase of a plot of state-owned land; Thaksin announced that he would not return to Thailand, claiming that the charges were politically motivated and that he would not be tried fairly. The Supreme Court issued a second arrest warrant for Thaksin in September, after he failed to appear at the beginning of his trial on charges related to allegations that he had instructed a state-controlled bank to offer a low-interest loan to Myanmar in 2004 for the purchase of telecommunications equipment from a subsidiary of Shin Corp. In October 2008 the Supreme Court convicted Thaksin *in absentia* of violating an article of the Constitution concerning conflict of interest in relation to his involvement in Pojaman's purchase of state land in 2003, sentencing him to two years' imprisonment; Pojaman was acquitted of the corruption charges against her in this case.

Meanwhile, a cabinet reorganization was effected in August 2008; notable changes included the appointment of Kowit Wattana, the national police chief during 2004–07, as Deputy Prime Minister and Minister of the Interior. Anti-Government protests in Bangkok escalated later that month, with the number of demonstrators rising to an estimated 30,000, as PAD supporters invaded several government buildings and the studios of the state-run National Broadcasting Services of Thailand, before occupying the grounds of Government House and refusing to leave. About 85 people were detained, and arrest warrants were subsequently issued for nine PAD leaders who were accused of illegal assembly and inciting unrest. Samak, who was forced to move his office initially to the military's headquarters and later to the former international airport at Don Muang, rejected demands for his resignation. As tensions mounted, with police reportedly using tear gas to repel 2,000 demonstrators attempting to enter the police headquarters in Bangkok, the protests extended beyond the capital, resulting in the temporary closure of three blockaded regional airports and disruption to rail services. On 2 September the Prime Minister declared a state of emergency in Bangkok, after one person died in confrontations between rival protesters from the PAD and the United Front for Democracy against Dictatorship (UDD—whose supporters were popularly dubbed 'the Red Shirts'). In a further setback for the Government, on the following day Tej Bunnag resigned as Minister of Foreign Affairs, just over a month after his appointment. Moreover, the Election Commission recommended that the Constitutional Court dissolve the PPP on the grounds of the electoral fraud committed by former Speaker Yongyuth.

Successive governments

On 9 September 2008 the Constitutional Court ordered Samak Sundaravej and his Cabinet to resign, ruling that the Prime Minister had violated the Constitution by accepting payment for presenting a television cookery programme while in office. After a failed attempt by the PPP to secure the re-election of Samak as Prime Minister, owing to opposition from the party's coalition partners, on 17 September Somchai Wongsawat, a brother-in-law of Thaksin Shinawatra as well as Deputy Prime Minister and Minister of Education in the outgoing Cabinet, was elected to the premiership. A new Cabinet was sworn in on 25 September, with Prime Minister Somchai assuming responsibility for the defence portfolio. Somchai replaced Samak as leader of the PPP at the end of the month. Meanwhile, the state of emergency in Bangkok was rescinded on 14 September, but the PAD-led protesters continued their occupation of the Government House compound, vowing to remain as long as the PPP retained power. Two of the nine protest organizers for whom arrest warrants had been issued were detained in early October, and the remaining seven PAD leaders sought by police surrendered later that month after treason charges against them were withdrawn; all nine were subsequently released on bail, still charged with lesser offences. Meanwhile, Deputy Prime Minister Chavalit Yongchaiyudh, the Government's chief negotiator with the PAD, resigned on 7 October, after two people died and more than 400 were injured during violent clashes that occurred when police used tear gas to disperse several thousand PAD demonstrators who were besieging the legislative building.

An estimated 40,000 people attended a rally in Bangkok in support of Thaksin and the PPP-led Government at the beginning of November 2008. Also in early November two bomb explosions in Narathiwat killed one person and injured more than 70 people. A week earlier Prime Minister Somchai had visited the southern provinces, noting that separatist violence in the region, which had caused more than 3,400 deaths since January 2004, appeared to have eased. The United Kingdom revoked the visas of Thaksin and Pojaman in November 2008, while they were both out of the country; later that month it was announced that the couple had divorced.

Several thousand PAD demonstrators again surrounded the parliament building, on 24 November 2008, before moving to the Cabinet's temporary offices at Don Muang airport, in what they described as a 'final battle' to oust the Government. Thousands of PAD protesters then seized control of Suvarnabhumi, Bangkok's main international airport, which led to the cancellation of all flights, severely damaging the tourism industry. The PAD declared that its occupation of Suvarnabhumi would continue until Somchai resigned, and subsequently also forced the closure of Don Muang airport. On 27 November Somchai declared a state of emergency around Bangkok's two airports; a stand-off subsequently ensued between police surrounding the airports and the protesters within. At the end of November some 20,000 government supporters attended a rally in the capital. Meanwhile, after three months, PAD protesters began to disperse from their encampment at Government House, where several small bomb attacks in late October and November had resulted in one death and injured around 90 people.

On 2 December 2008 the PAD announced that it was ceasing its protests and airport occupations, after the Constitutional Court ordered the dissolution of the PPP, Chart Thai and Matchimathipataya on the grounds of electoral fraud and barred the executives of the three parties from engaging in politics for five years, thus forcing Somchai to leave office. Many PPP deputies who were not disqualified from participating in politics joined Puea Thai, which had been formed in anticipation of the Court's decision; Yongyuth Wichaidith was elected as the new party's leader. Chart Thai and Matchimathipataya were similarly regrouped, as Chart Thai Pattana and Bhum Jai Thai (BJT), respectively. However, the DP succeeded in securing the support of a significant number of deputies from the dissolved parties, as well as that of several former coalition partners of the PPP, and on 15 December the DP's leader, Abhisit Vejjajiva, was elected as the new Prime Minister by a margin of 37 votes, defeating Police Gen. Pracha Promnok, the leader of Puea Pandin, who was supported by Puea Thai. In response to

Abhisit's election, supporters of Somchai's outgoing administration protested outside the parliament building and the DP's headquarters. The new Prime Minister appealed for national unity, pledging to address the country's economic difficulties and to continue some of the more populist policies pursued by previous governments. A new Cabinet took office on 22 December, comprising members of the DP, Friends of Newin (a breakaway faction of the former PPP, led by Newin Chidchob), Chart Thai Pattana, Puea Pandin (12 deputies from which had voted for Abhisit's election as Prime Minister), Ruam Jai Thai Chart Pattana, BJT and the SAP. Observers expressed concern regarding the lack of experience of several new ministers, while the selection of Kasit Piromya as Minister of Foreign Affairs was also controversial owing to his prominent support for the PAD protests. Thousands of demonstrators loyal to Thaksin and his allies, led by the UDD, took part in protests against the legitimacy of Abhisit's Government in late December, forcing the Prime Minister to make his inaugural policy speech to the National Assembly at the offices of the Ministry of Foreign Affairs; the parliament building was surrounded by protesters for two days.

By-elections were held on 11 January 2009 to fill the seats made vacant by the disqualification of deputies from the parties dissolved in the previous month. The governing coalition increased its majority in the House of Representatives, with the DP winning seven of the 29 seats contested, Chart Thai Pattana 10 and Puea Pandin three, while Puea Thai secured five seats and Pracharaj four. During its first few weeks in office the new Government focused its attention on measures to stimulate the economy and expressed its determination to protect the monarchy. Also in January the Friends of Newin grouping merged with BJT.

The UDD organized several anti-Government rallies at Government House in January–March 2009 demanding the resignation of Abhisit's Cabinet, the dissolution of the House of Representatives, the organization of new elections, the reinstatement of the 1997 Constitution, and the prosecution of the PAD leadership (for the damage caused to the economy by the occupation of Bangkok's airports in 2008). In March the Government defeated motions of no confidence in Abhisit and five of his ministers, which had been tabled in the House of Representatives by Puea Thai. In April UDD protesters forced the postponement of an Association of Southeast Asian Nations (ASEAN, see p. 218) summit meeting being held in Pattaya after blocking the route to the conference hall. Abhisit declared an extreme state of emergency as visiting Asian leaders were airlifted from the venue. The Government also invoked the Internal Security Act, affording the authorities additional powers to impose curfews and restrict gatherings. In the same month violent altercations took place in Bangkok between UDD protesters and the authorities, resulting in the deaths of two protesters, with more than 120 injured. In response to the violence, thousands of soldiers were mobilized to implement a security cordon around the demonstrators gathered outside Government House, ultimately prompting protest leaders to appeal for an end to the demonstrations. Arrest warrants were subsequently issued for 13 protest leaders on charges of inciting public disturbance and illegal assembly. Shortly after the ending of the protests, PAD founder Sondhi Limthongkul survived an apparent assassination attempt in Bangkok; in October he was selected as leader of the recently established Karn Muang Mai party.

In December 2009 Abhisit was forced to deny claims of a government plot to assassinate the exiled Thaksin, following the public disclosure of an ambiguously worded classified document, alleged to have been prepared by Minister of Foreign Affairs Kasit, which referred to Thaksin as a major factor in the destabilization of the Government that 'needed to be tackled'. The Prime Minister adamantly refuted that this was an indirect demand for Thaksin's permanent removal, insisting that the Government wished only to bring Thaksin back to Thailand, using legal means, to serve his two-year prison sentence for corruption.

In early January 2010 DP deputy leader Witthaya Kaewparadai resigned as Minister of Public Health amid allegations of spending irregularities committed by the health ministry. The outgoing minister was under investigation by the National Anti-Corruption Commission (as the NCCC had been renamed in July 2008) for his alleged involvement in the scandal. In mid-January Abhisit announced a government reorganization, which was endorsed by King Bhumibol from his hospital bed. (The King had been admitted to hospital apparently owing to respiratory problems in September 2009, prompting concern among many who viewed the long-standing monarch as the sole unifying figure within the deeply divided country.) Among the five cabinet changes effected, Jurin Laksanawisit, hitherto Minister of Education, was transferred to the public health portfolio, while Trairong Suwannakhiri replaced Korbsak Sabhavasu as a Deputy Prime Minister.

The UDD protests of 2010

In early February 2010 Maj.-Gen. Khattiya Sawasdipol, an outspoken supporter of former premier Thaksin Shinawatra, was charged with illegal arms possession amid allegations of involvement in a grenade attack on the army headquarters in late January. Khattiya had been suspended from the army a few days prior to the attack for insubordination. A group of about 500 UDD protesters gathered outside the police building in which Khattiya was being questioned, while Prime Minister Abhisit warned of the potential for more attacks on government buildings; UDD demonstrators had pledged to stage mass protests ahead of a court ruling, due later that month, on the Shinawatra family's assets, which had been frozen in June 2007 (see The ousting of Thaksin and imposition of military rule). The Government moved swiftly to deploy thousands of additional security personnel across the country in advance of the delivery of the verdict. A minor explosion near the Office of the Prime Minister in mid-February, and the discovery of an unexploded bomb within the compound of the Supreme Court on the following day, resulted in a further elevation of security around the capital. In late February the Supreme Court delivered its verdict in the asset seizure case, ruling that more than one-half of the Shinawatras' assets had been amassed as a result of Thaksin abusing his authority while Prime Minister in order to benefit Shin Corp (allegations that Thaksin had categorically rebutted throughout the court proceedings) and was therefore to be confiscated. The UDD contended that the ruling had been contrived to punish Thaksin while allowing the Court to maintain the appearance of due adherence to the proper judicial process, despite the judiciary remaining beholden to the agenda of the military-dominated élite. Two bomb attacks at separate branches of Bangkok Bank Public Co Ltd in the capital on the following day were attributed by the authorities to the UDD, which denied any involvement.

The Government invoked the Internal Security Act in Bangkok and seven surrounding provinces, as well as implementing additional security measures, for a two-week period from 11 March 2010 (and subsequently extended) in preparation for the anticipated protests. An estimated 40,000 security troops were deployed, and many checkpoints were erected, in and around the capital. Between 100,000 and 150,000 people attended a UDD mass rally, claiming that Prime Minister Abhisit had come to power illegitimately and demanding his resignation and the holding of fresh elections. The demonstrators marched through the streets of Bangkok, before surrounding Government House, whereupon they demanded that Abhisit tender his resignation and dissolve the House of Representatives by midday on 15 March. Upon learning that Abhisit had been transferred to army barracks in the north of the city (a development that served to reinforce the popular perception that he had come to power as an agent of the military), throngs of protesters gathered at the barracks to demand that the Prime Minister acquiesce to their demands. When the UDD's deadline passed, Abhisit issued a live statement on national television in which he announced that the coalition Government had agreed that it could not meet the demonstrators' demands.

In mid-March 2010 UDD protesters daubed the gates of Government House with blood, donated by hundreds of UDD supporters, a small number of whom had been allowed to pass through the security cordon around the House, in an apparent indication of the police force's commitment to ensuring a continuation of the hitherto peaceful nature of the protests. UDD leaders described the protest as a symbolic demonstration of the sacrifices that they were prepared to make for democracy. Protesters also threw blood at the headquarters of the DP and the private residence of Abhisit, who remained entrenched in the army barracks. About 65,000 UDD protesters were estimated to have participated in a subsequent mass rally. Thaksin urged the instigation of a campaign of 'civil disobedience', a comment that was criticized by many for appearing to incite further unrest. Towards the end of March Abhisit agreed to meet with UDD leaders for direct talks in order to 'restore peace and minimize the chance of violence'. Earlier that day four soldiers had been injured when grenades were thrown into the compound of the

army barracks in which Abhisit was staying. During the direct talks, which were broadcast live on national television, the UDD repeated its demands for fresh elections, while Abhisit highlighted the need to make a decision based on 'a consensus from the entire country' rather than capitulating to the UDD's demands. Abhisit's offer of early elections in 2011 was rejected by the UDD, which continued to press for the immediate dissolution of the legislature.

Mass rallies continued to be held every few days, despite warnings from the authorities that demonstrators would be arrested, as Abhisit came under increasing pressure to adopt a stronger stance and restore order. The non-violent nature of the protests was jeopardized when UDD protesters surrounded the parliamentary compound in early April 2010, accompanied by thousands of riot police. Legislators were forced to abandon their parliamentary session and were ushered out of the building amid high security, some having to be rescued from the compound by a military helicopter. A small group of protesters then breached security and entered the compound, although there was no report of any violence and the group soon retreated. Later that day Abhisit declared a state of emergency in Bangkok and surrounding areas for a period of three months, the fourth time that a state of emergency had been imposed in the capital since 2008; emergency rule was subsequently extended to encompass 24 of Thailand's 76 provinces. However, the declaration had no discernible effect on the protesters, who reiterated their resolve to remain encamped in Bangkok until their demands had been met.

Under the new state of emergency laws, the Government shut down the People Channel, a television station that the authorities had accused of inciting violence, on 8 April 2010. On the following day UDD protesters seized control of the station and compelled officials to allow the channel to recommence transmissions; the security forces' attempts to repel the demonstrators using water cannons and tear gas—the first time that force had been used during the four weeks of protest—proved unsuccessful. Any hopes of a peaceful resolution to the impasse were quashed when soldiers and police officers clashed violently with demonstrators on 10 April, during an unsuccessful attempt by the Government to reclaim an area of the capital held by the UDD. Security personnel fired tear gas and rubber bullets to disperse the crowds. Furthermore, the UDD alleged that troops had fired live ammunition at the protesters; although this was denied by the authorities, the testimony of independent witnesses to the violence appeared to confirm the veracity of such claims. According to local media, some protesters responded by throwing petrol bombs at advancing soldiers. Nineteen protesters, five soldiers and a Japanese cameraman working for the Reuters news agency were reported to have been killed during the clashes, and more than 800 others were injured in what constituted the worst incident of political violence in Thailand since May 1992.

In mid-April 2010 the Electoral Commission unexpectedly announced that it recommended the dissolution of the ruling DP owing to 'funding irregularities'; UDD leaders welcomed the development but stated that it had no bearing on their protests. An offer from the Government to dissolve the legislature within six months was rejected. Abhisit announced that Gen. Anupong Paojinda, the Commander-in-Chief of the Army, was to assume responsibility for restoring order from Deputy Prime Minister Suthep Thaugsuban, following a mismanaged attempt, overseen by Suthep, to arrest several UDD leaders, who were filmed escaping from the authorities. After the army explicitly stated that live ammunition would be used against protesters in certain circumstances, the UDD abandoned plans to march through Silom later that day, stating that it wished to avoid a confrontation. A series of grenade attacks in the capital's business district later in April resulted in the deaths of three people, with more than 80 others injured; neither side claimed responsibility for the blasts.

The unrest was not restricted to the capital. Several hand grenade attacks were reported in Chiang Mai during March and April 2010, and an improvised explosive device was detonated in the city in late March. Further bomb attacks, targeting the provincial police headquarters and banks, took place in mid-April. Also in mid-April pro-Government protests took place in numerous locations around the country, including Pattaya, Lampang and Ubon Ratchathani; the protests in Pattaya led to violent clashes between pro-Government groups and UDD supporters.

In early May 2010 Abhisit announced a 'road map' for reconciliation, which included the holding of elections in mid-November, subject to certain conditions, if the UDD agreed to call off its protests. The UDD accepted the offer of elections in November, but pledged to remain encamped in Bangkok until Deputy Prime Minister Suthep surrendered himself to the police for his involvement, as head of security operations at that time, in the clashes of 10 April that had left 25 people dead. Abhisit withdrew the offer of elections in November, insisting that an election date could only be reconsidered after the UDD had ended its mass protests and dispersed from the streets of Bangkok. In mid-May at least one person was killed and dozens of others were injured during clashes between the UDD and the authorities in which a series of explosions and heavy gunfire was reported. Among the injured was Maj.-Gen. Khattiya, who had been advising the protesters on military strategies since mid-March; Khattiya was admitted to hospital in a critical condition after being shot in the head, and died a few days later. The authorities moved in to seal off the protesters' camp in central Bangkok, allowing people out, but not in, and shutting off the power and water supplies to the area. As the violence escalated, more than 40 people were killed during sporadic altercations, prompting the closure of several foreign embassies.

An offer extended by the Senate on 18 May 2010 to mediate in talks between the two factions was welcomed by the UDD; however, the Government stated that it would enter into no further negotiations until the protesters had left their camp. On the following day, in response to the UDD's continued refusal to depart, troops were dispatched in armoured vehicles to break through the barricades that the protesters had erected around their camp, as the Government made a decisive effort to regain control; six people were believed to have been killed in the operation. Shortly thereafter, the UDD leaders announced their decision to surrender from a stage erected within the camp, stating that they did not want any more lives to be lost and urging the protesters to go home. Although the majority of the protesters dispersed peacefully from the streets of Bangkok, at least eight people were killed during exchanges of gunfire between retreating protesters and the authorities; furthermore, more than 30 buildings, including the stock exchange, were set on fire by protesters, and isolated pockets of resistance remained scattered around central Bangkok. The Government announced an overnight curfew for the capital and 23 provinces, the first time in 15 years that a curfew had been imposed in the country; the curfew remained in place until 29 May, by which time the vast majority of the UDD leadership had been detained by the authorities. The official death toll since the beginning of the protests in March was 92, with a further 1,800 injured. Meanwhile, the High Court approved an application by the police for a warrant to arrest Thaksin on terrorism charges, amid government allegations that the former premier, who remained in self-imposed exile, had provided financial and planning support to the UDD demonstrators.

Ongoing discord and UDD rallies

Although the UDD had ultimately failed in its bid to force Abhisit and his Government from office, the protests had served further to highlight the deep political divisions within Thailand. Such divisions were further underscored at the beginning of June 2010 by the results of no-confidence motions lodged by opposition legislators against Abhisit and Deputy Prime Minister Suthep, who were alleged to have abused their respective positions of power and to have authorized the use of excessive force to quell the protest movement. Although the motion against Abhisit was defeated by 246 votes to 186, while that against Suthep was defeated by 245 votes to 187, the strength of opposition to both leaders was a cause for concern for the Government. Motions of no confidence were also tabled against four other ministers, for reasons unrelated to the protests; all survived the action against them. In a government reorganization effected by Abhisit a few days later, notable appointments included that of Chalermchai Sri-on as Minister of Labour, in place of Phaithoon Kaeothong, about whom corruption allegations had been reported. Rumours that the reorganization was due to a rift within the DP were denied.

The nomination by Abhisit of Khanit na Nakhon, a former Attorney-General, as the head of the so-called Independent Truth and Reconciliation Commission of Thailand (ITRC), a fact-finding committee charged with investigating the violence surrounding the UDD protests, was approved by the Cabinet in June 2010. Later that month a bomb exploded outside the headquarters of BJT. Prior to the scheduled expiry of the three-month state of emergency in July, the Government extended emergency rule in the capital and 19 provinces for a further three months, citing concerns about a renewal of violence; by mid-August emergency rule had been revoked in 11 other provinces. Some opponents of the Government claimed that the attack outside the BJT headquarters in June had been contrived in order to provide a pretext for extending the state of emergency. A bomb explosion in Bangkok in late July, which killed one person and injured 10 others, was attributed by the authorities to elements loyal to the UDD; the attack came a few hours after the closing of polls in a by-election in the capital, in which the DP's candidate defeated Korkaew Pikulthong of Puea Thai, a UDD leader who had been imprisoned since his arrest in May and had, therefore, been unable to campaign. In August an appeal by Thaksin against the court order in February that more than one-half of the Shinawatras' assets be confiscated (see The UDD protests of 2010) was rejected by the Supreme Court. In the September the trial commenced of 17 of 19 UDD leaders, including Korkaew, indicted on charges of terrorist activity and inciting violence; Weng Tojirakarn and Nattawut Saikua, former Thai Rak Thai party executives who were prominent members of the UDD leadership, were also among the accused.

Tensions in the capital were exacerbated by the discovery in mid-September 2010 of three unexploded bombs in separate locations around the city. Again, critics of the Government alleged that the authorities had fabricated the apparent plot, together with a series of explosions reported in Bangkok in July–October, in order to justify the continued state of emergency in the capital and surrounding provinces. On 19 September the UDD defied the state of emergency to stage rallies in Bangkok and Thaksin's home town of Chiang Mai to commemorate the fourth anniversary of the coup that had ousted Thaksin from power, as well as to mark four months since the violent suppression of the anti-Government protests on 19 May. An estimated 15,000 UDD supporters attended a further rally in Bangkok on 19 November to commemorate the six-month anniversary of the final suppression of the protests. Later that month the Constitutional Court dismissed a petition filed by the Election Commission appealing for the dissolution of the DP owing to the alleged misuse of a 29m. baht state grant in 2005; the Court ruled that the petition had not been filed within the stipulated time scale and was therefore illegal. A second petition, which had been submitted by the Office of the Attorney-General in mid-July and which urged the dissolution of the DP, relating to illegal donations received by the party, was also dismissed by the Court on a legal technicality, in early December 2010.

A report leaked in mid-December 2010, detailing the findings of a preliminary official investigation into the deaths on 19 May of six people inside Wat Pathum Wanaram—a Buddhist temple in Bangkok that had been designated a safe zone for women, children, the elderly and the infirm, in which hundreds of people had sought refuge when the authorities moved in to clear the protesters' camp—indicated that security forces had fired into the temple and were responsible for at least three of the six deaths. The report uncovered insufficient evidence to determine the circumstances surrounding the deaths of the remaining three people, although all six were found to have been killed by high-velocity bullets. The Government, which had denied that soldiers were present at the scene of the killings, had previously blamed the deaths on retreating UDD supporters. A separate report leaked in the same month indicated that the death of the Japanese cameraman in April had also been the result of a high-velocity bullet, most likely fired by a member of the security forces. Later in December the state of emergency in Bangkok and surrounding provinces was finally removed; however, it was replaced by the Internal Security Act.

As many as 40,000 people were estimated to have attended the UDD's first rally since the revocation of emergency rule, in mid-January 2011. Thaksin addressed the protesters via a telephone link, praising their dedication to democracy. The UDD pledged to hold twice-monthly protests appealing for the resignation of Abhisit and the immediate release of UDD members arrested in the aftermath of the protests of 2010. At the end of January 2011 the UDD lodged a formal complaint with the International Criminal Court against Abhisit, claiming that he was guilty of crimes against humanity in his Government's handling of the protests and was criminally liable for the deaths of those killed during the unrest. Meanwhile, in mid-January Gen. Sonthi Boonyaratglin, the leader of the coup that had deposed Thaksin in September 2006, was elected Leader of the Matubhum Party, which was founded in 2008 and predominantly comprised members of the Muslim Wadah and Pak Nam factions.

In February 2011 constitutional amendments were approved by the legislature providing for a transfer to a single-seat constituency system, and an increase in the number of parliamentary members elected through party-list proportional representation; under the new legislation, approved by the Senate in late April, there were to be 375 constituency-based members and 125 party-list members. Also in February seven of the UDD leaders on trial for terrorism charges, including Korkaew, Weng and Nattawut, were granted bail on the condition that they refrain from any political activity and remain in Thailand. In March a civil court ordered 13 PAD leaders to pay 522m. baht (US $17.2m.) in damages to the operators of the Suvarnabhumi and Don Muang airports that the Alliance had occupied for a week in 2008. An estimated 30,000 UDD supporters attended a rally in Bangkok in mid-March 2011 to mark the anniversary of the beginning of their two-month protest in the previous year. A further UDD rally was held on 10 April to commemorate the anniversary of the clash that had killed 25 people one year previously; while the rally, which was attended by an estimated 20,000 people, passed off peacefully, shortly thereafter the authorities filed *lèse-majesté* complaints against 18 UDD members (including the seven bailed UDD leaders), all of whom were alleged to have insulted the monarchy during speeches given at the rally. In late April the offices of 13 radio broadcasting stations that were reported to have aired these speeches were raided by the police, on the grounds that they were operating without the requisite licences; all but one of the stations were shut down, equipment was seized and three radio station personnel were arrested. The UDD claimed that the raids represented part of a wider attempt by the Government to silence its critics.

The legislative elections of 2011

In mid-March 2011 Abhisit announced that he would dissolve the legislature in the first week of May, in advance of early elections expected to be held in July. Later in March Chart Thai Pattana and BJT announced that they were to form an alliance after the forthcoming polls, pledging to work together in order to 'protect the monarchy' and to 'bring reconciliation' among the Thai people. In April Ruam Chart Pattana and Puea Pandin agreed to merge into a new party, Chart Pattana Puea Pandin, while former Deputy Prime Minister Purachai Piumsombun, a close ally of Thaksin, was selected as Chairman of the newly established Rak Santi Party. The Senate was partially renewed in mid-April, when the Election Commission announced the list of senators newly appointed by the selection committee for a six-year term, the incumbent indirectly elected members having exceptionally served a three-year term (see The restoration of civilian rule). The number of appointed senators was reduced to 73 as a result of the creation in the previous month of a new province, for which a new senator would be elected at the next direct elections to the Senate (which were due to be held by March 2014), thus increasing the number of directly elected senators to 77. In late April Gen. Theeradet Meepian, a former ombudsman, was elected as the new Speaker of the Senate.

On 9 May 2011 Abhisit announced the dissolution, approved by King Bhumibol earlier that day, of the House of Representatives, with effect from the following day, and called elections for 3 July. On 12 May the Criminal Court revoked the bail of two of the seven bailed UDD leaders (see Ongoing discord and UDD rallies)—Jatuporn Prompan (a Puea Thai legislator) and Nisit Sinthuprai—both of whom were consequently returned to prison. The ruling followed the expiry of Jatuporn's parliamentary immunity from criminal prosecution upon the dissolution of the House of Representatives.

Yingluck Shinawatra, the younger sister of Thaksin (who was now living in exile in Dubai, the United Arab Emirates), was nominated as the prime ministerial candidate of Puea Thai on 16 May 2011, a decision that attracted fierce criticism from members of the ruling DP, who argued that Yingluck—who, although a successful businesswoman in her own right, had limited political experience—was merely a 'puppet' of the former premier. Many observers contended that the elections would effectively serve as a popular referendum on Thaksin's own legacy.

Abhisit repeatedly claimed that electoral success for Puea Thai would serve only to extend the country's protracted period of political instability, and, as the elections drew closer, the Prime Minister and the DP resorted increasingly to depicting Thaksin and the UDD as the main cause of the civil unrest in 2010. In mid-June 2011, despite previous assurances that the military would remain neutral in the election process, Commander-in-Chief of the Army Gen. Prayuth Chan-ocha claimed that the authorities had evidence of 'rampant' anti-monarchism committed by 'Thais living abroad' (widely interpreted as a reference to Thaksin) and urged the Thai people to vote for 'good' candidates.

By contrast, Yingluck appeared keen to distance herself and Puea Thai from the deep divisions that had come to characterize Thai politics, refraining from direct criticism of Abhisit and the DP, and instead striking a reconciliatory tone, promising to focus on the achievement of genuine, lasting national reunification should Puea Thai secure election. Among her electoral pledges were a general amnesty for all those involved in major politically motivated incidents since the September 2006 coup that had ousted Thaksin; the provision of greater powers to the ITRC, which had complained of interference from the Government and the military since its inception; actions to combat public corruption; the elimination of poverty by 2020; an increase in the minimum daily wage; and a phased reduction of the rate of corporate tax. The DP was fiercely critical of the proposed amnesty, alleging that the measure was intended specifically as a means of securing Thaksin's return to Thailand, as well as the restoration to the Shinawatra family of the assets seized in accordance with the Supreme Court's ruling in February 2010 (see The UDD protests of 2010).

Despite the fears of widespread electoral violence, the legislative elections, which were held as planned on 3 July 2011, passed off peacefully. Puea Thai secured a convincing victory, winning 265 seats in the 500-seat House of Representatives, thereby securing an absolute majority over the DP, which took only 159 seats. BJT and Chart Thai Pattana won 34 and 19 seats, respectively, while Palang Chon and Chart Pattana Puea Pandin each secured seven seats. On 4 July Yingluck announced that Puea Thai had concluded an agreement to form a coalition Government with Chart Thai Pattana, Palang Chon, Chart Pattana Puea Pandin and Mahachon (which had won one seat); the new administration thus controlled 299 seats in the lower legislative chamber. On the same day Abhisit tendered his resignation as leader of the DP. (However, he was re-elected to the post in mid-August, while Chalermchai Sri-on was elected as the party's Secretary-General in place of Suthep, who had also announced his resignation in the immediate aftermath of the DP's defeat.)

Recent developments: the premiership of Yingluck Shinawatra

A parliamentary vote on 5 August 2011 duly confirmed Yingluck as Thailand's inaugural female Prime Minister. Yingluck received royal endorsement as the new premier on 8 August, and her new Cabinet was approved by the King on the following day. Kittirat Na-Ranong, former President of the Stock Exchange of Thailand, was designated Deputy Prime Minister and Minister of Commerce; Yongyuth Wichaidit was appointed Deputy Prime Minister and Minister of the Interior; Chumpol Silpa-archa, leader of Chart Thai Pattana, was appointed Deputy Prime Minister and Minister of Tourism and Sports; and Capt. Chalerm Yubamrung and Gen. Kowit Wattana were appointed Deputy Prime Ministers without Portfolio. Other significant appointments included those of Gen. Yutthasak Sasiprapha as Minister of Defence and Thirachai Phuvanatnaranubala, formerly Secretary-General of the Securities and Exchange Commission, as Minister of Finance. Senior UDD leaders were notably absent from the Cabinet, in an apparent indication of Yingluck's desire not to alienate further the opposition, although the inclusion of Surapong Towijakchaikul, who was related to Thaksin through marriage, as the new Minister of Foreign Affairs elicited strong censure from the incoming Government's critics. Meanwhile, on 2 August the House of Representatives elected Somsak Kaitsuranont of Puea Thai as its new Speaker.

The Yingluck administration's first major controversy emerged before the end of its first month in office. In late August 2011 Thaksin paid a visit to Japan, during which he delivered a number of public speeches, in which he stated that he would return to the Thai premiership if it proved to be 'the wish of the people'. Critics of the former premier and the new Government gathered outside the Japanese embassy in Bangkok in protest, demanding the impeachment of Minister of Foreign Affairs Surapong, who they alleged had assisted Thaksin in obtaining a visa for his visit. (Under Japanese law, the granting of visas is prohibited for convicted criminals who have been awarded prison terms in excess of one year.) Also in late August, Thaksin's former wife, Pojaman, was acquitted of tax evasion, following a successful appeal against the three-year gaol term conferred on her in July 2008 (see The restoration of civilian rule). In mid-September 2011 Yingluck courted further controversy when she allowed Thaksin to summon the Puea Thai members of the Cabinet for a meeting via webcam, a development that the opposition argued lent weight to their claims that Yingluck was merely a proxy leader filling the role until Thaksin was able to return to Thailand. Further foreign visits conducted by Thaksin, including, notably, a trip to Cambodia in mid-September, during which the former premier met with Cambodian Prime Minister Hun Sen, prompted additional censure from detractors of the Yingluck administration.

The Government attracted further criticism in late August 2011 when it pledged to clamp down on websites deemed to be insulting to the monarchy; a 'war room' was subsequently established within the police headquarters in Bangkok to oversee the surveillance operation. The announcement prompted expressions of disappointment by human rights groups, many of which had hoped that the incoming Government might adopt a less rigid stance on the issue of *lèse-majesté* than previous administrations. (The number of *lèse-majesté* charges presented to the courts was reported to have increased from 30 in 2006 to some 478 in 2010.)

Severe flooding affected much of Thailand during the latter half of 2011, claiming the lives of more than 800 people and prompting the authorities to declare 65 of the country's 77 provinces as disaster zones; flooding persisted in some areas until mid-January 2012. At the beginning of December 2011 the World Bank estimated the total cost of the natural disaster at some 1,425,000m. baht (US $45,700m.). The Yingluck administration was criticized by the opposition for its perceived mishandling of the emergency situation—particularly from October as the flooding in and around the capital became more severe, prompting the authorities to urge people to evacuate low-lying areas of Bangkok. The criticism centred on claims that the Government had underestimated the extent of the flooding and that the various agencies involved in the disaster response operation had failed properly to share data and co-operate with one another, leading to the issuing of, at times, contradictory advice to the public; there were, in addition, allegations that financial aid had been embezzled by Puea Thai officials. Nevertheless, in late November the Minister of Justice, Police Gen. Pracha Promnok, who had been appointed director of the Government's Flood Relief Operation Command, survived a motion of no confidence filed against him by members of the opposition.

A major cabinet reorganization effected by Yingluck in mid-January 2012 was widely interpreted as a response to popular discontent with the Government's handling of the flood relief operation, as well as an attempt to increase loyalty towards the Prime Minister among cabinet ministers. (Covert plans to secure a royal pardon for Thaksin had been divulged in November 2011, apparently by members of the Cabinet, and, following the ensuing outcry among certain quarters of the public, the Government had been forced to declare that it would not endorse any such pardon for the former premier.) Among the notable cabinet changes was the promotion of Gen. Yutthasak Sasiprapha to the position of Deputy Prime Minister without Portfolio, in place of Gen. Kawit, while the defence portfolio was transferred to Air Chief Marshal Sukampol Suwannathat and Deputy Prime Minister Kittirat was transferred from the commerce portfolio to that of finance. Nalinee Taweesin, one of three newly appointed Ministers in the Prime Minister's Office, was a particularly controversial addition to the Cabinet on account of her personal links to the Zimbabwean dictator Robert Mugabe. Criticism was also prompted by the appointment of UDD leader Nattawut Saikua as Deputy Minister of Agriculture and Co-operatives.

In mid-January 2012 the Government approved the establishment of a 2,000m. baht compensation fund for victims of political unrest in the country since the September 2006 coup, as recommended by the ITRC. Compensation was to be paid to those injured or 'unfairly detained', as well as to relatives of those killed. In February PAD founder Sondhi Limthongkul was sentenced to 20 years' imprisonment following his conviction by the Criminal Court on 17 counts of corporate fraud pertaining to the Manager Media Group. Sondhi, who dismissed the charges against him as politically motivated, was released on bail pending an appeal against the sentence.

Following the expiry, at the end of May 2012, of the five-year ban implemented by the Constitutional Tribunal in 2007 on the participation in politics of 111 members of the disbanded Thai Rak Thai (see The ousting of Thaksin and imposition of military rule), Yingluck made a number of cabinet changes during the remainder of the year involving the appointment of a significant number of former members of the defunct party. In late May parliamentary debate on the ruling party's four proposed reconciliation bills, which would provide a general amnesty for all those involved in major political events since the September 2006 coup, was postponed indefinitely owing to fierce protests by PAD supporters who blocked access to the parliamentary building. The Government's plans to amend the 2007 Constitution, a charter that Puea Thai considered to be undemocratic, having been implemented following a military coup, proved more successful when, in July 2012, the Constitutional Court rejected opposition petitions claiming that the proposed amendments would undermine the monarchy and posed a threat to the political system. However, the Court ruled that government legislation on a comprehensive rewriting of the Constitution would have to be approved by referendum.

A report published by the ITRC in September 2012 apportioned blame on both sides—the security forces and the UDD demonstrators—for the escalation in violence during the 2010 protests, which led to the deaths of 92 people. The document did not, however, specify who was actually responsible for the deaths.

The Government suffered a setback in September 2012 following the resignation from office of the Deputy Prime Minister and Minister of the Interior, Yongyuth Wichaidit, after the National Anti-Corruption Commission found him guilty of malfeasance in connection with a ruling that he had made in 2002, while he was acting permanent secretary of the Ministry of the Interior, that the controversial sale, in 1997, of a plot of legally religious land to a company owned by then Deputy Prime Minister Thaksin Shinawatra had been legitimate. Shortly after standing down from his cabinet posts, Yongyuth also resigned from his seat in the House of Representatives and from the leadership of Puea Thai. Yongyuth was succeeded as Minister of the Interior in October 2012 by the erstwhile Minister of Transport, Charupong Ruangsuwan. A few days later Charupong, who had held the position of Secretary-General of Puea Thai since May 2011, was appointed as the party's new leader.

Relations between the Government and the opposition were further antagonized in late November 2012 when police fired tear gas at a gathering of at least 10,000 protesters in Bangkok demanding the overthrow of Yingluck, whom they accused of being a 'puppet' of her brother Thaksin. The protest had been organized by a new group entitled Pitak Siam (Protect Thailand), which was led by a retired army officer, Gen. Boonlert Laewprasit, and which was supported by a number of royalist groups, including the PAD. In the following month several PAD leaders were charged with invading a government building and blocking access to parliament during an anti-Government rally in August 2008 (see The restoration of civilian rule).

In January 2013 Chumpol Silpa-archa, who held the posts of Deputy Prime Minister and Minister of Tourism and Sports, as well as being the leader of Chart Thai Pattana, died. Former Minister of Agriculture and Co-operatives Theera Wongsamut was appointed as the new party leader in March, and in the following month Somsak Pureesrisak was assigned responsibility for the tourism and sports portfolio.

Meanwhile, the insurgency in the restive southern provinces continued unabated. In a report published in September 2011 the human rights organization Amnesty International accused insurgents in the south of deliberately targeting civilians and contended that some of the attacks might constitute war crimes. The report also reiterated claims made previously by Amnesty that the use of torture by the security forces in the counter-insurgency campaign was widespread. Three near-simultaneous bomb attacks in Narathiwat in that month claimed the lives of at least four people and injured more than 60 others. Narathiwat was the scene of further carnage in October, when seven people were killed and 10 others injured after gunmen opened fire and two bombs were detonated in apparently co-ordinated attacks. In the same month suspected insurgents launched a series of assaults at more than 30 locations across Yala, killing three people and injuring more than 50 others. Attacks continued to be reported throughout late 2011 and 2012. By the end of 2012 more than 5,000 people (including about 550 members of the security forces) were reported to have been killed in numerous incidents related to the insurrection since January 2004, with thousands more injured. Despite the continued deployment of tens of thousands of troops in the troubled region and the imposition of curfews, among other measures aimed at curbing the unrest, there appeared to be no abatement in the levels of violence during the first half of 2013. However, in late February there appeared some cause for optimism following the signing in the Malaysian capital of Kuala Lumpur of an agreement to launch peace talks by the Thai Government and one of the many insurgent groups—Barisan Revolusi Nasional (BRN)—under the auspices of the Malaysian Government. The talks commenced in Kuala Lumpur at the end of March; the BRN was represented by Hassan Taib, a veteran campaigner for autonomy for the southern provinces. In the second round of talks, held at the end of April, the government negotiators urged the rebel leaders to demonstrate their credibility by reducing the number of attacks.

Foreign Affairs

Thailand's former dependence on the USA has been greatly reduced by the increasing importance of regional trade and diplomatic relations. In the late 1980s Prime Minister Chatichai Choonhavan adopted a new business-orientated policy towards Cambodia, Laos, Viet Nam and Myanmar, encouraging investment in their developing economies; this policy was successfully pursued by subsequent premiers. In April 1995, following lengthy discussions with Viet Nam, Cambodia and Laos, the four countries established the Mekong River Commission (see p. 462) to promote the joint development of the Mekong's resources. In September 2008 Thailand ratified the ASEAN Charter, which codified the principles and purposes of the Association and came into effect in December of that year. Relations with the People's Republic of China also improved as Thailand became one of China's most significant trading partners. Thailand's foreign relations with a number of countries, particularly Cambodia, suffered a marked deterioration under the administration of Abhisit Vejjajiva (2008–11). Upon assuming the premiership in August 2011, Yingluck Shinawatra pledged her administration's commitment to restoring Thailand's foreign relations as a matter of urgency. Following the killing of 13 Chinese sailors by suspected Myanma drugs-traffickers in waters near the Thai–Myanma border in October, China urged Thailand and Myanmar to intensify efforts to improve security in the area. The three countries, together with Laos, commenced joint security patrols of the Mekong River in December.

Relations with Cambodia

Thai-Cambodian relations were severely undermined during the early 1990s by the provision of transport, medical care and other support to the Party of the Democratic Kampuchea (known as the Khmers Rouges—see Cambodia) by the Thai armed forces, which enjoyed lucrative business relations with the communist Cambodian insurgent group, despite the Thai Government's official policy of supporting the elected Government of Cambodia. In the latter half of 1997 intense fighting in Cambodia between forces loyal to the First Prime Minister, Hun Sen, and those of the former Second Prime Minister, Prince Norodom Ranariddh, resulted in an influx of refugees to Thailand. In January 1997, meanwhile, the Thai Government adopted a controversial resolution unilaterally to extend Thailand's maritime jurisdiction over waters that were also claimed by Cambodia and Viet Nam. However, the Thai Government insisted that its decision was legal under international practice.

In January 2003 Thai-Cambodian relations were severely strained when the Thai embassy and several Thai businesses situated in the Cambodian capital, Phnom Penh, were attacked by Cambodian demonstrators. Those who perpetrated the attacks were protesting against remarks, allegedly made by a Thai actress, claiming that the temples at Angkor Wat in Cambodia in fact belonged to Thailand. In response to the rioting, Prime Minister Thaksin Shinawatra downgraded diplomatic relations with Cambodia and the joint border was subsequently closed. The Cambodian Government issued a formal apology for the incident and promised compensation for those who had been affected by the violence. The Thai Government permitted a limited reopening of the border for commercial activities in February. In the following month the border was fully reopened and, in April, diplomatic relations were upgraded.

Tension arose between Thailand and Cambodia in July 2008, when the Preah Vihear temple, located on the border between the two countries, was declared a World Heritage Site by UNESCO, and both countries subsequently deployed troops to the area. Although the International Court of Justice (ICJ) had awarded ownership of the temple to Cambodia in a ruling in 1962, sovereignty of the surrounding area remained contentious, and the Thai Government's endorsement of Cambodia's application to UNESCO had provoked considerable controversy within Thailand. Bilateral talks aimed at resolving the situation commenced in July 2008, leading to agreement in August on the withdrawal of the majority of the soldiers deployed in the region, but in October at least two Cambodian troops were killed in exchanges of gunfire in the area. In November, following three days of talks, the two governments agreed on plans for a border demarcation process and a full withdrawal of troops. Four Thai soldiers were reported to have been killed during an exchange of fire across the border in April 2009. A partial withdrawal of troops was reported to have begun in August, but minor skirmishes in the disputed area continued to be reported during the latter half of 2009 and into 2010, while little discernible progress appeared to have been made with regard to demarcation of the border.

Meanwhile, Thai officials had been angered by statements made by Hun Sen at the ASEAN summit meeting, held in the Thai town of Hua Hin, in October 2009; the Cambodian premier had declared that Thaksin (who had been convicted *in absentia* of corruption and sentenced to two years' imprisonment by the Thai Supreme Court in the previous year—see Domestic Political Affairs) was welcome to seek refuge in Cambodia. In late October the Cambodian Government's decision to appoint Thaksin as an economic adviser further escalated the diplomatic dispute. Thailand recalled its ambassador from Phnom Penh in early November, accusing the Cambodian Government of interfering in Thailand's internal affairs; Cambodia responded by recalling its own ambassador from Bangkok on the following day. In mid-November Thai diplomats presented Cambodian officials with an extradition request for Thaksin, a request that was summarily rejected by the Cambodian Government on the grounds that Thaksin's conviction had been 'politically motivated'. In December a Thai government spokesman announced that the Thai ambassador would return to Phnom Penh if Cambodia 'corrected its stated opinions' of Thai politics and of the Thai justice system, and if it rescinded the appointment of Thaksin as economic adviser. Hun Sen responded by stating that normal bilateral relations would not be restored until Thailand's current Government had been removed from office, accusing the Abhisit administration of using the dispute over Thaksin as a distraction from the more serious issue of border demarcation. In February 2010 Hun Sen paid an official visit to the disputed area around the Preah Vihear temple, during which he accused Thailand of planning to invade Cambodia and urged Cambodian troops to continue to protect the country's borders from 'the enemy'. In March Cambodia was reported to have fired live rounds from rocket launchers in the mountainous province of Kampong Chhnang; Thailand played down the ASEAN Secretary-General's ensuing expressions of concern, dismissing the event as a routine military exercise. The announcement in August that Thaksin had resigned from his advisory position in Cambodia, citing personal difficulties, led to the restoration of diplomatic relations soon after, and, following several rounds of negotiations between Abhisit and Hun Sen, the two countries announced in December the full restoration of normal relations.

However, tensions once again escalated in October 2010, when a senior Thai investigator alleged that 11 members of the anti-Government Red Shirt movement who had been arrested earlier that month on suspicion of involvement in alleged assassination plots—the intended targets of which had included Abhisit—had received training at a Cambodian military base. The Cambodian Government adamantly denied the claims, which were based on witness statements arising from the arrest earlier in October of 11 men in Chiang Mai. Relations further deteriorated in early 2011. At the beginning of February Veera Somkwamkid, a former leader of the PAD, who had been arrested together with his secretary and five others in December 2010 a short distance inside Cambodian territory, was imprisoned for eight years, after being convicted by a Cambodian court on charges of spying for Thailand and illegally entering Cambodia; his secretary was convicted on the same charges and sentenced to six years' imprisonment. The five other detainees, among them a DP legislator, had been convicted of illegal entry in January 2011, received suspended prison sentences and were deported to Thailand. All seven denied the charges against them. Later in February clashes broke out close to the contested Preah Vihear site; four days of heavy exchanges of gunfire between Thai and

Cambodian troops claimed the lives of three Thai nationals (including one civilian) and eight Cambodians (including four civilians). About 30,000 local villagers were reported to have been displaced by the violence. UN Secretary-General Ban Ki-Moon urged both countries to exercise 'maximum restraint', while Hun Sen appealed to Ban to address urgently the issue of 'Thailand's aggression' and claimed that part of the Preah Vihear temple had been damaged by Thai artillery fire, a claim denied by the Thai Government, which insisted that it was merely protecting its own sovereignty.

At a meeting of ASEAN ministers responsible for foreign affairs held in the Indonesian capital, Jakarta, in February 2011, Thailand and Cambodia agreed to allow a team of unarmed Indonesian observers to monitor the disputed border territory. However, tensions were rekindled following the admission by Thailand in early April that Thai soldiers had used cluster bombs during the fighting in February, prompting expressions of outrage from the Cambodian Government. Fighting broke out again in contested border areas in mid-April, and by the end of that month at least a dozen Thai and eight Cambodian soldiers were reported to have been killed in the latest bout of violence. The ASEAN Secretary-General appealed for the immediate holding of formal dialogue, cautioning that the reputation of the regional bloc would be jeopardized should a complete cessation of hostilities not be swiftly secured. A tentative truce was declared in May, and the Thai–Cambodian border crossing near the Preah Vihear site was reopened. In the same month representatives from the two countries appeared before the ICJ in connection with the border dispute, with both sides stating that they would respect the ultimate decision of the Court. In July the ICJ ordered the withdrawal of all Cambodian and Thai military personnel from the disputed area around the Preah Vihear site and the establishment of a provisional demilitarized zone (PDZ) therein, which would be monitored by ASEAN-appointed observers.

The accession to the Thai premiership of Yingluck Shinawatra in August 2011 (see Domestic Political Affairs) appeared to precipitate a marked amelioration in Thailand's relations with Cambodia. During an official visit by Yingluck to Cambodia in September, it was agreed that both countries must adhere to the ICJ's rulings on the bilateral border dispute, including the redeployment of all military personnel away from the Preah Vihear site. Furthermore, the two neighbours pledged to bolster co-operation in the fields of trade and investment and cross-border crime. Following a meeting in Phnom Penh between the Thai Minister of Defence, Yuthasak Sasiprapha, and his Cambodian counterpart in December, the two sides agreed to establish a joint working group (JWG) on the simultaneous withdrawal of troops under the observance of Indonesian monitors. In April 2012 the JWG agreed to commence mine-clearing operations around the Preah Vihear site, and, following a meeting between Yingluck and Hun Sen in Siem Reap, Cambodia, in July, the two sides began withdrawing their military personnel from the disputed area to the PDZ, in accordance with the ICJ ruling. The Court commenced hearings on the ownership of the land around the Preah Vihear temple in April 2013.

Relations with Myanmar

Relations between Thailand and Myanmar were severely impaired during the 1980s and 1990s by persistent border incursions into Thailand by forces of the Myanma Government, during their offensive against the rebel Karen (Kayin) National Union (KNU)—see Myanmar—which led to a huge influx of Kayin refugees into Thailand. Bilateral relations were further strained when a group of armed Myanma student activists seized control of the Myanma embassy in Bangkok in October 1999, taking 89 people hostage and demanding the release of all political prisoners in Myanmar and the opening of a dialogue between the military Government and the opposition. All the hostages were released within 24 hours, in exchange for the Thai Government's provision of helicopter transport to give the hostage-takers safe passage to the Thai–Myanma border. The Thai Government's release of the assailants angered the ruling military junta in Myanmar, prompting the country to close its border with Thailand. In November Thai forces expelled thousands of illegal Myanma migrant workers from the border town of Mae Sot, despite threats made by Myanma government troops to shoot the returnees. Although the border was reopened to commerce in late November, relations between the two countries remained fraught.

In January 2000 10 armed Myanma rebels took control of a hospital in Ratchaburi, Thailand, holding hundreds of people hostage. The hostage-takers, reported by some sources to be linked to God's Army (a small breakaway faction of the KNU), issued several demands, including that the shelling of their base on the Thai–Myanma border by the Thai military be halted, that co-operation between Thai and Myanma government forces against the Kayins should cease, and that their people be allowed to seek refuge in Thailand. Thai government forces stormed the hospital, killing all 10 of the hostage-takers but releasing all of the hostages unharmed. This uncompromising resolution of the incident was praised by the military Government in Myanmar, and appeared to indicate a hardening of the Thai authorities' stance on Myanma dissident activity in Thailand. In February 2001 Myanma forces pursued Shan State Army (SSA) rebels into the northern Thai province of Chiang Rai, prompting reprisals by Thai troops. Despite the agreement of a cease-fire, Thailand sealed its border with Myanmar, and the situation was aggravated by Myanmar's assertion that Thailand was assisting the SSA. In April it was estimated that the number of refugees of Myanma origin in Thailand totalled almost 131,000. In May the United Wa State Army (UWSA), a Myanma ethnic militia, captured Hua Lone Hill near Chiang Mai; Thai troops retook the hill following a four-day battle in which at least 20 members of the UWSA were killed. The Government later lodged a formal protest with the Myanma Government after the latter's forces allegedly bombed a Thai outpost situated near the hill. The Myanma Government responded by accusing the Thai armed forces of having launched air-strikes into its territory.

In June 2001 Thaksin Shinawatra became the first Thai Prime Minister to visit Yangon, the Myanma capital, since 1997. While the subsequent discussions defused the immediate tensions, the two sides failed to reach any firm agreement as to how they would overcome the problems affecting bilateral relations. In January 2002 a joint Thai-Myanma commission met for the first time since 1999 to discuss plans to establish a task force that would aid in the repatriation of illegal Myanma immigrants. Further talks were held in February 2002, intended to facilitate bilateral co-operation in controlling the cross-border narcotics trade.

Relations were placed under severe strain in March 2002 when Thai soldiers clashed with members of the UWSA in Chiang Mai. Following the incident, in which one Thai soldier and 12 UWSA guerrillas were killed, the Thai Government lodged a formal protest with Myanmar's ruling military junta. In April a bomb exploded on the so-called 'Friendship Bridge' linking the two countries, resulting in the deaths of at least seven people. Later in the same month the Vice-Chairman of Myanmar's ruling State Peace and Development Council (SPDC) visited Thailand to hold talks with the Government concerning drugs-smuggling and the continued border tensions. However, in May fresh fighting broke out along the joint border between Myanma government troops, together with their UWSA allies, and the SSA; subsequently, the SPDC again accused the Thai Government of supporting the SSA, after which it closed the shared border. Meanwhile, following the commencement of a Myanma military campaign on the border, intended to reclaim outposts and camps in the country's Shan State, Thai troops fired across the frontier when two Thai soldiers were allegedly injured by Myanma shells. The Government denied that it supported Myanma insurgent ethnic militias but admitted that it had allowed refugees from Myanmar to cross into Thailand. The joint border finally reopened in October and relations continued to improve in 2003. In July of that year the Thai Government announced plans to relocate all Myanma political refugees resident in Thailand to refugee camps near the joint border, where it was believed they could more easily be controlled and would thus present less of a threat to bilateral relations. In June 2004 Myanma Prime Minister Gen. Khin Nyunt visited Thailand and discussed various economic, development and border issues with Thaksin. Following the ousting of Khin Nyunt in October, Thaksin held talks with the new Prime Minister, Lt-Gen. Soe Win, in December. In January 2005 Thailand increased security along the border with Myanmar, amid concerns that fighting between Myanma troops and insurgents might encroach upon Thai territory. In March the Thai Government ordered the relocation of about 3,000 Myanma political refugees to camps near the joint border. However, about 1,000 of the refugees failed to meet a deadline to register with the Thai authorities and were deported to Myanmar. In April Thailand again heightened security along the border with Myanmar, in response to renewed fighting between rival Myanma ethnic rebel groups close to Thai territory.

In January 2009 the office of the UN High Commissioner for Refugees (UNHCR, see p. 69) expressed concern regarding allegations that in the previous month Thai troops had intercepted about 1,000 Rohingya refugees from Myanmar who had been attempting to reach Thailand and forced them back out to sea in boats without engines; about 450 migrants were rescued by the Indonesian navy, but the remainder were unaccounted for. A decision by the Myanma junta in July 2010 to close a border crossing at Myawaddy, adjacent to the Thai border town of Mae Sot, was a source of considerable irritation to the Thai Government; the closure of the crossing was estimated to be costing Thailand nearly US $3m. daily in lost trade. The escalation of tensions in Myanmar's ethnic border areas in the immediate aftermath of the November legislative elections was reported to have led to more than 20,000 Myanma people fleeing into Thailand to escape the violence. Three Thai nationals were injured when mortar and grenade attacks strayed across the Myanma–Thai border during fighting between Myanma government troops and insurgents, causing Mae Sot to be evacuated. Prime Minister Abhisit Vejjajiva announced the deployment of additional Thai troops to the area to reinforce border security, and offered assurances that Myanma refugees arriving in Thailand would be treated in a humane manner. In early December the Myanma and Thai Ministers of Foreign Affairs met in the Myanma border town of Tachilek, reportedly to discuss the possible reopening of the border crossing at Myawaddy. In an unexpected development a few days later the border crossing at the Three Pagodas Pass, a prominent 'black market' trade route between Thailand and Myanmar, was reopened after a three-year closure. In January 2011 Myanmar eased border control restrictions between Myawaddy and Mae Sot, allowing the transit of goods via cross-border trading posts to resume. Cross-border trade was briefly suspended again in February, following two bomb explosions in neighbouring Myawaddy on the Myanma side of the border, which reportedly killed three people and injured six others. However, normal service was reported to have resumed later that month, although the land border crossing between Myawaddy and Mae Sot remained closed until December 2011. (The new Thai Prime Minister, Yingluck Shinawatra, had urged the Myanma authorities to reopen the crossing, the closure of which had continued to have a significantly detrimental impact on cross-border trade, during a visit to Myanmar in October.) Meanwhile, bilateral relations appeared to improve substantially following the adoption of a series of democratic reforms by the new, nominally civilian administration of Myanma President Thein Sein, who was inaugurated in March. On her first trip outside Myanmar since 1988, opposition leader Aung San Suu Kyi visited Thailand to attend the World Economic Forum in May 2012; during her visit Suu Kyi vowed to help the thousands of Myanma migrant workers in Thailand and held talks with Prime Minister Yingluck. President Thein Sein undertook his first official visit to Thailand in July, during which he met with Yingluck; the two leaders signed three Memorandums of Understanding on economic co-operation (including the development of Myanmar's deep-sea port at Dawei).

In February 2011 Amnesty International appealed for a full investigation to be launched into claims made by a group of 91 Rohingya refugees that they had been intercepted by the Thai navy in January and returned to sea in a boat without an engine and with limited food and water supplies. The Thai authorities denied the accusation, asserting that they had deported the group to Myanmar through official channels. According to the findings of an investigation conducted by the British Broadcasting Corporation, which were reported in January 2013, a number of Thai officials had allegedly sold Rohingya refugees to human traffickers in Malaysia in recent months. In response, the Thai Government pledged to launch an official inquiry into these allegations. The Thai authorities came under further scrutiny in March when it was claimed that Thai naval personnel had opened fire on a boat carrying about 20 Rohingya refugees off the west coast of Thailand, killing at least two. According to UNHCR, at early 2013 there were around 84,900 registered and an estimated 62,000 unregistered Myanma refugees resident in nine camps in Thailand. More than 70,000 refugees had been resettled in third countries between January 2005 and December 2011, a large proportion of whom had been accepted by the USA.

Relations with Laos

Thai-Laotian relations have been dominated in recent years by the issue of Laotian Hmong refugees living in Thailand. In December 2003 the USA agreed to accept around 15,000 of these refugees. The first group was resettled in the USA in June 2004, under the aegis of the International Organization for Migration. In August 2006 the Ministries of Foreign Affairs of Thailand and of Laos indicated that the two countries would co-operate to find a solution to the Hmong refugee issue, although neither side claimed responsibility. Through a joint process, the two countries were later reported to be verifying the origin of the migrants. In December a second 'Friendship Bridge' connecting Laos and Thailand over the Mekong River was inaugurated (the first having been opened in April 1994). In January 2007 the Thai Government decided against the forcible repatriation to Laos of some 153 Hmong migrants who had been arrested in Bangkok in 2006, following offers of asylum from several Western countries. However, the group of Hmong, now numbering 158, and all recognized as refugees, remained in an immigration detention centre in Thailand until December 2009 (see below). Meanwhile, in February 2008, following a visit to Laos, the Thai Minister of Foreign Affairs announced that the Thai authorities had almost completed the process of verifying the identity of the Hmong remaining in refugee camps in Phetchabun province (estimated at some 7,000). In June UNHCR expressed concern regarding the conditions under which a group of 837 Hmong had recently been returned to Laos from Ban Huay Nam Khao camp in Phetchabun province, amid reports that they had been forcibly deported following a mass protest at the camp; in July, after a further 391 Hmong were repatriated, UNHCR urged the Thai authorities to allow it access to the camp. A total of 1,809 Hmong were returned to Laos during 2008. In May 2009 the international medical aid organization Médecins Sans Frontières (MSF) announced that it was to withdraw from Ban Huay Nam Khao camp, citing ongoing intimidation and coercive tactics employed by the Thai military. MSF was the sole international agency allowed to operate in the camp and was responsible for providing food and medical treatment to the refugees. In December the Thai Government deported some 4,000 Hmong refugees at the camp back to Laos, including the 158 UNHCR-recognized political refugees, despite protests by UNHCR, the USA and human rights organizations. Following the repatriation, the Thai Government stated that it had concerns for the safety of about 100 of those who had been deported but had been assured by the Laotian Government that they would be granted pardons upon their return to Laos (q.v.).

Meanwhile, in January 2009, in an indication that the new administration in Thailand hoped to strengthen relations with Laos, Thai Prime Minister Abhisit Vejjajiva and Minister of Foreign Affairs Kasit Piromya both chose that country as the destination of their first official foreign visits. Kasit and his Lao counterpart agreed to make efforts to finalize the demarcation of their land border in 2009, followed by that of the inland water border (along the Mekong River) in 2010. However, with a number of difficult points of contention remaining unresolved, neither of these deadlines were met, and in March 2012 the two countries agreed on two new deadlines: 2014 for the land border and 2016 for the water border. A rail link constructed on the first Mekong 'Friendship Bridge' was opened in March 2009, connecting Thailand and Laos by rail for the first time. A third 'Friendship Bridge' over the Mekong was inaugurated in November 2011 and a fourth such bridge was expected to be opened by the end of 2013. Plans to construct a fifth 'Friendship Bridge' over the Mekong were under way at mid-2013 (see Laos). Meanwhile, following the meeting of a bilateral commission on co-operation co-chaired in October 2010 by Kasit and the Laotian Deputy Prime Minister and Minister of Foreign Affairs, Thongloun Sisolit, the two countries reiterated their ongoing commitment to strengthen relations; Thailand confirmed a prior agreement to purchase 7,000 MW of electricity from Laos by 2015. Lao Prime Minister Thongsing Thammavong held talks with Prime Minister Yingluck during a visit to Thailand in May–June 2012, when the two sides pledged to increase co-operation in combating human-trafficking and illegal drugs-smuggling, and to boost bilateral trade and investment; it was also agreed that Thailand would help to fund further infrastructure development (including road construction) in Laos.

Other regional relations

Relations with Malaysia, which had been strained by sporadic incidents in previous years, improved markedly from 1997. In February of that year Malaysia and Thailand established the Kolok River as the border demarcation between the two countries. In January 1998 the Malaysian authorities arrested, and transferred to the Thai authorities, three alleged Muslim separatist leaders wanted in Thailand in connection with terrorist activities in the southern provinces of the country. In April 2001 Prime Minister Thaksin paid an official visit to Malaysia, during which the two countries discussed border demarcation issues and agreed that the planned construction of a gas pipeline between Thailand and Malaysia would proceed as originally intended. Relations remained cordial and, in December 2002, the cabinets of the two countries held an historic joint meeting, during which trade and security issues were discussed. In early 2004 the Malaysian Government co-operated with Thailand in efforts to combat violence in the Thai southern provinces. In February the Thai Government mooted plans to construct a security fence along parts of the joint border, in the hope of preventing militants from seeking refuge in Malaysia. As unrest in southern Thailand continued, Prime Minister Thaksin visited Malaysia in April for talks with his counterpart, Abdullah Badawi, on border security and the economic development of the surrounding area. Bilateral relations were strained in December, when the Thai Government claimed to have photographic evidence that militants in southern Thailand had received training in Malaysia. In January 2005 the Malaysian authorities arrested Abdul Rahman Ahmad, whom Thailand held responsible for organizing much of the separatist violence in the south. A diplomatic dispute arose between the two countries in October concerning the fate of 131 Muslim asylum seekers, who had fled from the violence-stricken southern province of Narathiwat to neighbouring Malaysia (q.v.). Although the issue was eventually resolved in February 2006 when the Thai Government announced that it was to allow the refugees to remain in Malaysia, relations between the two countries had by that stage descended to their lowest point in recent years. In November 2005 former Malaysian Prime Minister Mahathir Mohamad visited Thailand for discussions with Thaksin, which helped to ease the tension that had been caused by Thai security officials' accusations that the Malaysian authorities were failing to prevent insurgents from crossing the border into Thailand. Thaksin and Mahathir agreed that the two countries should cease their 'war of words' and Mahathir was to stop advocating autonomy for Thailand's southern regions. In December Manasae Saeloh, a suspected leader of PULO, was arrested in Malaysia and handed over to the Thai authorities, by whom he was wanted in connection with numerous bomb attacks and other acts of violence. Relations became more cordial following the ousting from power of Thaksin in 2006. In December 2007 the interim Prime Minister, Gen. (retd) Surayud Chulanont, and Abdullah Badawi officially opened a new bridge across the Kolok River, which it was hoped would lead to a reduction in violence in the border region by improving economic prospects. In December 2009 Malaysian Prime Minister Najib Tun Razak became the first head of government formally to visit Thailand under the administration of Prime Minister Abhisit Vejjajiva. The two countries announced plans to foster closer co-ordination in anti-narcotics operations in June 2010. In February 2013 Malaysia acted as a mediator in the signing of an agreement on the commencement of peace talks between the Thai Government and one of the Muslim insurgent groups, the BRN (see Domestic Political Affairs).

Thailand also maintains cordial relations with Indonesia, as well as with the Philippines and Singapore. Under the Singapore-Thailand Third Country Training Programme (TCTP), introduced in 1997, Thailand and Singapore have jointly provided technical assistance to, *inter alia*, Cambodia, Laos, Myanmar and Viet Nam. In July 2010 Minister of Foreign Affairs Kasit met with his Indonesian counterpart in Jakarta, whereupon the two ministers pledged to extend bilateral co-operation in the fields of agriculture, fisheries, energy and investment; other issues discussed included co-operation on disaster management, and Kasit voiced the appreciation of the Thai Government for Indonesian support for Thailand's successful bid in May to secure election to the UN Human Rights Council.

Other external relations

In December 2001 Prime Minister Thaksin Shinawatra paid an official visit to the USA, during which he met with US President George W. Bush and assured him that Thailand would remain a strong ally in the US-led 'war on terror' following the September terrorist attacks. The US President praised the Thai Government for its consistent support throughout the campaign. In June 2003 Thaksin met with President Bush again in Washington, DC, to discuss counter-terrorism issues. In October President Bush attended an Asia Pacific Economic Cooperation (APEC, see p. 208) summit meeting in Bangkok, having paid an official state visit to Thailand in the days preceding the summit. The two heads of state announced that they were to enter into

formal negotiations with regard to the signing of a comprehensive bilateral free trade agreement. However, negotiations were postponed owing to the political upheaval of 2006–08 and remained suspended at mid-2013. None the less, representatives of the two countries convened in Washington, DC, for discussions on trade and investment matters in June 2008 and again in March 2009. Meanwhile, in February 2008, following the return to civilian rule in Thailand, the USA announced the resumption of military aid to Thailand, which it had suspended following the coup of September 2006. Relations were strained in December 2009 by the forced repatriation to Laos of some 4,000 Hmong refugees, which the USA had vehemently opposed (see Relations with Laos). Tensions were further exacerbated by reports in early December 2010 that former premier Thaksin, now a fugitive, had been invited by the US Commission on Security and Co-operation in Europe (CSCE) to Washington, DC, to address a forum entitled 'Thailand: Democracy, Governance and Human Rights'. In mid-December the CSCE announced that the forum had been postponed.

Following the victory of Puea Thai in legislative elections held in July 2011, and the subsequent accession to the premiership of Yingluck Shinawatra, the Administration of US President Barack Obama expressed its readiness to work with the new Thai Government in further fostering bilateral ties. However, the inclusion of Thailand on a 'watchlist' of so-called Specially Designated Countries that 'promote, produce, or protect terrorists', published by the US Department of Homeland Security later in July, prompted anger from the South-East Asian country. The sentencing to two-and-a-half-years' imprisonment of a Thai-born US citizen in December 2011, following his conviction on *lèse-majesté* charges after he had admitted translating and posting on the internet sections of a banned biography of King Bhumibol, prompted expressions of concern from US officials. The man had posted the offending material several years previously while resident in the USA and had been arrested in May 2011 during a visit to Thailand for medical treatment. However, the US Department of State maintained that the conviction would not adversely affect US-Thai relations. During a tour of South-East Asia in November 2012, President Obama and US Secretary of State Hillary Clinton both visited Thailand, where they held talks with Prime Minister Yingluck.

In February 2009 it was announced that a Thai military contingent was to join the African Union/United Nations Mission in Darfur (UNAMID) in western Sudan. In November 2010 the first deployment of Thai soldiers, comprising 409 personnel, was dispatched to join the peace-keeping mission; a further 403 Thai troops were deployed in early 2011. Despite a number of fatal attacks targeting UNAMID personnel in 2011–13, the Thai deployment remained in Darfur at mid-2013. (See Sudan for details of the Darfur conflict.)

Responsibility for a series of bomb explosions in February 2012, apparently targeting those affiliated with the Israeli embassies in Bangkok, New Delhi (India) and Tbilisi (Georgia), and in which nine people were injured, was attributed by the Israeli authorities to Iran and the militant Islamist organization Hezbollah (claims that were adamantly denied by the Iranian Government). Several arrests were made in connection with the incident in Bangkok, in which the bomb appeared to have been detonated prematurely. The trial of two Iranian nationals on charges of possession of unlawful explosives and causing explosions commenced in Bangkok in December.

CONSTITUTION AND GOVERNMENT

A new Constitution was adopted in 2007. Thailand is a constitutional monarchy. The King appoints the Prime Minister, who leads the Cabinet. The bicameral National Assembly of Thailand consists of the House of Representatives (Sapha Poothaen Rassadorn) and the Senate (Woothi Sapha). The House of Representatives has 500 members, of whom 375 are elected in multi-member constituencies, while the remainder are elected by a party list system of proportional representation. Members are elected for a term of four years. The Senate consists of 150 members, of whom 76 are elected (one from each of Thailand's 75 provinces and Bangkok) and the remainder are appointed by a selection committee. Senators serve six-year terms. With the creation of a 76th province in 2011, an additional directly elected seat was created in the Senate (although it was to remain vacant until the elections due to be held by March 2014), thus reducing the number of appointed members to 73.

REGIONAL AND INTERNATIONAL CO-OPERATION

Thailand is a member of the Association of Southeast Asian Nations (ASEAN, see p. 218), the Asia-Pacific Economic Cooperation (APEC, see p. 208), the Asian Development Bank (ADB, see p. 214), the UN's Economic and Social Commission for Asia and the Pacific (ESCAP, see p. 31), the Colombo Plan (see p. 460) and the Mekong River Commission (see p. 462).

Thailand became a member of the UN in 1946. As a contracting party to the General Agreement on Tariffs and Trade, Thailand joined the World Trade Organization (WTO, see p. 444) on its establishment in 1995. The country is also a member of the International Labour Organization (ILO, see p. 142) and the Non-aligned Movement (see p. 477).

ECONOMIC AFFAIRS

In 2011, according to estimates by the World Bank, Thailand's gross national income (GNI), measured at average 2009–11 prices, was US $307,129m., equivalent to $4,420 per head (or $8,390 per head on an international purchasing-power parity basis). During 2002–11, it was estimated, the population increased at an average annual rate of 0.8%, while gross domestic product (GDP) per head grew, in real terms, by an average of 3.1% per year. Overall GDP increased, in real terms, at an average annual rate of 4.2% in 2002–12; GDP rose by 0.1% in 2011 and by 6.4% in 2012.

According to preliminary figures, agriculture (including forestry, hunting and fishing) contributed 12.2% of GDP in 2012; 42.1% of the employed labour force were engaged in the sector in that year. Thailand's staple crop and principal agricultural export commodity is rice (Thailand became the world's largest exporter of rice in 1981). Rice exports accounted for 2.8% of the total value of exports in 2011. Other major crops include sugar cane, cassava (tapioca), oil palm fruit, maize, natural rubber, bananas, mangoes and pineapples. Fisheries products and livestock (mainly cattle, buffaloes, pigs and poultry) are also important. Thailand is one of the world's largest exporters of farmed shrimp. During 2002–12 agricultural GDP increased at an average annual rate of 2.4%; agricultural GDP rose by 3.1% in 2012.

In 2012 industry (including mining, manufacturing, construction and utilities) provided 43.6% of GDP, according to preliminary figures, and engaged 19.9% of the employed labour force. During 2002–12 industrial GDP increased at an average annual rate of 4.7%; the GDP of the industrial sector declined by 3.9% in 2011, but expanded by 7.2% in 2012.

According to preliminary figures, mining and quarrying contributed 4.0% of GDP in 2012, engaging 0.2% of the employed labour force in that year. Gemstones, notably diamonds, are the principal mineral export. Natural gas and, to a lesser extent, petroleum are also exploited, and production of these fuels increased substantially from the late 1990s. Tin, lignite, gypsum, tungsten, antimony, manganese, gold, zinc, iron and fluorite are also mined. During 2002–12 the GDP of the mining sector increased at an average annual rate of 4.0%; mining and quarrying GDP declined by 2.1% in 2011, but grew by 7.4% in 2012.

In 2012 manufacturing provided 34.0% of GDP, according to preliminary figures, and engaged 13.5% of the employed labour force. Textiles and garments, and electronics and electrical goods (particularly semiconductors) constitute Thailand's principal branches of manufacturing. Other manufacturing activities include the production of cigarettes, chemicals, cement and beer, sugar and petroleum refining, motor vehicle production, rubber production, and the production of iron and steel. During 2002–12 manufacturing GDP increased at an average annual rate of 4.9%; the GDP of the sector decreased by 4.3% in 2011, but rose by 7.0% in 2012.

According to preliminary figures, construction provided 2.7% of GDP in 2012, engaging 5.9% of the employed labour force in that year. During 2002–12 construction GDP increased at an average annual rate of 2.6%; the sector's GDP declined by 5.1% in 2011, but expanded by 7.8% in 2012.

Energy is derived principally from hydrocarbons. In 2011 51.0m. barrels of crude petroleum and an estimated 32,000m. cu m of natural gas were produced. In 2009 natural gas accounted for 70.7% of total electricity output and coal for 19.9%. Solar and wind energy have been introduced, but Thailand remains dependent on imported petroleum and electricity. In 2012 imports of mineral fuels comprised 19.3% of the value of merchandise imports.

Services (including transport and communications, commerce, banking and finance, public administration and other services) contributed 44.2% of GDP in 2012, according to preliminary figures. In that year 37.9% of the employed labour force were engaged in the services sector. Tourism has become a major source of foreign exchange, although the sector has been intermittently affected by unrest in Bangkok and by the violence in southern Thailand (see Contemporary Political History). Tourism receipts (excluding passenger transport) increased by 30.5% in 2011, to reach an estimated total of US $26,256m. The number of tourist arrivals rose by 16.0% in 2012, to reach 22.3m. During 2002–12 the GDP of the services sector expanded at an average annual rate of 4.0%; the GDP of the sector rose by 6.2% in 2012.

In 2011 Thailand recorded a visible merchandise trade surplus of US $16,991m. and there was a surplus of $5,918m. on the current account of the balance of payments. In 2012 the principal source of imports was Japan (providing 20.0% of the total); other major suppliers in that year were the People's Republic of China, the United Arab Emirates, Malaysia and the USA. The principal market for exports in that year was China (accounting for 11.7% of the total); other major purchasers were Japan, the USA, Hong Kong and Malaysia. The principal imports in 2012 were machinery, mineral fuels and lubricants, basic manufactures and chemical products. The principal exports were machinery, food, basic manufactures, chemicals and related products, mineral fuels and lubricants, and crude materials (inedible) except fuels.

A budget deficit of 281,305.5m. baht, on a cash basis, was recorded in 2011/12, equivalent to 2.6% of GDP. According to the Asian Development Bank (ADB), Thailand's external debt totalled US $130,500m. at the end of 2012; in that year the cost of debt-servicing was equivalent to 4.3% of the value of exports of goods and services. The annual rate of inflation averaged 2.8% in 2007–12. Consumer prices increased by 2.2% in 2012. At January 2013 only 0.8% of the labour force were unemployed.

In an effort to mitigate the repercussions of global recessionary conditions, in January 2009 the Government announced an economic stimulus plan envisaging expenditure of 116,700m. baht. In an attempt to boost domestic demand and sustain growth, the Bank of Thailand's interest rate was decreased by a total of 2.50 percentage points between December 2008 and April 2009, to 1.25%, thereafter remaining unchanged until mid-2010. Following a series of subsequent increases, the rate peaked at 3.50% in August 2011, before being reduced (in three stages) to 2.75% in October 2012 (at which level it remained at April 2013). Meanwhile, the country's resumption of robust growth, of 7.8%, in 2010 from a contraction in GDP of 2.3% in 2009 was due largely to the substantial recovery in manufacturing output, higher investment inflows, an improvement in consumer confidence and growing external demand. Subsidies and price controls on energy and other essential commodities announced by the Government in early 2011 enjoyed considerable success, with the rate of inflation decreasing from a peak of 4.3% in August 2011 to an overall annual average of 2.2% in 2012 (the lowest rate in three years). This fall in inflation occurred in spite of a rise in rice prices resulting from the destruction of some 25% of the annual paddy harvest as a result of severe flooding during the latter half of 2011. Despite pessimistic forecasts of a downturn in the tourism sector, tourist arrivals and receipts recorded substantial increases in 2011. However, the rate of GDP growth in that year decelerated drastically to just 0.1%, largely as a result of the debilitating effect of the flooding on the manufacturing industry. Nevertheless, partly owing to the relative political stability arising from the election in July 2011 of the Puea Thai-led coalition Government, combined with a strong rebound in domestic demand, real GDP growth reached 6.4% in 2012. The economic recovery was bolstered by a rise in employment and salaries, continuing expansion in the tourism sector, the introduction of new government subsidies (including for rice) and tax concessions, and increased public expenditure on infrastructure in the wake of the floods. The 11th National Economic and Social Development Plan, encompassing the 2012–16 period, placed a renewed focus on human and social development as well as the need for more effective management of natural resources and the environment. The ADB forecast a moderation in real GDP growth to 4.9% in 2013 and a rise in inflation to 3.2%, recommending that the Government address the widening disparities in income and access to basic services, public sector corruption and insufficient state investment in areas such as transport, water management and education.

Statistical Survey

Source (unless otherwise stated): National Statistical Office, Thanon Larn Luang, Bangkok 10100; tel. (2) 281-0333; fax (2) 281-3815; e-mail onsoadm@nso.go.th; internet www.nso.go.th.

Area and Population

AREA, POPULATION AND DENSITY

Area (sq km)	513,120*
Population (census results)	
1 April 2000	60,606,947
1 September 2010 (preliminary)	
Males	32,109,371
Females	33,370,082
Total	65,479,453
Population (official projections at mid-year)† . . .	
2012	67,912,000
2013	68,251,000
Density (per sq km) at mid-2012	133.0

* 198,117 sq miles.

† Figures rounded to the nearest one thousand persons; projections not adjusted to take account of results of the 2010 census.

POPULATION BY AGE AND SEX
('000 persons, official projections at mid-2013)

	Males	Females	Total
0–14	6,744	6,455	13,199
15–64	24,219	24,894	49,114
65 and over	2,517	3,420	5,937
Total	33,481	34,770	68,251

Note: Totals may not be equal to the sum of components, owing to rounding; estimates not adjusted to take account of results of 2010 census.

REGIONS
('000 persons, official projections at mid-2013)

	Area (sq km)	Population	Density (per sq km)
Bangkok	1,568.7	11,630	7,413.8
Central Region	102,336.0	11,500	112.4
Northern Region	169,644.3	12,273	72.3
Northeastern Region . .	168,855.3	23,153	137.1
Southern Region	70,715.2	9,696	137.0
Total	513,119.5	68,251	133.0

Note: Totals may not be equal to the sum of components, owing to rounding.

PRINCIPAL TOWNS
('000 persons, official projections at mid-2012)

Bangkok Metropolis*	6,846	Samut Prakan . .	1,341
Nakhon Ratchasima	2,840	Chon Buri . . .	1,226
Khon Kaen . .	1,909	Surat Thani . .	1,041
Ubon Ratchathani .	1,887	Nakhon Pathom .	991
Nakhon Si			
Thammarat . .	1,787	Nanthaburi . . .	987
Udon Thani . .	1,651	Lampang . . .	820
Chiang Mai . .	1,609	Rayong	613

* Formerly Bangkok and Thonburi.

BIRTHS, MARRIAGES AND DEATHS*

		Registered live births		Registered marriages	Registered deaths	
		Number	Rate (per 1,000)	Number	Number	Rate (per 1,000)
2003	. .	742,183	11.8	328,356	384,131	6.1
2004	. .	813,069	13.0	365,721	393,592	6.3
2005	. .	809,485	13.0	345,234	395,374	6.4
2006	. .	793,623	12.7	358,505	391,126	6.2
2007	. .	797,588	12.7	307,910	393,255	6.3
2008	. .	784,256	12.4	318,496	397,327	6.3
2009	. .	765,047	12.1	300,878	393,916	6.2
2010	. .	761,689	12.0	285,944	411,331	6.5

* Registration is incomplete. According to UN estimates, the average annual rates in 1995–2000: Births 15.6 per 1,000; Deaths 6.1 per 1,000; in 2000–05: Births 14.1 per 1,000; Deaths 6.6 per 1,000; in 2005–10: Births 12.9 per 1,000; Deaths 7.2 per 1,000 (Source: UN, *World Population Prospects: The 2010 Revision*).

2011: Registered marriages 308,048.

Source: partly UN, *Demographic Yearbook*.

Life expectancy (years at birth): 74.1 (males 70.8; females 77.5) in 2011 (Source: World Bank, World Development Indicators database).

ECONOMICALLY ACTIVE POPULATION*
('000 persons aged 15 years and over, July–September of each year)

	2010	2011	2012
Agriculture, hunting and forestry .	15,406	15,687	16,296
Fishing	339	428	367
Mining and quarrying	33	49	63
Manufacturing	5,189	5,299	5,343
Electricity, gas and water . . .	99	167	128
Construction	2,083	2,173	2,340
Wholesale and retail trade; repair of motor vehicles, motorcycles and personal and household goods . .	6,110	5,995	5,862
Hotels and restaurants . . .	2,558	2,618	2,319
Transport, storage and communications	1,048	1,014	1,129
Financial intermediation . . .	373	396	386
Real estate, renting and business activities	809	778	742
Public administration and defence; compulsory social security . .	1,618	1,555	1,657
Education	1,289	1,284	1,177
Health and social work . . .	703	723	657
Other community, social and personal service activities . .	793	895	820
Private households with employed persons	221	229	247
Extra-territorial organizations and bodies	0	4	6
Sub-total	38,672	39,294	39,539
Activities not adequately defined .	20	23	38
Total employed	38,692	39,317	39,578
Unemployed	341	262	231
Total labour force	39,033	39,580	39,809

* Excluding the armed forces.

Note: Totals may not be equal to the sum of components, owing to rounding.

Health and Welfare

KEY INDICATORS

Total fertility rate (children per woman, 2010)	1.6
Under-5 mortality rate (per 1,000 live births, 2010) . . .	13
HIV/AIDS (% of persons aged 15–49, 2009)	1.3
Physicians (per 1,000 head, 2004)	0.3
Hospital beds (per 1,000 head, 2010)	2.1
Health expenditure (2009): US $ per head (PPP)	327
Health expenditure (2009): % of GDP	4.2
Health expenditure (2009): public (% of total)	74.6
Access to water (% of persons, 2010)	96
Access to sanitation (% of persons, 2010)	96
Total carbon dioxide emissions ('000 metric tons, 2008) . .	285,732.6
Carbon dioxide emissions per head (metric tons, 2008) . .	4.2
Human Development Index (2011): ranking	103
Human Development Index (2011): value	0.682

For sources and definitions, see explanatory note on p. vi.

Agriculture

PRINCIPAL CROPS
('000 metric tons)

	2009	2010	2011
Rice, paddy	32,116	35,584	34,588
Maize	4,616	4,861	4,817
Sorghum	54	54	52
Cassava (Manioc, Tapioca) . .	30,088	22,006	21,912
Sugar cane	66,816	68,808	95,950
Beans, dry	103	104*	122*
Soybeans (Soya beans) . . .	176	177	176
Groundnuts, with shell . . .	46	45	48
Coconuts	1,381	1,298	1,055
Oil palm fruit	8,163	8,223	10,777
Cabbages and other brassicas .	496	550	491
Tomatoes	146	125	118
Pumpkins, squash, gourds . .	195	207	203*
Cucumbers and gherkins . .	234	237	261
Onions, dry	45	46	46*
Garlic	71	68	76
Maize, green	268	260	255*
Watermelons	580	528	518
Bananas	1,528	1,585	2,036*
Oranges*	396	373	425
Tangerines, mandarins, clementines, satsumas . .	515	280	360
Mangoes, mangosteens and guavas	2,470	2,551	3,277
Pineapples	1,895	1,925	2,593
Papayas	207	212	272
Tobacco, unmanufactured . .	62	59	68
Natural rubber	3,091	3,052	3,348

* FAO estimate(s).

Aggregate production ('000 metric tons, may include official, semi-official or estimated data): Total cereals 37,040 in 2009, 40,765 in 2010, 39,716 in 2011; Total roots and tubers 30,541 in 2009, 22,455 in 2010, 22,373 in 2011; Total vegetables (incl. melons) 3,817 in 2009, 3,812 in 2010, 3,739 in 2011; Total fruits (excl. melons) 10,148 in 2009, 10,274 in 2010, 13,090 in 2011.

Source: FAO.

LIVESTOCK
('000 head, year ending September)

	2009	2010	2011
Horses	5	6	7
Cattle	6,647	6,498	6,680*
Buffaloes	1,671	1,623	1,698
Pigs	7,481	7,624	7,660†
Sheep	40	43	52
Goats	384	380	428
Chickens	228,207	231,918	235,000
Ducks	16,347	29,233	32,179
Geese and guinea fowl . . .	132	136†	140†

* Unofficial figure.
† FAO estimate.

Source: FAO.

LIVESTOCK PRODUCTS
('000 metric tons)

	2009	2010	2011
Cattle meat	177.4	176.8	170.0
Buffalo meat	33.7	46.1	23.2
Pig meat	808.7	862.0	867.3*
Chicken meat	1,153.6	1,220.3	1,257.6
Duck meat*	77.3	80.0	81.8
Cows' milk	840.7	850.8	850.8*
Hen eggs	577.0†	585.5*	585.5*
Other poultry eggs*	393	395	395

* FAO estimate(s).
† Unofficial figure.

Source: FAO.

Forestry

ROUNDWOOD REMOVALS
('000 cubic metres, excl. bark, FAO estimates)

	2009	2010	2011
Sawlogs, veneer logs and logs for sleepers	300	300	300
Pulpwood	2,900	2,900	2,900
Other industrial wood . . .	5,500	5,500	5,500
Fuel wood	19,398	19,301	19,187
Total	28,098	28,001	27,887

Source: FAO.

SAWNWOOD PRODUCTION
('000 cubic metres, incl. railway sleepers)

	2003	2004	2005
Coniferous (softwood)* . . .	18	18	18
Broadleaved (hardwood) . . .	270*	2,796†	2,850*
Total*	288	2,814	2,868

* FAO estimate(s).
† Unofficial figure.

2006–11: Production assumed to be unchanged from 2005 (FAO estimates).

Source: FAO.

Fishing

('000 metric tons, live weight)

	2008	2009	2010
Capture	1,873.4	1,870.7	1,827.2
Freshwater fishes . . .	59.7	50.4	79.2
Bigeyes	32.3	31.0	31.6
Sardinellas	96.5	100.0	98.2
Anchovies, etc.	144.1	144.7	137.2
Indian mackerels . . .	112.6	115.4	114.0
Other marine fishes . .	538.8	573.5	556.1
Aquaculture*	1,330.9	1,416.7	1,286.1
Nile tilapia	217.3	221.0	179.2
Catfish (hybrid) . . .	136.5	130.1	116.9
Whiteleg shrimp . . .	501.4	571.2	561.1
Green mussel	203.2	193.6	166.9
Total catch*	3,204.3	3,287.4	3,113.3

* FAO estimates.

Source: FAO.

Mining

(metric tons unless otherwise indicated)

	2009	2010	2011
Lignite ('000 metric tons) . . .	16,360	17,907	18,000*
Crude petroleum ('000 barrels) .	56,302	55,906	51,000
Natural gas—gross production (million cu m)	30,625	31,730	32,000*
Iron ore—gross weight . . .	1,400,800	969,937	970,000*
Iron ore—metal content* . . .	800,000	485,000	485,000
Zinc ore—metal content . . .	34,000	25,529	29,664*
Tin concentrates—metal content .	166	291	282
Manganese ore—metal content .	31,200	24,200*	24,000*
Tungsten concentrates—metal content*	600	600	600
Tantalum—metal and oxide powder	50	50	50*
Silver (kg)	15,300	17,092	17,098
Gold (kg)	5,400	4,125	2,372
Marble—dimension stone ('000 cu m)	760.0	760.0*	760.0*
Granite—dimension stone ('000 cu m)*	10.0	10.0	10.0
Granite—industrial ('000 metric tons)*	5,000	5,000	5,000
Limestone ('000 metric tons) . .	150,200	150,200*	150,200*
Dolomite ('000 metric tons) . .	1,200.0	1,200.0*	1,200.0*
Calcite ('000 metric tons) . . .	750.0	750.0*	750.0*
Silica sand ('000 metric tons)* .	500.0	500.0	500.0
Ball clay ('000 metric tons) . .	1,000.0	1,000.0*	1,000.0*
Kaolin—marketable production ('000 metric tons)	500.0	500.0*	500.0*
Phosphate rock, crude* . . .	3,000	3,000	3,000
Fluorspar—metallurgical grade ('000 metric tons)	86,365	2,222	2,000*
Feldspar ('000 metric tons) . .	600.0	600.0*	600.0*
Barite ('000 metric tons) . . .	51.9	33.5	35.0*
Perlite*	7,000	7,000	7,000
Gypsum ('000 metric tons) . .	8,679	9,985	10,000*
Gemstones ('000 carats) . . .	30	30*	30*

* Estimate(s).

Source: US Geological Survey.

Industry

SELECTED PRODUCTS

('000 metric tons, unless otherwise indicated)

	2007	2008	2009*
Raw sugar	7,344	8,194	8,747
Beer (million litres)	2,161	2,160	1,837
Spirits (million litres) . . .	551	631	666
Synthetic fibre	674.6	592.7	601.6
Wood pulp	1,037.4	948.5	880.3
Petroleum products (million litres)	49,856	51,216	53,393
Cement	35,668	31,651	31,180
Galvanized iron sheets . . .	247.2	207.5	169.7
Integrated circuits (million units)	14,334	13,758	13,277
Computer monitors ('000 units) .	942	705	660
Computer keyboards ('000 units) .	931	633	109
Hard disk drives ('000 units) . .	205,277	246,986	258,271
Printers ('000 units)	17,439	15,693	8,177

* Provisional.

2010: Raw sugar 5,404; Beer (million litres) 1,948; Cement 36,496; Galvanized iron sheets 512.0.

2011: Raw sugar 7,972; Beer (million litres) 1,814; Cement 36,602; Galvanized iron sheets 531.3.

2012: Raw sugar 7,932; Beer (million litres) 2,085; Cement 41,047; Galvanized iron sheets 564.4.

Source: Bank of Thailand, Bangkok.

Finance

CURRENCY AND EXCHANGE RATES

Monetary Units
100 satangs = 1 baht.

Sterling, Dollar and Euro Equivalents (31 December 2012)
£1 sterling = 48.337 baht;
US $1 = 30.632 baht;
€1 = 40.415 baht;
1,000 baht = £20.69 = $32.65 = €24.74.

Average Exchange Rate (baht per US $)
2010   31.686
2011   30.492
2012   31.083

Note: Figures refer to the average mid-point rate of exchange available from commercial banks. In July 1997 the Bank of Thailand began operating a managed 'float' of the baht. In addition, a two-tier market was introduced, creating separate exchange rates for purchasers of baht in domestic markets and those who buy the currency overseas.

GOVERNMENT FINANCE

(central government transactions, non-cash basis, '000 million baht, year ending 30 September)

Summary of Balances

	2009/10	2010/11	2011/12
Revenue	1,804.0	2,019.5	2,120.6
Less Expense	1,826.2	1,996.9	2,200.8
Net operating balance . . .	22.2	22.6	−80.2
Less Net acquisition of non-financial assets	234.4	201.8	201.1
Net lending/borrowing . . .	−256.6	−179.2	−281.3

Revenue

	2009/10	2010/11	2011/12
Taxes	1,567.9	1,799.7	1,832.5
Taxes on income, profits and			
capital gains	682.9	852.7	843.6
Taxes on goods and services .	780.7	834.5	859.7
Social contributions	0.0	0.0	0.0
Grants	1.3	1.3	1.6
Other revenue	234.8	218.5	286.5
Total	1,804.0	2,019.5	2,120.6

Expense/Outlays

Expense by economic type	2009/10	2010/11	2011/12
Compensation of employees . .	752.8	727.7	801.3
Use of goods and services . .	488.4	395.0	406.7
Consumption of fixed capital . .	53.7	63.3	69.7
Interest	126.2	133.3	146.2
Subsidies	6.7	106.5	111.5
Grants	357.5	429.6	512.7
Social benefits	36.8	73.7	73.4
Other expense	4.2	67.7	79.2
Total	1,826.2	1,996.9	2,200.8

Outlays by functions of government*	2009/10	2010/11	2011/12
General public services . .	549.8	568.5	650.5
Defence	167.3	190.5	167.0
Public order and safety . . .	121.2	135.7	133.3
Economic affairs	380.1	375.8	425.1
Agriculture, forestry and fishing	115.3	43.3	112.5
Fuel and energy	2.8	6.3	13.7
Transport	103.6	33.5	40.0
Environmental protection . .	4.4	2.5	1.8
Housing and community amenities	42.7	48.6	164.0
Health	199.8	236.7	236.0
Recreation, culture and religion .	20.4	20.9	24.7
Education	423.4	480.4	460.1
Social protection	151.5	202.5	209.2
Total	2,060.6	2,262.1	2,471.8

* Including net acquisition of non-financial assets.

Source: Ministry of Finance, Bangkok.

INTERNATIONAL RESERVES
(US $ million at 31 December)

	2009	2010	2011
Gold (national valuation) . . .	2,935	4,599	7,735
IMF special drawing rights . .	1,523	1,497	1,494
Reserve position in IMF . . .	361	377	695
Foreign exchange	133,599	165,656	165,200
Total	138,418	172,129	175,124

Source: IMF, *International Financial Statistics*.

MONEY SUPPLY
('000 million baht at 31 December)

	2009	2010	2011
Currency outside depository			
corporations	804.6	895.1	990.0
Transferable deposits . . .	330.6	365.2	378.3
Other deposits	8,726.8	9,484.0	10,569.7
Securities other than shares . .	715.7	990.0	1,582.1
Broad money	10,577.6	11,734.3	13,520.0

Source: IMF, *International Financial Statistics*.

COST OF LIVING
(Consumer Price Index; base: 2007 = 100)

	2010	2011	2012
Food (incl. non-alcoholic beverages)	122.8	132.6	137.7
Tobacco and alcoholic beverages .	117.1	117.2	117.6
Energy	102.9	108.7	114.2
Clothing (incl. footwear) . . .	97.1	97.7	98.4
Housing and furnishing . . .	97.1	98.4	100.2
All items (incl. others) . . .	108.0	112.1	114.6

Source: Bank of Thailand, Bangkok.

NATIONAL ACCOUNTS
(million baht at current prices, preliminary)

Expenditure on the Gross Domestic Product

	2010	2011	2012
Government final consumption			
expenditure	1,310,027	1,397,530	1,543,626
Private final consumption			
expenditure	5,429,683	5,742,852	6,293,151
Changes in inventories . . .	121,382	37,451	141,092
Gross fixed capital formation . .	2,499,311	2,769,018	3,249,909
Total domestic expenditure .	9,360,403	9,946,851	11,227,778
Exports of goods and services . .	7,203,299	8,109,950	8,517,018
Less Imports of goods and services	6,452,512	7,631,792	8,399,185
Statistical discrepancy	−6,369	115,125	17,260
GDP in market prices . . .	10,104,821	10,540,134	11,362,871
GDP at constant 1988 prices .	4,596,112	4,599,655	4,895,634

Gross Domestic Product by Economic Activity

	2010	2011	2012
Agriculture, hunting and forestry .	1,142,671	1,295,682	1,276,994
Fishing	109,136	110,598	108,357
Mining and quarrying	346,631	384,641	449,193
Manufacturing	3,599,713	3,583,033	3,866,695
Electricity, gas and water . . .	296,583	291,226	335,845
Construction	269,273	269,762	303,472
Wholesale and retail trade; repair			
of motor vehicles, motorcycles			
and personal and household			
goods	1,323,916	1,354,399	1,461,803
Hotels and restaurants . . .	479,145	518,517	592,374
Transport, storage and			
communications	688,136	716,200	781,663
Financial intermediation . . .	410,048	482,449	529,591
Real estate, renting and business			
activities	228,770	239,893	252,248
Public administration and defence;			
compulsory social security . .	441,420	475,393	517,161
Education	435,246	459,831	503,947
Health and social work . . .	185,932	198,705	215,732
Other community, social and			
personal service activities . .	138,039	149,363	156,695
Private households with employed			
persons	10,162	10,442	11,101
GDP in market prices . . .	10,104,821	10,540,134	11,362,871

Source: National Economic and Social Development Board, Bangkok.

BALANCE OF PAYMENTS
(US $ million)

	2009	2010	2011
Exports of goods	150,788	191,600	219,119
Imports of goods	−118,180	−161,933	−202,129
Trade balance	32,607	29,667	16,991
Exports of services	30,102	34,288	41,528
Imports of services	−36,484	−44,975	−52,020
Balance on goods and services	26,226	18,980	6,500
Primary income received . .	5,084	5,102	7,187
Primary income paid	−14,790	−20,167	−18,532
Balance on goods, services and			
primary income	16,520	3,915	−4,845
Secondary income received . .	6,911	7,688	12,714
Secondary income paid . . .	−1,540	−1,656	−1,951
Current balance	21,891	9,946	5,918

—continued	2009	2010	2011
Capital account (net)	68	245	−40
Direct investment assets . . .	−4,171	−4,616	−8,240
Direct investment liabilities . .	4,854	9,104	7,780
Portfolio investment assets . .	−8,246	687	−887
Portfolio investment liabilities .	2,695	9,118	4,426
Financial derivatives and employee stock options (net)	1,117	−61	−550
Other investment assets . . .	1,944	−5,505	−7,739
Other investment liabilities . .	−771	16,164	−21
Net errors and omissions . . .	4,749	−3,837	545
Reserves and related items .	24,131	31,246	1,191

Source: IMF, *International Financial Statistics*.

External Trade

PRINCIPAL COMMODITIES
(distribution by SITC, '000 million baht)

Imports c.i.f.	2010	2011	2012
Food	226.9	268.9	324.4
Crude materials (inedible) except fuels	180.7	226.0	224.1
Mineral fuels, lubricants, etc. .	1,027.2	1,334.6	1,496.1
Chemicals and related products .	640.1	724.1	749.8
Basic manufactures	1,060.6	1,196.7	1,264.3
Machinery	2,057.6	2,278.9	2,835.3
Total (incl. others)	5,856.6	6,982.7	7,738.5

Exports f.o.b.	2010	2011	2012
Food	757.6	895.5	893.0
Crude materials (inedible) except fuels	352.4	511.6	394.1
Mineral fuels and lubricants . .	304.4	387.0	461.4
Chemicals and related products .	536.2	689.1	716.6
Basic manufactures	753.0	825.2	891.6
Machinery	2,604.0	2,572.9	2,865.9
Miscellaneous manufactured articles	204.4	179.2	208.4
Total (incl. others)	6,113.3	6,708.0	7,091.3

Source: Bank of Thailand, Bangkok.

PRINCIPAL TRADING PARTNERS
('000 million baht)

Imports c.i.f.	2010	2011	2012
Australia	189.1	242.1	170.2
China, People's Republic . . .	775.4	930.8	1,155.3
France	46.2	66.7	100.1
Germany	148.3	165.2	186.9
Hong Kong	58.2	71.3	54.0
India	72.1	92.2	100.0
Indonesia	182.2	225.3	252.7
Italy	46.8	64.2	69.0
Japan	1,211.5	1,288.1	1,549.4
Korea, Republic	258.5	281.0	280.8
Malaysia	343.9	376.2	409.6
Myanmar	90.0	106.5	114.8
Oman	80.1	79.9	73.2
Philippines	76.0	82.5	85.2
Qatar	68.3	76.8	82.7
Russia	102.7	137.7	126.6
Saudi Arabia	186.3	225.2	257.6
Singapore	201.9	237.7	244.9
Switzerland	166.5	270.9	227.7
Taiwan	218.2	229.0	256.8
United Arab Emirates . . .	280.2	442.5	489.2
United Kingdom	61.2	59.6	86.3
USA	342.1	408.7	403.6
Viet Nam	44.7	62.0	93.4
Total (incl. others)	5,856.6	6,982.7	7,738.5

Exports f.o.b.	2010	2011	2012
Australia	297.1	241.0	301.8
Cambodia	74.3	81.2	116.9
China, People's Republic . . .	678.6	791.2	830.8
France	55.7	56.7	50.0
Germany	104.4	113.4	111.4
Hong Kong	354.8	360.1	405.0
India	139.2	156.3	169.1
Indonesia	232.9	303.9	346.3
Italy	54.1	56.2	43.8
Japan	641.9	719.4	725.5
Korea, Republic	114.3	137.9	147.6
Laos	67.6	83.5	111.5
Malaysia	334.6	373.6	383.7
Myanmar	65.6	85.9	96.5
Netherlands	115.3	137.4	129.0
Philippines	154.9	139.8	150.1
Saudi Arabia	67.2	67.9	86.6
Singapore	284.7	344.0	334.6
South Africa	55.6	66.3	87.7
Switzerland	129.3	143.1	158.1
Taiwan	101.8	116.4	105.6
United Arab Emirates . . .	90.1	83.2	88.7
United Kingdom	115.7	117.1	117.5
USA	638.8	656.6	703.9
Viet Nam	184.5	212.7	206.7
Total (incl. others)	6,113.3	6,708.0	7,091.3

Source: Bank of Thailand, Bangkok.

Transport

RAILWAYS
(year ending 30 September)

	2008/09	2009/10	2010/11
Passengers carried ('000) . . .	46,978	45,153	45,833
Passenger-kilometres (million) .	8,814	8,246	8,032
Freight carried ('000 metric tons) .	11,534	11,623	n.a.

2005/06: Freight ton-kilometres (million) 3,508.

ROAD TRAFFIC
('000 motor vehicles in use at 31 December)

	2009	2010	2011
Passenger cars	4,078.5	4,496.8	5,001.4
Buses and trucks	926.3	954.8	990.4
Vans and pick-ups	4,696.9	4,894.7	5,137.6
Motorcycles	16,549.3	17,156.7	18,018.1
Total (incl. others)	27,184.6	28,484.8	30,194.9

SHIPPING

Flag Registered Fleet
(at 31 December)

	2010	2011	2012
Number of vessels	745	745	750
Total displacement ('000 grt) . .	2,960.7	2,867.9	3,096.1

Source: Lloyd's List Intelligence (www.lloydslistintelligence.com).

International Sea-borne Freight Traffic
(Port of Bangkok only, year ending 30 September)

	2008/09	2009/10	2010/11
Goods loaded ('000 metric tons) . .	1,310	1,453	1,455
Goods unloaded ('000 metric tons).	7,852	9,984	10,853
Vessels entered	2,541	2,681	2,991

Source: Port Authority of Thailand, Bangkok.

CIVIL AVIATION
(traffic on scheduled services)

	2007	2008	2009
Kilometres flown (million) . .	270	259	249
Passengers carried ('000) . .	21,192	19,993	19,619
Passenger-km (million) . . .	62,479	57,185	53,478
Total ton-km (million) . . .	8,156	7,509	6,970

Sources: UN, *Statistical Yearbook*.

2010: Passengers carried ('000) 20,303 (Source: World Bank, World Development Indicators database).

Tourism

FOREIGN TOURIST ARRIVALS BY COUNTRY OF RESIDENCE*

Country of origin	2009	2010	2011
Australia	646,705	698,046	829,855
China, People's Republic . .	777,508	1,122,219	1,721,247
France	427,067	461,670	515,572
Germany	573,473	606,874	619,133
Hong Kong	318,762	316,476	411,834
India	n.a.	760,371	914,971
Japan	1,004,453	993,674	1,127,893
Korea, Republic	618,227	805,445	1,006,283
Malaysia	1,757,813	2,058,956	2,500,280
Singapore	563,575	603,538	682,364
Sweden	350,819	355,214	373,856
Taiwan	362,783	369,220	447,610
United Kingdom	841,425	810,727	844,972
USA	627,074	611,792	681,748
Viet Nam	363,029	380,368	496,768
Total (incl. others)	14,149,841	15,936,400	19,230,470

* Includes Thai nationals resident abroad.

Receipts from tourism (US $ million, excl. passenger transport): 16,056 in 2009; 20,115 in 2010; 26,256 in 2011 (provisional) (Source: World Tourism Organization).

Communications Media

	2009	2010	2011
Telephones ('000 main lines in use)	7,204.9	6,924.8	6,61.2
Mobile cellular telephones ('000 subscribers)	65,952.3	71,624.2	77,604.7
Internet users ('000)	2,295.6	n.a.	3,846.0
Broadband subscribers ('000) . .	2,295.6	3,188.6	3,496.0

Source: International Telecommunication Union.

Education

(2009, unless otherwise indicated)

	Institutions	Teachers	Students
Ministry of Education:			
Office of the Permanent Secretary	3,968	125,678	2,345,282
Office of the Basic Education Commission	31,508	408,692	7,894,875
Office of the Higher Education Commission	174	60,554	1,926,414
Office of Vocational Education Commission	415	27,745	695,096
Mahidol Wittayanusorn School .	1	95	784
Mahamakut Buddhist University*	8	150	6,436
Mahachulalongkornrajavidyalaya University*	12	373	8,999
Bangkok Metropolitan Education Department	437	15,417	339,787
Royal Thai Police	183	1,979	26,090
Department of Local Administration	1,187	32,646	656,449
Ministry of Social Development and Human Security	3	55	483
Ministry of Public Health . . .	37	1,887	19,697
Merchant Marine Training Centre .	1	106	1,114
Civil Aviation Training Centre . .	1	30	2,207
National Bureau of Buddhism . .	400	4,706	56,109
Fine Arts Department	16	1,219	11,359
Office of Sports and Recreational Development	28	1,000	14,675
Armed Forces	15	1,899	7,967

* Figures for 2004.

Source: Ministry of Education, Bangkok.

Pupil-teacher ratio (primary education, UNESCO estimate): 16.0 in 2007/08 (Source: UNESCO Institute for Statistics).

Adult literacy rate (UNESCO estimates): 94.1% (males 95.9%; females 92.6%) in 2007 (Source: UNESCO Institute for Statistics).

Directory

The Government

HEAD OF STATE

King: HM King BHUMIBOL ADULYADEJ (King Rama IX—succeeded to the throne June 1946).

PRIVY COUNCIL

The Privy Council comprises a President and not more than 18 Privy Councillors, all of whom are appointed by the King. The Privy Council advises the King on all matters pertaining to his functions.
President: Gen. (retd) PREM TINSULANONDA.

CABINET
(May 2013)

The Cabinet comprises members of Puea Thai, Chart Thai Pattana, Palang Chon and the Chart Pattana Party.
Prime Minister: YINGLUCK SHINAWATRA.
Deputy Prime Minister and Minister of Foreign Affairs: SURAPONG TOWIJAKCHAIKUL.

Deputy Prime Minister and Minister of Finance: KITTIRAT NA-RANONG.
Deputy Prime Minister and Minister of Agriculture and Co-operatives: YUKOL LIM-LAEMTHONG.
Deputy Prime Minister and Minister of Education: PHONGTHEP THEPKANJANA.
Deputy Prime Ministers without Portfolio: Capt. CHALERM YOOBAMRUNG, PLODPRASOP SURASWADI.
Ministers in the Prime Minister's Office: VARATHEP RATTANAKORN, SANSANEE NAKPONG, NIWATTHAMRONG BOONSONGPAISAN.
Minister of the Interior: CHARUPONG RUANGSUWAN.
Minister of Defence: Air Chief Marshal SUKAMPOL SUWANNATHAT.
Minister of Tourism and Sports: SOMSAK PUREESRISAK.
Minister of Commerce: BOONSONG TERIYAPIROM.
Minister of Information and Communications Technology: Group Capt. ANUDITH NAKORNTHAP.
Minister of Industry: PRASERT BOONCHAISUK.
Minister of Social Development and Human Security: SANTI PROMPAT.

Minister of Transport: CHADCHART SITTIPUNT.

Minister of Natural Resources and Environment: PREECHA RENGSOMBOONSUK.

Minister of Energy: PONGSAK RUKTAPONGPISAL.

Minister of Justice: Police Gen. PRACHA PROMNOK.

Minister of Labour: PADERMCHAI SASOMSAP.

Minister of Culture: SONTAYA KHUNPLOEM.

Minister of Science and Technology: WORAVAT AU-APINYAKUL.

Minister of Public Health: PRADIT SINTAVANARONG.

MINISTRIES

Office of the Prime Minister: Government House, Thanon Phitsanulok, Dusit, Bangkok 10300; tel. (2) 281-4040; fax (2) 282-5131; e-mail opm@opm.go.th; internet www.opm.go.th.

Ministry of Agriculture and Co-operatives: Thanon Ratchadamnoen Nok, Bangkok 10200; tel. (2) 281-5955; fax (2) 282-1425; e-mail webmaster@moac.go.th; internet www.moac.go.th.

Ministry of Commerce: 44/100 Thanon Nonthaburi 1, Amphur Muang, Nonthaburi, Bangkok 11000; tel. (2) 507-7000; fax (2) 547-5210; e-mail webmaster@moc.go.th; internet www.moc.go.th.

Ministry of Culture: 666 Thanon Borommaratchachonnani, Bang Bumru, Bang Plat, Bangkok 10700; tel. (2) 422-8888; e-mail webmaster@m-culture.go.th; internet www.m-culture.go.th.

Ministry of Defence: Thanon Sanam Chai, Bangkok 10200; tel. (2) 222-1121; fax (2) 226-3117; e-mail webmaster@mod.go.th; internet www.mod.go.th.

Ministry of Education: Wang Chankasem, Thanon Ratchadamnoen Nok, Bangkok 10300; tel. (2) 281-9264; fax (2) 281-1753; e-mail website@emisc.moe.go.th; internet www.moe.go.th.

Ministry of Energy: 17 Kasatsuk Bridge, Thanon Rama I, Rong Muang, Pathumwan, Bangkok 10330; tel. (2) 223-3344; fax (2) 222-4495; e-mail moen@energy.go.th; internet www.energy.go.th.

Ministry of Finance: Thanon Rama VI, Samsennai, Phaya Thai, Rajatevi, Bangkok 10400; tel. (2) 273-9021; fax (2) 273-9408; e-mail webmaster-eng@mof.go.th; internet www.mof.go.th.

Ministry of Foreign Affairs: 443 Thanon Sri Ayudhya, Bangkok 10400; tel. (2) 643-5000; fax (2) 643-5102; e-mail information01@mfa.go.th; internet www.mfa.go.th.

Ministry of Industry: Thanon Rama VI, Ratchathewi, Bangkok 10400; tel. (2) 202-3000; fax (2) 202-3048; e-mail info@industry.go.th; internet www.industry.go.th.

Ministry of Information and Communications Technology: 120 Moo 3, Government Offices, Bldg B, 6th–9th Floors, Thanon Chaengwattana, Thung Song Hong, Laksi, Bangkok 10210; tel. (2) 141-6747; fax (2) 143-8019; e-mail pr@mict.go.th; internet www.mict.go.th.

Ministry of the Interior: Thanon Atsadang, Bangkok 10200; tel. (2) 222-1141; fax (2) 223-8851; e-mail webmaster@moi.go.th; internet www.moi.go.th.

Ministry of Justice: Thanon Chaengwattana, Pakkred, Nonthaburi, Bangkok 11120; tel. (2) 502-8051; fax (2) 502-8059; e-mail webmaster@moj.go.th; internet www.moj.go.th.

Ministry of Labour: Thanon Mitmaitri, Dindaeng, Bangkok 10400; tel. (2) 232-1421; fax (2) 246-1520; e-mail webmaster@mol.go.th; internet www.mol.go.th.

Ministry of Natural Resources and Environment: 92 Phaholyothin Soi 7, Samsen Nai, Phaya Thai, Bangkok 10400; tel. (2) 278-8500; fax (2) 278-8698; e-mail webmaster@mnre.mail.go.th; internet www.mnre.go.th.

Ministry of Public Health: Thanon Tiwanon, Amphur Muang, Nonthaburi 11000; tel. (2) 590-1000; fax (2) 591-8492; e-mail webmaster@health.moph.go.th; internet www.moph.go.th.

Ministry of Science and Technology: 75/47 Thanon Rama VI, Phaya Thai, Bangkok 10400; tel. (2) 333-3700; fax (2) 333-3833; e-mail webmaster@most.go.th; internet www.most.go.th.

Ministry of Social Development and Human Security: 1034 Thanon Krungkasem, Mahanak, Khet Pom Prab Sattruphai, Bangkok 10100; tel. (2) 659-6399; fax 659-6529; e-mail society@m-society.go.th; internet www.m-society.go.th.

Ministry of Tourism and Sports: 4 Ratchadamnoen Nok, Khet Pom Prab Sattruphai, Bangkok 10100; tel. (2) 283-1500; fax (2) 356-0746; e-mail webmaster@mots.go.th; internet www.mots.go.th.

Ministry of Transport: 38 Thanon Ratchadamnoen Nok, Khet Pom Prab Sattruphai, Bangkok 10100; tel. (2) 283-3000; fax (2) 283-3959; e-mail mot@mot.go.th; internet www.mot.go.th.

Legislature

RATHA SAPHA (NATIONAL ASSEMBLY)

Woothi Sapha (Senate)

The Senate consists of 150 members, of whom 76 members are elected to represent each of Thailand's 75 provinces and Bangkok, and the remainder are selected by a committee consisting primarily of judicial officials. Senators thus selected are drawn from lists of nominees made by organizations in various sectors.

Elections to the Senate were held on 2 March 2008. In accordance with transitional measures included in the 2007 Constitution, the 74 senators selected by committee in 2008 exceptionally served a three-year term. On 12 April 2011 the Election Commission announced the list of newly selected senators, who would serve a six-year term. The number of indirectly elected senators was reduced to 73 as a result of the creation in the previous month of a new province, for which a new senator would be elected at the next direct elections to the Senate (which were due to be held by March 2014), thus increasing the number of directly elected senators to 77.

Speaker of the Senate: NIKOM WAIRATPANIJ.

Sapha Poothaen Rassadorn (House of Representatives)

Speaker of the House of Representatives and President of the National Assembly: SOMSAK KAITSURANONT.

Election, 3 July 2011

Party	Seats
Puea Thai	265
Democrat Party	159
Bhum Jai Thai	34
Chart Thai Pattana	19
Palang Chon	7
Chart Pattana Puea Pandin	7
Rak Thailand	4
Matubhum Party	2
Rak Santi Party	1
New Democratic Party	1
Mahachon	1
Total	**500***

* A total of 375 candidates were elected in multi-member constituencies and the remaining 125 through a party-list system.

Election Commission

Election Commission of Thailand (ECT): 120 Moo 3, Government Offices, Bldg B, 2nd Floor, Thanon Chaengwattana, Thung Song Hong, Laksi, Bangkok 10210; tel. (2) 141-8888; fax (2) 219-3411; e-mail dav@ect.go.th; internet www.ect.go.th; Chair. APHICHART SUKHAGGANOND.

Political Organizations

Bhum Jai Thai (BJT) (Thai Pride Party): Suite 2159, 11 Thanon Phaholyothin, Chatuchak, Bangkok 10900; tel. (2) 940-6999; internet www.bhumjaithai.com; f. 2008; est. by fmr mems of Matchimathipataya (f. 2006) in anticipation of that party's dissolution, in Dec. 2008, by Constitutional Court; merged in Jan. 2009 with Friends of Newin (f. 2008 by NEWIN CHIDCHOB and other defectors from People's Power Party); in alliance with Chart Thai Pattana for 2011 elections; Leader ANUTHIN CHANWEERAKUL; Sec.-Gen. SAKYASAM CHITCHOB.

Chart Pattana Party: c/o House of Representatives, Bangkok; f. 2007; est. as Ruam Jai Thai Chart Pattana; renamed Ruam Chart Pattana in 2008; renamed Chart Pattana Puea Pandin Party following merger with Puea Pandin in 2011; present name adopted in Sept. 2011; Leader WANNARAT CHARNNUKUL.

Chart Thai Pattana (Thai Nation Development): 37/157 Moo 11, Sansab, Minburi, Bangkok; tel. (2) 243-8072; fax (2) 243-8074; e-mail chartthaipattana@chartthaipattana.or.th; internet www.chartthaipattana.or.th; f. 2008; est. by fmr mems of Chart Thai (f. 1981) in anticipation of that party's dissolution, in Dec. 2008, by Constitutional Court; right-wing; announced alliance with Bhum Jai Thai in 2011; Leader THEERA WONGSAMUT.

Democrat Party (DP) (Prachatipat): 67 Thanon Setsiri, Samsen Nai, Phaya Thai, Bangkok 10400; tel. (2) 270-0036; fax (2) 279-6086; e-mail public@democrat.or.th; internet www.democrat.or.th; f. 1946; liberal; Leader ABHISIT VEJJAJIVA; Sec.-Gen. CHALERMCHAI SRI-ON.

Karn Muang Mai (New Politics Party—NPP): Phra Nakhon Region, Bangkok 10200; tel. (2) 282-9844; fax (2) 282-9850; internet www.npp.or.th; f. 2009; est. by members of the People's Alliance for Democracy (PAD); Leader SOMSAK KOSAISUK; Sec.-Gen. SURIYASAI KATASILA.

Mahachon: 35,37 Soi Nonthaburi 32, Thanon Nonthaburi, Thasai, Muang District, Nonthaburi 11000; tel. (2) 525-48857; fax (2) 525-4887; f. 2004 following split in Democrat Party; Leader APIRAT SIRINAWIN.

Matubhum Party: Benjamas Bldg, 5th Floor, 555 Soi Ruam Chit, Dusit, Bangkok 10300; tel. (2) 715-3870; fax (2) 715-3790; f. 2008; comprises predominantly members of the Muslim Wadah and Pak Nam factions; Leader Gen. SONTHI BOONYARATGLIN.

New Democratic Party: c/o House of Representatives, Bangkok; Leader SUTHIN PICHARN.

Palang Chon (Force of Chon Buri): c/o House of Representatives, Bangkok; internet www.phalangchon.or.th; f. 2011; est. by fmr mems of Bhum Jai Thai; Leader SONTAYA KHUNPLOEM.

Pracha Santi Party: Thanon Amnuay Songkhram, Bangkok; f. 2011; supports formation of a national govt and eradication of corruption; Leader SERI SUWANNAPHANONT.

Pracharaj (Royal People Party): TPI Tower, 18th Floor, 26/56 Thanon Chan Tat Mai, Tungmahamek, Sathorn, Bangkok 10120; f. 2006; est. by breakaway faction of Thai Rak Thai (f. 1998); Leader SNOH THIENTHONG; Sec.-Gen. CHIENGCHUANG KANLAYANAMITH.

Puea Thai (For Thais): 1770 Thanon Phetchaburi, Bangkapi, Huay Kwang, Bangkok 10310; internet www.ptp.or.th; f. 2008; est. by fmr mems of People's Power Party (f. 2007) in anticipation of that party's dissolution, in Dec. 2008, by Constitutional Court; Leader CHARUPONG RUANGSUWAN; Sec.-Gen. PHUMTHAM WECHAYACHAI.

Rak Santi Party: 8 Thanon Sukonthasawat, Ladprao, Bangkok 10230; e-mail info@raksanti.org; internet www.raksanti.org; tel. (2) 907-7205; fax (2) 907-7203; f. 2011; Chair. PURACHAI PIUMSOMBUN; Sec.-Gen. PORNPEN PHETSUKSIRI.

Rak Thailand Party: c/o House of Representatives, Bangkok; f. 2011; Leader CHUWIT KAMOLVISIT; Sec.-Gen. CHAIWAT JUTI KRAIRIKSH.

Social Action Party (SAP) (Kij Sangkhom): 381/28–29 Thanon Mitrapap, Naimuang, Muang, Khon-kaen 40000; tel. and fax (2) 325-2234; f. 1981; disbanded in 2003; revived in mid-2008 by former leader Suwit Khunkitti, following his defection from Puea Pandin; conservative; Sec.-Gen. SUWIT KHUNKITTI.

Other parties that contested the 2011 elections included Thai Citizen, Prachathum, Dumrong Thai, Mass Power, Thai Por Pieng, Thai Pen Suk, Thais Is Thai, Thaen Khun Phaendin, Heaven and Earth, the Farmer Network of Thailand, New Politics, Liberal, Chart Samuccee, Bamrungmueang, Kasikorn Thai, Better Life, Palung Sungkom Thai, Thai Party for Thai People, Prachachon Chow Thai, Rakpandin, Civil Peace, New Aspiration, Asamatupoom, Sport Party of Thailand, Parung Chowna Thai, Thai Sangsun, Puen Kaset Thai and Maharatpattana.

Two popular movements, which staged large-scale political rallies and became involved in civil unrest from 2008, emerged in response to the political crises: the **People's Alliance for Democracy (PAD)**, a coalition of groups and individuals, including royalists, opposed to Thaksin Shinawatra, established in 2005 by Sondhi Limthongkul and popularly known as the 'Yellow Shirts' (internet www.padnet.net); and the **United Front for Democracy against Dictatorship (UDD)**, a coalition of broadly pro-Thaksin activists, popularly known as the 'Red Shirts', who rejected the legitimacy of the Government of Abhisit Vejjajiva (internet www.uddthailand.com). A new group named **Pitak Siam (Protect Thailand)** was established in 2012, with the support of a number of royalist groups, including the PAD, and organized a protest against the Government of Yingluck Shinawatra in November that year.

Groupings that were or are in armed conflict with the Government include:

Barisan Revolusi Nasional (BRN) (National Revolutionary Front): Yala; f. 1963; was organized into three principal factions— the BRN Congress (its military wing); the BRN Co-ordinate (its political wing); and the BRN Uram (its religious wing)—in the 1980s; Muslim secessionists; commenced peace talks with the Govt was in March 2013.

Bersatu (Council of the Muslim People of Pattani): Pattani; f. 1989; umbrella org. incl. the BRN and the PULO; Pattani secessionists.

Gerakan Mujahidin Islam Patani (GMIP): Pattani; f. 1986; dissolved in 1993 following internal disagreement, but re-formed in 1995; seeks the transformation of Pattani into an Islamic state; Leader KARIM KARUBANG.

Patani United Liberation Organization (PULO): e-mail infopulo@gmail.com; internet www.puloinfo.net; f. 1968; subsequently divided into factions; advocates secession of the five southern provinces (Satun, Narathiwat, Yala, Pattani and Songkhla); was engaged in peace talks with the Govt in early 2013; Pres. KASTURI MAHKOTA.

Runda Kumpulan Kecil (RKK): Yala; f. 2005; splinter group of the BRN Congress; seeks the implementation of an independent Islamic state in Thailand's southern provinces; Leader USTAZ RORHING AHSONG.

Diplomatic Representation

EMBASSIES IN THAILAND

Argentina: Glas Haus Bldg, 16th Floor, Suite 1601, 1 Soi Sukhumvit 25, Wattana, Bangkok 10110; tel. (2) 259-0401; fax (2) 259-0402; e-mail etal@mrecic.gov.ar; Ambassador ANA MARÍA RAMÍREZ.

Australia: 37 Thanon Sathorn Tai, Bangkok 10120; tel. (2) 344-6300; fax (2) 344-6593; e-mail austembassy.bangkok@dfat.gov.au; internet www.thailand.embassy.gov.au; Ambassador JAMES WISE.

Austria: 14 Soi Nandha, off Thanon Sathorn Tai, Soi 1, Bangkok 10120; tel. (2) 303-6257; fax (2) 303-6260; e-mail bangkok-ob@bmeia.gv.at; internet www.aussenministerium.at/botschaft/bangkok; Ambassador Dr JOHANNES PETERLIK.

Bahrain: 100/66–67 Sathorn Nakorn Tower, Thanon Sathorn Nua, Silom, Bangrak, Bangkok 10500; tel. (2) 636-7892; fax (2) 636-7459; e-mail bangkok.mission@mofa.gov.bh; Ambassador ADIL YOUSIF SATER.

Bangladesh: 47/8 Ekamai Soi 30, Thanon Sukhumvit 63, Khlong Tan Nua, Wattana, Bangkok 10110; tel. (2) 390-5107; fax (2) 390-5106; e-mail bdootbkk@truemail.co.th; internet www.bdembassybangkok.org; Ambassador KAZI IMTIAZ HOSSAIN.

Belgium: Sathorn Sq. Bldg, 16th Floor, 98 Thanon Sathorn Nua, Silom, Bangkok 10120; tel. (2) 108-1800; fax (2) 108-1807; e-mail bangkok@diplobel.fed.be; internet www.diplomatie.be/bangkok; Ambassador MARC MICHELSEN.

Bhutan: 375/1 Soi Ratchadanivej, Thanon Pracha-Uthit, Huay Kwang, Bangkok 10320; tel. (2) 274-4740; fax (2) 274-4743; e-mail bht_emb_bkk@yahoo.com; Ambassador KESANG WANGDI.

Brazil: Lumpini Tower, 34th Floor, 1168/101 Thanon Rama IV, Tungmahamek, Sathorn, Bangkok 10120; tel. (2) 679-8567; fax (2) 679-8569; e-mail brasemb.bangkok@itamaraty.gov.br; internet www.brazilembassy.or.th; Ambassador PAULO CESAR MEIRA DE VASCONCELLOS.

Brunei: 12 Soi Ekamai 2, Thanon Sukhumvit 63, Prakanong Nua, Wattana, Bangkok 10110; tel. (2) 714-7395; fax (2) 714-7382; e-mail bangkok.thailand@mfa.gov.bn; Ambassador Pengiran Dato' Paduka Haji KAMIS BIN Haji TAMIN.

Bulgaria: 83/24 Soi Witthayu 1, Thanon Witthayu, Lumpini, Pathumwan, Bangkok 10330; tel. (2) 627-3872; fax (2) 627-3874; e-mail bulgemth@csloxinfo.com; internet www.mfa.bg/bangkok; Ambassador KAMEN VELICHKOV.

Cambodia: 518/4 Thanon Pracha Uthit, Ramkhamhaeng Soi 39, Wangtonglang, Bangkok 10310; tel. (2) 957-5851; fax (2) 957-5850; e-mail camemb.tha@mfa.gov.kh; Ambassador YOU AY.

Canada: Abdulrahim Pl., 15th Floor, 990 Thanon Rama IV, Bangrak, Bangkok 10500; tel. (2) 636-0540; fax (2) 636-0566; e-mail bngkk@international.gc.ca; internet www.canadainternational.gc.ca/thailand-thailande; Ambassador PHILIP CALVERT.

Chile: 193/67 Lake Rajada Office Complex, 17th Floor, Thanon Ratchadaphisek, Klongtoey, Bangkok 10110; tel. (2) 251-9470; fax (2) 251-9475; e-mail embajada@chile-thai.com; internet www.chile-thai.com; Ambassador JAVIER BECKER MARSHALL.

China, People's Republic: 57 Thanon Ratchadaphisek, Bangkok 10310; tel. (2) 245-7043; fax (2) 246-8247; e-mail chinaemb_th@mfa.gov.cn; internet www.chinaembassy.or.th/eng; Ambassador GUAN MU.

Cuba: Mela Mansion Apt 7Ac, 5 Soi Sukhumvit 27, Klongtoey Nua, Wattana, Bangkok 10110; tel. (2) 665-2803; fax (2) 661-6560; e-mail embajada@th.embacuba.cu; internet embacuba.cubaminrex.cu/tailandiaing; Ambassador LÁZARO HERRERA MARTÍNEZ.

Czech Republic: 71/6 Soi Ruamrudi 2, Thanon Ploenchit, Bangkok 10330; tel. (2) 255-3027; fax (2) 253-7637; e-mail bangkok@embassy.mzv.cz; internet www.mfa.cz/bangkok; Ambassador VÍTĚZSLAV GREPL.

Denmark: 10 Soi Sathorn, Thanon Sathorn Tai, Bangkok 10120; tel. (2) 343-1100; fax (2) 213-1752; e-mail bkkamb@um.dk; internet www.ambbangkok.um.dk; Ambassador MIKAEL HEMNITI WINTHER.

Egypt: Sorachai Bldg, 31st Floor, 23/122–125 Sukhumvit 63, Wattana, Bangkok 10110; tel. (2) 726-9831; fax (2) 726-9834; e-mail egyptemb@truemail.co.th; Ambassador SHAMEL AL-SAYED NASSER.

Finland: Amarin Tower, 16th Floor, 500 Thanon Ploenchit, Bangkok 10330; tel. (2) 250-8801; fax (2) 250-8802; e-mail sanomat.ban@formin.fi; internet www.finland.or.th; Ambassador SIRPA MÄENPÄÄ.

France: CAT Tower, 23rd Floor, 72 Thanon Charoenkrung, Soi 36, Bangkok 10500; tel. (2) 657-5100; fax (2) 657-5111; e-mail ambassade@ambafrance-th.org; internet www.ambafrance-th.org; Ambassador THIERRY VITEAU.

Germany: 9 Thanon Sathorn Tai, Bangkok 10120; tel. (2) 287-9000; fax (2) 287-1776; e-mail info@bangkok.diplo.de; internet www.bangkok.diplo.de; Ambassador ROLF PETER GOTTFRIED SCHULZE.

Greece: 100/41 Sathorn Nakorn Tower, 23rd Floor, 100 Thanon Sathorn Nua, Bangkok 10500; tel. (2) 667-0090; fax (2) 667-0093; e-mail gremb.ban@mfa.gr; internet www.mfa.gr/bangkok; Ambassador NIKOLAOS VAMVOUNAKIS.

Holy See: 217/1 Thanon Sathorn Tai, Bangkok 10120 (Apostolic Nunciature); tel. (2) 212-5853; fax (2) 212-0932; e-mail nuntiusth@csloxinfo.com; Apostolic Nuncio Most Rev. PAUL TSCHANG IN-NAM (Titular Archbishop of Amantia).

Hungary: Oak Tower, 20th Floor, President Park Condominium, 99 Sukhumvit Soi 24, Klongtoey, Prakanong, Bangkok 10110; tel. (2) 661-1150; fax (2) 661-1153; e-mail mission.bgk@kum.gov.hu; internet www.mfa.gov.hu/emb/bangkok; Ambassador DENES TOMAJ.

India: 46 Soi Prasarnmitr, Thanon Sukhumvit, Soi 23, Bangkok 10110; tel. (2) 258-0300; fax (2) 258-4627; e-mail indiaemb@indianembassy.in.th; internet indianembassy.in.th; Ambassador ANIL WADHWA.

Indonesia: 600–602 Thanon Phetchaburi, Ratchathewi, Bangkok 10400; tel. (2) 252-3135; fax (2) 255-1267; e-mail kukbkk@ksc.th.com; internet www.bangkok.deplu.go.id; Ambassador LUTFI RAUF.

Iran: 215 Thanon Sukhumvit, Soi 49, Klongtan Nua, Wattana, Bangkok 10110; tel. (2) 390-0871; fax (2) 390-0867; e-mail info@iranembassy.or.th; Ambassador HOSSEIN KAMALIAN.

Israel: Ocean Tower II, 25th Floor, 75 Sukhumvit, Soi 19, Thanon Asoke, Bangkok 10110; tel. (2) 204-9200; fax (2) 204-9255; e-mail info@bangkok.mfa.gov.il; internet bangkok.mfa.gov.il; Ambassador SIMON RODED.

Italy: CRC Tower, 40th Floor, All Season Pl., 87 Thanon Witthaya, Lumpini, Bangkok 10330; tel. (2) 285-4090; fax (2) 285-4985; e-mail ambasciata.bangkok@esteri.it; internet www.ambbangkok.esteri.it; Ambassador MICHELANGELO PIPAN.

Japan: 177 Thanon Witthaya, Lumpini, Pathumwan, Bangkok 10330; tel. (2) 207-8500; fax (2) 207-8510; e-mail jis@bg.mofa.go.jp; internet www.th.emb-japan.go.jp; Ambassador SHIGEKAZU SATO.

Kazakhstan: GPF Witthayu Towers, Bldg A, Unit 804A, 93/1 Thanon Witthayu, Lumpini, Bangkok 10330; tel. (2) 254-3043; fax (2) 254-3042; e-mail mail@kazembassythailand.org; internet www.kazembassythailand.org; Chargé d'affaires a.i. ALIMZHAN TOKHTASSUNOV.

Kenya: 62 Thonglor Soi 5, Thanon Sukhumvit 55, Klongtan, Wattana, Bangkok 10110; tel. (2) 712-5721; fax (2) 712-5720; Ambassador RICHARD TITUS EKAI.

Korea, Democratic People's Republic: 14 Mooban Suanlaemthong 2, Soi 28, Thanon Pattanakarn, Suan Luang, Bangkok 10250; tel. (2) 319-2686; fax (2) 318-6333; Ambassador AN SONG NAM.

Korea, Republic: 23 Thanon Thiam-Ruammit, Ratchadaphisek, Huay Kwang, Bangkok 10320; tel. (2) 247-7537; fax (2) 247-7535; e-mail korea_emb_th@yahoo.co.kr; internet tha.mofat.go.kr; Ambassador JEON JAE-MAN.

Kuwait: 100/44 Sathorn Nakhorn Tower, Level 24A, Thanon Sathorn Nua, Bangrak, Bangkok 10500; tel. (2) 636-6600; fax (2) 636-7360; e-mail kwembassy_th @hotmail.com; Ambassador FAHAD AL-JAMAIZ.

Laos: 502/502/1–3 Soi Sahakarnpramoon, Thanon Pracha Uthit, Wangthonglang, Bangkok 10310; tel. (2) 539-6667; fax (2) 539-3827; e-mail embalao@bkklaoembassy.com; internet laoembassybkk.com; Ambassador LY BOUNKHAM.

Luxembourg: Q House Lumpini, 17th Floor, Thanon Sathorn Tai, Tungmahamek, Sathorn, Bangkok 10120; tel. (2) 677-7360; fax (2) 677-7364; e-mail bangkok.amb@mae.etat.lu; internet bangkok.mae.lu; Ambassador MARC THILL.

Malaysia: 35 Thanon Sathorn Tai, Tungmahamek, Sathorn, Bangkok 10120; tel. (2) 629-6800; fax (2) 679-2208; e-mail malbangkok@kln.gov.my; internet www.kln.gov.my/web/tha_bangkok; Ambassador Dato' NAZIRAH BINTI HUSSAIN.

Mexico: 21/60–62 Thai Wah Tower I, 20th Floor, Thanon Sathorn Tai, Sathorn, Bangkok 10120; tel. (2) 285-0995; fax (2) 285-0667; e-mail consular@mexicanembassythailand.com; internet www.sre.gob.mx/tailandia; Ambassador JORGE EDUARDO CHEN CHARPENTIER.

Mongolia: 100/3, Soi Ekamai 22, 63 Thanon Sukhumvit, Klongtan Nua, Wattana, Bangkok 10110; tel. (2) 381-1400; fax (2) 392-4199;

e-mail mongemb@loxinfo.co.th; Ambassador CHIMIDDORJIIN BATTÖMÖR.

Morocco: Sathorn City Tower, 12th Floor, 175 Thanon Sathorn Tai, Sathorn, Bangkok 10120; tel. (2) 679-5604; fax (2) 679-5603; e-mail ambmaroc@truemail.co.th; internet www.moroccoembassybangkok.org; Ambassador ABDELILAH AL-HASSANI.

Myanmar: 132 Thanon Sathorn Nua, Bangkok 10500; tel. (2) 233-2237; fax (2) 236-6898; e-mail myanmarembassybkk@gmail.com; Ambassador TIN WIN.

Nepal: 189 Soi 71, Thanon Sukhumvit, Prakanong, Bangkok 10110; tel. (2) 390-2280; fax (2) 381-2406; e-mail nepembkk@asiaaccess.net.th; Ambassador DORNATH ARYAL.

Netherlands: 15 Soi Tonson, Thanon Ploenchit, Lumpini, Pathumwan, Bangkok 10330; tel. (2) 309-5200; fax (2) 309-5205; e-mail ban@minbuza.nl; internet www.mfa.nl/ban; Ambassador JOAN BOER.

New Zealand: M Thai Tower, 14th Floor, All Seasons Pl., 87 Thanon Witthayu, Lumpini, Pathumwan, Bangkok 10330; tel. (2) 254-2530; fax (2) 253-9045; e-mail nzembbkk@loxinfo.co.th; internet www.nzembassy.com/thailand; Ambassador TONY LYNCH.

Nigeria: 412 Thanon Sukhumvit, Soi 71, Prakanong, Wattana, Bangkok 10110; tel. (2) 711-3076; fax (2) 392-6398; e-mail info@embnigeriabkk.com; Ambassador CHUKWUDI OKAFOR.

Norway: UBC II Bldg, 18th Floor, 591 Thanon Sukhumvit, Soi 33, Bangkok 10110; tel. (2) 204-6500; fax (2) 262-0218; e-mail emb.bangkok@mfa.no; internet www.emb-norway.or.th; Ambassador KATJA NORDGAARD.

Oman: Saeng Thong Thani Tower, 32nd Floor, 82 Thanon Sathorn Nua, Bangkok 10500; tel. (2) 639-9380; fax (2) 639-9390; e-mail embassyoman@yahoo.com; Ambassador HAFEEDH SALIM MOHAMED BA-OMAR.

Pakistan: 31 Soi Nana Nua, Thanon Sukhumvit 3, Bangkok 10110; tel. (2) 253-0288; fax (2) 253-0290; e-mail parepbangkok@gmail.com; internet www.mofa.gov.pk/thailand; Ambassador SOHAIL MAHMOOD.

Panama: 1168/37 Lumpini Tower, 16th Floor, Tungmahamek, Sathorn, Bangkok 10120; tel. (2) 679-7988; fax (2) 679-7991; e-mail embajada@panathai.com; internet www.panathai.com; Ambassador ISAURO RAMON MORA BORRERO.

Peru: Glas Haus Bldg, 16th Floor, 1 Thanon Sukhumvit, Soi 25, Wattana, Bangkok 10110; tel. (2) 260-6243; fax (2) 260-6244; e-mail peru@peruthai.or.th; internet www.peruthai.or.th; Ambassador JORGE CASTAÑEDA MÉNDEZ.

Philippines: 760 Thanon Sukhumvit, cnr Soi 30/1, Klongtan, Klongtoey, Bangkok 10110; tel. (2) 259-0139; fax (2) 259-2809; e-mail bangkokpe@gmail.com; internet www.philembassy-bangkok.net; Ambassador JOCELYNN SINGSON BATOON-GARCIA (designate).

Poland: 100/81–82, Vongvanij Bldg B, 25th Floor, Thanon Rama IX, Huay Kwang, Bangkok 10310; tel. (2) 645-0367; fax (2) 645-0365; e-mail bangkok.amb.sekretariat@msz.gov.pl; internet www.bangkok.polemb.net; Ambassador JERZY BAYER.

Portugal: 26 Bush Lane, Thanon Charoenkrung, Bangkok 10500; tel. (2) 234-2123; fax (2) 238-4275; e-mail mail@scban.dgaccp.pt; Ambassador JORGE RYDER TORRES PEREIRA.

Qatar: Capital Tower, 14th Floor, All Seasons Pl., 87/1 Thanon Witthayu, Lumpini, Pathumwan, Bangkok 10330; tel. (2) 660-1111; fax (2) 660-1122; e-mail info@qatarembassy.or.th; internet www.qatarembassy.or.th; Ambassador JABOR ALI HUSSEIN AL-DOUSARI.

Romania: 20/1 Soi Rajakhru, Phaholyothin Soi 5, Thanon Phaholyothin, Phaya Thai, Bangkok 10400; tel. (2) 617-1551; fax (2) 617-1113; e-mail romembnk@ksc.th.com; Chargé d'affaires a.i. GRUIA JACOTĂ.

Russia: 78 Thanon Sap, Bangrak, Bangkok 10500; tel. (2) 234-9824; fax (2) 237-8488; e-mail rusembbangkok@rambler.ru; internet www.thailand.mid.ru; Ambassador ALEKSANDR MARIYASOV.

Saudi Arabia: 82 Saengthong Thani Bldg, 23rd & 24th Floors, Thanon Sathorn Nua, Silom, Bangrak, Bangkok 10500; tel. (2) 639-2999; fax (2) 639-2950; Chargé d'affaires ABDELAH MUHAMMAD AL-SHAIBI.

Singapore: 129 Thanon Sathorn Tai, Bangkok 10120; tel. (2) 286-2111; fax (2) 286-6966; e-mail singemb_bkk@sgmfa.gov.sg; internet www.mfa.gov.sg/bangkok; Ambassador CHUA SIEW SAN.

Slovakia: 25/9-4 BKI/YWCA Bldg, 9th Floor, Thanon Sathorn Tai, Thungmahamek, Bangkok 10120; tel. (2) 677-3445; fax (2) 677-3447; e-mail emb.bangkok@mzv.sk; Ambassador VLADIMIR HALGAS.

South Africa: M-Thai Tower, Floor 12A, All Seasons Pl., 87 Thanon Witthayu, Pathumwan, Lumpini, Bangkok 10330; tel. (2) 659-2900; fax (2) 685-3500; e-mail saembbkk@loxinfo.co.th; internet www.saembbangkok.com; Ambassador DOUGLAS ROBINA PATRICIA MARKS.

Spain: Lake Rajada Office Complex, 23rd Floor, Suite 98–99, 193 Thanon Ratchadaphisek, Klongtoey, Bangkok 10110; tel. (2) 661-8284; fax (2) 661-9220; e-mail emb.bangkok@maec.es; internet www

.maec.es/subwebs/embajadas/bangkok; Ambassador DON IGNACIO SAGAZ.

Sri Lanka: Ocean Tower II, 13th Floor, 75/6–7 Sukhumvit, Soi 19, Klongtoey, Wattana, Bangkok 10110; tel. (2) 261-1934; fax (2) 261-1936; e-mail slemb@ksc.th.com; Ambassador Gen. (retd) SUWANDA HENNADIGE SHANTHA KOTTEGODA.

Sweden: First Pacific Pl., 20th Floor, 140 Thanon Sukhumvit, Bangkok 10110; tel. (2) 263-7200; fax (2) 263-7260; e-mail ambassaden.bangkok@gov.se; internet www.swedenabroad.com/bangkok; Ambassador KLAS MOLIN.

Switzerland: 35 Thanon Witthayu Nua, Lumpini, Pathumwan, Bangkok 10330; tel. (2) 253-0156; fax (2) 255-4481; e-mail ban.vertretung@eda.admin.ch; internet www.eda.admin.ch/bangkok; Ambassador CHRISTINE SCHRANER BURGENER.

Timor-Leste: Thanapoom Tower, 7th Floor, 1550 Thanon Phetchaburi, Makasan, Ratchathewi, Bangkok 10400; tel. (2) 654-7501; fax (2) 654-7504; e-mail embdrtl.bkk@gmail.com; Ambassador JOÃO FREITAS DE CÁMARA.

Turkey: 61/1 Soi Chatsan, Thanon Suthisarn, Huay Kwang, Bangkok 10310; tel. and fax (2) 355-5486; e-mail embassy.bangkok@mfa.gov.tr; internet www.bangkok.be.mfa.gov.tr; Ambassador OSMAN BÜLENT TULUN.

Ukraine: CRC Tower, 33rd Floor, All Seasons Pl., 87 Thanon Witthayu, Lumpini, Pathumwan, Bangkok 10330; tel. (2) 685-3216; fax (2) 685-3217; e-mail emb_th@mfa.gov.ua; internet www.mfa.gov.ua/thailand; Ambassador MARKIIAN CHUCHUK.

United Arab Emirates: CRC Tower, 29th Floor, All Seasons Pl., 87/2 Thanon Witthayu, Lumpini, Pathumwan, Bangkok 10330; tel. (2) 402-4000; fax (2) 402-4005; Ambassador MUHAMMAD ALI AHMAD OMRAN AL-SHAMSI.

United Kingdom: 14 Thanon Witthayu, Lumpini, Pathumwan, Bangkok 10330; tel. (2) 305-8333; fax (2) 255-8619; e-mail info.bangkok@fco.gov.uk; internet ukinthailand.fco.gov.uk; Ambassador MARK KENT.

USA: 95 Thanon Witthayu, Lumpini, Pathumwan, Bangkok 10330; tel. (2) 205-4000; fax (2) 254-1171; e-mail acsbkk@state.gov; internet bangkok.usembassy.gov; Ambassador KRISTIE KENNEY.

Viet Nam: 83/1 Thanon Witthayu, Lumpini, Pathumwan, Bangkok 10330; tel. (2) 251-5836; fax (2) 251-7203; e-mail vnemb.th@mofa.gov.vn; internet www.vietnamembassy-thailand.org; Ambassador NGO DUC THANG.

Judicial System

Supreme Court (Sarn Dika): 6 Thanon Ratchadamnoen Nai, Bangkok 10200; tel. (2) 221-3161; fax (2) 226-4389; e-mail supremc@judiciary.go.th; internet www.supremecourt.or.th; final court of appeal in all civil, bankruptcy, labour, juvenile and criminal cases; the Court's quorum consists of three judges, except in cases of exceptional importance or where there are reasons for reconsideration or overruling of its own precedents, when it sits in plenary session and the quorum is one-half of the total number of judges; Pres. (Chief Justice) PAIROTE WAYUPAP.

Court of Appeals (Sarn Uthorn): Thanon Ratchadaphisek, Chatuchak, Bangkok 10900; has appellate jurisdiction in all civil, bankruptcy, juvenile and criminal matters; hears appeals from all the Courts of First Instance, except the central Labour Court; two judges form a quorum; Chief Justice KAIT CHATANIBAND.

The Courts of First Instance (Sarn Chunton) include the categories of general courts (Civil Courts, Criminal Courts, Provincial Courts and Kwaeng Courts), juvenile and family courts, and specialized courts (Central Labour Court, Central Tax Court, Central Intellectual Property and International Trade Court, and Central Bankruptcy Court).

Religion

Buddhism is the predominant religion, professed by more than 95% of Thailand's total population. About 4% of the population are Muslims, being ethnic Malays, mainly in the south. Most of the immigrant Chinese are Confucians. Christians number about 427,000, mainly in Bangkok and northern Thailand. Brahmins and other Hindus and Sikhs number about 85,000.

BUDDHISM

Sangha Supreme Council

The Religious Affairs Dept, Thanon Ratchadamnoen Nok, Bangkok 10300; tel. (2) 281-6080; fax (2) 281-5415.

Governing body of Thailand's 350,000 monks, nuns and novices.

Supreme Patriarch of Thailand: NYANASAMVARA SUVADDHANA.

Buddhist Association of Thailand: 41 Thanon Phra Aditya, Bangkok 10200; tel. (2) 281-5693; fax (2) 281-9564; f. 1934; under royal patronage; 7,139 mems; Pres. NUTTAPASH INTUPUTI.

CHRISTIANITY

The Roman Catholic Church

For ecclesiastical purposes, Thailand comprises two archdioceses and eight dioceses. At 31 December 2006 there were an estimated 326,978 adherents in the country, representing about 0.5% of the population.

Catholic Bishops' Conference of Thailand

122/11 Soi Naksuwan, Thanon Nonsi, Yannawa, Bangkok 10120; tel. (2) 681-3900; fax (2) 681-5370; e-mail cbct_th@hotmail.com; internet www.cbct.net.

f. 1969; Pres. Rev. LOUIS CHAMNIERN SANTISUKNIRAN (Archbishop of Thare and Nonseng).

Archbishop of Bangkok: Most Rev. FRANCIS XAVIER KRIENGSAK KOVITHAVANIJ, Assumption Cathedral, 51 Thanon Oriental, Charoenkrung 40, Bangrak, Bangkok 10500; tel. (2) 237-5277; fax (2) 237-1033; e-mail webmaster@catholic.or.th; internet www.catholic.or.th.

Archbishop of Tharé and Nonseng: Bishop LOUIS CHAMNIERN SANTISUKNIRAN, POB 6, Amphur Muang, Sakon Nakhon 47000; tel. (42) 711-272; fax (42) 712-023.

The Anglican Communion

Thailand is within the jurisdiction of the Anglican Bishop of Singapore (q.v.).

Other Christian Churches

Baptist Church Foundation (Foreign Mission Board): 90 Soi 2, Thanon Sukhumvit, Bangkok 10110; tel. (2) 252-7078; Mission Admin. TOM WILLIAMS (POB 832, Bangkok 10501).

Church of Christ in Thailand: 328 Thanon Phaya Thai, Phaya Thai, Bangkok 10400; tel. (2) 214-6001; fax (2) 214-6010; e-mail secretary@cct.or.th; internet www.cct.or.th; f. 1934; 116,322 communicants; Moderator Rev. Dr BOONRATNA BOAYEN; Gen. Sec. Rev. SAYAM MAUNGSAK.

ISLAM

Office of the Chularajmontri: 100 Soi Prom Pak, Thanon Sukhumvit, Bangkok 10110; Sheikh Al-Islam (Chularajmontri) Haji ASIS PITHAKKHUMPOL.

BAHÁ'Í FAITH

Spiritual Assembly of the Baha'is of Thailand: 1415 Sriwara Soi 3/4, Ladprao Soi 94, Wangthonglang, Bangkapi, Bangkok 10310; tel. (2) 530-7417; fax (2) 935-6515; e-mail nsa@bahai.or.th; internet www.bahai.or.th; f. 1964; c. 15,000 mems.

The Press

DAILIES

Thai Language

Baan Muang: 1 Soi Pluem-Manee, Thanon Vibhavadi Rangsit, Bangkok 10900; tel. (2) 513-3101; fax (2) 513-3106; internet www.banmuang.co.th; f. 1972; Editor MANA PRAEBHAND; circ. 200,000.

Daily News: 1/4 Thanon Vibhavadi Rangsit, Laksi, Bangkok 10210; tel. (2) 790-1111; fax (2) 579-9983; e-mail editor@dailynews.co.th; internet www.dailynews.co.th; f. 1964; Editor-in-Chief PRAPA HETRAKUL SRINUALNAD; circ. 800,000.

Khao Sod (Fresh News): 12 Thanon Tethsaban Naruaman, Prachanivate 1, Chatuchak, Bangkok 10900; tel. (2) 580-0021; fax (2) 580-2301; e-mail matisale@matichon.co.th; internet www.matichon.co.th/khaosod; Editor-in-Chief KIATICHAI PONGPANICH; circ. 650,000.

Kom Chad Luek (Sharp, Clear, Deep): 44 Moo 10, Thanon Bangna Trad, Km 4.5, Bang Na, Bangkok 10260; tel. (2) 325-5555; fax (2) 317-2071; internet www.komchadluek.com; Editor ADISAL LIMPRUNGPATAKIT.

Krungthep Turakij Daily: Nation Multimedia Group Public Co Ltd, 44 Moo 10, Thanon Bangna Trad, Bang Na, Phra Khanong, Bangkok 10260; tel. (2) 317-0042; fax (2) 317-1489; e-mail kteditor@nationgroup.com; internet www.bangkokbiznews.com; f. 1987; Publr and Group Editor SUTHICHAI YOON; Editor DUANGKAMOL CHOTANA; circ. 75,882.

Manager Daily: Baan Phra Atit, 102/1 Thanon Phra Atit, Phra Nakorn, Bangkok; internet www.manager.co.th; f. 1990; Editor KHUNTHONG LORSERIVANICH.

Matichon: 12 Thanon Tethsaban Naruaman, Prachanivate 1, Chatuchak, Bangkok 10900; tel. (2) 580-0021; fax (2) 580-2301; e-mail matisale@matichon.co.th; internet www.matichon.co.th; f. 1977; Man. Editor PRASONG LERTRATANAVISUTH; circ. 550,000.

Naew Na (Frontline): 96 Moo 3, Thanon Vibhavadi Rangsit, Talaat Bang Khen, Bangkok 10210; tel. (2) 973-4250; fax (2) 552-3800; e-mail naewna@naewna.com; internet www.naewna.com; Editor WANCHAI WONGMEECHAI; circ. 200,000.

Post Today: 136 Thanon Na Ranong, Sonthorn Kosa, Klongtoey, Bangkok 10110; tel. (2) 240-3700; fax (2) 671-3147; e-mail nhakranl@ posttoday.com; internet www.posttoday.com; f. 2003; business news; Editor NA KAL LAOHAWILAI; circ. 100,000.

Siam Keela (Siam Sport): 66/26–29, Moo 12, Soi Ram Indra 40, Thanon Ram Indra, Klong Kum, Bueng Kum, Bangkok 10230; tel. (2) 508-8000; e-mail webmaster@siamsport.co.th; internet www .siamsport.co.th; f. 1973.

Siam Rath (Siam Nation): 12 Mansion 6, Thanon Ratchadamnoen, Bangkok 10200; tel. (2) 622-1810; fax (2) 224-1982; e-mail siamrath@ siamrath.co.th; internet www.siamrath.co.th; f. 1950; Editor CHACHAWAN KHONGUDOM; circ. 120,000.

Thai Post: 1852 Thanon Kasemrat, Klongtoey, Bangkok 10110; tel. (2) 240-2612; fax (2) 249-0295; internet www.thaipost.net; Editor ROJ NGAMMAEN.

Thai Rath: 1 Thanon Vibhavadi Rangsit, Bangkok 10900; tel. (2) 272-1030; fax (2) 272-1324; e-mail feedback@thairath.co.th; internet www.thairath.co.th; f. 1948; Editor SORAWUT WACHARAPHOL; circ. 800,000.

Than Setakij (Economic Base): 222 Than Setakij Bldg, Thanon Vibhavadi Rangsit, Chatuchak, Bangkok 10900; tel. (2) 513-9896; e-mail webmaster@thannews.th.com; internet www.thannews.th .com.

English Language

Bangkok Post: Bangkok Post Bldg, 136 Soi Na Ranong, Klongtoey, Bangkok 10110; tel. (2) 240-3700; fax (2) 240-3665; e-mail bpadmin@ bangkokpost.co.th; internet www.bangkokpost.com; f. 1946; morning; Editor-in-Chief PICHAI CHUENSUKSAWADI.

Business Day: Olympia Thai Tower, 22nd Floor, 444 Thanon Ratchadaphisek, Huay Kwang, Bangkok 10310; tel. (2) 512-3579; fax (2) 512-3565; e-mail info@bday.net; internet www.biz-day.com; f. 1994; business news; Man. Editor CHATCHAI YENBAMROONG.

The Nation: 44 Moo 10, Editorial Bldg, 6th Floor, Thanon Bangna Trad, Km 4.5, Bang Na, Phra Khanong, Bangkok 10260; tel. (2) 338-3333; fax (2) 338-3334; e-mail editor@nationgroup.com; internet www.nationmultimedia.com; f. 1971; morning; Publr and Group Editor SUTHICHAI YOON; Editor TULSATHIT TAPTIM; circ. 55,000.

Chinese Language

Sing Sian Yit Pao Daily News: 267 Thanon Charoenkrung, Talad-Noi, Bangkok 10100; tel. (2) 222-6601; fax (2) 225-4663; e-mail info@ singsian.com; internet www.singsian.com; f. 1950; Man. Dir NETRA RUTHAIYANONT; Editor TAWEE YODPETCH; circ. 70,000.

Tong Hua Daily News: 877–879 Thanon Charoenkrung, Talad-Noi, Bangkok 10100; tel. (2) 236-9172; fax (2) 238-5286; Editor CHART PAYONITHIKARN; circ. 85,000.

WEEKLIES

Thai Language

Bangkok Weekly: 533–539 Thanon Sri Ayudhya, Bangkok 10400; tel. (2) 245-2546; fax (2) 247-3410; Editor VICHIT ROJANAPRABHA.

Mathichon Weekly Review: 12 Thanon Tethsaban Naruaman, Prachanivate 1, Chatuchak, Bangkok 10900; tel. (2) 580-0021; fax (2) 580-2301; e-mail weekly@matichon.co.th; internet www.matichon .co.th/weekly; Editor RUANGCHAI SABNIRAND; circ. 300,000.

Sakul Thai: 58 Soi 36, Thanon Sukhumvit, Bangkok 10110; tel. (2) 258-5861; fax (2) 258-9130; internet www.sakulthai.com; Editor SANTI SONGSEMSAWAS.

Siam Rath Weekly Review: 12 Mansion 6, Thanon Rajdamnern, Bangkok 10200; Editor PRACHUAB THONGURAI.

English Language

Bangkok Post Weekly Review: U-Chuliang Bldg, 3rd Floor, 968 Thanon Phra Ram Si, Bangkok 10500; tel. (2) 233-8030; fax (2) 238-5430; f. 1989; Editor ANUSSORN THAVISIN; circ. 10,782.

FORTNIGHTLIES

Thai Language

Darathai: 9-9/1 Soi Sri Ak-Sorn, Thanon Chuapleung, Tungmahamek, Sathorn, Bangkok 10120; tel. (2) 249-1576; fax (2) 249-1575;

f. 1954; television and entertainment; Editor USA BUKKAVESA; circ. 80,000.

Dichan: 1400 Thai Bldg, Thanon Phra Ram Si, Bangkok; tel. (2) 249-0351; fax (2) 249-9455; e-mail dichan@pacific.co.th; Man. Editor KHUNYING TIPYAVADI PRAMOJ NA AYUDHYA.

Praew: 65/101–103 Thanon Chaiyaphruk, Taling Chan, Bangkok; tel. (2) 422-9999; fax (2) 434-3555; e-mail chantana@amarin.co.th; internet www.praew.com; f. 1979; women and fashion; Editorial Dir SUPAWADEE KOMARADAT; Editor CHANTANA YUTDHANAPHUM; circ. 150,000.

MONTHLIES

Bangkok 30: 98/5–6 Thanon Phra Arthit, Bangkok 10200; tel. (2) 282-5467; fax (2) 280-1302; f. 1986; Thai; business; Publr SONCHAI LIMTHONGKUL; Editor BOONSIRI NAMBOONSRI; circ. 65,000.

Chao Krung: 12 Mansion 6, Thanon Rajdamnern, Bangkok 10200; Thai; Editor NOPPHORN BUNYARIT.

The Dharmachaksu (Dharma-vision): Foundation of Mahamakut Rajavidyalai, 241 Thanon Phra Sumeru, Bangkok 10200; tel. and fax (2) 629-1391; e-mail books@mahamakuta.inet.co.th; internet www .mahamakuta.inet.co.th; f. 1894; Thai; Buddhism and related subjects; Editor SAENG CHANDR-NGAM; circ. 5,000.

Grand Prix: 4/299 Moo 5, Soi Ladplakhao 66, Thanon Ladplakhao, Bangkhen, Bangkok 10220; tel. (2) 971-6450; fax (2) 971-6469; e-mail pinyo@grandprixgroup.com; internet www.grandprixgroup.com/ gpi/maggrandprix/grandprix.asp; f. 1970; Editor PINYO SILPASART-DUMRONG; circ. 80,000.

The Investor: Pansak Bldg, 4th Floor, 138/1 Thanon Phetchaburi, Ratchathawi, Bangkok 10400; tel. (2) 282-8166; f. 1968; English language; business, industry, finance and economics; Editor TOS PATUMSEN; circ. 6,000.

Kasikorn: Dept of Agriculture, Catuchak, Bangkok 10900; tel. (2) 561-2825; fax (2) 579-4406; e-mail pannee.v@doa.in.th; internet www.doa.go.th; f. 1928; Thai; agriculture and agricultural research; Editor-in-Chief SOPIDA HE-MAKOM; Editor PANNEE WICHACHOO.

Look: 1/54 Thanon Sukhumvit 30, Pra Khanong, Bangkok 10110; tel. (2) 258-1265; Editor KANOKWAN MILINDAVANIJ.

Look East: 52/38 Soi Saladaeng 2, Silom Condominium, 12th Floor, Thanon Silom, Bangkok 10500; tel. (2) 235-6185; fax (2) 236-6764; f. 1969; English; Editor ASHA SEHGAL; circ. 30,000.

Metro Magazine: 109 Moo 8, 7th Floor, Srithepthai Bldg, Thanon Bangna Trad, Bang Na, Bangkok 10260; tel. (2) 746-7250; fax (2) 746-7266; e-mail mon@bkkmetro.com; internet www.bkkmetro.com; f. 1996; English language; lifestyle, events listings and consumer-oriented articles; Publr and Editor-in-Chief MUNINTRA SAENGSUVIMOL; circ. 35,000.

Motorcycle Magazine: 4/299 Moo 5, Soi Ladplakhao 66, Thanon Ladplakhao, Anusawari, Bangkhen, Bangkok 10220; tel. (2) 522-1731; fax (2) 522-1730; e-mail webmaster@grandprixgroup.com; internet www.grandprixgroup.com; f. 1972; publ. by Grand Prix Int. Co Ltd; Publr PRACHIN EAMLAMNOW; Editor PRAWIT PRAKEENWINCHA; circ. 55,000.

Saen Sanuk: 50 Soi Saeng Chan, Thanon Sukhumvit 42, Bangkok 10110; tel. (2) 392-0052; fax (2) 391-1486; English; travel and tourist attractions in Thailand; Editor SOMTAWIN KONGSAWATKIAT; circ. 85,000.

Sarakadee Magazine: 28–30 Soi Parinayok, Bangkok 10200; tel. (2) 281-6110; fax (2) 282-7003; e-mail admin@sarakadee.com; internet www.sarakadee.com; Thai; events, culture and nature.

Satawa Liang: 689 Thanon Wang Burapa, Bangkok; Thai; Editor THAMRONGSAK SRICHAND.

Villa Wina Magazine: Chalerm Ketr Theatre Bldg, 3rd Floor, Bangkok; Thai; Editor BHONGSAKDI PIAMLAP.

NEWS AGENCY

Thai News Agency (TNA): 63/1 Thanon Phra Rama 9, Huay Kwang, Bangkok 10320; operated by MCOT PCL; news service in Thai and English.

PRESS ASSOCIATIONS

Confederation of Thai Journalists: 299 Thanon Ratchasima, Dusit, Bangkok 10300; tel. (2) 668-9422; fax (2) 668-7505; internet www.ctj.in.th; Pres. CHATRI LIMCHAROON; Sec.-Gen. NATTAYA CHETCHOTIROS.

Press Association of Thailand: 299 Thanon Ratchasima, Dusit, Bangkok 10300; tel. (2) 537-3777; fax (2) 537-3888; e-mail webmaster@thaipressasso.com; internet www.thaipressasso.com; f. 1941; Pres. MANIT LUEPRAPHAI.

Thai Journalists' Association: 538/1 Thanon Samsen, Dusit, Bangkok 10300; tel. (2) 668-9422; fax (2) 668-7505; e-mail reporter@inet.co.th; internet www.tja.or.th; Pres. CHAVARONG LIMPATTAMAPANEE.

There are also regional press organizations and journalists' organizations.

Publishers

Advance Publishing Co Ltd: 1400 Rama IV Shopping Centre, Klongtoey, Bangkok 10110; tel. (2) 249-1824; fax (2) 249-2301; e-mail sirirat@pacific.co.th; Man. PRASERTSAK SIVASAHONG.

Amarin Printing and Publishing Public Co Ltd: 378 Thanon Chaiyaphruk, Taling Chan, Bangkok 10170; tel. (2) 422-9999; fax (2) 422-9905; e-mail info@amarin.co.th; internet www.amarin.com; f. 1976; general books and magazines; CEO RARIN UTAKAPAN PUNJARUNGROJ.

Bhannakij Trading: 34–42 Thanon Nakornsawan, Wat Sommanas, Bangkok 10100; tel. (2) 282-0282; fax (2) 629-9801; internet www.bhannakij.com; Thai fiction, school textbooks; Man. SOMSAK TECHAKASHEM.

Chalermnit Publishing Co Ltd: 108 Thanon Sukhumvit, Soi 53, Bangkok 10110; tel. (2) 662-6264; fax (2) 662-6265; e-mail chalermnit@hotmail.com; internet www.chalermnit.com; f. 1937; dictionaries, history, literature, guides to Thai language, works on Thailand and South-East Asia; Man. Dir Dr PARICHART JUMSAI.

Prae Pittaya Ltd: POB 914, 716–718 Wangburabha, Bangkok 10200; tel. (2) 221-4283; fax (2) 222-1286; general Thai books; Man. CHIT PRAEPANICH.

Praphansarn: 668–676 Thanon Charansanitwong, Bang Yee Khan, Bang Plat, Bangkok 10700; tel. (2) 435-1671; fax (2) 434-6812; e-mail editer@praphansarn.com; internet www.praphansarn.com; f. 1961; children's, comics, reference books; Man. Dir SUPHOL TAECHATADA.

Ruamsarn (1977): 864 Wangburabha, Thanon Panurangsri, Bangkok 10200; tel. (2) 221-6483; fax (2) 222-2036; f. 1951; fiction and history; Man. PITI TAWEWATANASARN.

Silkworm Books: 6 Thanon Sukkasem, T. Suthep, Muang, Chiang Mai 50200; tel. (53) 226-161; fax (53) 226-643; e-mail info@silkwormbooks.com; internet www.silkwormbooks.com; f. 1991; South-East Asian studies; English language.

Suksapan Panit (Business Organization of Teachers' Institute): 2249 Thanon Ratchasima, Bangkok 10300; tel. (2) 538-3033; e-mail suksapan99@hotmail.com; internet www.suksapan.or.th; f. 1950; general, textbooks, children's, pocket books; Pres. PANOM KAW KAMNERD.

Thai Watana Panich: 1991/129-130 Thanon Sukhumvit 77, Suan-Luang, Bangkok 10250; tel. (2) 320-3271; fax (2) 320-3729; e-mail webmaster@twp.co.th; internet www.twp.co.th; children's, school textbooks; Man. Dir INTIRA BUNNAG.

White Lotus Co Ltd: GPOB 1141, Bangkok 10501; tel. (3) 823-9883; fax (3) 823-9885; e-mail ande@loxinfo.co.th; internet whitelotusbooks.com; f. 1972; regional interests, incl. art and culture, history, sociology and natural history; Publr DIETHARD ANDE.

PUBLISHERS' ASSOCIATION

Publishers' and Booksellers' Association of Thailand (PUBAT): 83/159 Moo 6, Thanon Ngam Wong Wan, Thung Song Hong, Lak Si, Bangkok 10210; tel. (2) 954-9560; fax (2) 954-9565; e-mail info@pubat.or.th; internet www.pubat.or.th; f. 1960; organizes national book fairs and provides promotional opportunities for publishers; Pres. WORAPAN LOKITSATHAPORN.

Broadcasting and Communications

REGULATORY AUTHORITY

National Broadcasting and Telecommunications Commission: 87 Thanon Phaholyothin, Soi 8, Samsen Nai, Phaya Thai, Bangkok 10400; tel. (2) 271-0151; fax (2) 271-3516; e-mail 1200@nbtc.go.th; internet www.nbtc.go.th; f. 2010; est. as the sole regulator for both telecommunications and broadcasting sectors; replaced National Telecommunications Commission; Chair. THARES PUNSRI.

TELECOMMUNICATIONS

Advanced Info Service Public Co Ltd: 414 Thanon Phaholyothin, Shinawatra Tower I, Phaya Thai, Bangkok 10400; tel. (2) 299-5014; fax (2) 299-5165; e-mail callcenter@ais.co.th; internet www.ais.co.th; mobile telephone network operator providing 3G (third generation) cellular services; Chair. ALLEN LEW KEONG; CEO WICHIAN MEKTRAKARN.

CAT Telecom Public Co Ltd: 99 Thanon Chaengwattana, Moo 3, Laksi, Bangkok 10210-0298; tel. (2) 104-3000; fax (2) 104-3088; e-mail pr@cattelecom.com; internet www.cattelecom.com; f. 2003; est. following division of Communications Authority of Thailand (CAT); originally state-owned; corporatized in 2003; telecommunications and related services; Chair. DUSSADEE SINCHIRMSIRI; Pres. KITTISAK SRIPRASERT.

Samart Corpn Public Co Ltd: 99/1 Moo 4, Software Park Bldg, 35th Floor, Thanon Chaengwattana, Pakkred, Nonthaburi, Bangkok 11120; tel. (2) 502-6000; fax (2) 502-6186; e-mail pongthep.v@samartcorp.com; internet www.samartcorp.com; f. 1952; telecommunications installation and distribution; Chair. TONGCHAT HONGLADAROMP; Exec. Chair. and CEO CHAROENRATH VILAILUCK.

Thai Telephone and Telecommunication Public Co Ltd (TT&T): 252/30 Muang Thai Phatra Complex Tower 1, 24th Floor, Thanon Ratchadaphisek, Huay Kwang, Bangkok 10320; tel. (2) 693-2100; fax (2) 693-2124; e-mail icare@ttt.co.th; internet www.ttt.co.th; f. 1992; distributors of telecommunications equipment and services; Chair. PANTHEP JAMRADROAMRUN; Pres. DON BHASAVANICH.

TOT Public Co Ltd: 89/2 Moo 3, Thanon Chaengwattana, Thung Song Hong, Laksi, Bangkok 10210; tel. (2) 240-0701; e-mail prtot@tot.co.th; internet www.tot.co.th; f. 2002; state-owned; fmrly Telephone Organization of Thailand; name changed to TOT Corpn Public Co Ltd; name changed as above in 2005; telephone operator; de facto regulator; Chair. PANTHEP JAMRADROAMRUN; Pres. VARUT SUWAKORN.

Total Access Communications Public Co Ltd: 319 Chamchuri Sq. Bldg, 22nd–41st Floors, Thanon Phaya Thai, Pathumwan, Bangkok 10330; tel. (2) 202-8000; fax (2) 202-8929; e-mail ir@dtac.co.th; internet www.dtac.co.th; f. 1989; mobile telephone network operator; Chair. BOONCHAI BENCHARONGKUL; CEO JON ABDULLAH.

True Corpn PCL: 18 True Tower, Thanon Ratchadaphisek, Huay Kwang, Bangkok 10310; tel. (2) 643-1111; fax (2) 643-1651; internet www.truecorp.co.th/eng/index.jsp; f. 1990; est. under the name Telecomasia Corpn PCL; name changed as above in 2004; telecommunications services; Chair. DHANIN CHEARAVANONT; Pres. and CEO SUPHACHAI CHEARAVANONT.

True Move: 18 True Tower, Thanon Ratchadaphisek, Huay Kwang, Bangkok 10310; tel. (2) 647-5000; e-mail tmv_corp@truecorp.co.th; internet www.truemove.com; f. 2002; fmrly TA Orange Co Ltd; name changed as above in 2005; mobile telephone network operator; Chief Exec. SUPHACHAI CHEARAVANONT.

United Communication Industry Public Co Ltd (UCOM): 333/3 Chai Bldg, 18th Floor, Thanon Vibhavadi Rangsit, Ladyao, Chatuchak, Bangkok 10900; tel. (2) 202-8000; fax (2) 202-8929; e-mail ir.ucom@dtac.co.th; internet www.ucom.co.th; telecommunications service provider; Chair. SRIBHUMI SUKHANETR.

BROADCASTING

In 2005 the Government announced plans for nation-wide migration to digital technology for free-to-air television broadcasting. The switch from analogue to digital television was scheduled to take place by 2015.

Radio

National Broadcasting Services of Thailand (NBT): 236 Thanon Vibhavadi Rangsit, Huay Kwang, Bangkok 10320; tel. (2) 277-1966; fax (2) 277-8182; internet nbt.prd.go.th; f. 1930; govt-controlled; broadcasts educational, entertainment, cultural and news programmes on six national networks; operates more than 150 stations throughout Thailand; external services in French and English commenced in 1938; currently broadcasts in 12 languages; Dir RATTANA CHAROENSAK.

Ministry of Education Broadcasting Service: Centre for Innovation and Technology, Ministry of Education, Bangkok; tel. (2) 246-0026; f. 1954; morning programmes for schools (Mon.–Fri.); afternoon and evening programmes for general public (daily); Dir of Centre PISAN SIWAYABRAHM.

Pituksuntirad Radio Stations: stations at Bangkok, Nakhon Ratchasima, Chiang Mai, Pitsanuloke and Songkla; programmes in Thai; Dir-Gen. PAITOON WAIJANYA.

Radio Saranrom: Thanon Ratchadamnoen, POB 2-131, Bangkok 10200; tel. (2) 224-4904; fax (2) 226-1825; internet www.mfa.go.th/web/151.php; f. 1968; est. as Voice of Free Asia; name changed as above in 1998; operated by the Ministry of Foreign Affairs; broadcasts in Thai; Dir of Broadcasting PAIBOON KUSKUL.

Television

Bangkok Broadcasting & TV Co Ltd (Channel 7): 998/1 Soi Sirimitr, Phaholyothin 18/1, Chatuchak, Bangkok 10900; tel. (2) 610-0777; fax (2) 272-0010; e-mail prdept@ch7.com; internet www.ch7.com; commercial; Chair. KRIT RATANARAK.

Bangkok Entertainment Co Ltd (Channel 3): 3199 Maleenont Tower, Thanon Phra Rama IV, Klong Ton, Klongtoey, Bangkok 10110; tel. (2) 204-3333; fax (2) 204-1384; e-mail info@thaitv3.com; internet www.thaitv3.com; f. 1970; Man. Dir PRAVIT MALEENONT.

MCOT Public Co Ltd: 63/1 Thanon Phra Rama IX, Huay Kuang, Bangkok 10310; tel. (2) 201-6388; fax (2) 245-1854; e-mail ir@mcot .net; internet www.mcot.net; f. 1955; est. as Thai Television Co Ltd; named changed to The Mass Communication Org. of Thailand in 1977; present name adopted 2004; operates Modernine TV (fmrly Channel 9) and a satellite television channel; also operates radio stations and Thai News Agency; Chair. SORAJAK KASEMSUVAN; Pres. CHAKRAPHAN YOMCHINDA (acting).

National Broadcasting Services of Thailand (NBT): internet nbttv.prd.go.th; (see radio); operates TV Channel 11; parent station of eight regional TV networks.

Royal Thai Army Television HSA-TV (Channel 5): 210 Thanon Phaholyothin, Sanam Pao, Bangkok 10400; tel. (2) 279-2397; fax (2) 271-0930; e-mail webadmin@tv5.co.th; internet www.tv5.co.th; f. 1958; operates channels nation-wide; Dir-Gen. Maj.-Gen. KITTITAT PANECHAPHAN.

Thai Public Broadcasting Service: 145 Thanon Vibhavadi Rangsit, Talaat Bang Khen, Laksi, Bangkok 10210; tel. (2) 790-2000; fax (2) 790-2020; e-mail people@thaipbs.or.th; internet www.thaipbs.or .th; f. 2008; succeeded the former iTV; Man. Dir THEPCHAI YONG.

Thai TV Global Network: c/o Royal Thai Army HSA-TV, 210 Thanon Phaholyothin, Phaya Thai, Bangkok 10400; tel. (2) 278-1697; fax (2) 615-2066; e-mail tgn_mail@yahoo.com; internet www .thaitvglobal.com; established with the co-operation of all stations; distributes selected news, information and entertainment programmes from domestic stations for transmission to 170 countries world-wide via six satellite networks; Chair. Maj.-Gen. SOONTHORN SOPHONSIRI.

Finance

(cap. = capital; p.u. = paid up; res = reserves; dep. = deposits; m. = million; brs = branches; amounts in baht)

BANKING

Central Bank

Bank of Thailand: 273 Thanon Samsen, Wat Sam Phraya, Phra Nakhon, Bangkok 10200; tel. (2) 283-5353; fax (2) 280-0449; e-mail IRTeam@bot.or.th; internet www.bot.or.th; f. 1942; bank of issue; cap. 20m., res 5,562,107m., dep. 10,330,717m. (Dec. 2012); Gov. Dr PRASARN TRAIRATVORAKUL; 4 brs.

Commercial Banks

In 2012 14 commercial banks were operating in Thailand.

Bangkok Bank Public Co Ltd: 333 Thanon Silom, Bangrak, Bangkok 10500; tel. (2) 231-4333; fax (2) 231-4742; e-mail info@ bangkokbank.com; internet www.bangkokbank.com; f. 1944; cap. 19,088.4m., res 181,034m., dep. 1,678,651.5m. (Dec. 2011); 49% foreign-owned; Chair. KOSIT PANPIEMRAS; Pres. CHARTSIRI SOPHONPANICH; 656 local brs, 22 overseas brs.

Bank of Ayudhya Public Co Ltd: 1222 Thanon Rama III, Bang Phongphang, Yan Nawa, Bangkok 10120; tel. (2) 296-2000; fax (2) 683-1484; e-mail webmaster@krungsri.com; internet www.krungsri .com; f. 1945; cap. 60,741.4m., res 20,621.6m., dep. 744,139.5m. (Dec. 2011); Pres. MARK JOHN ARNOLD; Chair. VERAPHAN TEEPSUWAN; 384 local brs, 3 overseas brs.

CIMB Thai Bank Public Co Ltd: 44 Thanon Langsuan, Lumpini, Pathumwan, Bangkok 10330; tel. (2) 626-7000; fax (2) 657-3333; e-mail cimbthai.carecenter@cimbthai.com; internet www.cimbthai .com; f. 1998; fmrly BankThai Public Co Ltd, name changed as above 2009; cap. 8,158m., res 2,960.3m., dep. 139,170.5m. (Dec. 2011); Chair. CHAKRAMON PHASUKAVANICH; Pres. SUBHAK SIRAWAKSA; 98 brs.

Kasikorn Bank Public Co Ltd: 1 Soi Ratburana 27/1, Thanon Ratburana, Bangkok 10140; tel. (2) 888-8800; fax (2) 888-8882; e-mail info@kasikornbank.com; internet www.kasikornbank.com; f. 1945; fmrly Thai Farmers Bank PCL; name changed as above April 2003; cap. 23,932.6m., res 32,087.4m., dep. 1,295,570m. (Dec. 2011); 48.98% foreign-owned; Chair., Pres. and CEO BANTHOON LAMSAM; 824 local brs, 8 overseas brs.

Kiatnakin Bank Public Co Ltd: Amarin Tower, 11th Floor, 500 Thanon Ploenchit, Pathumwan, Bangkok 10330; tel. (2) 680-3333; fax (2) 256-9933; internet www.kiatnakinbank.com; f. 1971; est. as Kiatnakin Finance and Securities Co Ltd; name changed in 1999 to Kiatnakin Finance Public Co Ltd following separation of its finance and securities businesses; present name adopted 2005; cap. 5,658.2m., res 5,085.5m., dep. 100,999m. (Dec. 2010); Chair. SUPOL WATTANAVEKIN; Pres. BANYONG PONGPANICH; 16 brs.

Krung Thai Bank Public Co Ltd (State Commercial Bank of Thailand): 35 Thanon Sukhumvit, Klongtoey, Bangkok 10110; tel. (2) 255-2222; fax (2) 255-9391; e-mail call@contactcenter.ktb.co.th; internet www.ktb.co.th; f. 1966; cap. 57,604m., res 16,535.3m., dep. 1,446,892.1m. (Dec. 2011); taken under the control of the central bank in 1998, pending transfer to private sector; merged with First Bangkok City Bank PCL in 1999; Chair. Dr SATHIT LIMPONGPAN; Pres. APISAK TANTIVORAWONG; 719 local brs, 7 overseas brs.

Siam Commercial Bank Public Co Ltd: 9 Thanon Ratchadaphisek, Ladyao, Chatuchak, Bangkok 10900; tel. (2) 544-1000; fax (2) 937-7754; e-mail investor.relations@scb.co.th; internet www.scb.co .th; f. 1906; cap. 33,991.9m., res 39,045.3m., dep. 1,238,206m. (Dec. 2011); Exec. Chair. Dr VICHIT SURAPHONGCHAI; Pres. KANNIKAR CHALITAPORN; 1,112 local brs, 3 overseas brs.

Standard Chartered Bank (Thai) Public Co Ltd: 90 Thanon Sathorn Nua, Silom, Bangkok 10500; tel. (2) 724-4000; fax (2) 724-4444; internet www.standardchartered.co.th; f. 1933 as Wang Lee Bank Ltd, renamed 1985; cap. 14,837m., res 9,786.3m., dep. 181,675.3m. (Dec. 2011); taken under the control of the central bank in July 1999, 75% share sold to Standard Chartered Bank (United Kingdom); name changed to Standard Chartered Nakornthon Bank PCL in 1999; name changed as above in 2005; Chair. RAY FERGUSON; Pres. and CEO LYN KOK; 31 brs.

Thanachart Bank Public Co Ltd: 900 Tonson Tower, Thanon Ploenchit, Lumpini, Pathumwan, Bangkok 10330; tel. (2) 655-9000; fax (2) 655-9001; e-mail tcap_ir@thanachart.co.th; internet www .thanachartbank.co.th; f. 2002; 49% owned by Bank of Nova Scotia—Scotiabank (Canada); cap. 55,136.6m., res 3,703.0m., dep. 714,128.4m. (Dec. 2011); Chair. BANTERNG TANTIVIT; Man. Dir SOMJATE MOOSIRILERT; 670 brs.

TMB Bank Public Co Ltd: 3000 Thanon Phaholyothin, Chompon, Chatuchak, Bangkok 10900; tel. (2) 299-1111; fax (2) 273-7121; e-mail ir@tmbbank.com; internet www.tmbbank.com; f. 1957; fmrly Thai Military Bank Public Co Ltd; present name adopted 2005; merged with DBS Thai Danu Bank Public Co Ltd and Industrial Finance Corpn of Thailand in 2004; cap. 41,352.3m., res 5,266.5m., dep. 574,396m. (Dec. 2011); Chair. PHILIPPE DAMAS; CEO BOONTUCK WUNGCHAROEN; 431 local brs, 3 overseas brs.

United Overseas Bank (Thai) Public Co Ltd (UOBT): 191 Thanon Sathorn Tai, Bangkok 10120; tel. (2) 343-3000; fax (2) 287-2973; e-mail webmaster@uob.co.th; internet www.uob.co.th; f. 1998; est. by the merger of Laem Thong Bank Ltd with Radanasin Bank; name changed to UOB Radanasin Bank Public Co Ltd in Nov. 1999; name changed as above in 2005 following merger with Bank of Asia Public Co Ltd; cap. 24,856.6m., res 2,131m., dep. 211,205.4m. (Dec. 2011); Chair. WEE CHO YAW; Pres. and CEO WONG KIM CHOONG; 154 brs.

Development Banks

Bank for Agriculture and Agricultural Co-operatives (BAAC): 469 Thanon Nakorn Sawan, Dusit, Bangkok 10300; tel. (2) 280-0180; fax (2) 280-0442; e-mail train@baac.or.th; internet www.baac.or.th; f. 1966 to provide credit for agriculture; cap. 49,244m., res 5,795m., dep. 887,259m. (March 2012); Chair. KITTIRAT NA-RANONG; Pres. LUCK WAJANANAWAT; 491 brs.

Export-Import Bank of Thailand (EXIM Thailand): EXIM Bldg, 1193 Thanon Phaholyothin, Phaya Thai, Bangkok 10400; tel. (2) 271-3700; fax (2) 271-3204; e-mail info@exim.go.th; internet www.exim.go.th; f. 1993; govt-owned; provides financial services to support and promote Thailand's export-import trade and domestic and overseas investment; cap. 12,800m., res 3,126.9m., dep. 8,119.6m. (Dec. 2012); Chair. PRASONG POONTANEAT; Pres. KANIT SUKONTHAMAN; 9 brs.

Government Housing Bank: 63 Thanon Rama IX, Huay Kwang, Bangkok 10310; tel. (2) 645-9000; fax (2) 645-9001; e-mail crm@ghb .co.th; internet www.ghb.co.th; f. 1953 to provide housing finance; cap. 20,320.3m., res 11,129m., dep. 546,276.6m. (Dec. 2010); Chair. AREEPONG BHOOCHA-OOM; Pres. WORAVIT CHAILIMPAMONTRI; 120 brs.

Small and Medium Enterprise Development Bank of Thailand: SME Bank Tower, 310 Thanon Phaholyothin, Phaya Thai, Bangkok 10400; tel. (2) 265-3000; fax (2) 265-4000; e-mail sme@ smebank.co.th; internet www.smebank.co.th; fmrly Small Industries Finance Office, which became Small Industrial Finance Co Ltd in 1991; present name adopted 2002; cap. 11,600m., res 348.5m., dep. 71,676.3m. (Dec. 2010); Chair. PICHAI CHUNHAVAJIRA; Pres. PONGSAK CHAJIAMJAN (acting).

Savings Bank

Government Savings Bank: 470 Thanon Phaholyothin, Phaya Thai, Bangkok 10400; tel. (2) 299-8000; fax (2) 299-8490; e-mail salak@gsb.or.th; internet www.gsb.or.th; f. 1913; res 21,750.1m., dep. 1,272,085.6m. (Dec. 2010); Chair. PANNEE SATHAVARODOM; 578 brs.

Foreign Banks

In 2012 there were 15 foreign bank branches and 30 foreign representative offices in Thailand.

Bankers' Association

Thai Bankers' Association: Lake Rachada Office Complex, Bldg 2, 4th Floor, 195/5–7 Thanon Ratchadaphisek, Klongtoey, Bangkok 10110; tel. (2) 264-0883; fax (2) 264-0888; e-mail infodesk@tba.or.th; internet www.tba.or.th; f. 1958; Chair. CHARTSIRI SOPHOPANICH.

STOCK EXCHANGES

Stock Exchange of Thailand (SET): The Stock Exchange of Thailand Bldg, 62 Thanon Ratchadaphisek, Klongtoey, Bangkok 10110; tel. (2) 229-2000; fax (2) 654-5649; e-mail contact.tsd@set.or.th; internet www.set.or.th; f. 1975; 27 mems; Pres. CHARAMPORN JOTIKASTHIRA; Chair. SOMPOL KIATPHAIBOOL.

Securities and Exchange Commission: GPF Witthayu Towers, 16th Floor, 93/1 Thanon Witthayu, Lumpini, Pathumwan, Bangkok 10330; tel. (2) 695-9506; fax (2) 256-7755; e-mail info@sec.or.th; internet www.sec.or.th; f. 1992; supervises new share issues and trading in existing shares; chaired by Minister of Finance; Chair. CHAIKASEM NITISIRI; Sec.-Gen. VORAPOL SOCATIYANURAK.

INSURANCE

Selected Insurance Companies

Aioi Bangkok Insurance Co Ltd: Bangkok Insurance/YWCA Bldg, 22nd Floor, 25 Thanon Sathorn Tai, Tungmahamek, Sathorn, Bangkok 10120; tel. (2) 620-8000; fax (2) 677-3979; e-mail pr@aioibkkins.co.th; internet www.aioibkkins.co.th; f. 1951; fmrly Wilson Insurance Co Ltd; fire, marine, motor car, general; CEO YOSHIHIKO FUKASAWA; Pres. NOPADOL SANTIPAKORN.

American International Assurance Co Ltd: American International Tower, 181 Thanon Surawongse, Bangrak, Bangkok 10500; tel. (2) 634-8888; fax (2) 236-6452; e-mail th.customer@aia.com; internet www.aia.co.th; f. 1983; ordinary and group life, group and personal accident, credit, life; CEO RON VAN OIJEN.

Ayudhya Insurance Public Co Ltd: 898 Ploenchit Tower, 7th Floor, Thanon Ploenchit, Pathumwan, Bangkok 10330; tel. (2) 263-0335; fax (2) 263-0589; e-mail info@sagi.co.th; internet www.ayud.co.th; non-life; Chair. VERAPHAN TEEPSUWAN; Pres. ROWAN D'ARCY.

Bangkok Insurance Public Co Ltd: Bangkok Insurance Bldg, 25 Thanon Sathorn Tai, Bangkok 10120; tel. (2) 285-8888; fax (2) 610-2100; e-mail corp.comm1@bangkokinsurance.com; internet www.bangkokinsurance.com; f. 1947; non-life; Chair. and CEO CHAI SOPHONPANICH.

Bangkok Union Insurance Public Co Ltd: 175–177 Bangkok Union Insurance Bldg, Thanon Surawongse, Bangrak, Bangkok 10500; tel. (2) 233-6920; fax (2) 237-1856; e-mail bui@bui.co.th; internet www.bui.co.th; f. 1929; non-life; Chair. MANU LIEWPAIROT.

China Insurance Co (Siam) Ltd: 36/68–69, PS Tower, 20th Floor, Thanon Asoke, Sukhumvit 21, Bangkok 10110; tel. (2) 259-3718; fax (2) 259-1402; f. 1948; non-life; Chair. JAMES C. CHENG; Man. Dir FANG RONG-CHENG.

Indara Insurance Public Co Ltd: 364/29 Thanon Sri Ayudhya, Ratchathewi, Bangkok 10400; tel. (2) 247-9261; fax (2) 247-9260; e-mail contact@indara.co.th; internet www.indara.co.th; f. 1949; non-life; Chair. PRATIP WONGNIRUND; Man. Dir SUCHART TRISIRIWETAWATTANA.

Mittare Insurance Co Ltd: 295 Thanon Si Phraya, Bangrak, Bangkok 10500; tel. (2) 640-7777; fax (2) 640-7799; internet www.mittare.com; f. 1947; life, fire, marine, health, personal accident, automobile and general; fmrly Thai Prasit Insurance Co Ltd; Chair. SURACHAN CHANSRICHAWLA; Man. Dir SUKHATHEP CHANSRICHAWLA.

Navakij Insurance Public Co Ltd: 90/3–6, 100/50–55 Sathorn Nakorn Tower, Thanon Sathorn Nua, Silom, Bangrak, Bangkok 10500; tel. (2) 664-7777; fax (2) 636-7999; internet www.navakij.co.th; f. 1933; Chair. NIPHON TANGJEERAWONGSA.

Ocean Life Insurance Co Ltd: 170/74–83 Ocean Tower I Bldg, Thanon Ratchadaphisek, Klongtoey, Bangkok 10110; tel. (2) 261-2300; fax (2) 261-3344; e-mail info@ocean.co.th; internet www.ocean.co.th; f. 1949; life; Chair. KIRATI ASSAKUL; Man. Dir DAYANA BUNNAG.

Paiboon Insurance Co Ltd: Thai Life Insurance Bldg, 19th–20th Floors, 123 Thanon Ratchadaphisek, Bangkok 10310; tel. (2) 246-9635; fax (2) 246-9660; f. 1927; non-life; Chair. ANUTHRA ASSAWANONDA; Pres. VANICH CHAIYAWAN.

Prudential Life Assurance (Thailand) Public Co Ltd: Sengthong Thani Tower, 28th, 30th and 31st Floors, 82 Thanon Sathorn Nua, Bangkok 10500; tel. (2) 353-4999; fax (2) 353-4888; e-mail customer.service.ptsl@ibm.net; internet www.prudential.co.th; f. 1983; Chair. BURAPHA ATTHAKON; CEO BINAYAK DUTTA.

Siam Commercial New York Life Insurance Public Co Ltd: 4th Floor, SCB Bldg 1, 1060 Thanon Phetchaburi, SCB Chidlom, Ratchathewi, Bangkok 10400; tel. (2) 655-4000; fax (2) 256-1666; e-mail customerservice@scnyl.com; internet www.scnyl.com; f. 1976; life; Chair. and CEO KHUNYING JADA WATTANASIRITHAM.

Southeast Insurance (2000) Co Ltd (Arkanay Prakan Pai Co Ltd): Southeast Insurance Bldg, Unit 315G, 1–3 Thanon Silom, Bangrak, Bangkok 10500; tel. (2) 631-1331; internet www.seic2000.com; f. 1946; life and non-life; Chair. CHAYUT CHIRALERSPONG; Gen. Man. WICHAI INTARANUKULAKIJ.

Syn Mun Kong Insurance Public Co Ltd: 279 Thanon Srinakarin, Bangkapi, Bangkok 10240; tel. (2) 379-3140; fax (2) 377-5043; e-mail info@smk.co.th; internet www.smk.co.th; f. 1951; fire, marine, automobile and personal accident; Chair. RUENGWIT DUSADEESURAPOJ; Man. Dir RUENGDEJ DUSADEESURAPOJ.

Thai Health Insurance Public Co Ltd: RS Tower, 31st Floor, 121/89 Thanon Ratchadaphisek, Din-Daeng, Bangkok 10400; tel. (2) 202-9200; fax (2) 642-3130; e-mail buy@thaihealth.co.th; internet www.thaihealth.co.th; f. 1979; Chair. Dr APIRAK THAIPATANAKUL; Man. Dir VARANG CHAIYAWAN.

Thai Insurance Public Co Ltd: 34/3 Soi Lang Suan, Thanon Ploenchit, Lumpini, Pathumwan, Bangkok 10330; tel. (2) 613-0100; fax (2) 652-2870; e-mail tic@thaiins.com; internet www.thaiins.com; f. 1938; non-life; Chair. KAVI ANSVANANDA.

Thai Life Insurance Public Co Ltd: 123 Thanon Ratchadaphisek, Din-Daeng, Bangkok 10400; tel. (2) 247-0247; fax (2) 246-9946; e-mail thailife@thailife.com; internet www.thailife.com; f. 1942; life; Chair. VANICH CHAIYAWAN; CEO Dr APIRAK THAIPATANAGUL.

ThaiSri Insurance Co Ltd: 126/2 Thanon Krunthonburi, Klongsam, Bangkok 10600; tel. (2) 878-7111; fax (2) 439-4940; e-mail info@thaisri.com; internet www.thaisri.com; f. 1997; personal accident, automobile, fire, marine; jt venture between Thai Metropole Insurance and Zurich Financial Services Group (Switzerland); Chair. TAWEE BUTSUNTORN; CEO NATEE PANICHEWA.

Viriyah Insurance Co Ltd: RS Tower, 121/7 Thanon Ratchadaphisek, Din-Daeng, Bangkok 10320; tel. (2) 239-1000; fax (2) 641-3580; e-mail info@viriyah.co.th; internet www.viriyah.co.th; f. 1947; Chair. JARE CHUTHARATTANAKUL; Man. Dir SUVAPORN THONGTHEW.

Associations

The General Insurance Association: 223 Soi Ruamrudee, Thanon Witthayu, Bangkok 10330; tel. (2) 256-6032; fax (2) 256-6039; e-mail general@thaigia.com; internet www.thaigia.com; Pres. JEERAPHAN ASAWATHANAKUL; Sec.-Gen. ANON VANGVASU; 63 mems.

Thai Life Assurance Association: 36/1 Soi Sapanku, Thanon Rama IV, Tungmahamek, Sathorn, Bangkok 10120; tel. (2) 679-8080; fax (2) 679-8082; e-mail tlaa@tlaa.org; internet www.tlaa.org; f. 1956; Pres. SUTTI RAJITRANGSON; Sec.-Gen. NUSARA BANYATPIYAPHOD; 25 mems.

Trade and Industry

GOVERNMENT AGENCIES

Board of Investment (BOI): 555 Thanon Vibhavadi Rangsit, Chatuchak, Bangkok 10900; tel. (2) 553-8111; fax (2) 553-8222; e-mail head@boi.go.th; internet www.boi.go.th; f. 1958; formed to publicize investment potential and encourage economically and socially beneficial investments and also to provide investment information; chaired by the Prime Minister; Sec.-Gen. ATCHAKA SIBUNRUANG BRIMBLE.

Board of Trade of Thailand: 150/2 Thanon Rajbopit, Bangkok 10200; tel. (2) 622-1860; fax (2) 225-3372; internet www.thaichamber.org; f. 1955; mems: chambers of commerce, trade asscns, state enterprises and co-operative societies (large and medium-sized cos have associate membership); Chair. DUSIT NONTANAKORN.

Financial Sector Restructuring Authority (FSRA): 130–132 Tower 3, Thanon Witthayu, Pathumwan, Bangkok 10330; tel. (2) 263-2620; fax (2) 650-9872; f. 1997 to oversee the restructuring of Thailand's financial system; Chair. KAMOL JUNTIMA; Sec.-Gen. MONTRI CHENVIDAYAKAM.

Forest Industry Organization: 76 Thanon Ratchadamnoen Nok, Bangkok 10100; tel. (2) 282-3243; fax (2) 282-5197; e-mail fio@fio.co.th; internet www.fio.co.th; f. 1947; oversees all aspects of forestry and wood industries; Man. MANOONSAK TONTIWIWATTANA.

Office of the Cane and Sugar Board: Ministry of Industry, 6 Thanon Phra Ram Hok, Bangkok 10400; tel. (2) 202-3075; fax (2) 202-3070; e-mail ocsb0601@ocsb.go.th; internet www.ocsb.go.th; Sec.-Gen. PRASERT TAPANEEYANGKUL.

Rubber Estate Organization: 16 Moo, Nabon Station, Nakhon Si Thammarat Province 80220; tel. (75) 491-570; fax (75) 491-339;

e-mail reothai@reothai.co.th; internet www.reothai.co.th; Man. Dir CHAIROJ THAMMARATTANA (acting).

DEVELOPMENT AGENCIES

National Economic and Social Development Board: 962 Thanon Krung Kasem, Bangkok 10100; tel. (2) 280-4085; fax (2) 281-3938; e-mail pr@nesdb.go.th; internet www.nesdb.go.th; economic and social planning agency; Sec.-Gen. AKHOM TERMPITTHAYAPAISIT.

Royal Development Projects Board: Office of the Prime Minister, Government House, Thanon Nakhon Pathom, Bangkok 10300; tel. (2) 280-6193; e-mail rdpbict.g@rdpb.mail.go.th; internet www.rdpb.go.th; Sec.-Gen. SOMPOL PANMANEE.

CHAMBER OF COMMERCE

Thai Chamber of Commerce (TCC): 150 Thanon Rajbopit, Bangkok 10200; tel. (2) 622-1860; fax (2) 225-3372; e-mail tcc@thaichamber.org; internet www.thaichamber.org; f. 1946; Chair. DUSIT NONTANAKORN.

INDUSTRIAL AND TRADE ASSOCIATIONS

The Federation of Thai Industries: Queen Sirikit National Convention Center, Zone C, 4th Floor, 60 Thanon Ratchadaphisek Tadmai, Klongtoey, Bangkok 10110; tel. (2) 345-1000; fax (2) 345-1296; e-mail information@fti.or.th; internet www.fti.or.th; f. 1987; fmrly The Association of Thai Industries; 4,800 mems; Chair. PAYUNGSAK CHARTSUTHIPOL.

Mining Industry Council of Thailand: Soi 222/2, Thai Chamber of Commerce University, Thanon Vibhavadi Rangsit, Din-Daeng, Bangkok 10400; tel. (2) 275-7684; fax (2) 692-3321; e-mail miningthai@miningthai.org; internet www.miningthai.org; f. 1983; intermediary between govt organizations and private mining enterprises; Chair. YONGYOTH PETCHSUWAN; Sec.-Gen. ORANUCH RAMAKOMUT.

Rice Exporters' Association of Thailand: 37 Soi Ngamdupli, Thanon Phra Rama IV, Tungmahamek, Sathorn, Bangkok 10120; tel. (2) 287-2674; fax (2) 287-2678; e-mail contact@thairiceexporters .or.th; internet www.thairiceexporters.or.th; Pres. KORBSUK IEM-SURI; Sec.-Gen. THARNKASEM VANICHJAKVONG.

Sawmills Association: 101 Thanon Amnuaysongkhram, Dusit, Bangkok 10300; tel. (2) 243-4754; fax (2) 243-8629; e-mail info@thaisawmills.com; internet www.thaisawmills.com; Pres. SURASAK IEMDEENGAMLERT.

Thai Coffee Exporters' Association: 1302–1306 Thanon Songwad, Samphanthawong, Bangkok 10100; tel. (2) 221-1264; fax (2) 225-1962; e-mail cofexpo@cscoms.com.

Thai Contractors' Association: 2013 Italthai House, 12A Floor, Thanon Petchburi, Huay Kwang, Bangkok 10310; tel. (2) 318-8321; fax (2) 318-8325; e-mail webmaster@tca.or.th; internet www.tca.or .th; f. 1928 as The Engineering Association of Siam; name changed to The Engineering Contractors Assn in 1967 and as above in 1983; Pres. POLPAT KARNASUTA; Sec.-Gen. ANGSURAS AREEKUL.

Thai Diamond Manufacturers' Association: 87/139–40, Modern Town Bldg, 18th Floor, Soi Ekamai 3, Thanon Sukhumvit 63, Klong Ton Nua, Wattana, Bangkok 10110; tel. (2) 390-0341; fax (2) 711-4039; e-mail odtcbkk@loxinfo.co.th; internet www.thaidiamonds .org; 11-mem. board; Pres. CHIRAKITTI TANGKATHAC.

Thai Food Processors' Association: Tower 1, Ocean Bldg, 9th Floor, 170/21–22 Thanon Ratchadaphisek Tadmai, Klongtoey, Bangkok 10110; tel. (2) 261-2684; fax (2) 261-2996; e-mail thaifood@thaifood.org; internet www.thaifood.org; Pres. NAT ONSRI.

Thai Lac Association: 57/1 Soi Saphantia, Thanon Sipraya, Mahapreuktaram, Bangrak, Bangkok 10500; tel. (2) 233-4583; fax (2) 633-2913.

Thai Maize and Produce Traders' Association: Sathorn Thani II Bldg, 11th Floor, 92/26–27 Thanon Sathorn Nua, Bangrak, Bangkok 10500; tel. (2) 234-4387; fax (2) 667-0178; e-mail thaimaize@tmpta.org; internet www.thaimaizeandproduce.org; Pres. SUNAN SINGSOMBOON.

Thai Pharmaceutical Manufacturers' Association: 188/107 Thanon Charan Sanit Wong, Banchanglaw, Bangkoknoi, Bangkok 10700; tel. (2) 863-5106; fax (2) 863-5108; e-mail tpma@truemail.co .th; internet www.tpma.or.th; f. 1969; Pres. CHERNPORN TENGAM-NUAY.

Thai Rice Mills Association: 81–81/1 Trok Rongnamkheng, 24 Thanon Charoenkrung, Talad-Noi, Samphanthawong, Bangkok 10100; internet www.thairicemillers.com; tel. (2) 234-7289; fax (2) 234-7286; Pres. CHANCHAI RAKTHANANON.

Thai Rubber Association: 45–47 Thanon Chotivithayakun 3, Hat Yai, Songkhla 90110; tel. (74) 429-011; fax (74) 429-312; e-mail tra@csloxinfo.com; internet www.thainr.com; f. 1951; est. as Thai Rubber Traders' Asscn; Pres. LUKCHAI KITTIPHOL.

Thai Silk Association: Textile Industry Division, Small Industries Bldg, 5th Floor, Soi Trimitr, Thanon Rama IV, Klongtoey, Bangkok 10110; tel. (2) 712-4328; fax (2) 391-2896; e-mail thsilkas@thaitextile .org; internet www.thaitextile.org/tsa; f. 1962; Pres. BUNTOON WONGSEELASHOTE.

Thai Sugar and Bio-energy Producers' Association: SM Tower, 22nd Floor, 979/56 Thanon Phaholyothin, Phaya Thai, Bangkok 10400; tel. (2) 298-0167; fax (2) 298-0169; e-mail tsma2000@cscoms .com; internet www.thaisugar.org.

Thai Sugar Producers' Association: Thai Ruam Toon Bldg, 8th Floor, 794 Thanon Krung Kasem, Pomprap, Bangkok 10100; tel. (2) 282-0990; fax (2) 281-0342.

Thai Tapioca Trade Association: Sathorn Thani II Bldg, 20th Floor, 92/58 Thanon Sathorn Nua, Silom, Bangkok 10500; tel. (2) 234-4724; fax (2) 236-6084; e-mail ttta@loxinfo.co.th; internet www .ttta-tapioca.org; f. 1963; Pres. SEREE DENWORALAK.

Thai Textile Manufacturing Association: Panjit Tower, 4th Floor, 117/7 Thanon Sukhumvit (22), Soi 55, Klongton Nua, Klongtoey, Bangkok 10110; tel. (2) 392-0753-55; fax (2) 712-5440; e-mail ttma@thaitextile.org; internet www.thaitextile.org/ttma; f. 1960; Pres. PHONGSAK ASSAKUL.

Union Textile Merchants' Association (Thai Textile Merchants' Association): 562 Espreme Bldg, 4th Floor, Thanon Rajchawong, Samphanthawong, Bangkok 10100; tel. (2) 622-6711; fax (2) 622-6714; e-mail tma@thaitextile.org; internet www.thaitextile.org/tma; Chair. SUCHAI PORNSIRIKUL.

UTILITIES
Electricity

Electricity Generating Authority of Thailand (EGAT): 53 Moo 2, Thanon Charan Sanit Wong, Bang Kruai, Nothaburi, Bangkok 11130; tel. (2) 436-0000; fax (2) 436-4723; e-mail correspondence@egat.co.th; internet www.egat.co.th; f. 1969; Chair. PORNCHAI RUJIPRAPA.

Electricity Generating Public Co Ltd (EGCO): EGCO Tower, 222 Moo 5, Thanon Vibhavadi Rangsit, Thung Song Hong, Laksi, Bangkok 10210; tel. (2) 998-5999; fax (2) 955-0956; e-mail corp_com@egco.com; internet www.egco.com; subsidiary of EGAT; 59% transferred to the private sector in 1994–96; 14.9% owned by China Light and Power Co (Hong Kong); Chair. PORNCHAI RUJIPRAPA; Pres. SAHUST PRATUKNUKUL.

The Metropolitan Electricity Authority: 30 Soi Chidlom, Thanon Ploenchit, Lumpini, Pathumwan, Bangkok 10330; tel. (2) 254-9550; fax (2) 251-9586; e-mail webmaster@mea.or.th; internet www .mea.or.th; f. 1958; one of the two main power distribution agencies in Thailand; Gov. ARTHORN SINSAWASDI.

The Provincial Electricity Authority: 200 Thanon Ngam Wongwan, Chatuchak, Bangkok 10900; tel. (2) 589-0100; fax (2) 589-4850; e-mail webmaster@pea.co.th; internet www.pea.co.th; f. 1960; one of the two main power distribution agencies in Thailand; Gov. NARONGSAK KAMMALES.

Water

Metropolitan Waterworks Authority: 400 Thanon Prachachuen, Laksi, Bangkok 10210; tel. (2) 504-0123; fax (2) 503-9493; e-mail mwa1125@mwa.co.th; internet www.mwa.co.th; f. 1967; state-owned; provides water supply systems in Bangkok, Nanthaburi and Samut Prakan; Gov. CHAROEN PASSARA.

Provincial Waterworks Authority: 72 Thanon Chaengwattana, Don Muang, Bangkok 10210; tel. (2) 551-1020; fax (2) 552-1547; e-mail pr@pwa.co.th; internet www.pwa.co.th; f. 1979; provides water supply systems except in Bangkok Metropolis; Gov. RATANA KITCHAWAN; Chair. SURA-AT THONGNIRAMOL.

TRADE UNIONS

Confederation of Thai Labour (CTL): 25/59 Thanon Sukhumvit, Viphavill Village, Tambol Paknam, Amphur Muang, Samutprakarn, Bangkok 10270; tel. (2) 756-5346; fax (2) 755-2165; e-mail ctl_manas@hotmail.com; internet www.ctl.or.th; represents 44 labour unions; Pres. MANAS PHOSORN.

Labour Congress of Thailand (LCT): 420/393–394 Thippavan Village 1, Thanon Teparak, Samrong-Nua, Muang, Samutprakarn, Bangkok 10270; tel. and fax (2) 384-6789; e-mail lct_org@hotmail .com; f. 1978; represents 224 labour unions, four labour federations and approx. 140,000 mems; Pres. CHINCHOTE SAENGSANG; Gen. Sec. SAMAM THOMYA.

National Congress of Private Employees of Thailand (NPET): 142/6 Thanon Phrathoonam Phrakanong, Phrakanong, Klongtoey, Bangkok 10110; tel. and fax (2) 392-9955; represents 31 labour unions; Pres. BANJONG PORNPATTANANIKOM.

National Congress of Thai Labour (NCTL): 1614/876 Samutprakarn Community Housing Project, Sukhumvit Highway Km 30, Tai Baan, Muang, Samutprakarn, Bangkok 10280; tel. (2) 389-5134; fax (2) 385-8975; represents 171 unions; Pres. PANAS THAILUAN.

National Free Labour Union Congress (NFLUC): 277 Moo 3, Thanon Ratburana, Bangkok 10140; tel. (2) 427-6506; fax (2) 428-4543; represents 51 labour unions; Pres. ANUSSAKDI BOONYAPRANAI.

National Labour Congress (NLC): 586/248–250 Moo 2, Mooban City Village, Thanon Sukhumvit, Bang Phu Mai, Muang, Samutprakarn, Bangkok 10280; tel. and fax (2) 709-9426; represents 41 labour unions; Pres. CHIN THAPPHLI.

Thai Trade Union Congress (TTUC): 420/393–394 Thippavan Village 1, Thanon Teparak, Tambol Samrong-nua, Amphur Muang, Samutprakarn, Bangkok 10270; tel. and fax (2) 384-0438; e-mail thai-tuc@hotmail.com; f. 1983; represents 172 unions; Pres. PANIT CHAROENPHAO.

Thailand Council of Industrial Labour (TCIL): 99 Moo 4, Thanon Sukhaphibarn 2, Khannayao, Bungkum, Bangkok; tel. (2) 517-0022; fax (2) 517-0628; represents 23 labour unions; Pres. TAVEE DEEYING.

Transport

RAILWAYS

Thailand has a railway network of 4,429 km, connecting Bangkok with Chiang Mai, Nong Khai, Ubon Ratchathani, Nam Tok and towns on the isthmus.

State Railway of Thailand: 1 Thanon Rong Muang, Rong Muang, Pathumwan, Bangkok 10330; tel. (2) 220-4567; fax (2) 225-3801; e-mail info@railway.co.th; internet www.railway.co.th; f. 1897; 4,429 km of track in 2007; responsible for licensing a 4,044-km passenger and freight rail system, above ground; Chair. TAWANRAT ORNSIRA; Gov. PRAPAT CHONGSANGUAN.

Bangkok Mass Transit System Public Co Ltd: 1000 Thanon Phahonyothin, Chom Phon, Chatuchak, Bangkok 10900; tel. (2) 617-7300; fax (2) 617-7133; e-mail nuduan@bts.co.th; internet www.bts.co.th; f. 1992; responsible for the construction and management of the Skytrain, a two-line, 23.5-km elevated rail system, under the supervision of the Bangkok Metropolitan Area, the initial stage of which was opened in Dec. 1999; Exec. Chair. and CEO KEEREE KANJANAPAS.

Mass Rapid Transit Authority of Thailand (MRTA): 175 Thanon Rama IX, Huay Kwang, Bangkok 10320; tel. (2) 612-2444; fax (2) 612-2436; e-mail pr@mrta.co.th; internet www.mrta.co.th; a 20-km subway system was opened in Bangkok in July 2004; as part of the planned extension of the mass rapid transit system, was charged with the construction of three new lines, totalling 91 km in length: 27-km Blue Line (Hua Lamphong–Bang Khae; Bang Sue–Tha Phra); 24-km Orange Line (Bang Kapi–Bang Bumru); and 40-km Purple Line (Bang Yai–Rat Burana); Chair. SUPOTH SUBLOM; Gov. CHUKIAT PHOTA-YANUVAT.

ROADS

The total length of the road network was an estimated 180,053 km in 2010. A network of toll roads has been introduced in Bangkok in an attempt to alleviate the city's severe congestion problems.

Bangkok Mass Transit Authority (BMTA): 131 Thanon Thiam Ruammit, Huay Kwang, Bangkok 10310; tel. (2) 246-0973; fax (2) 247-2189; e-mail webmaster@bmta.co.th; internet www.bmta.co.th; controls Bangkok's urban transport system; Chair. SOMCHAI SIRIWATANACHOKE.

Department of Highways: Thanon Sri Ayudhya, Ratchathewi, Bangkok 10400; tel. (2) 354-6668; e-mail webmaster@doh.go.th; internet www.doh.go.th; Dir-Gen. CHATCHAWAN BOONJAROENKIT.

Department of Land Transport: 1032 Thanon Phaholyothin, Chatuchak, Bangkok 10900; tel. (2) 272-5671; fax (2) 272-5680; e-mail chairat@dlt.go.th; internet www.dlt.go.th; Dir-Gen. SOMCHAI SIRIWATANACHOKE.

Department of Rural Roads: 218/1, Thanon Phra Rama VI, Phaya Thai, Bangkok 10400; tel. (2) 299-4591; fax (2) 299-4606; e-mail webmaster@dor.go.th; internet www.dor.go.th; f. 2002; Dir-Gen. CHARTCHAI TIPSUNAVE.

Expressway and Rapid Transit Authority of Thailand (ETA): 2380 Thanon Phaholyothin, Senanikhom, Chatuchak, Bangkok 10900; tel. (2) 579-5380; e-mail webmasters@eta.co.th; internet www.eta.co.th; f. 1972; Dir-Gen. PHACHOEN PHAIROJSAK.

SHIPPING

There is an extensive network of canals, providing transport for bulk goods. The port of Bangkok is an important shipping junction for South-East Asia, and consists of 37 berths for conventional and container vessels. At the end of 2012 the Thai flag registered fleet (750 vessels) had a combined displacement totalling 3,096,083 grt.

Marine Department: 1278 Thanon Yotha, Talardnoi, Samphanthawong, Bangkok 10100; tel. (2) 233-1311; fax (2) 236-7148; e-mail marine@md.go.th; internet www.md.go.th; Dir-Gen. TAWANRAT ONSIRA.

Port Authority of Thailand: 444 Thanon Tarua, Klongtoey, Bangkok 10110; tel. (2) 269-3000; fax (2) 249-0885; e-mail info@port.co.th; internet www.port.co.th; 18 berths at Bangkok Port, 15 berths at Laem Chabang Port; originally scheduled for transfer to private sector in 1999, but plans have been repeatedly delayed; Chair. COMRONWIT THOOPGRAJANK; Dir-Gen. Capt. ITTHICHAI SUPHANKUL (acting).

Principal Shipping Companies

Jutha Maritime Public Co Ltd: Mano Tower, 2nd Floor, 153 Soi 39, Thanon Sukhumvit, Wattana, Bangkok 10110; tel. (2) 260-0050; fax (2) 259-9825; e-mail office@jutha.co.th; internet www.jutha.co.th; services between Thailand, Malaysia, Korea, Japan and Viet Nam; Chair. Rear-Adm. CHANO PHENJATI; Man. Dir CHANET PHENJATI.

Precious Shipping Public Co Ltd: Cathay House, 7th Floor, 8/30 Thanon Sathorn Nua, Bangrak, Bangkok 10500; tel. (2) 696-8800; fax (2) 633-8460; e-mail psl@preciousshipping.com; internet www.preciousshipping.com; Chair. THIRA WIPUCHANIN; Man. Dir KHALID MOINNUDIN HASHIM.

Regional Container Lines Public Co Ltd: Panjathani Tower, 30th Floor, 127/35 Thanon Ratchadaphisek, Chongnonsee Yannawa, Bangkok 10120; tel. (2) 296-1096; fax (2) 296-1098; e-mail rclbkk@rclgroup.com; internet www.rclgroup.com; Chair. KUA PHEK LONG; Pres. SUMATE TANTHUWANIT.

Thai International Maritime Enterprises Ltd: Sarasin Bldg, 5th Floor, 14 Thanon Surasak, Bangkok 10500; tel. (2) 236-8835; services from Bangkok to Japan; Chair. and Man. Dir SUN SUNDISAMRIT.

Thai Maritime Navigation Co Ltd: Manorom Bldg, 15th Floor, 51 Thanon Rama IV, Klongtoey, Bangkok 10110; tel. (2) 672-8690; fax (2) 249-0108; e-mail tmn@tmn.co.th; internet www.tmn.co.th; f. 1940; state-owned; services from Bangkok to Japan, the USA, Europe and ASEAN countries; Chair. NIPHON CHAKSUDUL; Sec.-Gen. SUWAPHAT SUVANNAKIJBORIHAN.

Thai Mercantile Marine Ltd: 599/1 Thanon Chua Phloeng, Klongtoey, Bangkok 10110; tel. (2) 240-2582; fax (2) 249-5656; e-mail tmmbkk@asiaaccess.net.th; f. 1967; services between Japan and Thailand; Chair. SUTHAM TANPHAIBUL; Man. Dir TANAN TANPHAIBUL.

Thoresen Thai Agencies Public Co Ltd: 26/26–27 Orakarn Bldg, 8th Floor, Soi Chidlom, Thanon Ploenchit, Kwang Lumpinee, Khet Pathumwan, Bangkok 10330; tel. (2) 254-8437; fax (2) 655-5631; e-mail tta@thoresen.com; internet www.thoresen.com; shipowner, liner operator, shipping agent (in Thailand and Viet Nam); ship repairs, offshore and diving services; Chair. PRASERT BUNSUMPUN; Man. Dir M. L. CHANDCHUTHA CHANDRATAT.

Unithai Group: 25 Alma Link Bldg, 11th Floor, Soi Chidlom, Thanon Ploenchit, Pathumwan, Bangkok 10330; tel. (2) 254-8400; fax (2) 254-8424; e-mail paporn.t@unithai.com; internet www.unithai.com; regular containerized/break-bulk services to Europe, Africa and Far East; also bulk shipping/chartering; Man. Dir ARTHIT PRATOOMSUVARN.

CIVIL AVIATION

Bangkok, Chiang Mai, Chiang Rai, Hat Yai, Phuket and Surat Thani airports are of international standard. U-Tapao is an alternative airport. Suvarnabhumi International Airport, a new facility located south-east of Bangkok, opened in September 2006, with an eventual capacity of 45m. passengers a year. Bangkok's former international airport at Don Muang was subsequently reopened to domestic commercial flights.

Airports of Thailand Public Co Ltd (AOT): 333 Thanon Cherdwutagard, Don Muang, Bangkok 10210; tel. (2) 535-1111; fax (2) 535-4061; e-mail aotpr@airportthai.co.th; internet www.airportthai.co.th; f. 1998; develops and manages airports; Chair. SUMET PHOTIMANEE; Pres. SOMCHAI SAWASDEEPON.

Department of Civil Aviation: 71 Soi Ngarmduplee, Thanon Rama IV, Tung Mahamek, Sathorn District, Bangkok 10120; tel. (2) 287-0320; fax (2) 286-3373; e-mail dca@aviation.go.th; internet www.aviation.go.th; f. 1963; Dir-Gen. VORADEJ HARNPRASERT.

Bangkok Airways: 99 Moo 14, Thanon Vibhavadi Rangsit, Chom Phon, Chatuchak, Bangkok 10900; tel. (2) 270-6699; fax (2) 265-5522; e-mail reservation@bangkokair.com; internet www.bangkokair.com; f. 1968; est. as Sahakol Air; present name adopted 1989; privately owned; scheduled and charter passenger services to 8 domestic and 8 international destinations; Pres. PUTTIPONG PRASARTTONG-OSOTH; CEO Dr PRASERT PRASARTTONG-OSOTH.

Nok Air: 183 Rajanakarn Bldg, 17th Floor, Thanon Sathorn Tai, Yannawa, Bangkok 10120; tel. (2) 627-2000; fax (2) 627-9830; e-mail public.info@thaiairways.co.th; internet www.nokair.com; f. 2004; 39%-owned by Thai Airways International Public Co Ltd; flights to six domestic destinations; CEO PATEE SARASIN.

Nok Mini Airlines: 19/18–19 Royal City Ave, Blk A, Thanon Phra Ram 9, Bangkapi, Huay Kwang, Bangkok 10310; tel. (2) 641-4190; fax (2) 641-4807; e-mail info@sga.aero; internet www.nokmini.com; f. 2002; est. as SGA Airlines; rebranded 2009; scheduled and chartered domestic services; Pres. JAIN CHARNNARONG.

One-Two-Go: 18 Thanon Ratchadapisek, Klongtoey, Bangkok 10110; tel. (2) 229-4260; fax (2) 229-4278; e-mail customer_relation@orient-thai.com; internet www.flyorientthai .com; f. 2003; subsidiary of Orient Thai Airlines; low-cost domestic flights; Chair. and Man. Dir KAJIT HABANANANDA.

Orient Thai Airlines: 18 Thanon Ratchadapisek, Klongtoey, Bangkok 10110; tel. (2) 229-4260; fax (2) 229-4278; e-mail customer_relation@orient-thai.com; internet www.flyorientthai .com; f. 1993; est. as Orient Express Air; domestic and international flights; Chair. and Man. Dir KAJIT HABANANANDA.

Phuket Air: 1168/71, Lumpini Tower Bldg, 25th Floor, Thanon Rama IV, Tungmahamek, Bangkok 10120; tel. (62) 679-8999; fax (62) 285-6480; e-mail info@phuketairlines.com; internet www .phuketairlines.com; f. 1999; international charter services; Pres. VIKROM AISIRI.

Thai AirAsia Co Ltd: Suvarnabhumi Int. Airport, 999 Moo 1, Departure Hall, 4th Floor, Rm T4-B01/01-04, Bangplee, Samutprakarn 10540; internet www.airasia.com; f. 2004; 50% owned by Asia Aviation, 49% owned by Air Asia Sdn Bhd (Malaysia); low-cost domestic flights; Group Chair. Dr PONGSATHORN SIRIYODHIN; CEO TASSAPON BIJLEVELD.

Thai Airways International Public Co Ltd (THAI): 89 Thanon Vibhavadi Rangsit, Bangkok 10900; tel. (2) 545-3321; fax (2) 545-3322; e-mail public.info@thaiairways.co.th; internet www.thaiair .com; f. 1960; 51% owned by Ministry of Finance; shares listed in July 1991, began trading in July 1992; merged with Thai Airways Co in 1988; domestic services from Bangkok to 20 cities; international services to over 50 destinations in Asia, Australasia, Europe and North America; Chair. AMPON KITTIAMPON; Pres. SORAJAK KASEMSU-VAN.

Thai Smile: 6 Thanon Larn Luang, Bangkok 10100; tel. (2) 356-1111; fax (2) 356-2222; e-mail contact@service.thaiairways.com; internet www.thaismileair.com; f. 2012; subsidiary of Thai Airways International Public Co Ltd; low-cost domestic and international flights; Man. Dir WORANATE LAPRABANG.

Tourism

Thailand is a popular tourist destination, noted for its temples, palaces, beaches and islands. Tourist arrivals totalled 22.3m. in 2012. Revenue from tourism (excluding passenger transport) was an estimated US $26,256m. in 2011.

Tourism Authority of Thailand (TAT): 1600 Thanon Phetchaburi Tat Mai, Makkasan, Ratchathewi, Bangkok 10400; tel. (2) 250-5500; fax (2) 250-5511; e-mail center@tat.or.th; internet www .tourismthailand.org; f. 1960; Gov. SURAPHON SVETASRENI.

Tourism Council of Thailand: 17th Floor, 1600 Thanon Phetchaburi Tat Mai, Makkasan, Ratchathewi, Bangkok 10400; tel. (2) 250-5500; fax (2) 250-0797; e-mail info@thailandtourismcouncil.org; internet www.thailandtourismcouncil.org; co-ordinates policy and projects between private sector and govt; membership comprises more than 60 tourism asscns; Pres. PIYAMAN TEJAPAIBUL.

Defence

As assessed at November 2012, the total strength of the armed forces was 360,850: army 245,000 (including an estimated 115,000 conscripts), navy 69,850 (25,850 conscripts), air force an estimated 46,000. Paramilitary forces numbered approximately 113,700, including a National Security Volunteer Corps of 45,000. Military service lasts for two years between the ages of 21 and 30 and is compulsory.

Defence Expenditure: Budget for 2013 was estimated at 181,000m. baht.

Chief of the Defence Forces: Gen. THANASAK PATIMAPRAKORN.

Commander-in-Chief of the Army: Gen. PRAYUTH CHAN-OCHA.

Commander-in-Chief of the Air Force: Air Chief Marshal PRAJIN JUNTONG.

Commander-in-Chief of the Navy: Adm. SURASAK RUNROENGROM.

Education

Education in Thailand is free and compulsory for nine years, following the implementation of the Compulsory Education Act of 2003, which extended the period from six years. In 2002 12 years of free basic education was granted to all students throughout the country, and in 2004 this was extended to 14 years, with the two years of pre-primary schooling henceforth also being offered free to all.

Pre-primary education begins at three years and enrolment was equivalent to 93% of the relevant age-group (males 92%, females 93%) in 2011. Primary education starts at the age of six and lasts for six years. In 2009 enrolment at primary level included 90% (males 90%, females 89%) of the relevant age-group. Secondary education, which also lasts for six years, is divided into two three-year cycles. Enrolment at secondary schools in 2011 included 74% (males 70%, females 78%) of students in the relevant age-group. There are numerous public and private universities in Thailand, including 41 Rajabhat Universities (formerly teacher-training colleges) and nine branches of the Rajamangala University of Technology. In 2006 enrolment in tertiary institutions was equivalent to 46% (males 44%, females 47%) of students in the relevant age-group. According to preliminary figures, government expenditure on education amounted to 460,100m. baht (18.6% of total government expenditure) in 2011/12.

TIMOR-LESTE
(EAST TIMOR)

Introductory Survey

LOCATION, CLIMATE, LANGUAGE, RELIGION, FLAG, CAPITAL

The Democratic Republic of Timor-Leste, which is styled Timor Loro Sa'e (Timor of the rising sun) in the principal indigenous language, Tetum, occupies the eastern half of the island of Timor, which lies off the north coast of Western Australia. The western half of the island is Indonesian territory and constitutes part of the East Nusa Tenggara Province. In addition to the eastern half of Timor island, the territory also includes an enclave around Oecusse (Oekussi) Ambeno on the north-west coast of the island, and the islands of Ataúro (Pulo Cambing) and Jaco (Pulo Jako). Timor's climate is dominated by intense monsoon rain, succeeded by a pronounced dry season. The north coast of the island has a brief rainy season from December to February; the south coast a double rainy season from December to June, with a respite in March. The mountainous spine of the island has heavy rains that feed torrential floods. Tetum and Portuguese are the official languages. More than 30 languages are in use in Timor-Leste. The predominant religion is Christianity; about 96.5% of the population were adherents of Roman Catholicism in 2009. Islam and animism are also practised. The national flag (proportions 1 by 2) displays a black triangle at the hoist (approximately one-third of the length of the flag) overlapping a yellow triangle (approximately one-half of the length of the flag) on a red background. The black triangle bears a five-pointed white star with one point aimed at the upper hoist corner. The capital is Dili.

CONTEMPORARY POLITICAL HISTORY

Historical Context

The Portuguese began trading in Timor in about 1520, principally for sandalwood, and they later established settlements and several ports on the island. They were forced to move to the north and east of the island by the Dutch, who had arrived in the early part of the 18th century and had established themselves at Kupana in the south-west. The division of the island between Portugal and the Netherlands was formalized in a treaty of 1859, although the boundaries were modified slightly in 1904. Portuguese Timor and Macao were administered as a single entity until 1896, when Portuguese Timor became a separate province. The eastern half remained a Portuguese overseas province when the Dutch recognized the western area as part of Indonesia in 1949.

The military coup in Portugal in April 1974 was followed by increased political activity in Portuguese Timor. In August 1975 the União Democrática Timorense (UDT—Timorese Democratic Union) demanded independence for Timor. The UDT allied with two other parties, the Associação Popular Democrática de Timor (Apodeti—Popular Democratic Association of Timor) and the Klibur Oan Timor Asuwain (KOTA—Association of Timorese Heroes), against the alleged threat of a communist regime being established by the Frente Revolucionária do Timor Leste Independente (Fretilin—Revolutionary Front for an Independent East Timor), and fighting broke out. The UDT forces were supported by the Indonesians. Gains on both sides were uneven, with Fretilin in control of Dili in mid-September. In the same month the Portuguese administration abandoned the capital and moved to the offshore island of Ataúro. The Indonesians intervened directly and by the beginning of December Indonesian troops controlled the capital. In November Portuguese-Indonesian peace talks in Italy were unsuccessful, and diplomatic relations were suspended after Indonesian military involvement. Two meetings of the UN Security Council voted for the immediate withdrawal of Indonesian troops. Fretilin's unilateral declaration of independence in November was recognized in December by the People's Republic of China. In December the enclave of Oecusse (Oekussi) Ambeno in West Timor was declared part of Indonesian territory. In May 1976 the People's Representative Council of East Timor voted for integration with Indonesia. However, the UN did not recognize the composition of the Indonesian-sponsored Council as being representative, and by mid-1976 the Portuguese had not formally ceded the right to govern, although they had no remaining presence in the territory.

In July 1976 East Timor was declared the 27th province of Indonesia. It is estimated that about 100,000 people, from a total population of 650,000, were killed or died of famine during the Indonesian occupation which lasted until 1999. In February 1983 the UN Commission on Human Rights adopted a resolution affirming East Timor's right to independence and self-determination.

Domestic Political Affairs

In September 1983, following a five-month cease-fire (during which government representatives negotiated with Fretilin), the armed forces launched a major new offensive. The rebels suffered a serious setback in August 1985, when the Australian Government recognized Indonesia's incorporation of East Timor. In November 1988 Gen. Suharto, the President of Indonesia, visited East Timor, prior to announcing that travel restrictions (in force since the annexation in 1976) were to be withdrawn. The territory was opened to visitors in December 1988. In October 1989 the Pope visited East Timor, as part of a tour of Indonesia, and made a plea to the Government to halt violations of human rights. In November 1990 the Government rejected proposals by the military commander of Fretilin, José Alexandre 'Xanana' Gusmão (later known as Kay Rala Xanana Gusmão), for unconditional peace negotiations aimed at ending the armed struggle in East Timor.

In November 1991 the armed forces fired on a peaceful demonstration at the funeral of a separatist sympathizer in Dili. The Indonesian Armed Forces (ABRI), which admitted killing 20 civilians, claimed that the attack had been provoked by armed Fretilin activists. Independent observers and human rights groups refuted this and estimated the number of deaths at between 100 and 180. There were also subsequent allegations of the summary execution of as many as 100 witnesses. Under intense international pressure, Suharto established a National Investigation Commission. Although the impartiality of the Commission was challenged on the grounds that it excluded non-governmental organizations, its findings received cautious foreign approbation, as they were mildly critical of ABRI and stated that 50 people had died, and 90 disappeared, in the massacre. The senior military officers in East Timor were replaced, and 14 members of the armed forces were tried by a military tribunal. The most severe penalty received by any of the soldiers involved was 18 months' imprisonment; this contrasted starkly with the sentences of convicted demonstrators, which ranged from five years' to life imprisonment.

In July 1992 Indonesia and Portugal agreed to resume discussions on East Timor under the auspices of the UN Secretary-General. In August the UN General Assembly adopted its first resolution condemning Indonesia's violations of fundamental human rights in East Timor. In September the appointment of Abílio Soares as Governor of East Timor provoked widespread criticism in the province; although Soares was a native of East Timor, he was a leading advocate of the Indonesian occupation. In October the US Congress suspended defence training aid to Indonesia, in protest at the killing of separatist demonstrators in November 1991. In October 1992, prior to the anniversary of the massacre, the human rights organization Amnesty International reported that hundreds of suspected supporters of independence had been arrested and tortured to prevent a commemorative demonstration.

Gusmão was arrested in November 1992 and, and was subsequently taken to Jakarta. In May 1993 Gusmão was found guilty of rebellion, conspiracy, attempting to establish a separate state and illegal possession of weapons, and was condemned to life imprisonment. The sentence was commuted to 20 years by Suharto in August. During the same month it was announced that all government combat forces were to be withdrawn from East Timor, leaving only troops involved in development projects. In September, however, the acting leader of Fretilin, Konis Santana, declared that, contrary to announcements, the Indonesians were actually renewing their forces in East Timor and that killings and atrocities continued.

In January 1994 Indonesia informed the UN Secretary-General's envoy that it would facilitate access to East Timor by human rights and UN organizations. In July the Indonesian authorities suppressed a demonstration in Dili, following weeks of increasing tension in the capital; at least three people were reportedly killed during the protest. Discussions between the armed forces and Gusmão in August were reported to have included consideration of the possibility of holding a referendum under the auspices of the UN to determine the future status of the disputed territory. The Indonesian Minister of Foreign Affairs, Ali Alatas, held discussions in October in New York, USA, with José Ramos Horta, the Secretary for International Relations of Fretilin, the first such talks to be officially recognized. At the beginning of November President Suharto agreed to hold talks with exiled East Timorese dissidents. However, the Government's increasingly conciliatory position on East Timor was reported largely to be a superficial attempt to improve Indonesia's human rights image prior to its hosting of the Asia-Pacific Economic Cooperation (APEC, see p. 208) summit meeting in mid-November.

In September 1995 the worst rioting that year took place in protest against Indonesian Muslim immigrants, following an Indonesian prison official's alleged insult to Roman Catholicism. Mosques and Muslim businesses were burned, and some Muslims were forced to flee the island. Further riots erupted in October, in which rival groups of separatists and integrationists clashed on the streets. The Roman Catholic Apostolic Administrator in Dili, the Rt Rev. Carlos Filipe Ximenes Belo, persuaded the rioters to return home following an agreement with ABRI; however, the agreement was subsequently broken by the armed forces, who arrested more than 250 alleged rioters.

From September 1995 East Timorese activists began forcing entry into foreign embassies in Jakarta and appealing for political asylum. They were granted asylum by the Portuguese, who were still officially recognized by the UN as the administrative power in East Timor. The Indonesian Government permitted the asylum seekers to leave, but denied that there was any persecution in East Timor. The culmination of the successful campaign was the storming by activists of the Dutch and Russian embassies in December. The demonstrators, some of whom were non-Timorese and belonged to a radical group called the People's Democratic Union, unsuccessfully demanded a meeting with the UN High Commissioner for Human Rights (see p. 45), José Ayala Lasso, who was visiting Indonesia and who, following a brief visit to East Timor, confirmed the occurrence of severe violations of human rights in the province.

In February 1996 President Suharto and the Portuguese Prime Minister met in Bangkok, Thailand (the first meeting on the subject of East Timor by heads of government). During the negotiations Portugal offered to re-establish diplomatic links in return for the release of Gusmão and the guarantee of human rights in East Timor. International awareness of East Timor was heightened in October, when Bishop Belo and José Ramos Horta were jointly awarded the Nobel Peace Prize. Ramos Horta declared that the award should have been made to Gusmão and invited the Indonesian Government to enter into serious negotiations on the future of East Timor. Four days after the announcement of the award, Suharto visited East Timor for the first time in eight years.

In November 1996 the Indonesian Government withdrew permission for foreign journalists to visit East Timor, where they had planned to attend a press conference conducted by Belo. In December Ramos Horta and Belo attended the Nobel Prize ceremony in Oslo, Norway. Riots in Dili (following a gathering of Belo's supporters to welcome him upon his return) resulted in the death of a member of ABRI; it was reported later in the month that at least one East Timorese citizen had been killed by the Indonesian authorities in a raid to capture those believed to be responsible for the soldier's death.

Following an increase in clashes between resistance forces and ABRI prior to the general election, in June 1997 a military commander of Fretilin, David Alex, was apprehended by the Indonesian armed forces. His subsequent death in custody was highly controversial; resistance groups rejected the official explanation that he had been fatally injured in a clash with security forces and claimed that he had been tortured to death. Guerrilla activity subsequently intensified, and in September at least seven Indonesian soldiers were killed in a clash with resistance forces. Further fighting took place in November and December.

In November 1997 the Australia-East Timor Association released a report cataloguing human rights abuses allegedly perpetrated by members of the Indonesian armed forces against Timorese women; abuses cited in the report included enforced prostitution, rape and compulsory sterilization programmes. In the same month shots were fired when Indonesian troops stormed the campus of the University of East Timor in Dili, following a vigil held by students to commemorate the massacre in Dili in 1991. According to reports, at least one student was killed in the incident, a number of others were injured and many were arrested. Belo accused the Indonesian security forces of having used 'excessive force', and this was confirmed by a report published by the Indonesian National Commission on Human Rights in December 1997. Also in December the Commission demanded the abolition of the country's anti-subversion legislation. In the same month two Timorese were sentenced to death under the legislation for their part in an ambush of election security officials earlier in the year, prompting threats of increased guerrilla activities by separatist forces, and a further four were sentenced to 12 years' imprisonment for taking part in armed resistance operations.

In January 1998 it was announced that a Timorese resistance congress that was due to be held in Portugal in March was to be replaced by a national convention to ensure the participation of the UDT. The convention, held in April, unanimously approved the 'Magna Carta' of East Timor, a charter intended to provide the basis for the constitution of future self-determination within the territory, and ratified plans for the establishment of the Conselho Nacional de Resistência Timorense (National Council of Timorese Resistance), a body intended to give the Timorese resistance movement a single national structure and to bring together representatives of the defunct Conselho Nacional da Resistência Maubere (National Council of Maubere Resistance), Fretilin and the UDT. Gusmão was appointed President of the new Conselho Nacional de Resistência Timorense, and Ramos Horta was named as Vice-President.

Following his accession to the Indonesian presidency in May 1998, B. J. Habibie publicly suggested that the territory might be given a new 'special' status within Indonesia and that troops might be withdrawn. While a number of prominent political prisoners were released soon after Habibie replaced Suharto as President, Gusmão's 20-year sentence was reduced by a mere four months. Following the killing of an East Timorese youth by Indonesian soldiers in June, the Government renewed efforts to demonstrate its conciliatory position and, in July, effected a much-publicized withdrawal of a limited number of troops from the territory. However, as in 1993, opposition groups subsequently claimed that fresh troops were being sent by the Indonesian Government to replace those leaving (a claim denied by Indonesian military leaders). An outbreak of severe violence in the Alas region of East Timor in November 1998 was reported to have claimed the lives of 82 people.

The 1999 vote for independence and subsequent events

On 27 January 1999 the Indonesian Government unexpectedly announced that, if the East Timorese voted to reject Indonesia's proposals for autonomy, it would consider granting independence to the province. As a result of a request from the UN Secretary-General, Kofi Annan, the Government also announced that it was to allow Gusmão to serve the remainder of his 20-year prison sentence under house arrest in Jakarta. Although the Indonesian Government was initially opposed to a referendum on the issue of independence for East Timor, it signed an agreement with Portugal on 5 May, giving its assent to a process of 'popular consultation' taking the form of a UN-supervised poll to determine the future status of East Timor. (In an Australian television interview in November 2008, Habibie revealed that his decision to allow a referendum was due to heavy influence from the Australian Prime Minister, John Howard.) The UN Mission in East Timor (UNAMET) was established by the UN Security Council in June 1999 to organize the poll in which the East Timorese could opt for a form of political autonomy or for independence. The 'popular consultation' was initially scheduled to be held on 8 August, and all East Timorese, including those living in exile, were to be allowed to participate in the ballot.

Following the announcement of the scheduled referendum, violence in the territory escalated. In advance of the poll, anti-independence militia groups based within East Timor initiated a campaign of violence and intimidation, which included summary killings, kidnappings, harassment and the forced recruitment of young East Timorese. The Indonesian military itself was discovered to be not only supporting but also recruiting, training and organizing many of the militias. Violence continued to escalate throughout the territory during April and May 1999. In one incident, in April, anti-independence militia members massacred 57 people in a churchyard in the town of Liquiça (Likisia); further massacres were reported to have occurred in other areas, including Dili. Also in April Gusmão (now under house arrest in Jakarta) responded to the increasing violence from anti-independence militias by reversing his previous position and urging guerrillas in Fretilin's military wing, the Forças Armadas Libertação Nacional de Timor Leste (Falintil), to resume their struggle. Although rival pro-independence and integrationist factions signed a peace accord in June supporting a cease-fire and disarmament in advance of the scheduled referendum, the violence continued unabated.

The escalating violence in the territory, together with logistical difficulties, led the UN to postpone the referendum to 21 August 1999 and then to 30 August. Although intimidation and violence by the militias continued, the referendum proceeded on 30 August. About 98.5% of those eligible to vote participated in the poll, which resulted in an overwhelming rejection, by 78.5% of voters, of the Indonesian Government's proposals for autonomy and in the endorsement of independence for East Timor. However, the announcement of the result of the referendum precipitated a rapid descent into anarchy. Pro-Jakarta militias embarked upon a campaign of murder and destruction in which hundreds of civilians were killed; as many as 500,000 (according to the UN) were forced to flee their homes, and many buildings were destroyed in arson attacks. While many of those who were displaced from their homes sought refuge in the hills, about one-half were estimated by the UN to have left the territory (a large number having entered West Timor), some involuntarily. In one incident during the campaign of extreme violence that followed the announcement of the result of the referendum, anti-independence militia members stormed the residence of Bishop Belo, evicting at gunpoint some 6,000 refugees who had sought shelter in the compound; the home of the bishop was burned down and dozens of East Timorese were reported to have been killed in the attack. Bishop Belo was evacuated to Australia, while Gusmão (who was released from house arrest in Jakarta by the Indonesian Government on 7 September) took refuge in the British embassy in Jakarta. Thousands of civilians besieged the UN compound in Dili, the premises of other international agencies, churches and police stations, seeking protection from the indiscriminate attacks of the militias. On 7 September martial law was declared in the territory and a curfew was imposed (although to no avail), and in mid-September, following international condemnation of the situation and intense diplomatic pressure, the Indonesian Government reversed its earlier opposition to a proposal by the Australian Government and agreed to permit the deployment of a multinational peace-keeping force. As the massacre of civilians continued, thousands of refugees were airlifted to safety in northern Australia, along with the remaining employees of the UN (many local staff members of UNAMET were among the victims of the violence); shortly after the UN withdrew its staff, anti-independence militia members set fire to the UN compound in Dili. Meanwhile, aid agencies warned that as many as 300,000 East Timorese people would starve if humanitarian assistance were not urgently provided.

The first contingent of several thousand UN peace-keeping troops, forming the International Force for East Timor (Interfet), was deployed in the territory on 20 September 1999. Led by Australia, which committed 4,500 troops, the force gradually restored order. A week later the Indonesian armed forces formally relinquished responsibility for security to the multinational force. At the end of October, after 24 years as an occupying force, the last Indonesian soldiers left East Timor. Meanwhile, in late September Indonesia and Portugal reiterated their agreement for the transfer of authority in East Timor to the UN. On 19 October the result of the referendum was ratified by the Indonesian legislature, the Majelis Permusyawaratan Rakyat (MPR—People's Consultative Assembly), thus permitting East Timor's accession to independence to proceed. Shortly thereafter, on 25 October, the UN Security Council established the UN Transitional Administration in East Timor (UNTAET) as an integrated peace-keeping operation fully responsible for the administration of East Timor during its transition to independence. UNTAET, with an initial mandate until 31 January 2001, was to exercise all judicial and executive authority in East Timor, to undertake the establishment and training of a new police force, and to assume responsibility for the co-ordination and provision of humanitarian assistance and emergency rehabilitation; the transfer of command of military operations in the territory from Interfet to the UNTAET peace-keeping force was completed on 23 February 2000. Meanwhile, the UN also began a large-scale emergency humanitarian relief effort; however, many displaced and homeless East Timorese remained without access to adequate food supplies, shelter and basic health care facilities.

Following reports that in mid-October 1999 Indonesian troops and militias had entered the isolated East Timorese enclave of Oecusse and allegedly massacred around 50 people, Interfet troops were deployed in Oecusse; most of the enclave's population of 57,000 were believed to have been removed to refugee camps in West Timor, and by early November only 10,000 of its citizens had been accounted for. Following his popularly acclaimed return to Dili in October, Gusmão met with the UNTAET Transitional Administrator, Sérgio Vieira de Mello, in November, and reportedly communicated the concerns of local East Timorese organizations that they were being marginalized by UNTAET officials. In November he visited Jakarta in order to establish relations with the Indonesian Government, and in December he visited Australia, where he met with representatives of the Australian Government to discuss the Timor Gap Treaty. The Treaty, which had been concluded between Australia and Indonesia in 1991, provided a framework for petroleum and gas exploration in the maritime zone between Australia and East Timor and for the division of any resulting royalties between Australia and Indonesia. However, Indonesia ceased to be party to the original Treaty when it relinquished control of East Timor in October 1999, and the transitional administration in East Timor subsequently expressed a desire to renegotiate the terms of the Treaty, which the UN considered to have no legal standing, as Indonesian sovereignty over East Timor had never been recognized by the international body. In February 2000 a Memorandum of Understanding (MOU) relating to the Treaty was signed by the Australian Government and East Timor's UN administrators, temporarily maintaining the arrangement for the division of royalties (although between Australia and East Timor rather than Australia and Indonesia). East Timor received its first payment of royalties from Australia under the MOU in October 2000. In the same month, however, the formal renegotiation of the Treaty began, with East Timor requesting the redrawing of the boundaries covered by the Treaty and a larger share of petroleum and gas royalties. Following independence in May 2002, both countries formally signed the Treaty. However, owing to prolonged negotiations over the division of royalties, Australia did not ratify the agreement until March 2003.

On 1 December 1999 José Ramos Horta returned to East Timor after 24 years of exile. Ramos Horta, who commanded much popular support, urged the East Timorese people to show forgiveness towards their former oppressors and appealed for reconciliation between Indonesia and East Timor. On 11 December Vieira de Mello convened the first meeting of the National Consultative Council (NCC) in Dili; the 15-member Council, comprising members of the Conselho Nacional de Resistência Timorense and other East Timorese political representatives as well as UNTAET officials, was established in late 1999 to advise UNTAET.

A number of mass graves containing the bodies of suspected victims of the violence perpetrated by the anti-independence militias both before and after the holding of the referendum in August 1999 were discovered in East Timor (including two in the Oecusse enclave) in late 1999 and early 2000. In December 1999 the International Commission of Inquiry in East Timor confirmed that the team of UN investigators had discovered evidence of 'systematic killing'.

In January 2000 a panel appointed by the Indonesian Government to investigate human rights abuses in East Timor delivered its report to the Indonesian Attorney-General. The report named 24 individuals whom it recommended should be prosecuted for their alleged involvement in violations of human rights in the territory. One of those named was the former Minister of Defence and Security and Commander-in-Chief of the Indonesian armed forces, Gen. Wiranto, who had since been appointed Co-ordinating Minister for Political, Legal and Security Affairs in the Indonesian Government; also named were a number of senior military officers, as well as leaders of the pro-Jakarta militias responsible for the extreme violence perpetrated during the period following the referendum. However, pro-independence leaders in East Timor strongly criticized the report as inadequate. In February the recently appointed President of Indonesia, Abdurrahman Wahid, visited East Timor and publicly apologized for the atrocities committed by the Indonesian armed forces during the Republic's occupation of the territory. Wahid reaffirmed the commitment of the Indonesian Government to the prosecution of any individuals implicated in the violation of human rights in East Timor. In the same month Wahid suspended Gen. Wiranto from the Indonesian Government. (Wiranto subsequently resigned in May.) The UN Secretary-General, Kofi Annan, made an official visit to East Timor in mid-February, during which he pledged that investigations into violations of human rights in the territory would be carried out.

In April 2000 UNTAET signed an agreement with the Indonesian Government regarding the extradition to East Timor of Indonesian citizens who were to be charged in connection with the violence of 1999. In July 2000 a team from the Indonesian Attorney-General's Office visited East Timor to investigate a limited number of cases of human rights violations. However, relations between East Timor and Indonesia remained tense, and the introduction in August 2000 of an amendment to Indonesia's Constitution providing for the exclusion of military personnel from retroactive prosecution prompted fears among many international observers that the possibility of the prosecution of members of the Indonesian military believed responsible for recent human rights abuses in East Timor would be placed in serious jeopardy (despite the suggestions of senior Indonesian legislators that the amendment would probably not apply to crimes such as genocide, war crimes and terrorism). In September the Indonesian Attorney-General's Office named 19 people whom it suspected of involvement in the violence of 1999. While human rights groups in both East Timor and Indonesia welcomed the publication of the list, which included the names of several former high-ranking members of the Indonesian armed forces, there was widespread disappointment that Gen. Wiranto was not among those named.

Progression towards sovereignty

In June 2000 an agreement was reached between UNTAET and East Timorese leaders on the formation of a new transitional coalition Government, in which the two sides were to share political responsibility. The Cabinet of the new transitional Government, which was formally appointed in July, initially incorporated four East Timorese cabinet ministers, including João Carrascalão, President of the UDT and a Vice-President of the Conselho Nacional de Resistência Timorense, who was allocated responsibility for infrastructure, and Mari Alkatiri, Secretary-General of Fretilin, who was appointed Minister of Economic Affairs. The new Cabinet also included four international representatives. Mariano Lopes da Cruz, an East Timorese national, was appointed Inspector-General. It was reported that Gusmão, while holding no formal position in the new Government, was to be consulted on an informal basis by the UNTAET Transitional Administrator, Sérgio Vieira de Mello (who was to retain ultimate control over the approval of any draft legislation proposed to the Cabinet), with respect to all political decisions. In October the Cabinet was expanded to nine members, with the appointment of José Ramos Horta as Minister of Foreign Affairs and Co-operation.

In July 2000 UNTAET approved the establishment of a 'National Council' to advise the new Cabinet. The East Timorese National Council, which consisted of a selection of 36 East Timorese representatives from the political, religious and private sectors, was inaugurated on 23 October, replacing the NCC. In the same month Gusmão was elected to lead the National Council.

In August 2000, meanwhile, Gusmão retired as the military commander of Falintil, in order to concentrate on his political role in the process of guiding East Timor towards full independence, relinquishing control of the guerrilla army to his deputy, José Maria Vasconcelos (alias Taur Matan Ruak). Initially, the future of Falintil appeared uncertain, and the refusal of the UN to allow the active involvement of the unit in attempts to combat incursions by Indonesian paramilitaries into East Timor led Gusmão to voice indirect criticism of the international organ-

ization in his resignation speech. In February 2001, however, a new East Timor Defence Force (Forças Defesa Timor Lorosae—Falintil-FDTL) was established, consisting of an initial 650 recruits drawn exclusively from the ranks of Falintil, which was itself to be dissolved. Taur Matan Ruak was promoted to the rank of Brigadier-General and appointed to command the new force. Meanwhile, a fund was established to finance the support and retraining of an estimated 1,000 Falintil veterans who were to be demobilized. Training of the new Defence Force was to be conducted by Portugal and Australia; its role was described as that of 'policing', with the defence of the territory remaining the responsibility of UNTAET peace-keeping troops.

In December 2000 four of the five East Timorese members of the transitional Cabinet threatened to resign, reportedly in protest at their treatment by the UN. The ministers, who allegedly claimed that they were merely 'puppet ministers' in the new coalition Government, demanded further clarification of the legal status of the Cabinet and of their authority as individual cabinet ministers, and called for the establishment of a more clearly defined relationship between UNTAET and the Cabinet. Further complaints about UNTAET's treatment of East Timorese officials were voiced at a donors' conference for East Timor held in the same month, and press reports suggested the existence of a level of public resentment of the UN's presence in East Timor. However, in January 2001 Ramos Horta warned that any attempt to scale down the UN's presence in East Timor would destabilize the territory's progression towards independence.

In late January 2001 the UN Security Council extended UNTAET's mandate (which had initially been scheduled to expire on 31 January 2001) until 31 January 2002. However, it was acknowledged that modifications of the mandate might be necessary to take into account developments in East Timor's progression towards full independence. From August 2000, meanwhile, in a move that allowed for greater formal East Timorese influence in the governing of the territory during the period preceding the territory's accession to full independence, a process commenced whereby the transitional Government began to be redefined as the East Timorese Transitional Administration (ETTA). Consisting of both UNTAET and East Timorese staff, ETTA was composed of the transitional Cabinet, the National Council and the judiciary. Final authority over ETTA rested with Vieira de Mello.

In February 2001 legislation providing for an election to an 88-seat Constituent Assembly, to be conducted on 30 August, was approved. The single chamber was to comprise 75 deputies elected on a national basis, using proportional representation, and one elected delegate from each of East Timor's 13 districts, chosen on a 'first-past-the-post' basis. The members of the Constituent Assembly were to be responsible for the preparation and adoption of a constitution, which would require the endorsement of at least 60 members.

In March 2001 Gusmão tendered his resignation as Speaker of the National Council, having become disaffected by the stagnation of the political process. At the same time he announced that he would not stand for President in the forthcoming election for the post, despite commanding an overwhelming level of public support for his candidacy. In April UNTAET announced that Ramos Horta would serve as Gusmão's replacement on the National Council, prompting his resignation as the Minister of Foreign Affairs and Co-operation (the two posts could not be held simultaneously). However, in the 9 April election for the post of Speaker, Manuel Carrascalão emerged victorious, defeating Ramos Horta, and criticized UNTAET for supporting his rival. Two weeks later Ramos Horta resigned from the National Council and resumed his position in the transitional Cabinet. In June the Conselho Nacional de Resistência Timorense announced its dissolution, reportedly in order to enable its constituent groups to evolve into fully independent political parties, and, in August, Gusmão finally yielded to immense popular pressure and international encouragement and announced his intention to stand for the presidency in 2002.

On 30 August 2001 91.3% of the eligible populace turned out to vote in the country's first free parliamentary elections. Fretilin secured 55 of the 88 seats available in the Constituent Assembly, commanding 57% of the votes cast. In second place, with seven seats, was the Partido Democrático (PD—Democratic Party). The Partido Social Democrata (PSD—Social Democrat Party) and the Associação Social-Democrata Timorense (ASDT—Timor Social Democratic Association) won six seats each. In September Vieira de Mello swore in the members of the Constituent Assembly, and five days later the second transitional Government was appointed. Mari Alkatiri of Fretilin was appointed leader of the Cabinet and retained the economy portfolio. Ramos Horta continued as Minister of Foreign Affairs and Co-operation. Of 20 available government positions, nine were allocated to Fretilin, two to the PD and the remaining nine to independents and various experts. In October the Constituent Assembly appointed a committee to oversee the drafting of the Constitution, taking into account the views of over 36,000 East Timorese summarized in reports presented by 13 constitutional commissions. In November 2001 the Assembly approved the structure of the draft Constitution.

In December 2000 UNTAET issued its first indictments for crimes committed against humanity in connection with the violence that had surrounded the referendum in 1999, charging 11 people (including an officer of the Indonesian special forces) with the murder of nine civilians in September 1999. In January 2001 an East Timor court sentenced a former pro-Jakarta militia member to 12 years' imprisonment for the murder of a village chief in September 1999, marking the first successful prosecution related to the violence of 1999. In September 2001 the UN filed 'extermination' charges against nine militiamen and two Indonesian soldiers accused of murdering 65 people two years previously. In October, in the first civil case of its kind, a US federal court awarded six East Timorese a total of US $66m. in damages after Indonesian Gen. Johny Lumintang was found to bear responsibility for human rights abuses. In December 2001 a UN tribunal took the first step in bringing those responsible for the atrocities committed in 1999 to justice. Of the 11 individuals indicted in December 2000, 10 were convicted of crimes against humanity and sentenced to prison terms of up to 33 years. However, the Jakarta authorities resisted the extradition of the indicted Indonesian Special Forces Officer to stand trial.

In February 2000 the UN expressed its concern that very few of the tens of thousands of East Timorese refugees remaining in camps across the border in West Timor were returning to East Timor; it had earlier been reported that pro-Jakarta militias had been intimidating the refugees in West Timor and preventing them from coming back home. In September the UN temporarily suspended its relief work among East Timorese refugees in West Timor, following the murder by pro-Jakarta militias of three UN aid workers in the territory earlier in the month. The murders prompted international criticism of the Indonesian Government for its failure to control the militia groups operating in West Timor. In November Ramos Horta alleged that estimates of the number of East Timorese refugees residing in West Timor (reported by some sources to be as high as 130,000) were being deliberately exaggerated by the Indonesian Government, and estimated the actual number of refugees to be no higher than 70,000.

In June 2001 refugees from East Timor participated in a process of registration through which they were permitted to decide whether or not they wished to return to the newly independent state. Of the 113,791 refugees who took part, 98% wished to remain in Indonesia. However, it was thought that intimidation by pro-Indonesia militias might have influenced the result and that the survey did not necessarily reflect the participants' long-term intentions. In the same month the six men accused of the murder of the three UN aid workers in September 2000 were found guilty of violence against people and property rather than murder and given light sentences. The UN criticized the verdicts and pressed for a review. In October 2001 the Indonesian authorities announced the imminent halting of aid to an estimated 80,000 East Timorese who remained in refugee camps in West Timor, and in November Gusmão visited West Timor in an effort to promote reconciliation and encourage the remaining refugees to return home.

In October 2001 the newly elected Constituent Assembly requested that the UN formally grant East Timor independence on 20 May 2002. The UN Security Council endorsed the Assembly's request, and agreed to maintain a peace-keeping presence in the region for between six months and two years after the granting of independence. In January 2002 UNTAET's mandate was extended until 20 May.

On 22 March 2002 the Constituent Assembly finally promulgated East Timor's first Constitution, which was to become effective upon independence on 20 May. The document provided for the adoption of Tetum and Portuguese as the country's official languages. On 14 April East Timor held its first presidential election, which resulted in an overwhelming victory for Gusmão, who secured almost 83% of the votes cast to defeat the only other candidate, Francisco Xavier do Amaral.

On 20 May 2002 East Timor celebrated its formal accession to independence, upon which it became known officially as the Democratic Republic of Timor-Leste. UNTAET was replaced by a smaller mission, the UN Mission of Support in East Timor (UNMISET), which was to remain in the country for two years to support administrative development and to assist in the maintenance of law and order, while downsizing its military presence as rapidly as possible. Gusmão was officially inaugurated as President and swore in the country's first Government. The National Parliament, as the Constituent Assembly had become, then held its inaugural session. Prime Minister Alkatiri stressed that the new Government would give priority to spending on health and education. The President of Indonesia, Megawati Sukarnoputri, attended the independence day celebrations, despite criticism from several members of the Indonesian legislature. Tension developed between Gusmão and Alkatiri after the latter was considered to have used Fretilin's parliamentary majority to secure the passage of a new Constitution that rendered Gusmão a largely symbolic head of state. The ill feeling persisted for several months, but relations between the President and the Prime Minister subsequently appeared to improve somewhat.

Continuing unrest and other concerns

In September 2002 Timor-Leste became a member of the UN. In the same month the Indonesian Government announced that the remaining refugee camps in West Timor would be closed at the end of 2002; Gusmão visited the province in November in an effort to encourage the estimated 30,000 remaining refugees to return to their homeland. In the following month the Government declared a state of alert in the country following an outbreak of rioting in Dili during which two people were killed. The protests had begun when a police officer allegedly shot at a student participating in a peaceful demonstration outside the police headquarters in the city. The violence was the worst to have occurred in the country since independence. In January 2003 further violence ensued when a group of armed men attacked villages near the town of Atsabe in the Ermera district, resulting in the deaths of five people. In the following month a bus travelling to Dili was ambushed by a group of armed men; two people subsequently died.

In March 2003 Prime Minister Alkatiri announced the appointment of Ana Pessôa, hitherto Minister of Justice, to the newly created post of Deputy Prime Minister. In the following month, owing to an increase in violence in Timor-Leste over the preceding months, the UN Security Council announced that UNMISET would no longer follow its original downsizing plan (under which the phased withdrawal of UN troops from the country would have commenced in July 2003) and would instead implement an alternative two-phase plan. Under the new strategy, UNMISET would retain primary responsibility for national security until December 2003, maintaining its peace-keeping force at its existing level, before preparing to hand over full responsibility for national defence to Falintil-FDTL on 20 May 2004. In May 2003 the UN Security Council formally extended the mandate of UNMISET until 20 May 2004. In October 2003 the Timorese authorities assumed responsibility for the administration of border crossings in the country from the UN. In May 2004 the UN Security Council voted unanimously to renew UNMISET's mandate, in a modified form and with a reduced military presence, until 20 May 2005. In March 2005 UN Secretary-General Kofi Annan recommended that UNMISET be deployed for an additional year, extending the mandate until 20 May 2006, a suggestion opposed by both the USA and Australia, which insisted that peace-keeping forces were no longer required in the country.

From mid-2002, at a specially created court in Jakarta (the Ad Hoc Indonesian Human Rights Tribunal on East Timor), the trials took place of 18 officers, government officials and militiamen believed to have participated in the violence that had surrounded the referendum for independence in 1999. In August 2002 Abílio Soares, the former Governor of East Timor, was found guilty of two charges of 'gross rights violations' and was sentenced to a three-year prison term. The sentence was widely criticized for its perceived leniency. In the same month the former chief of police in East Timor, Timbul Silaen, was acquitted of charges of failing to control his subordinates; five other Indonesian police and army officers were acquitted shortly afterwards. In November former Indonesian militia leader Eurico Guterres was sentenced to 10 years in prison, having been convicted of crimes against humanity. In the following month the former military chief of Dili, Lt-Col Soedjarwo, was sentenced to a five-year prison term for his role in the violence. In March 2003 the court sentenced Brig.-Gen. Noer Muis, a former army chief in East Timor, to five years in prison for crimes against humanity. In August Indonesian armed forces officer Maj.-Gen. Adam Damiri, the last and most senior official to be tried by the tribunal, was convicted of having failed to prevent atrocities in East Timor and sentenced to three years in prison. The court was subjected to widespread international criticism, owing to the fact that only six of those tried were convicted of the charges against them. In April 2004, following an appeal, the Indonesian Supreme Court upheld the conviction of Abílio Soares. However, in July the Jakarta High Court overruled the guilty verdicts of Lt-Col Soedjarwo, Brig.-Gen. Muis, Maj.-Gen. Damiri and Col Hulman Gultom (a former Dili police chief), and also halved the sentence of Eurico Guterres to five years. The decision meant that all of the police and military officials indicted by the Tribunal had been released, leaving only the two civilians (Soares and Guterres) serving sentences. The USA and the European Union (EU, see p. 281) denounced the acquittals as massive failings of justice. In November, moreover, Soares was cleared of the charges against him by Indonesia's Supreme Court, leaving only the conviction of Guterres standing. However, having reinstated his 10-year sentence in March 2006, the Supreme Court decided to rescind Guterres' conviction in April 2008, and he was released from prison.

Meanwhile, in early 2003 a UN-sponsored Special Panel for Serious Crimes (SPSC) that had been established in Dili began to issue indictments for crimes against humanity against several military officials in relation to the violence surrounding the referendum in 1999, including the former chief of the Indonesian armed forces, Gen. Wiranto, who awaited prosecution for the first time. Wiranto denied the charges against him. However, the Indonesian Government stated that it would refuse to permit the extradition of those charged to face trial. In April 2003 the SPSC sentenced José Cardosa Fereira, an East Timorese militia leader, to a 12-year prison term following his conviction for crimes against humanity. In June Quelo Mauno, a former leader of a pro-Indonesia militia, was convicted of the murder of an independence supporter in Oecusse in 1999 and sentenced to seven years in prison. By February 2004, some 47 people had been convicted of crimes relating to the referendum period. Meanwhile, the total number of people indicted by the court had risen to approximately 350, many of whom were resident in Indonesia; the Indonesian Government continued to refuse to extradite those indicted to stand trial. In May the SPSC finally issued an arrest warrant for Wiranto, who had been nominated in the previous month as a candidate for Indonesia's presidential election, the first round of which was scheduled for July. Fearing a breach in relations with Indonesia, President Gusmão and the Prosecutor-General, Longuinhos Monteiro, both acted to distance themselves from the warrant, insisting that a good rapport with neighbouring countries should take precedence over court proceedings to hold people accountable for crimes committed during the emergence of their nation. In December Timor-Leste and Indonesia agreed to establish the joint Commission of Truth and Friendship (CTF) to investigate the killings carried out during the period of the Timorese vote for independence, and this was formally approved by their respective Governments in March 2005. However, the CTF was rapidly dismissed by the international community; none of the crimes committed during Indonesian occupation prior to 1999 was to be investigated, and the CTF process was not intended to lead to prosecution. Furthermore, offenders who co-operated 'fully in revealing the truth' were to be guaranteed impunity, irrespective of the nature of their crimes. Despite the overwhelmingly negative response to the Commission, the 10-member panel was formally inaugurated in August 2005. Meanwhile, in February of that year the UN established the Commission of Experts, which was to review the judicial processes of the Ad Hoc Indonesian Human Rights Tribunal on East Timor, as well as the Serious Crimes Investigation Unit and the SPSC in Timor-Leste.

In February 2004, as sporadic outbreaks of violence, reportedly perpetrated by rebel militias based in rural areas, continued to occur in Timor-Leste, Cristiano da Costa, the leader of the Conselho Popular pela Defesa da República Democrática de Timor Leste (CPD-RDTL—Popular Council for the Defence of the Democratic Republic of East Timor), announced that his organization intended to challenge the legitimacy of the established Government in Timor-Leste following the planned withdrawal of UNMISET in May of that year. However, UNMISET's mandate was subsequently extended for an additional year,

although its presence was reduced to a mere 604 officers, while responsibility for law and order in the capital and for external security was transferred to the Government in advance of the formal full transfer of power. It was feared that the methods employed by the Government to suppress insurgents might result in further instability in the country. The use of the police to suppress political opposition was a particular cause for concern. In July the National Union of Resistance Staff and Veterans held a rally in Dili, demanding a cabinet reorganization and the dismissal of the unpopular Minister of Interior Affairs, Rogério Lobato. Police officers were drafted in, and resorted to beatings and the use of tear gas to disperse the crowd; some witnesses also claimed that guns were fired.

In December 2004 the first local elections since Timorese independence were held in Bobonaro and in the enclave of Oecusse. There was a high turn-out, exceeding 90% in some areas, and, despite numerous logistical problems, voters were able to cast their ballots in a calm and orderly manner, free from intimidation. By October 2005 elections had been held in the remaining 11 districts. While local councils held extremely limited authority, the election results revealed a considerable decline in popular support for Fretilin, with its share of the vote having decreased to less than 50% in some regions.

Meanwhile, on 20 May 2005 the mandate of UNMISET was officially concluded, and the last remaining UN troops were withdrawn from Timor-Leste in the following month. The UN Office in Timor-Leste (UNOTIL) was established to facilitate the transfer of complete power to the Timorese authorities; its mandate was due to be concluded on 19 May 2006, although this was subsequently extended until 25 August.

In July 2005 Prime Minister Alkatiri effected a cabinet reorganization, providing for an enlarged Government. Four state secretariats, including those responsible for defence and public works, were transformed into full ministries.

In early February 2006 an estimated 400 soldiers (approximately one-quarter of Timor-Leste's 1,600-strong army) staged a protest about living conditions in their barracks and about alleged discrimination against soldiers from western regions of the country; they claimed that army officers, who were predominantly from Timor-Leste's eastern regions, frequently passed over for promotion soldiers from western regions in favour of those from their own localities. Having deserted their duties, the protesting soldiers presented a petition to President Gusmão, who promised a government inquiry into their complaints and urged them to return to their barracks. However, the rebellion escalated in late February when more than 170 additional soldiers deserted their barracks. The military leadership issued an ultimatum, demanding that they return to duty or be dismissed; when they had failed to return by March, the Commander-in-Chief of the armed forces, Brig.-Gen. Taur Matan Ruak, sanctioned their dismissal. Ruak's action precipitated a series of large-scale protests, which escalated into violence in April, when supporters of the dismissed soldiers clashed with the police. The demonstrations, said to involve gangs, developed into looting, the destruction of property and eventually ethnic violence between eastern and western Timorese, which had claimed at least 37 lives and caused the displacement of an estimated 100,000 people by the following month. Prime Minister Alkatiri was criticized over his Government's handling of the situation, and anti-Government sentiments were increasingly voiced among protesters, who demanded Alkatiri's resignation. The turmoil led to the resignation of the Minister of Development, Abel Ximenes, at the beginning of May. At a Fretilin congress in mid-May, José Luís Guterres, the Timorese ambassador to the USA and Permanent Representative to the UN, withdrew his leadership challenge against Alkatiri after it emerged that the vote was to be determined by a show of hands rather than a secret ballot. At the end of May, in response to a request from Alkatiri, Australia deployed troops to Timor-Leste as part of the International Stabilisation Force, a multinational effort to aid the UN mission in the restoration of order and stability; Malaysia and New Zealand also contributed troops, while Portugal dispatched a contingent of police officers.

President Gusmão subsequently acted to curb the violence by assuming emergency powers and control of the country's security from the Minister of Defence and Security, Roque Rodrigues, and the Minister of Interior Affairs, Rogério Lobato, both of whom resigned. Gusmão later assigned their portfolios to Ramos Horta, who engaged in dialogue with leaders of the rebel troops. Alkatiri finally yielded to considerable pressure to resign, including from Gusmão, at the end of June 2006. Ramos Horta was appointed Prime Minister, retaining the defence portfolio, in July, in advance of the swearing in of a new Cabinet comprising several ministers of the previous administration, including the Minister of Agriculture, Forestry and Fisheries, Estanislau Aleixo da Silva, as Deputy Prime Minister, while José Luís Guterres became Minister of Foreign Affairs and Co-operation. The new Government was to remain in power until parliamentary elections, scheduled for mid-2007, were held.

In an indication that the security situation had improved significantly, in July 2006 Australia began to reduce its deployment in Timor-Leste, although some 2,000 personnel were projected to remain; in September Malaysia withdrew its remaining forces. Maj. Alfredo Reinado, the leader of the rebel troops, was apprehended at the end of July following the expiry of a weapons amnesty, but escaped from prison in August. In the same month UNOTIL was replaced by the UN Integrated Mission in Timor-Leste (UNMIT) for an initial period of six months. With an authorized strength of up to 1,608 police personnel and up to 34 military liaison and staff officers, supported by civilian staff, UNMIT aimed to maintain security and promote reconciliation and good governance. (UNMIT's mandate was subsequently extended on several occasions, until the mission completed its operation on 31 December 2012—see Recent developments: the 2012 elections.)

In October 2006 the UN Independent Special Commission of Inquiry for Timor-Leste released its report on the recent unrest: among other conclusions, it found that Rodrigues, Lobato and Ruak had unlawfully transferred weapons to civilians and that, although Alkatiri was not necessarily directly implicated in the transfer, he had failed to denounce it. The Commission consequently recommended further investigation into Alkatiri's involvement. The findings followed allegations that Alkatiri had formed a militia to consolidate his power base and to take action against opponents. Lobato's trial began in January 2007. In March he was found guilty of arming a group of civilians, led by a former Falintil guerrilla, and was sentenced to seven-and-a-half years' imprisonment. Although stability had been largely restored, outbreaks of violence continued, and some 70,000 internally displaced people were estimated to remain in refugee camps at the end of 2006.

The 2007 elections

In February 2007 Prime Minister Ramos Horta declared his candidacy for the forthcoming presidential election. In March President Gusmão indicated his desire to become Prime Minister and announced that he intended to join the Congresso Nacional da Reconstrução de Timor-Leste (CNRT—National Congress for the Reconstruction of Timor-Leste), a new political party, following the expiry of his presidential term. The first stage of the presidential election, held on 9 April, was contested by eight candidates. Francisco Guterres, the President of Fretilin, secured 27.9% of the votes cast, followed by Ramos Horta, who was favoured by Gusmão, with 21.8%, and Fernando de Araújo, President of the PD, with 19.2%. As no candidate achieved the requisite overall majority, the two leading contenders proceeded to a second round of voting, which was conducted on 9 May 2007: Ramos Horta received 69.2% of the votes cast. Unlike the first round, which had been marred by widespread violence and intimidation, the second stage of polling was conducted peacefully with no reports of any serious irregularities. Turn-out was high in both the first and second rounds, at 81.8% and 81.0%, respectively.

The electoral victory of Ramos Horta, who formally took office on 20 May 2007, was attributed to the support of the five non-Fretilin candidates who had been defeated in the first round of voting. Following Ramos Horta's assumption of the presidency, Estanislau Aleixo da Silva, hitherto the Deputy Prime Minister, assumed the role of Prime Minister in an interim capacity. Among the incoming President's priorities were plans for radical reform of the police force and judiciary. He also pledged to address the issue of the nearly 600 so-called 'petitioner soldiers' who had abandoned their barracks in February 2006 in protest against low pay and discrimination (see Continuing unrest and other concerns).

The legislative elections held on 30 June 2007 were contested by 14 political organizations and alliances. The number of seats in the National Parliament was reduced from 88 to 65. International observers declared their satisfaction with the conduct of the polls, in which 80.5% of the electorate participated. The electoral campaign had been generally peaceful, with the notable exception of the killing of two CNRT supporters in early June. Fretilin remained the largest party in the legislature following the elections, winning 21 seats, although its share of the vote declined to 29%, compared with 57% at the 2001 elections. The CNRT came a close second, with 24% of the vote and 18 seats, while an alliance of the ASDT and the PSD took 11 seats and the PD eight. Fretilin's relatively poor performance was attributed to public disillusionment with the pace of reform since independence.

As none of the parties had secured sufficient seats to govern alone, talks aimed at forming a coalition government ensued. On 6 July 2007 the CNRT, the ASDT-PSD alliance and the PD announced their intention to establish a coalition. However, Fretilin insisted on its right, as the largest parliamentary party, to participate in government, initially suggesting that it could form a minority administration and later proposing the creation of a 'government of national unity'. After weeks of deadlock, on 6 August Ramos Horta invited the CNRT-led coalition to form a government. The President's decision was denounced as unconstitutional by Fretilin and prompted violent protests by party supporters. Nevertheless, Gusmão was inaugurated as Prime Minister on 8 August; his new Cabinet included José Luís Guterres as Deputy Prime Minister. Gusmão pledged to improve security, to combat corruption and to facilitate the return to their homes of the thousands of refugees who remained in camps following their displacement during the unrest of April–May 2006. Meanwhile, Fernando de Araújo was elected Speaker of the National Parliament at its first session at the end of July.

President Ramos Horta held a meeting with the leader of the 'petitioner soldiers', Maj. Alfredo Reinado, in August 2007, under the mediation of the Swiss-based Centre for Humanitarian Dialogue. However, Reinado subsequently rejected attempts by the Timorese Government to initiate further talks aimed at achieving a negotiated settlement, insisting that the dismissed troops be reinstated into the armed forces and threatening to mount further attacks in Dili if the Government did not comply. He also demanded the withdrawal of foreign troops and judges from Timor-Leste. Four former soldiers were convicted of murder and sentenced to up to 12 years' imprisonment in late November for shooting dead eight unarmed police officers in April 2006. Reinado's trial on charges of murder, attempted murder and revolt commenced *in absentia* in early December 2007, after he refused to surrender to the authorities. None the less, the Government persisted in its efforts to maintain contact with the rebel soldiers.

The UN Secretary-General, Ban Ki-Moon, visited Timor-Leste in mid-December 2007, pledging continued UN assistance for the reform of the security forces and the judiciary.

The attempted assassinations of Ramos Horta and Gusmão

On 11 February 2008 President Ramos Horta was shot by renegade soldiers in an attack on his residence in Dili, during which Maj. Reinado and another rebel were killed by presidential guards. Seriously injured, the President was evacuated to Darwin, Australia, for medical treatment. Prime Minister Gusmão, who was reported to have been targeted shortly afterwards in a separate assault reportedly led by another leader of the rebel soldiers, Lt Gastão Salsinha, but was unharmed, announced a 48-hour state of emergency (subsequently extended) in response to what he described as an attempted coup, imposing a night-time curfew in Dili and a ban on public gatherings and protests. Australia swiftly dispatched around 200 additional troops to Timor-Leste, amid fears of renewed conflict, although no further violent incidents were reported in the days that followed. Speaker Fernando de Araújo assumed the role of acting President on 13 February after returning from overseas. On the same day arrest warrants were issued for several people suspected of involvement in the shootings, including Salsinha, who subsequently announced that he had assumed the leadership of the group of 'petitioner soldiers' and denied that they had attempted to murder Ramos Horta and Gusmão. Several days later Australian citizen Angelita Pires, reported to be Reinado's legal adviser and former partner, and alleged to have been with the rebel leader in the hours before the attacks, was arrested on suspicion of conspiracy, but was released on bail. Gusmão ordered the Timorese military and police forces temporarily to form a joint command to boost efforts to apprehend the perpetrators of the shootings. Meanwhile, the Prosecutor-General, Longuinhos Monteiro, stated that the authorities now believed that the rebels had intended to kidnap the President and Prime Minister rather than kill them. UNMIT's mandate was extended for another year in February 2008.

By the end of February 2008 most of the 'petitioner soldiers' had agreed to hold talks with the Government aimed at resolving their situation and were being held in a camp in Dili. A number of suspects surrendered to the joint command in March, although several others, including Lt Salsinha and Marcelo Caetano, whom Ramos Horta had apparently identified as the gunman who had shot him, remained at large. Having undergone a series of operations in Australia, on 17 April Ramos Horta returned to Dili, where he was welcomed by several thousand supporters, and resumed office immediately, urging Salsinha and his followers to surrender. Four former Timorese soldiers suspected of involvement in the shootings were detained in Indonesia and later extradited to Timor-Leste. In the week after Ramos Horta's return, the National Parliament agreed to his request to rescind the state of emergency, although in the district in which the rebels were believed to be in hiding it was extended for a further month, to 22 May. On 23 April Ramos Horta announced his intention to pardon former government minister Rogério Lobato (see Continuing unrest and other concerns), a decision that was widely seen as a tactic to encourage Salsinha and his followers to surrender, and which was received with alarm by international groups. In late April, following several days of negotiations with security officials, Salsinha, Caetano and 10 other rebels surrendered, relinquishing their weapons at a formal ceremony in Dili attended by Ramos Horta and Deputy Prime Minister José Luís Guterres. Meanwhile, the Australian Government announced the withdrawal of the additional troops that had been deployed to Timor-Leste in February. None the less, some 750 troops from Australia and 170 from New Zealand remained in the country to support UNMIT in its efforts to maintain security.

In May 2008, on the sixth anniversary of Timor-Leste's accession to independence, President Ramos Horta announced 80 presidential pardons. Among the recipients was Joni Marques, former leader of the Alfa militia group, who in 2001 had been given a prison sentence of more than 33 years for an attack on a convoy in 1999 in which a group of people, including nuns and priests, had been killed. International monitoring agencies expressed concern at the President's actions, and suggested that such pardons might undermine the rule of law.

In February 2009 Prime Minister Gusmão appointed the former Governor of Dili and ex-leader of the PSD, Mário Viegas Carrascalão, to the new position of second Deputy Prime Minister. Carrascalão was charged with the task of auditing government departments to identify corruption and financial mismanagement. Later in that month a draft of the World Bank's annual report, obtained by an Australian newspaper, was alleged to have warned that poor decision-making and financial management by the Government, as well as ongoing corruption and the politicization of the security forces and civil service, were undermining Timor-Leste's development and jeopardizing political stability and peace. In March Timorese investigators and Australian forensic scientists discovered the remains of 16 people in unmarked graves on the outskirts of Dili, believed to be the bodies of protesters killed during the 1991 Dili massacre.

The UN Security Council voted to extend the mandate of UNMIT for a further 12 months in February 2009. In March the head of UNMIT, Atul Khare, announced that the mission was to begin the phased transfer of responsibility to the Timor-Leste police, stating that in the preceding months significant progress had been made towards the restoration of stability. Longuinhos Monteiro, hitherto the Prosecutor-General, was appointed to command the new police force. (He was replaced as Prosecutor-General by Ana Pessôa, the former Deputy Prime Minister, who had also served as Minister of Justice.) The phased transition commenced in May, in the eastern district of Lautem.

In July 2009 the trial commenced of 27 people, mostly former members of the army or the police force, charged with involvement in the attempted assassinations of President Ramos Horta and Prime Minister Gusmão. Following protracted court proceedings, 24 of those charged were convicted in March 2010 and were sentenced to varying prison terms of up to 16 years. Contrary to the expectation of many observers, Angelita Pires was among the defendants who were acquitted. Despite the conclusion of the trial, significant doubts continued to be expressed by many observers as to the veracity of the official version of events. Particular suspicions were voiced in relation to the apparent attack on Gusmão, which some, notably including former Prime Minister Mari Alkatiri, argued had been fabricated. Furthermore, a report on the autopsy carried out on Maj. Reinado's corpse concluded that he had been shot in the back of the head at 'very close range', prompting speculation that he had

been executed rather than shot in defence as had been claimed by the authorities.

Meanwhile, local elections were successfully held in October 2009. While local councils remained restricted in their remit, it was hoped that the smooth conduct of the polls augured well for the forthcoming presidential and legislative elections, due to be held in mid-2012. The Government announced in April 2010 that municipal elections, due to take place in late 2010, were to be postponed until 2013 or 2014.

UNMIT's mandate was formally extended for a further year in February 2010, with its police contingent to be reduced from 1,488 personnel at early 2010 (already reduced from 1,608 in February 2009) to 1,280 by mid-2011. The transition of primary policing responsibilities to the Timorese police force was completed in March 2011; however, UN troops were to remain in the country until the end of 2012, in order to monitor developments, to oversee the holding of presidential and legislative elections, and to provide logistical support if necessary. UNMIT's mandate was formally extended for an additional year in February 2011.

Government corruption claims

The issue of public corruption became increasingly prominent during 2010–11. In January 2010 President Ramos Horta urged Prime Minister Gusmão to reorganize the Cabinet, amid ongoing allegations of rampant government corruption. However, he stressed that he could only recommend, rather than demand, action from Gusmão, whom he would continue to support in whatever decisions he might make as Prime Minister. In February the legislature elected Aderito Soares as Timor-Leste's first anti-corruption commissioner. Upon assuming office, Soares insisted that high-profile prosecutions alone would not be sufficient to address the problem of corruption, stating that a long-term re-education campaign would be required. Shortly thereafter, Gusmão announced that he would not be effecting any changes to his Cabinet, repudiating the claims of corruption within his Government and professing his full confidence in the conduct and integrity of his ministers, thereby prompting scepticism among some observers with regard to the Government's commitment to curbing vice. In September Mário Viegas Carrascalão resigned from the post of Deputy Prime Minister after publicly being described as 'stupid' and 'a liar' by Gusmão; the Prime Minister's comment followed a claim made by Carrascalão that Gusmão had been involved in an alleged corruption scandal at the Ministry of Foreign Affairs and Co-operation. Announcing his resignation, Carrascalão alleged that 'corruption, collusion and nepotism' remained rampant within the Timorese Government.

Later in September 2010 the Government announced that Deputy Prime Minister José Luís Guterres and Minister of Foreign Affairs and Co-operation Zacarias da Costa had both been formally indicted on corruption charges; Guterres was accused of nepotism and abuse of power in appointing his wife as counsel to the Timorese ambassador to the UN in New York, USA, in 2006 and subsequently authorizing a substantial increase in her salary, an arrangement in which da Costa was alleged to have been complicit. Da Costa was cleared of any wrongdoing by Dili District Court in November 2010. Ramos Horta announced later in that month that he had received instruction from the court to suspend Guterres from the National Parliament in order to remove the deputy premier's parliamentary immunity from prosecution so that he might stand trial; however, no immediate action was taken to this end. In March 2011 Dili District Court announced that the trial of Guterres, scheduled to commence later in the month, had been postponed until April, since his parliamentary immunity remained in place. In early April the legislature approved a resolution suspending Guterres from office for the day of his preliminary hearing; the limited nature of the resolution elicited widespread criticism, with some observers contending that anything less than a full suspension from office until and unless Guterres was exonerated of any wrongdoing was in flagrant violation of the Constitution. In May the court acquitted Guterres, ruling the charges to be baseless. Critics of the Government claimed that it had interfered in the judicial process.

In a report published in June 2010, Amnesty International urged the Timorese Government to address a legal loophole that allowed amnesties and presidential pardons to be granted to those convicted of war crimes and/or crimes against humanity, arguing that the authorities' 'routine use' of such action meant that the Government was failing to fulfil its obligations under international law and threatened to create a 'culture of impunity' among the Timorese population. Ramos Horta's decision in

October 2010 to grant pardons 'on humanitarian grounds' to the 24 people convicted in March of involvement in the attacks against himself and Gusmão in 2008 prompted concern from the UN Special Representative for Timor-Leste; the men and women had spent less than six months in prison and were reported to have shown no contrition for their part in the apparent assassination attempt. Some observers contended that the pardons indicated that Ramos Horta did not consider those convicted to pose any threat to himself or national security, which, it was argued, appeared to suggest that he might not subscribe to the official version of events that they had attempted to kill him and Gusmão. Some opponents of the Government claimed that the apparent plot had been wholly contrived so as to provide a cover for the execution of Reinado, a claim that was adamantly refuted by the authorities. A draft report released in January 2011 by the UN Development Programme was similarly critical of the Timorese Government's apparent opposition to pursuing the perpetrators of war crimes and of crimes against humanity, while also accusing the Government of failing adequately to address persistently high youth unemployment or to alleviate rural poverty. Meanwhile, in June 2010 the Court of Appeal upheld the acquittal of Angelita Pires in connection with the attempted assassinations of the President and Prime Minister in 2008, concluding that there was not enough evidence to support the Prosecutor-General's case against her.

Sporadic outbreaks of violence during 2010–11 were widely attributed to rivalries between martial arts groups, primarily comprising disaffected youth, elements of which were believed to be engaged in a variety of criminal activities. In mid-December 2011 one person was killed and three others injured in clashes between rival martial arts groups in Dili. Twenty police officers were subsequently reported to be under investigation for involvement in the clashes. Allegations that the police force had links to martial arts groups at an institutional level were robustly denied by the authorities. Amid mounting concerns about the risks posed to national security by the martial arts groups, in late December Prime Minister Gusmão issued a directive ordering the suspension of all activities by such groups for a period of one year.

Recent developments: the 2012 elections

Amendments to electoral legislation in advance of the presidential and legislative polls due to be held in mid-2012 were promulgated in June 2011, having secured approval by the National Parliament following their endorsement by the Cabinet in the latter half of 2010. In early September 2011 Taur Matan Ruak, who had been promoted to the rank of Major-General in 2009, announced his resignation as Commander-in-Chief of the armed forces and retirement from the military; he was succeeded by Maj.-Gen. Lere Anan Timur, a well-respected former member of Falintil with a reputation for a hardline military stance. In mid-October Ruak confirmed his intention to contest the presidential election in 2012.

In mid-January 2012 President Ramos Horta announced that the presidential election was to be held on 17 March. Ramos Horta, who was reported initially to have been reluctant to contest the poll, confirmed his candidacy in late January, following the signing of a petition by around 120,000 supporters urging him to seek re-election. As well as Ramos Horta and Ruak, who both stood as independents, although the latter was supported by the CNRT, 10 other presidential candidates—including, notably, Deputy Prime Minister José Luís Guterres, who was representing Frenti-Mudança (FM, a breakaway party from Fretilin), the PD's Fernando de Araújo, Fretilin's Francisco Guterres, former government minister Rogério Lobato and Angelita Pires—were approved by the National Electoral Commission. UNMIT's mandate was extended in February 2012 until the end of that year, with UN troops to be withdrawn in stages following the presidential and legislative elections.

Voting in the presidential election, which was held as scheduled on 17 March 2012, was reported to have been conducted in a calm, peaceful manner, furthering hopes that the phased withdrawal of UNMIT troops would be able to proceed as planned following the parliamentary polls. According to official results announced by the National Electoral Commission, Francisco Guterres emerged with the largest number of votes, attracting 28.8% of the ballot, while Ruak secured 25.7%; Ramos Horta was placed third, with 17.5% of the vote, just ahead of de Araújo, who took 17.3%. With no candidate securing a sufficient share of the vote to secure victory outright, a run-off election between Guterres and Ruak took place on 16 April, at which Ruak was elected President, winning 61.2% of the votes cast. A turn-out of

73.1% was recorded at the second ballot, declining from 78.2% at the first round. Ruak took office on 20 May, and the parliamentary elections were subsequently scheduled to be held on 7 July. Meanwhile, Prime Minister Gusmão assumed temporary responsibility for the justice portfolio in late April, while the Minister of Justice, Maria Lúcia Lobato, stood trial on charges of corruption, abuse of power and forgery; in June Lobato was found guilty and sentenced to five years' imprisonment.

In the legislative elections, which proceeded smoothly and peacefully on 7 July 2012, the CNRT, led by Prime Minister Gusmão, won the largest representation, but failed to secure a majority, taking 30 of the 65 seats in the National Parliament. Fretilin, which was the largest single party in the outgoing legislature but not represented in the Cabinet, won 25 seats, while the PD, a member of the incumbent ruling coalition, obtained eight and FM two. On 8 August a new coalition Government, comprising members of the CNRT, the PD and FM, was sworn into office. Gusmão retained the premiership, while Fernando de Araújo, the President of the PD, was appointed as Deputy Prime Minister and Co-ordinator of Social Affairs, and José Luís Guterres, the President of FM, became Minister of State and of Foreign Affairs and Co-operation. The CNRT's decision once again to exclude Fretilin from the Cabinet prompted minor outbreaks of violent protests in mid-July in and around Dili, during which one person was killed and several others injured, but the unrest was swiftly quelled by the security forces.

Following the successful conduct of the elections in mid-2012, UNMIT completed its withdrawal from Timor-Leste at the end of December (having formally restored full policing duties to the national security forces in October), and in March 2013 the few remaining personnel of the Australian-led International Stabilisation Force left the country (the force's mission having been completed in November 2012). The achievement by the country of a peaceful transfer of power was praised by US Secretary of State Hillary Clinton during her landmark visit to Timor-Leste in September 2012, when she met both Ruak and Gusmão.

Regional Affairs
Relations with Indonesia

Following its formal accession to independence in May 2002, Timor-Leste accorded high priority to the development of cordial relations with Indonesia. In July President Xanana Gusmão visited Indonesia on his first official trip abroad since assuming the presidency. Prime Minister Mari Alkatiri paid his first official visit to Indonesia in June 2003, holding talks with President Megawati Sukarnoputri. In June 2004 the Timorese Minister of Foreign Affairs and Co-operation, José Ramos Horta, and his Indonesian counterpart, Hassan Wirayuda, signed an agreement that resolved 90% of the border demarcation question. The remaining nine disputed land segments included territory in the Oecusse enclave; however, six of the nine segments were subsequently agreed upon in October, leaving just three areas still to be resolved. A formal border agreement between the two countries was signed by the respective heads of state during a visit by Indonesian President Susilo Bambang Yudhoyono to Dili in April 2005. During his stay Yudhoyono paid his respects at the cemetery in which victims from the 1991 Dili massacre (see Domestic Political Affairs) were buried. In October 2005, however, tensions arose between the two countries after clashes in the Oecusse enclave, allegedly involving gangs supported by Indonesian troops. Both the Timorese and the Indonesian Ministers of Foreign Affairs dismissed the violence as mere civilian land disputes arising from confusion over the delineation of the border.

Relations were further sullied by the final report, published in January 2006, of the Commission for Reception, Truth and Reconciliation (a national body created in 2002, charged with investigating alleged human rights violations during Indonesia's occupation of Timor-Leste). The report documented a catalogue of abuses allegedly carried out by Indonesian security forces in Timor-Leste between April 1974 and October 1999, claiming that as many as 180,000 Timorese civilians had died as a result of the Indonesian army's alleged deliberate policy of starvation. The cancellation of a scheduled meeting between Presidents Gusmão and Yudhoyono later in January 2006 was widely perceived to be as a result of the latter's displeasure with the findings of the report. Between February and September 2007 the CTF (Commission of Truth and Friendship—see Domestic Political Affairs), jointly formed by Indonesia and Timor-Leste in 2004 to establish the truth about the events of

1999, held five sessions of hearings, before retiring to prepare its recommendations. Prominent figures who appeared before the Commission included Gen. Wiranto, Gusmão and Brig.-Gen. Ruak. In July the UN prohibited its officials from testifying, owing to the decision to grant amnesty to perpetrators of serious crimes, while human rights organizations continued to criticize the process, claiming that insufficient numbers of victims had been summoned to give evidence. Meanwhile, in June, two weeks after taking office as President of Timor-Leste, Ramos Horta visited Indonesia. Ramos Horta and Yudhoyono reaffirmed their commitment to the CTF, extending its mandate by six months, and emphasized the importance of further improving bilateral relations. In July 2008 the CTF released its report, which found the Indonesian army responsible for the human rights crimes owing to its role in funding the pro-Indonesia militia groups that were the main perpetrators of the violence that occurred. Many international human rights organizations dismissed the report because its remit did not include the prosecution of individuals. The Presidents of Indonesia and Timor-Leste formally accepted the report's findings; however, President Yudhoyono stopped short of an official apology, instead expressing his 'deepest remorse'. In October President Ramos Horta urged the UN, which had boycotted the CTF, to end its ongoing investigation into the crimes committed during and after the 1999 independence vote, reportedly stating that maintaining strong relations with Indonesia was Timor-Leste's first priority.

During a visit to Indonesia in March 2011, Timorese Minister of Foreign Affairs and Co-operation Zacarias da Costa stated his Government's resolve to conclude the demarcation of the land border before the end of the year (an aim that was not, however, achieved). Gusmão, now Prime Minister and Minister of Defence and Security, met with the Indonesian Minister of Defence, Dr Ir Purnomo Yusgiantoro, in mid-August, whereupon the two signed an MOU pertaining to defence and security issues, which notably provided for the establishment of a bilateral joint defence committee.

Relations with Australia

Meanwhile, Timor-Leste's relations with Australia were strained by ongoing discussions relating to the Timor Sea Treaty, which entered into force in April 2003 (and was backdated to May 2002), covering the subject of joint exploration for mineral resources in the Timor Sea. In November 2003 bilateral negotiations began concerning the demarcation of the maritime boundary between the two countries, an important issue owing to its ramifications for the allocation of revenues from oil- and gasfields in the Timor Sea. Australia refused to recognize the boundary delineated by the UN Convention on the Law of the Sea. Prime Minister Mari Alkatiri accused Australia of deliberately attempting to stall the negotiations, following its refusal to agree to the holding of monthly discussions in order to bring about a more rapid resolution to the boundary issues. Months of acrimonious dispute ensued, during which numerous aid agencies, including the British-based Oxfam, accused Australia of pushing Timor-Leste to the point of ruin; Oxfam declared that if a maritime boundary were established between the two countries under international law, 'most, if not all' of the petroleum reserves would be allocated to Timor-Leste. In September 2004 the two countries appeared finally to have agreed upon a revenue-sharing arrangement, which over a period of 30 years would afford Timor-Leste \$A5,000m. in tax and royalty payments from the natural gas project in the Timor Sea. However, the negotiations again broke down, principally owing to the two countries' failure to agree on the contentious boundary issues. In February 2005 further acrimony arose when the Australian Government agreed to a mid-point boundary with New Zealand but still refused to consider a similar arrangement with Timor-Leste, provoking widespread accusations of blatant hypocrisy. In November a revenue-sharing deal was finally reached, with both countries agreeing to share equally the petroleum and gas revenues from the disputed region, which included the Greater Sunrise oil- and gasfields; as part of the arrangement, a final decision on the contentious issue of the delineation of a maritime boundary was deferred for 50 years in order to allow petroleum and gas projects to proceed. The 50-year agreement (the Treaty between Australia and the Democratic Republic of Timor-Leste on Certain Maritime Arrangements in the Timor Sea—CMATS) was formally signed in the Australian city of Sydney in January 2006 and entered into force in February 2007, following ratification by Timor-Leste's National Parliament. Since CMATS replaced one of the articles of the Timor Sea Treaty, the validity period of the latter charter was extended until 2057 (previously,

the Treaty had been due to expire after 30 years, i.e. in 2032). According to one of the provisions of CMATS, either Timor-Leste or Australia could terminate most of the agreement if no development plan for the Greater Sunrise field had been drawn up within six years of the treaty's entry into force. At the end of February 2013, with no such plan having been formulated, Timor-Leste was reported to be considering this termination option.

Despite the tensions arising from the boundary dispute, the Australian Government remained a major source of financial assistance for Timor-Leste, and announced a \$A240m. four-year aid programme in August 2007. After taking office in late 2007, Australian Prime Minister Kevin Rudd visited Dili in February 2008, whereupon he pledged additional support for Timor-Leste in the area of security in order to support long-term reform. Australia dispatched additional troops to the country following the attacks on President José Ramos Horta and Prime Minister Xanana Gusmão in February 2008 (see Domestic Political Affairs). In October the Australian Government recalled 100 troops from Timor-Leste, but reaffirmed its commitment to providing military support until political stability had been achieved. In March 2009 the Australian Minister for Defence opened an Australian-funded specialist military training centre on the outskirts of Dili. In June 2010 the Timorese embassy in the Australian capital, Canberra, moved from its temporary premises to a new, permanent building, construction of which had been funded by charitable fund-raising in Australia; the opening of the new premises was hailed by both sides as a reflection of the consolidation of sound bilateral relations. In the following month the Timorese legislature unanimously rejected a proposal, initiated by Australian Prime Minister Julia Gillard, to open a refugee-processing centre in Timor-Leste. The peaceful nature of the Timorese presidential and legislative elections, held in mid-2012 (see Domestic Political Affairs), was welcomed by the Australian Government as an indication of Timor-Leste's much-improved security situation, and facilitated the withdrawal of the remaining Australian troops from the country by the end of March 2013.

Other regional relations

Timor-Leste has continued to strengthen its relations with the rest of the Asia-Pacific region. In September 2007 President José Ramos Horta announced that he had established a task force to prepare for Timor-Leste's anticipated accession to the Association of Southeast Asian Nations (ASEAN, see p. 218), with a view to securing membership within around five years. Timor-Leste submitted its formal application to join the regional grouping in March 2011 and received strong support in its bid from a number of member states, including Indonesia, Cambodia, Malaysia and the Philippines. However, Singapore announced its intention to block the Timorese accession bid, arguing that the plan to create an ASEAN economic community by 2015 would be jeopardized by the inclusion of Timor-Leste, and that the new state lacked the necessary institutions and experienced officials to attend the hundreds of ASEAN meetings held annually. Following the submission of a revised membership application by Timor-Leste in November 2011, it was announced that ASEAN had established a working group to evaluate the country's bid. Meanwhile, Timor-Leste was granted observer status by the Melanesian Spearhead Group (comprising Fiji, Papua New Guinea, Solomon Islands and Vanuatu) in March of that year.

During a visit to Timor-Leste by the Myanma Minister of Foreign Affairs in August 2010, President Ramos Horta stated that Timor-Leste was keen to expand relations with Myanmar and had urged the Myanma military junta to open a dialogue with detained opposition leader Aung San Suu Kyi. The President welcomed Suu Kyi's release from house arrest shortly after the holding of legislative elections in Myanmar in November, as well as the reformist agenda subsequently adopted by the administration of President Thein Sein following his inauguration at the end of March 2011, and urged the USA and the EU fully to remove their sanctions against the country.

In October 2008 an agreement was signed to allow the Republic of Korea (South Korea) to import gas from Timor-Leste's Greater Sunrise fields by 2013, the first such energy accord to be concluded by Timor-Leste. In November 2010 it was announced that the two countries had signed an agreement providing for the supply to Timor-Leste of two navy patrol boats, together with an undisclosed quantity of munitions, from South Korea; the agreement was interpreted by some analysts as a reflection of Timor-

Leste's resolve to distance itself from Australia's sphere of military influence.

In March 2009 Prime Minister Gusmão paid a four-day visit to Japan, during which he met with his Japanese counterpart, Taro Aso, and other government officials. President Ramos Horta visited Japan in March 2010, meeting with the new Japanese Prime Minister, Yukio Hatoyama; issues discussed included financial aid, nuclear non-proliferation and climate change. During a meeting in the Japanese capital, Tokyo, in March 2012, Prime Minister Gusmão and his new Japanese counterpart, Yoshihiko Noda, presided over the signing of a bilateral agreement on the provision by Japan of a loan intended to facilitate the upgrading of a 118-km stretch of highway between Dili and Baucau—a key trade and tourism corridor—which it was hoped would help to boost Timor-Leste's economic development. Noda also expressed his support for Timor-Leste's application for membership of ASEAN.

CONSTITUTION AND GOVERNMENT

In March 2002 the Constituent Assembly promulgated East Timor's first Constitution and, on 14 April, the territory held its first presidential election. The President serves a five-year term. Upon the territory's accession to independence in May 2002, the Constituent Assembly was transformed into the National Parliament. (The number of seats in the National Parliament was reduced from 88 to 65 at the 2007 elections.) In 2002 the UN Transitional Administration in East Timor (UNTAET) formally relinquished its responsibility for the administration of the country and was succeeded by the UN Mission of Support in East Timor (UNMISET), which remained in the country, in a supporting role, ultimately for three years. UNMISET was replaced in May 2005 by the UN Office in Timor-Leste (UNOTIL), which was superseded by the UN Integrated Mission in Timor-Leste (UNMIT) in August 2006. Following the successful conduct of presidential and legislative elections in mid-2012, UNMIT completed its mandate and withdrew from Timor-Leste on 31 December 2012.

REGIONAL AND INTERNATIONAL CO-OPERATION

Timor-Leste is a member of the Asian Development Bank (ADB, see p. 214), the Comunidade dos Países de Língua Portuguesa (Community of Portuguese-Speaking Countries, see p. 475) and the UN's Economic and Social Commission for Asia and the Pacific (ESCAP, see p. 31). The country has been granted observer status at the Association of Southeast Asian Nations (ASEAN, see p. 218), and submitted a formal application for full membership of the regional grouping in March 2011. Timor-Leste was also granted observer status by the Melanesian Spearhead Group in that month.

Timor-Leste became a member of the UN in September 2002. The country is also a member of the International Labour Organization (ILO, see p. 142) and the Non-aligned Movement (see p. 477).

ECONOMIC AFFAIRS

In 2010, according to estimates by the World Bank, Timor-Leste's gross national income (GNI), measured at average 2008–10 prices, was US $3,123m., equivalent to $2,730 per head (or $5,210 per head on an international purchasing-power parity basis). During 2002–11, it was estimated, the population increased at an average annual rate of 3.2%, while gross domestic product (GDP) per head rose, in real terms, by an average of 3.9% per year. According to figures from the Asian Development Bank (ADB), overall GDP grew, in real terms, at an average annual rate of 16.6% during 2004–10; however, a decline of 1.5% was recorded in 2010. Non-oil GDP increased by 10.8% in 2011 and by 10.6% in 2012.

The agricultural sector (including forestry and fishing) contributed 4.5% of GDP in 2010, according to the ADB. The sector engaged an estimated 78.9% of the Timorese labour force in mid-2013, according to FAO. Coffee is a significant export commodity. However, the coffee sector remains extremely susceptible to climatic conditions, which, combined with poor irrigation systems, are primarily responsible for significant fluctuations in annual output. The value of coffee exports amounted to US $11.9m. in 2011. There are small plantations of coconuts, cloves and cinnamon. Subsistence crops include rice, maize and cassava. Livestock raised includes cattle and water buffalo. There is some small-scale fishing, and the forestry sector may yield as yet undeveloped potential. According to ADB figures, the GDP of the agricultural sector increased, in real terms, at an

average annual rate of 3.1% in 2004–10. Agricultural GDP remained constant in 2011 and 2012.

The industrial sector (including mining and quarrying, manufacturing, utilities and construction) accounted for 81.2% of GDP in 2010, according to the ADB. Industrial GDP increased at an average annual rate of 19.3% in 2004–10. The industrial sector's GDP contracted by 3.7% in 2010.

The mining sector contributed 78.8% of GDP in 2010, according to ADB figures. In the 1990s sizeable natural gasfields were discovered in and around the Timor Gap zone, and petroleum reserves in the region were estimated by some sources to total a potential 500m. barrels. The Timor Sea Treaty, relating to the sharing of petroleum and gas royalties with Australia, was signed in 2002 (see Contemporary Political History). In 2003 a US company was granted permission to develop the Bayu-Undan liquefied natural gasfield in the Timor Sea. In addition to offshore petroleum and gas, mineral resources include high-grade marble. The GDP of the mining sector increased at an average annual rate of 19.8% in 2004–10. However, the sector's GDP contracted by 4.1% in 2010.

There is a small manufacturing sector, which is mainly concerned with the production of textiles, the bottling of water and coffee-processing. In 2010 the manufacturing sector provided an estimated 0.7% of GDP, according to ADB figures. In May 2004 one of the world's largest wet-processing coffee factories was opened in Estado, which, together with expanded production at the existing Maubisse factory, was expected to increase significantly Timor-Leste's annual coffee output. Manufacturing GDP expanded, in real terms, at an average annual rate of 7.0% in 2004–10. The GDP of the manufacturing sector increased by 8.9% in 2010.

Construction provided 1.6% of GDP in 2010, according to ADB figures. Construction GDP increased, in real terms, at an average annual rate of 10.5% in 2004–10. The GDP of the sector grew by 13.1% in 2010.

In 2002 the Government elected to transfer control of the national power authority, Electricidade de Timor-Leste, to external management. Although the basic rehabilitation of the existing rural power infrastructure was largely complete by 2003, supplies of electricity subsequently remained intermittent, and the country's total generating capacity stood at only 40 MW in 2008. However, a major programme of electrification was undertaken in 2011–13. According to IMF figures, in the 2011 and 2012 budgets a total of US $729m. in capital expenditure was allocated to the expansion of the electricity grid and the construction of power plants.

According to ADB figures, the services sector contributed 14.3% of GDP in 2010. The development of the tourism sector has been hampered by a lack of facilities, as well as prohibitively high air fares from Indonesia and Australia. The services sector's GDP expanded, in real terms, at an average annual rate of 11.0% in 2004–10. The sector's GDP increased by 12.9% in 2010.

In 2010 Timor-Leste recorded a visible merchandise trade deficit of US $421.2m., while there was a surplus of $1,717.3m. on the current account of the balance of payments (largely owing to the allocation of petroleum and gas export revenues to the income and transfers accounts). The principal source of imports in 2011 was Indonesia, which supplied 30.7% of the total. Other leading suppliers were the People's Republic of China and Singapore. The principal destinations for exports (excluding oil and gas) were Germany (which purchased 42.6% of the total), the USA and Japan. The main imports in 2011 were electrical machinery and equipment, mineral fuels, vehicles (excluding railway or tramway rolling stock), iron or steel articles, and boilers, machinery and mechanical appliances. Reliable data for exports of oil and gas were not available (see above), but these, together with coffee, constituted the most significant merchandise exports in that year.

An overall budget surplus of US $1,066.0m. was estimated in 2012. Australia is a major provider of development assistance, with emphasis on governance, law, training, security and public sector services. Australia's aid budget for Timor-Leste was projected at $A116.7m. in 2012/13, to cover a variety of areas including the rehabilitation of rural roads, greater access to safe water supplies and the provision of good quality basic education. Consumer prices increased at an average annual rate of 6.6% in 2004–11, according to ADB figures. The rate of inflation was 10.9% in 2012. In 2010 the rate of unemployment was estimated by the ADB at 3.6%. According to the census of 2004, those recorded as unemployed, or deterred from seeking work, accounted for one-half of Dili residents aged between 15 and 24 years.

Upon independence in 2002 Timor-Leste's first National Development Plan was implemented. Its objectives, over an 18-year period, included the reduction of poverty and the introduction of a phased programme of development. External aid remained of vital importance. The implementation in February 2007 of an agreement between Timor-Leste and Australia regarding the allocation of revenue from the Greater Sunrise petroleum and gas project (see Contemporary Political History) was a major development; however, at April 2013 no development plan for the Greater Sunrise oil- and gasfields had yet been formulated. Nearly all of the Government's own revenue is derived from its Petroleum Fund, which serves as a long-term repository for all petroleum revenues, most of its assets being invested in US government bonds. The value of the Petroleum Fund rose from US $6,904m. at the end of 2010 to $11,054m. at 30 September 2012. Timor-Leste benefited greatly from the strength of international oil prices that prevailed until mid-2008 and again from late 2010. Meanwhile, the incidence of poverty was reportedly reduced from 50% in 2007 to 41% in 2009, during which year inflationary pressures eased considerably. By late 2010, however, inflationary pressures had re-emerged, and, following a steep increase in the final quarter of 2011, owing to rising food and fuel prices, strong domestic demand and a weakening of the US dollar (Timor-Leste's official currency), the annual average rate of inflation amounted to 13.1% in that year, according to the ADB. As a result of an easing in global food prices and lower import costs (arising from a strengthening US dollar), inflation moderated to 10.9% in 2012. Spending on infrastructural projects was expected to exceed $3,000m. in 2011–15, although the Government has encountered difficulties in utilizing budget allocations owing to capacity constraints.

Government expenditure totalled $1,807m. in 2012, representing an increase of 64.9% from the previous year. A major challenge remained the provision of basic services, particularly in rural areas, and more than 50% of the capital budget for the period 2009–12 was allocated to a national programme of electrification. Private sector development was expected to be stimulated by the approval in February 2012 of new legislation governing public-private partnerships; it was hoped that the creation of new business opportunities would encourage economic diversification, thus reducing the country's reliance on the petroleum sector. Following impressive GDP (non-petroleum) expansion of 10.8% in 2011 and 10.6% in 2012, largely driven by substantial increases in government expenditure (notably on public infrastructure), the ADB projected that the growth rate would moderate slightly to 10.0% in 2013 and 2014. Despite continuing high levels of planned public spending, the ADB forcast that the rate of inflation would decline to 9.0% in 2013 and to 7.7% in 2014.

PUBLIC HOLIDAYS

2014: 1 January (New Year's Day), 18 April (Good Friday), 1 May (Labour Day), 20 May (Independence Restoration Day), 19 June (Corpus Christi), 28 July* (Id al-Fitr, end of Ramadan), 30 August (Constitution Day), 4 October* (Id al-Adha, Feast of the Sacrifice), 1 November (All Saints' Day), 2 November (All Souls' Day), 12 November (National Youth Day), 28 November (Proclamation of Independence Day), 7 December (National Heroes' Day), 8 December (Immaculate Conception), 25 December (Christmas Day).

* These holidays are dependent on the Islamic lunar calendar and may vary by one or two days from the dates given.

Statistical Survey

Source (unless otherwise stated): Direcção Nacional de Estatística, Rua de Caicoli, PO Box 10, Dili, Timor-Leste; tel. 6703339527; e-mail dne@mof.gov.tl; internet www.dne.mof.gov.tl.

Area and Population

AREA, POPULATION AND DENSITY

Area (sq km)	14,954*
Population (census results)	
31 July 2004	923,198
11 July 2010	
Males	544,198
Females	522,211
Total	1,066,409
Population (UN estimates at mid-year)†	
2011	1,153,835
2012	1,187,195
2013	1,223,662
Density (per sq km) at mid-2013	81.8

* 5,774 sq miles.
† Source: UN, *World Population Prospects: The 2010 Revision*.

POPULATION BY AGE AND SEX
(UN estimates at mid-2013)

	Males	Females	Total
0–14	278,430	265,774	544,204
15–64	328,004	314,105	642,109
65 and over	17,247	20,102	37,349
Total	**623,681**	**599,981**	**1,223,662**

Source: UN, *World Population Prospects: The 2010 Revision*.

ADMINISTRATIVE DIVISIONS
(population at 2010 census)

Division	Area (sq km)	Population	Density (per sq km)
Aileu	676	44,325	65.6
Ainaro	870	59,175	68.0
Baucau	1,508	111,694	74.1
Bobonaro	1,381	92,049	66.7
Covalima	1,207	59,455	49.3
Dili	368	234,026	635.9
Ermera	771	117,064	151.8
Lautem	1,813	59,787	33.0
Liquiça	551	63,403	115.1
Manatuto	1,786	42,742	23.9
Manufahi	1,327	48,628	36.6
Oecusse	817	64,025	78.4
Viqueque	1,880	70,036	37.3
Total	**14,954**	**1,066,409**	**71.3**

PRINCIPAL TOWNS
(population at 2010 census)

Dili (capital) . .	234,026		Ermera	33,530
Baucau	46,500		Maliana	25,234

BIRTHS AND DEATHS
(annual averages, UN estimates)

	1995–2000	2000–05	2005–10
Birth rate (per 1,000)	46.1	40.4	39.4
Death rate (per 1,000)	12.9	10.0	8.7

Source: UN, *World Population Prospects: The 2010 Revision.*

Life expectancy (years at birth): 62.5 (males 61.5; females 63.5) in 2011 (Source: World Bank, World Development Indicators database).

Health and Welfare

KEY INDICATORS

Total fertility rate (children per woman, 2010) . . .	6.2
Under-5 mortality rate (per 1,000 live births, 2010) . . .	55
Physicians (per 1,000 head, 2004)	0.10
Hospital beds (per 1,000 head, 2010)	5.90
Health expenditure (2009): US $ per head	103
Health expenditure (2009): % of GDP	11.9
Health expenditure (2009): public (% of total)	66.1
Access to water (% of persons, 2010)	69
Access to sanitation (% of persons, 2010)	47
Total carbon dioxide emissions ('000 metric tons, 2008) . .	190.7
Carbon dioxide emissions per head (metric tons, 2008) . .	0.2
Human development index (2011): ranking	147
Human development index (2011): value	0.495

For sources and definitions, see explanatory note on p. vi.

Agriculture

PRINCIPAL CROPS
('000 metric tons)

	2009	2010	2011
Maize	134.7	148.9	30.7
Cassava (Manioc)	37.3	27.9	22.2
Rice, paddy	120.8	112.9	98.3
Sweet potatoes	12.8	9.6	9.6
Beans, dry*	8.1	8.2	9.6
Groundnuts, with shell* . . .	6.3	1.6	4.1
Coconuts	8.7	8.9	8.9
Bananas	0.7	0.7	0.7*
Guavas, mangoes and mangosteens	6.4	6.1	7.9*
Coffee, green	10.1	12.7	8.3

* FAO estimate(s).

Aggregate production ('000 metric tons, may include official, semi-official or estimated data): Total cereals 255.5 in 2009, 261.8 in 2010, 129.0 in 2011; Total roots and tubers 94.9 in 2009, 70.5 in 2010, 59.7 in 2011; Total vegetables (incl. melons) 28.6 in 2009, 25.8 in 2010, 31.3 in 2011; Total fruits (excl. melons) 15.4 in 2009, 14.9 in 2010, 18.1 in 2011.

Source: FAO.

LIVESTOCK
('000 head)

	2009	2010	2011*
Cattle	148	153	155
Buffaloes	104	107	107
Pigs	403	415	420
Horses	66	58	55
Goats	140	144	147
Sheep	42	43	45
Chickens	801	702	750

* FAO estimates.

Source: FAO.

LIVESTOCK PRODUCTS
('000 metric tons, estimates)

	2009	2010	2011
Cattle meat	1.0	1.0	1.1
Pig meat	9.5	9.8	9.9
Chicken meat	0.8	0.7	0.7
Hen eggs	1.2	1.1	1.1

Source: FAO.

Fishing

(metric tons, live weight, FAO estimates)

	2006	2007	2008
Total catch	2,573	2,944	3,177

2009–10: Catch assumed to be unchanged from 2008 (FAO estimates).

Source: FAO.

Finance

CURRENCY AND EXCHANGE RATES (US currency is used)

Monetary Units
100 cents (centavos) = 1 United States dollar ($).

Sterling and Euro Equivalents (31 December 2012)
£1 sterling = US $1.578;
€1 = $1.319;
US $100 = £63.37 = €75.79.

BUDGET
(US $ million)

Revenue	2011	2012*	2013†
Domestic revenue	109	134	147
Direct taxes	28	39	42
Indirect taxes	51	57	64
Fees and charges	12	13	15
Sales of rice and local produce .	1	5	3
Autonomous agencies and other	17	20	23
Oil and gas revenues	3,461	2,961	2,797
Oil and gas receipts . . .	3,240	2,753	2,309
Interest	221	208	488
Total	**3,570**	**3,095**	**2,944**

Expenditure‡	2011	2012*	2013†
Core Fund of Timor-Leste	605	894	1,002
Recurrent expenditure . .	491	720	816
Salaries and wages . .	112	139	160
Goods and services . .	237	347	419
Transfers	143	234	237
Capital expenditure and net lending	114	174	186
Human Capital Development Fund	17	38	42
Infrastructure Fund	474	875	753
Total	**1,096**	**1,807**	**1,798**

* Estimates.
† Projections.
‡ Excluding Development Partner Commitments (US $ million): 284 in 2011; 222 in 2012 (estimate); 203 in 2012 (projection).

Note: Totals may not be equal to the sum of components, owing to rounding.

Source: Ministry of Finance, Dili.

INTERNATIONAL RESERVES
(US $ million at 31 December)

	2009	2010	2011
IMF special drawing rights . .	12.115	11.901	11.864
Reserve position in IMF . . .	0.002	0.002	0.002
Foreign exchange	237.812	394.286	449.745
Total	249.929	406.189	461.611

Source: IMF, *International Financial Statistics.*

MONEY SUPPLY
(US $ million at 31 December)

	2009	2010	2011
Currency outside depository corporations	2.801	3.374	3.863
Transferable deposits . . .	154.642	138.012	158.821
Other deposits	110.913	153.639	159.744
Broad money	268.356	295.025	322.428

Source: IMF, *International Financial Statistics.*

COST OF LIVING
(Consumer Price Index; base: 2005 = 100)

	2009	2010	2011
All items	125.9	134.4	152.5

Source: IMF, *International Financial Statistics.*

NATIONAL ACCOUNTS
(US $ million at current prices)

Expenditure on the Gross Domestic Product

	2008	2009	2010
Government final consumption expenditure	791.2	860.9	964.9
Private final consumption expenditure	533.0	583.4	608.7
Change in stocks	1.7	1.9	2.1
Gross fixed capital formation . .	208.7	488.0	578.8
Total domestic expenditure	1,534.6	1,934.2	2,154.5
Exports of goods and services . .	4,267.3	3,094.2	3,940.1
Less Imports of goods and services	1,426.3	1,743.4	1,963.5
Statistical discrepancy	39.1	−1.6	−0.6
GDP in purchasers' values .	4,414.7	3,283.4	4,130.5
GDP at constant 2010 prices .	4,509.4	4,194.0	4,130.5

Gross Domestic Product by Economic Activity

	2008	2009	2010
Agriculture, forestry and fishing .	164.8	181.0	187.5
Mining	3,751.7	2,497.1	3,257.2
Manufacturing	17.1	21.7	27.0
Electricity, gas and water . . .	5.2	9.2	8.0
Construction	47.2	52.8	64.1
Trade	145.5	159.2	172.9
Transport and communications .	53.0	68.4	82.7
Finance	11.8	12.7	15.0
Public administration . . .	106.8	153.1	177.8
Other service activities . . .	122.6	128.2	142.2
Gross Value Added . . .	4,425.8	3,283.3	4,134.3
Taxes, *less* subsidies on production	−11.1	0.1	−3.8
GDP in purchasers' values .	4,414.7	3,283.4	4,130.5

Source: Asian Development Bank.

BALANCE OF PAYMENTS
(US $ million)

	2008	2009	2010
Exports of goods f.o.b.	14.1	9.2	17.8
Imports of goods f.o.b.	−310.9	−370.3	−439.1
Trade balance	−296.9	−361.1	−421.2
Services and income (net) . .	1,962.1	1,326.5	1,882.9
Balance on goods, services and income	1,665.2	965.4	1,461.7
Current transfers (net) . .	356.5	359.3	255.6
Current balance	2,021.7	1,324.7	1,717.3
Capital account (net) . . .	17.2	27.3	31.3
Direct investment (net) . .	39.7	49.9	26.9
Portfolio investment (net) . .	−2,003.1	−1,325.1	−1,509.0
Other investment (net) . .	−88.1	2.6	−56.0
Net errors and omissions . .	−7.3	−39.9	−54.3
Overall balance	−19.9	39.5	156.5

Source: Asian Development Bank.

External Trade

SELECTED COMMODITIES
(US $ '000)

Imports c.i.f.	2009	2010	2011
Cereals	35,169	14,123	9,182
Beverages, spirits and vinegar .	7,793	12,197	9,275
Mineral fuels, mineral oils and products of their distillation; bituminous substances; mineral waxes	38,040	41,151	47,654
Boilers, machinery and mechanical appliances; parts thereof . .	22,770	23,742	20,714
Vehicles, other than railway or tramway rolling stock, and parts thereof	58,486	23,404	33,711
Electrical machinery and equipment and parts thereof; sound recorders and reproducers; televisions, etc. .	25,198	23,404	99,381
Pharmaceutical products . .	5,269	3,736	3,414
Iron or steel articles . . .	5,149	11,121	23,493
Total (incl. others)	282,595	246,311	318,776

Exports f.o.b. (excl. oil and gas)	2009	2010	2011
Coffee	8,291	15,987	11,923
Total (incl. others) . . .	8,491	16,395	13,202

Re-exports (US $ '000): 26,021 in 2009; 25,265 in 2010; 40,050 in 2011. Note: The significance of re-exports may appear overstated owing to the inclusion of data connected with the outflow of foreign personnel and equipment as peace-keeping operations were scaled down.

Source: Ministério do Plano e das Finanças, Dili.

PRINCIPAL TRADING PARTNERS
(US $ '000)

Imports c.i.f.	2009	2010	2011
Australia	47,196	25,063	15,365
China, People's Republic . .	11,572	21,531	59,913
Germany	314	249	243
India	1,439	6,083	3,711
Indonesia	92,105	95,976	97,810
Japan	7,750	10,054	5,872
Korea, Republic	1,821	685	1,400
Malaysia	8,052	5,208	13,751
Portugal	9,487	7,060	4,768
Singapore	53,513	44,958	21,524
Thailand	3,346	3,198	8,069
Viet Nam	34,602	14,028	7,449
Total (incl. others)	282,594	246,311	318,776

Exports f.o.b. (excl. oil and gas)*	2009	2010	2011
Australia	250	691	557
British Indian Ocean Territory .	142	n.a.	n.a.
Canada	255	n.a.	n.a.
China, People's Republic . . .	57	233	417
Germany	2,372	4,215	5,629
Indonesia	412	702	463
Japan	402	617	670
Korea, Republic	106	176	299
New Zealand	86	71	n.a.
Portugal	755	722	118
Singapore	289	1,499	614
USA	2,873	7,196	2,911
Total (incl. others)	8,491	16,394	13,202

* Excluding re-exports (US $ million): 26.0 in 2009; 25.3 in 2010; 40.1 in 2011.
Note: The significance of re-exports may appear overstated owing to the inclusion of data connected with the outflow of foreign personnel and equipment as peace-keeping operations were scaled down.

Source: Ministério do Plano e das Finanças, Dili.

SHIPPING

Flag Registered Fleet
(at 31 December)

	2010	2011	2012
Number of vessels	1	1	1
Total displacement ('000 grt) . .	1,134	1,134	1,134

Source: Lloyd's List Intelligence (www.lloydslistintelligence.com).

Tourism

TOURIST ARRIVALS BY COUNTRY OF RESIDENCE

	2009	2010	2011
Australia	11,207	11,262	12,419
Brazil	849	803	978
China, People's Republic . . .	1,991	2,659	3,464
India	1,464	2,027	1,158
Indonesia	5,443	6,744	11,179
Japan	1,106	1,208	1,232
Malaysia	1,956	1,756	1,829
New Zealand	822	800	711
Philippines	1,709	2,177	2,413
Portugal	4,501	996	5,916
Singapore	1,393	1,495	1,519
United Kingdom	806	929	1,002
USA	1,802	1,720	2,207
Total (incl. others)	44,131	39,825	50,239

Tourism receipts (US $ million, excl. passenger transport): 14.0 in 2008; 13.2 in 2009; 21.4 in 2010 (Source: World Tourism Organization).

Communications Media

	2009	2010	2011
Telephones ('000 main lines in use)	2.9	2.9	3.1
Mobile cellular telephones ('000 subscribers)	350.9	600.6	614.2
Internet users	1,100	n.a.	n.a.
Broadband subscribers . . .	500	500	600

Source: International Telecommunication Union.

Education

(2009/10 unless otherwise indicated)

	Teachers	Students
Pre-primary*	237	6,987
Primary	7,622	230,175
Lower Secondary	2,343	60,591
Upper Secondary	2,072	40,910
Tertiary†	1,196	16,727

* 2004/05.
† 2008/09.
Source: UNESCO Institute for Statistics.

2011: *Institutions:* Basic education 1,273; Secondary education 74; Technical secondary education 17. *Teachers:* Basic education 8,832; Secondary education 1,445; Technical secondary education 318. *Students:* Basic education 304,057; Secondary education 37,782; Technical secondary education 6,586.

Pupil-teacher ratio (primary education, UNESCO estimate): 30.2 for 2009/10 (Source: UNESCO Institute for Statistics).

Adult literacy rate (UNESCO estimate): 58.3% (males 63.6%; females 53.0%) in 2010 (Source: UNESCO Institute for Statistics).

Directory

The Government

HEAD OF STATE

President: TAUR MATAN RUAK (elected 16 April 2012; inaugurated 20 May 2012).

CABINET
(May 2013)

The coalition Government comprises members of the Congresso Nacional da Reconstrução de Timor-Leste, the Partido Democrático and Frenti-Mudança.

Prime Minister and Minister of Defence and Security: KAY RALA XANANA GUSMÃO.

Deputy Prime Minister and Co-ordinator of Social Affairs: FERNANDO DE ARAÚJO.

Minister of State Administration: JORGE DA CONCEIÇÃO TEME.

Minister of State and of Foreign Affairs and Co-operation: JOSÉ LUÍS GUTERRES.

Minister of State and of the Presidency of the Council of Ministers: AGIO PEREIRA.

Minister of Justice: DIONÍSIO BABO SOARES.

Minister of Finance: MARIA MADALENA EMÍLIA PIRES.

Minister of Education: BENDITO DOS SANTOS FREITAS.

Minister of Health: SÉRGIO GAMA DA C. LOBO.

Minister of Trade, Industry and Environment: ANTÓNIO DA CONCEIÇÃO.

Minister of Agriculture and Fisheries: MARIANO SABINO.

Minister of Public Works: GASTÃO FRANCISCO DE SOUSA.

Minister of Petroleum and Mineral Resources: ALFREDO PIRES.

Minister of Social Solidarity: ISABEL AMARAL GUTERRES.

Minister of Tourism: FRANCISCO KALBUADI LAY.

Minister of Transport and Communications: PEDRO LAY.

MINISTRIES

Office of the President: Palácio das Cinzas, Caicoli, Dili; tel. 7840594; e-mail admin@presidencia.tl; internet www.presidencia.tl.

Office of the Prime Minister: Palácio do Governo, Av. Presidente Nicolau Lobato, Dili; tel. 7243559; fax 3339503; e-mail mail@ primeministerandcabinet.gov.tp; internet timor-leste.gov.tl.

Ministry of Agriculture and Fisheries: Edif. 5, Av. Presidente Nicolau Lobato, Dili; tel. 3310418; internet www.maf.gov.tl.

Ministry of Defence and Security: Palácio do Governo, Edif. 2, 1°, Av. Presidente Nicolau Lobato, Dili; tel. 3331190.

Ministry of Economy and Development: Rua D. Aleixo Corte Real, Edif. Fomento, 2°, Mandarin, Dili; tel. 3339039.

Ministry of Education: Rua de Vila Verde, Dili; tel. 3339654.

Ministry of Finance: Palácio do Governo, Edif. 5, Av. Presidente Nicolau Lobato, Dili; tel. 3339646; e-mail info@mof.gov.tl; internet www.mof.gov.tl.

Ministry of Foreign Affairs and Co-operation: Edif. 1, Av. Presidente Nicolau Lobato, POB 6, Dili; tel. 3339600; fax 3339025; internet www.mfac.gov.tp.

Ministry of Health: Edif. dos Serviços Centrais do Ministério da Saúde, Rua de Caicoli, POB 374, Dili; tel. 3331113; fax 3325189; e-mail carinton.salazar@moh.gov.tl; internet www.moh.gov.tl.

Ministry of Infrastructure: 8 Av. Bispo de Medeiros, Mercado Lama, Dili; tel. 3339355.

Ministry of Justice: Av. Jacinto Cândido, Dili; tel. 77230131; e-mail mj@mj.gov.tl; internet www.mj.gov.tl.

Ministry of Social Solidarity: Rua de Caicoli, Dili; tel. 3312256; fax 3310392; e-mail info@mss.gov.tl; internet www.mss.gov.tl.

Ministry of State Administration: Rua Jacinto Cândido, Caicoli, Dili; tel. 3339077; e-mail komunikasaun@estatal.gov.tl; internet www.estatal.gov.tl.

Ministry of Tourism, Trade and Industry: Edif. Fomento, Rua Dom Aleixo Corte Real, Mandarin, Dili; tel. 3331202; e-mail gab@ mtci-timorleste.com; internet www.mtci-timorleste.com.

President and Legislature

PRESIDENT

Presidential Election, First Ballot, 17 March 2012

Candidate	Votes	% of votes
Francisco Guterres (Fretilin)	133,635	28.76
Taur Matan Ruak (Independent)	119,462	25.71
José Ramos Horta (Independent)	81,231	17.48
Fernando de Araújo (PD)	80,381	17.30
Rogério Tiago de Fátima Lobato (Fretilin)	16,219	3.49
José Luís Guterres (Frenti-Mudança)	9,235	1.99
Manuel Tilman (KOTA)	7,226	1.56
Abílio de Araújo (PNT)	6,294	1.35
Lucas da Costa (PD)	3,862	0.83
Francisco Gomes (PLPA)	3,531	0.76
Maria do C. Lopes da Silva (Independent)	1,843	0.40
Angelita M. F. Pires (Independent)	1,742	0.37
Total	**464,661**	**100.00**

Presidential Election, Second Ballot, 16 April 2012

Candidate	Votes	% of votes
Taur Matan Ruak	275,471	61.23
Francisco Guterres	174,408	38.77
Total*	**449,879**	**100.00**

* Excluding 2,203 blank votes and 6,801 invalid votes.

NATIONAL PARLIAMENT

Speaker: VICENTE DA SILVA GUTERRES.

General Election, 7 July 2012

	Seats
Congresso Nacional da Reconstrução de Timor-Leste (CNRT)	30
Frente Revolucionária do Timor Leste Independente (Fretilin)	25
Partido Democrático (PD)	8
Frenti-Mudança	2
Total	**65**

Election Commission

National Electoral Commission (Comissão Nacional de Eleições—CNE): Av. Bispo Medeiros-Kintal, Dili; tel. 3310082; internet www.cne.tl; f. 2004; govt body; Chair. Dr FAUSTINO CARDOSO.

Political Organizations

There were 24 registered political parties in 2012.

Associação Popular Democrática de Timor Pro Referendo (Apodeti Pro Referendo) (Pro-Referendum Popular Democratic Association of Timor): c/o Frederico Almeida Santos Costa, CNRT Office, Balide, Dili; tel. 3324994; f. 1974 as Apodeti; present name adopted Aug. 2000; fmrly supported autonomous integration with Indonesia; Pres. FREDERICO ALMEIDA SANTOS COSTA.

Associação Social-Democrata Timorense (ASDT) (Timor Social Democratic Association): Av. Direitos Humanos Lecidere, Dili; tel. 3983331; f. 2001; Leader JOÃO CORREIA.

Barisan Rakyat Timor Timur (BRTT) (East Timor People's Front): fmrly supported autonomous integration with Indonesia; Pres. FRANCISCO LOPES DA CRUZ.

Congresso Nacional da Reconstrução de Timor-Leste (CNRT) (National Congress for the Reconstruction of Timor-Leste): Rua Nu Laran, Bairro dos Grilos, Dili; tel. 7358696; e-mail info@partidocnrt .com; internet partidocnrt.com; f. 2007; Pres. KAY RALA XANANA GUSMÃO.

Conselho Popular pela Defesa da República Democrática de Timor Leste (CPD-RDTL) (Popular Council for the Defence of the Democratic Republic of East Timor): opp. the Church, Balide, Dili; tel. 3481462; f. 1999; promotes adoption of 1975 Constitution of Democratic Republic of East Timor; Spokesperson CRISTIANO DA COSTA.

Frente Revolucionária do Timor Leste Independente (Fretilin) (Revolutionary Front for an Independent East Timor): Rua dos Mártires da Pátria, Dili; tel. 3321409; e-mail fretilin.media@gmail .com; internet fretilinmedia.blogspot.com; f. 1974; est. to seek full independence for East Timor; entered into alliance with the UDT in 1986; Pres. FRANCISCO GUTERRES; Sec.-Gen. MARI ALKATIRI.

Frenti-Mudança (Frente Reconstrução Nacional de Timor-Leste-Mudança—FM): Dili; f. 2011 by José Luís Guterres and fmr mems of Fretilin; Pres. JOSÉ LUÍS GUTERRES; Sec.-Gen. JORGE DA CONCEIÇÃO TEME.

Klibur Oan Timor Asuwain (KOTA) (Association of Timorese Heroes): Rua dos Mártires da Pátria, Fatuhada, Dili; tel. 3324661; e-mail clementinoamaral@hotmail.com; f. 1974 as pro-integration party; supported independence with Timorese traditions; Pres. MANUEL TILMAN.

Partai Democratik Maubere (PDM) (Maubere Democratic Party): Blk B-II, 16 Surikmas Lama Kraik, Fatumeta, Dili; tel. 3184508; e-mail pdm_party@hotmail.com; f. 2000; Pres. PAOLO PINTO.

Partai Liberal (PL) (Liberal Party): Talbessi Sentral, Dili; tel. 3786448; Pres. ARMANDO JOSÉ DOURADO DA SILVA.

Partido Democrata Cristão (PDC) (Christian Democrat Party): Former Escola Cartilha, Rua Quintal Kiik, Bairro Economico, Dili; tel. 3324683; e-mail marson60@yahoo.com; f. 2000; Pres. ANTÓNIO XIMENES.

Partido Democrático (PD) (Democratic Party): 1 Rua Democracia, Pantai Kelapa, Dili; tel. 3608421; e-mail flazama@hotmail.com; Pres. FERNANDO DE ARAÚJO; Sec.-Gen. MARIANO SABINO.

Partido Nacionalista Timorense (PNT) (Nationalist Party of Timor): Dili; tel. 3323518; internet pnt-timor-leste.planetaclix.pt; Pres. Dr ABÍLIO DE ARAÚJO.

Partido do Povo de Timor (PPT) (Timorese People's Party): Dili; tel. 3568325; f. 2000; pro-integration; Pres. Dr JACOB XAVIER.

Partido Republika National Timor Leste (PARENTIL) (National Republic Party of East Timor): Perumnar Bairopite Bob Madey Ran, Fahan Jalam, Ailobu Laran RTK; tel. 3361393; Pres. FLAVIANO PEREIRA LOPEZ.

Partido Social Democrata Timor Lorosae (PSD) (Social Democrat Party of East Timor): Apdo 312, Correios de Dili, Dili; tel. 3357027; e-mail psdtimor@hotmail.com; f. 2000; Pres. ZACARIAS ALBANO DA COSTA; Sec.-Gen. MARITO MAGONO.

Partido Socialista de Timor (PST) (Socialist Party of Timor): Rua Colegio das Madras, Balide, Dili; tel. 3560246; e-mail kaynaga@hotmail.com; Marxist-Leninist Fretilin splinter group; Pres. AVELINO COELHO DA SILVA.

Partido Trabalhista Timorense (PTT) (Timor Labour Party): 2B Rua Travessa de Befonte, 2 Bairro Formosa, Dili; tel. 3322807; f. 1974; Pres. ANGELA FREITAS.

Partido Unidade Nacional (PUN) (United National Party): c/o National Parliament, Dili; f. 2005; Pres. FERNANDA BORGES.

Partido Unidade Nacional Democrática da Resistência Timorense (UNDERTIM): c/o National Parliament, Dili; Pres. CORNELIO GAMA.

Partidu Liberta Puvu Aileba (PLPA): Dili; Pres. FRANCISCO GOMES.

União Democrata-Cristão de Timor (UDC/PDC) (Christian Democratic Union of Timor): 62 Rua Almirante Américo Thomás, Mandarin, Dili; tel. 3325042; f. 1998; Pres. VICENTE DA SILVA GUTERRES.

União Democrática Timorense (UDT) (Timorese Democratic Union): Palapagoa Rua da India, Dili; tel. 3881453; e-mail joaocarrascalao@msn.com; internet fitini.net/udttimor; f. 1974; allied itself with Fretilin in 1986; Pres. JOÃO VIEGAS CARRASCALÃO; Sec.-Gen. DOMINGOS OLIVEIRA.

Diplomatic Representation

EMBASSIES IN TIMOR-LESTE

Australia: Av. dos Mártires da Pátria, Dili; tel. 3322111; fax 3322247; e-mail austemb_dili@dfat.gov.au; internet www.easttimor.embassy.gov.au; Ambassador MILES ARMITAGE.

Brazil: Av. Governador Serpa Rosa, POB 157, Farol, Dili; tel. 3324203; fax 3324620; e-mail brasemb.dili@itamaraty.gov.br; internet dili.itamaraty.gov.br/pt-br; Ambassador EDSON MARINHO DUARTE MONTEIRO.

China, People's Republic: Av. Governador Serpa Rosa, POB 131, Farol, Dili; tel. 3325168; fax 3325166; e-mail chinaembassy2002@yahoo.com; internet tl.chineseembassy.org; Ambassador TIAN GUANGFENG.

Indonesia: Farol, Palapaco, POB 207, Dili; tel. 3317107; fax 3323684; e-mail kukridil@hotmail.com; internet www.dili.deplu.go.id; Ambassador MARCELLINUS PRIMANTO HENDRASMORO.

Japan: Av. de Portugal, Pantai Kelapa, POB 175, Dili; tel. 3323131; fax 3323130; e-mail japan.embassy.in.timor-leste@mofa.go.jp; internet www.timor-leste.emb-japan.go.jp; Ambassador KITAHARA IWAO.

Korea, Republic: Av. de Portugal, Motael, Dili; tel. 3321635; fax 3323636; e-mail koreadili@mofat.go.kr; internet tls.mofat.go.kr; Ambassador OH HYANG-KYUN.

Malaysia: Av. de Portugal, Praia dos Coqueiros, Dili; tel. 3321804; fax 3321805; e-mail maldili@kln.gov.my; internet www.kln.gov.my/web/tls_dili; Ambassador (vacant).

New Zealand: Rua Geremias do Amaral, Montael, Dili; tel. 3310087; fax 3324982; e-mail dili@mfat.gov.nz; Ambassador TONY FAUTUA.

Philippines: Av. Governador Serpa Rosa, Farol, Dili; tel. 33310408; fax 3310407; e-mail pe.dili@dfa.gov.ph; Ambassador MARIA H. BUGARIN.

Portugal: Edif. ACAIT, Av. Presidente Nicolau Lobato, Dili; tel. 3312533; fax 3312526; e-mail embaixada.portugal@embpor.tp; Ambassador LUÍS MANUEL BARREIRA DE SOUSA.

Thailand: Av. de Portugal, Motael, Dili; tel. 3310609; fax 3322179; e-mail thaidli@mfa.go.th; Ambassador TAWATCHAI KOOPIROM.

USA: Av. de Portugal, Praia dos Coqueiros, Dili; tel. 3324684; fax 3313206; e-mail ConsDili@state.gov; internet timor-leste.usembassy.gov; Ambassador JUDITH R. FERGIN.

Judicial System

Until independence was granted on 20 May 2002 all legislative and executive authority with respect to the administration of the judiciary in East Timor was vested in the UN Transitional Administration in East Timor (UNTAET). During the transitional period of administration a two-tier court structure was established, consisting of District Courts and a Court of Appeal. The Constitution, promulgated in March 2002, specified that Timor-Leste should have three categories of courts: the Supreme Court of Justice and other law courts; the High Administrative, Tax and Audit Court and other administrative courts of first instance; and military courts. The judiciary would be regulated by the Superior Council of the Judiciary, the function of which would be to oversee the judicial sector and, in particular, to control the appointment, promotion, discipline and dismissal of judges. In July 2003 the Court of Appeal was reconstituted. A new penal code was promulgated in March 2009. At that time a code based on Indonesian law remained in place for civil cases, but it was scheduled for replacement by civil codes based on Portuguese law.

Court of Appeal: Caicoli, Dili; tel. 3331149; e-mail tribunal.recurso@tribunais.tl; internet www.tribunais.tl; Pres. CLAUDIO XIMENES.

District Courts: there are four district courts, located in Dili, Baucau, Oecusse and Suai.

Office of the Prosecutor-General: Dili; Prosecutor-General ANA MARIA PESSÔA PEREIRA DA SILVA PINTO.

Religion

In 2009 it was estimated that about 96.5% of the total population were Roman Catholic.

CHRISTIANITY

The Roman Catholic Church

Timor-Leste comprises the dioceses of Dili and Baucau, directly responsible to the Holy See. In December 2007 there were an estimated 958,383 Roman Catholics.

Bishop of Baucau: Most Rev. BASILIO DO NASCIMENTO, Largo da Catedral, Baucau 88810; tel. 4121209; fax 4121380.

Bishop of Dili: Most Rev. ALBERTO RICARDO DA SILVA, Av. dos Direitos Humanos, Bidau Lecidere, CP 4, Dili 88010; tel. 3324850; fax 3321177.

Bishop of Maliana: Fr NORBERTO DO AMARAL.

Protestant Church

Igreja Protestante iha Timor Lorosa'e (Protestant Church in Timor-Leste): Jl. Raya Comoro, POB 1186, Dili 88110; tel. and fax 3323128; f. 1988 as Gereja Kristen Timor Timur (GKTT); adopted present name 2000; Moderator Rev. MOISES A. DA SILVA; 30,000 mems.

The Press

The Constitution promulgated in March 2002 guarantees freedom of the press in Timor-Leste.

Guide Post Magazine: Dili; tel. 7267160; e-mail advertising@guideposttimor.com; internet www.guideposttimor.com; monthly; Editor LEITH CARROLL.

Jornal da República (The Official Gazette of Timor-Leste): Dili; e-mail jornal_republica@mj.gov.tl; internet www.jornal.gov.tl; forum for publication of all govt regulations and directives, acts of national organs or institutions, and other acts of public interest requiring general notification; Portuguese.

Lalenok (Mirror): Rua Gov. Celestino da Silva, Farol, Dili; tel. 3321607; e-mail lalenok@hotmail.com; f. 2000; publ. by Kamelin Media Group; Tetum; 3 a week; Dir-Gen. and Chief Editor VIRGÍLIO DA SILVA GUTERRES; Editor JOSÉ MARIA POMPELA; circ. 300.

Lian Maubere: Dili; f. 1999; weekly.

Suara Timor Lorosae: STL Park, Surik Mas, Dili; tel. 3322824; fax 3322823; e-mail stl_redaksi@yahoo.com; internet suara-timorlorosae.com; f. 2000; daily; Editor-in-Chief and Publr SALVADOR J. XIMENES SOARES.

Timor Post: 6 Rua Dom Aleixo Corte-Real, Dili; f. 2000; managed by editors and staff of the fmr Suara Timor Timur; Tetum, English, Portuguese and Bahasa Indonesia; daily; Man. Editor OTELIO OTE; Chief Editor and Dir ADERITO HUGO DA COSTA; circ. 600.

PRESS AGENCY

Timornewsline: Rua Sebastian da Costa, Colmera, Dili; tel. 3324475; e-mail alberico@tlmc.org; internet www.timornewsline .com; operated by Timor-Leste Media Development Center.

PRESS ASSOCIATIONS

Sindicato dos Jornalistas de Timor-Leste (SJTL): Rua Dom Aleixo Corte-Real, Bebora, Dili; tel. 7248549; e-mail sjti@yahoo.com; f. 2001; Pres. RODOLFO DE SOUSA.

Timor Lorosae Journalists' Association (TLJA): Rua de Caicoli, Dili; tel. 3324047; fax 3327505; e-mail ajtl_tlja@hotmail.com; f. 1999; Co-ordinator OTELIO OTE; Pres. VIRGÍLIO DA SILVA GUTERRES.

Broadcasting and Communications

TELECOMMUNICATIONS

In July 2002 the Government granted a consortium led by Portugal Telecom a 15-year concession permitting it to establish and operate Timor-Leste's telecommunications systems. Under the terms of the concession, the consortium agreed to provide every district in Timor-Leste with telecommunications services at the most inexpensive tariffs viable within 15 months. At the expiry of the concession in 2017, the telecommunications system was to be transferred to government control. In 2011 the Government announced plans for the liberalization of the telecommunications sector. Having reached an agreement with Timor-Leste Telecom on ending the latter's monopoly, in July 2012 the Government granted telecommunications licences to two companies: Viettel Global Investment JSC (Viettel) and PT Telekomunikasi Indonesia International (Telin). Both companies reportedly commenced operating in early 2013. A new regulatory authority, the Autoridade Nacional de Communicações, was also to be created.

Telin Timor-Leste: Timor Plaza, 4th Floor, Rua Presidente Nicolau Lobato, Comoro, Dili; tel. 737373; fax 747474; internet www .telkomcel.tl; f. 2012; subsidiary of PT Telekomunikasi Indonesia International; commenced provision of mobile telecommunications services under the brand Telkomcel in early 2013.

Timor-Leste Telecom (TT): Sala No. 7, Hotel Timor, Av. dos Mártires da Pátria, POB 135, Dili; tel. 3303000; fax 3303419; e-mail info@timortelecom.tp; internet www.timortelecom.tp; f. 2002; jt venture mainly operated by Portugal Telecom; provides telecommunications services in Timor-Leste; Chair. FRANCISCO PADINHA; CEO Capt. MANUEL AMARO; 114 employees.

BROADCASTING

Following independence, the UN Mission of Support in East Timor (UNMISET) transferred control of public television and radio in Timor-Leste to the new Government. In 2003 a Public Broadcasting Service was established, controlled by an independent board of directors.

Radio

There are 18 radio stations operating in Timor-Leste, including community radio stations for each of the country's 13 districts. In addition to the public service, Radio Timor-Leste, the Roman Catholic Church operates a radio station, Radio Kamanak, while a third populist station, Voz Esperança, broadcasts in Dili. A fourth radio station, Radio Falintil FM, also operates in Dili and in October 2003 the Christian station Voice FM was established. In 2000 the US radio station Voice of America began broadcasting to Timor-Leste seven days a week in English, Portuguese and Bahasa Indonesia.

Radio Timor-Leste (RTL): Rua de Caicoli, Dili; tel. 3321826; e-mail radio@rttl.org; internet www.radiotvtl.com; fmrly Radio UNTAET; name changed as above in 2002; broadcasts mainly in Bahasa Indonesia, but also in English, Portuguese and Tetum, to an estimated 90% of Timor-Leste's population; Dir of Programming ROSARIO MARTINS.

Television

TV Timor-Leste (TVTL): Rua de Caicoli, Dili; tel. 3321825; e-mail tv@rttl.org; internet www.radiotvtl.com; f. 2000 as Televisaun Timor Lorosa'e by UNTAET; adopted present name in May 2002; broadcasts in Tetum and Portuguese; Gen. Man. ANTONIO DIAZ.

Finance

(cap. = capital; res = reserves; dep. = deposits; brs = branches)

BANKING

The Banco Central de Timor-Leste (Central Bank of Timor-Leste) was established in September 2011. Central banking functions were previously carried out by the Banking & Payments Authority of East Timor (from 2001–11) and the Central Payments Office (2000-01).

Banco Central de Timor-Leste: Av. Bispo Medeiros, POB 59, Dili; tel. 3313712; fax 3313713; e-mail info@bancocentral.tl; internet www .bancocentral.tl; f. 2011; regulates and supervises Timor-Leste's financial system, formulates and implements payments system policies, provides banking services to Timor-Leste's administration and foreign official institutions, manages fiscal reserves; Gov. ABRAÃO F. DE VASCONSELOS.

Banco Nacional de Comércio de Timor-Leste (BNCTL): Av. Martires da Patria, Mandarin, Dili; tel. 3339186; fax 3310444; e-mail mail@bnctl.com; internet www.bnctl.com; f. 2002.

Foreign Banks

Australia and New Zealand Banking Group Ltd (ANZ) (Australia): Av. Bidau Lecidere, POB 264, Dili; tel. 3324800; fax 3324822; e-mail easttimor@anz.com; internet www.anz.com/timorleste; retail and commercial banking services; Country Head CHRIS DURMAN; CEO BRIAN ROBB.

Banco Nacional Ultramarino (Portugal): Edif. BNU, 12–13 Av. Presidente Nicolau Lobato, Dili; tel. 3300000; fax 3323994; e-mail cgd.timor@cgd.pt; internet www.bnu.tl; wholly owned subsidiary of Caixa Geral de Depósitos, Portugal; Gen. Man. FERNANDO TORRÃO ALVES; 9 brs.

PT Bank Mandiri (Persero) (Indonesia): 12 Av. Presidente Nicolau Lobato, Colmera, Dili; tel. 3317777; fax 3317444; e-mail dili_timorleste@bankmandiri.co.id; Group Chair. EDWIN GERUNGAN.

Trade and Industry

GOVERNMENT AGENCIES

Autoridade Nacional do Petróleo—ANP (National Petroleum Authority): Ground Floor, East Wing, Pálacio do Governo, POB 113, Farol, Dili; tel. 3324098; fax 3324082; e-mail info@anp-tl.org; internet www.anp-tl.org; f. 2008; responsible for management of govt petroleum revenues; Pres. GUALDINO DO CARMO DA SILVA.

Direcção Nacional Politica do Recursos Naturais: 1st Floor, Fomento Bldg, Mandarin, POB 171, Dili; tel. and fax 3317143; e-mail amandio_gusmao@yahoo.com.au; internet www.timor-leste.gov.tl/ EMRD; Dir AMANDIO GUSMÃO SOARES.

Timor Gás & Petróleo Empresa Pública (Timor GAP EP): Dili; f. 2011; responsible for management of the country's petroleum resources.

TradeInvest Timor-Leste: Memorial Hall, Av. Praia dos Coqueros Farol, Dili 8000; tel. 3331084; fax 3331087; e-mail tradeinvest_tl@ yahoo.com; f. 2005 to encourage devt of entrepreneurship within Timor-Leste.

UTILITIES

As a result of the civil conflict in 1999, some 13–23 power stations were reported to require repairs ranging from moderate maintenance to almost complete rehabilitation. The rehabilitation of the power sector was funded largely by foreign donors. By July 2003 31 generators had been restored, supplying electricity to Dili, as well as to 12 districts and 33 sub-districts, but supplies of electricity remained intermittent. More than 50% of the capital budget for the period 2009–12 was allocated to a national programme of electrification.

Electricidade de Timor-Leste (EDTL): EDTL Bldg, Rua Estrada de Balide, Caicoli, Dili; tel. 3339254; fax 7230095; e-mail virgiliofguterres@hotmail.com; govt dept; responsible for power generation, distribution and financial management of power sector in Timor-Leste; transferred to external management in 2002; Dir VIRGILIO GUTERRES.

CO-OPERATIVES

Cooperativa Café Timor (CCT): 16 Rua Barros Gomes, Dili; tel. 3313139; e-mail boycedjs@gmail.com; f. 2000; produces and exports organic coffee, cacao, cassava, vanilla, cloves and pepper; also provides information and advisory services for mem. farmers; Gen. Man. SISTO MONIZ PIEDADE; 21,558 mems.

Cooperativa Fera Nakukun: Rua Vila Guico, Loes, Guico, Maubara; tel. 07358236 (mobile); 100% Timor-owned; fresh food supplier.

TRADE UNIONS

Konfederasaun Sindikatu Timor-Leste (KSTL) (Timor-Leste Trade Union Confederation): Av. Presidente Nicolao Lobato, Colmera, Dili; tel. 7239824; e-mail kstl.union@gmail.com; f. 2001; represents seven unions, comprising c. 4,700 workers within the press, teaching, nursing, construction, agricultural, maritime and transport sectors; Pres. JOSÉ DA CONCEIÇÃO DA COSTA.

Transport

ROADS

In 2010 the World Bank reported that the road network in Timor-Leste was an estimated 6,040 km in length, of which 1,430 km linked district centres and 870 km connected to larger administrative areas. There were 3,020 km of roads providing access to rural areas. In 2009 the Asian Development Bank approved the Road Network Development Sector Project for Timor-Leste, which included plans for rehabilitating 230 km of national roads and the development of a programme of road maintenance.

SHIPPING

Timor-Leste's maritime infrastructure includes ports at Dili, Carabela and Com, smaller wharves at Oecusse (Oekussi) and Liquiça (Likisia), and slip-landing structures in Oecusse, Batugade and Suai. In November 2001, following its reconstruction, the management of the port at Dili was transferred to the Government.

Port Authority of Timor-Leste (APORTIL): Av. de Portugal, Dili; tel. 3317264; f. 2003.

Principal Shipping Companies

Everise Freight Forwarding Inc: 2 Rua Belarmino Lobo, Dili; tel. 3324844; fax 3312856; e-mail everisedili@yahoo.com.

SDV Logistics (East Timor): Av. Presidente Nicolau Lobato, Bairro dos Grilos, POB 398, Dili; tel. 3322818; fax 3324077; e-mail dili@sdv.com; internet www.sdv.com; f. 1999; freight forwarder, shipping agent and customs broker; Ferguson Seacabs (a subsidiary of the Ferguson Group) and Swire Shipping (operated by China Navigation Company Pte Ltd) announced partnerships with SDV in 2012; Gen. Man. JÉRÔME PETIT.

CIVIL AVIATION

Timor-Leste has two international airports and eight grass runways. In June 2001 Dili Express Pte was the first Timor-based company to begin international flights, with a service to Singapore. Air North operates regular flights from Australia (Darwin) to Dili.

Civil Aviation Authority (AACTL): Dili; tel. 3317110; fax 3317111; e-mail henriques_sabino@yahoo.com; govt authority responsible for overall planning, implementation and operation of aviation services in Timor-Leste; Dir ROMUALDO DA SILVA.

Air Timor: Aeroporto Presidente Nicolau Lobato, POB 888, Dili; tel. 3312777; fax 3312888; e-mail maria.dacosta@air-timor.com; internet www.air-timor.com; f. 2008 as Austasia Airlines; name changed as above in 2010; operates services between Dili and Singapore in collaboration with SilkAir.

Tourism

In 2011 some 50,239 people visited the country. Although the tourism sector remains relatively undeveloped, the capital Dili and Atauro Island are popular tourist destinations. The country's first national park, Nino Konis Santana National Park, was established in 2007 and aims to protect a number of endangered species, including 25 endemic birds. The park encompasses more than 123,600 ha, including a marine area of 55,600 ha, which contains a globally important biodiversity of coral and reef fish.

Turismo de Timor-Leste: Rua Dom Aleixo Corte-Real, Bebora, Dili; tel. 3310371; fax 3339179; e-mail info@tourismtimorleste.com; internet www.tourismtimorleste.com; f. 2002; National Dir of Tourism JOSÉ QUINTAS.

Defence

As assessed at November 2012, the Timor-Leste Defence Force (Forças Defesa Timor Lorosae—Falintil-FDTL) comprised 1,250 army personnel and a naval element of 80. Following the successful conduct of presidential and legislative elections in mid-2012, the UN Integrated Mission in Timor-Leste (UNMIT) formally restored full policing duties to the national security forces in October. UNMIT completed its mandate and withdrew from Timor-Leste on 31 December that year. In March 2013 the few remaining personnel of the Australian-led International Stabilisation Force also left the country (the force's mission having been completed in November 2012).

Commander-in-Chief: Maj.-Gen. LERE ANAN TIMUR.

Education

According to UN estimates, the adult literacy rate was 58.3% in 2010. In 2004/05 there were 6,987 pre-primary school students, 177,970 primary school students, 50,014 lower secondary school students and 24,808 upper secondary school students in the country. By 2009/10 the number of students enrolled in primary schools had increased to 230,175, the number of lower secondary school students had risen to 60,591, and the number of upper secondary school students had reached 40,910. In 2008/09 there were an estimated 16,727 students engaged in tertiary education, principally at the National University of Timor-Leste. In 2011 enrolment in primary schools included 90% (males 91%, females 90%) of students in the relevant age-group, while the comparable ratio for secondary education was 39% (males 37%, females 41%). Expenditure by central government on education in 2011 was US $99.4m., equivalent to 6.2% of total central government expenditure. In 2007 the Government introduced an Education Reform Plan with the aim of providing nine years of free and compulsory education.

TOGO

Introductory Survey

LOCATION, CLIMATE, LANGUAGE, RELIGION, FLAG, CAPITAL

The Togolese Republic lies in West Africa, forming a narrow strip stretching north from a coastline of about 50 km (30 miles) on the Gulf of Guinea. It is bordered by Ghana to the west, by Benin to the east, and by Burkina Faso to the north. The climate in the coastal area is hot and humid, with an annual average temperature of 27°C (81°F); rainfall in this zone averages 875 mm (34.4 ins) per year, and is heaviest during May–October. Precipitation in the central region is heaviest in May–June and in October, and in the north, where the average annual temperature is 30°C (86°F), there is a rainy season from July to September. The official languages are French, Kabiyé and Ewe. About one-half of the population follows animist beliefs, while about 35% are Christians and 15% Muslims. The national flag (approximate proportions 3 by 5) has five equal horizontal stripes, alternately green and yellow, with a square red canton, containing a five-pointed white star, in the upper hoist. The capital is Lomé.

CONTEMPORARY POLITICAL HISTORY

Historical Context

Togoland, of which modern Togo was formerly a part, became a German colony in 1894. Shortly after the outbreak of the First World War, the colony was occupied by French and British forces. After the war, a League of Nations mandate divided Togoland into two administrative zones, with France controlling the larger eastern section, while the United Kingdom governed the west. The partition of Togoland split the homeland of the Ewe people, who inhabit the southern part of the territory, and this has been a continuing source of friction. After the Second World War, French and British Togoland became UN Trust Territories. In May 1956 a UN-supervised plebiscite in British Togoland produced, despite Ewe opposition, majority support for a merger with the neighbouring territory of the Gold Coast, then a British colony, in an independent state. The region accordingly became part of Ghana in the following year. In October 1956, in another plebiscite, French Togoland voted to become an autonomous republic, with internal self-government, within the French Community. Togo's foremost political parties at that time were the Comité de l'Unité Togolaise (usually known as the Unité Togolaise—UT), led by Sylvanus Olympio, and the Parti Togolais du Progrès (PTP), led by Nicolas Grunitzky, Olympio's brother-in-law. In 1956 Grunitzky became Prime Minister in the first autonomous Government, but in April 1958 a UN-supervised election was won by the UT. Olympio became Prime Minister and led Togo to full independence on 27 April 1960.

At elections in April 1961 Olympio became Togo's first President, while the UT was elected (unopposed) to all 51 seats in the Assemblée nationale. At the same time a referendum approved a new Constitution. On 13 January 1963 the UT regime was overthrown by a military revolt, in which Olympio was killed. Grunitzky subsequently assumed the presidency on a provisional basis. A referendum in May approved another Constitution, confirmed Grunitzky as President and elected a new legislature from a single list of candidates, giving equal representation to the four main political parties.

Grunitzky was deposed by a bloodless military coup, led by Lt-Col (later Gen.) Etienne (Gnassingbé) Eyadéma, the Army Chief of Staff, on 13 January 1967. Eyadéma, a member of the Kabiyé ethnic group, who had taken a prominent part in the 1963 rising, assumed the office of President in April. Political parties were banned, and the President ruled by decree. In November 1969 a new ruling party, the Rassemblement du Peuple Togolais (RPT), was founded, led by Eyadéma.

In Togo's first elections for 16 years, held on 30 December 1979, Eyadéma (the sole candidate) was confirmed as President of the Republic for a seven-year term. At the same time a new Constitution was overwhelmingly endorsed, while the list of 67 candidates for a single-party Assemblée nationale was approved by 96% of votes cast. On 13 January 1980 Eyadéma proclaimed the 'Third Republic'. In December 1986 President Eyadéma was re-elected, unopposed, for a further seven-year term.

Domestic Political Affairs

In December 1990 a new constitution was drafted, which envisaged, inter alia, a plurality of political parties. Meanwhile, several recently established, unofficial opposition movements formed a co-ordinating organization, the Front des Associations pour le Renouveau (FAR), led by Yawovi Agboyibo, to campaign for the immediate introduction of a multi-party political system. Eyadéma subsequently agreed to implement a general amnesty for political dissidents and to permit the legalization of political organizations. Following instances of violent unrest in April 1991, Eyadéma, fearing a civil conflict between the Kabiyé and Ewe ethnic groups (the Government and armed forces were composed overwhelmingly of members of the first group, while opposition groups for the most part represented the Ewe people), announced that a new constitution would be introduced within one year, and that multi-party legislative elections would be organized. At the end of the month it was announced that the FAR was to be disbanded. Agboyibo subsequently formed his own party, the Comité d'Action pour le Renouveau (CAR), which in May became one of 10 parties to enter into a Front de l'Opposition Démocratique (FOD, later renamed the Coalition de l'Opposition Démocratique—COD).

Following the organization of a general strike by the FOD, the Government agreed, in June 1991, that a 'national conference' would be held, with the power to choose a transitional Prime Minister and to establish a transitional legislative body. The conference opened in July; however, when it adopted resolutions suspending the Constitution, dissolving the Assemblée nationale and giving the conference sovereign power, government representatives withdrew. Subsequently the conference resolved to freeze the assets of the RPT, to transfer most of the powers of the President to a Prime Minister, and to prevent Eyadéma from contesting future elections. In defiance of a decree issued by Eyadéma temporarily suspending proceedings, the conference elected a Prime Minister, Joseph Kokou Koffigoh (a senior lawyer and prominent human rights activist), announced the dissolution of the RPT and the formation of a transitional legislature, the Haut Conseil de la République (HCR). Eyadéma capitulated, signing a decree that proclaimed Koffigoh as transitional Prime Minister. In September Koffigoh formed a transitional Government, most of the members of which had not previously held office: he himself assumed the defence portfolio.

Following a number of interventions by members of the armed forces, in August 1992 the HCR restored to Eyadéma the power to preside over the Council of Ministers and on 1 September the transitional Government was dissolved. Later that month a new transitional Government, led by Koffigoh, was appointed, including representatives of 10 parties; the most influential ministries were allocated to members of the RPT. On 27 September a new Constitution was approved in a referendum by 98.1% of the votes cast. At the end of the month, however, it was announced that local, legislative and presidential elections, initially scheduled to have been held in June, were to be further postponed. In October eight opposition parties announced the formation of a 'Patriotic Front', to be led by the leader of the Union Togolaise pour la Démocratie (UTD), Edem Kodjo, and Agboyibo.

In January 1993 Eyadéma dissolved the Government, reappointing Koffigoh as Prime Minister, and stated that he would appoint a new government of national unity to organize elections. His action provoked protests by the opposition parties, who claimed that, according to the Constitution, the HCR should appoint a Prime Minister since the transition period had now expired. In the same month two ministers representing the French and German Governments visited Togo to offer mediation in the political crisis. During their visit at least 20 people were killed when police opened fire on anti-Government protesters. Thousands of Togolese subsequently fled from Lomé, many seeking refuge in Benin or Ghana. In February inter-Togolese discussions organized by the French and German Governments in France failed when the presidential delegation withdrew after one day. In that month the French, German and US Governments suspended their programmes of aid to Togo. A new Government, in which supporters of Eyadéma retained the principal posts, was formed in February.

In April 1993 a new electoral schedule was announced, envisaging elections to the presidency and the legislature in July and August, respectively. The RPT designated Eyadéma as its presidential candidate. An independent, nine-member Commission Electorale Nationale (CEN) was to be established, to include three members nominated by the opposition parties. Three candidates eventually contested the presidential election held on 25 August at which Eyadéma was reported to have obtained 96.5% of the votes cast. French election observers concluded that the poll had not been satisfactorily conducted.

1994 legislative elections

Legislative elections were finally held on 6 and 20 February 1994. Despite the murder of an elected CAR representative after the first round, and violent incidents at polling stations during the second round, international observers expressed themselves satisfied with the conduct of the elections. The opposition won a narrow victory in the polls, with the CAR winning 36 seats and the UTD seven; the RPT obtained 35 seats and two other smaller pro-Eyadéma parties won three. During March Eyadéma consulted the main opposition parties on the formation of a new government. In late March the CAR and the UTD reached an agreement on the terms of their alliance and jointly proposed the candidacy of Agboyibo for Prime Minister. In March and April the Supreme Court declared the results of the legislative elections invalid in three constituencies (in which the CAR had won two seats and the UTD one) and ordered by-elections. In April Eyadéma nominated Kodjo as Prime Minister. The CAR subsequently declared that it would not participate in an administration formed by Kodjo. Kodjo took office on 25 April; his Government, appointed in May, comprised eight members of the RPT and other pro-Eyadéma parties, three members of the UTD, and eight independents.

At the by-elections, conducted on 4 and 18 August 1996 in the presence of 22 international observers, the RPT won control of all three constituencies. Consequently, the RPT and its allies were able to command a majority in the legislature, thus precipitating the resignation of the Kodjo administration. On 20 August Eyadéma appointed Kwassi Klutse, hitherto Minister of Planning and Territorial Development, as Prime Minister, and the new Council of Ministers, appointed in late August, comprised almost exclusively supporters of Eyadéma. In November the Union pour la justice et la démocratie, which held two seats in the legislature, announced that it was officially to merge with the RPT, thus giving the RPT an overall majority, with 41 seats.

In September 1997 a new electoral code was approved, providing for a CEN comprising nine members, chaired by the President of the Court of Appeal and including four members appointed by the opposition. The CAR, however, boycotted the legislative session in protest at the Government's refusal to reveal the findings of a report by a mission of the European Union (EU, see p. 281) on the country's electoral process. Later that month opposition parties, led by the CAR and the Union des Forces de Changement (UFC), organized a demonstration in Lomé in protest at the new electoral law and condemned as fraudulent the Government's preparations for the forthcoming presidential election.

The presidential election held on 21 June 1998 proceeded amid accusations of electoral malpractice, and on the following day counting of votes was halted without explanation, reportedly when the early returns showed Eyadéma to be in second place. Four members of the CEN resigned the same day, alleging intimidation. The Minister of the Interior and Security, Gen. Seyi Memene, announced that he had assumed responsibility for the ballot count, and that Eyadéma had been re-elected President with 52.1% of the valid votes cast. Following the announcement of the result, violent protests erupted throughout Lomé. The USA condemned the conduct of the election, and appealed to the Government to respect its own laws and electoral code, while the EU decided not to recognize the result, which was, none the less, confirmed by the Constitutional Court.

In September 1998 Klutse announced his new Council of Ministers. Despite Eyadéma's stated intention to form a government of national unity, no opposition figures were willing to be included.

Elections to the Assemblée nationale took place on 21 March 1999, contested only by the RPT and by two small parties loyal to Eyadéma, as well as by 12 independent candidates. (The principal opposition parties had boycotted the polling.) The Constitutional Court ruled that the RPT had won 77 seats, and that independent candidates had taken two seats. By-elections were to take place in two constituencies in which voting had been invalidated. (Both of these seats were subsequently won by the RPT.) Despite international criticism, Eyadéma rejected demands for fresh elections. In April Klutse tendered his Government's resignation; in May Eugene Koffi Adoboli was appointed Prime Minister.

In May 1999 the human rights organization Amnesty International published a report detailing numerous abuses of human rights committed by Togolese security forces, alleging that hundreds of political opponents of Eyadéma had been killed following the 1998 presidential election. In late July 1999 Eyadéma (who rejected the validity of the report) urged the UN and the Organization of African Unity (OAU, now the African Union—AU, see p. 191) to assist in the establishment of an international commission of inquiry into the allegations; such a commission was established in June 2000.

Opposition to Eyadéma

Discussions between the Government and opposition began in Lomé in July 1999, with the assistance of four international facilitators, representing France, Germany, the EU and La Francophonie. Eyadéma's announcement that he would not stand for re-election in 2003 and that new legislative elections would be held was widely credited with breaking the deadlock in negotiations. After the opposition had agreed to accept Eyadéma's victory in the presidential election, an accord was signed on 29 July 1999 by all the parties involved in negotiations. The accord made provision for the creation of an independent electoral body and for the establishment of a code of conduct to regulate political activity.

The first meeting took place in August 1999 of the 24-member Comité Paritaire de Suivi (CPS) responsible for the implementation of the accord, composed of an equal number of opposition and pro-Eyadéma representatives, and also including intermediaries from the EU. Harry Octavianus Olympio, the Minister for the Promotion of Democracy and the Rule of Law, was appointed to head the CPS. An agreement on announcing election results was reached in September, and in December agreement was achieved on a revised electoral code, providing for the establishment of an independent electoral commission. In April 2000 Eyadéma obliged the Assemblée nationale to accept the new electoral code. The EU subsequently offered to provide financial support for the elections, which were scheduled to be held later in 2000. The 20 members of the new Commission Electorale Nationale Indépendante (CENI) were named in June, and in July Arthème Ahoomey-Zounou of the Convergence Patriotique Panafricaine (CPP—formed in 1999 by the amalgamation of the UTD and three smaller parties, and headed by Edem Kodjo) was elected as President of the CENI.

In August 2000 Adoboli was overwhelmingly defeated in a legislative vote of no confidence and resigned. Eyadéma appointed Agbéyomé Kodjo, hitherto President of the Assemblée nationale, and regarded as a close ally of the President, as Prime Minister. In January 2001 the CENI announced that the legislative elections would be held in two rounds, on 14 and 28 October 2001, using the disputed electoral registers from the 1998 presidential election.

In February 2002 the Assemblée nationale approved amendments to electoral legislation; notably, henceforth all candidates for legislative elections were required to have been continuously resident in Togo for six months prior to elections, with presidential candidates to have been resident for a continuous 12 months. The CENI was also to be reduced in size from 20 to 10 members, and decisions were to be taken by a two-thirds' majority, instead of the four-fifths' majority required hitherto. These amendments led to a further postponement of the elections, which had been scheduled to take place in March. These measures attracted international disapproval, notably prompting the EU to suspend aid intended to finance the polls. In February five opposition parties issued a joint communiqué accusing the Government of having broken the conditions of the accord signed in July 1999, and in early March 2002 they rejected an invitation by Kodjo to nominate representatives to the CENI. The Government consequently announced that no date for the legislative elections could be announced until a complete electoral commission had been formed. In late March 10 opposition parties, which had not been party to the accord signed in 1999 and were therefore excluded from the CPS, announced the formation of the Coordination des Partis Politiques de l'Opposition Constructive, headed by Harry

Octavianus Olympio, who had also assumed the leadership of the Rassemblement pour le Soutien de la Démocratie et du Développement (RSDD). These 'constructive opposition' parties were prepared to participate in the electoral process and form alliances with the RPT. In mid-May 2002 a committee of seven judges (the Comité de Sept Magistrats—C-7), charged with monitoring the proposed legislative elections, was appointed. At the end of May the EU announced that it would not renew funding for the three facilitators it supported in Togo, in view of the continued lack of progress towards democracy.

In June 2002 Eyadéma dismissed Kodjo as Prime Minister and replaced him with Koffi Sama, the erstwhile Secretary-General of the RPT; a new Government, which included several principal members of the former administration, was appointed in July. Kodjo subsequently issued a statement criticizing the 'monarchic, despotic' regime of Eyadéma. The state prosecutor filed a suit against Kodjo on charges of disseminating false information and demeaning the honour of the President; Kodjo was expelled from the RPT and subsequently left Togo, taking up residence in France.

In early October 2002 the Assemblée nationale was dissolved, pending elections on 27 October. Prior to this date nine opposition parties that had declined to participate in the elections announced the formation of a new alliance, the Coalition des Forces Démocrates (CFD); members of the grouping included the CAR, the CPP and the UFC, in addition to a faction of 'renovators' within the RPT (which subsequently became the Pacte Socialiste pour le Renouveau—PSR). In the event, the RPT won 72 seats (46 unopposed) and the RSDD three, while three other parties won a total of five seats, and one independent candidate was elected. The C-7 estimated electoral turn-out at 67.4%, although the CFD claimed that only 10% of the electorate had voted. Eyadéma reappointed Sama as Prime Minister in mid-November; a new Government was formed in early December. All ministers were members of the RPT, with the exception of Harry Octavianus Olympio, who was appointed Minister responsible for Relations with Parliament.

In December 2002 the Assemblée nationale approved several constitutional amendments regarding the eligibility of presidential candidates. The restriction that had limited the President to serving two terms of office was removed, and the age of eligibility was reduced from 45 to 35 years. (It was widely believed that these measures were intended to permit Eyadéma to serve a further term of office, and also to permit the possible presidential candidacy of Eyadéma's son, Faure Gnassingbé.) Candidates were henceforth to be required to hold solely Togolese citizenship. In February 2003 the UFC, having opposed the constitutional amendments, announced its withdrawal from the CFD, after other parties within the grouping agreed to appoint representatives to the CENI prior to the holding of a presidential election later in the year. In April Eyadéma confirmed that he was to seek re-election; however, in May the CENI rejected the candidacy of Gilchrist Olympio, the son of the former President who had recently returned to Togo. Emmanuel Bob Akitani, the First Vice-President of the UFC, was announced as his party's candidate, following Olympio's debarment.

Eyadéma was returned to office in the presidential election held on 1 June 2003, receiving 57.8% of the votes cast. His nearest rival was Bob Akitani, with 33.7% of votes. Several of the defeated candidates declared that the election had been conducted fraudulently, although observers from the Economic Community of West African States (ECOWAS), the AU and the Conseil de l'Entente refuted these claims. Eyadéma was inaugurated for a further term of office on 20 June. Sama was reappointed as premier on 1 July, apparently with instructions from Eyadéma to form a government of national unity. However, most opposition parties reportedly declined representation in the administration, and the new Government, formed on 29 July, included only two representatives of the 'constructive opposition'. Faure Gnassingbé received his first ministerial posting, as Minister of Equipment, Mines, Posts and Telecommunications.

Talks between the EU and the Government on the conditions for a resumption of economic co-operation commenced in April 2004; the Government pledged to implement 22 measures, including the introduction of more transparent conditions for elections, the revision of the press code and a guarantee that political parties would be granted the freedom to conduct their activities without fear of harassment. In August the Assemblée nationale adopted amendments to the press code, notably repealing the powers of the Ministry of the Interior, Security and Decentralization to order the closure or seizure of newspapers.

In November 2004 the EU announced that it was to resume partial economic co-operation with Togo, in view of progress towards fulfilment of the 22 conditions established in April. It was emphasized, however, that the full resumption of development aid was dependent on the holding of free and fair elections within six months. In December Eyadéma announced that legislative elections would be held during the first half of 2005. In January 2005 the Assemblée nationale adopted legislation introducing several amendments to the electoral code in accordance with the demands of the EU, notably strengthening the powers of the CENI and increasing its membership to 13, to include two representatives of civil society.

The death of Eyadéma

On 5 February 2005 Prime Minister Sama announced that President Eyadéma had died while being transported out of the country for medical treatment. The Togolese military closed the country's borders, thus preventing Fambaré Natchaba, the President of the Assemblée nationale, who, according to the Constitution, was to assume the functions of head of state pending elections to be held within 60 days, from returning to Togo from a visit to Europe. Hours later it was announced that the Constitution had been suspended and that the armed forces had pledged their allegiance to Eyadéma's son, Faure Gnassingbé, as the new head of state. The following day an extraordinary session of the Assemblée nationale was convened, at which deputies voted to remove Natchaba from his post as President of the legislature and appoint Gnassingbé in his place. The Assemblée also approved a constitutional amendment authorizing an interim President to serve the remainder of the deceased predecessor's term, rather than arranging elections within 60 days (Eyadéma's term was due to expire in June 2008).

Gnassingbé was formally sworn in as President of Togo on 7 February 2005. The circumstances of his succession provoked domestic and international condemnation: the inauguration ceremony was boycotted by diplomats from Nigeria, the EU, the USA and the UN, while the AU and ECOWAS demanded that Gnassingbé stand down to allow fair and democratic elections to be held. Meanwhile, the Togolese opposition called a two-day strike for 8 and 9 February, in protest at the perceived coup; however, the strike was only partially observed. Subsequent protests resulted in at least four deaths and several injuries from clashes with security forces, who allegedly used tear gas and live ammunition to disperse protesters.

Following intense diplomatic pressure from ECOWAS, and from Nigeria in particular, Gnassingbé announced on 18 February 2005 that elections would be held within 60 days—however, he declined to stand down before that time. On 21 February the Assemblée nationale voted to reverse the constitutional amendments adopted on 6 February. Judging these concessions to be insufficient, ECOWAS imposed an arms embargo on Togo and travel restrictions on members of the Government, while the ambassadors of ECOWAS states were withdrawn from Lomé. The AU declared its support for the imposition of sanctions, while the USA announced that it would terminate all military assistance to Togo unless Gnassingbé stood down. On 25 February it was revealed that Gnassingbé had been appointed President of the RPT, and endorsed as the party's candidate in the forthcoming presidential election. Later that day Gnassingbé announced that he was resigning from the post of President of the Assemblée nationale, and hence from the position of interim President, stating that he did not wish to compromise the transparency and fairness of the election. Abass Bonfoh, Vice-President of the Assemblée nationale, became the acting head of state. The announcement was welcomed by ECOWAS, which lifted its sanctions.

The date of the election was subsequently set for 24 April 2005, although the opposition protested that it would be impossible to organize fair and transparent elections in such a brief period of time. (The EU also expressed doubts that fair elections could be held so promptly, and declined to send electoral observers.) Nevertheless, the radical opposition, which had grouped itself into a coalition of six parties (including, in addition to the four parties of the Front Uni de l'Opposition, the PSR and the UFC), subsequently announced that it would present a single candidate, Bob Akitani. Gnassingbé's candidature was supported by five small parties of the 'constructive opposition' as well as by the RPT.

On 11 April 2005 a peaceful demonstration in the capital was reported to have been attended by several thousand supporters of the opposition, who demanded that polling be postponed. On 16 April at least seven people were reported to have been killed, and some 150 injured, in clashes between supporters of the opposition and supporters of the youth wing of the RPT in Lomé.

The presidential election was held, as scheduled, on 24 April 2005, amid ongoing tensions. Although widespread violence was not reported on polling day, the seizure of ballot boxes, following the closure of polls, in areas of Lomé in which the opposition was known to have considerable support, and in other areas of the interior, was reported. Preliminary results, issued by the CENI on 26 April, indicated that Gnassingbé had been elected as President by a significant majority. The announcement of Gnassingbé's victory precipitated widespread rioting, particularly in Lomé and in southern regions, with some reports suggesting that as many as 100 people had died in the violence. (According to official figures, 22 people were killed in the rioting.) Meanwhile, Gilchrist Olympio, who had returned to Togo in March, declared that Bob Akitani had been the legitimate winner of polling, claiming that the opposition candidate had received more than 70% of the votes cast. However, on 27 April ECOWAS observers stated that the irregularities in the conduct of the election had not been such as to invalidate the declared results. By early May more than 20,000 Togolese were reported to have fled the country for either Benin or Ghana. On 3 May the Constitutional Court announced the final results of the election, which were not substantially different from the preliminary figures declared by the CENI; Gnassingbé was attributed 60.2% of the votes cast, compared with the 38.3% awarded to Bob Akitani. Some 63% of the electorate were reported to have voted. Gnassingbé was inaugurated as President on 4 May. Although the European Parliament adopted a resolution criticizing the conduct of the election, the election result was generally accepted by the international community.

The Gnassingbé presidency

On 19 May 2005 President Olusegun Obasanjo of Nigeria chaired a reconciliation summit in Abuja, the Nigerian capital, under the aegis of ECOWAS and the AU, which was attended by Gnassingbé, Gilchrist Olympio and other opposition leaders, as well as the heads of state of Benin, Burkina Faso, Gabon, Ghana and Niger. (Bob Akitani was unable to participate owing to ill health.) The talks ended without agreement, however, as the radical opposition continued to reject the legitimacy of Gnassingbé's victory and demanded a full investigation of alleged election irregularities as a precondition for entering into any power-sharing arrangement. In late May the AU removed sanctions against Togo, declaring that it considered conditions in Togo to be constitutional. Meanwhile, refugees continued to flee Togo, amid reports that opposition supporters were being arrested or kidnapped by the security forces. By late May 34,416 Togolese refugees (19,272 in Benin and 15,144 in Ghana) had been registered by the office of the UN High Commissioner for Refugees (UNHCR). It was estimated that a further 10,000 people had been internally displaced within Togo. Several thousand more people were reported to have fled Togo in subsequent months.

On 8 June 2005 Gnassingbé announced the appointment of former premier Edem Kodjo, regarded as a member of the moderate opposition, as Prime Minister. Later in June the formation of a 30-member Council of Ministers, dominated by the RPT, but also including several representatives of the opposition and of civil society, was announced. Notably, Tchessa Abi of the PSR was appointed as Keeper of the Seals, Minister of Justice; the other five members of the six-party coalition refused to participate and later condemned Abi's acceptance of a ministerial position, deciding to expel the PSR from the coalition. Zarifou Ayéva, the leader of the moderate opposition Parti pour la Démocratie et le Renouveau (which was absorbed into the RPT later in the year), was appointed as Minister of State, Minister of Foreign Affairs and African Integration, while the President's half-brother, Kpatcha Gnassingbé, became Minister-delegate at the Presidency of the Republic, responsible for Defence and Veterans.

The return of refugees was discussed by Gnassingbé and Gilchrist Olympio at a meeting in Rome, Italy, in July 2005, at which the two men also condemned violence and agreed that political prisoners arrested during the electoral process should be released. In September Gnassingbé announced that the holding of legislative elections was to be expedited, and that, in a measure intended to promote national unity, the country's first President, Sylvanus Olympio, was to be officially rehabilitated. In November some 460 political prisoners were released.

In March 2006 the Government announced that, to encourage Togolese refugees to return to their country, no legal proceedings were to be taken against opposition activists suspected of involvement in the unrest in 2005, excepting those involved in 'bloody crimes'; moreover, President Gnassingbé appealed for a formal resumption of the national dialogue between the authorities and the opposition. The inter-Togolese national dialogue, which had broken down following the death of Eyadéma, finally resumed in Lomé in April 2006, with the participation of six political parties (the CAR, the Convention Démocratique des Peuples Africains—Branche Togolaise, the CPP, the Parti pour la Démocratie et le Renouveau, the RPT and the UFC), as well as two civil society organizations and the Government.

On 20 August 2006, following negotiations chaired by the President of Burkina Faso, Blaise Compaoré, the Government signed a comprehensive political accord with the main opposition parties in Lomé that provided for the establishment of a transitional government, which would include members of opposition parties. It also called for the re-establishment of the CENI, which would organize and supervise transparent and democratic elections. (In January 2007 the CENI was approved as the official decision-making body for national elections.) Agboyibo replaced Kodjo as Prime Minister in September 2006 and was tasked with forming a government of national unity and organizing elections for 2007. He announced the formation of his new Council of Ministers later that month. In June 2007 the EU agreed to provide funding to support the forthcoming elections (initially scheduled to take place that month but subsequently postponed until August).

After further delays, legislative elections finally took place on 14 October 2007; the RPT secured 50 of the available 81 seats, the UFC took 27 seats and the CAR four. Voter turn-out was estimated at 95%, and international observers declared the election to have been largely free and fair, despite allegations by opposition parties of procedural irregularities. In November Agboyibo, having completed his task of leading the country through legitimate legislative elections, submitted his resignation; Komlan Mally, hitherto Minister of Towns and Town Planning, was appointed Prime Minister in December and named a new Council of Ministers. Notable dismissals included that of Kpatcha Gnassingbé. The EU had announced in November its resumption of full co-operation with Togo and granted the country €123m. in development aid.

In April 2008 the UN Office of the High Commissioner for Human Rights initiated the process of establishing a truth and reconciliation commission to investigate the political violence that took place in 2005. The commission was finally inaugurated in May 2009, and the first hearings commenced in September 2011. In its final report, released in April 2012, the commission recommended the implementation of electoral, judicial, police and military reforms, with the aim of combating impunity, strengthening human rights, reconciling disparate communities and, ultimately, averting further outbreaks of violence. The commission also urged the authorities to investigate those accused of committing rights abuses.

Mally resigned as Prime Minister on 5 September 2008, and two days later Gnassingbé appointed Gilbert Houngbo, who had previously served as the head of the UN Development Programme in Africa, as his replacement. Houngbo formed a new Council of Ministers later that month.

Kpatcha Gnassingbé was arrested in mid-April 2009 and charged with attempting to overthrow the Government. He had unsuccessfully sought refuge at the US embassy in Lomé after a raid by security forces on his residence, which reportedly resulted in the deaths of two soldiers. Legislation abolishing capital punishment and commuting existing death penalties to life imprisonment was approved by the Assemblée nationale in June.

Recent developments: the 2010 presidential election

Preparations for the presidential election, scheduled to be held in early 2010, dominated political affairs in 2009, and several amendments were made to the electoral law during that year. Some, such as a loosening of the stringent conditions for candidature, were welcomed by the opposition parties, while others, such as the extension, in April, of the mandate of the CENI, were met with considerable disapproval. In August the Assemblée nationale appointed a newly composed CENI to organize the election; however, the UFC and the CAR contested the manner in which the new commission had been appointed and appealed for popular protests. In October the CENI appointment was annulled and, after lengthy discussions, Issifou Taffa Tabiou was chosen by consensus to preside over the body. The opposition parties then threatened to boycott the election if two rounds of voting were not held, and again called for protests, which duly took place in late November. Gilchrist Olympio appealed for renewed demonstrations in January 2010, following talks between all parties and Compaoré's recommendation that a single round of voting be held; however, despite the announcement of a slight delay to the election (from 28 February to 4 March), it was confirmed that the election was to take place in a single round of voting.

In February 2010 the UFC announced the withdrawal of its three members from the CENI, stating that it did not wish to be associated with an 'electoral masquerade'. The party claimed that large numbers of those ineligible to vote, including minors and foreigners, had been added to the electoral register. In an attempt to alleviate opposition concerns over possible electoral fraud, monitors from the EU, the AU and ECOWAS were dispatched to Togo to oversee the election. Gilchrist Olympio, who remained in the USA where he was receiving medical treatment, had confirmed in mid-January that he would not stand in the election, and later that month the Secretary-General of the UFC, Jean-Pierre Fabre, was named as the party's candidate.

The presidential election was duly held on 4 March 2010. According to provisional results released by the CENI on 6 March, Gnassingbé received 60.9% of votes cast, while Fabre was placed second with 33.9%. Agboyibo, representing the CAR, won just 3.0% of the votes. Some 64.5% of the eligible electorate participated in the ballot. The results were immediately disputed by Fabre and several days of protests by supporters of both the UFC and the CAR ensued, necessitating the deployment of an estimated 6,000 police officers. Nevertheless, observers from ECOWAS praised the conduct of the election, while those from the EU declared the poll to have been 'free and transparent'. In mid-March the Constitutional Court announced that it had rejected the appeals of five of the defeated candidates and confirmed Gnassingbé's re-election to the presidency. At the end of March the Government issued a decree prohibiting the staging of any further demonstrations against the results of the elections, although this did not prevent 4,000 protesters from demonstrating in April in Lomé.

Gnassingbé was sworn in to serve a second presidential term on 3 May 2010, and two days later Prime Minister Houngbo announced his resignation and that of the Government. On 9 May Houngbo was reappointed to the premiership and was requested to form a new administration. In late May Gilchrist Olympio signed a political accord on behalf of the UFC on the party's participation in Houngbo's Government, a move that was denounced by Fabre. The composition of the new Council of Ministers was announced two days later; the UFC was allocated seven posts, the most senior being that of Minister of State, Minister of Foreign Affairs and Co-operation, to which Elliott Ohin was appointed. In response, the UFC national bureau, in a statement signed by Fabre, claimed that it had not been consulted on the accord and temporarily suspended Olympio and the seven government ministers from the party. The UFC subsequently split into two factions, led by Fabre and Olympio; the Government announced its recognition of the Olympio faction. In October Fabre proceeded to form a new party, the Alliance Nationale pour le Changement (ANC). In the following month, however, the Constitutional Court ruled that Fabre and eight other deputies belonging to the ANC should relinquish their seats in the Assemblée nationale, based on letters of resignation that they had allegedly sent to the President of the legislature, Abass Bonfoh. Fabre denied the existence of such letters and pledged to challenge the Court's decision. In October 2011 the ECOWAS Court of Justice ruled against the Constitutional Court's actions and appealed to the Government to pay compensation to the nine expelled deputies. The ANC claimed that the ECOWAS directive also ordered the reinstatement of the deputies (and demonstrations were held in the following month in support of this demand), although the RPT disputed this interpretation.

Col Gnama Latta was appointed as Minister of Security and Civil Protection in February 2011, following the designation of the incumbent, Col Atcha Titikpina, as Chief of General Staff of the armed forces two months earlier. Further government changes were effected in March. Following prolonged industrial action by medical professionals demanding better working conditions and the payment of promised bonuses, in June Minister of Health Komlan Mally was replaced by Charles Kondi Agba, who successfully negotiated a settlement to the dispute later that month.

Proposed restrictions on public protests—which would oblige organizers, under the threat of imprisonment, to secure

government approval before staging such events—attracted strong criticism from opposition parties and prompted anti-Government demonstrations during March 2011. The protests were suppressed by the security forces, leading to violent clashes between the demonstrators and the police. The opposition refused to participate in the legislative vote on the new regulations, but the ruling party's majority in the Assemblée nationale ensured that the bill was approved in May. Cross-party discussions on constitutional and electoral reform, in abeyance since early 2010, recommenced in September 2011, although the ANC and the CAR boycotted the talks.

Former Prime Minister Adoboli received a five-year prison sentence in July 2011 after being convicted, *in absentia*, of embezzling €1.2m. of public funds during his premiership, although he continued to protest his innocence. Two other government officials, including former Minister of Urbanization and Housing Hope Agboli, were found guilty of similar charges and were each sentenced, *in absentia*, to eight years' imprisonment. In September Kpatcha Gnassingbé and Gen. Assani Tidjani, the former Chief of Staff of the National Army, were convicted of orchestrating an attempted coup in 2009 and sentenced to prison terms of 20 years. A further 31 co-defendants, some of whom claimed that they had been tortured while in detention, were also given prison sentences of up to 20 years for their involvement in the alleged coup plot. Kpatcha Gnassingbé vehemently denied the charges, and some commentators expressed their suspicion that the 'coup' had been fabricated by the President in order to remove a potential political rival.

In April 2012 President Gnassingbé announced the dissolution of the RPT and its replacement by a new political party, the Union pour la République. Arthème Kwesi Séléagodji Ahoomey-Zunu of the CPP, the erstwhile minister responsible for trade, was appointed as Prime Minister in July after the resignation of Houngbo earlier that month. Ahoomey-Zunu duly formed a new Government.

In May 2012, in preparation for the forthcoming general election, the Assemblée nationale approved new constituency boundaries and the expansion of the 81-seat legislature to 91 seats. Opposition parties criticized the changes, arguing that they were designed to benefit the governing party, and in June a series of demonstrations were organized in Lomé by the Collectif Sauvons le Togo (CST—'Let's Save Togo' Collective), comprising the ANC and a variety of other political groups. However, the protests soon degenerated into violence, after the police used tear-gas against the demonstrators. Several prominent members of the CST, including former Prime Minister Agbéyomé Kodjo, were arrested in the aftermath of the disorder. Fabre's residence was raided by the police in July, precipitating another anti-Government demonstration later that month. Although the authorities introduced new restrictions on public gatherings in August, further opposition-led protests continued to be held throughout 2012. In January 2013 Kodjo and Fabre were held for questioning, along with other members of the opposition, in connection with two alleged arson attacks; Fabre, who denied any involvement, was charged with conspiracy and destruction of public property in March. The opposition regarded the investigation as politically motivated. Journalists staged protests in early 2013 in response to recently adopted legislation that bestowed the authorities with additional powers over the media. The Constitutional Court abrogated the legislation in March.

In May 2013 the President of the CENI announced that the legislative elections would take place in the first week of July.

Foreign Affairs

Relations with neighbouring Ghana have frequently become strained, as the common border with Togo has periodically been closed in an effort to combat smuggling and to curb political activity by exiles on both sides. In March 1993 and January 1994 the Togolese Government accused Ghana of supporting armed attacks on Eyadéma's residence, reflecting earlier accusations of Ghanaian involvement in unrest in Togo in early 1991. Full diplomatic relations between the two countries, suspended since 1982, were formally resumed in November 1994. In August 2009 the two countries agreed to reconvene their Joint Border Demarcation Commission as a matter of urgency to deal with transborder crime. Following ethnic clashes and land disputes in northern Ghana in May 2010, the Togolese Minister of Security and Civil Protection announced that some 3,500 Ghanaian refugees had fled into Togo and required shelter and food. The UN responded by providing emergency assistance.

Relations with fellow ECOWAS members were jeopardized by the perceived coup by which Gnassingbé assumed power following the death of his father Eyadéma (see The death of Eyadéma). Relations with Nigeria, in particular, were further compromised when the Togolese authorities refused to grant an aeroplane carrying the advance delegation of President Oluse-gun Obasanjo permission to land in Lomé. Nigeria withdrew its ambassador to Togo and imposed restrictions on visits of Togo-lese officials to Nigeria following the incident, anticipating the sanctions imposed by ECOWAS after Gnassingbé initially declined to stand down as interim President in advance of a presidential election. Following Gnassingbé's resignation on 25 February 2005, Nigeria and the other ECOWAS member states lifted their sanctions, returned their ambassadors to Lomé and resumed co-operation with Togo, approving the 24 April date for the presidential election and pledging to provide assistance to ensure the fairness and transparency of the poll.

Political instability and factional violence in Côte d'Ivoire following a disputed presidential election in late 2010 precipi-tated the inflow of up to 7,500 Ivorian refugees into Togo. Alassane Ouattara, who had been sworn in as the new Ivorian President in May 2011 after months of fighting, visited Togo in November and urged the refugees to return home. A repatriation accord was also signed by Togo, Côte d'Ivoire and UNHCR, to expedite the voluntary return of Ivorian refugees.

Togolese military personnel began to arrive in Mali during January 2013 as part of the UN's African-led International Support Mission in Mali (AFISMA). The Togolese Government had pledged to deploy over 700 soldiers to bolster the inter-national effort to suppress the rebel uprising in that country.

CONSTITUTION AND GOVERNMENT

Under the terms of the Constitution that was approved in a national referendum on 27 September 1992, and modified on 31 December 2002, executive power is vested in the President of the Republic, who is directly elected, by universal adult suffrage, for a period of five years and may serve an unlimited number of terms. The legislature is the unicameral Assemblée nationale, whose 81 members are also elected, by universal suffrage, for a five-year period. The Prime Minister is appointed by the Presi-dent from among the majority in the legislature, and the Prime Minister, in consultation with the President, nominates other ministers. For administrative purposes, the country is divided into five regions. It is further divided into 30 prefectures and sub-prefectures.

REGIONAL AND INTERNATIONAL CO-OPERATION

Togo is a member of the African Union (see p. 191), of the Economic Community of West African States (see p. 268) and of the West African organs of the Franc Zone (see p. 339).

Togo became a member of the UN in 1960, and was admitted to the World Trade Organization (WTO, see p. 444) in 1995. The country was elected as a non-permanent member of the UN Security Council in October 2011 and commenced its two-year mandate on 1 January 2012. Togo participates in the Group of 77 (G77, see p. 461) developing countries and is also a member of the International Cocoa Organization (see p. 456) and of the Inter-national Coffee Organization (see p. 456).

ECONOMIC AFFAIRS

In 2011, according to estimates by the World Bank, Togo's gross national income (GNI), measured at average 2009–11 prices, was US $3,441m., equivalent to $560 per head (or $1,030 on an international purchasing-power parity basis). During 2002–11, it was estimated, the population increased at an average annual rate of 2.2%, while gross domestic product (GDP) per head declined by an average of 0.8% per year. Overall GDP increased, in real terms, at an average annual rate of 3.1% in 2002–11; real GDP grew by 3.9% in 2011.

According to World Bank estimates, agriculture (including forestry and fishing) contributed 43.2% of GDP in 2011; in mid-2013 51.5% of the working population were employed in the sector, according to FAO estimates. The principal cash crops are cotton (which contributed 31.5% of earnings from merchandise exports in 2011), coffee and cocoa. Togo has generally been self-sufficient in basic foodstuffs: the principal subsistence crops are cassava, yams, maize, sorghum and rice. Imports of livestock products and fish are necessary to satisfy domestic needs. According to World Bank estimates, during 2002–11 agricultural GDP increased at an average annual rate of 4.5%; agricultural GDP grew by 4.7% in 2011.

According to World Bank estimates, industry (including min-ing, manufacturing, construction and power) contributed 15.9%

of GDP in 2011, and employed 10.1% of the working population in 1990. During 2002–11 industrial GDP increased by an average of 2.6% per year; industrial GDP rose by 4.8% in 2011.

Mining and quarrying contributed 2.9% of GDP in 2010. Togo has the world's richest reserves of first-grade calcium phos-phates. Concerns regarding the high cadmium content of Togo-lese phosphate rock have prompted interest in the development of lower-grade carbon phosphates, which have a less significant cadmium content. Exports of fertilizers provided 5.3% of earn-ings from merchandise exports in 2011. Limestone, diamonds, cement, gold and marble are also exploited. There are, in add-ition, smaller deposits of iron ore, zinc, rutile and platinum. In 1998 marine exploration revealed petroleum and gas deposits within Togo's territorial waters. In October 2002 the Togolese Government, the Hunt Oil Co of the USA and Petronas Carigali of Malaysia signed a joint-venture oil-production agreement, providing for the first offshore drilling in Togolese territorial waters. In October 2010 the Togolese Government and the Italian hydrocarbons company Eni signed two agreements on the exploration of the offshore area around the Dahomey Basin. The GDP of the mining sector was estimated to have declined at an average annual rate of 3.2% in 1991–95. According to the African Development Bank, mining GDP decreased by 0.2% in 2009, but increased by 3.4% in 2010.

According to World Bank estimates, manufacturing contrib-uted 7.8% of GDP in 2011. About 6.6% of the labour force were employed in the sector in 1990. Major companies are engaged in agro-industrial activities, the processing of phosphates, steel-rolling and in the production of cement. An industrial 'free zone' was inaugurated in Lomé in 1990, with the aim of attracting investment by local and foreign interests by offering certain (notably fiscal) advantages in return for guarantees regarding export levels and employment; a second 'free zone' was subse-quently opened, and provision was made for 'free zone' terms to apply to certain businesses operating outside the regions. Manu-facturing GDP increased by an average of 1.8% per year in 2002–11; manufacturing GDP grew by 4.0% in 2011.

Construction contributed 2.9% of GDP in 2010, and employed 2.5% of the working population according to the 1981 census. The sector's GDP increased by 12.2% in 2009 and by 7.2% in 2010, according to the AfDB.

Togo's dependence on imports of electrical energy from Ghana was reduced following the completion, in 1988, of a 65-MW hydroelectric installation (constructed in co-operation with Benin) at Nangbeto, on the Mono river. In March 2009 the Chinese company Sinohydro signed an agreement in Lomé on the development of a second hydroelectric installation on the Mono river, at Adjarala; the 147-MW plant, again to be operated jointly with Benin, was expected to commence operations in 2013. Meanwhile, a project to construct a pipeline to supply natural gas from Nigeria to Togo (and also to Benin and Ghana) had suffered numerous delays. In 2009 some 24.6% of electricity produced in Togo was generated from petroleum, while 73.8% was generated from hydroelectric sources. In 2011 fuel imports constituted 15.5% of all merchandise imports by value.

According to World Bank estimates, the services sector con-tributed 40.9% of GDP in 2011, and engaged 24.4% of the employed labour force in 1990. Lomé has been of considerable importance as an entrepôt for the foreign trade of land-locked countries of the region. However, political instability in the early 1990s and in 2005 resulted in the diversion of a large part of this activity to neighbouring Benin and undermined the tourism industry (previously an important source of foreign exchange). The GDP of the services sector increased by an average of 1.9% per year in 2002–11; services GDP increased by 2.6% in 2011.

In 2010 Togo recorded a visible merchandise trade deficit of US $448.2m. and there was a deficit of $199.7m. on the current account of the balance of payments. In 2011 the principal source of imports was the People's Republic of China (providing 18.1% of total imports); other major suppliers were France and Belgium. The principal market for exports in that year was also the People's Republic of China (which took 12.5% of Togo's exports); other significant purchasers were Burkina Faso, Benin, Niger, Ghana, and Nigeria. The principal exports in 2011 were cotton (mainly raw cotton), cement, plastics and articles thereof, and fertilizers. The principal imports in that year were mineral fuels and lubricants (mainly petroleum oils), cement, electrical and electronic equipment, and nuclear reactors and machinery.

Togo's estimated overall budget deficit for 2010 was 25,300m. francs CFA, equivalent to 1.6% of GDP. According to projections, Togo's overall budget deficit in 2011 was 66,200m. francs CFA.

Togo's general government gross debt was 1,010,420m. francs CFA in 2009, equivalent to 67.8% of GDP. Total external debt in 2010 was US $1,728m., of which $1,534m. was public and publicly guaranteed debt. In 2009, the cost of servicing long-term public and publicly guaranteed debt and repayments to the IMF was equivalent to 4.4% of the value of exports of goods, services and income (excluding workers' remittances). According to the ILO, consumer prices increased at an average annual rate of 2.9% in 2002–12. Consumer prices rose by 2.6% in 2012.

Togo's economy is dominated by the agricultural sector, with the main cash crops being coffee, cocoa and cotton. A sustained decline in the output of phosphates, traditionally one of the major sources of export earnings, and high international prices for petroleum imports have negatively impacted the trade balance in recent years, while the country's history of political instability and authoritarianism has deterred foreign investment. As a result, Togo continues to rely heavily on external assistance, particularly from the European Union, France and China, although relations with Western donor nations have often been strained due to the country's slow democratic transition. The AfDB and China have also invested in the construction of roads to reinforce Togo's position as a trade corridor linking land-locked countries to ports. Togo reached the completion point of the heavily indebted poor countries initiative in December 2010,

thus qualifying for debt relief of US $1,800m., representing an 82% reduction in the country's external debt in nominal terms. According to the IMF, real GDP rose by 4.0% in 2010, driven by expansion in the mining and construction sectors, as well as a good harvest. The economy grew by a further 4.9% in 2011, again supported by the agricultural sector and government investment in public works projects. Cotton output rose sharply in 2012, and the IMF estimated that economic expansion of 5.0% had been achieved in that year. Real GDP growth of 5.3% was forecast for 2013, although the economy remained susceptible to fluctuations in international commodity prices.

PUBLIC HOLIDAYS

2014: 1 January (New Year's Day), 13 January (Liberation Day, anniversary of the 1967 coup), 21 April (Easter Monday), 27 April (Independence Day), 1 May (Labour Day), 29 May (Ascension Day), 9 June (Whit Monday), 21 June (Martyr's Day), 28 July* (Id al-Fitr, end of Ramadan), 15 August (Assumption), 4 October* (Tabaski, Feast of the Sacrifice), 1 November (All Saints' Day), 25 December (Christmas).

*These holidays are dependent on the Islamic lunar calendar and may vary by one or two days from the dates given.

Statistical Survey

Source (except where otherwise indicated): Direction de la Statistique, BP 118, Lomé; tel. 22-21-62-24; fax 22-21-27-75; e-mail dgscn_tg@yahoo.fr; internet www .stat-togo.org.

Area and Population

AREA, POPULATION AND DENSITY

Area (sq km)	56,600*
Population (census results)	
22 November 1981	2,719,567
19 November 2010	
Males	3,009,095
Females	3,182,060
Total	6,191,155
Population (UN estimates at mid-year)†	
2011	6,154,812
2012	6,283,091
2013	6,412,560
Density (per sq km) at mid-2013	113.3

* 21,853 sq miles.
† Source: UN, *World Population Prospects: The 2010 Revision.*

POPULATION BY AGE AND SEX
(UN estimates at mid-2013)

	Males	Females	Total
0–14	1,233,787	1,233,905	2,467,692
15–64	1,840,394	1,880,140	3,720,534
65 and over	101,847	122,487	224,334
Total	3,176,028	3,236,532	6,412,560

Source: UN, *World Population Prospects: The 2010 Revision.*

Ethnic Groups (percentage of total, 1995): Kabré 23.7; Ewe 21.9; Kabiyé 12.9; Watchi 10.1; Guin 6.0; Tem 6.0; Mobamba 4.9; Gourmantché 3.9; Lamba 3.2; Ncam 2.4; Fon 1.2; Adja 0.9; Others 2.9 (Source: La Francophonie).

ADMINISTRATIVE DIVISIONS
(2010 census)

Region	Area (sq km)	Population	Density (per sq km)	Principal city
Centrale . .	13,317	617,871	46.4	Sokodé
Kara . . .	11,738	769,940	65.6	Kara
Maritime .	6,100	2,599,955	426.2	Lomé
Plateaux . .	16,975	1,375,165	81.0	Atakpamé
Savanes .	8,470	828,224	97.8	Dapaong
Total . .	56,600	6,191,155	109.4	

PRINCIPAL TOWNS
(at 2010 census)

Lomé (capital) . .	837,437	Atakpamé . . .		69,261
Sokodé	95,070	Dapaong . . .		58,071
Kara	94,878	Tsevie		54,474
Kpalimé	75,084			

Mid-2011 (urban population, incl. suburbs, UN estimate): Lomé (capital) 1,523,930 (Source: UN, *World Urbanization Prospects: The 2011 Revision*).

BIRTHS AND DEATHS
(annual averages, UN estimates)

	1995–2000	2000–05	2005–10
Birth rate (per 1,000)	38.5	35.9	33.2
Death rate (per 1,000)	12.3	11.7	11.3

Source: UN, *World Population Prospects: The 2010 Revision.*

Life expectancy (years at birth): 57.0 (males 55.5; females 58.6) in 2011 (Source: World Bank, World Development Indicators database).

ECONOMICALLY ACTIVE POPULATION
(census of 22 November 1981)

	Males	Females	Total
Agriculture, hunting, forestry and fishing	324,870	254,491	579,361
Mining and quarrying	2,781	91	2,872
Manufacturing	29,307	25,065	54,372
Electricity, gas and water	2,107	96	2,203
Construction	20,847	301	21,148
Trade, restaurants and hotels	17,427	87,415	104,842
Transport, storage and communications	20,337	529	20,866
Financing, insurance, real estate and business services	1,650	413	2,063
Community, social and personal services	50,750	12,859	63,609
Sub-total	470,076	381,260	851,336
Activities not adequately defined	14,607	6,346	20,953
Total employed	484,683	387,606	872,289
Unemployed	21,666	7,588	29,254
Total labour force	506,349	395,194	901,543

Mid-2013 (estimates in '000): Agriculture, etc. 1,346; Total labour force 2,612 (Source: FAO).

Health and Welfare

KEY INDICATORS

Total fertility rate (children per woman, 2010)	4.1
Under-5 mortality rate (per 1,000 live births, 2010)	103
HIV/AIDS (% of persons aged 15–49, 2009)	3.2
Physicians (per 1,000 head, 2008)	0.05
Hospital beds (per 1,000 head, 2005)	0.9
Health expenditure (2009): US $ per head (PPP)	74
Health expenditure (2009): % of GDP	7.4
Health expenditure (2009): public (% of total)	43.0
Access to water (% of persons, 2010)	61
Access to sanitation (% of persons, 2010)	13
Total carbon dioxide emissions ('000 metric tons, 2007)	1,419.1
Carbon dioxide emissions per head (metric tons, 2007)	0.2
Human Development Index (2011): ranking	162
Human Development Index (2011): value	0.435

For sources and definitions, see explanatory note on p. vi.

Agriculture

PRINCIPAL CROPS
('000 metric tons)

	2009	2010	2011
Rice, paddy	121.3	110.1	112.2
Maize	651.7	638.1	650.8
Millet	49.1	51.3	50.4
Sorghum	237.7	244.7	243.2
Cassava (Manioc)	895.7	908.8	998.5
Taro (Cocoyam)	19.5	20.2	20.4
Yams	704.4	710.4	727.7
Beans, dry	72.4	76.2	76.5
Groundnuts, with shell	44.5	46.5	47.4
Coconuts	12.8*	13.9*	13.8†
Oil palm fruit†	138	147	146
Seed cotton	27.9	43.0	83.6
Bananas†	21.6	21.0	22.0
Oranges†	14.0	13.8	14.0
Coffee, green	11.7	11.5	12.5
Cocoa beans	105.0*	101.5*	100.0†

* Unofficial figure.
† FAO estimate(s).

Aggregate production ('000 metric tons, may include official, semi-official or estimated data): Total cereals 1,061 in 2009, 1,046 in 2010, 1,058 in 2011; Total roots and tubers 1,625 in 2009, 1,645 in 2010, 1,753 in 2011; Total vegetables (incl. melons) 116 in 2009, 144 in 2010, 141 in 2011; Total fruits (excl. melons) 58 in 2009, 60 in 2010, 62 in 2011.

Source: FAO.

LIVESTOCK
('000 head, year ending September)

	2009	2010	2011
Cattle	308	309	311
Sheep*	2,054	2,108	2,109
Pigs†	561	565	569
Goats	1,870	1,916	1,962
Horses*	2	2	2
Asses*	3	3	3
Chickens	19,800†	21,650†	23,000*

* FAO estimate(s).
† Unofficial figure(s).

Source: FAO.

LIVESTOCK PRODUCTS
('000 metric tons, FAO estimates)

	2009	2010	2011
Cattle meat	9.1	9.3	9.4
Sheep meat	5.5	5.6	5.9
Goat meat	5.0	5.2	5.4
Pig meat	9.4	9.8	10.1
Chicken meat	26.0	28.4	29.6
Game meat	5.4	5.6	5.7
Cows' milk	12.7	12.8	12.8
Hen eggs	9.3	9.3	9.3

Source: FAO.

Forestry

ROUNDWOOD REMOVALS
('000 cubic metres, excluding bark)

	2003	2004	2005
Sawlogs, veneer logs and logs for sleepers	43	44	86
Other industrial wood	191	210	80
Fuel wood	5,653	4,424	4,424*
Total	5,887	4,678	4,590

* FAO estimate.

2006–11: Production assumed to be unchanged from 2005 (FAO estimates).

Source: FAO.

Fishing

('000 metric tons, live weight)

	2008	2009	2010
Capture	23.5	27.0	27.5
Tilapias	3.5	3.5	3.5
Other freshwater fishes	1.5	1.5	1.5
West African ilisha	0.8	1.0	1.3
Bigeye grunt	1.7	2.4	1.4
Round sardinella	1.8	2.4	2.7
European anchovy	2.7	2.7	5.1
Atlantic bonito	1.2	2.0	0.3
Jack and horse mackerels	0.5	n.a.	—
Jacks, crevalles	3.3	3.7	4.4
Aquaculture	0.1	0.1	0.1
Total catch	23.6	27.1	27.6

Source: FAO.

Mining

('000 metric tons unless otherwise indicated)

	2008	2009	2010
Diamonds (carats)	8,787	125	96
Limestone	1,824	1,704	1,700
Phosphate rock (gross weight) .	842	726	720
Phosphate content	303	260	260

Source: US Geological Survey.

Industry

SELECTED PRODUCTS
('000 metric tons unless otherwise indicated)

	2008	2009	2010
Palm oil*	7.8	8.2	8.8
Cement	360	283	283
Electric energy (million kWh) .	123	126	n.a.

* FAO estimate.

Palm oil (FAO estimate): 8.8 in 2011.

Sources: FAO; US Geological Survey; UN Industrial Commodity Statistics Database.

Finance

CURRENCY AND EXCHANGE RATES

Monetary Units
100 centimes = 1 franc de la Communauté Financière Africaine (CFA).

Sterling, Dollar and Euro Equivalents (31 December 2012)
£1 sterling = 784.523 francs CFA;
US $1 = 497.163 francs CFA;
€1 = 655.957 francs CFA;
10,000 francs CFA = £12.75 = $20.11 = €15.24.

Average Exchange Rate (francs CFA per US $)
2010   495.28
2011   471.87
2012   510.29

Note: An exchange rate of 1 French franc = 50 francs CFA, established in 1948, remained in force until January 1994, when the CFA franc was devalued by 50%, with the exchange rate adjusted to 1 French franc = 100 francs CFA. This relationship to French currency remained in effect with the introduction of the euro on 1 January 1999. From that date, accordingly, a fixed exchange rate of €1 = 655.957 francs CFA has been in operation.

BUDGET
('000 million francs CFA)

Revenue*	2009	2010	2011†
Tax revenue	229.0	246.6	268.8
Tax administration . . .	105.7	113.4	118.1
Customs administration . .	123.3	133.2	150.7
Non-tax revenue	23.4	50.2	51.0
Total	252.4	296.9	319.8

Expenditure‡	2009	2010	2011†
Current expenditure . . .	235.0	230.8	292.5
Salaries and wages . . .	94.2	82.6	98.7
Goods and services . .	64.5	59.5	70.6
Transfers and subsidies . .	59.2	69.4	109.2
Capital expenditure . . .	82.3	123.6	150.7
Externally financed . . .	44.4	77.3	83.0
Total‡	317.3	354.4	443.3

* Excluding grants received ('000 million francs CFA): 22.8 in 2009; 32.2 in 2010; 57.3 in 2011 (projection).
† Projections.
‡ Including lending minus repayments.

Source: IMF, *Togo: 2011 Article IV Consultation and Sixth Review Under the Extended Credit Facility Arrangement—Staff Report; Public Information Notice and Press Release on the Executive Board Discussion; and Statement by the Executive Director for Togo* (August 2011).

INTERNATIONAL RESERVES
(excluding gold, US $ million at 31 December)

	2009	2010	2011
IMF special drawing rights . .	92.9	91.4	91.0
Reserve position in IMF . . .	0.5	0.6	0.7
Foreign exchange	609.8	622.9	682.6
Total	703.2	714.9	774.3

Source: IMF, *International Financial Statistics*.

MONEY SUPPLY
('000 million francs CFA at 31 December)

	2009	2010	2011
Currency outside banks . . .	140.3	183.3	193.8
Demand deposits at deposit money banks	224.5	227.4	293.1
Total money (incl. others) . .	372.9	419.4	497.8

Source: IMF, *International Financial Statistics*.

COST OF LIVING
(Consumer Price Index; base: 2000 = 100)

	2008	2009	2010
Food, beverages and tobacco . .	138.3	141.7	150.9
Clothing	110.2	109.4	110.2
Housing, water, electricity and gas	121.3	124.9	124.8
All items (incl. others) . . .	127.5	130.0	134.1

2011: Food 153.8; All items (incl. others) 139.0.
2012: Food 159.0; All items (incl. others) 142.6.
Source: ILO.

NATIONAL ACCOUNTS
(million francs CFA at current prices)

Expenditure on the Gross Domestic Product

	2008	2009	2010
Government final consumption expenditure	190,304	211,456	190,229
Private final consumption expenditure	1,215,199	1,236,263	1,338,858
Changes in inventories . . .	47,379	30,083	13,370
Gross fixed capital formation . .	203,294	248,678	283,250
Total domestic expenditure .	1,656,176	1,726,480	1,825,707
Exports of goods and services . .	508,641	565,007	609,191
Less Imports of goods and services	746,288	797,938	857,013
GDP in purchasers' values .	1,418,529	1,493,550	1,577,885

Gross Domestic Product by Economic Activity

	2008	2009	2010
Agriculture, hunting, forestry and fishing	578,603	639,378	642,436
Mining and quarrying	59,114	48,187	41,247
Manufacturing	120,089	118,087	122,733
Electricity, gas and water	38,861	38,937	43,700
Construction	39,382	33,508	53,711
Wholesale and retail trade, restaurants and hotels	131,060	116,032	139,745
Transport and communications	73,285	78,626	91,546
Finance and insurance, real estate and business services	128,519	128,228	147,417
Public administration and defence	103,204	138,932	120,362
Other services	28,653	29,704	30,813
Sub-total	**1,300,770**	**1,369,619**	**1,433,710**
Less Imputed bank service charge	25,482	26,783	28,412
Indirect taxes, less subsidies	143,240	150,714	172,586
GDP in purchasers' values	**1,418,529**	**1,493,550**	**1,577,885**

Source: African Development Bank.

BALANCE OF PAYMENTS

(US $ million)

	2008	2009	2010
Exports of goods	852.6	903.0	976.2
Imports of goods	−1,307.2	−1,315.2	−1,424.4
Balance on goods	**−454.6**	**−412.1**	**−448.2**
Exports of services	283.1	293.6	320.2
Imports of services	−359.2	−374.7	−404.0
Balance on goods and services	**−530.7**	**−493.3**	**−532.0**
Primary income received	81.1	68.4	99.5
Primary income paid	−96.2	−87.4	−122.9
Balance on goods, services and primary income	**−545.8**	**−512.3**	**−555.4**
Secondary income received	385.2	412.9	416.7
Secondary income paid	−61.4	−77.2	−61.0
Current balance	**−222.0**	**−176.7**	**−199.7**
Capital account (net)	655.8	135.2	1,388.1
Direct investment assets	−10.9	−35.0	−76.3
Direct investment liabilities	50.7	46.1	124.9
Portfolio investment assets	−6.8	−1.4	−27.9
Portfolio investment liabilities	18.9	−29.2	6.0
Financial derivatives and employee stock options (net)	—	0.1	—
Other investment assets	28.4	−176.8	3.1
Other investment liabilities	−824.4	282.6	−1,206.9
Net errors and omissions	8.0	14.1	2.5
Reserves and related items	**−302.2**	**59.0**	**13.9**

Source: IMF, International Financial Statistics.

External Trade

PRINCIPAL COMMODITIES
(distribution by HS, US $ million)

Imports c.i.f.	2009	2010	2011
Cereals	61.5	74.9	55.6
Wheat and meslin, unmilled	20.3	14.4	29.5
Cotton	28.0	20.3	32.1
Mineral fuels, lubricants and related materials	147.4	139.2	186.7
Petroleum oils	144.0	132.1	174.6
Salt, sulphur, earth, stone, plaster, lime and cement	91.9	83.9	110.2
Cement	78.3	71.1	93.3
Electrical, electronic equipment	115.5	95.4	82.0
Boilers, machinery, etc.	82.9	52.3	79.9
Iron and steel	41.5	40.3	63.6
Pharmaceutical products	61.5	74.9	55.6
Medicament mixtures	56.5	70.6	48.8
Vehicles other than railway, tramway	76.0	77.4	105.0
Total (incl. others)	983.9	989.5	1,207.7

Exports f.o.b.	2009	2010	2011
Cotton	138.3	143.3	272.3
Raw cotton, excl. linters, not carded or combed	136.1	141.7	268.2
Salt, sulphur, earth, stone, plaster, lime and cement	275.7	164.6	165.3
Cement	119.0	117.4	121.7
Plastics and articles thereof	45.3	45.9	64.8
Plastic packing goods	33.1	30.9	47.8
Fertilizers	24.8	30.4	46.0
Essential oils, perfumes, cosmetics, toiletries	31.4	30.2	38.6
Pearls, precious stones, metals, coins, etc.	4.3	21.5	33.3
Iron and steel	25.5	31.1	25.5
Total (incl. others)	734.7	667.2	865.5

Source: Trade Map-Trade Competitiveness Map, International Trade Centre, www.intracen.org/marketanalysis.

PRINCIPAL TRADING PARTNERS
(US $ million)

Imports c.i.f.	2009	2010	2011
Belgium	43.8	67.3	65.2
Brazil	28.7	10.3	24.7
Canada	9.6	8.3	13.2
China, People's Repub.	168.4	162.0	218.2
Côte d'Ivoire	39.6	32.1	29.6
France (incl. Monaco)	127.6	174.7	162.4
Germany	34.5	28.0	37.2
Ghana	44.5	34.8	39.4
India	16.5	51.8	32.1
Indonesia	15.8	20.0	8.5
Italy	13.6	23.0	21.1
Japan	20.8	20.9	22.9
Netherlands	53.1	37.1	49.8
Nigeria	28.1	10.9	15.8
Senegal	8.5	11.2	10.5
South Africa	23.0	13.1	18.4
Spain	15.9	12.6	28.7
Ukraine	3.6	5.1	15.6
United Kingdom	12.5	8.9	20.7
USA	14.5	34.2	29.7
Total (incl. others)	983.9	989.5	1,207.7

Exports f.o.b.	2009	2010	2011
Bangladesh	1.0	12.1	11.8
Benin	84.8	89.3	97.0
Burkina Faso	78.6	76.8	99.2
China, People's Repub. . . .	59.7	56.6	108.5
Côte d'Ivoire	17.9	23.7	31.4
France (incl. Monaco)	6.3	5.5	9.9
Germany	3.7	3.9	9.2
Ghana	84.1	65.9	55.4
India	143.2	31.2	26.3
Indonesia	11.3	22.0	38.1
Malaysia	29.1	6.0	29.6
Mali	18.2	20.5	25.6
Niger	40.3	47.2	75.2
Nigeria	40.6	34.0	45.7
Senegal	8.0	5.7	7.8
Switzerland	4.0	13.0	26.9
Thailand	10.9	11.8	20.7
Viet Nam	5.7	8.9	24.5
Total (incl. others)	734.7	667.2	865.5

Source: Trade Map-Trade Competitiveness Map, International Trade Centre, www.intracen.org/marketanalysis.

Transport

RAILWAYS
(traffic)

	1997	1998	1999
Passengers carried ('000) . . .	152.0	35.0	4.4
Freight carried ('000 metric tons) .	250	759	1,090
Passenger-km (million) . . .	12.7	3.4	0.4
Freight ton-km (million) . . .	28.8	70.6	92.4

Source: Société Nationale des Chemins de Fer du Togo, Lomé.

ROAD TRAFFIC
(motor vehicles registered at 31 December)

	1994	1995	1996*
Passenger cars	67,936	74,662	79,200
Buses and coaches	529	547	580
Goods vehicles	31,457	32,514	33,660
Tractors (road)	1,466	1,544	1,620
Motorcycles and scooters . . .	39,019	52,902	59,000

* Estimates.

2007: Passenger cars 10,611; Buses and coaches 193; Lorries and vans 2,219; Motorcycles and scooters 34,246.

Source: IRF, *World Road Statistics*.

SHIPPING

Flag Registered Fleet
(at 31 December)

	2010	2011	2012
Number of vessels	127	154	208
Total displacement ('000 grt) . .	263.5	466.7	782.6

Source: Lloyd's List Intelligence (www.lloydslistintelligence.com).

International Sea-borne Freight Traffic
('000 metric tons)

Port Lomé	1997	1998	1999
Goods loaded	432.4	794.6	1,021.4
Goods unloaded	1,913.9	1,912.9	1,812.4

Source: Port Autonome de Lomé.

CIVIL AVIATION
(traffic on scheduled services)*

	1999	2000	2001
Kilometres flown (million) . .	3	3	1
Passengers carried ('000) . . .	84	77	46
Passenger-km (million) . . .	235	216	130
Total ton-km (million)	36	32	19

* Including an apportionment of the traffic of Air Afrique.

Source: UN, *Statistical Yearbook*.

Tourism

FOREIGN TOURIST ARRIVALS*

	2008	2009	2010
Belgium, Luxembourg and the Netherlands	708	1,515	2,696
Benin	5,465	12,520	13,788
Burkina Faso, Mali and Niger .	5,104	10,258	13,618
Côte d'Ivoire	3,607	6,780	8,933
France	13,480	28,229	37,911
Germany	1,305	3,034	3,029
Ghana	1,795	3,800	4,553
Italy	723	2,286	2,655
Nigeria	3,303	6,873	7,845
United Kingdom	747	1,073	1,545
USA	1,480	4,502	4,460
Total (incl. others)	73,982	149,945	202,044

* Arrivals at hotels and similar establishments, by country of residence.

Receipts from tourism (US $ million, excl. passenger transport): 68 in 2009; 66 in 2010.

Source: World Tourism Organization.

Communications Media

	2009	2010	2011
Telephones ('000 main lines in use)	178.7	213.6	240.0
Mobile cellular telephones ('000 subscribers)	2,187.3	2,452.4	3,104.8
Internet subscribers ('000) . .	59.6	60.6	n.a.
Broadband subscribers ('000) . .	2.7	3.8	4.8

Source: International Telecommunication Union.

Education

(2009/10 unless otherwise indicated)

	Institutions*	Teachers	Students Males	Students Females	Students Total
Pre-primary .	319*	1,646	21,206	21,684	42,890
Primary . .	4,701*	31,712	677,250	609,403	1,286,653
Secondary . .	n.a.	11,518†	n.a.	n.a.	482,877
Tertiary† . .	n.a.	470	n.a.	n.a.	32,502

* 1999/2000 figure.
† 2006/07 figures.

Source: UNESCO Institute for Statistics.

Pupil-teacher ratio (primary education, UNESCO estimate): 40.6 in 2009/10 (Source: UNESCO Institute for Statistics).

Adult literacy rate (UNESCO estimates): 57.1% (males 71.2%; females 43.6%) in 2009 (Source: UNESCO Institute for Statistics).

Directory

The Government

HEAD OF STATE

President: FAURE ESSOZIMNA GNASSINGBÉ (inaugurated 4 May 2005; re-elected 4 March 2010).

COUNCIL OF MINISTERS
(May 2013)

The Government is formed by the Union pour la République and the Union des Forces de Changement.

Prime Minister: ARTHÈME KWESI SÉLÉAGODJI AHOOMEY-ZUNU.

Minister of State, Minister of Primary and Secondary Education and Literacy: SOLITOKI MAGNIM ESSO.

Minister of State, Minister of Foreign Affairs and Co-operation: ELLIOTT OHIN.

Minister of the Economy and Finance: ADJI OTÉTH AYASSOR.

Minister of Basic Development, Handicrafts, Youth and Youth Employment: VICTOIRE SIDÉMEHO TOMÉGAH-DOGBÉ.

Minister of Health: CHARLES KONDI AGBA.

Minister of Higher Education and Research: OCTAVE NICOUÉ BROOHM.

Minister of Territorial Administration, Decentralization and Local Communities: GILBERT BAWARA.

Keeper of the Seals, Minister of Justice: TCHITCHAO TCHALIM.

Minister of Transport: DAMMIPI NOUPOKOU.

Minister of Labour, Employment and Social Security: YACOU-BOU KOUMADJO HAMADOU.

Minister of Public Works: NINSAO GNOFAM.

Minister of Technical Education and Professional Training: HAMADOU BRIM BOURAÏMA-DIABACTE.

Minister of Post and Telecommunications: CINA LAWSON.

Minister of Trade and the Promotion of the Private Sector: BERNADETTE ESSOZIMNA LEGUEZIM-BALOUKI.

Minister of Industry, the Free Zone and Technological Innovation: FRANÇOIS AGBÉVIADÉ GALLEY.

Minister of Security and Civil Protection: Col DAMEHANE YARK.

Minister of the Environment and Forest Resources: DÉDÉ AHOÉFA EKOUÉ.

Minister of Tourism: PADUMHÈKOU CHRISTOPHE TCHAO.

Minister of Social Affairs and National Solidarity: AFI NTIFA AMENYO.

Minister of Human Rights, the Consolidation of Democracy and Civic Education: LEONARDINA RITA DORIS WILSON-DE SOUZA.

Minister of the Civil Service and Administrative Reform: KOKOU DZIFA ADJEODA.

Minister of Sport and Leisure: BAKALAWA FOFANA.

Minister to the President of the Republic, responsible for Planning, Development and Land Settlement: MAWUSSI DJOSSOU SEMODJI.

Minister of the Promotion of Women: PATRICIA DAGBAN-ZONVIDÉ.

Minister of Agriculture, Stockbreeding and Fisheries: Col OURO KOURA AGADAZI.

Minister of Town Planning and Housing: KOMLAN NUNYABU.

Minister of Arts and Culture: FIATUWO KWADJO SÉSSÉNOU.

Minister of Communication: DJIMON ORÉ.

Minister of Water, Sanitation and Rural Water Supply: BISSOUNE NABAGOU.

Minister-delegate to the Minister of Agriculture, Stockbreeding and Fisheries, responsible for Rural Infrastructure: GOURDIGOU KOLANI.

MINISTRIES

Office of the President: Palais Présidentiel, ave de la Marina, Lomé; tel. 22-21-27-01; fax 22-21-18-97; e-mail presidence@republicoftogo.com; internet www.presidencetogo.com.

Office of the Prime Minister: Palais de la Primature, BP 1161, Lomé; tel. 22-21-15-64; fax 22-21-37-53; internet www.primature.gouv.tg.

Ministry of Agriculture, Stockbreeding and Fisheries: 5 ave de Duisburg, BP 385, Lomé; tel. 22-20-40-20; fax 22-20-44-99; internet ministereagriculture.com.

Ministry of Arts and Culture: Lomé.

Ministry of Basic Development, Handicrafts, Youth and Youth Employment: Lomé.

Ministry of the Civil Service and Administrative Reform: angle ave de la Marina et rue Kpalimé, BP 372, Lomé; tel. 22-21-41-83; fax 22-22-56-85; internet fonctionpubliquetogo.com.

Ministry of Communication: BP 40, Lomé; tel. 22-21-29-30; fax 22-21-43-80; e-mail info@republicoftogo.com.

Ministry of the Economy and Finance: CASEF, ave Sarakawa, BP 387, Lomé; tel. 22-21-35-54; fax 22-21-09-05; e-mail eco@republicoftogo.com; internet www.finances.gouv.tg.

Ministry of the Environment and Forest Resources: Lomé; tel. 22-21-56-58; fax 22-21-03-33.

Ministry of Foreign Affairs and Co-operation: pl. du Monument aux Morts, ave Georges Pompidou, BP 900, Lomé; tel. 22-21-29-10; fax 22-21-39-74; e-mail maeirtgce@yahoo.fr; internet www.diplomatie.gouv.tg.

Ministry of Health: rue Branly, BP 386, Lomé; tel. 22-21-35-24; fax 22-22-20-73; internet ministeresante.com.

Ministry of Higher Education and Research: rue Col de Roux, BP 12175, Lomé; tel. 22-22-09-83; fax 22-22-07-83; internet www.ministereeducation.org.

Ministry of Human Rights, the Consolidation of Democracy and Civic Education: BP 1325, Lomé; tel. 22-22-60-63; fax 22-20-07-74; e-mail mdhdcab@yahoo.fr.

Ministry of Industry, the Free Zone and Technological Innovation: Lomé.

Ministry of Justice: ave de la Marina, rue Colonel de Roux, Lomé; tel. 22-21-26-53; fax 22-22-29-06; internet ministerejustice.com.

Ministry of Labour, Employment and Social Security: Lomé.

Ministry of Mines and Energy: Lomé.

Ministry of Post and Telecommunications: ave de Sarakawa, BP 389, Lomé; tel. 22-23-14-00; fax 22-21-68-12; e-mail eco@republicoftogo.com; internet ministeretelecom.com.

Ministry of Primary and Secondary Education and Literacy: BP 398, Lomé; tel. 22-21-20-97; fax 22-21-89-34.

Ministry of the Promotion of Women: Lomé.

Ministry of Public Works: Lomé.

Ministry of Security and Civil Protection: rue Albert Sarraut, Lomé; tel. 22-22-57-12; fax 22-22-61-50; e-mail info@republicoftogo.com.

Ministry of Social Affairs and National Solidarity: Lomé.

Ministry of Sport and Leisure: BP 40, Lomé; tel. 22-21-22-47; fax 22-22-42-28.

Ministry of Technical Education and Professional Training: Lomé.

Ministry of Territorial Administration, Decentralization and Local Communities: Lomé.

Ministry of Tourism: Lomé.

Ministry of Town Planning and Housing: Lomé.

Ministry of Trade and the Promotion of the Private Sector: 1 ave de Sarakawa, face au Monument aux Morts, BP 383, Lomé; tel. 22-21-20-25; fax 22-21-05-72; e-mail ministereducommercetogo@yahoo.fr.

Ministry of Transport: Lomé.

Ministry of Water, Sanitation and Rural Water Supply: Lomé.

President and Legislature

PRESIDENT

Presidential Election, 4 March 2010

Candidate	Valid votes	% of valid votes
Faure Gnassingbé (RPT)	1,242,409	60.89
Jean-Pierre Fabre (UFC)	692,554	33.94
Yawovi Agboyibo (CAR)	60,370	2.96
Agbéyomé Kodjo (OBUTS)	17,393	0.85
Brigitte Kafui Adjamagbo-Johnson (CDPA—BT)	13,452	0.66
Bassabi Kagbara (PDP)	8,341	0.41
Jean Nicolas Messan Lawson (PRR)	6,027	0.30
Total	2,040,546	100.00

LEGISLATURE

Assemblée nationale

Palais des Congrès, BP 327, Lomé; tel. 22-22-57-91; fax 22-22-11-68; e-mail assemblee.nationale@syfed.tg.refer.org; internet www.assemblee-nationale.tg.

President: El Hadj ABASS BONFOH.

General Election, 14 October 2007

Party	Votes	% of votes	Seats
RPT	922,636	32.71	50
UFC	867,507	30.75	27
CAR	192,218	6.81	4
Others	838,484	29.72	—
Total	2,820,845	100.00	81

Election Commission

Commission Electorale Nationale Indépendante (CENI): 198 rue des Echis, BP 7005, Lomé; tel. 22-22-29-51; fax 22-22-39-61; e-mail info@cenitogo.tg; internet www.cenitogo.tg; 19 mems; Pres. ANGÈLE DOLA AGUIGAH.

Political Organizations

Alliance Nationale pour le Changement (ANC): Lomé; f. 2010; Leader JEAN-PIERRE FABRE; Sec.-Gen. JEAN-CLAUDE CODJO DÉLAVA.

Comité d'Action pour le Renouveau (CAR): 58 ave du 24 janvier, BP06, Lomé; tel. 22-22-05-66; fax 22-21-62-54; e-mail yagboyibo@bibway.com; moderately conservative; Pres. DODJI APEVON; 251,349 mems (Dec. 1999).

Convention Démocratique des Peuples Africains—Branche Togolaise (CDPA—BT): 5 rue Djidjollé, BP 13963, Lomé; tel. and fax 22-25-38-46; e-mail cdpa-bt.cdpa-bt@orange.fr; internet www.cdpa-bt.net; f. 1991; socialist; Gen. Sec. LÉOPOLD GNININVI; First Sec. Prof. EMMANUEL Y. GU-KONU.

Convergence Patriotique Panafricaine (CPP): BP 12703, Lomé; tel. 22-21-58-43; f. 1999; Pres. EDEM KODJO; First Vice-Pres. JEAN-LUCIEN SAVI DE TOVÉ.

Organisation pour Bâtir dans l'Union un Togo Solidaire (OBUTS): Quartier Djidjole, 686 rue 19 Tosti, Lomé; tel. 22-51-95-95; internet www.obuts.org; f. 2008; Pres. AGBÉYOMÉ KODJO; Sec.-Gen. YAWOVI BOESSI.

Parti Démocratique Panafricain (PDP): Lomé; f. 2005; Pres. BASSABI KAGBARA.

Parti du Renouveau et de la Rédemption (PRR): Quartier Kodjoviakopé, 34 rue Alédjo, Lomé; tel. 22-32-98-49; e-mail lerenouveau2003@yahoo.fr; internet www.prr-togo.com; Pres. JEAN NICOLAS MESSAN LAWSON.

Parti des Travailleurs (PT): 49 ave de Calais, BP 13974, Nyékonakpoé, Lomé; tel. 90-13-65-54 (mobile); socialist; Co-ordinating Sec. CLAUDE AMEGANVI.

Union des Forces de Changement (UFC): 59 rue Koudadzé, Lom-Nava, BP 62168, Lomé; tel. and fax 22-31-01-70; e-mail contact-togo@ufctogo.com; internet www.ufctogo.com; f. 1992; social-democratic; Pres. GILCHRIST OLYMPIO; First Vice-Pres. HAMADOU BRIM BOURAÏMA-DIABACTE; Sec.-Gen. Dr PIERRE JIMONGOU.

Union des Libéraux Indépendants (ULI): f. 1993 to succeed Union des Démocrates pour le Renouveau; Leader KWAMI MENSAN JACQUES AMOUZOU.

Union pour la République (UNIR): 572 rue Pydal Tokoin Wuiti, BP 1208, Lomé; tel. 22-26-04-95; fax 22-61-00-33; e-mail rpttogo@yahoo.fr; internet www.rpt.tg; f. 1969 as Rassemblement du Peuple Togolais; sole legal party 1969–91; name changed as above in 2012; Pres. FAURE GNASSINGBÉ; Sec.-Gen. SOLITOKI ESSO.

Diplomatic Representation

EMBASSIES IN TOGO

Brazil: Cité OUA, près de la Primature, BP 916, Lomé; tel. 22-61-56-58; fax 22-61-56-83; e-mail brasembtogo@helim.tg; Ambassador MIGUEL GUSTAVO DE PAIVA TORRES.

China, People's Republic: 1381 rue de l'Entente, BP 2690, Lomé; tel. 22-22-38-56; fax 22-21-40-75; e-mail chinaemb_tg@mfa.gov.cn; internet tg.chineseembassy.org/chn; Ambassador WANG ZUOFENG.

Congo, Democratic Republic: Lomé; tel. 22-21-51-55; Ambassador LOKOKA IKUKELE BOMOLO.

Egypt: 1163 rue de l'OCAM, BP 8, Lomé; tel. 22-21-24-43; fax 22-21-10-22; Ambassador MORTADA ALI MOHAMED LASHIN.

France: 13 ave du Golfe, BP 337, Lomé; tel. 22-23-46-00; fax 22-23-46-01; e-mail eric.bosc@diplomatie.fr; internet www.ambafrance-tg.org; Ambassador NICOLAS WARNERY.

Gabon: Lomé; tel. 22-22-18-93; fax 22-22-18-92; Ambassador JOSEPH AIMÉ OBIANG NDOUTOUME.

Germany: blvd de la République, BP 1175, Lomé; tel. 22-23-32-32; fax 22-23-32-46; e-mail amballtogo@cafe.tg; internet www.lome.diplo.de; Ambassador JOSEPH ALBERT WEIß.

Ghana: 38 rue Moyana, Tokoin-Ouest, BP 92, Lomé; tel. 22-21-31-94; fax 22-21-77-36; e-mail ghmfa01@cafe.tg; Ambassador JOHN MAXWELL KWADJO.

Holy See: BP 20790, Lomé; tel. 22-26-03-06; fax 22-26-68-80; e-mail noncia.tg@gmail.com; Apostolic Nuncio MICHAEL AUGUST BLUME (Titular Archbishop of Alessano).

Libya: Cite OUA, BP 4872, Lomé; tel. 22-61-47-08; fax 22-61-47-10; Ambassador AHMED BALLUZ.

Nigeria: 311 blvd du 13 janvier, BP 1189, Lomé; tel. and fax 22-21-59-76; Ambassador MATHEW SUNDAY ADOLI.

USA: Blvd Eyadema, BP 852, Lomé; tel. 22-61-54-70; fax 22-61-55-01; e-mail RobertsonJJ2@state.gov; internet togo.usembassy.gov; Ambassador ROBERT E. WHITEHEAD.

Judicial System

Justice is administered by the Constitutional Court, the Supreme Court, two Appeal Courts and the Tribunaux de Première Instance, which hear civil, commercial and criminal cases. There is a labour tribunal and a tribunal for children's rights. In addition, there are two exceptional courts, the Cour de Sûreté de l'Etat, which judges crimes against internal and external state security, and the Tribunal Spécial Chargé de la Répression des Détournements de Deniers Publics, which deals with cases of misuse of public funds.

Constitutional Court: BP 1331, Lomé; tel. 22-61-06-40; fax 22-61-05-45; internet www.courconstitutionnelle.tg; f. 1997; seven mems; Pres. ABOUDOU ASSOUMA.

Supreme Court: BP 906, Lomé; tel. 22-21-22-58; f. 1961; consists of three chambers (judicial, administrative and auditing); Chair. ABALO PIGNAKIWÉ PETCHELEBIA; Attorney-General KOUAMI AMADOS-DJOKO.

Audit Court (Cour des Comptes): Lomé; f. 2009; Pres. LALLE TANKPANDJA.

State Attorney: ATARA NDAKENA.

Religion

It is estimated that about 50% of the population follow traditional animist beliefs, some 35% are Christians and 15% are Muslims.

CHRISTIANITY

The Roman Catholic Church

Togo comprises one archdiocese and six dioceses. An estimated 25% of the total population was Roman Catholic.

Bishops' Conference

Conférence Episcopale du Togo, 561 rue Aniko Palako, BP 348, Lomé; tel. 22-21-22-72; fax 22-22-48-08.

statutes approved 1979; Pres. Most Rev. AMBROISE KOTAMBA DJOLIBA (Bishop of Sokodé).

Archbishop of Lomé: Most Rev. DENIS KOMIVI AMUZU-DZAKPAH, Archevêché, 561 rue Aniko Palako, BP 348, Lomé; tel. 22-21-22-72; fax 22-21-02-46; e-mail archlom@yahoo.cfr.

Protestant Churches

There are about 250 mission centres, with a personnel of some 250, affiliated to European and US societies and administered by a Conseil Synodal, presided over by a moderator.

Directorate of Protestant Churches: 1 rue Maréchal Foch, BP 378, Lomé; Moderator Pastor AGBI-AWUME (acting).

Église Evangélique Luthérienne au Togo: POB 80780, Lome; tel. 22-25-23-51; fax 22-25-32-52; e-mail elca_togo@hotmail.com; Pres. Rev. KOFFI GAWU SALLAH HUKPORTI.

Eglise Evangélique Presbytérienne du Togo: 1 rue Tokmake, BP 2, Lomé; tel. 22-21-46-69; fax 22-22-23-63; e-mail eeptbs@laposte.tg; internet www.eept-online.org; Moderator Rev. IMANUEL KOFFI AWANYOH.

Fédération des Evangéliques du Togo: Lomé; Co-ordinator HAPPY AZIADEKEY.

BAHÁ'Í FAITH

Assemblée Spirituelle Nationale: BP 1659, Lomé; tel. 22-21-21-99; e-mail asnbaha@yahoo.fr; Sec. ALLADOUM NGOMNA; 19,002 adherents (2006).

The Press

DAILIES

Forum de la Semaine: BP 81129, Lomé; tel. 99-53-54-55; fax 22-22-09-51; e-mail forumhebdo7@yahoo.fr; internet www .forumdelasemaine.com; Dir JEAN-BAPTISTE K. D. DZILAN.

Liberté: BP 80744, Lomé; tel. 23-36-88-16; fax 22-22-09-55; internet www.libertetg.com; Dir of Publication ZEUS AZIADOUVO; Editorial Dir MÉDARD AMETEPE.

Togo-Presse: BP 891, Lomé; tel. 22-21-53-95; fax 22-22-37-66; internet www.editogo.tg/presse.php; f. 1961; official govt publ; French, Kabiyé and Ewe; political, economic and cultural; circ. 8,000.

PERIODICALS

L'Alternative: BP 4132, Lomé; tel. 90-09-41-33 (mobile); fax 22-51-86-94; e-mail info@alternative-togo.com; internet www .lalternative-togo.com; Dir of Publication FERDINAND MENSAH AYITE; Editor-in-Chief MAXIME DOMEGNI.

Carrefour: 596 rue Ablogame, BP 6125, Lomé; tel. 99-44-45-43 (mobile); f. 1991; pro-opposition; weekly; Dir HOLONOU HOUKPATI.

Cité Magazine: 50 ave Pas de Souza, BP 6275, Lomé; tel. and fax 22-22-67-40; e-mail citemag@cafe.tg; internet www.cafe.tg/citemag; monthly; Editor-in-Chief GAËTAN K. GNATCHIKO.

Le Combat du Peuple: 62 rue Blagogee, BP 4682, Lomé; tel. 90-04-53-83 (mobile); fax 22-22-65-89; f. 1994; pro-opposition weekly; Editor LUCIEN DJOSSOU MESSAN; circ. 3,500 (2000).

Crocodile News: 909 rue Kuévidjin, no 27 Bé-Château, BP 61049, Lomé; tel. 99-46-00-36 (mobile); e-mail crocodilenews@yahoo.fr; internet crocodilenews.net; f. 1993; pro-opposition; weekly; Dir of Publication ASSIONGBON FRANCIS PEDRO AMAZUN; circ. 3,500 (2000).

La Dépêche: BP 20039, Lomé; tel. and fax 22-21-09-32; e-mail ladepeche@hotmail.com; f. 1993; 2 a week; Editor ESSO-WE APPOLINAIRE MÈWÈNAMÈSSÈ; circ. 3,000.

L'Etoile du Matin: S/C Maison du journalisme, Casier no 50, Lomé; e-mail wielfridsewa18@hotmail.com; f. 2000; weekly; Dir WIELFRID SÉWA TCHOUKOULI.

Etudes Togolaises (Revue Togolaise des Sciences): Institut National de la Recherche Scientifique, BP 2240, Lomé; tel. 22-21-01-39; fax 22-21-21-59; e-mail inrs@tg.refer.org; f. 1965; 2 a year; scientific review, mainly anthropology.

L'Exilé: Maison du journalisme, Casier no 28, Lomé; e-mail jexil@ hotmail.com; f. 2000; weekly; independent; Editor HIPPOLYTE AGBOH.

Journal Officiel de la République du Togo (JORT): BP 891, Lomé; tel. 22-21-37-18; fax 22-22-14-89; govt acts, laws, decrees and decisions.

Kyrielle: BP 823, Lomé; tel. 99-48-13-69; fax 90-05-38-35; e-mail kyriellj@yahoo.fr; f. 1999; monthly; culture, sport; Dir CRÉDO TETTEH; circ. 3,000 (2000).

Libre Togovi: BP 81190, Lomé; tel. 90-04-43-36; e-mail libretogovi@ mail.com; 2 a week; pro-democracy; distributed by the Comité Presse et Communication de la Concertation Nationale de la Société Civile.

Le Miroir du Peuple: 48 rue Defale, BP 81231, Lomé; tel. 99-46-60-24; e-mail nouveau90@hotmail.com; f. 1998; fmrly Le Nouveau Combat; weekly; independent; Dir ELIAS EDOH HOUNKANLY; circ. 1,000 (2000).

Nouvel Echo: BP 3681, Lomé; tel. 99-47-72-40 (mobile); f. 1997; pro-opposition; weekly; Dir ALPHONSE NEVAME KLU; Editor CLAUDE AMEGANVI.

Nouvel Eclat: Lomé; tel. 22-25-51-60; e-mail charlpass@hotmail .com; f. 2000; weekly; Dir CHARLES PASSOU; circ. 2,500 (2000).

La Nouvelle République: Lomé; tel. 99-45-55-43 (mobile); e-mail nouvelle.republique@caramail.com; f. 1999; Dir WIELFRID SÉWA TCHOUKOULI; circ. 2,500 (2000).

Le Regard: BP 81213, Lomé; tel. 90-04-09-09 (mobile); fax 22-26-13-70; e-mail leregard13@caramail.com; f. 1996; weekly; pro-opposition; supports promotion of human rights; Editor ABASS DURMAN MIKAÏLA; circ. 3,000 (2000).

Le Reporter des Temps Nouveaux: Maison du journalisme, Casier no 22, BP 1800, Lomé; tel. and fax 22-26-18-22; e-mail lereporter39@hotmail.com; f. 1998; weekly; independent; political criticism and analysis; Dir AUGUSTIN AMÉGAH; circ. 3,000 (2000).

Le Scorpion—Akéklé: S/C Maison du journalisme, BP 81213, Lomé; tel. 99-44-43-80 (mobile); fax 22-26-13-70; e-mail lescorpion@webmails.com; f. 1998; opposition weekly; Dir DIDIER AGBLETO; circ. 3,500 (2000).

Le Soleil: Lomé; tel. 90-04-41-97 (mobile); fax 90-04-89-10 (mobile); e-mail lesoleil@francemail.com; f. 1999; weekly; Dir YVES LACLÉ; circ. 2,000 (2000).

Témoin de la Nation: Maison du journalisme, Casier no 48, BP 434, Lomé; tel. 22-21-24-92; f. 2000; weekly; Dir ELIAS EBOH.

Tingo Tingo: 44–50 rue Douka, Kotokoucondji, BP 80419, Lomé; tel. and fax 22-22-17-53; e-mail jtingo-tingo@yahoo.fr; f. 1996; weekly; independent; Editor AUGUSTIN ASIONBO; circ. 3,500 (2000).

L'Union: Lomé; tel. 22-26-12-10; e-mail letambour@yahoo.fr; Dir of Publication ERIC JOHNSON.

PRESS ASSOCIATION

Syndicat National des Journalistes Indépendants du Togo (SYNJIT): Lomé; f. 2011; Sec.-Gen. MAXIME DOMEGNI.

Union des Journalistes Indépendants du Togo: BP 81213, Lomé; tel. 22-26-13-00; fax 22-21-38-21; e-mail maison-du-journalisme@ids.tg; also operates Maison de Presse; Sec.-Gen. CRÉDO TÉTTEH.

NEWS AGENCIES

Agence Togolaise de Presse (ATOP): 35 rue des Medias, BP 2327, Lomé; tel. 22-21-24-90; fax 22-22-28-02; e-mail atop.togo@gmail.com; internet www.atoptogo.blogspot.com; f. 1975; Dir-Gen. CLAUDINE ASSIBA AKAKPO.

Savoir News: Lomé; tel. 23-36-40-58; e-mail info@savoirnews.com; internet www.savoirnews.com.

Publishers

Centre Togolais de Communication Evangélique—Editions Haho (CTCE—Editions Haho): 1 rue Sylvanus Olympio, BP 378, Lomé; tel. 22-21-45-82; fax 22-21-29-67; e-mail ctce_ctce@yahoo.fr; f. 1983; general literature, popular science, poetry, school textbooks, Christian interest; Dir TOMPY KUDZO NAKOU.

Editions Akpagnon: BP 3531, Lomé; tel. and fax 22-22-02-44; e-mail yedogbe@yahoo.fr; f. 1978; general literature and non-fiction; Man. Dir YVES-EMMANUEL DOGBÉ.

Editions de la Rose Bleue: BP 12452, Lomé; tel. 22-22-93-39; fax 22-22-96-69; e-mail dorkenoo_ephrem@yahoo.fr; general literature, poetry; Dir EPHREM SETH DORKENOO.

Les Nouvelles Editions Africaines du Togo (NEA-TOGO): 239 blvd du 13 janvier, BP 4862, Lomé; tel. and fax 22-22-10-19; e-mail neatogo@yahoo.fr; general fiction, non-fiction and textbooks; Dir-Gen. KOKOU A. KALIPE; Editorial Dir TCHOTCHO CHRISTIANE EKUE.

Les Presses de l'Université du Lomé: BP 1515, Lomé; tel. 22-25-48-44; fax 22-25-87-84.

Société Nationale des Editions du Togo (EDITOGO): BP 891, Lomé; tel. 22-21-61-06; f. 1961; govt-owned; general and educational; Pres. BIOSSEY KOKOU TOZOUN; Man. Dir WIYAO DADJA POUWI.

Broadcasting and Communications

TELECOMMUNICATIONS

In early 2012 the Togo telecommunications sector comprised one fixed-line operator and two mobile operators. At the end of 2010 there were 56,446 subscribers to fixed–line telephone services and 2.5m. subscribers to mobile telephone services.

Moov Togo: 225 blvd du 13 janvier, BP 14511, Lomé; tel. 22-20-13-20; fax 22-20-13-23; e-mail moovcontact@moov.tg; internet www .moov.tg; operates mobile cellular telecommunications in 80 localities; Dir-Gen. DJIBRIL OUATTARA.

Togo Télécom: pl. de la Réconciliation, Quartier Atchante, BP 333, Lomé; tel. 22-21-44-01; fax 22-21-03-73; e-mail contact@togotelecom .tg; internet www.togotelecom.tg; Dir-Gen. PÈTCHÈTIBADI BIKASSAM.

Togo Cellulaire—Togocel: Immeubble CFAO, 219 ave du 24 Janvier, BP 924, Lomé; tel. 22-22-66-11; fax 22-22-59-00; e-mail togocel@togocel.tg; internet www.togocel.tg; f. 2001; provides mobile cellular communications services to more than 70% of the territory of Togo; Dir-Gen. AFFOH ATCHA-DEDJI.

Regulatory Authority

Autorité de Réglementation des Secteurs de Postes et de Télécommunications (ART&P): blvd Léopold Sédar Senghor, Tokoin Tamé Côté Est, S.O.S. Village d'Enfants, BP 358, Lomé;

tel. 22-23-63-80; fax 22-23-63-94; e-mail artp@artp.tg; internet www
.artp.tg; Dir-Gen. PALOUKI MASSINA.

BROADCASTING

**Haute Autorité de l'Audiovisuel et de la Communication
(HAAC):** BP 8697, Lomé; tel. 22-50-16-78; fax 22-50-16-80; e-mail
infos@haactogo.tg; internet www.haactogo.tg; Pres. BIOSSEY KOKOU
TOZOUN.

Radio

Radiodiffusion du Togo (Internationale)—Radio Lomé: BP
434, Lomé; tel. 22-21-24-93; fax 22-21-36-73; e-mail radiolome@
radiolome.tg; internet www.radiolome.tg; f. 1953; state-controlled;
radio programmes in French, English and vernacular languages;
Dir-Gen. WILLIBRONDE TELOU.

Radiodiffusion du Togo (Nationale): BP 21, Kara; tel. 26-60-60-
60; f. 1974 as Radiodiffusion Kara (Togo); state-controlled; radio
programmes in French and vernacular languages; Dir M'BA KPE-
NOUGOU.

Radio Carré Jeunes: BP 2550, Adidogomé, Lomé; tel. 22-25-77-44;
e-mail carrejeunes@yahoo.fr; f. 1999; community radio station;
popular education, cultural information; broadcasts in French, Ewe,
Kabiyé and other local languages; Dir KOUBATINE MANJAMIE.

Radio de l'Evangile-Jésus Aime (JVA): Klikamé, Bretelle
Atikoumé, BP 2313, Lomé; tel. 22-25-44-95; fax 22-25-92-81; e-mail
radio.jva@fatad.org; f. 1995; owned by the West Africa Advanced
School of Theology (Assemblies of God); Christian; education and
development; broadcasts on FM frequencies in Lomé and Agou in
French, English and 12 local languages; Dir Pastor DOUTI LALLEBILI
FLINDJA.

Radio Kanal FM: Immeuble de CAMPOS, ave Champs de Course,
BP 61554, Lomé; tel. 22-21-33-74; fax 22-20-19-68; e-mail kanalfm@
cafe.tg; internet www.kanalfm.tg; f. 1997; broadcasts in French and
Mina; independent; Dir MODESTE MESSAVUSSU-AKUE.

Radio Maria Togo: BP 30162, 155 de la rue 158, Hédzranawoé,
Lomé; tel. 22-26-11-31; fax 22-26-35-00; e-mail info.tog@radiomaria
.org; internet www.radiomaria.tg; f. 1997; Roman Catholic; broadcasts in French, English and six local languages; Dir BENU EFOEVI
PENOUKOU.

Radio Nana FM: 29 rue Béeniglato, BP 6212, Lomé; tel. 22-20-12-
02; e-mail nanafm_tg@yahoo.fr; internet www.nanafm.org; f. 1999;
broadcasts in French and Mina; community station; political,
economic and cultural information; Dir FERDINAND AFFOGNON.

Radio Nostalgie: 14 ave de la Victoire, Quartier Tokoin-Hôpital, BP
13836, Lomé; tel. 22-22-25-41; fax 22-21-07-82; e-mail
nostalgietogo@yahoo.fr; internet www.nostalgie.tg; f. 1995; broadcasts in French, Ewe and Mina; Pres. and Dir-Gen. FLAVIEN JOHNSON.

Radio X-Solaire: Kodjoviakopé; tel. 22-22-30-48; f. 2000; Dir MIWO-
NOVI AKUÉ.

Radio Zion: BP 13853, Kpalimé, Lomé; tel. 24-41-09-15; f. 1999;
religious; broadcasts in French, Ewe and Kabiyé; Dir EMMANUEL
KOUNOUGNA.

Broadcasts from Radio France Internationale, the British Broadcasting Corpn, Voice of America, Radio Deutsche Welle and Radio
Nederland are also received in Togo.

Television

Télévision Togolaise: BP 3286, Lomé; tel. 22-21-53-57; fax 22-21-
57-86; e-mail televisiontogolaise@yahoo.fr; internet www.tvt.tg;
f. 1973; state-controlled; three stations; programmes in French
and vernacular languages; Dir KUESSAN YOVODEVI.

TV2: BP 13100, Agoe; tel. 22-51-49-93; fax 22-54-49-05; e-mail
tg_tv2@yahoo.fr; f. 2001; Dir YOUWESSODJO OURO BANG'NA.

TV7: BP 81104, Lomé; tel. 22-21-06-07; Dir JOËL SODJI.

Other television channels include La Chaîne du Futur, TV Jabal
Nour al-Islamia and Télé Sport. Many foreign channels, such as TV 5,
France 2, France 3, France 24, France 5/Arte, RTI, ORTB, RTS,
ORTM, Canal Horizons, Direct 8 and Télésud, are also broadcast to
Togo.

Broadcasting Association

**Organisation Togolaise des Radios et Télévisions Indépen-
dantes (ORTI):** Lomé; tel. 22-21-33-74; e-mail kawokou@syfed.tg
.refer.org; Pres. RAYMOND AWOKOU KOUKOU.

Finance

(cap. = capital; res = reserves; dep. = deposits; m. = million;
br(s). = branch(es); amounts in francs CFA, unless otherwise
indicated)

BANKING

In 2009 there were 11 banks and two other financial institutions in
Togo.

Central Bank

Banque Centrale des Etats de l'Afrique de l'Ouest (BCEAO):
rue Branly, BP 120, Lomé; tel. 22-21-25-12; fax 22-21-76-02; e-mail
ocourrier@lome.bceao.int; internet www.bceao.int; HQ in Dakar,
Senegal; f. 1962; bank of issue for the mem. states of the Union
Economique et Monétaire Ouest-Africaine (UEMOA, comprising
Benin, Burkina Faso, Côte d'Ivoire, Guinea-Bissau, Mali, Niger,
Senegal and Togo); cap. 134,120m., res 1,474,195m., dep.
2,124,051m. (Dec. 2009); Gov. KONÉ TIÉMOKO MEYLIET; Dir in Togo
KOSSI TÉNOU; br. at Kara.

Commercial Banks

Banque Internationale pour l'Afrique au Togo (BIA—Togo):
13 rue de Commerce, BP 346, Lomé; tel. 22-21-32-86; fax 22-21-10-19;
e-mail bia-togo@cafe.tg; internet www.biat.tg; f. 1965; fmrly
Meridien BIAO—Togo; 55% owned by Attijariwafa Bank (Morocco);
cap. and res 567m., total assets 51,793m. (Dec. 2003); Pres. VICTOR
ALIPUI; Gen. Man. JEAN-PAUL LE CALM; 7 brs.

Banque Togolaise pour le Commerce et l'Industrie (BTCI):
169 blvd du 13 janvier, BP 363, Lomé; tel. 22-21-46-41; fax 22-21-32-
65; e-mail btci@btci.tg; internet www.btci.tg; f. 1974; 23.8% owned by
Groupe BNP Paribas (France), 24.8% owned by Société Financière
pour les Pays d'Outre-mer (Switzerland); cap. 1,700m., res 1,706m.,
dep. 91,564m. (Dec. 2006); Pres. BARRY MOUSSA BARQUÉ; Dir-Gen.
YAO PATRICE KANEKATOUA; 9 brs.

Ecobank Togo (EBT): 20 rue du Commerce, BP 3302, Lomé; tel. 22-
21-72-14; fax 22-21-42-37; e-mail ecobanktg@ecobank.com; internet
www.ecobank.com; f. 1988; 80.7% owned by Ecobank Transnational
Inc (operating under the auspices of the Economic Community of
West African States), 14.0% by Togolese private investors; cap.
5,000.0m., res 7,201.9m., dep. 155,807.2m. (Dec. 2009); Chair.
MICHEL KOMLANVI KLOUSSEH; Man. Dir DIDIER ALEXANDRE LAMINE
CORREA; 3 brs.

Ecobank Transnational Inc: 2 ave Sylvanus Olympio, BP 3261,
Lomé; tel. 22-21-03-03; fax 22-21-51-19; e-mail info@ecobank.com;
internet www.ecobank.com; f. 1985; holding co for banking cos in
Benin, Burkina Faso, Cameroon, Côte d'Ivoire, Ghana, Guinea,
Liberia, Mali, Niger, Nigeria, Senegal and Togo, Ecobank Develop-
ment Corpn and EIC Bourse; cap. and res US $105.5m., total assets
$1,523.1m. (Dec. 2003); Chair. KOLAPO LAWSON; CEO ARNOLD EKPE.

Orabank Bank Togo: 11 ave du 24 janvier, BP 325, Lomé; tel. 22-
21-62-21; fax 22-21-62-25; e-mail info-tg@orabank.net; internet www
.orabank.net; f. 2004; fmrly Financial Bank Togo, present name
adopted 2012; 97.38% owned by Oragroup SA; cap. 6,516m. (Dec.
2011); Dir-Gen. PATRICK MESTRALLET; 8 brs.

Société Interafricaine de Banque (SIAB): 14 ave Sylvanus
Olympio, BP 4874, Lomé; tel. 22-21-28-30; fax 22-21-58-29; e-mail
info@siabtogo.com; internet www.siabtogo.com; f. 1975; fmrly
Banque Arabe Libyenne-Togolaise du Commerce Extérieur; 86%
owned by Libyan Arab Foreign Bank, 14% state-owned; cap. and res
181m., total assets 6,999m. (Dec. 2003); Pres. AYAWOVI DEMBA
TIGNOKPA; CEO RABIE YOUSSEF ABUSHAWASHI.

Union Togolaise de Banque (UTB): UTB Circulaire, blvd du 13
janvier, Nyékonakpoè, BP 359, Lomé; tel. 22-23-43-00; fax 22-21-22-
06; e-mail utbsg@cafe.tg; internet www.utb.tg; f. 1964; 100% state-
owned; transfer to majority private ownership proposed; cap. and res
−12.3m., total assets 49.0m. (Dec. 2003); Chair. BADAWASSO GNARO;
Dir-Gen. YAOVI ATTIGBÉ IHOU; 11 brs.

Development Banks

Banque Ouest-Africaine de Développement (BOAD): 68 ave de
la Libération, BP 1172, Lomé; tel. 22-21-42-44; fax 22-21-72-69;
e-mail boadsiege@boad.org; internet www.boad.org; f. 1973; promotes West African economic development and integration; cap.
682,100m., total assets 849,993m. (Dec. 2004); Pres. CHRISTIAN
ADOVÈLANDÉ.

Banque Togolaise de Développement (BTD): ave des Nîmes X,
angle ave N. Grunitzky, BP 65, Lomé; tel. 22-21-36-41; fax 22-21-44-
56; e-mail togo_devbank@btd.tg; internet www.btd.tg; f. 1966; f. 43%
state-owned, 20% owned by BCEAO, 13% by BOAD; transfer to
majority private ownership pending; cap. 3,065m., res 7,591m., dep.
34,514m. (Dec. 2006); Chair. and Pres. ESSO KANDJA; Dir-Gen. ZAKARI
DAROU-SALIM; 8 brs.

Savings Bank

Caisse d'Epargne du Togo (CET): 23 ave de Kléber Dadjo, Lomé; tel. 22-21-20-60; fax 22-21-85-83; e-mail cet@ids.tg; internet www.cet.tg; state-owned; privatization proposed; cap. and res 544m., total assets 27,988m. (Dec. 2006); Pres. DJOSSOU SEMONDJI.

Credit Institution

Société Togolaise de Crédit Automobile (STOCA): 3 rue du Mono, BP 899, Lomé; tel. 22-21-37-59; fax 22-21-08-28; e-mail stoca@ids.tg; f. 1962; 93.3% owned by SAFCA; cap. and res −112m., total assets 1,677m. (Dec. 2003); Pres. DIACK DIAWAR; Dir-Gen. DÉLALI AGBALE.

Bankers' Association

Association Professionnelle des Banques et Etablissements Financiers du Togo (APBEF): rue Docteur Kaolo-Tokoin Tamé, près de la Résidence du Bénin, BP 4863, Lomé; tel. 22-26-69-13; fax 22-21-85-83; e-mail info@apbeftogo.com; internet apbeftogo.com.

STOCK EXCHANGE

Bourse Régionale des Valeurs Mobilières (BRVM): BP 3263, Lomé; tel. 22-21-23-05; fax 22-21-23-41; e-mail brvm@brvm.org; internet www.brvm.org; f. 1998; national branch of BRVM (regional stock exchange based in Abidjan, Côte d'Ivoire, serving the member states of UEMOA); Man. in Togo NATHALIE BITHO ATCHOLI.

INSURANCE

In 2009 there were 12 insurance companies in Togo.

Allianz Togo: 21 blvd du 13 janvier, angle ave Duisburg, BP 3703, Lomé; tel. 22-21-97-73; fax 22-21-97-75; e-mail allianz.togo@allianz-tg.com; f. 2000; Dir-Gen. OLIVIER PICARD.

Beneficial Life Insurance Togo: BP 1115, Lomé; tel. 22-22-06-07; fax 22-22-06-27; f. 2000; Dir-Gen. ALYSON BROWN.

Colina Togo: 10 rue du Commerce, BP 1349, Lomé; tel. 22-22-93-65; fax 22-21-73-58; e-mail togo@groupecolina.com; internet www.groupecolina.com; affiliated to Colina SA (Côte d'Ivoire); Dir-Gen. LOUIS KAKRE BADOBRE.

Compagnie Commune de Réassurance des Etats Membres de la CICA (CICA—RE): 43 ave du 24 janvier, 07 BP 12410, Lomé; tel. 22-23-62-69; fax 22-61-35-94; e-mail cica-re@cica-re.com; f. 1981; reinsurance co-operating in 12 West and Central African states; Pres. ALBERT PAMSY; Dir-Gen. N'GUESSAN JEAN BAPTISTE KOUAME.

Fidelia Assurances: 01 BP 1679, Lomé; tel. 22-20-74-94; fax 22-20-76-16; e-mail fideliaass@helim.tg; f. 2004; Dir-Gen. AKOÈTÈ DATÈ ADAMAH-TASSAH.

Groupement Togolais d'Assurances (GTA): route d'Atakpamé, BP 3298, Lomé; tel. 22-25-60-75; fax 22-25-26-78; e-mail gta@laposte.tg; f. 1974; 62.9% state-owned; non-life insurance; Man. Dir GUY CAMARA; also **Groupement Togolais d'Assurances Vie**, life insurance; Man. Dir YAO CLAUDE GBIKPI DATE.

Nouvelle Société Interafricaine d'Assurances Togo (NSIA Togo): rue Brazza, BP 1120, Lomé; tel. 22-20-81-50; fax 22-20-81-52; e-mail nsia.tg@groupensia.com; f. 2005; Dir-Gen. JOSÉ KWASSI SYMENOUH.

Sicar Gras Savoye Togo: 140 blvd du 13 janvier, BP 2932, Lomé; tel. 22-21-35-38; fax 22-21-82-11; e-mail sicargs@sicargs.tg; internet www.grassavoye.com; affiliated to Gras Savoye (France); Dir GUY BIHANNIC.

Union des Assurances du Togo (UAT): Immeuble BICI, 169 blvd du 13 janvier, BP 495, Lomé; tel. 22-21-10-34; fax 22-21-87-24; e-mail unatinfo@cafe.tg; also **Union des Assurances du Togo—Vie** (UAT—Vie) ; Dir-Gen. LOCOH THÉOPHILE KODJO.

Trade and Industry

ECONOMIC AND SOCIAL COUNCIL

Conseil Economique et Social: Lomé; tel. 22-21-53-01; f. 1967; advisory body of 25 mems, comprising five trade unionists, five reps of industry and commerce, five reps of agriculture, five economists and sociologists, and five technologists; Pres. KOFFI GBODZIDI DJONDO.

GOVERNMENT AGENCIES

Direction Générale des Mines et de la Géologie: BP 356, Lomé; tel. 22-21-30-01; fax 22-21-31-93; organization and administration of mining in Togo; Dir-Gen. MATTHIAS BANIMPO GBENGBARTANE.

Société d'Administration des Zones Franches (SAZOF): 2564 ave de la Chance, BP 3250, Lomé; tel. 22-53-53-53; fax 22-51-43-18; e-mail sazof@zonefranchetogo.tg; internet zonefranchetogo.tg;

administers and promotes export processing zones; Dir-Gen. YAZAZ EGBARÉ; Asst Dir-Gen. ATSOUVI YAWO SIKPA.

Société Nationale de Commerce (SONACOM): 29 blvd Circulaire, BP 3009, Lomé; tel. 22-21-31-18; f. 1972; cap. 2,000m. francs CFA; importer of staple foods; Dir-Gen. JEAN LADOUX.

DEVELOPMENT ORGANIZATIONS

Agricultural development is under the supervision of five regional development authorities, the Sociétés Régionales d'Aménagement et de Développement.

Agence Française de Développement (AFD): 437 ave de Sarakawa, BP 33, Lomé; tel. 22-21-04-98; fax 22-21-79-32; e-mail afdlome@groupe-afd.org; internet www.afd.fr; Country Dir PHILIPPE COLLIGNON.

Association Villages Entreprises: BP 23, Kpalimé; tel. and fax 24-41-00-62; e-mail averafp@hotmail.com; Dir KOMI AFELETE JULIEN NYUIADZI.

France Volontaires: BP 1511, Lomé; tel. 22-21-09-45; fax 22-21-85-04; e-mail afvp@togo-imet.com; internet www.france-volontaires.org; f. 1965; fmrly Association Française des Volontaires du Progrès; name changed as above in 2009; Nat. Del. MARC LESCAUDRON.

Office de Développement et d'Exploitation des Forêts (ODEF): 59 QAD rue de la Kozah, BP 334, Lomé; tel. 22-21-79-86; fax 22-21-34-91; e-mail kodefly@yahoo.fr; f. 1971; develops and manages forest resources; Man. Dir EDJIDOMÉLÉ GBADOE.

Recherche, Appui et Formation aux Initiatives d'Autodéveloppement (RAFIA): BP 43, Dapaong; tel. 27-70-80-89; fax 27-70-82-37; f. 1992; Dir NOIGUE TAMBILA LENNE.

Service de Coopération et d'Action Culturelle: ave de la Présidence, BP 91, Lomé; tel. 22-23-46-60; fax 22-23-46-75; e-mail scac-lome@tg.refer.org; administers bilateral aid from the French Ministry of Foreign Affairs; Dir ETIENNE CAZIN.

Société d'Appui a la Filière Café-Cacao-Coton (SAFICC): Lomé; f. 1992; development of coffee, cocoa and cotton production.

CHAMBER OF COMMERCE

Chambre de Commerce et d'Industrie du Togo (CCIT): ave de la Présidence, angle ave Georges Pompidou, BP 360, Lomé; tel. 22-21-70-65; fax 22-21-47-30; e-mail ccit@ccit.tg; internet www.ccit.tg; f. 1921; Pres. JONATHAN FIAWOO; br. at Kara.

EMPLOYERS' ORGANIZATIONS

Association des Grandes Entreprises du Togo (AGET): Immeuble UAT, 3e étage, 812 blvd du 13 janvier, Lomé; internet 22-21-95-85; internet www.aget-togo.org; f. 2007; Pres. JOSÉ SYMENOUH; Sec.-Gen. PASCAL COTI.

Conseil National du Patronat du Togo: 60 blvd du Mono, BP 12429, Lomé; tel. 22-21-08-30; fax 22-21-71-11; e-mail cnptogo@gmail.com; internet www.cnp-togo.tg; f. 1963 as Groupement Interprofessionnel des Entreprises du Togo; renamed as above in 1990; Pres. ALBERT KOSSIVI NAKU; Sec.-Gen. MOCKTAR SOW.

Syndicat des Commerçants, Industriels, Importateur et Exportateurs du Togo (SCIMPEXTO): BP 1166, Lomé; tel. 22-22-59-86; Pres. AMA JUSTIN D'ALMEIDA.

Syndicat des Entrepreneurs de Travaux Publics, Bâtiments et Mines du Togo: BP 12429, Lomé; tel. 22-21-19-06; fax 22-21-08-30; Pres. JOSÈPHE NAKU.

UTILITIES

Electricity

Communauté Electrique du Bénin: ave de la Kozah, BP 1368, Lomé; tel. 22-21-61-32; fax 22-21-37-64; e-mail dg@cebnet.org; f. 1968 as a jt venture between Togo and Benin to exploit the energy resources in the two countries; Chairs TCHAMDJA ANDJO, Z. MARIUS HOUNKPATIN; Man. DJIBRIL SALIFOU.

Compagnie Energie Electrique du Togo (CEET): Lomé; tel. 22-20-82-20; e-mail ceet@ceet.tg; internet www.ceet.tg; f. 1963; production, transportation and distribution of electricity; Dir-Gen. GNANDÉ DJÉTÉLI.

Gas

Société Togolaise de Gaz SA (Togogaz): BP 1082, Lomé; tel. 22-21-44-31; fax 22-21-55-30; 71% privatization pending; Dir-Gen. JOËL POMPA.

Water

Société Togolaise des Eaux (TdE): 53 ave de la Libération, BP 1301, Lomé; tel. 22-21-34-81; fax 22-21-46-13; f. 2003 to replace Régie Nationale des Eaux du Togo; production and distribution of drinking water; Pres. MARC AKLESSO AQUITEME.

TRADE UNIONS

Collectif des Syndicats Indépendants (CSI): Lomé; f. 1992 as co-ordinating org. for three trade union confederations.

Confédération Générale des Cadres du Togo (CGCT): BP 12837, Lomé; tel. 22-23-13-09; Sec.-Gen. MOLI EPHREM TSIKPLONOU.

Confédération Nationale des Travailleurs du Togo (CNTT): Bourse du Travail, BP 163, 160 blvd du 13 janvier, Lomé; tel. 22-22-02-55; fax 22-21-48-33; f. 1973; Sec.-Gen. AGUI YVES PALANGA; 35,000 mems (2007).

Confédération Syndicale des Travailleurs du Togo (CSTT): 14 rue Van Lare, BP 3058, Lomé; tel. 22-22-11-17; fax 22-22-44-41; e-mail cstt_cstt@yahoo.fr; internet www.csttogo.org; f. 1949, dissolved 1972, re-established 1991; comprises 36 unions and 7 professional federations (Agro-Alimentation, Education, General Employees, Industry, Public Services, Transport, Woodwork and Construction); Sec.-Gen. TÉVI SÉBASTIEN AYIKOÉ; 55,266 mems (2007).

Groupe des Syndicats Autonomes: BP 1728, Lomé; f. 1991; Sec.-Gen. PAP EDOUARD AGLAMEY.

Union Générale des Syndicats Libre du Togo (UGSL): BP 30137, Lomé; tel. 22-25-32-28; Sec.-Gen. MATHIAS HLOMADOR.

Union Nationale des Syndicats Indépendants du Togo (UNSIT): Tokoin-Wuiti, BP 30082, Lomé; tel. 22-21-32-88; fax 22-21-95-66; e-mail unsit@netcom.tg; f. 1991; Sec.-Gen. NORBERT GBIKPI-BENISSAN; 17 affiliated unions; 8,061 mems (2007).

Transport

RAILWAYS

Société Nationale des Chemins de Fer du Togo (SNCT): BP 340, Lomé; tel. 22-21-43-01; fax 22-21-22-19; e-mail togorail@yahoo.com; f. 1900; owned by West African Cement (Wacem) since Jan. 2003; total length 519 km, incl. lines running inland from Lomé to Atakpamé and Blitta (276 km), and Lomé to Tabligbo (77 km); a coastal line, running through Lomé and Aného, was closed to passenger traffic in 1987 (a service from Lomé to Kpalimé—119 km—has also been suspended); passengers carried (1999): 4,400 (compared with 628,200 in 1990); freight handled (2007): 631,798 metric tons; Gen. Man. M. M. REDDY.

ROADS

In 2007 there were an estimated 11,652 km of roads, of which some 21% were paved. The rehabilitation in the late 1990s of the 675-km axis road that links the port of Lomé with Burkina Faso, and thus provides an important transport corridor for land-locked West African countries, was considered essential to Togo's economic competitiveness. Other principal roads run from Lomé to the borders of Ghana, Nigeria and Benin.

Africa Route International (ARI—La Gazelle): Lomé; tel. 22-25-27-32; f. 1991 to succeed Société Nationale de Transports Routiers; Pres. and Man. Dir BAWA S. MANKOUBI.

SHIPPING

The major port, at Lomé, generally handles a substantial volume of transit trade for the land-locked countries of Mali, Niger and Burkina Faso. There is another port at Kpémé for the export of phosphates. At the end of 2012 Togo's merchant fleet comprised 208 vessels, with a total displacement of 782,626 grt.

Conseil National des Chargeurs Togolais (CNCT): BP 2991, Lomé; tel. 22-23-71-00; fax 22-27-08-40; e-mail cnct@cnct.tg; internet www.cnct.tg; f. 1980; restructured 2001; Dir-Gen. TOÏ GNASSINGBÉ.

Ecomarine International (Togo): Immeuble Ecomarine, Zone Portuaire, BP 6014, Lomé; tel. 22-27-48-04; fax 22-27-48-06; e-mail ecomarine@ecomarineint.com; f. 2001 to develop container-handling facility at Lomé Port; operates maritime transport between Togo, Senegal and Angola; Chair. Alhaji BAMANGA TUKUR.

Port Autonome de Lomé: BP 1225, Lomé; tel. 22-27-47-42; fax 22-27-08-18; e-mail togoport@togoport.tg; internet www.togoport.tg; f. 1968; transferred to private management in Jan. 2002; Pres. ASSIBA AMOUSSOU-GUENOU; Man. Dir Adm. ADEGNON KODJO FOGAN; 1,600 employees (2003).

Société Ouest-Africaine d'Entreprises Maritimes Togo (SOAEM—Togo): Zone Industrielle Portuaire, BP 3285, Lomé; tel. 22-21-07-20; fax 22-21-34-17; f. 1959; forwarding agents, warehousing, sea and road freight transport; Pres. JEAN FABRY; Man. Dir JOHN M. AQUEREBURU.

Société Togolaise de Navigation Maritime (SOTONAM): pl. des Quatre Étoiles, rond-point du Port, BP 4086, Lomé; tel. 22-21-51-73; fax 22-27-69-38; state-owned; privatization pending; Man. PAKOUM KPEMA.

SOCOPAO—Togo: 18 rue du Commerce, BP 821, Lomé; tel. 22-21-55-88; fax 22-21-73-17; f. 1959; freight transport, shipping agents; Pres. GUY MIRABAUD; Man. Dir HENRI CHAULIER.

SORINCO—Marine: 110 rue de l'OCAM, BP 2806, Lomé; tel. 22-21-56-94; freight transport, forwarding agents, warehousing, etc.; Man. AHMED EDGAR COLLINGWOOD WILLIAMS.

Togolaise d'Affrètements et d'Agence de Lignes SA (TAAL): 21 blvd du Mono, BP 9089, Lomé; tel. 22-23-19-00; fax 22-21-06-09; e-mail taalsa@togo-imet.com; internet www.taal.tg; f. 1992; shipping agents, haulage management, crewing agency, forwarding agents; Pres. and Man. Dir PAUL KOKOU EDJAMFEILE.

CIVIL AVIATION

There are international airports at Tokoin, near Lomé (Gnassingbé Eyadéma International Airport), and at Niamtougou. In addition, there are smaller airfields at Sokodé, Sansanné-Mango, Dapaong and Atakpamé.

Africa West Cargo: route de l'Aéroport, Zone Franche Aéroportuaire, BP 10019, Lomé; tel. 22-26-88-10; fax 22-26-17-49; e-mail info@africawestcargo.com; internet www.africawestcargo.com; f. 1997; air freight operator; CEO YANNICK ERBS.

Agence Nationale de l'Aviation Nationale du Togo: BP 2699, Lomé; tel. 22-26-37-40; fax 22-26-08-60; e-mail latta@togo-imet.com; internet www.anac-togo.tg; Dir-Gen. LATTA GNAMA.

ASKY Airlines: BP 2988, Lomé; tel. 22-23-05-10; fax 22-20-89-00; e-mail headoffice@flyasky.com; internet www.flyasky.com; f. 2008; commenced operations in 2010; 25% owned by Ethiopian Airlines; regional services; Chair. GERVAIS KOFFI DJONDO.

Société Aéroportuaire de Lomé-Tokoin (SALT): Aéroport International de Lomé-Tokoin, BP 10112, Lomé; tel. 22-23-60-60; fax 22-26-88-95; e-mail salt@cafe.tg; internet www.salt-togo.com; f. 1987; Dir-Gen. Dr AKRIMA KOGOE.

Tourism

Some 202,044 foreign tourist arrivals were reported in 2010. In that year receipts from tourism totalled US $66m.

Office National Togolais du Tourisme (ONTT): BP 1289, Lomé; tel. 22-21-43-13; fax 22-21-89-27; e-mail angelodjiss@yahoo.fr; internet www.togo-tourisme.com; f. 1963; Dir ANGELO DJISSODEY.

Defence

As assessed at November 2012, Togo's armed forces officially numbered about 8,550 (army 8,100, air force 250, naval force 200). Paramilitary forces comprised a 750-strong gendarmerie. Military service is by selective conscription and lasts for two years. Togo receives assistance with training and equipment from France.

Defence Expenditure: Budgeted at 27,800m. francs CFA in 2011.

Chief of General Staff: Col ATCHA MOHAMMED TITIKPINA.

Chief of Staff of the Land Army: Col BALI WIYAO.

Education

Education is officially compulsory between the ages of six and 15. Primary education is free, begins at six years of age and lasts for six years. It is divided into three cycles, each of two years. Secondary education, beginning at the age of 12, lasts for a further seven years, comprising a first cycle of four years and a second of three years. According to UNESCO estimates, in 2008/09 enrolment at primary schools included 94% of children in the relevant age-group (98% of boys; 89% of girls), while in 2009/10 secondary enrolment was equivalent to 51% of the relevant age-group. Proficiency in the two national languages, Ewe and Kabiyé, is compulsory. Mission schools are important, educating almost one-half of all pupils. In 2006/07 32,502 students were enrolled in institutions providing tertiary education. The Université du Lomé (formerly the University du Bénin) had about 14,000 students in the early 2000s, and scholarships to French universities are available. A second university opened in Kara, in the north of Togo, in early 2004. In 2010 spending on education represented 13.9% of total budgetary expenditure.

TONGA

Introductory Survey

LOCATION, CLIMATE, LANGUAGE, RELIGION, FLAG, CAPITAL

The Kingdom of Tonga comprises about 170 islands in the south-western Pacific Ocean, about 650 km (400 miles) east of Fiji. The Tonga (or Friendly) Islands are divided into three main groups: Vava'u, Ha'apai and Tongatapu. Only 36 of the islands are permanently inhabited. The climate is mild (16°–21°C or 61°–71°F) for most of the year, though usually hotter (27°C or 81°F) in December and January. The languages are Tongan, which is a Polynesian language, and English. Tongans are predominantly Christians, with some 36% being of the Wesleyan Methodist faith, 15% Roman Catholics and 15% Latter-day Saints (Mormons). The national flag (proportions 1 by 2) is red, with a rectangular white canton, containing a red cross, in the upper hoist. The capital is Nuku'alofa, on Tongatapu Island.

CONTEMPORARY POLITICAL HISTORY

Historical Context

The basis of the constitutional monarchy was established in the 19th century. The kingdom was neutral until 1900, when it became a British Protected State. The treaty establishing the Protectorate was revised in 1958 and 1967, giving Tonga increasing control over its affairs. Prince Tupouto'a Tungi, who had been Prime Minister since 1949, succeeded to the throne as King Taufa'ahau Tupou IV in December 1965 and appointed his brother, Prince Fatafehi Tu'ipelehake, as Prime Minister. Tonga achieved full independence, within the Commonwealth, on 4 June 1970.

Domestic Political Affairs

Elections to the Legislative Assembly held in May 1981 resulted unexpectedly in the new Assembly becoming dominated by traditionalist conservatives. In March 1982 the Minister of Finance, Mahe Tupouniua, resigned at the King's request after refusing to grant him extra-budgetary travel funds. Further elections to the Legislative Assembly took place in May 1984. In September 1985 the King declared his support for the French Government's programme of testing nuclear weapons in the South Pacific, on the grounds that it was in the broader interests of the Western alliance. However, he upheld his former statement of opposition to the tests in French Polynesia.

Elections were held in February 1987 to the nine commoner seats in the Legislative Assembly; among the six newcomers to the legislature were reported to be some of the Government's harshest critics. In July 1988 the Supreme Court awarded 26,500 pa'anga in damages to 'Akilisi Pohiva, the editor of a local independent journal and an elected member of the Legislative Assembly, after the Government had been found guilty of unfairly dismissing him from his post in the Ministry of Education in 1985, because he had reported on controversial issues. The court ruling intensified opposition demands for the abolition of perceived feudal aspects within Tongan society.

In September 1989 the commoner members of the Legislative Assembly (people's representatives) boycotted the Assembly, leaving it without a quorum, in protest at the absence of the Minister of Finance, whom they had wanted to question about the proceeds of the Government's sale of Tongan passports to foreign nationals, a process that had begun in 1983 as a means of acquiring revenue. Upon resuming their seats in the Assembly later in the month, the commoners introduced a motion demanding the reform of the Assembly to make it more accountable to the people. The motion proposed the creation of a more balanced legislature by increasing elected representation from nine to 15 seats and reducing noble representation to three seats (the Cabinet's 12 members were also members of the Assembly). In March 1990 a group of Tongan conservatives submitted an electoral petition, alleging bribery and corruption by Pohiva, the leader of the pro-reform commoners, and his colleagues, who had been re-elected by substantial majorities in the February general election. (In July 1988 the King had indicated his opposition to majority rule, claiming that the monarchical Government

reacted more quickly to the needs of the people than the Government of a parliamentary democracy.)

In October 1990 Pohiva initiated a court case against the Government, claiming that its controversial sale of passports to foreign citizens was unconstitutional and illegal. The passports were sold mainly in Hong Kong, for as much as US $30,000 each, allowing the purchasers, in theory, to avoid travel restrictions imposed on mainland Chinese passport-holders. However, in February 1991 a constitutional amendment to legalize the naturalization of the new passport-holders was adopted at an emergency session of the Legislative Assembly, and the case was therefore dismissed. In March a large demonstration was held in protest against the Government's actions, and a petition urging the King to invalidate the 426 passports in question and to dismiss the Minister of Police (who was responsible for their sale) was presented by prominent commoners and church leaders. In the following month the Government admitted that the former President of the Philippines, Ferdinand Marcos, and his family had been given Tongan passports as gifts, after his removal from power in 1986. The events that ensued from the sale of passports were widely viewed as indicative of the growing support for reform and for greater accountability in the government of the country. By 1996 most of the 6,600 passports sold under the scheme had expired.

In August 1991 the Prime Minister, Prince Fatafehi Tu'ipelehake, retired from office, owing to ill health (the Prince died in April 1999), and was succeeded by the King's cousin, Baron Vaea of Houma, who had previously held the position of Minister of Labour, Commerce and Industries.

Pressure for democratic reform

Plans by campaigners for democratic reform to establish a formal political organization were realized in November 1992, when the Pro-Democracy Movement was recognized, the group having been formed in the early 1970s as the Human Rights and Democracy Movement in Tonga. The group, led by Father Seluini 'Akau'ola (a Roman Catholic priest), organized a constitutional convention in the same month, at which options for the introduction of democratic reform were discussed. The Government refused to recognize or to participate in the convention, prohibiting any publicity of the event and denying visas to invited speakers from abroad. Nevertheless, at elections in February 1993 the pro-democracy reformists won six of the nine elective seats in the Legislative Assembly. In August 1994 Tonga's first political party was formed when the Pro-Democracy Movement launched the People's Party, under the chairmanship of a local businessman, Huliki Watab.

At elections in January 1996 pro-democracy candidates retained six seats in the Legislative Assembly. In March three journalists, including the editor of *The Times of Tonga*, were arrested and imprisoned in connection with an article in the newspaper that criticized the newly appointed Minister of Police, Fire Services and Prisons, Clive Edwards, for unfavourable remarks that he had made regarding the People's Party. All three were subsequently released, but were found guilty in April under a law against angering a civil servant.

In July 1996 the Legislative Assembly voted to resume the sale of Tongan passports to Hong Kong Chinese, despite the controversy caused by the similar scheme operated in the early 1990s. As many as 7,000 citizenships were to be made available for between 10,000 and 20,000 pa'anga, granting purchasers all the rights of Tongan nationality, except ownership of land.

In September 1996 a motion to impeach the Minister of Justice and Attorney-General, Tevita Topou, was proposed in the Legislative Assembly, following allegations that Topou had continued to receive his daily parliamentary allowance during an unauthorized absence from the Assembly. Moreover, the publication of details of the impeachment motion, which had been reported to *The Times of Tonga* by Pohiva, before it had been submitted to the Legislative Assembly, resulted in the imprisonment of Pohiva and of the newspaper's editor, Kalafi Moala, and deputy editor, Filakalafi Akau'ola, for contempt of parliament. The three were subsequently released, although in October Moala was found guilty on a further charge of contempt. In the same month the King closed the Assembly (which had been expected to sit until mid-November) until further notice. He denied that he had taken this decision in order to prevent further impeachment proceedings against Topou. Furthermore, in February 1997 the Speaker of the Legislative Assembly was found guilty of contempt of court for criticizing the Chief Justice's decision to release the three journalists imprisoned in September of the previous year. The Government rejected accusations that it was attempting to force the closure of *The Times of Tonga*, despite forbidding Moala (who was resident in New Zealand) to enter Tonga without written permission from the Government, banning all government-funded advertising in the publication and forbidding all government employees to give interviews to its journalists. Parliament reopened in late May. In June Akau'ola was arrested once again and charged with sedition for publishing a letter in *The Times of Tonga* that questioned government policy. However, in the same month the Government suffered a significant reverse when the Court of Appeal ruled that the imprisonment of Pohiva and the two journalists in late 1996 had been unlawful.

In September 1997, following a formal apology from Topou, the Legislative Assembly voted to abandon impeachment proceedings against him. In September 1998 the King closed the Legislative Assembly in response to a petition, signed by more than 1,000 people, that sought the removal from office of the Speaker, Eseta Fusitu'a, who was accused of misappropriating public funds and of abusing his position. Pohiva and other pro-democracy activists commended the King for his decisive action in response to the petition.

At a general election in March 1999 five members of the reformist Tonga Human Rights and Democracy Movement (formerly the Pro-Democracy Movement/People's Party) were returned to the Legislative Assembly. In January 2000 the King appointed his youngest son, Prince 'Ulukalala-Lavaka-Ata, as Prime Minister, replacing Baron Vaea who had in 1995 announced his intention to retire. It had been expected that Crown Prince Tupouto'a would take up the position, but his support for constitutional reform in Tonga (notably the abolition of life-time terms for the Prime Minister and ministers) contrasted with the King's more conservative approach. In March 2000 a report published by the US Department of State claimed that Tonga's system of government, whereby most members of the Legislative Assembly were not directly elected, was in breach of UN and Commonwealth human rights guidelines. The report was welcomed by the leader of the Tonga Human Rights and Democracy Movement, 'Akilisi Pohiva.

Financial scandals and other controversy

In September 2000 protests took place in Nuku'alofa, prompted by concerns that Chinese immigrant businesses, encouraged by the Government to establish themselves in Tonga, were creating unfavourable economic conditions for Tongan enterprises. The Tonga Human Rights and Democracy Movement appealed to the Government to cease issuing work permits to foreign (predominantly Chinese) business people and to end the sale of Tongan passports, which had raised an estimated US $30m. during the 1980s. In order to protect this money, the King had requested that the funds be placed in the Tonga Trust Fund, held in a cheque account at a branch of the Bank of America in the US city of San Francisco, California. In June 1999 Jesse Bogdonoff, a Bank of America employee, had successfully sought royal approval to invest the money in a company in the US state of Nevada, Millennium Asset Management, where Bogdonoff was named as the Fund's Advising Officer. The balance of the Fund and the interest it had accrued (totalling some $40m.) was due to be returned to Tonga in June 2001; instead, the money appeared to have vanished, while the company had seemingly ceased to exist. Bogdonoff denied any wrongdoing, claiming to have been deliberately misled with regard to the value of the funds. In September Princess Pilolevu, acting as Regent in the absence of the King and the Crown Prince, dismissed the Minister of Education, Kinikinilau Tutoatasi Fakafanua, who at the time of the incident had been Minister of Finance, along with the Deputy Prime Minister and Minister of Justice, Tevita Tupou, both of whom were trustees of the Fund. In October the acting Deputy Prime Minister, Clive Edwards, denied that the Privy Council had directed the transfers from the Fund or that any ministers were implicated. However, in June 2002 the Government admitted that about $26m. had been lost as a result of Bogdonoff's actions and that legal proceedings had been initiated in the USA. In February 2003 the Legislative Assembly began

impeachment proceedings against the ministers implicated in the matter. In February 2004 it was reported that the Government had agreed to settle out of court with Bogdonoff, who was to pay just $1m. in compensation to the Tongan authorities.

In January 2002 Pohiva published allegations that the King held a secret 'offshore' bank account containing US $350m., some of which was believed to be the proceeds of gold recovered from an 18th-century shipwreck. A letter written to the King from within the palace referring to the account was dismissed by the Government as a forgery. Pohiva was briefly held in custody in February, while police searched the offices of the Tonga Human Rights and Democracy Movement and confiscated computer equipment, in an attempt to find the source material of the allegations. New Zealand's Minister of Foreign Affairs and Trade condemned Tonga as being endemically corrupt, implying that New Zealand's annual aid of $NZ6m. profited the élite rather than the Tongan people as a whole. The King admitted that he did possess an overseas account, with the Bank of Hawaii, but claimed that it contained the profits of vanilla sales from his own plantation. Nevertheless, Pohiva was formally charged with the use and publication of a forged document. In May 2002 he was acquitted of charges of sedition.

Increasing criticism of the Government

At a general election in March 2002 52 candidates competed for the nine commoners' seats in the Legislative Assembly. The Tonga Human Rights and Democracy Movement won seven seats. In September, having repeatedly failed since 1998 to secure government approval for the group's registration under this name, the organization once again became known as the Human Rights and Democracy Movement in Tonga (HRDMT). However, in November 2005 the Government gave approval for a licence to be granted under the Incorporated Societies Act as Friendly Islands Human Rights and Democracy Movement Inc (FIHRDM Inc).

Concerns for the freedom of the media re-emerged in February 2003 when the Government declared *The Times of Tonga*, the twice-weekly newspaper printed in New Zealand, to be a 'prohibited import', describing it as a foreign publication with a political agenda. In April Tonga's Chief Justice, Gordon Ward, ruled that the ban was both illegal and unconstitutional. However, within hours of the ruling the Government ordered a new ban under different legislation. Ward overruled the ban in the following month, describing it as 'an ill-disguised attempt to restrict the freedom of the press', but on arrival from New Zealand 2,000 copies of the paper were seized by the Tongan customs authorities. In early June the Supreme Court granted an injunction to *The Times of Tonga* ordering the Government to allow its distribution. The Government once again defied the order, stating that it would appeal. In mid-June the newspaper (which had been banned in Tonga since February) was finally allowed to go on sale within the country, after Ward had threatened each individual member of the Cabinet with contempt of court if they did not permit its distribution.

One of the most vocal critics of the affair was the King's nephew, Prince 'Uluvalu Tu'ipelehake, who in June 2003 expressed concern that the attempts to legislate against the freedom of the press and to restrict the right to seek judicial review would bring Tonga into disrepute. However, in the following month the Legislative Assembly approved the Media Operators' Bill, which introduced restrictions on the involvement of foreign nationals in Tonga's media. The legislation was widely viewed as a further attempt to ban *The Times of Tonga*, the editor of which resided in New Zealand. In October Tonga's Roman Catholic bishop led a march by some 8,600 people to the government buildings in Nuku'alofa. The demonstration, which was the largest of its kind in Tonga's history, aimed to persuade the Government not to introduce any further restrictions on media freedom. However, a few days later the Legislative Assembly voted in favour of a constitutional amendment allowing for greater control of the media, and shortly afterwards introduced the Newspaper Act, which gave the Government increased powers to regulate the content of newspapers in the country.

The failure of Royal Tongan Airlines in early 2004 caused considerable disquiet, particularly in the tourism industry. At the opening session of the Legislative Assembly in May seven of the nine elected representatives staged a boycott, demanding the resignation of the Prime Minister, who they claimed had allowed millions of pa'anga to be wasted during his tenure as chairman of the airline. A legal challenge to the constitutional amendments governing media freedom, introduced by the Government in

2003, was begun in the Supreme Court in August 2004, and in October the Court declared the Media Operators' Act, the Newspaper Act and the associated constitutional amendments invalid. Shortly before the legal hearing began the Prime Minister announced the dismissal of three cabinet ministers, including the Minister of Police, Fire Services and Prisons, Clive Edwards, who had been one of the principal proponents of the constitutional amendments. In November the Prime Minister announced that four new cabinet ministers would be appointed from among the elected members of the Legislative Assembly (two from the nobles and two from the people's representatives) following the elections in March 2005. The announcement, which represented a departure from the usual procedure whereby ministers were selected from outside the legislature, was seen by many as a welcome concession towards democratic reform. However, Clive Edwards criticized the proposals, claiming that they were anti-democratic, as they required two members of the Legislative Assembly, elected by the people, to relinquish their seats in order to assume the new positions from which they could be dismissed at the discretion of the King.

Elections for the nine nobles' and nine commoners' seats took place on 16 and 17 March 2005, respectively. The latter were contested by a record number of 60 candidates. Two newly elected members from each group were appointed to positions in the Cabinet, and a by-election for the four vacated seats took place on 3–5 May. The Minister of Defence, 'Aloua Fetu'utolu Tupou, died suddenly in mid-April. At the subsequent by-election Clive Edwards was elected under the banner of the People's Democratic Party (PDP). The PDP had been launched in April by a breakaway group from the HRDMT, which had stated its intention to pursue political reform in a more aggressive manner. The new organization was registered in July, despite fears that this might be deemed illegal, as no provision existed in the Constitution for the establishment of political parties.

In May 2005 some 8,000 people marched to Tonga's Royal Palace in one of the largest demonstrations of its kind to take place in the country. The protesters presented a petition to the King expressing discontent at high electricity prices charged by the Shoreline Power Group and the excessive salaries reportedly paid to the company's executives.

In July 2005 public servants of the Public Service Association (PSA) voted to approve the first national strike in Tonga's history, following the Government's refusal to reconsider large disparities in public sector salary increases in the recent budget. Almost all of the country's teachers, numerous health care workers and employees from many other public services, totalling some 3,000 workers, joined the strike. Accusations of government attempts to restrict the PSA's access to the media were made when the power supply of a private television station was cut shortly before a statement by the PSA was due to be broadcast. During the third week of the strike some 10,000 people marched to the Royal Palace in support of the PSA. Subsequent reports of vandalism against school property and government vehicles were received, and an attempt had apparently been made to burn down the house of a senior executive of the Shoreline Power Group. The strike ended in September when the two sides signed an agreement allowing for salary increases of between 60% and 80%. More significantly, the agreement also provided for the establishment of a commission to review the country's Constitution and to examine possibilities for a more democratic form of government. Shortly afterwards a further demonstration by more than 10,000 people took place, appealing to the King to dismiss the entire Government and to conduct a constitutional review within 12 months. Protesters also reiterated their demands for the renationalization of former government assets, particularly power generation, but also Tonga's orbital satellite positions and its internet domain address.

Proposals for constitutional change and the riots of 2006

In October 2005 the King agreed to the establishment of a parliamentary committee to examine the issue of constitutional reform. In February 2006 the Prime Minister, Prince 'Ulukalala-Lavaka-Ata, resigned from office, relinquishing all his portfolios. People's Representative Dr Feleti (Fred) Sevele, a commoner and advocate of constitutional reform, was appointed acting Prime Minister. Prince 'Ulukalala had confronted increasing demands for his resignation, amid accusations of incompetence and inefficiency. In view of his pro-democracy stance, the appointment of Sevele was widely welcomed. He was expected to be influential in the establishment of democratic government in Tonga, partly owing to his close relationship with the progressive Crown Prince. During the course of his first official visit to New Zealand, Sevele confirmed that about one-quarter of posts in the civil service were to be abolished, as part of the Government's commitment to reduce budgetary expenditure. The National Committee for Political Reform (NCPR) submitted a report detailing its findings in August.

On 11 September 2006, after a protracted illness, King Taufa'ahau Tupou IV died in New Zealand, prompting a month of national mourning. Crown Prince Tupouto'a succeeded to the throne as King George Tupou V. In October the NCPR's report on political reform was discussed by members of the Legislative Assembly. The report envisaged a 26-member legislature, comprising 17 representatives elected by the people and nine representatives elected by nobles; the King would nominate a Prime Minister from the legislature, who would in turn select the Cabinet from among the elected representatives. Prime Minister Sevele subsequently stated that the Cabinet had proposed the establishment of a new parliamentary tripartite committee composed of cabinet members and nobles' and people's representatives, which would deliberate on the political reform process and present its conclusions in the following year. As part of its 'roadmap for political reform', the Cabinet made the following recommendations: that the Legislative Assembly should comprise between 23 and 28 representatives, nine of whom would be nobles' representatives and 14 people's representatives, elected according to constituency; the Cabinet should comprise between 12 and 14 members, including two Governors, with at least two-thirds being elected representatives of the Legislative Assembly; the King should appoint two-thirds of the Cabinet on the advice of the Prime Minister and the remaining one-third independently; and the Prime Minister should be an elected representative of the Legislative Assembly, appointed by the King on the advice of the Legislative Assembly, and with responsibility for choosing ministers.

In November 2006 demonstrations in Nuku'alofa against the slow pace of democratic reform developed into riots, with protesters engaging in widespread looting and destruction. Approximately 80% of the buildings in the business area of the city were reported to have been burned down, and police later verified that at least six bodies had been found in the ruins. Security forces from Australia and New Zealand arrived to help restore stability. In the aftermath of the violence hundreds of people were arrested. A modified programme of reform was approved later in the month, apparently in response to the unrest. The new programme envisaged a 30-member legislature comprising 21 people's representatives and nine nobles' representatives, with the Prime Minister to be elected by the legislature. King Tupou V had in fact endorsed the reforms in the previous month, but the final decision had been delayed pending the conclusions of the tripartite committee. In an address to the Legislative Assembly, the King highlighted the reconstruction efforts necessary after the 'shame' of the unrest, and reiterated the importance of democratic reform that was 'appropriate' for Tonga.

In early 2007 five pro-reform people's representatives, including Clive Edwards, were detained on charges that included sedition, in connection with their alleged involvement in the riots of November 2006. The state of emergency measures proclaimed following the unrest remained in effect until February 2011. In June 2008 an independent anti-corruption commission was established to investigate alleged financial wrongdoing within the Government; however, the commission was reportedly criticized by Pohiva, as it did not have the power to investigate the activities of the King.

The elections of 2008

On 23 April 2008 29 nobles elected nine representatives to the Legislative Assembly, and on the following day elections were held to determine the nine people's representatives. Approximately 48% of the electorate voted in the latter polls, in which 71 candidates participated. Pro-democracy candidates, including several awaiting trial on sedition charges, secured a majority of the commoners' seats, indicating continuing popular support for the reform movement. Although the elections were described as the last to be held under the prevailing system (with forthcoming constitutional changes expected to increase the proportions of democratically elected seats), reformists urged the King to formalize the process at his coronation. In July legislation was approved that provided for the establishment of a Constitutional and Electoral Commission. The Commission was to be composed of five commissioners nominated by the Cabinet, nobles, people's representatives and Judicial Services Commission (two), respectively. It met for the first time in January 2009, under the chairmanship of former Chief Justice Gordon Ward, and conducted a series of public forums on the nature of the proposed political reforms throughout the country.

In July 2008, in accordance with the undertaking of King Tupou V to relinquish his private business interests as soon as possible, the Tongan Government agreed to purchase the Shoreline Power Group. The Minister of Finance, National Planning, Public Enterprises and Information, Afu'alo Matoto, confirmed that the Government was to pay US $25m. for ownership of Shoreline, the country's only electric power generation facility, using funds derived from the sale of government shares in the Westpac Bank of Tonga. The new King also undertook to divest himself of his interests in the telecommunications sector and elsewhere.

Shortly before his coronation in August 2008, King Tupou V announced that he was voluntarily surrendering certain powers in favour of the Prime Minister, although the King was to retain judicial powers granting him the right to commute prison sentences and to appoint judges. The King also reiterated his commitment to parliamentary reform.

In May 2009 Sevele dismissed reported criticisms from Clive Edwards that the process of political reform was being obstructed by the Government. Edwards allegedly claimed that the tabling of the Constitutional and Electoral Commission's first report had been delayed, in order that recommended changes would not be in place in time for the elections scheduled for 2010. Meanwhile, in March 2009 five men (including Sione Teisina Fuko, the President of the PDP) were found not guilty of sedition, having been accused of inciting the unrest of November 2006. In September 2009 five people's representatives were acquitted by the Court of Appeal on charges of seditious conspiracy related to the unrest, but an appeal by Edwards against a conviction of inciting violence was dismissed.

In August 2009 the Minister of Civil Aviation, Marine and Ports, Paul Karalus, resigned, following the sinking of a ferry, the *Princess Ashika*, with the loss of 74 lives, earlier in that month. A commission of inquiry into the disaster concluded in March 2010 that the Government had been responsible for buying an unseaworthy vessel, and that Karalus had provided false information following the sinking.

Constitutional reform

In November 2009 the final report of the Constitutional and Electoral Commission was submitted to the Legislative Assembly. The Commission recommended that, effective from the next legislative elections, due to take place in late 2010, the elected membership of the Assembly should be increased to 26, of whom nine would be elected by and from among the hereditary nobles (as before), and 17 would be chosen in a general election (compared with nine previously). The term of the legislature was to be increased from three to four years. The executive power of the King was to be considerably reduced. The Prime Minister was to be appointed by the King, but nominated by the legislature, and cabinet ministers were to be selected by the Prime Minister, and not to number more than one-half of the members of the legislature; a maximum of four ministers could be appointed from outside the legislature. The King was to retain the power to approve or veto legislation and to dismiss the legislature. By the end of December the Legislative Assembly had approved most of the recommendations, and in early 2010 it debated the division of the country into 17 constituencies. Some pro-democracy members, including 'Akilisi Pohiva, opposed the adoption of single-member constituencies, arguing that traditional kinship ties might compromise the fairness of the voting system and might encourage bribery. The Assembly gave its approval to the Constitutional Amendment Act and the Constituency Boundaries Act in April 2010.

The Attorney-General, John Cauchi, resigned in April 2010, complaining of government interference in the judiciary; it was reported that this referred to judicial appointments, in particular the appointment of two independent prosecutors to investigate the sinking of the *Princess Ashika* (see The elections of 2008). Cauchi's predecessor in the post, 'Alisi Taumoepeau, then stated that she too had been forced to resign in May 2009 after objecting to political interference in judicial appointments.

The 2011 budget prompted controversy owing to the apparent disclosure that the level of state funding allocated to the King was to increase by nearly 200%, to in excess of US $700,000 annually, with a similar amount reserved each year for the King's travel expenses; a further $7m. was reported to have been allocated to the planned extension and renovation of the royal

palace. The revelation provoked considerable consternation among politicians and the general public alike. Isileli Pulu, a member of the newly established Democratic Party of the Friendly Islands (DPFI), argued that such an increase was both morally wrong and financially imprudent, given the beleaguered state of the national economy. In response to the suggestion that about one-half of the proposed increase was to be funded by foreign aid, New Zealand officials stated categorically that no funding provided by the New Zealand Government could be divested to this end. However, the Tongan Government insisted that no such increase was planned and that the figure of $700,000 was an estimate of the current cost to Tonga of the monarchy.

In a further controversial development that critics argued risked compromising the independence of the judiciary, the Judicial Services Commission Act was repealed in July 2010, thereby abolishing the Commission that hitherto had appointed Tonga's judges, responsibility for which was henceforth to be transferred to the (royally appointed) Lord Chancellor. In August the Government announced the formation by the Privy Council (appointed by the King and including the members of the Cabinet) of a Royal Commission of Inquiry into allegations that the Government had attempted to undermine the independence of the judiciary.

Recent developments: the 2010 elections and death of King Tupou V

Elections were held for the Legislative Assembly on 25 November 2010; for the first time in Tongan history, the majority of legislators were elected by the general populace. A total of 147 candidates contested the 17 elected seats, of which 12 were secured by DPFI, led by Pohiva, while independent candidates accounted for the remaining five. The nine noble representatives were elected on the same day by 34 nobles (including three of the King's four Law Lords).

Former cabinet minister Lord Tu'ivakano, a member of the nobility, was elected Prime Minister in December 2010, having secured 14 parliamentary votes (including those of the five independent members of the newly elected Legislative Assembly), thereby defeating Pohiva, who received only 12 votes. Lord Lasike was appointed as the new parliamentary Speaker. The inclusion within the Cabinet of two non-elected persons prompted criticism from some observers, who argued that such inclusions were inappropriate and undemocratic. Pohiva resigned as Minister of Health only one week after his nomination, reportedly in protest against the allocation of just two portfolios to members of the DPFI despite its strong performance in the elections, and against the inclusion of the two non-elected members. The Prime Minister stated that improving the performance of the national economy would be the main priority of his administration.

In April 2011 the managing director of Shipping Corporation of Polynesia (the operating firm of the *Princess Ashika*, which sank in August 2009) was convicted on charges of manslaughter, forgery and sending an unseaworthy ship to sea; he was sentenced to five years' imprisonment (reduced in September 2011 to three years and six months, of which three years were suspended), and the firm was fined US $2m. The captain and a former director at the Ministry of Transport were both convicted of manslaughter and of sending an unseaworthy ship to sea; the captain was sentenced to a four-year prison term, while the latter received a three-year suspended prison sentence. Another senior member of the ferry's crew was convicted of manslaughter and sentenced to five years' imprisonment.

At the opening of a new parliamentary session in June 2011 King Tupou V announced proposed legislation that would give the King greater control over appointments to the judiciary. In August opposition members tabled a parliamentary motion protesting against the Deputy Prime Minister's assumption of the role of Attorney-General, stating that the Constitution required those in senior legal positions to be independent of the Government. The dispute was resolved with the interim appointment of two foreign lawyers as Attorney-General and Lord Chancellor (a newly created position), pending the appointment of permanent officials.

Accusations of anti-democratic practice were, once again, levelled against the Government in October 2011, when legislation reducing the maximum penalty for illegal firearms possession from five years' imprisonment to a one-year term and from a fine of US $5,000 to $1,000 was approved. Members of the opposition claimed that the changes were designed to benefit two noble members, including Speaker Lord Lasike, who were awaiting trial on charges relating to illegal possession of firearms and ammunition. Moreover, critics asserted that the new legislation did not take account of increasing rates of gun crime in Tonga. The King refused to give his assent to the legislation. Criticism escalated into demands for Lasike's resignation in December, when it was revealed that he had breached the conditions of his bail and travelled to the USA. At the same time reports in the Australian press indicated that Australian police were investigating allegations that Lasike had accepted bribes in order to obtain a visa for the head of a Colombian drugs cartel, which apparently aimed to use Tonga as a hub for its cocaine-smuggling operations into Australia and the People's Republic of China. On Lasike's return from the USA in January 2012, he declared that he would resign as Speaker if the Supreme Court found him guilty of the charges against him; he was convicted in July and was removed as Speaker (being replaced by Lord Fakafanua), although his subsequent appeal against the conviction was successful in October.

On 18 March 2012, following a brief illness, King George Tupou V died in a hospital in Hong Kong. The King was succeeded by his brother, Crown Prince Tupouto'a Lavaka, hitherto High Commissioner to Australia and Prime Minister in 2000–06 (when, prior to being confirmed as his brother's heir, he had been known as Prince 'Ulukalala-Lavaka-Ata), who took the title King Tupou VI. Tupou VI's eldest son was invested as Crown Prince Tupouto'a 'Ulukalala in late March.

A series of cabinet reorganizations, together with the instigation of criminal investigations into several members of the Legislative Assembly (mostly on firearms offences), appeared to undermine the Government's stability during the first half of 2012. In June, for the first time in the country's political history, a motion of no confidence in the Prime Minister and his Cabinet was presented to parliament. The motion, which was submitted by the DPFI, was signed by 10 people's representatives and appeared to have the support of a total of 13 members of the Legislative Assembly. An independent and two ministers belonging to the DPFI resigned from the Cabinet shortly afterwards. However, uncertainty over the correct procedure for debating the motion, and questions over its constitutional validity, led to a number of delays and deferrals in the tabling of a debate and subsequent vote. When the vote finally took place in early October, it was defeated by 13 votes to 11, one of its previous supporters, People's Representative Sangster Saulala, of the DPFI, having reversed his position and accepted a cabinet post as Minister of Agriculture, Food, Forestry and Fisheries in July, and another being overseas receiving medical treatment. The opposition reiterated its view that the Prime Minister had lost the confidence of the Tongan people and announced its intention to investigate the possibility of initiating impeachment proceedings against him.

Meanwhile, in August 2012 a report was presented to the Legislative Assembly by an independent parliamentary committee, following its investigation into the disbursement of a 119m. pa'anga loan from the People's Republic of China, intended to assist Tonga's reconstruction programme in the aftermath of the 2006 riots. The loan had apparently increased levels of debt in the country to such an extent that the World Bank had stated that Tonga's access to overseas borrowing should be severely curtailed. Moreover, the report alleged that the transfer and allocation of the Chinese loan had been illegal and recommended that the Government pursue criminal charges against those involved.

Foreign Affairs

Although never colonized by a European power, Tonga, as a former British protectorate, is a member of the Commonwealth, and belongs to numerous other regional and international organizations (see Regional and International Co-operation). Large numbers of Tongans live and work abroad, mainly in New Zealand, Australia and the USA.

A friendship treaty that Tonga signed with the USA in July 1988 provided for the safe transit within Tongan waters of US ships capable of carrying nuclear weapons. Tonga was virtually alone in the region in failing to condemn the French Government for its decision to resume nuclear weapons tests in the South Pacific in mid-1995. However, in May 1996 it was announced that Tonga was finally to accede to the South Pacific Nuclear-Free Zone Treaty (see p. 125).

Regional relations

Australia and New Zealand are major trading partners and sources of financial and technical assistance for Tonga. Many Tongans are educated in New Zealand, and at the 2006 New Zealand census more than 50,000 residents identified themselves as Tongan. Under a 10-year aid strategy initiated in September 2008, New Zealand agreed to give priority to governance (allocating an initial $NZ5m. to Tonga's police development programme and $1.5m. to finance the work of the Constitutional and Electoral Commission: see Domestic Political Affairs), education, technical and vocational training, and tourism. The New Zealand Tonga Business Council was inaugurated in 2011 with the aim of promoting and enhancing bilateral business relations.

Meanwhile, following the introduction of legislation restricting media freedom in the country in late 2003, the New Zealand Government announced that it was to review its relationship with Tonga. The Tongan Government summoned New Zealand's ambassador to the islands to register its displeasure. However, in January 2004 Prince 'Uluvalu Tu'ipelehake appealed to Australia's Minister for Foreign Affairs, Alexander Downer, to encourage political reform and to support attempts to increase democratic representation in Tonga. In March 2009 Tonga named its first High Commissioner to New Zealand, and the High Commission of Tonga subsequently opened in Wellington. New Zealand has worked with the Tongan Government on a number of bilateral aid projects, focusing in particular on strengthening governance and improving education and economic performance. The New Zealand Government notably financed Tonga's first solar power farm, which opened in mid-2012, providing $NZ7.9m. for the project.

In November 2008, following the success of a similar scheme in New Zealand, the Australian Government signed a memorandum of understanding with Tonga, Kiribati, Vanuatu and Papua New Guinea, whereby 2,500 Pacific islanders would be permitted to work in Australia's horticultural industry, on a seasonal basis. An agreement on the Tonga-Australia Partnership for Development was signed by the two countries' Prime Ministers in August: Australian assistance under the programme was to give priority to improving infrastructure, primary health care and training for employment, and to developing a more efficient public sector. The new Tongan Prime Minister, Lord Tu'ivakano, made a two-week visit to Australia in August 2011, during which he held bilateral discussions with the Presidents of the World Bank and the Asian Development Bank, as well as meeting Australian Prime Minister Julia Gillard, who commended Tonga on its recent political reforms.

In November 1998 Tonga announced that it had decided to terminate its diplomatic links with Taiwan and to establish relations with the People's Republic of China. Tonga opened a consulate in China in May 2005. Several Chinese businesses were targeted in the Nuku'alofa riots of November 2006, prompting China to evacuate hundreds of its citizens. Tonga renewed a bilateral trade agreement with China in 2005, and an agreement on joint technical and economic co-operation was signed in 2007. Economic and technical co-operation agreements signed by the two countries in 2011 provided for US $19m. in Chinese aid to Tonga. In June 2012 the Chinese Government announced that it was to provide $25m. for two new aircraft in order to improve domestic air services in Tonga. The service was to be supported for three years with technical expertise from China.

Japan is also an important provider of aid for Tonga. In February 2010 the Japanese Government agreed to fund a project to introduce solar energy to Tonga; the project envisaged the installation of 500 solar home energy units, and was expected to make a sizeable contribution to meeting the Tongan Government's target of deriving 50% of electricity generation from renewable energy sources by 2015. Meanwhile, Japan opened an embassy in Tonga in March 2009. In September 2012 the Japanese Government announced that it was to provide more than 1m. pa'anga for community projects, including the upgrading of rural water supplies on Tongatapu.

Tonga's relations with Fiji suffered a reversal in May 2011, when Fiji's Prime Minister, Cdre Frank Bainimarama, lodged a formal complaint with the Tongan Prime Minister, accusing him of assisting a person charged with sedition of escaping from Fiji. In a statement the Tongan Government confirmed that it had sent a navy patrol boat to answer a distress call and had rescued one individual. It was subsequently reported that the person in question was Lt-Col Tevita Mara, Fiji's former army Chief of Staff, a former ally of Bainimarama, and the son of one of Fiji's most prominent political figures, the late Prime Minister Ratu

Sir Kamisese Mara. Reports later confirmed that Mara, who was related to the Tongan royal family, had been granted a Tongan passport. The Tongan Government rejected a Fijian request for Lt-Col Mara's extradition.

In November 2011 Tonga was one of eight Pacific states and territories that jointly established the Polynesian Leaders Group (see p. 478), which pledged to enhance co-operation among its members across a wide range of fields, including trade and investment, education, climate change and health. The first formal meeting of the Group was held on the sidelines of the annual Pacific Islands Forum summit in August 2012.

CONSTITUTION AND GOVERNMENT

Tonga is an hereditary monarchy, and the Constitution is based on that of 1875. Under constitutional reforms implemented in 2010, the King remained as head of state but relinquished many of his direct executive powers. Although executive authority has been transferred to the Cabinet, the King retains the power of veto. The King continues to preside over the Privy Council, which has advisory powers. The Legislative Assembly is unicameral. The number of seats determined by direct popular election was increased from a minority of nine People's Representatives to 17 of the 26 seats in 2010. A system of single-seat constituencies, replacing the previous multi-member constituencies, was introduced at the 2010 elections. Nine parliamentary seats continue to be reserved for hereditary nobles, chosen as previously from among their peers. In addition to the 26 elected members of the Legislative Assembly, a further four may be nominated by the incoming Prime Minister, who is elected by the Legislative Assembly. The legislature's term of office was increased from three to four years in 2010.

REGIONAL AND INTERNATIONAL CO-OPERATION

Tonga is a member of the Pacific Community (see p. 422), the Pacific Islands Forum (see p. 426), the Asian Development Bank (ADB, see p. 214) and the UN's Economic and Social Commission for Asia and the Pacific (ESCAP, see p. 31). The country is a signatory of the Lomé Conventions and the successor Cotonou Agreement (see p. 334) with the European Union (EU).

Tonga joined the UN in 1999 and was formally admitted to the World Trade Organization (WTO, see p. 444) in July 2007. It is also a member of the Commonwealth.

ECONOMIC AFFAIRS

In 2011, according to estimates by the World Bank, Tonga's gross national income (GNI), measured at average 2009–11 prices, was US $374m., equivalent to $3,580 per head (or $4,690 per head on an international purchasing-power parity basis). During 2002–11, it was estimated, the population increased at an average annual rate of 0.6%, while gross domestic product (GDP) per head declined marginally, in real terms. Overall GDP increased, in real terms, at an average annual rate of 1.2% in 2002–11, according to the Asian Development Bank (ADB). GDP expanded by 0.8% in the fiscal year ended June 2012.

Agriculture (including forestry and fishing) contributed a preliminary 18.9% of GDP in 2010/11, and the sector was expected by FAO to engage 25.6% of the employed labour force in mid-2013. The principal cash crops are coconuts, squash (pumpkin) and vanilla beans. Yams, taro, sweet potatoes, watermelons, tomatoes, cassava, lemons and limes, oranges, groundnuts and breadfruit are also cultivated as food crops, while the islanders keep pigs, goats, poultry and cattle. Exports of vegetable products accounted for 52.5% of export receipts (including re-exports) in 2011 and animals and animal products for a further 33.0%. According to figures from the ADB, agricultural GDP decreased at an average annual rate of 0.9% in 2002–11. Agricultural GDP increased by 0.5% in 2011/12.

Industry (including mining, manufacturing, construction and utilities) provided a preliminary 22.0% of GDP in 2010/11 and engaged 30.6% of the employed labour force in 2003. According to the ADB, industrial GDP increased at an average annual rate of 2.7% in 2002–11. Industrial GDP rose by 1.2% in 2011/12.

Mining contributed a preliminary 0.8% of GDP in 2010/11; the sector engaged 0.2% of the employed labour force in 2003. The mining sector is largely undeveloped, as Tonga possesses no known mineral resources on land. However, the Tongan Government has permitted several companies to explore its waters for deep sea minerals in recent years. In late 2012 Nautilus Minerals Tonga (a subsidiary of a Canadian-based company) announced the discovery of high-grade undersea deposits of gold, silver, copper and zinc in Tonga's exclusive economic zone.

According to figures from the ADB, during 2002–11 the sector's GDP increased, in real terms, at an average annual rate of 16.1%; following a rise of 137.7% in 2009/10, mining GDP contracted by 1.8% in 2010/11.

Manufacturing contributed a preliminary 6.5% of GDP in 2010/11, and (with mining) engaged 24.7% of the employed labour force in 2003. Output of food products and beverages dominates the manufacturing sector. Other manufacturing activities include the production of concrete blocks, small excavators, furniture, handicrafts, textiles, leather goods, sports equipment (including small boats), brewing and coconut oil. There is also a factory for processing sandalwood. According to figures from the ADB, during 2002–11 the sector's GDP declined, in real terms, at an average annual rate of 0.4%; manufacturing GDP declined by 2.5% in 2009/10, but increased by 7.2% in 2010/11.

Construction contributed a preliminary 11.8% of GDP in 2010/11; the sector engaged 4.2% of the employed labour force in 2003. According to figures from the ADB, during 2002–11 construction GDP increased, in real terms, at an average annual rate of 4.7%; the sector's GDP increased by 16.9% in 2010/11.

In an attempt to reduce fuel imports, a 2-MW wave-energy power plant was constructed in the early 1990s. The use of solar power is also of increasing significance, having been introduced with assistance from Japan and New Zealand, and the feasibility of wind power is also under consideration. In mid-2012 Tonga opened its first solar power farm, which was expected to generate some 4% of Tonga's energy demand and significantly reduce imports of diesel. Tonga aims to derive 50% of electricity generation from renewable energy sources by 2015. Imports of mineral products accounted for 25.7% of total import costs in 2011.

Service industries contributed a preliminary 59.1% of GDP in 2010/11; the sector engaged 37.5% of the employed labour force in 2003. Tourism makes a significant contribution to the economy. Visitor arrivals rose to 50,645 in 2009, but declined to 45,430 in 2010, before rising again to 46,005 in 2011. Tourism receipts totalled US $31m. in 2010. According to ADB figures, the GDP of the services sector increased at an average annual rate of 0.8% in 2002–11. Sectoral GDP expanded by 0.5% in 2011/12.

In 2010/11, according to the ADB, Tonga recorded a visible merchandise trade deficit of US $119.0m. and a deficit of $38.0m. on the current account of the balance of payments. In 2011 the principal source of imports was New Zealand (providing 30.2% of the total); other important suppliers were the USA, Fiji, Australia and the People's Republic of China. New Zealand was also the principal market for exports (purchasing 19.5% of the total); Japan, the USA and Australia were also significant purchasers. The principal exports in that year were vegetable products, animals and animal products, and wood pulp, paper and paperboard. The principal imports were mineral products, prepared foodstuffs, animals and animal products, machinery, mechanical appliances and electrical equipment, and base metals.

According to the ADB, in the financial year ending 30 June 2010 there was a budgetary deficit of 35.0m. pa'anga, equivalent to 4.9% of GDP. Tonga's total external debt reached US $186m. in 2012. In that year the cost of debt-servicing was equivalent to 9.0% of the total revenue from exports of goods and services. In 2012/13 official development assistance from Australia was projected at $A32.1m., while aid from New Zealand was estimated to total $NZ18.0m. The annual rate of inflation averaged 7.2% in 2002–11. Consumer prices increased by an average of 4.6% in 2011/12, according to the ADB. Some 1.1% of the labour force were unemployed in 2006, according to the ADB. However, the unemployment rate was estimated at 13% in 2012, although among certain groups the figure was believed to be much higher.

The constraints on Tonga's economic development have included large-scale emigration (and a consequent reliance on remittances from overseas, primarily New Zealand, Australia and the USA) and the weakness of international prices for squash, a major export commodity. Riots in the capital of Nuku'alofa in 2006 had a profound impact on the economy, as did the global financial crisis and tsunami and cyclone disasters of 2009 and 2010. The deterioration in the global economy in 2008/09 reduced the availability of employment opportunities in countries such as the USA and New Zealand, leading to a sharp decline in remittances from Tongans resident overseas, which contributed some 150m. pa'anga (equivalent to 22% of GDP) in 2009/10, compared with 200m. pa'anga (31% of GDP) in 2007/08, and decreased further, to 109m. pa'anga, in 2011/12. Observers suggested that Tonga's capacity to service its large public debt might be increased if the country's efforts to reform the public sector and state enterprises were to be more actively pursued. Much of the public debt, which was estimated at 45% of GDP in 2011/12, was due to the cost of financing reconstruction projects following the riots of 2006 and natural disasters of 2009 and 2010. A report published by the ADB in early 2013 suggested that emigration was crucial to Tonga's economic survival, owing to a lack of domestic employment and an ongoing reliance on remittances from overseas. These had continued to decline during 2012 and had not been offset by higher revenues from tourism. GDP growth slowed to 0.8% in 2011/12 (the lowest rate of economic growth in the Pacific region), owing to the completion of reconstruction projects and the continued decline in remittances. The ADB predicted a further deceleration in growth in

2012/13, to 0.5%. It was hoped that Tonga's successful bid to host the Pacific Games in 2019, announced in late 2012, would stimulate the economy, particularly the construction and tourism sectors.

PUBLIC HOLIDAYS

2014: 1 January (New Year's Day), 18–21 April (Easter), 25 April (ANZAC Day), 4 June (Independence Day), 4 July (Official Birthday of King Tupou VI), 17 September (Birthday of the Heir to the Crown of Tonga), 4 November (Tonga National Day), 4 December (Tupou I Day), 25–26 December (Christmas Day and Boxing Day).

Statistical Survey

Source (unless otherwise indicated): Tonga Government Department of Statistics, POB 149, Nuku'alofa; tel. (676) 23300; fax (676) 24303; e-mail dept@stats.gov.to; internet www.spc.int/prism/country/to/stats.

AREA AND POPULATION

Area: 748 sq km (289 sq miles).

Population: 101,991 at census of 30 November 2006; 103,036 (males 52,001, females 51,035) at census of 30 November 2011 (preliminary). *By Island Group* (2011 census, preliminary): Tongatapu 75,158; Vava'u 14,936; Ha'apai 6,650; 'Eua 5,011; Niuas 1,281; Total 103,036.

Density (at 2011 census): 137.7 per sq km.

Population by Age and Sex (Secretariat of the Pacific Community estimates at mid-2012): *0–14:* 39,141 (males 20,361, females 18,779); *15–64:* 58,803 (males 29,745, females 28,058); *65 and over:* 6,037 (males 2,643, females 3,394); *Total* 103,981 (males 52,750, females 51,231). Note: Estimates not adjusted to take account of 2011 census (Source: Pacific Regional Information System).

Principal Towns (population at 2011 census, preliminary): Nuku'alofa (capital) 24,158; Neiafu 4,045; Haveluloto 3,476; Tofoa-Koloua 3,358; Vaini 3,234.

Births, Marriages and Deaths (Secretariat of the Pacific Community estimates, 2010, unless otherwise indicated): Registered live births 2,735 (birth rate 26.5 per 1,000); Registered marriages (2004, provisional) 677 (marriage rate 6.6 per 1,000); Registered deaths 683 (death rate 6.6 per 1,000). Source: mainly Pacific Regional Information System.

Life Expectancy (years at birth): 72.3 (males 69.5; females 75.2) in 2011. Source: World Bank, World Development Indicators database.

Economically Active Population (persons aged 15 years and over, 2003): Agriculture, forestry and fishing 11,000; Mining and quarrying 60; Manufacturing 8,530; Electricity, gas and water 530; Construction 1,440; Trade, restaurants and hotels 3,560; Transport, storage and communications 1,580; Financing, insurance, real estate and business services 770; Public administration and defence 2,590; Education 1,780; Health and social work 660; Other community, social and personal services 1,330; Private households with employed persons 610; Extra-territorial organizations 90; Not adequately defined 30; *Total employed* 34,560 (males 20,420, females 14,140); Unemployed 1,890 (males 760, females 1,130); *Total labour force* 36,450 (males 21,180, females 15,270). Note: Figures are rounded to the nearest 10 persons. *Mid-2013* (estimates): Agriculture, etc. 11,000; Total labour force 43,000 (Source: FAO).

HEALTH AND WELFARE

Key Indicators

Total Fertility Rate (children per woman, 2010): 3.9.

Under-5 Mortality Rate (per 1,000 live births, 2010): 16.

Physicians (per 1,000 head, 2010): 0.6.

Hospital Beds (per 1,000 head, 2010): 2.6.

Health Expenditure (2009): US $ per head (PPP): 207.

Health Expenditure (2009): % of GDP: 4.6.

Health Expenditure (2009): public (% of total): 79.3.

Access to Sanitation (% of persons, 2010): 96.

Total Carbon Dioxide Emissions ('000 metric tons, 2008): 176.0.

Carbon Dioxide Emissions Per Head (metric tons, 2008): 1.7.

Human Development Index (2011): ranking 90.

Human Development Index (2011): value 0.704.

For sources and definitions, see explanatory note on p. vi.

AGRICULTURE, ETC.

Principal Crops ('000 metric tons, 2011, FAO estimates): Sweet potatoes 6.0; Cassava 7.2; Taro 3.2; Yams 4.9; Other roots and tubers 2.0; Coconuts 61.0; Pumpkins, squash and gourds 18.7; Other vegetables and melons 5.6; Bananas 0.8; Plantains 2.6; Oranges 0.7; Lemons and limes 1.8.

Livestock ('000 head, year ending September 2011, FAO estimates): Pigs 81; Horses 12; Cattle 11; Goats 13; Chickens 330.

Livestock Products (metric tons, 2011, FAO estimates): Pig meat 1,600; Hen eggs 280; Honey 11; Cows' milk 370.

Forestry ('000 cu m, 2000): *Roundwood Removals* (excl. bark): 4; *Sawnwood Production:* 2 (FAO estimate). *2001–11:* Annual output as in 2000 (FAO estimates).

Fishing (metric tons, live weight, 2010): Marine fishes 1,000 (FAO estimate) (Snappers and jobfishes 182; Albacore 57; Bigeye tuna 24; Yellowfin tuna 47); Marine crustaceans 401 (FAO estimate); Total catch (incl. others, FAO estimate) 2,150.

Source: FAO.

INDUSTRY

Electric Energy (production, million kWh): 51 in 2009; 51 in 2010; 51 in 2011. Source: Asian Development Bank.

FINANCE

Currency and Exchange Rates: 100 seniti (cents) = 1 pa'anga (Tongan dollar or $T). *Sterling, US Dollar and Euro Equivalents* (31 October 2012): £1 sterling = $T2.774; US $1 = $T1.721; €1 = $T2.236; $T100 = £36.05 = US $58.10 = €44.72. *Average Exchange Rate* (pa'anga per US $): 2.0345 in 2009; 1.9060 in 2010; 1.7290 in 2011.

Budget ('000 pa'anga, year ending 30 June 2010): *Revenue:* Taxation 116,242; Non-tax revenue 27,313; Capital receipts 3,050; Total 146,604 (excl. grants received from abroad 48,565). *Expenditure:* Current expenditure 183,838; Capital expenditure 18,446; Total 202,284 (excl. net lending 27,866). Source: Asian Development Bank.

International Reserves (US $ million at 31 December 2011): IMF special drawing rights 10.88; Reserve position in the IMF 2.63; Foreign exchange 129.79; *Total* 143.29. Source: IMF, *International Financial Statistics*.

Money Supply ('000 pa'anga at 31 December 2011): Currency outside depository corporations 30,048; Transferable deposits 92,718; Other deposits 183,278; *Broad money* 306,044. Source: IMF, *International Financial Statistics*.

Cost of Living (Consumer Price Index, excl. rent; base: 2005 = 100): All items 126.2 in 2009; 130.7 in 2010; 139.4 in 2011. Source: IMF, *International Financial Statistics*.

Gross Domestic Product (million pa'anga at constant 2010/11 prices, year ending 30 June): 728.5 in 2008/09; 748.4 in 2009/10; 783.4 in 2011 (preliminary).

Expenditure on the Gross Domestic Product (million pa'anga at current prices, year ending 30 June 2011, preliminary): Government final consumption expenditure 134.3; Private final consumption expenditure 660.5; Non-profit institutions serving households 51.3; Gross fixed capital formation 240.9; Change in stocks 55.7; *Total domestic expenditure* 1,142.7; Exports of goods and services 135.8; *Less* Imports of goods and services 477.0; Statistical discrepancy –18.1; *GDP in purchasers' values* 783.4.

Gross Domestic Product by Economic Activity (million pa'anga at current prices, year ending 30 June 2011, preliminary): Agriculture, forestry and fishing 133.3; Mining and quarrying 5.8; Manufacturing 46.1; Electricity, gas and water 20.4; Construction 82.9; Trade, restaurants and hotels 101.4; Transport, storage and communications 48.5; Finance and real estate 57.6; Public administration 91.8; Other services 117.3; *Sub-total* 705.2; *Less* Imputed bank service charges 13.4; *Gross value added in basic prices* 691.8; Indirect taxes, less subsidies 91.5; *GDP at market prices* 783.4.

Balance of Payments (US $ '000, 2009): Exports of goods 7,334; Imports of goods –139,640; *Trade balance* –132,306; Exports of services 34,511; Imports of services –46,871; *Balance on goods and services* –144,665; Primary income received 10,037; Primary income paid –6,190; *Balance on goods, services and primary income* –140,819; Secondary income received 96,669; Secondary income paid –10,066; *Current balance* –54,216; Capital account (net) 54,867; Direct investment liabilities –36; Financial derivatives and employee stock options (net) 1,657; Other investment assets 10,381; Other investment liabilities 5,649; Net errors and omissions –37,266; *Reserves and related items* –18,965. Source, IMF, *International Financial Statistics*.

EXTERNAL TRADE

Principal Commodities ('000 pa'anga, 2011): *Imports:* Animals and animal products 40,253; Vegetable products 10,797; Prepared foodstuffs 46,471; Mineral products 85,212; Chemical products 14,701; Wood and wood products 9,166; Wood pulp, paper and paperboard 11,511; Base metals and articles thereof 25,139; Machinery, mechanical appliances and electrical equipment 37,568; Transportation equipment 15,568; Miscellaneous manufactured articles 5,838; Works of art, collectors' pieces and antiques 918; Total (incl. others) 332,210. *Exports* (including re-exports): Animals and animal products 8,144; Vegetable products 12,935; Chemical products 508; Wood pulp, paper and paperboard 1,383; Base metals and articles thereof 791; Total (incl. others) 24,661.

Principal Trading Partners ('000 pa'anga, 2011): *Imports:* Australia 21,737; China, People's Republic 21,260; Fiji 29,419; Japan 16,472; New Zealand 100,477; USA 39,839; Total (incl. others) 332,210. *Exports:* Australia 2,290; Japan 5,161; New Zealand 4,819; USA 2,657; Total (incl. others) 24,661.

TRANSPORT

Road Traffic (registered motor vehicles, 2004): Passenger cars 6,580; Light goods vehicles 5,183; Heavy goods vehicles 2,698; Buses 114; Taxis 845; Total (incl. others) 16,748.

Shipping: *International Traffic* ('000 metric tons, 1998, unless otherwise indicated): Goods loaded 13.8; Goods unloaded 80.4. Vessels entered ('000 net registered tons) 1,950 in 1991 (Source: UN, *Statistical Yearbook*). *Flag Registered Fleet* (at 31 December 2009): Vessels 34; Total displacement ('000 grt) 42.4 (Source: Lloyd's List Intelligence—www.lloydslistintelligence.com).

Civil Aviation (traffic on scheduled services, 2004): Kilometres flown 1 million; Passengers carried 75,000; Passenger-km 19 million; Total ton-km 2 million. Source: UN, *Statistical Yearbook*.

TOURISM

Foreign Tourist Arrivals (excl. cruise-ship passengers): 50,645 in 2009; 45,430 in 2010; 46,005 in 2011.

Tourist Arrivals by Country (2011): Australia 10,320; New Zealand 22,253; USA 5,508; Total (incl. others) 46,005.

Tourism Receipts (US $ million, excl. passenger transport): 16 in 2009; 31 in 2010 (Source: World Tourism Organization).

COMMUNICATIONS MEDIA

Telephones (2011): 30,000 main lines in use.

Mobile Cellular Telephones (2011): 55,000 subscribers.

Internet Users (2009): 8,400.

Broadband Subscribers (2011): 1,300.

Source: International Telecommunication Union.

EDUCATION

Primary (2007 unless otherwise indicated, provisional): 117 schools (1999); 665 teachers; 16,892 pupils.

General Secondary (2007 unless otherwise indicated, provisional): 39 schools (1999); 982 teachers; 14,580 pupils.

Technical and Vocational: 4 colleges (2001); 84 teachers (2004); 1,121 students (2004).

Teacher-training (1999 unless otherwise indicated): 1 college; 22 teachers (1994); 288 students.

Universities, etc. (1985): 17 teachers; 85 students.

Other Higher Education: 36 teachers (1980); 620 students (1985); 230 students were studying overseas on government scholarships (1990).

Pupil-teacher Ratio (primary education, UNESCO estimate): 25.4 in 2006/07 (Source: UNESCO Institute for Statistics).

Adult Literacy Rate: 99.0% (males 99.0%; females 99.1%) in 2006 (Source: UNESCO Institute for Statistics).

Directory

The Government

HEAD OF STATE

Sovereign: HM King TUPOU VI (succeeded to the throne 18 March 2012).

CABINET
(May 2013)

Prime Minister and Minister of Foreign Affairs and Trade, of Defence and of Information and Communication: Lord TU'IVAKANO.

Deputy Prime Minister and Minister of Infrastructure: SAMIU KUITA VAIPULU.

Minister of Finance and National Planning: LISIATE 'ALOVEITA 'AKOLO.

Minister of Internal Affairs: Lord VAEA.

Minister of Revenue Services and of Police, Prisons and Fire Services: SIOSIFA TU'UTAFAIVA.

Minister of Justice: WILLIAM CLIVE EDWARDS.

Minister of Public Enterprises: FE'AOMOEATA VAKATA.

Minister of Education and Training: Dr ANA MAUI TAUFE'ULUNGAKI.

Minister of Commerce, Tourism and Labour: Dr VILIAMI UASIKE LATU.

Minister of Lands, Environment, Climate Change and Natural Resources: Lord MA'AFU.

Minister of Health: Lord TUTAFITU.

Minister of Agriculture, Food, Forestry and Fisheries: SANGSTER SAULALA.

The Governors of Ha'apai and of Vava'u serve as ex officio members of the Cabinet.

GOVERNMENT MINISTRIES AND OFFICES

Office of the Prime Minister: POB 62, Nuku'alofa; tel. 24644; fax 23888; e-mail pmomail@pmo.gov.to; internet www.pmo.gov.to.

Palace Office: Salote Rd, Kolofo'ou, Nuku'alofa; tel. 21000; fax 24102; internet www.palaceoffice.gov.to.

Ministry of Agriculture, Food, Forestry and Fisheries: POB 14, Administration Office, Vuna Rd, Kolofo'ou, Nuku'alofa; tel. 23038; fax 24271; internet www.mafff.gov.to.

Ministry of Commerce, Tourism and Labour: POB 110, Nuku'alofa; tel. 23688; fax 23887; e-mail info@mlci.gov.to; internet www.mctl.gov.to.

Ministry of Defence: POB 72, Nuku'alofa; tel. 23099; fax 23934; e-mail info@defence.gov.to; internet www.mic.gov.to.

Ministry of Education and Training: POB 61, Vuna Rd, Kolofo'ou, Nuku'alofa; tel. 24220; fax 23596; internet www.tongaeducation.gov.to.

Ministry of Finance and National Planning: POB 87, Treasury Bldg, Vuna Rd, Nuku'alofa; tel. 23066; fax 26011; e-mail info@finance.gov.to; internet www.finance.gov.to.

Ministry of Foreign Affairs and Trade: National Reserve Bank Bldg, 4th Floor, Salote Rd, Kolofo'ou, Nuku'alofa; tel. 23600; fax 23360; e-mail secfo@candw.to.

Ministry of Health: POB 59, Taufa'ahau Rd, Tofoa, Nuku'alofa; tel. 28233; fax 24921; e-mail tatuekaho@health.gov.to; internet www.health.gov.to.

Ministry of Information and Communications: POB 1380, Nuku'alofa; tel. 28170; fax 24861; e-mail enquiries@mic.gov.to; internet www.mic.gov.to.

Ministry of Infrastructure: Nuku'alofa.

Ministry of Internal Affairs: Tungi Collonade Bldg, Nuku'alofa; tel. 27145; fax 27099.

Ministry of Justice: POB 130, Railway Rd, Kolofo'ou, Nuku'alofa; tel. 21055; fax 23098; internet www.justice.gov.to.

Ministry of Lands, Environment, Climate Change and Natural Resources: POB 5, Vuna Rd, Nuku'alofa; tel. 23611; e-mail ceo@lands.gov.to; internet www.lands.gov.to.

Ministry of Police, Prisons and Fire Services: POB 8, Mauikisikisi Rd, Nuku'alofa; tel. 23233; fax 23036; e-mail polcombr@kalianet.to.

Ministry of Public Enterprises: Nuku'alofa.

Ministry of Revenue Services: POB 7, Railway Rd, Nuku'alofa; tel. 23444; fax 26638; internet www.revenue.gov.to.

Legislative Assembly

The number of directly elective seats was increased from a minority of nine to a majority of 17 at the 2010 election. The term of the Legislative Assembly was increased from three to four years.

Speaker: Lord FAKAFANUA.

Election, 25 November 2010

Party	Seats
Democratic Party of the Friendly Islands (DPFI) . .	12
Independents	5
Nobles' Representatives	9
Total	**26**

The nine Nobles' Representatives were elected from among their peers in a separate ballot. An additional four members may be appointed by the Prime Minister.

Election Commission

Electoral Commission: GPOB 1200, Nuku'alofa; tel. 26884; fax 28668; e-mail enquiries@tongaelections.com; internet www.tongaelections.com; f. 2010; Chair. BARRIE SWEETMAN; Supervisor of Elections PITA VUKI.

Political Organizations

Democratic Party of the Friendly Islands (DPFI): c/o Legislative Assembly, Nuku'alofa; f. 2010; est. as electoral vehicle by mems of Human Rights and Democracy Movement; advocates transparent government, further constitutional reform, greater accountability and economic reform; Leader 'AKILISI POHIVA.

Friendly Islands Human Rights and Democracy Movement Inc (FIHRDM Inc): POB 843, Nuku'alofa; tel. 25501; e-mail demo@kalianet.to; f. late 1970s; est. and recognized in 1992 as the Pro-Democracy Movement; application in 1998 for incorporation under new name of Tonga Human Rights and Democracy Movement refused by Govt; reverted to the name of Human Rights and Democracy Movement in Tonga (HRDMT) in 2002; assumed present name in Nov. 2005; advocates democratic reform and democratic process; Chair. SIMOTE MESUILAME VEA.

Paati Langafonua Tu'uloa (PLT) (Sustainable Nation-Building Party): f. 2007; Pres. SIONE FONUA.

People's Democratic Party: Nuku'alofa; f. 2005; breakaway group from HRDMT; Pres. SIONE TEISINA FUKO; Vice-Pres. SIONE TEISINA FUKO.

Tongan Democratic Labour Party: Nuku'alofa; f. 2010; Chair. Dr PITA TAUFATOFUA.

Diplomatic Representation

EMBASSIES AND HIGH COMMISSIONS IN TONGA

Australia: Salote Rd, Private Bag 35, Nuku'alofa; tel. 23244; fax 23243; e-mail ahctonga@dfat.gov.au; internet www.tonga.embassy .gov.au; High Commissioner BRETT ALDAM.

China, People's Republic: Vuna Rd, POB 877, Nuku'alofa; tel. 24554; fax 24595; e-mail chinaemb_to@mfa.gov.cn; Ambassador WANG DONGHUA.

Japan: NRBT Bldg, 5th Floor, POB 330, Nuku'alofa; tel. 22221; fax 27025; e-mail emb-japan@nu.mofa.go.jp; internet www.ton .emb-japan.go.jp; Ambassador Dr KAZUCHIKA HAMURO.

New Zealand: cnr Taufa'ahau and Salote Rds, POB 830, Nuku'alofa; tel. 23122; fax 23487; e-mail nzhcnuk@kalianet.to; High Commissioner MARK TALBOT.

Judicial System

There are eight Magistrates' Courts, the Land Court, the Supreme Court and the Court of Appeal. Appeal from the Magistrates' Courts lies to the Supreme Court, and from the Supreme Court and Land Court to the Court of Appeal (except in certain matters relating to hereditary estates, where appeal lies to the Privy Council). The Chief Justice and Puisne Judge are resident in Tonga and are judges of the Supreme Court and Land Court. The Court of Appeal is presided over by the Chief Justice and consists of three judges from other Commonwealth countries. In the Supreme Court, the accused in criminal cases, and either party in civil suits, may elect trial by jury. In the Land Court, the judge sits with a Tongan assessor. Proceedings in the Magistrates' Courts are in Tongan, and in the Supreme Court and Court of Appeal in Tongan and English. In 2011 the position was created of Lord Chancellor, who was charged with protecting the courts and the judges while preserving the integrity and impartiality of the judiciary.

Supreme Court: POB 11, Nuku'alofa; tel. 23599; fax 22380; e-mail cj_tonga@kalianet.to; Chief Justice MICHAEL DISHINGTON SCOTT; Chief Registrar MANAKOVI PAHULU.

Office of the Attorney-General: POB 85, Lavinia Road, Nuku'alofa; tel. 25347; fax 24005; Attorney-General NEIL ADSETT.

Lord Chancellor: ALBERT HARISON WAALKENS.

Religion

The Tongans are almost all Christians, and about 36% of the population belong to Wesleyan Methodist communities. There are also significant numbers of Roman Catholics (15%) and Latter-day Saints (Mormons—15%). Anglicans (1%) and Seventh-day Adventists (5%) are also represented. Fourteen churches are represented in total.

CHRISTIANITY

Kosilio 'ae Ngaahi Siasi 'i Tonga (Tonga National Council of Churches): POB 1205, Nuku'alofa; tel. 23291; fax 27506; e-mail tncc@kalianet.to; f. 1973; 3 mem. churches (Free Wesleyan, Roman Catholic and Anglican); Chair. Rt Rev. ALIFALETI MONE; Gen. Sec. Rev. SIKETI TONGA.

The Anglican Communion

Tonga lies within the diocese of Polynesia, part of the Church of the Province of New Zealand. The Bishop of Polynesia is resident in Fiji.

Archdeacon of Tonga and Samoa: Ven. SAM KOY, The Vicarage, POB 31, Nuku'alofa; tel. 22136.

The Roman Catholic Church

The diocese of Tonga, directly responsible to the Holy See, comprises Tonga and the New Zealand dependency of Niue. At 31 December 2007 there were an estimated 15,384 adherents in the diocese. The Bishop participates in the Catholic Bishops' Conference of the Pacific, based in Fiji.

Bishop of Tonga: SOANE PATITA MAFI, Toutaimana Catholic Centre, POB 1, Nuku'alofa; tel. 23822; fax 23854; e-mail cathbish@kalianet .to.

Other Churches

Church of Jesus Christ of Latter-day Saints (Mormon): Mission Centre, POB 58, Nukuʻalofa; tel. 23437; fax 23763; 53,000 mems; Pres. LYNN C. MCMURRAY.

Church of Tonga: Nukuʻalofa; f. 1928; a branch of Methodism; 6,912 mems; Pres. Rev. FINAU KATOANGA.

Free Church of Tonga: POB 23, Nukuʻalofa; tel. 23896; fax 24458; e-mail kmakakaufaki@yahoo.co.nz; f. 1885; 21,264 mems (2012; brs in Australia, New Zealand and USA; Pres. Rev. SEMISI FONUA.

Free Wesleyan Church of Tonga (Koe Siasi Uesiliana Tauʻataina ʻo Tonga): POB 57, Nukuʻalofa; tel. 23522; fax 24020; e-mail fwc@kalianet.to; internet www.fwc.to; f. 1826; 36,500 mems; Pres. Rev. Dr FINAU ʻAHIO.

Tokaikolo Christian Fellowship: Nukuʻalofa; f. 1978; breakaway group from Free Wesleyan Church; 5,000 mems.

BAHÁʼÍ FAITH

National Spiritual Assembly: POB 133, Nukuʻalofa; tel. 21568; fax 23120; e-mail nsatonga@patco.to; mems resident in 142 localities.

The Press

Eva, Your Guide to Tonga: POB 958, Nukuʻalofa; tel. 25779; fax 24749; e-mail editor@matangitonga.to; internet www.matangitonga.to; f. 1989; 4 a year; publication suspended under media restrictions in Jan. 2004; Publr and Editor PESI FONUA; circ. 4,500.

Ko e ITA: Nukuʻalofa; tel. 26282; e-mail koeita12@gmail.com; f. 2012; weekly; Tongan and English edns; Editor ILIESA TORA.

Ko e Keleʻa (Conch Shell): POB 1567, Nukuʻalofa; tel. 25501; fax 26330; internet www.planet-tonga.com/tongatimes/kelea; f. 1986; monthly; activist-orientated publication, economic and political; Editor MATENI TAPUELUELU; circ. 3,500.

Lali: Nukuʻalofa; f. 1994; monthly; English; national business magazine; Publr KALAFI MOALA.

Lao and Hia: POB 2808, Nukuʻalofa; tel. 14105; weekly; Tongan; legal newspaper; Editor SIONE HAFOKA.

Matangi Tonga Online: POB 958, Nukuʻalofa; tel. 25779; fax 24749; e-mail editor@matangitonga.to; internet www.matangitonga.to; f. 1986; monthly; national news magazine ceased publication following suspension of licence in Jan. 2004 and subsequently published solely on internet; Man. Editor MARY FONUA.

ʻOfa ki Tonga: c/o Tokaikolo Fellowship, POB 2055, Nukuʻalofa; tel. 24190; monthly; newspaper of Tokaikolo Christian Fellowship; Editor Rev. LIUFAU VAILEA SAULALA.

Taumuʻa Lelei: POB 1, Nukuʻalofa; tel. 27161; fax 23854; e-mail tmlcath@yahoo.com; f. 1929; monthly; Roman Catholic; Editor SOANE PATITA PAINI MAFI.

Times of Tonga/Ko e Taimiʻo Tonga: POB 880, Nukuʻalofa; tel. 27477; e-mail times@kalianet.to; internet www.taimionline.com; f. 1989; twice-weekly; English edn covers Pacific and world news, Tongan edn covers local news; part of Taimi Media Network; Publr KALAFI MOALA; Editor TELESIA ADAMS; circ. 8,000.

Tohi Fanongonongo: POB 57, Nukuʻalofa; tel. 26533; fax 24020; e-mail fwctf@kalianet.to; monthly; Wesleyan; Editor Rev. TEVITA PAUKAMEA TIUETI.

Publisher

Vavaʻu Press Ltd: POB 958, Nukuʻalofa; tel. 25779; fax 24749; e-mail vapress@matangitonga.to; internet www.matangitonga.to; f. 1980; books and magazines; Pres. PESI FONUA.

Broadcasting and Communications

TELECOMMUNICATIONS

Tonga Communications Corporation: Private Bag 4, Nukuʻalofa; tel. 20000; fax 26701; internet www.tcc.to; f. 2000; responsible for domestic and international telecommunications services; services include fixed telephone lines, broadband internet and mobile telephone services; Man. Dir TIMOTE KATOANGA.

Digicel Tonga Ltd: Fatafehi Rd, POB 875, Nukuʻalofa; fax 24978; e-mail customercare.tonga@digicelgroup.com; internet www.digiceltonga.com; f. 2008; Man. JACK BOURKE.

Tongasat—Friendly Islands Satellite Communications Ltd: POB 2921, Nukuʻalofa; tel. 24160; fax 23322; e-mail info@tongasat.com; internet www.tongasat.com; f. 1988; 80% Tongan-owned; private co but co-operates with Govt in management and leasing of orbital satellite positions; Chair. Princess SALOTE MAFILEʻO PILOLEVU TUITA; Man. Dir SEMISI PANUVE.

BROADCASTING

Radio

Tonga Broadcasting Commission (TBC): Tungi Rd, Fasi-moe-afi, POB 36, Nukuʻalofa; tel. 23555; fax 24417; e-mail tbc_news@tonga-broadcasting.net; internet www.tonga-broadcasting.net; independent statutory board; commercially operated; operates 2 free-to-air TV channels and 2 radio stations, with programmes in Tongan and English; Gen. Man. ELENOA AMANAKI.

93FM: Pacific Partners Trust, POB 478, Nukuʻalofa; tel. 27327; fax 27328; e-mail tonga@pacificpartners.org; broadcasts in English, Tongan, German, Mandarin and Hindi; Man. WILLY FLORIAN.

98FM (Voice of the People): Maʻa Fafine mo e Famili Centre, Fasi, Nukuʻalofa; f. 2012; aimed at women.

A3V The Millennium Radio 2000: POB 838, Nukuʻalofa; tel. 25891; fax 24195; e-mail a3v@pobox.alaska.net; broadcasts on FM; musical programmes; Gen. Man. SAM VEA.

BroadCom Broadcasting: POB 970, Nukuʻalofa; tel. 23550; fax 24417; e-mail broadcomradio89.5fm@gmail.com; f. 2009; operates 1 radio station, FM 89.5, and 1 TV channel, TMN TV2; Man. Dir KATALINA TOHI.

Tonga News Association: Nukuʻalofa; Pres. PESI FONUA.

Television

DigiTV: Fatafehi Rd, POB 875, Nukuʻalofa; fax 24978; e-mail customercaretonga@digicelgroup.com; internet www.digiceltonga.com; fmrly Tonfon TV; acquired by Digicel Group and renamed as above in 2007; operates 20 terrestrial channels; CEO (Digicel Tonga) STEPHEN BANNON.

Television Tonga: Fasi-moe-afi, Nukuʻalofa; f. 2000; 60% of programmes in English; 40% of programmes in Tongan.

Finance

(cap. = capital; res = reserves; dep. = deposits; m. = million; brs = branches; amounts in Tongan dollars)

BANKING

Central Bank

National Reserve Bank of Tonga: Private Bag 25, Nukuʻalofa; tel. 24057; fax 24201; e-mail nrbt@reservebank.to; internet www.reservebank.to; f. 1989; assumed central bank functions of Bank of Tonga; issues currency; manages exchange rates and international reserves; cap. 5.0m., res 13.1m., dep. 101.1m. (June 2009); Gov. SIOSI MAFI; Chair. STEVE EDWARDS.

Other Banks

Australia and New Zealand Banking Group Ltd: POB 910, Nukuʻalofa; tel. 20500; fax 23870; e-mail anztonga@anz.com; internet www.anz.com/tonga; Gen. Man. OWEN THOMSON.

MBf Bank Ltd: POB 3118, Taufaʻahau Rd, Nukuʻalofa; tel. 24600; fax 24662; e-mail info@mbfbank.to; internet www.mbfbank.to; f. 1993; 93.35% owned by MBf Asia Capital Corpn Holdings Ltd, 4.75% owned hitherto by King George Tupou V, 0.95% owned by Tonga Investments Ltd, 0.95% owned by Tonga Co-operative Federation Society; Gen. Man. H. K. YEOH.

Tonga Development Bank: Fatafehi Rd, POB 126, Nukuʻalofa; tel. 23333; fax 23775; e-mail ssefanaia@tdb.to; e-mail tdevbank@tdb.to; internet www.tdb.to; f. 1977; est. to provide credit for developmental purposes, mainly in agriculture, fishery, tourism and housing; cap. 10.5m., res 6.9m. (Dec. 2010); Man. Dir SIMIONE SEFANAIA; 6 brs.

Westpac Bank of Tonga: Taufaʻahau Rd, Nukuʻalofa; tel. 23933; fax 25066; e-mail westpactonga@westpac.com.au; internet www.westpac.to; f. 1973; est. as Bank of Tonga; name changed as above in 2002; owned by Westpac Banking Corpn (Australia); cap. 23.5m., res 10.6m., dep. 168.8m. (Sept. 2009); Gen. Man. MISHKA TUʻIFUA; 4 brs.

Trade and Industry

DEVELOPMENT ORGANIZATIONS

Tonga Investments Ltd: POB 27, Nukuʻalofa; tel. 24388; fax 24313; f. 1992; est. to replace Commodities Board; govt-owned; manages 5 subsidiary cos; Chair. TIOFILUSI TUETI; Man. Dir ANTHONY WAYNE MADDEN.

Tonga Association of Small Businesses: Nuku'alofa; f. 1990; est. to cater for the needs of small businesses; Chair. SIMI SILAPELU.

CHAMBER OF COMMERCE

Tonga Chamber of Commerce and Industry: FWC Bldg, Fasimoe-afi, POB 1704, Nuku'alofa; tel. 25168; fax 26039; e-mail chamber@kalianet.to; internet www.tongachamber.org; Pres. ALOMA JOHANSSON.

TRADE ASSOCIATIONS

Tonga Kava Council: Nuku'alofa; promotes the development of the industry both locally and abroad; Chair. TO'IMOANA TAKATAKA.

Tonga Squash Council: Nuku'alofa; promotes the development of the industry; introduced a quota system for exports in 2004; Pres. TSUTOMU NAKAO; Sec. STEVEN EDWARDS.

UTILITIES

Tonga Power Ltd: POB 429, cnr Taufa'ahau and Mateialona Rds, Kolofo'ou, Nuku'alofa; tel. 21400; fax 23047; internet www.tongapower.to; provides electricity via diesel motor generation; distributes and sells electricity commercially and domestically; state-owned; CEO JOHAN VAN BRINK.

Tonga Water Board: POB 92, Taufa'ahau Rd, Kolofo'ou, Nuku'alofa; tel. 23298; fax 23518; operates 4 urban water systems, serving about 25% of the population; Man. SAIMONE P. HELU.

TRADE UNIONS

Association of Tongatapu Squash Pumpkin Growers: Nuku'alofa; f. 1998.

Public Servants' Association (PSA): Nuku'alofa; Pres. FINAU TUTONE; Gen. Sec. MELE AMANAKI.

Tonga Nurses' Association and Friendly Islands Teachers' Association (TNA/FITA): POB 859, Nuku'alofa; tel. and fax 23972; e-mail fita@candw.to; Pres. FINAU TUTONE; Gen. Sec. TOKANKAMEA PULEIKU.

Transport

ROADS

Total road length was estimated at 680 km in 2000, of which some 27% were all-weather paved roads. Most of the network comprises fair-weather-only dirt or coral roads.

SHIPPING

The chief ports are Nuku'alofa, on Tongatapu, and Neiafu, on Vava'u, with two smaller ports at Pangai and Niuatoputapu.

Shipping Corporation of Polynesia Ltd: Queen Salote Wharf, Vuna Rd, POB 453, Nuku'alofa; tel. 23853; fax 23250; e-mail info@olovaha.com; internet www.olovaha.com; govt-owned; regular inter-islands passenger and cargo services; Chair. 'ALISI TAUMOEPEAU.

Warner Pacific Line: POB 93, Nuku'alofa; tel. 21088; services to Samoa, American Samoa, Australia and New Zealand; Man. Dir MA'AKE FAKA'OSIFOLAU.

CIVIL AVIATION

Tonga is served by Fua'amotu International Airport, 22 km from Nuku'alofa, and airstrips at Vava'u, Ha'apai, Niuatoputapu, Niua-

fo'ou and 'Eua. A government agency, Tonga Airports Ltd, assumed responsibility for the management of all airports in 2007. Air New Zealand provides a regular service to Australia and New Zealand and a regional carrier, Reef Air, operates between Tonga, Niue and Fiji. Virgin Australia (NZ) Ltd operates direct flights to Tonga from Sydney, Australia, and from Auckland, New Zealand. A domestic airline, Real Tonga, was launched in March 2013. Additionally, Air Samoa was expected to begin a weekly service from the Samoan island of Upolu to Niuatoputapu and Vava'u, linking with Niuafo'o in the north-west every second week.

Real Tonga: Tungi Colonnade, Nuku'alofa; tel. 23777; e-mail booking@realtonga.to; internet www.realtonga.to; f. 2013; operates domestic services; CEO TEVITA PALU.

Tourism

Tonga's attractions include scenic beauty, a pleasant climate and whale-watching opportunities. Visitor arrivals rose from to 50,645 in 2009, but declined to 45,430 in 2010, before increasing to 46,005 in 2011. The majority of tourists in that year were from New Zealand, Australia and the USA. In 2010 revenue from the industry totalled US $31m.

Tonga Tourist Association: POB 74, Nuku'alofa; tel. 23344; fax 23833; e-mail royale@kalianet.to; Pres. SAIA MOEHAU; Sec. SIMOTE POULIVAATI.

Tonga Visitors' Bureau: Vuna Rd, POB 37, Nuku'alofa; tel. 25334; fax 23507; e-mail info@thekingdomoftonga.com; internet www.thekingdomoftonga.com; f. 1978; Dir TATAFU MOEAKI.

Tourism Tonga Inc: Nuku'alofa; f. 2009.

Defence

Tonga has its own defence force, the Tonga Defence Services, consisting of both regular and reserve units. The island also has a defence co-operation agreement with Australia. As part of the multinational operation, a contingent of 55 Tongan soldiers was serving in Afghanistan in early 2013. Government expenditure on defence in 2004/05 was $T3.9m.; in 2012 military spending accounted for 0.9% of gross domestic product.

Commander of the Tonga Defence Services: Brig.-Gen. TAU'AIKA 'UTA'ATU.

Education

Free state education is compulsory for children between five and 14 years of age, while the Government and other Commonwealth countries offer scholarship schemes enabling students to go abroad for higher education. In 2007 there were 16,892 primary pupils and 14,580 secondary pupils, according to provisional figures. In 2004 a total of 1,121 students attended technical and vocational colleges, of which there were four in 2001. There was one teacher-training college in 1999, with 288 students. Some degree courses are offered at the university division of 'Atenisi Institute. A new establishment offering higher education, the 'Unuaki 'o Tonga Royal Institute, opened in 2004. Recurrent government expenditure on education in 2004/05 was an estimated $T19.0m.

TRINIDAD AND TOBAGO

Introductory Survey

LOCATION, CLIMATE, LANGUAGE, RELIGION, FLAG, CAPITAL

The Republic of Trinidad and Tobago consists of Trinidad, the southernmost of the Caribbean islands, and Tobago, which is 32 km (20 miles) to the north-east. Trinidad, which accounts for 94% of the total area, lies just off the north coast of Venezuela, on the South American mainland, while the country's nearest neighbour to the north is Grenada. The climate is tropical, with a dry season from January to May. Rainfall averages 1,561 mm (61.5 ins) per year. Annual average daytime temperatures range between 21°C (70°F) and 32°C (90°F). The official and main language is English, but French, Spanish, Hindi and Chinese are also spoken. In 2000 some 55% of the population were Christians, mainly Roman Catholics (29%) and Anglicans (8%), while 22% were Hindus and 6% Muslims. The national flag (proportions 3 by 5) is deep red, divided by a white-edged black diagonal stripe from upper hoist to lower fly. The capital is Port of Spain, on the island of Trinidad.

CONTEMPORARY POLITICAL HISTORY

Historical Context

Trinidad was first colonized by the Spanish in 1532, but was ceded to the British in 1802. Africans were transported to the island to work as slaves, but slavery was abolished in 1834. Shortage of labour led to the arrival of large numbers of Indian and Chinese immigrants, as indentured labourers, during the second half of the 19th century. In 1888 the island of Tobago, which had finally been ceded to the British in 1814, was joined with Trinidad as one political and administrative unit, and the territory remained a British colony until its independence on 31 August 1962.

Modern politics emerged in the 1930s with the formation of a trade union movement. The first political party, the People's National Movement (PNM), was founded in 1956 by Dr Eric Williams. It campaigned successfully at the elections to the Legislative Council in September 1956, and Williams became the colony's first Chief Minister in October. In 1958 the territory became a member of the newly established Federation of the West Indies, and in the following year achieved full internal self-government, with Williams as Premier. The Federation collapsed in 1961, however, following the secession of Jamaica and, subsequently, Trinidad and Tobago. After independence, in 1962, Williams was restyled Prime Minister, and the Governor became Governor-General.

Domestic Political Affairs

In April 1970 the Government declared a state of emergency, following several weeks of violent demonstrations by supporters of 'Black Power', protesting against unemployment and foreign influence in the country's economy. On the day that the emergency was proclaimed, part of the Trinidad and Tobago Regiment (the country's army) mutinied, but the mutiny collapsed after only three days. At a general election in May 1971, the PNM won all 36 seats in the House of Representatives.

A new Constitution came into effect on 1 August 1976, whereby Trinidad and Tobago became a republic, within the Commonwealth. At parliamentary elections in September, the PNM won two-thirds of the seats in the House of Representatives. The former Governor-General, Ellis Clarke, was sworn in as the country's first President in December 1976. A parliamentary resolution in 1977 to grant Tobago self-rule resulted, after long resistance from the Government, in the formation in 1980 of a Tobago House of Assembly, giving the island limited autonomy. Tobago was granted full internal self-government in January 1987.

Williams died in March 1981. George Chambers, a deputy leader of the PNM, was formally adopted as party leader in May and confirmed as Prime Minister. The PNM increased its majority in the House of Representatives in a general election in November. The United Labour Front (ULF), the Democratic Action Congress (DAC) and the Tapia House Movement, cam-

paigning jointly as the Trinidad and Tobago National Alliance, succeeded in retaining only 10 seats.

Co-operation between the four opposition parties increased, and, at local elections in August 1983, they successfully combined to defeat the PNM. In August 1984 the National Alliance and the Organization for National Reconstruction established the National Alliance for Reconstruction (NAR). Arthur Napoleon Raymond (A. N. R.) Robinson was elected leader of the new party in the following year. In 1986 the four parties merged to form one opposition party, still known as the NAR.

The stringent economic policies of the PNM Government provoked labour unrest over wage restraint and the general election of December 1986 resulted in a decisive victory for the NAR. Robinson was appointed Prime Minister.

The NAR experienced internal difficulties during 1987–88. In February 1988 more than 100 NAR members met to discuss the leadership of the alliance and the direction of its policies. Two cabinet ministers (including Basdeo Panday, the Minister of External Affairs) and one junior minister were subsequently dismissed from the Government. All three were former members of the ULF, which derived most of its support from the 'East' Indian community. Despite their accusations of racism against the NAR leadership, they were expelled from the party in October. In April 1989 Panday and the other dissidents announced the formation of a left-wing opposition party, the United National Congress (UNC).

In July 1990 members of the Jamaat al Muslimeen, a small Muslim group led by Yasin Abu Bakr, attempted to seize power. The rebels destroyed the capital's police headquarters and took control of the parliament building and the state television station. Some 45 people were taken hostage, among them Robinson and several cabinet ministers. The rebels demanded Robinson's resignation, elections within 90 days and an amnesty for those taking part in the attempted coup. On 28 July a state of emergency was declared and a curfew was imposed. On 31 July the Prime Minister, who had sustained gunshot wounds, was released from captivity by the rebels. A day later the rebels surrendered unconditionally. An amnesty pardoning them, signed by the President of the Senate, Joseph Emmanuel Carter, in his capacity as acting Head of State, was proclaimed invalid, on the grounds that it had been signed under duress. Bakr and his followers were charged with treason, a capital offence.

In November 1991 the imprisoned Jamaat al Muslimeen rebels won an appeal to the Judicial Committee of the Privy Council in the United Kingdom (the final court of appeal for Trinidad and Tobago), which ruled that the validity of the presidential pardon should be determined before the rebels were brought to trial, and that an application for their release should be heard by the High Court of Trinidad and Tobago immediately. On 30 June 1992 the High Court ruled that the pardon was valid, and ordered the immediate release of the 114 defendants. In October 1993 the Court of Appeal ruled to uphold the decision of the High Court. In October 1994 the Privy Council ruled to overturn the decisions of the High Court and the Court of Appeal, declaring the pardon invalid. However, it was also ruled that to rearrest the rebels and try them for offences committed during the insurrection would constitute an abuse of the legal process. The Jamaat al Muslimeen was subsequently awarded some TT $2.1m. in compensation for the destruction of its buildings following the coup attempt.

1991 election: PNM victorious

A general election, held in December 1991, resulted in a decisive victory for the PNM. The implementation of unpopular austerity measures was widely acknowledged as the main cause of the defeat of the NAR, and Robinson resigned as leader. A notable feature of the elections was the re-emergence of ethnic voting, with the vast majority of the votes divided between the Afro-Trinidadian-orientated PNM and the largely Indo-Trinidadian UNC. Patrick Manning was sworn in as Prime Minister. In spite of the change of government, industrial unrest continued.

The NAR retained control of the Tobago House of Assembly following elections in 1992. In July 1993 the Government and the

Tobago House of Assembly agreed to begin discussions concerning the upgrading of Tobago's constitutional status. Measures subsequently submitted for consideration by the legislature included the establishment of an executive council on Tobago and the appointment of an independent senator to represent the island.

Appeals for the restoration of capital punishment, prompted by growing public concern at the increasing rate of murder and violent crime, gained considerable impetus in August 1993 following the murder of the country's Prison Commissioner. In July 1994 Trinidad and Tobago conducted its first execution since 1979. However, the convicted murderer, Glen Ashby, was hanged only minutes before notice from the Privy Council in the United Kingdom was sent to the Court of Appeal in Trinidad granting a stay of execution. Following Ashby's execution, the Privy Council issued a conservatory order whereby, in the case of two men due to be heard by the Trinidad Court of Appeal, should their execution be ordered, it could not be conducted until the case had been heard by the Privy Council itself. This decision provoked protest from the Chief Justice of Trinidad and Tobago, who accused the Privy Council of pre-empting the Court of Appeal's exercise of its jurisdiction. Subsequently, the Government announced its intention to introduce legislation establishing the Court of Appeal as the final appeal court for criminal cases, pending regional agreement on a Caribbean appeal court.

1995 election: coalition Government

A general election was held in November 1995. The PNM and the UNC each secured 17 seats, while the NAR won the remaining two. Following discussions between the leader of the UNC, Basdeo Panday, and Robinson, who had resumed the leadership of the NAR in October, a coalition Government was established, with Panday as Prime Minister. It was widely understood that the NAR's support for the UNC in forming the Government had been dependent on undertakings concerning the prompt upgrading of Tobago's constitutional status. The NAR increased its majority in elections to the Tobago House of Assembly in December 1996.

In January 2000 Hanraj Sumairsingh, a member of the UNC, was found murdered. It was subsequently reported that Sumairsingh had written to the Prime Minister several times regarding threats by the Minister of Local Government, Dhanraj Singh, following Sumairsingh's revelation of alleged corruption in the unemployment relief programme administered by Singh's ministry. In October Singh was dismissed from his government post. Singh was charged with the murder of Sumairsingh, but in October 2003 he was exonerated.

In October 1997 it was announced that the Government had approved a proposal by the Attorney-General to expedite executions of persons convicted of murder, whereby the Government would allow only 18 months for completion of a hearing before the UN Human Rights Committee (UNHRC) and the Inter-American Commission on Human Rights (IACHR), in the event of the Privy Council rejecting an appeal. The Government hoped, by imposing a time limit on the UNHRC and the IACHR, to complete the appeals process within the five years allowed by the Privy Council as the maximum length of time between sentencing and execution. In April 1998 the Government refused to grant leave for the hearing of appeals against the death penalty made by nine men convicted of murder (the so-called Chadee gang). The nine subsequently appealed to the UNHRC. In May the Government announced that it was withdrawing from the UNHRC and the IACHR, as neither body had been able to guarantee the hearing of appeals within the 18 months requested by the Government. Many Caribbean states expressed their support for Trinidad and Tobago, although the PNM criticized the withdrawals as damaging the islands' international reputation. In June the IACHR ordered Trinidad and Tobago not to execute five people whose cases it had been scheduled to review; however, the authorities announced that the IACHR no longer had any jurisdiction over the cases, and that the executions would be carried out.

In October 1998, in what was considered a landmark case, the Privy Council rejected the appeals of two convicted murderers, who had claimed that their constitutional rights had been infringed by the conditions in which they had been imprisoned. In January 1999, in a further landmark judgment, the Privy Council ruled that, even though Trinidad and Tobago had withdrawn from the IACHR, two convicted killers could not be executed while their appeals were being considered by the Commission, since the appeals had been made prior to the withdrawal. In April the Privy Council ordered the release of three prisoners who had spent almost four years awaiting execution.

In May 1999 the Privy Council rejected an appeal for clemency made by the nine members of the Chadee gang, but granted a stay of execution to allow time to consider the legality of hanging as a means of administering the death penalty. At the end of May the Privy Council ruled that Trinidad and Tobago could legally proceed with the nine executions, which, despite international protests, were carried out in June.

In April 2000 the Government announced that it was to withdraw from the first optional protocol to the International Covenant on Civil and Political Rights, following a judgment from the UNHRC that Trinidad and Tobago could not continue to adhere to the resolution while differing on the subject of the death sentence. The announcement attracted widespread international condemnation. The Government also announced the introduction of a constitutional amendment, which would allow executions to proceed before the IACHR and the UNHRC had ruled on the cases. On 14 February 2001, at a Caribbean Community and Common Market (CARICOM, see p. 231) summit in Barbados, the leaders of 11 Caribbean states signed an agreement to establish the Caribbean Court of Justice (CCJ). The Court was to replace the Privy Council as the final court of appeal, and was to be based in Trinidad and Tobago. The CCJ would be financed by a US $100m. trust fund raised by the Caribbean Development Bank. In February 2005 Parliament voted to accept the authority of the new Court to settle CARICOM matters. The Court was eventually inaugurated on 16 April. However, owing to UNC opposition to adopting the appellate jurisdiction of the CCJ, the new Court was only to have jurisdiction in Trinidad and Tobago over CARICOM matters.

Elections of 2000 and 2001

The UNC secured a narrow majority in the House of Representatives at a general election in December 2000. Panday was inaugurated as Prime Minister for the second time. At elections to the Tobago House of Assembly in January 2001 the PNM secured eight of the 12 elective seats, ending the traditional domination of the House by the NAR.

The Government was beset by allegations of corruption in mid-2001 regarding the receipt of payments in exchange for supporting tenders for contracts with the state-owned oil company, Petrotrin, and irregularities in the accounts of the North West Regional Health Authority. A faction within the UNC, Team Unity, emerged in protest at the perceived corruption. Team Unity subsequently gained control of the party's national executive, but despite attempts by Team Unity to prevent UNC constituent elections from taking place in September, supporters of Panday were victorious in 30 of the 34 constituencies. Nevertheless, the Government's legislative majority was effectively lost in October when the three ministers formed a coalition with the PNM and the NAR. Amid increasing pressure from the opposition for his resignation, Panday asked the President to dissolve Parliament.

In the ensuing general election of December 2001 the UNC and the PNM secured an equal number of seats in the House of Representatives. The two party leaders reached an agreement on political collaboration in government (although not a coalition arrangement) that would allow the President to appoint the Prime Minister and Speaker in the House of Representatives and to reform the electoral process. However, following the appointment of Manning as Prime Minister and PNM nominee Max Richards as Speaker of the House of Representatives, the UNC withdrew from the post-election agreement.

Panday's refusal to be sworn in as Leader of the Opposition and to agree to elect a Speaker in the House of Representatives (Richards had withdrawn from the position after his impartiality was questioned) prevented the convening of the new Parliament in January 2002. Panday announced the UNC's intention to prevent Parliament from sitting for the next six months, thereby forcing Manning to call a new election, according to the provisions of the Constitution. Manning and Panday met for discussions at the end of January, but neither these meetings, nor negotiations mediated by CARICOM leaders in February, provided a solution to the dispute. Later in February Manning agreed to put the UNC's proposals for an executive comprising equal numbers of PNM and UNC representatives to the PNM party council. The UNC accused the Prime Minister of deliberately delaying the process. The first session of the new House of Representatives was reconvened in April; however, owing to the failure of the two parties to elect a Speaker, proceedings were adjourned.

Meanwhile, in March 2002 Panday's former finance minister, Brian Kuei Tung, and several senior government officials and prominent businessmen were arrested on charges of fraud and misbehaviour in public office with regard to the construction of a new terminal at Piarco Airport. Manning ordered a Commission of Inquiry into the project. In July the Commission accused two more UNC members of Parliament of criminal activity. Former Minister of Works and Transport Carlos John was accused of ignoring tender procedures during his time in office, and in the same month cocaine worth US $246,000 and two missiles were apparently found at the home of the former housing minister, Sadiq Baksh.

A report by the Commission of Inquiry into the Elections and Boundaries Commission in June 2002 documented countless flaws in its practices and recommended that all its members should resign. However, its members failed to relinquish their posts, despite Manning's pledge to implement the recommended reforms. In July Manning announced that if Parliament failed to elect a Speaker by 31 October, further elections would be held. Manning made a final, unsuccessful, attempt to convene Parliament in August before dissolving Parliament and announcing that elections would take place on 7 October.

2002 election: Manning returned to office

The PNM won a small majority in the election of October 2002. Manning again acceded to the office of Prime Minister.

Despite government efforts, in 2003 and 2004 there were increasing concerns over the continuing rise in crime rates, particularly kidnapping and murder. In 2003 the Senate approved legislation imposing a minimum 25-year prison sentence on those convicted of kidnap. In a landmark ruling, in November the Privy Council ruled that Trinidad and Tobago's mandatory death sentence for convicted murderers was unconstitutional and inconsistent with the country's international obligations. However, in July 2004 the Privy Council overturned its earlier ruling. A panel of judges decreed that the Trinidadian Constitution did not allow outside intervention to abolish the mandatory death penalty. However, the judges further ruled that this would not apply to the estimated 100 prisoners who had benefited from the November judgment.

Despite continuing concerns about the rise in criminal activity and allegations of government corruption, at an election to the Tobago House of Assembly in January 2005 the governing PNM increased its majority.

In May 2005 corruption charges were filed against Panday, his wife, and the former UNC Minister of Works and Transport, Carlos John, in relation to the construction project at Piarco Airport. In November former Minister of Works and Transport Franklin Khan was charged with six counts of corruption, while in January 2006 Minister of Energy and Energy Industries Eric Williams was charged with accepting bribes from a potential contractor. Both Williams and Khan denied the allegations, and the charges against them were dismissed in December 2007 and September 2010, respectively.

In July–October 2005 five bombs exploded in Port of Spain, injuring at least 30 people. Police suggested that the bombs may have been planted by criminals to distract attention from drugs-related activities. The authorities' perceived failure to find the perpetrators prompted widespread anger throughout the country. Mounting public pressure on the Government to curb the deterioration in law and order culminated on 22 October in a demonstration in the capital, attended by thousands of protesters.

In November 2005 the Government announced a number of initiatives aimed at stemming the rise in violent crime. Proposed reforms to the police force increased Parliament's role in selecting members of the Police Service Commission and the Police Commissioner. Another proposal was the establishment of a court expressly for hearing cases involving gun-related crime and kidnapping. Furthermore, legislation would prevent kidnappers and alleged perpetrators of more than three violent crimes from securing bail, and allow suspected kidnappers to be held for up to 60 days before being charged.

In November 2005 Yasin Abu Bakr was arrested and charged with seditious speech, incitement and terrorism, after allegedly preaching a sermon that called for a war on affluent Muslims who refused to pay *zakat*, a tithe for the poor, to his organization. In February 2006 the Attorney-General sought high court authorization for the state to confiscate 12 properties from members of the Jamaat al Muslimeen in compensation for damage caused during the attempted coup in 1990.

In April 2006 Panday was sentenced to two years' imprisonment, after being convicted of failing to make accurate declarations regarding a bank account held in London, United Kingdom. He was released on bail pending an appeal, but suspended as a member of Parliament and removed as Leader of the Opposition. Kamla Persad-Bissessar, a former Attorney-General, replaced him as opposition leader. In September Winston Dookeran, who had succeeded Panday as political leader of the UNC in 2005, resigned from this post to launch a new political organization, the Congress of the People (COP). Panday's appeal against his conviction was upheld in March 2007, and he was reinstated as UNC political leader in April; however, Persad-Bissessar remained Leader of the Opposition. A retrial was subsequently ordered, but the case was dismissed on procedural grounds in June 2012.

2007 election: the PNM re-elected

At a general election held on 5 November 2007 the PNM secured 26 seats in the enlarged 41-seat House of Representatives. The UNC—Alliance, comprising the UNC and several smaller parties, won the remaining 15 seats. Manning continued as Prime Minister. His administration was confronted with the problem of increasing public concern over the level of crime; the number of murders in 2007 was subsequently recorded as the highest on record at 395, rising further in 2008, to 547. Following the election, Panday, who had been re-elected to Parliament, replaced Persad-Bissessar as Leader of the Opposition.

Elections to the Tobago House of Assembly were held in January 2009, at which the incumbent PNM obtained eight of the 12 seats, while the opposition Tobago Organisation of the People (TOP), formed in 2008, won four seats.

In January 2009 Manning announced plans for significant constitutional reforms, which included the establishment of an executive president as head of government and head of state, an expansion of the Senate (from 31 to 37 members) and a reorganization of the judiciary. The proposals were to undergo a two-year public consultation period before being debated by Parliament.

Manning and Panday held discussions on constitutional reform in November 2009, agreeing to continue their collaboration on the issue. However, their views on the amendments required differed substantially, with Panday advocating the direct election of an executive president by the electorate (rather than by the House of Representatives, as proposed by the Government) and the election of a unicameral parliament by a system of proportional representation.

Recent developments: Persad-Bissessar in office

In January 2010 Panday was defeated by Persad-Bissessar in elections to the leadership of the UNC. In the following month, having secured the support of a majority of opposition deputies, Persad-Bissessar also replaced Panday as Leader of the Opposition. Persad-Bissessar proceeded to dismiss five UNC senators who had been appointed by Panday, and in early March filed a motion of no confidence against Manning, accusing the Prime Minister of 'questionable conduct' in a number of matters, including the alleged corruption at the state-owned Urban Development Corporation of Trinidad and Tobago. In late March, however, the Prime Minister announced that a general election, which was not constitutionally due to be held until 2012, would take place, and in April the President dissolved Parliament at Manning's request. The UNC, the COP, the TOP, the Movement for Social Justice and the National Joint Action Committee subsequently formed a coalition, the People's Partnership, to contest the forthcoming election, with Persad-Bissessar as the alliance's prime ministerial candidate.

The People's Partnership secured a comprehensive victory at the general election of 24 May 2010, attracting 60.0% of the votes cast and gaining control of 29 of the 41 seats in the House of Representatives (21 of which were won by the UNC, six by the COP and two by the TOP). The PNM, undermined by persistently high levels of violent crime and allegations of corruption, obtained the remaining 12 seats. The rate of participation by the electorate, at just under 70%, was the highest on record. Persad-Bissessar was inaugurated as the country's first female Prime Minister on 26 May, and her Cabinet took office two days later. The COP leader Winston Dookeran became Minister of Finance, Surujattan Rambachan received the foreign affairs portfolio, Jack Warner was appointed as Minister of Works and Transport, and Brig. John Sandy was given responsibility for national security. Manning resigned as PNM leader following the party's poor electoral performance and was replaced by Keith Rowley in

June. The People's Partnership strengthened its position further in July, when it overwhelmingly defeated the PNM in local elections, taking control of 11 of the country's 14 local authorities.

In July 2010, on the occasion of the 20th anniversary of the 1990 coup attempt, the Government revealed plans to form a commission to investigate the events surrounding the rebellion. To recover partially the cost of damages incurred during the uprising, in the following month the Government sold nine Jamaat al Muslimeen properties, raising over US $800,000, an act denounced as 'unlawful' by Bakr. The Government announced its intention to seize further property belonging to Jamaat al Muslimeen members involved in the failed coup. The inquiry into the attempted coup commenced proceedings in January 2011; these were ongoing in early 2013.

Legislation that defined the legal parameters for the interception of communications by the security services came into effect in January 2011 following Persad-Bissessar's revelation in November 2010 that the Security Intelligence Agency (SIA), a secretive branch of the Ministry of National Security, had implemented a campaign of illegal wire-tapping operations over the previous five years, seemingly with the approval of the Manning administration. Documents recovered from a police raid of SIA offices revealed that the Agency had unlawfully monitored the telephone calls and e-mails of a wide range of prominent individuals, including Persad-Bissessar, President George Maxwell Richards, PNM leader Keith Rowley, COP leader Winston Dookeran, high-ranking judicial figures, trade union leaders and journalists. Persad-Bissessar accused Manning's Government of an 'abuse of democracy', while Rowley attempted to distance the PNM from the former Prime Minister. In late November Attorney-General Anand Ramlogan announced in the Senate that the former head of the SIA, Nigel Clement, had admitted to receiving direct orders from Manning to carry out certain wire-tapping operations. Manning, who had defended the SIA's actions, denounced Ramlogan's allegation as 'utterly false'. Persad-Bissessar stated her intention of initiating an investigation into the scandal, although progress was expected to be hindered by the reported destruction by SIA operatives of much of the wire-tapping evidence.

With concern over crime still widespread among the public, the Government introduced new proposals in late 2010 to combat gang activity, illegal firearms, and corruption within the police force. Moves were also made to abrogate preliminary inquiries in order to expedite criminal trials. The number of murders in 2010 totalled 473, slightly lower than the 507 recorded in 2009, although the number of gangs operating in the country was reported to have increased from 66 in 2005 to over 100 by 2010. A proposed amendment to the Constitution to remove the legal obstacles that prevented the death penalty from being carried out prompted criticism from the United Kingdom and human rights groups in early 2011. The Government argued that capital punishment was necessary to deter criminality. However, PNM opposition to the legislation meant that the Government was unable to secure the three-quarters' majority in the House of Representatives required to modify the Constitution, and the bill was consequently rejected by the lower chamber in March. Anti-gang legislation received parliamentary approval in May, and in August Persad-Bissessar declared a state of emergency in several high-crime areas in response to a recent upsurge in the murder rate. An overnight curfew was imposed (although this was withdrawn in November, reportedly owing to pressure from the business sector), and the security forces were granted expanded powers until December, when the state of emergency expired. The Government claimed that these measures had dramatically reduced the crime rate, although the opposition criticized the state of emergency as an over-reaction. The number of murders declined to 352 in 2011, before rising again to 377 in 2012. In April 2012, in response to the continuing high rate of violent crime, Persad-Bissessar announced her Government's intention to replace the Privy Council with the CCJ as Trinidad and Tobago's final court of appeal in criminal cases. Furthermore, in January 2013 the Government announced proposals to bestow arrest powers on military personnel participating in police operations. The number of soldiers involved in domestic security activities was also to be increased, and joint police-military patrols were to be expanded across the country.

Mary King, the Minister of Planning, Economic and Social Restructuring and Gender Affairs, was dismissed in May 2011 following the publication of press reports accusing her of nepotism; King was succeeded by Bhoendradatt Tewarie. Also in that month, Manning was suspended from the House of Representatives for acting in contempt of Parliament. The former Prime Minister had claimed, without providing any evidence, that Persad-Bissessar had received funds from criminals linked to the illegal drugs trade, a charge that she had rejected. Jack Warner was suspended from his position as a senior official within the Fédération Internationale de Football Association (FIFA) in late May after being accused of involvement in a bribery scandal at the organization. The investigation into Warner's activities was discontinued in June following his resignation from FIFA. In spite of the controversy generated by these allegations, Warner retained his ministerial status in a cabinet reorganization implemented by Persad-Bissessar later that month, although he lost control of the transport portfolio, which was transferred to Devant Maharaj. Meanwhile, Minister of Legal Affairs Prakash Ramadhar was elected as the leader of the COP in July.

In November 2011 Persad-Bissessar proclaimed that a conspiracy to assassinate her, along with three other members of the Government, had been uncovered by the security services and that a number of suspects had been arrested. The Prime Minister speculated that the alleged plot had been formulated by criminals in retaliation for the Government's declaration of a state of emergency. However, the opposition questioned the veracity of her claims, amid suspicions that the assassination plot had been fabricated to allow the extension of the state of emergency, which was scheduled to end in December. In the event, no extension was sought by the Government, and all the detained suspects were released in early December owing to a lack of evidence. A motion of no confidence in the Persad-Bissessar administration, which had been proposed by Rowley, was overwhelmingly rejected by the House of Representatives in March 2012.

Persad-Bissessar effected an extensive cabinet reorganization in June 2012. Most notably, Larry Howai was appointed as Minister of Finance and Economy, replacing Dookeran, who became Minister of Foreign Affairs, while Warner received the high-profile national security portfolio.

In August 2012 the legislature adopted a highly controversial act that effectively annulled all legal cases not brought to trial within 10 years. Among the initial petitioners seeking to take advantage of this new law were two UNC-affiliated businessmen charged with corruption, prompting allegations that the legislation had been formulated to allow the UNC's allies to evade justice. Amid widespread public outrage, Parliament abrogated the law in September, while Persad-Bissessar issued an apology and dismissed Minister of Justice Herbert Volney, whom she accused of misleading the Government over the matter. Ramlogan, meanwhile, was the subject of an opposition-sponsored motion of censure, and demonstrations were held in November to demand his resignation as Attorney-General.

The PNM gained control of all 12 elective seats in the Tobago House of Assembly in polls conducted on 21 January 2013.

Anthony Carmona was inaugurated as national President on 18 March 2013.

Warner resigned as Minister of National Security and as UNC Chairman in April 2013 shortly after the dissemination of a report by the Integrity Committee of the Confederation of North, Central American and Caribbean Association Football (CONCACAF). The report's authors accused Warner, who had held the position of CONCACAF President during 1990–2011, of various fraudulent activities. Emmanuel George was named as the new Minister of National Security while Surujrattan Rambachan took on George's former responsibilities as Minister of Works and Infrastructure in addition to his existing local government portfolio.

Foreign Affairs

Trinidad and Tobago and Venezuela ratified a joint declaration on maritime boundaries in 1991, under which Trinidad and Tobago's maritime boundary was to be extended from 200 nautical miles (370 km) to 350 nautical miles (648 km). In 2003 the two countries signed a memorandum of understanding on the joint exploitation of cross-border oil and gas fields. Negotiations recommenced in 2006. The discussions stalled temporarily following Trinidad and Tobago's refusal to sign Venezuela's PetroCaribe energy accord, launched the previous year, which offered oil concessions and favourable financing terms to Caribbean nations. However, in early 2007 an agreement in principle was reached on the division of the cross-border Loran-Manatee natural gas field, which apportioned some 75% of the gas to Venezuela. Negotiations were suspended again later that year, however, and did not resume until 2009. A final agreement on the Loran-Manatee field was concluded in 2010, although discussions regarding the other fields had stalled by mid-2013.

In 2000 talks were held to find a solution to the maritime border dispute between Trinidad and Barbados. Despite further talks being held over the next two years, little progress was made. Bilateral relations deteriorated in February 2004 after several Barbadian fishermen were arrested in Trinidad and Tobago's waters; Barbados subsequently imposed economic sanctions on imports from Trinidad and Tobago, which they were later ordered to lift by CARICOM's Council for Trade and Economic Development. In April 2006 the UN Convention on the Law of the Sea handed down a decision establishing a median line between the two exclusive economic zones. The UN rejected Trinidad and Tobago's claim to a large area to the south-east of Barbados and instructed the two countries to negotiate a fishing agreement for a large disputed area to the north of Tobago, which would remain in Trinidad and Tobago's possession. Although the Prime Ministers of the two countries expressed their commitment to achieve a resolution, none had been reached by mid-2013. Meanwhile, a treaty on the delimitation of Trinidad and Tobago's maritime border with Grenada was ratified by both nations in April 2010.

CONSTITUTION AND GOVERNMENT

A new Constitution came into effect on 1 August 1976. Legislative power is vested in the bicameral Parliament, consisting of the Senate, with 31 members, and the House of Representatives, with 41 members. Representatives are elected for a five-year term by universal adult suffrage. The President is a constitutional Head of State, chosen by an electoral college of members of both the Senate and the House of Representatives. Members of the Senate are nominated by the President in consultation with, and on the advice of, the Prime Minister and the Leader of the Opposition. The Cabinet has effective control of the Government and is responsible to Parliament. Tobago Island was granted its own House of Assembly in 1980 and given full internal self-government in 1987. The Tobago House of Assembly has 15 members, of whom 12 are elected; the remaining three members are selected by the majority party.

REGIONAL AND INTERNATIONAL CO-OPERATION

Trinidad and Tobago is a member of the Caribbean Community and Common Market (CARICOM, see p. 231), of the Inter-American Development Bank (see p. 341), of the Latin American Economic System (see p. 462), of the Association of Caribbean States (see p. 459), of the Organization of American States (see p. 404), and of the Community of Latin American and Caribbean States (see p. 475), which was formally inaugurated in December 2011. Trinidad and Tobago is also host to the Caribbean Court of Justice (see p. 231), although the country retains the Privy Council in the United Kingdom as its final appellate court. Trinidad and Tobago was one of the six founder members of CARICOM's Caribbean Single Market and Economy, which was inaugurated on 1 January 2006. In September 2008 the Organisation of Eastern Caribbean States (see p. 477) approved a proposal for the establishment of an economic union with Trinidad and Tobago by 2011, followed by political union by 2013, but no substantive progress towards these objectives had been achieved by mid-2013.

Trinidad and Tobago was admitted to the UN in 1962. As a contracting party to the General Agreement on Tariffs and Trade, Trinidad and Tobago joined the World Trade Organization (see p. 444) shortly after its establishment in 1995. The country is a member of the Commonwealth (see p. 244).

ECONOMIC AFFAIRS

In 2011, according to estimates by the World Bank, Trinidad and Tobago's gross national income (GNI), measured at average 2009–11 prices, was US $20,249m., equivalent to US $15,040 per head (or US $24,940 on an international purchasing-power parity basis). During 2002–11, it was estimated, the population increased at an average annual rate of 0.4%, while gross domestic product (GDP) per head increased, in real terms, by an average of 4.3% per year. According to the World Bank, overall GDP increased, in real terms, at an average annual rate of 4.7% in 2002–11. According to the official figures, the economy contracted by 2.6% in 2011, but grew by 1.2% in 2012.

According to provisional figures, agriculture (including forestry, hunting and fishing) contributed 0.6% of GDP in 2012, and employed 3.5% (excluding unclassified activities) of the working population in 2011. The principal cash crops are sugar cane,

coffee, cocoa and citrus fruits. The fishing sector is small-scale, but is an important local source of food. During 2002–10, according to the World Bank, agricultural GDP declined by an average of 11.8% per year. The sector declined by 0.1% in 2011 and further by 4.9% in 2012, according to official provisional figures.

Industry (including mining and quarrying, manufacturing, construction and power) provided 56.2% of GDP in 2012, according to provisional figures and employed 30.6% (excluding undefined activities) of the working population in 2011. During 2002–10, according to the World Bank, industrial GDP increased at an average annual rate of 8.4%. According to official provisional figures, industrial GDP decreased by 0.9% in 2012.

In 2011 the mining and quarrying sector (including petroleum production) employed some 3.0% of the working population (excluding undefined activities). The petroleum sector provided 43.8% of GDP in 2012. Trinidad has the world's largest deposits of natural asphalt, and substantial reserves of natural gas. Trinidad and Tobago was one of the world's largest producers of methanol, a by-product of natural gas. Cement, limestone and sulphur are also mined. According to official provisional figures, the GDP of the sector declined by 1.0% in 2012.

According to provisional figures, manufacturing contributed 6.1% of GDP in 2012 and employed 8.1% (excluding undefined activities) of the working population in 2011. During 2002–10 manufacturing GDP increased at an average annual rate of 7.9%, according to the World Bank. According to official provisional figures, manufacturing GDP decreased by 0.4% in 2012.

Construction contributed 5.0% of GDP in 2012, according to provisional figures, and engaged 15.9% (excluding undefined activities) of the employed labour force in 2011. Sectoral GDP decreased by 2.0% in 2012.

Almost all of the country's energy is derived from natural gas (it provided 99.4% of total electricity production in 2009). Natural gas is also used as fuel for the country's two petroleum refineries and several manufacturing plants. Imports of mineral fuels and lubricants comprised 33.3% of the value of merchandise imports in 2010. In the same year exports of mineral fuels accounted for 61.5% of total exports.

According to provisional figures, the services sector contributed 43.2% of GDP in 2012 and employed some 65.9% (excluding unclassified activities) of the working population in 2011. Tourism is a major source of foreign exchange; in 2010 receipts from tourism totalled US $393m. and some 385,510 tourists visited the islands. According to the World Bank, the GDP of the services sector increased at an average annual rate of 4.8% in 2002–10. According to official figures, sectoral GDP increased by 2.9% in 2012.

In 2010 Trinidad and Tobago recorded a visible merchandise trade surplus of US $4,737.9m., and there was a surplus of US $4,172.3m. on the current account of the balance of payments. In 2010 the principal source of imports was the USA (27.7%). The USA was also the principal market for exports (47.6%) in that year; other major buyers were Jamaica and Canada. The principal exports in 2010 were mineral fuels and lubricants, chemicals, manufactured goods and crude materials. The principal imports were mineral fuels and lubricants (33.3% of the total), machinery and transport equipment, manufactured goods, and food and live animals.

There was a provisional budgetary deficit of TT $6,675.8m. in 2011/12. Trinidad and Tobago's general government gross debt was TT $44,819m. in 2011, equivalent to 31.7% of GDP. At the end of 2004 Trinidad and Tobago's total external debt was US $2,652m., of which US $1,197m. was public and publicly guaranteed debt. In 2004 the cost of debt-servicing was equivalent to 5.4% of the value of exports of goods and services. The annual rate of inflation averaged 7.2% in 2002–11. Retail prices increased by an estimated average of 5.1% in 2011. Some 5.8% of the labour force was unemployed in 2011.

The presence of significant petroleum and natural gas deposits, combined with substantial foreign investment, meant that the energy sector was a major contributor to Trinidad and Tobago's economy. The development of a major liquefied natural gas (LNG) plant at Point Fortin from 2001 made Trinidad and Tobago one of the world's leading suppliers of LNG. Substantial foreign investment allowed increased industrialization, which, combined with high international fuel prices, contributed to rapid economic expansion and a large trade surplus in 2002–08. However, concerns about rising crime rates damaged investor confidence, increased security costs for businesses and threatened the tourism industry. The economy entered recession in 2009, owing to the negative impact of the global economic crisis upon the price of Trinidad and Tobago's fuel exports. Although the energy industry recovered in 2010, activity in the non-energy sector remained stagnant, and zero growth was recorded in that year. The economy decreased by a further 2.6% in 2011, partly owing to production difficulties in the hydrocarbons sector, although high oil and gas prices helped to cushion the impact. Real GDP grew by 1.2% in 2012, with large-scale maintenance works hampering hydrocarbons output. In March the Government announced the discovery of a significant offshore petroleum deposit, potentially containing 48m. barrels of oil, while in November exploratory offshore drilling yielded a 1,000,000m. cu ft gas reservoir. Nevertheless, given the economic prominence of the energy sector, dwindling hydrocarbons

reserves remained a long-term concern. The IMF forecast real GDP growth of around 1.5% in 2013.

PUBLIC HOLIDAYS

2014: 1 January (New Year's Day), 30 March (Spiritual Baptist Shouters' Liberation Day), 18–21 April (Easter), 30 May (Indian Arrival Day), 19–20 June (Labour Day and Corpus Christi), 28 July* (Id al-Fitr, end of Ramadan), 1 August (Emancipation Day), 31 August (Independence Day), 24 September (Republic Day), 23 October† (Diwali), 25–26 December (Christmas).

* These holidays are dependent on the Islamic lunar calendar and may vary by one or two days from the dates given.

† Dependent on lunar sightings.

Statistical Survey

Sources (unless otherwise stated): Central Statistical Office, National Statistics Bldg, 80 Independence Sq., POB 98, Port of Spain; tel. 623-6945; fax 625-3802; e-mail info@cso.gov.tt; internet www.cso.gov.tt; Central Bank of Trinidad and Tobago, POB 1250, Port of Spain; tel. 625-4835; fax 627-4696; e-mail info@central-bank.org.tt; internet www.central-bank.org.tt.

Area and Population

AREA, POPULATION AND DENSITY

Area (sq km)	5,128*
Population (census results)	
15 May 2000	1,262,366
9 January 2011	
Males	666,305
Females	661,714
Total	1,328,019
Density (per sq km) at 2011 census	259.0

* 1,980 sq miles. Of the total area, Trinidad is 4,828 sq km (1,864 sq miles) and Tobago 300 sq km (116 sq miles).

POPULATION BY AGE AND SEX
(at 2011 census)

	Males	Females	Total
0–14	139,179	134,236	273,415
15–64	472,664	462,915	935,579
65 and over	54,462	64,563	119,025
Total	666,305	661,714	1,328,019

POPULATION BY ETHNIC GROUP
(at 2011 census)*

	Males	Females	Total	%
'East' Indian	236,823	231,701	468,524	35.43
African	228,068	224,469	452,537	34.22
Mixed	146,850	155,016	301,866	22.82
White	4,174	3,657	7,831	0.59
Other	4,918	4,624	9,542	0.72
Not stated	41,517	40,729	82,246	6.22
Total	662,350	660,196	1,322,546	100.00

* Excludes some institutional population and members of unenumerated households.

ADMINISTRATIVE DIVISIONS
(population at 2011 census)

	Population ('000)	Capital
Trinidad	1,267.1	Port of Spain
Port of Spain (city, capital) . .	37.1	—
San Fernando (city)	48.8	—
Arima (borough)	33.6	Arima
Chaguanas (borough)	83.5	Chaguanas
Point Fortin (borough)	20.2	Point Fortin
Diego Martin	103.0	Petit Valley
San Juan/Laventille	157.3	Laventille
Tunapuna/Piarco	215.1	Tunapuna
Couva/Tabaquite/Talparo . . .	178.4	Couva
Mayaro/Rio Claro	35.7	Rio Claro
Sangre Grande	75.8	Sangre Grande
Princes Town	102.4	Princes Town
Penal/Debe	89.4	Penal
Siparia	86.9	Siparia
Tobago	60.9	Scarborough
Total	1,328.0	—

BIRTHS AND DEATHS
(annual averages, UN estimates)

	1995–2000	2000–05	2005–10
Birth rate (per 1,000)	15.1	14.5	14.9
Death rate (per 1,000)	7.2	7.9	8.0

Source: UN, *World Population Prospects: The 2010 Revision*.

Life expectancy (years at birth): 70.0 (males 66.6, females 73.5) in 2011 (Source: World Bank, World Development Indicators database).

ECONOMICALLY ACTIVE POPULATION
('000 persons aged 15 years and over)

	2006	2007	2008
Agriculture, forestry, hunting and fishing	25.8	22.4	22.9
Mining and quarrying	20.4	22.8	21.1
Manufacturing	55.5	54.1	55.1
Electricity, gas and water . . .	7.7	7.2	7.9
Construction	96.7	103.0	108.5
Wholesale and retail trade, restaurants and hotels . .	106.6	108.3	108.2
Transport, storage and communication	42.7	41.5	41.2
Finance, insurance, real estate and business services	48.1	49.6	52.5
Community, social and personal services	181.1	178.6	179.5
Sub-total	584.6	587.5	596.9
Activities not adequately defined .	1.6	0.3	0.7
Total employed	586.2	587.8	597.6
Unemployed	39.0	34.5	29.0
Total labour force	625.2	622.3	626.6
Males	364.9	368.6	n.a.
Females	260.3	253.7	n.a.

Source: ILO.

2011 ('000 persons aged 15 years and over): Total employed 581.9 (Agriculture 20.5; Petroleum and gas 17.6; Construction and utilities 92.8; Manufacturing 47.1); Unemployed 35.9; *Total labour force* 617.8.

Health and Welfare

KEY INDICATORS

Total fertility rate (children per woman, 2010)	1.6
Under-5 mortality rate (per 1,000 live births, 2010) . .	27
HIV/AIDS (% of persons, aged 15–49, 2009)	1.5
Physicians (per 1,000 head, 2007)	1.2
Hospital beds (per 1,000 head, 2008)	2.5
Health expenditure (2009): US $ per head (PPP) . . .	1,465
Health expenditure (2009): % of GDP	5.8
Health expenditure (2009): public (% of total)	60.6
Access to water (% of persons, 2010)	94
Access to sanitation (% of persons, 2010)	92
Total carbon dioxide emissions ('000 metric tons, 2008) . .	49,772.2
Carbon dioxide emissions per head (metric tons, 2008) . .	37.4
Human Development Index (2011): ranking	62
Human Development Index (2011): value	0.760

For sources and definitions, see explanatory note on p. vi.

Agriculture

PRINCIPAL CROPS
('000 metric tons)

	2009	2010	2011
Rice, paddy*	2.5	2.3	2.5
Maize*	3.0	3.2	3.4
Taro (Cocoyam)*	5.6	5.7	5.4
Sugar cane	810.0*	n.a.	n.a.
Pigeon peas*	1.4	1.3	1.3
Coconuts	15.6†	16.6†	17.8*
Cabbages*	1.1	1.0	1.1
Lettuce*	1.7	1.5	1.6
Tomatoes*	2.2	1.7	2.0
Pumpkins, squash and gourds* .	2.1	1.8	1.8

—continued	2009	2010	2011
Cucumbers and gherkins* . .	1.6	1.3	1.4
Aubergines*	4.1	3.6	3.7
Watermelons*	1.3	1.1	1.1
Bananas*	7.0	8.1	8.9
Plantains*	5.5	5.7	6.4
Oranges*	5.6	5.2	4.3
Lemons and limes*	1.9	2.2	2.3
Grapefruit and pomelo* . . .	2.0	2.4	1.9
Pineapples*	6.8	6.2	8.0
Cocoa beans†	0.6	0.7	0.4

* FAO estimate(s).
† Unofficial figure(s).

Aggregate production ('000 metric tons, may include official, semi-official or estimated data): Total cereals 5.5 in 2009–10, 5.9 in 2011; Total roots and tubers 10.8 in 2009, 11.7 in 2010, 11.9 in 2011; Total vegetables (incl. melons) 19.5 in 2009, 17.2 in 2010, 17.6 in 2011; Total fruits (excl. melons) 84.8 in 2009, 97.1 in 2010, 114.2 in 2011.

Source: FAO.

LIVESTOCK
('000 head year ending September, FAO estimates)

	2009	2010	2011
Horses	1.4	1.4	1.4
Asses	2.3	2.3	2.3
Mules	2.0	2.0	2.0
Cattle	32.0	32.5	33.0
Buffaloes	5.9	5.9	5.9
Pigs	47.0	48.0	49.0
Chickens	32,000	33,000	34,000
Sheep	3.7	3.8	3.8
Goats	61.4	62.2	63.0

Source: FAO.

LIVESTOCK PRODUCTS
('000 metric tons, FAO estimates)

	2009	2010	2011
Cattle meat	1.0	1.0	1.1
Pig meat	3.1	3.2	3.2
Chicken meat	65.0	67.0	69.0
Cows' milk	4.8	5.0	5.0
Hen eggs	4.0	4.3	4.3

Source: FAO.

Forestry

ROUNDWOOD REMOVALS
('000 cubic metres, excl. bark, FAO estimates)

	2009	2010	2011
Sawlogs, veneer logs and logs for sleepers	47.0	47.0	47.0
Fuel wood	33.1	32.8	32.5
Total	80.1	79.8	79.5

Source: FAO.

SAWNWOOD PRODUCTION
('000 cubic metres, incl. railway sleepers, unofficial figures)

	2009	2010	2011
Total (all broadleaved) . . .	31	31	31

Source: FAO.

Fishing

('000 metric tons, live weight of capture)

	2008	2009	2010
Demersal percomorphs . .	2.0	2.2	2.4
King mackerel	1.0	1.0	0.8
Serra Spanish mackerel . .	1.5	1.5	1.2
Tuna-like fishes	0.2	0.2	0.3
Sharks, rays, skates, etc. . .	0.3	0.3	0.3
Other marine fishes . .	6.3	6.3	6.2
Penaeus shrimps	0.8	0.7	0.9
Total catch (incl. others) . . .	13.8	13.9	13.9

Source: FAO.

Mining

('000 barrels, unless otherwise indicated)

	2009	2010	2011
Crude petroleum	40,821	36,300	33,550
Natural gas liquids . . .	14,400	15,700	14,800
Natural gas (million cu m)* . .	42,903	44,565	42,883

* Figures refer to the gross volume of output.

Source: US Geological Survey.

Industry

SELECTED PRODUCTS
('000 metric tons unless otherwise indicated)

	2009	2010	2011
Sugar	28	n.a.	n.a.
Beer ('000 litres)	50,377	n.a.	n.a.
Fertilizers	6,168	6,262	5,715
Methanol	6,111	5,932	5,904
Cement	870	791	827
Iron (direct reduced)	1,182	1,752	1,706
Steel:			
billets	417	572	604
wire rods	238	361	427
Electric energy (million kWh) . .	7,873.3	n.a.	n.a.

Finance

CURRENCY AND EXCHANGE RATES

Monetary Units
100 cents = 1 Trinidad and Tobago dollar (TT $).

Sterling, US Dollar and Euro Equivalents (31 December 2012)
£1 sterling = TT $10.131;
US $1 = TT $6.420;
€1 = TT $8.471;
TT $100 = £9.87= US $15.58 = €11.81.

Average Exchange Rate (TT $ per US $)
2010   6.3755
2011   6.4093
2012   6.4158

CENTRAL GOVERNMENT BUDGET
(TT $ million)

Revenue	2009/10	2010/11	2011/12*
Current revenue	43,632.0	47,213.6	47,631.6
Tax revenue	37,074.4	42,017.3	41,156.6
Taxes on income and profit . .	27,516.4	33,245.1	30,644.5
Taxes on property . . .	44.1	32.0	35.1
Taxes on goods and services .	7,436.8	6,387.7	8,041.4
Taxes on international trade .	1,905.5	2,167.8	2,248.1
Other taxes	171.6	184.7	187.5
Non-tax revenue	6,557.6	5,196.3	6,475.0
Royalties on petroleum . .	1,900.5	2,416.7	2,528.5
Profits	2,086.6	1,695.1	2,192.3
Non-financial enterprises .	1,165.1	1,213.8	1,704.6
Financial enterprises . .	921.5	481.3	487.7
Interest	170.8	50.0	26.1
Capital revenue and grants . .	230.9	287.0	41.2
Total	43,862.9	47,500.6	47,672.8

Expenditure	2009/10	2010/11	2011/12*
Current expenditure	40,302.2	43,914.9	46,057.2
Wages and salaries . . .	6,711.0	7,179.7	7,556.4
Goods and services . . .	6,441.2	6,504.3	7,909.0
Interest payments	3,290.3	2,866.4	3,253.1
Domestic	2,846.1	2,486.9	2,824.5
External	444.2	379.5	428.6
Transfers and subsidies . .	23,859.7	27,364.5	27,338.7
Capital expenditure and net			
lending	6,399.2	7,577.5	8,291.4
Total	46,701.4	51,492.4	54,348.6

* Provisional figures.

Source: Ministry of Finance, Trinidad and Tobago.

INTERNATIONAL RESERVES
(US $ million at 31 December)

	2009	2010	2011
Gold (national valuation) . . .	67.9	86.7	97.4
IMF special drawing rights . .	431.9	424.3	423.2
Reserve position in IMF . . .	94.4	111.2	160.2
Foreign exchange	8,651.6	9,070.0	9,822.7
Total	9,245.8	9,692.2	10,503.5

Source: IMF, *International Financial Statistics*.

MONEY SUPPLY
(TT $ million at 31 December)

	2007	2008	2009
Currency outside banks . .	3,182.8	3,433.7	3,850.0
Demand deposits at commercial			
banks	11,083.6	12,399.9	17,413.3
Total money (incl. others) . .	16,777.2	19,226.9	26,655.0

Demand deposits at commercial banks: 19,228.3 in 2010; 19,146.9 in 2011.

Source: IMF, *International Financial Statistics*.

COST OF LIVING
(Retail Price Index; base: January 2003 = 100)

	2009	2010	2011
Food (incl. non-alcoholic beverages)	308.7	377.1	416.3
Clothing	95.3	94.6	95.0
Transport	125.5	139.8	140.9
Housing and utilities . . .	125.2	125.6	127.3
All items (incl. others) . . .	158.2	174.9	183.8

NATIONAL ACCOUNTS
(TT $ million at current prices)

Expenditure on the Gross Domestic Product

	2006	2007	2008*
Government final consumption expenditure	12,801.9	14,328.1	16,665.2
Private final consumption expenditure	56,339.4	65,690.9	68,668.1
Gross capital formation	18,146.0	17,666.0	19,418.0
Total domestic expenditure	87,287.3	97,685.0	104,751.3
Exports of goods and services	79,417.6	88,792.1	111,688.1
Less Imports of goods and services	44,596.9	49,050.5	64,324.1
GDP in purchasers' values	122,108.0	137,426.7	152,115.2

* Provisional.

Gross Domestic Product by Economic Activity

	2010	2011	2012*
Agriculture, hunting, forestry and fishing	816.0	902.8	888.0
Mining and hydrocarbons	56,015.3	70,313.7	67,105.4
Manufacturing	7,024.2	8,661.8	9,260.3
Electricity and water	1,809.7	2,000.1	1,930.2
Construction	9,410.5	8,772.3	7,642.7
Transport, storage and communication	6,903.1	7,193.4	8,235.2
Distribution	17,942.1	19,449.2	21,180.2
Finance, insurance and real estate	14,812.5	16,710.2	16,936.3
Government	10,423.9	11,219.8	13,302.8
Other services	5,912.3	5,954.7	6,559.6
Sub-total	131,069.6	151,178.0	153,040.7
Less Financial intermediation services indirectly measured	5,812.5	5,721.8	5,950.6
Value-added tax	6,032.3	4,917.0	6,497.6
GDP in purchaser's values	131,289.4	150,373.2	153,587.7

* Provisional figures.

BALANCE OF PAYMENTS
(US $ million)

	2008	2009	2010
Exports of goods	18,620.7	9,204.0	11,219.3
Imports of goods	−9,551.1	−6,962.6	−6,481.4
Balance on goods	9,069.6	2,241.4	4,737.9
Exports of services	936.5	764.8	874.2
Imports of services	−326.0	−383.3	−389.1
Balance on goods and services	9,680.1	2,622.9	5,223.0
Primary income received	309.9	297.6	299.7
Primary income paid	−1,537.9	−1,314.7	−1,379.2
Balance on goods, services and primary income	8,452.1	1,605.8	4,143.5
Secondary income received	108.7	137.3	108.8
Secondary income paid	−61.8	−110.3	−80.0
Current balance	8,499.0	1,632.8	4,172.3
Direct investment (net)	2,100.8	709.1	549.4
Portfolio investment (net)	−81.8	−120.0	—
Other investment (net)	−7,983.8	−3,027.1	−4,312.5
Net errors and omissions	197.4	131.3	26.9
Reserves and related items	2,731.6	−674.0	436.2

External Trade

PRINCIPAL COMMODITIES
(TT $ million)

Imports c.i.f.	2009	2010
Food and live animals	3,806.1	3,968.0
Beverages and tobacco	340.2	348.0
Crude materials except fuels	1,353.3	2,084.9
Mineral fuels and lubricants	14,481.4	13,755.4
Animal and vegetable oils and fats	207.3	230.6
Chemicals	3,442.5	3,158.1
Manufactured goods	5,744.8	4,739.4
Machinery and transport equipment	12,119.5	10,704.6
Miscellaneous manufactured articles	2,383.5	2,261.9
Total (incl. others)	43,935.7	41,283.0

Exports f.o.b.*	2009	2010
Food and live animals	965.0	927.7
Beverages and tobacco	881.2	739.7
Crude materials except fuels	1,750.7	3,668.4
Mineral fuels and lubricants	43,744.9	43,725.6
Animal and vegetable oils and fats	16.2	12.1
Chemicals	5,542.3	15,187.1
Manufactured goods	2,702.2	4,195.6
Machinery and transport equipment	1,661.0	2,259.0
Miscellaneous manufactured articles	441.8	408.1
Miscellaneous transactions and commodities	2.7	3.2
Total	57,708.0	71,126.5

* Including ships' stores and bunkers.

PRINCIPAL TRADING PARTNERS
(TT $ million)

Imports c.i.f.	2008	2009	2010
Barbados	228.1	190.0	242.5
Canada	1,636.1	941.6	1,172.9
Central and South America*	15,719.6	8,756.7	8,570.0
Venezuela	1,445.5	412.1	78.9
European Free Trade Association (EFTA)	228.2	181.0	190.7
European Union (EU)†	6,603.3	3,794.1	2,857.7
Guyana	197.9	163.1	160.6
Jamaica	100.3	139.3	69.0
United Kingdom	1,368.7	1,210.4	872.9
USA	14,299.5	13,531.6	11,426.6
Total (incl. others)	60,197.8	43,935.7	41,283.0

Exports f.o.b.‡	2008	2009	2010
Barbados	3,385.1	1,706.7	2,362.3
Canada	1,205.0	418.9	4,176.7
Central and South America*	10,216.8	3,398.9	7,955.2
European Free Trade Association (EFTA)	136.7	20.3	475.5
European Union (EU)†	13,271.8	5,570.9	4,176.7
Guyana	1,940.4	1,026.9	1,669.0
Jamaica	7,811.1	2,993.5	4,520.5
United Kingdom	2,093.0	2,344.5	1,417.1
USA	51,832.7	30,639.6	33,351.0
Total (incl. others)	115,093.4	57,365.9	70,367.9

* Excluding Belize, French Guiana, Guyana and Suriname.
† Excluding the United Kingdom, listed separately.
‡ Excluding ships' stores and bunkers.

Transport

ROAD TRAFFIC
(motor vehicles in use)

	1997	1998	1999
Passenger cars	194,300	213,400	229,400
Commercial vehicles	47,700	51,100	53,900

Source: UN, *Statistical Yearbook*.

Total number of registered vehicles: 441,541 in 2006; 468,255 in 2007; 471,749 in 2008.

SHIPPING
Flag Registered Fleet
(at 31 December)

	2010	2011	2012
Number of vessels	79	81	82
Total displacement (grt)	38,788	38,835	39,085

Source: Lloyd's List Intelligence (www.lloydslistintelligence.com).

International Sea-borne Freight Traffic
(estimates, '000 metric tons)

	1988	1989	1990
Goods loaded	7,736	7,992	9,622
Goods unloaded	4,076	4,091	10,961

Source: UN, *Monthly Bulletin of Statistics*.

1998: Port of Spain handled 3.3m. metric tons of cargo.

CIVIL AVIATION
(traffic on scheduled services)

	2007	2008	2009
Kilometres flown (million)	29	30	30
Passengers carried ('000)	1,086	1,103	1,014
Passenger-km (million)	3,184	3,312	3,106
Total ton-km (million)	337	351	325

Source: UN, *Statistical Yearbook*.

Passengers carried ('000): 1,720.8 in 2010 (Source: World Bank, World Development Indicators database).

Tourism

FOREIGN TOURIST ARRIVALS

Country of origin	2008	2009	2010
Barbados	19,350	15,672	13,676
Canada	54,205	49,514	46,390
Germany	4,876	4,895	4,657
Grenada	9,162	7,339	7,269
Guyana	25,097	20,679	18,339
Saint Lucia	5,071	4,429	4,187
Saint Vincent and Grenadines	8,064	7,421	6,726
United Kingdom	42,924	38,400	34,179
USA	189,553	195,438	183,171
Venezuela	12,252	11,521	9,543
Total (incl. others)	437,279	418,864	385,510

Tourism receipts (US $ million, excl. passenger transport): 367 in 2009; 393 in 2010.

Source: World Tourism Organization.

Communications Media

	2009	2010	2011
Telephones ('000 main lines in use)	303.2	293.3	292.0
Mobile cellular telephones ('000 subscribers)	1,846.3	1,894.2	1,826.2
Internet subscribers ('000)	145.0	149.8	157.2
Broadband subscribers ('000)	125.6	145.0	155.0

Personal computers: 175,500 in 2007 (132.1 per 1,000 persons).

Source: International Telecommunication Union.

Education
(2009/10 unless otherwise indicated)

	Institutions	Teachers	Students Males	Females	Total
Pre-primary	50*	2,186	15,121†	14,564†	29,685†
Primary	480‡	7,447	67,698	63,652	131,350
Secondary	101‡	7,045§	46,613§	48,662§	95,275§
Tertiary	3‖	1,800¶	7,515¶	9,405¶	16,920¶

* Government schools and assisted schools only, in 1992/93.
† 2006/07.
‡ 2001/02.
§ 2007/08.
‖ 2003/04; university and equivalent institutions.
¶ 2004/05.

Source: UNESCO Institute for Statistics.

Pupil-teacher ratio (primary education, UNESCO estimate): 17.6 in 2009/10 (Source: UNESCO Institute for Statistics).

Adult literacy rate (UNESCO estimates): 98.8% (males 99.2%, females 98.4%) in 2010 (Source: UNESCO Institute for Statistics).

Directory

The Government

HEAD OF STATE

President: ANTHONY THOMAS AQUINAS CARMONA (took office on 18 March 2013).

THE CABINET
(May 2013)

The Government is formed by the People's Partnership coalition, comprising the United National Congress, the Congress of the People and the Tobago Organisation of the People.

Prime Minister: KAMLA PERSAD-BISSESSAR.

Minister of Finance and the Economy: LARRY HOWAI.

Minister of National Security: EMMANUEL GEORGE.

Minister of Energy and Energy Affairs: KEVIN RAMNARINE.

Minister of Foreign Affairs: WINSTON DOOKERAN.

Minister of Public Administration: CAROLYN SEEPERSAD-BACHAN.

Minister of Tertiary Education and Skills Training: FAZAL KARIM.

Minister of Health: Dr FUAD KHAN.

Minister of Public Utilities: NIZAM BAKSH.

Minister of Food Production: DEVANT MAHARAJ.

Minister of Planning and Sustainable Development: Dr BHOENDRADATT TEWARIE.

Minister of Local Government and of Works and Infrastructure: Dr SURUJRATTAN RAMBACHAN.

Minister of Housing: Dr ROODAL MOONILAL.

Minister of Trade, Industry and Investment: VASANT BHARATH.

Minister of Tourism: STEPHEN CADIZ.

Minister of Justice: CHRISTLYN MOORE.

Minister of the People and Social Development: Dr GLENN RAMADHARSINGH.

Minister of Education: Dr TIM GOPEESINGH.

Minister of Community Development: WINSTON PETERS.

Minister of Legal Affairs: PRAKASH RAMADHAR.

Minister of Labour and Small and Micro Enterprise Development: ERROL MCLEOD.

Minister of Sport: ANIL ROBERTS.

Minister of Tobago Development: Dr DELMON BAKER.

Minister of the Arts and Multiculturalism: Dr LINCOLN DOUGLAS.

Minister of Gender, Youth and Child Development: MARLENE COUDRAY.

Minister of Transport: CHANDRESH SHARMA.

Minister of Science and Technology: Dr RUBERT GRIFFITH.

Minister of Environment and Water Resources: GANGA SINGH.

Minister of Communications: JAMAL MOHAMMED.

Minister of National Diversity and Social Integration: CLIFTON DECOTEAU.

Minister in the Ministry of National Diversity and Social Integration: EMBAU MOHENI.

Minister in the Ministry of National Security: (vacant).

Minister in the Ministry of People and Social Development: VERNELLA ALLEYNE-TOPPIN.

Minister in the Ministry of Works and Infrastructure: STACY ROOPNARINE.

Minister of State in the Ministry of Finance: RUDRANATH INDARSINGH.

Minister of State in the Ministry of Food Production: JAIRAM SEEMUNGAL.

Minister of State in the Office of the Prime Minister: RODGER SAMUEL.

Attorney-General: ANAND RAMLOGAN.

MINISTRIES

Office of the President: President's House, Circular Rd, St Ann's, Port of Spain; tel. 624-1261; fax 625-7950; e-mail info@thepresident .tt; internet www.thepresident.tt.

Office of the Prime Minister: Whitehall, 13–15 St Clair Ave, St Clair, Port of Spain; tel. 622-1625; fax 622-0055; e-mail permsec@ opm.gov.tt; internet www.opm.gov.tt.

Ministry of the Arts and Multiculturalism: JOBCO Bldg, 51–55 Frederick St, Port of Spain; tel. 625-8519; fax 627-4991; e-mail culturedivision.tt@gmail.com; internet www.culture.gov.tt.

Ministry of the Attorney-General: Cabildo Chambers, 23–27 St Vincent St, Port of Spain; tel. 623-7010; fax 625-0470; e-mail communication@ag.gov.tt; internet www.ag.gov.tt.

Ministry of Communications: Level 5, Nicholas Tower, 63–65 Independence Sq., Port-of-Spain; tel. 627-2664; fax 623-4731.

Ministry of Community Development: ALGICO Bldg, cnr Jerningham Ave and Queens Park East, Belmont, Port of Spain; tel. 625-3012; fax 625-5954; e-mail communications@community.gov.tt; internet www.community.gov.tt.

Ministry of Education: 18 Alexandra St, St Clair; tel. 622-2181; fax 622-4892; e-mail mined@tstt.net.tt; internet www.moe.gov.tt.

Ministry of Energy and Energy Affairs: Energy Tower, Levels 15 and 22–26, International Waterfront Centre, 1 Wrightson Rd, Port of Spain; tel. 623-6708; fax 625-6878; e-mail info@energy.gov.tt; internet www.energy.gov.tt.

Ministry of Environment and Water Resources: c/o Water and Sewerage Authority, Farm Rd, St Joseph; tel. 663-2762.

Ministry of Finance and the Economy: Eric Williams Finance Bldg, Level 18, Independence Sq., Port of Spain; tel. 627-9700; fax 627-5882; e-mail comm.finance@gov.tt; internet www.finance.gov.tt.

Ministry of Food Production: St Clair Circle, St Clair, Port of Spain; tel. 662-1221; fax 622-8202; e-mail info@fplma.gov.tt; internet agriculture.gov.tt.

Ministry of Foreign Affairs: Tower C, Levels 10–14, Waterfront Complex, 1 Wrightson Rd, Port of Spain; tel. 623-6894; fax 623-5853; e-mail website@foreign.gov.tt; internet www.foreign.gov.tt.

Ministry of Gender, Youth and Child Development: Level 21, Tower D, International Waterfront Complex, 1 Wrightson Rd, Port of Spain; tel. 627-1163.

Ministry of Health: 63 Park St, Port of Spain; tel. 627-0010; fax 623-9528; e-mail suggestions@health.gov.tt; internet www.health.gov.tt.

Ministry of Housing: NHA Bldg, 44–46 South Quay, Port of Spain; tel. 623-4663; fax 625-2793; e-mail info@housing.gov.tt; internet www.mphe.gov.tt.

Ministry of Justice: Tower C, Level 19–21, International Waterfront Complex, 1 Wrightson Rd, Port of Spain; tel. 625-5878; fax 623-5596; internet www.moj.gov.tt.

Ministry of Labour and Small and Micro Enterprise Development: Levels 5 and 6, Tower C, International Waterfront Centre, 1 Wrightson Rd, Port of Spain; tel. 625-8478; fax 624-9126; e-mail communicationsmolsmed@gov.tt; internet www.molsmed.gov.tt.

Ministry of Legal Affairs: Registration House, Huggins Bldg, 72–74 South Quay, Port of Spain; tel. 624-9971; fax 625-9803; e-mail info@legalaffairs.gov.tt; internet www.legalaffairs.gov.tt.

Ministry of Local Government: Kent House, Long Circular Rd, Maraval, Port of Spain; tel. 622-1669; fax 628-7283; e-mail localgovminister@gov.tt; internet www.localgov.gov.tt.

Ministry of National Diversity and Social Integration: JOBCO Bldg, Level 2, 51–55 Frederick St, Port of Spain; tel. 623-9311.

Ministry of National Security: Temple Court, 31–33 Abercromby St, Port of Spain; tel. 623-2441; fax 627-8044; e-mail info@mns.gov.tt; internet www.nationalsecurity.gov.tt.

Ministry of the People and Social Development: ANSA Bldg, Cnr Independence Sq. and Abercromby St, Port of Spain; tel. 625-9221; fax 627-4853; e-mail people@mpsd.gov.tt; internet www2 .mpsd.gov.tt.

Ministry of Planning and Sustainable Development: Eric Williams Financial Complex, Level 14, Independence Sq., Port of Spain; tel. 627-9700; fax 623-8123; e-mail mpesrga@phe.gov.tt; internet pesrga.gov.tt.

Ministry of Public Administration: National Library Bldg, Level 7, cnr Hart and Abercromby Sts, Port of Spain; tel. 625-6724; fax 623-6027; e-mail communicationsdivision@mpa.gov.tt; internet www .mpa.gov.tt.

Ministry of Public Utilities: 2 Elizabeth St, St Clair, Port of Spain; tel. 628-0749; fax 628-6067; e-mail cgeorge@mpu.gov.tt; internet www.mpu.gov.tt.

Ministry of Science and Technology: International Water Front Center, Level 19, Tower D, 1A Wrightson Rd, Port of Spain; tel. 625-5776; fax 627-1720; e-mail communicationstte@gov.tt.

Ministry of Sport: 12 Abercromby St, Port of Spain; tel. 625-5622; fax 623-0174; internet www.msya.gov.tt.

Ministry of Tertiary Education and Skills Training: International Water Front Center, Level 16-18, Tower C, 1A Wrightson

Rd, Port of Spain; tel. 623-9922; e-mail mtestcommunications@gov
.tt; internet www.stte.gov.tt.

Ministry of Tobago Development: Jerningham St, Scarborough,
Tobago; tel. 639-2652; fax 639-2655.

Ministry of Tourism: Levels 8 and 9, Tower C, International
Waterfront Complex, 1 Wrightson Rd, Port of Spain; tel. 624-1403;
fax 625-3894; e-mail mintourism@tourism.gov.tt; internet www
.tourism.gov.tt.

Ministry of Trade, Industry and Investment: Nicholas Tower,
Levels 11–17, 63–65 Independence Sq., Port of Spain; tel. 623-2931;
fax 627-8488; e-mail mti-info@gov.tt; internet www.tradeind.gov.tt.

Ministry of Transport: Level 23, Tower D, International Waterfront Complex, 1 Wrightson Rd, Port of Spain; tel. 625-4701; fax 623-
8261.

Ministry of Works and Infrastructure: Main Administrative
Bldg, cnr Richmond and London Sts, Port of Spain; tel. 625-1225;
fax 625-8070; internet www.mowt.gov.tt.

Legislature
PARLIAMENT
Senate

President: TIMOTHY HAMEL-SMITH.

The Senate consists of 31 members appointed by the President of the
Republic.

House of Representatives

Speaker: WADE MARK.
Election, 24 May 2010

Party	Valid votes	% of valid votes cast	Seats
People's Partnership* . . .	432,026	60.03	29
People's National Movement .	285,354	39.65	12
Others	2,347	0.32	—
Total†	719,727	100.00	41

* An electoral alliance comprising the United National Congress, the
  Congress of the People, the Tobago Organisation of the People, the
  National Joint Action Committee and the Movement for Social
  Justice.
† In addition, there were 2,595 invalid votes.

TOBAGO HOUSE OF ASSEMBLY

The House is elected for a four-year term of office and consists of 12
elected members and three members selected by the majority party.

Chief Secretary: ORVILLE LONDON.
Election, 21 January 2013

Party	% of valid votes cast	Seats
People's National Movement	61.0	12
Tobago Organisation of the People	36.5	—
Tobago Platform of the People	2.1	—
Total	100.0	12

Election Commission

Elections and Boundaries Commission (EBC): Scott House,
134–138 Frederick St, Port of Spain; tel. 623-4622; fax 627-7881;
e-mail ebc.research@gmail.com; internet www.ebctt.com; Chair. Dr
NORBERT J. MASSON; Chief Election Officer RAMESH NANAN.

Political Organizations

Congress of the People (COP): 2 Broome St, Woodbrook, cnr
Tragarete Rd, Port of Spain; tel. 622-5817; e-mail secretariat@coptnt
.com; internet www.coptnt.com; f. 2006; contested the 2010 general
election as a mem. of the People's Partnership coalition; Leader
PRAKASH RAMADHAR; Chair. CAROLYN SEEPERSAD-BACHAN.

Movement for Social Justice: Bay Rd Junction, 74 Southern Main
Rd, Marabella, Port of Spain; tel. 762-0133; e-mail msjtnt@gmail

.com; internet msjtnt.org; contested the 2010 election as a mem. of
the People's Partnership, left coalition in 2012; Leader DAVID
ABDULLAH; Chair. VINCENT CABRERA.

National Joint Action Committee (NJAC): 40 Duke St, Port of
Spain; tel. 623-5470; e-mail njaccommunications@gmail.com;
internet www.njactt.org; f. 1969; contested the 2010 general election
as a mem. of the People's Partnership coalition; Leader MAKANDAL
DAAGA; Pres. AIYEGORO OME.

National Transformation Movement (NTM): Port of Spain;
f. 2006; Leader LLOYD ELCOCK.

New National Vision (NNV): Freedom House, 30 Victoria Sq., Port
of Spain; tel. 221-0807; f. 1994; Leader FUAD ABU BAKR.

People's National Movement (PNM): Balisier House, 1 Tran-
quility St, Port of Spain; tel. 625-1533; fax 627-3311; e-mail info@
pnmtt.org; internet www.pnm.org.tt; f. 1956; moderate nationalist
party; Leader Dr KEITH ROWLEY; Chair. FRANKLIN KHAN.

The Platform of Truth: Breeze Hall, Scarborough, Tobago; tel. 639-
5135; e-mail tpttobago@gmail.com; internet www.tpttobago.com;
f. 2011; Leader HOCHOY CHARLES.

Tobago Organisation of the People (TOP): 2 Picton St, Scarborough, Tobago; tel. 635-1003; e-mail toptobago@gmail.com; internet
www.top.org.tt; f. 2007; only active in Tobago; contested the 2010
general election as a mem. of the People's Partnership coalition;
Leader ASHWORTH JACK.

United National Congress (UNC): Rienzi Complex, 78–81 Southern Main Rd, Couva; tel. 636-8145; e-mail info@unc.org.tt; internet
unctt.org; f. 1988; contested the 2010 general election as a mem. of
the People's Partnership coalition; social democratic; Leader KAMLA
PERSAD-BISSESSAR; Gen. Sec. DAVE TANCOO.

Diplomatic Representation
EMBASSIES AND HIGH COMMISSIONS IN TRINIDAD AND TOBAGO

Argentina: TATIL Bldg, 4th Floor, 11 Maraval Rd, POB 162, Port of
Spain; tel. 628-7557; fax 628-7544; e-mail etrin@mrecic.gov.ar;
internet www.etrin.mrecic.gov.ar; Ambassador MARCELO ALDO
SALVIOLO.

Australia: 18 Herbert St, St Clair, Port of Spain; tel. and fax 822-
5450; fax 822-5490; e-mail australianhighcommission.pos@gmail
.com; internet www.trinidadandtobago.embassy.gov.au; High Commissioner ROSS TYSOE.

Brazil: 18 Sweet Briar Rd, St Clair, POB 382, Port of Spain; tel. 622-
5779; fax 622-4323; e-mail brasil@tstt.net.tt; internet portofspain
.itamaraty.gov.br; Ambassador PAULO SERGIO TRABALLI BOZZI.

Canada: Maple House, 3–3A Sweet Briar Rd, St Clair, POB 1246,
Port of Spain; tel. 622-6232; fax 628-1830; e-mail pspan@
international.gc.ca; internet www.canadainternational.gc.ca/
trinidad_and_tobago-trinite_et_tobago; High Commissioner GÉRARD
LATULIPPE.

Chile: 4 Alexandra St, Saint Clair, POB 5099, Port of Spain; tel. 628-
0540; fax 622-9894; e-mail echile@tstt.net.tt; internet chileabroad
.gov.cl/trinidad-y-tobago; Ambassador FERNANDO AYALA GONZÁLEZ.

China, People's Republic: 39 Alexandra St, St Clair, Port of Spain;
tel. 622-6976; fax 622-7613; e-mail chinaemb_tt@mfa.gov.cn;
internet tt.china-embassy.org; Ambassador YANG YOUMING.

Colombia: 9–11 Fitt St, Woodbrook, Port of Spain; tel. 628-5656;
e-mail eptoespana@cancilleria.gov.co; Ambassador ALFREDO RAFAEL
RIASCOS NOGUERA.

Costa Rica: 38 Carlos St, Woodbrook, Port of Spain; tel. 628-9201;
fax 628-9203; e-mail embrctt1@tstt.net.tt; Ambassador EDGAR
GARCÍA MIRANDA.

Cuba: 92 Tragarete Rd, 2nd Floor, POB 1779, Port of Spain; tel. 622-
6075; fax 628-4186; e-mail embacubatrinidad@tstt.net.tt; internet
www.cubadiplomatica.cu/trinidadtobago; Ambassador HUMBERTO
RIVERO ROSARIO.

Dominican Republic: Suite 101, 10B Queen's Park West, Port of
Spain; tel. 624-7930; fax 623-7779; e-mail embdomtrinidadytobago@
serex.gov.do; Ambassador JOSÉ A. SERULLE RAMIA.

El Salvador: 29 Long Circular Rd, St James, Port of Spain; tel. 628-
4454; fax 622-8314; e-mail elsalvadortt@gmail.com; Ambassador
RAYMUNDO ERNESTO RODRIGUEZ DÍAZ.

France: TATIL Bldg, 6th Floor, 11 Maraval Rd, POB 1242, Port of
Spain; tel. 622-7447; fax 628-2632; e-mail cad
.port-d-espagne-amba@diplomatie.gouv.fr; internet www
.ambafrance-tt.org; Ambassador JACQUES STURM.

Germany: 19 St Clair Ave, St Clair, POB 828, Port of Spain; tel. 628-
1630; fax 628-5278; e-mail info@ports.diplo.de; internet www
.port-of-spain.diplo.de; Ambassador STEFAN SCHLÜTER.

Guatemala: Regents Towers, Apt 701, Westmoorings-by-the-Sea, Westmoorings; tel. and fax 632-7629; e-mail embtrintobago@minex .gob.gt; Ambassador GUISELA ATALIDA GODÍNEZ SAZO.

Holy See: 11 Mary St, St Clair, POB 854, Port of Spain; tel. 622-5009; fax 628-5457; e-mail apnuntt@googlemail.com; Apostolic Nuncio NICOLAS GIRASOLI.

India: 6 Victoria Ave, POB 530, Port of Spain; tel. 627-7480; fax 627-6985; e-mail hc@hcipos.org; internet www.hcipos.org; High Commissioner MALAY MISHRA.

Jamaica: 2 Newbold St, St Clair, Port of Spain; tel. 622-4995; fax 628-9043; e-mail jhctnt@tstt.net.tt; High Commissioner SHARON SAUNDERS.

Japan: 5 Hayes St, St Clair, POB 1039, Port of Spain; tel. 628-5991; fax 622-0858; e-mail embassyofjapan@tstt.net.tt; internet www.tt .emb-japan.go.jp; Ambassador YOSHIMASA TEZUKA.

Korea, Republic: 60 Eagle Crescent, Fairways, Maraval, Port of Spain; tel. 622-9081; fax 627-6317; e-mail koremb.tt@gmail.com; internet tto.mofat.go.kr; Ambassador WONKUN HWANG.

Mexico: 12 Hayes St, St Clair, Port of Spain; tel. 622-1422; fax 628-8488; e-mail info@mexico.tt; internet www.mexico.tt; Ambassador MARIO ARREOLA WOOG.

Netherlands: 69–71 Edward St, POB 870, Port of Spain; tel. 625-1210; fax 625-1704; e-mail por@minbuza.nl; internet tt.nlembassy .org; Ambassador LUCITA MOENIRALAM.

Nigeria: 3 Maxwell-Phillip St, St Clair, POB 140, Newtown, Port of Spain; tel. 622-4002; fax 622-7162; e-mail contact@ nigerianhighcommission-tt.org; internet www.nigerian highcommission-tt.org; High Commissioner MUSA JOHN JEN.

Panama: Suite 6, 1A Dere St, Port of Spain; tel. 623-3435; fax 623-3440; e-mail embapatt@wow.net; Ambassador ARLINE GONZÁLEZ COSTA.

South Africa: 4 Scott St, St Clair, POB 7111, Port of Spain; tel. 622-9869; fax 622-7089; e-mail betsie.erasmus@southafrica.org.tt; High Commissioner MAUREEN ISABELLA MODISELLE.

Spain: TATIL Bldg, 7th Floor, 11 Maraval Rd, Port of Spain; tel. 625-7938; fax 624-4983; e-mail emb.trinidad@mae.es; Ambassador JOAQUÍN DE ARÍSTEGUI.

Suriname: TATIL Bldg, 5th Floor, 11 Maraval Rd, Port of Spain; tel. 628-0704; fax 628-0086; e-mail surinameembassy@tstt.net.tt; Ambassador FIDELIA GRAAND-GALON.

United Kingdom: 19 St Clair Ave, St Clair, POB 778, Port of Spain; tel. 350-0444; fax 350-0425; e-mail generalenquiries.ptofs@fco.gov .uk; internet ukintt.fco.gov.uk; High Commissioner ARTHUR SNELL.

USA: 15 Queen's Park West, POB 752, Port of Spain; tel. 622-6371; fax 822-5905; e-mail ircpos@state.gov; internet trinidad.usembassy .gov; Chargé d'affaires a.i. THOMAS SMITHAM.

Venezuela: 16 Victoria Ave, POB 1300, Port of Spain; tel. 627-9821; fax 624-2508; e-mail embaveneztt@tstt.net.tt; Ambassador CORO-MOTO GODOY.

Judicial System

The Chief Justice, who has overall responsibility for the administration of justice in Trinidad and Tobago, is appointed by the President after consultation with the Prime Minister and the Leader of the Opposition. The President appoints and promotes judges on the advice of the Judicial and Legal Service Commission. The Judicial and Legal Service Commission, which comprises the Chief Justice as chairman, the chairman of the Public Service Commission, two former judges and a senior member of the bar, appoints all judicial and legal officers. The Judiciary comprises the Supreme Court and the Magistracy. The Supreme Court consists of the High Court of Justice and the Court of Appeal. The Court of Appeal hears appeals against decisions of the Magistracy and the High Court. Further appeals are directed to the Judicial Committee of the Privy Council of the United Kingdom. The Court of Appeal consists of the Chief Justice, who is President, and six other Justices.

The Magistracy and the High Court exercise original jurisdiction in civil and criminal matters. The High Court hears indictable criminal matters, family matters where the parties are married, and civil matters involving sums over the petty civil court limit. High Court judges are referred to as either Judges of the High Court or Puisne Judges. The Masters of the High Court, of which there are four, have the jurisdiction of judges in civil chamber courts. The Magistracy exercises summary jurisdiction in criminal matters and hears preliminary inquiries in indictable matters.

In 2005 Parliament voted to accept the authority of the Caribbean Court of Justice to settle international trade disputes. The Court was formally inaugurated in Port of Spain in April of that year.

Chief Justice: IVOR ARCHIE.

Supreme Court of Judicature: Hall of Justice, Knox St, Port of Spain; tel. 628-8529; fax 627-5477; e-mail cpiu@ttlawcourts.org; internet www.ttlawcourts.org; consists of the High Court of Justice and the Court of Appeal. Three locations: Port of Spain, San Fernando and Tobago. There are 23 Supreme Court Puisne Judges who sit in criminal, civil, and matrimonial divisions; Registrar EVELYN ANN PETERSEN.

Magistracy: St Vincent St, Port of Spain; tel. 625-2781; divided into 13 districts; consists of a Chief Magistrate, a Deputy Chief Magistrate, 13 Senior Magistrates and 29 Magistrates; Chief Magistrate MARCIA AYERS-CAESAR.

Director of Public Prosecutions: ROGER GASPARD.

Religion
CHRISTIANITY

Caribbean Conference of Churches: POB 876, Curepe; tel. 662-2979; fax 662-1303; e-mail ccchq@tstt.net.tt; internet www .ccc-caribe.org; f. 1973; Pres. Rev. Dr LESLEY G. ANDERSON; Gen. Sec. GERARD A. J. GRANADO.

Christian Council of Trinidad and Tobago: Hayes Court, 21 Maraval Rd, Port of Spain; tel. 637-9329; f. 1967; church unity org. formed by the Roman Catholic, Anglican, Presbyterian, Methodist, African Methodist, Spiritual Baptist and Moravian Churches, the Church of Scotland and the Salvation Army, with the Ethiopian Orthodox Church and the Baptist Union as observers; Pres. ADRIANA NOEL (acting); Sec. GRACE STEELE.

The Anglican Communion
Anglicans are adherents of the Church in the Province of the West Indies, comprising eight dioceses. The Archbishop of the West Indies is the Bishop of Nassau and the Bahamas. According to figures from the latest available census (2000), some 8% of the population were Anglicans.

Bishop of Trinidad and Tobago: CLAUDE BERKLEY, Hayes Court, 21 Maraval Rd, Port of Spain; tel. 622-7387; fax 628-1319; e-mail diocesett@tstt.net.tt; internet www.trinidad.anglican.org.

Protestant Churches
According to the 2000 census, 7% of the population were (Orthodox) Baptists, 7% were Pentecostalists, 4% were Seventh-day Adventists and 3% were Presbyterians.

Baptist Union of Trinidad and Tobago: 104 High St, Princes Town; tel. 655-2291; e-mail baptuni@tstt.net.tt; f. 1816; Pres. Rev. FRANCIS IVAN BAPTISTE; Gen. Sec. Rev. ANSLEM WARRICK; 24 churches, 3,600 mems.

Presbyterian Church of Trinidad and Tobago: POB 187, Paradise Hill, San Fernando; tel. and fax 652-4829; e-mail pctt@tstt.net .tt; internet www.presbyterianchurchtt.org; f. 1868; Moderator Rt Rev. BRENDA BULLOCK; Gen. Sec. APHZAL SELWYN ACKBARALI; 40,000 mems.

The Roman Catholic Church
For ecclesiastical purposes, Trinidad and Tobago comprises the single archdiocese of Port of Spain. According to the 2000 census, 26% of the population were Roman Catholics.

Antilles Episcopal Conference: 9A Gray St, Port of Spain; tel. 622-2932; fax 628-3688; e-mail secretariat@aec.org; internet www.aecrc .org; f. 1975; 21 mems from the Caribbean and Central American regions; Pres. Most Rev. PATRICK PINDER (Archbishop of Nassau in Bahamas).

Archbishop of Port of Spain: 27 Maraval Rd, Port of Spain; tel. 622-1103; fax 622-1165; e-mail abishop@carib-link.net; JOSEPH EVERARD HARRIS.

HINDUISM
Hindu immigrants from India first arrived in Trinidad and Tobago in 1845. The vast majority of migrants, who were generally from Uttar Pradesh, were Vishnavite Hindus, who belonged to sects such as the Ramanandi, the Kabir and the Sieunaraini. The majority of Hindus currently subscribe to the doctrine of Sanathan Dharma, which evolved from Ramanandi teaching. According to the 2000 census, 22% of the population were Hindus.

Arya Pratinidhi Sabha of Trinidad Inc (Arya Samaj): Seer-eeram Memorial Vedic School, Old Southern Main Rd, Montrose Village, Chaguanas; tel. 663-1721; e-mail president@ trinidadaryasamaj.org; Pres. LAKHRAM VIJAY BACHAN.

Pandits' Parishad (Council of Pandits): Maha Sabha Headquarters, Eastern Main Rd, St Augustine; tel. 645-3240; works towards the co-ordination of temple activities and the standardization of ritual procedure; affiliated to the Maha Sabha; 200 mems.

Sanathan Dharma Maha Sabha of Trinidad and Tobago Inc: Maha Sabha Headquarters, Eastern Main Rd, St Augustine; tel. 645-3240; e-mail mahasabha@ttemail.com; f. 1952; Hindu pressure group and public org.; organizes the provision of Hindu education; Pres. Dr D. OMAH MAHARAJH; Sec. Gen. SATNARAYAN MAHARAJ.

ISLAM

According to the 2000 census, 6% of the population were Muslims.

The Press
DAILIES

Newsday: 23A Chacon St, Port of Spain; tel. 623-2459; fax 625-8362; e-mail newsday@newsday.co.tt; internet www.newsday.co.tt; f. 1993; CEO and Editor-in-Chief THERESE MILLS; circ. 2,200,000.

Trinidad Guardian: 22 St Vincent St, POB 122, Port of Spain; tel. 623-8871; fax 625-5702; e-mail letters@ttol.co.tt; internet guardian.co.tt; f. 1917; morning; independent; Editor-in-Chief JUDY RAYMOND; circ. 52,617.

Trinidad and Tobago Express: 35 Independence Sq., Port of Spain; tel. 623-1711; fax 627-1451; e-mail express@trinidadexpress.com; internet www.trinidadexpress.com; f. 1967; morning; Editor-in-Chief OMATIE LYDER; circ. 55,000.

PERIODICALS

The Boca: 27A Saddle Rd, Maraval; tel. 634-2055; fax 622-6580; e-mail sales@boatersenterprise.com; internet www.boatersenterprise.com; 6 a year; magazine of the sailing and boating community.

The Bomb: Southern Main Rd, Curepe; tel. 645-2744; weekly; Publr SAT MAHARAJ.

Caribbean Beat Magazine: MEP Publishers, 6 Prospect Ave, Maraval, Port of Spain; tel. 622-3821; fax 628-0639; e-mail caribbean-beat@meppublishers.com; internet www.caribbean-beat.com; f. 1992; 6 a year; inflight magazine of Caribbean Airlines; Publr JEREMY TAYLOR; Editor NICHOLAS LAUGHLIN.

Catholic News: 31 Independence Sq., Port of Spain; tel. 623-6093; fax 623-9468; e-mail mail@catholicnews-tt.net; internet www.catholicnews-tt.net; f. 1892; weekly; Editor JUNE JOHNSTON; circ. 18,000.

Energy Caribbean: 6 Prospect Ave, Maraval, Port of Spain; tel. 622-3821; fax 628-0639; e-mail dchin@meppublishers.com; internet www.meppublishers.com; f. 2002; 6 a year; Editor JEREMY TAYLOR.

Sunday Guardian: 22 St Vincent St, POB 122, Port of Spain; tel. 623-8870; fax 625-7211; e-mail esunday@ttol.co.tt; internet www.guardian.co.tt; f. 1917; independent; morning; Editor-in-Chief JUDY RAYMOND; Editor DEBRA WANSER; circ. 48,324.

Tobago News: 18 eTeck Mall, Sangster's Hill, Scarborough; tel. 660-7107; fax 639-5565; e-mail ccngroupc@tstt.net.tt; internet www.thetobagonews.com; f. 1985; 2 a month; Editor CORDELL MCCLURE.

Trinidad and Tobago Gazette: 2–4 Victoria Ave, Port of Spain; tel. 625-4139; internet www.news.gov.tt; weekly; official govt paper; circ. 3,300.

Trinidad and Tobago Mirror: Cnr Ninth St and Ninth Ave, Barataria; tel. 674-1692; fax 674-3228; internet www.tntmirror.com; f. 1981; 2 a week; bought by Integrated Media Co Ltd in 2011; Publr MAXIE CUFFIE; circ. 35,000.

Publishers

Caribbean Children's Press: 7 Coronation St, St James; tel. and fax 628-4248; f. 1987; educational publishers for primary schools.

Caribbean Educational Publishers: Gulf View Link Rd, La Romaine; tel. 657-9613; fax 652-5620; e-mail mbscep@tstt.net.tt; Pres. TEDDY MOHAMMED.

Charran Publishing House Ltd: Wrightson Road, POB 126, Port of Spain; tel. 638-9205; fax 674-0817; e-mail siras@charranpublishers.com; internet www.charranpublishers.com; Man. Dir REGINALD CHARRAN.

Lexicon Trinidad Ltd: Lot 87, Frederick Settlement Industrial Estate, Caroni; tel. 662-1863; fax 663-0081; e-mail lexiconadmin@gmail.com; Dir KEN JAIKARANSINGH.

Morton Publishing: 97 Saddle Rd, Maraval; tel. 348-3777; fax 762-9923; e-mail morton@morton-pub.com; internet www.morton-pub.com; f. 1977; educational books; Pres. DOUG MORTON; Dir JULIE MORTON.

Paria Publishing Co Ltd: Third Ave, Cascade; tel. 624-4187; e-mail pariapublishing@gmail.com; internet www.pariapublishing.com; f. 1981; Dir DOMINIC BESSON.

Royards Publishing Co: 7A Macoya Industrial Estate, Macoya; tel. 663-6002; fax 663-3616; e-mail royards@aol.com; internet www.royards.com; f. 1984; educational publishers; Dirs CLIFFORD NARINESINGH, DWIGHT NARINESINGH.

Toute Bagai Publishing: 26 Kelly Kenny St, Woodbrook, Port of Spain; tel. 622-0519; fax 628-6909; e-mail info@macomag.com; internet www.macomag.com; f. 1999; magazines; publ. *MACO Caribbean Living*; Man. Dir NEYSHA SOODEEN.

Trinidad Publishing Co Ltd: 22–24 St Vincent St, Port of Spain; tel. 623-8870; fax 625-7211; e-mail business@ttol.co.tt; internet guardian.co.tt; f. 1917; Man. Dir GRENFELL KISSOON; Gen. Man. DOUGLAS WILSON.

University of the West Indies: Marketing and Communications Office, St Augustine; tel. 662-9387; fax 662-3858; e-mail marketing.communications@sta.uwi.edu; internet sta.uwi.edu/news/periodicals; f. 1960; journals, magazines, newsletters and periodicals; Editor ANNA WALCOTT-HARDY.

Sir Arthur Lewis Institute of Social and Economic Studies (SALISES): University of the West Indies, St Augustine; tel. 662-2002; fax 645-6329; e-mail salises@sta.uwi.edu; internet sta.uwi.edu/salises; f. 1999 by the merger of the Institute of Social and Economic Research (ISER), est. 1948, and the Consortium Graduate School of Social Sciences (CGSSS), est. 1985; books, journals and monographs; Dir PATRICK KENT WATSON.

Broadcasting and Communications
REGULATORY BODY

Telecommunications Authority of Trinidad and Tobago (TATT): 5 Eighth Ave Ext., off 12th St, Barataria; tel. 675-8288; fax 674-1055; e-mail info@tatt.org.tt; internet www.tatt.org.tt; f. 2001 to oversee the liberalization of the telecommunications sector; regulates the telecommunications and broadcasting sectors; Chair. SELBY WILSON; CEO CHRIS SEECHERAN.

TELECOMMUNICATIONS

Columbus Communications Trinidad Ltd (Flow): 29 Victoria Sq., Port of Spain; tel. 223-3569; fax 624-9584; e-mail mediainquiries@columbustrinidad.com; internet discoverflow.co/trinidad; f. 2005; digital cable television, internet and local telephone service providers; mobile cellular telephone licence granted in 2006; Man. Dir BRIAN COLLINS; 250 employees (2007).

Digicel Trinidad and Tobago: Ansa Centre, 11C Maraval Rd, Port of Spain; tel. 628-7000; fax 628-9540; e-mail tt.customer.care@digicelgroup.com; internet www.digiceltrinidadandtobago.com; owned by an Irish consortium; f. 2001; mobile cellular telephone licence granted in 2005; Chair. DENIS O'BRIEN; CEO JOHN DELVES.

One Caribbean Media Ltd (OCM): 35 Independence Sq., Port of Spain; tel. 623-1711; fax 627-4886; e-mail john.lumyoung@ocmnews.com; internet www.onecaribbeanmedia.net; f. 2006 by merger of Caribbean Communications Network (CCN) and The Nation Corpn (Barbados); Chair. Sir FRED GOLLOP; CEO DAWN THOMAS.

Open Telecom Ltd: 88 Edward St, Port of Spain; tel. 627-6559; e-mail sales@opentelecomtt.com; internet www.opentelecomtt.com; f. 1992; Chair. PETER GILLETTE; Chief Operations Man. NICHOLAS LOOK HONG.

Telecommunication Services of Trinidad and Tobago (TSTT) Ltd: 1 Edward St, POB 3, Port of Spain; tel. 625-4431; fax 627-0856; e-mail tsttceo@tstt.net.tt; internet www.tstt.co.tt; 51% state-owned, 49% by Cable & Wireless (UK); 51% privatization pending; CEO GEORGE HILL (acting).

blink Broadband: TSTT Broadband Marketing, 12 Richmond St, Port of Spain; tel. 824-8788; fax 623-6501; e-mail support@tstt.net.tt; internet www.blinkbroadband.tt; f. 2007; internet service provider; Exec. Vice-Pres. DIANNA DE SOUSA.

bmobile: 52 Jerningham Ave, Belmont; fax 627-1534; e-mail service@tstt.co.tt; internet www.bmobile.co.tt; f. 1991 as TSTT Cellnet; name changed as above 2006; mobile cellular telephone operator; Exec. Vice-Pres. RONALD WALCOTT (acting).

BROADCASTING
Radio

The Caribbean New Media Group (CNMG): 11A Maraval, Port of Spain; tel. 622-4141; fax 622-0344; e-mail webmaster@ctntworld.com; internet www.ctntworld.com; state-owned; operates three radio stations: Talk City 91.1 FM, Next 99.1 FM and Sweet 100.1 FM; and three television channels: 6 (cable), 9 and 13; CEO INGRID ISAAC.

i95.5 FM: 47 Tragarete Rd, New Town, Port of Spain; tel. 628-4955; fax 628-0251; e-mail info@i955fm.com; internet www.i955fm.com; Exec. Chair. and CEO LOUIS LEE SING.

I.S.A.A.C. 98.1 FM: 115A Woodford St, Newtown, Port of Spain; tel. 628-0904; fax 628-3108; e-mail info@isaac981.com; internet www .isaac981.com; f. 2002; 24-hour Christian radio station; CEO MARGARET ELCOCK.

Power 102 FM: Radio Vision Ltd, 88–90 Abercromby St, Port of Spain; tel. 627-6937; fax 627-9320; e-mail power102fm@gmail.com; internet www.power102fm.com; CEO O'BRIAN HAYNES; Man. SHARON PITT.

Radio Jaagriti 102.7 FM: cnr Pasea Main Rd Ext. and Churchill Roosevelt Hwy, Tunapuna; tel. 645-0613; fax 663-8961; e-mail comments@jaagriti.com; internet www.jaagriti.com; f. 2007; Hindu broadcasting network; Man. Dir SAT MAHARAJ; CEO DEVANT MAHARAJ.

Radio Tambrin 92.7: 3 Picton St, Scarborough, Tobago; tel. 639-3437; fax 660-7351; e-mail tambrin@tstt.net.tt; internet www .tambrintobago.com; f. 1998; CEO GEORGE LEACOCK.

Red 96.7: 47 Tragarete Rd, New Town, Port of Spain; tel. 628-4967; fax 628-0251; e-mail info@citadel.co.tt; internet www.red967fm.com; f. 2005; Exec. Chair. and CEO LOUIS LEE SING.

Soca 91.9 FM (Trini Bashment): 56A, Maraval Rd, Port of Spain; tel. 628-3460; fax 622-7674; e-mail info@soca919.com; internet www .919socafm.com; Man. Dir ANTHONY DEVON GEORGE.

Telemedia Ltd: Long Circular Mall, 4th Floor, Long Circular Rd, St James; tel. 622-4124; fax 622-6693; operates three commercial radio stations: Music Radio 97 FM (www.musicradio97.com), Ebony Radio 104 FM (www.ebony104.com) and Heartbeat 103.5 FM (www.heart-beatradiott.com); Gen. Man. KIRAN MAHARAJ.

Trinidad Broadcasting Co Ltd: Guardian Bldg, 2nd Floor, 22–24 St Vincent St, Port of Spain; tel. 623-9202; fax 623-8972; e-mail tbcnews@ttol.co.tt; operates five radio stations: Inspirational Radio 730 AM, Mix 95.1 FM, Vibe CT 105 FM, Sangeet 106 FM and Aakash Vani 106.5 FM; Gen. Man. BRANDON KHAN.

Trinidad and Tobago Radio Network: 153 Tragarete Rd, Port of Spain; tel. 628-6937; internet www.1077musicforlife.com; operates two stations: 96.1 WEFM and 107.7 FM.

Wack Radio 90.1 FM: 129C Coffee St, San Fernando; tel. 652-9774; fax 657-1888; e-mail contact@wackradio901fm.com; internet www .wackradio901fm.com; CEO KENNY PHILLIPS; Man. Dir DIANNE PHILLIPS.

WMJX 100.5 FM: 9 Long Circular Rd, St James; tel. 628-9516; fax 622-2756; e-mail comments@wmjxfm.com; internet www.wmjxfm .com; Gen. Man. KEITH CADET.

Television

ieTV Channel 1: 76 Tragarete Rd, Port of Spain; tel. 622-3541; fax 622-3097; e-mail ietv@tstt.net.tt; internet www.ietv1.com; owned by CL Communications Group; Indian entertainment-programming; CEO ANTHONY MAHARAJ.

TV6: 35 Independence Sq., Port of Spain; tel. 627-8806; fax 623-0785; e-mail enquiries@tv6tnt.com; internet www.tv6tnt.com; f. 1991; operates channels 6 and 18; owned by One Caribbean Media Ltd (OCM); Chair. Sir FRED GOLLOP; Gen. Man. SHIDA BOLAI.

Finance

(cap. = capital; res = reserves; dep. = deposits; m. = million; brs = branches; amounts in TT $)

BANKING

Central Bank

Central Bank of Trinidad and Tobago: Eric Williams Plaza, Brian Lara Promenade, POB 1250, Port of Spain; tel. 625-4835; fax 627-4696; e-mail info@central-bank.org.tt; internet www .central-bank.org.tt; f. 1964; cap. 800.0m., res 534.8m., dep. 53.5m. (Sept. 2009); Gov. JWALA RAMBARRAN.

Commercial Banks

Citibank (Trinidad and Tobago) Ltd: 12 Queen's Park East, POB 1249, Port of Spain; tel. 625-1046; fax 624-8131; internet www .citibank.com/trinidad; f. 1983; fmrly The United Bank of Trinidad and Tobago Ltd; name changed as above 1989; owned by Citicorp Merchant Bank Ltd; cap. 157.8m., res 94.4m., dep. 3,727.6m. (Dec. 2010); Chair. SURESH MAHARAJ; Country Man. DENNIS EVANS; 2 brs.

Citicorp Merchant Bank Ltd: 12 Queen's Park East, POB 1249, Port of Spain; tel. 623-3344; fax 624-8131; cap. 57.1m., res 151.8m., dep. 3,796.7m. (Dec. 2010); owned by Citibank Overseas Investment Corpn; Man. Dir KAREN DARBASIE.

First Citizens Bank Ltd: 9 Queen's Park East, Port of Spain; tel. 624-3178; fax 627-4548; e-mail enquiries@simplyfirst.net; internet www.firstcitizenstt.com; f. 1993 following merger of National Commercial Bank of Trinidad and Tobago Ltd, Trinidad Co-operative Bank Ltd and Workers' Bank of Trinidad and Tobago; state-owned; cap. 643.6m., res 1,838.4m., dep. 18,894.5m. (Sept. 2012); Chair. NYREE D. ALFONSO; CEO LARRY NATH; 25 brs.

RBC Royal Bank Trinidad and Tobago Ltd: Royal Court, 19–21 Park St, POB 287, Port of Spain; tel. 623-1322; fax 625-3764; e-mail royalinfo@rbtt.co.tt; internet www.rbtt.com/tt/personal; f. 1972 as Royal Bank of Trinidad and Tobago to take over local brs of Royal Bank of Canada; changed name to RBTT Bank Ltd in 2002, present name adopted 2011; bought by Royal Bank of Canada in 2007; cap. 404m., res 540m., dep. 17,511.4m. (Oct. 2011); CEO, Caribbean SURESH SOOKOO; 21 brs.

Republic Bank Ltd: 9–17 Park St, POB 1153, Port of Spain; tel. 623-1056; fax 624-1323; e-mail email@republictt.com; internet www .republictt.com; f. 1837 as Colonial Bank; became Barclays Bank in 1972; name changed as above 1981; merged with Bank of Commerce Trinidad and Tobago Ltd 1997; cap. 596.5m., res 1,371m., dep. 33,072.4m. (Sept. 2011); Chair. RONALD F. HARFORD; Man. Dir DAVID DULAL-WHITEWAY; 34 brs.

Republic Finance & Merchant Bank Ltd: 9–17 Park St, POB 1153, Port of Spain; tel. 623-1056; fax 624-1323; e-mail email@ republictt.com; internet www.republictt.com; f. 1965; owned by Republic Bank Ltd; cap. 30.0m., res 44.5m., dep. 1,836.5m. (Sept. 2004); Chair. RONALD F. HARFORD; Man. Dir CHERYL F. GREAVES.

Scotiabank Trinidad and Tobago Ltd: 56–58 Richmond St, POB 621, Port of Spain; tel. 625-3566; fax 627-5278; e-mail scotiamain@ tstt.net.tt; internet www.scotiabanktt.com; cap. 267.6m., res 454.4m., dep. 13,003m. (Oct. 2012); Chair. SYLVIA D. CHROMINSKA; Man. Dir ANYA M. SCHNOOR; 27 brs.

Development Banks

Agricultural Development Bank of Trinidad and Tobago: 87 Henry St, POB 154, Port of Spain; tel. 623-6261; fax 624-3087; e-mail northbranch@adbtt.com; internet www.adbtt.com; f. 1968; provides long-, medium- and short-term loans to farmers and the agri-business sector; Chair. RUDY MAHARAJ; CEO JACQUELINE RAWLINS.

DFL Caribbean: 10 Cipriani Blvd, POB 187, Port of Spain; tel. 623-4665; fax 624-3563; e-mail dfl@dflcaribbean.com; internet www .dflcaribbean.com; provides short- and long-term finance, and equity financing for projects in manufacturing, agro-processing, tourism, industrial and commercial enterprises; total assets 427.2m. (Dec. 2012); Chair. ANDREW FERGUSON; Gen. Man. SIEW PALTOO.

Credit Union

Co-operative Credit Union League of Trinidad and Tobago Ltd: 3 Cnr John and De Verteuil Sts, Montrose, Chaguanas; tel. 671-4711; fax 672-0164; e-mail culeague@tstt.net.tt; internet www.ccultt .org; Pres. BRIAN MOORE; Man. DIANNE JOSEPH; 400,000 mems.

STOCK EXCHANGE

Trinidad and Tobago Stock Exchange Ltd: Nicholas Tower, 10th Floor, 63–65 Independence Sq., Port of Spain; tel. 625-5107; fax 623-0089; e-mail ttstockx@stockex.co.tt; internet www.stockex.co.tt; f. 1981; 23 cos listed (2012); electronic depository system came into operation in 2003; Chair. RANJIT JEEWAN; CEO C. WAINWRIGHT ITON.

INSURANCE

ALGICO Trinidad and Tobago: ALGICO Plaza, 91–93 St Vincent St, POB 943, Port of Spain; tel. 625-4426; fax 623-4923; internet www .algico.com; f. 1977; fmrly known as American Life and General Insurance Co; bought by MetLife in 2010; Man. Dir ENRIQUE GONZALEZ.

Bankers Insurance Co of Trinidad and Tobago Ltd: 5 Mulchan Seuchan Rd, Chaguanas; tel. 672-1057; fax 672-2808; e-mail joan@ bankers-tt.com; internet www.bankerstt.com; CEO ZAMANATH ALI.

Beacon Insurance Co Ltd: 13 Stanmore Ave, POB 837, Port of Spain; tel. 623-2266; fax 623-9900; e-mail info@beacon.co.tt; internet www.beacon.co.tt; f. 1996; Man. Dir GERALD S HADEED.

CUNA Caribbean Insurance Society Ltd: 7 Gray St, St Clair, Port of Spain; tel. 628-2862; fax 628-3506; e-mail cunains@trinidad .net; internet www.cunacaribbean.com; f. 1991; marine aviation and transport; motor vehicle, personal accident, property; Man. Dir and CEO ANDRE GOINDOO; 3 brs.

Furness Anchorage General Insurance Ltd: 11–13 Milling Ave, Sea Lots, POB 283, Port of Spain; tel. 625-1746; fax 625-1243; e-mail furness@tstt.net.tt; internet www.furnessgroup.com; f. 1979; general; Chair. IGNATIUS SEVEIRANO FERREIRA; Exec. Chair. WILLIAM A. FERREIRA.

Guardian General Insurance Ltd: Newtown Centre, 30–36 Maraval Rd, Port of Spain; tel. 625-4445; fax 622-9994; e-mail guardian .general@ggil.biz; internet www.ggil.biz; founded by merger of NEMWIL and Caribbean Home; CEO RICHARD ESPINET; Vice-Pres. (Trinidad Operations) JOAN MITCHELL.

Guardian Life of the Caribbean: 1 Guardian Dr., West Moorings, Port of Spain; tel. 625-5433; fax 632-5695; e-mail guardian@gloc.biz; internet www.gloc.biz; f. 1980; Group Pres. RAVI TEWARI.

Gulf Insurance Ltd: 1 Gray St, St Clair, Port of Spain; tel. 622-5878; fax 628-0272; e-mail info@gulfinsuranceltd.com; internet www .gulfinsuranceltd.com; f. 1974; general; Chair. JASON CLARKE.

Maritime Financial Group: Maritime Centre, 10th Ave, POB 710, Barataria; tel. 674-0130; fax 638-6663; e-mail email@ maritimefinancial.com; internet www.maritimefinancial.com; f. 1978; property and casualty; CEO JOHN H. SMITH.

New India Assurance Co (T & T) Ltd: Guardian Bldg, 3rd Floor, 22–24 St Vincent St, POB 884, Port of Spain; tel. 623-1326; fax 625-0670; e-mail hoffice@newindiatt.com; tel. www.newindia.co.in; f. 1919; Man. Dir Mr ASWATHANARAYANA.

Sagicor Life Inc: Sagicor Financial Centre, 16 Queen's Park West, Port of Spain; tel. 628-1636; fax 628-1639; e-mail comments@sagicor .com; internet www.sagicorlife.com; f. 1840 as Barbados Mutual Life Assurance Society, name changed as above in 2002; Gen. Man. (Trinidad and Tobago) ROBERT TRESTRAIL.

Trinidad and Tobago Insurance Ltd (TATIL): 11A Maraval Rd, POB 1004, Port of Spain; tel. 628-2845; fax 628-0035; e-mail info@ tatil.co.tt; internet www.tatil.co.tt; acquired by ANSA McAL in 2004; Man. Dir MUSA IBRAHIM (TATIL General); Man. Dir STAFFORD YORKE (TATIL Life).

United Insurance Co (Trinidad): 18–20 London St, Port of Spain; tel. 627-7530; fax 627-3674; e-mail trinidad@unitedinsure.com; internet unitedinsure.com; 95.0% owned by Barbados Shipping and Trading Co; Gen. Man. DENNIS BENISAR.

INSURANCE ORGANIZATIONS

Association of Trinidad and Tobago Insurance Companies: 9A Stanmore Ave, POB 208, Port of Spain; tel. 624-2817; fax 625-5132; e-mail mail@attic.org.tt; internet www.attic.org.tt; Chair. DOUGLAS CAMACHO.

National Insurance Board: NIB House, Cipriani Pl., 2A Cipriani Blvd, Port of Spain; tel. 625-2171; fax 627-1787; e-mail info@nibtt .net; internet www.nibtt.net; f. 1971; statutory corpn; Chair. RAVI RAMOUTAR; Exec. Dir LORNA CHARLES.

Trade and Industry

GOVERNMENT AGENCIES

Cocoa and Coffee Industry Board: 27 Frederick St, POB 1, Port of Spain; tel. 625-0298; fax 627-4172; e-mail ccib@tstt.net.tt; f. 1962; marketing of coffee and cocoa beans, regulation of cocoa and coffee industry; Man. BARRY JOEFIELD.

Export-Import Bank of Trinidad and Tobago Ltd (EXIM-BANK): 30 Queen's Park West, Port of Spain; tel. 628-2762; fax 622-3545; e-mail eximbank@wow.net; internet www.eximbanktt .com; Chair. CLARRY BENN; CEO BRIAN AWANG.

Trinidad and Tobago Forest Products Ltd (TANTEAK): Connector Rd, Carlsen Field, Chaguanas; tel. 665-0078; fax 665-6645; f. 1975; harvesting, processing and marketing of state plantation-grown teak and pine; privatization pending; Chair. RUSKIN PUNCH; Man. Dir CLARENCE BACCHUS.

DEVELOPMENT ORGANIZATIONS

Housing Development Corporation: 44–46 South Quay, POB 555, Port of Spain; tel. 623-4663; fax 627-6940; e-mail info@housing .gov.tt; internet www.housing.gov.tt; f. 1962 as Nat. Housing Authority; Chair. HENCKLE LALL; Man. Dir JEARLEAN JOHN.

National Energy Corporation of Trinidad and Tobago Ltd: PLIPDECO House, Orinoco Dr., POB 191, Point Lisas, Couva; tel. 636-4662; fax 679-2384; e-mail infocent@carib-link.net; internet www.ngc.co.tt; owned by the Nat. Gas Co of Trinidad and Tobago Ltd; f. 1979; Chair. LARRY HOWAI; Pres. ANDREW MCINTOSH.

Point Lisas Industrial Port Development Corporation Ltd (PLIPDECO): PLIPDECO House, Orinoco Dr., POB 191, Point Lisas, Couva; tel. 636-2201; fax 636-4008; e-mail plipdeco@plipdeco .com; internet www.plipdeco.com; f. 1966; privatized in the late 1990s; deep-water port handling general cargo, liquid and dry bulk, to serve adjacent industrial estate, which now includes iron and steel complex, methanol, ammonia, urea and related downstream industries; Chair. IAN ATHERLY; Pres. ERNEST ASHLEY TAYLOR.

Urban Development Corporation of Trinidad and Tobago (UDeCOTT): 38–40 Sackville St, Port of Spain; tel. 627-0083; fax 623-5358; e-mail contact@udecott.com; internet www.udecott.com; f. 1994; reports to the Ministry of Housing; Chair. JEARLEAN JOHN.

CHAMBERS OF COMMERCE

The Energy Chamber of Trinidad and Tobago: Suite B2.03, Atlantic Plaza, Atlantic Ave, Point Lisas; tel. 652-5613; fax 653-4983; e-mail execoffice@energy.tt; internet www.energy.tt; f. 1956; Pres. CHARLES PERCY; CEO Dr THACKWRAY DRIVER.

Trinidad and Tobago Chamber of Industry and Commerce (Inc): Chamber Bldg, Columbus Circle, Westmoorings, POB 499, Port of Spain; tel. 637-6966; fax 637-7425; e-mail chamber@chamber .org.tt; internet www.chamber.org.tt; f. 1891; Pres. ANDREW SABGA; CEO CATHERINE KUMAR; 600 mems.

INDUSTRIAL AND TRADE ASSOCIATIONS

Agricultural Society of Trinidad and Tobago: 52 Penco St, Penco Court, Lange Park, Chaguanas; e-mail agrisocietytt@gmail .com; f. 1839; represents farmers' interests; Pres. DHANO SOOKOO.

Coconut Growers' Association (CGA) Ltd: Eastern Main Rd, POB 229, Laventille, Port of Spain; tel. 623-5207; fax 623-2359; e-mail cgaltd@tstt.net.tt; f. 1936; 354 mems; Exec. Chair. PHILIPPE AGOSTINI.

Co-operative Citrus Growers' Association of Trinidad and Tobago Ltd: Eastern Main Rd, POB 174, Laventille, Port of Spain; tel. 623-5127; fax 623-2487; e-mail ccga@wow.net; f. 1932; Gen. Man. GARY PRENTICE; 437 mems.

Pan Trinbago Inc: Victoria Park Suites, 14–17 Park St, Port of Spain; tel. 623-4486; fax 625-6715; e-mail panadmin@pantrinbago.co .tt; internet www.pantrinbago.co.tt; f. 1971; official body for Trinidad and Tobago steelbands; Pres. KEITH DIAZ; Sec. RICHARD FORTEAU.

Sugar Association of the Caribbean: Brechin Castle, Couva; tel. 636-2449; fax 636-2847; f. 1942; promotes and protects sugar industry in the Caribbean; Chair. KARL JAMES; 6 mem. asscns.

Trinidad and Tobago Contractors' Association: The Professional Centre, Unit B 203, 11–13 Fitzblackman Dr., Wrightson Rd Extension, Port of Spain; tel. 627-1266; fax 623-2949; e-mail ttcaservice@rave-tt.net; internet www.ttca.com; f. 1968; represents contractors, manufacturers and suppliers to the sector; Pres. MERVYN J. CHIN.

Trinidad and Tobago Manufacturers' Association: TTMA Bldg, 42 10th Ave, Barataria; tel. 675-8862; fax 675-9000; e-mail info@ttma.com; internet www.ttma.com; f. 1956; Pres. DOMINIC HADEED; 337 mems.

EMPLOYERS' ORGANIZATION

Employers' Consultative Association of Trinidad and Tobago (ECA): 17 Samaroo Rd, Aranguez Roundabout North, Aranguez; tel. 675-9388; fax 675-4866; e-mail ecatt@tstt.net.tt; internet www.ecatt .org; f. 1959; Chair. KESTON NANCOO; Exec. Dir LINDA BESSON; 700 mems.

STATE HYDROCARBONS COMPANIES

National Gas Co of Trinidad and Tobago Ltd (NGC): Orinoco Dr., Point Lisas Industrial Estate, POB 1127, Port of Spain; tel. 636-4662; fax 679-2384; e-mail ngc@ngc.co.tt; internet www.ngc.co.tt; f. 1975; purchases, sells, compresses, transmits and distributes natural gas to consumers; Chair. LARRY HOWAI; Pres. S. ANDREW MCINTOSH.

Petroleum Co of Trinidad and Tobago Ltd (Petrotrin): Petrotrin Administration Bldg, Southern Main Rd, Pointe-à-Pierre; tel. 658-3336; fax 658-2513; e-mail ken.allum@petrotrin.com; internet www.petrotrin.com; f. 1993 following merger between Trinidad and Tobago Oil Co Ltd (Trintoc) and Trinidad and Tobago Petroleum Co Ltd (Trintopec); govt-owned; petroleum and gas exploration and production; operates refineries and a manufacturing complex, producing a variety of petroleum and petrochemical products; Chair. LINDSAY GILLETTE; Pres. KHALID HASSANALI.

UTILITIES

Regulatory Authority

Regulated Industries Commission: Furness House, Corner Wrightson Rd & Independence Sq., Port of Spain; tel. 625-5384; fax 624-2027; e-mail complaints@ric.org.tt; internet www.ric.org.tt; f. 2000; Chair. ANNE-MARIE MOHAMMED; Exec. Dir HARJINDER S. ATWAL.

Electricity

Power Generation Co of Trinidad and Tobago (PowerGen): 6A Queen's Park West, Port of Spain; tel. 624-0383; fax 624-0983; e-mail pgcinfo@powergen.co.tt; internet www.powergen.co.tt; f. 1994; 51% owned by The Trinidad and Tobago Electricity Commission (T&TEC); operates 3 generation plants in Point Lisas, Port of Spain and Penal; Gen. Man. GARTH CHATOOR.

Trinidad and Tobago Electricity Commission (T&TEC): 63 Frederick St, Port of Spain; tel. 623-2611; fax 623-3759; e-mail comments@ttec.co.tt; internet www.ttec.co.tt; state-owned electricity transmission and distribution co; Chair. SUSILLA RAMKISSOON-MARK; Gen. Man. INDARJIT SINGH.

Trinity Power Ltd: Railway Rd, Dow Village, Couva; tel. 679-4542; fax 679-4463; e-mail gthompson@trinitypm.com; f. 1999; fmrly Inncogen Ltd; owned by York Research Corpn; Gen. Man. JACQUE-LINE LOOK LOY.

Gas

National Gas Co of Trinidad and Tobago Ltd: see State Hydrocarbons Companies.

Water

Water and Sewerage Authority (WASA): Farm Rd, St Joseph; tel. 662-2302; e-mail contact@wasa.gov.tt; internet www.wasa.gov.tt; f. 1965; Chair. INDAR MAHARAJ; CEO GANGA SINGH.

TRADE UNIONS

Federation of Independent Trade Unions and NGOs (FITUN): Paramount Bldg, 99A Circular Rd, San Fernando; tel. 652-2701; fax 652-7170; e-mail fitun_tt@yahoo.com; f. 2003; Pres. DAVID ABDULLAH; Gen. Sec. MICHAEL DEFREITAS.

National Trade Union Centre (NATUC): 16 New St, Port of Spain; tel. 625-3023; fax 627-7588; e-mail natuc@carib-link.net; f. 1991 as umbrella org. unifying entire trade union movt, incl. fmr Trinidad and Tobago Labour Congress and Council of Progressive Trade Unions; Pres. MICHAEL ANNISETTE; Gen. Sec. JACQUELINE JACK.

Transport

RAILWAYS

The Government in 2005 announced plans to reintroduce a railway service, which had been discontinued in 1968. The design phase of the project began in 2008 and construction was expected to take 10–15 years, costing an estimated TT $15,000m.

ROADS

There were 8,320 km (5,170 miles) of roads in Trinidad and Tobago in 2001, of which 51.1% were paved.

Public Transport Service Corporation: 60 Railway Bldg, South Quay, POB 391, Port of Spain; tel. 623-2341; fax 625-6502; e-mail ptscpos@ptsc.co.tt; internet www.ptsc.co.tt; f. 1965; national bus services, operates a fleet of buses; Chair. Dr VINCENT LASSE; Gen. Man. SELWYN SYLVESTER.

SHIPPING

The chief ports are Port of Spain, Pointe-à-Pierre and Point Lisas in Trinidad, and Scarborough in Tobago. Port of Spain handles 85% of all container traffic, and all international cruise arrivals. Port of Spain and Scarborough each have a deep-water wharf. Port of Spain possesses a dedicated container terminal, with two large overhead cranes. At December 2012 the flag registered fleet comprised 82 vessels, totalling 39,085 grt.

Point Lisas Industrial Port Development Corporation Ltd (PLIPDECO): see Trade and Industry—Development Organizations.

Port Authority of Trinidad and Tobago: Dock Rd, POB 549, Port of Spain; tel. 623-2901; fax 627-2666; e-mail vilmal@patnt.com; internet www.patnt.com; f. 1962; Chair. JOSEPH TONEY; CEO COLIN LUCAS.

Shipping Association of Trinidad and Tobago: 15 Scott Bushe St, Port of Spain; tel. 623-3355; fax 623-8570; e-mail satt@wow.net; internet shipping.co.tt; f. 1938; Pres. RHETT CHEE PING; Gen. Man. E. JOANNE EDWARDS-ALLEYNE.

CIVIL AVIATION

Piarco International Airport is situated 25.7 km (16 miles) south-east of Port of Spain and is used by numerous airlines. There is also an international airport at Crown Point, 13 km from Scarborough. There is a domestic service between Trinidad and Tobago. The regional airline LIAT (based in Antigua and Barbuda, and in which Trinidad and Tobago is a shareholder) operates scheduled flights connecting it with other islands in the Eastern Caribbean.

Airports Authority of Trinidad and Tobago (AATT): Airport Administration Centre, Piarco Int. Airport, South Terminal, Golden Grove Rd, Piarco; tel. 669-5311; fax 669-2319; e-mail aatt@tntairports.com; internet www.tntairports.com; administers Piarco and Crown Point International Airports; Chair. GERALD HADEED; Gen. Man. DAYANAND BIRJU (acting).

Caribbean Airlines Ltd (CAL): Sunjet House, 30 Edward St, Port of Spain; tel. 625-7200; e-mail mail@caribbean-airlines.com; internet www.caribbean-airlines.com; f. 2007 as successor to BWIA (f. 1940); operates scheduled passenger and cargo services linking destinations in the Caribbean region, South America, North America and Europe; Chair. RABINDRA MOONAN; CEO ROBERT CORBIE (acting).

Tourism

The climate and coastline attract visitors to Trinidad and Tobago. The latter island is generally believed to be the more beautiful and is less developed. The annual pre-Lenten carnival is a major attraction. Total tourist arrivals numbered an estimated 385,510 in 2010, while tourism receipts were estimated at US $393m. There were 3,815 hotel rooms in Trinidad and Tobago in 2008, of which 57.5% were on Tobago.

Tobago Department of Tourism: 12 Sangster Hill, Scarborough; tel. 639-2125; fax 639-3566; internet www.visittobago.gov.tt; Administrator ETHEL HECTOR-BERKLEY SYLVESTER.

Tourism Development Co of Trinidad and Tobago (TDC): Maritime Centre, Level 1, 29 10th Ave, Barataria; tel. 675-7034; fax 675-7722; e-mail info@tdc.co.tt; internet www.tdc.co.tt; f. 1993 as Tourism and Industrial Devt Co of Trinidad and Tobago; restructured and renamed as above in 2005; govt-owned; Chair. BRIAN FRONTIN; CEO SANDRA PERKINS.

Trinidad Hotels, Restaurants and Tourism Association (THRTA): c/o Trinidad & Tobago Hospitality and Tourism Institute, Airway Rd, Chaguaramas; tel. 634-1174; fax 634-1176; e-mail info@tnthotels.com; internet www.tnthotels.com; Pres. MICHELLE PALMER KEIZER; Exec. Dir LOUANNA CHAI-ALVES.

Tobago Hotel and Tourism Association (THTA): Apt 1, Lambeau Credit Union Bldg, Auchenskeoch Rd, Carnbee; POB 295, Scarborough; tel. and fax 639-9543; e-mail thta@tstt.net.tt; internet www.tobagohoteltourism.com; Pres. NICHOLAS HARDWICKE.

Defence

As assessed at November 2012, the Trinidad and Tobago Defence Force consisted of an army of an estimated 3,000 men and a coastguard of 1,050. Included in the coastguard was an air wing of 50.

Defence Budget: TT $2,840m. (US $446m.) in 2012.

Chief of Defence Staff: Brig.-Gen. KENRICK MAHARAJ.

Education

Primary and secondary education is provided free of charge. Many schools are run jointly by state and religious bodies. Attendance at school is officially compulsory for children between five and 12 years of age. Primary education begins at the age of five and lasts for seven years. In 2009/10 some 94% of children in this age-group were enrolled at primary schools. Secondary education, beginning at 12 years of age, lasts for up to five years, comprising a first cycle of three years and a second of two years. The ratio for secondary enrolment in 2008 was 74% of those in the relevant age-group (males 71%, females 76%), according to UNESCO estimates. Entrance to secondary schools is determined by the Common Entrance Examination.

Free tertiary tuition was introduced in 2006. The Trinidad campus of the University of the West Indies (UWI), at St Augustine, offers undergraduate and postgraduate programmes and includes an engineering faculty. The UWI Institute of Business offers postgraduate courses and develops programmes for local companies. The University of Trinidad and Tobago was established in 2004. The country has one teacher-training college and three government technical institutes and vocational centres. Budgeted expenditure on education and training by the central Government in 2013 was projected at TT $9,149.1m.

TUNISIA

Introductory Survey

LOCATION, CLIMATE, LANGUAGE, RELIGION, FLAG, CAPITAL

The Republic of Tunisia lies in north Africa, bordered by Algeria to the west and by Libya to the south-east. To the north and east, Tunisia has a coastline on the Mediterranean Sea. The climate is temperate on the coast, with winter rain, but hot and dry inland. Temperatures in Tunis are generally between 6°C (43°F) and 33°C (91°F). The country's highest recorded temperature is 55°C. Average annual rainfall is up to 1,500 mm in the north, but less than 200 mm in the southern desert. The official language is Arabic, and there is a small Berber Tamazight-speaking minority. French is widely used as a second language. Islam is the state religion, and almost all of the inhabitants are Muslims. There are small minorities of Christians and Jews. The national flag (proportions 2 by 3) is red, with a white disc, containing a red crescent moon and a five-pointed red star, in the centre. The capital is Tunis.

CONTEMPORARY POLITICAL HISTORY

Historical Context

Formerly a French protectorate, Tunisia was granted internal self-government by France in September 1955 and full independence on 20 March 1956. Five days later elections were held for a Constitutional Assembly, which met in April and appointed Habib Bourguiba as Prime Minister in a Government dominated by members of his Néo-Destour (New Constitution) Party. In July 1957 a republic was established, with Bourguiba as Head of State, and a new Constitution was promulgated in June 1959. At elections held in November, Bourguiba was elected unopposed to the new office of President, and the Néo-Destour Party won all 90 seats in the new National Assembly.

By 1964 the Néo-Destour Party had become the only legal political organization, and in November it was renamed the Parti socialiste destourien (PSD). A moderate socialist economic programme was introduced, which began with the expropriation of foreign-owned lands. However, attempts to introduce agricultural collectivization in 1964–69, under the direction of Ahmad Ben Salah, Minister of Finance and Planning, were abandoned following resistance from the rural population. Ben Salah was dismissed, arrested and subsequently sentenced to 10 years' hard labour. He escaped in 1973 and fled to Europe, from where he organized the radical Mouvement de l'unité populaire (MUP). In 1970 Hédi Nouira, hitherto Governor of the Banque Centrale de Tunisie, was appointed Prime Minister. He began to reverse Ben Salah's socialist economic policies, with the introduction of liberal economic reforms in the sectors of industry and agriculture. Liberalization of the economy was not accompanied by political reform, and the extensive powers of Nouira and Bourguiba were increasingly challenged by younger PSD members in the early 1970s. However, at the 1974 PSD Congress, Bourguiba was elected President-for-Life of the PSD and Nouira was confirmed as Secretary-General. In 1975, after approving the necessary amendments to the Constitution, the National Assembly elected Bourguiba President-for-Life of Tunisia. In 1980 Nouira resigned, owing to ill health, and was succeeded as Prime Minister and Secretary-General of the PSD by Muhammad Mzali.

The one-party system ended in mid-1981, when the Parti communiste tunisien (PCT), which had been proscribed in 1963, was granted legal status. The Government announced that any political group that gained more than 5% of the votes cast in the forthcoming legislative elections would also be officially recognized. Many of the Union générale Tunisienne du travail (UGTT) leaders imprisoned in 1978 after clashes between protesting workers and troops were pardoned. At elections to the National Assembly in November 1981, the PSD and the UGTT formed an electoral alliance, the Front national, which won all 126 seats in the new Assembly. In July 1986 Muhammad Mzali was replaced as Prime Minister by Rachid Sfar, and was dismissed as Secretary-General of the PSD. Mzali subsequently fled to Algeria, and was sentenced *in absentia* to terms of imprisonment and hard labour for defamatory comments against

Tunisian leaders and mismanagement of public funds. Elections to the National Assembly in November were boycotted by the opposition parties, with the result that the PSD, opposed only by 15 independent candidates, won all 125 seats.

Domestic Political Affairs

During late 1987 President Bourguiba's behaviour became increasingly erratic. In October he revoked several of his recent appointments of leading state officials, and dismissed Sfar from the premiership. Zine al-Abidine Ben Ali was appointed Prime Minister and Secretary-General of the PSD. On 7 November seven doctors declared that President Bourguiba was unfit to govern, owing to senility and ill health. In accordance with the Constitution, Ben Ali was sworn in as President. Hédi Baccouche was appointed Prime Minister, and a new Council of Ministers was formed, which excluded several close associates of Bourguiba. Ben Ali announced plans to reform the Constitution and to permit greater political freedom. In the same month the Government permitted the publication of previously suspended opposition newspapers, and by early 1988 some 3,000 political and non-political detainees had been released. In February the PSD was renamed the Rassemblement constitutionnel démocratique (RCD).

In April 1988 legislation was enacted by the National Assembly to institute a multi-party political system, and in July the Assembly approved a series of proposals to reform the Constitution. The office of President-for-Life was abolished, and the President was, henceforth, to be elected by universal suffrage every five years and limited to two consecutive terms of office. In September two further opposition parties, the left-wing Rassemblement socialiste progressiste and the liberal Parti social pour le progrès (renamed the Parti social libéral—PSL—in 1993), were legalized. In November the Government claimed that there were no longer any political prisoners in Tunisia, a total of 8,000 people having been released during the first year of Ben Ali's regime.

Ben Ali was nominated as the sole candidate (supported by all the officially recognized parties) for the presidential election of 2 April 1989, and was duly elected President, receiving 99.3% of the votes cast. In legislative elections the RCD won all 141 seats in the National Assembly, with some 80% of the votes cast. The Islamist-orientated Hizb al-Nahdah/Parti de la renaissance (the candidates of which contested the election as independents, since the party was not officially recognized) won some 13% of the votes cast, but failed to win any seats under an electoral system that favoured the ruling party. In September Ben Ali dismissed Prime Minister Baccouche and appointed Hamed Karoui, the former Minister of Justice, in his place.

In May 1990 the National Assembly approved the introduction of a system of partial proportional representation for forthcoming municipal elections. The winning party was to receive 50% of the seats, while the remainder were to be distributed among all the parties, according to the number of votes received by each one. However, the six legal opposition parties boycotted the elections, held in June, arguing that they were neither free nor fair. Consequently, the RCD won control of all but one of the 245 municipal councils.

In December 1992 Ben Ali announced a further revision of the electoral code, to include the introduction of partial proportional representation at legislative elections scheduled for March 1994. However, this apparent willingness to co-operate with the legalized opposition was accompanied by further repression of the Islamist movement, with increased censorship of publications sympathetic to their cause. In March 1992 the human rights organization Amnesty International published a report that detailed the arrests of some 8,000 suspected al-Nahdah members over an 18-month period, and cited 200 cases of torture and ill-treatment of detainees. It also claimed that at least seven Islamists had died while in custody. The Government reluctantly conceded that some violations of human rights had occurred. In the same month new restrictions were imposed on the activities of unofficial, quasi-political groups such as the Ligue tunisienne des droits de l'homme (LTDH). Meanwhile, an amnesty was granted to more than 1,000 detainees. In July and August the trials were held in Tunis of 171 alleged members of al-Nahdah, and of 108 alleged members of the organization's military wing, who were all accused of conspiring to overthrow the Government; 46 of the defendants were sentenced to life imprisonment, 16, including Rachid Ghannouchi, the leader of al-Nahdah, *in absentia*. (In 1993 Ghannouchi was granted political asylum in the United Kingdom.) Prison sentences of between one and 24 years were imposed on the remainder. In October appeals on behalf of 265 of those convicted were rejected, and another 20 al-Nahdah sympathizers were reportedly arrested in police raids.

There were indications in 1993 of a revival of political activity, and in April a new political organization, the Mouvement du renouveau (MR—Ettajdid, now known as the Mouvement ettajdid), held its first Congress. In January 1994 the National Assembly adopted reforms to the electoral code: thenceforth, 19 of the 163 seats in the enlarged Assembly were to be allocated to opposition parties in proportion to their overall national vote. At the presidential election, which took place concurrently with the legislative elections in March, Ben Ali was re-elected President, receiving 99.9% of the votes cast. The RCD received 97.7% of the total votes cast in the legislative elections, securing all 144 seats that were contested under a simple majority system. Of the 19 seats reserved for opposition candidates, the Mouvement des démocrates socialistes (MDS) secured 10, the MR four, the Union démocratique unioniste (UDU) three and the Parti de l'unité populaire (PUP) two.

In October 1995 Muhammad Mouada, the MDS Secretary-General, was arrested and accused of having received money from an unnamed foreign country. The previous day Mouada had, in an open letter to the President, criticized the lack of political freedom in Tunisia. In late October the Tunisian authorities prevented Khemais Chamari, an MDS member of the National Assembly, from travelling to Malta to attend an international conference on human rights. Chamari's parliamentary immunity was subsequently withdrawn, in order to allow judicial charges (relating to Mouada's trial) to be brought against him. In February 1996 Mouada was sentenced to two years' imprisonment for 'illegal detention of currency'. Although a court of appeal subsequently reduced his term by one year, at the end of the month Mouada was sentenced to 11 years' imprisonment for maintaining links with, and receiving money from, Libya. In July Chamari was sentenced to a further five years' imprisonment for breaching security proceedings relating to Mouada's trial. Human rights organizations protested at the severity of the sentence and appealed to the Tunisian authorities to release all political detainees. In December Mouada and Chamari were released conditionally on humanitarian grounds.

In December 1996 Ben Ali announced plans to amend the electoral law, which, *inter alia*, would lower the minimum eligible age of candidates for the National Assembly (from 25 to 23 years) and increase the representation of legal opposition parties in the Assembly and in municipal councils. Political parties would not be permitted to be based on religion, language, race or region, nor to have foreign links. The scope of referendums was also to be widened. In December 1997 the Council of Ministers reached consensus on draft legislation to amend the electoral law.

In March 1999 draft legislation was approved by the National Assembly to introduce extraordinary provisions to the Constitution that would allow pluralism in the presidential election scheduled for that year. The amendments allowed for the leaders of all political parties to contest the presidency provided that they had held their current leadership position for at least five consecutive years, and that their party was represented by one or more deputies in the legislature. (Hitherto, opposition parties had been unable to present candidates, owing to the requirement that they be supported by at least 30 deputies in the Assembly.) Despite the new provisions, only two leaders of opposition parties were eligible to contest the presidency, namely Abderrahmane Tlili (UDU) and Muhammad Belhadj Amor (PUP).

The 1999 presidential election

The first contested presidential election since independence took place in October 1999. As expected, Ben Ali comprehensively defeated his two rivals, securing 99.5% of the vote. At concurrent elections to the National Assembly, the RCD won all of the 148 seats contested under a simple majority system. Of the 34 seats reserved for opposition candidates, 13 were won by the MDS, the UDU and the PUP both took seven seats, the MR won five, and

the PSL two. In November Hamed Karoui was replaced as Prime Minister by Muhammad Ghannouchi.

In June 2000 the President of the Conseil national pour les libertés en Tunisie (CNLT), Moncef Marzouki, visited London, United Kingdom, where he reportedly held talks with the leader of al-Nahdah, Rachid Ghannouchi, and proposed future co-operation between secular and Islamist factions of the Tunisian opposition. In December Marzouki received a one-year prison sentence, having been convicted of belonging to an illegal group and of disseminating false information. His sentence was suspended in September 2001 by the court of appeal, although his civil rights were not restored.

Meanwhile, in November 2000 President Ben Ali announced a number of initiatives aimed at furthering the democratization process and promoting human rights in Tunisia. The measures included: state compensation for detainees held in police custody without reasonable grounds; the transfer of responsibility for the prison system from the Ministry of the Interior to the Ministry of Justice; new legislation to improve conditions in prisons and to reduce censorship of the press; and an increase, by 50%, in government subsidies allocated for other political parties and their publications.

At the fifth congress of the LTDH, held in October 2000, a new executive board was elected, with Mokhtar Trifi, an outspoken critic of the Ben Ali regime, as President. Four former members of the board subsequently filed a suit against the new leadership, citing procedural irregularities, and in November a court imposed a moratorium on the LTDH's activities. Trial proceedings against the LTDH began in January 2001, and in the following month the results of the October 2000 congress were ruled invalid. In March 2001 Trifi was charged with dissemination of false information and violation of the recent court ruling; however, in June the court of appeal ruled that the LTDH could resume its activities and ordered it to hold another congress within a year.

In March 2001 more than 250 human rights activists in Tunisia produced a petition that demanded wide-ranging democratic reforms prior to the presidential and legislative elections scheduled for 2004. In the same month some 100 moderate figures in civil society signed a separate petition accusing Ben Ali of corruption and nepotism, and denouncing his plans to amend the Constitution so as to permit him to seek a fourth term in office. In April al-Nahdah released a joint communiqué with Mouada's faction of the MDS, proposing the formation of an opposition coalition to unite Islamists and liberals against the Ben Ali regime.

The central committee of the ruling RCD announced in September 2001 that it would formally propose changes to the country's Constitution in order to enable Ben Ali to seek a fourth presidential term. In April 2002 members of the National Assembly overwhelmingly approved a constitutional reform bill, and at a referendum in May, according to official figures, the constitutional changes were approved by 99.5% of voters. The amendments raised the upper age limit for presidential candidates from 70 to 75 years, and removed the limit on the number of terms that could be served by a President. In August 2003 the changes were promulgated, and Ben Ali formally announced his intention to stand for a fourth term at elections scheduled for late 2004. Provision was also made for the creation of a second legislative chamber, to be called the Chamber of Advisers, for the establishment of a two-round presidential election system, and for a number of measures that would improve civil liberties and public freedoms. In January 2003 Ben Ali had reduced the number of ministries from 29 to 25, notably creating a Ministry of Justice and Human Rights and a Ministry of Employment.

In April 2002 a tanker lorry exploded outside a synagogue on the island of Djerba, causing the deaths of 21 people, most of whom were German tourists. The driver of the lorry was among those killed. The Tunisian authorities initially claimed that the explosion had been an accident, but a spokesman for the Israeli Ministry of Foreign Affairs insisted that it was an anti-Semitic terrorist attack. The Tunisian authorities subsequently confirmed that the explosion had been a 'premeditated criminal act'. A number of Arabic newspapers immediately carried claims that al-Qa'ida was responsible. In June 2002 the Qatar-based satellite television station *Al Jazeera* broadcast a statement by a spokesman for al-Qa'ida, asserting that the attack had been perpetrated in protest against Israel's recent military offensive against Palestinian-controlled areas of the West Bank. In November eight people were arrested in Lyon, France, in connection with the explosion, while in early 2003 several arrests took place in Spain, France and Saudi Arabia. In May 2007 two men were sentenced to five years' imprisonment each by a court in Madrid, Spain, for their role in the financing of the attack; in June the uncle of the lorry driver was sentenced to 20 years in gaol by a court in Tunis for helping to prepare the explosion. The trial of three men (including the principal suspect in the September 2001 attacks on the USA, Khalid Sheikh Muhammad) for their alleged involvement in the Djerba synagogue explosion began in France in January 2009; two of the men were subsequently sentenced to prison sentences of 18 and 12 years. However, it was ordered that a ruling on Khalid Sheikh Muhammad, who was in US custody in Guantánamo Bay, Cuba, be postponed until he could appear before the court in person.

President Ben Ali re-elected

By September 2004 three opposition candidates had officially registered to contest the presidential election scheduled to take place in October—Muhammad Bouchiha of the PUP, Mounir Béji of the PSL and Muhammad Ali Halouani of the MR. The Parti démocrate progressiste (PDP) announced in mid-October that it was withdrawing its candidates for the legislative elections in protest at what it considered an illegitimate electoral process in which it was denied access to the media and faced serious delays in having its manifesto approved. At the presidential election in the following month Ben Ali received 94.5% of the votes cast, while Bouchiha secured 3.8%, Halouani 1.0% and Béji 0.8%. At concurrent legislative elections the RCD won all of the 152 seats contested under a simple majority system, 25% of which would be occupied by women under new legislation, while, of the 37 reserved for the opposition, the MDS won 14 seats, the PUP 11, the UDU seven, and the MR and PSL three and two seats, respectively.

A report published in July 2004 by the US-based Human Rights Watch criticized the Government's treatment of political prisoners, many of whom, it claimed, had spent several years in solitary confinement, and urged the Tunisian authorities to allow domestic and international monitors to inspect prison standards. In June the leader of the UDU, Abderrahmane Tlili, was imprisoned for nine years, after being convicted of abusing his position while he was head of the Office de l'aviation civile et des aéroports. In November President Ben Ali pardoned 80 Islamist prisoners. A further 20 Islamist convicts were freed in July 2007 as part of an amnesty to mark the 50th anniversary of the Tunisian republic, including three former leaders of the banned al-Nahdah party.

In February 2005 Ben Ali announced plans to create a national electoral observatory in time for the forthcoming municipal elections. At those elections, held in May, the RCD won 4,098 of the 4,366 council seats contested. In July elections were first held to the new Chamber of Advisers, as provided for by the constitutional amendments of 2002. The new second chamber was composed of 126 members, of whom 43 were indirectly elected by municipal councillors and parliamentary deputies (as representatives of the regions) and 42 by the main professional federations and trade unions; the remaining 41 members were appointed by the President. All 43 regional representatives elected were RCD candidates. The Chamber of Advisers held its inaugural session in October 2005, and Abdullah Kallel was elected as Speaker; however, 14 seats remained vacant after the UGTT refused to elect its members to the new chamber. Meanwhile, in August Ben Ali effected a major reorganization of the Council of Ministers: Abdelwahab Abdallah, a former principal adviser to the President, was appointed Minister of Foreign Affairs and Kamel Morjane received the defence portfolio; Ali Chaouch, the former interior minister, assumed the post of Minister of Social Affairs, Solidarity and Tunisians Abroad and was succeeded as Secretary-General of the RCD by Hédi M'henni.

In September and October 2006 the Tunisian authorities increasingly began to take action against the wearing of the Islamic headscarf, following public comments by Ben Ali and other senior politicians that it was a 'sectarian' form of dress that was not native to the country. (President Bourguiba had introduced a ban on headscarves in schools and government offices in 1981.) Also in October 2006 Tunisia closed its embassy in Qatar in protest at an interview with Moncef Marzouki broadcast by *Al Jazeera*, in which he spoke against the Government's human rights record and advocated a campaign of civil resistance. In January 2007 the Minister of the Interior and Local Development, Rafik Belhaj Kacem, confirmed that police had shot dead 14 members of a suspected militant Islamist organization and arrested a number of others in Soliman, near Tunis. Two

members of the security forces were killed during the operation. Kacem reported that the group, which was suspected of having links to the Algerian Groupe salafiste pour la prédication et le combat (which in that month restyled itself as the al-Qa'ida Organization in the Land of the Islamic Maghreb—AQIM), had been in possession of explosives and details of foreign embassies and diplomatic staff in Tunis. In January 2008 a court in Tunisia sentenced two of the defendants to death; eight further defendants were sentenced to life imprisonment, while 20 others received prison terms ranging from five to 30 years.

Meanwhile, in November 2007 Ben Ali announced a range of measures designed to promote democracy and human rights in the country in a speech marking the 20th anniversary of his accession to the presidency; these included increasing the level of funding allocated to opposition parties and their press. None the less, in May 2008 the recently founded Syndicat national des journalistes Tunisiens (SNJT—which replaced the pro-Government Association des journalistes Tunisiens) made renewed demands for a review of media regulations in line with international standards of press freedom. This followed the publication of an SNJT report that detailed the various alleged violations of journalists' rights that had occurred in the previous year. The SNJT repeated its demands in February 2009, after the Government banned an edition of the daily newspaper *Attariq al-Jadid* that reproduced the transcript of a legal case. This, together with the forced closure of a Tunisian radio station a few days earlier, was considered to be further evidence of a significantly compromised level of media freedom in the country.

President Ben Ali was unanimously re-elected by the RCD congress as party Chairman in July 2008 thereby effectively becoming the RCD candidate for the next presidential election. Ben Ali's apparent intention to run for a fifth presidential term immediately began to provoke speculation regarding his intention to make himself President-for-Life (a designation abolished in 1988). In August 2008 Ben Ali effected a significant reorganization of the Council of Ministers.

As part of celebrations to mark the 21st anniversary of his accession to the presidency, in November 2008 Ben Ali pardoned 21 imprisoned members of al-Nahdah (said to be the last remaining group of detainees from the banned party); a further 23 prisoners were also reported to have been pardoned. While human rights organizations generally responded with cautious optimism to the release of prisoners, they none the less urged a wider amnesty for all detainees imprisoned for non-violent political convictions and practices.

The 2009 presidential and legislative elections

In anticipation of the legislative and presidential elections due later in the year, in March 2009 the National Assembly adopted a series of amendments to the electoral code. The amendments, which were subsequently promulgated by the President in April, were intended to promote greater plurality and ensure increased electoral transparency and participation. Notable among the new measures were an increase in the proportion of seats allocated to the opposition in the Chamber of Deputies from 20% to 25%, and the imposition of a 75% upper limit on the share of seats that could be obtained by any one list in the municipal councils (regardless of the number of votes obtained). The age of eligibility to vote was to be reduced from 20 to 18 years.

Ben Ali formally announced his intention to stand for a fifth consecutive elected term of office in August 2009. Ahmed Néjib Chebbi, a prominent member of the PDP, had previously announced that he was withdrawing from the presidential contest, citing a lack of transparency. Chebbi's candidature had been declared illegal in July 2008, when electoral legislation was amended to introduce a requirement for all presidential candidates to have been the elected leader of a recognized party for at least two years prior to the election. Indeed, this amendment rendered illegal the candidatures of all but three potential challengers—the PUP's Muhammad Bouchiha, Ahmed Inoubli of the UDU, and Ahmed Brahim of the Mouvement ettajdid.

At the presidential election of October 2009 Ben Ali was overwhelmingly returned to office, winning 89.6% of the valid votes cast. Bouchiha was placed second, with 5.0% of the vote, while Inoubli secured 3.8% and Brahim 1.6%. The rate of voter participation was officially estimated at 89.5%. At concurrent legislative elections, the RCD increased its representation, winning 161 of the 214 seats in the Chamber of Deputies. In accordance with the electoral code, the remaining seats were allocated to opposition parties. The MDS obtained 16 seats, the PUP 12 and the UDU nine. The remaining 16 seats were divided among the PSL (eight), the Parti des verts pour le progrès (six) and the Mouvement ettajdid (two). Turn-out at the legislative elections was officially estimated at 89.4%. International observers subsequently declared that the elections had been carried out in a transparent and neutral manner, although many commentators voiced criticism of the credibility of these observers. Ben Ali was sworn in as President the following month. He vowed to tackle unemployment and develop the media sector to allow for greater freedom of speech; however, he also warned against foreign interference in the country's internal affairs.

In January 2010 Ben Ali effected a reorganization of the Council of Ministers. Among the most notable appointments were those of Kamel Morjane (hitherto Minister of National Defence) as Minister of Foreign Affairs, and of Lazhar Bououni as Minister of Justice and Human Rights. Muhammad Ridha Chalghoum became Minister of Finance, while Ridha Grira assumed the national defence portfolio vacated by Morjane. At municipal elections held in May, the RCD won 90.7% of the votes cast, retaining control of all 264 of Tunisia's municipal councils.

The removal from office of Ben Ali

In mid-December 2010 Muhammad Bouazizi set himself alight, following the confiscation by the authorities of produce that he was selling, without a permit, in the central town of Sidi Bouzid. Upon attempting to pay the required fine, Bouazizi was initially reported to have been assaulted and verbally abused by a police officer. (However, charges brought against the police officer in respect of the incident were later dropped.) Bouazizi subsequently died of his injuries in early January 2011. The incident prompted angry demonstrations in Sidi Bouzid, which soon spread to neighbouring areas. Hundreds of Tunisians began protesting against unemployment, escalating prices for basic goods, poor living standards, state corruption, and a lack of freedom of expression and of other human and political rights. In an attempt to appease the protesters, on 20 December 2010 the Government announced a US $10m. employment programme; however, the demonstrations continued unabated, and the authorities responded with significant force and large-scale arrests of protesters. During demonstrations on 22 December in Sidi Bouzid, a youth fatally electrocuted himself in an act of desperation concerning the lack of job opportunities. The incident prompted a further intensification of the unrest, and additional police officers were deployed to a number of cities, including to the capital.

On 24 December 2010 one protester was killed, and several others were seriously injured, when police officers fired into a crowd of demonstrators in Menzel Bouzaiene, a town in the Sidi Bouzid governorate; one of those wounded subsequently died of his injuries. The Government claimed that the officers had been acting in self-defence after warning shots had been ignored by protesters, some of whom had thrown petrol bombs at a police station; however, protesters and the opposition accused the police of firing indiscriminately at unarmed protesters who posed no immediate risk. From late December trade union members and lawyers staged rallies, adding their voices to the escalating calls for immediate government action to address the issues raised by the protesters.

President Ben Ali addressed the nation in a televised broadcast on 28 December 2010, during which he condemned the violence of protesters, and vowed to hold to account all those involved; he also criticized foreign media for its coverage of the protests. Local media made no mention of the unfolding national crisis until 29 December, when a private news television channel first broadcast news and video footage of the protests. Meanwhile, on 28 December Ben Ali dismissed the Ministers of Communication Technologies, of Trade and Handicrafts, of Religious Affairs, and of Youth and Sports, as well as the governors of Sidi Bouzid, Jendouba and Zaghouan provinces, in connection with the unrest.

The protests continued to escalate in early January 2011, becoming increasingly marred by violent clashes between the authorities and the protesters. On 6 January Tunisian legal professionals staged a general strike in protest at the perceived use of excessive force by the authorities. Two days later nine protesters were killed, and many more injured, in clashes between the protesters and authorities in the Kasserine governorate and in Thala; in the latter, police used water cannons and live ammunition after protesters threw petrol bombs and set fire to a government building. On 9 January two protesters were fatally shot by police in Maknassy, in Sidi Bouzid governorate, and on 11 January the first serious clashes between security forces and demonstrators occurred in the centre of Tunis.

Ben Ali dismissed the Minister of the Interior and Local Development, Rafik Belhaj Kacem, on 12 January 2011, and ordered that all protesters within police custody be released; Kacem had been regarded by many to be primarily responsible for the violent police response to the protests. In a second televised speech on 13 January, Ben Ali pledged: not to seek re-election at the next presidential poll, due in 2014; to reduce the prices of staple foods; to allow greater freedoms of speech and of assembly; and to establish a committee of investigation into public corruption and the conduct of certain government officials. The President also promised to initiate a comprehensive investigation into the deaths of protesters. Almost immediately thereafter, opposition figures were permitted to appear on national television, and blocks on a number of internet sites were removed.

While the political opposition and some protesters cautiously welcomed the concessions, Ben Ali's speech did nothing to quell the unrest, with many protesters now demanding his immediate resignation. In response, on 14 January 2011 Ben Ali announced the dissolution of the Chamber of Deputies; declared the imposition of emergency rule, thereby outlawing gatherings of more than three people; and dismissed the Government, pledging to hold parliamentary elections within six months. Protests outside the Ministry of the Interior later that day, during which protesters reiterated their demands for Ben Ali to step down with immediate effect, were dispersed by the police using tear gas. Later that day it was announced that the President had fled the country, and on 15 January Saudi Arabia revealed that it had offered asylum to Ben Ali and his family; it was reported that Ben Ali had intended to fly to France but had been refused entry by the French Government. On 14 January Tunisian Prime Minister Muhammad Ghannouchi, citing Article 56 of the Constitution, had declared himself interim President, a declaration that was met with anger by the protesters, who criticized Ghannouchi's role as Prime Minister under Ben Ali; however, on 15 January the Constitutional Court ruled that, in the absence of an elected President, the parliamentary Speaker, rather than the Prime Minister, was the legitimate interim head of state; Fouad Mebazaa was duly sworn in as interim President later that day.

The announcement of an interim 'national unity' Government on 17 January 2011 provoked further ire, owing to the inclusion of RCD members. As well as former members of the Ben Ali administration, the new Council of Ministers included representatives of the UGTT, opposition leaders and independents. Opposition leaders named in the cabinet included Ahmed Brahim as Minister of Higher Education and Scientific Research, and Dr Mustapha Ben Jaâfar, leader of the Forum démocratique pour le travail et les libertés (Ettakatol), as Minister of Public Health. On the following day, however, it was announced that the UGTT had withdrawn its participation in the Government, while Ben Jaâfar also resigned as Minister of Public Health. Following several days of angry protests against the composition of the new cabinet, and demands for the dissolution of the RCD, on 20 January all RCD cabinet ministers resigned from the party. On the following day the new Council of Ministers announced an amnesty for all political detainees, including those from the previously outlawed Islamist movement al-Nahdah. The party's leader, Rachid Ghannouchi, returned to Tunisia from exile in the United Kingdom on 30 January, and al-Nahdah was awarded legal status on 1 March; other hitherto banned parties were also to be legalized.

On 27 January 2011 Muhammad Ghannouchi, who a few days earlier had stated his intention to resign after the holding of free and fair elections, announced a further cabinet reorganization that was widely interpreted as a bid to appease the protesters: six former RCD members, including, *inter alia*, the Ministers of Finance, Foreign Affairs, the Interior and National Defence, were replaced. On 13 February, however, it was announced that the newly appointed Minister of Foreign Affairs, Ahmed Ounaies, had resigned owing to controversy regarding complimentary comments that he had made to his French counterpart, Michèle Alliot-Marie. The French Government and, in particular, Alliot-Marie were the subject of considerable criticism for initially having indicated willingness to assist the Tunisian security forces in quelling the protests; Muhammad Mouldi Kéfi was appointed in his place. Meanwhile, after an international arrest warrant was issued for the ousted President on 26 January, in late January and early February about 30 members of Ben Ali's extended family were arrested, together with former Minister of the Interior Kacem; a number of senior security officials were removed, and all 24 regional governors were dismissed. Charges were subsequently drawn up by the Ministry of Justice against Ben Ali, his family and other close associates, while their extensive assets were confiscated by the authorities.

Violent clashes in late February 2011 between security forces and protesters demanding the ouster of those members of the Government who had served under Ben Ali prompted Ghannouchi's resignation as Prime Minister on 27 February. He was replaced later that day by Béji Caïd Essebsi, a former Minister of Foreign Affairs during the presidency of Habib Bourguiba. On 28 February the Minister of Industry and Technology, Muhammad Afif Chelbi, and the Minister of Planning and International Co-operation, Muhammad Nouri Jouini, both of whom had been government ministers during Ben Ali's presidency, also resigned. On 1 March a further three ministers—including Minister of Higher Education and Scientific Research Brahim and Minister of Regional and Local Development Ahmad Néjib Chebbi—also left the Government. Essebsi named his new Council of Ministers on 7 March, replacing those who had resigned, while retaining ministers from the outgoing interim administration in key posts. On the same day the interim Government announced that the secret police force was to be disbanded, and on 9 March the RCD was formally dissolved, and its assets liquidized, by court order. The party announced its intention to appeal against the ruling prior to the staging of elections to a constituent assembly, which interim President Mebazaa had announced, on 3 March, were to be held on 24 July. (However, for logistical reasons the polls were subsequently postponed until October 2011—see Ben Ali convicted and al-Nahdah comes to power.) Upon its election, one of the immediate priorities for the new assembly would be the drafting of a new constitution.

On 8 March 2011 Muhammad Bouchiha stood down as Secretary-General of the PUP, and was subsequently replaced by Hassine Hammami. The new Minister of the Interior, Farhat Rajhi, resigned on 28 March; his post was assumed by Habib Essid. In late April it was announced that certain former RCD officials were to be barred from contesting elections for a period of 10 years, following a recommendation by the High Authority for the Achievement of the Objectives of the Revolution, Political Reform and Democratic Transition, formed after Ben Ali's departure to oversee the implementation of reforms during the transitional period. Sporadic unrest continued, however: in early May an evening curfew was imposed in the capital, following renewed protests amid speculation that former supporters of Ben Ali were planning to stage a coup in the event that al-Nahdah emerged victorious at the forthcoming elections. Some demonstrations again called for the Government's resignation owing to the perceived delay in implementing reforms, and there was renewed criticism of the use of force against protesters by some members of the security forces.

Ben Ali convicted and al-Nahdah comes to power

In May 2011 it was agreed that the elections to a new National Constituent Assembly (NCA) would take place according to a system of proportional representation based on party lists; 50% of the candidates were to be female. The Instance supérieure indépendente pour les élections was established to monitor the polls. Following a recommendation by the commission later that month that the polls should be postponed from July to October in order to allow sufficient time to prepare voting lists and ensure that the ballot would be held fairly and efficiently, on 8 June 2011 Prime Minister Essebsi announced a new date of 23 October. The election postponement provoked another series of street demonstrations. On 27 June al-Nahdah withdrew its support from the High Authority, claiming that its composition was unrepresentative and unduly favoured left-wing parties. In July, with opinion polls showing that al-Nahdah was likely to emerge victorious at the elections in October, party spokespeople sought to reassure liberal Tunisians and concerned Western officials that it had no intention of imposing a strict Islamic order if it was invited to form the country's next government. Nevertheless, some five civil associations and four political parties, led by the Mouvement ettajdid, formed a coalition, the Pôle démocratique moderniste (al-Qotb—PDM), to counter the Islamist challenge.

Meanwhile, on 20 June 2011 Ben Ali, together with his second wife, Leila Trabelsi, was found guilty by a court in Tunis of the embezzlement of state funds during his time in office, and of possessing large amounts of foreign currency. The couple were sentenced *in absentia* to 35 years in prison, and were also required to pay fines of some US $66m. Ben Ali had described

some of the many charges against him as 'shameful lies and fabrications'. On 4 July the former President and his wife were additionally given 15-year prison terms for possessing illegal drugs, weapons and archaeological artifacts, and on 28 July Ben Ali was sentenced to 16 years in prison for abuse of power relating to corrupt property transactions. One of his daughters, Nesrine, and her husband were also given prison terms of eight years and 16 years, respectively, at the conclusion of the latter trial. Other trial proceedings were ongoing, including those which accused Ben Ali of having been responsible for the deaths of anti-Government protesters during Tunisia's recent revolution. On 12 August 23 members of Ben Ali's family and inner circle, including his wife (again *in absentia*) were convicted of having tried to leave Tunisia by illegal means or of assisting the President to flee in January 2011; they were given prison sentences of between four months and six years. However, Ben Ali's former security chief, Ali Seriati, was acquitted of the charges against him in that trial, although he faced other proceedings relating to allegations of conspiring against the state. Efforts made by the new Tunisian leadership to secure the extradition of Ben Ali from Saudi Arabia had not succeeded by the end of April 2013.

As intermittent protests and acts of violence continued to be reported across Tunisia, the state of emergency imposed in January 2011 was extended for an indefinite period from 1 August. On 15 September Tunisia's main political parties reached an agreement which stated that the NCA would have a one-year mandate to draft a new constitution, and that polls to elect a new President and Chamber of Deputies would take place no later than October 2012. Despite ongoing protests and strikes, elections to the 217-member NCA were duly held on 23 October 2011. At the polls, in which an estimated 60% of eligible voters reportedly participated, al-Nahdah secured the largest number representation, winning 89 seats; the secular Congrès pour la République (CPR), led by Moncef Marzouki, were placed second, with 29 seats. The recently formed, populist Pétition populaire pour la liberté, la justice et le développement (al-Aridha), led by businessman Muhammad Hechmi Hamdi, came third, with 26 seats; the Forum démocratique pour le travail et les libertés (Ettakatol) fourth, with 20 seats; and the PDP fifth, receiving 16 seats. The remaining seats were won by smaller parties or independents, including five by the newly formed PDM. Since al-Nahdah had failed to win an outright majority, it was required to seek potential coalition partners among secular parties such as Ettakatol and the CPR.

At the inaugural session of the NCA, held on 22 November 2011, Mustapha Ben Jaâfar of Ettakatol was elected Speaker. The following day the Government under Prime Minister Essebsi resigned. On 12 December members of the NCA elected the leader of the CPR, Marzouki, to replace Mebazaa as interim President; he was sworn into office on the following day. On 14 December al-Nahdah's Secretary-General, Hamadi Jebali, was asked to form a new government. Having succeeded in reaching a coalition agreement with Ettakatol and the CPR, Jebali announced his new Council of Ministers on 22 December; notable appointees included Ali Laârayedh as Minister of the Interior, Rafik Ben Abdessalem as Minister of Foreign Affairs and Houcine Dimassi as Minister of Finance. Having been approved by the NCA, Tunisia's new Islamist-led Government, which also included several independents, was inaugurated on 24 December.

In early 2012 concerns were raised by Tunisian reformists that some hardline Islamists in the country, particularly those of the Salafi movement, were seeking to undermine newly enjoyed media freedoms and to impose stricter censorship with regard to publications and websites that were deemed to be un-Islamic. On 16 March the umbrella grouping of 120 smaller Islamic organizations, the Tunisian Islamic Associations Front, organized a large protest in front of the NCA to persuade those involved with drawing up the new constitution to make Islam the only source of legislation; however, leading al-Nahdah officials insisted that it was not in favour of imposing *Shari'a* law. On 20 March up to 30,000 people attended a rally in central Tunis to commemorate Tunisia's Independence Day and to urge the Government to accelerate its implementation of promised political and economic reforms.

Interim President Marzouki extended the state of emergency for another month on 31 March 2012; it was extended again, by presidential decree, from 1 May to 31 July. Meanwhile, on 26 April 2012 the interim Prime Minister, Hamadi Jebali, stated that legislative elections would be held in early or mid-2013, in which year the presidential poll was also expected to take place. However, the proposed deadline for the holding of the elections was subsequently postponed (see Recent developments). On 30 April 2012 Ben Jaâfar announced that a special commission was being established to examine the circumstances of the violence that had taken place on 9 April, when some police officers in the centre of Tunis were alleged to have attacked demonstrators who were marking the annual Martyrs' Day, as well as journalists assigned to report on the protest. On the same day a reported 2,470 prisoners were granted an amnesty by Marzouki.

At the beginning of May 2012 two police officers were sentenced by a military court in Sfax to prison terms of 20 years and were also handed down fines, having been convicted of shooting dead a protester on 14 January 2011. According to the National Fact-Finding Commission on Abuses Committed during Recent Events, established by the interim Government to investigate the deaths that had occurred during Tunisia's revolution, 338 people were killed and 2,147 wounded as a result of the events between 17 December 2010 and 23 October 2011. The Commission's final report, issued on 4 May 2012, was non-binding and referred responsibility to the relevant ministries or legal authorities for bringing any relevant culprits to justice. Despite the fact that the new authorities were embarking on the transition to democratic rule and had stated their intention to allow greater individual freedoms than had been permitted during Ben Ali's presidency, in early May Amnesty International expressed concerns that security forces were continuing to use repressive measures against human rights activists, journalists and other specific minority groups. Such criticism of the Tunisian authorities, including claims that they were preventing freedom of expression, persisted into 2013.

Recent developments: increasing political instability leads to Jebali's resignation

Muhammad Abbou, the Secretary-General of the CPR, tendered his resignation as Minister-delegate to the Prime Minister, in charge of Administrative Reform on 30 June 2012, prompting rumours that divisions were widening among members of the interim Government. On 16 July Rachid Ghannouchi was decisively re-elected as the leader of al-Nahdah. On 27 July the Minister of Finance, Houcine Dimassi, tendered his resignation; he was replaced on a temporary basis by the Secretary of State for Finance, Slim Besbes, until Élyès Fakhfekh was formally appointed to the post on 19 December. Meanwhile, on 31 July 2012 interim President Marzouki extended the state of emergency until the end of August. It was extended for further one-month periods by Marzouki on 31 August, 30 September and 31 October, before being extended for three months on the latter date. The interim President cited as the reason behind the longer extension period the ongoing threat of Islamist violence in certain parts of the country. On 14 September 2012 a group of hardline Salafis had staged an attack on the US embassy in Tunis in protest against an anti-Islamic film produced in the USA, which had led to at least two deaths. A radical Islamist believed to have incited violence by encouraging demonstrators to attack the embassy building was convicted in late October and given a one-year prison sentence. Marzouki extended the emergency legislation for another month on 1 February 2013, and then, on 2 March, for a further three months until 3 June.

On 6 February 2013 Chokri Belaid, a secular, left-wing politician and lawyer who was openly critical of al-Nahdah and the Government, was assassinated. His murder, which was believed to have been carried out by a radical Salafist, provoked violent clashes between anti-Government demonstrators and security forces. As the security situation across the country worsened, Prime Minister Jebali announced his resignation on 19 February, owing to his failure to persuade al-Nahdah to join a new, technocratic coalition government. Many Tunisians accused the party of having to bear responsibility for Belaid's assassination, claiming that it had allowed hardline Islamist elements to take root in the country. On 22 February interim President Marzouki appointed the Minister of the Interior, Ali Laârayedh, as Prime Minister-designate. Laârayedh's first Council of Ministers—a coalition of al-Nahdah, the CPR, Ettakatol and independents—received the approval of the NCA on 13 March and was duly sworn in on the following day. Notable appointees were independents Rachid Sabbagh as Minister of National Defence, Lotfi Ben Jeddou as Minister of the Interior and Othman Jarandi as Minister of Foreign Affairs.

Having already received two terms of life imprisonment, *in absentia*, in June and July 2012, on 30 April 2013 Ben Ali was given a third life term, after being convicted by a military court in Sfax of causing death and injury through his order to the security forces to suppress anti-Government protests in early 2011. Rafik Belhaj Kacem was sentenced to 10 years in prison for his involvement in the deaths of protesters, while Ben Ali's former security chief, Ali Seriati, was again acquitted by the court owing to a lack of evidence. It was announced earlier in April 2013 that a UN recovery unit established to recover state funds that had allegedly been stolen by the leaders of ousted Arab regimes had been given some US $29m. of assets seized while Ben Ali was in power.

The drafting of Tunisia's new constitution was a source of considerable disagreement among the various political factions as the deadline for its presentation approached. Besides significant divisions regarding the political system that the country should adopt and concerns about the provision to be given for religious minorities, in August 2012 there were large-scale demonstrations in Tunis after reports had emerged that women's rights were to be restricted in the new document. Many secular political groupings continued to hold fears that the Islamist-led Government was seeking to draft a new constitution to further its Islamist agenda. A previous deadline for both presidential and legislative elections to be held on 23 June 2013 was missed, since the first draft of the new constitution was required to have been presented to the NCA in November 2012. On 15 March 2013 members of the NCA agreed a new timeframe concerning the drafting of the constitution and subsequent convening of legislative elections: the document was to be prepared by 8 July, and polls to be held between 15 October and 15 December.

Foreign Affairs
Regional relations
Relations with the other countries of the Maghreb improved considerably in the 1980s. A meeting between President Bourguiba and President Ben Djedid Chadli of Algeria in March 1983 led to the drafting of the Maghreb Fraternity and Co-operation Treaty, which envisaged the eventual creation of a Greater Maghreb Union, and was signed by Mauritania in December. In February 1989, at a meeting of North African heads of state in Morocco, a treaty was concluded that proclaimed the Union of the Arab Maghreb (Union du Maghreb arabe—UMA, see p. 464), comprising Algeria, Libya, Mauritania, Morocco and Tunisia. The treaty envisaged: the establishment of a council of heads of state; regular meetings of ministers responsible for foreign affairs; and, eventually, the free movement of goods, people, services and capital throughout the countries of the region.

In 1982 President Bourguiba permitted the Palestine Liberation Organization (PLO) to establish its headquarters near Tunis. In October 1985 Israeli aircraft attacked the PLO headquarters, causing the deaths of some 72 people, including 12 Tunisians. US support for the right of Israel to retaliate (the attack was a reprisal for the murder of three Israeli citizens in Cyprus) severely strained relations between Tunisia and the USA. In April 1988 Abu Jihad, the military commander of the PLO, was assassinated at his home in Tunis. The Tunisian Government blamed Israel for the murder, and complained to the UN Security Council. The PLO transferred its offices to Gaza in mid-1994, following the signing of the PLO-Israeli Cairo Agreement on implementing Palestinian self-rule in the Gaza Strip and Jericho.

In January 1988 the Tunisian Government announced that diplomatic relations with Egypt, which had been severed in 1979, would be resumed. In March 1990 Ben Ali made the first visit to the Egyptian capital, Cairo, by a Tunisian President since 1965, and signed several agreements on bilateral co-operation. In September 1990 a majority of members of the League of Arab States (Arab League, see p. 372) resolved to move the League's headquarters from Tunis (where it had been established 'temporarily' in 1979) to its original site in Cairo: the Tunisian Government protested at the decision.

Tunisia assumed the annual presidency of the UMA in January 1993. The Government made clear its determination to reactivate the process of Maghreb union, as well as dialogue with the European Community (now European Union—EU, see p. 281). In April 1994 the UMA ratified 11 agreements designed to improve co-operation and trade within the Maghreb. However, tensions between the UMA's member states subsequently undermined the activities of the Union. In March 1999 Ben Ali made his first official visit to Morocco, during which he pledged to strengthen relations with that country, and to revive the UMA. A summit meeting of ministers responsible for foreign affairs of the five UMA member states proceeded in the Algerian capital in March 2001. However, the meeting quickly broke down owing to disagreements between Moroccan and Algerian representatives. Following several further unsuccessful attempts to co-ordinate a summit meeting, in April 2008 celebrations were held in Tangier, Morocco, to mark the 50th anniversary of the summit at which the idea of a union of Arab Maghreb states was first proposed. The event ended with renewed calls for greater regional collaboration and a regalvanized UMA. A year later delegates responsible for foreign affairs from the UMA member states met in Tripoli, Libya, where they reiterated their commitment to improving political and economic co-operation among the countries of North Africa. In January 2012 Tunisia's new interim President, Moncef Marzouki, undertook his first foreign visit to Libya, where he raised hopes for a reactivation of the UMA by urging far closer co-operation and integration between Tunisia and Libya. During mid-2012 bilateral agreements were signed in the fields of security and technological co-operation.

Relations with Algeria were threatened in May 2000, when Tunisian security forces responded to an attack by Algerian Islamists; three of the Islamists were killed and two Tunisian soldiers wounded. The attack followed the signing of a bilateral customs agreement aimed at ending cross-border smuggling, considered by the Algerian Government to facilitate the activities of Islamist groups in Algeria. A number of bilateral agreements were signed during a visit to Algeria by Ben Ali in February 2002; most notably, the two countries pledged to formalize delineation of their maritime border. In August 2009 it was announced that nine bilateral co-operation agreements were to be signed between the two countries in the areas of the economy, commerce, culture and education. The Tunisian Secretary of State in charge of Maghreb, Arab and African Affairs, Abdelhafidh Harguem, announced that the introduction of a legal framework to allow for co-operation in the banking and financial sector was to be accelerated. Meanwhile, a preferential trade agreement was signed between Tunisia and Algeria in December 2008, and implemented in April 2010. The agreement paved the way for the establishment of a bilateral free trade zone, negotiations on which were ongoing in mid-2013. During a visit to Algeria by the Tunisian Prime Minister Essebsi in March 2012, Essebsi announced his intention to 'consolidate the countries' brotherly relations'. At the same time, the Algerian Government pledged some US $100m. in financial assistance to Tunisia, as it entered a transitional phase following the departure of former President Ben Ali. In April 2013 the first foreign visit by the newly appointed Tunisian Prime Minister, Ali Laârayedh, was to Algeria. His discussions with the Algerian premier, Abdelmalek Sellal, focused on joint efforts to tackle organized crime and the ongoing problem of Islamist militant activity in the border region.

As the crisis in Libya intensified in late February 2011 amid an uprising against the rule of Col Muammar al-Qaddafi, a reported 95,000 refugees—many of whom were African or Asian migrant workers—had crossed the border into Tunisia by early March. In April Libyan government forces engaged in heavy fighting with rebel soldiers strayed into Tunisian territory; it was subsequently reported that Tunisians who were already seeking entry to the EU (see Other external relations) began to flee to Italy in increasing numbers. In April 2012 Tunisia's Minister of National Defence, Abdelkarim Zebidi, demanded that the Libyan Government take firmer action along their joint border to prevent the trafficking of weapons, which had become a serious problem in the aftermath of the Libyan conflict. Meanwhile, in September 2011 Dr al-Baghdadi Ali al-Mahmoudi, who had been Secretary of the Libyan General People's Committee since March 2006, fled Libya and sought refuge in Tunisia. In late June 2012 he was extradited by Tunisia, following a ruling by the court of appeal, despite concerns among senior officials in the country that he might not receive a fair trial and might suffer torture if returned to Libyan custody. Al-Mahmoudi faced charges including involvement in the 'unjust killing' of pro-democracy protesters during the Libyan uprising, and of using his base in Tunisia to provide some US $25m. in funds to pro-Qaddafi forces during the subsequent civil conflict.

Other external relations

In July 1995 Tunisia concluded an association agreement with the EU, designed to foster closer commercial and political co-operation. Several Tunisian deputies demanded a suspension of the agreement in June 2000, after EU member states, particularly France, criticized the Tunisian authorities' failure to protect human rights. Relations between France and Tunisia deteriorated further during 2001, when the French Government again criticized the growing use of violence against human rights activists and voiced its concern at gaol sentences imposed upon prominent opposition figures. Relations improved, however, during 2002–04, and, during a visit by President Jacques Chirac to Tunisia in December 2003, the two countries signed a number of co-operation agreements relating to tourism and bilateral social security arrangements. In April 2008 the French President, Nicolas Sarkozy, made his first state visit to Tunisia since taking office in May 2007. During the visit Sarkozy and Ben Ali supervised the signing of several agreements designed to increase civilian nuclear and aviation co-operation between the two countries. Ben Ali also expressed support for Sarkozy's proposed community of EU member states and countries bordering the Mediterranean Sea. When the Union for the Mediterranean (as it came to be known) was officially inaugurated at a summit meeting in the French capital in July 2008, President Ben Ali was among the many leaders of the 43 member nations to be in attendance. After the ouster of Ben Ali in early 2011, French officials were firmly in support of Tunisia's application for its relations with the EU to be granted 'advanced partner' status (see below).

In March 2010 Tunisia formally applied to the EU for 'advanced partner' status, and duly commenced negotiations with the Union on the upgrading of relations. The Tunisian application proved divisive among EU member states, with some, including France and Italy, pledging support to the North African country in recognition of the strengthening economic, political and social partnership, while others argued that Tunisia must first do more to improve its human rights record. Meanwhile, initial offers of assistance by the French Government to the Tunisian security forces in their efforts to contain the protesters had attracted considerable criticism in January, both within Tunisia and among the international community. In mid-February 2011 thousands of Tunisians began to flee to Italy, in response to their poor employment opportunities and the instability arising from the change of regime. By the end of March, after large numbers of refugees had been taken to the Italian mainland or to France, an estimated 6,000 remained on the small Italian island of Lampedusa, provoking concerns among Italian and other EU officials. An agreement was reached between the Italian and Tunisian Governments on 5 April whereby those migrants who had arrived prior to that date were to be granted short-term visas to remain in Italy, while subsequent arrivals were to be deported. Since the overthrow of the Ben Ali regime, the Italian Government has made efforts to improve relations with its Tunisian counterpart. During 2012 the EU promised large increases in its provision of aid to Tunisia, while, on 19 November, Tunisia was formally granted 'advanced partner' status. As part of the agreement, EU member states pledged to support the interim Government's ongoing programme of economic and political reforms.

In December 2003 the US Secretary of State, Colin Powell, visited Tunisia for talks with President Ben Ali and the Tunisian Minister of Foreign Affairs, Habib Ben Yahia. Powell praised the excellent relations between the two countries and Tunisia's contribution to the US Administration's 'war on terror', which had been launched in response to the attacks of September 2001. However, he urged the Tunisian Government to pursue further political and economic reforms. In February 2004 Ben Ali visited Washington, DC, where he met with the US President, George W. Bush, to discuss a number of trade-related issues. During the talks Bush also stressed that, while the USA applauded Tunisia's efforts to liberalize its society, it remained critical of the country's human rights record and the continued oppression of the Tunisian media. Bilateral relations were further consolidated in September 2008, when US Secretary of State Condoleezza Rice visited Tunisia as part of a tour of Maghreb states. She met with Ben Ali and held discussions with Tunisian officials on issues including counter-terrorism and domestic reform. In a statement to the press, Rice commended the progress that Tunisia had made in promoting women's rights.

Despite US support over the years for the Ben Ali regime, in response to the popular protests of early 2011 US President Barack Obama hailed the courage and dignity of the Tunisian protesters in January, but urged all parties to eschew violence. Obama also appealed to the Tunisian Government to respect human rights and to commit to allowing free and fair elections. The US Assistant Secretary of State for Near Eastern Affairs expressed the Obama Administration's hope that the 'example' of Tunisia would bring reform to the rest of the region. In March US Secretary of State Hillary Clinton made an official visit to Tunisia, during which she met with Mebazaa, Prime Minister Essebsi and other members of the interim Government, and pledged US assistance to facilitate the implementation of social and political reforms. Nevertheless, Clinton's visit was marked by protests, with hundreds of people gathering in Tunis to warn against US intervention in Tunisia's internal affairs, and reports of anti-US slogans being shouted. In an effort to encourage the new Tunisian authorities to meet their pledges on reform following the overthrow of Ben Ali in January 2011, the US Administration was reported to have provided some US $32m. in financial assistance to the country by the end of April 2012. During subsequent months the USA continued to support Tunisia's progress towards becoming a democratic state, and the two countries engaged in close security co-operation.

CONSTITUTION AND GOVERNMENT

Following the removal from power of former President Zine al-Abidine Ben Ali in January 2011, the Constitution promulgated in 1959 (with subsequent amendments in 1988 and 2002) was annulled on 23 March 2011. A legal decree issued on that date stipulated that executive power was to be exercised by an interim President, who was to appoint a Council of Ministers, led by an interim Prime Minister. However, this was superseded by the Law on the Provisional Organization of State Powers, which was approved by the National Constituent Assembly (NCA) on 10 December and promulgated on 16 December. Accordingly, legislative power is exercised by the NCA, which also elects the President of the Republic. Executive power (except for those functions attributed to the President) is held by a Council of Ministers, led by the chosen representative of the largest party in the NCA. The NCA was expected to formulate a new, permanent Constitution in advance of presidential and legislative elections to be held in 2013.

REGIONAL AND INTERNATIONAL CO-OPERATION

Tunisia is a member of the Union of the Arab Maghreb (Union du Maghreb arabe—UMA, see p. 464), African Union (AU, see p. 191), the League of Arab States (the Arab League, see p. 372) and the Community of Sahel-Saharan States (CEN-SAD, see p. 460).

Tunisia joined the UN in November 1956, having gained independence in March of that year. As a contracting party to the General Agreement on Trade and Tariffs, Tunisia became a member of the World Trade Organization (WTO, see p. 444) on its establishment in 1995. The country also participates in the Organization of Islamic Cooperation (OIC, see p. 413).

ECONOMIC AFFAIRS

In 2011, according to estimates by the World Bank, Tunisia's gross national income, measured at average 2009–11 prices, was US $43,443m., equivalent to $4,070 per head (or $9,090 per head on an international purchasing-power parity basis). During 2002–11, it was estimated, the population increased at an average annual rate of 1.0%, while gross domestic product (GDP) per head increased, in real terms, by an average of 3.0%. According to official estimates, overall GDP increased, in real terms, at an average annual rate of 4.2% per year in 2002–12; real GDP declined by 0.2% in 2011, but increased by 4.1% in 2012.

Agriculture (including forestry and fishing) contributed 8.7% of GDP in 2011 and employed 17.7% of the working population in 2010. The principal crops are wheat, barley, potatoes, olives, tomatoes and watermelons. However, Tunisia imports large quantities of cereals, dairy produce, meat and sugar. The country's main agricultural export is olive oil; olives, citrus fruit and dates are also grown for export. During 2002–12, according to official estimates, agricultural GDP increased at an average annual rate of 4.3%; agricultural GDP increased by 3.9% in 2012.

Industry (including mining, manufacturing, construction and power) contributed 30.0% of GDP in 2011 and engaged 33.0% of the employed labour force in 2010. According to official figures, industrial GDP increased by an average of 2.6% per year during 2002–12; industrial GDP decreased by 2.8% in 2011, but increased by 1.9% in 2012.

Mining (excluding hydrocarbons) contributed an estimated 0.3% of GDP in 2011. In 1994 mining (with gas, electricity and water) employed 1.6% of the working population. In 2010 the principal mineral export was petroleum (which accounted for 14.1% of total export earnings). Tunisia's proven published oil reserves at the end of 2011 were estimated at 425m. barrels, sufficient to maintain production (at 2011 levels—averaging an estimated 78,000 barrels per day) for more than 15 years. Iron, zinc, lead, barite, gypsum, phosphate, fluorspar and sea salt are also mined. In addition, Tunisia possesses large reserves of natural gas. According to official estimates, the GDP of the mining sector (excluding hydrocarbons) decreased by 6.9% during 2002–12; mining GDP decreased by 53.7% in 2011, but increased by 1.4% in 2012.

Manufacturing (excluding hydrocarbons) contributed 17.3% of GDP in 2011, and employed 19.6% of the working population in 1994. Manufacturing is based on the processing of the country's principal agricultural and mineral products. Other important sectors include textiles, construction materials, machinery, chemicals, and paper and wood. In 2002–12, according to official estimates, manufacturing GDP increased at an average annual rate of 3.5%; sectoral GDP expanded by 3.3% in 2012.

Construction (including civil engineering) contributed 4.4% of GDP in 2011, and employed 13.2% of the working population in 1994. According to official estimates, GDP of the construction sector increased by 3.3% during 2002–12; sectoral GDP declined by 2.8% in 2011, but grew by 1.5% in 2012.

Energy is derived principally from gas (which contributed 89.7% of total electricity output in 2009) and petroleum (9.2%), although Tunisia also has several hydroelectric plants (which contributed just 0.5% of total output in 2009). Imports of mineral fuels and lubricants comprised 12.6% of the value of total imports in 2010. In the mid-2000s the Tunisian electricity grid was interconnected with that of Libya.

The services sector accounted for 61.4% of GDP in 2011 and employed 49.3% of the working population in 2010. Tourism represents an important source of revenue: receipts from tourism in 2011 totalled an estimated US $1,805m. (excl. passenger transport), and there were some 4.8m. tourist arrivals in that year, according to provisional figures. The GDP of the services sector increased by an average of 5.2% per year in 2002–12, according to official estimates; the sector's GDP increased by 5.6% in 2012.

In 2011 Tunisia recorded a visible merchandise trade deficit of US $4,747m., and a deficit of $3,386m. on the current account of the balance of payments. In 2011 the principal sources of imports were France, including Monaco (accounting for 18.3% of the total), Italy, Germany, the People's Republic of China and Russia. The principal market for Tunisian exports in that year was also France, including Monaco (taking 30.7%); other major purchasers were Italy and Germany. Tunisia's principal exports in 2011 were machinery and transport equipment (especially electrical equipment), textiles, food products, chemicals and related products, and mineral fuels and lubricants. The principal imports in that year were machinery and transport equipment, mineral fuels and lubricants, textiles, base metals and articles thereof, vehicles, chemicals and related products, food products, and plastics, rubbers and articles thereof.

In 2011 there was an estimated budgetary deficit of TD 1,678m. The 2012 budget forecast a deficit of TD 3,187m. Tunisia's general government gross debt was TD 28,769m. in 2011, equivalent to 44.4% of GDP. At the end of 2010 Tunisia's total external debt was US $21,584m., of which $14,609m. was public and publicly guaranteed debt. In that year the cost of servicing long-term public and publicly guaranteed debt and repayments to the IMF was equivalent to 10.4% of the value of exports of goods, services and income (excluding workers' remittances). The average annual rate of inflation was 3.8% in 2002–12; consumer prices increased by 5.6% in 2012. A reported 16.7% of the labour force were unemployed during October–December 2012.

The civil unrest and installation of a new administration in early 2011 had a profound impact on the national economy. The principal aims of the first interim Government after the ouster of President Ben Ali were to restore confidence in the Tunisian economy to ensure strong long-term growth and lower rates of unemployment; this required the authorities to seek additional financial assistance to support their extensive programme of political and economic reforms. In May the Group of Eight (G8) leading industrialized nations pledged loans worth US $25,000m. for the period 2011–16, while the World Bank and the African Development Bank also gave $1,500m. in emergency aid. The Government's draft supplementary budget for 2012—based on estimated GDP growth of 3.5%—forecast a

21.6% increase in spending, leading to a predicted deficit of some 6.6% of GDP. In fact, growth for 2012 was estimated at 4.1% in 2012, compared with a contraction of 0.2% in 2011. During 2012 the Tunisian economy continued to be deeply affected by the financial crisis among eurozone countries, with the European Union (see p. 281) not only being its principal trading partner (Tunisia was granted 'advanced partner' status in November), but also accounting for much of its vital tourism industry. Tourism revenues declined by 32% in 2011, compared with 2010, and, although there was evidence of a partial recovery during 2012, the industry was damaged by ongoing fears of attacks by radical Islamist groups. Moreover, protests against the lack of job opportunities and other economic hardships persisted into 2013. The draft supplementary budget for that year forecast a further rise in government expenditure, leading an anticipated deficit of around 5.3% of GDP. The budget—based on estimated GDP growth of 4.5%—included measures aimed at creating jobs (including 23,000 in the public sector) as well as improving employment and vocational training. In April 2013 the IMF agreed in principle to a loan for Tunisia worth an estimated $1,780m., to support the economic and political reform programme being implemented by the interim Islamist-led Government appointed following the legislative elections of October 2011.

PUBLIC HOLIDAYS

2014: 1 January (New Year's Day), 13 January (Mouloud, Birth of the Prophet), 14 January (Revolution and Youth Day), 20 March (Independence Day), 9 April (Martyrs' Day), 1 May (Labour Day), 25 July (Republic Day), 28 July* (Aid el-Seghir—Id al-Fitr, end of Ramadan), 13 August (Women's Day), 4 October* (Aid el-Kebir—Id al-Adha, Feast of the Sacrifice), 15 October (Evacuation of Bizerta).

* These holidays are dependent on the Islamic lunar calendar and may differ by one or two days from the dates given.

Statistical Survey

Source (unless otherwise stated): Institut National de la Statistique, BP 265, 70 rue el-Cham, 1002 Tunis; tel. (71) 891-002; fax (71) 792-559; e-mail ins@ins.tn; internet www.ins.nat.tn.

Area and Population

AREA, POPULATION AND DENSITY

Area (sq km)	
Land	154,530
Inland waters	9,080
Total	163,610*
Population (census results)	
20 April 1994	8,785,364
28 April 2004	
Males	4,965,435
Females	4,945,437
Total	9,910,872
Population (official estimates at 1 July)†	
2010	10,549,100
2011	10,673,800
2012	10,777,500
Density (per sq km) at 1 July 2012	69.7‡

* 63,170 sq miles.
† Estimates are rounded to the nearest 100 persons.
‡ Land area only.

POPULATION BY AGE AND SEX
(UN estimates at mid-2013)

	Males	Females	Total
0–14	1,268,928	1,216,684	2,485,612
15–64	3,770,891	3,786,832	7,557,723
65 and over	361,091	409,252	770,343
Total	5,400,910	5,412,768	10,813,678

Source: UN, *World Population Prospects: The 2010 Revision*.

GOVERNORATES
(population estimates at 1 July 2012)

	Area (sq km)*	Population†	Density (per sq km)
Tunis	346	1,003,700	2,900.9
Ariana	498	528,500	1,061.2
Ben Arous	761	600,900	789.6
Manouba	1,060	375,700	354.4
Nabeul	2,788	773,100	277.3
Zaghouan	2,768	174,000	62.9
Bizerte	3,685	556,000	150.9
Béja	3,558	305,400	85.8
Jendouba	3,102	424,200	136.8
Le Kef	4,965	255,100	51.4
Siliana	4,631	234,000	50.5
Kairouan	6,712	566,700	84.4
Kasserine	8,066	438,400	54.4

—continued	Area (sq km)*	Population†	Density (per sq km)
Sidi Bouzid	6,994	417,900	59.8
Sousse	2,621	641,700	244.8
Monastir	1,019	539,400	529.3
Mahdia	2,966	400,500	135.0
Sfax	7,545	955,500	126.6
Gafsa	8,990	344,500	38.3
Tozeur	4,719	105,900	22.4
Kébili	22,084	154,300	7.0
Gabès	7,175	367,500	51.2
Médenine	8,588	466,700	54.3
Tataouine	38,889	147,900	3.8
Total	154,530	10,777,500	69.7

* Land area only.
† Estimates are rounded to the nearest 100 persons, therefore total may not be equal to the sum of components.

PRINCIPAL TOWNS
(2004, census results)

Tunis (capital)	728,453	Ettadhamen	118,487
Sfax (Safaqis)	265,131	Kairouan (Qairawan)	117,930
Ariana	240,749	Gabès	116,323
Sousse	173,047	Bizerta (Bizerte)	114,371

Source: Thomas Brinkhoff, *City Population* (internet www.citypopulation.de).

Mid-2011 (incl. suburbs, UN estimate): Tunis 790,205 (Source: UN, *World Urbanization Prospects: The 2011 Revision*).

BIRTHS, MARRIAGES AND DEATHS

	Registered live births		Registered marriages		Registered deaths	
	Number	Rate (per 1,000)	Number	Rate (per 1,000)	Number	Rate (per 1,000)
2004	166,551	16.8	68,976	6.9	48,651	4.9
2005	170,999	17.1	73,971	7.4	49,768	5.0
2006	173,390	17.1	81,340	8.0	48,529	4.8
2007	177,503	17.4	76,809	7.5	48,308	4.7
2008	182,990	17.7	78,748	7.6	51,258	5.0
2009	184,282	17.7	81,605	7.8	51,082	4.9
2010	196,039	18.6	87,081	8.3	51,728	4.9
2011	201,599	18.9	95,537	9.0	58,037	5.4

Life expectancy (years at birth): 74.9 (males 72.9; females 76.9) in 2011.

EMPLOYMENT

('000 persons aged 15 years and over at 20 April 1994)

	Males	Females	Total
Agriculture, forestry and fishing .	393.7	107.3	501.0
Manufacturing	244.7	211.0	455.7
Electricity, gas and water* . .	34.4	2.4	36.8
Construction	302.6	3.2	305.8
Trade, restaurants and hotels† .	277.8	37.8	315.6
Community, social and personal services‡	503.9	163.2	667.1
Activities not adequately defined .	28.6	10.0	38.6
Total employed	**1,785.7**	**534.9**	**2,320.6**

* Including mining and quarrying.
† Including financing, insurance, real estate and business services.
‡ Including transport, storage and communications.

2010 (percentage distribution by sector): Agriculture and fishing 17.7; Industry 33.0; Services 49.3.

Health and Welfare

KEY INDICATORS

Total fertility rate (children per woman, 2010)	2.0
Under-5 mortality rate (per 1,000 live births, 2010) . . .	16
HIV/AIDS (% of persons aged 15–49, 2007) . . .	0.1
Physicians (per 1,000 head, 2009)	1.2
Hospital beds (per 1,000 head, 2010)	2.1
Health expenditure (2009): US $ per head (PPP) . . .	479
Health expenditure (2009): % of GDP	6.4
Health expenditure (2009): public (% of total)	54.9
Access to water (% of persons, 2008)	94
Access to sanitation (% of persons, 2008)	85
Total carbon dioxide emissions ('000 metric tons, 2008) . .	25,012.6
Carbon dioxide emissions per head (metric tons, 2008) . .	2.4
Human Development Index (2011): ranking	94
Human Development Index (2011): value	0.698

For sources and definitions, see explanatory note on p. vi.

Agriculture

PRINCIPAL CROPS

('000 metric tons)

	2009	2010	2011
Wheat	1,654	822	1,606
Barley	850	237	681
Potatoes	324	370	367
Broad beans, horse beans, dry .	70	48	73
Almonds, with shell . . .	60	52	61
Olives	800	750	863
Artichokes	16	14	18
Tomatoes	1,135	1,296	1,284
Pumpkins, squash and gourds .	51	49	48*
Cucumbers and gherkins . .	38	42	41*
Chillies and peppers, green . .	281	304	268
Onions and shallots, green† . .	210	217	210
Onions, dry†	140	145	140
Peas, green	14	11	11*
Carrots and turnips . . .	62	57	55*
Watermelons	570	498	470*
Oranges	116	137	139*
Tangerines, mandarins, clementines and satsumas . .	44	37	48
Lemons and limes	42	37	48

—continued	2009	2010	2011
Grapefruit and pomelos* . . .	84	87	93
Apples	110	126	128
Pears	60	66	61
Apricots	30	24	30
Peaches and nectarines . . .	118	117	123*
Grapes	97	97	114
Figs	28	26	26
Dates	162	174	180

* FAO estimate(s).
† Unofficial figures.

Aggregate production ('000 metric tons, may include official, semi-official or estimated data): Total cereals 2,564 in 2009, 1,109 in 2010, 2,342 in 2011; Total roots and tubers 324 in 2009, 370 in 2010, 367 in 2011; Total pulses 116 in 2009, 93 in 2010, 127 in 2011; Total vegetables (incl. melons) 2,825 in 2009, 2,961 in 2010, 2,860 in 2011; Total fruits (excl. melons) 1,180 in 2009, 1,221 in 2010, 1,314 in 2011.

Source: FAO.

LIVESTOCK

('000 head, year ending September)

	2009	2010	2011
Horses*	57	57	57
Asses*	240	240	240
Cattle	679	671	656
Camels*	235	235	237
Sheep	7,362	7,234	6,999
Goats	1,455	1,296	1,282
Chickens*	70,000	80,000	82,000
Turkeys*	5,800	5,800	6,100

* FAO estimates.

Source: FAO.

LIVESTOCK PRODUCTS

('000 metric tons)

	2009	2010	2011
Cattle meat	51.6	55.8	54.6
Sheep meat	49.1	50.0	51.5
Chicken meat	103.0	113.2	120.0
Cows' milk	1,048	1,059	1,054
Sheep's milk*	19.0	19.5	19.5
Goats' milk*	13.2	13.4	13.4
Hen eggs*	88	91	91
Wool, greasy*	10.3	10.4	10.4

* FAO estimates.

Source: FAO.

Forestry

ROUNDWOOD REMOVALS

('000 cu m, excl. bark, FAO estimates)

	2009	2010	2011
Sawlogs, veneer logs and logs for sleepers	25	25	25
Pulpwood	75	75	75
Other industrial wood . . .	118	118	118
Fuel wood	2,177	2,185	2,188
Total	**2,395**	**2,403**	**2,406**

Source: FAO.

SAWNWOOD PRODUCTION
('000 cu m, incl. sleepers)

	1992	1993	1994
Coniferous (softwood)	2.2	5.8	6.8
Broadleaved (hardwood) . . .	4.0	13.6	13.6
Total	6.2	19.4	20.4

1995–2011: Production as in 1994 (FAO estimates).

Source: FAO.

Fishing

('000 metric tons, live weight)

	2008	2009	2010
Capture	97.9	97.9	97.7
Mullets	6.6	7.1	7.3
Common pandora . . .	2.9	3.3	3.9
Sargo breams	0.3	0.4	0.4
Bogue	2.7	2.9	2.8
Jack and horse mackerels . .	8.9	8.2	9.4
Sardinellas	16.6	14.2	15.1
European pilchard . . .	18.4	19.0	14.4
Chub mackerel	3.5	3.1	3.4
Common cuttlefish . . .	4.9	3.9	4.7
Aquaculture	3.6	4.9	5.4
Total catch (incl. others) . . .	101.5	102.8	103.1

Source: FAO.

Mining

('000 metric tons unless otherwise indicated)

	2008	2009	2010
Crude petroleum	4,210	3,905	3,765
Natural gas (million cu m) . .	2,068	2,540	2,540
Iron ore: gross weight . .	108	151	150
Iron ore: metal content* . .	110	79	79
Phosphate rock†	7,692	7,409	7,281
Salt (marine)	1,063	1,260	1,300
Gypsum (crude)	177	360	360

* Estimated production.

† Figures refer to gross weight. The estimated phosphoric acid content (in '000 metric tons) was: 1,009 in 2008; 1,115 in 2009; 1,214 in 2010.

Lead concentrates (metric tons): 8,708 in 2005 (figure refers to metal content of concentrates).

Zinc concentrates (metric tons): 15,889 in 2005 (figure refers to metal content of concentrates).

Source: mostly US Geological Survey.

Industry

SELECTED PRODUCTS
('000 metric tons unless otherwise indicated)

	2008	2009	2010
Superphosphates	863	747	740
Cement	7,243	7,181	7,200
Crude steel	82	155	194
Quicklime	369	366	370
Motor gasoline ('000 barrels) . .	1,350	1,106	1,106
Kerosene	120	85	n.a.
Distillate fuel oil ('000 barrels) .	4,110	4,387	4,387
Residual fuel oil ('000 barrels) .	4,450	4,330	4,300
Electric energy (million kWh) .	14,662	15,693	n.a.

Sources: partly UN Industrial Commodity Statistics Database; US Geological Survey.

Finance

CURRENCY AND EXCHANGE RATES

Monetary Units
  1,000 millimes = 1 Tunisian dinar (TD).

Sterling, Dollar and Euro Equivalents (30 November 2012)
  £1 sterling = 2.525 dinars;
  US $1 = 1.572 dinars;
  €1 = 2.042 dinars;
  100 Tunisian dinars = £39.61 = $63.60 = €48.98.

Average Exchange Rate (dinars per US $)
  2009 1.3503
  2010 1.4314
  2011 1.4078

BUDGET
(million dinars)*

Revenue†	2010	2011‡	2012§
Tax revenue	12,699	13,668	14,653
Direct taxes	5,033	5,936	6,238
Trade taxes	564	564	589
Value-added tax . . .	3,750	3,818	4,177
Excise	1,563	1,512	1,559
Other taxes	1,789	1,839	2,091
Non-tax revenue	2,070	2,362	2,080
Capital revenue	—	—	8
Total	14,769	16,030	16,741

Expenditure‖	2010	2011‡	2012§
Current expenditure . . .	11,153	13,660	16,175
Wages and salaries . .	6,785	7,679	8,614
Goods and services . .	841	860	1,151
Interest payments . . .	1,152	1,190	1,286
Domestic	557	592	646
External	595	598	640
Transfers and subsidies . .	2,375	3,931	4,524
Non-allocated	—	—	600
Capital expenditure . . .	4,326	4,727	5,446
Direct investment . . .	1,450	1,459	2,806
Capital transfers and equity .	2,876	3,269	2,640
Total	15,479	18,387	21,621

* Figures refer to the consolidated accounts of the central Government, including administrative agencies and social security funds. The data exclude the operations of economic and social agencies with their own budgets.

† Excluding grants from abroad and receipts from privatization (million dinars): 84 in 2010; 591 in 2011 (estimate); 1,739 in 2012 (projected).

‡ Estimates.

§ Projected figures.

‖ Excluding net lending (million dinars): –35 in 2010; –88 in 2011 (estimate); 46 in 2012 (projected).

Source: IMF, *Tunisia: 2012 Article IV Consultation—Staff Report; Public Information Notice on the Executive Board Discussion; and Statement by the Executive Director for Tunisia* (September 2012).

CENTRAL BANK RESERVES
(US $ million at 31 December)

	2008	2009	2010
Gold (national valuation) . . .	3.4	3.3	3.0
IMF special drawing rights . .	5.2	379.1	372.3
Reserve position in IMF . . .	31.2	31.7	86.6
Foreign exchange	8,812.9	10,646.5	9,000.3
Total	8,852.7	11,060.6	9,462.2

2011: Gold (national valuation) 2.9; IMF special drawing rights 371.3; Reserve position in IMF 86.4.

Source: IMF, *International Financial Statistics*.

MONEY SUPPLY
(million dinars at 31 December)

	2009	2010	2011
Currency outside banks . . .	5,010	5,518	6,816
Demand deposits at commercial banks	8,835	10,012	11,300
Total money (incl. others) . .	14,874	16,454	19,733

Source: IMF, *International Financial Statistics*.

COST OF LIVING
(Consumer Price Index; base: 2000 = 100)

	2008	2009	2010
Food	132.6	138.3	147.2
Electricity, gas and other fuels .	146.7	150.0	167.8
Clothing	118.4	121.0	125.3
Rent	131.3	136.1	141.3
All items (incl. others) . . .	128.8	133.6	139.1

2011: Food 152.6; All items (incl. others) 143.9.

2012: Food 164.1; All items (incl. others) 152.0.

Source: ILO.

NATIONAL ACCOUNTS
(million dinars at current prices)

Expenditure on the Gross Domestic Product

	2008	2009	2010
Government final consumption expenditure	8,917.0	9,680.1	10,507.8
Private final consumption expenditure	33,922.3	36,390.4	39,643.7
Gross fixed capital formation . .	13,060.4	14,308.2	15,498.1
Change in inventories	1,047.3	235.1	1,140.3
Total domestic expenditure .	56,947.0	60,613.8	66,789.9
Exports of goods and services . .	30,761.1	26,428.1	31,210.9
Less Imports of goods and services	32,440.3	28,151.6	34,460.6
GDP in purchasers' values .	55,267.8	58,890.3	63,540.2
GDP at constant 2005 prices .	49,218.9	50,994.0	52,833.9

2011 (million dinars): GDP in purchasers' values 65,360.7; GDP at constant 2005 prices 52,710.1.

Gross Domestic Product by Economic Activity

	2009	2010	2011
Agriculture and fishing . .	4,873.6	4,659.0	5,315.3
Mining (excluding hydrocarbons) .	426.0	521.3	172.8
Manufacturing (excluding hydrocarbons)	9,878.6	10,735.3	10,635.5
Hydrocarbons, electricity and water	3,462.1	4,275.6	4,919.3
Construction and public works .	2,522.1	2,625.5	2,692.5
Maintenance and repair . . .	211.2	230.8	244.7
Transport and telecommunications	7,331.3	8,120.0	7,773.0
Hotels and restaurants . . .	2,933.3	3,204.0	2,681.9
Trade, finance, etc.	13,966.5	15,273.7	15,991.3
Non-market services	8,996.0	9,739.8	11,008.5
Sub-total	54,600.7	59,385.0	61,434.9
Less Imputed bank service charges	867.0	942.3	1,024.5
Gross value added at factor cost	53,733.7	58,442.7	60,410.4
Indirect taxes, *less* subsidies . .	5,156.5	5,097.5	4,950.2
GDP in purchasers' values .	58890.3	63,540.2	65,360.7

BALANCE OF PAYMENTS
(US $ million)

	2009	2010	2011
Exports of goods	14,481	16,493	17,876
Imports of goods	−18,117	−21,005	−22,623
Balance on goods	−3,636	−4,512	−4,747
Exports of services	5,334	5,632	4,618
Imports of services	−2,872	−3,234	3,178
Balance on goods and services	−1,174	−2,115	−3,306
Primary income received . . .	318	431	455
Primary income paid	−2,328	−2,355	−2,434
Balance on goods, services and primary income	−3,185	−4,039	−5,285
Secondary income received . .	1,979	1,972	1,946
Secondary income paid . . .	−28	−37	−47
Current balance	−1,234	−2,104	−3,386
Capital account (net)	164	82	184
Direct investment liabilities . .	1,525	1,335	433
Portfolio investment liabilities .	−89	−26	−44
Other investment assets . . .	−13	−240	−33
Other investment liabilities . .	1,217	700	1,063
Net errors and omissions . . .	67	33	74
Reserves and related items .	1,639	−222	−1,709

Source: IMF, *International Financial Statistics*.

External Trade

PRINCIPAL COMMODITIES
(US $ million)

Imports c.i.f.	2008	2009	2010
Food and live animals . . .	1,912.7	1,128.4	1,452.4
Cereal and cereal preparations .	1,229.0	484.0	777.2
Mineral fuels, lubricants, etc. .	4,151.0	2,178.2	2,793.7
Petroleum and related products .	3,299.3	1,686.9	2,160.5
Gas, natural and manufactured .	844.7	487.0	623.3
Chemicals and related products	2,345.6	2,065.3	2,301.6
Plastics in primary forms . . .	531.0	416.7	507.7
Basic manufactures	5,598.2	4,334.1	4,797.3
Textile yarn, fabrics and related products	2,087.6	1,749.0	1,844.7
Cotton fabrics, woven . .	987.0	829.3	844.7
Machinery and transport equipment	6,725.9	6,604.1	7,751.4
General industrial machinery and equipment	1,048.0	983.0	1,099.3
Electrical machinery, apparatus and appliances	1,920.0	1,756.6	2,239.3
Road vehicles	1,454.4	1,408.4	1,604.3
Miscellaneous manufactured articles	1,778.6	1,684.7	1,764.4
Total	24,638.4	19,096.2	22,215.4

Exports f.o.b.	2008	2009	2010
Food and live animals . . .	856.6	758.6	769.1
Mineral fuels, lubricants, etc. .	3,345.2	1,969.2	2,328.0
Petroleum and related products .	3,345.0	1,969.0	2,320.3
Petroleum oils and oils obtained from bituminous materials, crude	2,630.8	1,553.1	2,080.8
Animal and vegetable oils . .	771.2	497.6	428.0
Chemicals and related products	2,942.8	1,521.1	1,790.4
Fertilizers	1,525.4	661.2	812.8
Basic manufactures . . .	1,786.1	1,474.0	1,630.6
Machinery and transport equipment	4,044.1	3,624.9	4,678.2
Electrical machinery, apparatus and appliances	2,538.8	2,214.7	2,651.1
Miscellaneous manufactured articles	5,111.4	4,319.1	4,461.1
Articles of clothing and clothing accessories	3,765.6	3,120.3	3,089.2
Men's or boy's outerwear . .	1,020.7	760.5	722.5
Footwear	608.0	512.3	566.4
Total	19,320.0	14,445.1	16,426.6

Source: UN, *International Trade Statistics Yearbook.*

2011 (distribution by HS, million dinars): *Imports c.i.f.:* Food products 1,953.6 (Cereals 1,267.1); Mineral products 5,315.3; Chemicals and related products 2,371.8; Rubber and plastic articles 1,913.3 (Plastic articles 1,687.1); Textiles 3,827.2; Base metals and articles thereof 3,153.1; Machinery and mechanical appliances 8,137.1 (Boilers, etc. 3,665.3, Electrical equipment 4,471.8); Vehicles 2,377.7; Total imports (incl. others) 33,695.4; *Exports f.o.b.:* Food products 1,599.2; Mineral products 1,330.0; Chemicals and related products 1,453.3; Textiles 5,305.8; Footwear, headgear, etc. 834.3; Base metals and articles thereof 989.4; Machinery and mechanical appliances 7,012.5 (Electrical equipment 6,300.4); Vehicles 830.3; Total exports (incl. others) 25,091.9.

2012 (million dinars): Total imports 38,182.7; Total exports 26,547.6.

PRINCIPAL TRADING PARTNERS
(US $ million)*

Imports c.i.f.	2008	2009	2010
Algeria	724.3	501.2	621.5
Argentina	404.5	161.7	149.9
Belgium	444.2	383.1	466.0
Brazil	303.3	197.7	259.0
China, People's Republic . . .	919.6	956.6	1,344.1
Egypt	249.6	167.8	172.8
France (incl. Monaco) . . .	4,546.3	3,832.1	4,203.2
Germany	1,717.0	1,672.5	1,696.6
India	218.4	223.9	279.7
Italy	4,245.4	3,108.9	3,907.3
Japan	325.9	237.9	312.6
Korea, Republic	173.1	159.7	346.4
Libya	1,073.7	560.6	283.7
Malta	126.8	267.2	197.2
Netherlands	345.0	285.3	441.6
Russia	1,855.7	688.1	1,034.4
Spain	951.2	867.0	1,025.3
Turkey	732.3	576.6	631.7
Ukraine	516.4	327.4	303.0
United Kingdom	456.0	341.3	377.3
USA	748.8	764.8	905.2
Total (incl. others)	24,638.4	19,096.2	22,215.4

Exports f.o.b.	2008	2009	2010
Algeria	408.1	451.2	474.7
Belgium	430.0	319.6	320.3
France (incl. Monaco) . . .	5,507.5	4,283.3	4,717.3
Germany	1,338.0	1,270.1	1,388.1
India	595.2	238.3	307.2
Iran	234.7	127.8	53.2
Italy	3,991.7	3,038.4	3,264.9
Libya	871.2	831.8	732.3
Morocco	234.2	209.4	232.0
Netherlands	422.3	232.7	360.1
Spain	946.1	486.9	637.1
Switzerland (incl. Liechtenstein) .	456.0	133.3	263.7
Turkey	309.4	170.8	214.2
United Kingdom	898.6	686.7	824.8
USA	323.1	196.8	388.5
Total (incl. others)	19,320.0	14,445.1	16,426.6

* Imports by country of production; exports by country of last destination.

Source: UN, *International Trade Statistics Yearbook.*

2011 (million dinars): *Imports c.i.f.:* Algeria 896.4; Argentina 433.7; Belgium 599.0; Brazil 642.7; China, People's Republic 2,048.3; France 6,164.7; Germany 2,487.7; India 493.6; Italy 5,331.8; Japan 412.9; Russia 1,936.9; Spain 1,593.1; Turkey 1,195.9; Ukraine 468.8; USA 1,232.6; Total imports (incl. others) 33,695.4; *Exports f.o.b.:* Algeria 656.0; Belgium 473.4; France 7,695.4; Germany 2,271.4; Italy 5,432.3; Libya 1,103.3; Netherlands 587.2; Spain 1,079.4; USA 388.9; Total exports (incl. others) 25,091.9.

2012 (million dinars): Total imports 38,182.7; Total exports 26,547.6.

Transport

RAILWAYS
(traffic)

	2008	2009	2010
Passengers carried ('000) . . .	39,226	38,576	40,153
Passenger-km (million) . . .	1,494	1,486	1,534
Freight carried ('000 metric tons) .	10,528	9,318	10,446
Freight net ton-km (million) . .	2,073	1,821	2,024

ROAD TRAFFIC
(estimates, motor vehicles in use at 31 December)

	2000	2001	2002
Passenger cars	516,525	552,897	585,194
Buses and coaches	11,143	11,973	12,181
Lorries and vans	240,421	253,760	266,499
Road tractors	8,307	9,165	9,605

2010: Passenger cars 915,926; Buses and coaches 16,818; Lorries and vans 381,154; Motorcycles 6,724.

Source: IRF, *World Road Statistics.*

SHIPPING

Flag Registered Fleet
(at 31 December)

	2010	2011	2012
Number of vessels	61	62	62
Total displacement ('000 grt) . .	266.6	311.8	358.5

Source: Lloyd's List Intelligence (www.lloydslistintelligence.com).

International Sea-borne Freight Traffic
('000 metric tons)

	2008	2009	2010
Goods loaded*	7,939	7,817	8,145
Goods unloaded	16,520	14,553	16,326

* Excluding Algerian crude petroleum loaded at La Skhirra.

CIVIL AVIATION
(traffic on scheduled services)

	2007	2008	2009
Kilometres flown (million) . .	34	37	35
Passengers carried ('000) . . .	2,055	2,275	2,279
Passenger-km (million) . . .	2,960	3,357	3,220
Total ton-km (million)	303	343	326

Source: UN, *Statistical Yearbook*.

Passengers carried ('000): 5,464 in 2010 (Source: World Bank, World Development Indicators database).

Tourism

FOREIGN TOURIST ARRIVALS BY NATIONALITY
('000)

	2008	2009	2010
Algeria	968.5	961.3	1,060.0
Belgium	169.1	168.1	163.1
France	1,395.3	1,344.7	1,385.3
Germany	521.5	484.2	458.6
Italy	444.5	383.9	354.1
Libya	1,766.9	1,995.2	1,825.5
Poland	207.5	175.3	151.4
United Kingdom	254.9	275.7	353.3
Total (incl. others)	7,050.4	6,901.4	6,902.7

Total tourist arrivals ('000): 6,902 in 2010; 4,782 in 2011 (provisional).

Receipts from tourism (US $ million, excl. passenger transport): 2,773 in 2009; 2,645 in 2010; 1,805 in 2011 (provisional).

Source: World Tourism Organization.

Communications Media

	2009	2010	2011
Telephones ('000 main lines in use)	1,278.5	1,289.6	1,217.8
Mobile cellular telephones ('000 subscribers)	9,797.0	11,114.2	12,387.7
Internet subscribers ('000) . .	414.0	543.3	604.1
Broadband subscribers ('000) . .	372.8	481.8	544.4

Personal computers: 997,150 (96.6 per 1,000 persons) in 2008.

Source: International Telecommunication Union.

Education

(2010/11)

	Institutions	Teachers	Students
Primary (public)			
1st cycle	4,517	57,349	1,003,017
2nd cycle	2,154	37,900	469,459
Secondary (public)	511	37,416	466,939
Higher	193	21,552*	336,017*

* Full-time equivalent.

Pupil-teacher ratio (primary education, UNESCO estimate): 17.0 in 2008/09 (Source: UNESCO Institute for Statistics).

Adult literacy rate (UNESCO estimates): 77.6% (males 86.4%; females 71.0%) in 2008 (Source: UNESCO Institute for Statistics).

Directory

The Government

HEAD OF STATE

President: MONCEF MARZOUKI (ad interim; sworn in on 13 December 2011).

COUNCIL OF MINISTERS
(May 2013)

A coalition of the Parti de la renaissance/Hizb al-Nahdah, Congrès pour la République (CPR), Forum démocratique pour le travail et les libertés (Ettakatol) and independents (Ind.).

Prime Minister: ALI LAÂRAYEDH (Hizb al-Nahdah).

Minister of Justice: NADHIR BEN AMMOU (Ind.).

Minister of National Defence: RACHID SABBAGH (Ind.).

Minister of the Interior: LOTFI BEN JEDDOU (Ind.).

Minister of Foreign Affairs: OTHMAN JARANDI (Ind.).

Minister of Human Rights and Transitional Justice: SAMIR DILOU (Hizb al-Nahdah).

Minister of Social Affairs: KHALIL ZAOUIA (Ettakatol).

Minister of Finance: ELYÈS FAKHFEKH (Ettakatol).

Minister of Religious Affairs: NOUREDDINE KHADEMI (Ind.).

Minister of Education: SALEM LABYADH (Ind.).

Minister of Culture: MEHDI MABROUK (Ind.).

Minister of Higher Education and Scientific Research: MONCEF BEN SALEM (Hizb al-Nahdah).

Minister of Industry: MEHDI JOMAÂ (Ind.).

Minister of Trade and Handicrafts: ABDELWAHEB MAÂTAR (CPR).

Minister of Tourism: JAMEL GHAMRA (Ind.).

Minister of Agriculture: MUHAMMAD BEN SALEM (Hizb al-Nahdah).

Minister of Family and Women's Affairs: SIHEM BADI (CPR).

Minister of State Properties and Real Estate Affairs: SLIM BEN HMIDANE (CPR).

Minister of Professional Training and Employment: NAOUFEL JAMMELI (Ind.).

Minister of Development and International Co-operation: LAMINE DOGHRI (Ind.).

Minister of Youth and Sports: TAREK DHIAB (Ind.).

Minister of Public Works and the Environment: MUHAMMAD SALMANE (Ind.).

Minister of Transport: ABD AL-KARIM HAROUNI (Hizb al-Nahdah).

Minister of Public Health: ABDELLATIF MEKKI (Hizb al-Nahdah).

Minister of Information and Communication Technologies: MONGI MARZOUK (Hizb al-Nahdah).

Minister-delegate to the Prime Minister: NOUREDDINE BHIRI (Hizb al-Nahdah).

Minister-delegate to the Prime Minister, in charge of Economic Affairs: RIDHA SAIDI (Hizb al-Nahdah).

Minister-delegate to the Prime Minister, in charge of Governance and Anti-Corruption: ABDERRAHMANE LADGHAM (Ettakatol).

There are, in addition, 10 Secretaries of State. The Governor of the Central Bank also has full ministerial status.

MINISTRIES

Office of the President: Palais de Carthage, 2016 Carthage; tel. (71) 242-038; e-mail contact@carthage.tn; internet www.carthage .tn.

Office of the Prime Minister: pl. du Gouvernement, La Kasbah, 1030 Tunis; tel. (71) 565-400; e-mail boc@pm.gov.tn; internet www .pm.gov.tn.

Ministry of Agriculture: 30 rue Alain Savary, 1002 Tunis; tel. (71) 786-833; fax (71) 780-391; e-mail mag@ministeres.tn.

Ministry of Culture: 8 rue 2 mars 1934, la Kasbah, 1006 Tunis; tel. (71) 563-006; fax (71) 563-816; e-mail minculture@email.ati.tn; internet www.culture.tn.

Ministry of Development and International Co-operation: Tunis.

Ministry of Education: blvd Bab Benat, 1030 Tunis; tel. (71) 568-768; e-mail ministere@minedu.edunet.tn; internet www.education .gov.tn.

Ministry of Family and Women's Affairs: 2 rue d'Alger, 1001 Tunis; tel. (71) 252-514; fax (71) 349-900; e-mail maffepa@email.ati.tn; internet www.femmes.tn.

Ministry of Finance: pl. du Gouvernement, La Kasbah, 1008 Tunis; tel. (71) 571-888; fax (71) 572-390; e-mail pcontenu@finances.gov.tn; internet www.portail.finances.gov.tn.

Ministry of Foreign Affairs: ave de la Ligue des états arabes, 1030 Tunis; tel. (71) 847-500; fax (71) 785-025; e-mail mae@diplomatie.gov.tn; internet www.diplomatie.gov.tn.

Ministry of Higher Education and Scientific Research: ave Ouled Haffouz, 1030 Tunis; tel. (71) 786-300; fax (71) 786-701; e-mail mes@mes.rnu.tn; internet www.mes.tn.

Ministry of Human Rights and Transitional Justice: ave 2 Mars 1934, 2000 Bardo, Tunis; tel. (71) 702-288; fax (71) 702-822.

Ministry of Industry: Immeuble Beya, 40 Rue 8011, Montplaisir, 1002 Tunis; tel. (71) 905-132; fax (71) 902-742; e-mail contact@mit.gov.tn; internet www.industrie.gov.tn.

Ministry of Information and Communication Technologies: 3 bis rue d'Angleterre, 1000 Tunis; tel. (71) 359-000; fax (71) 352-353; e-mail info@infocom.tn; internet www.infocom.tn.

Ministry of the Interior: ave Habib Bourguiba, 1000 Tunis; tel. (71) 333-000; fax (71) 340-888; e-mail mint@ministeres.tn.

Ministry of Justice: 31 ave Bab Benat, 1019 Tunis; tel. (71) 561-440; fax (71) 586-106; e-mail info@e-justice.tn; internet www.e-justice.tn.

Ministry of National Defence: blvd Bab Menara, 1008 Tunis; tel. (71) 560-240; fax (71) 561-804; e-mail defnat@defense.tn; internet www.defense.tn.

Ministry of Professional Training and Employment: 10 blvd Ouled Haffouz, 1002 Tunis; tel. (71) 798-196; fax (71) 794-615; e-mail webmaster@mfpe.gov.tn; internet www.emploi.gov.tn.

Ministry of Public Health: Bab Saâdoun, 1006 Tunis; tel. (71) 577-000; fax (71) 567-100; e-mail msp@ministeres.tn; internet www.santetunisie.rns.tn.

Ministry of Public Works and the Environment: blvd de la terre, Centre Urbain Nord, 1080 Tunis; tel. (71) 728-644; fax (71) 728-655; e-mail webmaster@environnement.nat.tn; internet www.environnement.gov.tn.

Ministry of Religious Affairs: 76 ave Bab Benat, 1019 Tunis; tel. (71) 570-147; fax (71) 572-296; e-mail mar@ministeres.tn; internet www.affaires-religieuses.tn.

Ministry of Social Affairs: 27 blvd Bab Benat, 1006 Tunis; tel. (71) 567-502; fax (71) 150-000; e-mail masste@rnas.gov.tn; internet www.social.tn.

Ministry of State Properties and Real Estate Affairs: 19 ave de Paris, 1000 Tunis; tel. (71) 340-265; fax (71) 342-552; e-mail brc@mdeaf.gov.tn; internet www.mdeaf.gov.tn.

Ministry of Tourism: 1 ave Muhammad V, 1001 Tunis; tel. (71) 341-077; fax (71) 354-223; e-mail boc@tourisme.gov.tn; internet www.tourisme.gov.tn.

Ministry of Trade and Handicrafts: Tunis.

Ministry of Transport: ave Muhammad Bouazizi, 2035 Tunis; tel. (71) 772-110; fax (71) 807-203; e-mail mtr@ministeres.tn; internet www.transport.tn.

Ministry of Youth and Sports: ave Med Ali Akid, Cité El Khadhra, 1003 Tunis; tel. (71) 841-433; fax (71) 800-267; e-mail mjsep@sport.tn; internet www.sport.tn.

President and Legislature

PRESIDENT

On 12 December 2011 the National Constituent Assembly elected Moncef Marzouki to serve as interim President of the Republic. Marzouki—a long-standing opponent of former President Zine al-Abidine Ben Ali and leader of the Congrès pour la République party—was sworn into office the following day.

Presidential Election, 25 October 2009

Candidate	Votes	% of votes
Zine al-Abidine Ben Ali	4,238,711	89.62
Muhammad Bouchiha	236,955	5.01
Ahmed Inoubli	176,726	3.80
Ahmed Brahim	74,257	1.57
Total*	**4,729,649**	**100.00**

* Excluding 7,718 invalid votes.

LEGISLATURE

Majlis al-Watani al-Taasisi
(National Constituent Assembly)

Palais du Bardo, 2000 Tunis; tel. (71) 510-200; fax (71) 514-608; e-mail anc@anc.tn; internet www.anc.tn.

President: MUSTAPHA BEN JAÂFAR.

General Election, 23 October 2011

	Seats
Parti de la renaissance/Hizb al-Nahdah	89
Congrès pour la République (CPR)	29
Pétition populaire pour la liberté, la justice et le développement (al-Aridha)	26
Forum démocratique pour le travail et les libertés (Ettakatol)	20
Parti démocrate progressiste (PDP)	16
L'Initiative (al-Moubadara)	5
Pôle démocratique moderniste (al-Qotb)*	5
Afek Tounes	4
Parti communiste des ouvriers tunisiens (PCOT)	3
Movement du peuple (Echaâb)	2
Mouvement des démocrates socialistes (MDS)	2
Others	16
Total	**217**

* Coalition of five civil associations and four parties, led by Mouvement ettajdid.

Political Organizations

Following the removal from office of former President Zine al-Abidine Ben Ali in January 2011, a number of previously outlawed political organizations—including the Islamist Parti de la renaissance/Hizb al-Nahdah—were granted legal status, while several new parties also participated in elections to the National Constituent Assembly held on 23 October.

Congrès pour la République (CPR): 45 rue Ali Dargouth, 1001 Tunis; tel. (71) 346-001; fax (71) 346-002; e-mail cprtunisie@yahoo.fr; internet www.cprtunisie.net; f. 2001; Sec.-Gen. IMAD ALDAIMI.

Forum démocratique pour le travail et les libertés (Ettakatol—FDTL): 4 rue d'Angleterre, 1001 Tunis; tel. and fax (71) 320-258; e-mail contact@fdtl.org; internet www.ettakatol.org; f. 1994; Sec.-Gen. Dr MUSTAPHA BEN JAÂFAR.

L'Initiative (al-Moubadara): Tunis; internet www.almoubadara.tn; f. 2011; Leader KAMEL MORJANE.

Mouvement des démocrates socialistes (MDS): Tunis; in favour of a pluralist political system; participated in 1981 election and was officially recognized in Nov. 1983; 11-mem Political Bureau and 60-mem Nat. Council, normally elected by the party Congress; Sec.-Gen. AHMED KHASKHOUSSI.

Mouvement ettajdid: 7 ave de la liberté, Tunis; tel. (71) 349-307; fax (71) 350-748; internet ettajdid.org; f. 1993 as Mouvement du renouveau, successor to Parti communiste tunisien; leading party in the Pôle démocratique moderniste coalition; Sec.-Gen. AHMAD BRAHIM; Pres. of Nat. Council MUHAMMAD ALI HALOUANI.

Parti de la renaissance/Hizb al-Nahdah: Montplaisir, Tunis; tel. (71) 900-907; fax (71) 901-679; e-mail webmaster@nahdha.tn; internet www.ennahdha.tn; fmrly Mouvement de la tendance islamique (banned in 1981); awarded legal status in March 2011; Islamist-orientated; Leader RACHID GHANNOUCHI; Sec.-Gen. HAMADI JEBALI.

Parti républicain: Tunis; f. 2012 by merger of fmr Parti démocrate progressiste, Afek Tounes and 7 others; centrist; promotes freedom of expression and seeks to uphold democratic process; Sec.-Gen. MAYA JRIBI; Exec. Sec. YASSINE BRAHIM.

Parti social libéral (PSL): 42 ave Hédi Chaker, 1002 Tunis; tel. (71) 789-089; fax (71) 789-060; e-mail p.s.l@gnet.tn; f. 1988; officially recognized in Sept. 1988 as the Parti social pour le progrès; adopted present name in 1993; liberal; Pres. Dr MONDHER THABET.

Parti des travailleurs tunisiens (POT): Tunis; e-mail pcot@albadil.org; internet www.albadil.org; f. 1986; as Parti communiste des ouvriers tunisiens; name changed as above 2012; legalized 2011; Sec.-Gen. HAMMA HAMMAMI.

Parti de l'unité populaire (PUP): 7 rue d'Autriche, 1002 Tunis; tel. (71) 791-436; fax (71) 835-152; internet www.elwahda.org.tn; breakaway faction from Mouvement de l'unité populaire; officially recognized in Nov. 1983; Sec.-Gen. HASSINE HAMMAMI.

Parti des verts pour le progrès (PVP): 2 ave de France, bureau 335, 3ème étage, 1000 Tunis; tel. (71) 328-439; fax (71) 328-438; e-mail contact@partivert-tunisie.com; internet www

.partivert-tunisie.com; f. 2006; seeks to promote awareness of the environment; Sec.-Gen. MONGI KHAMASSI.

Pétition populaire pour la liberté, la justice et le développement (al-Aridha): Tunis; f. 2011; key demands include formation of a democratic constitution, adoption of a system of free health care and dispensation of grants to the unemployed; Leader MUHAMMAD HECHMI HAMDI.

Pôle démocratique moderniste (PDM) (al-Qotb): Tunis; internet www.pole.tn; f. 2011; coalition of 5 civil associations and 4 parties, led by Mouvement ettajdid; Leaders RIADH BEN FADL, MUSTAPHA BEN AHMED.

Union démocratique unioniste (UDU): Tunis; officially recognized in Nov. 1988; supports Arab unity; Sec.-Gen. AHMED INOUBLI.

Diplomatic Representation

EMBASSIES IN TUNISIA

Algeria: 18 rue de Niger, 1002 Tunis; tel. (71) 783-166; fax (71) 788-804; e-mail ambalg@gnet.tn; Ambassador ABD EL-KADER HADJAR.

Argentina: rue du Lac Victoria, BP 12, 1053 Tunis; tel. (71) 964-871; fax (71) 963-006; e-mail etune@mrecic.gov.ar; Ambassador SERGIO ALBERTO BAUR.

Austria: 16 rue ibn Hamdiss, BP 23, al-Menzah, 1004 Tunis; tel. (71) 239-038; fax (71) 755-427; e-mail tunis-ob@bmeia.gv.at; Ambassador Dr GERHARD WEINBERGER.

Bahrain: 72 Mouaouia ibn Soufiane Ave, Almanzah Althamen, 2037 Tunis; tel. (71) 750-865; fax (71) 766-549; e-mail tunis.mission@mofa.gov.bh; Ambassador Sheikh MUHAMMAD BIN ALI BIN HAMAD AL KHALIFA.

Belgium: 47 rue du 1er juin, BP 24, 1002 Tunis; tel. (71) 781-655; fax (71) 792-797; e-mail tunis@diplobel.fed.be; internet www.diplomatie.be/tunis; Ambassador PATRICK DE BEYTER.

Brazil: rue du Lac Léman, Les Berges du Lac, BP 93, 1053 Tunis; tel. (71) 965-455; fax (71) 846-995; e-mail brasemb.tunis@gnet.tn; internet www.ambassadedubresil.com; Ambassador LUIZ ANTONIO FACHINI GOMES.

Bulgaria: 5 rue Ryhane, BP 6, Cité Mahragène, 1082 Tunis; tel. (71) 798-962; fax (71) 791-667; e-mail embassy.tunis@mfa.bg; internet www.mfa.bg/embassies/tunisia; Ambassador MIHAIL NIKOLOVSKI.

Canada: rue de la Feuille d'Erable, Les Berges du Lac II, BP 48, 1053 Tunis; tel. (71) 010-200; fax (71) 010-393; e-mail tunis@international.gc.ca; internet www.canadainternational.gc.ca/tunisia-tunisie; Ambassador SÉBASTIEN BEAULIEU.

China, People's Republic: 22 rue Dr Burnet, 1002 Tunis; tel. (71) 780-064; fax (71) 792-631; e-mail chinaemb_tn@mfa.gov.cn; internet tn.china-embassy.org; Ambassador HUO ZHENGDE.

Congo, Democratic Republic: 11 rue Tertullien, Notre Dame, Tunis; tel. (71) 281-833; Ambassador MBOLADINGA KATAKO.

Côte d'Ivoire: 17 rue el-Mansoura, BP 21, Belvédère, 1002 Tunis; tel. (71) 755-911; fax (71) 755-901; e-mail acitn@ambaci-tunis.org; Ambassador YAPO ATCHAPO THOMAS.

Cuba: 1 rue Amilcar, al-Menzah VIII, 1004 Tunis; tel. (71) 767-235; fax (71) 755-922; e-mail embajador-tunez@topnet.tn; internet emba.cubaminrex.cu/tunezar; Ambassador (vacant).

Czech Republic: 98 rue de Palestine, BP 53, Belvédère, 1002 Tunis; tel. (71) 781-916; fax (71) 793-228; e-mail tunis@embassy.mzv.cz; internet www.mzv.cz/tunis; Ambassador ALEXANDR SLABÝ.

Egypt: ave Muhammad V, Quartier Montplaisir, no 8007, Tunis; tel. (71) 792-233; fax (71) 794-389; e-mail egyembassy.tunis@planet.tn; Ambassador AYMEN JAMELEDDINE ABD EL-FATTEH MACHRAFA.

Finland: Dar Nordique, rue du Lac Neuchâtel, Les Berges du Lac, 1053 Tunis; tel. (71) 861-777; fax (71) 961-080; e-mail sanomat.tun@formin.fi; internet www.finlandtunis.org; Ambassador TIINA JORTIKKA-LAITINEN.

France: 2 pl. de l'Indépendance, 1000 Tunis; tel. (71) 105-111; fax (71) 105-100; e-mail courier@ambassadefrance-tn.org; internet www.ambassadefrance-tn.org; Ambassador FRANÇOIS GOUYETTE.

Germany: 1 rue al-Hamra, BP 35, Mutuelleville, 1002 Tunis; tel. (71) 143-200; fax (71) 788-242; e-mail reg1@tunis.diplo.de; internet www.tunis.diplo.de; Ambassador JENS UWE PLÖTNER.

Greece: 6 rue Saint Fulgence, Notre Dame, 1082 Tunis; tel. (71) 288-411; fax (71) 285-849; e-mail gremb.tun@mfa.gr; internet www.mfa.gr/tunis; Ambassador THEODORA GROSOMANIDOU.

Hungary: 12 rue Achtart, BP 572, Nord Hilton, 1082 Tunis; tel. (71) 780-544; fax (71) 781-246; e-mail mission.tun@kum.hu; internet www.mfa.gov.hu/emb/tunis; Ambassador GYÖRGY PÁNTOS.

India: 4 pl. Didon, Notre Dame, 1002 Tunis; tel. (71) 787-819; fax (71) 783-394; e-mail amb.tunis@mea.gov.in; internet www.indianembassytunis.com; Ambassador NAGMA MUHAMMAD MALLICK.

Indonesia: 15 rue du Lac Malaren, BP 58, 1053 Tunis; tel. (71) 860-377; fax (71) 861-758; e-mail kbritun@gnet.tn; Ambassador MOHAMMAD IBNU SAID.

Iran: 10 rue de Docteur Burnet, Belvédère, 1002 Tunis; tel. (71) 790-084; fax (71) 793-177; Ambassador Dr PEIMAN DJEBELLI.

Iraq: ave Tahar B. Achour, route X2 m 10, Mutuelleville, Tunis; tel. (71) 965-824; fax (71) 964-750; e-mail tunemb@iraqmofamail.net; Ambassador SAAD JASSEM AL-HAYANI.

Italy: 37 rue Gamal Abd al-Nasser, 1000 Tunis; tel. (71) 321-811; fax (71) 324-155; e-mail ambitalia.tunisi@esteri.it; internet www.ambtunisi.esteri.it; Ambassador PIETRO BENASSI.

Japan: 9 rue Apollo XI, BP 163, Cité Mahrajène, 1082 Tunis; tel. (71) 791-251; fax (71) 786-625; e-mail eoj.tunis@tn.mofa.go.jp; internet www.tn.emb-japan.go.jp; Ambassador JUICHI TAKAHARA.

Jordan: 10 Nahj al-Shankiti, 1002 Tunis; tel. (71) 785-829; fax (71) 786-461; e-mail emb.jordan@planet.tn; Ambassador ZUHEIR DMOUR.

Korea, Republic: 3 rue de l'Alhambra, BP 297, Mutuelleville, 1002 Tunis; tel. (71) 799-905; fax (71) 791-923; e-mail tunisie@mofat.go.kr; internet tun.mofat.go.kr; Ambassador JOO BOK-RYONG.

Kuwait: 40 route Ariane, al-Menzah, Tunis; tel. (71) 754-811; fax (71) 767-659; e-mail tunis@mofa.gov.kw; Ambassador FAHAD AL-AWADHI.

Lebanon: rue d'Ormia, 1053 Les Berges du Lac, Tunis; tel. and fax (71) 960-001; e-mail ambassadeliban@planet.tn; Ambassador FARID ABBOUD.

Libya: 48 bis rue du 1er juin, Mutuelleville, 1002 Tunis; tel. (71) 780-866; fax (71) 795-338; Ambassador JEMAL JARNAZ.

Mali: 3 impasse Aboul Atahya, rue Dr Burnet, Mutueville, 1002 Tunis; BP 109, Cité Mahrajène, 1082 Tunis; tel. (71) 792-589; fax (71) 791-453; e-mail ambamali@planet.tn; Ambassador (vacant).

Malta: Immeuble Carthage Centre, rue du Lac de Constance, BP 71, Les Berges du Lac, Tunis; tel. (71) 965-811; fax (71) 965-977; e-mail maltaembassy.tunis@gov.mt; Ambassador Dr VICTORIA ANN CREMONA.

Mauritania: 17 rue Fatma Ennechi, BP 62, al-Menzah, Tunis; tel. (71) 234-935; Ambassador MAHFOUDH OULD MUHAMMAD AHMED.

Morocco: 39 rue du 1er juin, Mutuelle Ville, 1002 Tunis; tel. (71) 782-775; fax (71) 787-103; e-mail ambamaroc@sifamatunis.net; Ambassador MUHAMMAD FARAJ DOUKKALI.

Netherlands: 6–8 rue Meycen, Cité Mahrajène, 1082 Tunis; tel. (71) 155-300; fax (71) 155-330; e-mail tun@minbuza.nl; internet tunesie.nlambassade.org; Ambassador JOHANNES GERARDUS VAN VLOTEN DISSEVELT.

Pakistan: 35 rue Ali Ayari, al-Menzah 9A, Tunis; tel. (71) 871-330; fax (71) 871-410; e-mail pareptunis@yahoo.com; Ambassador MUSHTAQ ALI SHAH.

Poland: Le Grand Blvd de la Corniche, 2045 Les Berges du Lac II, Tunis; tel. (71) 196-193; fax (71) 196-203; e-mail tunis.amb.sekretariat@msz.gov.pl; internet www.tunis.polemb.net; Chargé d'affaires a.i. IWO BYCZEWSKI.

Portugal: 2 rue Sufétula, Belvédère, 1002 Tunis; tel. (71) 893-981; fax (71) 791-008; e-mail ambport@hexabyte.tn; Ambassador LUIS FARO RAMOS.

Qatar: rue Alhadi Krai, Northern al-Omran Quarter, 1082 Tunis; tel. (71) 849-600; fax (71) 749-073; e-mail tunis.amb@mofa.gov.qa; internet www.qatarembassy.tn; Ambassador SAAD BIN NASSER AL-HUMAIDI.

Romania: 18 ave d'Afrique, BP 57, al-Menzah V, 1004 Tunis; tel. (71) 766-926; fax (71) 767-695; e-mail ambroum@planet.tn; internet tunis.mae.ro; Ambassador NICOLAE NÄSTASE.

Russia: 4 rue Bergamotes, BP 48, el-Manar I, 2092 Tunis; tel. (71) 882-446; fax (71) 882-478; e-mail ambrustn@mail.ru; internet www.tunisie.mid.ru; Ambassador ALEKSANDR P. SHENI.

Saudi Arabia: ave Muhammad Bouazizi, Centre Urbain Nord C, Mahrajène, 1080 Tunis; tel. (71) 233-466; fax (71) 751-441; Ambassador Dr KHALED BIN MUSAID AL-ANQARI.

Senegal: BP 22, Belvédère, 1002 Tunis; tel. (71) 802-397; fax (71) 780-770; e-mail ambassene@planet.tn; internet www.ambasenegal.intl.tn; Ambassador MOUHAMADOU DOUDOU LO.

Serbia: 4 rue de Libéria, Belvédère, 1002 Tunis; tel. (71) 783-057; fax (71) 796-482; e-mail amb.serbia@gnet.tn; Ambassador MILICA CUBRILO FILIPOVIĆ.

Somalia: 6 rue Hadramout, Mutuelleville, Tunis; tel. (71) 289-505; Ambassador AHMAD ABDALLAH MUHAMMAD.

South Africa: 7 rue Achtart, Nord Hilton, BP 251, 1082 Tunis; tel. (71) 800-311; fax (71) 796-742; e-mail sa@emb-safrica.intl.tn; internet www.southafrica.intl.tn; Ambassador NONCEBA NANCY LOSI-TUTU.

Spain: 24 ave Dr Ernest Conseil, Cité Jardin, 1002 Tunis; tel. (71) 782-217; fax (71) 786-267; e-mail emb.tunez@maec.es; Ambassador ANTONIO COSANO PÉREZ.

Sudan: 37 rue d'Afrique, al-Menzah V, 1008 Tunis; tel. (71) 231-322; fax (71) 751-756; e-mail contact@soudanembassy-tn.com; Ambassador FADHEL ABDALLAH FADL IDRISS.

Switzerland: BP 56, Les Berges du Lac, 1053 Tunis; tel. (71) 962-997; fax (71) 965-796; e-mail tun.vertretung@eda.admin.ch; internet www.eda.admin.ch/tunis; Ambassador PIERRE COMBERNOUS.

Syria: 119 Azzouz Ribai-Almanar 3, Tunis; tel. (71) 888-188; Ambassador (vacant).

Turkey: 4 ave Hédi Karay, Centre Urbain Nord, BP 134, 1082 Tunis; tel. (71) 132-300; fax (71) 767-045; e-mail ambassade.tunis@mfa.gov.tr; internet tunis.emb.mfa.gov.tr; Ambassador ÖMER GÜCÜK.

Ukraine: 7 rue Saint Fulgence, Notre Dame, 1002 Tunis; tel. (71) 845-861; fax (71) 840-866; e-mail emb_tn@mfa.gov.ua; internet www.mfa.gov.ua/tunis; Ambassador VALERII RYLACH.

United Arab Emirates: 9 rue Achtart, Nord Hilton, Belvédère, 1002 Tunis; tel. (71) 788-888; fax (71) 788-777; e-mail media.tunis@mofa.gov.ae; Ambassador ABDULLAH IBRAHIM GHANIM SULTAN AL-SUWAIDI.

United Kingdom: rue du Lac Windermere, Les Berges du Lac, 1053 Tunis; tel. (71) 108-700; fax (71) 108-749; e-mail british.embassy@planet.tn; internet ukintunisia.fco.gov.uk; Ambassador CHRISTOPHER PAUL O'CONNOR.

USA: Les Berges du Lac, 1053 Tunis; tel. (71) 107-000; fax (71) 963-263; e-mail tuniswebsitecontact@state.gov; internet tunisia.usembassy.gov; Ambassador JACOB WALLES.

Yemen: rue Mouaouia ibn Soufiane, al-Menzah VI, Tunis; tel. (71) 237-933; Ambassador HUSSEIN DHAIFULLAH AL-AWADHI.

Judicial System

The **Cour de Cassation** in Tunis has three civil and one criminal sections. There are three **Cours d'Appel** at Tunis, Sousse and Sfax, and 13 **Cours de Première Instance**, each having three chambers, except the **Cour de Première Instance** at Tunis, which has eight chambers. **Justices Cantonales** exist in 51 areas.

Religion

The Constitution of 1959 recognizes Islam as the state religion, with the introduction of certain reforms, such as the abolition of polygamy. An estimated 99% of the population are Muslims. Minority religions include Judaism (an estimated 1,500 adherents in 2008) and Christianity. The Christian population comprises Roman Catholics, Greek Orthodox, and French and English Protestants.

ISLAM

Grand Mufti of Tunisia: Sheikh KAMAL AL-DIN JA'EIT.

CHRISTIANITY

The Roman Catholic Church

There were an estimated 20,500 adherents in Tunisia in December 2007.

Archbishop of Tunis: Most Rev. MAROUN ELIAS LAHHAM, Evêché, 4 rue d'Alger, 1000 Tunis; tel. (71) 335-831; fax (71) 335-832; e-mail eveche.tunisie@evechetunisie.org; internet www.diocesetunisie.org.

The Protestant Church

Reformed Church of Tunisia: 36 rue Charles de Gaulle, 1000 Tunis; tel. (71) 327-886; e-mail eglisereformee@yahoo.fr; f. 1880; c. 220 mems; Pastor WILLIAM BROWN.

The Press

DAILIES

Al-Chourouk (Sunrise): 25 rue Jean Jaurès, BP 36619, Tunis; tel. (71) 331-000; fax (71) 253-024; e-mail directiongenerale@alchourouk.com; internet www.alchourouk.com; Arabic; Dir SLAHEDDINE AL-AMRI; Editor-in-Chief ABD AL-HAMID RIAHI; circ. 70,000.

Essahafa: 6 rue Ali Bach-Hamba, 1000 Tunis; tel. (71) 341-066; fax (71) 349-720; e-mail contact@essahafa.info.tn; internet www.essahafa.info.tn; f. 1936; Arabic; Editor-in-Chief NEJI ABBASSI.

La Presse de Tunisie: 6 rue Ali Bach-Hamba, 1000 Tunis; tel. (71) 341-066; fax (71) 349-720; e-mail contact@lapresse.tn; internet www.lapresse.tn; f. 1936; French; Editors-in-Chief MONGI GHARBI, FAOUZIA MEZZI; circ. 40,000.

Le Quotidien: 25 rue Jean Jaurès, 1000 Tunis; tel. (71) 331-000; fax (71) 253-02; e-mail directiongenerale@lequotidien-tn.com; internet www.lequotidien-tn.com; f. 2001; French; Dir SLAHEDDINE AL-AMRI; Editor-in-Chief CHOUKRY BAKOUCHE; circ. 20,000.

As-Sabah (The Morning): ave Muhammad Bouazizi, BP 441, al-Menzah, 1004 Tunis; tel. (71) 238-222; fax (71) 232-761; e-mail redaction@assabah.com.tn; internet www.assabah.com.tn; f. 1951; Arabic; Dir MUSTAPHA AL-JABER; Editor-in-Chief NOUREDDINE ACHOUR; circ. 30,000.

Le Temps: ave Muhammad Bouazizi, al-Menzah, 1004 Tunis; tel. (71) 238-222; fax (71) 232-761; e-mail redaction@letemps.com.tn; internet www.letemps.com.tn; f. 1975; French; Dir MUSTAPHA AL-JABER; Editor-in-Chief RAOUF KHALSI; circ. 42,000.

Tunisia Live: 17 rue Charles de Gaulle, Tunis; tel. (71) 324-703; e-mail contact@tunisialive.net; internet www.tunisia-live.net; f. 2011; English; online only; Founders RAMLA JABER, YOUSSEF GAIGI, ZIED MHIRSI.

PERIODICALS

Afrique Economie: 16 rue de Rome, BP 61, 1015 Tunis; tel. (71) 347-441; fax (71) 353-172; e-mail iea@planet.tn; f. 1970; monthly; Dir MUHAMMAD ZERZERI.

Al-Akhbar (The News): 1 passage d'al-Houdaybiyah, 1000 Tunis; tel. (71) 344-100; fax (71) 355-079; internet www.akhbar.tn; f. 1984; weekly; Arabic; general; Dir MUHAMMAD BEN YOUSUF; circ. 75,000.

Al-Anouar al-Tounissia (Tunisian Lights): 25 rue al-Cham, 5000 Tunis; tel. (71) 331-000; fax (71) 253-024; internet www.alanouar.com; Arabic; Dir SLAHEDDINE AL-AMRI; circ. 165,000.

Attariq al-Jadid (New Road): 6 rue Metouia, 1069 Tunis; tel. (71) 256-400; fax (71) 240-981; internet www.attariq.org; f. 1981; weekly; Arabic; organ of the Mouvement ettajdid; Editor-in-Chief HATEM CHAÂBOUNI.

Al-Bayan (The Manifesto): 61 rue Abderrazek, Chraïbi, 1001 Tunis; tel. (71) 339-633; fax (71) 338-533; e-mail darelbayane@gnet.tn; f. 1976; weekly; general; organ of the Union tunisienne de l'industrie, du commerce et de l'artisanat; Dir HÉDI DJILANI; circ. 100,000.

Al-Biladi (My Country): 15 rue 2 mars 1934, Tunis; f. 1974; Arabic; political and general weekly for Tunisian workers abroad; Dir HÉDI AL-GHALI; circ. 90,000.

Bulletin Mensuel de Statistiques: Institut National de la Statistique, 70 rue al-Cham, BP 265, 1080 Tunis; tel. (71) 891-002; fax (71) 792-559; e-mail ins@mdci.gov.tn; internet www.ins.nat.tn; monthly.

Conjoncture: 37 ave Kheireddine Pacha, 1002 Tunis; tel. (71) 891-826; fax (71) 200-706; e-mail conjoncture2003@yahoo.fr; f. 1974; monthly; economic and financial surveys; Dir HABIB BEDHIAFI; circ. 5,000.

Démocratie: Tunis; f. 1978; monthly; French; organ of the MDS; Dir HASSIB BEN AMMAR; circ. 5,000.

Echaâb: 41 ave Ali Dargouth, 1001 Tunis; tel. (71) 255-020; fax (71) 355-139; e-mail journal.echaab@planet.tn; internet www.echaab.info.tn; weekly; Dirs HUSSAIN ABBASI, SAMI TAHIRI.

L'Economiste Maghrébin: 3 rue el-Kewekibi, 1002 Tunis; tel. (71) 790-773; fax (71) 793-707; e-mail info@leconomistemaghrebin.com; internet www.leconomiste.com.tn; f. 1990; bi-weekly; French; Dir HÉDI MÉCHRI; circ. 30,000.

L'Expert: 69 rue Echam, 1002 Tunis; tel. (71) 784-970; fax (71) 794-130; internet www.lexpertjournal.com.tn.

El-Fallah: 8451 rue Alain Savary, al-Khadra, 1003 Tunis; tel. (71) 806-800; fax (71) 809-181; e-mail utap.tunis@email.ati.tn; internet www.utap.org.tn; weekly; organ of the Union tunisienne de l'agriculture et de la pêche (UTAP); Dir MABROUK BAHRI; Editor GHARBI HAMOUDA; circ. 7,000.

L'Hebdo Touristique: rue 8601, 40, Zone Industrielle, La Charguia 2, 2035 Tunis; tel. (71) 786-866; fax (71) 794-891; e-mail haddad.tijani@planet.tn; f. 1971; weekly; French; tourism; Dir TIJANI HADDAD; circ. 5,000.

IBLA: Institut des Belles Lettres Arabes, 12 rue Jemaâ el-Haoua, 1008 Tunis; tel. (71) 560-133; fax (71) 572-683; e-mail ibla@gnet.tn; internet www.iblatunis.org; f. 1937; 2 a year; French, Arabic and English; social and cultural review on Maghreb and Muslim-Arab affairs; Dir JEAN FONTAINE; circ. 600.

Irfane (Children): 6 rue Muhammad Ali, 1000 Tunis; tel. (71) 256-877; fax (71) 351-521; f. 1965; monthly; Arabic; Dir-Gen. RIDHA EL-OUADI; circ. 100,000.

Jeunesse Magazine: 6 rue Muhammad Ali, 1000 Tunis; tel. (71) 256-877; fax (71) 351-521; f. 1980; monthly; Arabic; Dir-Gen. RIDHA EL-OUADI; circ. 30,000.

Journal Les Annonces: 6 rue de Sparte, BP 1343, Tunis; tel. (71) 350-177; fax (71) 347-184; e-mail nejib.azouz@planet.tn; internet www.elilane.com; f. 1978; 2 a week; French and Arabic; Dir MUHAMMAD NEJIB AZOUZ; circ. 170,000.

Journal Officiel de la République Tunisienne: ave Farhat Hached, 2040 Radès; tel. (71) 299-914; fax (71) 297-234; f. 1860; official gazette; Arabic and French; 2 a week; publ. by Imprimerie Officielle (State Press); Pres. and Dir-Gen. ROMDHANE BEN MIMOUN; circ. 20,000.

Al-Mawkif: 10 rue Eve Nohelle, 1001 Tunis; tel. (71) 332-271; fax (71) 332-194; e-mail mawkef_21@yahoo.fr; f. 1984; weekly; organ of the Parti démocrate progressiste; Man. Dir AHMED NÉJIB CHEBBI; Editor-in-Chief RACHID KHECHANA.

Al-Moussawar: 10 rue al-Cham, Tunis; tel. (71) 289-000; fax (71) 289-357; internet www.almoussawar.com; weekly; circ. 75,000.

Mouwatinoun (Citizens): Tunis; internet www.fdtl.org; f. 2007; weekly; Arabic; organ of the Forum démocratique pour le travail et les libertés (FDTL).

Réalités: 6–7 rue de Cameroun, 1002 Tunis; tel. (71) 893-489; fax (71) 787-160; e-mail redaction@realites.com.tn; internet www.realites.com.tn; f. 1979; weekly; Arabic and French; Dir TAÏEB ZAHAR; Editor-in-Chief ZYED KRICHEN; circ. 25,000.

Tounes el Khadra: 8451 rue Alain Savary, al-Khadra, 1003 Tunis; tel. (71) 806-800; fax (71) 809-181; e-mail utap.tunis@email.ati.tn; internet www.utap.org.tn; f. 1976; bi-monthly; agricultural, scientific and technical; organ of the UTAP; Dir MABROUK BAHRI; Editor GHARBI HAMOUDA; circ. 5,000.

Tunis Hebdo: 1 passage d'al-Houdaybiyah, 1000 Tunis; tel. (71) 344-100; fax (71) 355-079; e-mail tunishebdo@tunishebdo.com.tn; internet www.tunishebdo.com.tn; f. 1973; weekly; French; general and sport; Dir and Editor-in-Chief MUHAMMAD BEN YOUSUF; circ. 35,000.

NEWS AGENCY

Tunis Afrique Presse (TAP): 7 ave Slimane Ben Slimane, al-Manar, 2092 Tunis; tel. (71) 889-000; fax (71) 883-500; e-mail dg.tap@tap.info.tn; internet www.tap.info.tn; f. 1961; Arabic, French and English; offices in Algiers (Algeria), Rabat (Morocco), Paris (France) and New York (USA); daily news services; Pres. and Man. Dir MUHAMMAD TAIEB YOUSEFFI.

Publishers

Al-Dar al-Arabia Lil Kitab: 4 ave Mohieddine el-Klibi, BP 32, al-Manar 2, 2092 Tunis; tel. (71) 888-255; fax (71) 888-365; e-mail mal@gnet.tn; f. 1975; general literature, children's books, non-fiction; Chief Officer LOTFI BEN MBAREK.

Centre de Publications Universitaires: Campus Universitaire, BP 255, 1080 Tunis; tel. (71) 874-000; fax (71) 871-677; e-mail cpu@cpu.rnu.tn; internet www.mes.tn/cpu; educational books, journals.

Cérès Editions: 6 rue Alain Savary, Belvédère, 1002 Tunis; tel. (71) 280-505; fax (71) 287-216; e-mail info@ceres-editions.com; internet www.ceres-editions.com; f. 1964; social sciences, art books, literature, novels; Man. Editor KARIM BEN SMAÏL.

Dar Cheraït: Centre Culturel et Touristique Dar Cheraït, Route Touristique, 2200 Tozeur; tel. (76) 452-100; fax (76) 452-329; e-mail darcherait@planet.tn; internet www.darcherait.com.tn.

Dar al-Kitab: 5 ave Bourguiba, 4000 Sousse; tel. (73) 25097; f. 1950; literature, children's books, legal studies, foreign books; Pres. TAÏEB KACEM; Dir FAYÇAL KACEM.

Dar as-Sabah: ave Muhammad Bouazizi, BP 441, al-Menzah, 1004 Tunis; tel. (71) 717-222; fax (71) 232-761; e-mail redaction@assabah.com.tn; internet www.assabah.com.tn; f. 1951; 200 mems; publishes daily and weekly papers, including the dailies *As-Sabah* and *Le Temps*, which circulate throughout Tunisia, North Africa, France, Belgium, Luxembourg and Germany; Chair. MUHAMMAD SAKHER EL MATERI; Dir-Gen. MUSTAPHA al-JABER.

Editions Apollonia: 4 rue Claude Bernard, 1002 Tunis; tel. (71) 786-381; fax (71) 799-190; e-mail apolloniaeditions@gmail.com; internet www.apollonia.com.tn; art, literature, essays, poetry.

Editions Bouslama: 15 ave de France, 1000 Tunis; tel. (71) 240-056; fax (71) 381-100; f. 1960; history, children's books; Man. Dir ALI BOUSLAMA.

Institut National de la Statistique: 70 rue al-Cham, BP 265, 1080 Tunis; tel. (71) 891-002; fax (71) 792-559; e-mail ins@mdci.gov.tn; internet www.ins.nat.tn; publishes a variety of annuals, periodicals and papers concerned with the economic policy and devt of Tunisia.

Librairie al-Manar: 60 ave Bab Djedid, BP 179, 1008 Tunis; tel. (71) 253-224; fax (71) 336-565; e-mail librairie.almanar@planet.tn; f. 1938; general, educational, Islam; Man. Dir HABIB M'HAMDI.

Société d'Arts Graphiques, d'Edition et de Presse (SAGEP): 15 rue 2 mars 1934, La Kasbah, 1000 Tunis; tel. (71) 564-988; fax (71) 569-736; f. 1974; prints and publishes daily papers, magazines, books, etc.; Dir-Gen. MAHMOUD MEFTAH.

Sud Editions: 79 rue de Palestine, 1002 Tunis; tel. (71) 785-179; fax (71) 848-664; e-mail sud.editions@planet.tn; f. 1976; Arab literature, art and art history, history, sociology, religion; Man. Dir MUHAMMAD MASMOUDI.

GOVERNMENT PUBLISHING HOUSE

Imprimerie Officielle de la République Tunisienne: 40 ave Farhat Hached, 2098 Radès; tel. (71) 434-211; fax (71) 434-234; e-mail iort@iort.gov.tn; internet www.iort.gov.tn; f. 1860; Pres. and Dir-Gen. AHMED ZARROUK.

Broadcasting and Communications

TELECOMMUNICATIONS

Orange Tunisie: rue du Lac de Côme, Les Berges du Lac, 1053 Tunis; tel. (71) 167-900; fax (71) 961-808; internet www.orange.tn; f. 2010; launched mobile telephone network in May 2010; 49% stake owned by France Télécom; Chair. MARWAN MABROUK.

Orascom Telecom Tunisia (Tunisiana): Immeuble Zénith, Les Jardins du Lac, 1053 Tunis; tel. (22) 120-000; e-mail servicerp@tunisiana.com; internet www.tunisiana.com; f. 2002; Chair. TAWFIQ JELASSI; CEO KENNETH CAMPBELL.

Société Tunisienne d'Entreprises de Télécommunications (SOTETEL): rue des Entrepreneurs, Zone Industrielle, BP 640, La Charguia 2, 1080 Tunis; tel. (71) 941-100; fax (71) 940-584; e-mail contact@sotetel.net; internet www.sotetel.net; f. 1981; privatized in 1998; Pres. ALI GHODBANI; Dir-Gen. JAMEL MHEDHBI.

Tunisie Télécom: Jardins du Lac II, 1053 Tunis; tel. (71) 901-717; fax (71) 900-777; e-mail actel.virtuelle@ttnet.tn; internet www.tunisietelecom.tn; 65% state-owned, 35% owned by Tecom-Dig (Dubai, United Arab Emirates); CEO RAOUF CHKIR.

Regulatory Authority

Instance Nationale des Télécommunications (INT): Rue Echabia, Montplaisir, 1073 Tunis; tel. (71) 900-868; fax (71) 909-435; e-mail contact@intt.tn; internet www.intt.tn; f. 2001; Pres. KAMEL SAADAOUI.

BROADCASTING

Office National de la Télédiffusion (ONT) (National Broadcasting Corporation of Tunisia): Cité Ennassim 1, Montplaisir, BP 399, 1080 Tunis; tel. (71) 908-177; fax (71) 904-923; e-mail ont@telediffusion.net.tn; internet www.telediffusion.net.tn; f. 1993; supervision and management of the radio and television broadcasting networks.

Radio

Etablissement de la Radiodiffusion Tunisienne: 71 ave de la Liberté, 1002 Tunis; tel. (71) 847-300; fax (71) 780-993; e-mail portail@radiotunisienne.tn; internet www.radiotunisienne.tn; govt service; originally merged with Télévision Tunisienne; became independent 2006; broadcasts in Arabic, French, German, Italian, Spanish and English; radio stations at Gafsa, El-Kef, Monastir, Sfax, Tataouine and Tunis (3); television stations Tunis 7 and Canal 21; Pres. and Man. Dir MUHAMMAD MEDDEB.

Express FM: 1 rue Monastir 2045, l'Aouina Tunis; tel. (71) 760-769; e-mail contact@expressfm.tn; internet www.radioexpressfm.com; f. 2010; Gen. Man. NAJOUA RAHOUI.

Jawhara FM: rue des Orangers, Khzema Est, BP 120, 4051 Sousse; tel. (73) 275-800; fax (73) 275-810; e-mail direction@jawharafm.net; internet www.jawharafm.net; Dir Gen. ALI BELHAJ YOUSSEF.

Mosaïque FM: Tunis; tel. (71) 287-246; e-mail dg@mosaiquefm.net; internet www.mosaiquefm.net; f. 2003; first privately owned radio station when launched in 2003; broadcasts in Arabic and French to Tunis and the north-east of the country; Dir-Gen. NOUREDDINE BOUTAR.

Shems FM: 5 rue du Lac d'Annecy, Les Berges du Lac, Tunis; tel. (71) 167-070; e-mail contact@shemsfm.net; internet www.shemsfm.net; f. 2010; Dir-Gen. FATHI BHOURY.

Zitouna FM: 61 ave Habib Bourguiba, 2016 Carthage Hannibal; internet www.zitounafm.net; f. 2007.

Television

Etablissement de la Télévision Tunisienne: ave de la Ligue des Etats Arabes, Notre Dame, 1030 Tunis; e-mail info@tunisiatv.com; internet www.tunisie7.tn; formerly merged with Radiodiffusion Tunisienne; became independent 2006; Pres. and Man. Dir ADNENE KHEDR.

Hannibal TV: 85 ave du 13 Août, Choutrana II, Soukra, 2036 Tunis; e-mail contact@hannibaltv.com; internet www.hannibaltv.com.tn; f. 2005; privately owned channel; CEO LARBI NASRA.

Nessma TV: 14, rue 8006, Montplaisir, 1073 Tunis; tel. (71) 909-222; fax (71) 893-503; e-mail communication@nessmatv.tv; internet www.nessma.tv; f. 2009; covers Maghreb region; 50% owned by Karoui Group and rest by Quinta Communication and Mediaset Group; Pres. and CEO NABIL KAROUI.

Finance

(cap. = capital; dep. = deposits; res = reserves; m. = million; br(s) = branch(es); amounts in dinars, unless otherwise stated)

BANKING

Central Bank

Banque Centrale de Tunisie (BCT): 25 rue Hédi Nouira, BP 777, 1080 Tunis; tel. (71) 340-588; fax (71) 354-214; e-mail boc@bct.gov.tn; internet www.bct.gov.tn; f. 1958; cap. 6m., res 90m., dep. 5,752m. (Dec. 2009); Gov. CHÉDLI AYARI; 12 brs.

Commercial Banks

Amen Bank: ave Muhammad V, 1002 Tunis; tel. (71) 835-500; fax (71) 833-517; e-mail amenbank@amenbank.com.tn; internet www.amenbank.com.tn; f. 1967 as Crédit Foncier et Commercial de Tunisie; name changed as above in 1995; cap. 100m., res 241m., dep. 3,783m. (Dec. 2010); Chair. RACHID BEN YEDDER; Gen. Man. AHMAD EL-KARM; 81 brs.

Arab Banking Corpn Tunisie (ABC Tunisie): Immeuble ABC, rue du Lac d'Annecy, Les Berges du Lac, 1053 Tunis; tel. (71) 861-861; fax (71) 860-921; e-mail abc.tunis@arabbanking.com; internet www.arabbanking.com; f. 2000; cap. 50m., res −22m., dep. 189m. (Dec. 2009); Chair. MUHAMMAD HUSSAIN LAYAS; Pres. and Chief Exec. HASSAN ALI JUMA; 4 brs.

Arab Tunisian Bank: 9 rue Hédi Nouira, BP 520, 1001 Tunis; tel. (71) 351-155; fax (71) 342-852; e-mail atbbank@atb.com.tn; internet www.atb.com.tn; f. 1982; 64.2% owned by Arab Bank PLC (Jordan); cap. 100m., res 260m., dep. 2,926m. (Dec. 2010); Pres. Dr SAMAR EL-MOLLA; Dir-Gen. MUHAMMAD FERID BEN TANFOUS; 107 brs.

Attijari Bank: 14 ave de la Liberté, Tunis; tel. (71) 141-400; fax (71) 782-663; e-mail courrier@attijaribank.com.tn; internet www.attijaribank.com.tn; f. 1968 as Banque du Sud; present name adopted 2006; 37.11% owned by Attijariwafa bank (Morocco), 17.46% by Banco Santander (Spain); cap. 168m., res 102m., dep. 3,465m. (Dec. 2010); Pres. MONCEF CHAFFAR; CEO MUHAMMAD EL-KETTANI; Dir-Gen. HICHAM SEFFA; 93 brs.

Banque de l'Habitat: 21 ave Kheireddine Pacha, BP 242, 1002 Tunis; tel. (71) 001-800; fax (71) 951-048; e-mail banquehabitat@bh.fin.tn; internet www.bh.com.tn; f. 1984; 32.62% govt-owned; cap. 89m., res 312m., dep. 3,436m. (Dec. 2010); CEO BRAHIM HAJJI; 79 brs.

Banque Internationale Arabe de Tunisie (BIAT): 70–72 ave Habib Bourguiba, BP 520, 1080 Tunis; tel. (71) 340-733; fax (71) 346-454; e-mail correspondent.banking@biat.com.tn; internet www.biat.com.tn; f. 1976; cap. 170m., res 287m., dep. 5,509m. (Dec. 2010); Chair. ISMAIL MABROUK; Gen. Man. SLAHEDDINE LADJIMI; 138 brs.

Banque Nationale Agricole (BNA): rue Hédi Nouira, 1001 Tunis; tel. (71) 831-000; fax (71) 832-807; e-mail bna@bna.com.tn; internet www.bna.com.tn; f. 1989 by merger of Banque Nationale du Développement Agricole and Banque Nationale de Tunisie; cap. 160m., res 175m., dep. 4,887m. (Dec. 2010); Chair. and CEO JAAFAR KHATTECHE; 157 brs.

Banque de Tunisie SA: 2 rue de Turquie, BP 289, 1001 Tunis; tel. (71) 125-510; fax (71) 125-410; e-mail finance@bt.com.tn; internet www.bt.com.tn; f. 1884; cap. 112m., res −3m., dep. 2,219m. (Dec. 2010); CEO HABIB BEN SAAD; 103 agencies.

Société Tunisienne de Banque (STB): rue Hédi Nouira, BP 638, 1001 Tunis; tel. (71) 340-477; fax (71) 348-400; e-mail stb@stb.com.tn; internet www.stb.com.tn; f. 1957; 24.81% govt-owned; merged with Banque Nationale de Développement Touristique and Banque de Développement Economique de Tunisie in 2000; cap. 124m., res 378m., dep. 5,200m. (Dec. 2010); Chair. and Gen. Man. SAMIRA GHRIBI; 119 brs.

Union Bancaire pour le Commerce et l'Industrie (UBCI): 139 ave de la Liberté, Belvédère, 1002 Tunis; tel. (71) 842-000; fax (71) 849-338; e-mail saber.mensi@bnpparibas.com; internet www.ubcinet.net; f. 1961; affiliated with, and 50% owned by, BNP Paribas (France); cap. 50m., res 114m., dep. 1,525m. (Dec. 2009); Pres. and Gen. Man. PATRICK POUPON; 110 brs.

Union Internationale de Banques SA: 65 ave Habib Bourguiba, BP 109, 1000 Tunis; tel. (71) 347-000; fax (71) 353-090; e-mail lilia.meddeb@uib.fin.tn; internet www.uib.com.tn; f. 1963 as a merging of Tunisian interests by the Société Franco-Tunisienne de Banque et

de Crédit with Crédit Lyonnais (France) and other foreign banks, incl. Banca Commerciale Italiana; 52.3% owned by Société Générale (France); cap. 196m., res −123m., dep. 2,009m. (Dec. 2009); Chair. DAVID BERNARD; Dir-Gen. KAMEL NEJI; 94 brs.

Merchant Banks

Banque d'Affaires de Tunisie (BAT): 10 bis rue Mahmoud El Matri, Mutuelleville, 1002 Tunis; tel. (71) 143-800; fax (71) 891-678; e-mail bat@bat.com.tn; internet www.bat-tunisie.com; f. 1997; cap. 4.5m.; Pres. and CEO MUHAMMAD HABIB KARAOULI.

International Maghreb Merchant Bank (IM Bank): Immeuble Maghrebia, Bloc B, 3ème étage, Les Berges du Lac, 2045 Tunis; tel. (71) 860-816; fax (71) 860-057; e-mail imbank@imbank.com.tn; internet www.imbank.com.tn; f. 1995; Pres. OLIVIER PASTRÉ; Exec. Dirs NASREDINE DEKLI, AHMED BESBES.

Development Banks

Banque de Tunisie et des Emirats (BTE): 5 bis blvd Muhammad Badra, 1002 Tunis; tel. (71) 112-000; fax (71) 286-409; e-mail dg@bte.com.tn; internet www.bte.com.tn; f. 1982 as Banque de Tunisie et des Emirats d'Investissement; name changed as above in 2005; owned by the Govt of Tunisia and Abu Dhabi Investment Authority; cap. 90m., res 41m., dep. 258m. (Dec. 2010); Chair. SALAM RACHID AL-MOHANNADI; Gen. Man. GOLSOM JAZIRI; 12 brs.

Banque Tunisienne de Solidarité (BTS): 56 ave Muhammad V, 1002 Tunis; tel. (71) 844-040; fax (71) 845-537; e-mail bts@email.ati.tn; internet www.bts.com.tn; f. 1997; provides short- and medium-term finance for small-scale projects; cap. 40m.; Man. Dir LAMINE HAFSAOUI; 25 brs.

Banque Tuniso-Libyenne: 25 ave Kheireddine Pacha, BP 150, Montplaisir, 1007 Tunis; tel. (71) 901-350; fax (71) 902-818; e-mail btl@gnet.tn; internet www.btl.com.tn; f. 1983 as Banque Arabe Tuniso-Libyenne de Développement et de Commerce; present name adopted 2005; promotes trade and devt projects between Tunisia and Libya, and provides funds for investment in poorer areas; cap. 70.0m., res 2.2m., dep. 309.1m. (Dec. 2008); Chair. and Gen. Man. BADREDDINE BARKIA.

Société Tuniso-Séoudienne d'Investissement et de Développement (STUSID): 32 rue Hédi Karray, BP 20, 1082 Tunis; tel. (71) 718-233; fax (71) 719-233; e-mail commercial@stusid.com.tn; internet www.stusid.com.tn; f. 1981; provides long-term finance for devt projects; cap. 100.0m., res 84.4m., dep. 10.5m. (Dec. 2002); Chair. Dr ABD AL-AZIZ A. AL-NASRALLAH; Pres. and Dir-Gen. ABD AL-WAHEB NACHI.

'Offshore' Banks

Albaraka Bank Tunisia: 88 ave Hédi Chaker, 1002 Tunis; tel. (71) 790-000; fax (71) 780-235; e-mail bestbank@planet.tn; f. 1983; as Beit Ettamouil Saoudi Tounsi; name changed to above in 2009; Islamic bank; Chair. ABDELILAH SOUBAHI; Vice-Chair. and Man. Dir AISSA HIDOUSSI.

Alubaf International Bank: 8007 rue Montplaisir, BP 51, Belvédère, 1002 Tunis; tel. (71) 783-500; fax (71) 793-905; e-mail alub@alubaf.com.tn; internet www.alubaf.com.tn; f. 1985; 100% owned by Libyan Arab Foreign Bank; cap. US $25m., res $5m., dep. $333m. (Dec. 2010); Chair. Dr AHMAD MNEISSI ABD EL-HAMID; Gen. Man. ALTAHER M. AL-SHAMES.

North Africa International Bank (NAIB): ave Kheireddine Pacha, BP 485, 1002 Tunis; tel. (71) 950-800; fax (71) 950-840; e-mail naib@naibank.com; internet www.naibank.com; f. 1984; cap. US $30m., res $17m., dep. $365m. (Dec. 2010); Chair. and Gen. Man. GIUMA M. WAHEBA; 1 br.

Tunis International Bank: 18 ave des Etats-Unis d'Amérique, BP 81, 1002 Tunis; tel. (71) 782-411; fax (71) 782-479; e-mail tib1.tib@planet.tn; internet www.tib.com.tn; f. 1982; 86.6% owned by United Gulf Bank (Bahrain); cap. US $50m., res $22m., dep. $433m. (Dec. 2010); Chair. MASOUD J. HAYAT; Dep. Chair. and Man. Dir MUHAMMAD FEKIH; 3 brs.

STOCK EXCHANGE

Bourse des Valeurs Mobilières de Tunis (Bourse de Tunis): 34 ave de la Bourse, Les Berges du Lac II, 1053 Tunis; tel. (71) 197-910; fax (71) 197-903; e-mail info@bvmt.com.tn; internet www.bvmt.com.tn; f. 1969; Chair. MUHAMMAD FADHEL ABD EL-KEFI; Dir-Gen. MUHAMMAD BICHIOU.

INSURANCE

BEST Reinsurance (BEST Re): Rue du Lac de Côme, Les Berges du lac, BP 484, 1080 Tunis; tel. (71) 860-355; fax (71) 861-011; e-mail general@best-re.com; internet www.best-re.com; f. 1985; operates according to Islamic principles; cap. US $100m.; Chair. Dr SALEH J. MALAIKAH.

Caisse Tunisienne d'Assurances Mutuelles Agricoles—Mutuelle Générale d'Assurances (CTAMA—MGA): 6 ave Habib Thameur, 1069 Tunis; tel. (71) 340-933; fax (71) 332-276; e-mail ctama@planet.tn; internet www.ctamamga.com; f. 1912; Pres. NEJI HANNACHI; Dir-Gen. MANSOUR NASRI.

Cie d'Assurances Tous Risques et de Réassurance (ASTREE): 45 ave Kheireddine Pacha, BP 780, 1002 Tunis; tel. (71) 792-211; fax (71) 794-723; e-mail courrier@astree.com.tn; internet www.astree.com.tn; f. 1949; cap. 4m.; Pres. and Dir-Gen. MUHAMMAD HABIB BEN SAAD.

Cie Tunisienne pour l'Assurance du Commerce Extérieur (COTUNACE): ave Muhammad V, Montplaisir I, rue 8006, 1002 Tunis; tel. (71) 783-000; fax (71) 782-539; e-mail cotunace.ddc@planet.tn; internet www.cotunace.com.tn; f. 1984; cap. 5m.; 65 mem. cos; Pres. and Dir-Gen. MONCEF ZOUARI.

Société Tunisienne d'Assurance et de Réassurance (STAR): ave de Paris, 1000 Tunis; tel. (71) 340-866; fax (71) 340-835; e-mail star@star.com.tn; internet www.star.com.tn; f. 1958; Pres. and Dir-Gen. LASSAAD ZARROUK.

Tunis Re (Société Tunisienne de Réassurance): 12 ave du Japon, Montplaisir 1, BP 29, 1073 Tunis; tel. (71) 904-911; fax (71) 904-930; e-mail tunisre@tunisre.com.tn; internet www.tunisre.com.tn; f. 1981; various kinds of reinsurance; cap. 45m. (2011); Chair. and Gen. Man. LAMIA BEN MAHMOUD.

Trade and Industry

GOVERNMENT AGENCIES

Centre de Promotion des Exportations (CEPEX): Centre Urbain, BP 225, 1080 Tunis; tel. (71) 234-200; fax (71) 237-325; e-mail info@cepex.nat.tn; internet www.cepex.nat.tn; f. 1973; state export promotion org.; Pres. and Dir-Gen. ABDELLATIF HAMMEM.

Foreign Investment Promotion Agency (FIPA): rue Slaheddine al-Ammami, Centre Urbain Nord, 1004 Tunis; tel. (71) 752-540; fax (71) 231-400; e-mail fipa.tunisia@fipa.tn; internet www.investintunisia.tn; f. 1995; Dir-Gen. NOUREDDINE ZEKRI.

Office du Commerce de la Tunisie (OCT): 65 rue de Syrie, 1002 Tunis; tel. (71) 785-619; fax (71) 784-491; e-mail OCT@Email.ati.tn; internet www.infocommerce.gov.tn; f. 1962; Pres. and Dir-Gen. SLAHEDDINE MAKHLOUF; Sec.-Gen. MUSTAPHA DEBBABI.

CHAMBERS OF COMMERCE AND INDUSTRY

Chambre de Commerce et d'Industrie du Centre: rue Chadli Khaznadar, 4000 Sousse; tel. (73) 225-044; fax (73) 224-227; e-mail ccis.sousse@planet.tn; internet www.ccicentre.org.tn; f. 1895; 30 mems; Pres. NÉJIB MELLOULI; Dir FATEN BASLY.

Chambre de Commerce et d'Industrie du Nord-Est: Tom Bereaux Bizerte Center, angle rues 1er mai, Med Ali, 7000 Bizerte; tel. (72) 431-044; fax (72) 431-922; e-mail ccine.biz@gnet.tn; internet www.ccibizerte.org.tn; f. 1902; 30 mems; Pres. FAOUZI BEN AISSA; Dir MOUFIDA CHAKROUN.

Chambre de Commerce et d'Industrie de Sfax: rue du Lieutenant Hammadi Tej, BP 794, 3000 Sfax; tel. (74) 296-120; fax (74) 296-121; e-mail ccis@ccis.org.tn; internet www.ccis.org.tn; f. 1895; 35,000 mems; Pres. ABDESSALEM BEN AYED; Dir SOFIENE SALLEMI.

Chambre de Commerce et d'Industrie de Tunis: 31 ave de Paris, 1000 Tunis; tel. (71) 247-322; fax (71) 354-744; e-mail ccitunis@planet.tn; internet www.ccitunis.org.tn; f. 1885; 30 mems; Pres. MOUNIR MOUAKHAR.

INDUSTRIAL AND TRADE ASSOCIATIONS

Agence des Ports et des Installations de Pêches (APIP): Port de Pêche de La Goulette, BP 64, 2060 Tunis; tel. (71) 736-012; fax (71) 735-396; e-mail apip@apip.com.tn; internet www.apip.nat.tn; fishing ports authority; Pres. and Dir-Gen. SGHAÏER HOUCINE.

Agence de Promotion de l'Industrie (API): 63 rue de Syrie, 1002 Tunis; tel. (71) 792-144; fax (71) 782-482; e-mail api@api.com.tn; internet www.tunisieindustrie.nat.tn; f. 1987 by merger; co-ordinates industrial policy, undertakes feasibility studies, organizes industrial training and establishes industrial zones; overseas offices in Belgium, France, Germany, Italy, Sweden, the United Kingdom and the USA; 24 regional offices; Gen. Man. MUHAMMAD BEN ABDALLAH.

Centre Technique du Textile (CETTEX): ave des Industries, Zone Industrielle, Bir el-Kassaâ, BP 279, Ben Arous, 2013 Tunis; tel. (71) 381-133; fax (71) 382-558; e-mail cettex@cettex.com.tn; internet www.cettex.com.tn; f. 1992; responsible for the textile industry; Dir-Gen. SAMIR HAOUET.

Cie des Phosphates de Gafsa (CPG): Cité Bayech, 2100 Gafsa; tel. (76) 226-022; fax (76) 224-132; e-mail cpg.gafsa@cpg.com.tn; internet www.gct.com.tn; f. 1897; production and marketing of phosphates; Pres. and Dir-Gen. MUHAMMAD FADHEL ZRELLI.

Entreprise Tunisienne d'Activités Pétrolières (ETAP): 27 ave Kheireddine Pacha, BP 83, 1073 Tunis; tel. (71) 902-688; fax (71) 906-141; e-mail dexprom@etap.com.tn; internet www.etap.com.tn; f. 1974; state-owned; responsible for exploration, production, trade and investment in hydrocarbons; Pres. and CEO KHALED BECHEIKH.

Office des Céréales: Ministry of Agriculture and Environment, 30 rue Alain Savary, 1002 Tunis; tel. (71) 780-550; fax (71) 794-152; e-mail office.cereales@email.ati.tn; f. 1962; responsible for the cereals industry; Chair. and Dir-Gen. YOUSUF NEJI.

Office National des Mines: 24 rue 8601, BP 215, 1080 Tunis; tel. (71) 788-242; fax (71) 794-016; e-mail contact@onm.nat.tn; internet www.onm.nat.tn; f. 1963; mining of iron ores; research and study of mineral wealth; Dir-Gen. ABDELBAKI MANSOURI.

Office des Terres Domaniales (OTD): 60 rue Alain Savary, 1002 Tunis; tel. (71) 771-086; fax (71) 795-026; e-mail boc@otd.nat.tn; internet www.otd.nat.tn; f. 1961; responsible for agricultural production and the management of state-owned lands; Pres. and Dir-Gen. ABDELHAKIM KHALDI.

UTILITIES

Electricity and Gas

Société Tunisienne de l'Electricité et du Gaz (STEG): 38 rue Kemal Atatürk, BP 190, 1080 Tunis; tel. (71) 341-311; fax (71) 349-981; e-mail dpsc@steg.com.tn; internet www.steg.com.tn; f. 1962; responsible for generation and distribution of electricity and for production of natural gas; Pres. and Dir-Gen. OTHMAN BEN ARFA; 35 brs.

Water

Société Nationale d'Exploitation et de Distribution des Eaux (SONEDE): ave Slimane Ben Slimane, el-Manar 2, 2092 Tunis; tel. (71) 887-000; fax (71) 871-000; e-mail sonede@sonede.com.tn; internet www.sonede.com.tn; f. 1968; production and supply of drinking water; Pres. and Dir-Gen. HÉDI BELHAJ.

TRADE UNION

Union Générale Tunisienne du Travail (UGTT): 29 pl. Muhammad Ali, 1000 Tunis; tel. (71) 332-400; fax (71) 354-114; e-mail ugtt.tunis@email.ati.tn; internet www.ugtt.org.tn; f. 1946 by Farhat Hached; affiliated to ITUC; 360,000 mems in 24 affiliated unions; 18-mem. exec. bureau; Gen. Sec. ABDESSALEM JERAD.

Transport

RAILWAYS

In 2010 the total length of Tunisian railways was 1,119 route-km; 38.6m. passengers travelled by rail in Tunisia in 2009.

Société Nationale des Chemins de Fer Tunisiens (SNCFT): Gare de Tunis ville, pl. Barcelone, 1001 Tunis; tel. (71) 334-444; fax (71) 254-320; e-mail sncft@sncft.com.tn; internet www.sncft.com.tn; f. 1956; state org. controlling all Tunisian railways; Pres. and Dir-Gen. MUHAMMAD NAJIB FITOURI.

Société des Transports de Tunis (TRANSTU): 1 ave Habib Bourgiba, BP 660, 1025 Tunis; tel. (71) 259-422; fax (71) 342-727; e-mail contact@snt.com.tn; internet www.snt.com.tn; f. 2003 following merger of the Société Nationale des Transports and the Société du Métro Léger de Tunis; operates 5 light train routes with 136 trains, and 206 local bus routes with 1,050 buses; also operates in the suburbs of Tunis-Goulette-Marsa, with 18 trains; plans approved in 2006 for expansion of the light rail system, with 5 new express lines; Pres. and Dir-Gen. CHEDLY HAJRI.

ROADS

In 2010 there were 356 km of motorways, 4,746 km of highways, main or national roads, 6,496 km of secondary or regional roads and 7,820 km of other roads. The total length of the road network was 19,418 km.

Société Nationale de Transport Interurbain (SNTRI): ave Muhammad V, BP 40, Belvédère, 1002 Tunis; tel. (71) 784-433; fax (71) 791-621; e-mail marketing@sntri.com.tn; internet www.sntri.com.tn; f. 1981; Dir-Gen. SASSI YAHIA.

Société des Transports de Tunis: see Railways.

There are 12 **Sociétés Régionales des Transports**, responsible for road transport, operating in different regions in Tunisia.

SHIPPING

Tunisia has seven major ports: Tunis-La Goulette, Radès, Bizerta, Sousse, Sfax, Gabès and Zarzis. There is a special petroleum port at

La Skhirra. In April 2009 the Government invited bids for the construction of a new deep-water port at Enfidha.

At 31 December 2012 Tunisia's flag registered fleet totalled 62 vessels, with an aggregate displacement of 358,504 grt, of which one was a bulk carrier, five were fish carriers and two were general cargo ships.

Port Authority

Office de la Marine Marchande et des Ports (OMMP): Bâtiment Administratif, Port de la Goulette, 2060 La Goulette; tel. (71) 735-300; fax (71) 735-812; e-mail ommp@ommp.nat.tn; internet www .ommp.nat.tn; maritime port administration; Pres. and Dir-Gen. OMAR MAJDOUB.

CIVIL AVIATION

There are international airports at Tunis-Carthage, Sfax, Djerba, Monastir, Tabarka, Gafsa and Tozeur. Zine al-Abidine Ben Ali airport, located at Enfidha, 100 km south of Tunis, began operations in December 2009. The airport, with an initial annual capacity of 7m. passengers, was officially inaugurated by Zine al-Abidine Ben Ali in early 2010. However, following Ben Ali's ouster in January 2011, the airport was renamed Enfidha-Hammamet International Airport.

Office de l'Aviation Civile et des Aéroports: BP 137 and 147, Aéroport International de Tunis-Carthage, 1080 Tunis; tel. (71) 755-000; fax (71) 755-133; e-mail relations.exterieures@oaca.nat.tn; internet www.oaca.nat.tn; f. 1970; civil aviation and airport authority; Pres. and Gen. Dir SALAH GHARSALLAH.

Nouvelair Tunisie: Zone Touristique Dkhila, 5065 Monastir; tel. (73) 520-600; fax (73) 520-650; e-mail info@nouvelair.com.tn; internet www.nouvelair.com; f. 1989 as Air Liberté Tunisie; name changed as above in 1996; Tunisian charter co; flights from Tunis, Djerba and Monastir airports to Scandinavia and other European countries; Chair. AZIZ MILAD.

Sevenair: 10 rue de l'Artisanat, La Charguia 11, Tunis; tel. (71) 942-323; fax (71) 942-272; e-mail info@sevenair.com.tn; internet www .sevenair.com.tn; f. 1992 as Tuninter; Tunisian charter co; Gen. Man. MONCEF ZOUARI.

TunisAir (Société Tunisienne de l'Air): ave Muhammad Bouazizi, 2035 Tunis; tel. (71) 700-100; fax (71) 700-897; e-mail Resaonline@ tunisair.com.tn; internet www.tunisair.com; f. 1948; 45.2% govt-owned; 20% of assets privatized in 1995; flights to Africa, Europe and the Middle East; Pres. and Dir-Gen. NABIL CHETTAOUI.

Tunisavia (Société de Transports, Services et Travaux Aériens): blvd du leader Yasser Arafat, Tunis-Carthage International Airport, 2035 Tunis; tel. (71) 280-555; fax (71) 281-333; e-mail siege@ tunisavia.com.tn; internet www.tunisavia.com.tn; f. 1974; helicopter and charter operator; CEO MUHAMMAD AZIZ MILAD; Gen. Man. MOHSEN NASRA.

Tourism

The main tourist attractions are the magnificent sandy beaches, Moorish architecture and remains of the Roman Empire. Tunisia contains the site of the ancient Phoenician city of Carthage. Tourism, a principal source of foreign exchange, has expanded rapidly, following extensive government investment in hotels, improved roads and other facilities. The number of hotel beds increased from 71,529 in 1980 to 188,600 in 1999. The political uncertainty following the ouster of former President Zine al-Abidine Ben Ali in February 2011 had a significant effect on the tourism industry. According to provisional figures, there were 4.8m. foreign tourist arrivals in 2011, compared with 6.9m. in the previous year. Receipts from tourism were estimated at US $1,805m. in 2011, compared with $2,645m. in 2010.

Office National du Tourisme Tunisien: 1 ave Muhammad V, 1001 Tunis; tel. (71) 341-077; fax (71) 350-997; e-mail ontt@email.ati .tn; internet www.bonjour-tunisie.com; f. 1958; Dir-Gen. KHALED CHEIKH.

Defence

Chief of Staff of the Army: Gen. RACHID AMMAR.

Chief of Staff of the Navy: Adm. TAREK FAOUZI LARBI.

Chief of Staff of the Air Force: Gen. TAIEB LAADJIMI.

Estimated Defence Budget (2012): TD 1,900m.

Military Service: 1 year (selective).

Total Armed Forces (as assessed at November 2012): 35,800; army 27,000 (22,000 conscripts); navy est. 4,800; air force 4,000.

Paramilitary Forces (as assessed at November 2012): 12,000 National Guard.

Education

Education is compulsory in Tunisia for a period of nine years between the ages of six and 16. Primary education begins at six years of age and normally lasts for six years. Secondary education begins at 12 years of age and lasts for seven years, comprising a first cycle of three years and a second cycle of four years. In 2008/09, according to UNESCO estimates, the total enrolment at primary schools included 98% of children in the relevant age-group. In that year the total enrolment at secondary schools was equivalent to 90% of children in the relevant age-group. In 2011 some TD 3,000.2m. was allocated to education and professional training (equivalent to 14.9% of budgeted government expenditure).

In early 2012 there were 13 universities, including a virtual university, and a General Directorate of Technological Studies. Arabic is the first language of instruction in primary and secondary schools, but French is also used. French is used almost exclusively in higher education. The University of Tunis was opened in 1959/60. In 1988 the university was divided into two separate institutions: one for science, the other for arts. It has 54 faculties and institutes. In 1986 two new universities were opened, at Monastir and Sfax. In 2010/11 the number of full-time students enrolled at higher educational establishments in Tunisia was 336,017.

TURKEY

Introductory Survey

LOCATION, CLIMATE, LANGUAGE, RELIGION, FLAG, CAPITAL

The Republic of Turkey lies partly in south-eastern Europe and partly in western Asia. The European and Asian portions of the country (known, respectively, as Thrace and Anatolia) are separated by the Sea of Marmara, linking the Black Sea and the Aegean Sea. Turkey has an extensive coastline: on the Black Sea, to the north; on the Mediterranean Sea, to the south; and on the Aegean Sea, to the west. Most of Turkey lies in Asia, the vast Anatolian peninsula being bordered to the east by Georgia, Armenia, the Nakhichevan Autonomous Republic (part of Azerbaijan) and Iran, and to the south by Iraq and Syria. The smaller European part of the country is bordered to the west by Greece and Bulgaria. In the Asian interior the climate is one of great extremes, with hot dry summers and cold, snowy winters on the plateau. Temperatures in Ankara are generally between −4°C (25°F) and 30°C (86°F). On the Mediterranean coast it is more equable, with mild winters and warm summers. The principal language is Turkish, spoken by 90% of the population. About 7% speak Kurdish, mainly in the south-east. In 1928 the Arabic characters of the written Turkish language were superseded by Western-style script. Islam is the religion of 99% of the population. The national flag (proportions 2 by 3) is red, with a white crescent and a five-pointed white star to the left of centre. The capital is Ankara.

CONTEMPORARY POLITICAL HISTORY

Historical Context

Turkey was formerly a monarchy, ruled by a Sultan, with his capital in Constantinople (now İstanbul). At its zenith, the Turkish Empire, under the Osmanlı (Ottoman) dynasty, extended from the Persian (Arabian) Gulf to Morocco, including most Arab regions and south-eastern Europe. Following the dissolution of the Ottoman Empire after the First World War, political control of Turkey itself passed to the nationalist movement led by Mustafa Kemal, a distinguished army officer. On 23 April 1920, in defiance of the Sultan, a newly elected assembly established a provisional Government, led by Kemal, in Ankara, then a minor provincial town. Kemal's forces waged war against the Greek army in 1920–22, forcing the Greeks to evacuate Smyrna (İzmir) and eastern Thrace (the European portion of Turkey). The new regime abolished the sultanate in November 1922 and declared Turkey a republic, with Ankara as its capital and Kemal as its first President, on 29 October 1923. The Ottoman caliphate (the former monarch's position as Islamic religious leader) was abolished in March 1924.

Kemal pursued a radical programme of far-reaching reform and modernization, including: secularization of the state (in 1928); abolition of Islamic courts and religious instruction in schools; emancipation of women (enfranchised in 1934); banning of polygamy; development of industry; introduction of a Latin alphabet; adoption of the Gregorian (in place of the Islamic) calendar; and encouragement of European culture and technology. Another Westernizing reform was the introduction of surnames in 1934: Kemal assumed the name Atatürk ('Father of the Turks'). His autocratic regime attempted, with considerable success, to replace the country's Islamic traditions by the principles of republicanism, nationalism, populism and state control.

Following Atatürk's death in 1938, his Cumhuriyet Halk Partisi (CHP—Republican People's Party), the only authorized political grouping, remained in power under his close associate, İsmet İnönü, who had been Prime Minister in 1923–24 and 1925–37. İnönü was President from 1938 to 1950, and maintained Turkey's neutrality during most of the Second World War (Turkey declared war on Germany in February 1945). After the war İnönü introduced some liberalization of the regime. The one-party system was ended in 1946, when opposition leaders, including Celâl Bayar and Adnan Menderes, registered the Demokratik Parti (DP—Democratic Party); numerous other parties were subsequently formed. The DP won Turkey's first free election in 1950, and ruled for the next decade. Bayar became President, with Menderes as Prime Minister.

In May 1960 the Government was overthrown by a military coup, led by Gen. Cemal Gürsel, who assumed the presidency, claiming that the DP regime had betrayed Atatürk's principle of secularism. A series of coalition governments, mostly led by İnönü, held office from November 1961 until October 1965, when an election was won by the conservative Adalet Partisi (Justice Party), led by Süleyman Demirel, which appealed to supporters of the former DP. The Demirel Government remained in power until March 1971, when escalating student and labour unrest caused the armed forces to demand its resignation. 'Guided democracy', under military supervision, continued until October 1973, with a succession of right-wing 'non-party' administrations, martial law and the rigorous suppression of all left-wing activities.

Domestic Political Affairs

The return to civilian rule began in April 1973, when the Turkish Grand National Assembly (TGNA—the legislative body established in 1961) chose Adm. Fahri Korutürk as President, in preference to a candidate supported by the armed forces. Military participation in government was ended by an election in October 1973. No single party received sufficient support to form a government, and it was not until January 1974 that Bülent Ecevit, leader of the CHP (which had become a left-of-centre party), took office as Prime Minister, having negotiated a coalition with the Milli Selamet Partisi (MSP—National Salvation Party), a pro-Islamic right-wing group. Deteriorating relations with Greece were exacerbated by the Greek-backed coup in Cyprus (q.v.) in July 1974, when Turkey responded by dispatching troops, and occupying the northern part of the island, to protect the Turkish Cypriot population. Despite the failure of the coup, Turkish forces retained control of northern Cyprus, and the island remained effectively partitioned.

A long period of political instability was fostered by a succession of unsuccessful coalitions, and prompted an escalation in political violence, mainly involving clashes between left-wing and right-wing groups. On 12 September 1980, as the violence neared the scale of a civil war, the armed forces, led by Gen. Kenan Evren, Chief of the General Staff, seized power in a bloodless coup; a five-member National Security Council (NSC) was formed, which appointed a mainly civilian Cabinet. Martial law was declared throughout the country. In December the NSC published a decree endowing the military regime with unlimited powers. During 1981–83 a campaign to eradicate all possible sources of political violence was undertaken. In April 1981 former politicians were banned from future political activity, and in October all political parties were disbanded.

The new Government succeeded in reducing the level of political violence in Turkey and in restoring law and order. However, that this had been achieved at the expense of respect for human rights caused concern among Western governments: Turkey was banned from the Parliamentary Assembly of the Council of Europe (see p. 260), and aid from the European Community (EC, now European Union—EU, see p. 281) was suspended, and fellow members of the North Atlantic Treaty Organization (NATO, see p. 380) urged Turkey to return to democratic rule as soon as possible. In October 1981 a Consultative Assembly was established to draft a new constitution, which was approved by referendum in November 1982; objections were widely expressed that the President was to be accorded excessive powers while judicial powers and the rights of trade unions and the press were to be curtailed. An appended 'temporary article' installed Evren as President for a seven-year term.

In May 1983 the NSC revoked the ban on political organizations, permitting the formation of parties, subject to strict rules, in preparation for the first election to be held under the new Constitution. All the former political parties remained proscribed, and 723 former members of the TGNA and leading party officials were banned from political activity for up to 10 years. Followers of the former parties thus regrouped under new names and with new leaders. However, of the 15 new parties, only three were allowed to take part in the election: the Milliyetçi Demokrasi Partisi (MDP—Nationalist Democracy Party) and the Halkçı Partisi (HP—Populist Party), both of which had the tacit support of the NSC, and the conservative Anavatan Partisi (ANAVATAN—Motherland Party), led by Turgut Özal. In the November election ANAVATAN won 211 of the 400 seats in the unicameral legislature, and Özal was appointed Prime Minister in December. This result, which was followed by the holding of local government elections in March 1984, suggested a decisive rejection of military rule. Turkey was readmitted to the Parliamentary Assembly of the Council of Europe in May, but the Assembly continued to advocate the establishment of full democracy and political freedom in the country.

In November 1985 the HP and the Sosyal Demokrasi Partisi (Social Democratic Party), respectively the main opposition parties within and outside the National Assembly, merged to form the Sosyal Demokrat Halkçı Parti (SHP—Social Democratic Populist Party). However, the left-wing opposition was split as a result of the immediate formation of the Demokratik Sol Parti (DSP—Democratic Left Party), which drew support from the former CHP. The MDP voted to disband in May 1986.

In July 1987 all martial law decrees were repealed when martial law was replaced with a state of emergency in several provinces. At a national referendum in September 1987 a narrow majority approved the repeal of the ban on participation in political affairs, imposed on more than 200 politicians in 1981. This enabled Ecevit to assume the leadership of the DSP, while Demirel was elected as leader of the Doğru Yol Partisi (DYP—True Path Party). In a general election conducted in November 1987 ANAVATAN obtained 292 of the 450 seats in the enlarged TGNA, while the SHP won 99 seats and the DYP 59.

Özal succeeded Evren as President in November 1989, having secured the support of the simple majority required in a third round of voting by the TGNA in October. Yıldırım Akbulut, the Speaker of the TGNA and a former Minister of the Interior, was subsequently appointed Prime Minister. However, having been defeated by former Minister of Foreign Affairs Mesut Yılmaz in a contest for the ANAVATAN leadership in June 1991, Akbulut subsequently resigned as premier. In accordance with the Constitution, President Özal invited Yılmaz to head a new administration.

Legislative elections, October 1991 and April 1995

In a general election held on 20 October 1991 the DYP, under Demirel's leadership, received an estimated 27.3% of the votes cast, narrowly defeating ANAVATAN (with 23.9%) and the SHP (20.6%). Demirel formed a coalition administration with the SHP. However, by September 1992, following a succession of political defections from the SHP, the representation of the coalition parties in the TGNA had been reduced to 229. Furthermore, the reactivation of the CHP in September (following a relaxation of guidelines for the formation of political parties) threatened to undermine left-wing support for the Government.

Following the death of President Özal, Süleyman Demirel was elected to the presidency in May 1993. Tansu Çiller was elected to the DYP party leadership in June and promptly assumed the premiership, thereby becoming Turkey's first female Prime Minister. The new administration was strained by a sharp escalation of violence on the part of the outlawed Partiya Karkeren Kurdistan (PKK—Kurdistan Workers' Party). Plans to extend cultural and educational rights to the Kurds were abandoned following strong opposition from Demirel, right-wing members of the DYP and military leaders, who, in October 1993, effectively resisted a proposal to discuss the establishment of local autonomy for the Kurdish population in the south-east of the country.

A significant increase in terrorist attacks by Islamist and left-wing groups, especially the Dev-Sol (Revolutionary Left), in early 1990 was exacerbated by the Government's stance in the Gulf crisis of 1990–91, and both factions unleashed a series of attacks against Western targets in Turkey, including US civilians, diplomatic missions and offices of several national airlines and banks in İstanbul and Ankara. In September 1994 a former Minister of Justice, Mehmet Topaç, was shot dead by Dev-Sol members in Ankara. In January 1996 a faction of Dev-Sol, Devrimci Halk Kurtuluş Partisi—Cephesi (DHKP—C, the Revolutionary People's Liberation Party—Front), claimed responsibility for the murder of two leading Turkish business executives in İstanbul. In late 1996 it was reported that Dev-Sol had been subsumed by the DHKP—C.

In February 1995 a special conference of the SHP voted to merge with the CHP, consequently increasing the Government's parliamentary majority but forcing a renegotiation of the conditions of the coalition. Agreement was reached by Çiller and

Hikmet Çetin, the CHP leader, in March, and an extensive reorganization of the Government was undertaken in order to accommodate the party. Çetin became Deputy Prime Minister and Minister of State. Efforts by the Prime Minister to extend democratic rights within the Constitution encountered considerable opposition, both from conservative elements within her own party and from the fundamentalist Islamist Refah Partisi (RP—Welfare Party). Certain constitutional reforms, including the removal of restrictions on political associations and trade unions, the lowering of the age of eligibility to vote from 21 to 18 years and the expansion of the TGNA by 100 parliamentary seats to 550, were finally approved in July.

Deniz Baykal was elected leader of the CHP in September 1995. All CHP ministers subsequently resigned their cabinet positions, and ensuing coalition negotiations with Çiller failed as it became apparent that the political differences between the two leaders were insurmountable. Later in September Demirel was forced to accept the Prime Minister's resignation, but Çiller was immediately invited to form a new government. A DYP-CHP Government, headed by Çiller, with Baykal as Deputy Prime Minister and Minister of Foreign Affairs, took office in November.

At the general election held in December 1995 the RP secured the largest number of parliamentary seats (158), with 21.4% of the votes cast. The DYP won 135 seats, with 19.2% of the votes, while ANAVATAN took 132, with 19.7% of the votes. A new administration comprising ANAVATAN, led by Mesut Yılmaz, and the DYP was appointed in March 1996; Çiller conceded the premiership to Yılmaz, under a rotating arrangement. The new Government was soon strained by tensions between the two leaders, and allegations of corruption against Çiller, and in May Çiller announced the withdrawal of DYP support for the Government. In June Yılmaz announced the resignation of his Government, following a Constitutional Court ruling that annulled the parliamentary vote of confidence in his administration in March. A new coalition administration comprising the DYP and the RP, led by Necmettin Erbakan and with Çiller assuming the deputy premiership and foreign affairs portfolio, took office in July 1996. In August the military dismissed 13 officers on disciplinary charges relating to Islamist practices (50 officers had been dismissed on similar grounds in December 1995). In January 1997 the TGNA cleared Çiller of the final corruption charges against her.

In February 1997, following pressure from the military and DYP members of the Government, the RP was forced to withdraw proposals to extend Muslim education and to allow religious garments to be worn by public workers. At a meeting of the NSC held on 28 February, the military leadership presented an 18-point memorandum that set out to ensure the protection of Turkish secular state traditions, including greater supervision of Islamic financial and media operations, the removal of Islamists from public administration and closure of all unauthorized Islamic groupings; the military warned of punitive action if the proposals were not implemented. The Council of Ministers agreed in March to implement the NSC proposals, which had been endorsed by Erbakan, but the subsequent failure of the Government to act on the measures prompted charges from the military, opposition parties and dissident members of the DYP that it was undermining the modern secular tradition. By June the coalition had lost its majority in the TGNA as a result of defections, principally from the DYP, and Erbakan resigned as premier later that month. President Demirel asked the ANAVATAN leader, Mesut Yılmaz, to form a new administration, and a coalition with the DSP and the Democratic Turkey Party was inaugurated in July; the coalition controlled only a minority of seats in the TGNA, and was dependent on the support of the CHP. The tripartite Government pledged to improve law and order, implement previously proposed changes to the education system, and vigorously pursue EU membership. Defections from the DYP continued, and by the end of July its representation in the TGNA had been reduced from 135 to 93.

In August 1997 the TGNA approved legislation extending the duration of compulsory education from five to eight years. This was intended to raise the entry age to Islamic schools from 11 to 14, thus reducing attendance at such schools and lessening Islamic influence. Public demonstrations were organized in protests against the legislation, and against the military's insistence on the strict enforcement of the ban on wearing Islamic dress in public buildings, notably educational establishments.

In January 1998 the Constitutional Court ordered the dissolution of the RP on the grounds that it was responsible for undermining the secular regime, and banned seven of its members, including Erbakan, from holding political office for five years. Many former RP deputies joined the Fazilet Partisi (FP—Virtue Party), which had been established in December 1997. By March 1998 the FP's representation in the TGNA had risen to 140 seats, making it the largest parliamentary party (ANAVATAN controlled 139 seats).

In August 1998 12 former RP politicians, including Erbakan, were charged with illegally diverting funds from the party prior to its dissolution. An investigation into Çiller's assets was begun in September. Further investigations were launched in that month into Çiller and the former Minister of Finance for financial irregularities, and the immunity of the former TGNA Speaker was revoked, to allow an investigation, at his request, into his conduct following corruption allegations. Meanwhile, the Court of Appeal upheld a 10-month prison sentence imposed in April on the mayor of İstanbul, Recep Tayyip Erdoğan, upon his conviction for inciting hatred. As a result of his conviction, Erdoğan was deprived of his position of mayor; he also resigned from the FP. In December new charges were filed against him for insulting the judiciary in a speech following his sentencing. In the previous month corruption charges against Çiller were dismissed by a parliamentary commission, owing to insufficient evidence, while Erbakan was acquitted on charges of slandering the judiciary.

The April 1999 legislative elections

The Government resigned in November 1998, after the TGNA approved a motion of no confidence submitted by the CHP in response to accusations of corruption against Yılmaz. In January 1999, following protracted political manoeuvring, Bülent Ecevit of the DSP formed a Government, comprising DSP and independent deputies, which was to hold office until early elections in April. In February the trial began of 79 alleged Islamists, including Erbakan. Meanwhile, the High Electoral Board ruled that former RP deputies would not be allowed to take part in the forthcoming elections as independent candidates.

At the elections held in April 1999 no party secured an outright majority in the TGNA. The DSP won 136 of the 550 seats, and subsequently formed a coalition with the Milliyetçi Hareket Partisi (MHP—Nationalist Movement Party), which had won 129 seats, and ANAVATAN, with 86 seats. The remaining seats in the TGNA were won by the FP (111) and the DYP (85), with three seats won by independent candidates. The CHP leader, Deniz Baykal, resigned following the poor performance of his party. The new Government, led by Bülent Ecevit, was approved by a parliamentary vote of confidence in June.

Several articles of a political parties act relating to the closure of parties were approved in August 1999: no party would be permitted to re-form, even under a different name; party officials would be prohibited from active politics for five years and would be forbidden from standing as candidates for the party, although they would be permitted to stand as independent candidates. In September the FP submitted its preliminary defence against the motion to ban it. In October the assets of Erbakan and nine other former RP officials were frozen as part of the continuing trial of a case brought by the Treasury demanding the repayment of aid given to the RP in 1997, as well as the repayment of allegedly unregistered party funds. In March 2000 Erbakan was sentenced to one year in prison and a lifetime ban from politics for provoking animosity and hatred in a speech made in 1994. (In January 2001, however, his sentence was suspended, under penal legislation allowing conditional release for certain convictions. Moreover, in July 2006 the European Court of Human Rights—ECHR—ruled that Erbakan had not received a fair trial.) In December 1999, meanwhile, 300 people were detained following protests over the ban on wearing headscarves in universities; the Court of Appeals ruled that the prerogative to wear Islamic headscarves was not a democratic right. In April 2000 the parties of the governing coalition agreed to nominate the Chairman of the Constitutional Court, Ahmet Necdet Sezer, as their joint candidate for the presidency; he was elected in a third round of voting.

In December 2000 two police officers were killed following an attack on a police bus in İstanbul. In January 2001 the DHKP—C claimed responsibility for a suicide bomb attack on a police building, which killed two people. In April Sahil Izzet Erdis, the leader of the outlawed Great Eastern Islamic Raiders' Front (IBDA—C), was sentenced to death on charges of seeking to overthrow the secular state. In September a suicide bomber, believed to be acting on behalf of the DHKP—C, killed two policemen and a foreign tourist in central İstanbul. In May 2002

the EU designated the DHKP—C as a terrorist organization. Security forces arrested several members of DHKP—C in two attempted military operations during November 2004. In June 2006 four members of the organization were arrested following the shooting of a police officer in İstanbul. In January 2007 a further five DHKP—C members were detained by the Turkish authorities.

Meanwhile, despite the implementation of structural reform measures by the Ecevit Government, in November 2000 a severe banking crisis was provoked by an investigation by the Banking and Supervision Agency into 10 failed banks. The investigation exposed the vulnerability of the banking sector and the lack of confidence of foreign investors in the Turkish economy, as a result of a widening current account deficit and delays to the structural reform programme. The IMF and the World Bank agreed to emergency loans in order to support the programme. In February 2001 a second economic crisis was precipitated following a dispute between the President and Prime Minister: Sezer had accused Ecevit of not responding adequately to allegations of government corruption. Opposition parties and the business community had demanded the dismissal of Deputy Prime Minister Hüsamettin Özkan, the Minister of Energy and Natural Resources, Cumhur Ersümer, and the Minister of Public Works, Koray Aydin, and the initiation of a parliamentary investigation into the two ministers' affairs. The precarious balance of power within the governing coalition was, however, thought to have dissuaded Ecevit from undertaking any action against the alleged corruption. Later in February Turkey, with the support of the IMF, abandoned its exchange rate controls and allowed the lira to float, while empowering the Central Bank to pursue a rigorous monetary policy to control inflation.

Following the banking crisis, in March 2001 Ecevit replaced the Governor of the Central Bank and appointed Kemal Derviş, a senior economist at the World Bank, as Minister of Finance, in an attempt to salvage Turkey's economic reforms and restore confidence in the financial markets. Derviş announced an emergency plan for economic stabilization, which included the restructuring of three state-owned banks under one supervisory board, and succeeded in securing the financial support of the IMF and the World Bank. Yet the political implications of the financial crisis continued to be felt in April, as anti-Government demonstrations involving tens of thousands of people degenerated into riots in Ankara and İzmir. Ecevit, however, rejected demands for his Government to resign. Later in the month it was announced that 15 officials and business executives were to be tried on conspiracy and bribery charges, following a high-profile investigation into corruption in the state energy sector. The testimonies of the defendants resulted in the resignation of Ersümer, who was succeeded by Zeki Cakan of ANAVATAN in May.

In May 2001 the TGNA approved legislation designed to meet conditions demanded by the IMF before the latter was to release US $10,000m. in financial aid. At the end of the month the Minister of State for Privatization, Yuksel Yalova, resigned, owing to disagreements within the Government over the liberalization of the tobacco industry stipulated by the IMF. In July the Minister of Communications, Enis Öksüz, resigned, owing to his opposition to IMF-imposed plans to privatize the telecommunications sector. In September Aydin also resigned from his government post and from the TGNA, after corruption charges were brought against him with regard to his alleged receipt of funds from contracts relating to reconstruction in the aftermath of the 1999 earthquake in İzmit.

The rise to prominence of the AKP

In June 2001 the Constitutional Court banned the FP, on the grounds that it was essentially a continuation of the banned Islamist RP and was thus regarded as seeking to undermine the secular system. The Court expelled two FP members from the TGNA; however, it refrained from ordering the mass expulsions of the 100 remaining FP members from the legislature, who were allowed to remain in place as independents or join two planned successor parties. The ban was, nevertheless, opposed by most TGNA members, who were reportedly concerned that it would lead to more political instability. In July the ECHR upheld the Government's 1998 decision to ban the RP. Also in July 2001 a new Islamist party, Saadet Partisi (SP—Felicity Party), was established, incorporating about one-half of the former members of the FP. As with the FP, Erbakan was the main force in the party. In August the remaining members of the FP joined the new reformist Islamist Adalet ve Kalkınma (AKP—Justice and Development Party), established by former mayor of İstanbul

Erdoğan and FP member Abdullah Gül as an alternative to the SP. Shortly afterwards Erdoğan came under investigation for comments he had reportedly made in 1994 that allegedly insulted the Turkish state.

Meanwhile, in March 2001 the Government announced a new programme aimed at facilitating EU membership that entailed, *inter alia*, the eventual abolition of the death penalty and ending restrictions on freedom of expression, as well as improving the rights of minorities, but EU officials criticized the programme for its lack of specifics. Despite such plans, the TGNA approved a four-month extension of the state of emergency in the predominantly Kurdish south-east of the country, and in May the Turkish Radio and Television Supreme Council ordered the closure of 89 radio and television stations for broadcasting separatist and disruptive programmes. The TGNA in October overwhelmingly approved a number of constitutional amendments designed to facilitate Turkey's admission to the EU. The changes largely pertained to political freedoms and civil liberties, including minority rights (notably regarding the use of the Kurdish language). Significantly, the number of civilians on the powerful NSC would rise from five to nine, thereby lessening the power of the military (which would retain five members). Improved rights for women were approved in November. In August 2002 the TGNA formally abolished the death penalty in peacetime; in September, however, Amnesty International released a report alleging the widespread use of torture by police, citing testimony from more than 60 individuals during the first half of 2002.

In January 2002 the Constitutional Court imposed restrictions on the political activities of AKP leader Erdoğan, owing to his earlier allegedly seditious activities. The Court banned him from contesting the elections to the TGNA, and ordered his party to remove him from its leadership within six months. In March Ankara's Higher Criminal Court sentenced Erbakan to two years and four months in prison for embezzling party funds. (In December 2003 the Court of Appeals in Ankara upheld this sentence, although it was deferred for one year on medical grounds.)

In February 2002 the TGNA approved additional laws on freedom of thought and expression by means of a 'mini-reform' programme designed to satisfy EU standards. In July Prime Minister Ecevit was forced to call early elections to the TGNA for November, after several of his ministers, including Deputy Prime Minister and Minister of State Hüsamettin Özkan and Minister of Foreign Affairs İsmail Cem, and numerous DSP party legislators resigned, thereby denying the ruling coalition a majority in the TGNA. Cem formed a new party, the Yeni Türkiye Partisi (YTP—New Turkey Party), with 62 defectors from the DSP, whose representation in the TGNA had fallen from 128 seats to 65 seats. In early August the Minister of Finance, Kemal Derviş, resigned, and subsequently agreed to co-operate with the CHP. In September the AKP, which was leading in opinion polls, underwent a reverse, when Turkey's highest election board confirmed the Constitutional Court's decision to ban Erdoğan from holding public office. Although he had publicly professed secular and pro-European views, Erdoğan retained the distrust of the secularist military and judiciary, and in October the chief prosecutor sought to obtain an outright ban on the AKP, although this was not implemented.

The AKP comes to power

The elections to the TGNA held in November 2002 significantly transformed Turkish politics. With voter participation of 79.0%, the AKP won 34.3% of the votes cast, securing 363 seats in the TGNA. Only one other party, the CHP, achieved the 10% of the vote required for representation in the TGNA, winning 19.4% of the votes cast and securing 178 seats. Following the election, President Sezer appointed AKP deputy leader Abdullah Gül as Prime Minister, since Erdoğan was ineligible for the position. None the less, Erdoğan exerted a strong influence on the new Government. In December the AKP-dominated legislature approved constitutional reforms allowing Erdoğan to contest a forthcoming by-election. Initially vetoed by Sezer, these changes were subsequently re-endorsed by the TGNA, forcing the President to accept them.

In January 2003 Erdoğan was re-elected leader of the AKP and immediately announced plans to contest the by-election for the TGNA, membership of which would allow him to become Prime Minister. In February the electoral commission endorsed his candidacy, and Erdoğan was duly elected. President Sezer subsequently appointed Erdoğan as Prime Minister, and approved a

new Council of Ministers, in which Gül took the post of Deputy Prime Minister and Minister of Foreign Affairs.

In March 2003 a ruling by Turkey's Constitutional Court (subsequently upheld, in September, by the Court of Appeals) banned the pro-Kurdish nationalist Halkın Demokrasi Partisi (HADEP—People's Democracy Party) from political activity on the grounds that it had been aiding the PKK (a charge denied by the party). Some 46 members of the party were also subjected to a five-year ban. Shortly afterwards HADEP was reconstituted as the Democratik Halkın Partisi (DEHAP—Democratic People's Party). In June the TGNA adopted a further series of human rights reforms, including additional legislation to permit education and broadcasting in Kurdish and other minority languages, and to amend the existing legal definition of terrorism, in order to qualify for accession negotiations with the EU. At the end of that month Sezer vetoed one of the amendments, under which peaceful advocacy of an independent Kurdish state would no longer be illegal. However, the TGNA utilized its power to overrule the veto by returning the legislation to the President without amendment. Further reforms approved in July included provisions for the prompt investigation of allegations of torture and for prohibiting the trial of civilians in military courts in peacetime, as well as the reconstitution of the NSC as an advisory body, and the offer of a qualified amnesty to supporters of KADEK (the Congress for Freedom and Democracy in Kurdistan—see The Kurdish Issue).

Some 25 people were killed and about 300 injured in suicide bombings outside two of İstanbul's largest synagogues on 15 November 2003. On 20 November a further two suicide bombs exploded outside the Hong Kong and Shanghai Banking Corporation and the British consulate in İstanbul, killing some 31 people (including the Consul-General) and injuring more than 450. Although several extremist Turkish Islamist groups, including IBDA—C, claimed responsibility for the attacks, the involvement of al-Qa'ida was immediately suspected. Erdoğan condemned all acts of terrorism, and demonstrations were staged in Turkey against the bombings. By the end of that month a total of 62 people had been killed in the four bomb attacks, and 159 had been arrested on suspicion of involvement, of whom a number had been charged. The Turkish authorities announced that the bombings had been organized by a cell of Turkish nationals connected to al-Qa'ida, all of whom had been trained outside the country.

Local government elections, which were held on 28 March 2004, resulted in an increase in support for the AKP, which secured 42% of the votes cast and 58 of the country's 81 provinces. In May, as part of the series of reforms intended to bring Turkey into conformity with EU human rights and democratic standards, the TGNA adopted draft constitutional amendments to: abolish the death penalty and anti-terrorist state security courts; guarantee equality for women; and establish full parliamentary control over the budget of the armed forces. However, new education legislation, ending restrictions on university entrance for those trained in religious schools, was suspended in early June, following a veto by President Sezer. Also that month Turkey's stated commitment to new human rights standards, in compliance with EU requirements, appeared to be demonstrated by the Supreme Court's decision to order the release of the four Kurdish former parliamentary deputies, who had been sentenced to 15 years' imprisonment in 1994 for supporting the PKK. Following their release, a court in July 2004 overturned their convictions and ordered retrials. In a further significant measure, the TGNA in July authorized the prosecution for corruption of former Prime Minister Mesut Yılmaz and three other former ministers.

In January 2005, following the provisional offer by the EU in December 2004 to commence accession negotiations, Islamist party leaders criticized the conditions imposed and demanded that the Government organize a referendum on EU membership; protests were organized in İstanbul and in İzmit. In February 2005 the Chairman of the Human Rights Consultative Council tendered his resignation, citing continuing impediments posed by the Government (which had rejected a previous critical report of the Council over the stance on human rights). Turkey's new penal code, adopted as a precondition for the commencement of EU accession talks (see Foreign Affairs), entered into force in June, after a two-month postponement. Sezer subsequently vetoed an amendment reducing the penalties for anti-secular teaching in illegal religious schools; however, that veto was overruled by the TGNA later that month.

The murder of a prominent Armenian-Turkish journalist and human rights campaigner, Hrant Dink, in İstanbul in January 2007 provoked considerable outrage among the population. Eight suspects, some with close links to nationalist organizations, were arrested following Dink's killing, while several local police officers were suspended from duty for allegedly having failed to offer sufficient protection to the journalist after he had received death threats, or for apparently having shown support to the incarcerated principal suspect, Ögün Samast. Trial proceedings against Samast, together with 17 others suspected of involvement in the killing, commenced in İstanbul in July. In September 2010 the ECHR ruled that the Turkish Government had contravened two, three and 13 of the European Convention on Human Rights in relation to Dink's murder and ordered Turkey to compensate Dink's family for its failure to act upon information that it had received regarding plots to murder the journalist. At the trial's 15th hearing in October, judges ruled that Samast should be tried as a minor (the youth had been 17 years of age at the time of the killing); the trial finally commenced at a juvenile court in İstanbul on 28 February 2011. In July Samast was convicted of Dink's killing and illegal possession of a firearm, and was sentenced to 22 years and 10 months' imprisonment. Three other defendants were convicted of involvement in the killing in January 2012, one of whom was sentenced to life imprisonment, while the remaining two each received a 10-year gaol term. All other suspects were released. The judge acquitted all defendants of the charge of being members of a criminal organization and rejected allegations of official negligence or state collusion in the murder. Following his verdict, at least 20,000 demonstrators took to the streets in İstanbul to commemorate the fifth anniversary of Dink's death. After an appeal on the ruling by a prosecutor on 10 March the court verdict was sent to the Supreme Court of Appeals in early June. On 10 January 2013 the chief prosecutor of the Supreme Court of Appeals asked for the verdict on the Dink case to be annulled, describing the murder as an 'organized assassination'.

Meanwhile, in May 2006 an Islamist extremist, angered at a ruling barring the promotion of a teacher who wore the Islamic headscarf, entered the Council of State building and assassinated a senior judge. Large demonstrations followed in Ankara, supported by the judiciary and the Chief of the General Staff, Gen. Hilmi Özkök; protesters demanded the protection of secularism in Turkey. (The Islamist extremist was given two terms of life imprisonment by an Ankara court in February 2008, having been one of four defendants convicted of involvement in the murder.) In August 2006 Gen. Yaşar Büyükanıt succeeded Özkök as Chief of the General Staff.

In mid-April 2007, as the TGNA began preparations to elect a successor to President Sezer (whose term of office was to end on 16 May), some 300,000 people held a demonstration in Ankara to demand that Turkey remain a secular state. In late April the Minister of Foreign Affairs, Abdullah Gül, was nominated as the ruling AKP's presidential candidate and pledged to retain Turkey's secular status should he be elected. His assurance was met with scepticism, however, not least because his wife chose to wear the headscarf.

The initial round of voting in the TGNA was boycotted by the CHP and other opposition parties, which complained that they had not been consulted about Gül's application; they lodged an appeal with the Constitutional Court for the voting process to be cancelled. Since Gül secured only 357 out of 550 votes at the first round—10 fewer than the requisite number—it was announced at the end of the month that the Constitutional Court had annulled the initial vote. Prime Minister Erdoğan subsequently asked the legislature to approve proposals initiated by his party to endorse a constitutional amendment enabling the President henceforth to be directly elected for a five-year term and that a general election (scheduled for November) be brought forward to June in order to resolve the political crisis. The High Electoral Board ruled in May that an election should be held on 22 July. Meanwhile, the AKP's legislation was approved by the TGNA on 11 May, but subsequently vetoed by President Sezer. Following the re-endorsement of the legislation by the TGNA at the end of May, in a final bid to delay its passage the President exercised his right to refer the decision to a referendum.

The elections of 2007 and 2009

The AKP obtained 46.7% of the votes and 341 seats at the legislative elections of July 2007, against the CHP's 20.9% and 112 seats. The MHP came third, with 14.3% and 71 seats; however, one of the party's elected representatives died days later, resulting in one seat remaining vacant. Pro-Kurdish

deputies entered the TGNA as independents—the first time that there had been Kurdish representation in the legislature for 13 years. Shortly afterwards Abdullah Gül signalled his desire to remain a candidate for the presidency, and he was endorsed unanimously by his party. Following a third round of voting, in August, Gül secured the requisite simple majority and was elected as Turkey's 11th President. At his inauguration Gül reiterated his commitment to secularism, pluralism and freedom of belief. A new Council of Ministers was approved at the end of the month. The new Government's programme, which won a vote of confidence in early September, included proposals to reform and modernize the Turkish Constitution, and measures aimed at increasing economic prosperity. At the nation-wide referendum held on 21 October, a reported 69.0% of eligible voters approved the constitutional reforms regarding the direct election of future Turkish Presidents. The serving term of a President was also reduced from seven to five years (renewable once), while that of TGNA deputies was reduced from five to four years.

In January 2008 the AKP and the MHP together submitted a motion to the TGNA that would end the ban on the wearing of the Islamic headscarf by women at universities. The two constitutional amendments were passed into law by President Gül in February, having received parliamentary approval, provoking anger among Turkish secularists, who protested against the decision in Ankara and elsewhere. In June the Constitutional Court rescinded the legislation, on the grounds that it was unconstitutional. Meanwhile, in March 2008 an indictment was filed at the Constitutional Court by Abdurrahman Yalçınkaya, a prosecutor at the Court of Appeals, which presented detailed evidence of alleged 'anti-secular activities' of the AKP and urged the closure of the party and a five-year suspension from politics of 71 senior party officials, including the incumbent President and Prime Minister. In July the Constitutional Court found the party guilty of being a 'focal point of anti-secular activity', and ordered that its state funding be halved for a year, but only six of the 11 judges voted to disband the party, one short of the stipulated minimum.

A major reorganization of the Council of Ministers, involving 17 ministerial changes, was announced in May 2009. Significant changes included the appointment of Ali Babacan, hitherto Minister of Foreign Affairs, as Deputy Prime Minister with concurrent responsibility for economic co-ordination, while the foreign affairs portfolio was reassigned to Ahmet Davutoğlu, a foreign affairs adviser to the Prime Minister who had played a central role in Turkey's mediation of indirect peace talks between Israel and Syria during 2008.

In November 2009 the merger of ANAVATAN with the Demokrat Parti was announced. Supporters of the two centre-right parties were hopeful that the merger would help to restore their political influence; neither party had secured representation in the TGNA since the success of the AKP at the 2002 legislative elections.

Referendum on constitutional reform

The Government announced a package of proposed constitutional reforms in March, which were aimed at resolving persistent constitutional disputes between the executive, legislative, judicial and military branches of the Turkish state, and at expediting Turkey's accession to the EU. The Government embarked on a series of consultations with opposition parties in an effort to secure the required two-thirds' parliamentary majority for the legislation. However, CHP leader Deniz Baykal rejected the package of reforms, accusing the ruling party of seeking to consolidate its own power base.

In May 2010 the TGNA voted, by 336 votes to 72, to approve a revised package of constitutional reforms, thus falling short of the two-thirds' majority required to secure its passage outright, but exceeding the minimum number of votes necessary to put the legislation to a public referendum. It was subsequently announced that a referendum on the reforms was to be held on 12 September, a date of considerable symbolic importance, being the 30th anniversary of the 1980 military coup, an event that had precipitated the drafting of the existing, deeply unpopular Constitution.

In mid-May 2010 the CHP filed a petition with the Supreme Court appealing for the annulment of the package of reforms; the petition cited 'procedural errors'. Also in mid-May Deniz Baykal was forced to resign as CHP leader following allegations published in the media regarding his private life; Kemal Kılıçdaroğlu was elected unopposed as party leader at a conference in Ankara later that month. In early July the Supreme Court rejected the CHP's bid to have the entire package of reforms annulled, but did overturn some of the proposals relating to the judicial system, including the proposed restructuring of the Supreme Council of Judges and Public Prosecutors.

Keen to secure the backing of the Kurdish minority, which was identified as potentially holding the balance of power in the referendum, in early September 2010 Prime Minister Erdoğan pledged to effect a more comprehensive overhaul of the Constitution after the 2011 legislative elections. However, Kurdish politicians urged Kurds to boycott the referendum in protest at Erdoğan's failure to protect Kurdish rights more effectively. The referendum was duly held in September 2010, with the rate of participation recorded at 73.7% of the registered electorate. The package of reforms was approved by 57.9% of the valid votes cast. Erdoğan welcomed the result as a mandate for deeper reform, and pledged the Government's commitment to redrafting the 1982 Constitution.

The 'Ergenekon' investigation

Following the discovery of a hoard of munitions at a property belonging to a retired army officer in İstanbul in June 2007, an investigation was launched into the existence of a clandestine nationalist organization, known as Ergenekon, with alleged links to senior military, police, judicial and media figures. From early 2008 a series of high-profile arrests were made in connection with the investigation. In August Gen. İlker Başbuğ succeeded Büyükanıt as Chief of the General Staff; Başbuğ was replaced as Ground Forces Commander by Gen. Işık Koşaner, who, in a speech in late August, denied allegations of links between the military and Ergenekon, and reiterated the army's readiness to take action, if needed, to protect Turkey's secular Constitution. Trial proceedings against 86 suspected members of Ergenekon were initiated in October. Suspects were charged with various offences, which included belonging to a terrorist organization and plotting to overthrow the Government. According to the prosecution, the organization had plotted to foment disorder through a series of violent incidents, including high-profile assassinations, in order to undermine the Government and provoke a military coup. The organization was also indicted with responsibility for several violent incidents, previously attributed to Islamist militants, such as the murder of the judge at the Council of State in May 2006 (see The AKP comes to power) and a bomb attack at the offices of *Cumhuriyet* newspaper in the same month. As many as 40 additional suspects, including three retired generals and a former police chief, were arrested in January 2009. In March charges against an additional 56 suspects were appended to the ongoing trial proceedings. In April the Supreme Court of Appeals ordered that the trial relating to the Council of State attack of 2006 be merged with the Ergenekon trial. The proliferation of arrests during 2008–09 prompted some critics to accuse the Government of exploiting the case to discredit their political rivals.

In June 2009 the daily newspaper *Taraf* published a document, purported to have been drafted by a senior naval officer, containing details of a military plot to undermine the Government. Although an internal military inquiry concluded later that month that the document was a forgery, prosecutors assigned to the ongoing Ergenekon investigation none the less ordered the arrest of the accused officer. Also that month an amendment to Turkey's code of criminal procedure, endorsing the holding of civilian trials for military personnel accused of constitutional offences or crimes against national security, was approved by parliament. (The establishment of civil jurisdiction over the military was an important condition of Turkey's EU accession process.) However, the legislation was referred to the Constitutional Court by the CHP. A second Ergenekon trial, involving 56 suspects including two retired army generals, the highest ranking officials to face trial thus far, commenced on 20 July. In January 2010 the Constitutional Court issued an annulment of the legislation concerning civil trials for military personnel. Nevertheless, later that month the 12th High Criminal Court in İstanbul ruled that the Constitutional Court annulment would not affect the conduct of the ongoing Ergenekon trials.

A further series of arrests relating to two alleged coup plots (code-named 'Sledgehammer' and 'Cage') was carried out in 2010; detainees included former and serving military officers, with around 50 senior officers reported to have been detained on 22 February. In July 196 people—including 30 serving or retired military officers, among them a former army commander, Gen. (retd) Çetin Doğan, who the authorities alleged was the primary orchestrator of the plot—were indicted of conspiracy to overthrow the Government in relation to the Sledgehammer investigation. The 196 defendants, who remained free pending trial,

were formally charged during a preliminary hearing in December. The arrest in early 2011 of a number of media employees who had previously been critical of the Government's performance—including eight journalists employed by the internet television channel OdaTV, who were detained in February, and well-known journalists Ahmet Şık and Nedim Şener, who were apprehended in March—on suspicion of belonging to Ergenekon, heightened concerns that the Government was exploiting the ongoing coup investigations to discredit its critics and the opposition prior to legislative elections due in June. The arrest of the OdaTV journalists came a few days after the channel had claimed to possess video footage depicting police officers involved in the Ergenekon investigation planting evidence in premises associated with some of the accused. The most senior Ergenekon prosecutor, Zekeriya Öz, defended the arrests and denied that they were related to the journalists' work or personal views. However, in an unexpected development, Öz was transferred to the position of deputy chief public prosecutor and removed from the Ergenekon investigation. By mid-2011 more than 600 people had been charged in relation to Ergenekon and its associated investigations. Trial proceedings against Şık, Şener, the eight OdaTV journalists and four others, including former police chief Hanefi Avcıoğlu, who had been arrested in September 2010 on suspicion of belonging to Ergenekon, commenced in November 2011. Şık and Şener, together with two of the OdaTV journalists, Sait Çakır and Coşkun Musluk, were released in March 2012. Gen. Başbuğ, who had retired in 2010, became the most senior official to be arrested in connection with the Ergenekon investigation when he was detained in January 2012. The former Chief of the General Staff was alleged, *inter alia*, to have established or administered a terrorist organization and to have sought forcefully to unseat the Government. The trial of Gen. Başbuğ, who denied the charges against him, opened in March. By February 2013 some 67 suspects in the Ergenekon case were still in detention; prosecutors summed up their case in March, but by early May a verdict had still not been announced. Meanwhile, in September 2012 three army generals, including Doğan, were sentenced to 20 years' imprisonment for their alleged involvement in the 'Sledgehammer' plot; nearly 300 other officers were also convicted and 36 defendants acquitted; however, the prosecutor of the case subsequently filed an objection to the court's acquittal of the defendants.

The 2011 legislative elections

The campaigning period prior to legislative elections scheduled for June 2011 was marked by apparent attempts by the ruling AKP to discredit its opponents. Erdoğan had previously announced that, if the AKP were re-elected, it would seek to introduce a new constitution, which would include amending Turkey's system of government from a parliamentary to a presidential system. (It was widely believed that the Prime Minister intended to seek election to the presidency following the completion of Abdullah Gül's term.) In order to approve such a charter, the AKP would need to secure 367 of the 550 seats in the TGNA; in order to put it to a vote by means of a popular referendum, the incumbent party would need to secure 330 seats. Consequently, the AKP appeared determined to castigate its opponents while presenting itself as the protector of political and economic stability. The dissemination via the internet from May of video images purporting to depict a number of MHP members engaged in extramarital sexual activity, led to 10 of the opposition party's parliamentary candidates withdrawing from the contest. MHP leader Devlet Bahçeli accused the AKP of having funded the anonymous group responsible for the recording of the footage, while some pointed to the high-quality and sheer number of the videos as an indication of the involvement of the police. The Government adamantly denied any wrongdoing; however, little appeared to be done by the authorities to apprehend those responsible for the covert footage. Meanwhile, in April 2011 the BDP (which had decided not to contest the elections directly, owing to the stipulation that political parties must win at least 10% of the national vote in order to secure parliamentary representation) threatened to boycott the legislative elections after 12 independent candidates it had supported were barred from participating in the poll.

At the June 2011 elections the AKP won by a comfortable margin, although it fell short of the targeted 367 (or even 330) seats, securing 326 seats and 49.8% of the national vote. Its closest rival, the CHP, won 135 seats (26.0% of the vote). Despite the controversy surrounding the MHP, the party exceeded expectations, securing 53 seats (13.0% of the vote), while independent candidates endorsed by the BDP won 36 seats (6.6%).

However, one of the winning BDP-backed candidates was prevented from taking his seat owing to a previous criminal conviction for having links to the PKK; the seat was subsequently awarded to an AKP candidate by the High Electoral Board. As a result, the final number of seats won by the AKP increased to 327, while that of BDP-backed independents was reduced to 35.

Of further consternation to the opposition was the authorities' refusal to release from prison two winning CHP candidates, who were being held on remand in connection with the Ergenekon investigation, as well as five successful BDP-backed candidates, who were being held on suspicion of belonging to Koma Civakên Kurdistan (KCK—Union of Communities of Kurdistan), an organization allegedly linked to the PKK. In protest, the CHP and the BDP (whose members together constituted more than one-third of the legislature) boycotted the inaugural legislative session in late June 2011 and pledged to boycott further parliamentary proceedings until their members were released from gaol. However, in the event, the CHP and the BDP announced an end to their boycotts in July and September, respectively, with members of both parties acknowledging that the action had failed to have any tangible impact on the Government. Cemil Çiçek was elected as the new parliamentary Speaker in July 2011. In April 2012 Çiçek launched an initiative to release the eight imprisoned deputies; the three opposition parties agreed on a legal amendment under which members of parliament would be included among those exempt from pre-trial detention. President Gül confirmed his support for the deputies' release the following month. Erdoğan rejected the proposal, however, stating that it was an issue for the courts. In October 30 deputies from the European Council expressed concern over the detained deputies in a signed declaration.

Meanwhile, in July 2011 Prime Minister Erdoğan announced the composition of his new Cabinet. Mehmet Vecdi Gönül, Minister of National Defence in the outgoing administration, was replaced by İsmet Yılmaz. Egemen Bağış was appointed to head the newly formed Ministry of European Union Affairs, and former AKP Secretary-General İdris Naim Şahin was designated Minister of Internal Affairs.

Following the arrest of some 250 serving and retired army officials in connection with the ongoing Ergenekon investigation, and the Government's refusal to acquiesce to demands that the officials be released, in July 2011 the Chief of the General Staff resigned, together with the commanders of the ground forces, the navy and the air force. The mass resignations of the country's military leadership were widely interpreted as reflecting a paradigm shift in the power balance between the military and the civilian establishment, in favour of the latter. In August Gen. Necdet Özel was appointed as the new Chief of the General Staff.

As the PKK intensified its armed struggle against the Government in the aftermath of the legislative election (see The Kurdish Issue), an increasing number of arrests were made in the latter half of 2011 both of BDP members and of journalists who had reported critically on Kurdish issues. By the end of September more than 3,000 BDP officials were reported to have been arrested. In a series of police raids in İstanbul, Ankara and a number of other cities in December, some 40 journalists, most of whom were employed by pro-Kurdish media, were arrested on suspicion of belonging to the KCK; the first hearing against them began in September 2012, by which time an estimated 8,000 pro-Kurdish politicians, lawyers, academics, writers and journalists had been arrested on terrorism charges relating to the KCK. Some 63 prisoners who were part of the KCK investigation subsequently joined a hunger-strike to demand an end to the isolation of the PKK leader, Abdullah Öcalan (see The Kurdish issue). As the hunger-strike reached its 50th day, a group of protesters attempted to stage a demonstration in support of the prisoners at an Ankara university, while the BDP organized a day of action which was strongly supported in the south-eastern province of Diyarbakır. After an appeal by Öcalan, the hunger strike came to an end later that month.

Some 34 Kurdish civilians were killed in an air-strike in Diyarbakır in late December 2011. It was alleged that they had been attempting illegally to transport goods across the border with Iraq. In May 2012 a CHP deputy filed a criminal complaint against Erdoğan and Gen. Özel, claiming that the military had been aware that those killed were not in fact members of the PKK, and that Erdoğan and Özel were thus guilty of a crime against humanity. In late December the parliamentary Human Rights Inquiry Commission completed its report on the incident, but postponed the release of its findings to avoid coinciding with the first anniversary of the air-strike. The report concluded that the killings were not intentional, but occurred as a result of a lack of co-ordination between military and security officials. The adoption of the findings of the report in March 2013 prompted outrage among the families of the victims, as well as the three opposition parties.

In mid-April 2012 a number of retired generals, the most senior being former Deputy Chief of Staff Gen. Çevik Bir, were arrested as part of an investigation by the parliamentary Coup and Military Memorandum Commission into the memorandum presented by the military leadership at a meeting of the NSC in February 1997 aimed at preserving Turkey's secular traditions, an incident subsequently referred to as the 'post-modern coup'. The Commission also conducted an investigation into the coup of 1980, but this suffered a setback when Gen. (retd) Kenan Evren and the only other surviving member of the NSC at that time refused to answer questions. However, in November 2012 Evren denied any role in the torture of thousands after the 1980 coup. On 28 November the Commission submitted its final report to parliament amid claims by the BHP that its findings failed to address the expectations of the public or to advance democracy in Turkey. In February 2013 there was a further series of arrests of in connection with the 1997 memorandum, bringing the total number of generals in detention to more than 70.

Recent developments: moves towards a new constitution

In May 2012 the Constitutional Reconciliation Commission, comprising three members each from the four parties represented in the TGNA, plus the Speaker, began drafting the country's first non-military constitution, with an initial deadline for finalizing the draft set at the end of December 2012. During the months that ensued it was apparent that political differences were obstructing the progress of the Commission, with such fundamental issues as the definition of secularism, the medium of instruction in schools and the independence of the judiciary raising major disagreement across party lines. A further major issue of contention was the system of government, with Erdoğan's AKP espousing the adoption of a presidential system, which was unpopular with the CHP and the MHP, both of which accused the premier of aiming to establish authoritarian rule. By the end of December the Commission had only reached consensus on 28 of the 150 articles examined, and its term was subsequently extended until the end of April 2013. In March the Supreme Board of Judges and Public Prosecutors approved the AKP's proposal for a presidential system of government; the issue was subsequently to be discussed by the Commission. At a meeting of the Commission in early May it was decided that, with consensus having been reached on just 30 articles, the deadline would again be extended, until the end of June. However, the AKP announced that, owing to its frustration with the delays imposed by the opposition, it would submit its own constitutional proposal to the TGNA.

Meanwhile, relations between President Gül and Erdoğan appeared to have deteriorated. Owing to the constitutional amendment enacted shortly after his election, providing for popular elections to a five-year presidency and a maximum of two terms of office, Gül's position had been ambiguous. Erdoğan, who was widely rumoured to have ambitions to the presidency himself, used his influence to push an amendment through the TGNA in January 2012 stating that Gül should stand down in 2014 and not seek re-election. The CHP subsequently attempted to annul the law, and in June the Constitutional Court ruled that President Gül was eligible to serve a seven-year term and to stand for re-election.

In October 2012 the Constitutional Court deemed as unlawful the creation of several new ministries in 2011—the Ministry of Science, Industry and Technology, the Ministry of Forestry and Water Affairs, and the Ministry of Family and Social Policies—as they had been established by government decree rather than parliamentary law. The Court ruled that the Government had six months in which to submit draft laws on the ministries to the TGNA. In a further setback to the Government, President Gül on the same day vetoed a constitutional amendment facilitating early municipal elections, claiming that this would impose too great a burden on Turkey's economy.

Amid peace talks with Öcalan (see The Kurdish issue) in January 2013, Erdoğan instituted several cabinet changes, most notably the replacement of İdris Naim Şahin as interior minister with Muammer Güler, a former Governor of İstanbul. This move was thought to be linked to the peace process as Şahin's ultra-nationalist views had angered the Kurdish community in the past. In early February a suicide bomb attack outside the US embassy in Ankara resulted in the death of a security guard. It was alleged that the perpetrator, Ecevit Şanli, was a former member of the DHKP—C. In March a bomb was exploded at the Ministry of Justice building in the capital, while another incendiary device was set off at the AKP headquarters. As the Kurdish peace talks got under way, opposition to the process became increasingly apparent; in April the deputy chairman of the CHP, Gülşeren Onanc, resigned, having suggested that the party did not fully support the negotiations, while the MHP organized a large rally against the talks in İzmir.

The Kurdish Issue

In 1984 the outlawed PKK, seeking the creation of a Kurdish national homeland in Turkey, launched a violent guerrilla campaign against the Turkish authorities in the south-eastern provinces. The Government responded by arresting suspected Kurdish leaders, sending in more security forces, establishing local militia groups and imposing martial law (and later states of emergency) in the troubled provinces. However, violence continued to escalate, and in April and May 1990 clashes between rebel Kurds, security forces and civilians resulted in the deaths of 140 people. The conflict entered a new phase when, in August and October 1991, and March 1992 (in retaliation for continuing cross-border attacks on Turkish troops), government fighter planes conducted numerous sorties into northern Iraq in order to attack suspected PKK bases there. In late 1992 Turkish air and ground forces (in excess of 20,000 troops) conducted further attacks upon PKK bases inside northern Iraq. In the course of these raids many civilians and refugees (including Iraqi Kurds) were reportedly killed, prompting international observers and relief workers publicly to question the integrity of the exercises. The Iraqi Government lodged formal complaints with the UN, denouncing Turkish violations of Iraq's territorial integrity.

Hopes that a negotiated resolution to the conflict might be achieved, following the unilateral declaration of a cease-fire by the PKK in March 1993, were frustrated by renewed fighting in May and an intensification of the conflict in June. The bombing of several coastal resorts and of tourist attractions in central İstanbul confirmed the PKK's intention to disrupt the country's economy and to attract international attention to the conflict.

In November 1993 a 10,000-strong élite anti-terrorist force was created to counter the PKK forces, in addition to the estimated 150,000–200,000 troops already positioned in the area of conflict. In 1994 the security forces mounted a heavy offensive against the separatists, and again conducted air attacks on suspected PKK strongholds in south-eastern Turkey and in northern Iraq. In November a Kurdish proposal for a cease-fire, accompanied by international mediation, to achieve a peaceful settlement to the conflict was rejected by the Government, which emphasized the success of its anti-terrorist campaign.

A massive offensive, involving 35,000 air and ground force troops, was initiated against PKK targets in northern Iraq in March 1995. Turkish forces advanced some 40 km across the border, prompting protests from the Iraqi Government. Under increasing international pressure, Turkey undertook a complete withdrawal of its troops by May. Official figures stated that 555 Kurdish separatists and 58 Turkish soldiers were killed as a result of the operation. Earlier, in April, the PKK had obtained permission to convene in the Netherlands, in an attempt to establish a Kurdish parliament-in-exile, prompting Turkey temporarily to recall its ambassador from The Hague. Fighting was resumed in the south-east of the country in June, and in July a further week-long offensive was conducted against Kurdish bases in northern Iraq. In December the PKK leader, Abdullah Öcalan, announced a unilateral cease-fire on the part of his organization. By March 1996, having received no assurances of a cease-fire from the Turkish authorities, Öcalan advised tourists against visiting the country, warning of possible renewed attacks against major tourist sites. During April an estimated 400 PKK members were killed in the renewed military operation. In the following months PKK activists were frequently pursued into northern Iraq by Turkish ground and air forces, provoking protests from the Iraqi Government, and fighting in the south-eastern provinces escalated. In response, Turkish security forces conducted air raids against PKK targets in northern Iraq, which continued into early 1997. An estimated 2,800 PKK activists were killed during 1996 as a result of the conflict, in addition to 532 members of the security forces and 145 civilians.

In May 1997 Turkey again launched a massive military offensive against the PKK in northern Iraq, involving the

mobilization of 50,000 troops. Turkey claimed that the incursion was in response to an appeal by the Iraqi-based Kurdistan Democratic Party (KDP), which co-operated with the Turkish attack. The operation elicited rigorous condemnation from Iraq, Iran and Syria, but the response from members of NATO was muted. By June Turkish military officials claimed that the attack had achieved its objectives of destroying several PKK bases in northern Iraq and estimated that more than 3,000 PKK troops had been killed. A further offensive, launched in September, was speculated to be part of a Turkish plan to establish a security zone in northern Iraq to prevent cross-border attacks by the PKK. This assumption was apparently confirmed by the lifting of the state of emergency in three of the nine south-eastern provinces in October.

Relations with Syria, which had already deteriorated in July 1998 (owing to Syria's repeated claim to the Hatay region of Turkey), worsened in October, after Turkey threatened the use of force if Syria did not expel Öcalan and close down terrorist training camps in both Syria and the Beqa'a valley in Lebanon. It was reported that 10,000 Turkish troops had been deployed near the border; the Turkish ambassador to Syria was also recalled. Egypt and Iran both attempted to mediate in the dispute, and, following a meeting of Turkish and Syrian officials in late October, an agreement was signed under which Syria would not allow the PKK to operate on its territory; Öcalan was thus forced to leave the country, and he arrived in Italy in November. Turkey had already temporarily recalled its ambassador to Italy in October, after a meeting of the Kurdish parliament-in-exile was hosted there. Relations deteriorated further owing to Italy's refusal to extradite Öcalan and his subsequent application for asylum. However, in January 1999 Öcalan was reported to have left Italy after that application was rejected. In the following month he was captured at the Greek embassy in Kenya and returned to Turkey, prompting protests by Kurdish activists throughout Europe.

At the end of February 1999 Öcalan was formally charged, in the absence of defence counsel. PKK violence in protest at the trial, which commenced in March, continued, and there were also threats of violence against tourists in Turkey. In April a further operation was launched against the PKK, involving the deployment of some 15,000 Turkish troops in northern Iraq. In June Öcalan was convicted on treason charges and sentenced to death; violent demonstrations were held in protest at his sentence.

The PKK agreed to a cease-fire in August 1999, at which time Öcalan announced that the PKK was prepared to surrender its arms in exchange for Kurdish rights; PKK fighters withdrew from Turkey at the end of the month. However, the Government insisted that the PKK cease hostilities entirely in order for Turkey to reassess the situation. Following a statement issued by Öcalan in September in which he urged PKK rebels to show their commitment to the end of hostilities by surrendering to Turkish forces, two eight-member PKK delegations travelled to Ankara, where they were arrested and detained by the authorities.

In September 1999 the Kurdish parliament-in-exile convened in Brussels, Belgium, where it voted to dissolve and to join the Kurdistan National Congress. Following the cease-fire, the number of armed confrontations in the south-east had declined substantially and in October the Government reduced the number of checkpoints in the region. In November Öcalan's death sentence was upheld on appeal and the chief prosecutor rejected his application for a final appeal; his lawyers referred the case to the ECHR. A second trial against Öcalan, together with 101 other defendants, began in Ankara in December for a series of offences including extortion and murder allegedly carried out in the 1970s; the trial was adjourned until February 2000. In January 2000 the parties of the governing coalition announced that they had agreed to delay Öcalan's execution until a ruling had been given by the ECHR.

The PKK announced a formal end to its war against Turkey in February 2000, and stated that it would campaign for Kurdish rights within a framework of peace and democracy. In February three HADEP mayors were arrested and charged with aiding the PKK; they were released on bail, following protests both from within Turkey and internationally. Relations with the EU deteriorated further in February, when Turkey denied EU politicians permission to visit Öcalan in prison. At that time 18 people, including the HADEP leader, Ahmet Turan Demir, were sentenced to almost four years' imprisonment for organizing demonstrations in support of Öcalan. Despite the PKK's cease-fire declaration, Turkish troops continued to push into Kurdish strongholds throughout the year, and in early 2001 Turkish troops advanced into northern Iraq in an attempt to suppress PKK activities. Meanwhile, the hearing of the appeal against Öcalan's death sentence began at the ECHR in November 2000. Öcalan's appeal was based on the grounds that he had not received a fair trial in Turkey under the terms of the European Convention on Human Rights.

In April 2002 the PKK formally announced a change of name to the Congress for Freedom and Democracy in Kurdistan (KADEK), under Öcalan's leadership, and asserted its wish to campaign peacefully for Kurdish rights. Although the movement had abandoned its initiative for an independent Kurdish state, the announcement was received with scepticism on the part of the Turkish Government. However, KADEK was not included in the EU's list of organizations designated as 'terrorist', and it was believed that its agenda had been designed to win support from the EU. In November 2002, in a sign that the Government had acknowledged the conversion of the PKK, the state of emergency that prevailed in the two remaining south-eastern provinces of Diyarbakır and Sirnak was finally ended.

In October 2002, meanwhile, the State Security Court officially commuted Öcalan's death sentence to life imprisonment, in accordance with the abolition of the death penalty in peacetime by the TGNA in August. In March 2003 the ECHR issued a non-binding ruling that Öcalan had not received a fair trial, and criticized Turkey for violating some of Öcalan's rights; however, the ECHR rejected accusations by Öcalan's lawyers of inhumane treatment and illegal detention. Turkey immediately appealed against the ECHR, fearing renewed pressure from the EU to hold a retrial if the ruling was upheld. Despite its success in defeating Kurdish separatism, the Government continued to fear the possible emergence of a Kurdish state in northern Iraq after the ouster of Iraqi President Saddam Hussain's regime by US-led coalition forces in March–April 2003. In September, following renewed attacks by the organization in eastern Turkey, KADEK formally ended the cease-fire declared in February 2000, accusing the authorities of failing to address demands for improved Kurdish rights and freedom of expression. In November 2003 KADEK was reconstituted as the Kongreya Gelê Kurdistanê (KONGRA-GEL—Kurdistan People's Congress), which, in January 2004, the US Administration added to its list of designated terrorist organizations.

After revoking its cease-fire, KONGRA-GEL organized sporadic attacks during 2004. In July government troops launched an offensive against KONGRA-GEL positions at the border with Iraq. In late 2004 and early 2005 further clashes erupted between KONGRA-GEL militants and Turkish security forces, and in April the KONGRA-GEL leadership announced that the organization was to revert to its original name, PKK (although it appeared that not all elements of the movement did so). In May the ECHR ruled that the trial of Öcalan had been unfair, on the grounds that he had not been tried by an independent tribunal (owing to the presence of a military judge on the panel); the Turkish Government indicated that a further trial would be conducted.

In September 2005 some 88 PKK supporters were arrested in İstanbul, after protesting at being prevented from attending a rally in support of Öcalan (who was said to have been placed in solitary confinement). Despite the PKK's extension until early October of a unilateral cease-fire, which it had declared in August, clashes between rebels and government forces continued in the east of the country. Security forces, meanwhile, staged several operations in eastern Turkey against members of the PKK and its military wing, Hezên Parastina Gel (HPG—People's Defence Forces). In April 2006 a series of bomb attacks in İstanbul resulted in three deaths, and in August the coastal resorts of Marmaris and Antalya were also targeted: a further three people were killed in the Antalya blast and in both bombings there were dozens of casualties, including many foreign nationals. Responsibility for the attacks was claimed by a group calling itself Teyrêbazên Azadiya Kurdistan (TAK—Kurdistan Freedom Falcons), which purported to be linked to the PKK.

Amid the intensification of violence in south-eastern Turkey during 2006, the likelihood grew of a large-scale Turkish military incursion to attempt to defeat PKK rebels in northern Iraq. By July 2007, according to Hoshyar al-Zibari, the Iraqi Minister of Foreign Affairs, Turkish armed forces along the countries' mutual border amounted to some 140,000 personnel. In August, after a reported 12 Turkish soldiers had died during fighting with PKK militants in that month, Erdoğan and the Iraqi Prime

Minister, Nuri al-Maliki, reached a memorandum of understanding aimed at ending the 'safe haven' of the PKK in northern Iraq. A further security co-operation pact was signed in late September, although the Iraqi Government refused Turkey's principal demand that its military be permitted to enter Iraqi territory in pursuit of Kurdish fighters. A large number of Turkish soldiers were reported to have been killed during clashes with the PKK in subsequent weeks. In October the TGNA endorsed a decision to allow Turkish military raids into northern Iraq, despite US President George W. Bush and al-Maliki urging the Turkish leadership to show restraint. In November Bush pledged that the USA would increase its military co-operation with Turkey, in an apparent effort to dissuade the Turkish Government from launching a major incursion into Iraqi territory. Nevertheless, in December Turkish troops began an offensive against PKK bases in Iraq's northern region, in response to a series of cross-border raids by armed Kurdish separatists. The Iraqi Government protested to its Turkish counterpart that it had not been consulted over the military action, while the President of the Kurdish Autonomous Region, Masoud Barzani, described Turkey's actions as a violation of Iraqi sovereignty. It was reported at the end of February that several hundred troops had participated in the military campaign, despite initial claims that around 10,000 troops had been involved. Nevertheless, dozens of PKK militants were killed in the week-long offensive, together with several Turkish soldiers. (The Turkish military claimed by this time to have killed at least 230 PKK fighters, and to have lost 27 of its soldiers; however, PKK sources alleged that around 90 Turkish soldiers had died in the recent incursion.)

Sporadic cross-border clashes between Turkish forces and PKK rebels continued throughout 2008. At least 45 PKK fighters were reportedly killed in air-strikes between March and June. Prime Minister Erdoğan visited Iraq in July, the first visit by a Turkish premier in some 18 years, holding talks with his Iraqi counterpart on strengthening economic and political ties; the Iraqi authorities also indicated their support for Turkey's campaign against the PKK in northern Iraq. The military offensive against PKK positions in northern Iraq intensified following an attack on a Turkish army border camp in the Şemdinli district in early October, in which at least 15 soldiers were killed. In that month the TGNA voted to extend the Government's mandate to launch military operations against targets in northern Iraq. In January 2009 the establishment of a joint command centre to combat PKK operations in northern Iraq was announced, involving Turkish, Iraqi and US intelligence authorities. Despite a decrease in the intensity of the conflict at the beginning of 2009, renewed air-strikes were launched against PKK targets in northern Iraq from early February.

Meanwhile, as many as 10,000 people took part in a demonstration in İstanbul in June 2008 to demand fresh initiatives to resolve the Kurdish conflict. Erdoğan embarked on a tour of the mainly Kurdish south-eastern provinces in November, calling for national unity and solidarity in the face of separatism and terrorism; his presence provoked violent demonstrations in several towns. According to Turkish military sources, 696 PKK rebels had been killed and 177 captured during the conflict in 2008, while 171 members of the security forces and 51 civilians were killed in that year. In February 2009 at least 50 people were arrested in various south-eastern towns as demonstrations marking the 10th anniversary of the imprisonment of Öcalan escalated into violent clashes with security forces. The Demokratik Toplum Partisi (DTP—Democratic Society Party), a pro-Kurdish political party formed in 2005 to replace DEHAP, performed strongly in south-eastern Turkey in the municipal elections in March 2009, retaining control of local councils in Diyarbakır, Hakkari and Şırnak provinces, and gaining control of Van and Siirt at the expense of the AKP.

Hopes for a breakthrough in the Kurdish conflict were raised significantly in April 2009 when the PKK announced it was suspending all offensive operations until 1 June, in order to facilitate peace negotiations with the Government. In a series of newspaper interviews in May, PKK leaders revealed that the organization was willing to relinquish its demand for an independent Kurdish state and to seek a peaceful settlement to the conflict, in return for the recognition of Kurdish rights and the establishment of a regional legislature. At the beginning of June the PKK extended its truce for a further six weeks; an additional six-week extension was announced in mid-July. Meanwhile, the Turkish authorities refused to recognize the PKK's unilateral cease-fire, and military operations against Kurdish rebels continued. Six Turkish soldiers were killed when a roadside bomb exploded in Hakkari province in late May 2009; in response, the security forces launched air attacks on suspected PKK bases in northern Iraq at the end of May and in June. In July Prime Minister Erdoğan launched a major new initiative aimed at solving the Kurdish conflict. While specific details of the Government's Kurdish initiative were not publicly announced, the plan was believed to encompass greater political and cultural rights for Kurds, as well as incentives for militants to relinquish their armed resistance. In October the TGNA endorsed for a further year the Government's mandate to launch military operations against PKK targets in northern Iraq.

In what was designed to serve as a confidence-building measure, in mid-October 2009 a group of 34 PKK militants and supporters surrendered to a Turkish delegation close to Turkey's border with Iraq; following a brief interrogation all of the group were reported to have been released within 24 hours. Days later the returning PKK members were guests of honour at a rally in Diyarbakır attended by up to 100,000 supporters, prompting criticism from nationalist opposition parties. Further planned PKK repatriations were postponed, apparently in response to the widespread public opposition to the initiative. In November the Government announced plans to remove long-standing bans on private television channels broadcasting in Kurdish and the use of Kurdish names for towns and villages.

The Constitutional Court ordered the dissolution of the DTP in December 2009. The ruling stemmed from an indictment, first lodged in 2007, that accused the party of promoting separatism and of supporting the PKK. Some 37 DTP members were banned from political activity for five years, while the party's Chairman and another senior member were expelled from the TGNA. The party's leadership initially indicated that the remaining 19 DTP deputies would be withdrawn from the legislature. However, it was subsequently announced that the 19 former DTP deputies were to maintain their parliamentary participation as members of the Barış ve Demokrasi Partisi (BDP—Peace and Democracy Party). The ruling drew expressions of concern from the EU, and Erdoğan stated that he was opposed to the judicial closure of political parties.

The security forces mounted renewed operations against suspected Kurdish separatists from December 2009, with more than 30 people, including some municipal officials, arrested on 23 December; more than 140 people were reported to have been detained during further operations in south-eastern provinces on 21 January and 14 February 2010. In April it was reported that state prosecutors in Diyarbakır had filed indictments against 30 of the PKK contingent that had returned in October 2009, accusing them of disseminating propaganda or membership of a terrorist organization. In July 2010 PKK leader Murat Karayilan declared that he would order his group to lay down its weapons under UN supervision if the Turkish Government agreed to a cease-fire and his demands for greater political and cultural rights for Turkey's Kurds.

Meanwhile, a roadside bomb attack on a police bus in İstanbul in June 2010, which was attributed to Kurdish separatists, was reported to have injured 15 people; a second bomb attack on a military bus later in the month, for which the TAK claimed responsibility, claimed the lives of five people and injured 12 others. A suicide bomb attack on a police post in central Istanbul at the end of October, also thought to have been carried out by Kurdish rebels, injured more than 30 people, including 15 police officers. Sporadic ground- and air-strikes against alleged PKK militants in northern Iraq continued to be reported throughout 2010 and 2011. In March 2011 Erdoğan became the first Turkish premier to visit the Kurdish Autonomous Region of Iraq, where he held talks with Masoud Barzani regarding co-operation in combating the PKK.

Shortly prior to the June 2011 legislative elections, the BDP, angered by anti-Kurdish statements from members of the ruling AKP, threatened a campaign of 'civil disobedience' if the new administration failed comprehensively to address Kurdish demands for greater autonomy and rights. Following the polls, at which BDP-endorsed candidates secured 36 seats, Kurdish rebels intensified their armed campaign against government forces. By September more than 100 people were reported to have been killed in PKK-related violence since the elections. Following the deaths of eight soldiers during an attack on their convoy by rebels in Hakkari province in August, Erdoğan ordered a series of air-strikes against PKK targets in northern Iraq, in which the Government claimed some 100 militants were killed, although the PKK acknowledged the deaths of only three rebels.

A bomb explosion in central Ankara in September, which killed three civilians, was attributed to the PKK; however, the group denied responsibility. After approximately 100 PKK rebels launched a co-ordinated series of attacks on border posts and military targets in south-eastern Turkey in October, in which 24 Turkish soldiers were reported to have been killed and a further 18 injured, a contingent of Turkish soldiers made a ground incursion into northern Iraq and further air-strikes were launched against PKK targets therein; 15 Kurdish militants were reported to have been killed in the operation. By early 2012 hundreds of Kurdish activists were reported to have been arrested on suspicion of having links to the PKK since the escalation of violence.

Violent incidents between Turkish security forces and PKK militants continued throughout the first half of 2012. In May members of the PKK abducted Veysel Çelik, an AKP district chairman, in Diyarbakır. Meanwhile, in a major breakthrough supported by the BDP, Erdoğan and CHP leader Kemal Kılıçdaroğlu agreed on a 'road map' to end the Kurdish problem, which included the establishment of a non-parliamentary commission to lead the negotiations. In June eight soldiers were killed and 19 wounded in clashes with the PKK in the south-eastern province of Hakkari; some 18 militants were injured in a subsequent counter-offensive. Both Erdoğan and Selahattin Demirtaş, leader of the BDP, appealed to the PKK to end its use of violence. In July a rally organized by the BDP took place in Diyarbakır, despite a government ban. Police used pepper spray and water cannons to disperse the crowds, and a BDP deputy was injured during altercations. In August, in the heaviest fighting in several years, nearly 130 PKK militants and eight members of the security forces were killed in Hakkari province; seven zones of Hakkari were subsequently declared under military provision until early October. In October 10 schools in south-eastern Turkey were attacked by suspected PKK militants; the TGNA subsequently approved a motion to extend Turkey's military authority for cross-border operations against PKK members. In November Turkish forces launched a campaign of air-strikes against PKK camps in northern Iraq.

Officials from Turkey's National Intelligence Organization began talks with Öcalan in December 2012, in an attempt to end the hostilities. It was reported that the negotiations were focused on a gradual agenda of conflict resolution, which included, *inter alia*, a cease-fire, the deportation of PKK militants, and the transfer of Öcalan to house arrest. In January 2013 three female members of the PKK were assassinated in Paris, France; large crowds of mourners attended their funerals in Diyarbakır. French intelligence sources blamed the killings on internal conflict within the PKK. The incident, however, did not derail the peace process; in early February Erdoğan offered safe passage to any PKK militant prepared to withdraw from Turkey. At the end of that month Öcalan called for all PKK militants to leave the country by August. In mid-March the PKK released eight hostages in northern Iraq—all public officials captured in 2011 and 2012. In late March, on the occasion of *Nowruz* (Kurdish New Year), a statement from Öcalan was read out to crowds gathered in Diyarbakır, in which he called for a formal cease-fire and for PKK militants to withdraw from Turkey. In April the 63 members of the non-parliamentary commission to lead negotiations over the Kurdish issue were appointed, and in early May PKK militants began to leave Turkey, in accordance with the plan for a phased withdrawal of fighters outlined earlier that year.

Foreign Affairs

Relations with the USA and regional relations

During the 1990s Turkey's importance to its key ally, the USA, increased as its strategic location allowed it to co-operate with the USA in regional security issues. The Turkish Government responded positively to requests from the USA for logistical aid, following the forcible annexation of Kuwait by Iraq in August 1990, and closed its border with Iraq to all non-essential trade and, later, to traffic. In September Turkey and the USA extended an agreement to allow the USA access to more than 25 military establishments, in return for military and economic aid, that had been initially signed in 1980, and renewed in 1987. In January 1991 a resolution to extend the war powers of the Government and effectively endorse the unrestricted use of Turkish airbases by coalition forces was agreed by the TGNA. US aircraft subsequently embarked upon bombing missions into north-eastern Iraq from NATO bases inside south-eastern Turkey. In February and March the US Government announced substantial increases in military and economic aid to Turkey. In April an estimated 600,000 Kurds attempted to flee northern Iraq into Turkey. Following a massive international relief effort and the subsequent repatriation of the majority of refugees, the Turkish Government agreed to the deployment in south-east Turkey of a 3,000-strong multi-national 'rapid reaction force', which would respond to any further acts of aggression by Iraq against the Kurds in the newly created 'safe havens'. While all ground forces were withdrawn in October, the Turkish Government agreed to the continued use of its airbases by a small allied air-strike force to conduct patrols of northern Iraq under the mandate of 'Operation Provide Comfort'. The mandate was granted six-month extensions, despite increasing unease on the part of the Turkish authorities that the Kurdish enclave was providing a refuge for PKK separatists. Difficulties in Turkey's relations with the USA arose in 1994, following a decision by the US Congress to withhold some military and economic aid in order to encourage greater respect for human rights in the Turkish Government's treatment of Kurdish separatists.

In July 1996, in spite of his earlier election pledge to conclude the mandate for the use of Turkish bases for allied aircraft engaged in 'Operation Provide Comfort', the new RP Prime Minister, Necmettin Erbakan, secured a final extension of the operation's mandate until the end of the year. In September the Turkish Government refused permission for the use of its airbases for a US military operation against Iraqi forces that had violated the Kurdish area in northern Iraq. Turkey amassed an estimated additional 20,000 troops along the border and revealed proposals to establish a temporary security zone in the region in order to stem any influx of refugees from Iraq and to prevent the PKK from exploiting the situation. The Government also undertook to relocate the military co-ordination centre of 'Operation Provide Comfort' from Zakho in northern Iraq to Silopi in south-eastern Turkey. ('Operation Provide Comfort' was superseded by the more limited aerial surveillance operation 'Northern Watch' in January 1997.) During 1996 Turkey pursued diplomatic efforts to secure the reopening of the petroleum pipeline from Kirkuk in northern Iraq to Yumurtalik in Turkey, which had been closed since August 1990 as a result of UN-imposed economic sanctions. The pipeline was finally reactivated in December, in accordance with a UN agreement permitting the export of US $2,000m. of petroleum by Iraq over a six-month period in order to fund the purchase of essential medical and other humanitarian supplies. As relations between Iraq and the UN deteriorated from the end of 1997, Turkey announced that it opposed the use of its Incirlik airbase for potential US-led strikes against Iraq and urged a peaceful solution to the crisis. Although Turkey was informed of the air-strikes against Iraq in December, in January 1999 it announced that Turkish airbases would not be used in any new operation against Iraq.

Following the suicide attacks on the USA in September 2001, attributed to al-Qa'ida, Turkey emerged as a crucial ally in the former's 'war on terror', immediately pledging its co-operation. In October the TGNA agreed in principle to send troops to Afghanistan and allow foreign forces to be stationed in Turkey, and in December US Secretary of State Colin Powell visited Turkey to discuss security and bilateral trade issues. Meanwhile, hundreds of Turkish commandos were deployed in Uzbekistan in preparation for possible combat in Afghanistan, and 90 of these entered northern Afghanistan to train the opposition United National Islamic Front for the Salvation of Afghanistan (the United Front—UF, or 'Northern Alliance'). Turkey assumed command of the International Security Assistance Force (ISAF) in Afghanistan in June 2002, raising its troop presence in that country to 1,000. (Turkish command of the ISAF ended in February 2003.)

In 2002 Turkish leaders became increasingly concerned about the possibility that the USA would open a 'second front' in its military campaign to overthrow the regime of Saddam Hussein. In particular, the Government feared a break-up of the Iraqi state and the creation of a Kurdish state in northern Iraq that could be used to foster Kurdish nationalism in its own territory, and the possible mass exodus of Iraqi Kurds into Turkey. There were also concerns about the disruption to Turkish-Iraqi trade and economic co-operation that any US-led attack would bring. Prime Minister Ecevit's illness and subsequent preparations for elections to the TGNA in November meant that no agreements between Turkey and the USA were reached over the latter's planned invasion of Iraq. Relations between the two countries were further complicated by the victory of the AKP in the elections, and overwhelming public opposition to war against

Iraq. By January 2003 a number of senior US officials had visited Turkey to persuade the Government to accept the deployment of 62,000 US troops in the south-east of the country, and the use of the region as a staging post for a 'northern front' in the planned conflict. Following lengthy negotiations, the US Government offered a financial package of US $6,000m. in direct grants and an additional $20,000m. in loans and trade concessions in compensation for any economic losses incurred during the war; however, the Turkish authorities considered this sum to be insufficient. President Sezer warned in February that US forces could only be deployed in Turkey if the USA obtained a second UN resolution from the UN Security Council authorizing the use of force against Iraq.

In early March 2003 the TGNA rejected a motion allowing the USA to deploy troops in Turkey. As many as 50 AKP legislators voted against the Government, underscoring the level of opposition to US plans for a military campaign to oust the Iraqi regime. Later that month the TGNA voted only to allow the use of Turkish airspace for the conflict, but endorsed the deployment of Turkish troops in Iraq if considered necessary. The US-led coalition forces initiated attacks against the Iraqi regime shortly thereafter, and subsequently abandoned attempts to negotiate the use of Turkish bases. The aid package was withdrawn following the TGNA vote, but in April the USA offered a new, reduced loan package totalling US $8,500m. in order to repair bilateral relations. US Secretary of State Powell visited Ankara at that time and secured Turkish permission for humanitarian aid and US logistical supplies to be delivered to coalition troops in Iraq via Turkish territory. In September the Turkish and US Governments signed an agreement approving the loan to compensate for the adverse effects of the conflict in Iraq. In October a motion proposed by the Council of Ministers in favour of contributing peace-keeping troops to the US-led coalition in Iraq was endorsed by the TGNA. Following widespread protests in both Turkey and Iraq, however, the planned deployment of Turkish forces in Iraq was cancelled.

In October 2007 Turkey temporarily withdrew its ambassador to Washington, DC, in protest against the adoption by the Committee on Foreign Affairs of the US House of Representatives of a non-binding resolution describing as 'genocide' the killing of an estimated 1.5m. Armenians following the First World War. In his first visit to a Muslim country since becoming US President, Barack Obama travelled to Turkey in April 2009. In a speech to the TGNA he emphasized the importance of US-Turkish ties, and stated that the USA was not 'at war with Islam'. He also urged the EU to admit Turkey as a full member. In a statement issued on Armenian Remembrance Day later that month, Obama described the killing of an estimated 1.5m. Armenians in 1915–23 as a 'great atrocity' but, crucially, refrained from using the term 'genocide', despite a pre-election pledge to do so. The Turkish Ministry of Foreign Affairs issued a statement that described some aspects of the President's statement as 'unacceptable'; however, Obama's careful choice of words was widely believed to reflect his Administration's desire to expedite the normalization of Turkish-Armenian ties (see Other external relations).

Despite opposition from the Obama Administration, in March 2010 the US House of Representatives Committee on Foreign Affairs narrowly adopted a further non-binding resolution that called for the formal recognition of the Turkish 'genocide' against the Armenians. In response, Turkey recalled its ambassador from Washington, DC, for consultations, warning that the resolution could be detrimental to US-Turkish relations and to the Turkish-Armenian normalization process. None the less, in April the Turkish authorities expressed their satisfaction with US assurances concerning the 'genocide' dispute, and the Turkish ambassador returned to his post. However, concerned at Turkey's perceived shift closer towards Iran and further away from Israel, in August the US Senate took an unprecedented step when it blocked Obama's ambassadorial nomination to Ankara, while the House of Representatives Committee on Foreign Affairs conducted a special hearing on Turkey to discuss whether its orientation was indeed shifting in ways that might be unfavourable to bilateral relations. Later in the month the US Department of State held a publicly announced high-level policy discussion on Turkey, chaired by Secretary of State Hillary Clinton and with the participation of senior department officials. Although Obama, capitalizing on a legislative 'loophole', circumvented the Senate and unilaterally installed the two nominees during a congressional recess in December, the series of events in mid-2010 appeared to indicate a sense of deepening US mistrust of Turkish foreign policy. Nevertheless, in October 2011, Secretary of State Clinton welcomed Turkey's growing role in the Middle East and within the wider international community, and hailed deepening bilateral co-operation in areas including trade and security. However, Clinton also urged the Turkish Government to address its long-standing disputes with Cyprus, Greece and Israel, and to ratify the protocols concerning the normalization of relations with Armenia (see Other external relations), noting that these served as obstacles to regional progress and development. In May 2012 it was announced that the parliamentary Coup and Memorandum Commission would investigate US intervention into the 1980 military coup and the series of assassinations which preceded it. The US Government thanked the Turkish authorities for their response to the suicide bombing by a left-wing extremist of the US embassy in Ankara in February 2013.

In late 1995 a long-standing dispute with Syria and Iraq concerning the water supply from the Euphrates and Tigris rivers re-emerged as a major source of tension in Turkey's external relations. (Hostilities with Syria had already intensified during the year over that country's apparent support for the PKK, with the Turkish Government accusing Syria of supplying armaments to the separatist organization.) Protests by Syria and Iraq that Turkey was storing their share of water from the two rivers and restricting flow, in contravention of previous agreements, resulted in a ruling, in March 1996, by the Council of the League of Arab States (the Arab League, see p. 372) that the waters of the rivers should be shared equally between the three countries. However, in August 1998 the Turkish Government refused to revive water talks with Syria and Iraq, citing issues that had first to be improved between the countries, primarily that of terrorism. Relations between Syria and Turkey improved during 1999 and in October officials from the two countries reportedly agreed to open a new border crossing. However, in January 2000 Turkey appealed to the USA not to remove Syria from its list of nations accused of sponsoring terrorism, until such time as all PKK bases had been removed from Syria, and ruled out any concessions on the water issue in order to aid talks between Israel and Syria. A major rapprochement materialized in early 2002 when Turkey signed an agreement with Syria allowing for joint military exercises.

Turkish-Syrian relations continued significantly to improve following the success of the AKP in the Turkish legislative elections in November 2002, with the incoming Government swiftly adopting a formal policy of 'zero problems with neighbours'. President Bashar al-Assad became the first Syrian head of state to undertake an official visit to Turkey in January 2004. A bilateral agreement providing for visa-free travel between Turkey and Syria by both countries' nationals, for visits of up to 90 days, was signed in September 2009. Moreover, following a meeting of Arab and Turkish ministers in İstanbul in June 2010, an agreement to establish a free trade zone between Turkey, Syria, Jordan and Lebanon was announced. However, the agreement was terminated following the imposition by Turkey of economic and financial sanctions against Syria, in late November 2011, in response to the Syrian authorities' handling of civil unrest in that country. Announcing the sanctions, the Turkish Minister of Foreign Affairs, Ahmet Davutoğlu, declared that the Syrian Government had reached 'the end of the road', further stating that, while the Turkish Government did not support military action against Syria, it would not exclude the possibility of establishing a 'buffer zone' on the bilateral border in order to contain the thousands of refugees who had fled into Turkey to escape the violent crackdown by the Assad regime. The imposition of sanctions—which included travel bans on Syrian officials deemed responsible for violence against civilians or with close links to President Assad, and a freeze on their assets held in Turkey—followed repeated appeals by Turkey from mid-2011 urging the Assad regime to implement meaningful domestic reforms and to end its operations against anti-Government protesters. Such appeals remained unheeded, appearing somewhat to undermine Turkey's reputation as an influential regional power broker.

Following the massacre of more than 100 civilians in the Syrian region of Houla, in May 2012 the Turkish Government ordered Syrian diplomats to leave the country. In June a Turkish reconnaissance jet was shot down by Syrian air defence forces; the Syrian Government claimed that the plane had been guilty of a 'breach of sovereignty'. Turkey responded by deploying a convoy of military vehicles to the Syrian border. Military activity between the two countries continued; in early July Turkish jets

were deployed to repel Syrian helicopters in an incident close to the border. Later that month it was announced that all border gates with Syria were to be closed as they were deemed too hazardous for traffic. In August as the fighting in Syria intensified an estimated 4,000 Syrian refugees entered Turkey over a period of three days, bringing the total to some 60,000. The following month a Syrian mortar bomb hit a border town in the south-eastern province of Akçakale, killing five civilians; Turkey retaliated by bombing targets in Syria over a period of several days. In early October the TGNA passed a motion allowing the Turkish military to conduct cross-border raids into Syria. Turkey also increased its naval presence in the Mediterranean Sea. The NATO Secretary-General, Anders Fogh Rasmussen, announced that the organization was prepared to defend Turkey against attack if required. As intense fighting broke out between rebels and Syrian Government forces around the Syrian town of Azmarin, Turkey deployed two fighter planes to the border, while in Akçakale Turkish soldiers dug trenches near the border for the further deployment of troops and armoured vehicles. Following the interception of a Syrian passenger plane en route from Moscow, which the Turkish authorities claimed was being used to transport military equipment and ammunition to Syria, Syrian civilian flights were banned from using Turkish air space. In December NATO approved Turkey's request for *Patriot* missiles to defend its border against Syria. In February 2013 a car bomb exploded at the border town of Hatay, killing 14 people. Five people were subsequently detained over the incident (three additional suspects having been released), of whom four were of Syrian nationality and one Turkish. A further car bombing in Reyhanlı in early May, in which some 51 people were killed, was attributed by the Turkish Government to a left-wing group under the direction of the Syrian intelligence services. Some 13 people were subsequently detained for their alleged involvement in the bombing, while six further suspects were sought. The Syrian Government denied any involvement in the attack.

Meanwhile, in July 2008 Erdoğan became the first Turkish premier to visit Iraq in almost 20 years. During the two-day visit the Prime Minister held talks on bilateral trade and regional security issues with his Iraqi counterpart, Nuri al-Maliki, and the establishment of a strategic co-operation council was announced. Minister of Foreign Affairs Davutoğlu acted as a mediator, apparently with some success, during a diplomatic dispute between Iraq and Syria from late August 2009, which resulted from allegations of Syrian involvement in a series of bomb attacks in the Iraqi capital, Baghdad, earlier in August. Davutoğlu hosted a tripartite summit in Ankara in September aimed at resolving the dispute. Following a meeting of the Turkey-Iraq strategic co-operation council in October in Baghdad, 48 memorandums of understanding on co-operation in areas including trade, security, energy, water resources and agriculture were signed by the Iraqi and Turkish Prime Ministers. However, Prime Minister al-Maliki expressed his concern regarding Turkish military operations against PKK targets in northern Iraq and urged Turkey to respect Iraq's territorial integrity.

Provisional plans to open two new border crossings and to create a free trade and industrial zone inside Iraqi land on the Turkish border were announced in June 2010, and both sides stated their resolve to not allow an escalation in PKK violence to compromise bilateral relations. In March 2011 Prime Minister Erdoğan led a high-level Turkish delegation on a two-day visit to Iraq, during which he visited the Kurdish Autonomous Region, Baghdad and Najaf, holding discussions with al-Maliki and Iraq's most senior Shi'ite cleric, Grand Ayatollah Ali al-Sistani, as well as other Iraqi political and religious figures. However, the dispute concerning the supply of water to Iraq from the Euphrates and Tigris rivers remained unresolved. In May the Iraqi Government declared that the Turkish authorities' restriction of the water supply was 'unacceptable', claiming that a series of dams constructed on both rivers allowed Turkey to monopolize the rivers' waters, to the detriment of Iraq and Syria. An Iraqi government spokesperson insisted that the Iraqi legislature would not recognize the strategic co-operation council with Turkey until a bilateral water-sharing agreement was successfully concluded. In October the TGNA voted to extend for a further year the decree authorizing cross-border military operations against PKK militants in Iraq (this had previously been extended in October 2009 and again in October 2010). Turkey's relations with Iraq came under strain in May 2012 after Turkey refused to extradite Iraq's Vice-President, Tariq al-Hashimi, who had been found guilty *in absentia* of planning and facilitating murder. Later that month some 200 protesters in Basra, Iraq, demanded al-Hashimi's immediate extradition. At early May 2013 al-Hashimi was still residing in Turkey.

Meanwhile, in September 2011, following the AKP's re-election to a third term in government, Prime Minister Erdoğan embarked on a tour of Egypt, Tunisia and Libya, meeting with the new administrations following the ouster earlier in the year of the respective regimes of Hosni Mubarak, Zine al-Abidine Ben Ali and Muammar al-Qaddafi. Turkey's reputation within the Arab world had recently been buoyed by the Erdoğan Government's support for the Palestinian application for full membership of the UN, as well as Turkey's increasingly firm stance against Israel, and the Turkish premier appeared keen further to advance his status as a regional leader. During the three-nation tour, Erdoğan presented Turkey as an example for the Arab world, offering advice on achieving a successful fusion of the sometimes competing demands of democracy, development and Islam.

Following the imposition of economic and financial sanctions against Syria in November 2011, the Turkish Government announced that it was considering opening new border crossings with Iraq to enable trade with Saudi Arabia and Gulf states to go via Iraq and Jordan, thereby bypassing Syria, should the security situation in the latter country further deteriorate. However, Turkish–Iraqi tensions re-emerged in early 2012, following expressions of concern by the Iraqi Minister of Foreign Affairs over Turkish and Iranian competition to fill the power vacuum in Iraq in the absence of a representative, strong, national unity government in Iraq. The comment appeared to reflect a wider concern among some Arab states over Turkey's growing influence in the region. This fear, together with an apparent desire to distance itself from increasingly aggressive Turkish rhetoric demanding the resignation of the Assad regime, was considered to be behind the decision of the Arab League to exclude Turkey, together with Iran, from a summit meeting, convened in Baghdad in late March, on the issue of the Syrian unrest. Iraqi Prime Minister al-Maliki was also reported to have objected to the participation in the meeting of Turkey, which held observer status at the Arab League and which had participated in the vast majority of its previous major summits.

In early 1996 Turkey signed a new military and intelligence co-operation agreement with Israel, which permitted the use of Turkish airbases and airspace for military training purposes. The pact stemmed from common concerns about Iran, Iraq and Syria, and received support from the USA, a strong ally of both Turkey and Israel. The Arab League denounced the agreement as 'an act of aggression'. Business deals quickly followed, especially those concerning the supply of Turkish water to Israel. However, the gradual improvement in Turkey's relations with its Arab neighbours from 2000 made the pact with Israel less significant, and, in response to the increasing violence between Israelis and Palestinians in the West Bank and Gaza, Prime Minister Ecevit in April 2002 accused Israel of 'genocide' against the Palestinians. None the less, in August Turkey signed an agreement with Israel according to which it would sell the latter 50m. cu m of water every year for the next 20 years. In May 2004 relations with Israel became further strained, when Prime Minister Erdoğan condemned an Israeli offensive in Gaza. In January 2005, however, the Turkish Deputy Prime Minister and Minister of Foreign Affairs made an official visit to Israel—the first by a Turkish politician since the AKP Government was elected in November 2002.

Turkey received praise for its role as host and mediator for indirect peace talks between Syria and Israel during 2008. The talks, several rounds of which took place in İstanbul in mid-2008, were believed to be making progress towards a possible settlement of Israel and Syria's territorial dispute over the Golan Heights. However, negotiations were suspended following the launch of Israel's military offensive against Islamic Resistance Movement (Hamas) targets in Gaza in late December. Turkey, along with most other Muslim countries, voiced strong condemnation of Israel's actions. In late January 2009 there was an angry exchange between Erdoğan and Israeli President Shimon Peres during a debate on Gaza at the World Economic Forum in Davos, Switzerland. Erdoğan accused Israel of having committed crimes against humanity, and walked out when he was not afforded as much time to speak on the matter as the Israeli President. Nevertheless, a meeting between the foreign ministers of Israel and Turkey, which took place in Brussels, Belgium, in early March at the time of a NATO foreign ministers summit, signalled some improvement in relations.

However, relations between Israel and Turkey grew increasingly tense in the months following the formation in March 2009 of a new, predominantly right-wing Israeli Government led by Prime Minister Binyamin Netanyahu. In October Turkey announced the cancellation of Israel's involvement in a major military exercise. Despite initial denials that the cancellation was a political measure, Davutoğlu acknowledged in November that the decision stemmed from Turkish disapproval of Israel's military operation in Gaza. Meanwhile, in response, Netanyahu declared his opposition to Turkey resuming its role as mediator in the stalled Syrian-Israeli peace talks. Relations deteriorated further in January 2010 when Israel's Deputy Minister of Foreign Affairs, Danny Ayalon, was deemed to have 'humiliated' Turkey's ambassador to Israel, Ahmet Çelikkol, during a meeting that was attended by journalists and cameramen. Ayalon had summoned the ambassador officially to complain about the broadcast on Turkish state television of programmes depicting Israeli security forces in a manner considered offensive to Israel. The Turkish authorities summoned the Israeli ambassador in Ankara to protest at the mistreatment of their representative and threatened to suspend bilateral relations unless an unequivocal apology was issued. Following the subsequent issue of two separate apologies, the dispute was declared officially to be finished.

Relations declined markedly in May 2010, following the deaths of nine Turkish citizens during a raid by Israeli troops on a ship that had been chartered by a Turkish charitable organization, as part of a flotilla of vessels attempting to break the Israeli blockade of Gaza and deliver humanitarian supplies to the territory. On the evening of the raid, hundreds of Israelis gathered outside the Turkish embassy in Tel-Aviv to protest at what they perceived to be a Turkish ploy to cast Israel in a negative light, claiming that the flotilla of ships had been dispatched with the express intention of provoking a response from the Israeli military, allegations that were adamantly denied by the Turkish authorities. Although the Israeli Government insisted that its troops had acted in self-defence after being attacked by pro-Palestinian activists on board the ship, Erdoğan branded the incident an act of 'state terror' and in June Turkey suspended its diplomatic and military ties with Israel, withdrawing its ambassador from Tel-Aviv and insisting that it would not restore full relations until Israel publicly apologized for the incident, compensated the relatives of the victims and agreed to the holding of a full and independent international inquiry. Israel refused to acquiesce to the demands. It was reported in July that Davutoğlu and the Israeli Minister of Industry, Trade and Labour, Binyamin Ben-Eliezer, had conducted covert discussions aimed at securing an improvement in relations following the incident, seemingly at the behest of the US Administration. However, the publication by the UN in early September 2011 of a report detailing the findings of an inquiry into the circumstances surrounding the raid precipitated a significant deterioration in Israeli-Turkish relations. The report criticized the conduct of both countries over the incident, determining that the decision by the Israeli soldiers to board the vessel 'with such substantial force and with no final warning' constituted an 'excessive and unreasonable' action, while recognizing the 'legitimacy' of Israel's blockade as a means of stemming the flow of weapons into Gaza by sea. The Turkish Government was swift to condemn the report's conclusions, and, citing Israel's continued refusal formally to apologize for the incident, both the Israeli ambassador and his deputy were expelled from Ankara, while Turkey's remaining senior diplomats were recalled from its embassy in Tel-Aviv, as diplomatic relations with Israel were downgraded to the level of second secretary. Bilateral military and trade ties were also suspended.

In April 2012 Turkey blocked the participation of Israel in a NATO summit scheduled to take place the following month. In May a Turkish court voted unanimously to proceed with charges against senior military figures in Israel, as well as those members of the military who carried out the raid on the ship. In November the trial, *in absentia*, of members of the Israeli military involved in the incident began. Following a visit to Israel by US President Barack Obama in March 2013, Israeli Prime Minister Netanyahu issued an apology to his Turkish counterpart for 'errors' during the raid on the ship in 2010. Erdoğan was reported to have accepted the apology, and the two leaders apparently agreed to work to restore full diplomatic relations between their countries. In May 2013 a second round of talks on compensation for the families of the victims took place in

Tel-Aviv, the first round having occurred in Ankara in the previous month.

In April 1996 the Turkish and Iranian authorities ordered the expulsion of diplomatic personnel following accusations of Iranian involvement in Islamist terrorist attacks committed in Turkey in the early 1990s. In August 1996 relations with Iran were strengthened by the conclusion of an agreement providing for the construction of a 320-km pipeline between the two countries and the export of substantial supplies of natural gas from Iran. In December the Presidents of Turkey and Iran agreed to pursue greater economic and security co-operation. A trade agreement was concluded granting each other the status of most favoured nation. In February 1997 the Iranian ambassador to Turkey provoked a diplomatic crisis by advocating the introduction of Islamic law in Turkey. Criticism of the actions of the Turkish military by an Iranian consul-general later in that month resulted in both men being asked to leave the country. Iran responded by expelling two Turkish diplomats. However, both countries immediately undertook diplomatic initiatives to restore relations, and in March it was agreed that all bilateral agreements were to be pursued. Following negotiations, it was announced in September that full diplomatic relations were to be resumed.

In October 1998 Iran and Turkey established a committee to demarcate their joint border; they later signed a memorandum to increase customs co-operation at their main border crossing. In June 1999 a meeting of the Turkish-Iranian border committee was held for the first time since 1994; a number of issues were discussed and it was agreed that the committee should meet every year. In July, however, the Turkish chargé d'affaires was twice summoned to the Iranian Ministry of Foreign Affairs following the alleged bombing of an Iranian border region by Turkey in which five people died. In October Turkey announced it would contribute to compensation for the Iranian bomb damage; a Turkish report into the incident concluded that Turkey had bombed Iraq not Iran, although some people with Iranian citizenship, living in northern Iraq, might have been affected. However, from 2001 rising tensions between Azerbaijan and Iran over claims to the Caspian Sea, Turkey's strong support for Azerbaijan, its continuing alliance with Israel, and competition for influence in the Caucasus and Central Asia threatened to strain the relationship.

After coming to power in 2002 the AKP Government endeavoured to improve relations with Turkey's Muslim neighbours. This policy encompassed a significant strengthening of ties with Iran. Iranian President Mahmoud Ahmadinejad undertook a working visit to Turkey in August 2008, holding discussions with Prime Minister Erdoğan. In 2009 Turkey represented the largest consumer of Iranian natural gas exports, and negotiations concerning Turkish investment in the development of Iran's South Pars gasfield, which commenced in 2008, were ongoing. Meanwhile, amid growing tensions between Iran and Western nations over Iran's nuclear activities, Erdoğan made his second official visit to Iran in October 2009 for further discussions on bilateral trade and energy projects. During the visit Erdoğan emphatically defended Iran's entitlement to pursue a civil nuclear programme and called for the crisis to be resolved through international diplomacy. The Turkish Prime Minister subsequently rejected growing demands from the USA and other Western powers for a new round of UN sanctions in response to Iran's nuclear programme. Nevertheless, during an official visit to Washington, DC, in December Erdoğan indicated to US President Barack Obama his willingness to act as a mediator in the international dispute over Iran's nuclear programme—a proposal that secured Qatari and Syrian support in May 2010. Also in May Turkey and Iran, together with Brazil, signed an agreement under the terms of which Iran was to transfer the majority of its low-enriched uranium stockpiles to Turkey, to be kept under the supervision of the International Atomic Energy Agency and Iran, in exchange for the supply to Iran by Turkey of nuclear fuel rods. In June Turkey and Brazil voted against a UN Security Council resolution to impose fresh sanctions on Iran in response to that country's nuclear programme; however, the resolution was approved, having secured the support of 12 members of the Council. In February 2011 President Gül embarked on his inaugural state visit to Iran, during which he met with Ahmadinejad and reiterated Turkey's continued support for the resolution of the dispute over Iran's nuclear programme through negotiation. During a visit to Tehran in March 2012, Erdoğan stressed Turkey's readiness to host and mediate in talks, to be held between Iran, the UN Security Council's five

permanent members and Germany, aimed at resolving the ongoing nuclear dispute; talks were duly convened in İstanbul in mid-April.

The Cyprus question and relations with Greece

Although Turkey and Greece are both members of NATO, long-standing disputes over sovereignty in the Aegean Sea and concerning Cyprus have strained relations between the two countries, and tension was exacerbated when Turkey granted recognition to the 'Turkish Republic of Northern Cyprus' ('TRNC'), proclaimed in November 1983 (see the chapter on Cyprus). Throughout the early 1990s Turkey and Greece maintained strong support for their respective communities in Cyprus during the ongoing, but frequently interrupted, negotiations to resolve the issue. From mid-1996 an escalation in intercommunal tension in Cyprus emphasized divisions between the two countries. Turkey remained committed in its support for the 'TRNC' authorities and resolved to respond with military action to the proposed deployment of an anti-aircraft missile system in the Greek Cypriot territory. A joint defence doctrine was agreed by the Turkish and 'TRNC' authorities in January 1997, and in March a co-operation accord, providing for some US $250m. in economic assistance to the 'TRNC', was ratified by the two sides.

In April 1997, following Greece's continued refusal to conduct bilateral discussions with Turkey over sovereignty rights in the Aegean, Turkey rejected proposals to refer a dispute over Imia (Kardak), a small, uninhabited island of which both countries claimed sovereignty, to the International Court of Justice (ICJ). At the end of April the Greek and Turkish ministers responsible for foreign affairs held bilateral talks in Malta under EU auspices, during which it was agreed that each country would establish a committee of experts to help resolve bilateral disputes. In July, at a NATO summit in Madrid, Spain, direct talks took place between Demirel and the Greek Prime Minister, Konstantinos Simitis. The so-called Madrid agreement was signed, in which both sides pledged to respect the other's sovereign rights and to renounce violence, and the threat of violence, in their dealings with each other.

In July 1997 Turkey announced the formation of a joint committee to implement partial integration between Turkey and the 'TRNC', in response to the EU's agreement to commence accession talks with Cyprus. Turkey also declared in September that should the EU continue to conduct membership talks with the Greek Cypriot Government, then it would seek further integration with the 'TRNC'. Shortly afterwards Turkey banned all Greek Cypriot ships from entering Turkish ports.

In early 1999 Greece denied Turkish accusations of Greek support for the PKK, although Öcalan was later captured at the Greek embassy in Kenya. In August relations between the two countries improved markedly, after Greece offered assistance to Turkey following an earthquake that occurred in north-west Turkey at the end of that month. In January 2000 the Greek Minister of Foreign Affairs made the first official visit to Turkey by a Greek foreign minister for 38 years, during which it was agreed that direct talks would be held to reduce military tensions in the Aegean. In February his Turkish counterpart made an equally historic visit, becoming the first Turkish foreign minister to visit Greece in 40 years. In October, however, Greece withdrew from a joint NATO military exercise in the Aegean, after it accused Turkey of preventing Greek aircraft from flying over the disputed islands of Limnos and Ikaria. This followed a joint NATO military exercise with Greek and Turkish troops on a Greek beach in June, which had been considered to be a mark of considerable progress in Greek-Turkish relations. In February 2001 the Greek parliament decreed a 'Genocide Day' to commemorate the Turkish assault on the Greek community in eastern Turkey by Atatürk's forces in 1922. However, in April 2001 both Turkey and Greece announced major reductions in their weapons-procurement programmes, and in May Greece announced measures to improve the rights of its ethnic Turks (mainly in Thrace). In June the two countries discussed the possibility of allowing Turkish nationals to visit Greek islands in the Aegean for day trips without the need for visas, and the Minister of Foreign Affairs, İsmail Cem, received his Greek counterpart, Georgios Papandreou, to discuss friendship-building measures such as the de-mining of their mutual border and submitting a joint bid to host the 2008 European Football Championship.

None the less, Cyprus continued to overshadow bilateral relations, and in May 2001 Cem warned that there would be 'no limits' to Turkey's response were Cyprus to be admitted to EU membership before a political settlement had been reached; in

November Ecevit warned that Turkey could annex the 'TRNC' if this were to occur. In February 2002 the Turkish and Greek foreign ministers recommended talks, following the resumption of negotiations between the Greek and Turkish Cypriot sides on the island. In mid-March Turkey and Greece discussed ongoing disputes over the Aegean Sea, including the control of the continental shelves and the resources beneath them. Later in the month the two Governments signed an agreement to build a 285-km natural gas pipeline from Ankara to Komotini, Greece, thereby allowing Iranian gas to flow to the EU via the existing Tabriz–Ankara pipeline.

Following the elections to the TGNA in November 2002, Recep Tayyip Erdoğan stated that a final peace agreement over Cyprus would accelerate Turkey's chances of joining the EU. Erdoğan, whose political priority was Turkey's EU membership, was increasingly in conflict with Turkish Cypriot leader Rauf Denktaş's unyielding stance on reaching a political solution. In January 2003 Erdoğan publicly criticized Denktaş and stated that he was in favour of a new policy for Cyprus, with a view to achieving a solution by 28 February 2003 in order to allow the 'TRNC' to join the EU in 2004 at the same time as the Greek part of the island. During late 2002 and early 2003 the Turkish- and Greek-Cypriot leaders had made significant progress towards reaching a final agreement, which would permit the entire island to accede to the EU on 1 May 2004. However, negotiations on the peace plan failed in March 2003. Following further UN-sponsored discussions in New York, USA, on 13 February 2004 agreement was reached on a reunification plan based on proposals drafted by the UN Secretary-General, Kofi Annan. The Greek Cypriot President, Tassos Papadopoulos, and Denktaş resumed UN-sponsored negotiations in the Cypriot capital, Nicosia, on 19 February. Greece and Turkey joined the negotiations later in March; however, both Papadopoulos and Denktaş subsequently opposed a final resolution, which was to be submitted for approval by both the Greek- and Turkish-Cypriot communities at a referendum. On 24 April the reunification plan was endorsed by Turkish Cypriots by 64.9% of votes cast at the referendum, but rejected by Greek Cypriots by an overwhelming majority of 75.8% of the votes; consequently, only the Greek part of Cyprus was admitted to the EU on 1 May.

In April 2005 the Turkish Cypriot Prime Minister, Mehmet Ali Talat, who strongly supported reunification of the island and full participation in the EU, was elected to the 'TRNC' presidency, replacing Denktaş. In late January 2008 the Greek Prime Minister, Kostas Karamanlis, undertook an official three-day visit to Turkey—the first such visit by a Greek premier since 1959. In February 2008 Papadopoulos was defeated at the first round of the Greek Cypriot presidential elections, and at the second round Demetris Christofias was elected to succeed him. It was strongly hoped that the election of Christofias would facilitate the procurement of a swift and lasting resolution to Cyprus's long-running division, and, therefore, prove advantageous to Turkish hopes of EU accession. UN-sponsored reunification talks involving Christofias and Talat commenced in Nicosia in March, during which convergence was reached on a number of issues, including arrangements for the opening of a Green Line crossing-point in the heart of Nicosia as a symbol of reconciliation between their two communities (this occurred on 3 April). By August 2009 the two leaders had held 40 meetings and a second round of negotiations commenced in September.

In his first overseas visit since becoming Prime Minister of Greece, Georgios Papandreou visited Turkey on 9 October 2009 for a meeting of the South-East European Cooperation Process. During his visit Papandreou held discussions encompassing bilateral relations and the Cyprus dispute with Turkey's Prime Minister and Minister of Foreign Affairs. Nevertheless, in mid-October Papandreou declared that the withdrawal of Turkish troops from Cyprus remained a precondition for Turkey's accession to the EU. Talks on the reunification of Cyprus continued in early 2010; however, although agreement had been reached on several technical aspects of the negotiations, as well as various confidence-building initiatives, several core issues remained unresolved and, following the victory of Dr Derviş Eroğlu—who was regarded as an opponent of reunification—at the 'TRNC' presidential election in April, the prospect of a settlement appeared to be receding.

During a visit by Erdoğan to Greece in May 2010, an unprecedented joint cabinet meeting was held by the Greek Government and the Turkish Prime Minister (and 10 Turkish government ministers accompanying him on the visit), and 21 bilateral accords providing for increased mutual co-operation in

the fields of, *inter alia*, energy, technology, tourism and transportation, were signed. During the meeting, the two sides were reported to have discussed a reduction in arms spending, including a proposal suggested by Erdoğan for both countries to disarm in the Aegean, a suggestion that the Greek Government claimed it would seriously consider when Turkey proved that it was no longer a military threat. In November, following a request from the Greek Government, the European Commission dispatched more than 150 border guards from EU member countries to assist in controlling Greece's border with Turkey, in response to an increasing flow of migrants into the former country. (In early 2011 the Council of Europe and other bodies criticized the Greek authorities' treatment of immigrants, including chronically poor conditions in detention centres at the border.) In March 2011 the Turkish Minister of Foreign Affairs, Ahmet Davutoğlu, travelled to the Greek capital, Athens, where he met his Greek counterpart; both sides pledged to strive for a continued improvement in bilateral relations. Relations between Turkey and Cyprus were threatened in September after Turkey began exploratory activities in waters near Cyprus, after the latter had started drilling for gas in the area in the previous week. Turkey had contended that Cyprus should not proceed with such actions until the division of the island had been resolved. Meanwhile, in June the Turkish Government had announced the provision of US $16,500m. to the 'TRNC', to be disbursed on improvements to transport infrastructure. In October 2012 Turkey and Greece expressed their commitment to restarting confidence-building procedures, and in March 2013 Davutoğlu announced that Turkey was prepared to negotiate a two-state solution to the Cyprus question should negotiations on reunification fail.

Turkey's application for membership of the European Union

Following the 1980 military coup, the EC-Turkish Association Council (which had been established in 1963) was suspended, together with all community aid to the country. Turkey was readmitted to associate membership of the EC in September 1986, but failed to gain access to the suspended EC aid or to extend the rights of the large number of Turkish workers in Europe. In April 1987 Turkey made a formal application to become a full member of the EC. In December 1989 the application was effectively rejected, at least until 1993, by the Commission of the European Communities. The Commission cited factors including Turkey's unsatisfactory human rights record, high rate of inflation, dependence upon the rural population and inadequate social security provisions as falling short of EC expectations.

The Turkish Government began to implement measures to construct a customs union with the EU, which was to become effective on 1 January 1995. Human rights issues remained the main obstacle to securing an agreement, and in December 1994 the customs union was postponed on these grounds. In February 1995 Greece withdrew its veto on the customs union, having received assurance on the accession of Cyprus to the EU, and the agreement was signed in March. The Turkish Government subsequently pursued efforts to introduce new democratization legislation and to secure the support of European leaders for the customs union by extending guarantees on human rights and treatment of its Kurdish population. The final terms of the arrangement were agreed at a meeting of the EU-Turkish Association Council in October, and were approved by the European Parliament in December. The EU was expected to provide a total of ECU 1,800m. over a five-year period, in order to assist the implementation of the new trade regime and to alleviate any initial hardships resulting from the agreement. The customs union came into effect on 1 January 1996. Its implementation was, however, delayed, owing to Greek opposition to the release of ECU 375m. in aid, claiming that Turkish action in the Aegean was a violation of the agreement. In July Greece withdrew its opposition to Turkey's participation in an EU-Mediterranean assistance programme, although the block on funds from the customs union remained in effect. Throughout 1996 the Turkish Government criticized the EU for its failure to adhere to the terms of the economic agreement. In January 1997 Turkey warned that it would disrupt any expansion of NATO if the EU refused to consider the Turkish membership application. Previously, Turkey had prevented the use of NATO facilities by members of Western European Union, owing to Greek opposition to Turkey's full participation in the regional defence grouping.

Relations with the EU were tense in 1997 as the next group of EU applicants was selected. In December, following EU announcements that Turkey would not be invited to join the EU, but that it would be invited to a newly created EU Conference, which was to include both EU and non-EU states, Turkey stated that it would not attend such a conference and that it would also cease negotiations on Cyprus, human rights and the Aegean disputes. It further threatened to boycott EU goods and to withdraw its application to the EU if it was not included in a list of candidates by June. On 20 December Turkey announced a six-month freeze in relations with the EU, which later announced it was withholding all aid to Turkey for the following year, owing to the situation in the south-east of the country and its human rights problems. Turkey officially declined its invitation to the EU Conference in March 1998 and in May also declined to attend a scheduled meeting of the EU-Turkish Association Council. Relations with France deteriorated in May when the French National Assembly adopted a motion recognizing the Turkish 'genocide' against Armenians in 1915–23; a number of bilateral military and commercial contracts were suspended as a result.

In October 1999 an EU report declared Turkey to be a suitable candidate to join the union, although Turkey stated that it would not accept any extraordinary conditions attached to such a candidacy, particularly with relation to Öcalan and the Kurdish problem. A number of EU member states offered their support to Turkey in late 1999, including Greece and Italy. In December Turkey was invited to attend the EU summit in Helsinki, Finland, and to accept formal status as a candidate for membership. The Government initially objected, owing to attached conditions concerning Cyprus and the Aegean dispute with Greece, but following a visit to Turkey by Javier Solana, the Secretary-General of the Council of the European Union, decided to accept. Turkey announced at that time that it would seek an end to its territorial disputes with Greece by 2004, the deadline set by the EU for a review.

In August 2000 Turkey signed the International Covenant of Civil and Political Rights and the International Covenant on Economic, Social and Cultural Rights. This was described as a positive step by the EU in its 'progress to accession' report on Turkey in November, although it pointed out that Turkey had not yet acceded to a number of other major human rights instruments, such as the abolition of the death penalty and the Convention on the Elimination of All Forms of Racial Discrimination. The report concluded that Turkey did not yet meet the Copenhagen criteria (which state that a country must have achieved 'stability of institutions guaranteeing democracy, the rule of law, human rights and respect for and protection of minorities'), thus making accession negotiations impossible, and described the overall human rights record in Turkey as worrying. It also stated that although Turkey had the basic features of a democratic system, it was slow to implement institutional reforms. Accession was also conditional on a satisfactory settlement of the Cyprus problem. This condition led to the Turkish withdrawal from the UN-sponsored proximity talks in protest. Prime Minister Ecevit accused the EU of 'deception' over Turkey's membership application, stating that it had reneged on a promise not to link Turkey's application to a resolution of the Cyprus problem and disputes with Greece over territorial rights in the Aegean Sea. A rewording of the Cyprus condition was later approved by Turkey; however, further tension was caused by Turkey's obstruction of an EU-NATO agreement enabling the EU's planned Rapid Reaction Force to use NATO assets, despite Turkey's offer to contribute up to 6,000 troops to the force.

Meanwhile, the Armenian 'genocide' question continued to provoke tension between Turkey and the EU. The European Parliament adopted a resolution in November 2000 that formally accused Turkey of genocide against Armenians in 1915 (at the same time it also urged Turkey to withdraw its forces from the 'TRNC'). Turkey reacted angrily, with the Fazilet Partisi (FP—Virtue Party) proposing a legislative investigation 'with the aim of removing wrong and biased opinions'. Relations received a further setback in early May 2001 when the ECHR ruled that Turkey had grossly violated the human rights of thousands of Greek Cypriots during its 1974 invasion, and subsequent occupation, of northern Cyprus. The court highlighted the failure of the Turkish Government to investigate the fate of missing Greek Cypriots, their forcible eviction from the north and the subsequent confiscation of their property.

In late May 2001 Turkey nominally agreed to grant the EU's Rapid Reaction Force access to NATO assets for future operations. Although Turkey would be consulted on such matters, it would not have the same participation rights or veto powers as

the existing 15 EU members. However, Turkish officials remained dissatisfied at the arrangements, having lobbied strongly for a greater influence in EU security planning. Turkey also feared that an upsurge of violence in Cyprus would necessitate the deployment of the Rapid Reaction Force on the island, placing the EU directly against itself, and had unsuccessfully sought guarantees against such an eventuality. In December Turkey finally reached agreement with the EU regarding the Rapid Reaction Force after months of British diplomacy.

In August 2001, meanwhile, the ECHR ruled that the Government's decision to ban the Islamist FP did not violate human rights laws. In October the TGNA passed constitutional amendments designed to facilitate EU membership but stopped short of abolishing the death penalty, a crucial EU demand. The issue of capital punishment placed the EU at odds with the ultra-nationalist MHP in the ruling coalition, which had pledged to exact the death penalty imposed on PKK leader Abdullah Öcalan. In August 2002 the EU welcomed the TGNA's vote to abolish the death penalty in peacetime, as part of a broader package of reforms. The new AKP Government elected in November pledged to accelerate efforts to join the EU. However, in that month Valéry Giscard d'Estaing, the Chairman of the Convention on the Future of Europe, stated publicly that Turkey should never be allowed to join the EU, and that its accession would mean the 'end of the European Union'. Senior EU officials distanced themselves from the remarks, which were also dismissed by Erdoğan. At the EU summit in Copenhagen, Denmark, in December, EU leaders agreed to delay negotiations on Turkish membership until after December 2004, and to resume discussions only if Turkey had fulfilled all the entry obligations. Several EU members, notably France and Germany, remained less enthusiastic about Turkish membership, citing its poor human rights record, which Turkey again pledged to improve.

A further complication to Turkish ambitions for EU membership emerged with the failure of a UN plan for the reunification of Cyprus in April 2004 (see The Cyprus question and relations with Greece). The resultant accession of only Greek Cypriot Cyprus to the EU on 1 May presented complications for Turkey's EU aspirations, although the Greek Cypriot Government declared that it would not veto Turkey's membership application, provided that it met the standards stipulated by the EU. An official visit to Greece by Erdoğan in May—the first by a Turkish premier in 16 years—reflected the improvement in relations between the two countries.

In May 2004 the TGNA approved a number of constitutional amendments, in accordance with EU requirements, which included the removal of references to the death penalty and the abolition of the country's system of State Security Courts (which was used to try dissidents). An EU summit in Brussels in June reaffirmed that a decision would be taken in December on whether Turkey had made sufficient progress on the EU's criteria for membership and that formal accession negotiations would be initiated if standards were considered to have been met. However, severe doubts about Turkey's qualifications had been presented in a European Parliament resolution, which had been adopted overwhelmingly in April, drawing attention to Turkey's continued use of torture, to the persecution of minorities, and other contraventions.

Nevertheless, in October 2004 the European Commission announced its approval of Turkey's qualification for accession negotiations, on condition that reforms continued. In many EU member states, however, there was increasing opposition to the admission of Turkey, especially in Germany and France, where the opposition was believed to reflect concern over the accession of a predominantly Muslim country; some favoured an option that Turkey be offered 'privileged member' status, rather than full membership. On 17 December the EU extended a provisional invitation to Turkey to commence accession negotiations on 3 October 2005, subject to the Turkish Government's fulfilment of a number of criteria, including continued progress in political and economic reforms. Erdoğan accepted an EU requirement to sign a customs accord with member states by that date, but insisted that the protocol would not constitute official Turkish recognition of the authorities of Greek Cyprus; instead he agreed to a compromise arrangement, whereby Turkey made a commitment for future recognition. The British Prime Minister welcomed the agreement; however, both the French and Austrian Governments pledged to conduct national referendums on Turkish entry, while a demonstration in protest at Turkish membership was conducted in Italy. In June 2005 the German Bundestag (Federal Assembly) became the latest EU legislature to attract

Turkish anger by condemning the Armenian 'genocide' and accusing the Turkish Government of failing to address the issue.

In July 2005, pending an EU decision on the opening of accession negotiations in October, the Turkish Government signed the requisite customs protocol with Cyprus and the other nine new EU member states, but appended a declaration reaffirming that the accord did not constitute official recognition of Greek Cyprus. In September EU member states adopted a draft declaration stating that Turkish recognition of Cyprus was necessary to the accession process, but without stipulating a date for this (thereby posing no obstacle to the beginning of negotiations). At the beginning of October intensive debate took place between EU member states to resolve the impasse over Austria's insistence that Turkey be offered the lesser option of 'privileged partnership' (to which the Turkish Government remained opposed), rather than full membership. Austria withdrew its veto to the admission of Turkey, after Croatia was unexpectedly declared eligible to enter into membership negotiations. Turkey's accession negotiations with the EU were officially approved on 3 October, and opened on the following day.

In November 2005 an EU report, while welcoming Turkey's economic performance, criticized a lack of progress in political reforms, citing continued human rights violations, including torture, and the necessity for further judicial reforms. Furthermore, the subsequent reluctance of the Turkish authorities to open ports and airports to Greek Cypriot-registered traffic, in adherence to the customs protocol and as a condition to progress in the accession negotiations, prompted criticism from EU officials and repeated threats from the Greek Cypriot Government to veto Turkey's membership. Nevertheless, EU ministers responsible for foreign affairs formally opened the first chapter of accession negotiations with Turkey in June. Attempts by the Finnish presidency of the EU to broker a deal under which the EU would take charge of the port of Famagusta in the 'TRNC' while the nearby town of Varosha would be returned to Greek Cypriot control were eventually abandoned in November. Meanwhile, in October 2006 the EU advised Turkey that safeguarding freedom of expression in the country was to be regarded as a matter of urgency. During 2005–06 court proceedings were initiated against several prominent novelists who were accused of 'insulting Turkishness' under Article 301 of the penal code.

In November 2006 the European Commission recommended the suspension of negotiations on eight of 35 chapters of the accession talks (these included trade, financial services and transport), a decision that was endorsed at the summit meeting of the European Council in early December. At the end of December Turkey pledged to implement a six-year 'roadmap' and reform programme and to continue implementing all the required judicial and military reforms, even in those areas where negotiations had been suspended. In March 2007 the EU resumed negotiations with Turkey on the accession chapter relating to enterprise and industry. However, in June, following the inauguration as French President of Nicolas Sarkozy in the previous month, France blocked the commencement of negotiations on the accession chapter relating to economic and monetary union, apparently in a further move to prevent Turkey's eventual accession to the EU. (French officials later asserted that they were not opposed to the commencement of further negotiating chapters with Turkey, but that they believed that all options, including that of 'preferential partnership', should be considered.) Later in June the EU did extend membership discussions with Turkey on two new, smaller chapters concerning financial controls and statistics. In November the European Commission urged the Turkish Government to accelerate its political and social reform process, citing the treatment of the minority Kurdish population and Article 301 as particular areas where further progress was required. Accession talks concerning health and consumer affairs, as well as inter-European transport links, were initiated in December. The TGNA approved amendments to Article 301 in April 2008, although critics of the Government countered that the changes were not as far-reaching as they had hoped. Under the newly revised legislation, it would become a crime to insult 'the Turkish nation' rather than 'Turkishness', while the maximum sentence for someone convicted of such a crime was to be shortened from three to two years.

Despite the European Commission expressing concern at the lack of progress on key reforms in Turkey, two new negotiating chapters, concerning free movement of capital, and information and media, commenced in December 2008. Turkey created its first post within the Council of Ministers dedicated exclusively to

EU negotiations in January 2009. Egemen Bağış, a former AKP Vice-Chairman in charge of Foreign Affairs, was appointed Minister of State and Chief Negotiator for EU Affairs, the responsibilities of which role had hitherto been undertaken by the Minister of Foreign Affairs. During a Franco-German summit in May, President Sarkozy and German Chancellor Angela Merkel reiterated their opposition to Turkey's full membership of the EU, stating their preference for the negotiation of a 'privileged partnership' arrangement. Turkish officials again rejected this proposal and urged all European states to adhere to the ongoing accession process. An additional negotiating chapter, concerning taxation, commenced in June.

In its latest progress report on Turkey's EU accession, published in November 2009, the European Commission recognized that substantial progress had been made on judicial reform, civil-military relations and Kurdish rights. However, the report highlighted continuing concerns with regard to freedom of expression and referred specifically to tax fines levied against Doğan Media Holding, Turkey's largest media group, which it described as disproportionate and potentially politically motivated. (Critical coverage of the Government in newspapers and television stations owned by the Doğan group had led to increasing tensions with the AKP; in 2008 the Prime Minister called for a boycott of the media group.) A new negotiating chapter, concerning environmental issues, opened in December 2009, bringing to 12 the number of chapters under discussion. In January 2010 the European Parliament adopted a resolution on the 2009 progress report that urged Turkey to begin withdrawing its troops from northern Cyprus in order to facilitate reunification negotiations.

The approval by referendum of the Government's package of constitutional reforms in September 2010 (see Domestic Political Affairs) was expected to bolster Turkish hopes of acceding to the EU. However, while the EU had expressed support for the reforms, on the grounds that they afforded the democratically elected Turkish Government greater control over the military, the Union also voiced concern that the reforms gave the Government excessive control over the judiciary.

Meanwhile, in a two-day state visit to Turkey in March 2010 Chancellor Merkel reiterated her support for a 'privileged partnership' arrangement; however, she insisted that negotiations on Turkey's EU accession were 'open-ended'. During a visit to Berlin intended to strengthen Turkey's EU accession bid in February 2011, Erdoğan issued an unexpectedly stern rebuke to the German Government's efforts to integrate Turkish immigrants into German society, arguing that 'any policy which seeks to revoke the language and culture of migrants violates international law'. The criticism appeared to have been in retaliation for a comment made by a senior German government official urging that the Turkish accession bid be suspended owing to the failure of the Erdoğan Government to protect religious freedoms. Erdoğan also accused Merkel of using 'stalling tactics' to appease those among the German electorate who were opposed to Turkey's bid to join the EU.

During a visit to Ankara by Sarkozy in February 2011, the French President reiterated his Government's opposition to Turkish accession. Following the rejection in May of that year by the French Senate of draft legislation, endorsed by the French National Assembly in October 2006, that would have rendered it a crime to deny that the Armenians suffered genocide in 1915–23, in December 2011 the French lower chamber endorsed a revised proposal to outlaw the denial of genocide per se (with no explicit reference to Armenia or the Ottoman Empire), which was again referred to the Senate. (France had previously, in 2001, approved a law recognizing the killing of Armenians by the Turks as genocide.) In response, Turkey recalled its ambassador from France for consultations and suspended all bilateral political, economic and military ties. In January 2012 the Turkish Government urged the French Senate to reject the revived bill, under the terms of which those publicly denying genocide would be awarded a mandatory one year's imprisonment and fine of €45,000, with Minister of Foreign Affairs Ahmet Davutoğlu contending that approval of the legislation would leave a 'black stain on France's intellectual history'. In mid-January a French Senate committee issued a non-binding resolution suggesting that the bill was unconstitutional. Nevertheless, the French Senate approved the legislation in the following week, prompting the Turkish Government to state that it would take 'all necessary steps' against France, with the Turkish ambassador to France suggesting that this might include the permanent downgrading of diplomatic relations to the level of chargés d'affaires. In late

February France's highest legal authority, the Constitutional Court, ruled that the new law, which was due to have been ratified by Sarkozy by the end of that month, was unconstitutional—a development welcomed by Turkey. However, the Office of the French President swiftly announced that Sarkozy had asked the Government to draft a new version of the legislation that would take the Court's ruling into account, appearing to indicate that the issue had not yet run its course.

In July 2011 Minister of Foreign Affairs Davutoğlu declared that Turkey's relations with the EU would be suspended if Greek Cyprus assumed the rotating EU presidency as scheduled in July 2012, while the island remained divided. Draft legislation providing for reform of the judiciary and the media, approved by the Turkish Cabinet and referred to the TGNA in February 2012, was welcomed by the EU. However, the Union stressed that the Turkish Government needed to implement further reforms, particularly with regard to freedom of expression and the right to a fair trial. Amid ongoing tensions between the Turkish and Cypriot Governments and Turkey's continued refusal to open its ports and airports to Greek Cypriot-registered traffic, Turkey's accession bid remained effectively stalled at mid-2013. However, following the victory of Francois Hollande in the French presidential elections in May 2012, the Turkish Government expressed its desire to repair its relations with France, thus enabling renewed negotiations with the EU. (Turkey ended its sanctions against France the following month.) Later in May the Government launched a 'positive agenda' involving the establishment of eight working groups, each devoted to a specific chapter of the EU accession criteria. However, an EU report published in October expressed serious concerns about Turkey's progress in meeting those criteria.

Other external relations

Following the formal dissolution of the USSR in December 1991, the Turkish Government sought to further its political, economic and cultural influence in the Caucasus and Central Asia, in particular with Azerbaijan, Kazakhstan, Kyrgyzstan, Turkmenistan and Uzbekistan, all of which share ethno-linguistic ties with Turkey. Following the outbreak of war between Armenia and Azerbaijan in 1991, Turkey blockaded Armenia and provided support to its 'Turkic' ally, Azerbaijan. In June 1992 leaders of 11 nations, including Turkey, Greece, Albania and six former Soviet republics, established the Organization of the Black Sea Economic Cooperation (BSEC, see p. 411). In October 1994 a meeting of the heads of state of Turkey, Azerbaijan, Turkmenistan, Uzbekistan, Kazakhstan and Kyrgyzstan took place in Istanbul, in an effort to develop and improve relations among the 'Turkic' republics. Summit meetings have subsequently been convened each year. In the late 1990s Turkey sought to encourage Western firms to build a new petroleum pipeline from Baku, Azerbaijan, to the Turkish port of Ceyhan, via Tbilisi, Georgia, thereby allowing the transportation of petroleum from the Caspian Sea to the Mediterranean. Such a scheme would also increase Turkey's importance to the EU by making it the centre of the Transport Corridor Europe–Caucasus–Asia (TRACECA) project. Construction of the pipeline, which commenced in April 2003, was estimated to have cost some US $3,900m. The Turkish section of the project, the last of the three sections to be completed, was inaugurated in July 2006.

In mid-2001 work began on a new natural gas pipeline from Dzhubga, Russia, to Samsun, Turkey, beneath the Black Sea. Gas flows from Russia to Turkey commenced in early 2003; however, the pipeline, constructed at a cost of some US $3,500m., was not formally inaugurated until November 2005, owing to a protracted pricing dispute between the two countries. Meanwhile, during a significant visit to Turkey in December 2004 the Russian President, Vladimir Putin, signed co-operation agreements in the fields of trade, defence and finance. In May 2009 Prime Minister Erdoğan visited Russia and held talks with his counterpart, Putin, on energy co-operation and regional affairs; the premiers announced the extension of a contract for the supply of Russian natural gas to Turkey. In May 2010 the two countries signed a $20,000m. agreement under the terms of which Russia was to construct Turkey's first nuclear energy plant, in Akkuyu, Mersin province, comprising four 1,200-MW reactors, and was to hold a controlling stake in the project. During a state visit to Russia in March 2011, Erdoğan met with President Dmitrii Medvedev and Prime Minister Putin, and reaffirmed Turkish commitment to the project; construction was expected to commence during 2013 and the first reactor was expected to become operational in 2019, with completion of the project scheduled for 2022. In December 2011 a bilateral

agreement was signed under the terms of which Russia was to be allowed to construct the South Stream pipeline through Turkish territorial waters, enabling access to European markets via the Black Sea, and thereby bypassing Ukraine, while two long-standing contracts for the supply of Russian gas to Turkey were extended until 2021 and 2025, respectively; as a result of the renegotiated contracts, Russia was to supply Turkey with an additional 2,000m. cu m of gas annually. Construction of the pipeline was scheduled for completion by 2015.

Following the installation of Serge Sarkissian as President of Armenia in April 2008, there were renewed hopes of a rapprochement with Turkey, diplomatic relations with which had been suspended since Turkey closed its border with Armenia in 1993, in response to Armenia's conflict with Azerbaijan. President Gül became the first Turkish head of state to visit Armenia when he accepted an invitation from President Sarkissian to attend the first football match between the national teams in the Armenian capital, Yerevan, in September 2008. Turkey's Minister of Foreign Affairs, Ali Babacan, held direct talks on bilateral relations with his Armenian counterpart in April 2009 during a BSEC conference in Yerevan. In the same month the Turkish Ministry of Foreign Affairs announced that Swiss-mediated negotiations, underway since 2007, had resulted in an agreement on a comprehensive framework for the normalization of bilateral ties. In May 2009, during a visit to Baku, Prime Minister Erdoğan insisted that the reopening of the Turkish–Armenian border was conditional on Armenia withdrawing its troops from the Nagornyi Karabakh region. (Nagornyi Karabakh is the subject of a long-standing territorial dispute between Armenia and Azerbaijan.) Erdoğan's statement was widely interpreted as an attempt to appease Azerbaijan, which is a major supplier of natural gas to Turkey. Nevertheless, with US mediation, in October Turkey and Armenia signed two protocol agreements under the terms of which diplomatic relations were to be restored, the common border was to be reopened and an impartial commission to examine historical disputes between the two nations was to be established. However, a ruling by the Armenian Constitutional Court in January 2010 concerning the irrevocability of the term 'genocide' in reference to the Turkish massacre of Armenians after the First World War, and Turkey's continuing attempts to link the normalization process to the Nagornyi Karabakh issue, represented critical obstacles to normalization. In April the Armenian legislature suspended ratification of the protocols until such time as Turkey was 'prepared to continue the process without preconditions'. In April 2011 Turkish Deputy Prime Minister Bülent Arınç referred to ties with Armenia as 'the only missing part in our diplomatic relations'. The protocols had yet to be ratified as of early 2013.

CONSTITUTION AND GOVERNMENT

In October 1981 the National Security Council (NSC), which took power in September 1980, announced the formation of a Consultative Assembly to draft a new constitution, replacing that of 1961. The Assembly consisted of 40 members appointed directly by the NSC and 120 members chosen by the NSC from candidates put forward by the governors of the 67 provinces; all former politicians were excluded. The draft Constitution was approved by the Assembly in September 1982 and by a national referendum in November. Under the terms of the Constitution approved in 1982 (with subsequent amendments), legislative power is vested in the unicameral Turkish Grand National Assembly (TGNA), with 550 deputies, who are elected by universal adult suffrage for a four-year term. Executive power is vested in the President of the Republic, to be elected by universal adult suffrage for a term of five years (although no one candidate may serve more than two terms of office). The President is empowered to appoint a Prime Minister and senior members of the judiciary, the Central Bank and broadcasting organizations; to dissolve the TGNA; and to declare a state of emergency entailing rule by decree. Further changes to the Constitution were approved at a national referendum in September 2010 (see Contemporary Political History). For administrative purposes, Turkey comprises 81 provinces and 2,934 municipalities.

REGIONAL AND INTERNATIONAL CO-OPERATION

Turkey is a member of several regional organizations, including the Economic Cooperation Organization (ECO, see p. 274), and the Organization of the Black Sea Economic Cooperation (BSEC, see p. 411), which has its headquarters in Istanbul. Turkey also adheres to both the Council of Europe (see p. 260) and the

Organisation for Security and Co-operation in Europe (OSCE, see p. 397), and in December 1999 was accepted as a candidate for membership of the European Union (EU, see p. 281). (For details regarding Turkey's accession negotiations with the EU, see Contemporary Political History.)

Turkey was a founder member of the UN in October 1945. As a contracting party to the General Agreement on Tariffs and Trade, Turkey joined the World Trade Organization (WTO, see p. 444) on its establishment in 1995. It became a member of the North Atlantic Treaty Organization (NATO, see p. 380) in 1952. Turkey participates in the Organisation of Islamic Cooperation (OIC, see p. 413), as well as several development and economic co-operation bodies, including the Organisation for Economic Co-operation and Development (OECD, see p. 388), the Group of 20 (G20, see p. 466), and the Developing Eight (D-8, see p. 460).

ECONOMIC AFFAIRS

In 2011, according to estimates by the World Bank, Turkey's gross national income (GNI), measured at average 2009–11 prices, was US $766,441m., equivalent to $10,410 per head (or $17,340 per head on an international purchasing-power parity basis). During 2002–11, it was estimated, the population increased at an average annual rate of 1.3%, while gross domestic product (GDP) per head rose, in real terms, by an average of 3.9% per year. According to official figures, overall GDP increased, in real terms, by an annual average of 5.2% in 2002–11; GDP increased by 8.5% in 2011.

Agriculture (including forestry and fishing) contributed 9.0% to GDP in 2011 and engaged 24.6% of the employed population in 2012. The country is self-sufficient in most basic foodstuffs. The principal agricultural exports are cotton, tobacco, wheat, fruit and nuts. Other important crops are sugar beet, barley, potatoes, maize, and onions. The raising of sheep, goats, cattle and poultry is also an important economic activity. During 2002–11 agricultural GDP increased by an annual average rate of 2.0%; the agricultural sector grew by 5.6% in 2011.

Industry (including mining, manufacturing, construction and power) contributed 27.5% to GDP in 2011, and engaged 26.0% of the employed population in 2012. During 2002–11 industrial GDP increased by an annual average rate of 6.2%; the industrial sector contracted by 8.6% in 2009, before expanding by 13.8% in 2010 and further by 9.7% in 2011.

Mining contributed 1.7% to GDP in 2011 and engaged 0.5% of the employed population in 2012. Chromium, copper and borax are the major mineral exports. Coal, petroleum, natural gas, bauxite, iron ore, manganese and sulphur are also mined. The development and expansion of Turkey's gold-mining facilities was in progress in the early 21st century. During 2002–11 mining GDP increased by an annual average rate of 3.3%; mining GDP contracted by 6.7% in 2009, but expanded by 4.7% in 2010 and further by 3.9% in 2011.

Manufacturing contributed 18.3% to GDP in 2011 and engaged 17.8% of the employed population in 2012. The most important branches, measured by gross value of output, are textiles, food-processing, petroleum refineries, iron and steel, and industrial chemicals. During 2002–11 manufacturing GDP increased by an annual average rate of 6.3%; sectoral GDP declined by 7.2% in 2009, but grew by some 13.6% in 2010 and further by 9.6% in 2011.

Construction contributed 5.0% to GDP in 2011, and engaged 6.9% of the employed population in 2012. During 2002–11 construction GDP increased by an annual average rate of 6.1%; the construction sector contracted by some 16.1% in 2009, but increased by 18.3% in 2010 and further by 11.3% in 2011.

Energy is derived principally from thermal power plants. In 2010 46.5% of energy was derived from natural gas, 26.1% from coal, 24.5% from hydroelectric power and a further 1.0% from petroleum. The energy sector (including water) contributed 2.5% to GDP in 2011 and engaged 0.9% of the employed population in 2012. Total domestic output of crude petroleum and natural gas accounts for some 12% of the country's hydrocarbon requirements. Imports of petroleum and its products comprised 6.8% of the value of total imports in 2012. A major development project for south-eastern Anatolia, initially scheduled for completion in 2010, was expected to increase Turkey's energy production by 70% and to irrigate 1.6m. ha of uncultivable or inadequately irrigated land, by constructing dams and hydroelectric plants on the Tigris and Euphrates rivers and their tributaries. However, progress was delayed by the withholding of funding by the World Bank owing to the lack of an official agreement between Turkey,

Iraq and Syria on water-sharing pertaining to the Tigris and Euphrates rivers, and the anticipated completion date was revised to 2013. In March 2010 parliamentary approval was granted for the construction by a multilateral European consortium, including a subsidiary of Turkey's Türkiye Petrolleri Anonim Ortaklığı, of a 3,300-km pipeline from Erzurum in eastern Turkey to Austria; the US $10,700m. Nabucco project was designed to transport natural gas from the Caspian Sea region to central Europe, thus reducing Europe's dependency on gas supplies from Russia. Construction of the project was due to commence in the second half of 2013 and it was expected to become operational by 2017. Work on Turkey's first nuclear power plant, at Akkuyu, in Mersin province, with Russian involvement (see Contemporary Political History), was expected to commence in 2014; two other nuclear plants, in the Black Sea province of Sinop and at İğneada, in Kırklareli province, were scheduled to be built by 2023.

The services sector contributed 63.5% of GDP in 2011 and engaged 49.4% of the employed population in 2012. Tourism is one of Turkey's fastest growing sources of revenue. Total tourist arrivals increased to more than 31.8m. in 2012 and tourists generated some US $23,440.4m. in revenue in that year. Remittances from Turkish workers abroad also make an important contribution to the economy, amounting to $1,936m. in 2002. During 2002–11 the GDP of the services sector increased by an annual average rate of 5.8%; services GDP contracted by 1.8% in 2009, but expanded by 7.7% in 2010 and further by 8.7% in 2011.

In 2011 Turkey recorded a visible merchandise trade deficit of US $88,989m., and there was a deficit of $76,986m. on the current account of the balance of payments. In 2012 the principal source of imports (11.3% of the total) was Russia; other major suppliers were Germany, the People's Republic of China, the USA, Italy and Iran. Germany was the principal market for exports in that year (8.6% of the total); other important purchasers were Iraq, Iran, the United Kingdom and the United Arab Emirates. Exports in 2012 were dominated by basic manufactures (mainly textiles), machinery and transport equipment (mainly road vehicles), miscellaneous manufactured articles, food and live animals, and chemicals and related products. In that year the principal imports were machinery and transport equipment, mineral fuels (particularly petroleum), basic manufactures, chemical products, crude materials (inedible) except fuels, and miscellaneous manufactured articles.

In 2012 there was a provisional budgetary deficit of 14,188m. Turkish liras. Turkey's general government gross debt was 465,848m. Turkish liras in 2010, equivalent to 42.4% of GDP. Turkey's external debt at the end of 2010 was US $293,872m., of which $93,088m. was public and publicly guaranteed debt. In that year, the cost of servicing long-term public and publicly guaranteed debt and repayments to the IMF was equivalent to 36.7% of the value of exports of goods, services and income (excluding workers' remittances). The annual rate of inflation averaged 8.4% in 2003–12. Consumer prices increased by 8.9% in 2012. In 2012 the rate of unemployment was 9.2%.

The Government's national development plan for 2007–13 had as its principal aim the achievement of the levels of macroeconomic stability required for attaining membership of the European Union (EU, see p. 281). From the latter part of 2008 the impact of the global financial crisis resulted in negative growth, exacerbated by declining export revenues owing to the effects of adverse economic conditions on Turkey's main trading partners, and a sharp decline in output, particularly in the manufacturing sector. The economy returned to positive growth in 2010, buoyed by structural reforms to increase productivity and create new jobs. In a sign of growing domestic confidence in Turkey's economic recovery, in March 2010 the Government withdrew from negotiations with the IMF for a new stand-by arrangement, with Prime Minister Recep Tayyip Erdoğan declaring that the country could henceforth 'stand on its own feet'. (Turkey was scheduled to repay the final, US $431m. instalment of its IMF loan in May 2013.) Nevertheless, in March 2012 the Government successfully concluded an agreement with the World Bank providing for a new Country Partnership Strategy (CPS) for the period 2012–15. Under the terms of the CPS, the Bank was to provide funding of some US $4,450m. for public development projects, in support of Turkey's bid to become one of the world's 10 largest economies by 2023 (the centennial anniversary of the founding of the Turkish Republic). In April 2013 the World Bank praised Turkey's positive performance since the global economic crisis, but emphasized the need for continued structural reforms in order to avoid slow growth rates. The economy grew by 8.5% in

2011, but growth slowed to an estimated 3% in 2012; a slightly increased rate, of 3.5%, was predicted for 2013. The country's relatively impressive rate of growth was partly attributed to a tightening of monetary policy, and increased regulation in the banking sector. It was also seen as contributing to the considerable reduction in Turkey's current account deficit, which stood at an estimated 6.8% of GDP at the end of that year, down from 9.9% in 2011. At the start of 2013, despite increased economic stability, Turkey remained vulnerable to external influences such as the eurozone crisis and political turmoil in neighbouring countries.

PUBLIC HOLIDAYS

2014: 1 January (New Year's Day), 23 April (National Sovereignty and Children's Day), 1 May (Labour and Solidarity Day), 19 May (Commemoration of Atatürk, and Youth and Sports Day), 29–31 July* (Ramazan Bayram—End of Ramadan), 30 August (Victory Day), 5–8 October* (Kurban Bayram—Feast of the Sacrifice), 29 October (Republic Day).

* These holidays are dependent on the Islamic lunar calendar and may vary by one or two days from the dates given.

Statistical Survey

Source (unless otherwise stated): T. C. Başbakanlık Türkiye İstatistik Kurumu (Turkish Statistical Institute), Necatibey Cad. 114, 06580-Yücetepe/Ankara; tel. (312) 400410; internet www.turkstat.gov.tr.

Area and Population

AREA, POPULATION AND DENSITY

Area (sq km)	
Land	769,604
Inland water	13,958
Total	783,562*
Population (periodic census results)	
21 October 1990	56,473,035
22 October 2000	
Males	34,346,735
Females	33,457,192
Total	67,803,927
Population (annual census results at 31 December)†	
2010	73,722,988
2011	74,724,269
2012	75,627,384
Density (per sq km) at 31 December 2012	98.3‡

* 302,535 sq miles.
† In accordance with new methodology employing Address Based Population Registration System introduced in 2007.
‡ Land area only.

POPULATION BY AGE AND SEX
(annual population census at 31 December 2012)

	Males	Females	Total
0–14	9,678,382	9,178,797	18,857,179
15–64	25,803,873	25,284,329	51,088,202
65 and over	2,473,913	3,208,090	5,682,003
Total	37,956,168	37,671,216	75,627,384

PROVINCES
(annual population census at 31 December 2012)

	Area (sq km)	Population	Density (per sq km)
Adana	14,046	2,125,635	151.3
Adıyaman	7,606	595,261	78.3
Afyon	14,719	703,948	47.8
Ağrı	11,499	552,404	48.0
Aksaray	7,966	379,915	47.7
Amasya	5,704	322,283	56.5
Ankara	25,402	4,965,542	195.5
Antalya	20,791	2,092,537	100.6
Ardahan	4,968	106,643	21.5
Artvin	7,367	167,082	22.7
Aydın	7,904	1,006,541	127.3
Balıkesir	14,473	1,160,731	80.2
Bartın	2,080	188,436	90.6
Batman	4,659	534,205	114.7
Bayburt	3,739	75,797	20.3
Bilecik	4,307	204,116	47.4
Bingöl	8,254	262,507	31.8
Bitlis	7,095	337,253	47.5
Bolu	8,323	281,080	33.8
Burdur	7,135	254,341	35.6

—continued	Area (sq km)	Population	Density (per sq km)
Bursa	10,886	2,688,171	246.9
Çanakkale	9,950	493,691	49.6
Çankırı	7,492	184,406	24.6
Çorum	12,796	529,975	41.4
Denizli	11,804	950,557	80.5
Diyarbakır	15,204	1,592,167	104.7
Düzce	2,593	346,493	133.6
Edirne	6,098	399,708	65.5
Elazığ	9,281	562,703	60.6
Erzincan	11,728	217,886	18.6
Erzurum	25,331	778,195	30.7
Eskişehir	13,902	789,750	56.8
Gaziantep	6,845	1,799,558	262.9
Giresun	6,832	419,555	61.4
Gümüşhane	6,437	135,216	21.0
Hakkari	7,179	279,982	39.0
Hatay	5,831	1,483,674	254.4
Iğdir	3,588	190,409	53.1
Isparta	8,871	416,663	47.0
İstanbul	5,315	13,854,740	2,606.7
İzmir	12,016	4,005,459	333.3
Kahramanmaraş	14,457	1,063,174	73.5
Karabük	4,109	225,145	54.8
Karaman	8,869	235,424	26.5
Kars	10,139	304,821	30.1
Kastamonu	13,158	359,808	27.3
Kayseri	17,109	1,274,968	74.5
Kırıkkale	4,570	274,727	60.1
Kırklareli	6,300	341,218	54.2
Kırşehir	6,530	221,209	33.9
Kilis	1,428	124,320	87.1
Kocaeli	3,625	1,634,691	450.9
Konya	40,814	2,052,281	50.3
Kütahya	12,014	573,421	47.7
Malatya	12,103	762,366	63.0
Manisa	13,229	1,346,162	101.8
Mardin	8,806	773,026	87.8
Mersin	15,512	1,682,848	108.5
Muğla	12,949	851,145	65.7
Muş	8,067	413,260	51.2
Nevşehir	5,392	285,190	52.9
Niğde	7,365	340,270	46.2
Ordu	5,952	741,371	124.6
Osmaniye	3,196	492,135	154.0
Rize	3,922	324,152	82.6
Sakarya	4,880	902,267	184.9
Samsun	9,364	1,251,722	133.7
Siirt	5,473	310,879	56.8
Sinop	5,817	201,311	34.6
Sivas	28,567	623,535	21.8
Şanlıurfa	19,336	1,762,075	91.1
Şırnak	7,152	466,982	65.3
Tekirdağ	6,342	852,321	134.4
Tokat	10,073	613,990	61.0
Trabzon	4,664	757,898	162.5
Tunceli	7,686	86,276	11.2
Uşak	5,363	342,269	63.8
Van	22,983	1,051,975	45.8
Yalova	850	211,799	249.2
Yozgat	14,074	453,211	32.2

—continued	Area (sq km)	Population	Density (per sq km)
Zonguldak	3,310	606,527	183.2
Total	783,562	75,627,384	96.5

PRINCIPAL TOWNS
(population at annual census of 31 December 2012)

İstanbul . . .	13,710,512	Hatay . . .	742,590
Ankara (capital) .	4,842,136	Balıkesir . . .	711,743
İzmir (Smyrna) .	3,661,930	Eskişehir . . .	710,830
Bursa	2,402,012	Sakarya	680,637
Adana	1,886,624	Kahramanmaraş . .	675,589
Gaziantep . . .	1,604,933	Denizli	670,812
Konya	1,563,863	Aydın	611,846
Kocaeli	1,527,407	Tekirdağ . . .	589,049
Antalya	1,492,674	Van	548,717
Mersin	1,327,870	Erzurum . . .	509,474
Diyarbakır . . .	1,155,258	Malatya	504,793
Kayseri	1,116,393	Mardin	458,112
Şanlıurfa . . .	975,455	Sivas	428,426
Manisa	904,513	Trabzon	426,882
Samsun	840,399	Ordu	423,295

BIRTHS, MARRIAGES AND DEATHS

	Live births		Marriages		Deaths	
	Number	Rate (per 1,000)	Number	Rate (per 1,000)	Number*	Rate (per 1,000)
2004 .	1,213,545	17.9	615,357	8.6	433,000	6.1
2005 .	1,231,678	18.0	641,241	8.9	436,000	6.1
2006 .	1,238,725	17.8	636,121	8.7	440,000	6.0
2007 .	1,266,503	18.0	638,311	8.6	447,000	6.1
2008 .	1,262,333	17.8	641,973	9.0	454,000	6.4
2009 .	1,270,000	17.7	591,742	8.2	461,000	6.4
2010 .	1,279,000	17.6	582,715	8.0	459,000	6.3
2011 .	1,278,000	17.2	592,775	8.0	465,000	6.3

* Figures are estimates derived from address-based population registration.

Sources: partly UN, *Demographic Yearbook* and *Population and Vital Statistics Report*.

Recorded births (province and district centres only): 1,261,299 in 2009; 1,253,309 in 2010; 1,237,172 in 2011.

Recorded deaths (province and district centres only): 368,826 in 2009; 365,646 in 2010; 375,281 in 2011.

Life expectancy (years at birth): 73.9 (males 71.7; females 76.3) in 2011 (Source: World Bank, World Development Indicators database).

ECONOMICALLY ACTIVE POPULATION
(sample surveys, '000 persons aged 15 years and over)

	2010	2011	2012
Agriculture, hunting, forestry and fishing	5,683	6,143	6,097
Mining and quarrying . . .	115	125	113
Manufacturing	4,216	4,367	4,420
Electricity, gas and water . . .	165	212	218
Construction	1,431	1,676	1,709
Wholesale and retail trade; repair of motor vehicles, motorcycles and personal and household goods	3,326	3,476	3,502
Hotels and restaurants . . .	1,084	1,141	1,206
Transport, storage and communications	1,213	1,255	1,333
Financial intermediation . . .	273	280	264
Real estate, renting and business activities	490	581	691

—continued	2010	2011	2012
Public administration and defence; compulsory social security . .	1,292	1,337	1,458
Education	1,019	1,106	1,224
Health and social work . . .	590	693	808
Other community, social and personal service activities . .	1,699	1,717	1,780
Total employed	22,594	24,110	24,821
Unemployed	3,046	2,615	2,518
Total labour force	25,641	26,725	27,339
Males	18,257	18,867	19,147
Females	7,383	7,859	8,192

Note: Totals may not be equal to the sum of components, owing to rounding.

Health and Welfare

KEY INDICATORS

Total fertility rate (children per woman, 2010)	2.1
Under-5 mortality rate (per 1,000 live births, 2010) . . .	13
HIV/AIDS (% of persons aged 15–49, 2009)	<0.1
Physicians (per 1,000 head, 2009)	1.5
Hospital beds (per 1,000 head, 2009)	2.5
Health expenditure (2009): US $ per head (PPP)	957
Health expenditure (2009): % of GDP	6.7
Health expenditure (2009): public (% of total)	75.1
Access to water (% of persons, 2008)	99
Access to sanitation (% of persons, 2010)	90
Total carbon dioxide emissions ('000 metric tons, 2008) . .	283,979.8
Carbon dioxide emissions per head (metric tons, 2008) . .	4.0
Human Development Index (2011): ranking	92
Human Development Index (2011): value	0.699

For sources and definitions, see explanatory note on p. vi.

Agriculture

PRINCIPAL CROPS
('000 metric tons)

	2009	2010	2011
Wheat	20,600	19,674	21,800
Rice, paddy	750	860	900
Barley	7,300	7,250	7,600
Maize	4,250	4,310	4,200
Rye	343	367	366
Oats	218	204	218
Potatoes	4,398	4,548	4,613
Sugar beet	17,275	17,942	16,127
Beans, dry	181	213	201
Chick peas	563	531	487
Lentils	302	447	406
Walnuts	177	178	183
Hazelnuts, with shell	500	600	430
Olives	1,291	1,415	1,750
Sunflower seed	1,057	1,320	1,335
Cabbages and other brassicas .	707	693	710
Lettuce and chicory	438	419	424
Spinach	225	218	222
Tomatoes	10,746	10,052	11,003
Cauliflowers and broccoli . .	157	159	162
Pumpkins, squash and gourds .	412	430	411
Cucumbers and gherkins . .	1,735	1,739	1,749
Aubergines (Eggplants) . . .	816	847	822
Chillies and peppers, green . .	1,837	1,987	1,975
Onions and shallots, green . .	169	165	154
Onions, dry	1,850	1,900	2,141
Garlic	105	77	79
Beans, green	604	588	615
Carrots and turnips	594	533	602
Watermelons	3,810	3,683	3,864
Cantaloupes and other melons .	1,679	1,612	1,648
Bananas	205	210	207
Oranges	1,690	1,711	1,730
Tangerines, mandarins, etc. . .	846	859	872
Lemons and limes	784	787	790

—continued			2009	2010	2011
Grapefruit and pomelos	. . .		191	214	219
Apples	. . . . .		2,782	2,600	2,680
Pears	. . . . .		384	380	386
Quinces	. . . .		96	121	128
Apricots	. . . .		695	476	676
Sweet cherries	. . .		418	418	439
Sour cherries	. . .		193	195	182
Peaches and nectarines	. .		547	535	546
Plums and sloes	. .		246	241	269
Strawberries	. . .		292	300	302
Grapes	. . . .		4,265	4,255	4,296
Figs	. . . .		244	255	261
Tea	. . . .		199	235	222
Anise, badian, fennel and coriander			9	14	15
Tobacco, unmanufactured	. . .		85	55	45

Aggregate production ('000 metric tons, may include official, semi-official or estimated data): Total cereals 33,570 in 2009, 32,765 in 2010, 35,195 in 2011; Total roots and tubers 4,399 in 2009, 4,549 in 2010, 4,614 in 2011; Total pulses 1,237 in 2009, 1,345 in 2010, 1,234 in 2011; Total vegetables (incl. melons) 26,702 in 2009, 25,901 in 2010, 27,407 in 2011; Total fruits (excl. melons) 14,223 in 2009, 13,946 in 2010, 14,388 in 2011.

Source: FAO.

LIVESTOCK
('000 head, year ending September)

		2009	2010	2011
Horses	. . . . . .	180	167	155
Asses	. . . . . .	274	234	212
Cattle	. . . . . .	10,860	10,724	11,370
Buffaloes	. . . .	86	87	85
Camels	. . . . .	1	1	1
Pigs	. . . . .	2	2	2
Sheep	. . . . .	23,975	21,795	23,090
Goats	. . . .	5,594	5,128	6,293
Chickens	. . . .	244,280	229,969	234,918
Ducks	. . . . .	470	413	397
Geese and guinea fowls	. .	1,063	945	716
Turkeys	. . . .	3,230	2,755	2,942

Source: FAO.

LIVESTOCK PRODUCTS
('000 metric tons)

		2009	2010	2011
Cattle meat	. . . . . .	325.3	618.6	644.9
Buffalo meat	. . . .	1.0	3.4	1.6
Sheep meat*	. . . .	262	240	253
Goat meat*	. . . .	37.0	33.9	41.6
Horse meat*	. . . .	1.8	1.8	1.8
Chicken meat	. . . .	1,293.3	1,444.1	1,613.3
Cows' milk	. . . .	11,583.3	12,480.5	13,802.4
Buffalo milk	. . . .	32.4	35.5	40.4
Sheep milk	. . . .	734.2	816.8	892.8
Goats' milk	. . . .	192.2	272.8	320.6
Hen eggs	. . . .	864.5	740.0	810.0†
Honey	. . . .	82.0	81.1	94.2

* FAO estimates.
† Unofficial figure.
Source: FAO.

Forestry

ROUNDWOOD REMOVALS
('000 cubic metres, excl. bark)

		2009	2010	2011
Sawlogs, veneer logs and logs for				
sleepers	. . . . .	7,805	8,321	8,719
Pulpwood	. . . .	6,200	7,027	7,288
Other industrial wood	. . . .	247	347	416
Fuel wood	. . . .	5,048	4,859	4,616
Total	. . . .	19,300	20,554	21,039

Source: FAO.

SAWNWOOD PRODUCTION
('000 cubic metres, incl. railway sleepers)

		2009	2010	2011
Coniferous (softwood)	. . . .	3,777	3,984	4,192
Broadleaved (hardwood)	. . .	2,076	2,259	2,269
Total	. . . .	5,853	6,243	6,461

Source: FAO.

Fishing
('000 metric tons, live weight)

	2008	2009	2010
Capture	494.1	464.2	485.9
Common carp	11.6	11.0	12.1
Tarek	11.8	10.7	11.4
Whiting (incl. Poutassou)	13.5	12.7	14.8
Mullets	8.4	9.6	11.9
European pilchard	17.5	30.1	27.6
European sprat	39.3	53.4	57.0
European anchovy	251.7	204.7	229.0
Atlantic bonito	6.4	7.0	9.4
Bluefish	4.0	6.0	4.7
Atlantic horse mackerel	10.0	8.0	6.1
Mediterranean horse mackerel	22.1	20.4	14.4
Sand smelts (Silversides)	7.8	7.9	5.9
Striped venus	36.9	24.6	26.9
Marine molluscs	52.7	39.6	41.2
Aquaculture	153.0	159.6	167.7
Trout	68.6	80.9	85.2
Gilthead seabream	31.7	28.4	28.2
Seabasses	49.3	46.6	50.8
Total catch	647.0	623.9	653.7

Source: FAO.

Mining
('000 metric tons unless otherwise indicated)

		2009	2010	2011
Hard coal	. . . . .	3,774	3,667	5,619
Lignite	. . . .	82,263	74,437	89,806
Iron ore: gross weight	. . .	4,170	5,188	5,754
Iron ore: metal content[1]	. .	2,200	2,700	3,000
Copper[1,2]	. . . .	105	97	80
Bauxite	. . . .	1,473.2	1,311.1	1,500.0[1]
Lead: mine output[1,2]	. . .	26	23	26
Lead: concentrates[1,2]	. . .	23	21	23
Chromium[3]	. . . .	1,574.0	1,904.5	1,900.0[1]
Silver (kilograms)	. . .	351,600	363,520	450,000[1]
Gold (kilograms)[2,4]	. . .	14,469	16,890	25,000[1]
Marble ('000 cu m)	. . .	2,715.6	3,352.1	3,500.0[1]
Limestone[5]	. . .	243,184	270,441	270,000[1]
Quartzite	. . .	1,943.9	2,500.0	2,500.0[1]
Dolomite	. . .	11,152.1	15,224.5	15,000.0[1]
Bentonite	. . .	932.4	798.4	379.9
Kaolin	. . .	727.6	711.5	1,002.4
Silica sand[6]	. . .	4,499.2	4,022.4	3,250.0[1]
Gypsum	. . .	4,369.6	6,321.9	6,400.0[1]
Magnesite: mine output	. .	861.2	2,316.8	2,300.0[1]
Feldspar: mine output	. .	4,212.5	6,281.6	4,478.0
Borate minerals: mine output	.	3,923.5	4,442.9	6,306.6

—continued		2009	2010	2011
Borate minerals: concentrates	.	1,800.0[1]	2,200.0[1]	2,273.1
Nitrogen[1,7]	. . . .	100.0	200.0	200.0
Perlite: mine output	. . .	522.8	545.6	429.8
Pumice	. . . . . .	4,322.5	4,000.0[1]	4,000.0[1]
Pyrites[6]	. . . . . .	124.1	131.3	130.0[1]
Sodium sulphate: concentrates	.	4,592.0	1,600.6	1,500.0[1]

[1] Estimated production.
[2] Figures refer to metal content of ores and concentrates.
[3] Figures refer to gross weight of ores.
[4] Figures include estimated output from the by-products of refining other base metals.
[5] Excluding production used for making cement.
[6] Figures refer to gross weight of minerals.
[7] Nitrogen content of ammonia.

Source: US Geological Survey.

Crude petroleum ('000 metric tons): 2,490 in 2009; 2,602 in 2010; 2,427 in 2011.

Natural gas (million cu metres): 660.4 in 2009; 625.7 in 2010; 669.8 in 2011.

Industry

SELECTED PRODUCTS
('000 metric tons, unless otherwise indicated)

		2008	2009	2010*
Margarine	. . . . .	619.3	702.9	599.7
Flour	. . . . .	3,934.9	4,194.8	4,460.0
Sugar	. . . . .	2,132.2	2,522.4	2,465.6
Beer (million litres)	. .	1,030.8	1,009.3	1,024.0
Alcoholic spirits (million litres)	.	71.0	68.9	72.2
Cigarettes (with filter)	. .	134.9	132.9	115.2
Cotton yarn	. . . .	677.1	619.1	711.4
Wool yarn	. . . .	41.4	32.5	34.8
Products of the paper industry	.	4,303.2	4,190.9	5,001.9
Wood block flooring ('000 sq m)	.	30,739.8	44,498.7	64,801.8
Crude steel	. . . .	26,809.1	25,303.7	29,029.8
Cement	. . . . .	54,027.3	55,741.2	60,580.7
Sulphuric acid	. . . .	843.1	n.a.	n.a.
Motor oil	. . . . .	6,819.3	4,769.8	4,976.2
Motor gasoline	. . . .	4,509.1	3,878.3	3,882.8
Liquefied petroleum gas	. .	n.a.	621.8	683.3
Asphalt	. . . . .	2,241.9	2,056.7	2,789.0
Fuel oil (No. 6)	. . . .	n.a.	2,730.2	n.a.
Kerosene	. . . . .	80.9	13.5	n.a.
Fertilizers (incl. mineral or chemical)	. . . .	2,994.6	2,957.1	3,551.7
Domestic refrigerators and freezers ('000)	. . . .	5,640.6	5,348.5	7,161.5
Domestic washing machines ('000)		4,791.3	4,804.3	5,167.8
Ovens ('000)	. . . .	7,688.0	7,439.5	8,301.0
Vacuum cleaners ('000)	. .	1,819.6	1,633.3	2,249.3
Television receivers ('000, colour)	.	9,287.4	9,144.9	9,209.6
Tyres for automobiles ('000 units)		16,813.9	15,373.9	17,991.2
Tractors (number)	. . .	31,016	21,041	43,406
Passenger motor cars (number)	.	899,338	752,365	885,135
Pick-up trucks (number)	. .	162,742	84,243	n.a.
Buses and minibuses (number)	.	42,376	22,500	28,463
Electric energy (gross production, million kWh)	. . . . .	198,418.0	194,812.9	211,207.7

* Provisional figures.

2011: Electric energy 229,395.1.

Finance

CURRENCY AND EXCHANGE RATES

Monetary Units
100 kuruş = 1 Turkish lira.

Sterling, Dollar and Euro Equivalents (31 December 2012)
£1 sterling = 2.812 liras;
US $1 = 1.782 liras;
€1 = 2.351 liras;
100 Turkish liras = £35.56 = US $56.12 = €42.53.

Average Exchange Rate (Turkish liras per US $)
2010   1.5029
2011   1.6749
2012   1.7960

Note: A new currency, the new Turkish lira, equivalent to 1,000,000 of the former units, was introduced on 1 January 2005. Figures in this survey have been converted retrospectively to reflect this development. (The name of the currency reverted to Turkish lira on 1 January 2009, although new Turkish lira banknotes and coins remained in circulation for a further year.).

CONSOLIDATED BUDGET
(million Turkish liras)

Revenue		2010	2011	2012*
Tax revenue	. . . . .	216,109	260,262	286,117
Direct taxes	. . .	61,295	76,012	85,530
Indirect taxes	. . .	147,422	175,155	190,891
Taxes on wealth	. . .	7,392	9,095	9,696
Non-tax revenue	. . . .	19,447	23,836	27,449
Special revenues and funds	. .	150,263	184,254	215,762
Total	. . . . . .	385,819	468,352	529,328

Expenditure		2010	2011	2012*
Current expenditure	. . .	187,871	215,946	251,041
Investment expenditure	. .	37,545	43,322	49,848
Fixed capital	. . . .	37,712	43,136	49,672
Inventory variation	. . .	−166	187	176
Transfers	. . . . .	197,317	217,801	252,627
Current transfers	. . .	184,540	205,841	241,403
Capital transfers	. . .	12,777	11,960	11,224
Total	. . . . . .	422,734	477,070	553,516

* Provisional figures.

Source: Ministry of Development, Ankara.

INTERNATIONAL RESERVES
(US $ million at 31 December)

		2009	2010	2011
Gold (national valuation)	. .	4,121	5,258	9,888
IMF special drawing rights	. .	1,519	1,494	1,490
Reserve position in IMF	. . .	177	174	173
Foreign exchange	. . . .	69,178	79,046	76,659
Total	. . . . . .	74,995	85,972	88,210

Source: IMF, *International Financial Statistics*.

MONEY SUPPLY
(million Turkish liras at 31 December)

		2009	2010	2011
Currency outside depository corporations	. . . . .	33,845	43,623	48,592
Transferable deposits	. . .	95,503	114,031	132,168
Other deposits	. . . .	391,069	457,908	519,298
Securities other than shares	. .	—	1,113	10,338
Broad money	. . . . .	520,417	616,674	710,395

Source: IMF, *International Financial Statistics*.

COST OF LIVING
(Consumer Price Index; base: 2003 = 100)

	2010	2011	2012
Food and non-alcoholic beverages .	186.2	197.8	214.5
Alcoholic beverages and tobacco .	292.4	302.8	345.2
Clothing and footwear	124.6	132.8	143.6
Housing, water, electricity, gas and other fuels	208.0	220.1	245.3
Household goods	142.3	153.4	167.4
Health	127.6	128.3	130.1
Transport	171.0	188.0	202.4
Communications	112.1	112.6	116.2
Recreation and culture . . .	146.0	148.2	156.4
Education	185.9	196.0	207.8
Restaurants and hotels . . .	229.1	247.5	270.2
Miscellaneous goods and services .	191.7	216.2	244.2
All items	178.4	190.0	206.8

NATIONAL ACCOUNTS
(million Turkish liras at current prices)

Expenditure on the Gross Domestic Product

	2009	2010	2011
Government final consumption expenditure	140,028.9	157,513.6	180,670.2
Private final consumption expenditure	680,768.3	787,752.8	923,632.5
Increase in stocks	−18,427.3	6,707.7	26,364.8
Gross fixed capital formation . .	160,718.0	207,815.6	282,839.9
Total domestic expenditure .	963,087.9	1,159,789.7	1,413,507.4
Exports of goods and services . .	222,102.6	233,045.9	308,170.8
Less Imports of goods and services	232,632.1	294,036.3	423,616.2
GDP in purchasers' values .	952,558.6	1,098,799.3	1,298,062.0
GDP at constant 1998 prices .	97,003.1	105,885.6	114,889.0

Gross Domestic Product by Economic Activity

	2009	2010	2011
Agriculture, forestry and fishing .	78,775.9	92,739.0	103,643.9
Mining and quarrying . . .	14,235.4	15,785.4	19,175.1
Manufacturing	144,992.2	172,112.1	210,751.9
Electricity, gas and water . . .	22,818.1	25,455.0	28,752.6
Construction	36,577.6	45,669.5	57,294.5
Wholesale and retail trade . .	103,452.3	120,869.4	156,119.9
Hotels and restaurants . . .	23,714.1	25,589.6	29,547.4
Transport, storage and communications	127,283.5	144,427.5	176,132.1
Financial institutions . . .	42,687.8	40,501.6	40,662.8
Ownership of dwellings . . .	117,287.0	123,028.9	129,513.6
Real estate, renting and business activities	45,167.5	52,742.8	61,039.3
Public administration and defence; compulsory social security . .	41,270.6	46,090.3	52,310.5
Education	31,813.4	36,802.7	42,789.9
Health and social work . . .	16,448.8	17,939.5	19,415.5
Other community, social and personal services	16,078.2	18,696.6	21,420.4
Private households with employed persons	1,847.3	2,097.0	2,383.2
Sub-total	864,449.7	980,547.0	1,150,952.5
Taxes, *less* subsidies . . .	109,817.0	137,671.7	164,583.7
Less Financial intermediation services indirectly measured .	21,708.1	19,419.3	17,474.2
GDP in purchasers' values .	952,558.6	1,098,799.3	1,298,062.0

BALANCE OF PAYMENTS
(US $ million)

	2009	2010	2011
Exports of goods	109,729	120,991	143,497
Imports of goods	−134,497	−177,347	−232,486
Balance on goods . . .	−24,768	−56,356	−88,989
Exports of services	34,029	34,915	38,881
Imports of services	−16,795	−19,511	−20,986
Balance on goods and services	−7,534	−40,952	−71,094
Primary income received . . .	5,164	4,477	3,952
Primary income paid	−13,355	−11,616	−11,578
Balance on goods, services and primary income	−15,725	−48,091	−78,720
Secondary income received . .	2,889	2,104	2,523
Secondary income paid . . .	−534	−656	−789
Current balance	−13,370	−46,643	−76,986
Capital account (net) . . .	−51	−51	−30
Direct investment assets . . .	−1,553	−1,464	−2,466
Direct investment liabilities . .	8,411	9,038	16,085
Portfolio investment assets . .	−2,711	−3,524	2,688
Portfolio investment liabilities .	2,938	19,617	19,298
Other investment assets . .	10,987	7,012	11,310
Other investment liabilities . .	−8,006	28,250	19,877
Net errors and omissions . . .	4,274	2,736	11,232
Reserves and related items .	919	14,971	1,008

Source: IMF, *International Financial Statistics*.

External Trade

PRINCIPAL COMMODITIES
(distribution by SITC, US $ million, excl. military goods)

Imports c.i.f.	2010	2011	2012
Crude materials (inedible) except fuels	15,394.6	20,051.9	18,630.4
Metalliferous ores and metal scrap	8,201.8	11,141.6	10,754.1
Mineral fuels, lubricants, etc. .	38,497.0	54,116.8	60,115.2
Petroleum, petroleum products, etc.	11,390.6	15,245.9	16,178.7
Chemicals and related products	25,446.3	31,191.1	29,685.9
Organic chemicals	4,172.2	5,282.9	4,882.8
Medicinal and pharmaceutical products	4,777.7	5,083.1	4,343.1
Plastics in primary forms . .	7,650.0	9,932.2	9,928.9
Basic manufactures . . .	31,802.2	38,429.5	36,040.6
Textile yarn, fabrics, etc. . . .	6,701.8	7,719.4	6,593.6
Iron and steel	9,720.8	11,544.6	11,095.9
Machinery and transport equipment	53,875.8	67,076.8	61,604.4
Power-generating machinery and equipment	6,716.8	6,894.6	6,806.2
Machinery specialized for particular industries . . .	5,138.9	7,789.9	7,522.9
General industrial machinery, equipment and parts . . .	6,873.2	8,985.5	8,709.4
Road vehicles	13,174.4	16,782.2	14,184.6
Miscellaneous manufactured articles	11,638.1	14,137.6	13,154.2
Non-monetary gold, unwrought or semi-manufactured	2,523.5	6,726.3	8,392.1
Total (incl. others)	185,544.3	240,841.7	236,544.5

Exports f.o.b.		2010	2011	2012
Food and live animals	. . .	10,498.6	12,285.6	12,692.1
Vegetables and fruit	. . . .	6,152.5	6,695.7	6,554.5
Chemicals and related products	. . . . .	6,805.8	8,047.2	8,917.2
Basic manufactures	. . . .	33,181.5	40,327.7	41,289.0
Textile yarn, fabrics, etc.	. . .	8,969.6	10,783.2	11,091.1
Non-metallic mineral manufactures	. . .	3,708.4	3,729.3	3,761.8
Iron and steel	. . . .	10,199.5	12,836.9	13,100.1
Machinery and transport equipment	. . . . .	31,811.2	37,441.6	37,448.5
Road vehicles	. . . .	13,522.2	15,444.5	14,666.3
Miscellaneous manufactured articles	. . . . .	19,763.1	22,463.9	24,337.4
Clothing and accessories (excl. footwear)	. . . . .	12,745.6	13,945.0	14,290.8
Total (incl. others)	. . . .	113,883.2	134,906.9	152,536.7

PRINCIPAL TRADING PARTNERS
(US $ million, excl. military goods*)

Imports c.i.f. (excl. grants)	2010	2011	2012
Algeria	2,276.0	1,150.3	925.2
Belgium	3,213.6	3,959.3	3,690.3
Bulgaria	1,702.5	2,474.6	2,753.8
China, People's Republic . .	17,180.8	21,693.3	21,295.1
France	8,176.6	9,229.6	8,589.9
Germany	17,549.1	22,985.6	21,400.2
Greece	1,541.6	2,568.8	3,539.9
India	3,409.9	6,498.7	5,843.6
Iran	7,645.0	12,461.5	11,964.6
Italy	10,203.7	13,449.9	13,344.4
Japan	3,297.8	4,263.7	3,601.4
Korea, Republic	4,764.1	6,298.5	5,660.1
Netherlands	3,156.0	4,005.0	3,660.6
Poland	2,621.0	3,496.2	3,058.1
Romania	3,449.2	3,801.3	3,236.4
Russia	21,600.6	23,952.9	26,625.0
Saudi Arabia	2,437.2	2,001.5	2,171.1
Spain	4,840.1	6,196.5	6,022.8
Sweden	1,922.8	2,284.4	2,135.4
Switzerland	3,153.7	5,019.0	4,304.9
Ukraine	3,832.7	4,812.1	4,394.2
United Arab Emirates . .	698.4	1,649.5	3,596.5
United Kingdom . . .	4,680.6	5,840.4	5,629.4
USA	12,318.7	16,034.1	14,131.3
Total (incl. others)	185,544.3	240,841.7	236,544.5

Exports f.o.b.	2010	2011	2012
Algeria	1,504.6	1,470.5	1,813.3
Azerbaijan	1,550.5	2,064.0	2,587.5
Belgium	1,960.4	2,451.0	2,360.3
Bulgaria	1,497.4	1,622.8	1,682.0
China, People's Republic . .	2,269.2	2,466.3	2,833.4
Egypt	2,250.6	2,759.3	3,679.7
France	6,054.5	6,805.8	6,202.1
Germany	11,479.1	13,950.8	13,132.2
Greece	1,455.7	1,553.3	1,402.5
Iran	3,044.2	3,589.6	9,922.6
Iraq	6,036.4	8,310.1	10,827.7
Israel	2,080.1	2,391.1	2,330.3
Italy	6,505.3	7,851.5	6,375.9
Libya	1,932.4	747.6	2,140.1
Netherlands	2,461.4	3,243.1	3,248.4
Poland	1,504.3	1,758.3	1,854.5
Romania	2,599.4	2,878.8	2,497.0
Russia	4,628.2	5,992.6	6,683.0
Saudi Arabia	2,217.7	2,763.5	3,677.7
Spain	3,536.2	3,917.6	3,721.0
Switzerland	2,056.9	1,484.3	2,124.7
Ukraine	1,260.4	1,729.8	1,830.4
United Arab Emirates . .	3,332.9	3,706.7	8,175.5
United Kingdom . . .	7,235.9	8,151.4	8,700.8
USA	3,762.9	4,584.0	5,611.8
Total (incl. others)	113,883.2	134,906.9	152,536.7

* Imports by country of origin, exports by country of last consignment.

Transport

RAILWAYS
(traffic)

	2009	2010	2011
Passengers carried ('000) . . .	80,092	84,173	85,752
Passenger-km (million) . . .	5,374	5,491	5,882
Freight carried ('000 metric tons)*	21,813	24,355	25,421
Freight ton-km (million) . . .	10,326	11,462	11,677

* Excluding parcels and departmental traffic.

ROAD TRAFFIC
(motor vehicles by use)

	2009	2010	2011
Passenger cars	7,093,964	7,544,871	8,113,111
Minibuses	384,053	386,973	389,435
Buses and coaches . . .	201,033	208,510	219,906
Small trucks	2,204,951	2,399,038	2,611,104
Trucks	727,302	726,359	728,458
Motorcycles and mopeds . .	2,303,261	2,389,488	2,527,190
Special purpose vehicles . .	34,104	35,492	34,116

SHIPPING

Flag Registered Fleet
(at 31 December)

	2010	2011	2012
Number of vessels	1,291	1,297	1,325
Total displacement ('000 grt) . .	6,070.6	6,457.3	6,680.1

Source: Lloyd's List Intelligence (www.lloydslistintelligence.com).

International Sea-borne Traffic

	2005	2006	2007
Vessels entered (number) . . .	33,181	32,810	33,477
Passengers disembarked (number)	698,915	613,533	588,108
Goods unloaded ('000 metric tons)*	107,526	n.a.	n.a.
Vessels cleared (number) . .	23,245	23,564	24,941
Passengers embarked (number). .	705,937	608,654	594,385
Goods loaded ('000 metric tons)*	36,601	n.a.	n.a.

* Including timber.

CIVIL AVIATION
(scheduled services)

	2003	2004	2005
Domestic services:			
Kilometres flown ('000) . . .	28,180	28,489	35,886
Number of passengers . . .	4,991,517	5,805,291	7,151,491
Passenger-km ('000) . . .	2,751,910	3,223,299	3,991,885
Freight handled (metric tons) .	29,146	30,710	31,504
Total ton-km ('000)	275,681	321,118	392,055
International services:			
Kilometres flown ('000) . . .	101,738	109,038	122,899
Number of passengers . .	4,802,897	5,617,506	6,486,320
Passenger-km ('000)	12,223,997	14,227,375	16,359,597
Freight handled (metric tons) .	88,993	93,736	87,851
Total ton-km ('000)	1,617,729	1,849,177	2,104,407

Passengers carried (million): 78.7 in 2009; 102.8 in 2010; 117.6 in 2011.

Freight handled ('000 metric tons): 1,597.7 in 2009; 2,021.1 in 2010; 2,249.5 in 2011.

Tourism

VISITOR ARRIVALS BY NATIONALITY

Country	2010	2011	2012
Austria	500,321	528,966	505,560
Azerbaijan	486,381	578,685	593,238
Belgium	543,003	585,860	608,071
Bulgaria	1,433,970	1,491,561	1,492,073
France	928,376	1,140,459	1,032,565
Georgia	1,112,193	1,152,661	1,404,882
Germany	4,385,263	4,826,315	5,028,745
Greece	670,297	702,017	669,823
Iran	1,885,097	1,879,304	1,186,343
Israel	109,559	79,140	83,740
Italy	671,060	752,238	714,041
Netherlands	1,073,064	1,222,823	1,273,593
Russia	3,107,043	3,468,214	3,599,925
Sweden	447,270	571,917	617,811
Ukraine	568,227	602,404	634,663
United Kingdom	2,673,605	2,582,054	2,456,519
USA	642,768	757,143	771,837
Total (incl. others)	28,632,204	31,456,076	31,782,832

Tourism receipts (million US $, excl. passenger transport, incl. expenditure of Turkish nationals residing abroad): 20,806.7 in 2010; 23,020.4 in 2011; 23,440.4 in 2012.

Communications Media

	2009	2010	2011
Telephones ('000 main lines in use)	16,534.4	16,201.5	15,210.8
Mobile cellular telephones ('000 subscribers)	62,779.6	61,769.6	65,321.7
Internet subscribers ('000)	6,456.4	7,224.4	7,652.2
Broadband subscribers ('000)	6,443.2	7,087.7	7,554.7

Personal computers: 4,400,000 (61.0 per 1,000 persons) in 2006.

Source: International Telecommunication Union.

Education

(2011/12, unless otherwise indicated, provisional figures)

	Institutions	Teachers	Students
Pre-primary	28,625	55,883	1,169,556
Primary	32,108	515,852	10,979,301
Secondary:			
general	4,171	122,716	2,666,066
vocational and teacher training	5,501	113,098	2,090,220
Higher*	1,306	84,785	2,181,217

* Figures for 2005/06.

Adult literacy rate (UNESCO estimates): 90.8% (males 96.4%, females 85.3%) in 2009 (Source: UNESCO Institute for Statistics).

Directory

The Government

HEAD OF STATE

President: ABDULLAH GÜL (took office 28 August 2007).

COUNCIL OF MINISTERS
(May 2013)

The executive is formed by the Adalet ve Kalkınma Partisi (AKP).

Prime Minister: RECEP TAYYIP ERDOĞAN.

Deputy Prime Ministers: BÜLENT ARINÇ, ALI BABACAN, BEŞIR ATALAY, BEKIR BOZDAĞ.

Minister of Foreign Affairs: Prof. Dr AHMET DAVUTOĞLU.

Minister of Justice: SADULLAH ERGIN.

Minister of Family and Social Policy: FATMA ŞAHIN.

Minister of European Union Affairs: EGEMEN BAĞIŞ.

Minister of Science, Industry and Technology: NIHAT ERGÜN.

Minister of Economy: MEHMET ZAFER ÇAĞLAYAN.

Minister of National Defence: İSMET YILMAZ.

Minister of Internal Affairs: MUAMMER GÜLER.

Minister of Development: CEVDET YILMAZ.

Minister of Finance: MEHMET ŞIMŞEK.

Minister of National Education: NABI AVCI.

Minister of Health: Dr MEHMET MÜEZZINOĞLU.

Minister of Transport, Maritime Affairs and Communications: BINALI YILDIRIM.

Minister of Food, Agriculture and Livestock: Dr MEHMET MEHDI EKER.

Minister of Customs and Trade: HAYATI YAZICI.

Minister of Forestry and Water Works: VEYSEL EROĞLU.

Minister of Labour and Social Security: FARUK ÇELIK.

Minister of Energy and Natural Resources: Dr TANER YILDIZ.

Minister of Youth and Sports: SUAT KILIÇ.

Minister of Culture and Tourism: ÖMER ÇELIK.

Minister of the Environment and Urban Planning: ERDOĞAN BAYRAKTAR.

MINISTRIES

President's Office: Cumhurbaşkanlığı Genel Sekreterliği, 06689 Çankaya, Ankara; tel. (312) 4702308; fax (312) 4701316; e-mail cumhurbaskanligi@tccb.gov.tr; internet www.cankaya.gov.tr.

Prime Minister's Office: Vekaletler Cad., Başbakanlık Merkez Bina, 06573 Kızılay, Ankara; tel. (312) 4221000; fax (312) 4180476; e-mail bimer@basbakanlik.gov.tr; internet www.basbakanlik.gov.tr.

Deputy Prime Ministers' Office: Başbakan yard. ve Devlet Bakanı, Bakanlıklar, Ankara; tel. (312) 4191621; fax (312) 4191547.

Ministry of Culture and Tourism: Kültür ve Turizm Bakanlığı, Atatürk Bul. 29, 06050 Opera, Ankara; tel. (312) 3090850; fax (312) 3124359; e-mail info@kulturturizm.gov.tr; internet www.kultur.gov.tr.

Ministry of Customs and Trade: Ankara.

Ministry of Development: Ankara.

Ministry of Economy: Ankara.

Ministry of Energy and Natural Resources: Enerji ve Tabii Kaynaklar Bakanlığı, Türk Ocağı Cad. 2, 06100 Ankara; tel. (312) 2126420; fax (312) 2225760; e-mail bilgi@enerji.gov.tr; internet www.enerji.gov.tr.

Ministry of the Environment and Urban Planning: Ankara.

Ministry of European Union Affairs: Mustafa Kemal Mah. 2082 Cad. 4, 06510 Bilkent, Ankara; tel. (312) 2181300; fax (312) 2181464; e-mail bilgiedinme@ab.gov.tr; internet www.abgs.gov.tr.

Ministry of Family and Social Policy: Ankara.

Ministry of Finance: Maliye Bakanlığı, Dikmen Cad. 06450, Ankara; tel. (312) 4152900; fax (312) 4257816; e-mail bilgi@sgb.gov.tr; internet www.maliye.gov.tr.

Ministry of Food, Agriculture and Livestock: Tarım ve Hayvancılık Bakanlığı, Kampüsü Eskişehir Yolu 9 km Lodumlu, Ankara; tel. (312) 2873360; fax (312) 2863964; e-mail admin@tarim.gov.tr; internet www.tarim.gov.tr.

Ministry of Foreign Affairs: Dr Sadık Ahmet Cad. 8, 06100 Balgat, Ankara; tel. (312) 2921000; fax (312) 2873869; e-mail info@mfa.gov.tr; internet www.mfa.gov.tr.

Ministry of Forestry and Water Works: Çevre ve Orman Bakanlığı, Söğütözü Cad. 14E, Ankara; tel. (312) 2075000; fax (312) 2076299; e-mail webmaster@cevreorman.gov.tr; internet www.cevreorman.gov.tr.

Ministry of Health: Sağlık Bakanlığı, Mithatpaşa Cad. 3 Sihhiye, 06434 Ankara; tel. (312) 5852250; fax (312) 4339885; e-mail info@saglik.gov.tr; internet www.saglik.gov.tr.

Ministry of Internal Affairs: İçişleri Bakanlığı, Bakanlıklar, Ankara; tel. (312) 4224000; fax (312) 4181795; e-mail basin@icisleri.gov.tr; internet www.icisleri.gov.tr.

Ministry of Justice: Adalet Bakanlığı, 06659 Kizilay, Ankara; tel. (312) 4177770; fax (312) 4193370; e-mail akilic1@adalet.gov.tr; internet www.adalet.gov.tr.

Ministry of Labour and Social Security: Çalışma ve Sosyal Güvenlik Bakanlığı, İnönü Bul. 42, 06520 Emek, Ankara; tel. (312) 2966000; fax (312) 4179765; e-mail iletisim@csgb.gov.tr; internet www.csgb.gov.tr.

Ministry of National Defence: Milli Savunma Bakanlığı, 06100 Ankara; tel. (312) 4026100; fax (312) 4184737; internet www.msb .gov.tr.

Ministry of National Education: Milli Eğitim Bakanlığı, Atatürk Bul., Bakanlıklar, Ankara; tel. (312) 4191410; fax (312) 4177027; e-mail meb@meb.gov.tr; internet www.meb.gov.tr.

Ministry of Science, Industry and Technology: Sanayi ve Ticaret Bakanlığı, Eskişehir Yolu üzeri 7 km 2151 Cad. 154, 06510 Ankara; tel. (312) 2015000; fax (312) 2196738; e-mail webmaster@sanayi.gov.tr; internet www.sanayi.gov.tr.

Ministry of Transport, Maritime Affairs and Communications: T.C. Ulaştırma Denizcilik ve Haberleşme Bakanlığı, Hakkı Turayliç Cad. 5, 06338 Emek, Ankara; tel. (312) 2031116; fax (212) 2124930; e-mail okm@ubak.gov.tr; internet www.ubak.gov.tr.

Ministry of Youth and Sports: Ankara.

Legislature

Büyük Millet Meclisi
(Grand National Assembly)

TBMM 06543, Bakanlıklar, Ankara; tel. (312) 4205151; fax (312) 4206756; e-mail assembly@tbmm.gov.tr; internet www.tbmm.gov .tr.

Speaker: CEMIL ÇIÇEK.

General Election, 12 June 2011

Party	Valid votes cast	% of valid votes	Seats
Adalet ve Kalkınma Partisi (AKP)	21,399,082	49.83	327
Cumhuriyet Halk Partisi (CHP)	11,155,972	25.98	135
Milliyetçi Hareket Partisi (MHP)	5,585,513	13.01	53
Independents*	2,819,917	6.57	35
Saadet Partisi (SP)	543,454	1.27	0
Total (incl. others)	**42,941,763†**	**100.00**	**550**

* Affiliated to the Bariş ve Demokrasi Partisi (BDP).
† Excluding 973,185 invalid votes.

Election Commission

Yüksek Seçim Kurulu (YSK) (High Electoral Board): Kızılırmak Cad. 9, 06640 Küçükesat, Ankara; tel. (312) 4191040; fax (312) 4195308; e-mail bilgiedinme@ysk.gov.tr; internet www.ysk.gov.tr; independent; Chair. SADI GÜVEN.

Political Organizations

Political parties were banned from 1980–83. Legislation enacted in March 1986 stipulated that a party must have organizations in at least 45 provinces, and in two-thirds of the districts in each of these provinces, in order to take part in an election. A political party is recognized by the Government as a legitimate parliamentary group only if it has at least 20 deputies in the Grand National Assembly.

In mid-1992, following the adoption of less restrictive legislation concerning the formation of political parties, several new parties were established, and the left-wing CHP, dissolved in 1981, was reactivated.

In December 2009 the Kurdish nationalist Demokratik Toplum Partisi (DTP—Democratic Society Party) was banned by the Constitutional Court due to its alleged links to the proscribed Partiya Karkeren Kurdistan (PKK—Kurdistan Workers' Party).

Adalet ve Kalkınma Partisi (AKP) (Justice and Development Party): Söğütözü Cad. 6, Çankaya, Ankara; tel. (312) 2045000; fax

(312) 2045000; e-mail rte@akparti.org.tr; internet www.akparti.org .tr; f. 2001; Islamist-orientated; Leader RECEP TAYYIP ERDOĞAN.

Bağımsız Türkiye Partisi (BTP) (Independent Turkey Party): Cankiri Cad. 24, Kat 5 Ulus, Ankara; tel. (312) 3092001; fax (312) 3092003; e-mail btp@btp.org.tr; internet www.btp.org.tr; f. 2001; Chair. Prof. Dr HAYDAR BAŞ.

Bariş ve Demokrasi Partisi (BDP) (Peace and Democracy Party): Oguz Mah., Baris Manco Cad. 1388, Sok 37, Balgat, Ankara; tel. (312) 2201950; fax (312) 2201977; e-mail bdpbasin@gmail.com; internet www.bdp.org.tr; f. 2008; Kurdish nationalist, social democratic; following the dissolution of the pro-Kurdish Demokratik Toplum Partisi (DTP), its representatives in the Grand National Assembly and some elected officials at the provincial and local levels joined the BDP; Chair. SELAHATTIN DEMIRTAŞ, GÜLTEN KIŞANAK.

Büyük Birlik Partisi (BBP) (Great Unity Party): Gazi Mah., Silahtar Cad. 90, BBP Genel Merkezi Yenimahalle, Ankara; tel. (312) 4340923; fax (312) 4355818; e-mail bbp.duyuru@gmail.com; internet www.bbp.org.tr; f. 1993; Pres. MUSTAFA DESTICI; Sec.-Gen. ÜZEYIR TUNÇ.

Cumhuriyet Halk Partisi (CHP) (Republican People's Party): Anadolu Bul. 12, Söğütözü, Ankara; tel. (312) 2074000; fax (312) 2074039; e-mail chp@chp.org.tr; internet www.chp.org.tr; f. 1923 by Mustafa Kemal (Atatürk); dissolved in 1981 and reactivated in 1992; merged with Sosyal Demokrat Halkçı Parti (Social Democratic Populist Party) in Feb. 1995 and with the Yeni Türkiye Partisi in Oct. 2004; left-wing; Chair. KEMAL KILIÇDAROĞLU; Sec.-Gen. BIHLUN TAMAYLIGIL.

Demokrat Parti (DP) (Democratic Party): Akay Cad. 16, Kızılay, Ankara; tel. (312) 4441946; fax (312) 4168683; e-mail dp@dp.org.tr; internet www.dp.org.tr; f. 1983 as Doğru Yol Partisi (True Path Party); renamed as above in May 2007; merged with Anavatan Partisi (Motherland Party) in Nov. 2009; centre-right; Chair. GÜLTEKIN UYSAL.

Demokratik Sol Parti (DSP) (Democratic Left Party): Mareşal Fevzi Çakmak Cad. 17, Ankara; tel. (312) 2124950; fax (312) 2124188; e-mail dsp@dsp.org.tr; internet www.dsp.org.tr; f. 1985, drawing support from mems of the fmr Republican People's Party; centre-left; Chair. MASUM TÜRKER; Gen.-Sec. HASAN ERÇELEBI.

Emek Partisi (EMEP) (Labour Party of Turkey): Fevzi Çakmak 1 Sok. 15/5, Kızılay, Ankara; tel. (312) 2324198; fax (312) 2324197; e-mail emekpartisi@emep.org; internet www.emep.org; f. 1996; advocates scientific socialism; Chair. SELMA GURKAN.

Genç Parti (GP) (Youth Party): İller Sok. 7, Mebusevleri, 06580 Tandoğan, Ankara; fax (312) 2969757; f. 2002; populist, nationalist; Leader CEM UZAN.

Halkın Sesi Partisi (HAS Parti) (People's Voice Party): Oğuzlar Mah. 1397, Sok. 14, 06520 Balgat, Ankara; tel. (312) 2852484; fax (312) 2852480; e-mail iletisim@hasparti.org.tr; internet www .hasparti.org.tr; f. 2010 by fmr Chair. of Saadet Partisi; Chair. Prof. Dr NUMAN KURTULMUŞ.

Halkın Yükselişi Partisi (HYP) (People's Ascent Party): Filistin Sok. 30, Gaziosmanpaşa, Ankara; tel. (312) 4480621; fax (312) 4476968; e-mail hypgenelmerkez@hyp.org.tr; internet www.hyp .org.tr; f. 2005; advocates social democratic principles; Pres. RAGIP ÖNDER GÜNAY.

İşçi Partisi (IP) (Workers' Party): Toros Sok. 9, Sıhhiye, Ankara; tel. (312) 2318111; fax (312) 2292994; e-mail int@ip.org.tr; internet www.ip.org.tr; f. 1992; Chair. DOĞU PERINÇEK.

Liberal Demokrat Parti (LDP) (Liberal Democrat Party): İstanbul; tel. (533) 3323165; fax (212) 2550291; e-mail ldp@ldp.org; internet www.ldp.org.tr; f. 1994; Chair. CEM TOKER.

Millet Partisi (MP) (Nation Party): Atatürk Bul. 72/37, Kızılay, Ankara; tel. (312) 4194060; fax (312) 3127651; e-mail milletpartisi@hotmail.com; internet www.milletpartisi.org; f. 1992; Chair. AYKUT EDIBALI.

Milliyetçi Hareket Partisi (MHP) (Nationalist Action Party): Ceyhun Atif Kansu Cad. 128, Balgat, Ankara; tel. (312) 4725555; fax (312) 4731544; e-mail bilgi@mhp.org.tr; internet www.mhp.org .tr; f. 1983; fmrly the Democratic and Conservative Party; Leader DEVLET BAHÇELI; Sec.-Gen. İSMET BÜYÜKATAMAN.

Özgürlük ve Dayanisma Partisi (ODP) (Freedom and Solidarity Party): GMK Bul. 87/18, Maltepe, Ankara; tel. (312) 2317232; fax 2320347; e-mail odp@odp.org.tr; internet www.odp.org.tr; f. 1996; Chairs ALPER TAŞ, BILGE SEÇKIN ÇETINKAYA.

Özgür Toplum Parti (OTP) (Free Society Party): f. 2003; associated with Halkın Demokrasi Partisi; Leader AHMET TURAN DEMIR.

Saadet Partisi (SP) (Felicity Party): Ziyabey Cad. 2, Sok. 15, 06520 Balgat, Ankara; tel. (312) 2848800; fax (312) 2856246; e-mail bilgi@saadet.org.tr; internet www.saadet.org.tr; f. 2001; replaced conservative wing of Islamist fundamentalist and free-market advocating Fazilet Partisi (Virtue Party), which was banned in that year; Chair. Prof. Dr MUSTAFA KAMALAK.

Türkiye Komünist Partisi (TKP) (Communist Party of Turkey): Osmanağa Mah. Serasker Cad. Kazasker Sok. 10, Kadıköy, İstanbul; tel. (216) 4146504; fax (216) 3461137; e-mail tkp@tkp.org.tr; internet www.tkp.org.tr; f. 1981 as the Party of Socialist Power; name changed as above in 2001; Chair. ERKAN BAŞ.

Yurt Partisi (Homeland Party): Meşrutiyet Cad. Bayındır 2, Sok. 59/5, Kızılay, Ankara; tel. (312) 4189034; fax (312) 4189364; e-mail iletisim@yurtpartisi.org.tr; internet www.yurtpartisi.org.tr; f. 2002; nationalist and conservative party; Leader SAADETTIN TANTAN.

The following proscribed organizations were engaged in an armed struggle against the Government:

Devrimci Halk Kurtuluş Partisi—Cephesi (DHKP—C) (Revolutionary People's Liberation Party—Front): e-mail dhkc@ozgurluk .org; faction of Dev-Sol; subsumed parent org. in 1996.

Partiya Karkeren Kurdistan (PKK) (Kurdistan Workers' Party): internet www.pkkonline.net; f. 1978; 57-mem. directorate; launched struggle for an independent Kurdistan in 1984; declared cease-fire 2000; renamed Congress for Freedom and Democracy in Kurdistan (KADEK) April 2002 and KONGRA-GEL Nov. 2003; return to fmr name, PKK, announced April 2005, following resumption of armed struggle; name KONGRA-GEL continued to be used by some elements; military wing, Hezên Parastina Gel (HPG—People's Defence Forces), re-emerged 2004; Chair. MURAT KARAYILAN; Leader ABDULLAH ÖCALAN.

Diplomatic Representation

EMBASSIES IN TURKEY

Afghanistan: Cinnah Cad. 88, 06550 Çankaya, Ankara; tel. (312) 4422325; fax (312) 4426256; e-mail info@afghanembassy.org.tr; internet afghanembassy.org.tr; Ambassador Dr AMANULLAH JAYHOON.

Albania: Ebu Ziya Tevfik Sok. 17, Çankaya, Ankara; tel. (312) 4416103; fax (312) 4416109; e-mail embassy.ankara@mfa.gov.al; Ambassador GENCI MUÇAJ.

Algeria: Şehit Ersan Cad. 42, 06680 Çankaya, Ankara; tel. (312) 4687719; fax (312) 4687593; e-mail cezayirbe@yahoo.fr; Ambassador MOULOUD HAMAI.

Angola: Kennedy Cad. 155, 1-2-3 Gaziosmanpaşa, Ankara; tel. (312) 4282770; fax (312) 4282772; e-mail embaixada.turquia@mirex.gov .ao; Ambassador JOSÉ GUERREIRO ALVES PRIMO.

Argentina: Uğur Mumcu Cad. 60/1, 06700 Gaziosmanpaşa, Ankara; tel. (312) 4462062; fax (312) 4462063; e-mail embargturquia@yahoo .com.ar; Chargé d'affaires a.i. RAIMUNDO MARCELO APPELHANS.

Australia: Uğur Mumcu Cad. 88, 7th Floor, 06700 Gaziosmanpaşa, Ankara; tel. (312) 4599500; fax (312) 4464827; e-mail info-ankara@ dfat.gov.au; internet www.turkey.embassy.gov.au; Ambassador IAN BIGGS.

Austria: Atatürk Bul. 189, 06680 Kavaklıdere, Ankara; tel. (312) 4055190; fax (312) 4189454; e-mail ankara-ob@bmeia.gv.at; internet www.aussenministerium.at/botschaft/ankara.html; Ambassador KLAUS WÖLFER.

Azerbaijan: Diplomatik Site, Bakü Sok. 1, 06450 Oran, Ankara; tel. (312) 4911681; fax (312) 4920430; e-mail ankara@mission.mfa.gov .az; Ambassador FAIG BAGIROV.

Bahrain: İlkbahar Mah. 606, Sok. 19, Oran-Çankaya, Ankara; tel. (312) 4912656; fax (312) 4912676; e-mail ankara.mission@mofa.gov .bh; Ambassador IBRAHIM YOUSUF AL-ABDULLAH.

Bangladesh: Birlik Mah. 391, Cad. 16, 06610 Çankaya, Ankara; tel. (312) 4952719; fax (312) 4952744; e-mail bdootankara@ttmail.com; Ambassador ZULFIQUR RAHMAN.

Belarus: Abidin Daver Sok. 17, 06550 Çankaya, Ankara; tel. (312) 4416769; fax (312) 4416674; e-mail turkey@mfa.gov.by; internet www.turkey.mfa.gov.by; Ambassador VALERY KOLESNIK.

Belgium: Mahatma Gandhi Cad. 55, 06700 Gaziosmanpaşa, Ankara; tel. (312) 4056166; fax (312) 4468251; e-mail ankara@ diplobel.fed.be; internet www.diplomatie.be/ankara; Ambassador POL DE WITTE.

Bosnia and Herzegovina: Turan Emeksiz Sok., Park Bloklan, B Blok 3/9–10, Gaziosmanpaşa, Ankara; tel. (312) 4273602; fax (312) 4273604; e-mail bh_emba@ttmail.com; Ambassador DAMIR DZANKO.

Brazil: Reşit Galip Cad., İlkadım Sok. 1, 06700 Gaziosmanpaşa, Ankara; tel. (312) 4481840; fax (312) 4481838; e-mail brasemb@ brasembancara.org; internet www.brasembancara.org; Ambassador MARCELO JARDIM.

Bulgaria: Atatürk Bul. 124, 06680 Kavaklıdere, Ankara; tel. (312) 4672071; fax (312) 4686956; e-mail Embassy.Ankara@mfa.bg; internet www.mfa.bg/embassies/turkey; Ambassador KRASIMIR TULECHKI.

Canada: Cinnah Cad. 58, 06690 Çankaya, Ankara; tel. (312) 4092700; fax (312) 4092712; e-mail ankara@international.gc.ca; internet www.turkey.gc.ca; Ambassador JOHN HOLMES.

Chile: Reşit Galip Cad., İrfanli Sok. 14/1–3, 06700 Gaziosmanpaşa, Ankara; tel. (312) 4473418; fax (312) 4474725; e-mail embassy@chile .org.tr; internet www.chile.org.tr; Ambassador JORGE PATRICIO ARANCIBIA REYES.

China, People's Republic: Gölgeli Sok. 34, 06700 Gaziosmanpaşa, Ankara; tel. (312) 4360628; fax (312) 4464248; e-mail chinaemb_tr@ mfa.gov.cn; internet www.chinaembassy.org.tr; Ambassador GONG XIAOSHENG.

Colombia: Koza Sok. 91/5, 06570 Gaziosmanpaşa, Ankara; tel. (312) 4464388; fax (312) 4464399; e-mail eankara@cancilleria.gov.co; Ambassador FERNANDO PANESSO.

Congo, Democratic Republic: Turan Emeksiz Sok. 16/1, Gaziosmanpaşa, Ankara; tel. (312) 4660916; fax (312) 4660918; e-mail missionrdcankara@gmail.com; Ambassador MARCEL MULUMBA TSHIDIMBA.

Croatia: Kelebek Sok. 15/A, 06700 Gaziosmanpaşa, Ankara; tel. (312) 4469460; fax (312) 4464700; e-mail ankara@mvep.hr; internet tr.mvp.hr; Ambassador DRAŽEN HRASTIĆ.

Cuba: Şölen Sok. 8, 06550 Çankaya, Ankara; tel. (312) 4428970; fax (312) 4426115; e-mail embacubatur@tr.net; Ambassador JORGE QUESADA CONCEPCIÓN.

Czech Republic: Kaptanpaşa Sok. 15, Gaziosmanpaşa, Ankara; tel. (312) 4056139; fax (312) 4463084; e-mail ankara@embassy.mzv.cz; internet www.mzv.cz/ankara; Ambassador VÁCLAV HUBINGER.

Denmark: Mahatma Gandhi Cad. 74, 06700 Gaziosmanpaşa, Ankara; tel. (312) 4466141; fax (312) 4472498; e-mail ankamb@um .dk; internet www.ambankara.um.dk; Ambassador RUBEN MADSEN.

Djibouti: İlkbahar Mah. Galip Erdem Cad. 613, Sok. 6, Yıldız-Çankaya, Ankara; tel. (312) 4919513; fax (312) 4919510; e-mail djib .embassytr@gmail.com; Ambassador ADEN HOUSSEIN ABDILLAHI.

Ecuador: Kelebek Sok. 21/1, Gaziosmanpaşa, Ankara; tel. (312) 4460160; fax (312) 4460173; e-mail eecuturquia@mmrree.gov.ec; Ambassador SAA AUGUSTO CORRIERE.

Egypt: Atatürk Bul. 126, 06680 Kavaklıdere, Ankara; tel. (312) 4261026; fax (312) 4270099; e-mail embassy_egypt@yahoo.com; internet www.egyptturkey.com; Ambassador ABD AL-RAHMAN SALAH EL-DIN.

Estonia: Gölgeli Sok. 16, 06700 Gaziosmanpaşa, Ankara; tel. (312) 4056970; fax (312) 4056976; e-mail embassy.ankara@mfa.ee; internet www.estemb.org.tr/embassy; Ambassador MIKO HALJAS.

Ethiopia: Uğur Mumcu Sok. 74/1–2, 06700 Gaziosmanpaşa, Ankara; tel. (312) 4360400; fax (312) 4481938; e-mail ethembank@ ttnet.net.tr; Ambassador MULATU TESHOME WIRTU.

Finland: Kader Sok. 44, 06700 Gaziosmanpaşa, Ankara; tel. (312) 4574400; fax (312) 4680072; e-mail sanomat.ank@formin.fi; internet www.finland.org.tr; Ambassador NINA VASKUNLAHTI.

France: Paris Cad. 70, 06540 Kavaklıdere, Ankara; tel. (312) 4554545; fax (312) 4554527; e-mail ambaank@yahoo.fr; internet www.ambafrance-tr.org; Ambassador LAURENT BILI.

The Gambia: Hilal Mah., Hollanda Cad., 31 Yıldız, Ankara; tel. (312) 4425771; fax (312) 4425707; Ambassador GIBRIL JOOF.

Georgia: Kılıç Ali Sok. 12, Oran, Ankara; tel. (312) 4918030; fax (312) 4918032; e-mail ankara.emb@mfa.gov.ge; internet www .turkey.mfa.gov.ge; Ambassador TARIEL LEBANIDZE.

Germany: Atatürk Bul. 114, 06690 Kavaklıdere, Ankara; tel. (312) 4555100; fax (312) 4555337; e-mail info@ankara.diplo.de; internet www.ankara.diplo.de; Ambassador EBHARD POHL.

Ghana: Gölgeli Sok. 9, Gaziosmanpaşa, Çankaya, Ankara; tel. (312) 4425479; fax (312) 4418569; e-mail ghanaembassyturkey@yahoo .com; Ambassador İBRAHIM ABASS.

Greece: Zia ür-Rahman Cad. 9–11, 06670 Gaziosmanpaşa, Ankara; tel. (312) 4480873; fax (312) 4463191; e-mail gremb.ank@mfa.gr; Ambassador KYRIAKOS LOUKAKIS.

Holy See: Apostolic Nunciature, Birlik Mah. 3, Cad. 37, PK 33, 06552 Çankaya, Ankara; tel. (312) 4953514; fax (312) 4953540; e-mail vatican@tr.net; Apostolic Nuncio Most Rev. ANTONIO LUCI-BELLO (Titular Archbishop of Thurio).

Hungary: Sancak Mah. Layoş, Koşut Cad. 2, 06550 Yıldız, Çankaya, Ankara; tel. (312) 4422273; fax (312) 4415049; e-mail mission.ank@ mfa.gov.hu; internet www.mfa.gov.hu/kulkepviselet/tr/hu; Ambassador Dr JÁNOS HÓVÁRI.

India: Cinnah Cad. 77A, 06680 Çankaya, Ankara; tel. (312) 4382195; fax (312) 4403429; e-mail chancery@indembassy.org.tr; internet www.indembassy.org.tr; Ambassador SUSMITA GONGULEE THOMAS.

Indonesia: Abdullah Cevdet Sok. 10, 06680 Çankaya, Ankara; tel. (312) 4382190; fax (312) 4382193; e-mail kbriank@ttmail.com; Ambassador NAHARI AGUSTINI.

Iran: Tahran Cad. 10, 06700 Kavaklıdere, Ankara; tel. (312) 4682821; fax (312) 4682823; e-mail iranemb.ank@mfa.gov.ir; Ambassador ALIREZA BIGDELI.

Iraq: Turan Emeksiz Sok. 11, 06700 Gaziosmanpaşa, Ankara; tel. (312) 4687421; fax (312) 4684832; e-mail ankemb@iraqmofamail .com; Ambassador ABD AL-AMIR KAMAL ABU TABIKH.

Ireland: Uğur Mumcu Cad. 88, MNG Binası B Blok Kat 3, 06700 Gaziosmanpaşa, Ankara; tel. (312) 4591000; fax (312) 4468061; e-mail ankaraembassy@dfa.ie; internet www.embassyofireland.org .tr; Ambassador KENNETH THOMPSON.

Israel: Mahatma Gandhi Cad. 85, 06700 Gaziosmanpaşa, Ankara; tel. (312) 4597500; fax (312) 4597555; e-mail info@ankara.mfa.gov.il; internet ankara.mfa.gov.il; Chargé d'affaires a.i. YOSEF LEVY SFARI.

Italy: Atatürk Bul. 118, 06680 Kavaklıdere, Ankara; tel. (312) 4574200; fax (312) 4574280; e-mail ambasciata.ankara@esteri.it; internet www.ambankara.esteri.it; Ambassador GIANPAOLO SCARANTE.

Japan: Reşit Galip Cad. 81, 06692 Gaziosmanpaşa, Ankara; tel. (312) 4460500; fax (312) 4371812; e-mail culture@jpn-emb.org.tr; internet www.tr.emb-japan.go.jp; Ambassador KIYOSHI ARAKI.

Jordan: Dede Korkut Sok. 18 Mesnevi, 06690 Çankaya, Ankara; tel. (312) 4402054; fax (312) 4404327; e-mail ankara@fm.gov.jo; Ambassador AMJAD AL-ADAILEH.

Kazakhstan: Kiliç Ali Sok. 6, Diplomatik Site, 06450 Oran, Ankara; tel. (312) 4919100; fax (312) 4904455; e-mail ankara@mfa.kz; Ambassador ZHANSEIT TUIMEBAYEV.

Kenya: İlkbahar Mah., Turan Güneş Bul. 571, Cad. 612, Sok. 10, 06550 Yıldız, Ankara; tel. (312) 4914508; fax (312) 4914516; Chargé d'affaires LINDSAY KIPTINESS.

Korea, Republic: Cinnah Cad., Alaçam Sok. 5, 06690 Çankaya, Ankara; tel. (312) 4684822; fax (312) 4267872; e-mail turkey@mofat .go.kr; internet tur-ankara.mofat.go.kr; Ambassador LEE SANG-KYU.

Kosovo: Hirfanli Sok. 14/2, Gaziosmanpaşa, Ankara; tel. (312) 4467054; fax (312) 4467055; e-mail embassy.turkey@ks-gov.net; Ambassador AVNI SPAHIU.

Kuwait: Reşit Galip Cad., Kelebek Sok. 110, Gaziosmanpaşa, Ankara; tel. (312) 4450576; fax (312) 4462826; e-mail kuwait@ada .net.tr; Ambassador ABDULLAH ABD AL-AZIZ AL-DUWAIKH.

Kyrgyzstan: İlkbahar Mah., Galip Erdem Cad. 25, Çankaya, Ankara; tel. (312) 4913056; fax (312) 4913513; e-mail info@ kgembassy.org.tr; Ambassador ERMEK IBRAIMOV.

Latvia: Reşit Galip Cad. 95, Çankaya, Ankara; tel. (312) 4056136; fax (312) 4056137; e-mail embassy.turkey@mfa.gov.lv; Ambassador ATIS SJANITS.

Lebanon: Kızkulesi Sok. 44, Gaziosmanpaşa, 06700 Ankara; tel. (312) 4467485; fax (312) 4461023; e-mail lebembas@ttnet.net.tr; Ambassador MANSOUR ABDALLAH.

Libya: Cinnah Cad. 60, 06690 Çankaya, Ankara; tel. (312) 4381110; fax (312) 4403862; e-mail infolibya@yahoo.com; Ambassador ABD UL-RAZAQ MUKHTAR AHMED ABD AL-GADER.

Lithuania: Mahatma Gandhi Cad. 17/8–9, 06700 Gaziosmanpaşa, Ankara; tel. (312) 4470766; fax (312) 4470663; e-mail amb.tr@urm.lt; internet tr.mfa.lt; Ambassador KESTUTIS KUDZMANAS.

Luxembourg: Reşit Galip Cad. 70/2, 2 Gaziosmanpaşa, Ankara; tel. (312) 4591400; fax (312) 4365055; e-mail ankara.amb@mae.etat.lu; Ambassador ARLETTE CONZEMIUS.

Macedonia, former Yugoslav republic: Karaca Sok. 24/5–6, 06700 Gaziosmanpaşa, Ankara; tel. (312) 4399204; fax (312) 4399206; e-mail ankara@mfa.gov.mk; Ambassador GORAN TASKOVSKI.

Malaysia: Mahatma Gandhi Cad. 58, 06700 Gaziosmanpaşa, Ankara; tel. (312) 4463547; fax (312) 4464130; e-mail malankara@ kln.gov.my; internet www.kln.gov.my/perwakilan/ankara; Ambassador Dato' SAIPUL ANUAR ABD AL-MUIN.

Mauritania: Oran Mah. Şemsettin Bayramoğlu Sok. 7, Çankaya, Ankara; tel. (312) 4917063; fax (312) 4917064; e-mail moritanya .buyukelciligi@gmail.com; Ambassador MUHAMMAD AHMED LEHWEIRTHI.

Mexico: Kırkpınar Sok. 18/6, 06540 Çankaya, Ankara; tel. (312) 4423033; fax (312) 4420221; e-mail mexico@embamextur.com; internet www.mexico.org.tr; Ambassador JAIME GARCÍA AMARAL.

Moldova: Kaptanpaşa Sok. 49, 06700 Gaziosmanpaşa, Ankara; tel. (312) 4465527; fax (312) 4465816; e-mail ankara@mfa.md; internet www.turcia.mfa.md; Ambassador IGOR BOLBOCEANU.

Mongolia: A. Fethi Okyar Sok. 4, Oran Diplomatik Sitesi, 06700 Oran, Ankara; tel. (312) 4921027; fax (312) 4921064; e-mail ankara@ mfat.gov.mn; Ambassador BATKHISHIG BADAMDORJ.

Montenegro: Büyükesat, Gökçek Sok. 11, 06700 Ankara; tel. (312) 4364698; fax (312) 4361546; e-mail turkey@mfa.gov.me; Ambassador RAMO BRALIĆ.

Morocco: Reşit Galip Cad., Rabat Sok. 11, 06700 Gaziosmanpaşa, Ankara; tel. (312) 4376020; fax (312) 4468430; e-mail sifamatr@tr .net; Ambassador MUHAMMAD LOTFI AOUAD.

Netherlands: Hollanda Cad. 5, 06550 Yıldız, Ankara; tel. (312) 4091800; fax (312) 4091898; e-mail ank@minbuza.nl; internet turkey .nlembassy.org; Ambassador JAN PAUL DIRKSE.

New Zealand: Kizkulesi Sok. 11, Gaziosmanpaşa, Ankara; tel. (312) 4463333; fax (312) 4463317; e-mail nzembassyankara@ttmail.com; internet www.nzembassy.com/turkey; Ambassador TAHAMOANA (TAHA) AISEA MACPHERSON.

Niger: Mahatma Gandhi Cad. 40, Gaziosmanpaşa, Ankara; tel. (312) 4361013; fax (312) 4361017; e-mail niger@ambassadeturquie .org; Ambassador ADAM ABDOULAYE DAN-MARADI.

Nigeria: Uğur Mumcu Sok. 56, 06700 Gaziosmanpaşa, Ankara; tel. (312) 4481077; fax (312) 4481082; e-mail embassynigeriaturkey@ yahoo.co.uk; Ambassador AHMED A. M. MADORI.

Norway: Kirkpinar Sok. 18/3–4, 06540 Çankaya, Ankara; tel. (312) 4084800; fax (312) 4084899; e-mail emb.ankara@mfa.no; internet www.norway.org.tr; Ambassador JANIS BJØRN KANAVIN.

Oman: Diplomatik Alan, Besim Atalay Sok. 7, Oran, Ankara; tel. (312) 4910940; fax (312) 4900682; e-mail omanembassy@yahoo.com; Ambassador Sayyid QAIS BIN SALIM BIN ALI AL-SAID.

Pakistan: İran Cad. 37, Çankaya, Ankara; tel. (312) 4271410; fax (312) 4671023; e-mail perepankhara@yahoo.com; internet www .pakembassyankara.com; Ambassador MUHAMMAD HAROON SHAU-KAT.

Peru: Reşit Galip Cad. 70/1, 06700 Ankara; tel. (312) 4469039; fax (312) 4474026; e-mail peruankara@gmail.com; Ambassador JORGE ABARCA DEL CARPIO.

Philippines: Mahatma Gandhi Cad. 56, 06700 Gaziosmanpaşa, Ankara; tel. (312) 4465831; fax (312) 4465733; e-mail ankara_pe@ yahoo.com; Ambassador MARILYN JUSAYAN ALARILLA.

Poland: Atatürk Bul. 241, 06650 Kavaklıdere, Ankara; tel. (312) 4572000; fax (312) 4678963; e-mail ankara.amb.sekretariat@msz .gov.pl; internet ankara.msz.gov.pl; Chargé d'affaires PIOTR KRAWCZYK.

Portugal: Kuleli Sok. 39, Gaziosmanpaşa, Ankara; tel. (312) 4056028; fax (312) 4463670; e-mail embaixada@portugal.org.tr; internet www.portugalembassy.org.tr; Ambassador JORGE TITO DE VASCONCELES NOGUEIRA DIAS CABRAL.

Qatar: Bakü Sok. 6, Diplomatik Site, Oran, Ankara; tel. (312) 4907274; fax (312) 4906757; e-mail qeank@yahoo.com; Ambassador ABD AL-RAZAK ABD AL-GHANI.

Romania: Bükreş Sok. 4, 06680 Çankaya, Ankara; tel. (312) 4663706; fax (312) 4271530; e-mail romanyabyk@dsl.ttmail.com; internet ankara.mae.ro; Ambassador RADU ONOFREI.

Russia: Karyağdı Sok. 5, 06692 Çankaya, Ankara; tel. (312) 4392122; fax (312) 4383952; e-mail rus-ankara@yandex.ru; internet www.turkey.mid.ru; Ambassador VLADIMIR E. IVANOVSKII.

Saudi Arabia: Turan Emeksiz Sok. 6, 06700 Gaziosmanpaşa, Ankara; tel. (312) 4685540; fax (312) 4274886; e-mail tremb@mofa .gov.sa; Chargé d'affaires a.i. ABDULLAH M. A. AL-SHAFI.

Senegal: Hilal Mah., Alexander Dubcek Cad. 8, Yıldız, Ankara; tel. (312) 4420046; fax (312) 4420056; e-mail senegalbuyukelciligi@ gmail.com; Ambassador ISSAKHA MBACKE.

Serbia: Paris Cad. 47, 06691 Kavaklıdere, Ankara; tel. (312) 4260236; fax (312) 4278345; e-mail embserank@gmail.com; Ambassador DUŠAN SPASOJEVIĆ.

Singapore: Yıldızevler Mah., 4. Cad., 718 Sok. 13/14, 06550 Çankaya, Ankara; tel. (312) 4424330; fax (312) 4426144; e-mail singemb_ank@sgmfa.gov.sg; internet www.mfa.gov.sg/ankara; Chargé d'affaires LORLING LEE.

Slovakia: Atatürk Bul. 245, 06692 Kavaklıdere, Ankara; tel. (312) 4675075; fax (312) 4682689; e-mail emb.ankara@mzv.sk; Ambassador MILAN ZACHAR.

Slovenia: Kırlangıç Sok. 36, 06700 Gaziosmanpaşa, Ankara; tel. (312) 4054980; fax (312) 4260216; e-mail van@gov.si; Ambassador MILAN JAZBEC.

Somalia: Rabat Sok. 24/2, 06700 Gaziosmanpaşa, Ankara; tel. (312) 4364028; fax (312) 4364029; e-mail somemb.ankara@gmail.com; Chargé d'affaires a.i. NUR SHIEK HAMUD.

South Africa: Filistin Sok. 27, 06700 Gaziosmanpaşa, Ankara; tel. (312) 4056861; fax (312) 4466434; e-mail general.ankara@foreign .gov.za; internet www.southafrica.org.tr; Ambassador VIKA M. KHUMALO.

South Sudan: Kız Kulesi Sok. 1, Gaziosmanpaşa, Ankara; tel. (312) 4360285; fax (312) 4360284; e-mail info@southsudanankara.org; internet www.southsudanankara.org; Ambassador JOHN GAI YOH.

Spain: Abdullah Cevdet Sok. 8, 06550 Çankaya, Ankara; tel. (312) 4401796; fax (312) 4395170; e-mail emb.ankara@maec.es; internet www.maec.es/embajadas/ankara; Ambassador CRISTOBAL GONZÁLEZ-ALLER JURADO.

Sri Lanka: Kırlangıç Sok. 41, 06700, Gaziosmanpaşa, Ankara; tel. (312) 4271021; fax (312) 4271026; Ambassador BHARATHI DAVINA WIJERATNE.

Sudan: Mahatma Gandhi Cad. 48, Gaziosmanpaşa, Çankaya, 06700 Ankara; tel. (312) 4466327; fax (312) 4468506; e-mail ankara@mfa .gov.sd; Ambassador OMER HAIDAR ABU ZAID.

Sweden: Katip Çelebi Sok. 7, 06692 Kavaklıdere, Ankara; tel. (312) 4554100; fax (312) 4554120; e-mail ambassaden.ankara@gov.se; internet www.swedenabroad.com/ankara; Ambassador HÅKAN ÅKESSON.

Switzerland: Atatürk Bul. 247, 06692 Kavaklıdere, Ankara; tel. (312) 4573100; fax (312) 4671199; e-mail ank.vertretung@eda.admin .ch; internet www.eda.admin.ch/ankara; Ambassador RAIMUND KUNZ.

Syria: Sedat Simavi Sok. 40, 06550 Çankaya, Ankara; tel. (312) 4409657; fax (312) 4385609; Chargé d'affaires a.i. MOUNZER MOUNZER.

Tajikistan: Ferit Recai Ertuğrul Cad. 20, 25009 Oran, Ankara; tel. (312) 4911607; fax (312) 4911603; e-mail tajemb_turkey@yahoo.com; Ambassador FARRUH SHARIPOV.

Thailand: Koza Sok. 87, 06700 Gaziosmanpaşa, Ankara; tel. (312) 4374318; fax (312) 4378495; e-mail thaiank@ttmail.com; Ambassador RATHAKIT MANATHAT.

Tunisia: Ferit Recai Ertuğrul Cad. 19, Oran Diplomatic Site, Ankara; tel. (312) 4919635; fax (312) 4919634; e-mail at.ankara@ superonline.com; Chargé d'affaires a.i. NEYLA CHALA EP CHEBAANE.

'Turkish Republic of Northern Cyprus': Rabat Sok. 20, 06700 Gaziosmanpaşa, Ankara; tel. (312) 4461036; fax (312) 4465238; e-mail info@kktcbe.org.tr; internet www.kktcbe.org; Ambassador MUSTAFA LAKADAMYALI.

Turkmenistan: Koza Sok. 28, 06700 Çankaya, Ankara; tel. (312) 4416122; fax (312) 4417125; e-mail tmankara@ttnet.net.tr; Ambassador ATA SERDAROV.

Uganda: Uğur Mumcu Sok. 59, Gaziosmanpaşa, Ankara; tel. (312) 4370194; fax (312) 4370178; e-mail ugandaembassyturkey@gmail .com; Chargé d'affaires a.i. SANTA MARY LAKER KINYERA.

Ukraine: Sancak Mah. 512 Sok. 17, 06550 Çankaya, Ankara; tel. (312) 4415499; fax (312) 4406815; e-mail emb_tr@mfa.gov.ua; internet www.mfa.gov.ua/turkey; Ambassador SERGEI KORSUNSKII.

United Arab Emirates: Turan Güneş Bul. 13, Galip ERdem Cad. 613, Ylkbahar Mah., Çankaya, Ankara; tel. (312) 4901414; fax (312) 4912333; e-mail uaeemb@uaeemb.net; internet www.uaeemb.net; Ambassador KHALID KHALIFA A. RASHED AL-MU'ALLA.

United Kingdom: Şehit Ersan Cad. 46/A, 06680 Çankaya, Ankara; tel. (312) 4553344; fax (312) 4553352; e-mail info.officer@fco.gov.uk; internet ukinturkey.fco.gov.uk; Ambassador DAVID REDDAWAY.

USA: Atatürk Bul. 110, 06100 Kavaklıdere, Ankara; tel. (312) 4555555; fax (312) 4670019; e-mail webmaster_ankara@state.gov; internet turkey.usembassy.gov; Ambassador FRANCIS J. RICCIARDONE, Jr.

Uzbekistan: Sancak Mah. 549 Sok. 3, Yıldız, 06550 Çankaya, Ankara; tel. (312) 4413871; fax (312) 4427058; e-mail uzemb_ankara@yahoo.com; Ambassador ULFAT S. KADYROV.

Venezuela: Hilal Mah., Hollanda Cad., 696. Sok. 20A, Yıldız, 06550 Çankaya, Ankara; tel. (312) 4412145; fax (312) 4406755; e-mail mision-ankara@embavenez-turquia.com; Ambassador JOSÉ GREGORIO BRACHO REYES.

Viet Nam: Koza Sok. 109, Gaziosmanpaşa, Çankaya, Ankara; tel. (312) 4468049; fax (312) 4465623; e-mail dsqvnturkey@yahoo.com; internet www.vietnamembassy-turkey.org; Ambassador NGUYEN THE CUONG.

Yemen: Fethiye Sok. 2, 06700 Gaziosmanpaşa, Ankara; tel. (312) 4462637; fax (312) 4461778; e-mail yemenemb@superonline.com; Chargé d'affaires a.i. MAHDI SALEH NASSER AL-ODAMI.

Judicial System

Until the foundation of the Turkish Republic, a large part of the Turkish civil law—the laws affecting the family, inheritance, property, obligations, etc.—was based on the Koran, and this holy law was administered by special religious (*Shari'a*) courts. The legal reform of 1926 was not only a process of secularization, but also a radical change of the legal system. The Swiss Civil Code and the Code of Obligation, the Italian Penal Code and the Neuchâtel (Cantonal) Code of Civil Procedure were adopted and modified to fit Turkish customs and traditions.

According to current Turkish law, the power of the judiciary is exercised by judicial (criminal), military and administrative courts.

These courts render their verdicts in the first instance, while superior courts examine the verdict for subsequent rulings.

Constitutional Court: Consists of 17 members, appointed by the President. Reviews the constitutionality of laws, at the request of the President of the Republic, parliamentary groups of the governing party or of the main opposition party, or of one-fifth of the members of the National Assembly, and sits as a high council empowered to try senior members of state. The rulings of the Constitutional Court are final. Decisions of the Court are published immediately in the Official Gazette, and shall be binding on the legislative, executive and judicial organs of the state; Chief Justice HAŞIM KILIÇ.

Court of Appeals: The court of the last instance for reviewing the decisions and verdicts rendered by judicial courts. It has original and final jurisdiction in specific cases defined by law. Members are elected by the Supreme Council of Judges and Public Prosecutors; Chief Justice ALI ALKAN.

Council of State: An administrative court of the first and last instance in matters not referred by law to other administrative courts, and an administrative court of the last instance in general. Hears and settles administrative disputes and expresses opinions on draft laws submitted by the Council of Ministers. Three-quarters of the members are appointed by the Supreme Council of Judges and Public Prosecutors; the remaining quarter is selected by the President of the Republic.

Military Court of Appeals: A court of the last instance to review decisions and verdicts rendered by military courts, and a court of first and last instance with jurisdiction over certain military persons, stipulated by law, with responsibility for the specific trials of these persons. Members are selected by the President of the Republic from nominations made by the Military Court of Appeals.

Supreme Military Administrative Court: A military court for the judicial control of administrative acts concerning military personnel. Members are selected by the President of the Republic from nominations made by the Court.

Court of Jurisdictional Disputes: Settles disputes among judicial, administrative and military courts arising from disagreements on jurisdictional matters and verdicts.

Court of Accounts: A court charged with the auditing of all accounts of revenue, expenditure and government property, which renders rulings related to transactions and accounts of authorized bodies on behalf of the National Assembly.

Supreme Council of Judges and Public Prosecutors: The Minister of Justice serves as the President of the Supreme Council, while the Under-Secretary to the Minister of Justice is an ex officio member. The remaining 20 members of the Council comprise four appointed directly by the President of the Republic, three nominated by the Court of Appeals, two by the Council of State, one by the Justice Academy and 10 elected by judges and prosecutors; each of these members is appointed for a four-year term. Decides all personnel matters relating to judges and public prosecutors.

Public Prosecutor: The law shall make provision for the tenure of public prosecutors and attorneys of the Council of State and their functions. The Chief Prosecutor of the Republic, the Chief Attorney of the Council of State and the Chief Prosecutor of the Military Court of Appeals are subject to the provisions applicable to judges of higher courts.

Military Trial: Military trials are conducted by military and disciplinary courts. These courts are entitled to try the military offences of military personnel and those offences committed against military personnel or in military areas, or offences connected with military service and duties. Military courts may try non-military persons only for military offences prescribed by special laws.

Religion

ISLAM

More than 99% of the Turkish people are Muslims. However, Turkey is a secular state. Although Islam was stated to be the official religion in the Constitution of 1924, an amendment in 1928 removed this privilege. Since 1950 subsequent Governments have tried to re-establish links between religion and state affairs, but secularity was protected by the revolution of 1960, the 1980 military takeover and the 1982 Constitution.

Diyanet İşleri Başkanlığı (Presidency of Religious Affairs): Eskişehir Yolu 9 km Çankaya, Ankara; tel. (312) 2957000; e-mail protokol@diyanet.gov.tr; internet www.diyanet.gov.tr; Pres. Prof. Dr ALI BARDAKOĞLU.

CHRISTIANITY

The town of Antioch (now Antakya) was one of the earliest strongholds of Christianity, and by the 4th century had become a patriarchal see. Formerly in Syria, the town was incorporated into Turkey in 1939. Constantinople (now İstanbul) was also a patriarchal see, and by the 6th century the Patriarch of Constantinople was recognized as the Ecumenical Patriarch in the East. Gradual estrangement from Rome developed, leading to the final breach between the Catholic West and the Orthodox East, usually assigned to the year 1054.

There are estimated to be about 100,000 Christians in Turkey.

The Orthodox Churches

Armenian Patriarchate: Ermeni Patrikliği, Sevgi Sok. 6, 34130 Kumkapı, İstanbul; tel. (212) 5170970; fax (212) 5164833; e-mail haybadtivan@gmail.com; internet www.lraper.org; f. 1461; 100,000 adherents (incl. workers from Armenia—2007); Patriarch MUTAFYAN II; Deputy Patriarch ARAM ATESHIAN.

Bulgarian Orthodox Church: Bulgar Ortodoks Kilisesi, Halâskâr Gazi Cad. 319, Şişli, İstanbul; Rev. Archimandrite GANCO ÇOBANOF.

Greek Orthodox Church: The Ecumenical Patriarchate (Rum Ortodoks Patrikhanesi), Sadrazam Ali Paşa Cad. 35, 34220 Fener-Haliç, İstanbul; tel. (212) 5255416; fax (212) 5316533; e-mail patriarchate@ec-patr.org; internet www.ec-patr.org; Archbishop of Constantinople (New Rome) and Ecumenical Patriarch BARTHOLOMEW I.

The Roman Catholic Church

Turkey Catholic Bishops' Conference: Conferenza Episcopale di Turchia, Satırcı Sok. 2, Harbiye, 34373 İstanbul; tel. (212) 2307312; fax (212) 2303195; e-mail v.cancellarius@yahoo.com; internet www.katolikkilisesi.org; f. 1987; Pres. Most Rev. RUGGERO FRANCESCHINI (Archbishop of İzmir).

Armenian Rite

Patriarchate of Cilicia: f. 1742; Patriarch NERSES BEDROS TARMOUNI XIX (resident in Beirut, Lebanon).

Archdiocese of İstanbul: Sakızağacı Cad. 31, PK 183, 80072 Beyoğlu, İstanbul; tel. (212) 2441258; fax (212) 2432364; f. 1928; Archbishop HOVHANNES TCHOLAKIAN.

Byzantine Rite

Apostolic Exarchate of İstanbul: Hamalbaşı Cad. 44, PK 259, 80070 Beyoğlu, İstanbul; tel. (212) 2440351; fax (212) 2411543; f. 1911; Apostolic Admin. LOUIS PELÂTRE (Titular Bishop of Sasima).

Bulgarian Catholic Church: Bulgar Katolik Kilisesi, Eski Parmakkapı Sok. 15, Galata, İstanbul.

Latin Rite

Metropolitan Archdiocese of İzmir: Church of St Polycarp, Necatibey Bul. 2, PK 267, 35210 İzmir; tel. (232) 4840531; fax (232) 4845358; e-mail curiaves@yahoo.it; f. 1818; Archbishop of İzmir Most Rev. RUGGERO FRANCESCHINI.

Apostolic Vicariate of Anatolia: Mithat Paša Cad. 5, PK 75, 31200 Iskenderun; tel. (326) 6175916; fax (326) 6139291; e-mail curiaves@yahoo.it; f. 1990; Vicar Apostolic (vacant).

Apostolic Vicariate of İstanbul: Papa Roncalli Sok. 83, 80230 Harbiye, İstanbul; tel. (212) 2480775; fax (212) 2411543; e-mail vapostolique@yahoo.fr; f. 1742; Vicar Apostolic LOUIS PELÂTRE (Titular Bishop of Sasima).

Maronite Rite

The Maronite Patriarch of Antioch, Cardinal Nasrallah Pierre Sfeir, is resident in Bkerké, Lebanon.

Melkite Rite

The Greek Melkite Patriarch of Antioch, Grégoire III Laham, is resident in Damascus, Syria.

Syrian Rite

The Syrian Catholic Patriarch of Antioch, Ignace Pierre VIII Abdel Ahad, is resident in Beirut, Lebanon.

Patriarchal Exarchate of Turkey: Sarayarkası Sok. 15, PK 84, 34437 Ayazpaşa, İstanbul; tel. (212) 2432521; fax (212) 2490261; e-mail info@suryanikatolikkilisesi.com; f. 1908; Patriarchal Exarch Fr YUSUF SAĞ.

The Anglican Communion

Within the Church of England, Turkey forms part of the diocese of Gibraltar in Europe. The Bishop is resident in the United Kingdom.

Anglican Chaplaincy in İstanbul: Christ Church, Serdar Ekram Sok. 82, Karaköy, İstanbul; tel. (212) 2515616; fax (212) 2435702; e-mail parson@tnn.net; internet www.anglicanistanbul.com; Chaplain Rev. Canon IAN SHERWOOD.

JUDAISM

There are estimated to be about 23,000 Jews in Turkey.

Jewish Community of Turkey: Türkiye Hahambaşılığı, Yemenici Sok. 21, Beyoğlu, 34430 Tünel, İstanbul; tel. (212) 2938794; fax (212) 2441980; e-mail info@musevicemaati.com; internet www.musevicemaati.com; Chief Rabbi ISAK HALEVA.

The Press

Almost all İstanbul papers are also printed in Ankara and İzmir on the same day, and some in Adana. The most popular national dailies are *Zaman, Posta, Hürriyet* and *Sabah; Yeni Asır*, published in İzmir, is the best-selling quality daily of the Aegean region. There are numerous provincial newspapers with a limited circulation.

PRINCIPAL DAILIES

Akşam (Evening): Davutpaşa Cad. 34, 34020 Zeytinburnu, İstanbul; tel. (212) 4493000; fax (212) 4819561; e-mail editor@aksam.com.tr; internet www.aksam.com.tr; publ. by Türkmedya AŞ; Man. Dir MUSTAFA DOLU; circ. 150,053 (April 2009).

Bugün (Today): Meliha Avni Sozen Cad. 17, Block B, Mecidiyeköy, Sisli, İstanbul; tel. (212) 3558580; fax (212) 2730954; e-mail bugun@bugun.com.tr; internet www.bugun.com.tr; f. 2003; publ. by Koza Davetiye; Editor-in-Chief SELAHATTIN SADIKOĞLU; circ. 60,770 (April 2009).

Cumhuriyet (Republic): Prof. Nurettin Mazhar Öktel Sok. 2, 34381 Şişli, İstanbul; tel. (212) 3437274; fax (212) 2914976; e-mail portal@cumhuriyet.com.tr; internet www.cumhuriyet.com.tr; f. 1924; morning; left-wing, nationalist; Editor-in-Chief IBRAHIM YILDIZ; circ. 65,132 (April 2009).

Fotomaç: Barbaros Bul. 153, Cam Han, Beşiktaş, İstanbul; tel. (212) 3543368; fax (212) 3543557; e-mail spor@fotomac.com.tr; internet www.fotomac.com.tr; f. 1991; sport; publ. by Turkuvaz Radyo Televizyon Gazetecilik ve Yayıncılık AŞ (a subsidiary of Çalık Holding); Editor-in-Chief ZEKI UZUNDURUKAN; circ. 214,441 (April 2009).

Gazete Haberturk: Abdülhakhamit Cad. 25, Beyoğlu, İstanbul; tel. (212) 3136000; fax (212) 3136590; internet www.htgazete.com; f. March 2009; publ. by Ciner Yayın Holding; Editor-in-Chief FATIH ALTAYLI; weekly circ. 297,709 (April 2009).

Günes (Sun): Merkezefendi Mah. Davutpaşa Cad. 34, 34020 Zeytinburnu, İstanbul; tel. (212) 4493010; fax (212) 4819571; internet www.gunes.com; f. 1997; publ. by Türkmedya AŞ; Editor-in-Chief MURAT BÜYÜKÇELEBI; circ. 128,619 (April 2009).

Hürriyet (Freedom): Hürriyet Medya Towers, 34212 Güneşli, İstanbul; tel. (212) 6770000; fax (212) 6770846; e-mail interneteditor@hurriyet.com.tr; internet www.hurriyet.com.tr; f. 1948; morning; political; independent; publ. by Doğan Yayın Holding (Doğan Media Group); Chief Editor ENIS BERBEROĞLU; circ. 495,567 (April 2009).

Hürriyet Daily News and Economic Review: Sogutozu Mah., Dumlupinar Bul. 102, 06510 Çankaya, Ankara; tel. (312) 2070090; fax (312) 2070094; e-mail hdn@hurriyet.com.tr; internet www.turkishdailynews.com; f. 1961 as Daily News; later renamed Turkish Daily News; renamed as above 2008; English language; publ. by Doğan Yayın Holding (Doğan Media Group); CEO RAGIP NEBIL ILSEVEN; Editor-in-Chief DAVID JUDSON; circ. 6,106 (April 2009).

Milliyet: Doğan Medya Center, Bağcilar, 34204 İstanbul; tel. (212) 5056111; fax (212) 5056233; e-mail webadmin@milliyet.com.tr; internet www.milliyet.com.tr; f. 1950; morning; political; publ. by Doğan Yayın Holding (Doğan Media Group); Editor-in-Chief DERYA SAZAK; circ. 200,532 (April 2009).

Posta (Post): Yüzyıl Mah., Doğan Medya Center, 34204 Bağcılar, İstanbul; tel. (212) 5056111; fax (212) 5056520; e-mail internet@posta.com.tr; internet www.posta.com.tr; f. 1995; publ. by Doğan Yayın Holding (Doğan Media Group); Editor-in-Chief RIFAT ABABAY; circ. 516,136 (April 2009).

Radikal: Hürriyet Medya Towers, 34212 Güneşli, İstanbul; tel. (212) 6770000; fax (212) 4496047; e-mail iletisim@radikal.com.tr; internet www.radikal.com.tr; f. 1996; liberal; merged with economics and business daily *Referans* in 2010; publ. by Doğan Yayın Holding (Doğan Media Group); Man. Editor EYÜP CAN SAĞLIK.

Sabah (Morning): Barbaros Bul. 153, Cam Han, Beşiktaş, İstanbul; tel. (212) 3543000; e-mail editor@sabah.com.tr; internet www.sabah.com.tr; publ. by Turkuvaz Radyo Televizyon ve Gazetecilik AŞ (a subsidiary of Çalık Holding); Exec. Editor ERDAL ŞAFAK; circ. 380,851 (April 2009).

Star: Yeni Bosna Merkez Mah., Kavak Sok. 3/2, Ser Plaza, İstanbul; tel. (212) 4962020; fax (212) 4962179; e-mail editor@stargazete.com;

internet www.stargazete.com; f. 1999; Man. Editor MUSTAFA KARAALIOĞLU; circ. 102,706 (April 2009).

Takvim (Calendar): Barbaros Bul. 153, Cam Han 5, Beşiktaş, İstanbul; tel. (212) 3543000; fax (212) 3470677; e-mail takvim@takvim.com.tr; internet www.takvim.com.tr; lifestyle, entertainment and sport; publ. by Turkuvaz Radyo Televizyon ve Gazetecilik AŞ (a subsidiary of Çalık Holding); Man. Editor ERGÜN DILER; circ. 150,053 (April 2009).

Today's Zaman: Ahmet Taner Kışlalı Cad. 6, 34194 Yenibosna, İstanbul; tel. (212) 4541454; fax (212) 4541497; e-mail editor@todayszaman.com; internet www.todayszaman.com; f. 2007; English language; publ. by Zaman Media Group; Editor-in-Chief BÜLENT KENEŞ; circ. 4,677 (April 2009).

Türkiye (Turkey): Ekim Cad. 29, 34197 Yenibosna, İstanbul; tel. (212) 4543000; fax (212) 4543100; e-mail info@tg.com.tr; internet www.turkiyegazetesi.com.tr; f. 1970; nationalist, pro-Islamic; Editor-in-Chief NUH ALBAYRAK; circ. 141,313 (April 2009).

Vakit (Time): Ada 55, İstoç Bağcılar, İstanbul; tel. (212) 6592056; fax (212) 4474209; e-mail haber@vakit.com.tr; internet www.vakit.com.tr; f. 1978; Editor-in-Chief AHMET KARAHASANOĞLU; circ. 52,204 (April 2009).

Vatan (Homeland): Büyükdere Cad. 123, 34349 Gayrettepe, İstanbul; tel. (212) 3545454; internet www.gazetevatan.com; f. 2002; publ. by Doğan Yayın Holding (Doğan Media Group); Man. Editor İSMAIL YUVACAN; circ. 204,819 (April 2009).

Yeni Asır (New Century): Gaziosmanpaşa Bul. 5, 35260 Çankaya, İzmir; tel. (232) 4415000; fax (232) 4464222; e-mail yasir@yeniasir.com.tr; internet www.yeniasir.com.tr; f. 1895; political; publ. by Turkuvaz İzmir Gazete Dergi Basın Yayın AŞ (subsidiary of Çalik Holding); Chair. AHMET ÇALIK; Man. Editor ŞEBNEM BURSALI; circ. 38,760 (April 2009).

Yeni Çağ (New Age): Çobançeşme Mah., Kalender Sok. 12, 34550 Yenibosna, İstanbul; tel. (212) 4524040; fax (212) 4524055; e-mail yenicag@yenicaggazetesi.com.tr; internet www.yg.yenicaggazetesi.com.tr; f. 2002; nationalist; Man. Editor HAYRI KÖKLÜ; circ. 51,190 (April 2009).

Yeni Şafak (New Dawn): Yenidoğan Mah., Kızılay Sok. 39, Bayrampaşa, İstanbul; tel. (212) 6122930; fax (212) 6121903; e-mail halklailiskiler@yenisafak.com.tr; internet yenisafak.com.tr; f. 1995; Editor-in-Chief YUSUF ZIYA CÖMERT; circ. 103,598 (April 2009).

Zaman (Era): Ahmet Taner Kislali Cad. 6, 34194 Yenibosna, İstanbul; tel. (212) 4541454; fax (212) 4541467; e-mail h.dikmen@zaman.com.tr; internet www.zaman.com.tr; f. 1962; morning; Man. Editor EKREM DUMANLI; circ. 773,228 (April 2009).

WEEKLIES

Aksiyon: Fevzi Çakmak Mah., A. Taner Kışlalı Cad. 6, 34194 Yenibosna, İstanbul; tel. (212) 4541400; fax (212) 4548625; e-mail okur@aksiyon.com.tr; internet www.aksiyon.com.tr/aksiyon; f. 1994; news, politics, economics; Man. Editor BÜLENT KORUCU; circ. 38,184 (Nov. 2009).

BusinessWeek Türkiye: Ebulula Mardin Cad. 4, Gazeteciler Sitesi A8-1, 34330 Akatlar, İstanbul; tel. (212) 3245515; fax (212) 3245505; internet www.businessweek.com.tr; business and economics; publ. by Infomag Publishing Ltd and Bloomberg LP (USA); Man. Editor SERDAR TURAN.

Ekonomist: Hürriyet Medya Towers, 34212 Güneşli, İstanbul; tel. (212) 4103256; fax (212) 4103255; e-mail ekonomist@doganburda.com; internet www.ekonomist.com.tr; f. 1991; business and economics; publ. by Doğan Burda Dergi Yayıncılık ve Pazarlama AŞ; Man. Editor TALAT YEŞILOĞLU; circ. 9,505 (Nov. 2009).

Newsweek Türkiye: Abdülhakhamit Cad. 25, Beyoğlu, İstanbul; tel. (212) 3136000; fax (212) 3137455; internet www.newsweek.com.tr; news, business, economics; publ. by Ciner Gazete Dergi Basım Yayıncılık Sanayi ve Ticaret AŞ; Man. Editor SELÇUK TEPELI; circ. 4,500 (Nov. 2009).

Para: Toprak Center, Ihlamur Yıldız Cad. 10, 34353 Beşiktaş, İstanbul; tel. (212) 3263333; fax (212) 3543792; e-mail para@paradergi.com.tr; internet www.paradergi.com.tr; business and economics; publ. by Turkuvaz Gazete Dergi Basım AŞ; Man. Editor OĞUZ DEMIR; circ. 8,380 (Nov. 2009).

Tempo: Hürriyet Medya Towers, 34212 Güneşli, İstanbul; tel. (212) 4103282; fax (212) 4103311; internet www.tempoonline.com.tr; f. 1987; celebrity gossip, lifestyle; publ. by Doğan Burda Dergi Yayıncılık ve Pazarlama AŞ; Editor-in-Chief AYŞEGÜL SAVUR.

Yeni Aktüel: Toprak Center, Ihlamur Yıldız Cad. 10, 34353 Beşiktaş, İstanbul; tel. (212) 3263334; fax (212) 3543792; internet www.yeniaktuel.com.tr; culture; publ. by Turkuvaz Gazete Dergi Basım AŞ; Man. Editor DEFNE ASAL ER; circ. 6,381 (Nov. 2009).

PERIODICALS

Atlas: Hürriyet Medya Towers, 34212 Güneşli, İstanbul; tel. (212) 4103566; fax (212) 4103564; e-mail atlas@doganburda.com; internet www.kesfetmekicinbak.com; f. 1993; monthly; archaeology, geography; publ. by Doğan Burda Dergi Yayıncılık ve Pazarlama AŞ; Man. Editor ÖZCAN YÜKSEK.

Capital: Hürriyet Medya Towers, 34212 Güneşli, İstanbul; tel. (212) 4103228; fax (212) 4103227; e-mail capital@doganburda.com; internet www.capital.com.tr; f. 1993; monthly; business, economics; publ. by Doğan Burda Dergi Yayıncılık ve Pazarlama AŞ; Man. Editor SEDEF SEÇKIN BÜYÜK.

Chip: Hürriyet Medya Towers, 34212 Güneşli, İstanbul; tel. (212) 4103200; fax (212) 4103357; internet www.chip.com.tr; f. 1996; monthly; computing; publ. by Doğan Burda Dergi Yayıncılık ve Pazarlama AŞ; Man. Editor MAHMUT KARSLIOĞLU.

Global: Büyükdere Cad. 65, Saadet Apt 8/15, Mecidiyeköy, İstanbul; tel. (212) 2133881; fax (212) 2133884; e-mail info@globaldergisi.com; internet www.globaldergisi.com; business, economics; Man. Editor MÜGE MEŞE.

Güncel Hukuk: Hürriyet Medya Towers, 34212 Güneşli, İstanbul; tel. (212) 4103534; fax (212) 4103531; e-mail guncelhukuk@doganburda.com; internet www.guncelhukuk.com.tr; monthly; law; publ. by Doğan Burda Dergi Yayıncılık ve Pazarlama AŞ; Man. Editor Prof. Dr KÖKSAL BAYRAKTAR.

Infomag: Ebulula Mardin Cad. 4, Gazeteciler Sitesi A-8/1, Akatlar 1, Levent, İstanbul; tel. (212) 3245515; fax (212) 3245505; e-mail info@infomag.com.tr; internet www.infomag.com.tr; monthly; business; Man. Editor SERDAR TURAN.

Platin: Davutpaşa Cad. 34, 34020 Topkapı, İstanbul; tel. (212) 4493400; fax (212) 4819581; e-mail info@platinonline.com; internet www.platinonline.com; monthly; business, economics; publ. by Türkmedya AŞ; Editor LEVENT ERTEM.

NEWS AGENCIES

Anadolu Ajansı: Mustafa Kemal Bul. 128/C, Tandoğan, Ankara; tel. (312) 2317000; fax (312) 2312174; e-mail ozelbulten@aa.com.tr; internet www.aa.com.tr; f. 1920; Chair. and Dir-Gen. S. HILMI BENGI.

ANKA Ajansı: Cinnah Cad. 11/5 Kavaklıdere, Ankara; tel. (312) 4682500; fax (312) 4268471; e-mail anka@ankaajansi.com.tr; internet www.ankaajansi.com.tr; Dir-Gen. VELI ÖZDEMIR.

Bagımsiz Basın Ajansı (BBA): Saglam Fikir Sok. 9, Esentepe, 34394 İstanbul; tel. (212) 2122936; fax (212) 2122940; e-mail bba@bba.tv; internet www.bba.tv; f. 1971; provides camera crewing, editing and satellite services in Turkey, the Balkans, the Middle East and the former Soviet republics to broadcasters world-wide; Pres. BEDRI KAYABAL.

Cihan News Agency: Çobançeşme Mah. Kalender Sok. 16, 34530 Yenibosna, Bahçelievler, İstanbul; tel. (212) 5524057; fax (212) 4541456; e-mail newssales@cihan.com.tr; internet www.cihanmedia.com; f. 1992; part of Feza Media Corpn; Production Man. HAKAN ÇIDAL.

Doğan Haber Ajansı (Doğan News Agency): Doğan TV Center, 34204 Bağcılar, İstanbul; tel. (212) 4135555; fax (212) 4135598; internet www.dha.com.tr; f. 1999 by merger of Hürriyet Haber Ajansı and Milliyet Haber Ajansı; subsidiary of Doğan Yayın Holding (Doğan Media Group); 34 bureaux world-wide; Dir-Gen. UĞUR ÇEBECI.

İKA Haber Ajansı (Economic and Commercial News Agency): Atatürk Bul. 199/A-45, Kavaklıdere, Ankara; f. 1954; Dir ZIYA TANSU.

TEBA—Türk Ekonomik Basın Ajansı (Turkish Economic Press Agency): Süleyman Hacı Abdullahoğlu Cad. 5, D3 Balgat, Ankara; tel. (312) 2842006; fax (312) 2840638; e-mail teba@tebahaber.com.tr; internet www.tebahaber.com.tr; f. 1981; private economic news service; Propr YELDA CALTAS; Editor AKIN TOKATLI.

Ulusal Basın Ajansı (UBA): Meşrutiyet Cad. 5/10, Ankara; Man. Editor OĞUZ SEREN.

JOURNALISTS' ASSOCIATION

Türkiye Gazeteciler Cemiyeti: Türkocağı Cad. 1, Cağaloğlu, İstanbul; tel. (212) 5138300; fax (212) 5268046; e-mail tgc@tgc.org.tr; internet www.tgc.org.tr; f. 1946; Pres. ORHAN ERINÇ; Sec.-Gen. CELAL TOPRAK.

Publishers

Altın Kitaplar Yayınevi Anonim ŞTİ: Göztepe Mah. Kazım Karabekir Cad., İstanbul; tel. (212) 4463888; e-mail iletisim@altinkitaplar.tr; internet www.altinkitaplar.com.tr; f. 1959; fiction, non-fiction, biography, children's books, encyclopedias, dictionaries; Publrs FETHI UL, TURHAN BOZKURT; Chief Editor MÜRSIT UL.

Arkadas Co Ltd: Yuva Mah. 3702, Sok. 4, 06105 Yenimahalle, Ankara; tel. (312) 3960111; fax (312) 3960141; e-mail info@arkadas .com.tr; internet www.arkadas.com.tr; f. 1980; fiction, educational and reference books; Gen. Man. CUMHUR OZDEMIR.

Arkeoloji ve Sanat Yayınları (Archaeology and Art Publications): Hayriye Cad. 5/2 Mateo Mratoviç Apt., 34425 Beyoğlu, İstanbul; tel. (212) 2930378; fax (212) 2456877; e-mail info@arkeolojisanat.com; internet www.arkeolojisanat.com; f. 1978; classical, Byzantine and Turkish studies, art and archaeology, numismatics and ethnography books; Publr NEZIH BASGELEN; Senior Editor BRIAN JOHNSON.

Bilgi Yayınevi: Meşrutiyet Cad. 46/A, Yenişehir, 06420 Ankara; tel. (312) 4318122; fax (312) 4317758; e-mail info@bilgiyayinevi.com.tr; internet www.bilgiyayinevi.com.tr.

Doğan Burda Dergi Yayıncılık ve Pazarlama AŞ: Hürriyet Medya Towers, 34212 Güneşli, İstanbul; tel. (212) 4780300; fax (212) 4103581; e-mail dalan@doganburda.com; internet www .doganburda.com; jt venture between Doğan Yayın Holding (Doğan Media Group) and Hubert Burda Media Holding GmbH & Co KG (Germany); publishes 27 magazines and periodicals; Chair. PAUL-BERNHARD KALLEN; CEO MEHMET Y. YILMAZ.

Iletisim Yayınları: Binbirdirek Meydanı Sok., Iletisim Han 7/2, 34122 Cağaloğlu, İstanbul; tel. (212) 5162260; fax (212) 5161258; e-mail iletisim@iletisim.com.tr; internet www.iletisim.com.tr; f. 1984; fiction, non-fiction, encyclopedias, reference; Gen. Man. NIHAT TUNA.

Inkilap Kitabevi: Çobançeşme Mah. Altay Sok. 8 Yenibosna, İstanbul; tel. (212) 4961111; fax (212) 4961112; e-mail info@ inkilap.com; internet www.inkilap.com; f. 1935; general reference and fiction; Man. Dir A. FIKRI; Dir of Foreign Rights S. DIKER.

Kabalci Yayınevi: Ankara Cad. 47, Cağaloğlu, İstanbul; tel. (212) 5226305; fax (212) 5268495; e-mail info@kabalci.com.tr; internet www.kabalci.com.tr; art, history, literature, social sciences; Pres. SABRI KABALCI.

Metis Yayınları: Ipek Sok. 5, 34433 Beyoğlu, İstanbul; tel. (212) 2454696; fax (212) 2454519; e-mail rights@metisbooks.com; internet www.metisbooks.com; f. 1982; fiction, literature, non-fiction, social sciences; Dir SEMIH SÖKMEN.

Nobel Medical Publishing: Millet Cad. 111 Çapa, İstanbul; tel. (212) 6328333; fax (212) 5870217; e-mail info@nobeltip.com; internet www.nobeltip.com; f. 1974; medical books and journals; CEO ERSAL BINGÖL.

Nurdan Yayınları Sanayi ve Ticaret Ltd Sti: Prof. Kâzim Ismail Gürkan Cad. 13, Kat 1, 34410 Cağaloğlu, İstanbul; tel. (212) 5225504; fax (212) 5125186; e-mail nurdan@nurdan.com.tr; internet www.nurdan.com.tr; f. 1980; children's and educational; Dir NURDAN TÜZÜNER; Editor ÇIĞDEM TÜZÜNER.

Parantez Yayınları AŞ: Asmalı Mescid Mah. Tünel Meydanı, Tünel Geçidi İşhanı C Blok, D 424 Beyoğlu, İstanbul; tel. and fax (212) 2526516; e-mail parantez@yahoo.com; internet www.parantez .net; f. 1991; Publr METIN ZEYNIOĞLU.

Payel Yayınevi: Cağaloğlu Yokusu Evren han Kat 3/51, 34400 Cağaloğlu, İstanbul; tel. (212) 5284409; fax (212) 5124353; f. 1966; science, history, literature; Editor AHMET ÖZTÜRK.

Remzi Kitabevi AŞ: Akmerkez E3 Blok Kat. 14, Etiler, İstanbul; tel. (212) 2822080; fax (212) 2822090; e-mail post@remzi.com.tr; internet www.remzi.com.tr; f. 1927; general and educational; Dirs EROL ERDURAN, ÖMER ERDURAN, AHMET ERDURAN.

Seckin Yayınevi, Inc.: Saglik Sok. 21, 06410 Sihhiye, Ankara; tel. (312) 4353030; fax (312) 4352472; e-mail satis@seckin.com.tr; internet www.seckin.com.tr; f. 1959; accounting, computer science, economics, law, engineering; CEO KORAY SEÇKIN.

Türk Dil Kurumu (Turkish Language Institute): Atatürk Bul. 217, 06680 Kavaklıdere, Ankara; tel. (312) 4575200; fax (312) 4680783; e-mail bilgi@tdk.org.tr; internet tdk.gov.tr; f. 1932; non-fiction, research, language; Pres. Prof. Dr MUSTAFA S. KAÇALIN.

Varlık Yayınları AŞ: Ayberk Ap. Piyerloti Cad. 7–9, Çemberlitaş, 34400 İstanbul; tel. (212) 5162004; fax (212) 5162005; e-mail varlik@ varlik.com.tr; internet www.varlik.com.tr; f. 1933; fiction and non-fiction books, and cultural monthly review; Dirs FILIZ NAYIR DENIZTEKIN, OSMAN DENIZTEKIN.

GOVERNMENT PUBLISHING HOUSE

Ministry of Culture and Tourism: Directorate of Publications, Necatibey Cad. 55, 06440 Kızılay, Ankara; tel. (312) 2315450; fax (312) 2315036; e-mail yayimlar@kutuphanelergm.gov.tr; internet www.kultur.gov.tr; f. 1973; Dir ALI OSMAN GÜZEL.

PUBLISHERS' ASSOCIATION

Türkiye Yayıncılar Birliği Derneği (Publishers' Association of Turkey): Kazım Ismail Gürkan Cad. 12/3, Ortaklar Han, 34440 Cağaloğlu, İstanbul; tel. (212) 5125602; fax (212) 5117794; e-mail info@turkyaybir.org.tr; internet www.turkyaybir.org.tr; f. 1985;

Pres. METIN CELÂL ZEYNIOĞLU, NIYAZI ŞIMŞEK; Sec. KENAN KOCATÜRK; 300 mems.

Broadcasting and Communications

TELECOMMUNICATIONS

Avea İletşim Hizmetleri AŞ: Abdi İpekçi Cad. 75, 34367 Maçka, İstanbul; tel. (212) 4601500; internet www.avea.com.tr; f. Feb. 2004 as TT&TIM İletişim Hizmetleri AŞ; present name adopted Oct. 2004; 81.13% stake owned by Türk Telekom, 18.87% owned by İş Bankası; provides mobile cellular telecommunications services; 11.4m. subscribers (2010); Chair. MUHAMMAD HARIRI; CEO ERKAN AKDEMIR.

Turkcell İletişim Hizmetleri AŞ: Turkcell Plaza, Mesrutiyet Cad. 71, 34430 Tepebaşi, İstanbul; tel. (212) 3131000; fax (212) 2925393; e-mail musteri.hizmetleri@turkcell.com.tr; internet www.turkcell .com.tr; f. 1994; provides mobile cellular telecommunications services; 13.07% by TeliaSonera AB (Sweden); 33.9m. subscribers at Sept. 2010; Chair. COLIN J. WILLIAMS; CEO SÜREYYA CILIV.

Türksat AŞ: Konya Yolu 40 km, Gölbaşi, Ankara; tel. (312) 6153000; fax (312) 4995115; e-mail info@turksat.com.tr; internet www .turksat.com.tr; satellite and cable telecommunications services; CEO ÖZKAN DALBAY.

Türk Telekomünikasyon AŞ (Türk Telekom): Turgut Özal Bul., 06103 Aydınlıkevler, Ankara; tel. (312) 3060733; fax (312) 3245311; e-mail iletisim@turktelekom.com.tr; internet www.turktelekom .com.tr; 55% owned by Oger Telecoms Joint Venture Group, 30% by Turkish Govt and 15% by private investors; fixed-line telecommunications services; Chair. MUHAMMAD HARIRI; CEO Dr K. GÖRKHAN BOZKURT.

Vodafone Telekomünikasyon AŞ (Vodafone Türkiye): Vodafone Plaza, Büyükdere Cad. 67, 34398 Maslak, İstanbul; tel. (212) 3670000; fax (212) 3670010; internet www.vodafone.com.tr; f. 1994 as Telsim; name changed 2006, following acquisition by Vodafone Group PLC (United Kingdom); offers mobile cellular telecommunications services; CEO SERPIL TIMURAY.

Regulatory Authorities

Bilgi Teknolojileri ve İletişim Kurumu (Information and Communication Technologies Authority): Yeşilırmak Sok., 16 Demirtepe, 06430 Ankara; tel. (312) 2947200; fax (312) 2947145; e-mail info@tk .gov.tr; internet www.tk.gov.tr; f. 2000; Chair. Dr TAYFUN ACARER.

General Directorate of Communications: Hakkı Turayliç Cad. 5 Kat 7–8, Emek, Ankara; tel. (312) 2031000; fax (312) 2121775; e-mail soytas@ubak.opr.tr; internet hgm.ubak.gov.tr; Dir-Gen. ATILLA ÇELIK.

BROADCASTING

Regulatory Authority

Radyo ve Televizyon Üst Kurulu (RTÜK) (Radio and Television Supreme Council): Bilkent Plaza B2 Blok, Bilkent, 06530 Ankara; tel. (312) 2975000; fax (312) 2661985; e-mail rtuk@rtuk.org.tr; internet www.rtuk.org.tr; f. 1994; responsible for assignment of channels, frequencies and bands, controls transmitting facilities of radio stations and TV networks, draws up regulations on related matters, monitors broadcasting and issues warnings in case of violation of the Broadcasting law; Pres. DAVUT DURSUN.

Radio

Türkiye Radyo ve Televizyon Kurumu (TRT) (Turkish Radio and Television Corpn): Turan Güneş Bul., 06450 Oran, Ankara; tel. (312) 4632330; fax (312) 4632335; e-mail aktifhat@trt.net.tr; internet www.trt.net.tr; f. 1964; controls Turkish radio and television services, incl. four national radio channels; Dir-Gen. İBRAHIM ŞAHIN; Head of Radio ÇETIN TEZCAN.

Voice of Turkey: PK 333, 06443 Yenişehir, Ankara; tel. (312) 4633270; fax (312) 4633277; e-mail tsr@trt.net.tr; internet www .trt.net.tr; f. 1937; external service of the TRT; Head of Dept SULEYMAN KOKSOY.

There are also more than 50 local radio stations, an educational radio service for schools and a station run by the Turkish State Meteorological Service. The US forces have their own radio and television service.

Television

Digitürk: tel. (212) 4737373; fax (212) 3260099; e-mail destek@ digiturk.com.tr; internet www.digiturk.gen.tr; f. 1999; subsidiary of Çukurova Holding; subscription-based satellite television service offering 170 channels; also internet service provider; CEO ERTAN ÖZERDEM.

Türkiye Radyo ve Televizyon Kurumu (TRT): (Turkish Radio and Television Corpn): Oran Sitesi Turan Güneş Bul. A Blok Kat 6, 06450 Oran, Ankara; tel. (212) 2597275; e-mail aktifhat@trt.net.tr; internet www.trt.net.tr; four national, one regional and two international channels in 2008; Kurdish-language channel (TRT 6) launched January 2009; Arabic-language service (TRT 7) launched April 2010; Dir-Gen. İBRAHIM ŞAHIN; Head of Television NILGÜN ARTUN; Dir Ankara TV GÜRKAN ELÇI.

As of 2008 there were 23 national, 16 regional and 212 local terrestrial television broadcasters. There are also cable and satellite channels.

Finance

(cap. = capital; res = reserves; dep. = deposits; m. = million; br(s) = branch(es); amounts in Turkish liras; note: figures have been converted retrospectively to reflect the introduction on 1 January 2005 of the new unit of currency, equivalent to 1,000,000 of the old Turkish lira)

The Central Bank of the Republic of Turkey (Türkiye Cumhuriyet Merkez Bankası AŞ) was founded in 1931, and constituted in its present form in 1970. The Central Bank is the bank of issue and is also responsible for the execution of monetary and credit policies, the regulation of the foreign and domestic value of the Turkish lira jointly with the Government, and the supervision of the credit system. In 1987 a decree was issued to bring the governorship of the Central Bank under direct government control. In 2001 the Central Bank was granted policy independence.

In June 1999 an independent supervisory body, the Regulatory and Supervisory Board for Banking, was established by law to monitor the financial sector. The treasury, the Ministry of Finance, the Central Bank, the state planning organization, the Capital Markets Board and the Banks' Association of Turkey were each to nominate one member to the Board for a six-year term. The Board was operational from mid-2000. Other legislation passed in June 1999 incorporated core principles of the Basle Committee on Banking Supervision relating to risk-based capital requirements, loan administration procedures, auditing practices and credit risk issues.

The largest of the private-sector Turkish banks is the Türkiye İş Bankası AŞ, which operates 1,088 branches in the country.

There are several credit institutions in Turkey, including the Türkiye Sınai Kalkınma Bankası AŞ (Industrial Development Bank of Turkey), which was founded in 1950, with the assistance of the World Bank, to encourage private investment in industry by acting as underwriter in the issue of share capital.

There are numerous co-operative organizations, including agricultural co-operatives in rural areas. There are also a number of savings institutions.

In 1990 the Turkish Government announced plans to establish a structure for offshore banking. A decree issued in October of that year exempted foreign banks, operating in six designated free zones, from local banking obligations.

At the end of 1999 the number of banks operating in Turkey (excluding the Central Bank) totalled 81, of which seven were state-owned. Following a number of liquidations, mergers and acquisitions in the banking system after 2000, the number of banks had been reduced to 43 by the end of 2008. Of this total, 13 were development and investment banks; the number of state-owned banks had been reduced to three, with the control of Birleşik Fon Bankası AŞ (formerly Bayindirbank) passing to the Savings Deposit Insurance Fund. There were 11 private commercial banks and 16 foreign-owned banks.

BANKING

Regulatory Authority

Bancacılık Düzenleme ve Denetleme Kurumu (BDDK) (Banking Regulation and Supervisory Agency): Atatürk Bul. 191, 06680 Kavaklidere, Ankara; tel. (312) 4556500; fax (312) 4240879; e-mail bilgi@bddk.org.tr; internet www.bddk.org.tr; Chair. MUKIM ÖZTEKIN.

Central Bank

Türkiye Cumhuriyet Merkez Bankası AŞ (Central Bank of the Republic of Turkey): Head Office, İstiklal Cad. 10 Ulus, 06100 Ankara; tel. (312) 5075000; fax (312) 5075640; e-mail iletisimbilgi@tcmb.gov.tr; internet www.tcmb.gov.tr; f. 1931; bank of issue; cap. 46.2m., res 3,691.2m., dep. 89,359.6m. (Dec. 2009); Gov. Dr ERDEM BAŞÇI; 21 brs.

State Banks

Türkiye Cumhuriyeti Ziraat Bankası (Agricultural Bank of the Turkish Republic): Doğanbey Mah., Atatürk Bul. 8, 06107 Ulus, Ankara; tel. (312) 5842000; fax (312) 5844053; e-mail zbmail@

ziraatbank.com.tr; internet www.ziraat.com.tr; f. 1863; absorbed Türkiye Emlâk Bankası AŞ (Real Estate Bank of Turkey) in July 2001; cap. 2,500m., res 8,457m., dep. 113,771m. (Dec. 2011); Chair. MUHARREM KARSLI; Gen. Man. CAN AKIN ÇAĞLAR; 1,225 brs in Turkey, 11 brs abroad.

Türkiye Halk Bankası AŞ: Esikişehir Yolu, 2 Cad. 63, Söğütözü, 06520 Ankara; tel. (312) 2892000; fax (312) 2893575; e-mail info@ halkbank.com.tr; internet www.halkbank.com.tr; f. 1938; absorbed Türkiye Öğretmenler Bankası TAŞ in 1992; acquired 96 brs of Türkiye Emlak Bankası in 2001; merged with Pamukbank TAŞ in 2004; cap. 2,578m., res 506m., dep. 66,724m. (Dec. 2011); Chair. HASAN CEBECI; Gen. Man. SÜLEYMAN ASLAN; 705 brs in Turkey, 4 brs abroad.

Türkiye Vakıflar Bankası TAO (Vakifbank) (Foundation Bank of Turkey): Camlik Cad. Cayir Cimen Sok. 2, 34330 1 Levent, İstanbul; tel. (212) 3167116; fax (212) 3167126; e-mail international@vakifbank.com.tr; internet www.vakifbank.com.tr; f. 1954; cap. 3,300m., res 1,411m., dep. 62,260m. (Dec. 2011); Chair. HALIL AYDOĞAN; Gen. Man. SÜLEYMAN KALKAN; 603 brs in Turkey, 2 brs abroad.

Principal Commercial Banks

Akbank TAŞ: Sabancı Center, 34330 4 Levent, 80745 İstanbul; tel. (212) 3855555; fax (212) 2697787; e-mail investor.relations@akbank .com; internet www.akbank.com.tr; f. 1948; absorbed Ak Uluslararası Bankası AŞ in Sept. 2005; 20% owned by Citigroup; cap. 4,000m., res 3,003m., dep. 81,411m. (Dec. 2011); Chair. SUZAN SABANCI DINÇER; CEO HAKAN BINBAŞGIL; 926 brs in Turkey, 1 br. abroad.

Alternatifbank AŞ: Cumhuriyet Cad. 22–24, Elmadağ, 34367 İstanbul; tel. (212) 3156500; fax (212) 2331500; e-mail kalite@ abank.com.tr; internet www.abank.com.tr; f. 1991; 95.6% owned by Anadolu Group; cap. 300m., res 3m., dep. 3,642m. (Dec. 2011); Chair. TUNCAY ÖZILHAN; CEO HAMIT AYDOĞAN; 56 brs.

ING Bank AS: Eski Büyükdere Cad., Ayazaga Köyyolu 6, Maslak, 34398 İstanbul; tel. and fax (212) 4440600; internet www.ingbank .com.tr; f. 1990; fmrly Oyak Bank; owned by ING Groep NV (Netherlands); name changed as above in 2008; cap. 2,159m., res 117m., dep. 11,385m. (Dec. 2011); Chair. JOHN T. MCCARTHY; CEO PINAR ABAY; 365 brs in Turkey, 1 br. in Bahrain.

Şekerbank TAŞ: Büyükdere Cad. 171, Metrocity İş Merkezi, A Blok 34330 1 Levent, İstanbul; tel. (212) 3440737; fax (212) 3197162; e-mail intdiv@sekerbank.com.tr; internet www.sekerbank.com.tr; f. 1953; 33.98% owned by TuranAlem Securities (Kazakhstan); cap. 1,000m., res 24m., dep. 9,192m. (Dec. 2011); Chair. HASAN BASRI GÖKTAN; Gen. Man. MERIÇ ULUŞAHIN; 250 brs.

Tekstil Bankası AŞ (Tekstilbank): Büyükdere Cad. 63, 34398 Maslak, İstanbul; tel. (212) 3355335; fax (212) 3281328; e-mail ir@ tekstilbank.com.tr; internet www.tekstilbank.com.tr; f. 1986; cap. 420m., res 29m. dep. 2,687m. (Dec. 2011); 75.4% owned by GSD Holdings; Chair. AKGÜN TÜRER; Gen. Man. ÇIM GÜZELAYDINLI; 44 brs.

Türk Ekonomi Bankası AŞ (TEB): Meclisi Mebusan Cad. 57, 34427 Fındıklı, İstanbul; tel. (212) 2512121; fax (212) 2525058; internet www.teb.com.tr; f. 1927; fmrly Kocaeli Bankası TAŞ; jt venture between Colakoğlu Group and BNP Paribas SA (France); Fortis Bank AS merged into TEB in 2011; cap. 2,204m., res 102m., dep. 30,710m. (Dec. 2011); Chair. YAVUZ CANEVI; Exec. Dir and Gen. Man. VAROL CIVIL; 275 brs in Turkey, 1 br. in Bahrain.

Türkiye Garanti Bankası AŞ (Garantibank): Nispetiye Mah, Aytar Cad. 2, 34340 Levent Beşiktaş, İstanbul; tel. (212) 3181818; fax (212) 3181888; e-mail mutlus@garanti.com.tr; internet www .garantibank.com; f. 1946; owned by Doğuş Group; cap. 5,145m., res 845m., dep. 93,235m. (Dec. 2011); Chair. FERIT FAIK ŞAHENK; Pres. and CEO ERGUN ÖZEN; 808 brs in Turkey, 2 brs abroad.

Türkiye İş Bankası AŞ (İşbank): İş Kuleleri, 34330 Levent, İstanbul; tel. (212) 3160000; fax (212) 3160900; e-mail halkla .iliskiler@isbank.com.tr; internet www.isbank.com.tr; f. 1924; cap. 6,115m., res 2,156m., dep. 100,090m. (Dec. 2011); Chair. ERSIN ÖZINCE; CEO and Dir ADNAN BALI; 1,088 brs in Turkey, 15 abroad.

Yapı ve Kredi Bankası AŞ: Yapı Kredi Plaza, Blok D, 80620 İstanbul; tel. (212) 3397000; fax (212) 3396000; internet www.ykb .com.tr; f. 1944; cap. 4,286m., res 536m., dep. 78,264m. (Dec. 2011); merged with Koçbank AŞ in 2006; Exec. Dir and Dep. CEO CARLO VIVALDI; CEO FAIK AÇIKALIN; 838 brs.

Development and Investment Banks

İller Bankası Genel Müdürülügü: Atatürk Bul. 21, 06053 Opera, Ankara; tel. (312) 5087000; fax (312) 5087399; e-mail ilbank@ilbank .gov.tr; internet www.ilbank.gov.tr; Chair. and Gen. Man. HIDAYET ATASOY; 19 brs.

Türkiye Kalkınma Bankası (Development Bank of Turkey): İzmir Cad. 35, 06440 Kızılay Ankara; tel. (312) 4179200; fax (312) 4183967; e-mail rkalkinmahaberlesme@kalkinma.com.tr; internet www

.kalkinma.com.tr; cap. 160m., res 346m. (Dec. 2011); Chair. AHMET YAMAN (acting); Gen. Man. METIN PEHLIVAN (acting).

Türkiye Sınai Kalkınma Bankası AŞ (Industrial Development Bank of Turkey): Meclisi Mebusan Cad. 81, Findikli, 34427 İstanbul; tel. (212) 3345050; fax (212) 3345234; e-mail info@tskb.com.tr; internet www.tskb.com; f. 1950; cap. 613.5m., res 58.0m., dep. 1,395.6m. (Dec. 2009); Chair. ADNAN BALI; CEO H. FEVZI ONAT; 2 brs.

Savings Deposit Insurance Fund Bank

Birleşik Fon Bankası AŞ: Büyükdere Cad. 143, 34394 Esentepe, İstanbul; tel. (212) 3401000; fax (212) 3473217; e-mail callcenter@fonbank.com.tr; internet www.fonbank.com.tr; fmrly Bayindirbank; name changed as above 2005; control passed to Savings Deposit Insurance Fund in 2001; Chair. SALIM ALKAN; Gen. Man. RECEP SÜLEYMAN ÖZDIL.

Banking Organization

Banks' Association of Turkey: Nıspetıye Cad. Akmerkez B3 Blok. Kat 13–14, 34340 Etiler, İstanbul; tel. (212) 2820973; fax (212) 2820946; e-mail gensek@tbb.org.tr; internet www.tbb.org.tr; f. 1958; Chair. HUSEYIN AYDIN.

STOCK EXCHANGE

İstanbul Menkul Kıymetler Borsası (İMKB): Resitpaşa Mah., Tuncay Artun Cad., 34467 Emirgan, İstanbul; tel. (212) 2982100; fax (212) 2982500; e-mail international@imkb.gov.tr; internet www.ise.org; f. 1866; revived in 1986 after being dormant for about 60 years; 104 mems of stock market, 132 mems of bond and bills market (April 2008); Chair. and CEO HÜSEYIN ERKAN; Senior Vice-Chair. ARIL SEREN.

INSURANCE

Principal Companies

AKSigorta AŞ: Meclis-i Mebusan Cad. 67, 34427 Fındıklı, İstanbul; tel. (212) 3934300; fax (212) 3343900; e-mail info@aksigorta.com.tr; internet www.aksigorta.com.tr; f. 1960; life and non-life; Chair. AHMET CEMAL DÖRDÜNCÜ; Gen. Man. UĞUR GÜLEN.

Allianz Sigorta AŞ: Bağlarbaşı, Kısıklı Cad. 13, 34662 Altunizade, İstanbul; tel. (216) 5566666; fax (216) 5566777; e-mail info@allianz.com.tr; internet www.allianz.com.tr; f. 1923; general, non-life; also offers life insurance through its subsidiary, Allianz Hayat ve Emeklilik; fmrly Koç Allianz Sigorta AŞ; 84% owned by Allianz AG (Germany); Chair. Dr RÜŞDÜ SARAÇOĞLU; CEO GEORGE D. SARTOREL.

Anadolu Sigorta TAŞ (Anadolu Insurance Co): Büyükdere Cad. İş Kuleleri Kule 2 Kat. 23–26 34330 4 Levent, İstanbul; tel. (212) 3500350; fax (212) 3500355; e-mail bilgi@anadolusigorta.com.tr; internet www.anadolusigorta.com.tr; f. 1925; life and non-life; 35.53% owned by Türkiye İş Bankası AŞ; Chair. BURHAN KARAGÖZ, CEO MUSTAFA ALI SU.

AvivaSA Emeklilik ve Hayat AŞ (AvivaSA): İnkılap Mah., Küçüksu Cad., Akçakoca Sk. 8, 34768 Ümraniye, İstanbul; tel. (216) 6333333; fax (216) 6343888; e-mail musteri@avivasa.com.tr; internet www.aviva.com.tr; f. 2007 by merger of Aviva Hayat ve Emeklilik and AK Emeklilik; life; 49.7% stakes owned by AK Sigorta AŞ and Aviva PLC (United Kingdom); Chair. HAKAN AKBAŞ; Gen. Man. MERAL EGEMEN.

AXA Sigorta AŞ: Meclis-i Mebusan Cad. Oyak İş Hanı 15, 34427 Salıpazarı, İstanbul; tel. (212) 3342424; fax (212) 2521515; e-mail iletisim@axasigorta.com.tr; internet www.axasigorta.com.tr; life and non-life; Chair. and CEO HAKKI CEMAL ERERDI; 10 brs.

ERGO Sigorta AŞ: Saray Mah., Dr Adnan Büyükdeniz Cad. 4, Akkom Ofis Park, Blok Kat. 10–14, Ümraniye, İstanbul; tel. (216) 5548100; fax (216) 6667777; e-mail ergoisvicre@ergoisvicre.com.tr; internet www.ergoturkiye.com; f. 1926 as La Suisse Umum Sigorta, acquired by İsviçre in 1981; acquired by ERGO Versicherungsgrüppe AG (Germany) in 2008; name changed as above 2010; fire, accident, marine, engineering, agricultural; Chair. AKIN KOZANOĞLU; Gen. Man. Dr THOMAS BARON; 11 regional brs.

Eureko Sigorta: Büyükdere Cad., Nurol Plaza 257, 34398 Maslak, İstanbul; tel. (212) 3041000; fax (212) 2854424; e-mail esmusterihizmetleri@eurekosigorta.com.tr; internet www .eurekosigorta.com.tr; f. 1989 as Garanti Sigorta; renamed as above in Oct. 2007; 80% owned by Eureko BV (Netherlands) and 20% by Türkiye Garanti Bankası AŞ; non-life; Chair. ERGUN ÖZEN; CEO OKAN UTKUERI.

Groupama Sigorta AŞ: Groupama Plaza, Eski Büyükdere Cad. 2, 34398 Maslak, İstanbul; tel. (212) 3676767; fax (212) 3676868; e-mail sigorta@groupama.com.tr; internet www.groupama.com.tr; f. 1959 as Başak Sigorta; 56.67% stake acquired by Groupama SA (France) in 2006; adopted present name 2009, following merger with Güven

Sigorta TAŞ; life and non-life; Chair. PIERRE LEFEVRE; Gen. Man. ALAIN BAUDRY.

Güneş Sigorta: Güneş Plaza, Büyükdere Cad. 110, 34394 Esentepe-Şişli, İstanbul; tel. (212) 4441957; fax (212) 3556464; e-mail gunes@gunessigorta.com.tr; internet www.gunessigorta.com.tr; f. 1957; non-life; 51.3% stake owned by Türkiye Vakıflar Bankası TAO, 45% owned by Groupama (France); Chair. BILAL KARAMAN; Gen. Man. MEHMET İLKER AVCI.

Yapı Kredi Sigorta AŞ: Yapı Kredi Plaza, A Blok, Büyükdere Cad., 34330 Levent, İstanbul; tel. (212) 3360606; fax (212) 3360808; e-mail yksigorta@yksigorta.com.tr; internet www.yksigorta.com.tr; f. 1943 as Halk Sigorta; present name adopted 2000; life and non-life; 53.1% stake owned by Yapı ve Kredi Bankası AŞ; Chair. TAYFUN BAYAZIT; Gen. Man. Dr S. GIRAY VELIOĞLU.

Insurance Organization

Türkiye Sigorta ve Reasürans Şirketleri Birliği (Asscn of the Insurance and Reinsurance Companies of Turkey): Büyükdere Cad., Büyükdere Plaza 195, 1-2, 34394 Levent, İstanbul; tel. (212) 3241950; fax (212) 3256108; e-mail genel@tsrsb.org.tr; internet www.tsrsb.org.tr; f. 1954 by merger of the Association of the Insurance Companies of Turkey and the Central Office of Insurers; present name adopted 1975; 57 mems (2009); Pres. HULUSI TAŞKIRAN; Sec.-Gen. ERHAN TUNÇAY.

Trade and Industry

GOVERNMENT AGENCIES

Özelleştirme İdaresi Başkanlığı (ÖİB) (Privatization Administration): Ziya Gökalp Cad. 80, Kurtuluş, 06600 Ankara; tel. (312) 4304560; fax (312) 4359342; e-mail info@oib.gov.tr; internet www.oib .gov.tr; co-ordinates privatization programme; Pres. METIN KILCI.

Rekabet Kurumu (Turkish Competition Authority): Bilkent Plaza B3 Blok, 06800 Bilkent, Ankara; tel. (312) 2914444; fax (312) 2667920; e-mail rek@rekabet.gov.tr; internet www.rekabet.gov.tr; f. 1997; prevents restriction of competition, oversees mergers and monitors state aid; Pres. and Chair. Prof. Dr NURETTIN KALDIRIMCI.

Türkiye Atom Enerjisi Kurumu (Turkish Atomic Energy Authority): Eskişehir Yolu 9km, 06530 Lodumlu, Ankara; tel. (312) 2958700; fax (312) 2878761; e-mail bilgi_taek@taek.gov.tr; internet www.taek.gov.tr; f. 1956; controls the development of peaceful uses of atomic energy; 7 mems; Pres. Prof. Dr ÜNER ÇOLAK.

CHAMBERS OF COMMERCE AND INDUSTRY

Türkiye Odalar ve Borsalar Birliği (TOBB) (Union of Chambers and Commodity Exchanges of Turkey): Dumlupınar Bul. 252, Eskişehir Yolu 9 Km, 06530 Ankara; tel. (312) 2182000; fax (312) 2194090; e-mail info@tobb.org.tr; internet www.tobb.org.tr; f. 1950; represents 365 chambers and commodity exchanges; Pres. RIFAT HISARCIKLIOĞLU.

Ankara Sanayi Odası (ASO) (Ankara Chamber of Industry): Atatürk Bul. 193, Kavaklıdere, Ankara; tel. (312) 4171200; fax (312) 4175205; e-mail aso@aso.org.tr; internet www.aso.org.tr; f. 1963; Pres. M. NURETTIN ÖZDEBIR.

Ankara Tabip Odası (ATO) (Ankara Chamber of Commerce): Mithatpaşa Cad. 62/18 Kızılay, 06420 Ankara; tel. (312) 4188700; fax (312) 4187794; e-mail ato@ato.org.tr; internet www.ato.org.tr; Pres. Prof. Dr GÜLRIZ ERSÖZ.

İstanbul Sanayi Odası (İSO) (İstanbul Chamber of Industry): Meşrutiyet Cad. 62, 34430 Tepebaşı, İstanbul; tel. (212) 2522900; fax (212) 2495084; e-mail info@iso.org.tr; internet www.iso.org.tr; f. 1952; more than 12,500 mems (2006); Chair. C. TANIL KÜÇÜK; Gen. Sec. METE MELEKSOY.

İstanbul Ticaret Odası (İstanbul Chamber of Commerce): Reşadiye Cad. 34112 Eminönü, İstanbul; tel. (212) 4556000; fax (212) 5131565; e-mail info@us-istanbul.com; internet www.ito.org.tr; f. 1952; more than 300,000 mems; Pres. MURAT YALÇINTAŞ.

EMPLOYERS' ASSOCIATIONS

Türk Sanayicileri ve İşadamları Derneği (TÜSİAD) (Turkish Industrialists' and Businessmen's Association): Meşrutiyet Cad. 74, 34420 Tepebaşı, İstanbul; tel. (212) 2491929; fax (212) 2491350; e-mail tusiad@tusiad.org; internet www.tusiad.org; f. 1971; c. 600 mems; Chair. ÜMIT BOYNER; Sec.-Gen. ZAFER ALI YAVAN.

Türkiye İşveren Sendikaları Konfederasyonu (TİSK) (Turkish Confederation of Employer Associations): Hoşdere Cad. Reşat Nuri Sok. 108, 06540 Çankaya, Ankara; tel. (312) 4397717; fax (312) 4397502; e-mail tisk@tisk.org.tr; internet www.tisk.org.tr; f. 1962; represents (on national level) 23 employers' asscns; official representative in labour relations; Pres. TUĞRUL KUDATGOBILIK; Sec.-Gen. BÜLENT PIRLER.

UTILITIES

Plans for the privatization of the electricity distribution grid were announced in 2004. Following numerous delays, the privatization process resumed in 2008, under the supervision of the Privatization Administration.

Electricity

Elektrik Üretim Anonim Şirketi (EÜAŞ) (Electricity Generation Co Inc): İnönü Bul. 27, Bahçelievler, 06490 Ankara; tel. (312) 2126900; fax (312) 2130103; e-mail basinhalk@euas.gov.tr; internet www.euas.gov.tr; f. 2001, following devolution of responsibilities of fmr Elektrik Üretim-İletim AŞ into separate entities for generation, transmission and wholesale activities; responsible for electricity generation; Chair. SEFER BÜTÜN.

Türkiye Elektrik Dağıtım AŞ (TEDAŞ): İnönü Bulv. 27, Bahçelievler, 06490 Ankara; tel. (312) 2126915; fax (312) 2138873; e-mail bilgi@tedas.gov.tr; internet www.tedas.gov.tr; responsible for distribution and sale of electricity; owns 20 regional distribution cos; Pres. and Man. Dir HAŞIM KEKLIK.

Türkiye Elektrik İletim Anonim Şirketi (TEİAŞ) (Turkish Electricity Transmission Company): İnönü Bul. 27, Bahçelievler, 06490 Ankara; tel. (312) 2038061; fax (312) 2228160; e-mail basinmail@teias.gov.tr; internet www.teias.gov.tr; f. 2001 (see EÜAŞ); responsible for electricity transmission; Chair. and Gen. Man. KEMAL YILDIR.

Water

Devlet Su İşleri Genel Müdürlüğü (DSİ) (General Directorate of State Hydraulic Works): İnönü Bul., Yücetepe, 06100 Ankara; tel. (312) 4178300; fax (312) 4182498; e-mail idarim@dsi.gov.tr; internet www.dsi.gov.tr; f. 1954; controlled by the Ministry of Energy and Natural Resources; responsible for the planning and devt of water resources; Dir-Gen. HAYDAR KOÇAKER.

TRADE UNIONS

(Note: Statistics correct to July 2009)

DİSK (Türkiye Devrimci İşçi Sendikaları Konfederasyonu) (Confederation of Progressive Trade Unions of Turkey): Cad. Abide-I Hürriyet 117, Nakiye Elgün Sok. 91, Şişli, İstanbul; tel. (212) 2910005; fax (212) 2342075; e-mail disk@disk.org.tr; internet www.disk.org.tr; f. 1967; member of ITUC and European Trade Union Confed; Pres. EROL EKICI; Sec.-Gen. ADNAN SERDAROĞLU; 17 affiliated unions with 400,000 mems.

Hak-İş (Hak İşçi Sendikaları Konfederasyonu) (Confederation of Turkish Real Trade Unions): Tunus Cad. 37, 06680 Kavaklıdere, Ankara; tel. (312) 4178002; fax (312) 4250552; e-mail hakis@hakis.org.tr; internet www.hakis.org.tr; f. 1976; mem. of ITUC and European Trade Union Confed; Pres. MAHMUT ARSLAN; Gen. Sec. Dr OSMAN YILDIZ; 13 affiliated unions with 550,000 mems.

KESK (Kamu Emekçileri Sendikaları Konfederasyonu) (Confederation of Public Employees' Trade Unions): Çehre Sok. 6/1, Gaziosmanpaşa, Ankara; tel. (312) 4367111; fax (312) 4367470; e-mail kesk@kesk.org.tr; internet www.kesk.org.tr; f. 1995; mem. of ITUC and European Trade Union Confed; Pres. LAMI ÖZGEN; Gen. Sec. ISMAIL HAKKI TOMBUL; 11 affiliated unions with 224,413 mems.

Memur-Sen (Memur Sendikaları Konfederasyonu) (Confederation of Public Servants' Trade Unions): Özveren Sok. 9, 4 Demirtepe, Ankara; tel. (312) 2304898; fax (312) 2303989; e-mail info@memursen.org.tr; internet www.memursen.org.tr; f. 1995; Pres. AHMET GÜNDOĞDU; Gen. Sec. MAHMUT KAÇAR; 12 affiliated unions with 376,355 mems.

Türk-İş (Türkiye İşçi Sendikaları Konfederasyonu) (Confederation of Turkish Trade Unions): Bayındır Sok. 10, 06410 Kizilay, Ankara; tel. (312) 4333125; fax (312) 4336809; e-mail turkis@turkis.org.tr; internet www.turkis.org.tr; f. 1952; mem. of ITUC, European Trade Union Confed. and OECD/Trade Union Advisory Cttee; Pres. MUSTAFA KUMLU; Gen. Sec. PEVRUL KAVLAK; 33 affiliated unions and federations with 2.2m. mems.

Türkiye Kamu-Sen (Türkiye Kamu Çalışanları Sendikaları Konfederasyonu) (Confederation of Turkish Public Employees' Unions): Dr Mediha Eldem Sok. 85, Kocatepe, Çankaya, Ankara; tel. (312) 4242200; fax (312) 4242208; e-mail kamusen@kamusen.org.tr; internet www.kamusen.org.tr; f. 1992; Pres. ISMAIL KONCUK; Gen. Sec. ÖNDER KAHVECI; 13 affiliated unions with 400,000 mems.

Transport

RAILWAYS

The total length of the railways in operation within the national frontiers was 12,000 km in 2011, of which 9,642 km were main lines. There are direct rail links with Bulgaria, Iran and Syria.

Construction work on a new line connecting Turkey with Georgia and Azerbaijan commenced in late 2007. However, construction was temporarily suspended in August 2008, owing to military conflict between Georgia and Russia in the Georgian secessionist region of South Ossetia. Environmental concerns further delayed the project, which consequently was not expected to be completed until at least 2013. Construction work on a 533-km high-speed rail link between Ankara and İstanbul commenced in 2003. A 245-km section of the line between Ankara and Eskişehir became operational in March 2009; the line was scheduled to be fully operational by 2013. Construction work on the Marmaray Project, a 76-km suburban line between the European and Asian sections of İstanbul, incorporating a 13.6-km tunnel under the Bosphorus strait, commenced in 2004. Following several delays, the project was expected to be completed in 2015. İstanbul operates a two-line, 34.7-km light railway system and two metro lines totalling 42 km in length. The second of those lines, servicing 16 stations between Kadıköy and Kartal in the Asian part of the city, was inaugurated in mid-August 2012. Ankara, Adana, Bursa and İzmir also operate metro and light railway systems.

Türkiye Cumhuriyeti Devlet Demiryolları (TCDD) (Turkish State Railways): Talatpaşa Bul., 06330 Gar, Ankara; tel. (312) 3090515; fax (312) 3126247; e-mail byhim@tcdd.gov.tr; internet www.tcdd.gov.tr; f. 1924; operates all railways and connecting ports of the State Railway Admin., which acquired the status of a state economic enterprise in 1953, and a state economic establishment in 1984; Chair. of Bd and Dir-Gen. SÜLEYMAN KARAMAN.

ROADS

In January 2012 the total road network was estimated at 65,049 km of classified roads, of which 2,119 km were motorways, 31,372 km were highways and 31,558 km were secondary roads.

Karayolları Genel Müdürlüğü (KGM) (General Directorate of Highways): İnönü Bul., Yücetepe, 06100 Ankara; tel. (312) 4157000; fax (312) 4172851; e-mail info@kgm.gov.tr; internet www.kgm.gov.tr; f. 1950; Dir-Gen. MEHMET CAHIT TURHAN.

SHIPPING

At 31 December 2012 Turkey's merchant fleet comprised 1,325 vessels and had an aggregate displacement of 6,680,140 grt, of which 111 were bulk carriers, 27 were fish carriers, seven were gas tankers and 437 were general cargo ships.

The ports of Bandırma, Derince, Haydarpaşa (İstanbul), İskenderun and İzmir, all of which are connected to the railway network, are operated by Turkish State Railways (TCDD), while the port of İstanbul and five smaller ports are operated by the Turkish Maritime Organization. Responsibility for some 13 ports, including those of Antalya and Trabzon, was transferred from the Turkish Maritime Organization to private companies under separate 30-year agreements in 1997–2003. In 2007 control of the port of Mersin was transferred from TCDD to the private sector under a 36-year concession agreement. A similar arrangement involving the port of Samsun commenced in April 2010. In 2011 Prime Minister Recep Tayyip Erdoğan announced plans to construct a 50-km canal through the European portion of the country, connecting the Black and Mediterranean Seas. The 'Canal İstanbul' project was intended to relieve congestion on the Bosphorus Strait.

Regulatory and Port Authorities

Turkish Maritime Organization (TDI): Genel Müdürlüğü, Rıhtım Cad. Merkez Han 32, 34425 Karaköy, İstanbul; tel. (212) 2515000; fax (212) 2495391; e-mail tdibasin@tdi.gov.tr; internet www.tdi.com.tr; Gen. Man. BURHAN KÜLÜNK.

Port of Bandırma: TCDD Liman İşletme Müdürlüğü, Bandırma; tel. (266) 7187530; fax (266) 7136011; e-mail bandirmaliman@tcdd.gov.tr; Port Man. OKKES DEMIREL; Harbour Master RUSEN OKAN.

Port of Derince: TCDD Liman İşletme Müdürlüğü, Derince; tel. (262) 2399021; e-mail derinceliman@tcdd.gov.tr; Port Man. ALI ARIF AYTAÇ; Harbour Master HAYDAR DOĞAN.

Port of Haydarpaşa (İstanbul): TCDD Liman İşletme Müdürlüğü Haydarpaşa, İstanbul; tel. (216) 3488020; fax (216) 3451705; e-mail haydarpasaliman@tcdd.gov.tr; Port Man. NEDIM OZCAN; Harbour Master İSMAIL SAFAER.

Port of İskenderun: TCDD Liman İşletme Müdürlüğü, İskenderun; tel. (326) 6140044; fax (326) 6132424; e-mail iskenderunliman@tcdd.gov.tr; Port Man. HILMI SÖNMEZ; Harbour Master İSHAK ÖZDEMIR.

Port of İzmir: TCDD Liman İşletme Müdürlüğü, İzmir; tel. (232) 4631600; fax (232) 4632248; e-mail izmirliman@tcdd.gov.tr; Port Man. TURAN YALÇIN.

Port of Mersin: Yeni Mah. 101, Cad. 5307, Sok. 5, 33100 Mersin; tel. (324) 2412920; fax (324) 2290849; e-mail marketing@mersinport.com.tr; internet www.mersinport.com.tr; f. 2007; managed by a consortium of PSA Int. (Singapore) and Akfen (Turkey) under a 36-yr concession; Gen. Man. JOHN PHILLIPS; Harbour Master RACI TARHUSOĞLU.

Port of Samsun: TCDD Liman İşletme Müdürlüğü, Samsun; tel. (362) 2332293; fax (362) 4451626; e-mail samsunliman@tcdd.gov.tr; managed since April 2010 by Cey Group (Turkey) under a 36-year concession; Port Man. SAFFET YAMAK; Harbour Master Capt. ARIF H. UZUNOĞLU.

Principal Shipping Companies

Akmar Shipping Group: Küçükbakkalköy Mah. Cicek Sok. 4, Aksoy Plaza, 34750 Kadıköy, İstanbul; tel. (216) 5762666; fax (216) 5727195; e-mail info@akmar.com.tr; internet www.akmar .com.tr; f. 2004; Chair. NECDET AKSOY.

Deniz Nakliyatı TAŞ (Turkish Cargo Lines): Fahrettin Kerim Gökay Cad. Denizciler İş Merkezi No. 18, 1A Blok Kat. 1, Altunizade/Üsküdar, İstanbul; tel. (216) 4747400; fax (216) 4747430; e-mail tcl@tcl.com.tr; internet www.tcl.com.tr; f. 1955; bulk carriers; Chair. M. GÜNDÜZ KAPTANOĞLU; Gen. Man. CEMIL GÜCÜYENER; 2 large and 2 small handy bulk/ore carriers.

İstanbul Deniz Otobusleri Sanayi ve Ticaret AŞ: Kennedy Cad., Hizli Feribot Iskelesi Yenikapi, İstanbul; tel. (212) 4556900; fax (212) 5173958; e-mail info@ido.com.tr; internet www.ido.com.tr; f. 1987; state-owned; ferry co; scheduled for privatization; Gen. Man. Dr AHMET PAKSOY; 90 vessels.

Kiran Group of Shipping Companies: Fahrettin Kerim Gorkay Cad. 18, Denizciler İş Merkezi, B Blok Kat. 2, 34662 Altunizade, İstanbul; tel. (216) 5541400; fax (216) 5541414; e-mail kiran@kiran .com.tr; internet www.kiran.com.tr; f. 1959; Chair. TURGUT KIRAN; Man. Dir TAMER KIRAN; 19 vessels.

Ozsay Deniz Elektroniği AŞ: Güzelyalı, E-5 Üzeri 18, 34903 Pendik, İstanbul; tel. (216) 4933610; fax (216) 4930306; e-mail ozsay@tnn.net; internet www.ozsay.com; f. 1976; Pres. RECEP KALKAVAN; Man. Dir OMER KALKAVAN; 10 vessels.

Türkiye Denizcilik İşletmeleri Denizyolları İşletmesi Müdürlüğü (TDI): Meclısı Mebusan Cad. 18, 80040 Salıpazarı, İstanbul; tel. (212) 2521700; fax (212) 2515767; e-mail bilgiedinme@tdi.gov.tr; internet www.tdi.com.tr; ferry co; Chair. ERKAN ARIKAN; Man. Dir KADIR KURTOĞLU; 5 vessels.

Yardimci Shipping Group of Companies: Aydintepe Mah. Tersaneler Cad. 50 Sok. 7, 34947 Tuzla, İstanbul; tel. (216) 4938000; fax (216) 4928080; e-mail info@yardimci.gen.tr; internet www.yardimci .gen.tr; f. 1976; Chair. KEMAL YARDIMCI; Man. Dir HUSEYIN YARDIMCI; 9 vessels.

CIVIL AVIATION

There are 40 airports for international and domestic flights in Turkey. The largest of these are Atatürk and Sabiha Gökçen (both serving İstanbul), Esenboğa (Ankara), Adnan Menderes (İzmir), Antalya, Dalaman, Milas–Bodrum, Adana, Trabzon, Isparta Süleyman Demirel and Nevşehir–Kapadokya. A second terminal building at Sabiha Gökçen International Airport was inaugurated in October 2009. Earlier that year plans were announced to increase total passenger capacity at the airport to 20m. by 2018. In August 2012 the Government confirmed that it would seek to build a third international airport to serve İstanbul, located in the European part of the city. The first phase of the project, which was intended to accommodate up to 90m. passengers per year, was scheduled for completion by 2015.

Devlet Hava Meydanları İşletmesi Genel Müdürlüğü (General Directorate of State Airports Authority): Konya Yolu Üzeri No. 66, 06330 Etiler, Ankara; tel. (312) 2042000; fax (312) 2123917; e-mail dhmi@dhmi.gov.tr; internet www.dhmi.gov.tr; f. 1984; manages 36 airports nation-wide; responsible for air traffic control in Turkish airspace; Chair. of Bd and Dir-Gen. ORHAN BIRDAL.

Sivil Havacılık Genel Müdürlüğü (Directorate General of Civil Aviation): Bosna Hersek Cad. 5, 06510 Emek, Ankara; tel. (312) 2036000; fax (312) 2124684; e-mail ozelkalem@shgm.gov.tr; internet web.shgm.gov.tr; Dir-Gen. BILAL EKŞI.

Atlasjet Havacilik AŞ: Yeşilyurt Mah. Eski Halkali Yolu Alacati Evleri Yani 5B, 34153 Florya, İstanbul; tel. (212) 6632000; fax (212) 6632751; e-mail info@atlasjet.com; internet www.atlasjet.com; f. 2001; passenger and cargo; 17 aircraft; CEO ORHAN COŞKUN.

Onur Air Taşımacılık AŞ: Atatürk Havalimanı B Kapısı, Teknik Hangar Yanı 34149, Yeşilköy, İstanbul; tel. (212) 4686687; fax (212) 4686696; e-mail info@onurair.com.tr; internet www.onurair.com.tr; f. 1992; international and domestic passenger and cargo charter services; 22 aircraft; Gen. Man. ŞAHABETTIN BOLUKÇU.

Pegasus Hava Taşımacılığı AŞ (Pegasus Airlines): Basın Ekspres Yolu 2, Halkalı, İstanbul; tel. (212) 6977777; fax (212) 6939777; internet www.flypgs.com; f. 1990; domestic and international scheduled and charter services; 23 aircraft; Chair. ALI SABANCI; Gen. Man. SERTAÇ HAYBAT.

SunExpress (Güneş Ekspres Havacilik AŞ): Mehmetçik Mah. Aspendos Bul. Aspendos İş Merkezi 63/1–2, 07300 Antalya; tel. (242) 3102626; fax (242) 3102650; e-mail travelcenter@sunexpress .com; internet www.sunexpress.com; f. 1989; 50% owned by Deutsche Lufthansa AG (Germany) and 50% by Turkish Airlines; charter and scheduled passenger and freight; serves European destinations; 26 aircraft; Man. Dir PAUL SCHWAIGER.

TAV Havalimanları Holding AŞ: İstanbul Atatürk Havalimanı, Dış Hatlar Terminali, 34149 Yeşilköy, İstanbul; tel. (212) 4633000; fax (212) 4655050; e-mail info@tav.aero; internet www.tavairports .com; f. 1997; construction and management of airport facilities; manages Atatürk (İstanbul), Esenboğa (Ankara), Adnan Menderes (İzmir) and Gazipaşa (Antalya) airports, as well as airports in Georgia and Tunisia; Chair. HAMDI AKIN; Pres. and CEO Dr MUSTAFA SANI ŞENER.

Türk Hava Yolları AO (THY) (Turkish Airlines Inc): Genel Müdürlük Binas, Atatürk Hava Limanı, 34830 Yeşilköy, İstanbul; tel. (212) 4636363; fax (212) 4652388; e-mail customer@thy.com; internet www.thy.com.tr; f. 1933; 49.12% state-owned; extensive internal network and scheduled and charter flights to destinations in the Middle East, Africa, the Far East, Cen. Asia, the USA and Europe; 133 aircraft; Chair. HAMDI TOPÇU; Gen. Man. TEMEL KOTIL.

Tourism

Visitors to Turkey are attracted by the climate, fine beaches and ancient monuments. With government investment, the country has rapidly become a leading holiday destination for European tourists (particularly from the United Kingdom and Germany). In 2012 the number of tourists increased to 31.8m. (compared with 7.5m. in 1999); receipts from tourism reached US $23,440m. in 2012.

Ministry of Culture and Tourism: See The Government—Ministries; Dir-Gen. of Information MUSTAFA SYAHHAN; Dir-Gen. of Investments and Establishments KUDRET ASLAN.

Defence

Chief of the General Staff: Gen. NECDET ÖZEL.

Ground Forces Commander: Gen. HAYRI KIVRIKOĞLU.

Navy Commander: Adm. EMIN MURAT BILGEL.

Air Force Commander: Gen. MEHMET ERTEN.

Gendarmerie Commander: Gen. BEKIR KALYONCU.

Defence Budget (2012): TL 30,700m.

Military Service: 15 months.

Total Armed Forces (as assessed at November 2012): 510,600: army 402,000 (est. 325,000 conscripts); navy 48,600 (34,500 conscripts); air force 60,000. Reserves 378,700.

Paramilitary Forces (as assessed at November 2012): 150,000 gendarmerie; 3,250 coast guard.

Education

When the Turkish Republic was formed, the Ministry of Education became the sole authority in educational matters, replacing the dual system of religious schools and other schools. One of the main obstacles to literacy was the Arabic script, which required years of study before proficiency could be attained. In 1928, therefore, a Turkish alphabet was introduced, using Latin characters. At the same time the literary language was simplified, and purged of some of its foreign elements. In 2012 government expenditure on education was budgeted at about TL 39,100m.

PRIMARY EDUCATION

Primary education may be preceded by an optional pre-school establishment for children between three and six years of age. In the 2011/12 academic year, according to provisional figures, there were 28,625 such schools, with 55,883 teachers. In the same year 1,169,556 children were enrolled at pre-schools.

An education reform bill approved in March 2012 extended the duration of compulsory education from eight to 12 years. It includes four years of elementary school, four years of middle school and four years of high school. Elementary school starts from the age of six.

Primary education is now entirely free, and co-education is the accepted basis for universal education. According to provisional figures, the number of primary schools has risen from 12,511 in 1950 to 32,108 in 2011/12, and the number of teachers from 27,144 to 515,852. In the same year 10,979,301 children were enrolled at primary schools. In 2008/09, according to UNESCO estimates, 97% of children in the relevant age-group were enrolled in primary education.

SECONDARY EDUCATION

Secondary education lasts for a minimum of four years after primary education, and provides for students intending to proceed to higher educational institutions. The secondary education system encompasses general high schools, and vocational and technical high schools. In addition, since 1992/93 'open' high schools have provided secondary education opportunities to young working people through the media and other new technologies.

Those students who wish to proceed to an institute of higher education must pass the state matriculation examination. The study of a modern language (English, French or German) is compulsory. In 2011/12, according to provisional figures, there were 4,171 general high schools, with 122,716 teachers. In that year 2,666,066 children were enrolled in general secondary education. In 2008/09, according to UNESCO estimates, 74% of children in the relevant age-group were enrolled in secondary education.

VOCATIONAL EDUCATION

In 2011/12, according to provisional figures, a total of 2,090,220 students attended 5,501 vocational and teacher-training high schools, with 113,098 teachers. In addition, there are colleges for commerce, tourism, communication, local administration and secretarial skills.

HIGHER EDUCATION

Higher educational institutions in Turkey were established, and are administered, by the state. In early 2012 there were 139 universities, 45 of which were private. The main university at İstanbul, originally established in 1453, was attended by 73,061 students in 2003. A total of 2,181,217 students were enrolled at institutes of higher education in the 2005/06 academic year.

TURKMENISTAN

Introductory Survey

LOCATION, CLIMATE, LANGUAGE, RELIGION, FLAG, CAPITAL

Turkmenistan is situated in the south-west of Central Asia. It is bordered to the north by Uzbekistan, to the north-west by Kazakhstan, to the west by the Caspian Sea, to the south by Iran and to the south-east by Afghanistan. The climate is severely continental, with extremely hot summers and cold winters. The average temperature in January is –4°C (25°F), but winter temperatures can fall as low as –33°C (–27°F). In summer temperatures often reach 50°C (122°F) in the south-eastern Kara-Kum desert; the average temperature in July is 28°C (82°F). Precipitation is slight throughout much of the country: average annual rainfall ranges from only 80 mm (3.1 ins) in the north-west to about 300 mm (11.8 ins) in mountainous regions. Turkmen, a member of the Southern Turkic group, is the official language. Most of the population are Sunni Muslims. Islam in Turkmenistan has traditionally featured elements of Sufi mysticism and shamanism, and pilgrimages to local religious sites are reported to be common. The national flag (proportions 2 by 3) consists of a maroon stripe bearing a vertical design of five different carpet patterns above a wreath of olive branches on a green background, with five white, five-pointed stars framed by a narrow white crescent moon, in its upper dexter corner. The capital is Aşgabat.

CONTEMPORARY POLITICAL HISTORY

Historical Context

In 1877 Russia began a campaign against the Turkmen, which culminated in the battle of Gök Tepe in 1881, at which some 20,000 Turkmen are estimated to have been killed. In 1895 the Russian conquest was confirmed by agreement with the British; the international boundary thus established divided some Turkmen under Russian rule from others in the British sphere of influence. In 1917 the Bolsheviks attempted to take power in the region, but found limited local support. An anti-Bolshevik Russian Provisional Government of Transcaspia was formed, and a Turkmen Congress was also established. Soviet forces were sent to Aşgabat, and a Turkestan Autonomous Soviet Socialist Republic was declared on 30 April 1918. In July nationalists, aided by British forces, ousted the Bolshevik Government and established an independent Government in Aşgabat, protected by a British garrison. After the British withdrew, however, the Government was soon removed, and by 1920 Red Army troops were in control of Aşgabat. A Turkmen Soviet Socialist Republic (SSR) was established on 27 October 1924. In May 1925 it became a constituent republic of the USSR, and political power in the republic was held by the Communist Party of Turkmenistan (CPT).

In 1928 all Islamic institutions in Turkmenistan were closed. A programme of agricultural collectivization, which was begun in 1929 and entailed the forcible settlement of traditionally nomadic people in collective farms, provoked military resistance, and guerrilla warfare against Soviet power continued until 1936. In the 1930s many Turkmen intellectuals, and subsequently government and CPT officials, were imprisoned or executed. The development of extensive irrigation projects enabled rapid development of cotton-growing, particularly after 1945.

In the late 1980s the geographical remoteness of Turkmenistan inhibited its involvement in the political changes occurring in some other Soviet republics, and the CPT dominated the republic's elections to the all-Union Congress of People's Deputies in the Soviet and Russian capital, Moscow, in early 1989. A 'popular front' organization concerned with the status of Turkmen language and culture and environmental matters, Unity (Agzybirlik), was formed in September; however, it was banned in January 1990. Only the CPT and its approved organizations were permitted to participate in elections to the republican Supreme Soviet on 7 January. When the new Supreme Soviet convened, Saparmyrat Niyazov, the First Secretary of the CPT since 1985, was elected Chairman of the Supreme Soviet, the highest government office in the republic.

In May 1990 Turkmen officially became the state language, replacing Russian. On 22 August the Turkmenistani Supreme Soviet adopted a declaration of sovereignty. On 27 October Niyazov was elected, unopposed, by direct ballot, to the new post of executive President of Turkmenistan, reportedly receiving 98.3% of the votes cast. In late 1990 and early 1991 Turkmenistan participated in negotiations towards a new Union Treaty, which was to provide a new framework for the continuation of the USSR. At the referendum on the status of the USSR in March 1991, 95.7% of eligible voters in Turkmenistan—a higher proportion than in any other Soviet republic—approved the preservation of the USSR as a 'renewed federation'.

Domestic Political Affairs

President Niyazov made no public announcements in reaction to the attempted coup by conservative communists in Moscow of August 1991. On 18 October Turkmenistan was among the signatories of the treaty establishing an economic community of eight republics. At a national referendum held on 26 October, according to the official results, 94.1% of the electorate voted for independence. On the following day the Turkmenistani Supreme Council adopted a law on independence. The name of the republic was changed from the Turkmen SSR to Turkmenistan. In December the CPT changed its name to the Democratic Party of Turkmenistan (DPT). On 21 December Turkmenistan was one of 11 republics to sign the Almatı (Alma-Ata) Declaration, which formally established the Commonwealth of Independent States (CIS, see p. 251).

The DPT and Niyazov came to dominate independent Turkmenistan, and severe restrictions were placed on the media and opposition activity. The promotion of a presidential 'cult of personality' was reported to have prompted the resignation, in mid-1992, of the Minister of Foreign Affairs, Abdy Kuliyev. The new Constitution, adopted on 18 May, further enhanced presidential authority, making Niyazov Chairman of the Government (prime minister), as well as head of state. In June Niyazov was re-elected, again unopposed, to the presidency, receiving a purported 99.5% of the votes cast.

Other significant structural changes were introduced under the new Constitution. The Supreme Council was to be replaced as Turkmenistan's legislature by a 50-member Majlis (Assembly); however, until the expiry of its five-year term, the Supreme Soviet elected in 1990 (although renamed the Majlis) was to be retained as the republican legislature. The Khalk Maslakhaty (People's Council) was established as the 'supreme representative body of popular power', which was empowered to decide important political and economic issues, to demand changes to the Constitution, and to vote to express no confidence in the President, if it found his actions to be at variance with the law. The Khalk Maslakhaty was to comprise the 50 deputies of the Majlis, in addition to 50 elected and 10 appointed representatives from the electoral districts of Turkmenistan (the former were directly elected in November–December 1992); it was also to include the members of the Government and the Chairman of the Supreme Court, and was to be headed by the President.

After the new Constitution was adopted, there were fears that the rights of members of Turkmenistan's minority ethnic groups (the most numerous of which, Russians and Uzbeks, represented some 10% and 9%, respectively, of the total population in the early 1990s) were in jeopardy, as the document stipulated that only ethnic Turkmen would be eligible for employment in state enterprises, and removed the status of 'language of inter-ethnic communication' hitherto granted to Russian. The Constitution guaranteed state secularism.

The presidential 'cult of personality' was strengthened during 1993, with numerous institutions, streets and public buildings being named after Niyazov, while the Caspian Sea port of Krasnovodsk was renamed Türkmenbaşi ('Head of the Turkmen', a recently introduced mode of address for Niyazov). In December the Majlis voted to extend Niyazov's term of office until 2002, a decision that was endorsed by a reported 99.99% of the electorate in a referendum held on 15 January 1994.

Elections to the new, 50-member Majlis were held in December 1994, officially with the participation of 99.8% of the registered electorate. It was reported that 49 of the 50 deputies had been elected unopposed. The Majlis convened later in the month; the overwhelming majority of the deputies were believed to be members of the DPT.

Despite the result of the referendum of January 1994, elements of opposition to Niyazov were believed to be active in Turkmenistan, as well as in exile in other republics of the CIS, in particular Russia, where Abdy Kuliyev led an opposition group, the Turkmenistan Foundation. In June 1995 the Turkmenistani Supreme Court sentenced two opposition leaders to respective terms of 12 and 15 years' imprisonment in a labour colony, having found them guilty of involvement in a plot to assassinate Niyazov. In July 1995 a protest rally took place in Aşgabat, at which up to 1,000 demonstrators criticized Niyazov's leadership and the continuing economic hardships. In August Niyazov dismissed 10 of Turkmenistan's 50 local etrap (district or raion) administrative leaders. In October the President dismissed several senior members of the Council of Ministers. In 1996 and 1997 Niyazov effected widespread dismissals of government officials, as well as local administrative leaders and members of the judiciary. In April 1998 elections to the Khalk Maslakhaty were held, with the reported participation of 99.5% of the electorate.

Turkmenistan continued to attract the censure of international human rights organizations. In April 1998 a delegation of the Organization for Security and Co-operation in Europe (OSCE, see p. 397) appealed to Niyazov to release eight political prisoners who had been detained since the July 1995 demonstration. Niyazov agreed to their release, following which he made his first official visit to the USA where he met President Bill Clinton. Niyazov's systematic purging of government and other officials continued in May 1998. An attempted military rebellion in western Turkmenistan in September was followed by the dismissal of the Minister of Defence, and the comprehensive reorganization of senior personnel of the armed forces.

The promotion of public veneration for Niyazov appeared further to intensify during 1998: in December a giant ceremonial arch, surmounted by a revolving gold-plated statue of the President, was inaugurated in central Aşgabat. In what was interpreted as an effort to counter growing international accusations of dictatorial methods, the President declared, in December, that the elections to the Majlis scheduled for late 1999 would be contested on a multi-party basis, and that the establishment of new political parties would be permitted in advance of the poll. In December the Khalk Maslakhaty voted to abolish the death penalty, Turkmenistan thus becoming the first state in post-Soviet Central Asia to proscribe capital punishment.

Extension of Niyazov's presidential term

Elections to the Majlis were conducted on 12 December 1999. According to official reports, some 99% of the registered electorate participated in the poll. The DPT was the only party to obtain representation. In late December the new Majlis approved an amendment to the Constitution, extending Niyazov's presidential term indefinitely. Niyazov subsequently announced that the creation of opposition political parties would not be contemplated before 2010. The international community expressed outrage when, in March 2000, the leader of the unofficial popular opposition front, Unity, Nurberdi Nurmämmet, was sentenced to five years' imprisonment on charges of hooliganism and intent to murder, after he protested that the constitutional amendment was undemocratic.

On 1 January 2000 Turkmenistan formally adopted a revised form of the Latin script for the Turkmen language, replacing the Cyrillic script introduced in the 1920s. In July Niyazov issued an order declaring that, henceforth, knowledge of the Turkmen language would be a mandatory requirement for all government officials. Furthermore, all candidates for leadership posts were to have their genealogies over the previous three generations verified. Meanwhile, Niyazov dismissed a number of prominent government officials, including Boris Shikhmuradov, the Minister of Foreign Affairs, in July; Shikhmuradov was succeeded by Batyr Berdyyev. It was also announced that all officials, including government ministers, would henceforth be appointed for a six-month probationary period, prior to being confirmed in office.

In the early 2000s Niyazov oversaw the introduction of a number of policies intended to develop a strong Turkmen national identity, including the closure of the opera and ballet theatre in Aşgabat. A principal element of these policies was the publication of the *Ruhnama*, or national code of spiritual conduct

purportedly written by the President. The *Ruhnama* became fundamental to the school curriculum, and was in effect elevated to the status of a holy text, with display of the volume required in mosques, citations from the work included in inscriptions in religious and public buildings, and with knowledge of the text, moreover, becoming a prerequisite for entry into various professions. (A second volume of the *Ruhnama* was published in September 2004.)

In July 2001 Berdyyev was dismissed as Minister of Foreign Affairs, and replaced by Rashid Meredov. In late October Shikhmuradov was dismissed as ambassador to the People's Republic of China. He fled to Moscow from where, in November, he issued a statement condemning Niyazov's rule. Meanwhile, the Prosecutor-General, Gurbanbibi Atajanova, issued a warrant for Shikhmuradov's arrest on charges of the misappropriation of state property, along with a request for his extradition from Russia. In January 2002 Shikhmuradov established the People's Democratic Movement of Turkmenistan. In early February Nurmukhammet Hanamov resigned as ambassador to Turkey in order to join the opposition movement. In mid-February a former deputy premier, Hudayberdy Orazov, announced his support for the opposition-in-exile. The Turkmenistani authorities subsequently issued a request for the extradition of Hanamov and accused Orazov of embezzling state funds. Meanwhile, in March Niyazov dismissed a number of senior officials from the defence, intelligence and security services (including the Minister of Defence), whom he accused of plotting to remove him from power. In addition, the State Border Service was placed under the direct control of the President. A new Minister of Internal Affairs was appointed in May, and in the same month Seitbay Gandimov was dismissed as Deputy Chairman of the Government and Chairman of the Central Bank, following allegations that he had links with Orazov. Further cabinet reorganizations followed in August and September. In September the newly appointed Chairman of the Central Bank was dismissed, following the reported misappropriation from the bank of US $41.5m. In the same month Niyazov announced the creation of so-called 'labour armies', comprising 20,000 men under the age of 35, who were to be drafted to work without remuneration on public projects for a period of two years. Further government changes took place in mid-November, when Ovezgeldy Atayev was elected Chairman of the Majlis.

On 25 November 2002 an assassination attempt was made against the presidential motorcade, as it travelled through Aşgabat. Niyazov publicly accused Shikhmuradov and Hanamov, among others, of involvement in the organization of what they termed an attempted coup, and Shikhmuradov, who had clandestinely returned to Turkmenistan, was immediately arrested in Aşgabat. On the following day it was announced that 16 suspects had been arrested, although international human rights organizations reported that hundreds of people were detained in subsequent days. Following a televised confession, a one-day trial at the Supreme Court on 30 December found Shikhmuradov guilty of the attempt on Niyazov's life, and he was sentenced to 25 years' imprisonment (subsequently increased to a life sentence by the Majlis). Orazov and Hanamov were convicted *in absentia*, and another former Minister of Foreign Affairs, Berdyyev, was detained and sentenced in early 2003 to 25 years' imprisonment for his involvement in the assassination attempt; the opposition-in-exile subsequently indicated that both Shikhmuradov and Berdyyev may have died while in detention, although these claims remained unconfirmed. Meanwhile, opposition leader Murad Esenov, in exile in Sweden, claimed that the assassination attempt had been staged as a pretext for the arrest of Shikhmuradov and other members of the opposition, and the OSCE, concerned at the circumstances surrounding Shikhmuradov's trial and confession, sent a fact-finding mission to Aşgabat. In late December the Uzbekistani ambassador to Turkmenistan (the embassy of which country had been searched, in violation of the Vienna Convention on Diplomatic Relations) was expelled from the country, having been accused of harbouring Shikhmuradov immediately after the attack.

In February 2003 Niyazov issued decrees that temporarily reinstated the requirement for exit visas (which had been abolished in December 2001). (The requirement for exit visas was removed again in March 2004.) The import of foreign periodicals was prohibited, and the restrictions imposed on journalists were intensified. On 6 April 2003 elections to the Khalk Maslakhaty and to district and village councils took place, with the participation of some 89.3% of the electorate. The OSCE, which had accused the authorities of widespread human rights abuses in a report issued in March, questioned the legitimacy of the electoral process.

Constitutional amendments

On 15 August 2003 amendments to the Constitution elevated the Khalk Maslakhaty, which was henceforth to comprise 2,507 members, to the status of a 'permanently functioning supreme representative body of popular authority', and required it to remain in continuous session. The Khalk Maslakhaty was also accorded a number of legislative powers, which enabled it to adopt constitutional laws, thus effectively displacing the Majlis as the country's leading legislative body. Other changes to the Constitution forbade Turkmenistani citizens from holding dual nationality, superseding an agreement on dual nationality reached with Russia in December 1993.

Government changes in September 2003 included the appointment of Maj.-Gen. Agageldy Mamatgeldiyev as Minister of Defence. In November two new Deputy Chairmen and a new Minister of National Security were appointed. In the same month a new law came into force, which severely restricted the activities of non-governmental organizations, imposing fines, prison sentences and periods of 'corrective labour' for those convicted under the new guidelines. Also in November a new law was approved, restricting the activities of religious groups by criminalizing any confession not registered with the Ministry of Justice (at that time the only state-registered faiths were Sunni Islam and Russian Orthodox Christianity). The formation of political parties on religious grounds was also prohibited. (These laws were revised in March 2004.) In late November the UN General Assembly adopted a resolution (which was, notably, supported by Russia), expressing grave concerns over human rights violations in Turkmenistan. At the end of the month Niyazov pardoned more than 7,000 prisoners.

In February 2004 President Niyazov replaced 15,000 medical workers with army conscripts, in an attempt to reduce government expenditure on health care. In April the Minister of the Economy and Finance, the Minister of Education and the heads of two state-controlled banks were dismissed. In May Niyazov signed a decree prohibiting the use of child labour in the cotton industry. A further presidential decree, issued in June, invalidated all higher-education degrees received abroad; all teachers with such degrees were to be dismissed. In August Geldymuhammet Ashirkulov was appointed Minister of Internal Affairs, although he only remained in office until December, when he was succeeded by Akmamed Rahmanov. Meanwhile, in October Niyazov removed Enebai Atayeva as Deputy Chairman of the Government and Governor of the cotton-producing Ahal Velayat (Region), reportedly owing to official dissatisfaction with the nation-wide cotton harvest; the regional deputy governor and four heads of cotton-producing associations were also replaced. In the same month the UN General Assembly adopted a second resolution criticizing human rights violations in Turkmenistan; on this occasion, Russia abstained from voting.

Elections to the Majlis were conducted on 19 December 2004. According to official reports, 76.9% of the registered electorate participated in the poll, at which the DPT was the only party represented. (A second round of voting took place on 9 January 2005 in seven districts where candidates had failed to obtain the required 50% plus one of the votes cast.) In February 2005 Niyazov announced plans to close all hospitals outside Aşgabat, stating that the provision of hospitals outside the capital was unnecessary. In April the President prohibited the import and circulation of all foreign print media and refused to renew the licences of international shipping firms and express couriers operating in Turkmenistan.

Throughout 2005 and early 2006 President Niyazov frequently replaced state officials; many of those dismissed were accused of corruption or other abuses of office, and were sentenced to long custodial terms. Notably, in July 2005 the former Deputy Chairman of the Government, responsible for the Fuel and Energy Sector, Yolly Gurbanmuradov, was sentenced to 25 years' imprisonment, on charges of having abused his previous position as head of the State Bank for Foreign Economic Activities in 1993–2001. Meanwhile, in May 2005 Niyazov dismissed the Chairman of the Central Bank, who was accused of corruption. Niyazov further reorganized the energy sector in August and September of that year. In April 2006 Niyazov appointed Muhammetguly Ogshukov, previously First Deputy Prosecutor-General, to succeed Atajanova as Prosecutor-General. Later in the month Atajanova admitted to allegations, made by Niyazov, that she had taken bribes and stolen state property, after which

it was decreed that she had been relieved of her duties for having committed 'shameful' deeds and having damaged the reputation of the office of Prosecutor-General. Elections to the 625 gengeşes (municipalities) took place on 23 July.

Death of President Niyazov

On 21 December 2006 President Niyazov died, after suffering a heart attack. The Chairman of the Majlis, Ovezgeldy Atayev, who under the terms of the Constitution would become acting President, was dismissed from his post shortly after Niyazov's death, when state prosecutors announced that they would be investigating criminal charges against him. Subsequently, the State Security Council appointed the Deputy Chairman of the Government and Minister of Health and the Medical Industry, Gurbanguly Berdymuhamedov, as acting President, while Akja Nurberdiyeva succeeded Atayev as Chairman of the Majlis. Six candidates contested the presidential elections held on 11 February 2007. Berdymuhamedov won by an overwhelming majority, receiving 89.2% of the votes cast; the rate of participation by the electorate was officially recorded at 98.6%. (It was subsequently reported that at least three of the candidates had been dismissed from their state posts by 2009.) Berdymuhamedov was inaugurated as President on 14 February 2007. From mid-February the appointment of government ministers and other senior state officials was announced, including several ministers who had served under Niyazov. Among the principal appointments were those of Rashid Meredov as deputy premier and Minister of Foreign Affairs, Mamatgeldiyev as Minister of Defence and Myrat Karryyev as Minister of Justice; Muhammetgeldy Annaamanov was appointed Minister of Education, replacing Hydyr Saparliyev, who was promoted to the position of deputy premier. New appointments were also made to regional governorships and to the chairmanship of the Supreme Court and to the Office of the Prosecutor-General. Also in February Atayev and his wife were sentenced to five years' imprisonment on charges relating to the suicide of their daughter-in-law.

The most significant of President Berdymuhamedov's early decrees was the Code of Social Guarantees, signed into law on 19 March 2007, which restored pension rights that had been removed from an estimated 100,000 senior citizens in the previous year. Berdymuhamedov announced a programme of agricultural reforms and plans to extend public access to the internet, which hitherto had been severely restricted in Turkmenistan. (The first public access point to the internet in the country had been opened in February in Aşgabat.) In April the recently appointed Minister of Internal Affairs was dismissed, reportedly on the grounds that he had failed to address corruption within the ministry and to combat an increase in drug abuse within the country; he was succeeded by Khodjamyrat Annagurbanov. In October Berdymuhamedov removed Annagurbanov and the Minister of National Security, both of whom, according to an official announcement, were to be subject to criminal proceedings on undisclosed charges. Charymyrat Amanov was appointed to the Ministry of National Security, while Orazgeldy Amanmyradov received the internal affairs portfolio. On 9 December elections were conducted to councils in each of Turkmenistan's velayats. In April 2008 Hojamyrat Geldimyradov, hitherto Minister of Finance, was appointed as Deputy Chairman of the Government, responsible for Economic Affairs, while the Chairman of the Central Bank was also replaced. Later in April Berdymuhamedov established a special commission to revise the Constitution, and officially abolished the names of the months introduced by Niyazov (which had included various titles of Niyazov and his parents). On 21 July the text of a new draft constitution was announced.

New Constitution

On 26 September 2008 the new Constitution was approved at an extraordinary session of the Khalk Maslakhaty; it provided, *inter alia*, for the dissolution of the Khalk Maslakhaty, and the division of its powers between the President and the Majlis, which was to be enlarged to number 125 deputies. The President was henceforth to be responsible for appointing regional governors and mayors directly. Elections to the Majlis were conducted on 14 December, with a second round of voting following in one district on 28 December. A CIS observer mission stated that the poll had been conducted in accordance with the country's legislation and democratic standards. However, human rights groups and the OSCE, which had also dispatched a small monitoring mission to Turkmenistan, criticized the absence of democratic alternatives for the electorate. Opposition parties disputed the official voter participation figure of 93.8%, and claimed that participation amounted to only about 30% of the electorate. The new Majlis was convened on 9 January 2009. Reports stated that around 90% of the elected deputies were members of the DPT, and that the remainder were independent candidates endorsed by the party.

In January 2009 Tuvakmammed Japarov, hitherto the head of the Supreme Control Chamber of Turkmenistan (a financial regulatory body created in 2007), was appointed Deputy Chairman of the Government, responsible for Economic Affairs, following the resignation of Geldimyradov on the grounds of ill health. Berdymuhamedov also replaced a number of ministers, governors and senior managers of state concerns; these included the Minister of Energy and Industry and the Chairman of government petroleum agency Turkmenneft, after investigations conducted by the Supreme Control Chamber and the Office of the Prosecutor-General were reported to have revealed financial irregularities. Later that month Mamatgeldiyev tendered his resignation as Minister of Defence, on grounds of ill health; Yalym Berdyyev, hitherto Secretary of the State Security Council, was appointed to succeed him. In March the head of the presidential administration was replaced. In May it was announced that Berdymuhamedov had ordered the release of large numbers of prisoners, including Muhammetguly Aymuradov, who had served more than 14 years' imprisonment for anti-state crimes.

Ministerial changes

In late May 2009 Berdymuhamedov dismissed Amanmyradov as Minister of Internal Affairs, with the stated intention of addressing endemic corrupt practices within interior ministry bodies; Iskander Mulikov, hitherto head of a regional police department in the north of the country, was appointed to the post. A number of ministerial changes were effected in July: notably, Baymyrat Hojamuhammedov, hitherto Chairman of the state natural gas agency Türkmengaz, was appointed to replace Tachberdy Tagiyev as Deputy Chairman of the Government, responsible for Petroleum and Natural Gas. In August Berdymuhamedov signed a decree providing for the establishment of a naval force by 2015 (the existing maritime contingent comprising only coastal guard units). In January 2010 Berdymuhamedov announced a number of appointments to state enterprises and to the Government, appointing a new Mayor of Aşgabat. Also in January Berdymuhamedov's order that the giant ceremonial arch surmounted by a statue of Niyazov, which had been constructed in 1998, be removed from central Aşgabat was widely viewed as a further disassociation from the former regime. (The statue was duly dismantled in August 2010 and relocated to the outskirts of the city.) In April Berdymuhamedov carried out a further reorganization of government and other state officials. In September the Government announced the publication of the inaugural edition of what was deemed to be the first nominally independent newspaper in Turkmenistan since the early 1990s. However, the publication, *Rysgal* (Welfare), was published by the Union of Industrialists and Entrepreneurs, an organization regarded as closely allied with President Berdymuhamedov, and the first edition of the publication included an editorial feature written by the President.

In February 2011 Saparliyev was removed as deputy premier, in connection with his appointment as the Rector of the national polytechnic institute. In March Berdymuhamedov dismissed Charymyrat Amanov as Minister of National Security. Amanov was succeeded by the hitherto Minister of Defence, Yilym Berdyyev, who was, in turn, replaced by his hitherto deputy, Begench Gundogdyyev. Meanwhile, in April it was announced that the examination based on knowledge of the *Ruhnama*, which had formed a compulsory part of the curriculum at all state secondary schools, had been abolished, while compulsory courses on the text at universities were also to be withdrawn. Meanwhile, evidence of a developing 'cult of personality' around Berdymuhamedov included the granting to him of a new honorific title, 'Arkadag' ('Protective Mountain').

In May 2011 Berdymuhamedov appointed Orazmyrat Nyyazlyev as Chairman of the Central Commission for Elections and Referendums, replacing Myrat Garriyev, a longstanding supporter of the President, who became a Deputy Chairman of the advisory Council of Elders. On 1 June new legislation regulating presidential elections was promulgated; candidates were henceforth required either to be supported by a political party or to collect at least 50,000 signatures, to have resided in Turkmenistan for the previous 15 years, and to have served on a state body or organization. On 9 July Tuvakammad Japarov, hitherto Deputy Chairman of the Government, responsible for Economic

Affairs, was appointed as Chairman of the Central Bank, following the dismissal of Guvanchmyrat Geklenov from the post. Later that month, in a public display by the authorities of addressing corruption, the Supreme Court convicted 10 former employees of the Central Bank for bribe-taking and sentenced them to lengthy terms of imprisonment. Meanwhile, in early July an armaments depot exploded in the town of Abadan, outside Aşgabat, causing widespread damage; the Government stated that 15 people had been killed, although some reports indicated that the number of casualties totalled several hundred. In early August 40 officers received custodial sentences in connection with the explosion in July, while a further two explosions occurred in Abadan, killing eight people. On 4 August it was announced that a presidential election was to be conducted on 12 February 2012.

Recent developments: the 2012 presidential election

On 11 January 2012 President Berdymuhamedov signed into force legislation permitting the establishment of new political parties (in accordance with provisions in the 2008 Constitution). Also in January, however, the OSCE declared that it would not dispatch electoral observers to Turkmenistan in view of the continued lack of democratic freedom; an assessment mission report subsequently issued by the OSCE criticized, *inter alia*, the restrictions imposed on the registration of presidential candidates, and on the media. The other seven candidates who had emerged to contest the presidential election all expressed support for Berdymuhamedov. According to official results, Berdymuhamedov was overwhelmingly re-elected on 12 February, receiving 97.1% of the votes cast, with a participation rate of 96.7% of the electorate. (The candidates placed second and third, each of whom received around 1% of the vote, were both government ministers.) Berdymuhamedov was inaugurated as President on 17 February. In March the Government announced that preparations were under way for the creation of two new political parties, of which one was to be agrarian and the other was to represent entrepreneurs.

In April 2012 Berdymuhamedov dismissed Yarmuhammed Orazgulyyev (the third-placed candidate in the recent presidential election) as Minister of Energy and Industry, on the grounds that he was, as a parent, responsible for his son's involvement in car-racing that had resulted in a traffic accident. Shortly afterwards, Berdymuhamedov appointed Myrat Artykov as Orazgulyyev's successor. In May Berdymuhamedov dismissed Bayramgeldy Nedirov as Minister of the Petroleum and Gas Industry and Mineral Resources, appointing Kakageldy Abdullayev to the post in an acting capacity. Merdan Bayramov was dismissed as Minister of Agriculture in July, after a poor harvest had been recorded; he was succeeded by Rejep Bazarov. Shortly afterwards, it was announced that separate ministries for Energy and for Industry had been created, with Artykov becoming Minister of Energy, while Babaniyaz Italmazov was appointed as Minister of Industry. On 21 August the founding conference of a new political party, the Party of Industrialists and Entrepreneurs, was held in Aşgabat, prior to the official registration of the party.

On 4 January 2013 Berdymuhamedov signed into force new legislation that officially prohibited 'monopolization of the media', permitting any member of the public to own a media company, and provided for freedom of expression and a ban on all media censorship. Later in the month he accordingly transferred ownership of many of the country's newspapers to the Council of Ministers, while other publications were purportedly to be controlled by trade unions and the Ministry of Education. However, international media organizations, notably Reporters without Borders, denounced the reform as a deceptive measure designed to secure favour with the international community, and noted moreover that it made domestic internet sites subject to the same registration processes as other media. On 12 January Berdymuhamedov reorganized the Government, dismissing several ministers, including the Deputy Chairman, responsible for Transport and Communications, Rozymyrat Seyitkulyev, who was replaced by Akmyrat Yegeleyev, and the Minister of the Economy and Development, Byashimmyrat Hojamammedov, who became Hakim (Governor) of Balkan Velayat, and was succeeded by Babamyrat Taganov. The hitherto Mayor of Aşgabat (and a former Minister of Construction), Shamuhammet Durdylyev, was appointed Deputy Chairman, responsible for the Construction Sector, while Abdullayev became head of Türkmengaz, and was succeeded as Minister of the Petroleum and Gas Industry and Mineral Resources by Muhammetnur Halylov. Later in January six Deputy Chairmen were also awarded responsibility for overseeing the country's five velayats and the capital city. At a meeting of the UN Human Rights Council in April, the Turkmenistani authorities were strenuously criticized by US and Western European representatives for continued repression and the use of torture.

Foreign Affairs

Regional relations

One of the fundamental, constitutionally enshrined, principles of Turkmenistan's foreign policy is that of 'permanent neutrality'. The republic's neutral status was recognized by the UN General Assembly in December 1995, two months after Turkmenistan became the first of the former Soviet republics to join the Non-aligned Movement (see p. 477). Turkmenistan also adopted an equivocal attitude towards its membership of the CIS. The country refused to sign a number of CIS agreements on closer political, military and economic integration, and in September 2005 Niyazov confirmed that Turkmenistan intended to withdraw from full membership of the CIS, while remaining an associated member of the organization.

None the less, Turkmenistan's most important political ally and economic partner remains Russia. In December 1993 Turkmenistan became the first of the former Soviet republics to sign an agreement on dual citizenship with Russia, in the hope that this would help to stem the exodus of ethnic Russians from Turkmenistan. However, at a meeting in Moscow in April 2003, Niyazov and President Vladimir Putin of Russia agreed to rescind the agreement. In the same month Niyazov decreed that the estimated 95,000 dual passport holders in Turkmenistan should renounce either their Russian or Turkmenistani citizenship within two months, prompting protests from the Russian Ministry of Foreign Affairs, which insisted that the new agreement was not meant to apply with retroactive effect and, moreover, had not yet been ratified by Russia. Nevertheless, in August the Khalk Maslakhaty adopted constitutional amendments forbidding Turkmenistani citizens from holding dual citizenship, and placing any dual citizens remaining in the country in breach of the law.

Meanwhile, Turkmenistan's natural gas exports were a persistent cause of friction between Turkmenistan and Russia. The transport of natural gas from Turkmenistan was dependent on the use of the former Soviet pipeline system, which remained largely under Russian control. In 1993 Turkmenistan's access to European markets through this system was effectively curbed by Russia's decision to direct Turkmenistani gas exports to Ukraine and the South Caucasus. However, as a result of the recipient countries' delay in paying for their gas imports, Turkmenistan suspended all deliveries in 1993–95. Although gas exports to Ukraine and the South Caucasus were resumed in 1996, in the following year Niyazov announced the dissolution of the Turkmenistani-Russian company Turkmenrosgaz (which held a monopoly on the sale and export of Turkmenistani gas) because the company was in severe debt. In response, the Russian Government denied Turkmenistan access to the regional pipeline system. In subsequent years, delivery of natural gas supplies to both Russia and Ukraine has been interrupted on numerous occasions, as a result of disputes over tariffs and payments.

Following Niyazov's death in December 2006, in May 2007 President Berdymuhamedov met Presidents Putin of Russia and Nursultan Nazarbayev of Kazakhstan in Türkmenbaşi, where an agreement was reached to export Turkmenistani gas to Russia by way of Kazakhstan; Russia accepted a 40% price increase for imports of Turkmenistani gas over the following year. In April 2009 the Turkmenistani Government accused the Russian state-controlled natural gas monopoly Gazprom of having caused an explosion on a natural gas pipeline in Turkmenistan (thereby disrupting the country's exports), by unexpectedly reducing the flow of imported gas; Russian energy officials claimed that the blast had resulted from negligence on the part of the Turkmenistani authorities. Berdymuhamedov ordered that an investigation be conducted into the explosion, which had significantly strained relations between the two states, while Gazprom suspended gas imports from Turkmenistan. At an energy security conference, convened in Aşgabat later in April, Berdymuhamedov declared that Turkmenistan would seek to diversify the country's export partners for gas and that it intended to increase co-operation with the countries of Europe (thereby appearing to assert an energy policy independent of that of Russia). The dispute was resolved in December, when Russian President Dmitrii Medvedev and Berdymuhamedov, meeting in Aşgabat, signed a further agreement, under which Gazprom was to purchase reduced quantities of natural gas from Turkmenistan; the two heads of state also signed an accord intended to expand bilateral strategic energy co-operation. Exports of Turkmenistani gas to Russia resumed in January 2010.

Turkmenistan and Uzbekistan signed a treaty defining their common border in September 2000, and, under President Niyazov's orders, a 1,700-km fence was installed along the border in 2001. Bilateral relations deteriorated sharply in late 2002, following the alleged coup attempt in Turkmenistan on 25 November. In December the Uzbekistani embassy in Aşgabat was searched for evidence of complicity in the plot, and Uzbekistan's ambassador to Turkmenistan was subsequently declared *persona non grata*. The Uzbekistani authorities reacted with hostility, and troops from both countries were deployed along their common border. Stricter border controls were subsequently implemented. In November 2004 President Niyazov and President Islam Karimov of Uzbekistan met for their first presidential summit in more than four years in Buxoro, Uzbekistan, where they signed three bilateral agreements, pledging friendship between the two countries, mutual trust, and co-operation, agreeing the simplification of cross-border travel regulations for residents of border zones and establishing a framework for the sharing of regional water resources. The two Presidents subsequently declared that all bilateral disputes had been resolved. A new Uzbekistani ambassador to Turkmenistan was appointed in January 2005.

The legal status of the Caspian Sea, and the ownership of the extensive deposits of petroleum and natural gas beneath it, provoked controversy from the mid-1990s between all five of the littoral states (Turkmenistan, Azerbaijan, Iran, Kazakhstan and Russia). In early 1997 Turkmenistan and Azerbaijan became engaged in a dispute over the status of two Caspian oilfields (the Azeri and Çirağ fields—known as the Khazar and Kaverochkin fields in Turkmenistan), which were being developed by Azerbaijan and a consortium of international companies. The situation deteriorated in July, when Azerbaijan announced its intention to develop, in conjunction with a consortium of Russian companies, a third oilfield, which both countries laid claim to, known as Kyapaz to the Azeris and as Serdar to the Turkmen. Although Russia subsequently withdrew from the project, Azerbaijan refused to abandon its claim to the field. Apparently in response, in September Turkmenistan launched its first international tender for petroleum and gas exploration in the Caspian Sea, and announced that it expected Azerbaijan to compensate it for developing the Azeri and Çirağ fields. Although Kazakhstan and Russia signed an agreement in 2000 defining the legal status of the Caspian Sea, the remaining littoral states made limited progress. In January 2005 President Niyazov approved a proposal from a Canadian company, Buried Hill Energy and Petroleum, to develop the Serdar oilfield, prompting protests from Azerbaijan. In June 2008 President Berdymuhamedov and his Azerbaijani counterpart, meeting in St Petersburg, Russia, reached agreement on the reopening of the Turkmenistani embassy in the Azerbaijani capital, Baku (Bakı), which had been closed since 2001, and announced the establishment of an intergovernmental commission on bilateral co-operation. In July 2009 negotiations began between Turkmenistan and Azerbaijan, in an attempt to resolve ownership of energy resources in the Caspian Sea, but were rapidly abandoned, causing Berdymuhamedov to announce his intention to refer the dispute to an international arbitration court. In August Turkmenistani plans to establish a naval base at the Caspian Sea port of Türkmenbaşi prompted criticism from Azerbaijani officials. In September 2011 Russia reiterated its opposition to the proposed construction of a trans-Caspian pipeline, following the European Commission's declared support (see other external relations), maintaining that the agreement of all the littoral states was necessary for the project to proceed and citing environmental concerns. In November a working group of the five states, convening in Astana, Kazakhstan, made little progress towards reaching agreement on a draft of the Caspian Convention, a treaty that was to determine the division of the Caspian Sea. In December 2012 a summit meeting of CIS heads of state was convened in Aşgabat, when increased co-operation in measures to address drugs-trafficking, terrorism and organized crime was pledged.

Tensions over the disputed Serdar (Kyapaz) oilfield intensified in June 2012, when the Azerbaijani Government officially protested to Turkmenistan's ambassador in Baku at Turkmenistani exploration activities in the region; the Turkmenistani authorities responded by contending that Azerbaijani coastal guards had taken illegal action against a vessel that was conducting scientific research. In September Turkmenistan held its first naval exercises in the Caspian Sea. In April 2013 it was reported that Azerbaijan had appealed to Russia for military assistance, claiming that Turkmenistan's naval forces had fired on Azerbaijani offshore oil facilities. In the same month the Russian Minister of Foreign Affairs visited Aşgabat, where he discussed issues concerning the Caspian Sea with Berdymuhamedov.

Iran plays the most important role in Turkmenistan's foreign relations outside the CIS. In 1992 a number of agreements on closer political, economic and cultural integration were signed, including an accord to construct a railway line between Iran and Turkmenistan. The line, which linked the Turkmenistani city of Tejen with the northern Iranian city of Mashad, was opened in May 1996, thus affording Turkmenistan access both to the Persian (Arabian) Gulf and to İstanbul, Turkey. Turkmenistan and Iran also signed an agreement on the construction of a 140-km gas pipeline between the Korpeje natural gas deposit in south-western Turkmenistan and the city of Kord Kuy in northern Iran, as part of a network that would eventually transport Turkmenistani gas via Iran to Turkey and thence to Western Europe. The inauguration of the pipeline in December 1997 opened the first alternative export route for Turkmenistan's natural gas, and thus promised greater economic independence for the country from Russia. Following an agreement in July 2009, a second gas pipeline connecting Turkmenistan and Iran, which was to increase the volume of natural gas exports to Iran to 20,000m. cu m annually, entered into operation in January 2010.

In April 2006 Turkmenistan and the People's Republic of China signed an agreement to construct a natural gas pipeline between the two countries, by way of Uzbekistan and Kazakhstan; China was to purchase 30,000m. cu m of Turkmenistani gas each year for a period of 30 years from 2009. In August 2007 the Turkmenistani Government awarded China rights to develop gas reserves in eastern Turkmenistan in association with this project. Chinese President Hu Jintao made an official visit to Turkmenistan in August 2008, and in June 2009 the Turkmenistani and Chinese Governments signed an agreement increasing the amount of natural gas that China would purchase annually from Turkmenistan over a 30-year period to 40,000m. cu m. The new pipeline was officially inaugurated in December, at a ceremony attended by Berdymuhamedov, Hu Jintao, and the Presidents of Kazakhstan and Uzbekistan.

President Niyazov maintained the country's neutrality in the civil war in Afghanistan that followed the large-scale suicide attacks in the USA in September 2001 by the Islamist militant al-Qa'ida organization of Osama bin Laden. Niyazov refused US troops access to Turkmenistan's military bases, but gave his consent to the use of Turkmenistan's ground and air transport 'corridors' for the delivery of humanitarian aid to Afghanistan during US air-strikes. In December 2010 President Berdymuhamedov, President Hamid Karzai of Afghanistan, President Asif Ali Zardari of Pakistan and the Indian Minister of Petroleum and Natural Gas, Murli Deora, meeting in Aşgabat, signed a framework agreement on the construction of a pipeline, known as Tapi (Turkmenistan–Afghanistan–Pakistan–India), to carry Turkmenistani natural gas from Dauletabad in Turkmenistan to Fazilka, on the Pakistan–India border, via Afghanistan. Work on the US-supported project, which had been initially proposed in 1995, but had been delayed as a result of ongoing insecurity in Afghanistan and the border regions of Pakistan, was to be developed by the Asian Development Bank (ADB, see p. 214). A final agreement on the Tapi pipeline was signed in Avaza, Turkmenistan, in May 2012. US Assistant Secretary of State Robert Blake visited Turkmenistan in January 2013, when he discussed the impending withdrawal of US forces from Afghanistan, and commended the Turkmenistani Government's assistance in allowing the use of its airspace by transport planes.

Other external relations

In September 2007 President Berdymuhamedov, addressing the UN General Assembly, announced that he planned to develop co-operation with the international community in all areas of activity; he and other members of the Turkmenistani Government also met with US officials to discuss reforms and private investment. In February 2008 further discussions on energy co-operation were conducted during a visit to Aşgabat by a senior US official. In November 2010 the Government pledged to supply gas for the planned Nabucco Turkey–Austria pipeline project, supported by the European Union (EU, see p. 281), which was expected to commence operations in 2015. On 22 April 2009 the European Parliament approved the conclusion of an interim trade agreement with Turkmenistan, following delays owing to concern over the human rights situation in Turkmenistan, stating that this might be used to influence the authorities in strengthening the reform process. In September 2011 the EU Council mandated the European Commission to negotiate a treaty between the EU, Azerbaijan and Turkmenistan for the construction of a trans-Caspian pipeline, which would transport natural gas to Europe to supply the Nabucco pipeline. (A project to construct an underwater trans-Caspian gas pipeline to Turkey, via Azerbaijan and Georgia, had been suspended in 2000, owing to disagreements between Turkmenistan and Azerbaijan.) Negotiations continued in 2012 and it was announced that two framework agreements were being drafted on the project (which was strongly opposed by Russia and Iran). A meeting between Turkmenistani, Azerbaijani, Turkish and EU officials took place in Aşgabat in September, after which it was announced that Turkey would purchase gas from Turkmenistan. In February 2013 the Azerbaijani Government announced that preparation of the framework agreements was near completion.

CONSTITUTION AND GOVERNMENT

Under the terms of the 2008 Constitution, the President of the Republic is directly elected, by universal adult suffrage, for five years, for a maximum of two terms. The President is both head of state and head of government (Chairman of the Council of Ministers), holding executive power in conjunction with the Council of Ministers (which is appointed by the President), and is concurrently Supreme Commander of the Armed Forces. The supreme legislative body is the Majlis (Assembly), which is directly elected for a term of five years. Judicial power is exercised by the Supreme Court, the High Commercial Court, and military and other courts. Judges, who are independent, are appointed by the President for a term of five years. Turkmenistan is divided into five velayats (regions), which are subdivided into 50 etraps (districts) and 625 gengeşes (municipalities).

REGIONAL AND INTERNATIONAL CO-OPERATION

Turkmenistan is a member of the Non-aligned Movement (see p. 477), the European Bank for Reconstruction and Development (EBRD, see p. 276), the Economic Cooperation Organization (ECO, see p. 274) and the Organization of Islamic Cooperation (OIC, see p. 413). Turkmenistan is an associate member of the Commonwealth of Independent States (CIS, see p. 251).

Turkmenistan was admitted to the UN in 1992. In May 1994 Turkmenistan became the first Central Asian republic of the former USSR to join the 'Partnership for Peace' programme (see p. 383) of the North Atlantic Treaty Organization (NATO, see p. 380). The country's constitutional principle of 'permanent neutrality' was recognized by the UN General Assembly in December 1995.

ECONOMIC AFFAIRS

In 2011, according to estimates by the World Bank, Turkmenistan's gross national income (GNI), measured at average 2009–11 prices, was US $20,995m., equivalent to $4,110 per head (or $8,350 on an international purchasing-power parity basis). During 2002–11, it was estimated, the population increased at an average annual rate of 1.2%. Gross domestic product (GDP) per head increased, in real terms, by an average of 10.9% per year in 2002–11. Overall GDP increased, in real terms, at an average annual rate of 12.2% per year in 2002–11, according to the World Bank. GDP increased by 9.9% in 2011.

Agriculture contributed 14.5% of GDP in 2010, according to the Asian Development Bank (ADB, see p. 188). The sector employed 48.2% of the labour force in 2004 and, according to FAO, was forecast to employ an estimated 28.6% of the total economically active population at mid-2013. Although the Kara-Kum desert covers some 80% of the country's territory, widespread irrigation has enabled rapid agricultural development; however, over-intensive cultivation of the principal crop, cotton, together with massive irrigation projects, have led to serious ecological damage. In 1996 cotton contributed an estimated 11.5% of GDP, although the Government subsequently planned to reduce cotton production in favour of food production. Other important crops include grain, vegetables and fruit (in particular grapes and melons), although the country remains heavily dependent on imports of foodstuffs. Livestock husbandry (including the production of astrakhan and karakul wools) plays a central role in the sector, and silkworms are bred. According to the ADB, agricultural GDP increased, in real terms, at an average annual rate of 4.1% in 2002–10. Real agricultural GDP increased by 29.8% in 2010.

Industry (including mining, manufacturing, construction and power) contributed 48.4% of GDP in 2010, according to the ADB. In 2004 13.8% of the employed labour force were engaged in the sector. During 2002–10 industrial GDP increased, in real terms, at an average annual rate of 11.4%. Real industrial GDP increased by 5.8% in 2009, but decreased by 1.0% in 2010.

Turkmenistan is richly endowed with mineral resources, in particular natural gas and petroleum (recoverable reserves of which were estimated at some 24,318,552m. cu m and 600m. barrels, respectively, at the end of 2011). In 2011 Turkmenistan produced approximately 59,500m. cu m of gas and 10.7m. metric tons of petroleum. A new power installation, constructed at a cost of US $120m. in the town of Daşoguz, commenced production in December 2007; it was expected to generate more than 1,500m. kWh of electricity per year. In addition, Turkmenistan has large deposits of iodine, bromine, sodium sulphate, clay, gypsum and different types of salt.

The manufacturing sector contributed 46.6% of GDP in 2009, according to the World Bank. The principal branches of manufacturing are the processing of mineral resources (predominantly petroleum and natural gas) and textiles (mainly cotton products). Petroleum is refined at three refineries, at Türkmenbaşi, Seidi and Türkmenabat. According to the World Bank, manufacturing GDP increased by an annual average rate of 24.0% in 1998–2003. Sectoral growth was estimated at 25.6% in 2002 and 34.7% in 2003.

The construction sector contributed 8.1% of GDP in 2010, according to the ADB. Construction GDP increased by 9.6% in 2002–10. The sector grew by 4.9% in 2009, but declined by 0.7% in 2010.

In 2009 an estimated 15,980m. kWh of electricity was produced domestically; of electricity produced in 1994, some 20% was reported to have been exported, while a proportion of the remainder was distributed free of charge to domestic users. (Some charges for domestic electricity use were introduced in 1996, although free distribution was provided for in some subsequent annual budgets.) In 2003 mineral fuels accounted for just 0.7% of the value of merchandise imports, according to ADB estimates.

The services sector provided 37.0% of GDP in 2010, according to the ADB. The sector employed some 38.0% of the working population in 2004. Services GDP increased, in real terms, at an average annual rate of 10.1% in 2002–10. Real services GDP increased by 18.4% in 2010.

According to the ADB, in 2011 Turkmenistan recorded a trade surplus of US $1,400.0m., while there was deficit of $935.3m. on the current account of the balance of payments in 2010. In 2011 the principal source of imports (accounting for 21.1% of the total) was Turkey; other major suppliers were Russia, the People's Republic of China, the United Arab Emirates and Germany. The principal market for exports was the People's Republic of China (which took 58.4% of total exports). In 2003 the principal exports were basic manufactures. The principal imports in that year were machinery and transport equipment, basic manufactures, chemicals, miscellaneous manufactured articles, and food and live animals.

In 2010 Turkmenistan recorded an overall budgetary surplus of an estimated 1,167.0m. manats (equivalent to some 1.8% of GDP). Turkmenistan's general government gross debt was 5,826m. manats in 2011, equivalent to 7.3% of GDP. At the end of 2010 total external debt was US $422m., of which $359m. was public and publicly guaranteed debt. The annual average inflation rate declined from 1,748% in 1994 to 24.2% in 1999. According to the ADB, inflation averaged 6.6% per year in 2002–10. Consumer prices decreased by an annual average of 2.7% in 2009, but increased by 5.0% in 2010. In 2004 some 62,000 people were registered as unemployed (about 2.6% of the labour force); however, unofficial sources estimated the rate to be considerably higher.

In 2007 the country's new President, Gurbanguly Berdymuhamedov, indicated his intention to undertake significant economic reforms. In June 2008 restrictions on foreign exchange transactions were ended. Although a new Constitution protected private property rights and committed the country to the principles of the market economy, the Government, which maintained control over the financial system, was deemed to restrict foreign participation, and a lack of transparency continued to impede private sector development. A major natural gas pipeline linking Turkmenistan and the People's Republic of China entered into operation in December 2009, followed by the opening a second gas pipeline to Iran in January 2010. In May construction began on an East–West pipeline, which was to connect the fields of eastern Turkmenistan to the Caspian coast (and thereby facilitate Turkmenistan's access to European gas markets). In September 2011, moreover, the European Union (EU, see p. 281) began negotiations on a treaty between the EU, Azerbaijan and Turkmenistan for the construction of a trans-Caspian pipeline, which would transport gas to Europe to supply the planned Nabucco pipeline. An agreement on the construction of a pipeline to supply natural gas to Afghanistan, Pakistan and India was officially signed in May 2012. Particularly high GDP growth in 2011 was attributed to increasing gas exports to China and a rise in public investment. However, while Berdymuhamedov reaffirmed the necessity of attracting foreign and domestic investment, only the China National Petroleum Co had been granted a production-sharing agreement for onshore gas development. A new political party representing the interests of entrepreneurs was established in August 2012. In January 2013 Berdymuhamedov adopted a privatization programme for 2013–16, and established a government commission entasked with initiating membership negotiations with the World Trade Organization (WTO, see p. 444), although these plans were received with caution by international analysts. In March 2013 an international conference on Turkmenistan's potential accession to the WTO took place in the capital, Aşgabat. Also in March amendments to housing legislation as part of the pledged privatization reforms were announced, under which the purchase of state-owned homes was permitted from July.

PUBLIC HOLIDAYS

2014: 1 January (New Year's Day), 12 January (Memorial Day), 19 February (Flag Day), 8 March (International Women's Day), 21 March (Novrus Bairam, Spring Holiday), 9 May (Victory Day), 18 May (Constitution Day), 28 July* (Oraza Bairam—Id al-Fitr, end of Ramadan), 4 October* (Kurban Bairam—Id al-Adha, Feast of the Sacrifice), 6 October (Remembrance Day), 27 October (Independence Day), 12 December (Neutrality Day).

* These holidays are dependent on the Islamic calendar and may vary by one or two days from the dates given.

Statistical Survey

Principal sources (unless otherwise stated): IMF, *Turkmenistan, Economic Review, Turkmenistan—Recent Economic Developments* (December 1999); World Bank, *Statistical Handbook: States of the Former USSR.*

Area and Population

AREA, POPULATION AND DENSITY

Area (sq km)	488,100*
Population (census results)	
12 January 1989	3,533,925
10 January 1995	
Males	2,225,331
Females	2,257,920
Total	4,483,251
Population (UN estimates at mid-year)†	
2011	5,105,301
2012	5,169,657
2013	5,234,640
Density (per sq km) at mid-2013	10.7

* 188,456 sq miles.

† Source: UN, *World Population Prospects: The 2010 Revision*; these estimates are substantially lower than those produced by the state statistics institute (see below).

Population (official estimate): 6,800,200 at 1 April 2006 (Source: National Institute of State Statistics and Information).

POPULATION BY AGE AND SEX
(UN estimates at mid-2013)

	Males	Females	Total
0–14	755,107	733,558	1,488,665
15–64	1,733,386	1,799,766	3,533,152
65 and over	86,185	126,638	212,823
Total	2,574,678	2,659,962	5,234,640

Source: UN, *World Population Prospects: The 2010 Revision.*

POPULATION BY ETHNIC GROUP
(official estimates at 1 January 1993)

	Number	%
Turkmen	3,118,000	73.3
Russian	419,000	9.8
Uzbek	382,000	9.0
Kazakh	87,000	2.0
Others	248,000	5.8
Total	4,254,000	100.0

Ethnic groups (percentage of total, at census of 1995): Turkmen 77.0; Uzbek 9.2; Russian 6.7; Kazakh 2.0; Others 5.1 (Source: US embassy in Turkmenistan).

PRINCIPAL TOWNS
(estimated population at 1 January 1999)

Aşgabat (capital) .	605,000	Türkmenbaşı‡ . .	70,000
Türkmenabat* . .	203,000	Bayramaly . . .	60,000
Daşoguz . . .	165,000	Tejen	54,000
Mari	123,000	Serdar§ . . .	51,000
Balkanabat† . .	119,000		

* Formerly Charjew (Chardzhou).

† Formerly Nebit-Dag.

‡ Formerly Krasnovodsk.

§ Formerly Gyzylarbat (Kizyl-Arvat).

1 July 2002 (official estimate): Aşgabat 743,000.

Mid-2011 (incl. suburbs, UN estimate): Aşgabat 683,260 (Source: UN, *World Urbanization Prospects: The 2011 Revision*).

BIRTHS AND DEATHS
(annual averages, UN estimates)

	1995–2000	2000–05	2005–10
Birth rate (per 1,000)	24.5	23.3	22.0
Death rate (per 1,000)	7.8	7.7	7.7

Source: UN, *World Population Prospects: The 2010 Revision.*

Marriages (1998, provisional): 26,361 (marriage rate 5.4 per 1,000) (Source: UN, *Demographic Yearbook*).

2010: Birth rate 21.6 per 1,000; death rate 7.8 per 1,000 (Source: UN, *Statistical Yearbook for Asia and the Pacific*).

Life expectancy (years at birth): 65.0 (males 61.0; females 69.2) in 2011 (Source: World Bank, World Development Indicators database).

EMPLOYMENT
('000 persons at 31 December)

	1996	1997	1998*
Agriculture	769.8	778.8	890.5
Forestry	2.5	2.9	1.9
Industry†	172.0	188.1	226.8
Construction	136.2	122.8	108.2
Trade and catering . . .	91.8	101.2	115.8
Transport and communications .	77.7	77.9	90.7
Information-computing services .	1.3	1.0	1.2
Housing and municipal services .	50.2	46.8	48.3
Health care and social security .	97.4	100.4	89.2
Education, culture and arts . .	183.8	185.9	190.5
Science, research and development	9.2	6.9	5.2
General administration . . .	24.7	25.3	28.8
Finance and insurance . . .	8.7	9.6	12.6
Other activities	41.5	28.3	29.0
Total	1,666.8	1,675.9	1,838.7

* Provisional.

† Comprising manufacturing (except printing and publishing), mining and quarrying, electricity, gas, water, logging, and fishing.

2004 ('000 persons at 31 December, estimates): Employed 2,110 (Agriculture 1,017, Industry 291, Other 802); Unemployed 62; Total labour force (incl. those not registered) 2,389 (Source: Asian Development Bank, *Key Indicators of Developing Asian and Pacific Countries*).

Mid-2013 ('000 persons, estimates): Agriculture, etc. 728; Total (incl. others) 2,542 (Source: FAO).

Health and Welfare

KEY INDICATORS

Total fertility rate (children per woman, 2010)	2.4
Under-5 mortality rate (per 1,000 live births, 2010)	56
HIV/AIDS (% of persons aged 15–49, 2007)	<0.1
Physicians (per 1,000 head, 2009)	2.4
Hospital beds (per 1,000 head, 2009)	4.0
Health expenditure (2009): US $ per head (PPP) . . .	181
Health expenditure (2009): % of GDP	2.5
Health expenditure (2009): public (% of total)	59.2
Access to water (% of persons, 2004)	71
Access to sanitation (% of persons, 2010)	98
Total carbon dioxide emissions ('000 metric tons, 2008) . .	47,839.7
Carbon dioxide emissions per head (metric tons, 2008) . .	9.7
Human Development Index (2011): ranking	102
Human Development Index (2011): value	0.686

For sources and definitions, see explanatory note on p. vi.

Agriculture

PRINCIPAL CROPS
('000 metric tons)

	2009	2010	2011
Wheat*	2,900	3,000	3,273
Rice, paddy*	110	145	145
Barley*	63	73	97
Potatoes	247	245*	274*
Sugar beet*	234	234	234
Seed cotton	667†	1,000†	950*
Cabbages and other brassicas	68†	68†	75*
Tomatoes	327†	325*	354*
Onions, dry	112†	123*	122*
Carrots and turnips	70†	76*	75*
Watermelons	281	329*	450*
Grapes*	230	242	235
Apples	64†	70*	77*

* FAO estimate(s).
† Unofficial figure.

Aggregate production ('000 metric tons, may include official, semi-official or estimated data): Total cereals 3,090 in 2009, 3,235 in 2010, 3,531 in 2011; Total roots and tubers 247 in 2009, 245 in 2010, 274 in 2011; Total vegetables (incl. melons) 937 in 2009, 1,001 in 2010, 1,161 in 2011; Total fruits (excl. melons) 390 in 2009, 405 in 2010, 413 in 2011.

Source: FAO.

LIVESTOCK
('000 head at 1 January)

	2009	2010*	2011*
Horses	25	25	26
Asses	25*	25	25
Camels	122	120	120
Cattle	2,154	2,200	2,200
Pigs	30*	30	30
Sheep	13,513	13,600	13,650
Goats	2,848	2,800	2,750
Chickens	14,570†	15,000	15,500
Turkeys	500†	500	500

* FAO estimate(s).
† Unofficial figure.

Source: FAO.

LIVESTOCK PRODUCTS
('000 metric tons)

	2009	2010*	2011*
Cattle meat	140†	148	140
Sheep meat	128†	130	130
Goat meat	10†	10	10
Chicken meat	20†	20	20
Cows' milk	2,146	2,150	2,150
Hen eggs	50†	50	50
Honey	1*	1	1
Wool, greasy	38	38	38

* FAO estimate(s).
† Unofficial figure.

Source: FAO.

Fishing

(metric tons, live weight)

	2003	2004	2005*
Capture	14,543	14,992	15,000
Azov sea sprat	14,276	14,674	14,680
Aquaculture	24	16	16
Total catch	14,567	15,008	15,016

* FAO estimates.

2006–10: Catch assumed to be unchanged from 2005 (FAO estimates).

Source: FAO.

Mining

('000 metric tons unless otherwise indicated)

	2008	2009	2010
Crude petroleum*	10,300	10,400	10,700
Natural gas (million cu m)*	66,100	36,400	42,400
Bentonite†	50	50	50
Salt (unrefined)†	215	215	215
Gypsum (crude)†	100	100	100

* Source: BP, *Statistical Review of World Energy*.
† Estimates from US Geological Survey.

2011 ('000 metric tons unless otherwise indicated): Crude petroleum 10,700; Natural gas (million cu m) 59,500 (Source: BP, *Statistical Review of World Energy*).

Industry

SELECTED PRODUCTS
('000 metric tons unless otherwise indicated)

	2000	2001	2002
Cottonseed oil	48	45	26
Wheat flour	544	561	537
Woven cotton fabrics (million sq m)	34	61	78
Woven silk fabrics ('000 sq m)	216	115	283
Blankets	14	7	10
Knotted wool carpets and rugs ('000 sq m)	1,040	1,434	1,475
Footwear, excl. rubber ('000 pairs)	478	444	253
Nitric acid (100%)	192	151	212
Ammonia (nitrogen content)	117	99	130
Nitrogenous fertilizers (a)*	89	72	103
Phosphate fertilizers (b)*†	11	11	17
Soap	3.0	2.5	1.6
Motor spirit (petrol)	1,132	1,283	1,154
Gas-diesel (distillate fuel) oil	2,247	2,547	2,290
Residual fuel oils	1,536	1,586	1,591
Clay building bricks (million)	309	269	279
Quicklime	17	17	15
Cement	420	448	486
Electric energy (million kWh)	9,845	10,610	10,700

* Production in terms of (a) nitrogen or (b) phosphoric acid.
† Official figures.

2003 ('000 metric tons, unless otherwise indicated, estimates): Wheat flour 503; Nitrogenous fertilizers 96. (Source: Asian Development Bank, *Key Indicators of Developing Asian and Pacific Countries*.).

Electric energy (million kWh): 14,880 in 2007; 15,040 in 2008; 15,980 in 2009.

Motor spirit (petrol) ('000 metric tons): 1,414 in 2007; 1,549 in 2008; 1,414 in 2009.

Residual fuel oils ('000 metric tons): 1,951 in 2007; 2,137 in 2008; 1,951 in 2009.

Gas-diesel (distillate fuel) oil ('000 metric tons): 2,809 in 2007; 3,077 in 2008; 2,809 in 2009.

Cottonseed oil ('000 metric tons): 51 in 2006; 61 in 2007; 63 in 2008.

Source: mainly UN Industrial Commodity Statistics Database.

Cement ('000 metric tons, estimates): 1,025 in 2008; 1,100 in 2009; 1,140,000 in 2010. (Source: US Geological Survey.).

Finance

CURRENCY AND EXCHANGE RATES

Monetary Units
100 tenge = 1 Turkmenistani manat.

Sterling, Dollar and Euro Equivalents (30 November 2012)
£1 sterling = 4.576 new manats;
US $1 = 2.850 new manats;
€1 = 3.701 new manats;
100 new manats = £21.85 = $35.09 = €27.02.

Note: The Turkmenistani manat was introduced on 1 November 1993, replacing the Russian (formerly Soviet) rouble at a rate of 1 manat = 500 roubles. Following the introduction of the Turkmenistani manat, a multiple exchange rate system was established. The foregoing information refers to the official rate of exchange. This rate was maintained at US $1 = 4,165 manats between May 1997 and April 1998. It was adjusted to $1 = 5,200 manats in April 1998. In addition to the official rate, there was a commercial bank rate of exchange until this market was closed in December 1998. There was also a 'parallel' market rate, which averaged $1 = 6,493 manats in 1998 and reached $1 = 14,200 manats at mid-1999. In January 2008 foreign exchange bureaux (the operations of which had been suspended in 1998) re-opened and two exchange rates were fixed: the state exchange rate of $1 = 6,250 manats and the commercial rate of $1 = 19,800 manats for the general population, thereby virtually eradicating the unofficial market. In May of that year a unified 'floating' exchange rate of $1 = 14,250 manats was introduced. A new manat, equivalent to 5,000 of the former currency, was introduced on 1 January 2009, whereupon the unified exchange rate became $1 = 2.85 new manats.

BUDGET
('000 million manats)

Revenue*	1997	1998	1999†
State budget	2,067.3	1,867.5	2,382.3
Personal income tax	108.3	157.4	224.9
Profit tax	579.6	412.0	422.0
Value-added tax	797.9	714.9	946.3
Natural resources tax	231.2	43.1	201.1
Excise tax	92.4	221.3	377.8
Other receipts*	257.9	318.8	210.1
Pension and Social Security Fund	471.0	711.0	832.5
Medical Insurance Fund	32.7	8.2	0.0
Repayments on rescheduled gas debt	246.6	474.1	478.3
Total	2,817.6	3,060.8	3,693.1

Expenditure	1997	1998	1999†
National economy	843.9	461.1	623.3
Agriculture	632.5	331.4	223.2
Transport and communications	121.1	63.4	190.0
Other	90.3	66.3	210.1
Socio-cultural services‡	975.7	1,850.0	1,907.9
Education	435.3	919.2	1,048.7
Health	443.1	493.8	550.6
Communal services	9.1	337.9	188.6
Culture, recreation and other purposes	88.2	99.1	120.0
Defence§	440.2	435.8	582.0
Pension and Social Security Fund	387.8	511.5	605.9
Interest payments	72.1	11.1	18.0
Public administration and other purposes	94.3	153.4	157.2
Total	2,814.0	3,422.8	3,894.3

* Including grants received and road fund revenues.
† Approved budget.
‡ Excluding expenditure of the Pension and Social Security Fund.
§ Variable coverage, owing to changes in classification.

2008 (million new manats): Revenue 9,129.7; Expenditure 4,761.4 (Source: Asian Development Bank).

2009 (million new manats): Revenue 10,931.7; Expenditure 7,172.4 (Source: Asian Development Bank).

2010 (million new manats): Revenue 9,442.1; Expenditure 8,275.1 (Source: Asian Development Bank).

INTERNATIONAL RESERVES
(US $ million at 31 December)

	2005	2006	2007
Total	4,457.0	8,059.2	13,221.5

Source: Asian Development Bank.

MONEY SUPPLY
('000 million manats at 31 December)

	1996	1997	1998
Currency in circulation	270.2	407.7	1,040.2
Demand deposits at banks	130.0	423.4	259.8

Total money ('000 million manats at 31 December): 2,552 in 1999; 4,965 in 2000; 5,792 in 2001; 5,877 in 2002; 7,840 in 2003; 8,906 in 2004; 9,405 in 2005; 10,411 in 2006; 20,448 in 2007; 18,894 in 2008; 26,477 in 2009 (Source: Asian Development Bank).

COST OF LIVING
(Consumer Price Index; base: 2000 = 100)

	2008	2009	2010
All items	198.0	192.6	202.2

Source: Asian Development Bank.

NATIONAL ACCOUNTS
(million new manats at current prices)

Expenditure on the Gross Domestic Product

	2008	2009	2010
Government final consumption expenditure	3,619.7	5,642.0	5,990.4
Private final consumption expenditure	22,446.3	27,804.8	29,966.0
Changes in inventories	5,901.2	6,491.3	9,471.4
Gross fixed capital formation			
Total domestic expenditure	31,967.2	39,938.1	45,427.8
Exports of goods and services	31,689.6	42,975.2	49,118.2
Less Imports of goods and services	19,973.8	26,063.3	28,625.0
GDP in purchasers' values	43,683.0	56,850.0	65,920.9

Gross Domestic Product by Economic Activity

	2008	2009	2010
Agriculture	5,288.3	6,861.3	9,455.3
Mining and quarrying	19,203.3	24,954.5	26,208.0
Manufacturing			
Electricity, gas and water			
Construction	3,887.7	5,004.5	5,273.3
Trade, hotels and restaurants	1,719.5	2,248.1	2,829.9
Transport and communications	2,635.0	3,434.5	4,318.1
Finance	10,286.3	13,452.3	16,905.5
Public administration			
Other activities			
Sub-total	43,020.2	55,955.2	64,990.0
Taxes, less subsidies, on products	662.8	894.8	930.9
GDP in purchasers' values	43,683.0	56,850.0	65,920.9

Note: Deduction for financial intermediation services indirectly measured and adjustment for indirect taxes assumed to be distributed at origin.

Source: Asian Development Bank.

BALANCE OF PAYMENTS
(US $ million)

	1996	1997	1998
Exports of goods f.o.b.	1,692.0	774.0	614.1
Imports of goods f.o.b.	−1,388.3	−1,005.0	−1,137.1
Trade balance	303.7	−230.9	−523.0
Services (net)	−323.4	−402.5	−471.0
Balance on goods and services	−19.7	−633.5	−994.0
Other income (net)	16.7	84.8	32.6
Balance on goods, services and income	−3.0	−548.7	−961.4
Current transfers (net) . . .	4.8	−31.2	26.9
Current account	1.8	−579.9	−934.5
Direct investment	108.1	102.4	64.1
Trade credit (net)	60.8	−266.5	56.5
Other (net)	−211.6	1,035.9	749.7
Net errors and omissions . .	46.4	−71.4	33.9
Overall balance	5.4	220.6	−30.3

Current balance (US $ million): 3,553.0 in 2008; −2,978.5 in 2009; −935.3 in 2010 (Source: Asian Development Bank).

External Trade

PRINCIPAL COMMODITIES
(US $ million)

Imports c.i.f.	2001	2002	2003
Food and live animals	129.4	114.3	130.3
Beverages and tobacco . . .	56.8	70.1	67.4
Mineral fuels, lubricants, etc. .	39.1	25.7	17.7
Chemicals	178.6	210.8	271.2
Basic manufactures . . .	448.7	394.2	487.7
Machinery and transport equipment . . .	1,204.7	857.6	1,125.6
Miscellaneous manufactured articles . . .	128.1	112.7	165.2
Total (incl. others)	2,348.8	2,119.4	2,450.0*

Exports f.o.b.	2001	2002	2003
Food and live animals	4.7	3.4	2.9
Beverages and tobacco . . .	—	0.6	0.3
Mineral fuels, lubricants, etc. .	123.7	83.8	152.4
Chemicals	7.0	28.4	55.0
Basic manufactures . . .	141.6	150.6	169.6
Machinery and transport equipment	14.5	17.1	16.9
Miscellaneous manufactured articles	52.8	74.1	80.8
Total (incl. others)	2,620.2	2,855.6	3,320.0*

* Estimate.

2009 (US $ million): Total imports 6,473.0; Total exports 3,136.4.

2010 (US $ million): Total imports 5,603.9; Total exports 3,368.0.

2011 (US $ million): Total imports 7,780.7; Total exports 7,237.4.

Source: Asian Development Bank.

PRINCIPAL TRADING PARTNERS
(US $ million)

Imports	2009	2010	2011
China, People's Republic . . .	1,007.5	574.3	864.3
France	271.5	183.0	134.9
Germany	393.2	362.3	450.9
Iran	179.1	234.7	302.7
Russia	1,031.3	791.1	1,093.6
Turkey	1,039.6	1,253.8	1,643.4
Ukraine	357.7	229.8	224.8
United Arab Emirates . . .	366.4	479.9	619.1
USA	341.1	43.9	77.9
Uzbekistan	105.5	134.0	150.1
Total (incl. others)	6,473.0	5,603.9	7,780.7

Exports	2009	2010	2011
Afghanistan	169.6	215.3	241.2
China, People's Republic . . .	35.0	949.5	4,266.5
Hungary	197.8	0.1	0.1
Iran	335.0	159.5	205.7
Italy	56.0	177.9	335.3
Kazakhstan	114.6	150.1	193.7
Poland	180.3	3.5	0.9
Turkey	297.8	351.2	357.0
Ukraine	653.0	28.6	147.6
United Arab Emirates . . .	182.9	239.6	309.1
Total (incl. others) . . .	3,136.4	3,368.0	7,237.4

Note: Data reflect the IMF's direction of trade methodology, and, as a result, the totals may not be equal to those presented for trade in commodities.

Source: Asian Development Bank.

Transport

RAILWAYS
(traffic)

	1996	1997	1999*
Passenger journeys (million) . .	7.8	6.4	3.1
Passenger-km (million) . . .	2,104	958	701
Freight transported (million metric tons)	15.9	18.5	17.2
Freight ton-km (million) . . .	6,779	7,445	7,337

* Data for 1998 were not available.

Source: *Railway Directory*.

SHIPPING

Flag Registered Fleet
(at 31 December)

	2010	2011	2012
Number of vessels . . .	50	57	68
Total displacement ('000 grt) . .	72.0	86.2	111.9

Source: Lloyd's List Intelligence (www.lloydslistintelligence.com).

CIVIL AVIATION
(estimated traffic on scheduled services)

	2007	2008	2009
Kilometres flown (million) . . .	18	18	18
Passengers carried ('000) . .	1,851	1,823	1,706
Passenger-km (million) . . .	2,134	2,104	1,955
Total ton-km (million) . . .	204	200	186

Source: UN, *Statistical Yearbook*.

Passengers carried ('000): 399.5 in 2010 (Source: World Bank, World Development Indicators database).

Tourism

FOREIGN VISITOR ARRIVALS*

Country of nationality	2005	2006	2007
France	683	398	682
Germany	1,028	870	1,338
Iran	7,173	1,478	2,133
Japan	428	523	537
Netherlands	453	328	402
Russia	13	6	80
USA	332	441	566
Total (incl. others)	11,611	5,620	8,177

* Arrivals of non-resident tourists at national borders.

Tourism receipts (US $ million): 66 in 1996; 74 in 1997; 192 in 1998.

Source: World Tourism Organization.

Communications Media

	2009	2010	2011
Telephones ('000 main lines in use)	494.3	520.0	547.0
Mobile cellular telephones ('000 subscribers)	2,132.9	3,197.6	3,511.0
Internet users ('000)	80.4	n.a.	n.a.
Broadband subscribers ('000)	0.5	0.7	1.1

Source: International Telecommunication Union.

Education

1990/91: 76,000 students at higher schools (Source: UNESCO, *Statistical Yearbook*).

Institutions (2005): Secondary schools 1,704; Secondary specialized schools 15; Higher schools (incl. universities) 16 (Source: Permanent Mission of Turkmenistan to the United Nations).

Students enrolled at universities (2003): 14,859 (Source: UNICEF).

Adult literacy rate (UNESCO estimates): 99.6% (males 99.7%; females 99.5%) in 2010 (Source: UNESCO Institute for Statistics).

Directory

The Government

HEAD OF STATE

President of the Republic: GURBANGULY BERDYMUHAMEDOV (elected 11 February 2007; inaugurated 14 February 2007; re-elected 12 February 2012; inaugurated 17 February 2012).

COUNCIL OF MINISTERS
(May 2013)

Chairman of the Government: GURBANGULY BERDYMUHAMEDOV.

Deputy Chairman, Chief of the Government and Presidential Staff: HOJAMUHAMMED MUJAMMEDOV.

Deputy Chairman and Minister of Foreign Affairs: RASHID MEREDOV.

Deputy Chairman, responsible for Culture: BYAGUL NURMURADOVA.

Deputy Chairman, responsible for Economic Affairs: ANNAMUHAMMET GOCHIYEV.

Deputy Chairman, responsible for the Oil and Gas Sector and Fisheries: BAYMYRAT HOJAMUHAMMEDOV.

Deputy Chairman, responsible for Transport and Communications: AKMYRAT YEGELEYEV.

Deputy Chairman, responsible for the Construction Sector: SHAMUHAMMET DURDYLYEV.

Deputy Chairman: ANNAGELDY YAZMYRADOV.

Deputy Chairman: YAGSHYGELDY KAKAYEV.

Minister of Agriculture: REJEP BAZAROV.

Minister of Communications: BAYRAMGELDY OVEZOV.

Minister of Construction: JUMAGELDY BAYRAMOV.

Minister of Culture: GUNCHA MAMMEDOVA.

Minister of Defence: BEGENCH GUNDOGDYYEV.

Minister of the Economy and Development: BABAMYRAT TAGANOV.

Minister of Education: GULSHAT MAMMEDOVA.

Minister of Energy: MYRAT ARTYKOV.

Minister of Environmental Protection: BABAGELDY ANNABAYRAMOV.

Minister of Health and the Medical Industry: GURBANMAMMET ELYASOV.

Minister of Industry: BABANIYAZ ITALMAZOV.

Minister of Internal Affairs: ISKANDER MULIKOV.

Minister of Justice: MYRAT KARRYYEV.

Minister of Labour and Social Welfare: BEKMYRAT SHAMYRADOV.

Minister of National Security: YILYM BERDYYEV.

Minister of the Petroleum and Gas Industry and Mineral Resources: MUHAMMETNUR HALYLOV.

Minister of Public Utilities: SATLYKA SATLYKOVA.

Minister of Railways: BAYRAM ANNAMEREDOV.

Minister of Road Transport: MELE GURBANDURDYEV.

Minister of the Textile Industry: SAPARMYRAT BATYROV.

Minister of Trade and Foreign Economic Relations: BAYAR ABAYEV.

Minister of Water Resources: SEYITMYRAT TAGANOV.

Note: The following positions also form part of the Council of Ministers: the Prosecutor-General; the Chairmen of three state concerns, Türkmennebit/Turkmenneft (Turkmen Oil), Türkmengaz/Turkmengaz (Turkmen Gas) and Türkmennebitgazgurlushyk/Turkmenneftegazstroi (Turkmen Oil and Gas Construction), and of the state joint-stock corporation Türkmenhaky/Turkmenkover (Turkmen Carpets); the Chairmen of the Board of the Central Bank of Turkmenistan and of Türkmenvnesheconombank (State Bank for Foreign Economic Affairs of Turkmenistan); and the Chairman of the following bodies: the Supreme Court; the Supreme Economic Court; the State Borders Service; the State Customs Service; and the National Committee for Hydrometeorology at the Council of Ministers.

MINISTRIES

Office of the President and the Council of Ministers: 744004 Aşgabat, Galkynyş köç. 20; tel. (12) 35-45-34; fax (12) 35-51-12; e-mail nt@online.tm; internet www.turkmenistan.gov.tm.

Ministry of Agriculture: 744000 Aşgabat, Azad köç. 63; tel. (12) 35-66-91; fax (12) 35-01-18; e-mail minselhoz@online.tm.

Ministry of Communications: 744000 Aşgabat, Bitarap Türkmenistan köç. 40; tel. (12) 35-21-52; fax (12) 39-04-20; e-mail mincom@telecom.tm.

Ministry of Construction: 744000 Aşgabat, Navoi köç. 56; tel. (12) 35-60-60; fax (12) 39-35-90; e-mail mpsmt@online.tm; internet www.construction.gov.tm.

Ministry of Culture: 744000 Aşgabat, Puşkin köç. 14; tel. (12) 35-41-05; fax (12) 35-35-00.

Ministry of Defence: 744000 Aşgabat, Galkynyş köç. 4; tel. (12) 40-27-64; fax (12) 39-37-39.

Ministry of the Economy and Development: 744000 Aşgabat, 2008 köç. 4/1; tel. (12) 51-11-34; fax (12) 35-09-39; e-mail minekonom@online.tm; internet www.mineconom.gov.tm.

Ministry of Education: 744000 Aşgabat, Gerogly köç. 2; tel. (12) 35-58-03; fax (12) 39-88-11.

Ministry of Energy: 744000 Aşgabat, N. Pomma köç. 6; tel. (12) 37-94-59; fax (12) 39-61-20; e-mail kuwwat@online.tm; internet www.test.tm-style.com.

Ministry of Environmental Protection: 744036 Aşgabat, Arçabil Şaýoly 92; tel. (12) 44-80-02; fax (12) 44-80-29; e-mail mail@natureprotection.gov.tm; internet www.natureprotection.gov.tm.

Ministry of Foreign Affairs: 744000 Aşgabat, Arçabil Şaýoly 108; tel. (12) 44-56-94; fax (12) 21-86-75; e-mail fmatm@online.tm.

Ministry of Health and the Medical Industry: 744000 Aşgabat, Magtymguly Şaýoly 90; tel. (12) 35-10-63; fax (12) 35-50-32; e-mail healthtm@online.tm.

Ministry of Industry: Aşgabat.

Ministry of Internal Affairs: 744000 Aşgabat, Magtymguly Şaýoly 85; tel. (12) 35-13-28; fax (12) 39-19-44.

Ministry of Justice: 744000 Aşgabat, Navoi köç. 86; tel. (12) 38-08-91; fax (12) 39-44-10.

Ministry of Labour and Social Welfare: 744000 Aşgabat, Magtymguly Şaýoly 91; tel. (12) 39-71-58; fax (12) 51-07-55.

Ministry of National Security: 744000 Aşgabat, Magtymguly Şaýoly 93; tel. (12) 39-71-58.

Ministry of the Petroleum and Gas Industry and Mineral Resources: 744000 Aşgabat, Arçabil Saýoly 56; tel. (12) 40-30-01; fax (12) 40-30-44; e-mail ministryoilgas@online.tm; internet www.oilgas.gov.tm.

Ministry of Public Utilities: 744000 Aşgabat.

Ministry of Railways: 744000 Aşgabat, S. Türkmenbaşi köç. 7; tel. (12) 39-43-34; fax (12) 39-28-74; e-mail tde@online.tm.

Ministry of Road Transport: 744000 Aşgabat, B. Annanov köç. 2; tel. (12) 35-05-36; fax (12) 51-11-03; e-mail tcentr@online.tm.

Ministry of the Textile Industry: 744000 Aşgabat, Garaşyslyk Şaýoly 96; tel. (12) 21-03-03; fax (12) 21-09-06; e-mail tmtextile@mail.ru.

Ministry of Trade and Foreign Economic Relations: 744000 Aşgabat, Gerogly köç. 44; tel. (12) 35-10-47; fax (12) 35-34-91; e-mail mtfer@online.tm.

Ministry of Water Resources: 744000 Aşgabat, S. Niyazov Şaýoly 142; tel. (12) 39-06-15; fax (12) 39-85-39; e-mail sarmos@online.tm.

President

Presidential Election, 12 February 2012

Candidate	%
Gurbanguly Berdymuhamedov	97.14
Annageldy Yazmyradov	1.07
Yarmuhammed Orazgulyyev	1.02
Others	0.77
Total	100.00

Legislature

Majlis
(Assembly)

744000 Aşgabat, Garaşyslyk Şaýoly 110; tel. (12) 35-31-25; fax (12) 35-31-47.

Chairman: AKJA NURBERDIYEVA.

The Majlis is directly elected for a term of five years. Elections to an expanded 125-member Majlis were conducted on 14 December 2008, with a second round of voting following in one district on 28 December. It was reported that about 90% of the elected deputies were members of the ruling Democratic Party of Turkmenistan, while the remainder were independent candidates endorsed by the party. Following the resignation of a deputy, a poll was repeated in one district on 8 February 2009.

Election Commission

Central Commission for Elections and Referendums: Aşgabat; comprises a chairman, two vice-chairmen, a secretary and 12 mems, all appointed by the President of the Republic; Chair. ORAZMYRAT NYYAZLYEV; Sec. JEREN TAIMOVA.

Political Organizations

Democratic Party of Turkmenistan: 744014 Aşgabat, Gerogly köç. 28; tel. (12) 25-12-12; name changed from Communist Party of Turkmenistan in 1991; Chair. GURBANGULY BERDYMUHAMEDOV; Sec. ONJIK MUSAYEV.

Party of Industrialists and Entrepreneurs: Aşgabat; tel. (12) 22-74-12; f. 2012; Leader ORAZMAMMED MAMMADOV.

Unity (Agzybirlik): 744000 Aşgabat; e-mail agzybirlik@hotmail.com; internet www.agzybirlik.com; f. 1989; unregistered popular front organization; Leader NURBERDI NURMÄMMET.

Turkmenistan has effectively functioned as a one-party state, with the **Democratic Party of Turkmenistan** (led by the President of the Republic) dominant in all areas of government. However, in January 2012 legislation on the creation of a second political party was adopted; and the **Party of Industrialists and Entrepreneurs** was duly registered in August of that year; the party was largely to be dependent on state funding. The President of the Republic is also the leader of the **Galkynyş National Revival Movement of Turkmenistan**. There are, however, several unregistered opposition groups, such as **Unity (Agzybirlik)** .

Other opposition elements are based in other republics of the Commonwealth of Independent States, in particular Russia. A leading opposition figure in exile is a former Minister of Foreign Affairs, ABDY KULIYEV, whose **United Democratic Opposition of Turkmenistan (ODOT)** is based in Moscow, Russia, while the **Movement for Democratic Reform**, founded in 1996, is based in Sweden. The **Fatherland (Watan) Social Political Movement** is also based in Sweden (e-mail info@watan.ru; internet watan.ru) and comprises Turkmen and other Central Asian oppositionists. In January 2002 a former Minister of Foreign Affairs, BORIS SHIKHMURADOV, established the opposition **People's Democratic Movement of Turkmenistan** (PDMT; internet gundogar.org); however, he was imprisoned in December, having been convicted of orchestrating the attempted assassination of President Saparmyrat Niyazov in November. Another opposition leader accused of conspiring with Shikhmuradov was NURMUKHAMMET HANAMOV, founder of the **Republican Party of Turkmenistan** (RPT; internet tmrepublican.org; Co-Chair. NURMUKHAMMET HANAMOV, SAPAR YKLYMOV).

Opposition leaders met in Prague, Czech Republic, in September 2003 and announced the formation of the **Union of Democratic Forces of Turkmenistan (UDFT)**, comprising four main groups: the RPT; Fatherland; the ODOT; and the **Revival Social Political Movement**.

Diplomatic Representation

EMBASSIES IN TURKMENISTAN

Afghanistan: 744000 Aşgabat, Gerogly köç. 14; tel. (12) 39-58-21; fax (12) 39-58-20; e-mail eira.tm@gmail.com; Ambassador Dr MOHAMMAD FASEL SAIFI.

Armenia: 744000 Aşgabat, Gerogly köç. 14; tel. (12) 35-44-18; fax (12) 33-14-19; e-mail eat@online.tm; Ambassador VLADIMIR BADALIAN.

Azerbaijan: 744020 Aşgabat, Ata Govshudov köç. 112; tel. (12) 39-11-02; fax (12) 35-56-25; e-mail azsefir_ashg@online.tm; internet www.azembassyashg.com; Ambassador VAHDET SULTANZADE.

Belarus: 744000 Aşgabat, Gorky köç. 51; tel. (12) 97-11-83; fax (12) 97-11-85; e-mail turkmenistan@mfa.gov.by; internet www.turkmenistan.mfa.gov.by; Ambassador ENVER BARIYEV.

China, People's Republic: 744036 Aşgabat, Arçabil köç. 45; tel. (12) 48-81-05; fax (12) 21-06-70; e-mail chinaemb_tkm@mfa.gov.cn; internet tm.china-embassy.org; Ambassador XIAO QINGHUA.

France: 744000 Aşgabat, Esgerler köç. 35; tel. (12) 36-34-68; fax (12) 36-35-46; e-mail cad.achgabat-amba@diplomatie.gouv.fr; internet www.ambafrance-achgabat.org; Ambassador PIERRE LEBOVICS.

Georgia: 744000 Aşgabat, Azad köç. 139A; tel. (12) 97-08-28; fax (12) 97-02-48; e-mail ashgabat.emb@mfa.gov.ge; internet www.turkmenistan.mfa.gov.ge; Ambassador IOSEB CHAKHVASHVILI.

Germany: 744000 Aşgabat, Hydyr Derzhazhev köç., Hotel 'Ak Altin'; tel. (12) 36-35-15; fax (12) 36-35-22; e-mail info@aschgabat.diplo.de; Ambassador HELMUT-WOLFGANG BRETT.

India: 744000 Aşgabat, Yu. Emre köç. 2/1, Imperial International Business Centre; tel. (12) 45-24-25; fax (12) 45-61-56; e-mail indembhoc@online.tm; internet www.indianembassy-tm.org; Ambassador SUNIL JAIN.

Iran: 744000 Aşgabat, 2072 köç. 3; tel. (12) 34-93-61; fax (12) 35-05-65; Ambassador MOHAMMAD-MOUSA HASHEMI GOLPAYEGANI.

Israel: Aşgabat; Ambassador (vacant).

Japan: 744017 Aşgabat, 1945 köç. 60, Paytagt Trading Centre; tel. (12) 47-70-82; fax (12) 47-70-83; e-mail jp-embassy@ah.mofa.go.jp; internet www.tm.emb-japan.go.jp; Ambassador HARADA TIKAHITO.

Kazakhstan: 744036 Aşgabat, Garaşyslyk köç. 11/13; tel. (12) 48-04-68; fax (12) 48-04-75; e-mail office@embkaztm.org; Ambassador ORMAN NURBAYEV.

Korea, Democratic People's Republic: 744000 Aşgabat; Ambassador KIM YON CHJE.

Korea, Republic: 744005 Aşgabat, Azad köç. 17A; tel. (12) 94-72-86; fax (12) 94-72-89; e-mail korembtm@mofat.go.kr; internet tkm.mofat.go.kr; Ambassador AHN MYUNG-SOO.

Kyrgyzstan: 744000 Aşgabat, Gerogly köç. 85; tel. (12) 48-22-95; fax (12) 48-22-94; e-mail kg@online.tm; Ambassador BAZARBAY MAMBE-TOV.

Libya: 744000 Aşgabat, Azad köç. 17A; tel. (12) 35-49-17; fax (12) 39-35-26; Ambassador ZIAD ADHAM AL-MUNTASIR.

Romania: 744000 Aşgabat, Kusayev köç. 122; tel. (12) 34-76-55; fax (12) 34-76-20; e-mail ashabat@mae.ro; Ambassador RADU LIVIU HORUMBA.

Russia: 744005 Aşgabat, S. Türkmenbaşi Şaýoly 11; tel. (12) 94-15-05; fax (12) 94-28-66; e-mail embrus@online.tm; internet www.turkmenistan.mid.ru; Ambassador ALEKSANDR BLOKHIN.

Saudi Arabia: 744017 Aşgabat, Yu. Emre köç. 2/1, Imperial International Business Centre; tel. (12) 45-49-63; fax (12) 45-49-70; e-mail tmemb@mofa.gov.sa; Ambassador TURKI BIN KHALID BIN FAISAL AL-HASHR.

Tajikistan: 744000 Aşgabat, Gerogly köç. 19; tel. (12) 48-18-18; fax (12) 48-18-77; e-mail tadjemb_tm@mail.ru; Ambassador ABDURAHIM ASHUR.

Turkey: 744000 Aşgabat, Şevçenko köç. 9; tel. (12) 94-00-95; fax (12) 94-19-15; e-mail embassy.ashgabat@mfa.gov.tr; internet ashgabat.emb.mfa.gov.tr; Ambassador ŞEVKI MÜTEVELLIOĞLU.

Ukraine: 744001 Aşgabat, Azad köç. 49; tel. (12) 39-13-73; fax (12) 92-42-79; e-mail ukremb@online.tm; internet turkmenistan.mfa.gov.ua; Ambassador VALENTIN SHEVALEV.

United Arab Emirates: 744000 Aşgabat, Archabil 41/1; tel. (12) 48-10-28; fax (12) 48-10-29; e-mail uaembassy@online.tm; Ambassador HASSAN ABDULLAH AL-ADHAB.

United Kingdom: 744001 Aşgabat, Four Points Ak Altin Hotel, 3rd Floor, Offices 301–308; tel. (12) 36-34-62; fax (12) 36-34-65; e-mail beasb@online.tm; internet ukinturkmenistan.fco.gov.uk; Ambassador KEITH RENNIE ALLAN.

USA: 744000 Aşgabat, Puşkin köç. 9; tel. (12) 94-00-45; fax (12) 94-26-14; e-mail consularashgab@state.gov; internet turkmenistan.usembassy.gov; Ambassador ROBERT PATTERSON, Jr.

Uzbekistan: 744006 Aşgabat, Gerogly köç. 50A; tel. (12) 33-10-55; fax (12) 33-10-57; e-mail embashgabat@yahoo.com; Ambassador JAWHAR ISAMOV.

Judicial System

Judicial power is exercised by the Supreme Court, the High Commercial Court, and military and other courts. Judges are appointed by the President for a term of five years.

Supreme Court: 744000 Aşgabat, Navoi köç. 86; tel. (12) 39-09-32; fax (12) 35-50-50; Chair. AMANMYRAT HALLIYEV.

Office of the Prosecutor-General: 744000 Aşgabat, Seidi köç. 4; tel. (12) 35-25-56; fax (12) 35-44-82; Prosecutor-General YARANMYRAT YAZMYRADOV.

Religion

The majority of the population are adherents of Islam. In June 1991 the Supreme Soviet of the Turkmen SSR adopted a Law on Freedom of Conscience and Religious Organizations. In April 1994 a council for religious affairs, the Genğeş, was established, within the Office of the President; it was chaired by the qazi (supreme Islamic judge) of Turkmenistan, with the head of the Russian Orthodox Church (Moscow Patriarchate) in Turkmenistan serving as Deputy Chairman. In November 2003 new legislation, replacing that of 1991, was approved, restricting the activities of religious groups, although registration requirements for religious communities were made more flexible by a presidential decree, issued in early 2004. Further legislation, approved in March of that year, reduced the membership threshold required for a group to register from 500 to five. Prior to these amendments, only Sunni Muslim and Russian Orthodox Christian groups had been permitted to register. By mid-2004 groups of Seventh-day Adventist and Baptist Christians, Hare Krishnas, and Bahá'ís had also registered.

ISLAM

Turkmen are traditionally Sunni Muslims, but with elements of Sufism. Islam was severely persecuted by the Soviet regime from the late 1920s. Until July 1989 Aşgabat was the only Central Asian capital without a functioning mosque. The Muslims of Turkmenistan are officially under the jurisdiction of the Muslim Board of Central Asia, based in Tashkent, Uzbekistan, but, in practice, the Government permits little external influence in religious affairs. The Board is represented in Turkmenistan by a qazi, who is responsible for appointing Muslim clerics in all rural areas.

Qazi of Turkmenistan: ROVSHEN ALLABERDIYEV.

CHRISTIANITY

The Russian Orthodox Church (Moscow Patriarchate)

The Church in Turkmenistan comes under the jurisdiction of the Eparchy of Tashkent and Central Asia, headed by the Metropolitan of Tashkent and Central Asia, VIKENTII (MORAR), based in Uzbekistan.

Roman Catholic Church

The Church is represented in Turkmenistan by a Mission, established in September 1997. There were 85 adherents at 31 December 2007.

Superior: Fr ANDRZEJ MADEJ, 744000 Aşgabat, Gerogly köç. 20A, POB 98; tel. (12) 39-11-40; fax (12) 35-36-83; e-mail amadej@oblaci.pl.

The Press

In 2012 some 25 newspapers and 15 periodicals, all of which were state-owned, were published in Turkmenistan. The first privately owned publication in the country, *Rysgal*, was launched in September 2010. All publications listed below are in Turkmen, except where otherwise stated.

PRINCIPAL NEWSPAPERS

Adalat (Justice): 744005 Aşgabat, Magtymguly Saýoly 1/4; tel. (12) 39-79-04; weekly; Editor-in-Chief DOVLET H. GURBANGELDIYEV.

Beyik Türkmenbaşiyn Nesli (Generation of Türkmenbaşi the Great): 744064 Aşgabat, Galkynyş köç. 20; tel. (12) 22-33-78; f. 1922; 3 a week; for young people; Editor ANNAGUL NARLIEVA; circ. 21,591.

Edebiyat we sungat (Literature and Art): 744004 Aşgabat, Galkynyş köç. 20; tel. (12) 35-30-34; f. 1958; weekly; Editor ANNAMYRAT POLADOV; circ. 19,111.

Esger (Soldier): 744004 Aşgabat, 2038 köç. 29; tel. (12) 35-68-09; f. 1993; weekly; organ of the Council of Ministers; military newspaper; Editor-in-Chief AGAMYRAT GELDYEV; circ. 40,200.

Galkynyş (Revival): 744604 Aşgabat, Galkynyş köç. 20; tel. (12) 22-34-23; weekly; organ of the Democratic Party of Turkmenistan; Editor-in-Chief HUDAIBURDY DIVANGULIYEV; circ. 44,586.

Habarlar: 744004 Aşgabat, Galkynyş köç. 20; tel. (12) 46-84-70; weekly; in Russian and Turkmen; television and radio; business; advertisements; Editor-in-Chief R. BALABAN; circ. 3,596.

Mugallymlar gazeti (Teachers' Newspaper): 744004 Aşgabat, G. Kuliyev köç. 20; tel. (12) 38-61-45; f. 1952; 3 a week; organ of the Ministry of Education; Editor REJEPNUR GURBANNAZAROV; circ. 75,226.

Neitralnyi Turkmenistan (Neutral Turkmenistan): 744004 Aşgabat, Galkynyş köç. 20; tel. (12) 38-61-18; fax (12) 39-42-76; e-mail nt@online.tm; f. 1924; 6 a week; organ of the Majlis and the Council of Ministers; in Russian; Editor-in-Chief BEKDURDY AMANSARIYEV; circ. 30,091.

Novosti Turkmenistana (Turkmenistan News): 744000 Aşgabat, Bitarap Türkmenistan köç. 24A; tel. (12) 39-12-21; fax (12) 51-02-34; e-mail tpress@online.tm; f. 1994; weekly; in Russian, English and Turkmen; publ. by Türkmen Dowlet Khabarlar Gullugy news agency; Chair. BEKDURDY AMANSARIYEV; circ. 500.

Syyasy sokhbetdeş (Political Symposium): 744604 Aşgabat, Galkynyş köç. 20; tel. (12) 25-10-84; f. 1992; weekly; organ of the Democratic Party of Turkmenistan; Editor AKBIBI YUSUPOVA; circ. 14,500.

Türkmening yupekyoli (Turkmen Railwayman): 744007 Aşgabat, Chary Nurymov köç. 3; tel. and fax (12) 35-06-52; f. 1936; weekly; organ of the Turkmenistan State Railways; covers transport and communications; Editor BAYRAM SAHEDOV; circ. 11,500 (March 2010).

Türkmenistan: 744004 Aşgabat, Galkynyş köç. 20; tel. (12) 39-14-55; f. 1920; 6 a week; organ of the Council of Ministers and the Majlis; Editor-in-Chief ANNAMYRAT POLADOV; circ. 25,591.

Türkmenistan—Altyn Asar / Turkmenistan—Zolotoi Vek / Turkmenistan—The Golden Age: 744004 Aşgabat, Galkynyş köç. 20; tel. (12) 22-33-38; e-mail nt@online.tm; internet turkmenistan.gov.tm/_tm; f. 2003; online only; publ. by Govt and President; in Turkmen, Russian and English.

Watan (Fatherland): 744604 Aşgabat, Galkynyş köç. 20; tel. (12) 22-34-56; f. 1925; 3 a week; Editor-in-Chief (vacant); circ. 25,419.

PRINCIPAL PERIODICALS

Monthly, unless otherwise indicated.

Diyar: 744604 Aşgabat, Galkynyş köç. 20; tel. (12) 35-53-97; f. 1992; foreign policy and international relations; publ. by the President of the Republic and the Council of Ministers; Editor-in-Chief ASHIR-BERDY GURBANOV; circ. 12,881.

Garagum (Kara-Kum): 744005 Aşgabat, Galkynyş köç. 20; tel. (12) 35-11-15; f. 1928; literary; Editor SAPAR ORAYEV; circ. 2,546.

Guneş (The Sun): 744000 Aşgabat, Galkynyş köç. 20; tel. (12) 22-33-05; for children; Editor-in-Chief SHADURDY CHARYGYLLYEV; circ. 44,696.

Neft, gaz i mineralnye resursy Turkmenistana (Oil, Gas and Natural Resources of Turkmenistan): 744036 Aşgabat, Arçabil Saýoly 56; tel. (12) 40-33-01; fax (12) 40-38-28; e-mail magazine@oilgas.gov.tm; publ. by Ministry of the Petroleum and Gas Industry and Mineral Resources; in Russian.

Obrazovaniye (Education): Aşgabat; f. 2010; six a year; in Russian; organ of the Ministry of Education.

Rysgal (Welfare): 744000 Aşgabat, Ostrovsky köç. 26; f. 2010; in Turkmen and Russian; publ. by Union of Industrialists and Entrepreneurs; business.

Saglyk (Health): 744000 Aşgabat, Kerbabayev köç. 39/57; tel. (12) 39-16-21; f. 1990; 6 a year; publ. by the Ministry of Health and the Medical Industry; Editor-in-Chief BAYRAMAMMED TACHMAMEDOV.

Taze oba (New Countryside): 744000 Aşgabat, Azad köç. 63; tel. (12) 35-19-38; f. 1929; fmrly *Türkmenistanyň oba khozhalygy*; monthly; Editor BYASHIM TALLYKOV; circ. 9,450.

Türkmen dunyasi: 744004 Aşgabat, Azad köç. 20; tel. (12) 47-81-18; monthly; organ of the Humanitarian Association of World Turkmen; Editor-in-Chief ANNABERDY AGABAYEV; circ. 11,956.

Türkmen medeniyeti (Turkmen Culture): 744007 Aşgabat, O. Kuliyev köç. 21; tel. (12) 25-37-22; f. 1993; 2 a year; publ. by the Ministry of Culture; Editor GELDYMYRAT NURMUKHAMMEDOV.

Türkmen sporty/Sport Turkmenistana (Turkmen Sport): 744004 Aşgabat, Galkynyş köç. 20; tel. (12) 22-33-72; weekly; in Turkmen and Russian; Editor-in-Chief VIKTOR MIHAYLOV; circ. 2,500.

Turkmenistanda Ylym We Tekhnika (Science and Engineering of Turkmenistan): 744000 Aşgabat, Azad köç. 59; f. 1995 as *Izvestiya Akademii Nauk Turkmenistana*; 6 a year.

Türkmenistanyň Lukmancykygy: 744004 Aşgabat, A. Gulmammedov köç. 4A; tel. (12) 35-25-40; f. 2002; every two months; health policy; Editor-in-Chief O. SERDAROV.

Türkmenistanyňg Mejlisining Maglumatlary (Bulletin of the Majlis of Turkmenistan): 744000 Aşgabat, Garaşyslyk köç. 110; tel. (12) 35-50-39; fax (12) 35-31-47; e-mail mejlis@online.tm; f. 1960; 4 a year; proceedings of the Turkmenistani parliament; in Russian and Turkmen.

Vozrozhdeniye (Rebirth): 744604 Aşgabat, Galkynyş köç. 20; tel. (12) 35-10-84; f. 1937; fmrly *Politicheskii sobesednik* (Political Colloquium); in Russian; publ. by the Democratic Party of Turkmenistan; circ. 2,300.

Zenan Kalby (Female Soul): 744604 Aşgabat, Galkynyş köç. 20; tel. (12) 22-33-09; f. 1931; fmrly *Ovadan* (Beautiful), then *Gurbansoltan Eje* (Mother of Türkmenbaşi); for women; Editor AKBIBI YUSUBOVA; circ. 56,626.

NEWS AGENCY

TDH—Türkmen Dowlet Habarlar Gullugy (Turkmen State News Service): 744000 Aşgabat, Bitarap Türkmenistan köç. 24A; tel. (12) 39-12-21; fax (12) 51-02-34; e-mail tpress@online.tm; internet tdh.gov.tm; f. 1967; Chair. BEKDURDY AMANSARYEV.

Publishers

Magaryf Publishing House: 744000 Aşgabat; Dir N. ATAYEV.

Turkmenistan State Publishing Service: 744000 Aşgabat, Galkynyş köç. 100; tel. (12) 38-60-20; f. 1965; politics, science and fiction; Chair. (vacant).

Ylym Publishing House: 744000 Aşgabat, Azad köç. 59; tel. (12) 29-04-84; f. 1952; desert devt, science; Dir N. I. FAIZULAYEVA.

Broadcasting and Communications

TELECOMMUNICATIONS

The principal provider of telecommunications services is the state-owned Türkmentelekom, while mobile cellular communications have been provided by its subsidiary company, Altyn Asyr. In 2011 there were 547,000 fixed telephone lines and 3.5m. subscriptions to mobile telephone services in the country. A local subsidiary of the Russian company Mobile TeleSystems (MTS) provided mobile communications and internet services in Turkmenistan from 2007, but was obliged to withdraw from the country following the expiry of its contract at the end of 2010. MTS was permitted to recommence operations in Turkmenistan in August 2012. In April 2011 the Government announced that it was to establish a new mobile telecommunications company in co-operation with Huawaei Technologies (of the People's Republic of China) and Nokia Siemens Networks (of Finland and Germany).

Altyn Asyr: 744000 Aşgabat, Chary Nuriev köç. 3; tel. (12) 39-88-26; fax (12) 39-88-91; e-mail altynasyrgsm@online.tm; f. 2004; subsidiary of Türkmentelekom; provides mobile communications services; Gen. Dir KHAJIMURAD KHUDAIKULIEV.

MTS Turkmenistan: Aşgabat, Atamurata Nijazova köç. 85; tel. (12) 42-52-05; fax (12) 49-80-35; internet www.mts.tm; majority-owned by Mobile TeleSystems (Russia); wireless internet services introduced in 2008; operations suspended from late 2010 to August 2012; Gen. Dir OLEG ATAMANOV.

Türkmentelekom: 744013 Aşgabat, Asudalyk köç. 36; tel. (12) 35-21-52; fax (12) 39-60-55; e-mail admin@telecom.tm; internet www.telecom.tm; f. 1993; state-owned; subsidiary co, Altyn Asyr, provides mobile telecommunications and internet services; Dir-Gen. ANNA-DOVLET MUHAMMEDOV.

BROADCASTING

In 2012 there were seven state television channels and four state radio stations.

Turkmen State Information Agency (Türkmen Dovlet Habarlary): 744004 Aşgabat, Gerogly köç.; tel. (12) 35-68-12; fax (12) 51-02-34; e-mail tpress@online.tm; Dir JEREN TAIMOVA.

Radio

Turkmen National Radio Co: 744000 Aşgabat, Navoi köç. 5; tel. (12) 39-25-20; Chair. MURAD ORAZOV.

  Char Tarapdan (From All Sides): tel. (12) 39-86-72; Dir BYASHIM ATAYEV.

  Miras (Heritage): tel. (12) 35-20-43; Dir GURBANDURDY REJEPOV.

  Watan (Fatherland): tel. (12) 51-12-96; Dir NURBERDI DADEBAYEV.

Television

Turkmen National Television Co: 744000 Aşgabat, Navoi köç. 5; tel. (12) 39-25-20; Chair. MURAD ORAZOV.

  Altyn Asar (Golden Age): tel. (12) 39-85-06; Dir (vacant).

  Miras (Heritage): tel. (12) 35-20-43; Dir BYASHIM ATAYEV.

  Türkmenistan: tel. (12) 35-00-86; Dir MURAD A. ORAZOV.

  Yaşlyk (Youth): tel. (12) 35-00-86; Dir BEGENCH ABAEV.

Finance

(cap. = capital; res = reserves; dep. = deposits; m. = million; brs = branches; amounts in Turkmen manats, unless otherwise specified)

BANKING

In late 2002 there were 12 commercial banks operating in Turkmenistan. The state retains substantial interests and involvement in banking.

Central Bank

Central Bank of Turkmenistan (Türkmenistanyň Merkezi Banky): 744000 Aşgabat, Bitarap Türkmenistan köç. 36; tel. (12) 38-10-27; fax (12) 51-08-12; e-mail merkezb2@online.tm; internet www.cbt.tm; f. 1991; central monetary authority, issuing bank and supervisory authority; Chair. TUVAKMAMMED JAPAROV; 5 brs.

Other Banks

Daýhanbank: 744000 Aşgabat, Galkynyş köç. 12; tel. and fax (12) 41-98-68; e-mail daybank@online.tm; internet www.dayhanbank.gov.tm; f. 1989 as independent bank, Agroprombank, reorganized 1999; specializes in agricultural sector; Chair. of Bd TUMAR MAMMEDOV; 70 brs.

Garagum International Joint-Stock Bank: 744000 Aşgabat, S. Türkmenbaşi Şaýoly 126; tel. (12) 45-63-66; fax (12) 45-18-97; e-mail garagumbank@gmail.com; internet www.garagumbank.gov.tm; f. 1993 as International Bank for Reconstruction, Development and Support of Entrepreneurship, name changed 2000; Chair. MYRAT BABAYEV.

Garaşyslyk Bank: 744000 Aşgabat, Gerogly köç. 30A; tel. (12) 35-48-75; fax (12) 39-01-24; e-mail garash@cbtm.net; f. 1999 following merger of Gas Bank and Aşgabat Bank; cap. US $5m. (Oct. 2003); Chair. (vacant); 5 brs.

Halkbank State Commercial Bank of Turkmenistan: 744000 Aşgabat, Karliyev köç. 130; tel. (12) 35-07-50; fax (12) 35-00-31; internet www.cbt.tm/halkbank/www.halkbank.tm.htm; f. 1923, reorganized 1989; fmrly Savings Bank (Sberbank) of Turkmenistan; name changed as above in 2001; wholly state-owned; Chair. BEGENCH BAYMUKHAMEDOV; 120 brs.

President Bank of Turkmenistan (Türkmenistanyň Prezidentbank): 744005 Aşgabat, A. Karliyev köç. 132; tel. (12) 27-19-90; fax (12) 27-20-10; e-mail presidentbank@cbtm.net; internet www .presidentbank.gov.tm; f. 2000; cap. US $60m.; state-owned; Chair. of Bd NURGELDI SAZAKOV.

Senagatbank: 744013 Aşgabat, S. Türkmenbaşi Şaýoly 42; tel. (12) 45-31-33; fax (12) 45-44-09; e-mail senagat@online.tm; f. 1989; cap. 31,200m., res 1,394m., dep. 32,547m. (Feb. 2005); Chair. AKMYRAT ORAZOV; 5 brs.

Turkmen-Turkish Joint-Stock Commercial Bank (Türkmen-Türk paýdarlar täjirçilik banky): 744000 Aşgabat, Magtymguly Şaýoly 111/2, POB 15; tel. (12) 51-10-09; fax (12) 51-11-23; e-mail ttcb@online.tm; internet www.turkmenturkbank.com; f. 1993; 50% owned by Türkiye Cumhuriyeti Ziraat Bankasi, AŞ (Turkey), and 50% by Daihanbank; cap. 14.3m., dep. 130.7m., total assets 156.4m. (Dec. 2011); Gen. Man. AVNI DEMIRCI.

Türkmenbank—State Commercial Bank 'Türkmenistan': 744000 Aşgabat, Gerogly köç. 10A; tel. and fax (12) 39-67-35; e-mail info@tnbk.tm; internet www.tnbk.tm; f. 1992; Chair. ATAMYRAT ATALYKOV.

Türkmenbaşi Bank: 744000 Aşgabat, Annadurdiyev köç. 54; tel. (12) 51-11-26; e-mail mail@investbank.org; internet www.tbbank .gov.tm; f. 1992 as Investbank, renamed in 2000; Chair. BATIR DURDUMAMMADOV; 23 brs.

Türkmenvnesheconombank—State Bank for Foreign Economic Affairs of Turkmenistan: 744036 Aşgabat, Garaşyslyk Şaýoly 32; tel. (12) 40-60-40; fax (12) 40-65-63; e-mail tveb@online .tm; internet www.tfeb.gov.tm; f. 1992 as independent bank, from Soviet Vneshekonombank; wholly state-owned; cap. 119.9m., dep. 3,483.2m., total assets 6,216.6m. (Dec. 2011); Chair. of Bd RAHYMBERDI JEPBAROV.

COMMODITY EXCHANGE

State Commodity and Raw Materials Exchange of Turkmenistan (GTSBT): 744000 Aşgabat, Magtymguly Şaýoly 111; tel. (12) 35-43-21; fax (12) 51-03-04; e-mail info@exchange.gov.tm; internet www .exchange.gov.tm; f. 1994; Chair. ŞABERDY MEREDOV.

INSURANCE

State Insurance Org. of Turkmenistan (Türkmenistanyň Döwlet Ätiýaçlandyryş Guramasy): 744000 Aşgabat, Beyik Saparmyrat Türkmenbaşy Saýoly 42/1; tel. (12) 22-19-55; fax (12) 22-19-17; e-mail datig@online.tm; internet www.insurance.gov.tm; f. 1992; state-owned insurance monopoly; Dir-Gen. AMANBIBI AMANMEDOVA.

Trade and Industry

GOVERNMENT AGENCIES

National Institute of State Statistics and Information on Turkmenistan (Türkmenmillihasabat): 744000 Aşgabat, Magtymguly Saýoly 72; tel. (12) 39-42-65; fax (12) 35-43-79; e-mail staff@ natstat.gov.tm; f. 1997; Dir KAKAMYRAT MOMMADOV.

State Agency for Foreign Investment (SAFI): 744000 Aşgabat, Azad köç. 53; tel. and fax (12) 35-04-16; e-mail saffi@online.tm; f. 1996; monitors and regulates all foreign investment in Turkmenistan; registers foreign cos in Turkmenistan; Dir (vacant).

DEVELOPMENT ORGANIZATION

Small and Medium Enterprise Development Agency (SMEDA): 744000 Aşgabat, 2015 köç. 8; tel. (12) 34-42-59; fax (12) 34-51-49; e-mail smeda@cat.glasnet.ru; jt venture between Govt and the European Union; Dir SERDAR BABAYEV.

CHAMBER OF COMMERCE

Chamber of Commerce and Industry of Turkmenistan: 744000 Aşgabat, B. Karryyev köç. 17; tel. (12) 35-45-94; fax (12) 35-13-52; e-mail mission@online.tm; internet cci.gov.tm; f. 1959; Chair. PALVAN TAGANOVA.

EMPLOYERS' ORGANIZATION

Union of Industrialists and Entrepreneurs: 744000 Aşgabat, Ostrovsky köç. 26; f. 2008; Dir ALEKSANDR DADAYEV.

UTILITIES

Electricity

Kuvvat Turkmen State Energy Technology Corpn: 744000 Aşgabat, N. Pomma köç. 6; tel. (12) 35-68-04; fax (12) 39-06-82; e-mail kuvvat@online.tm; state electrical power generation co and agency; Chair. YUSUP DAVYDOV.

STATE HYDROCARBONS COMPANIES

Türkmenbaşi Complex of Oil-refining Plants (TNPZ): 745005 Balkan Velayat, Türkmenbaşi, TNPZ, POB 5; tel. (8243) 9-62-00; fax (8243) 2-45-44; e-mail tnpzdiryest@online.tm; internet www.oilgas .gov.tm; production and refining of petroleum; sales of petroleum and liquefied natural gas; Dir-Gen. SAHETMYRAT MAMMEDOV.

Türkmengaz/Turkmengaz (Turkmen Gas): 744036 Aşgabat, Arçabil Saýoly 56; tel. (12) 40-32-01; fax (12) 40-32-54; e-mail tmgas@online.tm; internet www.oilgas.gov.tm; f. 1996; govt agency responsible for natural gas operations, incl. development of system of extraction, processing of gas and gas concentrate, and gas transportation and sale; Chair. KAKAGELDY ABDULLAYEV.

Türkmengeologiya: 744000 Aşgabat, Arçabil Saýoly 56; tel. (12) 40-34-01; fax (12) 40-34-39; e-mail turkmengeology@online.tm; internet www.oilgas.gov.tm; govt agency responsible for natural gas and petroleum exploration; Chair. TORE YAGSHIMURAADOV.

Türkmennebit/Turkmenneft (Turkmen Oil): 744036 Aşgabat, Arçabil Saýoly 56; tel. (12) 40-36-01; fax (12) 40-31-84; internet www.oilgas.gov.tm; govt agency responsible for petroleum operations and production; Chair. ANNAGULY DERYAYEV.

Türkmennebitgazgurlushyk/Turkmenneftegazstroi (Turkmen Oil and Gas Construction): 744036 Aşgabat, Arçabil Saýoly. 56; tel. and fax (12) 40-35-01; e-mail tngg@online.tm; internet www .oilgas.gov.tm; govt agency for construction projects in the hydrocarbons sector; Chair. AMAN KURBANOV.

TRADE UNIONS

National Centre of Trade Unions of Turkmenistan: 744000 Aşgabat, S. Türkmenbaşi Şaýoly 13; tel. (12) 35-48-68; fax (12) 35-21-30; Chair. ENEBAY G. ATAYEVA.

Transport

RAILWAYS

The main railway line in the country runs from Türkmenbaşi (formerly Krasnovodsk), on the Caspian Sea, in the west, via Aşgabat and Mari, to Türkmenabat (formerly Charjew) in the east. From Türkmenabat, one line runs further east, to the other Central Asian countries of the former USSR, while another runs north-west, via Uzbekistan and Kazakhstan, to join the Russian rail network. In 2010 the total length of rail track in use in Turkmenistan was 3,115 km. A 203-km rail link from Türkmenabat to Atamarut was opened in 1999. In 1996 a rail link was established with Iran (on the route Tejen–Serakhs–Mashad), thus providing the possibility of rail travel and transportation between Turkmenistan and İstanbul, Turkey, as well as giving access to the Persian (Arabian) Gulf. A 540-km railway line, running south–north across the country from Aşgabat to Daşoguz, via Garagum, was completed in early 2006.

Turkmenistan State Railways (Türkmendemorjollari): 744007 Aşgabat, S. Türkmenbaşi Şaýoly 7; tel. (12) 35-55-45; fax (12) 51-06-32; f. 1992; Pres. B. P. REDJEPOV.

ROADS

In 2000 there was an estimated total of 24,000 km of roads, of which some 19,500 km were hard-surfaced. In the late 2000s construction was under way on a principal road of 1,200 km, which was to link Türkmenbaşi with the eastern towns of Türkmenabat and Farap.

SHIPPING

Shipping services link Türkmenbaşi (formerly Krasnovodsk) with Baku (Bakı, Azerbaijan), Makhachkala (Dagestan, Russia) and the major Iranian ports on the Caspian Sea. The Amu Dar'ya river is an important inland waterway. From 2000 Türkmenbaşi port was undergoing an extensive process of modernization. In 2012 the Turkmenistani merchant fleet comprised 68 vessels, with a combined displacement of 111,870 grt.

Shipowning Companies

Neftec: 745100 Balkan Velayat, Türkmenbaşi; tel. (2) 765-81; fax (2) 766-89.

Turkmen Maritime Steamship Co: 745100 Balkan Velayat, Türkmenbaşi, Şagadam köç. 8; tel. (2) 767-34.

Turkmen Shipping Co: 745100 Balkan Velayat, Türkmenbaşi, Şagadam köç. 8; tel. (2) 972-67; fax (2) 767-85.

Türkmenderyayollary: 746000 Lebap Velayat, Türkmenabat, ul. Gyamichiler 8; tel. (2) 223-12; fax (2) 23-46-88; f. 1992 as Turkmen River Shipping Co; renamed as above in 1998.

Türkmennefteflot: 745100 Balkan Velayat, Türkmenbaşi, POB 6; tel. (2) 762-62.

CIVIL AVIATION

Turkmenistan's principal international airport is at Aşgabat. A second international airport, at Türkmenbaşi, opened in April 2010.

National Civil Aviation Authority of Turkmenistan (Türkmenhovayollary): 744000 Aşgabat, Nurymov köç. 3A; tel. (12) 35-10-52; fax (12) 35-44-02; e-mail aviahead@online.tm; f. 1992; Dir-Gen. BATYR KAKALIEV.

Türkmenhovayollary—Turkmenistan Airlines: 744000 Aşgabat, Magtymguly köç. 80; tel. (12) 35-10-52; fax (12) 35-44-02; f. 1992; state-owned; domestic and international scheduled and charter passenger flights, incl. services to Europe, Central and South-East Asia, and the Middle East; three divisions: Ahal Air Co, Khazar Air Co and Lebap Air Co; Chair. IMAMBERDY IMAMBERDYYEVA (acting).

Tourism

Although the tourism sector in Turkmenistan remains relatively undeveloped, owing, in part, to the vast expanse of the Garagum (Kara-Kum) desert (which constitutes some 80% of the country's total area), the Government has made efforts to improve the standard of visitor accommodation (there are a number of new luxury hotels in Aşgabat) and to improve the capacity and efficiency of the capital's international airport. The scenic Kopet Dagh mountains, the Caspian Sea coast, the archaeological sites and mountain caves of Kugitang, and the hot subterranean mineral lake at Kov-Ata are among the country's natural attractions, while the ancient cities of Mari and Nisa—former capitals of the Seljuk and Parthian empires, respectively—are of considerable historical interest. In addition, Kunya-Urgench is an important site of Muslim pilgrimage. In 2007, according to the World Tourism Organization, there were 8,177 visitors from abroad; receipts from tourism totalled US $192m. in 1998.

Defence

The National Armed Forces of Turkmenistan began to be formed in mid-1992, initially under joint Turkmen and Russian command. As assessed at November 2012, the estimated strength of the armed forces was 22,000, consisting of an army of 18,500, an air force of 3,000 and a navy of 500. Military service is for a period of 24 months. In August 2009 President Gurbanguly Berdymuhamedov signed a decree providing for the establishment of a naval force by 2015 (the existing navy comprised only coastguard units). In May 1994 Turkmenistan became the first Central Asian republic of the former USSR to join the North Atlantic Treaty Organization's 'Partnership for Peace' programme.

Defence Expenditure: Budgeted at 599m. manats in 2011.

Chief of the General Staff: ISMAIL ISMAILOV.

Commander of the Ground Forces: BATIR MOLLAYEV.

Education

In September 2005 it was reported that all former Russian-language schools had adopted Turkmen as the main language of instruction, although one class with instruction in Russian was to be maintained in each school. In 2004 there was also one Turkish university and 14 Turkish schools. In 1995 34.4% of 15-to-18-year-olds were enrolled in general secondary education; in 1997 7.9% of those aged between 15 and 18 years were enrolled in technical and vocational schools. In 1997 83.1% of children aged between seven and 15 years were enrolled in basic education. The 1999 budget allocated 26.9% of total expenditure (1,048,700m. manats) to education.

From the second half of the 1990s reform of the education system left many children without access to free education, and free education at Turkmenistan's 16 universities was reportedly abolished from 2003. In 2004 a presidential decree invalidating all higher-education degrees received abroad came into effect; all teachers with such degrees were to be dismissed. Between 2002 and 2005 more than 12,000 teachers were removed from their posts. In March 2007 the new President, Gurbanguly Berdymuhamedov, increased the period of compulsory primary and secondary education from nine to 10 years and extended the period of higher education from two to five years (effective from the beginning of the 2007/08 school year). Students were no longer required to complete two years of practical work experience before applying to universities, and foreign degrees were given recognition. Some 13,800 students were enrolled at the country's 18 institutions of higher education in 2007/08.

TUVALU

Introductory Survey

LOCATION, CLIMATE, LANGUAGE, RELIGION, FLAG, CAPITAL

Tuvalu is a scattered group of nine small atolls (five of which enclose sizeable lagoons), extending about 560 km (350 miles) from north to south, in the western Pacific Ocean. Its nearest neighbours are Fiji to the south, Kiribati to the north and Solomon Islands to the west. The climate is warm and pleasant, with a mean annual temperature of 30°C (86°F), and there is very little seasonal variation. The average annual rainfall is about 3,500 mm (140 ins), the wettest months being November to February. The inhabitants speak Tuvaluan and English. Almost all of them profess Christianity, and about 98% are Protestants. The national flag (proportions 1 by 2) is light blue with the United Kingdom flag as a rectangular canton in the upper hoist, occupying one-quarter of the area, and nine five-pointed yellow stars (arranged to symbolize a map of the archipelago) in the fly. The flag was reintroduced in February 1997 to replace a design, adopted in October 1995, omitting the British union flag. The capital is on Funafuti Atoll.

CONTEMPORARY POLITICAL HISTORY

Historical Context

Tuvalu was formerly known as the Ellice (or Lagoon) Islands. Between about 1850 and 1875 many of the islanders were captured by slave-traders and this, together with European diseases, reduced the population from about 20,000 to 3,000. In 1877 the United Kingdom established the Western Pacific High Commission (WPHC), with its headquarters in Fiji, and the Ellice Islands and other groups were placed under its jurisdiction. In 1892 a British protectorate was declared over the Ellice Islands, and the group was linked administratively with the Gilbert Islands to the north. In 1916 the United Kingdom annexed the protectorate, which was renamed the Gilbert and Ellice Islands Colony (GEIC). During the Japanese occupation of the Gilbert Islands in 1942–43, the administration of the GEIC was temporarily moved to Funafuti in the Ellice Islands. (For more details of the history of the GEIC, see Kiribati.)

A series of advisory and legislative bodies prepared the GEIC for self-government. In May 1974 the last of these, the Legislative Council, was replaced by the House of Assembly, with 28 elected members (including eight Ellice Islanders) and three official members. A Chief Minister was elected by the House and chose between four and six other ministers, one of whom had to be from the Ellice Islands.

In January 1972 the appointment of a separate GEIC Governor, who assumed most of the functions previously exercised by the High Commissioner for the Western Pacific, increased the long-standing anxiety of the Ellice Islanders over their minority position as Polynesians in the colony, dominated by the Micronesians of the Gilbert Islands. In a referendum held in the Ellice Islands in August and September 1974, more than 90% of the voters favoured separate status for the group, and in October 1975 the Ellice Islands, under the old native name of Tuvalu ('eight standing together', which referred to the eight populated atolls), became a separate British dependency. The Deputy Governor of the GEIC took office as Her Majesty's Commissioner for Tuvalu. The eight Ellice representatives in the GEIC House of Assembly became the first elected members of the new Tuvalu House of Assembly. They elected one of their number, Toaripi Lauti, to be Chief Minister. Tuvalu was completely separated from the GEIC administration in January 1976. The remainder of the GEIC was renamed the Gilbert Islands and achieved independence, as Kiribati, in July 1979.

Tuvalu's first separate elections took place in August 1977, when the number of elective seats in the House of Assembly was increased to 12. An independence Constitution was finalized at a conference in the United Kingdom in February 1978. After five months of internal self-government, Tuvalu became independent on 1 October 1978, with Lauti as the first Prime Minister. The pre-independence House of Assembly was redesignated Parliament. In September 2000 Tuvalu was formally admitted to the UN.

Domestic Political Affairs

In 1983 the USA formally renounced its claim, dating from 1856, to Tuvalu's four southernmost atolls. Following elections to Parliament in September 1981, Lauti was replaced as Prime Minister by Dr Tomasi (later Sir Tomasi) Puapua. Puapua was re-elected Prime Minister following subsequent elections in September 1985.

In February 1986 a nation-wide poll was conducted to establish public opinion as to whether Tuvalu should remain an independent constitutional monarchy, with the British monarch at its head, or become a republic. Only on one atoll did the community appear to be in favour of the adoption of republican status. In March Tupua (later Sir Tupua) Leupena, a former Speaker of Parliament, was appointed Governor-General, replacing Sir Penitala Teo, who had occupied the post since independence in 1978.

At a general election in September 1989 an opponent of Puapua, Bikenibeu Paeniu (who had been appointed Minister of Community Services within the previous year), was elected Prime Minister. In October 1990 Toaripi Lauti succeeded Sir Tupua Leupena as Governor-General.

Relations with the United Kingdom, already tense, deteriorated further in late 1992, when the British Government harshly criticized the financial policy of Paeniu's Government. Paeniu defended his Government's policies, and stated that continued delays in the approval of aid projects from the United Kingdom meant that Tuvalu would not be seeking further development funds from the British Government.

The two elections of 1993 and subsequent events

At a general election held in September 1993, three of the 12 incumbent members of Parliament lost their seats. However, at elections to the premiership held in the same month, Paeniu and Puapua received six votes each. When a second vote produced a similar result, the Governor-General dissolved Parliament, in accordance with the Constitution. Paeniu and his Cabinet remained in office until the holding of a further general election in November. At elections to the premiership in the following month Kamuta Latasi defeated Paeniu by seven votes to five. Puapua, who had agreed not to challenge Paeniu in the contest in favour of supporting Latasi, was elected Speaker of Parliament. In June 1994 Latasi removed the Governor-General, Toomu Malaefono Sione, from office, only seven months after he had been appointed to the position, and replaced him with Tulaga (later Sir Tulaga) Manuella. Latasi alleged that Paeniu's appointment of Sione had been politically motivated.

In December 1994, in what was widely regarded as a significant rejection of its political links with the United Kingdom, the Tuvaluan Parliament voted to remove the British union flag from the Tuvaluan national flag. Despite considerable public opposition, a new design was selected and the new flag was inaugurated in October 1995.

In late 1996 the Deputy Prime Minister, Otinielu Tausi, and the parliamentary Speaker, Dr Tomasi Puapua, both withdrew their support for Latasi's Government, apparently owing to increasing popular dissatisfaction with his administration, thereby increasing the number of opposition members in Parliament from five to seven. A parliamentary motion of no confidence in the Government was approved in December by seven votes to five. Paeniu subsequently defeated Latasi, by a similar margin, to become Prime Minister, and a new Cabinet was appointed. In February 1997 the new premier proposed a parliamentary motion to restore the country's original flag, which was approved by seven votes to five.

A total of 35 candidates contested a general election on 26 March 1998. The period prior to the election had been characterized by a series of bitter disputes between Paeniu and Latasi, in which both had made serious accusations of sexual and financial misconduct against the other. Five members of the previous Parliament were returned to office, although Latasi unexpectedly failed to secure re-election. Paeniu was subsequently re-elected Prime Minister by 10 votes to two. Also in

1998 Puapua was appointed Governor-General, replacing Manuella.

On 13 April 1999 Paeniu lost a parliamentary vote of confidence and was forced to resign. Later in the month Ionatana Ionatana, hitherto the Minister of Health, Education, Culture, Women and Community Affairs, was elected by Parliament as the new Prime Minister. On his appointment Ionatana immediately effected a reorganization of the Cabinet.

It was announced in February 2000 that a US $50m. agreement on the sale of the country's national internet '.tv' suffix had been concluded with a US company, which intended to market the internet address to international television companies. The sale was expected to generate some $10m. annually in revenue for Tuvalu. The funds generated from the sale enabled Tuvalu officially to join the UN. Proceeds from the internet domain sale were also used to develop the islands' infrastructure.

In December 2000 Prime Minister Ionatana died unexpectedly. The Deputy Prime Minister, Lagitupu Tuilimu, became interim Prime Minister until February 2001, when Parliament elected as Prime Minister the Minister of Internal Affairs and Rural and Urban Development, Faimalaga Luka, who immediately named a new Cabinet. A vote of no confidence was upheld against Luka in December while he was in New Zealand, undergoing a medical examination. Koloa Talake, a former Minister of Finance, was elected Prime Minister in the same month, winning eight of the 15 votes cast (the number of parliamentary seats having been increased from 12 to 15). He appointed an entirely new Cabinet.

Following the general election held on 25 July 2002, Saufatu Sopoanga, a former Minister of Finance, defeated Amasone Kilei, the opposition candidate, by eight votes to seven to become the new Prime Minister. Sopoanga subsequently announced his intention to hold a referendum on the adoption of a republican system of government in Tuvalu.

In May 2003 two by-elections resulted in the loss of the Government's one-seat majority. The Government's subsequent refusal to convene Parliament (allegedly in order to evade a vote of no confidence) was strongly criticized by the opposition. The Government maintained that it would regain its majority with an imminent defection from the opposition and would then convene Parliament. In July, however, with the situation remaining unchanged, the opposition sought a court order obliging Sopoanga to convene Parliament. The appointment, in early September, of former Prime Minister Luka, hitherto Speaker and a member of Parliament, as the country's new Governor-General necessitated an additional by-election, which resulted in a further delay to Parliament being convened. However, following the success of its candidate at the by-election, and (as anticipated) the defection of an opposition member, the Government regained its majority in October. Parliament was finally convened in November. In April 2004 the Government announced that a team of officials was touring the outer islands to canvas opinion on the adoption of republican status for Tuvalu.

In August 2004 Prime Minister Sopoanga was ousted by nine parliamentary votes to five in a vote of no confidence after a member of the Government crossed the floor to vote with the opposition and was joined by the Speaker. Owing to Sopoanga's subsequent decision to relinquish his seat, thus necessitating the organization of a by-election before Parliament could elect a new premier, Deputy Prime Minister Maatia Toafa assumed the role of acting Prime Minister in the interim. Sopoanga regained his seat at the by-election in early October, and on 11 October acting Prime Minister Toafa was elected to the premiership, defeating Sopoanga by eight votes to seven.

In April 2005 Governor-General Luka resigned, having reached the maximum permitted age for the post of 65, and was replaced by Filoimea Telito. Meanwhile, the Government's majority was further consolidated by the results of three by-elections held during 2005.

Recent developments

The legislative election held on 3 August 2006 resulted in major changes to the composition of Parliament, with the entry of eight new members. Maatia Toafa was the only cabinet member to retain a seat, but was subsequently replaced as Prime Minister by Apisai Ielemia in mid-August. Ielemia assumed additional responsibility for the foreign affairs portfolio, while Taavau Teii was appointed Deputy Prime Minister and Minister of Natural Resources and Environment, and Lotoala Metia was named Minister of Finance, Economic Planning and Industries.

On 30 April 2008 a referendum on Tuvalu's system of government was conducted. The level of participation was low, at approximately 21% of the electorate. The majority of voters rejected proposals for a republican system, with a president as head of state: according to reports, 1,260 voters (or 65%) out of a total of 1,939 preferred the retention of the existing system of constitutional monarchy.

A total of 26 candidates registered to contest the 15 available seats at legislative elections held on 16 September 2010. Ten incumbent legislators, including Prime Minister Ielemia and the Speaker, former premier Kamuta Latasi, were returned to office; however, Teii unexpectedly lost his seat. On 29 September Toafa was elected Prime Minister, narrowly defeating Kausea Natano, the Minister for Public Utilities and Industries in the outgoing Government, by eight votes to seven. Toafa's Cabinet included Enele Sopoaga as Deputy Prime Minister and Minister of Foreign Affairs, Environment and Labour, and Monise Laafai as Minister of Finance. Isaia Taeia was appointed parliamentary Speaker.

On 22 December 2010 Prime Minister Toafa was removed from office following his defeat, by eight votes to seven, in a parliamentary motion of no confidence, reportedly filed in response to members' concerns about his management of the budget—a particular issue being indications that the Government was no longer to fund the cost of medical treatment abroad for Tuvaluans. The Minister of Home Affairs, Willie Telavi, had withdrawn his support for Toafa and defected to the opposition, reportedly in exchange for support for his candidacy for the premiership. Telavi was sworn in as the new Prime Minister on 24 December, having defeated Sopoaga in the contest for the premiership, securing eight votes to Sopoaga's seven. Telavi appointed his Cabinet on the same day, allocating himself the home affairs portfolio, while former premier Ielemia was appointed Minister for Foreign Affairs, Environment, Trade, Labour and Tourism; Metia was returned to the finance portfolio.

Following a demonstration by about 50 residents on Funafuti, a state of emergency, limiting meetings to a maximum of 10 people, was declared on 13 January 2011. The protesters, members of the Nukufetau community, demanded the resignation of their parliamentary representative, Minister of Finance Metia. A challenge to the Government's invocation of emergency rule lodged with the magistrate's court by local village leaders was dismissed in the following week. Prime Minister Telavi subsequently claimed that the state of emergency had been declared in response to the authorities' fears that the homes of parliamentary members might be targeted in arson attacks; constituents were alleged to have sent an intimidatory letter to Metia demanding his immediate resignation and threatening to do all in their power to remove him from office should he refuse to step down. The restriction on public gatherings was eased in late January to allow people to apply for approval from the police commissioner for gatherings of more than 10 people. The state of emergency was rescinded in February, amid opposition claims that it had been imposed in order to silence dissenters, rather than in response to any genuine security concerns.

The Minister of Works and Natural Resources, Isaia Italeli Taeia, died unexpectedly in July 2011 while attending a meeting of the Pacific Islands Forum Fisheries Committee in the Samoan capital, Apia. He was replaced at the resultant by-election held in the Nui constituency in August by his widow, Pelenike Tekinene Isaia, who thus became only the second woman ever to secure election to the Tuvaluan Parliament, following Naama Maheu Latasi, in Nanumea constituency, in 1989. (The issue of the lack of female members in Parliament had previously come to the fore in May 2010, when a consultation group, arranged by the Department of Women with support from the Pacific Islands Forum Secretariat and other regional organizations, had recommended the creation of two seats specifically to be reserved for women.) As a result of Pelenike Tekinene Isaia's election, the Government maintained its legislative majority of one. Isaia was subsequently appointed to the position of Minister of Home Affairs and Rural Development.

Opposition deputies commenced legal proceedings against the Government in April 2013 in an attempt to expedite a crucial by-election, which had been due to be organized since December 2012 as a consequence of the death of Minister of Finance, Economic Planning and Industries Metia, the member of Parliament for Nukufetau. The opposition contended that the Government was intentionally procrastinating on this matter as a defeat would result in the loss of the latter's legislative majority. Telavi repudiated this allegation, arguing that the delay had been provoked by a political dispute on Nukufetau. The by-election was expected to be conducted in mid-2013.

Environmental Concerns

In 1989 a UN report on the greenhouse effect (the heating of the earth's atmosphere as a result of pollution) listed Tuvalu as one of the island groups that would completely disappear beneath the sea in the 21st century, unless drastic action were taken. At the UN World Climate Conference, held in Switzerland in late 1990, Prime Minister Bikenibeu Paeniu appealed for urgent action by developed nations to combat the environmental changes caused by the greenhouse effect, which were believed to include a 10-fold increase in cyclone frequency (from two in 1940 to 21 in 1990), an increase in salinity in ground water and a considerable decrease in the average annual rainfall. The subsequent Prime Minister, Kamuta Latasi, was similarly critical of the industrial world's apparent disregard for the plight of small island nations vulnerable to the effects of climate change, particularly after Tuvalu was struck by tidal waves in 1994 (believed to be the first experienced by the islands). The Government of Tuvalu was strongly critical of Australia's refusal to reduce its emission of pollutant gases (known to contribute to the greenhouse effect) at the Conference of the Parties to the UN Framework Convention on Climate Change (UNFCCC—UN Environment Programme, see p. 61) in Kyoto, Japan, in late 1997.

In January 2002 it was reported that the Tuvaluan Government had engaged a US law firm to prosecute the USA and other nations for failing to meet their commitments to the UNFCCC. In September 2003 Tuvalu's Prime Minister addressed the 58th session of the UN General Assembly in New York, USA, and appealed for collective action to mitigate the impact of climate change and rising sea levels on the islands. He urged all industrialized nations, particularly the USA, to sign the Kyoto Protocol, which required industrial nations to reduce carbon dioxide emissions by an average of 5.2% during the five-year period 2008–12, to pre-1990 levels. The option of resettlement on neighbouring islands, including Fiji, was under consideration, but only as a last resort, and the Government was also considering the purchase of land in other countries, while declaring that this might be a useful long-term solution should the problems caused by climate change worsen. In December 2007 it was reported that water from wells was becoming increasingly unsuitable for consumption, while high tides were causing frequent flooding.

Although the Kyoto Protocol was finally ratified by Australia in December 2007, in April 2010 Tuvalu expressed its profound disappointment at the delay in Australia's plans to implement a carbon emissions trading scheme, owing to the Government's parliamentary difficulties in enacting the requisite legislation. At a climate change convention held in the Australian city of Cairns in April 2011, the Tuvaluan delegate stated that Tuvalu was experiencing flooding from high tides more frequently each year and asked for regional assistance in addressing the issue. At a UN climate change convention held in Bangkok, Thailand, later in April, the Tuvaluan delegate warned that discussions on climate change were becoming stagnant and urged those in attendance to make securing an extension to the Kyoto Protocol beyond its scheduled expiry in 2012 their principal priority. (In December 2012 the Kyoto Protocol was extended until 2020, with signatories committed to reducing greenhouse gas emissions by at least 18% below 1990 levels during 2013–20.)

A severe shortage of fresh drinking water on the islands, following a period of nearly six months without rainfall, prompted the Tuvaluan Government to declare a state of emergency in late September 2011. Strict rationing of water supplies was implemented on the Funafuti and Nukulaelae atolls, and local food crops were badly affected. In response to a request made by the Tuvaluan Government for external assistance, fresh water supplies and desalination units were dispatched to Funafuti and Nukulaelae by the New Zealand, Australian and Japanese authorities in October, while Australia also provided two delivery trucks to facilitate the distribution of water to communities, schools and hospitals. In addition, the Republic of Korea sent fresh water supplies. The Secretariat of the Pacific Regional Environment Programme (SPREP) disbursed funding in mid-October through its Small Grants Scheme to enable the Tuvaluan authorities to provide an urgent response to the challenges posed by the ongoing drought. Heavy rainfall, the first in nearly six months, later in October helped to ease the immediate crisis and the state of emergency was rescinded in late October. In the longer term, SPREP affirmed its commitment to providing assistance to improve water storage capacity in

Tuvalu (which had hitherto relied primarily on the collection of rainfall for its water supplies), including funding a project to construct a community water reservoir on Funafuti, which was to be designed so as to be resilient to flooding from high tides.

Foreign Affairs

Tuvalu has been subject to considerable international criticism regarding its stance on whaling. Its decision in mid-2004 to join the International Whaling Commission (IWC, see p. 453) was met with considerable disappointment. Environmental and animal welfare groups have on numerous occasions subsequently accused the Tuvaluan Government of accepting financial incentives from Japan in return for agreeing to use its vote to support a removal of the ban on commercial whaling at the commission's annual meetings.

It was reported in September 2010 that a new four-year fisheries initiative, intended to facilitate the management and development of the Tuvaluan fisheries industry in order to ease the problem of food security, was expected to be funded by New Zealand. New Zealand, together with Australia, led international efforts to provide significant support, in the form of fresh water supplies and desalination units, to alleviate the effects of severe drought in Tuvalu in late 2011 (see Environmental Concerns). In September of that year Australian Prime Minister Julia Gillard announced that Tuvalu was among the countries to be included in the expanded Pacific Seasonal Workers Pilot Scheme, an initiative intended to facilitate the recruitment of seasonal horticultural workers from Pacific countries by Australian enterprises in order to meet their seasonal harvest needs.

During a visit to Taiwan in December 2006 Prime Minister Apisai Ielemia declared that Tuvalu was Taiwan's staunchest international ally and would continue to offer its support to Taiwanese efforts to secure international recognition. During another visit to Taiwan in February 2009, Ielemia held discussions with Taiwanese President Ma Ying-jeou, following which the two leaders pledged their commitment to the development of bilateral relations. President Ma also expressed Taiwan's support for Tuvalu in addressing the problems arising from global warming (see Environmental Concerns). On a tour of Taiwan's six Pacific allies in March 2010, President Ma included a brief stop in Tuvalu; the focus of the visit was vocational training, and President Ma reiterated support for Tuvalu in its efforts to address the increasingly pressing issue of rising sea levels. Tuvalu established an embassy in Taiwan in March 2013.

In November 2011 Tuvalu was one of eight Pacific states and territories that jointly established the Polynesian Leaders Group (see p. 478), which was widely viewed as a counterfoil to the Melanesian Spearhead Group. The first formal meeting of the Group, which pledged to enhance co-operation among its members across a wide range of fields, including trade and investment, education, climate change and health, was held in the Cook Islands, on the sidelines of the annual Pacific Islands Forum (see p. 426) summit, in August 2012.

After enrolling with the Tuvaluan shipping register, in July 2012 approximately 20 Iranian oil tankers began sailing under the Tuvaluan flag as part of a strategy to circumvent the Western sanctions regime against Iranian petroleum exports. However, in response to US pressure, the ships were deregistered in August.

CONSTITUTION AND GOVERNMENT

Tuvalu is a constitutional monarchy. Under the Constitution of 1978, executive authority is vested in the British sovereign, as head of state, and is exercisable by her representative, the Governor-General, who is appointed on the recommendation of the Prime Minister and acts, in almost all cases, on the advice of the Cabinet. Legislative power is vested in the unicameral Parliament, with 15 members elected by universal adult suffrage for four years (subject to dissolution). The Cabinet is led by the Prime Minister, who is elected by and from the members of Parliament. On the Prime Minister's recommendation, other ministers are appointed by the Governor-General. The Cabinet is responsible to Parliament. Judicial power is exercised by Magistrates' and Island Courts and the High Court. Each of the inhabited atolls has its own elected Island Council, which is responsible for local government.

REGIONAL AND INTERNATIONAL CO-OPERATION

Tuvalu is a member of the Pacific Community (see p. 422), the Pacific Islands Forum (see p. 426) and the UN's Economic and

Social Commission for Asia and the Pacific (ESCAP, see p. 31). In 1993 the country was admitted to the Asian Development Bank (ADB, see p. 214). Tuvalu was one of eight founding members of the Polynesian Leaders Group, which was established in November 2011.

Tuvalu joined the UN in 2000. The country is also a member of the Commonwealth (see p. 244) and joined the International Monetary Fund (IMF, see p. 148) in June 2010.

ECONOMIC AFFAIRS

In 2011, according to estimates by the World Bank, Tuvalu's gross national income (GNI), measured at average 2009–11 prices, was US $49m., equivalent to $5,010 per head. During 2002–11, it was estimated, the population increased at an average annual rate of 0.4%, while gross domestic product (GDP) per head decreased, in real terms, by an average of 0.3% per year. According to figures from the Asian Development Bank (ADB), overall GDP grew, in real terms, at an average annual rate of 0.7% in 2002–11. GDP contracted by 0.6% in 2011, but increased by 1.2% in 2012.

Agriculture (including fishing) is, with the exception of copra production, of a basic subsistence nature. The sector contributed 23.2% of GDP in 2011. In mid-2013, according to FAO estimates, the sector engaged some 25% of the labour force. Coconuts (the source of copra) are the only cash crop. Pulaka, taro, papayas, the screw-pine (*Pandanus*) and bananas are cultivated as food crops, and honey is produced. From the 1990s agriculture was increasingly affected by climate change and rising sea levels. More frequent high tides caused flooding and damaged crops, particularly the important taro crop; such floods also killed tree roots, which reduced the harvest of coconuts and other fruits. Livestock comprises pigs, poultry and goats. Fish and other sea products are staple constituents of the islanders' diet. Although revenue from the sale of fishing licences to foreign fleets has declined in recent years, owing to decreasing catches, it remains an important source of income, earning $A5.6m. in 2011 (compared with $A11.8m. in 2001), equivalent to 17.1% of total revenue. A new licensing arrangement was expected to contribute to an increase in income from fishing licence fees to a projected $A6.8m. in 2012. The GDP of the agricultural sector increased at an average annual rate of 2.0% in 2002–11, according to ADB figures. Sectoral GDP rose by 0.5% in 2011.

Industry (including mining, manufacturing, construction and utilities) accounted for 9.3% of GDP in 2011. In 2002–11, according to ADB figures, industrial GDP expanded at an average annual rate of 3.3%. However, industrial GDP contracted by 28.7% in 2011. Manufacturing is confined to the small-scale production of coconut-based products, soap and handicrafts. The manufacturing sector contributed some 1.1% of GDP in 2011. In the same year the construction sector provided around 8.3% of GDP. According to ADB figures, between 2002 and 2011 the construction sector increased at an average annual rate of 3.8%. However, sectoral GDP declined by 35.4% in 2011.

Energy is derived principally from a power plant (fuelled by oil) and, on the outer islands, solar power. Tuvalu has announced its intention to reduce its carbon output to zero by 2020 through increased use of solar and wind power. In 2009 it was reported that the commencement of a programme to install solar power had resulted in a significant reduction in the country's fuel imports.

The Government is an important employer (engaging 1,185 people in 2001, equivalent to about one-half of the labour force), and consequently the services sector makes a relatively large contribution to Tuvalu's economy, providing some 67.4% of GDP in 2011. The islands' remote situation and lack of amenities have hindered the development of a tourism industry. Visitor arrivals totalled some 2,000 in 2011, according to provisional official figures. In 2011 receipts from the leasing of the islands' internet domain address reached US $A2.4m. The GDP of the services sector increased at an average annual rate of 0.9% in 2002–11, according to ADB figures. Growth of 6.4% was recorded in 2011.

In 2011 Tuvalu recorded a visible merchandise trade deficit of $A19.5m. and the deficit on the balance of payments reached $A14.9m. In 2011, according to ADB preliminary figures, the cost of imports totalled US $97.4m., while export revenue reached US $5.3m. The principal sources of imports in 2011 were Japan (providing 32.8% of the total) and the People's Republic of China. The principal markets for exports were Japan (taking 71.1% of the total), Switzerland and Australia. The main imports in 2005 were mineral products, prepared foodstuffs, machinery, mechanical appliances and electrical equipment, and transport equipment. An important source of support for the balance of payments has been remittances from Tuvaluan emigrant workers. Remittances from Tuvaluan seafarers employed on foreign vessels have weakened since around 2008, although this decline has been offset to some extent by remittances from workers engaged in seasonal harvesting in New Zealand and Australia. Gross workers' remittances declined from US $4.1m. in 2009 to US $3.1m. in 2010, but rose to US $3.4m. in 2011.

According to ADB figures, the 2011 budget allowed for expenditure of $A35.0m. (excluding net lending of $A–1.7m.), while revenue (including grants of $A12.2m.) totalled $A33.3m. The Tuvalu Trust Fund (TTF) was established in 1987, with assistance from New Zealand, Australia and the United Kingdom, to generate funding, through overseas investment, for development projects. At March 2012 the market value of the TTF stood at $A122.9m., according to the IMF, which projected that the balance of the CIF would decline to only $A2.1m. in 2013 (from $A15.3m in 2009). The market value of the TTF stood below its required maintained value throughout 2008–12, meaning that resources could not be transferred to the Consolidated Investment Fund (a depository of the TTF), which was used to finance budget deficits. In 2011/12 New Zealand budgeted for bilateral assistance worth $NZ5m., while aid from Australia was budgeted at $A9.8m. in 2012/13. Tuvalu has also received significant financial assistance from Taiwan. Other donors have included Japan and the European Union. According to the ADB, Tuvalu's external debt totalled US $13m. at the end of 2012; in 2011 the cost of servicing the debt was equivalent to 9.9% of the value of exports of goods and services. The annual rate of inflation averaged 2.6% in 2002–11, according to ADB figures; consumer prices rose by 1.4% in 2012.

Tuvalu has continued to suffer from the increasing impact of climate change. However, in an attempt to turn the arrival of the annual high tide to the islands' advantage by raising awareness of the issue of rising sea levels, in February 2010 Tuvalu held its first King Tide Festival; through initiatives such as this, the Government hoped to increase revenue from tourism. Receipts from the sale of fishing licences have become more vulnerable to variations in fish stocks. Amid reports that in the previous year Tuvalu had received only 5% of the revenue derived from local fishing activities, in late 2010 New Zealand expressed its support for a four-year fisheries programme that was expected to require funding of nearly US $3m. In 2011 the country reportedly signed a new agreement with VeriSign, the company to which the '.tv' internet domain facility had been leased, extending the arrangement, which had been due to expire in 2016, until the end of 2021. With numerous Tuvaluan seafarers having lost their jobs as a result of the global economic downturn, remittances were subdued, and the level of household poverty was reported to have increased to 20% in 2010. A priority for successive governments has been the need to reduce the disparities in living standards between Funafuti and the outer islands. The high level of public debt, estimated by the ADB at 44% of GDP in 2010, has become an issue of some concern, although this figure moderated to 29% in 2011. According to ADB data, GDP rose by 1.2% in 2012, following three successive years of contraction. This recovery was driven by increased activity in the retail and fishing sectors (a new licensing scheme having been introduced in the latter), as well as investment in infrastructure and education. Consumer prices expanded slightly in 2011–12, while remittance inflows from seafarers continued to deteriorate. These trends were expected to continue during 2013, and the ADB forecast GDP growth of 1.3% in that year.

PUBLIC HOLIDAYS

2014: 1 January (New Year's Day), 10 March (Commonwealth Day), 18 April (Good Friday), 21 April (Easter Monday), 12 May (Gospel Day), 9 June (Queen's Official Birthday), 4 August (National Children's Day), 1–2 October (Tuvalu Day, anniversary of independence), 10 November (Prince of Wales's Birthday), 25–26 December (Christmas).

Statistical Survey

Source (unless otherwise indicated): Central Statistics Division, Ministry of Finance, Economic Planning and Industries, PMB, Vaiaku, Funafuti; tel. 20107; fax 21210; e-mail statistics@tuvalu.tv; internet www.spc.int/prism/country/tv/stats/.

AREA AND POPULATION

Land Area: 25.6 sq km (9.9 sq miles).

Population: 9,043 at census of 17 November 1991; 9,561 (males 4,729, females 4,832) at census of 1 November 2002. *By Atoll* (2002 census): Funafuti 4,492; Vaitupu 1,591; Nanumea 664; Niutao 663; Nanumaga 589; Nukufetau 586; Nui 548; Nukulaelae 393; Niulakita 35. *Mid-2013* (Secretariat of the Pacific Community estimate): 11,323 (Source: Pacific Regional Information System).

Density (at mid-2013): 442 per sq km.

Population by Age and Sex (Secretariat of the Pacific Community estimates at mid-2013): *0–14:* 3,517 (males 1,827, females 1,690); *15–64:* 7,189 (males 3,574, females 3,615); *65 and over:* 617 (males 246, females 371); *Total* 11,323 (males 5647, females 5,676) (Source: Pacific Regional Information System).

Principal Towns (population at 2002 census): Alapi 1,024; Fakaifou 1,007; Senala 589; Teone 540; Vaiaku (capital) 516; Motufoua 506. Source: Thomas Brinkhoff, *City Population* (internet www.citypopulation.de).

Births and Deaths (Secretariat of the Pacific Community estimates, 2010, estimates): Registered live births 255 (birth rate 22.9 per 1,000); Registered deaths 100 (death rate 9.0 per 1,000). Source: Pacific Regional Information System.

Life Expectancy (years at birth, WHO estimates): 64 (males 64; females 63) in 2009. Source: WHO, *World Health Statistics*.

Economically Active Population: In 1979 there were 936 people in paid employment, 50% of them in government service. In 1979 114 Tuvaluans were employed by the Nauru Phosphate Co, with a smaller number employed in Kiribati and about 255 on foreign ships. At the 1991 census the total economically active population (aged 15 years and over) stood at 2,383 (males 1,605, females 778). *Mid-2013* (estimates): Agriculture, etc. 1,000; Total labour force 4,000 (Source: FAO).

HEALTH AND WELFARE
Key Indicators

Total Fertility Rate (children per woman, 2010): 3.1.

Under-5 Mortality Rate (per 1,000 live births, 2010): 33.

Physicians (per 1,000 head, 2009): 1.1.

Hospital Beds (per 1,000 head, 2001): 5.6.

Health Expenditure (2009): US $ per head (PPP): 382.

Health Expenditure (2009): % of GDP: 14.3.

Health Expenditure (2009): public (% of total): 84.7.

Access to Sanitation (% of persons, 2010): 85.

For sources and definitions, see explanatory note on p. vi.

AGRICULTURE, ETC.

Principal Crops (metric tons, 2011, FAO estimates): Coconuts 2,075; Roots and tubers 138; Vegetables 531; Bananas 265.

Livestock ('000 head, year ending September 2011, unless otherwise indicated, FAO estimates): Pigs 13.6; Chickens 45; Ducks 15 (2008).

Livestock Products (metric tons, 2011, FAO estimates): Chicken meat 50; Pig meat 114; Hen eggs 30; Honey 6.

Fishing (metric tons, live weight, 2010, FAO estimates): Total catch 11,324 (Skipjack tuna 7,480; Yellowfin tuna 950).

Source: FAO.

FINANCE

Currency and Exchange Rates: Australian and Tuvaluan currencies are both in use. Australian currency: 100 cents = 1 Australian dollar ($A). *Sterling, US Dollar and Euro Equivalents* (31 December 2012): £1 sterling = $A1.517; US $1 = $A0.961; €1 = $A1.268; $A100 = £65.94 = US $104.1 = €78.86. *Average Exchange Rate* ($A per US dollar): 1.0902 in 2010; 0.9695 in 2011; 0.9658 in 2012.

Budget ($A '000, 2008): Current revenue 16,790 (Revenue from taxation 6,772, Non-tax revenue 10,018); Grants 28,567; *Total revenue and grants* 45,357; Total expenditure 42,936. *2011:* Total revenue and grants 33,278; Total expenditure 35,004 (excl. net lending −1,726) (Source: Asian Development Bank).

Official Development Assistance (US $ million, 2002): Bilateral 11.2; Multilateral 0.5; Total 11.7 (all grants). *2008:* Total assistance 17.0. Source: UN, *Statistical Yearbook for Asia and the Pacific*.

Cost of Living (Consumer Price Index; base: November 2010 = 100): All items 102.6 in 2009; 100.7 in 2010; 101.2 in 2011. Source: Asian Development Bank.

Gross Domestic Product ($A '000 at constant 2005 prices): 33,886 in 2009; 33,413 in 2010; 33,223 in 2011.

Expenditure on the Gross Domestic Product ($A '000 at current prices, 2011): Government final consumption expenditure 24,918.8; Private final consumption expenditure 8,427.3; Gross fixed capital formation 18,407.7; *Total domestic expenditure* 51,753.8; Exports of goods and services 600.9; *Less* Imports of goods and services 16,828.6; *GDP in purchasers' values* 35,526.2. Source: UN Statistics Division, National Accounts Main Aggregates Database.

Gross Domestic Product by Economic Activity ($A '000 at current prices, 2011): Agriculture, hunting, forestry and fishing 8,450.6; Mining and quarrying 36.8; Manufacturing 390.1; Electricity, gas and water −48.0; Construction 3,016.3; Trade, restaurants and hotels 4,082.7; Transport, storage and communications 1,994.8; Finance and real estate 5,937.0; Public administration 6,326.4; Education 3,013.7; Health 1,866.3; Community and personal services 1,305.7; *Gross value added* 36,372.4; Taxes, less subsidies, on products 2,484.4; *Less* Imputed bank service charge 1,339.7; *GDP in purchasers' values* 37,517.1.

Balance of Payments ($A '000, 2011): Exports of goods f.o.b. 642; Imports of goods f.o.b. −20,155; *Trade balance* −19,512; Exports of services 3,381; Imports of services −32,235; *Balance on goods and services* −48,366; Primary income assets 19,492; Primary income liabilities −694; *Balance on goods, services and primary income* −29,568; Secondary income (net) 14,631; *Current balance* −14,939.

EXTERNAL TRADE

Principal Commodities ($A '000, 2005): *Imports:* Animals and animal products 1,473.8; Vegetable products 1,224.2; Prepared foodstuffs 2,385.1; Mineral products 3,661.2; Chemical products 734.5; Textiles and textile articles 759.2; Base metals and articles thereof 695.1; Machinery, mechanical appliances and electrical equipment 2,318.9; Transportation equipment 884.8; Total (incl. others) 16,908.3. *Exports:* Mineral products 5.9; Wood and wood products 10.0; Base metals and articles thereof 12.3; Machinery, mechanical appliances and electrical equipment 13.9; Transportation equipment 9.3; Instruments—measuring, musical 14.9; Total (incl. others) 80.0. *2006:* Total imports 17,903.0; Total exports 130.0. *2007:* Total imports 18,503.0; Total exports 120.0. Source: Asian Development Bank.

Principal Trading Partners (US $ million, 2011, preliminary): *Imports:* Australia 1.84; China, People's Republic 14.83; Japan 32.04; Malaysia 5.76; New Zealand 3.15; Total (incl. others) 97.42. *Exports:* Australia 0.22; Japan 3.79; Switzerland 0.33; Total (incl. others) 5.33.

Source: Asian Development Bank.

TRANSPORT

Shipping: *Flag Registered Fleet* (at 31 December 2012): Number of vessels 238; Total displacement ('000 grt) 1,309.6. Source: Lloyd's List Intelligence (www.lloydslistintelligence.com).

TOURISM

Tourist Arrivals: 1,651 in 2008; 1,580 in 2009; 2,000 in 2010–11 (provisional).

Tourist Arrivals by Country of Residence (2009): Australia 194; Fiji 251; Japan 397; New Zealand 188; United Kingdom 54; USA 70; Total (incl. others) 1,580.

Source: mainly World Tourism Organization.

COMMUNICATIONS MEDIA

Telephones (main lines, 2011): 1,400 in use.

Mobile Cellular Telephones (subscribers, 2011): 2,100.

Internet Users (2009): 4,300.

Broadband Subscribers (2011): 400.

Source: International Telecommunication Union.

EDUCATION

Pre-school (2005/06 unless otherwise indicated): 57 teachers (2004/05); 711 pupils.

Primary (2001 unless otherwise indicated): 9 government schools, 1 private school; 103 teachers (2006); 2,093 pupils (2007).

General Secondary (2005): 2 government schools; 56 teachers; 593 pupils..

Pupil-teacher Ratio (primary education, UNESCO estimate): 19.2 in 2003/04. Source: UNESCO Institute for Statistics.

Directory

The Government

HEAD OF STATE

Sovereign: HM Queen ELIZABETH II.
Governor-General: Sir IAKOBA TAEIA ITALELI (took office May 2010).

CABINET
(May 2013)

Prime Minister: WILLIE TELAVI.

Minister of Foreign Affairs, Environment, Trade, Labour and Tourism: APISAI IELEMIA.

Minister of Finance, Economic Planning and Industries: (vacant).

Minister of Communications, Transport and Public Utilities: KAUSEA NATANO.

Minister of Education, Youth and Sports: FALESA PITOI.

Minister of Health: TAOM TANUKALE.

Minister of Works and Natural Resources: (vacant).

Minister of Home Affairs and Rural Development: PELENIKE TEKINENE ISAIA.

MINISTRIES

Office of the Prime Minister: PMB, Vaiaku, Funafuti; tel. 20101; fax 20820.

Ministry of Education, Youth and Sports: POB 37, Vaiaku, Funafuti; tel. 20405; fax 20832; e-mail ses@tuvalu.tv.

Ministry of Finance, Economic Planning and Industries: PMB, Vaiaku, Funafuti; tel. 20202; fax 20210; e-mail secfin@tuvalu.tv.

Ministry of Foreign Affairs: Vaiaku, Funafuti; tel. 20102; fax 20820.

Ministry of Health: PMB, Vaiaku, Funafuti; tel. 20403; fax 20832; e-mail soh@tuvalu.tv.

Ministry of Home Affairs and Rural Development: PMB, Vaiaku, Funafuti; tel. 20172; fax 20821.

Ministry of Natural Resources and Environment: PMB, Vaiaku, Funafuti; tel. 20827; fax 20826.

Ministry of Public Utilities and Industries: PMB, Vaiaku, Funafuti.

Ministry of Works, Communications and Transport: PMB, Vaiaku, Funafuti; tel. 20052; fax 20772; e-mail tuvmet@tuvalu.tv.

Legislature

PARLIAMENT

Parliament has 15 members, who hold office for a term of up to four years. At the general election held on 16 September 2010, 10 of the 15 previous incumbents were re-elected. There are no political parties.

Speaker: Sir KAMUTA LATASI.

Diplomatic Representation

There are no embassies or high commissions in Tuvalu. The British High Commissioner in Fiji is also accredited as High Commissioner to Tuvalu. Other Ambassadors or High Commissioners accredited to Tuvalu include the Australian, New Zealand, US, French and Japanese Ambassadors in Fiji.

Judicial System

The Supreme Law is embodied in the Constitution. The High Court is the superior court of record, presided over by the Chief Justice, and has jurisdiction to consider appeals from judgments of the Magistrates' Courts and the Island Courts. Appeals from the High Court have traditionally been heard by the Court of Appeal in Fiji or, in the ultimate case, with the Judicial Committee of the Privy Council in the United Kingdom.

There are eight Island Courts with limited jurisdiction in criminal and civil cases.

High Court: Vaiaku, Funafuti; tel. 20837; Chief Justice FREDERICK GORDON WARD.

Office of the Attorney-General: Funafuti; tel. 20823; fax 20819; e-mail agoffice@tuvalu.tv; Attorney-General ESELEALOFA APINELU.

Religion

CHRISTIANITY

Te Ekalesia Kelisiano Tuvalu (The Christian Church of Tuvalu): POB 2, Funafuti; tel. 20755; fax 20651; f. 1861; autonomous since 1968; derived from the Congregationalist foundation of the London Missionary Society; some 91% of the population are adherents; Pres. Rev. TOFIGA FALANI; Gen. Sec. Rev. TAFUE M. LUSAMA.

Roman Catholic Church: Catholic Centre, POB 58, Funafuti; tel. and fax 20527; e-mail cathcent@tuvalu.tv; 131 adherents (31 Dec. 2006); Superior Fr JOHN IKATAERE RARIKIN.

Other churches with adherents in Tuvalu include the Church of Jesus Christ of Latter-day Saints (Mormons), the Jehovah's Witnesses, the New Apostolic Church and the Seventh-day Adventists.

BAHÁ'Í FAITH

National Spiritual Assembly: POB 48, Vaiaku Side, Funafuti; tel. 20645; e-mail natsectuv@yahoo.com; mems resident in 8 localities; Sec. MELALI TAAPE.

The Press

Te Lama: Ekalesia Kelisiano Tuvalu, POB 2, Valuku, Funafuti; tel. and fax 20755; e-mail gs_ekt@yahoo.com; quarterly; religious; Pres. Rev. TOFIGA FALANI; Editor Rev. KITIONA TAUSI; circ. 1,000.

Tuvalu Echoes: Broadcasting and Information Office, Vaiaku, Funafuti; tel. 20138; fax 20732; f. 1984; fortnightly; English; Editor MELAKI TAEPE; circ. 250.

Broadcasting and Communications

TELECOMMUNICATIONS

Tuvalu Telecommunications Corporation: Vaiaku, Funafuti; tel. 20001; fax 20800; f. 1994; Gen. Man. SIMETI LOPATI.

BROADCASTING

Tuvalu Media Corporation: PMB, Vaiaku, Funafuti; tel. 20731; fax 20732; e-mail media@tuvalu.tv; internet www.tuvalu-news.tv/tmc; f. 1999; govt-owned.

Radio

Radio Tuvalu: Broadcasting and Information Office, PMB, Vaiaku, Funafuti; tel. 20138; fax 20732; f. 1975; daily broadcasts in Tuvaluan and English, 43 hours per week; Programme Producer RUBY S. ALEFAIO.

Finance

BANKS

(cap. = capital; dep. = deposits; m. = million)

Development Bank of Tuvalu: POB 9, Vaiaku, Funafuti; tel. 20199; fax 20850; f. 1993; replaced the Business Development Advisory Bureau; Gen. Man. TAUKAVE POOLO.

National Bank of Tuvalu: POB 13, Vaiaku, Funafuti; tel. 20803; fax 20802; e-mail nationalbankoftuvalu@gmail.com; f. 1980; commercial bank; govt-owned; ($A '000) cap. 471.0, dep. 21,207 (Dec. 2011); Chair. MINUTE TAUPO; Gen. Man. SIOSE P. TEO; brs on all atolls.

Trade and Industry

GOVERNMENT AGENCIES

National Fishing Corporation of Tuvalu (NAFICOT): POB 93, Funafuti; tel. 20724; fax 20152; fishing vessel operators; seafood-processing and -marketing; agents for diesel engine spare parts, fishing supplies and marine electronics; Gen. Man. SEMU SOPOANGA TAAFAKI.

Tuvalu Philatelic Bureau: POB 24, Funafuti; tel. 20224; fax 20712.

CHAMBER OF COMMERCE

Tuvalu Chamber of Commerce: POB 27, Vaiaku, Funafuti; tel. 20846; fax 20800; Chair. MATANILE IOSEFA; Sec. TEO PASEFIKA.

UTILITIES

Electricity

Tuvalu Electricity Corporation (TEC): POB 32, Vaiaku, Funafuti; tel. 20352; fax 20351; e-mail mlotolua@tectuvalu.tv; internet www.tectuvalu.tv; Gen. Man. MAFALU LOTOLUA.

CO-OPERATIVE

Tuvalu Co-operative Society Ltd: POB 11, Funafuti; tel. 20747; fax 20748; e-mail mlaafai@tuvalu.tv; f. 1979; est. by amalgamation of the 8 island socs; controls retail trade in the islands; Gen. Man. MONISE LAAFAI; Registrar AUNESE MAKOI.

TRADE UNION

Tuvalu Overseas Seamen's Union (TOSU): POB 99, Funafuti; tel. 20609; fax 20610; e-mail tosu@tuvalu.tv; f. 1988; Sec.-Gen. FEPUALI KITISENI.

Transport

ROADS

Funafuti has some impacted-coral roads totalling around 8 km in length; elsewhere, tracks exist.

SHIPPING

There is a deep-water lagoon at the point of entry, Funafuti, and ships are able to enter the lagoon at Nukufetau. Irregular shipping services connect Tuvalu with Fiji and elsewhere. The Government operates an inter-island vessel.

CIVIL AVIATION

In 1992 a new runway was constructed with aid from the European Union to replace the grass landing strip on Funafuti. Air Marshall Islands operates a three-weekly service between Funafuti, Nadi (Fiji) and Majuro (Marshall Islands). The Government of Tuvalu purchased a substantial shareholding in Air Fiji in 2001, but the carrier terminated all operations in 2009. Air Pacific commenced a twice-weekly service from Fiji in August 2008.

Tourism

In 2004 there was one hotel, with 16 rooms, on Funafuti and three guest houses. Visitor arrivals were estimated to total 1,580 in 2009 and, according to provisional figures, some 2,000 in 2010–11. The majority of visitors in 2009 were from Japan, Fiji, Australia and New Zealand. In a new initiative to attract tourists, in February 2010 Tuvalu held its first King Tide Festival, celebrating the arrival of the annual high tide.

Tuvalu Tourism Office: PMB, Funafuti; tel. 20840; fax 20722; e-mail silaatitofuola@ymail.com; internet www.timelesstuvalu.com; Tourism Officer SILAATI TOFUOLA FILIAKE.

Education

Education is provided by the Government, and is compulsory between the ages of six and 15 years. In 2001 there were nine government and one private primary schools, with a total of 2,093 pupils in 2007 and 103 teachers in 2006. There were two secondary schools with 56 teachers and 593 pupils in 2005. The only tertiary institution is the Maritime Training School at Amatuku on Funafuti, with vocational, technical and commerce-related courses. About 60 people graduate from the school annually. Further training or vocational courses are available in Fiji and Kiribati. The University of the South Pacific (based in Suva, Fiji) has an extension centre on Funafuti offering diploma and vocational courses and the first two years of degree courses (the latter requiring completion in Suva). A programme of major reforms in the education system in Tuvalu, begun in the early 1990s, resulted in the lengthening of primary schooling (from six to eight years) and a compulsory two years of secondary education, as well as the introduction of courses at the Maritime Training School. Total government expenditure on education in 2001 was equivalent to some 35% of total budgetary expenditure.

UGANDA

Introductory Survey

LOCATION, CLIMATE, LANGUAGE, RELIGION, FLAG, CAPITAL

The Republic of Uganda is a land-locked equatorial country in East Africa, bordered by South Sudan to the north, the Democratic Republic of the Congo (DRC) to the west, Kenya to the east and Rwanda, Tanzania and Lake Victoria to the south. The climate is tropical, with temperatures, moderated by the altitude of the country, varying between 15°C and 30°C. The official language is English and there are many local languages, the most important of which is Luganda. About 75% of the population follow Christian beliefs, while some 15% are Muslims. The national flag (proportions 2 by 3) has six horizontal stripes: black, gold, red, black, gold and red. In the centre is a white disc containing a crested crane. The capital is Kampala.

CONTEMPORARY POLITICAL HISTORY

Historical Context

Formerly a British protectorate, Uganda became an independent member of the Commonwealth on 9 October 1962. The Government was led by Dr Milton Obote, leader of the Uganda People's Congress (UPC) from 1960 and Prime Minister from April 1962. At independence the country comprised four regions, including the kingdom of Buganda, which had federal status. Exactly one year after independence Uganda became a republic, with Mutesa II, Kabaka (King) of Buganda, (a region bordering Lake Victoria in southern Uganda) as first President. In February 1966 Obote led a successful coup against the Kabaka, and in April he became executive President. In September 1967 a new Constitution was introduced, establishing a unitary republic, and Buganda was brought under the control of the central Government. In 1969 all opposition parties were banned.

Obote was overthrown in January 1971 by the army, led by Maj.-Gen. (later Field Marshal) Idi Amin Dada, who assumed full executive powers and suspended political activity. Amin declared himself Head of State, took over legislative powers and suspended parts of the 1967 Constitution. In August 1972 Amin, proclaiming an 'economic war' to free Uganda from foreign domination, undertook a mass expulsion of non-citizen Asians (who comprised the majority of the resident Asian population), thereby incurring widespread international condemnation.

Amin's regime was characterized by the ruthless elimination of suspected opponents, mass flights of refugees to neighbouring countries and periodic purges of the army (which, in turn, perpetrated numerous atrocities). In February 1976 Amin claimed that large areas of western Kenya were historically part of Uganda, and in November 1978 Uganda annexed the Kagera salient from Tanzania. In early 1979 an invasion force comprising Tanzanian troops and the Uganda National Liberation Army (UNLA) gained control of the southern region of Uganda. Amin's forces capitulated, and in April a Tanzanian assault force entered Kampala. The remaining pro-Amin troops were defeated in June. Amin fled initially to Libya and in 1980 took up permanent residence in Saudi Arabia. He remained in exile there until his death in August 2003.

Domestic Political Affairs

A provisional Government, the National Executive Council (NEC), was established in April 1979 from the ranks of the Uganda National Liberation Front (UNLF, a coalition of 18 previously exiled groups), with Dr Yusuf Lule, a former vice-chancellor of Makerere University, as President. Lule was succeeded in June by Godfrey Binaisa (a former Attorney-General), who was, in turn, overthrown by the Military Commission of the UNLF in May 1980. The elections, in December, were contested by four parties and won by the UPC, with Obote, who remained its leader, becoming President for the second time. The defeated parties complained of gross electoral malpractice by UPC supporters.

The Obote Government was subject to constant attack from guerrilla groups operating inside the country. Hundreds of Obote's opponents were detained, including Democratic Party (DP) members of the National Assembly. Following the

withdrawal of Tanzanian troops in June 1981, there were reports from the West Nile Region of further atrocities by Ugandan soldiers. In January 1982 the Uganda Popular Front was formed to co-ordinate, from abroad, the activities of the main opposition groups in exile: the Uganda Freedom Movement (UFM), the Uganda National Rescue Front and the National Resistance Movement (NRM), led by Lule and his former Minister of Defence, Lt-Gen. (later Gen.) Yoweri Museveni. The NRM had a military wing, the National Resistance Army (NRA), led by Museveni. Lule died in 1985, whereupon Museveni became sole leader of the NRM and NRA.

In July 1985 Obote was overthrown in a military coup, led by Brig. (later Lt-Gen.) Basilio Okello. (Obote was subsequently granted political asylum by Zambia.) A Military Council, headed by Lt-Gen. (later Gen.) Tito Okello, the Commander-in-Chief of the army, was established to govern the country, pending elections to be held one year later. In subsequent months groups that had been in opposition to Obote, with the exception of the NRA and the NRM, reached agreement with the new administration and accepted positions on the Military Council. An amnesty was declared for exiles who had supported Amin.

In August 1985 the NRA, led by Museveni, entered into negotiations with the Government (under the auspices of President Daniel arap Moi of Kenya), while conducting a simultaneous military campaign to overthrow Okello. During the following two months the NRA gained control of large areas of the country and in January 1986 the NRA took control of Kampala by force and dissolved the Military Council. Okello fled to Sudan, and then to Tanzania. On 29 January Museveni was sworn in as President, and in February he announced the formation of a new Cabinet, comprising mainly members of the NRA and NRM, but also representatives of other political groups including the DP, the UPC, the UFM, the Federal Democratic Movement (FEDEMO), and three members of the previous administration. A National Resistance Council (NRC) was formed to act in place of a legislature for an indefinite period. All party political activity was banned in March. At a summit meeting in March the Heads of State of all neighbouring countries pledged their support for Museveni.

In late 1986 a rebellion by members of a so-called 'Holy Spirit' movement began in northern and eastern Uganda; between December 1986 and November 1987 some 5,000 ill-equipped 'Holy Spirit' fighters were reportedly killed in clashes with the NRA. By December 1987 the rebellion had been suppressed and its leader had escaped to Kenya. Surviving members of the movement, however, regrouped as the Lord's Resistance Army (LRA).

In February 1989 the first national election since 1980 was held. The NRC, hitherto composed solely of presidential nominees, was expanded from 98 to 278 members, to include 210 elected representatives. While 20 ministerial posts were reserved for nominated members of the NRC, 50 were allocated to elected members. Also in February Museveni appointed a Constitutional Commission to assess public opinion on Uganda's political future and to draft a new constitution.

In October 1989 (despite opposition from the DP) the NRC approved draft legislation to prolong the Government's term of office by five years from January 1990 (when its mandate had been due to expire); the NRM justified the extension of its rule by claiming that it required further time in which to organize elections and complete other preparations. In March 1990 the NRM extended the national ban on party political activity for a further five years. In May 1991 Museveni formally invited all former resident Asians expelled at the time of the Amin regime to return, pledging the restitution of expropriated property.

In December 1992 the Constitutional Commission presented its draft constitution to the Government. The draft was published in March 1993, and in the following month the NRC approved legislation authorizing the establishment of a Constituent Assembly. In July the NRC adopted a constitutional amendment revoking the abolition of traditional rulers, as provided for under the 1967 Constitution. Restored traditional rulers would, however, have only ceremonial significance.

In January 1994 the Ugandan National Democratic Alliance and the Ugandan Federal Army agreed to suspend hostilities, under the provisions of a government amnesty, and in March senior members of the Ruwenzururu Kingdom Freedom Movement in the south-west formally surrendered to the authorities. However, following the collapse of negotiations with the Government, the LRA intensified guerrilla activities in northern Uganda. From 1994 large numbers of security forces were deployed in the region, but failed to suppress the rebellion.

At elections to the 288-member Constituent Assembly, which took place on 28 March 1994, more than 1,500 candidates contested the 214 elective seats. Although the elections were officially conducted on a non-party basis, NRM members were believed to have secured the majority of votes in the centre, west and south-west of the country, whereas UPC and DP members, who advocated an immediate return to multi-party politics, secured the most seats in the north and east. The Constituent Assembly, which also comprised nominated representatives of the armed forces, political parties, trade unions, and civic organizations, debated and amended the draft constitution, finally enacting it in September 1995. The Constitution, under the terms of which a national referendum on the future introduction of a multi-party political system was scheduled to take place in 2000, was promulgated in October 1995.

A presidential election took place in May 1996, at which Museveni was returned to office, winning 74.2% of the votes cast. The election was pronounced free and fair by international observers. Legislative elections took place in June at which the total membership of the NRC, redesignated the Parliament under the new Constitution, was reduced from 278 to 276, comprising 214 elected and 62 nominated representatives.

During 1993–98 the LRA was alleged to have killed as many as 10,000 people, while some 220,000 sought refuge in protected camps. The LRA's use of abducted children as soldiers (reportedly some 10,000 by early 1999) attracted widespread international condemnation. The Government strongly resisted pressure to resume negotiations with the LRA, but in May 1999, appeared to modify its policy towards the rebel movement by offering it an amnesty and promising its leader, Joseph Kony, a cabinet post in the event of his being democratically elected. In the west, meanwhile, the Uganda People's Defence Forces (UPDF, as the NRA had been restyled) fought intermittently with two rebel groups: the Allied Democratic Forces (ADF), mainly comprising Ugandan Islamist fundamentalist rebels, exiled Rwandan Hutu militiamen and former soldiers from Zaire (which became the DRC in May 1997), and the West Nile Bank Front (WNBF). Although WNBF activities subsided in mid-1997, following the killing of several hundred of its members by Sudanese rebels, the ADF mounted a persistent terrorism campaign against western Ugandan targets.

Towards multi-party politics

In July 1999 legislation was enacted providing for a referendum on a multi-party political system to take place in the following year. However, most political parties announced that they would boycott the referendum on the grounds that it would be manipulated by the NRM for its own objectives. Ugandan party leaders had criticized the readiness of some Western donors to support the referendum process, claiming that by so doing they were legitimizing the prevailing suspension of active political opposition. At the referendum, which proceeded on 29 June 2000, 90.7% of participants voted in favour of retaining the existing 'no-party' political system. (However, the result was effectively nullified by the Constitutional Court in 2004—see below.)

A presidential election was held on 12 March 2001, following a delay of five days after it was revealed that the electoral register contained some 2.5m. more voters than there were citizens eligible to vote. At the election, which had a participation rate of 70%, Museveni was re-elected President, winning 69.3% of the votes cast. His main challenger, Kizza Besigye, won 27.8%. Legislative elections were held on 26 June. The rate of voter participation was reported as being low. The total number of seats in Parliament was increased to 292 (comprising 214 elected and 78 nominated representatives), of which the NRM reportedly secured more than 70%. In July Museveni appointed a new Cabinet, again under the premiership of Apollo Nsibambi, Prime Minister since April 1999, and including 10 ministers who had failed to retain their parliamentary seats in June 2001. Notably, Amama Mbabazi was appointed as Minister of Defence, a portfolio hitherto held by Museveni.

In May 2002 Parliament approved the Political Parties and Organizations Act 2002, which severely curtailed the activities of political parties, while classifying the NRM as a 'political system' rather than a party. The Act also provided for the dissolution of all parties not registered by 17 January 2003. However, in March 2003 opposition leaders successfully challenged two clauses of the Act in the Constitutional Court, which ruled that the NRM was not a system, but a political party, and suspended the section of the Act that required parties to register, pending the outcome of a further petition against the Act. (The Attorney-General later clarified that parties would still be obliged to register, but not by a particular time.) The ruling allowed political parties to operate nationally for the first time in 17 years. The NRM became the first party to apply for registration, in June. Meanwhile, in May Museveni effected a cabinet reorganization, notably appointing Prof. Gilbert Bukenya as Vice-President, following the resignation of the incumbent, Dr Speciosa Kazibwe, and dismissing a number of ministers who had recently expressed opposition to a proposal to revoke the current two-term limit on the presidential mandate. This proposal was endorsed by the Cabinet in August. By April 2004 some 60 new political parties had emerged, although only 13 had applied for registration.

In June 2004 the Constitutional Court issued a ruling that annulled the Referendum (Political System) Act of 2000 and effectively nullified the June 2000 referendum at which a return to a multi-party system had been rejected. Thus, legislative elections, scheduled to be held concurrently with the presidential election in 2006, would be held under the new system—subject to approval at a referendum, which was to be held in July 2005. In November 2004 the Constitutional Court repealed legislation preventing political parties from contesting elections. The Court also rejected an appeal from opposition parties against mandatory registration and ruled that parties would have six months to register prior to the 2006 elections. Meanwhile, it was reported in August 2004 that a new opposition party, the Forum for Democratic Change (FDC), had been formed by a merger of the Reform Agenda, the Parliamentary Advocacy Forum and the National Democratic Forum. Several parliamentarians affiliated to the UPC had apparently joined the new party.

In February 2005 the Constitution (Amendment) Bill, which provided for a return to multi-party democracy, was presented to the Parliament. The Bill also contained a provision for the removal of the two-term limit on the presidency. Parliament approved the removal of the two-term limit in June, and voted in favour of the holding of a national referendum on the restoration of multi-party democracy. At the referendum, which took place on 28 July, 92.5% of participants approved the motion. However, the rate of voter participation was low, at just 47%.

The 2006 presidential election

In October 2005 Besigye returned from four years of self-imposed exile in South Africa in order to contest the presidential election as the FDC's candidate. (He had left Uganda following the presidential election of 2001 claiming to fear for his safety.) Besigye was arrested in November 2005 and charged with rape and treason and later that month also appeared before a military tribunal on charges of terrorism and illegally possessing weapons. In January 2006 the High Court ruled that the military tribunal's authority to detain Besigye had expired and ordered his release; his trial was adjourned until after the election.

At the presidential election on 23 February 2006, Museveni, securing 59.3% of votes cast, was elected for a third term. Besigye was the only other candidate to mount a credible challenge, receiving 37.4% of the votes. International observers reported a number of serious flaws in the electoral process and concluded that a law adopted in 1997 that effectively granted the NRM access to public funds for campaigning did not provide a fair basis for multi-party elections. Legislative elections were held concurrently with the presidential election; the NRM secured 191 seats in the 319-member Parliament, while the FDC took 37 seats.

In March 2006 Besigye was acquitted of rape. The military conceded that Besigye would not have to face a court martial while on trial for treason, but did not drop the charges against him and appealed against the ruling that the terrorism and weapons charges must be heard in the High Court. In April Besigye challenged the results of the presidential election in the Supreme Court. The Court unanimously decided that the Electoral Commission had not conducted the election in compliance with the Constitution and other relevant legislation. However, it further ruled (by four votes to three) that this had not substantially affected the final outcome of the election. Besigye's trial for treason commenced in April; he and his 22 co-defendants denied the charges. In late May Museveni named his new Cabinet, again under the premiership of Nsibambi. Most notably, Gen. Ali Moses was replaced as First Deputy Prime Minister by Eriya Kategaya.

In March 2007 security agents raided the High Court and arrested six supporters of Besigye who had been granted bail. In response, the judiciary commenced industrial action and only agreed to return to work after Museveni expressed regret for the incident one week later. In April violence erupted in Kampala during protests against plans to allocate one-third of the Mabira forest to an Asian-owned sugar company, forcing police to protect Asian businesses and a Hindu temple; three people, including one Asian, were killed. In February 2009 Besigye was re-elected as President of the FDC, and indicated that he would once again challenge Museveni in the next presidential election in 2011. (In October 2010 the Constitutional Court dismissed the charges of treason against Besigye and 10 others, on the grounds that their fundamental rights had been violated by state agents.)

In February 2009 Museveni reorganized his Cabinet, replacing the Minister of Finance, Planning and Economic Development, Ezra Suruma, with Sydda Bbumba, who had previously held the gender, labour and social services portfolio. There were several new appointments to the Government, including that of Museveni's wife, Janet Museveni, as Minister of State for the Karamoja region. In September tensions arose between President Museveni and Ronald Muwenda Mutebi II, the Kabaka (King) of Buganda, after the President prohibited Mutebi from visiting an area of the region inhabited by ethnic minorities and suspended the operations of four local language radio stations. The President's decision to prevent the visit, prompted by Mutebi's hard-line stance on controversial issues, including land settlement and relations with ethnic minorities, prompted violence in Buganda and also in Kampala, where it was reported that at least 21 people had been killed. In November the Government approved land legislation that it claimed would grant greater rights to long-standing tenants in Buganda.

Amid emerging divisions within the NRM, in December 2009 four opposition parties (the UPC, the Justice Forum, the Conservative Party and the FDC) launched a 'Change 2011' strategy and pledged to field single presidential and parliamentary candidates in the 2011 elections in an attempt to remove Museveni from power. Museveni was confirmed as the NRM's presidential candidate in January 2010, and in April the FDC selected Besigye to contest the presidential election on behalf of the opposition coalition. However, in August the UPC withdrew from the alliance and threatened to boycott the elections, owing to dissatisfaction with the Electoral Commission.

On 11 July 2010 76 people were killed and a further 70 injured in two suicide bomb attacks in Kampala. The insurgent radical Islamist movement al-Shabaab claimed responsibility for the attacks, stating that they were in response to Uganda's support for the Somali Transitional Federal Government and the presence of Ugandan armed forces in Somalia. In January 2011 Human Rights Watch urged the Government to organize an independent investigation into the killing of a prominent homosexual rights activist, David Kato, who had suffered severe harassment and threats following his successful legal appeal against the anti-homosexual campaigning of a local newspaper. (In October 2009 proposed legislation seeking to increase the punishments for homosexuality, and including provision for the death penalty for the offence of 'aggravated homosexuality', had provoked international criticism and concern from donor Governments.) In early February 2011 the police announced the arrest of a suspect in Kato's murder.

The 2011 elections and popular protests

In January 2011 Besigye threatened to withdraw from the presidential poll, owing to suspicions that its conduct would be fraudulent. The presidential and legislative elections took place on 18 February 2011, as scheduled. Museveni was re-elected for a fourth term with about 68.4% of votes cast, while Besigye received 26.0% of the votes, according to official results. In the elections to the Parliament, the NRM secured 164 of the 238 directly elected seats; the FDC received 24 seats, the DP 11 seats and the UPC only seven seats. A voter turn-out of about 59% of the registered electorate was recorded. However, Commonwealth observers reported both bias during the electoral campaign and irregularities in the conduct of the voting, while a European Union (EU, see p. 281) monitoring group stated that the process had been marred by administrative failures. Besigye subsequently released a statement rejecting the results and complaining of widespread malpractice perpetrated by the authorities, and several opposition leaders declared support for him. Later in February Besigye, together with Mao and a further prominent opposition leader, Olara Otunnu, announced a campaign of peaceful protests against Museveni's Government; however, the Inspector General of Police announced that such demonstrations would be regarded as illegal. In the same month Museveni signed into force legislation authorizing the clandestine surveillance of telephones and other private communications for security purposes. At the end of February Prime Minister Nsibambi suspended from office nine government members who had contested the legislative elections as independent candidates, following a ruling by the Constitutional Court that it was illegal for party members to do so; a Minister of State subsequently resigned.

In early April 2011 Besigye was arrested in Kampala, after participating in a prohibited 'walk to work' campaign, which had been organized by opposition leaders in protest against sharp rises in fuel and commodity prices. Nevertheless, a further civil protest proceeded as planned a few days later, and was violently suppressed by the military police, prompting demonstrations in several towns; it was reported that 49 people, including Besigye, had been injured and some 220 demonstrators detained. Besigye's arrest later in April precipitated violent protests in Kampala, which were suppressed by security forces using live ammunition: two people were killed, 120 were injured and some 360 were arrested. On 12 May Museveni was inaugurated for a fourth term in office, while supporters of Besigye, who had returned to the country from Kenya on the same day following treatment for his injuries, gathered in Kampala, and were forcibly dispersed by police; one protester was reportedly killed in the disturbances. Citing concerns about Besigye's intention to mobilize his supporters for further protests (following the death of at least nine demonstrators in April), the authorities placed him under preventive house arrest later in May; he and three supporters were subsequently charged with holding an illegal assembly and inciting violence in connection with the protests.

On 27 May 2011 Museveni announced the formation of a new Government; Amama Mbabazi, the Minister of Security in the previous Cabinet, was appointed as the new Prime Minister. Edward Ssekandi, hitherto the parliamentary Speaker, became Vice-President, replacing Bukenya, who at the end of May was formally charged with abuse of office for illegally awarding a contract to a car supply company prior to a 2007 Commonwealth summit meeting in Kampala. In June 2011 it was announced that Mbabazi, who had also been under investigation for corruption relating to the occasion of the summit meeting, had been exonerated of wrongdoing.

In August 2011 Besigye was acquitted of all charges brought against him. In September two Ugandans were sentenced, respectively, to 25 and five years' imprisonment, after pleading guilty to involvement in the July 2010 bomb attacks perpetrated in Kampala by al-Shabaab. Although the FDC had announced, in mid-2011, that it would end the 'walk to work' campaign in order to prevent further supporters being killed in police reprisals, the protests resumed in October, at the initiative of the Activists for Change pressure group; a number of demonstrators were arrested, including Besigye.

Recent developments: corruption allegations

In October 2011 the Minister of Foreign Affairs, Sam Kutesa, and a further two government members tendered their resignation, after being charged at the country's anti-corruption court with abuse of office and causing the loss of state funds in the arrangement of construction projects prior to the Commonwealth summit meeting. In December the Minister in Charge of the Presidency, Masiko Kabakumba, also resigned, following allegations of corruption against her relating to her previous post as Minister of Communication and Information Communication Technology. In the same month the anti-corruption court acquitted Bukenya of all charges against him. In February 2012 the Minister of Gender, Labour and Social Affairs, Syda Bhumba, and the Minister in the Office of the Prime Minister, in charge of General Duties, Khiddu Makubuya, also ceded to pressure to resign, after an official investigation was initiated into corruption allegations against them regarding the payment of compensation to a businessman in 2010 (in which Museveni himself was implicated). Museveni was, nevertheless, confronted by increasing rebellion from parliamentary deputies who demanded the removal of other allegedly corrupt ministers.

Meanwhile, in February 2012 Besigye (who in January had been detained by the authorities in an effort to prevent the organization of a renewed protest campaign) was again injured during the police's suppression of a further opposition protest in

Kampala. In March a senior police official was killed by opposition supporters, who reacted violently after the police attempted to disperse an unauthorized visit in central Kampala by the capital's mayor, accompanied by many opposition leaders. In October Besigye was again arrested, after participating in a renewed campaign of anti-Government protests, entitled For God and Country (4GC), which was violently suppressed by police.

In April 2012 the Constitutional Court annulled legal proceedings against the ministers charged with corruption, on the grounds of irregularities in the Office of the Inspectorate of Government. In a government reorganization in August, Museveni reinstated to the Cabinet most of the officials who had resigned, including Kutesa (who was reappointed Minister of Foreign Affairs), and John Mwoono Nasasira (who received the post of Minister in the Office of the Prime Minister, in charge of General Duties). Also in August Museveni promoted his son, Muhoozi Kainerugaba, who headed a special army unit, to the rank of Brigadier-General. Following continued controversy over the proposed adoption of legislation criminalizing homosexuality, in December Museveni publicly declared that homosexuals should not be persecuted.

Meanwhile, the country's Auditor-General reported in October 2012 that about US $13m. intended for a rehabilitation programme in northern Uganda had been misappropriated by the Office of the Prime Minister. Twelve government officials were subsequently suspended from their posts, and two were formally charged, in connection with the allegations. After major donor nations responded with the suspension of aid to Uganda, in December the EU ambassador to Uganda announced that the Union had also frozen budgetary support for an initial period of six months, during which the Ugandan authorities were to return the misappropriated funds to donors, reform the public finance system and prosecute the officials responsible. In January 2013 the Irish Government announced that Uganda had reimbursed some €4m. in misappropriated Irish donor funds; the Ugandan authorities subsequently expressed confidence that donor assistance would be restored later that year, although by April external budgetary support had been completely suspended (see Economic Affairs). In March Kategaya, the First Deputy Prime Minister and Minister in Charge of East African Community Affairs, died in hospital in Nairobi.

Foreign Affairs

In March 1996 Museveni, Moi and President Benjamin Mkapa of Tanzania, meeting in Nairobi, Kenya, formally inaugurated the Secretariat of the Permanent Tripartite Commission for East African Co-operation, which aimed to revive the East African Community (EAC, see p. 460). A treaty for the re-establishment of the EAC, providing for the creation of a free trade area (with the eventual introduction of a single currency), for the development of infrastructure, tourism and agriculture within the Community and for the establishment of a regional legislature and court was ratified by the three Heads of State in November 1999. Museveni, Mkapa and President Mwai Kibaki of Kenya signed a protocol in March 2004 on the creation of a customs union, whereby most duties on goods within the EAC would be eliminated. The customs union was established on 1 January 2005. Following a two-day summit in Nairobi in December 2006, the Presidents of Burundi, the DRC, Kenya, Zambia, Tanzania and Uganda signed a regional security, stability and development treaty. The EAC was expanded to include Rwanda and Burundi in 2007. In November 2009 the Heads of State of Tanzania, Kenya, Uganda, Rwanda and Burundi signed a common market protocol, allowing the free movement of goods, services, people and capital within the EAC; the protocol entered into force in July 2010.

The regime of Laurent-Désiré Kabila, which took power in Zaire (subsequently the DRC) in May 1997, accused Uganda and Rwanda of creating, with DRC rebels, a Tutsi-dominated alliance with expansionist ambitions; it was also alleged that the DRC's two eastern neighbours were illegally exploiting mineral interests in the area occupied by their forces. In July 1999 a comprehensive cease-fire agreement was concluded in Lusaka, Zambia, by the Heads of State of all the countries engaged militarily in the civil war in the DRC, including those of Angola, Namibia and Zimbabwe, who had supported the DRC Government. In August tensions escalated into hostilities between Ugandan and Rwandan armed forces around the city of Kisangani. In May 2000 the DRC Government signed an agreement consenting to the deployment of the UN Mission in the Democratic Republic of the Congo (MONUC, see p. 94), to monitor the

frequently violated cease-fire that had been inaugurated by the Lusaka accord. After further clashes, Uganda and Rwanda withdrew their troops from Kisangani to allow its eventual cession to the control of MONUC. Following the publication of a UN report in April 2001, alleging that Burundi, Rwanda and Uganda were illegally exploiting the DRC's mineral reserves, Museveni announced that Uganda would withdraw its remaining troops from the DRC and pull out of the UN-sponsored Lusaka accord. Despite the redeployment of Ugandan troops in the north-east of the DRC in January 2002, to prevent escalating fighting between the rebel factions from reaching the border with Uganda, negotiations between Uganda and Rwanda continued, with British mediation, and in April the two countries signed a peace agreement in Kigali, Rwanda. In September a peace accord was signed by Uganda and the DRC in Luanda, Angola, providing for the normalization of relations between the two countries and the complete withdrawal of Ugandan troops from the DRC. Uganda subsequently began the withdrawal of its troops, although the UN permitted some of them to remain near the north-eastern town of Bunia to assist with maintaining security. In March 2003 the Governments of Uganda and the DRC, and local rebel groups, signed a cease-fire agreement. In response to the continuing violence around Bunia, the UN Security Council issued a resolution appealing for increased numbers of military and humanitarian observers to be stationed in the DRC under the MONUC mandate, and the immediate withdrawal of Ugandan troops. The Ugandan Government subsequently pledged to withdraw forces from the DRC, and all remaining Ugandan troops left the north-east of the country in May. In December 2005 the International Court of Justice (ICJ, see p. 26), in The Hague, Netherlands, upheld an appeal by the DRC against Uganda, submitted in April, and ordered the Ugandan Government to pay reparations for violations of international law perpetrated by its forces deployed in the country during 1998–2003.

Relations with the DRC became strained in 2007 due to a dispute over the ownership of Rukwanzi island in Lake Albert, on the border between the two countries; tension had increased in the area following the recent discovery of petroleum in the Lake Albert basin. In August a British national working for a Canadian oil company was killed in a clash involving Congolese and Ugandan security forces, and in the following month Museveni and the DRC President, Joseph Kabila, held a meeting in which they agreed to carry out a joint demarcation of the border. None the less, there were further violent incidents in late 2007, and in May 2008 Congolese troops occupied a disputed border area; Museveni and Kabila subsequently agreed to implement joint administration of Rukwanzi island.

In October 2012 the Ugandan Government, which had undertaken to mediate negotiations between the DRC Government and an insurgent group known as M23, denied accusations in a UN report that it had provided support to M23, and threatened to withdraw its peace-keeping troops from Somalia in protest. In December DRC government representatives and M23 leaders began peace negotiations, mediated by Ugandan Minister of Defence Crispus Kiyonga, in Kampala.

The victory in Rwanda of the Front Patriotique Rwandais (FPR) in mid-1994 brought about a significant improvement in bilateral relations; Maj.-Gen. Paul Kagame, Rwandan Vice-President and Minister of National Defence, had previously served in the Ugandan NRA, as had other members of the FPR administration. In August 1995 Museveni made an official visit to Rwanda, and both countries made commitments to enhance economic and social co-operation. In August 1998 Uganda and Rwanda jointly deployed troops in the DRC (see above), and relations between the two countries worsened during their involvement in the hostilities there, with frequent reports of clashes, especially around the town of Kisangani. However, this tension eased when both armies withdrew from Kisangani during May 2000, and in July Museveni and Kagame met to discuss relations between their respective countries. In July 2003 the Rwandan Government signed a tripartite agreement with the Ugandan authorities and the office of the UN High Commissioner for Refugees (UNHCR), providing for the voluntary repatriation of some 26,000 Rwandans resident in refugee camps in western Uganda. In February 2004 an improvement in diplomatic relations between Rwanda and Uganda (following progress in the situation in the DRC) was demonstrated by a bilateral agreement to strengthen co-operation in several fields.

From the late 1980s Sudanese troops reportedly made repeated incursions into Ugandan territory in pursuit of Sudanese rebels. Relations between the two countries deteriorated seriously in 1994, when each Government accused the other of harbouring and supporting their respective outlawed guerrilla groups; in April 1995 Uganda severed diplomatic relations with Sudan. In February 1998 Uganda deployed troops along the Uganda–Sudan border, with the aim of preventing LRA rebels from taking captives over the frontier into Sudan. In December, in Nairobi, the Presidents of Uganda and Sudan unexpectedly signed an accord that set out a comprehensive resolution of the two countries' differences. The Nairobi Agreement committed Uganda and Sudan to: the renunciation of force as a means of settling disputes; to the disarmament and disbandment of terrorist groups and the cessation of support for rebel groups; to the repatriation of prisoners of war; and to the restoration of full diplomatic relations by the end of February 2000. In September 2000 Uganda and Sudan agreed to disarm the LRA, which had been active throughout the earlier part of the year, and to relocate it at least 1,000 km deeper within Sudanese territory. Rebel attacks continued in northern Uganda, however, and in January 2001 President Museveni threatened to send troops to pursue rebel groups into Sudanese territory. Following a Libyan diplomatic initiative in that month, Sudan and Uganda agreed to restore diplomatic relations. In August the Ugandan embassy reopened in the Sudanese capital, Khartoum, and a chargé d'affaires was appointed; relations were upgraded to ambassadorial level in April 2002. In August 2001 the Sudanese President, Lt-Gen. Omar Hassan Ahmad al-Bashir, announced that his Government would no longer provide support for the LRA, and in December bank accounts used by the LRA in London, United Kingdom, were frozen. In March 2002 it was announced that Sudan was to allow the UPDF to deploy forces within its borders in order to pursue operations against the LRA, and later that month the Ugandan Government announced that its troops had captured all four main bases in Sudan belonging to the LRA. In November the Sudanese authorities agreed to extend permission for Ugandan troops to remain on its territory for as long as Uganda deemed necessary.

In early 2003 Museveni agreed to a cease-fire and appointed a delegation to commence peace negotiations with the LRA, but these soon collapsed. The Government ordered 800,000 people in northern Uganda to enter refugee camps for their protection; however, the LRA continued to attack the camps. In October LRA attacks, which had begun to spread further south and east, intensified, and a counter-offensive by the UPDF in December had little success. In February 2004 the LRA massacred more than 200 civilians sheltering in a refugee camp near Lira, in northern Uganda. Thousands demonstrated in Lira against the Government's failure to protect civilians, and the protests rapidly became violent. The Government introduced legislation in mid-2004 that allowed the prosecution by the International Criminal Court (ICC, see p. 349) of Ugandans suspected of war crimes. In June it was reported that at least 12 high-ranking LRA commanders had taken advantage of an amnesty offered by the Government and surrendered.

In November 2004 an LRA spokesman stated that the group no longer believed a military end to the conflict was possible, and that the LRA was thus willing to negotiate towards a peace accord. A cease-fire was agreed, although fighting continued outside the cease-fire zone. Although there were indications at the end of December that the Government and LRA were close to agreeing a permanent truce, the LRA postponed the signing of a memorandum of understanding in order to continue internal consultations. Shortly afterwards a UPDF force was ambushed, for which Museveni blamed the LRA. The Government refused to extend the cease-fire, and UPDF troops re-occupied the cease-fire zone in order to prevent attacks on civilians. A cease-fire was agreed in February 2005, during which an amnesty was offered to LRA fighters who wished to surrender. Later that month Brig. Sam Kolo, the LRA's chief negotiator in the recent peace talks, escaped an attack by LRA combatants with the help of the UPDF, to whom he surrendered. The UPDF stated that Kolo's life was in danger following a dispute with the LRA's deputy leader, Vincent Otti. The Government's chief negotiator confirmed that Otti would take Kolo's place in any future negotiations. In March, following a government request, the ICC agreed to delay issuing arrest warrants for LRA commanders after concerns were raised that they would be reluctant to negotiate if they feared arrest once peace had been established. The cease-fire agreed in February lapsed in March and fighting resumed.

In October 2005 the ICC issued arrest warrants for Kony, Otti and three other LRA commanders. Kony was indicted on 12 counts of crimes against humanity, including sexual enslavement, and 21 counts of war crimes. The UPDF claimed to have recently killed one of the five indicted LRA commanders. Shortly after the warrants were issued the LRA altered its tactics and began to attack humanitarian workers. In April 2006 the Ugandan Parliament approved legislation that enabled the Government to exclude Kony and others from the amnesty offered to the LRA.

In July 2006 peace talks between the LRA and the Government commenced in Juba, southern Sudan. On 26 August both sides agreed on a truce and a cease-fire came into force on 29 August. However, it emerged in October that both the Ugandan army and the LRA had violated the terms of their truce, according to a report by a peace process monitoring team. In December President Museveni held direct talks with a member of the LRA for the first time when he spoke by satellite telephone with Otti. A cessation of hostilities agreement, signed by both sides, was also extended in the same month for a second time, until 28 February 2007. However, the LRA withdrew from the talks in January, citing security fears after al-Bashir apparently indicated that he sought to eradicate the LRA from Sudan. Following a meeting between the UN Special Envoy for areas affected by the LRA, the former President of Mozambique, Joaquim Chissano, and Kony in mid-March, the LRA agreed to resume negotiations on condition that other African mediators join the talks along with Sudan. In mid-April the LRA signed a new cease-fire agreement with the Government. Peace talks resumed in Juba at the end of May. In November Kony appointed Okot Odhiambo as deputy leader of the LRA, amid unconfirmed reports that Otti had been executed alongside his family and several commanders who remained loyal to him. In January 2008 Otti's death was confirmed, although the cause of death remained unclear. A new cease-fire was agreed between the Government and the LRA in late January, and peace negotiations were subsequently resumed.

In April 2008, however, the peace talks ended in failure; Kony indicated that he was not willing to sign a full peace agreement until the ICC arrest warrant for him was lifted, and later dismissed his chief negotiator. In May a new War Crimes Court was established as a special division of the Uganda High Court, to deal specifically with human rights violations committed during the LRA insurgency in northern Uganda; the measure was widely regarded as an attempt to persuade the ICC to withdraw indictments against LRA commanders, following the breakdown in negotiations. (In March President Museveni had refused to hand over LRA leaders to stand trial at the ICC, stating that they should instead be tried by northern Uganda's traditional justice system.) In May a report by Human Rights Watch claimed that the LRA had taken advantage of the cease-fire to resume abduction and enslavement of civilians, including children, from neighbouring countries; Kony was believed to be rearming and preparing for a renewed conflict. In late 2008 the situation deteriorated further, after Kony failed to appear at a meeting of representatives, having committed himself to a peace agreement, effectively ending any prospect of a negotiated settlement. In December Ugandan, Sudanese and Congolese forces launched a joint offensive against LRA positions in north-eastern DRC. The LRA launched attacks on Congolese villages in response; by March 2009 as many as 1,000 civilians were believed to have been killed in reprisal for the offensive. In March a senior LRA commander, Thomas Kwoyelo, was captured in eastern DRC, while later that month Ugandan troops began to withdraw from the country as the joint offensive came to an end.

In November 2009 the Ugandan army claimed to have killed one of the principal commanders of the LRA, Lt-Col Okello Ogutti. Shortly afterwards, the US Senate approved the LRA Disarmament and Northern Uganda Recovery Act of 2009, which outlined the provision of military, intelligence and humanitarian assistance to countries in the region in support of action against the LRA. In October 2011 US President Barack Obama announced the deployment of some 100 troops to Uganda to assist regional forces in the location of Kony and his supporters. In early 2012 plans were finalized for the establishment of a military contingent led by the African Union (AU), under the aegis of the UN, to counter LRA operations; the proposed mission was to comprise troops from Uganda, South Sudan (which had seceded from Sudan in July 2011), the Central African Republic (CAR) and the DRC. Meanwhile, it was reported that several thousand people had been displaced as a result of a series of further attacks by the LRA in north-eastern DRC and in the CAR during early 2012. (At that time Kony was believed to be located in the CAR and to have only 200–700 combatants under his command.) The four-nation Regional Task Force was officially established in the South Sudanese capital, Juba, in March, under a UN-supported Regional Cooperation Initiative. Uganda contributed 3,000 troops of the 5,000-member AU contingent, which was subsequently deployed in the CAR with the aim of capturing Kony. Following a coup in the CAR by rebels who demanded the withdrawal of foreign forces from the country, however, in April 2013 the Ugandan Government suspended participation in the operation to arrest Kony. In the same month the US Administration offered a reward of US $5m. for information resulting in the capture of Kony or two other LRA leaders.

In the late 2000s LRA operations caused further displacement of civilians from neighbouring countries. In mid-2011 increased conflict in eastern DRC resulted in further large influxes of refugees, which reached emergency levels; according to UNHCR estimates, the number of refugees and asylum seekers in Uganda totalled 190,000 by August 2012. From early 2011 some 5,200 Ugandan troops were deployed in Somalia as part of the AU (see p. 191) Mission in Somalia (AMISOM), which was mandated to support peace-keeping operations in that country.

CONSTITUTION AND GOVERNMENT

Amendments to the Constitution of October 1995, introducing a multi-party political system and removing the two-term limit on the President, were endorsed at a national referendum held on 28 July 2005. Under the amended Constitution, the President (who had an unlimited number of mandates) and the unicameral legislature, the Parliament, were directly elected for a five-year term. Following elections in February 2011, the number of seats in Parliament totalled 375, comprising 238 directly elected representatives and 137 nominated members, including 112 women.

For the purposes of local administration, Uganda is divided into four regions and 80 districts.

REGIONAL AND INTERNATIONAL CO-OPERATION

Uganda is a member of the African Union (see p. 191), of the Common Market for Eastern and Southern Africa (COMESA, see p. 241), and the East African Community (EAC, see p. 460).

Uganda became a member of the UN in 1962. As a contracting party to the General Agreement on Tariffs and Trade, Uganda joined the World Trade Organization (WTO, see p. 444) on its establishment in 1995. Uganda participates in the Group of 77 (G77, see p. 461) developing countries. In October 2008 Uganda was elected as a non-permanent member of the UN Security Council for 2009 and 2010.

ECONOMIC AFFAIRS

In 2011, according to estimates by the World Bank, Uganda's gross national income (GNI), measured at average 2009–11 prices, was US $17,458m., equivalent to $510 per head (or $1,320 per head on an international purchasing-power parity basis). During 2002–11, it was estimated, the population increased at an average annual rate of 3.3%, while gross domestic product (GDP) per head grew, in real terms, by an average of 4.0% per year. According to official figures, overall GDP increased, in real terms, at an average annual rate of 7.2% in 2003–11; growth was 5.9% in 2011.

Agriculture (including hunting, forestry and fishing) contributed 24.4% of GDP in 2011, and engaged 68.7% of the employed labour force in 2003. According to the FAO, the sector was estimated to employ 73.0% of the total labour force in mid-2013. The principal cash crops are coffee, cotton, tea and tobacco. Cassava, sweet potatoes, maize, sugar cane and cocoa are also cultivated, and the production of cut flowers is an important activity. Together, coffee, tea, cocoa and spices provided 27.5% of export earnings in 2011. The main subsistence crops are plantains, cassava, sweet potatoes, maize, millet, sorghum, beans, groundnuts and rice. In addition, livestock (chiefly cattle, goats, sheep and poultry) are reared, and freshwater fishing is an important rural activity. Agricultural GDP increased by an average of 1.3% per year in 2003–11, according to official figures; sectoral growth was 0.5% in 2011.

Industry (including mining, manufacturing, construction and power) contributed 26.8% of GDP in 2011, and employed 7.8% of the working population in 2003. Industrial GDP increased at an average annual rate of 8.8% in 2003–11; it grew by 8.0% in both 2010 and 2011.

Mining has made a negligible contribution to GDP since the 1970s (0.4% in 2011), and in 2003 it employed just 0.3% of the working population. The Government aims to encourage renewed investment in the sector. Output of copper, formerly an important export, virtually ceased during the late 1970s. However, in 2012 the Government was seeking potential investors to revive production at the state-owned Kilembe copper mine in western Uganda. The production of cobalt from stockpiled copper pyrites commenced in 1999. Uganda is believed to possess the world's second largest deposit of gold, which began to be exploited again in the mid-1990s, and in mid-2010 a Russian-owned gold refinery, capable of refining 60 kg of gold per day, commenced operations. Apatite and limestone are also mined, while petroleum production—initially of some 500–1,000 barrels per day (b/d), but projected to reach 150,000 b/d—was expected to commence in 2013. There are, in addition, reserves of iron ore, magnetite, tin, tungsten, beryllium, bismuth, asbestos, graphite, phosphate and tantalite. Mining GDP increased at an average annual rate of 12.8% in 2003–11; it grew by 37.3% in 2010 and by 13.6% in 2011.

Manufacturing contributed 9.0% of GDP in 2011, and in 2003 it employed 6.1% of the working population. The most important manufacturing activities are the processing of agricultural commodities, brewing, vehicle assembly and the production of textiles, cement, soap, fertilizers, paper products, metal products, shoes, paints, matches and batteries. Manufacturing GDP increased by an average of 6.5% per year in 2003–11; it grew by 4.0% in 2011.

Construction contributed 14.0% of GDP in 2011, and employed 1.3% of the working population in 2003. Construction GDP increased at an average annual rate of 11.2% in 2003–11; it grew by 10.5% in 2011.

Energy is derived principally from hydroelectric power, although Uganda generates only about two-thirds of national energy requirements. Significant investment has, however, been made in hydroelectric power projects in recent years: in October 2012 a 250-MW hydroelectric power station at Bujagali was officially inaugurated, and plans to construct a 600-MW hydroelectric power station at Karuma, with funding from the People's Republic of China, were under way in early 2013. Imports of petroleum and petroleum products accounted for 22.9% of the value of Uganda's merchandise imports in 2011.

The services sector contributed 48.8% of GDP in 2011, and engaged 23.5% of the employed labour force in 2003. Trade is the most important aspect of the sector. Services GDP increased by an average of 8.1% per year in 2003–11. Services GDP grew by 6.6% in 2011.

In 2011 Uganda recorded a visible merchandise trade deficit of US $2,678.6m. and there was a deficit of $2,275.8m. on the current account of the balance of payments. In 2010 the principal sources of imports were India (providing 14.7% of the total), Kenya, China, the United Arab Emirates (UAE), Japan, South Africa and Saudi Arabia. The main markets for exports in that year were Sudan (accounting for 12.9% of the total), Kenya, the Democratic Republic of the Congo, Rwanda, the UAE and the Netherlands. COMESA and the European Union (EU, see p. 281) are important trading partners: in 2003 they took 28.3% and 17.7%, respectively, of total imports and provided 27.7% and 26.3%, respectively, of total exports. The principal exports in 2011 were food and live animals (mainly coffee, tea, cocoa, spices, fish, cereals and sugar), basic manufactures, machinery and transport equipment, inedible crude materials, and petroleum and petroleum products; the main imports in that year were machinery and transport equipment, petroleum products, basic manufactures, chemicals and related products, road vehicles, and food and live animals.

In the financial year ending 30 June 2012 Uganda's central government budgetary deficit was projected at 1,804,100m. shillings. Uganda's general government gross debt was 9,993,431m. shillings in 2010, equivalent to 27.0% of GDP. Uganda's external debt totalled US $2,994m. at the end of 2010, of which $2,671m. was public and publicly guaranteed debt. In that year, the cost of servicing long-term public and publicly guaranteed debt and repayments to the IMF was equivalent to 1.8% of the value of exports of goods, services and income (excluding workers' remittances). The average annual rate of inflation was 9.5% in 2002–12; consumer prices increased by 14.0% in 2012.

Uganda secured international aid and debt-relief, including assistance under the IMF's initiative for heavily indebted poor countries during 1998–2000. Despite subsequent high levels of economic growth, Uganda remained dependent on foreign aid, which financed around one-half of the country's expenditure. A five-year National Development Programme, which emphasized investment in public infrastructure, was introduced by the Government in April 2010. In May the IMF approved a new three-year programme, which was designed to support the strengthening of the country's institutions prior to anticipated large-scale petroleum production. Uganda participated in the common market that was established by the East African Community (EAC, see p. 460) in July. From early 2011, however, a rapid rise in inflation contributed to social discontent, prompting civil protests and strikes, while allegations of endemic corruption within the administration of President Yoweri Museveni subsequently emerged (see Domestic Political Affairs). In an effort to curb the rate of inflation, the Central Bank progressively raised interest rates during the second half of 2011. In January 2012 high interest rates and the Government's reduction of subsidies to the power sector (in accordance with IMF recommendations) precipitated further strike action. The budget for 2012/13, adopted in June 2012, projected lower growth of 3.2%, and provided for salary increases for public sector employees, balanced by tax rises. However, after the Auditor-General reported in October that US $13m. intended to finance a rehabilitation programme in northern Uganda had been misappropriated, major donor nations (notably the United Kingdom) withheld budgetary assistance for Uganda. In December the EU announced that it was also to suspend aid, for an initial period of six months, during which the Ugandan authorities were required to return the misappropriated funds to donors, reform the public finance system and prosecute the officials responsible. In January 2013 the IMF urged implementation of a government action plan to strengthen public financial management; the Fund also stated that the authorities' tightening of monetary policies had proved successful in restraining the inflation rate, but had, at the same time, contributed to a decline in GDP growth. The Government estimated that the suspension of aid would result in a budgetary shortfall of $260m. and reduce growth by 0.7 percentage points in the 2012/13 financial year, and announced plans for the introduction of new taxes. Although the Ugandan authorities anticipated that funding would be restored in the second half of 2013, in April the World Bank confirmed that it was to suspend budgetary support, and donors requested evidence of the required financial management reform.

PUBLIC HOLIDAYS

2014: 1 January (New Year's Day), 26 January (Liberation Day), 8 March (International Women's Day), 18–21 April (Easter), 1 May (Labour Day), 3 June (Martyrs' Day), 9 June (National Heroes' Day), 28 July* (Id al-Fitr, end of Ramadan), 4 October* (Id al-Adha, Feast of the Sacrifice), 9 October (Independence Day), 25 December (Christmas), 26 December (Boxing Day).

* These holidays are dependent on the Islamic lunar calendar and the exact dates may vary by one or two days from those given.

Statistical Survey

Sources (unless otherwise stated): Uganda Bureau of Statistics, POB 13, Entebbe; tel. (41) 320165; fax (41) 320147; e-mail ubos@infocom.co.ug; internet www .ubos.org; Statistics Department, Ministry of Finance, Planning and Economic Development, POB 8147, Kampala.

Area and Population

AREA, POPULATION AND DENSITY

Area (sq km)	
Land	199,807
Inland water and swamp	41,743
Total	241,551*
Population (census results)	
12 January 1991	16,671,705
12 September 2002	
Males	11,929,803
Females	12,512,281
Total	24,442,084
Population (official projections at mid-year)	
2010	31,784,600
2011	32,939,800
2012	34,131,400
Density (per sq km) at mid-2012	141.3

* 93,263 sq miles.

POPULATION BY AGE AND SEX
('000, official estimates at mid-2012)

	Males	Females	Total
0–14	8,635	8,676	17,311
15–64	7,911	8,447	16,358
65 and over	195	268	463
Total	**16,741**	**17,391**	**34,131**

Note: Totals may not be equal to the sum of components, owing to rounding.

PRINCIPAL ETHNIC GROUPS
(at census of 12 September 2002)*

Acholi	. . .	1,145,357	Basoga	. . . .	2,062,920
Baganda	. . .	4,126,370	Iteso	. . . .	1,568,763
Bagisu	. . .	1,117,661	Langi	. . . .	1,485,437
Bakiga	. . .	1,679,519	Lugbara	. . . .	1,022,240
Banyakole	. . .	2,330,212			

* Ethnic groups numbering more than 1m. persons, excluding population enumerated in hotels.

SUB-REGIONS
(population projections at mid-2012)

Region	Area (sq km)	Population	Density (per sq km)
Central	61,403	8,715,800	141.9
Western	55,277	8,487,200	153.5
Northern	85,392	7,972,200	93.4
Eastern	39,479	8,956,200	226.9
Total	**241,551**	**34,131,400**	**141.3**

PRINCIPAL TOWNS
('000, official population estimates at mid-2012)

Kampala (capital)	.	1,723.3	Kasese	. . . .	77.0
Gulu	. . . .	158.7	Masaka	. . .	74.8
Lira	. . . . .	112.1	Njeru	. . .	66.8
Mbale	. . . .	94.4	Kitgum	. . .	62.0
Jinja	. . . .	92.1	Arua	. . .	61.4
Mbarara	. . .	85.5	Mukono	. . .	60.6
Entebbe	. . .	83.2	Kabale	. . .	45.0

BIRTHS AND DEATHS
(annual averages, UN estimates)

	1995–2000	2000–05	2005–10
Birth rate (per 1,000)	48.7	47.9	46.3
Death rate (per 1,000)	18.2	15.8	13.2

Source: UN, *World Population Prospects: The 2010 Revision*.

2011: Birth rate 44.7 per 1,000; Death rate 12.0 per 1,000 (Source: African Development Bank).

Life expectancy (years at birth): 54.1 (males 53.4; females 54.8) in 2011 (Source: World Bank, World Development Indicators database).

EMPLOYMENT

(persons aged 10 years and over, census of 12 September 2002)*

	Males	Females	Total
Agriculture, hunting and forestry.	2,545,962	2,649,779	5,195,741
Fishing	102,043	16,743	118,786
Mining and quarrying	13,613	6,127	19,740
Manufacturing	108,653	45,594	154,247
Electricity, gas and water supply	12,860	1,509	14,369
Construction	105,769	2,939	108,708
Wholesale and retail trade, repair of motor vehicles, motorcycles and personal and household goods	191,191	143,145	334,336
Hotels and restaurants	23,741	64,099	87,840
Transport, storage and communications	119,437	5,798	125,235
Financial intermediation			
Real estate, renting and business activities	14,539	7,562	22,101
Public administration and defence, compulsory social security	146,319	27,278	173,597
Education	124,167	85,015	209,182
Health and social work	54,327	53,108	107,435
Other community, social and personal service activities	22,736	26,734	49,470
Private households with employed persons	14,019	19,115	33,134
Not classifiable by economic activity	120,219	76,167	196,386
Total employed	3,719,595	3,230,712	6,950,307

* Excluding population enumerated at hotels.

2003 ('000 persons aged 10 years and over): Agriculture, hunting and forestry 6,278.3; Fishing 83.3; Mining and quarrying 27.8; Manufacturing 564.9; Electricity, gas and water supply 9.3; Construction 120.4; Wholesale and retail trade, repair of motor vehicles, motorcycles and personal and household goods 1,074.2; Hotels and restaurants 240.8; Transport, storage and communications 175.9; Real estate, renting and business activities 37.0; Public administration and defence, compulsory social security 74.1; Education 240.8; Health and social work 74.1; Other community, social and personal service activities 148.2; Private households with employed persons 111.1; *Total employed* 9,260.0; Unemployed 346.0; *Total labour force* 9,606.0 (Source: ILO).

Mid-2013 ('000, estimates): Agriculture, etc. 11,930; Total labour force 16,349 (Source: FAO).

Health and Welfare

KEY INDICATORS

Total fertility rate (children per woman, 2010)	6.1
Under-5 mortality rate (per 1,000 live births, 2010)	99
HIV/AIDS (% of persons aged 15–49, 2009)	6.5
Physicians (per 1,000 head, 2005)	0.1
Hospital beds (per 1,000 head, 2010)	0.5
Health expenditure (2009): US $ per head (PPP)	118
Health expenditure (2009): % of GDP	8.5
Health expenditure (2009): public (% of total)	21.8
Access to water (% of persons, 2010)	72
Access to sanitation (% of persons, 2010)	34
Total carbon dioxide emissions ('000 metric tons, 2008)	3,747.7
Carbon dioxide emissions per head (metric tons, 2008)	0.1
Human Development Index (2011): ranking	161
Human Development Index (2011): value	0.446

For sources and definitions, see explanatory note on p. vi.

Agriculture

PRINCIPAL CROPS

('000 metric tons)

	2009	2010	2011
Rice, paddy	206	218	233
Maize	2,355	2,374	2,551
Millet	841	903	984*
Sorghum	374	391	437
Potatoes	689	695†	625†
Sweet potatoes	2,766	2,838*	2,554
Cassava (Manioc)	5,179	5,282*	4,753†
Sugar cane†	3,300	2,400	2,400
Beans, dry	452	455†	464†
Cow peas, dry	84	85†	87†
Pigeon peas	91	93†	95†
Soybeans	180	175*	180*
Groundnuts, with shell	185	172†	175†
Sesame seed	178	170*	173*
Seed cotton†	53	82	120
Onions, dry†	173	195	254
Bananas†	592	600	523
Plantains	9,512	9,550	10,547
Coffee, green	196	167	191
Tea	49	49	35
Tobacco, unmanufactured	19	27	28

* Unofficial figure.
† FAO estimate(s).

Aggregate production ('000 metric tons, may include official, semi-official or estimated data): Total cereals 3,796 in 2009, 3,905 in 2010, 4,228 in 2011; Total roots and tubers 8,634 in 2009, 8,815 in 2010, 7,933 in 2011; Total vegetables (incl. melons) 737 in 2009, 986 in 2010, 1,160 in 2011; Total fruits (excl. melons) 10,157 in 2009, 10,204 in 2010, 11,123 in 2011.

Source: FAO.

LIVESTOCK

('000 head, year ending September)

	2009	2010	2011
Asses*	18	18	18
Cattle†	7,521	7,746	8,103
Sheep†	1,800	1,847	1,902
Goats†	8,720	8,981	9,251
Pigs†	2,229	2,297	2,377
Chickens†	31,500	34,680	34,660

* FAO estimates.
† Unofficial figures.

Source: FAO.

LIVESTOCK PRODUCTS

('000 metric tons, FAO estimates)

	2009	2010	2011
Cattle meat	129	130	130
Sheep meat	9	9	9
Goat meat	32	32	33
Pig meat	111	113	117
Chicken meat	52	62	62
Cows' milk	1,155	1,190	1,190
Hen eggs	23	23	23

Source: FAO.

Forestry

ROUNDWOOD REMOVALS
('000 cubic metres, excl. bark)

	2009	2010	2011
Sawlogs, veneer logs and logs for sleepers	1,863*	1,973*	1,973†
Other industrial wood† . . .	2,120	2,120	2,120
Fuel wood†	39,046	39,636	40,176
Total	43,029	43,729	44,269

* Unofficial figure.
† FAO estimate(s).
Source: FAO.

SAWNWOOD PRODUCTION
('000 cubic metres, incl. railway sleepers)

	2004	2005	2006
Coniferous (softwood)	67	24	24
Broadleaved (hardwood) . . .	197	101	93
Total	264	125	117

2007–11: Figures assumed to be unchanged from 2006 (FAO estimates).
Source: FAO.

Fishing

('000 metric tons, live weight)

	2008*	2009	2010
Capture	403.5	412.0*	413.8
Cyprinids	35.0	52.5*	73.2
Tilapias	150.0	123.0*	83.5
African lungfishes	13.0	10.0*	6.3
Characins	42.0	74.0*	113.4
Nile perch	139.0	131.0*	120.4
Aquaculture	52.3	76.7	95.0*
Total catch	455.8	488.7*	508.8*

* FAO estimate(s).

Note: Figures exclude aquatic animals, recorded by number rather than weight. The number of Nile crocodiles captured was: 290 in 2008; n.a. in 2009; n.a. in 2010.
Source: FAO.

Mining

('000 metric tons unless otherwise indicated)

	2009	2010	2011
Cement (hydraulic)	1,162.2	1,347.3	1,666.2
Tantalum and niobium (columbium) concentrates (kilograms)	50	10	10*
Cobalt (metric tons)	673	624	661
Limestone	588.9	634.7	932.3
Salt (unrefined)*	15	15	15

* Estimate(s).

Gold (kilograms): 20 in 2008.
Source: US Geological Survey.

Industry

SELECTED PRODUCTS
('000 metric tons unless otherwise indicated)

	2003	2004	2005
Soft drinks (million litres) . . .	78.5	111.5	163.5
Sugar	139.5	189.5	182.9
Soap	101.3	93.4	127.6
Cement	507.1	559.0	692.7
Paint (million litres)	1.9	2.2	8.2
Edible oil and fat	56.0	58.1	43.3
Animal feed	20.9	19.6	17.3
Footwear (million pairs) . . .	3.4	3.6	46.3
Wheat flour	42.2	25.7	20.3
Processed milk (million litres) .	14.9	19.6	18.5
Cotton and rayon fabrics (million sq m)	11.1	10.1	13.6
Clay bricks, tiles, etc.	33.3	15.4	36.2
Corrugated iron sheets . . .	39.2	48.8	61.6

Cement ('000 metric tons): 1,162 in 2009; 1,347 in 2010; 1,666 in 2011.
Processed milk (million litres): 1,337 in 2009–10; 1,418 in 2011.
Source: Bank of Uganda.

Electric energy (million kWh): 1,953 in 2007; 2,088 in 2008; 2,186 in 2009 (Source: UN Industrial Commodity Statistics Database).

Finance

CURRENCY AND EXCHANGE RATES

Monetary Units
    100 cents = 1 new Uganda shilling.

Sterling, Dollar and Euro Equivalents (30 November 2012)
    £1 sterling = 4,317 new Uganda shillings;
    US $1 = 2,688 new Uganda shillings;
    €1 = 3,491 new Uganda shillings;
    10,000 new Uganda shillings = £2.32 = $3.72 = €2.86.

Average Exchange Rate (new Uganda shillings per US $)
    2009   2,030.3
    2010   2,177.6
    2011   2,522.7

Note: Between December 1985 and May 1987 the official exchange rate was fixed at US $1 = 1,400 shillings. In May 1987 a new shilling, equivalent to 100 of the former units, was introduced. At the same time, the currency was devalued by 76.7%, with the exchange rate set at $1 = 60 new shillings. Further adjustments were implemented in subsequent years. Foreign exchange controls were mostly abolished in 1993.

BUDGET
('000 million new shillings, year ending 30 June)

Revenue	2009/10	2010/11	2011/12*
Taxes	4,205.7	5,114.3	6,169.1
Grants	863.0	890.4	1,726.3
Other revenue	113.8	95.1	120.6
Oil revenue	—	1,192.7	—
Total	5,182.6	7,292.5	8,016.0

Expenditure	2009/10	2010/11	2011/12*
Compensation of employees . .	1,308.4	1,659.5	1,860.4
Interest payments	385.1	423.5	519.6
Non wage expenditure . . .	2,222.3	3,162.1	2,075.4
Statutory expenditure	391.3	712.9	515.9
Development expenditure . .	2,478.4	2,850.9	4,816.2
Domestic	1,591.4	1,808.9	2,674.3
External	887.0	1,042.0	2,142.0
Statistical discrepancy . . .	45.6	163.6	32.6
Total	6,831.1	8,972.5	9,820.1

* Projections.

INTERNATIONAL RESERVES
(US $ million at 31 December)

	2009	2010	2011
IMF special drawing rights . .	225.2	220.8	218.4
Foreign exchange	2,769.3	2,485.2	2,399.0
Total	2,994.5	2,706.0	2,617.4

Source: IMF, *International Financial Statistics*.

MONEY SUPPLY
('000 million new shillings at 31 December)

	2009	2010	2011
Currency outside depository corporations	1,329.75	1,776.68	2,091.95
Transferable deposits	3,071.21	4,146.83	4,268.57
Other deposits	2,396.74	3,442.96	4,006.73
Broad money	6,797.70	9,366.47	10,367.25

Source: IMF, *International Financial Statistics*.

COST OF LIVING
(Consumer Price Index for all urban households; base: 2000 = 100)

	2008	2009	2010
Food	171.1	213.9	218.4
Clothing	121.5	131.3	135.1
Rent, fuel and light . . .	181.1	193.2	203.1
All items (incl. others) . . .	158.5	179.2	186.3

2011: Food 289.0; All items (incl. others) 221.0.

2012: Food 313.7; All items (incl. others) 252.0.

Source: ILO.

NATIONAL ACCOUNTS
('000 million new shillings at current prices)

Expenditure on the Gross Domestic Product

	2009	2010	2011
Government final consumption expenditure	3,209	3,555	4,039
Private final consumption expenditure	26,315	32,131	38,736
Increase in stocks	92	101	144
Gross fixed capital formation . .	7,309	8,528	11,251
Total domestic expenditure .	36,925	44,315	54,170
Exports of goods and services . .	7,229	7,572	9,817
Less Imports of goods and services	10,557	13,304	18,379
GDP in purchasers' values .	33,596	38,584	45,607
GDP at constant 2002 prices .	19,707	20,933	22,174

Gross Domestic Product by Economic Activity

	2009	2010	2011
Agriculture, hunting, forestry and fishing	7,908	8,114	10,440
Mining and quarrying . . .	84	119	158
Manufacturing	2,595	2,933	3,861
Electricity and water . . .	1,243	1,472	1,461
Construction	4,058	4,620	5,968
Wholesale and retail trade . .	5,132	6,043	7,873
Hotels and restaurants . . .	1,513	1,772	2,259
Transport, storage and communications	2,120	3,422	2,064
Financial intermediation . . .	1,022	1,160	1,331
Real estate	1,446	1,609	1,814

—*continued*	2009	2010	2011
Business services	503	594	675
Public administration and defence	1,035	1,232	1,563
Education	1,745	1,937	1,894
Health	311	337	335
Other services	737	865	1,054
Sub-total	31,452	36,229	42,750
Less Financial intermediation services indirectly measured .	654	765	845
Gross value added at basic prices	30,798	35,464	41,905
Net taxes on products . . .	2,799	3,119	3,702
GDP at market prices . . .	33,596	38,584	45,607

BALANCE OF PAYMENTS
(US $ million)

	2009	2010	2011
Exports of goods	2,326.6	2,164.0	2,576.2
Imports of goods	−3,915.2	−4,540.4	−5,254.9
Balance on goods	−1,588.7	−2,376.4	−2,678.6
Exports of services	983.8	1,375.5	1,451.6
Imports of services	−1,417.1	−1,880.1	−2,280.0
Balance on goods and services	−2,021.9	−2,881.0	−3,507.1
Primary income received . .	41.9	21.3	28.1
Primary income paid . . .	−418.2	−312.8	−361.8
Balance on goods, services and primary income	−2,398.3	−3,172.4	−3,840.8
Secondary income received . .	1,541.2	1,563.0	1,843.6
Secondary income paid . .	−393.8	−250.0	−278.7
Current balance	−1,250.8	−1,859.4	−2,275.8
Capital account (net) . . .	—	—	5.7
Direct investment assets . .	—	3.4	
Direct investment liabilities . .	841.6	543.9	796.9
Portfolio investment assets . .	—	—	−0.1
Portfolio investment liabilities .	28.7	−110.5	256.8
Financial derivatives and employee stock options liabilities . . .	−6.2	−1.4	5.5
Other investment assets . .	−1.6	−132.2	154.8
Other investment liabilities . .	834.3	710.0	482.2
Net errors and omissions . .	−161.5	593.1	385.9
Reserves and related items .	284.5	−253.1	−188.2

Source: IMF, *International Financial Statistics*.

External Trade

PRINCIPAL COMMODITIES
(distribution by SITC, US $ million)

Imports c.i.f.	2009	2010	2011*
Food and live animals . . .	329.3	333.6	448.5
Cereals and cereal preparations .	203.0	187.1	231.1
Mineral fuels, lubricants, etc. .	743.7	932.4	1,317.3
Petroleum, petroleum products and related materials . . .	728.6	917.0	1,288.4
Animal and vegetable oils, fats and waxes	139.6	195.4	256.9
Fixed vegetable fats and oils . .	126.3	179.9	229.0
Chemicals and related products	558.4	574.5	725.5
Medicinal and pharmaceutical products	213.8	204.4	259.2
Basic manufactures . . .	761.5	769.8	809.9
Non-metallic mineral manufactures	158.2	151.2	159.3

Imports c.i.f.—*continued*	2009	2010	2011*
Iron and steel	220.0	228.8	271.0
Machinery and transport equipment	1,269.0	1,339.7	1,574.7
Telecommunications and sound recording/reproducing apparatus	229.0	227.9	343.4
Electrical machinery, apparatus, etc.	174.8	145.4	141.7
Road vehicles (incl. air-cushion vehicles) and parts (excl. tyres, engines and electrical parts) .	369.7	418.8	499.7
Miscellaneous manufactured articles	314.4	323.0	348.4
Total (incl. others)	4,257.6	4,664.3	5,630.9

Exports f.o.b.	2009	2010	2011*
Food and live animals . . .	633.5	717.9	951.2
Fish, crustaceans, molluscs and preparations thereof . . .	109.2	129.1	136.5
Cereals and cereal preparations .	58.3	76.7	69.0
Sugar, sugar preparations and honey	42.8	60.2	81.9
Coffee, tea, cocoa, spices and manufactures	375.3	395.4	593.1
Beverages and tobacco . . .	103.7	101.4	89.6
Tobacco and tobacco manufactures . . .	62.5	68.8	55.2
Crude materials (inedible) except fuels	120.3	106.0	188.4
Textile fibres (not wool tops) and their wastes (not in yarn) . .	29.9	32.1	91.6
Crude animal and vegetable materials n.e.s.	56.1	52.8	61.0
Mineral fuels, lubricants and related materials . . .	115.9	88.3	124.0
Petroleum, petroleum products and related materials . .	102.7	75.7	107.7
Animal and vegetable oils, fats and waxes	48.9	54.0	99.9
Chemicals and related products	61.3	53.4	68.6
Basic manufactures . . .	224.5	228.1	308.9
Non-metallic mineral manufactures	85.4	74.1	104.3
Iron and steel	86.2	78.5	103.1
Machinery and transport equipment	205.2	197.4	266.4
Telecommunications and sound recording/reproducing apparatus	62.4	84.9	130.8
Road vehicles (incl. air-cushion vehicles) and parts (excl. tyres, engines and electrical parts) .	47.6	51.8	60.8
Miscellaneous manufactured articles	59.2	42.1	55.3
Total (incl. others)	1,567.6	1,618.6	2,159.1

* Provisional.

PRINCIPAL TRADING PARTNERS
(US $ million)

Imports c.i.f.	2008	2009	2010
Bahrain	46.8	18.9	16.7
Belgium	52.8	35.9	34.8
China, People's Republic . . .	365.8	379.2	414.7
France (incl. Monaco) . . .	179.6	158.6	64.5
Germany	88.4	95.9	128.6
Hong Kong	46.9	37.1	35.6
India	470.5	521.1	684.4
Italy	87.5	56.6	69.1
Japan	268.7	270.0	305.5
Kenya	511.3	502.7	511.5
Korea, Republic	47.6	65.2	80.7
Malaysia	146.0	76.9	100.5
Netherlands	75.5	87.3	133.2

Imports c.i.f.—*continued*	2008	2009	2010
Saudi Arabia	115.7	169.5	239.3
Singapore	94.2	89.7	89.9
South Africa	305.2	245.3	250.4
Sweden	96.5	40.3	45.5
Tanzania	55.5	40.8	56.5
Thailand	27.3	39.2	49.0
United Arab Emirates . . .	515.5	416.6	391.0
United Kingdom	137.6	140.3	134.5
USA	117.4	87.0	105.5
Total (incl. others)	4,525.9	4,247.4	4,664.3

Exports f.o.b.	2008	2009	2010
Belgium	63.7	42.0	41.8
Burundi	45.4	55.8	51.3
China, People's Republic . .	12.8	17.1	22.0
Congo, Democratic Republic . .	125.0	156.6	184.0
Congo, Republic	22.0	8.3	—
France (incl. Monaco) . . .	33.7	22.7	12.4
Germany	75.0	62.9	73.6
Hong Kong	16.1	16.2	18.9
India	18.7	19.7	13.9
Italy	33.6	31.0	31.4
Kenya	164.6	174.0	190.3
Netherlands	81.8	79.0	89.9
Rwanda	136.9	135.3	149.3
Singapore	26.0	23.5	24.0
South Africa	14.9	23.0	10.3
Spain	26.9	26.0	36.4
Sudan	245.9	184.6	208.6
Switzerland-Liechtenstein . .	155.7	86.5	57.5
Tanzania	30.5	33.8	37.6
United Arab Emirates . . .	128.1	85.8	120.9
United Kingdom	118.4	52.4	36.9
USA	15.7	37.2	21.4
Total (incl. others)	1,724.3	1,567.6	1,618.6

Source: UN, *International Trade Statistics Yearbook*.

2011 (US $ million, provisional): Total imports 5,630.9; Total exports 2,159.1.

Transport

RAILWAYS
(traffic)

	1994	1995	1996
Passenger-km (million) . . .	35	30	28
Freight ton-km (million) . . .	208	236	187

Freight traffic ('000 ton-km): 212,616 in 2003; 229,439 in 2004; 185,559 in 2005.

ROAD TRAFFIC
(vehicles in use)

	2007	2008	2009
Passenger cars	81,320	90,856	96,575
Buses and coaches	40,471	50,472	63,789
Lorries and vans	79,273	86,818	93,172
Motorcycles	176,516	236,452	292,263

CIVIL AVIATION
(traffic on scheduled services)

	2007	2008	2009
Kilometres flown (million) . . .	3	3	3
Passengers carried ('000) . . .	60	63	64
Passenger-km (million) . . .	346	355	344
Total ton-km (million) . . .	63	61	58

Source: UN, *Statistical Yearbook*.

Passengers carried ('000, Entebbe international airport): 1,111 in 2010; 1,167 in 2011.

Tourism

FOREIGN TOURIST ARRIVALS

Country of residence	2009	2010	2011
Austria	897	20,304	53,820
Germany	6,778	8,650	8,960
India	12,946	16,747	19,419
Kenya	261,329	294,170	344,210
Netherlands	6,017	7,651	8,380
Rwanda	199,530	177,043	266,221
Sudan	15,088	22,909	39,333
Tanzania	48,948	42,289	59,013
United Kingdom	35,716	39,171	37,702
USA	37,971	45,856	47,869
Total (incl. others)	806,655	945,899	1,151,356

Tourism receipts (US $ million): 564 in 2009; 662 in 2010; 805 in 2011.

Communications Media

	2009	2010	2011
Telephones ('000 main lines in use)	233.5	327.1	464.8
Mobile cellular telephones ('000 subscribers)	9,383.7	12,828.3	16,697.0
Internet subscribers ('000) . .	30.0	134.0	88.8
Broadband subscribers . . .	6,000	54,800	35,500

Source: International Telecommunication Union.

Education

(2009/10 unless otherwise indicated)

	Institutions	Teachers	Students
Pre-primary	n.a.	19,844	498,644
Primary	n.a.	172,403	8,374,648
Secondary	n.a.	68,089	1,225,692
Tertiary*	n.a.	3,939	123,887
Teacher-training colleges† . .	10	n.a.	16,170
Technical schools and institutes†	25	n.a.	7,999
Universities†	18	n.a.	58,823

* 2008/09.
† 2003/04.

Source: mainly UNESCO Institute for Statistics.

Pupil-teacher ratio (primary education, UNESCO estimate): 49 in 2009/10.

Adult literacy rate (UNESCO estimates): 73.2% (males 82.6%; females 64.6%) in 2010 (Source: UNESCO Institute for Statistics).

Directory

The Government

HEAD OF STATE

President: Gen. (retd) YOWERI KAGUTA MUSEVENI (took office 29 January 1986; elected 9 May 1996, re-elected 12 March 2001, 23 February 2006 and 18 February 2011).

Vice-President: EDWARD KIWANUKA SSEKANDI.

THE CABINET
(May 2013)

Prime Minister: JOHN PATRICK AMAMA MBABAZI.

First Deputy Prime Minister and Minister in Charge of East African Community Affairs: (vacant).

Second Deputy Prime Minister and Minister of Public Service: HENRY MUGANWA KAJURA.

Third Deputy Prime Minister and Deputy Leader of Government Business: Gen. MOSES ALI.

Minister of Security: WILSON MURULI MUKASA.

Minister in Charge of the Presidency: FRANK TUMWEBAZE.

Minister for Karamoja: JANET KATAAHA MUSEVENI.

Minister in the Office of the Prime Minister, in charge of General Duties: JOHN MWOONO NASASIRA.

Minister of Relief and Disaster Preparedness: Dr STEVEN MALLINGA.

Minister of Information and National Guidance: MARY KAROORO OKURUT BUSINGYE.

Minister of Agriculture, Animal Industry and Fisheries: TRESS BUCYANAYANDI.

Minister of Defence: CRISPUS KIYONGA.

Minister of Education and Sports: JESSICA ROSE EPEL ALUPO.

Minister of Energy and Mineral Development: IRENE MULONI.

Minister of Finance, Planning and Economic Development: MARIA KIWANUKA.

Minister of Works and Transport: Eng. JAMES ABRAHAM BYANDAALA.

Minister of Justice and Constitutional Affairs: KAHINDA OTAFIIRE.

Minister of Gender, Labour and Social Affairs: TARSIS KABWEGYERE.

Minister of Trade, Industry and Co-operatives: AMELIA ANNE KYAMBADDE.

Minister of Water and Environment: Prof. EPHRAIM KAMUNTU.

Minister of Lands, Housing and Urban Development: DAUDI MIGEREKO.

Minister of Health: Dr DRADIDI JOYCE CHRISTINE ONDOA.

Minister of Foreign Affairs: SAM KUTESAKAHAMBA.

Minister of Information and Communication Technology: Dr RUHAKANA RUGUNDA.

Minister of Local Government: ADOLF MWESIGYE.

Minister without Portfolio, in charge of Political Mobilization: RICHARD TODWONG.

Minister of Tourism, Wildlife and Heritage: MARIA EMILY LUBEGA MUTAGAMBA.

Minister of Internal Affairs: HILARY ONEK.

In addition to the Cabinet Ministers, there were 48 Ministers of State. The Chief Whip and Attorney-General are also members of the Cabinet.

MINISTRIES

Office of the President: Parliament Bldg, POB 7168, Kampala; tel. (41) 4258441; fax (41) 4256143; e-mail aak@statehouse.go.ug; internet www.statehouse.go.ug.

Office of the Prime Minister: Post Office Bldg, Yusuf Lule Rd, POB 341, Kampala; tel. (41) 4236252; fax (41) 4341139; e-mail ps@opm.go.ug; internet www.opm.go.ug.

Ministry of Agriculture, Animal Industry and Fisheries: POB 102, Entebbe; tel. (41) 4320987; fax (41) 4321255; e-mail mosagr@hotmail.com; internet www.agriculture.go.ug.

Ministry of Communication and Information Communication Technology: NSSF House, Jinja Rd, POB 7817, Kampala; tel. (41) 4236262; fax (41) 4231314; internet www.ict.go.ug.

Ministry of Defence: Bombo, POB 7069, Kampala; tel. (41) 4270331; fax (41) 4245911; e-mail spokesman@defenceuganda.mil.ug; internet www.defence.go.ug.

Ministry of East African Community Affairs: Postel Bldg, 2nd Floor, 67/75 Yusuf Lule Rd, POB 7343, Kampala; tel. (41) 4340100; fax (41) 4348171; e-mail meaca@meaca.go.ug; internet www.meaca .go.ug.

Ministry of Education and Sports: Embassy House and Development Bldg, Plot 9/11, Parliament Ave, POB 7063, Kampala; tel. (41) 4234451; fax (41) 42230437; e-mail pro@education.go.ug; internet www.education.go.ug.

Ministry of Energy and Mineral Development: Amber House, Kampala Rd, Kampala; tel. (41) 4311111; fax (41) 4234732; e-mail psmemd@energy.go.ug; internet www.energyandminerals.go.ug.

Ministry of Finance, Planning and Economic Development: Appollo Kaggwa Rd, Plot 2-12, POB 8147, Kampala; tel. (41) 4707000; fax (41) 4230163; e-mail webmaster@finance.go.ug; internet www.finance.go.ug.

Ministry of Foreign Affairs: 2A/B Apollo Kaggwa Rd, POB 7048, Kampala; tel. (41) 4345661; fax (41) 4258722; e-mail info@mofa.go .ug; internet www.mofa.go.ug.

Ministry of Gender, Labour and Social Affairs: Plot 2, Lumumba Ave, Simbamanyo House, POB 7136, Kampala; tel. (41) 347854; fax (41) 256374; e-mail ps@mglsd.go.ug; internet www .mglsd.go.ug.

Ministry of Health: Plot 6, Lourdel Rd, Nakasero, POB 7272, Kampala; tel. (41) 4340874; fax (41) 4231584; e-mail info@health .go.ug; internet www.health.go.ug.

Ministry of Information and National Guidance: Kampala.

Ministry of Internal Affairs: Plot 75, Jinja Rd, POB 7191, Kampala; tel. (41) 4231103; fax (41) 4343088; e-mail info@mia.go .ug; internet www.mia.go.ug.

Ministry of Justice and Constitutional Affairs: Plot 1, Parliament Ave, Queens Chambers, POB 7183, Kampala; tel. (41) 4230538; fax (41) 4254829; e-mail mojca@africaonline.co.ug; internet www .justice.go.ug.

Ministry of Lands, Housing and Urban Development: POB 7096, Kampala; tel. (41) 4342931; internet www.mlhud.go.ug.

Ministry of Local Government: Uganda House, 8/10 Kampala Rd, POB 7037, Kampala; tel. (41) 4341224; fax (41) 4258127; e-mail info@ molg.go.ug; internet www.molg.go.ug.

Ministry of Public Service: Plot 12, Nakasero Hill Rd, Wandegeya, POB 7003, Kampala; tel. (41) 4250534; e-mail info@ publicservice.go.ug; internet www.publicservice.go.ug.

Ministry of Relief and Disaster Preparedness: POB 341, Kampala; tel. (41) 4236967.

Ministry of Security: Kampala.

Ministry of Tourism, Wildlife and Heritage: 6/8 Parliament Ave, POB 7103, Kampala; tel. (41) 4341076; fax (41) 4347286; internet www.mtti.go.ug.

Ministry of Trade, Industry and Co-operatives: 6/8 Parliament Ave, POB 7103, Kampala; tel. (41) 4314000; fax (41) 4347286; e-mail mintrade@mtti.go.ug; internet www.mtti.go.ug.

Ministry of Water and Environment: POB 20026, Kampala; tel. (41) 4505942; e-mail mwle@mwle.go.ug; internet www.mwle.go.ug.

Ministry of Works and Transport: Plot 4/6, Airport Rd, POB 10, Entebbe; tel. (42) 4320101; fax (42) 4321364; e-mail mowt@works.go .ug; internet www.works.go.ug.

President and Legislature

PRESIDENT

Election, 18 February 2011

Candidate	Votes	% of votes
Gen. (retd) Yoweri Kaguta Museveni (NRM)	5,428,368	68.38
Kizza Besigye (FDC)	2,064,963	26.01
Norbert Mao (DP)	147,917	1.86
Olara Otunnu (UPC)	125,059	1.58
Beti Olive Namisango Kamya (UFA)	52,782	0.66
Abed Bwanika (PDP)	51,708	0.65
Jaberi Bidandi Ssali (PPP)	34,688	0.44
Samuel Lubega Walter Mukaaku (Ind.)	32,726	0.41
Total	**7,938,211**	**100.00**

PARLIAMENT

Speaker: Rebecca Alitwala Kadaga.

Deputy Speaker: Jacob Oulanyah.

General Election, 18 February 2011

Party	Directly elected seats	Women members	Total seats
NRM	164	85	249
FDC	24	11	35
DP	11	1	12
UPC	7	3	10
CP	1	—	1
JEEMA	1	—	1
Ind.	30	12	42
Others*	—	—	25
Total	**238**	**112**	**375**

* Comprises 10 nominated representatives from the Uganda People's Defence Forces, five nominated representatives for young people (four from the NRM and one independent), five nominated representatives for people with disabilities (all from the NRM) and five nominated representatives for workers (four from the NRM and one independent).

Election Commission

Electoral Commission: 53–56 Jinja Rd, POB 22678, Kampala; tel. (41) 4337500; fax (41) 4337595; e-mail info@ec.or.ug; internet www .ec.or.ug; f. 1997; independent; Chair. Dr Badru M. Kiggundu.

Political Organizations

Political parties were ordered to suspend active operations, although not formally banned, in March 1986. In mid-2005 legislation was adopted allowing for a return to full multi-party democracy; the legislation was approved by 92.5% of voters in a national referendum held on 28 July 2005. A total of 38 political parties had been officially registered by 2011.

Conservative Party (CP): POB 5145, Kampala; f. 1979; Leader Ken Lukyamuzi.

Democratic Party (DP): City House, Plot 2/3, William St, POB 7098, Kampala; tel. and fax (41) 4252536; e-mail info@dpuganda.org; f. 1954; main support in southern Uganda; Pres. Norbert Mao; Vice-Pres. Zachary Olum.

Forum for Democratic Change (FDC): Plot 1944, Najjankumbi, Entebbe Rd, POB 26928, Kampala; tel. 757693020 (mobile); e-mail info@fdcuganda.org; internet fdc-uganda.org; f. 2004 by a merger of the Reform Agenda, the Parliamentary Advocacy Forum and the National Democratic Forum; Pres. Maj.–Gen. Gregory Mugisha Muntu.

Forum for Integrity in Leadership (FIL): Plot 48B, Ntinda Rd, POB 7606, Kampala; Chair. Emmanuel Tumusiime.

Justice Forum (JEEMA): POB 3999, Kampala; Leader Muhammad Kibirige Mayanja; Sec.-Gen. Hussein Kyanjo.

National Resistance Movement (NRM): Plot 10, Kyadondo Rd, POB 7778, Kampala; tel. (41) 346295; e-mail info@nrm.ug; internet www.nrm.ug; f. as National Resistance Movement to oppose the UPC Govt 1980–85; also opposed the mil. Govt in power from July 1985 to Jan. 1986; its fmr mil. wing, the National Resistance Army (NRA), led by Lt-Gen. (later Gen. retd) Yoweri Kaguta Museveni, took power in Jan. 1986; name changed as above on registration in 2003; Chair. Yoweri Museveni; Sec.-Gen. Amama Mbabazi.

People's Development Party (PDP): Makerere Hill Rd, Relief Bldg (opp. LDC), POB 25765, Kampala; f. 2007; Pres. Dr Abed Bwanika.

People's Progressive Party (PPP): Plot 6, Commercial St, Luzira, POB 9252, Kampala; tel. (41) 4505178; internet www.ppp.ug; f. 2004; Chair. Jaberi Bidandi Ssali.

Uganda Federal Alliance (UFA): POB 14196, Kampala; f. 2010; Leader Beti Olive Namissango Kamya.

Uganda Patriotic Movement (UPM): POB 2083, Kampala; tel. 752654524 (mobile); fax (41) 4236781; e-mail lubegabyayida@yahoo .com; f. 1980; Nat. Chair. D. A. Lubega Byay; Sec.-Gen. Mariam Ssempijja.

Uganda People's Congress (UPC): Plot 8–10, Kampala Rd, Uganda House, POB 37047, Kampala; tel. and fax (41) 236748; e-mail upcsecretariat@upcparty.net; internet www.upcparty.net; f. 1960; socialist-based philosophy; ruling party 1962–71 and 1980–85, sole legal political party 1969–71; Pres. Olara Otunnu; Sec.-Gen. Rev. Fr Jacinto Ogwal.

The following organizations are in armed conflict with the Government:

Allied Democratic Forces (ADF): active since 1996 in southeastern Uganda; combines Ugandan Islamic fundamentalist rebels, exiled Rwandan Hutus and guerrillas from the Democratic Republic of the Congo; Pres. Sheikh JAMIL MUKULU.

Lord's Resistance Army (LRA): f. 1987; claims to be conducting a Christian fundamentalist 'holy war' against the Govt; forces est. to number up to 1,500, operating mainly from bases in Sudan; Leader JOSEPH KONY; a breakaway faction (LRA—Democratic) is led by RONALD OTIM KOMAKECH.

Uganda People's Freedom Movement (UPFM): based in Tororo and Kenya; f. 1994 by mems of the fmr Uganda People's Army; Leader PETER OTAI.

West Nile Bank Front (WNBF): operates in northern Uganda.

Diplomatic Representation

EMBASSIES AND HIGH COMMISSIONS IN UGANDA

Algeria: 14 Acacia Ave, Kololo, POB 4025, Kampala; tel. (41) 4232918; fax (41) 4341015; e-mail ambalgka@imul.com; Ambassador ABDERRAHMANE BENMOKHTAR.

Belgium: Rwenzori Towers, 6th Floor, Plot 6, Nakasero Rd, POB 7043, Kampala; tel. (41) 4349559; fax (41) 4347212; e-mail kampala@diplobel.fed.be; internet www.diplomatie.be/kampala; Ambassador ALAIN HANSSEN.

China, People's Republic: 37 Malcolm X Ave, Kololo, POB 4106, Kampala; tel. (41) 4259881; fax (41) 4235087; e-mail chinaemb_ug@mfa.gov.cn; internet ug.china-embassy.org; Ambassador ZHAO YA-LI.

Congo, Democratic Republic: 20 Philip Rd, Kololo, POB 4972, Kampala; tel. (41) 4250099; fax (41) 4340140; Ambassador JEAN-CHARLES OKOTO LOLAKOMBE.

Cuba: KAR Dr., 10 Lower Kololo Terrace, POB 9226, Kampala; tel. (41) 4233742; fax (41) 4233320; e-mail embajador@africaonline.co.ug; internet www.cubadiplomatica.cu; Ambassador FRANCISCO JAVIER VIAMONTES CORREA.

Denmark: Plot 3, Lumumba Ave, POB 11243, Kampala; tel. (31) 2263211; fax (31) 2264624; e-mail kmtamb@um.dk; internet www.ambkampala.um.dk; Ambassador DAN E. FREDERIKSEN.

Egypt: 33 Kololo Hill Dr., POB 4280, Kampala; tel. (41) 4254525; fax (41) 4232103; e-mail egyembug@utlonline.co.ug; Ambassador SABRI MAGDI.

Ethiopia: 3L Kitante Close, off Kira Rd, POB 7745, Kampala; tel. (41) 4348340; fax (41) 4341885; Ambassador Ato TERFA MENEGESHA.

France: 16 Lumumba Ave, Nakasero, POB 7212, Kampala; tel. (41) 4304500; fax (41) 4304520; e-mail ambafrance.kampala@diplomatie.gouv.fr; internet www.ambafrance-ug.org; Ambassador ALINE KUSTER-MÉNAGER.

Germany: 15 Philip Rd, Kololo, POB 7016, Kampala; tel. (41) 4501111; fax (41) 4501115; e-mail info@kampala.diplo.de; internet www.kampala.diplo.de; Ambassador KLAUS DIETER DÜXMANN.

Holy See: Chwa II Rd, Mbuya Hill, POB 7177, Kampala (Apostolic Nunciature); tel. (41) 4505619; fax (41) 4441774; e-mail nuntius@imul.com; Apostolic Nuncio MICHAEL AUGUST BLUME (Titular Archbishop of Alexanum).

India: 11 Kyaddondo Rd, Nakasero, POB 7040, Kampala; tel. (41) 4257368; fax (41) 4254943; e-mail hoc@hicomindkampala.org; High Commissioner S. N. RAY.

Iran: 9 Bandali Rise, Bugolobi, POB 24529, Kampala; tel. (41) 4441689; fax (41) 4443590; Ambassador AMIR HUSSEIN NIKBIN.

Ireland: 25 Yusuf Lule Rd, Nakasero, POB 7791, Kampala; tel. (41) 7713000; fax (41) 4344353; e-mail kampalaembassy@dfa.ie; internet www.embassyofireland.ug; Ambassador ANNE WEBSTER.

Italy: 11 Lourdel Rd, Nakasero, POB 4646, Kampala; tel. (41) 4250442; fax (41) 4250448; e-mail segreteria.kampala@esteri.it; internet www.ambkampala.esteri.it; Ambassador STEFANO ANTONIO DEJAK.

Japan: Plot 8, Kyaddondo Rd, Nakasero, POB 23553, Kampala; tel. (41) 4349542; fax (41) 4349547; e-mail jembassy@jembassy.co.ug; internet www.ug.emb-japan.go.jp; Ambassador KAZUO MINAGAWA.

Kenya: 41 Nakasero Rd, POB 5220, Kampala; tel. (41) 4458235; fax (41) 4458239; e-mail kenyahicom@africaonline.co.ug; High Commissioner Maj.-Gen. (retd) GEOFFREY OKANGA LUKALE.

Korea, Democratic People's Republic: 10 Prince Charles Dr., Kololo, POB 5885, Kampala; tel. (41) 4546033; fax (41) 4450224; Ambassador JONG THAE YANG.

Libya: 26 Kololo Hill Dr., POB 6079, Kampala; tel. (41) 4344924; fax (41) 4344969; Ambassador (vacant).

Netherlands: Rwenzori Courts, 4th Floor, Plot 2, Nakasero Rd, POB 7728, Kampala; tel. (41) 4346000; fax (41) 4231861; e-mail kam@minbuza.nl; internet uganda.nlembassy.org; Ambassador ALPHONS JEAN ANTOINE JOSEPH MARIE GERTRUDE HENNEKENS.

Nigeria: 33 Nakasero Rd, POB 4338, Kampala; tel. (41) 4433691; fax (41) 4432543; e-mail nighicom-sgu@africaonline.co.ug; High Commissioner CORNELIUS OMOLADE OLUWATERU.

Norway: 18B Akii-Bua Rd, Nakasero, POB 22770, Kampala; tel. (41) 7112000; fax (41) 4343936; e-mail emb.kampala@mfa.no; internet www.norway.go.ug; Ambassador THORBJØRN GAUSTADSÆTHER.

Russia: 28 Malcolm X Ave, Kololo, POB 7022, Kampala; tel. (41) 4433676; fax (41) 4345798; Ambassador SERGEI SHISHKIN.

Rwanda: 2 Nakaima Rd, POB 2468, Kampala; tel. (41) 4344045; fax (41) 4458547; e-mail Ambakampala@minaffet.gov.rw; internet www.uganda.embassy.gov.rw; High Commissioner Maj.-Gen. FRANK MUGAMBAGE.

Saudi Arabia: 3 Okurut Close, Kololo, POB 22558, Kampala; tel. (41) 4340614; fax (41) 4454017; Ambassador AHMAD BIN MUHAMMAD AL-BAHLAL.

South Africa: Plot 15A, Nakasero Rd, POB 22667, Kampala; tel. (41) 4343543; fax (41) 4348216; e-mail kampala.sahc@foreign.gov.za; High Commissioner D. J. QWELANE.

South Sudan: Kampala; Ambassador LAURE SAMUEL LOMINSUK.

Sweden: 24 Lumumba Ave, Nakasero, POB 22669, Kampala; tel. (41) 7700800; fax (41) 7700801; e-mail ambassaden.kampala@foreign.ministry.se; internet www.swedenabroad.com/kampala; Ambassador URBAN ANDERSSON.

Tanzania: 6 Kagera Rd, Nakasero, POB 5750, Kampala; tel. (41) 4456272; fax (41) 4343973; High Commissioner LADISLAUS COLUMBAN KOMBA.

United Arab Emirates: Kampala; Ambassador HASSAN MOHAMMED OBAID AL-SUWAIDI.

United Kingdom: Plot 4, Windsor Loop Rd, POB 7070, Kampala; tel. (31) 2312000; fax (41) 4257304; e-mail bhcinfo@starcom.co.ug; internet ukinuganda.fco.gov.uk; High Commissioner ALISON BLACKBURNE.

USA: Plot 1577, Ggaba Rd, POB 7007, Kampala; tel. (41) 4259791; fax (41) 4259794; e-mail kampalawebcontact@state.gov; internet kampala.usembassy.gov; Ambassador SCOTT DELISI.

Zambia: Kampala; High Commissioner JUDITH K. K. KANGOMA KAPIJIMPANGA.

Judicial System

The judicial system comprises a Supreme Court, a Court of Appeal, a High Court and Magistrates' Courts. The Court of Appeal sits, whenever necessary, as a Constitutional Court to determine matters of a constitutional nature. There are also quasi-judicial institutions, such as Local Council Courts, Family and Children Courts and Land Courts. The Chief Justice is the head of the judiciary and is responsible for the administration and supervision of all courts in Uganda; he may issue orders and directions to the courts necessary for proper and efficient administration of justice.

Supreme Court: Plot 10, Upper Koloko, Seenu Awasthi Terrace, Mengo, Kampala; internet www.judicature.go.ug; hears appeals from the Court of Appeal and the Constitutional Court; consists of the Chief Justice and seven other judges; Chief Justice BENJAMIN ODOKI.

Court of Appeal: 5 Parliament Ave, Kampala; hears appeals from the High Court; acts as a Constitutional Court; consists of the Deputy Chief Justice and no fewer than seven Justices of Appeal, the number thereof being prescribed by Parliament; Deputy Chief Justice STEVEN KAVUMA (acting).

High Court: Plot 1, The Square, POB 7085, Kampala; tel. (41) 4233422; the court's services are also available from 11 High Court circuits, located at Fort Portal, Mbarara, Masaka, Masindi, Jinja, Soroti, Mbale, Gulu, Lira, Arua and Kabale; has full criminal and civil jurisdiction; Principal Judge YOROKAMU BAMWINE.

Magistrates' Courts: These were established under the Magistrates' Courts Act of 1970 and exercise limited jurisdiction in criminal and civil matters. The country is divided into magisterial areas, presided over by a Chief Magistrate. Under the Chief Magistrate there are two categories of Magistrates. The Magistrates preside alone over their courts. Appeals from the first category of Magistrates' Court lie directly to the High Court, while appeals from the second categories of Magistrates' Court lie to the Chief Magistrate's Court, and from there to the High Court. There are 27 Chief Magistrates' Courts, 52 Magistrates' Grade I Courts and 428 Magistrates' Grade II Courts.

Religion

Christianity is the majority religion—its adherents constitute approximately 75% of the population. Muslims account for some 15% of the population. A variety of other religions, including traditional indigenous religions, several branches of Hinduism, the Bahá'í Faith and Judaism, are practised freely and, combined, make up around 10% of the population. There are few atheists in the country. In many areas, particularly in rural settings, some religions tend to be syncretistic: deeply held traditional indigenous beliefs are blended into or observed alongside the rites of recognized religions, particularly in areas that are predominantly Christian. Missionary groups of several denominations are present and active in the country, including the Pentecostal Church, the Baptist Church, the Episcopal Church/Church of Uganda, the Church of Christ and the Mormons.

CHRISTIANITY

The Roman Catholic and Anglican Churches claim approximately the same number of followers, accounting for 90% of the country's professed Christians. The Seventh-day Adventist Church, the Church of Jesus Christ of Latter-day Saints (Mormons), the Orthodox Church, Jehovah's Witnesses, the Baptist Church, the Unification Church and the Pentecostal Church, among others, are also active.

The Anglican Communion

Anglicans are adherents of the Church of the Province of Uganda, comprising 29 dioceses. In 2002 there were about 8m. adherents.

Archbishop of Uganda and Bishop of Kampala: Most Rev. HENRY LUKE OROMBI, POB 14123, Kampala; tel. (41) 4270218; fax (41) 4251925; e-mail couab@uol.co.ug.

Greek Orthodox Church

Archbishop of East Africa: NICADEMUS OF IRINOUPOULIS (resident in Nairobi, Kenya); jurisdiction covers Kenya, Tanzania and Uganda.

The Roman Catholic Church

Uganda comprises four archdioceses and 15 dioceses. An estimated 43% of the total population is Roman Catholic.

Uganda Episcopal Conference

Uganda Catholic Secretariat, POB 2886, Kampala; tel. (41) 4510398; fax (41) 4510545.

f. 1974; Pres. Most Rev. JOHN BAPTIST ODAMA (Archbishop of Gulu).

Archbishop of Gulu: Most Rev. JOHN BAPTIST ODAMA, Archbishop's House, POB 200, Gulu; tel. (47) 4132026; fax (47) 4132860; e-mail metrog@archdioceseofgulu.org.

Archbishop of Kampala: CYPRIAN KIZITO LWANGA, Archbishop's House, POB 14125, Mengo, Kampala; tel. (41) 4270183; fax (41) 4345441; e-mail klarchdioc@utlonline.co.ug.

Archbishop of Mbarara: Most Rev. PAUL BAKYENGA, POB 150, Mbarara; tel. (48) 5420052; fax (48) 5421249; e-mail mbarchd@utlonline.co.ug.

Archbishop of Tororo: Most Rev. DENIS KIWANUKA LOTE, Archbishop's House, Plot 17 Boma Ave, POB 933, Mbale; tel. (45) 4433269; fax (45) 4433754; e-mail tororoad@africaonline.co.ug.

ISLAM

Muslims are mainly Sunni, although there are Shi'a followers of the Aga Khan among the Asian community.

The Uganda Muslim Supreme Council: POB 1146, Kampala; tel. (41) 4344499; fax (41) 4256500; Mufti of Uganda Sheikh SHABAN MUBAJJE; Chief Kadi and Pres. of Council HUSAYN RAJAB KAKOOZA.

BAHÁ'Í FAITH

National Spiritual Assembly: Kikaaya Hill Mile 4, Gayaza Rd, Kawempe Division, POB 2662, Kampala; tel. (31) 2262681; e-mail ugandabahai@gmail.com; f. 1951; mems resident in 2,721 localities.

JUDAISM

There is a small Jewish community, the Abayudaya, in central Uganda, with some 600 members and six synagogues.

The Press

DAILY AND OTHER NEWSPAPERS

The Citizen: Kampala; tel. 7846097708 (mobile); internet www.theugandacitizen.com; f. 2007; English.

The Daily Monitor: Plot 29–35, 8th St, POB 12141, Kampala; tel. (41) 7744100; fax (41) 4232369; e-mail editorial@ug.nationmedia.com; internet www.monitor.co.ug; f. 1992; daily; English; Man. Editor DANIEL KALINAKI; circ. 22,000 (Mon.–Sat.), 24,000 (Sun.).

Financial Times: Plot 17/19, Station Rd, POB 31399, Kampala; tel. (41) 4245798; bi-weekly; English; Editor G. A. ONEGI OBEL.

Focus: POB 268, Kampala; tel. (41) 4235086; fax (41) 4242796; f. 1983; publ. by Islamic Information Service and Material Centre; 4 a week; English; Editor HAJJI KATENDE; circ. 12,000.

Guide: POB 5350, Kampala; tel. (41) 4233486; fax (41) 4268045; f. 1989; weekly; English; Editor-in-Chief A. A. KALIISA; circ. 30,000.

Munnansi News Bulletin: POB 7098, Kampala; f. 1980; weekly; English; owned by the Democratic Party; Editor ANTHONY SGEKWEYAMA.

Munno: POB 4027, Kampala; f. 1911; daily; Luganda; publ. by the Roman Catholic Church; Editor ANTHONY SSEKWEYAMA; circ. 7,000.

New Vision: POB 9815, Kampala; tel. (41) 4337000; fax (41) 4232050; e-mail editorial@newvision.co.ug; internet www.newvision.co.ug; f. 1986; official govt newspaper; daily; English; Editor-in-Chief BARBARA KAIJA; Man. Editor BEN OPOLOT; circ. 34,000 (Mon.–Sat.), 42,000 (Sun.).

  Bukedde: e-mail bukeddekussande@newvision.co.ug; internet www.bukedde.co.ug; daily; Luganda; Editor GEOFFREY KULUBYA; circ. 16,000.

  Etop: e-mail etop@newvision.co.ug; weekly; vernacular; Editor KENNETH OLUKA; circ. 5,000.

  Orumuri: tel. (48) 5421265; internet www.orumuri.co.ug; weekly; vernacular; circ. 11,000.

  Rupiny: e-mail rupiny@newvision.co.ug; internet www.rupiny.co.ug; weekly; vernacular; Editor NANCY ANEK-OBITA; circ. 5,000.

Ngabo: POB 9362, Kampala; tel. (41) 4242637; f. 1979; daily; Luganda; Editor MAURICE SEKAWUNGU; circ. 7,000.

The Star: POB 9362, Kampala; tel. (41) 4242637; f. 1980; revived 1984; daily; English; Editor SAMUEL KATWERE; circ. 5,000.

Taifa Uganda Empya: POB 1986, Kampala; tel. (41) 4254652; f. 1953; daily; Luganda; Editor A. SEMBOGA; circ. 24,000.

Weekly Topic: POB 1725, Kampala; tel. (41) 4233834; weekly; English; Editor JOHN WASSWA; circ. 13,000.

PERIODICALS

Eastern Africa Journal of Rural Development: Dept of Agricultural Economics and Agribusiness, Makerere University, POB 7062, Kampala; tel. 772616540 (mobile); fax (41) 4530858; e-mail bkiiza@infocom.co.ug; annual; Editor BARNABAS KIIZA; circ. 800.

The Exposure: POB 3179, Kampala; tel. (41) 4267203; fax (41) 4259549; monthly; politics.

The Independent: Kampala; internet www.independent.co.ug; f. 2007; weekly; Editor ANDREW MWENDA.

Leadership: POB 2522, Kampala; tel. (41) 4422407; fax (41) 4421576; f. 1956; 11 a year; English; Roman Catholic; circ. 7,400; Editor Fr CARLOS RODRÍGUEZ.

Mkombozi: c/o Ministry of Defence, Republic House, POB 3798, Kampala; tel. (41) 4270331; f. 1982; military affairs; Editor A. OPOLOTT.

Musizi: POB 4027, Mengo, Kampala; f. 1955; monthly; Luganda; Roman Catholic; Editor F. GITTA; circ. 30,000.

Uganda Confidential: POB 5576, Kampala; tel. (41) 4250273; fax (41) 4255288; e-mail ucl@swiftuganda.com; internet www.swiftuganda.com/~confidential; f. 1990; monthly; Editor TEDDY SSEZI-CHEEYE.

NEWS AGENCY

Uganda News Agency (UNA): POB 7142, Kampala; tel. (41) 4232734; fax (41) 4342259; Dir CRISPUS MUNDUA (acting).

Publishers

Centenary Publishing House Ltd: POB 6246, Kampala; tel. (41) 4241599; fax (41) 4250427; f. 1977; religious (Anglican); Man. Dir Rev. SAM KAKIZA.

Fountain Publishers Ltd: POB 488, Kampala; tel. (41) 4259163; fax (41) 4251160; e-mail fountain@starcom.co.ug; internet www.fountainpublishers.co.ug; f. 1989; general, school textbooks, children's books, academic, scholarly; Man. Dir JAMES TUMUSIIME.

Longman Uganda Ltd: POB 3409, Kampala; tel. (41) 4242940; f. 1965; Man. Dir M. K. L. MUTYABA.

Uganda Printing and Publishing Corporation (UPPC): POB 33, Entebbe; tel. (41) 4220639; fax (41) 4220530; e-mail info@uppc.co

.ug; internet www.uppc.co.ug; f. 1993; Man. Dir LEVI MALINZI (acting).

Broadcasting and Communications

REGULATORY AUTHORITY

Uganda Communications Commission: UCC House, 42–44 Spring Rd, Bugolobi, POB 7376, Kampala; tel. (41) 4339000; fax (41) 4348832; e-mail ucc@ucc.co.ug; internet www.ucc.co.ug; f. 1998; regulatory body; Exec. Dir GODFREY MUTABAZI.

TELECOMMUNICATIONS

In 2011 there were seven providers of telecommunications services in Uganda.

Airtel Uganda Ltd: Celtel House, 40 Wampewo Ave, Kololo, POB 6771, Kampala; tel. 752230110 (mobile); fax (41) 4230106; e-mail info.africa@airtel.com; internet africa.airtel.com/uganda; f. 1995; fmrly Celtel Uganda, subsequently Zain Uganda, present name adopted 2010; Man. Dir V. G. SOMASEKHAR.

MTN Uganda Ltd: MTN Towers, 22 Hannington Rd, POB 24624, Kampala; tel. and fax (31) 2212333; e-mail mtn@mtn.co.ug; internet www.mtn.co.ug; f. 1998; CEO THEMBA KHUMALO.

Orange Uganda: Plot 28–30, Clement Hill Rd, POB 24144, Kampala; tel. 790000100 (mobile); e-mail care@orange.co.ug; internet www.orange.ug; f. 2009 following acquisition by France Telecom of a 53% stake in the Ugandan mobile phone operator Hits Telecom Uganda Ltd; provides mobile cellular telecommunications services; CEO PHILIPPE LUXCEY.

Uganda Telecom Ltd (UTL): Rwenzori Courts, Plot 2/4A, Nakasero Rd, POB 7171, Kampala; tel. (41) 4333200; fax (41) 4345907; e-mail info@utlonline.co.ug; internet www.utl.co.ug; f. 1998; state-owned; privatization pending; Man. Dir ABDULBASET ELAZZABI.

WARID Telecom: Plot 16A, Clement Hill Rd, POB 70665, Kampala; tel. 700100100 (mobile); fax 200221111; e-mail customercare@waridtel.co.ug; internet waridtel.co.ug; f. 2006; CEO SRIRAM YARLAGADDA.

BROADCASTING

Radio

91.3 Capital FM: POB 7638, Kampala; tel. (41) 4235092; fax (41) 4344556; f. 1993; independent music station broadcasting from Kampala, Mbarara and Mbale; Chief Officers WILLIAM PIKE, PATRICK QUARCOO.

Central Broadcasting Service (CBS): POB 12760, Kampala; tel. (41) 4272993; fax (41) 4340031; f. 1996; independent station broadcasting in local languages and English to most of Uganda; Man. Dir KAAYA KAVUMA.

Radio One: Duster St, POB 4589, Kampala; tel. (41) 4348211; fax (41) 4344385; e-mail info@radioonefm90.com; internet www.radioonefm90.com.

Sanyu Radio: Katto Plaza, Nkrumah Rd, Kampala; f. 1993; independent station broadcasting to Kampala and its environs.

UBC Radio: Plot 17/19, Nile Ave, POB 2038, Kampala; tel. (41) 4257257; fax (41) 4257252; e-mail ubc@ubconline.co.ug; internet ubconline.co.ug; f. 1954; state-controlled; under Uganda Broadcasting Corpn (UBC), formed by merger of Radio Uganda and Uganda Television in 2005; broadcasts in 23 languages, including English and Ugandan vernacular languages, through five stations, Red, Blue, Butebo, Magic and Star FM; Man. Dir PAUL KIHIIKA.

Voice of Toro: POB 2203, Kampala.

Television

Sanyu Television: Naguru; f. 1994; independent station broadcasting to Kampala and its environs.

UBC TV: Plot 17/19, Nile Ave, POB 2038, Kampala; tel. (41) 4257897; fax (41) 4257252; e-mail ubc@ubconline.co.ug; internet ubconline.co.ug; f. 1962; state-controlled commercial service; under Uganda Broadcasting Corpn (UBC), formed by merger of Radio Uganda and Uganda Television in 2005; programmes mainly in English, also in Swahili and Luganda; transmits over a radius of 320 km from Kampala; five relay stations are in operation, others are under construction; Man. Dir PAUL KIHIIKA.

Finance

(cap. = capital; res = reserves; dep. = deposits; m. = million; brs = branches; amounts in new Uganda shillings, unless otherwise indicated)

BANKING

In 2010 there were 22 commercial banks, three credit institutions and three microfinance deposit-taking institutions in Uganda.

Central Bank

Bank of Uganda: 37–43 Kampala Rd, POB 7120, Kampala; tel. (41) 4258441; fax (41) 4230878; e-mail info@bou.or.ug; internet www.bou.or.ug; f. 1966; bank of issue; cap. 20,000m., res 1,099,687m., dep. 5,416,569m. (June 2009); Gov. EMMANUEL TUMUSIIME-MUTEBILE; Dep. Gov. Dr LOUIS A. KASEKENDE.

State Bank

Uganda Development Bank Ltd (UDBL): 15A Clement Hill Rd, Ruth Towers, POB 7210, Kampala; tel. (41) 4355555; fax (41) 4355556; e-mail info@udbl.co.ug; internet www.udbl.co.ug; f. 1972; state-owned; reorg. 2001; CEO GABRIEL OTUDA ETOU.

Commercial Banks

ABC Capital Bank (U) Ltd: Colline House, Plot 4, Pilkington Rd, POB 21091, Kampala; tel. (41) 4345200; fax (41) 4258310; e-mail abc@abccapitalbank.com; f. 2009.

Bank of Africa—Uganda Ltd: Plot 45, Jinja Rd, POB 2750, Kampala; tel. (41) 4302001; fax (41) 4230902; e-mail boa@boa-uganda.com; internet www.boa-uganda.com; f. 1986 as Allied Bank International (Uganda); name changed as above in 2005; 47.7% owned by Bank of Africa—Kenya, 21.9% by Aureos East Africa Fund, 19.8% by The Netherlands Development Finance Co, 10.6% by Central Holdings Ltd; cap. 7,508m., res 9,599m., dep. 174,631m. (Dec. 2009); Chair. JOHN CARRUTHERS; Man. Dir MICHEL KAHN; 5 brs.

Cairo International Bank: 30 Kampala Rd, POB 7052, Kampala; tel. (41) 4230132; fax (41) 4230130; e-mail moona@cib.co.ug; internet www.cairointernationalbank.co.ug; 44.4% owned by Banque du Caire, 36.1% owned by Kato Aromatics SAE, 6.5% each owned by Bank of Egypt, Bank Misr and Bank of Alexandria; cap. 7,135m. (Dec. 2003); Chair. JOHN ELANGOT; Man. Dir NABIL GHANEM.

Crane Bank Ltd: Crane Chambers, 38 Kampala Rd, POB 22572, Kampala; tel. (41) 4345345; fax (41) 4231578; e-mail cranebank@cranebanklimited.com; internet www.cranebanklimited.com; f. 1995; wholly owned by various private investors; cap. 50,000m., res 9,948m., dep. 418,768m. (Dec. 2009); Chair. J. BIRIBONWA; Man. Dir A. R. KALAN.

DFCU Bank Ltd: Plot 2, Jinja Rd, POB 70, Kampala; tel. (41) 4256891; fax (41) 4231687; e-mail dfcubank@dfcugroup.com; internet www.dfcugroup.com; f. 1984 as Gold Trust Bank Ltd; current name adopted 2000; 60.02% owned by Commonwealth Development Corpn; total assets US $114.3m. (Dec. 2006); Chair. NKOSANA MOYO; Man. Dir GEORGE E. MORTIMER.

Diamond Trust Bank (Uganda) Ltd: Diamond Trust Bldg, Plot 17–19, Kampala Rd, POB 7155, Kampala; tel. (41) 4259331; fax (41) 4342286; e-mail info@dtbuganda.co.ug; internet www.dtbafrica.com; f. 1995; 40% owned by The Diamond Jubilee Investment Trust, 33.3% owned by Aga Khan Fund for Economic Development, 26.7% owned by Diamond Trust Bank Kenya Ltd; cap. 6,000m., res 3,400m., dep. 182,961m. (Dec. 2009); Chair. MAHMOOD MANJI; CEO VARGHESE THAMBI.

Ecobank Uganda Ltd: Plot 4, Parliament Ave, POB 7368, Kampala; tel. (41) 7700231; fax (31) 2266079; e-mail ecobankug@ecobank.com; internet www.ecobank.com; f. 2008; Chair. DAVID TWAHIRWA; Man. Dir OLADELE ADEBIYI ALABI.

Equity Bank Uganda Ltd: Plot 390, Muteesa 1 Rd, Katwe, POB 10184, Kampala; tel. (31) 2262437; fax (31) 2262436; e-mail info@equitybank.co.ug; internet www.equitybank.co.ug; Chair. PETER MUNGA; Exec. Dir APOLLO N. NJOROGE.

Fina Bank Uganda Ltd: Plot 7, Buganda Rd, POB 7323, Kampala; tel. (41) 4237305; fax (41) 4237305; e-mail banking@finabank.co.ug; internet www.finabank.com/ug/; f. 2008; Chair. DHANU HANSRAJ CHANDARIA; CEO CHARLES NALYAALI.

Global Trust Bank (U) Ltd: Plot 2A, Kampala Rd, POB 72747, Kampala; tel. (41) 7100700; fax (41) 4254007; e-mail globaltrust@bankglobaltrust.com; internet www.bankglobaltrust.com; f. 2008; Man. Dir MORENIKEJI OLUDOTUN ADEPOJU.

Mercantile Credit Bank Ltd: Plot 10, Old Port Bell Rd, POB 620, Kampala; tel. and fax (41) 4235967; e-mail mcb@afsat.com; cap. 1,000m. (Dec. 2003); Chair. PALLE MOELLER; Man. NELSON LUGOLOBI.

National Bank of Commerce (Uganda) Ltd: Cargen House, Plot 13A, Parliament Ave, POB 23232, Kampala; tel. (41) 2347699; fax (41) 2347701; e-mail nbc@swiftuganda.com; cap. 4,631m. (Dec.

2003); acquired by Crane Bank Ltd in Sep. 2012; Chair. AMOS NZEYI; Man. Dir G. BANGERA.

Orient Bank Ltd: Orient Plaza, Plot 6/6A, Kampala Rd, POB 3072, Kampala; tel. (41) 4236012; fax (41) 4236066; e-mail mail@orient-bank.com; internet www.orient-bank.com; f. 1993; cap. 5,000m., res 2,440m., dep. 205,920m. (Dec. 2009); Chair. MICHAEL COOK; CEO MAXWELL IBEANUSI; 6 brs.

Post Bank Uganda Ltd: Plot 11/13, Nkrumah Rd, POB 7189, Kampala; tel. (41) 4258551; fax (41) 4347107; e-mail postbank@imul .com; wholly state-owned; cap. 2,000m. (Dec. 2003); Chair. STEPHEN MWANJE.

Development Banks

Capital Finance Corpn Ltd: 4 Pilkington Rd, POB 21091, Kampala; tel. (41) 4345200; fax (41) 4258310; 70% owned by City Credit Bank Ltd; Chair. KEMAL LALANI; Man. Dir and CEO GHULAM HAIDER DAUDANI.

Centenary Rural Development Bank: 7 Entebbe Rd, POB 1892, Kampala; tel. (41) 4251276; fax (41) 4251273; e-mail info@centenarybank.co.ug; internet www.centenarybank.co.ug; cap. 4,020.5m., res 6,675.5m., dep. 448,308.5m. (Dec. 2009); Chair. Dr JOHN DDUMBA SSENTAMU; Man. Dir FABIAN KASI.

Development Finance Co of Uganda Ltd: Rwenzori House, 1 Lumumba Ave, POB 2767, Kampala; tel. (41) 4231215; fax (41) 4259435; e-mail dfcu@dfcugroup.com; internet www.dfcugroup.com; owned by Commonwealth Devt Corpn (60%), Uganda Devt Corpn (18.5%) and International Finance Corpn (21.5%); cap. 3,978m. (Dec. 2003); Chair. WILLIAM S. KALEMA; Man. Dir C. MCCORMACK.

East African Development Bank (EADB): East African Development Bank Bldg, 4 Nile Ave, POB 7128, Kampala; tel. (41) 4230021; fax (41) 4259763; e-mail admin@eadb.org; internet www .eadb.org; f. 1967; majority stake held by the Govts of Kenya, Tanzania and Uganda; provides financial and tech. assistance to promote industrial development within Uganda, Kenya, Rwanda and Tanzania; regional offices in Nairobi (Kenya), Kigali (Rwanda) and Dar es Salaam (Tanzania); cap. US $99.8m., res US $11.1m., dep. US $118.7m. (Dec. 2009); Dir-Gen. APOPO VIVIENNE.

Housing Finance Bank Ltd: Investment House, 25 Kampala Rd, POB 1539, Kampala; tel. (41) 4259651; fax (41) 4341429; internet www.housingfinance.co.ug; f. 1967; 45% owned by Govt, 50% owned by National Social Security Fund, 5% owned by National Housing and Construction Corpn; cap. 61,000.0m., res 6,475.4m., dep. 109,411.7m. (Dec. 2009); Chair. KEITH MUHAKANIZI; Man. Dir NICHOLAS OKWIR.

Foreign Banks

Bank of Baroda (Uganda) Ltd (India): 18 Kampala Rd, POB 7197, Kampala; tel. (41) 4233680; fax (41) 4230781; e-mail bobho@spacenet .co.ug; internet www.bankofbaroda.com; f. 1953; 80% owned by Bank of Baroda (India); cap. 4,000m., res 5,647m., dep. 126,995m. (Dec. 2004); Chair. and Man. Dir M. D. MALLYA; 6 brs.

Barclays Bank of Uganda Ltd (United Kingdom): Barclay House, Plot 4, Hannington Rd, POB 7101, Kampala; tel. (31) 4218300; fax (31) 4259467; e-mail barclays.uganda@barclays.com; internet www .barclays.com; f. 1969; wholly owned by Barclays Bank PLC (United Kingdom); cap. 4,000m., res 15,236m., dep. 328,553m. (Dec. 2005); Chair. GEORGE EGADU; Man. Dir CHARLES ONGWAE; 4 brs.

Citibank (Uganda) Ltd (USA): Plot 4, Centre Court, Ternan Ave, Nakasero, POB 7505, Kampala; tel. (41) 4305500; fax (41) 4340624; internet www.citibank.com/eastafrica/uganda.htm; 99.9% owned by Citicorp Overseas Investment Corpn, 0.1% owned by Foremost Investment; cap. 21,285m. (Dec. 2003); Chair. Prof. J. M. L. SSEBUWUUFU; Man. Dir SHIRISH BHIDE.

Stanbic Bank Uganda Ltd (United Kingdom): Crested Towers, Short Tower, 17 Hannington Rd, POB 7131, Kampala; tel. (31) 4224111; fax (41) 4231116; e-mail ugandainfo@stanbic.com; internet www.stanbicbank.co.ug; f. 1906 as National Bank of India Uganda; adopted present name 1993; 80% owned by Stanbic Africa Holdings Ltd (United Kingdom); merged with Uganda Commercial Bank Ltd 2002; cap. 5,119m., res 67,880m., dep. 1,539,873m. (Dec. 2009); Chair. Dr MARTIN ALIKER; Man. Dir KITILI MBATHI; 2 brs.

Standard Chartered Bank Uganda Ltd (United Kingdom): 5 Speke Rd, POB 7111, Kampala; tel. (41) 44258211; fax (41) 44231473; e-mail scb.uganda@ug.standardchartered.com; internet www .standardchartered.com/ug; f. 1912; wholly owned by Standard Chartered Bank PLC; cap. 4,000m., res 22,806m., dep. 604,380m. (Dec. 2006); Chair. JAMES MULWANA; Man. Dir LAMIN MANJANG; 7 brs.

Tropical Bank (Libya): Plot 27, Kampala Rd, POB 9485, Kampala; tel. (41) 4313100; fax (31) 2264494; e-mail admin@trobank.com; internet www.trobank.com; f. 1972; 99.7% owned by Libyan Arab Foreign Bank; cap. 30,000m., res 8,433m., dep. 125,314m. (Dec. 2009); acquired GERALD SENDAULA; Man. Dir PRINCE KASSIM NAKIBINGE.

United Bank for Africa (Uganda) Ltd: Spear House, Plot 22, Jinja Rd, POB 7396, Kampala; tel. (41) 7715122; fax (41) 7715117; f. 2008; CEO MARGARET MWANAKATWE; 5 brs.

STOCK EXCHANGE

Uganda Securities Exchange: Workers' House, 2nd Floor, Northern Wing, 1 Pilkington Rd, POB 23552, Kampala; tel. (41) 4343297; fax (41) 4343841; internet www.use.or.ug; f. 1997; Chair. CHARLES MBIRE; Chief Exec. JOSEPH S. KITAMIRIKE.

INSURANCE

In March 2011 there were 22 insurance companies licensed to operate in Uganda.

APA Insurance (Uganda) Ltd: Crown House, 1st Floor, Plot 4A, Kampala Rd, POB 7651, Kampala; tel. (41) 4250087; e-mail apa .uganda@apainsurance.org.

Chartis Uganda Insurance Co Ltd: Plot 60, Bombo Rd, POB 7077, Kampala; tel. (41) 4533781; fax (41) 4541572; e-mail chartisuganda@chartisinsurance.com; internet www.chartisinsurance.com/ug-about-us_918_210594.html; f. 1962; fmrly AIG Uganda Insurance Co Ltd; name changed as above in 2009; Man. Dir ALEX WANJOHI; 3 brs.

East Africa General Insurance Co Ltd: Plot 14, Kampala Rd, POB 1392, Kampala; tel. (31) 22262221; fax (41) 4343234; e-mail vkrishna@eagen.co.ug; internet www.eagen.co.ug; f. 1949; public shareholding co; fire, life, motor, marine and accident; CEO VYASA KRISHNA.

Excel Insurance Co Ltd: Crest House, Plot 2D, Nkurumah Rd, POB 7213, Kampala; tel. (41) 4348595; fax (41) 4342304; e-mail excelins@infocom.co.ug; internet www.excelinsurance.co.ug; Man. Dir JOHN SSENTAMU DDUMBA.

First Insurance Co Ltd: King Fahd Plaza, 2nd Floor, Plot 52, Kampala Rd, POB 5254, Kampala; tel. (41) 4342863; fax (41) 345923.

GoldStar Insurance Co Ltd: Plot 38, Kampala Rd, Crane Chambers, POB 7781, Kampala; tel. (41) 4250110; fax (41) 4254956; e-mail goldstar@goldstarinsurance.com; Man. Dir AZIM THARANI.

Lion Assurance Co Ltd: Tall Tower, 12th Floor, Crested Towers Bldg, POB 7658, Kampala; tel. (41) 4341450; fax (41) 4257027; e-mail insure@lion.co.ug; fmrly Pan World Insurance Co Ltd; Chair. OWEK. GODFREY K. KAVUMA; Gen. Man. GEORGE ALANDE.

National Insurance Corporation: Plot 3, Pilkington Rd, POB 7134, Kampala; tel. (41) 4258001; fax (41) 4259925; e-mail nic@nic.co .ug; internet www.nic.co.ug; f. 1964; 60% owned by IGI PLC, Nigeria; general and life; Chair. REMI OLOWUDE; Man. Dir SAM JEFF NJOROGE.

NICO Insurance (Uganda) Ltd: 3rd Floor, Greenland Towers, Kampala Rd, opposite Bank of Uganda, POB 24256, Kampala; tel. (31) 2264720; fax (31) 2264723; internet www.nicomw.com; subsidiary of NICO Holdings Ltd (based in Malawi); Man. Dir RONALD ZAKE.

Phoenix of Uganda Assurance Co Ltd: Workers House, Northern Wing, 8th Floor, Pilkington Rd, POB 70149, Kampala; tel. (41) 349664; fax (41) 349662; e-mail info@phoenixuganda.com; internet phoenixassurancegroup.com; f. 2003; Chair. MAHEBOOB ALIBHAI; Gen. Man. V. PARTHASARATHI.

Rio Insurance Co Ltd: Plot 20, Kampala Rd, POB 5710, Kampala; tel. (41) 4341264; fax (41) 4235292.

Statewide Insurance Co Ltd (SWICO): Sure House, Plot 1, Bombo Rd, POB 9393, Kampala; tel. (41) 4345996; fax (41) 4343403; e-mail swico@infocom.co.ug; internet www.swico.co.ug; f. 1982; Man. Dir JOSEPH KIWANUKA.

TransaAfrica Assurance Co Ltd: Impala House, Plot 13/15, Kimathi Ave, POB 7601, Kampala; tel. (41) 4251411; fax (41) 4254511; e-mail taacl@spacenet.co.ug.

UAP Insurance Co Ltd: Plot 1, Kimathi Ave, POB 7185, Kampala; tel. (41) 4234190; fax (41) 4256388; e-mail uac@starcom.co.ug; internet www.uap.co.ug; Chair. RONALD KALYANGO.

Uganda Co-operative Insurance Ltd: Plot 10, Bombo Rd, POB 6176, Kampala; tel. (41) 4241836; fax (41) 4258231; f. 1982; general; Chair. EPHRAIM KAKURU; Gen. Man. (vacant).

Regulatory Authority

Uganda Insurance Commission: NIC Building Annexe, 3rd Floor, Plot 3, Pilkington Rd, POB 22855; tel. (41) 4346712; fax (41) 4349260; e-mail uic@uginscom.go.ug; Chair. ELIAS B. KASOZI.

Insurance Association

Uganda Insurers' Association: Plot 24A, Acacia Ave, Kololo, POB 8912, Kampala; tel. (41) 4230469; fax (41) 4500944; internet www.uia .co.ug; f. 1965; Chair. SOLOMON RUBONDO.

Trade and Industry

GOVERNMENT AGENCIES

Capital Markets Authority: 8th Floor, Jubilee Insurance Centre, 14 Parliament Ave, POB 24565, Kampala; tel. (41) 4342788; fax (41) 4342803; e-mail info@cmauganda.co.ug; internet www.cmauganda .co.ug; f. 1996 to develop, promote and regulate capital markets sector; Chair. GRACE JETHRO KAVUMA; CEO JAPHETH KATTO.

Enterprise Uganda: 38 Lumumba Ave, Nakasero, POB 24581, Kampala; tel. (41) 4251810; fax (41) 4250968; e-mail info@enterprise .co.ug; internet www.enterprise.co.ug; Exec. Dir CHARLES OCICI.

Export and Import Licensing Division: POB 7000, Kampala; tel. (41) 4258795; f. 1987; advises importers and exporters and issues import and export licences; Prin. Commercial Officer JOHN MUHWEZI.

Privatization Unit: Kampala; f. 2001; oversees privatization programme.

Uganda Advisory Board of Trade: POB 6877, Kampala; tel. (41) 4233311; f. 1974; issues trade licences and services for exporters.

Uganda Export Promotion Board: POB 5045, Kampala; tel. (41) 4230233; fax (41) 4259779; e-mail uepc@starcom.co.ug; internet www.ugandaexportsonline.com; f. 1983; provides market intelligence, organizes training, trade exhibitions, etc.; Exec. Dir FLORENCE KATE.

Uganda Investment Authority (UIA): Investment Centre, TWED Plaza, Plot 22, Lumumba Ave, POB 7418, Kampala; tel. (41) 4301000; fax (41) 4342903; e-mail info@ugandainvest.com; internet www.ugandainvest.go.ug; f. 1991; promotes foreign and local investment, assists investors, provides business information, issues investment licences; Exec. Dir FRANK SEBOWA; Dep. Exec. Dir TOM BURINGURIZA (acting).

DEVELOPMENT ORGANIZATIONS

Dairy Development Authority (DDA): Plot 1, Kafu Rd, POB 256, Kampala; tel. (41) 343883; fax (41) 250270; internet www.dda.or.ug; f. 2000.

National Agricultural Research Organisation (NARO): Plot 3, Lugard Ave, POB 295, Entebbe; tel. (41) 320512; fax (41) 321070; e-mail dgnaro@infocom.co.ug; internet www.naro.go.ug; f. 2005.

National Housing and Construction Corpn: Crested Towers, POB 659, Kampala; tel. (41) 4330002; fax (41) 4258708; e-mail sales@ nhcc.co.ug; internet www.nhcc.co.ug; f. 1964; govt agent for building works; also develops residential housing; Chair. Dr COLIN SENTONGO; Gen. Man. M. S. KASEKENDE.

Uganda Industrial Development Corpn Ltd: 9–11 Parliament Ave, POB 7042, Kampala; tel. (41) 4234381; fax (41) 4241588; f. 1952; Chair. SAM RUTEGA.

CHAMBER OF COMMERCE

Uganda National Chamber of Commerce and Industry: Plot 1A, Kira Rd, POB 3809, Kampala; tel. (41) 4503024; fax (41) 4230310; e-mail info@chamberuganda.com; internet www.chamberuganda .com; Chair. OLIVE Z. KIGONGO.

INDUSTRIAL AND TRADE ASSOCIATIONS

CMB Ltd (Coffee Marketing Board): POB 7154, Kampala; tel. (41) 4254051; fax (41) 4230790; state-owned; privatization pending; purchases and exports coffee; Chair. Dr DDUMBA SSENTAMU; Man. Dir SAM KIGGUNDU.

Cotton Development Organization: POB 7018, Kampala; tel. (41) 4232968; fax (41) 4232975; Man. Dir JOLLY SABUNE.

Horticultural Exporters' Association of Uganda (HORTEXA): POB 29392, Kampala; tel. (77) 2364389; e-mail hortexa@yahoo.com; f. 1990; Chair. DAVID LULE.

Produce Marketing Board: Plot 15, Clement Hill Rd, POB 3705, Kampala; tel. (41) 232968; fax (41) 232975; internet cdouga.org; Gen. Man. ESTHER KAMPAMPARA.

Uganda Coffee Development Authority (UCDA): Coffee House, Plot 35, Jinja Rd, POB 7267, Kampala; tel. (41) 4256940; fax (41) 4256994; e-mail ucdajc@ugandacoffee.org; internet www .ugandacoffee.org; f. 1991; enforces quality control and promotes coffee exports, maintains statistical data, advises Govt on local and world prices and trains processors and quality controllers; Chair. FABIANO R. TIBEITA; Man. Dir HENRY A. NGABIRANO.

Uganda Flowers Exporters' Association (UFEA): Plot 92, Ssebugwawo Dr., Old Airport, Entebbe, POB 29558, Kampala; tel. (31) 2263320; fax (31) 2263321; e-mail ufea@ufea.co.ug; internet ufea.co .ug; f. 1995; Chair. JACQUE SCHRIER.

Uganda Manufacturers' Association (UMA): Lugogo Show Grounds, POB 6966, Kampala; tel. (41) 4221034; fax (41) 4220285; e-mail administration@uma.or.ug; internet uma.or.ug; f. 1988; promotes mfrs' interests; Chair. KADDU KIBERU.

Uganda National Farmers' Federation: Plot 27, Nakasero Rd, POB 6213, Kampala; tel. (41) 4340249; fax (41) 4230748; internet www.unffe.org; f. 1992 as Uganda National Farmers' Association; Pres. CHARLES OGANG; Sec.-Gen. HENRY MUTEBI KITYO.

Uganda Tea Authority: POB 4161, Kampala; tel. (41) 4231003; state-owned; controls and co-ordinates activities of the tea industry; Gen. Man. MIRIA MARGARITA MUGABI.

Uganda Tea Development Ltd (UTDAL): 821 Rubaga Rd, off Kabaka Anjagala Roundabout, POB 6204, Kampala; tel. (41) 4343633; fax (41) 4343634; e-mail marketing@ugatea.com; internet ugatea.com; f. 2001; Gen. Man. BYARUGABA IGNATIUS.

EMPLOYERS' ORGANIZATION

Federation of Uganda Employers (FUE): Plot 60, Veron House, Ntinda, POB 3820, Kampala; tel. (41) 4220201; fax (41) 4286290; e-mail info@fuemployers.org; internet www.fuemployers.org; f. 1958; Chair. MARTIN KASEKENDE; Exec. Dir ROSEMARY N. SSENABULYA.

UTILITIES

Electricity

Electricity Regulatory Authority (ERA): ERA House, Plot 15, Shimon Rd, Nakasero, POB 10332, Kampala; tel. (41) 4341852; fax (41) 4341624; e-mail era@africaonline.co.ug; internet www.era.or .ug; f. 1999; Chair. RICHARD SANTO APIRE; CEO Eng. Dr F. B. SEBBOWA.

Rural Electrification Agency: 1 Pilkington Rd, Worker's House, 10th Floor, POB 7317, Kampala,; tel. (31) 2264095; fax (41) 4346013; e-mail rea@rea.or.ug; internet www.rea.or.ug; Exec. Dir GODFREY TURYAHIKAYO.

Uganda Electricity Distribution Co Ltd (UEDCL): Nakasero Towers, 6th Floor, 37 Nakasero Rd, Kampala; tel. (31) 2330300; fax (41) 4255600; e-mail contact@uedcl.co.ug; internet www.uedcl.co.ug; f. 2001 as one of the successor bodies of the Uganda Electricity Board; privatized and operations handed over to UMEME Uganda Ltd in 2005 under a 20-year concession agreement; functions as a statutory body overseeing the operations of UMEME Uganda Ltd; Chair. GAD GASAATURA; Man. Dir JOSEPH KATERA.

UMEME Uganda Ltd: Rwenzori House, Plot 1, 2nd Floor, Lumumba Ave, POB 23841, Kampala; tel. (41) 2360600; e-mail info@umeme.co.ug; internet www.umeme.co.ug; f. 2005; develops, operates and maintains the electricity distribution network on behalf of Uganda Electricity Distribution Co Ltd; Chair. PATRICK BITATURE; Man. Dir CHARLES CHAPMAN.

Uganda Electricity Generation Co Ltd: Plot 2–8, Faraday Rd, Ambercourt, POB 1101, Jinja; tel. (43) 4120891; fax (43) 4123064; internet www.uegcl.com; f. 2001 as one of the successor bodies of the Uganda Electricity Board; Chair. SANDY S. TICKODRI-TOGBOA; Man. Dir JOHN MUGYENZI.

Uganda Electricity Transmission Co Ltd: Plot 10, Hannington Rd, POB 7625, Kampala; tel. (41) 7802000; fax (41) 3441789; e-mail transco@uetcl.com; internet www.uetcl.com; f. 2001; as one of the successor bodies of the Uganda Electricity Board; Man. Dir ERIASI KIYEMBA.

Water

National Water & Sewerage Corpn: Plot 39, Jinja Rd, POB 7053, Kampala; tel. (41) 4315100; fax (41) 4234802; e-mail info@nwsc.co .ug; internet www.nwsc.co.ug; f. 1972; serves 22 towns; privatization pending; Chair. WILLIAM OKECHO; Man. Dir ALEX GISAGARA (acting).

CO-OPERATIVES

In 2000 there were 6,313 co-operative societies, grouped in 34 unions. There is at least one co-operative union in each administrative district.

Uganda Co-operative Alliance: Plot 47/49, Nkurumah Rd, Kampala; tel. (41) 4258898; fax (41) 4258556; e-mail ucainfocen@uca.co .ug; internet www.uca.co.ug; co-ordinating body for co-operative unions.

TRADE UNIONS

National Organization of Trade Unions (NOTU): Plot 64, Ntinda Rd, POB 2150, Kampala; tel. (41) 4256295; fax (41) 4259833; e-mail notu@ifocom.co.ug; internet www.notu.or.ug; f. 1973; Chair. OWERE USHER WILSON; Sec.-Gen. PETER CHRISTOPHER WERIKHE; 89,500 mems (2007).

    Amalgamated Transport and General Workers' Union: POB 30407, Kampala; tel. (41) 232508; fax (41) 341541; e-mail atgwu@ utlonline.co.ug; internet www.atgwu.org.ug; f. 1938; Gen. Sec. OJIAMBO-OCHIENG ROMANO.

Transport

RAILWAYS

In 2002 there was 260 km of track in operation. A programme to rehabilitate the railway network is under way. A 725-km railway project to link Gulu in northern Uganda with Juba, South Sudan, has been under consideration since 2004. There are also plans to upgrade and reopen the 333-km Kampala–Kasese railway line.

Uganda Railways Corporation (URC): Plot 53, 1st Floor, Nasser Rd, POB 7150, Kampala; tel. (41) 4254961; fax (41) 4344405; f. 1977 following the dissolution of East African Railways; management of operations assumed by Rift Valley Railways consortium in Nov. 2006; CEO I. IYAMULEMYE.

ROADS

In 2006 Uganda's road network consisted of approximately 10,800 km of national or trunk roads (of which some 2,200 km were bituminized, the rest being gravel), 27,500 km of district or feeder roads, 4,300 km of urban roads (comprising roads in Kampala City, the 13 municipal councils and the 50 town councils in the country) and 30,000 km of community roads. There are also private roads, some of which are open to the general travelling public. Road transport remains the dominant mode of transport in terms of scale of infrastructure and the volume of freight and passenger movement. The National (Trunk) Road Network carries 80% of Uganda's passenger and freight traffic and includes international routes linking Uganda to neighbouring countries and to the sea (via Kenya and Tanzania), and internal roads linking areas of high population and large administrative and commercial centres. It provides the only form of access to most rural communities. The Government is implementing a programme of continuous upgrading of key gravel roads to bitumen standard.

Uganda National Roads Authority (UNRA): Plot 5, Lourdel Road, Nakasero, POB 28487, Kampala; tel. (31) 2233100; fax (41) 4232807; e-mail roadinfo@unra.go.ug; internet www.unra.go.ug; f. 2006; Exec. Dir Eng. PETER SSEBANAKITTA.

Uganda Road Fund: 5th Floor, Soliz House, Plot 23, Lumumba Ave, POB 7501, Kampala; tel. (41) 4257072; e-mail info@roadfund .ug; internet www.roadfund.ug; f. 2008; Chair. Eng. Dr FRANCIS BAZIRAAKE; Exec. Dir Eng. Dr MICHAEL M. ODONGO.

INLAND WATERWAYS

A rail wagon ferry service connecting Jinja with the Tanzanian port of Tanga, via Mwanza, was inaugurated in 1983, thus reducing Uganda's dependence on the Kenyan port of Mombasa. In 1986 the Uganda and Kenya Railways Corporations began the joint operation of Lake Victoria Marine Services, to ferry goods between the two countries via Lake Victoria.

CIVIL AVIATION

The international airport is at Entebbe, on Lake Victoria, some 40 km from Kampala. There are also several small airfields.

Civil Aviation Authority (CAA): POB 5536, Kampala; Airport Rd, Entebbe International Airport; tel. (41) 4352000; fax (41) 4321401; e-mail aviation@caa.co.ug; internet www.caa.co.ug; Man. Dir WENCESLAUS RAMA MAKUZA.

Principal Airlines

Air Uganda (AU): Plot 11/13, Lower Kololo Terrace, POB 36591, Kampala; tel. (41) 4258262; fax (41) 4500932; e-mail info@air-uganda .com; internet www.air-uganda.com; f. 2007; services to Africa; CEO HUGH FRASER.

Eagle Air Ltd: Adam House, Plot 11, Portal Ave, POB 7392, Kampala; tel. (41) 4344292; fax (41) 4344501; e-mail admin@ eagleair-ug.com; internet www.eagleair-ug.com; f. 1994; domestic services, charter flights to neighbouring countries; Man. Dir Capt. ANTHONY RUBOMBORA.

Royal Daisy Airlines: Plot 13, Buganda Rd, POB 35177, Kampala; tel. (41) 4256213; fax (41) 4256137; e-mail admin@royaldaisy.com; internet www.royaldaisy.com; f. 2005; Man. Dir and CEO DAISY ROY.

Tourism

Uganda's principal attractions for tourists are the forests, lakes, mountains and wildlife (including its mountain gorillas) and an equable climate. A programme to revive the tourist industry by building or improving hotels and creating new national parks began in the late 1980s. There were 1.15m. tourist arrivals in 2011 (compared with 12,786 in 1983). Revenue from the sector in that year was estimated at US $805m.

Uganda Tourist Board: Impala House, 13/15 Kimatti Ave, POB 7211, Kampala; tel. (41) 4342196; fax (41) 4342188; e-mail utb@ visituganda.com; internet www.visituganda.com; Chair. PETER KAMYA; Gen. Man. IGNATIUS NAKISHERO.

Defence

As assessed at November 2012, the Uganda People's Defence Forces (UPDF, formerly the National Resistance Army) was estimated to number 45,000 men, including paramilitary forces (a border defence unit of about 600 men, a police air wing of about 800 men, and around 400 marines and local defence units totalling about 3,000 men). In 2012 a total of 6,708 Ugandan troops were stationed abroad, of whom six were observers.

Defence Expenditure: Budgeted at US 622,000m. in 2013.

Chief of Defence Forces: Gen. ARONDA NYAKARIMA.

Commander of the Air Force: Maj.-Gen. JIM OWOYESIGIRE.

Commander of the Land Forces: Lt-Gen. KATUMBA WAMALA.

Education

Most schools are supported by the Government, although a small proportion are sponsored by missions. Traditionally, all schools have charged fees. In 1997, however, the Government introduced an initiative known as Universal Primary Education (UPE), whereby free primary education was phased in for up to four children per family. In January 2007 the Government initiated free secondary school education in 700 public schools as part of a phased programme to introduce universal free education. Primary education, which is in principle free and compulsory, begins at six years of age and lasts for seven years. Secondary education, beginning at the age of 13, lasts for a further six years, comprising a first cycle of four years and a second of two years. In 2009/10, according to UNESCO, enrolment at primary level included 91% (males 90%; females 92%) of children in the relevant age-group, while in that year enrolment at secondary schools was equivalent to 28% (males 30%; females 26%) of children in the relevant age-group. In 2004/05 just 3.5% (males 4.3%; females 2.7%) of those in the relevant age-group were enrolled in tertiary education. In addition to Makerere University in Kampala, there is a university of science and technology at Mbarara, and a small Islamic university is located at Mbale. In 2003/04 58,823 students were enrolled in Ugandan universities. In 2010 spending on education represented 15% of total budgetary expenditure.

UKRAINE

Introductory Survey

LOCATION, CLIMATE, LANGUAGE, RELIGION, FLAG, CAPITAL

Ukraine is situated in east-central Europe. It is bordered by Poland, Slovakia, Hungary, Romania and Moldova to the west, by Belarus to the north, and by Russia to the north-east and east. To the south lie the Black Sea and the Sea of Azov. The climate is temperate, especially in the south. The north and north-west share many of the continental climatic features of Poland or Belarus. Average temperatures in Kyiv (Kiev) range from −6.1°C (21°F) in January to 20.4°C (69°F) in July, and average annual rainfall is 615 mm (24 ins). The official state language is Ukrainian, although Russian is widely spoken, except in the west. Most of the population are adherents of Orthodox Christianity, and there are many adherents of the Catholic Church (mostly followers of Eastern rites), predominantly in western regions. There are also a number of Protestant churches and small communities of Jews and Muslims, the latter principally comprising Crimean Tatars. The national flag (proportions 2 by 3) has two equal horizontal stripes, of pale blue over yellow. The capital is Kyiv.

CONTEMPORARY POLITICAL HISTORY

Historical Context

The original East Slavic state, Kyivan (Kievan) Rus, founded in the late 10th century, was based in what is now Ukraine, and is claimed as the precursor of Russia, Belarus and Ukraine. Following the fall of the Rus principalities, in the 13th and 14th centuries, during the Mongol invasions, the Ukrainians (sometimes known as Little Russians or Ruthenians), mainly under Polish and Lithuanian rulers, developed distinctively from the other Eastern Slavs. Ukrainians first entered the Russian Empire in 1654, when a Cossack state east of the Dnipro (Dniepr) River, led by Hetman Bohdan Khmelnytsky, sought Russian protection from Polish invasion. In 1667 Ukraine was divided: the regions east of the Dnipro became part of Russia, while Western Ukraine was annexed by Poland. Russia gained more Ukrainian lands as a result of subsequent partitions of Poland (1793 and 1795) and, in the south, from the Ottoman Empire; the western regions were acquired by Austria.

When the Russian Empire collapsed, in 1917, Ukrainian nationalists set up a central Rada (council or soviet) in Kyiv and demanded autonomy from the Provisional Government in Petrograd (St Petersburg). After the Bolshevik coup, in November, the Rada proclaimed a Ukrainian People's Republic. In December the Bolsheviks established a rival Government in Kharkiv, and by February 1918 much of Ukraine was occupied by Soviet forces. In March, however, the Bolsheviks were forced to cede Ukraine to Germany, under the terms of the Treaty of Brest-Litovsk. Ukraine was the battleground for much of the fighting in the Civil War over the next two years, but in December 1920 a Ukrainian Soviet Socialist Republic (SSR) was established.

The Treaty of Rīga, which formally ended the Soviet–Polish War in 1921, assigned territories in western Ukraine to Poland, Czechoslovakia and Romania. Eastern and central lands formed the Ukrainian SSR, one of the founding members of the Union of Soviet Socialist Republics (USSR), in December 1922. The collectivization of agriculture from 1929 had severe consequences for the republic; at least 5m. Ukrainians were estimated to have died in a famine in 1933, which resulted from collectivization. By the late 1930s almost the entire Ukrainian cultural and political élite had been imprisoned, killed or exiled. Ukraine also suffered greatly during the Second World War, during which an estimated 6m. people died in the republic. Soviet victory in the war, and the annexing of territories from Czechoslovakia, Poland and Romania led to the uniting of western and eastern Ukraine. In 1954 Crimea (hitherto part of Russia), the Tatar inhabitants of which had been deported *en masse* to Soviet Central Asia in 1944, was transferred to Ukrainian control. During the 1960s there was an increase in covert opposition to the regime. In 1973 Petro Shelest, the First Secretary (leader) of the Communist Party of Ukraine (CPU), was dismissed and replaced by Vladimir Shcherbitsky, a loyal ally of the Soviet leader, Leonid Brezhnev, whose conservatism was such that the accession of the reformist Mikhail Gorbachev to the Soviet leadership, in 1985, had little initial effect in Ukraine.

On 26 April 1986 a serious explosion occurred at the Chornobyl (Chernobyl) nuclear power station, in northern Ukraine. Some 135,000 people were evacuated from a 50-km (30-mile) exclusion zone around Chornobyl (much of which was within Belarus). Thirty-one people were killed in the initial explosion, but in 1996 it was reported that an estimated 2,500 deaths in Ukraine may have been caused by the accident, while a further 3.2m. people had been affected by the disaster, as a result of increased incidence of cancers and other related illnesses. Official secrecy surrounding the Chornobyl accident led to greater public support for Ukrainian opposition movements, such as the liberal nationalist Ukrainian People's Movement for Restructuring (Rukh), founded in 1988 by a group of prominent writers and intellectuals. Meanwhile, economic problems contributed to a growing militancy among mining communities in the Donbass region (around Donetsk, in eastern Ukraine) in early 1989, and the revival of hitherto 'underground' religious groups resulted in the re-legalization, in December 1989, of the Ukrainian Byzantine rite ('Greek') Catholic Church, which had been suppressed in 1946.

Shcherbitsky was dismissed in September 1989; he was replaced by Volodymyr Ivashko. In local and republican elections, held on 4 March 1990, candidates supported by the Democratic Bloc, led by Rukh, won 108 of the 450 seats in the Verkhovna Rada (Supreme Council—republican legislature). Independents supported by the Bloc won about 60 seats, although an estimated 280 independent candidates supported the CPU leadership. In June Ivashko was elected Chairman of the Verkhovna Rada (the highest state post in Ukraine); he resigned later in the month as First Secretary of the CPU. On 16 July the Verkhovna Rada adopted a declaration of sovereignty. Later in the month Ivashko resigned as Chairman of the Verkhovna Rada, following his appointment as Deputy General Secretary of the Communist Party of the Soviet Union; he was replaced by Leonid Kravchuk, hitherto Second Secretary of the CPU. In October Vitold Fokin, a moderate reformist, succeeded Vitaliy Masol as Chairman of the Council of Ministers (Prime Minister).

The Government participated in negotiations on a new union treaty and signed the protocol to a draft treaty in March 1991. The Government also agreed to conduct the all-Union referendum on the future of the USSR (see the Russian Federation), but appended a further question, asking if Ukraine's declaration of sovereignty should form the basis for participation in a renewed federation. Of the electorate, 84% participated in the referendum, 70% of whom approved Gorbachev's proposal to preserve the USSR as a 'renewed federation'. However, Ukraine's own question received greater support (80%), and an additional question in certain western regions, which asked voters if they supported a fully independent Ukraine, secured the support of 90% of those voting.

Domestic Political Affairs

Following the attempted coup by conservative communists in Moscow, the Russian and Soviet capital, on 19 August 1991, the Verkhovna Rada, on 24 August, adopted a declaration of independence, pending confirmation by a referendum on 1 December, when a direct presidential election was also scheduled. The CPU was banned in late August. Kravchuk was elected President of the Republic on 1 December, with 62% of the votes cast. In the referendum, some 90% of votes were cast in favour of independence (84% of the electorate participated), which thereby took effect. In early December an independent Ukrainian armed forces was established. In January 1992 a new interim currency coupon, which retained the Ukrainian name of the Soviet currency, the karbovanets, was introduced.

The Government was subject to intense criticism as inflation increased sharply. It resigned in September 1992, having been conclusively defeated in a vote of no confidence. In October Leonid Kuchma, hitherto director-general of a missile factory in Dnipropetrovsk, was appointed Prime Minister, and a new Government was formed. Kuchma proposed a programme of economic reform, which was strongly opposed by left-wing groups, including the Socialist Party of Ukraine (SPU), which had been formed from elements of the CPU. As Ukraine began to experience 'hyperinflation', more than 2m. miners and factory workers, mainly in the Donbass region, joined a strike, in June 1993, demanding a referendum of confidence in the President and in the Verkhovna Rada. In September Kuchma tendered his resignation, which was accepted by the legislature; Yufym Zvyahylsky was appointed as Prime Minister, in an acting capacity, although after several days President Kravchuk assumed direct control of the Government.

Elections to the new, 450-member Verkhovna Rada were held on 27 March 1994, with two subsequent rounds of voting staged in constituencies where candidates had failed to secure at least 50% of the votes cast. The CPU was permitted to contest the elections and won 86 seats, more than any other group, and, in alliance with the SPU and the Peasants' Party of Ukraine (PPU), formed the largest bloc in the Verkhovna Rada; 170 nominally independent candidates were elected. A notable political division between eastern (where left-wing parties obtained greater support) and western (where moderate nationalist parties won the greatest share of the votes) regions was evident in the election results. Further rounds of voting, held in late 1994 to fill the 112 vacant seats, failed to elect candidates in more than 50 seats. In May Oleksandr Moroz, the leader of the SPU, was elected Chairman of the Verkhovna Rada, which in June elected Masol as Prime Minister.

A presidential election held on 26 June 1994 was inconclusive, as no candidate secured the minimum 50% of the votes necessary for election. Kravchuk received the greatest share of votes cast, with 37.7%, followed by Kuchma, with 31.3%. In a second round of voting, held on 10 July, Kuchma was elected President, securing 52.1% of the votes. A continuing polarity in voting patterns was recorded between the east, where voters largely supported Kuchma, and the west, where Kravchuk secured a majority of votes cast. In March 1995 Masol resigned as Prime Minister and was replaced, in an acting capacity, by Yevhen Marchuk. In June the President and the Verkhovna Rada granted the President additional powers, including the right to issue decrees with the force of legislation, until the adoption of a new constitution.

In May 1996 Kuchma dismissed Marchuk as premier, appointing Pavlo Lazarenko in his place. The new Constitution, providing extensive powers of appointment to the President, was adopted on 28 June. In July the Cabinet of Ministers resigned; Lazarenko retained the premiership in the new Government. The Government commenced a structural reorganization of the coal-mining sector, and in mid-July an agreement was reached with the trade unions to end an ongoing strike. The attempted assassination of Lazarenko, shortly after the signing of the agreement, was linked by some observers to his role in resolving the dispute. Lazarenko resigned in July 1997. In mid-July the legislature approved Valeriy Pustovoytenko as Prime Minister. In September the legislature approved a new electoral law, which provided for 225 seats in the 450-member Verkhovna Rada to be allocated by proportional representation on the basis of party lists, subject to a minimum threshold of 4% of the total votes cast, and for the remaining 225 to be elected from single-seat constituencies. Meanwhile, it was announced that Lazarenko was to be prosecuted on charges of embezzlement.

Some 30 parties and blocs contested the legislative elections held on 29 March 1998, in which 70.8% of the electorate participated. The CPU obtained 123 seats, becoming the largest party in the legislature. Eight parties secured representation on the basis of party lists, and 136 independent deputies were elected. Oleksandr Tkachenko, the leader of the PPU, was elected as legislative Chairman in July. Lazarenko was arrested in December as he attempted to enter Switzerland, and charged with money-laundering (he was later released on bail). In February 1999 the Verkhovna Rada endorsed a resolution allowing for Lazarenko to be charged, and shortly afterwards he was detained in the USA. (In June 2004 Lazarenko was convicted of money-laundering, fraud and extortion by a federal court in Los Angeles, California, USA, and in August 2006 a US court sentenced Lazarenko to nine years' imprisonment.)

Kuchma is re-elected

In the first round of voting in the presidential election, held on 31 October 1999, Kuchma was placed first, with 36.5% of the votes cast, followed by Petro Symonenko of the CPU, who

obtained 22.2% of the votes. In early November Kuchma undertook a number of measures that were regarded as being intended to ensure his re-election, including the dismissal of governors of three oblasts (regions) in which he not been the first-placed candidate. In the second ballot, on 14 November, Kuchma defeated Symonenko, receiving some 57.7% of the votes cast; he was inaugurated on 30 November. In December the Verkhovna Rada endorsed the nomination of Viktor Yushchenko (Governor of the National Bank of Ukraine—NBU—since 1993) as premier. In January 2000 left-wing factions in the legislature prevented a vote on Tkachenko's dismissal as legislative Chairman, compelling the new centrist parliamentary majority led by Kravchuk to hold a session in a separate building, where it voted unanimously to remove Tkachenko and his deputy from the chairmanship of the legislature. In February the majority faction elected Ivan Plyushch, an ally of Pustovoytenko, as legislative Chairman. After several days, deputies of the majority grouping gained entry to the parliamentary building, and normal activity resumed.

Meanwhile, a presidential decree, issued in January 2000, scheduled a referendum on proposed constitutional amendments for 16 April. Four questions—on the dissolution of the Verkhovna Rada should deputies fail to approve the state budget within three months of its submission; the reduction of the number of deputies from 450 to 300; the establishment of a bicameral legislature; and the placing of limitations on the immunity enjoyed by deputies—were approved by a majority of the 81% of the electorate that participated in the referendum. However, as no implementation of these decisions ensued, it appeared that the referendum had served primarily to increase the President's authority over the legislature.

In July 2000 the Deputy Prime Minister, responsible for Energy Issues, Yuliya Tymoshenko, a prominent instigator of reforms in the energy sector and the leader of the Fatherland party, was charged with corruption, as a result of investigations into her former ally, Lazarenko, in the USA. In early November police discovered near Kyiv a decapitated corpse, believed to be that of an investigative opposition journalist, Heorhiy Gongadze, missing since September. In late November Moroz released audio recordings of a discussion, allegedly between Kuchma, the Head of the Presidential Administration, Volodymyr Lytvyn, and the Minister of Internal Affairs, Yuriy Kravchenko, on possible means of killing Gongadze. Controversy surrounded the authenticity of the recordings, which a former presidential security adviser had made over a period of several months, prior to fleeing Ukraine.

In January 2001 Kuchma dismissed Tymoshenko, as an investigation into her alleged involvement in tax evasion and the smuggling of Russian gas proceeded. After further audio recordings were made public, in February Kuchma admitted that the recordings were of his voice, but stated that they had been edited in an attempt to incriminate him. Tymoshenko, heading a loose coalition of opposition movements, the National Salvation Forum (NSF), became the most prominent leader of a series of demonstrations staged in Kyiv to demand Kuchma's resignation. In February Kuchma dismissed the head of the Security Service of Ukraine (SBU), Gen. Leonid Derkach, and the head of the presidential bodyguard. In mid-February Tymoshenko was arrested on charges of tax evasion. In March Kuchma dismissed Kravchenko as Minister of Internal Affairs, replacing him with Yuriy Smirnov. At the end of that month Tymoshenko was released from prison, although the charges against her remained under investigation. In May Gongadze's death was officially attributed to a criminal attack, and it was announced that the investigation into his death was to be closed.

In April 2001 the Verkhovna Rada approved a motion of no confidence in the Prime Minister and his Cabinet of Ministers, despite the achievement during Yushchenko's premiership of the first economic growth since independence. In May Anatoliy Kinakh, hitherto First Deputy Prime Minister, responsible for Economic Policy, was appointed Prime Minister. In September Tymoshenko rejected the suggestion that the NSF unite with the Our Ukraine bloc of centrist and nationalist parties headed by Yushchenko, and her movement subsequently became known as the Yuliya Tymoshenko Bloc (BYuT). Meanwhile, in advance of legislative elections, supporters of Kuchma formed the For a United Ukraine (FUU) bloc, headed by Lytvyn.

In February 2002 Ukrainian prosecutors charged Lazarenko, *in absentia*, with having ordered the murders of two parliamentary deputies in 1996 and 1998; in March 2002 the Government's director of arms exports, Valeriy Malev, was killed in an automobile collision. It subsequently emerged that several days before Malev's death Kuchma had been informed of the discovery of further audio recordings, in which Kuchma and Malev were allegedly heard to discuss the sale of air-defence equipment to Iraq, in violation of UN sanctions.

The 2002 legislative elections

In the legislative elections, held on 31 March 2002, Our Ukraine, then comprising 10 parties, obtained both the largest share of the votes (23.6%) and the largest number of seats to be won by any party (112); FUU received the second largest number of seats (101), but only 11.8% of the votes cast. The CPU obtained 20.0% of the votes cast, but received only 66 seats. The Social-Democratic Party of Ukraine—United (SDPU—U) received 24 seats and 6.3% of the votes cast, the SPU 23 seats and 6.9% of the votes, and the BYuT 22 seats and 7.3% of the votes. Ninety-three independent candidates were elected. A report by observers from the Organization for Security and Co-operation in Europe (OSCE, see p. 397) indicated 'important flaws' in the organization of the elections. Lyvtyn was subsequently elected Chairman of the Verkhovna Rada.

In August 2002 Kuchma announced that a Constitutional Commission was to be formed to investigate the possibility of introducing constitutional reforms. In October a senior judge in Kyiv opened a criminal investigation into Kuchma, who was charged with violating 11 articles of the criminal code. However, in November an ally of Kuchma was elected as Chairman of the Supreme Court, and in late December the Court ruled that the investigation into Kuchma had been opened illegally. Meanwhile, on 16 November, following the dismissal of Kinakh, Kuchma appointed Viktor Yanukovych of the Party of the Regions (PR—one of the parties affiliated to FUU), latterly Governor of Donetsk Oblast, as Prime Minister. A new Government assumed office later in the month. In December a stable pro-presidential majority was established in the Verkhovna Rada.

In February 2003 Yushchenko issued a public statement urging the authorities to end what he described as 'political terror', including physical assaults against a number of political activists and the unsolved murders of several journalists. In the same month the Verkhovna Rada rejected draft legislation on constitutional reform presented by deputies of the SDPU—U and the SPU, providing for the election of all 450 deputies by proportional representation; the Verkhovna Rada again rejected the draft in April. Meanwhile, in March Kuchma submitted a draft on constitutional reform to the legislature, providing for the replacement of the Verkhovna Rada by a State Assembly elected under a party list system and a House of the Regions; parliament was to be granted the power to dismiss the Prime Minister, and the President the power to dissolve parliament. In April Yanukovych was elected as Chairman of the PR, while the First Deputy Prime Minister and Minister of Finance, Mykola Azarov, became the party's Chairman of the Political Council. Following the failure of the Verkhovna Rada to support either of the constitutional amendments, the President stated in June that he was prepared to co-operate with members of the legislative opposition. In September a new draft, prepared by members of the pro-presidential and CPU legislative factions (widely known as the Medvedchuk-Symonenko draft, after the Head of the Presidential Administration, Viktor Medvedchuk and the CPU leader, respectively), was presented to the Verkhovna Rada; the text envisaged the extension of the mandate of the existing legislature until 2007, when its replacement would be elected by proportional representation, and the introduction of a system under which the President would be elected by the Verkhovna Rada. In September 2003 Anatoliy Zlenko retired as Minister of Foreign Affairs. He was succeeded by Kostyantyn Hryshchenko, hitherto ambassador to the USA. In October Kuchma dismissed the Prosecutor-General, Svyatoslav Pyskun, nominating Hennadiy Vasilyev, a former Chief Prosecutor in Donetsk Oblast, as his replacement; the legislature approved the appointment in November. There were renewed concerns about the use of force to inhibit political debate, after Our Ukraine was forcibly prevented from holding a conference in Donetsk at the end of October.

In late December 2003 the Verkhovna Rada provisionally approved the Medvedchuk-Symonenko draft on constitutional reform (however, the 274 votes cast in favour of the proposals, although sufficient to enable the bill to receive a second reading in the legislature, fell short of the 300 votes required for its approval), although the leadership of the Our Ukraine, BYuT and SPU factions did not support the proposals. (The draft was not approved on a second reader in April 2004.) Meanwhile, on 30 December 2003 the Constitutional Court declared that Kuchma would be eligible to seek re-election upon the expiry of his term of office in October 2004. On 3 February 2004 the Verkhovna Rada voted to amend the Medvedchuk-Symonenko draft on constitutional reform, removing those proposals pertaining to the election of the President by the legislature. In March the Verkhovna Rada approved legislation, supported by the SPU and the CPU, introducing a proportional representation system for the election of all 450 parliamentary deputies; the percentage of the votes required for a party to obtain election was to be reduced from 4% to 3%. The legislation was signed into law by Kuchma in early April.

The 'orange revolution'

Politics in 2004 were dominated by preparations for the presidential election. In April the pro-presidential bloc named Yanukovych as their candidate. On 20 August two bombs exploded in a Kyiv market, and a further explosion occurred on 3 September; the authorities suggested that the explosions were connected to members of Our Ukraine, while the opposition claimed that the secret services had orchestrated the attacks in an attempt to discredit them. In September Yushchenko, the principal opposition presidential candidate, was admitted to a clinic in Vienna, Austria. He subsequently emerged with his skin severely scarred by lesions, apparently the result of having been poisoned during a meal with senior members of the secret services. Shortly before the first round of the election Yanukovych, in his capacity as Prime Minister, announced that the rate of state pensions was to be increased. Yanukovych also pledged to grant Russian the status of a joint official language and work towards permitting dual Ukrainian-Russian citizenship. Yushchenko, conversely, made it clear that he would, if elected, seek the closer integration of Ukraine into the European Union (EU, see p. 281) and the North Atlantic Treaty Organization (NATO, see p. 380).

At the first round of voting, held on 31 October 2004 and contested by 26 candidates, Yushchenko received 39.9% of the votes cast, and Yanukovych 39.3% of the votes, according to results released by the Central Electoral Commission (CEC); Yushchenko and Yanukovych consequently proceeded to a second round on 21 November. The CEC initially indicated that Yanukovych led by nearly 3% in the second round, with more than 99% of the votes counted, contradicting several exit polls endorsed by the opposition. Large-scale protests at the allegedly fraudulent conduct of the count, in support of Yushchenko, in which Tymoshenko played a prominent part, commenced in central Kyiv on 22 November, focused around Maidan Nezalezhnosti (Independence Square). The youth group Pora! (Enough!) played a major role in the organization of the protests, which were almost entirely peaceful and attracted several hundreds of thousands of people. The demonstrators established a tent settlement, and adopted the colour orange as a unifying symbol, leading what became known as the 'orange revolution'. Meanwhile, a number of local administrations, including the city councils of Kyiv and Lviv, declared that they did not accept the results announced by the CEC and that they regarded Yushchenko as the legitimate head of state. The OSCE condemned the conduct of both rounds of voting. On 23 November Yushchenko took a symbolic oath of office in front of the Verkhovna Rada. On 24 November the CEC officially announced the preliminary results of the second round: Yanukovych was declared the winner, with 49.5% of the votes cast, while Yushchenko was deemed to have received 46.6%. However, speeches and demonstrations, led by Yushchenko and Tymoshenko, continued in freezing conditions in central Kyiv, and protesters blockaded numerous government buildings. In eastern Ukraine the administrations of several oblasts (notably Donetsk and Luhansk) threatened to hold referendums on autonomy or secession should Yushchenko be declared President.

Following an appeal to the Supreme Court regarding the conduct of the second round of voting, on 25 November 2004 the Court announced that it would suspend the publication of the election results until the opposition's complaints could be considered. A significant shift in the allegiances of the state-owned broadcasting outlets, which had hitherto demonstrated a pro-Yanukovych bias, was also observed. On 27 November the Verkhovna Rada voted to declare the 21 November ballot invalid and to express a lack of confidence in the CEC, while a subsequent motion of no confidence in Yanukovych's Government was adopted on 1 December (these resolutions, however, required the signature of President Kuchma to be binding). On 29 November Serhiy Tihipko resigned as NBU Governor and as the manager of

Yanukovych's presidential campaign. Meanwhile, Polish President Aleksander Kwaśniewski, Lithuanian President Valdas Adamkus and the EU High Representative for Common Foreign and Security Policy, Javier Solana, arrived in Kyiv to attempt mediation between Yushchenko and Yanukovych, in the presence of Kuchma. On 3 December the Supreme Court ruled that the declared results of the second round of voting were invalid, and ordered that a repeat election be conducted within three weeks.

Viktor Yushchenko becomes President

On 8 December 2004, following extensive negotiations, the Verkhovna Rada voted to support a series of amendments to the Constitution and electoral law, with 420 deputies voting in favour of the proposals. The constitutional amendments provided for the transfer of several powers of appointment from the President to the Prime Minister and the legislature and for the expulsion from the legislature of any deputy who left the party or bloc on whose list he had been elected. Kuchma signed the amendments into law, although they were not fully to take effect until after the legislative elections due to be held in March 2006. Kuchma also announced the dismissal of the Prosecutor-General, Hennadiy Vasilyev (who was replaced by his predecessor, Pyskun, who had won a court case declaring his dismissal in 2003 to be illegal), and approved a reconstitution of the CEC. Yanukovych took leave from his position as Prime Minister in order to campaign for the repeated second round of voting; he was replaced in an acting capacity by Azarov. The ballot was held on 26 December 2004. After preliminary results suggested a victory for Yushchenko, Yanukovych lodged complaints against the conduct of the election with the CEC and, subsequently, the Supreme Court, causing the official publication of the results to be delayed. Meanwhile, on 27 December Minister of Transport and Communications Heorhiy Kirpa was found dead, with multiple bullet wounds. Earlier in the month Yuriy Lyakh, Chairman of the Ukrainian Credit Bank, had been found dead in his office, from neck wounds apparently inflicted with a paper knife. Both cases were officially described as suicide, despite widespread speculation that the deaths had been political assassinations. On 31 December Yanukovych resigned as Prime Minister, and on 6 January 2005 Kuchma signed a decree dismissing the Cabinet of Ministers. On the latter date Yanukovych's complaints were rejected by the Supreme Court, and four days later Yushchenko was officially declared to have won the ballot of 26 December 2004, receiving 51.99% of the votes cast, compared with the 44.2% awarded to Yanukovych. A clear regional divide was evident in the results, with Yushchenko obtaining more than 75% of the votes cast in 12 administrative divisions of western and central Ukraine, including Kyiv City, while Yanukovych received similarly overwhelming majorities in four divisions of eastern Ukraine and Crimea. Following the Supreme Court's rejection of Yanukovych's final appeal, Yushchenko was inaugurated as President on 23 January 2005.

On 4 February 2005 the Verkhovna Rada approved Yushchenko's nomination of Tymoshenko as Prime Minister and a new Cabinet of Ministers was announced, notably including Kinakh as First Deputy Prime Minister. Other ministerial appointments included Yuriy Lutsenko as Minister of Internal Affairs and Anatoliy Hrytsenko as Minister of Defence. Yushchenko also appointed many new regional governors, and named Petro Poroshenko, a prominent business executive, as Chairman of the National Security and Defence Council. The new Government declared combating corruption to be a priority, and several privatizations conducted during Kuchma's presidency were targeted for investigation. Tensions over this and other policy matters existed between the three main political groupings represented within the Government: nationalists and populists, associated chiefly with Tymoshenko; statist socialists linked with the SPU; and those elements regarded as more sympathetic to business interests, associated more closely with Yushchenko. The latter formed a new political party, People's Union Our Ukraine.

Yushchenko also endorsed a reopening of the investigation into the death of Gongadze. On 4 March 2005 former Minister of Internal Affairs Kravchenko was found dead, reportedly as the result of suicide, shortly before he had been due to be questioned at the office of the Prosecutor-General in connection with Gongadze's death. The trial of three men on charges related to the case, all former police officers, commenced in January 2006; a fourth man, suspected of being Gongadze's killer, was believed to have fled Ukraine. (In March 2008 the three men were found guilty of murdering Gongadze, each receiving custodial sentences of 12–13 years, although the investigations failed to discover who had ordered the killing.)

Meanwhile, it soon became apparent that some of the new administration's policy decisions had been instrumental in reducing the hitherto strong rate of economic growth. Increases in social spending led to heightened inflation. Moreover, Tymoshenko's decision, in April 2005, to maintain at existing levels the retail prices of petroleum (for which Ukraine was heavily dependent on Russia) resulted in several Russian companies limiting their supplies to Ukraine, causing severe shortages. In May Yushchenko issued a decree criticizing the Government's action in restraining prices, ordering that the restraints be removed as a matter of urgency. Meanwhile, interfactional disagreements in the Verkhovna Rada meant that several items of legislation, which had been intended to expedite Ukraine's application for membership of the World Trade Organization (WTO, see p. 444), were not approved by the legislature before the beginning of its summer recess.

The collapse of the orange coalition

The growing tensions between the constituent groupings within the ruling authorities resulted in a series of resignations in September 2005. On 2 September the Chief of the Presidential Staff, Oleksandr Zinchenko, resigned, criticizing the allegedly corrupt actions of Poroshenko and other officials. On 8 September, after Mykola Tomenko stepped down as Deputy Prime Minister, Yushchenko dismissed Tymoshenko and her Government, and also announced that Poroshenko had resigned from the National Security and Defence Council. Tymoshenko stated that, as a result of her dismissal, the BYuT would effectively go into opposition. On 20 September the Verkhovna Rada narrowly failed to approve Yushchenko's nomination of a senior member of People's Union Our Ukraine, Yuriy Yekhanurov, as Prime Minister. In order to obtain support from the PR, Yushchenko agreed a 10-point memorandum with Yanukovych, the terms of which included an amnesty for all those involved in electoral fraud at the annulled second round of presidential voting in 2004, and an extension of the immunity from prosecution enjoyed by legislative deputies to members of regional and local councils. On 22 September 2005 Yekhanurov was confirmed as Prime Minister. New appointments in his administration included that of Arseniy Yatsenyuk as Minister of the Economy. Pyskun was dismissed as Prosecutor-General, on 14 October, after which it was announced that all criminal charges against Poroshenko had been abandoned. On 31 October the Verkhovna Rada approved the appointment of Oleksandr Medvedko as Prosecutor-General. New arrangements for the purchase of natural gas (following a dispute with Russia—see Foreign Affairs) were a source of considerable controversy within Ukraine and were instrumental in bringing about a vote of no confidence in the Government on 10 January 2006, which was approved by 250 votes to 50 against. However, President Yushchenko requested that the Yekhanurov administration remain in office until after the forthcoming legislative elections.

The legislative elections were contested by 45 parties and blocs on 26 March 2006, under a system of full proportional representation and excluding nominally independent deputies. Yanukovych's PR became the largest party, with 32.1% of the total votes cast, receiving 186 seats. The BYuT was placed second, with 22.3% and 129 seats, while the Our Ukraine bloc (comprising several smaller, generally liberal or nationalist parties, in addition to Our Ukraine) obtained 14.0% and 81 seats. The SPU, with 5.7% (33 seats), and the CPU, with 3.7% (21 seats), also surpassed the 3% quota required for representation. The conduct of the elections was described by international monitors as generally free and fair. In late June it was announced that Our Ukraine, the BYuT and the SPU were to form a governing coalition supportive of Yushchenko, with Tymoshenko as premier. However, when the coalition declined to nominate Moroz as legislative Chairman, the SPU announced its withdrawal from the coalition, and instead announced that it would support a so-called 'anti-crisis coalition', headed by the PR and including the CPU, although this agreement also collapsed before a government could be formed. At the end of July a 'national unity coalition' was formed after Yushchenko and leaders of four of the five parliamentary parties (with the BYuT the exception) signed a document that outlined various domestic and foreign policy aims, including the retention of Ukrainian as the sole official language (outwith Crimea) and the eventual incorporation of Ukraine into European and Atlantic organizations. On 4 August the Verkhovna Rada approved the nomination of Yanukovych as Prime Minister and the formation of a new

Government, comprising representatives of the PR, Our Ukraine, the SPU and (for the first time in post-Soviet Ukraine) the CPU.

Tensions between Yushchenko and Yanukovych continued to be evident, while the balance of powers between the President, Prime Minister and Verkhovna Rada, following the enactment of the 2004 constitutional amendments, remained uncertain; in particular, several of Yanukovych's actions as Prime Minister exceeded the official remit of that office. In September 2006 Yanukovych refused to sign several presidential decrees (which, in order to become valid, required the approval of the Prime Minister and Chairman of the Verkhovna Rada). In the same month Yanukovych expressed Ukraine's unpreparedness to enter into a closer relationship with NATO at a meeting of the Alliance in Brussels, Belgium, despite such remarks being contrary to the terms of the coalition policy document. Later that month the Verkhovna Rada voted to abolish the prohibition on parliamentary deputies transferring party allegiance or becoming independent. At the end of September Yanukovych demanded the dismissal of the governors of five eastern regions who were members of Our Ukraine, a demand that required presidential endorsement.

On 1 December 2006 the Verkhovna Rada voted in favour of the dismissal of the Minister of Foreign Affairs, Borys Tarasyuk, and the Minister of Internal Affairs, Lutsenko. Tarasyuk resigned from the Government at the end of January 2007, after his dismissal was upheld by the appeals court in Kyiv. On 20 March the Verkhovna Rada rejected Yushchenko's nomination of Volodymyr Ohryzko as Minister of Foreign Affairs, and one day later approved the appointment of Yatsenyuk to that position. Later in the month a group of deputies hitherto loyal to Yushchenko announced that they would henceforth form part of the PR faction in the Verkhovna Rada.

The 2007 pre-term legislative elections

Frustrated at the inability to govern effectively, on 2 April 2007 Yushchenko issued a decree dissolving the Verkhovna Rada and scheduling pre-term parliamentary elections for 27 May. Yanukovych initially refused to accept the presidential decree and asked the Constitutional Court to rule on the constitutionality of the dissolution of parliament. Meanwhile, the Verkhovna Rada continued to meet, refusing to recognize the legitimacy of its dissolution. On 25 April Yushchenko announced that the parliamentary elections were to be delayed until 24 June. On 30 April the Verkhovna Rada approved a resolution calling for the concurrent holding of fresh presidential and legislative elections, to be held no later than December and subject to the introduction of a number of constitutional amendments. Meanwhile, the Constitutional Court had failed to issue any ruling on the legitimacy of the dissolution of the legislature; the acting Chairman of the Court resigned in May, while several other judges of the Court were absent, effectively rendering the Court unable to conduct its work. On 1 June Yushchenko again dismissed Pyskun, who had been reappointed to the Office of Prosecutor-General in April, and replaced him, again, with Medvedko. On 5 June Yushchenko rescheduled the legislative elections to 30 September. Our Ukraine and BYuT deputies subsequently withdrew from the Verkhovna Rada. In early July Our Ukraine formed an electoral alliance with the People's Self-Defence group of Lutsenko and several smaller parties, which became known as the Our Ukraine-People's Self-defence bloc. Tymoshenko demanded that a national referendum to resolve the constitutional impasse be conducted to coincide with the elections, and began to organize a petition to that end.

According to results of the legislative elections on 30 September 2007, published by the CEC in mid-October, the PR won 34.4% of the votes and 175 seats, the BYuT 30.7% and 156 seats, the Our Ukraine-People's Self-defence bloc 14.2% and 72 seats, the CPU 5.4% and 27 seats, and the Lytvyn bloc 4.0% and 20 seats. The SPU failed to secure representation. International observers described the elections as having met democratic standards. Tymoshenko and the leader of the Our Ukraine-People's Self-defence bloc, Vyacheslav Kyrylenko, subsequently announced their intention to sign a coalition agreement, which would allow the two groupings a narrow parliamentary majority. The Verkhovna Rada was convened on 23 November, when Yanukovych formally relinquished the premiership. Yatsenyuk was appointed legislative Chairman on 4 December, and on 18 December, after two failed attempts, Tymoshenko's nomination as Prime Minister was approved by 226 votes in the Verkhovna Rada. Her Government comprised 12 representatives of the BYuT and 11 of the Our Ukraine-People's Self-

defence bloc; the Minister of Foreign Affairs, Volodymyr Ohryzko, who, together with the Minister of Defence, had been nominated by the President in accordance with the Constitution, was independent.

In January 2008 it was reported that Lutsenko, who had been reappointed Minister of Internal Affairs, had assaulted the Mayor of Kyiv, Leonid Chernovetsky. In March tensions between the President and Prime Minister were heightened, as Yushchenko criticized the Government's economic policies and accused Tymoshenko of permitting corrupt practices in land auctions. Following continued denunciations of Tymoshenko by Yushchenko, in May BYuT deputies blockaded the Verkhovna Rada, preventing Yushchenko from making his annual parliamentary address.

Continuing tensions between Our Ukraine and the Tymoshenko Bloc

In June 2008 the coalition of the BYuT and the Our Ukraine-People's Self-defence bloc lost its narrow parliamentary majority, following the resignation of one deputy from each faction. A parliamentary motion expressing no confidence in Tymoshenko's Government was defeated in July. In early September PR parliamentary faction leader Raisa Bohatyryova, the Secretary of the National Security and Defence Council, was expelled from the party, after refusing to endorse Yanukovych's support for the declared independence of South Ossetia and Abkhazia from Georgia following the military conflict between Georgia and Russia in the previous month. On the following day Yushchenko announced the withdrawal of the Our Ukraine-People's Self-defence bloc from the ruling coalition, after the BYuT supported the PR in voting for a parliamentary motion approving legislation that would reduced presidential powers. Yatsenyuk subsequently tendered his resignation as Chairman of the Verkhovna Rada, and on 8 October Yushchenko officially dissolved the Verkhovna Rada and announced that further legislative elections would take place on 7 December. Later in October Yushchenko reconvened the Verkhovna Rada to debate financial austerity measures required for the disbursement of IMF assistance (following the onset of the international financial crisis) and rescheduled the elections for 14 December. The Verkhovna Rada accepted Yatsenyuk's resignation on 12 November; after attempts to adopt legislation allocating funds to the organization of the elections failed, Yushchenko announced that it would not, in fact, be possible to organize legislative elections in 2008.

On 9 December 2008 Lytvyn was re-elected to his former position of Chairman of the Verkhovna Rada. A new coalition agreement between Our Ukraine-People's Self-defence bloc, the BYuT and the Lytvyn bloc was signed on 16 December. However, Kyrylenko, who opposed the coalition agreement, withdrew from Our Ukraine-People's Self-defence bloc and formed a breakaway movement, For Ukraine. In February 2009 Viktor Pynzenyk, who had expressed opposition to the Government's plan for economic recovery, resigned as Minister of Finance. In the same month the Ministry of Foreign Affairs threatened to expel the Russian ambassador in Ukraine (and former Russian premier), Viktor Chernomyrdin, following a newspaper interview in which he made a number of disparaging comments about the Ukrainian political leadership. In early March the Verkhovna Rada voted in favour of removing Ohryzko from the post of Minister of Foreign Affairs.

In April 2009 the Verkhovna Rada voted in favour of scheduling the first round of the forthcoming presidential election for 25 October (rather than on 17 January 2010, as provided for by the Constitution). In early May 2009 the Constitutional Court overturned the proposed rescheduling of the election. Also in May Lutsenko offered his resignation from the post of Minister of Internal Affairs, at the request of Yushchenko, after he had been detained by police at the airport of Frankfurt, Germany, for apparently intoxicated and violent behaviour. After parliamentary deputies belonging to the BYuT opposed the acceptance of his resignation (which was likely to precipitate the collapse of the ruling coalition), the Verkhovna Rada voted in favour of a motion requesting his suspension from office while the incident was investigated. In early June the Verkhovna Rada approved the dismissal of Yekhanurov as Minister of Defence, a development strongly supported by Tymoshenko. On 7 June negotiations between the PR and the BYuT on the formation of a parliamentary 'grand coalition' failed when Yanukovych withdrew.

In July 2009 Oleksiy Pukach, the former head of the interior ministry's external surveillance directorate, was arrested for suspected involvement in the murder in 2000 of journalist

Heorhiy Gongadze (after being charged *in absentia* in 2003). In September 2009 PR deputies began a blockade of parliamentary sessions, after the Verkhovna Rada rejected a PR proposal for increases in salaries and pensions. Meanwhile, Lutsenko (who remained in post as Minister of Internal Affairs) claimed that senior NBU officials had been involved in plans to weaken the national currency, on the instructions of the Ukrainian presidency, in order to damage Tymoshenko's Government. At the end of September the privatization of one of Ukraine's largest petrochemical factories, in Odesa, which Yushchenko had strenuously opposed, was invalidated by the State Property Fund, on the grounds that the highest tendered price represented an undervaluing of the factory. In October the Verkhovna Rada approved Yushchenko's nomination of Poroshenko, as Minister of Foreign Affairs. In the following month the legislature approved budgetary amendments (opposed by Tymoshenko) providing for increases in salaries and pensions; in consequence, the IMF suspended lending to Ukraine.

Viktor Yanukovych elected President

At the first round of the presidential election, which was contested by 18 candidates on 17 January 2010, Yanukovych won 35.3% of the votes cast and Tymoshenko 25.1%; Tihipko received 13.1%, ahead of Yatsenyuk, with 7.0%, and Yushchenko, who received only 5.5% of the votes. Some 70.4% of the electorate participated in the poll. On 28 January the Verkhovna Rada voted in favour of removing Lutsenko from his post, on the grounds that police had disrupted voting (he claimed that members of the police service had intervened to prevent electoral malpractice); one day later Tymoshenko reinstated him as acting Minister of Internal Affairs, although his reinstatement was subsequently suspended by a Kyiv court. In early February Yushchenko signed into law recently adopted amendments to electoral legislation, proposed by the PR, abolishing the requirement for representatives of candidates to endorse vote counts at polling stations, with effect from the second round of the presidential election.

The second round of the presidential election, which was conducted on 7 February 2010, was narrowly won by Yanukovych, with 49.0% of votes cast, compared with the 45.5% awarded to Tymoshenko. Although OSCE observers declared that the poll had been fair, Tymoshenko claimed that widespread malpractice had been perpetrated. Although she withdrew a legal challenge against the election results after a few days, Tymoshenko stated that she continued to refuse to recognize the legitimacy of Yanukovych's election as President and boycotted his inaugural ceremony, which took place on 25 February. On 3 March the Verkhovna Rada adopted a motion of no confidence in Tymoshenko's Government. A new parliamentary coalition was negotiated on 11 March between the PR, the Lytvyn bloc and the CPU, which (following a number of defections) controlled a total of 235 of the 450 seats in the Verkhovna Rada (further defections to the coalition ensued). On the same day the legislature voted to approve the nomination of Azarov as Prime Minister; a new Government, dominated by the PR, was formed. Andriy Klyuyev, became First Deputy Prime Minister. Tihipko (who had recently announced the revival of the Working Ukraine political party that he headed, under the new name, A Strong Ukraine) became Deputy Prime Minister, responsible for Economic Affairs. Five other Deputy Prime Ministers were prominent members of the PR. Other appointments included that of Anatoliy Mohilyov, a senior police official, as Minister of Internal Affairs, while Hryshchenko returned to the position of Minister of Foreign Affairs that he had held in 2003–05. Following discussions between Azarov and an IMF delegation on conditions for the resumption of the IMF credit agreement, the CPU indicated that it would withdraw from the ruling coalition should the Government adopt economic austerity measures. On 23 April Azarov was elected Chairman of the PR.

An agreement was reached with Russia in April 2010, whereby Ukraine was to obtain natural gas at reduced prices, in exchange for the extension, by a further 25 years until 2042, of the Russian lease on the base of the Black Sea Fleet in the Crimean peninsula. Despite violent disturbances by opposition deputies, the Verkhovna Rada approved the agreement on 27 April 2010. Tymoshenko denounced the agreement as a violation of national sovereignty and urged a mass opposition protest outside the Verkhovna Rada in early May to demand the removal of Yanukovych and early elections. In May the Office of the Prosecutor-General announced the resumption of a 2004 criminal case against Tymoshenko relating to the alleged bribery of Supreme

Court judges, which had been abandoned with her installation as premier in January 2005.

In early July 2010 the Verkhovna Rada voted to dismiss Volodymyr Semynozhenko as Deputy Prime Minister, responsible for Humanitarian Affairs, in response to a motion proposed by a BYuT deputy. (Semynozhenko was appointed later in the month as an adviser to the Prime Minister.) In the same month President Yanukovych appointed a close ally, Nestor Shufrych, hitherto the Minister of Emergency Situations, as Deputy Chairman of the National Security Council. Later in July the IMF approved the resumption of lending to Ukraine, after the Government pledged to adhere to fiscal austerity measures. In early August the International Press Institute, in an open letter to Yanukovych, urged him to address what it described as the significant deterioration in press freedom since his election. In September the Office of the Prosecutor-General announced that the official investigation into the killing of Gongadze in 2000 had concluded that former Minister of Internal Affairs Kravchenko had ordered his murder.

The trial and conviction of Tymoshenko

On 1 October 2010 the Constitutional Court ruled that the constitutional amendments agreed in December 2004 were unlawful; consequently, the power to appoint the Prime Minister and other members of the Government, which since 2006 had been shared between the President, Prime Minister and the Verkhovna Rada, was again to be vested solely in the President. On 13 October 2010 Yanukovych dismissed two Deputy Prime Ministers, appointing both to other senior positions. On 31 October local elections were conducted on the basis of a mixed singlemandate and proportional representation electoral system, under new regulations, which had been adopted by the Verkhovna Rada in July; parties that had been established less than one year beforehand and political alliances (notably the BYuT) were prohibited from contesting the elections. International election monitors concluded that the organization of the elections failed to meet democratic standards and cited numerous procedural violations, many of which were related to the new electoral regulations. A low voter turn-out, of about 50%, was recorded; the PR secured 11 of the 24 contested mayoral posts, while Fatherland (which contested the elections in place of the BYuT) obtained only two. In early November Yanukovych appointed Viktor Pshonka as Prosecutor-General, replacing Medvedko. At the end of that month Yanukovych vetoed legislation providing for reforms to the tax code and returned it to the Verkhovna Rada for revision, in response to large-scale protests in Kyiv and other towns that had been organized by owners of small and medium-sized enterprises. Amended legislation on a new tax code was adopted by the Verkhovna Rada on 2 December. On 9 December Yanukovych signed a decree effecting a government reorganization, in which several ministries were abolished.

On 20 December 2010 Tymoshenko was formally charged with abuse of power during her term as premier; she denied all charges, which related to the misappropriation of carbon credit funds amounting to €320m. Five BYuT parliamentary deputies, having staged a protest in the Verkhovna Rada, were slightly injured in an ensuing clash with PR deputies. A number of former members of Tymoshenko's administration were also accused of abuse of office, including Lutsenko, who was arrested later that month. In January 2011 Tymoshenko's former Minister of the Economy, Bohdan Danylyshyn, who had been arrested in the Czech Republic in October 2010 in response to an international arrest warrant, was granted political asylum by the Czech Government and released from custody, owing to concerns that the charges against him and other opposition members were politically motivated.

On 1 February 2011 the Verkhovna Rada approved legislation scheduling the next parliamentary elections (which had been due in March) for 28 October 2012, while the next presidential election was scheduled for March 2015. While the rescheduling of the elections had been proposed on grounds of cost, it was also expected to benefit the PR. In March 2011 former President Kuchma was officially charged with abuse of office in connection with the killing of Gongadze. In April the IMF again suspended funding to Ukraine, after the Government failed to adopt pension reforms. In June President Yanukovych dismissed Viktor Tykhonov as Deputy Prime Minister and Minister of Regional Development, Construction and Communal Services and Municipal Economy; he was replaced in July by the hitherto Governor of Donetsk Oblast, Anatoliy Blyznyuk.

Meanwhile, in May 2011 further charges of abuse of office were brought against Tymoshenko, on the grounds that in January

2009 she had signed an unfavourable agreement with Russia for the supply of gas (see Foreign Affairs) without consulting the Council of Ministers; her trial on charges relating to this case began in June 2011. On 5 August Tymoshenko was arrested on charges of contempt of court and denied bail; her subsequent detention in a prison in Kyiv prompted a series of protests by her followers in the capital. However, former President Yushchenko, testifying at Tymoshenko's trial, stated that she had been motivated in negotiating the agreement by the wish to increase her personal popularity. On 11 October Tymoshenko was found guilty on charges of abuse of office, the judge stating that she had deliberately exceeded her authority in signing the gas agreement. She was sentenced to seven years' imprisonment, fined the equivalent of US \$188m., and was to be prohibited from seeking public office for the duration of her imprisonment and for a further period of three years following her release. The verdict prompted violent protests by her supporters in Kyiv, which were rapidly dispersed by police. Tymoshenko's imprisonment prompted international controversy, and was widely described as politically motivated. In early November further charges were officially brought against Tymoshenko, relating to offences of embezzlement and tax evasion allegedly committed while she was head of gas trading company United Energy Systems during the 1990s. In mid-November the Verkhovna Rada rejected legislative amendments that would have decriminalized the offences for which Tymoshenko had been sentenced. (The amendments were again rejected in February 2012.) Meanwhile, on 7 November 2011, following the appointment of Mohilyov as Prime Minister of Crimea, Vitaliy Zakharchenko, hitherto head of the State Tax Service, was chosen to replace him as Minister of Internal Affairs. In late December the appeals court in Kyiv upheld the sentence imposed on Tymoshenko, and she was transferred to a prison in Kharkiv. In the same month a Kyiv court ordered that the case against Kuchma for involvement in the killing of Gongadze be abandoned, after the Constitutional Court ruled in October that it could not proceed since the alleged evidence of the clandestine audio recordings had been obtained illegally. (The trial of Pukach on charges related to the murder of Gongadze had officially commenced in July, and testimony provided during the ongoing proceedings also implicated Kuchma and Lytvyn.)

Further imprisonments

In January 2012 Yanukovych appointed Valeriy Khoroshkovsky, hitherto the Chairman of the SBU, as Minister of Finance, following the resignation of Fedir Yaroshenko. In early February Yanukovych appointed Dmytro Salamatin, the head of the state defence industry company Ukoboronprom since 2011, and who was reported to have held Russian citizenship until 1999, as Minister of Defence, and the Chief of the General Staff was also replaced. During February 2011 Yanukovych continued the government reorganization, removing Klyuyev from the post of First Deputy Prime Minister and appointing him as Secretary of the National Security Council; his predecessor in that role, Bohatyrova, became Deputy Prime Minister and Minister of the Protection of Health. Khoroshkovsky became First Deputy Prime Minister, and was succeeded as Minister of Finance by Yuriy Kolobov. Poroshenko was appointed Minister of Economic Development and Trade. It was reported, meanwhile, that Yanukovych had agreed to the introduction of Russian advisers in the SBU and to consultation with the Russian Government over future security service appointments. In early March Yanukovych announced the introduction of a number of social initiatives, including an increase in certain pensions, to enter into effect from mid-2012, seemingly in an attempt to increase his personal popularity prior to the elections later that year. In the same month Tihipko dissolved A Strong Ukraine and urged its former members to join the PR, of which party he subsequently became Deputy Chairman.

Meanwhile, in February 2012 Lutsenko was sentenced to four years' imprisonment on charges of abuse of office and embezzlement. In April two ministers who had served under Tymoshenko were also imprisoned: a former environment minister, Heorgiy Filipchuk, received a sentence of three years for having exceeded his authority in preparing a ministry contract, while a former acting Minister of Defence, Valeriy Ivashchenko (who had been detained since August 2010), was sentenced to a term of five years, also for having exceeded his authority, in connection with the allegedly fraudulent privatization of a ship-building plant in Crimea. The Russian authorities announced, meanwhile, that Tymoshenko was suspected of involvement in the 1996 murder of parliamentary deputy and businessman Yevhen Shcherban. On 27 April 2012 at least 29 people were injured in four explosions in Dnipropetrovsk (one person had been killed in a similar explosion in the town in November 2011); the Ukrainian authorities announced an investigation into the attacks, which were most generally attributed to disputes between rival organized crime groups. In May 2012 Tymoshenko was transferred to a hospital, where she ended a hunger strike that she had begun in late April in protest at her alleged ill-treatment in prison.

On 8 August 2012 President Yanukovych signed controversial legislation (which had prompted protests in Kyiv) permitting languages spoken by more than 10% of the population in any administrative region to be granted official status therein. The measure was opposed by Ukrainian nationalists, in particular owing to concerns that the status of the Ukrainian language would be threatened by the increased official use of Russian that the law would permit. Several days later Odesa City Council voted to grant Russian official status in the city, representing the first application of this new legislation. Later in August Ivashchenko was released on appeal, with a one-year suspended sentence. However, Lutsenko was sentenced to a further two years' imprisonment on charges of negligence, while the country's highest appeal court upheld the verdict imposed on Tymoshenko.

Recent developments: the 2012 legislative elections

Under legislation that had been adopted in late 2011, the legislative elections on 28 October 2012 were held under a mixed single-mandate and party-list electoral system; the participation of electoral blocs was not permitted and the threshold for parliamentary representation was raised from 3% to 5% of votes cast. OSCE and local observers criticized the conduct of the elections, particularly citing irregularities in vote-counting in single-mandate constituencies. Tymoshenko began a further hunger strike on the following day, and opposition parties staged protests in early November against alleged government malpractice. According to official preliminary results, which were announced by the CEC on 13 November, PR secured 30.0% of the votes cast on the basis of party lists, winning 186 seats overall, while Fatherland took 25.5% of the party-list votes and 101 seats. The newly established Ukrainian Democratic Alliance for Reform (UDAR), led by international boxing champion Vitaliy Klychko, received 14.0% of the party-list votes and 40 seats, while the nationalist Freedom party demonstrated a strong increase in support, with 10.4% and 37 seats (the party was the most popular in the western Lviv Oblast). The CPU obtained 13.2% and 32 seats. Voter turn-out of about 58% was recorded. The CEC upheld complaints of violations in five single-mandate constituencies, where the results were annulled. In the re-run elections in these districts the PR won a further seat, and Fatherland obtained another four.

Following the resignation of the incumbent Government, on 9 December 2012 Yanukovych reappointed Azarov as Prime Minister; his new administration was approved in the Verkhovna Rada on 13 December. Serhiy Arbuzov, hitherto the NBU Governor, became the First Deputy Prime Minister, while the three Deputy Prime Ministers included the hitherto Minister of Energy and the Coal Industry, Yuriy Boyko, and the hitherto long-standing Minister of Foreign Affairs, Kostyantyn Hryshchenko, who was succeeded in his former post by Leonid Kozhara. While several non-party ministers were appointed, the only representative in the Cabinet of Ministers of any party other than the PR was the leader of the pro-business Forward, Ukraine! party, Nataliya Korolevska, who was appointed Minister of Social Policy. On the same day Volodymyr Rybak was elected as the new Chairman of the Verkhovna Rada, replacing Lytvyn; the parliamentary session was disrupted by Freedom deputies, who clashed with PR members after accusing them of violating voting regulations.

On 29 January 2013 Pukach was sentenced to life imprisonment for ordering the killing of Gongadze. Meanwhile, proceedings by the Ukrainian authorities against Tymoshenko continued; in January Pshonka publicly declared that she was suspected of ordering the killing of Shcherban. In February Ivashchenko fled Ukraine, and was granted political asylum in Denmark. In March a Ukrainian court removed the parliamentary mandate of Serhiy Vlasenko, a prominent member of Fatherland, on the grounds that he had concurrently worked as a lawyer. The trial of Tymoshenko on the embezzlement and tax evasion charges was repeatedly postponed, after she refused to attend hearings on grounds of ill health. In early April Yanukovych signed a decree issuing formal pardons to seven prisoners, among them Lutsenko and Filipchuk. Meanwhile, in early March Our Ukraine (which had obtained under 1% of the votes cast at the recent legislative elections) voted to dissolve itself during a congress in Kyiv; however, this decision was disputed by a faction of the party, who announced that they would hold an alternative congress in May, while retaining members of the officially registered party.

Crimea

Despite the political differences between the Ukrainian-speaking western regions and the Russian-speaking eastern regions that were evident during the 1990s and 2000s, only in the Crimean peninsula did any significant movement for reunification with Russia emerge. The situation was further complicated by the status of the Crimean Tatars, who had been forcibly deported to Soviet Central Asia in 1944, and who began to return to Crimea from late 1989. In a referendum held in January 1991, residents of Crimea (which then had the status of an ordinary oblast) voted to restore it to the status of a nominally autonomous republic. The decision, although it had no legal basis, was ratified by the Verkhovna Rada. In June Crimean Tatars established 'parallel' institutions to those of the state, without any constitutional or legal status. The Kurultay (Assembly) was a popular assembly that was intended to convene once a year, the Qırımtatar Milly Meclisi (Crimean Tatar National Assembly) was to meet throughout the year, and a number of local assemblies were also established. In February 1992 the Crimean Supreme Council, the regional legislature, voted to transform the region into the Republic of Crimea, and in May declared Crimea an independent state, adopting a new Constitution. However, following threats from the Verkhovna Rada to impose an economic blockade and direct rule on Crimea, this declaration was rescinded. In June the Ukrainian Government confirmed the status of Crimea (except for Sevastopol city) as an autonomous republic within Ukraine. Meanwhile, relations between the local leadership and Crimean Tatars, some 250,000 of whom had returned to Crimea by late 1992, deteriorated steadily, primarily as a result of disputes over the ownership of land and property, and the right to gain Ukrainian citizenship. In October a Tatar encampment was dispersed on the orders of the Crimean Government, and in response some 6,000 Tatars stormed the Crimean parliament building.

With the election of Yurii Meshkov as President of Crimea in January 1994, it appeared likely that the region would renew efforts towards sovereignty, as well as establishing closer links with Russia. In response, the Verkhovna Rada approved constitutional amendments, according to which the Ukrainian President could nullify any measures taken by the Crimean authorities he deemed to be illegal. In March a referendum was held in Crimea, simultaneously with the Ukrainian legislative elections; 70% of those voting in the referendum supported broader autonomous powers for Crimea. In May, following a vote by the Crimean parliament to restore the suspended Constitution of May 1992, the Ukrainian Government ordered the Crimean legislature to rescind its decision. In September 1994 the Crimean legislature voted to restrict the Crimean President's executive authority. Meanwhile, the Verkhovna Rada approved a constitutional amendment, permitting it to nullify any legislation adopted by the Crimean parliament that contravened the Ukrainian Constitution. In March 1995 the Ukrainian legislature voted to abolish both the Crimean Constitution of May 1992 and the Crimean presidency, and in April 1995 Kuchma imposed direct rule on Crimea.

In October 1995 the Crimean legislature approved a new Constitution. Before its final adoption by the Verkhovna Rada in December 1996, the Constitution underwent several amendments; notably, Ukrainian was recognized as the state language, although Russian was to be the language of all official correspondence of the autonomous republic. In February 1997, contrary to national law, which stipulates that the appointment of the Crimean Prime Minister is the prerogative of the Ukrainian President, the Crimean parliament arrogated to itself the power to appoint the regional Government. In April it appointed Anatolii Franchuk as the new Crimean premier, in place of Arkadii Demydenko. Kuchma suspended this resolution, declaring it to be a violation of the Ukrainian Constitution, but, following the approval of a second motion of no confidence in Demydenko, in June Kuchma consented to his dismissal. The Crimean legislature subsequently approved a new Council of Ministers headed by Franchuk. In October Kuchma exercised his veto over items of legislation approved by the Crimean Supreme Council—the adoption of Russian as the peninsula's official language of business communication, and the realignment of

Crimea's time zone with that of Moscow—that were regarded as an assertion of the primacy of Crimea's links with Russia. Further conflict arose between the national Government and the Crimean legislature in February 1998, following the approval of legislation by the Verkhovna Rada, whereby all Ukrainian citizens were to be eligible to contest the seats in the Crimean legislature—hitherto, only citizens resident in Crimea had been eligible. In addition, the new legislation stated that elections to the Crimean parliament were to be held simultaneously with the elections to the Verkhovna Rada in March, rather than in September, as had previously been decided by the Crimean Supreme Council.

Elections to the Crimean legislature in March 1998 brought the issue of the status of the Crimean Tatars to the fore, when demonstrations were staged by Tatars appealing for the right to vote. The OSCE estimated that about one-half of the 165,000 Tatars resident in Crimea did not have Ukrainian citizenship and were, therefore, ineligible to vote. Leonid Grach, the leader of the CPU in Crimea, was elected Chairman of the new Crimean Supreme Council. In May a new Council of Ministers was appointed, with Sergei Kunitsyn as Chairman. In January 1999 a new Crimean Constitution came into effect. Although citizenship had recently been granted to a number of Crimean Tatars, representatives of the group held a demonstration in May in Simferopol, demanding constitutional changes to ensure better representation and rights for Crimean Tatars and for the Crimean Tatar language to be recognized as a state language; subsequent protests culminated in a 20,000-strong demonstration in Simferopol in May 2000. In July 2001 the Supreme Council dismissed Kunitsyn from the premiership for the third time. Although Kuchma had refused to recognize the previous dismissals, in late July Kuchma accepted Kunitsyn's removal from office, and expressed support for the new premier elected by the Crimean Supreme Council, Valerii Gorbatov.

As campaigning for the concurrent elections to the Verkhovna Rada and the Crimean Supreme Council, to be held on 31 March 2002, commenced, controversy was provoked at the end of February by the invalidation of Grach's candidacy for a seat in the Supreme Council on technical grounds. Despite his disqualification, Grach's name appeared on ballot papers and he was re-elected to the Supreme Council in defiance of the decision of the Crimean Court of Appeal. The elections to the Crimean Supreme Council demonstrated a sizeable shift in support away from the communists towards the centrist Kunitsyn Team, named after its leader, which won 39 of the 100 seats in the Council; a pro-communist electoral alliance, the Grach bloc, received 28 seats. Three other parties obtained representation and 29 independent candidates were elected. In late April the Ukrainian Supreme Court approved Grach's appeal, thereby serving to legitimize his status as a deputy of the Crimean legislature, although he failed to be re-elected as Chairman of the Crimean legislature. The new parliament also voted for the dismissal of Gorbatov and the reappointment of Kunitsyn as Prime Minister, and allies of Kunitsyn established a legislative majority. None the less, in the concurrent elections to the Verkhovna Rada, the CPU remained the most popular party on the peninsula. For the first time, Crimean Tatar deputies were elected to the Verkhovna Rada, within the Our Ukraine bloc.

In early 2004 an increase in ethnic tension between Crimean Tatars and the Slavic inhabitants of the peninsula was reported. Although it appeared that disputes over land were the principal source of tension, some reports suggested that violence had been provoked by groups of Russian extremist nationalists and Cossack groups resident in neighbouring regions of Russia. In the first few months of the year, in advance of the 60th anniversary of the deportation of the Tatars from the peninsula, several clashes and violent incidents occurred, and in early April a petition, signed by over 35,000 Crimean Tatars, which alleged that the police force in Crimea were ignoring incidents of inter-ethnic violence against Tatars, was presented to President Kuchma. In April 2005 Kunitsyn resigned as Prime Minister of Crimea, following his appointment as an adviser to President Yushchenko; the Crimean Supreme Council voted to approve Anatolii Matviyenko as his replacement. Following the dismissal of Tymoshenko as Prime Minister of Ukraine in early September, the Crimean Supreme Council voted to dismiss the republican Government; Matviyenko duly resigned on 20 September. On 23 September the Crimean Supreme Council approved the appointment of Anatolii Burdyugov, the leader of the Crimean branch of Yushchenko's People's Union Our Ukraine party, as Prime Minister, and a new Government was formed at the end of the month. In late February 2006 the Crimean legislature voted to hold a referendum on the proposed introduction of Russian as a state language within the peninsula; however, President Yushchenko stated that the referendum would be unconstitutional, and this ruling was subsequently confirmed by the CEC.

Elections to the Crimean Supreme Council, held concurrently with local elections and with those to the Verkhovna Rada on 26 March 2006, were marred by allegations of electoral fraud; moreover, one candidate was killed on polling day. At the end of March the President's Representative in Crimea, Volodomyr Kulich, announced that a commission comprising senior officials of several ministries and law enforcement bodies was to be established to investigate the apparent electoral violations. Meanwhile, protesters outside the Crimean parliamentary building demanded that elections in districts where violations were found be declared null and void. The results of the elections were finally announced on 19 April. The For Yanukovych bloc (principally comprising the PR) obtained the largest proportion of the votes cast, with 32.6%; it was awarded 44 of the 100 seats in the Supreme Council. The second-placed party was the pro-Russian Union party, with 7.6% of the votes and 10 seats. The Kunitsyn bloc obtained 10 seats, the CPU nine, the People's Movement of Ukraine-Rukh and the BYuT each obtained eight seats, the far left Nataliya Vitrenko People's Opposition bloc obtained seven seats, and the 'Ne Tak' Opposition bloc (which comprised several centrist parties associated with allies of former President Kuchma) obtained four. In early June Viktor Plakida, a former energy sector executive and a member of the PR, was elected Prime Minister by the Supreme Council.

In late May 2006 the proposed staging of military exercises off the coast of Crimea, under the aegis of NATO and with the participation of the defence forces of 12 countries, was a focus for protests in the port of Feodosiya, in the east of Crimea, principally by Russian nationalists opposed to Ukrainian involvement with NATO. It was also reported that the local branches of the CPU and the PR supported the protests. Although similar exercises had taken place in the region on an annual basis since 1997, on each occasion, in accordance with the national Constitution, they had required the specific approval of the Verkhovna Rada. As political turmoil had prevented the Verkhovna Rada from approving the forthcoming exercises in early 2006, it became apparent that they had no legal standing. On 11 June some 200 US reserve troops began to leave Crimea, having been prevented from undertaking the construction work for which they had been contracted, and the proposed exercises were abandoned.

Meanwhile, there were heightened ethnic tensions on the peninsula during 2006, mostly relating to questions of land ownership. In the first half of the year clashes broke out on several occasions in protest against the operations of a market located on a traditional Crimean Tatar burial site. (The market was moved to a new location later in the year.) In December the Crimean branch of the CPU organized a 'people's referendum' on the peninsula (which was not, however, recognized as having any official status) on Ukraine's aspirations towards NATO membership. According to the results of the poll issued by the CPU, some 58% of eligible voters participated in the 'referendum', of whom almost 99% rejected the notion of Ukrainian accession to NATO.

Following the dissolution of the Verkhovna Rada and scheduling of pre-term elections for 30 September 2007, it was announced in July that Kunitsyn was again to head the pro-presidential coalition, reconstituted as Our Ukraine-People's Self-defence bloc, in Crimea. A number of electoral irregularities were reported in the Republic on 30 September; at the elections to the Verkhovna Rada, Yanukovych's PR secured some 61.0% of votes cast in the Republic, followed by the Our Ukraine-People's Self-defence bloc, with only 8.2%, the CPU, with 7.6%, and the BYuT, with about 6.9%.

Russia's military operation in Georgia in early August 2008, and recognition of the separatist regimes in South Ossetia and Abkhazia on 26 August, increased fears, both in Ukraine and internationally, of a similar conflict eventually breaking out in Crimea. In early September the Ukrainian Government expressed concern that Russian passports had been issued to (ethnically Russian) residents of Crimea, and accused Russia of encouraging instability. The Ukrainian authorities formally protested to the Russian consulate in Sevastopol; however, the Representative of the President of Ukraine in Crimea, Leonid Zhunko, denied that a large-scale issuance of Russian passports had been conducted. On 17 September the Crimean legislature approved an appeal to the Ukrainian Verkhovna Rada for the

recognition of the independence of Abkhazia and South Ossetia, while pro-Russian groups demonstrated outside the parliamentary building in support of the separatist authorities in those territories.

The election of Viktor Yanukovych to the presidency in early 2010 was reported to have encouraged separatist sentiments in Crimea; in February the republican legislature voted to adopt the Russian, rather than Ukrainian, variant of its name as its official designation, in infringement of the Ukrainian Constitution. In mid-March premier Plakida and the parliamentary Chairman submitted their resignations. On 17 March the Supreme Council elected the leader of the PR in Crimea, Vladimir Konstantinov, as the new Chairman. With the agreement of Yanukovych, Konstantinov's nomination of Vasilii Dzharty, also a prominent local member of the PR, as Prime Minister was approved by 82 deputies in the legislature on the same day. Yanukovych subsequently appointed Kunitsyn as his representative in the Republic. In May the Crimean legislature adopted a resolution requiring that the Russian language be used, together with Ukrainian, in official processes in the peninsula. Elections to the Supreme Council were conducted concurrently with local elections throughout Ukraine, on 31 October, under a new mixed single-mandate and proportional representation electoral system. The PR markedly strengthened its position in the Republic, obtaining 48.9% of the votes cast on the basis of party list votes and a total of 80 seats in the legislature, ahead of the CPU, with only 7.4% of the votes cast and five seats. The other parties represented in the new Crimean Supreme Council were the People's Movement of Ukraine-Rukh (with 7.0% of the votes cast and five seats), Union (5.3%, five seats), Russian Unity (4.0%, three seats) and A Strong Ukraine (3.6%, two seats). Konstantinov was re-elected as legislative Chairman.

Meanwhile, in October 2010 President Yanukovych appointed Plakida, initially in an acting capacity, as his representative in Crimea. Vladimir Yatsuba, a former minister in the Ukrainian Government and a PR member, was appointed to the position in January 2011. However, in June Yatsuba was appointed Head of Sevastopol City Administration, and Plakida again became the acting envoy of the President in the Republic. Dzharty died in August; he was succeeded as Prime Minister in an interim capacity by Pavel Burlakov. On 7 November Yanukovych appointed Anatoliy Mohilyov (Mogilev), hitherto Ukraine's Minister of Internal Affairs, and also a member of the PR, as premier. The appointment of Mohilyov prompted some concerns, since, as chief of police in Crimea in 2007–10, he had undertaken the suppression of Crimean Tatar protests over land rights.

Following the adoption, in July 2012, by the Ukrainian authorities of legislation permitting official status to be granted to minority languages in regions of Ukraine where they were spoken by at least 10% of the local population, the long-established but unofficial representative group of the Crimean Tatar population, the Mejlis, led by Mustafa Cemil, intensified its campaign for the Crimean Tatar language to receive official status in the Autonomous Republic. In September Supreme Council deputies made speeches in the legislature in Crimean Tatar (which were then translated into Russian) for the first time. The PR was again the most successful party in Crimea at elections to the Verkhovna Rada held on 28 October 2012, obtaining 51.2% of the votes cast in the Autonomous Republic.

Considerable controversy was caused in relation to the creation by presidential decree, in late January 2013, of a Council of Representatives of Crimean Tatars, which was intended to provide a means of representing Crimean Tatar interests to the republican and Ukrainian authorities. In that month Lentun Bezazi, a member of the Supreme Council and a former member of the CPU, was elected Head of the Council. Members of the existing Crimean Tatar representative bodies, the Mejlis and the Quriltay, refused to recognize the legitimacy of, or participate in, the Council. In March Cemil stated that any attempts by the state authorities to abolish the Mejlis (which Mohilyov had recently referred to as existing outside the legal framework of Ukraine) would provoke a violent response. Tensions were heightened further when the republican Government announced that, for the first time, members of the Mejlis (who had previously played a leading part in such commemorations) would effectively be excluded from the organization of official commemorations to mark the anniversary on 17–18 May of the 1944 deportation of the Crimean Tatars; Cemil announced the intention of leading an unofficial commemoration in the event that the exclusion was maintained.

Foreign Affairs

Regional relations

Following the collapse of the USSR in 1991, the Ukrainian leadership was notably reluctant to sign any union agreement with the other former Soviet republics that might compromise its declaration of independence. It was this reluctance to enter into a renewed political union that led to the establishment of the Commonwealth of Independent States (CIS, see p. 251) by President Kravchuk, and the leaders of Russia and Belarus, on 8 December. Uniquely among the states associated with the organization, Ukraine declined to ratify the agreement providing for its membership of the CIS (but remained a participating country). Although relations with Russia remained generally good following independence, tensions existed between those who sought to renew closer links with Russia and countries of 'Eurasia' and those who sought to emphasize Ukraine's independence and 'European' status. Ukraine agreed to a unified command for the strategic (principally nuclear-armed) forces of the former USSR, but began to establish its own conventional armed forces. In January 1994 a trilateral agreement on the removal of nuclear weapons from Ukraine was signed by Ukraine, Russia and the USA, and in November the Verkhovna Rada voted to ratify the Treaty on the Non-Proliferation of Nuclear Weapons (see p. 122). In December Ukraine formally signed the Treaty, and the Strategic Arms' Reduction Treaty (START) I entered into force. The transfer to Russia of Ukraine's nuclear weapons was completed by June 1996.

Throughout the 1990s Ukraine consistently refused to participate in organizations that it perceived as being dominated by Russia, although it became an associate member of the CIS Air Defence Agreement in 1995. In 1997 Ukraine initiated the establishment of the GUAM (Georgia-Ukraine-Azerbaijan-Moldova) grouping. In 2001 a permanent office of the grouping (known as GUUAM in 1999–2005, when Uzbekistan was also a member) was opened in Yalta, Crimea. In 2006, at a summit held in Kyiv, the grouping was formally inaugurated as a full international organization concerned with the promotion of democracy, energy security and strengthening relations; it was also redesignated as the Organization for Democracy and Economic Development—GUAM (see p. 477). As the Kuchma administration became increasingly isolated internationally in the early 2000s, Ukraine's relationship with Russia appeared to strengthen. In January 2003 Kuchma was elected as Chairman of the CIS, becoming the first non-Russian to hold that post. (He was, however, replaced by Russian President Vladimir Putin in 2004.) Proposals to join a 'single economic zone' with Belarus, Kazakhstan and Russia were approved by the Verkhovna Rada in September 2003, on the condition that participation did not contravene the Ukrainian Constitution, although interest in Ukraine's participation in such a zone waned following the election of Yushchenko as President in late 2004. In August 2005 Yushchenko and President Mikheil Saakashvili of Georgia, meeting in Borjomi, Georgia, signed a declaration on the creation of a nine-country Community of Democratic Choice. The alliance was officially launched in December at a meeting in Kyiv.

The principal controversy between Ukraine and Russia concerned ownership of the former Soviet Black Sea Fleet, based in Sevastopol, on the Crimean peninsula. Although both countries agreed in July 1992 to exercise joint control over the fleet for a transitional period of three years, in April 1995 the Russian parliament imposed a moratorium on plans to divide the fleet. Nevertheless, in June Russian President Boris Yeltsin and Kuchma agreed to the equal division of the fleet, with separate Ukrainian and Russian bases. The main Russian base was to be at Sevastopol, although the exact legal status of the city was left unresolved. Yeltsin and Kuchma signed an agreement on 31 May 1997, in accordance with which the Russian fleet was to lease three bays in Sevastopol for 20 years, while the Ukrainian fleet was to use the remainder. Upon expiry the treaty could be renewed for five years, but would then be subject to renegotiation. A bilateral Treaty of Friendship, Co-operation and Partnership was also signed, in which Russia for the first time recognized the sovereignty of Ukraine. Russia finally ratified the treaty in February 1999, and later that year and in March 2000 further agreements were signed between Russia and Ukraine pertaining to the fleet. In January 2003 a treaty delineating the land boundary between Russia and Ukraine was signed by Kuchma and Putin, although discussions on the status of the Sea of Azov, which lies between the two countries, remained unresolved. Work on the construction of a Russian dam in the Sea precipitated considerable controversy, and raised concerns that the territorial integrity of Ukraine was being violated. In December Presidents Kuchma and Putin signed an agreement on the use of the Sea of Azov, the entirety of which was defined as comprising the internal waters of both countries. Agreement was also reached on the maritime state boundary of Russia and Ukraine in the region.

The Ukrainian presidential election of 2004 caused considerable upheaval in diplomatic relations with Russia. During the course of the campaign, the Russian Government was accused of interference in favour of Yanukovych; notably, President Putin visited Ukraine before each round of voting to appear publicly with Yanukovych and Kuchma. Symbolically, and in accordance with promises made during his election campaign, President Yushchenko visited Moscow one day after his inauguration in January 2005, and emphasized the importance of maintaining co-operative relations with Russia. However, further diplomatic tension was caused by the appointment of Tymoshenko as Prime Minister in February, in part as a result of a warrant existing in Russia for her arrest on charges of the attempted bribery of Russian officials during her time as head of a Ukrainian natural gas trading company in the 1990s. In late 2005 the Russian state-controlled gas monopoly, Gazprom, issued demands that Ukraine pay market prices for the supply of natural gas, rather than the heavily subsidized rate (of US $50 per 1,000 cu m) that it had paid hitherto. Following the failure of the Ukrainian authorities and Gazprom to reach agreement, on 1 January 2006 Gazprom suspended supplies to Ukraine, a measure that caused considerable hardship in Ukraine, as well as resulting in the loss of supplies to other European countries that received gas from pipelines traversing Ukraine. On 4 January supplies of natural gas to Ukraine were restored, after Ukraine agreed to pay $95 per 1,000 cu m for a mixture of Russian and Turkmenistani natural gas, which was to be supplied to Ukraine by a Swiss-registered company, RosUkrEnergo.

The appointment of Yanukovych as Prime Minister in August 2006 facilitated an improvement in relations between Ukraine and Russia: on 15 August Yanukovych met Chairman of the Russian Government, Mikhail Fradkov, in Sochi, Russia, and on 22 December President Putin visited Ukraine for the first time since Yushchenko's election. On 3 October Gazprom threatened again to suspend natural gas supplies to Ukraine, on the grounds that it was owed US $1,300m.; on 9 October, however, it was announced that a compromise agreement had been reached, whereby Ukraine was to repay $1,200m. by transferring gas from underground storage facilities in Ukraine to Gazprom for further export. Tymoshenko, who had recently returned to the office of Prime Minister, strenuously criticized an agreement reached between Russia and Ukraine, which retained the intermediary trading company in gas supplies to Ukraine, RosUkrEnergo (jointly owned by Gazprom and a consortium of Ukrainian businessmen). Meanwhile, Russia strongly opposed Ukraine's formal request for NATO membership (see Other external relations). Putin subsequently warned that, in the event that Ukraine joined NATO and agreed to the deployment on its territory of elements of the planned US national missile defence system, Russia would be prepared to target its missiles at Ukraine. In February 2008 Gazprom warned that it would reduce supplies to Ukraine, in response to debts incurred during the previous month; it was subsequently announced that Ukraine and Russia had reached a debt settlement, and also agreed to discontinue use of RosUkrEnergo as an intermediary. Later in February, however, Gazprom claimed that Ukraine had failed to sign the negotiated agreements. After further discussions, in April the Ukrainian Government announced that agreement had been reached on a new payment scheme; at the insistence of the Russian authorities, RosUkrEnergo was to remain the intermediary company, operating within Russia.

Following Russia's military operation against Georgia in early August 2008, Yushchenko, together with the Presidents of Estonia, Lithuania and Poland and the Prime Minister of Latvia, visited Georgia in a demonstration of solidarity, where he attended a rally in support of President Saakashvili in Tbilisi, the Georgian capital. On 13 August Yushchenko issued a ruling, based on a resolution by the National Security and Defence Council, requiring Russia to request prior permission for movements of its Black Sea Fleet based at Sevastopol (after Russian vessels belonging to the Fleet participated in the conflict). Later in August he officially ended a bilateral agreement reached in 1992 (which had been abrogated by Russia in February) on Russian use of two Ukrainian radar stations, and offered to make them available to European nations.

In December 2008 a further dispute erupted with Russia, after Gazprom demanded some US $2,100m. owed by Ukraine for the non-payment of natural gas and incurred fines; although Ukrainian state utility Naftogaz Ukrainy announced at the end of that month that it was to pay $1,500m., continuing disagreement over the price Ukraine would pay for Russian gas and the level of transit fees to be paid by Gazprom during 2009 resulted in Russia's suspension of gas supplies to Ukraine on 1 January. After accusing Ukraine of abstracting Russian gas intended for export to Europe, Russia also halted supplies to Europe by way of Ukraine on 7 January (resulting in severe disruptions to supplies to some 18 European countries). Following intensive EU mediation and emergency discussions between Gazprom and Naftogaz, on 19 January Putin (as Russian premier) and Tymoshenko signed an agreement in Moscow whereby Ukraine would pay an average price for Russian gas in 2009 that would be 20% lower than that charged to European countries, while the transit price would remain unchanged (with both converging to market levels in 2010). Gas supplies to Europe by way of Ukraine were finally restored on 21 January. Following further discussions between Putin and Tymoshenko in Moscow at the end of April, it was agreed that Gazprom would not penalize Ukraine for failure to accept the contracted amount of gas in 2009 and would assist in payment of the transit fee to ensure supply.

In February 2009 Ukraine threatened to expel the Russian ambassador, former Russian premier Viktor Chernomyrdin, after he criticized the Ukrainian authorities; Chernomyrdin was transferred from the post in June. In an open letter in August, Russian President Dmitrii Medvedev accused Yushchenko of pursuing 'anti-Russian' policies and of supplying armaments to Georgian forces in the conflict of the previous year, and attributed responsibility to Ukraine for the periodic disruption of Russian gas supplies to Europe via Ukraine. At the beginning of September discussions between Tymoshenko and Putin resulted in a concession to allow Ukraine to pay only for the natural gas it consumed, rather than the amount that it was contracted to import from Russia. In November, following discussions in Yalta between Tymoshenko and Putin, it was confirmed that the gas transit fees paid by Russia to Ukraine would be increased significantly in the following year, while Ukraine would be charged the European market price for Russian gas. In January 2010, shortly after the defeat of Yushchenko in the first round of a presidential election, Medvedev finalized the appointment of a new Russian ambassador to Ukraine. Following his election to the presidency in February, Yanukovych pledged to restore cordial relations between Ukraine and Russia and to end the recurrent disputes over gas supplies. In mid-February Medvedev invited Yanukovych to Moscow. In March the new Ukrainian Prime Minister, Mykola Azarov, met Putin and Gazprom officials for discussions in Moscow, when Putin consented to further negotiations on gas prices. On 21 April Medvedev and Yanukovych, meeting in Kharkiv, reached an agreement whereby Russia was to grant Ukraine a substantial discount on the price of Russian gas, while Ukraine was to extend the lease on the base of the Black Sea Fleet in the Crimean peninsula (due to expire in 2017) for a further 25 years. (The Verkhovna Rada ratified the agreement on 27 April 2010.) Following a meeting in Sochi between Azarov and Putin at the end of April, Putin announced proposals for the merger of Gazprom and Naftogaz Ukrainy, and the integration of the two countries' nuclear industries. In May, during Medvedev's first official state visit to Ukraine, he signed a number of further agreements with Yanukovych, including one confirming the border between the two countries.

In April 2011 it was reported that the Ukrainian Government had failed to respond to an invitation, extended by Putin during a visit to Ukraine, to join Russia's newly established customs union with Belarus and Kazakhstan. In October Yanukovych and Medvedev met for discussions in eastern Ukraine; the Russian Government expressed displeasure at the sentence imposed earlier that month on former premier Tymoshenko in connection with the January 2009 gas agreement (see Domestic Political Affairs).

In February 2012 the Ukrainian Government threatened to lower substantially the level of gas imports from Russia, after failing to negotiate a further reduction in Russian gas prices. Later that month Ukrainian officials issued strenuous protests, after Russian quality control agency Rospotrebnadzor suspended imports of cheese from three major Ukrainian producers, on the grounds that they used excessive quantities of palm oil; the ban was ended in April. In March President Yanukovych and Putin issued pledges to deepen co-operation in a number of areas, following discussions in Moscow. It was reported, meanwhile, that Yanukovych had established closer links with the Russian authorities prior to elections in October, including agreement to the introduction of Russian advisers in the SBU and to consultation with the Russian Government over future security service appointments. After a proposed arrangement whereby Ukraine would purchase gas at Russian domestic prices, in exchange for the acquisition of Naftogaz Ukrainy by Gazprom, was abandoned, further disagreements arose with Gazprom over Russian gas prices and the level of supplies. In July Putin (who had returned to the Russian presidency) met Yanukovych in Yalta, and undertook negotiations on the possible admission of Ukraine to the Russian-led customs union. In February 2013 the Ukrainian Government refused to pay US $7,000m. demanded by Gazprom for unused gas that it had been contracted to purchase in 2012. Further discussions between Yanukovych and Putin took place in Moscow in March 2013; it was reported that the Ukrainian leader sought greater concessions on the price of Russian gas, in exchange for a new agreement favourable to Russia regarding the movements of its Black Sea Fleet. Despite Russian pressure, however, the Ukrainian Government failed to pledge to join the customs union, following statements issued by EU officials that membership of such a body was incompatible with an envisaged EU free trade agreement (see Other external relations).

Other external relations

Ukraine sought to counterbalance its close relations with Russia during the 1990s by a policy of engagement with Western nations and organizations, as part of what was termed a 'multi-vector' foreign policy. In 1994 Ukraine joined NATO's 'Partnership for Peace' (see p. 383) programme; a 'Charter on a Distinctive Relationship' was signed with the Organization in 1997, envisaging enhanced co-operation with the Alliance. The 'orange revolution' that brought Yushchenko to power was generally welcomed in the USA; in early April 2005 he visited the USA, meeting President George W. Bush and addressing the US Senate. During a visit to Kyiv in July 2009, US Vice-President Joseph Biden reaffirmed US support for Ukraine's aspirations for integration into Western institutions, emphasizing that this would not be affected by recent US efforts to achieve a rapprochement with Russia, but also urged reform of the energy sector.

Ukraine signed a trade agreement with the EU in June 1995, and was formally admitted to the Council of Europe (see p. 260) in November. The Ukrainian leadership had long expressed an intention to pursue full membership of the EU; however, the failure to abolish capital punishment (which is prohibited by the conditions of membership of the organization) before March 2000 was a source of tension, as was the slow pace of political and economic reform. President Yushchenko, who was elected in late 2004, emphasized in his earliest diplomatic pronouncements that he regarded the integration of Ukraine into both the EU and NATO as fundamental goals of his presidency. However, the return of Yanukovych as Prime Minister in August 2006 proved detrimental to Ukraine's attempts to enter into a Membership Action Plan with NATO. Ukraine's membership application to the WTO (see p. 444), submitted in 1993, was formally approved on 5 February 2008 and was ratified by the legislature in April. Meanwhile, in January 2008 Ukraine formally requested a NATO Membership Action Plan (MAP), which was regarded as preparatory to membership. (Opposition parties, notably the PR and the CPU, strongly criticized Ukraine's request for NATO membership.) At a NATO summit meeting, which was convened in Bucharest, Romania, on 2 April, Ukraine and Georgia were not offered a MAP, although the Alliance made clear that it welcomed a closer relationship with both countries. Following Russia's military action in Georgia in early August, an EU summit meeting on Ukraine, which was conducted in Paris, France, on 9 September, resulted in an offer of an Association Agreement, replacing a 10-year Partnership and Co-operation Agreement and providing for trade benefits and increased energy co-operation; negotiations on visa-free entry to EU states for Ukrainian citizens began in late October. In May 2009 Ukraine was included in the EU's Eastern Partnership programme, which envisaged the introduction of enhanced free trade and visa arrangements. In January 2010 Ukraine became the first non-member state to contribute forces to the multinational NATO Response Force. Following his installation as President, Yanukovych's first state visit in March was to Brussels, Belgium, where he discussed with EU officials a programme for the adoption of the Association Agreement, including the establishment of a free trade area. In July the Verkhovna Rada approved legislation, which was subsequently signed into force by Yanukovych, defining Ukrainian foreign policy as being based upon the 'non-bloc' status of the country (thereby excluding it from NATO membership), while emphasizing that it would seek to maintain constructive co-operation with a range of partners, including NATO, the EU, the CIS and Russia. The first summit meeting between the EU and Ukraine under the Yanukovych Government took place in Brussels in November, when the President issued assurances that Ukraine's closer relations with Russia would benefit Euro-Atlantic security and also sought to allay concerns regarding a perceived deterioration in democratic conditions in the country.

The sentence of imprisonment imposed on former premier Tymoshenko in October 2011 (see Domestic Political Affairs) attracted international criticism and prompted the EU to cancel a planned visit to Brussels by Yanukovych that had been scheduled to take place that month. In December negotiations on the Association Agreement were concluded at a meeting between Ukrainian and EU officials in Kyiv. In January 2012 the Parliamentary Assembly of the Council of Europe adopted a resolution demanding the release of political prisoners in Ukraine, notably including Tymoshenko. On 30 March, however, the EU and Ukraine initialled the Association Agreement, which included provisions for the establishment of a free trade area. In April the imprisonment of a former minister who had served under Tymoshenko, Valeriy Ivashchenko, prompted further critical statements from the US Administration and from EU High Representative for Foreign Affairs and Security Policy Catherine Ashton. In May international pressure over the case of Tymoshenko intensified following alleged mistreatment of her in prison; the Ukrainian Government was obliged to postpone a summit meeting in Yalta, after several European heads of state cancelled planned visits to the country. EU foreign ministers, meeting in Brussels in May, decided to postpone the signature of the Association Agreement. In addition, a number of EU government leaders, including those of Germany, the United Kingdom and France, in June boycotted 2012 football European Championship events in Kyiv; the tournament, which was co-hosted by Ukraine (with Poland), had been anticipated as an opportunity to improve Ukraine's international standing. In September the US Senate adopted a resolution urging the imposition of visa sanctions on officials involved in the imprisonment of Tymoshenko. Although the US Administration failed to implement the resolution, in October it withdrew the visa of Ukrainian Deputy Prosecutor-General Renat Kuzmin, after he reportedly conducted clandestine investigations relating to Tymoshenko during a visit to the USA in July. Despite alleged violations in the conduct of the legislative elections in October and the continued detention of Tymoshenko, on 10 December EU foreign ministers announced that they were prepared to sign the Association Agreement at the next Eastern Partnership summit meeting in November 2013; however, it was stipulated that the Ukrainian authorities were required to meet a number of conditions, including the redress of political convictions and extensive reforms of the judicial system in co-operation with the Council of Europe. Following discussions with Yanukovych in Brussels in February 2013, European Council President Herman Van Rompuy declared that the Ukrainian authorities were required to demonstrate progress in reforms by May, and the granting of a presidential pardon to seven prisoners in April, including former Minister of Internal Affairs Yuriy Lutsenko, was stated as having occurred in part in response to European lobbying efforts.

CONSTITUTION AND GOVERNMENT

Executive power is vested in the President and the Prime Minister, and legislative power is the prerogative of the 450-member Verkhovna Rada (Supreme Council), which is directly elected for a five-year term. The President is elected by direct, popular vote for a five-year term. The President appoints the Prime Minister and the members of the Cabinet of Ministers and may, in certain circumstances, order the dissolution of the legislature. Judicial power is exercised by the Supreme Court and by courts of general jurisdiction. Ukraine is a unitary state, divided for administrative purposes into 24 oblasts (regions), one autonomous republic (Crimea), and two metropolitan areas (Kyiv and Sevastopol). The Constitution guarantees local self-government to regions, cities, settlements and villages. Regional governors are appointed by the President.

REGIONAL AND INTERNATIONAL CO-OPERATION

Ukraine is a founder member of the Commonwealth of Independent States (CIS, see p. 251), but has not ratified the CIS Charter. Ukraine is a member of the European Bank for Reconstruction and Development (EBRD, see p. 276), the Organization of the Black Sea Economic Cooperation (BSEC, see p. 411) and the Organization for Democracy and Economic Development—GUAM (see p. 477). In June 1994 Ukraine signed an agreement of partnership and co-operation with the European Union (EU, see p. 281), which was ratified in 1998. Ukraine was admitted to the Organization for Security and Co-operation in Europe (OSCE, see p. 397) and the Council of Europe (see p. 260) in 1995. In 1994 Ukraine joined the 'Partnership for Peace' (see p. 383) programme of the North Atlantic Treaty Organization (NATO, see p. 380).

Ukraine was, as the Ukrainian Soviet Socialist Republic, a founder member of the UN. Prior to the dissolution of the USSR in 1991, both Ukraine and Belarus had formally separate UN membership from that of the USSR, despite both republics forming integral parts of the Union. Ukraine acceded to the World Trade Organization (WTO, see p. 444) in 2008.

ECONOMIC AFFAIRS

In 2011, according to the World Bank, Ukraine's gross national income (GNI), measured at average 2009–11 prices, was US $142,812m., equivalent to $3,120 per head (or $7,080 per head, on an international purchasing-power parity basis). During 2002–11 gross domestic product (GDP) per head increased, in real terms, at an average annual rate of 4.4% per year, while the population decreased by an average annual rate of 0.6%. Ukraine's GDP increased, in real terms, at an average annual rate of 3.7% in 2002–11. Real GDP increased by 5.2% in 2011.

Agriculture (including forestry and fishing) contributed 9.5% of GDP in 2011, and the sector provided 15.8% of employment in 2008. Ukraine has large areas of extremely fertile land, forming part of the 'black earth' belt, and the country is self-sufficient in almost all aspects of agricultural production. The principal crops are grain, potatoes, sugar beet and other vegetables. A programme to transfer state collective farms to private ownership was initiated in 1991, although by 1997 only 14% of land was managed by private farms, which, in that year, contributed some 46% of total agricultural output. During 2002–11, according to the World Bank, agricultural GDP increased at an average annual rate of 2.4%, in real terms. The GDP of the sector decreased by 1.3% in 2010, but increased by 4.5% in 2011.

Industry (including mining, manufacturing, construction and power) contributed an estimated 28.8% of GDP in 2011, and provided 23.4% of employment in 2008. Heavy industry dominates the sector, particularly metal-working, mechanical engineering, chemicals and machinery products. According to the World Bank, industrial GDP increased by an annual average rate of 1.9%, in real terms, in 2002–11. Real industrial GDP increased by 4.5% in 2011.

In 2003 some 3.7% of the work-force were engaged in mining and quarrying; the sector contributed 7.5% of GDP in 2011. Ukraine has large deposits of coal (mainly in the huge Donbass coal basin) and high-grade iron ore, and there are also significant reserves of manganese, titanium, graphite, natural gas and petroleum. Production of coal declined by some 53% in 1989–95, and in 1996 the Government implemented a major reorganization of the coal-mining industry, including the closure of several loss-making mines. According to UN estimates, during 2002–11, the GDP of the mining sector (including utilities) increased at an average annual rate of 1.5%, in real terms; the GDP of the sector (including utilities) increased by 6.2% in 2011.

The manufacturing sector provided 17.6% of employment in 2003, and the sector contributed 14.3% of GDP in 2011. According to the World Bank, during 2002–11 real manufacturing GDP increased by an average annual rate of 5.0%. The GDP of the sector increased by 4.5% in 2011.

The construction sector contributed 3.2% of GDP in 2011, and the sector provided 5.0% of employment in 2008. According to UN estimates, during 2002–11 construction GDP decreased, in real terms, at an average annual rate of 3.8%; the sector's GDP increased by 10.9% in 2011.

Ukraine is highly dependent on imports of energy products, of which Russia and Turkmenistan are the principal suppliers. Imports of mineral fuels comprised 34.6% of the value of total imports in 2011. Ukraine is also vitally important as an energy transit country, situated as it is between the mineral resource-rich countries of the former USSR and the developed economies of Europe. A pipeline from a new oil terminal at Odesa, on the Black Sea coast, to Brody, near the border with Poland, which was originally intended to carry petroleum from the Caspian Sea to Central and Western Europe, was completed in 2001; however, following Ukraine's failure to secure petroleum suppliers from the Caspian region, the pipeline entered operation in reverse direction, permitting Russian companies to pump their petroleum to the Black Sea for export. Two new nuclear reactors began energy production in 2004. In 2009 nuclear power accounted for 48.0% of Ukraine's electricity production; coal accounted for 36.6% and natural gas for 8.1%.

The services sector contributed 61.7% of GDP in 2011 and engaged 60.7% of the employed labour force in 2008. According to the World Bank, during 2002–11 the GDP of the sector increased, in real terms, by an average annual rate of 3.3%; the sector's GDP increased by 1.2% in 2011. A significant event for the development of the tourism sector in Ukraine was the announcement, in April 2007, that the country was to co-host, with Poland, the 2012 football European Championship finals.

In 2011 Ukraine recorded a merchandise trade deficit of US $18,031m., while there was a deficit of $10,233m. on the current account of the balance of payments. In 2011 the principal market for exports was Russia (accounting for 29.0% of the value of total exports). Turkey was another important export market. Russia was also the principal source of imports in 2011, providing 35.3% of all imports. Other significant suppliers of imports included Germany, the People's Republic of China and Belarus. The principal imports in 2011 were mineral products, machinery, mechanical and electrical equipment, chemical products, vehicles and transportation equipment, base metals, and plastics and rubber. The principal exports in that year were base metals and products of base metals, mineral products, machinery, mechanical and electrical equipment, vegetable products, chemical products and vehicles and transportation equipment.

In 2011 a consolidated budgetary deficit of 18,300m. hryvnyas was recorded, equivalent to 1.4% of GDP in that year. Ukraine's general government gross debt was 473,815m. hryvnyas in 2011, equivalent to 36.4% of GDP. Ukraine's total external debt was US $116,808m. at the end of 2010, of which $16,246m. was public and publicly guaranteed debt. In that year, the cost of servicing long-term public and publicly guaranteed debt and repayments to the IMF was equivalent to 40.7% of the value of exports of goods, services and income (excluding workers' remittances). According to International Labour Organization (ILO) estimates, in 2002–09 the average annual inflation rate was 12.8%. According to official figures, consumer prices decreased by 0.2% in 2012. Some 7.5% of the labour force were unemployed in 2012.

Ukraine's reliance on imported energy supplies, and its over-dependence on steel exports, were among the principal reasons that it was severely affected by the international financial crisis from 2008. In July 2010, following the announcement of an extensive programme of economic reforms, the IMF approved a new stand-by credit agreement for Ukraine, totalling US $15,100m. over a period of 29 months. In April 2011, however, the IMF suspended the disbursement of funds under the stand-by agreement, in response to the Government's failure to implement numerous reforms, including to the pensions system. With the aim of reducing dependence on Russian fuel imports, amid further disagreements with Russian state-controlled enterprise Gazprom over Russian gas prices, in early 2012 the Government launched a tender for hydrocarbons exploration and production in western Ukraine. In March the Government initialled an Association Agreement with the European Union (EU, see p. 281), which included provisions for a free trade area; however, EU objections to the imprisonment of several political opponents of the Yanukovych Government, notably Yuliya Tymoshenko (see Domestic Political Affairs), presented an impediment to ratification of the Agreement. In response to severe drought during 2012, in October the Government announced a ban on wheat exports. Growth slowed to 3.0% in that year (according to IMF projections), following a strong recovery in 2010–11. Despite continuing concerns over political imprisonments and other democratic conditions in Ukraine, in December 2012 the EU envisaged the signature of the Association Agreement in November 2013; however, it was stipulated that the Ukrainian authorities were required to demonstrate progress in a number of areas, including the redress of political convictions and extensive reforms of the judicial system. In February 2013 the EU agreed to provide Ukraine with some €610m. in financial assistance, contingent on the adoption of IMF-recommended policies. Although the Ukrainian Government was engaged in negotiations with the IMF in an effort to secure a new $15,000m. credit arrangement, it displayed continued reluctance to comply with requirements; the Fund particularly criticized large subsidies on gas and domestic heating, which were deemed to have placed considerable strains on the budget and contributed to a rapidly widening current account deficit.

PUBLIC HOLIDAYS

2014: 1 January (New Year), 7 January (Orthodox Christmas), 8 March (International Women's Day), 21 April (Orthodox Easter Monday), 1 May (Labour Day), 9 May (Victory Day), 9 June (Pentecost Monday), 28 June (Constitution Day), 24 August (Independence Day).

Statistical Survey

Principal source (unless otherwise stated): State Committee for Statistics, 01023 Kyiv, vul. Sh. Rustaveli 3; tel. (44) 226-20-21; fax (44) 235-37-39; e-mail info@ukrstat.gov.ua; internet www.ukrstat.gov.ua.

Area and Population

AREA, POPULATION AND DENSITY

Area (sq km)	603,700*
Population (census results)	
12 January 1989	51,706,742
5 December 2001	
Males	22,441,344
Females	26,015,758
Total	48,457,102
Population (official estimates at 1 January, rounded)	
2011	45,778,500
2012	45,633,600
2013	45,553,000
Density (per sq km) at 1 January 2013	75.5

* 233,090 sq miles.

POPULATION BY AGE AND SEX
(UN estimates at mid-2013)

	Males	Females	Total
0–14	3,386,840	3,206,125	6,592,965
15–64	14,910,727	16,325,694	31,236,421
65 and over	2,253,817	4,613,541	6,867,358
Total	20,551,384	24,145,360	44,696,744

Source: UN, *World Population Prospects: The 2010 Revision.*

POPULATION BY ETHNIC GROUP
(permanent inhabitants, census of 5 December 2001)

	'000	%
Ukrainian	37,541.7	78.13
Russian	8,334.1	17.34
Belarusian	275.8	0.57
Moldovan	258.6	0.54
Crimean Tatar	248.2	0.52
Others	1,393.9	2.90
Total	48,052.3	100.00

ADMINISTRATIVE DIVISIONS

	Area ('000 sq km)	Population (at 1 January 2013)*	Density (per sq km)
Oblasts			
Cherkasy	20.9	1,268,900	60.7
Chernihiv	31.9	1,077,800	33.8
Chernivtsi	8.1	907,200	112.0
Dnipropetrovsk	31.9	3,307,800	103.7
Donetsk	26.5	4,375,400	165.1
Ivano-Frankivsk	13.9	1,381,800	99.4
Kharkiv	31.4	2,744,400	87.4
Kherson	28.5	1,078,200	37.8
Khmelnytsky	20.6	1,314,000	63.8
Kirovohrad	24.6	995,200	40.5
Kyiv	28.1	1,722,100	61.3
Luhansk	26.7	2,256,500	84.5
Lviv	21.8	2,540,700	116.5
Mykolayiv	24.6	1,173,500	47.7
Odesa	33.3	2,395,200	71.9
Poltava	28.8	1,467,800	51.0
Rivne	20.1	1,156,900	57.6
Sumy	23.8	1,143,200	48.0
Ternopil	13.8	1,077,300	78.1
Transcarpathia	12.8	1,254,400	98.0
Vinnytsya	26.5	1,627,000	61.4
Volyn	20.2	1,040,000	51.5
Zaporizhzhya	27.2	1,785,200	65.6
Zhytomyr	29.9	1,268,900	42.4
Cities			
Kyiv	0.8	2,845,000	3,556.3
Sevastopol	0.9	383,400	426.0
Autonomous Republic			
Crimea	26.1	1,965,200	75.3
Total	603.7	45,553,000	75.5

* Official estimates, rounded.

PRINCIPAL TOWNS
(official estimates at 1 January 2012)

Kyiv (Kiev, capital)	2,814,858	Poltava	297,589
Kharkiv	1,441,362	Chernihiv	296,723
Odesa	1,008,162	Cherkasy	286,163
Dnipropetrovsk	999,577	Zhytomyr	271,895
Donetsk	955,041	Sumy	269,663
Zaporizhzhya	772,627	Khmelnytsky	263,703
Lviv	729,842	Horlivka	258,879
Kryvyi Rih	660,203	Chernivtsi	255,929
Mykolayiv	497,032	Rivne	250,174
Mariupol	464,457	Dniprodzerzhynsk	242,646
Luhansk	427,187	Kirovohrad	234,919
Vinnytsya	370,814	Kremenchuk	226,434
Makiyivka	356,118	Ivano-Frankivsk	224,600
Sevastopol	340,559	Ternopil	217,300
Simferopol	335,582	Lutsk	213,063
Kherson	300,666	Bila Tserkva	210,551

BIRTHS, MARRIAGES AND DEATHS

	Registered live births		Registered marriages		Registered deaths	
	Number	Rate (per 1,000)	Number	Rate (per 1,000)	Number	Rate (per 1,000)
2004	427,259	9.0	278,230	5.9	761,263	16.0
2005	426,085	9.0	332,138	7.1	781,964	16.6
2006	460,368	9.8	354,959	7.6	758,093	16.2
2007	472,657	10.2	416,427	9.0	762,877	16.4
2008	510,588	11.0	321,992	7.0	754,462	16.3
2009	512,526	11.1	318,199	6.9	706,740	15.3
2010	497,689	10.8	305,933	6.7	698,235	15.2
2011	502,595	11.0	355,900	7.8	664,588	14.5

Life expectancy (years at birth, official estimates): 71.0 (males 66.0; females 75.9) in 2011.

IMMIGRATION AND EMIGRATION

	2009	2010	2011
Immigrants	32,917	30,810	31,684
Emigrants	19,470	14,677	14,588

ECONOMICALLY ACTIVE POPULATION
(annual averages, '000 persons aged 15–70 years)

	2006	2007	2008
Agriculture, hunting, forestry and fishing	3,649.1	3,484.5	3,322.1
Mining and quarrying; manufacturing; electricity, gas and water supply	4,036.9	3,973.0	3,871.4
Construction	987.1	1,030.2	1,043.4
Wholesale and retail trade; repair of motor vehicles, motorcycles and personal and household goods; hotels and restaurants	4,406.9	4,564.4	4,744.4
Transport, storage and communications	1,428.8	1,451.9	1,465.8
Financial intermediation	286.0	344.4	394.9
Real estate, renting and business activities	1,041.9	1,134.7	1,150.4
Public administration and defence; compulsory social security	1,033.7	1,036.4	1,067.5
Education	1,690.5	1,693.7	1,702.4
Health and social work	1,356.7	1,359.0	1,369.9
Other community, social and personal service activities; private households with employed persons; extra-territorial organizations and bodies	812.8	832.5	840.1
Total employed	20,730.4	20,904.7	20,972.3
Total unemployed	1,515.0	1,417.6	1,425.1
Total labour force	22,245.4	22,322.3	22,397.4

Source: ILO.

2012 (annual averages, '000 persons aged 15–70 years): Total employed 20,354.3; Unemployed 1,657.2; Total labour force 22,011.5.

Health and Welfare

KEY INDICATORS

Total fertility rate (children per woman, 2010)	1.4
Under-5 mortality rate (per 1,000 live births, 2010) . . .	13
HIV/AIDS (% of persons aged 15–49, 2009)	1.1
Physicians (per 1,000 head, 2009)	3.2
Hospital beds (per 1,000 head, 2009)	8.7
Health expenditure (2009): US $ per head (PPP)	495
Health expenditure (2009): % of GDP	7.8
Health expenditure (2009): public (% of total)	55.0
Access to water (% of persons, 2010)	98
Access to sanitation (% of persons, 2010)	94
Total carbon dioxide emissions ('000 metric tons, 2008) . .	323,532.1
Carbon dioxide emissions per head (metric tons, 2008) . .	7.0
Human Development Index (2011): ranking	76
Human Development Index (2011): value	0.729

For sources and definitions, see explanatory note on p. vi.

Agriculture

PRINCIPAL CROPS
('000 metric tons)

	2009	2010	2011
Wheat	20,886.4	16,851.3	22,323.6
Barley	11,833.1	8,484.9	9,097.7
Maize	10,486.3	11,953.0	22,837.9
Rye	953.5	464.9	578.9
Oats	730.7	458.5	505.6
Millet	139.3	117.1	278.8
Buckwheat	188.6	133.7	281.6
Potatoes	19,666.1	18,705.0	24,248.0
Sugar beet	10,067.5	13,749.0	18,740.0
Peas, dry	493.6	452.4	364.3
Sunflower seed	6,364.0	6,771.5	8,670.5
Cabbages and other brassicas .	1,509.3	1,497.4	2,004.0
Tomatoes	2,040.8	1,824.7	2,111.6
Pumpkins, squash and gourds .	559.9	516.9	626.9
Cucumbers and gherkins . .	883.0	860.1	966.0
Chillies and peppers, green . .	155.3	163.6	185.2
Onions, dry	875.6	908.9	1,174.9
Garlic	150.1	157.4	171.9
Carrots and turnips . . .	686.4	714.6	864.2
Watermelons	531.0	626.5	617.6
Apples	853.4	897.0	954.1
Pears	145.9	141.7	153.1
Apricots	73.4	77.2	119.9
Sweet cherries	53.0	73.0	72.8
Sour (Morello) cherries . . .	115.8	154.5	172.9
Plums and sloes	136.7	154.5	134.7
Grapes	468.7	407.9	521.9

Aggregate production ('000 metric tons, may include official, semi-official or estimated data): Total cereals 45,406 in 2009, 38,679 in 2010, 56,256 in 2011; Total roots and tubers 19,666 in 2009, 18,705 in 2010, 24,248 in 2011; Total vegetables (incl. melons) 9,011 in 2009, 8,911 in 2010, 10,608 in 2011; Total fruits (excl. melons) 2,003 in 2009, 2,068 in 2010, 2,307 in 2011.

Source: FAO.

LIVESTOCK
('000 head at 1 January)

	2009	2010	2011
Horses	466	443	414
Cattle	5,079	4,827	4,494
Pigs	6,526	7,577	7,960
Sheep	1,096	1,197	1,101
Goats	631	636	631
Chickens	158,800	172,600	183,600
Ducks	8,720	9,780	10,777
Geese and guinea fowls . . .	6,820	5,940	6,270
Turkeys	2,200	1,800	1,880

Source: FAO.

LIVESTOCK PRODUCTS
('000 metric tons)

	2009	2010	2011
Cattle meat	453.5	427.7	399.1
Pig meat	526.5	631.2	704.4
Chicken meat	894.2	953.4	995.2
Cows' milk	11,363.5	10,977.2	10,804.0
Sheep's milk	27.9	51.6	49.2
Goats' milk	218.2	219.7	232.8
Poultry eggs	938.2	1,017.8	1,089.8
Hen eggs	883.8	973.9	1,064.2
Honey	74.1	70.9	70.3

Source: FAO.

Forestry

ROUNDWOOD REMOVALS
('000 cubic metres, excl. bark)

	2009	2010	2011
Sawlogs, veneer logs and logs for sleepers	4,801	5,735	6,300
Pulpwood	737	1,101	1,118
Other industrial wood* . . .	644	700	572
Fuel wood*	8,040	8,610	9,521
Total	14,221	16,146	17,511

* Unofficial figures.
Source: FAO.

SAWNWOOD PRODUCTION
('000 cubic metres, incl. railway sleepers)

	2009	2010	2011
Coniferous (softwood)	1,299	1,290	1,408
Broadleaved (hardwood) . . .	454	445	490
Total	1,753	1,735	1,898

Source: FAO.

Fishing

('000 metric tons, live weight)

	2008	2009	2010
Capture	195.4	213.2	186.0
Azov sea sprat	12.1	12.3	10.0
Gobies	8.7	7.7	8.8
Sardinellas	5.9	32.8	4.2
European pilchard (sardine) . .	27.6	13.6	14.4
European sprat	21.1	24.6	24.7
European anchovy	11.0	14.6	22.4
Other jack and horse mackerels.	0.5	8.1	26.8
Other mackerels	0.3	1.1	—
Antarctic krill	8.1	—	—
Aquaculture	24.3	24.1	23.0
Common carp	20.0	20.0	20.0
Silver carp	2.8	2.2	1.4
Total catch	219.8	237.3	209.0

Source: FAO.

Mining

('000 metric tons unless otherwise indicated)

	2008	2009	2010
Coal (Anthracite)*	14,000	13,000	14,000
Coal (Bituminous)*	63,400	59,000	61,000
Coal (Lignite)*	200	200	200
Crude petroleum	4,168	3,917	4,149
Natural gas (million cu m)	21.5	21.5	20.5
Iron ore: gross weight	72,688	66,476	78,171
Manganese ore†	1,446.6	932.0	1,589.3
Ilmenite concentrate*	520	500	500
Rutile concentrate*	60	60	60
Zirconium concentrates*	36	31	30
Uranium concentrate (metric tons)*†	830	830	850
Bentonite*	200	195	185
Kaolin	1,775	1,119	1,391
Potash salts (crude)*‡	12.0	12.0	n.a.
Native sulphur*	135	120	130
Salt (unrefined)	4,425	5,395	4,908
Graphite (metric tons)*	5,800	5,500	6,000
Peat	358	449	430

* Estimated production.
† Figures refer to the metal content of ores and concentrates.
‡ Figures refer to potassium oxide content.

Source: US Geological Survey.

2011 ('000 metric tons unless otherwise indicated): Coal (available) 61,756; Crude petroleum 2,424; Natural gas (million cu m) 19,214; Iron ore (gross weight) 80,581.

Industry

SELECTED PRODUCTS
('000 metric tons unless otherwise indicated)

	2009	2010	2011
Flour	2,734	2,632	2,587
Margarine, etc.	353	363	356
Sunflower oil (unrefined)	2,796	3,030	3,174
Fruit and vegetable juices	710	749	593
Sugar (white, crystalline)	1,275	1,805	2,586
Vodka and similar spirits ('000 hectolitres)	4,230	4,250	3,320
Beer ('000 hectolitres)	30,000	31,000	30,520
Soft drinks ('000 hectolitres)	14,700	1,480	1,420
Cigarettes (million)	114,000	103,000	95,400
Cotton yarn	6.7	5.0	2.5
Textiles (million sq m)	86.8	88.2	88.1
Coats for women and girls ('000)	1,783	1,874	1,567
Jackets, blazers, pullovers, etc. for women and girls ('000)	2,036	1,802	1,911
Trousers for men and boys ('000)	4,671	4,572	4,790
Trousers for women and girls ('000)	3,255	3,785	3,251
Knitted outerwear ('000 pieces)	3,119	3,897	2,670
Footwear (million pairs)	20.4	25.7	23.9
Particle board (unprocessed, '000 cu m)	1,295	1,471	1,642
Paper for household, sanitary and hygiene purposes	120	126	130
Boxes, cabinets and bags from paper and cardboard (million sq m)	783	867	875
Coke-oven coke	17,400	18,600	19,599
Coal-tar pitch	785	845	878
Motor spirit (petrol)	3,259	2,875	2,835
Gas-diesel (distillate fuel) oil	3,903	3,709	2,664
Residual fuel (Mazout) oils	2,600	2,464	2,148
Ammonia (synthetic)	3,033	4,163	5,264
Sulphuric acid	890	1,295	1,537
Nitric mineral or chemical fertilizers	2,166	2,285	2,940
Caustic soda (Sodium hydroxide)	78	86	159
Rubber tyres ('000)	4,805	5,430	3,586
Quicklime	4,101	4,241	4,253
Cement	9,500	9,500	10,515
Ceramic building bricks (million)	1,109	1,017	1,022
Cement building blocks (million)	1,057	1,297	1,139

—continued	2009	2010	2011
Cast iron	25,700	27,400	28,881
Steel (incl. semi-finished products)	30,300	33,300	35,511
Finished rolled ferrous metals	16,100	17,600	19,511
Pipes of ferrous metals	1,742	1,957	2,372
Tractors (number)	1,445	5,189	6,355
Household refrigerators ('000)	157	164	108
Household washing machines ('000)	164	167	312
AC motors and generators, universal motors, etc. ('000)	460	592	466
Electrical transformers ('000)	12,100	4,000	5,000
Low-tension electrical facilities ('000)	51,200	52,800	60,700
Television receivers ('000)	238	69	45
Passenger motor cars ('000)	66	75	97
Buses (number)	1,500	2,700	3,744
Trucks (incl. other than self-propelled, number)	15,200	44,500	55,900
Trailers and semi-trailers (number)	23,100	21,500	26,200
Electric energy ('000 million kWh)	174	189	194

Finance

CURRENCY AND EXCHANGE RATES

Monetary Units
100 kopiykas = 1 hryvnya.

Sterling, Dollar and Euro Equivalents (31 December 2012)
£1 sterling = 12.613 hryvnyas;
US $1 = 7.993 hryvnyas;
€1 = 10.546 hryvnyas;
100 hryvnyas = £7.93 = $12.51 = €9.48.

Average Exchange Rate (hryvnyas per US $)
2010   7.9356
2011   7.9676
2012   7.9910

GOVERNMENT FINANCE
(general government transactions, million hryvnyas)

Summary of Balances

	2009	2010	2011
Revenue	384,909	449,977	557,363
Less Expense	429,691	507,697	567,853
Net operating balance	−44,782	−57,720	−10,491
Less Net acquisition of non-financial assets	8,111	13,253	19,152
Net lending/borrowing	−52,893	−70,973	−29,642

Revenue

	2009	2010	2011
Taxes	208,758	235,713	313,678
Taxes on income, profits and capital gains	77,533	91,388	115,322
Taxes on goods and services	114,391	124,180	174,670
Social contributions	115,334	136,542	159,453
Grants	677	342	521
Other revenue	60,142	77,379	83,711
Total	384,909	449,977	557,363

Expense/Outlays

Expense by economic type	2007	2008	2009
Compensation of employees . .	74,454	100,433	108,768
Use of goods and services . . .	47,328	61,878	69,979
Interest	4,063	4,906	10,644
Subsidies	20,684	35,315	27,799
Grants	249	177	119
Social benefits	125,040	185,199	202,796
Other expense	20,715	19,296	9,587
Total	292,533	407,205	429,691

Outlays by functions of government*	2009	2010	2011
General public services . . .	34,264	46,213	149,030
Defence	9,663	11,347	13,242
Public order and safety . . .	24,346	28,826	32,638
Economic affairs	39,522	44,444	57,887
Environmental protection . .	2,539	2,872	3,891
Housing and community amenities	7,498	5,431	8,679
Health	37,933	46,119	49,787
Recreation, culture and religion .	8,471	11,680	10,909
Education	66,783	79,840	86,269
Social protection	210,435	247,320	177,020
Total	441,454	524,093	589,353

* Including net acquisition of non-financial assets.

Source: IMF, *Government Finance Statistics Yearbook*.

Consolidated budget (million hryvnyas): *Total revenue:* 272,967 in 2009; 314,506 in 2010; 398,554 in 2011. *Total expenditure:* 307,399 in 2009; 377,843 in 2010; 416,854 in 2011 (Source: Ministry of Finance, Kyiv).

INTERNATIONAL RESERVES
(US $ million at 31 December)

	2010	2011	2012
Gold (national valuation) . .	1,249.0	1,385.3	1,890.4
IMF special drawing rights . .	8.0	17.9	9.2
Foreign exchange	33,319.4	30,391.4	22,646.6
Total	34,576.4	31,794.6	24,546.2

Source: IMF, *International Financial Statistics*.

MONEY SUPPLY
(million hryvnyas at 31 December)

	2009	2010	2011
Currency outside depository corporations	157,029.4	182,989.9	192,664.8
Transferable deposits . . .	118,161.9	148,469.2	170,293.3
Other deposits	209,580.6	265,381.7	318,842.8
Securities other than shares . .	2,526.3	1,030.7	3,713.7
Broad money	487,298.2	597,871.6	685,514.6

Source: IMF, *International Financial Statistics*.

COST OF LIVING
(Consumer Price Index at December; base: December previous year = 100)

	2010	2011	2012
Food and non-alcoholic beverages .	110.6	101.7	97.7
Alcoholic and tobacco products .	122.1	108.8	107.0
Clothing and footwear	102.2	101.0	97.7
Housing, water, electricity, gas and other fuels	113.8	111.0	100.7
Furnishings, household equipment and routine maintenance of the house	101.2	103.5	100.5
Health	105.8	106.4	102.0
Transport	106.6	120.9	104.1
Communication	91.1	103.5	101.4
Recreation and culture . . .	102.5	103.2	100.2
Education	110.3	105.7	104.4
Restaurants and hotels . . .	107.4	107.2	102.8
Miscellaneous goods and services .	108.7	105.4	102.2
All goods and services . . .	109.1	104.6	99.8

NATIONAL ACCOUNTS
(million hryvnyas at current prices)

National Income and Product

	2009	2010	2011
Compensation of employees . .	451,343	540,651	636,722
Net operating surplus and mixed income	239,472	295,241	352,974
Domestic primary incomes	690,815	835,892	989,696
Consumption of fixed capital .	107,204	115,338	125,809
Gross domestic product (GDP) at factor cost	798,019	951,230	1,115,505
Taxes on production and imports .	134,842	149,602	204,136
Less Subsidies	19,516	18,263	17,562
GDP in market prices . . .	913,345	1,082,569	1,302,079
Primary incomes received from abroad	35,938	49,607	54,589
Less Primary incomes paid abroad	54,977	53,259	73,851
Gross national income (GNI) .	894,306	1,078,917	1,282,817
Less Consumption of fixed capital .	107,204	115,338	125,809
Net national income	787,102	963,579	1,157,008
Current taxes and transfers from abroad	34,967	39,777	45,187
Less Current transfers paid abroad	4,701	6,815	6,590
Net national disposable income	817,368	996,541	1,195,605

Expenditure on the Gross Domestic Product

	2009	2010	2011
Final consumption expenditure .	772,826	914,230	1,113,008
Gross capital formation . .	155,815	199,918	270,019
Gross fixed capital formation .	167,644	195,927	241,785
Changes in inventories . .	−12,274	3,616	27,714
Acquisitions, less disposals, of valuables	445	375	520
Total domestic expenditure .	928,641	1,114,148	1,383,027
Exports of goods and services . .	423,564	549,365	707,953
Less Imports of goods and services	438,860	580,944	788,901
GDP in market prices . . .	913,345	1,082,569	1,302,079

Gross Domestic Product by Economic Activity

	2009	2010	2011
Agriculture, hunting, forestry and fishing	65,758	82,641	110,564
Mining and quarrying	40,676	65,551	87,077
Manufacturing	141,878	158,483	166,382
Electricity, gas and water supply .	31,804	34,984	45,012
Construction	21,528	32,518	37,232
Wholesale and retail trade; repair of motor vehicles, motorcycles and personal goods . . .	129,997	164,826	203,755
Transport, storage and communications	97,050	111,013	133,196
Education	49,239	55,678	62,099
Health and social work . . .	34,573	42,181	45,825
Other economic activities . . .	234,827	252,098	274,308
Sub-total	847,330	999,973	1,165,450
Less Financial intermediation services indirectly measured .	50,849	45,814	45,649
Gross value added in basic prices	796,481	954,159	1,119,801
Taxes on products	119,988	130,957	184,195
Less Subsidies on products . .	3,124	2,547	1,917
GDP in market prices . . .	913,345	1,082,569	1,302,079

BALANCE OF PAYMENTS
(US $ million)

	2009	2010	2011
Exports of goods	37,134	47,299	62,383
Imports of goods	−42,477	−56,896	−80,414
Balance on goods	−5,343	−9,597	−18,031
Exports of services	14,946	18,327	21,269
Imports of services	−11,560	−12,712	−13,383
Balance on goods and services	−1,957	−3,982	−10,145
Primary income received . .	4,624	4,715	5,485
Primary income paid	−7,064	−6,724	−9,281
Balance on goods, services and primary income	−4,397	−5,991	−13,941
Secondary income received . .	3,460	4,042	4,751
Secondary income paid . . .	−799	−1,067	−1,043
Current balance	−1,736	−3,016	−10,233
Capital account (net)	595	187	98
Direct investment assets . .	−115	−692	−192
Direct investment liabilities . .	4,769	6,451	7,207
Portfolio investment assets . .	−8	−17	−48
Portfolio investment liabilities . .	−1,525	4,359	1,617
Other investment assets . .	−10,822	−10,748	−9,883
Other investment liabilities . .	−3,183	7,155	8,005
Net errors and omissions . . .	310	1,366	975
Reserves and related items .	−11,715	5,045	−2,454

Source: IMF, *International Financial Statistics*.

External Trade

PRINCIPAL COMMODITIES
(distribution by Harmonized System, US $ million)

Imports f.o.b.	2009	2010	2011
Prepared food, beverages, spirits and tobacco . .	2,034.3	2,504.9	3,026.7
Mineral products	15,695.1	21,127.9	30,029.6
Mineral fuels, oils, waxes and bituminous substances . . .	14,638.7	19,602.7	28,605.3
Crude petroleum	2,989.6	4,171.3	4,272.4
Natural gas	7,979.4	9,392.9	14,046.0
Chemicals and related products	5,319.3	6,441.7	8,020.8
Pharmaceutical products . . .	2,130.3	2,445.8	2,879.0
Plastics, rubbers, and articles thereof	2,663.8	3,661.4	4,498.4
Plastic and articles thereof . .	2,141.6	2,867.3	3,413.6
Textiles and textile articles .	1,416.9	1,974.8	1,989.8
Base metals and articles thereof	2,676.6	4,128.0	5,697.1
Iron and steel	1,117.5	1,921.4	2,776.8
Machinery and mechanical appliances, electrical equipment and appliances, parts and accessories .	6,257.0	8,167.0	12,795.1
Machinery and mechanical appliances, computers, etc. . .	3,947.8	4,563.8	7,112.4
Electrical machinery, equipment and parts, etc.	2,309.3	3,603.2	5,682.6
Vehicles, aircraft, vessels and associated transportation equipment	2,163.8	3,664.3	6,204.2
Vehicles other than railway or tramway rolling stock . . .	1,963.2	3,320.6	5,443.5
Total (incl. others)	45,435.6	60,740.0	82,608.2

Exports f.o.b.	2009	2010	2011
Vegetable products	5,034.9	3,976.3	5,532.0
Cereals	3,556.2	2,467.1	3,617.2
Animal or vegetable fats and oils, etc.	1,796.0	2,617.3	3,396.4
Prepared food, beverages, spirits, tobacco	2,088.0	2,571.1	2,939.0
Mineral products	3,900.1	6,731.3	10,259.7
Ores, slag and ash	1,340.1	2,576.2	3,916.7
Mineral fuels, oils, waxes and bituminous substances . . .	2,130.8	3,661.4	5,691.1
Chemicals and related products	2,515.2	3,479.2	5,390.3
Base metals and articles thereof	12,816.8	17,332.5	22,111.0
Iron and steel	10,252.5	14,626.6	18,466.1
Articles of iron and steel . . .	1,946.9	1,993.7	2,844.3
Machinery and mechanical appliances, electrical equipment and appliances, parts and accessories . .	5,014.3	5,670.4	6,759.0
Machinery and mechanical appliances, computers, etc. . . .	2,787.0	3,135.3	3,569.8
Electrical machinery, equipment and parts, etc.	2,227.4	2,535.1	3,189.2
Vehicles, aircraft, vessels and associated transportation equipment	5,014.3	3,262.4	4,854.8
Railway or tramway locomotives, rolling stock, track fixtures and fittings, signals, etc.	777.1	2,400.9	3,806.7
Total (incl. others)	39,702.9	51,430.5	68,394.2

PRINCIPAL TRADING PARTNERS
(US $ million)

Imports f.o.b.	2009	2010	2011
Austria	612.2	697.6	713.3
Belarus	1,692.8	2,567.6	4,211.8
China, People's Republic . . .	2,734.3	4,700.4	6,268.3
Czech Republic	622.1	747.9	1,181.3
France (incl. Monaco)	971.5	1,106.7	1,501.5
Germany	3,852.1	4,603.1	6,865.7
Hungary	678.3	1,214.3	1,326.7
Italy	1,139.8	1,390.3	2,005.8
Japan	519.5	801.8	1,014.1
Kazakhstan	2,033.9	766.2	1,675.9
Korea, Republic	567.6	786.0	1,236.0
Netherlands	677.5	837.9	1,186.8
Poland	2,170.3	2,788.8	3,183.3
Romania	488.1	682.2	1,125.7
Russia	13,235.8	22,198.0	29,132.2
Turkey	952.2	1,298.3	1,481.2
Turkmenistan	718.3	31.4	736.0
United Kingdom	651.1	821.0	1,128.6
USA	1,286.3	1,766.8	2,591.2
Uzbekistan	1,640.8	81.7	643.9
Total (incl. others)	45,435.6	60,740.0	82,608.2

Exports f.o.b.	2009	2010	2011
Azerbaijan	546.6	610.8	708.3
Belarus	1,258.9	1,899.2	1,922.3
Bulgaria	395.5	450.9	755.4
China, People's Republic . . .	1,434.4	1,316.6	2,180.0
Czech Republic	340.7	626.2	842.4
Egypt	1,013.3	1,328.0	1,335.6
Germany	1,248.1	1,499.5	1,763.8
Hungary	730.2	860.1	1,340.7
India	1,152.5	1,426.1	2,265.3
Iran	755.8	1,030.7	1,127.5
Italy	1,227.6	2,412.3	3,039.5
Jordan	474.5	519.0	448.5
Kazakhstan	1,418.4	1,300.5	1,857.5
Moldova	693.6	713.5	874.4
Netherlands	594.9	563.2	833.4
Poland	1,213.1	1,787.2	2,794.1

Exports f.o.b.—*continued*	2009	2010	2011
Romania	319.5	705.9	950.7
Russia	8,495.1	13,431.9	19,819.6
Saudi Arabia	498.2	644.5	817.0
Slovakia	433.7	568.2	843.0
Spain	570.4	411.7	970.6
Switzerland	453.3	472.2	62.5
Syria	753.3	646.8	920.6
Turkey	2,126.5	3,026.7	3,748.6
USA	250.6	812.2	1,113.8
Total (incl. others)	39,702.9	51,430.5	68,394.2

Transport

RAILWAYS
(traffic)

	2009	2010	2011
Passengers carried ('000 journeys)	425,975	427,241	429,785
Freight carried ('000 metric tons) .	391,523	432,897	469,308
Passenger-km (million) . . .	48,274	50,038	50,837
Freight ton-km (million) . . .	195,979	218,038	243,556

ROAD TRAFFIC
(motor vehicles in use)

	2007	2008	2009
Passenger cars	5,939,598	6,393,903	6,518,678
Motorcycles and mopeds . .	714,345	650,938	554,544
Buses and coaches	185,503	188,008	180,379
Lorries and vans	406,441	451,106	965,437

Source: IRF, *World Road Statistics*.

INLAND WATERWAYS

	2009	2010	2011
Passengers carried ('000 journeys)	7,734	7,631	8,027
Freight carried ('000 metric tons) .	9,798	11,057	9,867
Passenger-km (million) . . .	123	95	92
Freight ton-km (million) . . .	7,927	9,015	7,365

SHIPPING

Flag Registered Fleet
(at 31 December)

	2010	2011	2012
Number of vessels	625	606	595
Total displacement ('000 grt) . .	1,006.0	921.1	829.8

Source: Lloyd's List Intelligence (www.lloydslistintelligence.com).

International Sea-borne Freight Traffic
('000 metric tons)

	2009	2010	2011
Goods loaded	88,081.9	84,037.6	84,895.0
Goods unloaded	12,839.4	17,440.6	19,417.4

CIVIL AVIATION
(traffic on scheduled services)

	2009	2010	2011
Passengers carried ('000) . . .	5,131	6,105	7,505
Passenger-km (million) . . .	9,021	10,969	13,761
Total ton-km (million)	350	378	369

Kilometres flown (million): 35 in 2007; 68 in 2008; 71 in 2009 (Source: UN, *Statistical Yearbook*).

Tourism

TOURIST ARRIVALS

Country of residence	2010	2011	2012
Belarus	3,058,023	2,643,988	3,091,780
Hungary	944,777	862,051	742,445
Moldova	4,063,459	4,071,785	4,849,115
Poland	2,089,647	1,720,104	1,404,086
Romania	910,450	735,233	791,281
Russia	7,900,436	9,018,487	9,526,695
Slovakia	609,994	564,337	476,574
Total (incl. others)	21,203,327	21,415,296	23,012,823

Receipts from tourism (US $ million, excl. passenger transport): 3,576 in 2009; 3,788 in 2010; 4,294 in 2011 (provisional) (Source: World Tourism Organization).

Communications Media

	2009	2010	2011
Book production (titles) . . .	22,491	22,557	22,826
Newspapers (titles)	2,499	2,347	2,266
Magazines and other periodicals (titles)	2,515	2,822	2,886
Telephones ('000 main lines in use)	13,026.3	12,941.3	12,680.9
Mobile cellular telephones ('000 subscribers)	55,333.2	53,928.8	55,576.5
Internet subscribers ('000) . .	2,650	3,661	4,178
Broadband subscribers ('000) . .	1,908	2,955	3,168

Source: mainly International Telecommunication Union.

Education

(2012/13 unless otherwise indicated)

	Institutions	Teachers	Students
Pre-primary	16,100*	191,500†	1,428,000
Primary *and* General secondary .	19,700	510,000	4,222,000
Specialized secondary: vocational	972	265,100‡	423,300
Higher	823	121,300†	2,170,100

* Including some 900 with activities suspended.
† 1993/94 figure.
‡ 2008/09 figure.

Note: Most figures are rounded.

Pupil-teacher ratio (primary education, UNESCO estimate): 15.7 in 2009/10 (Source: UNESCO Institute for Statistics).

Adult literacy rate (UNESCO estimates): 99.7% (males 99.8%; females 99.6%) in 2010 (Source: UNESCO Institute for Statistics).

Directory

The Government

HEAD OF STATE

President: VIKTOR F. YANUKOVYCH (elected 7 February 2010; inaugurated 25 February).

CABINET OF MINISTERS
(May 2013)

The Cabinet of Ministers principally comprises representatives of the Party of the Regions.

Prime Minister: MYKOLA YA. AZAROV.

First Deputy Prime Minister: SERHIY H. ARBUZOV.

Deputy Prime Minister: YURIY A. BOYKO.

Deputy Prime Minister: KOSTYANTYN I. HRYSHCHENKO.

Deputy Prime Minister: OLEKSANDR YU. VILKUL.

Minister of the Cabinet of Ministers: OLENA L. LUKASH.

Minister of Agrarian Policy and Production: MYKOLA V. PRYSYAZHNYUK.

Minister of Culture: LEONID M. NOVOKHATKO.

Minister of Defence: PAVLO A. LEBEDEV.

Minister of Ecology and Natural Resources: OLEH V. PROSKURYAKOV.

Minister of Economic Development and Trade: IHOR M. PRASOLOV.

Minister of Education and Science: DMYTRO V. TABACHNYK.

Minister of Energy and the Coal Industry: EDUARD A. STAVYTSKY.

Minister of Finance: YURIY V. KOLOBOV.

Minister of Foreign Affairs: LEONID O. KOZHARA.

Minister of Health: RAISA V. BOHATYROVA.

Minister of Industrial Policy: MIKHAILO K. KOROLENKO.

Minister of Infrastructure: VOLODYMYR V. KOZAK.

Minister of Internal Affairs: VITALIY YU. ZAKHARCHENKO.

Minister of Justice: OLEKSANDR V. LAVRYNOVYCH.

Minister of Regional Development, Construction and Communal Services: HENNADIY P. TEMNYK.

Minister of Revenues and Duties: OLEKSANDR V. KLYMENKO.

Minister of Social Policy: NATALIA YU. KOROLEVSKA.

Minister of Youth and Sport: RAVIL S. SAFIULLIN.

MINISTRIES

Office of the President: 01220 Kyiv, vul. Bankova 11; tel. (44) 255-73-33; fax (44) 255-78-44; e-mail press@apu.gov.ua; internet www.president.gov.ua.

Office of the Cabinet of Ministers: 01008 Kyiv, vul. M. Hrushevskoho 12/2; tel. (44) 256-63-33; e-mail web@kmu.gov.ua; internet www.kmu.gov.ua.

Ministry of Agrarian Policy and Production: 01001 Kyiv, vul. Khreshchatik 24; tel. (44) 226-25-39; fax (44) 278-76-02; e-mail ministr@minapk.gov.ua; internet www.minagro.gov.ua.

Ministry of Culture: 01601 Kyiv, vul. Ivana Franka 19; tel. (44) 235-23-78; fax (44) 235-21-80; e-mail info@mincult.gov.ua; internet www.mincult.kmu.gov.ua.

Ministry of Defence: 01021 Kyiv, vul. M. Hrushevskoho 30/1; tel. (44) 253-04-71; fax (44) 226-20-15; e-mail admou@mil.gov.ua; internet www.mil.gov.ua.

Ministry of Ecology and Natural Resources: 03035 Kyiv, vul. Uritskoho 35; tel. (44) 206-31-15; fax (44) 206-31-07; e-mail press@menr.gov.ua; internet www.menr.gov.ua.

Ministry of Economic Development and Trade: 01008 Kyiv, vul. M. Hrushevskoho 12/2; tel. (44) 253-93-94; fax (44) 226-31-81; e-mail meconomy@me.gov.ua; internet www.me.gov.ua.

Ministry of Education and Science: 01135 Kyiv, pr. Peremohi 10; tel. (44) 486-24-42; fax (44) 236-10-49; e-mail ministry@mon.gov.ua; internet www.mon.gov.ua.

Ministry of Energy and the Coal Industry: 01601 Kyiv, vul. Khreshchatik 30; tel. (44) 531-36-89; fax (44) 239-44-30; e-mail kanc@mintop.energy.gov.ua; internet mpe.kmu.gov.ua.

Ministry of Finance: 01008 Kyiv, vul. M. Hrushevskoho 12/2; tel. (44) 206-59-47; fax (44) 425-90-26; e-mail infomf@minfin.gov.ua; internet www.minfin.gov.ua.

Ministry of Foreign Affairs: 01018 Kyiv, pl. Mykhailivska 1; tel. (44) 238-16-57; fax (44) 226-31-69; e-mail zsmfa@mfa.gov.ua; internet www.mfa.gov.ua.

Ministry of Health: 01601 Kyiv, vul. M. Hrushevskoho 7; tel. (44) 253-61-94; fax (44) 253-40-17; e-mail moz@moz.gov.ua; internet www.moz.gov.ua.

Ministry of Industrial Policy: 03035 Kyiv, vul. Surikova 3; tel. (44) 246-32-20; fax (44) 245-62-09; e-mail info@ppa.gov.ua; internet industry.kmu.gov.ua.

Ministry of Infrastructure: 01135 Kyiv, pr. Peremohy 14; tel. (44) 226-22-04; fax (44) 486-72-06; e-mail portal@mtu.gov.ua; internet www.mtu.gov.ua.

Ministry of Internal Affairs: 01024 Kyiv, vul. Ak. Bohomoltsya 10; tel. (44) 256-03-33; fax (44) 256-16-33; e-mail mail@centrmia.gov.ua; internet mvs.gov.ua.

Ministry of Justice: 01001 Kyiv, vul. Horodetskoho 13; tel. and fax (44) 228-37-23; e-mail themis@minjust.gov.ua; internet www.minjust.gov.ua.

Ministry of Regional Development, Construction and Communal Services: 01205 Kyiv, vul. V. Zhytomyrska 9; tel. (44) 284-05-11; fax (44) 226-22-08; e-mail minregion@minregion.gov.ua; internet www.minregionbud.gov.ua.

Ministry of Revenues and Duties: 04655 Kyiv-53, Lvivska pl. 8; tel. (44) 272-51-59; fax (44) 272-08-41; e-mail gromada@sta.gov.ua.

Ministry of Social Policy: 01601 Kyiv, vul. Esplanadna 8/10; tel. (44) 226-24-45; fax (44) 289-00-98; e-mail press@mlsp.gov.ua; internet www.mlsp.gov.ua.

Ministry of Youth and Sport: 01601 Kyiv, vul. Esplanadna 42; tel. (44) 289-12-64; fax (44) 289-12-94; e-mail press2@msms.gov.ua.

President

Presidential Election, First Ballot, 17 January 2010

Candidates	Votes	%
Viktor F. Yanukovych (Party of the Regions)	8,686,751	35.33
Yuliya V. Tymoshenko (Fatherland)	6,159,829	25.05
Serhiy L. Tihipko (Independent)	3,211,257	13.06
Arseniy P. Yatsenyuk (Independent)	1,711,749	6.96
Viktor A. Yushchenko (Independent)	1,341,539	5.46
Others	2,528,766	10.28
Against all candidates	542,824	2.21
Total*	24,588,257	100.00

* Including 405,542 invalid votes (1.65% of the total).

Second Ballot, 7 February 2010

Candidates	Votes	%
Viktor F. Yanukovych (Party of the Regions)	12,481,266	48.96
Yuliya V. Tymoshenko (Fatherland)	11,593,357	45.48
Against all candidates	1,113,069	4.37
Total*	25,493,529	100.00

* Including 305,837 invalid votes (1.20% of the total).

Legislature

Verkhovna Rada
(Supreme Council)

01008 Kyiv, vul. M. Hrushevskoho 5; tel. (44) 255-21-15; fax (44) 253-32-17; e-mail umz@rada.gov.ua; internet www.rada.gov.ua.

Chairman: VOLODYMYR V. RYBAK.

General Election, 28 October 2012*

Parties and blocs	A†	B†	Total
Party of the Regions	72	115	187
Fatherland	62	43	105
Ukrainian Democratic Alliance for Reform	34	6	40
Freedom	25	12	37
Communist Party of Ukraine	32	—	32
United Centre	—	3	3
Ukrainian People's Party	—	2	2
Radical Party of Oleh Lyashko	—	1	1
Independent candidates	—	43	43
Total	**225**	**225**	**450**

* Including the results of re-run elections in five single mandate constituencies in which the initial results were annulled.

† Of the 450 seats in the Verkhovna Rada, 225 (A) are awarded according to proportional representation on the basis of party lists, and 225 (B) are elected in single-mandate constituencies.

Election Commission

Central Electoral Commission of Ukraine (CEC) (Tsentralna vyborcha Komisiya Ukrainy): 01196 Kyiv, pl. L. Ukrainky 1; tel. (44) 286-84-62; e-mail post@cvk.gov.ua; internet www.cvk.gov.ua; Head VOLODYMYR SHAPOVAL.

Political Organizations

Since the 1990s Ukrainian politics has been characterized by frequent changes of formation and allegiance within and between various factions or blocs. In mid–November 2012 there were 200 political parties registered in Ukraine, of which the following were the most important:

Communist Party of Ukraine (CPU) (Komunistychna Partiya Ukrainy): 04070 Kyiv, vul. Borysohlibska 7; tel. (44) 238-93-76; e-mail press@kpu.net.ua; internet www.kpu.net.ua; banned 1991–93; advocates state control of economy and confederation with Russia; Sec. of Cen. Cttee PETRO M. SYMONENKO.

Fatherland (Batkivshchyna): 01133 Kyiv, bulv. Lesi Ukrainky 26/615; tel. (44) 286-42-36; fax (44) 285-69-07; e-mail sector@byti.org.ua; internet www.byut.com.ua; f. 1999; merged with Conservative Republican Party in 2002, and with Yabluko party in 2004; nationalist, populist, supportive of socially orientated economics; Chair. YULIYA V. TYMOSHENKO; 275,000 mems (2005).

Forward, Ukraine! (Ukraina—Vpered!): Kyiv, vul. M. Zhytomyrska 18B; e-mail a.gorbenko@korolevska.com.ua; internet ukraina-vpered.com; f. 1998; supports small and medium-sized business interests and modernization; Leader NATALIYA KOROLEVSKA.

Freedom (Svoboda): 02140 Kyiv, vul. Vyshnyakivska 6A/70; e-mail vo@svoboda.org.ua; internet www.svoboda.org.ua; f. 1995 as a political party; fmrly Social Nationalist Party of Ukraine; extreme nationalist; Chair. OLEH YA. TYAHNIBOK.

Front of Changes (Front Zmin): 04071 Kyiv, vul. Verkhniy Val 4A/17; tel. (44) 220-07-73; fax (44) 220-07-72; e-mail office@frontzmin.org; internet frontzmin.org; f. 2007; Pres. ARSENIY P. YATSENYUK.

Green Party of Ukraine (Partiya Zelenykh Ukrainy): 01001 Kyiv, vul. Chapayeva 2/16, POB 535B; e-mail sekretariat@greenparty.ua; internet www.greenparty.ua; f. 1990; Pres. DENIS D. MOSKAL.

Our Ukraine (Nasha Ukraina): 04070 Kyiv, vul. Borychiv Tik 22A; tel. and fax (44) 278-26-79; e-mail info@nasha-ukraina.org; internet www.razom.org.ua; f. 2005 as People's Union Our Ukraine to support administration of Pres. Viktor Yushchenko; renamed Our Ukraine People's Union 2007; present name adopted 2009; party voted in support of self-dissolution in March 2013; however, this was disputed by a faction, who announced that they would hold an alternative congress in May of that year; Chair. VIKTOR A. YUSHCHENKO.

Party of the Regions (PR) (Partiya Rehioniv): 01021 Kyiv, vul. Lypska 10; tel. (44) 594-95-31; fax (44) 594-74-30; e-mail partreg@ln.ua; internet www.partyofregions.org.ua; f. 1997 as the Workers' Solidarity Party of Regional Rebirth of Ukraine; present name adopted 2001; absorbed A Strong Ukraine in March 2012; Chair. MYKOLA AZAROV.

People's Movement of Ukraine-Rukh (PMU-R) (Narodnyi Rukh Ukrainy): 01034 Kyiv, vul. O. Honchara 33; tel. (44) 246-47-67; fax (44) 531-30-42; e-mail info@nru.org.ua; internet www.nru.org.ua; f. 1989 as popular movement (Ukrainian People's Movement for Restructuring); registered as political party in 1993; national democratic party; Chair. BORYS I. TARASYUK.

People's Party (Narodna Partiya): 01601 Kyiv, vul. Reitarska 6A; tel. (44) 270-61-86; fax (44) 270-65-91; e-mail info@narodna.org.ua; internet narodna.org.ua; f. 1996 as Agrarian Party of Ukraine; renamed People's Agrarian Party of Ukraine in 2004; present name adopted 2005; centrist; Leader VOLODYMYR M. LYTVYN.

People's Self-defence (Narodna Samooborona): 01133 Kyiv, vul. Lesi Ukrainky 10A; tel. (44) 529-31-31; fax (44) 451-47-29; e-mail edit@samooborona.in.ua; internet www.nso.org.ua; f. 1999 as Forward, Ukraine!; present name adopted 2010; Leader YURIY V. LUTSENKO.

Progressive Socialist Party of Ukraine (Prohresyvna Sotsialistychna Partiya Ukrainy): Kyiv, ul. Kreshchatik 42A; tel. and fax (44) 483-32-57; e-mail pspu@tsu.net.ua; internet www.vitrenko.org; f. 1996 by members of the Socialist Party of Ukraine; favours extension of Belarus-Russia Union to incorporate Ukraine; opposed to Ukraine seeking membership of NATO; Chair. NATALIYA M. VITRENKO.

Radical Party of Oleh Lyashko (RPL) (Radikalna Partiya Oleha Lyashka): 01008 Kyiv, vul. Hrushevskoho 5; tel. (44) 255-44-62; e-mail info@liashko.ua; internet www.rpl.kiev.ua; f. 2010; supports greater integration of Ukraine into the European Union; Leader OLEH LYASHKO.

Reforms and Order Party (Partiya 'Reformy i poryadok'): 01021 Kyiv, vul. Institutska 28; tel. (44) 536-91-26; fax (44) 536-91-27; e-mail ref_ord@i.com.ua; internet www.prp.org.ua; f. 1997 as Reforms and Order Party; changed name to Our Ukraine in mid-2004; in July 2005 the Ministry of Justice ruled that the party had acted unlawfully in adopting the name 'Our Ukraine', and the party reverted to its original name; Chair. SERHIY V. SOBOLYEV.

Socialist Party of Ukraine (SPU) (Sotsialistychna Partiya Ukrainy): 02100 Kyiv, vul. Bazhova 12; tel. and fax (44) 296-68-27; e-mail zegal@socialist.in.ua; internet www.spu.in.ua; f. 1991; formed as partial successor to the CPU; advocates democratic socialism; Chair. PETRO I. USTENKO.

Ukrainian Democratic Alliance for Reform (UDAR) (Ukrainsky Demokratychny Alyans za Reformy): Kyiv, vul. Hrushevskoho 3; tel. (44) 481-22-29; e-mail press.klichko@gmail.com; internet klichko.org; supportive of establishment of Ukraine as a democratic, social-market state under the rule of law; Leader VITALIY V. KLYCHKO.

Ukrainian People's Party (UPP) (Ukrainska Narodna Partiya): 01601 Kyiv, vul. Pushkinska 28A; tel. (44) 234-59-17; fax (44) 234-05-68; e-mail analit@unp.ua; internet www.unp.ua; f. 1999 as breakaway faction of People's Movement of Ukraine-Rukh by fmr leader Vyacheslav Chornovil; fmrly Ukrainian People's Movement-Rukh; present name adopted 2003; Chair. YURIY I. KOSTENKO.

Union Party (Partiya 'Soyuz'): Kyiv, vul. Pochaynyska 28A; internet mir.im; f. 1997; left-of-centre; supports closer relationship between Ukraine and Russia; Leader LEV YU. MIRIMSKII.

United Centre (Yedyny Tsentr): 04071 Kyiv, vul. Yaroslavska 56A; tel. (44) 207-44-77; fax (44) 207-44-72; e-mail press@edc.org.ua; internet www.edc.org.ua; f. 1999; fmrly Party of Private Property; Chair. VIKTOR BALOHA.

Diplomatic Representation

EMBASSIES IN UKRAINE

Afghanistan: 03037 Kyiv, vul. Hromovoi 14; tel. (44) 249-66-63; fax (44) 249-66-62; e-mail afembkiev@yahoo.com; internet www.afghanembassy.com.ua; Ambassador FAZLURRAHMAN FAZIL.

Algeria: 01014 Kyiv, vul. Zvirenetska 76A; tel. (44) 286-76-88; fax (44) 286-77-86; e-mail ambalgukr@gmail.com; Ambassador MOHAMED BACHIR MAZOUZ.

Argentina: 01901 Kyiv, vul. Fedorova 12; tel. (44) 581-33-27; fax (44) 238-69-22; e-mail eucra@mrecic.gov.ar; Ambassador LILA ROLDÁN VÁZQUEZ DE MOINE.

Armenia: 01901 Kyiv, vul. Volodymyrska 45; tel. (44) 234-90-05; fax (44) 235-43-55; e-mail armukraineembassy@mfa.am; internet www.armembassy.com.ua; Ambassador ANDRANIK MANOUKIAN.

Austria: 01901 Kyiv, vul. Ivana Franka 33; tel. (44) 277-27-90; fax (44) 230-23-52; e-mail kiew-ob@bmeia.gv.at; internet www.bmeia.gv.at/kiew; Ambassador WOLF DIETRICH HEIM.

Azerbaijan: 01901 Kyiv, vul. Hlubochytska 24; tel. (44) 484-69-40; fax (44) 484-69-46; e-mail kiev@mission.mfa.gov.az; internet www.azembassy.com.ua; Ambassador EYNULLA MADATLI.

Belarus: 01901 Kyiv, vul. M. Kotsyubynskoho 3; tel. (44) 537-52-00; fax (44) 537-52-13; e-mail ukraine@mfa.gov.ua; internet www.ukraine.mfa.gov.by; Ambassador VALENTYN V. VELICHKO.

Belgium: 01030 Kyiv, vul. Leontovicha 4; tel. (44) 238-26-00; fax (44) 238-26-01; e-mail kiev@diplobel.fed.be; internet www.diplomatie.be/kiev; Ambassador JANA ZIKMUNDOVA.

Brazil: 04070 Kyiv, vul. Borychiv Tik 22A; tel. (44) 425-93-64; fax (44) 425-95-40; e-mail kievbrem@brasil.kiev.ua; internet brasil.kiev.ua; Ambassador ANTÓNIO FERNANDO CRUZ DE MELLO.

Bulgaria: 01023 Kyiv, vul. Hospitalna 1; tel. (44) 246-72-37; fax (44) 235-51-19; e-mail embuln@i.kiev.ua; Ambassador KRASIMIR MIN-CHEV.

Canada: 01901 Kyiv, vul. Yaroslaviv Val 31; tel. (44) 590-31-00; fax (44) 590-31-09; e-mail kyiv@international.gc.ca; Ambassador TROY LULASHNYK.

China, People's Republic: 01901 Kyiv, vul. M. Hrushevskoho 32; tel. (44) 253-13-29; fax (44) 253-73-71; internet ua.china-embassy.org; Ambassador ZHANG XIYUN.

Croatia: 01901 Kyiv, vul. Artema 51/50; tel. (44) 486-21-22; fax (44) 484-69-43; e-mail croemb.ukraine mvpei.hr; internet ua.mvp.hr; Ambassador TOMISLAV VIDOŠEVIĆ.

Cuba: 01901 Kyiv, prov. Byekhtyerevsky 5; tel. (44) 486-57-43; fax (44) 486-19-07; e-mail secretaria@embcuba.com.ua; Ambassador ERNESTO ANTONIO SENTÍ DARIAS.

Czech Republic: 01901 Kyiv, vul. Yaroslaviv Val 34A; tel. (44) 272-21-10; fax (44) 272-62-04; e-mail kiev@embassy.mzv.cz; internet www.mzv.cz/kiev; Ambassador IVAN POČUCH.

Denmark: 01054 Kyiv, vul. Hoholivska 8; tel. (44) 200-12-60; fax (44) 200-12-81; e-mail ievamb@um.dk; internet www.ukraine.um.dk; Ambassador MICHAEL BORG-HANSEN.

Egypt: 01901 Kyiv, vul. Observatorna 19; tel. (44) 212-13-27; fax (44) 486-94-28; e-mail eg.emb_kiev@mfa.gov.eg; Ambassador OSAMA TAWFIQ YOUSEF BADR.

Estonia: 01901 Kyiv, vul. Pushkinska 43B; tel. (44) 590-07-80; fax (44) 590-07-81; e-mail embassy.kyiv@mfa.ee; internet www.estemb.kiev.ua; Ambassador SULEV KANNIK.

Finland: 01901 Kyiv, vul. Striletska 14; tel. (44) 278-70-49; fax (44) 278-20-32; e-mail sanomat.kio@formin.fi; internet www.finland.org.ua; Ambassador ARJA INKERI MAKKONEN.

France: 01901 Kyiv, vul. Reitarska 39; tel. (44) 590-36-00; fax (44) 590-36-24; e-mail ambafrance.kiev@ukrpost.ua; internet www.ambafrance-ua.org; Ambassador ALAIN REMY.

Georgia: 01032 Kyiv, bulv. T. Shevchenko 25; tel. (44) 220-03-40; fax (44) 220-03-48; e-mail kyiv.emb@mfa.gov.ge; internet www.ukraine.mfa.gov.ge; Ambassador MIKHEIL UKLEBA.

Germany: 01901 Kyiv, vul. B. Khmelnytskoho 25; tel. (44) 247-68-00; fax (44) 247-68-18; e-mail info@kiew.diplo.de; internet kiew.diplo.de; Ambassador CHRISTOPH WEIL.

Greece: 01901 Kyiv, vul. Panfilovtsiv 10; tel. (44) 254-54-71; fax (44) 254-39-98; e-mail greece@kiev.relc.com; internet www.mfa.gr/kiev; Ambassador GEORGIOS GEORGOUNTZOS.

Holy See: 01901 Kyiv, vul. Turhenyevska 40; tel. (44) 482-35-57; fax (44) 482-35-53; e-mail nuntiusua@gmail.com; internet www.nuntiatura.kiev.ua; Apostolic Nuncio THOMAS EDWARD GULLICKSON (Titular Archbishop of Polymartium).

Hungary: 01034 Kyiv, vul. Reitarska 33; tel. (44) 230-80-01; fax (44) 272-20-90; e-mail kev@li.hu; internet www.mfa.gov.hu/emb/kiev; Ambassador MIHÁLY BAYER.

India: Kyiv, vul. M. Berlinskoho 20B; tel. (44) 468-66-61; fax (44) 468-66-19; e-mail india@indianembassy.org.ua; internet www.indianembassy.org.ua; Ambassador RAJIV K. CHANDER.

Indonesia: 04107 Kyiv, vul. Otto Shmidta 8B; tel. (44) 206-54-90; fax (44) 206-54-97; e-mail kbri@indo.ru.kiev.ua; internet www.kemlu.go.id/kyiv; Ambassador NINIEK KUN NARYATIE.

Iran: 01901 Kyiv, vul. Kruhlouniversytetska 12; tel. (44) 253-85-43; fax (44) 254-02-53; internet www.iranembassy.com.ua; Ambassador AKBAR QASEMI-ALIABADI.

Iraq: 01014 Kyiv, vul. Zvirynetska 35; tel. (44) 268-04-40; fax (44) 286-04-45; e-mail kefemb@iraqmofamail.com; Ambassador SHORSH KHALID SAID.

Israel: 01901 Kyiv, bulv. L. Ukrainky 34; tel. (44) 586-15-00; fax (44) 586-15-56; e-mail info@kiev.mfa.gov.il; internet ukraine.mfa.gov.il; Ambassador REUVEN DINEL.

Italy: 01901 Kyiv, vul. Yaroslaviv Val 32B; tel. (44) 230-31-00; fax (44) 230-31-03; e-mail ambasciata.kiev@esteri.it; internet www.ambkiev.esteri.it; Ambassador FABRIZIO ROMANO.

Japan: 01901 Kyiv, prov. Muzeiniy 4; tel. (44) 490-55-00; fax (44) 490-55-02; e-mail jpembua7f@sovamua.com; internet www.ua.emb-japan.go.jp; Ambassador TADASHI IDZAVA.

Kazakhstan: 04050 Kyiv, vul. Melnykova 26; tel. (44) 489-18-58; fax (44) 483-11-98; e-mail post@kazakh.kiev.ua; internet www.kazembassy.com.ua; Ambassador ZAUTBEK K. TURISBEKOV.

Korea, Republic: 01034 Kyiv, vul. Volodymyrska 43; tel. (44) 246-37-59; fax (44) 246-37-57; e-mail korea@koremb.kiev.ua; internet ukr.mofat.go.kr; Ambassador KIM EUN-JOONG.

Kuwait: 04210 Kyiv, vul. Obolonska nab. 19; tel. (44) 391-51-60; fax (44) 391-51-63; e-mail kiev@mofa.gov.kw; Ambassador YOUSEF HUSSAIN AL-GABANDI.

Kyrgyzstan: 01901 Kyiv, vul. Malo-kitayevska 48A; tel. and fax (44) 500-59-36; e-mail embassy.kg.kiev@silvercom.net; internet kyrgyzembassy.com.ua; Ambassador ULUKBEK CHINALIEV.

Latvia: 01901 Kyiv, vul. I. Mazepy 6B; tel. (44) 490-70-30; fax (44) 490-70-35; e-mail embassy.ukraine@mfa.gov.lv; internet www.latemb.kiev.ua; Ambassador ATIS SJANITS.

Lebanon: 01030 Kyiv, vul. Chapayeva 4/3; tel. (44) 234-15-91; fax (44) 234-15-65; e-mail lebembukr@foreigh.gov.lb; Ambassador YOUSSEF SADAKA.

Libya: 04050 Kyiv, vul. Ovrutska 6; tel. (44) 238-60-70; fax (44) 238-60-66; Ambassador FEISAL AL-SHAARI.

Lithuania: 01901 Kyiv, vul. Buslivska 21; tel. (44) 254-09-20; fax (44) 254-09-28; e-mail amb.ua@urm.lt; internet ua.mfa.lt; Ambassador PETRAS VAITIEKŪNAS.

Macedonia, former Yugoslav republic: 03150 Kyiv, vul. I. Fedorova 12; tel. (44) 238-66-16; fax (44) 238-66-17; e-mail embmac@carrier.kiev.ua; Ambassador ACO SPASENOVSKI.

Malaysia: 01901 Kyiv, vul. Buslivksa 25; tel. (44) 286-89-40; fax (44) 286-89-42; e-mail malkiev@kln.gov.my; internet www.kln.gov.my/perwakilan/kiev; Ambassador CHUAH TEONG BAN.

Mexico: 03150 Kyiv, vul. A. Barbusa 5; tel. (44) 220-07-23; fax (44) 220-07-24; e-mail embamexucrania@mexico.kiev.ua; Ambassador BERENICE RENDON TALAVERA.

Moldova: 01901 Kyiv, vul. Yagotinska 2; tel. (44) 521-22-80; fax (44) 521-22-72; e-mail kiev@mfa.md; internet www.ucraina.mfa.md; Ambassador ION STĂVILĂ.

Morocco: 03680 Kyiv, vul. I. Fedorova 12; tel. (44) 284-33-26; fax (44) 568-58-84; e-mail morocco@kiev.farlep.net; Ambassador ABDEL-JALIL SAUBRY.

Netherlands: 01901 Kyiv, Kontraktova pl. 7; tel. (44) 490-82-00; fax (44) 490-82-09; e-mail kie@minbuza.nl; Ambassador PIETER JAN WOLTHERS.

Nigeria: 01015 Kyiv, bulv. Panfilovtsiv 36; tel. (44) 254-58-50; fax (44) 254-53-71; e-mail nigeriakyiv@yahoo.com; Ambassador FRANK NGOZI ISOH.

Norway: 01901 Kyiv, vul. Striletska 15; tel. (44) 590-04-70; fax (44) 234-06-55; e-mail emb.kiev@mfa.no; internet www.norway.com.ua; Ambassador JON ELVEDAL FREDRIKSEN.

Pakistan: 01015 Kyiv, pr. Panfilovtsiv 7; tel. (44) 280-25-77; fax (44) 254-45-30; e-mail parepkyiv@mail.kar.net; Ambassador AHMAD NAWAZ SALIM MELA.

Poland: 01034 Kyiv, vul. Yaroslaviv Val 12; tel. (44) 230-07-00; fax (44) 270-63-36; e-mail kijow.amb.sekretariat@msz.gov.pl; internet www.kijow.polemb.net; Ambassador GENRIK LITVIN.

Portugal: 01901 Kyiv, vul. I. Fedorova 12; tel. (44) 287-58-61; fax (44) 230-26-25; e-mail geral@embport.kiev.ua; Ambassador MÁRIO JESUS DOS SANTOS.

Romania: 01030 Kyiv, vul. M. Kotsyubynskoho 8; tel. (44) 234-00-40; fax (44) 235-20-25; e-mail romania@adamant.net; Ambassador CORNEL IONESCU.

Russia: 03049 Kyiv, Povitroflotskyi pr. 27; tel. (44) 244-09-61; fax (44) 246-34-69; e-mail rusemb@kv.ukrtel.net; internet www.embrus.org.ua; Ambassador MIKHAIL YU. ZUBAROV.

Serbia: 04070 Kyiv, vul. Voloska 4; tel. (44) 425-60-60; fax (44) 417-55-10; e-mail ambars@ukr.net; Ambassador DUŠAN LAZIĆ.

Slovakia: 01901 Kyiv, vul. Yaroslaviv Val 34; tel. (44) 272-03-10; fax (44) 272-32-71; e-mail embassy@kiev.mfa.sk; Ambassador PAVOL HAMŽÍK.

Slovenia: 01030 Kyiv, vul. B. Khmelnytskoho 48; tel. (44) 585-23-31; fax 585-23-43; e-mail vki@gov.si; internet www.kijev.veleposlanistvo.si; Ambassador NATAŠA PRAH.

South Africa: 01004 Kyiv, vul. V. Vasylkivska 9/2, POB 7; tel. (44) 287-71-72; fax (44) 287-72-06; e-mail saemb@utel.net.ua; Ambassador CHUPU STENLEY MATHABATHA.

Spain: 01901 Kyiv, vul. Khoriva 46; tel. (44) 492-73-20; fax (44) 492-73-27; e-mail embespua@mail.mae.es; Ambassador JOSÉ RODRÍGUEZ MOYANO.

Sweden: 01901 Kyiv, vul. Ivana Franka 34/33; tel. (44) 494-42-70; fax (44) 494-42-71; e-mail ambassaden.kiev@foreign.ministry.se; internet www.swedenabroad.com/kiev; Ambassador STEFAN GULLGREN.

Switzerland: 01015 Kyiv, vul. Kozyatynska 12, POB 114; tel. (44) 281-61-28; fax (44) 280-14-48; e-mail kie.vertretung@eda.admin.ch;

internet www.eda.admin.ch/kiev; Ambassador Dr CHRISTIAN SCHOE-NENBERGER.

Syria: 01901 Kyiv, vul. Biloruska 5; tel. (44) 489-55-51; fax (44) 483-97-88; e-mail syrian-emb@ukr.net; Ambassador MOHAMED SAID AKIL.

Turkey: 01901 Kyiv, vul. Arsenalna 18; tel. (44) 281-07-51; fax (44) 285-64-23; e-mail embassy.kiev@mfa.gov.tr; internet www.kiev.be.mfa.gov.tr; Ambassador MEHMET SAMSAR.

Turkmenistan: 01901 Kyiv, vul. Pushkinska 6; tel. (44) 278-68-70; fax (44) 279-30-34; e-mail embassy@ambturkm.org.ua; internet www.ambturkm.org.ua; Ambassador NURBERDI AMANMYRADOV.

United Kingdom: 01025 Kyiv, vul. Desyatynna 9; tel. (44) 490-36-60; fax (44) 490-36-62; e-mail ukembinf@gmail.com; internet ukinukraine.fco.gov.uk; Ambassador SIMON SMITH.

USA: 04112 Kyiv, vul. I. Sikorskoho 4; tel. (44) 490-40-00; fax (44) 521-51-55; e-mail press@usembassy.kiev.ua; internet ukraine.usembassy.gov; Ambassador JOHN F. TEFFT.

Uzbekistan: 01901 Kyiv, vul. Volodymyrska 16; tel. (44) 501-50-00; fax 501-50-01; e-mail embassy@uzbekistan.org.ua; internet www.uzbekistan.org.ua; Ambassador ALISHER ABDUALIEV.

Viet Nam: 01011 Kyiv, vul. Tovarna 51A; tel. (44) 284-57-40; fax (44) 284-55-42; e-mail vnemb.ua@mofa.gov.vn; internet www.mofa.gov.vn/vnemb.ua; Ambassador NGUYET HO DAC MINH.

Judicial System

The judicial system in Ukraine is implemented by local courts, courts of appeal, high courts, and the Supreme Court. Ukraine has no jury system; most cases are heard by either a single judge or two judges accompanied by assessors.

Constitutional Court of Ukraine (Konstytutsiynyi Sud Ukrayiny): 01033 Kyiv, vul. Zhylianska 14; tel. (44) 289-05-53; fax (44) 287-20-01; e-mail inbox@ccu.gov.ua; internet www.ccu.gov.ua; f. 1996; Chair. ANATOLIY S. HOLOVIN.

Supreme Court (Verkhovnyi sud Ukraini): 01024 Kyiv, vul. P. Orlyka 4; tel. (44) 253-33-13; internet www.scourt.gov.ua; composed of 20 judges; Chair. PETRO PYLYPCHUK.

Supreme Economic Court (Vyshyi hospodarskyi sud Ukraini): 01016 Kyiv, vul. Kopylenka 6; tel. (44) 536-18-01; fax (44) 536-18-18; e-mail public@vasu.arbitr.gov.ua; internet www.vgsu.arbitr.gov.ua; Chair. VIKTOR I. TATKOV.

Office of the Prosecutor-General: 01011 Kyiv, vul. Riznytska 13/15; tel. (44) 288-84-71; fax (44) 280-28-51; e-mail interel@gp.gov.ua; internet www.gp.gov.ua; Prosecutor-General VIKTOR P. PSHONKA.

Religion

State Department for Ethnic and Religious Affairs (Derzhavnyi departament u spravakh nationalnostei ta religii): 01025 Kyiv, vul. Volodymyrska 9; tel. (44) 278-17-18; e-mail mail@scnm.gov.ua; internet www.scnm.gov.ua; Chair. YURIY YE. RESHETNIKOV.

CHRISTIANITY

The Eastern Orthodox Church

Eastern Orthodoxy is the principal religious affiliation in Ukraine. Until 1990 all legally constituted Orthodox church communities in Ukraine were part of the Ukrainian Exarchate of the Russian Orthodox Church (Moscow Patriarchate). In that year the Russian Orthodox Church in Ukraine was renamed the Ukrainian Orthodox Church (UOC), partly to counter the growing influence of the previously prohibited Ukrainian Autocephalous Orthodox Church (UAOC). A new ecclesiastical organization was formed in June 1992, when Filaret (Denisenko), the former Metropolitan of Kyiv, united with a faction of the UAOC to form the Kyiv Patriarchate. In July 1995 Filaret was elected as Patriarch, prompting some senior clergy to leave the church and join the UAOC. In the late 2000s the UOC (Moscow Patriarchate) remained the largest church organization in Ukraine.

Ukrainian Autocephalous Orthodox Church: 01001 Kyiv, vul. Tryohsvyatytelska 8A; tel. (44) 228-02-00; e-mail uaocinfo@ukr.net; internet www.uaoc.info; f. 1921; forcibly incorporated into the Russian Orthodox Church (Moscow Patriarchate) in 1930; continued to operate clandestinely; formally revived in 1990; 600 parishes in 2013; Primate Metropolitan of Kyiv and All Ukraine MEFODIY (KUDRYAKOV).

Ukrainian Orthodox Church (Kyiv Patriarchate): 01004 Kyiv, vul. Pushkinska 36; tel. (44) 234-10-96; fax (44) 234-30-55; e-mail patb@ukrpack.net; internet www.cerkva.info; f. 1992 by factions of the Ukrainian Orthodox Church (Moscow Patriarchate) and Ukrainian Autocephalous Orthodox Church; 4,221 parishes in 2009; Patriarch of Kyiv and All Rus-Ukraine FILARET (DENISENKO).

Ukrainian Orthodox Church (Moscow Patriarchate): 01015 Kyiv, vul. Sichnevoho Povstannya 25/34; tel. (44) 255-12-04; fax (44) 254-53-01; e-mail press@orthodox.org.ua; internet www.pravoslavye.org.ua; exarchate of the Russian Orthodox Church (Moscow Patriarchate); 11,738 parishes in 2009; Metropolitan of Kyiv and All Ukraine VLADIMIR (SABODAN).

Russian Orthodox Old Belief (Old Ritual) Church (Russkaya Pravoslavnaya Staroobryadcheskaya Tserkov): 49017 Dnipropetrovsk, pr. K. Marksa 60/8; tel. (562) 52-17-75; internet www.staroobryad.narod.ru; f. 1652 by separation from the Moscow Patriarchate; divided into two main branches: the *popovtsi* (which have priests) and the *bezpopovtsi* (which reject the notion of ordained priests and the use of all sacraments, other than that of baptism). Both branches are further divided into various groupings. The largest group of *popovtsi* are those of the Belokrinitskii Concord; there were 56 parishes of the Belokrinitskii Concord in Ukraine in 2009, and 10 parishes of *bezpopovtsi* at that time; Bishop of Kyiv and all Ukraine SAVVAYIYE.

The Roman Catholic Church

Most Catholics in Ukraine are adherents of the Byzantine rites observed by the so-called 'Greek' Catholic Church, which is based principally in western Ukraine and Transcarpathia. In 2005 the seat of the head of the Byzantine-rite Church was relocated from Lviv to Kyiv. In 2009 there were 3,728 parishes of the Byzantine rites in Ukraine, 1,064 parishes of the Latin rite and 27 parishes of the Armenian rite. Ukraine comprises one archbishopric-major (of the Byzantine rite), three archdioceses (including one each for Catholics of the Latin, Byzantine and Armenian rites), three archiepiscopal exarchates, eight dioceses of the Byzantine rite (of which one is directly responsible to the Holy See) and six dioceses of the Latin rite. At 31 December 2007 there were an estimated 4,801,879 adherents (excluding adherents of the Armenian rite, for whom figures were not available), equivalent to some 8.8% of the population. Of that number, around 83% followed the Byzantine rite.

Bishops' Conference of Ukraine: 79008 Lviv, pl. Katedralna 1; tel. (32) 276-94-15; fax (32) 296-61-14; f. 1992; Pres. Most Rev. MIECZYSŁAW MOKRZYCKI (Latin Rite Archbishop of Lviv).

Byzantine Ukrainian Rite

Archbishop-Major of Kyiv and Halych: Most Rev. SVYATOSLAV SHEVCHUK, 01000 Kyiv, vul. Riznytska 11 B/28–29; tel. and fax (44) 254-56-10; e-mail arkyrparh-kv@voliacable.com; internet www.ugcc.org.ua; head of Ukrainian Greek Catholic Church; established in 1596 by the Union of Brest; forcibly integrated into the Russian Orthodox Church (Moscow Patriarchate) in 1946, but continued to function in an 'underground' capacity; relegalized in 1989; in 2005 the seat of the head of the Church was relocated from Lviv, in western Ukraine, to Kyiv.

Byzantine Ukrainian Rite Archbishop of Lviv: Most Rev. IHOR VOZNIAK, 79000 Lviv, pl. Sv. Yura 5; tel. and fax (32) 261-08-94; e-mail cerkvalviv@ugcc.org.ua.

Latin Rite

Latin Rite Archbishop of Lviv: Most Rev. MIECZYSŁAW MOKRZYCKI, 79011 Lviv, vul. Samchuka 14 A; tel. (32) 240-37-47; fax (32) 240-37-48; e-mail rka@lviv.farlep.net; internet www.rkc.lviv.ua.

Armenian Rite

Armenian Rite Archbishop of Lviv: (vacant).

Protestant Churches

There were 9,069 Protestant communities registered in Ukraine in 2009.

All-Ukrainian Union of Associations of Evangelical Christians-Baptists: 01004 Kyiv, vul. L. Tolstoho 3B; tel. (44) 234-82-41; fax (44) 234-16-76; e-mail office@ecbua.info; internet www.ecbua.info; 2,391 churches in Ukraine (2010); the Baptist Union of Ukraine is a part of the Euro-Asiatic Baptist Federation; Pres. VYACHESLAV V. NESTERUK.

All-Ukrainian Union of Christians of the Evangelical Faith—Pentecostals: 03115 Kyiv, vul. Oniskevycha 3; tel. (44) 452-21-40; fax (44) 424-25-80; e-mail mail@uupc.org; internet www.chve.org.ua; 1,553 parishes in 2009; Pres. MYKHAILO S. PANOCHKO.

Embassy of the Blessed Kingdom of God for All Nations: 02152 Kyiv, vul. Tychchyny 18, Legkoatletletichesky manezh; tel. (44) 553-15-38; e-mail mail@godembassy.org; internet www.godembassy.org; f. 1994 as Word of Faith (Slovo Very); Pastor SUNDAY ADELAJA; 25,000 mems (2005).

Ukrainian Lutheran Church: 01004 Kyiv, vul. O. Honchara 41A; tel. and fax (44) 234-08-04; 43 parishes in 2009; Leader of Church Bishop Dr VYACHESLAV HORPYNCHUK.

ISLAM

In 2009 there were 535 Islamic communities officially registered in Ukraine, of which 352 were members of the Religious Administration of Muslims of Crimea. An Islamic University was established in Donetsk in 1998.

All-Ukrainian Association of Muslim Social Organizations (Arraid): 04119 Kyiv, vul. Dekhtyarivska 25A; tel. (44) 490-99-00; fax (44) 490-99-22; e-mail office@arraid.org; internet www.arraid .org; f. 1997; brs in Dnipropetrovsk, Donetsk, Kharkiv, Luhansk, Lviv, Odesa, Simferopol, Vinnytsya, Sumy and Zaporizhzhya; publishes periodical *Arraid (Pioneer)* in Arabic and Russian and educational material in Russian, Tatar and Ukrainian; undertakes charitable and educational work; Chair. BASSIL MAREEI.

Religious Administration of Muslims of Ukraine: 04071 Kyiv, vul. Lukyanovska; tel. (44) 465-18-77; fax (44) 456-17-70; e-mail islam@i.kiev.ua; internet www.islamyat.org; f. 1992; 112 communities in Ukraine (excluding Crimea) in 2009; Mufti Sheikh AKHMED TAMIM.

JUDAISM

In 2001 there were 103,600 Jews in Ukraine (according to census results), despite high levels of emigration from the 1970s. From 1989 there was a considerable revival in the activities of Jewish communities. In 2009 there were 295 Jewish religious communities registered in Ukraine (of which 124 were members of the Chabad-Lubavitch sect), compared with 12 synagogues in 1989.

All-Ukrainian Jewish Congress: 01023 Kyiv, vul. Mechnykova 14/1; tel. (44) 235-71-20; fax (44) 235-10-67; e-mail vek@i.kiev.ua; internet www.jewish.kiev.ua; f. 1997; affiliated to the Federation of Jewish Communities of the CIS and the Baltic states; unites 183 communities; Chief Rabbi of Ukraine AZRIEL CHAIKIN.

Jewish Confederation of Ukraine: 04071 Kyiv, vul. Shekavystka 29; tel. (44) 463-70-75; fax (44) 463-70-88; e-mail eku@jewukr.org; internet www.jewukr.org; f. 1999; Chief Rabbi of Kyiv and All Ukraine YAAKOV DOV BLEICH.

The Press

In 2009 there were a total of 2,499 newspapers and 2,515 periodicals published in Ukraine. In addition to newspapers published in Ukraine, several newspapers and magazines published in Russia have a large circulation in Ukraine.

The publications listed below are in Ukrainian, except where otherwise stated.

PRINCIPAL NEWSPAPERS

Demokratychna Ukraina (Democratic Ukraine): 03047 Kyiv, pr. Peremohy 50; tel. (44) 454-88-30; fax (44) 456-91-21; e-mail dua@dua .com.ua; internet www.dua.com.ua; f. 1918; fmrly *Radyanska Ukraina* (Soviet Ukraine); 4 a week; Editor VITALIY ADAMENKO; circ. 62,400 (2005).

Den (The Day): 04212 Kyiv, vul. Marshala Tymoshenka 2L; tel. (44) 414-40-66; fax (44) 414-49-20; e-mail master@day.kiev.ua; internet www.day.kiev.ua; f. 1998; in Ukrainian and Russian; 5 a week; publ. by the Presa Ukrainy (Press of Ukraine) Publishing House; Editor-in-Chief LARYSA IVSHYNA.

Fakty i Kommentarii (Facts and Commentaries): 04116 Kyiv, vul. V. Vasylevskoy 27–29; tel. (44) 484-17-81; fax (44) 482-05-50; e-mail info@fakty.ua; internet www.facts.kiev.ua; f. 1997; daily; politics, economics, sport, law, culture; in Russian; Chief Editor ALEKSANDR SHVETS.

Gazeta po-Kiyevski (Kyiv Newspaper): 04080 Kyiv, vul. Frunze 104A; tel. (44) 205-43-85; e-mail online@pk.kiev.ua; internet pk.kiev .ua; in Russian; 6 a week; Chief Editor SERGEI TIKHII.

Holos Ukrayiny/Golos Ukrayiny (Voice of Ukraine): 03047 Kyiv, vul. Nesterova 4; tel. (44) 503-68-72; fax (44) 224-72-54; e-mail mail@ golos.com.ua; internet www.golos.com.ua; f. 1990; organ of the Verkhovna Rada; in Ukrainian and Russian; 5 a week; Editor ANATOLIY F. GORLOV; circ. 150,000 (2011).

Kommersant-Ukrayina (Businessman-Ukraine): 01011 Kyiv, vul. Rybalska 22; tel. and fax (44) 497-37-20; internet www.kommersant .ua; f. 2005; owned by Kommersant Publishing House (Russia); in Russian; Dir-Gen. and Chief Editor ANDREI GOGOLEV.

Kyiv Post: 01034 Kyiv, vul. Prorizna 22B; tel. (44) 234-65-00; fax (44) 234-30-62; e-mail letters@kyivpost.com; internet www.kyivpost .com; f. 1995; weekly; in English; Chief Editor BRIAN BONNER; circ. 25,000 (2010).

Literaturna Ukrayina (Literary Ukraine): 01061 Kyiv, bulv. L. Ukrainky 20; tel. (44) 286-36-39; e-mail lit_ukraine@ukr.net; f. 1927; weekly; organ of Union of Writers of Ukraine; Editor PETRO PEREBYJNIS; circ. 7,150 (2007).

Molod Ukrayiny (The Youth of Ukraine): 03047 Kyiv, pr. Peremohy 50; tel. (44) 454-83-90; fax (44) 235-31-52; e-mail mu@pressa.kiev.ua; f. 1925; 3 a week; Editor-in-Chief T. M. FEDORENKO; circ. 8,000 (2010).

Pravda Ukrayiny (The Truth of Ukraine): 01032 Kyiv, vul. Starovokzalna 17; tel. (44) 270-62-16; e-mail vyasnopolska@pravda-ua .info; internet www.pravda-ua.info; f. 1938; weekly; in Russian; Editor-in-Chief VIKTORIYA YASNOPOLSKAYA; circ. 187,000.

Robitnycha Hazeta/Rabochaya Gazeta (Workers' Gazette): 03047 Kyiv, pr. Peremohy 50; tel. (44) 454-84-94; fax (44) 456-68-85; e-mail mail@rg.kiev.ua; internet www.rg.kiev.ua; f. 1957; 5 a week; publ. by the Cabinet of Ministers and Inter-regional Association of Manufacturers; Ukrainian and Russian edns; Dir-Gen. and Chief Editor ANATOLIY KRYVOLAPOV.

Silski Visti (Rural News): 03047 Kyiv, pr. Peremohy 50; tel. (44) 441-86-32; fax (44) 446-93-71; e-mail ssk@silvist.kiev.ua; internet www.silskivisti.kiev.ua; f. 1920; 3 a week; Chief Editor V. D. HRUZIN.

Ukrayina Moloda (Ukraine The Young): 03047 Kyiv, pr. Peremohy 50; tel. and fax (44) 454-83-92; e-mail natali@umoloda.kiev.ua; internet www.umoloda.kiev.ua; f. 1991; 5 a week; independent; Editor MYKHAYLO DOROSHENKO; circ. 131,657 (2008).

Ukrayinska Pravda (Ukrainian Truth): Kyiv; e-mail ukrpravda@ gmail.com; internet www.pravda.com.ua; online only; in Russian and Ukrainian; Editor-in-Chief OLENA PRYTULA.

Ukrayinske Slovo (The Ukrainian Word): 01010 Kyiv, vul. I. Mazepy 6; tel. (44) 280-70-59; fax (44) 280-62-65; e-mail ukrslovo@ ukr.net; internet www.ukrslovo.com.ua; f. 1933; weekly; nationalist; Editor-in-Chief HRYHORIY KRYMCHUK.

Uryadoviy Kuryer (Official Courier): 01008 Kyiv, vul. Sadova 1; tel. (44) 253-12-95; fax (44) 253-39-50; e-mail letter@ukcc.com.ua; internet ukurier.gov.ua; f. 1990; 5 a week; organ of the Cabinet of Ministers; Editor-in-Chief ALLA KOVTUR; circ. 83,000 (2008).

Vechirniy Kyiv (Evening Kyiv): 04136 Kyiv, vul. Marshala Hrechka 13; tel. (44) 434-61-09; fax (44) 443-96-09; f. 1932; 5 a week; Editor-in-Chief OLEKSANDR BALABKO; circ. 45,000 (2005).

PRINCIPAL PERIODICALS

Barvinok (Periwinkle): 04119 Kyiv, vul. Dekhtyarivska 38–44; tel. (44) 213-99-13; fax (44) 211-04-36; e-mail barvinok@kievweb.com.ua; f. 1928; fortnightly; illustrated popular fiction for school-age children; in Ukrainian; Editor VASYL VORONOVYCH; circ. 40,000.

Berezil: 61002 Kharkiv, vul. Chernyshevskoho 59; tel. (57) 700-54-34; fax (57) 700-54-37; e-mail berezil@ukr.net; internet www.berezil .kh.ua; f. 1956; fmrly *Prapor*; monthly; journal of Union of Writers of Ukraine; fiction and socio-political articles; Editor-in-Chief VOLODYMYR NAUMENKO; circ. 5,000.

Delovaya Stolitsya (Capital City Business): 01135 Kyiv, vul. Pavlovska 29; tel. (44) 502-02-21; fax (44) 502-02-27; e-mail editor@dsnews.ua; internet www.dsnews.ua; f. 2001; weekly; in Russian; Editor-in-Chief INNA KOVTUN; circ. 67,500 (2008).

Dnipro (The Dnieper): 04119 Kyiv, vul. Dekhtyarivska 38–44; tel. (44) 446-11-42; f. 1927; 2 a month; novels, short stories, essays, poetry, social and political topics; Editor MYKOLA LUKIV.

Dzerkalo Tyzhnya/Zerkalo Nedyeli (Mirror of the Week): 03150 Kyiv, vul. Tverska 6; tel. (44) 529-78-22; fax (44) 269-74-52; e-mail info@mirror.kiev.ua; internet www.mw.ua/; f. 1994; weekly; politics, economics, the arts; Ukrainian and Russian edns; also English edition (online only); Editor-in-Chief VLADIMIR MOSTOVOI; circ. 57,000 (2006).

Fokus (Focus): 04080 Kyiv, vul. Frunze 104; tel. and fax (44) 207-45-54; internet www.focus.ua; f. 2006; political, weekly; Editor NADEZHDA SHALOMOVA; circ. 34,390 (2012).

Kompanyon (Companion): 01010 Kyiv, vul. I. Mazepy 10A; tel. (44) 494-25-01; fax (44) 494-25-05; e-mail administrator@companion.ua; internet www.companion.ua; f. 1996; weekly; in Russian; economics, politics, business; Editor-in-Chief A. POHORELOV; circ. 25,000 (2004).

Kyiv: 01025 Kyiv, vul. Desyatinna 11; tel. (44) 229-02-80; f. 1983; monthly; journal of the Union of Writers of Ukraine and the Kyiv Writers' Organization; fiction; Editor-in-Chief PETRO M. PEREBYJNIS.

Malyatko (Child): 04119 Kyiv, vul. Dekhtyarivska 38–44; tel. (44) 483-96-26; fax (44) 483-98-91; e-mail malyatko_1@online.com.ua; f. 1960; monthly; illustrated; for pre-school children; Editor-in-Chief ZINAIDA LESHENKO; circ. 35,000 (2012).

Nataly: 02156 Kyiv, vul. Kyoto 25; tel. (44) 593-05-85; e-mail natali@ blitz.kiev.ua; internet www.natali.ua; monthly; women's interest; Editor-in-Chief ZHANNA LAVROVA; circ. 679,115 (2002).

Natsionalna Bezpeka i Oborona (National Security and Defence): 01015 Kyiv, vul. Mazepy 34, Oleksander Razumkov

Ukrainian Centre for Economic and Political Studies; tel. (44) 201-11-98; fax (44) 201-11-99; e-mail info@uceps.com.ua; internet www.uceps.com.ua; f. 2000; monthly; energy, security, politics, economics, international relations; in Ukrainian and English; Chief Editor LYUDMYLA SHANHINA.

Politychna Dumka/Politicheskaya Mysl/Political Thought: 01030 Kyiv, vul. Leontovycha 5; tel. and fax (98) 413-62-17; e-mail politdumka@bigmir.net; internet www.politdumka.kiev.ua; f. 1993; current affairs and political analysis; Ukrainian, Russian and English edns; Editor MARINA PYROZHUK.

PostPostup (PostProgress): Lviv; f. 2006 as revival of earlier publication, itself a successor to the self-published (*samvydav/samizdat*) Soviet-era *Postup*; monthly; satirical, politics, culture; Chief Editor YURIY VYNNYCHUK; circ. 90,100 (2012).

Vitchyzna (Fatherland): 01021 Kyiv, vul. M. Hrushevskoho 34; tel. (44) 253-28-51; internet www.vitchyzna.ukrlife.org; f. 1933; 6 a year; Ukrainian prose and poetry; Editor OLEKSANDR HLUSHKO; circ. 50,100.

Vsesvit (The Universe): 01030 Kyiv, vul. Zolotovoritska 6A; tel. and fax (44) 235-63-41; e-mail myk@vsesvit-review.kiev.ua; internet www.vsesvit-journal.com; f. 1925; monthly; foreign fiction, literary criticism and reviews of foreign literature and art; Exec. Editor YURIY MYKYTENKO; circ. 2,000 (2012).

Yi (Ji): Lviv; e-mail info@ji.lviv.ua; internet www.ji-magazine.lviv.ua; f. 1989; independent; literature and literary criticism, culture, politics, philosophy; Chief Editor IRYNA MAGDYSH.

Zhinka (Woman): 03047 Kyiv, pr. Peremohy 50; tel. (44) 226-30-55; fax (44) 456-36-94; e-mail zhinka@cki.ipri.kiev.ua; f. 1920; monthly; publ. by Presa Ukrainy Publishing House; social and political subjects, fiction; for women; Editor LIDIYA MAZUR; circ. 55,000.

NEWS AGENCIES

Interfax-Ukrayina (Interfax-Ukraine): 01034 Kyiv, vul. Reitarska 8/5A; tel. (44) 270-74-65; fax (44) 270-65-69; e-mail pr@interfax.kiev.ua; internet www.interfax.kiev.ua; f. 1992; Dir OLEKSANDR MARTY-NENKO.

Respublika Ukrainian Independent Information Agency (UNIAR): 02005 Kyiv, vul. Mechnykova 14/1; tel. (44) 246-46-34; e-mail naboka@uniar.kiev.ua; internet www.uniar.kiev.ua; independent press agency; Dir S. NABOKA.

Ukrainian Independent Information and News Agency (UNIAN): 01001 Kyiv, vul. Khreshchatyk 4; tel. (44) 279-31-31; fax (44) 461-91-11; e-mail iviu@unian.net; internet www.unian.net; f. 1993; press agency and monitoring service; selected services are provided in Ukrainian, Russian and English; Gen. Dir OLEH I. NALIVAIKO; Editor-in-Chief OLEKSANDR A. KHARCHENKO.

Ukrayinski Novyni Informatsyonnoye Ahentstvo (Ukrainian News Information Agency): 01033 Kyiv, vul. Volodymyrska 61/11/41; tel. (44) 494-31-60; fax (44) 494-31-67; e-mail office@ukranews.com; internet www.ukranews.com; f. 1993; economic and political news; in Ukrainian, Russian and English.

UkrInform–Ukrainian National Information Agency: 01001 Kyiv, vul. B. Khmelnytskoho 8/16B; tel. (44) 279-81-52; fax (44) 279-86-65; e-mail office@ukrinform.com; internet news.ukrinform.com.ua; f. 1918; Dir-Gen. VIKTOR CHAMARA.

Publishers

In 1996 there were 6,460 book titles (including pamphlets and brochures) published in Ukraine (total circulation 50.9m.). By 2009 the number of book titles published in Ukraine had increased to 22,491.

Abetka (ABC): 32300 Khmelnitsky obl., Kamyanets-Podilsky, vul. Knyaziv Koriatovychiv 9A, POB 111; tel. and fax (3849) 2-73-84; e-mail abetka2006@mail.ru; internet www.abetka.in.ua; f. 1997; educational and reference literature for secondary schools; Dir YAROSLAV I. SYSYN.

Alerta (Alert): 04210 Kyiv, vul. Luhova 13, POB 112; tel. (44) 223-15-25; e-mail alerta@ukr.net; internet www.alerta.kiev.ua; f. 2001; economic and legal literature for higher education; Dir OLEKSANDR V. DIORDIYCHUK.

Avers: 79097 Lviv, vul. Furmanska 5/28; tel. (32) 240-30-41; fax (32) 240-30-40; e-mail avers@lviv.farlep.net; internet www.avers-books.com.ua; children's literature; f. 1994.

Diasoft: 03055 Kyiv, POB 100; tel. (44) 212-12-54; fax (44) 216-35-64; e-mail admin@diasoft.kiev.ua; internet www.diasoft.kiev.ua; f. 1993; computer studies and related literature.

Folio: 61002 Kharkiv, vul. Chubarya 11; tel. (57) 700-42-29; fax (57) 715-64-92; e-mail trade@folio.com.ua; internet folio.com.ua; f. 1991; classic and contemporary fiction in Russian, Ukrainian and French; Gen. Man. OLEKSANDR V. KRASOVYTSKIY.

Kalvariya (Calvary): 01054 Kyiv, POB 108; tel. and fax (38) 486-03-30; e-mail anetta@calvaria.org; internet www.calvaria.org; f. 1991; modern Ukrainian poetry and prose, and popular literature for children and adolescents; Dir ANETTA ANTONENKO.

Kamenyar (Stonemason): 79008 Lviv, vul. Pidvalna 3; tel. and fax (32) 235-59-49; e-mail vyd_kamenyar@mail.lviv.ua; internet www.kamenyar.com.ua; f. 1939; state-owned; fiction and criticism; in Ukrainian, Russian and Polish; Dir DMYTRO I. SAPIHA.

Karpaty (The Carpathians): 88000 Transcarpathian obl., Uzhhorod, pl. Zhupanatska 3; tel. (312) 23-23-66; fiction and criticism; Dir V. V. BRASLAVETS.

Lybid (Swan): 01004 Kyiv, vul. Pushkinska 32; tel. and fax (44) 279-11-71; e-mail info@lybid.org.ua; internet www.lybid.org.ua; f. 1835; University of Kyiv press; educational, scientific and reference literature; Dir OLENA A. BOYKO.

Medytsyna Svitu (Medicines of the World): 79071 Lviv, vul. Kulparkivska 131, POB 3566; tel. and fax (32) 224-47-15; e-mail msvitu@mail.lviv.ua; internet www.msvitu.com; f. 1997; medical journals, history, art and religion; Dir ZINOVIY MATCHAK.

Molod (Youth): 04119 Kyiv, vul. Dekhtyarivska 38–44; tel. (44) 211-02-18; in Ukrainian; Dir OLHA I. POLONSKA.

Muzichna Ukraina (Musical Ukraine): 01034 Kyiv, vul. Pushkinska 32; tel. (44) 235-11-08; fax (44) 279-66-54; f. 1966; books on music; in Ukrainian; Dir ANATOLIY K. ANDRIYCHUK.

Mystetstvo: 01034 Kyiv, vul. Zolotovoritska 11; tel. (44) 235-53-92; fax (44) 279-05-64; e-mail mystetstvo@ukr.net; f. 1932; fine art criticism, theatre and screen art, tourism, Ukrainian culture; in Ukrainian, Russian, English, French and German; Dir NINA D. PRYBEHA.

Naukova Dumka (Scientific Thought): 01601 Kyiv, vul. Tereshchenkivska 3; tel. (44) 234-40-68; fax (44) 234-70-60; e-mail info@ndumka.kiev.ua; internet www.ndumka.kiev.ua; f. 1922; scientific books and periodicals; research monographs; Ukrainian literature; dictionaries and reference books; in Ukrainian, Russian and English; Dir IHOR R. ALEKSEYENKO.

Osvita (Education): 04053 Kyiv, vul. Yu. Kotsyubynski 5; tel. and fax (44) 486-93-46; e-mail osvita@kv.ukrtel.net; internet www.osvitapublish.com.ua; f. 1920; state-owned; educational books for schools of all levels; Dir-Gen. BORYS MAKSYMETS.

Prapor (Flag): 61002 Kharkiv, vul. Chubarya 11; tel. (57) 706-15-84; fax (57) 706-15-81; e-mail prapor.kniga@mail.ru; internet www.prapor.kharkov.ua; fmrly Berezil; general; in Ukrainian and Russian; Dir LARISA O. BOBROVNIKOVA.

Prosvita (Enlightenment): 01032 Kyiv, bulv. Shevchenka 46; tel. (44) 234-15-86; fax (44) 234-95-23; e-mail office@prosvita.kiev.ua; internet www.prosvita.kiev.ua; f. 1990; textbooks for all levels of education from pre-school to higher education.

Takson: 04050 Kyiv, POB 25; tel. (44) 483-27-46; fax (44) 483-55-70; e-mail taxon@voliacable.com; internet www.taxon.kiev.ua; f. 1992; international law, politics, economics; Gen. Dir NINA FINIKOVA.

Ukrainskiy Pysmennyk (Ukrainian Writer): 01054 Kyiv, vul. O. Honchara 52; tel. and fax (44) 216-25-92; e-mail ukps@ln.ua; f. 1933; publishing house of the National Union of Writers of Ukraine; fiction; in Ukrainian; Chair. VOLODYMYR YAVORIVSKY.

Veselka (Rainbow): 04050 Kyiv, vul. Melnikova 63; tel. (44) 483-92-65; fax (44) 483-33-59; e-mail veskiev@iptelecom.net.ua; internet www.veselka-ua.com; f. 1934; books for pre-school and school-age children; in Ukrainian and foreign languages; Dir YAREMA P. HOYAN.

Znannya Ukrainy (Knowledge of Ukraine): 01034 Kyiv, vul. Striletska 28; tel. (44) 537-63-61; fax (44) 537-63-62; e-mail znannia@znannia.com.ua; internet www.znannia.com.ua; f. 1948; general non-fiction; Dir VOLODYMYR I. KARASOV.

Broadcasting and Communications

TELECOMMUNICATIONS

Regulatory Authority

State Committee for Communication and Information: 01001 Kyiv, vul. Khreshchatyk 22; tel. (44) 228-15-00; fax (44) 228-61-41; e-mail mailbox@stc.gov.ua; internet www.stc.gov.ua; Chair. YURIY O. PLAKSYUK.

Major Service Providers

Astelit: 03110 Kyiv, vul. Solomyanska 11A; tel. (44) 233-63-63; internet www.life.com.ua; f. 2005; 51% owned by TurkCell (Turkey) (q.v.); provides mobile cellular telecommunications services under the brand name 'Life'.

Golden Telecom GSM: 01021 Kyiv, vul. Khreshchatyk 19A; tel. (44) 490-55-55; fax (44) 490-00-70; e-mail info@goldentele.com;

internet www.goldentele.com; fixed-line and mobile cellular telephone services; CEO ANDRIY MILINEVSKY.

KyivStar GSM: Kyiv, vul. I. Mazepy 24; tel. (44) 466-04-66; internet www.kyivstar.net; f. 1997; 54.2% owned by Telenor (Norway); provides mobile cellular telecommunications services under the brand names 'Ace & Base' and 'Djuice' in major cities and other regions across Ukraine; Pres. IHOR LITOVCHENKO; 20m. subscribers (2007).

MTS Ukraina: 01601 Kyiv, vul. Leiptsizka 15; tel. (44) 240-00-00; fax (44) 230-02-56; e-mail slavik@umc.com.ua; internet www.umc.com.ua; f. 1991; fmrly Ukrainian Mobile Communications; present name adopted 2007; 100% owned by MTS (Russia); Gen. Man. VASILIY LATSANICH.

UkrTelecom: 01601 Kyiv, bulv. Shevchenka 18; tel. (44) 235-00-01; fax (44) 234-12-49; e-mail info@ukrtelecom.ua; internet www.ukrtelecom.ua; f. 1993; national fixed telecommunications network operator; provides national and international telecommunications services; Chair. of Bd HEORHIY B. DZEKON.

BROADCASTING

Regulatory Authorities

National Television and Radio Broadcasting Council of Ukraine: 01601 Kyiv, vul. Prorizna 2; tel. and fax (44) 278-75-75; e-mail pressa@nrada.gov.ua; internet www.nrada.gov.ua; f. 1994; monitoring and supervisory; issues broadcasting licences; Chair. VOLODYMYR A. MANZHOSOV.

State Committee for Television and Radio Broadcasting (Derzhavnyi komitet telebachennya i radiomovlennya Ukrainy): 01001 Kyiv, vul. Khreshchatyk 26/206; tel. (44) 239-63-89; fax (44) 279-44-50; e-mail office@comin.gov.ua; internet comin.kmu.gov.ua; responsibilities include the supervision of 27 state-controlled television and radio companies; Chair. OLEKSANDR V. KURDINOVICH.

Radio

Hromadske (Community) Radio: 01025 Kyiv, vul. Volodymyrska 61/11/50; tel. (44) 494-40-14; information, news and discussion programmes.

National Radio Co of Ukraine-Ukrainian Radio (Natsionalna Radiokompaniya Ukrainy-Ukrainske Radio): 01001 Kyiv, vul. Khreshchatyk 26; tel. (44) 279-17-57; fax (44) 279-34-77; e-mail krutouz@nrcu.gov.ua; internet www.nrcu.gov.ua; state-owned; domestic broadcasts; also international broadcasts in English, German, Romanian and Ukrainian; Gen. Dir TARAS AVRAKHOV.

Several independent radio stations broadcast to the major cities of Ukraine.

Television

National Television Co of Ukraine (Natsionalna telekompaniya Ukrainy): 04119 Kyiv, vul. Melnykova 42; tel. (44) 481-43-86; f. 1965; owns Pershy Natsionalny TV channel (q.v.); Chair. YEGOR A. BENKENDORF.

1+1: 01001 Kyiv, vul. Khreshchatyk 7/11; tel. and fax (44) 490-01-01; e-mail contact@1plus1.tv; internet www.1plus1.tv; f. 1995; independent; broadcasts for 24 hours daily to 95% of Ukrainian population; Chair. of Bd of Dirs OLEKSANDR YU. RODNYANSKY.

5 Kanal: 04176 Kyiv, vul. Elektrykiv 26; tel. and fax (44) 239-16-86; internet 5.ua; f. 2003; terrestrial broadcasts to 14 cities, and cable and satellite broadcasts; 24-hour news broadcasts; Dir-Gen. IVAN ADAMCHUK.

ICTV: 01033 Kyiv, vul. Pankivska 11; tel. (44) 288-19-19; internet ictv.ua; f. 1992.

Inter: 01054 Kyiv, vul. Dmitriyevska 30; tel. and fax (44) 490-67-65; e-mail pr@inter.ua; internet www.inter.ua; f. 1996; Chair. YAROSLAV POROKHNYAK.

Novy Kanal (New Channel): 01054 Kyiv, vul. Turhenevska 25; tel. (44) 501-99-28; fax (44) 501-99-20; e-mail post@novy.tv; internet www.novy.tv; f. 1998; broadcasts in Ukrainian and Russian; Dir-Gen. IRYNA LYSENKO.

Pershy Natsionalny (First National): 04119 Kyiv, vul. Melnykova 42; tel. (44) 241-39-09; fax (44) 246-88-48; internet 1tv.com.ua; f. 1965; owned by the National Television Co of Ukraine; Gen. Dir (Pres.) YEGOR A. BENKENDORF.

STB: 03113 Kyiv, vul. Shevtsova 1; tel. (44) 501-98-99; e-mail info@stb.ua; internet stb.ua; f. 1997; Chair. of Bd VOLODYMYR BORODYANSKY.

Telekanal 'Ukraina': 03148 Kyiv, vul. Heroyiv Kosmosu 4; tel. (44) 495-85-55; internet kanalukraina.tv; 100% owned by System Capital Management; offices in Kyiv and Donetsk; Dir MARYNA MYRGORODSKA.

TVi: Kyiv; tel. (44) 277-95-30; fax (44) 277-95-31; e-mail web@tvi.ua; internet tvi.ua; f. 2008; independent; news, current affairs; Chief Editor VITALIY E. PORTNIKOV.

Finance

(cap. = capital; res = reserves; dep. = deposits; brs = branches; m. = million; amounts in hryvnyas, unless otherwise indicated)

BANKING

Central Bank

National Bank of Ukraine (Natsionalny Bank Ukrainy): 01601 Kyiv, vul. Institutska 9; tel. (44) 253-01-80; fax (44) 230-20-33; e-mail webmaster@bank.gov.ua; internet www.bank.gov.ua; f. 1991; cap. 100m., res 89,871m., dep. 39,308m. (Dec. 2008); Gov. IHOR SORKIN.

Other State Bank

UkrExImBank—State Export-Import Bank of Ukraine: 03150 Kyiv, vul. Horkoho 127; tel. (44) 247-89-48; fax (44) 247-80-82; e-mail bank@eximb.com; internet www.eximb.com; f. 1992; fmrly br. of USSR Vneshekonombank (External Trade Bank); state-owned; cap. 17,126.7m., res 919.6m., dep. 32,663.6m. (Dec. 2011); Chair. of Bd VITALIY V. BILOUS; 29 brs.

Commercial Banks

Aktyv-Bank (Active-Bank): 04070 Kyiv, vul. Borysohlibska 3; tel. (44) 390-25-91; fax (44) 390-25-72; e-mail bank@activebank.com.ua; internet www.activebank.com.ua; f. 2002; cap. 312.8m., res 206.0m., dep. 1,758.7m. (Dec. 2010); Chair. of Managing Bd IHOR M. SOLNTSEV.

Alfa-Bank (Ukraine): 01025 Kyiv, vul. Desyatinna 4/6; tel. (44) 490-46-00; fax (44) 490-46-01; e-mail ccd@alfabank.kiev.ua; internet www.alfabank.com.ua; f. 1993; cap. US $631.3m., res −$242.6m., dep. $1,729.5m. (Dec. 2009); CEO RUSHAN KHVESYUK; Pres. OLEKSANDR LUKANOV.

Bank Kredyt Dnipro/ Bank Kredit Dnepr (Credit Dnepr Bank): 49600 Dnipropetrovsk, vul. Pysarzhevskoho 1A; tel. (562) 36-73-16; fax (562) 33-39-77; e-mail info@creditdnepr.com; internet creditdnepr.com.ua; f. 1993; 99.99% owned by Brancroft Enterprises (Cyprus); cap. 338.7m., res 115.1m., dep. 6,669.5m. (Dec. 2011); Chair. PAVEL MAKAROV.

Brokbiznesbank: 03057 Kyiv, pr. Peremohy 41; tel. (44) 206-22-06; fax (44) 459-67-80; e-mail bank@bankbb.com; internet www.bankbb.com; f. 1991; cap. 1,981.8m., res 246.5m., dep. 9,143.6m. (Dec. 2010); Chair. of Council OLEKSANDR V. BURYAK; Chair. of Bd NATALIYA B. HAVRILYUK (acting); 235 brs.

Credit Agricole Bank: 01004 Kyiv, vul. Pushkinska 42/4; tel. (44) 393-76-37; fax (44) 581-07-66; e-mail viktoriia.volkhina@credit-agricole.com.ua; internet www.credit-agricole.com.ua; f. 1993 as Industrial Export Bank; name changed as above in 2011; absorbed Calyon Bank Ukraine in 2013; 99.99% owned by Crédit Agricole (France); cap. 1,050.0m., res 24.3m., dep. 5,715.5m. (Dec. 2011); Chair. of Bd YEVHENIYA S. CHEMERIS.

Finance and Credit Bank (Bank 'Financy ta Kredyt'): 04050 Kyiv, vul. Artema 60; tel. (44) 490-68-70; fax (44) 201-42-90; e-mail info.contactcenter@fcbank.com.ua; internet www.fcbank.com.ua; f. 1990; cap. 2,000.0m., res 32.9m., dep. 10,763.1m. (Dec. 2011); Chair. VLADIMIR H. KHLYVNYUK; 11 brs.

First Ukrainian International Bank/Pershyi Ukrainskyi Mizhnarodnyi Bank (FUIB): 83001 Donetsk, vul. Universitetska 2A; tel. (623) 32-45-00; fax (623) 32-47-00; e-mail info@fuib.com; internet www.pumb.ua; f. 1991; cap. US $429.0m., res $72.0m., dep. $2,596.5m. (Dec. 2011); absorbed Dongorbank in 2011; Chair. of Bd SERHIY CHERNENKO.

Forum Bank (Bank Forum): 02100 Kyiv, bulv. Verkhovnoi Rady 7; tel. (44) 205-35-59; fax (44) 200-24-52; e-mail info@forum.ua; internet www.forum.ua; f. 1994; present name adopted 2010; 98.77% owned by Yernamio Consulting Ltd (Cyprus); cap. 5,953.4m., res 88.8m., dep. 6,689.3m. (Dec. 2011); Chair. OLEKSIY V. PERTIN; 194 brs (Dec. 2010).

Khreshchatyk Bank: 01001 Kyiv, vul. Khreshchatyk 8A; tel. and fax (44) 428-97-55; e-mail bank@xbank.com.ua; internet www.xcitybank.com.ua; f. 1993; present name adopted 1998; 23.7% owned by Kyiv City Administration; cap. US $133.0m., res −$43.4m., dep. $690.0m. (Dec. 2011); Chair. of Bd DMYTRO M. GRYDZHYK; 160 brs.

Klyrynhovy Dom AB (Clearing House Joint-Stock Bank): 04070 Kyiv, vul. Borysohlibska 5A; tel. (44) 593-10-30; fax (44) 593-10-31; e-mail info@clhs.kiev.ua; internet www.clhs.kiev.ua; f. 1996; cap. 439.7m., res 136.4m., dep. 2,853.4m. (Dec. 2011); Chair. of Bd VIKTORIYA ANDREYIVSKA.

Kredobank: 79026 Lviv, vul. Sakharova 78; tel. (32) 297-23-20; fax (32) 297-08-37; e-mail office@kredobank.com.ua; internet www

.kredobank.com.ua; f. 1990; present name adopted 2006; 98.6% owned by PKO Bank Polski SA (Poland); cap. 1,919.0m., res 0.3m., dep. 2,637.0m. (Dec. 2011); Chair. DMITRO KREPAK.

Kredytprombank: 01014 Kyiv, bulv. Druzhby Narodiv 38; tel. (44) 490-27-77; fax (44) 490-72-28; e-mail kpb@kreditprombank.com; internet www.kreditprombank.com; f. 1997; cap. 1,865.5m., res 1,054.2m., dep. 6,776.4m. (Dec. 2010); Chair. of Bd VITALIY O. MASYURA.

Kyivska Rus Bank: 04071 Kyiv, vul. Khoryva 11A; tel. and fax (44) 467-64-00; e-mail info@kruss.kiev.ua; internet www.kruss.kiev.ua; f. 1996; 47.7% owned by Sharp Arrow Holdings (Cyprus); cap. 276.1m., res 97.8m., dep. 3,798.7m. (Dec. 2010); Chair. VIKTOR BRATKO.

Megabank: 61002 Kharkiv, vul. Artema 30; tel. (572) 14-33-63; fax (572) 47-20-78; e-mail mega@megabank.net; internet www .megabank.net; f. 1990; present name adopted 2001; cap. 550.1m., res 50.5m., dep. 2,726.4m. (Dec. 2011); Chair. of Supervisory Council VIKTOR G. SUBOTIN; Chair. of Bd OLENA ZHUKOVA; 8 brs.

OTP Bank: 01033 Kyiv, vul. Zhylyanska 43; tel. (44) 490-05-00; fax (44) 490-05-59; e-mail office@otpbank.com.ua; internet www .otpbank.com.ua; f. 1998; present name adopted 2006; 100% owned by OTP Bank (Hungary); cap. 2,888.3m., res 1,196.4m., dep. 8,649.0m. (Dec. 2011); Chair. of Bd TAMASH KHAK-KOVACH.

Pivdennyi Bank: 65059 Odesa, vul. Krasnova 6/1; tel. and fax (482) 30-70-30; e-mail in@pivdenny.ua; internet www.bank.com.ua; f. 1993; cap. 965.8m., res 537.0m., dep. 10,631.2m. (Dec. 2011); Chair. of Bd VADYM V. MOROKHOVSKIY; 26 brs.

PrivatBank: 49094 Dnipropetrovsk, nab. Peremohy 50; tel. (562) 716-10-00; fax (56) 716-12-71; e-mail privatbank@pbank.dp.ua; internet www.privatbank.ua; cap. 13,545m., res 920m., dep. 105,888m. (Dec. 2011); Chair. of Bd ALEKSANDR V. DUBILET; 51 brs.

ProCredit Bank Ukraine (ProKredyt Bank Ukraine): 03115 Kyiv, pr. Peremohy 107A; tel. (44) 590-10-00; fax (44) 590-10-01; e-mail info@procreditbank.com.ua; internet www.procreditbank.com.ua; f. 2000; present name adopted 2003; 60% owned by ProCredit Holding AG (Germany), 20% by Western NIS Enterprise Fund (Germany), 20% by European Bank for Reconstruction and Development (United Kingdom); cap. US \$37.3m., res –\$3.3m., dep. \$190.5m. (Dec. 2011); Gen. Man. VIKTOR PONOMARENKO.

Prominvestbank (Industrial-Investment Bank): 01001 Kyiv, prov. Shevchenka 12; tel. (44) 201-51-20; fax (44) 201-50-44; e-mail bank@ pib.com.ua; internet www.pib.com.ua; f. 1922 as Stroibank, name changed 1992; 97.85% owned by Vnesheconombank (Russia); cap. 6,231.5m., res 2,248.3m., dep. 18,430.8m. (Dec. 2011); Chair. VIKTOR BASHKIROV; 600 brs.

Raiffeisen Bank Aval: 01011 Kyiv, vul. Leskova 9; tel. (44) 490-88-88; fax (44) 490-87-55; e-mail info@aval.ua; internet www.aval.ua; f. 1992 as Aval Bank; present name adopted 2006; 96.3% owned by Raiffeisen International Bank Holding AG (Austria); cap. 3,002.4m., res 4,268.3m., dep. 43,226.5m. (Dec. 2011); Pres. VOLODYMYR I. LAVRENCHUK; 1,400 brs and sub-brs.

Sberbank Rossii (Ukraine): 01034 Kyiv, vul. Volodymyrska 46; tel. and fax (44) 247-45-45; e-mail sbrf@sbrf.com.ua; internet www .sbrf.com.ua; f. 2001; fmrly Bank NRB, present name adopted 2008; 100% owned by Sberbank—Savings Bank of the Russian Federation; cap. 3,392.5m., res 404.3m., dep. 22,118.9m. (Dec. 2012); Chair. of Bd IGOR YUSHKO.

Swedbank: 01032 Kyiv, vul. Kominterna 30; tel. (44) 481-48-67; fax (44) 481-48-85; e-mail info@swedbank.ua; internet www.swedbank .ua; f. 1991; present name adopted 2007; wholly owned by Swedbank (Sweden); cap. US \$815.2m., res –\$131.9m., dep. \$77.9m. (Dec. 2011); Chair. of Bd RAINER MULLER-HANKO.

Ukrgazbank: 01004 Kyiv, vul. Chervonoarmiyska 39; tel. (44) 494-46-50; fax (44) 239-28-44; e-mail office@ukrgasbank.com; internet www.ukrgasbank.com; f. 1993; 93% owned by the Ministry of Finance; cap. 10,012.8m., res 319.8m., dep. 7,076.0m. (Dec. 2011); Chair. OLEKSANDR MOROZOV.

UkrSibbank: 04070 Kyiv, vul. Andriyevksa 2/12; tel. (44) 590-06-75; fax (44) 230-48-98; e-mail info@ukrsibbank.com; internet www .ukrsibbank.com; f. 1990; commercial and investment banking, non-banking financial services; 84.99% owned by BNP Paribas SA (France); cap. 7,511.7m., res 743.2m., dep. 20,970.6m. (Dec. 2011); Gen. Man. PHILIP ZHOANE; 1,000 brs and sub-brs.

UkrSotsBank (UniCredit Bank): 03150 Kyiv, vul. Kovpaka 29; tel. (44) 230-32-99; fax (44) 529-13-07; e-mail info@unicredit.ua; internet www.unicredit.com.ua; f. 1990; 94.2% owned by UniCredit Group (Italy); cap. 1,396.6m., res 2,931.1m., dep. 18,903.5m. (Dec. 2011); Chair. of Supervisory Council WILLIBALD CERNKO; Chair. of Bd BORIS TIMONKIN; over 500 brs.

VAB Bank-Vseukrainsky Aktsionerny Bank (All-Ukrainian Share Bank): 04119 Kyiv, vul. Zoolohichna 5; tel. (44) 496-33-96; fax (44) 489-01-45; e-mail info@vab.ua; internet www.vab.ua; f. 1992;

present name adopted 2007; cap. US \$239.3m., res \$20.3m., dep. \$700.3m. (2011); CEO DENIS MALTSEV; 170 brs.

VTB Bank: 01004 Kyiv, vul. Pushkinska 8/26; tel. (44) 486-04-90; e-mail info@vtb.com.ua; internet www.vtb.com.ua; f. 2005; present name adopted 2007; cap. 5,415.8m., res 254.4m., dep. 28,919.2m. (Dec. 2011); Chair. of Bd VADYM PUSHKAROV; 20 brs.

Savings Bank

State Savings Bank of Ukraine—Oschadbank (Derzhavnyi Oshchadnyi Bank Ukrainy): 01023 Kyiv, vul. Hospitalna 12G; tel. (44) 363-01-33; fax (44) 247-85-68; e-mail contact-centre@ oschadnybank.com; internet www.oschadnybank.com; f. 1991; cap. 878.5m., res 484.7m., dep. 7,400m. (2006); Chair. SERHIY O. PODRYEZOV; 6,000 brs.

Banking Association

Association of Ukrainian Banks (Asotsiatsiya Ukrainskykh Bankiv): 02660 Kyiv, vul. M. Raskova 15/703; tel. (44) 516-87-75; fax (44) 516-87-76; e-mail kanc@aub.com.ua; internet www.aub.org .ua; f. 1990; fmrly Commercial Bank Asscn; Pres. OLEKSANDR SUGONIAKO.

COMMODITY EXCHANGES

Carpathian Commodity Exchange: 78200 Ivano-Frankivsk obl., Kolomiya, vul. Vahylevycha 1, POB 210; tel. and fax (343) 34-76-25; fax (343) 32-19-61; e-mail prtb@list.ru; internet prtb.com.ua; f. 1991; Gen. Man. IHOR SHEVCHUK.

Donetsk Commodity Exchange: 83086 Donetsk, vul. Pershotravnevska 12; tel. (62) 338-10-93; fax (62) 335-92-91; e-mail oltradex@ pub.dn.ua; f. 1991; Gen. Man. PETRO O. VYSHNEVSKYI.

Kharkiv Commodity Exchange: 61058 Kharkiv, vul. Lenina 5; tel. (57) 701-36-02; fax (57) 701-37-03; e-mail ss@htb.kharkov.ua; f. 1993; Pres. IHOR V. ZOTOV.

Kyiv Universal Exchange: 01103 Kyiv, Zaliznychne shose 57; tel. and fax (44) 295-11-29; e-mail nva@iptelecom.net.ua; internet www .kue.kiev.ua; f. 1990; Pres. KONSTANTIN LAPUSHEN.

Odesa Commodity Exchange: 65114 Odesa, vul. Lyustdorfska doroha 140A; tel. (482) 61-89-92; fax (482) 47-72-84; e-mail yuri@oce .odessa.ua; f. 1796; re-established 1990; Gen. Man. MYKOLA O. NIKOLISHEN.

Pridniprovska Commodity Exchange: 49000 Dnipropetrovsk, vul. Nab. Lenina 15a; tel. (562) 35-77-11; fax (56) 35-77-45; e-mail ptb@pce.dp.ua; internet pce.co.ua; originally founded 1908 as Katerinoslav Commodity Exchange; re-established with present name in 1991; brs in Dniprodzerzhynsk, Kryvyi Rih, Marhanets, Pavlohrad and Synelnykove; Dir-Gen. VADYM F. KAMEKO.

Ukrainian Universal Commodity Exchange: 03680 Kyiv, pr. Akademika Hlushkova 1/6; tel. (44) 596-94-94; fax (44) 251-95-40; e-mail birga@uutb.kiev.ua; internet www.uutb.com.ua; f. 1991; Gen. Man. A. A. KAZAKOV.

Zaporizhzhya Commodity Exchange 'Hileya': 69037 Zaporizhzhya, vul. 40 rokiv Radyanskoyi Ukrainy 41; tel. (612) 33-32-73; fax (612) 34-76-62; f. 1991; re-established 1996; Gen. Man. ANTON A. KHULAKHSIZ.

INSURANCE

State Insurance Companies

DASK UkrinMedStrakh: 01601 Kyiv, vul. O. Honshara 65; tel. (44) 216-30-21; fax (44) 216-96-92; e-mail ukrmed@ukrpack.com; f. 1999; provides compulsory medical insurance to foreigners and stateless persons temporarily resident in Ukraine.

Oranta Insurance Co: 01015 Kyiv, vul. Zhylyanska 75; tel. (44) 537-58-00; fax (44) 537-58-83; e-mail oranta@oranta.ua; internet www.oranta.ua; f. 1921; Chair. of Bd OLEG SPILKA.

Commercial Insurance Companies

AKB Garant Insurance Co: 03062 Kyiv, pr. Peremohy 67; tel. (44) 454-75-25; e-mail akb@garant.kiev.ua; internet www.garant.kiev .ua; f. 1994; general insurance services; Gen. Man. OLEKSANDR I. DYACHENKO.

ECCO Insurance Co: 01034 Kyiv, vul. Prorizna 4/23; tel. (44) 278-40-84; fax (44) 278-10-82; e-mail insurance@ecco-alpha.kiev.ua; internet www.ecco-insurance.at; f. 1991; affiliated to ECCO (Austria); life and non-life insurance; Chair. JACOB KUESS.

EnergoPolis Insurance Co: 01033 Kyiv, vul. Sh. Rustaveli 39–41; tel. (44) 244-02-36; fax (44) 244-05-94; e-mail office@enpolis.com.ua; internet www.enpolis.com.ua; Chair. VIKTOR V. PROTSENKO (acting).

HDI Insurance: 03150 Kyiv, vul. Chervonoarmiyska 102; tel. (44) 247-44-77; fax (44) 529-08-94; e-mail hdi@hdi.ua; internet www.hdi .ua; f. 1992; fmrly Alkona Insurance Co, present name adopted 2008; insurance and reinsurance; Chair. KOSTYANTYN KSYENICH.

Ingo Ukraina Insurance Co: 01054 Kyiv, vul. Vorovskogo 33; tel. (44) 490-27-44; fax (44) 490-27-48; e-mail office@ingo.ua; internet www.ingo.com.ua; f. 1994; fmrly Ostra-Kyiv Insurance Co; re-insurance, medical, travel, property and cargo insurance; Chair. of Bd IHOR N. HORDYENKO.

Inter-Policy Insurance Co: 01033 Kyiv, vul. Volodymyrska 69; tel. (44) 465-30-48; fax (44) 289-14-84; e-mail info@inter-policy.com; internet www.inter-policy.com; f. 1993.

Investservis Insurance Co: 04050 Kyiv, Kudryavsky uzviz 5–6/208; tel. (44) 531-90-09; fax (44) 502-99-61; e-mail postbox@inserv.kiev.ua; internet www.inserv.com.ua; f. 1995; general insurance services; Chair. of Bd PAVOL NORULAK.

Kyiv Insurance Co: 04053 Kyiv, vul. Yu. Kotsubynskoho 20; tel. (44) 461-92-41; fax (44) 461-92-43; f. 1998.

Ostra Insurance Co: 65026 Odesa, vul. Pushkinska 13; tel. (48) 724-68-30; fax (48) 724-38-41; e-mail main@ostra.com.ua; internet www.ostra.com.ua; f. 1990; non-life; Chair. KHYRACH MAHDYEV.

PZU Ukraine Insurance Co: 04112 Kyiv, vul. Dehtyarivska 62; tel. (44) 238-62-38; fax (44) 581-04-55; e-mail mail@pzu.com.ua; internet www.pzu.com.ua; 100% owned by PZU (Poland); 4 subsidiary cos; life and non-life; Pres. IRENEUSZ WESOŁOWSKI.

QBE Ukraina Insurance: 04070 Kyiv, vul. Illinska 8; tel. (44) 537-53-90; fax (44) 537-53-99; e-mail info.ukraine@qbe.com; internet www.qbeeurope.com/ukraine; f. 1998; affiliate of QBE Insurance (New Zealand); Gen. Dir OLEH SOSNOVSKY.

Skide Insurance Co: 04050 Kyiv, vul. Hlybochytska 72; tel. (44) 417-40-04; fax (44) 228-40-33; e-mail skide@iptelecom.net.ua; f. 1991; Pres. VOLODYMYR BESARAB.

Sun Life Ukraine: 01032 Kyiv, vul. Starovokzalna 17; tel. (44) 235-20-02; fax (44) 235-89-17; e-mail office@sunlife.com.ua; f. 1993; life; Pres. ROSTYSLAV B. TALSKYI.

UkrGazPromPolis Insurance Co: 01034 Kyiv, vul. O. Honshara 41; tel. (44) 235-25-00; fax (44) 235-31-13; e-mail office@ugpp.com.ua; internet www.ugpp.com.ua; f. 1996; jointly owned by UkrGazProm, UkrGazPromBank and KyivTransGaz; Pres. KONSTANTYN O. YEFYMENKO.

Insurance Association

League of Insurance Organizations of Ukraine: 02660 Kyiv, vul. M. Roskovoyi 11; tel. and fax (44) 516-82-30; e-mail liga@uainsur.com; internet www.uainsur.com; f. 1992; non-profit asscn of insurance cos; Pres. NATALIYA HUDYMA.

Trade and Industry

GOVERNMENT AGENCY

State Property Fund of Ukraine (Fond Derzhavnoho Maina Ukrainy): 01133 Kyiv, vul. Kutuzova 18/9; tel. (44) 200-33-33; fax (44) 286-79-85; e-mail marketing@spfu.kiev.ua; internet www.spfu.gov.ua; Head OLEKSANDR V. RYABCHENKO (acting).

NATIONAL CHAMBER OF COMMERCE

Ukrainian Chamber of Commerce and Industry (Torgovo-Promyslova Palata Ukrainy/Torgovo-Promyshlennaya Palata Ukrainy): 01601 Kyiv, vul. V. Zhytomyrska 33; tel. (44) 272-28-04; fax (44) 272-33-53; e-mail ucci@ucci.org.ua; internet www.ucci.org.ua; f. 1972; Pres. GENNADIY D. CHYZHYKOV; 27 regional brs with a total of c. 10,000 mems.

REGIONAL CHAMBERS OF COMMERCE

Chambers of Commerce are located in every administrative region of Ukraine, including the following:

Dnipropetrovsk Chamber of Commerce: 49044 Dnipropetrovsk, vul. Shevchenka 4; tel. (562) 36-22-58; fax (562) 36-22-59; e-mail dcci@dcci.org.ua; internet www.dcci.org.ua; f. 1995; brs at Kryvyi Rih and Dniprodzerzhynsk; Pres. VYTALIY H. ZHMURENKO.

Donetsk Chamber of Commerce: 83007 Donetsk, pr. Kyivsky 87; tel. (62) 387-80-00; fax (62) 387-80-01; e-mail info@dttp.donetsk.ua; internet www.cci.donbass.com; f. 1964; brs at Artemovsk, Horlivka, Kramatorsk, Makiyivka and Mariupol; Pres. GENNADII D. CHIZHIKOV.

Kharkiv Chamber of Commerce: 61037 Kharkiv, pr. Moskovsky 122; tel. (57) 714-96-90; fax (57) 738-64-79; e-mail info@kcci.kharkov.ua; internet www.kcci.kharkov.ua; Pres. VIKTOR I. LOBODA.

Kyiv Chamber of Commerce and Industry: 01504 Kyiv, vul. B. Khmelnytskoho 55; tel. (44) 246-83-01; fax (44) 246-99-66; e-mail info@kiev-chamber.org.ua; internet www.kiev-chamber.org.ua; Pres. MYKOLA V. ZASULSKIY.

Lviv Chamber of Commerce and Industry: 79011 Lviv, Stryiskiy park 14; tel. and fax (32) 276-46-11; e-mail lcci@cci.com.ua; internet www.lcci.com.ua; f. 1850; Pres. DMYTRO D. AFTANAS.

Odesa Chamber of Commerce and Industry: 65125 Odesa, vul. Bazarna 47; tel. (48) 38-04-82; fax (482) 49-63-07; e-mail orcci@orcci.odessa.ua; internet www.orcci.odessa.ua; f. 1924; brs at Illichivsk, Izmayil and Reni; Pres. SERHIY SHUVALOV.

Sevastopol Chamber of Commerce and Industry: 99011 Sevastopol, ul. B. Morskaya 34; tel. (692) 54-61-51; fax (692) 54-06-44; e-mail members@stpp.org.ua; internet www.stpp.org.ua; f. 1963; Pres. LYUDMILA I. VISHNYA.

Transcarpathian (Zakarpatska) Chamber of Commerce and Industry: 88015 Transcarpathian obl., Uzhhorod, vul. Hrushevskoho 62; tel. (312) 66-94-50; fax (312) 66-94-60; e-mail tpp@tpp.uzhgorod.ua; internet www.tpp.uzhgorod.ua; br. at Mukachevo; Pres. OTTO O. KOVCHAR.

Zaporizhzhya Chamber of Commerce: 69000 Zaporizhzhya, bulv. Tsentralnyi 4; tel. (612) 13-50-24; fax (612) 33-11-72; e-mail cci@cci.zp.ua; internet www.cci.zp.ua; brs at Berdyansk and Melitopol; Pres. VOLODOMYR I. SHAMYLOV.

EMPLOYERS' ORGANIZATION

Congress of Business Circles of Ukraine: 01061 Kyiv, vul. Prorizna 15; tel. (44) 228-64-81; fax (44) 229-52-84; Pres. VALERIY G. BABICH.

UTILITIES

Regulatory Bodies

National Electricity Regulatory Commission of Ukraine: 03057 Kyiv, vul. Smolenska 19; tel. (44) 241-90-01; fax (44) 241-90-47; e-mail box@nerc.gov.ua; f. 1994; promotion of competition and protection of consumer interests; Chair. YURIY PRODAN.

State Inspectorate for Nuclear Regulation (Derzhavna inspektsiya yadernoho rehulyuvannya Ukrainy): 01011 Kyiv, vul. Arsenalna 9/11; tel. (44) 254-33-47; fax (44) 254-33-11; e-mail pr@hq.snrc.gov.ua; internet www.snrc.gov.ua; Chair. OLENA A. MYKOLAICHUK.

Electricity

EnergoAtom: 01032 Kyiv, vul. Vetrova 3; tel. (44) 281-48-83; e-mail pr@nae.atom.gov.ua; internet www.energoatom.kiev.ua; f. 1996; responsible for scientific and technical policy within the nuclear power industry; manages all five nuclear power producing installations in Ukraine; Pres. ANDRIY L. DERKACH.

Kyivenergo: 01001 Kyiv, pl. Ivana Franka 5; tel. (44) 201-58-67; fax (44) 239-47-06; e-mail pubrel@kievenergo.com.ua; internet www.kievenergo.com.ua; power generation and distribution; Chair. SERHIY M. TITENKO.

Zakhidenergo (West Energy): 79026 Lviv, vul. Kozelnytska 15; tel. (322) 39-07-10; fax (322) 39-07-17; e-mail kanc@gwce.energy.gov.ua; internet www.zakhidenergo.ua; f. 1995; power generation; Dir-Gen. PETRO I. OMELYANOVSKIY.

Gas

Naftogaz Ukrainy (Oil and Gas of Ukraine): 01001 Kyiv, vul. B. Khmelnytskoho 6B; tel. (44) 461-25-37; fax (44) 220-15-26; e-mail ngu@naftogaz.net; internet www.naftogaz.com; f. 1998; state-owned; production and distribution of gas and petroleum; storage of gas; gas- and condensate-processing; Chair. of Bd OLEH DUBYNA.

TRADE UNION FEDERATIONS

Confederation of Free Trade Unions of Ukraine (CFTUU) (Konfederatsiya Vilnykh Profspilok Ukrainy—KVPU): 03150 Kyiv, vul. V. Vasylkivska 54; tel. (44) 287-33-38; fax (44) 287-72-83; e-mail info@kvpu.org.ua; internet www.kvpu.org.ua; f. 1997; independent; Chair. MYKHAYLO YA. VOLYNETS.

Federation of Trade Unions of Ukraine (FTUU): 01012 Kyiv, Maidan Nezalezhnosti 2; tel. (44) 278-06-08; fax (44) 279-48-62; e-mail fpsu@fpsu.org.ua; internet www.fpsu.org.ua; f. 1990; fmr Ukrainian branch of General Confederation of Trade Unions of the USSR; 46 sectoral and 27 regional member bodies; Chair. YURIY KULYK.

Transport

RAILWAYS

In 2010 there were 21,705 km of railway track in use, of which 9,877 km were electrified.

State Railway Transport Administration—Ukrzaliznytsia: 03680 Kyiv, vul. Tverska 5; tel. (44) 223-00-10; fax (44) 258-80-11; e-mail ci@uz.gov.ua; internet www.uz.gov.ua; Dir-Gen. (vacant).

Ukrreftrans: 08502 Kyiv, vul. Chervoniy; tel. (45) 656-91-92; e-mail sekretar1@ukrref.uz.gov.ua; internet www.ukrreftrans.gov.ua; state-owned freight transportation service; Dir VASILIY M. ILCHISHIN.

Dnipropetrovsk Metro: 49038 Dnipropetrovsk, vul. Kurchatova 8; tel. and fax (562) 778-65-33; e-mail metrodp@ukr.net; internet gorod .dp.ua/metro; f. 1995; one line with six stations; total length 8 km; total planned network of 74 km.

Kharkiv Metro: 61052 Kharkiv, vul. Engelsa 29; tel. (57) 730-34-13; fax (57) 731-21-41; e-mail s@metro.kharkov.ua; internet www.metro .kharkov.ua; f. 1975; three lines with 28 stations; total length 35.5 km; CEO MYKHAYLO F. KARAMSHUK.

Kyiv Metro: 03055 Kyiv, pr. Peremohy 35; tel. and fax (44) 238-54-63; e-mail nto@metro.kiev.ua; internet www.metro.kiev.ua; f. 1960; three lines with 42 stations; Dir VOLODYMYR I. FEDORENKO.

ROADS

In 2010 the total length of roads in Ukraine was 169,496 km, including 21,129 km of main roads and 78,930 km of secondary roads. Some 97.8% of the total network was hard-surfaced.

INLAND WATERWAYS

The Dnipro (Dniepr—Dnieper) river is the most important route for river freight.

SHIPPING

The main ports are Yalta and Yevpatoriya in Crimea, and Odesa. In addition to long-distance international shipping lines, there are services to Russia and Georgia. At December 2012 Ukraine's flag registered fleet comprised 595 vessels, totalling 829,812 grt.

Port Authority

Odesa Commercial Sea Port: 65026 Odesa, pl. Mytna 1; tel. (48) 729-35-55; fax (48) 729-36-27; e-mail vyy@port.odessa.ua; internet www.port.odessa.ua; f. 1794; state-owned; cargo handling and storage, marine passenger terminal services; Gen. Man. YURIY VASKOV.

Shipping Companies

Azov Shipping Co: 87510 Donetsk obl., Mariupol, pr. Admirala Lunina 89; tel. (629) 37-83-73; fax (629) 37-83-59; e-mail admin@ c2smtp.azsco.anet.donetsk.ua; f. 1871; Pres. SERHIY V. PRUSIKOV.

State Black Sea Shipping Co: 65026 Odesa, vul. Lanzheronovska 1; tel. (482) 25-21-60; fax (482) 60-57-33; Pres. BORIS SCHERBAK.

Ukrainian Danube Shipping Co: 68600 Odesa obl., Izmayil, vul. Chervonaflotska 28; tel. (4841) 7-25-46; fax (4841) 2-53-55; e-mail udp_t@udp.izmail.uptel.net; internet www.oaoudp.com.ua; f. 1944; cargo and passenger services; Pres. PETR S. SUVOROV.

Ukrainian Shipping Co (UkrShip): 65014 Odesa, vul. Marazlyevska 8; tel. (48) 734-73-50; fax (48) 777-07-00; e-mail admin@ ukrship.odessa.ua; f. 1996; Pres. A. SAVITSKIY.

Ukrrechflot Co: 04071 Kyiv, Nizhny val. 51; tel. and fax (44) 417-44-41; fax (44) 417-15-93; e-mail info@ukrrichflot.com.ua; f. 1992; jt-stock co; Pres. PAVEL PODLESNY.

CIVIL AVIATION

The principal international airport is at Boryspil (Kyiv), but several other airports, including those at Dnipropetrovsk and Odesa, also service international flights.

AeroSvit Airlines: 01032 Kyiv, Boryspil 7; tel. (44) 490-34-90; fax (44) 246-50-46; e-mail info@aerosvit.com; internet www.aerosvit .com; f. 1994; operates scheduled and charter passenger services to domestic and international destinations; Chief Exec. and Dir-Gen. GRYGORIY GURTOVOY.

ARP 410: 03151 Kyiv, Vozdukhoflotsky pr. 94; tel. (44) 246-99-26; fax (44) 243-40-33; e-mail arp410-cs@svitonline.com; f. 1999; domestic passenger and international cargo flights; Dir-Gen. ANATOLIY P. KUDRIN.

Donbassaero Airlines (Donbass-Vostochnye Aviyalinii Ukrainy—Donbassaero): 83021 Donetsk, vul. Vzlyotna 1, Donetsk International Airport; tel. (62) 388-51-03; fax (62) 332-00-55; e-mail info@donbass.aero; internet www.donbass.aero; f. 1933 as Donetsk State Airline; present name adopted 2007; passenger and cargo flights between Donetsk and domestic and international destinations; Dir-Gen. OLEG B. NOVIKOV.

Khors Air Company: 03035 Kyiv, vul. Mekhanizatorov 10; tel. (44) 246-28-88; fax (44) 494-32-86; e-mail ors@khors.kiev.ua; internet www.khors.com.ua; f. 1990; operates international, regional and domestic cargo and passenger services; Gen. Dir ANATOLIY VYSO-CHANSKIY.

Ukraine International Airlines (Mizhnarodni Avialinyi Ukraini): 02121 Kyiv, Kharkivske shose 201-203; tel. (44) 461-56-56; fax (44) 230-88-66; e-mail uia@flyuia.com; internet www .ukraine-international.com; f. 1992; 61.6% state-owned; operates domestic services, and international services to European and Middle Eastern destinations from Kyiv, Dnipropetrovsk, Kharkiv, Lviv, Odesa and Simferopol; Pres. YURIY MIROSHNIKOV.

Tourism

The Black Sea coast of Ukraine has several popular resorts, including Odesa and Yalta. The Crimean peninsula is a popular tourist centre in both summer and winter, owing to its temperate climate. Kyiv, Lviv and Odesa have important historical attractions, and there are many archaeological monuments on the Black Sea coast, including the remains of ancient Greek and Ottoman settlements. However, the tourism industry remains relatively undeveloped. There were 23.0m. foreign tourist arrivals in Ukraine in 2012; according to provisional data, receipts from tourism totalled US $4,294m. in 2011.

Ministry of Culture: see The Government (Ministries).

State Tourism Administration of Ukraine (Derzhavna turystychna administratsiya Ukrainy): 01034 Kyiv, vul. Yaroslaviv val 36; tel. (44) 272-42-15; fax (44) 272-42-77; e-mail info@tourism.gov.ua; internet www.tourism.gov.ua; f. 1999; Chair. VALERIY I. TSYBUKH.

Defence

In December 1991 an independent Ukrainian military was established. As assessed at November 2012, there were an estimated 129,950 active personnel in the Ukrainian Armed Forces (excluding the Black Sea Fleet), including 70,750 ground forces, an air force of 45,250 and a navy of an estimated 13,950. There were also paramilitary forces, comprising some 45,000 in the Border Guard and 39,900 serving under the Ministry of Internal Affairs. In addition, some 9,500 were serving in civil defence troops. There were, additionally, some 1m. reserves. Military service is compulsory for males over 18 years of age, for a period of 18 months in the ground forces and air forces, and for 24 months in the navy.

In 1993–94 a programme of nuclear disarmament was agreed with the USA and Russia, involving the dismantling and surrender of the ex-Soviet warheads. The transfer of strategic nuclear weapons to Russia for dismantling was completed in mid-1996. On 31 May 1997 Ukraine and Russia signed an agreement on the division of the Soviet Black Sea Fleet, on the terms of its deployment and on the status of its base, Sevastopol. In 2010 an agreement was reached to extend Russia's lease on the Black Sea Fleet base for a further 25-year period from 2017.

Defence Expenditure: Budgeted at an estimated 16,400m. hryvnyas in 2012.

Chief of the General Staff and Commander-in-Chief of the Land Forces: Col-Gen. VOLODYMYR ZAMANA.

Commander-in-Chief of the Air Defence: Col-Gen. IVAN RUSNAK.

Commander-in-Chief of the Land Forces: Col-Gen. MYKOLA PETRUK.

Commander-in-Chief of the Navy: Vice-Adm. VIKTOR MAKSIMOV.

Education

The reversal of the 'Russification' of the education system was one of the principal demands of the opposition movements that emerged in the late 1980s. In the early 1990s there were significant changes to the curriculum, with greater emphasis on Ukrainian history and literature, while some religious and private educational institutions were established.

Education is compulsory between seven and 15 years of age. Primary education lasts for four years, while secondary education comprises two cycles, of five years and two years, respectively. In 2012/13 there were 16,100 pre-primary educational establishments in Ukraine (although 900 of these had their operations suspended), providing for 1,428,000 students. Some 4,222,000 students attended 19,700 primary and general secondary institutions, and 423,300 students attended 972 vocational secondary educational institutions. In 2009/10 enrolment at primary schools included 91% of children in the relevant age-group, while enrolment at secondary level included 86% of children in the relevant age-group. In 2012/13 there were 2,170,100 students enrolled in higher education. Government expenditure on education in 2011 was 86,269m. hryvnyas (14.6% of total budgetary expenditure).

THE UNITED ARAB EMIRATES

Introductory Survey

LOCATION, CLIMATE, LANGUAGE, RELIGION, FLAG, CAPITAL

The United Arab Emirates (UAE) lies in the east of the Arabian peninsula. It is bordered by Saudi Arabia to the west and south, and by Oman to the east. In the north the UAE has a short frontier with Qatar and a coastline of about 650 km (400 miles) on the southern shore of the Persian (Arabian) Gulf, separated by a detached portion of Omani territory from a small section of coast on the western shore of the Gulf of Oman. The climate is exceptionally hot in summer, with average maximum temperatures exceeding 40°C, and humidity is very high. Winter is mild, with temperatures ranging from 17°C to 20°C. Average annual rainfall is very low: between 100 mm and 200 mm. The official language is Arabic, spoken by almost all of the native population. Arabs are, however, outnumbered by non-Arab immigrants, mainly from India, Pakistan, Bangladesh and Iran. According to official census results, UAE nationals represented about 20% of the total population in 2005. Official figures published in late 2008 indicated that non-nationals made up more than 80% of the UAE's population and constituted over 90% of the workforce. Most of the inhabitants are Muslims, mainly of the Sunni sect. The national flag (proportions 1 by 2) has three equal horizontal stripes, of green, white and black, with a vertical red stripe at the hoist. The capital is Abu Dhabi.

CONTEMPORARY POLITICAL HISTORY

Historical Context

Prior to independence the UAE was Trucial Oman, also known as the Trucial States, and the component sheikhdoms of the territory were under British protection. Although from 1892 the United Kingdom assumed responsibility for the sheikhdoms' defence and external relations, they were otherwise autonomous and followed the traditional form of Arab monarchy, with each ruler having virtually absolute power over his subjects.

In 1952 the Trucial Council, comprising the rulers of the seven sheikhdoms, was established in order to encourage the adoption of common policies in administrative matters. Petroleum, the basis of the area's modern prosperity, was first discovered in 1958, when deposits were located beneath the coastal waters of Abu Dhabi, the largest of the sheikhdoms. Onshore petroleum was found in Abu Dhabi in 1960, and commercial exploitation of petroleum began in 1962, providing the state with greatly increased revenue. However, Sheikh Shakhbut bin Sultan Al Nahyan, the Ruler of Abu Dhabi since 1928, failed to use the income from petroleum royalties to develop his domain. As a result, the ruling family deposed him in August 1966 and installed his younger brother, Sheikh Zayed bin Sultan. Under the rule of Sheikh Zayed, Abu Dhabi was transformed, with considerable income from the petroleum industry allocated for public works and the provision of welfare services. In 1966 petroleum was discovered in neighbouring Dubai (the second largest of the Trucial States), which also underwent a rapid development.

In January 1968 the United Kingdom announced its intention to withdraw British military forces from the area by 1971. In March 1968 the Trucial States formed the Federation of Arab Emirates, along with nearby Bahrain and Qatar. However, both Bahrain and Qatar seceded from the Federation in August 1971 to become separate independent states. In July six of the Trucial States (Abu Dhabi, Dubai, Sharjah, Umm al-Qaiwain, Ajman and Fujairah) had agreed on a federal Constitution for achieving independence as the United Arab Emirates (UAE). The United Kingdom accordingly terminated its special treaty relationship with the States, and the UAE became independent on 2 December 1971. The remaining sheikhdom, Ras al-Khaimah, joined the UAE in February 1972. At independence Sheikh Zayed of Abu Dhabi took office as the first President of the UAE. Sheikh Rashid bin Said Al Maktoum, the Ruler of Dubai since 1958, became Vice-President, while his eldest son, Sheikh Maktoum bin Rashid Al Maktoum (Crown Prince of Dubai), became Prime Minister in the federal Council of Ministers. A 40-member consultative assembly, the Federal National Council (FNC), was also inaugurated.

Domestic Political Affairs

In January 1972 the Ruler of Sharjah, Sheikh Khalid bin Muhammad al-Qasimi, was killed by rebels under the leadership of his cousin, Sheikh Saqr bin Sultan, who had been deposed as the sheikhdom's Ruler in June 1965. However, the rebels were defeated, and Sheikh Khalid was succeeded by his brother, Sheikh Sultan bin Muhammad al-Qasimi.

Sheikh Zayed of Abu Dhabi, disappointed with progress towards centralization, reportedly announced in August 1976 that he was not prepared to accept another five-year term as President. In November, however, the highest federal authority, the Supreme Council of Rulers (comprising the Rulers of the seven emirates), re-elected him unanimously, following agreements granting the federal Government greater control over defence, intelligence services, immigration, public security and border control.

Owing to a dispute over a senior appointment in February 1978, the forces of Dubai and Ras al-Khaimah refused to accept orders from the Federal Defence Force. Although Ras al-Khaimah later reintegrated with the Federal Defence Force, Dubai's armed forces effectively remained a separate entity. In March 1979 a 10-point memorandum from the National Council, containing proposals for increased unity, was rejected by Dubai, which, together with Ras al-Khaimah, boycotted a meeting of the Supreme Council. In April Sheikh Maktoum resigned as Prime Minister; he was replaced by his father, Sheikh Rashid, who formed a new Council of Ministers in July, while retaining the post of Vice-President. Sheikh Ahmad bin Rashid al-Mu'alla, the Ruler of Umm al-Qaiwain (the smallest of the emirates) since 1929, died in February 1981, and was succeeded by his son, Rashid. Sheikh Rashid bin Humaid al-Nuaimi, the Ruler of Ajman since 1928, died in September 1981, and was succeeded by his son, Humaid.

There was an attempted coup in Sharjah in June 1987, when Sheikh Abd al-Aziz, a brother of Sheikh Sultan, announced (in his brother's absence) the abdication of the Ruler, on the grounds that he had mismanaged the economy. The Supreme Council of Rulers intervened to endorse Sheikh Sultan's claim to be the legitimate Ruler of Sharjah, effectively restoring him to power. Sheikh Abd al-Aziz was given the title of Crown Prince and was granted a seat on the Supreme Council. In February 1990, however, Sheikh Sultan removed his brother from the post of Crown Prince and revoked his right to succeed him as Ruler. In July Sheikh Sultan appointed Sheikh Ahmad bin Muhammad al-Qasimi, the head of Sharjah's petroleum and mineral affairs office, as Deputy Ruler of Sharjah, although he was not given the title of Crown Prince.

In October 1990, upon the death of his father, Sheikh Maktoum acceded to the positions of Ruler of Dubai and Vice-President and Prime Minister of the UAE. In January 1995 Sheikh Maktoum issued a decree naming Sheikh Muhammad bin Rashid Al Maktoum as Crown Prince, and Sheikh Hamdan bin Rashid Al Maktoum as Deputy Ruler of Dubai. In June 1996 legislation designed to make the provisional Constitution permanent was endorsed by the FNC, following its approval by the Supreme Council of Rulers. At the same time Abu Dhabi was formally designated capital of the UAE.

In October 2003 Sheikh Zayed appointed Sheikh Hamdan bin Zayed Al Nahyan as a Deputy Prime Minister, in addition to his existing responsibilities as Minister of State for Foreign Affairs. In the following month Sheikh Zayed issued a decree installing Sheikh Muhammad bin Zayed Al Nahyan, the Chief of Staff of Federal Armed Forces, as Deputy Crown Prince of Abu Dhabi. Meanwhile, in June Sheikh Saqr bin Muhammad al-Qasimi, the ruler of Ras al-Khaimah, deposed his eldest son, Khalid (who subsequently departed to Oman), as Crown Prince and appointed a younger son, Saud, in his place.

Sheikh Khalifa accedes to the presidency

Sheikh Zayed died on 2 November 2004, following several years of ill health. His son, Sheikh Khalifa bin Zayed Al Nahyan, automatically succeeded him as Ruler of Abu Dhabi and was elected by the Supreme Council to the presidency the following day. On the day before Sheikh Zayed's death a restructuring had been implemented of the Council of Ministers (the first such reorganization since 1997). The most significant changes were the appointment as Minister of Economy and Planning of Sheikha Lubna bint Khalid al-Qasimi, who became the first woman to hold a cabinet position in the UAE, and the combining of the petroleum and mineral resources ministry with the electricity and water portfolio to form a new Ministry of Energy, headed by Muhammad bin Dhaen al-Hamili. In December Sheikh Khalifa announced a similarly rare restructuring of the Abu Dhabi Executive Council, to be chaired by the new Crown Prince, Sheikh Muhammad, who also remained the Chief of Staff of Federal Armed Forces.

Sheikh Maktoum, who had reportedly suffered from heart problems, died suddenly in January 2006. He was immediately succeeded as Ruler of Dubai by his brother, Sheikh Muhammad bin Rashid Al Maktoum, who had been Dubai's Crown Prince since 1995. Sheikh Muhammad replaced Sheikh Maktoum as Vice-President and Prime Minister of the UAE, while also retaining control of the Ministry of Defence, a position that he had held since 1971.

In December 2005 Sheikh Khalifa announced proposals to open one-half of the 40 seats in the FNC to indirect election via new national councils in each of the emirates. The President envisaged that this represented the first step towards wider participatory democracy and the federation's first general election. The partial elections to the FNC were held on 16, 18 and 20 December 2006: four members of the Council were elected from each of Abu Dhabi and Dubai, three each from Sharjah and Ras al-Khaimah, and two each from Fujairah, Umm al-Qaiwain and Ajman. The 20 seats were contested by 450 candidates, including 65 women. Just 6,689 selected UAE nationals (among them 1,189 women) were eligible to participate in the polls as members of the new electoral colleges (these had been chosen by the National Electoral Committee, established in August). The elected members included one woman, selected in Abu Dhabi. Overall voter turn-out in the seven emirates was reported to be 74.4%. The new FNC was inaugurated in February 2007. (Of its 20 appointed members, nine were women.) At the opening session, Abd al-Aziz Abdullah al-Ghurair was elected Speaker.

In February 2008 Sheikh Muhammad issued a decree appointing his son, Sheikh Hamdan bin Muhammad bin Rashid Al Maktoum, as Crown Prince of Dubai. The new Crown Prince and his younger brother, Sheikh Maktoum, were also named as Deputy Rulers of Dubai. (Sheikh Hamdan had been appointed Chairman of the Dubai Executive Council in September 2006.) The appointments were followed in the same month by a reorganization of the federal Council of Ministers. While the strategic portfolios of energy, foreign affairs and defence remained unchanged, other appointments, which included the transfer of Sheikha Lubna al-Qasimi from the economy portfolio to that of foreign trade, were regarded as reflecting Sheikh Muhammad's policy priorities in further developing the business sector.

The UAE's record on human rights was reviewed under the UN Human Rights Council's Universal Periodic Review (UPR) process during 2008. A national report, outlining the Emirates' achievements and plans regarding human rights, with contributions from several government ministries and domestic non-governmental organizations, was published in September. At a Council session in Geneva, Switzerland, in December, the UAE's Minister of State for Foreign Affairs announced that the UAE had agreed to adopt 36 recommendations on human rights made by other member states: these included proposals on human-trafficking, working conditions, freedom of the press and children's rights; 21 recommendations were rejected, including those on corporal and capital punishment, trade unions, and women's rights; while a further 17 recommendations were reserved for further review. Of these, nine had been rejected and eight either accepted or placed under consideration by the time of the final UPR session in March 2009, at which the Human Rights Council voted unanimously to endorse the UAE's national report. Nevertheless, the US Department of State's 2008 Human Rights Report on the UAE, published in February 2009, contained several negative observations on the human rights situation in the UAE, including its record on issues such as the mistreatment of prisoners, media censorship, people-trafficking and working conditions, as well as the allegation that a member of the royal family had tortured a foreign national because of a

business dispute. The Ministry of Foreign Affairs issued a statement rejecting much of the criticism in the report, which, it claimed, contained 'generalities and unsubstantiated statements', and was the result of the application of a foreign value system to an Islamic state. In April a US television channel broadcast segments of a video recording, which, it claimed, showed the alleged torture incident, and named the royal family member as Sheikh Issa bin Zayed Al Nahyan, a brother of Sheikh Khalifa. In May Sheikh Issa was detained in connection with the investigation into the incident. At his trial, which began in December, Sheikh Issa pleaded not guilty to all charges; his lawyer alleged that his client was the victim of a conspiracy and that the video recording had been manipulated. In January 2010 Sheikh Issa was acquitted on all charges, although full details of the judge's decision were not published. Two US-Lebanese brothers, who had been involved in recording the incident and smuggling the tape to the USA, were convicted, *in absentia*, on charges of blackmail and of drugging the prince; each was sentenced to five years' imprisonment.

A number of constitutional amendments were endorsed by the Supreme Council of Rulers in December 2008 and approved by the FNC in January 2009, including the extension of the FNC's legislative term from two to four years and an article prohibiting FNC members from conducting business arrangements with government agencies during their legislative term.

Sheikh Rashid bin Ahmad al-Mu'alla, Ruler of Umm al-Qaiwain since 1981, died in January 2009. His son, Sheikh Saud bin Rashid al-Mu'alla, was immediately appointed to succeed him. Sheikh Rashid bin Saud bin Rashid al-Mu'alla was appointed Crown Prince.

Government changes and the 2011 elections

Sheikh Khalifa effected a reorganization of the Council of Ministers in May 2009. Lt-Gen. Sheikh Saif bin Zayed Al Nahyan, the Minister of the Interior, and Sheikh Mansour bin Zayed Al Nahyan, the Minister of Presidential Affairs, were both appointed Deputy Prime Ministers, in addition to their existing responsibilities. Humaid Muhammad Obaid al-Qattami, hitherto Minister of Health, was accorded the education portfolio, replacing Dr Hanif Hassan Ali, who assumed the health portfolio. The former Deputy Prime Ministers, Sheikh Sultan bin Zayed Al Nahyan and Sheikh Hamdan bin Zayed Al Nahyan, both left the Government. In November the members of the Supreme Council of Rulers re-elected Sheikh Khalifa as President for a further five-year term.

Meanwhile, from late 2008 the negative impact of the global economic downturn on the UAE's economy, particularly in the construction, property, financial services and tourism sectors, began to result in job losses, the cancellation of thousands of work permits for foreign workers, and the postponement or scaling down of numerous infrastructure projects. From December 2009 the authorities in Dubai introduced a number of administrative reforms in an effort to prevent a recurrence of the debt crisis that had emerged in November following the announcement of a six-month moratorium on debt repayments by Dubai World, a government-owned investment company. In January 2010 Sheikh Hamdan, the Crown Prince, announced a significant reorganization of Dubai's Executive Council, involving the establishment of new committees to oversee government policy in five key sectors: economic development; security and justice; infrastructure and environment; social development; and health and safety.

In October 2010 the death was announced of Sheikh Saqr bin Muhammad al-Qasimi, the Ruler of Ras al-Khaimah since 1948. He was immediately succeeded by Crown Prince Sheikh Saud, despite a counter-claim by his half-brother, Khalid, who had been deposed as Crown Prince in 2003. Sheikh Saud in turn was succeeded as Crown Prince by Sheikh Muhammad bin Saud bin Saqr al-Qasimi. In July 2012 it was announced that an Executive Council was to be established in Ras al-Khaimah to be chaired by the Crown Prince.

In March 2011 it was announced that indirect elections for one-half of the 40 seats in the FNC would take place on 24 September. In the previous month the membership of the electoral colleges used to allocate those 20 seats had been expanded to include 129,274 people, compared with a membership of just 6,689 at the elections held in December 2006. However, the newly expanded membership still represented less than 20% of the local population, and there were increasing appeals for the right to vote to be granted to all UAE nationals. The announcement of the election date followed the submission of an online petition to the President earlier in March by 133 academics, journalists and political activists, in which they appealed for the introduction of direct elections and for the advisory FNC to be given full legislative powers.

Some 468 candidates, of whom just under one-fifth were women, registered to take part in the elections. In the event, a total of 35,877 voters turned out to cast their ballots, representing a participation rate of just 27.8% of eligible voters. Some observers contended that the low voter turn-out indicated growing disenfranchisement in the context of the limited nature of the reform process within the UAE. However, others contended that the low level of participation in the polls was as much a reflection of general satisfaction with the Government as a result of the high standards of living enjoyed by the majority of the population. One female candidate, in Umm al-Qaiwain, was among the 20 newly elected members, while the 20 appointed members included a further six women. The new FNC was inaugurated by Sheikh Khalifa in November 2011.

Recent developments: arrests of alleged dissidents

Amid anti-Government protests and unrest across the Middle East and North Africa, in April 2011 five signatories to the online petition circulated in March—including Ahmed Mansour, the organizer of an online forum promoting political reforms—were arrested, and subsequently denied bail, by the UAE authorities. In June the five were charged with publicly insulting government officials, which carried a maximum penalty of five years' imprisonment, despite appeals from international rights groups, including Amnesty International and Human Rights Watch, for their immediate release. Mansour was additionally charged with appealing for anti-Government demonstrations. All five pleaded not guilty to the charges against them at a preliminary hearing later in June. The first four sessions of their trial, which commenced at the Supreme Court in September, were held *in camera*, prompting appeals for greater transparency of the judicial process within the UAE from rights groups. Amnesty International alleged that the defence was not granted access to all of the prosecution's evidence and was prohibited from calling back witnesses for cross-examination. All five defendants were convicted in November, with Mansour being sentenced to three years' imprisonment, and his co-defendants each receiving a two-year gaol term. However, in what was widely interpreted as a response to the increasing external criticism of the authorities' treatment of pro-democracy activists, on the following day Sheikh Khalifa granted the five men an official pardon, and they were released from custody shortly thereafter.

Numerous alleged dissidents were arrested in the UAE during 2012, among whom were included human rights lawyers, judges, teachers and student leaders. Many of those detained were members of al-Islah, a conservative religious society with suspected links to the Muslim Brotherhood. In July al-Islah publicly affirmed its loyalty to the UAE Government and called for the release of the 41 detainees who, it claimed, had been subject to false allegations. In late October the European Parliament adopted a resolution on the human rights situation in the UAE in which it expressed concern regarding the country's treatment of those who had exercised their right to freedom of expression. None the less, on 12 November UAE was elected to the UN Human Rights Council for a three-year term; while the following day Sheikh Khalifa issued a decree amending the country's law on internet crime, under the terms of which citizens who were found to have derided or damaged the state and its institutions via the internet would be subject to imprisonment. On 26 January 2013 six international human rights organizations called for an end to the crackdown against human rights campaigners and political activists. Two days later it was announced that a total of 94 UAE nationals (including 13 women and 10 who were abroad) would be tried on charges of attempting to seize power. Among their number was Sheikh Sultan bin Kayed al-Qasimi, a member of one of UAE's seven ruling families and Chairman of al-Islah. Their trial began on 4 March. On 22 March Abdullah al-Hadidi, the son of one of the detainees, was arrested after communicating details of the trial via the internet: he was charged the following month and sentenced to 10 months' imprisonment.

Meanwhile, on 17 March 2013 five new members of the Council of Ministers were appointed: most notably Abd al-Rahman Muhammad al-Owais became Minister of Health, Suhail bin Muhammad al-Mazroui Minister of Energy and Abdullah bin Muhammad al-Nuaimi Minister of Public Works.

Foreign Affairs
Regional relations

During the early 1990s relations between the UAE and Iran were impeded by a protracted dispute concerning the sovereignty of Abu Musa, an island situated between the states in the Persian (Arabian) Gulf. The island had been administered since 1991 under a joint agreement between Iran and Sharjah, in accordance with which an Iranian garrison was stationed on the island. In that year Iran had also seized the smaller neighbouring islands of Greater and Lesser Tunb. In March–April 1996 bilateral relations deteriorated further when Iran opened an airport on Abu Musa and a power station on Greater Tunb. In February 1999 the UAE protested at the construction by Iran of municipal facilities on Abu Musa and at recent Iranian military exercises near the disputed islands. Iran subsequently complained to the UN that, in disputing the location of its military exercises, the UAE was interfering in Iranian internal affairs. Commercial links between the two countries remained strong, meanwhile, with the UAE having particular importance as the largest supplier of imports to Iran. In May 2007 President Mahmoud Ahmadinejad of Iran made the first ever visit to the UAE by an Iranian head of state. Sheikh Muhammad visited Iran in February 2008, thus becoming the most senior UAE official to visit the country since the Iranian Revolution in 1979.

Reports in August 2008 that Iran had established two maritime administrative offices on Abu Musa provoked strong condemnation from the UAE authorities and the GCC. None the less, an official visit to the Iranian capital, Tehran, in October by the UAE's Minister of Foreign Affairs, Sheikh Abdullah bin Zayed Al Nahyan, culminated in the signing of an agreement to establish a joint UAE-Iran commission to promote bilateral relations. While both countries were committed to the advancement of their political and economic ties, neither side showed any inclination to retreat from their stance on the disputed islands. In March 2009 a spokesperson for Iran's Ministry of Foreign Affairs, in response to repeated GCC statements on the UAE's claims to sovereignty over the islands, described them as 'inseparable parts of Iran'. This duly provoked further condemnation from the UAE and the GCC, as well as renewed calls for the issue to be referred to the International Court of Justice in The Hague, Netherlands. Bilateral tensions were fuelled by UAE objections to what it perceived to be Iranian attempts to influence anti-Government demonstrations that erupted in Bahrain (q.v.) from February 2011. During a visit to the UAE in March 2012 by the Iranian Minister of Economic Affairs and Finance, Sayed Shamseddin Hosseini, the two countries affirmed the importance of the bilateral relationship and pledged further to enhance trade and economic ties. However, relations were further strained in mid-April, following a visit by President Ahmadinejad to Abu Musa. The UAE withdrew its ambassador from Iran in protest, while the GCC issued a statement in which it condemned Ahmadinejad's visit as a provocation. In February 2013 the UAE reacted angrily to Iran's announcement that it was to conduct an inspection tour of the islands prior to establishing a national security and foreign affairs policy for the disputed territory.

Meanwhile, relations between the UAE and Saudi Arabia had also become strained by the UAE's trade negotiations with the USA; Saudi Arabia considered that the GCC should negotiate any trade agreement as a single body. In December 2005 the relationship was weakened further in relation to a long-standing border dispute between the UAE and Saudi Arabia concerning the Shaybah oilfield in the Rub al-Khali desert region. Bilateral tensions were exacerbated by a naval clash in March 2010, during which two Saudi sailors were reported to have been injured when UAE naval officers opened fire on a Saudi patrol vessel in disputed waters between the coasts of Saudi Arabia and Abu Dhabi. The vessel's sailors were detained in Abu Dhabi for several days before being handed over to the Saudi embassy later in the month.

At the summit meeting of the Council of the League of Arab States (the Arab League, see p. 372) convened in Beirut, Lebanon, in March 2002, the Minister of State for Foreign Affairs, Sheikh Hamdan bin Zayed Al Nahyan, declared the UAE to be opposed to any future US-led campaign to oust the regime of Saddam Hussein in Iraq as a potential second phase in the USA's declared 'war on terror'. However, in March 2003 the UAE disregarded appeals by some members of the Arab League to refuse to provide facilities for military action in Iraq; at the commencement of the conflict later in that month some 3,000 US air force personnel and 72 combat aircraft were stationed in the UAE. In the immediate aftermath of the ousting of the regime of

Saddam Hussain in April, the UAE provided significant humanitarian aid to Iraq, and made clear its intention to participate in the reconstruction of the country. In early 2004 the UAE agreed to write off most of Iraq's bilateral debt. Following the kidnapping of a member of its diplomatic staff in Iraq in May 2006, the UAE withdrew its chargé d'affaires from Baghdad, the Iraqi capital. In June 2008, however, the UAE's Minister of Foreign Affairs visited Baghdad, becoming the first senior government official from a GCC country to do so since the US-led invasion of Iraq in 2003. This was followed, in July 2008, by the visit of Iraqi Prime Minister Nuri al-Maliki to Abu Dhabi, during which Sheikh Khalifa announced plans to reinstate full diplomatic relations and approved the cancellation of some US $7,000m. of Iraqi debt. A new UAE ambassador to Iraq, the first since 1990, took up his post in September. In January 2012 the two countries announced that bilateral economic relations were to be normalized. Following a meeting in April between the UAE Minister of Foreign Affairs, Sheikh Abdullah bin Zayed Al Nahyan, and his Iraqi counterpart, Hoshyar al-Zibari, it was announced that a further $5,800m. of Iraqi debt owed to the UAE was to be waived.

In May 2009 there was some uncertainty regarding the future of plans to create a GCC monetary union, with a common currency, by 2010, after the UAE announced that it was to withdraw from the project. The UAE's apparent abandonment of proposed monetary union arose from a recent decision of the GCC to locate key financial institutions, including the future central bank, in the Saudi Arabian capital, Riyadh, rather than in the UAE.

The assassination in Dubai of a senior member of the Palestinian Islamic Resistance Movement (Hamas), Mahmoud al-Mabhouh, in January 2010 provoked an international diplomatic dispute, after Hamas accused the Israeli external intelligence service, Mossad, of involvement in al-Mabhouh's death. In February the Dubai authorities issued details of 11 individuals suspected of carrying out the assassination, all of whom had travelled to the emirate using false Australian, British, Irish, French and German passports. The head of Dubai's police force subsequently stated that he was almost certain of Mossad's responsibility for the killing, although the Israeli Government continued to deny any involvement.

In March 2011 a contingent of 500 UAE police officers was deployed to Bahrain as part of a GCC 'Peninsula Shield' force, which also comprised troops from Saudi Arabia and Qatar. The deployment was effected in response to a request from King Hamad bin Isa Al Khalifa of Bahrain and followed several weeks of unrest and anti-Government protests in the kingdom. UAE-Bahraini relations were further consolidated by a visit to Bahrain by a UAE delegation, headed by Crown Prince Gen. Sheikh Muhammad bin Zayed Al Nahyan and the Deputy Prime Minister and Minister of Presidential Affairs, Sheikh Mansour bin Zayed Al Nahyan, in July, during which the visiting UAE officials met with King Hamad and Bahraini Prime Minister Sheikh Khalifa bin Sulman Al Khalifa.

The UAE Government had traditionally been strongly allied with the regime of Egyptian President Hosni Mubarak before his ouster in February 2011. In December 2012, however, the two countries' historic ties were threatened by claims in the Egyptian media that the UAE was involved in a plot against Mubarak's Islamist successor, Muhammad Mursi. Relations became further strained in early 2013 when it was announced that 11 Egyptian nationals had been arrested and detained in the UAE on charges of recruiting members to the Muslim Brotherhood, the ruling party in Egypt (see Domestic Political Affairs); despite appeals by the Egyptian authorities, the detainees had not been released by April 2013.

The UAE adopted a firm stance in favour of the opposition forces in the conflict in Libya from early 2011 that ultimately led to the ousting, in August, of the regime of Col Muammar al-Qaddafi, and to the eventual capture and killing, in October, of Qaddafi himself. The UAE was one of the first states to recognize the legitimacy of the National Transitional Council established by rebel forces, and contributed aircraft to the NATO operation against the Libyan government forces, as well as offering financial assistance to the rebels.

Other external relations

In common with other GCC members, the UAE pledged support for the USA in its efforts to bring to justice the perpetrators of terrorism, following the suicide attacks against New York and Washington, DC, USA, on 11 September 2001. (Hitherto, the UAE had been one of only three states to maintain official relations with the Taliban regime in Afghanistan.) None the less, the UAE emphasized that the success of the US-led 'coalition against terror' must be linked to a resumption of the Arab-Israeli peace process, and expressed concerns that military action should not target any Arab state. The UAE's banking sector came under international scrutiny after US investigators claimed to have evidence of transactions between banks in the UAE and the USA linking the Saudi-born dissident Osama bin Laden with the suicide attacks. At the end of September the Emirates' Central Bank ordered that the assets in the UAE of 27 individuals and organizations accused by the USA of involvement in terrorism be frozen; in November the Central Bank reportedly ordered a freeze on the assets of a further 62 entities. In November 2002 the Central Bank tightened regulations on the informal money-transfer system known as *hawala*, after the practice was criticized by Western law enforcement agencies as an important element in the financing of terrorism.

The UAE signed a Trade and Investment Framework Agreement with the USA—regarded as a preliminary step towards a bilateral free trade agreement—in July 2004. Free trade negotiations with the USA duly commenced in March 2005. In late 2007, however, the Office of the US Trade Representative announced that the two countries had agreed that they would be unable to conclude a free trade accord during the tenure of the incumbent US Administration. Despite the inauguration of Barack Obama as the new US President in January 2009, substantive negotiations on a free trade agreement had not recommenced by early 2013.

In April 2008 the UAE's Minister of Foreign Affairs, Sheikh Abdullah bin Zayed Al Nahyan, and the US Secretary of State, Condoleezza Rice, meeting in Bahrain in advance of a GCC-US summit, signed a memorandum of understanding governing co-operation in the peaceful use of nuclear energy. Prior to this agreement, the UAE (which had in January ratified the International Convention for the Suppression of Acts of Nuclear Terrorism) issued a policy document regarding plans for the potential development of nuclear energy for civilian use, including a commitment to forgo any domestic enrichment or reprocessing capability in exchange for the long-term supply of fuel from external sources. Military co-operation with the USA increased in December with the signing of a contract, worth over US $3,000m., for the provision of a US-made medium-range defensive missile system. This was followed, in January 2009, by the signing of an agreement on civilian nuclear co-operation; having achieved US congressional approval, the so-called 123 Agreement entered into effect in December. Statements released by both parties expressed the hope that the UAE's nuclear energy programme would serve as a model for similar projects throughout the region. Also in December the contract to construct four civil nuclear power plants in the UAE, at a reported cost of some $40,000m., was awarded to a consortium from the Republic of Korea (South Korea); the first of the plants was expected to commence operations in 2017, with the remaining three scheduled for completion by 2020.

Bilateral co-operation accords signed during the course of a visit to the UAE by President Nicolas Sarkozy of France in January 2008 included an arrangement whereby France would assist in the development of a civilian nuclear energy programme in the UAE. Agreement was also reached on the establishment by France of a permanent military base in Abu Dhabi, capable of accommodating some 500 armed forces personnel. The base was officially inaugurated by Sarkozy during a visit to the UAE in May 2009. The importance of the bilateral relationship was underscored by the UAE Minister of Foreign Affairs, Sheikh Abdullah bin Zayed Al Nahyan, during a meeting with his French counterpart, Alain Juppé, in March 2012. The ministers' discussions were reported to have included the proposed sale to the UAE of 60 French-manufactured fighter jets, as well as regional issues including the ongoing civil unrest in Syria (q.v.).

CONSTITUTION AND GOVERNMENT

A provisional Constitution for the UAE took effect in December 1971. This laid the foundation for the federal structure of the Union of the seven emirates, previously known as the Trucial States. In July 1975 a committee was appointed to draft a permanent federal constitution, but in 1976 the provisional document was extended for five years. The provisional Constitution was extended for further five-year periods in 1981, 1986 and 1991. Legislation designed to make the provisional Constitution permanent was endorsed in June 1996, after it had been approved by the Supreme Council of Rulers.

The highest federal authority is the Supreme Council of Rulers, comprising the hereditary rulers of the seven emirates, each of whom is virtually an absolute monarch in his own domain. Decisions of the Supreme Council require the approval of at least five members, including the rulers of both Abu Dhabi and Dubai. From its seven members, the Supreme Council elects a President and a Vice-President. The President appoints the Prime Minister and the federal Council of Ministers, responsible to the Supreme Council, to hold executive authority. The legislature is the Federal National Council (FNC), a consultative assembly that considers laws proposed by the Council of Ministers. The FNC comprises 40 members, of whom one-half are appointed by the emirates, with the remainder chosen by electoral colleges comprising UAE nationals selected by the National Electoral Committee. A constitutional amendment extending the FNC's term from two to four years was endorsed by the Supreme Council of Rulers in December 2008 and approved by the FNC in January 2009. Partial elections to the FNC took place on 24 September 2011. There are no political parties.

REGIONAL AND INTERNATIONAL CO-OPERATION

The UAE was a founder member of the Cooperation Council for the Arab States of the Gulf (the Gulf Cooperation Council—GCC, see p. 255) in May 1981. GCC member states established a unified regional customs tariff in January 2003, and agreed to create a single market and currency. The economic convergence criteria for the monetary union were agreed at a GCC summit in Abu Dhabi in December 2005, and in January 2008 the GCC common market was launched. However, there was doubt regarding prospects for monetary union after the UAE announced in May 2009 that it was to withdraw from the project. The country also participates in the League of Arab States (the Arab League) and the Organization of the Arab Petroleum Exporting Countries (OAPEC, see p. 410).

The UAE joined the UN in December 1971 and became a member of the World Trade Organization (WTO, see p. 444) in 1996. It is also a participant in the Organization of Islamic Cooperation (OIC, see p. 413). The International Renewable Energy Agency (IRENA, see p. 472), established in 2009, has its headquarters in Abu Dhabi.

ECONOMIC AFFAIRS

In 2011, according to estimates by the World Bank, the UAE's gross national income (GNI), measured at average 2009–11 prices, was US $321,665m., equivalent to $40,760 per head (or $48,220 on an international purchasing-power parity basis). During 2002–11, it was estimated, the population increased by an average annual rate of 10.3%. Gross domestic product (GDP) per head decreased, in real terms, by an average of 5.0% per year during. Overall GDP increased, in real terms, by an average annual rate of 4.4% in 2002–11, according to official estimates; real GDP increased by an estimated 4.2% in 2011.

According to official estimates, agriculture (including livestock and fishing) contributed 0.8% of GDP in 2011, and engaged 6.9% of the employed population in 2008. The principal crops are dates, tomatoes, pumpkins, squash and gourds, cucumber and gherkins, and aubergines. The UAE imports some 70% of food requirements. Some agricultural products are exported on a small scale. Livestock-rearing and fishing are also important. During 2002–11 agricultural GDP, according to official estimates, decreased, in real terms, at an average annual rate of 3.7%; the GDP of the sector decreased by 1.8% in 2010, but increased by 0.3% in 2011.

Industry (including mining, manufacturing, construction and power) contributed 56.7% of GDP in 2011, according to official estimates, and engaged 37.5% of the working population in 2008. During 2002–11, according to official estimates, industrial GDP increased by an average of 3.7% per year; the GDP of the sector expanded by 1.7% in 2010 and by 5.3% in 2011.

Mining and quarrying contributed 37.1% of GDP in 2011, according to official estimates, and employed only 1.4% of the working population in 2008. Petroleum production is the most important industry in the UAE, with balance of payments data as published by the IMF indicating that exports of crude petroleum and related products contributed 30.1% of total export revenues in 2010. At the end of 2011 the UAE's proven recoverable reserves of petroleum were 97,800m. barrels, representing 5.9% of world reserves. Production levels in 2011 averaged 3.32m. barrels per day (b/d). As a member of the Organization of the Petroleum Exporting Countries (OPEC, see p. 418), the UAE is subject to production quotas agreed by the Organization's Conference. The UAE has large natural gas reserves, estimated at 6,089,900m. cu m at the end of 2011 (2.9% of world reserves). Most petroleum and natural gas reserves are concentrated in Abu Dhabi. Dubai is the UAE's second largest producer of petroleum. Marble and sand are also quarried. According to official estimates, the GDP of the mining sector increased by an average annual rate of 1.7% during 2002–11; mining GDP increased by 1.0% in 2010 and by 6.7% in 2011.

Manufacturing contributed 7.7% of GDP in 2011, according to official estimates, and employed 12.7% of the working population in 2008. The major heavy industries in the UAE are related to hydrocarbons, and activities are concentrated in the Jebel Ali Free Zone in Dubai and the Jebel Dhanna-Ruwais industrial zone in Abu Dhabi. The most important products are liquefied petroleum gas, distillate fuel oils and jet fuels. There are two petroleum refineries in Abu Dhabi, and the emirate has 'downstream' interests abroad. The most important activities in the non-hydrocarbons manufacturing sector are aluminium, steel and chemicals. During 2002–11, according to official estimates, manufacturing GDP increased at an average annual rate of 3.5%; the GDP of the sector decreased by 6.9% in 2010 and by 3.1% in 2011.

Construction contributed 10.1% of GDP in 2011, according to official estimates, and engaged 22.3% of the working population in 2008. During 2002–11, according to official estimates, the GDP of the construction sector increased by an average of 11.3% per year; the construction sector grew by 3.2% in 2011.

Each of the emirates is responsible for its own energy production. Electric energy is generated largely by thermal power stations, utilizing the UAE's own hydrocarbons resources. In December 2009 an agreement with the USA regarding co-operation in the development of a civilian nuclear power programme entered into effect. In the same month the contract to construct four civil nuclear power plants was awarded to a South Korean consortium.

The services sector contributed 42.5% of GDP in 2011, according to official estimates, and engaged 55.7% of the working population in 2008. The establishment of the Jebel Ali Free Zone in 1985 enhanced Dubai's reputation as a well-equipped entrepôt for regional trade, and significant growth in both re-exports and tourism has been recorded in recent years. The financial services and real estate sectors have also expanded rapidly as the UAE has pursued economic diversification. During 2002–11, according to official estimates, the GDP of the services sector increased by an average of 6.1% per year; the sector's GDP increased by 2.9% in 2011.

In 2011, according to preliminary Central Bank figures, the UAE recorded a visible trade surplus of AED 291,950m., and there was a surplus of AED 112,700m. on the current account of the balance of payments. In 2011 the principal source of imports was India, which supplied 17.4% of total imports; other important suppliers were the People's Republic of China, the USA and Germany. India was also the principal market for non-petroleum exports in that year, taking 31.8% of the total. The other member states of the Cooperation Council for the Arab States of the Gulf (the Gulf Cooperation Council—GCC, see p. 255) together took 11.6% of non-petroleum exports in that year. Largely through its re-export trade, the UAE is of particular importance as a supplier of goods to Iran. Excluding hydrocarbons and free trade exports, the principal exports in 2011 were base metals and articles of base metal, vehicles and other transport equipment, plastics, rubber and related articles, and prepared foodstuffs, beverages, spirits and tobacco. The principal imports in that year were pearls, precious or semi-precious stones and precious metals, machinery and electrical equipment, vehicles and other transport equipment, base metals and articles of base metal, and chemical products.

According to Central Bank estimates the UAE recorded a deficit of AED 31,964m. on the consolidated government budget in 2010, equivalent to 2.9% of GDP. The federal budget, to which Abu Dhabi is the major contributor, represents about one-quarter of the country's total public expenditure, as the individual emirates have their own budgets for municipal expenditure and local projects. In 2011 the UAE's gross government debt was AED 223,382m., equivalent to 17.8% of GDP. Annual inflation averaged 3.2% in 2007–12. Consumer prices increased by an annual average of just 0.7% in 2012, compared with 12.3% in 2008. Some 4% of the labour force were recorded as unemployed in 2008. More than 90% of the workforce are estimated to be non-UAE nationals.

The economy of the UAE was negatively affected by the international financial crisis and the sharp decline in international oil prices from late 2008. By the final quarter of the year, the impact of the global economic downturn was particularly pronounced in Dubai, the heavily services-based economic model of which came under intense scrutiny. In February 2009 the Central Bank acquired US $10,000m. of a sovereign bond issue by the Government of Dubai (one-half of the total issue), thereby assisting Dubai in meeting its debt-servicing obligations for that year. Federal intervention in the economy was particularly notable in view of the traditional autonomy retained by each emirate in its economic affairs. The announcement in November of a six-month postponement of repayments on the estimated $59,000m. of debt held by the government-owned investment company Dubai World provoked fears of a major default on Dubai's sovereign debt, leading to a sharp decline in international share prices. In response, the Central Bank introduced additional liquidity facilities to support the banking sector, while Dubai World announced plans to restructure some of its liabilities. However, the authorities in Abu Dhabi and Dubai declined to offer state guarantees for Dubai World's debt. In December the acquisition by Abu Dhabi-controlled institutions of the remaining $10,000m. of Dubai's sovereign bond issue was completed, and the provision in March 2010 of a $9,500m. fund to support Dubai World's debt-servicing obligations provided further reassurance to the company's creditors. A steady recovery was brought about by high oil prices and nominal growth in the tourism, services and manufacturing sectors, all of which showed an increase of around 3% in 2012, according to official figures. In the same year in Dubai the real estate sector began to gain momentum for the first time since the financial crisis. In May 2012, in an attempt to safeguard the UAE's financial sector from further global crises, a government committee proposed that a new federal agency, the Emirates Financial Services Authority, should be created to oversee the sector's day-to-day operations, duties that had previously been carried out by the Central Bank, which would remain the prudential regulator of the financial system. In February 2013 the UAE's legislature, the Federal National Council (FNC), rejected draft legislation under the terms of which foreign parties would have been permitted 100% ownership of companies outside the UAE's free trade zones, as opposed to owning a minority stake as demanded by the existing company law.

PUBLIC HOLIDAYS

2014: 1 January (New Year's Day), 13 January* (Mouloud, Birth of Muhammad), 26 May* (Leilat al-Meiraj, Ascension of Muhammad), 28 July* (Id al-Fitr, end of Ramadan), 4 October* (Id al-Adha, Feast of the Sacrifice), 24 October* (Muharram, Islamic New Year), 2 December (National Day).

* These holidays are dependent on the Islamic lunar calendar and may vary slightly from the dates given.

Statistical Survey

Source (unless otherwise stated): Central Bank of the UAE, POB 854, Abu Dhabi; tel. (2) 6652220; fax (2) 6652504; e-mail admin@cbuae.gov.ae; internet www .centralbank.ae; National Bureau of Statistics, POB 93000, Abu Dhabi; tel. (2) 6271100; fax (2) 6261344; e-mail contactus@nbs.gov.ae; internet www .uaestatistics.gov.ae.

Area and Population

AREA, POPULATION AND DENSITY

Area (sq km)	77,700*
Population (census results)	
17 December 1995	2,411,041
5 December 2005	
UAE nationals	825,495
Males	417,917
Females	407,578
Non-UAE nationals	3,280,932
Total	4,106,427
Population (official estimate at mid-year)	
2010	8,264,070†
Density (per sq km) at mid-2010	106.4

* 30,000 sq miles.
† Comprising 947,997 UAE nationals and 7,316,073 non-UAE nationals.

Mid-2013 (UN estimate): Total population 8,207,939 (Source: UN, *World Population Prospects: The 2010 Revision*).

POPULATION BY AGE AND SEX
(UN estimates at mid-2013)

	Males	Females	Total
0–14	700,615	653,617	1,354,232
15–64	4,939,900	1,867,918	6,807,818
65 and over	32,999	12,890	45,889
Total	5,673,514	2,534,425	8,207,939

Source: UN, *World Population Prospects: The 2010 Revision*.

Population by Sex (official estimates at mid-2010): Total 8,264,070 (males 6,161,820, females 2,102,250).

POPULATION BY EMIRATE
(official estimates at mid-2010, UAE nationals only)

	Area (sq km)	Population	Density (per sq km)
Abu Dhabi	67,340	404,546	6.0
Dubai	3,885	168,029	43.3
Sharjah	2,590	153,365	59.2
Ajman	259	42,186	162.9
Ras al-Khaimah	1,684	97,529	57.9
Fujairah	1,166	64,860	55.6
Umm al-Qaiwain . . .	777	17,482	22.5
Total	77,700	947,997	12.2

Note: Figures for non-nationals, totalling 7,316,073, were not available.

PRINCIPAL TOWNS
(estimated population at mid-2003)

Dubai	1,171,000	Ras al-Khaimah .	102,000
Abu Dhabi (capital).	552,000	Fujairah .	54,000
Sharjah	519,000	Umm al-Qaiwain .	38,000
Al-Ain	348,000	Khor Fakkan . .	32,000
Ajman	225,000		

2011 (official estimate at 31 December): Dubai 2,003,170 (Source: Statistics Centre, Municipality of Dubai, *Dubai in Figures*).

BIRTHS, MARRIAGES AND DEATHS

	Live births		Marriages*		Deaths	
	Number	Rate (per 1,000)	Number	Rate (per 1,000)	Number	Rate (per 1,000)
2003 . .	61,165	15.1	12,277	3.0	6,002	1.5
2004 . .	63,113	14.6	12,794	2.9	6,123	1.4
2005 . .	64,623	15.7	12,984	3.2	6,361	1.5
2006 . .	62,969	14.9	13,190	3.1	6,483	1.5
2007 . .	67,689	15.1	12,987	2.9	7,414	1.7
2008 . .	68,779	14.4	15,041	3.2	7,755	1.6
2009 . .	76,366	15.1	15,155	3.0	7,788	1.5
2010 . .	79,625	n.a.	15,104	n.a.	7,414	n.a.
2011 . .	83,950	n.a.	15,105	n.a.	7,350	n.a.

* Muslim marriages only.

Life expectancy (years at birth): 76.7 (males 75.8; females 77.7) in 2011 (Source: World Bank, World Development Indicators database).

EMPLOYMENT
(persons aged 15 years and over)

	2005	2006*	2007†
Agriculture, hunting, forestry and fishing	193,044	209,066	225,499
Mining and quarrying	38,694	41,906	45,199
Oil and gas	33,200	35,956	38,783
Manufacturing	336,585	364,521	393,173
Electricity, gas and water supply .	34,207	37,046	39,958
Construction	534,398	578,753	624,242
Wholesale and retail trade; repair of motor vehicles, motorcycles and personal and household goods	502,427	544,129	586,897
Hotels and restaurants . .	116,615	126,294	136,220
Transport, storage and communications	162,768	176,278	190,133
Financial intermediation . .	31,015	33,589	36,229
Real estate, renting and business activities	77,858	84,320	90,947
Public administration and defence; compulsory social security . .	286,105	309,851	334,207
Community, social and personal service activities	114,736	124,259	134,026
Private households with employed persons	222,506	240,975	259,916
Total employed	2,650,958	2,870,987	3,096,646

* Preliminary figures.
† Estimates.

2008 ('000 persons aged 15 years and over): Agriculture, hunting, forestry and fishing 233; Mining and quarrying 47 (Oil and gas 40); Manufacturing 431; Electricity, gas and water 39; Construction 757; Wholesale and retail trade; repair of motor vehicles, motorcycles and personal and household goods 643; Hotels and restaurants 146; Transport, storage and communications 204; Financial intermediation 42; Real estate, renting and business activities 97; Public administration and defence; compulsory social security 353; Community, social and personal service activities 142; Private households with employed persons 264; *Total employed* 3,397.

Health and Welfare

KEY INDICATORS

Total fertility rate (children per woman, 2010)	1.7
Under-5 mortality rate (per 1,000 live births, 2010) . . .	7.0
HIV/AIDS (% of persons aged 15–49, 1994)	0.18
Physicians (per 1,000 head, 2007)	1.9
Hospital beds (per 1,000 head, 2008)	1.9
Health expenditure (2009): US $ per head (PPP)	1,956
Health expenditure (2009): % of GDP	4.4
Health expenditure (2009): public (% of total)	76.9
Access to sanitation (% of persons, 2010)	98
Total carbon dioxide emissions ('000 metric tons, 2008) . .	155,066.4
Carbon dioxide emissions per head (metric tons, 2008) . .	25.0
Human Development Index (2011): ranking	30
Human Development Index (2011): value	0.846

For sources and definitions, see explanatory note on p. vi.

Agriculture

PRINCIPAL CROPS
('000 metric tons, FAO estimates)

	2009	2010	2011
Potatoes	7.1	7.8	9.5
Cabbages	9.5	9.3	8.4
Lettuce	1.1	1.2	1.1
Spinach	1.1	1.1	0.9
Tomatoes	150.0	165.0	159.6
Cauliflowers and broccoli . .	8.5	9.0	11.9
Pumpkins, squash and gourds .	30.5	32.0	32.6
Cucumbers and gherkins . .	23.0	24.0	26.2
Aubergines (Eggplants) . .	13.5	14.0	14.0
Chillies and peppers, green . .	7.5	8.2	8.2
Onions and shallots, green . .	15.1	14.1	15.2
Beans, green	1.0	1.4	1.6
Carrots and turnips	8.6	8.3	9.5
Watermelons	1.0	1.2	1.2
Cantaloupes and other melons .	2.5	2.8	2.8
Lemons and limes	5.0	4.6	4.6
Mangoes, mangosteens and guavas	11.0	10.6	13.0
Dates	759.0	825.3	900.0

Aggregate production ('000 metric tons, may include official, semi-official or estimated data): Total fruits (excl. melons) 795.7 in 2009, 861.1 in 2010, 940.8 in 2011.

Source: FAO.

LIVESTOCK
('000 head, year ending September)

	2009	2010	2011*
Cattle	62†	62†	64
Camels	380†	380†	390
Sheep	1,475	1,450*	1,400
Goats	1,941	1,988†	2,000
Chickens*	18,000	20,000	21,000

* FAO estimate(s).
† Unofficial figure.

Source: FAO.

LIVESTOCK PRODUCTS
('000 metric tons, FAO estimates)

	2009	2010	2011
Cattle meat	14.8	15.0	15.4
Camel meat	29.7	30.1	30.2
Sheep meat	12.1	7.0	6.9
Goat meat	37.6	38.1	38.4
Chicken meat	39.6	40.8	41.4
Cows' milk	22.0	23.5	23.5
Camels' milk	40.4	42.4	42.4
Sheep's milk	15.8	17.5	17.5
Goats' milk	40.0	42.0	42.0
Hen eggs	30.0	26.1	26.1

Source: FAO.

Fishing
('000 metric tons, live weight)

	2008	2009	2010
Capture	74.1	77.7	79.6
Groupers and seabasses . .	9.0	9.1	8.1
Grunts and sweetlips . .	1.3	2.5	2.1
Emperors (Scavengers) . . .	22.0	24.8	22.8
King soldier bream . . .	3.4	3.6	3.1
Sardinellas	4.1	0.8	0.8
Narrow-barred Spanish mackerel	3.3	4.9	8.7
Jacks and crevalles . . .	1.6	1.5	1.0
Carangids	7.9	9.0	8.7
Indian mackerel . . .	0.6	0.6	1.5
Aquaculture	1.2	—	—
Total catch (incl. others) . . .	75.3	77.7	79.6

Source: FAO.

Mining

	2009	2010	2011
Crude petroleum (million metric tons)	126.3	131.4	150.1
Natural gas (million cu metres)* .	48,820	51,280	51,730

* Excluding gas flared or recycled.

Source: BP, *Statistical Review of World Energy*.

Industry

SELECTED PRODUCTS
('000 barrels, unless otherwise indicated)

	2008	2009	2010
Cement ('000 metric tons) . . .	21,885	18,997	18,000
Aluminium ('000 metric tons) . .	945	955	1,400
Motor spirit (petrol)	18,000	16,000	18,000
Kerosene	37,000	42,000	45,000
Gas-diesel (distillate fuel) oil . .	28,000	32,300	35,000
Residual fuel oils	5,000	7,000	6,000
Liquefied petroleum gas . . .	4,000	6,000	7,000

Source: US Geological Survey.

Electric energy (million kWh): 76,106 in 2007; 86,260 in 2008; 90,573 in 2009 (Source: UN Industrial Commodity Statistics Database).

Finance

CURRENCY AND EXCHANGE RATES

Monetary Units
100 fils = 1 UAE dirham (AED).

Sterling, Dollar and Euro Equivalents (31 December 2012)
£1 sterling = 5.795 dirhams;
US $1 = 3.673 dirhams;
€1 = 4.845 dirhams;
100 UAE dirhams = £17.26 = $27.23 = €20.64.

Exchange Rate: The Central Bank's official rate was set at US $1 = 3.671 dirhams in November 1980. This remained in force until December 1997, when the rate was adjusted to $1 = 3.6725 dirhams.

BUDGET OF THE CONSOLIDATED GOVERNMENTS
(million UAE dirhams)

Revenue	2008	2009*	2010†
Tax revenue	17,735	18,366	17,319
Custom revenue	8,686	8,186	8,588
Non-tax revenue	412,868	217,048	279,697
Revenue from petroleum and natural gas	361,515	174,091	239,271
Profit of joint stock corporations	23,167	16,596	13,106
Total	430,603	235,414	297,016

Expenditure	2008	2009*	2010†
Current expenditure	191,636	291,708	255,033
Salaries and wages	29,001	32,711	33,377
Goods and services	49,179	67,738	84,953
Subsidies and transfers . .	41,154	45,479	37,943
Development expenditure . .	31,485	45,083	38,746
Loans and equity	51,844	67,787	35,201
Total	274,965	404,578	328,980

* Preliminary.
† Estimates.

2011 (consolidated accounts of the federal governments of Abu Dhabi, Dubai and Sharjah, '000 million UAE dirhams, estimates): *Revenue* (including IMF estimates of revenues from other government entities operating in the oil and gas sector): Total 439.6 (Hydrocarbons 362.6, Non-hydrocarbon 77.0). *Expenditure and grants:* Total 227.8 (Foreign grants 5.6) (Source: IMF, see below)

2012 (consolidated accounts of the federal governments of Abu Dhabi, Dubai and Sharjah, '000 million UAE dirhams, projections): *Revenue* (including IMF estimates of revenues from other government entities operating in the oil and gas sector): Total 490.4 (Hydrocarbons 404.3, Non-hydrocarbon 86.1). *Expenditure and grants:* Total 231.2 (Foreign grants 5.9) (Source (2011–12): IMF, *United Arab Emirates: Staff Report for the 2012 Article IV Consultation*—May 2012).

INTERNATIONAL RESERVES
(excluding gold, US $ million at 31 December)

	2009	2010	2011
IMF special drawing rights . .	848.2	833.5	831.8
Reserve position in IMF . . .	185.6	200.8	347.0
Foreign exchange*	25,070.4	31,750.9	36,090.5
Total	26,104.2	32,785.3	37,269.3

* Figures exclude the Central Bank's foreign assets and accrued interest attributable to the governments of individual emirates.

Source: IMF, *International Financial Statistics*.

MONEY SUPPLY
(million UAE dirhams at 31 December)

	2009	2010	2011
Currency outside banks . . .	37,217	38,560	41,591
Demand deposits at commercial banks	186,265	194,401	222,505
Total money	223,482	232,961	264,096

Source: IMF, *International Financial Statistics*.

COST OF LIVING
(Consumer Price Index; base: 2007 = 100)

	2010	2011	2012
Food, beverages and tobacco . .	122.4	129.6	136.4
Clothing and footwear	108.4	106.4	108.9
Housing (incl. rent)	113.6	110.8	108.0
Furniture, etc.	118.9	123.1	125.7
Medical care and health services .	105.3	105.7	106.9
Transport	114.5	118.8	119.0
Communication	98.1	98.2	98.2
Recreation and culture	109.3	114.3	114.6
Education	128.9	133.6	139.6
All items (incl. others) . . .	115.0	116.0	116.8

NATIONAL ACCOUNTS
(million UAE dirhams at current prices)

Gross Domestic Product by Emirate

	2007	2008	2009*
Abu Dhabi	545,368	705,159	596,434
Dubai	310,056	342,900	294,158
Sharjah	54,002	65,026	60,946
Ajman	12,633	14,441	13,885
Ras al-Khaimah	14,580	16,413	15,738
Fujairah	9,172	9,904	9,330
Umm al-Qaiwain	2,246	2,424	2,314
Total	948,056	1,156,267	992,805

* Preliminary figures.

Expenditure on the Gross Domestic Product

	2009	2010*	2011†
Government final consumption expenditure	89,301	90,141	93,657
Private final consumption expenditure	554,453	575,650	640,938
Increase in stocks	12,228	12,123	12,201
Gross fixed capital formation	243,466	296,408	340,225
Total domestic expenditure	899,448	974,322	1,087,021
Exports of goods and services	741,694	827,322	1,081,323
Less Imports of goods and services	687,271	758,962	924,505
GDP in purchasers' values	953,871	1,042,682	1,243,839
GDP at constant 2007 prices	930,475	942,397	981,659

* Preliminary figures.
† Estimates.

Gross Domestic Product by Economic Activity

	2009	2010*	2011†
Agriculture, livestock and fishing	9,620	9,873	10,481
Mining and quarrying	254,252	324,832	479,982
Oil and gas	251,818	322,369	477,304
Manufacturing	85,623	92,275	99,425
Electricity and water	23,908	22,485	24,216
Construction	117,673	120,496	131,210
Wholesale and retail trade, and repairs	134,190	138,347	146,472
Restaurants and hotels	21,142	20,589	22,403
Transport, storage and communications	92,592	90,934	99,007
Financial institutions and insurance	73,808	79,431	85,464
Real estate and business services	109,134	111,001	110,200
Government services	50,251	52,027	54,058
Community, social and personal services	22,682	23,511	27,103
Private households with employed persons	4,266	4,425	5,088
Sub-total	999,141	1,090,226	1,295,108
Less Imputed bank service charge	45,270	47,544	51,270
GDP in purchasers' values	953,871	1,042,682	1,243,839

* Preliminary figures.
† Estimates.

BALANCE OF PAYMENTS
('000 million UAE dirhams)

	2009	2010	2011*
Exports of goods f.o.b.	704.39	784.22	1,034.32
Imports of goods f.o.b.	−549.80	−604.35	−742.37
Trade balance	154.60	179.87	291.95
Services (net)	−100.17	−111.51	−135.13
Income (net)	11.80	−0.37	0.08
Balance on goods, services and income	66.23	67.99	156.90
Current transfers (net)	−37.40	−41.40	−44.20
Current balance	28.81	26.59	112.70
Capital and financial accounts (net)	−35.58	18.46	−60.35
Net errors and omissions	−15.76	−18.12	−35.72
Overall balance	−22.52	26.93	16.62

* Preliminary estimates.

External Trade

PRINCIPAL COMMODITIES
(distribution by HS, million UAE dirhams)

Imports c.i.f.	2009	2010	2011
Vegetable products	18,683.9	20,187.3	24,299.6
Prepared foodstuffs, beverages, spirits and tobacco	8,868.2	10,423.5	12,283.7
Chemical products, etc.	24,063.4	27,122.0	33,044.7
Plastics, rubber and articles thereof	13,720.2	15,368.2	17,730.1
Textiles and textile articles	17,494.7	17,826.8	20,683.6
Pearls, precious or semi-precious stones, precious metals, etc.	101,497.7	139,191.3	188,431.7
Base metals and articles of base metal	41,206.3	41,755.7	55,814.9
Machinery and electrical equipment	108,134.3	94,294.2	106,099.7
Vehicles and other transport equipment	57,205.1	60,346.2	72,184.4
Total (incl. others)	447,393.8	485,413.9	602,757.3

Exports f.o.b.*	2009	2010	2011
Animals and animal products	773.4	923.4	1,180.9
Prepared foodstuffs, beverages, spirits and tobacco	4,265.1	5,825.8	6,281.2
Mineral products	3,713.3	3,330.4	6,299.4
Chemical products, etc.	1,692.9	2,198.7	2,979.8
Plastics, rubber and articles thereof	5,211.4	5,909.7	6,828.1
Textiles and textile articles	1,005.0	1,177.2	1,057.0
Stone, plaster, cement, ceramic and glassware	1,903.6	2,329.8	2,440.0
Base metals and articles of base metal	8,019.5	7,633.4	11,155.1
Machinery and electrical equipment	1,386.9	1,504.4	1,439.6
Vehicles and other transport equipment	1,718.4	6,190.6	5,094.8
Total (incl. others)†	65,278.9	83,077.7	114,038.3

* Excluding petroleum exports and excluding re-exports; re-exports amounted to 147,693.4m. dirhams in 2009; 185,863.3m. dirhams in 2010; 210,842.8m. dirhams in 2011.
† Excluding free zone exports.

SELECTED MAJOR TRADING PARTNERS
(million UAE dirhams)

Imports		2009	2010	2011
Australia	. . . .	6,365.4	7,500.0	8,956.8
Belgium	. . . .	6,496.8	6,718.8	10,819.2
Brazil	. . . .	3,750.2	4,471.3	5,773.2
Canada	. . . .	4,323.7	3,525.1	5,435.0
China, People's Republic	. . .	47,825.6	49,905.3	54,960.0
France (incl. Monaco)	. . .	14,027.1	12,779.3	15,982.9
GCC countries	. . . . .	21,537.6	22,336.3	27,821.8
Germany	. . . . . .	29,998.0	29,679.5	30,656.1
Hong Kong	. . . . .	4,054.6	3,853.0	6,305.5
India	. . . .	61,564.8	83,187.4	105,132.2
Italy (incl. San Marino)	. .	17,417.6	15,150.9	19,966.9
Japan	. . . .	26,903.7	28,501.6	30,010.1
Korea, Republic	. . . .	16,899.2	12,140.3	22,919.2
Netherlands	. . . . .	4,800.7	4,925.2	5,064.8
Pakistan	. . . . . .	5,764.9	6,547.5	7,201.8
Saudi Arabia	. . . . .	12,179.3	11,969.9	15,048.3
Sudan	. . . .	2,334.3	4,962.0	7,442.3
Switzerland	. . . . .	9,819.9	11,488.4	15,289.6
Thailand	. . . . . .	7,518.4	7,785.4	8,975.4
Turkey	. . . .	9,362.3	9,108.9	8,962.5
United Kingdom	. . . .	18,762.4	17,238.8	21,477.5
USA	. . . .	41,524.9	41,303.6	53,274.9
Total (incl. others)	. . . .	**447,393.8**	**485,413.9**	**602,757.3**

Exports*		2009	2010	2011
Bahrain	. . . .	669.5	905.0	1,239.6
Belgium	. . . .	3,451.2	4,014.5	556.3
Brazil	. . . .	256.7	3,079.3	1,903.9
Canada	. . . .	316.1	197.1	2,935.9
Egypt	. . . .	801.8	1,243.7	1,403.3
GCC countries	. . . . .	33,311.3	32,365.1	13,217.8
Hong Kong	. . . . .	188.0	611.5	1,751.3
India	. . . .	46,497.0	80,218.0	36,234.9
Kuwait	. . . .	1,161.7	1,667.5	3,252.9
Oman	. . . .	1,858.9	1,818.3	1,194.3
Pakistan	. . . . . .	1,806.5	2,100.7	1,316.3
Qatar	. . . .	4,897.4	1,817.9	1,870.6
Saudi Arabia	. . . . .	3,007.0	3,743.5	5,660.4
Singapore	. . . . . .	475.2	612.1	3,284.4
Switzerland	. . . . .	8,727.0	13,418.5	14,457.6
Thailand	. . . . . .	260.7	380.2	2,130.0
Turkey	. . . .	681.8	586.1	3,241.8
United Kingdom	. . . .	1,551.2	2,618.3	594.9
USA	. . . .	3,323.1	3,331.4	1,177.8
Total (incl. others)	. . . .	**212,972.3**	**268,940.9**	**114,038.3**

* Data for non-petroleum exports and all re-exports.

Transport

ROAD TRAFFIC
('000 registered motor vehicles in use)

		2000	2001	2002
Passenger cars (incl. taxis)	. .	561.9	654.2	606.1
Trucks (incl. public)	. . .	83.3	66.2	66.2
Buses (incl. public)	. . . .	14.7	13.3	16.0
Other	. . . .	13.2	11.2	13.1

Total vehicles in use ('000): 767 in 2002; 792 in 2003.

2007 (motor vehicles registered at 31 December): Passenger cars 1,279,098; Buses and coaches 48,205; Vans and lorries 39,424; Motorcycles and mopeds 13,639 (Source: IRF, *World Road Statistics*).

SHIPPING
Flag Registered Fleet
(at 31 December)

	2010	2011	2012
Number of vessels	. . . . .	716	730	738
Total displacement ('000 grt)	. .	1,572.8	1,515.3	1,348.8

Source: Lloyd's List Intelligence (www.lloydslistintelligence.com).

International Sea-borne Shipping
(estimated freight traffic, '000 metric tons)

	1988	1989	1990
Goods loaded	. . . . .	63,380	72,896	88,153
Crude petroleum	. . . .	54,159	63,387	78,927
Other cargo	. . . .	9,221	9,509	9,226
Goods unloaded	. . . . .	8,973	8,960	9,595

Source: UN, *Monthly Bulletin of Statistics*.

CIVIL AVIATION
(traffic on scheduled services)*

		2007	2008	2009
Kilometres flown (million)	. .	483	573	655
Passengers carried ('000)	. . .	25,088	28,432	31,762
Passenger-km (million)	. . .	108,262	124,831	143,849
Total ton-km (million)	. . .	16,971	19,337	21,823

* Figures include an apportionment (one-quarter) of the traffic of Gulf Air, a multinational airline with its headquarters in Bahrain.

Source: UN, *Statistical Yearbook*.

2010 ('000): Passengers carried 42,555 (Source: World Bank, World Development Indicators database).

Tourism

FOREIGN TOURIST ARRIVALS*

Country		2002	2003	2004
Canada	. . . .	95,878	55,297	57,718
Egypt	. . . .	111,822	121,221	131,635
France	. . . .	90,735	98,624	112,429
Germany	. . . . . .	236,660	235,147	337,594
India	. . . .	336,046	357,941	356,446
Iran	. . . .	270,350	334,453	336,734
Jordan	. . . .	73,140	76,553	76,308
Lebanon	. . . . . .	74,225	83,137	90,409
Pakistan	. . . . . .	154,711	183,724	173,152
Russia	. . . .	267,655	324,484	340,716
United Kingdom	. . . .	491,604	496,147	644,688
USA	. . . .	123,112	175,116	192,948
Total (incl. others)†	. . . .	**5,445,367**	**5,871,023**	**6,195,006**

* Figures refer to international arrivals at hotels and similar establishments.
† Total includes domestic tourists.

Total tourist arrivals ('000): 6,812 in 2009; 7,432 in 2010; 8,129 in 2011 (provisional).

Receipts from tourism (US $ million, excl. passenger transport): 7,352 in 2009; 8,577 in 2010; 9,204 in 2011 (provisional).

Source: World Tourism Organization.

Communications Media

	2009	2010	2011
Telephones ('000 main lines in use)	1,580.1	1,479.5	1,825.5
Mobile cellular telephones ('000 subscribers)	10,671.9	10,926.0	11,727.4
Internet subscribers ('000) . .	1,404.4	1,374.9	1,324.1
Broadband subscribers ('000) . .	687.7	786.8	867.0

Personal computers: 1,400,000 (330.8 per 1,000 persons) in 2006.

Source: International Telecommunication Union.

Education

(Government schools only)

	2008/09	2009/10	2010/11
Institutions	721	725	718
Teachers*	27,469	28,832	28,886
Students			
Pre-primary	23,910	24,821	26,733
Primary	175,761	175,968	177,911
Secondary	60,903	63,032	61,061
Other schools	1,799	1,610	n.a.

*Includes administrative and technical staff.

Source: Ministry of Education, United Arab Emirates.

Pupil-teacher ratio (primary education, UNESCO estimate): 16.8 in 2009/10 (Source: UNESCO Institute for Statistics).

Adult literacy rate (UNESCO estimates): 90.4% (males 90.9%; females 89.2%) in 2007 (Source: UNESCO Institute for Statistics).

Directory

The Government

HEAD OF STATE

President: Sheikh KHALIFA BIN ZAYED AL NAHYAN (Ruler of Abu Dhabi, elected by the Supreme Council of Rulers as President of the UAE on 3 November 2004; re-elected 3 November 2009).

Vice-President: Sheikh MUHAMMAD BIN RASHID AL MAKTOUM (Ruler of Dubai).

SUPREME COUNCIL OF RULERS
(with each Ruler's date of accession)

Ruler of Abu Dhabi: Sheikh KHALIFA BIN ZAYED AL NAHYAN (2004).

Ruler of Dubai: Sheikh MUHAMMAD BIN RASHID AL MAKTOUM (2006).

Ruler of Sharjah: Sheikh SULTAN BIN MUHAMMAD AL-QASIMI (1972).

Ruler of Ras al-Khaimah: Sheikh SAUD BIN SAQR AL-QASIMI (2010).

Ruler of Umm al-Qaiwain: Sheikh SAUD BIN RASHID AL-MU'ALLA (2009).

Ruler of Ajman: Sheikh HUMAID BIN RASHID AL-NUAIMI (1981).

Ruler of Fujairah: Sheikh HAMAD BIN MUHAMMAD AL-SHARQI (1974).

COUNCIL OF MINISTERS
(May 2013)

Prime Minister and Minister of Defence: Sheikh MUHAMMAD BIN RASHID AL MAKTOUM.

Deputy Prime Minister and Minister of the Interior: Lt-Gen. Sheikh SAIF BIN ZAYED AL NAHYAN.

Deputy Prime Minister and Minister of Presidential Affairs: Sheikh MANSOUR BIN ZAYED AL NAHYAN.

Minister of Finance: Sheikh HAMDAN BIN RASHID AL MAKTOUM.

Minister of Foreign Affairs: Sheikh ABDULLAH BIN ZAYED AL NAHYAN.

Minister of Higher Education and Scientific Research: Sheikh HAMDAN BIN MUBARAK AL NAHYAN.

Minister of Public Works: ABDULLAH BIN MUHAMMAD AL-NUAIMI.

Minister of Economy: SULTAN BIN SAID AL-MANSOURI.

Minister of Development and International Co-operation: Sheikha LUBNA BINT KHALID AL-QASIMI.

Minister of Justice: Dr HADIF JOWAN AL-DHAHIRI.

Minister of Energy: SUHAIL BIN MUHAMMAD AL-MAZROUI.

Minister of Labour: SAQR GHOBASH SAID GHOBASH.

Minister of Social Affairs: Dr MARIAM MUHAMMAD KHALFAN AL-ROUMI.

Minister of Education: HUMAID MUHAMMAD OBAID AL-QATTAMI.

Minister of the Environment and Water: Dr RASHID AHMAD AL-FAHD.

Minister of Culture, Youth and Community Development: Sheikh NAHYAN BIN MUBARAK AL NAHYAN.

Minister of Health: ABD AL-RAHMAN BIN MUHAMMAD AL-OWAIS.

Minister of Cabinet Affairs: MUHAMMAD BIN ABDULLAH AL-GARGAWI.

Minister of State for Financial Affairs: OBAID HUMAID AL-TAYER.

Minister of State for Foreign Affairs and for Federal National Council Affairs: Dr ANWAR MUHAMMAD GARGASH.

Ministers of State: REEM IBRAHIM AL-HASHEMI, Dr MAITHA SALIM AL-SHAMSI, SULTAN AHMAD AL-JABER, ABDULLAH BIN MUHAMMAD GOBASH.

FEDERAL MINISTRIES

Office of the Prime Minister: POB 12848, Dubai; tel. (4) 3534550; fax (4) 3530111; e-mail info@primeminister.ae; internet www.uaepm.ae.

Office of the Deputy Prime Minister: POB 831, Abu Dhabi; tel. (2) 4451000; fax (2) 4450066.

Ministry of Cabinet Affairs: POB 899, Abu Dhabi; tel. (2) 6811113; fax (2) 6812968; e-mail moca@uae.gov.ae; internet www.moca.gov.ae.

Ministry of Culture, Youth and Community Development: POB 17, Abu Dhabi; tel. (2) 4466145; fax (2) 4452504; e-mail info@mcycd.gov.ae; internet www.mcycd.ae.

Ministry of Defence: POB 46616, Abu Dhabi; tel. (4) 3532222; fax (4) 3531974; e-mail mod@mod.gov.ae; internet www.mod.gov.ae.

Ministry of Development and International Co-operation: POB 110555, Abu Dhabi; tel. (2) 4956000; fax (2) 4499164.

Ministry of Economy: POB 901, Abu Dhabi; tel. (2) 3161111; fax (2) 6260000; e-mail economy@economy.ae; internet www.economy.ae.

Ministry of Education: POB 3962, Abu Dhabi; tel. (2) 4089999; fax (4) 2176006; e-mail ccc.moe@moe.gov.ae; internet www.moe.gov.ae.

Ministry of Energy: POB 59, Abu Dhabi; tel. (2) 6126500; fax (2) 6272291; e-mail moenr@moenr.ae; internet www.moenr.gov.ae.

Ministry of the Environment and Water: POB 213, Abu Dhabi; tel. (2) 4444747; fax (2) 4490444; e-mail archives@moew.gov.ae; internet www.moew.gov.ae.

Ministry of Finance: POB 433, Abu Dhabi; tel. (2) 6726000; fax (2) 6768414; e-mail webmaster@mof.gov.ae; internet www.mof.gov.ae.

Ministry of Foreign Affairs: POB 1, Abu Dhabi; tel. and fax (2) 2222000; e-mail info@mofa.gov.ae; internet www.mofa.gov.ae.

Ministry of Health: POB 848, Abu Dhabi; tel. (2) 6330000; fax (2) 6726000; e-mail info@moh.gov.ae; internet www.moh.gov.ae.

Ministry of Higher Education and Scientific Research: POB 45253, Abu Dhabi; tel. (2) 6428000; fax (2) 6428778; e-mail mohe@uae.gov.ae; internet www.mohesr.ae.

Ministry of the Interior: POB 398, Abu Dhabi; tel. (2) 4414666; fax (2) 4022776; e-mail moi@moi.gov.ae; internet www.moi.gov.ae.

Ministry of Justice: POB 260, Abu Dhabi; tel. (2) 6921000; fax (2) 6810680; e-mail moj@uae.gov.ae; internet ejustice.gov.ae.

Ministry of Labour: POB 809, Abu Dhabi; tel. (2) 6671700; fax (2) 4494293; e-mail minister@mol.gov.ae; internet www.mol.gov.ae.

Ministry of Presidential Affairs: POB 280, Abu Dhabi; tel. (2) 6222221; fax (2) 6222228; e-mail ihtimam@mopa.ae; internet www.mopa.ae.

Ministry of Public Works: POB 878, Abu Dhabi; tel. (4) 2610001; fax (4) 2125544; e-mail info@mopw.gov.ae; internet www.mopw.gov.ae.

Ministry of Social Affairs: POB 809, Abu Dhabi; tel. (4) 2637777; fax (4) 2633525; e-mail info@msa.gov.ae; internet www.msa.gov.ae.

Ministry of State for Federal National Council Affairs: POB 130000, Abu Dhabi; tel. (2) 4041000; fax (2) 4041155; e-mail mfnca@mfnca.gov.ae; internet www.mfnca.gov.ae.

Ministry of State for Financial Affairs: POB 433, Abu Dhabi; tel. (2) 771133; fax (2) 793255.

Ministry of State for Foreign Affairs: POB 1, Abu Dhabi; tel. (2) 6660888; fax (2) 6652883.

Legislature

Federal National Council (FNC)

POB 836, Abu Dhabi; tel. (2) 6812000; fax (2) 6812846; e-mail info@almajles.gov.ae; internet www.almajles.gov.ae.

Formed under the provisional Constitution, the Council is composed of 40 members from the various emirates (eight each from Abu Dhabi and Dubai, six each from Sharjah and Ras al-Khaimah, and four each from Ajman, Fujairah and Umm al-Qaiwain). Each emirate appoints its own representatives separately. The Council studies laws proposed by the Council of Ministers and can reject them or suggest amendments. In December 2005 Sheikh Khalifa announced that elections would be introduced to choose one-half of the members of the FNC, which would also be expanded and granted enhanced powers. In August 2006 a National Electoral Committee was established to preside over the elections, which were held during 16–20 December. A constitutional amendment extending the Council's term from two to four years was endorsed by the Supreme Council of Rulers in December 2008 and approved by the FNC in January 2009. A further round of elections took place on 24 September 2011.

Speaker: MUHAMMAD AHMAD AL-MURR.

Diplomatic Representation

EMBASSIES IN THE UNITED ARAB EMIRATES

Afghanistan: POB 5687, Abu Dhabi; tel. (2) 4472666; fax (2) 4472660; e-mail afgem555@emirates.net.ae; internet www.afghanembassy-uae.com; Ambassador Dr NAJIBULLAH MOJADIDI.

Algeria: POB 3070, Abu Dhabi; tel. (2) 448949; fax (2) 4447068; e-mail emalgadhabi@hotmail.com; Ambassador HAMID CHEBIRA.

Angola: POB 36532, Abu Dhabi; tel. (2) 4477042; fax (2) 4477043; e-mail info@adangola.ae; internet www.adangola.ae; Ambassador FLÁVIO SARAIVA DE CARVALHO FONSECA.

Argentina: POB 3325, Abu Dhabi; tel. (2) 4436838; fax (2) 4431392; e-mail info_eearb@mrecic.gov.ar; Ambassador RUBÉN EDUARDO CARO.

Armenia: POB 6358, Abu Dhabi; tel. (2) 4444196; fax (2) 4444197; e-mail armemiratesembassy@mfa.am; internet uae.mfa.am; Ambassador GEGHAM GHARIBJANYAN.

Australia: POB 32711, al-Muhairy Centre, 8th Floor, Sheikh Zayed I St, Abu Dhabi; tel. (2) 4017500; fax (2) 4017501; e-mail abudhabi.embassy@dfat.gov.au; internet www.uae.embassy.gov.au; Ambassador PABLO KANG.

Austria: POB 35539, Abu Dhabi; tel. (2) 6944999; fax (2) 6944988; e-mail abu-dhabi-ob@bmeia.gv.at; internet www.bmeia.gv.at/en/embassy/abu-dhabi; Ambassador PETER ELSNER-MACKAY.

Azerbaijan: POB 45766, Plot N-297, W-16, al-Bateen Area, Abu Dhabi; tel. (2) 6662848; fax (2) 6663150; e-mail azembasy@eim.ae; internet www.azembassy.ae; Ambassador ELKHAN GAHRAMANOV.

Bahrain: POB 3367, Abu Dhabi; tel. (2) 6657500; fax (2) 6674141; e-mail abudhabi.mission@mofa.gov.bh; Ambassador MUHAMMAD SAQR AL-MAAWDA.

Bangladesh: POB 2504, Villa 21, Delma St, al-Rowdha, Abu Dhabi; tel. (2) 4465100; fax (2) 4464733; e-mail bdootabudhabi@bdembassy.ae; internet www.bdembassyuae.org; Ambassador MUHAMMAD NUZMUL QAWNAIN.

Belarus: POB 30337, Plot 111, Villa 2, East 19, Sharq Area, Abu Dhabi; tel. (2) 4453399; fax (2) 4451131; e-mail uae@mfa.gov.by; internet uae.mfa.gov.by; Ambassador ALEXANDER SEMESHKO.

Belgium: POB 3686, al-Masood Tower, 6th Floor, Hamdan St, Abu Dhabi; tel. (2) 6319449; fax (2) 6319353; e-mail abudhabi@diplobel.fed.be; internet www.diplomatie.be/abudhabi; Ambassador CHRISTIAAN TANGHE.

Bosnia and Herzegovina: POB 43362, Abu Dhabi; tel. (2) 6444164; fax (2) 6443619; e-mail ambassador.rk@bhmc.ae; internet www.bhmc.ae; Ambassador MILUTIN VASILJEVIĆ.

Brazil: POB 3027, Villa 3, St 5, Madinat Zayed, Abu Dhabi; tel. (2) 6320606; fax (2) 6327727; e-mail brasemb.abudhabi@itamaraty.gov.br; internet abudhabi.itamaraty.gov.br; Ambassador JOSÉ DE MENDONÇA E LIMA.

Brunei: POB 5836, Abu Dhabi; tel. (2) 4486999; fax (2) 4486333; e-mail kbdauh98@amirates.net.ae; Ambassador (vacant).

Canada: POB 6970, Abu Dhabi Trade Towers, West Tower, 9th and 10th Floors, Abu Dhabi; tel. (2) 6940300; fax (2) 6940399; e-mail abdbi@international.gc.ca; internet www.dfait-maeci.gc.ca/abudhabi; Ambassador ARIF LALANI.

Chile: St 4, nr St 23, al-Mushrif, Abu Dhabi; tel. (2) 4472022; fax (2) 4472023; e-mail info@chile-uae.com; internet chile-uae.com; Ambassador JEAN-PAUL TARUD KUBORN.

China, People's Republic: POB 2741, Plot 26, W-22, Abu Dhabi; tel. (2) 4434276; fax (2) 4436835; e-mail chinaemb_ae@mfa.gov.cn; internet ae.chineseembassy.org; Ambassador HUANG JIEMIN.

Cyprus: POB 63013, 426 al-Khaleej al-Arabi St, Abu Dhabi; tel. (2) 6654480; fax (2) 6657870; e-mail cyembadb@eim.ae; Ambassador ELPIDOFOROS ECONOMOU.

Czech Republic: POB 27009, City Bank Bldg, Corniche Plaza, Abu Dhabi; tel. (2) 6782800; fax (2) 6795716; e-mail abudhabi@embassy.mzv.cz; internet www.mzv.cz/abudhabi; Ambassador JAROSLAV LUDVA.

Denmark: POB 105415, Abu Dhabi; tel. (2)4410104; fax (2) 4410021; e-mail auhamb@um.dk; internet fae.um.dk; Ambassador POUL O. G. HOINESS.

Egypt: POB 4026, Abu Dhabi; tel. (2) 4445566; fax (2) 4449878; e-mail egyptembassyabudhabi@live.com; Ambassador TAMER MANSOUR.

Eritrea: POB 2597, Abu Dhabi; tel. (2) 6331838; fax (2) 6790060; e-mail erimb75@emirates.net.ae; Chargé d'affaires a.i. ALAMIN NAFIE YOUSEF.

Fiji: Abu Dhabi; Ambassador ROBIN NAIR.

Finland: POB 3634, al-Masood Tower, Hamdan St, Abu Dhabi; tel. (2) 6328927; fax (2) 6325063; e-mail sanomat.abo@formin.fi; internet www.finland.ae; Ambassador ILKKA-PEKKA SIMILÄ.

France: POB 4014, Abu Dhabi; tel. (2) 4435100; fax (2) 4434158; e-mail contact@ambafrance.ae; internet www.ambafrance-eau.org; Ambassador ALAIN AZOUAOU.

The Gambia: POB 3675, Abu Dhabi; tel. (2) 6433955; fax (2) 6433963; e-mail gamsyuae@emirates.net.ae; Ambassador (vacant).

Germany: POB 2591, Abu Dhabi Mall, West Tower, 14th Floor, Abu Dhabi; tel. (2) 6446693; fax (2) 6446942; e-mail info@abu-dhabi.diplo.de; internet www.abu-dhabi.diplo.de; Ambassador NIKOLAI VON SCHOEPFF.

Greece: POB 5483, Abu Dhabi; tel. (2) 4492550; fax (2) 4492455; e-mail gremb.abd@mfa.gr; internet www.mfa.gr/abu; Ambassador DIONISIOS ZOIS.

Hungary: POB 44450, Abu Dhabi; tel. (2) 6766190; fax (2) 6766215; e-mail mission.abu@mfa.gov.hu; internet www.mfa.gov.hu/emb/abudhabi; Ambassador JÁNOS GYURIS.

India: POB 4090, Abu Dhabi; tel. (2) 4492700; fax (2) 4444685; e-mail ambassador@indembassyuae.org; internet www.indembassyuae.org; Ambassador M. K. LOKESH.

Indonesia: POB 7256, Abu Dhabi; tel. (2) 4454448; fax (2) 4455453; e-mail indoemb@emirates.net.ae; internet www.kemlu.go.id/abudhabi; Ambassador SALMAN AL-FARISI.

Iran: POB 4080, Abu Dhabi; tel. (2) 4447618; fax (2) 4448714; e-mail iranemb@emirates.net.ae; internet www.iranembassy.org.ae; Ambassador MUHAMMAD REZA FAYYAZ.

Iraq: Embassies Area, 41 West 59/2, Abu Dhabi; tel. (2) 4418022; fax (2) 4418155; e-mail ademb@iraqmfamail.com; Ambassador ARSHAD TAWFIQ.

Ireland: POB 61581, 1–2 Khalifa al-Suwaidi Development, 19th St (off 32nd St), al-Bateen Area, Abu Dhabi; tel. (2) 4958200; fax (2) 6819233; e-mail irishvisaofficedubai@gmail.com; internet www.embassyofireland.ae; Ambassador CIARÁN MADDEN.

Italy: POB 46752, Villa 438–439, St 26, al-Manaseer Area, Abu Dhabi; tel. (2) 4435622; fax (2) 4434337; e-mail italianembassy.abudhabi@esteri.it; internet www.ambabudhabi.esteri.it; Ambassador GIORGIO STARACE.

Japan: POB 2430, Abu Dhabi; tel. (2) 4435696; fax (2) 4434219; e-mail embjpn@ab.mofa.go.jp; internet www.uae.emb-japan.go.jp; Ambassador YOSHIHIKO KAMO.

Jordan: POB 4024, Abu Dhabi; tel. (2) 4447100; fax (2) 4449157; e-mail embjord1@emirates.net.ae; internet www.jordanembassy.ae; Ambassador NAYEF ZEIDAN.

Kazakhstan: 593 Rashid bin Said Al Maktoum St, al-Safarat District, Abu Dhabi; tel. (2) 4498778; fax (2) 4498775; e-mail abudhabi@mfa.kz; internet www.kazembemirates.net; Ambassador ASKAR A. MUSSINOV.

Kenya: POB 3854, Abu Dhabi; tel. (2) 6666300; fax (2) 6652827; e-mail kenyarep@emirates.net.ae; internet www.kenyaembassy.ae; Ambassador MUHAMMED ABDI GELLO.

Korea, Republic: POB 3270, Abu Dhabi; tel. (2) 6439122; fax (2) 6439130; e-mail uae@mofat.go.kr; internet are.mofat.go.kr; Ambassador KWON TAE-KYUN.

Kuwait: POB 926, Abu Dhabi; tel. (2) 4477146; fax (2) 4477675; e-mail q8embassy@gmail.com; Ambassador SALEH MUHAMMAD AL-BUAIJAN.

Lebanon: POB 4023, Abu Dhabi; tel. (2) 4492100; fax (2) 4493500; e-mail lebanon3@eim.ae; Chargé d'affaires a.i. FARAH AL-KHATIB AL-HARIRI.

Libya: POB 5739, Abu Dhabi; tel. (2) 4450030; fax (2) 4450033; e-mail libya_emb_ae@foreign.gov.ly; Ambassador Dr ARIF ALI AL-NAYEDH.

Malaysia: POB 3887, Abu Dhabi; tel. (2) 4482775; fax (2) 4482779; e-mail admin@malaysianembassy.ae; internet www.kln.gov.my/perwakilan/abudhabi; Ambassador AHMAD ANWAR BIN ADNAN.

Mauritania: POB 2714, Abu Dhabi; tel. (2) 4462724; fax (2) 4465772; e-mail mminejih@hotmail.com; Ambassador HAMID OULD AHMAD TALEB.

Mexico: POB 108543, Villa 1, Sector 23, Plot 7A, Bain al-Jessrain, Abu Dhabi; tel. (2) 5580088; fax (2) 5580077; e-mail embamex@eim.ae; internet embamex.sre.gob.mx/emiratosarabesunidos; Ambassador FRANCISCO JAVIER ALONSO ESCOBAR.

Morocco: POB 4066, Abu Dhabi; tel. (2) 4433973; fax (2) 4433917; e-mail sifmabo@yahoo.com; internet www.moroccan-emb.ae; Ambassador MUHAMMAD AIT OUALI.

Nepal: POB 38282, Abu Dhabi; tel. (2) 6344767; fax (2) 6344469; e-mail info@nepalembassyuae.org; internet www.nepalembassyuae.org; Ambassador DHANANJAYA JHA.

Netherlands: POB 46560, al-Masood Tower, 6th Floor, Sheikh Hamdan St, Abu Dhabi; tel. (2) 6958000; fax (2) 6313158; e-mail abu@minbuza.nl; internet www.netherlands.ae; Ambassador Dr GERALD MICHELS.

New Zealand: Villa 226/2, al-Karamah St (24th St, between 11th & 13th), al-Karamah Area, Abu Dhabi; tel. (2) 4411222; fax (2) 4411555; e-mail nzembassy.abu.dhabi@mfat.govt.nz; internet www.nzembassy.com/united-arab-emirates; Ambassador MALCOLM MILLAR.

Nigeria: POB 110171, Abu Dhabi; tel. (2) 4431503; fax (2) 4431792; e-mail nigerabudhabi@yahoo.co.uk; Ambassador OMOLADE OLUWATERU.

Norway: POB 47270, Abu Dhabi; tel. (2) 6211221; fax (2) 6213313; e-mail emb.abudhabi@mfa.no; internet www.norway.ae; Ambassador ÅSE ELIN BJERKE.

Oman: POB 2517, Said bin Tahnon Sq., al-Mushraf Area, Abu Dhabi; tel. (2) 4463333; fax (2) 4464633; e-mail abudhabi@mofa.gov.om; Ambassador Sheikh MUHAMMAD BIN ABDULLAH ALI AL-QATABI.

Pakistan: Plot 2, Sector W59, Embassies Area, Abu Dhabi; tel. (2) 4447800; fax (2) 4447172; e-mail parepabudhabi@pakistanembassyuae.org; internet www.pakistanembassyuae.org; Ambassador (vacant).

Philippines: POB 3215, Villa 8, St 8, Sector 94, Zone 2, Abu Dhabi; tel. (2) 6390006; fax (2) 6390002; e-mail auhpe@philembassy.ae; internet philembassy.ae; Ambassador GRACE RELUCIO PRINCESA.

Poland: POB 2334, Abu Dhabi; tel. (2) 4465200; fax (2) 4462967; e-mail polonez@emirates.net.ae; internet www.abuzabi.polemb.net; Ambassador ADAM KRZYMOWSKI.

Qatar: POB 3503, 26th St, al-Minaseer, Abu Dhabi; tel. (2) 4493300; fax (2) 4493311; e-mail qatar-embassy2009@hotmail.com; Ambassador ABDULLAH M. AL-UTHMAN.

Romania: POB 70416, Abu Dhabi; tel. (2) 4459919; fax (2) 4461143; e-mail romaniae@emirates.net.ae; internet abudhabi.mae.ro; Ambassador ADRIAN MĂCELARU.

Russia: POB 8211, Abu Dhabi; tel. (2) 6721797; fax (2) 6788731; e-mail rusembuae@gmail.com; internet www.uae.mid.ru; Ambassador ANDREI V. ANDREYEV.

Saudi Arabia: POB 4057, Abu Dhabi; tel. (2) 4445700; fax (2) 4448491; e-mail aeemb@mofa.gov.sa; Ambassador IBRAHIM AL-SAAD AL-IBRAHIM.

Somalia: POB 4155, Abu Dhabi; tel. and fax (2) 6651580; e-mail webmaster@somaligov.net; internet www.uae.somaligov.net; Ambassador AHMED MUHAMMAD IGAL.

South Africa: POB 29446, Abu Dhabi; tel. (2) 4473446; fax (2) 4473031; e-mail info@southafrica.ae; internet www.southafrica.ae; Ambassador YACOOB ABBA OMAR.

Spain: POB 46474, al-Saman Tower, Hamdan St, Abu Dhabi; tel. (2) 6269544; fax (2) 6274978; e-mail emb.abudhabi@maec.es; Ambassador JOSÉ EUGENIO SALARICH.

Sri Lanka: POB 46534, Abu Dhabi; tel. (2) 6316444; fax (2) 6331661; e-mail lankemba@emirates.net.ae; internet www.srilankaembassyuae.com; Ambassador SARATH WIJESINGHE.

Sudan: POB 4027, Abu Dhabi; tel. (2) 4446699; fax (2) 4490540; e-mail sudembll@emirates.net.ae; Ambassador AHMED AL-SIDDIQ ABD AL-HAI.

Sweden: POB 31867, Abu Dhabi; tel. (2) 4178800; fax (2) 4178850; e-mail ambassaden.abu-dhabi@gov.se; internet www.swedenabroad.com/abudhabi; Ambassador MAX BJUHR.

Switzerland: POB 46116, Abu Dhabi; tel. (2) 6274636; fax (2) 6269627; e-mail adh.vertretung@eda.admin.ch; internet www.eda.admin.ch/uae; Ambassador ANDREA REICHLIN.

Syria: POB 4011, Abu Dhabi; tel. (2) 4448768; fax (2) 4449387; Ambassador Dr ABD AL-LATIF AL-DABBAGH.

Thailand: POB 47466, Abu Dhabi; tel. (2) 5576551; fax (2) 5576552; e-mail thaiauh@emirates.net.ae; internet www.thaiembassy.org/abudhabi; Ambassador WARAWUDH CHUWIRACH.

Tunisia: POB 4166, Abu Dhabi; tel. (2) 6811331; fax (2) 6812707; e-mail pol_ambtunad@eim.ae; Ambassador TAREK BETTAIEB.

Turkey: POB 3204, Abu Dhabi; tel. (2) 4109999; fax (2) 4109905; e-mail embassy.abudhabi@mfa.gov.tr; internet abudhabi.emb.mfa.gov.tr; Ambassador Ş. VURAL ALTAY.

Uganda: Villa 28, West 17/02, al-Falah St 9, al-Bateen, Abu Dhabi; tel. (2) 6659931; fax (2) 6659934; e-mail info@ugandaembassyuae.com; internet www.ugandaembassyuae.com; Ambassador Prof. SEMAKULA KIWANUKA.

Ukraine: POB 35572, Abu Dhabi; tel. (2) 6327506; fax (2) 6327586; e-mail embua@embukr.ae; internet www.oae.mfa.gov.ua/oae; Ambassador YURIY V. POLUREZ.

United Kingdom: POB 248, Abu Dhabi; tel. (2) 6101100; fax (2) 6101586; e-mail consular.uae@fco.gov.uk; internet ukinuae.fco.gov.uk; Ambassador DOMINIC JERMEY.

USA: POB 4009, Abu Dhabi; tel. (2) 4142200; fax (2) 4142469; e-mail webmasterabudhabi@state.gov; internet abudhabi.usembassy.gov; Ambassador MICHAEL H. CORBIN.

Yemen: POB 2095, Abu Dhabi; tel. (2) 4448457; fax (2) 4443691; e-mail yemenemb@emirates.net.ae; Ambassador AHMAD ABDULLAH SALEH.

Judicial System

The 95th article of the Constitution of 1971 provided for the establishment of the Union Supreme Court and Union Primary Tribunals as the judicial organs of State.

The Union has exclusive legislative and executive jurisdiction over all matters that are concerned with the strengthening of the federation, such as foreign affairs, defence and Union armed forces, security, finance, communications, traffic control, education, currency, measures, standards and weights, matters relating to nationality and emigration, Union information, etc.

The late President Sheikh Zayed signed the law establishing the new federal courts on 9 June 1978. The new law effectively transferred local judicial authorities into the jurisdiction of the federal system.

Primary tribunals in Abu Dhabi, Sharjah, Ajman and Fujairah are now primary federal tribunals, and primary tribunals in other towns in those emirates have become circuits of the primary federal tribunals.

The primary federal tribunals may sit in any of the capitals of the four emirates and have jurisdiction on all administrative disputes between the Union and individuals, whether the Union is plaintiff or defendant. Civil disputes between Union and individuals will be heard by primary federal tribunals in the defendant's place of normal residence.

The law requires that all judges take a constitutional oath before the Minister of Justice and that the courts apply the rules of *Shari'a* (Islamic religious law) and that no judgment contradicts the *Shari'a*. All employees of the old judiciaries will be transferred to the federal authority without loss of salary or seniority.

Shari'a Court: In February 1994 President Sheikh Zayed ordered that an extensive range of crimes, including murder, theft and adultery, be tried in *Shari'a* courts rather than in civil courts; Chief Shari'a Justice AHMAD ABD AL-AZIZ AL-MUBARAK.

Federal Supreme Court: Pres. and Chief Justice ABD AL-WAHAB ABDUL.

Religion

ISLAM

Most of the inhabitants are Sunni Muslims, while about 16% of Muslims are Shi'ites.

CHRISTIANITY

Roman Catholic Church

Apostolic Vicariate of Southern Arabia: POB 54, Abu Dhabi; tel. (2) 4461895; fax (2) 4465177; e-mail info@ccsarabia.org; internet www.ccsarabia.org; f. 1889; fmrly Apostolic Vicariate of Arabia; renamed as above, following reorganization in 2011; responsible for most of the Arabian peninsula (incl. the UAE, Oman and Yemen), containing an estimated 850,000 Catholics (31 December 2011); Vicar Apostolic Bishop PAUL HINDER (Titular Bishop of Macon, Georgia).

The Anglican Communion

Within the Episcopal Church in Jerusalem and the Middle East, the UAE forms part of the diocese of Cyprus and the Gulf. The Anglican congregations in the UAE are entirely expatriate. The Bishop in Cyprus and the Gulf resides in Cyprus, while the Archdeacon in the Gulf is resident in Bahrain.

The Press

The state regulator for the sector is the National Media Council, under the Chairmanship of SAQR GHOBASH SAID GHOBASH (Minister of Labour).

ABU DHABI

Abu Dhabi Magazine: POB 662, Abu Dhabi; tel. (2) 6214000; fax (2) 6348954; f. 1969; Arabic, some articles in English; monthly; Editor ZUHAIR AL-QADI; circ. 18,000.

Abu Dhabi Official Gazette: POB 19, Abu Dhabi; tel. (2) 6688413; fax (2) 6669981; e-mail gazette@ecouncil.ae; f. 1965; Arabic; daily; official reports and papers.

Abu Dhabi Tempo: POB 33760, Abu Dhabi; tel. (2) 6673349; fax (2) 6673389; e-mail info@abudhabitempo.com; internet www .abudhabitempo.com; f. 2009; monthly; local community news; distributed free of charge; publ. by BrandMoxie; Editor SANA BAGERSH; circ. 30,000.

Al-Ain Times: POB 15229, al-Ain; tel. (3) 7671995; fax (3) 7671997; e-mail alaintimes@gmail.com; internet www.alaintimesuae.com; f. 2006; English and Arabic; weekly; publ. by Alpha Beta Publrs and Media Consultants; Chief Editor FADWA M. B. AL-MUGHARIBI.

Akhbar al-Arab: POB 54040, Abu Dhabi; tel. (2) 4486000; e-mail info@akhbaralarab.ae; internet www.akhbaralarab.co.ae; f. 1999; daily; political; circ. 50,000.

Alrroya Aleqtisadiya (Economic Vision): POB 112494, Abu Dhabi; tel. (2) 6517777; fax (2) 6517772; internet www.alrroya.com; f. 2009; Arabic; business daily; publ. by Imedia LLC; Man. Editor REFAAT JAAFAR.

Hiya (She): POB 2488, Abu Dhabi; tel. (2) 4474121; Arabic; weekly for women; publ. by Dar al-Wahdah.

Al-Ittihad (Unity): POB 791, Abu Dhabi; tel. (2) 4455555; fax (2) 4455126; e-mail editor@alittihad.co.ae; internet www.alittihad.ae; f. 1972; Arabic; daily and weekly; publ. by Abu Dhabi Media Co; Man. Editor ALI ABU AL-RISH; circ. 58,000 daily, 60,000 weekly.

Majid: POB 791, Abu Dhabi; tel. (2) 4451804; fax (2) 4451455; e-mail majid-magazine@emi.co.ae; internet www.majid.ae; f. 1979; Arabic; weekly; children's magazine; publ. by Abu Dhabi Media Co; Man. Editor AHMAD OMAR; circ. 164,000.

The National: Abu Dhabi Media Co, 4th St, Sector 18, Zone 1, Abu Dhabi; tel. (2) 4144000; fax (2) 4144001; internet www.thenational .ae; f. 2008; English; daily; publ. by Abu Dhabi Media Co; Editorial Dir MARTIN NEWLAND; Editor-in-Chief HASSAN FATTAH.

Zahrat al-Khaleej (Splendour of the Gulf): POB 791, Abu Dhabi; tel. (2) 4461600; fax (2) 4451653; e-mail abedrabbo@admedia.ae; f. 1979; Arabic; weekly; women's magazine; publ. by Abu Dhabi Media Co; Editor-in-Chief TALAL TOHME; circ. 10,000.

DUBAI

Al-Bayan (The Official Report): POB 2710, Dubai; tel. (4) 3444400; fax (4) 3447846; e-mail readers@albayan.ae; internet www.albayan .ae; f. 1980; Arabic; daily; publ. by Awraq Publishing, a subsidiary of Arab Media Group; CEO SAMI AL-QAMZI; Editor-in-Chief DA'EN SHAHIN; circ. 82,575.

Emarat Al-Youm: POB 502012, Dubai; e-mail 1971ey@gmail.com; internet www.emaratalyoum.com; Arabic; business daily; publ. by Awraq Publishing, a subsidiary of Arab Media Group; Editor SAMI AL-RIYAMI.

Emirates 24/7: POB 191919, Dubai; tel. (4) 3062222; fax (4) 3407698; e-mail news@emirates247.com; internet www .emirates247.com; f. 2005; English; online; Editor-in-Chief RIYAD MICKDADY.

Emirates Woman: POB 2331, Dubai; tel. (4) 2824060; fax (4) 2827593; e-mail faye@motivate.co.ae; f. 1981; English; monthly; fashion, health and beauty; publ. by Motivate Publishing; Editor FAYE JAMES; circ. 20,324.

Gulf News: Sheikh Zayed Rd, POB 6519, Dubai; tel. (4) 3447100; fax (4) 3441627; e-mail editor@gulfnews.com; internet www.gulfnews .com; f. 1978; English; daily; two weekly supplements, *Junior News* (Wed.), *Gulf Weekly* (Thur.); publ. by Al-Nisr Publishing; Editor-in-Chief ABD-AL HAMID AHMAD; circ. 103,000.

Al-Jundi (The Soldier): POB 2838, Dubai; tel. (4) 3532222; fax (4) 3744272; e-mail mod5@eim.ae; f. 1973; Arabic; monthly; military and cultural; Editor-in-Chief Brig. MUHAMMAD ALI ABDULLAH AL-EASSA; circ. 10,000.

Khaleej Times: POB 11243, Dubai; tel. (4) 3383535; fax (4) 3383345; e-mail ktimes@emirates.net.ae; internet www.khaleejtimes.com; f. 1978; a Galadari enterprise; English; daily; distributed throughout the region and in India, Pakistan and the United Kingdom; free weekly supplement, *Weekend* (Fri.); Publr and Editor-in-Chief MUHAMMAD A. R. GALADARI; Man. Dir QASSIM MUHAMMAD YOUSUF; circ. 70,000.

Al-Manara: Office 129, Bldg 10, Dubai Media City; tel. (4) 3901777; fax (4) 3904554; e-mail dar@almanaramagazine.ae; internet www .almanaramagazine.ae; Arabic; lifestyle; Editor WALID AL-SAADI.

Trade and Industry: POB 1457, Dubai; tel. (4) 2280000; fax (4) 2211646; e-mail dcciinfo@dcci.org; internet www.dubaichamber.ae; f. 1975; Arabic and English; monthly; publ. by Dubai Chamber of Commerce and Industry; circ. 26,000.

UAE Digest: POB 500595, Dubai; tel. (4) 3672245; fax (4) 3678613; e-mail info@sterlingp.ae; internet www.sterlingp.ae; English; monthly; publ. by Sterling Publications; current affairs; Man. Editor K. RAVEENDRAN.

Viva: POB 500024, Dubai; tel. (4) 2108000; fax (4) 2108080; e-mail vivaletters@itp.com; internet www.vivamagazine.ae; f. 2004; publ. by ITP; Editor MANDIE GOWER; circ. 23,000.

What's On: POB 2331, Dubai; tel. (4) 2824060; fax (4) 2827593; e-mail editor-wo@motivate.co.ae; internet www.whatsonlive.com; f. 1979; English; monthly; publ. by Motivate Publishing; Group Editor and Man. Partner IAN FAIRSERVICE; circ. 31,055.

Xpress: POB 6519, Dubai; tel. (4) 3447100; fax (4) 3420433; e-mail editor@alnisrmedia.com; internet www.xpress4me.com; f. 2007; English; weekly; publ. by Al-Nisr Publishing; Editor NIRMALA JANSSEN.

RAS AL-KHAIMAH

Akhbar Ras al-Khaimah (Ras al-Khaimah News): POB 87, Ras al-Khaimah; Arabic; monthly; local news.

Al-Ghorfa: POB 87, Ras al-Khaimah; tel. (7) 2333511; fax (7) 2330233; f. 1970; Arabic and English; free monthly; publ. by Ras al-Khaimah Chamber of Commerce and Industry; Editor ZAKI H. SAQR.

Ras al-Khaimah Magazine: POB 200, Ras al-Khaimah; Arabic; monthly; commerce and trade; Chief Editor AHMAD AL-TADMORI.

SHARJAH

Al-Azman al-Arabia (Times of Arabia): POB 5823, Sharjah; tel. (6) 5356034.

The Gulf Today: POB 30, Sharjah; tel. (6) 5777999; fax (6) 5777737; e-mail tgt@gulftoday.ae; internet gulftoday.ae; f. 1996; English; daily; Editor-in-Chief AYSHA TARYAM; circ. 38,000.

Al-Khaleej (The Gulf): POB 30, Sharjah; tel. (6) 5625304; fax (6) 5598547; e-mail kh_readers@alkhaleej.ae; internet www.alkhaleej .co.ae; f. 1970; Arabic; daily; political; independent; Editor GHASSAN TAHBOUB; circ. 82,750.

Al-Sharooq (Sunrise): POB 30, Sharjah; tel. (6) 5598777; fax (6) 5599336; f. 1970; Arabic; weekly; general interest; Editor YOUSUF AL-HASSAN.

Al-Tijarah (Commerce): Sharjah Chamber of Commerce and Industry, POB 580, Sharjah; tel. (6) 5116600; fax (6) 5681119; e-mail scci@ sharjah.gov.ae; internet www.sharjah.gov.ae; f. 1970; Arabic/English; monthly magazine; circ. 50,000; annual trade directory; circ. 100,000.

NEWS AGENCY

Emirates News Agency (WAM): POB 3790, Abu Dhabi; tel. (2) 4454545; fax (2) 4044200; e-mail wamnews@eim.ae; internet www

.wam.org.ae; f. 1977; operated by the Govt; Dir-Gen. IBRAHIM AL-ABED; Chief Editor JAMAL NASSER.

Publishers

All Prints: POB 857, Abu Dhabi; tel. (2) 6336999; fax (2) 6320844; e-mail allprints@allprints.co.ae; internet www.all-prints.com; f. 1968; publishing and distribution; Partners BUSHRA KHAYAT, TAHSEEN S. KHAYAT.

ITP: POB 500024, Dubai; tel. (4) 4443000; fax (4) 4443030; e-mail info@itp.com; internet www.itp.com; f. 1987; publishes more than 60 magazines, incl. *Ahlan!*, *Arabian Business*, *Time Out Dubai*, *Viva*; CEO WALID AKAWI.

Kalimat Publishing and Distribution: POB 21969, Sharjah; tel. (6) 5566696; fax (6) 5566691; e-mail info@kalimat.ae; internet www .kalimat.ae; f. 2007; children's books; CEO Sheikha BODOUR AL-QASIMI.

Motivate Publishing: POB 2331, Dubai; tel. (4) 2824060; fax (4) 2820428; e-mail motivate@motivate.ae; internet www .motivatepublishing.com; f. 1979; books and magazines; Man. Partner and Group Editor IAN FAIRSERVICE.

Sterling Publications: POB 500595, Dubai; tel. (4) 3672245; fax (4) 3678613; e-mail info@sterlingp.ae; publs include *UAE Digest*, *Banking*, *Business Review* and *Ajman Today*; Man. Dir SANKARA NARAYANAN; Man. Editor K. RAVEENDRAN.

Broadcasting and Communications

TELECOMMUNICATIONS

Emirates Integrated Telecommunications Co (du): POB 502666, Dubai; tel. (4) 3600000; fax (4) 3604440; e-mail talk-to-us@du.ae; internet www.du.ae; f. 2006; commenced operations under the brand name *du* in Feb. 2007; 40% owned by the federal Govt, 20% by TECOM Investment, 20% by Mubadala Devt Co and 20% by public shareholders; provides telecommunications services throughout the UAE; Chair. AHMAD BIN BYAT; CEO OSMAN SULTAN.

Emirates Telecommunications Corpn (Etisalat): POB 3838, Abu Dhabi; tel. (2) 6182091; fax (2) 6334448; e-mail prd@etisalat.co .ae; internet www.etisalat.co.ae; f. 1976; provides telecommunications services throughout the UAE; Chair. MUHAMMAD HASSAN OMRAN; CEO MUHAMMAD AL-QAMZI.

Regulatory Authority

Telecommunications Regulatory Authority (TRA): POB 26662, Abu Dhabi; tel. (2) 6269999; fax (2) 6118209; e-mail info@ tra.ae; internet www.tra.ae; f. 2004; Chair. MUHAMMAD BIN AHMAD AL-QAMZI; Dir-Gen. MUHAMMAD AL-GHANEM.

BROADCASTING

Radio

Abu Dhabi Radio: Abu Dhabi Media Co, 4th St, Sector 18, Zone 1, Abu Dhabi; tel. (2) 4144000; fax (2) 4144001; internet www.admedia .ae; f. 1969; broadcasts in Arabic over a wide area; also broadcasts in French, Bengali, Filipino and Urdu; affiliated channels include Emarat FM, Quran Kareem Radio, Sawt Al Musiqa; owned and operated by Abu Dhabi Media Co; Dir-Gen. ABD AL-WAHAB AL-RADWAN.

Arabian Radio Network: POB 502012, Dubai; tel. (4) 3912000; fax (4) 3912007; e-mail info@arn.ae; internet www.arn.ae; f. 2001; owned by Arab Media Group; operates 8 stations; CEO MUHAMMAD AL-MULLA.

Capital Radio: POB 63, Abu Dhabi; tel. (2) 4451000; fax (2) 4451155; govt-operated; English-language FM music and news station; Station Man. AIDA HAMZA.

Channel 4 Radio Network: POB 442, Ajman; tel. (6) 7461444; e-mail chris@channel4fm.com; internet www.channel4fm.com; operates 89.1 Radio 4, 104.8 Channel 4, 103.2 Coast, 101.3 Gold and 107.8 Radio Al Rabia stations; owned by Ajman Independent Studios LLC; Head CHRIS ROSE.

Ras al-Khaimah Broadcasting Station: POB 141, Ras al-Khaimah; tel. (7) 2851151; fax (7) 2352300; five transmitters broadcast in Arabic, Urdu, Malayalam, Telugu, Tamil and Bangla; Chair. ABD AL-MALIK BIN KAYED AL-QASSIMI.

Sharjah Radio and Television: POB 111, Sharjah; tel. (6) 5661111; fax (6) 5669999; e-mail info@sharjahtv.ae; internet www .sharjahtv.ae; Dir AMNA KHAMIS GHARIB AL-NAKHI.

Umm al-Qaiwain Broadcasting Station: POB 444, Umm al-Qaiwain; tel. (6) 7666044; fax (6) 7666055; e-mail uaqfm@emirates .net.ae; f. 1978; broadcasts music and news in Arabic, Malayalam, Sinhala and Urdu; Gen. Man. ALI JASSEM.

Television

Abu Dhabi Television: Abu Dhabi Media Co, 4th St, Sector 18, Zone 1, Abu Dhabi; tel. (2) 4144000; fax (2) 4144001; internet www .adtv.ae; f. 1969; reorg. 2008; broadcasts entertainment and news programmes; affiliated channels include Emirates Channel, Abu Dhabi Sports; owned by Abu Dhabi Media Co; Exec. Dir KARIM SARKIS.

Ajman Television Network: POB 442, Ajman; tel. (6) 7465000; fax (6) 7465135; e-mail progajtv@ajmantv.com; internet www.ajmantv .com; f. 1996; broadcasts in Arabic and English; Chair. ABDULLAH MUHAMMAD.

Arabian Television Network: Arab Media Group, POB 500666, Dubai; tel. (4) 3062222; fax (4) 3479965; e-mail info@ arabmediagrouponline.com; internet www.arnonline.com; f. 2007; broadcasts own entertainment channels, incl. SHOOFtv and Noor Dubai TV; also adapts international brands for Arab market, such as MTV Arabia; owned by Arab Media Group; Gen. Man. MARYAM AL-FALASI.

City 7 TV: POB 502209, Bldg 4, Dubai Media City, Dubai; tel. (4) 3678142; fax (4) 3678060; e-mail info@city7tv.com; internet www .city7tv.com; Pres. MOHI EL-DIN BIN HENDI.

Dubai Media Inc: POB 835, Dubai; tel. (4) 3369999; fax (4) 3360060; e-mail info@dmi.ae; internet www.dmi.gov.ae; f. 2004; channels include Dubai Television, Dubai One, Sama Dubai, Dubai Sports; state-owned; Chair. Sheikh MAKTOUM BIN MUHAMMAD BIN RASHID AL MAKTOUM; Man. Dir AHMAD ABDULLAH AL-SHEIKH.

Middle East Broadcasting Center (MBC): POB 76267, Dubai; tel. (4) 3919999; fax (4) 3919900; e-mail infotv@mbc.ae; internet www .mbc.net; f. 1991; broadcasts throughout region via satellite; channels include Al-Arabiya News Channel, MBC Persia (Farsi service), MBC 1, 2, 3 and 4 (entertainment); Chair. Sheikh WALID AL-IBRAHIM.

Sharjah Radio and Television: see Radio.

Finance

(cap. = capital; res = reserves; dep. = deposits; m. = million;
brs = branches; amounts in dirhams, unless otherwise indicated)

BANKING

Central Bank

Central Bank of the United Arab Emirates: POB 854, Abu Dhabi; tel. (2) 6652220; fax (2) 6652504; e-mail admin@cbuae.gov .ae; internet www.centralbank.ae; f. 1973; acts as issuing authority for local currency; superseded UAE Currency Bd in Dec. 1980; cap. 300m., res 1,200m., dep. 156,274m. (Dec. 2009); Chair. KHALIFA MUHAMMAD AL-KINDI; Gov. SULTAN BIN NASSER AL-SUWAIDI; 5 brs.

Principal Banks

Abu Dhabi Commercial Bank (ADCB): POB 939, Abu Dhabi; tel. (2) 6962222; fax (2) 6450384; e-mail info@adcb.com; internet www .adcb.com; f. 1985 by merger; 65% govt-owned, 35% owned by private investors; cap. 5,595m., res 12,768m., dep. 113,748m. (Dec. 2011); Chair. MUHAMMAD GHANIM AL-SUWAIDI; Exec. Dir ALA'A MUHAMMAD KHALIL ERAIQAT; 40 brs in the UAE, 2 brs in India.

Abu Dhabi Islamic Bank: POB 313, Abu Dhabi; tel. (2) 6100600; fax (2) 6656028; e-mail adib@adib.co.ae; internet www.adib.ae; f. 1997; cap. 4,364m., res 2,892m., dep. 57,103m. (Dec. 2011); Chair. JAWAN AWAIDHA SUHAIL AL-KHAILI; CEO TIRAD MAHMOUD; 60 brs.

Ajman Bank PJSC: POB 7770, Block C, 13th Floor, al-Mina Rd, Ajman Free Zone, Ajman; tel. (6) 7479999; fax (6) 7479990; e-mail info@ajmanbank.ae; internet www.ajmanbank.ae; f. 2008; 25% owned by Govt of Ajman; *Shari'a*-compliant services; cap. 1,000m., res −12m., dep. 2,897m. (Dec. 2011); Chair. Sheikh AMMAR BIN HUMAID AL-NUAIMI; CEO MUHAMMAD AMIRI (acting); 2 brs.

Bank of Sharjah: POB 1394, Sharjah; tel. (6) 5694411; fax (6) 5694422; e-mail enquire@bankofsharjah.com; internet www .bankofsharjah.com; f. 1973; cap. 2,100m., res 1,430m., dep. 14,801m. (Dec. 2010); Chair. AHMAD AL-NOMAN; Exec. Dir and Gen. Man. VAROUJAN NERGUIZIAN; 2 brs.

Commercial Bank of Dubai PSC: POB 2668, Mankhool St, Dubai; tel. (4) 2121000; fax (4) 2121911; e-mail cbd-ho@cbd.ae; internet www .cbd.ae; f. 1969; 20% owned by Govt of Dubai; cap. 1,941m., res 2,948m., dep. 30,380m. (Dec. 2011); Chair. SAEED AHMED GHOBASH; CEO PETER BALTUSSEN; 24 brs.

Commercial Bank International PSC: POB 4449, al-Riqah St, Dubai; tel. (4) 2275265; fax (4) 2279038; e-mail cbiho@emirates.net

.ae; internet www.cbiuae.com; f. 1991; cap. 1,407m., res 210m., dep. 9,139m. (Dec. 2011); Chair. MUHAMMAD SULTAN AL-QADI; CEO KRIS BABICCI; 9 brs.

Dubai Bank PJSC: POB 65555, Sheikh Zayed Rd, Dubai; e-mail info@dubaibank.ae; internet www.dubaibank.ae; tel. (4) 3328989; fax (4) 3290071; f. 2002 by Emaar Properties, a real estate developer; cap. 1,500m., res 113m., dep. 15,306m. (Dec. 2009); Chair. MUHAMMAD HADI AHMED AL-HUSSAINI.

Dubai Islamic Bank PJSC: POB 1080, Airport Rd, Deira, Dubai; tel. (4) 2953000; fax (4) 2954111; e-mail contactus@dib.ae; internet www.alislami.ae; f. 1975; cap. 3,797m., res 4,394m., dep. 68,823m. (Dec. 2011); Chair. Dr MUHAMMAD EBRAHIM AL-SHAIBANI; CEO ABDULLAH AL-HAMLI; 44 brs.

Emirates Investment Bank PJSC: POB 5503, Office 904, Twin Towers, Baniyas St, Deira, Dubai; tel. (4) 2328080; fax (4) 2328134; e-mail aeibank@emirates.net.ae; internet www.aeibank.com; f. 1976 as Arab Emirate Investment Bank Ltd; name changed as above in 2010; cap. 49m., res 54m., dep. 1,130m. (Dec. 2011); Chair. OMAR ABDULLAH AL-FUTTAIM.

Emirates Islamic Bank PJSC: POB 5547, Baniyas Rd, Deira, Dubai; tel. (4) 2287474; fax (4) 2272172; e-mail info@emiratesislamicbank.ae; internet www.emiratesislamicbank.ae; f. 1976 as Middle East Bank; became a Public Joint Stock Co (PJSC) in 1995; present name adopted 2004; subsidiary (99.8% owned) of Emirates Bank Int; cap. 2,430m., res 319m., dep. 27,934m. (Dec. 2010); Chair. HESHAM ABDULLA AL-QASSIM; CEO JAMAL SAEED BIN GHALAITA; 32 brs.

Emirates NBD PJSC: POB 2923, Baniyas Rd, Deira, Dubai; tel. (4) 2256256; fax (4) 2227662; e-mail ibrahims@emiratesbank.com; internet www.emiratesnbd.com; f. 2007 by merger of Emirates Bank Int. PJSC with Nat. Bank of Dubai PJSC; 56% owned by Govt of Dubai; cap. 9,557m., res 17,789m., dep. 219,419m. (Dec. 2011); Chair. Sheikh AHMAD BIN SAID AL MAKTOUM; CEO RICK PUDNER; 132 brs.

First Gulf Bank: POB 6316, Sheikh Zayed St, Abu Dhabi; tel. (2) 6816666; fax (2) 6814282; e-mail info@fgb.ae; internet www.fgb.ae; f. 1979; cap. 1,500m., res 16,894m., dep. 111,721m. (Dec. 2011); Chair. Sheikh MANSOUR BIN ZAYED AL NAHYAN; Man. Dir ABD AL-HAMID SAID; CEO ANDRÉ SAYEGH; 19 brs.

Investbank PSC: POB 1885, Sharjah; tel. (6) 5694440; fax (6) 5694442; e-mail custserv@invest-bank.ae; internet www .investbank.ae; f. 1975; cap. 1,155m., res 502m., dep. 7,657m. (Dec. 2011); Chair. Dr ABDULLAH OMRAN TARYAM; Gen. Man. SAMI R. FARHAT; 12 brs.

Mashreqbank PSC: POB 1250, Omer bin al-Khattab St, Deira, Dubai; tel. (4) 2223333; fax (4) 2226061; internet www.mashreqbank .com; f. 1967 as Bank of Oman; present name adopted 1993; cap. 1,690m., res 779m., dep. 52,640m. (Dec. 2011); Chair. and Pres. ABDULLAH BIN AHMAD AL-GHURAIR; CEO ABD AL-AZIZ ABDULLAH AL-GHURAIR; 57 brs in the UAE, 22 brs abroad.

Al-Masraf: POB 46733, ARBIFT Bldg, Hamdan St, Tourist Club Area, Abu Dhabi; tel. (2) 6721900; fax (2) 6777550; e-mail arbiftho@ emirates.net.ae; internet www.arbift.com; f. 1976 as Arab Bank for Investment and Foreign Trade; renamed as above in 2007; jointly owned by the UAE Federal Govt, the Libyan Arab Foreign Bank and the Banque Extérieure d'Algérie; cap. 1,500m., res 1,201m., dep. 9,333m. (Dec. 2011); Chair. MUHAMMAD SAIF AL-SUWAIDI; Gen. Man. A. S. PILLAI (acting); 7 brs in the UAE.

National Bank of Abu Dhabi (NBAD): POB 4, Tariq ibn Ziad St, Abu Dhabi; tel. (2) 6111111; fax (2) 6275738; e-mail CustomerSupport@nbad.com; internet www.nbad.com; f. 1968; 73% owned by Abu Dhabi Investment Council, 3% by foreign institutions and the remainder by UAE citizens; issued Islamic bonds for the first time in June 2010; cap. 2,870m., res 15,106m., dep. 191,612m. (Dec. 2011); Chair. NASSER AHMAD KHALIFA AL-SUWAIDI; Group Chief Exec. MICHAEL H. TOMALIN; 73 brs in the UAE, 31 brs abroad.

National Bank of Fujairah PSC: POB 2979, Dubai; tel. (4) 3971700; fax (4) 3973922; e-mail nbfho@nbf.ae; internet www.nbf .ae; f. 1982; owned jointly by Govt of Fujairah (36.78%), Govt of Dubai (9.78%), and UAE citizens and cos (51.25%); cap. 1,100m., res 563m., dep. 10,338m. (Dec. 2011); Chair. Sheikh SALEH BIN MUHAMMAD AL-SHARQI; CEO VINCE COOK; 11 brs.

National Bank of Ras al-Khaimah PSC (RAKBANK): POB 5300, Rakbank Bldg, Oman St, al-Nakheel, Ras al-Khaimah; tel. (7) 2281127; fax (7) 2283238; e-mail nbrakho@emirates.net.ae; internet www.rakbank.ae; f. 1976; 52.75% owned by Govt of Ras al-Khaimah; cap. 1,385m., res 2,154m., dep. 18,624m. (Dec. 2011); Chair. Sheikh OMAR BIN SAQR AL-QASIMI; CEO GRAHAM HONEYBILL; 16 brs.

National Bank of Umm al-Qaiwain PSC: POB 800, Umm al-Qaiwain Private Properties Dept Bldg, King Faisal St, Umm al-Qaiwain; tel. (6) 7655225; fax (6) 7655440; e-mail nbuq@nbq.ae; internet www.nbq.ae; f. 1982; cap. 1,600m., res 1,018m., dep. 7,090m.

(Dec. 2011); Chair. Sheikh SAUD BIN RASHID AL-MU'ALLA; Man. Dir and CEO Sheikh NASSER BIN RASHID AL-MU'ALLA; 16 brs.

Noor Islamic Bank PJSC: POB 8822, Dubai; tel. (4) 4268888; fax (4) 3456789; internet www.noorbank.com; f. 2008; *Shari'a*-compliant services; 25% owned by Investment Corpn of Dubai, 25% by Dubai Group, 5% by UAE Federal Govt, 45% by private investors; total assets 22,000m.; Chair. Sheikh AHMAD BIN SAEED AL MAKTOUM; CEO HUSSAIN AL-QEMZI; 10 brs.

Sharjah Islamic Bank: POB 4, Al-Borj Ave, Sharjah; tel. (6) 5115123; fax (6) 5681699; e-mail contact.center@sib.ae; internet www.sib.ae; f. 1976 as Nat. Bank of Sharjah; present name adopted 2005, reflecting the bank's conversion to *Shari'a*-compliant operations; commercial bank; cap. 2,425m., res 1,396m., dep. 11,299m. (Dec. 2011); Chair. Sheikh SULTAN BIN MUHAMMAD BIN SULTAN AL-QASSIMI; CEO MUHAMMAD AHMAD ABDULLAH; 13 brs.

Union National Bank (UNB): POB 3865, Salam St, Abu Dhabi; tel. (2) 6741600; fax (2) 6786080; e-mail feedback@unb.co.ae; internet www.unb.co.ae; f. 1983; fmrly Bank of Credit and Commerce (Emirates); cap. 4,495m., res 2,333m., dep. 60,884m. (Dec. 2011); Chair. Sheikh NAHYAN BIN MUBARAK AL NAHYAN; CEO MUHAMMAD NASR ABDEEN; 26 brs in the UAE.

United Arab Bank: POB 25022, HE Sheikh Abdullah bin Salem al-Qassimi Bldg, 6th Floor, al-Qassimi St, Sharjah; tel. (6) 5733900; fax (6) 5733907; e-mail uarbae@emirates.net.ae; internet www.uab.co.ae; f. 1975; affiliated to Société Générale, France; 35% owned by Commercial Bank of Qatar; cap. 996m., res 610m., dep. 8,693m. (Dec. 2011); Chair. Sheikh FAISAL BIN SULTAN BIN SALEM AL-QASSIMI; CEO PAUL TROWBRIDGE; 9 brs.

Development Bank

Emirates Industrial Bank: POB 2722, Arab Monetary Fund Bldg, 6th Floor, Corniche Rd, Abu Dhabi; tel. (2) 6339700; fax (2) 6319191; e-mail projects_auh@emiratesindustrialbank.net; internet www.eib .ae; f. 1982; offers low-cost loans to enterprises with at least 51% local ownership; 100% state-owned; cap. 200m.; Chair. OBAID HUMAID AL-TAYER; Gen. Man. MUHAMMAD ABD AL-BAKI MUHAMMAD.

Bankers' Association

United Arab Emirates Bankers' Association: POB 44307, Abu Dhabi; tel. (2) 4467706; fax (2) 4463718; e-mail ebauae@emirates.net .ae; internet www.eba-ae.com; f. 1983; Chair. AHMAD HUMAID AL-TAYER (Chair., Commercial Bank of Dubai); Gen. Man. FATHI M. SKAIK.

SOVEREIGN WEALTH FUNDS

Abu Dhabi Investment Authority (ADIA): POB 3600, 211 Corniche, Abu Dhabi; tel. (2) 4150000; fax (2) 4151000; internet www .adia.ae; f. 1976; manages Govt of Abu Dhabi's investment portfolio; Chair. Sheikh KHALIFA BIN ZAYED AL NAHYAN (President of the UAE and Ruler of Abu Dhabi); Man. Dir Sheikh HAMAD BIN ZAYED AL NAHYAN.

Abu Dhabi Investment Company (Invest AD): POB 46309, Abu Dhabi; tel. (2) 6658100; fax (2) 6650575; e-mail info@investad.ae; internet www.investad.ae; f. 1977; investment of govt funds, and advisory activities in the UAE and the Middle East; 98% owned by Abu Dhabi Investment Council and 2% by Nat. Bank of Abu Dhabi; Chair. KHALIFA M. AL-KINDI; CEO NAZEM FAWWAZ AL-KUDSI.

Emirates Investment Authority: POB 3235, Abu Dhabi; e-mail careers@eia.gov.ae; internet www.eia.gov.ae; f. 2007; federal sovereign wealth fund; Chair. Sheikh MANSOUR BIN ZAYED AL NAHYAN (Deputy Prime Minister and Minister of Presidential Affairs); CEO MUBARAK RASHID AL-MANSOURI.

Investment Corporation of Dubai: POB 333888, Dubai International Financial Center, 6th Floor, DIFC Gate Village, Dubai; tel. (4) 7071333; fax (4) 7071444; e-mail info@icd.gov.ae; internet www .icd.gov.ae; f. 2006; manages Govt of Dubai's investment portfolio; Chair. Sheikh MUHAMMAD BIN RASHID AL MAKTOUM (Ruler of Dubai); Exec. Dir and CEO MUHAMMAD I. AL-SHAIBANI.

RAK Investment Authority: POB 31291, Ras al-Khaimah; tel. (7) 2446533; fax (7) 2447202; e-mail gm@rakinvestmentauthority.com; internet www.rak-ia.com; f. 2005; sovereign wealth fund of Ras al-Khaimah Govt; cap. US $1,200m. (2009); CEO Dr KHATER MASAAD.

STOCK EXCHANGES

Abu Dhabi Securities Exchange (ADX): POB 54500, Abu Dhabi; tel. (2) 6277777; fax (2) 6128728; e-mail info@adx.ae; internet www .adx.ae; f. 2000 as Abu Dhabi Securities Market, renamed as above 2008; 67 listed cos (Jan. 2010); Chair. NASSER AHMAD AL-SUWAIDI; Dir-Gen. TOM HEALY.

Dubai Financial Market (DFM): POB 9700, Dubai; tel. (4) 3055555; fax (4) 3314924; e-mail helpdesk@dfm.co.ae; internet www.dfm.co.ae; f. 2000; restructured to comply with *Shari'a* principles in 2006; 63 listed cos, 7 bonds, 15 mutual funds (Sept. 2008); market capitalization AED 61,370m. (Feb. 2004); Chair. ABD AL-JALIL YOUSUF; CEO and Man. Dir ESSA ABD AL-FATTAH KAZIM.

NASDAQ Dubai: POB 53536, The Exchange Bldg, Level 7, Gate District, Dubai International Financial Centre, Dubai; tel. (4) 3612222; fax (4) 3612130; e-mail corpcomm@nasdaqdubai.com; internet www.nasdaqdubai.com; f. 2005 as Dubai Int. Financial Exchange; renamed as above 2008; Chair. ABD AL-WAHED AL-FAHIM; CEO HAMED ALI.

Regulatory Authority

Securities and Commodities Authority: POB 33733, Abu Dhabi; tel. (2) 6277888; fax (2) 6274600; e-mail contactus@sca.ae; internet sca-mo1.sca.ae; f. 2000; Chair. SULTAN BIN SAID AL-MANSOURI (Minister of Economy); CEO ABDULLAH SALEM AL-TURIFI.

INSURANCE

Abu Dhabi National Insurance Co (ADNIC): POB 839, Abu Dhabi; tel. (2) 8040100; fax (2) 6268600; e-mail adnic@adnic.ae; internet www.adnic.ae; f. 1972; subscribed 25% by the Govt of Abu Dhabi and 75% by UAE nationals; all classes of insurance; Chair. KHALIFA MUHAMMAD AL-KINDI.

Al-Ahlia Insurance Co: POB 128, Ras al-Khaimah; tel. (7) 2221479; e-mail contactus@alahli.com; internet www.alahli.com; f. 1977; Chair. ABDULLAH S. BAHAMDAN; Gen. Man. YAHYA NOUR EL-DIN; 3 brs.

Al-Ain Ahlia Insurance Co: POB 3077, Abu Dhabi; tel. (2) 4459900; fax (2) 4456685; e-mail alainins@emirates.net.ae; internet www.alaininsurance.com; f. 1975; Chair. MUHAMMAD BIN J. R. AL-BADIE AL-DHAHIRI; Gen. Man. MUHAMMAD MAZHAR HAMADEH; brs in Dubai, Sharjah, Tarif, Ghouifat and al-Ain.

Dubai Insurance Co PSC: POB 3027, Dubai; tel. (4) 2693030; fax (4) 2693727; e-mail info@dubins.ae; internet www.dubins.ae; f. 1970; Chair. BUTI OBAID AL-MULLA.

Al-Fujairah National Insurance Co PSC: POB 277, Fujairah; tel. (9) 2233355; fax (9) 2224344; e-mail ho@fujinsco.ae; internet www.afnic.ae; f. 1976; 84.75% owned by Govt of Fujairah; cap. 75m.; Chair. ABD AL-GHAFOUR BAHROUZIAN; Gen. Man. ANTOINE MAALOULI.

Sharjah Insurance Co: POB 792, Sharjah; tel. (6) 5686690; fax (6) 5686545; e-mail sico@emirates.net.ae; internet www.shjins.com; f. 1970; Chair. Sheikh MUHAMMAD BIN SAOUD AL-QASSIMI; Gen. Man. AHMED KHATER.

Union Insurance Co PSC: POB 1225, Ajman; tel. (6) 7466996; fax (6) 7466997; e-mail unins@emirates.net.ae; internet www.unioninsuranceuae.com; national insurance co of Ajman emirate; Chair. ABDULLAH HUMAID AL-MAZROUI; Gen. Man. SAMER S. BUSHNAQ.

Trade and Industry

DEVELOPMENT ORGANIZATIONS

Abu Dhabi Fund for Development (ADFD): POB 814, al-Salam St, Abu Dhabi; tel. (2) 6441000; fax (2) 6440800; e-mail ifo@adfd.ae; internet www.adfd.ae; f. 1971; offers economic aid to other Arab states and developing countries in support of their development; cap. AED 4,000m.; Dir-Gen. SAID KHALFAN MATAR AL-ROMAITHI.

Abu Dhabi Investment Council (ADIC): POB 3600, Abu Dhabi; tel. (2) 4150000; fax (2) 4151000; f. 2007; responsible for co-ordinating Abu Dhabi's investment policy; Chair. Sheikh KHALIFA BIN ZAYED AL NAHYAN; 1 br. overseas.

Department of Economic Development Abu Dhabi: POB 12, Abu Dhabi; tel. (2) 6727200; fax (2) 6727749; e-mail ier@adeconomy.ae; internet www.adeconomy.ae; f. 1974; supervises Abu Dhabi's Economic Vision 2030 programme; Chair. NASSER AL-SOWAIDI; Under-Sec. MUHAMMAD OMAR ABDULLAH.

General Holding Corpn (GHC): POB 4499, Abu Dhabi; tel. (2) 6144444; fax (2) 6312857; e-mail info@ghc.ae; internet www.ghc.ae; f. 1979 as Gen. Industry Corpn; name changed as above 2004; responsible for the promotion of non-petroleum-related industry; Chair. Sheikh HAMAD BIN ZAYED AL NAHYAN; Vice-Chair. NASSER AHMAD AL-SOWAIDI.

CHAMBERS OF COMMERCE

Federation of UAE Chambers of Commerce and Industry: POB 3014, Abu Dhabi; tel. (2) 6214144; fax (2) 6339210; POB 8886, Dubai; tel. (4) 2955500; fax (4) 2941212; e-mail info@fcciuae.ae; internet www.fcciuae.ae; f. 1976; seven mem. chambers; Chair. SALAH SALEM BIN OMAIR AL-SHAMSI; Sec.-Gen. ABDULLAH SULTAN ABDULLAH.

Abu Dhabi Chamber of Commerce and Industry: POB 662, Abu Dhabi; tel. (2) 6214000; fax (2) 6215867; e-mail services@adcci.gov

.ae; internet www.abudhabichamber.ae; f. 1969; 45,000 mems; Pres. SALAH SALEM BIN OMAIR AL-SHAMSI; Dir-Gen. MUHAMMAD RASHID AL-HAMELI.

Ajman Chamber of Commerce and Industry: POB 662, Ajman; tel. (6) 7422177; fax (6) 7471666; e-mail info@ajcci.gov.ae; internet www.ajcci.gov.ae; f. 1977; Chair. OBEID BIN ALI AL-MUHAIRI; Dir-Gen. MUHAMMAD AL-HAMRANI.

Dubai Chamber of Commerce and Industry: POB 1457, Dubai; tel. (4) 2280000; fax (4) 2211646; e-mail customercare@dubaichamber.ae; internet www.dubaichamber.ae; f. 1965; 108,000 mems (2007); Chair. ABD AL-RAHMAN SAIF AL-GHURAIR; Dir-Gen. HAMAD BUAIMIM.

Fujairah Chamber of Commerce, Industry and Agriculture: POB 738, Fujairah; tel. (9) 2222400; fax (9) 2221464; internet www.fujcci.ae; Pres. SAID ALI KHAMAS; Dir-Gen. MUHAMMAD KHALID AL-JASSEM.

Ras al-Khaimah Chamber of Commerce and Industry: POB 87, Ras al-Khaimah; tel. (7) 2260000; fax (7) 2260112; e-mail rcci@rakchamber.ae; internet www.rakchamber.ae; f. 1967; 17,840 mems (Dec. 2007); Chair. YOUSUF AL-NEAIMI; Dir-Gen. Dr NASER AHMED SALMEEN.

Sharjah Chamber of Commerce and Industry: POB 580, Sharjah; tel. (6) 5116600; fax (6) 5681119; e-mail scci@sharjah.gov.ae; internet www.sharjah.gov.ae; f. 1970; 33,500 mems; Chair. AHMAD MUHAMMAD AL-MIDFA'A; Dir-Gen. SAID OBAID AL-JARWAN.

Umm al-Qaiwain Chamber of Commerce and Industry: POB 436, Umm al-Qaiwain; tel. (6) 7651111; fax (6) 7657056; e-mail uaqcci@emirates.net.ae; Pres. ABDULLAH RASHID AL-KHARJI; Man. Dir SHAKIR AL-ZAYANI.

STATE HYDROCARBONS COMPANIES

Abu Dhabi

Supreme Petroleum Council: POB 898, Abu Dhabi; tel. (2) 602000; fax (2) 6023389; f. 1988; assumed authority and responsibility for the administration and supervision of all petroleum affairs in Abu Dhabi; Chair. Sheikh KHALIFA BIN ZAYED AL NAHYAN; Sec.-Gen. YOUSUF BIN OMEIR BIN YOUSUF.

Abu Dhabi National Oil Co (ADNOC): POB 898, Abu Dhabi; tel. (2) 6020000; fax (2) 6023389; e-mail adnoc@adnoc.com; internet www.adnoc.ae; f. 1971; cap. AED 7,500m.; state co; deals in all phases of oil industry; owns two refineries: one on Umm al-Nar island and one at Ruwais; Habshan Gas Treatment Plant (scheduled for partial privatization); gas pipeline distribution network; a salt and chlorine plant; holds 60% participation in operations of ADMA-OPCO and ADCO, and 88% of ZADCO; has 100% control of Abu Dhabi Nat. Oil Co for Oil Distribution (ADNOC-FOD), Abu Dhabi Nat. Tanker Co (ADNATCO), Nat. Drilling Co (NDC) and interests in numerous other cos, both in the UAE and overseas; ADNOC is operated by Supreme Petroleum Council; Chair. Sheikh KHALIFA BIN ZAYED AL NAHYAN (Pres. of the UAE and Ruler of Abu Dhabi); CEO ABDULLAH NASSER AL-SUWAIDI.

Subsidiaries include:

Abu Dhabi Co for Onshore Oil Operations (ADCO): POB 270, Abu Dhabi; tel. (2) 6040000; fax (2) 6665523; e-mail webmaster@adco.ae; internet www.adco.ae; f. 1978; shareholders are ADNOC (60%), BP, Shell and Total (9.5% each), ExxonMobil (9.5%) and Partex (2%); oil exploration, production and export operations from onshore oilfields; average production (1990): 1.2m. b/d; Chair. YOUSUF BIN OMEIR BIN YOUSUF; Gen. Man. ABD AL-MUNIM SAIF AL-KINDI.

Abu Dhabi Drilling Chemicals and Products Ltd (ADDCAP): POB 46121, Abu Dhabi; tel. (2) 6029000; fax (2) 6029010; e-mail addcap@emirates.net.ae; f. 1975; production of drilling chemicals and provision of marine services; wholly owned subsidiary of ADNOC; Chair. YOUSUF BIN OMEIR BIN YOUSUF; Gen. Man. MAHFOUD A. DARBOUL AL-SHEHHI.

Abu Dhabi Gas Industries Co (GASCO): POB 665, Abu Dhabi; tel. (2) 6030000; fax (2) 6037414; e-mail info@gasco.ae; internet www.gasco.ae; f. 1978; started production in 1981; recovers condensate and LPG from Asab, Bab and Bu Hasa fields for delivery to Ruwais natural gas liquids fractionation plant; capacity of 22,000 metric tons per day; 68% owned by ADNOC; Total, Shell Gas and Partex have a minority interest; Chair. YOUSUF OMEIR BIN YOUSUF; Gen. Man. MUHAMMAD SAHOO AL-SUWAIDI.

Abu Dhabi Gas Liquefaction Co (ADGAS): POB 3500, Abu Dhabi; tel. (2) 6061111; fax (2) 6065500; e-mail info@adgas.com; internet www.adgas.com; f. 1973; 70% owned by ADNOC, 15% by Mitsui and Co, 10% by BP, 5% by Total; operates LGSC and the LNG plant on Das Island, which uses natural gas produced in association with oil from offshore fields and has a design capacity of approx. 2.3m. metric tons of LNG per year and 1.29m. tons of LPG per year; the liquefied gas is sold to the Tokyo Electric Power Co, Japan; Chair. ABDULLAH NASSER AL-SUWAIDI; Gen. Man. SAIF AHMAD AL-GHAFLI.

Abu Dhabi Marine Operating Co (ADMA-OPCO): POB 303, Abu Dhabi; tel. (2) 6060000; fax (2) 6064888; e-mail webmaster@adma.ae; internet www.adma-opco.com; operates a concession 60% owned by ADNOC, 40% by Abu Dhabi Marine Areas Ltd (BP, Total and Japan Oil Devt Co); f. 1977 as an operator for the concession; production (1984): 67.89m. barrels (8.96m. metric tons); Chair. YOUSUF BIN OMEIR BIN YOUSUF; Gen. Man. ALI R. AL-JARWAN.

Abu Dhabi Oil Refining Co (TAKREER): POB 3593, Abu Dhabi; tel. (2) 6027000; fax (2) 6027001; e-mail publicrelation@takreer.com; internet www.takreer.com; refining of crude petroleum; production of chlorine and related chemicals; Chair. YOUSUF BIN OMEIR BIN YOUSUF; Gen. Man. JASIM ALI AL-SAYEGH.

ADNOC Distribution: POB 4188, Abu Dhabi; tel. (2) 6771300; fax (2) 6722322; e-mail Information@adnoc-dist.ae; internet www .adnoc-dist.co.ae; 100% owned by ADNOC; distributes petroleum products in UAE and world-wide; Chair. YOUSUF BIN OMEIR BIN YOUSUF; Gen. Man. JAMAL JABER AL-DHAREEF.

National Drilling Co (NDC): POB 4017, Abu Dhabi; tel. (2) 6776100; fax (2) 6779937; e-mail webmaster@ndc.ae; internet www.ndc.ae; drilling operations; Chair. ABDULLAH NASSER AL-SUWAIDI; Gen. Man. ABDALLAH SAEED AL-SUWAIDI.

National Petroleum Construction Co (NPCC): POB 2058, Abu Dhabi; tel. (2) 5549000; fax (2) 5549111; e-mail npccnet@eim.ae; internet www.npcc.ae; f. 1973; 'turnkey' construction and maintenance of offshore facilities for the petroleum and gas industries; cap. AED 100m.; Chair. HUSSAIN JASEM AL-NOWAIS; CEO AQEEL A. MADHI.

Ajman

Ajman National Oil Co (AJNOC): POB 410, Ajman; tel. (6) 7421218; f. 1983; 50% govt-owned, 50% held by Canadian and private Arab interests.

Dubai

Dubai Petroleum Establishment: POB 2222, Dubai; tel. (4) 3432222; fax (4) 3012200; internet www.dubaipetroleum.ae; f. 1963 as Dubai Petroleum Co; reorg. and renamed as above 2007; wholly owned by Dubai authorities; responsible for managing Dubai's offshore petroleum assets; Gen. Man. JEFF SEVERIN.

DUGAS (Dubai Natural Gas Co Ltd): POB 4311, Dubai (Location: Jebel Ali); tel. (4) 8846000; fax (4) 8846118; wholly owned by Dubai authorities; Dep. Chair. and Dir SULTAN AHMAD BIN SULAYEM.

Emarat: POB 9400, Dubai; tel. (4) 3434444; fax (4) 3433393; e-mail info@emarat.ae; internet www.emarat.ae; f. 1981 as Emirates General Petroleum Corpn, renamed as above 1996; wholly owned by Ministry of Finance; marketing and distribution of petroleum; Chair. OBAID HUMAID AL-TAYER (Minister of State for Financial Affairs); Gen. Man. JAMAL AL-MIDFA.

Emirates National Oil Co (ENOC): POB 6442, ENOC Complex, Sheikh Rashid Rd, Dubai; tel. (4) 3374400; fax (4) 3134702; e-mail webmaster@enoc.com; internet www.enoc.com; f. 1993; responsible for management of Dubai-owned cos in petroleum-marketing sector; Chief Exec. SAEED KHOORY.

Emirates Petroleum Products Co Pvt. Ltd (EPPCO): POB 5589, Dubai; tel. (4) 372131; fax (4) 3031605; e-mail f&e@eppcouae .com; internet www.eppcouae.com; f. 1980; jt venture between Govt of Dubai and Caltex Alkhaleej Marketing; sales of petroleum products, bunkering fuel and bitumen; Chair. Sheikh HAMDAN BIN RASHID AL MAKTOUM.

Sedco-Houston Oil Group: POB 702, Dubai; tel. (4) 3224141; holds onshore concession of over 400,000 ha as well as the offshore concession fmrly held by Texas Pacific Oil; Pres. CARL F. THORNE.

Sharjah

Sharjah Petroleum Council: POB 188, Sharjah; f. 1999; Chair. Sheikh AHMAD BIN SULTAN AL-QASIMI (Deputy Ruler of Sharjah); Sec.-Gen. Eng. WALEED RASHID DEMAS.

Sharjah Liquefied Petroleum Gas Co (SHALCO): POB 787, Sharjah; tel. (6) 5286333; fax (6) 5286111; e-mail shalco@shalco.ae; f. 1984; 100% owned by Sharjah authorities; gas-processing; producer of liquified commercial propane and commercial butane; Dir-Gen. SALEH AL-ALI.

Umm al-Qaiwain

Petroleum and Mineral Affairs Department: POB 9, Umm al-Qaiwain; tel. (6) 7666034; Chair. Sheikh SULTAN BIN AHMAD AL-MU'ALLA.

UTILITIES
Abu Dhabi

Regulation and Supervision Bureau: POB 32800, Abu Dhabi; tel. (2) 4439333; fax (2) 4439334; e-mail bureau@rsb.gov.ae; internet www.rsb.gov.ae; f. 1998; regulatory authority; Chair. MUHAMMAD AHMAD AL-BOWARDI; Dir-Gen. NICK CARTER.

Abu Dhabi Water and Electricity Authority (ADWEA): POB 6120, Abu Dhabi; tel. (2) 6943333; fax (2) 6943192; e-mail pr@adwea .gov.ae; internet www.adwea.gov.ae; f. 1998 to manage the water and electricity sectors and oversee the privatization process; Chair. Dr AHMAD BIN MUBARAK AL-MAZROUI; Dir-Gen. ABDULLAH SAIF AL-NUAIMI.

Abu Dhabi Distribution Co: POB 219, Abu Dhabi; tel. (2) 6423000; fax (2) 6426033; e-mail contactcentre@addc.ae; internet www.addc.ae; f. 1998; distribution of water and electricity; Chair. Sheikh DIAB BIN ZAYED AL NAHYAN.

Abu Dhabi National Energy Co (TAQA): POB 55224, Abu Dhabi; tel. (2) 6943662; fax (2) 6422555; e-mail info@taqa.ae; internet www.taqa.ae; f. 2005; 51% owned by ADWEA; owns assets in power, water, petroleum and mineral sectors in the UAE and abroad; provides more than 85% of the water and electricity produced in Abu Dhabi; Chair. HAMAD AL-HURR AL-SUWAIDI; CEO CARL SHELDON.

Abu Dhabi Transmission and Dispatch Co: POB 173, Abu Dhabi; tel. (2) 6414000; fax (2) 6426333; internet www.transco.ae; f. 1999; operation and devt of the transmission network for water and electricity; Chair. Dr ABDULLAH AL-SUWAIDI; Man. Dir DAVID COPESTAKE.

Abu Dhabi Water and Electricity Co (ADWEC): POB 51111, Abu Dhabi; tel. (2) 6943333; fax (2) 6425773; e-mail webmaster@ adwec.ae; internet www.adwec.ae; f. 1999; responsible for forecasting and managing the supply and demand of electricity and water; Chair. AHMAD SAIF AL-DARMAKI; Man. Dir GERHARDT GLEISSNER.

Al-Ain Distribution Co: POB 1065, al-Ain; tel. (3) 7636000; fax (3) 7629949; e-mail customercare@aadc.ae; internet www.aadc.ae; f. 1999; distribution of water and electricity; Chair. Sheikh DIAB BIN ZAYED AL NAHYAN.

Bayounah Power Co: POB 33477, Abu Dhabi; tel. (2) 6731100; fax (2) 6730403; e-mail webmaster@adwea.gov.ae; internet www .bpc.ae; f. 1999; operates two power stations at Abu Dhabi (also water desalination) and al-Ain; Chair. AHMAD HILAL AL-KUWAITI; Man. Dir ABD AL-JALEEL AL-KHOURY.

Al-Mirfa Power Co: POB 32277, Abu Dhabi; tel. (2) 8833044; fax (2) 8833011; e-mail info@ampc.ae; internet www.ampc.ae; f. 1999 to control Mirfa and Madinat Zayed plants; capacity 300 MW electricity per day, 37m. gallons water per day; Chair. MUHAMMAD FOULAD; Gen. Man. PHILIP GRAHAM TILSON.

As part of the privatization programme, several independent power and water projects (IWPPs) have been established, including Arabian Power Co, Emirates CMS Power Co, Gulf Total Tractebel Power Co, Shuweihat CMS International Power Co, and Taweelah Asia Power Co (TAPCO). In each IWPP, ADWEA retains a 60% shareholding while the remaining 40% is owned by private investors.

Dubai

Dubai Electricity and Water Authority (DEWA): POB 564, Dubai; tel. (4) 3244444; fax (4) 3248111; e-mail customercare@ dewa.gov.ae; internet www.dewa.gov.ae; f. 1992 following merger of Dubai Electricity Co and Dubai Water Dept; management and devt of the water and electricity sectors; CEO and Man. Dir SAID MUHAMMAD AHMAD AL-TAYER.

Northern Emirates (Ajman, Fujairah, Ras al-Khaimah and Umm al-Qaiwain)

Federal Water and Electricity Authority: POB 1672, Dubai; tel. (4) 2315555; fax (4) 2809977; e-mail cs@fewa.gov.ae; internet www .fewa.gov.ae; generation and distribution of electricity and water in the northern emirates; operates six power-generating plants and three water desalination plants; scheduled for part-privatization; Gen. Man. MUHAMMAD MUHAMMAD SALEH.

Sharjah

Sharjah Electricity and Water Authority (SEWA): Sharjah; tel. (2) 5288888; fax (2) 5288000; e-mail contactus@sewa.gov.ae; internet www.sewa.gov.ae; Chair. Sheikh SULTAN BIN MUHAMMAD AL-QASSIMI.

Transport
RAILWAYS

The first phase of an urban light-railway system, Dubai Metro—with 10 of the 29 planned stations in operation on the Red Line—opened in September 2009. By early 2012 all 29 stations had been opened. The 23-km Green Line was inaugurated in September 2011, with 18 of its planned 20 stations in operation. In 2006 the Abu Dhabi authorities announced plans for the construction of a 130-km metro system, projected for completion by 2015. Plans for the construction of a federal railway network for passengers and freight, linking the seven emirates, gained final government approval in March 2009. The 1,000-km network was to be constructed in two phases, with the first phase expected to take five years to complete.

Etihad Rail: f. 2009 as Union Railway Co; current name adopted 2011; charged with construction of, and eventual operations of, a federal railway network for both passengers and freight, to extend throughout the UAE; first phase of construction—comprising a 264-km freight line between Ruwais and Habshan and Shah in Abu Dhabi—expected to commence in 2013; wholly state-owned; Chair. NASIR AL-SUWAIDI; CEO NASIR AL-MANSOURI.

ROADS

The road network in the UAE is undergoing rapid development. Abu Dhabi and Dubai are linked by a good road that is dual carriageway for most of its length. This road forms part of a west coast route from Shaam, at the UAE border with the northern enclave of Oman, through Dubai and Abu Dhabi to Tarif. An east coast route links Dibba with Muscat, Oman. Other roads include the Abu Dhabi–al-Ain highway and roads linking Sharjah and Ras al-Khaimah, and Sharjah and Dhaid. An underwater tunnel links Dubai Town and Deira by dual carriageway and pedestrian subway. An extensive development plan announced in July 2006—the Dubai Strategic Plan—was to allocate AED 44,000m. to road infrastructure up to 2020 and to include the construction of 500 km of new roads, and upgrades of the emirate's existing road network. Contracts for construction work on the 327-km Mafraq–Ghoueifat highway, linking the UAE with Qatar and Saudi Arabia, were expected to be awarded in 2013. In 2008 there was a total paved road network of 4,080 km.

SHIPPING

Dubai has been the main commercial centre in the Gulf for many years. Abu Dhabi has also become an important port since the opening of the first section of its artificial harbour, Port Zayed. The Khalifa Port and Industrial Zone in Abu Dhabi, with a capacity of 2.5m. 20-ft equivalent units (TEU) per year, was inaugurated in September 2012. There are smaller ports in Sharjah, Fujairah, Ras al-Khaimah and Umm al-Qaiwain. Dubai possesses two docks capable of handling 500,000-metric-ton tankers, seven repair berths and a third dock able to accommodate 1,000,000-ton tankers. The Dubai port of Mina Jebel Ali, which was to be expanded at a cost of some US $1,362m., has the largest man-made harbour in the world. Plans were under way to expand Ras al-Khaimah's Mina Saqr Port. The first phase of the Mina Saqr project was completed in 2007, increasing the port's annual capacity to 350,000 TEUs; upon completion of the second phase, capacity would increase to 1.7m. TEUs per year.

At 31 December 2012 the United Arab Emirates' flag registered fleet totalled 738 vessels, with an aggregate displacement of 1,348,804 grt, of which four were bulk carriers, two were fish carriers and 28 were general cargo ships.

Abu Dhabi

Abu Dhabi Ports Co (ADPC): POB 54477, Mina Zayed, Abu Dhabi; tel. (2) 6952000; fax (2) 6952177; e-mail info@adpc.ae; internet www.adpc.ae; responsible for the devt and regulation of Abu Dhabi's ports and related industrial zones; Chair. Dr SULTAN AHMAD AL-JABER; CEO (vacant).

Abu Dhabi Terminals (ADT): POB 422, Port Zayed, Abu Dhabi; tel. (2) 6730600; fax (2) 6731023; e-mail info@adterminals.ae; internet www.adterminals.ae; f. 2006; replaced Abu Dhabi Seaports Authority (f. 1972); administers Port Zayed, Musaffah port and Freeport; facilities at Port Zayed include 21 deep-water berths and 5 container gantry cranes of 40 metric tons capacity; cold storage 20,500 tons; handled a total of 390,087 TEUs in 2008; jt venture between ADPC and Mubadala; Chair. TAWFIQ YOUSUF AL-MUBARAK; CEO MUHAMMAD AL-MANNAEI.

Abu Dhabi National Tanker Co (ADNATCO): POB 2977, Sheikh Khalifa Energy Complex, Takreer Tower, Abu Dhabi; tel. (2) 6028400; fax (2) 6723999; e-mail info@adnatcongsco.com; internet www.adnatco.com; f. 1975; subsidiary co of ADNOC, operating owned and chartered tankships, and transporting crude petroleum, refined products and sulphur; Gen. Man. ALI OBAID AL-YABHOUNI.

Abu Dhabi Petroleum Ports Operating Co (IRSHAD): POB 61, Abu Dhabi; tel. (2) 6028000; fax (2) 6742094; e-mail info@irshad.ae; internet www.irshad.ae; f. 1979; 60% owned by ADNOC, 40% by LAMNALCO Kuwait; manages Jebel Dhanna, Ruwais, Das Island, Umm al-Nar and Zirku Island SPM terminal, Mubarraz; operates fleet of 36 vessels; cap. AED 50m.; Chair. YOUSUF BIN OMEIR BIN YOUSUF; Gen. Man. KHALIFA M. AL-GOBAISI.

Dubai

Dubai Ports World (DP World): POB 17000, JAFZA 17, 5th Floor, Dubai; tel. (4) 8811110; fax (4) 48811331; e-mail info@dpworld.com; internet www.dpworld.ae; f. 2005 by merger of Dubai Ports Authority (f. 1991 by merger of Mina Jebel Ali and Mina Rashid) and Dubai Ports Int. (f. 1999); subsidiary of state-controlled Dubai World; 23% sold via initial public offering Nov. 2007; storage areas and facilities for loading and discharge of vessels; operates ports of Mina Jebel Ali and Mina Rashid in Dubai, Port Zayed in Abu Dhabi, Fujairah Port and numerous other international facilities; handled 42m. TEUs world-wide in 2006; CEO MUHAMMAD SHARAF; Sr Vice-Pres. and Man. Dir, UAE Region MUHAMMAD AL-MUALLEM.

Drydocks World—Dubai: POB 8988, Dubai; tel. (4) 3450626; fax (4) 3450116; e-mail drydocks@drydocks.gov.ae; internet www.drydocks.gov.ae; f. 1983; state-owned; dry-docking and repairs, tank-cleaning, construction of vessels and floating docks, conversions, galvanizing, dredging, etc.; Chair. KHAMIS JUMA BUAMIM.

Fujairah

Port of Fujairah: POB 787, Fujairah; tel. (9) 2228800; fax (9) 2228811; e-mail info@fujairahport.ae; internet www.fujairahport.ae; f. 1983; operated by Dubai Ports World; offers facilities for handling container, general cargo and roll on, roll off (ro-ro) traffic; handled 565,723 TEUs in 1999; Chair. Sheikh SALEH BIN MUHAMMAD AL-SHARQI; Gen. Man. Capt. MOUSA MURAD.

Ras al-Khaimah

Saqr Port Authority: POB 5130, Ras al-Khaimah; tel. (7) 2668444; fax (7) 2668533; e-mail info@saqrport.ae; internet www.saqrport.ae; govt-owned; port operators handling bulk cargoes, containers, general cargo and ro-ro traffic; Gen. Man. Capt. COLIN CROOKSHANK.

Sharjah

Department of Seaports and Customs: POB 510, Sharjah; tel. (6) 5281666; fax (6) 5281425; e-mail shjports@eim.ae; internet www.sharjahports.ae; the authority administers Port Khalid, Hamriyah Port and Port Khor Fakkan and offers specialized facilities for container and ro-ro traffic, reefer cargo and project and general cargo; in 2003 Port Khalid handled 145,482 TEUs of containerized shipping, and Port Khor Fakkan 1,444,451 TEUs; Port Khalid and Hamriyah Port together handled over 4m. metric tons of non-containerized cargo; Chair. (Ports and Customs) Sheikh KHALID BIN ABDULLAH AL-QASIMI; Dir-Gen. ISSA JUMA AL-MUTAWA.

Umm al-Qaiwain

Ahmed bin Rashid Port and Free Zone Authority: POB 279, Umm al-Qaiwain; tel. (6) 7655882; fax (6) 7651552; e-mail abrpaftz@emirates.net.ae; Pres. KHALID BIN RASHID AL-MU'ALLA; Gen. Man. MURTAZA K. MOOSAJEE.

CIVIL AVIATION

There are seven international airports, two in Dubai, and one in each of Abu Dhabi, al-Ain, Fujairah and Ras al-Khaimah, as well as a smaller one at Sharjah, which forms part of Sharjah port, linking air, sea and overland transportation services. The second airport in Dubai, Al Maktoum International Airport, was officially inaugurated in June 2010. Initially, the airport was open exclusively to cargo carriers. Part of the Dubai World Central commercial and residential infrastructure development, the new airport was expected, upon completion of a secondary phase of construction, to have five runways, four terminal buildings and an annual capacity of 160m. passengers and 12m. metric tons of freight, rendering it the largest airport in the world. It was reported that passenger carriers would begin to serve the airport from October 2013. Meanwhile, an expansion project at the Dubai International Airport, to increase annual capacity from 60m. to 90m. passengers, was scheduled for completion in 2018. Plans for the construction of a new terminal at Abu Dhabi International Airport, with a projected annual passenger capacity of 30m., were under way in 2013; the terminal was expected to be completed by 2017. Plans to construct a new terminal at Sharjah International Airport, at a cost of US $354m., were announced in late 2008.

General Civil Aviation Authority: POB 6558, Abu Dhabi; tel. (2) 4447666; fax (2) 4054535; e-mail info@gcaa.ae; internet www.gcaa.ae; f. 1996; responsible for all aspects of civil aviation; Chair. SULTAN BIN SAID AL-MANSOURI (Minister of Economy); Dir-Gen. SAIF MUHAMMAD AL-SUWAIDI.

Abu Dhabi Aviation: POB 2723, Abu Dhabi; tel. (2) 5758000; fax (2) 5757775; e-mail adava@abudhabiaviation.com; internet www.abudhabiaviation.com; f. 1976; domestic charter flights; Chair. NADER AHMAD MUHAMMAD AL-HAMADI; Gen. Man. MUHAMMAD IBRAHIM AL-MAZROUI.

Air Arabia: POB 132, Sharjah; tel. (6) 5088888; fax (6) 5580244; e-mail hraydan@airarabia.com; internet www.airarabia.com; f. 2003; 55% owned by private investors, 45% by the Sharjah Govt; low-fare airline; serves 46 destinations across the Middle East, N. Africa, S. and Cen. Asia, and Europe; handled 3.6m. passengers in 2008; Chair. Sheikh ABDULLAH BIN MUHAMMAD AL THANI; CEO ADEL ALI.

Emirates Airline: POB 686, Dubai; tel. (4) 2951111; fax (4) 2955817; e-mail corpcom@emiratesairline.com; internet www.emirates.com; f. 1985; owned by the Dubai Govt; operates services to over 100 destinations in 61 countries; carried 21.2m. passengers and 1.3m. metric tons of freight in 2007/08; Chair. and Chief Exec. Sheikh AHMAD BIN SAID AL MAKTOUM; Exec. Vice-Chair. MAURICE FLANAGAN; Pres. TIM CLARK.

Etihad Airways: POB 35566, Khalifa City A, Abu Dhabi; tel. (2) 5110000; fax (2) 5111200; internet www.etihadairways.com; f. 2003; owned by the Abu Dhabi Govt; operates 56 aircraft serving more than 66 destinations in 43 countries; carried 4.6m. passengers in 2007; Chair. Sheikh HAMAD BIN ZAYED AL NAHYAN; CEO JAMES HOGAN.

Falcon Express Cargo Airlines (FECA): Dubai International Airport, POB 93722, Dubai; tel. (4) 2826886; fax (4) 2823125; e-mail admin@feca.bz; internet www.falcongroup.bz; f. 1995; dedicated courier freight.

RAK Airways: POB 31457, Ras al-Khaimah; tel. (7) 2075000; fax (7) 2447387; e-mail info@rakairways.com; internet www.rakairways.com; f. 2006; flights commenced 2007; owned by Govt of Ras al-Khaimah; operates from Ras al-Khaimah Int. Airport; serves destinations in Bangladesh, Egypt, India and Saudi Arabia; Chair. Sheikh OMAR BIN SAQR AL-QASIMI; CEO OMAR JAHAMEH.

Tourism

Each emirate develops and promotes its tourist attractions separately, although a federal tourism authority, the National Council of Tourism and Antiquities, commenced operations in late 2009. Dubai is the UAE's most popular tourist destination; its wide range of luxury hotels and resorts, and entertainment and shopping facilities attracted around 7m. visitors in 2008. Abu Dhabi is developing its tourism industry, with an emphasis on leisure, heritage and cultural facilities, as well as luxury hotels and resorts. An extensive commercial, residential and leisure project is being developed at Saadiyat Island, which will incorporate beaches, hotels, golf courses and a cultural district that will accommodate branches of the Louvre and Guggenheim museums, as well as the Sheikh Zayed National Museum. There are established tourism sectors in Sharjah and Ras al-Khaimah, and plans are being implemented to foster tourism in Ajman and Fujairah. According to provisional figures, in 2011 there were 8.1m. foreign visitors to the UAE, compared with 616,000 in 1990. Receipts from tourism totalled US $9,204m. in 2011, according to provisional figures.

National Council of Tourism and Antiquities (NCTA): Abu Dhabi; f. 2008; commenced operations 2009; Dir-Gen. MUHAMMAD KHAMIS BIN HARIB AL-MUHAIRI.

Abu Dhabi Tourism Authority (ADTA): POB 94000, Abu Dhabi; tel. (2) 4440444; fax (2) 4440400; e-mail contact@abudhabi.ae; internet www.abudhabitourism.ae; f. 2004; Chair. Sheikh SULTAN BIN TAHNUN AL NAHYAN; Dir-Gen. MUBARAK HAMAD AL-MUHEIRI.

   Tourism Development and Investment Authority (TDIC): POB 126888, Abu Dhabi; tel. (2) 4061400; e-mail info@tdic.ae; internet www.tdic.ae; 100% owned by ADTA; responsible for the devt of a range of major projects incl. Saadiyat Island; CEO LEE TABLER.

Dubai Department of Tourism and Commerce Marketing: POB 594, Dubai; tel. (4) 2230000; fax (4) 2230022; e-mail info@dubaitourism.co.ae; internet www.dubaitourism.co.ae; f. 1997; 18 offices abroad; Chair. Sheikh MUHAMMAD BIN RASHID AL MAKTOUM (Ruler of Dubai); Dir-Gen. HILAL AL-MARRI.

Fujairah Tourism and Antiquities Authority: POB 829, Fujairah; tel. (9) 2231554; fax (9) 2231006; e-mail fujtourb@emirates.net.ae; internet fujairah-tourism.gov.ae; f. 1995; Chair. Sheikh SAEED BIN SAEED AL-SHARQI; Gen. Man. SAEED AL-SAMAHI.

National Corporation for Tourism and Hotels (NCTH): POB 6942, Abu Dhabi; tel. (2) 4099999; fax (2) 4099990; e-mail ncth@emirates.net.ae; internet www.ncth.com; 20% owned by Govt of Abu Dhabi; Chair. HAMDAN BIN MUBARAK AL-NAYHAN.

Ras al-Khaimah Tourism Promotion Board: POB 31219, Ras al-Khaimah; tel. (7) 2445125; fax (7) 2447463; internet www.raktourism.com; f. 2006; Chair. Sheikh ABD AL-AZIZ BIN HUMAID AL-QASIMI; CEO Dr KHATER MASSAAD.

Sharjah Commerce and Tourism Development Authority: POB 26661, Crescent Tower, 9th Floor, Buheirah Corniche, Sharjah; tel. (6) 5566777; fax (6) 5563000; e-mail sctda@sharjah.org; internet www.sharjahtourism.ae; f. 1996; Dir-Gen. MUHAMMAD ALI AL-NOMAN.

Defence

The Union Defence Force and the armed forces of the various emirates were formally merged in May 1976. Abu Dhabi and Dubai retain a degree of independence. Military service is voluntary.

Chief of Staff of the Federal Armed Forces: Lt-Gen. HAMAD MUHAMMAD THANI AL-RUMAITHI.

Defence Budget (2011): AED 34,200m.; federal expenditure on defence has been substantially reduced since the early 1980s, but procurement and project costs are not affected, as individual emirates finance these separately.

Total armed forces (as assessed at November 2012): 51,000 (army 44,000; navy est. 2,500; air force 4,500).

In May 2009 a French military base, comprising naval, air force and army facilities, was inaugurated in Abu Dhabi; at November 2011, a force numbering 800 was deployed at the base.

Education

Primary education is compulsory, beginning at six years of age and lasting for six years. Secondary education, starting at the age of 12, lasts for three years. After one year, students can choose between science- or arts-based streams. According to UNESCO estimates, enrolment at primary schools included 90% of children in the relevant age-group in 2008/09, while the comparable ratio for secondary enrolment was 83%. In 2010/11 a total of 26,733 children attended government pre-primary schools, and 177,911 attended primary schools in the UAE. In the same year secondary enrolment in government schools totalled 61,061. There are primary and secondary schools in all the emirates, and further education in technical fields is available in the more advanced areas. Many students receive higher education abroad. The UAE has 14 universities. A branch of the Université Paris-Sorbonne opened in Abu Dhabi in October 2006, while a branch of New York University opened in 2009. Two American universities are in operation, in Sharjah and Dubai. A British university and a Canadian university operate in Dubai, which also hosts branches of universities from Australia, others from the United Kingdom, and the USA. Four higher colleges of technology (two for male and two for female students) in Abu Dhabi opened in 1988. According to UNESCO, in 2008/09 a total of 87,006 students were enrolled in university and other higher education; some 60% of students in tertiary education in that year were females. Budgeted federal government expenditure by the Ministries of Education and of Higher Education and Scientific Research in 2012 totalled an estimated AED 8,200m. (equivalent to 20% of total expenditure by the central Government).

THE UNITED KINGDOM

Introductory Survey

LOCATION, CLIMATE, LANGUAGE, RELIGION, FLAG, CAPITAL

The United Kingdom of Great Britain and Northern Ireland lies in north-western Europe, occupying the major portion of the British Isles. It is separated from the coast of Western Europe by the English Channel to the south and by the North Sea to the east. The United Kingdom comprises four countries: England, Scotland and Wales, which constitute the island of Great Britain; and Northern Ireland, situated in the north-east of the island of Ireland (comprising six of the nine counties in the historic Irish province of Ulster), which borders the state of Ireland and provides the United Kingdom with its only land boundary. The climate of the United Kingdom is generally temperate but variable. The average temperature is about 15°C (59°F) in summer and about 5°C (41°F) in winter. The average annual rainfall is 1,125 mm (44.3 ins). The principal language is English, but Welsh also has official status in Wales, where it is spoken by about one-fifth of the population. The Church of England is the established church in England. Other large Christian denominations are Roman Catholicism, Methodism, the United Reformed Church and the Baptists. The national flag (proportions 1 by 2), known as the Union Jack or Union Flag, is a superimposition of the red cross of Saint George of England, the white saltire of Saint Andrew of Scotland and the red saltire of Saint Patrick of Ireland, all on a blue background. The capital is London.

CONTEMPORARY POLITICAL HISTORY

Historical Context

The United Kingdom of Great Britain and Ireland was established in 1801 by the union of the Parliament of Ireland (hitherto in personal union with the British crown) with that of Great Britain. Throughout the 19th century the United Kingdom's imperial expansion across the globe consolidated its dominance in world affairs. Increasing demands from the Roman Catholic population in Ireland for home rule were eventually conceded to after the First World War (1914–18), following a guerrilla campaign waged by the clandestine Irish Republican Army (IRA) in an attempt to force British withdrawal. In 1920 two parliaments were created in Ireland: one in Belfast, for the six Protestant-dominated counties in the north-east (Northern Ireland), and one in Dublin for the rest of the island. The Parliament of Northern Ireland subsequently chose to remain an integral part of the United Kingdom when the Irish Free State (now Ireland) acceded to dominion status in 1922.

Following the Second World War (1939–45), successive British governments, in response both to nationalist aspirations and world pressure, gradually granted independence to the remaining overseas colonies; almost all of these became members of the Commonwealth (see p. 244). The United Kingdom's dominance diminished over the Commonwealth, which became a free association of states, and the country looked increasingly to the North Atlantic Treaty Organization (NATO, see p. 380) and to the European Community (EC, now European Union—EU, see p. 281) for its future security.

Domestic Political Affairs

Following the general election of 1945, the Labour Party formed a government under Clement Attlee. The general election of 1951 was won by the Conservative Party, which remained in power for 13 years. The election of 1964 gave a small parliamentary majority to the Labour Party, led by Harold Wilson. The Labour Party was re-elected in 1966, but in 1970 a Conservative government, under Edward Heath, was returned. After the general election of February 1974 Wilson formed a minority government; at a further election in October the Labour Party achieved a small majority in the House of Commons (the lower chamber of Parliament). Wilson resigned as Prime Minister in April 1976, and was succeeded by James Callaghan. The latter's Labour administration was immediately confronted by a serious monetary crisis and, following a series of by-election defeats, became a minority government again.

At the general election of May 1979 the Conservative Party won a parliamentary majority. A government was formed under Margaret Thatcher, who became the United Kingdom's first woman Prime Minister. Thatcher's policies proved controversial, owing to the austerity of certain economic measures and an accompanying increase in unemployment. Furthermore, new legislation restricted the power of the trade unions. Meanwhile, the Labour Party became increasingly divided, and in March 1981 four former ministers from the right wing of the party established the Social Democratic Party (SDP). The SDP formed a political alliance with the Liberals later that year. (The two parties formally merged in 1988 as the Social and Liberal Democrats, and became the Liberal Democrats in the following year.)

In April 1982 Argentine forces invaded the British dependency of the Falkland Islands (q.v.). The successful military campaign to recover the islands in June boosted the Government's popularity, despite rising unemployment and strict monetary control of the economy. In the general election of June 1983 the Conservative Party increased its majority in the House of Commons to 146 seats. The Labour Party's parliamentary representation decreased and Neil Kinnock subsequently replaced Michael Foot as the Labour leader. In June 1987 the Conservative Government was again re-elected, winning a majority of 102 seats in the House of Commons.

In mid-1990 the introduction of a local tax, the community charge (or 'poll tax'), in conjunction with an economic recession, contributed to considerable national dissatisfaction with the Thatcher administration. The Cabinet was also divided, chiefly over policy on integration with the EC. In November the Deputy Prime Minister, Sir Geoffrey Howe, resigned from the Government in protest against Thatcher's hostility towards economic and political union within the EC. Michael Heseltine (who had resigned as Secretary of State for Defence in 1986) announced that he would challenge Thatcher for the leadership of the Conservative Party. In the first ballot of the leadership election (conducted among Conservative Members of Parliament—MPs) Thatcher failed to achieve an outright victory and subsequently withdrew her candidacy. John Major, Chancellor of the Exchequer since October 1989, eventually won the contest and was officially appointed Prime Minister in November 1990. (The community charge was replaced with a local council tax, based on property values, in April 1993.)

At a general election held in April 1992 the Conservative Party was re-elected with an overall, but substantially reduced, majority in the House of Commons. Economic recession continued. Divisions within the Conservative Party over the provisions of the Treaty on European Union (the Maastricht Treaty) were exacerbated by the United Kingdom's departure from the exchange rate mechanism of the European Monetary System (see p. 318) in September.

John Smith replaced Kinnock as leader of the Labour Party in July 1992. Prior to his death, in May 1994, Smith reformed the relationship between the Labour Party and the trade unions, reducing the unions' influence over policy formulation and the election of party chiefs and parliamentary candidates. In July 1994 Tony Blair, Labour's parliamentary spokesman on home affairs, was elected leader by the party's electoral college. Blair's initiative to abandon Labour's socialist commitment to common ownership of the means of production provoked a much-publicized reassessment of party ideology, and became a test of support for the new leadership. In April 1995 a special party conference endorsed a draft text to replace the relevant clause of the party's constitution.

In June 1995 Major announced his resignation as leader of the Conservative Party, asserting that speculation regarding a challenge to his leadership was undermining both his authority as Prime Minister and that of the Government. The Secretary of State for Wales, John Redwood, resigned from the Cabinet in order to challenge Major as party leader. In the ballot for the leadership, held in July, Major was endorsed by a large majority of the parliamentary party. However, Major's authority within the party continued to be challenged by those MPs demanding a limitation in the country's convergence with the EU. In April Major committed a future Conservative administration to conducting a popular referendum on the country's participation in a European single currency, but in June more than 70 Conservative MPs declared their support for a wider referendum on EU membership, demonstrating the increasing prominence of the so-called Eurosceptic faction of the party.

The Government of Tony Blair

At a general election held on 1 May 1997 the Labour Party secured an overwhelming victory, winning 418 of the 659 parliamentary seats. The Conservative Party secured only 165 seats and failed to win any parliamentary representation in Scotland or Wales for the first time in its history. Major immediately announced his resignation as leader of the Conservative Party: William Hague, hitherto Secretary of State for Wales, was elected to the post (and thus as Leader of the Opposition) by Conservative MPs in June. In the new Labour Government Gordon Brown, who had been instrumental in Blair's modernization of the Labour Party, was named as Chancellor of the Exchequer and Robin Cook became Secretary of State for Foreign and Commonwealth Affairs. The new administration set out a series of radical policy proposals and government reforms, including a transfer of operational responsibility for monetary policy to the Bank of England, legislation intended to improve standards in education, the enshrinement of the European Convention on Human Rights in domestic law (which was effected by the implementation of the 1998 Human Rights Act in October 2000), the adoption of a national minimum wage, and constitutional reform.

In July 1997 the Government formally published its proposals for the establishment of devolved legislative authorities in Scotland and Wales. A proposed new elected parliament was envisaged for Scotland, with powers to legislate on all domestic matters, including education, health, local government, law and order, and a possible mandate to vary the rate of income tax set by the United Kingdom Government. An executive level of government was to be headed by a First Minister. The national assembly for Wales, like the Scottish body, was envisaged as assuming control of the annual block grant for the region from central government, and as undertaking responsibility for issues covered by the Welsh Office. In a referendum held in Scotland in September, 74.3% of those voting supported a new parliament, while 63.5% approved its having tax-varying powers. The referendum in Wales, held one week later, was less conclusive, with only 50.3% of participants (or some 25% of eligible voters) endorsing the national assembly; none the less, the Government declared its intention to implement the majority decision. Elections to the new legislative authorities were held in May 1999, and powers were transferred to both the Scottish and the Welsh legislatures on 1 July.

In October 1998 the Government announced that legislation was to be introduced to remove the voting rights of hereditary peers in the House of Lords (the upper chamber of Parliament), and that a Royal Commission was to be appointed to consider options for a definitive reform of the non-elected second chamber. Opposition from within the House of Lords was appeased in December when a compromise agreement was reached under which 92 hereditary peers were to retain their seats in an interim second chamber pending the definitive reform. Legislation for the abolition of hereditary peerages and the establishment of an interim chamber was approved by the Lords in October 1999 and received royal assent in November. In January 2000 the Royal Commission published its proposals for the definitive reform of the upper house, recommending that the new chamber should comprise some 550 members, the majority of whom would be chosen by an independent commission, while a 'significant minority' would be elected by regional proportional representation.

In February 2001 an outbreak of foot-and-mouth disease among British livestock prompted the European Commission to impose a temporary ban on the export of live animals, meat and dairy products from the United Kingdom. The rapid spread of the disease throughout the country, mounting pressure from agricultural interest groups and popular opposition to the timing of the polls led the Government to announce in April that emergency legislation would be introduced to provide for a five-week postponement of the local elections due to be held in May. Blair later confirmed that an early general election (which, prior to the epidemic, had been widely expected to be held concurrently with the local elections) would also be conducted in June. The last case of foot-and-mouth disease was identified in

September, and in February 2002 the European Commission lifted remaining restrictions on the import and export of British meat and livestock.

At the general election, held on 7 June 2001, the Labour Party won another comprehensive victory, securing 412 of the 659 parliamentary seats. The Conservative Party obtained 166 seats, while the Liberal Democrats increased their parliamentary representation to 52 seats. Following his party's poor performance, Hague announced his intention to resign the leadership of the Conservative Party; in September Iain Duncan Smith, hitherto the Conservative Party's parliamentary spokesman on defence, was elected to replace him. Meanwhile, in a major reorganization of the Cabinet, Jack Straw, hitherto Secretary of State for the Home Department, replaced Cook as Secretary of State for Foreign and Commonwealth Affairs and David Blunkett assumed Straw's portfolio. The Ministry of Agriculture, Fisheries and Food, which had been heavily criticized for its handling of the foot-and-mouth outbreak, was replaced by the Department for the Environment, Food and Rural Affairs.

Blair's support for the US-led campaign to oust the regime of Saddam Hussein in Iraq in 2003 (see Foreign Affairs) provoked considerable public opposition and caused division within the Labour Party and the Government. In February the proposed military action against Iraq precipitated nation-wide anti-war demonstrations, including a march in London reportedly attended by some 1m. people. Following the failure to secure a second UN resolution authorizing military action in Iraq and the announcement in March that British troops would be deployed as part of the US-led coalition, Cook resigned as Leader of the House of Commons, citing his unwillingness to accept collective responsibility for the decision to commit the United Kingdom to military action without international agreement or domestic support. However, despite the opposition of a significant number of Labour MPs, Blair's strategy was supported by the Conservative Party, and a motion endorsing military action was approved by a large majority in the Commons. In May Clare Short, the Secretary of State for International Development, also resigned from the Cabinet, accusing Blair of reneging on assurances he had made to her concerning the need for a UN mandate to establish a legitimate Iraqi government. The British Broadcasting Corporation (BBC) came into conflict with the Government in the same month, when a BBC journalist alleged that a dossier, published by the Government in September 2002 to explain the case for the removal of the Iraqi regime, had made exaggerated and misleading claims concerning Iraq's possession of chemical and biological weapons. In February 2004 an inquiry was established under Lord Butler of Brockwell, to investigate the accuracy of the intelligence gathered on the alleged existence of Iraqi weapons of mass destruction; in July 2004 it reported that intelligence surrounding the compilation of the September 2002 dossier was 'seriously flawed' and criticized the intelligence services for using unreliable sources of information within Iraq.

In June 2003, meanwhile, an extensive reorganization of the Cabinet included plans to effect major changes to the British legal and judicial system. Under the proposals, a supreme court was to replace the judicial function of the House of Lords as the United Kingdom's highest court of appeal and the post of Lord Chancellor was to be abolished. The decision to abolish such an historic position without prior consultation was heavily criticized by a number of parliamentarians, and in July the clause of the Constitutional Reform Bill providing for the removal of the Lord Chancellor was rejected by the House of Lords. The Government subsequently agreed only to modify the Lord Chancellor's role (by substantially reducing his judicial powers and divesting him of the functions of Speaker of the House of Lords), while retaining the office. The Constitutional Reform Act finally received royal assent in March 2005 and came into force in April, when the Lord Chief Justice of England and Wales assumed control of the judiciary in England and Wales from the Lord Chancellor; in January 2006 the House of Lords formally agreed to elect a Speaker (the Lord Speaker), the Lord Chancellor having hitherto traditionally presided over debates. The new Supreme Court commenced operations in October 2009.

At the general election on 5 May 2005 the Labour Party was re-elected for a third term with a substantially reduced majority, securing 355 of the 645 parliamentary seats contested. The Conservative Party and the Liberal Democrats both increased their representation in the House of Commons, securing 197 and 62 seats, respectively. The Labour Party's loss of popularity was attributed principally to a decline in personal support for Blair and the ongoing military action in Iraq. Following the election, the Conservative leader, Michael Howard, who had replaced Iain Duncan Smith in October 2003 after the latter lost a vote of confidence among Conservative MPs, announced his resignation; in December David Cameron was elected by the party membership to succeed him.

The London bombings

On 7 July 2005 52 people were killed and more than 700 injured in four attacks—three on London Underground trains and one on a bus—perpetrated by suicide bombers in London. Of the four bombers, all of whom also died in the attacks, three were subsequently discovered to have been native British Muslims of Pakistani descent, while the fourth was a convert to Islam of Jamaican origin. In September Al Jazeera, a Qatar-based television station, broadcast a videotaped communiqué, supplied to it by the militant Islamist al-Qa'ida organization, in which Mohammad Sidique Khan, who had been identified as one of the four bombers, cited the United Kingdom's participation in the invasion of Iraq in 2003 as one of the motivations for the attacks. On 21 July 2005 at least four further attempts to carry out bomb attacks on the London transport system were unsuccessful owing to the failure of the devices to explode. By the end of the month four men suspected of involvement in the failed attacks of 21 July had been arrested in the United Kingdom, while two other suspects were extradited from Italy and Ethiopia later that year. The trial of the six men on charges of conspiracy to murder commenced in January 2007. In July four of the defendants were found guilty and were each sentenced to life imprisonment. The two remaining defendants each admitted lesser charges in November, and both received prison terms.

In response to the attacks, the Government published a new Terrorism Bill in September 2005. The draft legislation sought to establish new offences of preparing, assisting in, encouraging or exalting terrorist acts, and proposed that the maximum period for which suspected terrorists could be detained without charge should be extended from 14 to 90 days. While a number of the bill's provisions were supported by both the Conservatives and the Liberal Democrats, representatives of those parties claimed that the Government had failed to justify the proposed extension of the maximum period of detention without charge, while civil liberties organizations claimed that such a measure would infringe suspects' human rights. In November the 90-day extension was emphatically rejected by the House of Commons. The dismissal of the proposed legislation, which 49 Labour MPs had also refused to support, marked the first defeat that the Labour Government had suffered in the Commons since assuming power in 1997. The defeat was followed by a vote in favour of extending the maximum permissible period of detention of terrorist suspects without charge to 28 days. In March 2006 the House of Lords finally approved the legislation, which came into force in April.

In March 2006, after the House of Lords Appointments Commission had expressed concern over a number of Labour nominations for peerages, it was revealed that four of the nominees had made unpublicized loans totalling at least £4.5m. to the Labour Party. A police investigation was subsequently launched into whether, effectively, the Labour Party had illegally sold 'titles of honour'. Although the investigation was widened to examine the funding of both the Conservatives and the Liberal Democrats, the nominations called into question the Labour Party's commitment to transparency in political party funding, the reform of which it had begun after its election in 1997. Labour had in fact been under no legal obligation—as it would have been had they been donations—to declare the loans, but the fact that the party's treasurer had been unaware of them strengthened the impression of duplicity. In July 2006 the Labour Party's principal fund-raiser, Lord Levy, was arrested in the course of the investigation, while during the year the Prime Minister was among about 90 others (including members of all three main political parties) who were interviewed by the police. However, in July 2007 the Crown Prosecution Service announced that no charges would be brought in relation to the allegations.

New legislative proposals on the reform of the House of Lords, published in February 2007, suggested the abolition (over a transitional period) of all hereditary and life peerages and the reduction of the total membership of the upper house to 540, while MPs were to choose between a range of options on the proportion of members that would be elected and appointed. In a non-binding vote on these options, conducted in March, a majority of MPs favoured an entirely elected upper house, while a smaller majority voted for one with 80% elected and 20% appoin-

ted members; in the House of Lords itself all the options were rejected and the house voted to retain a non-elected upper chamber.

At local and regional elections on 4 May 2007 the Labour Party incurred considerable losses. In Scotland, the Scottish National Party (SNP), which advocated independence for Scotland, gained 20 new seats, thus obtaining a total of 47 of the 129 seats in the legislature, while Labour won 46, the Conservatives 17, the Liberal Democrats 16 and the Scottish Green Party two. On 16 May members of the Scottish Parliament elected the SNP leader, Alex Salmond, as First Minister, at the head of a minority SNP administration (with partial support from the Green members); Nicola Sturgeon was appointed as Deputy First Minister in addition to receiving the post of Cabinet Secretary for Health and Wellbeing. In the election to the National Assembly for Wales Labour lost four seats, but remained the largest party in the legislature with 26 of the 60 seats, while the Welsh nationalist Plaid Cymru won 15, the Conservative Party 12 and the Liberal Democrats six. In June Labour and Plaid Cymru finally agreed to form a coalition administration, in which Rhodri Morgan remained as First Minister and Plaid Cymru leader Ieuan Wyn Jones became his Deputy. (Morgan retired in December 2009 and was replaced as leader of Welsh Labour and First Minister by Carwyn Jones.)

The Government of Gordon Brown

In May 2007 Blair made the long-anticipated announcement that he would resign as leader of the Labour Party, with effect from 27 June. As the sole candidate, Gordon Brown, Chancellor of the Exchequer since 1997, was confirmed as the new leader of the party on 24 June. Brown assumed the role of Prime Minister three days later, following Blair's resignation, and subsequently announced an extensive reorganization of the Cabinet. Alistair Darling, previously the Secretary of State for Trade and Industry, replaced Brown as Chancellor of the Exchequer, while David Miliband was appointed Secretary of State for Foreign and Commonwealth Affairs. Jack Straw was appointed Secretary of State for Justice (the Department for Constitutional Affairs having been renamed the Ministry of Justice in the previous month) and Lord Chancellor, and Jacqui Smith was named as Secretary of State for the Home Department.

The first week of Brown's premiership was marked by two failed bomb attacks perpetrated by Islamist extremists. At the end of June 2007 two car bombs placed in central London failed to detonate, while a day later two men were arrested after driving a vehicle containing explosive materials into a terminal building at Glasgow Airport. (One of the men arrested in Glasgow died in August, having sustained severe injuries during the attack.) The trials of two men suspected of plotting the attacks began in October 2008; in December one of the men was sentenced to 32 years' imprisonment, while the other defendant was acquitted of all charges.

Despite widespread cross-party opposition, in June 2008 the Government's controversial Counter-Terrorism Bill, which contained provisions for the extension of the maximum period of detention for terrorist suspects from 28 to 42 days in exceptional circumstances, was narrowly approved by the House of Commons, with the support of members of the Democratic Unionist Party. However, in October the House of Lords overwhelmingly rejected the proposals for an extension of the detention period, which were subsequently omitted from the Counter-Terrorism Bill; the bill was given royal assent in November.

Support for Brown's leadership within the parliamentary ranks of Labour declined further in July 2008, following the loss to the SNP of a by-election in Glasgow East, a constituency the Labour Party had won by a large majority at the general election of 2005. There ensued considerable media speculation regarding a potential leadership challenge, notably by Miliband. In a cabinet reorganization effected in October, Brown unexpectedly appointed Peter Mandelson to succeed John Hutton as Secretary of State for Business, Enterprise and Regulatory Reform. (Mandelson, a former close associate of Blair, had served in the latter's Cabinet from 1997–98 and 1999–2001, but had been forced to resign on two occasions owing to impropriety; since 2004 he had been a European Commissioner.) Hutton, in turn, was appointed as Secretary of State for Defence. The Prime Minister's political reputation was enhanced in late 2008 by his response to the global financial crisis, as he played a significant role in international efforts to co-ordinate measures to address the economic downturn.

Meanwhile, from early 2008 a campaign by sections of the media to force the disclosure of MPs' claims for parliamentary allowances began increasingly to damage the reputation of ministers and other parliamentarians. In 2005 a group of journalists had requested the disclosure of claims made by 14 prominent politicians, including Brown, Blair and Cameron, under the 2000 Freedom of Information Act; this request was endorsed by the Information Tribunal in February 2008, and in May the High Court of Justice rejected an appeal against this decision by the Speaker of the House of Commons, Michael Martin. The details of the expense claims were disclosed later that month, and the Commons authorities consequently prepared to publish details of claims made by all MPs since 2004. Meanwhile, successive revelations throughout 2008 and early 2009 regarding allowances for secondary residences implicated senior Conservative and Labour politicians (notably including Jacqui Smith) and precipitated calls for a comprehensive reform of the system of parliamentary expenses. New regulations requiring the submission of receipts for all items included in expense claims, as well as the publication of details regarding income earned by MPs from activities separate from their parliamentary role, were approved by the Commons in May 2009; however, no agreement was reached over a reform of second home allowances, which were the subject of an ongoing inquiry by the independent public advisory body, the Committee on Standards in Public Life.

In May 2009 a national newspaper, *Daily Telegraph*, disclosed that it had covertly obtained a copy of the digital file in preparation by the House of Commons authorities that was to detail the expense claims made by all MPs between 2004 and 2008, and which had been scheduled for official publication in July 2009. The newspaper published excerpts from the file over the course of the month, revealing what was commonly perceived to be extensive and widespread abuse of the parliamentary allowance system by MPs from all three main parties, and prompting intense public criticism of the members concerned. Later in May 2009 a substantial number of MPs from all three main parties expressed support for a proposed motion of no confidence in the Speaker, Martin, who had been heavily criticized for his handling of the issue. The following day Martin announced his resignation both as Speaker of the Commons and as an MP. Meanwhile, the details of all MPs' allowance claims were officially released ahead of schedule in late June; on the same day the Commons authorities announced that, since April, MPs had voluntarily repaid a total of nearly £500,000 arising from dubious expense claims.

The extent of public disaffection with the Government, and with the established political parties in general, was highlighted by the results of elections to local councils in England and to the European Parliament, held concurrently on 4 June 2009. In the local elections the Labour Party lost control of the four remaining county councils it had held, while the Conservative Party emerged with control of 30 of the 34 councils contested. In the European Parliament elections the Labour Party won just 15.7% of the votes cast in Great Britain and 13 of the 69 available seats (compared with 19 in 2004); the UK Independence Party, which advocated British withdrawal from the EU, secured 16.5% of the votes and also took 13 seats, while the Conservatives won 27.7% (25 seats) and the Liberal Democrats 13.7% (11 seats). The extreme right-wing British National Party secured representation for the first time at national or European level, winning two seats in the north of England. Participation in the European elections was recorded at just 34.7% of electors in the United Kingdom. Brown effected a government reorganization shortly after the elections, in response to the Labour Party's poor performance; his authority had been weakened in the preceding days by a series of ministerial resignations, including those of Smith (who had announced her intention to leave the Government on 2 June, as a result of the criticism she had received over her expense claims) and James Purnell (who resigned as Secretary of State for Work and Pensions shortly before polling closed on 4 June). Alan Johnson was appointed to replace Smith as Secretary of State for the Home Department, while Purnell was replaced by Yvette Cooper. Among other changes, Mandelson was appointed First Secretary of State, Secretary of State for Business, Innovation and Skills and Lord President of the Council, thus gaining additional responsibilities, including higher education.

In late June 2009 the Government introduced emergency legislation to effect a partial reform of the parliamentary allowances system: the Parliamentary Standards Act, which received cross-party support and came into force in July, introduced an Independent Parliamentary Standards Authority (IPSA) to regulate MPs' allowances, and made it a criminal offence for an MP to provide false or misleading information about a claim for expenses. In November the Committee on Standards in Public Life published the results of its inquiry into MPs' allowances. The proposals were largely adopted by IPSA, which published its new rules on parliamentary expenses (which were to take effect after the forthcoming general election) in March 2010. Meanwhile, in February Sir Thomas Legg, a former senior civil servant who had conducted an audit of the expenses disclosed in May and June 2009, published his report: 390 current and former MPs who were judged to have made excessive claims under the second homes allowance were asked to make repayments totalling some £1.1m. (including the Prime Minister, who was asked to return more than £12,000 claimed for home maintenance costs). During 2010–11 six parliamentarians (both Labour and Conservative) were charged and convicted of false accounting in relation to their expense claims; the six offenders received prison terms ranging from nine to 18 months.

In June 2009, following the withdrawal of British troops from Iraq in April, Brown announced the establishment of a long-awaited independent inquiry into the invasion and occupation of that country. The public hearings of the inquiry, chaired by Sir John Chilcot, commenced in November and were concluded in February 2011; the inquiry was not expected to submit its final report until at least mid-2013. In January 2010 the inquiry heard evidence from senior ministers and government advisers in office at the time of the invasion, including Blair, who defended his decision to participate in the US-led military action. Brown also testified before the inquiry in March, when he insisted that, as Chancellor of the Exchequer, he had not denied any request for funding of the military campaign. Blair appeared before the inquiry for a second time in January 2011, largely reiterating the arguments he had made during his first testimony. A few days earlier Chilcot had expressed disappointment at a decision made by the Cabinet Secretary, Sir Gus O'Donnell, following consultation with Blair, not to allow the inquiry to publish correspondence and records of discussions between the former Prime Minister and the US President in the period preceding the invasion of Iraq.

The 2010 election and the coalition Government

The general election of 6 May 2010 was the first since February 1974 at which no party won an outright majority in the House of Commons. The Conservative Party emerged as the largest grouping in the House, winning 305 of the 649 contested seats with 36.1% of the votes cast. The Labour Party secured 258 seats with 29.0% of the votes, while the Liberal Democrats took 57 seats with 23.0% of the votes, thus holding the balance of power. The rate of participation was 65.1%.

Following the election, the leader of the Liberal Democrats, Nick Clegg, declared that the Conservatives, as the party with the greatest number of seats and votes, had the right to seek to form a government first (contrary to the existing constitutional convention, which favoured the incumbent Prime Minister, and despite the fact that the Liberal Democrats were considered to be ideologically closer to the Labour Party). Accordingly, the Conservatives and the Liberal Democrats entered into negotiations with a view to forming a government that would command the support of the House of Commons. On 10 May 2010 Liberal Democrat negotiators began formal parallel talks with the Labour Party, following an announcement by Brown that he intended to resign as party leader by September; it was widely speculated that the Liberal Democrats would be more amenable to forming a coalition government with Labour if Brown were replaced as Prime Minister. However, on 11 May, following the collapse of negotiations between Labour and the Liberal Democrats, Brown resigned as both Prime Minister and Labour leader. He was succeeded as Prime Minister by the Conservative leader, David Cameron, who announced that the Conservatives and the Liberal Democrats had agreed to form a coalition government (the United Kingdom's first since the Second World War). The composition of the Cabinet was announced the following day; Clegg became Deputy Prime Minister and Lord President of the Council, while the majority of ministerial roles were assigned to Conservatives. Notably, William Hague, the former party leader, was appointed First Secretary of State and Secretary of State for Foreign and Commonwealth Affairs, George Osborne became Chancellor of the Exchequer, and Theresa May was named Secretary of State for the Home Department and Minister for Women and Equalities. In addition to Clegg, four other Liberal Democrats were appointed to the Cabinet, including Dr Vincent Cable as Secretary of State for Business, Innovation and Skills and Chris Huhne as Secretary of State for Energy and Climate

Change. The Labour leadership was assumed on an interim basis by Harriet Harman, hitherto deputy leader of the party, until September, when Ed Miliband, Secretary of State for Energy and Climate Change in Brown's administration, was elected leader of the Labour Party by the party's electoral college, only narrowly defeating his brother, David, the former Secretary of State for Foreign and Commonwealth Affairs, with strong support from trade union voters.

Shortly after taking office the Conservative-Liberal Democrat coalition published a document outlining its agreed programme for government, which included a commitment to reduce public expenditure by some £6,200m. in the current financial year as part of urgent measures to reduce the structural deficit, as well as proposals for parliamentary and electoral reform, a banking levy, an annual limit on immigration from outside the EU, education reforms and the cancellation of the previous Government's plans to introduce identity cards. The resignation of David Laws, the Liberal Democrat Chief Secretary to the Treasury, in late May 2010, after he admitted impropriety regarding his claims for parliamentary allowances, necessitated an early, but minor, reorganization of the Cabinet: Laws was succeeded by Danny Alexander, hitherto Secretary of State for Scotland, who was replaced in that post by Michael Moore.

With the primary focus of the Government being to eliminate the public deficit within five years, in June 2010 Osborne presented an emergency budget, providing for a combination of real-terms reductions in expenditure, to cover all areas with the exception of health and overseas development aid, and measures to increase revenue, including, from January 2011, a rise in the rate of value-added tax and the introduction of a banking levy. Meanwhile, an independent Office for Budget Responsibility was created to provide official growth and budget forecasts and to assess the Government's progress in achieving its fiscal targets. Also in June 2010, Osborne announced the Government's intention to reform the regulatory framework of the financial sector, with far greater responsibility being granted to the Bank of England. A comprehensive spending review presented in October expanded on the Government's plans to reduce expenditure: the budgets of all government departments (other than health and overseas aid) would be cut by an average of 19% over a period of four years. Particular focus was to be given to reducing the cost of social welfare payments, where net savings of some £7,000m. per year were envisaged. Overall, the reductions in expenditure were projected to amount to £81,000m. by 2014/15. Under his 'Big Society' initiative, Prime Minister Cameron aimed to decentralize the provision of many public services away from central government to voluntary groups and individuals, as well as to local authorities. Also published in October was a strategic defence and security review, which included provision for a reduction of 25,000 in the number of civilian staff employed by the Ministry of Defence.

In July 2010 Clegg announced the details of the Government's proposals for parliamentary and electoral reform: the introduction of fixed five-year parliamentary terms; a reduction in the number of seats in the House of Commons from 650 to 600 and amendments to the boundaries of constituencies in order to make them more equal in terms of the size of their electorate; and the organization of a national referendum in May 2011 on whether the alternative vote (AV) model should replace the current 'first-past-the-post' voting system in general elections. The two coalition parties were divided over the issue of electoral reform. The Conservatives strongly favoured the retention of existing voting procedures, while the Liberal Democrats advocated the AV system (whereby voters rank candidates in order of preference and the first candidate to secure 50% of the vote wins the seat), considering it to be a compromise that might eventually lead to a full version of proportional representation. Although the Labour Party had supported a referendum on AV during the election campaign, it opposed a reduction in the number of legislative seats and changes to constituency boundaries. As these measures were contained in the same bill, Labour peers sought to impede its passage through the House of Lords in early 2011. However, the proposed legislation was finally approved on 16 February, the legal deadline for it to be possible to organize a referendum on the planned date of 5 May. A separate bill on fixed five-year parliamentary terms received royal assent on 15 September, according to which it was legally required that parliamentary elections be held every five years on the first Thursday in May, beginning on 7 May 2015. The only circumstances that would allow for the holding of an early general election were if a motion for an early election was agreed either

by at least two-thirds of the whole House of Commons, or if a parliamentary motion of no confidence in the government was passed by a simple majority and no alternative administration was confirmed by the House within 14 days.

In November 2010 the Government proposed an annual limit of 21,700 (from April 2011) on the number of visas issued to skilled workers from outside the European Economic Area (EEA, comprising the EU, Iceland, Norway and Liechtenstein) who wished to work in the United Kingdom. However, in an apparent concession to opponents both within the coalition and within the business sector of a fixed limit, intra-company transfers of personnel with annual salaries exceeding £40,000 would be exempt. Cable, the Secretary of State for Business, Innovation and Skills, had notably raised concerns in September 2010 that an interim limit imposed in June was too restrictive and was damaging the economy. In April 2012 the Government announced that the annual cap on visas for non-EEA skilled workers would be maintained at 21,700 until April 2014. Immigration policy again prompted tensions within the Government in April 2011, when Cable publicly criticized a pledge by Cameron to reduce net migration levels from hundreds of thousands of people per year to tens of thousands, noting that such a target was Conservative, rather than coalition, policy and 'risked inflaming extremism'. According to official figures, net immigration fell from a record high of 252,000 in 2010 to an estimated 216,000 in 2011.

Government plans to raise the state-imposed limit on the tuition fees that universities in England could charge domestic students for undergraduate courses from £3,000 per year to £9,000 from September 2012 provoked significant opposition in late 2010. A series of demonstrations against the proposal took place in university towns nation-wide; one of these, held in central London on 10 November, escalated into rioting at the Conservative Party's headquarters. More than 120 people were arrested in connection with the violence and with further disorder that occurred at a second major protest later that month. Particular anger was directed towards the Liberal Democrats, who had pledged during the campaign for the May elections not to increase tuition fees. None the less, the legislation on tuition fees was adopted by Parliament in December, albeit by a majority of only 21 votes in the House of Commons.

Following a review of counter-terrorism policy, in January 2011 the Secretary of State for the Home Department, Theresa May, confirmed that the maximum period for which suspected terrorists could be detained without charge had reverted from 28 days to 14 days and announced the Government's intention to abolish control orders, which had been introduced in 2005 to place restrictions on the movements of terrorism suspects who could not be prosecuted owing to the sensitivity of the evidence against them. However, proposed new 'terrorism prevention and investigation measures' were deemed by civil liberties campaigners to be only slightly less restrictive than the control orders, which critics had claimed were effectively a form of house arrest and which had been subject to several legal challenges.

Also in January 2011 the Secretary of Health, Andrew Lansley, presented a bill for major reform of the National Health Service in England, which provided for a drastic reduction in the number of health bodies, in order to lower administration costs, and an increase in the powers of general practitioners (GPs, family doctors) to commission medical services for their patients. However, amid mounting criticism of the proposals, notably from the British Medical Association and the Royal College of Nursing (the two main organizations representing doctors and nurses), in April Lansley announced a 'pause' to allow further consultation on the bill. In June the Prime Minister outlined substantial amendments to the bill, including the gradual implementation of its provisions and the involvement of hospital staff (in addition to GPs) in the commissioning of patients' treatment. (The revised bill received royal assent in March 2012.)

The Labour Party comfortably retained two seats in the House of Commons at by-elections held in January and March 2011; the second ballot was notable for the poor performance of the Liberal Democrats, whose share of the vote for that constituency declined to a mere 4.2% from 17.3% at the general election in May 2010. In early March 2011, at a referendum held in Wales, 63.5% of those participating (35.3% of the electorate) voted in favour of the Welsh National Assembly being granted full legislative powers over domestic matters, without the requirement to seek the consent of the United Kingdom Parliament. More than 250,000 people participated in a march organized by the Trades Union Congress later that month in central London in protest against reductions in public spending; although the demonstration was largely peaceful, some 200 arrests were made after small groups of protesters attacked shops and banks, clashing with police officers.

On 5 May 2011 local and regional elections took place, together with a national referendum on the replacement of the 'first-past-the-post' electoral system with AV. The change in the voting system, which had been advocated by the Liberal Democrats, was defeated by a significant margin, with 67.9% of the valid votes cast against the proposal and only 32.1% in favour; turnout at the referendum was 42.2%. The Liberal Democrats also performed poorly at the local elections, where they lost almost one-half of their incumbent councillors whose seats were contested. The Conservatives, by contrast, (who had campaigned against the adoption of AV) slightly increased their already high number of councillors and won control of two further councils. The Labour Party, which had been divided over support for AV, obtained more than 800 council seats in England and won 30 of the 60 seats in the Welsh Assembly (thus missing a majority by just one seat), but suffered serious losses in the elections to the Scottish Assembly. The SNP, led by Alex Salmond, became the first party to win an overall majority in the Scottish Assembly, taking 69 seats (an increase of 22 seats from the previous elections), compared with 37 seats for the Labour Party (a loss of nine seats). While the Conservatives lost only one seat in Scotland, leaving its total at 15 seats, the Liberal Democrats' representation declined from 16 seats to five. Salmond, who was re-elected as First Minister later in May, announced that a referendum on Scottish independence would take place in the second half of the new parliamentary term (which had earlier been increased from four to five years—as a one-off for this term alone—to avoid a clash of dates with the 2015 general election to the Parliament in London).

In mid-May 2011 Clegg revealed the Government's latest proposals for reform of the House of Lords, according to which membership of the upper house would be reduced from almost 800 to 300, of whom 240 (80%) would be elected by popular vote to serve non-renewable terms of 15 years and the remaining 60 would be appointed. In addition, it was proposed that Church of England bishops would retain their right to sit in the House of Lords, but their number would be lowered from 26 to 12.

Recent developments: riots and the Leveson Inquiry

From early 2011 the British newspaper sector came under increasing scrutiny and criticism regarding revelations that journalists had engaged in illegal telephone hacking—i.e. the interception of private voice messages left on mobile telephones—and other unlawful methods to obtain information on a range of prominent figures (including Tony Blair, Peter Mandelson and members of the royal family). The main culprits of such impropriety were employees of the Sunday tabloid newspaper *News of the World*, which was owned by Rupert Murdoch's News International. As part of the inquiry into the 'hacking scandal' undertaken by the Metropolitan Police, a number of journalists were detained for questioning. In response to the relentless criticism, particularly in light of the disclosure that a private investigator working for the Sunday newspaper had hacked into the telephone messages of a murdered school-girl, News International ceased publication of *News of the World* (which had been founded in 1843) on 10 July. Later that week the Chief Executive of News International, Rebekah Brooks, stood down from her post. Two days later the Commissioner of the Metropolitan Police, Sir Paul Stephenson, resigned his position following allegations of his involvement in the scandal; a government inquiry was subsequently set up to investigate the nature of the relationship between the police and the media. On the same day as Stephenson's resignation Brooks was detained for questioning regarding the hacking affair and alleged corrupt practices. In their subsequent appearances before the Culture, Olympics, Media and Sport select committee Brooks, Murdoch and his son James Murdoch (the Chairman of News International Europe and Asia) claimed not to have been aware at the time of the large-scale use of telephone hacking by newspaper employees. The scandal had immediate repercussions for the Prime Minister whose former director of communications, Andy Coulson, had been forced to resign as editor of *News of the World* in 2007 (when the first instance of telephone hacking was disclosed); Coulson had stood down from his position in Cameron's office in January 2011 when further revelations regarding the scandal were beginning to emerge. Coulson was detained for questioning in July. In the same month the Prime Minister announced the establishment of a new inquiry, which was to be

headed by Lord Justice Brian Leveson and was to expand its investigations to cover the relationship between the police and journalists, the general ethics and culture of the British media sector and the existing system of regulation of print media by the Press Complaints Commission. In November the Metropolitan Police revealed that the total potential number of victims of telephone hacking stood at some 5,800. In the same month James Murdoch stood down from his position as Chairman of News International. In May 2012 Brooks (a personal friend of Prime Minister Cameron), together with her husband and four former employees of News International were charged with perverting the course of justice.

On 30 June 2011 considerable disruption was caused by a one-day strike organized by the public sector trade unions to protest against the Government's cuts in public expenditure and proposed changes to the pensions of state employees. The unions staged another strike on 30 November, claiming the participation of more than 2m. public sector workers (the Government asserted that the number was considerably lower).

On 4 August 2011 the controversial shooting of an unarmed man by police officers in north London prompted public protests, which within three or four days had escalated into violent rioting, arson and looting by large groups of disaffected youths in many parts of the capital; the unrest spread to a number of other towns and cities throughout England, including Manchester, Birmingham, Bristol, Oxford and Liverpool. The Government ordered the deployment of thousands of police officers to quash the disturbances and by 10 August the situation had, for the most part, been brought under control. The police had been given authorization to use plastic bullets and tear gas, but in the event refrained from doing so. Five people were killed during the rioting and several hundred were injured (the majority of whom were police officers). Much debate ensued regarding the identification of the underlying causes of the riots and a special session of the House of Commons was called to discuss the matter. By the end of August around 3,000 people had been arrested for their suspected involvement in the civil disorder. The sentences passed on those found guilty were generally much more stringent than the terms of imprisonment normally imposed for similar crimes.

In mid-October 2011 the Government suffered a further setback when the Secretary of State for Defence, Liam Fox, resigned his post following allegations regarding his potential abuse of office in his relations with a personal friend (who, although holding no position in the Government or Conservative Party, had, none the less, accompanied Fox on numerous official trips abroad and had made frequent visits to the Ministry of Defence). Fox was replaced by the erstwhile Secretary of State for Transport, Philip Hammond, who was himself succeeded by Justine Greening. In early February 2012 Huhne resigned from his post as Secretary of State for Energy and Climate Change following an announcement that he and his former wife, Vicky Pryce, were to be charged with conspiracy to pervert the course of justice with regard to an alleged driving offence. He was replaced by fellow Liberal Democrat Edward Davey. (In March 2013 Huhne and Pryce, having both been found guilty, were sentenced to short terms in prison.)

In mid-February 2012 Prime Minister Cameron and Scottish First Minister Salmond held talks in Edinburgh on the latter's plans to hold a referendum on Scottish independence. Cameron strongly supported the retention of the union of the United Kingdom, while conceding that greater devolved powers could be granted to the Scottish Assembly. The following month the SNP administration and the Secretary of State for Scotland, Michael Moore, reached agreement on the provisions of the Scotland Act 2012, according to which the Scottish Parliament was to be granted greater authority over Scotland's taxation and borrowing. The legislation received royal assent in May. In October Cameron and Salmond signed an agreement regarding the holding of a referendum before the end of 2014 on proposed independence for Scotland. As part of the agreement, the voting franchise of the poll was to be extended to 16- and 17-year-olds. In March 2013 Salmond announced that the referendum would be held on 18 September 2014.

In the course of the Leveson Inquiry it was revealed in mid-April 2012 that the Secretary of State for Culture, Olympics, Media and Sport, Jeremy Hunt, may have breached the ministerial code by reportedly helping Rupert Murdoch's News Corporation—through frequent briefings—in its bid fully to takeover British Sky Broadcasting (BSkyB) during 2011. Hunt had assumed quasi-judicial responsibility for adjudicating on the bid following the divestment of this role from Vince Cable in December 2010 (after the latter had made injudicious comments regarding the matter to journalists posing as constituents). The Labour Party demanded that Hunt resign immediately and that a separate independent investigation into the alleged wrong-doings be instigated. However, although his special adviser stood down in late April 2012, the Secretary of State, who enjoyed the support of Cameron, remained in office.

At local elections in England, Scotland and Wales, which took place on 3 May 2012, the Conservative Party and the Liberal Democrats performed poorly; the Conservative Party lost control of 12 councils and the Liberal Democrats one, while the Labour Party gained control of an additional 32 local councils. In Scotland, the SNP made substantial advances, winning the largest number of seats across the country, while in Wales, the Labour Party enjoyed its best local election results since 2008. The Conservative Party did, however, retain the mayoralty of London by a narrow margin. The following week, according to trade union estimates, some 400,000 public sector workers (including police officers) took part in another national one-day strike in protest against the Government's continuing austerity measures; government figures claimed that the number of participants totalled only some 100,000. At local elections to 35 councils in England and Wales in May 2013 the Conservative Party performed badly, losing control of 10 councils; the Liberal Democrats lost a number of council seats, while, notably, the populist UK Independence Party drew a large proportion of votes, winning an average of 25% of votes where it stood candidates.

Meanwhile, the House of Lords Reform Bill, which was based on the Government's proposals announced in May 2011 (although the proposed membership was now 450), was presented to the House of Commons by Clegg in June 2012. As a result of staunch opposition among backbench Conservative MPs, the bill was abandoned in August; Clegg claimed that, in blocking the passage of the legislation, the Conservatives had reneged on their 'coalition contract'.

The Leveson Inquiry concluded its process of evidence-gathering in late July 2012, having heard testimony from, among many others, Cameron and former prime ministers Blair and Brown. On the same day, seven former journalists of the *News of the World*, including Brooks and Coulson, were charged with illegal telephone hacking. The Leveson Inquiry published its final report in November; the document recommended the establishment of a new, independent press regulatory body (backed by law) to replace the existing Press Complaints Commission.

A substantial cabinet reorganization carried out by Cameron in early September 2012 led to a strengthening of the right-wing element in government and a concomitant weakening of the Liberal Democrats' authority. Among the notable changes was the promotion of Minister of State for Employment Christopher Grayling to the cabinet position of Lord Chancellor and Secretary of State for Justice, replacing Kenneth Clarke, who was appointed as a Minister without Portfolio. In an unexpected move, Hunt, despite the scandal surrounding him earlier in the year, replaced Andrew Lansley as Secretary of State for Health; Lansley was demoted to the position of Leader of the House of Commons and Lord Privy Seal. Later in the month Andrew Mitchell resigned as Parliamentary Secretary to the Treasury and Chief Whip, in the wake of the controversy surrounding a verbal altercation between himself and several police officers outside the Prime Minister's London residence in Downing Street; he was replaced by Conservative stalwart Sir George Young.

Although opposed by more than one-half of Conservative MPs, historic legislation was endorsed by the House of Commons in February 2013 which would offer same-sex couples the right to marry.

Allegations of Complicity in Torture

Following the NATO-led incursion into Afghanistan in October 2001, the United Kingdom became subject to allegations that its airspace and air transport facilities had been used in the transfer ('extraordinary rendition') of detainees, in particular terrorist suspects, by the US Central Intelligence Agency (CIA) to third countries where it was possible that they might be subjected to torture during interrogation. In December 2005 Blair dismissed calls by human rights organizations for an inquiry into the so-called rendition flights and insisted that he had no evidence to suggest that anything illegal had occurred. However, in February 2008 David Miliband, the Secretary of State for Foreign and Commonwealth Affairs, admitted to the House of Commons that

the US military base on Diego Garcia in the British Indian Ocean Territory had, in fact, been used in the rendition of detainees.

In October 2008 the Secretary of State for the Home Department asked the Attorney-General, Baroness Scotland of Asthal, to investigate allegations made by Binyam Mohamed, an Ethiopian national resident in the United Kingdom who had been detained in Afghanistan by the US authorities in 2002. Mohamed claimed that members of the British intelligence services had colluded in his torture during a period of detention in Morocco, prior to being transferred to the US camp for detained 'enemy combatants' at Guantánamo Bay, Cuba, in 2005; Miliband denied that the British authorities had been complicit in torture. Mohamed returned to the United Kingdom in February 2009, following his release from Guantánamo Bay, where all charges against him had been dropped. In March Baroness Scotland asked the Commissioner of the Metropolitan Police to investigate the allegations relating to Mohamed. Although human rights groups and lawyers welcomed the investigation, they continued to demand a judicial inquiry to establish the full extent of British collusion in acts of torture. In February 2010 the Court of Appeal ordered Miliband to authorize the publication of a document summarizing information, given to the Security Service (MI5) by the US Central Intelligence Agency (CIA), on Mohamed's treatment while in US custody. The information, which was subsequently released, indicated that MI5 had, at the very least, been aware of 'cruel, inhuman and degrading treatment' by the US authorities. In early May, moreover, the Court of Appeal overturned a High Court ruling, made the previous November, that evidence could be withheld from claimants seeking compensation for alleged British complicity in their mistreatment by foreign countries if disclosure would compromise national security. Later in May the new Secretary of State for Foreign and Commonwealth Affairs, William Hague, promised that an independent inquiry would be conducted into all unresolved allegations of British complicity in the torture of terrorist suspects abroad. The inquiry, headed by Sir Peter Gibson, the Intelligence Services Commissioner, was established in July, although it was not to commence work until all police investigations into the allegations had been completed. In November the Lord Chancellor and Secretary of State for Justice, Kenneth Clarke, announced that out-of-court settlements had been reached with 16 former detainees at Guantánamo Bay claiming to have been victims of British complicity in torture; no admission of culpability was made. By early January 2012 the Gibson Inquiry (or Detainee Inquiry) had made little progress as it continued to await the completion of lengthy preliminary police investigations, which were widely criticized by human rights organizations for their lack of credibility and transparency. Following the launch in that month of fresh investigations into allegations made by two Libyan erstwhile dissidents—Sami al-Saadi and Abdul Hakim Belhaj—that British intelligence agents had been complicit in their respective renditions to Libya and subsequent torture at the hands of the regime of Col Muammar al-Qaddafi in 2004, the Government announced the abandonment of the Gibson Inquiry. However, Clarke stated that, once the ongoing investigation procedures were completed, the Government was committed to establishing a new independent, judge-led inquiry. In December 2012 the Government agreed to pay £2.2m. in compensation to al-Saadi for its part in his illegal rendition to Libya.

Northern Ireland

Towards a peace settlement

During the late 1960s an active civil rights movement sought to end discrimination against Roman Catholics in Northern Ireland, where the Protestant-supported Ulster Unionist Party (UUP) had remained in permanent control of the Parliament and government since the partition of Ireland in 1922. However, Protestant extremists viewed the non-violent movement as a republican threat, and resorted to violence against Catholic activists. The Irish Republican Army (IRA) was originally a small element in the civil rights movement, but, after increasingly serious disturbances, a breakaway group, calling itself the Provisional IRA (generally known simply as the IRA), embarked on a campaign of violence with the aim of reuniting Ireland on its own terms. In April 1969 the Northern Ireland Government requested that British army units be assigned to protect important installations and in August the British and Northern Ireland governments agreed that all security forces in the territory would be placed under British command. In March 1972, as a result of increased violence, the British Government assumed direct responsibility for law and order. Finding this unacceptable, the Northern Ireland Government resigned. The British Government prorogued the Northern Ireland Parliament and introduced direct rule from London.

In 1973 new legislation abolished the office of Governor (the British monarch's representative) and the Northern Ireland Parliament, and provided for new constitutional arrangements. In June elections were conducted for a 78-member Northern Ireland Assembly, and an Executive was subsequently constituted from its members. An important part of this new 'power-sharing' arrangement was the establishment of a limited role for the Irish Government in Northern Ireland's affairs. Accordingly, in December, at Sunningdale (in southern England), the British and Irish governments and the Northern Ireland Executive finalized an agreement to form a Council of Ireland (with members drawn from the governments of Northern Ireland and Ireland), which would have a range of economic and cultural responsibilities in both parts of Ireland. However, the Sunningdale Agreement and the new devolved authority in Northern Ireland were rejected by many Protestants, and led, in 1974, to a general strike. A state of emergency was declared and the Executive was forced to resign. The Assembly was prorogued, and Northern Ireland returned to direct rule by the British Government. The collapse of the Sunningdale Agreement led to a rise in popularity of the more extreme Democratic Unionist Party (DUP—founded in 1971, and led by Rev. Dr Ian Paisley), which established itself as the main rival to the UUP.

Throughout the 1970s and 1980s the IRA and the Irish National Liberation Army (INLA, which emerged in 1975) perpetrated terrorist attacks on British military and civilian targets both in Northern Ireland and in England and continental Europe, while Protestant 'loyalist' paramilitary groups engaged in attacks on Roman Catholics.

Discussions between the governments of the United Kingdom and Ireland in 1984–85 culminated in the signing of the Anglo-Irish Agreement in November 1985. The Agreement established the Intergovernmental Conference, through which British and Irish ministers were to meet regularly to discuss political, security, legal and cross-border matters relating to Northern Ireland. While giving the Irish Government a formal consultative role in Northern Ireland affairs, the Agreement recognized that the constitutional status of Northern Ireland remained unchanged and would not be altered without the consent of a majority of Northern Ireland's population. The Agreement had the support of the predominantly Roman Catholic Social Democratic and Labour Party (SDLP), and was approved by the Irish and British parliaments. However, it was strongly opposed by most unionist politicians, who organized mass demonstrations and violent protests against the Agreement. In June 1986 the Northern Ireland Assembly was dissolved.

In January 1990 the British Government launched an initiative to convene meetings between representatives from the major political parties in Northern Ireland and the British and Irish governments to discuss devolution in Northern Ireland and the future of its relations with Ireland. Sinn Féin (the political wing of the IRA) was to be excluded from the talks because of its refusal to denounce the IRA's campaign of violence. Bilateral discussions between the British Government and the DUP, the UUP, the SDLP and the non-sectarian Alliance Party eventually began in April 1991, and talks subsequently commenced between all the Northern Ireland parties and the Irish Government. The principal point of contention was the unionists' demand that Ireland hold a referendum on Articles 2 and 3 of its Constitution, which laid claim to the territory of Northern Ireland. The Irish Government, however, remained unwilling to make such a concession except as part of an overall settlement. In the absence of an agreement, the negotiations formally ended in November 1992, and the Anglo-Irish Intergovernmental Conference resumed.

In December 1993 the British and Irish prime ministers, John Major and Albert Reynolds, made a joint declaration, known as the Downing Street Declaration (after the British Prime Minister's official residence in London), which provided a specific framework for a peace settlement. The initiative, which was widely supported by opposition parties in the United Kingdom and Ireland, referred to the possibility of a united Ireland and accepted the legitimacy of self-determination, while insisting on majority consent within Northern Ireland. The DUP, the UUP and Sinn Féin rejected the document, effectively removing any confidence of achieving an imminent peace settlement. However,

the British and Irish governments reiterated their intention to pursue the peace process.

In August 1994 the IRA announced 'a complete cessation of violence'. In October the loyalist paramilitary groups declared a suspension of military activity, which was effectively to be linked to that of the IRA. Later that month Major announced new measures to restart the peace process, adopting the 'working assumption' that the IRA cease-fire was permanent. The first public meeting between Sinn Féin and British government officials was held in December, marking the start of exploratory talks between the two sides. In February 1995 Major and the new Irish Prime Minister, John Bruton, presented a Framework Document containing proposals for cross-border co-operation, together with a separate British government paper outlining a new Northern Ireland Assembly with wide legislative and executive authority. Both governments emphasized that any final agreement about the proposals was to be subject to parliamentary approval and popular consent through the holding of a referendum. Despite a positive Sinn Féin response to the Framework Document, the issue of decommissioning paramilitary weapons remained the major obstacle to peace negotiations: the British Government objected to Sinn Féin's linking of IRA decommissioning with the demilitarization of Northern Ireland, while Sinn Féin rejected the Government's insistence that decommissioning by paramilitary organizations be a precondition to conducting all-party negotiations.

In November 1995 the British and Irish governments agreed to initiate preliminary talks with all the parties in Northern Ireland. An international commission to assess the practicalities of the decommissioning of armaments and other aspects of the peace process, chaired by George Mitchell, an adviser to US President Bill Clinton, began meetings with all sides involved in the process in December. The commission's final report, issued in January 1996, recommended proceeding with all-party talks on the condition that all sides endorse the eventual complete disarmament of paramilitary organizations, the renunciation of violence and the cessation of paramilitary 'punishment' attacks. According to the report, arms decommissioning was to be considered in parallel with the negotiations, while the eventual surrender of weaponry was to be conducted under international supervision, with those involved being free from prosecution. The report was generally supported by all sides.

In February 1996 the IRA abruptly terminated its cease-fire by exploding a large bomb in London. The organization blamed the British Government for the resumption of hostilities, citing its inflexible response to the Mitchell report. Bruton and Major declared that they would suspend all ministerial dialogue with Sinn Féin, but would intensify efforts to achieve a peaceful settlement. At the end of the month the leaders announced an initiative to pursue the peace process, involving the election of a forum for intersectoral dialogue that would subsequently engage in comprehensive political negotiations, to be based on the 1995 Framework Document. The election to the 110-member Northern Ireland Forum, under an electoral system intended to ensure a wide representation of the region's political groupings, was held in May; the UUP secured the largest number of seats, followed by the DUP, the SDLP and Sinn Féin. The Alliance Party and five smaller parties also won representation. The multi-party discussions, which commenced in June, were undermined by Sinn Féin's exclusion, in the absence of a new IRA cease-fire declaration, and by unionist opposition to the appointment of Mitchell as Chairman. Further political uncertainty followed an IRA bomb attack in Manchester in June. Moreover, sectarian disputes regarding the organization of traditional Protestant marches in July prompted the SDLP to withdraw from the Forum.

The election of the Labour Government in May 1997 generated renewed optimism that a peace settlement could be achieved. The new Prime Minister, Tony Blair, proposed a timetable for the talks, and stated that he envisaged their conclusion by no later than May 1998, when the results would be put to a popular referendum. In June 1997 the British and Irish governments announced a fresh initiative to accelerate the peace process, whereby the decommissioning of paramilitary weapons, together with other confidence-building measures, would be undertaken concurrently with political negotiations, in an attempt to facilitate Sinn Féin's participation in the process, and clarified that Sinn Féin would be eligible to join substantive negotiations six weeks after a new IRA cease-fire announcement.

In July 1997 the IRA announced the restoration of its cease-fire. A few days later the Irish and British governments jointly declared that the all-party negotiations would commence in September, with the participation of Sinn Féin. Accordingly, in September Sinn Féin endorsed the so-called 'Mitchell principles', which committed participants to accepting the outcome of the peace process and renouncing violence as a means of punishment or resolving problems. The UUP, together with the DUP and the United Kingdom Unionist Party (UKUP), which had already declared their boycott of any discussions with Sinn Féin, and other loyalist representatives, failed to attend the opening session of the talks when they resumed in September, owing partly to a statement by the IRA that undermined Sinn Féin's endorsement of the Mitchell principles. Nevertheless, the UUP rejoined the peace negotiations a few days later, and in late September all eight parties to the talks signed a procedural agreement to pursue substantive negotiations. At the same time the Independent International Commission on Decommissioning (IICD) was inaugurated, under the chairmanship of the former head of the Canadian armed forces, Gen. John de Chastelain.

The Good Friday Agreement

In January 1998 Blair and the Irish Prime Minister, Bertie Ahern, published a document outlining a framework for negotiations: this envisaged 'balanced constitutional change' by both governments and proposed a devolved form of government within Northern Ireland. After intensive negotiations, on 10 April a settlement was announced. The Good Friday Agreement (or Belfast Agreement) envisaged radical reform of the political structures of Northern Ireland, its relations with Ireland, and its constitutional standing within the United Kingdom. The main provisions of the Agreement were as follows: the establishment of a 108-member elected Northern Ireland Assembly, with authority to legislate on all domestic matters currently administered by the Northern Ireland Office; an Executive Committee, to be elected by the Assembly and headed by a First Minister and Deputy First Minister; an obligation that the Assembly establish, within one year, a North/South Ministerial Council at which representatives of the Irish Government and the executive authority in Northern Ireland might consider issues of cross-border concern; regular meetings of representatives of the Irish Government with members of the British Parliament, the Northern Ireland Assembly and other regional assemblies of the United Kingdom, under a new British-Irish Council, with the objective of promoting co-operation, information exchange and agreement on issues of mutual interest; amendment of Articles 2 and 3 of the Irish Constitution; replacement of the 1985 Anglo-Irish Agreement with a new bilateral accord, incorporating a British-Irish Intergovernmental Council to oversee the Assembly and North/South Council; and a commitment by all parties to achieve the decommissioning of paramilitary weapons within two years. The UUP, the SDLP, Sinn Féin and most of the smaller parties approved the settlement, although several dissident UUP politicians later joined the DUP and UKUP in their campaign to prevent an endorsement of the accord, and the Protestant Orange Order (a fraternal organization, based in Northern Ireland, which is strongly linked to unionism) urged its members to oppose the Agreement. Some 71.1% of voters in Northern Ireland approved the proposed peace settlement in a referendum conducted on 22 May 1998, while in a concurrent referendum in Ireland 94.4% of voters approved the proposed amendments to the Constitution.

The first election to the Northern Ireland Assembly was conducted on 25 June 1998, with the UUP and the SDLP emerging as the largest parties. At the inaugural meeting of the Assembly in July, David Trimble was elected as First Minister of the executive body, while Seamus Mallon of the SDLP was elected as Deputy First Minister. Sectarian violence soon threatened to disrupt the peace process following confrontations between the security forces and members of the Orange Order who, in defiance of the newly established Parades Commission, sought to march its traditional route along the predominantly Roman Catholic-inhabited Garvaghy Road in Portadown to the church at nearby Drumcree. (The Parades Commission—a quasi-judicial non-departmental public body—had been established earlier in the year, charged with placing restrictions on or banning outright any parade in Northern Ireland that it deemed contentious or offensive.) In August the peace process again came under threat when 29 people in Omagh, Co Tyrone, were killed by an explosive device planted by a dissident republican group, the Real IRA, representing the single largest toll of deaths in any incident since the onset of sectarian unrest in the 1960s.

The peace process continued to be obstructed throughout late 1998 by a dispute between unionists and Sinn Féin concerning the decommissioning of paramilitary weapons, with Trimble insisting that the admittance of Sinn Féin representatives to the Executive Committee be conditional on progress in the demilitarization of the IRA. For its part, Sinn Féin insisted that the Good Friday Agreement did not specify when decommissioning should begin, only that it should be completed by May 2000. As a result of the dispute the deadline of 21 October 1998 for the formation of the Executive Committee and the North/South bodies was not met. In December agreement was finally reached on the responsibilities of the 10 government departments of the Executive Committee and of six North/South 'implementation' bodies. This was endorsed by the Northern Ireland Assembly in February 1999.

During 1999 the date for the devolution of powers to the new Northern Ireland institutions, envisaged as 10 March in the Good Friday Agreement, was postponed several times, and negotiations were halted in July when Trimble announced that the UUP would not participate in a devolved administration with Sinn Féin until some decommissioning had taken place. A review of the peace process, headed by George Mitchell, began in September. In that month the former Chairman of the Conservative Party, Chris Patten, who had been appointed in April 1998 to head an independent commission charged with conducting a review of policing in Northern Ireland, published his report. Recommended changes to the Royal Ulster Constabulary (RUC) included the establishment of an elected body of representatives, drawn from all sections of the community, to which the new force would be accountable, the active recruitment of Roman Catholic officers in order that the force should achieve a balanced representation, and a reduction in the number of serving officers from 13,500 to 7,500, subject to the successful conclusion of the peace process. The report provoked anger from unionists, who particularly objected to plans to change the force's name, oath and symbols. Sinn Féin, meanwhile, renewed its demand that the force be disbanded.

In November 1999 Mitchell concluded the review of the peace process, producing an agreement providing for the devolution of powers to the Executive Committee. The agreement followed a statement by the IRA that it would appoint a representative to enter discussions with the IICD. Trimble persuaded his party to approve the agreement. On 29 November the Northern Ireland Assembly convened to appoint the 10-member Executive Committee. On 2 December power was officially transferred from London to the new Northern Ireland executive and, in accordance with the Good Friday Agreement, the Irish Government removed from the Irish Constitution its territorial claim over Northern Ireland. The North/South Ministerial Council and the British-Irish Council both held their inaugural meetings in that month. In late December the British Government announced a review of security procedures in Northern Ireland and the withdrawal of some 2,000 troops from Northern Ireland, and in January 2000 it adopted the majority of the recommendations contained in the Patten report, provoking an angry response from unionists. In that month the Sinn Féin President, Gerry Adams, dismissed the possibility of immediate IRA decommissioning, and a report by the IICD confirmed that there had been no disarmament. With the prospect of the collapse of the peace process, the British and Irish governments engaged in intensive negotiations. On 1 February the IRA released a statement giving assurances that its cease-fire would not be broken and expressing support for the peace process. However, it failed to comply with an 11 February deadline to begin decommissioning, and legislation came into effect on that day suspending the new executive, legislative and co-operative institutions and returning Northern Ireland to direct rule. The IRA subsequently announced its withdrawal from discussions with the IICD. Adams refused to participate in any further review of the peace process until the suspended institutions had been restored.

Continuing impasse over decommissioning

Direct talks between the British and Irish governments and the principal parties resumed in early May 2000, with the British Government promising to restore the Northern Ireland institutions on 22 May and postpone the deadline for decommissioning until June 2001, subject to a commitment by the IRA on the arms issue. On 6 May 2000 the IRA responded by offering to 'initiate a process that will completely and verifiably put arms beyond use'. Under the offer a number of IRA arms depositories were to be regularly inspected by two independent international figures, Martti Ahtisaari, the former President of Finland, and Cyril

Ramaphosa, a principal figure in the South African peace process. Trimble narrowly succeeded in securing the approval of the UUP of a return to power sharing, and on 30 May power was once again transferred from London to the new Northern Ireland institutions. In accordance with their continued policy of attempting to impede the functioning of the Assembly, DUP ministers agreed to retake their places in the Assembly but announced their intention periodically to resign their posts in order to disrupt parliamentary business. In June the IRA allowed three arms depositories to be inspected by Ramaphosa and Ahtisaari and announced that it had also resumed contact with the IICD.

In July 2000 the decision again to prohibit the Orange Order from marching along the Garvaghy Road in Portadown provoked renewed sectarian violence and numerous attacks on the security forces. Later in that month, under the terms of the Good Friday Agreement, the final group of 86 convicted terrorists was freed from prison in Northern Ireland. Their release was widely criticized as it had been conditionally linked to the commencement of IRA arms decommissioning, which had yet to begin. Feuding between loyalist paramilitary groups led to violent unrest in the second half of 2000, and in August troops were once again deployed on the streets of Belfast. In an attempt further to disrupt the peace process, the dissident Real IRA exploded two bombs outside the BBC's Television Centre building in London in March and April 2001.

On 1 July 2001 Trimble resigned as First Minister, fulfilling a pledge to step down if the IRA had not commenced a process of decommissioning by that date. (Mallon's position of Deputy First Minister also became vacant, although he continued to exercise the functions of his office.) Trimble's resignation triggered a six-week period at the end of which, barring the resolution of the impasse between the parties and the election of a First Minister and Deputy First Minister, new elections to the Assembly would have to be held. Later in July the IICD stated that the IRA had yet to decommission a single weapon, and had failed to outline how it intended to put its arms beyond use.

In August 2001 the British and Irish governments published their joint 'Proposals for the Implementation of the Good Friday Agreement'. The proposals stipulated that while decommissioning was not a precondition of the Agreement, it remained indispensable to a political resolution and must be resolved in a manner 'acceptable to and verified by the IICD'. However, Trimble remained adamant that in the continued absence of IRA decommissioning of weapons there would be no progress. A few days later both the IICD and the IRA confirmed that they had agreed upon a confidential decommissioning scheme, and de Chastelain announced that he was satisfied that the IRA had begun a process that would put arms 'completely and verifiably' beyond use. Trimble described the announcement as a 'step forward', but insisted that it was not sufficient for him to retract his resignation and demanded evidence of the destruction of weapons. Faced with the impending collapse of the Northern Ireland institutions, on 10 August the British Government suspended the institutions for a 24-hour period. Under a legal loophole contained within the Good Friday Agreement, this decision allowed for a six-week extension to the previously imposed deadline for the election of a First Minister and Deputy. In response to the suspension, the IRA withdrew the offer to commence the process of decommissioning. A further 24-hour suspension was effected on 22 September, thus granting the parties a further six weeks in which to attempt to resolve the continuing impasse.

Also in August 2001 the British Government announced revised policing proposals, which envisaged the equal division of recruitment to the police force between Protestants and Roman Catholics and allowed for the possibility of former paramilitary prisoners sitting on the 29 District Police Partnership Boards, providing that they relinquished their support for terrorist organizations. Sinn Féin had rejected the proposals before their publication and insisted that they would refuse to nominate members to the new 19-member Northern Ireland Policing Board (NIPB), which would be responsible for overseeing the police. In November the RUC was officially renamed the Police Service of Northern Ireland (PSNI) and the NIPB held its inaugural meeting. The two vacant Sinn Féin seats on the board were allocated to the DUP and the UUP.

In September 2001 Trimble announced that the UUP would introduce a motion in the Assembly to exclude the two Sinn Féin ministers from the Executive, and that if, as was almost certain, the motion was defeated and there was still no progress on the

decommissioning issue by the IRA, UUP ministers would begin to withdraw from the Executive, thus precipitating its collapse. The UUP exclusion motion was duly defeated in October and the three UUP ministers and the two DUP ministers resigned. Later that month the IRA and the IICD issued separate statements, which affirmed that the IRA had taken the unprecedented step of putting a significant quantity of arms, ammunition and explosives beyond use. The announcement prevented the imminent collapse of the Northern Ireland institutions and was widely welcomed by all pro-Agreement parties. Trimble immediately announced that he would seek re-election to the post of First Minister, and the UUP and DUP ministers subsequently resumed their posts. On 2 November, however, Trimble failed in his attempt to be re-elected as First Minister. Although he secured a majority of the total votes cast (including all 38 nationalist votes), two anti-Agreement members of the UUP voted against Trimble, thus preventing him from obtaining the constitutionally required majority of unionists in favour of his re-election. Following intensive negotiations, four members of non-aligned parties agreed to redesignate themselves temporarily as unionists, and on 6 November Trimble finally regained the post of First Minister. The new SDLP leader, Mark Durkan, was elected Deputy First Minister.

In mid-2002, despite the announcement in April that the IRA had put a further quantity of arms, ammunition and explosives beyond use, the fragility of the peace process was underscored by unprecedented levels of street violence in Belfast, for which the UUP maintained that the IRA was primarily responsible. Adams' refusal to testify before a US investigation into alleged IRA links with left-wing rebels in Colombia, allied with allegations of IRA involvement in the theft of documents from PSNI Special Branch offices in Belfast in March 2002 and the discovery, in June, of an IRA intelligence database listing details of more than 200 judges, politicians and members of the security forces, provoked unionist demands that Sinn Féin ministers be removed from the power-sharing Executive and further 'crisis' meetings between the British and Irish governments. In August the Real IRA was suspected to have been responsible for a bomb attack in which a Protestant man was killed—the first fatality caused by the organization since the Omagh bombing in August 1998—and a Roman Catholic was murdered in an apparent revenge act for the earlier wounding of a young Protestant. The situation was exacerbated by the escalation of a feud between rival loyalist paramilitary groups, which resulted in a number of shootings.

In October 2002 Sinn Féin's offices at the Northern Ireland Assembly were raided by police, who, as part of a major investigation into intelligence-gathering by republicans, suspected that the IRA had infiltrated the Northern Ireland Office and gained access to large numbers of confidential documents. Trimble accused Sinn Féin of a 'massive political conspiracy' and threatened to withdraw from the Executive unless the British Government proposed the expulsion of Sinn Féin from the Assembly. Emergency talks between the British and Irish governments and the Northern Ireland political leaders followed; however, Blair's demands for IRA concessions on the arms issue were not met. The two DUP ministers resigned from the Executive, and on 14 October the Assembly was suspended and direct rule imposed. In a joint statement, Blair and Ahern announced that the devolved institutions would be restored only if Sinn Féin severed its links with paramilitary organizations. Later that month the IRA announced the suspension of all contact with the IICD.

In May 2003 the British and Irish governments published a Joint Declaration, which included plans to reduce the security forces in Northern Ireland from 14,500 to 5,000 by April 2005, to repeal anti-terrorist legislation specific to Northern Ireland, to establish an independent monitoring body to assess any breaches of the Good Friday Agreement, and to transfer policing and judicial powers to a devolved government. The Declaration also urged a full and permanent cessation of all paramilitary activity. Talks between the British and Irish governments and the major Northern Ireland political parties continued during late 2003, and in September the four members of the Independent Monitoring Commission (IMC) were appointed. In an attempt to restart the process of devolution, Trimble and Adams met with Ahern and Blair in London in October, and it was revealed that elections to the Northern Ireland Assembly would take place in November. However, later on the same day Trimble declared that the acts of decommissioning of IRA weapons, witnessed by de Chastelain earlier that day, were not sufficiently transparent, and that the UUP was to withdraw from the peace process. The British Government later acknowledged that the devolved institutions would not be restored following the elections, and that a review of the Good Friday Agreement would take place in early 2004.

At the elections to the Northern Ireland Assembly in November 2003 the DUP, which remained opposed to the Good Friday Agreement, secured 30 of the 108 seats, thus becoming the largest party in the Assembly. The UUP won 27 seats, while Sinn Féin increased its parliamentary representation to 24 seats. The SDLP suffered a significant loss of support, winning just 18 seats. The election results increased the pressure on Trimble from anti-Agreement factions of the UUP, which called for his resignation. Furthermore, the DUP demanded a full renegotiation of the Good Friday Agreement. However, both Ahern and Blair reiterated that the 'principles and values' of the Agreement would not be changed.

The review of the Good Friday Agreement commenced in February 2004 with Paisley setting out his party's own proposals for power sharing. While acknowledging that the proposals signalled progress on the part of the DUP, they were generally negatively received by Sinn Féin, which feared that they would lead to a return to unionist majority rule. In March Trimble withdrew his party from the talks in protest against the alleged IRA involvement in the recent kidnapping of a dissident republican in Belfast. Further negotiations at Leeds Castle in England in September ended with no agreement. In November the Ulster Defence Association (UDA) indicated its intention to end violence and demilitarize following an announcement by the British Government that it would officially recognize the loyalist paramilitary group's February cease-fire. Later in November Paisley stated that the disarming of the IRA would be an acceptable starting point for the power-sharing agreement only if it was verified by photographic evidence. Paisley later issued an ultimatum to the IRA to the effect that if the peace accord were not restored in the current situation it would become an almost impossible task in the future, and demanded that the IRA repent of its past actions. Adams declared Paisley's comments to be offensive and stated that Sinn Féin would go no further in negotiations. In December, despite being resigned to the collapse of the peace process, Blair and Ahern met in Belfast to reveal their final proposals to restore devolution. On the following day the IRA declared that photographic proof of decommissioning had never been an option and that although the IRA was committed to the peace process, it would not be subjected to a perceived process of humiliation.

In December 2004 an estimated £26.5m. was stolen from the Belfast headquarters of Northern Bank. The PSNI immediately set up an investigation into the incident and later stated that the IRA had been responsible for the robbery. In a report published in February 2005 the IMC implicated not only the IRA but also Sinn Féin leaders (these accusations were vehemently denied by Adams). In early February Ahern and Blair warned the IRA that its failure to demilitarize was the only obstacle to an agreement on power sharing; on the following day the IRA withdrew its commitment to decommissioning. In April, in an initiative that aimed to break the deadlock over the restoration of devolution, Adams urged the IRA to embrace the political alternative to armed struggle that now existed.

At the general election to the British Parliament in May 2005 the UUP recorded its worst electoral performance since the formation of Northern Ireland's first government in 1921, retaining only one of the five seats it had previously held. Following the election, in which he had himself lost his seat, Trimble resigned as leader of the UUP; in June the party elected Sir Reg Empey as its new leader.

The IRA renounces violence

In July 2005 the IRA issued a communiqué in which it formally renounced its armed struggle and committed itself to the pursuit of its objectives, including the goal of a united Ireland, through peaceful means only. At the same time the IRA undertook to conclude the process of comprehensive, verifiable weapons decommissioning. The communiqué was cautiously welcomed by Blair and Ahern, as well as by leading unionists, including Paisley and Empey; however, the DUP condemned the Government's decision to begin removing security facilities in South Armagh on the day after it had been issued. In September the IRA formally declared that it had completed the process of weapons decommissioning. De Chastelain, who, together with two clergymen, one Roman Catholic and one Protestant, had witnessed the decommissioning, announced at the same time

that he was satisfied that the arms decommissioned represented the totality of the IRA's arsenal. In the following month the proscribed Loyalist Volunteer Force (LVF) responded to weapons decommissioning by the IRA by disbanding all of its paramilitary units. In December, in a further response to the IRA's abandonment of its armed struggle, the Government announced that British military strength in Northern Ireland would be reduced to below 9,000 in the following month.

The Northern Ireland Assembly was recalled on 15 May 2006. The Assembly's primary responsibility was to elect a First Minister and a Deputy First Minister as soon as possible, to allocate ministerial portfolios, and to make other preparations for government. Once the Assembly had elected a First Minister and a Deputy First Minister on a cross-community basis and formed an Executive, power would automatically be devolved to the Assembly and at that point the British Government's power to suspend the Assembly would lapse definitively. In the event of the Assembly's being unable to elect First and Deputy First Ministers within the normal six-week period, Blair and Ahern stated that they would be prepared to allow a further period of 12 weeks after the summer recess (i.e. up to 24 November) for the formation of an Executive.

In October 2006 discussions took place at St Andrews, in Scotland, between Blair, Ahern and the leaders of the principal Northern Ireland parties. The ensuing St Andrews Agreement declared the parties' commitment to stable power-sharing government, the rule of law (including support for the PSNI), and human rights and equality issues, and established a schedule for the restoration of devolved government by March 2007 and the devolution of criminal justice and policing by 2008. It also provided for changes to the functioning of the Northern Ireland Assembly and Executive, including the introduction of a statutory ministerial code and amendments to the procedure for the election of the First Minister and Deputy First Minister. Following qualified approval of the St Andrews Agreement by Sinn Féin and the DUP, legislation giving effect to the accord was adopted by Parliament in November 2006. The new law provided for the Northern Ireland Assembly to be redesignated as a transitional assembly and to be dissolved in January 2007, pending elections in March, after which parties would nominate assembly members to positions in a devolved executive, to take office on 26 March. In January Sinn Féin held a special party conference, at which delegates voted to support the PSNI and to take up the party's allocated places on the NIPB, thereby reversing the party's long-standing policy and removing the last obstacle to the process of devolution. In February the UDA announced that it would accept the participation of Sinn Féin in a future government, while in May the loyalist Ulster Volunteer Force (UVF) announced that it had renounced paramilitary activity.

At the elections to the Assembly, held on 7 March 2007, the DUP won 36 of the 108 seats, Sinn Féin 28, the UUP 18, the SDLP 16 and the Alliance Party seven. On 26 March Paisley and Adams committed themselves to forming a new power-sharing executive by 8 May, on which date Paisley was duly sworn in as First Minister and Sinn Féin's Martin McGuinness as Deputy First Minister. The remaining 10 ministries were allocated using the so-called D'Hondt method, in proportion to the number of seats obtained by each party in the Assembly.

During 2007 relations between the two main parties within the Executive were cordial. However, by 2008 the issue of the devolution of powers over the justice system and policing to the Executive had led to renewed disagreements between the DUP and Sinn Féin. Paisley insisted that the IRA disband its army council, that arson attacks on Orange Order buildings cease and that financing measures be agreed by the Executive and the British Government before powers could be transferred. Adams, however, welcomed the British Government's proposals to transfer powers by the end of the year and accused the DUP of reneging on its commitment to the St Andrews Agreement. In March a cross-party Assembly committee failed to reach an agreement over the devolution of powers.

In March 2008 Paisley announced his intention to resign as leader of the DUP and, thus, as First Minister at the end of May. At a meeting of the party's executive committee the following month, the Minister of Finance and Personnel, Peter Robinson, was nominated to succeed Paisley as party leader. Paisley duly resigned from both posts and in June Robinson, having assumed the party leadership, was elected as First Minister by the Assembly. (McGuinness was concurrently re-elected as Deputy First Minister.) However, continued disagreements between the

DUP and Sinn Féin, most notably regarding devolution, precipitated the latter's refusal to attend meetings of the Executive from June. In November, following the conclusion of protracted discussions between the two main parties, Robinson and McGuinness announced the details of an initial agreement outlining the process by which the transfer of powers over justice and policing to the Northern Ireland institutions could take place. Under the terms of the agreement, a temporary arrangement for the devolution of powers would be invoked, allowing the Assembly to elect by cross-community vote a single minister responsible for justice until May 2012, upon which date a permanent settlement would be enacted. The agreement also provided for the appointment of an independent Attorney-General for Northern Ireland (a role currently held by the Attorney-General for England and Wales). None the less, the parties failed to agree a timetable for the process of devolution.

In early 2009 a series of attacks against police officers and military personnel prompted concerns over the increased security threat from armed dissident republican groups. In March two British soldiers were shot dead at a barracks in Co Antrim, while two days later a Roman Catholic police officer was killed in Co Armagh; representatives of all the parties engaged in the democratic process condemned the killings, responsibility for which was claimed by two dissident republican groups, the Real IRA and the Continuity IRA. In May the IMC published a report in which it stated that the threat from dissident republican paramilitaries remained 'serious'. Incidents of violence and attempted bomb attacks attributed to such groups occurred throughout the remainder of 2009. Meanwhile, the IICD confirmed in June that the UVF and a related loyalist paramilitary organization, the Red Hand Commando, had completed the decommissioning of their weapons; the other main loyalist armed group, the UDA, completed its decommissioning process in January 2010. In October 2009 the republican INLA, which had declared a cease-fire in 1998, announced that its armed struggle was over; in February 2010 it announced that it had disposed of its arsenal, just one day before the mandate of the IICD was due to expire (and, with it, the immunity from prosecution for possession of weapons afforded to armed groups). The Official IRA (which had maintained a cease-fire since 1972) and a dissident faction of the UDA also completed their decommissioning on the same day.

Disagreements between the DUP and Sinn Féin over a timetable for the devolution of policing and justice powers continued to hinder the functioning of the Executive during 2009. Legislation providing for the appointment of a Minister of Justice within the Executive was approved by the Assembly in December; however, the DUP insisted on the establishment of measures to improve unionist 'community confidence', including the abolition of the Parades Commission, before it would agree to an immediate transfer of powers. After talks between the DUP and Sinn Féin over the transfer of policing and justice powers collapsed in January 2010, the British Prime Minister, Gordon Brown, and the Irish Prime Minister, Brian Cowen, held discussions in Belfast with all the Northern Irish parties, stressing the need for prompt and substantial progress in the devolution process. The DUP and Sinn Féin finally reached an agreement on 4 February, which, subject to approval by the Assembly, would lead to the transfer of powers and the appointment of a Minister of Justice (who would not be nominated by either party) on 12 April. As well as detailing the relationship between the Minister of Justice and the rest of the Executive, the agreement also provided for the establishment of a new mechanism to resolve disputes over marches by Protestant orders, which would replace the Parades Commission. The proposed timetable for devolution was approved by the Assembly in March. On 12 April David Ford, the leader of the Alliance Party, was elected Minister of Justice in a cross-community vote in the Assembly—despite the opposition of the UUP, which remained opposed to the immediate transfer of powers, and of the SDLP, which maintained that it was entitled to the ministerial post under the D'Hondt method.

At the general election to the House of Commons on 6 May 2010 Robinson unexpectedly lost his seat to the Alliance Party, which gained representation in the Commons for the first time. The DUP retained its remaining eight seats, while Sinn Féin and the SDLP also emerged with their representation unchanged, at five and three seats, respectively. The UUP, which contested the election in a controversial alliance with the Conservative Party as Ulster Conservatives and Unionists—New Force, failed to win any seats. Despite Robinson's personal defeat in the election, on

10 May he was endorsed as leader of the DUP and First Minister by the party's Assembly members. Following the UUP's poor electoral performance, Empey announced that he would resign as leader of the party later that year; in September Tom Elliott was elected as his successor.

The proposals of a working group established by the DUP and Sinn Féin to draft a new framework for resolving disputes over marches by Protestant orders were published in April 2010. Under the plan, the Parades Commission would be replaced by two new bodies: one to consider applications for permission to hold a parade or protest, and a second to adjudicate in the event of a dispute. A proposed code of conduct would enshrine the right to live in freedom from sectarian harassment, but would also make it an offence to prevent or disrupt a lawful public assembly or parade. However, at a meeting in early July, the Grand Orange Lodge of Ireland (a corporate body representing the whole structure of the Orange Order) voted in favour of rejecting the draft legislation. Later that month sectarian violence surrounding the Orange Order parades was described as the worst for a number of years, with the most serious rioting occurring in the Ardoyne district of north Belfast. In September Robinson announced that the bill on the marches had been put on hold, in view of the opposition of the Orange Order, and in December new members were appointed to the Parades Commission (with which the Order refused to engage).

Meanwhile, in June 2010 the report was finally published of an inquiry established in 1998 into the fatal shooting of 14 republican demonstrators by the security forces in Londonderry (Derry) on 30 January 1972 ('Bloody Sunday'). Conducted by Lord Saville of Newdigate, the inquiry, which had begun hearing evidence in March 2000 and concluded in November 2004, was the longest running and most expensive, at a cost of some £195m., in British history. The Saville report exonerated the civilians who were killed or wounded, noting that none of those shot was armed with a firearm or posed a threat of causing death or serious injury, and that some had been attempting to flee or aid others when shot. Contrary to the findings of a previous inquiry carried out by Lord Widgery of South Molton in 1972, the Saville report concluded that the deaths of the demonstrators resulted from a 'serious and widespread loss of discipline among the soldiers', who gave no warning before firing unjustifiably, and that some soldiers had knowingly given false evidence to seek to justify their actions. As regards allegations surrounding the IRA's involvement in events, the inquiry found that although there had been some shooting by republican paramilitaries, the soldiers had fired first, and that McGuinness, who had admitted being the IRA's adjutant (effectively second-in-command) in Londonderry in January 1972, had not 'engaged in any activity that provided any of the soldiers with any justification for opening fire', despite the unconfirmed possibility that he might have fired a weapon on the day. In a statement to the House of Commons on the day of the publication of the report, the Prime Minister, David Cameron, apologized, on behalf of the Government, for the conduct of the armed forces on 'Bloody Sunday'. In September 2011 the Government announced that relatives of those killed or wounded by the British forces in the course of 'Bloody Sunday' would receive financial compensation. In February 2013 the Government offered each of the affected families compensation of about £50,000, a sum that was dismissed by some as derisory.

Attacks by dissident republican paramilitaries in Northern Ireland increased in 2010, amid indications of greater co-operation between the various groups and their development of enhanced technical capabilities (notably improvised explosive devices), leading the British authorities to raise the official threat level to Great Britain from Northern Irish-related terrorism from moderate to substantial in September. However, in a report presented in November the IMC recorded a substantial increase during that year in the number of dissidents arrested and charged with terrorist offences and declines in the number of casualties from shootings and assaults. The IMC completed its mission in March 2011. In the following month the killing of a Roman Catholic police officer in a car bombing in Omagh was attributed to dissident republicans (who were increasingly targeting Catholic members of the PSNI in an attempt to deter others from enlisting in the traditionally Protestant-dominated force, around one-third of which now comprised Catholics); the murder provoked widespread cross-community condemnation. Despite concerns over security raised by the attack, the historic visit of Queen Elizabeth II to the Republic of Ireland in May proceeded as planned and was widely held to have been a notable diplomatic and political success. The state visit, which was the first to have been undertaken by a British monarch since the Irish Republic gained its independence in 1921, was strongly condemned by dissident republican groups, who claimed that the Queen was guilty of 'war crimes'.

In November 2010 Adams announced his resignation as a member of the Assembly in order to contest the forthcoming general election in the Republic of Ireland; he also relinquished his seat in the House of Commons in January 2011 and was duly elected to the Irish legislature in February. At the elections to the Northern Ireland Assembly on 5 May, the DUP and Sinn Féin retained their positions as the two principal parties in the legislature, winning 38 and 29 seats, respectively. Turn-out was low, at 55.6% of the electorate, compared with 62.9% in 2007. Following the elections, Robinson and Trimble retained their positions as First Minister and Deputy Prime Minister, while David Ford remained in the post of Minister of Justice.

There was an escalation in sectarian violence in June 2011 when Protestant youths attacked a Catholic enclave in east Belfast. The ensuing fighting lasted for two days and, although there were no serious injuries, shots were fired by both sides. The PSNI asserted that dissident members of the UVF had been responsible for orchestrating the disturbances. There were serious outbreaks of localized violence during the traditional Protestant marching season in the following month. In October the Real IRA claimed responsibility for detonating a bomb outside the UK City of Culture 2013 office in Londonderry and the fatal shooting of a prison officer near Portadown, in County Armagh, in November 2012 was believed to have been perpetrated by dissident republican paramilitaries.

A controversial decision taken by Belfast City Council in early December 2012 to restrict the flying of the Union Flag at Belfast City Hall provoked a series of demonstrations by loyalists and unionists who viewed the decision as an attack on their 'cultural identity'. Within days, the situation had deteriorated as sectarian violence and rioting erupted on the streets of the city. The unrest, some of which was allegedly orchestrated by dissident members of the UVF and the UDA, spread to other towns in January 2013, but had generally abated by the end of the month. A foiled mortar attack on a police station in Londonderry in early March prompted concerns that dissident republican groups were broadening their campaign of violence.

Foreign Affairs

Regional relations

The United Kingdom became a full member of the EC in January 1973. A referendum in 1975 endorsed British membership by a large majority. During the 1980s the Thatcher Government demanded controls on spending by the EC, and particularly reform of the Common Agricultural Policy (CAP), and expressed scepticism regarding proposals for greater European economic unity, on the grounds that this was likely to entail a loss of national sovereignty. Following Major's assumption of the British premiership, relations with individual members of the EC (particularly Germany) improved, and the Government adopted a more pragmatic approach towards European developments. Nevertheless, the British Government agreed to the terms of the Maastricht Treaty in 1992 only after substantial concessions had been granted for the United Kingdom. In particular, the United Kingdom's participation in the final stage of European Economic and Monetary Union (EMU), including the adoption of a single EC currency by 2000, was made optional.

On its election in May 1997, the Blair administration announced its intention to withdraw the country's option not to participate in the 'social chapter' of the Maastricht Treaty, and to promote completion of the internal economic market and enlargement of the EU. However, the new Government remained opposed to greater EU authority over national borders and immigration controls, and its demanded reform of the CAP. In June 1997 EU heads of state and of government signed the Treaty of Amsterdam, amending the Maastricht Treaty. The new agreement incorporated the social chapter, given the Labour Government's willingness to subscribe to the protocol. The United Kingdom, together with Ireland, secured an exemption from obligations with regard to immigration, asylum and visa policies; however, Blair negotiated an option to participate in certain co-operative aspects of the border arrangements.

In October 1997 the Chancellor of the Exchequer, Gordon Brown, attempted to clarify the Government's stance on the European single currency. He identified five key principles for participation in EMU, relating to its impact on the British economy and employment, and insisted that membership would have to be preceded by a sustained period of economic stability. In May 1999 Blair expressed his intention to end what he termed the United Kingdom's 'ambivalence' towards the EU and to make the country a 'leading partner' in the bloc. In June 2003 Brown announced that four of the five key principles for deciding British participation in EMU had not yet been fulfilled. Nevertheless, he stated that the Government remained in favour of joining the single currency once the conditions were in place.

A bill was published in January 2005 to allow for a referendum on a draft EU constitutional treaty, which had been approved by the leaders of the 25 member states of the EU in June 2004. In June 2005, however, following the failure of the French and Dutch electorates to endorse the treaty in referendums, the Government announced that it would not proceed with a second reading of the bill in the House of Commons. In December 2007 the Reform Treaty (later known as the Treaty of Lisbon), which replaced the defunct constitutional treaty, was signed in Lisbon, Portugal. A motion by the Conservative Party to ratify the treaty by national referendum was rejected by the House of Commons in March 2008. (Prior to the 2005 general election, all three main political parties had promised to ratify the constitutional treaty by means of a referendum.) The treaty was ratified by parliamentary vote in June 2008. By November 2009 the treaty had been ratified by all 27 EU member states and entered into force in December.

The coalition Government that took office under David Cameron in May 2010 pledged that, during the current parliamentary term, no further powers would be transferred to the EU and that the United Kingdom would not adopt or prepare to adopt the European single currency. In November 2010 the Government introduced a bill—subsequently entitled the European Act 2011—to Parliament that would notably incorporate a sovereignty clause into the European Communities Act of 1972 affirming that ultimate legal authority remained with the British Parliament rather than with the EU and would provide for a national referendum on any proposed new EU treaty or amendment to an existing EU treaty that would transfer powers from the United Kingdom to the EU. The bill was approved by the House of Commons in March 2011 and received royal assent in July. Meanwhile, in late 2010 Cameron failed to secure sufficient support from other member states for his demand that there should be no expansion in the EU budget for 2011, but succeeded in limiting the increase in expenditure. The Prime Minister also persuaded his French and German counterparts to join him in declaring their opposition to any rise in the EU budget in real terms during 2014–20 compared with expenditure in 2013. The British Government came into conflict with the European Court of Human Rights (ECHR) in early 2011 over its reluctance to comply with a 2005 ruling by the Court that the United Kingdom was in breach of the European Convention on Human Rights by disenfranchising all prisoners. In February 2011 the House of Commons overwhelmingly voted in favour of a non-binding motion to retain the current ban preventing convicted prisoners from voting, but in April the ECHR rejected an attempt by the Government to overturn the 2005 ruling, insisting that the United Kingdom draft proposals to grant prisoners the right to vote within six months; this demand was not heeded by the British authorities and the impasse on disenfranchisement continued. In October 2011 a parliamentary motion requesting the holding of a referendum on whether the United Kingdom should withdraw from the EU, retain the status quo or renegotiate the terms of its membership was rejected by 483 votes to 111. Although the motion was comfortably defeated, the number of those who had voted in favour of it (the majority of whom were Conservative MPs) revealed the strength of the Eurosceptic faction within parliament. In early December at an EU summit in Brussels, Belgium, Prime Minister Cameron vetoed a Franco-German proposal to draw up a new EU treaty to establish a closer fiscal union between the members of the eurozone. This action, which was taken following the rejection of Cameron's demands for the imposition of safeguards for British financial institutions, was widely condemned by other members of the EU (notably France) but was welcomed by the Eurosceptics in the Conservative Party. In April 2012 Secretary of State for Justice and Lord Chancellor Kenneth Clarke presided over a ministerial conference of the Council of Europe which had been convened in Brighton, England, to discuss proposals put forward by the Conservative Party to reform the operations of the ECHR (partly with a view to clearing the massive backlog of cases and to facilitating the extradition of alleged terrorists). Conservative plans to introduce a UK Bill of Rights collapsed at the end of the year in the face of opposition from the Liberal Democrats to the repeal of the Human Rights Act or to withdrawal from the ECHR. Also in December, Cameron pledged not to block the introduction of a treaty effecting closer economic and monetary union among the members of the eurozone, provided that the United Kingdom was permitted to renegotiate its EU membership terms. In January 2013 the British Prime Minister announced that a referendum on the United Kingdom's continuing membership of the EU would be held by the end of 2017 (if the Conservatives won the 2015 general election). Cameron himself favoured the United Kingdom remaining within the Union, on the condition that a new settlement on the terms of its membership was reached prior to the referendum.

The long-standing dispute with Spain over the sovereignty of Gibraltar has frequently strained relations between the two countries. In November 2001 the British Government announced that it would be willing to consider joint sovereignty of the territory with Spain. Despite widespread public opposition in Gibraltar, in March 2002 both the Spanish and British governments reiterated their determination to proceed with plans for a joint sovereignty agreement. However, in April the Spanish Prime Minister stated that Spain would never cede its claim to total sovereignty over the territory. In response to the joint sovereignty proposals, the Gibraltarian authorities organized a referendum which explicitly asked if Gibraltarians approved of 'the principle that Britain and Spain should share sovereignty over Gibraltar'. The referendum, held on 7 November, resulted in an overwhelming rejection of the Spanish and British proposals. Although both Spain and the United Kingdom condemned the referendum and refused to recognize its validity, the British Government subsequently acknowledged that any arrangements for joint sovereignty were practically unenforceable due to the strength of public opposition in Gibraltar. In June 2003 the Government announced that talks with Spain regarding the possibility of sharing the sovereignty of Gibraltar had failed and suspended any further negotiations over the issue indefinitely. In December 2004 a tripartite meeting between the United Kingdom, Spain and Gibraltar was held in the United Kingdom, and it was subsequently announced that, henceforth, decisions on the territory's future must be agreed by all three parties (the so-called Forum of Dialogue). In March 2006 the British Government stressed that a proposed new constitution for the territory did not diminish British sovereignty over Gibraltar, despite the inclusion of references to the right to self-determination of Gibraltarians. The new Constitution, which gave Gibraltar much greater control over its internal affairs, was approved in a referendum in November and entered into force in January 2007. Meanwhile, in September 2006 agreements were signed by representatives of the three governments allowing easier border crossings in and out of Gibraltar, direct commercial flights to Gibraltar from Spain, and improved telecommunications links. In January 2012 the new conservative Spanish Government stated that it was prepared to hold discussions with Gibraltar and the United Kingdom specifically on issues of co-operation, but it ruled out the future convention of the tripartite Forum of Dialogue to discuss the future status of Gibraltar. Henceforth, despite the British Government's firm support for continuing the trilateral forum, all talks concerning Gibraltar's sovereignty and jurisdiction would be conducted on a bilateral basis between Spain and the United Kingdom.

Other external relations

Following Iraq's forcible annexation of Kuwait in August 1990, the British Government promptly supported the efforts of the USA in defending Saudi Arabia from potential Iraqi aggression and deployed some 42,000 personnel in the subsequent engagement in hostilities against Iraq, under the auspices of the UN. British troops also participated in humanitarian efforts to protect the Kurdish population within Iraq from persecution by the Iraqi armed forces. In January 1993 British fighter aircraft took part in US-led attacks on military targets in Iraq, launched in response to renewed Iraqi incursions into Kuwait and obstruction of a UN investigation into a suspected Iraqi nuclear weapons programme. In September 1996 the British Government gave political and logistical support to a series of air-strikes by the USA against targets in Iraq. In December 1998, following Iraq's refusal to co-operate with weapons inspections by the UN Special Commission (UNSCOM), the USA and the United Kingdom conducted a further series of air-strikes in an effort to 'degrade' Iraq's military capabilities. More airborne attacks were carried out in early 1999 and mid-2000 in response to alleged violations

by Iraq of the UN air exclusion zone. In February 2001 the United Kingdom and the USA were again involved in the bombardment of a number of targets in Iraq, in response to a reportedly increased threat to aircraft from those countries in the preceding weeks. The action was, however, condemned by several Western and Arab countries.

In July 2002, as speculation mounted about the possibility of further military action against Iraq, Prime Minister Blair indicated that he had concerns about any potential military strikes and subsequently announced his support for the UN Security Council's proposal that UN weapons inspectors be readmitted to Iraq. He did, however, stress in August that the British Government was determined to deal with the threat posed by Iraq's alleged possession of weapons of mass destruction. In September, following a meeting with the US President, George W. Bush, Blair announced that the United Kingdom and the USA would attempt to secure a new UN Security Council resolution that would approve military action in Iraq, should the latter fail to comply with UN weapons inspectors. In the same month the British Government published a dossier outlining its case against the Iraqi regime and the perceived threat posed by that country's 'illicit weapons programmes' to the security of both the West and the Middle East. However, it appeared that the United Kingdom and the USA were becoming increasingly isolated in their attempts to secure approval for the use of military force against Iraq. In November, after a compromise had been reached between the five permanent members, the UN Security Council unanimously adopted Resolution 1441, which demanded, *inter alia*, that Iraq permit weapons inspectors from UNSCOM's replacement, the UN Monitoring, Verification and Inspection Commission (UNMOVIC), and the International Atomic Energy Agency (IAEA, see p. 122) unrestricted access to sites suspected of holding illegal weapons, and required the Iraqi leadership to make a full declaration of its chemical, biological, nuclear and ballistic weapons, as well as related materials used in civilian industries, within 30 days.

During January 2003 Blair, while asserting that conflict was not inevitable if Iraq complied with the UN's disarmament terms and insisting that UNMOVIC and the IAEA be granted sufficient time in order to complete their inspections, ordered large numbers of troops to the Persian (Arabian) Gulf region to join the increasing number of US forces already in position there. As the likelihood of a US-led military response to the crisis grew, the United Kingdom was one of eight European countries to sign a joint statement expressing support for the USA's stance on Iraq. Despite signs of progress being reported by UNMOVIC, on 24 February the United Kingdom, the USA and Spain presented a draft resolution to the Security Council effectively authorizing a US-led military campaign against Saddam Hussain's regime, in response to what the USA claimed was overwhelming evidence of Iraq's possession of weapons of mass destruction, its attempts to conceal such weapons from the UN inspectorate and its links with international terrorism, including the al-Qa'ida network. Officials from France, Russia and Germany presented an alternative proposal involving an extended timetable of weapons inspections in order to avert a war. On 7 March the United Kingdom submitted an amended draft resolution to the Security Council, which demanded that Iraq demonstrate 'full, unconditional, immediate and active co-operation with its disarmament obligations under resolution 1441' by 17 March.

On 16 March 2003 Blair attended a summit meeting in the Azores, Portugal, along with President Bush and the Spanish Prime Minister, José María Aznar. The following day the United Kingdom, the USA and Spain withdrew their resolution from the UN, stating that they reserved the right to take their own action to ensure Iraqi disarmament. Later that day Bush issued an ultimatum giving Saddam Hussain and his two sons 48 hours to leave Baghdad or face military action. Shortly after the expiry of Bush's 48-hour deadline, on 19 March US and British armed forces launched a campaign (code-named Operation Iraqi Freedom) to oust the regime of Saddam Hussain. British troops were principally engaged in securing towns in southern Iraq, including Iraq's second largest city, Basra, after the US-led coalition had seized control of the key southern port of Umm Qasr and the Al-Faw Peninsula. Baghdad was captured by US forces on 9 April and, following the collapse of the Iraqi regime, on 1 May President Bush officially declared an end to 'major combat operations' in Iraq.

On 22 May 2003 the UN Security Council approved Resolution 1483, which recognized the US- and British-led Coalition Provisional Authority (CPA) as the legal occupying power in Iraq, and mandated the CPA to establish a temporary Iraqi governing authority. UN sanctions imposed on Iraq in 1990 were also lifted. However, armed resistance to coalition forces continued unabated. In July 2003 the British Government formally assumed command of the multinational task force for south-eastern Iraq, with its headquarters in Basra, comprising some 16,000 troops, of whom 11,000 were British. In September the British Government agreed to dispatch a further 1,200 troops to Iraq while placing another 1,800 soldiers on stand-by. Meanwhile, there appeared to be little sign of the chemical, biological and nuclear weapons that had been the *raison d'être* of the US-led campaign. In September Blair apologized for the intelligence claim that Iraq possessed weapons of mass destruction; however, he refused to apologize for sending British troops to Iraq, stating that the removal of Saddam Hussein was sufficient justification.

In June 2004 the USA formally transferred sovereignty to the new Iraqi authorities. By the end of 2008 responsibility for the four provinces supervised by British forces had been handed over to the Iraqi security forces. The complete withdrawal of British troops commenced in March 2009, when responsibility for operations in the south of the country was transferred to US forces, and the British mission in Iraq formally ended on 30 April.

In early 1999 the United Kingdom was one of the principal participants in a NATO air offensive against the Federal Republic of Yugoslavia (now Serbia). The campaign, which began in March, was intended to end the atrocities committed by Serb forces against ethnic Albanians in the Serbian province of Kosovo. In June the Yugoslav President, Slobodan Milošević, accepted the NATO alliance's terms for a cessation of hostilities, and by the end of that month Serb forces had withdrawn from Kosovo. British troops formed part of the force that entered the province to instigate the peace process. In November diplomatic relations with Yugoslavia were restored. The United Kingdom was one of the first countries to afford diplomatic recognition to Kosovo following its declaration of independence from Serbia in February 2008.

The terrorist attacks on New York and Washington, DC, on 11 September 2001, for which the USA held the al-Qa'ida organization of Osama bin Laden responsible and in which 78 British citizens were killed, were denounced as an attack on the democratic world by Blair, who offered to provide military and diplomatic assistance to the US Administration in its quest to bring the perpetrators of the attacks to justice. The British Prime Minister, who by late October had held talks with more than 50 foreign heads of government, played a significant role in strengthening the international coalition against terrorism and obtaining support for military action against the Islamist Taliban regime in Afghanistan, which was suspected of harbouring senior al-Qa'ida figures, including bin Laden.

In October 2001 US and British armed forces commenced the aerial bombardment of suspected al-Qa'ida camps and strategic Taliban positions in Afghanistan, and in the following month British troops began ground operations in the country. In December it was announced that the United Kingdom had agreed to lead the International Security Assistance Force (ISAF), which was granted a six-month mandate by the UN to provide security in Kabul and its environs. The first British peace-keeping troops arrived in Afghanistan later in December. In March 2002 a separate force of 1,700 British combat troops was deployed in Afghanistan to assist US special forces with their pursuit of the remaining Taliban and al-Qa'ida fighters. By the end of 2006 around 5,300 British troops were stationed in Afghanistan, either participating in ISAF or assisting US special forces. British deployment was augmented in stages over the following few years; by December 2009 a total of 9,500 British troops were stationed in Afghanistan. At a NATO summit meeting in November 2010, at which a framework for transferring full military control of Afghanistan's national security to Afghan forces by the end of 2014 was endorsed, the British Prime Minister, David Cameron, stated that all British combat troops would be withdrawn from the country by 2015. The transition process commenced in July 2011. At April 2013 some 9,000 British troops remained stationed in Afghanistan, but this figure was scheduled to decrease to 5,200 by the end of the year.

In November 1991 the United Kingdom and the USA demanded that Libya extradite for trial, either in the United Kingdom or the USA, two suspected intelligence agents who were alleged to be responsible for an explosion that destroyed a US passenger aircraft over Lockerbie, Scotland, in 1988. The United Kingdom subsequently supported the imposition, by the UN, of economic and political sanctions against Libya. In view of

Libya's continued refusal to allow the suspects to be tried in Scotland, in August 1998 the United Kingdom and the USA conceded to a Libyan proposal, subsequently endorsed by the UN Security Council, that they be tried on neutral territory in the Netherlands. In March 1999 Libya finally agreed to the extradition of the suspects. The UN sanctions against Libya were subsequently suspended. The trial of Abd al-Baset Ali Muhammad al-Megrahi and Al-Amin Khalifa Fhimah, which was heard in the Netherlands under Scottish law by a panel of Scottish judges in the presence of international observers, commenced in May 2000. At the end of January 2001 the judges unanimously found al-Megrahi guilty of the murder of 270 people and sentenced him to life imprisonment. Fhimah was, however, acquitted, owing to lack of evidence, and was freed to return to Libya. Despite mounting pressure from Arab states, the United Kingdom maintained that sanctions against Libya would not be permanently revoked until Libya accepted responsibility for the bombing and paid 'substantial' compensation. In March 2002, following the unanimous rejection of an appeal, al-Megrahi was transferred to a prison in Scotland to begin his sentence; it was ruled in November 2003 that he would serve 27 years in prison before becoming eligible for parole. Also in March 2002 Libya appointed an ambassador to the United Kingdom for the first time in 17 years.

In March 2003 it was reported that, following negotiations in London, Libya had agreed to accept civil responsibility for the actions of its officials in the Lockerbie case and would pay compensation to the families of the victims, in stages, conditional upon the removal of UN and US sanctions. Following the transfer of US \$2,700m. in compensation to the International Bank of Settlements, the Security Council approved the formal lifting of UN sanctions against Libya in September.

In December 2003 Blair announced that Libya had agreed to disclose and dismantle its programme to develop weapons of mass destruction and long-range ballistic missiles. The statement was the culmination of nine months of clandestine negotiations between Libyan, British and US diplomats, during which the Libyan authorities had reportedly shown evidence of a 'well advanced' nuclear weapons programme, as well as the existence of large quantities of chemical weapons and bombs designed to carry poisonous gas. In March 2004 Blair visited Tripoli and held talks with Libyan leader Col Muammar al-Qaddafi, after which the British Prime Minister stated that there was genuine hope for a 'new relationship', while Qaddafi insisted that he was willing to join the international 'war against terror'. In September Qaddafi announced that Libya had dismantled its weapons of mass destruction programme and in December, with the unilateral sanctions imposed upon Libya by the USA having consequently been lifted, Libya paid the second instalment of its compensation to the families of those killed in the Lockerbie bombing. In May 2006 Libya was removed from the US list of states deemed to support international terrorism, the condition for the payment of the final instalment of compensation. In October 2005 a memorandum of understanding signed by Libya and the United Kingdom guaranteed that Libya would not subject to torture or execute any person who was repatriated to it from the United Kingdom. A further memorandum of understanding was signed by Qaddafi and Blair in May 2007, which provided for negotiations on the transfer of prisoners, extradition and mutual assistance in criminal law. A final agreement was signed in November 2008 and ratified by the British Government in April 2009.

A second appeal against al-Megrahi's conviction opened at the High Court in Edinburgh in April 2009. In May the Scottish Government rejected a request from the Libyan authorities to transfer al-Megrahi to Libya under the terms of the recently ratified prisoner transfer agreement, on the grounds that such a transfer could not take place while an appeal was in progress. However, in July al-Megrahi, who was suffering from a terminal illness, asked the Scottish Cabinet Secretary for Justice, Kenny MacAskill, to release him from gaol on compassionate grounds. Al-Megrahi's request was duly granted in August and he returned to Libya. His return caused considerable controversy in the United Kingdom and strained relations with the USA, especially after allegations emerged that the British Government had exerted pressure on the Scottish authorities to release al-Megrahi as part of a secret agreement with Libya. In September Brown insisted that no such assurances had been made to Libya and maintained that the decision to release al-Megrahi had been taken entirely by the Scottish Government. None the less, it was reported that the Secretary of State for Justice, Jack

Straw, had informed MacAskill in December 2007 that it would be contrary to British interests to seek to exclude al-Megrahi from the terms of the pending prisoner transfer agreement. Confidential US diplomatic cables published in December 2010 by WikiLeaks, an organization disseminating leaked private and classified content, claimed that Qaddafi had threatened a range of repercussions against the United Kingdom, including an immediate cessation of all British commercial activity in Libya, if al-Megrahi were not released. However, in February 2011 a report on al-Megrahi's release prepared by the Cabinet Secretary, Sir Gus O'Donnell, concluded that although the British Government had done 'all it could' to facilitate a Libyan appeal for al-Megrahi's transfer or release, there was no evidence that it had exerted pressure on the Scottish authorities to respond favourably to such an appeal.

The British Government arranged the voluntary evacuation of its nationals from Libya in February 2011, amid a series of violent clashes in that country between anti-Government protesters and armed forces loyal to Qaddafi. Following the adoption in late February of a resolution by the UN Security Council that demanded an end to the violence and the use of force against civilians in Libya, and imposed an embargo on the supply of arms to Libya, together with other sanctions against Qaddafi, his family and associates, the British Prime Minister, David Cameron, confirmed that assets held in the United Kingdom by the Libyan leader and his family had been frozen and their diplomatic immunity had been revoked. Cameron also strongly supported the imposition of a no-fly zone over Libya by the UN Security Council on 17 March in a resolution that also authorized member states to take 'all necessary measures' to enforce the ban on flights and to protect civilians under threat of attack, but excluded 'a foreign occupation force of any form on any part of Libyan territory'. Two days later, as part of a multinational coalition under US command, British, French and US forces commenced missile strikes against Libyan air defence systems. The House of Commons voted overwhelmingly in support of military action in Libya on 21 March, and on 27 March NATO member states agreed to assume full command of UN-authorized military operations in Libya from the USA. NATO-led operations to enforce the no-fly zone and to protect Libyan civilians continued during April and May. In late July the British Government gave official recognition to the Libyan rebels' interim governing body and in mid-September Prime Minister Cameron and President Nicolas Sarkozy of France visited the newly liberated Libyan capital, Tripoli, to hold talks with the country's new leaders. During another visit to Libya by the British Prime Minister, in February 2013, he pledged further aid to support greater improvements to the country's security situation, including specialized military training.

Diplomatic relations with Argentina, which had been severed in 1982 following the invasion of the Falkland Islands, were restored in 1990. While both countries continued to indicate that their respective claims to sovereignty over the Falkland Islands were not negotiable, political dialogue was able to proceed under a mutual arrangement to circumvent the issue of sovereignty. In September 1995 the two sides concluded an accord to allow exploration for offshore petroleum and gas deposits in the disputed waters around the Islands. A joint commission was to be established to supervise licensing and revenue sharing. (The first licences were awarded in October 1996.) In October 1995 Prime Minister Major met with the Argentine President, Carlos Menem, at the UN headquarters in New York, USA (the first such high-level meeting since the 1982 war). In October 1998 Menem made an official visit to the United Kingdom, the first by an Argentine President in almost 40 years, and in July 2001 Blair became the first serving British Prime Minister to visit Argentina. However, tensions between the two countries increased in the late 2000s; in March 2007 Argentina withdrew from the 1995 agreement on petroleum exploration, arguing that the United Kingdom had used it to justify its sovereignty claim. In February 2010 the commencement of prospecting operations in Falklands waters by a British oil company provoked strong protests from the Argentine Government, which asked the UN to initiate negotiations between the two countries on the sovereignty issue. The British Government defended the Islands' right to develop its petroleum industry and declared that the United Kingdom would take all necessary measures to defend the Islands. In October the Argentine Government formally protested to the British Government and to the UN, after the United Kingdom announced that it was to conduct military exercises, including the firing of missiles, off the coast of the Falklands; the British

Government insisted that the manoeuvres were 'routine'. Relations between the two countries deteriorated considerably in February 2012 when the Argentine Government lodged a formal complaint with the UN regarding the alleged militarization of the Falklands by the United Kingdom. The British Government countered this accusation by stating that the dispatch of a naval warship to the islands in March was part of routine operations. In March 2013 a referendum held in the Falklands that produced an overwhelming vote in favour of retaining the Islands' status as an overseas territory of the United Kingdom was dismissed as a 'parody' by Argentine President Cristina de Kirchner, who continued to demand that the United Kingdom surrender the Islands.

Relations with Iran were strained from 1989 as a result of the *fatwa* (edict) issued by the Iranian spiritual leader, Ayatollah Ruhollah Khomeini, demanding the execution of the British author Salman Rushdie for his novel *The Satanic Verses*, which contained material deemed to be blasphemous against Islam. Although tensions eased in the late 1990s following the establishment of a more moderate government in Iran, relations came under further strain in the mid-2000s. In May 2004 demonstrators in the Iranian capital, Tehran, demanded the closure of the British embassy in the city and the removal of the ambassador, in protest against British policy in Iraq, and threw petrol bombs at the building. Diplomatic relations deteriorated further in June when three British patrol crafts and eight Royal Navy personnel were captured on the Shatt al-Arab waterway by Iranian authorities who claimed the servicemen had entered Iranian territorial waters. After intense negotiations between British and Iranian diplomats, the men were released four days later and claimed that they had been forcibly escorted into Iranian waters. In October 2005 Blair warned Iran against supporting rebel factions in Iraq. The Iranian Government denied that it was doing so, and accused British forces stationed in Iraq of assisting Arab separatists responsible for recent bomb explosions in the Iranian city of Ahvaz. The United Kingdom, together with the USA and other Western governments, expressed suspicion during the early 2000s that Iran's programme of uranium enrichment was not, as Iran claimed, purely for peaceful purposes. In November 2004, after discussions with representatives of France, Germany and the United Kingdom, acting on behalf of the EU, Iran agreed to suspend its uranium enrichment programme, but in January 2006 it announced that it was resuming nuclear research and development. Between late 2006 and mid-2010 the UN Security Council imposed a number of sanctions on Iran for persistently refusing to comply with requests to desist from uranium enrichment. Meanwhile, in March 2007 the Iranian navy arrested 15 British naval personnel whom it accused of intruding into Iranian territorial waters; they were released after almost two weeks in captivity. Relations between Iran and the United Kingdom deteriorated further in mid-June 2009, when the Iranian authorities alleged British involvement in fomenting the civil unrest that followed a disputed presidential election held in Iran that month. Two British diplomats were expelled from Iran on the grounds that they had engaged in activities 'inconsistent with their diplomatic status', and the British Government responded with the expulsion of two Iranian diplomats. In late June nine Iranian employees of the United Kingdom's embassy in Tehran were arrested for their alleged role in the post-election disturbances. Although the majority were released without charge in July, Hossein Rassam, a senior political analyst, was convicted of espionage in October and sentenced to four years' imprisonment. An appeals court overturned the espionage conviction in October 2010, however, reducing Rassam's sentence to a one-year suspended prison term for the dissemination of propaganda against the authorities. Talks on Iran's nuclear programme involving the participation of the United Kingdom, the four other permanent members of the UN Security Council and Germany (the so-called P5+1 talks), as well as Iran, were conducted during 2011–12 and into the first half of 2013, but proved relatively fruitless. Meanwhile, relations between the United Kingdom and Iran came under increasing strain in late November 2011, when, in response to the imposition of new British sanctions against Iran in protest against the worsening human rights situation in that country, the British embassy compound in Tehran was attacked by Iranian demonstrators. A few days later the embassy was closed down and the British Government ordered the closure of the Iranian embassy in London.

In early 2011 the United Kingdom joined many other countries in condemning the ruthless military response of the Syrian armed forces to a popular uprising demanding the resignation of the Syrian President, Lt-Gen. Bashar al-Assad. As the confrontation descended into bloody civil war the United Kingdom was one of a number of countries to advocate the complete lifting of the EU's arms embargo on Syria in order to facilitate the provision of weaponry and equipment to the rebel forces.

CONSTITUTION AND GOVERNMENT

The United Kingdom is a constitutional monarchy. However, it has no written Constitution; its constitutional principles are determined by an accumulation of statutes, common law, convention and precedent. Among the most important statutes in the evolution of the British Constitution may be cited: Magna Carta of 1215, which began the process by which the law acquired a status of its own, independent of the Crown; the Bill of Rights of 1689, which established the rights of the people and Parliament in relation to the Crown; the Reform Act of 1832, the first in a series of Acts widening the electoral franchise, culminating in the Representation of the People Act of 1928, which granted universal suffrage; and the Parliament Act of 1911, which established the supremacy in Parliament of the elected House of Commons.

The sovereign is the head of state and the monarchy is hereditary. Parliament consists of the House of Commons and the House of Lords. The 650 members of the Commons are elected for a maximum of five years by direct suffrage by all citizens of 18 years and over, using single-member constituencies. The House of Lords is composed of hereditary Peers of the Realm and Life Peers created by the sovereign for outstanding public service. (Legislation providing for the abolition of all but 92 hereditary peers and the establishment of an interim second chamber pending a definitive reform of the House of Lords took effect in 1999.) Legislation may be initiated in either House but it usually originates in the Commons. Each bill has three readings in the Commons and it is then passed to the Lords, who may return it to the Commons with amendments or suggestions. The Lords may delay, but cannot prevent, any bill from becoming law once it has been passed by the Commons. Executive power is held by the Cabinet, headed by the Prime Minister. The Cabinet is responsible to the House of Commons.

The 108-member Northern Ireland Assembly was established in 1998, as part of the multi-party agreement on the future governance of Northern Ireland. An Executive Committee, headed by a First Minister, was constituted from among the legislative members. Responsibility for all matters formerly implemented by the Northern Ireland Office was transferred to the devolved authority under new parliamentary legislation implemented in December 1999. The 1998 Agreement also provided for the establishment of a North/South Ministerial Council, to facilitate co-operation between the Irish Government and representatives of the Northern Ireland Executive on specific cross-border and all-island concerns, and of a British-Irish Council, comprising representatives of British and Irish Governments, members of the devolved authorities in Northern Ireland, Scotland and Wales, and representatives of the Isle of Man and the Channel Islands. The new Northern Ireland institutions were suspended during 2000 and again from 2002 until 2007, when devolved government was restored. Full devolution under the terms of the agreement was completed in April 2010 with the transfer of powers over policing and justice.

In 1999 devolved legislative authorities were established in Scotland and Wales. In Scotland a new elected Parliament, based in Edinburgh, was established with powers to legislate on all domestic matters (including education, health, local government and law and order) and with a mandate to vary taxes set by the Government of the United Kingdom by 3%. The Scottish Parliament has 129 members, elected every four years by a combined system of direct voting and a form of proportional representation, whereby additional members are elected at large from a party list. In November 2010 a bill providing for the transfer of additional, mainly fiscal, powers to the Scottish Parliament was introduced in the House of Commons; the Scotland Act 2012 received royal assent in May 2012. The National Assembly for Wales, located in Cardiff, undertook responsibility for issues covered by the Welsh Office of the Government of the United Kingdom. The 60-member National Assembly is elected under the same system as in Scotland. In November 2009, in a report submitted to the Welsh First Minister, a 16-member All Wales Convention, appointed in mid-2008, concluded that the devolution of full legislative powers over domestic matters to the National Assembly for Wales would be desirable. In a referendum held in Wales on 3 March 2011, 63.5% of those participating (35.3% of the electorate) voted in favour of the Assembly being granted direct law-making powers in the currently devolved areas. Later that month the Welsh First Minister signed a commencement order giving the Assembly direct law-making powers, following its approval by the Assembly's members.

REGIONAL AND INTERNATIONAL CO-OPERATION

The United Kingdom is a member of the European Union (EU, see p. 281), but declined to participate in economic and monetary union, which introduced the single currency, or the Schengen Agreement on open borders. It is a member of the Council of Europe (see p. 260) and the Organization for Security and Co-operation in Europe (OSCE, see p. 397).

The United Kingdom joined the UN on its foundation in 1945, and is a permanent member of the UN Security Council. As a contracting party to the General Agreement on Tariffs and Trade, it joined the World Trade Organization (WTO, see p. 444) on its establishment in 1995. It was a founder member of the North Atlantic Treaty Organization (NATO, see p. 380). The Commonwealth (see p. 244), which developed as an association of the United Kingdom and its former dependencies, has its Secretariat in London. The United Kingdom also participates in the Organisation for Economic Co-operation and Development (OECD, see p. 388), the Group of Eight major industrialized nations (G8, see p. 475) and the Group of 20 major industrialized and systemically important emerging market nations (G20, see p. 466).

ECONOMIC AFFAIRS

In 2011, according to estimates by the World Bank, the United Kingdom's gross national income (GNI), measured at average 2009–11 prices, was US $2,366,544m., equivalent to $37,780 per head (or $35,940 per head on an international purchasing-power parity basis). During 2002–11, it was estimated, the population increased at an average annual rate of 0.6%, while gross domestic product (GDP) per head increased, in real terms, by an average of 0.7% per year over the same period. According to the World Bank, overall GDP increased, in real terms, at an average annual rate of 1.3% in 2002–11. Real GDP increased by 0.7% in 2011.

Agriculture (including hunting, forestry and fishing) contributed 0.6% of GDP in 2010, and accounted for 1.3% of work-force jobs in 2011. The principal crops include wheat, sugar beet, potatoes and barley. Livestock-rearing (particularly poultry and cattle) and animal products are important, as is fishing. The GDP of the agricultural sector decreased, in real terms, by an average of 0.7% per year during 2002–11; it declined by 2.0% in 2011.

Industry (including mining, manufacturing, construction and power) contributed 22.4% of GDP in 2010, and accounted for 15.7% of work-force jobs in 2011. Industrial GDP increased, in real terms, at an average annual rate of 1.3% during 2002–11; it grew by 3.4% in 2011.

Mining (including petroleum and gas extraction) contributed 2.7% of GDP in 2010, and accounted for 0.2% of work-force jobs in 2011. Natural gas, sand and gravel, limestone, crude petroleum, igneous rock and coal are the principal minerals produced. The GDP of the mining sector (together with utilities) increased, in real terms, at an average annual rate of 6.1% during 2002–11; the GDP of extractive and utilities industries increased by 6.2% in 2011.

Manufacturing provided 10.6% of GDP in 2010, and accounted for 8.0% of work-force jobs in 2011. The principal branches of manufacturing include transport equipment, food products, machinery, chemical products, and metals and metal products. In real terms, the GDP of the manufacturing sector decreased at an average annual rate of 0.3% during 2002–11; manufacturing GDP increased by 2.1% in 2011.

Construction provided 6.4% of GDP in 2011, and accounted for 6.5% of work-force jobs in 2011. In real terms, the GDP of the construction sector increased at an average annual rate of 0.4% during 2002–11; construction GDP increased by 8.3% in 2010 and by 3.1% in 2011.

Energy is derived principally from natural gas, petroleum and, to a lesser degree in recent years, coal. Of the United Kingdom's total consumption of energy in 2011, 47.8% was derived from petroleum, 29.3% from natural gas, 18.6% from electricity (including nuclear and hydroelectric power), 1.7% from renewable and waste sources (including geothermal and solar heat), and 1.1% from coal. At April 2013 there were 16 nuclear power reactors (at nine nuclear power plants) operating in the United

Kingdom; all of the plants were scheduled to be shut down by 2035 owing to their age. Energy companies were encouraged by the Government to build new nuclear power plants, and eight potential sites were identified in 2011. Permission was granted in March 2013 for two new reactors to be constructed, at Hinkley Point in Somerset, England. In 2012 mineral fuels accounted for 16.1% of the value of total merchandise imports.

Services accounted for 76.9% of GDP in 2010, and accounted for 83.0% of work-force jobs in 2011. The United Kingdom is an important international centre for business and financial services. Financial intermediation and other business services (including renting and real estate) contributed 29.0% of GDP in 2010. Receipts from tourism totalled £17,998m. in 2011. Wholesale and retail trade (including the motor trade) and repairs (11.2% of GDP in 2010) and transport and communications (10.4% of GDP in 2010) are also major contributors to the economy. In real terms, the GDP of the services sector increased at an average annual rate of 2.2% during 2002–11; the sector's GDP grew by 1.2% in 2011.

In 2012 the United Kingdom recorded a visible trade deficit of £106,343m. and there was a deficit of £57,679m. on the current account of the balance of payments. In 2012 the principal source of imports (12.9%) was Germany, while the principal market for exports was the USA (13.7%). Other major trading partners include the People's Republic of China, France, the Netherlands, Ireland, Norway and the USA. The principal imports in 2012 were machinery and transport equipment (including road vehicles), mineral fuels (especially petroleum and petroleum products), miscellaneous manufactured articles (notably clothing and footwear), basic manufactures, chemicals and related products, and food and live animals. Machinery and transport equipment (especially mechanical machinery equipment) were the principal exports in that year, followed by chemicals and chemical products (notably medicinal products), petroleum and petroleum products, and miscellaneous manufactured articles.

There was a budgetary deficit of £95,100m. in the financial year ending 31 March 2012, equivalent to 6.0% of GDP for the same period. Gross general government debt was £1,273,100m. (equivalent to 83.3% of GDP) at the end of the same financial year. The annual rate of inflation, according to the retail price index, averaged 3.3% in 2002–12; retail prices increased by 5.2% in 2011 and by 3.2% in 2012, while consumer prices (excluding owner-occupier housing costs and council tax) increased by 4.5% in 2011 and by 2.8% in 2012. The rate of unemployment averaged 7.8% in August–October 2012.

Following a period of recession in the early 1990s, the economy experienced a prolonged period of expansion, with sustained growth in GDP accompanied by declining unemployment and low rates of inflation. However, the world-wide economic crisis that began in 2007 had a severe effect on the British economy, which in 2008 entered its worst recession since the Second World War. The shortage of credit in the global financial system caused substantial losses in British financial institutions, and necessitated significant government intervention in the banking sector. As the availability of credit contracted, house prices and consumer spending declined and redundancies increased. In a bid to encourage spending and ease pressure on businesses, the Bank of England lowered its official interest rate from 5.0% in September 2008 to a historic low of 0.5% in March 2009. This emergency policy was augmented by 'quantitative easing', in which the Bank increased the money supply by some £200,000m. between March 2009 and January 2010 through the purchase of government and corporate bonds. Despite these measures, GDP contracted by 4.9% in 2009 and the budget deficit increased to 7.6% of GDP in 2009/10. The coalition Government that took office in May 2010 declared that it would implement a 'significantly accelerated' reduction of the deficit, to be achieved principally through lower spending. With the aim of balancing the budget by 2015/16, expenditure by government departments (other than health and overseas aid) was to be reduced by an average of 19% in real terms over four years, while tax-related measures included an increase in the rate of value-added tax from 17.5% to 20% from January 2011. The economy began to show signs of modest recovery. GDP grew by an estimated 1.3% in 2010, while the budget deficit declined to 6.7% of GDP in 2010/11 and further to 6.0% of GDP in 2011/12. In spite of further quantitative easing, the economy entered a 'double-dip' recession following two consecutive contractions in GDP, by 0.3% in the final quarter of 2011 and by 0.3% in the first quarter of 2012, largely owing to a notable decrease in manufacturing and construction output. The annual rate of real GDP growth moderated to 0.7% in 2011 and, despite the increase in economic activity arising from London's hosting of the 2012 Olympic Games, fell further to just 0.2% in 2012. The economy narrowly avoided a 'triple-dip' recession when GDP grew by 0.3% in the first quarter of 2013 following a contraction of 0.3% in the final quarter of 2012. In April 2013 the IMF forecast that overall GDP growth in that year would reach 0.7%. The Bank of England's official interest rate remained at 0.5% in April 2013 and was not expected to be raised until at least the end of 2015. The inflation rate (according to the consumer price index), which in September 2011 had matched its record high of 5.2% largely owing to an increase in energy prices, fell considerably in 2012. At February 2013, the rate, although still exceeding the target of 2%, stood at 2.8%. In December 2011 the unemployment rate rose to 8.4%, the highest level for 16 years; however, partly owing to substantial recruitment for the Olympic Games, unemployment declined to less than 8% in the latter half of 2012. In December 2012 the Government admitted that its aim of eliminating the structural budget deficit would not be achieved until 2017/18 (two years later than originally targeted). The rising gross general government debt (which increased from 76.7% of GDP at 31 March 2011 to 83.3% of GDP at 31 March 2012) was expected further to hinder economic recovery.

PUBLIC HOLIDAYS

2014: 1 January (New Year's Day), 2 January* (Scotland only), 17 March (St Patrick's Day, Northern Ireland only), 18 April (Good Friday), 21 April† (Easter Monday), 5 May* (May Bank Holiday), 26 May (Spring Bank Holiday), 12 July (Battle of the Boyne, Northern Ireland only), 4 August* (Summer Bank Holiday, Scotland only), 25 August† (Summer Bank Holiday), 25 December (Christmas Day), 26 December* (Boxing Day).

Additional public holidays may be established by local authorities in Scotland.

* Bank Holidays but not national holidays in Scotland.

† Excluding Scotland.

Statistical Survey

Source (unless otherwise stated): Office for National Statistics, 1 Drummond Gate, London, SW1V 2QQ; internet www.statistics.gov.uk.

Area and Population

AREA, POPULATION AND DENSITY

Land area (sq km)	242,495*
Population usually resident (census results)	
29 April 2001	58,789,194
27 March 2011	
Males	31,028,123
Females	32,154,040
Total	63,182,163
Density (per sq km) at 2011 census	260.6

* 93,628 sq miles.

POPULATION BY AGE AND SEX
('000, at 2011 census)

	Males	Females	Total
0–14	5,681.3	5,418.5	11,100.0
15–64	20,752.1	20,953.1	41,705.0
65 and over	4,594.7	5,782.6	10,377.0
Total	31,028.1	32,154.2	63,182.2

Note: Totals may not be equal to the sum of components, owing to rounding.

DISTRIBUTION OF POPULATION
('000 at 2011 census)

	Land area (sq km)	Population	Density (per sq km)
Great Britain	228,919	61,371.3	268.1
England	130,279	53,012.5	406.9
Wales	20,733	3,063.4	147.8
Scotland	77,907	5,295.4	68.0
Northern Ireland	13,576	1,810.9	133.4
Total	242,495	63,182.2	260.6

Note: Totals may not be equal to the sum of components, owing to rounding.

ADMINISTRATIVE AREAS
('000, population at 2011 census)

England			
Greater London . .	8,173.9	Redcar and Cleveland	135.2
Metropolitan		Rutland	37.4
Counties:			
		Shropshire[6] . . .	306.1
Greater Manchester .	2,682.5	Slough	140.2
Merseyside . .	1,381.2	South Gloucestershire	262.8
South Yorkshire . .	1,343.6	Southampton . .	236.9
Tyne and Wear . .	1,104.8	Southend-on-Sea . .	173.6
West Midlands . .	2,738.1	Stockton-on-Tees .	191.6
West Yorkshire . .	2,226.1	Stoke-on-Trent . .	249.0
Unitary Authorities:		Swindon	209.2
Bath and North East			
Somerset . . .	176.0	Telford and Wrekin .	166.6
Bedford[1]	157.5	Thurrock	157.7
Blackburn with			
Darwen . . .	147.5	Torbay	131.0
Blackpool . . .	142.1	Warrington . . .	202.2
Bournemouth . .	183.5	West Berkshire . .	153.8
		Windsor and	
Bracknell Forest . .	113.2	Maidenhead . .	144.6
Brighton and Hove .	273.4	Wiltshire[7]	471.0
Bristol	428.2	Wokingham . . .	154.4
Central Bedfordshire[1]	254.4	York	198.0
		Non-Metropolitan	
Cheshire East[2] . .	370.1	*Counties:*	
Cheshire West and			
Chester[2] . . .	329.6	Buckinghamshire . .	505.3
Cornwall[3]	532.3	Cambridgeshire . .	621.2
Darlington . . .	105.6	Cumbria	499.9
Derby	248.7	Derbyshire . . .	769.7
Durham[4]	513.2	Devon	746.4
East Riding of			
Yorkshire . . .	334.2	Dorset	412.9

Halton	125.8	East Sussex . . .	526.7
Hartlepool . . .	92.0	Essex	1,393.6
Herefordshire . .	183.5	Gloucestershire . .	597.0
Isle of Wight . .	138.3	Hampshire . . .	1,317.8
Isles of Scilly[3] . .	2.2	Hertfordshire . . .	1,116.0
Kingston upon Hull .	256.4	Kent	1,463.7
Leicester	329.9	Lancashire . . .	1,171.3
Luton	203.2	Leicestershire . .	650.5
Medway . . .	263.9	Lincolnshire . . .	713.7
Middlesbrough . .	138.4	Norfolk	857.9
Milton Keynes . .	248.8	North Yorkshire . .	598.4
North Lincolnshire .	167.4	Northamptonshire .	692.0
North Somerset . .	202.6	Nottinghamshire . .	785.8
North East			
Lincolnshire . .	159.6	Oxfordshire . . .	653.8
Northumberland[5] .	316.0	Somerset	530.0
Nottingham . . .	305.7	Staffordshire . . .	848.5
Peterborough . .	183.6	Suffolk	728.2
Plymouth . . .	256.4	Surrey	1,132.4
Poole	147.6	Warwickshire . .	543.8
Portsmouth . . .	205.1	West Sussex . . .	806.9
Reading	155.7	Worcestershire . .	566.2

[1] Formerly part of Non-Metropolitan County of Bedfordshire; became two new unitary authorities of Bedford and Central Bedfordshire on 1 April 2009.

[2] Formerly part of Non-Metropolitan County of Cheshire; became two new unitary authorities of Cheshire East and Cheshire West and Chester on 1 April 2009.

[3] Formerly part of Non-Metropolitan County of Cornwall/Isles of Scilly; became two new unitary authorities of Cornwall and Isles of Scilly on 1 April 2009.

[4] Formerly Non-Metropolitan County of Durham; became new unitary authority of Durham on 1 April 2009.

[5] Formerly Non-Metropolitan County of Northumberland; became new unitary authority of Northumberland on 1 April 2009.

[6] Formerly Non-Metropolitan County of Shropshire; became new unitary authority of Shropshire on 1 April 2009.

[7] Became new unitary authority of Wiltshire on 1 April 2009.

Wales		Isle of Anglesey . .	69.7
Unitary Authorities:		Merthyr Tydfil . .	58.8
Blaenau Gwent . .	69.8	Monmouthshire . .	91.3
Bridgend	139.2	Neath Port Talbot .	139.8
Caerphilly . . .	178.8	Newport	145.7
Cardiff	346.1	Pembrokeshire . .	122.4
Carmarthenshire . .	183.8	Powys	133.0
Ceredigion . . .	75.9	Rhondda, Cynon, Taff	234.4
Conwy	115.2	Swansea	239.0
Denbighshire . . .	93.7	Torfaen	91.1
Flintshire	152.5	Vale of Glamorgan .	126.3
Gwynedd	121.9	Wrexham	134.8

Scotland		Glasgow City . . .	593.2
Unitary Authorities:		Highland	232.1
Aberdeen City . .	222.8	Inverclyde . . .	81.5
Aberdeenshire . .	253.0	Midlothian . . .	83.2
Angus	116.0	Moray	93.3
Argyll and Bute . .	88.2	North Ayrshire . .	138.2
Clackmannanshire .	51.4	North Lanarkshire .	337.8
Comhairle nan Eilean			
Siar (Western Isles)	27.7	Orkney Islands . .	21.4
Dumfries and			
Galloway . . .	151.3	Perth and Kinross .	146.7
Dundee City . . .	147.3	Renfrewshire . . .	174.9
East Ayrshire . .	122.7	Scottish Borders . .	113.9
East Dunbartonshire .	105.0	Shetland Islands . .	23.2
East Lothian . . .	99.7	South Ayrshire . .	112.8
East Renfrewshire .	90.6	South Lanarkshire .	313.8
Edinburgh, City of .	476.6	Stirling	90.2
Falkirk	156.0	West Dunbartonshire .	90.7
Fife	365.2	West Lothian . . .	175.1

Northern Ireland

Unitary Authorities:

Antrim	53.4	Derry		107.9
Ards	78.1	Down		69.7
Armagh	59.3	Dungannon		57.9
Ballymena	64.0	Fermanagh		61.8
Ballymoney	31.2	Larne		32.2
Banbridge	48.3	Limavady		33.5
Belfast	281.0	Lisburn		120.2
Carrickfergus	39.1	Magherafelt		45.0
Castlereagh	67.2	Moyle		17.1
Coleraine	59.1	Newry and Mourne		99.5
Cookstown	37.0	Newtownabbey		85.1
Craigavon	93.0	North Down		78.9
		Omagh		51.4
		Strabane		39.8

PRINCIPAL LOCALITIES*

('000, population at 2011 census)

Greater London (capital)	8,173.9	Wigan		317.8
Birmingham	1,073.0	South Lanarkshire		313.8
Leeds	751.5	Dudley		312.9
Glasgow City	593.2	Sandwell		308.1
Sheffield	552.7	Nottingham		305.7
Bradford	522.5	Doncaster		302.4
Manchester	503.1	Stockport		283.3
Edinburgh	476.6	Belfast		281.0
Liverpool	466.4	Newcastle upon Tyne		280.2
Bristol	428.2	Bolton		276.8
Kirklees	422.5	Sunderland		275.5
Fife	365.2	Sefton		273.8
Cardiff	346.1	Brighton and Hove		273.4
North Lanarkshire	337.8	Walsall		269.3
East Riding of Yorkshire	334.2	Medway		263.9
Leicester	329.9	South Gloucestershire		262.8
Wakefield	325.8	Rotherham		257.3
Wirral	319.8	Plymouth		256.4
Coventry	318.6	Kingston upon Hull		256.3

* Local authority areas (excluding unitary authorities agglomerated in 2009) with populations greater than 250,000.

BIRTHS, MARRIAGES AND DEATHS*

	Registered live births		Registered marriages†		Registered deaths	
	Number	Rate (per 1,000)	Number	Rate (per 1,000)	Number	Rate (per 1,000)
2004	715,996	12.0	313,551	5.2	584,791	9.8
2005	722,549	12.0	286,826	4.8	582,964	9.7
2006	748,563	12.4	277,611	4.6	572,224	9.4
2007	772,245	12.7	273,920	4.5	574,685	9.4
2008	794,383	12.9	273,207	4.4	579,697	9.4
2009	790,204	12.8	267,898	4.4	559,617	9.1
2010	807,271	13.0	277,736‡	4.5.	561,666	9.0
2011	807,776	12.8	n.a.	n.a.	552,232	8.7

* In England and Wales, figures for births are tabulated by year of occurrence, while figures for Scotland and Northern Ireland are tabulated by year of registration. Births to non-resident mothers in Northern Ireland are excluded from the figures for the United Kingdom.

† Figures exclude civil partnerships (figures are rounded to nearest 10): 1,950 in 2005; 16,110 in 2006; 8,730 in 2007; 7,170 in 2008; 6,280 in 2009; 6,390 in 2010; 6,800 in 2011.

‡ Provisional figure.

Sources: Office for National Statistics; General Register Office for Scotland; Northern Ireland Statistics and Research Agency.

Life expectancy (years at birth): 80.4 (males 78.5; females 82.4) in 2010 (Source: World Bank, World Development Indicators database).

IMMIGRATION AND EMIGRATION*

Immigrants

('000)

Origin†	2009	2010	2011
EU‡	198	208	203
Commonwealth countries	204	219	204
Australia, New Zealand, Canada	45	50	43
Australia	29	30	26
South Africa	11	7	8
Other African Commonwealth	31	23	19
Bangladesh, India, Pakistan, Sri Lanka	101	121	122
Other	16	19	12
Other territories‡	164	163	159
USA	31	22	23
Middle East	26	24	26
Total	567	591	566

Emigrants

('000)

Destination†	2009	2010	2011
EU‡	144	136	124
Commonwealth countries	127	102	124
Australia, New Zealand, Canada	82	58	70
Australia	57	40	48
South Africa	6	7	3
Other African Commonwealth	8	8	7
Bangladesh, India, Pakistan, Sri Lanka	23	21	29
Other	8	8	13
Other territories‡	97	102	103
USA	27	25	24
Middle East	15	15	17
Total	368	339	351

* Figures were compiled in accordance with the Long-term International Migration (LTIM) methodology, which supplements International Passenger Survey (IPS) data (whereby small samples of detailed passenger numbers are extrapolated according to a weighting system) with data on migration between the UK and Northern Ireland supplied by the Northern Ireland Statistics and Research Agency (NISRA), and with Home Office data on asylum seekers and their dependents. In addition, two adjustments were estimated to account for 'visitor switchers' (who stay longer than their stated intention) and 'migrant switchers' (who stay for less time than intended).

† Figures refer to the country of immigrants' last permanent residence or emigrants' intended future residence.

‡ Figures for all years show the EU as it was constituted at 31 December of year shown, therefore figures for 'EU' and for 'Other territories' may not be comparable for all years.

WORK-FORCE JOBS BY INDUSTRY

('000, annual averages, seasonally adjusted)

	2009	2010	2011
Agriculture, hunting, forestry and fishing	390	437	421
Mining and quarrying	63	65	63
Manufacturing	2,609	2,551	2,524
Construction	2,176	2,038	2,048
Electricity, gas and water	283	305	326
Wholesale and retail trade; repair of motor vehicles and motorcycles	4,766	4,778	4,793
Hotels and restaurants	1,917	1,908	2,040
Transport, storage and communications	2,656	2,606	2,711
Real estate, renting and other business activities	5,105	5,169	5,377
Banking, finance, insurance, etc.	1,126	1,122	1,105
Public administration and defence; compulsory social security	1,783	1,722	1,615

—continued	2009	2010	2011
Education	2,763	2,758	2,698
Human health and social work	3,950	4,051	4,015
Other services	1,681	1,733	1,794
Total	31,269	31,242	31,528

Note: Since data correspond to jobs rather than employees, a single worker may be counted more than once; figures include armed forces personnel.

Economically active population (labour force survey, '000 persons aged 16 years and over, excl. armed forces, November–January 2013): Total employed 29,732; Unemployed 2,516; Total labour force 32,248 (males 17,353, females 14,895).

Health and Welfare

KEY INDICATORS

Total fertility rate (children per woman, 2010)	1.9
Under-5 mortality rate (per 1,000 live births, 2010)	5
HIV/AIDS (% of persons aged 15–49, 2009)	0.2
Physicians (per 1,000 head, 2010)	2.7
Hospital beds (per 1,000 head, 2009)	3.3
Health expenditure (2009): US $ per head (PPP)	3,438
Health expenditure (2009): % of GDP	9.8
Health expenditure (2009): public (% of total)	84.1
Total carbon dioxide emissions ('000 metric tons, 2008)	522,855.5
Carbon dioxide emissions per head (metric tons, 2008)	8.5
Human Development Index (2011): ranking	28
Human Development Index (2011): value	0.863

For sources and definitions, see explanatory note on p. vi.

Agriculture

PRINCIPAL CROPS
('000 metric tons)

	2009	2010	2011
Wheat	14,076	14,878	15,257
Barley	6,668	5,252	5,494
Oats	744	685	613
Rye	36	38	37
Triticale (wheat-rye hybrid)	65	70	60
Potatoes	6,396	6,056	6,115
Sugar beet	8,457	6,527	8,504
Rapeseed	1,912	2,230	2,758
Peas, dry	151	147	123
Broad beans, dry	180*	160*	134†
Onions, dry	355	365	301
Mushrooms and truffles	69	69	69
Carrots and turnips	719	763	694
Cabbages and other brassicas	278	291	279
Cauliflower and broccoli	186	188	181
Peas, green	401	373	425
Linseed	54	72	71
Lettuce and chicory	134	134	133
Tomatoes	87	89	90
Cucumbers and gherkins	58	65	67
Apples	229	235	234
Pears	21	33	30
Strawberries	110	103	107

* Unofficial figure.
† FAO estimate.

Aggregate production (may include official, semi-official or estimated data): Total cereals 21,619 in 2009, 20,946 in 2010, 21,485 in 2011; Total pulses 839 in 2009, 727 in 2010, 608 in 2011; Total roots and tubers 6,396 in 2009, 6,056 in 2010, 6,115 in 2011; Total vegetables (incl. melons) 2,609 in 2009, 2,679 in 2010, 2,569 in 2011; Total fruits (excl. melons) 414 in 2009, 429 in 2010, 423 in 2011.

Source: FAO.

LIVESTOCK
('000 head, year ending September)

	2009	2010	2011
Cattle	10,025	10,112	9,933
Sheep	31,445	31,084	31,634
Pigs	4,540	4,460	4,441
Chickens	159,288	164,000	166,000*
Ducks and geese*	2,195	2,318	2,405
Turkeys	4,400	3,900	3,900

* FAO estimate(s).
Source: FAO.

LIVESTOCK PRODUCTS
('000 metric tons unless otherwise indicated)

	2009	2010	2011
Cattle meat	833	908	936
Sheep meat	307	277	289
Pig meat	720	758	806
Chicken meat	1,270	1,376	1,354
Cows' milk	13,852	14,081	14,246
Butter and ghee	118	120	130
Cheese	360	370	390
Hen eggs	603	658	662
Wool, greasy*	65	67	67

* FAO estimates.
Source: FAO.

Forestry

ROUNDWOOD REMOVALS
('000 cubic metres, excl. bark)

	2009	2010	2011
Sawlogs, veneer logs and logs for sleepers	5,209	5,743	5,993
Pulpwood	1,860	2,071	2,248
Other industrial wood	566	524	547
Fuel wood	988	1,381	1,234
Total	8,623	9,718	10,022

Source: FAO.

SAWNWOOD PRODUCTION
('000 cubic metres, incl. railway sleepers)

	2009	2010	2011
Coniferous (softwood)	2,809	3,053	3,227
Broadleaved (hardwood)	48	48	52
Total	2,856	3,101	3,279

Source: FAO.

Fishing

('000 metric tons, live weight)

	2008	2009	2010
Capture	596.0	591.1	612.7
Haddock	33.1	36.3	33.6
Blue whiting	38.2	6.4	8.0
Atlantic herring	67.1	67.1	66.9
Atlantic mackerel	124.9	172.0	160.4
Edible crab	22.7	22.3	24.5
Norway lobster	43.5	42.9	38.7
Aquaculture	179.2	179.1*	201.1*
Atlantic salmon	128.7	133.4	154.6
Blue mussel	28.2	28.0*	30.2
Total	775.2	770.2*	813.7*

* FAO estimate.

Note: Figures exclude aquatic mammals, recorded by number rather than weight. The number of whales and porpoises caught was: 28 in 2008; nil in 2009; nil in 2010.

Source: FAO.

Mining and Quarrying

('000 metric tons unless otherwise indicated)

	2009	2010	2011*
Hard coal (incl. slurries) . .	17,874	18,416	18,492
Natural gas and petroleum:			
Methane—colliery . . .	67	63	60
Methane—onshore . . .	89	88	55,000
Methane—offshore . . .	59,581	57,036	
Crude petroleum	62,820	58,047	
Onshore	1,181	941	58,000
Offshore	61,639	57,106	
Condensates and others[1] .	5,378	4,915	5,000
China clay (sales)[2] . . .	1,060	1,000	1,000
Ball clay (sales)	727	1,000	1,000
Fireclay[3]	129	110	100
Common clay and shale[3] . .	5,310	5,934	5,483
Slate[4]	683	695	700
Limestone	60,110	60,207	65,000
Dolomite	3,164	4,540	
Chalk[3]	4,047	3,626	3,500
Sandstone	12,335	11,556	11,500
Common sand and gravel[5] . .	66,226	61,700	62,000
Igneous rock[6]	44,618	44,876	45,000
Gypsum*	1,700	1,700	1,700
Rock salt*	2,000	2,000	
Salt from brine*	1,000	1,000	7,000
Salt in brine*[7]	2,800	2,800	
Fluorspar*	19	26	—
Barytes	36	34	31
Talc	3	3	4
Potash[8]	700	700	770

* Estimates.
[1] Includes ethane, propane and butane, in addition to condensates (pentane and hydrocarbons).
[2] Dry weight.
[3] Excluding production in Northern Ireland.
[4] Including waste used for constructional fill and powder and granules used in industry.
[5] Including marine-dredged sand and gravel for both home consumption and export.
[6] Excluding production in Northern Ireland and the Channel Islands.
[7] Used for purposes other than salt-making.
[8] Chloride (K_2O content).

Source: British Geological Survey.

Industry

SELECTED PRODUCTS

('000 metric tons unless otherwise indicated)

	2008	2009	2010
Flour of wheat and meslin[1] . .	4,277	n.a.	n.a.
Beer ('000 hectolitres) . .	49,611	45,141	n.a.
Cigarettes ('000 million) . .	42.1	44.0	n.a.
Butane and propane[2] . . .	2,248	2,113	2,247
Petroleum naphtha[2] . . .	1,863	1,529	1,596
Motor spirit (petrol)[2] . . .	20,319	20,404	19,918
Aviation turbine fuel[2] . . .	6,549	6,022	5,781
Burning oil[2]	3,092	2,830	2,570
Diesel fuel and gas oil[2] . .	26,761	25,393	24,837
Fuel oil[2]	10,496	7,964	6,912
Lubricating oils[2]	514	510	578
Petroleum bitumen (asphalt)[2] .	1,485	1,338	1,276
Cement[3]	10,070	n.a.	n.a.
Pig iron[4]	10,137	7,671	7,233
Crude steel (usable) . . .	13,521	10,075	9,708
Aluminium—(wrought remelt) .	654.5	n.a.	n.a.
Refined lead—unwrought[5] . .	318.7	n.a.	n.a.
Electric energy (million kWh) .	389,649	n.a.	n.a.

[1] Source: UN Industrial Commodity Statistics Database.
[2] Refinery production only (excluding supplies from other sources).
[3] Excluding production in Northern Ireland.
[4] Including blast-furnace ferro-alloys.
[5] Lead reclaimed from secondary and scrap material, and lead refined from bullion and domestic ores; includes antimonial lead.

Passenger motor cars: 1,442,100 in 2006.

Road goods vehicles: 206,800 in 2005.

Finance

CURRENCY AND EXCHANGE RATES

Monetary Units
100 pence (pennies) = 1 pound sterling (£).

Dollar and Euro Equivalents (31 December 2012)
US $1 = 63.37 pence;
€1 = 83.61 pence;
£10 = $15.78 = €11.96.

Average Exchange Rate (pound sterling per US $)
2010 0.6472
2011 0.6241
2012 0.6330

BUDGET
(general government transactions, year ending 31 March, £ '000 million)

Current Revenue

	2009/10	2010/11	2011/12
Income tax (net)	147.5	153.3	152.7
National insurance contributions .	96.6	97.7	101.6
Value-added tax	73.5	86.3	98.1
Corporation tax	36.5	43.0	43.1
Petroleum revenue tax . . .	0.9	1.5	2.0
Fuel duties	26.2	27.3	26.8
Capital gains tax	2.5	3.6	4.3
Inheritance tax	2.4	2.7	2.9
Stamp duties	7.9	6.0	6.1
Tobacco duty	8.8	9.1	9.9
Spirits duties	2.7	2.7	2.9
Wine duties	3.0	3.1	3.4
Beer and cider duties . . .	3.5	3.7	3.8
Air passenger duty	1.9	2.2	2.6
Insurance premium tax . . .	2.3	2.5	3.0
Climate change levy . . .	0.7	0.7	0.7
Business rates	23.4	23.6	24.9
Council tax	25.3	25.7	26.0
Other HMRC taxes	5.4	5.9	5.9
Other taxes and royalties . .	19.3	28.3	28.7
Vehicle excise duty (VED) .	5.6	5.8	5.9
Interest and dividends . . .	3.4	2.4	5.7
Gross operating surplus and rent .	23.3	25.2	23.6
Other receipts and adjustments .	–3.7	–5.7	–6.2
Total current revenue . . .	**513.3**	**550.8**	**572.6**

Total current revenue (revised figures): 512.2 in 2009/10; 551.1 in 2010/11.

Source: HM Treasury, *Budget 2013* (March 2013).

Expenditure

By function of government	2009/10	2010/11	2011/12
General public services . . .	52.7	67.5	69.4
International services . . .	7.9	8.8	8.9
Public sector debt interest . .	31.1	46.0	48.6
Public and common services .	13.6	12.7	11.9
Defence	37.7	39.3	38.6
Public order and safety . . .	34.2	33.0	31.8
Economic affairs	46.3	38.9	37.2
Enterprise and economic development	11.8	4.8	4.3
Science and technology . . .	3.5	3.4	3.8
Employment policies . .	3.5	3.8	2.8
Agriculture, fisheries and forestry	5.5	5.4	5.8
Transport	23.0	21.5	20.4
Environment protection . . .	11.0	11.0	10.7
Housing and community amenities	16.4	12.9	10.3
Health	118.2	121.3	121.4
Recreation, culture and religion .	13.3	13.1	13.2
Education	88.4	91.6	93.1
Social protection	224.6	231.2	240.6
EU transactions	0.1	2.8	1.2
Accounting adjustments . .	28.7	29.9	26.1
Depreciation	19.4	20.3	21.1
Less Public sector gross investment	67.9	58.8	49.8
Total current expenditure .	**623.0**	**653.9**	**664.6**

Source: HM Treasury, *Statistical Bulletin: Public Spending Statistics* (February 2013).

OFFICIAL RESERVES
(US $ million at 31 December)*

	2009	2010	2011
Gold	11,012	14,067	15,272
IMF special drawing rights . .	14,344	14,118	14,593
Foreign currencies	35,618	43,489	49,691
Reserve position in IMF . . .	3,333	4,892	8,441
Other reserve assets	−169	1,303	5,543
Total	64,138	77,869	93,540

* Reserves are revalued at 31 March each year.

Source: Bank of England.

MONEY SUPPLY
(£ million at 31 December)

	2010	2011	2012
Retail deposits and cash . . .	14,485,752	14,959,952	15,608,886
Notes and coin in private sector.	606,678	633,970	662,034
Bank and building society deposits	13,879,074	14,325,982	14,946,853
Wholesale deposits	11,846,315	10,716,115	9,329,895
Total broad money	26,332,068	25,676,068	24,938,783

Source: Bank of England.

COST OF LIVING
(General Index of Retail Prices, annual averages; base: January 1987 = 100)

	2010	2011	2012
Food	195.0	206.6	213.3
Catering	279.8	291.2	300.2
Alcoholic drink	244.3	258.5	267.0
Tobacco	422.6	469.1	509.0
Housing	313.7	319.0	325.2
Fuel and light	262.1	289.9	311.9
Household goods	169.8	179.6	186.5
Household services	217.3	224.1	233.4
Clothing and footwear	91.9	102.5	110.4
Personal goods and services . .	237.1	247.5	255.8
Motoring expenditure . . .	219.1	238.4	240.3
Fares and other travel costs . .	287.6	308.5	323.2
Leisure goods	86.5	85.1	84.9
Leisure services	317.6	329.9	342.2
All items	223.6	235.2	242.7

NATIONAL ACCOUNTS
(£ million at current prices)

National Income and Product

	2009	2010	2011
Compensation of employees .	777,576	796,421	814,515
Gross operating surplus . .	388,788	405,536	422,514
Mixed income	81,018	85,281	85,602
Gross domestic product (GDP) at factor cost . .	1,247,382	1,287,238	1,322,631
Taxes on production and imports } *Less* Subsidies	154,481	179,330	194,129
Statistical discrepancy . . .	—	1	−607
GDP at market prices . .	1,401,863	1,466,569	1,516,153
Primary incomes received from abroad . . . . . . } *Less* Primary incomes paid abroad	17,162	12,474	15,174
Gross national income . .	1,419,025	1,479,043	1,531,327
Less Consumption of fixed capital .	159,859	164,006	170,986

	2009	2010	2011
—*continued*			
Net national income . . .	1,259,166	1,315,037	1,360,341
Current transfers from abroad . } *Less* Current transfers paid abroad	−14,340	−18,265	−20,291
Net national disposable income	1,244,826	1,296,772	1,340,050

2011 (revised figures): *GDP at factor cost* 1,324,405 (Compensation of employees 814,447); Taxes, less subsidies, on production and imports 196,392; Statistical discrepancy −4,969; *GDP at market prices* 1,515,828; Primary incomes from abroad (net) 23,905; *Gross national income* 1,539,733.

2012: *GDP at factor cost* 1,349,905 (Compensation of employees 838,918); Taxes, less subsidies, on production and imports 198,300; Statistical discrepancy −6,740; *GDP at market prices* 1,541,465; Primary incomes from abroad (net) −871; *Gross national income* 1,540,596.

Expenditure on the Gross Domestic Product

	2010	2011	2012
Final consumption expenditure .	1,276,578	1,311,615	1,354,152
Households (incl. non-profit institutions serving households)	941,537	975,906	1,013,606
General government	335,040	335,709	340,546
Gross capital formation . . .	221,493	225,313	223,282
Gross fixed capital formation .	218,631	213,216	218,239
Changes in inventories . . .	2,076	8,583	2,310
Acquisitions, less disposals of valuables	786	3,514	2,742
Total domestic expenditure .	1,498,071	1,536,926	1,577,434
Exports of goods and services . .	447,885	492,455	488,428
Less Imports of goods and services	479,387	516,602	524,582
Statistical discrepancy	—	3,049	185
GDP in purchasers' values .	1,466,569	1,515,828	1,541,465

Gross Domestic Product by Economic Activity

	2008	2009	2010
Agriculture, hunting, forestry and fishing	8,030	7,857	8,333
Mining and quarrying	36,789	30,431	35,589
Manufacturing	137,283	132,260	139,120
Electricity, gas and water supply .	31,974	34,760	35,626
Construction	98,469	85,575	83,280
Wholesale and retail trade; repair of motor vehicles, motorcycles and personal and household goods	142,359	140,716	147,203
Hotels and restaurants . .	37,740	36,736	38,044
Transport, storage and communication	139,941	134,299	136,598
Financial intermediation . . .	117,433	131,786	123,021
Real estate, renting and business activities	256,291	235,712	256,905
Public administration and defence	65,240	68,040	69,918
Education	83,203	85,340	87,408
Health and social work . . .	94,366	99,470	103,667
Other community, social and personal services*	41,827	42,028	44,249
Gross value added at basic prices	1,290,945	1,265,010	1,308,962
Value-added taxes on products .	91,952	79,900	95,888
Other taxes on products . . .	63,186	62,729	67,934
Less Subsidies on products . .	5,152	5,776	6,215
GDP in purchasers' values .	1,440,931	1,401,863	1,466,569

* Including private households with employees, and extra-territorial organizations.

BALANCE OF PAYMENTS
(£ million)

	2010	2011	2012
Exports of goods f.o.b.	265,708	299,073	300,456
Imports of goods f.o.b.	−364,217	−399,303	−406,799
Trade balance	−98,509	−100,230	−106,343
Exports of services	182,177	193,382	187,972
Imports of services	−115,170	−117,299	−117,783
Balance on goods and services	−31,502	−24,147	−36,154
Other income received . . .	160,466	192,634	161,915
Other income paid	−145,838	−166,763	−160,353
Balance on goods, services and income	−16,874	1,724	−34,592
Current transfers received . .	17,233	16,430	16,512
Current transfers paid	−37,643	−38,388	−39,599
Current balance	−37,284	−20,234	−57,679
Capital account (net) . . .	3,704	3,228	3,705
Direct investment abroad . .	−25,565	−66,579	−45,209
Direct investment from abroad .	32,750	31,917	39,471
Portfolio investment abroad . .	−76,843	−6,598	−125,414
Portfolio investment from abroad	77,934	−37,974	−77,961
Financial derivatives (net) . .	32,788	−2,911	30,759
Other investment abroad . . .	−224,094	−105,007	228,121
Other investment from abroad .	217,377	199,625	6,372
Net errors and omissions . . .	5,303	9,481	5,477
Overall balance	6,070	4,948	7,642

GROSS PUBLIC EXPENDITURE ON OVERSEAS AID
(£ million, year ending 31 March)

	2009/10	2010/11	2011/12
Total bilateral aid	4,765.7	5,311.9	5,178.6
DFID* bilateral programmes .	3,958.3	4,248.0	4,204.1
Poverty reduction budget support	634.1	643.7	536.7
Other financial aid . . .	518.8	550.7	544.8
Technical co-operation . .	419.9	467.9	527.9
Grants and other aid in kind .	1,898.8	2,168.5	2,225.5
Humanitarian assistance .	434.6	350.7	354.3
DFID debt relief . . .	52.1	66.5	15.0
Other bilateral programmes .	807.5	1,063.8	974.5
CDC investments . . .	354.4	416.2	284.3
Debt relief	7.2	54.3	91.0
Other	445.9	593.3	599.2
Total multilateral aid . . .	2,748.8	3,461.9	3,461.7
European Commission . .	1,424.1	1,431.8	1,355.6
World Bank Group . . .	559.8	926.7	1,038.6
UN agencies	278.6	417.3	434.5
Other	486.3	686.1	633.1
Administrative costs	252.1	233.2	309.3
Total gross expenditure on aid	7,766.6	9,007.0	8,949.6

* Department for International Development (DFID).

Source: Department for International Development, *Statistics on International Development*.

External Trade

(Note: Figures include the Isle of Man and the Channel Islands)

PRINCIPAL COMMODITIES
(£ million, seasonally adjusted)

Imports c.i.f.	2010	2011	2012
Food and live animals . . .	27,174	29,498	30,130
Mineral fuels, lubricants, etc. .	44,923	61,926	65,339
Petroleum, petroleum products, etc.	36,048	49,548	53,896
Chemicals and related products	44,756	48,920	49,388
Basic manufactures* . . .	43,591	49,223	49,878
Machinery and transport equipment	129,235	129,023	131,240
Mechanical machinery and equipment	28,781	32,851	34,348
Electrical machinery, apparatus, etc.	50,998	51,268	50,637
Road vehicles and parts† . . .	33,664	36,779	36,638
Other transport equipment . .	15,792	8,125	9,617
Miscellaneous manufactured articles	54,764	58,744	59,635
Clothing and footwear	18,453	19,889	19,695
Scientific and photographic apparatus	9,114	9,582	10,083
Total (incl. others)	364,217	399,301	406,562

Exports f.o.b.	2010	2011	2012
Food and live animals . . .	10,130	11,103	10,902
Mineral fuels, lubricants, etc. .	35,139	42,762	43,715
Petroleum, petroleum products, etc.	31,329	38,039	39,514
Chemicals and related products	50,916	53,176	52,949
Organic chemicals	8,859	9,187	9,013
Medicinal products	22,362	22,881	23,466
Basic manufactures* . . .	29,255	34,917	32,364
Machinery and transport equipment	92,736	103,519	104,426
Mechanical machinery and equipment	32,857	38,596	39,354
Electrical machinery, apparatus, etc.	25,770	26,190	24,210
Road vehicles and parts† . . .	23,373	27,420	28,947
Other transport equipment . .	10,736	11,313	11,915
Miscellaneous manufactured articles	31,446	33,751	35,870
Scientific and photographic apparatus	9,290	10,192	10,372
Total (incl. others)	265,708	299,073	299,948

* Sorted industrial diamonds, usually classified with natural abrasives (under 'crude materials'), are included with 'basic manufactures'.
† Excluding tyres, engines and electrical parts.

PRINCIPAL TRADING PARTNERS
(£ million, seasonally adjusted)

Imports c.i.f.	2010	2011	2012
Belgium-Luxembourg	18,017	20,078	18,863
Canada	5,770	6,152	5,550
China, People's Republic . . .	30,637	31,533	31,521
Czech Republic	3,992	4,247	4,471
Denmark	4,117	6,090	5,827
Finland	2,165	2,453	2,164
France	21,574	23,077	22,498
Germany	46,419	50,457	52,477
Hong Kong	8,172	7,640	7,411
India	5,812	6,097	6,210
Ireland	12,870	13,079	12,834
Italy	13,944	14,091	14,251
Japan	8,106	8,882	8,553
Korea, Republic	2,564	2,619	3,255

Imports c.i.f.—*continued*	2010	2011	2012
Netherlands	26,450	28,591	31,227
Norway	21,057	25,219	22,370
Poland	6,106	7,089	7,397
Russia	5,259	7,466	8,466
Singapore	4,145	3,887	3,742
South Africa	4,426	2,955	3,313
Spain (excl. Canary Is)	10,385	11,817	11,530
Sweden	6,809	7,726	9,056
Switzerland	7,432	7,595	9,037
Turkey	5,350	5,569	5,766
USA	26,998	28,793	29,935
Total (incl. others)	364,217	399,301	406,562

Exports f.o.b.	2010	2011	2012
Australia	3,368	4,394	4,737
Belgium-Luxembourg	13,603	16,252	14,622
Canada	4,132	4,752	4,154
China, People's Republic	7,623	9,298	10,540
Denmark	2,752	3,015	2,705
France	19,201	21,998	21,030
Germany	27,877	32,564	32,149
Hong Kong	4,463	5,382	5,382
India	4,074	5,699	4,665
Ireland	16,907	17,897	17,389
Italy	8,839	10,020	8,087
Japan	4,344	4,728	4,922
Netherlands	21,218	23,566	24,820
Norway	3,120	3,399	3,648
Poland	3,797	4,321	3,439
Russia	3,602	5,012	5,590
Singapore	3,453	3,822	4,483
Spain (excl. Canary Is)	9,925	9,739	8,530
Sweden	5,557	6,267	5,755
Switzerland	5,222	5,466	6,763
United Arab Emirates	4,066	4,864	5,370
USA	37,985	39,881	41,019
Total (incl. others)	265,708	299,073	299,948

Transport

RAILWAYS

	2007/08	2008/09	2009/10
Passenger journeys (million):			
National railways	1,218	1,266	1,258
Underground railways (London and Glasgow)	1,110	1,103	1,072
Light rail	201	203	199
Passenger-km (million):			
National railways	48,930	50,613	51,101
Underground railways (London and Glasgow)	8,398	8,691	8,499
Light rail	1,185	1,191	1,271
Freight carried (million metric tons)*	102	103	n.a.
Freight ton-km ('000 million)*	21	21	n.a.

* Great Britain only. Figures exclude parcels and materials for rail infrastructure.

ROAD TRAFFIC
('000 licensed vehicles in Great Britain at 31 December)

	2006	2007	2008
Private motor cars	26,508	26,878	27,021
Motorcycles, scooters and mopeds	1,094	1,133	1,160
Light goods vehicles*	3,137	3,261	3,303
Heavy goods vehicles	446	446	436
Public passenger vehicles	107	109	111
Crown property and tax exempt	1,991	2,043	2,091

* Goods vehicles less than 3,500 kg in weight.

2009: Private motor cars and light goods vehicles 30,352; Motorcycles, scooters and mopeds 1,160; Heavy goods 415; Total (incl. others) 34,258.

SHIPPING
Flag Registered Fleet
(at 31 December)

	2010	2011	2012
Number of vessels	2,455	2,461	2,453
Total displacement ('000 grt)	18,561.0	18,791.1	18,459.1

Source: Lloyd's List Intelligence (www.lloydslistintelligence.com).

International Sea-borne Freight Traffic
('000 metric tons)

	2004	2005	2006
Goods imported	342,425	354,391	365,112
Goods exported	230,645	230,529	218,627

Source: Department for Transport.

CIVIL AVIATION
(United Kingdom airlines)

	2008	2009	2010
All scheduled services:			
Aircraft stage flights (number)	1,056,298	1,001,504	978,269
Aircraft-km flown (million)	1,508	1,444	1,440
Passengers carried (million)	105	103	102
Passenger-km flown (million)	232,592	230,588	225,649
Total cargo carried (metric tons)	979,791	900,668	929,136
Total metric ton-km (million)	6,383	5,952	6,167
Freight metric ton-km (million)	6,284	5,864	6,072
Mail metric ton-km (million)	99	89	95
Domestic scheduled services:			
Aircraft stage flights (number)	369,499	341,207	329,341
Aircraft-km flown (million)	173	123	115
Passengers carried (million)	21	20	18
Passenger-km flown (million)	8,952	8,326	7,711
Total cargo carried (metric tons)	6,125	5,202	4,670
Total metric ton-km (million)	2	2	2
Freight metric ton-km (million)	2	2	1
Mail metric ton-km (million)	0	1	1
International scheduled services:			
Aircraft stage flights (number)	686,799	660,027	648,928
Aircraft-km flown (million)	1,371	1,320	1,293
Passengers carried (million)	84	83	83
Passenger-km flown (million)	233,640	222,262	217,938
Total cargo carried (metric tons)	973,665	895,466	924,465
Total metric ton-km (million)	6,381	5,951	6,165
Freight metric ton-km (million)	6,282	5,862	6,070
Mail metric ton-km (million)	99	89	95

Tourism

FOREIGN VISITORS BY REGION OF ORIGIN
('000 unless otherwise indicated)

	2009	2010	2011
Europe	22,083	22,046	22,438
North America	3,564	3,397	3,586
Other countries	4,242	4,360	4,774
Total	29,889	29,803	30,798
Total expenditure (£ million)	16,592	16,899	17,998

Source: International Passenger Survey, Office for National Statistics, *Travel Trends*.

VISITS BY COUNTRY OF PERMANENT RESIDENCE
('000)

	2009	2010	2011
Australia	912	986	1,093
Belgium	903	1,136	984
Canada	687	686	740
France	3,784	3,618	3,633
Germany	2,780	3,004	2,947
Ireland	2,948	2,629	2,574
Italy	1,221	1,472	1,526
Netherlands	1,715	1,758	1,789
Norway	573	649	739
Poland	1,041	1,101	1,057
Spain	2,164	1,809	1,836
Sweden	604	758	794
Switzerland	701	623	768
USA	2,877	2,711	2,846
Total (incl. others)	29,889	29,803	30,798

Source: International Passenger Survey, Office for National Statistics, *Travel Trends*.

Communications Media

	2009	2010	2011
Telephones ('000 main lines in use)	33,540	33,409	33,230
Mobile cellular telephones ('000 subscribers)	80,255	81,116	81,612
Internet users ('000)	19,238	20,528	20,438
Broadband subscribers ('000)*	18,222	19,130	20,438

* Excluding corporate connections.

Source: International Telecommunication Union.

Education

PRE-PRIMARY, PRIMARY AND SECONDARY EDUCATION

	2009/10	2010/11	2011/12
Schools	33,137	32,750	32,518
Public sector mainstream	28,742	28,569	28,332
Nursery*	3,166	3,130	3,095
Primary	21,427		21,165
Primary Academy converter	—	37	—
Secondary (incl. specialist)	4,149	4,121	4,072
Modern	160	137	n.a.
Selective (Grammar)	233	204	n.a.
City Technology Centres	3	3	n.a.
Academies	203	371	n.a.
Comprehensive	3,156	3,036	n.a.

—*continued*	2009/10	2010/11	2011/12
Not applicable	394	370	n.a.
Middle deemed secondary	225	225	196
Non-maintained mainstream	2,570	2,498	2,502
Special schools	1,373	1,293	1,281
Maintained	1,253	1,218	1,209
Non-maintained	120	75	72
Pupil Referral Units	452	427	403
Teachers ('000):[1]	491.5	489.6	n.a.
Maintained nursery and primary schools	200.5	199.4	n.a.
Maintained secondary schools	208.1	220.0	n.a.
Non-maintained mainstream	67.9	55.4	n.a.
All special schools	15.0	14.8	n.a.
Full-time and part-time pupils ('000):	9,676.8	9,654.1	9,712.8
Maintained schools	9,055.7	9,064.3	9,121.3
Nursery	152.5	138.3	141.6
Primary	4,882.1	4,922.0[2]	5,006.7[2]
Nursery classes	299.6	304.8	311.1
Other classes	4,582.4	4,358.1	4,433.5
Secondary	3,906.7	3,888.7	3,855.6
Special schools	101.5	102.8	105.0
Pupil referral units[3]	13.0	12.5	12.4
Non-maintained schools	621.2	589.8	591.4
Special schools	5.5	4.4	4.3
Other	615.7	585.4	587.1

* Excluding pre-school education centres not in partnership with a local authority.
[1] Qualified teachers only. Full-time teachers and the full-time equivalent of part-time teachers. Excluding Pupil Referral Unit teachers.
[2] Including total for Wales, for which breakdown by class type was not available.
[3] England and Wales only; excluding pupils registered elsewhere.

Source: partly Department for Education, London.

POST-COMPULSORY EDUCATION

	2008/09	2009/10	2010/11
Universities	127	126	126
Other higher education institutes	37	37	37
Further education institutes/colleges	434	427	416
Sixth-form colleges	94	94	93
Full-time teaching and research staff ('000)*	170	167	162
Students (incl. from overseas) taking higher education courses:			
full-time students ('000)	1,596.9	1,692.7	1,739.0
part-time students ('000)	959.7	965.5	920.3

* Excluding part-time academic staff in further and higher education institutes.

Note: Figures for institutions include, but for teaching staff exclude, the Open University.

Source: partly Department for Education, London.

Directory

The Government

HEAD OF STATE

Queen: HM Queen ELIZABETH II (succeeded to the throne 6 February 1952).

THE MINISTRY
(May 2013)

A coalition of the Conservative Party (Con.) and the Liberal Democrats (LD).

The Cabinet

Prime Minister, First Lord of the Treasury and Minister for the Civil Service: DAVID CAMERON (Con.).

Deputy Prime Minister and Lord President of the Council (with special responsibility for political and constitutional reform): NICK CLEGG (LD).

First Secretary of State and Secretary of State for Foreign and Commonwealth Affairs: WILLIAM HAGUE (Con.).

Chancellor of the Exchequer: GEORGE OSBORNE (Con.).

Chief Secretary to the Treasury: DANNY ALEXANDER (LD).

Secretary of State for the Home Department and Minister for Women and Equalities: THERESA MAY (Con.).

Secretary of State for Defence: PHILIP HAMMOND (Con.).

Secretary of State for Business, Innovation and Skills: Dr VINCENT (VINCE) CABLE (LD).

Secretary of State for Work and Pensions: IAIN DUNCAN SMITH (Con.).

Lord Chancellor and Secretary of State for Justice: CHRISTOPHER GRAYLING (Con.).

Secretary of State for Education: MICHAEL GOVE (Con.).

Secretary of State for Communities and Local Government: ERIC PICKLES (Con.).

Secretary of State for Health: JEREMY HUNT (Con.).

Secretary of State for Environment, Food and Rural Affairs: OWEN PATERSON (Con.).

Secretary of State for International Development: JUSTINE GREENING (Con.).

Secretary of State for Scotland: MICHAEL MOORE (LD).

Secretary of State for Energy and Climate Change: EDWARD DAVEY (LD).

Secretary of State for Transport: PATRICK MCLOUGHLIN (Con.).

Secretary of State for Culture, Media and Sport: MARIA MILLER (Con.).

Secretary of State for Northern Ireland: THERESA VILLIERS (Con.).

Secretary of State for Wales: DAVID JONES (Con.).

Leader of the House of Lords and Chancellor of the Duchy of Lancaster: Lord HILL (Con.).

Minister without Portfolio (Minister of State): KENNETH CLARKE (Con.).

Minister without Portfolio (Minister of State): GRANT SHAPPS (Con.).

Minister without Portfolio (Minister of State): JOHN HAYES (Con.).

Also attending Cabinet

Minister for the Cabinet Office and Paymaster General: FRANCIS MAUDE (Con.).

Minister for Government Policy, Cabinet Office: OLIVER LETWIN (Con.).

Minister of State for Universities and Science, Department for Business, Innovation and Skills: DAVID WILLETTS (Con.).

Minister of State, Department for Education and Cabinet Office: DAVID LAWS (LD).

Senior Minister of State at the Foreign and Commonwealth Office, and Senior Minister of State for Faith and Communities at the Department for Communities and Local Government: Baroness WARSI (Con.).

Leader of the House of Commons and Lord Privy Seal: ANDREW LANSLEY (Con.).

Parliamentary Secretary to the Treasury and Chief Whip: Sir GEORGE YOUNG (Con.).

Attending Cabinet when required

Attorney-General: DOMINIC GRIEVE (Con.).

Ministers not in the Cabinet

Ministers of State, Foreign and Commonwealth Office: DAVID LIDINGTON (Con.), HUGO SWIRE (Con.).

Financial Secretary to the Treasury: GREG CLARK (Con.).

Economic Secretary to the Treasury: SAJID JAVID (Con.).

Exchequer Secretary to the Treasury: DAVID GAUKE (Con.).

Minister of State, Ministry of Justice: Lord MCNALLY (LD).

Minister of State, Ministry of Justice and of Home Office: DAMIAN GREEN (Con.).

Ministers of State, Home Office: MARK HARPER (Con.), JEREMY BROWNE (LD).

Ministers of State, Ministry of Defence: ANDREW ROBATHAN (Con.), MARK FRANCOIS (Con.).

Ministers of State, Department for Business, Innovation and Skills: Lord GREEN (Con.), MICHAEL FALLON (Con.).

Ministers of State, Department for Work and Pensions: MARK HOBAN (Con.), STEVE WEBB (LD).

Ministers of State, Department of Energy and Climate Change: MICHAEL FALLON (Con.), GREGORY BARKER (Con.).

Minister of State, Department of Health: NORMAN LAMB (LD).

Minister of State, Department for Communities and Local Government: MARK PRISK (Con.).

Minister of State, Department for Culture Media and Sport: HUGH ROBERTSON (Con.).

Minister of State, Department for Transport: SIMON BURNS (Con.).

Minister of State, Department for Environment, Food and Rural Affairs: DAVID HEATH (LD).

Minister of State, Department for International Development: ALAN DUNCAN (Con.).

Minister of State, Northern Ireland Office: MIKE PENNING (Con.).

Solicitor-General: OLIVER HEALD (Con.).

Lords Chief Whip and Captain of the Honourable Corps of Gentlemen at Arms: Baroness ANELAY OF ST JOHNS (Con.).

MINISTRIES

Prime Minister's Office: 10 Downing St, London, SW1A 2AA; tel. (20) 7270-3000; fax (20) 7925-0918; internet www.number10.gov.uk.

Cabinet Office: 70 Whitehall, London, SW1A 2AS; tel. (20) 7276-1234; e-mail publiccorrespondence@cabinet-office.gsi.gov.uk; internet www.gov.uk/government/organisations/cabinet-office.

Attorney General's Office: 20 Victoria St, London, SW1H 0NF; tel. (20) 7271-2492; e-mail correspondence@attorneygeneral.gsi.gov.uk; internet www.gov.uk/government/organisations/attorney-generals-office.

Department for Business, Innovation and Skills: 1 Victoria St, London, SW1H 0ET; tel. (20) 7215-5000; e-mail enquiries@bis.gsi.gov.uk; internet www.gov.uk/government/organisations/department-for-business-innovation-skills.

Department for Communities and Local Government: Eland House, Bressenden Place, London, SW1E 5DU; tel. (30) 3444-0000; e-mail contactus@communities.gsi.gov.uk; internet www.gov.uk/government/organisations/department-for-communities-and-local-government.

Department for Culture, Media and Sport: 100 Parliament St, London, SW1A 2BQ; tel. (20) 7211-6000; e-mail enquiries@culture.gov.uk; internet www.gov.uk/government/organisations/department-for-culture-media-sport.

Ministry of Defence: Main Bldg, 5th Floor, Whitehall, London, SW1A 2HB; tel. (20) 7218-9000; e-mail ministerial-correspondence@mod.uk; internet www.gov.uk/government/organisations/ministry-of-defence.

Department for Education: Sanctuary Bldgs, Great Smith St, London, SW1P 3BT; tel. (870) 000-2288; internet www.gov.uk/government/organisations/department-for-education.

Department of Energy and Climate Change: 3 Whitehall Place, London, SW1A 2HH; tel. (300) 060-4000; e-mail correspondence@decc.gsi.gov.uk; internet www.gov.uk/government/organisations/department-of-energy-climate-change.

Department for Environment, Food and Rural Affairs: Nobel House, 17 Smith Sq., London, SW1P 3JR; tel. (20) 7238-6951; e-mail defra.helpline@defra.gsi.gov.uk; internet www.gov.uk/government/organisations/department-for-environment-food-rural-affairs.

Foreign and Commonwealth Office: King Charles St, London, SW1A 2AH; tel. (20) 7008-1500; e-mail fcocorrespondence@fco.gov.uk; internet www.gov.uk/government/organisations/foreign-commonwealth-office.

Government Equalities Office: 2–4 Cockspur Street, London, SW1Y 5DH; tel. (20) 7211-6000; e-mail enquiries@geo.gsi.gov.uk; internet www.gov.uk/government/organisations/government-equalities-office.

Department of Health: Richmond House, 79 Whitehall, London, SW1A 2NS; tel. (20) 7210-4850; fax (20) 7210-5952; internet www.gov.uk/government/organisations/department-of-health.

Home Office: 2 Marsham St, London, SW1P 4DF; tel. (20) 7035-4848; fax (20) 7035-4745; e-mail public.enquiries@homeoffice.gsi.gov.uk; internet www.gov.uk/government/organisations/home-office.

Department for International Development: 22 Whitehall, London, SW1A 2EG; tel. (20) 7023-0000; e-mail enquiry@dfid.gov.uk; internet www.gov.uk/government/organisations/department-for-international-development.

Ministry of Justice: 102 Petty France, London, SW1H 9AJ; tel. (20) 3334-3555; e-mail general.queries@justice.gsi.gov.uk; internet www.gov.uk/government/organisations/ministry-of-justice.

Northern Ireland Office: 1 Horse Guards Rd, London, SW1A 2HQ; tel. (28) 9052-0700; e-mail nioweb.editor@nio.x.gsi.gov.uk; internet www.gov.uk/government/organisations/northern-ireland-office.

Office of the Leader of the House of Commons: 1 Horse Guards Rd, London, SW1A 2HQ; tel. (20) 7276-1005; fax (20) 7276-1006; e-mail leader@commonsleader.x.gsi.gov.uk; internet www.gov.uk/government/organisations/the-office-of-the-leader-of-the-house-of-commons.

Office of the Leader of the House of Lords: 1 Horse Guards Rd, London, SW1A 2HQ; tel. (20) 7219-3200; fax (20) 7219-3051; e-mail psleaderofthelords@cabinet-office.x.gsi.gov.uk; internet www.gov.uk/government/organisations/office-of-the-leader-of-the-house-of-lords.

Scotland Office: Dover House, Whitehall, London, SW1A 2AU; tel. (20) 7270-6754; fax (20) 7270-6812; e-mail scottish.secretary@ scotland.gsi.gov.uk; internet www.gov.uk/government/ organisations/scotland-office.

Department for Transport: Great Minster House, 33 Horseferry Rd, London, SW1P 4DR; tel. (300) 330-3000; internet www.gov.uk/ government/organisations/department-for-transport.

HM Treasury: 1 Horse Guards Rd, London, SW1A 2HQ; tel. (20) 7270-5000; e-mail ministers@hmtreasury.gsi.gov.uk; internet www .hm-treasury.gov.uk.

Wales Office: Gwydyr House, Whitehall, London, SW1A 2NP; tel. (29) 2092-4220; fax (20) 7270-0578; e-mail correspondence@ walesoffice.gsi.gov.uk; internet www.gov.uk/government/ organisations/wales-office.

Department for Work and Pensions: Caxton House, Tothill St, London, SW1H 9DA; tel. (20) 3267-5144; e-mail ministers@dwp.gsi .gov.uk; internet www.gov.uk/government/organisations/ department-for-work-pensions.

Legislature

PARLIAMENT

House of Commons

House of Commons Information Office, Norman Shaw North, London, SW1A 2TT; tel. (20) 7219-4272; e-mail hcinfo@parliament.uk; internet www.parliament.uk.

Speaker: JOHN BERCOW.

Chairman of Ways and Means and Deputy Speaker: LINDSAY HOYLE.

General Election, 6 May 2010

	Votes	% of votes	Seats*
Conservative Party . . .	10,703,754	36.05	304
Labour Party	8,609,527	29.00	256
Liberal Democrats . . .	6,836,824	23.03	57
Democratic Unionist Party .	168,216	0.57	8
Scottish National Party .	491,386	1.65	6
Sinn Féin	171,942	0.58	5
Plaid Cymru	165,394	0.56	3
Social Democratic and Labour Party . . .	110,970	0.37	3
Others	2,433,367	8.20	8†
Total	29,691,380	100.00	650

* Seats as at April 2013.
† Including the Speaker and three deputies.

House of Lords
(May 2013)

Lord Speaker: Baroness D'SOUZA.

Lord Chairman of Committees and Deputy Speaker: Lord SEWEL.

Distribution of seats at May 2013

	Life Peers	Hereditary Peers	Archbishops and Bishops	Total
Labour Party . .	216	4	—	220
Conservative Party	162	48	—	210
Liberal Democrats .	85	4	—	89
Crossbench . .	150	31	—	181
Others . . .	33	1	25	59
Total . . .	646	88	25	759*

* Excluding 39 members on leave of absence, 10 disqualified as senior members of the judiciary and one disqualified as a member of the European Parliament.

The Legislative Authorities and Executive Bodies of Northern Ireland, Scotland and Wales

New constitutional arrangements for Northern Ireland entered into force in 1998, following their approval in a popular referendum. Responsibility for all matters formerly implemented by the Northern Ireland Office was transferred to the new devolved institutions in 1999; however, the institutions were suspended and direct rule by the British Government was reimposed in 2000 and from 2002–07, owing to a series of political impasses. Responsibility for justice and policing was transferred to the devolved institutions in April 2010. The 108-member Northern Ireland Assembly is elected for a term of four years under a form of proportional representation by means of the single transferable vote in multi-member constituencies. Members are required to designate themselves as 'Nationalist', 'Unionist', or 'Other', and certain decisions of the Assembly must be approved by a majority both of Nationalist and Unionist members. A power-sharing Executive Committee, headed by a First Minister and a Deputy First Minister (who must represent the largest party in each of the two main communities, respectively), is elected from among the Assembly members.

Devolved legislative authorities for Scotland and Wales were established in 1999. An executive level of government, headed by a First Minister, was also established for each country. The Scottish Parliament has powers to legislate on all domestic matters, including education, health, local government and law and order. It is also empowered to vary the rate of income tax set by the United Kingdom Government by up to 3%. The National Assembly for Wales (Cynulliad Cenedlaethol Cymru) exercises responsibility for issues formerly covered by the Wales Office of the United Kingdom Government. Initially the Assembly could only initiate secondary legislation in areas under its control, but in 2007 it was granted powers to initiate primary legislation—known as Assembly Measures—in its fields of competence, subject to prior approval by the British Parliament. At a referendum held in Wales on 3 March 2011, 63.5% of those participating (35.3% of the electorate) voted in favour of the Assembly being granted direct law-making powers in the currently devolved areas, including education, health and local government. Later that month the Welsh First Minister signed a commencement order giving the Assembly direct law-making powers, following its approval by the Assembly's members. In November 2010 a bill providing for the transfer of additional, mainly fiscal, powers to the Scottish Parliament was introduced in the House of Commons; under the terms of the Scotland Act 2012, the Scottish Parliament was, from 2016, to control the setting of levels of income tax within Scotland. (The control of certain other taxes was expected to be devolved to the Scottish Parliament in 2015.) Both the Scottish Parliament and the National Assembly for Wales are elected, for a term of four years, by a combined system of direct voting in single-member constituencies and a form of proportional representation, whereby additional members are elected from a party list on the basis of larger, multi-member constituencies.

NORTHERN IRELAND

Northern Ireland Assembly

Parliament Bldgs, Ballymiscaw, Belfast, BT4 3XX; tel. (28) 9052-1333; fax (28) 9052-1961; e-mail info.office@niassembly.gov.uk; internet www.niassembly.gov.uk.

Presiding Officer (Speaker): WILLIAM HAY.

Election, 5 May 2011

	First preference votes	% of first preference votes	Seats
Democratic Unionist Party	198,436	29.98	38
Sinn Féin	178,222	26.93	29
Ulster Unionist Party .	87,531	13.23	16
Social Democratic and Labour Party . . .	94,286	14.24	14
Alliance Party . . .	50,875	7.69	8
Traditional Unionist Voice	16,480	2.49	1
Green Party . . .	6,031	0.91	1
Independents . . .	3,003	0.45	1
Total (incl. others) . .	670,778	100.00	108

Executive Committee
(May 2013)

A power-sharing executive, comprising the Democratic Unionist Party (DUP), Sinn Féin (SF), the Ulster Unionist Party (UUP), the Social Democratic and Labour Party (SDLP) and the Alliance Party (AP).

First Minister: PETER ROBINSON (DUP).

Deputy First Minister: MARTIN McGUINNESS (SF).

Minister of Finance and Personnel: SAMMY WILSON (DUP).

Minister of Education: JOHN O'DOWD (SF).

Minister of Enterprise, Trade and Investment: ARLENE FOSTER (DUP).

Minister of Health, Social Services and Public Safety: EDWIN POOTS (DUP).

Minister for Social Development: NELSON MCCAUSLAND (DUP).

Minister for Employment and Learning: Dr STEPHEN FARRY (AP).

Minister of Justice: DAVID FORD (AP).

Minister of the Environment: ALEX ATTWOOD (SDLP).

Minister of Culture, Arts and Leisure: CARÁL NÍ CHUILÍN (SF).

Minister for Regional Development: DANNY KENNEDY (UUP).

Minister of Agriculture and Rural Development: MICHELLE O'NEILL (SF).

SCOTLAND

Scottish Parliament

Edinburgh, EH99 1SP; tel. (131) 348-5000; fax (131) 348-5601; e-mail sp.info@scottish.parliament.uk; internet www.scottish.parliament.uk.

Presiding Officer: TRICIA MARWICK.

Election, 5 May 2011

	Total votes	%	Seats
Scottish National Party	1,779,336	44.70	69
Labour Party	1,154,020	28.99	37
Conservative Party	522,619	13.13	15
Liberal Democrats	261,186	6.56	5
Others	263,112	6.61	3*
Total	3,980,273	100.00	129

Note: Table includes constituency and regional results.

* Comprises two seats for the Scottish Green Party and one for an independent candidate.

Scottish Government
(May 2013)

The Government is formed by the Scottish National Party.

First Minister: ALEX SALMOND.

Deputy First Minister and Cabinet Secretary for Infrastructure, Investment and Cities: NICOLA STURGEON.

Cabinet Secretary for Health and Wellbeing: ALEX NEIL.

Cabinet Secretary for Finance, Employment and Sustainable Growth: JOHN SWINNEY.

Cabinet Secretary for Education and Lifelong Learning: MICHAEL RUSSELL.

Cabinet Secretary for Justice: KENNY MACASKILL.

Cabinet Secretary for Rural Affairs and the Environment: RICHARD LOCHHEAD.

Cabinet Secretary for Culture and External Affairs: FIONA HYSLOP.

Minister for Transport and Veteran Affairs: KEITH BROWN.

Minister for Welfare and Housing: MARGARET BURGESS.

Minister for Commonwealth Games and Sport: SHONA ROBISON.

Minister for Public Health: MICHAEL MATHESON.

Minister for Energy, Enterprise and Tourism: FERGUS EWING.

Minister for Local Government and Planning: DEREK MACKAY.

Minister for Children and Young People: AILEEN CAMPBELL.

Minister for Youth Employment: ANGELA CONSTANCE.

Minister for Learning, Science and Scotland's Languages: Dr ALASDAIR ALLAN.

Minister for Parliamentary Business and Chief Whip: JOE FITZPATRICK.

Minister for Community Safety and Legal Affairs: ROSEANNA CUNNINGHAM.

Minister for Environment and Climate Change: PAUL WHEELHOUSE.

Minister for External Affairs and International Development: HUMZA YOUSAF.

Lord Advocate: FRANK MULHOLLAND.

Solicitor-General: LESLEY THOMSON.

WALES

National Assembly for Wales
(Cynulliad Cenedlaethol Cymru)

Cardiff Bay, Cardiff, CF99 1NA; tel. (800) 010-5500; e-mail assembly.info@wales.gov.uk; internet www.assemblywales.org.

Presiding Officer: ROSEMARY BUTLER.

Election, 5 May 2011

	Total votes	%	Seats
Labour Party	751,612	39.58	30
Conservative Party	451,161	23.76	14
Plaid Cymru	352,706	18.58	11
Liberal Democrats	176,608	9.30	5
Others	166,553	8.77	0
Total	1,898,640	100.00	60

Note: Table includes constituency and regional results.

Welsh Government
(May 2013)

The Government is formed by the Welsh Labour Party.

First Minister: CARWYN JONES.

Minister for Finance and Leader of the House: JANE HUTT.

Minister for Education and Skills: LEIGHTON ANDREWS.

Minister for Natural Resources and Food: ALUN DAVIES.

Minister for Health and Social Services: Prof. MARK DRAKEFORD.

Minister for Culture and Sport: JOHN GRIFFITHS.

Minister for Local Government and Government Business: LESLEY GRIFFITHS.

Minister for Economy, Science and Transport: EDWINA HART.

Minister for Communities and Tackling Poverty: HUW LEWIS.

Minister for Housing and Regeneration: CARL SARGEANT.

Counsel-General: THEODORE HUCKLE.

Election Commission

The Electoral Commission: 3 Bunhill Row, London, EC1Y 8YZ; tel. (20) 7271-0500; fax (20) 7271-0505; e-mail info@electoralcommission.org.uk; internet www.electoralcommission.org.uk; f. 2000; Chair. JENNY WATSON; Chief Exec. PETER WARDLE.

Political Organizations

Alliance Party of Northern Ireland: 88 University St, Belfast, BT7 1HE; tel. (28) 9032-4274; fax (28) 9033-3147; e-mail alliance@allianceparty.org; internet allianceparty.org; f. 1970; non-sectarian and non-doctrinaire party of the centre, attracting support from within both Catholic and Protestant sections of the community in Northern Ireland; 1,500 mems; Leader DAVID FORD.

British National Party: POB 213, Wigton, CA7 7AL; e-mail enquiries@bnp.org.uk; internet www.bnp.org.uk; f. 1982 as a breakaway faction from the National Front; Leader NICK GRIFFIN.

Conservative Party (Conservative and Unionist Party): 30 Millbank, London, SW1P 4DP; tel. (20) 7222-9000; fax (20) 7222-1135; internet www.conservatives.com; f. 1834; mem. of the International Democrat Union and the European Democrat Union; in the European Parliament part of the European Conservatives and Reformists; 320,000 mems (adherent on a local, rather than national, basis); Leader DAVID CAMERON; Co-Chairs GRANT SHAPPS, ANDREW FELDMAN.

Northern Ireland Conservatives (NI Conservatives): 84 High St, Bangor, Belfast, BT20 5BA; tel. (28) 9185-9073; internet www.niconservatives.com; party has no Assembly members, but is represented at council level; fmrly called Conservative Party in Northern Ireland; re-launched in 2012 under the present name; Chair. IRWIN ARMSTRONG.

Scottish Conservative & Unionist Party: 67 Northumberland St, Edinburgh, EH3 6JG; tel. (131) 524-0030; fax (131) 524-0049; e-mail info@scottishconservatives.com; internet www.scottishconservatives.com; Chair. DAVID MUNDELL; Leader RUTH DAVIDSON.

Welsh Conservative Party: Ground Floor, Rhymney House, 1–2 Copse Walk, Cardiff Gate Business Park, Cardiff, CF23 8RB; tel. (29) 2073-6562; e-mail info@welshconservatives.com; internet www.welshconservatives.com; Chair. JEFF JAMES; Assembly Leader ANDREW R. T. DAVIES.

Co-operative Party: 77 Weston St, London, SE1 3SD; tel. (20) 7367-4150; fax (20) 7407-4476; e-mail mail@party.coop; internet www.party.coop; f. 1917; under an Agreement with the Labour Party it is recognized as the political party representing the co-operative movement, and fields candidates, jtly with the Labour Party, who are Labour and Co-operative candidates at local and British parliamentary elections; promotes the principles of the co-operative movement;

seeks to extend co-operative enterprise and cares for the interests of the consumer; individual mems in 200 brs; 47 societies are affiliated; Chair. GARETH THOMAS; Gen. Sec. KARIN CHRISTIANSEN.

Democratic Unionist Party (DUP): 91 Dundela Ave, Belfast, BT4 3BU; tel. (28) 9047-1155; fax (28) 9052-1289; e-mail info@mydup .com; internet www.mydup.com; f. 1971 as the successor to the Protestant Unionist Party; upholds the union of Northern Ireland with the United Kingdom; Leader PETER ROBINSON.

Green Party: 56–64 Development House, Leonard St, London, EC2A 4LT; tel. (20) 7549-0310; fax (20) 7549-0318; e-mail office@ greenparty.org.uk; internet www.greenparty.org.uk; f. 1973 as People, adopted the name Ecology Party in 1975; present name adopted 1985; campaigns for the protection of the environment and the promotion of social justice; approx. 12,000 mems; Leader NATALIE BENNETT; Chair. TIM DAWES (2012–13).

Labour Party: One Brewer's Green, London SW1H 0RH; tel. (845) 092–2299; e-mail info@new.labour.org.uk; internet www2.labour .org.uk; f. 1900; affiliated to the Socialist International and the Party of European Socialists; 15 trade unions are affiliated to the party through the Trade Union and Labour Party Liaison Organisation; Leader ED MILIBAND; Dep. Leader and Chair. HARRIET HARMAN; Gen. Sec. IAIN MCNICOL.

> **Scottish Labour:** 290 Bath St, Glasgow, G2 4RE; tel. (141) 572-6900; fax (141) 572-2566; e-mail scotland@new.labour.org.uk; internet www.scottishlabour.org.uk; Leader JOHANN LAMONT; Gen. Sec. IAN PRICE.

> **Welsh Labour:** 1 Cathedral Rd, Cardiff, CF11 9HA; tel. (29) 2087-7700; fax (29) 2022-1153; e-mail wales@labour.org.uk; internet www.welshlabour.org.uk; Leader CARWYN JONES.

Liberal Democrats: 8–10 Great George St, London, SW1P 3AE; tel. (20) 7222-7999; fax (20) 7799-2170; internet www.libdems.org.uk; f. 1988, following the merger of the Liberal Party (f. 1877) and the Social Democratic Party (f. 1981, disbanded 1990); c. 65,000 mems; Leader NICK CLEGG; Pres. TIM FARRON.

> **Scottish Liberal Democrats:** 4 Clifton Terrace, Edinburgh, EH12 5DR; tel. (131) 337-2314; fax (131) 337-3566; e-mail administration@scotlibdems.org.uk; internet www.scotlibdems .org.uk; Leader WILLIE RENNIE.

> **Welsh Liberal Democrats:** Freedom Central, Blake Court, Schooner Way, Cardiff, CF10 4DW; tel. (29) 2031-3400; fax (29) 2031-3401; e-mail enquiries@welshlibdems.org.uk; internet www .welshlibdems.org.uk; Leader KIRSTY WILLIAMS.

Plaid Cymru—Party of Wales: Tŷ Gwynfor, Anson Court, Atlantic Wharf, Cardiff, CF10 4AL; tel. (29) 2047-2272; fax (29) 2064-6001; e-mail post@plaidcymru.org; internet www.plaidcymru.org; f. 1925; promotes Welsh interests and seeks independence for Wales; 10,000 mems; Leader LEANNE WOOD; Pres. JILL EVANS.

Progressive Unionist Party: 299 Newtownards Rd, Belfast, BT4 1AG; tel. (28) 9022-5040; fax (28) 9022-5041; e-mail info@pupni.com; internet progressiveunionistparty.org; loyalist party in Northern Ireland; Leader BILLY HUTCHINSON.

Respect: POB 167, Manchester, M19 0AH; tel. (7794) 192-670; e-mail office@respectparty.info; internet www.respectparty.org; f. 2004; left-wing; Nat. Sec. CHRIS CHILVERS.

Scottish Green Party: Bonnington Mill 72, Newhaven Rd, Edinburgh, EH6 5QG; tel. (870) 0772207; internet www.scottishgreens .org.uk; f. 1990; ecologist; Co-Convenors PATRICK HARVIE, MARTHA WARDROP.

Scottish National Party (SNP): Gordon Lamb House, 3 Jackson's Entry, Edinburgh, EH8 8PJ; tel. (800) 633-5432; fax (131) 525-8901; e-mail info@snp.org; internet www.snp.org; f. 1934; advocates independence for Scotland as a member of the EU and Scottish control of national resources; Leader ALEX SALMOND.

Scottish Socialist Party (SSP): Central Chambers, Suite 370, 4th Floor, 93 Hope St, Glasgow, G2 6LD; tel. (141) 221-7470; internet www.scottishsocialistparty.org; f. 1999; Co-Spokespersons COLIN FOX, SANDRA WEBSTER; Nat. Sec. KEVIN MCVEY.

Sinn Féin (We Ourselves): 53 Falls Rd, Belfast, BT12 4PD; tel. (28) 9034-7350; fax (28) 9022-3001; e-mail admin@sinnfein.ie; internet www.sinnfein.ie; f. 1905; seeks the reunification of Ireland and the establishment of a 32-county democratic socialist state; engages in community politics; Pres. GERRY ADAMS; Chair. DECLAN KEARNEY; Gen. Sec. DAWN DOYLE.

Social Democratic and Labour Party (SDLP): 121 Ormeau Rd, Belfast, BT7 1SH; tel. (28) 9024-7700; fax (28) 9023-6699; e-mail info@sdlp.ie; internet www.sdlp.ie; f. 1970; radical, left-of-centre principles with a view to the eventual reunification of Ireland by popular consent; Leader Dr ALASDAIR MCDONNELL.

Socialist Labour Party: POB 112, Leigh, WN7 4WS; tel. and fax (1942) 603335; e-mail info@socialist-labour-party.org.uk; internet www.socialist-labour-party.org.uk; f. 1996; supports renationaliza-

tion of industry, constitutional reform, withdrawal from the European Union; Pres. ANDREW JORDAN.

Socialist Party: POB 24697, London, E11 1YD; tel. (20) 8988-8777; e-mail info@socialistparty.org.uk; internet www.socialistparty.org .uk; f. 1991 as Militant Labour by fmr members of the Militant tendency (an extreme-left faction within the Labour Party); present name adopted 1997; registered with the Electoral Commission under the name Socialist Alternative; mem. of the Committee for a Workers' International (CWI); Gen. Sec. PETER TAAFFE.

Socialist Workers' Party (SWP): POB 42184, London, SW8 2WD; tel. (20) 7819-1170; fax (20) 7819-1179; e-mail enquiries@swp.org.uk; internet www.swp.org.uk; f. 1950; advocates workers' control through revolution, not reform; Nat. Sec. CHARLIE KIMBER.

Solidarity—Scotland's Socialist Movement: POB 7565, Glasgow, G42 2DN; e-mail info@solidarityscotland.org; internet www .solidarityscotland.org; f. 2006 by disaffected mems of the Scottish Socialist Party; Nat. Sec. GRAEME MCIVER.

Traditional Unionist Voice (TUV): 38 Henry St, Ballymena, Belfast, BT42 3AH; tel. (28) 2564-0250; internet www.tuv.org.uk; f. 2007 by fmr members of Democratic Unionist Party opposed to power sharing in Northern Ireland; Leader JIM ALLISTER.

UK Independence Party (UKIP): POB 408, Newton Abbot, Devon, TQ12 9BG; tel. (1626) 831290; fax (1626) 831348; e-mail mail@ukip.org; internet www.ukip.org; f. 1994; advocates withdrawal from the European Union; 27,000 mems; Leader NIGEL FARAGE; Exec. Chair. STEVE CROWTHER.

Ulster Unionist Party: Strandtown Hall, 2–4 Belmont Rd, Belfast, BT4 2AN; tel. (28) 9047-4630; fax (28) 9065-2149; e-mail uup@uup .org; internet www.uup.org; f. 1905; governed Northern Ireland 1921–72; supports parity and equality for Northern Ireland within the United Kingdom; Leader MIKE NESBITT.

Veritas: Albany House, Office 404, 4th Floor, 324–326 Regent St, London, W1B 3HH; tel. (870) 7606148; e-mail info@veritas-party .com; internet www.veritasparty.com; f. 2005; advocates withdrawal from the European Union; Leader THERESE MUCHEWICZ.

Diplomatic Representation

EMBASSIES AND HIGH COMMISSIONS IN THE UNITED KINGDOM

Afghanistan: 31 Prince's Gate, London, SW7 1QQ; tel. (20) 7589-8891; fax (20) 7584-4801; e-mail contacts@afghanistanembassy.org .uk; internet www.afghanistanembassy.org.uk; Ambassador MOHAMMAD DAUD YAAR.

Albania: 33 St George's Drive, London, SW1V 4DG; tel. (20) 7828-8897; fax (20) 7828-8869; e-mail embassy.london@mfa.gov.al; internet www.albanianembassy.co.uk; Ambassador MAL BERISHA.

Algeria: 54 Holland Park, London, W11 3RS; tel. (20) 7299-7077; fax (20) 7229-7076; e-mail info@algerianembassy.org.uk; internet www .algerianembassy.org.uk; Ambassador AMAR ABBA.

Angola: 22 Dorset St, London, W1U 6QY; tel. (20) 7299-9850; fax (20) 7486-9397; e-mail embassy@angola.org.uk; internet www.angola .org.uk; Ambassador MIGUEL GASPAR FERNANDES.

Antigua and Barbuda: 45 Crawford Pl., 2nd Floor, London, W1H 4LP; tel. (20) 7258-0070; fax (20) 7258-7486; e-mail enquiries@ antigua-barbuda.com; internet www.antigua-barbuda.com; High Commr Dr CARL ROBERTS.

Argentina: 65 Brook St, London, W1K 4AH; tel. (20) 7318-1300; fax (20) 7318-1301; e-mail info@argentine-embassy-uk.org; internet www.argentine-embassy-uk.org; Ambassador ALICIA AMALIA CASTRO.

Armenia: 25A Cheniston Gdns, London, W8 6TG; tel. (20) 7938-5435; fax (20) 7938-2595; e-mail armemb@armenianembassyuk .com; internet www.uk.mfa.am; Ambassador (vacant).

Australia: Australia House, Strand, London, WC2B 4LA; tel. (20) 7379-4334; fax (20) 7240-5333; internet www.uk.embassy.gov.au; High Commr MIKE RANN.

Austria: 18 Belgrave Mews West, London, SW1X 8HU; tel. (20) 7344-3250; fax (20) 7344-0292; e-mail london-ob@bmeia.gv.at; internet www.bmeia.gv.at/london; Ambassador Dr EMIL BRIX.

Azerbaijan: 4 Kensington Court, London, W8 5DL; tel. (20) 7938-3412; fax (20) 7937-1783; e-mail london@mission.mfa.gov.az; internet www.azembassy.org.uk; Ambassador FAKHRADDIN GURBANOV.

Bahamas: 10 Chesterfield St, London, W1J 5JL; tel. (20) 7408-4488; fax (20) 7499-9937; e-mail information@bahamashclondon.net; internet www.bahamashclondon.net; High Commr ELDRED EDISON BETHEL.

Bahrain: 30 Belgrave Sq., London, SW1X 8QB; tel. (20) 7201-9170; fax (20) 7201-9183; e-mail information@bahrainembassy.co.uk;

internet www.bahrainembassy.co.uk; Ambassador ALICE THOMAS SAMAAN.

Bangladesh: 28 Queen's Gate, London, SW7 5JA; tel. (20) 7584-0081; fax (20) 7581-7477; e-mail info@bhclondon.org.uk; internet www.bhclondon.org.uk; High Commr Dr MOHAMED MIJARUL QUAYES.

Barbados: 1 Great Russell St, London, WC1B 3ND; tel. (20) 7299-7150; fax (20) 7323-6872; e-mail london@foreign.gov.bb; High Commr HUGH ANTHONY ARTHUR.

Belarus: 6 Kensington Court, London, W8 5DL; tel. (20) 7937-3288; fax (20) 7361-0005; e-mail uk.london@mfa.gov.by; internet uk.mfa.gov.by; Ambassador SERGEI ALEINIK.

Belgium: 17 Grosvenor Cres., London, SW1X 7EE; tel. (20) 7470-3700; fax (20) 7470-3795; e-mail london@diplobel.fed.be; internet www.diplomatie.be/london; Ambassador JOHAN VERBEKE.

Belize: 45 Crawford Pl., 3rd Floor, London, W1H 4LP; tel. (20) 7723-3603; fax (20) 7723-9637; e-mail bzhc-lon@btconnect.com; internet www.belizehighcommission.com; High Commr PERLA PERDOMO.

Bolivia: 106 Eaton Sq., London, SW1W 9AD; tel. (20) 7235-4255; fax (20) 7235-1286; e-mail embol@bolivianembassy.co.uk; internet www.bolivianembassy.co.uk; Chargé d'affaires a.i. VERÓNICA PAOLA ARGOTE.

Bosnia and Herzegovina: 5–7 Lexham Gdns, London, W8 5JJ; tel. (20) 7373-0867; fax (20) 7373-0871; e-mail embassy@bhembassy.co.uk; internet www.bhembassy.co.uk; Ambassador MUSTAFA MUJEZINOVIĆ.

Botswana: 6 Stratford Pl., London, W1C 1AY; tel. (20) 7499-0031; fax (20) 7495-8595; e-mail bohico@govbw.com; High Commr ROY BLACKBEARD.

Brazil: 14–16 Cockspur St, London, SW1Y 5BL; tel. (20) 7399-9000; fax (20) 7399-9100; e-mail info@brazil.org.uk; internet www.brazil.org.uk; Ambassador ROBERTO JAGUARIBE.

Brunei: 19–20 Belgrave Sq., London, SW1X 8PG; tel. (20) 7581-0521; fax (20) 7235-9717; e-mail info@bdhcl.co.uk; High Commr MOHD AZIYAN bin ABDULLAH.

Bulgaria: 186–188 Queen's Gate, London, SW7 5HL; tel. (20) 7584-9400; fax (20) 7584-4948; e-mail ambass.office@bulgarianembassy.org.uk; internet www.bulgarianembassy-london.org; Ambassador KONSTANTIN DIMITROV.

Burundi: Uganda House, 2nd Floor, 58–59 Trafalgar Sq., London, WC2N 5DX; tel. (20) 7930-4958; fax (20) 7930-4957; e-mail info@burundiembassy.org.uk; internet www.burundiembassy.org.uk; Chargé d'affaires a.i. BERNARD NTAHIRAJA.

Cambodia: 64 Brondesbury Park, Willesden Green, London, NW6 7AT; tel. (20) 8451-7997; fax (20) 8451-7594; e-mail cambodianembassy@btconnect.com; internet www.cambodianembassy.org.uk; Ambassador HOR NAMBORA.

Cameroon: 84 Holland Park, London, W11 3SB; tel. (20) 7727-0771; fax (20) 7792-9353; e-mail info@cameroonhighcommission.co.uk; internet www.cameroonhighcommission.co.uk; High Commr NKWELLE EKANEY.

Canada: MacDonald House, 1 Grosvenor Sq., London, W1K 4AB; tel. (20) 7258-6600; fax (20) 7258-6333; e-mail ldn@international.gc.ca; internet www.london.gc.ca; High Commr GORDON CAMPBELL.

Chile: 37–41 Old Queen St, London, SW1H 9JA; tel. (20) 7222-2361; fax (20) 7222-0861; e-mail embachile@embachile.co.uk; Ambassador TOMAS MÜLLER.

China, People's Republic: 49–51 Portland Pl., London, W1B 4JL; tel. (20) 7299-4049; fax (20) 7636-5578; e-mail press_uk@mfa.gov.cn; internet www.chinese-embassy.org.uk; Ambassador LIU XIAOMING.

Colombia: 3 Hans Cres., London, SW1X OLN; tel. (20) 7589-9177; fax (20) 7581-1829; e-mail egranbretana@cancilleria.gov.co; internet www.colombianembassy.co.uk; Ambassador JOSÉ MAURICIO RODRÍGUEZ MÚNERA.

Congo, Democratic Republic: 45–49 Great Portland St, London, W1W 7LD; tel. (20) 7580-3931; fax (20) 7580-8713; e-mail info@ambardc-londres.gov.cd; internet www.ambardc-londres.gov.cd; Ambassador BARNABE KIKAYA BIN KARUBI.

Costa Rica: 14 Lancaster Gate, London, W2 3LH; tel. (20) 7706-8844; fax (20) 7706-8655; e-mail info@costaricaembassy.co.uk; Ambassador PILAR SABORÍO DE ROCAFORT.

Côte d'Ivoire: 2 Upper Belgrave St, London, SW1X 8BJ; tel. (20) 7235-6991; fax (20) 7259-5320; Ambassador CLAUDE STANISLAS BOUAH-KAMON.

Croatia: 21 Conway St, London, W1T 6BN; tel. (20) 7387-2022; fax (20) 7387-0310; e-mail vrhlon@mvep.hr; internet uk.mfa.hr; Ambassador Dr IVAN GRDEŠIC.

Cuba: 167 High Holborn, London, WC1V 6PA; tel. (20) 7240-2488; fax (20) 7836-2602; e-mail embacuba@cubaldn.com; Ambassador ESTHER ARMENTEROS.

Cyprus: 13 St James's Sq., London, SW1Y 4LB; tel. (20) 7321-4100; fax (20) 7321-4164; e-mail cyphclondon@btconnect.com; internet www.mfa.gov.cy/highcomlondon; High Commr ALEXANDROS N. ZENON.

Czech Republic: 26 Kensington Palace Gdns, London, W8 4QY; tel. (20) 7243-1115; fax (20) 7727-9654; e-mail london@embassy.mzv.cz; internet www.mzv.cz/london; Ambassador MICHAEL ŽANTOVSKÝ.

Denmark: 55 Sloane St, London, SW1X 9SR; tel. (20) 7333-0200; fax (20) 7333-0270; e-mail lonamb@um.dk; internet www.amblondon.um.dk; Ambassador ANNE HEDENSTED STEFFENSEN.

Dominica: 1 Collingham Gdns, London, SW5 0HW; tel. (20) 7370-5194; fax (20) 7373-8743; e-mail info@dominicahighcommission.co.uk; internet www.dominicahighcommission.co.uk; High Commr FRANCINE BARON.

Dominican Republic: 139 Inverness Terrace, London, W2 6JF; tel. (20) 7727-7091; fax (20) 7727-3693; e-mail info@dominicanembassy.org.uk; internet www.dominicanembassy.org.uk; Ambassador Dr FEDERICO ALBERTO CUELLO CAMILO.

Ecuador: Flat 3B, 3 Hans Cres., London, SW1X 0LS; tel. (20) 7584-1367; fax (20) 7590-2509; e-mail eecugranbretania@mmrree.gov.ec; Ambassador ANA ALBÁN MORA.

Egypt: 26 South St, London, W1K 1DW; tel. (20) 7499-3304; fax (20) 7491-1542; e-mail eg.emb_london@mfa.gov.eg; Ambassador MUHAMMAD ASHRAF EM KAMAL ELKHOLY.

El Salvador: 8 Dorset Sq., 1st and 2nd Floors, London, NW1 6PU; tel. (20) 7224-9800; fax (20) 7224-9878; e-mail elsalvador.embassy@gmail.com; Ambassador WERNER MATÍAS ROMERO.

Equatorial Guinea: 13 Park Pl., St James's, London, SW1A 1LP; tel. (20) 7499-6867; fax (20) 7499-6782; e-mail embarege-londres@embarege-londres.org; internet www.embarege-londres.org; Ambassador MARI-CRUZ EVUNA ANDEME.

Eritrea: 96 White Lion St, London, N1 9PF; tel. (20) 7713-0096; fax (20) 7713-0161; e-mail paamba@erimbauk.com; Ambassador TESFAMICAEL GERAHTU OGBAGHIORGHIS.

Estonia: 16 Hyde Park Gate, London, SW7 5DG; tel. (20) 7589-3428; fax (20) 7589-3430; e-mail london@mfa.ee; internet www.estonia.gov.uk; Ambassador Dr AINO VON WIRÉN.

Ethiopia: 17 Prince's Gate, London, SW7 1PZ; tel. (20) 7589-7212; fax (20) 7584-7054; e-mail info@ethioembassy.org.uk; internet www.ethioembassy.org.uk; Ambassador BERHANU KEBEDE.

Fiji: 34 Hyde Park Gate, London, SW7 5DN; tel. (20) 7584-3661; fax (20) 7584-2838; e-mail mail@fijihighcommission.org.uk; internet www.fijihighcommission.org.uk; High Commr SOLO MARA.

Finland: 38 Chesham Pl., London, SW1X 8HW; tel. (20) 7838-6200; fax (20) 7235-3680; e-mail sanomat.lon@formin.fi; internet www.finemb.org.uk; Ambassador PEKKA HUHTANIEMI.

France: 58 Knightsbridge, London, SW1X 7JT; tel. (20) 7073-1000; fax (20) 7073-1004; e-mail presse.londres-amba@diplomatie.gouv.fr; internet www.ambafrance-uk.org; Ambassador BERNARD EMIÉ.

Gabon: 27 Elvaston Pl., London, SW7 5NL; tel. (20) 7823-9986; fax (20) 7584-0047; Ambassador OMER PIANKALI.

The Gambia: 92 Ledbury Rd, London, W11 2AH; tel. (20) 7229-8066; fax (20) 7229-9225; e-mail gambiahighcomuk@btconnect.com; High Commr ELIZABETH YA ELI HARDING.

Georgia: 4 Russell Gdns, London, W14 8EZ; tel. (20) 7348-1941; fax (20) 7603-6682; e-mail embassy@geoemb.plus.com; internet www.uk.mfa.gov.ge; Ambassador (vacant).

Germany: 23 Belgrave Sq., London, SW1X 8PZ; tel. (20) 7824-1300; fax (20) 7824-1435; e-mail info@london.diplo.de; internet www.london.diplo.de; Ambassador GEORG BOOMGAARDEN.

Ghana: 13 Belgrave Sq., London, SW1X 8PN; tel. (20) 7201-5921; fax (20) 7245-9552; e-mail information@ghanahighcommissionuk.com; internet www.ghanahighcommissionuk.com; High Commr KWAKU DANSO-BOAFO.

Greece: 1A Holland Park, London, W11 3TP; tel. (20) 7229-3850; fax (20) 7229-7221; e-mail political@greekembassy.org.uk; internet www.greekembassy.org.uk; Ambassador KONSTANTINOS BIKAS.

Grenada: The Chapel, Archel Rd, London, W14 9QH; tel. (20) 7385-4415; fax (20) 7381-4807; e-mail office@grenada-highcommission.co.uk; internet www.grenadahclon.co.uk; High Commr RUTH ELIZABETH ROUSE.

Guatemala: 13 Fawcett St, London, SW10 9HN; tel. (20) 7351-3042; e-mail info@guatemalanembassy.co.uk; Ambassador ACISCLO VALLADARES MOLINA.

Guinea: 258 Belsize Rd, London, NW6 4BT; tel. (20) 7316-1861; e-mail office@ambaguinee-london.co.uk; Chargé d'affaires a.i. SANGARE RAMATOULAYE.

Guyana: 3 Palace Court, Bayswater Rd, London, W2 4LP; tel. (20) 7229-7684; fax (20) 7727-9809; e-mail guyanahc1@btconnect.com; internet www.guyanahclondon.co.uk; High Commr LALESHWAR K. N. SINGH.

Holy See: 54 Parkside, London, SW19 5NE (Apostolic Nunciature); tel. (20) 8944-7189; fax (20) 8947-2494; e-mail nuntius@globalnet.co .uk; Apostolic Nuncio Most Rev. ANTONIO MENNINI (Titular Archbishop of Ferentium).

Honduras: 115 Gloucester Pl., London, W1U 6JT; tel. (20) 7486-4880; fax (20) 7486-4550; e-mail hondurasuk@lineone.net; internet www.hondurasembassy.co.uk; Ambassador IVÁN ROMERO-MARTÍNEZ.

Hungary: 35 Eaton Pl., London, SW1X 8BY; tel. (20) 7201-3440; fax (20) 7823-1348; e-mail mission.lon@mfa.gov.hu; internet www.mfa .gov.hu/emb/london; Ambassador JÁNOS CSÁK.

Iceland: 2A Hans St, London, SW1X 0JE; tel. (20) 7259-3999; fax (20) 7245-9649; e-mail icemb.london@utn.stjr.is; internet www.iceland .is/uk; Ambassador BENEDIKT JÓNSSON.

India: India House, Aldwych, London, WC2B 4NA; tel. (20) 7836-8484; fax (20) 7836-4331; e-mail administrativewing@hcilondon.in; internet www.hcilondon.in; High Commr Dr JAIMINI BHAGWATI.

Indonesia: 38 Grosvenor Sq., London, W1X 2HW; tel. (20) 7499-7661; fax (20) 7491-4993; e-mail kbri@btconnect.com; internet www .indonesianembassy.org.uk; Ambassador HAMZAH THAYEB.

Iraq: 421 Queens Gate, London, SW7 5JE; tel. (20) 7590-7650; fax (20) 7590-7679; e-mail lonemb@iraqmofamail.net; internet www .iraqembassy.org.uk; Chargé d'affaires a.i. MUHIEDDIN HUSSEIN ABDALLAH.

Ireland: 17 Grosvenor Pl., London, SW1X 7HR; tel. (20) 7235-2171; fax (20) 7201-6961; e-mail londonembassymail@dfa.ie; internet www .embassyofireland.co.uk; Ambassador BOBBY MCDONAGH.

Israel: 2 Palace Green, London, W8 4QB; tel. (20) 7957-9500; fax (20) 7957-9555; e-mail info@london.mfa.gov.il; internet www .embassyofisrael.co.uk; Ambassador DANIEL TAUB.

Italy: 14 Three Kings Yard, London, W1K 4EH; tel. (20) 7312-2200; fax (20) 7312-2230; e-mail ambasciata.londra@esteri.it; internet www.amblondra.esteri.it; Chargé d'affaires a.i. MARCO MANCINI.

Jamaica: 1–2 Prince Consort Rd, London, SW7 2BZ; tel. (20) 7823-9911; fax (20) 7589-5154; e-mail jamhigh@jhcuk.com; internet www .jhcuk.com; High Commr ALOUN NDOMBET-ASSAMBA.

Japan: 101–104 Piccadilly, London, W1J 7JT; tel. (20) 7465-6500; fax (20) 7491-9348; e-mail info@ld.mofa.go.jp; internet www.uk .emb-japan.go.jp; Ambassador KEIICHI HAYASHI.

Jordan: 6 Upper Phillimore Gdns, London, W8 7HA; tel. (20) 7937-3685; fax (20) 7937-8795; e-mail london@fm.gov.jo; internet www .jordanembassy.org.uk; Ambassador MAZEN HOMOUD.

Kazakhstan: 33 Thurloe Sq., London, SW7 2SD; tel. (20) 7590-3490; fax (20) 7584-8481; e-mail london@kazembassy.org.uk; internet www.kazembassy.org.uk; Ambassador KAIRAT ABUSSEITOV.

Kenya: 45 Portland Pl., London, W1B 1AS; tel. (20) 7636-2371; fax (20) 7323-6717; e-mail info@kenyahighcommission.net; internet www.kenyahighcommission.net; High Commr EPHRAHIM W. NGARE.

Korea, Democratic People's Republic: 73 Gunnersbury Ave, London, W5 4LP; tel. (20) 8992-4965; fax (20) 8992-2053; e-mail dprkembassy@yahoo.co.uk; Ambassador HYON HAK BONG.

Korea, Republic: 60 Buckingham Gate, London, SW1E 6AJ; tel. (20) 7227-5500; fax (20) 7227-5503; e-mail koreanembinuk@mofat.go .kr; internet gbr.mofa.go.kr; Ambassador SUK HWAN PARK.

Kosovo: 100 Pall Mall, London SW1Y 5NQ; tel. (20) 7659-6140; fax (20) 7659-6137; e-mail embassy.uk@rks-gov.net; internet www .ambasada-ks.net/gb; Ambassador LIRIM GREIÇEVCI.

Kuwait: 2 Albert Gate, London, SW1X 7JU; tel. (20) 7590-3400; fax (20) 7823-1712; Ambassador KHALID AL-DUWAISAN.

Kyrgyzstan: Ascot House, 119 Crawford St, London, W1U 6BJ; tel. (20) 7935-1462; fax (20) 7935-7449; e-mail mail@kyrgyz-embassy.org .uk; internet www.kyrgyz-embassy.org.uk; Chargé d'affaires a.i. AIBEK TILEBALIEV.

Latvia: 45 Nottingham Pl., London, W1U 5LY; tel. (20) 7312-0041; fax (20) 7312-0042; e-mail embassy.uk@mfa.gov.lv; internet www .mfa.gov.lv/london; Ambassador EDUARDS STIPRAIS.

Lebanon: 21 Kensington Palace Gdns, London, W8 4RB; tel. (20) 7227-6696; fax (20) 7243-1699; e-mail emb.leb@btinternet.com; Ambassador INAAM OSSEIRAN.

Lesotho: 7 Chesham Pl., London, SW1 8HN; tel. (20) 7235-5686; fax (20) 7235-5023; e-mail lhc@lesotholondon.org.uk; internet www .lesotholondon.org.uk; High Commr MAANA MAPETJA (acting).

Liberia: 23 Fitzroy Sq., London, W1T 6EW; tel. (20) 7388-5489; fax (20) 7380-1593; e-mail info@embassyofliberia.org.uk; internet www .embassyofliberia.org.uk; Ambassador WESLEY MOMO JOHNSON.

Libya: 15 Knightsbridge, London, SW1X 7LY; tel. (20) 7201-8280; fax (20) 7245-0588; internet www.libyanembassy.org.uk; Ambassador MAHMOUD NACUA.

Lithuania: 2 Bessborough Gardens, London SW1V 2JE; tel. (20) 7592-2840; fax (20) 7592-2864; e-mail amb.uk@urm.lt; internet uk .mfa.lt; Ambassador ASTA SKAISGIRYTĖ LIAUŠKIENĖ.

Luxembourg: 27 Wilton Cres., London, SW1X 8SD; tel. (20) 7235-6961; fax (20) 7235-9734; e-mail londres.amb@mae.etat.lu; internet londres.mae.lu; Chargé d'affaires a.i. BÉATRICE KIRSCH.

Macedonia, former Yugoslav republic: Buckingham Court, Suites 2.1 and 2.2, 2nd Floor, 75–83 Buckingham Gate, London, SW1E 6PE; tel. (20) 7976-0535; fax (20) 7976-0539; e-mail sek .london@mfa.gov.mk; internet www.macedonianembassy.org.uk; Ambassador JOVAN DONEV.

Malawi: 36 John St, London, WC1N 2AT; tel. (20) 7421-6010; fax (20) 7831-9273; e-mail malawihighcom@btconnect.com; internet www .malawihighcommission.co.uk; High Commr BERNARD H. SANDE.

Malaysia: 45–46 Belgrave Sq., London, SW1X 8QT; tel. (20) 7235-8033; fax (20) 7235-5161; e-mail mwlon@btconnect.com; internet www.kln.gov.my/web/gbr_london; High Commr Dato' ZAKARIA SULONG.

Maldives: 22 Nottingham Pl., London, W1U 5NJ; tel. (20) 7224-2135; fax (20) 7224-2157; e-mail info@maldiveshighcommission.org; internet www.maldiveshighcommission.org; High Commr AHMED SHIAAN (acting).

Malta: Malta House, 36–38 Piccadilly, London, W1J 0LE; tel. (20) 7292-4800; fax (20) 7734-1831; e-mail maltahighcommission .london@gov.mt; High Commr JOSEPH ZAMMIT TABONA.

Mauritius: 32–33 Elvaston Pl., London, SW7 5NW; tel. (20) 7581-0294; fax (20) 7823-8437; e-mail londonmhc@btinternet.com; High Commr ABHIMANU MAHENDRA KUNDASAMY.

Mexico: 16 St George St, Hanover Sq., London, W1S 1FD; tel. (20) 7499-8586; fax (20) 7495-4035; e-mail mexuk@sre.gob.mx; internet www.sre.gob.mx/reinounido; Ambassador (vacant).

Moldova: 5 Dolphin Sq., Edensor Rd, London, W4 2ST; tel. (20) 8995-6818; fax (20) 8995-6927; e-mail embassy.london@mfa.md; internet www.britania.mfa.gov.md; Ambassador IULIAN FRUNTAŞU.

Monaco: 7 Upper Grosvenor St, London, W1K 2LX; tel. (20) 7318-1081; fax (20) 7493-4563; e-mail embassy@gouv.mc; Ambassador EVELYNE GENTA.

Mongolia: 7–8 Kensington Court, London, W8 5DL; tel. (20) 7937-0150; fax (20) 7937-1117; e-mail office@embassyofmongolia.co.uk; internet www.embassyofmongolia.co.uk; Ambassador BULGAA ALTANGEREL.

Montenegro: 18 Callcott St, London, W8 7SU; tel. (20) 7727-6007; fax (20) 7243-9358; e-mail unitedkingdom@mfa.gov.me; Ambassador LJUBIŠA STANKOVIĆ.

Morocco: 49 Queen's Gate Gdns, London, SW7 5NE; tel. (20) 7581-5001; fax (20) 7225-3862; e-mail ambalondres@maec.gov.ma; internet www.moroccanembassylondon.org.uk; Ambassador Princess CHRIFA LALLA JOUMALA ALAOUI.

Mozambique: 21 Fitzroy Sq., London, W1T 6EL; tel. (20) 7383-3800; fax (20) 7383-3801; internet www.mozambiquehighcommission.org .uk; High Commr CARLOS DOS SANTOS.

Myanmar: 19A Charles St, London, W1J 5DX; tel. (20) 7148-0740; fax (20) 7409-7043; e-mail melondon@btconnect.com; Ambassador KYAW MYO HTUT.

Namibia: 6 Chandos St, London, W1G 9LU; tel. (20) 7636-6244; fax (20) 7637-5694; e-mail info@namibiahc.org.uk; internet www .namibiahc.org.uk; High Commr GEORGE MBANGA LISWANISO.

Nepal: 12A Kensington Palace Gdns, London, W8 4QU; tel. (20) 7229-1594; fax (20) 7792-9861; e-mail eon@nepembassy.org.uk; internet www.nepembassy.org.uk; Ambassador Dr SURESH CHANDRA CHALISE.

Netherlands: 38 Hyde Park Gate, London, SW7 5DP; tel. (20) 7590-3200; fax (20) 7225-0947; e-mail lon@minbuza.nl; internet unitedkingdom.nlembassy.org; Ambassador LAETITIA VAN DEN ASSUM.

New Zealand: New Zealand House, 80 Haymarket, London, SW1Y 4TQ; tel. (20) 7930-8422; fax (20) 7839-4580; e-mail aboutnz@ newzealandhc.org.uk; internet www.nzembassy.com/uk; High Commr Dr LOCKWOOD SMITH.

Nicaragua: Vicarage House, Suite 31, 58–60 Kensington Church St, London, W8 4DB; tel. (20) 7938-2373; fax (20) 7937-0952; e-mail embaniclondon@btconnect.com; Ambassador CARLOS ARGÜELLO GÓMEZ.

Nigeria: Nigeria House, 9 Northumberland Ave, London, WC2N 5BX; tel. (20) 7839-1244; fax (20) 7839-8746; e-mail chancery@ nigeriahc.org; internet www.nigeriahc.org.uk; High Commr Dr DALHATU SARKI TAFIDA.

Norway: 25 Belgrave Sq., London, SW1X 8QD; tel. (20) 7591-5500; fax (20) 7591-5501; e-mail emb.london@mfa.no; internet www .norway.org.uk; Ambassador KIM TRAAVIK.

Oman: 167 Queen's Gate, London, SW7 5HE; tel. (20) 7225-0001; fax (20) 7589-2505; Ambassador ABD AL-AZIZ AL-HINAI.

Pakistan: 34–36 Lowndes Sq., London, SW1X 9JN; tel. (20) 7664-9200; fax (20) 7664-9224; e-mail poldiv@phclondon.org; internet www.phclondon.org; High Commr WAJID SHAMSUL HASAN.

Panama: 40 Hertford St, London, W1J 7SH; tel. (20) 7493-4646; fax (20) 7493-4333; e-mail panama1@btconnect.com; Ambassador ANA IRENE DELGADO.

Papua New Guinea: 14 Waterloo Pl., 3rd Floor, London, SW1R 4AR; tel. (20) 7930-0922; fax (20) 7930-0828; e-mail kunduldn3@btconnect.com; High Commr WINNIE A. KIAP.

Paraguay: 344 Kensington High St, 3rd Floor, London, W14 8NS; tel. (20) 7610-4180; fax (20) 7371-4297; e-mail embapar@btconnect.com; internet www.paraguayembassy.co.uk; Ambassador MIGUEL ANGEL SOLANO LÓPEZ CASCO.

Peru: 52 Sloane St, London, SW1X 9SP; tel. (20) 7235-1917; fax (20) 7235-4463; e-mail postmaster@peruembassy-uk.com; internet www.peruembassy-uk.com; Ambassador JULIO MUÑOZ.

Philippines: 6–8 Suffolk St, London, SW1Y 4HG; tel. (20) 7451-1780; fax (20) 7930-9787; e-mail embassy@philemb.co.uk; internet www.philembassy-uk.org; Ambassador ENRIQUE A. MANALO.

Poland: 47 Portland Pl., London, W1B 1JH; tel. (20) 7291-3520; fax (20) 7291-3575; e-mail london@msz.gov.pl; internet london.mfa.gov.pl; Ambassador WITOLD SOBKÓW.

Portugal: 11 Belgrave Sq., London, SW1X 8PP; tel. (20) 7235-5331; fax (20) 7235-0739; e-mail londres@mne.pt; internet www.portuguese-embassy.co.uk; Ambassador JOÃO DE VALLERA.

Qatar: 1 South Audley St, London, W1K 1NB; tel. (20) 7493-2200; fax (20) 7493-2661; Ambassador KHALID BIN RASHID BIN SALIM AL-HAMOUDI AL-MANSOURI.

Romania: Arundel House, 4 Palace Green, London, W8 4QD; tel. (20) 7937-9666; fax (20) 7937-8069; e-mail londra@mae.ro; internet londra.mae.ro; Ambassador ION JINGA.

Russia: 6–7 Kensington Palace Gdns, London, W8 4QX; tel. (20) 7229-6412; fax (20) 7727-8625; e-mail office@rusemblon.org; internet www.rusemb.org.uk; Ambassador ALEKSANDR YAKOVENKO.

Rwanda: 120–122 Seymour Pl., London, W1H 1NR; tel. (20) 7224-9832; fax (20) 7724-8642; e-mail uk@ambarwanda.org.uk; internet www.rwandahc.org; High Commr WILLIAMS NKURUNZIZA.

Saint Christopher and Nevis: 10 Kensington Court, 2nd Floor, London, W8 5DL; tel. (20) 7937-9718; fax (20) 7937-7484; e-mail info@sknhc.co.uk; High Commr KEVIN MONROE ISAAC.

Saint Lucia: 1 Collingham Gdns, London, SW5 0HW; tel. (20) 7370-7123; fax (20) 7370-1905; e-mail enquiries@stluciahcuk.org; High Commr Dr ERNEST HILAIRE.

Saint Vincent and the Grenadines: 10 Kensington Court, London, W8 5DL; tel. (20) 7565-2874; fax (20) 7937-6040; e-mail info@svghighcom.co.uk; internet www.svghighcom.co.uk; High Commr CENIO E. LEWIS.

Saudi Arabia: 30 Charles St, London, W1J 5DZ; tel. (20) 7917-3000; e-mail ukemb@mofa.gov.sa; internet www.saudiembassy.org.uk; Ambassador Prince MUHAMMAD BIN NAWAF BIN ABD AL-AZIZ.

Senegal: 39 Marloes Rd, London, W8 6LA; tel. (20) 7937-7237; fax (20) 7938-2546; e-mail senegalembassy@hotmail.co.uk; internet www.senegalembassy.co.uk; Ambassador ABDOU SOURANG.

Serbia: 28 Belgrave Sq., London, SW1X 8QB; tel. (20) 7235-9049; fax (20) 7235-7092; e-mail london@serbianembassy.org.uk; internet www.serbianembassy.org.uk; Ambassador Dr DEJAN POPOVIĆ.

Seychelles: 11 Grosvenor Cres., 4th Floor, London, SW1X 7EE; tel. (20) 7235-0680; fax (20) 7235-7509; e-mail seyhc.london@btconnect.com; High Commr MARIE-PIERRE LLOYD.

Sierra Leone: 41 Eagle St, London, WC1R 4TL; tel. (20) 7404-0140; fax (20) 7430-9862; e-mail info@slhc-uk.org.uk; internet www.slhc-uk.org.uk; High Commr EDWARD MOHAMED TURAY.

Singapore: 9 Wilton Cres., London, SW1X 8SP; tel. (20) 7235-8315; fax (20) 7245-6583; e-mail singhc_lon@sgmfa.gov.sg; internet www.mfa.gov.sg/london; High Commr THAMBYNATHAN JASUDASEN.

Slovakia: 25 Kensington Palace Gdns, London, W8 4QY; tel. (20) 7313-6470; fax (20) 7313-6481; e-mail emb.london@mzv.sk; internet www.mzv.sk/londyn; Ambassador MIROSLAV WLACHOVSKÝ.

Slovenia: 10 Little College St, London, SW1P 3SH; tel. (20) 7222-5700; fax (20) 7222-5277; e-mail vlo@gov.si; internet london.embassy.si; Ambassador IZTOK JARC.

South Africa: South Africa House, Trafalgar Sq., London, WC2N 5DP; tel. (20) 7451-7299; fax (20) 7451-7283; internet southafricahouseuk.com; High Commr Dr ZOLA SIDNEY THEMBA SKWEYIYA.

South Sudan: 28–32 Wellington Rd, London, NW8 9SF; tel. (20) 7554-8785; e-mail info@goss-london.com; Ambassador SABIT ABBE ALLEY.

Spain: 39 Chesham Pl., London, SW1X 8SB; tel. (20) 7235-5555; fax (20) 7259-5392; e-mail emb.londres@mail.maec.es; internet www.maec.es/embajadas/londres; Ambassador FEDERICO TRILLO-FIGUEROA MARTÍNEZ-CONDE.

Sri Lanka: 13 Hyde Park Gdns, London, W2 2LU; tel. (20) 7262-1841; fax (20) 7262-7970; e-mail mail@slhc-london.co.uk; internet www.slhclondon.org; High Commr Dr CHRIS NONIS.

Sudan: 3 Cleveland Row, St James's, London, SW1A 1DD; tel. (20) 7839-8080; fax (20) 7839-7560; e-mail admin@sudanembassy.co.uk; internet www.sudanembassy.co.uk; Ambassador ABDULLAHI HAMAD ALI.

Swaziland: 20 Buckingham Gate, London, SW1E 6LB; tel. (20) 7630-6611; fax (20) 7630-6564; e-mail enquiries@swaziland.org.uk; High Commr DUMSILE T. SUKATI.

Sweden: 11 Montagu Pl., London, W1H 2AL; tel. (20) 7917-6400; fax (20) 7724-4174; e-mail ambassaden.london@gov.se; internet www.swedenabroad.com/london; Ambassador NICOLA CLASE.

Switzerland: 16–18 Montagu Pl., London, W1H 2BQ; tel. (20) 7616-6000; fax (20) 7724-7001; e-mail lon.swissembassy@eda.admin.ch; internet www.swissembassy.org.uk; Ambassador ANTON THALMANN.

Syria: 8 Belgrave Sq., London, SW1X 8PH; tel. (20) 7245-9012; fax (20) 7235-4621; e-mail info@syrianembassy.co.uk; internet www.syrianembassy.co.uk; Chargé d'affaires a.i. GHASSAN DALLA.

Tajikistan: 26–28 Hammersmith Grove, London, W6 7BA; tel. (20) 8834-1003; fax (20) 8834-1100; e-mail info@tajembassy.org.uk; internet www.tajembassy.org.uk; Ambassador ERKIN S. KASYMOV.

Tanzania: 3 Stratford Pl., London, WIC 1AS; tel. (20) 7569-1470; fax (20) 7495-8817; e-mail balozi@tanzania-online.gov.uk; internet tanzaniahighcommission.co.uk; Ambassador PETER KALLAGHE.

Thailand: 29–30 Queen's Gate, London, SW7 5JB; tel. (20) 7589-2944; fax (20) 7823-7492; e-mail csinfo@thaiembassyuk.org.uk; internet www.thaiembassyuk.org.uk; Ambassador PASAN TEPARAK.

Tonga: 36 Molyneux St, London, W1H 5BQ; tel. (20) 7724-5828; fax (20) 7723-9074; e-mail office@tongahighcom.co.uk; High Commr SONATA TUPOU (acting).

Trinidad and Tobago: 42 Belgrave Sq., London, SW1X 8NT; tel. (20) 7245-9351; fax (20) 7823-1065; e-mail tthc@btconnect.com; internet tthighcommission.co.uk; High Commr GARVIN NICHOLAS.

Tunisia: 29 Prince's Gate, London, SW7 1QG; tel. (20) 7584-8117; fax (20) 7584-3205; e-mail london@tunisianembassy.co.uk; Ambassador NABIL AMMAR.

Turkey: 43 Belgrave Sq., London, SW1X 8PA; tel. (20) 7393-0202; fax (20) 7393-0066; e-mail embassy.london@mfa.gov.tr; Ambassador ÜNAL ÇEVIKÖZ.

Turkmenistan: 131 Holland Park Ave, London, W11 4UT; tel. (20) 7610-5239; fax (20) 7751-1903; e-mail tkm-embassy-uk@btconnect.org.uk; internet www.turkmenembassy.org.uk; Ambassador YAZMURAD SERYAEV.

Uganda: Uganda House, 58–59 Trafalgar Sq., London, WC2N 5DX; tel. (20) 7839-5783; fax (20) 7839-8925; e-mail info@ugandahighcomission.co.uk; internet www.ugandahighcommission.co.uk; High Commr JOAN KAKIMA NYAKATUURA RWABYOMERE.

Ukraine: 60 Holland Park, London, W11 3SJ; tel. (20) 7727-6312; fax (20) 7702-1708; e-mail emb_gb@mfa.gov.ua; internet uk.mfa.gov.ua; Ambassador VOLODYMYR KHANDOGIY.

United Arab Emirates: 30 Princes Gate, London, SW7 1PT; tel. (20) 7581-1281; fax (20) 7581-9616; e-mail informationuk@mofa.gov.ae; internet www.uae-embassy.ae/uk; Ambassador ABD AL-RAHMAN GHANIM AL-MUTAIWEE.

USA: 24–32 Grosvenor Sq., London, W1A 1AE; tel. (20) 7499-9000; internet london.usembassy.gov; Ambassador LOUIS B. SUSMAN.

Uruguay: 125 Kensington High St, London, W8 5SF; tel. (20) 7937-4170; fax (20) 7376-0502; e-mail emburuguay@emburuguay.org.uk; Ambassador JULIO MOREIRA MORÁN.

Uzbekistan: 41 Holland Park, London, W11 3RP; tel. (20) 7229-7679; fax (20) 7229-7029; e-mail info@uzbekembassy.org; internet www.uzbekembassy.org; Ambassador OTABEK AKBAROV.

Venezuela: 1 Cromwell Rd, London, SW7 2HW; tel. (20) 7584-4206; fax (20) 7589-8887; e-mail info@venezlon.co.uk; internet www.embavenez-uk.org; Ambassador SAMUEL MONCADA.

Viet Nam: 12–14 Victoria Rd, London, W8 5RD; tel. (20) 7937-1912; fax (20) 7937-6108; e-mail vanphong@vietnamembassy.org.uk; internet www.vietnamembassy.org.uk; Ambassador VU QUANG MINH.

Yemen: 57 Cromwell Rd, London, SW7 2ED; tel. (20) 7584-6607; fax (20) 7589-3350; e-mail yemenembassy@btconnect.com; internet www.yemenembassy.org.uk; Ambassador ABDULLAH AL-RADHI.

Zambia: Zambia House, 2 Palace Gate, London, W8 5NG; tel. (20) 7589-6655; fax (20) 7581-1353; e-mail zhc@btconnect.com; internet www.zambiahc.org.uk; High Commr BIZWAYO NEWTON NKUNIKA.

Zimbabwe: Zimbabwe House, 429 Strand, London, WC2R 0QE; tel. (20) 7836-7755; fax (20) 7379-1167; e-mail zimlondon@yahoo.co.uk; Ambassador GABRIEL MHARADZE MACHINGA.

Judicial System

There are, historically, three sources of the law as administered in the law courts of England and Wales: Statute Law, which is a written law and consists mainly of Acts of Parliament; Common Law, which originated in ancient usage and has not been formally enacted; and Equity, which was the system evolved by the Lord Chancellor's court (Court of Chancery) to mitigate the strictness of some of the common law rules. The law of the European Union has been added to these.

Scottish common and statute law differ in some respects from that current in England and Wales, owing to Scotland's retention of its own legal system under the Act of Union with England of 1707. Northern Ireland also retains a separate judicial structure, which closely resembles the English system.

Judicial independence is guaranteed by the Constitutional Reform Act 2005, which states that ministers of the Crown may not seek to influence judicial decisions through any special access to the judiciary. According to the Act of Settlement 1701, senior judges in England and Wales are appointed for life and can be removed from office only after an address from Parliament to the Sovereign. The participation of private citizens in all important criminal and some civil cases, in the form of a summoned jury of 12 persons, who judge, if necessary by a majority, the facts of a case (questions of law being decided by the judge), also helps to ensure a fair trial.

THE SUPREME COURT

The Supreme Court (which assumed the judicial functions formerly exercised by the House of Lords in 2009) is the final court of appeal for the whole of the United Kingdom in civil cases, and for England, Wales and Northern Ireland in criminal cases. It hears appeals from the Court of Appeal in England and Wales, the Court of Appeal in Northern Ireland and the Court of Session in Scotland, and in some limited cases from the High Court of Justice in England and Wales and the High Court in Northern Ireland. It also exercises jurisdiction in relation to devolution matters: that is, it decides on whether the actions of the legislative and executive bodies of Northern Ireland, Scotland and Wales are within their respective competencies.

The Justices of the Supreme Court additionally constitute the Judicial Committee of the Privy Council. This is the final court of appeal for appeals from the Overseas Territories and Crown Dependencies, and from certain Commonwealth countries; it also exercises domestic jurisdiction in ecclesiastical matters and appeals from disciplinary tribunals of certain professions.

Supreme Court: Parliament Sq., London, SW1P 3BD; tel. (20) 7960-1500; fax (20) 7960-1901; e-mail enquiries@supremecourt.gsi .gov.uk; internet www.supremecourt.gov.uk; Justices of the Supreme Court Lord NEUBERGER OF ABBOTSBURY (Pres.), Lord HOPE OF CRAIGHEAD (Deputy Pres.).

JUDICIAL SYSTEM OF ENGLAND AND WALES

The criminal courts of lowest jurisdiction in England and Wales are the magistrates' courts (or petty sessions), presided over by Justices of the Peace, who are unpaid lay citizens. They have power to try all non-indictable offences, and may try some of the less serious indictable offences if the defendant agrees. More serious criminal cases are heard initially in the magistrates' courts, whence they are committed for trial in the Crown Court. In London and in certain other large towns there are a small number of professional salaried magistrates, known as District Judges (Magistrates' Court), who sit alone, whereas lay justices normally sit in threes when acting judicially. Youth Courts, composed of specially trained justices, have the power to try most charges against children aged under 18 years.

More serious criminal cases are tried by jury in the Crown Court, which sits at various centres throughout England and Wales. Court centres are administratively divided into three tiers. The most serious offences are tried at first and second tier centres presided over by High Court Judges, Circuit Judges or Recorders. Circuit Judges or Recorders preside over third tier centres, where the less serious offences are tried. The Crown Court also hears appeals from the magistrates' courts.

Most civil actions are tried in the county courts, which have unlimited jurisdiction in civil matters. They are presided over by a Circuit Judge, or, in some cases, a District Judge, sitting alone.

Certain important civil cases are heard in the High Court of Justice, which has three divisions—Chancery, Queen's Bench and Family. The Chancery Division deals with litigation about property, patents, family trusts, companies, dissolution of partnerships and disputed estates. The Queen's Bench Division hears cases involving damage to property, personal injuries, etc., and also includes the Administrative, Commercial, Admiralty, and Technology and Con-struction Courts. The Family Division hears contested or complex divorce and separation cases and matters relating to children such as adoption, wardship or guardianship of minors.

The Court of Appeal hears appeals in civil cases from County Courts and the High Court of Justice and in criminal cases from the Crown Courts. Appeals from the High Court that involve important points of law occasionally go direct to the Supreme Court.

Court of Appeal: The Royal Courts of Justice, Strand, London, WC2A 2LL; tel. (20) 7947-6000; the Court of Appeal consists of a Civil Division and a Criminal Division, headed respectively by the Master of the Rolls and the Lord Chief Justice (who is also the head of the judiciary). The Master of the Rolls is the effective head of the court. The presidents of the three divisions of the High Court are also ex officio members of the Court of Appeal.

Master of the Rolls and Head of Civil Justice: Lord DYSON.

Lord Chief Justice of England and Wales and Head of Criminal Justice: Lord JUDGE.

High Court of Justice: The Royal Courts of Justice, Strand, London, WC2A 2LL; tel. (20) 7947-6000.

Chancellor of the High Court (President of the Chancery Division): Sir ROBERT ANDREW MORRITT.

President of the Queen's Bench Division and Judge in Charge of the Administrative Court: Sir JOHN THOMAS.

President of the Family Division and Head of Family Justice: Sir NICHOLAS PETER RATHBONE WALL.

JUDICIAL SYSTEM OF NORTHERN IRELAND

The judicial system of Northern Ireland closely resembles that of England and Wales. The senior courts, as in England and Wales, are the Court of Appeal, the High Court (which hears certain civil cases) and the Crown Court (which has jurisdiction in criminal matters). The county court system also corresponds to its English counterpart, with minor variations. County court judges share with the judges of the High Court the exercise of the jurisdiction of the Crown Court. The jurisdiction of the magistrates' courts (courts of summary jurisdiction) is exercised by a permanent judiciary of legally qualified resident magistrates. The Supreme Court in London is the final court of appeal for civil and criminal cases.

Lord Chief Justice of Northern Ireland: Sir DECLAN MORGAN, Royal Courts of Justice, Chichester St, Belfast, BT1 3JF; tel. (28) 9023-5111; fax (28) 9031-3508; e-mail adminoffice@courtsni.gov.uk; internet www.courtsni.gov.uk.

SCOTTISH JUDICIAL SYSTEM

Minor criminal offences are dealt with in the Justice of the Peace courts (formerly district courts), each headed by a lay Justice of the Peace assisted by a legally qualified Clerk. Most criminal actions, including all but the most serious offences, are tried in the Sheriff courts. Cases are usually heard by a Sheriff and a jury, but may be heard by a Sheriff alone. Sheriff courts also hear civil cases, in which they have practically unlimited jurisdiction. There are 49 Sheriff courts grouped in six regional sheriffdoms, each headed by a Sheriff Principal, to whom decisions of the Sheriffs in civil cases may be appealed.

The highest criminal court is the High Court of Justiciary, which sits in various locations around Scotland. It acts as a court of first instance for the most serious cases, which are tried by a judge and a jury of 15 members. It also functions as the supreme court of appeal in criminal matters, in which capacity it sits only in Edinburgh; appeal may be made to it from the Sheriff courts and from the Justice of the Peace courts. There is no further appeal to the Supreme Court in London.

The Court of Session is the supreme civil court in Scotland. It has an Inner House and an Outer House. The latter deals with the major civil cases and divorce actions, usually at first instance. The Inner House is mainly an appeal court, whence further appeal may be made to the Supreme Court in London.

The most senior members of the Scottish judiciary are the Senators of the College of Justice. They sit both in a criminal capacity as judges of the High Court of Justiciary, where they are known as Lords Commissioners of the Justiciary, and in a civil capacity as judges of the Court of Session, where they are known as Lords of Council and Session.

Court of Session: Parliament House, Parliament Sq., Edinburgh, EH1 1RQ; tel. (131) 225-2595; fax (131) 240-6755; e-mail supreme .courts@scotcourts.gov.uk; internet www.scotcourts.gov.uk.

Lord President of the Court of Session and Lord Justice General: Lord GILL.

Lord Justice Clerk: Lord CARLOWAY.

High Court of Justiciary: Lawnmarket, Edinburgh, EH1 2PE; tel. (131) 225-2595; fax (131) 240-6915; e-mail supreme.courts@ scotcourts.gov.uk; internet www.scotcourts.gov.uk; the head of the High Court of Justiciary is the Lord Justice General, who is also Lord

President of the Court of Session. The Lord Justice Clerk is the deputy head of the court. The ordinary judges are those of the Court of Session, sitting in a criminal capacity as Lords Commissioners of Justiciary.

Religion
CHRISTIANITY

Churches Together in Britain and Ireland: 39 Eccleston Sq., London, SW1V 1BX; tel. (845) 680-6851; fax (845) 680-6852; e-mail info@ctbi.org.uk; internet www.ctbi.org.uk; f. 1990 as successor to the British Council of Churches; co-ordinates the activities of its 38 member churches and liaises with ecumenical bodies in Britain and Ireland; provides a forum for joint decision-making and enables the churches to take action together; Gen. Sec. Rev. Canon BOB FYFFE.

Action of Churches Together in Scotland (ACTS): 7 Forrester Lodge, Inglewood, Alloa, FK10 2HU; tel. (1259) 216980; fax (1259) 215964; e-mail ecumenical@acts-scotland.org; internet www .acts-scotland.org; aims to encourage and express unity of Christian Churches in Scotland; 9 mem. churches; Convener Rev. Dr DOUGLAS GALBRAITH; Gen. Sec. STEPHEN SMYTH.

Churches Together in England (CTE): 27 Tavistock Sq., London, WC1H 9HH; tel. (20) 7529-8131; e-mail office@cte.org .uk; internet www.cte.org.uk; f. 1990; 40 mem. bodies; Pres Rev. MICHAEL HEANEY, Most Rev. VINCENT NICHOLS, Most Rev. JUSTIN WELBY, Rt Rev. JANA JERUMA-GRINBERGA, Archbishop GREGORIOS OF THYATEIRA AND GREAT BRITAIN (Pres.-elect); Gen. Sec. Rev. DAVID CORNICK.

Churches Together in Wales (Cytûn): 58 Richmond Rd, Cardiff, CF24 3UR; tel. (29) 2046-4204; e-mail post@cytun.org.uk; internet www.cytun.org.uk; fmrly the Council of Churches for Wales; Chief Exec. Rev. ALED EDWARDS.

Irish Council of Churches: Inter-Church Centre, 48 Elmwood Ave, Belfast, BT9 6AZ; tel. (28) 9066-3145; e-mail info@ irishchurches.org; internet www.irishchurches.org; f. 1922 (present name adopted 1966); 14 mem. churches; the organization of the churches in Ireland takes no account of the partition of the island into two separate political entities, with Ireland and Northern Ireland thus subject to a unified jurisdiction for ecclesiastical purposes; Pres. Fr GODFREY O'DONNELL; Exec. Officer MERVYN MCCULLAGH.

The Anglican Communion

The Church of England
The Church of England is the Established Church, and as such acknowledges the authority of Parliament in matters in which secular authority is competent to exercise control. Queen Elizabeth I was declared 'Supreme Governor on Earth' of the Church of England, and the Sovereign is consecrated to this office at coronation.

In England there are two Provinces, Canterbury and York. The former contains 30, the latter 14, dioceses. Each Province has its ancient Convocations, the Upper and Lower House. By the Enabling Act the Constitution of the National Assembly of the Church of England ('Church Assembly') received statutory recognition in 1920, with power, subject to the control and authority of Parliament, of initiating legislation on all matters concerning the Church of England. Measures passed by the Assembly and approved by Parliament were submitted for the Royal Assent, having the force of Acts of Parliament.

In 1970, by the Synodical Government Measure (1969), the Church Assembly was reconstituted as the General Synod and was also given authority to exercise most of the functions of the Convocations. The House of Bishops consists of members of the Upper House of the Convocations (53 persons). The House of Clergy consists of the Lower Houses (a maximum of 259 persons). The House of Laity consists almost entirely of representatives of the dioceses elected by the deanery synods (a maximum of 258 persons).

In 2010 there were 1,214,100 people on the Church's electoral rolls.

The Archbishops and the 24 senior Bishops sit in the House of Lords.

Archbishop of Canterbury, Primate of All England and Metropolitan: Rt Rev. JUSTIN WELBY, Lambeth Palace, London, SE1 7JU; tel. (20) 7898-1200; fax (20) 7261-9836; e-mail contact@ lambethpalace.org.uk; internet www.archbishopofcanterbury.org.

Archbishop of York, Primate of England and Metropolitan: Most Rev. Dr JOHN SENTAMU, Bishopthorpe Palace, Bishopthorpe, York, YO23 2GE; tel. (1904) 707021; fax (1904) 709204; e-mail office@ archbishopofyork.org; internet www.archbishopofyork.org.

General Synod of the Church of England: Church House, Great Smith St, London, SW1P 3AZ; tel. (20) 7898-1326; fax (20) 7898-1369; e-mail cofe.comms@churchofengland.org; internet www .churchofengland.org; f. 1970; Sec.-Gen. WILLIAM FITTALL.

The Church of Ireland
61–67 Donegall St, Belfast, BT1 2QH; tel. (28) 9023-2909; fax (28) 9032-3554; e-mail enquiries@ireland.anglican.org; internet www .ireland.anglican.org.

Ireland (including Northern Ireland) comprises two archdioceses and 10 dioceses; in 2011 there were 275,000 members of the Church of Ireland in Northern Ireland.

Archbishop of Armagh and Primate of All Ireland: Most Rev. Dr RICHARD CLARKE, Church House, 46 Abbey St, Armagh, BT61 7DZ; tel. (28) 3752-7144; fax (28) 3752-7823; e-mail archbishop@armagh .anglican.org.

The Church in Wales
39 Cathedral Rd, Cardiff, CF11 9XF; tel. (29) 2034-8200; fax (29) 2038-7835; e-mail information@churchinwales.org.uk; internet www.churchinwales.org.uk.

The Province of Wales was created as a result of the Welsh Church Act of 1914, which took effect on 31 March 1920 and separated the four Welsh dioceses from the Province of Canterbury. It is divided into six dioceses served by 620 stipendiary clerics. The number of Easter communicants is 60,827 (2011). The Church in Wales has an administrative governing body which is a legislative assembly composed of bishops, clergy and laity, and a representative body incorporated by Royal Charter, which holds and manages the property and central funds of the Church; Provincial Sec. JOHN SHIRLEY.

Archbishop of Wales: Most Rev. BARRY C. MORGAN, Llys Esgob, Cathedral Green, Llandaff, Cardiff, CF5 2YE; tel. (29) 2056-2400; fax (29) 2056-8410; e-mail archbishop@churchinwales.org.uk.

The Scottish Episcopal Church
21 Grosvenor Cres., Edinburgh, EH12 5EE; tel. (131) 225-6357; fax (131) 346-7247; e-mail office@scotland.anglican.org; internet www .scotland.anglican.org.

Formerly the Established Church of Scotland, was disestablished and disendowed in 1689; is in full communion with all branches of the Anglican Communion; seven dioceses: Aberdeen and Orkney, Argyll and The Isles, Brechin, Edinburgh, Glasgow and Galloway, Moray, Ross and Caithness, and St Andrews, Dunkeld and Dunblane. There is a Bishop in each diocese; one of them is elected by the other Bishops as the Primus; Churches, mission stations, etc. 310, clergy 402, communicants 29,810; Sec.-Gen. to the General Synod JOHN STUART.

Primus: Most Rev. DAVID CHILLINGWORTH (Bishop of St Andrew's, Dunkeld and Dunblane), Glasgow & Galloway Diocesan Centre, 5 St Vincent Pl., Glasgow, G1 2DH; tel. (141) 2215720; fax (141) 2216911; e-mail office@glasgow.anglican.org; internet www.glasgow.anglican .org.

The Roman Catholic Church
For ecclesiastical purposes Great Britain comprises seven archdioceses and 23 dioceses. There is also an eparchy (which was raised from the status of apostolic exarchate in January 2013) for the Ukrainian Rite. Ireland (including Northern Ireland) comprises four archdioceses and 22 dioceses. The dioceses of Down and Connor and Dromore are completely in Northern Ireland, while the archdiocese of Armagh and the dioceses of Derry and Clogher are partly in Northern Ireland and partly in Ireland. At 31 December 2006 there were an estimated 4,097,772 adherents in England and Wales, of whom about 50,000 were of the Ukrainian Rite, and an estimated 702,890 adherents in Scotland. At the 2011 census 40.8% of the population of Northern Ireland gave their religion as Catholic or Roman Catholic.

Latin Rite

Bishops' Conference of England and Wales
39 Eccleston Sq., London, SW1V 1BX; tel. (20) 7630-8220; fax (20) 7901-4821; e-mail ccn@cbcew.org.uk; internet www.catholic-ew.org .uk; Pres. Most Rev. VINCENT NICHOLS (Archbishop of Westminster); Gen. Sec. Rt. Rev. MARCUS STOCK.

Archbishop of Westminster: Most Rev. VINCENT NICHOLS, Archbishop's House, Vaughan House, 46 Francis St, London SW1P 1QN; tel. (20) 7798-9033; fax (20) 7798-9077; e-mail archbishop@rcdow.org .uk; internet www.rcdow.org.uk/archbishop.

Archbishop of Birmingham: Most Rev. BERNARD LONGLEY, Archbishop's House, 8 Shadwell St, Queensway, Birmingham, B4 6EY; tel. (121) 236-9090; fax (121) 212-0171; e-mail fr_dominic.cosslett@ rc-birmingham.org; internet www.birminghamdiocese.org.uk.

Archbishop of Liverpool: (vacant), Archbishop's House, Lowood, Carnatic Road, Mossley Hill, Liverpool, L18 8BY; tel. (151) 724-6398; fax (151) 724-6405; e-mail archbishop.liverpool@rcaolp.co.uk; internet www.liverpoolcatholic.org.uk.

Archbishop of Southwark: Most Rev. PETER DAVID SMITH, Archbishop's House, 150 St George's Rd, Southwark, London, SE1 6HX;

tel. (20) 7928-2495; fax (20) 7928-7833; e-mail secswk@rcsouthwark .co.uk; internet www.rcsouthwark.co.uk.

Archbishop of Cardiff: GEORGE STACK, Archbishop's House, 43 Cathedral Rd, Cardiff, CF11 9HD; tel. (29) 2022-0411; fax (29) 2037-9036; e-mail arch@rcadc.org; internet www.rcadc.org.

Archbishop of Armagh and Primate of All Ireland: Cardinal SEÁN B. BRADY, Ara Coeli, Cathedral Rd, Armagh, BT61 7QY; tel. (28) 3752-2045; fax (28) 3752-6182; e-mail admin@aracoeli.com; internet www.armagharchdiocese.org.

Bishops' Conference of Scotland

64 Aitken St, Airdrie, ML6 6LT; tel. (1236) 764061; fax (1236) 762489; e-mail gensec@bpsconfscot.com; internet www.bpsconfscot.com; Pres. HE Cardinal PHILIP TARTAGLIA (Archbishop of Glasgow); Gen. Sec. Rev. HUGH BRADLEY.

Archbishop of St Andrews and Edinburgh: (vacant), Archbishop's House, 42 Greenhill Gdns, Edinburgh, EH10 4BJ; tel. (131) 447-3337; fax (131) 447-0816; e-mail cardinal@staned.org.uk; internet www.archdiocese-edinburgh.com.

Archbishop of Glasgow: Most Rev. PHILIP TARTAGLIA, Curial Offices, 196 Clyde St, Glasgow, G1 4JY; tel. (141) 226-5898; fax (141) 225-2600; e-mail info@rcag.org.uk; internet www.rcag.org.uk.

Ukrainian Rite

Bishop: Rt Rev. HLIB LONCHYNA, Bishop's House, 21 and 22 Binney St, London, W1Y 1YN; tel. (20) 7629-1534; fax (20) 7355-3314; e-mail frben@catholic.org.

Protestant Churches

Association of Baptist Churches in Ireland: 19 Hillsborough Rd, Moira, Craigavon, BT67 0HG; tel. (28) 9261-9267; e-mail abc@ thebaptistcentre.org; internet www.baptistsinireland.org; 115 churches; 93 ministers; 8,500 mems; Pres. Pastor PHILIP BROWN; Dir Pastor WILLIAM COLVILLE.

Baptist Union of Great Britain: Baptist House, POB 44, 129 Broadway, Didcot, OX11 8RT; tel. (1235) 517700; fax (1235) 517715; e-mail info@baptist.org.uk; internet www.baptist.org.uk; f. 1813; the Baptist form of church government is congregational; baptism by immersion of believers is practised; the churches are grouped in associations; 135,000 mems (2011); Pres. CHRIS DUFFET; Gen. Sec. Rev. JONATHAN P. EDWARDS.

Church of Scotland: 121 George St, Edinburgh, EH2 4YN; tel. (131) 225-5722; fax (131) 220-3113; e-mail lturnbull@cofscotland.org .uk; internet www.churchofscotland.org.uk; the national Church of Scotland was reformed in 1560, and became Presbyterian in doctrine and constitution. In 1921 the Church of Scotland Act was passed, by which the articles declaring the full spiritual freedom of the Church are recognized as lawful. In 1925 the Church of Scotland (Property and Endowments) Act became law, and made over to the Church of Scotland places of worship, manses and endowments in absolute property, vesting the future control of them in Trustees. The union of the Church of Scotland and the United Free Church was effected in 1929; 600,000 mems; Moderator of the General Assembly (2012/13) Rt Rev. ALBERT BOGLE.

Elim Pentecostal Church: De Walden Rd, West Malvern WR14 4DF; tel. (845) 3026750; fax (845) 3026752; e-mail info@elimhq.net; internet www.elim.org.uk; f. 1915; c. 550 churches and 60,000 adherents in Great Britain; Gen. Superintendent Rev. JOHN GLASS.

Free Church of Scotland: 15 North Bank St, The Mound, Edinburgh, EH1 2LS; tel. (131) 226-5286; fax (131) 220-0597; e-mail offices@freechurchofscotland.org; internet www.freechurch.org; f. 1843; 103 congregations; Principal Clerk of Assembly Rev. JAMES MacÍVER.

Free Churches Group, Churches Together in England: 27 Tavistock Sq., London, WC1H 9HH; tel. (20) 7529-8131; fax (20) 7529-8134; e-mail office@cte.org.uk; internet www .churches-together.net; central body for the co-ordination of the work of the Free Churches throughout England and Wales; Moderator Rev. MICHAEL HEANEY; Exec. Sec. Rev. MARK FISHER.

Lutheran Council of Great Britain: 30 Thanet St, London, WC1H 9QH; tel. (20) 7554-2900; fax (20) 7383-3081; e-mail enquiries@ lutheran.org.uk; internet www.lutheran.org.uk; f. 1948; 179,300 mems (2010); Chair. Rev. TORBJØRN HOLT; Gen. Sec. JAMES LAING.

Methodist Church: Methodist Church House, 25 Marylebone Rd, London, NW1 5JR; tel. (20) 7486-5502; fax (20) 7224-5228; e-mail helpdesk@methodistchurch.org.uk; internet www.methodist.org .uk; f. 1739 by Rev. John Wesley, a priest of the Church of England; the governing body of the Church is the Annual Conference, which consists of ministers and lay representatives. The Church throughout Great Britain is divided into 31 Districts, and these hold their Synod Meetings in the autumn and the spring. The Districts are divided into Circuits, which hold regular Circuit Meetings, made up of representatives from the churches within the Circuit. There are

also local Church Councils; 219,988 mems (2011); Pres. of the Methodist Conference (2012/13) Rev. MARK WAKELIN; Gen. Sec. Rev. Dr MARTYN ATKINS.

Methodist Church in Ireland: 1 Fountainville Ave, Belfast, BT9 6AN; tel. (28) 9032-4554; fax (28) 9023-9467; e-mail secretary@ irishmethodist.org; internet www.irishmethodist.org; 230 churches; 207 ministers; 51,425 mems; Pres. Rev. KENNETH LINDSAY.

Moravian Church: 5 Muswell Hill, London, N10 3TJ; tel. (20) 8883-3409; fax (20) 8365-3371; e-mail office@moravian.org.uk; internet www.moravian.org.uk; f. 1457; Sec. Provincial Board JACKIE MORTEN.

Moravian Church in Ireland: 5 Locksley Park, Belfast, BT10 0AR; tel. (28) 9061-9755; e-mail paul.holdsworth@moravian.org.uk; f. 1746; Chair. of Conf. PAUL M. HOLDSWORTH.

Non-Subscribing Presbyterian Church of Ireland: 25 Weavers Meadow, Banbridge, BT32 4RL; tel. (28) 4062–6902; e-mail info@ nspresbyterian.org; internet www.nspresbyterian.org; Moderator Rt. Rev. SAM PEDEN; Clerk Rev. NORMAN HUTTON.

Presbyterian Church in Ireland: Church House, Fisherwick Pl., Belfast, BT1 6DW; tel. (28) 9032-2284; fax (28) 9041-7301; e-mail info@presbyterianireland.org; internet www.presbyterianireland .org; 549 churches; 381 ministers; 258,000 mems, 27,000 in 550 Sunday Schools; Moderator of the Gen. Assembly Rev. Dr ROY PATTON; Clerk of Assembly and Gen. Sec. Rev. Dr DONALD WATTS.

Presbyterian Church of Wales: Tabernacle Chapel, 81 Merthyr Rd, Whitchurch, Cardiff, CF14 1DD; tel. (29) 2062-7465; fax (29) 2061-6188; e-mail swyddfa.office@ebcpcw.org.uk; internet www .ebcpcw.org.uk; f. 1811; 650 churches, 77 full-time ministers, 28,000 mems; Moderator of General Assembly Rev. IAIN HODGINS; Gen. Sec. Rev. W. BRYN WILLIAMS.

Salvation Army: 101 Newington Causeway, London, SE1 6BN; tel. (20) 7367-4500; fax (20) 7367-4728; e-mail info@salvationarmy.org .uk; internet www.salvationarmy.org.uk; f. 1865; Territorial Commdr JOHN MATEAR.

Union of Welsh Independents: Tŷ John Penri, 5 Axis Court, Riverside Business Park, Swansea Vale, Swansea, SA7 0AJ; tel. (1792) 795888; fax (1792) 795376; e-mail undeb@annibynwyr.org; internet www.annibynwyr.org; f. 1872; Pres. RONALD WILLIAMS; Gen. Sec. Rev. Dr GERAINT TUDUR.

United Free Church of Scotland: 11 Newton Pl., Glasgow, G3 7PR; tel. (141) 332-3435; fax (141) 333-1973; e-mail gensec@ufcos.org .uk; internet www.ufcos.org.uk; f. 1900; 60 congregations, 34 ministers and pastors, 3,394 mems; Moderator I. F. R. LLOYD; Gen. Sec. Rev. JOHN O. FULTON.

United Reformed Church: United Reformed Church House, 86 Tavistock Pl., London, WC1H 9RT; tel. (20) 7916-2020; fax (20) 7916-2021; e-mail urc@urc.org.uk; internet www.urc.org.uk; f. 1972 by union of the Congregational Church in England and Wales and the Presbyterian Church of England; joined by the Churches of Christ 1981 and by the Scottish Congregational Church 2000; approx. 1,500 churches, 700 ministers and 250,000 mems; Co-Moderators Rev. VAL MORRISON, Rev. Dr MICHAEL JAGESSAR; Gen. Sec. Rev. Dr ROBERTA ROMINGER.

Orthodox Churches

Council of Oriental Orthodox Churches in the United Kingdom and the Republic of Ireland: 97 Cadogan Gdns, London, E18 1LY; e-mail freldhose@hotmail.com; comprises the Armenian, Coptic, Ethiopian, Eritrean, Indian and Syrian Orthodox Churches; Pres. Bishop ANGAELOS.

Armenian Community and Church Council of Great Britain: POB 46207, London, W5 1XX; e-mail info@accc.org.uk; internet www .accc.org.uk; Chair. ARA PALAMOUDIAN.

Greek Orthodox Church (Archdiocese of Thyateira and Great Britain of the Ecumenical Patriarchate): Thyateira House, 5 Craven Hill, London, W2 3EN; tel. (20) 7723-4787; fax (20) 7224-9301; e-mail mail@thyateira.org.uk; internet www.thyateira.org.uk; f. 1922; Archbishop of Thyateira and Great Britain GREGORIOS; Chancellor Bishop ATHANASIOS OF TROPAEOU.

Russian Orthodox Church in Great Britain and Ireland (Diocese of Sourozh of the Patriarchate of Moscow): Cathedral of the Dormition of the Mother of God, Ennismore Gdns, London, SW7 1NH; tel. (20) 7584-0096; fax (20) 7584-9864; e-mail office@sourozh .org; internet www.sourozh.org; f. 1962; Archbishop ELISEY OF SOUROZH.

Serbian Orthodox Church: 131 Cob Lane, Bournville, Birmingham, B30 1QE; tel. (121) 458-5273; fax (121) 458-4986; Patriach Bishop IRINEJ GAVRILOVICA.

Other Christian Churches

First Church of Christ, Scientist: 8 Wright's Lane, Kensington, London, W8 6TA; tel. (20) 7937-3389; fax (20) 7937-3341; e-mail hello@firstlondon.org; internet www.firstlondon.org; f. 1879; the Mother Church is the First Church of Christ, Scientist, in Boston, MA (USA); approx. 150 churches in Great Britain; District Man. for Great Britain and Ireland TONY LOBL.

Church of Jesus Christ of Latter-day Saints (Mormon): Public Affairs, 751 Warwick Rd, Solihull, West Midlands, B91 3DQ; tel. (121) 712-1161; e-mail adockmp@ldschurch.org; internet www.lds .org.uk; f. 1830; c. 186,082 mems; First Pres. THOMAS S. MONSON.

General Assembly of Unitarian and Free Christian Churches: Essex Hall, 1–6 Essex St, London, WC2R 3HY; tel. (20) 7240-2384; fax (20) 7240-3089; e-mail info@unitarian.org.uk; internet www .unitarian.org.uk; f. 1928; 200 congregations; Pres. LIS DYSON-JONES.

Jehovah's Witnesses: Watch Tower House, The Ridgeway, London, NW7 1RN; tel. (20) 8906-2211; fax (20) 8371-0051; internet www .jw.org; f. 1900; there were an estimated 130,000 Jehovah's Witnesses in the UK in 2007.

The Religious Society of Friends (Quakers) in Britain: Friends House, 173 Euston Rd, London, NW1 2BJ; tel. (20) 7663-1000; fax (20) 7663-1001; e-mail enquiries@quaker.org.uk; internet www .quaker.org.uk; f. mid-17th century by George Fox; the Quakers have 15,800 mems and 8,400 'attenders' in Great Britain; Recording Clerk PAUL PARKER.

Seventh-day Adventist Church Headquarters: Stanborough Park, Watford, Herts, WD25 9JZ; tel. (1923) 672251; fax (1923) 893212; e-mail info@adventist.org.uk; internet adventist.org.uk; f. 1863; there were 34,000 mems in approx. 360 congregations across the UK and Ireland in Dec. 2012; Pres. Pastor IAN SWEENEY.

Spiritualists' National Union: Redwoods, Stansted Hall, Stansted Mountfitchet, Essex, CM24 8UD; tel. (1279) 816363; fax (1279) 812034; e-mail charles.coulston@snu.org.uk; internet www .snu.org.uk; f. 1891 (and inc. 1901); for the advancement of Spiritualism as a religion and a religious philosophy, it is a trust corporation officially recognized as the central and national body representing the Spiritualists in the UK; manages the Arthur Findlay College of Psychic Science and the Arthur Findlay Learning and Conference Centre; c. 360 Spiritualist churches, societies and 20,000 mems; Pres. DAVID BRUTON; Gen. Sec. CHARLES S. COULSTON.

ISLAM

The Muslim community in the United Kingdom, which according to the 2011 census for England and Wales numbered 2.7m. (4.8% of the population), consists mainly of people from the Indian sub-continent and their British-born descendants. The chief concentrations of Muslims are in London, the Midlands, South Wales, Lancashire and Yorkshire.

London Central Mosque Trust and Islamic Cultural Centre: 146 Park Rd, London, NW8 7RG; tel. (20) 7725-2213; fax (20) 7724-0493; e-mail info@iccuk.org; internet www.iccuk.org; Dir-Gen. Dr AHMAD AL-DUBAYAN.

Muslim Council of Britain: POB 57330, London, E1 2WJ; tel. (845) 2626786; fax (20) 7247-7079; e-mail admin@mcb.org.uk; internet www.mcb.org.uk; f. 1997; Sec.-Gen. FAROOQ MURAD.

SIKHISM

According to the 2001 census, there were 336,000 Sikhs in the United Kingdom, who originally came from the Punjab region of the Indian sub-continent as well as from East Africa, although many are now British-born. Each gurdwara (temple) is independent, and there is no central national body.

Sikh Missionary Society, UK: 10 Featherstone Rd, Southall, Middlesex, UB2 5AA; tel. (20) 8574-1902; fax (20) 8574-1912; e-mail info@sikhmissionarysociety.org; internet www .sikhmissionarysociety.org; promotes Sikhism and acts as a resource centre for information and literature; Hon. Gen. Sec. SURINDER SINGH PUREWAL.

HINDUISM

According to the 2001 census, there were 559,000 Hindus in the United Kingdom, with their origins in India, East Africa and Sri Lanka, although many are now British by birth. Hindus in the United Kingdom are concentrated in London, the Midlands and Yorkshire.

JUDAISM

The Jewish community in the United Kingdom numbered 267,000, according to the 2001 census. Jewish congregations are concentrated in London and the South-East. The Chief Rabbi of the United Hebrew Congregations of the Commonwealth is the spiritual leader of United Synagogue, which is the largest synagogue organization and represents the mainstream Orthodox branch of Judaism in the United Kingdom. Other organizations represent the various other Jewish denominations.

Chief Rabbi of the United Hebrew Congregations of the Commonwealth: Lord SACKS, 305 Ballards Lane, London, N12 8GB; tel. (20) 8343-6301; fax (20) 8343-6310; e-mail info@chiefrabbi .org; internet www.chiefrabbi.org.

Liberal Judaism: The Montagu Centre, 21 Maple St, London, W1T 4BE; tel. (20) 7580-1663; fax (20) 7631-9838; e-mail montagu@ liberaljudaism.org; internet www.liberaljudaism.org; f. 1902; 9,300 mems, 31 affiliated synagogues, 3 assoc. communities; Chief Exec. Rabbi DANNY RICH.

Masorti Judaism: Alexander House, 3 Shakespeare Rd, Finchley, London, N3 1XE; tel. (20) 8349-6650; e-mail enquiries@masorti.org .uk; internet www.masorti.org.uk; 15 synagogues and communities; Senior Rabbi JONATHAN WITTENBERG.

Movement for Reform Judaism: The Sternberg Centre for Judaism, 80 East End Rd, London, N3 2SY; tel. (20) 8349-5640; fax (20) 8349-5699; e-mail admin@reformjudaism.org.uk; internet www .reformjudaism.org.uk; Chief Exec. BEN RICH.

Spanish and Portuguese Jews' Congregation: 2 Ashworth Rd, London, W9 1JY; tel. (20) 7289-2573; fax (20) 7289-2709; e-mail howardmiller@spsyn.org.uk; internet www.sandp.org; f. 1657; Pres. of the Bd DAVID DANGOOR.

Union of Orthodox Hebrew Congregations (UOHC): 140 Stamford Hill, London, N16 6QT; tel. (20) 8802-6226; fax (20) 8809-6590; e-mail ck@uohc.co.uk; f. 1926; over 100 affiliated synagogues in the United Kingdom and other Commonwealth countries; Gen. Sec. CHAYIM SCHNECK.

United Synagogue: 305 Ballards Lane, London, N12 8GB; tel. (20) 8343-8989; fax (20) 8343-6263; internet www.theus.org.uk; f. 1870 by Act of Parliament; Pres. STEPHEN PACK; Chief Exec. JEREMY JACOBS.

BUDDHISM

According to the 2001 census, the Buddhist community in the United Kingdom numbered 152,000.

Buddhist Society: 58 Eccleston Sq., London, SW1V 1PH; tel. (20) 7834-5858; fax (20) 7976-5238; e-mail info@thebuddhistsociety.org; internet www.thebuddhistsociety.org; f. 1924; Registrar LOUISE MARCHANT.

BAHÁ'Í FAITH

National Spiritual Assembly of the Bahá'ís of the United Kingdom: 27 Rutland Gate, London, SW7 1PD; tel. (20) 7584-2566; fax (20) 7584-9402; e-mail nsa@bahai.org.uk; internet www .bahai.org.uk; f. 1923; Sec. Dr KISHAN MANOCHA.

The Press

The United Kingdom has some of the highest circulation figures in the world for individual newspapers (*The Sun* 2.3m., and *Daily Mail* 1.8m. at March 2013). There are about 1,100 regional and local daily and weekly newspapers in the United Kingdom.

There is no law which specifies the operations of the press, but several items of legislation bear directly on press activities. Although exact reporting of legal proceedings appearing at the time of trial is protected from later charges of defamation, the freedom to report cases is subject to certain restrictions. The strict laws of contempt of court and of libel somewhat limit the scope of the press. Libel cases can involve the awarding of punitive damages against the press. The Official Secrets Act of 1911 prohibits the publication of secret information where this is judged not to be in the national interest.

The Press Complaints Commission, which replaced the Press Council in 1991, has an independent chairman and 16 members, drawn from the lay public and the press. It deals with complaints from the public and upholds a 16-point Code of Practice.

Among the most influential newspapers may be included: *The Times, The Guardian, The Independent, Daily Telegraph* and *Financial Times* (daily), *The Observer, The Independent on Sunday, The Sunday Times* and *Sunday Telegraph* (Sunday newspapers). Prominent among the popular press are: *Daily Express, Daily Mail, Daily Mirror* and *The Sun* (daily); and the *Sunday Mirror* (Sunday newspaper).

No important newspaper is directly owned by a political party. The industry has fostered the growth of large national groups or chains of papers controlled by a single organization or individual. The largest of these are as follows:

Daily Mail and General Trust PLC: Northcliffe House, 2 Derry St, London, W8 5TT; tel. (20) 3615-0000; fax (20) 7938-4626; e-mail enquiries@dmgt.com; internet www.dmgt.com; controls through Associated Newspapers 1 national daily, *Daily Mail,* 1 national Sunday, *The Mail on Sunday,* 1 London daily, the *Metro;* announced in Nov. 2012 that a new business, Local World, was to buy the more than 80 regional titles from its Northcliffe Media regional newspaper arm; Daily Mail group was to hold 38.7% of shares in Local World; Group Chair. Lord ROTHERMERE, IV; Group CEO MARTIN MORGAN.

Guardian Media Group PLC: Kings Pl., 90 York Way, London, N1 9GU; tel. (20) 3353-2000; internet www.gmgplc.co.uk; f. 1821; owned by the Scott Trust Ltd; subsidiary publishing cos include Guardian Newspapers Ltd (controls *The Guardian, The Observer*) and GMG Regional Media (controls *Manchester Evening News*); Chair. AMELIA FAWCETT; CEO ANDREW MILLER.

Independent News and Media (UK) Ltd: 2 Derry St, London, W8 5HF; tel. (20) 7005-2000; internet www.inmplc.com; publishes 2 national dailies, *The Independent* and a concise version, *i*, and one national Sunday paper, *The Independent on Sunday*; also publishes *Belfast Telegraph* and *Sunday Life* in Northern Ireland; British subsidiary of Ireland's Independent News & Media PLC; Chief Exec. VINCENT CROWLEY; Chief Exec., United Kingdom I. G. FALLON.

News International PLC: 3 Thomas More Sq., London, E98 1XY; tel. (20) 7782-6000; fax (20) 7782-6097; internet www.newsint.co.uk; British subsidiary of USA's News Corporation; subsidiary cos: News Group Newspapers Ltd (controls *The Sun*), Times Newspapers Ltd (controls *The Times* and *The Sunday Times*); CEO MIKE DARCEY.

Trinity Mirror PLC: 1 Canada Sq., Canary Wharf, London, E14 5AP; tel. (20) 7293-3000; fax (20) 7293-3280; internet www .trinitymirror.com; f. 1999; by merger of Mirror Group Newspapers Ltd and Trinity International Holdings; controls a total of over 200 newspapers, including 1 national daily paper, *Daily Mirror*, 2 national Sunday papers, *The People, Sunday Mirror*, 2 Scottish national papers, *Daily Record* and *Sunday Mail*, and numerous regional and local papers; Chair. DAVID GRIGSON; Chief Exec. SIMON FOX.

United Business Media Ltd: Ludgate House, 245 Blackfriars Rd, London, SE1 9UY; tel. (20) 7921-5000; e-mail communications@ubm .com; internet www.ubm.com; f. 1996 by merger of United Newspapers and MAI group; international media and information group; 3 core business divisions—professional media, market research, news distribution; Chair. JOHN BOTTS; CEO DAVID LEVIN.

PRINCIPAL NATIONAL DAILIES
(average net circulation figures, in the United Kingdom only, as at March 2012, unless otherwise stated)

Daily Express: The Northern & Shell Bldg, 10 Lower Thames St, London, EC3R 6EN; tel. (20) 8612-7000; e-mail expressletters@ express.co.uk; internet www.express.co.uk; f. 1900; Propr Northern and Shell Group; Editor HUGH WHITTOW; circ. 558,513.

Daily Mail: Northcliffe House, 2 Derry St, London, W8 5TT; tel. (20) 7938-6000; fax (20) 7937-4463; e-mail letters@dailymail.co.uk; internet www.dailymail.co.uk; f. 1896; inc. *News Chronicle* (1960) and *Daily Sketch* (1971); Propr Associated Newspaper Holdings; Editor-in-Chief PAUL DACRE; Man. Dir GUY ZITTER; circ. 1,952,524.

Daily Mirror: 1 Canada Sq., Canary Wharf, London, E14 5AP; tel. (20) 7293-3000; fax (20) 7293-3280; e-mail mailbox@mirror.co.uk; internet www.mirror.co.uk; f. 1903; Propr Trinity Mirror PLC; also publishes Sunday edn, *Sunday Mirror*; Editors PETER WILLIS (weekdays), ALISON PHILLIPS (weekend); circ. 1,083,938.

Daily Star: The Northern & Shell Bldg, 10 Lower Thames St, London, EC3R 6EN; tel. (20) 8612-7000; fax (20) 7922-7960; e-mail starletters@dailystar.co.uk; internet www.dailystar.co.uk; f. 1978; Propr Express Newspapers PLC; Editor DAWN NEESOM; circ. 617,305.

Daily Telegraph: 111 Buckingham Palace Rd, London, SW1W 0DT; tel. (20) 7931-2000; e-mail dtletters@telegraph.co.uk; internet www .telegraph.co.uk; *Daily Telegraph*, f. 1855, *Morning Post*, f. 1772; amalgamated 1937; Propr Press Acquisitions Ltd; Chief Exec. MURDOCH MACLENNAN; Editor TONY GALLAGHER; circ. 576,378.

Financial Times: Number One Southwark Bridge, London, SE1 9HL; tel. (20) 7873-3000; fax (20) 7873-3076; e-mail subscriptions@ft .com; internet www.ft.com; f. 1880; Propr Pearson PLC; CEO JOHN RIDDING; Editor LIONEL BARBER; circ. 319,381.

The Guardian: POB 61864, Kings Pl., 90 York Way, London, N1 9GU; tel. (20) 3353-2000; fax (20) 7837-2114; e-mail userhelp@ guardian.co.uk; internet www.guardian.co.uk; f. 1821; Propr Guardian News and Media Ltd; CEO ANDREW MILLER; Editor ALAN RUSBRIDGER; circ. 217,190.

i: 2 Derry St, London, W8 5HF; tel. (20) 7005-2000; fax (20) 7005-2999; e-mail i@independent.co.uk; internet www.independent.co.uk/ i; f. 2010; concise version of *The Independent*; Exec. Editor STEFANO HATFIELD; circ. 273,793.

The Independent: 2 Derry St, London, W8 5TT; tel. (20) 7005-2000; fax (20) 7005-3859; e-mail customerservices@independent.co.uk; internet www.independent.co.uk; f. 1986; Editor CHRIS BLACKHURST; circ. 100,672.

Racing Post: 1 Canada Sq., Canary Wharf, London, E14 5AP; tel. (20) 7293-3000; fax (20) 7293-3758; e-mail editor@racingpost.co.uk; internet www.racingpost.co.uk; f. 1986; covers national and inter-

national horse racing, greyhound racing, general sport and betting; Editor BRUCE MILLINGTON; circ. 58,629.

The Sun: 3 Thomas More Sq., London, E98 1XY; tel. (20) 7782-4000; fax (20) 7782-4108; e-mail letters@the-sun.co.uk; internet www .thesun.co.uk; f. 1921 as *Daily Herald*; present name since 1964; Propr News International PLC; also publishes *The Sun on Sunday*; Editor DOMINIC MOHAN; circ. 2,614,725.

The Times: 1 Virginia St, London, E98 1RL; tel. (20) 7782-5000; fax (20) 7782-5046; e-mail help@timesplus.co.uk; internet www .thetimes.co.uk; f. 1785; Propr News International PLC; Editor JOHN WITHEROW (acting); circ. 394,102.

LONDON DAILIES

London Evening Standard: Northcliffe House, 2 Derry St, London, W8 5EE; tel. (20) 3367-7000; fax (20) 7937-2648; internet www .standard.co.uk; f. 1827; merged with *Evening News* 1980; Mon.–Fri.; evening; distributed free of charge; 75% stake acquired by Evening Standard Ltd in Jan. 2009; Editor SARAH SANDS; Man. Dir ANDREW MULLINS; circ. 704,008 (2011).

Metro: Northcliffe House, 2 Derry St, London, W8 5TT; tel. (20) 7651-5200; fax (20) 7806-8338; e-mail mail@ukmetro.co.uk; internet www.metro.co.uk; f. 1999; Mon.–Fri.; morning; distributed free of charge; also distributed in Bath, Birmingham, Brighton, Bristol, Cardiff, Derby, Edinburgh, Glasgow, Leeds, Leicester, Liverpool, Manchester, Newcastle, Nottingham and Sheffield; Propr Associated Newspaper Holdings PLC; Editor KENNY CAMPBELL; Man. Dir LINDA GRANT; circ. 734,488 (London); 1,332,225 (total UK—2009).

PRINCIPAL PROVINCIAL DAILIES
(average net circulation figures as at June 2011, unless otherwise stated)

Aberdeen

Evening Express: Aberdeen Journals Ltd, Lang Stracht, Mastrick, Aberdeen, AB15 6DF; tel. (1224) 344150; e-mail ee.news@ajl.co.uk; internet www.eveningexpress.co.uk; f. 1879; Editor ALAN MCCABE; circ. 47,849.

Press and Journal: Aberdeen Journals Ltd, Lang Stracht, Mastrick, Aberdeen, AB15 6DF; tel. (1224) 343311; fax (1224) 663575; e-mail pj.editor@ajl.co.uk; internet www.pressandjournal.co.uk; f. 1747; morning; Editor DAMIAN BATES; circ. 67,781.

Belfast

Belfast Telegraph: 124–144 Royal Ave, Belfast, BT1 1EB; tel. (28) 9026-4000; fax (28) 9055-4506; e-mail newseditor@belfasttelegraph .co.uk; internet www.belfasttelegraph.co.uk; f. 1870; independent; evening; Proprs Independent News and Media PLC; Editor MIKE GILSON; circ. 58,491 (2010).

Irish News: 113–117 Donegall St, Belfast, BT1 2GE; tel. (28) 9032-2226; fax (28) 9033-5510; e-mail enquiries@irishnews.com; internet www.irishnews.com; f. 1855; Irish nationalist; morning; Editor NOEL DORAN; circ. 43,647.

News Letter: Metro Bldg, 6–9 Donegall Sq. South, Belfast, BT1 5JA; tel. (28) 3839-5577; e-mail newsdesk@newsletter.co.uk; internet www.newsletter.co.uk; f. 1737; unionist; morning; Editor DARWIN TEMPLETON; circ. 23,492.

Birmingham

Birmingham Mail: 6th Floor, Fort Dunlop, Fort Parkway, B24 9FF; tel. (121) 234-5536; e-mail newsdesk@birminghammail.net; internet www.birminghammail.net; f. 1870; morning; independent; Propr Trinity Mirror PLC; Editor DAVID BROOKES; circ. 47,217.

Bradford

Telegraph & Argus: Hall Ings, Bradford, BD1 1JR; tel. (1274) 729511; e-mail newsdesk@telegraphandargus.co.uk; internet www .telegraphandargus.co.uk; f. 1868; evening; Editor PERRY AUSTIN-CLARKE; circ. 26,766.

Brighton

The Argus: Argus House, Crowhurst Rd, Hollingbury, Brighton, BN1 8AR; tel. (1273) 544544; fax (1273) 566114; e-mail editor@ theargus.co.uk; internet www.theargus.co.uk; f. 1880; Propr Newsquest Media Group; Editor MICHAEL BEARD; circ. 24,949.

Bristol

Evening Post: Temple Way, Bristol, BS2 0BU; tel. (117) 934-3000; e-mail epnews@bepp.co.uk; internet www.thisisbristol.co.uk; f. 1932; inc. the *Evening World*; Propr Local World; independent; Editor-in-Chief MIKE NORTON; circ. 38,344.

Western Daily Press: Temple Way, Bristol, BS99 7HD; tel. (117) 934-3000; e-mail wdnews@bepp.co.uk; internet www.thisissomerset

.co.uk; f. 1858; Propr Local World; morning; independent; Editor TIM DIXON; circ. 28,322.

Cardiff

South Wales Echo: Six Park St, Cardiff, CF10 1XR; tel. (29) 2024-3630; e-mail echo.newsdesk@mediawales.co.uk; internet www .walesonline.co.uk; f. 1884; Propr Trinity Mirror PLC; evening; independent; Editor TIM GORDON; circ. 23,754.

Western Mail: Six Park St, Cardiff, CF10 1XR; tel. (29) 2024-3630; e-mail newsdesk@mediawales.co.uk; internet www.walesonline.co .uk; f. 1869; independent; Editor ALAN EDMUNDS; circ. 26,931.

Coventry

Coventry Telegraph: Corporation St, Coventry, CV1 1FP; tel. (24) 7663-3633; e-mail darren.parkin@coventrytelegraph.net; internet www.coventrytelegraph.net; f. 1891 as *Midland Daily Telegraph*; independent; Propr Trinity Mirror PLC; morning; Editor ALUN THORNE; circ. 34,359.

Darlington

Northern Echo: POB 14, Priestgate, Darlington, DL1 1NF; tel. (1325) 505065; e-mail newsdesk@nne.co.uk; internet www .thenorthernecho.co.uk; f. 1869; morning; independent; Editor PETER BARRON; circ. 41,181.

Derby

The Derby Telegraph: Northcliffe House, Meadow Rd, Derby, DE1 2BH; tel. (1332) 291111; fax (1332) 253027; e-mail newsdesk@ derbytelegraph.co.uk; internet www.thisisderbyshire.co.uk; f. 1932; incl. *Derby Daily Telegraph*, f. 1879, *Derby Daily Express*, f. 1884; Propr Local World; Editor NEIL WHITE; circ. 32,356.

Dundee

Courier and Advertiser: 80 Kingsway East, Dundee, DD4 8SL; tel. (1382) 223131; fax (1382) 225511; e-mail courier@dcthomson.co.uk; internet www.thecourier.co.uk; f. 1810; Propr DC Thomson; morning; Editor RICHARD NEVILLE; circ. 61,981.

Edinburgh

Edinburgh Evening News: Barclay House, 108 Holyrood Rd, Edinburgh, EH8 8AS; tel. (131) 620-8744; e-mail newsen@ edinburghnews.com; internet www.edinburghnews.com; f. 1873; Propr Johnston Press PLC; Man. Dir STUART BIRKETT; circ. 39,947.

The Scotsman: Barclay House, 108 Holyrood Rd, Edinburgh, EH8 8AS; tel. (131) 620-8620; fax (131) 620-8617; e-mail reception@ scotsman.com; internet www.scotsman.com; f. 1817; morning; Propr Johnston Press PLC; Editor IAN STEWART; circ. 37,731.

Glasgow

Daily Record: 1 Central Quay, Glasgow, G3 8DA; tel. (141) 309-3000; e-mail reporters@dailyrecord.co.uk; internet www.dailyrecord .co.uk; f. 1895; morning; independent; Propr Trinity Mirror PLC; Editor-in-Chief ALAN RENNIE; circ. 291,825 (Feb. 2012).

Glasgow Evening Times: 200 Renfield St, Glasgow, G2 3Q3; tel. (141) 302-7000; e-mail eveningtimescustomerservice@ heraldandtimes.co.uk; internet www.eveningtimes.co.uk; f. 1876; Propr Newsquest; Editor TONY CARLIN; circ. 47,000.

The Herald: 200 Renfield St, Glasgow, G2 3QB; tel. (141) 302-7000; e-mail news@theherald.co.uk; internet www.www.heraldscotland .com; f. 1783; morning; independent; Propr Newsquest; Editor-in-Chief JONATHAN RUSSELL; circ. 47,226.

Scottish Daily Express: Citypoint Z, 25 Tyndrum St, Glasgow, G4 0JY; tel. (141) 352-2521; e-mail scot.news@express.co.uk; internet www.express.co.uk/scottish; morning; regional edn of *Daily Express*; Propr Northern and Shell Group; Editor DAVID HAMILTON.

Grimsby

Grimsby Telegraph: 80 Cleethorpe Rd, Grimsby, DN31 3EH; tel. (1472) 360360; e-mail newsdesk@grimsbytelegraph.co.uk; internet www.thisisgrimsby.co.uk; f. 1898; evening; Editor MICHELLE LALOR; circ. 25,974.

Ipswich

East Anglian Daily Times: Press House, Lower Brook St, Ipswich, IP4 1AN; tel. (1473) 230023; e-mail news@eadt.co.uk; internet www .eadt.co.uk; f. 1874; Propr Archant; morning; Editor TERRY HUNT; circ. 29,932.

Kingston upon Hull

Hull Daily Mail: Blundell's Corner, Beverley Rd, Kingston upon Hull, HU3 1XS; tel. (1482) 327111; e-mail news@mailnewsmedia.co .uk; internet www.thisishullandeastriding.co.uk; f. 1885; evening; Editor NEIL HODGKINSON; circ. 43,523.

Leeds

Yorkshire Evening Post: No. 1 Leeds, 26 Whitehall Rd, Leeds, LS12 1BE; tel. (113) 238-8917; e-mail yep.newsdesk@ypn.co.uk; internet www.yorkshireeveningpost.co.uk; f. 1890; Propr Johnston Press PLC; Editorial Dir PETER CHARLTON; circ. 36,512.

Yorkshire Post: No. 1 Leeds, 26 Whitehall Rd, Leeds, LS12 1BE; tel. (113) 238-8432; e-mail yp.newsdesk@ypn.co.uk; internet www .yorkshirepost.co.uk; f. 1754; morning; Propr Johnston Press PLC; Editorial Dir PETER CHARLTON; circ. 39,698.

Leicester

Leicester Mercury: St George St, Leicester, LE1 9FQ; tel. (116) 251-2512; fax (116) 253-0645; e-mail newsdesk@leicestermercury.co .uk; internet www.thisisleicestershire.co.uk; f. 1874; evening; Editor RICHARD BETTSWORTH; circ. 51,153.

Liverpool

Liverpool Echo: POB 48, Old Hall St, Liverpool, L69 3EB; tel. (151) 227-2000; e-mail letters@liverpool.com; internet www.liverpoolecho .co.uk; f. 1879; evening; independent; Propr Trinity Mirror PLC; Editor ALASTAIR MACHRAY; circ. 85,463.

Manchester

Manchester Evening News: 1 Scott Pl., Hardman St, Manchester, M3 3RN; tel. (161) 832-7200; fax (161) 211-2034; e-mail newsdesk@ men-news.co.uk; internet www.manchestereveningnews.co.uk; f. 1868; independent; Editor ROB IRVINE; circ. 90,973.

Middlesbrough

Evening Gazette: Borough Rd, Middlesbrough, TS1 3AZ; tel. (1642) 245401; e-mail news@eveninggazette.co.uk; internet www .gazettelive.co.uk; f. 1869; Propr Trinity Mirror PLC; Editor CHRIS STYLES; circ. 40,563.

Newcastle upon Tyne

Evening Chronicle: Groat Market, Newcastle upon Tyne, NE1 1ED; tel. (191) 201-6429; e-mail ec.news@ncjmedia.co.uk; internet www.chroniclelive.co.uk; f. 1885; Propr Trinity Mirror PLC; Editor DARREN THWAITES; circ. 52,486.

The Journal: Groat Market, Newcastle upon Tyne, NE1 1ED; tel. (191) 201-6446; e-mail journal.editor@ncjmedia.co.uk; internet www .journallive.co.uk; f. 1832; morning; Propr Trinity Mirror PLC; Editor BRIAN AITKEN; circ. 26,280.

Norwich

Eastern Daily Press: Prospect House, Rouen Rd, Norwich, NR1 1RE; tel. (1603) 628311; e-mail edp@archant.co.uk; internet www .edp24.co.uk; f. 1870; independent; Propr Archant Regional Ltd; Editor PETER WATERS; circ. 59,490.

Nottingham

Nottingham Post: Castle Wharf House, Nottingham, NG1 7EU; tel. (115) 948-2000; fax (115) 964-4032; e-mail newsdesk@ nottinghameveningpost.co.uk; internet www.thisisnottingham.co .uk; f. 1878; Editor MEL COOK; circ. 35,361.

Plymouth

Western Morning News: 17 Brest Rd, Derriford Business Park, Plymouth, PL6 5AA; tel. (1752) 765500; fax (1752) 765535; e-mail wmnnewsdesk@westernmorningnews.co.uk; internet www .westernmorningnews.co.uk; f. 1860; Editor BILL MARTIN; circ. 31,058.

Portsmouth

The News: The News Centre, London Rd, Hilsea, Portsmouth, PO2 9SX; tel. (23) 9266-4488; e-mail lucy.varney@thenews.co.uk; internet www.portsmouth.co.uk; f. 1877; evening; Editor MARK WALDRON; circ. 41,442.

Sheffield

The Star: York St, Sheffield, S1 1PU; tel. (114) 252-1364; fax (114) 252-1225; e-mail jeremy.clifford@thestar.co.uk; internet www .thestar.co.uk; f. 1887; evening; independent; Propr Johnston Press PLC; Editor JEREMY CLIFFORD; circ. 37,255.

Southampton

Southern Daily Echo: Newspaper House, Test Lane, Redbridge, Southampton, SO16 9JX; tel. (23) 8042-4777; fax (23) 8042-4545; e-mail newsdesk@dailyecho.co.uk; internet www.dailyecho.co.uk; f. 1888; Propr Newsquest; Editor IAN MURRAY; circ. 31,964.

Stoke-on-Trent

The Sentinel: Sentinel House, Etruria, Stoke-on-Trent, ST1 5SS; tel. (1782) 602525; e-mail newsdesk@thesentinel.co.uk; internet www.thisisstaffordshire.co.uk; f. 1854; Editor-in-Chief MIKE SASSI; circ. 50,792.

Sunderland

Sunderland Echo: Echo House, Pennywell, Sunderland, SR4 9ER; tel. (191) 501-5800; fax (191) 534-3807; e-mail echo.news@northeast-press.co.uk; internet www.sunderlandecho.com; f. 1873; evening; Editor RICHARD ORD (acting); circ. 32,771.

Swansea

South Wales Evening Post: Adelaide St, Swansea, SA1 1QT; tel. (1792) 510000; e-mail postnews@swwmedia.co.uk; internet www.thisissouthwales.co.uk; f. 1930; Editor JONATHAN ROBERTS; circ. 40,149.

Telford

Shropshire Star: Waterloo Rd, Ketley, Telford, TF1 5HU; tel. (1952) 242424; fax (1952) 254605; e-mail newsroom@shropshirestar.co.uk; internet www.shropshirestar.com; f. 1964; evening; Propr Shropshire Newspapers Ltd; Editor KEITH HARRISON; circ. 55,606.

Wolverhampton

Express and Star: 51–53 Queen St, Wolverhampton, WV1 1ES; tel. (1902) 313131; e-mail newsdesk@expressandstar.co.uk; internet www.expressandstar.co.uk; f. 1874; evening; Propr The Midland News Association Ltd; Editor ADRIAN FABER; circ. 113,174.

York

The Press: POB 29, 76–86 Walmgate, York, YO1 9YN; tel. (1904) 567131; e-mail newsdesk@thepress.co.uk; internet www.thepress.co.uk; morning; Editor STEVE HUGHES; circ. 25,989.

PRINCIPAL WEEKLY NEWSPAPERS

(average net circulation figures as at February 2012, unless otherwise stated)

Asian Times: Garavi Gujarat House, 1 Silex St, London, SE1 0DW; tel. (20) 7928-1234; fax (20) 7261-0055; e-mail newsdesk@easterneyeuk.co.uk; internet www.asiantimesonline.co.uk; Editor HAMANT VERMA; Man. Dir WAYNE BOWER.

Daily Star Sunday: Ludgate House, 245 Blackfriars Rd, London, SE1 9UX; tel. (20) 7928-8000; fax (20) 7633-0244; e-mail dailystarnewsdesk@dailystar.co.uk; internet www.dailystar.co.uk/sunday; f. 1978; Propr Express Newspapers PLC; Editor GARETH MORGAN; circ. 599,078.

The Independent on Sunday: 2 Derry St, London, W8 5HF; tel. (20) 7005-2000; fax (20) 7005-2627; internet www.independent.co.uk; f. 1990; Propr Independent Newspapers UK; Editor JOHN MULLIN; circ. 124,260.

The Mail on Sunday: Northcliffe House, 2 Derry St, London, W8 5TS; tel. (20) 7938-6000; fax (20) 7937-3829; internet www.mailonsunday.co.uk; f. 1982; Propr Associated Newspapers Ltd; Editor GEORDIE GREIG; Man. Dir STEPHEN MIRON; circ. 1,882,469.

The Observer: Kings Pl., 90 York Way, London, N1 9GU; tel. (20) 3353-2000; fax (20) 7713-4250; e-mail letters@observer.co.uk; internet observer.guardian.co.uk; f. 1791; owned by Guardian Newspapers Ltd; Sun.; Editor JOHN MULHOLLAND; circ. 253,022.

The People: 1 Canada Sq., Canary Wharf, London, E14 5AP; tel. (20) 7293-3201; e-mail online@people.co.uk; internet www.people.co.uk; f. 1881; Propr Trinity Mirror PLC; Editor JAMES SCOTT; circ. 701,246.

Scotland on Sunday: Barclay House, 108 Holyrood Rd, Edinburgh, EH8 8AS; tel. (131) 620-8620; e-mail reception@scotsman.com; internet swww.scotsman.com/scotland-on-sunday; f. 1988; Propr Johnston Press PLC; Editor IAN STEWART; circ. 46,964.

The Sun on Sunday: 3 Thomas More Sq., London, E98 1XY; tel. (20) 7782-4100; fax (20) 7782-4108; e-mail custserv@the-sun.co.uk; internet www.thesun.co.uk; f. 2012; Propr News International PLC; Editor DOMINIC MOHAN; circ. 3,213,613.

Sunday Express: The Northern & Shell Bldg, 10 Lower Thames St, London, EC3R 6EN; tel. (20) 8612-7075; e-mail web.help@express.co.uk; internet www.express.co.uk/sunday; f. 1918; incl. *Sunday Despatch* 1961; independent; Propr Northern and Shell Group; Editor-in-Chief MARTIN TOWNSEND; circ. 567,800.

Sunday Herald: 200 Renfield St, Glasgow, G2 3QB; tel. (141) 302-7800; e-mail letters@sundayherald.com; internet www.sundayherald.com; f. 1999; Propr Newsquest Media Group; Editor RICHARD WALKER; circ. 30,771.

Sunday Life: 124–144 Royal Ave, Belfast, BT1 1DN; tel. (28) 9026-4312; fax (28) 9054-4507; e-mail slnews@sundaylife.co.uk; internet www.sundaylife.co.uk; f. 1988; Editor MARTIN BREEN.

Sunday Mail: 1 Central Quay, Glasgow, G3 8DA; tel. (141) 309-3000; e-mail reporters@dailyrecord.co.uk; internet www.sundaymail.co.uk; Propr Trinity Mirror PLC; Editor ALLAN RENNIE; circ. 376,898.

Sunday Mercury: Fort Dunlop, Fort Parkway, Birmingham, B24 9FF; tel. (121) 234-5493; e-mail paul.cole@sundaymercury.net; internet www.sundaymercury.net; Propr Trinity Mirror PLC; f. 1918; Exec. Editor PAUL COLE.

The Sunday Post: 80 Kingsway East, Dundee, DD4 8SL; tel. (1382) 223131; e-mail mail@sundaypost.com; internet www.sundaypost.com; f. 1919; DC Thomson & Co. Ltd; Editor DONALD MARTIN; circ. 300,000.

Sunday Sun: Groat Market, Newcastle upon Tyne, NE1 1ED; tel. (191) 201-6299; fax (191) 230-0238; e-mail matt.mckenzie@ncjmedia.co.uk; internet www.sundaysun.co.uk; f. 1919; Propr Trinity Mirror PLC; independent; north-east England; Editor MATT MCKENZIE; circ. 59,865 (June–Dec. 2011).

Sunday Telegraph: 111 Buckingham Palace Rd, London, SW1W 0DT; tel. (20) 7931-2000; e-mail stletters@telegraph.co.uk; internet www.telegraph.co.uk; f. 1961; Propr Press Acquisitions Ltd; Editor IAN MCGREGOR; circ. 461,280.

The Sunday Times: 3 Thomas More Sq., London, E98 1RL; tel. (20) 7782-5000; e-mail newsdesk@sunday-times.co.uk; internet www.sunday-times.co.uk; f. 1822; Propr News International; Editor MARTIN IVENS (acting); circ. 939,395.

Wales on Sunday: Media Wales Ltd, Six Park St, Cardiff, CF10 1XR; tel. (29) 2024-3671; e-mail simon.farrington@mediawales.co.uk; internet www.walesonline.co.uk; f. 1991; Editor SIMON FARRINGTON; circ. 35,955 (2008).

SELECTED PERIODICALS

Arts and Literature

Apollo: 22 Old Queen St, London, SW1H 9HP; tel. (20) 7961-0150; fax (20) 7961-0110; e-mail editorial@apollomag.com; internet www.apollo-magazine.com; f. 1925; owned by Press Holdings; monthly; fine and decorative art; Editor OSCAR HUMPHRIES.

Architects' Journal: Greater London House, Hampstead Rd, London, NW1 7EJ; tel. (20) 7728-4573; fax (20) 7391-3435; e-mail crystal.bennes@emap.com; internet www.architectsjournal.co.uk; f. 1895; Thur.; Editor CHRISTINE MURRAY; circ. 13,491 (July 2005).

Architectural Review: Greater London House, Hampstead Rd, London, NW1 7EJ; tel. (20) 7728-4589; e-mail paul.finch@emap.com; internet www.arplus.com; f. 1896; monthly; Editor CATHERINE SLESSOR; circ. 18,544 (May 2007).

The Artist: Caxton House, 63–65 High St, Tenterden, TN30 6BD; tel. (1580) 763673; fax (1580) 765411; e-mail sally@tapc.co.uk; internet www.painters-online.co.uk; f. 1931; 13 a year; Man. Editor SALLY BULGIN.

ArtReview: 1 Sekforde St, London, EC1R 0BE; tel. (20) 7107-2760; fax (20) 7107-2761; e-mail editorial@artreview.com; internet www.art-review.com; f. 1949; monthly; Editor MARK RAPPOLT.

BBC Music Magazine: Tower House, 14th Floor, Fairfax St, Bristol, BS1 3BN; tel. (117) 314-7355; fax (117) 934-9008; e-mail music@bbcmagazines.com; internet www.classical-music.com; f. 1992; monthly; classical music; Editor OLIVER CONDY; circ. 42,834 (Dec. 2010).

The Bookseller: Endeavour House, 189 Shaftesbury Ave, London, WC2H 8TJ; tel. (20) 7420-6006; fax (20) 7420-6103; e-mail letters.to.editor@bookseller.co.uk; internet www.thebookseller.com; f. 1858; incorporates *Bent's Literary Advertiser* (f. 1802); Fri.; Propr VNU Entertainment Media UK Ltd; Editor NEILL DENNY.

The Burlington Magazine: 14–16 Dukes Rd, London, WC1H 9SZ; tel. (20) 7388-8157; fax (20) 7388-1230; e-mail burlington@burlington.org.uk; internet www.burlington.org.uk; f. 1903; monthly; all forms of art, ancient and modern; Editor RICHARD SHONE.

Classical Music: Rhinegold Publishing Ltd, 241 Shaftesbury Ave, London, WC2H 8TF; tel. (20) 7333-1742; fax (20) 7333-1769; e-mail classical.music@rhinegold.co.uk; internet www.rhinegold.co.uk; f. 1976; fortnightly; Editor KIMON DALTAS; circ. 18,000 (July 2005).

Dancing Times: 45–47 Clerkenwell Green, London, EC1R 0EB; tel. (20) 7250-3006; fax (20) 7253-6679; e-mail dt@dancing-times.co.uk;

internet www.dancing-times.co.uk; f. 1910; monthly; ballet, modern dance and musical theatre; Editor JONATHAN GRAY.

Empire: Endeavour House, Shaftesbury Ave, WC2H 8JG; tel. (20) 7182-8781; internet www.empireonline.co.uk; monthly; film; Editor MARK DINNING; circ. 172,639 (July–Dec. 2010).

Film Review: Visual Imagination Ltd, 9 Blades Court, Deodar Rd, London, SW15 2NU; tel. (20) 8875-1520; fax (20) 8875-1588; e-mail filmreview@visimag.com; internet www.visimag.com/filmreview; f. 1955; monthly.

Folklore: The Folklore Society, c/o The Warburg Institute, Woburn Sq., London, WC1H 0AB; tel. (20) 7862-8564; e-mail enquiries@folklore-society.com; internet www.folklore-society.com; f. 1878; 3 a year; Editor Prof. PATRICIA LYSAGHT.

Gramophone: Teddington Studios, Broom Rd, Teddington, TW11 9BE; tel. (20) 8267-5000; fax (20) 8267-5844; e-mail gramophone@haymarket.com; internet www.gramophone.co.uk; f. 1923; monthly; Publr SIMON TEMLETT; Editor JAMES JOLLY; circ. 36,817 (2007).

Granta: 12 Addison Ave, London, W11 4QR; tel. (20) 7605-1360; fax (20) 7704-1361; e-mail editorial@granta.com; internet www.granta.com; f. 1889; quarterly; Editor JOHN FREEMAN; circ. 80,000 (2005).

Index on Censorship: Free Word Centre, 60 Farringdon Rd, London, EC1R 3GA; tel. (20) 7324-2522; fax (20) 7278-1878; e-mail contact@indexoncensorship.org; internet www.indexoncensorship.org; f. 1972; 4 a year; concerned with freedom of expression throughout the world; Editor JO GLANVILLE.

Jazz Journal: Jazz Journal, The Invicta Press, Queen's Rd, Ashford, TN24 8HH; tel. (20) 8516-0456; e-mail editor@jazzjournal.co.uk; internet www.jazzjournal.co.uk; f. 1948; monthly; Editor MARK GILBERT.

Language Learning Journal: Association for Language Learning, University of Leicester, University Rd, Leicester, LE1 7RH; tel. (116) 2297600; e-mail info@all-languages.org.uk; internet www.all-languages.org.uk; f. 1990; 2 a year; Editors Dr NORBERT PACHLER, Dr DOUGLAS ALLFORD.

mixmag: 90–92 Pentonville Rd, London, N1 9HS; tel. (20) 7078-8400; fax (20) 7833-9900; e-mail mixmag@mixmag.net; internet www.mixmag.net; f. 1983; publ. by Development Hell Ltd; monthly; dance music and club culture; Editor NICK DE COSEMO; circ. 34,073 (2008).

Mojo: Endeavour House, 189 Shaftesbury Ave, London, WC2H 8JG; tel. (20) 7208-3443; fax (20) 7182-8596; internet www.mojo4music.com; f. 1993; monthly; popular music; Editor PHIL ALEXANDER; circ. 94,617 (2010).

NME: IPC Media Ltd, The Blue Fin Bldg, 110 Southwark St, London, SE1 0SU; tel. (20) 3148-5000; e-mail krissi_murison@ipcmedia.com; internet www.nme.com; f. 1952; Wed.; popular music; Editor MIKE WILLIAMS; circ. 56,284.

Opera: 36 Black Lion Lane, London, W6 9BE; tel. (20) 8563-8893; fax (20) 8563-8635; e-mail editor@opera.co.uk; internet www.opera.co.uk; f. 1950; monthly; Editor JOHN ALLISON.

Poetry Review: 22 Betterton St, London, WC2H 9BX; tel. (20) 7420-9883; fax (20) 7240-4818; e-mail poetryreview@poetrysociety.co.uk; internet www.poetrysociety.org.uk; f. 1909; quarterly; Editor FIONA SAMPSON; circ. 4,500 (2008).

Q Magazine: Endeavour House, 189 Shaftesbury Ave, London, WC2H 8JG; tel. (20) 7182-8000; fax (20) 7182-8547; internet www.q4music.com; f. 1986; monthly; music, general features; Editor (vacant); circ. 88,240 (2010).

Sight and Sound: British Film Institute, 21 Stephen St, London, W1T 1LN; tel. (20) 7255-1444; fax (20) 7436-2327; e-mail s&s@bfi.org.uk; internet www.bfi.org.uk/sightandsound; f. 1932; monthly; international film review; Editor NICK JAMES; circ. 20,283 (2007).

The Stage: Stage House, 47 Bermondsey St, London, SE1 3XT; tel. (20) 7403-1818; fax (20) 7357-8478; e-mail editor@thestage.co.uk; internet www.thestage.co.uk; f. 1880; Thur.; theatre, light entertainment, television, opera, dance; Man. Dir CAROLINE COMERFORD; circ. 34,000 (2008).

The Times Literary Supplement: 3 Thomas More Sq., London, E98 1BS; tel. (20) 7782-4985; fax (20) 7782-4966; e-mail letters@the-tls.co.uk; internet www.the-tls.co.uk; f. 1902; Fri.; weekly journal of literary criticism; Editor Sir PETER STOTHARD; circ. 36,535 (2008).

Top of the Pops: Vineyard House, 44 Brook Green, London, W6 7BT; e-mail totp.magazine@bbc.com; internet www.totpmag.com; monthly; popular music; Editor PETER HART; circ. 119,739 (2009).

Current Affairs and History

Antiquity: Dept of Archaeology, Durham University, South Rd, Durham, DH1 3LE; tel. and fax (191) 334-1125; e-mail editor@antiquity.ac.uk; internet antiquity.ac.uk; f. 1927; quarterly; archaeology; Editor Prof. CHRIS SCARRE.

The Big Issue: 1–5 Wandsworth Rd, London, SW8 2LN; tel. (20) 7526-3200; fax (20) 7526-3201; e-mail info@bigissue.com; internet www.bigissue.com; also offices based in Bristol, Cardiff, Glasgow, Manchester and the Midlands producing regional weekly edns; f. 1991; weekly; current affairs, social issues; Editor-in-Chief A. JOHN BIRD; total circ. 134,456 (2008).

Classical Quarterly: Journals Group, Cambridge University Press, The Edinburgh Bldg, Shaftesbury Rd, Cambridge, CB2 2RU; tel. (1223) 326070; fax (1223) 325150; e-mail journals@cambridge.org; internet journals.cambridge.org/jid_caq; f. 1906; 2 a year; language, literature, history and philosophy; Editors BRUCE GIBSON, JOHN WILKINS.

Contemporary Review: POB 1242, Oxford, OX1 4FJ; tel. and fax (1865) 201529; e-mail editorial@contemporaryreview.co.uk; internet www.contemporaryreview.co.uk; f. 1866; quarterly; publ by Contemporary Review Co Ltd; politics, international affairs, social subjects, the arts; Editor Dr RICHARD MULLEN.

English Historical Review: Faculty of History, Old Boys' High School, George St, Oxford, OX1 2RL; e-mail ehr@history.ox.ac.uk; internet ehr.oxfordjournals.org; f. 1886; 6 a year; learned articles and book reviews; Editors MARTIN CONWAY, CATHERINE HOLMES.

The Historian: The Historical Association, 59A Kennington Park Rd, London, SE11 4JH; tel. (20) 7735-3901; fax (20) 7582-4989; e-mail enquiry@history.org.uk; internet www.history.org.uk; f. 1906; 4 a year; Editor Dr TREVOR JAMES; circ. 2,600 (2013).

History Today: 25 Bedford Ave, London, WC1B 3AT; tel. (20) 3219-7810; fax (20) 3219-7829; e-mail admin@historytoday.com; internet www.historytoday.com; f. 1951; monthly; illustrated general historical magazine; Editor PAUL LAY; circ. 25,274 (2007).

International Affairs: Royal Institute of International Affairs, Chatham House, 10 St James's Sq., London, SW1Y 4LE; tel. (20) 7957-5724; fax (20) 7957-5710; e-mail csoper@chathamhouse.org; internet www.chathamhouse.org; f. 1922; 6 a year; owned by Royal Institute of International Affairs; publ. by Wiley-Blackwell; original articles, and reviews of publications on international affairs; Editor CAROLINE SOPER.

Journal of Contemporary History: Unit 24, The Bardfield Centre, Great Bardfield, CM7 4SL; tel. (1371) 811608; fax (870) 288-9730; e-mail office@jch.org.uk; internet www.jch.org.uk; f. 1966; quarterly; publ. by SAGE Publications Ltd; Editors RICHARD J. EVANS, STANLEY G. PAYNE.

London Gazette: POB 7923, London, SE1 5ZH; tel. (20) 7394-4517; fax (20) 7394-4572; e-mail london.gazette@tso.co.uk; internet www.london-gazette.co.uk; f. 1665; 5 a week; the oldest continuously published newspaper in the UK; govt journal of official, legal and public notices.

New Left Review: 6 Meard St, London, W1F 0EG; tel. (20) 7734-8830; fax (20) 7439-3869; e-mail mail@newleftreview.org; internet www.newleftreview.org; f. 1960; 6 a year; international politics, economics and culture; Editor SUSAN WATKINS.

New Statesman: John Carpenter House, 7th Floor, John Carpenter St, London, EC4Y 0BY; tel. (20) 7936-6400; e-mail info@newstatesman.co.uk; internet www.newstatesman.com; f. 1913; weekly; current affairs, politics and the arts; publ. by New Statesman Ltd; Editor JASON COWLEY; circ. 23,909 (2011).

People in Power: Cambridge International Reference on Current Affairs Ltd (CIRCA), 13–17 Sturton St, Cambridge, CB1 2SN; tel. (1223) 564334; fax (1223) 354643; e-mail pip@circaworld.com; internet www.peopleinpower.com; f. 1987; bi-monthly; current world-wide government listings and health contacts; owned by CIRCA Ltd; Man. Dir ROGER EAST; Producer CATHERINE JAGGER.

The Political Quarterly: Wiley-Blackwell, 9600 Garsington Rd, Oxford, OX4 2DQ; tel. (1865) 476303; fax (1865) 476770; internet www.wiley.com; f. 1930; Editors ANDREW GAMBLE, ANTHONY WRIGHT.

Private Eye: 6 Carlisle St, London, W1D 3BN; tel. (20) 7437-4017; fax (20) 7437-0705; e-mail strobes@private-eye.co.uk; internet www.private-eye.co.uk; f. 1961; fortnightly; satirical; Editor IAN HISLOP; circ. 205,231 (2008).

Prospect: 2 Bloomsbury Pl., London, WC1A 2QA; tel. (20) 7255-1281; fax (20) 7255-1279; e-mail editorial@prospect-magazine.co.uk; internet www.prospect-magazine.co.uk; f. 1995; monthly; political and cultural; Editor BRONWEN MADDOX; circ. 27,552.

Race & Class: The Institute of Race Relations, 2–6 Leeke St, London, WC1X 9HS; tel. (20) 7837-0041; fax (20) 7278-0623; e-mail info@irr.org.uk; internet www.irr.org.uk; f. 1959; quarterly; journal on racism, empire and globalization; Editors A. SIVANANDAN, HAZEL WATERS.

The Spectator: 22 Old Queen St, London, SW1H 9HP; tel. (20) 7961-0200; fax (20) 7961-0058; e-mail editor@spectator.co.uk; internet www.spectator.co.uk; f. 1828; Propr Press Holdings; Thur.; independent political and literary review; Editor FRASER NELSON; circ. 76,952 (2008).

Tribune: 9 Arkwright Rd, London, NW3 6AN; tel. (20) 7433-6410; fax (20) 7433-6419; e-mail mail@tribunemagazine.co.uk; internet www.tribuneweb.co.uk; f. 1937; Fri.; Labour's independent weekly; politics, current affairs, arts; Editor CHRIS MCLAUGHLIN.

Economics and Business

Accountancy Age: Incisive Media, 32–34 Broadwick St, London, W1A 2HG; tel. (20) 7316-9000; fax (20) 7316-9250; e-mail news@accountancyage.com; internet www.accountancyage.co.uk; f. 1969; weekly; Editor KEVIN REED; circ. 60,337 (2007).

The Banker: Number One Southwark Bridge, London, SE1 9HL; tel. (20) 7873-3000; e-mail thebanker@ft.com; internet www.thebanker.com; f. 1926; monthly; international and domestic banking and finance, investment banking and capital markets, banking technology, monetary and economic policy; Propr Pearson PLC; Editor BRIAN CAPLEN; circ. 28,166 (2010).

Campaign: Haymarket Marketing Publications Ltd, 174 Hammersmith Rd, London, W6 7JP; tel. (20) 8267-4656; fax (20) 8267-4915; e-mail campaign@haymarket.com; internet www.brandrepublic.com/campaign; f. 1968; advertising, marketing and media; Thur.; Editor CLAIRE BEALE; circ. 10,012 (June 2008).

Crops: Farmers Weekly Group, Quadrant House, The Quadrant, Sutton, SM2 5AS; tel. (20) 8652-4934; fax (20) 8652-8928; e-mail crops@rbi.co.uk; internet www.fwi.co.uk; f. 1984; 8 a year; publ. by Reed Business Information; Editor RICHARD ALLISON; circ. 13,203 (Jan.-Dec. 2011).

The Economic Journal: Wiley, 9600 Garsington Rd, Oxford, OX4 2DQ; tel. (1865) 776868; fax (1865) 714591; e-mail rabbott@wiley.com; internet wileyonlinelibrary.com/journal/ecoj; f. 1891; 9 a year; owned by Royal Economic Society; Man. Editors WOUTER DEN HAAN, ANDREA GALEOTTI, RACHEL GRIFFITH, STEVE MACHIN, MARTIN CRIPPS, FREDERIC VERMEULEN, KJELL SALVANES.

The Economist: 25 St James's St, London, SW1A 1HG; tel. (20) 7830-7000; fax (20) 7839-2968; e-mail letters@economist.com; internet www.economist.com; f. 1843; 50% owned by Pearson PLC, 50% by individual shareholders; Fri.; Editor JOHN MICKLETHWAIT; CEO ANDREW RASHBASS; circ. 182,539 (June 2008).

Euromoney: Nestor House, Playhouse Yard, London, EC4V 5EX; tel. (20) 7779-8888; fax (20) 7779-8653; e-mail hotline@euromoneyplc.com; internet www.euromoney.com; f. 1969; monthly; Editor CLIVE HORWOOD; circ. 25,368 (June 2008).

Farmers Weekly: Farmers Weekly Group, Quadrant House, The Quadrant, Sutton, SM2 5AS; tel. (20) 8652-4911; fax (20) 8652-4005; e-mail farmers.weekly@rbi.co.uk; internet www.fwi.co.uk; f. 1934; Fri.; publ. by Reed Business Information; Editor JANE KING; circ. 68,897 (June 2008).

Investors Chronicle: Number One Southwark Bridge, London, SE1 9HL; tel. (20) 7382-3000; e-mail ic.cs@ft.com; internet www.investorschronicle.co.uk; f. as *Money Market Review* 1860; amalgamated with *Investors Chronicle* 1914; amalgamated with the *Stock Exchange Gazette* 1967; Fri.; independent financial and economic review; Editor JOHN HUGHMAN; circ. 30,027.

Management Today: 174 Hammersmith Rd, London, W6 7JP; tel. (20) 8267-4967; fax (20) 8267-4680; e-mail editorial@mtmagazine.co.uk; internet www.managementtoday.co.uk; f. 1966; monthly; Editor MATTHEW GWYTHER; circ. 100,002 (June 2008).

Education

Higher Education Quarterly: Wiley-Blackwell, 9600 Garsington Rd, Oxford, OX4 2DQ; tel. (1865) 776868; fax (1865) 714591; internet www.wileyonlinelibrary.com/journal/hequ; f. 1946; Editors LEE HARVEY, CELIA WHITCHURCH.

The Teacher: Hamilton House, Mabledon Pl., London, WC1H 9BD; tel. (20) 7380-4708; fax (20) 7387-8458; e-mail teacher@nut.org.uk; internet www.teachers.org.uk/theteacher; f. 1872; magazine of the NUT; news, comments and articles on all aspects of education; 6 a year; Editor ELLIE CAMPBELL-BARR.

The Times Educational Supplement (TES): 26 Red Lion Sq., London, WC1R 4HQ; tel. (20) 3194-3000; fax (20) 3194-3333; e-mail letters@tes.co.uk; internet www.tes.co.uk; f. 1910; Fri.; Editor GERARD KELLY; circ. 57,714.

Times Higher Education (THE): 26 Red Lion Sq., London, WC1R 4HQ; tel. (20) 3194-3000; fax (20) 3194-3300; e-mail editor@thes.co.uk; internet www.timeshighereducation.co.uk; f. 1971 as *The Times Higher Education Supplement*; Thur.; Editor ANN MROZ; circ. 21,140 (Dec. 2007).

Home, Fashion and General

Bella: H. Bauer Publishing Ltd, 1st Floor, 24–28 Oval Rd, London, NW1 7DT; tel. (20) 7241-8000; fax (20) 7241-8030; internet www.bauer.co.uk; f. 1987; Tue.; fashion, beauty, health, cookery, handicrafts; Editor JULIA DAVIS; circ. 246,446 (2010).

Best: National Magazine Company, 72 Broadwick St, London, W1F 9EP; tel. (20) 7439-5000; fax (20) 7439-4580; e-mail best@acp-natmag.co.uk; internet www.natmags.co.uk; f. 1987; weekly; women's interest; Editor JACKIE HATTON; circ. 302,309 (2010).

Chat: IPC Connect Ltd, The Blue Fin Bldg, 110 Southwark St, London, SE1 0SU; tel. (20) 3148-6153; fax (20) 3148-8111; e-mail ben_gelblum@ipcmedia.com; internet www.ipcmedia.com; weekly; women's interest; Editor GILLY SINCLAIR; circ. 430,674 (2010).

Company: National Magazine House, 72 Broadwick St, London, W1F 9EP; tel. (20) 7439-5000; fax (20) 7439-6886; e-mail company.mail@natmags.co.uk; internet www.natmags.co.uk; monthly; Editor VICTORIA WHITE; circ. 217,324 (2010).

Cosmopolitan: National Magazine House, 72 Broadwick St, London, W1F 9EP; tel. (20) 7439-5000; e-mail cosmo.mail@hearst.co.uk; internet www.cosmopolitan.co.uk; f. 1972; monthly; women's interest; Editor LOUISE COURT; circ. 401,750 (2010).

Elle: 64 North Row, London, W1K 7LL; tel. (20) 7150-7000; fax (20) 7150-7001; e-mail lorraine.candy@hf-uk.com; internet www.elleuk.com; f. 1985; monthly; women's interest; Editor-in-Chief LORRAINE CANDY; circ. 195,625 (2010).

Esquire: National Magazine House, 72 Broadwick St, London, W1F 9EP; tel. (20) 7439-5601; fax (20) 7439-5675; e-mail info@esquire.co.uk; internet www.esquire.co.uk; f. 1991; monthly; men's interest; Editor ALEX BILMES; circ. 52,705 (2009).

FHM: Endeavour House, 189 Shaftesbury Ave, London, WC2H 8JG; tel. (20) 7436-8534; fax (20) 7182-8021; e-mail help@fhm.com; internet www.fhm.com; f. 1987; monthly; men's interest; Editor JOE BARNES; circ. 192,586 (2010).

Glamour: Vogue House, Hanover Sq., London, W1S 1JU; tel. (20) 7499-9080; e-mail glamoureditorialmagazine@condenast.co.uk; internet www.glamour.com; f. 2001; monthly; women's interest; Editor JO ELVIN; circ. 526,216 (2010).

Good Housekeeping: National Magazine House, 72 Broadwick St, London, W1F 9EP; tel. (20) 7439-5000; fax (20) 7437-6886; e-mail goodh.mail@natmags.co.uk; internet www.goodhousekeeping.co.uk; f. 1922; monthly; Editor-in-Chief LINDSAY NICHOLSON; circ. 422,496 (2010).

GQ: The Condé Nast Publications Ltd, Vogue House, Hanover Sq., London, W1S 1JU; tel. (20) 7499-9080; fax (20) 7495-1679; internet www.gq-magazine.co.uk; f. 1988; monthly; Editor DYLAN JONES; circ. 120,019 (2009).

Grazia: Endeavour House, 189 Shaftesbury Ave, London, WC2H 8JG; tel. (20) 7437-9011; e-mail graziadaily@graziamagazine.co.uk; internet www.graziamagazine.co.uk; f. 2005; weekly; Editor JANE BRUTON; circ. 224,421 (2010).

Harper's Bazaar: National Magazine House, 72 Broadwick St, London, W1F 9EP; tel. (20) 7439-5000; fax (20) 7437-6886; internet www.harpersbazaar.co.uk; f. 1929; Propr National Magazine Co Ltd; monthly; international fashion, beauty, general features; Editor JUSTINE PICARDIE; circ. 109,646 (2009).

Heat: Endeavour House, 189 Shaftesbury Ave, London, WC2H 8JG; tel. (20) 7437-9011; internet www.heatworld.com; f. 1999; Tue.; celebrity news, TV, radio, films; Editor LUCIE CAVE; circ. 370,132 (2010).

Hello!: Hello! Ltd, Wellington House, 69–71 Upper Ground, London, SE1 9PQ; tel. (20) 7667-8700; fax (20) 7667-8716; e-mail hello@hellomagazine.com; internet www.hellomagazine.com; Propr, Hola, SA (Spain); weekly; Publishing Dir CHARLOTTE STOCKTING; Editor KAY GODDARD; circ. 373,225.

Homes and Gardens: The Blue Fin Bldg, 110 Southwark St, London, SE1 0SU; tel. (20) 7261-6202; fax (20) 7261-6247; e-mail homesandgardens@ipcmedia.com; internet www.homesandgardens.com; f. 1919; monthly; Editor DEBORAH BARKER; circ. 136,136 (2010).

House & Garden: The Condé Nast Publications Ltd, Vogue House, Hanover Sq., London, W1S 1JU; tel. (20) 7499-9080; fax (20) 7629-2907; e-mail harriet.bindloss@condenast.co.uk; internet www.houseandgarden.co.uk; f. 1920; monthly; Editor SUSAN CREWE; circ. 130,781 (2010).

Ideal Home: IPC Media Ltd, The Blue Fin Bldg, 110 Southwark St, London, SE1 0SU; tel. (20) 3148-5000; e-mail ideal_home@ipcmedia.com; internet www.idealhomemagazine.co.uk; f. 1920; 11 a year; Editor ISOBEL MCKENZIE-PRICE; circ. 205,659 (2010).

InStyle: The Blue Fin Bldg, 110 Southwark St, London, SE1 0SU; tel. (20) 7261-4747; fax (20) 7261-6664; internet www.instylemagazine.co.uk; f. 2001; monthly; fashion, beauty; Editor EILIDH MACASKILL; circ. 186,251 (2010).

The Lady: 39–40 Bedford St, London, WC2E 9ER; tel. (20) 7379-4717; fax (20) 7497-2137; e-mail editors@lady.co.uk; internet www.lady.co.uk; f. 1885; Fri.; Publr BEN BUDWORTH; circ. 29,095.

Marie Claire: IPC Media Ltd, The Blue Fin Bldg, 110 Southwark St, London, SE1 0SU; tel. (20) 3148-7481; e-mail marieclaire@ipcmedia

.com; internet www.marieclaire.co.uk; f. 1988; monthly; women's interest; Man. Editor TRISH HALPIN; circ. 266,881 (July–Dec. 2011).

My Weekly: D. C. Thomson & Co Ltd, 80 Kingsway East, Dundee, DD4 8SL; tel. (1382) 223131; fax (1382) 452491; e-mail myweekly@ dcthomson.co.uk; f. 1910; Thur.; women's interest; Editor SALLY HAMPTON; circ. 124,066 (2011).

Now: The Blue Fin Bldg, 110 Southwark St, London, SE1 0SU; tel. (20) 3148-6373; fax (20) 3148-8110; internet www.nowmagazine.co .uk; weekly; celebrity news, TV, radio, films; Editor SALLY EYDEN; circ. 338,080 (2010).

Nuts: The Blue Fin Bldg, 110 Southwark St, London, SE1 0SU; tel. (20) 7261-6174; e-mail nutsmagazine@ipcmedia.com; internet www .nutsmag.co.uk; f. 2004; weekly; Editor DOMINIC SMITH; circ. 147,134 (2010).

OK!: The Northern & Shell Bldg, 10 Lower Thames St, London, EC3R 6EN; tel. (871) 434-1010; e-mail editor@ok-magazine.com; internet www.ok-magazine.co.uk; weekly; Editor LISA BYRNE; circ. 478,878 (2010).

The People's Friend: D. C. Thomson & Co Ltd, 80 Kingsway East, Dundee, DD4 8SL; tel. (1382) 223131; fax (1382) 452491; e-mail peoplesfriend@dcthomson.co.uk; f. 1869; Wed.; women's fiction, home, crafts, general; Editor ANGELA GILCHRIST; circ. 330,093.

Prima: 72 Broadwick St, London, W1F 9EP; tel. (20) 7439-5000; fax (20) 7312-4100; e-mail prima@hearst.co.uk; internet www .allaboutyou.com/prima; f. 1986; owned by Hearst Magazines UK; monthly; Editor GABY HUDDART; circ. 256,053 (2012).

Reader's Digest: 157 Edgware Rd, London, W2 2HR; tel. (20) 7715-8000; fax (20) 7053-4500; e-mail theeditor@readersdigest.co.uk; internet www.readersdigest.co.uk; f. 1938; monthly; Editor CATHE-RINE HAUGHNEY; circ. 403,458 (2010).

The Scots Magazine: D. C. Thomson & Co. Ltd, 80 Kingsway East, Dundee, DD4 8SL; tel. (1382) 223131; fax (1382) 322214; e-mail mail@scotsmagazine.com; internet www.scotsmagazine.com; f. 1739; monthly; Scottish interest; Editor PHIL SMITH; circ. 36,049 (2008).

Take a Break: H. Bauer Publishing Ltd, 24–28 Oval Rd, London, NW1 7DT; tel. (20) 7241-8000; fax (20) 7241-8052; e-mail tab .features@bauer.co.uk; internet www.bauer.co.uk; f. 1990; Thur.; Editor REBECCA FLEMING; circ. 855,372 (2010).

Tatler: The Condé Nast Publications Ltd, Vogue House, Hanover Sq., London, W1S 1JU; tel. (20) 7499-9080; fax (20) 7409-0451; internet www.tatler.co.uk; f. 1709; monthly; Man. Editor KAREN HODKINSON; circ. 85,064 (2010).

That's Life!: H. Bauer Publishing Ltd, 24–28 Oval Rd, London, NW1 7DT; tel. (20) 7241-8000; fax (20) 7241-8008; e-mail sales@tpc-london .com; internet www.bauer.co.uk; f. 1995; Thur.; Editor SOPHIE HEARSEY; circ. 341,545 (2010).

Vanity Fair: The Condé Nast Publications Ltd, Vogue House, Hanover Sq., London, W1S IJU; tel. (20) 7499-9080; fax (20) 7499-4415; internet www.vanityfair.com; monthly; Editor HENRY PORTER; circ. 102,471 (2010).

Viz: Dennis Publishing Ltd, 30 Cleveland St, London, W1T 4JD; tel. (20) 7907-6000; fax (20) 7907-6020; e-mail viz@viz.co.uk; internet www.viz.co.uk; f. 1979; monthly; Editor SIMON DONALD; circ. 88,165 (2007).

Vogue: The Condé Nast Publications Ltd, Vogue House, Hanover Sq., London, W1S 1JU; tel. (20) 7499-9080; fax (20) 7408-0559; e-mail vogue.com.editor@condenast.co.uk; internet www.vogue.co.uk; f. 1916; monthly; Editor ALEXANDRA SHULMAN; circ. 210,561 (2010).

The Voice: GV Media Group Ltd, Moorfoot House, 221 Marsh Wall, London, E14 9FJ; tel. (20) 7510-0340; fax (20) 7510-0341; e-mail letters@gvmedia.co.uk; internet www.voice-online.co.uk; f. 1982; Mon.; black interest; Editor GEORGE RUDDOCK.

Wallpaper*: 7th Floor, The Blue Fin Bldg, 110 Southwark St, London, SE1 0SU; tel. (20) 3148-5000; fax (20) 3148-8119; e-mail contact@wallpaper.com; internet www.wallpaper.com; f. 1996; monthly; Editor TONY CHAMBERS; circ. 108,050 (2008).

Woman: The Blue Fin Bldg, 110 Southwark St, London, SE1 0SU; tel. (20) 3148-6491; e-mail woman@ipcmedia.com; internet www .ipcmedia.com/brands/woman; f. 1937; Tue.; Editor KAREN LIVER-MORE; circ. 338,577 (2010).

Woman and Home: The Blue Fin Bldg, 110 Southwark St, London, SE1 0SU; tel. (20) 3148-7836; e-mail woman&home@ipcmedia.com; internet www.ipcmedia.com/brands/womanhome; f. 1926; monthly; Editor SUE JAMES; circ. 369,321 (2010).

Woman's Own: The Blue Fin Bldg, 110 Southwark St, London, SE1 0SU; tel. (20) 3148-6552; fax (20) 3148-8112; internet www.ipcmedia .com/brands/womansown; f. 1932; Tue.; Editor CATHERINE WEST-WOOD; circ. 272,376 (2010).

Woman's Weekly: The Blue Fin Bldg, 110 Southwark St, London, SE1 0SU; tel. (20) 3148-6628; internet www.ipcmedia.com/brands/

womansweekly; f. 1911; Wed.; Editor DIANE KENWOOD; circ. 38,577 (2010).

Zoo: Mappin House, 4 Winsley St, London, W1W 8HF; tel. (20) 7182-8000; internet www.zootoday.com; f. 2004; weekly; Editor TOM ETHERINGTON; circ. 68,610 (2010).

Law

Law Quarterly Review: 100 Avenue Rd, London, NW3 3PF; tel. (20) 7393-7000; fax (20) 7393-7010; internet www.sweetandmaxwell .co.uk; f. 1885; quarterly; Editor Prof. FRANCIS M. B. REYNOLDS.

Law Society's Gazette: 113 Chancery Lane, London, WC2A 1PL; tel. (20) 7242-1222; e-mail gazette-editorial@lawsociety.org.uk; internet www.lawgazette.co.uk; f. 1903; weekly; Editor-in-Chief PAUL ROGERSON; circ. 118,927.

The Lawyer: St Giles House, 50 Poland St, London, W1V 7AX; tel. (20) 7970-4614; fax (20) 7970-4640; e-mail catrin.griffiths@ thelawyer.com; internet www.thelawyer.com; weekly; Editor CATRIN GRIFFITHS; circ. 31,571 (June 2008).

Leisure Interests and Sport

Autocar Magazine: Haymarket Publishing, Teddington Studios, Broom Rd, Teddington, TW11 9BE; tel. (20) 8267-5630; fax (20) 8267-5759; e-mail editorial@autocar.co.uk; internet www.autocar.co.uk; f. 1895; Wed.; Editor CHAS HALLETT; circ. 58,091 (2008).

Autosport: Haymarket Consumer Media, Broom Rd, Teddington, TW11 9BE; tel. (20) 8267-5118; e-mail rob.aherne@haymarket.com; internet www.autosport.com; f. 1950; Thur.; covers all aspects of motor sport; Editor-in-Chief ANDY VAN DE BURGT; circ. 38,324 (2007).

BBC Gardeners' World Magazine: Immediate Media, Vineyard House, 5th Floor, 44 Brook Green, Hammersmith, London, W6 7BT; tel. (20) 7150-5700; e-mail magazine@gardenersworld.com; internet www.gardenersworld.com; f. 1991; monthly; Editor LUCY HALL; circ. 260,133 (2010).

BBC Good Food: 44 Vineyard House, Brook Green, London W6 7BT; tel. (20) 150-5332; e-mail goodfood@bbc.com; internet www .bbcgoodfood.com; f. 1989; monthly; Editor GILLIAN CARTER; circ. 305,855 (2010).

Car: Media House, Lynchwood Business Park, Lynchwood, Peter-borough, PE2 6EA; tel. (1733) 468485; fax (1733) 468660; e-mail car@ bauermedia.co.uk; internet www.carmagazine.co.uk; f. 1962; monthly; Editor PHIL MCNAMARA; circ. 58,380 (2010).

Country Life: 9th Floor, The Blue Fin Bldg, 110 Southwark St, London, SE1 0SU; tel. (20) 3148-4435; fax (20) 3148-8129; e-mail milly_cumming@ipcmedia.com; internet www.countrylife.co.uk; f. 1897; Thur.; Editor MARK HEDGES; circ. 40,821 (2007).

The Countryman: The Water Mill, Broughton Hall, Skipton, BD23 3AG; tel. (1756) 701381; fax (1756) 701326; e-mail editorial@ thecountryman.co.uk; internet www.thecountryman.co.uk; f. 1927; monthly; independent; Editor PAUL JACKSON; circ. 19,817 (2007).

The Cricketer: The Cricketer Publishing Ltd, 70 Great Portland St, London, W1W 7UW; tel. (20) 7460-5200; e-mail magazine@ thecricketer.com; internet www.thecricketer.com; f. 1921; monthly; Editor ANDREW MILLER; circ. 32,098 (2010).

FourFourTwo: Haymarket Consumer Media, Broom Rd, Teddington, TW11 9BE; tel. (20) 8267-5848; fax (20) 8267-5354; e-mail martyn.jones@haymarket.com; internet www.fourfourtwo.com; f. 1994; monthly; football; Editor DAVID HALL; circ. 107,987 (2008).

Golf Monthly: The Blue Fin Bldg, 110 Southwark St, London, SE1 0SU; tel. (20) 7148-4530; e-mail golfmonthly@ipcmedia.com; internet www.golf-monthly.co.uk; f. 1911; monthly; Editor MICHAEL HARRIS; circ. 82,264 (2008).

Hi-Fi News: Leon House, 10th Floor, 233 High St, Croydon, CR9 1HZ; tel. (20) 8726-8310; fax (20) 8726-8397; e-mail hi-finews@ ipcmedia.com; internet www.hifinews.co.uk; f. 1956; monthly; all aspects of high-quality sound reproduction, record reviews; Editor PAUL MILLER; circ. 11,353 (2008).

Men's Health: 72 Broadwick St, London, W1F 9EP; tel. (20) 7339-4400; fax (20) 7339-4444; e-mail nicky.williams@natmag-rodale.co .uk; internet www.menshealth.co.uk; f. 1995; monthly; lifestyle, health, general features; Editor MORGAN REES; circ. 245,754 (2010).

Practical Photography: Media House, Lynchwood Business Park, Lynchwood, Peterborough, PE2 6EA; tel. (1733) 468546; fax (1733) 468387; e-mail practical.photography@bauerconsumer.co.uk; internet www.photoanswers.co.uk; monthly; Editor-in-Chief ANDREW JAMES; circ. 62,303 (2007).

Radio Times: Vineyard House, 44 Brook Green, London, W6 7BT; tel. (20) 7150-5000; e-mail feedback@radiotimes.com; internet www .radiotimes.com; f. 1923; weekly; programme guide to television and radio broadcasts; Editor BEN PRESTON; circ. 947,131 (2010).

Rugby World: The Blue Fin Bldg, 110 Southwark St, London, SE1 0SU; tel. (20) 3148-4702; e-mail paul_morgan@ipcmedia.com;

internet www.rugbyworld.com; monthly; Editor PAUL MORGAN; circ. 48,381 (2007).

Time Out: Time Out Magazine Ltd, Universal House, 251 Tottenham Court Rd, London, W1T 7AB; tel. (20) 7813-3000; fax (20) 7813-6001; e-mail net@timeout.co.uk; internet www.timeout.com; f. 1968; weekly; listings and reviews of events in London; Time Out Group also publishes city guides and specialized London guides; Editor MARK FRITH; circ. 76,356 (2008).

TVTimes: The Blue Fin Bldg, 110 Southwark St, London, SE1 0SU; tel. (20) 3148-5570; e-mail tvtimes_letters@ipcmedia.com; internet www.ipcmedia.com/brands/tvtimes; f. 1955; features and listings of all television broadcasts; Editor IAN ABBOTT; circ. 290,686 (2010).

What Car?: Teddington Studios, Broom Rd, Teddington, TW11 9BE; tel. (20) 8267-5688; fax (20) 8267-5750; e-mail whatcar@haymarket .com; internet www.whatcar.com; f. 1973; 13 a year; Group Editor STEVE FOWLER; circ. 83,102 (2009).

What's On TV: The Blue Fin Bldg, 110 Southwark St, London, SE1 0SU; tel. (20) 3148-5928; e-mail wotv-postbag@ipcmedia.com; internet www.ipcmedia.com/brands/whatsontv; f. 1991; weekly; television programme guide and features; Editor COLIN TOUGH; circ. 1,209,018 (2010).

Zest: 72 Broadwick St, London, W1F 9EP; tel. (20) 7439-5000; fax (20) 7437-6886; e-mail contact@zest.co.uk; internet www.zest.co.uk; health, beauty, fitness and nutrition; Editor MANDIE GOWER; circ. 104,636 (2008).

Medicine, Science and Technology

Biochemical Journal: Portland Press Ltd, Eagle House, 3rd Floor, 16 Procter St, London, WC1V 6NX; tel. (20) 7280-4110; fax (20) 7280-4169; e-mail editorial@portlandpress.com; internet www.biochemj .org; f. 1906; 2 a month; publ. by Portland Press on behalf of the Biochemical Society; Chair., Editorial Board PETER R. SHEPHERD.

British Journal of Psychiatry: 17 Belgrave Sq., London, SW1X 8PG; tel. (20) 7235-2351; fax (20) 7259-6507; e-mail bjp@rcpsych.ac .uk; internet bjp.rcpsych.org; monthly; original articles, reviews and correspondence; publ. by the Royal College of Psychiatrists; Editor PETER TYRER; circ. 14,100 (2005).

British Journal of Psychology: St Andrew's House, 48 Princess Rd East, Leicester, LE1 7DR; tel. (116) 252-9506; fax (116) 227-1314; e-mail bjop@wiley.com; internet www.bpsjournals.co.uk; f. 1904; quarterly; publ. by Wiley-Blackwell; Editor Dr STEFAN SCHWEINBERGER.

British Journal of Sociology: Wiley-Blackwell, 9600 Garsington Rd, Oxford, OX4 2DQ; tel. (1865) 776868; fax (1865) 714591; internet www.blackwellpublishing.com/bjos; f. 1950; quarterly; Editor RICHARD WRIGHT.

BMJ: BMA House, Tavistock Sq., London, WC1H 9JP; tel. (20) 7387-4410; fax (20) 7383-6418; e-mail editor@bmj.com; internet www.bmj .com; f. 1840; Sat.; 10 overseas edns; Editor Dr FIONA GODLEE; circ. 120,606 (2008).

Computer Weekly: Reed Business Information, Quadrant House, The Quadrant, Sutton, SM2 5AS; tel. (20) 8652-8642; fax (20) 8652-8979; e-mail cwnews@rbi.co.uk; internet www.computerweekly .com; f. 1966; Tue.; Editor BRIAN McKENNA.

Computing: Incisive Media, 32–34 Broadwick St, London, W1A 2HG; tel. (20) 7316-9000; fax (20) 7316-9160; e-mail computing@vnu .co.uk; internet www.computing.co.uk; f. 1973; Thur.; Editor ABIGAIL WARAKER; circ. 115,000 (2005).

Flight International: Reed Business Information, Quadrant House, The Quadrant, Sutton, SM2 5AS; tel. (20) 8652-3842; fax (20) 8652-3840; e-mail flight.international@rbi.co.uk; internet www .flightinternational.com; f. 1909; Tue.; Editor MURDO MORRISON.

Geographical Magazine: Circle Publishing, 1 Victoria Villas, Richmond, TW9 2GW; tel. (20) 8332-2713; fax (20) 8332-9307; e-mail magazine@geographical.co.uk; internet www.geographical .co.uk; f. 1935; monthly; Editor GEORDIE TORR; circ. 21,684 (2008).

The Lancet: 32 Jamestown Rd, London, NW1 7BY; tel. (20) 7424-4910; fax (20) 7424-4911; e-mail editorial@lancet.com; internet www .thelancet.com; f. 1823; Sat.; medical; Editor Dr RICHARD HORTON.

Nature: Macmillan Magazines Ltd, 4 Crinan St, London, N1 9XW; tel. (20) 7833-4000; fax (20) 7843-4640; e-mail nature@nature.com; internet www.nature.com/nature; f. 1869; Thur.; scientific; Editor-in-Chief Dr PHILIP CAMPBELL.

New Scientist: Lacon House, 84 Theobald's Rd, London, WC1X 8NS; tel. (20) 7611-1200; fax (20) 7611-1250; e-mail news@ newscientist.com; internet www.newscientist.com; f. 1956; Thur.; science and technology; Editor ROGER HIGHFIELD; circ. 144,401 (2010).

Nursing Times: Emap Inform, Greater London House, Hampstead Rd, London, NW1 7EJ; tel. (20) 728-3702; fax (20) 7874-0505; e-mail nt@emap.com; internet www.nursingtimes.net; f. 1905; Tue.; pro-fessional nursing journal; Editor JENNI MIDDLETON; circ. 35,754 (2008).

The Practitioner: 10 Fernthorpe Rd, London, SW16 6DR; tel. (20) 8677-3508; fax (20) 8664-7429; e-mail editor@thepractitioner.co.uk; internet www.thepractitioner.co.uk; f. 1868; monthly; medical journal for general practitioners; owned by Practitioner Medical Publishing Ltd; Editor CORINNE SHORT.

Religion and Philosophy

Catholic Herald: Herald House, 15 Lamb's Passage, Bunhill Row, London, EC1Y 8TQ; tel. (20) 7448-3602; fax (20) 7256-9728; e-mail editorial@catholicherald.co.uk; internet www.catholicherald.co.uk; f. 1888; Catholic weekly newspaper; Fri.; Editor LUKE COPPEN.

Church Times: 13–17 Long Lane, London, EC1A 9PN; tel. (20) 7776-1060; fax (20) 7776-1086; e-mail editor@churchtimes.co.uk; internet www.churchtimes.co.uk; f. 1863; owned by Hymns Ancient & Modern Trust; Church of England and world-wide Anglican news; Fri.; Man. Editor PAUL HANDLEY.

Jewish Chronicle: 25 Furnival St, London, EC4A 1JT; tel. (20) 7415-1500; fax (20) 7405-9040; e-mail editorial@thejc.com; internet www.thejc.com; f. 1841; Fri.; Editor STEPHEN POLLARD; circ. 32,875 (June 2008).

Methodist Recorder: 122 Golden Lane, London, EC1Y 0TL; tel. (20) 7251-8414; fax (20) 7251-8600; e-mail editorial@ methodistrecorder.co.uk; internet www.methodistrecorder.co.uk; f. 1861; Thur.; Man. Editor MOIRA SLEIGHT.

New Blackfriars: Blackfriars, Oxford, OX1 3LY; tel. (1865) 650-0901; e-mail nb.editor@english.op.org; internet www.wiley.com; f. 1920; 6 a year; religious and cultural; Editor Rev. FERGUS KERR.

Philosophy: Royal Institute of Philosophy, 14 Gordon Sq., London, WC1H 0AR; tel. (20) 7387-4130; e-mail editor@ royalinstitutephilosophy.org; internet www .royalinstitutephilosophy.org; f. 1925; quarterly; Editor Prof. ANTHONY O'HEAR.

The Universe: The Universe Media Group, Alberton House, St Mark's Parsonage, Manchester, M3 2WJ; tel. (161) 214-1200; e-mail joseph.kelly@thecatholicuniverse.com; internet www .thecatholicuniverse.com; f. 1860; Sun.; illustrated Catholic newspaper and review; Editorial Dir JOSEPH KELLY.

Woman Alive: Christian Publishing and Outreach, Garcia Estate, Canterbury Rd, Worthing, BN13 1BW; tel. (1903) 604352; e-mail womanalive@cpo.org.uk; internet www.womanalive.co.uk; f. 1982; monthly; Editor JACKIE HARRIS.

PRESS ORGANIZATION

Press Complaints Commission: Halton House, 20–23 Holborn, London, EC1 0022; tel. (20) 7831-0022; fax (20) 7831-0025; e-mail complaints@pcc.org.uk; internet www.pcc.org.uk; f. 1991 to replace the Press Council, following the report of the Committee on Privacy and Related Matters; an independent organization established by the newspaper and magazine industry through the Press Standards Board of Finance to deal with complaints from the public about the contents and conduct of newspapers and magazines; the Commission has an independent chairman and 16 members, drawn from the lay public (who are in the majority) and the press; it upholds a 16-point Code of Practice, agreed by a committee of editors representing the newspaper and magazine industry; it aims to ensure that the British press maintains the highest professional standards, having regard to generally established press freedoms; Chair. Lord HUNT.

NEWS AGENCIES

Press Association Ltd: 292 Vauxhall Bridge Rd, London, SW1V 1AE; tel. (870) 120-3200; fax (870) 120-3201; e-mail info@pa.press .net; internet www.pa.press.net; f. 1868; national news agency of the United Kingdom and Ireland; Exec. Chair. PAUL POTTS; Man. Dir TONY WATSON; Editor JONATHAN GRUN.

Thomson Reuters: The Thomson Reuters Bldg, 30 The South Colonnade, Canary Wharf, London, E14 5EP; tel. (20) 7250-1122; fax (20) 7324-5400; e-mail editor@reuters.com; internet uk.reuters .com; f. 2008 by merger of Reuters Group PLC (f. 1851) and Thomson Corpn; world-wide news and information service to media and business clients in 57,900 organizations and media clients in 157 countries; over 55,000 employees; Chair. DAVID THOMSON; CEO JAMES C. SMITH.

INSTITUTIONS

Chartered Institute of Journalists: 2 Dock Offices, Surrey Quays Rd, London, SE16 2XU; tel. (20) 7252-1187; fax (20) 7232-2302; e-mail memberservices@cioj.co.uk; internet www.cioj.co.uk; f. 1884; Pres. CHARLIE HARRIS; Gen. Sec. DOMINIC COOPER.

The Journalists' Charity (Newspaper Press Fund): Dickens House, 35 Wathen Rd, Dorking, RH4 1JY; tel. (1306) 887511; fax

(1306) 888212; e-mail enquiries@journalistscharity.org.uk; internet www.journalistscharity.org.uk; f. 1864; charity for journalists and their dependants; Chair. ROBERT WARREN; Dir DAVID ILOTT.

Newspaper Publishers' Association (NPA): St Andrew's House, 8th Floor, 18–20 St Andrew St, London, EC4A 3AY; tel. (20) 7636-7014; fax (20) 7631-5119; f. 1906; comprises 8 national newspaper groups; Chair. CLIVE MILNER; Dir DAVID NEWELL.

Newspaper Society (NS): St Andrew's House, 8th Floor, 18–20 St Andrew St, London, EC4A 3AY; tel. (20) 7632-7400; fax (20) 7632-7401; e-mail ns@newspapersoc.org.uk; internet www.newspapersoc.org.uk; f. 1836; represents the regional and local press; Pres. MICHAEL PELOSI; Dir DAVID NEWELL.

Professional Publishers' Association: Queen's House, 28 Kingsway, London, WC2B 6JR; tel. (20) 7404-4166; fax (20) 7404-4167; e-mail info@ppa.co.uk; internet www.ppa.co.uk; f. 1913; trade association for the British magazine industry; Chair. KEVIN HAND; CEO BARRY MCILHENEY; more than 200 mems.

Association of Publishing Agencies (APA): Queen's House, 3rd Floor, 55–56 Lincoln's Inn Fields, London, WC2A 3LJ; tel. (20) 7404-4166; fax (20) 7404-4167; e-mail info@apa.co.uk; internet www.apa.co.uk; f. 1993; trade association for the customer publishing industry; Chair. MARTIN MACCONNOL; CEO PATRICK FULLER.

UK Association of Online Publishers (AOP): Queen's House, 55–56 Lincoln's Inn Fields, London, WC2A 3LJ; tel. (20) 7404-4166; fax (20) 7404-4167; e-mail lee.baker@ukaop.org.uk; internet www.ukaop.org.uk; f. 2002; represents the interests of online content providers; Chair. TIM FAIRCLIFF; Dir LEE BAKER.

Scottish Newspaper Society: 21 Lansdowne Cres., Edinburgh, EH12 5EH; tel. (131) 535-1064; fax (131) 535-1063; e-mail info@scotns.org.uk; f. 2010 following merger of Scottish Daily Newspaper Society and Scottish Newspaper Publishers Association; Dir JAMES RAEBURN.

See also under Employers' Organizations.

Principal Publishers

Publishing firms in the United Kingdom are mainly located in London and many are members of large publishing groups, notably Random House, Reed Elsevier, the Pearson Group and Thomson Reuters. Fiction remains the largest category. The United Kingdom publishes more new titles every year than any other European country. In 2011 a total of 149,800 new and revised titles were issued.

Alma Books Ltd: London House, 243–253 Lower Mortlake Rd, Richmond, TW9 2LL; tel. (20) 8948-9550; fax (20) 8948-5599; e-mail info@almabooks.com; internet www.almabooks.com; f. 2005; acquired Oneworld Classics (now Alma Classics) in 2011; fiction, plays, music, opera, European classics, translations, general books, social sciences, politics; Calderbooks, Calder Collections, English National Opera guides; Man. Dir ALESSANDRO GALLENZI.

Anova Books Group Ltd: The Old Magistrates Court, 10 Southcombe St, London, W14 0RA; tel. (20) 7605-1400; fax (20) 7605-1401; e-mail info@anovabooks.com; internet www.anovabooks.com; f. 2005; fmrly Chrysalis Books; imprints: Batsford, Collins & Brown, Conway, National Trust Books, Paper Tiger, Pavilion, Portico, Robson, Salamander; Chair. ROBIN WOOD; Chief Exec. POLLY POWELL.

Asean Academic Press Ltd: POB 13945, London, E5 0XY; fax (20) 8533-5856; e-mail aapub@attglobal.net; internet www.aseanacademicpress.com; educational, technical, professional and scientific books on Asia.

Ashgate Publishing Ltd: Wey Court East, Union Rd, Farnham, GU9 7PT; tel. (1252) 736600; fax (1252) 736736; e-mail ashgate.online@ashgate.com; internet www.ashgate.com; f. 1967; social sciences and humanities, art, business and public sector management books; imprints: Ashgate, Gower, Lund Humphries, Variorum; Chair. N. FARROW.

Atlantic Books: Ormond House, 26–27 Boswell St, London, WC1N 3JZ; tel. (20) 7269-1610; fax (20) 7430-0916; e-mail enquiries@groveatlantic.co.uk; internet www.atlantic-books.co.uk; f. 2000; subsidiary of Grove/Atlantic, Inc (USA); mem. of Independent Alliance; imprints: Guardian Books, Observer Books, Portobello Press; CEO and Publr TOBY MUNDY.

Berlitz Publishing: 58 Borough High St, London, SE1 1XF; tel. (20) 7403-0284; fax (20) 7403-0290; e-mail publishing@berlitz.co.uk; internet www.berlitzpublishing.com; f. 1970; travel, languages, reference, leisure, children's books; owned by Apa Publications UK Ltd; Man. Dir KATHARINE LECK.

A. & C. Black Publishers Ltd: 37 Soho Sq., London, W1D 3QZ; tel. (20) 7758-0200; fax (20) 7758-0222; e-mail enquiries@acblack.com; internet www.acblack.com; f. 1807; inc. Adlard Coles Nautical, Christopher Helm, Herbert Press, Pica Press, T & AD Poyser,

Thomas Reed, Methuen Drama, Wisden; children's and educational books, music, arts and crafts, drama, reference, sport, theatre, travel, sailing, ornithology; owned by Bloomsbury Publishing PLC; Chair. NIGEL NEWTON; Editorial Dir JANET MURPHY.

Bloomsbury Publishing PLC: 36 Soho Sq., London, W1D 3QY; tel. (20) 7494-2111; fax (20) 7434-0151; e-mail csm@bloomsbury.com; internet www.bloomsbury.com; f. 1986; fiction, non-fiction and children's; Chair. JEREMY WILSON; CEO NIGEL NEWTON.

Bowker (UK) Ltd: St Andrew's House, 18–20 St Andrew's St, London, EC4A 3AG; tel. (20) 7832-1770; fax (20) 7832-1710; e-mail sales@bowker.co.uk; internet www.bowker.co.uk; part of ProQuest Group of Cos; bibliographic information, catalogue enrichment and general information; Man. Dir DOUG MCMILLAN.

Marion Boyars Publishers Ltd: 26 Parke Rd, London, SW13 9NG; tel. (20) 8788-9522; fax (20) 8789-8122; e-mail catheryn@marionboyars.com; internet www.marionboyars.co.uk; f. 1975; fiction, plays, cinema, music, translations, literary criticism, sociology; Man. Dir CATHERYN KILGARRIFF.

Boydell & Brewer Ltd: Whitwell House, St Audry's Park Rd, Melton, Woodbridge, IP12 1SY; tel. (1394) 610600; fax (1394) 610316; e-mail editorial@boydell.co.uk; internet www.boydellandbrewer.com; f. 1978; literature, art, history; Editorial Dir CAROLINE PALMER; Sr Commissioning Editor MICHAEL MIDDEKE.

Cambridge University Press: The Edinburgh Bldg, Shaftesbury Rd, Cambridge, CB2 2RU; tel. (1223) 312393; fax (1223) 315052; e-mail information@cambridge.org; internet www.cambridge.org; f. 1534; academic and scientific monographs and textbooks, educational, English language teaching materials, microsoftware, Bibles, prayer books and academic journals; Chief Exec. STEPHEN R. R. BOURNE.

Canongate Books: 14 High St, Edinburgh, EH1 1TE; tel. (131) 557-5111; fax (131) 557-5211; e-mail info@canongate.co.uk; internet www.canongate.net; f. 1973; general, fiction, non-fiction; mem. of Independent Alliance; Chair. JAMIE BYNG.

Jonathan Cape Ltd: Random House, 20 Vauxhall Bridge Rd, London, SW1V 2SA; tel. (20) 7840-8606; fax (20) 7233-6117; e-mail enquiries@randomhouse.co.uk; internet www.randomhouse.co.uk; f. 1921; imprint of The Random House Group Ltd; general, biography, travel, belles-lettres, fiction, history, poetry; subsidiary imprint: The Bodley Head (biography, current affairs, humour); Publishing Dir DAN FRANKLIN.

Carlton Books: 20 Mortimer St, London, W1T 3JW; tel. (20) 7612-0418; fax (20) 7612-0401; e-mail sales@carltonbooks.co.uk; internet www.carltonbooks.co.uk; f. 1992; Man. Dir JONATHAN GOODMAN.

Century: Random House, 20 Vauxhall Bridge Rd, London, SW1V 2SA; tel. (20) 7840-8569; fax (20) 7233-6127; e-mail enquiries@randomhouse.co.uk; internet www.randomhouse.co.uk; f. 1987; imprint of The Random House Group Ltd; general, biography, travel, current affairs, fiction, memoirs, music, philosophy; Man. Dir RICHARD CABLE.

Chatto and Windus: 20 Vauxhall Bridge Rd, London, SW1V 2SA; tel. (20) 7840-8745; fax (20) 7233-6117; internet www.randomhouse.co.uk; imprint of The Random House Group Ltd; general, academic, biography, memoirs, politics, history, literary criticism, current affairs, cultural studies and fiction; imprint: Hogarth Press; Dir CLARA FARMER.

Church House Publishing: Church House, Great Smith St, London, SW1P 3AZ; tel. (20) 7898-1451; fax (20) 7898-1449; e-mail publishing@c-of-e.org.uk; internet www.chpublishing.co.uk; Publ. Man. Dr THOMAS ALLAIN-CHAPMAN.

James Clarke and Co Ltd: POB 60, Cambridge, CB1 2NT; tel. (1223) 350865; fax (1223) 366951; e-mail publishing@jamesclarke.co.uk; internet www.jamesclarke.co.uk; f. 1859; academic and reference: history, philosophy, religion, theology; imprints: Acorn Editions, James Clarke, Lutterworth Press, Patrick Hardy Books; acquired James Nisbet & Co in 2008; Man. Dir ADRIAN BRINK.

Collins Bartholomew: Westerhill Rd, Bishopbriggs, Glasgow, G64 2QT; tel. (208) 307-4515; fax (141) 306-3245; e-mail collinsbartholomew@harpercollins.co.uk; internet www.bartholomewmaps.com; f. 1826; cartographic division of HarperCollins Publishers; maps, atlases, bespoke mapping services and data; Man. Dir SHEENA BARCLAY.

Conran Octopus: Endeavour House, 189 Shaftesbury Ave, London, WC2H 8JY; tel. (20) 7632-5400; fax (20) 7531-8627; e-mail info@octopus-publishing.co.uk; internet www.octopusbooks.co.uk; illustrated reference books; imprint of Octopus Publishing Group Ltd; Group CEO ALISON GOFF.

Constable and Robinson Ltd: 3 The Lanchesters, 162 Fulham Palace Rd, London, W6 9ER; tel. (20) 8741-3663; fax (20) 8748-7562; e-mail enquiries@constablerobinson.com; internet www.constablerobinson.com; biography and autobiography, general and military history, current affairs, psychology and self-help, health, popular science, and crime fiction; Man. Dir NICHOLAS ROBINSON.

Continuum International Publishing Group: The Tower Bldg, 11 York Rd, London, SE1 7NX; tel. (20) 7922-0880; fax (20) 7922-0881; e-mail info@continuumbooks.com; internet www.continuumbooks.com; f. 1994; popular culture, religion, humanities, social sciences, philosophy and education; imprints: Burns & Oates, Continuum, T&T Clark, Thoemmes Continuum, Hambledon Continuum and Network Continuum; Chair. PATRICK AUSTEN; CEO OLIVER GADSBY.

Darton, Longman and Todd Ltd: 1 Spencer Court, 140–142 Wandsworth High St, London, SW18 4JJ; tel. (20) 8875-0155; fax (20) 8875-0133; e-mail info@darton-longman-todd.co.uk; internet www.dltbooks.com; f. 1959; theology, spirituality, religious biography and history, Bibles; Editorial Dir DAVID MOLONEY.

David & Charles Ltd: Brunel House, Forde Close, Newton Abbot, TQ12 4PU; tel. (1626) 323200; fax (1526) 323319; e-mail postmaster@davidandcharles.co.uk; internet www.davidandcharles.co.uk; f. 1960; owned by F+W Publications, Inc. (USA); general, trade and reference; Group Chair. and CEO DAVID NUSSBAUM.

André Deutsch Ltd: 20 Mortimer St, London, W1T 3JW; tel. (20) 7612-0400; fax (20) 7612-0401; e-mail enquiries@carltonbooks.co.uk; internet www.carltonbooks.co.uk; f. 1950; biography, memoirs, humour, art, politics, history, travel, sport; imprint of Carlton Books.

Dorling Kindersley PLC: 80 Strand, London, WC2R ORL; tel. (20) 7010-3000; fax (20) 7010-6060; e-mail customerservice@dk.com; internet www.dorlingkindersley-uk.co.uk; f. 1974; holding co Pearson PLC; illustrated reference books; CEO PETER FIELD.

Gerald Duckworth and Co Ltd: Greenhill House, 1st Floor, East Wing, 90–93 Cowcross St, London, EC1M 6BF; tel. (20) 7490-7300; fax (20) 7490-0080; e-mail info@duckworth-publishers.co.uk; internet www.ducknet.co.uk; f. 1898; trade, academic; Propr PETER MAYER.

Edinburgh University Press: 22 George Sq., Edinburgh, EH8 9LF; tel. (131) 650-4218; fax (131) 650-3286; e-mail editorial@eup.ed.ac.uk; internet www.euppublishing.com; learned books and journals; Chair. IVON ASQUITH; Chief Exec. TIMOTHY WRIGHT.

Edward Elgar Publishing Ltd: The Lypiatts, 15 Lansdown Rd, Cheltenham, GL50 2JA; tel. (1242) 226934; fax (1242) 262111; e-mail info@e-elgar.co.uk; internet www.e-elgar.com; f. 1986; economics, law, business and management, public and social policy; Man. Dir E. ELGAR.

Elsevier Ltd: The Boulevard, Langford Lane, Kidlington, Oxford, OX5 1GB; tel. (1865) 843000; fax (1865) 843010; internet www.elsevier.com; f. 1958; academic and professional reference books; imprints: Academic Press, Architectural Press, Bailliere Tindall, Butterworth-Heinemann, Churchill Livingstone, Digital Press, Elsevier, Elsevier Advanced Technology, Focal Press, Gulf Professional, Made Simple Books, Morgan Kaufmann, Mosby, Newnes, North-Holland, Pergamon, Saunders; part of Reed Elsevier Group PLC; Man. Dir ANNA MOON.

Encyclopaedia Britannica UK Ltd: Unity Wharf, 2nd Floor, Mill St, London, SE1 2BH; tel. (20) 7500-7800; fax (20) 7500-7878; e-mail enquiries@britannica.co.uk; internet www.britannica.co.uk; f. 1768; publs Encyclopaedia Britannica, Britannica Book of the Year, Great Books of the Western World, Britannica Learning Library, Britannica Almanac; Man. Dir IAN GRANT.

Euromonitor International: 60–61 Britton St, London, EC1M 5UX; tel. (20) 7251-8024; fax (20) 7608-3149; e-mail info@euromonitor.com; internet www.euromonitor.com; f. 1972; business and commercial reference; Chair. R. N. SENIOR; Man. Dir T. J. FENWICK.

Evans Publishing Group: 2A Portman Mansions, Chiltern St, London, W1U 6NR; tel. (20) 7487-0920; fax (20) 7487-0921; e-mail sales@evansbrothers.co.uk; internet www.evansbooks.co.uk; f. 1906; educational, children's, general and overseas books; Man. Dir BRIAN JONES; Publr SU SWALLOW.

Everyman's Library: Northburgh House, 10 Northburgh St, London, EC1V 0AT; tel. (20) 7566-6350; fax (20) 7490-3708; e-mail books@everyman.uk.com; internet www.randomhouse.com/knopf/classics; f. 1906; publ. in United Kingdom by The Random House Group Ltd.

Faber and Faber Ltd: Bloomsbury House, 74–77 Great Russell St, London, WC1B 3DA; tel. (20) 7927-3800; fax (20) 7927-3801; internet www.faber.co.uk; f. 1929; biography, autobiography, children's, film, drama, popular science, economics, fiction, history, music, poetry; mem. of Independent Alliance; Man. Dir STEPHEN PAGE.

The Folio Society Ltd: 44 Eagle St, London, WC1R 4FS; tel. (20) 7400-4200; fax (20) 7400-4242; internet www.foliosociety.com; f. 1947; fine illustrated edns of children's, fiction, food, gardening, history, biographies, poetry and travel books; Publishing Dir DAVID HAYDEN.

Footprint Handbooks Ltd: 6 Riverside Court, Lower Bristol Rd, Bath, BA2 3DZ; tel. (1225) 469141; fax (1225) 469461; e-mail discover@footprintbooks.com; internet www.footprintbooks.com; Publr ALAN MURPHY; Dirs ANDY RIDDLE, PATRICK DAWSON.

W. Foulsham & Co Ltd: The Oriel, Capital Point, 33 Bath Rd, Slough, SL1 3UF; tel. (1753) 526769; fax (1753) 535003; e-mail reception@foulsham.com; internet www.foulsham.com; f. 1819; finance, reference; Man. Dir BARRY BELASCO.

Fourth Estate: 77–85 Fulham Palace Rd, London, W6 8JB; tel. (20) 8741-7070; fax (20) 8307-4440; e-mail general@4thestate.co.uk; internet www.4thestate.co.uk; f. 1984; literature, humour, general reference, current affairs, literary and commercial fiction, cookery; imprint of HarperCollins Publishers; Publishing Dir NICHOLAS PEARSON.

Samuel French Ltd: 52 Fitzroy St, London, W1T 5JR; tel. (20) 7387-9373; fax (20) 7387-2161; e-mail theatre@samuelfrench-london.co.uk; internet www.samuelfrench-london.co.uk; f. 1830; drama; Chair. (vacant); Man. Dir VIVIEN GOODWIN.

Granta Books: 12 Addison Ave, London, W11 4QR; tel. (20) 7605-1360; fax (20) 7605-1361; e-mail publicity@granta.com; internet www.granta.com; fiction, political non-fiction; mem. of Independent Alliance; Publr SIGRID RAUSING.

Gresham Books Ltd: 19–21 Sayers Lane, Tenterden, TN30 6BW; tel. (1580) 767596; fax (1580) 764142; e-mail info@gresham-books.co.uk; internet www.gresham-books.co.uk; f. 1978; hymn books, school histories, music folders; Chief Exec. NICHOLAS OULTON.

Guinness World Records Ltd: 184–192 Drummond St, 3rd Floor, London, NW1 3HP; tel. (20) 7891-4567; fax (20) 7891-4501; internet www.guinnessworldrecords.com; f. 1954; acquired by Jim Pattison Group in 2008; music and general interest; Man. Dir ALISTAIR RICHARDS.

Hachette UK: 338 Euston Rd, London, NW1 3BH; tel. (20) 7873-6000; fax (20) 7873-6124; internet www.hachette.co.uk; f. 1993 as Hodder Headline; acquired by Hachette Livre (France) in 2004; present name adopted 2008; divisions: Hodder Education, John Murray Ltd, Headline Publishing Group, Hodder and Stoughton Ltd, Hachette Children's Books, Orion, Octopus Publishing Group, Little, Brown Book Group, Chambers Harrap; Group Chief Exec. TIM HELY HUTCHINSON.

Robert Hale Ltd: Clerkenwell House, 45–47 Clerkenwell Green, London, EC1R 0HT; tel. (20) 7251-2661; fax (20) 7490-4958; e-mail enquire@halebooks.com; internet www.halebooks.com; f. 1936; memoirs, biography, travel, sport, fiction, belles-lettres, general non-fiction; Man. Dir JOHN HALE.

Hamlyn: Endeavour House, 189 Shaftesbury Ave, London, WC2H 8JY; tel. (20) 7632-5400; fax (20) 7531-8650; e-mail info@octopus-publishing.co.uk; internet www.hamlyn.co.uk; imprint of Octopus Publishing Group Ltd; cookery, DIY, gardening, sports, health, animals; Man. Dir DAVID INMAN.

Harlequin Mills and Boon Ltd: Eton House, 18–24 Paradise Rd, Richmond, TW9 1SR; tel. (20) 8288-2800; fax (20) 8288-2899; internet www.millsandboon.co.uk; f. 1908; romantic fiction; Man. Dir MANDY FERGUSON.

HarperCollins Publishers Ltd: 77–85 Fulham Palace Rd, London, W6 8JB; tel. (20) 8307-4000; fax (20) 8307-4440; e-mail contact@harpercollins.co.uk; internet www.harpercollins.co.uk; f. 1819; owned by News International; fiction and non-fiction of all classes, including biographies, history, travel, nature, sport, art, children's, classics, atlases, reference, religion; imprints: Armada, Bartholomew, Collins, Collins Bibles, Collins Cartographic, Collins Classics, Collins Crime, Collins English Dictionaries, Collins Liturgical, Flamingo, Fontana, HarperCollins, HarperCollins Audio, HarperCollins Paperbacks, HarperCollins Science Fiction and Fantasy, Jets, Lions, Marshall Pickering, Nicholson, Times Books, Tolkien, Tracks, Young Lions; CEO and Publr VICTORIA BARNSLEY.

Harvill Secker: The Random House Group Ltd, 20 Vauxhall Bridge Rd, London, SW1V 2SA; tel. (20) 7840-8540; fax (20) 7233-6117; e-mail enquiries@randomhouse.co.uk; internet www.randomhouse.co.uk/harvillsecker; fiction, non-fiction, illustrated books; imprint of The Random House Group Ltd.

Haynes Publishing: Sparkford, Yeovil, BA22 7JJ; tel. (1963) 440635; fax (1963) 440001; e-mail sales@haynes.co.uk; internet www.haynes.co.uk; f. 1960; transport, manuals etc.; Chair. J. H. C. HAYNES; CEO E. OAKLEY.

Headline Publishing Group: 338 Euston Rd, London, NW1 3BH; tel. (20) 7873-6000; fax (20) 7873-6124; e-mail enquiries@headline.co.uk; internet www.headline.co.uk; f. 1986; division of Hachette UK; fiction, autobiography, biography, food and wine, gardening, popular science, sport and TV tie-ins; Man. Dir JANE MORPETH; CEO KATE WILSON.

Heinemann: Halley Court, Jordan Hill, Oxford, OX2 8EJ; tel. (1865) 311366; fax (1865) 310043; e-mail enquiries@pearson.com; internet www.heinemann.co.uk; imprint of Pearson Education; educational textbooks for UK and abroad; Man. Dir JOHN FALLON.

William Heinemann: Random House, 20 Vauxhall Bridge Rd, London, SW1V 2SA; tel. (20) 7840-8707; fax (20) 7233-6127; e-mail enquiries@randomhouse.co.uk; internet www.randomhouse.co.uk; arts, biography, fiction, history, science, travel; imprint of The Random House Group Ltd.

Hodder Education: 338 Euston Rd, London, NW1 3BH; tel. (20) 7873-6000; fax (20) 7873-6299; e-mail educationenquiries@hodder.co.uk; internet www.hoddereducation.co.uk; f. 1906; imprints: Hodder Arnold, Hodder Gibson, Hodder Murray and Teach Yourself; division of Hachette UK; Chief Exec. THOMAS WEBSTER.

Hodder and Stoughton: 338 Euston Rd, London, NW1 3BH; tel. (20) 7873-6000; fax (20) 7873-6024; e-mail websiteadministrator@hodder.co.uk; internet www.hodder.co.uk; f. 1868; division of Hachette UK; imprints: Mobius, Sceptre; general, biography, travel, fiction, current affairs; Man. Dir JAMIE HODDER-WILLIAMS.

Icon Books Ltd: Omnibus Business Centre, 39–41 North Rd, London, N7 9DP; tel. (20) 7697-9695; fax (20) 7697-9501; e-mail info@iconbooks.co.uk; internet www.iconbooks.co.uk; f. 1991; non-fiction; mem. of Independent Alliance; Man. Dir SIMON FLYNN.

Informa PLC: Informa House, 30–32 Mortimer St, London, W1W 7RE; tel. (20) 7017-5000; internet www.informa.com; journals and books; commercial, professional, academic and scientific, reference; Chair. DEREK MAPP; Chief Exec. PETER RIGBY.

IOP Publishing: Dirac House, Temple Back, Bristol, BS1 6BE; tel. (117) 929-7481; fax (117) 929-4318; e-mail custserv@iop.org; internet publishing.iop.org; f. 1874; scientific and technical; Man. Dir STEVEN HALL.

Jane's Information Group Ltd: Sentinel House, 163 Brighton Rd, Coulsdon, CR5 2YH; tel. (20) 8700-3700; fax (20) 8763-1006; e-mail info.uk@janes.com; internet www.janes.com; owned by IHS, Inc (USA); intelligence and analysis on national and international defence, security and risk developments; Pres. and COO SCOTT KEY.

Jordan Publishing Ltd: 21 St Thomas St, Bristol, BS1 6JS; tel. (117) 923-0600; fax (117) 923-0486; e-mail achim.bosse@jordanpublishing.co.uk; internet www.jordanpublishing.co.uk; f. 1863; practical law books covering family law, litigation, company, property and private client law; Man. Dir CAROLINE VANDRIDGE-AMES.

Michael Joseph Ltd: 80 Strand, London, WC2R 0RL; tel. (20) 7010-3000; fax (20) 7010-6060; internet www.penguin.co.uk; f. 1936; general, fiction, non-fiction; division of Penguin; Publishing Dir LOUISE MOORE.

Richard Joseph Publishers Ltd: POB 15, Torrington, EX38 8ZJ; tel. (1805) 625750; fax (1805) 625376; e-mail info@sheppardsconfidential.com; internet www.sheppardsconfidential.com; f. 1990; reference and directories; publishes the weekly journal *Sheppard's Confidential*; Man. Dir RICHARD JOSEPH.

Kenyon-Deane: 10 Station Rd, Industrial Estate, Malvern, WR13 6RN; tel. and fax (1684) 540154; e-mail simon@cressrelles.co.uk; internet www.cressrelles.co.uk; f. 1971; owned by Cressrelles Publishing Company Ltd; incorporates Kenyon House Press, H. F. W. Deane Ltd; plays and drama textbooks, specialists in all-women plays and plays for young people; Man. Dir LESLIE SMITH.

Kingfisher Publications PLC: New Penderel House, 283–288 High Holborn, London, WC1V 7HZ; tel. (20) 7903-9999; fax (20) 7242-4979; e-mail sales@kingfisherpub.com; internet www.kingfisherpub.com; children's books; imprints: Kingfisher; owned by Pan Macmillan Ltd; Man. Dir JOHN PICKETT.

Kogan Page Ltd: 120 Pentonville Rd, London, N1 9JN; tel. (20) 7278-0433; fax (20) 7837-6348; e-mail kpinfo@koganpage.com; internet www.koganpage.co.uk; f. 1967; business, management, accountancy, textbooks, transport, careers, personal development, training, marketing, consumer, reference; Man. Dir HELEN KOGAN.

Lawrence and Wishart Ltd: 99A Wallis Rd, London, E9 5LN; tel. (20) 8533-2506; fax (20) 8533-7369; e-mail info@lwbooks.co.uk; internet www.lwbooks.co.uk; f. 1936; politics, history, feminism, race, economics, Marxist theory, cultural studies; Man. Editor SALLY DAVISON.

Letts and Lonsdale: Letts and Lonsdale, HarperCollins Publrs Ltd, Westerhill Rd, Bishopbriggs, Glasgow, G64 2QT; tel. (844) 576-8126; fax (844) 576-8131; e-mail education@harpercollins.co.uk; internet www.lettsandlonsdale.com; a division of HarperCollins Ltd; children's, educational, textbooks; Man. Dir ANDREW WARE.

LexisNexis Butterworths: Halsbury House, 35 Chancery Lane, London, WC2A 1EL; tel. (20) 7400-2500; fax (20) 7400-2842; internet www.lexisnexis.co.uk; f. 1818; part of Reed Elsevier PLC; law, tax, accountancy, banking books and journals; Group Man. Dir CHRISTIAN FLECK.

Frances Lincoln: 4 Torriano Mews, Torriano Ave, London, NW5 2RZ; tel. (20) 7485-0409; fax (20) 7485-0490; e-mail reception@frances-lincoln.com; internet www.franceslincoln.com; f. 1977; owned by Quaro Publishing plc; illustrated non-fiction, children's fiction and non-fiction; Man. Dir DAVID GRAHAM.

Little, Brown Book Group UK: 100 Victoria Embankment, London, EC4Y 0DY; tel. (20) 7911-8000; fax (20) 7911-8100; e-mail info@littlebrown.co.uk; internet www.littlebrown.co.uk; imprints: Abacus, Virago, Sphere, Orbit, Little Brown, Piatkus, Atom; division of Hachette UK; CEO and Publr URSULA MACKENZIE.

Liverpool University Press: 4 Cambridge St, Liverpool, L69 7ZU; tel. (151) 794-2233; fax (151) 794-2235; e-mail lup@liv.ac.uk; internet www.liverpool-unipress.co.uk; f. 1899; European and American literature, social, political, economic and ancient history, planning, hispanic studies, population studies, architecture, art, art history, cultural studies, science fiction criticism series; Dir ANTHONY COND.

Lonely Planet Publications: 2nd Floor, 186 City Rd, London, EC1V 2NT; tel. (20) 7106-2100; fax (20) 7106-2101; internet www.lonelyplanet.com; f. 1973; travel, languages; acquired by BBC Worldwide in 2011, which sold it in 2013; Publr STEPHEN PALMER.

Lund Humphries: Wey Court East, Union Rd, Farnham, GU9 7PT; tel. (1252) 736600; fax (1252) 736736; e-mail ashgate.online@ashgate.com; internet www.lundhumphries.com; f. 1967; arts, graphic arts, design, architecture, photography, scholarly, Arabic language; Chair. NIGEL FARROW.

McGraw-Hill Education: McGraw-Hill House, Shoppenhangers Rd, Maidenhead, SL6 2QL; tel. (1628) 502500; fax (1628) 635895; e-mail helpme@mcgraw-hill.com; internet www.mcgraw-hill.co.uk; f. 1909; technical, scientific, computer studies, professional reference, general and medical books; Pres. ROBERT BAHASH.

Macmillan Education Ltd: Between Towns Rd, Oxford, OX4 3PP; tel. (1865) 405700; fax (1865) 405701; e-mail help@macmillan.com; internet www.macmillaneducation.com; a division of Macmillan Publishers Ltd; English Language Teaching and educational books; Chief Exec. SIMON ALLEN; Man. Dir SUE JONES.

Manchester University Press: Oxford Rd, Manchester, M13 9NR; tel. (161) 275-2310; fax (161) 274-3346; e-mail d.rodgers@manchester.ac.uk; internet www.manchesteruniversitypress.co.uk; f. 1904; humanities and social sciences; Chief Exec. DAVID RODGERS.

Methuen: 8 Artillery Row, London, SW1P 1RZ; tel. (20) 7802-0018; fax (20) 7828-1244; e-mail info@methuen.co.uk; internet www.methuen.co.uk; f. 1889; fiction, non-fiction, biography, history, sport, theatre, drama, humour, politics, poetry, travel; Man. Dir PETER TUMMONS.

Mitchell Beazley: Endeavour House, 189 Shaftesbury Ave, London, WC2H 8JY; tel. (20) 7632-5400; fax (20) 7531-8650; e-mail info@mitchell-beazley.co.uk; internet www.mitchell-beazley.co.uk; f. 1969; imprint of Octopus Publishing Group Ltd; *Miller's* antiques, arts and design, interiors and style, gardening, reference, wine and food; Publr DAVID LAMB.

John Murray Publishers: 338 Euston Rd, London, NW1 3BH; tel. (20) 7873-6000; fax (20) 7873-6446; internet www.hachette.co.uk; f. 1768; division of Hachette UK; biography, autobiography, memoir, history, travel, fiction, current affairs; Man. Dir ROLAND PHILIPPS.

Nelson Thornes Ltd: Delta Pl., 27 Bath Rd, Cheltenham, GL53 7TH; tel. (1242) 267287; fax (1242) 253695; e-mail csupport@nelsonthornes.com; internet www.nelsonthornes.com; educational; Man. Dir RICHARD HODSON.

Novello and Co Ltd: 14–15 Berners St, London, W1T 3LJ; tel. (20) 7612-7400; fax (20) 7612-7545; e-mail promotion@musicsales.co.uk; internet www.chesternovello.com; music; Man. Dir JAMES RUSHTON.

Octopus Publishing Group Ltd: Endeavour House, 189 Shaftesbury Ave, London, WC2H 8JY; tel. (20) 632-5400; fax (20) 7531-8650; e-mail info@octopus-publishing.co.uk; internet www.octopus-publishing.co.uk; division of Hachette UK; imprints: Bounty, Cassell Illustrated, Conran Octopus, Gaia Books, Godsfield Press, Hamlyn, Miller's, Mitchell Beazley, Philip's, Spruce; Chief Exec. ALISON GOFF.

Open University Press, McGraw-Hill Education (UK): Shoppenhangers Rd, Maidenhead, SL6 2QL; tel. (1628) 502500; fax (1628) 635895; e-mail enquiries@openup.co.uk; internet www.openup.co.uk; academic, study skills, politics, sociology, psychology, education, higher education, media, film and cultural studies, health and social welfare, counselling and psychotherapy, management and public policy; Dir JIM VOUTE.

Orion Publishing Group: Orion House, 5 Upper St Martin's Lane, London, WC2H 9EA; tel. (20) 7240-3444; fax (20) 7240-4822; e-mail info@orionbooks.co.uk; internet www.orionbooks.co.uk; f. 1991; division of Hachette UK; imprints: Gollancz, Orion, Orion Children's, Phoenix, Weidenfeld & Nicolson; CEO PETER ROCHE.

Peter Owen Publishers: 20 Holland Park Ave, London, W11 3QU; tel. (20) 7373-5628; fax (20) 7221-0931; e-mail admin@peterowen.com; internet www.peterowen.com; f. 1951; fiction, autobiography, biography, translations, history, the arts, etc.; Man. Dir PETER OWEN; Editorial Dir ANTONIA OWEN.

Oxford University Press: Great Clarendon St, Oxford, OX2 6DP; tel. (1865) 556767; fax (1865) 556646; e-mail webenquiry.uk@oup.com; internet www.oup.com; f. c. 1478; Bibles, prayer books, the

Oxford English Dictionary, the *Oxford Dictionary of National Biography* and many other dictionaries and books of reference, learned and general works from the humanities to the sciences, educational, electronic, music and children's books and audio-visual and English language teaching material; Sec. to the Delegates of the Press and Chief Exec. NIGEL PORTWOOD.

Palgrave Macmillan Ltd: Houndmills, Basingstoke, RG21 6XS; tel. (1256) 329242; fax (1256) 479476; e-mail palgrave@palgrave .com; internet www.palgrave.com; academic, professional, textbooks and journals; Man. Dir DOMINIC KNIGHT.

Pan Macmillan Ltd: 20 New Wharf Rd, London, N1 9RR; tel. (20) 7014-6000; fax (20) 7014-6001; e-mail sales@macmillan.co.uk; internet www.panmacmillan.com; fiction and non-fiction, children's, general reference; imprints: Macmillan, Pan, Picador, Sidgwick & Jackson, Boxtree, Tor, Macmillan Children's Books, Campbell Books, Young Picador, Rodale; Man. Dir ANTHONY FORBES WATSON.

Pearson Education Ltd: Edinburgh Gate, Harlow, CM20 2JE; tel. (1279) 623623; fax (870) 850-5255; e-mail enquiries@pearson.com; internet www.pearsoned.co.uk; Propr Pearson PLC; acquired Harcourt Education International in 2007; imprints include: Ginn, Heinemann, Longman, Payne-Gallway, Prentice Hall, Raintree, Rigby and Scott Prentice; CEO JOHN FALLON.

Pearson Publishing Group: Pearson Publishing Group, Chesterton Mill, French's Rd, Cambridge, CB4 3NP; tel. (1223) 350555; fax (1223) 356484; e-mail info@pearson.co.uk; internet www.pearson.co .uk; f. 1991; Chair. GEORGE PEARSON.

Penguin Books Ltd: 80 The Strand, London, WC2R 0RL; tel. (20) 7010-3000; fax (20) 7416-3099; e-mail editor@penguin.co.uk; internet www.penguin.co.uk; f. 1936; holding co Pearson PLC; paperback imprints: Penguin and Puffin; reprints and original works of fiction and non-fiction including travel, biography, science and social studies, reference books, handbooks, plays, poetry, classics and children's books; Penguin Group UK is made up of Penguin Press (Allen Lane, Reference, Penguin Classics and Penguin Modern Classics), Penguin General (imprints: Viking, Hamish Hamilton, Fig Tree and Penguin Ireland), Michael Joseph and the children's division (imprints: Puffin, Ladybird, Frederick Warne and BBC Children); jt venture with Random House agreed Oct. 2012 to come into effect in 2013; Pearson PLC to hold 47% stake, Bertelsmann AG 53%; Chair. and Chief Exec. JOHN MAKINSON; CEO (UK) TOM WELDON.

Phaidon Press Ltd: Regent's Wharf, All Saints St, London, N1 9PA; tel. (20) 7843-1000; fax (20) 7843-1010; e-mail enquiries@phaidon .com; internet www.phaidon.com; art, architecture, children's, contemporary culture, cookery, design, decorative arts, fashion, photography and music, film, fine art; Chair. RICHARD SCHLAGMAN.

Philip's: 2–4 Heron Quays, London, E14 4JP; tel. (20) 7644-6940; fax (20) 7644-8464; e-mail philips@philips-maps.co.uk; internet www .philips-maps.co.uk; imprint of Octopus Publishing Group Ltd; maps, atlases, astronomy, encyclopaedias; Man. Dir JOHN GAISFORD.

Pluto Press: 345 Archway Rd, London, N6 5AA; tel. (20) 8348-2724; fax (20) 8348-9133; e-mail pluto@plutobooks.com; internet www .plutobooks.com; academic, scholarly, and current affairs; Chair. ROGER VAN ZWANENBERG; Man. Dir ANNE BEECH.

Profile Books Ltd: 3A Exmouth House, Pine St, Exmouth Market, London, EC1R 0JH; tel. (20) 7841-6300; fax (20) 7833-3969; e-mail info@profilebooks.co.uk; internet www.profilebooks.com; f. 1996; fiction, non-fiction; imprints: Economist Books, GreenProfile, Profile Business, Serpent's Tail; mem. of Independent Alliance; Man. Dir ANDREW FRANKLIN.

ProQuest Information and Learning: The Quorum, Barnwell Rd, Cambridge, CB5 8SW; tel. (1223) 215512; fax (1223) 215514; e-mail marketing@proquest.co.uk; internet www.proquest.com; f. 1973 as Chadwyck-Healey Ltd; changed name as above in 2001; academic; CEO KURT SANFORD.

Quercus Publishing PLC: 21 Bloomsbury Sq., London, WC1A 2NS; tel. (20) 7291-7200; e-mail richard.arcus@quercusbooks.co.uk; internet www.quercusbooks.co.uk; f. 2004; fiction, non-fiction; mem. of Independent Alliance; CEO MARK EVANS.

The Random House Group Ltd: Random House, 20 Vauxhall Bridge Rd, London, SW1V 2SA; tel. (20) 7840-8400; fax (20) 7840-8778; e-mail enquiries@randomhouse.co.uk; internet www .randomhouse.co.uk; holding co Bertelsmann AG; imprints: Arrow, Jonathan Cape, Cedar, Century, Chatto & Windus, Ebury Press, Everyman, Harvill Secker, William Heinemann, Hutchinson, Mainstream, Pimlico, Random House Children's Books, Rider, Vermilion, Vintage, Yellow Jersey; jt venture with Random House agreed in Oct 2012 to come into effect in 2013; Bertelsmann AG to hold 53%, Pearson 47%; Chair. and CEO MARKUS DOHLE.

Reader's Digest Association Ltd: 157 Edgware Rd, London, W2 2HR; tel. (20) 7053-4500; internet www.readersdigest.co.uk; various non-fiction, condensed and series fiction; Chair. RANDALL CURAN; CEO TOM WILLIAMS.

Reed Business Information: Quadrant House, The Quadrant, Sutton, SM2 5AS; tel. (20) 8652-3500; fax (20) 8652-8932; e-mail rbi .subscriptions@qss-uk.com; internet www.reedbusiness.co.uk; f. 1866; business directories and online services; CEO MARK KELSEY.

Reed Elsevier Group PLC: 1–3 Strand, London, WC2N 5JR; tel. (20) 7930-7077; fax (20) 7166-5799; e-mail london@reedelsevier.com; internet www.reedelsevier.com; f. 1992; books, journals, magazines and electronic resources; divisions: science and medical, education, legal and business; Chair. ANTHONY HABGOOD; CEO ERIK ENGSTROM.

Routledge: 2 Park Sq., Milton Park, Abingdon, OX14 4RN; tel. (20) 7017-6000; fax (20) 7017-6699; e-mail info@tandf.co.uk; internet www.routledge.com; f. 1836; imprint of Taylor & Francis Group; professional, academic, reference; Man. Dir JEREMY NORTH.

SAGE Publications Ltd: 1 Oliver's Yard, 55 City Rd, London, EC1Y 1SP; tel. (20) 7324-8500; fax (20) 7324-8600; e-mail info@ sagepub.co.uk; internet www.sagepub.co.uk; f. 1971; academic and professional social sciences, sciences and humanities; imprint: Sage Education; Pres. STEPHEN BARR.

Schofield and Sims Ltd: Dogley Mill, Penistone Rd, Fenay Bridge, Huddersfield, HD8 0NQ; tel. (1484) 607080; fax (1484) 606815; e-mail post@schofieldandsims.co.uk; internet www .schofieldandsims.co.uk; f. 1901; educational; Chair. NICK PLATTS.

Scholastic Ltd: Villiers House, Clarendon Ave, Leamington Spa, CV32 5PR; tel. (1926) 887799; fax (1926) 883331; e-mail enquiries@ scholastic.co.uk; internet www.scholastic.co.uk; f. 1964; direct marketing, educational and children's books; Group Man. Dir ALAN HURCOMBE.

SCM-Canterbury Press Ltd: Invicta House, 3rd Floor, 108–114 Golden Lane, London EC1Y 0TG; tel. (20) 7776-7540; fax (20) 7776-7556; e-mail admin@norwichbooksandmusic.co.uk; internet www .canterburypress.co.uk; f. 1929; imprint of Hymns Ancient and Modern Ltd; religious, theological; Group CEO DOMINIC VAUGHAN.

Scripture Union: 207–209 Queensway, Bletchley, Milton Keynes, MK2 2EB; tel. (1908) 856000; fax (1908) 856111; e-mail info@ scriptureunion.org.uk; internet www.scriptureunion.org.uk; f. 1867; Christian education and Bible reading guides; Nat. Dir Rev. TIM HASTIE-SMITH.

Short Books: 3A Exmouth House, Pine St, London, EC1R 0JH; tel. (20) 7833-9429; e-mail info@shortbooks.co.uk; internet www .shortbooks.co.uk; f. 2001; biography, fiction, non-fiction; mem. of Independent Alliance; Man. Dirs REBECCA NICOLSON, AUREA CARPENTER.

Simon & Schuster: 1st Floor, 222 Gray's Inn Rd, London, WC1X 8HB; tel. (20) 7316-1900; fax (20) 7316-0332; e-mail enquiries@ simonandschuster.co.uk; internet www.simonandschuster.co.uk; f. 1986; owned by CBS Corpn (USA); fiction, non-fiction, music, travel; imprints: Pocket Books, Touchstone, Scribner, Free Press; Man. Dir IAN S. CHAPMAN.

Society for Promoting Christian Knowledge: 36 Causton St, London, SW1P 4ST; tel. (20) 7592-3900; fax (20) 7592-3939; e-mail spck@spck.org.uk; internet www.spck.org.uk; f. 1698; religious; imprints: SPCK, Azure, Sheldon Press; Publishing Dir JOANNA MORIARTY.

Souvenir Press Ltd: 43 Great Russell St, London, WC1B 3PD; tel. (20) 7580-9307; fax (20) 7580-5064; e-mail souvenirpress@ukonline .co.uk; general; Man. Dir ERNEST HECHT.

The Stationery Office: St Crispins, Duke St, Norwich, NR3 1PD; tel. (1603) 622211; e-mail customer.services@tso.co.uk; internet www.tso.co.uk; f. 1786 as His Majesty's Stationery Office (govt publishing house); privatized in 1996; acquired by Williams Lea in 2007; business and publishing services; publishes *Hansard, Highway Code, British Pharmacopoeia*; Chief Exec. RICHARD DELL.

Sweet and Maxwell Ltd: 100 Avenue Rd, London, NW3 3PF; tel. (20) 7393-7000; fax (20) 7393-7010; e-mail customer.services@ sweetandmaxwell.co.uk; internet www.sweetandmaxwell.co.uk; f. 1799; imprints: Stevens and Sons Ltd, W. Green, Round Hall, ESC Publishing, the European Law Centre; holding co Thomson Reuters; law books; Pres. MARK SCHLAGETER.

Taylor & Francis Group Ltd: 2 Park Sq., Milton Park, Abingdon, OX14 4RN; tel. (20) 7017-6000; fax (20) 7017-6699; e-mail info@tandf .co.uk; internet www.taylorandfrancisgroup.com; division of Informa PLC; imprints: Taylor & Francis, Routledge, Garland Science, CRC Press and Psychology Press; professional, academic, scientific, technical, reference; books and journals; Chief Exec. ROGER HORTON.

Thames and Hudson Ltd: 181A High Holborn, London, WC1V 7QX; tel. (20) 7845-5000; fax (20) 7845-5050; e-mail sales@ thamesandhudson.co.uk; internet www.thamesandhudson.com; f. 1949; art, archaeology, history, etc.; Chair. THOMAS NEURATH; Man. Dir JAMIE CAMPLIN.

Thomson Reuters: The Thomson Reuters Bldg, South Colonnade, Canary Wharf, London, E14 5EP; tel. (20) 7250-1122; e-mail general .info@thomsonreuters.com; internet thomsonreuters.com; f. 2008 by merger of Thomson Corpn and Reuters Group PLC (f. 1865); legal, financial; also owns Reuters news agency; Chair. DAVID THOMSON; CEO THOMAS H. GLOCER.

Transworld Publishers Ltd: 61–63 Uxbridge Rd, London, W5 5SA; tel. (20) 8579-2652; fax (20) 8579-5479; e-mail info@transworld-publishers.co.uk; internet www.booksattransworld.co.uk; imprints: Corgi, Bantam Books, Black Swan, Bantam Press, Doubleday, Expert Books, Eden Project Books, Channel 4 Books; all types of fiction and non-fiction; division of The Random House Group Ltd; Publishing Dir SELINA WALKER.

University of Wales Press: 10 Columbus Walk, Brigantine Pl., Cardiff, CF10 4UP; tel. (29) 2049-6899; fax (29) 2049-6108; e-mail press@press.wales.ac.uk; internet www.uwp.co.uk; f. 1922; academic and educational (Welsh and English); Dir HELGARD KRAUSE.

Usborne Publishing: Usborne House, 83–85 Saffron Hill, London, EC1N 8RT; tel. (20) 7430-2800; fax (20) 7430-1562; e-mail mail@usborne.co.uk; internet www.usborne.com; f. 1973; children's publishing; Man. Dir PETER USBORNE.

Virgin Books: 20 Vauxhall Bridge Rd, London, SW1V 2SA; tel. (20) 7840-8400; e-mail editorial@virgin-books.co.uk; internet www.virginbooks.com; 90% owned by The Random House Group Ltd; general, popular culture, film, music, humour, biography, fiction, non-fiction, erotica; imprints: Virgin, Black Lace and Nexus; Chair. RICHARD CABLE.

Frederick Warne (Publishers) Ltd: 80 Strand, London, WC2R 0RL; tel. (20) 7010-3000; fax (20) 7010-6707; e-mail peterrabbit@uk.penguingroup.com; internet www.peterrabbit.com; f. 1865; a division of Penguin Books since 1983; classic illustrated children's books (including Beatrix Potter); Man. Dir STEPHANIE BARTON.

Wiley-Blackwell: 9600 Garsington Rd, Oxford, OX4 2DQ; tel. (1865) 776868; fax (1865) 714591; e-mail customer@wiley.co.uk; internet www.wiley.com; f. 2001 as Blackwell Publishing Ltd, by merger of Blackwell Publishing and Blackwell Science; acquired by John Wiley & Sons, Inc. (USA) in 2007; academic, professional, business, medical and science books and journals; Pres. and CEO WILLIAM J. PESCE.

The Women's Press: 27 Goodge St, London, W1T 2LD; tel. (20) 7636-3992; fax (20) 7637-1866; e-mail david@the-womens-press.com; internet www.the-womens-press.com; f. 1978; Dir DAVID ELLIOTT.

Yale University Press: 47 Bedford Sq., London, WC1B 3DP; tel. (20) 7079-4900; fax (20) 7079-4901; e-mail sales@yaleup.co.uk; internet www.yalebooks.co.uk; f. 1973; the only US university press to operate a separate publishing co in Europe; Man. Dir ROBERT BALDOCK.

Zed Books Ltd: 7 Cynthia St, London, N1 9JF; tel. (20) 7837-0384; fax (20) 7833-3960; e-mail editorial@zedbooks.net; internet www.zedbooks.co.uk; f. 1977; academic, current affairs; Editor TAMSINE O'RIORDAN.

PUBLISHERS' ORGANIZATIONS

Booktrust: Book House, 45 East Hill, London, SW18 2QZ; tel. (20) 8516-2977; fax (20) 8516-2978; e-mail query@booktrust.org.uk; internet www.booktrust.org.uk; non-profit-making organization funded by voluntary donations and membership fees; f. 1945; originally f. 1925 as The National Book Council to extend the use and enjoyment of books; renamed Book Trust 1986; publishes annotated book lists; postal book information service; administers book prizes, including the Orange Prize for Fiction and the John Llewellyn Rhys Prize; runs www.booktrusted.com, a website dedicated to children's books; Chair. SUE HORNER; Exec. Dir VIV BIRD.

The Publishers' Association: 29B Montague St, London, WC1B 5BW; tel. (20) 7691-9191; fax (20) 7691-9199; e-mail mail@publishers.org.uk; internet www.publishers.org.uk; f. 1896; represents book, journal and electronic publishers in the UK and seeks to promote the sales of British books; Pres. URSULA MACKENZIE; Chief Exec. RICHARD MOLLET; 127 mems.

Publishing Scotland: Scott House, 10 South St, Andrew St, Edinburgh, EH2 2AZ; tel. (131) 228-6866; fax (131) 524-8157; e-mail enquiries@publishingscotland.org; internet www.publishingscotland.org; f. 1973 as Scottish Publishers' Assocn; present name adopted 2007; network body for the book publishing industry in Scotland; provides information, support, training, book fair representation; Chair. KATY LOCKWOOD-HOLMES; Chief Exec. MARION SINCLAIR.

Broadcasting and Communications

REGULATORY AUTHORITY

Office of Communications (Ofcom): Riverside House, 2A Southwark Bridge Rd, London, SE1 9HA; tel. (20) 7981-3000; fax (20) 7981-3333; e-mail contact@ofcom.org.uk; internet www.ofcom.org.uk;

f. 2003 to replace the Office of Telecommunications, the Broadcasting Standards Commission, the Radio Authority, the Radiocommunications Agency and the Independent Television Commission; the independent regulator for the British communications industries, with responsibilities across television, radio, telecommunications and wireless communications services; promotes choice, quality and value in electronic communications services, where appropriate, by encouraging competition between the providers of those services; ensures the most efficient use of the radiocommunications spectrum (the airwaves used for the transmission of all non-military wireless communications services); ensures that a wide range of electronic communications services, including broadband, is available across the United Kingdom; ensures that a wide range of television and radio programmes of high quality and wide appeal are broadcast; maintains plurality in the media by ensuring a sufficiently broad range of ownership; protects audiences against offensive or harmful material, unfairness or the infringement of privacy on television and radio; Chair. COLETTE BOWE; Chief Exec. ED RICHARDS.

TELECOMMUNICATIONS

Arqiva Ltd: Crawley Court, Winchester, SO21 2QA; tel. (1962) 823434; internet www.arqiva.com; f. 2005; Chair. PETER SHORE; CEO JOHN CRESSWELL.

British Telecommunications PLC: BT Centre, 81 Newgate St, London, EC1A 7AJ; tel. (20) 7356-5000; fax (20) 7356-6630; e-mail btgroup@bt.com; internet www.bt.com; wholly owned subsidiary of BT Group PLC; Chair. Sir MICHAEL RAKE; Chief Exec. IAN LIVINGSTON.

Cable and Wireless Communications: 26 Red Lion Sq., 3rd Floor, London, WC1R 4HQA; tel. (20) 7315-4000; internet www.cwc.com; fixed-line, mobile and broadband services; Chair. Sir RICHARD LAPTHORNE; Chief Exec. TONY RICE.

Cable & Wireless Worldwide: Waterside House, Longshot Lane, Bracknell, RG12 1XL; tel. (19) 0884-5000; e-mail ir@cw.com; internet www.cw.com; f. 2010 following demerger from Cable and Wireless Communications; voice, data and internet telecommunications services; Chair. JOHN BARTON; Chief Exec. GAVIN DARBY.

EE (Everything Everywhere Ltd): Hatfield Business Park, Hatfield, AL10 9BW; tel. (1707) 315000; internet www.everythingeverywhere.com; f. 2010, with the merger of T-Mobile (UK) Ltd and Orange (UK); Chair. TIMOTHEUS HOTTGES; CEO OLAF SWANTEE.

Hutchison 3G UK Ltd (3): Star House, 20 Grenfell Rd, Maidenhead, SL6 1EH; tel. (1628) 765000; internet www.three.co.uk; f. 2003; mobile cellular telecommunications; owned by Hutchison Whampoa Ltd (Hong Kong); CEO DAVID DYSON.

KCOM Group PLC: 37 Carr Lane, Hull, HU1 3RE; tel. (1482) 602100; fax (1482) 219289; e-mail contactus@kcom.com; internet www.kcomplc.com; f. 1904; fmrly Kingston Communications; Chair. BILL HALBERT; Exec. Dir KEVIN WALSH.

Orange: St James Court, Gt Park Rd, Almondsbury Park, Bradley Stoke, Bristol, BS32 4QJ; tel. (870) 376-8888; internet www.orange.co.uk; f. 1994; acquired by France Telecom in 2000; part of the Orange SA (France) group; merged with T-Mobile (UK) Ltd in July 2010 to form EE (Everything Everywhere Ltd); Chief Exec. TOM ALEXANDER; Group Chair. DIDIER LOMBARD.

TalkTalk Telecom Group PLC: 11 Evesham St, London, W11 4AR; tel. (20) 3417-1000; fax (20) 3417-1001; internet www.talktalkgroup.com; TalkTalk demerged from Carphone Warehouse in 2010 to become TalkTalk Telecom Group PLC; acquired AOL's UK broadband business in 2007 and Tiscali UK in 2009; provides fixed-line telecommunications, digital television services and broadband internet access; markets under the TalkTalk and AOL brands to residential customers and the Opal brand to business customers; Chair. CHARLES DUNSTONE; CEO DIDO HARDING.

Telefónica O₂ UK: 260 Bath Rd, Slough, SL1 4DX; tel. (113) 2722000; e-mail feedback@o2.com; internet www.o2.co.uk; f. 2001 after demerging from BT Group as O₂; fmrly BT Cellnet; acquired by Telefónica, SA (Spain) in March 2006; CEO RONAN DUNNE.

THUS: 1–2 Berkeley Sq., 99 Berkeley St, Glasgow, G3 7HR; tel. (141) 567-1234; fax (141) 566-3035; e-mail thus.enquiries@thus.net; internet www.thus.net; f. 1994 as Scottish Power Telecommunications Holdings; demerged from ScottishPower and renamed THUS Group PLC 2002; acquired by Cable and Wireless 2008; offers fixed-line telecommunications services to business customers; also internet service provider; Man. Dir SEAN MAHON.

T-Mobile (UK) Ltd: Everything Everywhere Ltd, Hatfield Business Park, Hatfield, AL10 9BW; tel. (1707) 315000; internet www.t-mobile.co.uk; owned by Deutsche Telekom AG (Germany); fmrly One2One; merged with Orange in July 2010 to form EE (Everything Everywhere Ltd); Man. Dir RICHARD MOAT.

Virgin Media: Media House, Bartley Wood Business Park, Bartley Way, Hook, Reading, RG27 9UP; tel. (1256) 752000; fax (1256)

752100; internet www.virginmedia.com; f. 2007 by merger of NTL Inc and Virgin Mobile; Chair. JAMES F. MOONEY; CEO NEIL BERKETT.

Vodafone Group PLC: Vodafone House, The Connection, Newbury, RG14 2FN; tel. (1635) 33251; internet www.vodafone.com; Chair. GERARD KLEISTERLEE; Group Chief Exec. VITTORIO COLAO.

BROADCASTING

British Broadcasting Corporation (BBC): Broadcasting House, Portland Pl., London, W1A 1AA; tel. (20) 7580-4468; fax (20) 7637-1630; internet www.bbc.co.uk; f. 1922; operates under Royal Charter; financed by the television licence fees; governed by BBC Trust, which replaced fmr Board of Governors in 2007; Chair., BBC Trust Lord PATTEN; Dir-Gen. TONY HALL; Dir, Television DANNY COHEN; Dir, News FRANCESCA UNSWORTH (acting); Dir, Radio HELEN BOADEN; Dir, Strategy and Digital JAMES PURNELL; Dir, Future Media RALPH RIVERA; Dir, Marketing, Communications and Audiences SHARON BAYLAY; Chief Financial Officer ZARIN PATEL; CEO, BBC Worldwide and Dir, Global TIM DAVIE.

Radio

British Broadcasting Corporation

BBC Radio provides a service of five national networks throughout the United Kingdom, 40 local radio stations in England and the Channel Islands, Radio Scotland, Radio Wales, Radio Cymru, broadcasting in Welsh, and Radio Ulster and Radio Foyle (in Northern Ireland); it also offers a number of specialist digital services; Dir, Radio HELEN BOADEN.

Radio 1: broadcasts 24 hours a day of contemporary music programmes; Controller BEN COOPER.

Radio 2: broadcasts popular music and culture; Controller BOB SHENNAN.

Radio 3: provides 24-hour broadcasts of classical music, drama, talks and documentaries; Controller ROGER WRIGHT.

Radio 4: broadcasts news and current affairs and also provides a wide range of features, drama and discussions; Controller GWYNETH WILLIAMS.

Radio 5 Live: began broadcasting in March 1994, replacing Radio 5; provides a 24-hour service of news and sports programmes; also operates **5 Live Sports Extra**, a part-time digital network for sports events not broadcast elsewhere on BBC Radio; Controller JONATHAN WALL.

6 Music: began broadcasting in 2002, digital station playing pop and rock music; Controller BOB SHENNAN.

1Xtra: began broadcasting in 2002; digital station playing contemporary urban music for a young audience; Controller BEN COOPER.

Asian Network: began broadcasting in 2002, digital station aimed at the Asian communities in the United Kingdom; Controller BOB SHENNAN.

BBC Radio 4 Extra: began broadcasting in 2002; digital radio station featuring archive material and original spoken-word programming; Controller GWYNETH WILLIAMS.

BBC World Service: Bush House, Strand, London, WC2B 4PH; tel. (20) 7240-3456; fax (20) 7557-1258; e-mail worldservice@bbc.co.uk; internet www.bbc.co.uk/worldservice; the World Service in English is broadcast for 24 hours daily and is directed to all areas of the world. In addition, there are special services to: the Far East (in Cantonese, Burmese and Thai); the Indian sub-continent (in Bengali, Sinhala, Tamil and Urdu); the Caucasus and Central Asia (in Uzbek); the Middle East and North Africa (in Arabic, Pashto, Farsi and Turkish); Europe (in Romanian); and Africa (in Arabic, English, French, Hausa, Somali and Swahili); Dir PETER HORROCKS.

Independent Radio

Absolute Radio: 1 Golden Sq., London, W1F 9DJ; tel. (20) 7434-1215; internet www.absoluteradio.co.uk; began broadcasting April 1993 as Virgin Radio; present name adopted 2008; popular music; also operates 2 digital stations, **Absolute Classic Rock** and **Absolute Xtreme**; Propr TIML Radio Ltd; Chief Exec. DONNACH O'DRISCOLL.

Global Radio: 30 Leicester Sq., London, WC2H 7LA; tel. (20) 7766-6000; fax (20) 7766-6111; e-mail info@thisisglobal.com; internet www.thisisglobal.com; owns and operates radio stations across the United Kingdom, incl. 95.8 Capital FM, Choice FM, Classic FM, Galaxy, Gold, Heart, LBC and Xfm; Chair. CHARLES ALLEN; CEO STEPHEN MIRON.

Independent Radio News (IRN): Mappin House, 4 Winsley St, London, W1W 8HF; tel. (20) 7182-8591; fax (20) 7182-8594; e-mail news@irn.co.uk; internet www.irn.co.uk; f. 1973; produced by Sky Radio News; news agency for the independent local radio network; Chair. TERRY SMITH; Man. Dir TIM MOLLOY.

The Local Radio Company PLC: Carn Brea Studios, Barncoose Industrial Estate, Redruth, TR15 3RQ; tel. (1209) 310435; fax (1209) 310406; internet www.thelocalradiocompany.com; f. 2004 to purchase the entire share capital of Radio Investments Ltd; owns and operates 10 local radio stations across the UK; Chair TREVOR SMALLWOOD; Chief Exec. WILLIAM ROGERS.

TalkSport UK: 18 Hatfields, London, SE1 8DJ; tel. (20) 7959-7800; e-mail adam.bullock@talksport.co.uk; internet www.talksport.net; began broadcasting February 1995 as Talk Radio UK; name changed as above January 2000; Propr UTV PLC; Man. Dir ADAM BULLOCK.

Television

There are five principal television channels: BBC One and BBC Two, controlled by the British Broadcasting Corporation; and Channel 3 (ITV), Channel 4 and Five, operated by commercial broadcasters licensed by the Office for Communications (Ofcom). Channel 3 comprises 16 franchises allocated by a system of competitive tendering (15 on a regional basis—including one for the Channel Islands, q.v.—and one for the nation-wide breakfast-time programme), the majority of which are owned by ITV PLC. The central co-ordinating body for Channel 3 is ITV Network Ltd.

Digital television broadcasting in the United Kingdom began in 1998. The transition to digital television began in 2008 and was completed across the whole of the United Kingdom in 2012.

British Broadcasting Corporation

BBC Television: BBC Audience Services, POB 1922, Darlington, DL3 0UR; tel. (20) 8743-8000; internet www.bbc.co.uk; operates BBC One, BBC Two, BBC Three, BBC Four, CBeebies, CBBC, BBC News and BBC Parliament; Dir, Television DANNY COHEN.

BBC One: internet www.bbc.co.uk/bbcone; Controller CHARLOTTE MOORE (acting).

BBC Two: internet www.bbc.co.uk/bbctwo; began broadcasting in 1964; Controller JANICE HADLOW.

BBC Three: internet www.bbc.co.uk/bbcthree; launched in 2003; digital entertainment channel; Controller ZAI BENNETT.

BBC Four: internet www.bbc.co.uk/bbcfour; digital channel showing in-depth cultural programmes, dramas, documentaries, current affairs, etc.; Controller RICHARD KLEIN.

CBBC: internet www.bbc.co.uk/cbbc; digital service for children aged six to 13; Controller DAMIAN KAVANAGH.

CBeebies: internet www.bbc.co.uk/cbeebies; digital service aimed at under-fives; Controller KAY BENBOW.

BBC News: internet www.bbc.co.uk/news; 24-hour digital news service; Dir, News FRANCESCA UNSWORTH (acting); Controller SAM TAYLOR.

BBC Parliament: internet www.bbc.co.uk/parliament; provides coverage from the Houses of Parliament and the devolved Parliament and Assemblies in Scotland, Wales and Northern Ireland; Controller PETER KNOWLES.

BBC Alba: c/o MG Alba, Seaforth Rd, Stornoway, Isle of Lewis, HS1 2SD; tel. (1851) 705550; fax (1851) 706432; e-mail fios@mgalba.com; internet www.bbc.co.uk/alba; f. 2008 to provide radio and television programming in Scottish Gaelic; operates a free-to-air digital television channel, **BBC Alba**, and a radio station, **BBC Radio nan Gàidheal**; jtly managed by BBC and MG Alba (Gaelic Media Service); Chief Exec. DONALD CAMPBELL; Head of Content ALAN ESSLEMONT; Head of Service MARGARET MARY MURRAY.

Channel 3 (ITV)

ITV Network Ltd: ITV Network Centre, 200 Gray's Inn Rd, London, WC1V 8HF; tel. (20) 7156-6000; fax (20) 7843-8158; e-mail info@itv.co.uk; internet www.itv.com; f. 1956 as Independent Television Association; from 1992 the central co-ordinating body for Channel 3 (ITV); Dir, Television PETER FINCHAM.

ITV PLC: The London Television Centre, Upper Ground, London, SE1 9LT; tel. (20) 7157-3000; internet www.itvplc.com; f. 2004 following the merger of Carlton and Granada; through its subsidiary ITV Broadcasting Ltd, owns all of the regional Channel 3 licences in England, Wales and the border region of Scotland, comprising Anglia (East of England), Border (Northern England, Southern Scotland and Isle of Man), Central (East, West and South Midlands), Granada (North-West England), London (London Weekday), LWT (London Weekend), Meridian (South and South-East England), Tyne Tees (North-East England), Wales and West, Westcountry (South-West England), Yorkshire (Yorkshire and Lincolnshire) and ITV Breakfast Ltd (national breakfast-time service); broadcasts on Channel 3 as ITV1; its subsidiary ITV Digital Channels Ltd operates 5 free-to-air digital channels: ITV2, ITV3, ITV4, ITV1 HD and CITV; Chair. ARCHIE NORMAN; Chief Exec. ADAM CROZIER.

STV Group PLC: Pacific Quay, Glasgow, G51 1PQ; tel. (141) 300-3000; e-mail communication@stv.tv; internet www.stvplc.tv; fmrly

SMG PLC; owns the Channel 3 licences for Central and Northern Scotland; broadcasts as STV; Chair. RICHARD FINDLAY; Chief Exec. ROB WOODWARD; Man. Dir, Broadcasting Services and Regulatory Affairs BOBBY HAIN.

UTV PLC (Ulster Television): Havelock House, Ormeau Rd, Belfast, BT7 1EB; tel. (28) 9032-8122; fax (28) 9024-6695; e-mail info@u.tv; internet www.u.tv; started transmission 1959; owns Channel 3 licence for Northern Ireland; Chair. RICHARD HUNTINGFORD; Chief Exec. JOHN McCANN; Man. Dir, Television MICHAEL WILSON.

Other Independent Television Broadcasters

Channel 4 Television: 124 Horseferry Rd, London, SW1P 2TX; tel. (20) 7396-4444; internet www.channel4.com; f. 1980; began broadcasting 1982; national television service; also operates 4 free-to-air digital channels: E4, Film4, More4 and 4Music; financed by advertising; a publicly owned corporation with a remit to provide public service broadcasting that demonstrates innovation, experiment and creativity, appeals to the tastes and interests of a culturally diverse society, includes programmes of an educational nature and exhibits a distinctive character; Chair. Lord BURNS; Chief Exec. DAVID ABRAHAM.

Channel 5 Television: 10 Lower Thames Street, London, EC3R 6EN; tel. (20) 8612-7700; e-mail customerservices@channel5.com; internet www.channel5.com; awarded licence for fifth national terrestrial channel in October 1995; commenced broadcasting on 30 March 1997; also operates 2 digital channels: 5 and 5USA; owned by Northern & Shell; Dir, Programmes BEN FROW.

Freeview: DTV Services Ltd, Broadcast Centre, 27–29 Cursitor St, London, EC4A 1LT; tel. (8708) 809980; internet www.freeview.co.uk; f. 2002; a consortium of the BBC, Arqiva, ITV PLC, Channel 4 and BSkyB providing Freeview, a digital service offering more than 40 television stations and additional interactive services; commenced transmission in late 2002; Man. Dir ILSE HOWLING.

Independent Television News Ltd (ITN): 200 Gray's Inn Rd, London, WC1X 8XZ; tel. (20) 7833-3000; internet www.itn.co.uk; f. 1955; ITV PLC holds a 40% stake, with Daily Mail and General Trust PLC, Thomson Reuters and United Business Media each holding a 20% stake; provides all national and international news programming for ITV1 and the London region, plus news programming for Channel 4 and Independent Radio News (IRN); also operates the ITN Archive, ITN Factual, ITN On and ITN Source; became a profit-making company in 1993; Chair. MAGGIE CARVER; Chief Exec. JOHN HARDIE.

Sianel Pedwar Cymru (S4C) (Channel Four Wales): Parc Tŷ Glas, Llanishen, Cardiff, CF14 5DU; tel. (870) 6004141; e-mail s4c@s4c.co.uk; internet s4c.co.uk; f. 1980; commenced broadcasting in 1982; Welsh-language television service for Wales; English-language programming ceased in 2010 following the extension of Channel 4 programming to Wales; regulated by the Welsh Fourth Channel Authority, a public body appointed by the UK Secretary of State for Culture, Media and Sport; financed by Dept for Culture, Media and Sport and advertising revenue; Chair. HUW JONES; Chief Exec. IAN JONES.

Satellite and Cable Broadcasting

In early 2011 some 23.8m. households in the United Kingdom had taken up access to digital television services. The major satellite and cable television companies are listed below.

BBC Worldwide Television: Media Centre, 201 Wood Lane, London, W12 7TQ; tel. (20) 8433-2000; internet www.bbcworldwide.com; began broadcasting in 1991; part of BBC Worldwide Ltd; broadcasts 24-hour news and information ('BBC World') and light entertainment programmes to Europe ('BBC Prime'); other news programmes broadcast to Africa, Asia (including a Japanese-language service to Japan), the Middle East, North America, Australia and New Zealand; Chief Exec. TIM DAVIE.

British Sky Broadcasting Group PLC (BSkyB): Grant Way, Isleworth, TW7 5QD; tel. (20) 7705-3000; fax (20) 7705-3030; internet www.sky.com; f. 1990 by merger of British Satellite Broadcasting (BSB) and Sky TV PLC (a subsidiary of News International); satellite broadcaster and programme provider; multi-channel digital television service SkyDigital); Chair. NICHOLAS FERGUSON; CEO JEREMY DARROCH.

  SkyDigital: 6 Centaurs Business Park, Grant Way, Isleworth, TW7 5QD; tel. (20) 7705-3000; fax (20) 7705-3030; e-mail skydigital@sky.com; internet www.sky.com; owned by British Sky Broadcasting Group PLC; CEO JEREMY DARROCH.

Eurosport UK: 55 Drury Lane, London, WC2B 5SQ; tel. (20) 7468-7777; fax (20) 7468-0023; e-mail gcanardduchene@eurosport.com; internet www.eurosport.co.uk; began broadcasting in 1989; broadcasts sport events, sport news; Man. Dir SIMON CRANE.

Freesat: POB 6296, London, W1A 3FF; tel. (845) 313-0051; internet www.freesat.co.uk; f. 2007; commenced broadcasting in May 2008;

free-to-air digital satellite service, offering more than 130 digital television and radio channels; jtly owned by the BBC and ITV PLC; Man. Dir EMMA SCOTT.

MTV Networks UK and Ireland: 17–29 Hawley Cres., London, NW1 8TT; tel. (20) 7284-7777; fax (20) 7284-7755; e-mail info@mtv.co.uk; internet www.mtv.co.uk; began broadcasting in 1987; popular music; Man. Dir DAVID LYNN.

UKTV: 245 Hammersmith Rd, London, W6 8PW; tel. (20) 7299-6200; fax (20) 7299-6000; internet www.uktv.co.uk; f. 1997; 10 channels: Alibi, Blighty, Dave, Eden, G.O.L.D., Home, UKTV Food, UKTV Gardens, Watch and Yesterday; satellite, cable and DTT; co-owned by BBC Worldwide Ltd and Virgin Media; CEO DARREN CHILDS; Controller EMMA TENNANT.

Finance

BANKING
(cap. = capital; res = reserves; dep. = deposits; m. = million; brs = branches; amounts in pounds sterling)

Central Bank

Bank of England: Threadneedle St, London, EC2R 8AH; tel. (20) 7601-4444; fax (20) 7601-5460; e-mail enquiries@bankofengland.co.uk; internet www.bankofengland.co.uk; inc by Royal Charter in 1694, and nationalized by Act of Parliament on 1 March 1946; under the 1998 Bank of England Act, the Bank's Monetary Policy Committee is responsible for formulating monetary policy within the framework of maintaining price stability and supporting the Government's economic policies; ensures the stability of the financial markets and acts as a lender of last resort; runs the Prudential Regulation Authority (f. 2013), which regulates banks, building societies and other deposit-takers, insurers and major investment companies; mem. of the Cheque and Credit Clearing Company; office in Leeds; 12 regional agencies assess economic conditions and contribute to the formulation of monetary policy; cap. 15m., res 588m., dep. 218,073m. (Feb. 2010); Gov. Sir MERVYN KING; Dep. Govs PAUL TUCKER, CHARLES BEAN, ANDREW BAILEY.

Principal Banks Incorporated in the United Kingdom

Barclays Bank PLC: 1 Churchill Place, London, E14 5HP; tel. (20) 7116-1000; fax (20) 7699-3463; internet group.barclays.com; inc. 1896; clearing bank; principal operating co of Barclays PLC (group holding co); cap. 14,494m., res 3,308m., dep. 542,036m. (Dec. 2011); Group Chair. Sir DAVID WALKER; Group CEO ANTONY JENKINS.

Clydesdale Bank PLC: 30 St Vincent Pl., Glasgow, G1 2HL; tel. (141) 248-7070; fax (141) 204-0828; internet www.cbonline.co.uk; f. 1838; wholly owned by National Australia Bank Ltd; clearing bank; cap. 1,742m., res 723m., dep. 27,007m. (Sept. 2012); Chair. MALCOLM WILLIAMSON; Chief Exec. (Europe) DAVID THORBURN; 340 brs.

The Co-operative Bank PLC: POB 101, 1 Balloon St, Manchester, M60 4EP; tel. (161) 832-3456; fax (161) 829-4475; e-mail customerservice@co-operativebank.co.uk; internet www.co-operativebank.co.uk; f. 1872; clearing bank; merger with Britannia Building Society approved April 2009; cap. 410m., res 95.9m., dep. 39,975.2m. (Dec. 2011); Chair. PAUL FLOWERS; Chief Exec. ROD BULMER (acting); 158 brs.

Coutts and Co: 440 Strand, London, WC2R 0QS; tel. (20) 7753-1000; fax (20) 7753-1050; internet www.coutts.com; f. 1692; private clearing bank and asset management; parent co The Royal Bank of Scotland Group PLC; cap. 41.3m., dep. 22,095m., total assets 23,271.3m. (Dec. 2011); Chair. DAVID DOUGLAS-HOME, Earl of Home; Chief Exec. MICHAEL MORLEY; 27 brs.

Danske Bank: Donegall Sq. West, Belfast, BT1 6JS; tel. (28) 9004-5000; fax (28) 9089-3214; internet www.danskebank.co.uk; f. 1960; owned by Danske Bank Group; fmrly called Northern Bank Limited; name changed to present in 2012; cap. 204.6m., res 589.6m., dep. 5,462.2m. (Dec. 2011); Chair. PETER STRAARUP; CEO GERRY MALLON; 81 brs.

First Trust Bank: 4 Queens Sq., Belfast, BT1 3DJ; tel. (28) 9032-5599; fax (28) 9032-1754; internet www.firsttrustbank.co.uk; f. 1991 following merger of Northern Ireland operations of AIB Group, Ireland and TSB Northern Ireland; trading name of AIB Group (UK) PLC in Northern Ireland; Group Chair. (UK) DAVID PRITCHARD; Man. Dir TERRY McDAID; 57 brs.

HSBC Bank PLC: 8 Canada Sq., London, E14 5HQ; tel. (20) 7991-8888; fax (20) 7992-4880; internet www.hsbc.co.uk; f. 1836; from 1992 subsidiary of HSBC Holdings PLC; clearing bank; cap. 797m., res 20,419m., dep. 484,400m. (Dec. 2012); Chair. DOUGLAS FLINT; CEO BRIAN ROBERTSON; 1,700 brs.

Lloyds Banking Group PLC: 25 Gresham St, London, EC2V 7HN; tel. (20) 7626-1500; fax (20) 7356-2494; internet www.lloydsbankinggroup.com; f. 2009 by merger of Lloyds TSB Bank PLC and HBOS PLC; owns and operates Bank of Scotland, Cheltenham and Gloucester, Halifax and Lloyds TSB; 44.3% stake owned by UK Govt; cap. 1,513m., res –380m., dep. 347,316m. (Dec. 2008); Chair. Sir WINFRIED BISCHOFF; Group Chief Exec. ANTÓNIO HORTA OSÓRIO.

National Westminster Bank PLC (NatWest): 135 Bishopsgate, London, EC2M 3UR; tel. (20) 7726-1000; fax (20) 7375-5050; internet www.natwest.com; f. 1968; clearing bank; acquired by The Royal Bank of Scotland Group PLC in 2000; cap. 1,678m., res 3,931m., dep. 250,950m. (Dec. 2011); Group Chair. Sir PHILIP HAMPTON; Group Chief Exec. STEPHEN HESTER; 1,631 brs.

The Royal Bank of Scotland PLC: POB 1000, Gogaburn, Edinburgh, EH12 1HQ; tel. (131) 556-8555; fax (131) 557-6565; internet www.rbs.co.uk; f. 1985 as result of merger of Royal Bank of Scotland and Williams & Glyn's Bank. The Royal Bank of Scotland (est. by Royal Charter in 1727) merged with National Commercial Bank of Scotland in 1969. Williams & Glyn's Bank was result of merger of Glyn Mills & Co (est. 1753) and Williams Deacon's Bank (est. 1771); 81.5% stake held by UK Govt; cap. 6,609m., res 42,323m., dep. 515,050m. (Dec. 2011); Chair. Sir PHILIP HAMPTON; Group Chief Exec. STEPHEN HESTER; 639 brs.

Santander UK PLC: Abbey National House, 2 Triton Sq., Regent's Pl., London, NW1 3AN; tel. (870) 607-6000; e-mail feedback@abbey.com; internet www.santander.co.uk; f. 1944 as Abbey National Building Society; current status assumed in 1989; owned by Banco Santander, SA (Spain); cap. 3,999m., res 5,646m., dep. 169,602m. (Dec. 2011); Chair. Lord BURNS; Chief Exec. ANA BOTÍN; 793 brs.

Standard Chartered Bank: 1 Basinghall Ave, London, EC2V 5DD; tel. (20) 7885-8888; fax (20) 7885-9999; internet www.standardchartered.com; f. 1853; holding co Standard Chartered PLC; cap. US $1,192m., res $16,355m., dep. $439,780m. (Dec. 2011); Chair. JOHN PEACE; Group Chief Exec. PETER SANDS; 570 brs.

Ulster Bank Ltd: 11–16 Donegall Sq. East, Belfast, BT1 5UB; tel. (28) 9027-6000; fax (28) 9027-5661; e-mail morrow@ulsterbank.com; internet www.ulsterbank.co.uk; f. 1836; mem. of Royal Bank of Scotland Group; cap. 1,505m., res 11,447m., dep. 35,236m. (Dec. 2011); Chair. SEAN DORGAN; Group Chief Exec. CORMAC MCCARTHY; 214 brs.

Virgin Money PLC: Jubilee House, Gosforth, Newcastle upon Tyne, NE3 4PL; tel. (191) 285-7191; e-mail info@virginmoney.com; internet uk.virginmoney.com; f. 1995; cap. 1,400m., res –22.5m., dep. 16,781.4m. (Dec. 2011); Chair. DAVID CLEMENTI; CEO JAYNE-ANNE GADHIA.

Yorkshire Bank: 30 St Vincent Pl., Glasgow, G1 2HL; tel. (113) 247-2000; fax (113) 242-0733; internet www.ybonline.co.uk; f. 1859; wholly owned by National Australia Bank Ltd; trading name of Clydesdale Bank plc which is a subsidiary of National Australia Bank Group; Chief Exec. (Europe) DAVID THORBURN; 182 brs.

Principal Merchant Banks

Barclays Capital: 5 The North Colonnade, Canary Wharf, London, E14 4BB; tel. (20) 7623-2323; e-mail publisher@barclayscapital.com; internet www.barcap.com; investment banking division of Barclays PLC; Chief Exec. RICH RICCI.

Brown, Shipley & Co Ltd: Founders Court, Lothbury, London, EC2R 7HE; tel. (20) 7606-9833; fax (20) 7282-3399; e-mail info@brownshipley.co.uk; internet www.brownshipley.com; f. 1810; owned by KBC Group NV (Belgium); Chair. STEPHEN BLANEY; Man. Dir IAN SACKFIELD.

Butterfield Bank (UK) Ltd (Butterfield Private Bank): 99 Gresham St, London, EC2V 7NG; tel. (20) 7776-6700; fax (20) 7776-6701; e-mail info@uk.butterfieldgroup.com; internet www.uk.butterfieldgroup.com; f. 1919; acquired by Bermuda's Bank of Butterfield 2004; cap. 20m., res 13.7m., dep. 805.6m. (Dec. 2008); Man. Dir GEORGE BOGUCKI.

Cater Allen Private Bank: Abbey House, 9 Nelson St, Bradford, BD1 5AN; tel. (114) 228-2407; e-mail info@caterallen.co.uk; internet www.caterallen.co.uk; f. 1981 by merger of Cater Ryder and Co Ltd (f. 1816) and Allen Harvey and Ross Ltd (f. 1888); part of Santander Private Banking UK; Chair. MALCOLM MILLINGTON; Man. Dir RICHARD J. DUNN.

Citibank International PLC: POB 242, Citigroup Centre, 33 Canada Sq., Canary Wharf, London, E14 5LB; tel. (20) 7500-5000; fax (20) 7500-1695; internet www.citibank.co.uk; f. 1972; cap. 1,757m., res 1,266m., dep. 12,518m. (Dec. 2011); Chair. and Chief Exec. WILLIAM J. MILLS.

Citigroup: 33 Canada Sq., Canary Wharf, London, E14 5LB; tel. (20) 7986-4000; internet www.citigroup.com; f. 2000 by merger of J. Henry Schroder & Co Ltd and Salomon Smith Barney; present name adopted 2001; Chair. MICHAEL E. O'NEILL; CEO MICHAEL L. CORBAT.

Close Brothers Ltd: 10 Crown Pl., London, EC2A 4FT; tel. (20) 7426-4000; fax (20) 7426-4044; e-mail cblbank@closebrothers.co.uk; internet www.closebrothers.co.uk; cap. 82.5m., res –8m., dep. 3,531.1m. (July 2012); Man. Dir STEPHEN HODGES.

Commerzbank: 30 Gresham St, London, EC2V 7PG; tel. (20) 7623-8000; fax (20) 7623-4069; internet www.commerzbank.com; f. 1958; acquired Dresdner Kleinwort Ltd in 2009; share cap. 548.6m., res 67.5m., dep. 602.2m. (Dec. 2005); Chair. and CEO MARTIN BLESSING.

DB UK Bank Limited: 23 Great Winchester St, London, EC2P 2AX; tel. (20) 7545-8000; fax (20) 7545-6155; internet www.db.com/unitedkingdom; f. 1838; as George Peabody & Co; renamed Morgan Grenfell & Co Ltd in 1910; present name adopted 2004; acquired by Deutsche Bank Group in 1989; cap. 385m., res 4.3m., dep. 1,975.3m. (Dec. 2011); Chief Exec. COLIN GRASSIE; 1 br.

Investec Bank (UK) Ltd: 2 Gresham St, London, EC2V 7QP; tel. (20) 7597-4000; fax (20) 7597-4070; internet www.investec.com; f. 1977 as Allied Arab Bank Ltd, name changed as above 1997; acquired Guinness Mahon & Co Ltd 1998; cap. 1,070.7m., res 320.2m., dep. 12,358.4m. (March 2012); Chair. HUGH HERMAN; CEO STEPHEN KOSEFF.

Rothschild: New Court, St Swithin's Lane, London, EC4P 4DU; tel. (20) 7280-5000; fax (20) 7929-1643; internet www.rothschild.com; f. 1804; cap. 57.7m., res 66.6m., dep. 1,347.3m. (March 2012); Chair. Baron DAVID DE ROTHSCHILD; 4 brs.

UBS Limited (UBS Investment Bank): 100 Liverpool St, London, EC2M 2RH; tel. (20) 7567-8000; fax (20) 7568-4800; internet www.ubs.com/investmentbank; cap. 154m., res 2,120m., dep. 8,358m. (March 2011); Group Chair. KASPER VILLIGER; CEO ANDREA ORCEL.

Savings Organization

National Savings & Investments: 375 Kensington High St, London, W14 8SD; tel. (845) 9645-0000; e-mail pressoffice@nationalsavings.co.uk; internet www.nsandi.com; govt department and Executive Agency of the Chancellor of the Exchequer; money placed in National Savings and Investments is used by the Treasury to help cost-effectively manage the national debt and contribute towards the Government's financing needs; Chair. MARTIN GRAY; Chief Exec. JANE PLATT.

National Savings regional offices: Glasgow, G58 1SB; Durham, DH99 1NS; Blackpool, FY3 9ZW; Lytham St Annes, FY0 1YN; f. 1861; Chief Exec. PETER BAREAU.

Credit Institutions

ECI Ventures: Brettenham House, 1st Floor, Lancaster Pl., London, WC2E 7EN; tel. (20) 7606-1000; fax (20) 7240-5050; e-mail enquiries@ecipartners.com; internet www.eciv.co.uk; f. 1976; advises and manages ECI5 (£78m. UK Ltd Partnership), ECI6 (£100m. UK Ltd Partnership) and EC17 (£175m. UK Ltd Partnership) to provide equity capital, mainly for management buyouts; Chair. STEPHEN DAWSON.

Permira: 80 Pall Mall, London, SW1Y 5ES; tel. (20) 7632-1000; fax (20) 7930-3185; e-mail chris.davison@permira.com; internet www.permira.com; fmrly Schroder Ventures Europe; present name adopted 2001; advises 19 Permira Funds world-wide to provide equity capital for financial acquisitions, leveraged buyouts and buy-ins, growth buyouts, public-to-private transactions, 'turnarounds'; Chair. DAMON BUFFINI.

3i Group PLC: 16 Palace St, London, SW1E 5JD; tel. (20) 7928-3131; fax (20) 7928-0058; e-mail general_enquiries@3i.com; internet www.3i.com; f. 1945 as the Industrial and Commercial Finance Corpn Ltd by the English and Scottish clearing banks, renamed Finance for Industry PLC, renamed Investors in Industry Group PLC in 1983, and renamed as above in 1988; provides long-term and permanent financial advice; Chair. Sir ADRIAN MONTAGUE; Chief Exec. MICHAEL QUEEN.

Banking and Finance Organizations

Association for Financial Markets in Europe: 1 George Yard, St Michael's House, London, EC3V 9DH; tel. (20) 7743-9300; fax (20) 7743-9301; e-mail info@afme.eu; internet www.afme.eu; f. 2009 with the merger of London Investment Banking Asscn and Financial Market Asscn; approx. 150 mems include British and foreign banks and securities houses; CEO SIMON LEWIS.

Association of Foreign Banks (AFB): 1 Bengal Ct, London, EC3V 9DD; tel. (20) 7283-8300; fax (20) 7283-8302; e-mail secretariat@foreignbanks.org.uk; internet www.foreignbanks.org.uk; f. 1947; incorporated as the Foreign Banks and Affiliates Asscn; name changed as above in 2002; approx. 180 mem. banks; Chair. PAUL ORCHART; Chief Exec. JOHN TREADWELL.

British Bankers' Association (BBA): Pinners Hall, 105–108 Old Broad St, London, EC2N 1EX; tel. (20) 7216-8800; fax (20) 7216-8811; e-mail info@bba.org.uk; internet www.bba.org.uk; f. 1919; 225 mems; Chief Exec. ANTHONY BROWNE.

Building Societies Association (BSA): York House, 6th Floor, 23 Kingsway, London, WC2B 6UJ; tel. (20) 7520-5900; fax (20) 7240-5290; e-mail simon.rex@bsa.org.uk; internet www.bsa.org.uk; represents mutual lenders and deposit takers, including all UK building societies; Dir-Gen. ADRIAN COLES.

The Chartered Institute of Bankers in Scotland: Drumsheugh House, 38B Drumsheugh Gardens, Edinburgh, EH3 7SW; tel. (131) 473-7777; fax (131) 473-7788; e-mail info@charteredbanker.com; internet www.charteredbanker.com; f. 1875; professional examinations, courses and publications; approx. 13,000 mems; Pres. JAMES LINDSAY; Chief Exec. SIMON THOMPSON.

Lending Standards Board: Level 17, City Tower, 40 Basinghall St, London, EC2V 5DE; tel. (845) 230-9694; fax (20) 7374-4414; e-mail info@lstdb.org.uk; internet www.lendingstandardsboard.org.uk; self-regulatory body which monitors and enforces Banking Code (for personal customers) and Business Banking Code; fmrly known as Banking Code Standards Bd; name changed to present in 2009; Chair. GERARD LEMOS; Chief Exec. ROBERT SKINNER.

London Money Market Association: 2 Gresham St, London, EC2V 7QP; tel. (20) 7597-4492; fax (20) 7597-4491; e-mail itmconsulting@btinternet.com; internet www.lmma.org.uk; f. 1997; 24 mems include international banks, securities houses, building societies; Chair. IAN MAIR; Dep. Chair. IAN FOX.

STOCK EXCHANGE

The London Stock Exchange: 10 Paternoster Sq., London, EC4M 7LS; tel. (20) 7797-1000; fax (20) 7334-8916; e-mail enquiries@londonstockexchange.com; internet www.londonstockexchange.com; had its origins in the coffee houses of 17th-century London; formally constituted in 1801; became a public limited company in 2000; merged with TMX Group, operator of the Toronto Stock Exchange, in 2011; 55% shares held by The London Stock Exchange; 2,682 listed cos with a total value of £3,779,699m. (Sept. 2010); Chair. CHRIS GIBSON-SMITH; Chief Exec. XAVIER ROLET.

SUPERVISORY BODIES

The Financial Ombudsman Service: South Quay Plaza, 183 Marsh Wall, London, E14 9SR; tel. (20) 7964-1000; fax (20) 7964-1001; e-mail complaint.info@financial-ombudsman.org.uk; internet www.financial-ombudsman.org.uk; f. 2001 to replace The Personal Investment Authority Ombudsman Bureau, The Insurance Ombudsman Bureau, The Office of the Banking Ombudsman, The Office of the Building Societies Ombudsman, The Office of the Investment Ombudsman, The Securities and Futures Authority Complaints Bureau, The Financial Services Authority Complaints Unit and The Personal Insurance Arbitration Service; Chair. Sir CHRISTOPHER KELLY; Chief Ombudsman NATALIE CEENEY.

Financial Conduct Authority (FCA): 25 The North Colonnade, Canary Wharf, London, E14 5HS; tel. (20) 7066-1000; fax (20) 7066-1099; internet www.fca.org.uk; f. 2013; replaced the Financial Services Authority under the terms of the Financial Services Act 2012; regulates the financial services industry in the UK; Chair. JOHN GRIFFITH-JONES; Chief Exec. MARTIN WHEATLEY.

Securities & Investment Institute: 8 Eastcheap, London, EC3M 1AE; tel. (20) 7645-0600; fax (20) 7645-0601; e-mail info@sii.org.uk; internet www.sii.org.uk; f. 1992; aims to promote professional standards and ethics in the securities industry; Chair. SCOTT DOBBIE; Chief Exec. SIMON CULHANE.

INSURANCE

Lloyd's: 1 Lime St, London, EC3M 7HA; tel. (20) 7327-1000; fax (20) 7626-2389; e-mail enquiries@lloyds.com; internet www.lloyds.com; had its origins in the coffee house opened c. 1688 by Edward Lloyd and was incorporated by Act of Parliament (Lloyd's Acts 1871 and 1982); an international insurance market and Society of Underwriters, consisting of individual members ('Names') and corporate members grouped into syndicates who accept risks on the basis of unlimited and limited liability, respectively; business is effected through firms of brokers who are permitted to place insurances either directly or by way of reinsurance; administered by the Corporation of Lloyd's through an 18-member Council, mostly elected by and from the underwriting membership; regulated by the Financial Services Authority (FSA), under the Financial Services and Markets Act of 2000; capacity to accept insurance premiums of more than £17,000m. in 2010; 85 syndicates underwriting insurance in 2010, covering all classes of business from more than 200 countries and territories world-wide; Chair. JOHN NELSON; CEO RICHARD WARD.

Principal Insurance Companies

AEGON UK PLC: Edinburgh Park, Edinburgh, EH12 9SE; tel. (870) 600-0337; fax (131) 549-4225; e-mail enquiries@aegon.co.uk; internet www.aegon.co.uk; f. 1831 as Scottish Equitable Life Assurance Society; restyled Scottish Equitable PLC in 1994; acquired by AEGON NV (Netherlands) in 1998 and present name adopted 1999; Chief Exec. ADRIAN GRACE.

Allianz Insurance PLC: 57 Ladymead, Guildford, GU1 1DB; tel. (1483) 568161; fax (1483) 300952; internet www.allianz.co.uk; part of the Allianz Group (Germany); f. 1905, fmrly Cornhill Insurance Co PLC; Chair. CLEMENT B. BOOTH; Chief Exec. ANDREW TORRANCE.

AON Limited: 8 Devonshire Sq., London, EC2M 4PL; tel. (20) 7626-5500; fax (20) 7621-1511; e-mail aon.questions@aon.co.uk; internet www.aon.co.uk; subsidiary of AON Corpn, USA; Chair. PAUL MANDUCA; CEO ROBERT BROWN.

Aviva PLC: POB 420, St Helen's, 1 Undershaft, London, EC3P 3DQ; tel. (20) 7283-2000; e-mail aviva_info@aviva.com; internet www.aviva.com; formed by merger of Commercial Union and General Accident in 1998; merged with Norwich Union PLC in 2000; renamed as above in 2002; Chair. Lord SHARMAN OF REDLYNCH; Chief Exec. MARK WILSON.

AXA Insurance PLC: 5 Old Broad St, London, EC2N 1AD; tel. (20) 7702-3109; fax (20) 7369-3909; e-mail customerservice@axa-insurance.co.uk; internet www.axa.co.uk; f. 1903; Chair. ANTHONY HAMILTON; Group CEO HENRI DE CASTRIES.

Bupa: Bupa House, 15–19 Bloomsbury Way, London, WC1A 2BA; tel. (20) 7656-2000; e-mail companysecretary@bupa.com; internet www.bupa.co.uk; f. 1947; Chair. Lord ALEXANDER LEITCH; Chief Exec. STUART FLETCHER.

The Co-operative Insurance: POB 67, Mitcheldean, GL17 0ZA; tel. (800) 294-1021; fax (161) 837-4048; e-mail ibis@co-operativeinsurance.co.uk; internet www.co-operativeinsurance.co.uk; f. 1867; Chair. PAUL FLOWERS; Chief Exec. ROD BULMER (acting).

Direct Line Group: Churchill Court, Westmoreland Rd, Bromley, BR1 1DP; tel. (20) 8313-3030; fax (20) 8681-0512; internet www.directlinegroup.com; f. 1985; wholly owned by The Royal Bank of Scotland; CEO PAUL ROBERT GEDDES.

Ecclesiastical Insurance Office PLC: Beaufort House, Brunswick Rd, Gloucester, GL1 1JZ; tel. (845) 777-3322; fax (1452) 423557; e-mail information@eigmail.com; internet www.ecclesiastical.co.uk; f. 1887; Chair. WILL SAMUEL; Group Chief Exec. MICHAEL TRIPP.

Equitable Life Assurance Society: Walton St, Aylesbury, HP21 7QW; tel. (845) 603-6771; fax (1296) 386383; e-mail enquiries@equitable.co.uk; internet www.equitable.co.uk; f. 1762; Chair. IAN BRIMECOME; Chief Exec. CHRIS WISCARSON.

Friends Provident PLC: One New Change, London, EC4M 9EF; tel. (845) 641-7825; fax (1306) 740150; e-mail customer.services@friendsprovident.co.uk; internet www.friendslife.co.uk; f. 1832; Exec. Chair. Sir MALCOLM WILLIAMSON; Group CEO ANDY BRIGGS.

Legal and General Group PLC: 1 Coleman St, London, EC2R 5AA; tel. (20) 3124-2000; fax (20) 3124-2500; internet www.legalandgeneralgroup.com; f. 1836; Group CEO NIGEL WILSON; Group Chair. JOHN STEWART; Sec. G. J. TIMMS.

  Legal and General Insurance Ltd: 1 Coleman St, London, EC2R 5AA; tel. (20) 3124-2000; fax (20) 7528-6222; f. 1946 as British Commonwealth Insurance Co; Man. Dir PETER GRAHAM; Sec. JEAN WEBB.

Liverpool Victoria (LV): County Gates, Bournemouth, BH1 2NF; tel. (1202) 292333; fax (1202) 292253; internet www.lv.com; f. 1843; Chair. DENNIS HOLT; Group Chief Exec. MICHAEL (MIKE) ROGERS.

MGM Advantage: MGM House, Heene Rd, Worthing, BN11 3AT; tel. (1903) 836067; fax (1903) 836004; e-mail customers@mgmadvantage.com; internet www.mgmadvantage.com; f. 1852; Chair. Sir WILLIAM PROBY; CEO CHRIS EVANS.

Munich Re Life: 25 Canada Sq., Level 31, Canary Wharf, London, E14 5LQ; tel. (20) 7718-1000; fax (20) 7718-1010; internet www.munichre.co.uk; f. 1977; reinsurance; CEO ANDY REAR.

Munich Re Non-Life: Plantation Pl., 30 Fenchurch St, London, EC3M 3AJ; tel. (20) 3003-7000; fax (20) 3003-7010; e-mail 30fsreception@munichre.com; internet www.munichre.co.uk; f. 1890; reinsurance; Man. Dir and Gen. Man. FRANK BUCHSTEINER.

The National Farmers Union Mutual Insurance Society Ltd (NFU Mutual): Tiddington Rd, Stratford upon Avon, CV37 7BJ; tel. (1789) 204211; fax (1789) 298992; internet www.nfumutual.co.uk; f. 1910; Chair. RICHARD PERCY; Group Chief Exec. LINDSAY SINCLAIR.

Old Mutual Plc: 5th Floor, Old Mutual Pl., 2 Lambeth Hill, London, EC4V 4GG; tel. (20) 7002-7000; internet www.oldmutual.com; f. 1845; Chair. PATRICK O'SULLIVAN; Group CEO JULIAN ROBERTS.

Pearl: The Pearl Centre, Lynch Wood, Peterborough, PE2 6FY; tel. (1733) 470470; fax (1733) 472300; e-mail customersupport@pearl.co.uk; internet www.pearl.co.uk; f. 1864; part of Phoenix Group of Cos; present name adopted Dec. 2003; Chair. JONATHAN EVANS.

Phoenix Life Ltd: POB 1979, Liverpool, L69 3ED; tel. (151) 255-5180; fax (1733) 475116; internet www.phoenixlife.co.uk; f. 2005 by a merger of Swiss Life UK and Royal & Sun Alliance UK life business; merged with Britannic Assurance PLC in 2007; subsidiary of Resolution PLC; Chair. HOWARD DAVIES; CEO MIKE MERRICK.

The Prudential Assurance Co Ltd: Laurence Pountney Hill, London, EC4R 0HH; tel. (20) 7220-7588; fax (20) 7548-3465; e-mail media.relations@prudential.co.uk; internet www.prudential.co.uk; f. 1848; holding co: Prudential Corpn PLC; Group Chair. PAUL MANDUCA; Group CEO TIDJANE THIAM.

The Royal London Mutual Insurance Society Ltd: 55 Gracechurch St, London, EC3V 0RL; tel. (8450) 502020; fax (1625) 605400; e-mail info@royal-london.co.uk; internet www.royal-london.co.uk; f. 1861; Chair. TIM MELVILLE-ROSS; Group Chief Exec. PHIL LONEY.

> **Scottish Life:** St Andrew House, 1 Thistle St, Edinburgh, EH2 1DG; tel. (845) 605-0050; fax (131) 456-7880; e-mail e-face@scottishlife.co.uk; internet www.scottishlife.co.uk; f. 1881; inc. as a Mutual Company 1968; became part of Royal London Mutual Insurance Society in July 2001; Man. Dir EWAN SMITH.

RSA Insurance Group PLC: 9th Floor, 1 Plantation Place, 30 Fenchurch St, London, EC3M 3BD; tel. (20) 7111-7000; internet www.rsagroup.com; f. 1996 by merger of Royal Insurance Holdings PLC (f. 1845) and Sun Alliance Group PLC; present name adopted 2008; Chair. JOHN NAPIER; CEO SIMON LEE.

Scottish Widows PLC: Scottish Widows 15, Dalkeith Rd, Edinburgh, EH16 5BU; tel. (845) 767-8910; fax (131) 662-4053; e-mail cameron.walker@scottishwidows.co.uk; internet www.scottishwidows.co.uk; f. 1815 as Scottish Widows' Fund and Life Assurance Society; name changed as above March 2000 following acquisition by Lloyds TSB; mem. of Lloyds Banking Group; Chair. Lord BLACKWELL; Group Exec. Dir TOBY STRAUSS.

Standard Life PLC: Standard Life House, 30 Lothian Rd, Edinburgh, EH1 2DH; tel. (131) 225-2552; e-mail customer_service@standardlife.com; internet www.standardlife.com; f. 1825; present name adopted 2006; assets under management £156,800m. (2009); Chair. GERRY GRIMSTONE; Group CEO DAVID NISH.

Swiss Re UK Ltd: 30 St Mary Axe, London, EC3A 8EP; tel. (20) 7933-3000; fax (20) 7933-5000; internet www.swissre.com; f. 1863; Chair. WALTER B. KIELHOLZ; CEO MICHEL M. LIÈS.

Wesleyan Assurance Society: Colmore Circus, Birmingham, B4 6AR; tel. (121) 335-3487; fax (121) 200-2971; internet www.wesleyan.co.uk; f. 1841; Chair. BRYAN JACKSON; CEO CRAIG ERRINGTON.

Zurich Assurance Ltd: UK Life Centre, Station Rd, Swindon, SN1 1EL; tel. (1793) 511227; internet www.zurich.co.uk; f. 1872; Group Chair. JOSEF ACKERMANN; CEO MARTIN SENN.

Insurance Associations

Association of British Insurers: 51 Gresham St, London, EC2V 7HQ; tel. (20) 7600-3333; fax (20) 7696-8999; e-mail info@abi.org.uk; internet www.abi.org.uk; f. 1985; principal trade association for insurance companies; protection, promotion, and advancement of the common interests of all classes of insurance business; c. 390 mems; Chair. TIDJANE THIAM; Dir-Gen. OTTO THORESEN.

British Insurance Brokers' Association (BIBA): John Stow House, 8th Floor, 18 Bevis Marks, London, EC3A 7JB; tel. (870) 950-1790; fax (20) 7626-9676; e-mail enquiries@biba.org.uk; internet www.biba.org.uk; f. 1977; Chair. ANDY HOMER; Chief Exec. ERIC GALBRAITH.

Chartered Insurance Institute: 42–48 High Rd, South Woodford, London, E18 2JP; tel. (20) 8989-8464; fax (20) 8530-3052; e-mail customer.serv@cii.co.uk; internet www.cii.co.uk; f. 1897; inc 1912; approx. 100,000 mems; Pres. AMANDA BLANC; CEO Dr SANDY SCOTT.

Fire Protection Association: London Rd, Moreton-in-Marsh, GL56 0RH; tel. (1608) 812500; fax (1608) 812501; e-mail fpa@thefpa.co.uk; internet www.thefpa.co.uk; f. 1946; Man. Dir JONATHAN O'NEILL.

Insurance Institute of London: 5th Floor, 20 Aldermanbury, London, EC2V 7HY; tel. (20) 7600-1343; fax (20) 7600-6857; e-mail iil.london@cii.co.uk; internet www.iilondon.co.uk; f. 1907; Pres. MARTIN SOUTH.

International Underwriting Association (IUA): London Underwriting Centre, 3 Minster Ct, Mincing Lane, London, EC3R 7DD; tel. (20) 7617-4444; fax (20) 7617-4440; e-mail info@iua.co.uk; internet www.iua.co.uk; f. 1998; Chair. STEPHEN RILEY; Chief Exec. DAVE J. MATCHAM.

Associations of Actuaries

Faculty of Actuaries: 18 Dublin St, Edinburgh, EH1 3PP; tel. (20) 7632-2100; fax (131) 240-1313; e-mail faculty@actuaries.org.uk; internet www.actuaries.org.uk; f. 1856; 1,275 Fellows, 13 Honorary Fellows; Pres. PHILIP SCOTT; Chief Exec. DEREK CRIBB.

Institute of Actuaries: Staple Inn Hall, High Holborn, London, WC1V 7QJ; tel. (20) 7632-2100; fax (20) 7632-2111; e-mail institute@actuaries.org.uk; internet www.actuaries.org.uk; f. 1848; Royal Charter 1884; 16,287 mems (May 2008); Pres. PHILIP SCOTT; Chief Exec. DEREK CRIBB.

Trade and Industry
GOVERNMENT AGENCIES

Advisory, Conciliation and Arbitration Service (Acas): Euston Tower, 286 Euston Rd, London, NW1 3JJ; tel. (20) 7396-0022; fax (20) 7210-3615; internet www.acas.org.uk; f. 1975; an independent organization, under the direction of a council comprising employers, trade union representatives and independent members, appointed by the Secretary of State for Business, Innovation and Skills; aims to improve organizations and working life through good employment relations; provides collective conciliation, arbitration, mediation, advisory, training and information services, and conciliates in individual employment rights issues; Chair. ED SWEENEY; Chief Exec. JOHN TAYLOR.

Central Arbitration Committee: Euston Tower, 22nd Floor, 286 Euston Rd, London, NW1 3JJ; tel. (20) 7904-2300; fax (20) 7904-2301; e-mail enquiries@cac.gov.uk; internet www.cac.gov.uk; f. 1976 as an independent body under the 1975 Employment Protection Act, in succession to Industrial Court/Industrial Arbitration Board; adjudicates on claims for statutory trade union recognition and de-recognition under the 1999 Employment Relations Act; determines disclosure of information complaints and considers applications and complaints received under the Information and Consultation of Employees Regulations 2004; considers applications in relation to the establishment and operation of European Works Councils, European Companies and European Co-operative Societies; Chair. Sir MICHAEL BURTON; Chief Exec. SIMON GOULDSTONE.

Competition Appeal Tribunal: Victoria House, Bloomsbury Pl., London, WC1A 2EB; tel. (20) 7979-7979; fax (20) 7979-7978; e-mail info@catribunal.org.uk; internet www.catribunal.org.uk; f. 2002; a specialist tribunal established to hear certain cases in the sphere of UK competition and economic regulatory law; hears appeals against decisions of the Office of Fair Trading and the regulators in the telecommunications, electricity, gas, water, railways and air traffic services sectors under the Competition Act 1998; reviews decisions of the Office of Fair Trading, the Competition Commission and the Secretary of State made pursuant to the merger control and market investigation provisions of the Enterprise Act 2002; also has jurisdiction, under the Competition Act 1998, to award damages in respect of infringements of European or British competition law and, under the Communications Act 2003, to hear appeals against decisions of Ofcom; headed by the President and a panel of Chairmen and 14 mems with backgrounds in law, economics, business, accountancy and regulation who sit with the President or a mem. of the panel of Chairmen to hear cases; Pres. Sir GERALD BARLING; Registrar CHARLES DHANOWA.

Competition Commission: Victoria House, Southampton Row, London, WC1B 4AD; tel. (20) 7271-0100; fax (20) 7271-0367; e-mail info@cc.gsi.gov.uk; internet www.competition-commission.org.uk; conducts in-depth inquiries into mergers, markets and the regulation of the major regulated industries; Chair. ROGER WITCOMB; Chief Exec. DAVID SAUNDERS.

Competition Service: Victoria House, Bloomsbury Pl., London, WC1A 2EB; tel. (20) 7979-7979; fax (20) 7979-7978; e-mail info@catribunal.org.uk; internet www.catribunal.org.uk; f. 2003 under the Enterprise Act 2002; a corporate and executive non-departmental public body, whose purpose is to fund and provide support services to the Competition Appeal Tribunal.

Consumer Focus: Victoria House, Southampton Row, London, WC1B 4AD; tel. (20) 7799-7900; fax (20) 7799-7901; e-mail contact@consumerfocus.org.uk; internet www.consumerfocus.org.uk; f. 2008 by merger of Postwatch, energywatch and the National Consumer Council; advocacy body for consumer rights; Chair. CHRISTINE FARNISH.

Forestry Commission: Silvan House, 231 Corstorphine Rd, Edinburgh, EH12 7AT; tel. (131) 334-0303; fax (131) 334-3047; e-mail enquiries@forestry.gsi.gov.uk; internet www.forestry.gov.uk; govt dept responsible for protecting and expanding the forests and woodlands of England, Scotland and Wales and increasing their value to society and the environment; implements the Government's forestry policy within the framework of the Forestry Acts, administers the Woodland Grant Scheme, controls tree-felling through the issue of licences, administers plant health regulations to protect woodlands against tree pests and diseases, and conducts research; responsible for the management of the national forests; Chair. PAMELA WARHURST; Dir-Gen. TIM ROLLINSON.

Natural England: Foundry House, 3 Millsands, Riverside Exchange, Sheffield, S3 8NH; tel. and fax (300) 060-3900; e-mail enquiries@naturalengland.org.uk; internet www.naturalengland.org.uk; f. 2006 by merger of English Nature, landscape, access and recreation sections of the Countryside Agency and the environmental land management functions of the Rural Development Service; advises Government and acts on issues relating to the conservation and enhancement of the environmental, economic and social well-being of the English countryside; Chair. POUL CHRISTENSEN; Chief Exec. DAVE WEBSTER.

Office of Fair Trading: Fleetbank House, 2–6 Salisbury Sq., London, EC4Y 8JX; tel. (20) 7211-8000; fax (20) 7211-8800; e-mail enquiries@oft.gsi.gov.uk; internet www.oft.gov.uk; f. 1973; monitors consumer affairs, competition policy, consumer credit, estate agencies, etc.; Chair. PHILIP COLLINS; Chief Exec. CLIVE MAXWELL.

Skills Funding Agency: Cheylesmore House, Quinton Rd, Coventry, CV1 2WT; tel. (845) 377-5000; fax (24) 7682-3675; e-mail info@skillsfundingagency.bis.gov.uk; internet skillsfundingagency.bis.gov.uk; f. 2010; agency of the Department for Business, Innovation and Skills; funds and regulates adult further education and skills training in England; Chief Exec. KIM THORNEYWORK (acting).

DEVELOPMENT ORGANIZATIONS

GLE oneLondon: 10–12 Queen Elizabeth St, London, SE1 2JN; tel. (20) 7403-0300; fax (20) 7940-1742; e-mail info@gle.co.uk; internet www.gle.co.uk; f. 2001 following merger between London Enterprise Agency and Greater London Enterprise; jtly owned by all 33 London borough councils; Man. Dir NICHOLAS NICOLAOU.

Invest Northern Ireland (Invest NI): Bedford Sq., Bedford St, Belfast, BT2 7ES; tel. (28) 9069-8000; fax (28) 9043-6536; e-mail eo@investni.com; internet www.investni.com; f. 2002; Invest NI is the main economic development agency in Northern Ireland and, sponsored by the Dept of Enterprise, Trade and Investment, aims to strengthen the Northern Ireland economy; Chair. MARK ENNIS; Chief Exec. ALASTAIR HAMILTON.

London First: 3 Whitcomb St, London, WC2H 7HA; tel. (20) 7665-1500; fax (20) 7665-1501; e-mail staff@london-first.co.uk; internet www.london-first.co.uk; promotes London as a business centre; Chair. PHILIP DILLEY; Chief Exec. Baroness JO VALENTINE.

Overseas Development Institute: 111 Westminster Bridge Rd, London, SE1 7JD; tel. (20) 7922-0300; fax (20) 7922-0399; e-mail odi@odi.org.uk; internet www.odi.org.uk; f. 1960; independent policy unit on international development and humanitarian issues; Chair. Dr DALEEP MUKARJI; Dir Dr ALISON EVANS.

Scottish Enterprise: Atrium Court, 50 Waterloo St, Glasgow, G2 6HQ; tel. (141) 204-1111; fax (141) 248-1600; e-mail enquiries@scotent.co.uk; internet www.scottish-enterprise.com; economic development agency for lowland Scotland; Chair. CRAWFORD GILLIES; Chief Exec. LENA C. WILSON.

CHAMBERS OF COMMERCE

British Chambers of Commerce (BCC): 65 Petty France, London, SW1H 9EU; tel. (20) 7654-5800; fax (20) 7654-5819; e-mail info@britishchambers.org.uk; internet www.britishchambers.org.uk; f. 1860; in January 1993 subsumed National Chamber of Trade (f. 1897); represents the new Approved Chamber Network in the United Kingdom (comprising 51 Chambers); Pres. MARTYN PELLEW; Dir-Gen. JOHN LONGWORTH.

International Chamber of Commerce (ICC) United Kingdom: 12 Grosvenor Pl., London, SW1X 7HH; tel. (20) 7838-9363; fax (20) 7235-5447; e-mail info@iccorg.co.uk; internet www.iccuk.net; f. 1920; British affiliate of the world business org.; CEO and Dir NICHOLAS ARMOUR.

London Chamber of Commerce and Industry: 33 Queen St, London, EC4R 1AP; tel. (20) 7248-4444; fax (20) 7489-0391; e-mail lc@londonchamber.co.uk; internet www.londonchamber.co.uk; f. 1881; Pres. WILLIE WALSH; Chief Exec. COLIN STANBRIDGE.

Northern Ireland Chamber of Commerce (NICC): Chamber of Commerce House, 22 Great Victoria St, Belfast, BT2 7BJ; tel. (28) 9024-4113; fax (28) 9024-7024; e-mail mail@northernirelandchamber.com; internet www.nicci.co.uk; f. 1783; 4,000 mems; Pres. MARK NODDER; Chief Exec. ANN MCGREGOR.

INDUSTRIAL AND TRADE ASSOCIATIONS

ADS: Salamanca Sq, 9 Albert Embankment, London, SE1 7SP; tel. (20) 7091-4500; fax (20) 7091-4545; e-mail enquiries@adsgroup.org.uk; internet www.adsgroup.org.uk; f. 2009 by merger of Asscn of Police and Public Security Suppliers, Defence Mfrs Assscn and Soc. of British Aerospace Cos; national trade asscn for the British aerospace, defence and security industries; CEO REES WARD.

Aluminium Federation: National Metalforming Centre, 47 Birmingham Rd, West Bromwich, B70 6PY; tel. (121) 601-6363; fax (870) 138-9714; e-mail alfed@alfed.org.uk; internet www.alfed.org.uk; f. 1962; Pres. CARL TOMLINSON; Chief Exec. WILL SAVAGE.

Association of the British Pharmaceutical Industry: 7th Floor, Southside, 105 Victoria St, London SW1E 6QT; tel. (870) 890-4333; fax (20) 7747-1447; e-mail abpi@abpi.org.uk; internet www.abpi.org.uk; f. 1930; Pres. DEEPAK KHANNA; Dir-Gen. Dr STEPHEN WHITEHEAD.

Association of Manufacturers of Domestic Appliances: Rapier House, 40–46 Lamb's Conduit St, London, WC1N 3NW; tel. (20) 7405-0666; fax (20) 7405-6609; e-mail info@amdea.org.uk; internet www.amdea.org.uk; f. 1969; 28 mem. cos; Chief Exec. DOUGLAS HERBISON.

BFM (British Furniture Manufacturers' Association): Wycombe House, 9 Amersham Hill, High Wycombe, Bucks, HP13 6NR; tel. (149) 4523-021; fax (149) 4474-270; e-mail info@bfm.org.uk; internet www.bfm.org.uk; merged in January 1993 with BFM Exhibitions and BFM Exports; Man. Dir JACKIE BAZELEY.

British Beer and Pub Association: Ground Floor, Brewers' Hall, Aldermanbury Sq., London, EC2V 7HR; tel. (20) 7627-9191; fax (20) 7627-9123; e-mail contact@beerandpub.com; internet www.beerandpub.com; f. 1904; trade association for British brewing industry and multiple pub operators; Chair. JONATHAN NEAME; Chief Exec. BRIGID SIMMONDS.

British Cable Association: 3–30 Lingfield Rd, London, SW19 4PU; tel. and fax (20) 8946-6978; e-mail peter.smeeth@btconnect.com; internet www.bcauk.org; f. 1903; fmrly British Cable Makers' Confederation; Sec.-Gen. PETER SMEETH.

British Ceramic Confederation: Federation House, Station Rd, Stoke-on-Trent, Staffs., ST4 2SA; tel. (1782) 744631; fax (1782) 744102; e-mail bcc@ceramfed.co.uk; internet www.ceramfed.co.uk; f. 1984; 100 mems; Chief Exec. Dr LAURA COHEN.

British Electrotechnical and Allied Manufacturers' Association (BEAMA): Westminster Tower, 3 Albert Embankment, London, SE1 7SL; tel. (20) 7793-3000; fax (20) 7793-3003; e-mail info@beama.org.uk; internet www.beama.org.uk; f. 1905 as British Electrical and Allied Manufacturers' Association Ltd, present name from 2002; 250 mems; Pres. LES WOOLNER; CEO HOWARD PORTER.

British Exporters' Association: Broadway House, Tothill St, London, SW1H 9NQ; tel. (20) 7222-5419; fax (20) 7799-2468; e-mail hughbailey@bexa.co.uk; internet www.bexa.co.uk; Pres. Earl RICHARD OF KILMOREY; Chair. JON COLEMAN; Dir HUGH BAILEY.

British Footwear Association: 3 Burystead Pl., Wellingborough, Northants, NN8 1AH; tel. (1933) 229005; fax (1933) 225009; e-mail info@britishfootwearassociation.co.uk; internet www.britishfootwearassociation.co.uk; f. 1898; Sec. ELAINE DAVIES.

British Glass: 9 Churchill Way, Chapeltown, Sheffield, S35 2PY; tel. (114) 290-1850; fax (114) 290-1851; e-mail info@britglass.co.uk; internet www.britglass.org.uk; over 100 mems; Dir-Gen. DAVID DALTON.

British Hospitality Association: Queen's House, 55–56 Lincoln's Inn Fields, London, WC2A 3BH; tel. (20) 7404-7744; fax (20) 7404-7799; e-mail bha@bha.org.uk; internet www.bha.org.uk; f. 1907; Pres. ALAN PARKER; Chief Exec. UFI IBRAHIM.

The British Precast Concrete Federation Ltd: 60 Charles St, Leicester, LE1 1FB; tel. (116) 253-6161; fax (116) 251-4568; e-mail info@britishprecast.org; internet www.britishprecast.org; f. 1918; approx. 125 mems; Chief Exec. MARTIN A. CLARKE.

British Printing Industries Federation: 2 Villiers Court, Meriden Business Park, Copse Dr, Coventry, CV5 9RN; tel. (0845) 250-7050; fax (01676) 526-033; e-mail andrew.brown@bpif.org.uk; internet www.britishprint.com; f. 1900; 2,500 mems; Pres. TONY GARNISH; Chief Exec. KATHY WOODWARD.

British Rubber Manufacturers' Association: 6 Bath Pl., Rivington St, London, EC2A 3JE; tel. (20) 7457-5040; fax (20) 7972-9008; f. 1968; Pres. JAMES RICKARD; Dir A. J. DORKEN.

The Carpet Foundation: MFC Complex, 60 New Rd, Kidderminster, DY10 1AQ; tel. (1562) 755568; fax (1562) 865405; internet www.carpetfoundation.com; 11 manufacturer and 1,100 retailer mems; Chair. JOHN DUNCAN; Chief Exec. MIKE HARDIMAN.

CBI: Centre Point, 103 New Oxford St, London, WC1A 1DU; tel. (20) 7379-7400; fax (20) 7379-7200; e-mail webteam@cbi.org.uk; internet www.cbi.org.uk; f. 1965 as the Confederation of British Industry; adopted current name in 2001; acts as a national point of reference for all seeking views of industry and is recognized internationally as the representative organization of British industry and management; advises the Government on all aspects of policy affecting the interests of industry; has a direct corporate membership employing more than 4m., and a trade association membership representing more than 6m. of the work-force; Pres. Sir ROGER CARR; Dir-Gen. JOHN CRIDLAND.

Chemical Industries Association: King's Bldgs, Smith Sq., London, SW1P 3JJ; tel. (20) 7834-3399; fax (20) 7834-4469; e-mail enquiries@cia.org.uk; internet www.cia.org.uk; Chief Exec. STEVE ELLIOTT.

Dairy UK: 93 Baker St, London, W1U 6QQ; tel. (20) 7486-7244; fax (20) 7487-4734; e-mail info@dairyuk.org; internet www.dairyuk.org; f. 1933; Chair. ROBERT WISEMAN; Dir-Gen. JIM BEGG.

EEF—The Manufacturers' Oganization: Broadway House, Tothill St, London, SW1H 9NQ; tel. (20) 7222-7777; fax (20) 7222-2782; e-mail enquiries@eef-fed.org.uk; internet www.eef.org.uk; f. 1896 as

Engineering Employers' Federation; 6,000 mems through 14 associations; Pres. MARTIN J. TEMPLE; CEO TERRY C. SCUOLER.

Electrical Contractors' Association: ESCA House, 34 Palace Court, London, W2 4HY; tel. (20) 7313-4800; fax (20) 7221-7344; e-mail info@eca.co.uk; internet www.eca.co.uk; f. 1901; Pres. PAUL McNAUGHTON; Chief Exec. STEVE BRATT.

Energy Networks Association: Dean Bradley House, 6th Floor, 52 Horseferry Rd, London, SW1P 2AF; tel. (20) 7706-5100; e-mail info@energynetworks.org; internet www.energynetworks.org; f. 2003; represents British gas and electricity transmission and distribution licence holders; Chair. STEVE JOHNSON; Chief Exec. DAVID SMITH.

Farmers' Union of Wales: Llys Amaeth, Plas Gogerddan, Aberystwyth, SY23 3BT; tel. (1970) 820820; fax (1970) 820821; e-mail head.office@fuw.org.uk; internet www.fuw.org.uk; f. 1955; 14,000 mems; Pres. EMYR JONES.

Food and Drink Federation: 6 Catherine St, London, WC2B 5JJ; tel. (20) 7836-2460; fax (20) 7836-0580; e-mail generalenquiries@fdf.org.uk; internet www.fdf.org.uk; Dir-Gen. MELANIE LEECH.

Glass and Glazing Federation: 54 Ayres St, London, SE1 1EU; tel. (20) 7939-9101; fax (870) 042-4266; e-mail info@ggf.org.uk; internet www.ggf.org.uk; f. 1977; trade organization for employers and cos in the flat glass, glazing, home improvement, plastic and window film industries; Pres. MARK WARREN; Chief Exec. NIGEL REES.

Institute of Export: Export House, Minerva Business Park, Lynch Wood, Peterborough, PE2 6FT; tel. (1733) 404400; fax (1733) 404444; e-mail institute@export.org.uk; internet www.export.org.uk; f. 1935; professional educational organization devoted to the development of British export trade and the interests of those associated with it; more than 6,000 mems; Pres. JAMES DAVIES; Chair. DOUG TWEDDLE; Dir ANDY GIBSON.

Labour Relations Agency: 2–16 Gordon St, Belfast, BT1 2LG; tel. (28) 9032-1442; fax (28) 9033-0827; e-mail info@lra.org.uk; internet www.lra.org.uk; f. 1976; provides an impartial and confidential employment relations service to those engaged in industry, commerce and the public services in Northern Ireland; provides advice on good employment practices and assistance with the development and implementation of employment policies and procedures; also active in resolving disputes through its conciliation, mediation and arbitration services.

Mineral Products Association: Gillingham House, 38–44 Gillingham St, London, SW1V 1HU; tel. (20) 7963-8000; fax (20) 7963-8001; e-mail info@mineralproducts.org; internet www.mineralproducts.org; fmrly Quarry Products Asscn; Chair. DYFRIG JAMES; Chief Exec. NIGEL JACKSON.

Mineral Products Association—Cement: Riverside House, 4 Meadows Business Park, Station Approach, Blackwater, Camberley, GU17 9AB; tel. (1276) 608700; fax (1276) 608701; e-mail mpacement@mineralproducts.org; internet cement.mineralproducts.org/; Exec. Dir PAL CHANA.

National Association of British and Irish Millers Ltd: 21 Arlington St, London, SW1A 1RN; tel. (20) 7493-2521; fax (20) 7493-6785; e-mail info@nabim.org.uk; internet www.nabim.org.uk; trade assoc. of the British flour milling industry; f. 1878; Dir-Gen. ALEXANDER WAUGH; Sec. NIGEL BENNETT.

National Farmers' Union: Agriculture House, Stoneleigh Park, Warwickshire, CV8 2TZ; tel. (24) 7685-8500; fax (24) 7685-8501; e-mail nfu@nfu.org.uk; internet www.nfuonline.com; f. 1908; Pres. PETER KENDALL; Dir-Gen. KEVIN ROBERTS.

Northern Ireland Hotels Federation: The McCune Bldg, 1 Shore Rd, Belfast, BT15 3PG; tel. (28) 9077-6635; fax (28) 9077-1899; e-mail office@nihf.co.uk; internet www.nihf.co.uk; f. 1999; Pres. JAMES McGINN; Chief Exec. JANICE GAULT.

Northern Ireland Textiles and Apparel Asscn: 5C The Square, Hillsborough, BT26 6AG; tel. (28) 9268-9999; fax (28) 9268-9968; e-mail info@nita.co.uk; f. 1993; 30 mems.

Producers' Alliance for Cinema and Television (PACT) Ltd: Fitzrovia House, 3rd Floor, 153–157 Cleveland St, London, W1T 6QW; tel. (20) 7380-8230; fax (20) 7067-4377; e-mail enquiries@pact.co.uk; internet www.pact.co.uk; film and TV producers; represents 1,000 companies; Chair. DEBBIE MANNERS; Chief Exec. JOHN McVAY.

Scottish Building Federation: Crichton House, Crichton's Close, Edinburgh, EH8 8DT; tel. (131) 556-8866; e-mail info@scottish-building.co.uk; internet www.scottish-building.co.uk; f. 1895; Pres. ROBBIE COOKE; Chief Exec. MICHAEL LEVACK.

Scottish Enterprise—Textiles: Apex House, 99 Haymarket Terrace, Edinburgh, EH12 5DH; tel. (131) 313-6243; fax (131) 313-4231; internet www.scottish-textiles.co.uk; present name since 1991.

Sea Fish Industry Authority (Seafish): 18 Logie Mill, Logie Green Rd, Edinburgh, EH7 4HS; tel. (131) 558-3331; fax (131) 558-1442; e-mail seafish@seafish.co.uk; internet www.seafish.org; f. 1981; non-departmental public body sponsored by the 4 United Kingdom Government fisheries departments and funded by a levy on seafood; works with all sectors of the British seafood industry to satisfy consumers, raise standards, improve efficiency and secure a sustainable future; Chair. JOHN WHITEHEAD; Chief Exec. PAUL WILLIAMS.

Society of Motor Manufacturers and Traders: 71 Great Peter St, London, SW1P 2BN; tel. (20) 7235-7000; fax (20) 7235-7112; e-mail membership@smmt.co.uk; internet www.smmt.co.uk; f. 1902; Pres. NIGEL STEIN; Chief Exec. PAUL EVERITT.

Sugar Nutrition UK: 25 Floral St, London, WC2E 9DS; tel. (20) 7189-8301; fax (20) 7031-8101; e-mail info@sugarnutrition.org.uk; internet www.sugarnutrition.org.uk; f. 1964; represents sugar companies in the UK, provides technical, educational and consumer information about sugar and health; Dir Dr ALISON BOYD.

Timber Trade Federation: Building Centre, 26 Store St, London, WC1E 7BT; tel. (20) 3205-0067; fax (20) 7291-5379; e-mail ttf@ttf.co.uk; internet www.ttf.co.uk; Chief Exec. JOHN WHITE.

Ulster Chemists' Association: 5 Annadale Ave, Belfast, BT7 3JH; tel. (28) 9069-0456; fax (28) 9069-0457; e-mail adrienne@uca.org.uk; internet www.uca.org.uk; f. 1901; promotion and protection of interests of community pharmacies in Northern Ireland; Pres. JONATHAN LLOYD.

Ulster Farmers' Union: Dunedin, 475 Antrim Rd, Belfast, BT15 3DA; tel. (28) 9037-0222; fax (28) 9037-1231; e-mail info@ufuhq.com; internet www.ufuni.org; f. 1918; 11,500 mems; Pres. HARRY SINCLAIR; Chief Exec. CLARKE BLACK.

UK Fashion and Textile Association (UKFT): 3 Queen Sq., London WC1N 3AR; tel. (20) 7843-9460; fax (20) 7843-9478; e-mail info@ukft.org; internet www.ukft.org; f. 1982 as British Clothing Industry Asscn; renamed as above 2009; Chair. PETER LUCAS; Chief Exec. JOHN MILN.

United Kingdom Petroleum Industry Association: Quality House, Quality Court, Chancery Lane, London, WC2A 1HP; tel. (20) 7269-7600; e-mail info@ukpia.com; internet www.ukpia.com; f. 1978; Pres. GARY HAYWOOD; Dir-Gen. CHRIS HUNT.

EMPLOYERS' ASSOCIATIONS

British Retail Consortium: 21 Dartmouth St, London, SW1H 9BP; tel. (20) 7854-8900; fax (20) 7854-8901; e-mail info@brc.org.uk; internet www.brc.org.uk; f. 1975; represents retailers; Chair. ROB TEMPLEMAN; Dir-Gen. STEPHEN ROBERTSON.

Chartered Management Institute: Management House, Cottingham Rd, Corby, NN17 1TT; tel. (1536) 204222; fax (1536) 201651; e-mail enquiries@managers.org; internet www.managers.org.uk; f. 1992 as the Institute of Management by amalgamation of British Institute of Management (f. 1947) and Institution of Industrial Managers (f. 1931); changed name as above in 2002; represents 86,000 individual mems and 450 corporate mems; Pres. TERRY MORGAN; Chief Exec. ANN FRANCKE.

Federation of Small Businesses: Sir Frank Whittle Way, Blackpool Business Park, Blackpool, FY4 2FE; tel. (1253) 336000; fax (1253) 348046; e-mail membership@fsb.org.uk; internet www.fsb.org.uk; f. 1974; represents the interests of British small businesses and the self-employed; 213,000 mems; Nat. Chair. JOHN WALKER.

Institute of Directors: 116 Pall Mall, London, SW1Y 5ED; tel. (20) 7766-8866; fax (20) 7766-8833; e-mail enquiries@iod.com; internet www.iod.com; f. 1903; 43,000 mems; Chair. IAN DORMER; Dir-Gen. SIMON WALKER.

UTILITIES

Electricity and Gas

Regulatory Authorities

Northern Ireland Authority for Utility Regulation (Utility Regulator): Queens House, 14 Queens St, Belfast, BT1 6ED; tel. (28) 9031-1575; fax (28) 9031-1740; e-mail info@uregni.gov.uk; internet www.uregni.gov.uk; name changed from Northern Ireland Authority for Energy Regulation to present in 2007; independent public body to regulate the electricity, water, sewage, and natural gas industries in Northern Ireland; Chair. BILL EMERY; Chief Exec. SHANE LYNCH.

Office of Gas and Electricity Markets (Ofgem): 9 Millbank, London, SW1P 3GE; tel. (20) 7901-7000; fax (20) 7901-7066; e-mail consumeraffairs@ofgem.gov.uk; internet www.ofgem.gov.uk; f. 1999 following merger of Offer and Ofgas; regulates the gas and electricity industries in England, Scotland and Wales and aims to promote the interests of all gas and electricity customers by promoting competition and regulating monopolies; Chair. Lord MOGG; Chief Exec. ALISTAIR BUCHANAN.

Principal Companies

British Energy: GSO Business Park, East Kilbride, G74 5PG; tel. (1355) 846000; fax (1355) 846001; e-mail john.mcnamara@

british-energy.com; internet www.british-energy.com; production of electricity; operates 8 nuclear power stations and 1 coal-fired power station in the United Kingdom; acquired by EDF (France) Jan. 2009; 20% stake held by Centrica; Chief Exec. Dr ANDREW SPURR.

British Gas: Centrica PLC, Millstream, Maidenhead Rd, Windsor, SL4 5GD; tel. (1753) 494000; fax (1753) 494001; e-mail house@ britishgas.co.uk; internet www.britishgas.co.uk; part of Centrica Group; Chair. ROGER CARR; Man. Dir PHIL BENTLEY.

Central Networks: Herald Way, Pegasus Business Park, East Midlands Airport, Castle Donington, DE74 2TU; tel. (800) 0963080; internet www.central-networks.co.uk; distribution of electricity; fmrly East Midlands Electricity PLC; merged with Midlands Electricity PLC in 2004 and name changed to above; sold by E.ON UK to PPL Corpn in March 2011; Man. Dir JOHN CRACKETT.

EDF Energy: 40 Grosvenor Pl., London, SW1X 7GN; tel. (20) 7242-9050; e-mail info@edfenergy.com; internet www.edfenergy.com; producer and supplier of electricity and gas; Chair. HENRI PROGLIO; Chief Exec. VINCENT DE RIVAZ.

E.ON UK PLC: Westwood Way, Westwood Business Park, Coventry, CV4 8LG; tel. (24) 7642-4000; fax (24) 7642-5432; e-mail email .queries@eonenergy.com; internet www.eon-uk.com; f. 2004; fmrly Powergen UK PLC; supplies, distributes and sells electricity; also retailer of gas; subsidiary of E.ON AG (Germany); Chief Exec. Dr ANTHONY COCKER.

Green Energy (UK) PLC: Black Swan House, 23 Baldock St, Ware, SG12 9DH; tel. (1920) 486156; fax (1920) 484268; e-mail help@ greenenergyuk.com; internet www.greenenergyuk.com; Chair. Sir PETER THOMPSON; CEO DOUGLAS STEWART.

National Grid PLC: 1–3 Strand, London, WC2N 5EH; tel. (20) 7004-3000; fax (20) 7004-3004; internet www.nationalgrid.com; Chair. Sir PETER GERSHON; Chief Exec. STEVE HOLLIDAY.

Northern Ireland Electricity PLC (NIE): 120 Malone Rd, Belfast, BT9 5HT; tel. (28) 9066-1100; e-mail customercontact@nie.co .uk; internet www.nie.co.uk; holding co Viridian Group; acquired by Electricity Supply Board (ESB—Ireland) Dec. 2010; transmission and distribution of electricity in Northern Ireland; associated co NIE Energy supplies electricity; Man. Dir JOE O'MAHONY.

Northern Powergrid: Lloyds Court, 78 Grey St, Newcastle upon Tyne, NE1 6AF; tel. (800) 668877; e-mail cus.serv@ northernpowergrid.com; internet www.northernpowergrid.com; subsidiary of MidAmerican Energy Holdings Co; delivers electricity to 3.8m. homes in the north-east of England, Yorkshire and Humberside; Chief Exec. PHIL JONES.

npower: Oak House, Bridgwater Rd, Warndon, Worcester, WR4 9FP; tel. (1793) 877777; fax (1793) 892525; internet www.npower .com; f. 1999 to combine the electricity and gas supply business of 6 companies; launched in 2000; retail arm of RWE npower PLC; CEO VOLKER BECKERS.

Phoenix Natural Gas Ltd: 197 Airport Rd West, Belfast, BT3 9ED; tel. (28) 9055-5555; fax (28) 9055-5500; e-mail info@ phoenix-natural-gas.com; internet www.phoenix-natural-gas.com; f. 1996; CEO PETER DIXON.

RWE npower plc: Windmill Hill Business Park, Whitehill Way, Swindon, SN5 6PB; tel. (1793) 877777; fax (1793) 893955; internet www.rwenpower.com; Group CEO VOLKER BECKERS.

SSE PLC (Scottish and Southern Energy PLC): Inveralmond House, 200 Dunkeld Rd, Perth, PH1 3AQ; tel. (1738) 456660; fax (1738) 455281; e-mail info@scottish-southern.co.uk; internet www.sse.com; Chair. Lord SMITH OF KELVIN; CEO IAN MARCHANT.

Scottish Power Ltd: Corporate Office, 1 Atlantic Quay, Glasgow, G2 8SP; tel. (141) 248-8200; fax (141) 248-8300; internet www .scottishpower.com; subsidiary of Iberdrola, SA (Spain); Chair. JOSÉ IGNACIO SÁNCHEZ GALÁN.

South Wales Electricity PLC: POB 7506, Perth, PH1 3QR; tel. (800) 052-5252; internet www.swalec.co.uk; part of Scottish and Southern Energy Group; CEO JOHN ROBINS.

Southern Electric: 55 Vastern Rd, Reading, RG1 8BU; internet www.southern-electric.co.uk; part of Scottish and Southern Energy Group; Group CEO IAN MARCHANT.

Water

Regulatory Authority

Water Services Regulation Authority (Ofwat): Centre City Tower, 7 Hill St, Birmingham, B5 4UA; tel. (121) 644-7500; fax (121) 644-7559; e-mail mailbox@ofwat.gsi.gov.uk; internet www .ofwat.gov.uk; independent economic regulator of the water and sewerage cos in England and Wales; ensures compliance with the functions specified in the Water Industry Act of 2003; Chair. PHILIP FLETCHER; Chief Exec. REGINA FINN.

Principal Companies

Anglian Water Services Ltd: POB 770, Lincoln, LN5 7WX; tel. (8457) 919155; fax (1480) 326981; internet www.anglianwater.co.uk; Chair. Sir ADRIAN MONTAGUE; Man. Dir PETER SIMPSON.

Northern Ireland Water: Northland House, 3 Frederick St, Belfast, BT1 2NR; tel. (8457) 440088; e-mail waterline@niwater.com; internet www.niwater.com; Chair. SEÁN HOGAN; Chief Exec. TREVOR HASLETT.

Northumbrian Water Ltd: Abbey Rd, Pity Me, Durham, DH1 5FJ; tel. (870) 608-4820; fax (191) 301-6202; internet www.nwl.co.uk; Chair. ANDREW HUNTER; CEO HEIDI MOTTRAM.

Scottish Water: Castle House, 6 Castle Drive, Carnegie Campus, Dunfermline, KY11 8GG; tel. (845) 601 8855; e-mail customer .service@scottishwater.co.uk; internet www.scottishwater.co.uk; f. 2002; Chair. RONNIE MERCER; Chief Exec. RICHARD K. ACKROYD.

Severn Trent Water Ltd: Severn Trent Centre, 2 St John's St, Coventry, CV1 2LZ; tel. (121) 722-4000; fax (121) 722-4800; internet www.stwater.co.uk; Chair. Sir JOHN EGAN; Chief Exec. TONY WRAY.

South East Water Ltd: Rocfort Rd, Snodland, ME6 5AH; tel. (845) 301-8045; e-mail contactcentre@southeastwater.co.uk; internet www.southeastwater.co.uk; merged with Mid Kent Water 2007; owned by Hastings Diversified Utilities Fund and the Utilities Trust of Australia; Chair. GORDON MAXWELL; Man. Dir PAUL BUTLER.

South Staffordshire Water PLC: Green Lane, Walsall, WS2 7PD; tel. (1922) 616239; internet www.south-staffs-water.co.uk; f. 1853; Exec. Dir DAVID SANKEY; Man. Dir Dr ELIZABETH ANNE SWARBRICK.

South West Water Ltd: Peninsula House, Rydon Lane, Exeter, EX2 7HR; tel. (1392) 446688; fax (1392) 434966; internet www .southwestwater.co.uk; part of Pennon Group; Chair. KENNETH HARVEY; CEO CHRISTOPHER LOUGHLIN.

Southern Water PLC: POB 41, Worthing, BN13 3NZ; tel. (1903) 264444; fax (1903) 691435; e-mail customerservices@southernwater .co.uk; internet www.southernwater.co.uk; Chair. COLIN HOOD; CEO MATTHEW WRIGHT.

Thames Water Utilities Ltd: POB 286, Swindon, SN38 2RA; tel. (845) 920-0888; internet www.thameswater.co.uk; acquired by Kemble Water Ltd in 2006; Chair. Sir PETER MASON; CEO MARTIN BAGGS.

United Utilities PLC: Haweswater House, Lingley Mere Business Park, Great Sankey, Warrington, WA5 3LW; tel. (1925) 237000; fax (1925) 237066; internet www.uuplc.co.uk; Chair. Dr JOHN MCADAM; CEO STEVE MOGFORD.

Veolia Water Central Limited: Tamblin Way, Hatfield, AL10 9EZ; tel. (845) 782-3333; internet central.veoliawater.co.uk; fmrly known as Three Valley Waters PLC; name changed as above in 2009; Chair. OLIVIER BRET; Man. Dir RICHARD BIENFAIT.

Welsh Water (Dwr Cymru Cyfyngedig): Pentwyn Rd, Nelson, Treharris, CF46 6LY; tel. (1443) 452300; fax (1443) 452809; e-mail enquiries@dwrcymru.com; internet www.dwrcymru.com; f. 1989; Chair. ROBERT AYLING; Man. Dir NIGEL ANNETT.

Wessex Water Services Ltd: Claverton Down Rd, Bath, BA2 7WW; tel. (1225) 526000; e-mail info@wessexwater.co.uk; internet www .wessexwater.co.uk; Propr YTL (Malaysia); Chair. and CEO COLIN SKELLETT.

Yorkshire Water Services Ltd: POB 52, Bradford, BD6 2SZ; tel. (1274) 691111; fax (1274) 372800; internet www.yorkshirewater .com; Chair. KEVIN WHITEMAN; Chief Exec. RICHARD FLINT.

CO-OPERATIVE ORGANIZATIONS

Co-operatives UK: Holyoake House, Hanover St, Manchester, M60 0AS; tel. (161) 246-2900; fax (161) 831-7684; e-mail info@ cooperatives-uk.coop; internet www.cooperatives-uk.coop; f. 1869; co-ordinates, informs and advises the 45 retail consumer co-operative societies and 700 worker co-operatives and employee-owned businesses; Chair. DAVID BUTTON; Sec.-Gen. ED MAYO; Society Sec. HELEN BARBER.

Co-operative Group Ltd: New Century House, POB 53, Manchester, M60 4ES; tel. (161) 834-1212; fax (161) 834-4507; e-mail customer.relations@co-op.co.uk; internet www.co-operative.co.uk; f. 1863; merged with United Co-operatives in 2007; Chair. LEN WARDLE.

National Association of Co-operative Officials (NACO): 6A Clarendon Pl., Hyde, Cheshire, SK14 2QZ; tel. (161) 351-7900; fax (161) 366-6800; e-mail info@naco.coop; internet www.naco.coop; f. 1918; Nat. Pres. JACK DEVERS.

TRADE UNIONS

Central Organizations

Trades Union Congress (TUC): Congress House, Great Russell St, London, WC1B 3LS; tel. (20) 7636-4030; fax (20) 7636-0632; e-mail info@tuc.org.uk; internet www.tuc.org.uk; f. 1868; 53 affiliated unions, with a total membership of 6m. (2012); affiliated to the ITUC and the European Trade Union Confederation; nominates the British Workers' Delegate to the International Labour Organization; Gen. Sec. FRANCES O'GRADY.

Irish Congress of Trade Unions (Northern Ireland Committee): 4–6 Donegall Street Pl., Belfast, BT1 2FN; tel. (28) 9024-7940; fax (28) 9024-6898; e-mail info@ictuni.org; internet www.ictuni.org; 34 affiliated unions in Northern Ireland, with a membership of 215,000; Gen. Sec. DAVID BEGG.

Scottish Trades Union Congress: 333 Woodlands Rd, Glasgow, G3 6NG; tel. (141) 337-8100; fax (141) 337-8101; e-mail info@stuc.org .uk; internet www.stuc.org.uk; f. 1897; 630,000 individual mems affiliated through 37 trade unions and 22 trades union councils (2012); Gen. Sec. GRAHAME SMITH.

Wales Trades Union Council: 1 Cathedral Rd, Cardiff, CF11 9SD; tel. (29) 2034-7010; fax (29) 2022-1940; e-mail wtuc@tuc.org.uk; internet www.wtuc.org.uk; f. 1973; Gen. Sec. MARTIN MANSFIELD.

Unions not affiliated to the TUC

Irish National Teachers' Organization (INTO): 23 College Gardens, Belfast, BT9 6BS (headquarters in Dublin); tel. (28) 9038-1455; fax (28) 9066-2803; e-mail infoni@into.ie; internet www.into.ie; f. 1868; affiliated to the Irish Congress of Trade Unions (Northern Ireland Committee); Northern Sec. GERRY MURPHY; 6,800 mems (Jan. 2012).

National Farmers' Union (NFU): see Industrial and Trade Associations.

Northern Ireland Public Service Alliance: Harkin House, 54 Wellington Park, Belfast, BT9 6DP; tel. (28) 9066-1831; fax (28) 9066-5847; e-mail info@nipsa.org.uk; internet www.nipsa.org.uk; affiliated to the Irish Congress of Trade Unions; Pres. (2012/13) PATRICK MULHOLLAND; Gen. Sec. BRIAN CAMPFIELD; 45,000 mems.

Services Industrial Professional Technical Union (SIPTU): 3 Antrim Rd, Belfast, BT15 2BE; tel. (28) 9031-4000; fax (28) 9031-4044; e-mail athompson@siptu.ie; internet www.siptu.ie; affiliated to the Irish Congress of Trade Unions (Northern Ireland Committee); Regional Sec. JOE CUNNINGHAM; 7,000 mems.

Ulster Teachers' Union: 94 Malone Rd, Belfast, BT9 5HP; tel. (28) 9066-2216; fax (28) 9068-3296; e-mail office@utu.edu; internet www .utu.edu; f. 1919; affiliated to the Irish Congress of Trade Unions (Northern Ireland Committee); Pres. STEPHEN McCORD; Gen. Sec. AVRIL HALL-CALLAGHAN; 6,700 mems (Dec. 2012).

National Federations

Confederation of Shipbuilding and Engineering Unions: 218 Green Lanes, London, N4 2HB; tel. (20) 8826-2074; 750,000 mems in 6 affiliated trade unions; Gen. Sec. HUGH SCULLION.

Federation of Entertainment Unions: c/o Equity, Guild House, Upper St Martin's Lane, London, WC2H 9EG; tel. and fax (1962) 713134; e-mail harris.s@btconnect.com; f. 1990; 6 affiliated unions; Sec. CHRISTINE PAYNE.

General Federation of Trade Unions (GFTU): Headland House, 4th Floor, 308–312 Grays Inn Rd, London, WC1X 8DP; tel. (20) 7520-8340; fax (20) 7520-8350; e-mail gftuhq@gftu.org.uk; internet www .gftu.org; f. 1899 by the TUC; c. 215,000 mems affiliated through 21 unions; Gen. Sec. DOUG NICHOLLS.

Transport

RAILWAYS

The Railways Act 1993, providing for a process of rail privatization, received royal assent in November 1993. A separate, government-owned company, Railtrack, was set up on 1 April 1994 to take responsibility for infrastructure (track, signals and stations) and levy charges on train operators for track access. As a result of the 1993 Railways Act, 25 Train Operating Units (TOUs) came into being on 1 April 1994. The Director of Passenger Rail Franchises was responsible for awarding franchises for the 25 TOUs as early as practicable and was to monitor the franchises to ensure compliance with the agreed contracts. The first passenger train franchises were awarded in 1995, and two TOUs were transferred to private operators in 1996; the final TOU transferred to the private sector the following year. Railtrack was transferred to the private sector in 1996. In October 2001 the Government placed the heavily indebted Railtrack in administration. Railtrack remained in administration until October 2002, when Network Rail, a 'not-for-profit' government-supported company, completed a takeover.

In February 1986 the Treaty of Canterbury was signed between the Governments of France and the United Kingdom, providing the constitutional basis for the construction of a tunnel between the two countries under the English Channel. The Channel Tunnel opened in

May 1994, at an estimated cost of £4,700m., and comprises a fixed link of two rail tunnels and one service tunnel. Of the total length of 31 miles (50 km), 24 miles (38 km) are under the seabed. The rail services provider, Eurostar UK, moved all London operations from Waterloo International to St Pancras station in 2007. In the same year, a 109-km high speed railway line, connecting St Pancras International in London through Kent to the Channel Tunnel became operational. In 2012 the Government announced plans for the construction of the first phase of a high-speed line connecting London with the north of England. The first phase of the project, to link London with Birmingham, was expected to be completed by 2026. A second phase, announced in January 2013, linking Birmingham with Manchester and Leeds, was planned to become operational in 2033.

In 2010 the total length of track was 31,324 km, of which 12,566 km was electrified. A 50.5-km rail link, the Channel Tunnel, connects the United Kingdom with France beneath the English Channel (La Manche).

DfT Rail Group: Department for Transport, Great Minster House, 33 Horseferry Rd, London, SW1P 4DR; tel. (300) 330-3000; fax (20) 7944-9643; e-mail rail@dft.gsi.gov.uk; internet www.dft.gov.uk/pgr/rail; f. 2005 to assume many functions of the dissolved Strategic Rail Authority (SRA); has strategic and financial responsibility for the railways; Dir-Gen. MIKE MITCHELL.

Office of Rail Regulation: 1 Kemble St, London, WC2B 4AN; tel. (20) 7282-2000; fax (20) 7282-2040; e-mail rail.library@orr.gsi.gov .uk; internet www.rail-reg.gov.uk; f. 2004; Chair. ANNA WALKER.

Network Rail Ltd: Kings Pl., 90 York Way, London, N1 9AG; tel. (20) 7557-8000; internet www.networkrail.co.uk; f. 2002 as a 'not-for-profit' company by train operators, rail unions and passenger groups to take over responsibility for running the UK rail network from Railtrack PLC; Chair. RICHARD PARRY-JONES; Chief Exec. DAVID HIGGINS.

Northern Ireland Railways Co Ltd: Central Station, East Bridge St, Belfast, BT1 3PB; tel. (28) 9089-9400; fax (28) 9089-9401; internet www.nirailways.co.uk; f. 1967; subsidiary of Northern Ireland Transport Holding Co (see under Roads) and part of the Translink rail and bus network; operates rail services for passenger traffic over 342 km and for freight traffic over 268 km of railway track; a high-speed passenger service between Belfast and Dublin, launched in co-operation with Irish Rail, began operations in 1997; Chief Exec. CATHERINE MASON; Gen. Man., Rail Services MALACHY McGREEVY.

Channel Tunnel Rail Link

Eurotunnel Group: UK Terminal, Ashford Rd, Folkestone, Kent, CT18 8XX; tel. (1303) 282222; fax (1303) 850360; e-mail press@ eurotunnel.com; internet www.eurotunnel.com; f. 1986; Anglo-French consortium contracted to design, finance and construct the Channel Tunnel under a concession granted for a period up to 2052 (later extended to 2086); receives finance exclusively from the private sector; operates a service of road vehicle 'shuttle' trains and passenger and freight trains through the Channel Tunnel; Chair. and Chief Exec. JACQUES GOUNON.

Eurostar UK Ltd/Eurostar Group: Times House, Bravingtons Walk, Regent Quarter, London, N1 9AW; tel. (20) 7902-3658; e-mail press.office@eurostar.co.uk; internet www.eurostar.com; commenced international high-speed passenger rail services in 1994; provides services from London, and Ebbsfleet and Ashford (both in Kent), direct to Paris, Brussels, Lille, Calais-Frethun, Disneyland Paris, Avignon and Bourg St Maurice; Chair. RICHARD BROWN; CEO NICOLAS PETROVIC.

Associations

Railway Industry Association: 22 Headfort Pl., London, SW1X 7RY; tel. (20) 7201-0777; fax (20) 7235-5777; e-mail ria@riagb.org.uk; internet www.riagb.org.uk; f. 1875; represents UK-based railway suppliers, with a free sourcing service for products and services; 160 mems; Chair. DAVID TONKIN; Dir-Gen. JEREMY CANDFIELD.

Association of Train Operating Companies: 3rd Floor, 40 Bernard St, London, WC1N 1BY; tel. (20) 7841-8000; e-mail enquiry@atoc.org; internet www.atoc.org; f. 1994; Chair. TOM SMITH; CEO MICHAEL ROBERTS.

ROADS

Total road length in Great Britain in 2010 was 419,628 km, of which 3,673 km was motorways, 49,024 km highways and 122,620 km secondary roads. In 2005 there were 24,930 km (15,491 miles) of roads of all classes in Northern Ireland, including some 110 km (68 miles) of motorway.

Highways Agency: 123 Buckingham Palace Rd, London, SW1W 9HA; tel. and fax (8459) 556575; e-mail ha_info@highways.gsi.gov .uk; internet www.highways.gov.uk; executive agency of the Department for Transport; responsible for maintaining, operating and improving the motorway and trunk road network in England; Chair. ALAN COOK; Chief Exec. GRAHAM DALTON.

Northern Ireland Transport Holding Co: Chamber of Commerce House, 22 Great Victoria St, Belfast, BT2 7LX; tel. (28) 9024-3456; fax (28) 9033-3845; internet www.translink.co.uk; publicly owned; owns Metro, Northern Ireland Railways Co Ltd and Ulsterbus, all part of the Translink rail and bus network; Chair. JOHN TRETHOWAN; Chief Exec. CATHERINE MASON.

Ulsterbus Ltd: Milewater Rd, Belfast, BT3 9BG; Central Station, Belfast, BT1 3PB; tel. (28) 9089-9400; fax (28) 9035-1474; internet www.translink.co.uk/atulsterbus.asp; responsible for almost all bus transport in Northern Ireland, except Belfast city; services into Ireland; assoc. co Flexibus Ltd (minibus contract hire); Chief Exec. CATHERINE MASON; Gen. Man., Bus Services FRANK CLEGG.

METROPOLITAN TRANSPORT

Metro: Milewater Rd, Belfast, BT3 9BG; tel. (28) 9035-1201; fax (28) 9035-1474; internet www.translink.co.uk/metro.asp; responsible for operating municipal transport in the City of Belfast; subsidiary of Northern Ireland Transport Holding Co (see under Roads); Chief Exec. CATHERINE MASON.

Metrolink: Metrolink House, Queens Rd, Manchester, M8 0RY; tel. (161) 205-2000; e-mail customerservices@metrolink.co.uk; internet www.metrolink.co.uk; opened 1992; owned by the Transport for Greater Manchester (TfGM); operated by Serco Metrolink; 37-station hybrid tram (operated by RATP Dev UK) and rail network in Greater Manchester, bounded by Altrincham, Bury, Eccles and Manchester Piccadilly; Dir PHILIP PURDY.

Transport for London (TfL): Windsor House, 42–50 Victoria St, London, SW1H 0TL; tel. (20) 7941-4500; fax (20) 7649-9121; e-mail enquire@tfl.gov.uk; internet www.tfl.gov.uk; f. 2000; executive arm of Greater London Authority (GLA), responsible for activities of former London Transport; Chair. BORIS JOHNSON (Mayor of London); Commr PETER HENDY.

Docklands Light Railway: POB 154, Castor Lane, London, E14 0DS; tel. (20) 7363-9700; fax (20) 7363-9561; e-mail cservice@dlr.co.uk; internet www.dlr.co.uk; opened 1987; operations franchised to a private co, Serco Docklands; 34-km, 40-station system in east London; construction of an extension from Canning Town to Stratford International scheduled for completion in early 2011; Dir JONATHAN FOX.

London Underground: 55 Broadway, London, SW1H 0BD; tel. (20) 7222-5600; internet www.tfl.gov.uk/tube; f. 1985; however, underground railway network dates back to 1863; responsible for providing and securing the services of underground rail in Greater London; Man. Dir MIKE BROWN.

Strathclyde Partnership for Transport (Subway): Broomloan Depot, Robert St, Govan, G51 3HB; tel. (141) 332-6811; fax (141) 425-1023; e-mail enquiry@spt.co.uk; internet www.spt.co.uk/subway; f. opened 1896; electrified in 1923; owned and operated by Strathclyde Partnership for Transport (SPT); 10-km, 15-station underground rail network in central Glasgow; Chief Exec. GORDON MACLENNAN; Dir, Subway Operations BRIAN BELL.

Tyne and Wear Metro: Nexus House, St James Blvd, Newcastle upon Tyne, NE1 4AX; tel. (191) 203-3333; fax (191) 203-3180; e-mail metro.communications@nexus.org.uk; internet www.tyneandwearmetro.co.uk; opened 1980; 77.5-km, 60-station light rail network serving Newcastle, Gateshead, North Tyneside, South Tyneside and Sunderland; owned and operated by Tyne and Wear Passenger Transport Executive (Nexus); Dir-Gen. BERNARD GARNER.

INLAND WATERWAYS

There are some 3,220 km (2,000 miles) of inland waterways in Great Britain under the control of British Waterways, varying from the river navigations and wide waterways accommodating commercial craft to canals taking small holiday craft.

Canal & River Trust: Station House, 1st Floor, 500 Elder Gate, Milton Keynes, MK9 1BB; tel. (303) 040 4040; e-mail customer.services@canalrivertrust.org.uk; internet canalrivertrust.org.uk; f. 2012; charitable trust which took over from British Waterways (public corpn) in July 2012; responsible for waterways in England and Wales; Chief Exec. ROBIN EVANS.

Scottish Canals: Canal House, Applecross St, Glasgow, G4 9SP; tel. (141) 332-6936; e-mail enquiries@scottishcanals.co.uk; internet www.scottishcanals.co.uk; f. 2012; a public corpn of the Scottish government; took over from British Waterways in Scotland in 2012; responsible for the management of canals; Chief Exec. STEVE DUNLOP.

SHIPPING

There are more than 400 ports in the United Kingdom, of which Grimsby and Immingham, the Tees and Hartlepool ports, London (Tilbury), Southampton, Milford Haven, Liverpool, the Forth ports,

Felixstowe, Dover and Sullom Voe are the largest (in terms of the tonnage of goods traffic handled) In 2010 some 334.1m. metric tons of freight traffic were handled by the sea ports. Twenty-one ports, including Grimsby and Immingham, Hull, Southampton and five ports in South Wales, are owned and administered by Associated British Ports. The majority of the other large ports are owned and operated by public trusts, including London, which is administered by the Port of London Authority, and Belfast, administered by the Belfast Harbour Commissioners. At 31 December 2012 the flag registered fleet comprised 2,453 vessels, with a combined displacement of 18.5m. grt, of which 7 were gas tankers, 141 general cargo ships, 455 fishing vessels and 37 bulk ships.

Britain is linked to the rest of Europe by an extensive passenger and vehicle ship ferry service.

Associated British Ports (ABP): Aldwych House, 71–91 Aldwych, London, WC2B 4HN; tel. (20) 7430-1177; fax (20) 7406-7896; e-mail info@abports.co.uk; internet www.abports.co.uk; f. 1983; controls 21 UK ports; Chair. CHRIS CLARK; Chief Exec. PETER JONES.

The Baltic Exchange Ltd: 38 St Mary Axe, London, EC3A 8BH; tel. (20) 7283-9300; fax (20) 7369-1622; e-mail enquiries@balticexchange.co.uk; internet www.balticexchange.com; world market for chartering ships, charters aircraft, buys and sells ships and aircraft; 590 mems; Chair. QUENTIN SOANES; Chief Exec. JEREMY PENN.

British Ports Association (BPA): 30 Park St, 1st Floor, London, SE1 9EQ; tel. (20) 7260-1780; fax (20) 7260-1784; e-mail info@britishports.org.uk; internet www.britishports.org.uk; f. 1992; promotes and protects the general interests of port authorities, comments on proposed legislation and policy matters; Chair. COLIN PARKER; Dir DAVID WHITEHEAD.

Port of London Authority: London River House, Royal Pier Rd, Gravesend, DA12 2BG; tel. (1474) 562200; fax (1474) 562281; internet www.pla.co.uk; Chair. Dame HELEN ALEXANDER; Chief Exec. RICHARD EVERITT.

Principal Shipping Companies

Bibby Line Ltd: 105 Duke St, Liverpool, L1 5JQ; tel. (151) 708-8000; fax (151) 794-1099; e-mail info@bibbylinelimited.co.uk; internet www.bibbyline.co.uk; f. 1807; various shipping operations incl. chemical carriage and shallow water accommodation; Chair. S. P. SHERRARD; Man. Dir SIMON KITCHEN.

Boyd Line: The Orangery, Hesslewood Country Office Park, Ferriby Rd, Hessle, HU13 0LH; tel. (1482) 324024; fax (1482) 323737; vessel owners and managers; Man. Dir JONATHAN CARDEN; 2 vessels.

BP Shipping Ltd: Chertsey Rd, Sunbury on Thames, TW16 7LN; tel. (1932) 771652; internet www.bpshipping.co.uk; f. 1915; division of BP PLC; Chief Exec. JOHN RIDGWAY; 53 vessels.

CalMac Ferries Ltd (Caledonian MacBrayne): The Ferry Terminal, Gourock, PA19 1QP; tel. (1475) 650100; e-mail enquiries@calmac.co.uk; internet www.calmac.co.uk; f. 1851; fmrly Caledonian MacBrayne Ltd; adopted current name 2006; owned by Scottish Govt; extensive car and passenger services on Firth of Clyde and to Western Isles of Scotland; 29 ro-ro vessels; Chair. PETER K. TIMMS; Man. Dir MARTIN DORCHESTER.

Coastal Container Line Ltd: The Logistic Centre, Royal Seaforth Container Terminal, Port of Liverpool, Liverpool, L21 1JR; tel. (151) 949-1000; fax (151) 949-6551; e-mail shipping@ccl-seaforth.co.uk; internet www.coastalcontainer.co.uk; container services from Belfast and Dublin to Cardiff and Liverpool; Gen. Man. MARC CROOKES.

DFDS Seaways: International Passenger Terminal, Royal Quays, North Shields, Newcastle upon Tyne, NE29 6EE; tel. (151) 906-2700; fax (151) 906-2718; internet www.norfolkline.com; fmrly Norfolkline Irish Sea Ferries; owned by DFDS Group; ro-ro freight, car and passenger services from Birkenhead–Belfast and Dublin, and Dover–Dunkirk and Calais (France).

James Fisher & Sons PLC: Fisher House, POB 4, Barrow-in-Furness, LA14 1HR; tel. (1229) 615400; fax (1229) 836761; e-mail enquiries@james-fisher.com; internet www.james-fisher.co.uk; f. 1847; provider of marine services operating in all sectors; also supplier of engineering services to the nuclear energy industry; Exec. Chair. CHARLES J. RICE; CEO NICHOLAS P. HENRY.

Fyffes Group Ltd: Houndmills Rd, Houndmills Industrial Estate, Basingstoke, RG21 6XL; tel. (1256) 383200; fax (1256) 383259; e-mail info@fyffes.com; internet www.fyffes.com; f. 1901; Chair. DAVID McCANN.

Geest Line: Eaglepoint, Little Park Farm Rd, Segensworth, Fareham, PO15 5TD; tel. (1489) 873500; fax (1489) 873501; e-mail quotes@geestline.com; internet www.geestline.com; container cargo transportation between the UK and the Caribbean; Man. Dir PETER DIXON.

Goulandris Brothers (Chartering) Ltd: 34A Queen Anne's Gate, London, SW1H 9AB; tel. (20) 7222-5244; fax (20) 7222-6817; e-mail chartering@goulanbros.co.uk; internet www.goulanbros.com; f. 1968; ship chartering and brokerage; Man. Dir BASIL GOULANDRIS.

Heyn Shipping Solutions: 1 Corry Pl., Belfast Harbour, Belfast, BT3 9AH; tel. (28) 9035-0035; fax (28) 9035-0005; e-mail info@heyn.co.uk; internet www.heyn.co.uk; liner and port agency; Man. Dir DAVID CLARKE.

Holbud Ship Management Ltd: Hydery House, 66 Leman St, London, E1 8EU; tel. (20) 7488-4901; fax (20) 7265-0654; ship agents; Dir B. D. SABARWAL.

OSG Ship Management (UK) Ltd: Moreau House, 116 Brompton Rd, London, SW3 1JJ; tel. (20) 7591-6660; fax (870) 607-9546; internet www.osg.com; bulk carriers, parcels tankers, conventional tankers; transportation of crude petroleum, petroleum products and liquified natural gas; Chair. MICHAEL P. ZIMMERMAN; Man. Dir Capt. GEORGE DIENIS.

P & O Ferries: Channel House, Channel View Rd, Dover, CT17 9TJ; tel. (1304) 863000; fax (1304) 863223; e-mail customer.services@poferries.com; internet www.poferries.com; car and passenger services across the English Channel and North Sea; subsidiary of DP World (Dubai, UAE); parent co of P&O Irish Sea Ferries; fmrly P&O Stena Line; CEO HELEN DEEBLE.

Shell International Trading and Shipping Co Ltd: Shell Centre, London, SE1 7NA; tel. (20) 7934-1234; e-mail shelltradingcommunications@shell.com; internet www.shell.com/shipping; world-wide operations trading and transporting crude petroleum and supplying petroleum products; incorporates Shell Tankers (UK) Ltd.

Stena Line Ltd: Stena House, Station Approach, Holyhead, LL65 1DQ; tel. (1407) 606666; fax (1407) 606604; e-mail info.uk@stenaline.com; internet www.stenaline.com; parent co Stena AB (Sweden); services from Great Britain to Northern Ireland, Ireland and the Netherlands; Group CEO GUNNAR BLOMDAHL; Area Dir, Irish Sea MICHAEL McGRATH.

Stephenson Clarke Shipping Ltd: Eldon Court, Percy St, Newcastle upon Tyne, NE99 1TD; tel. (191) 232-2184; fax (191) 260-3208; e-mail all@scsbulk.co.uk; internet www.scsbulk.com; f. 1730; ship operators, agency and management services; Man. Dir TREVOR KINGSLEY-SMITH.

Andrew Weir Shipping Ltd: Dexter House, 2 Royal Mint Court, London, EC3N 4XX; tel. (20) 7575-6000; fax (20) 7481-4784; e-mail shipman@aws.co.uk; internet www.aws.co.uk; f. 1885; shipowners, ship managers; Man. Dir STEVE CORKHILL.

Shipping Associations

Passenger Shipping Association Ltd (PSA): 41–42 Eastcastle St, 1st Floor, London, W1W 8DU; tel. (20) 7436-2449; fax (20) 7636-9206; e-mail info@psa-ace.org; internet www.the-psa.co.uk; fmrly Ocean Travel Development (f. 1958); 74 mems; Chair. SIMON JOHNSON; Dir WILLIAM GIBBONS.

UK Chamber of Shipping: 30 Park St, London, SE1 9EQ; tel. (20) 7417-2800; fax (20) 7600-1534; e-mail query@ukchamberofshipping.com; internet www.ukchamberofshipping.com; Pres. HELEN DEEBLE; Dir-Gen. MARK BROWNRIGG.

CIVIL AVIATION

In 2010 there were 55 airports in the United Kingdom. In addition to many international air services into and out of the country, an internal air network operates from more than 20 main commercial airports.

The principal airports are Heathrow, Gatwick and Stansted serving London, and Manchester, Birmingham and Glasgow, which in 2010 handled 65.7m., 31.4m., 18.6m., 17.8m., 8.6m. and 6.5m. passengers, respectively. In 2010 London City Airport handled 2.8m. passengers. In March 2008 a fifth terminal building opened at Heathrow, increasing capacity at the airport to some 90m. passengers a year.

BAA PLC: The Compass Centre, Nelson Rd, London Heathrow Airport, Hounslow, TW6 2GW; tel. (20) 8745-9800; e-mail baamediacentre@baa.com; internet www.baa.com; f. 1966 as British Airports Authority; privatized in 1987; propr of Heathrow, Stansted, Southampton, Glasgow and Aberdeen airports; Chair. Sir NIGEL RUDD; CEO COLIN MATTHEWS.

Civil Aviation Authority (CAA): CAA House, 45–59 Kingsway, London, WC2B 6TE; tel. (20) 7379-7311; e-mail infoservices@caa.co.uk; internet www.caa.co.uk; f. 1972; public service enterprise and a regulatory body responsible for economic and safety regulation of civil aviation; advises Govt on aviation issues; conducts economic and scientific research; produces statistical data; regulates British airspace; represents consumer interests and manages airspace users' needs; Chair. Dame DEIRDRE HUTTON.

NATS Ltd: Corporate and Technical Centre, 4000 Parkway, Whiteley, Fareham, PO15 7FL; tel. (1489) 616001; fax (1489) 615734; e-mail press.office@nats.co.uk; internet www.nats.co.uk; f. 1962 as National Air Traffic Control Services; name changed as above in 1972 when the org. became part of the CAA (q.v.); public-private partnership between the Airline Group (a consortium of British Airways, BMI, easyJet, Monarch, MyTravel, Thomsonfly and Virgin Atlantic), BAA PLC, NATS employees and the British Govt; provides air traffic control services over the UK and North Atlantic, at 15 British airports and at Gibraltar Airport. It operates and maintains a nation-wide communications, surveillance and navigation network; Chair. JOHN DEVANEY; CEO RICHARD DEAKIN.

Principal Private Airlines

British Airways PLC: Waterside, POB 365, Harmondsworth, UB7 0GB; tel. (845) 779-9977; internet www.britishairways.com; f. 1972; operates extensive domestic, European and world-wide services, scheduled services to more than 250 destinations in 99 countries; British Airways and Iberia (Spain) merged to form International Airlines Group (IAG) in Jan. 2011; Chair. MARTIN BROUGHTON; Chief Exec. KEITH WILLIAMS.

easyJet PLC: Hangar 89, London Luton Airport, Luton, LU2 9LS; tel. (871) 244-2366; internet www.easyjet.com; f. 1995; low-cost scheduled domestic and European passenger services from 17 UK airports; Chair. Sir JOHN BARTON; CEO CAROLYN McCALL.

Flybe: Jack Walker House, Exeter International Airport, Exeter, EX5 2HL; tel. (1392) 366669; fax (1392) 366151; e-mail administration.hr@flybe.com; internet www.flybe.com; f. 1979 as Jersey European Airways; name changed as above 2002; acquired BA Connect in 2007; independent regional airline providing low-cost domestic and European services; Chair. and CEO JIM FRENCH.

Loganair Ltd: St Andrews Drive, Glasgow Airport, Abbotsinch, Paisley, PA3 2TG; tel. (141) 848-7594; fax (141) 887-6020; internet www.loganair.co.uk; f. 1962; signed franchise agreement with Flybe in 2008; Scottish domestic services and flights to Belfast, Birmingham, Londonderry and the Isle of Man; Chair. (vacant); CEO DAVID HARRISON.

Monarch Airlines: Prospect House, Prospect Way, London Luton Airport, Luton, LU2 9NU; tel. (1582) 400000; fax (1582) 411000; e-mail press.office@monarch.co.uk; internet www.monarch.co.uk; f. 1967; scheduled and charter services to the Mediterranean; CEO IAIN RAWLINSON; Man. Dir KEVIN GEORGE.

Thomson Airways: London Luton Airport, Luton, LU2 9ND; tel. (870) 190-0737; e-mail lynn.houghton@thomson.co.uk; internet www.thomson.co.uk; f. 1962 as Britannia Airways; renamed as present following merger of Thomsonfly and First Choice Airways; propr TUI AG (Germany); operates scheduled services from 20 UK airports to 80 destinations world-wide; Man. Dir CHRIS BROWNE.

Virgin Atlantic Airways: Manor Royal, Crawley, RH10 9NU; tel. (844) 811-0000; internet www.virgin-atlantic.com; f. 1984; operates services to destinations in the USA, Africa, the Caribbean and the Far East; Chair. Sir RICHARD BRANSON; Chief Exec. CRAIG KREEGER.

Tourism

In 2011 there were 30.8m. arrivals by foreign visitors to the United Kingdom; receipts from tourism totalled £17,998m. in that year.

Northern Ireland Tourist Board: St Anne's Court, 59 North St, Belfast, BT1 1NB; tel. (28) 9023-1221; fax (28) 9024-0960; e-mail info@nitb.com; internet www.discovernorthernireland.com; Chair. HOWARD HASTINGS; Chief Exec. ALAN CLARKE.

VisitBritain: 1 Palace St, London, SW1E 5HX; tel. (20) 7578-1000; fax (20) 8563-0302; e-mail corporatepr@visitbritain.org; internet www.visitbritain.com; markets Great Britain overseas; Chair. CHRISTOPHER RODRIGUES; CEO SANDIE DAWE.

VisitEngland: 1 Palace St, London, SW1E 5HE; tel. (20) 7578-1400; fax (20) 7578-1401; internet www.visitengland.com; f. 2009; promotes tourism in England to domestic visitors; Chair. Lady COBHAM; CEO JAMES BERRESFORD.

Visit London: 2 More London Riverside, 6th Floor, London, SE1 2RR; tel. (20) 7234-5800; fax (20) 7378-6525; e-mail info@visitlondon.com; internet www.visitlondon.com; f. 1963; promotes London to leisure and business visitors; Chair. TAMARA INGRAM; CEO JAMES BIDWELL.

VisitScotland: Ocean Point One, 94 Ocean Drive, Leith, Edinburgh, EH6 6JH; tel. (131) 472-2207; e-mail info@visitscotland.com; internet www.visitscotland.com; Chair. PETER LEDERER; Chief Exec. MALCOLM ROUGHEAD.

Visit Wales: Brunel House, 2 Fitzalan Rd, Cardiff, CF24 0UY; tel. (845) 2049-9909; fax (29) 2048-5031; e-mail info@visitwales.co.uk; internet www.visitwales.co.uk; Dir, Tourism and Marketing JONATHAN JONES.

Defence

The United Kingdom is a member of the North Atlantic Treaty Organization (NATO) and maintains a regular army. As assessed at November 2012, the total strength of the armed forces, including those enlisted outside Britain (3,520), was 165,650 (army 96,850, navy 32,000, air force 36,800). There was also a reserve force of 80,550. There is no compulsory military service. In November 2004 the European Union (EU) ministers responsible for defence agreed to create a number of 'battlegroups' (each numbering about 1,500 men), which could be deployed at short notice to crisis areas around the world. The EU battlegroups, two of which were to be ready for deployment at any one time, following a rotational schedule, reached full operational capacity from 1 January 2007. The United Kingdom was the sole contributor to one battlegroup and also participated in another in conjunction with the Netherlands. The United Kingdom possesses its own nuclear weapons.

Defence Expenditure: £38,700m. in 2011/12.

Chief of Defence Staff: Gen. Sir DAVID RICHARDS.

Vice-Chief of Defence Staff: Gen. Sir NICHOLAS HOUGHTON.

First Sea Lord and Chief of Naval Staff: Adm. Sir GEORGE ZAMBELLAS.

Chief of General Staff: Gen. Sir PETER WALL.

Chief of Air Staff: Air Chief Marshal Sir STEPHEN DALTON.

Education

Education is compulsory for all children between the ages of five (four in Northern Ireland) and 16, and is provided free of charge between the ages of three and 18 years. (From 2013 pupils in England will be compelled to remain in full-time education or training until the academic year in which they become 17, and from mid-2015 until they are 18 years.) In Northern Ireland, Scotland and Wales the devolved authorities are responsible for all levels of education. In England the Department for Education is responsible for schools, whereas responsibility for further and higher education rests with the Department for Business, Innovation and Skills. For historical reasons, the education system in Scotland differs considerably from that current in the rest of the United Kingdom.

All state schools in England, Wales and Northern Ireland must conform to the national curriculum, which is set by the competent government authority. Compulsory education in the state sector England and Wales comprises four Key Stages. Primary schools cover Key Stages 1 and 2, catering for children aged from five to seven years and seven to 11 years, respectively, while Key Stages 3 (ages 11–14) and 4 (14–16) are covered in secondary schools. (In some areas, middle schools, which may be classified as either primary or secondary, cater for various age ranges between eight and 14 years.) A similar system prevails in Northern Ireland, where the stages at primary level are designated Foundation Stage (ages 4–6), Key Stage 1 (6–8) and Key Stage 2 (8–11). Various provisions exist for pre-school education in nursery schools and playgroups, which may be state-run or provided by voluntary or private organizations. Most children in England and Wales enter primary school at the age of four and are grouped in reception classes (part of the Early Years Foundation Stage in England), where they receive up to one year of schooling prior to Key Stage 1. At secondary level, the system of comprehensive (mixed-ability) schools prevails in most areas; however, some localities (including Northern Ireland) additionally retain grammar schools, to which admission is determined through a test of ability. A number of academies and 'free schools', both of which operate outside of local authority control, have also been established. At the end of compulsory education at the age of 16 years, most pupils in England, Wales and Northern Ireland take examinations for the General Certificate of Secondary Education (GCSE). Thereafter, pupils may remain in secondary school for a further two years, where they may take the General Certificate of Education Advanced Level (A Level) in the subjects of their choice; alternatively, they may attend a sixth-form or further education college, where they may study for A Levels or vocational awards. The A Level consists of two units: the Advanced Subsidiary (AS) Level, examinations for which are taken after one year of study (at the age of 17 years); and the A2, which is taken after two years of study (aged 18 years). From 2008 pupils aged 14 years have been able to undertake a Diploma, comprising up to three stages, lasting up to five years, in one of five vocational subject areas in place of GCSE and A Level examinations. Further education colleges offer a wide range of vocational courses for students aged 16 years and over; among the most prominent of these are National Vocational Qualifications (NVQs), which consist of five defined levels of achievement.

In Scotland the curriculum in state schools is not prescribed by statute; however, the Scottish Government issues advice and guidance to schools and Scottish Local Authorities. From August 2010 all schools were expected to follow the Scottish Government's new curriculum for education at ages 3–18, known as the Curriculum for Excellence. Primary education begins at the age of five and lasts for seven years, with pupils entering secondary school at the age of 12. At the age of 16 most pupils are examined for Standard Grades, part of the system of National Qualifications (NQs). Some schools offer NQ Intermediate 1 and 2 qualifications as an alternative to Standard Grades; as part of the Curriculum for Excellence, Standard Grades and Intermediate awards were to be replaced by National awards from 2014. Pupils remaining at secondary school for post-compulsory education take the NQ Higher award (typically in up to five or six subjects) after one further year of study, after which they are eligible for higher education in Scotland; they may subsequently remain in school for an additional year and study for the NQ Advanced Higher award, which is generally required for entry into universities in England and Wales. As in the rest of the United Kingdom, further education colleges provide a variety of vocational qualifications; the Scottish equivalent of the NVQ is the Scottish Vocational Qualification (SVQ).

In 2010/11 100% of children in the relevant age-group were enrolled at primary school in the United Kingdom, while those enrolled at secondary school included 98% of the relevant age-group.

In 2007/08 there were 120 publicly funded universities (including the Open University) and 49 other higher education institutions offering courses of higher education in the United Kingdom. There is also one privately funded university, the University of Buckingham. The Open University provides degree and other courses predominantly through distance learning methods, and requires no formal qualifications for entry to its courses. The first degree course normally lasts for three years (four in Scotland) and leads to a Bachelor of Arts or Sciences (BA or BSc) degree. The second degree course lasts for one or two years and leads to a master's degree; the third lasts three years and leads to a doctoral degree. Many higher education institutions also offer a range of vocational qualifications below degree level, including the Higher National Diploma (HND), which requires two years of study. Publicly funded universities in England, Wales and Northern Ireland may charge domestic students tuition fees for undergraduate courses, subject to a state-imposed limit. Eligible full-time Scottish-domiciled or non-British European Union students who are studying in Scotland are not required to pay tuition fees. University fees for postgraduate courses, and those charged to foreign students, are unregulated.

Schools in the United Kingdom are administered and financed in several ways. Most schools are controlled by local authorities (Education and Library Boards in Northern Ireland). Academies are publicly funded schools within the state sector in England that receive direct funding from the Department of Education and have considerable operational autonomy. Alongside the state system, there are independent schools, which do not receive grants from public funds but are financed by fees and endowments; many of these schools are administered by charitable trusts and church organizations. Budgetary expenditure on education and training in 2010/11 totalled an estimated £92,300m., representing 14.2% of total current expenditure.

UNITED KINGDOM CROWN DEPENDENCIES

The Channel Islands and the Isle of Man lie off shore from the United Kingdom but are not integral parts of the country. They are dependencies of the British Crown and have considerable self-government in internal affairs.

THE CHANNEL ISLANDS

The Channel Islands lie off the north-west coast of France to the west of Normandy, in the English Channel (la Manche). The bailiwicks of the Channel Islands (Guernsey and its dependencies, and Jersey) are the remnants of the Duchy of Normandy, which was in permanent union with the English (now British) Crown from 1106. They do not, however, form part of the United Kingdom. The islands have their own legislative assemblies and legal and administrative systems, their laws depending for their validity on Orders made by the Queen in Council. Her Majesty's Government in the United Kingdom is responsible for the defence and international relations of the islands, and the Crown is ultimately responsible for their good government. The bailiwicks do not form part of the European Union.

Guernsey

Introduction

The civil flag of Guernsey is white, bearing a red cross of St George, with a yellow couped cross superimposed on the cross. The capital is St Peter Port. English is the language in common use, but the Norman *patois* is spoken in some rural parishes. According to official estimates, Guernsey's population totalled 62,915 at 31 March 2011.

The sovereign is represented in Guernsey by the Lieutenant-Governor, appointed by the Crown. Executive power is exercised by the Policy Council, headed by the Chief Minister. The legislature, the States of Deliberation, comprises the Bailiff, appointed by the Crown, who is President ex officio; HM Procureur and HM Comptroller, Law Officers of the Crown (who are entitled to speak, but not to vote); 45 People's Deputies, elected by popular franchise every four years; and two Alderney Representatives, elected by the States of Alderney. Dependencies of Guernsey are Alderney, Brecqhou, Herm, Jethou, Lihou and Sark.

In addition to the British public holidays, Guernsey celebrates 9 May (Liberation Day).

Statistical Survey

(including Herm and Jethou)

Source (unless otherwise stated): Policy and Research Unit, Sir Charles Frossard House, La Charroterie, St Peter Port, Guernsey, GY1 1FH; tel. (1481) 717012; fax (1481) 717157; internet www.gov .gg.

AREA AND POPULATION

Area: 63.6 sq km (24.6 sq miles).

Population: 59,807 (males 29,138, females 30,669) at census of 29 April 2001. *2011* (official estimate at 31 March): 62,915 (males 31,025, females 31,890).

Density (at 31 March 2011): 989.2 per sq km.

Population by Age and Sex (official estimates at 31 March 2011): *0–14:* 9,535 (males 4,939, females 4,596); *15–64:* 42,994 (males 21,497, females 21,497); *65 and over:* 10,386 (males 4,589, females 5,797); *Total* 62,915 (males 31,025, females 31,890).

Parishes (2001 census): St Peter Port 16,488; Vale 9,573; Castel 8,975; St Sampson 8,592; St Martin 6,267; St Saviour 2,696; St Andrew 2,409; St Pierre du Bois 2,188; Forest 1,549; Torteval 973; Herm 95; Jethou 2; Total 59,807.

Births and Deaths (2011): Live births 605; Deaths 503.

Immigration and Emigration (2011): Immigrants 4,631; emigrants 4,249.

Economically Active Population (at 31 March 2012): Horticulture and other primary 433; Manufacturing 698; Construction 3,030; Utilities 398; Transport and storage 1,022; Information and communication 1,051; Hostelry 1,831; Wholesale, retail and repairs 4,367; Finance 6,815; Real estate activities 230; Professional, business, scientific and technical activities 2,010; Administrative and support service activities 1,367; Public administration 5,558; Education 516; Human health, social and charitable work activities 1,695; Arts, entertainment and recreation 397; Other services 691; *Total employed* 32,109 (males 14,834, females 17,275); Unemployed 616; *Total labour force* 32,725.

AGRICULTURE

The principal crops are flowers, most of which are grown under glass. About 16.3 sq km (6.2 sq miles) are cultivated.

MINING

Production ('000 metric tons): 139 in 2009; 120 in 2010; 116 in 2011.

FINANCE

Currency and Exchange Rates: 100 pence = 1 pound sterling (£). *Dollar and Euro Equivalents* (31 December 2012): US $1 = 63.37 pence; €1 = 83.61 pence; £10 = $15.78 = €11.96.

Note: Guernsey is in monetary union with the United Kingdom. It has its own coins and notes but United Kingdom coins and notes are also legal tender.

Budget (£ million, 2011): General revenue income 346 (Income tax 270); General revenue expenditure 333 (Education 75; Health and Social Services 107).

Cost of Living (Retail Price Index at mid-year; base: 31 December 2008 = 100): All items 100.9 in 2010; 103.9 in 2011; 107.2 in 2012.

Gross Domestic Product (£ million at current prices, estimates): 1,882.3 in 2009; 1,886.1 in 2010; 1,895 in 2011.

Gross Domestic Product by Economic Activity (£ million at current prices, 2010): Horticulture 9.5; Other primary 15.2; Manufacturing 33.5; Construction 125.9; Utilities 15.6; Transport 32.9; Hostelry 49.5; Wholesale 29.7; Retail 111.4; Recreation 17.8; Information 55.6; Financial services 730.2; Legal, business and personal services 261.8; Health, education and public administration 272.8; Non-profit 6.8; Other 117.7; *Gross domestic product* 1,886.1.

EXTERNAL TRADE

Principal Commodities: *Imports* (1999): Petroleum and oil 168,026,000 litres. *Exports* (1998, £ million): Light industry 47.0; Total flowers 34.0; Total vegetables 5.0.

TRANSPORT

Road Traffic (vehicles registered, 2011): Private vehicles 62,918; Commercial vehicles 12,827; Motorcycles 11,141.

Shipping (2011): Passenger movements 384,258.

Civil Aviation (2011): Passenger movements 902,013.

TOURISM

Number of Visitors (2011): 358,700.

COMMUNICATIONS MEDIA

Telephones (2010): 45,100 main lines in use.

Mobile Cellular Telephones (2004): 43,800.

Internet Users (2009): 48,300.

Source: International Telecommunication Union.

EDUCATION

Primary (at January 2012): 4,389 pupils (males 2,288, females 2,101).

Secondary (incl. further education, at January 2012): 4,442 pupils (males 2,246, females 2,196).

Higher (2008/09): 889 students.

Directory

The Government

HEAD OF STATE

Queen: HM Queen ELIZABETH II.

Lieutenant-Governor and Commander-in-Chief of the Bailiwick of Guernsey: Air Marshal PETER WALKER.

POLICY COUNCIL
(May 2013)

Chief Minister: PETER HARWOOD.

Deputy Chief Minister and Minister of the Home Department: JONATHAN LE TOCQ.

Minister of the Treasury and Resources: GAVIN ST PIER.

Minister of Public Services: PAUL LUXON.

Minister of Education: ROBERT SILLARS.

Minister of Health and Social Services: MARK DOREY.

Minister of Housing: DAVID JONES.

Minister of Commerce and Employment: KEVIN STEWART.

Minister of Social Security: ALLISTER LANGLOIS.

Minister of the Environment: ROGER DOMAILLE.

Minister of Culture and Leisure: MICHAEL O'HARA.

OTHER OFFICIALS

Bailiff of Guernsey: RICHARD JOHN COLLAS.

Deputy Bailiff: RICHARD JAMES MCMAHON.

HM Procureur (Attorney-General): HOWARD EDWARD ROBERTS.

HM Comptroller (Solicitor-General): MEGAN M. E. PULLUM.

GOVERNMENT OFFICE

States of Guernsey: Sir Charles Frossard House, La Charroterie, St Peter Port, GY1 1FH; tel. (1481) 717000; fax (1481) 713787; internet www.gov.gg.

Judicial System

Justice is administered in Guernsey by the Royal Court, which consists of the Bailiff and the 12 Jurats. The Royal Court also deals with a wide variety of non-contentious matters. A Stipendiary Magistrate deals with minor civil and criminal cases. The Guernsey Court of Appeal deals with appeals from the Royal Court.

Religion

CHRISTIANITY

The Church of England

The Church of England in Guernsey is the established church. The Deanery includes the islands of Alderney, Sark, Herm and Jethou; it forms part of the diocese of Winchester.

Dean of Guernsey: Very Rev. Canon PAUL MELLOR, The Deanery, Cornet St, St Peter Port, GY1 1BZ; tel. (1481) 720036; fax (1481) 722948; e-mail kpaulmellor@cwgsy.net.

The Roman Catholic Church

The diocese of Portsmouth includes the Channel Islands and part of southern England. In Guernsey there are three Roman Catholic churches, of which the senior is St Joseph and St Mary, Cordier Hill, St Peter Port.

Catholic Dean of Guernsey: Fr MICHAEL HORE, Ampthill House, Cordier Hill, St Peter Port, GY1 1JH; tel. (1481) 720196; fax (1481) 711247; e-mail sjoss.guernsey@virgin.net; internet catholic.org.gg.

Other Christian Churches

The Presbyterian Church and the Church of Scotland are represented by St Andrew's Church, The Grange, St Peter Port. The Baptist, Congregational, Elim and Methodist Churches are also represented in the island.

The Press

Guernsey Press and Star: The Guernsey Press Co, POB 57, Braye Rd, Vale, GY1 3BW; tel. (1481) 240240; fax (1481) 240235; e-mail newsroom@guernsey-press.com; internet www.thisisguernsey.com/guernsey-press; f. 1897; daily; independent; Editor RICHARD DIGARD; circ. 15,022 (June 2012).

Guernsey Weekly Press: The Guernsey Press Co, POB 57, Braye Rd, Vale, GY1 3BW; tel. (1481) 240240; fax (1481) 240235; e-mail editorial@thisisguernsey.com; internet www.thisisguernsey.com; f. 1902; Thur; independent; Editor RICHARD DIGARD.

Publishers

Toucan Press: The White Cottage, route de Carteret, Castel, GY5 7YG; tel. (1481) 257017; f. 1850; history, Thomas Hardy, Channel Islands; Man. Dir G. STEVENS COX.

Broadcasting and Communications

TELECOMMUNICATIONS

Airtel-Vodafone (Guernsey): 45 The High St, St Peter Port, GY1 2JT; tel. 7839700121 (mobile); e-mail 121@airtel-vodafone.gg; internet www.airtel-vodafone.com; mobile phone services; jt venture between Bharti Airtel Ltd (India) and Vodafone PLC (United Kingdom); mobile telecommunications services; Chief Exec. IAIN WILLIAMS.

Join Together (JT): 24 High St, St Peter Port, GY1 2JU; tel. (1481) 882345; internet www.jtglobal.com; f. 2002; subsidiary of Jersey Telecom; offers fixed-line and mobile telecommunications services, off-island connectivity and hosting; Man. Dir PAUL D. TAYLOR.

Sure: Centenary House, POB 3, La Vrangue, St Peter Port, GY1 2EY; tel. (1481) 700700; fax (1481) 724640; e-mail contact@surecw.com; internet www.surecw.com/guernsey; part of Cable and Wireless; fixed-line and mobile telecommunications services, as well as broadband internet services; Chief Exec. DENIS MARTIN.

Regulatory Authority

Channel Islands Competition and Regulatory Authorities (CICRA): Suites B1 and B2, Hirzel Court, St Peter Port, GY1 2NH; tel. (1481) 711120; fax (1481) 711140; e-mail info@cicra.gg; f. 2001; regulates postal and telecommunications sectors and electricity; Chief Exec. ANDREW RISELEY.

BROADCASTING

Radio

BBC: Radio and Television (see United Kingdom).

BBC Radio Guernsey: Television House, Bulwer Ave, St Sampson, GY2 4LA; tel. (1481) 200600; fax (1481) 200361; e-mail radio.guernsey@bbc.co.uk; internet www.bbc.co.uk/guernsey; f. 1982; Man. Editor ROBERT WALLACE.

Island FM: 12 Westerbrook, St Sampson, GY2 4QQ; tel. (1481) 242000; fax (1481) 241120; e-mail studio@islandfm.com; internet www.islandfm.com.

Television

Channel Television: Television House, Bulwer Ave, St Sampson, GY2 4LA; tel. (1481) 241888; fax (1481) 241889; e-mail broadcast.gsy@channeltv.co.uk; internet www.channelonline.tv; Exec. Chair. MICK DESMOND.

(See also under Jersey.)

Finance

(cap. = capital; res = reserves; dep. = deposits; brs = branches; amounts in pounds sterling, unless otherwise indicated.)

Guernsey Financial Services Commission: POB 128, Glategny Court, Glategny Esplanade, St Peter Port, GY1 3HQ; tel. (1481) 712706; fax (1481) 712010; e-mail info@gfsc.gg; internet www.gfsc .gg; f. 1988; regulates banking, investment, insurance and fiduciary activities; Chair. CEES SCHRAUWERS; Dir-Gen. JOHN NIKOLAS (NIK) VAN LEUVEN.

BANKING

At December 2012 total bank deposits in Guernsey were £86,700m. in 32 financial institutions.

Adam and Company International Ltd: POB 402, Royal Bank Pl., 1 Glategny Esplanade, St Peter Port, GY1 3GB; tel. (1481) 715055; fax (1481) 726919; e-mail john.judge@adambank.com; internet www.adambank.com; f. 1990; cap. 0.5m., res 0.5m., dep. 185.4m. (Dec. 2011); Chair. S. FLETCHER; Man. Dir J. JUDGE.

Butterfield Bank (Guernsey) Ltd: POB 25, Regency Court, Glategny Esplanade, St Peter Port, GY1 3AP; tel. (1481) 711521; fax (1481) 714533; e-mail info@butterfield.gg; internet www .butterfieldbank.gg; f. 1989; subsidiary of Bank of N. T. Butterfield & Son Ltd (Bermuda); cap. 40m., res 0.2m., dep. 863.3m. (Dec. 2011); Man. Dir ROBERT MOORE.

Crédit Suisse (Guernsey) Ltd: POB 368, Helvetia Court, South Esplanade, St Peter Port, GY1 3JY; tel. (1481) 719000; fax (1481) 724676; e-mail csguernsey.info@credit-suisse.com; internet www .credit-suisse.com/guernsey; f. 1986; cap. US $6.1m., dep. $5,741.9m., total assets $6,150.1m. (Dec. 2011); CEO R. McGREGOR.

EFG Private Bank (Channel Islands) Ltd: POB 603, EFG House, St Julian's Ave, St Peter Port, GY1 4NN; tel. (1481) 723432; fax (1481) 723488; internet www.efggroup.com; f. 1992 as The Private Bank & Trust Co (Guernsey) Ltd; present name adopted 1997; cap. 5m., res 33.1m., dep. 818.5m. (Dec. 2006); Man. Dir D. G. GARDNER.

SG Hambros Bank (Channel Islands) Ltd: POB 6, Hambro House, St Julian's Ave, St Peter Port, GY1 3AE; tel. (1481) 726521; fax (1481) 727139; e-mail channelislands@sghambros.com; internet www.sghambros.com; f. 1967; fmrly SG Hambros Bank and Trust (Guernsey) Ltd; name changed in 2005 following merger with SG Hambros Bank and Trust (Jersey) Ltd; merchant bankers; cap. 4.5m., res 77.7m., dep. 1,840.9m. (Dec. 2011); Chair. WARWICK J. NEWBURY; Chief Exec. RICHARD A. OLLIVER.

HSBC Private Bank (CI) Ltd: HSBC Private Bank Bldg, Park Pl., Park St, St Peter Port, GY1 1EE; tel. (1481) 759000; fax (1481) 759020; internet www.hsbcprivatebank.com; f. 1985; present name adopted 2008, following merger with HSBC Private Bank (Jersey) Ltd; cap. US $25m., res $503.9m., dep. $13,677.1m. (Dec. 2011); CEO GARY MILLER.

Investec Bank (Channel Islands) Ltd: POB 188, La Vieille Cour, St Peter Port, GY1 3LP; tel. (1481) 711500; fax (1481) 741147; e-mail enquiries@investec-ci.com; internet www.investec.com; f. 1977 as Guinness Mahon Guernsey Ltd; present name adopted 1999; cap. 14.6m., res 21.8m., dep. 1,529m. (March 2012); Chair. A. TAPNACK; Gen. Man. MORT MIRGHAVAMEDDIN.

Lloyds TSB Offshore Ltd Private Banking Office: POB 136, Sarnia House, Le Truchot, St Peter Port, GY1 4EN; tel. (1481) 708000; fax (1481) 727416; e-mail pvtbankingg@lloydstsb-offshore .com; internet www.lloydstsb-offshore.com; Head of Sales and Relationships GARY BROWNBRIDGE.

Rothschild Bank International Ltd: St Julian's Court, St Peter Port, GY1 3BP; tel. (1481) 713713; fax (1481) 727705; e-mail private .banking@rothschild.com; internet www.rothschild.gg; f. 1967; present name adopted 2007; subsidiary of N. M. Rothschild & Sons Ltd, London; cap. 5m., res –0.7m., dep. 686.5m. (March 2012); Chair. CHRISTOPHER COLEMAN; Man. Dir PETER ROSE.

Royal Bank of Canada (Channel Islands) Ltd: POB 48, Canada Court, St Peter Port, GY1 3BQ; tel. (1481) 744000; fax (1481) 744001; e-mail infogpb@rbc.com; internet www.rbcprivatebanking.com; f. 1973; subsidiary of Royal Bank of Canada; cap. 5m., res 6m., dep. 6,590.2m. (Oct. 2011); Chair. DAVID P. O'BRIEN; Man. Dir C. C. BLAMPIED.

Schroders (CI) Ltd: POB 334, Regency Court, Glategny Esplanade, St Peter Port, GY1 3UF; tel. (1481) 703700; fax (1481) 703600; internet www.schroders.com/ci; f. 1992; cap. 0.5m., res 4.5m., dep. 716m. (Dec. 2009); Chief Exec. JULIAN WINSER.

Banking Organization

Association of Guernsey Banks: c/o Butterfield Bank (Guernsey) Ltd, St Peter Port, GY1 3AP; tel. (1481) 711521; fax (1481) 714533; e-mail John.Robinson@gg.butterfieldgroup.com; internet www.agb .org.gg; f. 1988; 37 mems; Chair. JOHN ROBINSON.

STOCK EXCHANGE

Channel Islands Stock Exchange (CISX): 1 Lefebvre St, St Peter Port, GY1 4PJ; tel. (1481) 713831; fax (1481) 714856; e-mail info@cisx .com; internet www.cisx.com; Chief Exec. TAMARA MENTESHVILI.

INSURANCE

At 31 March 2013 there were 242 international insurance companies and eight domestic insurers operating in Guernsey.

Generali Worldwide Insurance Co Ltd: POB 613, Generali House, Hirzel St, St Peter Port, GY1 4PA; tel. (1481) 715400; fax (1481) 715390; e-mail enquiries@generali-guernsey.com; internet www.generali-gw.com; CEO GAVIN TRADELIUS.

Heritage Group: POB 225, Heritage Hall, Le Marchant St, St Peter Port, GY1 4HY; tel. (1481) 716000; fax (1481) 712357; e-mail info@ heritage.co.gg; internet www.heritage.co.gg; Chair. MARTIN BELCHER; CEO RICHARD TEE.

Insurance Corpn of the Channel Islands Ltd: POB 160, Dixcart House, Sir William Pl., St Peter Port, GY1 4EY; tel. (1481) 713322; e-mail icci@insurancecorporation.com; internet www .insurancecorporation.com; mem. of the RSA Insurance Group; Man. Dir GLYN SMITH.

Islands' Insurance Brokers Ltd: Lancaster Court, Forest Lane, St Peter Port, GY1 1WJ; tel. (1481) 710731; fax (1481) 712223; e-mail insure@islandsinsurance.gg; internet www.islands-insurance.com; f. 1978; insurance broker; owned by National Farmers' Union Mutual Insurance Society Ltd; Dir PETER ROWE.

Trade and Industry

CHAMBER OF COMMERCE

Guernsey Chamber of Commerce: Suite 1, 16 Glategny Esplanade, St Peter Port, GY1 1WN; tel. (1481) 727483; fax (1481) 710755; e-mail office@guernseychamber.com; internet www .guernseychamber.com; f. 1808; Pres. RUPERT DOREY; Dir BARRY CASH.

UTILITIES

Electricity

Guernsey Electricity: POB 4, Electricity House, Northside, Vale, GY1 3AD; tel. (1481) 200700; fax (1481) 246942; e-mail admin@ electricity.gg; internet www.electricity.gg; Chair. IAN BEATTIE; Man. Dir ALAN BATES.

Gas

Guernsey Gas: The Energy Centre, Admiral Park, St Peter Port, GY1 2BB; tel. (1481) 724811; internet www.gsygas.com; Man. Dir PAUL GARLICK.

Water

Guernsey Water: POB 30, Brickfield House, St Andrew, GY1 3AS; tel. (1481) 239500; fax (1481) 234649; e-mail customer.service@water .gg; internet www.water.gg; fmrly States of Guernsey Waterboard; name changed as above 2004; Dir, Water Services ANDREW REDHEAD.

Transport

SHIPPING

Alderney Shipping Co Ltd: POB 77, White Rock, St Peter Port, GY1 4BN; tel. (1481) 724810; fax (1481) 712081; e-mail questions@ alderneyshipping.com; internet www.aldshp.co.uk; f. 1969; Man. Dir BRUNO KAY-MOUAT.

Condor Ltd: New Jetty Offices, White Rock, St Peter Port, GY1 2LL; tel. (1202) 207207; fax (1202) 685184; internet www.condorferries.co .uk; f. 1964; regular passenger service operating between the Channel Islands and St Malo (France), and between the Channel Islands and Poole, Weymouth and Portsmouth; Man. Dir ROGER NORMAN.

Condorferries Freight: La Plaiderie House, 3rd Floor, La Plaiderie, St Peter Port, GY1 1WD; tel. (1481) 728620; fax (1481) 728521; e-mail jeff.vidamour@condorferries.co.uk; internet www .condorferries.co.uk; regular ro-ro freight services between Portsmouth, Guernsey, Jersey and St Malo (France); Freight Dir JEFF VIDAMOUR.

Isle of Sark Shipping Co Ltd: White Rock, St Peter Port, GY1 2LN; tel. (1481) 724059; fax (1481) 713999; e-mail info@sarkshipping.info; internet www.sarkshipping.info; operates daily services between Guernsey and Sark.

Trident Charter Co Ltd: Woodville, Les Dicqs, Vale, GY6 8JW; tel. (1481) 245253; fax (1481) 700226; e-mail peterwilcox@cwgsy.net; internet www.traveltrident.com; f. 1968; Man. PETER WILCOX.

CIVIL AVIATION

Aurigny Air Services Ltd: States Airport, La Planque Lane, Forest, GY8 0DT; tel. (1481) 266444; fax (1481) 266446; e-mail customerrelations@aurigny.com; internet www.aurigny.com; f. 1968; scheduled passenger services from Guernsey to Alderney, Jersey, Bristol, East Midlands, London Gatwick, London Stansted, Manchester, Southampton and Dinard (France); freight services, tour operation, ambulance charters and third party handling; owned by the States of Guernsey; Man. Dir MALCOLM HART.

Blue Islands: Century House, 12 Victoria St, St Anne, Alderney, GY9 3UF; tel. (1481) 711321; fax (1481) 735235; e-mail enquiries@blueislands.com; internet www.blueislands.com; f. 1999 as Le Cocqs Air Link; name changed as above in 2006; scheduled passenger flights between Alderney, Guernsey and Jersey, and to Southampton, the Isle of Man, Geneva and Zürich (both Switzerland); Chair. DEREK COATES; Man. Dir PAUL SABIN.

Tourism

A total of 358,700 tourists visited Guernsey during 2011.

VisitGuernsey: POB 23, St Peter Port, GY1 3AN; tel. (1481) 723552; e-mail enquiries@visitguernsey.com; internet www.visitguernsey.com; Dir, Marketing and Tourism JASON MORIARTY.

Islands of the Bailiwick of Guernsey

Alderney

The area of Alderney is 7.9 sq km (3.1 sq miles) and at the 2001 census the population was 2,294; in March 2012 the population had decreased to an estimated 2,091. The principal town is St Anne's (or St Anne).

The President, who is directly elected for a four-year term, is the civic head of Alderney and has precedence on the island over all persons except the Lieutenant-Governor of Guernsey, and the Bailiff of Guernsey or his representative. He presides over meetings of the States of Alderney, which are responsible for the administration of the island with the exception of policing, public health and education, which are administered by the States of Guernsey. The States consist of 10 members who hold office for four years and are elected by universal suffrage of residents.

President of the States: STUART TROUGHT.

Chief Executive of the States: ROY BURKE.

Greffier: SARAH KELLY.

States of Alderney: POB 1001, Alderney, GY9 3AA; tel. (1481) 822811; fax (1481) 822436; e-mail info@alderney.gov.gg; internet www.alderney.gov.gg.

Brecqhou and Lihou

Brecqhou (measuring 1.2 km by 0.5 km) is a dependency of Sark. Lihou (area 0.2 sq km) is, for administrative purposes, part of Guernsey.

Herm

Herm is held on a 100-year lease from the States of Guernsey by Wood of Herm Island Ltd, with a duty to preserve the island's outstanding natural beauty and peacefulness. Farming and tourism are the chief sources of income. The island has an area of 2.0 sq km (0.8 sq miles). In 2002 the population of Herm was 60.

Herm Island Administration Office: Herm Island, Guernsey, GY1 3HR; tel. (1481) 722377; fax (1481) 700334; e-mail admin@herm-island.com; internet www.herm-island.com; Finance and Admin. Dir ANDREW BAILEY.

Jethou

Jethou has an area of 0.2 sq km (0.07 sq miles) and is leased by the Crown to a tenant who has no official functions. At the 2001 census the population of Jethou was two.

Sark

The area of the island is 5.5 sq km (2.1 sq miles) and at the 2001 census the population was 589. No motor vehicles are permitted apart from a small number of tractors. In summer a daily boat service runs between Guernsey and Sark, and in winter a limited service is provided. There are two harbours on the island.

The Seigneur of Sark is the hereditary civic head of the island and thereby entitled to certain privileges. The Seigneur is a member of the Chief Pleas of Sark, the island's parliament, and has a suspensory veto on its ordinances. The Seigneur traditionally had the right, subject to the approval of the Lieutenant-Governor of Guernsey, to appoint the Seneschal of Sark, who was President of Chief Pleas and Chairman of the Seneschal's Court (the local Court of Justice). In order to comply with human rights laws, in October 2010 the Chief Pleas voted to split the long-standing dual role of the Seneschal into two separate (parliamentary and judicial) roles—President of Chief Pleas and Seneschal (Chairman of the Seneschal's Court). The former officer would be elected by the members of the Chief Pleas, while the latter (who would not hold a seat in the Chief Pleas) would be appointed by the Seigneur. The division of roles officially entered into force on 26 February 2013.

In March 2006 the Chief Pleas voted in favour of reducing the number of its members from 54 (comprising the Seigneur, the Seneschal, the owners of the island's 40 tenements—known as tenants—and 12 elected 'deputies of the people') to 30 (the Seigneur, the Seneschal, 14 tenants and 14 residents). Under the reformed system the elected members of the Chief Pleas would be elected by universal suffrage of residents. An official opinion poll on the composition of the Chief Pleas was conducted between mid-August and early September. Some 56.0% of the valid votes cast (234 of a total of 418) supported open elections for all 28 elective seats in the Chief Pleas, while 44.0% of voters favoured the option of reserving 12 of the 28 seats specifically for residents and eight for tenants. A participation rate of 89.5% was recorded for the opinion poll, which was subsequently approved by the Chief Pleas. In February 2008 the Chief Pleas ratified the reform law, which would allow for the introduction of a mainly elected chamber. In addition, the law extended the term of office of the unelected Seneschal to the duration of his natural life. The Privy Council of the United Kingdom approved the proposed changes in April and elections for 28 of the seats in the Chief Pleas duly took place in December.

Seigneur of Sark: JOHN MICHAEL BEAUMONT.

President of Chief Pleas: Lt-Col REGINALD J. GUILLE.

Seneschal (Chairman of the Seneschal's Court): JEREMY LA TROBE-BATEMAN.

Greffier: TREVOR J. HAMON.

Sark Committee Office: La Chasse Marette, GY9 0SF; tel. (1481) 832118; fax (1481) 833086; e-mail seigneur@gov.sark.gg; internet www.gov.sark.gg.

Sark Tourism: Harbour Hill, Sark, GY9 0SB; tel. (1481) 832345; fax (1481) 832483; e-mail contact@sark.info; internet www.sark.info.

JERSEY

Introduction

Jersey, the largest of the Channel Islands, is situated to the south-east of Guernsey, from which it is separated by 27 km (17 miles) of sea. The official language of Jersey is English (since 1960), although French is still used in the courts. The state and civil flag is white with a red saltire and coat of arms bearing three yellow lions and surmounted by a yellow crown. The capital is St Helier. According to the census of 27 March 2011, Jersey's population was 97,857.

The sovereign is represented in Jersey by a Lieutenant-Governor, appointed by the Crown. Executive power is exercised by the 10-member Council of Ministers, headed by the Chief Minister, who is elected by the Assembly of the States (the insular legislature). The Assembly of the States, which is presided over by the Bailiff, includes 51 elected members—10 Senators (elected on an island-wide basis), 12 Connétables (heads of parishes), and 29 Deputies (representing constituencies), all elected by universal suffrage for four-year terms. It also includes five appointees of the Crown—the Lieutenant-Governor, the Bailiff, the Dean of Jersey, the Attorney-General and the Solicitor-General, all of whom are entitled to sit and speak in the States, but not to vote. From the legislative elections of October 2014 the number of Senators in the Assembly of the States was to be reduced to eight.

In addition to the British public holidays, Jersey celebrates 9 May (Liberation Day).

Statistical Survey

Source (unless otherwise stated): States of Jersey Statistics Department, Cyril Le Marquand House, POB 140, JE4 8QT; tel. (1534) 440426; fax (1534) 440409; e-mail statistics@gov.je; internet www.gov.je/statistics.

AREA AND POPULATION

Area: 118.2 sq km (45.6 sq miles).

Population (census of 27 March 2011): 97,857 (males 48,296, females 49,561).

Density (at 2011 census): 827.9 per sq km.

Population by Age and Sex (census of 27 March 2011): *0–14:* 15,169 (males 7,665, females 7,504); *15–64:* 68,215 (males 34,198, females 34,017); *65 and over:* 14,473 (males 6,433, females 8,040); *Total* 97,857 (males 48,296, females 49,561).

Principal Towns (2011): St Helier 33,522; St Saviour 13,580; St Brelade 10,568; St Clement 9,221.

Births and Deaths (2009): Live births 1,005 (10.9 per 1,000); Deaths 760 (8.2 per 1,000). *2011:* Live births 1,100; Deaths 716.

Employment (private sector employees at June 2012, rounded estimates): Agriculture and fishing 2,230; Manufacturing and utilities 1,630; Construction and quarrying 5,100; Wholesale and retail 8,420; Hotels, restaurants etc. 6,320; Transport, storage and communication 2,800; Financial services 12,590; Miscellaneous business activities (incl. computers) 4,610; Education, health and other services 5,930; *Total employed* 49,610. Note: In addition 6,770 employees were engaged in the public sector. *January 2013:* Registered unemployed and actively seeking work 2,020.

AGRICULTURE, ETC.

Principal Crops: Some 56% of total land area was classified as agricultural in 2010. The principal crops are potatoes, cauliflowers and tomatoes.

Livestock (2010): Cattle 5,200 (incl. 2,970 heifers in milk); Poultry 22,030.

Livestock Product (2010): Cows' milk 12.9m. litres.

Fishing (metric tons, 2010): Capture 1,818 (Skates and rays 37, Other wet fish 70, Brown crabs 409, Lobsters 225, Spider crabs 173, Scallops 401, Whelks 497, Others 5); Aquaculture 833 (Oysters 629, Scallops 2, Mussels 201); *Total catch* 2,651.

MINING

Production ('000 metric tons): Igneous rock 325 in 2008; 249 in 2009; 238 in 2010.

FINANCE

Currency and Exchange Rates: 100 pence = 1 pound sterling (£). *Dollar and Euro Equivalents* (31 December 2012): US $1 = 63.37 pence; €1 = 83.61 pence; £10 = $15.78 = €11.96.

Note: Jersey is in monetary union with the United Kingdom. It has its own coins and notes but United Kingdom coins and notes are also legal tender.

Budget (£ million, 2010): Net consolidated fund income 546 (Tax 394); Consolidated fund expenditure 631 (Recurrent expenditure 599, Capital 32).

Money Supply (currency in circulation, £ million at 31 December 2010): Notes 85.2; Coins 7.6; *Total* 92.8.

Cost of Living (Retail Price Index at December; base June 2000 = 100, all items): 143.2 in 2010; 150.4 in 2011; 153.5 in 2012.

Gross National Income (£ million at current prices): 3,620 in 2009; 4,050 in 2010; 4,010 in 2011 (provisional).

Gross Value Added by Economic Activity (£ million at current prices, 2011, provisional): Agriculture 48; Manufacturing 54; Electricity, gas and water 39; Construction 236; Wholesale and retail trade 270; Hotels, restaurants and bars 130; Transport, storage and communications 164; Finance 1,493; Other business activities 890; Public administration 321; *Total* 3,645.

TRANSPORT

Road Traffic (vehicles registered at 31 December 2001): Motor cars 71,059; Motorcycles 5,676; Mopeds 2,200; Buses and minibuses 691; Tractors 2,369; Vans 7,562; Trucks 3,617; Total (incl. others) 94,538. *2011* (vehicles registered at 31 December): Total 117,537.

Shipping (2011): Passenger movements 785,000; Containerized freight ('000 metric tons handled) 349.

Civil Aviation (2005): Aircraft movements 70,012; Total passengers carried 1,483,477 (Arrivals 741,969, Departures 741,508). *2011:* Total passenger arrivals 735,522 (of whom 624,792 were from the UK).

TOURISM

Tourist Arrivals (2004): *Holiday and Leisure Visitors* (staying in paid accommodation): 377,820 (UK mainland 301,460; Other Channel Islands 14,900; France 29,380; Germany 10,060; *Total*: 731,310. *2011:* Total visitor arrivals 689,700 (number staying in paid accommodation 334,400); Total revenues £242m.

COMMUNICATIONS MEDIA

Telephones (2010): 73,800 main lines in use.

Mobile Cellular Telephones (2006, estimate): 102,000.

Internet Users (2009): 29,500.

Source: partly International Telecommunication Union.

EDUCATION

Pupils (2011): Primary 7,000 (state schools 5,698, private 1,302); Secondary 6,280 (state schools 5,117, private 1,163).

Directory

The Government

HEAD OF STATE

Queen: HM Queen ELIZABETH II.

Lieutenant-Governor and Commander-in-Chief of Jersey: Sir JOHN McCOLL.

COUNCIL OF MINISTERS
(May 2013)

Chief Minister: IAN GORST.

Deputy Chief Minister and Minister for Home Affairs: IAN LE MARQUAND.

Minister for Economic Development: ALAN MACLEAN.

Minister for Education, Sport and Culture: PATRICK RYAN.

Minister for Health and Social Services: ANNE PRYKE.

Minister for Housing: ANDREW GREEN.

Minister for Planning and Environment: ROBERT DUHAMEL.

Minister for Social Security: FRANCIS LE GRESLEY.

Minister for Transport and Technical Services: KEVIN LEWIS.

Minister for Treasury and Resources: PHILIP OZOUF.

OTHER OFFICIALS

Bailiff: MICHAEL CAMERON ST JOHN BIRT.

Deputy Bailiff: WILLIAM JAMES BAILHACHE.

Dean of Jersey: Very Rev. ROBERT FREDERICK KEY.

Attorney-General: TIMOTHY LE COCQ.

Solicitor-General: HOWARD SHARP.

GOVERNMENT OFFICES

Chief Minister's Department: POB 140, Cyril Le Marquand House, St Helier, JE4 8QT; tel. (1534) 445500; fax (1534) 440409; e-mail cmdept@gov.je; internet www.gov.je.

Economic Development Department: Cyril Le Marquand House, JE4 8UL; tel. (1534) 448100; e-mail edgroup@gov.je.

Education, Sport and Culture Department: POB 142, Highlands Campus, JE4 8QJ; tel. (1534) 445504; fax (1534) 445524; e-mail esc@gov.je.

Environment Department: South Hill, St Helier, JE2 4US; tel. (1534) 445508; fax (1534) 445528; e-mail planning@gov.je.

Health and Social Services Department: Peter Crill House, Gloucester St, St Helier, JE1 3QS; tel. (1534) 442000; fax (1534) 444216; e-mail health@gov.je.

Home Affairs Department: 11 Royal Sq., St Helier, JE2 4WA; tel. (1534) 445507; fax (1534) 447933; e-mail homeaffairs@gov.je.

Housing Department: POB 587, Jubilee Wharf, 24 Esplanade, St Helier, JE4 8XT; tel. (1534) 445510; fax (1534) 445530; e-mail socialhousing@gov.je.

Social Security Department: POB 55, La Motte St, St Helier, JE4 8PE; tel. (1534) 445505; fax (1534) 445525; e-mail socialsecurity@gov.je.

Transport and Technical Services Department: POB 412, States Offices, Southern Hill, St Helier, JE4 8UY; tel. (1534) 445509; fax (1534) 445529; e-mail tts@gov.je.

Treasury and Resources Department: POB 353, Cyril Le Marquand House, St Helier, JE4 8UL; tel. (1534) 445502; e-mail treasury@gov.je.

States of Jersey Assembly: Morier House, St Helier, JE1 1DD; tel. (1534) 441020; fax (1534) 441098; e-mail statesgreffe@gov.je; internet www.statesassembly.gov.je.

Judicial System

Justice is administered in Jersey by the Royal Court, which consists of the Bailiff or Deputy Bailiff and 12 Jurats elected by an Electoral College. There is a Court of Appeal, which consists of the Bailiff (or Deputy Bailiff) and two judges, selected from a panel appointed by the Crown. A final appeal lies to the Privy Council in certain cases.

A Stipendiary Magistrate deals with minor civil and criminal cases. He also acts as an Examining Magistrate in some criminal matters.

Religion

CHRISTIANITY

The Church of England

The Church of England is the established church. The Deanery of Jersey is an Ecclesiastical Peculiar, governed by its own canons, the Dean being the Ordinary of the Island; it is attached to the diocese of Winchester for episcopal purposes.

Dean of Jersey: Very Rev. ROBERT FREDERICK KEY, The Deanery, David Place, St Helier, JE2 4TE; tel. (1534) 720001; fax (1534) 617488; e-mail deanofjersey@jerseymail.co.uk.

The Roman Catholic Church

The diocese of Portsmouth includes the Channel Islands and part of southern England. The Episcopal Vicar for the Channel Islands resides at St Peter Port, Guernsey. In Jersey there are 12 Roman Catholic churches, including St Mary and St Peter's, Wellington Rd, St Helier (English), and St Thomas's, Val Plaisant, St Helier (French).

Catholic Dean of Jersey: Fr NICHOLAS FRANCE, 17 Val Plaisant, St Helier, JE2 4TA; tel. (1534) 720235; fax (1534) 607991; e-mail sthelier@catholicchurch.org.je; internet www.catholicchurch.org.je.

Other Christian Churches

The Baptist, Congregational New Church, Methodist and Presbyterian churches are also represented.

The Press

Jersey Evening Post: Guiton House, Five Oaks, St Saviour, JE4 8XQ; tel. (1534) 611611; fax (1534) 611620; e-mail news@jerseyeveningpost.com; internet www.jerseyeveningpost.com; f. 1890; independent; Propr The Guiton Group; Editor CHRIS BRIGHT; circ. 18,088 (2011).

Jersey Weekly Post: POB 582, Guiton House, Five Oaks, St Saviour, JE4 8XQ; tel. (1534) 611611; fax (1534) 611620; e-mail news@jerseyeveningpost.com; internet www.thisisjersey.com; Thur; Propr The Guiton Group; Editor CHRIS BRIGHT; circ. 1,200.

Publishers

Ashton & Denton Publishing Co (CI) Ltd: 3 Burlington House, St Saviour's Rd, St Helier, JE2 4LA; tel. (1534) 735461; fax (1534) 875805; e-mail asden@supanet.com; f. 1957; local history, holiday guides, financial; Man. Dir A. MACKENZIE.

Barnes Publishing Ltd: 1 L'Anciennete, La Route de Ste Marie, St Mary, JE3 3DB; tel. (1534) 484649; e-mail ian@barnespublishing.com; internet barnespublishing.com; f. 1992 as Apache Publishing; present name adopted 1998; Man. Dir IAN BARNES.

Broadcasting and Communications

TELECOMMUNICATIONS

Jersey Competition Regulatory Authority: Salisbury House, 2nd Floor, 1–9 Union St, St Helier, JE2 3RF; tel. (1534) 514990; e-mail info@cicra.je; internet www.cicra.gg; f. 2001; part of the Channel Islands Competition and Regulatory Authorities (CICRA); enforces competition law; also regulates postal & telecom sectors; Chief Exec. ANDREW RISELEY.

Airtel-Vodafone (Jersey): 26 Queen St, St Helier, JE2 4WD; tel. 7829700121 (mobile); e-mail 121@airtel-vodafone.je; internet www.airtel-vodafone.com; f. 2007; mobile cellular telecommunications; jt venture between Bharti Airtel Ltd (India) and Vodafone PLC (United Kingdom); Chief Exec. VINOD SUD.

Jersey Telecom: POB 53, No. 1 The Forum, Grenville St, St Helier, JE4 8PB; tel. (1534) 882882; fax (1534) 882883; e-mail enquiries@jerseytelecom.com; internet www.jerseytelecom.com; Chair. JOHN BOOTHMAN; CEO GRAEME MILLAR.

Sure: King St, POB 366, St Helier, JE2 4WE; tel. (1534) 888291; fax (1534) 888292; e-mail hello@surecw.com; internet www.surecw.com/jersey; part of Cable and Wireless; Chief Exec., Sure Jersey GRAHAM HUGHES.

BROADCASTING

Radio

BBC: Radio and Television (see United Kingdom).

BBC Jersey: 18 and 21 Parade Rd, St Helier, JE2 3PL; tel. (1534) 870000; e-mail jersey@bbc.co.uk; internet www.bbc.co.uk/jersey; f. 1982; broadcasts 78 hours a week; Man. Editor JON GRIPTON.

Channel 103 FM: 6 Tunnell St, St Helier, JE2 4LU; tel. (1534) 888103; fax (1534) 877177; e-mail info@channel103.com; internet www.channel103.com; f. 1992; Man. Dir LINDA BURNHAM.

Television

Channel Television: Television Centre, La Pouquelaye, St Helier, JE1 3ZD; tel. (1534) 816816; fax (1534) 816777; e-mail broadcast@channeltv.co.uk; internet www.channelonline.tv; f. 1962; privately owned regional licence holder for Channel 3 (ITV1) in the United Kingdom; daily transmissions; Exec. Chair. MICK DESMOND.

Programmes are also received from the BBC, Channel 4 and Five in the United Kingdom and also from France.

Finance

Jersey Financial Services Commission: POB 267, 14–18 Castle St, St Helier, JE4 8TP; tel. (1534) 822000; fax (1534) 822002; e-mail info@jerseyfsc.org; internet www.jerseyfsc.org; f. 1998; financial services regulator; Dir-Gen. JOHN HARRIS.

BANKING

(cap. = capital; auth. = authorized; res = reserves; dep. = deposits; m. = million; br./brs = branch(es); amounts in pounds sterling, unless otherwise indicated)

In 2012 total bank deposits in Jersey were £152,145m. in 42 institutions.

Banks

ABN AMRO Private Banking: POB 255, 7 Castle St, St Helier, JE4 8TB; tel. (1534) 604000; fax (1534) 759041; e-mail pbclients@uk .abnamro.com; internet www.abnamroprivatebanking.com/jersey; f. 1997; Head of Private Banking PATRICK CROWLEY.

AIB Bank (CI) Ltd: POB 468, AIB House, 25 Esplanade, St Helier, JE1 2AB; tel. (1534) 883000; fax (1534) 883112; e-mail one@aib.je; internet www.aib.je; f. 1981; cap. 120m., dep. 2,030.5m., total assets 2,205.3m. (Dec. 2010); CEO D. J. MOYNIHAN.

Bank Leumi (Jersey) Ltd: POB 510, 2 Hill St, St Helier, JE4 5TR; tel. (1534) 702525; fax (1534) 617446; e-mail info@leumijersey.com; internet www.bankleumi.co.uk; f. 1993; cap. 15.5m., res 0.1m., dep. 317.8m. (Dec. 2012).

Citibank (Channel Islands) Ltd: POB 104, 38 The Esplanade, St Helier, JE4 8QB; tel. (1534) 608000; fax (1534) 608190; internet www .privatebank.citibank.com; f. 1969; Chair. RICHARD D. PARSONS.

Coutts & Co Channel Islands: POB 64, Royal Bank House, 71 Bath St, St Helier, JE4 8ND; tel. (1534) 282345; fax (1534) 282199; e-mail info@coutts.com; internet www.coutts.com.

Deutsche Bank International Ltd: POB 727, St Paul's Gate, New St, St Helier, JE4 8ZB; tel. (1534) 889900; fax (1534) 889911; internet www.dboffshore.com; f. 1972; cap. 15m., res 1.7m., dep. 2,180.2m. (Dec. 2011); Chief Country Officer ANDREAS TAUTSCHER.

SG Hambros Bank (Channel Islands) Ltd: POB 197, SG Hambros House, 18 The Esplanade, St Helier, JE4 8PR; tel. (1534) 815555; fax (1534) 815640; e-mail channelislands@sghambros.com; internet www.sghambros.com; f. 1967 as Hambros (Jersey) Ltd; previously SG Hambros Bank and Trust (Jersey) Ltd; name changed in 2005 following merger with SG Hambros Bank and Trust (Guernsey) Ltd; subsidiary of SG Hambros Bank and Trust Ltd, London; cap. 4.5m., res 77.7m., dep. 1,840.9m. (Dec. 2011); Chair. WARWICK J. NEWBURY; Man. Dir RICHARD A. OLLIVER.

HSBC Bank International Ltd: HSBC House, St Helier, JE1 1HS; tel. (1534) 616111; fax (1534) 616001; e-mail offshore@hsbc.com; internet www.offshore.hsbc.com; f. 1967 as Midland Bank Finance Corpn (Jersey) Ltd; cap. 1.4m., res 71.8m, dep. 7,391.1m. (Dec. 2011); Chief Exec. MARTIN DAVID SPURLING.

HSBC Bank Middle East Ltd: POB 315, HSBC House, The Esplanade, St Helier, JE4 8UB; tel. (1534) 606512; fax (1534) 606149; e-mail chris.keirle@hsbc.com; internet www.middleeast .hsbc.com; cap. US $931.1m., res $48.5m., dep. $31,196.5m. (Dec. 2011); Chair. YOUSSEF NASR.

Kleinwort Benson (Channel Islands) Ltd: POB 76, Kleinwort Benson House, Wests Centre, St Helier, JE4 8PQ; tel. (1534) 613000; fax (1534) 613141; internet www.kleinwortbenson.com; f. 1962; mem. of the Dresdner Bank Group; cap. 5m., res 20m., dep. 1,910m. (Dec. 2008); Man. Dir MARTIN ANGUS TAYLOR.

Lloyds TSB Offshore Ltd: POB 160, 25 New St, St Helier, JE4 8RG; tel. (1534) 854144; fax (1534) 503215; e-mail jerseyoffc@ lloydstsb-offshore.com; internet www.lloydstsb-offshore.com; part of Lloyds TSB banking group; cap. 446.9m., res 14.9m., dep. 13,224.6m. (Dec. 2011); Chair. MARTIN FREDERICK FRICKER.

JPMorgan Chase Bank: POB 127, JPMorgan House, Grenville St, St Helier, JE4 8QH; tel. (1534) 626262; fax (1534) 626301; Gen. Man. L. C. WORTHAM.

JP Morgan Trust Co (Jersey): POB 127, JPMorgan House, Grenville St, St Helier; tel. (1534) 626262; fax (1534) 626300; Chair. T. TODMAN; Man. Dir L. C. WORTHAM.

Nedbank Private Wealth Ltd: Fairbairn House, 31 The Esplanade, St Helier, JE1 1FB; tel. (1534) 887889; e-mail jer@ nedbankprivatewealth.com; internet www.nedbankprivatewealth .com; f. 2012 through the merger of several orgs; fmrly Fairbairn Private Bank; Man. Dir G. J. HORTON.

The Royal Bank of Scotland International Ltd: POB 64, 71 Bath St, St Helier, JE4 8PJ; tel. (1534) 285200; fax (1534) 285588; internet www.rbsint.com; f. 1966; cap. 96.5m., res 4.9m., dep. 23,521.8m. (Dec. 2011); Chief Exec. ADRIAN GILL.

Standard Bank Jersey Ltd: POB 583, Standard Bank House, 47–49 La Motte St, St Helier, JE4 8XR; tel. (1534) 881188; fax (1534) 881199; e-mail sboff@standardbank.com; internet www .standardbank.com/wealth; f. 1977 as Brown Shipley (Jersey); present name adopted 2000; cap. 26.5m., res 3.4m., dep. 1,294.3m. (Dec. 2011); Chair. R. A. G. LEITH; CEO IAN GIBSON.

Standard Chartered (Jersey) Ltd: POB 80, 15 Castle St, St Helier, JE4 8PT; tel. (1534) 704000; fax (1534) 704600; internet www.standardchartered.com/je; f. 1966 as Julian S. Hodge Bank (Jersey) Ltd; present name adopted 2004; cap.US $7.3m., res $83.2m., dep. $4,392.2m. (Dec. 2011); CEO RICHARD INGLE.

INSURANCE

Jersey Mutual Insurance Soc.: 74 Halkett Pl., St Helier, JE1 1BT; tel. (1534) 734246; fax (1534) 733381; e-mail info@jerseymutual.com; internet www.jerseymutual.com; f. 1869; general and household; Pres. A. MOLLET; Gen. Man. R. A. JEANNE.

Trade and Industry

CHAMBER OF COMMERCE

Jersey Chamber of Commerce: Chamber House, 25 Pier Rd, St Helier, JE1 4HF; tel. (1534) 724536; fax (1534) 724942; e-mail admin@jerseychamber.com; internet www.jerseychamber.com; f. 1768; Pres. RAY SHEAD; Head, Marketing and Operations CATHERINE HARGREAVES; 500 mems.

Utilities

Electricity

Jersey Electricity PLC: The Powerhouse, POB 45, Queen's Rd, St Helier, JE4 8NY; tel. (1534) 505460; fax (1534) 505565; e-mail jec@jec .co.uk; internet www.jec.co.uk; f. 1924; Chair. GEOFFREY GRIME; CEO CHRIS AMBLER.

Gas

Jersey Gas Co Ltd: POB 169, Tunnell St, St Helier, JE4 8RE; tel. (1534) 755500; fax (1534) 769822; e-mail jerseygas@jsy-gas.com; internet www.jsygas.com; Man. Dir PAUL GARLICK.

Water

Jersey New Waterworks Co Ltd (Jersey Water): Mulcaster House, Westmount Rd, St Helier, JE1 1DG; tel. (1534) 707300; fax (1534) 707400; e-mail info@jerseywater.je; internet www .jerseywater.je; 73.9% stake owned by States of Jersey; Chair. KEVIN KEEN; Man. Dir HOWARD SNOWDEN.

Transport

SHIPPING

The harbour of St Helier has 1,400 m of cargo working quays, with 10 berths in dredged portions (2.29 m) and eight drying berths.

Condor Ferries: The Elizabeth Terminal, St Helier; tel. (1534) 601000; e-mail reservations@condorferries.co.uk; internet www .condorferries.co.uk; head office in Guernsey; fast ferry and conventional ferry services between the UK, Channel Islands and France.

CIVIL AVIATION

The States of Jersey Airport is at St Peter, Jersey.

Tourism

In 2011 Jersey recorded some 689,700 tourist arrivals; 334,400 visitors stayed in paid accommodation. Tourist receipts in that year were £242m.

Jersey Tourism: Liberation Pl., St Helier, JE1 1BB; tel. (1534) 448800; fax (1534) 448898; e-mail info@jersey.com; internet www .jersey.com; Dir DAVID DE CARTERET.

THE ISLE OF MAN

Introduction

The Isle of Man lies in the Irish Sea between the Cumbrian coast of England and Northern Ireland. It is a dependency of the Crown and does not form part of the United Kingdom or the European Union. It has its own legislative assembly and legal and administrative systems, its laws depending for their validity on Orders made by the Queen in Council. Her Majesty's Government in the United Kingdom is responsible for the defence and international relations of the island, and the Crown is ultimately responsible for its good government. However, control of direct taxation is exercised by the Manx Government (headed by a Chief Minister) and, although most rates of indirect taxation are the same on the island as in the United Kingdom, there is some divergence of rates. The capital is Douglas. The population of the Isle of Man was 84,497, according to the census of 27 March 2011.

The head of state of the Isle of Man is the British monarch as the Lord of Mann. The Lieutenant-Governor, who is the Crown's personal representative on the island, is appointed by the head of state (on the advice of the Chief Minister, the President of Tynwald and the First Deemster/Head of the Judiciary) for a five-year term. The legislature is Tynwald, comprising two branches, the Legislative Council and the House of Keys, sitting together as one body, but voting separately on all questions except in certain eventualities. The House of Keys, the lower chamber, has 24 members, who represent single member and multi-member constituencies and are elected by adult suffrage for five years. Eight of the 11 members of the Legislative Council are elected by the House of Keys. The remainder are ex officio members: the Lord Bishop of Sodor and Man, the Attorney-General, and the President of Tynwald, who is elected by all the members of Tynwald.

In addition to the British public holidays, the Isle of Man also celebrates Senior Race Day of the annual Isle of Man Tourist Trophy (TT) Races (which falls on 14 June in 2013 and 13 June in 2014) and Tynwald Day (5 July).

Statistical Survey

Source: Isle of Man Government Offices, Bucks Rd, Douglas; tel. (1624) 685711; internet www.gov.im.

AREA AND POPULATION

Area: 572 sq km (221 sq miles).

Population (at census of 27 March 2011): 84,497 (males 41,971, females 42,526).

Density (at 2011 census): 147.7 per sq km.

Population by Age and Sex (census, 27–28 March 2011): *0–14:* 14,036 (males 7,302, females 6,734); *15–64:* 55,475 (males 27,877, females 27,598); *65 and over:* 14,986 (males 6,792, females 8,194); *Total* 84,497 (males 41,971, females 42,526).

Principal Localities (2011 census): Douglas (capital) 27,935; Onchan 9,283; Ramsey 7,809; Peel 5,092; Braddan 3,582; Port Erin 3,531; Castletown 3,093.

Births and Deaths (2011): Live births 938 (birth rate 11.1 per 1,000); Deaths 816 (death rate 9.7 per 1,000).

Economically Active Population (2011 census): Agriculture, etc. 850; Manufacturing 2,295; Construction 3,352; Electricity, gas and water 878; Transport and communication 3,037; Wholesale and retail trade 4,504; Entertainment, catering and tourist accommodation 2,808; Banking, finance and insurance 6,553; Real estate and renting 1,049; Other professional, business and scientific services 5,034; Education 2,795; Medical and health services 3,539; Public administration 3,058; Other services 3,382; *Total employed* 43,134 (males 23,126, females 20,008); Unemployed 1,475 (males 907, females 568); *Total labour force* 44,609 (males 24,033, females 20,576).

AGRICULTURE, ETC.

Crops (area in acres, 2011): Cereals and potatoes 10,674; Grass 65,332; Rough grazing 28,067.

Livestock (2011): Cattle 30,290; Sheep 133,703; Pigs 376; Poultry 12,751.

Fishing (2011): *Amount Landed* (metric tons): Scallops 1,534; Queen scallops 4,529; Crabs 554. *Value of Landings*: Scallops £2.6m.; Queen scallops £1.4m.; Crab £0.4m.

FINANCE

Currency and Exchange Rates: 100 pence = 1 pound sterling (£). *Dollar and Euro Equivalents* (31 December 2012): US $1 = 63.37 pence; €1 = 83.61 pence; £10 = $15.78 = €11.96.

Note: The Isle of Man is in monetary union with the United Kingdom. It has its own coins and notes, but United Kingdom coins and notes are also legal tender.

Budget (£ million, 2013/14, estimates): *Total Revenue* 516.9 (Customs and excise 312.0; Income and other taxes 191.0); *Total Expenditure* 502.5 (Health and social security 270.6).

Cost of Living (Retail Price Index; base: January 2000 = 100): All items 135.4 in 2009; 142.2 in 2010; 150.7 in 2011.

Gross National Income (GNI) (£ million at current factor cost): 3,414.8 in 2008/09; 3,417.3 in 2009/10; 3,647.7 in 2010/11.

Gross Domestic Product by Economic Activity (£ million at current factor cost, 2010/11): Agriculture, hunting, forestry and fishing 26.4; Mining and quarrying 13.4; Manufacturing 155.8; Electricity, gas and water supply 58.7; Construction 172.5; Wholesale and retail trade, repair of motor vehicles, motorcycles and personal and household goods 221.4; Transport and communications 237.3; Catering and entertainment and tourist accommodation 51.0; Financial services, real estate, renting and business activities 1,218.9; Other professional, educational, scientific and medical service activities 1,058.8; Public administration 143.4; Other services 111.3; *Sub-total* 3,468.7; Imputed rents, less adjustments for financial intermediation services indirectly measured, government depreciation of fixed assets and non-profit institutions serving households 39.2; *Total* 3,507.9.

TRANSPORT

Road Traffic (registered vehicles, 2001): Private 45,195; Engineering 385; Goods 4,489; Agricultural 931; Hackney 790; Public service 146; Motorcycles, scooters and tricycles 4,519.

Shipping (2010/11): Passengers handled 649,049; General freight handled 137,735 metric tons; Registered merchant vessels 373; Other registered vessels 686; Total displacement ('000 grt) 12,350.

Civil Aviation: Passengers handled 710,791 (2011); Freight carried 4,594 metric tons (2003).

TOURISM

Tourist Arrivals (2011): Staying visitors 223,371; Day visitors 7,785; Business travellers 68,622.

COMMUNICATIONS MEDIA

Telephone Connections (2001): Fixed 56,000; Mobile 32,000.

Television Licences (2000): 28,601.

EDUCATION

State Primary: 35 schools (2007/08), 6,578 students (2010/11).

State Secondary: 5 schools (2007/08), 4,679 students (2010/11).

Further and Higher Education: 1 college (2008/09), 960 students (2010/11).

There are, in addition, two private schools.

Directory

The Government

HEAD OF STATE

Lord of Mann: HM Queen ELIZABETH II.

Lieutenant-Governor: ADAM WOOD.

COUNCIL OF MINISTERS
(May 2013)

Chief Minister: ALLAN BELL.

Minister of Community, Culture and Leisure: GRAHAM CREGEEN.

Minister of Environment, Food and Agriculture: PHIL GAWNE.

Minister of Economic Development: JOHN SHIMMIN.

Minister of Education and Children: TIMOTHY CROOKALL.
Minister of Health: DAVID ANDERSON.
Minister of Home Affairs: JUAN WATTERSON.
Minister of Infrastructure: DAVID CRETNEY.
Minister of Social Care: CHRIS ROBERTSHAW.
Minister of the Treasury: EDDIE TEARE.

GOVERNMENT OFFICES

Isle of Man Government: Government Office, Bucks Rd, Douglas, IM1 3PN; tel. (1624) 685702; fax (1624) 685710; e-mail chief.minister@cso.gov.im; internet www.gov.im.

Department of Community, Culture and Leisure: Illiam Dhone House, 2 Circular Rd, Douglas, IM1 1PG; tel. (1624) 686817; fax (1624) 686709; e-mail dccl@gov.im; internet www.gov.im/dccl.

Department of Economic Development: St George's Court, Upper Church St, Douglas, IM1 1EX; tel. (1624) 686400; internet www.gov.im/ded.

Department of Education and Children: Hamilton House, Peel Rd, Douglas, IM1 5EZ; tel. (1624) 685820; fax (1624) 685834; e-mail admin@doe.gov.im; internet www.gov.im/education.

Department of Environment, Food and Agriculture: Thie Slieau Whallian, Foxdale Rd, St Johns, IM4 3AS; tel. (1624) 685835; e-mail defa@gov.im; internet www.gov.im/defa.

Department of Health: Crookall House, Demesne Rd, Douglas, IM1 3QA; tel. (1624) 642608; fax (1624) 685130; e-mail dh@gov.im; internet www.gov.im/health.

Department of Home Affairs: Homefield, 88 Woodbourne Rd, Douglas, IM2 3AP; tel. (1624) 694300; fax (1624) 621298; e-mail generalenquiries.dha@gov.im; internet www.gov.im/dha.

Department of Infrastructure: Sea Terminal, Douglas, IM1 2RF; tel. (1624) 686600; internet www.gov.im/transport.

Department of Social Care: Markwell House, Market St, Douglas, IM1 2RZ; tel. (1624) 685656; e-mail socialsecurity@gov.im; internet www.gov.im/socialcare.

Department of the Treasury: Government Office, Bucks Rd, Douglas, IM1 3PZ; tel. (1624) 685586; internet www.gov.im/treasury.

External Relations Division: Government Office, Bucks Rd, Douglas, IM1 3PN; tel. (1624) 685711; internet www.gov.im/cso.

Legislature

TYNWALD

President: CLARE CHRISTIAN.
Deputy President: STEPHEN CHARLES RODAN.

Legislative Council (Upper House)

President of the Council: CLARE CHRISTIAN.
Lord Bishop of Sodor and Man: Rt Rev. ROBERT M. E. PATERSON.
Attorney-General: JOHN QUINN (acting).
Members appointed by the House of Keys: ROBERT PHILIP BRAIDWOOD, EDWARD ALAN CROWE, MICHAEL COLEMAN, CHARLES GEOFFREY CORKISH, DUDLEY MICHAEL WILLIAM BUTT, ALEXANDER FRANK DOWNIE, JUAN RICHARD TURNER, T. P. WILD.
Clerk: JONATHAN KING.

House of Keys (Lower House)

Speaker: STEPHEN CHARLES RODAN.
Clerk of Tynwald, Secretary of the House and Counsel to the Speaker: ROGER IAN SEXTON PHILLIPS.

The House of Keys consists of 24 members, elected by adult suffrage for five years—eight for Douglas, three for Onchan, two for Ramsey, one each for Peel and Castletown, and nine for rural districts. Most members of the House of Keys are elected as independents. However, a small number are affiliated to political parties. The last general election took place on 29 September 2011, at which 21 seats were won by independents and three by the Liberal Vannin Party.

Political Organizations

Liberal Vannin: Troutbeck Strang Rd, Union Mills, IM4 4NP; tel. (1624) 853352; e-mail office@liberalvannin.org; internet www.liberalvannin.org; f. 2006; Chair. ROY REDMAYNE; Leader PETER KARRAN.

Manx Labour Party: f. 1918; Spokesperson DAVID CRETNEY.

Mec Vannin: internet www.mecvannin.im; f. 1962; advocates the establishment of the Isle of Man as a sovereign republic; Pres. BERNARD MOFFATT; Chair. MARK KERMODE.

Judicial System

The Isle of Man is, for legal purposes, an autonomous sovereign country under the British Crown, with its own legislature and its own independent judiciary administering its own common or customary and statute law. The law of the Isle of Man is, in most essential matters, the same as the law of England and general principles of equity administered by the English Courts are followed by the Courts of the Isle of Man unless they conflict with established local precedents. Her Majesty's High Court of Justice of the Isle of Man is based upon the English system but modified and simplified to meet local conditions. Justices of the Peace are appointed by the Lord Chancellor of Great Britain usually on the nomination of the Lieutenant-Governor. The Deemsters, the High Bailiff, the Mayor of Douglas, and the Chairmen of the Town and Village Commissioners are all ex officio Justices of the Peace. The Manx Court of Appeal consists of the Deemsters and the Judge of Appeal.

First Deemster and Clerk of the Rolls: DAVID DOYLE.
Second Deemster: ANDREW CORLETT.
Deemster: ALASTAIR MONTGOMERIE.
Judge of Appeal: GEOFFREY TATTERSALL.

Religion

CHRISTIANITY

The Church of England

The Isle of Man forms the diocese of Sodor and Man, comprising 28 parishes. The parish church of St German at Peel was designated a cathedral in 1980.

Lord Bishop of Sodor and Man: Rt Rev. ROBERT M. E. PATERSON, Bishop's House, The Falls, Tromode Rd, Douglas, IM4 4PZ; tel. (1624) 622108; fax (1624) 672890; e-mail bishop@sodorandman.im; internet www.gumbley.net/diocese.htm.

Roman Catholic Church

The deanery of the Isle of Man is part of the archdiocese of Liverpool. There are six Catholic churches on the island.

Dean of the Isle of Man: Very Rev. Canon PHILIP GILLESPIE, St Mary of the Isle, Hill St, Douglas, IM1 3EG; tel. (1624) 675509; fax (1624) 674359; e-mail bjpalger@yahoo.co.uk.

Other Churches

There are also congregations of the following denominations: Baptist, Bethel Non-Denominational, Christadelphian, Congregational, Greek Orthodox, Independent Methodist, Methodist, Presbyterian, Elim Pentecostal, United Reformed, and Religious Society of Friends (Quakers); also Christian Science, Jehovah's Witnesses and the Church of Jesus Christ of Latter-day Saints.

There are small Bahá'í, Jewish and Muslim communities on the island.

The Press

Isle of Man Courier: Publishing House, Peel Rd, Douglas, IM1 5PZ; tel. (1624) 670000; fax (1624) 661041; e-mail john.sherrocks@newsiom.co.im; internet www.iomonline.co.im; f. 1884; weekly; Editor RICHARD BUTT; circ. 37,102 (2009).

Isle of Man Examiner: Publishing House, Peel Rd, Douglas, IM1 5PZ; tel. (1624) 695695; fax (1624) 661041; internet www.iomtoday.co.im; f. 1880; owned by Johnston Press; weekly; Editor RICHARD BUTT; circ. 11,019 (2011).

The Manx Independent: Publishing House, Peel Rd, Douglas, IM1 5PZ; tel. (1624) 670000; fax (1624) 661041; e-mail john.sherrocks@newsiom.co.im; internet www.iomonline.co.im; f. 1987; Fri; Editor RICHARD BUTT; circ. 10,537 (2011).

Manx Tails Magazine: Media House, Cronkbourne, Douglas, IM4 4SB; tel. (1624) 696565; fax (1624) 625623; e-mail mail@manninmedia.co.im; internet www.manxtails.co.im; f. 1982 as in-flight magazine of Manx Airlines; launched as an all-island publication in 2002; monthly; distributed free of charge; Editor SIMON RICHARDSON; circ. 36,400.

Sea Breezes Magazine: Media House, Cronkbourne, Douglas, IM4 4SB; tel. (1624) 696573; fax (1624) 661655; e-mail sb.enquiries@seabreezes.co.im; internet www.seabreezes.co.im; f. 1919; Editor HAMISH C. ROSS.

Publishers

Amulree Publications: Lossan y Twoaie, Glen Rd, Laxey, IM4 7AN; tel. (1624) 862238; e-mail amulree@mcb.net; internet www.manxshop.com; f. 1993; Propr BILL SNELLING.

Electrochemical Publications Ltd: Asahi House, 10 Church Rd, Port Erin, IM9 6AQ; tel. (1624) 834941; fax (1624) 835400; Man. Dir WILLIAM GOLDIE.

Lily Publications Ltd: POB 33, Ramsey, IM99 4LP; tel. (1624) 898446; fax (1624) 898449; e-mail sales@lilypublications.co.uk; internet www.lilypublications.co.uk; f. 1991; Man. Dir MILES COWSILL.

Mannin Media Group Ltd: Media House, Cronkbourne, Douglas, IM4 4SB; tel. (1624) 696565; fax (1624) 625623; e-mail mail@manninmedia.co.im; internet www.manninmedia.co.im; Chief Exec. STEVEN BROWN.

The Manx Experience: Sunnybank Ave, Birch Hill, Onchan, IM3 3BW; tel. (1624) 627727; fax (1624) 663627; e-mail mail@manxexperience.co.uk; Man. Dir GWYNNETH BROWN, STEVEN BROWN.

Pines Press: The Pines, Ballelin, Maughold, Ramsey, IM7 1HJ; tel. (1624) 862030; f. 1987; Dir B. CLYNE.

Keith Uren Publishing: 12 Manor Lane, Farmhill, Braddan, IM2 2NX; tel. and fax (1624) 611100; e-mail portfolio@manx.net; internet keithurenpublishing.com; f. 1991; magazines; Man. Dir KEITH UREN.

Vathek Publishing Ltd: Bridge House, Dalby, IM5 3BP; tel. (1624) 844056; fax (1624) 845043; e-mail mlw@vathek.com; internet www.vathek.com; legal journals; Man. Dir MAIRWEN LLOYD-WILLIAMS.

Broadcasting and Communications

Isle of Man Communications Commission: St Andrew's House, 2nd Floor, Douglas, IM1 2PX; tel. (1624) 677022; fax (1624) 626499; e-mail margaret.king@iomcc.im; internet www.gov.im/government/boards/cc.xml; appointed by the Isle of Man Govt to represent the island's interests in all matters of telecommunications, radio and television; Chair. JUAN WATTERSON (Minister of Home Affairs); Dir CARMEL MCLAUGHLIN.

TELECOMMUNICATIONS

Manx Telecom Ltd: Isle of Man Business Park, Cooil Rd, Braddan, IM99 1HX; POB 100, Douglas, IM99 1HX; tel. (1624) 624624; fax (1624) 636011; e-mail mail@manx-telecom.com; internet www.manx-telecom.com; f. 1986; subsidiary of Telefónica O₂ UK PLC; Man. Dir MIKE DEE.

Sure: 14 Athol St, Douglas, IM1 1JA; tel. (1624) 247247; e-mail talk@surecw.com; internet www.surecw.com; owned by Batelco; part of Cable and Wireless; mobile, broadband and fixed-line services; operates under the brand name of Sure Mobile; CEO EDDIE SAINTS.

BROADCASTING
Radio and Television

BBC: Radio and Television (see United Kingdom).

Energy FM: 100 Market St, Douglas, IM1 2PH; tel. (1624) 611936; fax (1624) 664699; internet www.energyfm.net; f. 2001.

ITV Border: Television (see United Kingdom).

Manx Radio: Broadcasting House, POB 1368, Douglas, IM99 1SW; tel. (1624) 682600; fax (1624) 682604; e-mail reception@manxradio.com; internet www.manxradio.com; f. 1960; commercial station operated (by agreement with the Isle of Man Government) by Radio Manx Ltd; Chair. DAVID NORTH; Man. Dir ANTHONY PUGH.

3FM: 45 Victoria St, Douglas, IM1 3RS; tel. (1624) 616333; fax (1624) 614333; internet www.three.fm; music.

The Isle of Man also receives television programmes from Channel 4 and Five.

Finance

Financial Supervision Commission: POB 58, Finch Hill House, Bucks Rd, Douglas, IM99 1DT; tel. (1624) 689300; fax (1624) 689399; e-mail fsc@gov.im; internet www.fsc.gov.im; f. 1983; responsible for the licensing, authorization and supervision of banks, building societies, investment businesses, collective investment schemes and fiduciary service providers; Chair. ROSEMARY PENN; Chief Exec. JOHN ASPDEN.

Treasury: Government Office, Bucks Rd, Douglas, IM1 3PU; tel. (1624) 685586; fax (1624) 685662; e-mail treasuryadmin@gov.im; internet www.gov.im/treasury; Minister ANNE CRAINE; Chief Financial Officer P. M. SHIMMIN.

BANKING

(cap. = capital; res = reserves; dep. = deposits; m. = million; brs = branches; amounts in pounds sterling)

At 31 December 2012 there were 32 licensed banks and building societies in the Isle of Man. At 31 December 2012 total bank deposits amounted to some £50,192m. The Financial Supervision Commission may allow a major bank to establish a presence on the island on a managed bank basis, by awarding an 'offshore' banking licence.

AIB Bank (CI) Ltd: 10 Finch Rd, Douglas, IM1 2PT; tel. (1624) 639639; fax (1624) 639636; e-mail one@aib.im; internet www.aib.im; f. 1977; Dir CHRISTOPHER HOWLAND.

AIB International Savings Ltd: Jubilee Bldgs, Victoria St, Douglas, IM1 2SH; tel. (1624) 698000; fax (1624) 698001; e-mail enquiries@angloirishbank.co.im; internet www.angloirishbank.co.im; fmrly Anglo Irish Bank Corpn (International) PLC; name changed to present 2011; wholly owned subsidiary of Allied Irish Banks PLC (Ireland); cap. 135m., res 60.2m., dep. 3,217.4m. (Dec. 2009); f. 1988; Man. Dir DAVID MACGREGOR.

Alliance & Leicester International Ltd: POB 226, 19–21 Prospect Hill, Douglas, IM99 1RY; tel. (1624) 641888; fax (1624) 663577; internet www.alil.co.im; owned by Banco Santander, SA (Spain); cap. 125m., dep. 3,355.2m. (Dec. 2011); CEO TANIA SOBEY; Man. Dir JOHN PEARSON.

Bank of Ireland (IOM) Ltd: POB 246, Christian Rd, Douglas, IM99 1XF; tel. (1624) 644222; fax (1624) 644298; e-mail info@boioffshore.com; internet www.boioffshore.com; f. 1981; cap. 25m., res 10m., dep. 603.7m. (March 2011); Chair. J. L. M. QUINN; Man. Dir MICHAEL MCKAY.

Barclays Private Bank and Trust (Isle of Man) Ltd: POB 48, Queen Victoria House, Victoria St, Douglas, IM99 1DF; tel. (1624) 682828; fax (1624) 620905; internet www.barclays.co.uk/privatebank; cap. 5m., dep. 159.6m. (Dec. 2011); Man. Dir ALAN R. PATRICK.

Barclays Private Clients International Ltd: POB 213, Eagle Court, 25 Circular Rd, Douglas, IM99 1RH; tel. (1624) 684000; fax (1624) 684321; international banking services; cap. 50.2m., res 741.8m., dep. 17,163.7m. (Dec. 2011); Man. Dir GREG ELLISON; 6 brs.

Britannia International Ltd: POB 231, Britannia House, Athol St, Douglas, IM99 1SD; tel. (1624) 681100; fax (1624) 681105; e-mail enquiries@britanniainternational.com; internet www.britanniainternational.com; f. 1988; 'offshore' subsidiary of The Co-operative Bank PLC; cap. 10m., dep. 1,794.6m. (Dec. 2011); Man. Dir MARK BERESFORD.

Cayman National Bank and Trust Co (Isle of Man) Ltd: Cayman National House, 4–8 Hope St, Douglas, IM1 1AQ; tel. (1624) 646900; fax (1624) 662192; e-mail banking@caymannationalwealth.com; internet www.caymannationalwealth.com; f. 1985; subsidiary of Cayman National Corpn, Cayman Islands; cap. 3.5m., dep. 86.2m. (Sept. 2012); Man. Dir IAN BANCROFT.

Conister Bank Ltd: Conister House, Isle of Man Business Park, Cooil Rd, Braddan, IM2 2QZ; tel. (1624) 694694; fax (1624) 624278; e-mail info@conistertrust.com; internet www.conistertrust.com; f. 1935; specializes in asset finance; cap. 5m., dep. 55.9m. (Dec. 2011); Chair. PETER HAMMONDS; Man. Dir SIMON HULL; 1 br.

Duncan Lawrie (IOM) Ltd: 14–15 Mount Havelock, Douglas, IM1 2QG; tel. (1624) 620770; fax (1624) 676315; e-mail iom@duncanlawrie.com; internet www.duncanlawrie.com; cap. 6.8m., dep. 104.1m. (Dec. 2012); Chair. P. J. FIELD; Man. Dir ALAN M. MOLLOY.

Habib European Bank Ltd: 14 Athol St, Douglas, IM1 1JA; tel. (1624) 622554; fax (1624) 627135; e-mail habibbank@manx.net; internet www.habibbank.com; f. 1982; subsidiary of Habib Bank AG (Switzerland); cap. 5m., dep. 55.2m. (Dec. 2011); Sr Vice-Pres. A. SHAIKH.

Kleinwort Benson Bank (Isle of Man) Ltd: POB 203, St George's Court, Upper Church St, Douglas, IM99 1RB; tel. (1624) 643200; fax (1624) 622039; e-mail infoiom@closepb.com; internet www.closepb.com; f. 1976 as Rea Brothers (Isle of Man) Ltd; present name adopted 2011; merchant bank; cap. 5m., dep. 227.7m. (July 2010); Man. Dir GRAHAM SHEWARD.

Nationwide International Ltd: POB 217, 5–11 St George's St, Douglas, IM99 1RN; tel. (1624) 696000; fax (1624) 696001; internet www.nationwideinternational.com; f. 1990; Chair. CARL GANDY; Man. Dir PHILIP DUNNE.

Nedbank Private Wealth (IOM) Ltd: St Mary's Court, 20 Hill St, Douglas, IM1 1EU; tel. (1624) 645000; fax (1624) 627218; e-mail iom@nedbankprivatewealth.com; internet www.nedbankprivatewealth.com; f. 1987 as Robert Fleming (IOM) Ltd; present name adopted 2012; cap. 5m., res 0.3m., dep. 569.7m. (Dec. 2011); Chair. TOM BOARDMAN; Man. Dir GREG HORTON.

Standard Bank Isle of Man Ltd: Standard Bank House, 1 Circular Rd, Douglas, IM1 1SB; tel. (1624) 643643; fax (1624) 643800; e-mail sbiom@standardbank.com; internet www.sboff.com; f. 1972 as Standard Chartered Bank (Isle of Man) Ltd; present name adopted 1995; cap. 5m., res 0.9m., dep. 1,117.1m. (Dec. 2011); Man. Dir J. COYLE.

Zurich Bank International Ltd: POB 422, Lord St, Douglas, IM99 3AF; tel. (1624) 671666; fax (1624) 627526; e-mail relationship.banking@zurich.com; internet www.zurichbankinternational.com;

f. 1983 as Dunbar International Ltd; present name adopted 2003; cap. 10.5m., dep. 482.2m. (Dec. 2011); Chair. RICHARD DESMOND; Man. Dir DAVID PEACH.

'Offshore' Banks

Coutts & Co Isle of Man: POB 59, Royal Bank House, 2 Victoria St, Douglas, IM99 INJ; tel. (1624) 632222; fax (1624) 620988; e-mail info@coutts.com; internet www.coutts.com.

Isle of Man Bank Ltd: POB 13, 2 Athol St, Douglas, IM99 1AN; tel. (1624) 637000; fax (1624) 624686; internet www.iombank.com; f. 1865; cap. 7.5m., dep. 1,409.3m. (Dec. 2011); bankers to Isle of Man Govt; mem. of the Royal Bank of Scotland Group; Chair. JAMES MORRIS; 10 brs.

Lloyds TSB Offshore Ltd: POB 8, Victory House, Prospect Hill, Douglas, IM99 1AH; tel. (1624) 657848; fax (1624) 628267; e-mail cbiom@lloydstsb-offshore.com; internet www.lloydstsb-offshore.com.

The Royal Bank of Scotland International Ltd: POB 151, Royal Bank House, 2 Victoria St, Douglas, IM99 1NJ; tel. (1624) 646464; fax (1624) 646497; e-mail marketingiom@rbsint.com; internet www.rbsinternational.com; Chief Exec. IAN HENDERSON.

Restricted Banks

Merrill Lynch Bank and Trust Co (Cayman) Ltd: Belgravia House, 34–44 Circular Rd, Douglas, IM1 1QW; tel. (1624) 688600; fax (1624) 688601; internet www.ml.com; Man. N. ORDERS.

INSURANCE

There were 142 authorized insurance companies in the Isle of Man at 31 December 2012, including:

Canada Life International Ltd: Canada Life House, Alexandra Rd, Castletown, IM9 1RJ; tel. (1624) 820200; fax (1624) 820201; e-mail adviser.support@canadalifeint.com; internet www.canadalifeint.com; f. 1987; Man. Dir SEAN CHRISTIAN.

Castletown Insurance Services Ltd: Compton House, Parliament Sq., Castletown, IM9 1LA; tel. (1624) 827710; fax (1624) 827709; e-mail rdrinkwater@castletowninsurance.com; internet www.castletowninsurance.com; f. 1998; Man. Dir RICHARD DRINKWATER.

CMI Insurance Co Ltd: Clerical Medical House, Victoria Rd, Douglas, IM99 1LT; tel. (1624) 638888; fax (1624) 625900; e-mail iom.policyadministration1@clericalmedical.com; internet www.offshore.clericalmedical.com; part of Lloyds Banking Group (United Kingdom).

Friends Provident International Ltd: Royal Court, Castletown, IM9 1RA; tel. (1624) 821212; fax (1624) 824405; e-mail rowservicing@fpiom.com; internet www.fpinternational.com; Man. Dir PAUL TUNNICLIFFE.

Hansard International Ltd: POB 192, Harbour Court, Lord St, Douglas, IM99 1QL; tel. (1624) 688000; fax (1624) 688008; e-mail enquiries@hansard.com; internet www.hansard.com; f. 1986; Exec. Chair. Dr LEONARD S. POLONSKY.

Isle of Man Assurance Ltd: IOMA House, Hope St, Douglas, IM1 1AP; tel. (1624) 681200; fax (1624) 681390; e-mail info@ioma.co.im; internet www.ioma.co.im; Chair. ROBIN BIGLAND; Man. Dir NIGEL WOOD.

Royal Insurance Service Co (IOM) Ltd: Jubilee Bldgs, 1 Victoria St, Douglas, IM99 1BF; tel. (1624) 620625; fax (1624) 620934; Man. DAVID STACEY.

Royal London 360°: Royal London House, Isle of Man Business Park, Cooil Rd, Douglas, IM2 2SP; tel. (1624) 681681; fax (1624) 677336; e-mail csc@royallondon360.com; internet www.royallondon360.com; f. 2008 by merger of Scottish Life International Insurance Co Ltd and Scottish Provident International Life Assurance Ltd; subsidiary of Royal London Mutual Insurance Society Ltd; CEO DAVID KNEESHAW.

Royal Skandia Life Assurance Ltd: POB 159, Skandia House, King Edward Rd, Onchan, IM99 1NU; tel. (1624) 655555; fax (1624) 611715; e-mail support@royalskandia.com; internet www.royalskandia.com.

Tower Insurance Co Ltd: POB 27, Jubilee Bldgs, 1 Victoria St, Douglas, IM99 1BF; tel. (1624) 645900; fax (1624) 663864; e-mail tower.insurance@uk.rsagroup.com; internet www.towerinsurance.co.im; subsidiary of RSA Insurance Group PLC (United Kingdom); Man. Dir PETER GALLAGHER.

Zurich International Life Ltd: 43–51 Athol St, Douglas, IM99 1EF; tel. (1624) 662266; fax (1624) 662038; e-mail helppoint.iom@zurich.com; internet www.zurichintlife.com.

Supervisory Authority

Insurance and Pensions Authority: Finch Hill House, Ground Floor, Bucks Rd, Douglas, IM1 3DF; tel. (1624) 646000; fax (1624) 646001; e-mail ipa@gov.im; internet www.gov.im/ipa; Chief Exec. DAVID A. VICK.

Trade and Industry
CHAMBER OF COMMERCE

Isle of Man Chamber of Commerce: 1st Floor, Capital House, Circular Rd, Douglas, IMI 1AG; tel. (1624) 674941; fax (1624) 663367; e-mail enquiries@iomchamber.org.im; internet www.iomchamber.org.im; f. 1956; 300 mems; Pres. NICK VERARDI; Chair. MIKE SHAW; Chief Exec. MIKE HENNESSY.

UTILITIES
Electricity

Manx Electricity Authority: POB 177, Douglas, IM99 1PS; tel. (1624) 687687; fax (1624) 687612; e-mail mea@gov.im; internet www.gov.im/mea; Chair. EDDIE G. LOWEY; Chief Exec. P. E. KING.

Gas

Manx Gas Ltd: Murdoch House, South Quay, Douglas, IM1 5PA; tel. (1624) 644444; fax (1624) 626528; e-mail info@manxgas.co.im; internet www.manxgas.com; f. 1999 by merger of Douglas Gas and Calor Manx Gas; Man. Dir TONY NICHOLLS.

Water

Isle of Man Water and Sewage Authority: Drill Hall, Tromode Rd, Douglas, IM2 5PA; tel. (1624) 695949; fax (1624) 695956; e-mail water@gov.im; internet www.gov.im/water; also responsible for sewage system; Chair. JOHN HOUGHTON; Chief Exec. PETER WINSTANLEY.

TRADE UNIONS

In 1991 the Trade Union Act was approved by Tynwald, providing for the registration of trade unions. Although trade unions had been active previously on the Isle of Man, they had not received legal recognition.

Manx Fish Producers' Organization Ltd: Heritage Centre, The Quay, Peel, IM5 1TA; tel. (1624) 842144; fax (1624) 844395; e-mail manx.fa@lineone.net; Chair. MICHAEL MOORE.

Manx National Farmers' Union: Agriculture House, Ballafletcher Farm Rd, Tromode, IM4 4QE; tel. (1624) 662204; e-mail gensec@manx-nfu.org; internet www.manx-nfu.org; Pres. RAY CRAINE; Gen. Sec. BELINDA LEACH.

Unite: 25 Fort St, Douglas, IM2 2LJ; tel. (1624) 621156; fax (1624) 676998.

Transport
RAILWAYS

The total length of railways in Isle of Man is 63 km (39 miles), of which 35 km (22 miles) were electrified.

Isle of Man Transport: Transport Headquarters, Banks Circus, Douglas, IM1 5PT; tel. (1624) 662525; fax (1624) 663637; e-mail info@busandrail.dtl.gov.im; internet www.iombusandrail.info; 29 km (18 miles) of electric track; also 25 km (16 miles) of steam railway track, and Snaefell Mountain Railway (7 km of electric track); 85 buses; Head of Rail Services JOHN KENNAUGH; Head of Bus Services DAVE KINRADE.

ROADS

In 2008, there were 500 km (311 miles) of roads on the Isle of Man. Most of the buses are operated by Bus Vannin, a department of the Isle of Man Government.

Dept of Transport: Sea Terminal, Douglas, IM1 2RF; tel. (1624) 686600; fax (1624) 686617; e-mail enquiries@dot.gov.im; internet www.gov.im/transport; Chief Exec. IAN THOMPSON.

SHIPPING

At 31 December 2012 the flag registered fleet comprised 577 vessels, totalling 14.5m. grt. of which 83 were bulk vessels, 48 were gas tankers and 58 were general cargo ships.

Döhle (IOM) Ltd: Fort Anne, Douglas, IM1 5PD; tel. (1624) 649649; e-mail info@doehle-iom.com; internet www.doehle-iom.com; fmrly Midocean Maritime Ltd; present name adopted 2001; part of Peter Döhle Group (Germany); ship management; Chair. JÖRG VANSELOW; COO CLIFF DAVIES.

Isle of Man Steam Packet Co Ltd: Imperial Bldgs, Douglas, IM1 2BY; tel. (1624) 645700; fax (1624) 645703; internet www .steam-packet.com; f. 1830; daily services operate all the year round between Douglas and Heysham and Liverpool; during the summer there are frequent services between the island and Dublin and Belfast; Chair. ROBERT QUAYLE; Chief Exec. MARK WOODWARD.

Mezeron Ltd: East Quay, Ramsey, IM8 1BG; tel. (1624) 812302; fax (1624) 815613; e-mail info@mezeron.com; internet www.mezeron .com; f. 1983; cargo services; acquired by Döhle (IOM) Ltd in 2008; Man. Dir NORMAN LEECE.

Ramsey Steamship Co Ltd: 8 Auckland Terrace, Parliament St, Ramsey, IM8 1AF; tel. (1624) 816202; fax (1624) 816206; e-mail tony@ramsey-steamship.com; internet www.ramsey-steamship .com; f. 1913; cargo services; Man. Dir A. G. KENNISH.

Tufton Oceanic (Isle of Man) Ltd: 2nd Floor, St George's Court, Upper Church St, Douglas, IM1 1EE; tel. (1624) 663616; fax (1624) 663918; e-mail tufton@tuftonoceanic.com; internet www .tuftonoceanic.com; Chair. TAKIS KLERIDES; Man. Dir CATO BRAHDE.

CIVIL AVIATION

Citywing: Hangar 9, Isle of Man Airport, Ballasalla, IM9 2AY; tel. (1624) 822111; e-mail customer.services@citywing.com; internet www.citywing.com; f. 2006; fmrly called Manx2 Ltd; scheduled passenger flights to Belfast City and Belfast International, Blackpool, East Midlands, Gloucestershire, Jersey and Leeds/Bradford; Chair. NOEL HAYES; Man. Dir DAVID BUCK.

Island Aviation and Travel Ltd: Ronaldsway Airport, Ballasalla, IM9 2AS; tel. (1624) 824300; fax (1624) 824946; e-mail enquiries@ iaat.co.uk; internet www.iaat.co.uk; provides executive charters to world-wide destinations, runs air ambulance services, aircraft management, handling; Man. Dir JOHN CRITCHLEY.

Tourism

In 2011 a total of 223,371 tourists stayed at least one night on the Isle of Man.

Isle of Man Tourism Division: Dept of Economic Development, 1st Floor, St George's Court, Upper Church St, Douglas, IM1 1EX; tel. (1624) 686766; e-mail tourism@gov.im; internet www.visitisleofman .com; responsibilities of tourist board, also operates modern and vintage transport systems, a Victorian theatre and an indoor and outdoor sport and leisure complex; f. 1896; Head of Tourism ANGELA BYRNE.

UNITED KINGDOM OVERSEAS TERRITORIES

From February 1998 the British Dependent Territories were referred to as the United Kingdom Overseas Territories, following the announcement of the interim findings of a British government review of the United Kingdom's relations with the Overseas Territories. In March 1999 draft legislation confirming this change was published by the British Government: under the proposed legislation, the citizens of Overseas Territories would be granted the rights, already enjoyed by the citizens of Gibraltar and the Falkland Islands, to British citizenship and of residence in the United Kingdom. These entitlements were not reciprocal, and British citizens would not enjoy the same rights with regard to the Overseas Territories. The British Overseas Territories Act entered effect in May 2002. The British Government meanwhile announced its determination to ensure that legislation in the Overseas Territories adhered to British and European Union standards, particularly in the areas of financial regulation and human rights.

ANGUILLA

Introductory Survey

LOCATION, CLIMATE, LANGUAGE, RELIGION, FLAG, CAPITAL

Anguilla, a coralline island, is the most northerly of the Leeward Islands, lying 113 km (70 miles) to the north-west of Saint Christopher (St Kitts) and 8 km (5 miles) to the north of St Maarten/St Martin. Also included in the territory are the island of Sombrero, 48 km (30 miles) north of Anguilla, and several other uninhabited small islands. The climate is sub-tropical, the heat and humidity being tempered by the trade winds. Temperatures average 27°C (80°F) and mean annual rainfall is 914 mm (36 ins), the wettest months being September to December. English is the official language. Many Christian churches are represented, the principal denominations being the Anglican and Methodist Churches. The flag (proportions 3 by 5 on land, 1 by 2 at sea) has a dark blue field with the Union flag in the upper hoist corner and, in the centre of the fly, a white shield bearing three orange circling dolphins above a light blue base. The capital is The Valley.

CONTEMPORARY POLITICAL HISTORY

Historical Context

Anguilla, previously inhabited by Arawaks and Caribs, was a British colony from 1650 until 1967. From 1825 the island became increasingly associated with Saint Christopher (St Kitts) for administrative purposes (see chapter on Saint Christopher and Nevis). The inhabitants of Anguilla petitioned for separate status in 1875 and 1958. In February 1967, however, St Christopher-Nevis-Anguilla assumed the status of a State in Association with the United Kingdom, as did four other former British colonies in the Eastern Caribbean. These Associated States became independent internally, while the British Government retained responsibility for external affairs and defence.

Domestic Political Affairs

In May 1967 the Anguillans, under the leadership of Ronald Webster, a local businessman and head of the only political party, the People's Progressive Party (PPP), repudiated government from Saint Christopher. After attempts to repair the breach between Saint Christopher and Anguilla had failed, British security forces were deployed in Anguilla in March 1969 to install a British Commissioner. Members of London's Metropolitan Police Force remained on the island until the Anguilla Police Force was established in 1972. In July 1971 the British Parliament approved the Anguilla Act, one clause of which stipulated that, should Saint Christopher-Nevis-Anguilla decide to end its associated status, Anguilla could be separated from the other islands. In August the British Government's Anguilla Administration Order 1971 determined that the British Commissioner would continue to be responsible for the direct administration of the island, with the co-operation of a local elected council. The terms of this Order were superseded by the introduction of a new Constitution in February 1976. Anguilla formally separated from Saint Christopher-Nevis-Anguilla on 19 December 1980, assuming the status of British Dependent Territory. In accordance with the terms of the British Government's Anguilla Constitution Order of 1982, a new Constitution came into operation in Anguilla on 1 April 1982.

Legislative elections were held in March 1976, and Webster was appointed Chief Minister. In February 1977, following his defeat on a motion of confidence, he was replaced by Emile Gumbs as Chief Minister and as leader of the PPP (renamed the Anguilla National Alliance—ANA—in 1980). Webster was returned to power, to lead the recently formed Anguilla United Party (AUP), at a general election in May 1980. Webster's administration collapsed in May 1981 and Webster subsequently formed a new political party, the Anguilla People's Party (APP), which won a general election in June. A general election in March 1984, however, resulted in a conclusive defeat for the APP. Gumbs became Chief Minister, and pursued a policy of revitalizing the island's economy, mainly through tourism and attracting foreign investment. Webster resigned as leader of the APP, which was renamed the Anguilla Democratic Party (ADP).

The majority of the population expressed no desire for independence, but the new Government appealed for wider powers for the Executive Council, and for more aid and investment from the United Kingdom. In 1985 the Governor appointed a committee to review the Constitution, in response to an earlier unanimous request from the House of Assembly for modifications, particularly concerning the status of women and of persons born overseas of Anguillan parents. The amendments, which provided for the appointment of a Deputy Governor and designated international financial affairs (the 'offshore' banking sector) as the Governor's responsibility, came into effect in 1990.

Gumbs remained Chief Minister following a general election in February 1989. In 1991 the British Government abolished capital punishment for the crime of murder in Anguilla (as well as in several other British Dependent Territories).

A general election in March 1994 failed to produce a clear majority for any one party, and a coalition was subsequently formed by the ADP and the AUP. The AUP leader, Hubert Hughes, was subsequently appointed Chief Minister, replacing Sir Emile Gumbs (as he had become). On assuming the post, Hughes stated that he might seek Anguilla's independence from the United Kingdom.

The announcement by the British Government in January 1997 that it was considering the extension of its powers in the Dependent Territories of the Caribbean attracted criticism from Hughes. The proposed reintroduction of reserve powers, whereby the Governor (with the consent of the British Government) can amend, veto or introduce legislation without the agreement of the local legislature, provoked accusations from Hughes that the United Kingdom hoped to create a situation in which territories would be forced to seek independence. The British Government, however, maintained that the initiative had been prompted largely by a desire to secure Anguilla's financial services sector from exploitation by criminal organizations, particularly drugs-traffickers.

In May 1998 Hughes announced that public consultations would be undertaken on a proposal to reform Anguilla's constitutional status. Hughes criticized the current Constitution for vesting executive authority in the Governor rather than in locally elected ministers. In September, however, the British Government announced that its Overseas Dependencies were to be renamed United Kingdom Overseas Territories. In March 1999 the British Government issued a policy document confirming the change of name, and guaranteeing citizens of Overseas Dependencies the right to British citizenship. The proposals also included the requirement that the Constitutions of Overseas Territories should be revised in order to conform to British and international standards. The process of revision of the Anguillan Constitution began in September 1999.

The composition of the legislature remained unaltered following the March 1999 general election. The AUP-ADP coalition therefore kept control of the House of Assembly, and the four members of the Executive Council retained their portfolios.

In June 1999 the ADP leader, Victor Banks, resigned from his post as Minister of Finance and Economic Development, and withdrew from the ruling coalition, accusing Hughes of excluding his party from the decision-making process. The other ADP minister, Edison Baird, refused to resign his post, and was subsequently expelled from the party. Although Banks' resignation deprived the AUP-ADP coalition of its majority in the House of Assembly, Hughes announced that he did not intend to resign. Banks and the three members of the opposition ANA therefore withdrew from the House, demanding that fresh elections be held. Lacking the necessary quorum in the legislature, the Government was unable to implement policy or to introduce a budget for 1999/2000.

In January 2000 legal proceedings begun by Hughes, in an attempt to compel the Speaker to convene the House of Assembly, were rejected by the High Court. In the resulting general election, the ANA won three seats, the AUP two, and the ADP one, while Edison Baird was elected as an independent. The ANA and the ADP, which had formed an electoral alliance, the Anguilla United Front (AUF), therefore gained control of the House of Assembly. The leader of the ANA, Osbourne Fleming, was appointed the Chief Minister of an Executive Council that included two other ANA ministers.

Following Anguilla's inclusion on an Organisation for Economic Co-operation and Development (OECD, see p. 388) 'black list' of tax havens in 2000, the Government introduced legislation to combat money-laundering on the island, including the establishment of a Money Laundering Reporting Authority. OECD removed Anguilla from the list in 2002, declaring that the Government had made sufficient commitments to improve transparency and effective exchange of information on tax matters. In late 2002, however, the burgeoning financial sector faced further disruption when the United Kingdom, under pressure from the European Union (EU, see p. 281), as part of its efforts to investigate tax evasion, demanded that Anguilla disclose the identities and account details of Europeans holding private savings accounts on the island. Anguilla, along with some other British Overseas Territories facing similar demands, claimed it was being treated unfairly compared with more powerful European countries, such as Switzerland and Luxembourg. In 2004 a new financial regulatory body, the Anguilla Financial Services Commission, commenced operations. The Commission represented a further commitment to transparency within the sector. Nevertheless, in April 2009 Anguilla was included on OECD's so-called 'grey list' of territories that had committed to improving transparency in the financial sector but had not yet substantially implemented such change. In March 2010 Anguilla was removed from OECD's list after signing tax-sharing agreements with 13 other countries during the previous 12 months. A financial task force was established by the Government in September as a further measure to improve transparency. In May 2013 Anguilla reached agreement with the United Kingdom to share information about bank accounts held in the territory.

In May 2002 the British Overseas Territories Act, having received royal assent in the United Kingdom in February, came into force and granted British citizenship to the people of its Overseas Territories, including Anguilla. Under the new law Anguillans would be able to hold British passports and work in the United Kingdom and anywhere else in the EU.

At the general election of 21 February 2005, the AUF secured four seats; the remaining three seats were shared by the Anguilla United Movement (AUM—as the AUP had been renamed, with one seat) and the Anguilla National Strategic Alliance (formed by Edison Baird in the previous year—with two seats). The AUF campaigned strongly on the success of its infrastructural improvements, particularly the expansion of Anguilla's airport, during its previous administration.

Constitutional reform

In December 2005 the Government announced its intention to establish a new Constitutional and Electoral Reform Commission, to build on the work done by the previous electoral commission in 2001–04 in ascertaining the views of the people of Anguilla. The Commission began work in February 2006; key issues to be addressed were the fundamental rights and freedoms outlined in the Constitution, the powers of the Governor and the size of the House of Assembly. The Commission's recommendations were submitted to the Governor in August. It was announced in March 2007 that the Government was to receive a delegation from the British Foreign and Commonwealth Office (FCO) in July to facilitate discussions towards constitutional reform. This necessitated a preliminary review of the Commission's recommendations, together with public consultations, prior to the FCO representatives' arrival. The first in an extensive series of such reviews was convened in early March. While several sections of the extant Constitution were regarded by the Commission as still relevant and adequate, areas identified as problematic and in most urgent need of amendment included the administration of justice—particularly to reflect the abolition of the death penalty—transparency in judicial proceedings, enforcement of constitutional rights, and the appointment of the island Governor and deputies.

In addition, concern had been expressed that the existing number of ministers in the Executive Council (or Cabinet, in accordance with the Commission's proposals) was insufficient for the dispatch of governmental responsibilities and should be increased, but that the ratio of ministers to non-ministerial representatives in the House of Assembly should not exceed 50%; it was proposed that members of the Council be increased from three to five ministers, in addition to the Chief Minister (or Premier under the recommendations). The Cabinet would comprise these six members, each awarded a vote, together with the Deputy Governor and the Attorney-General, who would remain without voting authority. The Premier would replace the Governor as chairman of the Cabinet, although the latter would retain the right to be informed by, consult and advise the Cabinet. Further, it was suggested that the size of the Assembly be increased from seven elected members to 13. (Should it be concluded that seven ministers be appointed in addition to the Chief Minister, the Assembly should grow to 15 members in order to accommodate the recommended majority of non-ministerial members.) An existing provision, reportedly not yet exercised, affording the Governor alternative powers to force legislation through the House of Assembly was considered a threat to democracy and the Commission urged for its repeal; similarly, the rescision of powers previously vested in the Secretary of State to disallow legislation passed by the Governor was advised, on the basis that such a provision was no longer required.

The Commission also proposed extensive electoral reform: *inter alia*, the institution of an independent Boundaries Commission was put forward, as was thorough revision of the Election Act. The abolition of the Judicial Services Commission and establishment of a Judicial and Legal Services Commission as its successor, endowed with powers to influence the Governor's judicial appointments, was also suggested and constituted a measure more consistent with other Caribbean states under the jurisdiction of the Eastern Caribbean Supreme Court. The embedding of the Financial Services Commission and its regulatory authority within the constitution was also promulgated in order to enhance supervision of the financial services industry in Anguilla.

Interpreted broadly, the Commission's recommendations sought to advance Anguilla's ambitions towards greater self-determination and the democratic, inclusive administration of its own affairs, gradually reducing the influence of the Government of the United Kingdom—upon whose unilateral authority so many of its existing constitutional statutes were premised. The institution of independent public service and advisory bodies was intended to equip a future government with the appropriate consultative resources to generate more comprehensive and effective legislative proposals for the advancement of Anguilla and the protection of its people.

The proposed visit by an FCO delegation to discuss constitutional reform was postponed in July 2007 by the Anguillan Government in order that further public consultations might be conducted. The Government confirmed, however, that it would be seeking 'full internal self-government' for Anguilla, and at the end of April 2008 it announced the commencement of work on a draft constitution. The proposed document was scheduled for completion in mid-2009, after which consultations between representatives of the Governments of Anguilla and the United Kingdom were to begin, although the change of government in early 2010 meant discussions were delayed.

The 2010 election

A general election was held on 15 February 2010. The AUM, led by former Chief Minister Hubert Hughes, won four of the seven elected seats in the House of Assembly. The AUF's parliamentary representation was reduced to two seats while the remaining seat was secured by the APP. The AUF leader, Victor Banks, lost his seat in the Valley South constituency. Hughes' new administration included Edison Baird as Deputy Chief Minister and Minister of Social Development and Walcott Richardson in the key post of Minister of Home Affairs, including Labour, Natural Resources, Lands, Physical Planning and Immigration. Hughes took on the finance portfolio.

In February 2013, following the arrest of Richardson on charges of indecent assault, Hughes additionally assumed responsibility for the labour and immigration departments. Richardson resigned from the Executive Council later that month, and Jerome Roberts of the APP was appointed as his replacement.

Recent developments: United Kingdom relations

A political dispute arose in January 2011, when Governor Alistair Harrison rejected the 2011 budget on the grounds that it failed to address adequately the territory's precarious fiscal position. Harrison had urged the Government to increase taxes and to reduce drastically the number of public sector workers in order to return government finances to a sustainable level by 2013. Hughes claimed that these austerity measures would inflict unprecedented suffering upon the local population and demanded independence from the United Kingdom. Financial consultants, hired by the British Government, were sent to Anguilla in February 2011 to assist with the modification of the budget, which was finally approved in late March. Hughes declared that the delayed approval had led to the loss of a number of important revenue streams, prompting him to reiterate his desire for independence for Anguilla. Relations between Anguilla and the United Kingdom deteriorated further in April when the

Government accused the Governor of exceeding his powers after Harrison had instructed the Minister of Home Affairs, Walcott Richardson, to stop issuing visa waivers. The Governor claimed that too many waivers had been granted since Richardson took office and that the matter was a security concern. The British Government raised further doubts over the sustainability of Anguilla's fiscal position in September and ordered Hughes to implement measures to reduce the island's budget deficit. Bilateral tensions were exacerbated in December when Hughes organized a small demonstration to demand the replacement of Harrison as Governor on the grounds of his alleged interference in the affairs of the Government, the legislature and the judiciary; in particular, Hughes had condemned a proposal by Harrison to reorganize several senior members of the civil service. The British Government approved the 2012 budget in January. After lengthy negotiations with British officials, in April 2013 Hughes agreed to abide by new fiscal responsibility guidelines, as delineated in the Framework for Fiscal Sustainability and Development. The signing of this accord was expected to hasten British approval of the 2013 budget. Meanwhile, Christina Scott was due to succeed Harrison as Governor in mid-2013.

Foreign Affairs

In 2005 the Governments of Anguilla and the British Virgin Islands announced the formal establishment of the maritime boundary between the two territories. The boundary had been agreed in 2002 following discussions facilitated by the British Government. Co-operation between British Virgin Islands customs officials and their Anguillan counterparts enabled the recovery of a substantial quantity of drugs from a container vessel impounded in Anguilla in 2006; the haul was thought to be the largest ever seized on the island and an indication of the success of joint law enforcement initiatives in the region.

CONSTITUTION AND GOVERNMENT

The Constitution vests executive power in a Governor, appointed by the British monarch. The Governor is responsible for external affairs, international financial affairs, defence and internal security. In most other matters the Governor acts on the advice of the Executive Council, led by the Chief Minister. Legislative power is held by the House of Assembly, comprising 11 members: two ex officio, two nominated by the Governor, and seven elected for five years by universal adult suffrage. The Executive Council is responsible to the House. A review of the Constitution was ongoing in 2013.

REGIONAL AND INTERNATIONAL CO-OPERATION

In 1987 Anguilla became the eighth member of the Eastern Caribbean Central Bank (see p. 465) and in 2001 joined the new regional stock exchange, the Eastern Caribbean Securities Exchange (based in Saint Christopher and Nevis). In 1999 Anguilla was granted associate membership of the Caribbean Community and Common Market (CARICOM, see p. 231). The territory is also an associate member of the Organisation of Eastern Caribbean States (OECS, see p. 477) and the Economic Community for Latin America and the Caribbean (see p. 35). In 2007 the country joined the single market component of CARICOM's Single Market and Economy, full implementation of which was expected by 2015. The territory is a member of the Commonwealth (see p. 244). As a dependency of the United Kingdom, Anguilla has the status of Overseas Territory in association with the European Union (see p. 281).

ECONOMIC AFFAIRS

In 2010 the gross national income of Anguilla, measured at current prices, was EC $743.8m, equivalent to EC $45,123 per head. During 2002–11, it was estimated, the population increased at an average annual rate of 3.9%, while gross domestic product (GDP) per head increased, in real terms, by an average of 3.1% per year. According to estimates by the Eastern Caribbean Central Bank (ECCB, see p. 465), overall GDP increased, in real terms, at an average annual rate of 4.6% in 2002–11; real GDP decreased by 4.3% in 2010, but increased by 4.5% in 2011.

Agriculture (including crops, livestock and fishing) contributed 2.5% of GDP in 2011 and agriculture, fishing and mining engaged 3.2% of the employed labour force in 2001. Smallholders grow vegetables and fruit for domestic consumption; the principal crops are pigeon peas, sweet potatoes and maize. Livestock-rearing traditionally supplies significant export earnings, but the principal productive sector is the fishing industry (which is also a major employer). Real agricultural GDP increased by an annual average of 3.4% during 2002–11, according to ECCB estimates; sectoral GDP decreased by 3.6% in 2010, but increased by 27.2% in 2011.

Industry (including mining, manufacturing, construction and power) accounted for 13.7% of GDP in 2011 and (not including the small mining sector) engaged 18.8% of the employed labour force in 2001. The sector is traditionally based on salt production and shipbuilding, although the construction sector grew strongly in recent years. Real industrial GDP increased by an annual average of 2.8% in

2002–11, according to ECCB estimates; the sector contracted by 10.5% in 2011.

The mining and quarrying sector contributed 0.4% of GDP in 2011 and engaged only 0.2% of the working population in 1992. Anguilla's principal mineral product is salt. Mining GDP decreased by an annual average of 2.5% during 2002–11, according to ECCB estimates; sectoral GDP decreased by a massive 56.5% in 2010 and by a further 5.2% in 2011.

The manufacturing sector, accounting for 2.4% of employment in 2001 and for only 2.1% of GDP in 2011, consists almost entirely of boat-building and fisheries-processing. Real manufacturing GDP increased by an annual average of just 0.1% in 2002–11, according to the ECCB; sectoral GDP declined by 50.3% in 2010 and by 1.5% in 2011.

The construction industry, which engaged 14.9% of the employed labour force in 2001, accounted for 6.4% of GDP in 2011. GDP in the construction sector increased at an annual average of 2.1% during 2002–11; however, the sector declined by 18.0% in 2011.

Imported hydrocarbon fuels meet most energy needs; mineral fuels and lubricants accounted for 14.3% of the total value of imports in 2008. In 2012 the Government proposed to increase the use of renewable energy sources, particularly wind farms.

The services sector accounted for 83.9% of GDP in 2011 and engaged 77.9% of the employed labour force in 2001. Tourism is increasingly the dominant industry of the economy, and is a catalyst for growth in other areas. The hotel and restaurant sector is the largest contributor to GDP, accounting for 20.2% of GDP in 2011. The hotel and restaurant sector increased by 6.6% in 2011. Tourism expenditure totalled EC $283.4m. in 2011. The USA provided 54.2% of visitors (including excursionists) in 2012. The 'offshore' financial institutions are also important contributors to the GDP of the services industry, contributing 12.8% of GDP in 2011 and employing some 7.7% of the economically active population in 2001. The real GDP of the services sector increased at an annual average of 3.6% in 2002–11, according to ECCB estimates; sectoral growth increased by 0.5% in 2011.

In 2011 Anguilla recorded a merchandise trade deficit of EC $126.83m., and a deficit on the current account of the balance of payments of EC $99.21m. The trade deficit was partly offset by receipts from the 'invisibles' sector: tourism, financial services, remittances from Anguillans abroad and official assistance. The principal sources of imports are the USA (51.2% in 2008), Trinidad and Tobago and Puerto Rico. The principal markets for exports are Guyana (38.4% in 2008) and the USA (14.8%). The main commodity exports are lobsters, fish, livestock and salt. Imports, upon which Anguilla is highly dependent, consist of machinery and transport equipment, manufactures, foodstuffs, and construction materials.

In 2011, according to the ECCB (see p. 465), a budgetary surplus of EC $21.6m. was estimated. Anguilla's total public sector debt was an estimated EC $230.3m. at the end of 2011. According to ILO, consumer prices increased by an annual average of 4.3% in 2002–11; consumer prices rose by 6.2% in 2011. Some 7.8% of the labour force were unemployed in July 2002.

The onset of recession in 2008 brought to an end several years of robust growth, and the economy contracted dramatically in 2009. The island's two most important sectors, tourism and construction, both declined as a direct consequence of the global economic downturn. The contractions in the economies of Anguilla's two most significant sources of visitors, the USA and the United Kingdom, led to a decrease in tourist numbers and revenues. Real GDP contracted by a further 4.3% in 2010. Although a modest recovery in the tourism sector was evident in that year, a lack of investment in new developments meant that the construction industry contracted by 23.7%. The tourism recovery extended into 2011, and, in an attempt to stabilize the fiscal position, a temporary 6% income tax was introduced in April. The economy grew by 4.5%, according to ECCB estimates. The ECCB estimated further economic growth, of 6.8% in 2013, although the performance of the key tourism and construction industries were crucial to this expansion. A resurgence in tourism activity was expected in 2013. Anguilla's prospects for future growth were largely contingent upon an improvement in the international economic climate and the expansion of the island's transport infrastructure.

PUBLIC HOLIDAYS

2014: 1 January (New Year's Day), 3 March (for Birthday of James Ronald Webster), 18 April (Good Friday), 21 April (Easter Monday), 1 May (Labour Day), 30 May (Anguilla Day), 9 June (Whit Monday), 16 June (Queen's Official Birthday—provisional), 4 August (August Monday), 7 August (August Thursday), 8 August (Constitution Day), 19 December (National Heroes' and Heroines' Day), 25–26 December (Christmas).

Statistical Survey

Source (unless otherwise stated): Government of Anguilla, The Secretariat, The Valley; tel. 497-2451; fax 497-3389; e-mail stats@gov.ai; internet gov.ai/statistics.

AREA AND POPULATION

Area (sq km): 96 (Anguilla 91, Sombrero 5).

Population: 11,430 at census of 9 May 2001; 13,452 (males 6,659, females 6,793) at census of 11 May 2011 (preliminary).

Density (at 2011 census): 140.1 per sq km.

Population by Age and Sex (at 2001 census): *0–14:* 3,202 (males 1,590, females 1,612); *15–64:* 7,356 (males 3,632, females 3,724); *65 and over:* 872 (males 406, females 466); *Total* 11,430 (males 5,628, females 5,802).

Principal Towns (population at 2001 census): South Hill 1,495; North Side 1,195; The Valley (capital) 1,169; Stoney Ground 1,133. *Mid-2011* (UN estimate, incl. suburbs): The Valley 1,766 (Source: UN, *World Urbanization Prospects: The 2011 Revision*).

Births, Marriages and Deaths (2010): Registered live births 186 (birth rate 11.4 per 1,000); Registered marriages 62 (marriage rate 3.8 per 1,000); Registered deaths 66 (death rate 4.0 per 1,000). *2011:* Birth rate 12.9 per 1,000; Death rate 4.4 per 1,000 (Source: Pan American Health Organization).

Life Expectancy (years at birth): 80.9 (males 78.3; females 83.5) in 2011. Source: Pan American Health Organization.

Economically Active Population (persons aged 15 years and over, census of 9 May 2001): Agriculture, fishing and mining 183; Manufacturing 135; Electricity, gas and water 81; Construction 830; Trade 556; Restaurants and hotels 1,587; Transport, storage and communications 379; Finance, insurance, real estate and business services 433; Public administration, social security 662; Education, health and social work 383; Other community, social and personal services 164; Private households with employed persons 164; *Sub-total* 4,773; Activities not stated 871; *Total employed* 5,644 (males 3,014, females 2,630); Unemployed 406 (males 208, females 198); *Total labour force* 6,050 (males 3,222, females 2,828). *July 2002:* Total employed 5,496 (males 3,009, females 2,487); Unemployed 465 (males 204, females 261); Total labour force 5,961 (Source: ILO).

HEALTH AND WELFARE

Total Fertility Rate (children per woman, 2011): 1.8.

Under-5 Mortality Rate (per 1,000 live births, 1997): 34.0.

Physicians (per 1,000 head, 2003): 1.2.

Hospital Beds (per 1,000 head, 2009): 2.2.

Health Expenditure (% of GDP, 2007): 3.0.

Access to Water (% of persons, 2004): 60.

Access to Sanitation (% of persons, 2004): 99.

Sources: Caribbean Development Bank, *Social and Economic Indicators 2004* and Pan American Health Organization.

For definitions, see explanatory note on p. vi.

AGRICULTURE, ETC.

Fishing (metric tons, live weight, 2010): Marine fishes 309; Caribbean spiny lobster 115; Stromboid conchs 277; Total catch 701. Source: FAO.

INDUSTRY

Electric Energy ('000 kWh): 89,728 in 2008; 91,335 in 2009; 98,532 in 2010. Source: Eastern Caribbean Central Bank.

FINANCE

Currency and Exchange Rates: 100 cents = 1 Eastern Caribbean dollar (EC $). *Sterling, US Dollar and Euro Equivalents* (31 December 2012): £1 sterling = EC $4.261; US $1 = EC $2.700; €1 = EC $3.562; EC $100 = £23.47 = US $37.04 = €28.07. *Exchange Rate:* Fixed at US $1 = EC $2.70 since July 1976.

Budget (EC $ million, 2011): *Revenue:* Tax revenue 180.7 (Taxes on domestic goods and services 104.2, Taxes on international trade and transactions 65.5, Taxes on property 2.9, Taxes on income and profits 8.2); Non-tax revenue 24.3; Total 205.0 *Expenditure:* Current expenditure 173.9 (Personal emoluments 80.5, Other goods and services 38.7, Transfers and subsidies 45.5, Interest payments 9.1); Capital expenditure 9.6; Total 183.4. Source: Eastern Caribbean Central Bank, *Annual Economic and Financial Review 2014*.

Cost of Living (Consumer Price Index; base: 2005 = 100): All items 121.7 in 2008; 120.8 in 2009; 122.1 in 2010. Source: IMF, *International Financial Statistics*.

Gross Domestic Product (EC $ million at constant 2006 prices): 699.44 in 2009; 669.11 in 2010; 699.47 in 2011. Source: Eastern Caribbean Central Bank.

Expenditure on the Gross Domestic Product (EC $ million at current prices, 2010): Government final consumption expenditure 149.68; Private final consumption expenditure 605.55; Gross fixed capital formation 178.43; *Total domestic expenditure* 933.66; Exports of goods and services 334.94; *Less* Imports of goods and services 529.80; *GDP in purchasers' values* 738.80. Source: Eastern Caribbean Central Bank.

Gross Domestic Product by Economic Activity (EC $ million at current prices, 2011): Agriculture (including crops, livestock and fishing) 16.73; Mining and quarrying 2.93; Manufacturing 14.04; Electricity and water 32.29; Construction 43.16; Wholesale and retail trade 51.33; Hotels and restaurants 136.33; Transport and communications 58.91; Finance, insurance, real estate and business services 86.55; Real estate and housing 94.18; Public administration and defence 70.53; Education 22.93; Health 21.72; Other services 24.41; *Sub-total* 676.03; *Less* Financial intermediation services indirectly measured 33.94; *Gross value added in basic prices* 642.09; Taxes, *less* subsidies, on products 154.08; *GDP in purchasers' values* 796.18. Source: Eastern Caribbean Central Bank.

Balance of Payments (EC $ million, 2011): Goods (net) –328.76; Services (net) 201.76; *Balance on goods and services* –127.00; Income (net) 0.17; *Balance on goods, services and income* –126.83; Current transfers (net) 27.62; *Current balance* –99.21; Capital account (net) 24.82; Direct investment (net) 102.92; Portfolio investment –3.43; Other investments (net) –25.82; Net errors and omissions –5.67; *Overall balance* –6.39. Source: Eastern Caribbean Central Bank.

EXTERNAL TRADE

Principal Commodities (EC $ million, 2008): *Imports:* Food and live animals 56.4; Beverages and tobacco 39.7; Mineral fuels, lubricants, etc. 104.7; Chemicals and related products 53.2; Basic manufactures 215.1; Machinery and transport equipment 156.5; Miscellaneous manufactured articles 87.6; Total (incl. others) 733.7. *Exports* (incl. re-exports): Food and live animals 0.2; Beverages and tobacco 12.7; Basic manufactures 8.0; Machinery and transport equipment 8.1; Miscellaneous manufactured articles 0.2; Total (incl. others) 31.0. *2011* (estimates): Total imports 395.3; Total exports (incl. re-exports) 18.9 (Source: Eastern Caribbean Central Bank).

Principal Trading Partners (EC $ million, 2008): *Imports:* Barbados 4.7; Guyana 14.6; Puerto Rico 56.2; Trinidad and Tobago 106.2; United Kingdom 5.5; USA 375.9; US Virgin Islands 3.9; Total (incl. others) 733.7. *Exports* (incl. re-exports): British Virgin Islands 0.1; Guyana 11.9; United Kingdom 0.6; USA 4.6; Total (incl. others) 31.0. *2011* (estimates): Total imports 395.3; Total exports (incl. re-exports) 18.9 (Source: Eastern Caribbean Central Bank).

TRANSPORT

Road Traffic (motor vehicles in use at 31 December 2006): Passenger cars 4,155; Vans and lorries 92; Motorcycles and mopeds 22; Total 4,269 (Source: IRF, *World Road Statistics*).

Shipping: *Flag Registered Fleet* (at 31 December 2012): 5; Total displacement 1,127 grt. (Source: Lloyd's List Intelligence—www.lloydslistintelligence.com).

TOURISM

Visitor Arrivals: 118,411 (stop-overs 61,998, excursionists 56,413) in 2010; 123,558 (stop-overs 65,783, excursionists 57,775) in 2011; 129,391 (stop-overs 64,698, excursionists 64,693) in 2012.

Visitor Arrivals by Place of Residence (2012): Canada 7,994; Caribbean 7,958; United Kingdom 4,251; USA 70,190; Total (incl. others) 129,391.

Tourism Receipts (EC $ million): 250.5 in 2009; 258.6 in 2010; 283.4 in 2011. Source: Eastern Caribbean Central Bank.

COMMUNICATIONS MEDIA

Telephones (2011): 6,200 main lines in use.

Mobile Cellular Telephones (2011): 26,000 subscribers.

Internet Subscribers (2008): 3,700.

Broadband Subscribers (2011): 3,900.

Source: International Telecommunication Union.

EDUCATION

Pre-primary (2009/10 unless otherwise indicated): 11 schools (2003); 44 teachers; 444 pupils (males 243, females 201).

Primary (2009/10 unless otherwise indicated): 8 schools (2003); 112 teachers; 1,620 pupils (males 832, females 788).

Secondary (2009/10 unless otherwise indicated): 1 school (2002/03); 96 teachers (2006/07); 1,041 pupils (males 516, females 525).

Tertiary (2007/08): 14 teachers; 54 students (9 males, 45 females).

Pupil-teacher Ratio (primary education, UNESCO estimate): 14.5 in 2009/10.

Adult Literacy Rate (UNESCO estimates): 95.4% (males 95.1%; females 95.7%) in 1995. Source: UNESCO, *Statistical Yearbook*.

Source (unless otherwise indicated): UNESCO Institute for Statistics.

Directory

The Government

HEAD OF STATE

Queen: HM Queen ELIZABETH II.

Governor: WILLIAM ALISTAIR HARRISON (took office 21 April 2009).

Governor-designate: CHRISTINA MARTHA ELENA SCOTT (scheduled to take office in mid-2013).

EXECUTIVE COUNCIL
(May 2013)

The Government is formed by the Anguilla United Movement (AUM) and the Anguilla Progressive Party (APP).

Chief Minister and Minister of Finance, Economic Development, Investments and Tourism: HUBERT B. HUGHES (AUM).

Deputy Chief Minister and Minister of Social Development: EDISON BAIRD (AUM).

Minister of Home Affairs, Natural Resources, Lands and Physical Planning: JEROME C. ROBERTS (APP).

Minister of Infrastructure, Communications, Utilities and Housing: EVAN GUMBS (AUM).

Parliamentary Secretary with responsibility for Tourism: HAYDN HUGHES.

Deputy Governor: STANLEY EVERTON REID.

Attorney-General: JAMES WOOD.

MINISTRIES

Office of the Governor: Government House, POB 60, The Valley; tel. 497-2622; fax 497-3314; e-mail governorsoffice@gov.ai.

Office of the Chief Minister: The Secretariat, POB 60, The Valley; tel. 497-3518; fax 497-3389; e-mail chief-minister@gov.ai.

All ministries are based in The Valley, mostly at the Secretariat (tel. 497-2451; internet www.gov.ai).

Legislature

HOUSE OF ASSEMBLY

Speaker: BARBARA WEBSTER-BOURNE.

Clerk to House of Assembly: ADELLA RICHARDSON.

Election, 15 February 2010

Party	% of votes	Seats
Anguilla United Movement (AUM) .	32.67	4
Anguilla United Front (AUF) . .	39.39	2
Anguilla Progressive Party (APP) . .	14.71	1
Independent candidates	13.24	—
Total	100.00	7

There are also two ex officio members and two nominated members.

Political Organizations

Anguilla Progressive Party (APP): The Valley; Leader BRENT DAVIS.

Anguilla United Front (AUF): The Valley; tel. 497-4541; e-mail othlyn@unitedfront.ai; internet www.unitedfront.ai; f. 2000 by the alliance of the Anguilla Democratic Party and the Anguilla National Alliance; Leader VICTOR F. BANKS.

Anguilla United Movement (AUM): The Valley; tel. 497-0335; e-mail joanivy2002@yahoo.com; f. 1978; revived 1984; fmrly known as the Anguilla United Party—AUP; conservative; Leader HUBERT B. HUGHES.

Judicial System

Justice is administered by the High Court, Court of Appeal and Magistrates' Courts. Anguilla is under the jurisdiction of the Eastern Caribbean Supreme Court (ECSC). One of the ECSC's High Court Judges arbitrates in sittings of the territory's High Court.

High Court Judge: LOUISE ESTHER BLENMAN.

Registrar: VERNETTE S. RICHARDSON.

Religion

CHRISTIANITY

The Anglican Communion

Anglicans in Anguilla are adherents of the Church in the Province of the West Indies, comprising nine dioceses. Anguilla forms part of the diocese of the North Eastern Caribbean and Aruba. According to figures from the last census (2001), 29% of the population are Anglican.

Bishop of the North Eastern Caribbean and Aruba: Rt Rev. LEROY ERROL BROOKS, St Mary's Rectory, POB 180, The Valley; tel. 497-2235; fax 497-8555; e-mail brookx@anguilla.net.com.

The Roman Catholic Church

The diocese of St John's-Basseterre, suffragan to the archdiocese of Castries (Saint Lucia), includes Anguilla, Antigua and Barbuda, the British Virgin Islands, Montserrat and Saint Christopher and Nevis. The Bishop resides in St John's, Antigua. Some 6% of the population are Roman Catholic, according to census figures.

Roman Catholic Church: St Gerard's, POB 47, The Valley; tel. 497-2405; e-mail info@stgerards-anguilla.org; internet stgerards-anguilla.org; Pastor PAUL CZOCH.

Other Christian Churches

According to the last census, 24% of the population are Methodist.

Methodist Church: Epworth Manse, POB 5, 2640 The Valley; tel. 497-2612; fax 497-8460; e-mail methodism@anguillanet.com; internet www.lidmethodist.org; Supt Minister Rev. E. DUNSTAN RICHARDSON.

The Seventh-day Adventist, Baptist, Church of God, Pentecostal, Apostolic Faith and Jehovah's Witnesses Churches and sects are also represented.

The Press

Anguilla Life Magazine: POB 1622, The Valley; tel. 497-3080; fax 497-4196; e-mail anguillalife@anguillanet.com; internet www.anguillanews.com; f. 1998; 3 a year; Publr and Editor CLAIRE DEVENER; circ. 10,000.

Anguilla Official Gazette: House of Assembly, POB 60, The Valley AI-2640; tel. 497-5081; fax 498-2210; internet gazette.gov.ai; monthly; govt news-sheet.

The Anguillian Newspaper: POB 98, The Valley; tel. 497-3823; fax 497-8706; e-mail theanguillian@anguillanet.com; internet theanguillian.com; weekly; Editor A. NAT HODGE.

The Light: Sandy Hill, POB 1373, The Valley; tel. 497-5058; fax 497-5641; e-mail thelight@anguillanet.com; f. 1993; owned by Hodgeco Publishing Inc; weekly; newspaper; Editor GEORGE C. HODGE.

What We Do in Anguilla: Sandy Hill, POB 1373, The Valley; tel. 497-5058; e-mail thelight@anguillanet.com; f. 1987; monthly newsletter, annual magazine; tourism; Editor GEORGE C. HODGE; circ. 20,000.

Broadcasting and Communications

TELECOMMUNICATIONS

LIME: POB 77, The Valley; tel. 804-2994; e-mail customerservice@lime.com; internet www.time4lime.com/ai; fmrly Cable & Wireless (Anguilla) Ltd; name changed as above 2008; contact centres in Jamaica and Saint Lucia; fixed lines, mobile telecommunications and internet services provider; CEO DAVID SHAW; Exec. Vice-Pres. (Leeward Islands) DAVIDSON CHARLES.

Wireless Ventures (Anguilla) Ltd: Babrow Bldg, The Valley; tel. 498-7500; fax 498-7510; e-mail customercareanguilla@digicelgroup

.com; internet www.digicelanguilla.com; owned by Digicel Ltd (Bermuda); fmrly AT&T Wireless; Country Man. JOHN GIDHARRY.

BROADCASTING

Radio

The Caribbean Beacon: Long Rd, POB 690, The Valley; Head Office: POB 7008, Columbus, GA 31908, USA; tel. 338-3030; fax 497-4311; f. 1981; privately owned and operated; religious and commercial; broadcasts 24 hours daily; Pres. MELLISA SCOTT; CEO B. MONSELL HAZELL.

Klass 92.9 FM: POB 339, The Valley; tel. 497-3791; e-mail request@klass929.com; internet www.klass929.com; f. 2006; commercial; Owner ABNER BROOKS, Jr.

Kool FM: North Side, The Valley; tel. 497-0103; fax 497-0104; e-mail kool@koolfm103.com; internet www.koolfm103.com; commercial; Man. ASHLEY BROOKS.

Radio Anguilla: Dept of Information and Broadcasting, Secretariat, POB 60, The Valley; tel. 497-2218; fax 497-5432; e-mail radioaxa@anguillanet.com; internet www.radioaxa.com; f. 1969; owned by the Govt of Anguilla; 250,000 listeners throughout the north-eastern Caribbean; broadcasts 17 hours daily; Dir FARRAH BANKS; Programme Man. KEITHSTONE GREAVES.

UP Beat Radio 97.7 FM: Cedar Ave, Rey Hill, POB 5045, The Valley, AI 2640; tel. 498-3354; fax 497-5995; e-mail info@hbr1075.com; internet hbr1075.com; f. 2000; commercial; music and news programmes; Dirs IWANDAI I. GUMBS, WHALDOMA (RAS B.) BROOKS.

ZJF FM: POB 333, The Valley; tel. 497-3919; fax 497-3909; f. 1989; commercial; Man. SELWYN BROOKS.

Television

Anguilla TV: tel. 662-7365; e-mail donna@islandeyetv.com; internet www.islandeyetv.com; operated by Eye TV; terrestrial channels 3 and 9; 24-hour local and international English language programming; Exec. Producer DONNA DAVIS.

Caribbean Cable Communications (Anguilla): Edwin Wallace Rey Dr., POB 336, The Valley; tel. 497-3600; fax 497-3602; e-mail customersupport@caribcable.com; internet www.caribcable.com; also broadcasts to Nevis; Pres. LEE BERTMAN.

Finance

(cap. = capital; res = reserves; dep. = deposits; m. = million; amounts in EC dollars)

BANKING

Central Bank

Eastern Caribbean Central Bank: Fairplay Commercial Complex, POB 1385, The Valley; tel. 497-5050; fax 497-5150; e-mail eccbaxa@anguillanet.com; internet www.eccb-centralbank.org; HQ in Basseterre, Saint Christopher and Nevis; bank of issue and central monetary authority for Anguilla, Antigua and Barbuda, Dominica, Grenada, Montserrat, Saint Christopher and Nevis, Saint Lucia and Saint Vincent and the Grenadines; Gov. Sir K. DWIGHT VENNER; Man. Dir JENNIFER NERO.

Commercial Banks

Caribbean Commercial Bank (Anguilla) Ltd: POB 23, The Valley; tel. 497-3917; fax 497-3570; e-mail service@ccb.ai; internet www.ccb.ai; f. 1976; Chair. OSBOURNE B. FLEMING; Man. Dir STARRY WEBSTER-BENJAMIN.

CIBC FirstCaribbean International Bank Ltd: POB 140, The Valley; tel. 497-2301; fax 497-2980; e-mail care@firstcaribbeanbank.com; internet www.firstcaribbeanbank.com; f. 2002 as FirstCaribbean International Bank Ltd following merger of Caribbean operations of Barclays Bank PLC and CIBC; present name adopted 2011 after CIBC became the majority shareholder in Firstcaribbean; Exec. Chair. MICHAEL MANSOOR; CEO RIK PARKHILL.

National Bank of Anguilla Ltd (NBA): POB 44, The Valley; tel. 497-2101; fax 497-3310; e-mail nbabankl@anguillanet.com; internet www.nba.ai; f. 1985; 6% owned by Govt of Anguilla; cap. 30.6m., res 52.4m., dep. 915.4m. (March 2009); regulated by Eastern Caribbean Central Bank; Chair. CONRAD W. FLEMING; CEO E. VALENTINE BANKS.

Scotiabank Anguilla Ltd: Fairplay Commercial Centre, POB 250, The Valley; tel. 497-3333; fax 497-3344; e-mail bns.anguilla@scotiabank.com; internet www.anguilla.scotiabank.com; f. 1989; cap. 32,4m., res. 13,6m., dep. 225,5m. (Oct. 2010); Man. Dir KERWIN BAPTISTE.

'Offshore' Banks

Caribbean Commercial Investment Bank Ltd: 2 St Mary's St, POB 23, The Valley; tel. 497-2242; fax 497-7054.

Foreign Commerce Bank Ltd: The Anguilla Professional Complex, POB 1648, The Valley; tel. 498-5576; fax 498-5578.

National Bank of Anguilla (Private Banking and Trust) Ltd: Conrad W. Fleming Corporate Bldg, St Mary's Rd, POB 44, The Valley; tel. 497-7096; fax 497-2296.

Trust Companies

Codan Trust Co (Anguilla) Ltd: Mitchell House, POB 147, The Valley; tel. 498-6789; fax 498-8423; e-mail anguilla@conyersdill.com; internet www.conyersdill.com; subsidiary of Conyers, Dill and Pearman, Bermuda; Man. GARETH THOMAS.

First Anguilla Trust Co Ltd: Mitchell House, POB 174, The Valley, AI 2640; tel. and fax 498-8800; e-mail information@firstanguilla.com; internet www.firstanguilla.com; owned by Webster Dyrud Mitchell; f. 1995; Dir PAM WEBSTER.

GenevaTrust: 201 Rogers Office Bldg, Edwin Wallace Rey Dr., George Hill; tel. 518-1130; fax 870-3949; e-mail geneva@genevatrust.com; internet www.genevatrust.com; f. 2005; as the GenevaTrust Corpn; subsidiary of Geneva Assurance Ltd; CEO NADINE DE KOKER.

Global Trustees (Anguilla) Ltd: 201 The Rogers Office Bldg, Edwin Wallace Rey Dr., George Hill; tel. 498-5858; fax 497-5504; e-mail anguilla@gcsl.info; internet www.gcsl.info; fmrly Hansa Bank and Trust Co; Man. Dir CARLYLE K. ROGERS.

Intertrust (Anguilla) Ltd: National Bank Corporate Bldg, Airport Rd, POB 1388, The Valley; tel. 497-2189; fax 497-5007; e-mail toni.niekoop@intertrustgroup.com; internet www.intertrustgroup.com; fmrly Fortis Intertrust (Anguilla) Ltd; Dir TONI NIEKOOP.

Lutea (Anguilla) Ltd: S1 South, Auckland House, POB 1533, The Quarter; tel. 498-0340; fax 498-0341; e-mail acharles@lutea.com; internet www.lutea.com; owned by the Lutea Group of Cos, administered in Jersey (United Kingdom); Man. AINE CHARLES.

Mossack Fonseca & Co (British Anguilla) Ltd: Quantum Bldg, Suite 29, Caribbean Commercial Centre, The Valley; tel. 498-7777; fax 497-3727; e-mail britishanguilla@mossfon.com; internet www.mossfon.com; Administrator CUTELYN CARTY.

Sinel Trust (Anguilla) Ltd: POB 821, The Valley; fax 497-8289; e-mail arichardson@sineltrust.com; CEO ALEX RICHARDSON.

REGULATORY AUTHORITY

Anguilla Financial Services Commission: MAICO HQ Bldg, 2nd Floor, Cosley Dr., POB 1575, The Valley; tel. 497-5881; fax 497-5872; e-mail info@fsc.org.ai; internet www.fsc.org.ai; f. 2004; Dir KEITH BELL.

STOCK EXCHANGE

Eastern Caribbean Securities Exchange: Bird Rock, Basseterre, Saint Christopher and Nevis; tel. (869) 466-7192; fax (869) 465-3798; e-mail info@ecseonline.com; internet www.ecseonline.com; f. 2001; regional securities market designed to facilitate the buying and selling of financial products for the 8 mem. territories—Anguilla, Antigua and Barbuda, Dominica, Grenada, Montserrat, Saint Christopher and Nevis, Saint Lucia, and Saint Vincent and the Grenadines; Chair. Sir K. DWIGHT VENNER; Gen. Man. TREVOR E. BLAKE.

INSURANCE

At the end of December 2011 there were 252 captive insurance companies registered in Anguilla.

A-Affordable Insurance Services Inc: Maison Complex, Unit 21, Stoney Ground Rd, The Valley; tel. 497-5757; fax 497-2122; e-mail a_afins@anguillanet.com; Gen. Man. NICOLE ALLEYNE.

Alliance Insurance Services Ltd: POB PW 5236, George Hill; tel. 498-7788; fax 498-7780; e-mail info@aisanguilla.com; internet www.aisanguilla.com; f. 2006; Man. Dir HEATHER WALLACE; Man. SANDRA LOVELL.

Captiva Global Ltd: POB 941, Edwin Wallace Rey Dr., George Hill; tel. 498-5858; fax 497-5504; e-mail info@captivagroup.net; Group Dir NOELLA M. THOMPSON; Group Man.Dir HARRY J. THOMPSON.

D-3 Enterprises Ltd: Caribbean Commercial Center, POB 1377, The Valley; tel. 497-3525; fax 497-3526; e-mail d3@d3ent.com; internet www.d-3enterprises.com; represents the Atlantic Southern Insurance Co Ltd and the Caribbean Alliance Insurance Co Ltd; Gen. Man. CLEMENT RUAN.

Fidelity Insurance Co.: The Law Bldg POB 687, The Valley; tel. 497-0484; fax 497-5753; e-mail clientserv@fidinsco.com; internet www.fidinsco.com/about_anguilla.html.

Gulf Insurance Ltd: POB 1254, South Hill; tel. 498-4853; fax 498-5852; e-mail chantalpiazzi@yahoo.com; internet www.gulfinsuranceltd.com; Dirs CHANTAL PIAZZI, MICHAEL PERMUY.

Malliouhana-Anico Insurance Co Ltd (MAICO): Herbert's Commercial Centre, POB 492, The Valley; tel. 497-3712; fax 497-3710;

e-mail maico@anguillanet.com; internet www.maicoanguilla.com; f. 1988; wholly owned subsidiary of National Bank of Anguilla Ltd; Man. MONICA HODGE.

National Caribbean Insurance Co Ltd: Caribbean Commercial Complex, POB 323, The Valley; tel. 497-2865; fax 497-3783.

National General Insurance Co N.V. (NAGICO): Albert Lake Dr, The Valley; tel. 497-5940; fax 497-0510; e-mail info.anguilla@nagico.com; internet www.nagico.com; f. 1982; CEO IMRAN MCSOOD-AMJAD; Man. CARLYN CARTY.

Trade and Industry

DEVELOPMENT ORGANIZATION

Anguilla Development Board: Cannon Ball Office Complex, Wallblake Rd, POB 285, The Valley; tel. 497-2595; fax 497-2959; f. 1979; provides financial and technical assistance to fishing, agriculture, tourism and industry; Gen. Man. ALTHEA HODGE.

CHAMBER OF COMMERCE

Anguilla Chamber of Commerce and Industry: POB 321, The Valley; tel. 497-2839; fax 497-3880; e-mail acoci@caribcable.com; internet www.anguillachamber.com; Pres. KEITHLEY LAKE; Exec. Dir CARLTON PICKERING.

INDUSTRIAL AND TRADE ASSOCIATION

Anguilla Financial Services Association (AFSA): POB 1071, The Valley; tel. 498-4224; fax 498-4220; e-mail support@anguillafsd.com; internet www.anguillafsc.com; Registrar LANSTON CONNOR.

UTILITIES

Electricity

Anguilla Electricity Co Ltd: POB 400, The Valley; tel. 497-5200; fax 497-5440; e-mail info@anglec.com; internet www.anglec.com; f. 1991; operates a power station and 12 generators; Chair. JAMES RICHARDSON; Gen. Man. THOMAS HODGE.

Water

Water Corpn of Anguilla: The Valley; CEO ROMMEL HUGHES.

Transport

ROADS

Anguilla has 175 km (108 miles) of roads, of which 46.9% is paved. There are 63 km of main roads and 112 km of secondary roads.

SHIPPING

There are three main seaports. The principal port of entry is Sandy Ground on Road Bay. The Corito Bay port is used by two oil companies for the import of petroleum products and propane. The Blowing Point port is the passenger terminal for ferries operating between Anguilla and Marigot (St Martin). The other areas of entry are Cove, Forest, Island Harbour and Little Harbour.

Anguilla Air and Seaports Authority: c/o Permanent Secretary, MICUHAF, POB 60, The Valley; tel. 497-3476; fax 497-5258; e-mail larry.franklin@gov.ai; f. 2009; Chair. KENN BANKS; Supt. (Ports) EDWIN HARRIS.

Link Ferries: Little Harbour; tel. 497-2231; fax 497-3290; e-mail fbconnor@anguillanet.com; internet www.link.ai; f. 1992; daily services to Julianna International Airport (St Martin) and charter services to neighbouring islands and offshore quays; Capt. and Owner FRANKLYN CONNOR.

CIVIL AVIATION

Clayton J. Lloyd International Airport (known as Wallblake Airport until 2010), 3.2 km (2 miles) from The Valley, has an asphalt-surfaced runway with a length of 1,665 m (5,462 ft). Reconstruction and expansion of the airport in 2004 included an extension of the runway to accommodate mid-range aircraft. LIAT (see Civil Aviation, Antigua and Barbuda) and Winair regional airlines also operate from the airport.

Anguilla Air Services: POB 559, Clayton J. Lloyd International Airport; tel. 498-5922; fax 498-5921; e-mail info@anguillaairservices.com; internet www.anguillaairservices.com; f. Dec. 2006; operates passenger and cargo charter flights from Anguilla to neighbouring islands; official carrier for Winair (Winward Islands Airways) in Anguilla; Man. Dir CARL THOMAS.

Trans Anguilla Airways (2000) Ltd (TAA): POB 1329, Clayton J. Lloyd International Airport; tel. 497-8690; fax 497-8689; e-mail transang@anguillanet.com; internet www.transanguilla.com; f. 1996; air charter service in the Eastern Caribbean; Chair. JOSHUA GUMBS.

Tourism

Anguilla's sandy beaches and unspoilt natural beauty attract tourists and also day visitors from neighbouring St-Martin/St Maarten. Tourism receipts totalled an estimated EC $283.4m. in 2011 and visitor arrivals totalled 129,391 in 2012.

Anguilla Hotel and Tourism Association: Coronation Ave, POB 1020, The Valley; tel. 497-2944; fax 497-3091; e-mail ahtaadmin@anguillanet.com; internet www.anguillahta.com; f. 1981; Pres. DELROY LAKE; Exec. Dir GILDA GUMBS-SAMUEL.

Anguilla Tourist Board: Coronation Ave, POB 1388, The Valley, AI 2640; tel. 497-2759; fax 497-2710; e-mail atbtour@ivisitanguilla.com; internet ivisitanguilla.com; Dir CANDIS NILES.

Defence

The United Kingdom is responsible for the defence of Anguilla.

Education

Education is free and compulsory between the ages of five and 17 years. Primary education begins at five years of age and lasts for six years. Secondary education, beginning at 11 years of age, lasts for a further six years. There are six government primary schools and one government secondary school, on two campuses. According to UNESCO estimates, in 2007/08 enrolment at primary schools included 93% of children in the relevant age-group, while enrolment at secondary schools included 78% of pupils in the relevant age-group. Post-secondary education is undertaken abroad.

BERMUDA

Introductory Survey

LOCATION, CLIMATE, LANGUAGE, RELIGION, FLAG, CAPITAL

The Bermudas or Somers Islands are an isolated archipelago, comprising about 138 islands, in the Atlantic Ocean, about 917 km (570 miles) off the coast of South Carolina, USA. Bridges and causeways link seven of the islands to form the principal mainland. The climate is mild and humid. Temperatures are generally between 8°C (46°F) and 32°C (90°F), with an average annual rainfall of 1,470 mm (58 ins). The official language is English, but there is a small community of Portuguese speakers. Most of the inhabitants profess Christianity, and numerous denominations are represented, the principal one being the Anglican Church. The flag (proportions 1 by 2) is the British 'Red Ensign' (this usage being unique among the British colonies), with, in the fly, the colony's badge: a seated red lion holding a shield (with a gold baroque border), which depicts the wreck off Bermuda of the ship of the first settlers. The capital is Hamilton.

CONTEMPORARY POLITICAL HISTORY

Historical Context

Bermuda was first settled by the British in 1609. It has had a representative assembly since 1620 (and thus claims one of the oldest parliaments in the world), and became a British Crown Colony in 1684. Bermuda was granted internal self-government by the Constitution introduced in 1968, although the British Government retains responsibility in certain matters. Various amendments to the 1968 Constitution were made in 1973, the most important being the establishment of the Governor's Council, through which the Governor exercises responsibility for external affairs, defence, internal security and the police. In 1974 the Government Leader was restyled Premier and the Executive Council became the Cabinet.

Domestic Political Affairs

The first general election under the new Constitution, which took place in May 1968 against a background of rioting and racial tension (some 60% of the population are of African origin, the rest mostly of

European extraction), was won by the United Bermuda Party (UBP), a moderate, multiracial party whose policies were based on racial co-operation and continued support for dependent status. The underlying racial tensions were emphasized in 1972 and 1973 by shooting incidents which resulted in the deaths of the Governor, the Commissioner of Police and three others. In December 1977 the Governor's assassin and another convicted murderer were executed, and further rioting ensued. A state of emergency was declared, and British troops were flown to Bermuda to restore order.

At the general election of May 1976, the UBP was returned to power with a decreased majority. The mainly black, left-wing Progressive Labour Party (PLP), which campaigned for independence, increased its legislative presence. In August 1977 Sir John Sharpe, Premier and leader of the UBP since December 1975, resigned both posts and was succeeded by David Gibbons, the Minister of Finance.

In February 1978 a Royal Commission was established to investigate the causes of racial violence, and in August the Commission published a report which suggested the redrawing of constituency boundaries to improve the PLP's prospects for winning seats. Despite this, the UBP won the December 1980 election. Gibbons resigned as Premier and was succeeded by John Swan, the Minister of Home Affairs. Constitutional amendments introduced in 1979 included provision for closer consultation between the Premier and the Leader of the Opposition on the appointment of members of the Public Service Commission and the Boundaries Commission, and on the appointment of the Chief Justice. The 1978 Royal Commission recommended early independence for Bermuda, but the majority of the population at that time seemed to oppose such a policy. Swan had declared himself in favour of eventual independence for the colony, but only with the support of the Bermudian people.

The UBP increased its majority in the House of Assembly at a general election in February 1983. Internal divisions within the PLP led to the expulsion from the party of four PLP deputies. These members, after sitting as independents, formed a new centre party, the National Liberal Party (NLP), in August 1985. In October Swan called an early general election, hoping to take advantage of the divided opposition. The UBP was decisively returned to power. Following a general election in February 1989, the UBP remained in power, but with a reduced legislative representation.

The UBP was returned to power at a general election in October 1993. In February 1994 legislation providing for the organization of a referendum on independence for Bermuda was narrowly approved in the House of Assembly. The debate on independence was believed to have intensified as a result of the announcement in late 1993 that British and US forces would close their facilities and withdraw permanently from the island by April 1995 and September 1995, respectively. The PLP, which advocates independence for Bermuda, consistently opposed the organization of a referendum on the subject, believing that the independence issue should be determined by a general election. In May 1994 a PLP legislative motion to reject a proposed government inquiry into the possibilities for independence was narrowly approved, effectively halting further progress towards a referendum. However, the debate continued, and further legislation regarding the proposed referendum was narrowly approved in March 1995. The PLP encouraged its supporters to boycott the poll, which required not only a majority of votes, but also the approval of 40% of eligible voters in order to achieve a pro-independence result.

The referendum took place in August 1995. Some 59% of eligible voters participated in the poll, of which 74% registered their opposition to independence from the United Kingdom, and 26% expressed their support for it. The following day Swan resigned as Premier and as leader of the UBP. Factions within the governing party were perceived to have become considerably polarized during the independence debate, which had resulted in the division of opinion along racial lines. The Minister of Finance, David Saul (who had remained neutral on the independence issue), was subsequently elected leader of the UBP, and therefore became Premier. However, under his leadership divisions within the party appeared to deepen. In March 1997 Saul announced his resignation as Premier and as leader of the UBP. He was replaced by Pamela Gordon, who was elected to the party leadership (and thus as Premier) unopposed.

The PLP in power

Elections to the House of Assembly took place in November 1998. The PLP won its first ever majority in the House of Assembly. A new Cabinet was appointed and party leader Jennifer Smith was sworn in as Bermuda's first PLP Premier. Smith promised that, although independence for Bermuda remained a stated aim of her party, no immediate moves in that direction would be made.

In October 2000 the opposition UBP boycotted the opening of parliament in protest against government plans to reduce the number of seats in the House of Assembly. Gordon claimed that there had not been adequate public consultation on the matter. Premier Smith had rejected calls for a constitutional conference or a referendum on the proposals, which included replacing the two-member constituencies with single-member ones, although she did announce that the Government would hold a public meeting to discuss the issue. The

PLP believed that the existing system was weighted in favour of the UBP, which was considered the party of the white population. In December the House of Assembly approved a motion requesting that the British Government approve the establishment of a boundaries commission. Any changes would be subject to ratification by the United Kingdom's Foreign and Commonwealth Office (FCO). In January 2001 the UBP submitted an 8,500-signature petition to the British Government, demanding a constitutional conference or referendum before any changes were made. The FCO, however, stated that a constitutional conference was unnecessary, and in April it began consultations over the proposed changes. The commission recommended reducing the number of seats in the House of Assembly by four, to 36. In addition, whereas deputies had previously been elected from 20 two-member constituencies, under the proposed scheme each member of parliament would be elected by a separate constituency. The FCO approved the changes before the July 2003 general election.

In March 1999 the British Government published draft legislation redesignating its Dependencies as United Kingdom Overseas Territories, and guaranteeing their citizens' rights to a British passport and to residence in the United Kingdom. The document also stated, however, that the Overseas Territories would be obliged to reform their legislation to ensure compliance with European standards on human rights and on financial regulation. In October it was announced that in accordance with the proposed reforms, corporal and capital punishment were to be removed from the statute book. In May 2002 the British Overseas Territories Act, having received royal assent in the United Kingdom in February, came into force and granted British citizenship to the people of its Overseas Territories, including Bermuda. Under the new law Bermudians would be able to hold British passports and work in the United Kingdom and anywhere else in the European Union (see p. 281).

At an election to the smaller 36-seat House of Assembly in July 2003, the PLP retained its parliamentary majority, but its share of the popular vote was reduced. Smith resigned as Premier after it emerged that she had retained her seat, in what was regarded as a 'safe' PLP constituency, by just eight votes. She was replaced by William Alexander Scott.

In July 2005 the Misuse of Drugs Amendment Act introduced legislation allowing courts to fine those convicted of drugs offences up to US $1m. and to impose prison sentences of between 10 years and life. Despite the designation of a dedicated cabinet minister and employment of an eminent British police officer as Assistant Commissioner specializing in drugs crime prevention, drugs-related violent crime escalated during 2006.

In November 2005 a Bermuda Independence Commission, established by Scott in order to foment debate regarding the island's future, submitted its report. However, its findings were criticized for being biased, as they failed to include contributions from the UBP, including only the ruling PLP's submission. In an attempt to quell the criticism, Scott declared that discussions would take place in 2006 regarding the future status of Bermuda. However, public opinion remained strongly in favour of maintaining links with the United Kingdom. In March both the UN and the British Government indicated their support for a referendum on the issue; however, Scott maintained that the question of independence should be decided at the next general election, constitutionally due by 2008. The issue of independence created political tension between the population's black majority, from which the PLP drew much of its support, and the white minority.

Scott's premiership was abruptly curtailed in October 2006 after he was defeated in a PLP leadership contest; former Deputy Premier Ewart Brown succeeded him. Brown confirmed his commitment to addressing disruptive racial tensions among the island's communities by creating a ministerial post for matters of social rehabilitation. Racial tensions proved of particular pertinence to the opposition UBP, embroiled as it was in an internal racial discrimination controversy which, in January 2007, precipitated the resignations of House of Assembly member Jamahl Simmons and party Chairwoman Gwyneth Rawlins. Both alleged serious charges of racial discrimination against factions within the party. Simmons claimed that a white élite within the UBP was attempting to remove him from his seat; the departure of two black party members only exacerbated public scepticism about the party's professed allegiance to an integrated Bermudian society.

The unauthorized disclosure, from a source within the Bermuda police, of documents implicating the Premier and a number of other high-ranking government officials in a corruption scandal, served to compromise relations with the United Kingdom in May 2007. Brown maintained that a previous inquiry, in 2004, into the alleged dubious arrangement between government personnel (including himself) and the state-owned Bermuda Housing Corporation—whereby considerable public funds were appropriated for private enrichment—had discharged him of any misconduct.

The PLP secured a third consecutive term in office at a general election held on 18 December 2007, with 52.5% of the votes cast, while the UBP won 47.3% of the ballot. The parties' representation in the legislature remained as at the 2003 election: 22 seats for the PLP and 14 seats for the UBP. Allegations of corruption and issues of race featured prominently in the election campaign, with PLP candidates employing inflammatory rhetoric to suggest that the UBP, if elected, would install a regime oppressive to the black population. After failing to win the constituency seat he contested, Michael Dunkley was replaced as leader of the UBP by Kim Swan.

A political dispute developed in June 2009 after it was revealed that the PLP Government had agreed with US authorities to allow four Chinese Uygur (Uighur) Muslim separatists to settle in Bermuda following their release from the US detention centre at Guantánamo Bay, Cuba. The UBP claimed that Premier Brown had acted 'autocratically' by accepting the former detainees without consultation with either the Cabinet, the Governor or the British Government. On 20 June the Government survived a motion of no confidence in the House of Assembly. Following the vote, the Minister of Culture and Social Rehabilitation, Dale Butler, resigned in protest against the Premier's handling of the affair. The FCO also remonstrated with the Government for its lack of consultation, claiming that the matter fell outside the Bermudian authorities' remit. By early 2013 the Uygurs had yet to gain Bermudan citizenship.

The Cox Government

Brown resigned as Premier, and PLP leader, on 28 October 2010, in accordance with an earlier pledge to serve only one four-year term. Deputy Premier and Minister of Finance Paula Cox won the PLP leadership election on the same day, and was inaugurated as the new Premier on 29 October. Cox reorganized the Cabinet in November. Notably, Derrick Burgess, who succeeded Cox as Deputy Premier, was given responsibility for public works (one of several newly created portfolios), former Premier Dame Jennifer Smith was appointed as Minister of Education, David Burch took control of the new Ministry of National Security, and Michael Scott became Attorney-General and Minister of Justice; Cox retained the finance portfolio.Wayne Perinchief, a former Deputy Police Commissioner, was appointed as Minister of National Security in April 2011, following Burch's resignation earlier that month.

The planned merger of the UBP and the Bermuda Democratic Alliance (BDA—formed in 2009 following a split within the UBP) was postponed in May 2011 when Swan raised objections to the union, which would entail the replacement of the UBP and the BDA with a new party, the One Bermuda Alliance (OBA). Although Swan filed a successful legal challenge to prevent the dissolution of the UBP, the OBA was established later that month by seven of the nine UBP deputies and all three BDA representatives, thus displacing the UBP as the largest opposition bloc in the House of Assembly. Interim OBA leader John Barritt was inaugurated as leader of the opposition in mid-May. Craig Cannonier was elected as OBA leader in September and triumphed in a parliamentary by-election in November, becoming leader of the opposition shortly thereafter.

Cox effected a cabinet reorganization in November 2011. Among other changes, Burgess became Minister of Transport, Walter Roban was transferred to the Ministry of Public Works, Patrice Minors received the economy portfolio, and Kim Wilson was appointed as Attorney-General and Minister of Justice. However, Roban submitted his resignation later that month amid corruption allegations; he was replaced by Michael Weeks. Nevertheless, Roban was reappointed to the Cabinet in June 2012 as Minister of Transport following Burgess' resignation. George Fergusson succeeded Sir Richard Gozney as Governor in May.

Recent developments: the 2012 general election

Elections to the House of Assembly took place on 17 December 2012. The OBA emerged victorious, winning 51.7% of the ballot and 19 seats in the legislature, compared with 46.1% and 17 seats, respectively, for the PLP. Turn-out was recorded at 70.7%. Cannonier assumed the premiership on the following day. His Cabinet, which was installed on 20 December, included Everard Richards as Minister of Finance, Michael Fahy as Minister of Home Affairs, Michael Dunkley as Minister of Public Safety, and Mark Pettingill as Attorney-General and Minister of Justice. Promoting economic recovery was declared to be the main aim of the new Government. Cox failed to retain her seat in the election and consequently resigned as PLP leader; Marc Bean was elected as her replacement on 21 December. The UBP did not contest the election (Swan unsuccessfully stood as an independent), effectively marking the dissolution of the party.

The 'Offshore' Financial Sector

In 1999 Premier Smith reassured the Organisation for Economic Co-operation and Development (OECD, see p. 388) that Bermuda was determined to improve regulation of the 'offshore' financial services sector. A report by the Financial Action Task Force on Money Laundering (see p. 465) concluded in June 2000 that Bermuda appeared 'to have effective regulations and supervision' in place in its financial services sector. In the same month the Government agreed to co-operate with OECD in an international effort to reduce tax evasion, promising to end within five years the 'harmful' practices

that had given the island a reputation as a tax haven. Measures included a pledge to exchange information about tax in Bermuda with other nations, and the introduction of legislation for companies to audit accounts and for these to be made available to the Bermudian authorities. The Government had, however, pledged to maintain its existing tax system, which included no income tax. In December the members of the House of Assembly agreed, for the first time, to declare their assets and financial interests.

In mid-2002 the issue of financial transparency and corporate governance in Bermuda re-emerged following the disastrous collapse of several US multinationals. The indictment on tax evasion charges of Dennis Kozlowski, the former CEO of Tyco International Ltd, a manufacturer of electronic security systems with a nominal headquarters on the island, fuelled a growing campaign in the USA against the perceived lack of financial scrutiny in Bermuda. The USA's Corporate Patriot Enforcement Act of 2005 sought to discourage US corporations to relocate their headquarters from the USA to offshore sites such as Bermuda, by making them still liable to pay tax in the USA.

In December 2006 the House of Assembly ratified legislation to facilitate the registration and license of investment funds in the territory by eliminating 'unnecessary' administrative protocols and to encourage further expansion in a sector already attractive to international fund operators. Bermuda's financial sector was criticized in February 2007 for its resistance to regulatory mechanisms and reluctance to engage in transparency exercises. In April 2009 OECD included Bermuda on its 'grey list' of tax havens that had committed to, but not implemented, an internationally agreed standard of transparency measures. However, Bermuda was the first jurisdiction to be removed from the list two months later after it signed its 12th tax information-sharing agreement. By early 2013 the Government had signed a further 26 accords. In May Bermuda reached agreement with the United Kingdom to share information about bank accounts held in the territory.

CONSTITUTION AND GOVERNMENT

The Constitution was introduced in June 1968 and amended in 1973 and 1979. An appointed Governor, responsible for external affairs, defence and internal security, represents the British monarch. The bicameral legislature comprises the Senate (11 nominated members) and the House of Assembly, with 36 members representing separate constituencies elected for five years by universal adult suffrage. The Governor appoints the majority leader in the House as Premier, and the latter nominates other ministers. The Cabinet is responsible to the legislature. For the purposes of local government, the island has long been divided into nine parishes (originally known as 'tribes', except for the 'public land' of St George's, the capital until 1815). The town of St George's and the city of Hamilton constitute the two municipalities of the territory.

REGIONAL AND INTERNATIONAL CO-OPERATION

Bermuda, the oldest colony of the United Kingdom, has the status of Overseas Territory in association with the European Union (see p. 281) and has also been granted Designated Territory status by the British Government (this allows Bermudian-based funds and unit trusts access to the British market). Bermuda's financial services also benefit from a special tax treaty with the USA. A similar agreement was signed in November 2005 with Australia, in which both parties would share tax information on a specific subject under investigation or audit. In 2000 Bermuda joined the Caribbean Tourism Organization. In 2003 Bermuda became an associate member of the Caribbean Community and Common Market (CARICOM, see p. 231). The territory is a member of the Commonwealth (see p. 244).

ECONOMIC AFFAIRS

In 1997, according to estimates by the World Bank, Bermuda's gross national income, measured at average 1995–97 prices, was US $2,128m. During 2002–11, it was estimated, the population increased at an average annual rate of 0.3%. Overall gross domestic product (GDP) increased, in real terms, at an average annual rate of 0.4% in 2003–11; real GDP decreased by 2.8% in 2011.

Agriculture (including forestry, fishing, and mining and quarrying) engaged only 1.7% of the employed labour force in 2012. Agriculture, forestry and fishing contributed 0.8% of GDP in 2011. The principal crops were potatoes, carrots, bananas, vegetables and melons. Flowers are grown for export. Other vegetables and fruit are also grown, but Bermuda remains very dependent upon food imports, which, with beverages and tobacco, accounted for 17.4% of total imports in 2011. There is a small fishing industry, mainly for domestic consumption. In 2003–11, according to official figures, agricultural GDP increased by an annual average of 2.4%; the sector declined by 4.0% in 2011.

Industry (including manufacturing, construction, quarrying and public utilities) contributed 6.2% of GDP in 2011 and engaged 9.6% of the employed labour force in 2012. The principal industrial sector is construction. Industrial GDP decreased by an average of 1.8% per year in 2003–11; the sector decreased by 4.4% in 2011.

Manufacturing contributed 1.1% of GDP in 2011 and employed 2.1% of the active labour force in 2012. The main activities include ship repairs, boat-building and the manufacture of paints and pharmaceuticals. According to official figures, in real terms, the manufacturing sector declined at an average rate of 3.2% per year during 2003–11; the sector decreased by 5.8% in 2011.

The construction (including quarrying) sector contributed 3.4% of GDP in 2011 and engaged 6.4% of the employed labour force in 2012. In real terms, the construction sector decreased at an average rate of 0.7% per year during 2003–11; sectoral GDP decreased by 15.5% in 2010 and further by 5.6% in 2011.

Energy requirements are met mainly by the import of mineral fuels (fuels accounted for 8.9% of total imports in 2011). Most of Bermuda's water is provided by privately collected rainfall.

Bermuda is overwhelmingly a service economy, with service industries contributing 93.0% of GDP in 2011 and engaging 88.7% of the employed labour force in 2012. There is a significant commercial and 'offshore' financial sector. An estimated 18.9% of the employed labour force were engaged directly in the finance, insurance, real estate and business sectors in 2012. International business was estimated to account for 23.1% of GDP in 2011. At the end of 2012 the number of companies registered in Bermuda totalled 14,578, a 1.8% decline on the previous year's total. Another important source of income is the 'free flag' registration of shipping. Tourism is estimated to account for some 60% of all employment, directly and indirectly. The total number of tourists, particularly of cruise ship passengers, is strictly controlled, in order to maintain Bermuda's environment and its market for wealthier visitors. Most tourists come from the USA (some 73.2% of total arrivals by air in 2009). In 2012 some 610,230 tourists visited Bermuda, a 6.3% decline on the previous year's figure. Tourism revenues increased in 2011, to US $434.8m., compared with US $385.5m in 2010. The GDP of the hotel and restaurants sector grew by 4.1% in 2011. In 2003–11 the GDP of the services sector increased by an annual average of 0.5%; services GDP decreased by 1.8% in 2011.

Bermuda is almost entirely dependent upon imports, has very few commodity exports and, therefore, consistently records a large visible merchandise trade deficit (B $897m. in 2011). Receipts from the service industries normally ensure a surplus on the current account of the balance of payments (recorded at $679m. in 2011). The USA is the principal source of imports (providing 71.1% of total imports in 2011) and the principal market for exports. Canada is another important trading partner. The main exports are rum, flowers, medicinal and pharmaceutical products and the re-export of petroleum products. In 2011 the principal imports were machinery and transport equipment, food, beverages and tobacco, chemicals and related products, and mineral fuels and lubricants.

In 2012/13 there was an estimated budgetary deficit of some B $24.4m. (excluding capital expenditure). The average annual rate of inflation was 2.6% in 2002–12. The rate averaged 2.4% in 2012. In 2012 the official unemployment rate was recorded at 8.0%.

Bermudians enjoy a high standard of living, although there is considerable inequality in the distribution of wealth. Proximity to the USA and the parity of the US and Bermuda dollars help both tourism and financial industries, and Bermuda's status as a United Kingdom Overseas Territory remains a perceived contributor to political stability and financial integrity. The international business sector is the most significant component of the territory's economy, contributing about one-quarter of GDP. Following several years of rapid expansion, this sector contracted in 2008–12 owing to the global economic downturn. The international recession also had a negative impact on the tourism sector, which relied heavily on visitors from the USA, although the opening of a mega-cruise port in 2009 resulted in a steady increase in cruise ship arrivals during 2009–11; air arrivals rose in 2011 after three consecutive years of decline. In 2012 cruise ship and air arrivals both decreased, although the construction industry registered positive growth for the first time since 2008. The economy as a whole contracted by 5.1% in 2009, by 2.2% in 2010, by 2.8% in 2011 and, according to government estimates, by a further 2.0% in 2012. The Ministry of Finance projected that real GDP would decrease by a further 0.8% in 2013, but expected growth to resume from 2014; however, owing to the islands' heavy dependence on the tourism and 'offshore' finance sectors, this was conditional upon the continued recovery of the US economy.

PUBLIC HOLIDAYS

2014: 1 January (New Year's Day), 18 April (Good Friday), 24 May (Bermuda Day), 16 June (National Heroes' Day), 31 July (Emancipation Day), 1 August (Somers' Day), 1 September (Labour Day), 11 November (Remembrance Day), 25–26 December (Christmas).

Statistical Survey

Source: Dept of Statistics, Cabinet Office, POB HM 3015, Hamilton HM MX; tel. 297-7761; fax 295-8390; e-mail statistics@gov.bm; internet www.statistics.gov.bm.

AREA AND POPULATION

Area: 53.3 sq km (20.59 sq miles).

Population (civilian, non-institutional): 62,059 at census of 20 May 2000; 64,237 (males 30,858, females 33,379) at census of 20 May 2010. *Mid-2013* (official projection): 65,002.

Density (mid-2013): 1,219.5 per sq km.

Population by Age and Sex (official projections at mid-2013): *0–14:* 10,949 (males 5,586, females 5,363); *15–64:* 44,964 (males 21,571, females 23,393); *65 and over:* 9,089 (males 3,706, females 5,383); *Total* 65,002 (males 30,863, females 34,139).

Principal Town (2011, UN estimate): Hamilton (capital) 11,065. Source: UN, *World Urbanization Prospects: The 2011 Revision.*

Births, Marriages and Deaths (2009 unless otherwise indicated): Live births 819 (birth rate 12.7 per 1,000); Marriages 721 in 2008 (marriage rate 11.2 per 1,000); Deaths 470 (death rate 7.3 per 1,000) (Sources: UN, *Population and Vital Statistics Report*; UN, *Demographic Yearbook*). *2011:* Birth rate 11.4; Death rate 7.6 (Source: Pan American Health Organization).

Life Expectancy (years at birth, 2011): 80.7 (males 77.5; females 84.0). Source: Pan American Health Organization.

Employment (2012, preliminary): Agriculture, forestry, fishing, mining and quarrying 600; Manufacturing 753; Electricity, gas and water 386; Construction 2,274; Wholesale and retail trade 4,136; Hotels and restaurants 4,393; Transport and communications 2,178; Financial intermediation 2,508; Real estate 490; Business activities 3,720; Public administration 4,298; Education, health and social services 3,756; Other community, social and personal services 2,135; International business activity 3,867; *Total employed* 35,494.

HEALTH AND WELFARE

Total Fertility Rate (children per woman, 2011): 2.0.

Physicians (per 1,000 head, 2005): 2.1.

Hospital Beds (per 1,000 head, 2010): 5.3.

Health Expenditure (% of GDP, 2004): 4.3.

Health Expenditure (public, % of total, 1995): 53.2.

Total Carbon Dioxide Emissions ('000 metric tons, 2008): 388.7.

Carbon Dioxide Emissions Per Head (metric tons, 2008): 6.1.

Source: partly Pan American Health Organization.

For other sources and definitions, see explanatory note on p. vi.

AGRICULTURE, ETC.

Principal Crops (metric tons, 2011, FAO estimates): Potatoes 1,029; Carrots and turnips 374; Vegetables and melons 3,663; Bananas 320.

Livestock (2011, FAO estimates): Cattle 650; Horses 1,000; Pigs 800.

Livestock Products (metric tons, 2011, FAO estimates): Cows' milk 1,400; Hen eggs 360.

Fishing (metric tons, live weight, 2010): Groupers 45; Snappers and jobfishes 31; Wahoo 81; Yellowfin tuna 37; Carangids 56; Caribbean spiny lobster 39; Total catch (incl. others) 382.

Source: FAO.

INDUSTRY

Electric Energy (production, million kWh): 643 in 2007; 645 in 2008; 733 in 2009. Source: UN Industrial Commodity Statistics Database.

FINANCE

Currency and Exchange Rates: 100 cents = 1 Bermuda dollar (B $). *Sterling, US Dollar and Euro Equivalents* (31 December 2012): £1 sterling = B $1.578; US $1 = B $1.000; €1 = B $1.319; B $100 = £63.37 = US $100.00 = €75.79. *Exchange Rate:* The Bermuda dollar is at par with the US dollar. Note: US and Canadian currencies are also accepted.

Budget (B $ million, 2012/13, estimates): Total current account revenue 909.6; Total current account expenditure 934.0; Total capital expenditure 76.2.

Cost of Living (Consumer Price Index; base: 2000 = 100): All items 135.6 in 2010; 139.2 in 2011; 142.6 in 2012. Source: ILO.

Gross Domestic Product (US $ million at constant 1996 prices): 5,322.6 in 2009; 5,208.1 in 2010; 5,060.9 in 2011.

Expenditure on the Gross Domestic Product (B $ million at current prices, 2011, UN estimates): Government final consumption expenditure 1,188.6; Private final consumption expenditure 4,429.3; Gross fixed capital formation 1,122.2; Change in inventories 62.1; *Total domestic expenditure* 6,802.2; Exports of goods and services 2,458.5; *Less* Imports of goods and services 3,287.9; *GDP in purchasers' values* 5,972.7. Source: UN Statistics Division, National Accounts Main Aggregates Database.

Gross Domestic Product by Economic Activity (B $ million at current prices, 2011): Agriculture, forestry and fishing 43.8; Manufacturing 65.2; Electricity, gas and water 97.6; Construction and quarrying 200.0; Wholesale and retail trade and repair services 382.0; Restaurants and hotels 263.8; Transport and communications 265.3; Financial intermediation 735.6; Real estate and renting activities 965.0; Business activities 526.4; Public administration 343.1; Education, health and social work 458.5; Other community, social and personal services 122.7; International business activity 1,342.8; *Sub-total* 5,811.8; *Less* Imputed bank service charges 444.1; Taxes and duties on imports 189.5; *GDP in purchasers' values* 5,557.1.

Balance of Payments (B $ million, 2011): Exports of goods f.o.b. 13; Imports of goods f.o.b. –910; *Trade balance* –897; Receipts from services and income 3,274; Payments on services and income –1,698; *Current balance* 679; Direct investment (net) 444; Portfolio investment (net) –2,549; Other investments (net) 1,832; Reserve assets (net) 11; *Overall balance* 418.

EXTERNAL TRADE

Principal Commodities (US $ million, 2011): *Imports:* Food, beverages and tobacco 151.4; Mineral fuels and lubricants 77.2; Chemicals and related products 84.0; Basic manufactures 61.6; Machinery and transport equipment 168.9; Total (incl. others) 868.7. *Exports:* Total 13.5.

Principal Trading Partners (US $ million): *Imports* (2011): Canada 107.3; Caribbean countries 13.0; United Kingdom 27.4; USA 617.8; Total (incl. others) 868.7. *Exports* (1995): France 7.5; United Kingdom 3.9; USA 31.3; Total (incl. others) 62.9. *2011:* Total exports 13.5.

TRANSPORT

Road Traffic (vehicles in use, 2011): Private cars 21,991; Motorcycles 20,395; Buses, taxis and limousines 771; Trucks and tank wagons 3,969; Other 1,535; *Total* 48,661.

Shipping: *Ship Arrivals* (2004): Cruise ships 161; Cargo ships 186; Oil and gas tankers 21. *Flag Registered Fleet* (at 31 December 2012): Vessels 209; Total displacement 12,189,448 grt (Source: Lloyd's List Intelligence, www.lloydslistintelligence.com). *International Freight Traffic* ('000 metric tons, 1990): Goods loaded 130; Goods unloaded 470 (Source: UN, *Monthly Bulletin of Statistics*).

Civil Aviation (2011): Aircraft arrivals 13,252; Passengers 404,448; Air cargo 3,423,870 kg; Air mail 462,263 kg.

TOURISM

Visitor Arrivals: 580,193 (arrivals by air 232,262, cruise ship passengers 347,931) in 2010; 651,502 (arrivals by air 236,038, cruise ship passengers 415,464) in 2011; 610,230 (arrivals by air 231,968, cruise ship passengers 378,262) in 2012.

Tourism Receipts (US $ million, incl. passenger transport): 321.2 in 2009; 385.5 in 2010; 434.8 in 2011.

COMMUNICATIONS MEDIA

Telephones (2010): 57,800 main lines in use.

Mobile Cellular Telephones (2010): 88,200 subscribers.

Personal Computers: 14,250 (225 per 1,000 persons) in 2004.

Internet Users (2009): 54,000.

Broadband Subscribers (2010): 40,100.

Source: International Telecommunication Union.

EDUCATION

Pre-primary (1999, unless otherwise indicated): 12 schools (2006); 191 teachers; 429 pupils.

Primary: 17 (and 5 middle) schools (2006); 608 teachers (2009/10); 4,473 pupils (2009/10) (Source: partly UNESCO Institute for Statistics).

Senior: 18 schools (1999); 825 teachers (2009/10); 4,418 pupils (2009/10)*.

Higher: 1 institution (2002); 83 teachers (2009/10); 834 students (2009/10).
* Including 7 private schools.

2004: Local student enrolment 10,594 (government schools including pre-school 6,370, private schools excluding pre-school 3,512, Bermuda College 712); Teachers 1,310.

Pupil-teacher Ratio (primary education, UNESCO estimate): 7.4 in 2009/10. Source: UNESCO Institute for Statistics.

Adult Literacy Rate (UNESCO estimates): 99% (males 98%; females 99%) in 1998 (Source: UNESCO, *Statistical Yearbook*).

Directory

The Government

HEAD OF STATE

Queen: HM Queen ELIZABETH II.

Governor and Commander-in-Chief: GEORGE DUNCAN FERGUSSON (took office 23 May 2012).

Deputy Governor: DAVID ARKLEY.

CABINET
(May 2013)

The Government is formed by the One Bermuda Alliance.

Premier: CRAIG CANNONIER.

Minister of Public Works: TREVOR MONIZ.

Minister of Economic Development: Dr GRANT GIBBONS.

Minister of Finance: EVERARD TRENTON (BOB) RICHARDS.

Minister of Environment and Planning: SYLVAN DEVEAUX RICHARDS, Jr.

Minister of Education: Sen. NALTON SINCLAIR BRANGMAN.

Minister of Public Safety: MICHAEL HENRY DUNKLEY.

Minister of Tourism and Transport: SHAWN GRANVILLE CROCKWELL.

Minister of Health and Seniors: PATRICIA JASMINE GORDON PAMPLIN.

Minister of Community and Cultural Development: REGINALD WAYNE EUGENE SCOTT.

Minister without Portfolio: LEAH SCOTT.

Minister of Home Affairs: Sen. MICHAEL FAHY.

Attorney-General and Minister of Justice: MARK JAMES PETTINGILL.

MINISTRIES

Office of the Governor: Government House, 11 Langton Hill, Pembroke HM 13; tel. 292-3600; fax 292-6831; e-mail executiveofficer@gov.bm; internet www.gov.bm.

Office of the Premier: Cabinet Office, Cabinet Bldg, 105 Front St, Hamilton HM 12; tel. 292-5501; fax 292-8397; e-mail premier@gov.bm; internet www.gov.bm.

Ministry of Community and Cultural Development: Hamilton HM 12.

Ministry of Economic Development: Hamilton HM 12.

Ministry of Education: 14 Waller's Point Rd, St David's DD 03; tel. 278-3300; fax 278-3348; e-mail reve@gov.bm; internet www.moed.bm.

Ministry of Environment and Planning: Dame Lois Browne-Evans Bldg, 5th Floor, 58 Court St, Hamilton HM 12; tel. 297-7590; e-mail aftodd@gov.bm.

Ministry of Finance: 2nd Floor, Government Administration Bldg, 30 Parliament St, Hamilton HM 12; tel. 295-5151; fax 295-5727.

Ministry of Health and Seniors: Continental Bldg, 25 Church St, Hamilton HM 12; tel. 278-4900; fax 292-2622; e-mail wjones@gov.bm; internet www.health.gov.bm.

Ministry of Home Affairs: Hamilton HM12.

Ministry of Justice and Attorney-General's Chambers: Penthouse Floor, Global House, 43 Church St, Hamilton HM 12; tel. 292-2463; fax 292-3608; e-mail agc@gov.bm.

Ministry of Public Safety: Government Administration Bldg, 1st Floor, 30 Parliament St, POB HM 1364, Hamilton HM 12; tel. 297-7819; fax 295-4780; e-mail mtelemaque@gov.bm.

Ministry of Public Works: 3rd Floor, General Post Office Bldg, 56 Church St, Hamilton HM 12; tel. 295-5151; fax 295-0170; e-mail nfox@bdagov.bm.

Ministry of Tourism and Transport: Global House, 43 Church St, Hamilton HM12; tel. 295-3130; fax 295-1013; e-mail clwhitter@gov .bm.

Legislature

SENATE

President: CAROLANNE MARIE BASSETT.
Vice-President: JOAN DILLAS-WRIGHT.
There are 11 nominated members.

HOUSE OF ASSEMBLY

Speaker: K. H. (RANDOLPH) HORTON.
Deputy Speaker: SUZANN ROBERTS-HOLSHOUSER.
Clerk to the Legislature: SHERNETTE WOLFE; tel. 292-7408; fax 292-2006; e-mail smwolffe@gov.bm.
General Election, 17 December 2012

Party	% of votes	Seats
One Bermuda Alliance (OBA)	51.68	19
Progressive Labour Party (PLP) . . .	46.07	17
Independent	2.25	—
Total valid votes	100.00	36

Political Organizations

One Bermuda Alliance (OBA): 58 Reid St, POB 1940, Hamilton HM HX; tel. 294-3264; e-mail info@oba.bm; internet www.oba.bm; f. 2011 by fmr mems of the United Bermuda Party and the Bermuda Democratic Alliance; Leader CRAIG CANNONIER; Chair. THAD HOLLIS; Sec. KAREN MAGNUM.

Progressive Labour Party (PLP): Alaska Hall, 16 Court St, POB 1367, Hamilton HM 17; tel. 292-2264; fax 295-7890; e-mail info@plp .bm; internet www.plp.bm; f. 1963; advocates the 'Bermudianization' of the economy, more equitable taxation, a more developed system of welfare and preparation for independence; Leader MARC A. R. BEAN; Chair. MAYNARD DILL; Sec.-Gen. TULANI O. BULFORD.

Judicial System

Supreme Court: Parliament St, Hamilton HM 12; tel. 292-1350; fax 295-6594; unlimited civil jurisdiction and jurisdiction over all serious criminal matters; also hears civil and criminal appeals from the Magistrates' Courts; Chief Justice IAN R. C. KAWALEY; Registrar CHARLENE A. SCOTT.

Court of Appeal: Hamilton HM 12; f. 1964; Pres. EDWARD ZACCA.

Director of Public Prosecutions: RORY FIELD.

There are also three Magistrates' Courts with a limited civil jurisdiction and jurisdiction over all petty offences.

Religion

CHRISTIANITY

The Anglican Communion

According to the latest available census figures (2000), some 23% of the population are Anglicans. The Anglican Church of Bermuda consists of a single, extra-provincial diocese, directly under the metropolitan jurisdiction of the Archbishop of Canterbury, the Primate of All England.

Bishop of Bermuda: Rt Rev. PATRICK WHITE, Bishop's Lodge, 18 Ferrar's Lane, Pembroke HM 08, POB HM 769, Hamilton HM CX; tel. 292-6987; fax 292-5421; internet www.anglican.bm.

The Roman Catholic Church

According to the latest available census figures (2000), some 15% of the population are Roman Catholics. Bermuda forms a single diocese, suffragan to the archdiocese of Kingston in Jamaica. The Bishop participates in the Antilles Episcopal Conference (currently based in Port of Spain, Trinidad and Tobago).

Bishop of Hamilton in Bermuda: ROBERT JOSEPH KURTZ, 2 Astwood Rd, POB HM 1191, Hamilton HM EX; tel. 232-4414; fax 232-4447; e-mail rjkurtz@northrock.bm.

Protestant Churches

According to the 2000 census, 11% of the population are African Methodist Episcopalians, 7% are Seventh-day Adventists, 4% are Pentecostalists and 4% are Wesleyan Methodists. The Presbyterian Church, the Church of God, the Salvation Army, the Brethren Church and the Baptist Church are also active in Bermuda.

Baptist Church: Emmanuel Baptist Church, 35 Dundonald St, Hamilton HM 10; tel. 295-6555; fax 296-4491; Pastor RONALD K. SMITH.

Wesley Methodist Church: 41 Church St, Hamilton HM 12; tel. 292-0418; fax 295-9460; e-mail info@wesley.bm; internet www .wesley.bm; Rev. CALVIN STONE.

The Press

The Bermuda Sun: 19 Elliott St, POB HM 1241, Hamilton HM FX; tel. 295-3902; fax 292-5597; e-mail feedback@bermudasun.bm; internet www.bermudasun.bm; f. 1964; 2 a week; official govt gazette; Co-Publr and Editor-in-Chief TONY MCWILLIAM; Co-Publr and Gen. Man. LISA BEAUCHAMP; circ. 12,500.

The Bermudian: POB HM 283, Hamilton HM AX; tel. 232-7041; fax 232-7042; e-mail info@thebermudian.com; internet www .thebermudian.com; f. 1930; monthly; pictorial and lifestyle magazine; Editor TINA STEVENSON; circ. 7,500.

Bermudian Business: POB HM 283, Hamilton HM AX; tel. 232-7041; fax 232-7042; e-mail info@thebermudian.com; internet www .bermudianbusiness.com; f. 1996; publ. by The Bermudian Publishing Co Ltd; Publr TINA STEVENSON; circ. 2,500.

Preview Bermuda: 19 Elliott St, POB HM 3273, Hamilton HM PX; tel. 292-4155; fax 292-4156; e-mail info@previewbermuda.com; internet www.previewbermuda.com; monthly magazine; caters to tourists and visitors to Bermuda; Publr JACKIE STEVENSON; circ. 15,000 per month.

The Royal Gazette: 2 Par-la-Ville Rd, POB HM 1025, Hamilton HM DX; tel. 295-5881; fax 292-2498; e-mail letters@royalgazette.bm; internet www.theroyalgazette.com; f. 1828; morning daily; incorporates *The Colonist* and *Daily News* (f. 1866); Editor WILLIAM J. ZUILL; Man. Dir KEITH JENSEN; circ. 17,500.

The Worker's Voice: 49 Union Sq., Hamilton HM 12; tel. 292-0044; fax 295-7992; e-mail csmith@biu.bm; internet www.biu.bm/ #!publications; fortnightly; organ of the Bermuda Industrial Union; Editor-in-Chief CALVIN SMITH.

This Week in Bermuda: 13 Addendum Lane, Pembroke, POB 937, HM 07; tel. 295-1189; fax 295-3445; e-mail info@thisweek.bm; internet www.thisweek.bm; Editor CANDICE E. DICKINSON; Gen. Man. HORST AUGUSTIMOVIC.

Publishers

Bermuda Maritime Museum Press: POB MA 133, Sandys MA BX; tel. 234-1333; fax 234-1735; e-mail info@bmm.bm; internet www .bmm.bm; publishes books, *MARITimes* magazine, *Bermuda Journal of Archaeology and Maritime History*; Chair. ROBERT STEINHOFF.

Bermudian Publishing Co Ltd: POB HM 283, Hamilton HM AX; tel. 232-7041; fax 232-7042; e-mail info@thebermudian.com; internet www.thebermudian.com; social sciences, sociology, sports; Editor TINA STEVENSON.

MediaHouse Ltd: 19 Elliot St, Hamilton HM 10; tel. 295-1944; e-mail rfrench@mediahouse.com; internet www.mediahouse.com; f. 1959 as Island Press; rebranded as above in 2005; newspapers, magazines, directories; CEO RANDY FRENCH.

Broadcasting and Communications

TELECOMMUNICATIONS

Bermuda Digital Communications/CellularOne: 22 Reid St, Hamilton HM 3262; tel. 296-4010; fax 296-4020; e-mail info@ cellularone.bm; internet www.cellularone.bm; f. 1998; mobile cellular telephone operator; CEO KURT EVE.

Bermuda Telephone Co (BTC): 30 Victoria St, POB 1021, Hamilton HM DX; tel. 295-1001; fax 295-1192; e-mail customersupport@btc .bm; internet www.btc.bm; f. 1987; Pres. and CEO LLOYD FRAY.

Digicel Bermuda: Washington Mall, 22 Church St, Phase II, POB 896, Hamilton HM 11; tel. 500-5000; fax 295-3235; e-mail info .bermuda@digicelgroup.com; internet www.digicelbermuda.com; f. 2005; mobile telecommunications and internet services provider; CEO (Bermuda) WAYNE MICHAEL CAINES.

LinkBermuda Ltd: 1 Middle Rd, Smith's FL 03, POB HM 151, Hamilton HM AX; tel. 497-7000; fax 296-4490; e-mail helpdesk@ LinkBermuda.com; internet www.LinkBermuda.com; new fibre-optic submarine cable, Gemini Bermuda, installed in 2007; acquired by the Bragg Group, Canada, in 2011; CEO ANN PETLEY-JONES.

North Rock Communications Ltd: 22 Church St, Hamilton, HM 11; tel. 540-0585; fax 540-2701; e-mail info@northrock.bm; internet www.northrock.bm; f. 1997; wireless and dial-up internet services provider; Gen. Man. VICKI COELHO.

TeleBermuda International Ltd (TBI): Victoria Pl., 1st Floor, 31 Victoria St, POB HM 3043, Hamilton HM 10; POB HM 3043, Hamilton HM NX; tel. 296-9000; fax 298-9010; e-mail business@telebermuda.com; internet www.telebermuda.com; f. 1997; a division of GlobeNet Communications, provides an international voice and data service; owns a fibre-optic network connecting Bermuda, Cayman Islands and the USA; Pres. and COO GREGORY SWAN.

BROADCASTING

Radio

Bermuda Broadcasting Co: POB HM 452, Hamilton HM BX; tel. 295-2828; fax 295-4282; e-mail zbmzfb@bermudabroadcasting.com; f. 1982 as merger of ZBM (f. 1943) and ZFB (f. 1962); operates 4 radio stations; CEO ULRIC P. (RICK) RICHARDSON; Comptroller MALCOLM R. FLETCHER.

DeFontes Broadcasting Co Ltd (VSB): 94 Reid St, POB HM 1450, Hamilton HM FX; tel. 292-0050; fax 295-1658; e-mail news@vsbbermuda.com; internet www.vsbbermuda.com; f. 1981 as St George's Broadcasting Co; commercial; 4 radio stations; Pres. KENNETH DEFONTES; Station Man. MIKE BISHOP.

Television

Bermuda Broadcasting Co: see Radio; operates 2 TV stations (Channels 7 and 9).

Bermuda Cablevision Ltd: 19 Laffan St, POB 1642, Hamilton HM GX; tel. 292-5544; fax 295-3023; e-mail info@cablevision.bm; internet www.cablevision.bm; f. 1988; 180 channels; Gen. Man. TERRY ROBERSON.

DeFontes Broadcasting Co Ltd (VSB): see Radio; operates 1 TV station.

Finance

(cap. = capital; res = reserves; dep. = deposits; m. = million; brs = branches; amounts in Bermuda dollars, unless otherwise stated)

BANKING

Central Bank

Bermuda Monetary Authority: BMA House, 43 Victoria St, Hamilton HM 12; tel. 295-5278; fax 292-7471; e-mail info@bma.bm; internet www.bma.bm; f. 1969; central issuing and monetary authority; cap. 20.0m., res 24.7m., total assets 187.4m. (Dec. 2009); Chair. GERALD SIMONS; CEO JEREMY COX.

Commercial Banks

Bank of N. T. Butterfield & Son Ltd: 65 Front St, POB HM 195, Hamilton HM 12; tel. 295-1111; fax 292-4365; e-mail contact@bntb.bm; internet www.bm.butterfieldgroup.com; f. 1858; inc 1904; cap. 5.5m., res 1,313.2m., dep. 8,228m. (Dec. 2010); Chair. BRENDAN McDONAUGH; Pres. and CEO BRADFORD KOPP; 4 brs.

Bermuda Commercial Bank Ltd: Bermuda Commercial Bank Bldg, 19 Par-la-Ville Rd, POB 1748, Hamilton HM GX; tel. 295-5678; fax 295-8091; e-mail elambert@bcb.bm; internet www.bermuda-bcb.com; f. 1969; cap. US $16.8m., res US $8.3m., dep. US $457.5m. (Sept. 2012); COO HORST E. FINKBEINER, II; Chief Financial Officer GREG REID.

HSBC Bank Bermuda Ltd: 6 Front St, POB HM 1020, Hamilton HM 11; tel. 295-4000; fax 295-7093; e-mail customer.care@hsbc.bm; internet www.hsbc.bm; f. 1889; fmrly Bank of Bermuda Ltd; 100% acquired by HSBC Asia Holdings BV (Netherlands) in Feb. 2004; name changed as above in May 2010; cap. US $30.0m., res US $432.6m., dep. US $9,752.1m. (Dec. 2010); Chair. PHILLIP BUTTERFIELD; CEO RICHARD MOSELEY; 7 brs.

STOCK EXCHANGE

Bermuda Stock Exchange: 30 Victoria St, 3rd Floor, POB 1369, Hamilton HM FX; tel. 292-7212; fax 292-7619; e-mail info@bsx.com; internet www.bsx.com; f. 1971; more than 600 listed equities, funds, debt issues and depositary programmes; Chair. DAVID BROWN; Pres. and CEO GREG WOJCIECHOWSKI.

INSURANCE

The majority of insurance companies in Bermuda are subsidiaries of foreign insurance companies, or owned by foreign industrial or financial concerns.

Bermuda Insurance Market Information Office: Cedarpark Centre, 48 Cedar Ave, POB HM 2911, Hamilton HM LX; tel. 292-9829; fax 295-3532; e-mail biminfo@bii.bm; internet www.bermuda-insurance.org; publr of industry newsletter; Dir (Information Services) DAVID FOX.

Major Companies

ACE Bermuda: ACE Bldg, 17 Woodbourne Ave, POB HM 1015, Hamilton HM DX; tel. 295-5200; fax 298-9620; e-mail info@acebermuda.com; internet www.acebermuda.com; f. 1985; total revenue $14,154m. (Dec. 2007); Pres. G. REES FLETCHER; Regional Exec. and COO ALLISON TOWLSON.

American Safety Reinsurance Ltd (ASRE): The Boyle Bldg, 2nd Floor, 31 Queen St, Hamilton HM 11; tel. 296-8560; fax 296-8561; e-mail npascall@amsafety.bm; internet www.amsafety.bm; subsidiary of American Safety Insurance Holdings, Ltd; Chief Officer NICHOLAS PASCALL.

Argus Insurance Co Ltd: Argus Insurance Bldg, 14 Wesley St, POB HM 1064, Hamilton HM EX; tel. 295-2021; fax 295-6591; e-mail insurance@argus.bm; internet www.argus.bm; Chair. SHEILA E. NICOLL; CEO ALISON HILL.

BF&M Ltd: BF&M Insurance Bldg, 112 Pitts Bay Rd, Pembroke HM 08; tel. 295-5566; fax 292-8604; e-mail jwight@bfm.bm; internet www.bfm.bm; holding co for insurance and insurance related cos; CEO JOHN WIGHT.

Flagstone Reinsurance: Wellesley House, 2nd Floor, 90 Pitts Bay Rd, Pembroke HM 08; tel. 278-4300; fax 296-9879; e-mail info@flagstonere.com; internet www.flagstonere.bm; CEO DAVID BROWN.

Hiscox Insurance Co (Bermuda) Ltd (Hiscox Bermuda): Wessex House, 4th Floor, 45 Reid St, Hamilton, HM12; tel. 278-8300; fax 278-8301; e-mail jeremy.pinchin@hiscox.bm; internet www.hiscox.bm; CEO JEREMY PINCHIN.

Paumanock Insurance Co Ltd: Windsor Pl., 3rd Floor, 18 Queen St, Hamilton; tel. 292-2404; fax 292-2648.

Validus Reinsurance Ltd: 48 Par-la-Ville Rd, Suite 1790, Hamilton HM 11; tel. 278-9000; fax 278-9090; e-mail conan.ward@validusre.bm; internet www.validusre.bm; f. 2005; general reinsurance coverage; CEO CONAN M. WARD.

XL Insurance Co Ltd: Brian O'Hara House, 1 Bermudiana Rd, Hamilton HM 08; tel. 292-8515; fax 292-5280; e-mail contact.xli@xlgroup.com; internet www.xlinsurance.com; CEO DAVID B. DUCLOS.

ASSOCIATIONS

Association of Bermuda Insurers and Reinsurers (ABIR): XL House, 1 Bermudiana Rd, Hamilton HM 11; tel. 294-7221; fax 296-4207; e-mail leila.madeiros@abir.bm; internet www.abir.bm; represents international insurers and reinsurers; Pres. and Exec. Dir BRADLEY L. KADING.

Bermuda Insurance Management Association (BIMA): POB HM 824, Hamilton HM CX; tel. 295-6015; fax 295-1702; e-mail tmcmahon@cedar.bm; f. 1978; manages over 1,200 insurance and reinsurance cos; liaises with govt and other financial orgs; Pres. THOMAS McMAHON.

Trade and Industry

GOVERNMENT AGENCY

Bermuda Registrar of Companies: Government Administration Bldg, 30 Parliament St, Hamilton HM 12; tel. 297-7530; fax 292-6640; e-mail jfsmith@gov.bm; internet www.roc.gov.bm; Registrar of Companies STEPHEN LOWE.

DEVELOPMENT ORGANIZATIONS

Bermuda Business Development Corpn (BBDC): The Windsor Pl., 1st Floor, 22 Queen St, Hamilton HM 11; tel. 292-0632; fax 292-1797; e-mail info@businessbermuda.org; internet www.businessbermuda.org; f. 2013 following merger of BBDC with Business Bermuda and the Insurance Devt Council; Chair. CAROLINE FOULGER.

Bermuda Economic Development Corpn (BSBDC): Sofia House, 48 Church St, POB HM 637, Hamilton HM CX; tel. 292-5570; fax 295-1600; e-mail info@bsbdc.bm; internet www.bedc.bm; f. 1980; funded jtly by the Govt and private banks; guarantees loans to small businesses; responsible for establishing economic empowerment zones; Gen. Man. LUCRETIA MING.

CHAMBER OF COMMERCE

Bermuda Chamber of Commerce: 1 Point Pleasant Rd, POB HM 655, Hamilton HM CX; tel. 295-4201; fax 292-5779; e-mail info@bermudacommerce.com; internet www.bermudacommerce.com; f. 1907; Pres. RONNIE VIERA; Exec. Dir JOANNE MacPHEE; 750 mems.

EMPLOYERS' ASSOCIATIONS

Bermuda Employers' Council: 4 Park Rd, Hamilton HM 11; tel. 295-5070; fax 295-1966; e-mail kjensen@bec.bm; internet www.bec.bm; f. 1960; advisory body on employment and labour relations; Exec. Dir KEITH JENSEN (acting); 420 mems.

Construction Association of Bermuda: POB HM 238, Hamilton HM AX; tel. 292-0633; fax 292-0564; e-mail caob@logic.bm; internet www.constructionbermuda.com; f. 1968; Pres. CHARLES DUNSTAN; 90 mems.

Hotel Employers of Bermuda: c/o Bermuda Hotel Asscn, Carmel, 61 King St, Hamilton HM 19; tel. 295-2127; fax 292-6671; e-mail jharvey@bdahotels.bm; f. 1968; Pres. FRANK STOCEK; CEO JOHN HARVEY; 8 mems.

UTILITIES

Electricity

Bermuda Electric Light Co Ltd (BELCO): 27 Serpentine Rd, POB HM 1026, Hamilton HM DX; tel. 295-5111; fax 292-8975; e-mail info@belco.bm; internet www.belco.bm; f. 1904 as the Bermuda Electric Light, Power & Traction Co (BELPT); owned by Ascendant Group Ltd; Chair. REGINALD S. MINORS; Pres. WALTER M. HIGGINS.

Gas

Bermuda Gas & Utility Co Ltd: 25 Serpentine Rd, Pembroke, POB 373, HM BX; tel. 295-3111; fax 295-8311; e-mail info@bermudagas.bm; internet www.bermudagas.bm; f. 1936; owned by Ascendant Group Ltd; Gen. Man. JUDITH UDDIN.

TRADE UNION

In 2007 trade union membership was estimated at approximately 9,140. There are nine registered trade unions, eight of which profess membership of the Bermuda Trades Union Congress.

Bermuda Trades Union Congress (BTUC): POB 2080, Hamilton HM HX; tel. 292-6515; fax 292-0697; e-mail mcharles@ibl.bm; Pres. WENDELL (SHINE) HAYWARD; Gen. Sec. MICHAEL CHARLES.

Transport

ROADS

There are some 225 km (140 miles) of public highways and 222 km of private roads, with almost 6 km reserved for cyclists and pedestrians. All the roads are paved. Each household is permitted only one passenger vehicle, and visitors may only hire mopeds, to limit traffic congestion.

SHIPPING

The chief port of Bermuda is Hamilton, followed by St George's and King's Wharf. All three are used by freight and cruise ships. There is also a 'free' port, Freeport, on Ireland Island. In 2000 it was proposed to enlarge Hamilton docks in order to accommodate larger cruise ships. There remained, however, fears that such an enlargement would place excessive strain on the island's environment and infrastructure. Bermuda is a 'free flag' nation, and at December 2012 the shipping register comprised 209 vessels, totalling 12,189,448 grt, of which 29 were bulk carriers, 45 gas tankers and 34 were general cargo ships.

Department of Marine and Ports Services: 4 Crow Lane, Pembroke, POB HM 180, Hamilton HM AX; tel. 295-6575; fax 295-5523; e-mail marineports@bolagov.bm; internet www.marineandports.bm; Dir FRANCIS RICHARDSON; Harbour Master DAVID SIMMONS.

Department of Maritime Administration: Magnolia Pl., 2nd Floor, 45 Victoria St, POB HM 1628, Hamilton HM GX; tel. 295-7251; fax 295-3718; e-mail enquires.bermudashipping@gov.bm; internet www.bermudashipping.bm; f. 1789; Chief Surveyor SIMON HILL; Registrar of Shipping EDWARD ROBINSON.

Principal Shipping Companies

B & H Ocean Carriers Ltd: Par-la-Ville Pl., 3rd Floor, 14 Par-la-Ville Rd, POB HM 2257, Hamilton HM JX; tel. 295-6875; fax 295-6796; e-mail info@bhocsa.com; internet www.bhocean.com; f. 1988; Chair. MICHAEL S. HUDNER.

Bermuda Forwarders Ltd: 2 Mill Creek Park, POB HM 511, Hamilton HM CX; tel. 292-4600; fax 292-1859; e-mail info@bermudaforwarders.com; internet www.bermudaforwarders.com; f. 1955; international import and export handlers; Pres. TOBY KEMPE.

Bermuda Worldwide Shipping Ltd: 4 Mill Reach Lane, Pembroke, POB FL404, Flatts FLBX; tel. 292-9649; fax 292-4563; e-mail info@bdashipping.bm; internet www.bdashipping.bm; Pres. ROGER MONIZ.

Bernhard Schulte Shipmanagement (Bermuda) Ltd Partnership: Richmond House, 12 Par-la-Ville Rd, POB HM 2089, Hamilton HM HX; tel. 295-0614; fax 292-1549; e-mail management@amlp.bm; internet www.bs-shipmanagement.com; f. 2008 by the merger of Hanseatic Shipping, Dorchester Atlantic Marine, Eurasia Group and Vorsetzen Bereederungs- und Schiffahrtskontor; owned by the Schulte Group; CEO ANDREAS DROUSSIOTIS; CEO RAJESH BAJPAEE.

BEST Shipping: 3 Addendum Lane North, Pembroke, Hamilton HM 07; tel. 292-8080; fax 295-1713; e-mail info@best.bm; internet www.best.bm; f. 1987 as Bermuda Export Sea Transfer Ltd; sea and air freight services; Pres. and Man. Dir DAVID SOUSA.

Container Ship Management Ltd: 14 Par-la-Ville Rd, POB HM 2266, Hamilton HM JX; tel. 295-1624; fax 295-3781; e-mail bcl@csm.bm; internet www.bcl.bm; f. 1980; privately owned; Chair. JOHN H. K. WHITE; Pres. and CEO GEOFFREY FRITH.

Gearbulk Holding Ltd: Par-la-Ville Pl., 14 Par-la-Ville Rd, POB HM 2257, Hamilton HM JX; tel. 295-2184; fax 295-2234; internet www.gearbulk.com; f. 1968; Pres. ARTHUR E. M. JONES.

Golden Ocean Group Ltd: Par-la-Ville Pl., 14 Par-la-Ville Rd, POB HM 1593, Hamilton HM 08; tel. 295-6935; fax 295-3494; e-mail tor@frontmgt.no; internet www.goldenocean.no; Chair., Pres. and CEO JOHN FREDRIKSON; Exec. Dir HERMAN BILLUNG.

Meyer Shipping: Waverley Bldg, 35 Church St, Hamilton HM 12; tel. 296-9798; fax 295-4556; e-mail shipping@meyer.bm; internet www.meyer.bm; f. 1867; subsidiary of the Meyer Group of Companies; Exec. Vice-Pres. JOE SIMAS.

CIVIL AVIATION

The L. F. Wade International Airport is served by several international airlines. The former US Naval Air Station (the only airfield) was returned to the Government of Bermuda in 1995, following the closure of the base and the withdrawal of US forces from the islands.

Department of Civil Aviation: Channel House, Suite 2, 12 Longfield Rd, Southside, POB GE 218, St George's GE BX; tel. 293-1640; fax 293-2417; e-mail info@dca.gov.bm; internet www.dca.gov.bm; Dir THOMAS DUNSTAN.

L.F. Wade International Airport: 3 Cahow Way, St George's GE CX; tel. 293-2470; e-mail dao@gov.bm; internet www.bermudaairport.aero; fmrly Bermuda International Airport, adopted present name 2007; Gen. Man. AARON ADDERLEY.

Tourism

Tourism is the principal industry of Bermuda and is government-sponsored. The great attractions of the islands are the climate scenery, and facilities for outdoor entertainment of all types. In 2012 a total of 610,230 tourists (including 378,262 cruise ship passengers) visited Bermuda. The industry earned an estimated US $435m. in 2011. In 2010 there were 44 licensed hotels and 2,659 rooms.

Bermuda Department of Tourism: Global House, 43 Church St, Hamilton; tel. 292-0023; fax 292-7537; e-mail app@bermudatourism.com; internet www.bermudatourism.com; Dir BILLY GRIFFITH.

Bermuda Hotel Association: Carmel, 61 King St, Hamilton HM 19; tel. 295-2127; fax 292-6671; e-mail jharvey@bdahotels.bm; internet www.experiencebermuda.com; Pres. FRANK STOCEK; Exec. Dir JOHN HARVEY; 37 mem. hotels.

Defence

The local defence force is the Bermuda Regiment, with a strength of some 630 men and women in 1999. The Regiment employs selective conscription. According to the 2012/13 budget statement, some B $109m. of expenditure was allocated to national security, representing 10.1% of total government expenditure.

Education

There is free compulsory education in government schools between the ages of five and 16 years, and a number of scholarships are awarded for higher education and teacher training. There are also seven private secondary schools, which charge fees. In 2009/10 enrolment at primary level institutions was equivalent to an estimated 83% of children in the relevant age-group, while at the secondary level it was equivalent to an estimated 50% of pupils in the relevant age-group. The Bermuda College accepts students over the age of 16, and is the only post-secondary educational institution. Extramural degree courses are available through Queen's University, Canada, and Indiana and Maryland Universities, USA. A Career Pathways programme to prepare students for businesses and industries was introduced in 2012/13. Budgetary expenditure on education in the financial year 2012/13 was projected at B $134m., representing 12.4% of total government expenditure.

THE BRITISH ANTARCTIC TERRITORY

The British Antarctic Territory lies within the Antarctic Treaty area (i.e. south of latitude 60° S). The territory, created by an Order in Council which came into force on 3 March 1962, consists of all islands and territories south of latitude 60° S, between longitudes 20° W and 80° W, and includes the South Orkney Islands, the South Shetland Islands, the Antarctic Peninsula and areas south and east of the Weddell Sea. With the island of South Georgia and the South Sandwich Islands (now forming a separate territory, q.v.), this area had been constituted by the United Kingdom as the Falkland Islands Dependencies in 1908. In December 2012 the United Kingdom Government announced that about one-third of the territory, which was previously unnamed, was to be called Queen Elizabeth Land to mark Queen Elizabeth II's 60 years as British monarch. The flag of the British Antarctic Territory (proportions 1 by 2) has a white field bearing the union flag of the United Kingdom in the canton and, in the centre of the fly half of the flag, the arms of the territory, which consists of a white shield with three wavy blue horizontal lines at the top overlapped by a red triangle, apex downwards, bearing a brown and yellow torch with red-bordered yellow flames framed by golden rays, the shield supported by a golden lion and a black and white penguin with a yellow throat, both supporters surmounted by a scroll of yellow and light blue with a red reverse and the red inscription 'Research and Discovery'; above the shield, a helmet of grey, light blue and white supporting a torse, alternately of white and light blue, is depicted below a sailing ship of black flying the British Blue Ensign at the gaff. The territory has its own legal system and postal administration, and is financially self-sufficient owing to revenue derived from income tax and the sale of postage stamps.

Area: Land covers about 1,709,400 sq km (660,003 sq miles).

Population: There is no permanent population, but scientists and support personnel staff the British Antarctic Survey stations. In January 2013 a Dutch laboratory opened as part of the Rothera research base. *2005/06:* summer 200 (Rothera 148, Halley 37, Signy 15); winter 37.

High Commissioner, British Antarctic Territory: Dr PETER HAYES, Overseas Territories Directorate, Foreign and Commonwealth Office, King Charles St, London, SW1A 2AH, United Kingdom; tel. (20) 7008-2617; internet britishantarcticterritory.fco.gov.uk.

Administrator: HENRY BURGESS, Polar Regions Unit, Overseas Territories Directorate, Foreign and Commonwealth Office, King Charles St, London, SW1A 2AH, United Kingdom; tel. (20) 7008-2617; fax (20) 7008-2086; e-mail polarregions@fco.gov.uk.

British Antarctic Survey: High Cross, Madingley Rd, Cambridge, CB3 0ET, United Kingdom; tel. (1223) 221400; fax (1223) 362616; e-mail basweb@bas.ac.uk; internet www.antarctica.ac.uk; f. 1962 to replace Falkland Islands Dependencies Survey; responsible for almost all British scientific activities in Antarctica; operates two ice-strengthened ocean-going vessels (RRS *Ernest Shackleton* and RRS *James Clark Ross*), four de Havilland Twin Otter and one Dash-7 aircraft; total budget £48.8m. in 2012/13; Dir (acting) ALAN RODGER.

RESEARCH STATIONS

	Latitude	Longitude
Halley	75° 35' S	26° 34' W
King Edward Point	54° 17' S	36° 30' W
Rothera	67° 34' S	68° 08' W
Signy (summer only)	60° 43' S	45° 36' W

THE BRITISH INDIAN OCEAN TERRITORY (BIOT)

The British Indian Ocean Territory (BIOT) was formed in November 1965, through the amalgamation of the former Seychelles islands of Aldabra, Desroches and Farquhar with the Chagos Archipelago, a group of islands 1,930 km north-east of Mauritius, previously administered by the Governor of Mauritius. Aldabra, Desroches and Farquhar were ceded to Seychelles when that country was granted independence in June 1976. Since then BIOT has comprised only the Chagos Archipelago, including the coral atoll Diego Garcia, with a total land area of 60 sq km (23 sq miles).

BIOT was established to meet British and US defence requirements in the Indian Ocean. An agreement concluded in 1966 between the United Kingdom and the USA provided for BIOT to be used by both countries over an initial period of 50 years, with the option of extending this for a further 20 years. The United Kingdom undertook to cede the Chagos Archipelago to Mauritius when it was no longer required for defence purposes. Originally the US military presence was limited to a communications centre on Diego Garcia. In 1972, however, construction of a naval support facility was begun, apparently in response to the expansion of the Soviet maritime presence in the Indian Ocean.

Following the purchase of the islands' privately owned coconut plantations by the British Crown in 1966, they ceased to operate (production of copra was previously the principal economic function of the islands) and the inhabitants were offered the choice of resettlement in Mauritius or in Seychelles. The majority (numbering about 1,200 individuals) went to Mauritius, the resettlement taking place during 1969–73, prior to the construction of the military facility. Mauritius subsequently campaigned for the immediate return of the territory. A protracted dispute with the United Kingdom over compensation for those displaced ended in 1982 when the British Government agreed to an *ex gratia* payment of £4m. In July 2000 a judicial review of the validity of the Immigration Ordinance of 1971, under which the islanders were removed from BIOT, and which continued to prevent them from resettling in the territory, was instigated.

In November 2000 the British High Court ruled that the Chagos islanders (Chagossians or Îlois) had been illegally evicted from the Chagos Archipelago, and quashed Section 4 of the 1971 Ordinance, which prevented the return of the Chagossians to BIOT. During the case it transpired that the British Government had apparently termed the Chagossians 'contract workers' in order to persuade the UN that the islanders were not an indigenous population with democratic rights. However, memoranda of the Foreign and Commonwealth Office (FCO) revealed government knowledge of some of the Chagossians living in the Chagos Archipelago for two gener-

ations. The British Secretary of State for Foreign and Commonwealth Affairs declined an appeal, thereby granting the islanders an immediate right to return to BIOT. Despite this, a new ordinance, issued in January 2001, permitted the former residents to return to any of the islands in the Archipelago, except Diego Garcia. The British Overseas Territories Act came into effect in May 2002, allowing the displaced islanders to apply for British citizenship. In October 2003 the High Court ruled that although the islanders could claim to have been ill-treated, the British Government had not known at the time that its actions were unlawful and their claims for compensation were dismissed. Many of the islanders subsequently moved to the United Kingdom.

In June 2004 the British Government issued two decrees under the Royal Prerogative explicitly stating the country's resumption of full control of immigration services within the archipelago and banning the Chagossians from returning. In May 2006 the British High Court ruled that the exclusion of the islanders from their territory was irrational and unlawful. The British Government commenced proceedings to overturn the May ruling at the Court of Appeal in February 2007; however, in May that court confirmed that the residents of the Chagos Archipelago had been unlawfully removed and upheld the displaced islanders' immediate right to return. In November the House of Lords granted the British Government the right to appeal against the Court of Appeal's decision, on the condition that the Chagossians' costs were met by the British Government. The appeal was heard in mid-2008 and in November the House of Lords ruled in favour of the British Government, thus denying the Chagossians the right to return, and citing as its main reason the fact that the United Kingdom would have been obliged to meet the costs of economic, social and educational advancement of the residents. The ruling also stated that fair compensation had been agreed and paid, and that the British Government had no further obligations towards the Chagossians. Having exhausted the appeals process in the United Kingdom, the Chagossians announced that they would take their case to the European Court of Human Rights (ECHR); however, it was estimated that only approximately 700 of the 2,000 deported during the 1960s and 1970s were still alive.

In April 2010 the British Government announced that it had designated the Chagos archipelago a marine protection area (MPA), within which all fishing and other activities were to be prohibited. The conservation area, covering some 544,000 sq km, was to be patrolled by a ship vested with the powers to arrest fleets caught fishing illegally, to impose fines of up to £100,000 and to confiscate boats and fishing equipment. Although the British Government claimed that these plans were drawn up for purely environmental reasons, they were expected to have an impact on the Chagossians' hearing at the ECHR as the ban on fishing would remove the legal means by which they could sustain their standard of living. In December the Mauritian Government announced that it had taken a case against the United Kingdom to the UN International Tribunal for the Law of the Sea on the grounds that the MPA was not compatible with the UN Convention on the Law of the Sea. Furthermore, the Chagossians also appealed for a judicial review of the decision to create the MPA, although this was not to take place until after the ECHR had delivered its verdict. In December 2012 the ECHR ruled that it had no jurisdiction to examine the Chagossians' case, claiming that the islanders had 'effectively renounced' their claims when they received compensation in 1982 from the British authorities for their resettlement. Following an unsuccessful challenge by the British authorities, in January 2013 the UN International Tribunal for the Law of the Sea ruled that it was within its jurisdiction to hear the case against the United Kingdom's unilateral declaration of an MPA around the Chagos Islands.

In recent years Diego Garcia has frequently been used as a base for US aircraft carrying out air strikes on Iraq and Afghanistan. In March–April 2003 the base was used to launch bombing raids on Iraq in the US-led military campaign to oust the regime of Saddam Hussein. In February 2008 the British Secretary of State for the Foreign and Commonwealth Office admitted that, contrary to previous government statements, a number of so-called rendition flights (the transfer of detainees, in particular terrorist suspects, by the US Central Intelligence Agency to third countries where it was possible that they might be subjected to torture during interrogation) had used facilities at Diego Garcia.

In December 2000, following the British High Court's ruling, Mauritius again staked its claim for sovereignty over the Chagos Archipelago. In April 2004 Paul Bérenger, the recently installed Prime Minister of Mauritius, renewed the campaign to reclaim sovereignty after specialists in international law advised him that the decree by which the United Kingdom separated the Chagos Archipelago from Mauritius was illegal. An attempt was made to block the Mauritian Government from pursuing the case at the International Court of Justice on the basis of a long-standing ruling, whereby members of the Commonwealth could not take the United Kingdom to court; in July the ruling was extended to former members of the Commonwealth, in order to prevent Mauritius from circumventing the obstacle by withdrawing from that organization. Mauritius announced that it would pursue the matter at the General Assembly of the UN. The Mauritian case was strengthened by the fact that the 1966 agreement establishing the US base on Diego Garcia was due to expire in 2016. Although the accord included a 20-year optional extension, both parties were obliged to agree to extend, modify or terminate it by December 2014.

The civil administration of BIOT is the responsibility of a non-resident commissioner in the FCO in London, United Kingdom, represented on Diego Garcia by a Royal Navy commander and a small British naval presence. A chief justice, a senior magistrate and a principal legal adviser (who performs the functions of an attorney-general) are resident in the United Kingdom.

Land Area: about 60 sq km.

Population: There are no permanent inhabitants. In February 2012 there were about 2,800 US and British military personnel and civilian support staff stationed in the territory.

Currency: The official currency is the pound sterling, but the US dollar is also accepted.

Commissioner: Dr PETER RICHARD HAYES, Head of Overseas Territories Dept, Foreign and Commonwealth Office, King Charles St, London, SW1A 2AH, United Kingdom; tel. (20) 7008-2691.

Administrator: JOHN ANDREW MCMANUS, Overseas Territories Dept, Foreign and Commonwealth Office, King Charles St, London, SW1A 2AH, United Kingdom; tel. (20) 7008-2691; e-mail john.mcmanus@fco.gov.uk.

Commissioner's Representative: Commdr LEE HARDY, RN, Diego Garcia, c/o BFPO Ships.

THE BRITISH VIRGIN ISLANDS

Introductory Survey

LOCATION, CLIMATE, LANGUAGE, RELIGION, FLAG, CAPITAL

The British Virgin Islands consist of more than 60 islands and cays, of which only 16 are inhabited. The islands, most of which are mountainous and of volcanic origin (the only exception of any size is the coralline island of Anegada), lie at the northern end of the Leeward Islands, about 100 km (62 miles) to the east of Puerto Rico and adjoining the United States Virgin Islands. The climate is subtropical but extremes of heat are relieved by the trade winds. The average annual rainfall is 1,000 mm (39 ins). The official language is English. Most of the inhabitants profess Christianity. The flag is the British 'Blue Ensign', with the territory's badge (a green shield, with a white-clad virgin and 12 oil lamps, above a scroll bearing the motto 'vigilate') in the fly. The capital, Road Town, is situated on the island of Tortola.

CONTEMPORARY POLITICAL HISTORY

Historical Context

Previously peopled by Caribs, and named by the navigator Christopher Colombus after St Ursula and her 11,000 fellow-martyrs, the islands were settled by buccaneers and the Dutch, but were finally annexed by the British in 1672. In 1872 they became part of the British colony of the Leeward Islands, which was administered under a federal system. The federation was dissolved in July 1956, but the Governor of the Leeward Islands continued to administer the British Virgin Islands until 1960, when an appointed Administrator (restyled Governor in 1971) assumed direct responsibility. Unlike the other Leeward Islands, the British Virgin Islands did not join the Federation of the West Indies (1958–62), preferring to develop its links with the US Virgin Islands.

Domestic Political Affairs

A new Constitution was introduced in April 1967, when H. Lavity Stoutt became the islands' first Chief Minister. He was later replaced by Willard Wheatley. At an election in September 1975 Stoutt's Virgin Islands Party (VIP) and the United Party (UP) each won three of the seven elective seats on the Legislative Council. Wheatley, sitting as an independent member, held the balance of power and he continued in office, with Stoutt as Deputy Chief Minister.

An amended Constitution took effect in June 1977, giving more extensive internal self-government. In an election in November 1979 independent candidates won five of the nine elective seats on the enlarged Legislative Council, with the VIP winning the remainder. Stoutt secured enough support to be reinstated as Chief Minister. In the November 1983 election the VIP and the UP each secured four seats. The one successful independent candidate, Cyril Romney, became Chief Minister and formed a coalition Government with members of the UP.

In August 1986 the Governor dissolved the Legislative Council six days before a scheduled council debate on a motion of no confidence against Romney (who had allegedly been involved with a company under investigation by the British police and the US Department of Justice's Drug Enforcement Administration). At a general election in the following month the VIP won a majority of seats and Stoutt was appointed Chief Minister. The VIP increased its majority at a general election in 1990.

The principal concern of the Stoutt administration in the early 1990s was the trade in, and increasing local use of, illicit drugs. In late 1990 the Stoutt administration introduced legislation to impose more stringent regulations governing the 'offshore' financial sector, while plans to review immigration policy were under discussion, in an attempt to reduce the number of illegal immigrants entering the territory. Both areas had previously been considered to be insufficiently protected from exploitation by traffickers seeking to introduce illicit drugs into the islands or to divert funds from their sale through the financial sector.

In August 1993 the British Government appointed three commissioners to review the territory's Constitution at the request of the Legislative Council. Proposed changes included the introduction of direct elections for the position of Chief Minister, the enlargement of the Legislative Council and the adoption of a bill of rights. The British Government's decision in 1994 to accept the commission's proposal to enlarge the Legislative Council to 13 seats (by the creation of four seats representing the territory 'at large') was strongly criticized by Stoutt.

At elections to the legislature in February 1995 the VIP won six seats, the UP and the Concerned Citizens' Movement (CCM) each secured two seats and independent candidates won the remaining three seats. One of the successful independents subsequently gave his support to the VIP, thus providing the party with the majority required to form a Government, again headed by Stoutt. In May the Deputy Chief Minister, Ralph O'Neal, was appointed Chief Minister, following Stoutt's sudden death.

Elections to the Legislative Council took place in May 1999. The VIP retained control of the legislature, increasing its representation to seven seats. The recently founded National Democratic Party (NDP) took five seats, while the CCM retained one seat. O'Neal subsequently re-appointed the members of the previous Executive Council.

A general election was held on 16 June 2003. The NDP secured eight seats compared with the VIP's five. Orlando Smith became the new Chief Minister.

Relationship with the United Kingdom and financial transparency

In March 1999 the Government of the United Kingdom published draft legislation pertaining to its relationship with its Overseas Dependencies, which were to be renamed United Kingdom Overseas Territories (and had been referred to as such since February 1998). The legislation proposed the extension of British citizenship to the citizens of Overseas Territories, although it also required its Overseas Territories to amend their legislation on human rights and on the regulation of the financial services sector to meet international standards. In July the British Government appointed a consultant, Alan Hoole, a former Governor of Anguilla, to review the Constitution of the British Virgin Islands. In September Hoole proposed several changes to the Constitution, including the introduction of more frequent meetings of the Legislative Council and the removal of the Governor's powers to veto legislation. Under the terms of the proposed changes, the Governor was also to be obliged to consult with the Executive Council before implementing policy in his areas of special responsibility (foreign affairs, the civil service and defence). It was also suggested that members of the Legislative Council should be obliged to declare their interests.

In September 2000 the Legislative Council adopted legislation abolishing judicial corporal punishment, in keeping with the United Kingdom's acceptance of the European Convention of Human Rights.

The Organisation for Economic Co-operation and Development (OECD, see p. 388) announced in April 2002 that the British Virgin Islands had made sufficient commitments to improve the transparency of its tax and regulatory systems to be removed from an updated list of 'unco-operative' tax havens. In the same month, the financial secretary, L. Allen Wheatley, was arrested in connection with the mishandling of government contracts relating to the Beef Island Airport development project, and in May the Government survived a motion of no confidence brought against it in connection with the airport development project. The trial of Wheatley and four other men began in November 2003; four of the five defendants pleaded guilty to approving an airport telecommunications contract based on inflated prices that cost the Government some US \$450,000. In January 2004 Wheatley was sentenced to nine months in gaol. (Wheatley had already been sentenced to five years' imprisonment on separate corruption charges in February 2003.)

In late 2002 the recovering financial sector faced further disruption when the United Kingdom, under pressure from a European Union (EU, see p. 281) investigation into tax evasion, demanded that the British Virgin Islands disclose the identities and account details of Europeans holding private savings accounts on the islands. The British Virgin Islands, along with some other British Overseas Territories facing similar demands, claimed it was being treated unfairly compared with more powerful European countries, such as Switzerland and Luxembourg.

In May 2002 the British Overseas Territories Act, having received royal assent in the United Kingdom in February, came into force and granted British citizenship to the people of its Overseas Territories, including the British Virgin Islands. Under the new law British Virgin Islanders would be able to hold British passports and work in the United Kingdom and anywhere else in the EU.

A commission for constitutional review was appointed in April 2004, which was to consider, *inter alia*, the criteria for qualification for residency status, the reserve powers of the Governor, the duties of the Attorney-General and the introduction of an article relating to human rights into the Constitution. A Constitutional Review Report was released in 2005, based on the commission's findings. Among the suggestions included in the report were the reform of the legal system, and a move towards a cabinet system of government. A first round of negotiations to discuss the proposed constitutional reform, between representatives of the British Government and the Chief Minister, was held in March 2006. Negotiations continued throughout that year. A final forum, conducted in February 2007, sought to examine the provisions of a draft constitution document prepared by the Constitutional Review Commission and conclude debate upon the proposed new statutes. The British Foreign and Commonwealth Office endorsed the successful completion of negotiations, announcing the formulation of a new constitution for the territory that would

simultaneously afford greater autonomy to the country while maintaining harmonious relations with the United Kingdom; Chief Minister Smith expressed his satisfaction that '95 per cent' of the Review Commission's stated objectives for constitutional reform had been achieved.

The principal features of the proposed constitution included the institution of a cabinet system of government (whereby the Executive Council would be renamed 'the Cabinet'), within which the Premier (formerly Chief Minister) would command influence in the determination of the cabinet agenda, previously the subject of the Governor's sole arbitration, and a Cabinet Secretary would be appointed to set the Cabinet's agenda; the establishment of a National Security Council—to be comprised of the Governor, the Premier, a named government minister, the Attorney-General and the Commissioner of Police—conferring matters of internal security and policing of the islands from the sole remit of the British Government to that of the British Virgin Islands also, and upon whose recommendations the Governor would be obliged to act; the institution of an Office for Public Prosecutions; a reduction in the Governor's powers of veto; the inclusion of a Fundamental Rights Chapter to ensure the promotion and protection of citizens' human rights and freedoms; and provision for the creation of a sixth government ministry to accommodate the requirements of the territory's expanding population. The United Kingdom would retain some residual authority in order to regulate the development of the British Virgin Islands, embracing issues such as the observation of international standards in relation to the burgeoning financial services sector and the islands' natural disaster preparedness. After being approved by the United Kingdom Privy Council on 14 June, the Virgin Islands Constitutional Order 2007 became effective on 15 June, subsequent to the dissolution of the Legislative Council.

The VIP in power

The VIP achieved a convincing victory at a general election held on 20 August 2007, securing 10 seats while the NDP won two. An independent candidate won the remaining seat in the renamed legislature, the House of Assembly. The leader of the VIP, Ralph O'Neal, became the British Virgin Islands' first Premier.

It was announced in April 2009 that the Eastern Caribbean Supreme Court was to establish a new division, based on Tortola, to preside over all stages of litigation concerning major domestic, international or cross-border commercial claims. Tortola had been chosen as the location for this new body owing to its important role in the region's 'offshore' financial sector and because a number of multi-million dollar cases had been brought by commercial interests in the territory in recent years. Justice Edward Alexander Banner was sworn in to preside over the new court, which came into effect in May.

The British Virgin Islands was, in April 2009, included in OECD's so-called 'grey list' of territories that had yet substantially to implement moves towards transparency in the financial sector. The territory consequently increased efforts to reach internationally agreed standards of financial openness by signing tax information sharing agreements with other countries. In August, after reaching its 12th such accord, the British Virgin Islands was removed from the OECD list. By early 2013 the jurisdiction had secured a further 10 agreements.

In February 2010 the Government awarded a 16-year contract to supply drinking water on the islands to the British company Biwater. The contract, worth US \$43m., included the construction of a desalination plant and two sewage treatment plants, as well as a pipeline network and reservoirs. The opposition claimed that the terms of the contract were too generous to Biwater and that the Government was guaranteeing a loan to the company; these claims were denied by the Minister of Communications and Works, Julian Fraser, who insisted the contract would only be beneficial to the islands' economy and quality of life. In June the NDP demanded that an official inquiry be established to investigate the controversy surrounding the contract; the opposition were particularly concerned about the lack of a tender process. In October Minister of Education and Culture Andrew Fahie also publicly expressed reservations about the deal. Nevertheless, the Government and the Governor continued to resist this pressure and reiterated their support for Biwater. A final contract was signed by the Government and Biwater in July 2011.

William Boyd McCleary was inaugurated as the territory's new Governor in August 2010, following the retirement of David Pearey.

Recent developments: the NDP in power

In a general election conducted on 7 November 2011, the NDP secured a majority in the House of Assembly, winning nine seats; the VIP obtained the remaining four seats. The rate of voter participation was recorded at 68.8%. NDP leader Orlando Smith, who declared that his Government would focus primarily on reviving the islands' economy, was sworn in as Premier on 10 November. Kedrick Pickering was appointed as Deputy Premier and Minister of Natural Resources, while Smith assumed responsibility for finance. The new administration announced plans to reassess the Biwater agreement, and a full review was initiated later that month. In spite of the

Government's concerns, however, it was anticipated that Biwater would commence fresh water distribution in 2014.

Following discussions with British government officials, in April 2012 Smith agreed to abide by new fiscal responsibility guidelines, as delineated in the Protocols for Effective Financial Management. The 'offshore' financial sector came under fresh scrutiny in April 2013 after confidential documents concerning the industry were published by several major international media outlets. The leaked files, it was alleged, revealed that the British Virgin Islands' financial system was being used to facilitate various illegal practices such as tax avoidance, asset concealment and fraud. A number of high-profile politicians and businesspeople from around the world were linked to the scandal. Smith ordered an investigation into the affair, but continued to speak in defence of the islands' financial industry. The British Government announced in May 2013 that agreement had been reached on new banking transparency laws for the territory as part of efforts to combat international tax evasion.

CONSTITUTION AND GOVERNMENT

Under the provisions of the 2007 Constitution, the Governor is appointed by the British monarch and is responsible for external affairs, defence and internal security, terms and conditions of service of public officers, and the administration of the Courts. The Governor also fulfils the role of Presiding Officer at meetings of the Cabinet, which comprises the Premier and five other members. The House of Assembly comprises 15 members: a Speaker, one ex officio member, and 13 members elected by universal adult suffrage.

REGIONAL AND INTERNATIONAL CO-OPERATION

The British Virgin Islands became an associate member of the Caribbean Community and Common Market (CARICOM, see p. 231) in 1991; it is a member of CARICOM's Caribbean Development Bank (see p. 236) and an associate member of the Organisation of Eastern Caribbean States (see p. 477). The territory is also an associate member of the Economic Community for Latin America and the Caribbean (see p. 35). In economic affairs the territory has close affiliations with the neighbouring US Virgin Islands, and uses US currency. The territory is a member of the Commonwealth (see p. 244). As a dependency of the United Kingdom, the islands have the status of Overseas Territory in association with the European Union (see p. 281).

ECONOMIC AFFAIRS

In 2011, according to UN estimates, the British Virgin Islands' gross domestic product (GDP) was US $1,007m., equivalent to some $39,015 per head. During 2001–10, according to estimates, the population increased at an average annual rate of 2.7%. GDP increased, in real terms, by 2.0% per year during 2002–11, according to UN estimates; growth was estimated at 2.5% in 2011.

Agriculture (including forestry and fishing) contributed 1.0% of GDP in 2011, and engaged 0.6% of the employed labour force in 2005. The islands produce fruit and vegetables for domestic consumption or export to the US Virgin Islands, and some sugar cane (for the production of rum). Food imports accounted for 18.9% of total import costs in 1997. The fishing industry caters for local consumption and export, and provides a sporting activity for tourists. According to UN estimates, in 2002–11 agriculture GDP increased, in real terms, at an average annual rate of 0.1%; the sector declined by 2.8% in 2010, but increased by 3.4% in 2011.

Industry (including mining, manufacturing, construction and public utilities) accounted for 11.0% of GDP in 2011 and engaged 11.4% of the employed labour force in 2005. The mining sector is negligible, consisting of the extraction of materials for the construction industry and of some salt. Manufacturing, which provided 2.9% of GDP in 2011, consists mainly of light industry; there is one rum distillery, two factories for the production of ice, some plants producing concrete blocks and other construction materials, small boat manufacture and various cottage industries. Most energy requirements must be imported (mineral fuels accounted for an estimated 8.5% of total imports in 1997). According to UN estimates, in 2002–11 GDP of the industrial sector decreased, in real terms, at an average annual rate of 2.1%; industrial GDP grew by 0.4% in 2011.

The construction sector contributed 5.7% of GDP in 2011, according to UN estimates, and engaged 7.8% of the employed labour force in 2005. During 2002–11 the GDP of the sector decreased at an average annual rate of 4.2%; sectoral GDP decreased by 31.5% in 2010, before increasing by 38.2% in 2011.

Services, primarily tourism and financial services, constitute the principal economic sector of the British Virgin Islands, contributing 88.0% of GDP in 2011, and accounting for 88.1% in 2005. The tourism industry directly contributed some US $274m. to the economy in 2012, equivalent to 27% of GDP, according to the World Travel and Tourism Council (WTTC), and directly employed about 33% of the working population. The British Virgin Islands is the largest 'bareboat' chartering centre in the Caribbean, and approximately 60% of stop-over visitors stay aboard yachts. The number of stop-over visitors was 308,793 in 2009 (most of whom were from the USA), a 10.7% decrease on the previous year's total. This figure was estimated to rise to 372,000 in 2013, according to the WTTC. The financial services sector contributed about 60% of overall revenue in 2008. By the end of 2012 the number of active International Business Companies (IBCs) registered was 459,005. The islands have recorded significant growth in the establishment of mutual funds, which totalled 2,318 in 2012. During 2002–11 the GDP of the sector increased at an average annual rate of 2.6%; growth in the sector was estimated at 0.4% in 2011.

In 2003, according to the Caribbean Development Bank (CDB), the British Virgin Islands recorded a merchandise trade deficit of US $158.1m. The trade deficit is normally offset by receipts from tourism, development aid, remittances from islanders working abroad (many in the US Virgin Islands) and, increasingly, from the 'offshore' financial sector. The principal sources of imports (most of the islands' requirements must be imported) are the USA (which provided 56.9% of imports in 1997), Trinidad and Tobago, Antigua and Barbuda, and also the United Kingdom. The principal markets for the limited amount of exports are the US Virgin Islands and the USA and Puerto Rico; rum is exported to the USA. Machinery and transport equipment are the principal imports (accounting for 40.4% of total imports in 1997), and fruit and vegetables, rum, sand and gravel are the main exports.

The budget for the 2007 financial year projected revenue at US $265.0m. against recurrent and capital expenditure of $267.9m. In 2004 total external debt was calculated to be $44.1m. Central government debt to GDP ratio was estimated at below 10% in 2007, according to CDB estimates. The average annual rate of inflation was 2.8% in 2000–08; consumer prices increased by an average 3.3% in 2009. The rate of unemployment was estimated to be 3.1% in 2008.

The economy of the British Virgin Islands is largely dominated by tourism and the provision of international financial services, both of which are vulnerable to external pressures, in particular the performance of the US economy. The 'offshore' financial sector is an important source of employment and the single most important source of government revenue. International attempts to encourage the reform of 'offshore' financial centres are therefore of great concern to the British Virgin Islands, particularly as IBCs, which are not taxed and which are not obliged to disclose their directors or shareholders, have been singled out for particular criticism. The global economic downturn led to a decrease in visitor numbers to the islands in 2008 and 2009, which in turn affected other sectors of the economy, notably construction and retail. Financial services experienced a more significant decline during those years as a result of the world-wide recession, which was compounded by the greater international scrutiny of the sector. Nevertheless, owing to a recovery in the tourism and financial services industries, the economy grew by 4.5% in 2010 and by 2.5% in 2011. Legislation reducing customs and duties for the corporate sector was approved by the House of Assembly in February 2012; the Government hoped that these measures would encourage business activity and thus boost the employment rate. Notwithstanding the challenging global economic climate, GDP expanded by an estimated 4.0% in 2012, and the Government expected the growth rate to rise slightly in 2013.

PUBLIC HOLIDAYS

2014: 1 January (New Year's Day), 3 March (H. Lavity Stoutt's Birthday), 10 March (Commonwealth Day), 18 April (Good Friday), 21 April (Easter Monday), 7 June (Queen's Official Birthday), 9 June (Whit Monday), 1 July (Territory Day), 4–6 August (Festival Monday, Tuesday and Wednesday), 21 October (Saint Ursula's Day), 25–26 December (Christmas).

Statistical Survey

Source: Development Planning Unit, Central Administrative Complex, Road Town, Tortola VG1110; tel. 494-3701; fax 494-3947; e-mail dpu@dpu.org; internet dpu.gov.vg.

AREA AND POPULATION

Area: 153 sq km (59 sq miles). *Principal Islands* (sq km): Tortola 54.4; Anegada 38.8; Virgin Gorda 21.4; Jost Van Dyke 9.1.

Population: 16,115 at census of 12 May 1991; 23,161 (males 11,436, females 11,725) at census of 21 May 2001; 29,537 (official projection) in 2010; *By Island* (2001 census): Tortola 19,282; Virgin Gorda 3,203; Anegada 250; Jost Van Dyke 244; Other 182 (Other islands 86, Boats 96); Total 23,161.

Density (2010): 193.1 per sq km.

Population by Age (official projections, 2010): *0–14:* 7,404; *15–64:* 20,368; *65 and over:* 1,765; *Total* 29,537.

Principal Town: Road Town (capital), population 9,540 (UN estimate, incl. suburbs, mid-2011). Source: UN, *World Urbanization Prospects: The 2011 Revision.*

Births, Marriages and Deaths (2007 unless otherwise indicated): 279 live births (birth rate 10.1 per 1,000); 419 marriages (marriage rate 15.2 per 1,000); 109 deaths (2008—death rate 3.9 per 1,000). *2011:* Crude birth rate 14.5 per 1,000; Crude death rate 4.5 per 1,000 (Source: Pan American Health Organization).

Life Expectancy (years at birth, estimates): 77.6 (males 76.3; females 79.0) in 2011. Source: Pan American Health Organization.

Employment (2005): Agriculture, hunting and forestry 78; Fishing 14; Mining and quarrying 37; Manufacturing 404; Electricity, gas and water supply 145; Construction 1,260; Wholesale and retail trade 1,624; Hotels and restaurants 2,573; Transport, storage and communications 454; Financial intermediation 797; Real estate, renting and business activities 1,307; Public administration and social security 5,142; Education 1,119; Health and social work 141; Other community, social and personal service activities 724; Private households with employed persons 404; *Sub-total* 16,223; Not classifiable by economic activity 9; *Total* 16,232. *2010:* Total employed 18,796.

HEALTH AND WELFARE

Total Fertility Rate (children per woman, 2011): 1.7.

Physicians (per 1,000 head, 1999): 1.15.

Hospital Beds (per 1,000 head, 2006): 1.8.

Health Expenditure (% of GDP, 1995): 3.9. *2004* (public expenditure only): 2.3.

Health Expenditure (public, % of total, 1995): 36.5.

Source: Pan American Health Organization.

For definitions, see explanatory note on p. vi.

AGRICULTURE, ETC.

Livestock ('000 head, 2011, FAO estimates): Cattle 2.4; Sheep 6.1; Goats 10.0; Pigs 1.5.

Fishing (metric tons, live weight, 2010, FAO estimates): Snappers 70; Boxfishes 30; Jacks and crevalles 25; Caribbean spiny lobster 40; Marine fishes 770; Total catch (incl. others) 1,200.

Source: FAO.

INDUSTRY

Electric Energy (production, million kWh): 48 in 2007; 50 in 2008; 52 in 2009. Source: UN Industrial Commodity Statistics Database.

FINANCE

Currency and Exchange Rate: United States currency is used: 100 cents = 1 US dollar ($). *Sterling and Euro Equivalents* (31 December 2012): £1 sterling = US $1.578; €1 = US $1.319; US $100 = £63.37 = €75.79.

Budget (US $ million, 2006): *Revenue:* Total recurrent revenue 247.9. *Expenditure:* Recurrent expenditure 222.6; Capital expenditure 38.6; Total expenditure 261.2. *2007* (US $ million, projections): Total recurrent revenue 265.0; Total expenditure 267.9 (Recurrent expenditure 221.5, Capital expenditure 46.4).

Cost of Living (Consumer Price Index; base: 1995 = 100): All items 142.9 in 2007; 153.1 in 2008; 158.2 in 2009.

Gross Domestic Product (US $ million at constant 2005 prices): 940.8 in 2009; 982.7 in 2010; 1,007.0 in 2011. Source: UN Statistics Division, National Accounts Main Aggregates Database.

Expenditure on the Gross Domestic Product (US $ million at current prices, 2011): Government final consumption expenditure 87; Private final consumption expenditure 359; Gross fixed capital formation 241; Changes in inventories –18; *Total domestic expenditure* 669; Exports of goods and services 1,116; *Less* Imports of goods and services 778; *GDP in purchasers' values* 1,007. Source: UN Statistics Division, National Accounts Main Aggregates Database.

Gross Domestic Product by Economic Activity (US $ million at current prices, 2011): Agriculture, hunting, forestry and fishing 9; Mining, manufacturing and utilities 49 (Manufacturing 27); Construction 53; Wholesale, retail trade, restaurants and hotels 248; Transport, storage and communication 102; Other activities 465; *Total gross value added* 926; Net taxes on products 81 (figure obtained as a residual); *GDP in purchasers' values* 1,007 (Source: UN Statistics Division, National Accounts Main Aggregates Database).

EXTERNAL TRADE

Principal Commodities (US $ '000): *Imports c.i.f.* (1997): Food and live animals 31,515; Beverages and tobacco 8,797; Crude materials (inedible) except fuels 1,168; Mineral fuels, lubricants, etc. 9,847; Chemicals 8,816; Basic manufactures 31,715; Machinery and transport equipment 47,019; Total (incl. others) 116,379. *Exports f.o.b.* (1996): Food and live animals 368; Beverages and tobacco 3,967; Crude materials (inedible) except fuels 1,334; Total (incl. others) 5,862. *2001* (exports, US $ million): Animals 0.1; Fresh fish 0.7; Gravel and sand 1.4; Rum 3.6; Total 28.13.

Principal Trading Partners (US $ '000): *Imports c.i.f.* (1997): Antigua and Barbuda 1,807; Trinidad and Tobago 2,555; United Kingdom 406; USA 94,651; Total (incl. others) 166,379. *Exports f.o.b.* (1996): USA and Puerto Rico 1,077; US Virgin Islands 2,001; Total (incl. others) 5,862. *1999:* Imports 208,419; Exports 2,081.

Source: mainly UN, *International Trade Statistics Yearbook.*

TRANSPORT

Road Traffic (motor vehicles registered and licensed, 2005): 13,392 (Private vehicles 9,201, Commercial vehicles 2,102, Rental vehicles 1,196, Taxis 483, Government 275, Motorcycles 135).

Shipping: *International Freight Traffic* ('000 metric tons, 2002): Goods unloaded 145.6. *Cargo Ship Arrivals* (2002): 2,027 (Source: British Virgin Islands Ports Authority). *Flag Registered Fleet* (at 31 December 2012): Number of vessels 18; Total displacement 19,421 grt (Source: Lloyd's List Intelligence—www.lloydslistintelligence.com).

Civil Aviation (passenger arrivals): 153,391 in 2003; 220,239 in 2004 (estimate); 220,116 in 2005 (estimate).

TOURISM

Visitor Arrivals ('000): 345.9 stop-over visitors, 571.7 cruise ship passengers in 2008; 308.8 stop-over visitors, 530.3 cruise ship passengers in 2009; 330.3 stop-over visitors, 501.5 cruise ship passengers in 2010.

Tourism Revenue (US $ million, incl. passenger transport): 446 in 2008; 369 in 2009; 389 in 2010. Source: World Tourism Organization.

COMMUNICATIONS MEDIA

Telephones (2010): 25,500 main lines in use.

Mobile Cellular Telephones (2010): 94,200 subscribers.

Internet Subscribers (2010): 10,900.

Broadband Subscribers (2010): 10,900.

Source: International Telecommunication Union.

EDUCATION

Pre-primary (2008/09 unless otherwise indicated): 5 schools (1994/95); 55 teachers; 726 pupils.

Primary (2009/10 unless otherwise indicated): 21 schools (2006); 242 teachers; 3,201 pupils.

Secondary (2009/10 unless otherwise indicated): 7 schools (2006); 233 teachers; 2,029 pupils.

Tertiary (2008/09): 105 teachers; 1,211 pupils.

Pupil-teacher Ratio (primary education, UNESCO estimate): 13.2 in 2009/10.

Sources: UNESCO Institute for Statistics; Caribbean Development Bank, *Social and Economic Indicators.*

Directory

The Government

HEAD OF STATE

Queen: HM Queen ELIZABETH II.

Governor: WILLIAM BOYD MCCLEARY (assumed office 20 Aug. 2010).

Deputy Governor: INEZ ARCHIBALD.

CABINET
(May 2013)

The Government is formed by the National Democratic Party.

Premier and Minister of Finance: D. ORLANDO SMITH.

Deputy Premier and Minister of Natural Resources and Labour: KEDRICK PICKERING.

Minister of Health and Social Development: RONNIE W. SKELTON.

Minister of Education and Culture: MYRON V. WALWYN.

Minister of Communications and Works: MARK VANTERPOOL.

Attorney-General: Dr CHRISTOPHER PHILLIP MALCOLM.

MINISTRIES

Office of the Governor: 20 Waterfront Dr., POB 702, Road Town, Tortola VG1110; tel. 494-2345; fax 494-5582; e-mail bvigovernor@gov.vg; internet www.bvi.gov.vg.

Office of the Deputy Governor: Central Administration Bldg, West Wing, 33 Admin Dr., Road Town, Tortola VG1110; tel. 494-3701; fax 494-6481; e-mail webmaster@dgo.gov.vg; internet www.dgo.gov.vg.

Office of the Premier: 33 Admin Dr., Wickham's Cay 1, Road Town, Tortola VG1110; tel. 468-3701; fax 494-6413; e-mail premieroffice@gov.vg.

Ministry of Communications and Works: 33 Admin Dr., Wickham's Cay 1, Road Town, Tortola VG1110; tel. 468-2183; fax 494-3873; e-mail mcw@gov.vg.

Ministry of Education and Culture: 33 Admin Dr., Wickham's Cay 1, Road Town, Tortola VG1110; tel. 468-3358; fax 468-0021; e-mail mec@gov.vg.

Ministry of Finance: 33 Admin Dr., Wickham's Cay 1, Road Town, Tortola VG1110; tel. 494-3701; fax 494-6413; e-mail finance@gov.vg; internet www.finance.gov.vg.

Ministry of Health and Social Development: 33 Admin Dr., Wickham's Cay 1, Road Town, Tortola VG1110; tel. 468-3701; fax 494-5018; e-mail ministryofhealth@gov.vg.

Ministry of Natural Resources and Labour: 33 Admin Dr., Wickham's Cay 1, Road Town, Tortola VG1110; tel. 468-0675; fax 494-4283; e-mail nrl@gov.vg.

HOUSE OF ASSEMBLY

Speaker: INGRID MOSES-SCATLIFFE.

Clerk: PHYLLIS EVANS, Richard C. Stoutt Bldg, Wickham's Cay I, POB 2390, Road Town, Tortola VG1110; tel. 494-4757; fax 494-4544; e-mail JHodge@gov.vg; internet www.legco.gov.vg.

General Election, 7 November 2011

Party	Seats
National Democratic Party (NDP)	9
Virgin Islands Party (VIP)	4
Total	13

Election Commission

Office of the Supervisor of Elections: Ulric Dawson Bldg, 6 Russell Hill Rd, Road Town, Tortola VG1110; tel. 468-4380; fax 468-2779; e-mail electionsoffice@gov.vg; Supervisor of Elections JULIETTE PENN.

Political Organizations

National Democratic Party (NDP): Wickham Cay, Tortola VG1110; e-mail bvindp@gmail.com; internet bvindp.com; f. 1998; Chair. EILEEN PARSONS; Pres. D. ORLANDO SMITH.

People's Party (POP): Road Town, Tortola; f. 2011; Leader ALLEN WHEATLEY.

United Party (UP): POB 3068, Road Town, Tortola VG1110; tel. 495-2656; fax 494-1808; e-mail liberatebvi@msn.com; f. 1967; Chair. CONRAD MADURO.

Virgin Islands Party (VIP): Road Town, Tortola VG1110; e-mail info@viparty.com; Chair. RALPH T. O'NEAL.

Judicial System

Justice is administered by the Eastern Caribbean Supreme Court (ECSC), based in Saint Lucia, which consists of two divisions: the High Court of Justice and the Court of Appeal. There are two resident High Court Judges, as well as an Acting High Court Judge. A visiting Court of Appeal, comprised of the Chief Justice and two Judges of Appeal, sits twice a year in the British Virgin Islands. There is also a Magistrates' Court, which hears prescribed civil and criminal cases. The final Court of Appeal is the Privy Council in the United Kingdom. Under the terms of the 2007 Constitution, a Judicial and Legal Services Commission, chaired by the Chief Justice, was established to counsel the Governor in matters relating to judicial appointments and regulation of the territory's legal system. In 2009 the ECSC established a new division of the court, based on Tortola, to preside over all stages of litigation concerning major domestic, international or cross-border commercial claims.

High Court Judges: RITA JOSEPH-OLIVETTI, EDWARD BANNISTER.

Registrar: PAULA AJARIE.

Magistrate's Office: Magistrates Court, POB 140, Road Town, Tortola VG1110; tel. 494-3460; fax 494-2499; e-mail magistrate@vigilate.org; Magistrate VALERIE R. STEPHENS.

Religion

CHRISTIANITY

The Roman Catholic Church

The diocese of St John's-Basseterre, suffragan to the archdiocese of Castries (Saint Lucia), includes Anguilla, Antigua and Barbuda, the British Virgin Islands, Montserrat and Saint Christopher and Nevis. The Bishop is resident in St John's, Antigua. According to official estimates from 2005, 10% of the population are Roman Catholics.

The Anglican Communion

The British and US Virgin Islands form a single, missionary diocese of the Episcopal Church of the United States of America. The Bishop of the Virgin Islands is resident on St Thomas in the US Virgin Islands. According to official estimates from 2005, 17% of the population are Anglicans.

Protestant Churches

Various Protestant denominations are represented, principally the Methodist Church (an estimated 33% of the population in 2005). Others include the Church of God (9%), Seventh-day Adventist (6%), and Baptist Churches (5%).

The Press

The BVI Beacon: 10 Russell Hill Rd, POB 3030, Road Town, Tortola VG1110; tel. 494-3434; fax 494-6267; e-mail bvibeacn@surfbvi.com; internet www.bvibeacon.com; f. 1984; Thur.; local and international news; also operates from the US Virgin Islands; Editor FREEMAN ROGERS; circ. 3,400.

The BVI StandPoint: Wickham's Cay, POB 4311, Road Town, Tortola VG1110; tel. 494-8106; fax 494-8647; e-mail editorial@vistandpoint.com; internet www.vistandpoint.com; fmrly *BVI Penny Saver*, adopted current name in 2001; Tue. and Fri.; covers local and international news; Publr ELTON CALLWOOD; Editor FAREEZA HANIFF; circ. 18,000.

The Welcome (The Welcome Guide to the British Virgin Islands): POB 133, Road Town, Tortola; tel. 494-2413; fax 494-4413; e-mail info@bviwelcome.com; internet www.bviwelcome.com; f. 1971; every 2 months; general, tourist information; Publr and Editor CLAUDIA COLLI; circ. 165,000.

Publishers

aLookingGlass: 7 Road Reef Plaza, POB 3895, Sea Cow's Bay, Tortola, VG1110; tel. 494-7788; fax 494-8777; e-mail info@alookingglass.com; internet www.alookingglass.com; f. 2002; publishes *The BVI Property & Yacht* monthly; Man. Dir OWEN WATERS; Gen. Man. COLIN RATHBUN.

Global Directories (BVI) Ltd: Wickhams Cay 1, POB 3403, Road Town, Tortola VG1110; tel. 494-2060; fax 494-3060; e-mail bvi-sales@globaldirectories.com; internet bviyp.com; fmrly Caribbean Publishing Co (BVI) Ltd; subsidiary of MediaHouse Ltd, Bermuda; Publishes telephone directories, Caribbean Yellow Pages; Gen. Man. MICHAEL ARNOLD.

Island Publishing Services Ltd: Blackburn Hwy, POB 133, Road Town, Tortola VG1110; tel. 494-2413; fax 494-6589; e-mail info@bviwelcome.com; internet www.bviwelcome.com; publishes *The Welcome* (q.v.), *BVI Restaurant and Food Guide* (annual), *The Limin' Times* (weekly entertainment guide), and *The British Virgin Islands Cruise Ship Visitors' Guide* (annual); Gen. Man. KAREN BELL; Publr and CEO CLAUDIA COLLI.

Broadcasting and Communications

TELECOMMUNICATIONS

A Telecommunications Liberalization Act was ratified by the Government in 2007.

Caribbean Cellular Telephone (CCT Global Communications): Geneva Pl., 333 Waterfront Dr., POB 267, Road Town, Tortola VG1110; tel. 494-3825; fax 494-4933; internet www.cctwireless.com; f. 1986 as CCT Boatphone; mobile cellular telephone operator; Gen. Man. JOSE LUIS FERNANDEZ.

Digicel: POB 4168, Road Town, Tortola VG1110; tel. 494-2048; fax 494-0111; e-mail bvicustomercare@digicelgroup.com; internet www.digicelbvi.com; granted licence to operate mobile cellular telephone network in British Virgin Islands in Dec. 2007; mobile telecommunications and internet services provider; CEO DECLAN CASSIDY (British Virgin Islands).

LIME: Cutlass Bldg, Wickham's Cay 1, POB 440, Road Town, Tortola VG1110; tel. 494-4444; fax 494-2506; e-mail support@candwbvi.net; internet www.time4lime.com; f. 1967 as Cable & Wireless (WI) Ltd; name changed as above 2008; Group CEO TONY RICE; Regional CEO GERARD BORELY.

Regulatory Bodies

Telecommunications Regulatory Commission: LM Business Centre, 3rd Floor, 27 Fish Lock Rd, Road Town, POB 4401, Tortola; tel. 468-4165; fax 494-6786; e-mail contact@trc.vg; internet www.trc.vg; f. 2006; regulatory body; Chair. AYANA HULL-BRATHWAITE; CEO GUY L. MALONE.

Telephone Services Management Unit: Deputy Governor's Office, Central Administration Bldg, 2nd Floor, West Atrium, Road Town, Tortola VG1110; tel. 494-4728; fax 494-6551; e-mail tsmu@bvigovernment.org; govt agency; Man. REYNELL FRASER.

BROADCASTING

Radio

Virgin Islands Broadcasting Ltd—Radio ZBVI: Baughers Bay, POB 78, Road Town, Tortola VG1110; tel. 494-2250; fax 494-1139; e-mail zbvi@caribsurf.com; internet www.zbvi.vi; f. 1965; commercial; Gen. Man. HARVEY HERBERT; Operations Man. SANDRA POTTER WARRICAN.

Television

BVI Cable TV: Fishlock Rd, POB 644, Road Town, Tortola VG1110; tel. 494-3831; fax 494-3205; operated by Innovative Communication Corporation, based in the US Virgin Islands; programmes from US Virgin Islands and Puerto Rico; 53 channels; Gen. Man. LUANNE HODGE.

Finance

BANKING

Commercial Banks

Banco Popular de Puerto Rico: POB 67, Road Town, Tortola VG1110; tel. 494-2117; fax 494-5294; e-mail internet@bppr.com; internet www.bancopopular.com; Pres. and CEO RICHARD L. CARRIÓN; Man. SANDRA SCATLIFFE.

Bank of Nova Scotia (Canada): Wickham's Cay 1, POB 434, Road Town, Tortola VG1110; tel. 494-2526; fax 494-4657; e-mail joycelyn.murraine@scotiabank.com; internet www.bvi.scotiabank.com; f. 1967; Man. Dir JOYCELYN MURRAINE.

First Bank Virgin Islands: Road Town Business Centre, Wickham's Cay 1, Road Town, POB 435, Tortola VG1110; tel. 494-8899; fax 494-3863; e-mail e-firstbank@firstbankpr.com; internet www.firstbankvi.com; f. 1994; est. as a commercial bank in Puerto Rico; Pres. and CEO AURELIO ALEMÁN-BERMUDEZ.

FirstCaribbean International Bank Ltd: Wickham's Cay 1, POB 70, Road Town, Tortola VG1110; tel. 852-9900; fax 495-2361; e-mail barcbvi@surfbvi.com; internet www.firstcaribbeanbank.com; f. 2003 following merger of Caribbean operations of Barclays Bank PLC and CIBC; Barclays relinquished its stake in 2006; Chair. MICHAEL MANSOOR; CEO RIK PARKHILL; 2 brs.

VP Bank (BVI) Ltd: 3076 Sir Francis Drake's Highway, POB 3463, Road Town, Tortola VG1110; tel. 494-1100; fax 494-1199; e-mail info.bvi@vpbank.com; internet www.vpbank.vg; Chair. FREDY YOGT; CEO SIEGBERT NÄSCHER.

Development Bank

National Bank of the Virgin Islands Ltd: New Social Security Bldg, Wickham's Cay 1, POB 275, Road Town, Tortola VG1110; tel. 494-3737; fax 494-3119; e-mail admin@natbankvi.com; internet www.natbankvi.com; f. 1976; fmrly Development Bank of the British Virgin Islands; state-owned; Chair. KENNETH HODGE.

REGULATORY AUTHORITY

Financial Services Commission: Pasea Estate, POB 418, Road Town, Tortola VG1110; tel. 494-1324; fax 494-5016; e-mail enquiries@bvifsc.vg; internet www.bvifsc.vg; f. 2002; independent financial services regulator; Chair. ROBIN GAUL; Man. Dir and CEO ROBERT MATHAVIOUS.

TRUST COMPANIES

Abacus Trust and Management Services Ltd: 333 Waterfront Dr., Road Town, Tortola VG1110; tel. 494-4388; fax 494-3088; e-mail info@mwmabacus.com; internet www.mwmabacus.com; f. 1994; Man. MEADE MALONE.

AMS Trustees Ltd: Sea Meadow House, POB 116, Road Town, Tortola VG1110; tel. 494-3399; fax 494-3041; e-mail enquiries@amsbvi.com; internet www.amsbvi.com; f. 1985; privately owned; subsidiary of the AMS Group (British Virgin Islands); Man. Dir NICHOLAS CLARK.

Belmont Trust Ltd: Belmont Chambers, Tropic Isle Bldg, Nibbs St, POB 3443, Road Town, Tortola VG1110; tel. 494-5800; fax 494-2545; e-mail info@belmontbvi.net; internet www.belmontbvi.com; Man. Dir ANDREA DOUGLAS.

CCP Financial Consultants Ltd: Ellen Skelton Bldg, Fishers Lane, POB 681, Road Town, Tortola VG1110; tel. 494-6777; fax 494-6787; e-mail info@ccpbvi.com; internet www.ccpbvi.com; Dir JOSEPH ROBERTS.

Citco BVI Ltd: Wickham's Cay, POB 662, Road Town, Tortola VG1110; tel. 494-2217; fax 494-3917; e-mail bvi-trust@citco.com; internet www.citco.com; Man. NICOLA GILLESPIE.

HSBC International Trustee (BVI) Ltd: Woodbourne Hall, POB 916, Road Town, Tortola VG1110; tel. 494-5414; fax 494-5417; e-mail kenneth.morgan@htvg.vg; Dir KENNETH MORGAN.

Hunte & Co Services Ltd: Omar Hodge Bldg, 3rd Floor, Wickham's Cay I, POB 3504, Road Town, Tortola; tel. 495-0232; fax 495-0229; e-mail laura.arthur@hunteandco.com; internet www.hunteandco.com.

Maples and Calder BVI: Sea Meadow House, POB 173, Road Town, Tortola VG1110; tel. 852-3000; fax 852-3097; e-mail bviinfo@maplesandcalder.com; internet www.maplesandcalder.com; Man. Partner ARABELLA DI LORIO.

Midocean Management and Trust Services (BVI) Ltd: 9 Columbus Centre, Pelican Dr., POB 805, Road Town, Tortola VG1110; tel. 494-4567; fax 494-4568; e-mail midocean@maitlandgroup.com; owned by Maitland Group; Man. ELIZABETH WILKINSON.

Moore Stephens International Services (BVI) Ltd: Palm Grove House, Wickham's Cay I, POB 3186, Road Town, Tortola VG1110; tel. 494-3503; fax 494-3592; e-mail moorestephens@moorestephensbvi.com; internet www.moorestephens.com; Partner NICHOLAS LANE.

TMF (BVI) Ltd: Palm Grove House, 4th Floor, POB 438, Road Town, Tortola VG1110; tel. 494-2616; fax 494-2704; e-mail bvi@tmf-group.com; internet www.tmf-group.com; Dir GRAHAM COOK.

Totalserve Trust Company Ltd: 197 Main St, POB 3540, Road Town, Tortola VG1110; tel. 494-6900; fax 494-6990; e-mail bvi@totalserve.eu; internet www.totalservetrust.eu; f. 2003; Man. DENESHAR MEADE.

Tricor Services (BVI) Ltd: Palm Grove House, Wickham's Cay, POB 438, Road Town, Tortola VG1110; tel. 494-6004; fax 494-6404; e-mail info@bvi.tricorglobal.com; internet www.bvi.tricorglobal.com; f. 2000; Man. PATRICK A. NICHOLAS.

Trident Trust Company (BVI) Ltd: Trident Chambers, Wickham's Cay, POB 146, Road Town, Tortola VG1110; tel. 494-2434; fax 494-3754; e-mail bvi@tridenttrust.com; internet www.tridenttrust.com; Man. BARRY R. GOODMAN.

At the end of 2012 there were 2,318 active licensed mutual funds registered with the British Virgin Islands International Finance Centre.

INSURANCE

ALTA Insurance Management (BVI) Ltd: POB 4623, Road Town, Tortola VG1110; tel. 494-9670; fax 494-9690; e-mail gtaylor@altaholdings.com; internet www.altaholdings.com; Pres. DONALD B. ROUSSO; Man. Dir GREGORY M. TAYLOR.

AMS Insurance Management Services Ltd: Sea Meadow House, POB 116, Road Town, Tortola VG1110; tel. 494-3399; fax 494-3041; e-mail enquiries@amsbvi.com; internet www.amsbvi.com; f. 1982; Man. Dir NICHOLAS CLARK; Dir (Insurance) DEREK LLOYD.

Belmont Insurance Management Ltd: Belmont Chambers, Tropic Isle Bldg, Nibbs St, POB 3443, Road Town, Tortola VG1110; tel. 494-5800; fax 494-2545; e-mail info@belmontbvi.com; internet www.belmontbvi.com; Man. Dir ANDREA DOUGLAS.

Caledonian Global Insurance Services (BVI) Ltd: Rodus Bldg, 4th Floor, Road Town, Tortola VG1110; tel. 949-0050; fax 814-4875; e-mail insurance@caledonian.com; internet www.caledonian.com; f. 2005; acquired by New World Holdings Inc in 2011; Dir HARRY THOMPSON.

Captiva Global Ltd: Caribbean Chambers, POB 4428, Road Town, Tortola VG1110; tel. 494-4111; fax 494-4222; e-mail info@captivagroup.net; internet www.captiva.vg; Dir NOELLA M. THOMPSON; Man. Dir HARRY J. THOMPSON.

Caribbean Insurers Ltd (CIL): Mirage Bldg, POB 129, Road Town, Tortola VG1110; tel. 494-2728; fax 494-4393; e-mail pl@caribbins.com; internet www.caribbeaninsurers.com; f. 1973; part of the Caribbean Insurers Group; Chair. JOHN WILLIAMS; Man. Dir BRIAN JERMYN.

HWR Insurance Management Services Ltd (Harneys Insurance): Craigmuir Chambers, POB 71, Road Town, Tortola VG1110; tel. 494-2233; fax 494-3547; e-mail bvi@harneys.com; internet www.harneys.com; Man. Dir DAVID SPYER.

Marine Insurance Office (BVI) Ltd (MIO): Mill Mall, Wickham's Cay 1, POB 874, Road Town, Tortola VG1110; tel. 494-3795; fax 494-4540; e-mail info@mioinsurance.com; f. 1985; Man. WESLEY WOOLHOUSE.

Osiris Insurance Management Ltd: Coastal Bldg, Wickham's Cay 11, POB 2221, Road Town, Tortola VG1110; tel. 494-9820; fax 494-6934; e-mail miles@osiristrust.com; internet osiristrust.com; Man. Dir MILES WALTON.

Trident Insurance Management (BVI) Ltd: Trident Chambers, Wickham's Cay, POB 146, Road Town, Tortola VG1110; tel. 494-2434; fax 494-3754; e-mail bvi@tridenttrust.com; Man. DEREK LLOYD.

USA Risk Group (BVI) Inc: Columbus Centre, POB 4428, Road Town, Tortola; tel. 872-7475; fax 229-6280; e-mail rleadbetter@usarisk.ky; internet www.usarisk.com; Pres. GARY H. OSBORNE; Man. ROB LEADBETTER.

Several US and other foreign companies have agents in the British Virgin Islands. At the end of 2012 there were 157 'captive' insurance companies registered in the British Virgin Islands.

Trade and Industry

GOVERNMENT AGENCY

Trade and Investment Promotion Department: Chief Minister's Office, Central Administration Bldg, 33 Administration Dr., Road Town, Tortola VG1110; tel. 494-5007; fax 494-5657; e-mail trade@bvigovernment.org.

CHAMBER OF COMMERCE

British Virgin Islands Chamber of Commerce and Hotel Association: Tropic Aisle Bldg, Wickham's Cay 1, POB 376, Road Town, Tortola VG1110; tel. 494-3514; fax 494-6179; e-mail info@bviccha.org; internet www.bviccha.org; f. 1986; Chair. JAMAL S. SMITH; Pres. (Business and Commerce) DEBORAH O'NEAL; Pres. (Hotels and Tourism) ROMNEY PENN; 250 mems.

UTILITIES

Electricity

British Virgin Islands Electricity Corpn (BVIEC): Long Bush, POB 268, Road Town, Tortola VG1110; tel. 494-3911; fax 494-4291; e-mail bviecgm@bvielectricity.com; internet www.bvielectricity.com; f. 1979; privatization pending; Chair. ALLAN PARKER; Gen. Man. LEROY ABRAHAM.

Water

Water and Sewerage Dept: Water & Sewerage Compound, Baughers Bay, Road Town, POB 130, Tortola VG1110; tel. 494-3416; fax 494-6746; e-mail wsd@gov.vg; f. 1980; Dir MANOHERLAL KEROF (acting).

Transport

ROADS

In 2002 there were 132 km (82 miles) of access roads, 77 km of primary roads, 37 km of secondary roads and 90 km of tertiary roads.

Public Works Department: Baughers Bay, POB 284, Tortola VG1110; tel. 494-2722; fax 494-4740; e-mail pwd@bvigovernment.org; responsible for road maintenance; Dir JEFFREY SKELTON.

SHIPPING

There are two direct steamship services, one from the United Kingdom and one from the USA. Motor launches maintain daily mail and passenger services with St Thomas and St John, US Virgin Islands. Expansion of the cruise ship pier in Road Town was completed in 2008.

British Virgin Islands Ports Authority: Port Purcell, POB 4, Road Town, Tortola VG1110; tel. 494-3435; fax 494-2642; e-mail bviports@bviports.org; internet www.bviports.org; f. 1991; Chair. GREGORY ADAMS; Man. Dir VINCENT VICTOR O'NEAL.

Island Shipping & Trading Co Ltd: POB 61, Road Town, Tortola VG1110; tel. 494-2268; fax 494-4708; e-mail operations@islandshipping.com; internet www.islandshipping.com; Chair. PETER HAYCRAFT; Man. Dir CHRISTOPHER HAYCRAFT.

Tropical Shipping: Port Purcell Seaport, Island Shipping and Trading, POB 250, Road Town, Tortola VG1110; tel. 494-2674; fax 494-3505; e-mail lmoses@tropical.com; internet www.tropical.com; Pres. MIKE PELLICCI; Man. LEROY MOSES.

CIVIL AVIATION

Terrance B. Lettsome (formerly Beef Island) International Airport, about 16 km (10 miles) from Road Town, has a runway with a length of 1,500 m (4,921 ft). Captain Auguste George Airport on Anegada has been designated an international point of entry. In 2010 the airport on Virgin Gorda underwent major renovation, including an extension to the runway to allow larger aircraft to land.

British Virgin Islands Airports Authority: POB 4416, Road Town, Tortola VG1110; tel. 852-9000; fax 852-9045; internet www.bviaa.com; f. 2005; Chair. DEBRA ROMNEY-HODGE (acting); Man. Dir DENNISTON FRASER.

BVI Airways: Suite 234, Terrance B. Lettsome International Airport, Beef Island, Tortola VG1120; e-mail customerservice@bviairways.com; internet www.gobvi.com; f. 2010; flights to St Maarten, Dominica and Antigua; CEO LUKE SMITH.

Tourism

The main attraction of the islands is their tranquillity and clear waters, which provide excellent facilities for sailing, fishing, diving and other water sports. In 2010 there were an estimated 2,353 hotel rooms. There are also many charter yachts offering overnight accommodation. There were some 330,343 stop-over visitors and 501,451 cruise ship passengers in 2010. The majority of tourists are from the USA. Receipts from tourism totalled some US $389.4m. in 2010.

British Virgin Islands Chamber of Commerce and Hotel Association: see Chamber of Commerce.

British Virgin Islands Tourist Board: AKARA Bldg, 2nd Floor, DeCastro St, Road Town, Tortola VG1110; tel. 494-3134; fax 494-3866; e-mail info@bvitourism.com; internet www.bvitourism.com; Chair. RUSSEL HARRIGAN; Dir SHARON FLAX-MARS.

Defence

The United Kingdom is responsible for the defence of the islands.

Education

Primary education is free, universal and compulsory between the ages of five and 11. Secondary education is also free and lasts from 12 to 16 years of age. In 2008/09 some 726 pupils were attending pre-primary schools; in 2009/10, according to UNESCO estimates, enrolment at primary schools included 87% of children in the relevant age-group, while enrolment at secondary schools was equivalent to 98% of pupils in the relevant age category. Some 3,201 pupils attended primary schools in 2009/10, while 2,029 students attended secondary schools. Higher education is available at the University of the Virgin Islands (St Thomas, US Virgin Islands) and elsewhere in the Caribbean, in North America and in the United Kingdom. The 2012/13 budget allocated US $55.8m. to the Ministry of Education and Culture.

THE CAYMAN ISLANDS

Introductory Survey

LOCATION, CLIMATE, LANGUAGE, RELIGION, FLAG, CAPITAL

The Cayman Islands lie about 290 km (180 miles) west-north-west of Jamaica and consist of three main islands: Grand Cayman and, to the north-east, Little Cayman and Cayman Brac. The climate is tropical but is tempered by the trade winds, with a cool season between November and March, when temperatures average 24°C (75°F). The rainy season lasts from May until October. Mean annual rainfall is 1,524 mm (60 ins). The official language is English. Many Christian churches are represented. The flag is the British 'Blue Ensign', with the islands' coat of arms (a golden lion on a red background above three stars in green, representing the three main islands, superimposed on wavy lines of blue and white, the shield surmounted by a torse of white and blue bearing a yellow pineapple behind a green turtle, and with the motto 'He hath founded it upon the seas' on a scroll beneath) on a white roundel in the fly. The capital is George Town, on the island of Grand Cayman.

CONTEMPORARY POLITICAL HISTORY

Historical Context

The Cayman Islands came under acknowledged British rule in 1670 and were settled mainly from Jamaica and by privateers and buccaneers. The islands of Little Cayman and Cayman Brac were permanently settled only in 1833, and until 1877 there was no administrative connection between them and Grand Cayman. A representative assembly first sat in 1832. The islands formed a dependency of Jamaica until 1959, and the Governor of Jamaica held responsibility for the Cayman Islands until Jamaican independence in 1962, when a separate administrator was appointed (the title was changed to that of Governor in 1971). The 1959 Constitution was revised in 1972, 1992 and 1994, and a new Constitution introduced in 2009.

Domestic Political Affairs

For many years there have been no formal political parties on the islands, despite the emergence of a nascent party political system during the 1960s with the formation, in 1961, of the National Democratic Party (NDP), as part of a campaign for self-government. The Christian Democratic Party was formed as a conservative opposition. Both parties disappeared within a few years despite the electoral success of the NDP, largely owing to the system of gubernatorial nomination to the Executive Council. In the 1970s elections for the 12 elective seats in the Legislative Assembly came to be contested by 'teams' of candidates, as well as by independents. Two such teams were formed, Progress and Dignity (the more conservative) and Unity, but all candidates were committed to augmenting the economic success of the Caymans, and favoured continued dependent status. There are no plans for independence, and the majority of the population wish to maintain the islands' links with the United Kingdom.

At elections in 1980 the Unity team won a legislative majority. This majority was overturned in 1984, owing to public disquiet at the rapid growth of the immigrant work-force, and the implications of the recent US challenges to the Cayman Islands' bank secrecy laws. In 1987 the Legislative Assembly successfully sought stricter regulations of status and residency for those able to participate in elections, in an attempt to protect the political rights of native Caymanians (in view of the very large immigrant population). Prior to the November 1988 election the teams regrouped into more informal coalitions, indicating the primacy of personal over 'party' affiliations.

In July 1990 the Legislative Assembly approved proposals to review the Constitution. The implementation of most recommendations, including the appointment of a Chief Minister, was postponed pending a general election. One of the amendments, however, which involved increasing the number of elective seats in the Legislative Assembly to 15, was adopted in March 1992. The proposed reforms had prompted the formation, in mid-1991, of the territory's first political organization since the 1960s, the Progressive Democratic Party, later renamed the National Team. National Team members secured a majority in the Legislative Assembly in the November 1992 general election. In the same month James Ryan was appointed Chief Secretary, following the retirement of Lemuel Hurlston.

At a general election in November 1996 the governing National Team remained in power, although with a reduced majority. Two new groupings, the Democratic Alliance and Team Cayman, won parliamentary representation.

Emergence of new political parties

In a general election held on 8 November 2000 the governing National Team suffered a heavy defeat, losing six of its nine seats.

The newly elected Legislative Assembly appointed Kurt Tibbetts of the Democratic Alliance as Leader of Government Business.

In an unprecedented development in November 2001, several members of the Legislative Assembly, dissatisfied with the Government's leadership during the economic slowdown, formed the United Democratic Party (UDP). McKeeva Bush, the leader of the new party and Deputy Leader of Government Business and Minister of Tourism, Environment and Transport, claimed that at least 10 members of the 15-member Assembly were UDP supporters. Subsequently, the passing of a motion of no confidence against the Leader of Government Business resulted in Tibbetts and Edna Moyle, the Minister of Community Development, Women's Affairs, Youth and Sport, leaving the Executive Council. Bush became the new Leader of Government Business, while two other UDP legislators, Gilbert McLean and Frank McField, joined the Cabinet. In May 2002 the five opposition members of the legislative assembly formed a new political party, the People's Progressive Movement (PPM), led by Tibbetts.

The financial sector

In March 1999 the Government of the United Kingdom published draft legislation pertaining to its relationship with its Overseas Dependencies, which were to be renamed United Kingdom Overseas Territories (and had been referred to as such since February 1998). The legislation proposed the extension of British citizenship to the citizens of Overseas Territories, although it also required the Territories to amend their legislation on human rights and on the regulation of the financial services sector to meet international standards. The Cayman Islands were praised for the introduction in 1998 of laws on tax evasion, and for strengthening the regulatory powers of the Monetary Authority.

In January 2003 Bush accused the United Kingdom of undermining the course of Cayman Islands' justice, after a routine money-laundering case was dismissed amid allegations of espionage and obstruction of justice by British intelligence agents. The trial collapsed after it was alleged that the Director of the Cayman Islands Financial Reporting Unit (and a key witness in the trial) had passed information about the case to an unnamed agency of the British Government, understood to be the Secret Intelligence Service (MI6). It was claimed that MI6 wished to protect the names of its sources within the Caribbean 'offshore' banking community. Bush demanded that the British Government pay for the failed trial, estimated to cost some US $5m., and for any negative repercussions the affair might have for the reputation of the islands' banking sector. The United Kingdom, however, refused to compensate the Cayman Islands and maintained that although its intelligence agencies might have helped in the investigation, they had never interfered in the case. In March the Attorney-General, David Ballantyne, resigned amid accusations that he was aware that British intelligence agents were working covertly in the Cayman Islands.

The US Senate Finance Committee reported in June 2007 that it had identified more than 14,000 registered companies purportedly maintaining headquarters at a single address in the Cayman Islands, and subsequently commissioned an inquiry into the anomaly. It was estimated that evasion of US tax obligations by such entities—achieved by establishing 'offshore' subsidiaries on the islands—had resulted in a US $100,000m. shortfall in tax-based revenue and precipitated a growing sentiment of hostilities between the two nations' respective regulatory authorities. The inquiry reported its findings in July 2008: it concluded that although the Cayman Islands adhered to international financial standards, the use of the islands by US citizens was often indicative of illegal tax activities. The collapse in 2008 of several Cayman Island-based hedge funds, exacerbating the global financial crisis, caused increased attention to be focused on the territory's financial institutions. US President Barack Obama announced in May 2009 that he intended to implement stringent new laws governing tax havens, and called for more transparency from the 'offshore' sector; in January 2013 legislation was enacted in the USA requiring foreign banks to disclose to the USA all details of US account holders or face a punitive tax.

The Cayman Islands' inclusion, in April 2009, on an Organisation for Economic Co-operation and Development (OECD, see p. 388) 'grey list' of territories that had yet substantially to implement moves towards transparency in the financial sector was a set-back for the jurisdiction's reputation. However, in August the territory was removed from the list after signing 12 tax information-sharing agreements with other countries. (By early 2013 the Cayman Islands had signed a further 19 accords.) In October 2010 the territory received a broadly favourable assessment under OECD's Global Forum on Transparency and Exchange of Information for Tax Purposes peer review mechanism, although the need for further reform was highlighted. The Government created a task force to address money-laundering in March 2012. The British Government announced in May 2013 that agreement had been reached on new banking transparency laws for the territory as part of efforts to combat international tax evasion.

Constitutional reform

In March 2002 a three-member Constitutional Review Commission submitted a new draft constitution. The proposals included the creation of the office of Chief Minister, the establishment of a full ministerial government, and incorporated a bill of rights. The proposed document had to be debated by the Legislative Assembly and then approved by the British Parliament before being formally adopted. The opposition demanded a referendum on the recommendations, on the grounds that the UDP had rejected several of the proposals, despite strong public support for the changes, but Bush forwarded the proposals to the British Foreign and Commonwealth Office (FCO). In December Bush and the leader of the opposition, Tibbetts, travelled to the United Kingdom in order to review the proposed constitution with FCO officials. Consensus, however, proved impossible to achieve. While the PPM called for a public referendum on the issue, the UDP announced in February 2004 that it would not participate in the constitutional review process before the next election. In March 2006 an FCO delegation visited the Cayman Islands for informal discussions aimed at restarting the process of constitutional reform.

In May 2002 the British Overseas Territories Act, having received royal assent in the United Kingdom in February, came into force and granted British citizenship to the people of its Overseas Territories, including the Cayman Islands. Under the new law Caymanians would be able to hold British passports and work in the United Kingdom and elsewhere in the European Union (see p. 281).

The opposition PPM won a resounding victory at the general election of May 2005. The outgoing UDP Government had been criticized for its handling of the aftermath of Hurricane Ivan, which had caused an estimated CI $2,800m. of damage in September 2004, and also for its decision, in the same month, to grant 'belonger' status to some 3,000 people, a move interpreted by many as an attempt to increase the party's electoral support. The Leader of Government Business, Kurt Tibbetts, pledged to hold a referendum on increased autonomy for the islands. In November he announced a Freedom of Information Bill, to be debated in the Legislative Assembly, prior to a public consultation exercise. The proposed legislation was intended to promote government transparency and accountability, thus increasing constitutional democracy. Following several delays, the legislation was finally approved in August 2006 and in the following month the Freedom of Information Unit was officially opened. The law finally became effective in January 2009.

In February 2007 the Government announced the establishment of a Constitutional Review Secretariat to initiate renewed efforts towards constitutional reform in the territory. In January 2008 the Government launched a series of public consultations ahead of a referendum on the draft constitution scheduled to be held in May. The FCO affirmed in April that the new constitution must include a bill of rights and, in response, the Government postponed the referendum to allow a longer period of public deliberation. Discussions resumed in January 2009, and in April it was announced that the referendum would be held on 20 May, at the same time as the legislative election.

At the general election in May 2009, the opposition UDP defeated the incumbent PPM, securing nine of the 15 available seats. The PPM secured five seats and the remaining one was taken by an independent candidate. The rate of voter participation was 80.6% of the electorate. McKeeva Bush was sworn in as Leader of Government Business on 27 May.

In the concurrent referendum on the draft constitution some 62% of voters supported the changes. As a result, on 10 June 2009 the Privy Council approved the new charter. It came into force on 6 November. The new Constitution gave greater autonomy to the Cabinet, replacing the Governor-appointed Financial Secretary with an elected Minister of Finance (a portfolio assumed by Premier Bush). Although the Governor retained overall control of foreign affairs, certain aspects of external dealings were delegated to the Cabinet. A Bill of Rights, Freedoms and Responsibilities also came into effect in November 2012.

Recent developments: referendum and collapse of the Bush administration

Tibbetts resigned as leader of the opposition and PPM leader in February 2011. He was succeeded by Alden McLaughlin in the same month. In May the British Government declared that approval of the 2011/12 budget would only be granted after the Cayman authorities agreed to reduce their expenditure projections; a revised budget received British endorsement in the following month. During a meeting with British government officials in November 2011, Bush agreed to abide by new fiscal responsibility guidelines, as delineated in the Framework for Fiscal Responsibility (FFR). The United Kingdom finally approved the territory's 2012/13 budget in August 2012 after Bush pledged to implement further austerity

measures and to enact the FFR. However, in October, in spite of vehement opposition from the British Government, Bush announced his intention to modify certain clauses within the FFR. Amid speculation that the United Kingdom was preparing to impose direct rule on the territory, in November Bush agreed to submit the FFR to the legislature unaltered, and the document was approved later that month.

After coming under pressure from opposition-supported campaigners, the Premier announced in April 2012 that a referendum on electoral reform would be held on 18 July. Participants were to be asked the question 'Do you support an electoral system of single member constituencies with each elector being entitled to cast only one vote?' Bush disapproved of the proposed single member constituency system, which he argued would be destabilizing, expensive to implement and more susceptible to fraud than the existing multi-member constituency framework, while advocates of the proposal denounced the current electoral rules as undemocratic and inequitable. In the referendum, over 65% of the voters endorsed the proposal. However, turn-out was not high enough for the result to be considered binding.

Meanwhile, it was revealed in July 2011 that Premier Bush was under investigation by the police in relation to purported financial discrepancies. In 2004, while serving as Leader of Government Business, Bush had allegedly received some US $350,000 from a development company in return for favourable cabinet decisions on 're-zoning issues'. Bush rejected the accusations. However, in April 2012 it was revealed that Bush was under investigation in three separate cases of financial irregularities, and later that month details emerged of a police inquiry into the Premier's alleged connection to an illegal shipment of dynamite. Bush accused the opposition of colluding with British officials to end his premiership, although the United Kingdom strongly denied that the police investigations were politically motivated. Bush was placed under arrest on 11 December and was granted bail on the following day. In response, a no confidence motion against Bush was adopted by the Legislative Assembly on 18 December, and he was duly replaced as Premier by Julianna O'Connor-Connolly, the erstwhile Deputy Premier, the following day. O'Connor-Connolly formed a minority Government comprised of those UDP members who had endorsed the motion of no confidence, all of whom resigned from the party on 29 December. In March 2013 Bush was charged with theft, misconduct and breach of trust. A general election was scheduled to be conducted on 22 May.

CONSTITUTION AND GOVERNMENT

A new Constitution was adopted in 2009, granting greater autonomy to Cayman Islanders, although it extended many of the terms of the previous 1959 charter. The Governor, who is appointed by the British monarch, is responsible for external affairs, defence, internal security and the public service. The Governor is Chairman of the Cabinet, comprising three members appointed by the Governor and five members elected by the Legislative Assembly. The Legislative Assembly comprises three official members and 15 members elected by universal adult suffrage for a period of four years.

REGIONAL AND INTERNATIONAL CO-OPERATION

The Cayman Islands has been an associate member of the Caribbean Community and Common Market (CARICOM, see p. 231) since 2002; the territory is also a member of CARICOM's Caribbean Development Bank (see p. 236). The Cayman Islands has the status of Overseas Territory in association with the European Union (see p. 281). The territory is a member of the Commonwealth (see p. 244).

ECONOMIC AFFAIRS

In 2011, according to UN estimates, the Cayman Islands' gross domestic product (GDP) was CI $2,647.2m., equivalent to some US $57,610 per head. During 2002–11, according to official estimates, the population increased at an average annual rate of 3.0%, while GDP increased, in real terms, by 0.7% per year during 2002–11, according to UN estimates; overall GDP decreased by 2.9% in 2010, but increased by 0.9% in 2011.

Agriculture (which engaged only 0.8% of the employed labour force in October–November 2011 and accounted for 0.3% of GDP in 2011 as a whole) is limited by infertile soil, low rainfall and high labour costs. The principal crops are citrus fruits and bananas, and some other produce for local consumption. Flowers (particularly orchids) are produced for export. Livestock-rearing consists of beef cattle, poultry (mainly for eggs) and pigs. Fishing is mainly for lobster and shrimp. According to UN estimates, during 2002–11 the GDP of the agricultural sector increased, in real terms, by an average annual rate of 2.6%; real agricultural GDP decreased by 1.8% in 2010 and by a further 7.2% in 2011.

Industry, engaging 13.9% of the employed labour force in October–November 2011 and accounting for 7.5% of GDP in that year, consists mainly of construction and related manufacturing, some food-processing and tourism-related light industries. The construction sector contributed 2.9% of GDP in 2011, while manufacturing activities accounted for only about 0.8% of the total in that year. Energy requirements are satisfied by the import of petroleum products and gas (24.1% of total imports in 2011). According to UN estimates, during 2002–11 industrial GDP decreased, in real terms, by an average of 1.8% per year; real industrial GDP decreased by 12.8% in 2010 and by 1.0% in 2011.

Service industries dominate the Caymanian economy, accounting for 85.3% of employment (excluding unclassified activities) in October–November 2011 and contributing 92.2% of GDP in that year. The tourism industry is an important economic contributor. The industry was estimated to contribute 24.2% of GDP, directly and indirectly, in 2012, according to the World Travel and Tourism Council. The industry earned US $535m. in 2009, although this figure declined to $385m. in 2010. Most visitors are from the USA (78.6% of tourist arrivals in 2011). The Cayman Islands is one of the largest 'offshore' financial centres in the world; in March 2013 there were 222 banks and 142 active trust companies and 10,932 mutual funds on the islands, according to the Cayman Islands Monetary Authority. In October–November 2011 the financial services sector engaged 10.0% of the working population, and in the year as a whole insurance and finance contributed 36.9% of GDP. According to UN estimates, the GDP of the services sector increased, in real terms, by an average of 0.7% per year in 2002–11; real services GDP decreased by 2.9% in 2010, but increased by 1.3% in 2011.

In 2011 the Cayman Islands recorded a merchandise trade deficit of CI $743.9m. Receipts from tourism and the financial sector, remittances and capital inflows normally offset the trade deficit. The principal source of imports is the USA (which provided some 90.9% of total imports in 2011). The principal imports in 2011 were petroleum products and gas, miscellaneous manufactured articles, food and live animals, machinery and transport equipment, and basic manufactures. The principal exports in that year were crude materials, machinery and transport equipment, miscellaneous manufactured articles, and basic manufactures.

An estimated government budget deficit of CI $72.2m. was recorded in 2011. At the end of 1999 the public debt stood at US $114.8m. The average annual rate of inflation was 2.2% in 2002–11; consumer prices increased by 1.3% in 2011. According to official census figures, only 56.4% of the resident population of the islands were Caymanian in 2011 (compared with 79% in 1980). Some 6.3% of the labour force were unemployed in October–November 2011.

Both the principal economic sectors, 'offshore' finance and tourism, benefit from the Cayman Islands' political stability, good infrastructure and extensive development. The financial sector, which benefits from an absence of taxation and of foreign exchange regulations, as well as enjoying strict confidentiality laws, contracted in 2009, following the onset of the global financial crisis in the previous year. Tourist arrivals also declined in 2009, and real GDP contracted by 6.9%, according to government data. The economy contracted by a further 2.9% in 2010. The financial sector remained subdued in that year, and activity in the construction industry, which had been particularly badly affected by the recession, declined further. However, there was an increase in air arrivals and cruise ship visitors, indicating a recovery in the tourism sector. In spite of mixed results in the tourism and financial industries, as well as another year of negative growth in the construction sector, real GDP expanded by 0.9% in 2011. Preliminary data for 2012 indicated that, while financial services and construction had continued to struggle, rising tourist arrivals had supported real GDP growth of 1.2% in that year.

PUBLIC HOLIDAYS

2014: 1 January (New Year's Day), 27 January (National Heroes' Day), 5 March (Ash Wednesday), 18 April (Good Friday), 21 April (Easter Monday), 19 May (Discovery Day), 7 June (Queen's Official Birthday), 7 July (Constitution Day), 10 November (Remembrance Day), 25–26 December (Christmas),

Statistical Survey

Sources: Government Information Services, Cricket Sq., Elgin Ave, George Town, Grand Cayman; tel. 949-8092; fax 949-5936; The Information Centre, Economic and Statistics Office, Government Administration Bldg, Grand Cayman; tel. 949-0940; fax 949-8782; e-mail infostats@gov.ky; internet www.eso.ky.

AREA AND POPULATION

Area: 262 sq km (102 sq miles). The main island of Grand Cayman is about 197 sq km (76 sq miles), about one-half of which is swamp. Cayman Brac is 39 sq km (15 sq miles); Little Cayman is 26 sq km (11 sq miles).

Population: 39,410 at census of 10 October 1999; 55,036 (males 27,218, females 27,818) at census of 10 October 2010 (Grand Cayman 52,740, Cayman Brac 2,098, Little Cayman 198). *2011* (official estimate at 31 December): 55,517.

Density (at 2010 census): 210.1 per sq km.

Population by Age and Sex (official estimates at 31 December 2011): *0–14:* 10,067 (males 5,128, females 4,939); *15–64:* 42,726 (males 21,215; females 21,511); *65 and over:* 2,724 (males 1,111, females 1,613); *Total* 55,517 (males 27,454, females 28,063).

Principal Towns (at 2010 census): George Town (capital) 28,089; West Bay 11,222; Bodden Town 10,543.

Births, Marriages and Deaths (2011 unless otherwise indicated): Live births 800 (birth rate 14.5 per 1,000); Marriages 530 (marriage rate 9.6 per 1,000, 2010); Deaths 176 (death rate 3.2 per 1,000).

Life Expectancy (years at birth, 2011): 80.7 (males 78.0; females 83.4). Source: Pan American Health Organization.

Economically Active Population (sample survey, persons aged 15 years and over, October–November 2011): Agriculture and fishing 268; Manufacturing, mining, printing and publishing 763; Construction 3,707; Electricity, gas and water supply 438; Wholesale and retail trade 4,227; Restaurants and hotels 3,735; Transport, post and telecommunication 2,457; Financial services 3,535; Public administration, education, health and social work 5,478; Other community, social and personal service activities 1,931; Private households with employed persons 3,637; Real estate, renting and business services 5,017; *Sub-total* 35,193; Not classifiable by economic activity 74; *Total employed* 35,267; Unemployed 2,353; *Total labour force* 37,620 (Caymanian 17,701, non-Caymanian 19,919).

HEALTH AND WELFARE

Total Fertility Rate (children per woman, 2011): 1.9.

Physicians (per 1,000 head, 2008): 2.7.

Health Expenditure: % of GDP (1997): 4.2.

Health Expenditure: public (% of total, 1997): 53.2.

Total Carbon Dioxide Emissions ('000 metric tons, 2008): 557.4.

Total Carbon Dioxide Emissions Per Head (metric tons, 2008): 10.1.

Source: mainly Pan American Health Organization.

For definitions, see explanatory note on p. vi.

AGRICULTURE, ETC.

Livestock ('000 head, 2011, FAO estimates): Cattle 2.1; Goats 2.2; Pigs 1.1; Chickens 6.

Fishing (metric tons, live weight, 2010): Total catch 125 (all marine fishes).

Source: FAO.

INDUSTRY

Electric Energy (production, million kWh): 608.8 in 2009; 605.1 in 2010; 606.5 in 2011.

FINANCE

Currency and Exchange Rates: 100 cents = 1 Cayman Islands dollar (CI $). *Sterling, US Dollar and Euro Equivalents* (31 December 2012): £1 sterling = CI $1.315; US $1 = 0.833 CI cents; €1 = CI $1.100; CI $100 = £76.05 = US $120.00 = €90.95. *Exchange rate:* Fixed at CI $1 = US $1.20.

Budget (CI $ million, 2011): *Revenue:* Taxes on international trade and transactions 162.2; Taxes on other domestic goods and services 289.5; Taxes on property 36.4; Other tax revenue 1.2; Non-coercive revenue 60.6 (Sales of goods and services 55.8); Total 549.9. *Expenditure:* Current expenditure 519.9 (Personnel costs 216.3, Supplies and consumable goods 94.0, Subsidies 131.6, Transfer payments 31.0, Interest payments 32.9, Other 14.1); Other executive expenses 3.0; Capital expenditure and net lending 99.2; Total 622.1.

Cost of Living (Consumer Price Index; base: June 2008 = 100): All items 98.6 in 2009; 98.9 in 2010; 100.2 in 2011.

Gross Domestic Product (CI $ million at constant 2007 prices): 2,633.5 in 2009; 2,556.1 in 2010; 2,579.5 in 2011.

Gross Domestic Product by Economic Activity (CI $ million in current prices, 2011): Agriculture and fishing 9.2; Mining and quarrying 17.8; Manufacturing 23.5; Electricity and water supply 88.6; Construction 84.3; Wholesale and retail trade 211.6; Hotels and restaurants 145.2; Transport, storage and communication 202.2; Finance and insurance 1,055.0; Real estate, renting and business services 619.0; Public administration and defence 178.4; Education

67.7; Health and social work 79.5; Other services 79.6; *Sub-total* 2,861.6; *Less* Financial intermediation services indirectly measured 358.5; *GDP in basic prices* 2,503.0; Tax less subsidies on products 193.4; *GDP in purchasers' values* 2,696.4.

EXTERNAL TRADE

Principal Commodities (CI $ million, 2011): *Imports c.i.f.:* Food and live animals 118.4; Beverages and tobacco 27.6; Petroleum products and gas 183.4; Chemicals and related products 31.7; Basic manufactures 77.1; Machinery and transport equipment 107.4; Miscellaneous manufactured articles 134.0; Total (incl. others) 762.0. *Exports f.o.b.:* Crude materials 2.1; Basic manufactures 0.5; Machinery and transport equipment 1.5; Miscellaneous manufactured articles 1.0; Total (incl. others) 18.1.

Principal Trading Partners (CI $ million, 2011): *Imports c.i.f.:* Jamaica 5.4; Japan 3.5; United Kingdom 5.5; USA 692.4; Total (incl. others) 762.0. *Exports f.o.b.:* Total 18.1.

TRANSPORT

Road Traffic ('000 motor vehicles in use, 2002): Passenger cars 23.8; Commercial vehicles 6.4.

Shipping: *International Freight Traffic* ('000 metric tons): Goods loaded 735 (1990); Goods unloaded 239,138 (2000). *Cargo Vessels* (2011 unless otherwise indicated): Vessels 55 (2010); Calls at port 465. *Flag Registered Fleet* (at 31 December 2012): Number of vessels 804; Total displacement 3,835,950 grt. (Source: Lloyd's List Intelligence—www.lloydslistintelligence.com).

Civil Aviation (traffic at Owen Roberts International Airport and Gerrard Smith International Airport, 2011): Aircraft movements 29,100; Freight carried (metric tons) 1,030.8 (loaded 155.5, unloaded 875.3); Passengers carried 1,151,500 (arriving 577,600, departing 573,900).

TOURISM

Visitor Arrivals ('000): 1,792.4 (arrivals by air 272.0, cruise ship passengers 1,520.4) in 2009; 1,886.1 (arrivals by air 288.3, cruise ship passengers 1,597.8) in 2010; 1,710.6 (arrivals by air 309.1, cruise ship passengers 1,401.5) in 2011.

Stay-over Arrivals by Place of Origin ('000, 2011): Canada 24.6; Europe 21.1; USA 242.9; Total (incl. others) 309.1. Source: Cayman Islands Tourism Department, George Town.

Tourism Receipts (US $ million, excl. passenger transport): 535 in 2009; 385 in 2010. Source: World Tourism Organization.

COMMUNICATIONS MEDIA

Telephones: 37,200 main lines in use in 2011.

Mobile Cellular Telephones (subscribers): 95,100 in 2011.

Fixed and Mobile Telecommunication Lines (number in service): 132,349 in 2011.

Broadband Subscribers: 18,800 in 2011.

Internet Users: 24,000 in 2009.

Source: mainly International Telecommunication Union.

EDUCATION

(at 30 September 2011 unless otherwise indicated)

Institutions (excl. Lighthouse School): Government 17; Private 11; Total 28.

Enrolment (at 30 September 2010): *Government:* Primary 2,553; Middle 1,198; Secondary 1,111; Total 4,862. *Private:* Total 2,881. *Total:* 7,743 (excl. Lighthouse School 86). *2011:* Government 4,890; Private 2,756; Total 7,646.

Pupil-teacher Ratio (primary education, UNESCO estimate): 12.1 in 2007/08. Source: UNESCO Institute for Statistics.

Adult Literacy Rate: 98.9% in 2007 (males 98.7%, females 99.0%). Source: UNESCO Institute for Statistics.

Directory

The Government

HEAD OF STATE

Queen: HM Queen ELIZABETH II.
Governor: DUNCAN TAYLOR (assumed office 15 January 2010, until Aug. 2013).

CABINET
(May 2013)

The Government is formed by former members of the United Democratic Party.

Chairman: DUNCAN TAYLOR (The Governor).

Premier and Minister of Finance, District Administration, Works, Lands and Agriculture: JULIANNA O'CONNOR-CONNOLLY.

Deputy Governor, Head of the Civil Service and Minister of Internal and External Affairs*: FRANZ MANDERSON.

Attorney-General and Minister of Legal Affairs*: SAMUEL BULGIN.

Cabinet Secretary*: ORRETT CONNOR.

Minister of Health, Environment, Youth, Sports and Culture: MARK SCOTLAND.

Deputy Premier and Minister of Education, Training and Employment: ROLSTON ANGLIN.

Minister of Community Affairs, Gender and Housing: DWAYNE SEYMOUR.

Minister of Tourism and Development: CLINE GLIDDEN, Jr.

A District Commissioner, Ernie Scott, represents the Governor on Cayman Brac and Little Cayman.
* Appointed by the Governor.

GOVERNMENT OFFICES

Office of the Governor: Govt Admin Bldg, 133 Elgin Ave, George Town, Grand Cayman KY1-9000; tel. 244-2401; fax 945-4131; e-mail staffoff@candw.ky; internet www.ukincayman.fco.gov.uk.

All official government offices and ministries, unless otherwise stated, are located in the Government Administration Bldg, Elgin Ave, George Town, Grand Cayman.

Ministry of Community Affairs, Gender and Housing: tel. 244-2424; fax 949-3896; e-mail foi.mcw@gov.ky; internet www.mcagh.gov.k.

Ministry of District Administration, Works, Lands and Agriculture: tel. 244-2412; fax 949-2922; e-mail ministry.dawga@gov.ky; internet www.dapah.gov.ky.

Ministry of Education, Training and Employment: tel. 244-2417; fax 949-9343; e-mail education@gov.ky; internet www.education.gov.ky.

Ministry of Finance, Tourism and Development: tel. 244-2458; fax 945-1746; e-mail tedc@gov.ky; internet www.mtd.gov.ky.

Ministry of Health, Environment, Youth, Sports and Culture: tel. 244-2318; fax 949-1790; e-mail h&hs@gov.ky; internet www.ministryofhealth.gov.ky.

Ministry of Internal and External Affairs: tel. 244-3179; fax 946-5453; e-mail foi.pie@gov.ky; internet www.pie.gov.ky.

Ministry of Legal Affairs: Edward St, Albert Panton, POB 495, George Town, Grand Cayman KY1-1106; tel. 244-2405; fax 949-6079; e-mail agc@gov.ky; internet www.judicial.ky.

LEGISLATIVE ASSEMBLY

Legislative Assembly: 33 Fort St, POB 890, George Town, Grand Cayman KY1-1103; tel. 949-4236; fax 949-9514; internet www.legislativeassembly.ky; Clerk ZENA MERREN-CHIN.

Members: The Deputy Governor, the Attorney-General, the Financial Secretary and 15 elected members. According to the terms of the 2009 Constitution, the number of elected members was to be increased to 18 at the next dissolution of the Legislative Assembly, when the Deputy Governor was to give up his seat. An Electoral Boundaries Commission also was to be established to review constituency boundaries. An election was scheduled to be held on 22 May 2013.

Speaker: MARY J. LAWRENCE.

Election Commission

Elections Office: Smith Road Centre, 2nd Floor, 150 Smith Rd, George Town, Grand Cayman; tel. 949-8047; fax 946-2977; e-mail electionsoffice@candw.ky; internet www.electionsoffice.ky; Supervisor of Elections KEARNEY SIDNEY GOMEZ.

Political Organizations

People's Progressive Movement (PPM): 488 Crewe Rd, George Town, POB 10526, Grand Cayman; tel. 945-1776; fax 946-0184; e-mail info@ppm.ky; internet www.theprogressives.ky; f. 2002; Leader ALDEN MCLAUGHLIN; Gen. Sec. RAYBURN FARRINGTON.

United Democratic Party (UDP): Unit 15, 2nd Floor, Rankin's Plaza, Eastern Ave, POB 12417, Grand Cayman; tel. 943-3338; fax

943-3339; e-mail info@udp.ky; internet www.udp.ky; tel. 943-3338; fax 943-3339; f. 2001; Leader W. McKeeva Bush; Deputy Leader Ellio Solomon.

Judicial System

There is a Grand Court of the Islands (with Supreme Court status), a Summary Court, a Youth Court and a Coroner's Court. The Grand Court has jurisdiction in all civil matters, admiralty matters, and in trials on indictment. Appeals lie to the Court of Appeal of the Cayman Islands and beyond that to the Privy Council in the United Kingdom. The Summary Courts deal with criminal and civil matters (up to a certain limit defined by law) and appeals lie to the Grand Court.

The Grand Court: Edward St, George Town, POB 495, Grand Cayman KY1-1106; internet www.judicial.ky; Chief Justice Anthony Smellie; Chief Magistrate Nova G. A. Hall.

President of the Court of Appeal: Sir John Chadwick.

Director of Public Prosecutions: Cheryll Richards.

Clerk of the Courts of the Islands: Valdis Foldats, Court's Office, Edward St, George Town, POB 495, Grand Cayman KY1-1106; tel. 949-4296; fax 949-9856; e-mail valdis.foldats@gov.ky; internet www .judicial.ky.

Religion

CHRISTIANITY

The oldest established denominations are (on Grand Cayman) the United Church of Jamaica and Grand Cayman (Presbyterian), and (on Cayman Brac) the Baptist Church. Anglicans are adherents of the Church in the Province of the West Indies (Grand Cayman forms part of the diocese of Jamaica). Within the Roman Catholic Church, the Cayman Islands forms part of the archdiocese of Kingston in Jamaica. According to the latest available census figures (2007), some 26% of the population are adherents of the Church of God, 13% are Roman Catholics, 9% belong to the United Church, 8% are Baptists, 8% are Seventh-day Adventists, 7% are Pentecostalists and 4% are Anglicans.

The Press

The Cayman Islands Journal: The Compass Centre, Shedden Rd, POB 1365, George Town, Grand Cayman; tel. 949-5111; fax 949-7675; internet www.compasscayman.com/journal; publ. by Cayman Free Press; monthly; broadsheet business newspaper; Publr Brian Uzzell.

Cayman Net News: Mirco Centre, 85 North Sound Rd, Alissta Towers, POB 11063, Grand Cayman KY1-1008; tel. 623-6060; fax 949-0679; e-mail info@caymannetnews.com; internet www .caymannetnews.com; internet news service; publishes weekly newspaper (f. 2006); Publr and Editor-in-Chief Deon Ebanks.

Caymanian Compass: The Compass Centre, Shedden Rd, POB 1365, George Town, Grand Cayman; tel. 949-5111; fax 949-7675; e-mail tammie@cfp.ky; internet www.compasscayman.com; f. 1965; publ. by the Cayman Free Press; 5 a week; Editor Tammie Chisholm; circ. 10,000.

The Chamber: POB 1000, George Town, Grand Cayman; tel. 949-8090; fax 949-0220; e-mail info@caymanchamber.ky; internet www .caymanchamber.ky; f. 1965; monthly; newsletter of the Cayman Islands Chamber of Commerce; Editor Wil Pineau; circ. 5,000.

Christian Lifestyle: Bldg G, Unit 3, Countryside Shopping Village, POB 1217, Grand Cayman KY1 1108; tel. 926-2507; fax 946-1737; e-mail editor@cstylemagazine.com; internet www.christian lifestylemagazine.com; f. 2008; publ. every 2 months; Editor Karen Chin.

Gazette: Gazette Office, Government Information Service, Cayman Islands Government, Aqua World Mall, Merrendale Dr., Grand Cayman; tel. 949-8092; fax 949-5936; e-mail caymangazette@gov .ky; internet www.gazettes.gov.ky; official govt newspaper; publ. fortnightly on Mon; Editor-in-Chief Patricia Ebanks.

Key to Cayman: The Compass Centre, Shedden Rd, POB 1365, George Town, Grand Cayman KY1 1108; tel. 949-5111; fax 949-7675; e-mail cfp@candw.ky; internet keytocayman.com; 2 a year; free tourist magazine; publ. by the Cayman Free Press; Cayman Free Press also publs *Caymanian Compass* newspaper and accompanying supplements, *Cayman Islands Journal*, *Cayman Islands Yearbook & Business Directory*, *Cayman Islands Map*, and *Inside Out*, a home and living magazine; Editor Natasha Were.

Publishers

Acorn Publishing Co: Alissta Towers, North Sound Rd, Seven Mile Beach, POB 31403, Grand Cayman KY1-1206; tel. 916-2413; fax 946-

2830; e-mail info@acorn.ky; internet caymanyp.com/ Cayman-Islands/Publishers-Book; Publishes Good Taste Magazine, Explore Cayman.

Cayman Free Press Ltd: The Compass Centre, Shedden Rd, POB 1365, George Town, Grand Cayman; tel. 949-5111; fax 949-7675; e-mail info@cfp.ky; internet www.caymanfreepress.com; f. 1965; Publishes Caymanian Compass, The Journal, Observor on Sunday, Cayman Financial Review, What's Hot, Cayman Buzz Directory, Inside Out, Cayman Ashore, Hurricane Supplement; Gen. Man. Brian Uzzell.

CLM Publishing: POB 1217, Grand Cayman, KY1-1108; tel. 926-2507; e-mail clmpublishing@gmail.com; internet www .clmpublsihing.webs.com; publishes *Christian Lifestyle Magazine*; Chair. and CEO Karen E. Chin.

Global Directories (Cayman) Ltd: 62 Form Lane, 3rd Floor, Camana Bay, POB 688, George Town, Grand Cayman; tel. 949-7027; fax 949-8366; e-mail caysales@globaldirectories.com; internet caymanislandsyp.com; f. 1978; fmrly Caribbean Publishing Co (Cayman) Ltd; Dir Lester Garnett.

Government Information Service: Gazette Office, Government Information Services, Cayman Islands Govt, 2nd Floor Govt Admin. Bldg, George Town, Grand Cayman; tel. 949-8092; fax 949-5936; e-mail caymangazette@gov.ky; internet www.gazettes.gov.ky; publr of official govt releases, *Gazette*.

Tower Marketing: Grand Cayman; tel. 623-6700; fax 769-6700; e-mail lynne@tower.com.ky; internet www.tower.com.ky; f. 1999; Man. Dir Lynne Byles.

Broadcasting and Communications

REGULATORY AUTHORITY

Information and Communications Technology Authority (ICTA): Alissta Towers, 3rd Floor, 85 North Sound Rd, POB 2502, Grand Cayman KY1-1104; tel. 946-4282; fax 945-8284; e-mail info@ icta.ky; internet www.icta.ky; f. 2002; responsible for the regulation and licensing of telecommunications, broadcasting, and all forms of radio which includes ship, aircraft, mobile and amateur radio and the management of the Cayman Islands internet domain; Chair. Dale Crighton; Man. Dir David Archbold.

TELECOMMUNICATIONS

Digicel Cayman: Cayman Financial Centre, 36a Roys Dr., 3rd Floor, POB 700, George Town, Grand Cayman; tel. 623-3444; fax 623-3329; e-mail caycustomercare@digicelgroup.com; internet www .digicelcayman.com; f. 2003; owned by an Irish consortium; acquired the operations of Cingular Wireless (fmrly those of AT&T Wireless) in the country in 2005 (www.cingular.ky); Chair Denis O'Brien; CEO Chris Hayman.

LIME: Anderson Sq. Bldg, Anderson Sq., Shedden Rd, POB 293, George Town, Grand Cayman; tel. 949-7800; fax 949-7962; e-mail cs@candw.ky; internet www.time4lime.com; f. 1966 as Cable & Wireless (Cayman Islands) Ltd; name changed as above 2008; Cable & Wireless' monopoly over the telecommunications market ended in 2004; CEO Tony Rice; CEO (Jamaica and the Cayman Islands Garry Sinclair.

Logic Communications: Governors Sq., West Bay Rd, Seven Mile Beach, POB 31112, Grand Cayman, KY1-1205; tel. 743-4300; fax 743-4301; e-mail support@logic.ky; internet www.logic.ky; f. 2003 as WestTel Ltd; name changed as above in 2010; wholly owned subsidiary of KeyTech Ltd, Bermuda; provides telephone and internet services; CEO Michael Edenholm.

TeleCayman: Cayman Corporate Centre, 27 Hospital Rd, 4th Floor, POB 704 GT, Grand Cayman; tel. 769-1000; fax 769-0999; e-mail customer@telecayman.com; internet www.telecayman.com; f. 2003; provides telephone and internet services; Business Man. Chris Haydon.

BROADCASTING

Radio

Radio Cayman: Elgin Ave, POB 1110 GT, George Town, Grand Cayman KY1-1102; tel. 949-7799; fax 949-6536; e-mail radiocayman@gov.ky; internet www.radiocayman.gov.ky; started full-time broadcasting 1976; govt-owned commercial radio station; service in English; operates Radio Cayman One and Breeze FM; Dir Norma McField.

Radio Heaven 97 FM: Hurst Rd, Newlands, POB 31481, Grand Cayman, KY1-1206; tel. and fax 938-1082; e-mail pam@heaven97 .com; internet www.heaven97.com; f. 1997; owned by Christian Communications Asscn; commercial station; Christian broadcasting, music and news; Man. Dir Stephen Faucette.

Radio ICCI-FM: International College of the Cayman Islands, 595 Hirst Rd, POB 136, Grand Cayman KY1-1501; tel. 947-1100; fax 947-

1210; e-mail info@myicci.com; internet www.icci.edu.ky; f. 1973; radio station of the International College of the Cayman Islands; educational and cultural; Pres. TASHA EBANKS GARCIA.

Radio Vibe: 21 Eclipse Dr., POB 10236, George Town, Grand Cayman KY1-1002; tel. 949-8423; fax 946-9867; e-mail info@paramountmedia.ky; internet www.vibefm.ky; operated by Paramount Media Services, in addition to Spin FM; Man. KENNETH G. RANKINE.

Radio Z99.9 FM: Grand Harbour, Suite 21 and 22, Shamrock Rd, POB 30110, George Town, Grand Cayman KY1-1201; tel. 945-1166; fax 945-1006; e-mail info@z99.ky; internet www.z99.ky; owned by Hurley's Entertainment Corpn Ltd; Programs Dir JASON HOWARD.

Television

Cayman Adventist Television Network (CATN/TV): 209 Walkers Rd, POB 515, George Town, Grand Cayman KY1-1106; tel. 949-167; fax 949-6167; e-mail mission@candw.ky; internet caymanadventist.org; f. 1996; local and international programmes, mainly religious; Pres. SHIAN O'CONNOR; Exec. Sec. AL POWELL.

Cayman Christian TV Ltd: POB 964, Grand Cayman KY1-1102; tel. 947-2599; relays Christian broadcasting from the USA; Vice-Pres. FRED RUTTY.

CITN Cayman 27: 45 Eclipse Way, POB 30563, Grand Cayman KY1-1203; tel. 745-2739; fax 749-1002; e-mail hlofters@weststartv.com; internet www.cayman27.com.ky; f. 1992 as Cayman International Television Network; 24 hrs daily; local and international news and US entertainment; 10-channel cable service of international programmes by subscription; Gen. Man. APRIL CUMMINGS; News Dir BEN MEADE.

WestStar TV Ltd: 45 Eclipse Way, POB 31117, Grand Cayman KY1-1205; tel. 745-5555; fax 745-5554; e-mail support@weststartv.ky; internet www.weststartv.com; f. 1993; operates wireless cable television service; affiliated to WestTel Ltd; CEO BOB TAYLOR; Operations Man. TRACI BRADLEY.

Finance

(cap. = capital; res = reserves; dep. = deposits; m. = million; brs = branches)

Banking facilities are provided by commercial banks. The islands have become an important centre for 'offshore' companies and trusts. At the end of March 2013 there were 222 banks and 142 active trust companies and 10,932 mutual funds on the islands. The islands are well known as a tax haven owing to the absence of any form of direct taxation. In September 2011 assets held by banks registered in the Cayman Islands totalled US $1,607,000m.

Cayman Islands Monetary Authority (CIMA): 80E Shedden Rd, Elizabethan Sq., POB 10052 APO, George Town, Grand Cayman KY1-1001; tel. 949-7089; fax 946-4230; e-mail contactpublicrelations@cimoney.com.ky; internet www.cimoney.com.ky; f. 1997; responsible for managing the territory's currency and reserves and for regulating the financial services sector; cap. CI $2.3m., res CI $20.4m., dep. CI $88.7m. (June 2012); Chair. GEORGE McCARTHY; Man. Dir CINDY SCOTLAND.

PRINCIPAL BANKS AND TRUST COMPANIES

AALL Trust and Banking Corpn Ltd: AALL Bldg, POB 1166, George Town, Grand Cayman; tel. 949-5588; fax 945-5772; internet www.aall.com; Chair. ERIK MONSEN; Man. Dir KEVIN DOYLE.

Appleby Trust (Cayman) Ltd: Clifton House, 75 Fort St, POB 1350, Grand Cayman KY1-1108; tel. 949-4900; fax 949-4901; e-mail cayman@applebyglobal.com; internet www.applebyglobal.com; f. 2006 following acquisition of business interests of Ansbacher (Cayman) Ltd; offices in Bermuda; Dir GEORGE BASHFORTH.

Atlantic Security Bank: POB 10340, George Town 1097, Grand Cayman; internet www.asbnet.com; f. 1981 as Banco de Crédito del Peru International, name changed as above 1986; cap. US $70m. res US $13.9m. dep. US $1,320.6m. (Dec. 2011); Pres. DIONISIO ROMERO.

Banco Safra (Cayman Islands) Ltd: c/o Bank of Nova Scotia, POB 501, George Town, Grand Cayman; tel. 814-1574; fax 949-9512; f. 1993; res US $113.9m., dep. US $422.2m. (Dec. 2011); Pres. CARLOS ALBERTO VIEIRA.

BANIF-Banco Internaçional do Funchal (Cayman) Ltd: Genesis Bldg, 3rd Floor, POB 32338 SMB, George Town, Grand Cayman; tel. 945-8060; fax 945-8069; e-mail banifcay@candw.ky; internet www.banif.pt; Chair., Exec. Bd Dr JOAQUIM FILIPE MARQUES DOS SANTOS; Sec. BRUNO MIGUEL DOS SANTOS DE JESUS.

BNP Paribas Fortis Bank (Cayman) Ltd: Grand Pavilion Commercial Centre, 802 West Bay Rd, POB 2003, George Town, Grand Cayman; tel. 949-7942; fax 949-8340; e-mail phil.brown@ky.fortisbank.com; internet www.bnpparibas.com; f. 1984 as Pierson, Heldring & Pierson (Cayman) Ltd; name changed to Mees Pierson (Cayman) Ltd in 1993; present name adopted in June 2000; Chair. HERMAN DAEMS.

Butterfield Bank (Cayman) Ltd: Butterfield House, 68 Fort St, POB 705, George Town, Grand Cayman KY1-1107; tel. 949-7055; fax 949-7004; e-mail info@ky.butterfieldbank.com; internet www.ky.butterfieldgroup.com; f. 1967; name changed as above in 2004, fmrly Bank of Butterfield International (Cayman) Ltd; subsidiary of Bank of N. T. Butterfield & Son Ltd, Bermuda; cap. US $16.4m., res US $25.9m., dep. US $1,817.4m. (Dec. 2010); Chair. BRAD KOPP; Man. Dir CONOR O'DEA; 3 brs.

Caledonian Bank and Trust Ltd: Caledonian House, 69 Dr Roy's Dr., POB 1043, George Town, Grand Cayman KY1-1102; tel. 949-0050; fax 949-8062; e-mail info@caledonian.com; internet www.caledonian.com; f. 1970; CEO KOBI DORENBUSH.

Cayman National Bank Ltd: Cayman National Bank Bldg, 4th Floor, 200 Elgin Ave, POB 1097, George Town, Grand Cayman; tel. 949-4655; fax 949-7506; e-mail cnb@caymannational.com; internet www.caymannational.com; f. 1974; subsidiary of Cayman National Corpn; cap. CI $2.4m., res CI $41m., dep. CI $807.5m. (Sept. 2011); Chair. TRUMAN MURRAY BODDEN; Pres. STUART DACK; 8 brs.

CITCO Bank and Trust Co Ltd: 89 Nexus Way, 2nd Floor, Camana Bay, POB 31105, Grand Cayman KY1-1205; tel. 945-3838; fax 945-3888; e-mail cayman-bank@citco.com; internet www.citco.com; Pres. MIKE McWATT.

Coutts & Co (Cayman) Ltd: Coutts House, 1446 West Bay Rd, POB 707, George Town, Grand Cayman KY1-1107; tel. 945-4777; fax 945-4799; e-mail info@rbscoutts.com; internet www.rbscoutts.com; f. 1967; 100% owned by Royal Bank of Scotland International (Holdings) Ltd (Jersey); fmrly NatWest International Trust Corpn (Cayman) Ltd and RBS Coutts (Cayman) Ltd, present name adopted Nov. 2011; CEO ALEXANDER CLASSEN.

Deutsche Bank (Cayman) Ltd: Boundary Hall, Cricket Sq., 171 Elgin Ave, POB 1984, George Town, Grand Cayman KY1-1104; tel. 949-8244; fax 949-8178; e-mail dmg-cay@candw.ky; internet www.dboffshore.com; f. 1983 as Morgan Grenfell (Cayman) Ltd; name changed to Deutsche Morgan Grenfell (Cayman) Ltd in 1996; name changed as above in 1998; Chair. Dr JOSEF ACKERMANN; CEO HERMANN-JOSEF LAMBERTI.

Fidelity Bank (Cayman) Ltd: POB 914, George Town, Grand Cayman KY1-1103; tel. 949-7822; fax 949-6064; e-mail bank@fidelitycayman.com; internet www.fidelitycayman.com; f. 1979; Chair. WILLIAM ALLEN.

FirstCaribbean International Bank Ltd: POB 68, 25 Main St, George Town, Grand Cayman KY1-1102; tel. 949-7300; fax 949-7179; internet www.firstcaribbeanbank.com; f. 2002 following merger of Caribbean operations of Barclays Bank PLC and CIBC; Barclays relinquished its stake to CIBC in June 2006; Chair. MICHAEL MANSOOR; CEO RIK PARKHILL; Cayman Islands Contact MARK McINTYRE.

HSBC Bank Cayman: HSBC House, 68 West Bay Rd, POB 1109, George Town, Grand Cayman KY1-1102; tel. 949-7755; fax 949-7634; e-mail hbky.information@ky.hsbc.com; internet www.hsbc.ky; f. 1982; CEO GONZALO JALLES; Head of Corporate Banking MARK McINTYRE.

Intertrust Bank (Cayman) Ltd: Harbour Pl., 4th Floor, 103 South Church St, POB 1034, Grand Cayman; tel. 949-8455; fax 949-9717; e-mail cayman@ky.intertrustgroup.com; internet www.intertrustgroup.com; f. 1952 (Intertrust); took over operations of Close Bank (Cayman) Ltd in Aug. 2011; Man. Dir LINDBURGH MARTIN.

Merrill Lynch Bank and Trust Co (Cayman) Ltd: Harbour Centre, 4th Floor, North Church St, George Town, Grand Cayman; tel. 637-7455; fax 949-8895; internet www.ml.com.

Royal Bank of Canada: 24 Shedden Rd, POB 245, Grand Cayman KY1-1104; tel. 949-4600; fax 949-7396; internet www.royalbank.com; Vice-Pres. and Country Head JASON K. WATERS.

Royal Bank of Canada Trust Co (Cayman) Ltd: 24 Shedden Rd, POB 1586 GT, Grand Cayman KY1-1110; tel. 949-9107; fax 949-5777; internet www.rbcprivatebanking.com/cayman-islands.html; Man. Dir DEANNA BIDWELL.

Scotiabank and Trust (Cayman) Ltd: Scotia Centre, 6 Cardinal Ave, POB 689, George Town, Grand Cayman KY1-1107; tel. 949-7666; fax 949-0020; e-mail scotiaci@candw.ky; internet www.cayman.scotiabank.com; f. 1968; fmrly Bank of Nova Scotia Trust Company (Cayman) Ltd; present name adopted Dec. 2003; Man. Dir DOUG COCHRANE.

UBS Fund Services (Cayman Islands) Ltd: UBS House, 227 Elgin Ave, POB 852, George Town, Grand Cayman KY1-1103; tel. 914-1060; fax 914-4060; internet www.ubs.com/cayman-funds; Man. Dir DARREN STAINROD.

Development Bank

Cayman Islands Development Bank: Cayman Financial Centre, 36B Dr Roy's Dr., POB 2576 GT, George Town, Grand Cayman; tel. 949-7511; fax 949-6168; e-mail cidb.manager@cidb.ky; internet cidb.ky; f. 2002; replaced the Housing Devt Corpn and the Agricultural and Industrial Devt Bd; under the jurisdiction of the Ministry of Finance, Tourism and Devt; Gen. Man and CEO TRACY EBANKS.

Banking Association

Cayman Islands Bankers' Association: Caledonian House, 69 Dr Roy Dr., POB 676, George Town, Grand Cayman; tel. 949-0330; fax 945-1448; e-mail ciba@cibankers.org; internet www.cibankers.org; Pres. MIKE MCWATT; COO CECIL CHAN-A-SUE; 78 full mems, 200 assoc. mems.

STOCK EXCHANGE

Cayman Islands Stock Exchange (CSX): 4th Floor, Elizabethan Sq., POB 2408, George Town, Grand Cayman KY1-1105; tel. 945-6060; fax 945-6061; e-mail csx@csx.com.ky; internet www.csx.com.ky; f. 1996; more than 3,000 cos listed (Feb. 2011); govt-owned; Chair. ANTHONY B. TRAVERS; CEO VALIA THEODORAKI.

INSURANCE

Several foreign companies have agents in the islands. A total of 741 insurance companies were registered as of March 2013. In particular, the islands are a leading international market for health insurance. Locally incorporated companies include the following:

BAF Insurance Co (Cayman) Ltd: POB 10389, Grand Cayman KY1-1004; tel. 949-5089; fax 949-7192; e-mail spars-myles@mybafsolutions.com; internet www.cayman.mybafsolutions.com; Chair. HARVEY STEPHENSON; Gen. Man. TERENCE SPENCER.

Captiva Managers Ltd: Landmark Sq., 64 Earth Close, POB 32315, Grand Cayman KY1-1209; tel. 946-4111; fax 946-4222; e-mail info@captivagroup.net; internet www.captiva.vg; Group Dir NOELLA M. THOMPSON; Group Man. Dir HARRY J. THOMPSON.

Cayman First Insurance Co Ltd: 103 South Church St, POB 2171, Grand Cayman KY1-1105; tel. 949-7028; fax 949-7457; e-mail michael.gayle@caymanfirst.com; internet www.caymanfirst.com; Gen Man. MICHAEL GAYLE.

Cayman Islands National Insurance Co Ltd (CINICO): Cayman Centre, 1st Floor, Dorcy Dr, Airport Rd, George Town, POB 10112, Grand Cayman KY1-1001; tel. 949-8101; fax 949-8226; e-mail ltibbetts@cinico.ky; internet www.cinico.ky; govt-owned; Chair. SCOTT CUMMINGS; CEO LONNY TIBBETTS.

Insurance Company of the West Indies (Cayman) Ltd (ICWI): 93 Hospital Rd, POB 461, Grand Cayman KY1-1106; tel. 949-6970; fax 949-6929; e-mail icwi@candw.ky; internet www.icwi.com/cayman; subsidiary of Insurance Company of the West Indies, Jamaica; Chair. and CEO DENNIS LALOR; Man. HEATHER LANIGAN.

Island Heritage Insurance Co Ltd: Atlantic Star House, 128 Lawrence Blvd, POB 2501, Grand Cayman KY1-1104; tel. 949-7280; fax 945-6765; e-mail info@islandheritage.com.ky; internet www.islandheritageinsurance.com; general insurance; acquired by BF&M (Bermuda) in 2012; Pres. and CEO GARTH MACDONALD.

Sagicor Life of the Cayman Islands Ltd: 198 North Church St, POB 1087, George Town, Grand Cayman KY1-1102; tel. 949-8211; fax 949-8262; e-mail customerservice@sagicor.com; internet www.sagicorcayman.com; wholly owned subsidiary of Sagicor Life Jamaica Ltd; Chair. RICHARD O. BYLES; Pres. and CEO MICHAEL A. FRASER.

Trade and Industry

GOVERNMENT AGENCY

National Investment Council: Cayman Corporate Centre, 1st Floor, Hospital Rd, POB 10087 APO, Grand Cayman KY1-1001; tel. 945-0943; fax 945-0941; e-mail investment@dci.gov.ky; internet www.investcayman.ky; f. 2003 as Cayman Islands Investment Bureau; renamed 2010 and merged into Dept of Commerce and Investment; CEO JONATHAN PIERCY.

CHAMBER OF COMMERCE

Cayman Islands Chamber of Commerce: Unit 4-107, Governors Sq., 23 Lime Tree Bay Ave, West Bay Rd, POB 1000, West Bay, Grand Cayman KY1-1102; tel. 949-8090; fax 949-0220; e-mail info@caymanchamber.ky; internet www.caymanchamber.ky; f. 1965; Pres. CHRIS DUGGAN; CEO WIL PINEAU; 594 corporate mems and 78 associates.

TRADE ASSOCIATION

Cayman Finance: 94 Shedden Rd, Suite 2, POB 11048, Grand Cayman KY1-1008; tel. 946-6000; fax 946-6001; e-mail info@caymanfinances.com; internet www.caymanfinances.com; f. 2003 as Cayman Islands Financial Services Asscn; name changed as above in Oct. 2009; aims to promote the integrity and transparency of the financial services sector; Chair. RICHARD COLES; CEO GONZALO JALLES.

UTILITIES

Electricity

Electricity Regulatory Authority: Grand Pavilion, Suite 2, West Bay Rd, POB 10189, Grand Cayman KY1-1002; tel. 949-8372; fax 947-9598; e-mail general@caymanera.com; internet caymanera.com; f. 2005; Chair. SHERRI BODDEN-COWAN; Man. Dir LOUIS BOUCHER (acting).

Caribbean Utilities Co Ltd (CUC): Corporate HQ & Plant, 457 North Sound Rd, POB 38, George Town, Grand Cayman; tel. 949-5200; fax 949-5203; e-mail service@cuc.ky; internet www.cuc-cayman.com; Pres. and CEO J. F. RICHARD HEW; Chair. DAVID RITCH.

Cayman Brac Power and Light Co Ltd (CBP&L): Stake Bay Point, POB 95, Stake Bay, Cayman Brac; tel. 948-2224; fax 948-2204; e-mail braclite@candw.ky; Gen. Man. JONATHAN TIBBETTS.

Water

Cayman Islands Water Authority: 13G Red Gate Rd, POB 1104 GT, George Town, Grand Cayman KY1-1102; tel. 949-2837; fax 949-0094; e-mail info@waterauthority.ky; internet www.waterauthority.ky; Man. Dir Dr GELIA FREDERICK-VAN GENDEREN; Chair. JOHN LEMUEL HURLSTON.

Consolidated Water Co Ltd (CWCO): Windward 3, 4th Floor, Regatta Office Park, POB 1114, George Town, Grand Cayman KY1-1102; tel. 945-4277; fax 949-2957; e-mail info@cwco.com; internet ir.cwco.com; f. 1973; Pres. and CEO FREDERICK W. MCTAGGART; Dir and Chair. WILMER F. PERGANDE.

Transport

ROADS

There are some 406 km (252 miles) of motorable roads, of which 304 km are surfaced with tarmac. The road network connects all districts on Grand Cayman and Cayman Brac (which has 76 km of motorable roads), and there are 43 km of motorable roads on Little Cayman (of which about 18 km are paved). According to the 2012/13 budget address, US $1.6m. was to be allocated for ongoing improvements to the islands' road network and also for the planning and development of new public roads.

SHIPPING

George Town is the principal port. An agreement to build a new port facility in George Town was signed in April 2010. Cruise liners, container ships and smaller cargo vessels ply between the Cayman Islands, Florida, Jamaica and Costa Rica. There is no cruise ship dock in the Cayman Islands. Ships anchor off George Town and ferry passengers ashore to the North or South Dock Terminals in George Town. The number of cruise ship passengers is limited to 6,000 per day. The port of Cayman Brac is Creek; there are limited facilities on Little Cayman. In December 2012 the shipping register comprised 804 vessels, with combined displacement totalling 3,835,950 grt, of which 26 were bulk carriers and 28 were general cargo ships.

Maritime Authority of Cayman Islands (MACI): Strathvale House, 2nd Floor, 90 North Church St, POB 2256, Grand Cayman KY1-1107; tel. 949-8831; fax 949-8849; e-mail maci.consulting@cishipping.com; internet www.cishipping.com; f. 2005; wholly govt-owned; legal entity responsible for: enforcement of international maritime laws and conventions; implementation of maritime safety and security, Cayman Islands marine environment laws; formation of national maritime policy; representation and protection of national maritime interests at international forums; also undertakes vessel and mortgage registration, advisory and marine survey and audit services fmrly administered by Cayman Islands Shipping Registry; Chair. BRUCE BLAKE; CEO A. JOEL WALTON.

Port Authority of the Cayman Islands: Harbour Dr., POB 1358 GT, George Town, Grand Cayman KY1-1108; tel. 949-2055; fax 949-5820; e-mail support@caymanport.com; internet www.caymanport.com; Chair. JOHN HENRY EBANKS.

Principal Shipping Companies

Cayman Islands Shipping Registry: Govt Admnistration Bldg, 3rd Floor, 133 Elgin Ave, POB 2256, Grand Cayman KY1-110; tel. 949-8831; fax 949-8849; e-mail cisrky@cishipping.com; internet www.cishipping.com; f. 1993; division of Maritime Authority of Cayman Islands (MACI); CEO A. JOEL WALTON.

Seaboard Marine (Cayman): Mirco Commerce Centre, 2nd Floor, Industrial Park, POB 1372, George Town, Grand Cayman KY1-1108; tel. 949-4977; fax 949-8402; e-mail info@seaboardcayman.com; internet www.seaboardcayman.com; Man. Dir ROBERT FOSTER.

Thompson Shipping Co Ltd: 10 Shipping Lane, Off Portland Rd, Industrial Park, POB 188, George Town, Grand Cayman KY1-1104; tel. 949-8044; fax 949-8349; e-mail info@thompsonshipping.com; internet www.thompsonshipping.com; f. 1977; agent for Thompson Line, a div. of Tropical Shipping; Contact Person SUSAN GABRUCH.

CIVIL AVIATION

There are two international airports in the territory: Owen Roberts International Airport, 3.5 km (2 miles) from George Town, and Gerrard Smith International Airport on Cayman Brac. Both are capable of handling jet-engined aircraft. In 2011 the Government confirmed plans to triple capacity at Owen Roberts Airport and in 2012 it announced a project to expand terminal facilities at Gerrard Smith to accommodate long-haul international flights. Cayman Airways, American Airlines, Delta Airlines are few of the flights that operate in Cayman Islands.

Civil Aviation Authority of the Cayman Islands (CAACI): Unit 2, Cayman Grand Harbour Complex, Shamrock Rd, POB 10277, George Town, Grand Cayman KY1-1003; tel. 949-7811; fax 949-0761; e-mail civil.aviation@caacayman.com; internet www.caacayman .com; f. 1987; Dir-Gen. RICHARD SMITH; Chair. SHERIDAN BROOKS-HURST; Dir-Gen. RICHARD SMITH.

Cayman Airways Ltd: 91 Owen Roberts Dr., POB 10092, Grand Cayman KY1-1001; tel. 949-8200; fax 949-7607; e-mail customerrelations@caymanairways.net; internet www.cayman airways.com; f. 1968; wholly govt-owned since 1977; operates local services and scheduled flights to Jamaica, Honduras and the USA; Chair. PILAR BUSH (acting); Pres. and CEO FABIAN WHORMS.

Island Air: Airport Rd, POB 2433, George Town, Grand Cayman KY1-1105; tel. 949-5252; fax 949-1073; e-mail res@islandair.ky; internet islandair.ky; f. 1987; operates daily scheduled services between Grand Cayman, Cayman Brac and Little Cayman; Man. Dir MARCUS CUMBER.

Tourism

The Cayman Islands are a major tourist destination, the majority of visitors coming from North America. The beaches and opportunities for diving in the offshore reefs form the main attraction for most tourists. In 2010 there were an estimated 4,587 hotel rooms. In 2011 there were 309,100 arrivals by air (compared with 288,300 in 2010) and some 1,401,500 cruise visitors (compared with 1,597,800 in 2010). The USA remained the core market for stay-over visitors to the islands (78.6% in 2011). In 2010 the tourism industry earned an estimated US $385m.

Cayman Islands Department of Tourism (CIDOT): Windward 3, Regatta Office Park, POB 67, George Town, Grand Cayman KY1-1102; tel. 949-0623; fax 949-4053; e-mail pr@caymanislands.ky; internet www.caymanislands.ky; f. 1965; Dir SHOMARI SCOTT.

Cayman Islands Tourism Association (CITA): 1320 West Bay Rd, POB 31086 SMB, Grand Cayman KY1-1205; tel. 949-8522; fax 946-8522; e-mail info@cita.ky; internet www.cita.ky; f. 2001 as a result of the amalgamation of the Cayman Tourism Alliance and the Cayman Islands Hotel and Condominium Asscn; Pres. HARRY LALLI; Exec. Dir JANE VAN DER BOL.

Sister Islands Tourism Association (SITA): POB 187, Cayman Brac KY2-2101; tel. and fax 916-4874; e-mail sita@candw.ky; internet www.sisterislands.com; Pres. NEIL VAN NIEKERK.

Defence

The United Kingdom is responsible for the defence of the Cayman Islands.

Education

Schooling is compulsory for children between the ages of five and 17 years. It is provided free in 11 government-run primary schools and three secondary schools. There are also 10 private schools. Primary education, from five years of age, lasts for six years; in 2007/08 enrolment at primary schools included an estimated 90% of pupils in the relevant age-group. Secondary education is for seven years; enrolment at secondary-level institutions in 2007/08 included an estimated 83% of students in the relevant age-group. There were also 1,274 children enrolled at pre-primary schools in 20007/08. The Cayman Islands Law School, Community College of the Cayman Islands, University College of the Cayman Islands and the International College of the Cayman Islands number among providers of tertiary-level education in the territory. In 2013 the Government set out a five-year strategy for improving education. Budgetary spending on education in 2012/13 was approved at US $66.9m.

THE FALKLAND ISLANDS

Introductory Survey

LOCATION, CLIMATE, LANGUAGE, RELIGION, FLAG, CAPITAL

The Falkland Islands, comprising two large islands and about 200 smaller ones, are in the south-western Atlantic Ocean, about 770 km (480 miles) north-east of Cape Horn, South America. The climate is generally cool, with strong winds (mainly westerly) throughout the year. The mean annual temperature is 6°C (42°F), while average annual rainfall is 635 mm (25 ins). The language is English. Most of the inhabitants profess Christianity, with several denominations represented. The flag is the British 'Blue Ensign', with the territory's coat of arms (a shield showing a white and violet ram standing in green grass, on a blue background, above a sailing ship bearing red crosses on its pennants and five six-pointed stars on its central sail, on three white horizontal wavy lines, with the motto 'Desire the Right' on a scroll beneath) on a white disc in the centre of the flag. The capital is Stanley, on East Falkland Island.

CONTEMPORARY POLITICAL HISTORY

Historical Context

The first recorded landing on the islands was made from a British ship in 1690, when the group was named after Viscount Falkland, then Treasurer of the Royal Navy. French sailors named the islands 'Les Malouines' (after their home port of Saint-Malo), from which the Spanish name 'Islas Malvinas' is derived. A French settlement was established in 1764 on the island of East Falkland, but in 1767 France relinquished its rights to the territory to Spain, which then ruled the adjacent regions of South America. Meanwhile, a British expedition annexed West Falkland in 1765, and a garrison was established. The British settlement, formed in 1765–66, was recognized by Spain in 1771 but withdrawn in 1774. The Spanish garrison was withdrawn in 1811.

When the United Provinces of the River Plate (now Argentina) gained independence from Spain in 1816, the Falkland Islands had no permanent inhabitants, although they provided temporary bases for sealing and whaling activities by British and US vessels. In 1820 an Argentine ship was sent to the islands to proclaim Argentine sovereignty as successor to Spain. An Argentine settlement was founded in 1826 but most of its occupants were expelled by a US warship in 1831. The remaining Argentines were ejected by a British expedition in 1832, and British sovereignty was established in 1833.

Domestic Political Affairs

Conflict with Argentina

The islands became a Crown Colony of the United Kingdom, administered by a British-appointed Governor. However, Argentina did not relinquish its claim, and negotiations to resolve the dispute began in 1966 at the instigation of the UN. The inhabitants of the islands, nearly all British by descent, consistently expressed their desire to remain under British sovereignty.

After routine talks between delegations of the British and Argentine Governments in New York in February 1982, the Argentine foreign ministry announced that it would seek other means to resolve the dispute. Argentina's military regime took advantage of a British protest at the presence of a group of Argentine scrap merchants, who had made an unauthorized landing on South Georgia in March and had raised an Argentine flag, to invade the Falkland Islands on 2 April. A small contingent of British marines was overwhelmed, the British Governor was expelled and an Argentine military governorship was established. The USA and the UN attempted (unsuccessfully) to mediate, in an effort to prevent military escalation. British forces, which had been dispatched to the islands immediately after the Argentine invasion, recaptured South Georgia on 25 April. The Argentine forces on the Falklands formally surrendered on 14 June, after a conflict in the course of which about 750 Argentine, 255 British and three Falklanders' lives were lost.

The Governor returned to the islands as Civil Commissioner on 25 June 1982, and the United Kingdom established a 'protection zone' around the islands, extending 150 nautical miles (278 km) off shore, as well as a garrison of about 4,000 troops. The British Government began an investigation into the possibilities of developing the islands' economy, and in November agreed to grant the Falkland Islanders full British citizenship. In November 1983 the post of Chief Executive of the Falkland Islands Government was created, in combination with the executive vice-chairmanship of the newly formed Falkland Islands Development Corporation.

The issue of the sovereignty of the Falkland Islands remained a major impediment to the normalization of relations between Argentina and the United Kingdom. The Argentine Government refused to agree to a formal declaration that hostilities were ended until the United Kingdom agreed to participate in negotiations over sovereignty, while the United Kingdom refused to negotiate until Argentina had formally ended hostilities. In October 1984 the Argentine Government removed restrictions on British companies and interests in Argentina as a possible prelude to resuming negotiations. However, the British Government's refusal to discuss the issue of sovereignty, and its insistence on the paramountcy of the Falkland Islanders' wishes, were reflected in the new Constitution for the Falklands (approved by the islands' Legislative Council in January 1985), which guaranteed the islanders' right to self-determination.

The number of British troops stationed on the islands was reduced, following the opening, in mid-1985, of a new military airport at Mount Pleasant, about 30 km south-west of Stanley, enabling rapid reinforcement of the garrison, if necessary. In October elections took place on the Falklands for a new Legislative Council.

In 1986 parliamentary delegations from the United Kingdom and Argentina conducted exploratory talks. However, the British Government remained intransigent on the issue of sovereignty. In early 1986 Argentina's continued claim to the naval protection zone was manifested in attacks on foreign fishing vessels by Argentine gunboats. In October the United Kingdom unilaterally declared a fisheries conservation and management zone extending 150 nautical miles (278 km) around the islands, with effect from February 1987, to prevent the over-fishing of the waters. The imposition of this zone, whose radius coincided with that of the naval protection zone, was condemned by the majority of UN members, as was the United Kingdom's rejection, in November 1986, of an offer by Argentina to declare a formal end to hostilities in exchange for the abolition of the protection zone.

Beginning in 1982 the UN General Assembly voted annually, by an overwhelming majority, in favour of the resumption of negotiations between Argentina and the United Kingdom. The British Government consistently declined to engage in such dialogue. However, relations between Argentina and the United Kingdom improved, following the election, in May 1989, of a new Argentine President, Carlos Saúl Menem, who initially indicated that his country would be willing to suspend temporarily its demand that the issue of the sovereignty of the Falkland Islands be discussed, in the interests of the restoration of full diplomatic and commercial relations with the United Kingdom. In October a meeting of British and Argentine representatives, which took place in Madrid, Spain, culminated in the formal cessation of all hostilities, and the re-establishment of diplomatic relations at consular level. Restrictions on Argentine merchant vessels with regard to the naval protection zone around the Falkland Islands were also eased. In the following month, however, the United Kingdom announced that it was to increase the extent of its territorial waters around the islands from three to 12 nautical miles, in spite of protests from the Argentine authorities. In February 1990 Argentina and the United Kingdom conducted further negotiations in Madrid, as a result of which the two countries re-established full diplomatic relations. It was also announced that the naval protection zone around the Falkland Islands was to be modified in March, and that mutually agreed military procedures, which would ensure the security of the region, would take effect.

Following successful negotiations between Argentina and the United Kingdom in Madrid in November 1990, an agreement regarding the protection and conservation of the South Atlantic fishing area was announced. The two sides also agreed to establish a South Atlantic Fisheries Commission, to discuss fishing activity and conservation in the region.

In December 1993 the Argentine Government indicated its acceptance of the United Kingdom's proposed extension of fishing rights around the Falkland Islands from 150 to 200 miles, in order to allow the islanders to fulfil an annual squid-fishing quota of 150,000 metric tons. In August 1994 the British Government unilaterally decided to extend its fisheries conservation zone north of the islands, thereby annexing a small but lucrative fishing ground (not previously protected by British or Argentine legislation) that was being plundered by foreign fishing vessels. Following the release of a Joint Declar-

ation between the two Governments on 14 July 1999, both Governments agreed to co-operate to combat illegal fishing in the South-West Atlantic and to ensure the sustainability of fish stocks in the region.

In November 1991 the Governments of both Argentina and the United Kingdom claimed rights of exploration and exploitation of the seabed and the subsoil of the continental shelf around the Falkland Islands (which were believed to be rich in petroleum reserves). In December 1993 the British Geological Survey reported that preliminary seismic investigations indicated deposits in excess of those located in British North Sea oilfields. A bilateral agreement on petroleum and gas exploration in an area of 18,000 sq km, south-west of the islands, was concluded in New York in September 1994. A joint hydrocarbons commission would regulate licensing in the area. The successful conclusion of the agreement appeared to dissipate Argentine objections, voiced earlier in the year, to the Falkland Islands' unilateral offer of rights to drill in 19 areas (comprising 44,000 sq km not covered by the Anglo-Argentine agreement) to the north and south of the islands. Licences to explore for hydrocarbons were awarded to five international consortia in October 1996. The possibility that commercial quantities of petroleum might be discovered prompted renewed discussion as to the amount of any future royalties exacted by the Falkland Islands Government that should be returned to the Government of the United Kingdom. In early 1997 the British Government indicated that it expected to benefit considerably from any such royalties, while the Falkland Islands administration proposed that some of the revenue could be used to finance the islands' defence expenditure (currently funded by the United Kingdom). Meanwhile, the Argentine Government claimed that it should be entitled to benefit from the discovery of petroleum in the region.

In May 1999 formal negotiations between the Falkland Islands and Argentina took place in the United Kingdom. Issues under discussion included co-operation in fishing and petroleum exploration, Argentine access to the islands and the resumption of air links with mainland South America. (In March Chile had ended its country's regular air services to the islands in protest against the British Government's continued detention of the former Chilean President, Gen. Augusto Pinochet.) Four of the islands' councillors also attended the three days of talks, thereby occasioning the first direct talks between Falkland Islanders and the Argentine Government. The dialogue continued in July in New York and London. On 14 July a joint Argentine-British declaration was issued that eliminated the restrictions on travel by Argentine citizens to the Falkland Islands and re-established airline services by the Chilean carrier LanChile between South America and the Falkland Islands (with a stop-over in Argentina). It was also agreed to increase bilateral co-operation between Argentina and the Falkland Islands on combating illegal fishing and conservation of fish stocks. The agreement did not affect claims to sovereignty. Even so, the round of talks provoked demonstrations by an estimated 500 people on the Falkland Islands. The protests resumed on 16 October when the first flights carrying Argentine visitors arrived in the Falklands. In July 2000 the Anglo-Argentine dialogue on joint petroleum and gas exploration was suspended by mutual agreement for an indefinite period of time.

In May 2003 the new Argentine President, Néstor Carlos Kirchner, reiterated his country's claim to the Falkland Islands. In November Argentina began to demand that the increasingly frequent air charter services flying from the Falkland Islands to Chile obtain permission to use Argentine airspace. The decision was intended to exert pressure on the British Government into reversing its policy of not allowing Argentine airlines to fly to the Falkland Islands. The services were suspended in January 2004 after the British Government lodged objections to the Argentine demands. A reference to the islands was included in a draft of the constitutional treaty of the European Union, to which Argentina strongly objected. At a meeting of the UN's Special Committee on Decolonization, held in mid-2005, the Falkland Islands appealed for the right to self-determination; the Committee requested that the Governments of Argentina and the United Kingdom resume negotiations.

The Argentine Government formed a Congressional Observatory in June 2006 with the express function of actively reclaiming the Falkland Islands, which it continued to refer to as Argentine territory. In January 2007 the Argentine Minister of Foreign Affairs, International Trade and Worship, Jorge Taiana, had sought to enlist the support of the UN Secretary-General, Ban Ki-Moon, asserting that the United Kingdom had seized the archipelago by illegal means. President Kirchner maintained that the islanders possessed no right to self-determination, contending that the present population displaced indigenous Argentine residents upon settlement in 1833 with the intention of establishing a British colonial state, a claim strenuously refuted by the United Kingdom. In February Argentina rejected an invitation by the British Government to participate in joint commemorative celebrations to mark the 25th anniversary of the conflict's end. A joint hydrocarbon exploratory contract between Argentina and the United Kingdom was abandoned in the following month; the Argentine Government accused the British of pursuing a 'unilateral' approach to oil exploration initiatives and averred that there would be no further developments on the matter until the United Kingdom had agreed to resume negotiations over the islands' sovereignty. The original agreement, signed by former Argentine President Carlos Saúl Menem in 1995, followed the restoration of diplomatic relations between the two countries in 1990 and had been regarded as Argentine acknowledgment of the United Kingdom's claim to the sea floor surrounding the Falkland Islands. In April 2007 the Kirchner administration reiterated its claim to the territory and enjoined the British Government to cede to international demands to engage in dialogue over the future of the islands. The United Kingdom stated that it would not consider amendments to the governance or affiliations of the Falkland Islands unless and until a request to this effect was registered by the populace; it was asserted that no such request had been expressed by the islanders and, further, that they opposed Argentina's territorial offensive.

New legislation approved by the Argentine legislature on 11 April 2007 effectively required fishing companies wishing to operate in the maritime exclusion zone surrounding the islands to choose between Argentine or British authorities when making permit applications, and included restrictions against fishing in Argentine jurisdictional waters where a permit issued by the corresponding issuing authority was not held. A recent decision by the Falkland Islands authorities to begin issuing 25-year licences—as opposed to the one-year permits issued previously—had provoked protest from Argentina, which claimed its territorial rights had been disregarded.

The new President of Argentina, Cristina Fernández de Kirchner, stated in December 2007 that she was not prepared to make concessions in sovereignty claims, and her Government once again urged the United Kingdom to relaunch the negotiations process. However, two months earlier, in October, the British Government announced its intention to submit a claim to the UN Commission on the Limits of the Continental Shelf for Atlantic seabed territory around the Falkland Islands. Argentine foreign minister Taiana insisted that his Government would challenge any such claim made by the United Kingdom. Tensions between the two countries were exacerbated in May 2008 when Taiana accused the British Government of 'illegitimately' issuing licences for hydrocarbon exploration and extraction activities in an area north of the Falkland Islands, part of the Argentine continental shelf. The British Government refused to concede to any of the claims made by its Argentine counterpart and maintained that it held sovereignty over the disputed area. On 24 April 2009 Argentina lodged a hostile claim before the UN Commission to some 1.7m. sq km (660,000 sq miles) of seabed surrounding the territory, as well as an area north of Antarctica. This was formally countered by the United Kingdom, which presented its own claim to the disputed region. Tensions between Argentina and the United Kingdom rose further in September after a British company, Desire Petroleum, announced plans to commence drilling in an area north of the Falklands in 2010. In the weeks preceding the start of the operation in February, the Argentine Government asserted that the drilling was illegal, and reiterated its claim on the seabed surrounding the islands. In mid-February President Kirchner decreed that all ships sailing through Argentine waters must hold a permit, effectively blockading the area around the islands. Despite the escalation of the dispute, drilling went ahead as planned. In May 2010 Rockhopper Exploration of the United Kingdom announced that it had discovered oil in an offshore bloc to the north of the islands, prompting renewed Argentine criticism of the drilling operations. After further analysis of the deposit, Rockhopper Exploration confirmed in March 2011 the presence of a 'significant' amount of petroleum, and another large oil discovery was announced in September; the company anticipated that production would commence by 2016. Drilling by numerous oil firms was ongoing in early 2013, in spite of threats by Argentina to initiate legal action against the companies involved.

Landmine-clearing

In enforcing the statutes of the Ottawa Convention, adopted under the Landmines Act 1998, the United Kingdom was required to identify and eliminate all mine devices within its territory and overseas jurisdictions within 10 years of the Convention's enactment. The resultant deadline for the destruction of all anti-personnel landmines in the Falkland Islands was established as March 2009. An assessment of the feasibility of eliminating the remaining landmines was conducted in October 2007 and revealed that the process would be technically possible but was expected to require a considerable amount of funding. At a meeting of Ottawa Convention signatories in Geneva, Switzerland, in November 2008, the United Kingdom was granted a 10-year extension to the March 2009 deadline, with the proviso that research into modern methods of mine-clearing be undertaken. An operation, begun in 2009, to remove some 1,250 landmines from four minefields was completed successfully in June 2010. However, the British Government estimated in February 2011 that over 15,000 mines, in 83 minefields, were still deployed in the territory. In March 2012 another demining operation concluded

in Stanley, opening up a further 3.5 sq km of previously inaccessible land to residents and tourists. A third clearance operation was under way in early 2013.

A new Constitution

A new Constitution came into force on 1 January 2009. The charter was a culmination of a constitutional review process initiated by the British Government's Department of Overseas Territories in 1997, with the aim of according greater self-governance to the islands. A number of changes to the administration of the territory had been proposed; a Constitutional Select Committee was convened in February 2007 to complete the review discussions, and final proposals were submitted to the British Foreign and Commonwealth Office (FCO) for deliberation in June. Most notable among the amendments proposed were the insertion of the citizens' right to self-determination within the main body of the Constitution, the updating of provisions in accordance with the United Kingdom's obligations under the European Convention on Human Rights, and clarification of the Governor's and Chief Executive's roles as head of the Public Service and head of the Civil Service, respectively. Officials from the FCO held two rounds of talks with the Constitutional Select Committee in December 2007 and February 2008 to discuss the draft constitution. Following further public consultation, the new Constitution came into force in 2009. It asserted the islanders' right to self-determination and contained amendments to the rules under which British citizens would be eligible for Falklands Islands status, as well as provisions for a Public Accounts Committee and a Complaints Commissioner to improve transparency in the territory. It also provided further clarification of the division of powers between the Executive Council and the Governor, stating that the Governor must abide by the advice of the Executive Council on domestic policies, though not in matters of external affairs, defence and the administration of justice.

Recent developments: tensions rise again

In May 2010 Argentina expressed dissatisfaction that the new British Government had rejected a proposal to recommence sovereignty discussions. An escalating British naval presence in the region, as part of 'routine military exercises' in Falkland waters, including the firing of missiles, attracted criticism from Argentina, Brazil, Paraguay, Uruguay and Venezuela in October. In support of neighbouring Argentina's position on the Falklands Islands, in September Uruguay had refused to allow a British naval vessel, which was en route to the disputed archipelago, to refuel at a Uruguayan port. In a similar incident, Brazil also denied a British naval ship permission to dock in January 2011. The member nations of the Mercado Común del Sur (Southern Common Market—Mercosur) declared in December that vessels registered in the Falkland Islands would be prohibited from docking at Mercosur ports, prompting censure from the United Kingdom. The Unión de Naciones Suramericanas (Union of South American Nations) had announced a similar ban in November 2010. However, these moves, which formed part of Argentina's strategy of regionalizing the sovereignty dispute to put diplomatic pressure on the British Government, were viewed as largely symbolic owing to the small number of ships flying the Falkland Islands flag. Nevertheless, tensions had risen sharply during 2011 in response to Argentina's increasingly assertive rhetoric in relation to its claim over the Islands. British Prime Minister David Cameron repeatedly asserted that the United Kingdom would not engage in negotiations over the sovereignty of the Falkland Islands owing to the overwhelming desire of the islanders to remain under British control. Argentina accused the United Kingdom of 'militarization' in February 2012 following the announcement that a British destroyer would be stationed in the Falkland Islands to replace an older vessel and following the deployment of HRH Prince William, the Duke of Cambridge, to the South Atlantic for a brief military tour of duty. The Argentine Government also suspected that a British nuclear submarine had been sent to the region, although this was denied by the United Kingdom. The British embassy in Argentina came under attack by protesters on 2 April, the 30th anniversary of the start of the Falklands conflict; British and Argentine officials condemned the violence.

In June 2012 Kirchner gave an unprecedented speech to the UN's Special Committee on Decolonization, in which she strongly criticized an upcoming referendum on the future status of the Falklands and again appealed for sovereignty talks with the United Kingdom. A British offer to host trilateral discussions with the Falkland Islands and Argentina was rejected by the latter in January 2013. In the referendum, which was held on 10–11 March, 99.8% of voters endorsed the continuation of the territory's existing relationship with the United Kingdom. The rate of participation by the electorate was 92%. Argentina refused to recognize the results, and President Kirchner insisted that the plebiscite had no legal validity.

CONSTITUTION AND GOVERNMENT

A new Constitution came into force on 1 January 2009. Administration is conducted by the appointed Governor (who is the personal representative of the British monarch), aided by the Executive Council, comprising two ex officio members and three members elected by the Legislative Assembly. The Legislative Assembly is composed of the Governor, two ex officio members and eight elected members. Voting is by universal adult suffrage.

REGIONAL AND INTERNATIONAL CO-OPERATION

The Falkland Islands are a member of the Commonwealth (see p. 244).

ECONOMIC AFFAIRS

According to government estimates, gross domestic product (GDP) was some £104m. in 2007. In 2001 GDP per head was put at £24,030 and annual growth was estimated at 2%.

Most of the agricultural land on the Falkland Islands is devoted to the rearing of sheep. However, the land is poor and more than four acres are required to support one animal. In the late 1990s annual exports of wool were valued at some £3.5m. Declining international wool prices encouraged agricultural diversification, such as the pursuit of organic farming, the breeding of cashmere goats and also the development of meat production (an abattoir was constructed to meet European Union standards, incurring expenditure of £372,332 in 2002 and a further £678,371 in 2003). Some vegetables are produced (notably in a hydroponic market garden), and there are small dairy herds (500 dairy cows in May 2011). From 1987, when a licensing system was introduced for foreign vessels fishing within a 150-nautical-mile conservation and management zone (see Contemporary Political History), the economy was diversified and the islands' annual income increased considerably. Although revenue from the sale of licences declined in the 1990s following the Argentine Government's commencement of the sale of fishing licences in 1993, licences (and transshipments) totalled £18.0m. in 2009/10, equivalent to 42.5% of total budget revenue in that year. The revenue funds social provisions and economic development programmes. In the late 1980s about one-third of the world's total catch of *illex* and *loligo* squid was derived from this fishing zone. However, over-fishing in the area surrounding the conservation zone had a detrimental effect on stocks of fish in the islands' waters. The sector contracted in 2009. A recovery was evident in 2010, but squid numbers remained relatively low.

Manufacturing activity on the islands reflects the predominance of the agricultural sector: a wool mill on West Falkland produces yarns for machine knitting, hand knitting and weaving. Several small companies in the Falklands produce garments for local and export sales. Some fish-processing also takes place on East Falkland.

The Falkland Islands are heavily dependent on imports of all fuels, except peat; households primarily depend on kerosene and diesel for heating purposes. Wind power is used in many remote locations to offset this dependence and reduce pollution of the atmosphere. In 2011 a British oil company, Rockhopper Exploration, announced it had made a 'significant' discovery of petroleum in the waters to the north of the islands; drilling by numerous oil firms was ongoing in 2013.

The Falkland Islands Development Corporation oversees the islands' economic development on behalf of the Government. Since the 1980s the Government has sought to promote the development of the tourism sector. Tourism, and in particular eco-tourism, developed rapidly in the 2000s, and the number of visitors staying on the Falklands Islands had grown to some 3,000 a year, while around 40,000 tourists a year sailed through Stanley harbour on their way to Antarctica and sub-Antarctic islands such as South Georgia. In 2009/10 some 62,500 cruise ship passengers visited the Falkland Islands. The sale of postage stamps and coins represents a significant source of income; the value of sales of the former was £296,229 in 1996/97, while the value of sales of the latter totalled £49,351 in 1995/96.

In 2000 the islands recorded an estimated merchandise trade surplus of £28,041,897. Fish, most of which is purchased by the United Kingdom, Spain and Chile, is the islands' most significant export. The principal imports are fuel, provisions, alcoholic beverages, building materials and clothing. In 2001 the Government brought 100 reindeer from the South Georgia Islands (with the aim of increasing the number to 10,000 over the following 20 years) in order to export venison to Scandinavia and Chile. By 2011 there were 184 reindeer on the islands.

The budget for the financial year 2009/10 provided for revenue of £42.4m. and expenditure of £47.6m. The islands are generally self-sufficient in all areas of the economy (although expenditures associated with defence are the responsibility of the British Government). The annual rate of inflation averaged 2.5% in 1995–2003; consumer prices increased by 0.7% in 2002 and by 1.2% in 2003. There is a significant shortage of local labour on the islands.

The fisheries licensing sector accounted for about 60% of GDP. After a decline in fishing licence revenues in 2009, annual income from this source rose during 2010–12. The unstable nature of the fishing licence sector increased hopes that exploitation of hydrocar-

bons in the waters around the islands would yield positive results. Seismic surveys conducted in the waters around the Falkland Islands in 2008 suggested the area could yield as much as 18,000m. barrels of petroleum. Confirmation in 2011 of a 'significant' petroleum deposit raised expectations of further oil reserves being uncovered; exploration operations were ongoing in 2013. Nevertheless, the exploration of hydrocarbons in the area threatened other sectors of the economy. Argentina imposed several economic sanctions on the Falklands, including a ban on oil companies working in that country from any involvement in oil exploration around the Falkland Islands. It also prohibited Chilean flights to the islands from using Argentine airspace, a move that threatened the Falkland Islands' burgeoning tourism sector. Tourist numbers decreased slightly in 2010 following a sharper decline in 2009, although the sector recovered during the 2011/12 season. Several cruise lines cancelled their Falklands itineraries in 2012 after some vessels returning from the islands were subjected to harassment and obstruction while attempting to dock at Argentine ports. Poor weather conditions also led to further cancellations. Cruise ship arrivals were consequently projected to decline in 2012/13. According to government figures, the economy expanded by 5.3% in 2010. This followed a drastic contraction of about 9.0%, according to preliminary estimates, in 2009, mainly owing to the decrease in the squid catch and a reduction in tourist numbers.

PUBLIC HOLIDAYS

2014: 1 January (New Year's Day), 18 April (Good Friday), 21 April (HM the Queen's Birthday), 16 June (for Liberation Day), 6 October (Spring Holiday), 8 December (Anniversary of the Battle of the Falkland Islands in 1914), 25–27 December (Christmas).

Statistical Survey

Source (unless otherwise stated): The Treasury of the Falkland Islands Government, Stanley, FIQQ 1ZZ; tel. 27143; fax 27144; internet www.falklands.gov.fk.

AREA AND POPULATION

Area: approx. 12,173 sq km (4,700 sq miles): East Falkland and adjacent islands 6,760 sq km (2,610 sq miles); West Falkland and adjacent islands 5,413 sq km (2,090 sq miles).

Population*: 2,478 at census of 8 October 2006; 2,932 at census of 15 April 2012 (preliminary).

*Census data exclude military personnel and civilians based at Mount Pleasant military base, also excluded are residents absent on census night (84 in 2006; 91 in 2012).

Density (2012 census): 0.26 per sq km.

Population by Age and Sex (at 2006 census): *0–14:* 458 (males 222, females 236); *15–64:* 1,755 (males 903, females 852); *65 and over:* 265 (males 135, females 130); *Total* 2,478 (males 1,260, females 1,218).

Principal Town (2006 census): Stanley (capital), population 2,115.

Births and Deaths (2006): Live births 27; Deaths 20. Source: UN, *Population and Vital Statistics Report*.

Economically Active Population (persons aged 15 years and over, 2012 census): Agriculture and fishing 247; Mining and quarrying (incl. oil and gas exploration) 26; Manufacturing 30; Construction 143; Electricity, water and gas 74; Hospitality and tourism 183; Transport, storage and communications 203; Finance 41; Business services 38; Administration and support service activities 117; Community, social and personal services 99; Public service (local government) 485; Public service (other) 25; Other services 12; *Total employed* 1,723.

AGRICULTURE, ETC.

Livestock (2011, official figures at 31 May): Sheep 488,395; Cattle 4,688; Goats 145; Reindeer 184; Horses 494; Poultry 2,070.

Livestock Products (metric tons, 2011, FAO estimates): Cattle meat 157; Sheep meat 810; Cows' milk 1,500; Wool, greasy 2,200. Source: FAO.

Fishing ('000 metric tons, live weight of capture, 2010): Southern blue whiting 0.4; Argentine hake 6.3; Patagonian grenadier 4.1; Patagonian squid 58.1; Argentine shortfin squid 3.4; Total catch (incl. others) 99.6. Source: FAO.

FINANCE

Currency and Exchange Rates: 100 pence (pennies) = 1 Falkland Islands pound (FI £). *Sterling, Dollar and Euro Equivalents*

(31 December 2012): £1 sterling = FI £1.00; US $1 = 63.37 pence; €1 = 83.61 pence; FI £100 = £100.00 sterling = $157.80 = €1,196.00. *Average Exchange Rate* (FI £ per US dollar): 0.6472 in 2010; 0.6241 in 2011; 0.6330 in 2012. Note: The Falkland Islands pound is at par with the pound sterling.

Budget (FI £ million, 2009/10): *Revenue:* Sales and services 9.7; Fishing licences and transshipment 18.0; Investment income 4.5; Taxes and duties 10.2; Total 42.4. *Expenditure:* Operating expenditure 38.9 (Public works 8.5, Fisheries 5.2, Health care 7.5, Education 5.3, Aviation 2.5, Police and justice 1.5, Agriculture 1.0, Central administration 3.5, Other 3.9); Capital expenditure 8.7; Total 47.6.

Cost of Living (Consumer Price Index for Stanley; base: 2000 = 100): All items 101.3 in 2001; 102.0 in 2002; 103.2 in 2003. Source: ILO.

EXTERNAL TRADE

2000 (estimates): Total imports £18,958,103; Total exports £47,000,000. Fish is the principal export. Trade is mainly with the United Kingdom, Spain and Chile.

TRANSPORT

Shipping: *Flag Registered Fleet* (at 31 December 2012): Number of vessels 28; Total displacement 47,170 grt. (Source: Lloyd's List Intelligence—www.lloydslistintelligence.com).

Road Traffic: 3,065 vehicles in use in 1995.

TOURISM

Day Visitors (country of origin of cruise ship excursionists, 2006/07 season): Canada 4,862; United Kingdom 6,736; USA 21,298; Total (incl. others) 51,282. *2008/09:* Total 62,600 (Source: Falkland Islands Tourist Board).

EDUCATION

2003 (Stanley): *Primary:* Teachers 18; Pupils 203. *Secondary:* Teachers 18; Pupils 160.

Directory

The Government

(May 2013)

HEAD OF STATE

Queen: HM Queen ELIZABETH II.
Governor: NIGEL ROBERT HAYWOOD (took office 16 October 2010).

HEAD OF GOVERNMENT

Chief Executive of the Falkland Islands Government: KEITH PADGETT.

TERRITORIAL ADMINISTRATION

Government Secretary: PETER T. KING.
Attorney-General: DAVID PICKUP.
Commander, British Forces South Atlantic Islands: Brig. BILL ALDRIDGE.

EXECUTIVE COUNCIL

The Council consists of six members.

GOVERNMENT OFFICES

Office of the Governor: Government House, Stanley, FIQQ 1ZZ; tel. 28200; fax 27434; e-mail gov.house@horizon.co.fk.
London Office: Falkland Islands Government Office, Falkland House, 14 Broadway, London, SW1H 0BH, United Kingdom; tel. (20) 7222-2542; fax (20) 7222-2375; e-mail reception@falklands.gov.fk; internet www.falklands.gov.fk; f. 1983.

LEGISLATIVE ASSEMBLY

Comprises the Governor, two ex officio (non-voting) members and eight elected members. Elections to the Legislative Assembly are held every four years. The last election was held on 5 November 2009.
Speaker: KEITH BILES.
Office of the Legislative Assembly: Legislature Dept, Gilbert House, Stanley, FIQQ 1ZZ; tel. 27451; e-mail assembly@sec.gov.fk; internet www.falklands.gov.fk.

Judicial System

The judicial system of the Falkland Islands is administered by the Supreme Court (presided over by the non-resident Chief Justice), the Magistrate's Court (presided over by the Senior Magistrate) and the Court of Summary Jurisdiction. The Court of Appeal for the territory sits in the United Kingdom and appeals therefrom may be heard by the Judicial Committee of the Privy Council.

Supreme Court: Town Hall, Ross Rd, Stanley, FIQQ 1ZZ; tel. 27271; fax 27270; Chief Justice CHRISTOPHER GARDNER, QC; Registrar and Courts Administrator JAN PARKE.

Court of Appeal: Stanley, FIQQ 1ZZ; Pres. Judge BRIAN APPLEBY; Registrar MICHAEL J. ELKS.

Religion

CHRISTIANITY

The Anglican Communion, the Roman Catholic Church and the United Free Church predominate. Also represented are the Evangelist Church, Jehovah's Witnesses, the Lutheran Church, Seventh-day Adventists and the Bahá'í faith.

The Anglican Communion

The Archbishop of Canterbury, the Primate of All England, exercises episcopal jurisdiction over the Falkland Islands and South Georgia.

Rector: Rev. Dr RICHARD HINES, The Deanery, Christ Church Cathedral, Stanley, FIQQ 1ZZ; tel. 21100; fax 21842; e-mail deanery@horizon.co.fk.

The Roman Catholic Church

Prefect Apostolic of the Falkland Islands: MICHAEL BERNARD McPARTLAND, St Mary's Presbytery, 12 Ross Rd, Stanley, FIQQ 1ZZ; tel. 21204; fax 22242; e-mail stmarys@horizon.co.fk; internet www.southatlanticrcchurch.com; f. 1764; 300 adherents (2006).

The Press

Falkland Islands Gazette: Attorney-General's Chambers, POB 587, Stanley, FIQQ 1ZZ; tel. 28464; fax 27276; e-mail bsteen@sec.gov.fk; internet www.falklands.gov.fk; govt publ; Editor BARBARA STEEN.

Falkland Islands News Network: POB 141, Stanley, FIQQ 1ZZ; tel. and fax 21182; e-mail finn@horizon.co.fk; internet www.falklandnews.com; relays news daily online and via fax as FINN(COM) Service; Man. JUAN BROCK; publishes *Teaberry Express* (weekly).

Penguin News: Ross Rd, Stanley, FIQQ 1ZZ; tel. 22709; fax 22238; e-mail adverts@penguinnews.co.fk; internet www.penguin-news.com; f. 1979; weekly (Fri.); independent newspaper; Man. FRAN BIGGS; Editor LISA WATSON; circ. 1,450.

Broadcasting and Communications

TELECOMMUNICATIONS

In 1989 Cable & Wireless PLC installed a digital telecommunications network covering the entire Falkland Islands. The system provides international services as well as a new domestic network. The first mobile telephone network was introduced in 2005 and a broadband internet service in 2006.

Cable & Wireless South Atlantic Ltd: Ross Rd, POB 584, Stanley, FIQQ 1ZZ; tel. 20834; fax 20811; e-mail info@cwfi.co.fk; internet www.cwfi.co.fk; f. 1989; exclusive provider of national and international telecommunications and internet services in the Falkland Islands under a licence issued by the Falkland Islands Govt; CEO JUSTIN McPHEE.

BROADCASTING

Radio

British Forces Broadcasting Service (BFBS): BFBS Falkland Islands, Mount Pleasant, BFPO 655; tel. 32179; fax 32193; e-mail falklands@bfbs.com; internet www.bfbs-radio.com; 24-hour satellite service from the United Kingdom; Station Man. CHRIS PEARSON; Sr Engineer ADRIAN ALMOND.

Falkland Islands Radio Service: Broadcasting Studios, John St, Stanley, FIQQ 1ZZ; tel. 27277; fax 27279; e-mail cgoss@firs.co.fk; internet www.firs.co.fk; f. 1929; fmrly Falkland Islands Broadcasting Station; 24-hour service, partly financed by local Govt; broadcasts in English; Station Man. CORINA GOSS; Programme Controller LIZ ELLIOT.

Television

British Forces Broadcasting Service (BFBS): BFBS Falkland Islands, Mount Pleasant, BFPO 655; tel. 32179; fax 32193; internet www.bfbs.com/tv; daily four-hour transmissions of taped broadcasts from BBC and ITV of London, United Kingdom; Sr Engineer PETER NEALE.

KTV: Dean St, POB 68, Stanley, FIQQ 1ZZ; tel. 22349; fax 21049; e-mail kmzb@horizon.co.fk; internet www.ktv.co.fk; satellite television broadcasting services; Man. Dirs MARIO ZUVIC BULIC, SHARON ZUVIC BULIC.

Finance

BANK

Standard Chartered Bank: Ross Rd, POB 597, Stanley, FIQQ 1ZZ; tel. 22220; fax 22219; e-mail bank.info@sc.com; internet www.standardchartered.com/fk; branch opened in 1983; CEO (Americas) JULIO ROJAS.

INSURANCE

The British Commercial Union, Caribbean Alliance Insurance and Norman Tremellen companies maintain agencies in Stanley.

Consultancy Services Falklands Ltd: 44 John St, Stanley, FIQQ 1ZZ; tel. 22666; fax 22639; e-mail consultancy@horizon.co.fk; Man. ALISON BAKER.

Trade and Industry

DEVELOPMENT ORGANIZATION

Falkland Islands Development Corporation (FIDC): Shackleton House, West Hillside, Stanley, FIQQ 1ZZ; tel. 27211; fax 27210; e-mail dwaugh@fidc.co.fk; internet www.fidc.co.fk; f. 1983; provides loans and grants; encourages private sector investment, inward investment and technology transfer; Gen. Man. DAVID WAUGH.

CHAMBER OF COMMERCE

Chamber of Commerce: West Hillside, POB 378, Stanley, FIQQ 1ZZ; tel. 22264; fax 22265; e-mail manager@commerce.co.fk; internet www.falklandislandschamberofcommerce.com; f. 1993; promotes private industry; operates DHL courier service; runs an employment agency; Pres. ROGER SPINK; 87 mems.

TRADING COMPANIES

Falkland Islands Co Ltd (FIC): Crozier Pl., Stanley, FIQQ 1ZZ; tel. 27600; fax 27603; e-mail fic@horizon.co.fk; internet www.the-falkland-islands-co.com; f. 1851; part of Falkland Islands Holding PLC; the largest trading co; retailing, wholesaling, shipping, insurance and Land Rover sales and servicing; operates as agent for Lloyd's of London and general shipping concerns; travel services; wharf owners and operators; Dir and Gen. Man. ROGER KENNETH SPINK.

Falkland Islands Meat Co Ltd: Sand Bay, East Falklands, FIQQ 1ZZ; tel. 27013; fax 27113; e-mail info@falklandmeat.co.fk; internet www.falklands-meat.com; exporters of lamb, mutton and beef meat; Gen. Man. JOHN FERGUSON.

Falkland Oil and Gas Ltd (FOGL): 56 John St, Stanley, F1QQ 1ZZ; e-mail info@fogl.co.uk; internet www.fogl.co.uk; f. 2004; shareholders include Falkland Islands Holdings PLC (16%), Global Petroleum (14%) and RAB Capital PLC (33%); operates an offshore petroleum exploration programme with 8 licences covering 65,354 sq km; Chair. RICHARD LIDDELL; CEO TIM BUSHELL.

EMPLOYERS' ASSOCIATIONS

The Falkland Islands Sheep Owners' Association: Coast Ridge Farm, Fox Bay, FIQQ 1ZZ; tel. 42094; fax 42084; e-mail n.knight.coastridge@horizon.co.fk; f. 1967; asscn for sheep station owners; limited liability private co; Company Sec. N. KNIGHT.

Rural Business Association of the Falkland Islands: POB 296, Stanley, FIQQ 122; tel. 22432; fax 22660; e-mail secretary@rba.org.fk; internet www.rba.org.fk; f. 1999; farmers' org.; Chair. RICHARD EVANS.

TRADE UNION

Falkland Islands General Employees Union: Ross Rd, Stanley, FIQQ 1ZZ; tel. 21151; e-mail geu@horizon.co.fk; f. 1943; Chair. GAVIN SHORT; 400 mems.

Transport

RAILWAYS

There are no railways on the islands.

ROADS

There are 29 km (18 miles) of paved road in and around Stanley. There are 54 km of all-weather road linking Stanley and the Mount Pleasant airport (some of which has been surfaced with a bitumen substance), and a further 37 km of road as far as Goose Green. There are 300 km of arterial roads in the North Camp on East Falkland linking settlements, and a further 197 km of road on West Falkland. Where roads have still not been built, settlements are linked by tracks, which are passable by all-terrain motor vehicles or motorcycles except in the most severe weather conditions. Total expenditure on roads, improving the North Camp and Stanley road networks, was estimated at £1.13m. for the fiscal year 2011/12.

SHIPPING

There is a floating deep-water jetty in Stanley. There is a ship on charter to the Falkland Islands Co Ltd, which makes the round trip to the United Kingdom four or five times a year, carrying cargo. The British Ministry of Defence charters ships to the Falkland Islands once every three weeks. There are irregular cargo services between the islands and southern Chile and Uruguay. The Falkland Islands Development Corpn commissioned a port development plan in 2007 for the upgrade of existing facilities to reflect growth in containerized traffic and cruise ship arrivals, and to accommodate proposed further oil exploration in territorial waters.

The Falkland Islands flag registered fleet numbered 28 vessels, with a total displacement of 47,170 grt, at December 2012; the majority of vessels registered are deep-sea fishing vessels.

Stanley Harbour: c/o Dept of Fisheries, POB 598, Stanley, FIQQ 1ZZ; tel. 27260; fax 27265; e-mail Mjamieson@fisheries.gov.fk; Marine Officer and Harbour Master MALCOLM JAMIESON.

Private Companies

Byron Marine Ltd: Byron House, 3 H Jones Rd, Stanley, FIQQ 1ZZ; tel. 22245; fax 22246; e-mail info@byronmarine.com; internet www.byronmarine.com; f. 1992; additional activites include offshore oil and gas exploration support services, deep-sea fishing and property; contracted managers of the Falkland Islands Government Port Facility; island-wide pilotage services; vessel and port agency; Man. Dir LEWIS CLIFTON.

Falkland Islands Shipping Ltd: Crozier Pl., Stanley, FIQQ 1ZZ; tel. 27629; fax 27601; e-mail stanleyoffice@falklandislandshipping.com; internet www.falklandislandshipping.com; subsidiary of the Falkland Islands Co Ltd (q.v.); Man. JIMMY FORSTER.

Seaview Ltd: 37 Fitzroy Rd, POB 215, Stanley, FIQQ 1ZZ; tel. 22669; fax 22670; e-mail seaview.agent@horizon.co.fk; internet www.fis.com/polar; operates subsidiary co, Polar Ltd (f. 1989); Man. Dir ALEX REID.

Sulivan Shipping Services Ltd: Davis St, POB 159, Stanley, FIQQ 1ZZ; tel. 22626; fax 22625; e-mail sulivan@horizon.co.fk; internet www.sulivanshipping.com; f. 1987; provides port agency and ground-handling services; Man. Dir JOHN POLLARD; Operations Man. ELVIO (MIGS) COFRÉ.

CIVIL AVIATION

There are airports at Stanley and Mount Pleasant; the latter has a runway of 2,590 m (8,497 ft), and is capable of receiving wide-bodied jet aircraft. The British Royal Air Force operates two weekly flights from the United Kingdom. The Chilean carrier LAN Airlines operates weekly return flights from Punta Arenas. An 'air bridge', operated by charter carriers subcontracted to the British Ministry of Defence, provides a link via Ascension Island between the Falkland Islands and the United Kingdom.

Falkland Islands Government Air Service (FIGAS): Stanley Airport, Airport Rd, Stanley, FIQQ 1ZZ; tel. 27219; fax 27302; e-mail operations@figas.gov.fk; internet www.visitorfalklands.com/contents/view/116; f. 1948 to provide social, medical and postal services between the settlements and Stanley; aerial surveillance for Dept of Fisheries since 1990; operates five nine-seater aircraft to over 35 landing strips across the islands; Gen. Man. MORGAN GOSS.

Tourism

During the 2008/09 season some 62,600 day visitors from cruise ships visited the islands. US citizens constitute the primary visitor group. Wildlife photography, bird-watching and hiking are popular tourist activities. The Falkland Islands Development Corpn (FIDC) plans to develop the sector in collaboration with the Government and tourism operators in the territory.

Falkland Islands Tourist Board: Jetty Visitor Centre, POB 618, Stanley, FIQQ 1ZZ; tel. 22215; fax 27020; e-mail info@visitorfalklands.com; internet www.falklandislands.com; Gen. Man. JAKE DOWNING.

Defence

As assessed at November 2012, there were approximately 1,520 British troops stationed on the islands (420 army, 680 air force and 420 navy). The cost of maintaining the garrison totalled £75m. in 2010–11. There is a Falkland Islands Defence Force, composed of 75 islanders.

Education

Education is compulsory, and is provided free of charge, for children between the ages of five and 16 years. Facilities are available for further study beyond the statutory school-leaving age. In 2003 203 pupils were instructed by 18 teachers at the primary school in Stanley, while 160 pupils received instruction from 18 teachers at the secondary school in the capital; further facilities existed in rural areas, with six peripatetic teachers visiting younger children for two out of every six weeks (older children boarded in a hostel in Stanley). Total expenditure on education was estimated at £6.4m. for 2011/12 (equivalent to 14% of total government expenditure).

GIBRALTAR

Introductory Survey

LOCATION, CLIMATE, LANGUAGE, RELIGION, FLAG

The city of Gibraltar lies in southern Europe. The territory consists of a narrow peninsula of approximately 4.8 km (3 miles) in length, running southwards from the south-west coast of Spain, to which it is connected by an isthmus. About 8 km (5 miles) across the bay, to the west, lies the Spanish port of Algeciras, while 32 km (20 miles) to the south, across the Strait of Gibraltar, is Ceuta (a Spanish enclave within Morocco). The Mediterranean Sea lies to the east. The total area of the territory is 6.5 sq km (2.5 sq miles). The climate is temperate, and snow or frost are extremely rare. The mean minimum and maximum temperatures during the winter are 13°C (55°F) and 18°C (65°F), respectively, and during the summer they are 13°C (55°F) and 29°C (85°F), respectively; the average annual rainfall is 890 mm (35 ins). The official language is English, although most of the population is bilingual in English and Spanish. More than three-quarters of the population are Roman Catholic. The flag (proportions 1 by 2) bears the arms of Gibraltar (a red castle with a pendant golden key) on a background, the upper two-thirds of which are white and the lower one-third red.

CONTEMPORARY POLITICAL HISTORY

Historical Context

Since the Second World War, this Overseas Territory has achieved considerable social and economic progress, through intensive development of its social and economic infrastructure, and by the expansion of commerce and the encouragement of tourism. Gibraltar has exercised control over most internal matters since 1969.

The Spanish Government lays claim to Gibraltar as a part of its territory, while the United Kingdom maintains that the Treaty of Utrecht (1713) granted sovereignty over Gibraltar to the United Kingdom in perpetuity (with the stipulation that, if the United Kingdom relinquished the colony, it would be returned to Spain). In 1963 the Spanish Government launched a campaign, through the UN, for the cession of Gibraltar to Spain. It also imposed restrictions against Gibraltar, culminating in the closure of the frontier in 1969, the withdrawal of the Spanish labour force, and the severing of transport and communication links with Spain.

Following a referendum held in the territory in 1967, in which the overwhelming majority voted in favour of retaining British sovereignty, a new Constitution, promulgated in 1969, contained a provision that the British Government undertook never to enter into arrangements whereby the people of Gibraltar would pass under the sovereignty of another state against their freely and democratically expressed wishes. Gibraltar joined the European Community (EC, now European Union—EU, see p. 281) with the United Kingdom in 1973.

By 1977, Spain appeared to have adopted a more flexible attitude towards Gibraltar. At talks held between Spanish and British ministers in November representatives of the Gibraltar Government were included for the first time as part of the British delegation. Further negotiations took place in 1979 and 1980. In October 1980 the British Parliament granted Gibraltarians the right to retain full British citizenship. Negotiations for the reopening of the frontier continued in 1982, but a change of attitudes in both countries, following the war between the United Kingdom and Argentina over the sovereignty of the Falkland Islands (q.v.), resulted in an indefinite postponement. In December Spain reopened the border to pedestrians of Spanish nationality and to British subjects resident in Gibraltar.

Domestic Political Affairs

At the general election held in January 1984 the Gibraltar Labour Party—Association for the Advancement of Civil Rights (GLP—AACR), led by Sir Joshua Hassan, retained a majority of one seat in the House of Assembly. The Gibraltar Socialist Labour Party (GSLP), led by Joe Bossano, secured the remaining seven seats, replacing the Democratic Party of British Gibraltar as the opposition party in the House of Assembly. (Under the terms of the Constitution, the party with the largest share of the vote obtained a maximum of eight seats in the 15-seat House of Assembly.)

In November 1984 the British and Spanish Governments agreed to provide equal rights for Spaniards in Gibraltar and for Gibraltarians in Spain; to allow free movement for all traffic between Gibraltar and Spain; and to conduct negotiations on the future of the territory, including (for the first time) discussions on sovereignty. Border restrictions were finally ended in February 1985, and negotiations took place between the British and Spanish Governments to improve cross-border co-operation, especially in tourism and civil aviation. In December, however, Spanish proposals for an interim settlement of the territory's future were rejected by the British Government as unacceptable since they implied the eventual automatic cession of Gibraltar to Spain. Subsequent discussions concerning principally Spain's demands for access to the Gibraltar airport (which the Spanish Government claimed was situated on land not covered by the terms of the Treaty of Utrecht) were inconclusive, owing to the Gibraltar Government's insistence that the airport remain exclusively under the control of the British and Gibraltar authorities. In December 1987 British and Spanish government negotiators concluded an agreement that recommended increased co-operation between Spain and Gibraltar in the area of transport, in particular the joint administration of Gibraltar's airport. It was announced that Gibraltar's inclusion in an EC directive concerning air transport regulation was subject to the Gibraltar Government's approval of the transport agreement. However, the House of Assembly rejected the agreement, on the grounds that it would represent an infringement of British sovereignty, and voted unanimously to contest Gibraltar's exclusion from the EC directive.

The Government of Joe Bossano

At a general election held in March 1988, the GSLP received 58.2% of the votes cast, obtaining eight seats in the House of Assembly, and the GLP—AACR received 29.3% of the vote, securing seven seats. Bossano became Chief Minister, at the head of Gibraltar's first socialist Government. He announced that he would not participate in British-Spanish negotiations concerning Gibraltar, on the grounds that the territory's sovereignty was not a matter for negotiation between Spain and the United Kingdom, and that the December 1987 agreement would, in his view, result in the absorption of Gibraltar into Spain.

In February 1990 the British and Spanish Governments agreed to contest a legal action that was to be brought by Gibraltar in the European Court of Justice (ECJ) against Gibraltar's exclusion from the EC directive adopted to liberalize European air transport, which prevented the territory from expanding its air links with Europe. The decision to contest the action was considered to be a further attempt by the United Kingdom to persuade Gibraltar to co-operate with Spain. In March 1991 the United Kingdom withdrew the majority of British army personnel from Gibraltar, although the Royal Navy and Royal Air Force detachments remained.

In May 1991 the Spanish Prime Minister made an official visit to the United Kingdom, and was reported to have proposed a plan for joint sovereignty over Gibraltar, whereby the dependency would become effectively autonomous, with the British and Spanish monarchs as joint heads of state. Although it represented a significant concession by the Spanish Government (it had previously advocated only the return of total sovereignty to Spain), the plan was rejected by the Gibraltar Government. At the EC summit meeting held at Maastricht, Netherlands, in December, Spain continued to refuse to recognize Gibraltar's status as part of the EC, and remained determined to exclude it from the External Frontiers Convention (EFC), which was designed to strengthen common controls on entry into countries belonging to the EC. The continued failure to reach an agreement, particularly concerning the administration of Gibraltar airport, prevented the ratification of the EFC.

At a general election held in January 1992 the GSLP retained eight seats in the House of Assembly, and Bossano was returned for a second term as Chief Minister. The Gibraltar Social Democrats (GSD), which supported Gibraltar's participation in British-Spanish negotiations, secured the remaining seven seats. In February 1992, prior to discussions with British ministers in London, Bossano announced that Gibraltar was to attempt to obtain a revision of the 1969 Constitution, with the aim of achieving self-determination within four years. The British Government, however, stated that it would not consider granting independence to Gibraltar, unless the Spanish Government was prepared to accept the agreement, and excluded the possibility of formal negotiations on the issue.

In January 1993 Gibraltarians lodged a formal protest after increasingly strict monitoring of vehicles by Spanish customs officials resulted in severe delays at the frontier. In early 1994 Bossano accused the British Government of subordinating the interests of Gibraltar to the promotion of harmonious relations with Spain, and demanded a renegotiation of the 1987 airport agreement on the grounds that its provisions had subsequently become redundant and contrary to EU law.

In late 1994 Spain alleged that insufficient action was being taken by Gibraltar to curtail the smuggling of tobacco from Gibraltar to Spain and of illegal narcotics between Morocco and Spain by Gibraltar-based speedboats. The imposition in October of stringent border inspections by Spain prompted a protest by the British Government. The border checks were eased following assurances that measures were being taken against those involved in smuggling. Spain reimposed frontier controls in March 1995, precipitating renewed criticism by the British Government.

In July 1995, following the confiscation of more than 60 speedboats alleged to have been used in the transport of contraband, the Spanish Government eased frontier controls. The seizures provoked two days of riots and looting in Gibraltar, followed by a peaceful mass demonstration organized by Gibraltar business interests and trade unions in support of the continuing implementation of anti-smuggling measures. Although the British and Spanish Governments jointly agreed in September that the anti-smuggling measures were proving effective, the death of a Spanish civil guard in pursuit of smugglers in April 1996 led to the renewal of border controls by Spain.

Caruana becomes Chief Minister

Campaign debates in advance of legislative elections in May 1996 focused on Gibraltar's external relations. Bossano and the GSLP proposed that the territory's status be replaced before the year 2000 by a form of 'free association' with the United Kingdom, while the GSD declared as its aims the achievement of improved relations with both Spain and the United Kingdom and the modernization of Gibraltar's Constitution. The elections attracted an unusually high turn-out (87.7% of eligible voters), and resulted in the GSD receiving 48% of the vote and the maximum of eight seats in the House of Assembly; the GSD leader, Peter Caruana, became Chief Minister. The GSLP received 39% of the vote and the Gibraltar National Party obtained 13%.

In November 1996 Caruana renewed his demand that Gibraltar be accorded equal status with the United Kingdom in future negotiations concerning the territory's interests. In January 1997 Caruana refused to attend discussions on Gibraltar, held in Madrid, Spain, between the United Kingdom and Spain, on the grounds that Gibraltar would not be granted power of veto. A suggestion by Spain that sovereignty over Gibraltar be shared between Spain and the United Kingdom for a 100-year period, with full control then passing to Spain, was rejected by the British Government.

In October 1997 Caruana informed the Decolonization Committee of the UN General Assembly that he intended to seek from the British Government an extensive review of the territory's 1969 Constitution. It was to be proposed that Gibraltar would obtain additional autonomy in the conduct of its affairs while remaining in a close political and constitutional relationship with the United Kingdom, similar to that held by the Crown Dependencies of the Channel Islands and the Isle of Man (q.v.). During 1997 new tensions arose between the United Kingdom and Spanish Governments over the long-standing refusal by Spain to permit military aircraft from the United Kingdom and the North Atlantic Treaty Organization (NATO, see p. 380) to cross Spanish airspace on their approach to Gibraltar airport. In July the British Government indicated that it would oppose the full incorporation of Spain into NATO unless the ban were lifted. An indication by Spain of its willingness to open its airspace to these flights in return for joint military control of the airport was strongly opposed by Caruana and rejected by the British Government. In July

1998 Spain reversed its long-standing refusal to participate in NATO manoeuvres that were based in, or passed through, Gibraltar. In that month the Spanish Government unsuccessfully requested the British Government to consider a revived proposal for the shared sovereignty of Gibraltar for a period of 50 years, to be followed by the territory's full integration into Spain.

In November 1998 complaints by the Gibraltar Government arose over the conduct of Spanish fishing vessels in the Bay of Gibraltar, which were stated to be operating in violation of the territory's nature protection ordinance. In January 1999 a Spanish trawler was impounded by the Gibraltar authorities, and Spain began to intensify delays in road traffic crossing the frontier. An agreement reached in February between the Gibraltar authorities and the Spanish fishermen was not recognized by the Spanish Government.

At the general election held in February 2000 the GSD secured 58.7% of the vote, against 40.8% obtained by an electoral coalition of the GSLP and the Gibraltar Liberal Party (GLP). Caruana was reconfirmed as Chief Minister, and the GSD retained its eight seats in the House of Assembly. The rate of participation was again high, at 83.6%.

Extended negotiations between the Spanish and British Governments were concluded in April 2000 with a compromise agreement relating to the administrative status of Gibraltar whereby Spain was to recognize the validity of Gibraltar identity cards for travel within the EU and of the territory's financial institutions, provided that the 'competent authority' responsible for their supervision was the United Kingdom rather than the Gibraltar Government. It was also agreed that the British authorities would provide a facility, based in London, through which the Spanish and Gibraltar authorities could have indirect communication. An incidental effect of the agreement was to terminate the long-standing refusal by Spain to adopt any legislation by the EU that might have required it to deal directly with Gibraltar's police or financial regulatory authorities.

British-Spanish sovereignty negotiations

In July 2001 the British and Spanish Governments renewed discussions on Gibraltar's future status for the first time since 1998. At a subsequent meeting in October 2001, the British Secretary of State for Foreign and Commonwealth Affairs, Jack Straw, and his Spanish counterpart, Josep Piqué i Camps, agreed to work towards achieving a settlement on the issue by December 2002 (this was later modified to September 2002). Amid public criticism of proposals of joint British-Spanish sovereignty, Caruana rebuffed an invitation to attend the next round of negotiations, claiming that he would not be accorded equal status in the discussions. The Chief Minister also stated that the territory would not accept any change in sovereignty, the sharing of responsibility for its external affairs between Spain and the United Kingdom, nor any Spanish military presence.

At the negotiations in November 2001, Piqué announced that Spain was prepared to increase the number of telephone lines available to Gibraltar from 35,000 to 100,000 and provide greater access to the Spanish health care system. However, the issue of the right of the citizens of Gibraltar to vote on the terms of an agreement regarding the future status of the territory remained a point of contention between Spain and the United Kingdom. At the end of the month the British Government announced that Gibraltarians would be given the right to vote in elections to the European Parliament, but ruled out the possibility of the territory's further integration into the United Kingdom. In an open letter published in the local press, Piqué attempted to allay Gibraltarians' fears of the implications of Spanish rule and urged Caruana to attend the negotiations. The following month, however, most of the territory's 300,000 citizens took part in a public demonstration against the joint sovereignty proposals. Further public protests were held in March 2002 and Caruana threatened to organize a referendum on the subject of sovereignty.

In May 2002 the Overseas Territories Act, having received royal assent in the United Kingdom in February, came into force, granting British citizenship rights to the people of its Overseas Territories, including Gibraltar. Under the new law, Gibraltarians would be eligible to hold British passports and work in the United Kingdom and other EU countries.

Negotiations between the Spanish and British Governments progressed in mid-2002, although discussions stalled over Spain's claims to eventual sovereignty rather than permanent co-sovereignty and its refusal to allow British control over the military base. In response, Caruana called a referendum for November. Talks recommenced in September, but with no definite deadline. The referendum, held on 7 November, in which 87.9% of the electorate voted, demonstrated overwhelming (98.97%) opinion against the proposal for the United Kingdom and Spain to exert joint sovereignty over Gibraltar; however, the poll was not recognized by either Spain or the United Kingdom.

At a general election held on 28 November 2003 the GSD secured 51.5% of the vote, a significant decrease from the 2000 election, against 39.7% secured by the GSLP-GLP coalition; 79.2% of the electorate participated. The balance of seats in the House of Assembly remained unchanged, with the GSD holding eight seats and the opposition seven seats. Caruana continued in the post of Chief Minister.

For the purposes of the 2004 elections to the European Parliament, in late 2003 the British Parliament adopted legislation incorporating Gibraltar into the South-West electoral region of the United Kingdom; for the first time, Gibraltarians were thus eligible to vote in European elections. Approximately 58% of the Gibaltarian electorate participated in the poll. In June 2006 the ECJ rejected a complaint submitted by the Spanish Government, which insisted that Gibraltarians were ineligible to vote in European elections.

Trilateral talks and constitutional reform

In October 2004 Straw and his recently appointed Spanish counterpart, Miguel Angel Moratinos, held discussions in Madrid, at which they addressed the issue of the future format for talks on Gibraltar, which were to include Gibraltarian representation for the first time. Talks involving the three parties took place in the United Kingdom in December further to define this new forum, and in February 2005 the first official trilateral session took place in Málaga, Spain. As a result, a number of technical working groups were established to focus on the most significant issues: the airport, border control, nuclear submarines, telecommunications and pensions. Following several further rounds of discussions by the so-called Forum of Dialogue, in September 2006 Caruana, Moratinos and the British Minister of State for Europe, Geoff Hoon, signed a series of agreements in Córdoba, Spain: allowing for the operation of flights from Spain and the rest of Europe to Gibraltar; increasing the number of telephone lines to the territory; addressing the issue of outstanding pension payments to Spaniards formerly employed in Gibraltar; and easing border restrictions. Moratinos also stated that the Spanish Government had received written assurances from the United Kingdom that nuclear submarines would no longer be docked in Gibraltar. The question of sovereignty was not addressed.

Meanwhile, following lengthy negotiations between the United Kingdom and Gibraltar, it was announced in March 2006 that agreement had been reached on the main provisions of a new draft constitution for the territory. The British authorities stressed that the proposals did not diminish British sovereignty over Gibraltar, which would remain a United Kingdom Overseas Territory. The preamble to the new constitution also made clear that the British Government would never enter into arrangements under which the people of Gibraltar would pass under the sovereignty of another state against their freely and democratically expressed wishes. The draft constitution confirmed that the people of Gibraltar had the right of self-determination (according to the provisions of the UN Charter); this right was not constrained by the Treaty of Utrecht, except in so far as Spain would have the right of refusal should Britain ever renounce sovereignty. Thus, Gibraltarian independence would be an option only with Spanish consent. The remainder of the text introduced substantial reforms. The main elements included limiting the responsibilities of the Governor to the areas of external affairs, defence, internal security and public services, thereby reversing the existing practice and giving Gibraltar much greater control over its internal affairs. The House of Assembly was to be restyled the Gibraltar Parliament and would be allowed to determine its own size (subsequently set at 17 seats). The Governor's powers to withhold assent to legislation approved by the Gibraltarian authorities would be streamlined and his power to disallow proposed new laws would be removed (although his mandate to make Orders in Council would be retained). New commissions were to be created to deal with appointments to the judiciary and to public services, and a new Police Authority for Gibraltar was to be established. In a referendum held on 30 November 2006 the Constitution was approved by 60.2% of the valid votes cast, with 37.8% votes against, 1.7% blank ballots, and a participation rate of 60.4%. The new Constitution entered into force on 2 January 2007 (except for those provisions relating to the Parliament, which were to take effect following the next legislative elections).

In February 2007 Caruana created two new ministries, the Ministry of Finance and the Ministry of Justice. The Chief Minister, who already had responsibility for financial affairs, formally became Minister of Finance and also assumed ministerial responsibility for justice, which had been the preserve of the unelected Attorney-General under the previous Constitution. In July legislation was approved providing for the transfer of the post of head of the judiciary from the Chief Justice to the President of the Court of Appeal, as specified by the new Constitution.

At the general election held on 11 October 2007 the GSD remained the largest party in the enlarged legislature, holding the maximum of 10 of the 17 seats, having obtained 49.3% of the votes cast; 81.4% of the electorate voted. The only other grouping to obtain representation was the GSLP-GLP alliance, with seven seats and 45.5% of the votes cast. Caruana reassumed office as Chief Minister and Minister of Finance, but appointed Daniel Feetham as Minister of Justice as part of an extensive government reorganization. Upon his inauguration, Caruana made a speech to Parliament in which he described the new constitutional arrangements as having 'placed Gibraltar and the United Kingdom in a constitutional relationship with each other that is modern and non-colonial in nature', and pledged to explore the possibility of implementing further democratic reforms.

Dispute over territorial waters

A ministerial meeting of the trilateral Forum of Dialogue (which had continued to hold regular discussions since 2005) took place in Gibraltar in July 2009 between Caruana, Moratinos, and the British Secretary of State for Foreign and Commonwealth Affairs, David Miliband. Moratinos thus became the first Spanish minister to visit Gibraltar. The three ministers agreed to increase co-operation in matters including environmental protection, taxation, crime prevention, education, and maritime communication and safety; by mutual agreement, the issue of sovereignty was not raised. The meeting was overshadowed by a dispute between Gibraltar and Spain concerning the waters surrounding the territory, which Spain had recently designated a Site of Community Importance in accordance with EU legislation and with the approval of the European Commission. In May the Gibraltar Government had initiated proceedings against the Commission at the ECJ, claiming that waters within three nautical miles of the territory were under British sovereignty and that Spain thus had no right to make such a designation; Spain maintained that none of its territorial waters other than those within the port of Gibraltar had been ceded to the United Kingdom under the Peace of Utrecht. In March 2010 the Government of the United Kingdom filed a separate case before the ECJ against the Commission's decision to publish an updated list of Sites of Community Importance that maintained Spain's contested designation; however, in May 2011 the Court declared the United Kingdom's case inadmissible on technical grounds. Gibraltar and the United Kingdom made separate appeals against this decision, but both were rejected by the ECJ in August 2012.

Further tensions arose between Gibraltar and Spain in September 2010, when the Gibraltar Government accused the Spanish Civil Guard of forcibly preventing Gibraltarian police officers from exercising their duties by facilitating the escape of a suspected Spanish drugs-trafficker whom they had arrested in the waters surrounding the territory. Describing the incident as 'wholly unacceptable', in mid-October Caruana stated that technical discussions on matters relating to the waters surrounding Gibraltar would be 'pointless and inappropriate' and challenged Moratinos to agree to refer the dispute over sovereignty of these waters to the International Court of Justice. Later that month the participants in the trilateral Forum of Dialogue agreed to proceed with a series of technical meetings in five areas: visas; financial services and taxation; maritime communications and safety; environmental protection; and education. However, the issue of police, judicial and customs co-operation was to be addressed at a more senior, political level.

Recent developments: the Government of Fabián Picardo

In April 2011 Bossano retired as long-term leader of the GSLP and was replaced by Fabián Picardo. At the general election held on 8 December the GSLP-GLP alliance won a narrow majority, with 48.9% of the votes cast (taking 10 seats in the legislature), ousting the incumbent GSD, which received 46.8% of the votes and took the remaining seven seats. The Progressive Democratic Party, which had been established by former GSD deputy leader Keith Azopardi in 2006 following the GSD's merger with the Gibraltar Labour Party in 2005, received 4.4% of the votes. The turn-out at the poll was 82.5% of the electorate. Picardo was appointed as Chief Minister on 9 December. The new Council of Ministers included veteran politician Bossano, who assumed responsibility for the portfolio of enterprise, training and employment. Picardo expressed his willingness to continue tripartite talks with Spain and the United Kingdom, but stated that Gibraltar's sovereignty was not negotiable. There was widespread concern that the new conservative Government in Spain, which had defeated the incumbent socialist administration in a general election in November, would adopt a more hardline stance towards Gibraltar in any future talks. These fears appeared justified in January 2012 when the Spanish Government stated that it was prepared to hold discussions with Gibraltar and the United Kingdom specifically on issues of co-operation, but it ruled out the reconvention of the tripartite Forum of Dialogue to discuss the future status of Gibraltar. Henceforth, all talks concerning Gibraltar's sovereignty and jurisdiction would be conducted on a bilateral basis between Spain and the United Kingdom.

Tensions escalated following an incident in May 2012 when, on the orders of the Spanish Government, several Spanish Civil Guard boats acted as an escort to three Spanish trawlers, which, so the Gibraltarian authorities claimed, were fishing illegally (using large nets without a licence, in contravention of a 1991 environmental law) in British Gibraltar territorial waters. The Spanish boats reportedly left the area near Gibraltar harbour when requested to do so by a number of Royal Gibraltar Police boats and a Royal Navy support vessel. The dispute prompted the cancellation of a planned visit by the Spanish Queen to the United Kingdom later in May to celebrate the 60th anniversary of Queen Elizabeth II's reign. An official visit made by the British monarch's youngest son, Prince Edward, and his wife to Gibraltar in the following month also met with protests from the Spanish authorities.

In October 2012 relations between the United Kingdom and Spain were further strained by official complaints made by the British authorities that the Spanish police were causing 'unacceptable' delays (of up to six hours) for people crossing the border with Gibraltar. Spain claimed that the hold-ups had been caused by a police operation to counter tobacco smuggling. The following month the United Kingdom lodged an official protest regarding recent 'provocative' incursions by Spanish naval and customs vessels into Gibraltarian waters.

CONSTITUTION AND GOVERNMENT

Gibraltar is a United Kingdom Overseas Territory. The first Constitution, promulgated in 1969, was replaced by a new Constitution in 2007. Executive authority is vested in the British Sovereign and is exercised by the Council of Ministers, presided over by the Chief Minister, except in areas reserved to the Governor. These are defined by the Constitution as external affairs, defence, internal security and public offices. The Gibraltar Parliament comprises the Speaker (who is appointed by, but not from, the Parliament) and 17 members who are elected for a four-year term. The Parliament elects and appoints the Mayor, who represents the City of Gibraltar in a ceremonial capacity. Gibraltar has no administrative divisions but is divided into seven Major Residential Areas.

REGIONAL CO-OPERATION

Gibraltar joined the European Community, now European Union (EU, see p. 281), with the United Kingdom in 1973. However, Gibraltar is outside the customs union, is exempted from the Common Agricultural Policy and is not a signatory to the Schengen Agreement on border controls, although police co-operation rules apply.

ECONOMIC AFFAIRS

In 2010/11, according to provisional official estimates, Gibraltar's gross domestic product (GDP), measured at current prices, was G£1,050.54m. equivalent to some G£35,589 per head. Gibraltar's population totalled some 27,495 at the census of May 2001; in 2011 it stood at 29,752.

Gibraltar lacks agricultural land and natural resources, and the territory is dependent on imports of foodstuffs and fuels. Foodstuffs were estimated to account for 6% of total imports (excluding petroleum products) in 2004.

The industrial sector (including manufacturing, construction and power) employed 18.9% of the working population at October 2011.

Manufacturing employed 2.1% of the working population at October 2011. The most important sectors are shipbuilding and ship-repairs, and small-scale domestic manufacturing (mainly bottling, coffee-processing, pottery and handicrafts).

Gibraltar is dependent on imported petroleum for its energy supplies. Mineral fuels (excluding petroleum products) accounted for about 55% of the value of total imports in 2004.

Tourism and banking make a significant contribution to the economy. In 2011 revenue from tourism was estimated at G£279.41m. Visitor arrivals by air in 2011 rose to 164,428, according to official figures. The number of visitor arrivals via the land frontier also reached a record high in 2011; 11,940,543 people crossed into Gibraltar during that year. Many cross-border day visitors come to the country with the purpose of shopping. At October 2011 the financial sector employed about 8.9% of the working population. Several Spanish banks established offices in Gibraltar, encouraging the growth of the territory as an 'offshore' banking centre, while the absence of taxes for non-residents also encouraged the use of Gibraltar as a financial centre. In 2012 there were 16 banks and 65 licensed insurance companies operating in Gibraltar. In November 2002 the European Commission ruled that Gibraltar's tax-free status was illegal and ordered Gibraltar to end its system of granting tax exemption to companies, which was unique in the European Union (EU, see p. 281). The Commission ruled in 2005 that Gibraltar could extend the tax-exempt status of the 8,464 companies registered in the territory until the end of December 2010.

In 2011 Gibraltar recorded a visible trade deficit of £387.4m. In 2011 the principal sources of imports (excluding petroleum products) were the United Kingdom (accounting for 27.1% of the total) and Spain. The principal imports in 2004 were mineral fuels and manufactured goods. The principal re-exports in that year were petroleum products, manufactured goods and wines, spirits, malt and tobacco.

According to official estimates, the budgetary surplus was estimated to reach £27.4m in 2012/13. The annual rate of inflation averaged 2.9% during 2002–12. Retail prices increased by 2.0% in 2012. The rate of unemployment in 2011 was estimated to be 1.8% of the labour force; in 2010 some 49.9% of employees commuted to the territory from residences in Spain.

The Gibraltar economy is based on tourism, shipping, online gaming, and banking and finance. From the late 1980s the Gibraltar Government focused on developing the territory as an 'offshore' financial centre, stimulating private investment and promoting the tourism sector. A project to build a new financial district on land reclaimed from the sea commenced in 1990. Following the reduction in British military personnel in Gibraltar in the early 1990s, revenue from the British defence forces (which had accounted for some 60% of the economy in 1985) declined sharply; by 2012 revenue from the British military accounted for only around 7%. After 1999 there was a significant increase in gambling outlets in Gibraltar, as operations transferred from the United Kingdom to avoid high gambling taxation. By October 2010 the Government had issued 19 remote gambling licences, the territory having become a major centre for online gambling firms. The budget for 2012/13 forecast that gambling fees would contribute 2.7% of government revenue in that year. In November 2002 the European Commission ruled that Gibraltar's Exempt Company programme, which exempted 'offshore' companies from corporation tax, was illegal and ordered Gibraltar to close its tax haven. Consequently, the Gibraltar Government introduced a new taxation structure, which took effect in January 2011; this abolished the tax-exempt status enjoyed by more than 8,000 companies and introduced a uniform 10% rate of corporation tax (representing a significant reduction from the 20% and 35% rates hitherto levied on locally owned firms), in an effort to encourage businesses, particularly in the financial services sector, to locate in the territory. Meanwhile, Gibraltar's economy continued to expand in 2008–12, recording fiscal surpluses and maintaining low levels of public debt and high employment, despite less favourable global economic conditions (notably the fiscal crisis in the eurozone, with Spain being one of the worst affected of the EU member states).

PUBLIC HOLIDAYS

2014: 1 January (New Year's Day), 10 March (Commonwealth Day), 18 April (Good Friday), 21 April (Easter Monday), 1 May (May Day), 27 May (Spring Bank Holiday), 16 June (Queen's Official Birthday), 25 August (Late Summer Bank Holiday), 10 September (Gibraltar National Holiday), 25–26 December (Christmas).

Statistical Survey

Source (unless otherwise indicated): Statistics Office, 99 Harbours Walk, The New Harbours, Gibraltar; tel. 20075515; fax 20051160; e-mail gibstats@gibtelecom.net; internet www.gibraltar.gov.gi.

AREA AND POPULATION

Area: 6.5 sq km (2.5 sq miles).

Population (excl. armed forces): 27,495 (males 13,644, females 13,851) at census of 12 November 2001 (Gibraltarians 22,882, Other British 2,627, Non-British 1,986). *2011* (official figure): 29,752 (Gibraltarians 24,288, Other British 3,042, Non-British 2,422).

Density (2011): 4,577.2 per sq km.

Population by Age and Sex (at 2001 census): *0–14:* 5,062 (males 2,655, females 2,407); *15–64:* 18,127 (males 9,229, females 8,898); *65 and over:* 4,306 (males 1,760, females 2,546); *Total* 27,495 (males 13,644, females 13,851).

Births, Marriages and Deaths (2011, excl. armed forces): Live births 442 (birth rate 14.9 per 1,000); Marriages 990 (residents 176) (marriage rate for residents 5.9 per 1,000); Deaths 241 (death rate 8.1 per 1,000).

Life Expectancy (years at birth at census of 2001): Males 78.5; Females 83.3.

Employment (October 2011): Manufacturing 464 (Shipbuilding 243); Construction 3,434; Electricity, gas and water 299; Wholesale and retail trade, and repair of goods 3,044; Restaurants and hotels 1,180; Transport, storage and communications 1,326; Financial intermediation 1,974; Real estate, renting and business activities 2,377; Public administration and defence 1,937; Education 921; Health and social work 1,745; Other community, social and personal services 3,546; Total 22,247 (males 13,231, females 9,016). Figures cover only non-agricultural activities, excluding mining and quarrying.

INDUSTRY

Electric Energy (2011): 164.3m. kWh.

FINANCE

Currency and Exchange Rates: 100 pence (pennies) = 1 Gibraltar pound (G£). *Sterling, Dollar and Euro Equivalents* (31 December

2012): £1 sterling = G£1.0000; US $1 = 63.37 pence; €1 = 83.61 pence; G£10 = £10.00 sterling = $15.78 = €11.96. *Average Exchange Rate* (G£ per US dollar): 0.6472 in 2010; 0.6241 in 2011; 0.6330 in 2012. Note: The Gibraltar pound is at par with sterling.

Budget (G£ '000, year ending 31 March 2013, estimates): *Recurrent Revenue:* Taxes 190,000; Duties 123,790; Gambling fees 12,141; Rates 25,001; Departmental fees and receipts 100,309; Government earnings 6,512; Total 457,753. *Recurrent Expenditure:* Treasury 13,615; Health 85,283; Environment and tourism 16,545; Housing and administration 9,568; Family, youth and community affairs 21,870; Education, employment and training 50,595; Social security 36,108; Utilities 48,066; Culture, heritage and sport 6,381; Office of Principal Auditor 809; Supplementary provision 8,000; Consolidated fund charges 59,093; Miscellaneous expenditure 74,403; Total 430,336.

Cost of Living (Retail Price Index at January; base: April 1998 = 100): 132.9 in 2011; 137.9 in 2012; 140.7 in 2013.

Gross National Product (G£ million, at factor cost): 776.31 in 2008/09; 875.77 in 2009/10; 921.62 in 2010/11 (provisional estimate).

Gross Domestic Product (G£ million, at factor cost): 896.44 in 2008/09; 998.36 in 2009/10; 1,050.54 in 2010/11 (provisional estimate).

EXTERNAL TRADE

Imports c.i.f. (G£ million, excluding petroleum products): 479.3 in 2009; 482.5 in 2010; 541.2 in 2011.

Exports f.o.b. (G£ million, excluding petroleum products): 169.5 in 2009; 167.2 in 2010; 153.8 in 2011.

Principal Trading Partners (G£ '000, 2011, excluding petroleum products): *Imports:* France 7,209; Netherlands 14,999; Spain 121,789; United Kingdom 146,897; Total (incl. others) 541,211. Note: Figures for exports were not available.

TRANSPORT

Road Traffic (licences current at 31 December 2011): Private vehicles 15,086; Commercial vehicles 1,795; Motorcycles 8,572.

Shipping: *Flag Registered Fleet* (at 31 December 2012): Vessels 365; Total displacement 3,252,275 grt. Source: Lloyd's List Intelligence (www.lloydslistintelligence.com).

Civil Aviation (2011): Passenger arrivals ('000) 189.5; Passenger departures ('000) 193.5; Freight loaded 16 metric tons; Freight unloaded 111 metric tons. Figures exclude military passengers and freight.

TOURISM

Visitor Arrivals ('000): 10,302.2 in 2009; 11,530.8 in 2010; 11,940.5 in 2011.

Tourism Receipts (G£ million): 257.59 in 2009; 277.89 in 2010; 279.41 in 2011.

COMMUNICATIONS MEDIA

Television Licences (2005): 5,965.

Telephone Stations (2004): 34,476.

Telephones (main lines in use, 2011): 24,000 (Source: International Telecommunication Union).

Mobile Cellular Telephones (2011): 32,500 subscribers (Source: International Telecommunication Union).

Internet Subscribers (31 March 2011): 239.

Broadband Subscribers (31 March 2011): 10,221.

EDUCATION

Primary (state schools, 2011 unless otherwise indicated): 11 schools (1999), 2,933 pupils.

Secondary (state schools, 2011 unless otherwise indicated): 2 schools (1999), 2,077 pupils.

Total Teaching Staff at Primary and Secondary Schools (state schools, 2011): 397.

Technical and Vocational (1999): 1 college, 201 full-time students.

Pupil-teacher Ratio (primary education, UNESCO estimate): 16.0 in 2008/09 (Source: UNESCO Institute for Statistics).

Directory

The Government

HEAD OF STATE

Queen: HM Queen ELIZABETH II.

Governor and Commander-in-Chief: Vice-Adm. Sir ADRIAN JOHNS (took office 26 October 2009).

COUNCIL OF MINISTERS
(May 2013)

The Government is formed by the alliance of the Gibraltar Socialist Labour Party and the Gibraltar Liberal Party.

Chief Minister: FABIÁN PICARDO.

Deputy Chief Minister: Dr JOSEPH GARCIA.

Minister for Health and Environment: Dr JOHN CORTES.

Minister for Housing and the Elderly: CHARLES BRUZON.

Minister for Equality and Social Services: SAMANTHA SACRAMENTO.

Minister for Education, Financial Services, Gaming, Telecommunications and Justice: GILBERT LICUDI.

Minister for Enterprise, Training and Employment: JOE BOSSANO.

Minister for Tourism, Public Transport and the Port: NEIL COSTA.

Minister for Traffic, Health and Safety, and Technical Services: PAUL BALBAN.

Minister for Sports, Culture, Heritage and Youth: STEVEN LINARES.

MINISTRIES

Office of the Governor: The Convent, Main St; tel. 20045440; fax 20047823; e-mail enquiry.gibraltar@fco.gov.uk.

Office of the Chief Minister: 6 Convent Pl.; tel. 20070071; fax 20076396.

Ministry of Education, Financial Services, Gaming, Telecommunications and Justice: 23 Queensway; tel. 20077486; fax 20071564; e-mail info.edu@gibraltar.gov.gi.

Ministry of Enterprise, Training and Employment: Unit 76/77, Harbours Walk, New Harbours; tel. 2001100; fax 20073981; e-mail employment.service@gibraltar.gov.gi.

Ministry of Equality and Social Services: 14 Governor's Parade; tel. 20044070; e-mail mhe@gibraltar.gov.gi.

Ministry of Family, Youth and Community Affairs: 14 Governor's Parade; tel. 20051149; fax 20074941; e-mail dss@gibraltar.gov.gi.

Ministry of Finance: 6 Convent Pl.; tel. 20070071; fax 20076396; e-mail financeministry@gibtelecom.net.

Ministry of Housing and the Elderly: City Hall, John Mackintosh Sq.; tel. 20075603; fax 20052947.

Ministry of Justice: Suite 771, Europort; tel. 20052557; fax 20047677; e-mail mefs@gibraltar.gov.gi.

Ministry of Sports, Culture, Heritage and Youth: 310 Main St; tel. 20047592; fax 20052589; e-mail culture.minister@gibtelecom.net.

Ministry of Tourism, Public Transport and the Port: Suite 631, 3rd Floor, Europort; tel. 20078871; fax 20078899; e-mail info.mttp@gibraltar.gov.gi.

Ministry of Traffic, Health and Safety and Technical Services: Joshua Hassan House, Secretary's Lane; tel. 20059801; e-mail mthst@gibraltar.gov.gi.

Legislature

Gibraltar Parliament
156 Main St; tel. 200784200; fax 20042849; e-mail parliament@gibtelecom.net; internet www.gibraltar.gov.gi.

Speaker: HARESH K. BUDHRANI.

General Election, 8 December 2011

Party	Votes*	% of votes	Seats
Gibraltar Socialist Labour Party (GSLP)	85,414	48.9	10
Gibraltar Liberal Party (GLP)			
Gibraltar Social Democrats (GSD)	81,721	46.8	7
Progressive Democratic Party (PDP) . . .	7,622	4.4	—
Total	174,757	100.0	17

* Each voter was permitted to vote for a maximum of 10 candidates. The total number of ballots cast was 21,712.

Political Organizations

All political organizations in Gibraltar advocate self-determination for the territory.

Gibraltar Liberal Party (GLP): 95 Irish Town; tel. and fax 20076959; e-mail info@liberal.gi; internet www.liberal.gi; f. 1991 as the Gibraltar National Party; Leader Dr JOSEPH GARCIA; Sec.-Gen. STEVEN LINARES.

Gibraltar Social Democrats (GSD): 1A College Lane; tel. and fax 20044105; e-mail gsdhq@gibtelecom.net; internet www.gsd.gi; f. 1989; holds a majority of seats in the House of Assembly; absorbed the Gibraltar Labour Party in 2005; Leader PETER CARUANA.

Gibraltar Socialist Labour Party (GSLP): Suite 16, Block 3, Watergardens; tel. 20050700; fax 20078983; e-mail gslp.website@gmail.com; internet www.gslp.gi; f. 1978; Leader FABIÁN PICARDO.

New Gibraltar Democracy (NGD): f. 2005; Christian democratic; Leader CHARLES GOMEZ.

Progressive Democratic Party (PDP): POB 1373; tel. and fax 20049000; e-mail info@pdp.gi; internet www.pdp.gi; f. 2006; Leader KEITH AZOPARDI.

Judicial System

The 2006 Constitution provides for the protection of the fundamental rights and freedoms of the individual and the maintenance of a Supreme Court with unlimited jurisdiction to hear and determine any civil or criminal proceedings under any law. The Courts of Law of Gibraltar comprise a Court of Appeal, the Supreme Court and the Magistrates' Court.

The substantive law of Gibraltar is contained in Orders in Council which apply to Gibraltar, enactments of the Parliament of the United Kingdom which apply to or have been extended or applied to Gibraltar, locally enacted acts and subsidiary legislation, and common law and the rules of equity from time to time in force in England so far as they may be applicable and subject to all necessary modification.

Court of Appeal

The Law Courts, 277 Main St.

Holds three sessions each year; the Justices of Appeal are drawn from the English Court of Appeal.

President: Sir MURRAY STUART-SMITH.

Justices of Appeal: Sir PHILIP OTTON, Sir WILLIAM ALDOUS, Sir JONATHAN PARKER, Sir SIMON TOCKEY.

Supreme Court

The Law Courts, 277 Main St; tel. 20078808; fax 20077118.

Includes the office of Admiralty Marshal.

Chief Justice: ANTHONY E. DUDLEY.

Magistrates' Court

The Law Courts, 277 Main St; tel. 20075671; fax 20040483.

Stipendiary Magistrate: CHARLES PITTO.

Religion

At the 2001 census 78.1% of the population were Roman Catholic, 7.0% Church of England, 4.0% Muslim, 2.1% Jewish and 1.8% Hindu.

CHRISTIANITY

The Roman Catholic Church

Gibraltar forms a single diocese, directly responsible to the Holy See. At 31 December 2006 there were an estimated 21,470 adherents in the territory (78.1% of the total population).

Bishop of Gibraltar: Rt Rev. RALPH HESKETT, 215 Main St; tel. 20076688; fax 20043112; e-mail epis.carroca@gibnynex.gi; internet www.catholicdiocese.gi.

The Church of England

The diocese of Gibraltar in Europe, founded in 1980, has jurisdiction over the whole of continental Europe, Turkey and Morocco.

Bishop of Gibraltar in Europe: Rt Rev. GEOFFREY ROWELL, Bishop's Lodge, Church Rd, Worth, RH10 7RT, United Kingdom; tel. (1293) 883051; fax (1293) 884479; e-mail bishop@dioceseineurope.org.uk; internet europe.anglican.org.

Dean of the Cathedral of the Holy Trinity: Very Rev. JOHN PADDOCK, 4/1 Jumpers, Rosia Rd; tel. 20078377; fax 20078463; e-mail deangib@gibnet.gi; internet www.gibconnect.com/~holytrinity.

Other Christian Churches

Church of Scotland: St Andrew's Manse, 29 Scud Hill; tel. and fax 20077040; e-mail scotskirk@gibraltar.gi; internet www.scotskirkgibraltar.com; f. 1800; Minister Rev. EWEN MACLEAN; 50 mems.

Gibraltar Methodist Church: 297 Main St; tel. and fax 20040870; e-mail minister@methodist.org.gi; internet www.methodist.org.gi; f. 1769; Minister Rev. FIDEL PATRON; 80 mems.

ISLAM

A mosque to serve the Islamic community in Gibraltar and financed by the Government of Saudi Arabia was constructed in the late 1990s.

JUDAISM

Jewish Community: Managing Board, 91 Irish Town; tel. 20072606; fax 20040487; e-mail mbjc@gibtelecom.net; internet www.jewishgibraltar.com; Pres. HAIM LEVY; Admin. Sec. SUSAN LEVY; 600 mems.

The Press

Gibraltar Chronicle: POB 27, Watergate House, Casemates; tel. 20043596; fax 20079927; e-mail management@chronicle.gi; internet www.chronicle.gi; f. 1801; daily (except Sun.); English; Man. Editor DOMINIQUE SEARLE; circ. 6,000.

Gibraltar Gazette: Ministry of Justice, Legislation Support Unit, Treasury Bldg, 23 John Mackintosh Sq.; tel. 20051246; fax 20041822; f. 1949; weekly; publ. by *Gibraltar Chronicle*; official notices.

Gibraltar Magazine: POB 1124, 17 Turnbull's Lane; tel. and fax 20077748; e-mail gibmag@gibnet.gi; internet www.thegibraltarmagazine.com; f. 1995; monthly; English; business and leisure; Editor ANDREA MORTON.

Insight: 1st Floor, 77 Main St; tel. 20040913; fax 20048665; e-mail info@insightgibraltar.com; internet www.insightgibraltar.com; f. 1992; print and internet magazine; circ. 6,000.

Panorama: 95 Irish Town; tel. 20079797; fax 20074664; e-mail gibnews@panorama.gi; internet www.panorama.gi; f. 1975; Mon.–Fri.; English; news and features; Editor JOE GARCÍA; circ. 4,000.

The New People: Suite No. 6/608, Icom House, 1–5 Irish Town; tel. 54374000; e-mail thenewpeople@gibtelecom.net; internet www.thenewpeople.net; f. 1980; weekly; English with Spanish section; Editor JUAN CARLOS PÉREZ; circ. 1,000.

Vox: Unit 91, Harbours Walk, New Harbours, POB 306; tel. 20077414; fax 20072531; e-mail editor@vox.gi; internet www.vox.gi; f. 1955; weekly; independent; in English and Spanish; Editor DEREK MCGRAIL; circ. 1,800.

Broadcasting and Communications

REGULATORY AUTHORITY

Gibraltar Regulatory Authority (GRA): Suite 603, Europort; tel. 20074636; fax 20072166; e-mail info@gra.gi; internet www.gra.gi; f. 2000; statutory body responsible for the regulation of telecommunications, the radio spectrum, data protection, broadcasting and postal services; Chief Exec. PAUL CANESSA.

TELECOMMUNICATIONS

CTS Gibraltar Ltd: 48 Royal Ocean Ave, Royal Ocean Plaza; tel. 21651500; fax 21651502; e-mail customerservices@cts-europe.com; internet www.cts-europe.com; part of CTS Group; mobile and broadband internet services.

Gibtelecom: 15/21 John Mackintosh Sq., POB 929; tel. 20052200; fax 20071673; e-mail info@gibtele.com; internet www.gibtele.com; f. 1990; jtly owned by Govt of Gibraltar and Telekom Slovenije

(Slovenia); operates local and international telephone and telecommunications services; provides a range of digital, satellite, mobile and internet services; Chair. Dr JOSEPH GARCÍA (Deputy Chief Minister); CEO TIM BRISTOW.

Sapphire Networks: Suite 303, Eurotowers, POB 797; tel. 20047200; fax 20047272; e-mail info@sapphire.gi; internet www.sapphire.gi; f. 2005; internet service provider; Man. Dir LAWRENCE ISOLA.

BROADCASTING

Gibraltar Broadcasting Corporation (GBC): Broadcasting House, 18 South Barrack Rd; tel. 20079760; fax 20078673; e-mail gbc@gibraltar.gi; internet www.gbc.gi; f. 1963; responsible for television and radio broadcasting; CEO GERARD TEUMA (designate).

Radio

GBC—Radio (Radio Gibraltar): 24 hours daily in English and Spanish, including commercial broadcasting. In addition to local programmes, the BBC World Service programme is relayed.

Television

GBC—TV: operates in English for 24 hours daily; GBC and relayed BBC programmes are transmitted.

Finance

(cap. = capital; res = reserves; dep. = deposits; m. = million; brs = branches; amounts in G£)

BANKING

In September 2012 there were 16 banks operating in Gibraltar.

Regulatory Authority

Financial Services Commission: POB 940, Suite 943, Europort; tel. 20040283; fax 20040282; e-mail info@fsc.gi; internet www.fsc.gi; f. 1991; regulates the activities of the financial sector; CEO MARCUS KILLICK.

Banks

Credit Suisse (Gibraltar) Ltd: Neptune House, 1st Floor, Marina Bay, POB 556; tel. 20078399; fax 20076027; e-mail csg.mail@credit-suisse.com; f. 1987; cap. 5m., dep. 1,073.2m. (Dec. 2011); Chair. HANS-ULRICH DOERIG; Man. Dir THOMAS WESTH OLSEN.

EFG Bank (Gibraltar) Ltd: Eurolife Bldg, 1 Corral Rd, POB 561; tel. 20040117; fax 20040110; e-mail atlaco@gibnet.gi; fmrly Banco Atlántico (Gibraltar) Ltd; Man. EMILIO MARTÍNEZ PRIEGO.

SG Hambros Bank (Gibraltar) Ltd: Hambro House, 32 Line Wall Rd, POB 375; tel. 20002000; fax 20079037; e-mail gibraltar@sghambros.com; internet www.sghambros.com; f. 1981; acquired ABN AMRO Private Banking in 2008; owned by Société Générale (France); cap. 29.5m., res 1.1m., dep. 462.5m. (Dec. 2011); Chair. WARWICK J. NEWBURY; Man. Dir EMMA PÉREZ.

Jyske Bank (Gibraltar) Ltd: 76 Main St, POB 143; tel. 20072782; fax 20072732; e-mail jyskebank@jyskebank.gi; internet jyskebank.gi; f. 1855 as Galliano (A. L.) Bankers; in 1988 name changed as above; cap. 26.5m., res 2.1m., dep. 1,705.2m. (Dec. 2011); Chair. JENS LAURITZEN; Man. Dir CHRISTIAN BJØRLØW.

Lloyds TSB Bank PLC: 1st Floor, Royal Ocean Plaza, Ocean Village, POB 482; tel. 20077373; fax 20070023; internet www.lloydstsb.gi; f. 1986; Man. ALBERT DOUGLAS LANGSTON.

Lombard Odier and Cie Ltd: Suite 921, Europort, POB 407; tel. 20073350; fax 20073475; e-mail gibraltar@lombardodier.com; internet www.lombardodier.com; fmrly Lombard Odier Darier Hentsch Private Bank Ltd, name changed as above 2012; Man. Dir JAVIER DE MENDIETA.

NatWest Offshore Ltd: NatWest House, 57 Line Wall Rd, POB 707; tel. 20077737; fax 20074557; e-mail natwestgib@gibnynex.gi; internet www.natwestoffshore.com; f. 1988.

Royal Bank of Scotland (Gibraltar) Ltd: 1 Corral Rd, POB 766; tel. 20073200; fax 20070152; e-mail marvincartwright@rbsint.com; internet www.rbsinternational.com; Country Man. MARVIN CARTWRIGHT.

Turicum Private Bank Ltd: Turicum House, 315 Main St, POB 619; tel. 20044144; fax 20044145; e-mail info@turicum.com; internet www.turicumprivatebank.com; f. 1993; Chair. Dr RAYMOND BISANG; CEO URS HÜNI.

Savings Bank

Gibraltar Savings Bank: Treasury Dept, Treasury Bldg, 23 John Mackintosh Sq.; tel. 20048396; fax 20077147; e-mail treasury@gibtelecom.net; dep. 242.2m. (March 2007); Dir C. VICTORY.

Association

Gibraltar Bankers' Association (GBA): POB 380; tel. 20044144; fax 20044145; e-mail langham@mercuryin.es; internet www.gba.gi; f. 1982; Pres. CHRISTIAN GARCIA; 17 mem. banks.

INSURANCE

There were 65 licensed insurance companies operating in Gibraltar in April 2012.

BMI Insurance Services Limited: Unit 7, Portland House, Glacis Rd, POB 469; tel. 20051010; e-mail info@bmigroup.gi; internet www.bmigroup.gi.

Brit Insurance: Suite 913 Europort; tel. 20043882; fax 20048159; internet www.britinsurance.com; f. 2007.

Capurro Insurance and Investments Ltd: 20 Line Wall Rd, POB 130; tel. 20040850; fax 20040851; e-mail info@capurroinsurance.com; internet www.capurroinsurance.com; Man. MARIO J. ROVEGNO.

Castiel Winser Insurance and Financial Consultants: Natwest House, 57/63 Line Wall Rd, POB 464; tel. 20077723; fax 20079257; e-mail financialservices@castielwinser.com; internet www.castielwinser.com; f. 1985; Man. Dir SYDNEY ISAAC ATTIAS.

Eurolife Assurance (International) Ltd: 6A Queensway, POB 64; tel. 20045502; fax 20051071; e-mail enquiries@grantthornton.gi; Man. A. SMITH.

Eurolinx (Gibraltar) Ltd: Suites 21–22, Victoria House, 26 Main St, POB 671; tel. 20040240; fax 20040241; e-mail eurolinx@sapphirenet.gi; internet www.eurolinx.gi; f. 1990; Man. Dir JOHN LISTER.

Evolution Insurance Co Ltd: 23 Ocean Village Promenade, Level 2, Ocean Village Business Centre; tel. 20077065; fax 20062285; e-mail enquiries@evo-insurance.com; internet www.evo-insurance.com; f. 2003; Man. Dir CHRIS LE CONTE.

Gibro Insurance Services Ltd: Gibro House, 4 Giro's Passage, POB 693; tel. 20076222; fax 20071423; e-mail gibro@gibro.com; internet www.gibro.com; f. 1994; Chair. Hon. JOHN BRIAN PEREZ.

Middlesea Insurance PLC: Suite 1A, 143 Main St, POB 502; tel. 20076434; fax 20076741; f. 2000.

Ultimate Insurance Co Ltd: Suite 913 Europort; tel. 20043882; fax 20060762; e-mail enquiries@uicl.eu; internet www.ultimatepetpartners.co.uk; f. 2009; Man. Dir PAUL HAMPSHIRE.

Association

Gibraltar Insurance Association: c/o POB 371, 2nd Floor, 85 Main St; tel. 20045578; fax 20045579; internet www.gia.gi; f. 1997; approx. 71 mems; Chair. CHRIS JOHNSON.

Trade and Industry

GOVERNMENT AGENCY

InvestGibraltar: Suite 771, Europort; tel. 20052634; fax 20052635; e-mail info@investgibraltar.gov.gi; internet www.investgibraltar.gov.gi.

CHAMBER OF COMMERCE

Gibraltar Chamber of Commerce: Watergate House, 2–6 Casemates Sq., POB 29; tel. 20078376; fax 20078403; e-mail info@gibraltarchamberofcommerce.com; internet www.gibraltarchamberofcommerce.com; f. 1882; Pres. NICHOLAS RUSSO; 300 mems.

EMPLOYERS' ORGANIZATIONS

Gibraltar Federation of Small Businesses: GFSB House, POB 211, 112 Irish Town; tel. 20047722; fax 20047733; e-mail gfsb@gfsb.gi; internet www.gfsb.gi; f. 1996; Chair. STUART RODRIGUEZ.

Gibraltar Hotel Association: c/o Caleta Hotel; tel. 20076501; fax 20071050; e-mail caleta@gibnynex.gi; internet www.caletahotel.com; f. 1960; Chair. FRANCO OSTUNI; 7 mems.

Gibraltar Motor Traders' Association: POB 167; tel. 20079004; f. 1961; Gen. Sec. G. BASSADONE; 6 mems.

Hindu Merchants' Association: POB 1313; tel. 20079000; fax 20071966; e-mail vikram.nagrani@hassans.gi; f. 1979; Pres. VIKRAM NAGRANI; 720 mems.

PRINCIPAL TRADE UNIONS

Gibraltar Taxi Association: 19 Waterport Wharf; tel. 20070052; fax 20076986; e-mail gibtaxiass@gibtelecom.net; internet www.gibtaxi.com; f. 1957; Pres. RONALD IGNACIO; 100 mems.

Gibraltar Trades Council: 7 Hargraves Ramp, POB 279; tel. 20076930; fax 20079646; e-mail ggca@gibtelecom.net; comprises unions representing 70% of the working population; affiliated to the United Kingdom Trades Union Congress; Sec. MICHAEL J. A. TAMPIN. Affiliated unions:

Gibraltar General and Clerical Association (GGCA): 7 Hargrave's Ramp, POB 279; tel. 20076930; fax 20079646; e-mail ggca@gibtelecom.net; internet www.ggca.gi; f. 1947; Pres. WENDY CUMMING; Gen. Sec. MICHAEL J. A. TAMPIN; 1,205 mems (2009).

NASUWT (Gibraltar): 98 Harbours Walk, New Harbours; tel. 20076308; fax 20077608; e-mail gtateachers@gibtelecom.net; internet www.gibconnect.com/~gta/; f. 1962; fmrly the Gibraltar Teachers' Association; Pres. STUART BORASTERO; 400 mems.

Unite (United Kingdom) (Gibraltar District): tel. 20074185; fax 20071596; f. 1924; 4,239 mems.

UTILITIES
Electricity

Gibraltar Electricity Authority: Gibelec House, North Mole Rd; tel. 20048908; fax 20077408; e-mail enquiries@gibelec.gi; internet www.gibelec.gi; govt-owned; generation, distribution and supply of electricity.

Water

AquaGib Ltd: Suite 10B, Leanse Pl., 50 Town Range; tel. 20040880; fax 20040881; e-mail main.office@aquagib.gi; internet www.aquagib.gi; fmrly known as Lyonnais des Eaux (Gibraltar) Ltd; present name adopted 2003; f. 1991; 66.67% owned by Northumbrian Water Group (United Kingdom), 33.33% govt-owned; Man. Dir D. CANO.

Transport

RAILWAYS
There are no railways in Gibraltar.

ROADS
There is a total road length of 53.1 km, including 12.9 km of highways.

Ministry of Enterprise, Development, Technology and Transport: see Ministries.

SHIPPING
In 2012 the flag registered fleet totalled 365 vessels, with a combined displacement of 3.3m grt. The Strait of Gibraltar is a principal ocean route between the Mediterranean and Black Sea areas and the rest of the world.

Gibraltar is used by many long-distance liners, and has dry dock facilities and a commercial ship-repair yard. Tax concessions are available to ship owners who register their ships in Gibraltar.

A new passenger ferry service between Gibraltar and the Spanish port of Algeciras, across the Bay of Gibraltar, began operating in December 2009.

Gibdock Limited: Main Wharf Rd, The Dockyard; tel. 20059400; fax 20044404; e-mail mail@gibdock.com; internet www.gibdock.com; f. 1998; dry dock facilities and general ship-repairing; CEO JOSEPH CORVELLI.

Gibraltar Maritime Administration: Watergate House, 2/8 Casemate Sq.; tel. 20047771; fax 20047770; e-mail maritime.survey@gibraltar.gov.gi; internet www.gibraltarship.com; Administrator RICHARD MONTADO.

Gibraltar Port Authority: Port Office, North Mole; tel. 20046254; fax 20051513; e-mail gpa.enquiries@portofgibraltar.gi; internet www.gibraltarport.com; CEO Capt. PETER W. HALL.

M. H. Bland & Co Ltd: Cloister Bldg, POB 554, Market Lane; tel. 20079478; fax 20071608; internet www.mhbland.com; f. 1810; ship agents, stevedoring, warehousing; also operates cable-car service to peak of the Rock of Gibraltar; Chair. JOHN A. GAGGERO.

CIVIL AVIATION
The airport is at North Front, on the isthmus, 2.5 km from the city centre. An agreement reached in September 2006 between Gibraltar, the United Kingdom and Spain allowed for the operation of flights from Spain and the rest of Europe to Gibraltar. Hitherto Spain had blocked direct air links between Gibraltar and European countries other than the United Kingdom. Commercial flights between Gibraltar and Spain began in December 2006. In accordance with the 2006 agreement, plans were announced in 2007 for a new airport terminal adjoining the border with Spain; the new terminal opened in November 2011.

Tourism

Gibraltar's tourist attractions include its climate, beaches and a variety of amenities. Following the reopening of the border with Spain in February 1985, the resumption of traffic by day visitors contributed to the expansion of the tourist industry. In 2011 visitor arrivals numbered some 11.9m., while revenue from tourism was estimated at G£279.4m.

Gibraltar Tourist Board: Duke of Kent House, Cathedral Sq.; tel. 20074950; fax 20074943; e-mail information@tourism.gov.gi; internet www.visitgibraltar.gi; CEO NICHOLAS GUERRERO.

Defence

There is a local defence force, the Gibraltar Regiment, which, following the abolition of conscription, was reorganized as a predominantly volunteer reserve unit; as assessed at November 2011 it comprised 175 members. British army personnel stationed in Gibraltar numbered 95 and there were about 70 Royal Air Force personnel. There is one Royal Navy base located in Gibraltar.

Commander-in-Chief: Vice-Adm. Sir ADRIAN JOHNS.

Education

Education is compulsory between the ages of five and 15 years, and is provided free in government schools. The language of instruction is English. There are four nursery schools, 11 primary schools (of which one is private), one Service school (administered by the Ministry of Defence for the children of military personnel), two secondary comprehensive schools—one for boys and one for girls and one college of further education. In 2011 there were 2,933 pupils in state primary schools, 2,077 pupils in state secondary schools and 397 teaching staff in state primary and secondary schools. Higher national diploma and degree courses are offered by the universities in the United Kingdom. Scholarships for students in higher education are provided by both government and private sources. There is also one college providing technical and vocational training, and a school for children with special needs. Government expenditure on education, employment and training in 2011/12 was forecast at G£29.1m. (equivalent to 7.8% of total spending).

MONTSERRAT

Introductory Survey

LOCATION, CLIMATE, LANGUAGE, RELIGION, FLAG, CAPITAL

Montserrat is one of the Leeward Islands in the West Indies. A mountainous, volcanic island, it lies about 55 km (35 miles) north of Basse-Terre, Guadeloupe, and about 43 km south west of Antigua. The climate is generally warm, with a mean maximum temperature of 30°C (86°F) and a mean minimum of 23°C (73°F), but the island is fanned by sea breezes for most of the year. The average annual rainfall is about 1,475 mm (58 ins), although there is more rain in the central and western areas. English is the official language. Many Christian churches are represented, but the principal denominations are the Anglican, Roman Catholic and Methodist Churches. The flag is the British 'Blue Ensign', with the island's badge (a shield depicting a woman dressed in green holding a harp and a cross) on a white roundel in the fly. The interim capital is Brades.

CONTEMPORARY POLITICAL HISTORY
Historical Context

Montserrat was first settled by the British (initially Roman Catholic exiles) in 1632, by which time the few original Carib inhabitants had disappeared. It formed part of the federal colony of the Leeward Islands from 1871 until 1956, when the federation was dissolved and the presidency of Montserrat became a separate colony. Montserrat participated in the short-lived Federation of the West Indies (1958–62) and, from 1960, the island had its own Administrator (the title was changed to that of Governor in 1971). The Constitution (see below) came into force in 1960.

Domestic Political Affairs

The first priority of successive legislatures has been to improve infrastructure and maintain a healthy economy. Between 1952 and 1970 William Bramble dominated island politics. His son, Austin Bramble, leader of the Progressive Democratic Party (PDP), opposed and succeeded him as Chief Minister. In November 1978 the People's Liberation Movement (PLM) won all seven elective seats in the Legislative Council, and the PLM's leader, John Osborne, became Chief Minister. In the general election of February 1983 the PLM was returned to government.

Attempts to form an opposition alliance between the PDP and the National Development Party (formed by business interests and former members of the PDP) were unsuccessful. Against a divided opposition, the PLM won the general election of August 1987. Osborne was returned to office as Chief Minister.

Osborne was an advocate of independence from the United Kingdom, despite the apparent lack of popular support for this policy. A referendum on the issue was planned for 1990, but the devastation caused by Hurricane Hugo in September 1989 meant that any plans for independence were postponed. Furthermore, the Osborne Government and the British authorities were embarrassed by controversy surrounding the hitherto lucrative 'offshore' financial sector. In 1989 the Governor's office announced that the British police were investigating serious allegations against certain banks (involving the processing of illegal funds from a variety of criminal activities). Registration was suspended, several people were charged with criminal offences and most banking licences were revoked. The Montserrat Government agreed to introduce recommended provisions for the regulation of the financial services industry and responsibility for the sector was transferred from the Chief Minister to the Governor. In December 1991 the Legislative Council approved legislation allowing the re-establishment of a comprehensive 'offshore' financial centre. However, despite considerably improved regulation, more than 90% of the island's 'offshore' and commercial banks were again closed following further investigations by British inspectors in mid-1992.

The resignation of the Deputy Chief Minister, Benjamin Chalmers, in September 1991, following a dispute with Osborne, resulted in the loss of the Government's majority in the Legislative Council. This prompted an early election in the following month, when the National Progressive Party (NPP), formed only two months prior to the election, secured a majority of seats. The NPP leader, Reuben Meade, became Chief Minister.

Volcanic eruption

The eruption of Chances Peak volcano in July 1995, which had been dormant for more than 100 years, caused severe disruption to the island and threatened to devastate Plymouth and surrounding areas in southern Montserrat. In August the threat of a more serious eruption prompted the evacuation of some 5,000 people to the north of the island, and the declaration by the Government of a state of emergency and a night curfew. As volcanic activity subsided in September, evacuated islanders returned to Plymouth and villages near the volcano. However, by December the area was again deemed to be unsafe, and 4,000 people were evacuated for a period of several weeks. The Governor and Chief Minister secured an agreement from the British Government for the provision of assistance with evacuation and rehabilitation programmes. A third evacuation took place in April 1996, following another series of eruptions, and it was announced that some 5,000 evacuees living in 'safe areas' would remain there at least until the end of the year. In that month the British Government announced that Montserratians would be granted residency and the right to work in the United Kingdom for up to two years. In August the British Government announced that it was to provide assistance worth £25m. to finance housing construction projects, infrastructure development, the provision of temporary health and education facilities and other public services in the northern 'safe areas' of the island. By the end of 1996 it was estimated that some 5,000 islanders had left the territory since the onset of volcanic activity in mid-1995.

In September 1996 the Deputy Chief Minister, Noel Tuitt, resigned from his post and from the NPP, stating that he was disillusioned with Meade's leadership. Disagreement over the Government's management of the volcano crisis and its handling of aid funds led to the proposal, by an opposition member in October, of a motion of no confidence in the Chief Minister. Meade, however, avoided a vote on the motion by dissolving the Legislative Council.

No party won an overall majority at a general election in November 1996. A four-member coalition cabinet was subsequently formed under the leadership of Bertrand Osborne, who was sworn in as Chief Minister on 13 November.

In June 1997 the scale of volcanic activity on the island increased dramatically with the eruption of the Soufrière Hills volcano, which left some two-thirds of the island uninhabitable, destroyed Plymouth and resulted in 19 deaths. Islanders were evacuated to 'safe areas' in the north of the country. The British Government released emergency aid to finance the construction of emergency shelters for evacuees, and for repairs to temporary hospital facilities. In July it was announced that a package of options for Montserratians was being formulated, which would offer islanders resettlement grants and assisted passage either to other islands within the Caribbean or to the United Kingdom. The 'safe area' in the north was to be developed for those wishing to remain on the island. By the end of July the population of Montserrat was estimated to have declined to 5,800; in the month since the eruption of the Soufrière Hills volcano some 800 islanders had moved to Antigua, bringing the total number who had moved there since the onset of volcanic activity in 1995 to some 3,000. Many more had resettled on other Caribbean islands or in the United Kingdom.

In August 1997 Bertrand Osborne resigned as Chief Minister following four days of public demonstrations in protest at his handling of the volcano crisis. On the same day the British Government announced the financial details of its voluntary evacuation scheme for those wishing to leave Montserrat. The offer, which comprised a relocation grant of £2,400 for adults and £600 for minors, in addition to travel costs, provoked an angry response from islanders, who protested that the grants were severely inadequate. Osborne's successor as Chief Minister, David Brandt, an independent member of the Legislative Council, criticized the British Government's offer while also accusing it of attempting to depopulate Montserrat by showing insufficient commitment to the redevelopment of the island. The British Secretary of State for International Development, Clare Short, accused the island's leaders of making unreasonable demands, causing considerable offence to the island Government. The controversy was assuaged only when the British Secretary of State for Foreign and Commonwealth Affairs announced the formation of a special inter-departmental committee charged with co-ordinating assistance to Montserrat. At the end of August a five-year sustainable development plan for the north of the island was announced, to include finance for new housing, social services and improved infrastructure.

In January 1998 Brandt renewed his accusations that the British Government was attempting to depopulate Montserrat by delaying the release of development funds. It was subsequently announced that the United Kingdom would provide further finance of £4.8m. for housing on the island. The new funding brought the total amount committed by the British Government in 1995–98, since the beginning of the volcano crisis, to £59m. In May the British Government announced that all citizens of Montserrat, except those already resident in other countries, would be entitled to settle in the United Kingdom. The estimated 3,500 refugees already in the United Kingdom on temporary visas were to be allowed to apply for permanent residency. In July the Soufrière Hills volcano erupted again, covering much of the island in ash, and postponing plans to reopen parts of Plymouth to residents. In August part of the central zone of Montserrat was reopened, following operations to remove ash and debris.

In January 1999 an inquest into the 19 deaths during the eruptions found that in nine cases the British Government was in part to blame for the deaths. The jury criticized the public shelters provided, where conditions were described as 'deplorable', and the Government's failure to provide farming land in the 'safe area', which had led to some farmers choosing to risk their lives rather than abandon their farms. The Department for International Development denied culpability for the deaths, and announced that it was to spend a further £75m. on a three-year redevelopment programme in the north of the island.

In February 1999 studies were published confirming that the volcanic ash covering much of Montserrat contained significant amounts of silica, the cause of the lung disease silicosis. It was suggested that the threat to health from long-term exposure to the ash might further limit the number of areas of the island suitable for redevelopment. Further explosions of ash and minor eruptions of lava continued throughout the rest of the year.

In September 1999 public consultations took place to discuss government proposals to establish a new capital at Little Bay, in the north-west of the island. Progress on the project was finally achieved with the establishment of the Montserrat Development Corporation in 2007, whose mandate included the advancement of plans for the construction of the new capital, and the issuing of a contract to a local company to develop the infrastructure. Also in September 1999 the British Government announced further assistance for the construction of housing. In March 2000 the dome of lava, which had been covering the Soufrière Hills volcano, collapsed, producing lava flows and mudslides in the west of the island, and covering much of the 'safe zone' with ash.

In July 2001 there was a further partial collapse of the dome of lava covering the Soufrière Hills volcano. In the following month Montserrat signed up to a British mortgage assistance programme, which would provide housing subsidies and loans to residents who had been made homeless as a result of volcanic activity.

In February 2001 Chief Minister Brandt's coalition Government collapsed, following the resignations of two members. A general election, under a new, nine-member single constituency system, was held in April. Former Chief Minister John Osborne's newly formed New People's Liberation Movement (NPLM) won most seats. Osborne was sworn in as Chief Minister.

A massive volcanic eruption, the largest since 1995, occurred in July 2003, causing infrastructural damage, and the destruction of numerous buildings in Salem, which was on the edge of the 'safe zone'. In July 2008 the dome again partially collapsed, leading to the temporary evacuation of nearby residents.

Coalition government

No party won an overall majority in the general election of 31 May 2006. The Movement for Change and Prosperity (MCAP) secured the largest representation, with four seats, followed by the NPLM with three seats. The Montserrat Democratic Party (MDP) won one seat, as did former Chief Minister David Brandt, again standing as an independent. Lowell Lewis of the MDP assembled a coalition Government, which was sworn in on 2 June. Allegations of corruption and mismanagement levelled against candidates from both the former government and opposition overshadowed the election process and doubts were expressed about the new administration's compositional stability.

Lewis disbanded the coalition Government on 21 February 2008 and formed a new political alliance with the MCAP. Two NPLM ministers were replaced by MCAP members. At the end of March Lewis also ousted John Osborne, Minister of Education, Health and Community Services, assigning his portfolio to a member of the MCAP, and giving the new coalition Government a majority in the Legislative Council, with six seats.

In October 2008 opposition leader David Brandt filed a motion of no confidence against Chief Minister Lewis as a result of his perceived mismanagement of the island's economic affairs. Lewis avoided the motion by relinquishing the portfolios for finance and economic development to fellow minister Meade. However, in June 2009, faced with continuing dissatisfaction within the Council from MCAP members, Lewis dismissed Meade from government, as well as Roselyn Cassell-Sealy, the Minister of Education, Labour, Health and Community Services. Cassell-Sealy was succeeded by Osborne, whom she had replaced. The following day Lewis requested a dissolution of the Legislative Council so that a general election could be held, two years before it was constitutionally due.

In the general election of 8 September 2009 MCAP secured a majority in the Legislative Council, winning six of the nine seats and over 52% of the votes cast. Independent candidates were elected to the other three seats. One of these was outgoing Chief Minister Lewis, who contested the election as an independent after his party, the MDP, did not field any candidates. MCAP leader Reuben Meade was sworn in as Chief Minister on 10 September.

Recent developments: a new Constitution

Concerns emerged in November 2006 relating to the ongoing constitutional revision process, which had been under negotiation with the Government of the United Kingdom since 1997. A series of constitutional reform debates in the Legislative Council provoked an angry response from some members of the Chief Minister's Constitutional Advisory Committee. They alleged that Montserrat's increased reliance upon budgetary assistance from the United Kingdom—necessitated by volcanic disruption—was being exploited as a 'coercive tool' in the reform process. While the United Kingdom had encouraged Montserrat to express its preferences and recommendations towards the drafting of a new constitution, it was emphasized that ultimate authority would reside with the British Government, eliciting accusations that only a token democracy was being offered. Requests for a system of 'free association', permitting self-determination from the United Kingdom—drafting its own constitution without recourse to the administering nation, but retaining links with that country—and the appointment of an indigenous Deputy Governor who would assume some of the responsibilities of the British Governor in Montserrat, were declined.

Further meetings to discuss the constitutional reform process were conducted during 2009. In May 2010 a contingent of British government officials travelled to the island, and a final draft of the charter was agreed. The new Constitution was approved by the Legislative Council on 7 October and by the Privy Council in the United Kingdom on 13 October, and came into effect on 27 September 2011. In accordance with the new charter, Meade became the island's first Premier (as the position of Chief Minister had been redesignated), while the Executive Council and Legislative Council were replaced with an Executive Cabinet and a Legislative Assembly, respectively. A National Advisory Council was also created, giving the Government and the Leader of the Opposition the opportunity to present the Governor with recommendations on foreign affairs, defence and security, although the Governor would still retain overall responsibility for these areas. In addition, the Premier was granted control over the island's relations with regional organizations, while the Governor was henceforth obliged to consult with the local authorities

before appointing senior public officials. (Adrian Davis had been sworn in as Montserrat's new Governor in April.)

In May 2012 Meade requested the removal of Montserrat from the UN Special Committee on Decolonization's list of prospective colonies, arguing that Montserratians were satisfied with the territory's constitutional status and were not interested in pursuing independence in the near future. However, in mid-June Donaldson Romeo, the leader of the opposition, submitted a no confidence motion against the Government, citing concerns over Meade's decolonization statement and his fiscal policies. None the less, the motion was overwhelmingly defeated later that month.

Foreign Affairs

Following a Cuban Government-sponsored trip to Havana by Chief Minister Lowell in 2007, Montserrat and Cuba pledged to strengthen bilateral relations, particularly in consideration of the burgeoning threat posed by the Soufrière Hills volcanic dome.

In 2008 the Jamaican Prime Minister, Bruce Golding, visited Montserrat and signed a memorandum of understanding between the two countries. This pledged Jamaican support in areas such as cultural enhancement, tourism, economic development, education and health.

CONSTITUTION AND GOVERNMENT

A new Constitution was promulgated on 27 September 2011. Under its provisions, the Governor is appointed by the British monarch and is responsible for defence, external affairs and internal security. The Governor is President of the seven-member Executive Cabinet. The Legislative Assembly comprises nine members, elected for five years, and two ex officio members.

REGIONAL AND INTERNATIONAL CO-OPERATION

Montserrat is a member of the Eastern Caribbean Central Bank (ECCB) and the Organisation of Eastern Caribbean States (OECS, see p. 477). The territory is also a member of the regional stock exchange, the Eastern Caribbean Securities Exchange (based in Saint Christopher and Nevis), established in 2001. Montserrat is a founder member of the Caribbean Community and Common Market (CARICOM, see p. 231). In October 2003 the British Government formally backed plans for Montserrat to participate fully in the Caribbean Single Market and Economy (CSME) proposed by the CARICOM. The CSME came into force in 2006, although Montserrat was not a founding member. In December 2009 Montserrat was a signatory to the Treaty of the OECS, establishing an Economic Union among member states. The Economic Union, which involved the removal of barriers to trade and the movement of labour as a step towards a single financial and economic market, came into effect on 21 January 2011. Although Montserrat received British consent to participate in the Economic Union in December, the territory had not acceded to the regional initiative by April 2013.

The territory is a member of the Commonwealth (see p. 244). As a dependency of the United Kingdom, Montserrat has the status of Overseas Territory in association with the European Union (EU, see p. 281).

ECONOMIC AFFAIRS

In 2011, according to the Eastern Caribbean Central Bank (ECCB), Montserrat's gross domestic product (GDP) at market prices was a preliminary EC $157.41m., equivalent to approximately EC $31,981 per head. In 2002–11 real GDP increased by an annual average of 1.7%; GDP decreased by 3.8% in 2010, but increased by 1.8% in 2011.

Agriculture (including forestry and fishing) contributed 1.2% of GDP in 2011, and engaged 6.6% of the employed labour force in 1992. The sector was almost destroyed by the volcanic eruptions of 1997, which caused an 81.3% decline in agricultural production, and a return to subsistence farming. The sector's GDP fluctuated thereafter. Prior to the volcanic eruption the principal crops grown were white potatoes, onions, rice and sea island cotton. Cattle, goats, sheep and poultry were also farmed. Montserrat's fisheries are underexploited, owing to the absence of a sheltered harbour. During 2002–11 agricultural GDP, according to the ECCB, decreased, in real terms, at an average annual rate of 0.8%; the sector declined by 19.3% in 2010, but grew by 30.7% in 2011.

Industry (including mining, manufacturing, construction and public utilities) contributed 13.0% of GDP in 2011, and engaged some 30.9% of the employed labour force in 1987. Mining and quarrying contributed 0.8% of GDP in 2011. Manufacturing contributed 0.9% of GDP in 2011 and engaged 5.6% of the employed labour force (together with mining) in 1992. Light industries comprise the processing of agricultural produce (also cotton and tropical fruits), as well as spring water bottling and the manufacture of garments and plastic bags. In 2006 the Government signed a 25-year contract with a British plastics recycling company to supply volcanic ash, to be used in the blending of recycled plastics. The industrial sector declined by an average of 3.2% annually in 2002–11; sectoral GDP declined by 12.3% in 2010, but increased by 8.9% in 2011

Construction contributed 8.2% of GDP in 2011 and employed 17.5% of the working population in 1988. The sector enjoyed growth in the mid-1990s, owing to reconstruction programmes following the volcanic eruptions, but in 2002–11, according to the ECCB, declined at an average annual rate of 6.4%; the sector declined by 12.6% in 2010, but grew by 6.2% in 2011. Energy requirements are dependent upon the import of mineral fuels (26.8% of total imports in 2009).

Services contributed a preliminary 85.8% of GDP in 2011. The tourism sector, which in 2011 contributed an estimated EC $14.0m. in receipts, remains important to the island, and it is hoped to establish Montserrat as a centre for environmental tourism, with the volcano itself as the premier attraction. The GDP of the hotel and restaurant sector increased by an annual average of 0.7% between 2002–11. The sector grew by 4.1% in 2010, but declined by 8.3% in 2011. The real GDP of the services sector increased by an annual average of 2.7% during 2002–11; the sector declined by 2.3% in 2010, but grew by 0.8% in 2011.

In 2011 Montserrat recorded an estimated trade deficit of EC $73.6m. Earnings from the services sector, mainly tourism receipts and net transfers (in particular, the remittances from Montserratians abroad and the income of foreign retired people), generally offset persistent trade deficits. There was an estimated deficit on the current account of the balance of payments of EC $28.1m. in 2011. The principal trading partner is the USA (providing 68.5% of imports and receiving 12.2% of exports in 2009). Other trading partners of importance include Anguilla, Trinidad and Tobago, Saint Christopher and Nevis, the United Kingdom, and Antigua and Barbuda. Export receipts increased to some US $3.1m. by 2009. In addition to mineral fuels, the other principal imports were vehicles and nuclear reactors, boilers and machinery.

In 2011 there was a budgetary surplus of EC $20.7m (including grants of $100.5m.). The capital budget is funded almost entirely by overseas aid, notably from the United Kingdom and Canada. Financial assistance from the United Kingdom for 2011–12 was put at £24.6m. Montserrat's total external public debt was estimated at EC $4.7m. at the end of 2011, according to figures from the ECCB. Consumer prices increased by 4.4% in 2011. The Caribbean Development Bank (see p. 236) estimated the unemployment rate to stand at some 13% of the labour force in 2001.

The eruption of the Soufrière Hills volcano in 1997 destroyed much of Montserrat's infrastructure and devastated the island's agricultural heartland; the implications for the vital tourism industry were severe. Montserrat's inclusion, in April 2009, on the Organisation for Economic Co-operation and Development's (see p. 388) 'grey list' of territories that had yet substantially to implement moves towards transparency in the financial sector hindered efforts to re-establish the island as a centre for international financial services. (Montserrat was removed from the list in 2011 after signing tax information-sharing agreements with 12 other jurisdictions and in May 2013 the British Government announced that agreement had been reached on new banking transparency laws for the territory as part of efforts to combat international tax evasion.) While most of the Caribbean region struggled with recession in 2009, in Montserrat real GDP continued to rise. However, owing to the weak performance of the construction sector, which in turn negatively affected the sand-mining industry, the economy contracted by 3.8% in 2010. With the island suffering from drought during that year, agricultural activity was also subdued, although the tourism industry showed signs of recovery. During 2011, with the notable exception of tourism, there was a revival in most sectors of the economy, including construction, mining, agriculture and financial services. The ECCB put GDP growth at 1.8% in that year. The Government reported robust growth in the tourism, financial, agricultural and construction industries in 2012 and projected that the economy would expand by 1.6% in that year. It was hoped that exploratory drilling for geothermal energy, which was being conducted in 2013, would yield positive results. The United Kingdom had provided £8.6m. for the project, which was being undertaken by an Icelandic company. Prospects for continued economic recovery would be boosted by discovery of geothermal potential, as well as on improvements to sea and air links, an increase in tourist numbers and reform of the tax collection regime.

PUBLIC HOLIDAYS

2014: 1 January (New Year's Day), 17 March (St Patrick's Day), 18 April (Good Friday), 21 April (Easter Monday), 5 May (Labour Day), 9 June (Whit Monday), 14 June (Queen's Official Birthday), 4 August (August Monday), 23 November (Liberation Day), 25–26 December (Christmas), 31 December (Festival Day).

Statistical Survey

Sources (unless otherwise stated): Government Information Service, Media Centre, Chief Minister's Office, Old Towne; tel. 491-2702; fax 491-2711; Eastern Caribbean Central Bank, POB 89, Basseterre, Saint Christopher; internet www.eccb-centralbank.org; OECS Economic Affairs Secretariat, *Statistical Digest*.

AREA AND POPULATION

Area: 102 sq km (39.5 sq miles).

Population: 4,491 at census of 12 May 2001; 4,922 (males 2,546, females 2,376) at census of 12 May 2011.

Population by Age and Sex (at 2011 census): *0–14:* 971 (males 490, females 481); *15–64:* 3,260 (males 1,709, females 1,551); *65 and over:* 691 (males 347, females 344); *Total* 4,922 (males 2,546, females 2,376).

Density (at 2011 census): 48.3 per sq km.

Principal Towns: Plymouth, the former capital, was abandoned in 1997. Brades is the interim capital.

Births and Deaths (1999): 45 live births (birth rate 9.4 per 1,000); 59 deaths (death rate 12.4 per 1,000) (Source: UN, *Population and Vital Statistics Report*). *2003:* Crude birth rate 9.6 per 1,000; Crude death rate 12.3 per 1,000 (Source: Caribbean Development Bank, *Social and Economic Indicators*). *2011:* Crude birth rate 11.7 per 1,000; Crude death rate 7.2 per 1,000 (Source: Pan American Health Organization).

Life Expectancy (years at birth, estimates): 73.2 (males 75.0; females 71.2) in 2011. Source: Pan American Health Organization.

Employment (1992): Agriculture, forestry and fishing 298; Mining and manufacturing 254; Electricity, gas and water 68; Wholesale and retail trade 1,666; Restaurants and hotels 234; Transport and communication 417; Finance, insurance and business services 242; Public defence 390; Other community, social and personal services 952; *Total* 4,521 (Source: *The Commonwealth Yearbook*). *1998* (estimate): Total labour force 1,500.

HEALTH AND WELFARE

Physicians (per 1,000 head, 1999): 0.18.

Hospital Beds (per 1,000 head, 2010): 5.9.

Health Expenditure (public, % of GDP, 2007): 9.0.

Health Expenditure (public, % of total, 1995): 67.0.

Source: Pan American Health Organization.

For sources and definitions, see explanatory note on p. vi.

AGRICULTURE, ETC.

Principal Crops (metric tons, 2011, FAO estimates): Vegetables 766 (incl. melons); Fruit (excl. melons) 957.

Livestock ('000 head, 2011, FAO estimates): Cattle 9.8; Sheep 4.8; Goats 7.1; Pigs 1.2.

Livestock Products ('000 metric tons, 2011, FAO estimates): Cattle meat 0.7; Cows' milk 1.9.

Fishing (metric tons, live weight, 2010, FAO estimate): Total catch 24 (all marine fishes).

Source: FAO.

INDUSTRY

Electric Energy (million kWh): 11.6 in 2007; 11.7 in 2008; 11.8 in 2009.

FINANCE

Currency and Exchange Rates: 100 cents = 1 East Caribbean dollar (EC $). *Sterling, US Dollar and Euro Equivalents* (31 December 2012): £1 sterling = EC $4.261; US $1 = EC $2.700; €1 = EC $3.562; EC $100 = £23.47 = US $37.04 = €28.07. *Exchange Rate:* Fixed at US $1 = EC $2.70 since July 1976.

Budget (EC $ million, 2011): *Revenue:* Revenue from taxation 36.6 (Taxes on income and profits 18.1, Taxes on property 0.8, Taxes on domestic goods and services 3.2, Taxes on international trade and transactions 14.5); Non-tax revenue 4.6; Total 41.2 (excl. grants 100.5). *Expenditure:* Current expenditure 93.2 (Personal emoluments 42.7, Goods and services 19.8, Transfers and subsidies 30.6); Capital expenditure 27.8; Total 121.0.

International Reserves (US $ million at 31 December 2011): Foreign exchange 24.81. Source: IMF, *International Financial Statistics*.

Money Supply (EC $ million at 31 December 2011): Currency outside depository corporations 21.63; Transferable deposits 33.60; Other deposits 156.17; *Broad money* 211.40. Source: IMF, *International Financial Statistics*.

Cost of Living (Consumer Price Index at December; base: April 1984 = 100): All items 242.4 in 2009; 248.6 in 2010; 259.6 in 2011.

Gross Domestic Product (EC $ million at constant 2006 prices): 152.99 in 2009; 147.11 in 2010; 149.70 in 2011.

Expenditure on the Gross Domestic Product (EC $ million at current prices, 2010, preliminary): Government final consumption expenditure 74.24; Private final consumption expenditure 124.43; Gross fixed capital formation 40.00; *Total domestic expenditure* 238.67; Export of goods and services 33.05; *Less* Imports of goods and services 115.91; *GDP at market prices* 155.81.

Gross Domestic Product by Economic Activity (EC $ million at current prices, 2011): Agriculture, forestry and fishing 1.71; Mining and quarrying 1.20; Manufacturing 1.28; Electricity and water 4.60; Construction 11.81; Wholesale and retail trade 7.97; Restaurants and hotels 2.32; Transport 5.06; Communications 6.54; Banks and insurance 14.72; Real estate and housing 20.02; Government services 48.35; Other services 19.19; *Sub-total* 144.76; *Less* Financial intermediation services indirectly measured 2.13; *Gross value added at basic prices* 142.64; Taxes, less subsidies, on products 14.78; *GDP at market prices* 157.41.

Balance of Payments (EC $ million, 2011): Goods (net) –73.58; Services (net) –16.13; *Balance on goods and services* –89.72; Income (net) –9.58 *Balance on goods, services and income* –99.29; Current transfers (net) 71.18; *Current balance* –28.12; Capital account (net) 19.07; Direct investment (net) 6.65; Portfolio investment (net) 0.50; Public sector long-term investment –0.50; Commercial banks –23.57; Other investment assets 40.35; Other investment liabilities 2.14; Net errors and omissions 5.07; *Overall balance* 21.59.

EXTERNAL TRADE

Principal Commodities (US $ '000, 2009): *Imports c.i.f.:* Meat and edible meat offal 914; Beverages, spirits and vinegar 1,285; Mineral fuels, oils, distillation products, etc. 7,943 (Petroleum oils, not crude 7,444); Nuclear reactors, boilers, machinery, etc. 2,067; Electrical, electronic equipment 1,295; Vehicles other than railway, tramway 2,432 (Cars, incl. station wagon 1,445); Total (incl. others) 29,605. *Exports f.o.b.:* Salt, sulphur, earth, stone, plaster, lime and cement 1,404; Nuclear reactors, boilers, machinery, etc. 957; Electrical, electronic equipment 189; Optical, photo, technical, and medical apparatus 299; Total (incl. others) 3,148.

Principal Trading Partners (US $ '000, 2009): *Imports c.i.f.:* Barbados 128; Canada 415; China, People's Repub. 237; Dominican Republic 237; Jamaica 654; Japan 1,520; Netherlands 309; St Vincent and the Grenadines 295; Trinidad and Tobago 1,803; United Kingdom 1,666; USA 20,272; Total (incl. others) 29,605. *Exports f.o.b.:* Anguilla 480; Antigua and Barbuda 77; British Virgin Islands 208; Dominica 381; France (incl. Monaco) 133; Netherlands Antilles 211; New Zealand 247; St Christopher and Nevis 366; Trinidad and Tobago 481; United Kingdom 153; USA 384; Total (incl. others) 3,148.

Source: UN, *International Trade Statistics Yearbook*.

TOURISM

Tourist Arrivals (2011): Stay-over arrivals 5,395 (USA 1,526, Canada 320, United Kingdom 1,329, Caribbean 1,881, Others 339); Excursionists 1,997; Total visitor arrivals (incl. others) 10,472.

Tourism Receipts (EC $ million): 16.4 in 2009, 15.9 in 2010; 14.0 in 2011.

TRANSPORT

Road Traffic (vehicles in use, 1990): Passenger cars 1,823; Goods vehicles 54; Public service vehicles 4; Motorcycles 21; Miscellaneous 806.

Shipping: ('000 metric tons, 1990): *International Freight Traffic:* Goods loaded 6; Goods unloaded 49. Source: UN, *Monthly Bulletin of Statistics*.

Civil Aviation (1985): Aircraft arrivals 4,422; passengers 25,380; air cargo 132.4 metric tons.

COMMUNICATIONS MEDIA

Telephones (2011): 2,600 main lines in use.

Mobile Cellular Telephones (2011): 4,200 subscribers.

Broadband Subscribers: 300 in 2011.

Source: International Telecommunication Union.

EDUCATION

Pre-primary: 11 schools (1999); 14 teachers (2008/09); 128 pupils (2008/09).

Primary: 2 schools (1999); 37 teachers (2008/09); 485 pupils (2008/09).

Secondary: 1 school (1999); 27 teachers (2008/09); 358 pupils (2008/09).

Pupil-teacher Ratio (primary education, UNESCO estimate): 13.1 in 2008/09.

Sources: UNESCO, *Statistical Yearbook*; UNESCO Institute for Statistics.

Directory

The Government

HEAD OF STATE

Queen: HM Queen ELIZABETH II.

Governor: ADRIAN DEREK DAVIS (took office 8 April 2011).

Deputy Governor: ALRIC TAYLOR.

EXECUTIVE CABINET
(May 2013)

The Government is formed by the Movement for Change and Prosperity.

President: ADRIAN DEREK DAVIS (The Governor).

Attorney-General: ESCO HENRY.

Financial Secretary: JOHN SKERRITT.

Premier and Minister of Finance and Economic Management with responsibility for Local Government, Immigration, Information Communication, Regional and International Affairs, and Tourism: REUBEN T. MEADE.

Minister of Agriculture, Lands, Housing, the Environment, Consumer Affairs and Ecclesiastical Affairs: EASTON TAYLOR-FARRELL.

Minister of Communication, Works and Labour: CHARLES KIRNON.

Minister of Education, Health, Community Services, Youth Affairs, Sports and Culture: COLLIN RILEY.

Permanent Secretary to the Office of the Premier: BEVERLEY MENDES.

Cabinet Secretary: ANGELA GREENAWAY.

Clerk to the Executive Cabinet: JUDITH JEFFERS.

MINISTRIES

Office of the Governor: Unit 8, Farara Plaza, Brades; tel. 491-2688; fax 491-8867; e-mail govoffice.montserrat@fco.gov.uk; internet ukinmontserrat.fco.gov.uk.

Office of the Deputy Governor: No. 3, Farara Plaza, Brades; tel. 491-6524; fax 491-9751; e-mail odg@gov.ms; internet odg.gov.ms.

Office of the Attorney-General: POB 129, Valley View; tel. 491-4686; fax 491-4687; e-mail legal@gov.ms; internet agc.gov.ms.

Office of the Premier: Govt HQ, POB 292, Brades; tel. 491-3378; fax 491-6780; e-mail ocm@gov.ms; internet ocm.gov.ms.

Ministry of Agriculture, Lands, Housing and the Environment: Govt HQ, POB 272, Brades; tel. 491-2546; fax 491-9275; e-mail malhe@gov.ms; internet www.malhe.gov.ms.

Ministry of Communications and Works: Woodlands; tel. 491-2521; fax 491-3475; e-mail comworks@gov.ms.

Ministry of Education: Govt HQ, POB 103, Brades; tel. 491-2541; fax 491-6941; e-mail deped@gov.ms.

Ministry of Finance and Economic Management: Govt HQ, POB 292, Brades; tel. 491-2777; fax 491-2367; e-mail minfin@gov.ms; internet www.finance.gov.ms.

Ministry of Health and Community Services: Govt HQ, POB 24, Brades; tel. 491-2880; fax 491-3131; e-mail mehcs@gov.ms; internet moh.gov.ms.

LEGISLATIVE ASSEMBLY

Speaker: TERESINA BODKIN.

Clerk: JUDITH BAKERS.

Election, 8 September 2009

Party	Seats
Movement for Change and Prosperity (MCAP) . . .	6
Independent	3
Total	9

There are also two ex officio members (the Attorney-General and the Financial Secretary).

Political Organizations

Montserrat Democratic Party (MDP): c/o Kelsick & Kelsick, Woodlands Main Rd, POB 185, Brades; tel. 491-2379; e-mail lowell@mdp.ms; internet www.mdp.ms; f. 2006; Leader Dr LOWELL LEWIS.

Montserrat Labour Party (MLP): Brades; f. 2009 by fmr mems of the NPLM (q.v.); Leaders MARGARET DYER-HOWE, IDABELLE MEADE.

Montserrat Reformation Party (MRP): Brades; f. 2009; Leaders ADELINA TUITT, ALRIC TAYLOR.

Movement for Change and Prosperity (MCAP): POB 419, Brades; e-mail mail@mcap.ms; internet www.mcap.ms; f. 2005 by fmr mems of the National Progressive Party (NPP); Leader REUBEN T. MEADE; Chair. RANDOLPH RILEY.

New People's Liberation Movement (NPLM): f. 1997 as successor party to People's Progressive Alliance and the Movement for National Reconstruction (MNR); opposition party; Leader DAVID OSBORNE.

Judicial System

Justice is administered by the Eastern Caribbean Supreme Court (based in Saint Lucia—comprised of the Court of Appeal and the High Court), the Court of Summary Jurisdiction and the Magistrate's Court. A revised edition of the Laws of Montserrat came into force in 2005.

Registrar: AMILA DALEY.

Magistrate's Office: Govt HQ, Brades; tel. 491-4056; fax 491-8866; e-mail magoff@gov.ms; Magistrate CLIFTON WARNER.

Religion

CHRISTIANITY

The Montserrat Christian Council: St Peter's, POB 227; tel. 491-4864; fax 491-2139; Chair. Rev. B. RUTH ALLEN.

The Anglican Communion

Anglicans are adherents of the Church in the Province of the West Indies, comprising eight dioceses. Montserrat forms part of the diocese of the North Eastern Caribbean and Aruba. The Bishop is resident in The Valley, Anguilla.

The Roman Catholic Church

Montserrat forms part of the diocese of St John's-Basseterre, suffragan to the archdiocese of Castries (Saint Lucia). The Bishop is resident in St John's, Antigua and Barbuda.

Other Christian Churches

There are Baptist, Methodist, Pentecostal and Seventh-day Adventist churches and other places of worship on the island.

The Press

Montserrat Newsletter: Farara Plaza, Unit 8, Brades; tel. 491-2688; fax 491-8867; e-mail richard.aspin@fco.gov.uk; internet www.ukinmontserrat.fco.gov.uk; f. 1998; 4 a year; govt information publ; Publicity Officer RICHARD ASPIN.

The Montserrat Reporter: POB 306, Davy Hill; tel. 491-4715; fax 491-2430; e-mail editor@themontserratreporter.com; internet www.themontserratreporter.com; f. 1984; weekly on Fri.; Editor BENNETTE ROACH; circ. 2,000.

Broadcasting and Communications

TELECOMMUNICATIONS

LIME: POB 219, Sweeney's; internet www.time4lime.com/ms; fmrly known as Cable & Wireless (West Indies) Ltd; CEO TONY RICE; Regional CEO GERARD BORELY.

BROADCASTING

Radio

Radio Antilles: POB 35/930, Plymouth; tel. 491-2755; fax 491-2724; f. 1963; in 1989 the Govt of Montserrat, on behalf of the Org. of Eastern Caribbean States, acquired the station; has one of the most powerful transmitters in the region; commercial; regional; broadcasts in English and French; Chair. Dr H. FELLHAUER; Man. Dir KRISTIAN KNAACK; Gen. Man. KEITH GREAVES.

Radio Montserrat (ZJB): POB 51, Sweeney's; tel. 491-2885; fax 491-9250; e-mail zjb@gov.ms; internet www.zjb.gov.ms; f. 1952; first broadcast 1957; govt station; CEO LOWELL MASON.

Television

Television services can also be obtained from Saint Christopher and Nevis, Puerto Rico and from Antigua and Barbuda.

Cable Television of Montserrat Ltd: POB 447, Olveston; tel. 491-2507; fax 491-3081; Man. SYLVIA WHITE.

People's Television (PTV): Manjack; tel. 491-5110; e-mail deedge@candw.ms; internet www.ptvmontserrat.com; Man. DENZIL EDGECOMBE.

Finance

The Eastern Caribbean Central Bank, based in Saint Christopher and Nevis, is the central issuing and monetary authority for Montserrat.

Eastern Caribbean Central Bank—Montserrat Office: 2 Farara Plaza, POB 484, Brades; tel. 491-6877; fax 491-6878; e-mail eccbmni@candw.ms; internet www.eccb-centralbank.org; Resident Rep. CLAUDETTE WEEKES.

Financial Services Commission: Phoenix House, POB 188, Brades; tel. 491-6887; fax 491-9888; e-mail fscmrat@candw.ms; internet www.fscmontserrat.org; f. 2001; the Commission consists of the Commissioner and 4 other mems appointed by the Governor; Head DULCIE JAMES.

BANKING

Bank of Montserrat Ltd: POB 10, Brades; tel. 491-3843; fax 491-3163; e-mail bom@candw.ms; internet www.bankofmontserrat.ms; Gen. Man. MICHAEL JOSEPH.

Montserrat Building Society: POB 101, Brades Main Rd, Brades; tel. 491-2391; fax 491-6127; e-mail mbsl@candw.ms.

St Patrick's Co-operative Credit Union Ltd: Credit Union House, POB 337, Brades; tel. 491-3666; fax 491-6566; internet www.stpatrickscreditunion.cbt.cc/index.html; Accounting Man. KAREN WEST.

STOCK EXCHANGE

Eastern Caribbean Securities Exchange: based in Bird Rock, Basseterre, Saint Christopher and Nevis; tel. (869) 466-7192; fax (869) 465-3798; e-mail info@ecseonline.com; internet www.ecseonline.com; f. 2001; regional securities market designed to facilitate the buying and selling of financial products for the 8 mem. territories—Anguilla, Antigua and Barbuda, Dominica, Grenada, Montserrat, Saint Christopher and Nevis, Saint Lucia and Saint Vincent and the Grenadines; Chair. Sir K. DWIGHT VENNER; Gen. Man. TREVOR E. BLAKE.

INSURANCE

Insurance Services (Montserrat) Ltd: POB 185, Brades; tel. 491-2103; fax 491-9704; e-mail ismcall@candw.ag; Gen. Man. STEPHEN FRANCOIS.

NAGICO: Ryan Investments, POB 496, Brades; tel. 491-3403; fax 491-7307; e-mail info@ryaninvestments.ms; internet www.nagico.com.

N. E. M. (West Indies) Insurance Ltd (NEMWIL): POB 287, Brades; tel. 491-3813; fax 491-3815; acquired by Guardian Holdings Ld in 2001.

United Insurance Co Ltd: Jacquie Ryan Enterprises Ltd, POB 425, Brades; tel. 491-2055; fax 491-3257; e-mail united@candw.ms; internet unitedinsure.com; CEO JACQUIE RYAN.

Trade and Industry

GOVERNMENT AGENCIES

Montserrat Development Corporation (MDC): Brades; internet www.mdc.ms; f. 2007; overseeing plans for new capital in Little Bay; promotes private sector investment and economic growth; Chair. JOHN RYAN; CEO COLIN HEARTWELL.

Montserrat Economic Development Unit: Govt HQ, POB 292, Brades; tel. 491-2066; fax 491-4632; e-mail devunit@gov.ms; internet www.devunit.gov.ms.

CHAMBER OF COMMERCE

Montserrat Chamber of Commerce and Industry (MCCI): Ryan's Court, POB 384, Olveston; tel. 491-3640; fax 491-6602; e-mail chamber@candw.ms; refounded 1971; 31 company mems, 26 individual mems; Pres. FLORENCE GRIFFITH JOSEPH; Vice-Pres. GRACELYN CASSELL.

UTILITIES

Electricity and Water

Montserrat Utilities Ltd (MUL): POB 324, Davy Hill; tel. 491-2538; fax 491-4904; e-mail mul@mul.ms; internet www.mul.ms; f. 2008 by merger of Montserrat Electricity Services Ltd and Montserrat Water Authority; domestic electricity generation and supply; domestic water supply; Man. Dir PETER WHITE; Man. of Water and Sewerage EMILE DUBERRY.

Gas

Grant Enterprises and Trading: POB 350, Brades; tel. 491-9654; fax 491-4854; e-mail granten@candw.ms; domestic gas supplies.

Transport

ROADS

Prior to the 1997 volcanic eruption Montserrat had an extensive and well-constructed road network. There were 203 km (126 miles) of good surfaced main roads, 24 km of secondary unsurfaced roads and 42 km of rough tracks. The 2007 budget allocated funds of over $5m. for continued road and infrastructure improvements, particularly in areas to become more densely populated through resettlement. In 2008 a $5.9m. road reinstatement project from Salem to St John funded by the British Department for International Development was begun and was expected to be completed by 2013.

SHIPPING

Following the destruction of the principal port at Plymouth in 1997, an emergency jetty was constructed at Little Bay in the north of the island. In 2010 the European Union-funded Little Bay Port Development Project was begun. The project was to be executed in two phases, at an estimated cost of US $40m., although it remained delayed in 2013. There is a daily ferry service to and from Antigua.

Port Authority of Montserrat: Little Bay, POB 383, Plymouth; tel. 491-2791; fax 491-8063; e-mail monpa@candw.ms; Man. SHAWN O'GARRO.

Montserrat Shipping Services: POB 46, Brades; tel. 491-3614; fax 491-3617; e-mail customerservice@monship.org.

CIVIL AVIATION

The main airport, Blackburne at Trants, 13 km (8 miles) from Plymouth, was destroyed by the volcanic activity of 1997. A helicopter port at Gerald's in the north of the island was completed in 2000. A new, temporary international airport at Gerald's, financed at a cost of EC $51.95m. by the European Union and the British Department for International Development, was completed in 2005. In the longer term, the Government intended to construct a permanent international airport at Thatch Valley. Montserrat is linked to Antigua by a helicopter service, which operates three times a day. The island is also a shareholder in the regional airline, LIAT (based in Antigua and Barbuda). In 2008 LIAT and Carib Aviation (also based in Antigua and Barbuda) entered into an agreement to operate scheduled flights into and out of the airport at Gerald's, renamed the John A. Osborne Airport, in the same year.

Montserrat Airways Ltd: John A. Osborne Airport, POB 225, Gerald's; tel. 491-3434; e-mail info@flymontserrat.com; internet www.flymontserrat.com; charter services; subsidiary of Love Air, United Kingdom; Chair. Capt. NIGEL HARRIS.

> **FlyMontserrat:** John A. Osborne Airport, POB 225, Gerald's; tel. 491-3434; e-mail info@flymontserrat.com; internet www.flymontserrat.com; f. 2009; flights between Montserrat, Antigua and St Christopher and Nevis; Chair. Capt. NIGEL HARRIS.

Tourism

Since the 1997 volcanic activity, Montserrat has been marketed as an eco-tourism destination. Known as the Emerald Isle of the Caribbean, Montserrat is noted for its Irish connections, and for its range of flora and fauna. In 2011 there were 5,395 stop-over tourist arrivals, 34% of whom were from Caribbean countries, 28% from the USA and 25% from the United Kingdom. In addition, there were 1,997 excursionists. A large proportion of visitors are estimated to be Montserrat nationals residing overseas. Tourism earnings totalled an estimated EC $14m. in 2011.

Montserrat Tourist Board: Bldgs B and C, 7 Farara Plaza, POB 7, Brades; tel. 491-2230; fax 491-7430; e-mail info@montserrattourism.ms; internet www.visitmontserrat.com; f. 1993; Chair. ELIJAH SILCOTT; Dir ERNESTINE CASSELL.

Defence

The United Kingdom is responsible for the defence of Montserrat.

Education

Education, beginning at five years of age, is compulsory up to the age of 14. Secondary education begins at 12 years of age, and comprises a first cycle of five years and a second, two-year cycle. In 2008 enrolment in primary education included an estimated 92% of children in the relevant age-group, while enrolment in secondary education was an estimated 96% in 2007. Enrolment in tertiary education in the year 2008 was equivalent to 17%. In 2011 there were four primary schools, including two government schools and one government secondary school. In 1999 there were 11 nursery schools, sponsored by a government-financed organization, and a Technical College, which provided vocational and technical training for school-leavers. There was also an extra-mural department of the University of the West Indies in Plymouth. Construction of the Montserrat Community College was completed in 2003. Three 'off-shore' medical schools were licensed in 2003. The Ministry of Education was allocated a total of EC $8.9m. in the 2013 budget.

THE PITCAIRN ISLANDS

Introductory Survey

LOCATION, CLIMATE, LANGUAGE, RELIGION, CAPITAL

The Pitcairn Islands consist of Pitcairn Island and three uninhabited islands, Henderson, Ducie and Oeno. Pitcairn, situated in the Pacific Ocean about midway between Panama and New Zealand, has an area of less than 4.5 sq km (1.75 sq miles) and had a population of 48 permanent residents at the end of 2012. Mean monthly temperatures range from 19°C (66°F) in August to 24°C (75°F) in February, and average annual rainfall is 2,000 mm. The official language is English, but most of the islanders use Pitcairnese or Pitkern, a dialect based on 18th-century seafarers' English and Tahitian. The islanders are adherents of the Seventh-day Adventist Church. The chief settlement is Adamstown on Pitcairn Island.

CONTEMPORARY POLITICAL HISTORY

Discovered in 1767 and first settled by mutineers of *HMS Bounty* in 1790, Pitcairn officially became a British settlement in 1887. In 1893 a parliamentary form of government was adopted, and in 1898 responsibility for administration was assumed by the High Commissioner for the Western Pacific. Pitcairn came under the jurisdiction of the Governor of Fiji in 1952. In 1970 Pitcairn was placed within the remit of the British High Commissioner in New Zealand acting as Governor, in consultation with an Island Council. The 10-member Island Council is presided over by the Island Mayor (elected triennially by popular vote) and includes two other ex officio members (the Island Secretary, who is appointed by the Governor for an indefinite term, and the Chairman of the Island Council, who is directly elected), four members elected by popular vote, one co-opted by the Chairman, one appointed by the Governor and the 10th seat is held by the non-resident Commissioner (appointed by the Governor), who liaises between the Council and the Governor. Aside from the Island Mayor and the Island Secretary, the members of the Island Council serve two-year terms. The Island Magistrate, who presides over the Island Court, is appointed by the Governor for a three-year term. The British Overseas Territories Act, which took effect in May 2002, granted citizenship rights in the United Kingdom to residents of the Overseas Territories, including Pitcairn. The legislation also entitled Pitcairn Islanders to hold British passports and to work in the United Kingdom and elsewhere in the European Union.

In 1987 the British High Commissioner in Fiji, acting on behalf of Pitcairn, the United Kingdom's last remaining dependency in the South Pacific, joined representatives of the USA, France, New Zealand and six South Pacific island states in signing the South Pacific Regional Environment Protection Convention, the main objective of which was to prevent the dumping of nuclear waste in the region.

In early 2000 British detectives began an investigation into an alleged rape case on the island. The British team was joined by the New Zealand police force in early 2001, when the case was widened to include 15 alleged sexual assaults, amid reports claiming that sexual abuse, particularly of children, was commonplace on the island. In November 2000 Crown Solicitor Simon Moore, based in Auckland, New Zealand, was appointed as Pitcairn's first Public Prosecutor, with the task of deciding whether to bring charges against 20 Pitcairn Islanders. His decision was delayed by the fact that many of the complainants now lived in New Zealand and by the logistical problems of a trial that could potentially involve the entire populace. However, in April 2003 nine men on the island were charged with a total of 64 offences. Many islanders expressed serious concern that their community would not be able to function if the men (who constituted virtually the entire male work-force) were extradited to New Zealand to stand trial. In early June a further four men, who had all become resident in New Zealand, were charged with a total of 32 offences, including 10 charges of rape, which were alleged to have taken place on Pitcairn between five and 40 years previously. In April 2004 the Supreme Court of Pitcairn (sitting for only the second time in its history, at a special session in Auckland) rejected the application by the accused men resident on the island to be tried on Pitcairn. However, in June Pitcairn's Court of Appeal (sitting for the first time in its history) overruled this decision and stated that, despite the logistical problems involved, the trial would be conducted on Pitcairn. Meanwhile, lawyers for the accused men argued that the trial should be abandoned as the islanders were all descendants of the *Bounty* mutineers, who had renounced all allegiance to the British Crown. Their claims that Pitcairn Islanders were not subject to British jurisdiction appeared to be supported by historical documents discovered in London. Moreover, a group of women from Pitcairn issued a public statement claiming that sexual relations between men and girls below the British legal age of consent were commonplace on the island, and not considered to be a criminal offence by either party or by the community as a whole. Nevertheless, the trial of seven of the defendants began in September. Some 25 lawyers, police officers and journalists travelled to Pitcairn, and witnesses in New Zealand gave evidence via live satellite video link. In October six of the seven defendants were found guilty of many of the 51 charges against them, and one was acquitted. Among those convicted was the Mayor of Pitcairn, Steve Christian, who was found guilty of five counts of rape. (A separate trial for six Pitcairn Islanders resident abroad charged with 41 offences was held in Auckland in 2005.)

The convicted men on Pitcairn, four of whom were given prison sentences of between two and six years while two received non-custodial sentences, began a legal challenge against their convictions in February 2005. Their defence was based on the previous claim that Pitcairn Islanders were not subject to British jurisdiction. Their appeal was rejected by the Pitcairn Supreme Court, sitting in Auckland. In October 2006 the United Kingdom's highest court, the Privy Council, rejected a further appeal, declaring that Pitcairn had been ruled by the Crown as a British possession for more than 100 years, and was thus unable to reject a law affirming it as such. Furthermore, the judges decided that there was absolutely no doubt that the laws on sexual offences applied to the six men. The convicted men subsequently assisted in the construction of a new prison. Seven New Zealand prison officers were dispatched to staff the new facility.

Meanwhile, following some structural changes in the local government of Pitcairn, in December 1999 the position of Mayor, who was to preside over the Island Council, was created. The role had been fulfilled hitherto by the Island Magistrate, a post held by Jay Warren since 1991. The islands' first Mayor, Steve Christian, was dismissed in October 2004, following his conviction on charges of rape (see above). In December Jay Warren, the only defendant to be acquitted in the recent trials, was elected as the island's Mayor for a three-year term. In April 2006 George Fergusson, the newly appointed British High Commissioner to New Zealand, replaced Richard Fell as Governor of Pitcairn, Henderson, Ducie and Oeno Islands. Michael Warren was elected Mayor in December 2007, defeating the incumbent Jay Warren and one other candidate.

In April 2009, after the majority of islanders voted in favour of the proposal, the Governor signed a law to remove the ban on the consumption of alcohol, subject to various caveats. The prohibition had remained in force since the 1830s.

Consultations on amendments to the Constitution, which were explicitly to state Pitcairn Islanders' rights and responsibilities, commenced in 2009. Emphasis was to be placed on partnership values as the basis of Pitcairn's relationship with the United Kingdom. Advice on human rights and other constitutional matters was provided by the Commonwealth Foundation, and islanders' comments on the proposed revisions were to be submitted to the Governor by the end of October. Video-conference facilities were used during the consultation process, enabling the islanders to discuss the proceedings with officials in the United Kingdom and New Zealand. The constitutional amendments were enacted in February 2010. New provisions included the formal incorporation of the Island Council into the Constitution; a requirement that the Island Council be consulted by the Governor with regard to all draft legislation; the holding of elections to the Island Council every two years rather than every year; the creation of the role of Ombudsman, who was to be responsible for investigating any complaints of government maladministration; the permanent establishment of a Supreme Court; and the appointment of an independent Attorney-General. In March, at a ceremony in Adamstown attended by the Governor, the new Constitution was duly proclaimed. Victoria Treadell, the incoming British High Commissioner to New Zealand, was inaugurated as the new Governor of Pitcairn in June, replacing George Fergusson.

Michael Warren was re-elected as the island's Mayor in December 2010. In the same month, however, he was charged with possession of child pornography, although he refuted the allegations against him. At a hearing held at New Zealand's Papakura District Court in December 2011, at which Warren appeared via satellite video link, the Mayor's lawyers challenged the jurisdiction of New Zealand's courts to hear cases pertaining to Pitcairn, arguing that his case should be dealt with in Pitcairn. (Under the island's laws, the maximum penalty for which Warren could be liable was 100 days' imprisonment.) In October 2012 the Pitcairn Supreme Court rejected the constitutional challenges presented by Warren's defence (including his objection to the decision to hold his trial in New Zealand) and remanded the Mayor on bail to stand trial in a session of the Pitcairn Supreme Court in Auckland in the following year. Warren's subsequent appeal against this ruling was turned down by the Pitcairn Court of Appeal in March 2013.

ECONOMIC AFFAIRS

The economy has traditionally been based on fishing, handicrafts, horticulture and the sale of postage stamps. Attempts to increase revenue from the island's agricultural output by producing dried fruits (notably bananas, mangoes and pineapples) intensified from 1999. Diversification of this sector to include the production of jam, dried fish and coffee was subsequently under consideration. Pitcairn honey, which was pronounced to be 'exceptionally pure' by the New Zealand Ministry of Agriculture, began to be exported, largely through internet sales, in late 1999. The British Government subsequently provided funding for a bee-keeping expert to spend six months on Pitcairn and assist in the expansion of the honey industry. By 2010 the number of beehives had increased to 150, total output was estimated at around 1,000 jars annually, and the product was being supplied to New Zealand and exclusive food retailers in the United Kingdom.

A reafforestation scheme, begun in 1963, concentrated on the planting of miro trees, which provide a rosewood suitable for handicrafts. An exclusive economic zone (EEZ) extending 370 km (200 nautical miles) off shore was designated in 1980 and officially declared in 1992. In 1987 the Governor of the islands signed a one-year fishing agreement with Japan, whereby the Japan Tuna Fisheries Co-operative Association was granted a licence to operate vessels within Pitcairn's EEZ. The agreement was subsequently renewed, but lapsed in 1990.

In 1992 it was reported that significant mineral deposits, formed by underwater volcanoes, had been discovered within the islands' EEZ. The minerals, which were believed to include manganese, iron, copper, zinc, silver and gold, could (if exploited) dramatically affect the territory's economy.

Development projects have been focused on harbour improvements, power supplies, telecommunications and road-building. A new health clinic was established, with British finance, in 1996. Major improvements (financed by British and European Union aid) to the jetty and slipway at Bounty Bay and to the road between Bounty Bay and Adamstown (the Hill of Difficulty road), which leads to the landing area, were carried out in 2005.

In August 2004 the British Government announced the provision of US $6.5m. in emergency assistance for the territory in order to avert a financial crisis. In 2006 the British Government provided £1.9m. for a project to repair local infrastructure. Plans for infrastructural development included the building of a breakwater at Bounty Bay. It was hoped that the project, jointly funded by the British Government and the European Development Fund, would make the island more accessible to passenger and cargo ships. A project to instal wind power as an alternative energy source to the diesel-powered generators was initiated in 2007, with funding from the United Kingdom, but was abandoned in 2013 owing to organizational difficulties and financial mismanagement. Proposals to develop solar-powered energy on the island are currently under discussion.

Pitcairn's first radio-telephone link was established in 1985, and a new telecommunications unit was installed in 1992. It was hoped that Pitcairn might find an additional source of revenue through the sale of website addresses in early 2000 when the island won a legal victory to gain control of the internet domain name suffix '.pn'. In 2008 television services became available for the first time, and the telephone system was upgraded to give islanders constant internet access. In March of that year, however, an international software security company reported that in per caput terms Pitcairn had become one of the world's worst offenders with regard to the relaying of unsolicited e-mails.

New Zealand currency is used. There is no formal taxation (except for small licensing fees on guns and vehicles); instead, islanders between the ages of 16 and 65 years must, by law, carry out public work. Government revenue has been derived mainly from philatelic sales (one-half of current revenue in 1992/93), and from interest earned on investments. The island reported a deficit in the mid-2000s, as a result of which the British Government has since subsidized the island economy with assistance of £2m. annually. Projected British aid to Pitcairn for 2012/13 totalled some £2.9m. In 2004/05 revenue totalled US $746,000, while expenditure totalled US $1.0m. In 2012 exports from Pitcairn to New Zealand were worth $NZ149,252, while imports from that country cost $NZ709,575. Pitcairn's imports from the USA totalled US $40,527 in 2012, while exports to the USA were worth US $4,511.

Hopes have been expressed that the development of the tourism sector might provide some impetus to economic growth. In 2005 a museum was constructed on the island to house some of Pitcairn's historical artefacts, including the *Bounty* cannon, which was raised from Bounty Bay with assistance from an Australian team in 1999 and returned to the island in 2009. Since 2009 the Government has been operating the *MV Claymore II* as the island's only dedicated passenger/cargo vessel providing tourists with adventure tourism holidays to Pitcairn for three- or 10-day visits. Tourists stay with local families, and some families have invested in the construction of private self-contained units for tourists to rent. Other initiatives included the improvement of ship berthing facilities, and in August 2010 it was reported that Pitcairn had begun to derive much economic benefit from the increase in arrivals of cruise ships, bringing hundreds of tourists. In the early 2010s some 10–15 cruise ships visited Pitcairn every year, generating income for the local population from the sale of souvenirs, landing fees and the stamping of passports. It was hoped that this revitalization of the economy would encourage islanders resident overseas to return to Pitcairn. A steady decline in the population, owing mainly to emigration to New Zealand, has been a major problem. The islands' potential for eco-tourism, to include activities such as whale-watching, has also been identified as a possible source of revenue. In 1988, meanwhile, uninhabited Henderson Island, the largest of the island grouping and the world's only forested atoll with its ecology remaining virtually intact, was included on the UNESCO World Heritage List. The island, 168 km (104 miles) east-north-east of Pitcairn, was to be preserved as a bird sanctuary. There are five species of bird unique to the island: the flightless rail or Henderson chicken, the green Henderson fruit dove, the Henderson crake, the Henderson reed warbler and the Henderson lorikeet. However, concern was expressed in 1994 following claims by scientists studying the island that its unique flora and fauna were threatened by the accidental introduction of foreign plant species by visitors and by an increase in the rat population. In August 2010, with rats on Henderson Island estimated to number 30,000, UNESCO emphasized the need for urgent action to address the rodent issue and warned of the possibility of the removal of Henderson Island's World Heritage status. During the latter half of 2011 a delegation from the United Kingdom's Royal Society for the Protection of Birds implemented a rat eradication programme, partly funded by the British Government, on Henderson Island, amid reports that the growing rat population was killing thousands of newly hatched endangered birds each year. A monitoring expedition in mid-2012 confirmed that rats were still present on the island, albeit at greatly reduced levels. The fall in the number of the rats meant that there was a substantial rise in the reproduction rate of the island's native birds.

PUBLIC HOLIDAYS

2014: 1 January (New Year's Day), 23 January (Bounty Day), 18 April (Good Friday), 21 April (Easter Monday), 14 June (Queen's Birthday), 25 December (Christmas), 26 December (Boxing Day).

Statistical Survey

Source: Office of the Governor of Pitcairn, Henderson, Ducie and Oeno Islands, c/o British Consulate-General, Pitcairn Islands Administration, Private Box 105-696, Auckland, New Zealand; tel. (9) 366-0186; fax (9) 366-0187; e-mail pitcairn@iconz.co.nz.

AREA AND POPULATION

Area: 35.5 sq km (13.71 sq miles). *By Island*: Pitcairn 4.35 sq km; Henderson 30.0 sq km; Oeno is less than 1 sq km and Ducie is smaller.

Population: 66 at census of 31 December 1991. *31 December 2012* (annual census): 53. Note: Figure excludes 11 off-island residents.

Density (all residents, Pitcairn only, 31 December 2012): 14.7 per sq km.

Employment (able-bodied men, 2002): 9.

FINANCE

Currency and Exchange Rates: 100 cents = 1 Pitcairn dollar. The Pitcairn dollar is at par with the New Zealand dollar ($NZ). New Zealand currency is usually used.

Budget ($NZ, 1998/99): Revenue 492,000; Expenditure 667,000.

EXTERNAL TRADE

Trade with New Zealand ($NZ '000): *Imports:* 626.1 in 2010; 479.3 in 2011; 709.6 in 2012. *Exports:* 137.8 in 2010; 76.0 in 2011; 149.3 in 2012.

Trade with the USA (US $ '000): *Imports:* 3.7 in 2010; 15.7 in 2011; 40.5 in 2012. *Exports:* 4.1 in 2010; 2.8 in 2011; 4.5 in 2012.

TRANSPORT

Road Traffic (motor vehicles, 2002): Passenger vehicles 30 (two-wheeled 1, three-wheeled 6, four-wheeled 23); Tractors 3; Bulldozer 1; Digger 1.

Shipping: *Local Vessels* (communally owned open surf boats, 2000): 3. *International Shipping Arrivals* (visits by passing vessels, 1996): Ships 51; Yachts 30.

COMMUNICATIONS

Telephones (2002): a party-line service with 15 telephones in use; 2 public telephones; 2 digital telephones. Most homes also have VHF radio.

Directory

The Government

Governor of Pitcairn, Henderson, Ducie and Oeno Islands: VICTORIA TREADELL (British High Commissioner in New Zealand—took office May 2010).

Office of the Governor of Pitcairn, Henderson, Ducie and Oeno Islands: c/o British High Commission, 44 Hill St, POB 1812, Wellington 6011, New Zealand; tel. (4) 924-2888; fax (4) 473-4982; e-mail ppa.mailbox@fco.gov.uk; Gov. VICTORIA TREADELL.

Pitcairn Islands Office: Private Box 105-696, Auckland, New Zealand; tel. (9) 366-0186; fax (9) 366-0187; e-mail admin@pitcairn .gov.pn; internet www.government.pn.

ISLAND COUNCIL
(May 2013)

Mayor: MICHAEL WARREN.

Deputy Mayor: SIMON YOUNG.

Governor's Representative (ex officio): SAMANTHA SMITH.

Other Members: BRENDA CHRISTIAN, JACQUI CHRISTIAN, MICHELE CHRISTIAN, JAY WARREN, KERRY YOUNG.

Elections to the Island Council take place every two years, in December. Meetings are held at the Court House in Adamstown.

Office of the Island Secretary: The Square, Adamstown.

Judicial System

The constitutional amendments enacted in February 2010 provided for the establishment of the Pitcairn Supreme Court and for the appointment of an independent Attorney-General.

Chief Justice: CHARLES BLACKIE.

Island Magistrate: SIMON YOUNG.

Public Prosecutor: SIMON MOORE.

Public Defender: PAUL DACRE.

Attorney-General: PAUL RISHWORTH.

Religion

CHRISTIANITY

Since 1887 many of the islanders have been adherents of the Seventh-day Adventist Church.

Pastor: JOHN O'MALLEY, SDA Church, The Square, POB 24, Adamstown; fax 872-7620/9763.

The Press

Pitcairn Miscellany: tel. 15669595; e-mail admin@miscellany.pn; internet www.miscellany.pn; monthly online newsletter; f. 1959; edited by the Education Officer; Editors PAUL SHELLING, RUTH SHELLING; circ. 270 (2012).

Finance, Trade and Industry

There are no formal banking facilities. A co-operative trading store was established in 1967. Industry consists of handicrafts, and the production of honey and dried fruit.

Transport

ROADS

There are approximately 14 km (9 miles) of dirt road suitable for two-, three- and four-wheeled vehicles. In 2002 Pitcairn had one conventional motor cycle, six three-wheelers and 22 four-wheeled motor cycles, one four-wheel-drive motor car, three tractors, a five-ton digger and a bulldozer; traditional wheelbarrows are used occasionally. Work to concrete the road, known as the Hill of Difficulty, was completed in mid-2006.

SHIPPING

No passenger ships have called regularly since 1968, and sea communications are restricted to cargo vessels operating between New Zealand and Panama, which make scheduled calls at Pitcairn three times a year, as well as a number of unscheduled calls. A shipping route between French Polynesia and Pitcairn was opened in 2006. There are also occasional visits by private yachts. The number of cruise ships calling at Pitcairn increased in the late 1990s, and 10 such vessels visited the island in 2000 (compared with just two or three annually in previous years). Two cruise ships called at Pitcairn in April 2005 before stopping at Oeno Island for the tourists to witness a solar eclipse near the island. Bounty Bay, near Adamstown, is the only possible landing site, and there are no docking facilities; in mid-2007 plans to build a breakwater at Bounty Bay were announced. In 1993 the jetty derrick was refitted with an hydraulic system. Major work to repair the slipway and jetty was carried out by the islanders in mid-2005.

Tourism

The tourism sector has yet to be developed. The development of ecotourism, to include activities such as whale-watching, has been identified as offering particular potential for the islands. Henderson Island was declared a UNESCO World Heritage Site in 1988 and has been designated as a bird sanctuary.

Pitcairn Island Tourism Dept: Adamstown; e-mail tourism@pitcairn.pn; internet www.visitpitcairn.pn; Co-ordinator HEATHER MENZIES.

Education

Free primary education is provided on the island under the direction of a qualified schoolteacher, recruited in New Zealand. Scholarships, provided by the Pitcairn Government, are available for post-primary education or specialist training in New Zealand. In February 2004 there were seven children (four primary and three secondary) being educated on Pitcairn.

SAINT HELENA, ASCENSION AND TRISTAN DA CUNHA

Introductory Survey

LOCATION, CLIMATE, LANGUAGE, RELIGION, FLAG, CAPITAL

Saint Helena lies in the South Atlantic Ocean, about 1,930 km (1,200 miles) from the south-west coast of Africa, while the island of Ascension lies 1,131 km (703 miles) north-west of Saint Helena. The island of Tristan da Cunha lies 2,800 km (1,740 miles) west of Cape Town, South Africa: Saint Helena is 2,300 km (1,430 miles) to the north-east. Also in the group are Inaccessible Island, 37 km (23 miles) west of Tristan; the three Nightingale Islands, 37 km (23 miles) south; and Gough Island (Diego Alvarez), 425 km (264 miles) south. Saint Helena has a sub-tropical and mild climate, with a mean maximum temperature of 24°C (75°F) and a mean minimum of 19°C (66°F). The average annual rainfall is 113 mm (4.5 ins). The mean maximum temperature on Ascension is 30°C (86°F), while the mean minimum temperature is 24°C (75°F). Average annual rainfall is about 2,252 mm (89 ins). The climate on Tristan da Cunha is typically oceanic and temperate with rainfall averaging 1,675 mm (66 ins) per year. English is the official language. The majority of the population of the islands are Anglicans. The flag (proportions 1 by 2) is the British 'Blue Ensign' with the Saint Helena shield (depicting a ship of the British East India Co approaching the rocky shores of the island, above which in the yellow chief is a Saint Helena plover) in the fly. The capital is Jamestown, on Saint Helena.

SAINT HELENA

Contemporary Political History

Governed by the British East India Co from 1673, the island was brought under the direct control of the British Crown in 1834. At general elections held in September 1976, the Saint Helena Progressive Party, advocating the retention of close economic links with the United Kingdom, won 11 of the 12 elective seats in the Legislative Council. This policy has been advocated by almost all members of the Legislative Council brought to office at subsequent general elections (normally held every four years) up to and including that held in November 2009.

In October 1981 a commission was established by the Governor to review the island's constitutional arrangements. The commission reported in 1983 that it was unable to identify any proposal for constitutional change that would command the support of the majority of the islanders. In 1988, however, a formal Constitution was introduced to replace the Order in Council and Royal Instructions under which Saint Helena had been governed since 1967. The Constitution entered into force on 1 January 1989.

Owing to the limited range of economic activity on the island (see below), Saint Helena is dependent on development and budgetary aid from the United Kingdom. In 1981 the United Kingdom adopted the British Nationality Act, which effectively removed the islanders' traditional right of residence in Britain. An informal 'commission on citizenship' was established in 1992 by a number of islanders to examine Saint Helena's constitutional relationship with the United Kingdom, with special reference to the legal validity of the 1981 legislation as applied to Saint Helena. In April 1997 the commission obtained a legal opinion from a former Attorney-General of Saint Helena to the effect that the application of the Act to the population of Saint Helena was in contravention of the Royal Charter establishing British sovereignty in 1673. In 1998 the British Government indicated that it was considering arrangements under which islanders would be granted employment and residence rights in the United Kingdom. It was also announced that a review was to take place of the future constitutional status of the islands, and of means whereby their economies might be strengthened. It was subsequently agreed that the operation of the 1981 legislation in relation to Saint Helena would also be reviewed. As an immediate measure to ameliorate the isolation of Saint Helena, the British Government conceded permission for civilian air landing rights on Ascension Island, which, with the contemplated construction of a small airstrip on Saint Helena, could facilitate the future development of the islands as a tourist destination.

In May 2002 the British Overseas Territories Act, which granted British citizenship to the people of the United Kingdom Overseas Territories (as the British Dependent Territories had been restyled), including Saint Helena and dependencies, came into effect. Under the new legislation these citizens acquired the right to hold a British passport and to work in the United Kingdom, but not the other benefits of citizenship (such as reduced fees for education). The Act restored those rights removed by the British Nationality Act of 1981. In September 2002 an independent constitutional adviser visited Saint Helena and consulted extensively with the island's residents on the options for future constitutional development. A consultative poll on the draft for a new constitution, which, *inter alia*, proposed the creation of a ministerial form of government, took place on 25 May 2005. The draft document was rejected by 52.6% of voters. Concern was expressed at the low rate of voter participation, recorded at 43% of registered voters. Nevertheless, it was indicated that elements of the rejected constitution were expected to be adopted, including a change to the number of constituencies on Saint Helena. The British Government subsequently stated that it wished to identify any possible improvements to the existing Constitution in conjunction with the new Executive Council, which took office following the elections held on 31 August 2005. In April 2008 Governor Andrew Gurr outlined proposals for a new constitution to be drafted following a full consultation process, which he envisaged would be completed by mid-2009. He suggested that the previous draft constitution had been rejected due to the proposed introduction of ministerial government, and that consequently a number of potential improvements in other areas had been lost.

On 1 September 2009 the Saint Helena, Ascension and Tristan da Cunha Constitution Order 2009 entered into force. Under the new Constitution, Ascension and Tristan da Cunha were no longer referred to as 'Dependencies' and the territory was henceforth to be known as Saint Helena, Ascension and Tristan da Cunha. The new Constitution also established fundamental rights and freedoms for each of the three islands, which were to share the same Governor, Attorney-General, Supreme Court and Court of Appeal. Saint Helena was to be represented by an eight-member Executive Council and a 17-member Legislative Council, while Ascension and Tristan da Cunha were to be represented by Island Councils. Legislative elections were held in early November following which the new councils were formed. The Legislative Council subsequently appointed chairmen to head the eight Council Committees responsible for overseeing policy formation.

Meanwhile, in February 2002 a referendum was held by the Government in Saint Helena, Ascension Island, the Falkland Islands and on Royal Mail Ship (RMS) *St Helena* on future access to the island; 71.6% of the votes cast were in favour of the construction of an airport (28.4% opting for a shipping alternative). The project was expected to cost some £40m., of which the British Government was reported to have agreed to contribute some £26.3m., approximately equal to the cost of replacing the mail ship in 2010. Potential contractors for the airport project were invited to develop their proposals for the provision of air services to the island; however, in February 2008 it was revealed that none of the shortlisted companies had provided an appropriate solution, and further negotiations would be necessary for the commencement of the project. Despite an initial commitment to bringing the airport into operation by 2012, in April 2009 the British Department for International Development (DfID), in response to the worsening of the United Kingdom's economic climate, announced a further consultation on future access to Saint Helena. In December Douglas Alexander, the British Secretary of State for International Development, announced that as a result of 'current economic conditions' the British Government had decided it would not be appropriate to proceed with the project 'at this time'. The decision was vehemently criticized by the local authorities on Saint Helena and in July 2010 it was decided that construction of the airport would proceed. In December DfID and the Saint Helena Government signed a memorandum of understanding detailing the reforms required in order to prepare for the construction of the airport, and in November 2011 the Governor confirmed that DfID's conditions had been met. A contract for the construction of the airport was entered into with Basil Read (Pty) Ltd at a total cost of some £247m., a reduction of approximately 20% compared with the cost originally quoted in 2008 prior to the project's cancellation. The airport was expected to commence operations in early 2016, whereupon the RMS *St Helena* (one of the few ships regularly to call at the island) would be retired.

In May 2008 it was reported that the United Kingdom Government had registered claims with the UN Commission for the Limits of the Continental Shelf to extend its territorial waters surrounding Saint Helena, Ascension Island and Tristan da Cunha. It was hoped that these areas of seabed could be secured with the possibility of drilling for petroleum, gas and mineral resources in future years.

In a rationalization of the island's public services, on 1 April 2011 the 13 government departments were replaced by 10 government directorates and the Office of the Chief Secretary was replaced by a Secretariat.

On 23 March 2013 a referendum, which attracted a turn-out of just some 10%, was held on proposals to amend the Constitution whereby the members of the Legislative Council of Saint Helena would elect from among themselves a 'Chief Councillor' to head the Executive Council (a function currently performed by the Governor); the Chief Councillor would then nominate the other members of the Executive Council. The proposals, which were intended to improve democratic accountability, were defeated by 168 votes to 42.

Governor Mark Capes dissolved the Legislative Council in April 2013 pending the holding of a general election in July (shortly after the scheduled publication of a new and updated electoral register); the members of the Council were to continue to operate on an acting basis until the election. In a new development, each eligible voter was to be permitted to select up to 12 candidates for the poll.

Economic Affairs

The economy of Saint Helena is heavily reliant on British aid. In 2006/07 the assistance totalled £14.76m. and consisted of direct budgetary aid (£6.9m.), an annual subsidy for the operation of the RMS *St Helena* (£3.1m.) and support for bilateral development assistance. Total United Kingdom assistance to St Helena was £20.6m. in 2009/10 (direct budgetary aid was £7.7m., a decrease from £8.7m. in 2008/09). Local budget revenues totalled £9.4m. in 2009/10. According to official estimates, Saint Helena's gross national product (GNP) totalled £19.0m. in 2009/10; per capita GNP was estimated at £4,761 in the same financial year. Gross domestic product (GDP) was estimated to have increased, in real terms, by an average of 0.9% per year during 2005/06–2009/10; a decline of 13.1%, in real terms, was recorded for 2009/10. The population declined at an average annual rate of 0.4% during 2005/06–2009/10, and, largely as a result of this, per capita GDP increased, in real terms, by an average of 0.4% per year over the same period. The annual rate of inflation, according to retail prices, averaged 5.1% in 2002–09, and the rate, influenced to a large extent by the prevailing rates in its two most important trading partners, South Africa and the United Kingdom, had remained relatively stable (at around 3%–5%) during 2003–07, although consumer prices increased by 8.0% in both 2008 and 2009. Retail prices increased by 4.1% in 2012. In 2004 the rate of unemployment (including community work scheme placements) was estimated at 7.6%, but by November 2008 this rate was estimated to have fallen to 2.3% of the labour force.

At the 2008 census 7.3% of the employed labour force were engaged in agriculture and fishing, 20.0% in industry (predominantly construction) and 72.7% in services. Employment in the public sector was estimated to account for 60% of employment in the late 2000s. There is a significant visible trade deficit (£9.9m. in 2009/10), with the cost of imports amounting to £10.3m. (including almost 26% spent on importing food and live animals), compared with export revenues of just £321,000 (derived almost entirely from fish). In 2009 exports of fish (which, apart from a small quantity of coffee, is the only commodity exported) totalled 265.7 metric tons (compared with 27.2 tons in 1985). Improvements in vessel capacity have helped to increase fish exports in recent years. A rise in overseas philatelic sales has also generated significant revenues (£89,000 in 2008/09), as has a fledgling tourist industry (£707,000 in 2009/10). However, a large proportion of the labour force (approximately 1,000) must seek employment overseas, principally on Ascension and the Falkland Islands. According to the British Foreign and Commonwealth Office, approximately 1,700 members of the work-force were employed offshore at the beginning of 2005. Remittances from overseas contributed an estimated £3.4m. in 2009/10.

In early 2012 the Saint Helena authorities published a Sustainable Economic Development Plan (SEDP) for 2012/13–2021/22, which aimed to introduce a 'tourism driven economy' in conjunction with the construction of the airport. The SEDP stated that a 'relatively modest' number of visitors (totalling 30,000 per year) was required in order to make Saint Helena financially self-sustaining, and plans were already advanced with regard to the construction of a number of large tourism resorts on the island. Furthermore, based on the visitor number projections, average wages on the island were predicted to double in real terms by 2021/22, while an increase in GDP, to £117m. by 2022 (compared with £15.6m. in 2009/10), was also projected.

ASCENSION

Discovered by Portuguese navigators in 1501, the island is a semi-barren, rocky peak of purely volcanic origin. Britain took possession of Ascension in 1815, in connection with Napoleon's detention on Saint Helena. The island is famous for green turtles, and is also a breeding ground for the sooty tern. Under an agreement with the British Government, US forces occupy Wideawake Airfield, which is used as a tracking station for guided missiles. Ascension has no indigenous population, being inhabited by British and US military personnel, *émigré* workers and government administrative staff from Saint Helena. There are also a number of expatriate civilian personnel of Merlin Communications International (MCI), which operates the British Broadcasting Corporation (BBC) Overseas World Service Atlantic relay station, Cable and Wireless Worldwide PLC, which provides international communications services and operates the 'Ariane' satellite tracking station of the European Space Agency, and staff providing the island's common services. The island is an important communications centre and hosts one of the world's five ground antennae that assist in the operation of the global positioning system (GPS) navigational system. Ascension does not raise its own finance; the costs of administering the island are borne collectively by the user organizations, supplemented by income from philatelic sales and, in recent years, by the sale of the international internet domain code.ac. The island is developing a modest eco-tourism sector. Some revenue, which is remitted to the Saint Helena administration, is derived from fishing licences (estimated to be around £1m. in 1999). Facilities on Ascension underwent rapid development in 1982 to serve as a major staging post for British vessels and aircraft on their way to the Falkland Islands (q.v.), and the island has continued to provide a key link in British supply lines to the South Atlantic.

Dissent developed among the resident population in June 2002, following the decision of the Foreign and Commonwealth Office to impose taxes for the first time on the island (including income tax, property tax and tax on alcohol and tobacco). The primary objection of the population was that this was 'taxation without representation', as the islanders do not possess the right to vote, to own property or even to live on the island. The Governor responded with plans to introduce a democratically elected council that would have a purely advisory function and no decision-making powers, claiming that the islanders initially needed to acquire experience of governance. On 22–23 August a vote on the democratic options took place on the island, with 95% of the votes cast being in favour of an Island Council, rather than an Inter-Island Council plus Island Council structure; 50% of those eligible to vote did so. The Council was to be chaired by the Administrator, on behalf of the Governor, and was to comprise seven elected members, the Attorney-General, the Director of Finance and one or two appointed members. Elections for councillors took place in October, and the Island Council was inaugurated in the following month. A joint consultative council was also to be established, with representatives from both Ascension and Saint Helena, in order to develop policy relating to economic development and tourism common to both islands. (Elections to a new Island Council were held in November 2005.)

The British Government subsequently stated its intention to enact legislation granting the islanders right of abode and the right to own property. However, following a visit to the island by a delegation of British officials in November 2005, it was announced that the proposed reforms would not be carried out. The British Government cited its reluctance fundamentally to change the nature of the territory and also maintained that granting such rights would impose greater financial liabilities on British taxpayers and would incur an unacceptable level of risk for the United Kingdom. In January 2006 the Island Council announced that it intended to seek clarification regarding the legality of the British Government's decision and reiterated its commitment to securing the islanders' right to abode and the right to purchase property.

Following the resignation of six of the Island Council's members in January 2007, a general election was called. However, when only two candidates presented themselves for election, the Island Council was suspended in May 2007 and the Ascension Island Advisory Group was established to provide advice to the Administrator on certain policy issues. The suspension of the Council was expected to remain in place until May 2008, after which elections would be held. It was anticipated that the Advisory Group would meet on a monthly basis, to be supplemented by informal meetings as necessary. Consultation papers were to be issued to encourage the people of Ascension to participate in the decision-making process. In October elections were held (eight nominations having been received) and a new Island Council was sworn in later that month. Meanwhile, in May it was reported that the United Kingdom Government had submitted a claim to the UN Commission for the Limits of the Continental Shelf regarding the extension of its territorial waters around Ascension Island (see Saint Helena).

As of early 2004 Ascension Island had a balanced fiscal budget, although with minimal reserves. Government expenditure funds one school, one hospital (offering limited services), police and judicial services; these services are provided without charge to local taxpayers. The Saint Helena-based firm Solomons has a primary role in the incipient private sector and a lucrative sports-fishing industry has been established and developed in recent years. In December 2011 the 10th European Development Fund awarded a grant of some €16.6m. to Saint Helena and its dependencies for infrastructure and economic development projects over the next four years, including a road improvement initiative for Ascension Island.

TRISTAN DA CUNHA

Tristan da Cunha was discovered in 1506, but remained uninhabited until occupied by US whalers during 1790–1811. The British Navy took possession of the island in 1817. Tristan's population was evacuated to the United Kingdom in 1961, after volcanic eruptions, but the majority of families were resettled in 1963. The island's major source of revenue derives from a royalty for a crayfishing concession, supplemented by income from the sale of commemorative coins, postage stamps and other philatelic items, and handicrafts. The fishing industry and the local administration employ all of the working population. Some 20 power boats operating from the island land their catches to a canned crayfish factory built by the Atlantic Islands Development Corpn, whose fishing concession was transferred in January 1997 to a new holder, Premier Fishing (Pty) Ltd, of Cape Town, and later to another South African company, Ovenstone (Pty) Ltd. In June 2001 a hurricane in the main settlement of Edinburgh of the Seven Seas destroyed the hospital, community centre and numerous homes, and also killed many cattle; the satellite telephone link was lost and the island was without electricity for one week, although no serious injuries were sustained. DfID granted a £75,000 emergency aid package in response to the disaster. However, the cost of repairs surpassed that figure considerably. Furthermore, the problem of poaching in the island's waters resulted in much of Tristan da Cunha's limited resources being used to fund fishing patrols rather than swiftly restoring the damaged infrastructure. In February 2008 a fire destroyed the crayfish factory, along with the island's power plant; new generators were installed in the following month and a new factory was opened in July 2009. The island's harbour was also renovated in 2008, in a project paid for by DfID, and undertaken with the help of Royal Engineers from the United Kingdom. Budget estimates for 2005/06 projected a deficit of £147,507. Development aid from the United Kingdom ceased in 1980, since when the island has financed its own projects. In April 2008, prompted by concerns surrounding the island's dwindling capital reserves, Administrator David Morley warned that the island could be bankrupt within four years unless economic austerity measures were implemented immediately. Chief among these proposals was the introduction, with effect from 1 June 2008, of an incremental system of income tax (with a maximum rate of 13%). It was reported in May 2008 that the United Kingdom Government had registered a claim with the UN Commission for the Limits of the Continental Shelf to extend its territorial waters around Tristan da Cunha (see Saint Helena).

Statistical Survey

Sources (unless otherwise indicated): Development and Economic Planning Dept, Government of Saint Helena, Saint Helena Island, STHL 1ZZ; tel. 2777; fax 2830; e-mail depd@helanta.sh; Saint Helena Development Agency (SHDA), POB 117, No. 2 Main St, Jamestown, Saint Helena Island, STHL 1ZZ; tel. 2920; fax 2166; e-mail enquiries@shda.co.sh; internet www.shda.co.sh.

Note: Unless otherwise indicated, figures in this Statistical Survey relate only to the island of Saint Helena.

AREA AND POPULATION

Area: 411 sq km (159 sq miles). St Helena 121 sq km (47 sq miles); Ascension Island 88 sq km (34 sq miles); Tristan da Cunha 98 sq km (38 sq miles); Inaccessible Island 10 sq km (4 sq miles); Nightingale Islands 2 sq km (1 sq mile); Gough Island 91 sq km (35 sq miles).

Population: 5,157 at census of 8 March 1998; 4,257 (enumerated total) at census of 10 February 2008, 3,981 (resident population) at census of 10 February 2008. *Ascension Island* (St Helenians only, enumerated total at 2008 census): 710. *Tristan da Cunha* (enumerated total at 2008 census): 264. *2012* (official estimate at 31 December); Saint Helena 4,236. Note: There are no indigenous inhabitants on Ascension Island, but several hundred personnel and employees and their families are permanently resident (884 at 31 March 2010, comprising St Helena 696, UK 106, USA 70 and others 12). There is a small weather station on Gough Island, staffed, under agreement, by personnel employed by the South African Government.

Density (at 2008 census): 35.2 per sq km.

Population by Age and Sex (resident population at 2008 census): *0–14:* 600 (males 317, females 283); *15–64:* 2,677 (males 1,378, females 1,299); *65 and over:* 703 (males 326, females 377); *Total* 3,981 (males 2,022, females 1,959). Note: Total includes one male of undetermined age.

Principal Town (UN estimate, incl. suburbs): Jamestown (capital), population 673 in mid-2011 (Source: UN, *World Urbanization Prospects: The 2011 Revision*).

Births and Deaths (2012): Registered live births 31 (7.1 per 1,000); Registered deaths 62 (14.2 per 1,000).

Employment (2008 census): Agriculture, hunting and related activities 122; Fishing 33; Mining and quarrying 8; Manufacturing 115; Electricity, gas and water 113; Construction 190; Wholesale and retail trade, etc. 385; Hotels and restaurants 36; Transport, storage and communications 237; Financial intermediation 20; Real estate, renting and business activities 185; Public administration and defence 157; Education 112; Health and social work 178; Other community services 217; Private household 17; Extra-territorial organizations 5; *Total employed* 2,130 (males 1,174; females 956) (Source: ILO). *Unemployed* (2007/08, incl. community work scheme) 66.

AGRICULTURE, ETC.

Livestock (livestock census, 2009): Cattle 598; Sheep 651; Pigs 386; Goats 773; Asses 46; Chickens 4,421.

Livestock Products (metric tons, 2009): Cattle meat 40.9; Pig meat 67.2; Sheep meat 0.8.

Fishing (metric tons, live weight, including Ascension and Tristan da Cunha, 2010): Skipjack tuna 250; Yellowfin tuna 65; Tristan da Cunha rock lobster 403; Total catch (incl. others) 864. Figures include catches of rock lobster from Tristan da Cunha during the 12 months ending 30 April of the year stated (Source: FAO).

INDUSTRY

Electric Energy (production, kWh million): 8.5 in 2008; 8.8 in 2009; 9.1 in 2010.

FINANCE

Currency and Exchange Rate: 100 pence (pennies) = 1 Saint Helena pound (£). *Sterling, Dollar and Euro Equivalents* (31 December 2012): £1 sterling = Saint Helena £1; US $1 = 63.37 pence; €1 = 83.61 pence; £10 = $15.78 = €11.96. *Average Exchange Rate* (£ per US dollar): 0.6472 in 2010; 0.6241 in 2011; 0.6330 in 2012. Note: The Saint Helena pound is at par with the pound sterling.

Budget (£ million, 2009/10): Total revenue 9.4 (excluding United Kingdom budgetary aid 7.7); Total expenditure (incl. trading accounts) 23.4. *Ascension Island* (£ million, year ending 31 March 2004, estimates): Total revenue 4.3; Total expenditure 4.0 (recurrent 3.3, capital 0.7). *Tristan da Cunha* (£ million, 2005/06, estimates): Total revenue 0.7; Expenditure 0.9 (with excess expenditure financed from capital reserves of 1.2).

Gross National Product (£ million at current prices): 20.32 in 2007/08; 21.47 in 2008/09; 19.04 in 2009/10.

Gross Domestic Product (£ million at current prices): 17.28 in 2007/08; 17.39 in 2008/09; 15.55 in 2009/10.

Expenditure on the Gross Domestic Product (£ million at current prices, 2009/10): Government expenditure 20.22; Private expenditure 14.25; Changes in stocks 0.21; *Total domestic expenditure* 34.68; Exports of goods and services 1.19; *Less* Imports of goods and services 20.32; *GDP in purchasers' values* 15.55.

Money Supply (£ '000, 2006/07): Currency in circulation 3,618 (excl. commemorative coins valued at 514).

Cost of Living (Retail Price Index October–December; base: April–June 2010 = 100): 101.5 in 2010; 108.6 in 2011; 113.0 in 2012.

EXTERNAL TRADE

Principal Commodities (£ '000, 2009/10): *Imports:* Total 10,267 (Food and live animals 2,617; Beverages and tobacco 633; Mineral fuels, lubricants, etc. 1,349; Chemicals and related materials 680; Basic manufactures 1,371; Machinery and transport equipment 1,896; Miscellaneous manufactured articles 1,418). *Exports:* Total 321 (Fish 311). Note: Trade is mainly with the United Kingdom (imports 4,732 in 2009/10) and South Africa (imports 5,431 in 2009/10).

TRANSPORT

Road Traffic (2009): 2,391 licensed vehicles (incl. 1,459 passenger motor cars; 172 motorcycles; 90 buses; 541 vans and lorries).

Shipping: *Vessels Entered* (2009): 235. *Flag Registered Fleet* (at 31 December 2012): Vessels 2; Total displacement 2,232 grt (Source: Lloyd's List Intelligence—www.lloydslistintelligence.com).

TOURISM

Visitor Arrivals: 2,542 (tourists 778) in 2011; 2,731 (tourists 574) in 2012.

Receipts from Tourism (£ '000, estimates): 414 in 2007/08; 320 in 2008/09; 707 in 2009/10.

COMMUNICATIONS MEDIA

Television Subscribers (April 2007): 1,161.

Telephones (main lines in use, 2011): 2,400 (Source: International Telecommunication Union).

Internet Subscribers (2011): 900 (Source: International Telecommunication Union).

Broadband Subscribers (2011): 800 (Source: International Telecommunication Union).

EDUCATION

Primary (2006/07): 2 schools; 14 teachers; 115 pupils.

Amalgamated School (2006/07): 1 school; 15 teachers; 116 pupils.

Intermediate (2006/07): 2 schools; 17 teachers; 119 pupils.

Secondary (2006/07): 1 school; 42 teachers; 324 pupils.

2009/10 (all levels): 7 schools; 88 teachers; 516 enrolled pupils.

Directory

The Government

HEAD OF STATE

Queen: HM Queen ELIZABETH II.

Governor: MARK CAPES.

The Governor of Saint Helena, in his capacity as Governor of Ascension and Tristan da Cunha, is represented by an Administrator on those islands. The Governor, either directly, or through the Administrator, exercises executive authority on behalf of Her Majesty Queen Elizabeth II. The Governor, acting after consultation with the Island Councils, whose advice he or she is not obliged to follow, may make laws for the peace, order and good government of Ascension and Tristan da Cunha.

Administrator of Ascension: COLIN WELLS.

Administrator of Tristan da Cunha: SEAN BURNS.

EXECUTIVE COUNCIL
(May 2013)

President: MARK CAPES (The Governor).

Chief Secretary: OWEN O'SULLIVAN.

Financial Secretary: COLIN OWEN.

Attorney-General: KENNETH BADDON.

Elected Members: RODNEY BUCKLEY, CYRIL GUNNELL, MERVYN YON, ANTHONY GREEN, STEDSON FRANCIS.

LEGISLATIVE COUNCIL
(May 2013)

The Legislative Council consists of the Speaker, the Deputy Speaker, 12 elected members and three ex officio members (the Chief Secretary, the Financial Secretary and the Attorney-General). The Legislative Council was dissolved on 19 April 2013 by the Governor pending the holding of a general election in July; the members of the Council were to continue to operate on an acting basis until the election.

Speaker: CATHY HOPKINS.

Deputy Speaker: ERIC BENJAMIN.

Committee Chairmen

Access and Transport: JOHN CRANFIELD.

Economy and Finance: ANTHONY GREEN.

Education and Employment: RODNEY BUCKLEY.

Health and Social Welfare: CYRIL GUNNELL.

Home, Civil Society and International: DEREK THOMAS.

Infrastructure and Utilities: MERVYN YON.

Natural Resources, Development and Environment: RAYMOND WILLIAMS.

Tourism and Leisure: BERNICE OLSSON.

GOVERNMENT OFFICES

Office of the Governor: The Castle, Jamestown, STHL 1ZZ; tel. 2555; fax 2598; e-mail pagovernor@sainthelena.gov.sh; internet www.sainthelena.gov.sh.

Secretariat: The Castle, Jamestown, STHL 1ZZ; tel. 2470; fax 2598; e-mail secretariat@cwimail.sh.

Finance Directorate: The Castle, Jamestown, STHL 1ZZ; tel. 2470; fax 2020; e-mail directoroffinance@sainthelena.gov.sh.

Office of the Administrator of Ascension: The Residency, Georgetown, Ascension, ASCN 1ZZ; tel. 7000; fax 6152; e-mail aigenquiries@ascension.gov.ac; internet www.ascension-island.gov .ac.

Office of the Administrator of Tristan da Cunha: The Administrator's Office, Edinburgh of the Seven Seas, Tristan da Cunha, TDCU 1ZZ; tel. (20) 30142000; fax (satellite) (20) 30142000; e-mail tristandcadmin@gmail.com; internet www.tristandc.com/administator.php.

Political Organizations

There are no political parties in Saint Helena. Elections to the Legislative Council, the latest of which took place in November 2009, are conducted on a non-partisan basis.

Judicial System

The legal system is derived from English common law and statutes. There is a Supreme Court and a Court of Appeal, and provision was made in the 2009 Constitution for the establishment of other subordinate courts. The Supreme Court is presided over by a Chief Justice. The Court of Appeal consists of a President and two or more Justices of Appeal. There is also a four-member Judicial Services Commission, presided over by the Chief Justice.

The Attorney-General of Saint Helena is the principal legal adviser to the Government of Saint Helena. The Attorney-General of Ascension and of Tristan da Cunha is the principal legal adviser to the Government of Ascension and to the Government of Tristan da Cunha and is the person for the time being holding or acting in the office of Attorney-General of St Helena. The courts of Ascension and of Tristan da Cunha are the Supreme Court of St Helena, the Court of Appeal of St Helena, and such courts subordinate to the Supreme Court as may be established by law.

Chief Justice: CHARLES W. EKINS.

Attorney-General: KENNETH BADDON.

Sheriff: GRETA PAT MUSK.

Religion

The majority of the population belongs to the Anglican Communion. Ascension forms part of the Anglican diocese of Saint Helena, which normally provides a resident chaplain who is also available to minister to members of other denominations. There is a Roman Catholic chapel served by visiting priests, as well as a small mosque. Adherents of the Anglican church predominate on Tristan da Cunha, which is within the Anglican Church of Southern Africa, and is under the jurisdiction of the Archbishop of Cape Town, South Africa.

CHRISTIANITY

The Anglican Communion

Anglicans are adherents of the Anglican Church of Southern Africa (formerly the Church of the Province of Southern Africa). The Metropolitan of the Province is the Archbishop of Cape Town, South Africa. St Helena forms a single diocese.

Bishop of Saint Helena: Rt Rev. RICHARD FENWICK, Bishopsholme, POB 62, Saint Helena, STHL 1ZZ; tel. and fax 4471; e-mail bishop@helanta.sh; diocese f. 1859; has jurisdiction over the islands of Saint Helena and Ascension.

The Roman Catholic Church

The Church is represented in Saint Helena, Ascension and Tristan da Cunha by a Mission, established in August 1986. There were an estimated 100 adherents in the islands at 31 December 2007.

Superior: Rev. Fr MICHAEL MCPARTLAND (also Prefect Apostolic of the Falkland Islands); normally visits Tristan da Cunha once a year and Ascension Island two or three times a year; Rev. Fr MICHAEL DAVID GRIFFITHS, Sacred Heart Church, Jamestown, STHL 1ZZ; tel. and fax 2535.

Other Christian Churches

The Salvation Army, Seventh-day Adventists, Baptists, New Apostolics and Jehovah's Witnesses are active on the island.

BAHÁ'Í FAITH

There is a small Bahá'í community on the island.

The Bahá'í Community of St Helena: Moon Bldg, Napoleon St, POB 49, Jamestown; tel. 4525; fax 4924; e-mail enquiries@ sthelenabahai.org; internet www.sthelenabahai.org; f. 1954; Chair. BASIL GEORGE.

The Press

The St Helena Independent: St Helena Media Productions Ltd, 2nd Floor, Association Hall, Main St, Jamestown, STHL 1ZZ; tel. 2660; e-mail independent@cwimail.sh; internet www.saint.fm; f. 2005; independent; weekly.

The Sentinel: The Livery Stables, nr The Market Clock, Jamestown, STHL 1ZZ; tel. 2727; e-mail news@shbc.sh; internet www.shbc .sh/sentinel; f. 2012.

Broadcasting and Communications

TELECOMMUNICATIONS

Cable & Wireless (St Helena) PLC: POB 2, Bishops Rooms, Jamestown, STHL 1ZZ; tel. 2155; fax 2206; e-mail webmaster@ helanta.sh; internet www.cw.com/sthelena; f. 1899; provides national and international telecommunications.

BROADCASTING

In 2011 a new community-owned media services organization was established. The government-funded Saint Helena Broadcasting (Guarantee) Corporation (SHBC), which broadcasts three FM radio stations (one of which is a relay of the British Broadcasting Corporation's World Service), became operational in December 2012 when Radio St Helena ceased broadcasting. SHBC also introduced a weekly newspaper; the Sentinel published its first edition on 29 March 2012, replacing the Saint Helena Herald.

Cable & Wireless PLC: The Moon, Jamestown, STHL 1ZZ; tel. 2200; f. 1995; provides a 3-channel television service 24 hours daily from 5 satellite channels.

Saint Helena Broadcasting (Guarantee) Corporation (SHBC): The Livery Stables, nr The Market Clock, Jamestown, STHL 1ZZ; tel. 2727; e-mail news@shbc.sh; internet www.shbc.sh; f. 2011; CEO DARRIN HENRY.

Saint FM Community Radio (Guarantee) Ltd: Association Hall, Main St, Jamestown, STHL 1ZZ; tel. 2660; e-mail fm@helanta.sh; internet www.saint.fm; f. 2004; established as Saint FM; closed down Dec. 2012, but recommenced broadcasting, as Saint FM Community Radio, in March 2013; independent FM radio station; Dir LES BALDWIN; Station Man. DONNA CROWIE.

Finance

BANK

Bank of Saint Helena: Post Office Bldg, Main St, Jamestown, STHL 1ZZ; tel. 2390; fax 2553; e-mail jamestown@sthelenabank .com; internet www.sainthelenabank.com; f. 2004; replaced the Government Savings Bank; total assets £42,369,292 (31 March 2010); Chair. LYN THOMAS; Man. Dir ROSEMARY BARGO; 1 br. on Ascension.

INSURANCE

Solomon & Co PLC: Jamestown, STHL 1ZZ; tel. 2380; fax 2423; e-mail generalenquiries@solomons.co.sh; internet www .solomons-sthelena.com; f. 1790; business operating units include: mercantile, procurement, shipping and travel agents, stevedoring, insurance, livestock and arable farming (including coffee production), bakery, butchery, bulk fuel management, vehicle inspection, autoshop, construction works and information technology and administration services; CEO MANDY PETERS.

Trade and Industry

GOVERNMENT AGENCY

St Helena Development Agency: 2 Main St, POB 117, Jamestown, STHL 1ZZ; tel. 2920; fax 2166; e-mail enquiries@shda.co.sh; internet www.shda.co.sh; f. 1995; Chair. GEORGE STEVENS; Man. Dir LINDA HOUSTON.

CHAMBER OF COMMERCE

St Helena Chamber of Commerce: POB 34, Jamestown, STHL 1ZZ; tel. 2258; fax 2598; e-mail secretary@chamberofcommerce.org .sh; internet www.chamberofcommerce.org.sh; 60 mems; Pres. STUART MOORS; Sec. BRENDA MOORS-CLINGHAM.

CO-OPERATIVE

St Helena Growers' Co-operative Society: Jamestown, STHL 1ZZ; tel. and fax 2511; vegetable marketing; also suppliers of agricultural tools, seeds and animal feeding products; 108 mems (1999); Chair. STEDSON FRANCIS; Sec. PETER W. THORPE.

Transport

There are no railways in Saint Helena.

AIR

The construction of an airport on Saint Helena was first proposed in 2002. Despite an initial commitment to bringing the airport into operation by 2012, in April 2009 the British Department for International Development announced a further consultation on future access to Saint Helena. In December it was announced that as a result of 'current economic conditions' the British Government had decided that it would not be appropriate to proceed with the airport project 'at this time'. However, in July 2010 it was announced that construction of the airport would proceed, and it was expected to be operational by early 2016. A twice-weekly Royal Air Force Tristar service between the United Kingdom and the Falkland Islands transits Ascension Island both southbound and northbound. There is a weekly US Air Force military service linking the Patrick Air Force Base in Florida with Ascension Island, via Antigua and Barbuda. There is no airfield on Tristan da Cunha.

ROADS

In 2002 there were 118 km of bitumen-sealed roads, and a further 20 km of earth roads, which can be used by motor vehicles only in dry weather. All roads have steep gradients and sharp bends.

SHIPPING

The St Helena Line Ltd (RMS *St Helena*) provides a two-monthly passenger/cargo service from Cape Town, in South Africa, to Saint Helena and Ascension Island. The mail ship ceased its twice yearly visits to Portland, in the United Kingdom, in October 2011. A vessel under charter to the British Ministry of Defence visits the island monthly on its United Kingdom–Falkland Islands service. A US freighter from Cape Canaveral calls at three-monthly intervals. The St Helena Line Ltd, the MV *Hanseatic*, and MS *Explorer* and the SA *Agulhas* each visit Tristan da Cunha once each year, and two crayfish concession vessels each make three visits annually, remaining for between two and three months. Occasional cruise ships also visit the island.

St Helena Line Ltd: Andrew Weir Shipping, Dexter House, 2 Royal Mint Court, London, EC3N 4XX, United Kingdom; tel. (20) 7265-0808; fax (20) 7481-4784; internet www.aws.co.uk; internet www.rms-st-helena.com; service subsidized by the British Govt; operates 2-monthly passenger/cargo services by the RMS *St Helena* to and from Cape Town, South Africa, calling at Saint Helena and Ascension Island, and once a year at Tristan da Cunha; also operates programme of shuttle services between Saint Helena and Ascension Island and the St Helena Liner Shipping Service; Chair. GARRY HOPCROFT.

Tourism

Although Saint Helena possesses flora and fauna of considerable interest to naturalists, as well as the house (now an important museum) in which the French Emperor Napoleon I spent his final years in exile, the remoteness of the island, which is a two-day sea voyage from Ascension Island, has inhibited the development of tourism. The construction of an airport on Saint Helena (scheduled to be completed by early 2016) is expected greatly to increase the island's accessibility to the limited number of visitors that can currently be accommodated. A total of 847 tourists visited Saint Helena in 2009. There are three hotels and a range of self-catering facilities. Small-scale eco-tourism is encouraged on Ascension Island, although accommodation is limited and all visits require written permission from the Administrator. Access is available by twice weekly flights operated from the United Kingdom by the Royal Air Force (see above), and by the RMS *St Helena*. Permission from the Administrator and the Island Council is required for visits to Tristan da Cunha. Facilities for tourism are limited, although some accommodation is available in island homes.

St Helena Tourism: Main St, Jamestown, STHL 1ZZ; tel. 2158; fax 2159; e-mail melissa.fowler@tourism.gov.sh; internet www.sthelenatourism.com; f. 1998; provides general information about the island; Dir CATHY ALBERTS.

Education

Education is compulsory and free for all children between the ages of five and 15 years, although power to exempt after the age of 14 can be exercised by the Education Committee. The standard of work at the secondary comprehensive school is orientated towards the requirements of the General Certificate of Secondary Education and the General Certificate of Education Advanced Level of the United Kingdom. During the second half of the 1980s the educational structure was reorganized from a two-tier to a three-tier comprehensive system, for which a new upper-school building was constructed.

There is a free public library in Jamestown, financed by the Government and managed by a committee, and a mobile library service in the country districts. There is also a Teacher Education Centre in Jamestown.

SOUTH GEORGIA AND THE SOUTH SANDWICH ISLANDS

South Georgia, an island of 3,592 sq km (1,387 sq miles), lies in the South Atlantic Ocean, about 1,300 km (800 miles) east-south-east of the Falkland Islands. The South Sandwich Islands, which have an area of 311 sq km, lie about 750 km south-east of South Georgia.

The United Kingdom annexed South Georgia and the South Sandwich Islands in 1775. With a segment of the Antarctic mainland and other nearby islands (now the British Antarctic Territory), they were constituted as the Falkland Islands Dependencies in 1908. Argentina made formal claim to South Georgia in 1927, and to the South Sandwich Islands in 1948. In 1955 the United Kingdom unilaterally submitted the dispute over sovereignty to the International Court of Justice (based in the Netherlands), which decided not to hear the application in view of Argentina's refusal to submit to the Court's jurisdiction. South Georgia was the site of a British Antarctic Survey base (staffed by 22 scientists and support personnel) until it was invaded in April 1982 by Argentine forces, who occupied the island until its recapture by British forces three weeks later. The South Sandwich Islands were uninhabited until the occupation of Southern Thule in December 1976 by about 50 Argentines, reported to be scientists. Argentine personnel remained until removed by British forces in June 1982.

Under the provisions of the South Georgia and South Sandwich Islands Order of 1985, the islands ceased to be governed as dependencies of the Falkland Islands on 3 October 1985. The Governor of the Falkland Islands is, ex officio, Commissioner for the territory.

In May 1993, in response to the Argentine Government's decision to commence the sale of fishing licences for the region's waters, the British Government announced an extension, from 12 to 200 nautical miles, of its territorial jurisdiction in the waters surrounding the islands, in order to conserve crucial fishing stocks.

In September 1998 the British Government announced that it would withdraw its military detachment from South Georgia in 2000, while it would increase its scientific presence on the island with the installation of a permanent team from the British Antarctic Survey to investigate the fisheries around the island for possible exploitation. The small military detachment finally withdrew in March 2001. The British garrison stationed in the Falkland Islands would remain responsible for the security of South Georgia and the South Sandwich Islands.

Increased volcanic activity on Montagu Island, in the South Sandwich Islands, previously thought to be dormant, had been monitored closely by the British Antarctic Survey since 2001. In late 2005 Mount Belinda erupted, adding some 50 acres to the island's land area in just one month. The island is largely ice-covered and the eruption allowed scientists the rare opportunity to make direct observations of volcanic activity under ice sheets.

Budget revenue for 2010 amounted to £4.2m., while expenditure totalled £4.9m. The main sources of revenue are the sale of fishing licences (£3.2m.), incomes from visitor landing charges (£0.7m.), philatelic and commemorative coin sales, and customs and harbour duties.

At the close of the 2011/12 cruise ship season, South Georgia had recorded a total of 51 ship calls and 5,831 passengers to the island. Greater numbers of visitors to this inhospitable territory—coupled with a growing recognition of the climate change phenomenon—prompted the Government to review its existing biosecurity policy. In May 2011 Commissioner Nigel Haywood ratified the Wildlife and Protected Areas Ordinance, which outlined new measures to protect the territory's delicate ecosystem and to prevent the introduction of potentially destructive species of flora and fauna. Furthermore, in an effort to conserve maritime biodiversity, legislation was adopted in February 2012 that designated South Georgia and the South Sandwich Islands' territorial waters a Marine Protected Area. Colin

Roberts was scheduled to succeed Haywood as Commissioner in April 2014.

The British Antarctic Survey maintains two research stations on South Georgia, at King Edward Point (usually eight winter personnel, 12 summer personnel) and Bird Island (four winter personnel, 10 summer personnel). In 2009/10 summer personnel at the two bases and the Signy research station in the South Orkney Islands amounted to 46.

Commissioner: NIGEL ROBERT HAYWOOD (took office on 16 October 2010).

Senior Executive Officer and Director of Fisheries: Dr MARTIN COLLINS (Stanley, Falkland Islands).

THE TURKS AND CAICOS ISLANDS

Introductory Survey

LOCATION, CLIMATE, LANGUAGE, RELIGION, FLAG, CAPITAL

The Turks and Caicos Islands consist of more than 30 low-lying islands forming the south-eastern end of the Bahamas chain of islands, and lying about 145 km (90 miles) north of Haiti. Eight islands are inhabited: Grand Turk and Salt Cay (both in the smaller Turks group to the east of the Caicos), South Caicos, Middle (Grand) Caicos, North Caicos, Providenciales (Provo), Pine Cay and Parrot Cay. The climate is warm throughout the year but tempered by constant trade winds. The average annual temperature is 27°C (82°F) and rainfall ranges from 530 mm (21 ins) in the eastern islands to 1,000 mm (40 ins) in the west. The official language is English, though some Creole is spoken by Haitian immigrants. Many Christian churches are represented, the largest denomination being the Baptist Union (36% of the population at the 2001 census). The flag is the British 'Blue Ensign', with the shield from the islands' coat of arms, bearing a shell, a lobster and a cactus, in the fly. The capital is Cockburn Town, on Grand Turk island.

CONTEMPORARY POLITICAL HISTORY

Historical Context

The Turks and Caicos Islands were first settled by Amerindian peoples. The islands were then inhabited by privateers, and were settled from Bermuda and by exiled 'Loyalists' from the former British colonies in North America. A Jamaican dependency from 1874 to 1959, the Turks and Caicos Islands became a separate colony in 1962, following Jamaican independence. After an administrative association with the Bahamas, the islands received their own Governor in 1972. The first elections under the present Constitution took place in 1976, and were won by the pro-independence People's Democratic Movement (PDM).

Domestic Political Affairs

In 1980 an agreement was made with the United Kingdom whereby, if the governing PDM won the 1980 elections, the islands would receive independence and a payment of £12m. However, lacking the leadership of J. A. G. S. McCartney, the Chief Minister (who had been killed in an aircraft accident in May), the PDM lost the election in November to the Progressive National Party (PNP), which is committed to continued dependent status. At a subsequent general election, in May 1984, the PNP, led by the Chief Minister, Norman Saunders, won a further term in office.

In March 1985 the Chief Minister, the Minister for Development and Commerce and a PNP member of the Legislative Council were arrested in Miami, Florida, USA, on charges involving illicit drugs and violations of the US Travel Act. All three men were subsequently convicted and imprisoned. Saunders was replaced as Chief Minister by Nathaniel Francis.

In July 1986 a commission of inquiry into allegations of arson and administrative malpractice concluded that Francis and two of his ministers were unfit for ministerial office; all three ministers resigned. In the same month the Governor dissolved the Government, and the Executive Council was replaced by an interim advisory council, comprising the Governor and four members of the former Executive Council. A constitutional commission was appointed in September to review the future administration of the islands.

A general election, preceding the return to ministerial rule, took place in March 1988, following the British Government's acceptance of the principal recommendations of the constitutional commission in the previous year. Under a new multi-member system of representation, the PDM won a majority of seats on the Legislative Council. Oswald O. Skippings, the leader of the PDM, was appointed Chief

Minister. The new Constitution strengthened the reserve powers of the Governor, but otherwise the form of government was similar to the provisions of the 1976 Constitution.

In April 1991 a general election took place, at which the PNP defeated the PDM. Skippings was replaced as Chief Minister by C. Washington Misick, the leader of the PNP. However, the PDM was returned to office at a general election in January 1995. Derek Taylor, leader of the PDM, was appointed Chief Minister. The PDM increased its representation in the Legislative Council at a general election in March 1999.

A serious dispute arose between the Legislative Council and the Governor in August 1995, following the latter's decision to reappoint Kipling Douglas to the position of Chief Justice. Taylor, who claimed that Douglas did not enjoy the confidence of his Government, described the decision as provocative and disrespectful. Relations deteriorated in subsequent months, and in February 1996 a petition requesting the immediate removal of the Governor, signed by all members of the Government and opposition, was presented to the British Foreign and Commonwealth Office (FCO). The petition was rejected by the British Government, which deployed a frigate in the islands' waters and ordered 100 police officers to prepare for immediate transfer to the territory in the event of civil disturbance.

Constitutional reform

In April 2002 the Governor established a constitutional review body to discuss changes to the islands' Constitution. This all-party panel presented a report in September. Discussions on a new constitution took place in 2004 between representatives of the Turks and Caicos Islands and British Governments. Following further negotiations between government ministers in October 2005, it was agreed that a draft text of a modernized constitution would be drawn up by the FCO. This proposed document would be subject to approval by both the PDM and the PNP, after which a public consultation period would be held. Adoption of the amendments would be subject to approval by the Legislative Council.

In May 2002 the British Overseas Territories Act, having received royal assent in the United Kingdom in February, came into force and granted British citizenship rights to the people of its Overseas Territories, including the Turks and Caicos Islands. Under the new law, Turks and Caicos Islanders would be able to hold British passports and work in the United Kingdom and anywhere else in the European Union.

At a general election in April 2003 the PDM won seven of the 13 seats in the Legislative Council. The PNP took the remaining six seats, but challenged the results in two constituencies. By-elections were held in the two constituencies in August after evidence emerged of bribery and irregularities in voter registration lists; the PNP secured victory in both ballots and therefore wrested overall control of the Legislative Council from the PDM. Michael Misick replaced Taylor as Chief Minister.

A public consultation was conducted over a draft constitution, formulated pursuant to an agreement upon greater self-government for the territory, between United Kingdom and island representatives in October 2005, and approved by the Legislative Council on 28 June 2006. Following final submission to the FCO and endorsement by Queen Elizabeth II, the Council decreed the Turks and Caicos Constitutional Order 2006, adopting the new Constitution on 19 July. The Constitution was finally enacted on 9 August, when Chief Minister Misick and Deputy Chief Minister Floyd Hall were inaugurated as Premier and Deputy Premier, respectively. Former Chief Secretary Mahala Wynns was appointed to the new post of Deputy Governor; the assignment complied with a new constitutional requirement that the position be occupied by a 'belonger' of the Turks and Caicos Islands. Notable amendments under the new Constitution included the investiture of a unicameral parliament, which would replace and enlarge upon the former Legislative Council, and the inauguration of a Cabinet to replace the Executive Council.

A general election was held on 9 February 2007. The PNP was returned to office for a second term. Misick was reappointed Premier. The ballot followed a bitterly fought election campaign, in which the PDM made allegations of corruption against the ruling party. In December 2008 Misick avoided a debate on a motion of no confidence submitted by the PDM as a result of a dispute over parliamentary procedure. Parliament was subsequently prorogued by the Governor, Gordon Wetherell, to be reconvened in April 2009. Later in December nine members of the ruling PNP drafted a letter to Wetherell requesting that Misick resign, citing a loss of confidence from legislators.

Deputy Premier Floyd Hall resigned on 13 February 2009, citing the legislative stalemate caused by the ongoing suspension of Parliament. Galmo Williams, the Minister for Home Affairs, had resigned the previous day. Misick announced that he would resign as Premier by the end of March, and that he would not be seeking re-election as leader of the PNP. Misick stood down on 23 March, at which point Williams was sworn in as Premier. Williams promptly announced the formation of a new Cabinet.

Direct rule

The United Kingdom's House of Commons Foreign Affairs Committee published a report in July 2008 regarding the administration of its Overseas Territories, in which it detailed claims of corruption and intimidation made by residents of the Turks and Caicos Islands. The allegations of corruption referred to the sale of Crown land for unsustainable developments or for the personal gain of government members; nepotism in the distribution of development contracts and irregularities in the purchase of property for government use; the granting of 'belonger' status to individuals who were ineligible under the current law; and the misuse of public funds. The report criticized the Governor, who had failed to investigate the allegations. Although Premier Misick denied the allegations, a Commission of Inquiry was established later that month. In February 2009 Sir Robin Auld issued the Commission of Inquiry's interim report, which referred to a 'high probability of systemic corruption and serious dishonesty', 'political amorality and general incompetence' and contained 24 recommendations, including the partial or full suspension of the Constitution and direct rule of the islands by the United Kingdom, acting through the Governor, with the advice of an Advisory Council. The report also recommended that criminal investigations should be instigated against Misick and four of his former cabinet ministers. On 14 August the British Government announced the imposition of direct rule from the United Kingdom, the partial suspension of the Constitution and the removal of the Premier and Cabinet. The House of Assembly was also suspended. The FCO announced its intention to hold elections in the territory no later than July 2011 and stated that its aim was to establish a lasting basis for good governance, sound financial management and sustainable development.

The Advisory Council immediately instituted a Stabilization Plan to reduce expenditure and increase revenue, as well as to lower the debt. At the end of August 2009 a Special Prosecutor was also appointed to look into possible criminal charges against the former PNP Government. Former Premier Williams denounced the imposition of direct rule as a *coup d'état*. In early 2010 the FCO's Director of Overseas Territories indicated that following the elections, British government representatives would maintain an increased presence in the territory to ensure continuing good governance. The announcement called into question the plan to end direct rule following the ballot. A protest against British rule, held in March and supported by the PNP and the PDM, demonstrated the resentment harboured by some sections of the population.

The British Government announced in September 2010 that the 2011 elections would be postponed, citing a lack of progress on both the territory's reform programme and the investigation into alleged government corruption. Leaders of the PNP and the PDM, as well as the Caribbean Community and Common Market (CARICOM, see p. 231), expressed their opposition to the postponement of the ballot, and demonstrations were held during that month in protest against the delay. Further small-scale protest action, organized and funded by the PNP according to local media reports, was conducted in March 2011, and Providenciales airport was temporarily blockaded by demonstrators. It was expected that new elections would be held in late 2012, although this was contingent upon eight 'milestones' being reached, including constitutional, governmental, electoral and financial reform, a return to fiscal stability, and progress in the investigation into alleged government corruption.

A process of constitutional reform was initiated by the British Government in early 2010. A contingent of constitutional experts was sent to the territory, and public consultations on the content of a revised constitution were held. Among the most important proposals for inclusion in the new charter were a reduction in the number of cabinet ministers, the withdrawal of trial by jury in certain circumstances, the abrogation of the Advisory National Security Council and a stipulation that a budget surplus must be maintained. A

visiting FCO delegation held further meetings and public consultations in May 2011 to garner opinion on the draft constitution. A particular source of contention among the islanders was a proposal to grant the Governor additional powers, while planned changes to electoral rules, jury trials and regulations governing 'belonger' status were also criticized. The PDM denounced the document as an attempt by the United Kingdom to reimpose a colonial system on the territory. To address some of these concerns, talks between officials from the Turks and Caicos Islands and the United Kingdom took place in June. It was agreed that the existing 'first past the post' electoral framework would remain in place and that 'belonger' requirements would be modified, although the British Government refused to amend the proposals concerning jury trials and the increased powers of the Governor. Moreover, the United Kingdom added a new clause to the draft charter prohibiting the Premier from serving more than two consecutive terms.

Further details regarding the alleged corruption perpetrated by the previous PNP administration emerged throughout 2010. Documents recovered from the Land Registry Department indicated that large plots of Crown land had been sold at vastly reduced rates to certain individuals, allegedly favoured PNP associates, who then rapidly divested them to foreign companies for an enormous profit. It was also revealed that Clayton Greene, the leader of the PNP, had provided legal services for one of the foreign firms involved in the scandal while serving as Speaker of the House of Assembly. The British Government estimated that the territory had lost up to US $5,000m. as a result of this scheme. During late 2011 Floyd Hall and three other former ministers, along with several of their family members and associates, were detained and charged in connection with the fraudulent land sales, while in February 2012 Greene was also accused of involvement in the alleged conspiracy. In April he was charged with eight corruption offences. In addition, charges were filed in February against Misick's brother, Chalmers, for money-laundering and against McAllister Hanchell, another former PNP minister, for receiving bribes. In March an international arrest warrant was issued for former Premier Misick, who had been subjected to an assets freeze in June 2011 and had reportedly fled to the Dominican Republic. Also in March 2012, the interim Turks and Caicos authorities commenced legal action against the PNP: it was alleged that the party's headquarters were unlawfully situated on Crown land and hence should be demolished. In mid-2012 Oswald Skippings and Rufus Ewing were elected as leaders of the PDM and the PNP, respectively.

Recent developments: restoration of self-government

In June 2012 the British Government announced that, with the exception of achieving a fiscal surplus (which was expected in 2012/13), all the 'milestones' had now been reached. New ordinances governing, *inter alia*, elections, party funding, government transparency and public finances had been introduced, while substantive progress on the draft constitution and the corruption investigation had been achieved. In light of these positive developments, the United Kingdom declared that elections would be conducted in the territory in November. The new Constitution became effective on 15 October, although the PNP and the PDM continued to express concern about the Governor's new powers. The trial of the 13 people accused of corrupt practices (now including seven former ministers) was due to commence in late 2013.

In the general election, which took place as scheduled on 9 November 2012, the PNP secured eight of the 15 seats in the House of Assembly (despite losing the popular vote), while the PDM won the remaining seven. Turn-out was put at 84%. Ewing was inaugurated as Premier on 13 November, and he formed a new Government shortly thereafter. Charles Misick, the erstwhile Premier's brother, received the finance portfolio, and his cousin, Amanda, was given responsibility for health. Skippings failed to obtain a seat in the legislature, and in December he was replaced as PDM leader by Sharlene Cartwright-Robinson. Following an appeal by the PDM, in February 2013 Amanda Misick's election victory was annulled by the Supreme Court on the grounds that the participation of an ineligible candidate had potentially distorted the results in her district. Nevertheless, Misick was re-elected in the resulting by-election on 22 March and was reappointed to the Cabinet later that month as the Minister of Environment and Home Affairs.

In December 2012 former Premier Misick was detained in Brazil, where he had been residing since late 2011. The Brazilian authorities rejected Misick's application for political asylum, and extradition proceedings against him were under way in early 2013.

The British Government announced in May 2013 that agreement had been reached on new banking transparency laws for the territory as part of efforts to combat international tax evasion.

CONSTITUTION AND GOVERNMENT

The Constitution, which entered into force on 15 October 2012, provides for a Cabinet and a unicameral House of Assembly. Executive authority is vested in the British monarch and is exercised by the

Governor (the monarch's appointed representative). The Governor is responsible for external affairs, internal security, defence, international financial services and the appointment of public officers; other matters are resolved by the Governor upon the advice of the Cabinet. The Governor is President of the Cabinet, which comprises nine members: two ex officio (the Attorney-General and the Chief Financial Officer); the Premier; and six appointed by the Governor from among the elected members of the House of Assembly. The House of Assembly comprises 22 members: the Speaker; four nominated members; the two ex officio members of the Cabinet and 15 members elected by universal adult suffrage.

REGIONAL AND INTERNATIONAL CO-OPERATION

The Turks and Caicos Islands are a member of the Caribbean Development Bank (see p. 236) and an associate member of the Caribbean Community and Common Market (CARICOM, see p. 231). The territory became an associate member of the Association of Caribbean States (see p. 459) in April 2006. The Turks and Caicos Islands are a member of the Commonwealth (see p. 244). As a dependency of the United Kingdom, the Turks and Caicos have the status of Overseas Territory in association with the European Union (EU, see p. 281).

ECONOMIC AFFAIRS

In 2011, according to UN estimates, the Turks and Caicos Islands' gross national income was US $1,045m., equivalent to $26,658 per head. In 2009, according to official estimates, gross domestic product (GDP) was US $795.6m., equivalent to some $21,346 per head. According to the World Bank, during 2002–11, it was estimated, the population increased at an average annual rate of 6.1%. According to official figures, overall GDP increased in real terms, by an annual average of 7.4% in 2001–09; real GDP increased by 9.3% in 2008, but decreased by 11.1% in 2009.

Agriculture is not practised on any significant scale in the Turks Islands or on South Caicos (the most populous island of the territory). None the less, the sector (including fishing) contributed 0.6% to GDP in 2009 and engaged 1.2% of the employed labour force in 2008. The other islands of the Caicos group grow some beans, maize and a few fruits and vegetables. There is some livestock-rearing, but the islands' principal natural resource is fisheries, which accounts for almost all commodity exports, the principal species caught being the spiny lobster (an estimated 154 metric tons in 2010) and the conch (an estimated 5,446 tons in that year). Conchs were being developed commercially (on the largest conch farm in the world), and there was potential for larger-scale fishing. Exports of lobster and conch earned US $4.3m. in 2009, accounting for 20.7% of total export earnings in that year. The sector's GDP decreased, in real terms, by an annual average rate of 1.8% during 2001–09; agricultural GDP decreased by 23.5% in 2008, but increased by 3.2% in 2009.

Industrial activity consists mainly of construction (especially for the tourism industry) and fish-processing. Industry contributed 14.3% to GDP in 2009 and the sector engaged some 23.5% of the employed labour force in 2008. The sector's GDP increased, in real terms, by an annual average rate of 4.7% during 2001–09; industrial GDP increased by 12.0% in 2008, but declined by 34.3% in 2009.

Mining contributed some 0.6% of GDP in 2009, and the sector engaged 0.1% of the employed labour force in 2008. The islands possess plentiful supplies of aragonite, but mineral fuels are imported (accounting for some 11.3% of the value of total imports in 2009) to satisfy energy requirements. The sector's GDP decreased, in real terms, by an annual average rate of 15.8% during 2001–09; mining GDP increased by 2.8% in 2008, but declined by a dramatic 90.3% in 2009.

Manufacturing contributed some 1.5% of GDP in 2009, and the sector engaged 1.4% of the employed labour force in 2008. The sector's GDP decreased, in real terms, by an annual average rate of 2.0% during 2001–09; manufacturing GDP decreased by 10.7% in 2009.

Construction contributed some 7.8% of GDP in 2009, and the sector engaged 21.1% of the employed labour force in 2008. The sector's GDP increased, in real terms, by an annual average rate of 3.3% during 2001–09; construction GDP increased by 2.8% in 2008, but declined by 50.2% in 2009.

The principal economic sector is the services industry, which in 2009 contributed an estimated 85.1% to GDP and engaged 75.3% of the employed labour force in 2008. The sector is dominated by tourism, which is concentrated on the island of Providenciales. The market is for wealthier visitors, mostly from the USA. Tourist arrivals increased from approximately 117,600 in 1999 to a provisional 354,000 in 2011, while tourism receipts were estimated at US $355.1m. in 2005. A new $40m. cruise ship terminal, capable of receiving large passenger liners, was inaugurated in 2006. In 2007 nearly 380,000 cruise ship passengers visited the islands, compared with just 17,052 in 2004. The 'offshore' financial sector has grown in recent years. In 2012 there were some 11,134 overseas companies active in the islands. The sector's GDP increased, in real terms, by an

annual average rate of 8.9% during 2001–09; services GDP increased by 13.2% in 2008, but declined by 3.7% in 2009.

In 2009 the Turks and Caicos Islands recorded a merchandise trade deficit (including re-exports) of US $354.6m. This deficit is normally offset by receipts from tourism, aid from the United Kingdom and revenue from the 'offshore' financial sector. The USA is the principal trading partner (providing 98.7% of imports and receiving 99.5% of exports, in 2009), but some trade is conducted with the United Kingdom, Japan, and with neighbouring nations.

There was an overall budget deficit of US $33.4m. in 2007/08, and the deficit on the current account was estimated to be equivalent to 3.5% of GDP in 2007. The total external public debt was projected to be $43.0m. in 2008/09. The rate of inflation, which stood at about 3.7% in 2007, is dependent upon the movement of prices in the USA, the islands' principal trading partner. The unemployment rate was recorded at some 8.3% in 2008. A large number of Turks and Caicos 'belongers' have emigrated, many to the Bahamas, especially in search of skilled labour.

The perceived stability of the Turks and Caicos Islands as an United Kingdom Overseas Territory was called into question following the suspension of the Constitution and imposition of direct rule from the United Kingdom in 2009. After several years of rapid expansion, GDP contracted by 11.1% in that year, but rose by 1.0% in 2010 and by 4.1% in 2011. There was a sustained recovery in the tourism industry during 2009–11, with visitor numbers increasing each year, although the construction sector declined sharply over the same period. Economic growth—driven more by inward investment than by domestic production—remained highly dependent on external factors. The large fiscal deficit and unsustainable debt burden were the main economic problems confronting the authorities. A large proportion of the territory's debt was rescheduled in February 2011, after the British Government agreed to act as guarantor on a low-interest US $260m. loan (superseded by a bond issue in April), but public debt continued to rise. Plans were also under way to lower the budget deficit—by rationalizing the civil service, reducing public sector salaries, and increasing taxes and duties. Although expenditure in 2011/12 was higher than originally forecast owing to the discovery of further unpaid debts, the authorities anticipated that the budget would register a surplus by the end of the 2012/13 financial year. In April 2013 the Progressive National Party Government announced several revenue-generating measures, including increases in hotel tax and stamp duty.

PUBLIC HOLIDAYS

2014: 1 January (New Year's Day), 10 March (for Commonwealth Day), 18 April (Good Friday), 21 April (Easter Monday), 26 May (National Heroes' Day), 9 June (Queen's Official Birthday), 4 August (Emancipation Day), 26 September (National Youth Day), 13 October (Columbus Day), 17 October (International Human Rights Day), 25–26 December (Christmas).

Statistical Survey

Source: Department of Economic Planning and Statistics, Ministry of Finance, South Base, Grand Turk; tel. 946-2801; fax 946-2557; e-mail info@depstc.org; internet www.depstc.org.

AREA AND POPULATION

Area: 948 sq km (366 sq miles). Note: Area includes low water level for all islands, but excludes area to high water mark.

Population: 19,886 at census of 20 August 2001; 31,458 (males 16,037, females 15,421) at census of 25 January 2012 (preliminary). *By Island* (at 2012 census, preliminary): Grand Turk 4,831; South Caicos 1,139; Middle Caicos 168; North Caicos 1,312; Salt Cay 108; Parrot Cay 131; Providenciales 23,769.

Density (at 2012 census): 33.2 per sq km.

Population by Age and Sex (at 2001 census): *0–14:* 5,693 (males 2,736, females 2,957); *15–64:* 13,436 (males 6,826, females 6,610); *65 and over:* 758 (males 335, females 423); *Total* 19,886 (males 9,897, females 9,989) (Source: UN, *Demographic Yearbook*).

Principal Towns: Cockburn Town (capital, on Grand Turk), population 2,500 (1987 estimate); Cockburn Harbour (South Caicos), population 1,000. *Mid-2011* (UN estimate, incl. suburbs): Grand Turk 6,784 (Source: UN, *World Urbanization Prospects: The 2011 Revision*).

Births, Marriages and Deaths (2008): Live births 453 (birth rate 12.4 per 1,000); Marriages 486; Deaths 65 (death rate 1.8 per 1,000). *2011:* Crude birth rate 17.8; Crude death rate 3.0 (Source: Pan American Health Organization).

Life Expectancy (years at birth, 2011): 79.1 (males 76.4; females 82.0). Source: Pan American Health Organization.

Economically Active Population (2008): Agriculture and fishing 259; Mining and quarrying 18; Manufacturing 290; Utilities 183; Construction 4,468; Wholesale and retail trade 1,841; Hotels and restaurants 4,098; Transport, storage and communications 1,053 Financial intermediation 610; Real estate, renting and business services 2,920; Public administration 2,432; Education, health and social work 944; Other community, social and personal services 1,491; Private household employment 526; *Sub-total* 21,133; Activities not adequately defined 360; *Total employed* 21,493; Unemployed 1,945; *Total labour force* 23,438.

HEALTH AND WELFARE

Total Fertility Rate (children per woman, 2011): 1.7.

Under-5 Mortality Rate (per 1,000 live births, 1997): 22.0.

Hospital Beds (per 1,000 head, 2008): 1.4.

Physicians (per 1,000 head, 2001): 7.3.

Health Expenditure (public, % of total, 2004): 12.6.

Health Expenditure (US $ per head, 2004): 741.2.

Access to Water (% of persons, 2008): 98.

Access to Sanitation (% of persons, 2004): 96.

Source: partly Pan American Health Organization.

For other sources and definitions see explanatory note on p. vi.

AGRICULTURE, ETC.

Fishing (metric tons, live weight of capture, 2010): Caribbean spiny lobster 154; Stromboid conchs 5,286; Total catch (incl. others) 5,446.

Source: FAO.

INDUSTRY

Electric Energy (production, million kWh): 182 in 2007; 198 in 2008; 209 in 2009. Source: UN Industrial Commodity Statistics Database.

FINANCE

Currency and Exchange Rate: United States currency is used: 100 cents = 1 US dollar ($). *Sterling and Euro Equivalents* (31 December 2012): £1 sterling = US $1.578; €1 = US $1.319; $100 = £63.37 = €75.79.

Budget (US $ million, 2007/08): Total revenue and grants 280.31 (Current revenue 206.79, Capital revenue and grants 73.52); Total expenditure 313.73 (Current expenditure 235.85, Capital expenditure 77.89).

Gross Domestic Product (US $ million at constant 2000 prices): 622.0 in 2007; 679.6 in 2008; 604.2 in 2009.

Expenditure on the Gross Domestic Product (US $ million, 2007, preliminary): Government final consumption expenditure 143.0; Private final consumption expenditure 458.3; Gross capital formation 392.6; *Total domestic expenditure* 993.9; Exports of goods and services 522.6; *Less* Imports of goods and services 687.9; *GDP in market prices* 828.6.

Gross Domestic Product by Economic Activity (US $ million, 2009): Agriculture and fishing 4.6; Mining and quarrying 5.0; Manufacturing 11.7; Utilities 35.3; Construction 62.3; Wholesale and retail trade 26.4; Hotels and restaurants 275.8; Transport, storage and communications 78.7; Financial intermediation 104.4; Real estate, renting and business activities 76.0; Public administration, defence and social security 58.5; Education 23.7; Health and social work 17.6; Other community, social and personal services 19.0; *Sub-total* 799.0; *Less* Financial intermediation services indirectly measured 85.6; *Gross value added in basic prices* 713.4; Taxes, *less* subsidies, on products 82.3; *GDP in market prices* 795.6.

Balance of Payments (US $ million, 2002): Exports of goods f.o.b. 7.7; Imports of goods f.o.b. −177.5; *Trade balance* −169.8; Exports of services 163.1; Imports of services −81.8; *Balance on goods and services* −88.5. Source: Caribbean Development Bank, *Social and Economic Indicators*.

EXTERNAL TRADE

Principal Commodities (US $ million, 2009, provisional): *Imports:* Food and live animals 62.2; Beverages and tobacco 15.3; Crude materials (inedible) except fuels 9.9; Mineral fuels, lubricants, etc. 42.3 (Petroleum and petroleum products 40.9); Chemicals and related products 21.9; Basic manufactures 68.4; Machinery and transport equipment 75.8 (Road vehicles 16.4); Miscellaneous manufactured articles 78.2; Total (incl. others) 375.4. *Exports:* Food and live animals 4.4 (Conchs 3.2; Lobsters 1.1); Machinery and transport equipment 11.4; Total exports (incl. others) 19.4. Note: Figures for exports exclude re-exports valued at 1.4.

Principal Trading Partners (US $ million, 2009, provisional): *Imports c.i.f.:* Bahamas 3.2; USA 370.4; Total (incl. others) 375.4. *Exports f.o.b.:* USA 20.7; Total (incl. others) 20.8. Note: Figures for exports include re-exports valued at 1.4.

TRANSPORT

Road Traffic (1984): 1,563 registered motor vehicles.

Shipping: *International Freight Traffic* (estimates in '000 metric tons, 1990): Goods loaded 135; Goods unloaded 149. *Merchant Fleet* (vessels registered at 31 December 2009): 7; Total displacement 1,386 grt. Sources: UN, *Monthly Bulletin of Statistics*; IHS Fairplay, *World Fleet Statistics*.

TOURISM

Tourist Arrivals ('000): 351 in 2009; 281 in 2010; 354 in 2011 (provisional).

Tourism Receipts (US $ million, estimates): 275.6 in 2003; 317.9 in 2004; 355.1 in 2005.

Sources: World Tourism Organization; Caribbean Development Bank, *Social and Economic Indicators*.

COMMUNICATIONS MEDIA

Telephones (2010): 3,700 main lines in use.

Mobile Cellular Telephones (2008): 25,100 subscribers.

Internet Subscribers (2008): 3,000.

Source: International Telecommunication Union.

EDUCATION

Pre-primary (2008/09 unless otherwise indicated): 9 schools (2005/06); 87 teachers (2004/05, estimate); 1,174 pupils.

Primary (2008/09 unless otherwise indicated): 14 schools (2005/06); 126 teachers (state schools only, 2005/06); 2,891 pupils.

General Secondary (2008/09 unless otherwise indicated): 8 schools (2005/06); 135 teachers (state schools only, 2005/06); 2,095 pupils. Note: In addition, 6 further private schools offered both primary and secondary education to 674 pupils in 2005/06.

Tertiary Education (2005/06): 2 schools; 257 pupils.

Special Education (2005/06): 2 schools; 99 pupils.

Pupil-teacher Ratio (primary education, UNESCO estimate): 15.0 in 2004/05. Source: UNESCO Institute for Statistics.

Adult Literacy Rate (UNESCO estimates): 99% (males 99%; females 98%) in 1998.

Sources: partly UNESCO Institute for Statistics; Caribbean Development Bank, *Social and Economic Indicators*.

Directory

The Government

HEAD OF STATE

Queen: HM Queen ELIZABETH II.

Governor: DAMIAN RODERIC (RIC) TODD (took office 12 Sept. 2011).

Deputy Governor: ANYA WILLIAMS.

THE CABINET
(May 2013)

The Cabinet is formed by the Progressive National Party

Premier and Minister of Tourism: Dr RUFUS WASHINGTON EWING.

Deputy Premier and Minister of Education, Youth, Sports and Culture: AKIERRA MARY DEANNE MISSICK.

Minister of Finance with responsibility for Investment and Trade, Airport Authority and Government Computer Services: CHARLES WASHINGTON MISICK.

Minister of Health and Human Services (Gender Affairs, Social Services): PORSHA MONIQUE STUBBS-SMITH.

Minister of Agriculture, Environment and Home Affairs: AMANDA ANISHA MISICK.

Minister of Border Control and Labour: RICARDO DON-HUE GARDINER.

Minister of Government Support Services: GEORGE ALEXANDER LIGHTBOURNE.

Attorney-General*: HUW SHEPHEARD.

Chief Financial Officer*: STEPHEN TURNBULL (acting).
* Appointed by the Governor.

GOVERNMENT OFFICES

Office of the Governor: Govt House, Waterloo, Grand Turk; tel. 946-2308; fax 946-2903; e-mail governorgt@fco.gov.uk.

Office of the Premier: N. J. S. Francis Bldg, Govt Sq., Grand Turk; tel. 946-2801; fax 946-2777; e-mail premier@gov.tc.

Office of the Deputy Governor: South Base, Grand Turk; tel. 946-2702; fax 946-2886; e-mail cso@gov.tc.

Attorney-General's Chambers: South Base, Grand Turk; tel. 946-2096; fax 946-2588; e-mail attorneygeneral@tciway.tc; internet www.lawsconsolidated.tc.

All ministries are based on Grand Turk.

Legislature

HOUSE OF ASSEMBLY

Speaker: ROBERT HALL.
Election, 9 November 2012

Party	Seats
Progressive National Party (PNP)	8
People's Democratic Movement (PDM) . . .	7
Total	**15**

In addition to the 15 directly elected members, two members are appointed by the Governor, and one each by the Premier and the Leader of the Opposition, bringing the total members to 19.

Election Commission

Office of the Supervisor of Elections: Providenciales; Supervisor DUDLEY LEWIS.

Political Organizations

People's Democratic Movement (PDM): POB 309, Providenciales; tel. 231-6898; e-mail info@votepdm.com; internet votepdm.com; f. 1975; favours internal self-govt and eventual independence; Chair. LYNDEN HALL; Leader SHARLENE CARTWRIGHT -ROBINSON; Sec.-Gen. CYNCLAIR MUSGROVE.

Progressive National Party (PNP): Progress House, Airport Rd, Providenciales; tel. 442-5050; fax 946-8206; e-mail pnptci@me.com; internet www.pnp.tc; supports full internal self-govt; Chair. TREVOR COOKE; Leader RUFUS W. EWING; Sec.-Gen. SHARON SIMMONS.

People's Progressive Party (PPP): Providenciales; f. 2012; Leader HAROLD CHARLES; Treas. EDWARD SMITH.

Judicial System

Justice is administered by the Supreme Court of the islands, presided over by the Chief Justice. There is a Chief Magistrate resident on Grand Turk, who also acts as Judge of the Supreme Court. There are also three Deputy Magistrates.

The Court of Appeal comprises a President and two Justices of Appeal. In certain cases, appeals are made to the Judicial Committee of the Privy Council in the United Kingdom.

Judicial Department: Grand Turk; tel. 946-2114; fax 946-2720; Chief Justice EDWIN GOLDSBROUGH; Chief Magistrate CLIFTON WARNER (Providenciales).

Religion

CHRISTIANITY

The Anglican Communion

Within the Church in the Province of the West Indies, the territory forms part of the diocese of Nassau and the Bahamas. The Bishop is resident in Nassau. According to the latest census (2001), around 10% of the population are Anglicans.

Anglican Church: St Mary's Church, Front St, Grand Turk; tel. 946-2289; internet bahamas.anglican.org; Archbishop Rev. LAISH Z. BOYD.

The Roman Catholic Church

The Bishop of Nassau, Bahamas (suffragan to the archdiocese of Kingston in Jamaica), has jurisdiction in the Turks and Caicos Islands as Superior of the Mission to the Territory (founded in June 1984). According to the 2001 census, around 11% of the population are Roman Catholics.

Roman Catholic Mission: Leeward Hwy, POB 340, Providenciales; tel. and fax 941-5136; e-mail info_rcm@catholic.tc; internet www.catholic.tc; churches on Grand Turk, South and North Caicos, and on Providenciales; 132 adherents in 1990 (according to census results); Chancellor Fr PETER BALDACCHINO.

Other Christian Churches

According to the 2001 census, some 36% of the population are Baptists, 12% belong to the Church of God, 9% are Methodists, 6% are Seventh-day Adventists and 2% are Jehovah's Witnesses.

Baptist Union of the Turks and Caicos Islands: South Caicos; tel. 946-3220; Gen. Sec. Rev. GOLDSTONE WILLIAMS.

Jehovah's Witnesses: Kingdom Hall, Intersection 21 Bridge Rd, Turtle Cove, POB 400, Providenciales; tel. 941-5583; fax 941-3496; e-mail englishprovo@yahoo.com.

New Testament Church of God: POB N-1708, Orea Alley, Grand Turk; tel. 324-2582; fax 324-7891; e-mail info@churchofgodbtci.org; internet www.churchofgodbtci.org.

Seventh-day Adventists: Grand Turk; tel. 946-2065; Pastor PETER KERR.

The Press

Times of the Islands Magazine: Lucille Lightbourne Bldg 7, POB 234, Providenciales; tel. and fax 946-4788; e-mail timespub@tciway.tc; internet www.timespub.tc; f. 1988; quarterly; circ. 10,000; Man. Editor KATHY BORSUK.

Turks and Caicos Free Press: Market Pl., POB 179, Providenciales; tel. 332-5615; fax 941-3402; e-mail info@fptci.com; internet tcfreepress.com; f. 1991; publ. by Vox-Global Télématique; weekly; circ. 3,000; Editor Dr GILBERT MORRIS; Man. BARBARA SMITH.

Turks & Caicos Islands Real Estate Association Real Estate Magazine: Lucille Lightbourne Bldg, POB 234, Providenciales; tel. and fax 946-4788; e-mail timespub@tciway.tc; internet www.tcrea.com; publ. by Times Publ. Ltd; 2 a year; circ. 15,000; Man. Editor KATHY BORSUK.

Turks and Caicos Sun: Airport Plaza, Suite 5, POB 439, Providenciales; tel. 946-8542; fax 941-3281; e-mail turksandcaicossun@express.tc; internet www.suntci.com; f. 2005; publ. by Island Publishing Co Ltd; weekly; Publr and Editor-in-Chief HAYDEN BOYCE.

Turks and Caicos Weekly News: Leeward Hwy, Cheshire House, POB 52, Providenciales; tel. 946-4664; fax 946-4661; e-mail tcnews@tciway.tc; internet www.tcweeklynews.com; f. 1982; Editor BLYTHE DUNCANSON.

Where, When, How: Ad Vantage Ltd, J105 Regent Village, Grace Bay, Providenciales; tel. 946-4815; fax 941-3497; e-mail info@wwhtci.com; internet www.wherewhenhow.com; f. 1994; 5 a year; travel magazine; Co-Editors CHARLES ZDENEK, BRENDA ZDENEK; circ. 70,000 a year.

Publisher

Ad Vantage Ltd: J105 Regent Village, Grace Bay, Providenciales; tel. 946-4815; fax 941-3497; e-mail info@wwhtci.com; internet www.wherewhenhow.com; f. 1994; publr of *Where When How* magazine and *Providenciales Dining Guide*; Co-Editors CHARLES ZDENEK, BRENDA ZDENEK.

Broadcasting and Communications

TELECOMMUNICATIONS

Digicel: Graceway House, Unit 207, Leeward Hwy, Providenciales; tel. 941-7600; fax 941-7601; e-mail tcicustomercare@digicelgroup.com; internet www.digiceltci.com; owned by an Irish consortium; granted licence in 2006 to provide mobile telecommunications services in Turks and Caicos; Group CEO and Dir COLM DELVES; Country Man. E. JAY SAUNDERS.

LIME: Cable & Wireless (TCI) Ltd, Leeward Hwy, POB 78, Providenciales; tel. 946-2200; fax 941-3051; e-mail cwtci@tciway.tc; internet www.time4lime.com; f. 1973; monopoly ended in Jan. 2006; fmrly Cable & Wireless; name changed as above 2008; telecommunications and internet services provider; CEO TONY RICE.

Regulatory Authority

Telecommunication Commission: Business Solutions Bldg, Leeward Hwy, POB 203, Providenciales; tel. 946-1900; fax 946-1119; e-mail johnwilliams@tcitelecommission.tc; internet www.tcitelecom.com; f. 2004; Telecommunications Officer JOHN WILLIAMS.

BROADCASTING

Radio

Radio Turks and Caicos (RTC): POB 69, Grand Turk; tel. 946-2010; fax 946-1600; e-mail rtcdirector@rtc107fm.com; internet www.rtc107fm.com; f. 1972; govt-owned; commercial; broadcasts 105 hrs weekly; Dir CHRISTOPHER JARRETT.

Radio Visión Cristiana Internacional: North End, South Caicos; tel. and fax 946-6847; fax 946-3724; e-mail wns_72@hotmail.com; internet www.radiovision.net; commercial; Man. WENDELL SEYMOUR.

Television

TCI New Media Network: Leeward Hwy, Providenciales; e-mail news@tcinewmedianetwork.tc; internet tcinewmedianetwork.tc; f. 2008; govt-owned; Gen. Man. AVA-DAYNE KERR.

WIV Cable TV: Tower Raza, Leeward Hwy, POB 679, Providenciales; tel. 946-4866; fax 946-4790; e-mail info@wivgroup.com; internet wivtc.com; Chair. G. ROBERT BLANCHARD, Jr.

Finance

(cap. = capital; res = reserves; dep. = deposits; br(s). = branch(es);
amounts in US $ unless otherwise indicated)

BANKING

Bordier Bank (TCI) Ltd: Caribbean Pl., Leeward Hwy, POB 5, Providenciales; tel. 946-4335; fax 946-4540; e-mail enquiries@bibt.com; internet www.bibt.com; Chair. FRANÇOIS BOHN; Man. ELISE HARTSHORN.

British Caribbean Bank: Governors Rd, POB 270, Providenciales; tel. 941-5028; fax 941-5029; e-mail info@bcbtci.com; internet www.bcbtci.com; fmrly Belize Bank, Turks & Caicos; Man. Dir ANDREW ASHCROFT.

FirstCaribbean International Bank (Bahamas) Ltd: Leeward Hwy, POB 698, Providenciales; tel. 946-4007; fax 946-4573; e-mail care@firstcaribbeanbank.com; internet www.firstcaribbeanbank.com; f. 2002 following merger of Caribbean operations of Barclays Bank PLC and CIBC; Barclays relinquished its stake to CIBC in June 2006; Exec. Chair. MICHAEL MANSOOR; CEO RIK PARKHILL.

Scotiabank (Turks and Caicos) Ltd (Canada): Cherokee Rd, POB 15, Providenciales; tel. 339-7100; fax 946-4755; e-mail bns.turkscaicos@scotiabank.com; internet turksandcaicos.scotiabank.com; Man. Dir CECIL ARNOLD; brs on Grand Turk and Providenciales.

Turks and Caicos Banking Co Ltd (TCBC): H102 Regent Village, Grace Bay Rd, POB 777, Providenciales; tel. 941-4994; fax 941-5943; e-mail services@tcbc.tc; internet www.turksandcaicos-banking.com; f. 1980; dep. 71m., total assets 81.4m. (Dec. 2011); Pres. ANTON J. B. FAESSLER; CEO DAVID J. BEE.

REGULATORY AUTHORITY

Financial Services Commission (FSC): Harry E. Francis Bldg, Pond St, POB 173, Grand Turk; tel. 946-2791; fax 946-2821; e-mail fsc@tciway.tc; internet www.tcifsc.tc; f. 2002; regulates local and 'offshore' financial services sector; Chair. ERROL ALLEN; Man. Dir J. KEVIN HIGGINS.

TRUST COMPANIES

Berkshire Trust Co Ltd: Caribbean Pl., POB 657, Providenciales; tel. 946-4324; fax 946-4354; e-mail berkshire.trust@tciway.tc; internet www.berkshire.tc; Dir GORDON WILLIAMSON.

Chartered Trust Co: Town Centre Mall, Mezzanine Floor, Butterfield Sq., POB 125, Providenciales; tel. 946-4881; fax 946-4041; e-mail reception@chartered-tci.com; internet www.chartered-tci.com; Man. Dir PETER A. SAVORY.

M & S Trust Co Ltd: Butterfield Sq., POB 260, Providenciales; tel. 946-4650; fax 946-4663; e-mail sr@mslaw.tc; internet www.mslaw.tc/Trust; Man. Partner TIMOTHY P. O'SULLIVAN; Man. STEVE ROSS.

Meridian Trust Co Ltd: Caribbean Pl., Leeward Hwy, POB 599, Providenciales; tel. 941-3082; fax 941-3223; e-mail mtcl@tciway.tc; internet www.meridiantrust.tc; Man. Dir KEITH BURANT.

Temple Trust Co Ltd: 1143 Leeward Hwy, Providenciales; tel. 946-5740; fax 946-5739; e-mail info@temple-group.com; internet www.templefinancialgroup.com; f. 1985; CEO DAVID C. KNIPE.

INSURANCE

Turks and Caicos Association of Insurance Managers (TC-AIM): Southwinds Pl., Unit 6, Leeward Hwy, Providenciales; tel. 946-4987; fax 946-4621; internet turksandcaicos.tc/aim; f. 2000 as Asscn of Insurance Managers; name changed as above in 2003 when registered as a non-profit asscn; protects interests of domestic and 'offshore' insurance cos in the islands; Pres. ADRIAN CORR; Treas. ROSS BLUMENTRITT.

Turks and Caicos Islands National Insurance Board: Misick's Bldg, POB 250, Grand Turk; tel. 946-1048; fax 946-2701; internet www.tcinib.tc; f. 1992; 4 brs; Chair. LILLIAN MISSICK; Dir COLIN HEARTWELL.

Trade and Industry

GOVERNMENT AGENCIES

Financial Services Commission (FSC): see Finance.

General Trading Company (Turks and Caicos) Ltd: PMBI, Cockburn Town, Grand Turk; tel. 946-2464; fax 946-2799; shipping agents, importers, air freight handlers; wholesale distributor of petroleum products, wines and spirits.

Turks Islands Importers Ltd (TIMCO): Front St, POB 72, Grand Turk; tel. 946-2480; fax 946-2481; f. 1952; agents for Lloyds of London, importers and distributors of food, beer, liquor, building materials, hardware and appliances; Dir HUBERT MAGNUS.

DEVELOPMENT ORGANIZATION

Turks and Caicos Islands Investment Agency (TC Invest): Hon. Headley Durham Bldg, Church Folly, POB 105, Grand Turk; tel. 946-2058; fax 946-1464; e-mail tcinvest@tciway.tc; internet www.tcinvest.tc; f. 1974 as Devt Bd of the Turks and Caicos Islands; statutory body; devt finance for private sector; promotion and management of internal investment; Chair. CLAYTON GREENE; CEO HIGGS CONRAD.

CHAMBERS OF COMMERCE

Grand Turk Chamber of Commerce: POB 148, Grand Turk; tel. 946-2043; fax 946-2504; e-mail gtchamberofcomm@tciway.tc; f. 1974; 57 mem. cos; Pres. and Exec. Dir GLENNEVANS CLARKE; Hon. Sec. SHERLIN WILLIAMS.

North Caicos Chamber of Commerce: tel. 231-1232; Pres. FRANKLYN ROBINSON; Sec. LLEWYN HANDFIELD.

Providenciales Chamber of Commerce: POB 361, Providenciales; tel. 332-6418; e-mail provochambertci@gmail.com; internet www.provochamber.com; f. 1991; 131 mems (2006); Pres. TINA FENIMORE; Vice-Pres. E. JAY SAUNDERS.

UTILITIES

Electricity and Gas

Fortis TCI Ltd: 1030 Leeward Hwy, POB 132, Providenciales; tel. 946-4313; fax 946-4532; internet www.fortistci.com; Fortis Energy (Bermuda) completed its acquisition of 100% shares in the co in Aug. 2006; sole provider of electricity in South Caicos; Pres. and CEO EDDINTON POWELL.

Turks and Caicos Utilities Ltd: Pond St, POB 73, Grand Turk; tel. 946-2798; fax 946-2896; e-mail customerservice@tcu.tc; internet www.tcu.tc; Man. JOHN CHANNER.

Water

Provo Water Co Ltd: 197A, Grace Bay Rd, Providenciales; tel. 946-5202; fax 946-5204; e-mail provowater@tciway.tc; internet provowater.server279.com; owned by HAB Group; generation.

Turks and Caicos Water Co: Provo Golf Clubhouse, Grace Bay Rd, POB 124, Providenciales; tel. 946-5659; fax 946-5830; e-mail jared@habgroup.com; internet www.habgroup.com/TCWC/Turks_and_Caicos_Water_Co.html; production of desalinated water.

Transport

ROADS

There are 121 km (75 miles) of roads in the islands, of which 24 km, on Grand Turk, South Caicos and Providenciales, are surfaced with tarmac. A causeway linking the North and Middle Caicos islands was completed in 2007.

SHIPPING

There are regular freight services from Miami, FL, USA. The main sea ports are Grand Turk, Providenciales, Salt Cay and Cockburn

Harbour on South Caicos. A new US $40m. cruise ship terminal in Grand Turk, with capacity for large passenger liners, opened in 2006.

AL Services Ltd (AlServ): SDR Commercial Centre, 176 South Dock Rd, POB 253, Providenciales; tel. 941-3267; fax 941-3269; e-mail piper@tciway.tc; internet www.al-services.tc; freight forwarders; Man. Dir MCALLISTER (PIPER) HANCHELL.

Cargo Express Shipping Service Ltd: South Dock Rd, Bldg 70, Providenciales; tel. 941-5006; fax 941-5062; e-mail cargoexp@express.tc; represents Tropical Shipping.

Seacair Ltd: 1 Churchill Bldg, Front St, POB 170, Grand Turk; tel. 946-2591; fax 946-2226; e-mail seacairltd@tciway.tc; represents G & G Shipping; cargo and freight services; Gen. Man. ERIC SMITH.

CIVIL AVIATION

There are international airfields on Grand Turk, South Caicos, North Caicos and Providenciales, the last being the most important; there are also landing strips on Middle Caicos, Pine Cay, Parrot Cay and Salt Cay. An expansion project at Providenciales airport that included a new terminal building and the lengthening of the runway to accommodate transatlantic flights was completed in 2013. A second phase of the terminal expansion project was expected to begin by mid-2013.

Civil Aviation Authority: POB 168, Grand Turk; tel. 946-2137; fax 946-1185; e-mail info@tcicaa.org; internet tcicaa.org; Chair. BRIAN LIGHTBOURNE; Man. Dir THOMAS SWANN.

Air Turks and Caicos (2003) Ltd: 1 Interisland Plaza, Old Airport Rd, POB 191, Providenciales; tel. 946-4181; fax 946-4040; e-mail info@flyairtc.com; internet www.airturksandcaicos.com; also operates SkyKing Ltd; Chair. LYNDON R. GARDINER.

Caicos Express Airways: Southern Shores Bldg, Leeward Hwy, POB 18, Providenciales; tel. 941-5730; fax 946-8131; e-mail info@caicosexpressairways.com; internet www.caicosexpressairways.com; chartered flights; Man. Dir RICHARDSON ARTHUR.

Cairsea Services Ltd: Old Airport Rd, POB 138, Providenciales; tel. 946-4205; fax 946-4504; e-mail shipping@cairsea.com; internet www.cairsea.com; Man. Dir RODNEY THOMPSON.

Global Airways Ltd: POB 359, Providenciales; tel. 941-3222; fax 946-7290; e-mail global@tciway.tc; internet www.globalairways.tc; operates inter-island connections and Caribbean charter flights; Man. Dir LINDSEY GARDINER.

Turks and Caicos Islands Airport Authority (TCIAA): Providenciales International Airport, Providenciales; tel. 946-4420; fax 941-5996; e-mail info@tciairports.com; internet www.tciairports.com/web; CEO JOHN T. SMITH.

Tourism

The islands' main tourist attractions are the numerous unspoilt beaches, and the opportunities for diving. Salt Cay has been designated a World Heritage site by UNESCO. Hotel accommodation is available on Grand Turk, Salt Cay, South Caicos, Parrot Cay, Pine Cay and Providenciales. In 2011 there were some 354,000 tourist arrivals. In 2006 68.3% of stop-over tourists were from the USA. In 2007 there were 2,632 hotel rooms (some 87% of which were on Providenciales). Revenue from the sector in 2005 totalled an estimated US $355.1m.

Turks and Caicos Hotel and Tourism Association: POB 251, Ports of Call, Providenciales; tel. 941-5787; fax 946-4001; e-mail manager@turksandcaicoshta.com; internet www.turksandcaicoshta.com; fmrly Turks and Caicos Hotel Asscn; over 90 mem. orgs; Pres. MICHEL NEUTELINGS; CEO STACY COX.

Turks and Caicos Islands Tourist Board: Front St, POB 128, Grand Turk; tel. 946-2321; fax 946-2733; e-mail info@turksandcaicostourism.com; internet www.turksandcaicostourism.com; f. 1970; br. in Providenciales; Dir RALPH HIGGS.

Defence

The United Kingdom is responsible for the defence of the Turks and Caicos Islands.

Education

Primary education, beginning at seven years of age and lasting seven years, is compulsory, and is provided free of charge in government schools. Secondary education, from the age of 14, lasts for five years, and is also free. In 2004/05, according to UNESCO estimates, 78% of children in the relevant age-group were enrolled in primary education, while the comparable ratio for secondary education was 70%. In 2005/06 there were 14 government primary schools and eight government secondary schools. In 2003 government budgetary recurrent expenditure on scholarships, education, grants and contributions was US $8.2m. (8.8% of total recurrent expenditure). According to the 2011/12 government budget communication, $23.4m. was allocated to education and youth departments (accounting for 13.7% of government spending), of which $5.4m. was for tertiary education in the territory during that fiscal year.

THE UNITED STATES OF AMERICA

Introductory Survey

LOCATION, CLIMATE, LANGUAGE, RELIGION, FLAG, CAPITAL

The United States of America comprises mainly the North American continent between Canada and Mexico. Alaska, to the north-west of Canada, and Hawaii, in the central Pacific Ocean, are two of the 50 states of the USA. There is considerable climatic variation, with mean annual average temperatures ranging from 29°C (77°F) in Florida to −13.3°C (10°F) in Alaska. Average annual rainfall ranges from 1,831 mm (72.1 ins) in Arkansas to 191 mm (7.5 ins) in Nevada. Much of Texas, New Mexico, Arizona, Nevada and Utah is desert. The official language is English, although there are significant Spanish-speaking minorities. Christianity is the predominant religion. The national flag (proportions 10 by 19) has 13 alternating stripes (seven red and six white) with a dark blue rectangular canton, containing 50 white, five-pointed stars, in the upper hoist. The capital is Washington, DC.

CONTEMPORARY POLITICAL HISTORY

Historical Context

Concern at the spread of communist influence in Asia dominated US foreign policy during the 1960s and early 1970s. From 1961, until their termination in 1973 by President Richard Nixon, US military operations against communist forces in South Viet Nam led to considerable political division within the USA and were widely criticized internationally. Following a series of scandals involving Nixon and senior administration officials in allegations of corruption and obstruction of justice, known as the 'Watergate' affair, Nixon resigned in August 1974 and was replaced by the Vice-President, Gerald Ford. In November 1976 Jimmy Carter, a Democrat, was elected President. Domestically, economic recession and inflation preoccupied the Carter Administration, and the President's management of the economy was a decisive factor in his defeat by the Republican candidate, Ronald Reagan, in the 1980 presidential election.

Although economic recession and high unemployment persisted in the early period of the Reagan Administration, the Republicans retained their previous level of congressional representation in the November 1982 elections. With the resumption of economic growth in 1983, and its strong resurgence through 1984, unemployment and inflation fell, and in November Reagan was re-elected for a further four-year term, securing the largest majority of electoral votes in US history. However, the closing months of Reagan's presidency were clouded by political scandals involving senior presidential appointees.

Domestic Political Affairs

The Gulf War and the presidency of George Bush, 1989–93

At the November 1988 presidential election, Reagan was succeeded by his Vice-President, George Bush, although the Senate and House of Representatives both retained Democratic majorities. The initial months of the Bush Administration were dominated by concern over the formulation of effective measures to contain the federal budget deficit, and over the future course of arms reduction negotiations with the USSR (see Relations with the USSR and successor states).

Following the invasion of Kuwait by Iraqi forces on 2 August 1990, and the subsequent annexation of that country by Iraq, the US Government assumed a leading international role in the implementation of measures to bring about an Iraqi withdrawal. The imposition of mandatory economic sanctions against Iraq by the UN Security Council on 6 August was quickly followed by 'Operation Desert Shield', in which US combat troops and aircraft were dispatched to Saudi Arabia, at that country's request, to secure its borders against a possible attack by Iraq. In late August the UN Security Council endorsed the use of military action to enforce its economic sanctions. In early September President Bush and his USSR counterpart, Mikhail Gorbachev, jointly demanded an Iraqi withdrawal, and later that month the UN Security Council intensified its economic measures against

Iraq. However, the ineffectiveness both of economic sanctions and of diplomatic negotiation had become evident by late November, and the USSR gave its assent to the use of force against Iraq, although it did not participate in the multinational force that was now arrayed in the Persian (Arabian) Gulf region and included, under US command, air, sea and ground forces from the United Kingdom, France, Italy, Egypt, Morocco, Kuwait and the other Arab Gulf states. Jordan, which had sought to promote a negotiated settlement, was perceived by the US Government as sympathetic to Iraq, and US financial aid to that country was suspended.

On 29 November 1990 the UN Security Council authorized the use of 'all necessary means' to force Iraq to withdraw from Kuwait, unless it did so by 15 January 1991. By early January the USA had established a considerable military presence in the Gulf region, and on 17 January 'Operation Desert Storm' was launched, with massive air and missile attacks against Iraqi positions, both in Iraq and Kuwait. In the course of the conflict, more than 110,000 attacking air missions were flown over Kuwait and Iraq by multinational air forces, while naval support operations were conducted from the Gulf. In the following weeks severe damage was inflicted on Iraqi military and economic targets, while counter-attacks by its air force, and attempts to draw Israel into the conflict by launching missile attacks on population centres, proved ineffective. A ground offensive by the multinational force was launched on 23–24 February, and Iraqi positions were quickly overrun. Hostilities were suspended on 28 February. The Government of Iraq accepted cease-fire terms on 3 March, leaving the multinational forces in control of Kuwait and parts of southern Iraq. Troop withdrawals from the occupied area of Iraq commenced in March, with the remaining US troops evacuated in May, to be replaced by a UN peace-keeping force.

Following the termination of hostilities, in which 148 US troops died in combat, internal rebellions broke out within Iraq by groups opposed to President Saddam Hussain. The severity with which these were suppressed, particularly in the northern region among the Kurdish ethnic group, and the subsequent flight of refugees into neighbouring areas of Turkey and Iran, prompted large-scale international relief operations. The US Administration was widely criticized for its refusal to support the anti-Government insurgents and to take action to depose Saddam Hussain. In May 1991 the USA began airlifting troops to northern Iraq to establish 'safe' enclaves, to which Kurdish refugees were encouraged to return. The US military continued to monitor events in these Kurdish areas from operational bases in Turkey and other strategic points in the region. Relations with Iraq remained tense following the discovery in November by UN representatives that President Saddam Hussain's regime was seeking to conceal its continuing development of nuclear weapons capability. In July 1992 contention arose between the Government of Iraq and the UN over the rights of UN observers to inspect Iraqi nuclear facilities, and in the following month the US Government sought to limit internal military operations by the Iraqi Government by imposing an air exclusion zone south of latitude 32°N. This was followed, in January 1993, by US participation in selective bombings of Iraqi missile sites.

Following the conclusion of the Gulf War in early 1991, Bush's political popularity declined sharply, amid growing public perception that the Government was assigning greater priority to foreign affairs than to addressing the problems of the US economy, which had been in recession since early 1989. In April 1992 serious rioting broke out in Los Angeles, California, and spread briefly to several other cities. The underlying causes of the disorders were widely ascribed to the worsening economic and social plight of the impoverished urban black minority.

The 1992 presidential election campaign, in which Bush was opposed by Bill Clinton, a Democratic state governor, and Ross Perot, a populist independent, was dominated by social and economic issues. Bush's record of economic management, particularly in relation to the persistence of federal budget deficits, provided the major line of attack by the opposing candidates. Voter turn-out, at 55%, was the highest at any presidential election since 1968, and gave a decisive majority, of 43% to 37%, to Clinton. Perot obtained almost 19% of the popular vote.

The Clinton presidency, 1993–2001

The initial preoccupation of the Clinton Administration was the formulation of an economic recovery plan, to be phased over a five-year period, to reduce the federal budget deficit by means of increased taxation and economies in the cost of government, rather than by reduced levels of spending. Certain aspects of the economic recovery plan, particularly those relating to higher income tax and a new energy tax, encountered initial opposition in the Democrat-controlled Congress, but were eventually approved, in a modified form, by mid-1993. However, by this time the President's initial popularity had diminished, owing in part to perceptions of indecisiveness by Clinton in formulating effective policies.

The collapse of Clinton's plans for health care reform following congressional opposition in 1994, together with increasing public concern about the domestic economy and the effectiveness of Clinton's policies on social issues (notably in the areas of welfare expenditure, law enforcement and the protection of traditional social values), led to a sharp rise in support for the conservative doctrines of politicians representing the right wing of the Republican Party. At congressional elections in November 1994, the Republicans gained control both of the Senate (for the first time since 1986) and the House of Representatives (which had been controlled by the Democrats since 1954). As a result, in 1995 serious divisions began to emerge between President Clinton and Congress. In June tensions arose over proposals to achieve a balanced federal budget. In November Clinton, in an effort to resolve the deadlock, refused to renew the temporary funding arrangements, causing an eight-day shutdown of all non-essential operations of the federal Government. Agreement on the 1995/96 budget was eventually reached in April 1996.

Clinton decisively secured a second term in office in November 1996, gaining 49.2% of the popular vote, compared with 40.7% for his Republican challenger, Bob Dole, and 8.4% for Ross Perot, who stood as a representative of the Reform Party. The President announced proposals to achieve further reductions in welfare dependency, by providing tax credits and other incentives to employers. Financial savings were to be achieved by reductions in defence expenditure, and by the implementation of additional cuts in spending on health care for the elderly. Clinton reiterated his intention, however, of seeking improved provisions for insured health care, and of achieving a balanced federal budget by 2002. Agreement between Clinton and the Republican congressional leadership on the general terms of these budgetary measures was reached in May 1997.

During his second term as President, Clinton was confronted by a number of allegations, which he consistently denied, of perjury and obstruction of justice arising from accusations of sexual harassment, dating from prior to 1992 and extending throughout his presidency. These matters were brought within the ambit of a congressionally mandated, independent counsel, Kenneth Starr, who began in 1994 to examine the legal ramifications of the 'Whitewater' affair (President Clinton and his wife, Hillary, were accused of financial irregularities in their alleged involvement in a company that collapsed in 1989, during Clinton's tenure as Governor of Arkansas). In January 1998 Starr was authorized by the Attorney-General to investigate whether a sexual relationship alleged by a former White House intern, Monica Lewinsky, had taken place with the President in 1995. Clinton vehemently denied any improper conduct with Lewinsky; however, in August 1998, following an offer of immunity from prosecution by Starr to Lewinsky, the President admitted that an inappropriate relationship had taken place, although he had at no time sought to obstruct legal processes. Starr's report to Congress alleged that Clinton had committed 11 offences of perjury and obstruction of justice, constituting grounds for his removal from office. No evidence, however, was offered of wrongdoing by Clinton in relation to the 'Whitewater' affair. In October the House of Representatives voted to commence an impeachment inquiry against the President, but in February 1999 the Senate acquitted Clinton on the first and second articles of impeachment. A subsequent attempt in the Senate to obtain a vote of censure on Clinton was unsuccessful.

In August 1998 bomb attacks on US embassy buildings in Nairobi, Kenya, and Dar es Salaam, Tanzania, claimed 258 lives, and were followed by US air missile attacks on a factory site in Khartoum, Sudan (which was alleged to be a manufactory of chemicals for use in toxic gases), and on targets in Afghanistan, which were stated by the US Government to be operational centres for Osama bin Laden, a fugitive Saudi Arabian-born Islamist activist whom the USA believed to be responsible for past assaults on US forces and facilities in Somalia, Yemen and Saudi Arabia. Bin Laden was also held responsible for terrorist operations within the USA, including the 1993 bombing of the World Trade Center in New York. In October 2001 four associates of bin Laden were sentenced to life imprisonment by a US court for their involvement in the bomb attacks in Nairobi and Dar es Salaam. Meanwhile, in September 1996 Clinton sanctioned missile strikes from US naval vessels in the Gulf at military targets in Iraq, in retaliation for attacks by Iraqi forces against Kurds in northern Iraq. In December 1998, following the termination by Iraq of international weapons inspections in its territory, the USA and the United Kingdom conducted further missile raids on Iraqi military sites.

Presidential vote of 2000: George W. Bush elected

A presidential election was held on 7 November 2000. Vice-President Al Gore was the Democratic Party candidate, while George W. Bush, the Governor of Texas and a son of former President Bush, was the Republican Party's nominee. Following voting, it emerged that the possession of an overall majority in the presidential Electoral College would depend on the 25 college mandates from the state of Florida, where the result of the ballot was in dispute. The state was initially declared in favour of Governor Bush, pending the result of a mandatory automated recount of the votes; however, the Democrats challenged the declaration (and the state government's refusal to permit the ballots to be recounted by electoral staff following the automated recount) in the Florida Supreme Court, claiming that a significant number of votes in certain counties had been incorrectly registered by the automated counting system. The Court ruled that the ballots in the counties concerned should be recounted by electoral staff and allowed an additional 12 days for this process to be completed. The US Supreme Court disallowed this ruling, however, and returned the matter to the Florida Supreme Court for further consideration. Only one county completed its 'manual' recount and the result remained in Governor Bush's favour (by 537 votes). The Democrats began further legal action, claiming that the importance of recounting all disputed ballots transcended time limits. The Florida Supreme Court upheld the appeal and ordered the recounting of some 45,000 disputed ballots. The Republicans challenged the verdict, claiming that no provision for such 'manual' recounts was made in the electoral legislation. The US Supreme Court narrowly upheld the Republican appeal. With all legal options exhausted, and with the Florida legislature having voted to endorse a list of Republican electors irrespective of the outcome of further legal action, Vice-President Gore conceded defeat in Florida (and thereby nationally) on 13 December. Final results subsequently indicated that Vice-President Gore obtained 48.4% of the valid votes cast, compared with 47.9% obtained by Governor Bush. Thus, the latter became the first contender since 1876 to win a majority in the Electoral College while losing the national popular ballot.

The new Government immediately suspended the implementation of a number of environmental regulations issued by Clinton shortly before his departure from office. The Bush Administration's first budget, presented in February 2001, included provisions for reductions in levels of personal taxation.

Attacks of 11 September 2001

On 11 September 2001 four commercial passenger aircraft were hijacked shortly after take-off from Boston, New York and Washington, DC. The two aircraft originating in Boston, both bound for Los Angeles, were diverted to New York, and each was flown into one of the two towers of the World Trade Center, both of which subsequently collapsed. The third aircraft was flown into the Pentagon building (the headquarters of the Department of Defense) in Washington, DC, and the fourth aircraft, also apparently heading for Washington, DC, crashed in farmland near Pittsburgh, Pennsylvania. The death toll was eventually put at 2,752, including 266 passengers and crew (including the hijackers) on the four aircraft, 190 at the Pentagon, and the remainder in New York, principally those unable to escape from the towers before they collapsed, and members of the emergency services. On 13 September the Secretary of State, Gen. Colin Powell, identified Osama bin Laden and his al-Qa'ida organization, a network of fundamentalist Islamist militants, as responsible for the attacks. However, bin Laden, who was believed to be in Afghanistan, where he was harboured by the extremist Islamist Taliban regime, had already denied accusations that he had ordered the hijackings, although he expressed his approval of the attacks. In late 2002 an independent bipartisan inquiry, the National Commission on Terrorist Attacks Upon the United States, was established to investigate the circumstances surrounding the attacks. In March 2003 security forces in Rawalpindi, Pakistan, arrested the Kuwaiti-born Khalid Sheikh Mohammed, accused of being the operational planner behind the attacks, and released him into US custody for interrogation. In March 2006, in a court in Virginia, Moroccan-born Zacarias Moussaoui pleaded guilty to charges of conspiracy to commit acts of terrorism, in relation to the attacks. Moussaoui had pleaded guilty to conspiracy charges in July 2002, but subsequently retracted his plea. In May 2006 he was sentenced to life imprisonment without parole. In March 2007 Khalid Sheikh Mohammed, regarded as one of the principal agents of al-Qa'ida's operations, was tried by military commission, along with two other alleged key al-Qa'ida operatives. The US Department of Defense released a partial transcript of Sheikh Mohammed's trial at the detention centre in Guantánamo Bay, Cuba (see US-led military operations in Afghanistan, below), in which the suspect claimed involvement in 31 separate international terrorism plots and attacks, including orchestration of the 1993 and 2001 attacks on the World Trade Center, the beheading of US journalist Daniel Pearl in 2002 and numerous assassination attempts against international political leaders. However, speculation that such admissions had been obtained under duress, or torture, tarnished any belief in the international community that justice had been achieved and provoked further criticism of the interrogation methods employed at Guantánamo Bay. Charges brought by the US Government in February 2008 against five prisoners being held in Guantánamo Bay, including Khalid Sheikh Mohammed, elicited similar censure. The charges, for which military prosecutors were to seek the death penalty, related to the detainees' alleged involvement in the 2001 attacks and included conspiracy, murder, attacking civilians, destruction of property and terrorism. In November 2009 the Attorney-General, Eric Holder, announced that all five would be transferred to New York for a civilian trial (in which the death penalty would still be sought). The charges against the five within the military commissions were withdrawn in January 2010 in order to allow their future trial by a civilian court.

In the wake of the attacks on New York and Washington, DC, Congress unanimously approved emergency anti-terrorism legislation, which made provision for increased military spending and US $20,000m. for reconstruction in New York, and adopted a resolution authorizing the President to use 'all necessary and appropriate force' against those who organized the attacks. Congress also approved the so-called 'Patriot Act' (Uniting and Strengthening America by Providing the Appropriate Tools Required to Intercept and Obstruct Terrorism—PATRIOT—Act of 2001), which was signed into law in October 2001, giving wide-ranging powers to the Government to investigate citizens and non-citizens alike. The Act was viewed by critics as a threat to civil liberties. (The Patriot Act was scheduled to expire at the end of 2005, but was temporarily extended by Congress until February 2006. A continuance of the measure, the USA Patriot Act Improvement and Reauthorization Act of 2005, was signed into law by the President in March 2006.) The Government began to form an international coalition against terrorism, for which most Western Governments pledged their support. The North Atlantic Treaty Organization (NATO) invoked Article Five of the NATO Charter (which states that an attack on a member state is an attack on all 19 members), which required members to assist the USA; the Governments of the United Kingdom, France and Germany, among others, offered military and financial assistance. The Taliban regime in Afghanistan denied involvement in the terrorist attacks, and warned that it would retaliate if attacked. On 17 September 2001 the USA issued an ultimatum to the Taliban, via Pakistan (one of only three states with diplomatic links to the regime), to surrender bin Laden or face an imminent military assault. Several weeks of intense diplomatic activity ensued, during which time international support for the USA's so-called global 'war on terror' increased, and the US Government was apparently able to gather further evidence of the al-Qa'ida network's involvement in the attacks. Meanwhile, US military forces increased their presence in the region around Afghanistan. Pakistan and Uzbekistan agreed to grant the US-led forces use of their airbases for emergency operations, and Russia allowed access to its airspace for humanitarian missions. Saudi Arabia also granted access to its airspace.

US-led military operations in Afghanistan

On 2 October 2001 NATO declared that it had received evidence from the USA that confirmed bin Laden's responsibility for the terrorist attacks. On 7 October US and British armed forces commenced military operations ('Operation Enduring Freedom') against Taliban military targets and suspected al-Qa'ida training camps in Afghanistan. On 14 October a senior Taliban official offered to surrender bin Laden to a third country in return for a cessation of US bombing, if the USA provided evidence of his involvement in the terrorist attacks, an offer the USA rejected. The US-led forces co-ordinated operations with the military wing of the exiled Afghan Government, the United National Islamic Front for the Salvation of Afghanistan (also known as the Northern Alliance). During November the latter made substantial territorial gains in northern and western Afghanistan, including the Afghan capital, Kabul, and Mazar-i-Sharif, a strategically important town in the north. In late November US ground forces were deployed for the first time, near the southern city of Kandahar, in an attempt to locate bin Laden. Kandahar fell to the US-led forces in early December, leaving only localized areas of Taliban resistance. The USA refused, however, to deploy peace-keeping troops in Afghanistan to support the interim administration of Hamid Karzai, which replaced the Taliban regime in December, although in January 2002 the Bush Government pledged some US $296.8m. in funds for the reconstruction of Afghanistan.

In January 2002 the US military began transferring members of the Taliban and al-Qa'ida who had been captured in battle to the US naval base in Guantánamo Bay. Initially, the USA refused to grant the detainees (numbering almost 300) prisoner-of-war status under the Geneva Convention of 1949 (which guaranteed trial by court martial or a civilian court, as opposed to a military tribunal), prompting criticism from its coalition partners, which intensified following the publication of photographs showing prisoners shackled and blindfolded. In February, following pressure from the British and French Governments, President Bush accorded partial protection of the Convention to captured Taliban fighters (he denied full protection, claiming that the soldiers were members of an irregular militia); al-Qa'ida captives were offered no protection, as they were considered to be terrorists with no allegiance to any specific state or government. In June the Supreme Court ruled that, while the President as Commander-in-Chief had the power to detain enemy combatants, they were entitled to legal representation in a US federal court. The following day the first three prisoners from Guantánamo Bay appeared before a military tribunal.

In July 2004 the National Commission on Terrorist Attacks Upon the United States delivered its final report into intelligence failures in the months preceding the attacks of 11 September 2001. It asserted that both the Clinton and Bush Administrations had failed to realize the immediacy of the threat posed by the al-Qa'ida network. The report highlighted opportunities to uncover the plot that had been overlooked by both the Central Intelligence Agency (CIA) and the Federal Bureau of Investigation (FBI). However, it did not conclude that the attacks could have been prevented. It also found that, while Osama bin Laden had approved Khalid Sheikh Mohammed's plan in 1999, there was no evidence to link al-Qa'ida with Iraqi President Saddam Hussain. The report recommended, *inter alia*: the creation of a national director of intelligence with overall responsibility for all of the intelligence services; the formation of a national counter-terrorism centre to co-ordinate intelligence-gathering; a reduction in the number of congressional intelligence oversight committees; the establishment of an international network of intelligence-sharing; and the implementation of a national policy to address the threat of militant Islamism. On 17 December 2004, following its approval earlier in the month by both houses of Congress, President Bush enacted the Intelligence Reform and Terrorism Act, which drew on some of the recommendations of the Commission's report. The legislation was designed to restructure the security services and provided for a cabinet-level Director of National Intelligence, to be responsible for co-ordinating the activities of 15 different agencies, including the CIA and the FBI.

Prelude to the 2003 invasion of Iraq

In September 2002 the Republicans submitted a draft resolution to Congress, which would authorize President Bush to use 'any means necessary' to enforce existing UN resolutions against the regime of Saddam Hussain in Iraq and to defend US national interests by depriving Iraq of weapons of mass destruction. It was the first tangible evidence that the Administration was willing to deploy unilateral military action if the UN Security Council did not approve a new resolution authorizing military action against the Iraqi regime. The resolution was approved by Congress in October, with the provision that the Administration should first exhaust all available channels at the UN and other diplomatic means. As a result of US-led pressure, in November the UN Security Council passed unanimously Resolution 1441, which obliged Iraq, *inter alia*, to declare all weapons of mass destruction within 30 days, to comply with the UN Monitoring, Verification and Inspection Commission (UNMOVIC—the UN weapons inspectors, and successor to the UN Special Commission—UNSCOM), to allow UNMOVIC to resume its work within 45 days (UNSCOM had been expelled from Iraq in 1998), and to allow inspectors unrestricted access within Iraq. Later that month UNMOVIC resumed its operations and reported that the Iraqi Government was prepared to comply with Resolution 1441. In December Iraq presented its report on weapons of mass destruction to UNMOVIC; however, US officials declared Iraq to be in 'material breach' of Resolution 1441, for failing to comply with the demand for an accurate and complete account of its weapons programmes, and for resubmitting information that it had previously given to the UN. Following this development, the US and British Governments drew up a timetable to allow UNMOVIC to carry out intensified searches in early 2003, with the threat of military action against Saddam Hussain's regime for non-compliance.

In January 2003 some 70,000 US personnel joined the 60,000 troops already stationed in the Persian (Arabian) Gulf, and military exercises intensified. The French and German Governments expressed their opposition to any eventual conflict and called for a resolution to the problem by diplomatic means. However, the Administration took an increasingly uncompromising stance; President Bush stated that the USA would lead a 'coalition of the willing' if support was withheld by other UN Security Council members and its traditional allies. In February the USA, together with the United Kingdom, intensified its efforts to secure a second UN resolution that would authorize military intervention in Iraq; on 5 February Powell presented evidence of the alleged existence of weapons of mass destruction in Iraq, and possible links between Saddam Hussain's regime and al-Qa'ida. However, in mid-February UNMOVIC reported greater co-operation on the part of the Iraqi Government and that it had thus far failed to find any weapons of mass destruction. (On 13 February Saddam Hussain issued a presidential decree prohibiting weapons of mass destruction, although some *al-Samoud* missiles were found with a greater range than permitted under UN resolutions.) On 24 February the USA, with the United Kingdom and Spain, presented a draft resolution, reiterating that Iraq had been warned it would face serious consequences if it failed to disarm, and that it had failed to comply with Resolution 1441. In early March diplomatic efforts to resolve the crisis showed signs of breaking down when Russia and then France declared that they would employ their veto on any resolution leading to conflict, while the UN Secretary-General, Kofi Annan, questioned the legitimacy of a conflict in Iraq without UN approval. Nevertheless, Powell stated that the USA could go to war without a second UN resolution. UNMOVIC, meanwhile, reported that Iraq had destroyed part of its stock of *al-Samoud* missiles. An amended version of the draft for a second resolution was issued in mid-March and a deadline of 17 March given for Iraq to demonstrate full compliance with Resolution 1441. On 16 March President Bush, the British Prime Minister, Tony Blair, and the Spanish premier, José María Aznar, held an emergency summit in the Azores, Portugal, at the end of which the three leaders issued an ultimatum giving Saddam Hussain and his two sons 48 hours to leave Iraq or face invasion. The following day the USA, the United Kingdom and Spain decided not to seek a second UN resolution and condemned France for obstructing diplomatic efforts to reach a peaceful outcome. The President of France, Jacques Chirac, responded by criticizing the USA and the United Kingdom for making an 'unjustified' decision to resort to war, and for gravely undermining the UN. The USA announced that some 30 countries had expressed support for its 'coalition of the willing', although only the United Kingdom, Australia, the Czech Republic and Slovakia provided troops.

Iraqi regime of Saddam Hussain ousted

Shortly after the expiry of President Bush's 48-hour deadline, on 19 March 2003 US and British armed forces launched 'Operation Iraqi Freedom' to oust the regime of Saddam Hussain. A first

wave of air-strikes against targets in the southern suburbs of the Iraqi capital, Baghdad, apparently aimed at leading members of the Iraqi regime (including the President himself), failed to achieve their target. Soon afterwards British and US forces crossed into Iraq from Kuwait and generally made a swift advance towards the capital. At the same time, a concerted campaign of massive air-strikes was launched by US-led forces against the key symbols of the Iraqi regime in and around Baghdad, including selected military bases, communications sites, government buildings and broadcasting headquarters. Government and military sites in other prominent Iraqi cities were targeted by the US-led coalition in subsequent days. The US and British forces adopted a simultaneous campaign of issuing leaflets and broadcasting radio messages, in an attempt to persuade Iraqi citizens to abandon their support for Saddam Hussain: their declared intention was that Operation Iraqi Freedom would precipitate the disintegration of the regime 'from within'. By 9 April US forces reached the centre of Baghdad and on 1 May the conflict was officially declared over: Iraq did not formally offer its surrender. In mid-April US Gen. (retd) Jay Garner, Director of the USA's Office of Reconstruction and Humanitarian Assistance in Iraq, was appointed Civil Administrator in Iraq, with the intention of overseeing the peaceful transition to civilian rule by Iraqi nationals. An Iraq Survey Group was established to investigate the presence of illegal weapons in the country. In early May a US diplomat, L. Paul Bremer, succeeded Garner as Civil Administrator. In July US special forces killed Saddam Hussain's sons, Uday and Qusay, in Mosul, and on 13 December US special forces captured Saddam Hussain himself, in the village of Ad-Dawr near his birthplace, Tikrit: he was accorded prisoner-of-war status and held in US custody, pending his trial by a court to be convened by the Iraqi Governing Council. Legal custody of Saddam Hussain was transferred to the new Iraqi Interim Government in June 2004, but he remained under US guard. The former Iraqi President's trial began in Baghdad in October 2005, and on 30 December 2006 Saddam Hussain was executed by hanging, following the rejection of his appeal against the death sentence imposed by the Supreme Iraqi Criminal Tribunal on 5 November.

In July 2003 the US Administration admitted that claims, made in January, that the regime of Saddam Hussain had attempted to procure uranium from several African countries as part of its nuclear programme were 'possibly inaccurate'. The claims had formed part of the argument for declaring war on Iraq. In October the Iraq Survey Group published its first report, which stated that although no weapons of mass destruction had been found thus far, there was evidence of weapons-related programmes. However, in January 2004 David Kay, the head of the Iraq Survey Group, resigned, stating that he did not believe that any stockpiles of weapons of mass destruction ever existed. The Survey Group left Iraq in January 2005. In an interim report to Congress in October 2004, Kay's successor, Charles Duelfer, concluded that Saddam Hussain had destroyed his stocks of weapons of mass destruction 10 years previously. In a report in March 2005, the Survey Group was critical of the restructuring proposed at the CIA and FBI and also criticized the agencies' failure to provide accurate information on the state of unconventional weapons in Iraq. In July 2004 a Senate intelligence committee concluded that the CIA had provided the Bush Administration with flawed intelligence before the invasion of Iraq.

In April 2004 photographs were published of US soldiers allegedly abusing prisoners at the Abu Ghraib prison near Baghdad. As further evidence of maltreatment continued to emerge, in May the Department of Defense revealed that in September 2003 investigations had begun into some 20 cases of the deaths or alleged torture of prisoners in US custody in Iraq. President Bush publicly condemned the abuse of prisoners. The first prosecution of one of the soldiers involved began in the USA in June 2004. In August an internal military investigation directly implicated 27 soldiers in abuse at Abu Ghraib, while an independent civilian panel confirmed 66 out of some 300 reported cases of prisoner abuse in US-run prisons in Iraq, Afghanistan and at Guantánamo Bay. However, it did not find any systematic policy of abuse or instructions from senior military or government officials. In March 2005 it was announced that the USA was to hand over control of the prison to the Iraqi authorities.

Transfer of sovereignty in Iraq

In June 2004 Bremer officially handed over sovereignty to the Interim Government of Iraq. Full diplomatic relations were restored. In January 2005 the Department of Defense revealed that it planned fundamentally to restructure the armed forces, diverting funds from costly weapons systems to manpower. At that time the cost of the military operation in Iraq had already exceeded US $200,000m. In July 2006 Muthanna became the first of Iraq's 18 provinces to be transferred from military control to the full responsibility of the Iraqi Government, signalling a measure of progress in the efforts to achieve stability. Despite fears of an escalation in sectarian violence, in September authority over the Iraqi armed forces was formally conferred upon the Government of Iraq by the US-led coalition.

Concerns about the misuse of reconstruction funding in Iraq precipitated the cancellation of contracts with US companies Parsons, Halliburton and Bechtel during 2006. The Special Inspector General for Iraq Reconstruction (SIGIR) was, as of 30 April that year, pursuing 72 separate investigations into alleged fraudulence and profiteering by firms involved in the rebuilding efforts. In July the results of an audit into the practices of the United States Agency for International Development (USAID) concluded that an accounting scheme had been employed to conceal overspending on reconstruction ventures in Iraq. The disclosure in November by the *New York Times* that President Bush had endorsed a military authorization bill in October, which included a provision for the disbanding of the Office of the SIGIR, precipitated outrage among Democrats who regarded the measure as an attempt to conceal the Administration's mismanagement of reconstruction funds.

The bipartisan Iraq Study Group (ISG) was established in March 2006 to conduct an assessment of the situation in Iraq and generate proposals for a revised US strategy towards resolution of the conflict. The ISG submitted its report to Congress in December, declaring the climate in Iraq to be 'grave and deteriorating', and cautioning that stability and democracy, as opposed to 'victory', should constitute the emphasis of future US military, diplomatic and political initiatives. Meanwhile, in October the US military conceded that its efforts to secure the Iraqi capital had been unsuccessful, and the UN reported that the number of US and Iraqi fatalities was unremittingly high. President Bush and his Iraqi counterpart, Nouri al-Maliki, pledged their intention for the expeditious transfer of responsibility from military to Iraqi government authority, although no definite timetable was advanced.

Bush's new strategy for Iraq, 'A New Way Forward', was announced in January 2007. The new strategy was summarized as one that required greater commitment from the Iraqi Government to quell sectarian violence and establish democracy in the country through the attainment of a series of 'benchmarks', in return for US military reinforcements (numbering a further 21,500 troops) to assist in achieving the security and stability that would enable the Iraqi leaders to resume full responsibility for the territory. Bush cautioned that a withdrawal of US forces before this was accomplished would leave Iraq vulnerable to a 'contagion of violence' engulfing the whole region. Expansion of the USA's military capabilities was also requested, with the President asking Congress to authorize an increase of 92,000 personnel in the Army and Marine Corps over the next five years. The decision to expand US participation in what was increasingly regarded as a civil war met with strenuous opposition from Democrats. None the less, dispatch of US reinforcements began in February 2007.

President Bush's proposed budget for 2008, presented in February 2007, incorporated a request for supplemental funding of US $93,400m. in 2008, and $141,000m. in 2009, to augment the Department of Defense's operations in the ongoing 'war on terror'. In March 2007 the House of Representatives voted in favour of emergency spending legislation that would provide $124,000m. for the funding of military operations in Iraq and Afghanistan over the next six months; however, attached to the provision was a timetable for the withdrawal, by 1 September 2008, of combat troops not devoted to security or training functions in Iraq. The Senate subsequently approved a similar bill allowing $122,000m. in emergency funding and stipulating withdrawal of US troops by an earlier deadline of 31 March 2008. Both versions of the legislation, in harmony with the President's stated new strategy, recommended that 'benchmarks' be reached by the Iraqi Government in order to guarantee continued US support. A final version received congressional approval in April 2007. However, in May the President vetoed the law, stating that setting a timetable for troop withdrawal would undermine military efforts and foster further insurgency in Iraq.

At a joint hearing of the House of Congress armed services and foreign affairs committees in September 2007, Gen. David Petraeus, the leader of US forces in Iraq, testified that the objectives of the 'surge' in troop numbers—30,000 extra US troops were dispatched to Iraq between February and June—were largely being met. He claimed that the tactic had reduced sectarian violence, but he acknowledged the ongoing difficulties of the situation and warned that a premature reduction in troop levels would have 'devastating consequences'. Petraeus advised that the US military presence could be scaled down in December 2007 and still further in July 2008, to the 2006 level of 130,000 troops. President Bush subsequently announced that 5,700 troops would be withdrawn from Iraq by the end of 2007 and a total of 21,500 by July 2008, in accordance with Petraeus's recommendations. Bush declined to give a timetable for a full withdrawal of troops, leading Democrats to criticize the scope of the plans. In February 2008 the President's 2009 federal budget presentation to Congress included a proposed 7.5% increase in spending on defence from 2008, to US $515,000m. An additional $70,000m. was allocated to fund the conflicts in Iraq and Afghanistan between the start of the fiscal year in October and January 2009. In a speech on 19 March 2008 in recognition of the fifth anniversary of the invasion of Iraq, Bush hailed the success of the 'surge' tactic amid criticism over the rising cost of the war. Estimates in this respect differed widely, with the non-partisan Congressional Budget Office placing the figure at $600,000m., while economist Joseph Stiglitz calculated that the total cost of the war for the USA alone would be $3,000,000m. Democrat consternation was further incited in April when Petraeus advocated a suspension in troop withdrawals after July in order to undertake a 45-day period of reassessment, as a result of which the President ordered an indefinite suspension to the exit, leaving a US force of around 140,000 combat personnel in the country from August. Petraeus was replaced as leader of US forces in Iraq by Gen. Raymond T. Odierno in September.

Alleged torture of terrorist suspects

In November 2005 it was reported that US intelligence services maintained a network of secret prisons—referred to as 'black sites'—in locations that included eastern European Union (EU) countries. It was further alleged that terrorist suspects were taken from these prisons to countries where torture was tolerated, in a practice known as 'extraordinary rendition'. The following month Secretary of State Condoleezza Rice acknowledged the existence of rendition but denied any toleration of the torture of suspects. However, in January 2005 it had been revealed that, three years previously, the chief legal counsel to the President, Alberto Gonzales (who was appointed Attorney-General in January 2005), had issued a memorandum stating that the USA was not bound by the Geneva Conventions in its treatment of prisoners captured in Afghanistan. In another memorandum ordered by Gonzales in August 2002, it was proposed that CIA officers and other non-military personnel be exempted from a presidential directive for the humane treatment of prisoners. In February 2006 the UN Commission on Human Rights published a report that concluded that the methods used by the US military to interrogate prisoners at Guantánamo Bay amounted to torture, and appealed to the US Government to close the base and try the remaining detainees before courts on the US mainland. A military report to the Senate's armed forces committee in July found that treatment of the prisoners did not constitute torture, but that it was abusive and degrading. In December President Bush approved an amendment to ban the 'cruel, inhuman and degrading' treatment of prisoners, although he appended a presidential signing statement to the effect that the President's authority superseded the new legislation. Department of State officials were summoned to appear before the UN Committee Against Torture in Geneva, Switzerland, in May to answer enquiries relating to the alleged use of torture employed in extraordinary rendition. The Department of State delegation contended that it had sought assurances that detainees conveyed under this system would not be subjected to torture in their destination country and that US definitions of torture did not infringe those set out in the 1987 Convention. The UN concluded that interrogation methods involving 'waterboarding' (simulated drowning), sexual humiliation and the use of menacing dogs were unacceptable and should be eliminated. It also ruled that the detention of prisoners without charge for extended periods, the use of extraordinary rendition and reports of concealed prisons were issues of grave concern, and it urged the closure of the detention centre at Guantánamo Bay.

In June 2006 the US Supreme Court ruled that military tribunals established for the trial of prisoners at Guantánamo Bay contravened the US uniform code of military justice and Geneva Conventions, rejecting the Bush Administration's contention that the President's authority as Commander-in-Chief, and the resolution of Congress approved following the 11 September 2001 terrorist attacks, sanctioned the institution of such military tribunals. The Department of Defense issued a memorandum in July 2006 declaring that all prisoners at Guantánamo Bay and other US military detention centres world-wide would be protected under Article III of the Geneva Conventions, assuring humane treatment of and basic judicial defence for those facing trial. The announcement corrected previous assertions that the Military Commissions Act precluded invocation of Geneva Conventions articles. The Military Commissions Act of 2006, intended to 'bring to justice' terrorists and other unlawful enemy combatants by means of thorough, fair trials administered by military commissions, was approved by Congress in September and signed into law in the following month. In March 2007 an Australian, David Hicks (a convert to Islam), became the first detainee to be granted trial by such a commission at Guantánamo Bay and the first convicted of a terrorism offence since the camp's inauguration in 2002. An appeal by the legal representatives of approximately 60 Guantánamo detainees (facing similar military tribunals), contending that the prisoners had a constitutional right to contest their imprisonment in a US federal court, was rejected, by two votes to one, in the US Court of Appeal in February 2007. The Court's ruling stated that non-citizens without property or residency in the USA were not entitled to US constitutional rights. However, in June 2008 the Supreme Court issued a ruling that all detainees at Guantánamo Bay were entitled to challenge their detention through the US civilian courts. The decision did not bring to an end the military tribunals, which continued throughout 2008; however, in November a US court ruled that five Algerian detainees should be released from the prison camp after they successfully challenged their right to a civilian trial.

Alleged use of 'harsh interrogation' techniques, including waterboarding, caused controversy in October 2007, when a report by the *New York Times* claimed that the US Department of Justice had privately authorized their use by the CIA against terrorist suspects in 2005 while asserting that such methods did not contravene anti-torture legislation then before Congress. Later in the same month the Director of the CIA, Gen. Michael Hayden, defended the Agency's interrogation practices and use of extraordinary rendition as a lawful and indispensable means of obtaining information from suspects. However, on 6 December 2007—when an agreement was also reached by Congress negotiators on the terms of legislation to prohibit the use of 'harsh interrogation' techniques by the CIA—Hayden revealed that film tapes documenting the use of such procedures on two al-Qa'ida members in 2002 had been destroyed in November 2005, ostensibly to protect the identities of the CIA interrogators. Critics accused the Agency of destroying evidence that might provoke further allegations of torture in relation to their practices. A former CIA officer subsequently attested that waterboarding was used in the interrogation of Abu Zubaydah, the first high-ranking al-Qa'ida member to be captured after the terrorist attacks of 11 September 2001, and that he now considered the practice to constitute torture. In January 2008 a criminal investigation was launched by Attorney-General Michael B. Mukasey, and in February Hayden, for the first time, admitted the use of waterboarding on three al-Qa'ida detainees, including Khalid Sheikh Mohammed. He declared, however, that the method had not been used in the previous five years and that he had banned its use in 2006. Further, he did not rule out its future employment and admitted he was unsure of its legality under current laws. In March 2008 President Bush vetoed the legislation restricting 'harsh interrogation' techniques already approved by the House of Representatives in December 2007 and by the Senate in February 2008, claiming that such 'specialized interrogation procedures' were of proven effectiveness and, while not practised by the military, should remain available to the CIA. (For subsequent related developments, see the section on Legislative reform under the Obama Administration.)

Bush's second presidential term, 2005–09

Presidential and legislative elections were held on 2 November 2004. The elections were notable for being the first in which unregulated donations to the electoral campaigns of political parties from individuals, businesses and unions ('soft money') were banned. In the presidential ballot, President Bush was returned for a second term of office, taking some 51% of the popular vote. John Kerry, the Democratic challenger, conceded defeat before the final result was confirmed. In the concurrent legislative elections, the Republicans also increased their majority in both houses of Congress. The President was sworn in on 20 January 2005. His new Cabinet included Condoleezza Rice as Secretary of State and Alberto Gonzales as Attorney-General. In February Bush presented a 2006 budget plan to Congress, which proposed reductions in funding to 12 out of 23 government agencies. Spending cuts targeted subsidies to farmers and health care payments to the poor and military veterans, as well as education and environment programmes. In May a presidential request for a further US $82,000m., principally towards continued military involvement in Afghanistan and Iraq, was approved by Congress.

In late August 2005 Hurricane Katrina caused extensive damage to the Gulf coast states of Louisiana, Mississippi and Alabama. Louisiana was the worst affected state: an estimated 80% of the city of New Orleans was flooded. On 2 September President Bush declared a state of emergency in 13 states to release some US $10,500m. in emergency funding; on the same day Congress approved legislation for emergency aid amounting to $51,800m. Damage to infrastructure was blamed for delays in delivering relief to those affected by the hurricane. The US Government appealed to the EU, NATO and the UN for crisis assistance. On 6 September the mayor of New Orleans ordered the evacuation of the entire city, some 480,000 people; however, an estimated 10,000 people, either unable or unwilling to move, remained in the city. More than 38,000 members of the National Guard were deployed in affected areas; they were joined by 8,500 soldiers on active duty. The impact of another hurricane, Hurricane Rita, along the Gulf coast at the end of September, further affected relief efforts. By August 2006 the official death toll as a result of Hurricane Katrina, the USA's deadliest natural disaster in almost 80 years, was 1,836; a further 135 people remained missing.

A report by the Government Accountability Office, published in February 2006, criticized government at all levels for its failure adequately to respond to the emergency. It found that relief efforts had been hampered by the absence of a clear chain of command, and compounded by insufficient planning and preparation; it also identified examples of waste and fraud in the appropriation of relief and reconstruction funds. Meanwhile, President Bush appealed to Congress for a further US $19,600m. towards reconstruction along the Gulf coast, particularly the strengthening of the protective levees around New Orleans. In August, however, it emerged that of the $110,000m. designated by Congress to the cause, only $44,000m. had been disseminated.

The Republican Party faced a series of corruption scandals in 2005–06. In September 2005 the Republican Majority Leader in the House of Representatives, Tom DeLay, was indicted on charges of having illegally financed Republican candidates in the 2002 election campaign. In October I. 'Scooter' Lewis Libby, chief of staff to Vice-President Dick Cheney, was indicted on charges that included obstruction of justice and perjury during an investigation into the leaking of the identity of CIA agent Valerie Plame in mid-2003. It was held that Plame's identity had deliberately been made public as a reprisal against her husband, Senator Joseph Wilson, a former US Ambassador to Iraq, who had publicly accused the Administration of making selective use of intelligence to justify the invasion of Iraq in 2003. The Libby trial commenced in January 2007, although neither Libby nor Vice-President Cheney, also implicated in the scandal, testified. In March Libby was convicted of four charges of perjury, and in June was sentenced to 30 months in prison. In the following month President Bush commuted Libby's sentence to a two-year probation period and a US $250,000 fine, after describing the original sentence as 'excessive'.

At mid-term elections in November 2006, the Democrats secured control of both chambers of Congress. The Republican electoral defeat was regarded as indicative of citizens' loss of confidence in Bush's presidency, principally owing to the lack of progress in Iraq and escalating violence in Afghanistan, but also in regard to domestic policy, namely the perceived inadequacy of the federal Government's response to Hurricane Katrina, immigration policy, the erratic nature of economic recovery and the numerous cases of corruption within Republican ranks. Immediately following the elections, the Secretary of Defense, Donald

Rumsfeld, ceded to demands for his resignation, citing the need for a 'fresh perspective' on the ongoing conflict in Iraq. Robert M. Gates, a former CIA Director, succeeded him. Rumsfeld had attracted international opprobrium for his apparent approval of 'harsh interrogation' techniques in the examination of terrorism suspects.

Further controversy involving the Republican Administration emerged in early 2007, after it was revealed that eight US state attorneys had been summarily dismissed under the direction of Attorney-General Alberto Gonzales. It was claimed that the dismissals were politically motivated, the majority having allegedly resulted from the attorneys' failure sufficiently to pursue accusations of voting irregularities against Democratic candidates in the November 2006 elections. Gonzales testified before the Senate Judiciary Committee in April 2007, when inconsistencies between his various statements regarding his knowledge of, and motivation for, the dismissals were found seriously to undermine his integrity as an impartial arbiter of justice. Several senior officials at the White House and the Department of Justice (including the President's influential Deputy Chief of Staff, Karl Rove) were implicated in the controversy and subsequently resigned. In September Gonzales finally stood down from office while maintaining that he had committed no wrongdoing. Michael B. Mukasey was confirmed by the Senate as the new Attorney-General in November.

An unprecedented boom in the US housing market in the first half of the 2000s was fuelled by low interest rates and a highly competitive mortgage market. However, a downturn in house prices during 2007 activated a severe mortgage crisis, as interest rates rose and many low-income borrowers were unable to meet repayment obligations on lending, leaving a number of lending institutions facing bankruptcy. Housing and Urban Development Secretary Alphonso Jackson resigned in April 2008, amid an ongoing FBI investigation into allegations of favouritism in awarding housing contracts and as the US housing market continued to deteriorate. The crisis in the housing market moved Congress to approve legislation in mid-2008: the Housing and Economic Recovery Act provided for emergency funding for federal mortgage institutions and was intended to restore confidence in the sector. None the less, during 2008 the crisis intensified and a full-scale financial crisis emerged; with numerous major financial institutions under threat of collapse, the federal Government was obliged to intervene to save a number of large banks and insurance companies (see Economic Affairs).

Obama elected President

Presidential and congressional elections were held on 4 November 2008. Illinois senator Barack Obama had been selected as the Democratic Party's representative in June, thereby becoming its first African American presidential candidate, after a long campaign in which he had defeated New York senator Hillary Clinton. Joseph Biden, the Delaware senator, was Obama's vice-presidential nominee. The Republican Party's presidential candidate, John McCain, selected the Governor of Alaska, Sarah Palin, as his running mate. In the event, Obama secured a clear victory, winning 52.9% of the valid votes cast and 365 electoral college votes, compared with McCain's 45.7% and 173 electoral college votes. The Democrats also performed well in the concurrently held congressional elections. The party increased its majority in the House of Representatives to 256 seats, and to 57 seats in the Senate, although it lacked the 60-member so-called 'super majority' required to overcome Republican delaying tactics in the latter. However, the defection, in April 2009, of Arlen Specter from the Republican Party to the Democratic Party, increased the Democrats' representation in the Senate to 58. This, in effect, gave the Democrats the three-fifths' 'super majority', as the two independent senators routinely voted with the Democrats.

Obama was sworn in as President on 20 January 2009. Hillary Clinton was named Secretary of State in Obama's Cabinet, while Timothy F. Geithner was installed as Secretary of the Treasury, and Robert M. Gates, Secretary of Defense in the previous Bush Administration, was reappointed to that post. Obama's first choice for the commerce portfolio, Bill Richardson, was forced to withdraw in December 2008 owing to an ongoing investigation into financial irregularities, and a second nominee, Republican Judd Gregg, withdrew his candidacy in February 2009 after disagreements over economic policy; Gary F. Locke was subsequently confirmed as Secretary of Commerce in March. The President's candidate to take over the health and human services portfolio, former Senate majority leader Tom Daschle, had also retired from the nomination process at the end of January owing

to tax discrepancies; Kathleen Sebelius was confirmed as Secretary of Health and Human Services in April. Sonia Sotomayor became the first Hispanic American Associate Justice of the Supreme Court in August 2009, having been nominated to the post by Obama in May.

Legislative reform under the Obama Administration

One of the first priorities of the new Administration of Barack Obama was to gain congressional approval for a US $787,000m. economic stimulus programme aimed at alleviating the impact of the economic slowdown (see Economic Affairs). The series of measures, which included tax cuts, funding for infrastructural projects, the introduction of a cap on executive salaries, and several protectionist moves, was approved by Congress in February 2009. President Obama also announced a further $50,000m. in aid for homeowners struggling to meet mortgage payments.

Shortly after taking office, Obama had proposed a comprehensive reform of the health care system, with the aim of controlling rising costs, extending provision, improving the affordability of health insurance and increasing the accountability of health insurers. The House of Representatives and the Senate approved two separate, but broadly similar, health care reform bills in November and December 2009, respectively. However, the legislative process subsequently stalled, amid considerable opposition to the proposed changes from Republicans, who contended that the measures would, in fact, raise costs and entail excessive government intrusion. Moreover, the Democratic Party suffered a serious reverse in January 2010, when it lost a special election for the senate seat in Massachusetts previously held by senior Democrat Edward Kennedy, who had died in August 2009: Republican Scott Brown, who opposed the health care bill, defeated the Democratic candidate, Martha Coakley. The victory of the Republican Party, which followed its defeat of the Democratic Party in gubernatorial elections in New Jersey and Virginia in November, reflected not only public uncertainty regarding Obama's health care proposals, but also discontent over the country's economic difficulties, and deprived the Democrats of their 'super majority' in the Senate.

Undeterred, Obama renewed his efforts to secure the congressional passage of health care reforms, and on 21 March 2010, by a margin of 219 votes to 212, the House of Representatives approved the bill adopted by the Senate in December 2009, despite unanimous Republican opposition. Under the legislation, which Obama signed into law two days later, health care provision was to be extended to an estimated 32m. currently uninsured US residents through the expansion of Medicaid, a joint federal-state programme for certain low-income categories, and the creation of state-based 'exchanges' offering subsidized insurance. In addition, health insurers would henceforth be prohibited from denying coverage to those with pre-existing medical conditions. Amendments to the legislation, submitted under the budget reconciliation process, which meant that they required the approval of only a simple majority of senators, had been adopted by both houses and signed by Obama by the end of the month. The Congressional Budget Office estimated that the implementation of the reforms would cost some US $938,000m. in 2010–19 and result in a net reduction in the federal budget deficit of $143,000m. over the same period.

Meanwhile, financial reforms continued in 2010. In March Obama enacted legislation providing tax incentives for businesses hiring unemployed workers and funding for infrastructure projects, following its approval by both chambers of Congress, and in July Obama pledged an end to taxpayer-funded bail-outs as he signed into effect wide-ranging legislation that provided for a comprehensive overhaul of the financial regulatory system. *Inter alia*, the legislation afforded the Government new powers to shut down companies that were deemed to pose a threat to the national economy; granted enhanced powers to the Federal Reserve (the USA's central banking system), which was henceforth to be liable to greater congressional scrutiny; and offered greater protection to consumers from hidden borrowing fees and punitive rates of interest. The law was widely acclaimed as a second major legislative success for the Obama Administration, although Republicans contested that it would prove a burden on small banks and those companies and individuals reliant on them.

Upon taking office in January 2009, Obama had immediately instituted a 120-day hiatus on the military tribunals at Guantánamo Bay to allow for a thorough review of the situation. He also reiterated his pledge to close the prison camp within a year. The new President had already diverged significantly from the previous Administration by claiming that waterboarding constituted torture and by admitting the existence of secret CIA prisons. He also ordered that the CIA cease the torture of detainees. His decision was widely praised, although the presidential order stopped short of halting the CIA's right to use extraordinary rendition. However, in May Obama announced that military tribunals would be resumed for a number of detainees, following the implementation of measures to strengthen the legal rights of defendants, while others would be tried in US civilian courts. Later that month it emerged that Ahmed Ghailani, who was accused of involvement in the 1998 embassy bombings in Nairobi and Dar es Salaam, would be the first Guantánamo inmate to be tried by a US federal court. Ghailani's trial commenced in New York in June 2009, and in November 2010 he was convicted on one count of conspiracy to destroy US property with explosives but acquitted of 284 other counts of conspiracy and multiple murder charges, after the presiding judge ruled that the evidence of the main witness was not admissible because he had been held in a secret CIA prison 'under extreme duress'; nevertheless, Ghailani was sentenced to life imprisonment in January 2011.

Meanwhile, difficulties had arisen over the release of a number of Guantánamo detainees, some of whom were considered to be at risk of abuse if returned to their countries of origin. In addition, transfers of inmates to Yemen, where many of the prisoners originated, were suspended in January 2010, following a failed bombing attempt on a flight from the Netherlands' capital, Amsterdam, to Detroit, Michigan, on 25 December 2009 by a Nigerian, Umar Farouk Abdulmutallab, who claimed to have been trained by al-Qa'ida in Yemen. A review of the incident revealed a number of intelligence failures, concluding that the CIA and the National Counterterrorism Center had had access to sufficient information to have uncovered and potentially disrupted the plot; the Yemen-based al-Qa'ida in the Arabian Peninsula, which claimed responsibility for the failed attack, was subsequently designated a foreign terrorist organization by the US Administration. At his trial in October 2011, Abdulmutallab pleaded guilty to attempting to commit an act of terrorism, and he was sentenced to life imprisonment in February 2012.

With Obama's self-imposed deadline for securing the closure of Guantánamo Bay long passed, hopes of securing its closure in the foreseeable future were dealt a severe blow in December 2010, when the House of Representatives voted to prohibit the Administration from transferring Guantánamo inmates to US soil for trial or detention. A report partly declassified in December 2010, in which it was claimed that 81 of the 598 prisoners released thus far from Guantánamo Bay were known to have resumed involvement in terrorism-related activities, was cited by the Republicans as evidence of the need to provide for the continued detention of those prisoners whose release was deemed to be too dangerous but against whom there was insufficient presentable evidence for either a civilian or military trial. Approximately 170 detainees remained at the camp in early 2013.

Continued engagement in Iraq and Afghanistan

In February 2009 President Obama reiterated his electoral pledge to withdraw all US combat troops from Iraq by the end of August 2010. US combat troops commenced their withdrawal from urban areas in Iraq on 30 June 2009, having formally transferred responsibility for security to Iraqi forces. Some US forces were to remain in the cities, in a non-combative capacity, to train, advise and support the Iraqi security forces, while others would participate in Iraqi-led operations outside urban areas. In September 2010 Operation Iraqi Freedom was renamed 'Operation New Dawn' to reflect the revised role of the US forces following the withdrawal from Iraq of all remaining US combat troops, two weeks ahead of schedule, in mid-August. Operation New Dawn formally ended in mid-December 2011 with the withdrawal of all remaining US non-combat service personnel from the country. Total losses of US military personnel in Iraq had reached almost 4,500, while estimates of total Iraqi fatalities were a matter of dispute, ranging from 90,000 to as many as 650,000.

Meanwhile, in February 2009 President Obama announced that a further 17,000 US troops would be deployed in Afghanistan. The reinforcements were expected to facilitate a shift towards counter-insurgency tactics—a break from the US Army's traditional doctrine—including a greater emphasis on defending major population centres and bolstering support for the Government of Afghan President Hamid Karzai. At the end of March Obama confirmed his Administration's shift in policy towards combating insurgency in Afghanistan and neighbouring

Pakistan by announcing that an additional 4,000 troops were to be dispatched to the region to support the Afghan army and police force there. In June veteran Special Operations commander Lt-Gen. Stanley McChrystal, a strong advocate of the counter-insurgency strategy, was appointed as Commander of the International Security Assistance Force (ISAF) in Afghanistan.

As the security situation in Afghanistan continued to deteriorate, a further 30,000 US troops were dispatched to that country in early 2010, in order to reinforce counter-insurgency operations and to allow an expansion in the training of the Afghan security forces. In February US-led coalition forces and Afghan troops initiated a major counter-insurgency operation in Helmand province, 'Operation Moshtarak', which was described as the largest offensive since the Taliban regime was ousted in late 2001. In a notable change of approach, the offensive was widely publicized beforehand in order to warn the civilian population. In July 2010 Obama nominated Gen. David Petraeus as the new Commander of ISAF, in place of Gen. McChrystal, who had been recalled to Washington, DC, after negative comments pertaining to Vice-President Biden and other prominent figures within the Obama Administration were attributed to him in a prominent US publication.

In July 2010 President Karzai announced details of ambitious plans for Afghan forces to have assumed control of all military and law enforcement operations throughout Afghanistan by 2014; in November Karzai's plans gained the formal support of NATO. During a visit to Kabul in January 2011, Vice-President Biden pledged a continuation of US assistance beyond 2014, exclusively in a training and supportive, rather than military, capacity; during his visit, Biden also claimed that Taliban momentum had been 'largely arrested' in key areas, including Helmand and Qandahar, but acknowledged that such gains were 'fragile and reversible'.)

In June 2011 President Obama presented his plans for the phased withdrawal of the approximately 100,000 US troops deployed in Afghanistan. It was envisaged that all US military personnel would leave the country by 2014, with the first 10,000 troops to be recalled by the end of 2011 and a further 23,000 to be withdrawn by September 2012. Also in June 2011, the Government announced that it had held preliminary discussions with representatives of the Taliban in an attempt to negotiate an end to the conflict. In July Gen. John Allen replaced Gen. Petraeus as Commander of ISAF, following the latter's appointment as Director of the CIA.

There was outrage in Afghanistan after video footage emerged in January 2012 of US marines apparently desecrating the bodies of three deceased Taliban combatants, a potential breach of the Geneva Conventions. US officials, who condemned the soldiers, promptly announced an investigation into the incident. Anti-US sentiment increased further in the following month, when it was reported that copies of the Koran had been 'inadvertently' incinerated by US military personnel. Although Obama apologized for the indiscretion, protests were organized throughout Afghanistan, some of which degenerated into violence, resulting in the deaths of some 40 people (including six US troops). Further demonstrations were held in March after a US soldier allegedly massacred 17 Afghan civilians in Qandahar. Obama issued another apology, but the atrocity placed additional strain on relations between the USA and Afghan Government, while the Taliban announced that it was suspending its participation in negotiations with the US Administration.

In late April 2012, after lengthy negotiations, it was reported that the US and Afghan authorities had reached agreement on the terms of a long-term strategic partnership agreement, which would provide for a continued US military and civil presence in Afghanistan for a further 10 years after the planned 2014 withdrawal. Under the agreement, specific details of which were not made public, it was anticipated that the US military would continue to support the Afghan security forces in a training and advisory capacity, but would also be permitted to mount counter-terrorism and intelligence-gathering operations within the country. The agreement was also expected to provide for continued US financial support for education and governance in Afghanistan. In early May, exactly one year after the killing of bin Laden (see The 2010 mid-term elections), President Obama made an unannounced visit to Kabul during which the draft partnership agreement was signed by the US leader and President Karzai. Following talks between Obama and Karzai in January 2013, it was announced that US combat operations in Afghanistan would largely be brought to an end by mid-2013, with the remaining US military contingent adopting training and counter-terrorism roles. However, final agreement to a key demand of the US authorities—that US troops remaining in Afghanistan after 2014 would be granted immunity from prosecution—had yet to be granted by the Afghan Government. According to the Department of Defense, total losses of US military personnel in Operation Enduring Freedom had reached 2,190 by early April 2013, 2,068 deaths having occurred in Afghanistan.

The 2010 mid-term elections

Despite the legislative achievements of the Obama Administration, the immense public goodwill that had greeted the President's election had all but dissipated by mid-2010. The growing popularity of the Tea Party Movement—a broad-based anti-Government movement on the right of the political spectrum that had emerged in 2009—was indicative of increasing dissatisfaction with continued economic hardship and the Administration's legislative agenda.

Mid-term elections were held on 2 November 2010, and, as expected the Democrats suffered heavy losses: the Republicans gained 63 seats in the House of Representatives (the largest change of seats in the House following a mid-term election since 1938), and won six seats in the Senate. With the Republicans reclaiming the House majority and the Senate remaining under Democrat control, it was widely anticipated that efforts by the Obama Administration to push through further legislative reform would require a much greater level of compromise in order to bridge the divide between the Democratic and Republican political agendas. An example of this was provided by a tax bill that was approved by both congressional chambers and signed into law in December 2010. The legislation, which provided for a two-year extension to tax reductions for the wealthiest Americans that had been introduced during the presidency of George W. Bush, was the result of a deal brokered between the Obama Administration and the Republicans, by which Obama rescinded his electoral pledge to eliminate the tax reductions in exchange for Republican support for an extension to benefits for 2m. unemployed and low-income earners.

In January 2011 Gabrielle Giffords, a Democratic member of the House of Representatives for Arizona, was critically injured in an apparent assassination attempt perpetrated by a lone gunman; six people were fatally shot and 13 others (including Giffords) were injured in the incident. The killing prompted enormous public debate on the increasing polarization and hostility present in US politics, with many commentators suggesting that the vitriolic nature of right-wing opposition to the Obama Administration, notably from supporters of the Tea Party Movement, helped to foster a culture of violent political enmity and may have contributed to Giffords' shooting. In his State of the Union address later in that month, Obama paid tribute to Giffords and appealed for a bipartisan effort to heal the divisions caused by 'sharply polarized' political debate.

Meanwhile, in December 2010 a federal judge in Virginia ruled that the health care reform legislation approved in March was unconstitutional since it overstepped the 'boundaries of congressional power'. In January 2011 a second federal judge, in Florida, ruled that the health care reforms, specifically the requirement that all American citizens purchase health insurance, contravened the Constitution and should be rescinded. The Obama Administration dismissed the judgment as 'legal overreaching' and announced its intention to appeal against the ruling. In August a federal court of appeal in Georgia also adjudged the legislation to be in breach of the Constitution, prompting the Administration in September to petition the Supreme Court to rule on the constitutionality of the health reforms. In its final verdict, issued in June 2012, the Supreme Court ruled in favour of the Obama Administration, declaring the main provisions of the health care legislation to be constitutional. However, the Court ruled against a provision that effectively coerced the states into participation in the expansion of the Medicaid programme (by threatening them with the loss of existing federal funding); the states, therefore, were entitled to opt out of the proposed Medicaid expansion.

Controversy was generated in April 2011 by the announcement that Khalid Sheikh Mohammed (accused of planning the terrorist attacks of 11 September 2001, see above) would be tried by a military commission at Guantánamo Bay, following congressional opposition to an earlier decision that he would stand trial in a civilian court in the USA. Obama had previously expressed doubts that a fair trial could be conducted under the military commission system. (Mohammed and four other defendants were arraigned before a military tribunal at Guantánamo Bay in early May 2012.) The Obama Administration suffered embarrassment later in April 2011, when hundreds of classified US documents detailing conditions at Guantánamo Bay were released by the WikiLeaks organization (see Foreign Affairs—Other external relations). The documents contained evidence of the detention of suspects without charge and the imprisonment of innocent civilians.

At the beginning of May 2011 Osama bin Laden, the founder of al-Qa'ida and the FBI's 'most-wanted' terrorist target, was killed during a raid carried out by US special operations forces on a fortified compound in Abbottabad, Pakistan. Four other inhabitants of the compound, including one of bin Laden's sons, were reportedly killed during the operation. Following confirmation of his identity by DNA testing, bin Laden's body was buried at sea. The outcome of the operation resulted in a significant improvement in President Obama's domestic approval rating, according to several opinion polls. Furthermore, many observers suggested that the killing of bin Laden would provide the Administration with additional impetus in its efforts to extricate the USA from its military campaign in Afghanistan.

Differences in approach with regard to reducing the mounting federal budget deficit exacerbated divisions between the Democrats and the Republicans in early 2011. President Obama's draft budget for 2011/12, which was submitted to Congress in February 2011, proposed a range of deficit-reduction measures, including planned tax increases and a five-year freeze on non-military spending. However, the proposals were vehemently opposed by Republicans, in particular those associated with the Tea Party Movement, who demanded a far more radical programme of spending cuts, including reductions in social spending, particularly on health care, as well as lower taxation to stimulate economic growth. An impasse over federal spending for the remainder of the 2011 fiscal year, which almost resulted in a 'shutdown' of non-essential government services, was finally resolved in April when the House approved a hard-fought compromise arrangement. After further prolonged and acrimonious negotiations, a bipartisan agreement to raise the country's 'debt ceiling', the upper limit of permissible public debt, was concluded in late July, and the legislation was duly adopted by Congress in early August. In return for Republican congressional support, the Obama Administration had been forced to grant significant concessions, including a US $917,000m. reduction in government spending (without a concomitant rise in taxation) in order to lower the deficit over the following 10 years. A bipartisan Joint Select Committee on Deficit Reduction (commonly termed the 'super committee') was also to be formed to draft measures to reduce the deficit by a further $1,500,000m. over the same time period. The debt ceiling deal prevented a shutdown and also precluded the risk of the Government defaulting on its debt-repayment obligations, but the ideological divisions between the two parties raised fears of future legislative deadlock, which contributed to the unprecedented downgrading of the USA's credit rating by the Standard & Poor's agency later in August. Another government shutdown was averted in September, after Democrats and Republicans reached a late compromise over funding for the Federal Emergency Management Agency. In November it was announced that the 'super committee' had foundered, with Obama blaming the failure on Republican intransigence, particularly in relation to proposed tax increases; consequently, automatic budget reductions totalling $1,200,000m. (popularly termed the 'fiscal cliff') were scheduled to come into force from 2013. The threat of a government shutdown was narrowly avoided once again in mid-December 2011, when both parties reached a compromise agreement on federal spending for the remainder of the fiscal year (to 30 September 2012). None the less, acute disagreement remained over the means of funding proposed extensions of a payroll tax reduction and long-term unemployment payments. Despite lengthy negotiations, only a two-month deal on extending these politically sensitive benefits was reached by the rival parties in late December. However, in what was seen as a political success for President Obama, a cross-party agreement to extend the aforementioned measures until the end of the year was approved by Congress in February 2012. In July both parties assented to a six-month extension of the federal spending agreement, and legislation formalizing this arrangement received congressional approval in September.

Demonstrators commenced an occupation of Zuccotti Park, located close to New York's main financial district, Wall Street, in September 2011. The protest action was organized by the

'Occupy Wall Street' group, an informal coalition of mostly left-wing activists, to demonstrate against, *inter alia*, rising levels of income inequality, high unemployment, corruption, and the involvement of the corporate sector in US politics. President Obama expressed sympathy for the demonstrators in October, while Republicans were far more disapproving. Although the Zuccotti Park protesters were evicted by riot police in November, by this time the Occupy movement had spread to many other cities, both within the USA and world-wide. The demonstrations had subsided by early 2012, with many of the encampments having been raided by the security forces (sometimes resulting in violent clashes and mass arrests).

Gates was succeeded as Secretary of Defense by the erstwhile Director of the CIA, Leon Panetta, in July 2011, while Jacob Lew became the new Chief of Staff to the President in January 2012. Secretary of Commerce John Bryson resigned in June owing to ill health; he was replaced, on an interim basis, by Rebecca Blank. Meanwhile, in January a series of primary ballots commenced to select the Republican Party's candidate for the forthcoming presidential election. At the outset, 10 Republican candidates entered the contest, which was marked by vitriolic clashes between the contestants and by the increasingly influential role of independent campaign groups (the so-called 'super-PACs'), which were permitted to raise and spend unlimited funds in support of candidates, providing funds were not donated directly to the candidate's campaign. Willard Mitt Romney, a former governor of Massachusetts, formally received the Republican nomination in August, while Obama was endorsed by the Democratic Party in the following month. Campaigning was temporarily suspended in late October owing to the passage of Hurricane Sandy, which wrought significant devastation, particularly in north-eastern states. States of emergency were declared in eight states and the District of Columbia, more than 2.5m. homes experienced power cuts and at least 159 people lost their lives during the storm. A US $60,000m. relief package was approved in January 2013.

Recent developments: Obama's second term

In the presidential election, held on 6 November 2012, Obama was re-elected with 51.1% of the popular vote and 332 electoral college votes, while Romney secured 47.2% of the ballot and 206 electoral college votes. In the concurrent legislative polls, the Democratic Party retained control of the Senate, winning 53 seats (compared with 45 seats for the Republicans and two for independents). Although the Democrats increased their presence in the House of Representatives to 201 seats and won the popular vote nation-wide, the chamber remained under the leadership of the Republican party, which gained 234 seats. Obama was inaugurated on 20 January 2013.

The Cabinet was in the process of being reorganized in early 2013. The Senate confirmed three of Obama's key nominations in January–February (John Kerry as Secretary of State, Charles Hagel as Secretary of Defense and Jacob Lew as Secretary of the Treasury), and several further nominations were awaiting approval. Denis McDonough was appointed as Chief of Staff to the President in January; in March John Brennan was confirmed as the new Director of the CIA (Gen. Petraeus had resigned from the post in November 2012 following revelations about his private life).

With the December 2010 tax legislation scheduled to expire in early January 2013 and the automatic budget reductions resulting from the collapse of the 'super committee' due to come into effect in the same month, commentators warned that the economy was at risk of re-entering recession. Following several rounds of cross-party negotiations, on 31 December 2012 an agreement was finally concluded that, *inter alia*, indefinitely extended the tax cuts introduced by the Bush Administration (excluding those benefiting the highest income earners) and postponed the spending reductions for two months. Unemployment benefits and tax credits for certain low-income groups were maintained, but the payroll tax reduction was not renewed. Congress approved the deal on 1 January 2013 and later that month also voted to suspend the debt ceiling limitations until May. Subsequent talks, however, failed to yield an agreement on averting the automatic budget cuts, which duly entered into force on 1 March in a process known as 'sequestration'. Congress authorized a six-month federal spending plan in late March, thereby avoiding another conflict over a potential government shutdown.

In December 2012 a gunman murdered 20 young children and six adults at a school in Newtown, Connecticut. This tragedy, combined with a number of other high-profile mass shooting incidents during 2012, created a renewed impetus for the introduction of firmer gun control legislation, a perennially controversial issue within the USA. President Obama established a task force on gun violence later that month, and a bill was subsequently drafted providing for new restrictions on firearm purchases. However, in spite of widespread popular support for the proposed gun control measures, Republican senators overwhelmingly rejected the bill in April 2013 owing to the party's long-standing ideological opposition to firearm regulations.

Two bombs were detonated on 15 April 2013 during the annual Boston Marathon, resulting in the deaths of three spectators and over 250 injuries. Dzhokhar Tsarnaev, a naturalized US citizen born in Kyrgyzstan, was apprehended later that month and charged with terrorist offences in connection with the attack. His brother and suspected co-conspirator, Tamerlan, was killed during an armed confrontation with the police. Media reports alleged that the men had carried out the attack in retaliation for the US military interventions in Iraq and Afghanistan.

Immigration and Border Security

In January 2004 the US-Visit programme was implemented, requiring that all visa holders entering the USA were electronically fingerprinted and photographed on arrival. In April 2006 some 500,000 people in Los Angeles participated in a march in protest against restrictive new immigration legislation; other protest marches took place in Phoenix, Denver and Milwaukee. The legislation, approved by the House of Representatives in December 2005, made illegal immigration a criminal offence, and approved the Secure Border Initiative (SBI), which envisaged construction of 1,130 km (700 miles) of reinforced fencing along parts of the US–Mexican border, together with the implementation of surveillance cameras and motion sensors designed to act as a 'virtual fence' in those parts of the border without a physical barrier. The Senate ratified immigration legislation in May 2006 authorizing the establishment of a guest worker programme. Provisions were also made for immigrants to attain citizenship, subject to the satisfaction of certain criteria. In August the federal Government implemented 'Operation Jump Start', an immigration control initiative effected in the southern border regions, including Arizona, Texas, California and New Mexico. The initiative entailed the deployment of 6,000 National Guard personnel in support of the Border Patrol, and succeeded in curtailing the illegal border crossings by an estimated 30% by early 2007; Operation Jump Start was formally concluded in July 2008.

In March 2010, after some 1,035 km (643 miles) of the border fence had been erected, the Secretary of Homeland Security, Janet Napolitano, announced a freeze on new SBI funding and diverted US $50m. of its approved funding to other uses, amid escalating public debate as to the potential effectiveness of the initiative: after more than $1,000m. spent on the project, just 53 miles of the border had been covered by the surveillance technology by the end of 2010. In August the House of Representatives approved the disbursement of some $600m. on an additional 1,500 Border Patrol agents, as well as two unmanned surveillance 'drones', in a development heralded by many observers as a return to more traditional border security measures. In January 2011 Napolitano announced the cancellation of the SBI project, pledging to formulate a new strategy that would offer 'a more effective balance between cost and capability'. Researchers estimated that there were approximately 11m. undocumented immigrants in the USA in early 2013; a peak of about 12m. had been recorded in 2008.

The details of a cross-party immigration reform bill were revealed in April 2013. The proposals most notably included a normalization mechanism for undocumented immigrants, as well as an expansion of the work visa programme and new border security measures. The legislation was expected to be presented to the Senate in mid-2013.

Energy Security and Environmental Concerns

An energy policy report issued by the Administration of George W. Bush in May 2001, which included a proposal to introduce legislation authorizing exploratory drilling for oil in the Arctic National Wildlife Refuge in Alaska (ANWR), prompted criticism from the environmental lobby. In August the House of Representatives voted in favour of the proposal; however, the proposed legislation was rejected by the Senate in April 2002. The Administration subsequently introduced a provision to allow drilling to start in 2004, whereby federal revenue would be raised from the sale of leases to petroleum companies, but in March 2003 Congress removed the provision. In August the

Government proposed further controversial amendments to regulations governing carbon emissions; under the new legislation, energy companies would no longer be required to install anti-pollution measures when upgrading equipment. The announcement prompted criticism from environmental groups. In March–April 2005 Congress narrowly approved a proposal to begin drilling in the ANWR. However, in its final version, the relevant legislation was part of a wider budget reconciliation bill that was only approved by both houses in December once the ANWR provision had been removed. In what appeared to be a repetition of the previous year's events, in March 2006 the Senate narrowly approved legislation that would permit the opening of parts of the ANWR to drilling; however, the outcome was again contingent on congressional approval of another budget reconciliation bill. Despite ratification of minor amendments to existing ANWR legislation during 2007, and the President's reiteration in April 2008 of the Refuge's potential as a resource for bolstering the Strategic Petroleum Reserve—with regard to the effects of escalating international oil prices upon the domestic economy—the existing restrictions were still in place when Barack Obama, who was strongly opposed to any future exploration of the ANWR, took office in January 2009. Although Obama announced proposals in March 2010 to expand offshore oil and gas exploration off the Atlantic coast, notably off Virginia, a reversal of his position on the ANWR seemed unlikely. According to the US Geological Survey, recoverable oil reserves in the ANWR were estimated at 10,400m. barrels of oil in 2005; at that time US oil consumption totalled about 20m. barrels per day.

An explosion in April 2010 on the Deepwater Horizon offshore drilling rig, which was operating for the United Kingdom-based company BP in an oilfield about 60 km south-east of the Louisiana coast, precipitated the largest ever accidental offshore oil spill globally. The equivalent of an estimated 4.9m. barrels of oil seeped into the Gulf of Mexico between the time of the explosion, on 20 April, and the eventual capping of the well, after a number of failed attempts, on 15 July. The initial explosion claimed the lives of 11 oil workers. In May Obama established a bipartisan National Commission on the BP Deepwater Horizon Oil Spill and Offshore Drilling, which was charged with investigating the oil spill with a view to providing recommendations on how best to reduce the risk, and mitigate the impact, of any future spills as a result of offshore drilling. In November the Commission concluded that BP had not sacrificed safety in attempts to boost its profits but that some decisions had increased risks on the oil rig. BP established a US $20,000m. compensation fund from which to pay out damages to individuals and businesses affected by the oil spill; Obama also persuaded BP to create a separate $100m. fund from which to compensate oil rig employees who had been left unemployed as a result of the disaster. BP confirmed in November 2012 that it would pay $4,500m. in fines to settle the criminal charges that had been filed against the company in the wake of the accident, and a civil trial was ongoing in early 2013. The Department of Justice also concluded a settlement deal with the owner of Deepwater Horizon, the Switzerland-based firm Transocean, which pledged to pay $1,400m. in penalties in January 2013.

Meanwhile, in March 2001 the withdrawal of support by the Bush Administration for the ratification process of the Kyoto Protocol on climate change (UN Environment Programme, see p. 61), claiming that it would be detrimental to US economic interests, had prompted stern condemnation from environmental campaigners and numerous foreign governments and international organizations. In February 2002 Bush proposed voluntary, less far-reaching, measures to reduce emissions of greenhouse gases. In response to the heightened international concern over global warming and the depletion of energy resources, President Bush signed the Energy Independence and Security Act in December 2007, increasing fuel efficiency standards for passenger vehicles and stipulating that biofuels should account for 36,000m. gallons of motor fuel by 2022 in order to reduce the USA's dependence on imported petroleum.

Hopes of greater US co-operation in international efforts to counter the effects of man-made climate change were raised by Obama's election to the presidency, and in June 2009 the House of Representatives voted to commit the USA to reducing carbon emissions by 17% from 2005 levels by 2020 and by 83% by 2050; if approved by the Senate, the bill, which was hailed as the most important energy- and environment-related legislation in US history, would also provide for the establishment of a national 'cap and trade' system (an emissions trading programme with overall limits set by the federal Government). However, following the Democrats' loss of its 'super majority' in the Senate (see Domestic Political Affairs), the Obama Administration was forced to abandon the bill in June 2010, owing to continued opposition from Republican senators. In place of the abandoned bill, more limited legislation was proposed, the focus of which was on increasing firms' liability for oil spills, in response to public anger towards BP in the wake of the Gulf of Mexico spill. The new bill was approved by the House of Representatives in July. However, it stalled in the Senate, with many Democrats blaming Republican senators for wilfully obstructing the passage of the bill in order to deny a major legislative success to the Obama Administration. Forced to adapt, Obama announced a moderated environmental strategy in his State of the Union address in January, which included a plan to double the percentage of US electricity derived from clean energy sources, from about 40% to 80% by 2035.

In January 2012 the US Department of State rejected a plan to build a 2,700-km oil pipeline, Keystone XL, connecting oil sands fields in Canada with markets in the USA. It was announced that further time would be needed to assess the environmental impact of the project. The pipeline had been criticized by environmentalists since oil sands production is more polluting than conventional petroleum operations. Nevertheless, in February the Obama Administration endorsed the construction of the first section of the pipeline in the southern USA. A revised proposal for the remaining branches was submitted in May, and a final decision on the project was expected in the second half of 2013.

Foreign Affairs

Relations with Latin America

Ronald Reagan's Administration actively supported right-wing regimes in Latin America, where the US military occupation of Grenada in November 1983 attracted considerable international criticism. In December 1989, following the failure of an internal coup attempt that received non-military US support, the USA, under the presidency of Reagan's successor, George Bush, carried out an armed invasion of Panama and subsequently installed an elected government. US troops were withdrawn in February 1990.

The Administration of Bill Clinton made renewed efforts to restore to power Fr Jean-Bertrand Aristide, the first democratically elected President of Haiti, who had taken refuge in the USA following his overthrow by a military junta in 1991. An economic embargo imposed by the Organization of American States (OAS, see p. 404), together with implied threats of military intervention by the US Government, had failed to displace the military regime, and conditions within Haiti had led large numbers of refugees to seek asylum in the USA, many of whom were forcibly repatriated by the US authorities. In June 1994, following the imposition in the previous month of international sanctions against Haiti by the UN Security Council, Clinton announced the suspension of all commercial and financial transactions with Haiti. In September, following a diplomatic mission led by former President Carter, a UN-sponsored multinational force, composed almost entirely of US troops, arrived in Haiti with the agreement of the military junta, which relinquished power in October. US troops were withdrawn from the UN force in March 1995. In January 2004 the Administration of George W. Bush condemned attacks on thousands of demonstrators protesting against the Aristide Government. In March, in the face of growing violence and under international pressure, Aristide resigned and went into exile, although he claimed that he had been unconstitutionally removed from office by the USA. Several hundred US marines were deployed in Haiti in March–June 2004 as the vanguard of a multinational UN Stabilization Mission in Haiti to disarm rebel forces and stabilize the country. Following the earthquake that struck Haiti in January 2010, the USA dispatched some 12,000 military personnel to the country to assist in the distribution of relief supplies.

Successive US Governments remained unwilling to restore relations with Cuba. Relations between the two countries deteriorated in March 1996, after two civilian aircraft carrying Cuban exiles protesting against the Government of Fidel Castro were shot down by the Cuban air force over international waters. In response, Clinton acceded to congressional demands to strengthen the US commercial and economic embargo that has been in force since 1962. Under the new measure, the Cuban Liberty and Solidarity (Helms-Burton) Act, the USA was to penalize foreign investors whose business in any way involved property in Cuba that was confiscated from US citizens following the 1959 revolution. In July 1996 a number of Canadian, Mexican and Italian companies were informed that sanctions were to be imposed on them under the Helms-Burton legislation, barring their senior executives and certain shareholders from visiting the USA. In response to intense international pressure, Clinton declared a temporary moratorium on certain provisions of the Helms-Burton Act, and in April 1997 the US Government and the European Union (EU), which had opposed the measure, announced that a compromise had been agreed, subject to the abandonment by the US Government of certain sections of the Act. The moratorium on Title III of the Act was subsequently extended at six-monthly intervals and remained in operation in 2013. In late 2001 the USA lifted temporarily the trade embargo against Cuba to allow the purchase of food and medicines necessary for the reconstruction and aid effort following the devastation caused by Hurricane Michelle. In May 2002, however, the Bush Administration accused Cuba of maintaining a biological warfare programme and offering weapons technology to 'rogue states' (deemed by the Department of State to be those countries with the capabilities to use weapons of mass destruction without adherence to traditional international conventions). In April 2004 a motion, supported by the USA, condemning Cuba for human rights violations, was approved by the UN General Assembly; similar US-backed motions had been passed by the UN in 2002 and 2003. In April 2005 a milder, US-proposed motion requesting that the mandate of the UN's Special Rapporteur on Human Rights in Cuba be extended was approved by the General Assembly. In July Secretary of State Condoleezza Rice appointed Caleb McCarry Cuba Transition Co-ordinator, a position created at the behest of a special panel charged with directing the US Government's actions 'in support of a free Cuba' and hastening the end to Castro's presidency. Bilateral relations deteriorated further in 2007 following the release from a US prison of Luis Posada Carriles, who was wanted in Cuba on terrorism charges. The Cuban Government accused the Bush Administration of hypocrisy in its so-called 'war on terror'. In April 2009 the Administration of Barack Obama relaxed certain sanctions against Cuba, including travel restrictions on Cuban-American citizens and limits on remittances, and permitted US telecommunications companies to seek access to the Cuban market, prompting hopes of an amelioration in relations. However, any improvement in relations was halted by the imprisonment in December of a US contractor on suspicion of espionage; Alan Gross had been arrested while working as a business and economic development consultant despite only possessing a tourist visa, but both he and the Obama Administration strenuously refuted the claims against him. In March 2011 Gross was convicted in Cuba on charges of 'actions against the independence and territorial integrity of the state' and sentenced to 15 years' imprisonment. The verdict attracted criticism from the US authorities.

In December 1994 President Clinton proposed the formation, by 2006, of a Free Trade Area of the Americas (FTAA), comprising 34 countries of the Western hemisphere, although excluding Cuba. Negotiations were scheduled to conclude by January 2005, but stalled in November 2004; although it was agreed to resume talks in mid-2006, there had been no progress to this end by early 2013. Meanwhile, however, the Venezuelan President, Lt-Col (retd) Hugo Chávez Frías, had commenced implementation of an alternative free trade initiative for the Americas, the Bolivarian Alternative for the Americas (Alternativa Bolivariana para las Américas—ALBA), in direct challenge to the moribund FTAA. Relations between the Bush and Chávez Governments deteriorated markedly in the 2000s, and in September 2008 the Venezuelan President suspended diplomatic relations with the USA in solidarity with the Bolivian Government of Evo Morales. Morales had expelled the US ambassador, accusing him of fomenting opposition dissent in Bolivia. Secretary of State Hillary Clinton intimated in mid-2009 that the Obama Government wanted to improve relations with the left-wing administrations in Bolivia and Venezuela, and in June US-Venezuelan diplomatic relations were resumed. Formal relations with Bolivia were finally re-established in November 2011.

In January 2000 the Clinton Administration announced an aid package for the Andean region worth US $1,300m., the largest ever aid programme for Latin America. The main portion of the programme, which became known as the Plan Colombia, was to provide some $860m. to Colombia, three-quarters of which was allocated to the security forces in that country, to aid with the ongoing war against drugs-trafficking. The size of the military component of the Plan caused controversy internationally, as did

the proposed aerial destruction of crops in the region. The Bush Administration implemented an Andean Counterdrug Initiative in 2001 to complement Plan Colombia, the focus of which was on improving social and economic conditions in the region. Nevertheless, the objective remained the same: to reduce significantly the flow of drugs from the Andean region into the USA. An agreement signed by the USA and Colombia in October 2009, granting the US military access to seven Colombian bases, strengthened bilateral relations, but was criticized by other South American countries, most notably Venezuela. In February 2010 the Obama Administration proposed a reduction in funding for Plan Colombia in its budget plan for the 2011 fiscal year, partly on the grounds that the programme had progressed to less costly phases. Meanwhile, the USA signed bilateral free trade agreements with Colombia and Panama in 2006 and 2007, respectively. The two agreements (together with a free trade pact with the Republic of Korea—South Korea) were finally approved by Congress in October 2011.

In response to the removal from power of the President of Honduras, José Manuel Zelaya Rosales, in June 2009 the Obama Administration withdrew some development aid and suspended military co-operation with the Central American state. Further aid to Honduras was cancelled in September, and the visas of the acting President, Roberto Micheletti Baín, and several other senior officials in his administration were revoked. However, the USA recognized the results of presidential and legislative elections held in Honduras in November, describing them as an important step forward', and a US representative attended the inauguration of the new President, Porfirio Lobo Sosa, in January 2010. In March Secretary of State Hillary Clinton announced that US aid to Honduras would be restored and advocated the country's return to full participation in the OAS, its membership rights having been suspended since July 2009. Disbursement of US military and development aid to Honduras was restored from June 2010. Honduras was readmitted to the OAS in June 2011.

President Obama embarked on a tour of Latin America in March 2011, visiting Brazil, Chile and El Salvador, with the aim of promoting economic co-operation and improved regional security. The tour commenced with a meeting between Obama and Brazilian President Dilma Vana Rousseff, emphasizing the growing economic and strategic importance of US relations with Brazil, Latin America's largest economic power. An agreement between the USA and Chile on nuclear energy was signed, while in El Salvador Obama pledged US $200m. to help to address the dramatic rise in violent crime in that country.

Relations with the USSR and successor states

A summit meeting in December 1989 between President George Bush and Soviet head of state Mikhail Gorbachev, in Valletta, Malta, marked the opening of a new era in US-Soviet relations. The withdrawal by the USSR in late 1989 and early 1990 from the exercise of direct political influence on the internal affairs of the countries of Eastern Europe was accompanied by a further improvement in US-Soviet relations, and by the implementation of programmes of US economic aid for several of the former Soviet 'client' states. In September 1990 the USA and USSR, with France and the United Kingdom (the other powers that occupied Germany at the end of the Second World War), formally agreed terms for the unification of the two post-war German states, which took effect in the following month. In July the USA, together with the world's six largest industrial democracies, agreed to provide the USSR with economic and technical assistance in undertaking a transition to a market economy. This initiative was followed in November by the signing in Paris, France, by members of NATO and the Warsaw Pact, of a Treaty on Conventional Armed Forces in Europe (CFE), which provided for bilateral limits to be placed on the number of non-nuclear weapons sited between the Atlantic Ocean and the Ural Mountains. Immediately following the signing of the CFE Treaty, Presidents Bush and Gorbachev were present at a meeting of the Conference on Security and Co-operation in Europe (CSCE, now the Organization for Security and Co-operation in Europe— OSCE, see p. 397), at which the USA, the USSR and 32 other countries signed a charter declaring the end of the post-war era of confrontation and division in Europe. In July 1991 the USA and the USSR signed a Strategic Arms Reduction Treaty (START, renamed START I after negotiations commenced on START II— see below), providing for a 30% reduction in long-range nuclear weapons over a seven-year period.

In December 1991, following the replacement of the USSR by the Commonwealth of Independent States (CIS) comprising 11 of the former Soviet republics, the independence of each republic was recognized by the USA. In January 1992 a meeting was held between President Bush and President Boris Yeltsin of Russia, the dominant republic within the CIS. President Bush expressed concern that effective measures should be taken by the Russian Government to ensure that the nuclear weapons and related technical expertise of the former USSR did not become available to countries not in possession of nuclear weapons capability, or to nations in the Middle East or to the Democratic People's Republic of Korea (North Korea). At a subsequent meeting held in February, the Russian leader assured President Bush that immediate safeguards were in force, and that all short-range nuclear warheads would be moved into Russia from sites in other CIS republics. At a summit meeting held between Presidents Bush and Yeltsin in June in Washington, DC, agreement was reached on further substantial reductions in nuclear arms, under which, by 2003, total holdings of nuclear warheads would be reduced to less than one-half of the quotas contained in START.

In January 1993 Presidents Bush and Yeltsin met in Moscow to sign START II, which provided for the elimination by 2003 of almost 75% of all US and CIS-held nuclear warheads. Although ratified by the US Senate in 1993, START II remained unratified by the Russian legislature until April 2000. However, enactment of START II was contingent on the continuation of the Anti-Ballistic Missile (ABM) treaty (signed with the USSR in 1972). In December 2001 President George W. Bush announced the USA's intention to withdraw from the ABM Treaty after a six-month notice period, claiming that its adherence prevented the development of the US National Missile Defence (NMD) programme, a network of ground- and sea-based interceptor rockets with the capability of destroying intercontinental ballistic missiles launched by a hostile power. Meanwhile, in November 2001, following a summit meeting in Washington, DC, George W. Bush and Russian President Vladimir Putin pledged to reduce their nation's nuclear arsenals by approximately two-thirds over the following decade; a formal agreement, the Moscow Treaty, was signed in May 2002. In June the USA formally withdrew from the ABM. President Bush emphasized that the USA's withdrawal from the ABM would not undermine US-Russian relations. Russia immediately withdrew from START II, which had been effectively superseded by the treaty signed with the USA in the previous month.

The Administration of Barack Obama sought to improve US relations with Russia. In July 2009, during Obama's first official visit to Moscow since taking office, the President and his Russian counterpart, Dmitrii Medvedev, signed a joint understanding on the negotiation of a new nuclear arms control treaty to replace START I, which was due to expire at the end of 2009, and agreed to establish a bilateral presidential commission to enhance co-operation in areas including energy, counter-terrorism activities and drugs-trafficking. Furthermore, officials signed a new strategic framework for military co-operation, which had been suspended since August 2008 owing to the conflict between Russia and Georgia (q.v.), while the Russian Government also agreed to allow the USA to transport military personnel and equipment across its territory to Afghanistan. US-Russian relations were further improved in September 2009 when Obama announced the abandonment of plans initiated by his predecessor (and opposed by Russia) to construct missile defence facilities in the Czech Republic and Poland. However, the Administration intended to pursue other missile defence projects within Europe, using initially sea-based, but subsequently also land-based, interceptors. In March 2010 Obama and Medvedev reached agreement on a replacement for START I and the Moscow Treaty of 2002, which would commit both Russia and the USA to reducing their deployed nuclear warheads from a maximum allowable number of 2,200 to 1,550 within seven years of the new treaty coming into force. In addition, the maximum numbers of launchers and missiles were to be limited to 800 and 700, respectively, and a new inspection and verification regime was to be established. The New START Treaty was signed by Obama and Medvedev in the Czech Republic in April 2010. Having been ratified by the US Senate in December and by the Russian legislature in January 2011, the treaty came into effect in February. In September the Russian authorities expressed their disapproval of a US-Romanian accord providing for the establishment of interceptors in Romania by 2015. In September 2012 Russia ordered the discontinuation of all USAID operations in the country, which were primarily focused on supporting local human rights and civil society organizations. The Russian authorities accused the US agency of attempting to exert political influence through its operations. In December the US Congress approved legislation that would normalize bilateral trade relations with Russia; however, the legislation also included a provision authorizing the imposition of US sanctions on Russians accused of human rights violations, which placed further strain on bilateral relations.

Relations with the People's Republic of China

In December 1992 relations with the People's Republic of China were revived by the removal of a US embargo on sales of military equipment. However, relations with China pursued an uneven course under the Administration of Bill Clinton, owing to disagreements over trade matters and criticism by the USA of alleged abuses by the Chinese Government of human rights. Relations between the two countries declined sharply in February 1996, following US protests over Chinese military operations near Taiwan. Relations between the two countries were enhanced in October 1997 by a state visit to the USA by President Jiang Zemin, following which the US Government revoked a ban, in force since 1989, on the export of US nuclear technology to China. China, together with Russia and the USA, refused in December 1997 to sign an international treaty—the Ottawa Convention—banning the manufacture and use of anti-personnel land-mines; the US Government based its objection to the arrangements on its requirement for land-mines to protect its troops stationed in the Republic of Korea. (Following a review of land-mine policy, in February 2004 the Administration of George W. Bush announced that it would not sign the treaty and would continue to use, indefinitely, 'non-persistent' land-mines that would self-destruct or self-deactivate after a certain period of time.) Following the settlement in 1999 of a dispute over infringements of US copyright and other intellectual property rights, Chinese enhanced trading privileges were granted permanent status in 2000, opening the way for China to join the World Trade Organization (WTO, see p. 444). However, the accidental bombing by US aircraft of the Chinese diplomatic mission in the Yugoslav capital during NATO air attacks in May 1999 led to a period of strained relations, despite a subsequent apology and the payment of compensation by the US Government. In September 2001, in return for China's acceptance of its NMD programme (see Relations with the USSR and successor states), the USA pledged to keep China informed of its development and agreed to recognize that the Chinese might, in the future, want to resume nuclear weapons testing. The USA also urged China not to transfer ballistic missile technology to countries that the USA considered to be 'rogue states'.

President Barack Obama adopted a conciliatory approach during his first official visit to China, which took place in November 2009, emphasizing the need for joint action to confront global challenges. A joint statement, issued following Obama's talks with his Chinese counterpart, Hu Jintao, envisaged increased bilateral co-operation in areas such as climate change, security and trade. None the less, tensions arose in January 2010 when the Obama Administration confirmed plans to proceed with the sale of weapons to Taiwan under an agreement reached during George W. Bush's presidency. In retaliation, the Chinese Government announced its intention to suspend military exchanges with the USA, to review bilateral co-operation and to impose sanctions on US companies supplying the arms. US-Sino relations were further strained in February after Obama held a meeting with the Dalai Lama, the exiled spiritual leader of Tibet, in Washington, DC, despite Chinese objections. However, the USA and China agreed to restore full military ties in September. During an official visit to Washington, DC, by President Hu in January 2011, Obama urged the Chinese Government to take tougher action to improve China's human rights record, including in Tibet; during his visit Hu made a rare acknowledgement that 'a lot still needs to be done in China in terms of human rights'. Following private talks between the two heads of state, the Obama Administration announced bilateral trade and investment deals worth an estimated US $45,000m. However, bilateral relations suffered a reverse in July after Obama held a second meeting with the Dalai Lama, while in September a US pledge to renovate Taiwan's fleet of fighter aircraft attracted further Chinese criticism. An additional source of dispute was the announcement by Obama in November that 2,500 US troops would be gradually deployed to northern Australia during 2012–16. This development came at a time of heightened tensions resulting from the US Administration's increasingly assertive rhetoric with regard to its interests in the Asia-Pacific region: in June 2012 US military officials announced plans to base 60% of the US naval fleet in the Pacific region by 2020. Analysts viewed the USA's actions as part of a broader strategy to counterbalance

China's regional influence. In August 2012 the Chinese authorities issued strong objections to a statement by the US Department of State that was critical of China's establishment of a military garrison in a disputed area of the South China Sea. The US statement asserted that territorial disputes in the South China Sea involving China and several South-East Asian nations, including Viet Nam and the Philippines, posed a serious threat to regional security and US interests.

Nevertheless, despite the evident tensions, US and Chinese authorities endeavoured to maintain steady bilateral relations, and in April 2013 Gen. Martin Dempsey, Chairman of the US Joint Chiefs of Staff, travelled to Beijing for talks on expanding US-Sino military co-operation. It was hoped that the installation of a new leadership in China, in November 2012, would facilitate improved co-operation between the two world powers. Moreover, in mid-April 2013 the USA and China issued a joint statement, in which they pledged to work together to forge a peaceful solution to rising tensions on the Korean peninsula (see Relations with North Korea).

Relations with North Korea

The prevention of nuclear proliferation, which remained a prime objective of US foreign policy, led in 1993 and early 1994 to a serious confrontation between the USA and the Democratic People's Republic of Korea (North Korea). In March 1993 North Korea, which is a signatory of the Nuclear Non-Proliferation Treaty (NPT) and is subject, by virtue of its membership of the International Atomic Energy Agency (IAEA, see p. 122), to the monitoring of its nuclear installations, refused to grant the IAEA inspectorate full access to its nuclear power facility. It cited as its reasons the existence of joint military exercises between the Republic of Korea (South Korea) and the USA and 'unjust acts' by the IAEA. The US Government stated that it had reason to suspect that North Korea had been diverting nuclear plant material for the development of atomic weapons. In July President Bill Clinton visited South Korea, and warned North Korea that any use of nuclear weapons by them would be met with military force. The crisis steadily worsened during early 1994, and in June the US Government, after seeking unsuccessfully to offer North Korea economic aid, investment and diplomatic recognition, began to seek support for the imposition of UN economic sanctions. Later in the same month, following a visit to North Korea by former President Carter (acting as an unofficial representative of the Government), North Korea agreed to a temporary suspension of its nuclear programme, pending formal discussions with the US Government. These meetings were convened in July. Negotiations aimed at improving relations between the USA and North Korea, and at fostering a political settlement between North and South Korea, were pursued throughout both Clinton Administrations. In March 1999 the US and North Korean Governments agreed on terms whereby US officials would receive unrestricted access to inspect North Korean nuclear facilities.

In January 2002 President George W. Bush described North Korea, together with Iran and Iraq, as forming an 'axis of evil' that supported international terrorism and sought to develop weapons of mass destruction. Relations with North Korea were severely strained in late 2002 when it emerged that the North Korean Government had resumed its nuclear energy programme, effectively breaking the accord signed with the USA in 1994. In October 2002 North Korea demanded a treaty of non-aggression with the USA and asserted its right to possess nuclear weapons. In the following month the USA, South Korea, Japan and the EU suspended their supply of petroleum to North Korea until its Government promised to terminate its nuclear weapons programme, although North Korea denied it operated such a programme. However, in December it announced operations would resume at the Yongbyon nuclear plant, which was capable of producing weapons-grade plutonium. The USA considered that economic sanctions would be an effective means of containing North Korea, although this led to a more uncompromising stance from North Korea, which said it would consider UN sanctions an 'act of war', and subsequently withdrew from the NPT in January 2003. In July North Korea claimed that it had made enough plutonium to produce six nuclear bombs. In August six-party negotiations opened in the Chinese capital, Beijing, between the USA, North Korea, China, South Korea, Japan and Russia; however, little progress was achieved. In October President Bush announced that the USA would be prepared to offer security assurances to North Korea in exchange for verifiable dismantling of any weapons programmes. In February 2004 a further round of six-party talks took place in Beijing.

Talks in June ended unsuccessfully and in February 2005 North Korea admitted for the first time that it possessed nuclear weapons. Talks eventually resumed in August, and the following month it appeared that a breakthrough had been made when North Korea agreed in principle to end its weapons development programme in exchange for a civilian light-water reactor. However, North Korea refused to begin dismantling its nuclear programme until it had received the reactor. Meanwhile, US authorities froze the assets of eight North Korean companies, which were accused of supporting the North Korean weapons programme. In October the US Department of Justice charged North Korea with having forged millions of dollars worth of counterfeit US \$100 bills since 1989. The North Korean Government insisted that six-party negotiations would not resume until the economic sanctions against it were lifted.

In October 2006, after North Korea conducted its first nuclear test, the USA entered into further talks, and in February 2007 significant progress appeared to have been made when the Government of North Korea agreed to effect the disarmament programme agreed upon in 2005. The process was to begin with the closure of the nuclear reactor in Yongbyon within 60 days, but progress once again stalled when North Korea missed a deadline at the end of 2007 by which it was due to give a full account of its nuclear activities. North Korea eventually declared its nuclear activities in June 2008, and in October the country was removed from the US Department of State's list of state sponsors of terrorism. Nevertheless, six-party talks again broke down in December over verification of the disarmament programme, prompting the USA to suspend aid to the country. Tensions were heightened in April 2009, following the launch of a North Korean rocket. Following condemnation from the UN Security Council, the North Korean Government (which claimed to have been placing a communications satellite into orbit) announced its permanent withdrawal from the six-party talks and the restoration of its nuclear facilities at Yongbyon. In June the Security Council adopted a resolution strengthening sanctions against North Korea in response to the underground detonation of a nuclear device in May. Further nuclear tests conducted in July led to the imposition of sanctions against additional North Korean individuals and organizations. In December Stephen Bosworth, the US Special Representative for North Korea Policy, visited North Korea for the first time since his appointment in February, holding 'exploratory' discussions with the country's leaders (although not Kim Jong Il); Bosworth subsequently stated that a 'common understanding' on the importance of the disarmament process had been reached, although he had not secured a firm commitment on North Korea's return to the six-party talks. However, hopes of a thawing in bilateral relations appeared to be quashed by the announcement in May 2010 that the US military was to participate in new naval exercises with South Korea, following the sinking, allegedly by a North Korean torpedo, of a South Korean military vessel in March, in which 46 South Korean sailors had been killed. North Korea denied any involvement, and its state news agency counterclaimed that the USA had manipulated the incident to fabricate the appearance of North Korean involvement. The North Korean Government issued a bellicose warning to the Obama Administration in July, threatening to 'legitimately counter' the US-South Korean naval exercises with its 'powerful nuclear deterrence'.

In July 2011 the USA hosted discussions with senior North Korean officials in an attempt to restart the six-party talks, and a further round of negotiations took place in October. However, diplomatic relations with North Korea were complicated by the death of Kim Jong Il in December and the assumption of power by his son, Kim Jong Un. Nevertheless, bilateral talks resumed in February 2012, and it was subsequently announced that, in exchange for US food aid, North Korea had pledged to suspend its nuclear programme, to refrain from missile-testing activities and to permit IAEA investigators to return to the country. However, this rapprochement proved short-lived, owing to North Korea's efforts to launch a satellite into orbit in April. The operation, which was unsuccessful, was widely perceived as an attempted missile test and hence in breach of the recent arrangement with the USA (as well as earlier UN Security Council resolutions). The Obama Administration withdrew its offer of food aid and, in early May, the Security Council imposed sanctions on three state-run North Korean corporations and tightened up existing economic sanctions on the regime. Further UN sanctions were introduced in early 2013 in response to another North Korean satellite launch in December 2012 and a further nuclear test in February 2013. US-South Korean military exercises were conducted in March, prompting the North Korean authorities to issue a series of increasingly inflammatory statements, including threats against the USA and its interests in the region. The Obama Administration declared that, as a precautionary measure, missile defences in western US states would be reinforced and a new defence system would be installed on the US Pacific territory of Guam. Two US warships were also transferred to the Korean peninsula. In April North Korea announced its intention to resume operations at the Yongbyon nuclear facility.

Relations with the Middle East and North Africa

In the period following the Gulf War of 1990–91 (see Domestic Political Affairs) the US Government actively pursued initiatives to convene a regional conference to seek a permanent solution to the wider problems of the Middle East. In August 1991 Egypt, Israel, Jordan, Lebanon and Syria agreed to take part in such a conference, the opening session of which was convened in October. Successive negotiations failed to make any substantive progress, and traditionally close relations between Israel and the USA subsequently came under strain, following pressure by the US Government on Israel to suspend the construction of Jewish settlements in occupied territories, pending the eventual outcome of the peace negotiations.

During 1993 the Administration of Bill Clinton continued to foster efforts to promote a general resolution of tensions in the Middle East. With US assistance, but as a direct result of secret diplomatic mediation by Norway, the Palestine Liberation Organization (PLO) and the Government of Israel signed an agreement providing for Palestinian self-government in the Occupied Territories and for mutual recognition by Israel and the PLO. In January 1994, following a meeting held in Geneva, Switzerland, between Clinton and President Hafiz al-Assad of Syria, negotiations were initiated for a settlement between Israel and Syria. In December 1999, under Clinton's auspices, the first substantive negotiations since 1996 between the Governments of Israel and Syria took place in Washington, DC. In March 2000 the US Government sought to move towards a rapprochement with Iran with the announcement that it was to ease some of the trade sanctions against Iran that had been in force since 1979.

In his State of the Union address in January 2002, President George W. Bush described Iran and Iraq, together with North Korea, as forming an 'axis of evil' that supported international terrorism and sought to develop weapons of mass destruction, and hinted that the USA was considering pre-emptive strikes against them. US allies warned against attacking states unless firm evidence of a link to terrorism could be found. In May the 'axis of evil' was extended to include Libya and Syria (as well as Cuba). The Bush Administration claimed that Libya and Syria had violated international weapons treaties. In December the Iranian Government denied US allegations of evidence of the secret manufacture of nuclear weapons. In September 2003 the USA supported an IAEA resolution establishing a deadline of the end of October for Iran to disclose full details of its nuclear programme and provide evidence that it was not developing nuclear weapons. In December Libya agreed to disclose and dismantle its programme to develop weapons of mass destruction and long-range ballistic missiles, following nine months of secret negotiations between the Libyan leader, Col Muammar al-Qaddafi, and US and British diplomats. In February 2004 the USA ended the restrictions on its citizens travelling to Libya, in place since 1981, and in June diplomatic relations were officially re-established between the two countries for the first time in 23 years; however, Libya was not removed from the US list of state sponsors of terrorism until May 2006. (In September 2008 Condoleezza Rice became the first US Secretary of State in 50 years to visit Libya.) In February 2005, in protest against what it believed to be Syria's role in the assassination of the Prime Minister of Lebanon, Rafiq Hariri, the USA removed its ambassador to Syria for consultations, and later demanded that all Syrian troops withdraw from Lebanon. The Administration of President Barack Obama sought to renew diplomatic relations with Syria, and in February 2010 Obama nominated a new US ambassador to Syria, Robert Ford, although his nomination was blocked by Republicans in the Senate throughout 2010. Obama forced through Ford's appointment during a congressional recess in January 2011. However, in March the US Administration condemned the excessive use of force by Syrian security forces against anti-Government and pro-democracy protesters. High-ranking members of the Syrian regime were subjected to a US

assets freeze in April, and these economic sanctions were expanded in subsequent months. The US embassy in Damascus, the Syrian capital, came under attack by pro-Government supporters in July following a visit by Ford to the Syrian city of Hama to demonstrate solidarity with the protest movement. With the state-orchestrated violence continuing, in August Obama urged Syrian President Bashar al-Assad to relinquish power. Ford was recalled to the USA for consultations in October after threats of violence were made against him, prompting Syria to withdraw its ambassador to the USA in response. US-led efforts in late 2011 to secure a UN Security Council resolution censuring the Syrian authorities for their violent response to the demonstrations failed due to opposition from Russia and China. The Syrian chargé d'affaires was expelled from the USA in late May 2012 in protest against the massacre of 108 people in Houla earlier that month. The atrocity had allegedly been perpetrated by elements linked to the Assad regime. In December the USA, together with over 100 other countries, formally accorded recognition to the National Coalition for Opposition Forces and the Syrian Revolution.

In April 2006 the Iranian President, Mahmoud Ahmadinejad, announced that Iran had successfully achieved the enrichment of uranium for civilian purposes. The Iranian Government claimed that the enriched uranium was not weapons-grade, but was, rather, to be used as nuclear fuel. In May a draft UN resolution was promulgated, under which France, Germany, the United Kingdom and the USA again urged Iran to arrest its nuclear enrichment programme and to abandon construction of a heavy-water reactor by the end of August, or face economic sanctions. In return for compliance, a portfolio of incentives was offered, including the provision of light-water nuclear reactors for electricity generation. However, in August Iran's Supreme Leader, Ayatollah Ali Khamenei, declared that the country's nuclear programme would continue, and at the end of that month the heavy-water plant became operational.

A resolution was approved by the UN Security Council in December 2006 imposing sanctions against Iran, which prevented the import or export of materials and technology associated with uranium enrichment enterprises and froze the financial assets of 12 Iranians and 10 institutions associated with the country's nuclear development programme. Nevertheless, in January 2007 Iran announced that production of nuclear fuel for industrial purposes was to commence imminently and declared its intention to enhance economic and military co-operation with Iraq. US suspicions that the Iranian Government was supplying Iraqi Shi'ite militants with ammunition and weapons appeared substantiated in February when US military officials in the Iraqi capital reported the seizure of explosives components manufactured in Iran; however, links between the bomb materials and the Iranian administration could not be unequivocally proven. Furthermore, the National Intelligence Estimate, published in December 2007 and compiled using information supplied by the USA's 16 intelligence agencies, reported with 'high confidence' that Iran had ceased its nuclear weapons programme in 2003 and had not recommenced such activities by mid-2007, although it continued to enrich uranium.

President Obama extended US trade and investment sanctions against Iran for a further year in March 2009, but later that month called for a 'new beginning' in relations between the two countries in a video message to the Iranian people and leadership. The President's policy of engagement was jeopardized in the following month, when a journalist with dual US-Iranian citizenship was convicted by an Iranian court of spying for the USA and sentenced to eight years' imprisonment. However, in what was regarded as a conciliatory gesture, the journalist was released in May and permitted to return to the USA, her sentence having been commuted to a two-year suspended term. Bilateral talks between the USA's Undersecretary of State for Political Affairs, William Burns, and Iran's chief nuclear negotiator, Saeed Jalili, in October represented the most senior-level direct engagement between the two countries since the Islamic Revolution of 1979. The talks took place on the sidelines of negotiations in Geneva on Iran's nuclear programme, involving representatives of China, France, Germany, Russia and the United Kingdom, as well as the USA. However, the international negotiations reached an impasse in November, as Iran refused to accept a proposal that it transfer a large proportion of its enriched uranium to Russia and France for further processing to the level of enrichment required for medical research purposes and announced plans to expand its nuclear programme. Following protracted lobbying by the US Administration, in early June

2010 the UN Security Council adopted a resolution imposing further sanctions on Iran, owing to Iran's lack of compliance with previous resolutions related to its nuclear programme; the resolution expanded the scope of the existing arms embargo and tightened restrictions on certain financial and shipping enterprises. In the same month the US Congress approved the Comprehensive Iran Sanctions, Accountability, and Divestment Act of 2010, which Obama signed into law at the beginning of July; the law provided for, *inter alia*, the imposition against Iran of additional sanctions prohibiting specified foreign exchange, banking, and property transactions.

Tensions between the USA and Iran were exacerbated in August 2011, when two US tourists were sentenced to eight years' imprisonment after being found guilty by an Iranian court of espionage and entering Iran illegally. The US Administration criticized the convictions, although both men, who denied any wrongdoing, were released in the following month. Additional arrests of alleged CIA operatives were made by the Iranian security forces throughout the year. A further dispute erupted in October after the USA accused Iran of conspiring to attack the Saudi Arabian and Israeli embassies in the USA and to murder the Saudi Arabian ambassador; Iran rejected the allegations. Following the publication in November of an IAEA report noting the potential military applications of the Iranian nuclear programme, the USA (along with the United Kingdom and Canada) imposed sanctions upon the Iranian financial and hydrocarbons industries. In late December Obama announced sanctions against Iran's central bank, and these measures were expanded in February 2012. Nevertheless, the IAEA revealed in early 2012 that Iran was continuing to enrich uranium, prompting further censure from the USA, while in March Obama warned the Iranian authorities that military action remained an option to prevent their acquisition of a nuclear weapon. Iran subsequently agreed to participate in a new round of nuclear negotiations involving the members of the UN Security Council and Germany. Four meetings were duly held between April and July, and further talks were conducted in February and April 2013, but no substantive progress was reported. The USA continued to broaden its sanctions regime against Iran during 2012, largely targeting the country's energy sector.

Meanwhile, following an escalation in the ongoing conflict in the Middle East, from early 2002 the USA intensified its efforts towards brokering a peace agreement between Israel and the Palestinians. In April Secretary of State Colin Powell visited Israel and held separate talks with the Israeli Prime Minister, Ariel Sharon, and with Palestinian President Yasser Arafat. However, the mission failed to bring about a cease-fire or the withdrawal of Israeli forces from Palestinian areas. In April 2003 President Bush presented both the Israeli and Palestinian Prime Ministers with an internationally sponsored 'roadmap' for peace, envisaging the phased creation of a sovereign Palestinian state. However, despite acceptance of the plan, Israel continued work on the construction of a 'security fence' in the disputed West Bank region, begun in mid-2002. In July 2003 the US Administration threatened to withhold almost US $10,000m. in essential loan guarantees unless construction of the fence ceased. Following approval by the Israeli Government of a further phase of construction, in November the US Congress cut $290m. from a total $1,400m. in loan guarantees to Israel as a penalty for the continuing expansion of Jewish settlements in the West Bank and Gaza. At a meeting between Bush and Sharon in Crawford, Texas, in April 2005, the President gave his support to Israel's planned withdrawal from the Gaza Strip, but criticized the continued expansion of Jewish settlements in the West Bank. In April 2006 the EU and USA suspended financial aid provisions to the Palestinian Authority (PA), under the leadership of the militant Hamas movement, in response to its continued refusal to recognize the state of Israel. The US Administration's failure to demand an immediate end to the Israeli military offensive against the radical Hezbollah movement in southern Lebanon that began in July also strained US-Lebanese relations.

At a Middle East peace conference held in Annapolis, Maryland, in November 2007, Israeli Prime Minister Ehud Olmert and Palestinian President Mahmoud Abbas agreed mutually to a deadline of December 2008 for the formulation of a peace settlement. However, this deadline was not met, and at the end of that month Israel initiated a major offensive against Hamas targets in the Gaza Strip that continued until mid-January 2009. During separate meetings in Washington, DC, with the new Israeli Prime Minister, Binyamin Netanyahu, and Palestinian President Abbas in May President Obama sought to foster a

revival of the stalled peace process and declared his commitment to a two-state solution. He also urged Israel to halt the expansion of settlements in the West Bank and East Jerusalem. In the following month, during his first official visit to the Middle East, Obama delivered a speech in Cairo, Egypt, in which he advocated a 'new beginning' in the relationship between the USA and Muslims world-wide, based on 'mutual interest and mutual respect'. While describing the USA's bond with Israel as 'unbreakable', the President also asserted that the situation for Palestinians was 'intolerable'. However, subsequent efforts by senior US diplomats, notably George Mitchell, the special envoy for the Middle East, to revive the peace process faltered over the settlements issue, and a tripartite meeting of Obama, Abbas and Netanyahu in New York in September also failed to result in a resumption of negotiations, as did talks between Obama and Netanyahu in Washington, DC, in November. Tensions in US-Israeli relations arose in March 2010, when the Israeli authorities' approval of plans to construct 1,600 new housing units in East Jerusalem overshadowed a visit to Israel by US Vice-President Joseph Biden and jeopardized a recent US-brokered agreement to hold indirect Israeli-Palestinian talks.

Direct negotiations between Netanyahu and Abbas, chaired by US Secretary of State Hillary Clinton, commenced in Washington, DC, in early September 2010, although Hamas refused to recognize their legitimacy. During September Obama urged the Israeli Government to extend the 10-month moratorium on settlement-building in the West Bank, which was due to expire later that month; however, Netanyahu was unwilling to implement a complete freeze on construction. A second round of direct negotiations took place in Sharm el-Sheikh, Egypt, and in Jerusalem, in mid-September. However, little progress was achieved with regard to substantive issues and, following the expiry of Israel's temporary settlement ban on 26 September, the PA suspended its involvement in the peace process.

Obama provoked controversy in Israel in May 2011 by declaring his support for the establishment of a Palestinian state within the boundaries existing prior to the 1967 'Six-Day War' but incorporating negotiated land exchanges. Netanyahu, citing security and demographic concerns, firmly rejected this plan during a visit to the USA later that month in spite of widespread international support for Obama's proposals. In October Congress suspended US $200m. of US aid designated for the PA following a failed attempt by Abbas in the previous month to secure Palestinian membership of the UN. The USA had opposed this unilateral move, arguing that Palestinian independence could only be accomplished after entering into dialogue with Israel. Some $90m. of frozen Palestinian aid was released by Congress in March 2012. Despite continuing US opposition, an upgrade in the Palestinians' UN status (to that of non-member observer state) was overwhelming approved by the UN General Assembly in November. The USA was one of only nine nations that voted against the motion.

Egypt has traditionally been one of the USA's firmest allies across the Middle East and North Africa region. The Obama Administration's response to protracted popular protests in Cairo and other major Egyptian cities from January 2011, the aim of which was to force the resignation of President Muhammad Hosni Mubarak, was at first markedly measured, with US officials compelled to balance expressions of support for the pro-democracy demonstrations with the offer of continued support for its long-standing ally Mubarak. However, Mubarak's eventual decision to tender his resignation in mid-February was hailed by Obama as a crucial moment in the 'wheel of history'. The US President congratulated the Egyptian people for taking the first step in determining their own future. He also urged the interim military Government to revoke Egypt's controversial state of emergency legislation, which had been in place almost continuously since 1967; amend the Constitution so that democratic principles were enshrined; and provide for the staging of free and fair elections.

Similar protests erupted in several other countries in the Middle East and North Africa during early 2011. In February Obama expressed concern at the violent response of the security forces to pro-democracy demonstrations in Bahrain, a key US ally due to its hosting of the US Navy's Fifth Fleet. Obama urged the Bahraini authorities to implement democratic reforms but did not condemn the deployment of Gulf Co-operation Council troops in the country to maintain order and security. The Obama Administration also denounced the use of violence against anti-Government demonstrators in Yemen; however, US criticism was tempered by the Yemeni Government's role as a strategic ally in the region, especially with regard to US-led anti-terrorism initiatives. The US response to the excessive use of state force to quell anti-Government protests and rebel attacks in Libya was more robust. In February Obama demanded that Libyan leader Col Muammar al-Qaddafi relinquish power, and sanctions against the Libyan regime, including an assets freeze, were imposed. On 17 March the USA gave its support to UN Security Council Resolution 1973, which endorsed the establishment of an air exclusion zone over Libya, and also played a leading role in the subsequent military intervention in that country. The USA recognized the opposition National Transitional Council as the legitimate Libyan Government in July, and US military support precipitated the final overthrow of the Qaddafi regime in October.

Anti-US demonstrations took place in many Muslim countries during September 2012 in protest against a US-produced film deemed to be highly disrespectful to Islam. The US embassies in Egypt, Yemen, Tunisia and Sudan came under attack, with several deaths reported, while at least 20 people lost their lives in Pakistan during clashes between anti-US protesters and the security forces. Moreover, the US ambassador to Libya and three US consular employees were killed in an apparent terrorist attack on the US consulate in Benghazi.

Other external relations

Relations with Pakistan—regarded in the USA as vitally important due to that country's co-operation in combating Islamist militancy and its provision of logistical assistance to US-led coalition forces engaged in military operations in neighbouring Afghanistan—came under increasing strain during 2011. Bilateral ties deteriorated in January due to the commencement in Pakistan of legal action against Raymond Davis, a CIA operative accused of shooting and killing two Pakistani men in Lahore. Davis claimed that he had been defending himself against an attempted robbery. President Obama asserted that Davis had diplomatic immunity and demanded his release. Following the payment of compensation to the victims' relatives, Davis was acquitted in March, prompting violent protests in Pakistan. Meanwhile, attacks by US 'drones' (unmanned aircraft) against militants within Pakistan also damaged relations between the two countries. The frequency of such operations, which often resulted in civilian casualties, had increased significantly since 2010. In April 2011 press reports claimed that the Pakistani Government had demanded a reduction in drone attacks and a curtailment of CIA operations in the country. In the same month the US Chairman of the Joint Chiefs of Staff, Adm. Michael Mullen, alleged that Pakistan's Directorate for Inter-Services Intelligence was colluding with militants in Afghanistan. The problematic nature of US-Pakistani relations was further illustrated by the covert operation carried out by US special forces on Pakistani territory at the beginning of May in which al-Qa'ida founder Osama bin Laden was killed (see Domestic Political Affairs). While the Pakistani authorities welcomed bin Laden's demise, Prime Minister Yusuf Raza Gilani described the operation, which was carried out without consultation with the Pakistani authorities, as a violation of national sovereignty, and angrily rejected the widely held assumption that bin Laden's presence in the country must have been sanctioned by senior Pakistani officials. In late May Pakistan demanded the withdrawal of approximately 120 US troops who had been providing training to the Pakistani military, while in July the USA suspended US $800m. of military aid that it had earlier pledged to Pakistan. Bilateral relations declined further in November, when a US air-strike killed 24 Pakistani border officials who had allegedly opened fire on US soldiers operating in neighbouring Afghanistan. In retaliation, Pakistan, which rejected these allegations, denied NATO access to its road links with Afghanistan and expelled all US personnel from the Shamsi drone base in Baluchistan. US military assistance totalling $770m. was suspended in December due to Pakistan's lack of progress in combating militancy in the border area, and a further $900m. was withheld in May 2012 in protest against the closure of supply lines to Afghanistan. Nevertheless, Pakistan reopened its road network to NATO in July after the USA formally apologized for the border air-strike incident. Aid flows resumed later that year.

In March 2006 an agreement was reached between President George W. Bush and India's premier, Manmohan Singh, during discussions in New Delhi, India, under the terms of which India would be permitted to purchase nuclear fuel and technology from the USA in return for the separation of its military and civilian nuclear programmes and consent for UN inspection of its civilian nuclear facilities. US assistance for the advancement of India's nuclear programme, together with those of Pakistan and Israel, had previously been denied under US law as the three were not signatories of the NPT. Amendments to the US Atomic Energy Act of 1954, permitting nuclear co-operation with India, were signed into law in December. The agreement was enacted by Bush in October 2008, following its approval by Congress and earlier endorsement by the IAEA.

Following a revival of contacts between the USA and Viet Nam, in May 1992 there was a partial relaxation of a trade embargo in force since 1975. In February 1994 the US Government lifted the remaining sanctions on trade with Viet Nam, and in the following July the USA established full diplomatic relations with that country. In June 2012, during an Asian tour, US Secretary of Defense Leon Panetta completed the first high-level, official US visit to Viet Nam in more than 30 years; Panetta held talks on military co-operation and regional security with his Vietnamese counterpart. In the same week Panetta met with the Secretary of National Defense of the Philippines to discuss military co-operation and proposals for the deployment of US military troops in that country. Both Viet Nam and the Philippines were engaged in territorial disputes with China in the South China Sea.

The USA's relations with Myanmar, which had been strained for many years due to the latter's poor human rights record and history of authoritarianism, began to improve from 2011 due to the implementation of limited reforms to liberalize and democratize the Myanma political system. In recognition of these unexpected developments, US Secretary of State Hillary Clinton travelled to Myanmar in November to meet with the country's leadership, the first such visit since 1955. Long-standing US sanctions were to remain in force, although certain restrictions were retracted during 2012. The USA appointed an ambassador to Myanmar in mid-2012, and President Obama made an unprecedented visit to the country in November.

By mid-1993 the crisis in the former Yugoslavia had assumed increased importance as a foreign policy issue, leading to disagreements between the USA and the Western European powers, which opposed US proposals to launch direct air strikes against military positions held by Bosnian Serbs. The US Administration, while avoiding any direct military commitment, gave its support, through NATO, to peace-keeping operations in Bosnia and Herzegovina. In June 1994 the US Government endorsed proposals by EU countries for the tripartite partition of Bosnia and Herzegovina. In November 1995, following US-sponsored negotiations held in Dayton, Ohio, a peace agreement was reached by the opposing sides. As part of its implementation, the US Government agreed to contribute 20,000 troops to a multinational supervisory force of 60,000 troops under the command of NATO. The USA committed about 8,500 troops in an extended NATO peace-keeping operation in Bosnia and Herzegovina until mid-1998, and about 1,000 soldiers served as part of NATO's Stabilization Force until December 2004.

In March 1999 the US Government initiated and led, under NATO auspices, a sustained campaign of missile raids on military and related installations in Serbia and Montenegro, in support of international demands that the President of the Federal Republic of Yugoslavia, Slobodan Milošević, desist from the mass expulsion of members of the ethnic Albanian population of the Serbian province of Kosovo. Following the military withdrawal of Serbian forces from Kosovo in June, US forces took a leading role in subsequent UN peace-keeping operations in the region.

An escalation in the conflict between Arab *Janjaweed* militia and ethnic groups in the Darfur region of Sudan, which had been ongoing since 2003, prompted protests in Washington, DC, and 18 other US cities in April 2006 to demand that the US Administration intervene to alleviate the humanitarian crisis there. In May the Darfur Peace Agreement—negotiated by the US Deputy Secretary of State, Robert B. Zoellick, African Union representatives and other foreign officials working in Nigeria—was signed between the Sudanese Government and a faction of the Sudan Liberation Army. In October President Bush signed the Darfur Peace and Accountability Act into law, imposing sanctions against those responsible for genocide, crimes against humanity and war crimes, supporting strategies to defend civilians and humanitarian exercises, and promoting peace initiatives in Darfur. The legislation was augmented by an executive order—forbidding transactions with, and receipt of property of, the Sudanese Government—which came into effect simultaneously. The order, while specifically prohibiting transactions relating to the oil and petrochemical industries of Sudan, made provision for limited trade to continue with non-governmental concerns in other regions of Sudan. Further sanctions were imposed against Sudan in 2007, excluding additional companies owned or operated by the Sudanese Government from the US financial system and blocking the assets of individuals accused of instigating violence in Darfur. The Obama Administration praised the successful and relatively peaceful execution of a referendum on the secession of South Sudan in mid-January 2011, during which an overwhelming majority approved the formation of a sovereign state in the south of the country; however, the US authorities continued to express concerns regarding the pace of progress on security and humanitarian issues in Darfur. US sanctions against Sudan remained in force in early 2013.

The Obama Administration deployed some 100 troops to Uganda in October 2011 to support (in a non-combat capacity) the regional military effort to subjugate the militant Lord's Resistance Army (LRA) and capture its leader, Joseph Kony. An unspecified number of these US Special Forces were subsequently transferred to the Central African Republic, the Democratic Republic of the Congo and South Sudan to provide assistance to those countries' armed forces in suppressing LRA activity in the region. In a separate non-combat deployment, around 100 US soldiers were sent to Niger in February 2013 to support a French-led mission to quell a predominantly Islamist rebellion in neighbouring Mali. It was reported that a US drone base would also be established in Niger to monitor militant Islamist groups in the region.

The USA attracted international criticism by its refusal to sign up to the terms of the International Criminal Court (ICC), established to try war criminals, which was inaugurated at The Hague, Netherlands, in March 2003. The USA defended its position by claiming that members of its military could be put on trial on political grounds, and, in response, in the same month, Congress approved the American Service Member and Citizen Protection Act, which would enable the USA to free, by force if necessary, any member of its military arrested by the ICC. In July the USA reduced military aid to some 35 countries that refused to sign agreements that would give US citizens immunity from prosecution. By August 2006 some 101 Bilateral Immunity Agreements had been signed, exempting certain US citizens from referral to the ICC. In January 2008 legislation repealing the restrictions on military assistance to nations unwilling to enter into Bilateral Immunity Agreements was signed into law. Upon taking office, the Obama Administration initiated a full policy review of US-ICC relations. In November 2009 the USA attended an ICC assembly meeting in The Hague as an observer, the first time that it had participated in an ICC meeting since 2001. While the USA was not expected to accede to ICC membership in the short term, it repeatedly pledged its commitment to supporting the efforts of the Court to bring war criminals to justice.

In November 2010 WikiLeaks, an organization devoted to publishing leaked information, began to release a series of classified US diplomatic cables, allegedly secured through a source in the US Army. The documents contained candid assessments by US diplomats of foreign leaders and international affairs, as well as details of highly sensitive, private discussions with foreign officials. The cables emanated from more than 200 US overseas missions and caused significant embarrassment to the Government. US officials condemned the publication of the cables, claiming that this would damage relations with other countries, place US diplomats and soldiers in danger, and jeopardize future intelligence-gathering. Despite threats of legal action from US and other governments, in September 2011 WikiLeaks released all 251,000 uncensored cables in its possession, a move that attracted further criticism. In February 2013, during his court martial, US military intelligence analyst Bradley Manning admitted to being the source of the leaked cables. Legal proceedings were ongoing in early 2013.

CONSTITUTION AND GOVERNMENT

The Constitution of the USA was adopted on 4 March 1789; 27 amendments have since been ratified, the most recent in 1992. The USA is a federal republic. Each of the 50 constituent states and the District of Columbia exercises a measure of internal self-government. Defence, foreign affairs, coinage, posts, the higher levels of justice, and internal security are the responsibility of the federal Government. The President is head of the executive and is elected for a four-year term by a college of representatives elected directly from each state. The President appoints the other members of the executive, subject to the consent of the Senate. Congress is the seat of legislative power and consists of the Senate (100 members) and the House of Representatives (435 members). Two senators are chosen by direct election in each state, to serve a six-year term, and one-third of the membership is renewable every two years. Representatives are elected by direct and universal suffrage for a two-year term. The number of representatives of each state in Congress is determined by the size of the state's population. Ultimate judicial power is vested in the Supreme Court, which has the power to disallow legislation and to overturn executive actions that it deems unconstitutional.

REGIONAL AND INTERNATIONAL CO-OPERATION

The USA is a member of the Organization of American States (OAS, see p. 404) and of the Inter-American Development Bank (IDB, see p. 341). Together with Mexico and Canada, the USA is a signatory to the North American Free Trade Agreement (NAFTA, see p. 378), which entered into force in 1994 and had been fully implemented by 2008. Agreement on a free trade accord, to be known as the Central American Free Trade Agreement (CAFTA), between the USA and Guatemala, Costa Rica, El Salvador, Honduras and Nicaragua was signed in May 2004 in Washington, DC. The Agreement, which was restyled DR-CAFTA following the inclusion of the Dominican Republic later that year, was ratified by Congress in July 2005 and signed by President George W. Bush in August. DR-CAFTA came into effect in El Salvador, Honduras, Nicaragua and Guatemala in 2006, in the Dominican Republic in 2007, and in Costa Rica in 2009. Discussions to establish a Free Trade Area of the Americas, first proposed in 1995, stalled in late 2004, and (although it was agreed in mid-2006 to resume talks) no progress had been made by April 2013.

The USA was a founder member of the UN in 1945 and is a permanent member of the UN Security Council; the headquarters of the organization are located in New York. As a contracting party to the General Agreement on Tariffs and Trade (GATT), the USA joined the World Trade Organization (WTO, see p. 444) on its establishment in 1995. The USA is also a member of the North Atlantic Treaty Organization (NATO, see p. 380) and of the Organisation for Economic Co-operation and Development (OECD, see p. 388), and participates in the Group of Eight (G8, see p. 475) leading industrialized nations and in the Group of Twenty (G20, see p. 466).

ECONOMIC AFFAIRS

In 2011, according to estimates by the World Bank, the USA's gross national income (GNI), measured at average 2009–11 prices, was US $15,097,083m., equivalent to $48,450 per head (or $48,890 on an international purchasing-power parity basis). During 2002–11, it was estimated, the population increased at an average annual rate of 0.9%, while gross domestic product (GDP) per head increased, in real terms, by an average of 1.6% per year. During the same period, according to UN estimates, overall GDP increased, in real terms, at an average annual rate of 1.6%; GDP increased by 2.4% in 2010 and by 1.8% in 2011. According to chain linked methodologies, GDP increased by 1.8% in 2011 and by 2.2% in 2012.

Agriculture (including forestry, fishing and hunting) contributed 1.2% of GDP in 2011 and engaged 1.6% of the employed civilian population in 2010. The principal crops are hay, potatoes, sugar beet and citrus fruit, which, together with cereals, cotton and tobacco, are important export crops. In recent years the production and export of soybeans have also become significant. The principal livestock are cattle, pigs and poultry. Food and live animals provided an estimated 6.5% of total export revenue in 2012. The GDP of the sector increased, in real terms, by an average of 4.0% per year in 2002–11, according to UN estimates; sectoral GDP decreased by 3.6% in 2010, but increased by 4.7% in 2011. According to chain linked methodologies, sectoral GDP decreased by 2.8% in 2010 and further by 13.6% in 2011.

Industry (including mining, manufacturing, construction and utilities) provided 18.9% of GDP in 2011 and engaged 18.1% of the employed civilian population in 2010. According to UN estimates, industrial GDP increased, in real terms, at an average annual rate of 1.1% in 2002–11; the sector's GDP increased by 5.9% in 2010 and by 4.5% in 2011. According to chain linked methodologies, industrial GDP increased by 3.9% in 2010 and by 1.8% in 2011

Mining and quarrying contributed 1.9% of GDP in 2011 and engaged 0.5% of the employed civilian population in 2010. The USA has significant mineral deposits, specifically of petroleum, natural gas, coal (with 237,295m. metric tons at the end of 2011, the USA had the largest proven recoverable reserves of coal in the world), copper, iron, silver and uranium. At the end of 2010 the USA's proven recoverable reserves of petroleum were 30,872m. barrels, equivalent to 1.9% of the world's proven oil reserves, and sufficient to sustain production at 2011 levels for about 11 years. Crude petroleum production averaged 7.8m. barrels per day (b/d) in 2011. The USA's proven recoverable reserves of natural gas were estimated at 8,490,000m. cu m at the end of 2011, and production in that year totalled 651,293m. cu m (second only to Russia). Crude materials (excluding fuels) accounted for an estimated 5.9% of total export revenue in 2012; mineral fuels accounted for a further 8.9% of the value of exports in that year. In real terms, the GDP of the sector (including utilities) remained constant during 2002–11, according to UN estimates; mining (including utilities) GDP declined by 1.5% in 2010, but increased by 4.1% in 2011.

Manufacturing contributed 11.5% of GDP in 2011 and engaged 10.1% of the employed civilian population in 2010. In 2011 the principal branches of manufacturing (measured by value of shipments) were petroleum and coal products (15.2%), chemical products (14.1%), food (12.9%), transportation equipment (12.6%), machinery (6.7%), computer and electronic equipment (6.1%), fabricated metal products (5.9%), and primary metal industries (5.1%). According to UN estimates, manufacturing GDP increased, in real terms, by an average of 2.4% per year in 2002–11; sectoral GDP for manufacturing increased by 10.8% in 2010 and by 2.2% in 2011. According to chain linked methodologies, sectoral GDP increased by 6.9% in 2010 and by 2.5% in 2011.

The construction sector contributed 3.5% of GDP in 2011 and engaged 6.5% of the employed labour force in 2010. During 2002–11, according to UN estimates, the GDP of the sector decreased at an average annual rate of 1.7%; construction GDP decreased by 3.3% in 2010, but increased by 13.6% in 2011. According to chain linked methodologies, sectoral GDP decreased by 1.2% in 2010 and by 0.3% in 2011.

According to the US Energy Information Administration (EIA), the USA is the world's largest producer, consumer and net importer of energy. Energy is derived principally from domestic and imported hydrocarbons. The EIA estimated that in 2010 69.7% of total electricity production was provided by fossil fuels (coal 42.2%, natural gas 24.8% and petroleum 0.7%), 19.2% was provided by nuclear power, and some 4.7% was derived from renewable sources. In 2012 fuel imports amounted to an estimated 18.7% (petroleum and petroleum products 18.0%) of total merchandise import costs.

Services (including government services) provided 80.0% of GDP in 2011 and engaged 80.3% of the employed civilian population in 2010. The combined GDP of all service sectors rose, in real terms, at an average rate of 2.1% per year during 2002–11, according to UN estimates. Of non-government services subsectors, the contribution of professional and business services was most significant in 2011 (contributing 12.5% of the total GDP of non-government services). Services GDP increased by 2.5% in 2010 and by 5.1% in 2011. According to chain linked methodologies, sectoral GDP increased by 2.2% in 2010 and by 1.9% in 2011.

In 2011 the USA recorded a visible merchandise trade deficit of US $734,900m. (excluding military transactions), and there was a deficit of $465,920m. on the current account of the balance of payments. In 2012 the People's Republic of China was the principal provider of imports (supplying 18.7% of the total); other major suppliers were Canada, Mexico and Japan. Canada was the principal export market in that year, accounting for 18.9% of the total value of exports; Mexico was the second largest export market in that year, followed by the People's Republic of China. In 2012 machinery and transport equipment constituted the most significant category of both imports (accounting for 38.2% of the total value of imports) and exports (40.5% of the total).

A federal budget deficit of US $1,086,900m. was recorded for the financial year ending 30 September 2012, an amount equivalent to 7.8% of GDP in that year. The USA's general government gross debt was $14,764,222m. in 2011, equivalent to 98.7% of GDP. The annual rate of inflation averaged 2.5% in 2002–12. Consumer prices increased by 2.1% in 2012. The rate of unemployment averaged 9.6% in 2010.

The US economy grew throughout the early 2000s, fuelled by robust consumer consumption. However, the country suffered an economic shock in late 2006 when the sub-prime mortgage crisis emerged: after house prices began to collapse in that year, many individuals were left unable to refinance mortgages as interest rates rose, leading to unprecedented levels of repossessions, and creating a nation-wide, and eventually global, 'credit crunch' as banks and mortgage lenders cut back on offering credit. The financial crisis intensified dramatically after the collapse of Lehman Brothers, an investment bank, and other financial ventures in September 2008, which led to fears of a complete breakdown of the financial sector. A government-backed rescue plan for the banks, valued at US $700,000m., was approved by Congress in October. Following the inauguration of President Barack Obama in January 2009, Congress approved a $787,000m. fiscal stimulus package in February, which included tax cuts and large-scale government spending. These measures contributed to a return to growth in the third quarter of 2009, following four successive quarters of negative growth, although GDP for the year as a whole contracted by 3.5%. In November 2010 a fresh round of quantitative easing was launched by the Federal Reserve; the central bank was to buy long-term Treasury security bonds worth some $600,000m. in an attempt to support economic growth. The recovery continued in 2011, with exports showing signs of improvement, although real GDP growth slowed to 1.8% in that year (from 2.4% in 2010), according to the IMF. Rates of unemployment and poverty remained high, while sluggish activity in the construction and manufacturing sectors, depressed levels of domestic demand, and rising fuel prices acted as constraints on the economy. In an effort to reduce the unsustainably high budget deficit, in August Congress approved a plan to lower government spending by $917,000m. over the following 10 years. Nevertheless, in an unprecedented move later that month, the USA's credit rating was downgraded by the Standard & Poor's agency, which regarded the planned spending cuts as insufficient and also expressed concern about the deep divisions within Congress. The Federal Reserve resumed quantitative easing measures in September 2012. Some modest tax rises received congressional approval in January 2013, but the inability of the Democrats and Republicans to reach agreement on a comprehensive fiscal reform plan left the economy in a constant state of low-level crisis. Moreover, in March cross-party dialogue failed to prevent the onset of 'sequestration', the automatic implementation of austere budget cuts (totalling $1,100,000m. over 10 years, with some $85,000m. taking effect in 2013/14)—the measure had originally been devised to incentivize bipartisan co-operation rather than as a serious deficit reduction strategy. Analysts feared that failure to halt the sequestration process, by introducing a replacement programme with more gradual reductions in government spending, could undermine the country's fragile economic recovery. Meanwhile, unemployment rose from 4.9% in February 2008 to a peak of 10.0% in October 2009, before moderating gradually to 7.6% in March 2013. The IMF forecast economic growth of 1.9% in 2013.

PUBLIC HOLIDAYS*

2014: 1 January (New Year's Day), 20 January (Birthday of Martin Luther King, Jr), 17 February (Washington's Birthday/Presidents' Day), 26 May (Memorial Day), 4 July (Independence Day), 1 September (Labor Day), 13 October (Columbus Day), 11 November (for Veterans' Day), 27 November (Thanksgiving Day), 25 December (Christmas Day).

* Federal legal public holidays are designated by presidential proclamation or congressional enactment, but need not be observed in individual states, which have legal jurisdiction over their public holidays.

Statistical Survey

Source (unless otherwise stated): Statistical Information Office, Population Division, Bureau of the Census, US Dept of Commerce, Washington, DC 20233-0001; internet www.census.gov.

Area and Population

AREA, POPULATION AND DENSITY

Area (sq km)
Land	9,161,923
Water*	664,706
Total	9,826,630†

Population (census results)
1 April 2000‡	281,421,906

1 April 2010
Males	151,781,326
Females	156,964,212
Total	308,745,538

Population (official estimates at 1 January)
2011	310,544,109
2012	312,818,472
2013	315,090,923
Density (per sq km) at 1 January 2013§	34.4

* Comprises Great Lakes, and inland, territorial, and coastal waters.
† 3,794,083 sq miles.
‡ Excluding adjustment for underenumeration; the adjusted total was 281,424,602.
§ Land area only.

POPULATION BY AGE AND SEX
(population at census of 1 April 2010)

	Males	Females	Total
0–14	31,288,927	29,938,286	61,227,213
15–64	103,129,439	104,120,902	207,250,341
65 and over	17,362,960	22,905,024	40,267,984
Total	151,781,326	156,964,212	308,745,538

RACES
(population at 2010 census)

	Number	%
White	241,937,061	78.36
Black	40,250,635	13.04
Asian	15,159,516	4.91
American Indian and Alaska Native	3,739,506	1.21
Native Hawaiian and Pacific Islander	674,625	0.22
Others*	6,984,195	2.26
Total	308,745,538	100.00

* Includes those of two or more races.

Hispanic or Latino population (all races): 50,477,594 (16.4%).

STATES
(population at census of 1 April 2010*)

State	Land area (sq km)	Residents	Density (per sq km)	Capital
Alabama	131,426	4,779,736	36.4	Montgomery
Alaska	1,481,347	710,231	0.5	Juneau
Arizona	294,312	6,392,017	21.7	Phoenix
Arkansas	134,856	2,915,918	21.6	Little Rock
California	403,933	37,253,956	92.2	Sacramento
Colorado	268,627	5,029,196	18.7	Denver
Connecticut	12,548	3,574,097	284.8	Hartford
Delaware	5,060	897,934	177.5	Dover
District of Columbia	159	601,723	3,784.4	Washington
Florida	139,670	18,801,310	134.6	Tallahassee
Georgia	149,976	9,687,653	64.6	Atlanta
Hawaii	16,635	1,360,301	81.8	Honolulu
Idaho	214,314	1,567,582	7.3	Boise
Illinois	143,961	12,830,632	89.1	Springfield
Indiana	92,895	6,483,802	69.8	Indianapolis
Iowa	144,701	3,046,355	21.1	Des Moines
Kansas	211,900	2,853,118	13.5	Topeka

State—*continued*	Land area (sq km)	Residents	Density (per sq km)	Capital
Kentucky	102,896	4,339,367	42.2	Frankfort
Louisiana	112,825	4,533,372	40.2	Baton Rouge
Maine	79,931	1,328,361	16.6	Augusta
Maryland	25,314	5,773,552	228.1	Annapolis
Massachusetts	20,306	6,547,629	322.4	Boston
Michigan	147,121	9,883,640	67.2	Lansing
Minnesota	206,189	5,303,925	25.7	St Paul
Mississippi	121,488	2,967,297	24.4	Jackson
Missouri	178,414	5,988,927	33.6	Jefferson City
Montana	376,979	989,415	2.6	Helena
Nebraska	199,099	1,826,341	9.2	Lincoln
Nevada	284,448	2,700,551	9.5	Carson City
New Hampshire	23,227	1,316,470	56.7	Concord
New Jersey	19,211	8,791,894	457.6	Trenton
New Mexico	314,309	2,059,179	6.6	Santa Fe
New York	122,283	19,378,102	158.5	Albany
North Carolina	126,161	9,535,483	75.6	Raleigh
North Dakota	178,647	672,591	3.8	Bismarck
Ohio	106,056	11,536,504	108.8	Columbus
Oklahoma	177,847	3,751,351	21.1	Oklahoma City
Oregon	248,631	3,831,074	15.4	Salem
Pennsylvania	116,074	12,702,379	109.4	Harrisburg
Rhode Island	2,706	1,052,567	389.0	Providence
South Carolina	77,983	4,625,364	59.3	Columbia
South Dakota	196,540	814,180	4.1	Pierre
Tennessee	106,752	6,346,105	59.4	Nashville
Texas	678,051	25,145,561	37.1	Austin
Utah	212,751	2,763,885	13.0	Salt Lake City
Vermont	23,956	625,741	26.1	Montpelier
Virginia	102,548	8,001,024	78.0	Richmond
Washington	172,348	6,724,540	39.0	Olympia
West Virginia	62,361	1,852,994	29.7	Charleston
Wisconsin	140,663	5,686,986	40.4	Madison
Wyoming	251,489	563,626	2.2	Cheyenne
Total	9,161,923	308,745,538	33.7	

* Includes armed forces residing in each State.

PRINCIPAL TOWNS
(population at census of 1 April 2010)

Town	Population	Town	Population
New York	8,175,133	Las Vegas	583,756
Los Angeles	3,792,621	Oklahoma City	579,999
Chicago	2,695,598	Albuquerque	545,852
Houston	2,099,451	Tucson	520,116
Philadelphia	1,526,006	Fresno	494,665
Phoenix	1,445,632	Sacramento	466,488
San Antonio	1,327,407	Long Beach, CA	462,257
San Diego	1,307,402	Kansas City, MO	459,787
Dallas	1,197,816	Mesa City, AZ	439,041
San Jose	945,942	Virginia Beach, VA	437,994
Jacksonville	821,784	Atlanta	420,003
Indianapolis	820,445	Colorado Springs	416,427
San Francisco	805,235	Omaha	408,958
Austin	790,390	Cleveland	396,815
Columbus, OH	787,033	Tulsa	391,906
Fort Worth	741,206	Oakland	390,724
Charlotte	731,424	Minneapolis	382,578
Detroit	713,777	Wichita	382,368
El Paso	649,121	Arlington, TX	365,438
Memphis	646,889	New Orleans	343,829
Baltimore	620,961	Honolulu	337,256
Boston	617,594	Anaheim	336,265
Seattle	608,660	Tampa	335,709
Washington, DC (capital)	601,723	Santa Ana, CA	324,528
Nashville-Davidson	601,222	St Louis	319,294
Denver	600,158	Pittsburgh	305,704
Milwaukee	594,833	Cincinnati	296,943
Portland, OR	583,776	Toledo, OH	287,208

BIRTHS, MARRIAGES, DEATHS

	Registered live births		Registered marriages		Registered deaths	
	Number ('000)	Rate (per 1,000)	Number ('000)	Rate (per 1,000)	Number ('000)	Rate (per 1,000)
2003	4,090	14.1	2,245	7.7	2,448	8.4
2004	4,112	14.0	2,279	7.8	2,398	8.2
2005	4,143	14.0	2,249	7.6	2,448	8.3
2006	4,266	14.2	2,193*	7.4*	2,426	8.1
2007	4,316	14.3	2,197	7.3	2,424	8.0
2008	4,248	14.0	2,157	7.1	2,472	8.1
2009	4,131	13.5	2,077	6.8	2,437	7.9
2010	3,999	13.0	n.a.	n.a.	2,466	8.0

* Data for Louisiana were not available.

Source: National Center for Health Statistics, US Department of Health and Human Services.

Life expectancy (years at birth): 79 (males 76; females 81) in 2011 (Source: World Bank, World Development Indicators database).

IMMIGRATION
(year ending 30 September)

Country of birth	2008/09	2009/10	2010/11
Europe	105,476	88,801	83,850
Bosnia-Herzegovina	1,501	946	878
Poland	8,754	7,643	6,863
Russia	8,238	6,718	7,944
Ukraine	11,223	8,477	8,292
United Kingdom	15,748	12,792	11,572
Asia	413,312	422,063	451,593
Bangladesh	16,651	14,819	16,707
China, People's Republic . .	64,238	70,863	87,016
India	57,304	69,162	69,013
Iran	18,553	14,182	14,822
Korea, Republic	25,859	22,227	22,824
Pakistan	21,555	18,258	15,546
Philippines	60,029	58,173	57,011
Taiwan	8,038	6,732	6,154
Thailand	10,444	9,384	9,962
Viet Nam	29,234	30,632	34,157
Africa	127,046	101,355	100,374
Egypt	8,844	8,978	7,778
Ethiopia	15,462	14,266	13,793
Nigeria	15,253	13,376	11,824
Somalia	13,390	4,558	4,451
North America, Central America and the Caribbean	375,180	336,553	333,902
Canada	16,140	13,328	12,800
Mexico	164,920	139,120	143,446
Caribbean			
Cuba	38,954	33,573	36,452
Dominican Republic . . .	49,414	53,870	46,109
Haiti	24,280	22,582	22,111
Jamaica	21,783	19,825	19,662
Central America			
El Salvador	19,909	18,806	18,667
Guatemala	12,187	10,467	11,092
South America	102,860	87,178	86,096
Brazil	14,701	12,258	11,763
Colombia	27,849	22,406	22,635
Ecuador	12,128	11,492	11,103
Peru	16,957	14,247	14,064
Venezuela	11,154	9,409	9,183
Total (incl. others and unknown) .	1,130,818	1,042,625	1,062,040

Source: US Department of Homeland Security, *Yearbook of Immigration Statistics*.

ECONOMICALLY ACTIVE POPULATION
(annual averages, civilian labour force, '000 persons aged 16 years and over)

	2008	2009	2010
Agriculture, hunting, forestry and fishing	2,168	2,103	2,206
Mining and quarrying	819	707	731
Manufacturing	15,904	14,202	14,081
Electricity, gas and water . . .	1,225	1,233	1,253
Construction	10,974	9,702	9,077
Wholesale and retail trade; repair of motor vehicles, motorcycles and personal and household goods	20,585	19,685	19,739
Hotels and restaurants . . .	9,795	9,717	9,564
Transport, storage and communications	6,501	6,012	5,880
Financial intermediation . . .	7,279	6,826	6,605
Real estate, renting and business activities	18,489	17,804	17,998
Public administration and defence; compulsory social security . .	6,763	6,875	6,983
Education	13,169	13,188	13,155
Health and social work . . .	18,233	18,632	18,907
Other services	13,458	13,192	12,884
Total employed	145,362	139,877	139,064
Unemployed	8,924	14,265	14,825
Total labour force	154,286	154,142	153,889
Males	82,519	82,123	81,985
Females	71,767	72,019	71,904

Health and Welfare

KEY INDICATORS

Total fertility rate (children per woman, 2010)	2.1
Under-5 mortality rate (per 1,000 live births, 2010) . . .	8
HIV/AIDS (% of persons aged 15–49, 2009)	0.6
Physicians (per 1,000 head, 2000)	2.56
Hospital beds (per 1,000 head, 2005)	3.2
Health expenditure (2009): US $ per head (PPP)	7,960
Health expenditure (2009): % of GDP	17.6
Health expenditure (2009): public (% of total)	47.7
Total carbon dioxide emissions ('000 metric tons, 2008) . .	5,461,013.7
Carbon dioxide emissions per head (metric tons, 2008) . .	18.0
Human Development Index (2011): ranking	4
Human Development Index (2011): value	0.910

For sources and definitions, see explanatory note on p. vi.

Agriculture

PRINCIPAL CROPS
('000 metric tons)

	2009	2010	2011
Wheat	60,366	60,062	54,413
Rice, paddy	9,972	11,027	8,392
Barley	4,949	3,925	3,392
Maize	332,549	316,165	313,918
Oats	1,351	1,178	779
Sorghum	9,728	8,773	5,447
Potatoes	19,564	18,016	19,361
Sweet potatoes	883	1,082	1,223
Sugar cane	27,608	24,821	26,655
Sugar beet	27,019	29,060	26,152
Beans, dry	1,150	1,442	900
Soybeans (Soya beans) . . .	91,417	90,606	83,171
Groundnuts, with shell . . .	1,675	1,885	1,649
Sunflower seed	1,377	1,241	925
Rapeseed	669	1,113	699
Cabbages and other brassicas .	1,019	1,054	958
Lettuce and chicory . . .	3,827	4,106	390
Tomatoes	14,181	12,859	12,625
Cucumbers and gherkins . .	922	881	759
Onions, dry	3,429	3,338	3,353

—*continued*	2009	2010	2011
Peas, green	401	314	268
String beans	978	925	861
Carrots and turnips	1,327	1,342	1,306
Maize, green	4,242	3,788	3,658
Watermelons	1,765	1,893	1,769
Cantaloupes and other melons	1,037	1,036	1,000
Oranges	8,281	7,478	8,079
Tangerines, mandarins, etc.	402	541	571
Lemons and limes	827	800	835
Grapefruit and pomelos	1,183	1,123	1,147
Apples	4,402	4,210	4,273
Pears	868	738	853
Peaches and nectarines	1,201	1,255	1,171
Plums and sloes	568	493	560
Strawberries	1,271	1,294	1,313
Grapes	6,629	6,778	6,693
Tobacco, unmanufactured	373	326	273

Aggregate production (may include official, semi-official or estimated data): Total cereals 419,381 in 2009, 401,670 in 2010, 386,788 in 2011; Total fruits (excl. melons) 27,448 in 2009, 26,181 in 2010, 27,140 in 2011; Total oilcrops 18,500 in 2009, 18,855 in 2010, 16,943 in 2011; Total roots and tubers 20,507 in 2009, 19,421 in 2010, 20,586 in 2011; Total vegetables (incl. melons) 37,290 in 2009, 35,609 in 2010, 34,670 in 2011.

Source: FAO.

LIVESTOCK
('000 head at 1 January)

	2009	2010	2011
Cattle	94,521	93,881	92,682
Pigs	67,148	64,887	66,361
Sheep	5,747	5,620	5,480
Horses*	9,800	10,000	10,150
Chickens (million)*	2,100	2,100	2,100
Turkeys (million)	247	244	249

* FAO estimates.

Source: FAO.

LIVESTOCK PRODUCTS
('000 metric tons)

	2009	2010	2011
Cattle meat	11,891	12,046	11,988
Sheep meat	80	76	76
Pig meat	10,442	10,186	10,331
Chicken meat	16,334	16,971	17,110
Cows' milk	85,881	87,474	89,015
Hen eggs	5,349	5,412	5,419

Source: FAO.

Forestry

ROUNDWOOD REMOVALS
('000 cubic metres)

	2009	2010	2011
Sawlogs and veneer logs	147,228	148,119	144,331
Pulp wood	136,552	127,119	127,448
Other industrial wood	8,311	8,311	12,217
Fuel wood	40,437	40,437	40,437
Total	332,528	323,986	324,433

Source: FAO.

SAWNWOOD PRODUCTION
('000 cubic metres)

	2009	2010	2011
Coniferous	39,576	42,163	45,410
Broadleaved	16,494	15,466	16,284
Total	56,070	57,629	61,694

Source: FAO.

Fishing

('000 metric tons, live weight)

	2008	2009	2010
Capture	4,349.9	4,222.1	4,369.5
Humpback salmon	118.2	133.3	169.0
Pacific cod	224.1	222.8	244.8
Walleye pollock	1,032.5	846.5	883.4
North Pacific hake	241.1	114.8	161.2
Atlantic menhaden	187.7	182.2	229.0
Gulf menhaden	420.7	454.8	438.6
American sea scallop	202.3	218.1	215.3
Atlantic surf clam	138.6	122.3	98.4
Aquaculture*	500.1	480.3	495.5
Channel catfish	233.6	215.9	217.2
Total catch*	4,849.9	4,702.3	4,865.0

* FAO estimates.

Note: Figures exclude aquatic plants (metric tons): 6,951 in 2008; 8,207 in 2009; 9,027 in 2010, and sponges (metric tons): 210.1 in 2008; 121.1 in 2009; 116.7 in 2010. Also excluded are aquatic mammals (recorded by number rather than weight); the number of whales and dolphins caught was: 405 in 2008; 270 in 2009; n.a. in 2010. The number of seals and sea lions caught was: 1,608 in 2008; n.a. in 2009; n.a. in 2010. The number of American alligators caught was: 230,464 in 2008; 297,187 in 2009; 369,731 in 2010.

Source: FAO.

Mining

('000 metric tons unless otherwise indicated)

	2008	2009	2010
Crude petroleum (million barrels)[1]	1,812	1,957	1,998
Natural gas (million cu ft)[1,2]	21,112	21,648	22,382
Coal (million short tons)[1,3]	1,172	1,075	1,084
Iron ore[4]	53,600	27,600	50,600
Copper[5]	1,310	1,180	1,110
Lead[5]	399	395	356
Zinc[5]	748	710	723
Molybdenum (metric tons)[5]	55,900	47,800	59,400
Silver (metric tons)[5]	1,250	1,250	1,280
Uranium ('000 pounds)[1,6]	3,902	3,708	4,228
Gold (metric tons)[5]	233	223	231
Platinum group metals (kg):[5]			
Platinum	3,580	3,830	3,450
Palladium	11,900	12,700	11,600
Lime	19,800	15,800	18,300
Sand and gravel (million metric tons):			
Construction	1,060	831	795
Industrial	30,400	24,600	29,900
Stone, crushed (million metric tons)	1,460	1,160	1,160
Bentonite	4,910	3,650	4,630
Fuller's Earth	2,340	2,010	2,050
Kaolin	6,740	5,290	5,420
Phosphate rock[2]	30,200	26,400	25,800
Potash[2,7]	2,400	1,500	2,400
Soda ash	11,300	9,310	10,600
Diatomite	764	575	595
Salt	47,400	43,100	43,500

[1] Source: Energy Information Administration, US Department of Energy.
[2] Figures refer to marketable production.
[3] 1 short ton = 0.907185 metric tons.
[4] Figures refer to the gross weight of usable ore.
[5] Figures refer to metal content of ores and concentrates.
[6] Figures refer to gross weight of uranium oxide ore.
[7] Figures refer to the content of K_2O contained in minerals and compounds.

2011: Crude petroleum (million barrels) 2,063; Natural gas (million cu ft) 24,036; Uranium ('000 pounds, preliminary) 3,991.

2012: Crude petroleum (million barrels) 2,367; Natural gas (million cu ft) 25,298.

Source (unless otherwise indicated): US Geological Survey.

Industry

PRINCIPAL MANUFACTURES
(value of shipments in $ '000 million)

	2009	2010	2011
Food	627.2	649.3	710.4
Beverages and tobacco products	127.9	130.6	136.9
Wood products	65.0	69.6	70.6
Paper	161.6	170.0	175.9
Printing and related activities	82.9	82.4	82.7
Petroleum and coal products	495.8	627.1	836.8
Chemicals	624.4	697.8	776.8
Plastics and rubber products	171.1	188.8	204.5
Non-metallic mineral products	89.7	90.1	93.0
Primary metal industries	168.9	232.8	280.2
Fabricated metal products	280.9	293.9	326.8
Machinery	288.0	317.7	365.7
Computers and electronic products	320.7	331.3	337.9
Electrical equipment, appliances and components	105.4	110.0	120.0
Transportation equipment	539.9	636.8	690.4
Total (incl. others)	4,419.5	4,905.4	5,498.6

Source: Bureau of the Census, US Department of Commerce, *Annual Survey of Manufactures*.

Finance

CURRENCY AND EXCHANGE RATES

Monetary Units
100 cents = 1 United States dollar ($).

Sterling and Euro Equivalents (31 December 2012)
£1 sterling = US $1.578;
€1 = $1.319;
US $100 = £63.37 = €75.79.

FEDERAL BUDGET
('000 $ million, year ending 30 September)*

Revenue	2011	2012	2013†
Individual income taxes	1,091.5	1,132.2	1,234.0
Corporation income taxes	181.1	242.3	287.7
Social insurance taxes and contributions	818.8	845.3	951.1
Excise taxes	72.4	79.1	85.3
Estate and gift taxes	7.4	14.0	12.9
Customs duties and fees	29.5	30.3	33.6
Miscellaneous receipts	102.8	107.0	107.3
Total	2,303.5	2,450.2	2,712.0

Expenditure	2011	2012	2013†
National defence	705.6	677.9	660.0
International affairs	45.7	47.2	56.9
General science, space research and technology	29.5	29.1	30.7
Energy	12.2	14.9	15.1
Natural resources and environment	45.5	41.6	37.7
Agriculture	20.7	17.8	27.0
Commerce and housing credit	-12.6	40.8	17.7
Transportation	93.0	93.0	94.5
Community and regional development	23.8	25.1	38.0
Education, training, employment and social services	101.2	90.8	84.6

Expenditure—continued	2011	2012	2013†
Health	372.5	346.7	371.7
Medicare	485.7	471.8	510.5
Income security	597.4	541.3	564.0
Social security	730.8	773.3	818.4
Veterans' benefits and services	127.2	124.6	139.6
Administration of justice	56.1	56.3	60.6
General government	25.5	28.0	30.5
Net interest	230.0	220.4	222.8
Undistributed offsetting receipts	-86.5	-103.5	-95.1
Total	3,603.1	3,537.1	3,684.9

* Including social security and postal service receipts and expenditures, which are extrabudgetary.
† Estimates.

Sources: Office of Management and Budget, Executive Office of the President; and Financial Management Service, US Department of the Treasury.

STATE AND LOCAL GOVERNMENT FINANCES
($ million, fiscal years*)

Revenue	2007/08	2008/09	2009/10
From federal government	477,983	536,760	623,732
From state and local governments	2,176,152	1,529,906	2,547,648
General revenue from own sources	1,945,042	1,876,624	1,878,323
Taxes	1,331,012	1,271,356	1,269,650
Property	408,972	424,014	441,661
Sales and gross receipts	451,776	433,556	431,176
Individual income	304,901	270,518	260,338
Corporation income	56,932	45,980	42,860
Other	108,430	97,288	93,614
Charges and miscellaneous	614,030	605,268	608,674
Utility and liquor stores	145,768	151,260	153,496
Insurance trust revenue	85,342	-497,978	515,829
Employee retirement	26,875	-563,836	416,666
Unemployment compensation	34,489	42,115	75,191
Other	23,978	23,743	23,972
Total	2,654,134	2,066,666	3,171,380

Expenditure	2007/08	2008/09	2009/10
General expenditure	2,399,788	2,475,076	2,538,114
Education	825,486	850,674	859,965
Elementary and secondary	565,716	577,597	574,029
Institutions of higher education	222,631	234,387	242,730
Other	37,138	38,691	43,206
Libraries	11,543	11,378	12,024
Public welfare	403,697	431,098	456,708
Hospitals	129,370	136,461	142,854
Health	79,820	81,939	81,498
Social insurance administration	4,071	4,584	5,157
Veterans' services	1,080	933	794
Highways	153,734	152,067	155,870
Other transportations	27,868	29,809	30,137
Police	89,267	92,999	95,489
Fire protection	39,500	40,312	42,634
Correction	72,943	74,503	72,939
Protective inspection	14,951	14,846	14,282
Natural resources	29,876	30,563	29,106
Parks and recreation	40,652	40,578	40,284
Housing and community development	50,965	47,489	53,492
Sewerage	46,741	47,619	51,896
Solid waste management	23,702	24,390	23,766
Financial administration	40,462	40,319	39,978
Judicial and legal services	41,433	42,854	43,028
General public buildings	15,107	15,308	15,002

Expenditure—*continued*	2007/08	2008/09	2009/10
Other government administration	29,341	28,943	28,840
Interest on general debt . .	100,242	103,478	105,721
Miscellaneous commercial activities	7,277	7,520	6,944
Other and unallocable . .	120,661	124,412	129,706
Utility and liquor stores . .	198,673	211,239	212,599
Insurance trust expenditure . .	233,629	275,479	359,794
Unemployment compensation .	35,568	66,159	135,367
Employee retirement . . .	180,007	190,964	205,088
Other	18,054	18,355	19,339
Total†	2,836,852	2,966,614	3,114,847

* Figures refer to the fiscal year of individual state governments, normally ending 30 June, or, in the case of the following exceptions, ending on some date within the previous 12 months: the state government of Texas and Texas school districts (31 August); the state governments of Alabama and Michigan, all local governments in the District of Columbia, and Alabama school districts (30 September); and all state and local governments of New York (31 March).

† Including intergovernmental expenditure ($ million): 4,761 in 2007/08; 4,820 in 2008/09; 4,340 in 2009/10.

Source: Governments Division, Bureau of the Census, US Department of Commerce, *Survey of Government Finances.*

INTERNATIONAL RESERVES
($ '000 million at 31 December)

	2009	2010	2011
Gold (national valuation) . . .	11.04	11.04	11.04
IMF special drawing rights . .	57.81	56.82	54.95
Reserve position in IMF . . .	11.39	12.49	30.08
Foreign exchange	50.52	52.08	51.88
Total	130.76	132.43	147.95

Source: IMF, *International Financial Statistics.*

CURRENCY AND COIN IN CIRCULATION*
($ million at end of June)

	2010	2011	2012
Total	945,137.9	1,028,909.7	1,169,129.1

* Currency outside Treasury and Federal Reserve banks, including currency held by commercial banks.

Source: Financial Management Service, US Department of the Treasury.

COST OF LIVING
(Consumer Price Index for all urban consumers, average of monthly figures. Base: 1982–84 = 100, unless otherwise indicated)

	2010	2011	2012
Food and beverages	220.0	227.9	233.7
Housing	216.3	219.1	222.7
Clothing	119.5	122.1	126.3
Transport	193.4	212.4	217.3
Medical care	388.4	400.3	414.9
Recreation*	113.3	113.4	114.7
Education and communication* .	129.9	131.5	133.8
Other goods and services . . .	381.3	387.2	394.4
All items	218.1	224.9	229.6

* Base: December 1997 = 100.

Source: Bureau of Labor Statistics, US Department of Labor.

NATIONAL ACCOUNTS
($ '000 million at current prices)

National Income and Product

	2010	2011	2012
Compensation of employees . .	7,977.2	8,303.2	8,573.3
Operating surplus	3,627.0	3,767.6	3,963.4
Domestic factor incomes . .	11,604.2	12,070.8	12,536.7
Consumption of fixed capital . .	1,873.4	1,936.8	2,011.7
Statistical discrepancy	23.3	31.9	67.2
Gross domestic product (GDP) at factor cost	13,500.9	14,039.5	14,615.6
Taxes on production and imports .	1,055.0	1,097.9	1,130.0
Less Subsidies on production and imports	57.0	61.6	60.8
GDP in purchasers' values .	14,498.9	15,075.7	15,684.8
Factor income received from abroad	716.5	783.7	782.3
Less Factor income paid abroad .	507.2	531.8	539.3
Gross national product (GNP) .	14,708.2	15,327.5	15,927.8
Less Consumption of fixed capital .	1,873.4	1,936.8	2,011.7
Net national product . . .	12,834.8	13,390.8	13,916.1
Statistical discrepancy	−23.3	−31.9	−67.2
National income in market prices	12,811.4	13,358.9	13,848.8

Expenditure on Gross Domestic Product

	2010	2011	2012
Government final consumption expenditure	3,057.5	3,059.8	3,062.8
Private final consumption expenditure	10,215.7	10,729.0	11,119.6
Increase in stocks	58.4	36.6	58.1
Gross fixed investment . . .	1,679.0	1,818.3	2,004.2
Total domestic expenditure .	15,010.6	15,643.7	16,244.7
Exports of goods and services . .	1,844.4	2,094.2	2,184.0
Less Imports of goods and services	2,356.1	2,662.3	2,744.0
GDP in purchasers' values .	14,498.9	15,075.7	15,684.8

Gross Domestic Product by Economic Activity*

	2009	2010	2011
Private industries	12,056.7	12,532.3	13,081.8
Agriculture, forestry, fishing and hunting	142.4	157.6	173.5
Agriculture	113.2	124.8	138.7
Forestry, fishing and related activities	29.2	32.9	34.9
Mining	221.7	251.9	289.9
Electricity, gas and water . .	264.7	284.5	297.9
Construction	542.9	523.3	529.5
Manufacturing	1,540.1	1,630.5	1,731.5
Wholesale trade	766.3	799.0	845.1
Retail trade	846.8	876.0	905.7
Transport and storage . . .	396.6	422.6	447.9
Information	604.8	612.2	646.6
Finance and insurance . . .	1,093.6	1,157.3	1,159.3
Real estate and rental and leasing	1,848.3	1,864.5	1,898.8
Professional and business services	1,693.2	1,769.6	1,883.9
Professional, scientific and technical services . . .	1,045.8	1,084.0	1,151.5
Management of companies and enterprises	248.2	262.7	283.6
Administrative and waste management services . .	399.1	423.0	448.8
Education	163.1	166.4	174.2
Health care and social assistance	1,062.4	1,102.7	1,136.9
Arts, entertainment and recreation	130.6	139.4	148.0

—*continued*	2009	2010	2011
Hotels and restaurants . . .	394.8	418.6	443.1
Other private services . . .	344.4	356.0	369.9
Government	1,917.0	1,966.6	1,993.8
Federal	613.0	647.2	658.1
General government . . .	553.2	589.2	607.0
Government enterprises . .	59.8	57.9	51.1
State and local	1,304.0	1,319.5	1,335.8
General government . . .	1,208.6	1,222.5	1,235.4
Government enterprises . .	95.4	97.0	100.3
GDP in purchasers' values .	13,973.7	14,498.9	15,075.7

* Distribution is based on the 1997 North American Industry Classification System (NAICS), which differs from ISIC.

Source: Bureau of Economic Analysis, US Department of Commerce.

BALANCE OF PAYMENTS
($ '000 million)

	2009	2010	2011
Exports of goods	1,073.15	1,292.58	1,500.92
Imports of goods	−1,575.49	−1,934.01	−2,235.82
Balance on goods	−502.34	−641.43	−734.90
Exports of services	508.51	551.54	603.98
Imports of services	−385.29	−404.82	−428.92
Balance on goods and services	−379.12	−494.70	−559.84
Primary income received . . .	609.18	683.40	751.29
Primary income paid	−489.46	−499.54	−524.28
Balance on goods, services and primary income	−259.41	−310.84	−332.83
Secondary income received . .	85.26	86.53	97.67
Secondary income paid . . .	−207.75	−217.64	−230.76
Current balance	−381.90	−441.96	−465.92
Capital account (net)	−0.14	−0.16	−1.21
Direct investment assets . . .	−278.57	−393.03	−442.87
Direct investment liabilities . .	139.56	270.99	257.53
Portfolio investment assets . .	−375.11	−174.92	−82.96
Portfolio investment liabilities .	357.35	808.87	336.61
Financial derivatives and employee stock options (net) . . .	44.82	14.08	39.01
Other investment assets . . .	597.29	−434.85	34.52
Other investment liabilities . .	−193.50	293.58	430.39
Net errors and omissions . . .	142.39	59.23	−89.11
Reserves and related items .	52.18	1.82	15.98

Source: IMF, *International Financial Statistics*.

FOREIGN AID
($ million, year ending 30 September)

	2003/04*	2004/05*	2005/06†
Multilateral assistance . . .	1,464.7	1,702.8	1,797.2
Bilateral assistance . . .	15,554.7	31,546.9	14,364.0
Military assistance . . .	6,285.4	4,848.3	5,151.2

* Appropriated.
† Requested.

Source: US Agency for International Development.

External Trade

PRINCIPAL COMMODITIES
(distribution by SITC, $ million)

Imports	2010	2011	2012
Food and live animals . . .	70,322.8	82,474.4	84,554.2
Mineral fuels, lubricants, etc. . .	354,967.9	453,872.2	424,504.6
Petroleum, petroleum products, etc.	329,747.4	431,866.2	408,688.4
Chemicals and related products	173,314.3	198,339.0	195,619.9
Basic manufactures	194,503.0	230,771.3	234,836.2
Machinery and transport equipment	713,784.5	795,246.4	869,282.4
General industrial machinery, equipment and parts . . .	60,425.7	74,175.3	81,531.6
Office machines and automatic data-processing machines . .	113,476.0	116,490.0	118,867.4
Telecommunications and sound equipment	137,304.9	137,952.1	143,878.8
Other electrical machinery, apparatus, etc.	119,633.8	137,936.8	144,333.4
Motor vehicles	178,946.0	198,706.9	235,370.4
Miscellaneous manufactured articles	287,282.2	308,364.4	319,005.5
Clothing and accessories (excl. footwear)	78,518.4	85,558.9	84,916.8
Total (incl. others)	1,913,160.1	2,207,823.9	2,275,392.5

Exports	2010	2011	2012
Food and live animals . . .	82,665.5	101,601.9	100,291.8
Crude materials (inedible) except fuels	81,051.6	91,592.6	91,790.6
Mineral fuels, lubricants, etc. . .	81,285.6	129,873.7	137,339.5
Chemicals and related products	189,330.9	207,103.1	207,351.4
Basic manufactures	119,698.1	139,745.9	141,623.0
Machinery and transport equipment	521,871.7	581,973.3	625,782.0
Power-generating machinery and equipment	36,023.2	39,610.9	43,158.4
Machinery specialized for particular industries . . .	51,129.7	57,051.7	58,832.5
General industrial machinery, equipment and parts . . .	56,571.9	66,107.6	71,600.6
Office machines and automatic data-processing machines . .	44,532.2	48,862.1	49,871.2
Telecommunication equipment, parts and accessories . .	42,565.0	48,158.9	49,021.2
Other electrical machinery, apparatus, etc.	105,338.4	106,876.0	107,849.8
Motor vehicles	95,147.6	115,093.1	127,039.1
Transport equipment . . .	84,613.0	93,169.7	111,238.2
Miscellaneous manufactured articles	133,980.7	143,512.4	151,678.6
Professional, scientific and controlling instruments, etc. .	51,833.6	56,690.3	59,819.1
Total (incl. others)	1,278,263.2	1,480,431.9	1,546,455.2

Source: Office of Trade and Industry Information (OTII), Manufacturing and Services, International Trade Administration, US Department of Commerce.

PRINCIPAL TRADING PARTNERS
($ million)

Imports	2010	2011	2012
Brazil	23,957.9	31,736.2	32,096.8
Canada	277,647.5	315,346.5	324,246.3
China, People's Republic	364,943.9	399,361.9	425,643.6
Colombia	15,659.3	23,113.4	24,632.4
France (incl. Monaco)	38,354.5	40,039.6	41,600.6
Germany	82,429.1	98,662.6	108,524.5
India	29,532.6	36,167.4	40,518.3
Ireland	33,847.6	39,369.6	33,308.7
Israel	20,982.4	23,039.3	22,134.1
Italy	28,505.0	33,950.5	36,930.7
Japan	120,545.2	128,924.6	146,387.7
Korea, Republic	48,874.6	56,635.5	58,879.8
Malaysia	25,900.3	25,776.7	25,933.5
Mexico	229,907.9	262,864.4	277,652.7
Nigeria	30,515.9	33,854.2	19,130.0
Russia	25,691.0	34,619.0	29,273.5
Saudi Arabia	31,412.8	47,476.3	55,667.0
Switzerland	19,136.1	24,357.5	25,690.4
Taiwan	35,846.0	41,404.8	38,859.7
Thailand	22,693.2	24,830.0	26,126.5
United Kingdom	49,775.0	51,236.1	54,934.8
Venezuela	32,707.4	43,256.4	38,725.8
Total (incl. others)	1,913,160.1	2,207,823.9	2,275,392.5

Exports	2010	2011	2012
Australia	21,797.6	27,541.8	31,207.9
Belgium	25,455.7	29,876.9	29,397.8
Brazil	35,425.1	42,943.9	43,717.4
Canada	249,105.0	280,889.6	291,757.6
Chile	10,905.3	15,986.2	18,885.8
China, People's Republic	91,880.6	103,939.4	110,590.1
France (incl. Monaco)	26,968.5	27,803.0	30,835.9
Germany	48,160.7	49,155.8	48,785.8
Hong Kong	26,570.3	36,448.9	37,480.2
India	19,250.1	21,501.3	22,335.6
Israel	11,294.4	13,936.0	14,270.1
Italy	14,219.2	16,006.6	15,972.5
Japan	60,485.6	65,706.1	70,046.4
Korea, Republic	38,845.7	43,414.5	42,317.9
Malaysia	14,079.8	14,246.5	12,854.3
Mexico	163,473.0	198,377.6	216,330.9
Netherlands	34,939.2	42,350.6	40,679.8
Saudi Arabia	11,556.3	13,829.5	18,118.1
Singapore	29,017.4	31,223.3	30,560.6
Switzerland	20,687.3	24,425.2	26,165.1
Taiwan	26,043.4	25,898.4	24,369.9
United Arab Emirates	11,673.4	15,900.4	22,569.9
United Kingdom	48,413.5	55,880.7	54,817.0
Venezuela	10,649.4	12,343.4	17,631.2
Total (incl. others)	1,278,263.2	1,480,431.9	1,546,455.2

Source: Office of Trade and Industry Information (OTII), Manufacturing and Services, International Trade Administration, US Department of Commerce.

Transport

RAILWAYS
(revenue traffic on class I railroads only)

	2002	2003	2004
Passengers carried ('000)*	23,269	24,595	25,215
Passenger-miles (million)*	5,314	5,680	5,511
Freight carried (million short tons)	2,207	2,240	2,398
Freight ton-miles ('000 million)	1,507	1,551	1,663

*Amtrak passenger traffic only.

Freight ton-miles ('000 million): 1,691 in 2010; 1,885 in 2011.

Source: Association of American Railroads, Washington, DC.

Passengers carried (Amtrak passengers only, fiscal year ending 30 September, million): 27.8 in 2010; 30.2 in 2011 (Source: National Railroad Passenger Corporation (Amtrak), *Annual Report 2011*).

ROAD TRAFFIC
('000 motor vehicles registered at 31 December)

	2009	2010	2011
Passenger cars	134,880	130,892	125,657
Buses and coaches	842	846	666
Lorries (trucks) and vans	110,561	110,322	118,456
Motorcycles	7,930	8,010	8,438

Source: Federal Highway Administration.

INLAND WATERWAYS
(freight carried, million short tons)

	2008	2009	2010
Lake waterways	90.4	63.2	80.5
Coastal waterways	186.3	167.7	164.5
Internal waterways*	588.5	522.5	565.6
Total†	956.3	857.1	893.5

*Internal refers to freight moved solely within US boundaries, excluding traffic on the Great Lakes system. Figures also exclude waterway improvement materials and fish.
†Totals include intra-port and intra-territorial traffic.

Source: Waterborne Commerce Statistics Center, US Army Corps of Engineers.

OCEAN SHIPPING
Sea-going Merchant Vessels

	2001	2002	2003
Number:			
passenger	11	13	11
container	90	91	87
roll-on/roll-off	60	60	64
bulk	15	17	20
tanker	142	130	110
other*	136	132	124
Total	454	443	416
Capacity ('000 dwt):			
passenger	99	104	90
container	3,058	3,201	3,309
roll-on/roll-off	1,260	1,273	1,411
bulk	604	706	837
tanker	8,447	7,532	5,828
other*	2,362	2,162	1,818
Total	15,830	14,978	13,294

*Includes breakbulk, partial container, refrigerated cargo, barge carrier and specialized cargo vessels.

Source: Maritime Administration, US Department of Transportation.

Vessels Entered and Cleared in Foreign Trade in all Ports

	1998	1999	2000
Entered:			
number	61,417	58,374	60,064
displacement ('000 net tons)	619,071	621,204	672,834
Cleared:			
number	60,711	56,599	57,864
displacement ('000 net tons)	630,816	618,990	670,855

Source: Maritime Administration, US Department of Transportation.

CIVIL AVIATION
(US airlines, revenue traffic on scheduled services)

	2003	2004	2005*
Number of departures ('000) . .	10,839	11,398	11,475
Domestic traffic:			
Passengers enplaned ('000) .	592,412	640,683	670,152
Passenger-miles (million) . .	500,271	551,935	579,661
Freight ton-miles (million)† .	12,342	12,756	12,634
Mail ton-miles (million)† . .	880	819	719
International traffic:			
Passengers enplaned ('000) .	53,863	62,222	68,273
Passenger-miles (million) . .	156,638	181,743	199,326
Freight ton-miles (million)† .	13,021	13,926	14,178
Mail ton-miles (million)† . .	492	477	476

* Provisional figures.
† Short tons (1 short ton = 0.907185 metric tons).

Source: Air Transport Association of America.

Tourism

FOREIGN VISITOR ARRIVALS
(by country of residence, '000)

	2010	2011	2012
Australia	904	1,038	1,014
Canada	19,959	21,028	21,190
France	1,342	1,504	1,358
Germany	1,726	1,824	1,749
Italy	838	892	758
Japan	3,386	3,250	3,385
Korea, Republic	1,108	1,145	1,138
Mexico	13,423	13,414	12,764
United Kingdom	3,851	3,835	3,485
Total (incl. others)	59,745	62,325	61,150

Tourism receipts (incl. passenger transport, $ million): 134,463 in 2010; 152,745 in 2011; 168,076 in 2012.

Source: Office of Travel and Tourism Industries, International Trade Administration, US Department of Commerce.

Communications Media

	2009	2010	2011
Telephones ('000 main lines in use)	152,963	151,171	145,875
Mobile cellular telephones ('000			
subscribers)	274,300	278,900	290,304
Internet subscribers ('000) . .	81,939	86,125	n.a.
Broadband subscribers ('000) . .	80,698	81,744	85,630

Source: International Telecommunication Union.

Education

ENROLMENT
('000 students at September of each year)

	2008	2009	2010*
Public:			
elementary	34,285	34,440*	34,637
secondary	14,980	14,842*	14,668
higher	13,972	14,811	14,926
Private:			
elementary	4,335	4,151*	4,092
secondary	1,373	1,337*	1,306
higher	5,131	5,617	5,657

* Projection(s).

Total elementary and secondary school teaching staff ('000): 3,647 (public 3,210, private 437) in 2009; 3,542 (public 3,099, private 443) in 2010; 3,679 (public 3,246, private 433) (projections).

Total higher education teaching staff ('000, projections): 910 (public 603, private 306) in 2007; 927 (public 602, private 326) in 2008; 969 (public 633, private 336) in 2009.

Source: National Center for Education Statistics, US Department of Education.

Pupil-teacher ratio (primary education, UNESCO estimate): 13.6 in 2009/10 (Source: UNESCO Institute for Statistics).

Directory

The Executive

HEAD OF STATE

President: BARACK HUSSEIN OBAMA (took office 20 January 2009; re-elected 6 November 2012).
Vice-President: JOSEPH R. BIDEN, Jr.

THE CABINET
(May 2013)

The Government is formed by the Democratic Party.
Secretary of State: JOHN F. KERRY.
Secretary of the Treasury: JACOB (JACK) LEW.
Secretary of Defense: CHARLES (CHUCK) T. HAGEL.
Attorney-General: ERIC H. HOLDER, Jr.
Secretary of the Interior: SALLY JEWELL.
Secretary of Agriculture: THOMAS J. VILSACK.
Secretary of Commerce: REBECCA M. BLANK (acting).
Secretary of Labor: SETH D. HARRIS (acting).
Secretary of Health and Human Services: KATHLEEN SEBELIUS.
Secretary of Housing and Urban Development: SHAUN L. S. DONOVAN.
Secretary of Transportation: RAYMOND L. LaHOOD.
Secretary of Energy: ERNEST J. MONIZ.
Secretary of Education: ARNE DUNCAN.
Secretary of Veterans Affairs: Gen. (retd) ERIC K. SHINSEKI.
Secretary of Homeland Security: JANET NAPOLITANO.

Officials with Cabinet Rank

Vice-President: JOSEPH R. BIDEN, Jr.
Chief of Staff to the President: DENIS RICHARD McDONOUGH.
Chair of the Council of Economic Advisers: ALAN B. KRUEGER.
Director of the Office of Management and Budget: SYLVIA MATHEWS BURWELL.
US Trade Representative: DEMETRIOS MARANTIS.
Administrator of the Environmental Protection Agency: BOB PERCIASEPE (acting).
US Ambassador to the United Nations: SUSAN RICE.
Secretary of the Small Business Administration: KAREN G. MILLS.

GOVERNMENT DEPARTMENTS

Department of Agriculture: 1400 Independence Ave, SW, Washington, DC 20250; tel. (202) 720-8732; fax (202) 720-9997; e-mail chris.mather@usda.gov; internet www.usda.gov; f. 1889.

Department of Commerce: 1401 Constitution Ave, NW, Washington, DC 20230; tel. (202) 482-2000; e-mail thesec@doc.gov; internet www.commerce.gov; f. 1913.

Department of Defense: 1400 Defense Pentagon, Washington, DC 20301-1400; tel. (703) 571-3343; fax (703) 428-1982; internet www.defense.gov; f. 1947.

Department of Education: 400 Maryland Ave, SW, 7E-247, Washington, DC 20202; tel. (202) 401-2000; fax (202) 401-0596; internet www.ed.gov; f. 1979.

Department of Energy: Forrestal Bldg, 1000 Independence Ave, SW, Washington, DC 20585; tel. (202) 586-5000; fax (202) 586-4403; e-mail the.secretary@hq.doe.gov; internet www.energy.gov; f. 1977.

Department of Health and Human Services: Hubert H. Humphrey Bldg, 200 Independence Ave, SW, Washington, DC 20201; tel. (202) 696-6162; fax (202) 690-8715; internet www.hhs.gov; f. 1980.

Department of Homeland Security: 1600 Pennsylvania Ave, NW, Washington, DC 20528; tel. (202) 282-8000; e-mail john .minnick@dhs.gov; internet www.dhs.gov; f. 2002.

Department of Housing and Urban Development: 451 Seventh St, SW, Washington, DC 20410; tel. (202) 708-1112; fax (202) 708-3106; internet www.hud.gov; f. 1965.

Department of the Interior: 1849 C St, NW, Washington, DC 20240; tel. (202) 208-3100; fax (202) 208-5048; e-mail feedback@ios .doi.gov; internet www.doi.gov; f. 1849.

Department of Justice: 950 Pennsylvania Ave, NW, Washington, DC 20530-0001; tel. (202) 514-2000; fax (202) 307-6777; e-mail askdoj@usdoj.gov; internet www.usdoj.gov; f. 1870; incl. the Office of the Attorney-Gen.

Department of Labor: Frances Perkins Bldg, 200 Constitution Ave, NW, Washington, DC 20210; tel. (202) 693-6000; fax (202) 693-6111; e-mail contact-ocio@dol.gov; internet www.dol.gov; f. 1913.

Department of State: 2201 C St, NW, Washington, DC 20520; tel. (202) 647-4000; fax (202) 647-6738; internet www.state.gov; f. 1789.

Department of Transportation: 1200 New Jersey Ave, SE, Washington, DC 20590; tel. (202) 366-4000; fax (202) 366-7202; e-mail dot.comments@dot.gov; internet www.dot.gov; f. 1967.

Department of the Treasury: 1500 Pennsylvania Ave, NW, Washington, DC 20220; tel. (202) 622-2000; fax (202) 622-6415; e-mail dcfo@do.treas.gov; internet www.ustreas.gov; f. 1789.

Department of Veterans Affairs: 810 Vermont Ave, NW, Washington, DC 20420; tel. (202) 461-7600; internet www.va.gov; f. 1989.

EXECUTIVE OFFICE OF THE PRESIDENT

The White House Office: 1600 Pennsylvania Ave, NW, Washington, DC 20500; tel. (202) 456-1414; fax (202) 456-2461; e-mail vice_president@whitehouse.gov; internet www.whitehouse.gov; coordinates activities relating to the President's immediate office; Chief of Staff to the Pres. DENIS RICHARD MCDONOUGH.

Central Intelligence Agency: Office of Public Affairs, Washington, DC 20505; tel. (703) 482-0623; fax (703) 482-1739; internet www .cia.gov; f. 1947; Dir JOHN OWEN BRENNAN.

Council of Economic Advisers: Eisenhower Executive Office Bldg, 17th St and Pennsylvania Ave, NW, Washington, DC 20502; tel. (202) 395-5042; fax (202) 395-6958; internet www.whitehouse .gov/cea; f. 1946; Chair. ALAN B. KRUEGER.

Council on Environmental Quality: 722 Jackson Pl., Washington, DC 20503; tel. (202) 395-5750; fax (202) 456-0753; e-mail efoia@ ceq.eop.gov; internet www.whitehouse.gov/ceq; f. 1969; Chair. NANCY SUTLEY.

Domestic Policy Council: Eisenhower Executive Office Bldg, Rm 469, 1600 Pennsylvania Ave, NW, Washington, DC 20500; tel. (202) 456-5594; fax (202) 456-2878; internet www.whitehouse.gov/dpc; f. 1993; fmrly a part of the Office of Policy Devt; includes the Office of Social Innovation and Civic Participation; Dir CECILIA MUÑOZ.

National Economic Council: Eisenhower Executive Office Bldg, Rm 235, 1600 Pennsylvania Ave, NW, Washington, DC 20502; tel. (202) 456-2800; fax (202) 456-2878; internet www.whitehouse.gov/ nec; f. 1993; fmrly a part of the Office of Policy Devt; Dir GENE B. SPERLING.

National Security Council: Old Executive Office Bldg, 17th St and Pennsylvania Ave, NW, Washington, DC 20504; tel. (202) 456-1414; internet www.whitehouse.gov/nsc; f. 1947; Asst to the Pres. for Nat. Security Affairs TOM DONILON.

Office of Administration: Eisenhower Executive Office Bldg, 17th St, 1650 Pennsylvania Ave, NW, Washington, DC 20503; tel. (202) 456-2861; fax (202) 456-7921; internet www.whitehouse.gov/oa; f. 1977; Dir CAMERON MOODY.

Office of Faith-Based and Neighborhood Partnerships: The White House, 1600 Pennsylvania Ave, NW, Washington, DC 20502; tel. (202) 456-3394; e-mail whpartnerships@who.eop.gov; internet www.whitehouse.gov/ofbnp; f. 2001 as Office of Faith-Based and Community Initiatives; Dir MELISSA ROGERS.

Office of Management and Budget: 725 17th St, NW, Washington, DC 20503; tel. (202) 395-3080; fax (202) 395-3888; internet www .whitehouse.gov/omb; Dir SYLVIA MATHEWS BURWELL.

Office of National AIDS Policy: Eisenhower Executive Office Bldg, Rm 464, Washington, DC 20502; tel. (202) 456-4533; fax (202) 456-7315; e-mail aidspolicy@who.eop.gov; internet www .whitehouse.gov/onap/aids; Dir GRANT COLFAX.

Office of National Drug Control Policy: POB 6000, Rockville, MD 20849-6000; tel. (202) 395-6700; fax (301) 519-5212; internet www.ondcp.gov; f. 1988; Dir R. GIL KERLIKOWSKE.

Office of Public Engagement and Intergovernmental Affairs: The White House, 1600 Pennsylvania Ave, NW, Washington, DC 20500; tel. (202) 456-1414; internet www.whitehouse.gov/engage; internet www.whitehouse.gov/administration/eop/iga; internet www.whitehouse.gov/administration/eop/oua; includes the Council on Women and Girls and the Office of Urban Affairs; Asst to the Pres. for Public Engagement and Intergovernmental Affairs VALERIE JARRETT; Dir, Public Engagement JON CARSON; Dir, Intergovernmental Affairs DAVID AGNEW; Director, Urban Affairs DEREK R. B. DOUGLAS.

Office of Science and Technology Policy: 725 17th St, Rm 5228, NW, Washington, DC 20502; tel. (202) 456-7116; fax (202) 456-6021; e-mail info@ostp.gov; internet www.ostp.gov; f. 1993; Dir JOHN HOLDREN.

Office of the United States Trade Representative: Winder Bldg, 600 17th St, NW, Washington, DC 20508; tel. (202) 395-3230; fax (202) 395-6121; e-mail contactustr@ustr.eop.gov; internet www.ustr .gov; f. 1963.

Office of the Vice-President: The White House, 1600 Pennsylvania Ave NW, Washington, DC 20501; tel. (202) 456-1414; fax (202) 456-2461; internet www.whitehouse.gov.

United States Mission to the United Nations: Press and Public Diplomacy Section, 140 East 45th St, New York, NY 10017; tel. (212) 415-4062; fax (212) 415-4053; e-mail usa@un.int; internet www.un .int/usa; US Ambassador to the United Nations Dr SUSAN RICE.

White House Military Office: Executive Office of the President, 1600 Pennsylvania Ave, NW, Washington, DC 20500; internet www .whitehouse.gov/whmo; areas of responsibility include Camp David (f. 1942) and Air Force One (f. 1962); Dir GEORGE D. MULLIGAN, Jr.

President and Legislature

PRESIDENT

Election, 6 November 2012

	Popular votes	% of popular votes	Electoral College votes
Barack Obama (Democrat)	65,899,660	51.06	332
Mitt Romney (Republican)	60,932,152	47.21	206
Others*	2,235,850	1.73	—
Total	129,067,662	100.00	538

* Including write-in candidates, etc.

CONGRESS

The 113th US Congress convened on 3 January 2013.

Senate
(May 2013)

The Senate comprises 100 members. Senators' terms are for six years, one-third of the Senate being elected every two years.

President of the Senate: Vice-President JOSEPH R. BIDEN, Jr.

President Pro Tempore: PATRICK LEAHY.

Democrats: 53 seats.

Republicans: 45 seats.

Independents: 2 seats.

Majority Leader: HARRY M. REID.

Minority Leader: MITCH MCCONNELL.

House of Representatives
(May 2013)

A new House of Representatives, comprising 435 members, is elected every two years.

Speaker: JOHN A. BOEHNER.

Republicans: 233 seats.

Democrats: 201 seats.

Vacant: 1 seat.

Majority Leader: ERIC CANTOR.

Minority Leader: NANCY PELOSI.

Election Commission

Federal Election Commission: 999 E St, NW, Washington, DC 20463; tel. (202) 694-1100; fax (202) 219-1043; e-mail info@fec.gov; internet www.fec.gov; f. 1975; independent; Chair. ELLEN L. WEINTRAUB.

Independent Agencies

Advisory Council on Historic Preservation: 1100 Pennsylvania Ave, NW, Suite 803, Old Post Office Bldg, Washington, DC 20004; tel. (202) 606-8503; fax (202) 606-8647; e-mail achp@achp.gov; internet www.achp.gov; f. 1966; Chair. MILFORD WAYNE DONALDSON; Exec. Dir JOHN M. FOWLER.

African Development Foundation: 1400 I St, NW, Suite 1000, Washington, DC 20005-2248; tel. (202) 673-3916; fax (202) 673-3810; e-mail info@adf.gov; internet www.adf.gov; Chair. JACK LESLIE; Pres. and CEO SHARI BERENBACH.

American Battle Monuments Commission: Courthouse Plaza II, Suite 500, 2300 Clarendon Blvd, Arlington, VA 22201-3367; tel. (703) 696-6900; fax (703) 696-6666; e-mail info@abmc.gov; internet www.abmc.gov; f. 1923; Chair. MERRILL A. MCPEAK; Sec. MAX CLELAND.

Appalachian Regional Commission: 1666 Connecticut Ave, NW, Washington, DC 20009-1068; tel. (202) 884-7700; fax (202) 884-7682; e-mail info@arc.gov; internet www.arc.gov; f. 1965; Fed. Co-Chair. EARL F. GOHL; States' Co-Chair. EARL RAY TOMBLIN.

Commission on Civil Rights: 624 Ninth St, NW, Washington, DC 20425; tel. (202) 376-7700; fax (202) 376-7672; e-mail publications@usccr.gov; internet www.usccr.gov; f. 1957; Chair. MARTIN R. CASTRO.

Commission of Fine Arts: National Bldg Museum, Suite 312, 401 F St, NW, Washington, DC 20001-2728; tel. (202) 504-2200; fax (202) 504-2195; e-mail cfastaff@cfa.gov; internet www.cfa.gov; f. 1910; Chair. EARL A. POWELL, III; Sec. THOMAS LUEBKE.

Commodity Futures Trading Commission (CFTC): 3 Lafayette Centre, 1155 21st St, NW, Washington, DC 20581; tel. (202) 418-5000; fax (202) 418-5521; e-mail questions@cftc.gov; internet www.cftc.gov; f. 1974; Chair. GARY GENSLER.

Corporation for National and Community Service (CNS): 1201 New York Ave, NW, Washington, DC 20525; tel. (202) 606-5000; fax (202) 565-2799; e-mail info@cns.gov; internet www.nationalservice.gov; Chair. LAYSHA WARD; CEO WENDY SPENCER.

Defense Nuclear Facilities Safety Board: 625 Indiana Ave, Suite 700, NW, Washington, DC 20004-2901; tel. (202) 694-7000; fax (202) 208-6518; e-mail mailbox@dnfsb.gov; internet www.dnfsb.gov; f. 1988; Chair. PETER S. WINOKUR; Gen. Man. MARCELYN ATWOOD.

Environmental Protection Agency: Ariel Rios Bldg, 1200 Pennsylvania Ave, NW, Washington, DC 20460; tel. (202) 272-0167; internet www.epa.gov; f. 1970; Admin. BOB PERCIASEPE (acting).

Equal Employment Opportunity Commission: 1801 L St, NW, POB 7033, Washington, DC 20507; tel. (202) 663-4900; fax (202) 663-4639; e-mail info@ask.eeoc.gov; internet www.eeoc.gov; f. 1965; Chair. JACQUELINE A. BERRIEN.

Export-Import Bank of the United States (Ex-Im Bank): see Finance—Banking.

Farm Credit Administration (FCA): 1501 Farm Credit Dr., McLean, VA 22102-5090; tel. (703) 883-4000; fax (703) 790-3260; e-mail info-line@fca.gov; internet www.fca.gov; f. 1933; Chair. and CEO JILL LONG THOMPSON.

Federal Communications Commission (FCC): see Broadcasting and Communications.

Federal Deposit Insurance Corporation (FDIC): 550 17th St, NW, Washington, DC 20429; tel. (202) 736-0000; e-mail publicinfo@fdic.gov; internet www.fdic.gov; f. 1933; Chair. MARTIN J. GRUENBERG; Dir JEREMIAH O. NORTON.

Federal Election Commission: see Election Commission.

Federal Emergency Management Agency (FEMA): Federal Center Plaza, 500 C St, SW, Washington, DC 20472; tel. (202) 646-2500; fax (202) 646-2531; e-mail askfema@dhs.gov; internet www.fema.gov; f. 1979; part of the Dept of Homeland Security; Admin. WILLIAM CRAIG FUGATE.

Federal Home Loan Mortgage Corporation (Freddie Mac): 8200 Jones Branch Dr., MS 200, McLean, VA 22102-3110; tel. (703) 903-2000; internet www.freddiemac.com; f. 1970; CEO DONALD H. LAYTON.

Federal Housing Finance Agency: 1700 G St, NW, 4th Floor, Washington, DC 20552; tel. (202) 796-5595; fax (202) 408-1435; e-mail fhfainfo@fhfa.gov; internet www.fhfa.gov; Dir EDWARD DEMARCO (acting).

Federal Labor Relations Authority (FLRA): 1400 K St, 4th Floor, NW, Washington, DC 20424; tel. (202) 218-7770; fax (202) 343-1007; e-mail solmail@flra.gov; internet www.flra.gov; f. 1978; Chair. ERNEST DUBESTER.

Federal Maritime Commission: see Transport—Ocean Shipping.

Federal Mediation and Conciliation Service: 2100 K St, NW, Washington, DC 20427; tel. (202) 606-8100; fax (202) 606-4251; e-mail foia@fmcs.gov; internet www.fmcs.gov; f. 1947; Dir GEORGE H. COHEN.

Federal National Mortgage Association (Fannie Mae): 3900 Wisconsin Ave, NW, Washington, DC 20016-2892; tel. (202) 752-7000; internet www.fanniemae.com; f. 1938; Chair. PHILIP A. LASKAWY; Pres. and CEO TIMOTHY MAYOPOULOS.

Federal Reserve System: see Finance—Banking.

Federal Retirement Thrift Investment Board (FRTIB): 1250 H St, NW, Washington, DC 20005; tel. (202) 942-1600; fax (202) 942-1676; internet www.frtib.gov; f. 1986; Chair. MICHAEL KENNEDY; Exec. Dir GREGORY T. LONG.

Federal Trade Commission: 600 Pennsylvania Ave, NW, Washington, DC 20580; tel. (202) 326-2222; fax (202) 326-2396; internet www.ftc.gov; f. 1914; Chair. EDITH RAMIREZ; Exec. Dir PATRICIA F. BAK (acting).

General Services Administration: 1 Constitution Sq., 1275 First St, NE, Washington, DC 20417; tel. (202) 501-1231; fax (202) 465-1416; e-mail rodsm.ncsc@gsa.gov; internet www.gsa.gov; f. 1949; Admin. DANIEL M. TANGHERLINI (acting).

Inter-American Foundation: 901 North Stuart St, 10th Floor, Arlington, VA 22203; tel. (703) 306-4319; fax (703) 306-4365; e-mail info@iaf.gov; internet www.iaf.gov; f. 1969; provides grants to non-governmental and community-based orgs in Latin America and the Caribbean; Chair. JOHN P. SALAZAR; Pres. ROBERT N. KAPLAN.

Medicare Payment Advisory Commission (MedPAC): 601 New Jersey Ave, NW, Suite 9000, Washington, DC 20001; tel. (202) 220-3700; fax (202) 220-3759; e-mail webmaster@medpac.gov; internet www.medpac.gov; Chair. GLENN M. HACKBARTH; Exec. Dir MARK E. MILLER.

Merit Systems Protection Board: 1615 M St, NW, Washington, DC 20419; tel. (202) 653-7200; fax (202) 653-7130; e-mail mspb@mspb.gov; internet www.mspb.gov; f. 1979; Chair. SUSAN TSUI GRUNDMANN.

National Aeronautics and Space Administration (NASA): 300 E St, SW, Suite 5K39, Washington, DC 20546-0001; tel. (202) 358-0001; fax (202) 358-4338; e-mail info-center@hq.nasa.gov; internet www.nasa.gov; f. 1958; Admin. CHARLES F. BOLDEN, Jr.

National Archives and Records Administration: 8601 Adelphi Rd, College Park, MD 20740-6001; tel. (301) 837-1600; fax (301) 837-0483; internet www.archives.gov; f. 1934; Archivist of the United States DAVID FERRIERO.

National Capital Planning Commission: 401 Ninth St, NW, Suite 500, Washington, DC 20004; tel. (202) 482-7200; fax (202) 482-7272; e-mail info@ncpc.gov; internet www.ncpc.gov; f. 1924; Chair. L. PRESTON BRYANT, Jr; Exec. Dir MARCEL C. ACOSTA.

National Council on Disability: 1331 F St, NW, Suite 850, Washington, DC 20004-1107; tel. (202) 272-2004; fax (202) 272-2022; e-mail ncd@ncd.gov; internet www.ncd.gov; f. 1978; Chair. JEFF ROSEN; Exec. Dir (vacant).

National Credit Union Administration: 1775 Duke St, Alexandria, VA 22314-3428; tel. (703) 518-6300; fax (703) 518-6660; e-mail boardmail@ncua.gov; internet www.ncua.gov; f. 1970; Chair. DEBBIE MATZ; Exec. Dir DAVID M. MARQUIS.

National Endowment for the Arts: 1100 Pennsylvania Ave, NW, Washington, DC 20506-0001; tel. (202) 682-5400; fax (202) 682-5639; e-mail webmgr@arts.endow.gov; internet www.arts.gov; f. 1965; Chair. JOAN SHIGEKAWA (acting).

National Endowment for the Humanities: 1100 Pennsylvania Ave, NW, Rm 503, Washington, DC 20506; tel. (202) 634-1121; e-mail info@neh.gov; internet www.neh.gov; f. 1965; Chair. JAMES A. LEACH.

National Labor Relations Board: 1099 14th St, NW, Washington, DC 20570-0001; tel. (202) 273-1000; fax (202) 273-4270; internet www.nlrb.gov; f. 1935; Chair. MARK GASTON PEARCE.

National Mediation Board (NMB): 1301 K St, NW, Suite 250 East, Washington, DC 20005-7011; tel. (202) 692-5010; fax (202) 523-5080; internet www.nmb.gov; f. 1934; Chair. HARRY HOGLANDER.

National Science Foundation (NSF): 4201 Wilson Blvd, Arlington, VA 22230; tel. (703) 292-5111; e-mail info@nsf.gov; internet www.nsf.gov; f. 1950; supports basic scientific and engineering research and education; Chair. DAN E. ARVIZU; Dir Dr CORA MARRETT (acting).

National Transportation Safety Board: see Transport.

Nuclear Regulatory Commission (NRC): 1 White Flint North, 11545 Rockville Pike, Rockville, MD 20852-2738; tel. (301) 415-7000; fax (301) 415-3716; e-mail NRCExecSec@nrc.gov; internet www.nrc.gov; f. 1975; Chair. ALLISON M. MACFARLANE; Exec. Dir (Operations) BILL BORCHARDT.

Occupational Safety and Health Review Commission (OSHRC): 1120 20th St, 9th Floor, NW, Washington, DC 20036-3457; tel. (202) 606-5398; fax (202) 606-5052; internet www.oshrc.gov; f. 1970; Chair. THOMASINA V. ROGERS.

Office of Government Ethics: 1201 New York Ave, NW, Suite 500, Washington, DC 20005-3917; tel. (202) 482-9300; fax (202) 482-9237; e-mail contactoge@oge.gov; internet www.usoge.gov; f. 1978; Dir WALTER M. SHAUB, Jr.

Office of Personnel Management (OPM): Theodore Roosevelt Federal Bldg, 1900 E St, NW, Washington, DC 20415; tel. (202) 606-1800; fax (202) 606-2573; e-mail general@opm.gov; internet www.opm.gov; f. 1979; Dir JOHN BERRY.

Office of Special Counsel: 1730 M St, NW, Suite 300, Washington, DC 20036-4505; tel. (202) 254-3600; fax (202) 254-3711; e-mail adr@osc.gov; internet www.osc.gov; Special Counsel CAROLYN LERNER; Dep. Special Counsel MARK COHEN.

Peace Corps: Paul D. Coverdell Peace Corps HQ, 1111 20th St, NW, Washington, DC 20526; tel. (202) 692-2100; fax (202) 692-2101; e-mail webmaster@peacecorps.gov; internet www.peacecorps.gov; f. 1961; Dir CARRIE HESSLER-RADELET (acting).

Pension Benefit Guaranty Corporation: 1200 K St, NW, Suite 12201, Washington, DC 20005-4026; tel. (202) 326-4010; fax (202) 326-4016; e-mail participant.pro@pbgc.gov; internet www.pbgc.gov; f. 1974; Dir JOSHUA GOTBAUM.

Postal Regulatory Commission: 901 New York Ave, NW, Suite 200, Washington, DC 20268-0001; tel. (202) 789-6800; fax (202) 789-6891; e-mail prc-dockets@prc.gov; internet www.prc.gov; f. 1970; Chair. RUTH Y. GOLDWAY.

Railroad Retirement Board: 844 North Rush St, Chicago, IL 60611-2092; tel. (312) 751-4300; fax (312) 751-7154; e-mail opa@rrb.gov; internet www.rrb.gov; f. 1935; Chair. MICHAEL S. SCHWARTZ.

Securities and Exchange Commission: Station Pl., 100 F St, NE, Washington, DC 20549; tel. (202) 942-8088; e-mail publicinfo@sec.gov; internet www.sec.gov; f. 1935; Chair. ELISSE B. WALTER.

Selective Service System: 1515 Wilson Blvd, Arlington, VA 22209-2425; tel. (703) 605-4100; fax (703) 605-4106; e-mail information@sss.gov; internet www.sss.gov; f. 1940; Dir LAWRENCE G. ROMO.

Small Business Administration: 409 Third St, SW, Washington, DC 20416; tel. (202) 205-6650; fax (202) 205-6802; e-mail answerdesk@sba.gov; internet www.sba.gov; f. 1953; Admin. KAREN G. MILLS.

Smithsonian Institution: 1000 Jefferson Dr., SW, POB 37012, Washington, DC 20560-0001; tel. (202) 633-1000; e-mail info@si.edu; internet www.si.edu; f. 1846; Chair. FRANCE CÓRDOVA; Sec. G. WAYNE CLOUGH.

Social Security Administration: Office of Public Inquiries, Windsor Park Bldg, 6401 Security Blvd, Baltimore, MD 21235-0001; tel. (410) 965-3120; fax (410) 966-6166; internet www.ssa.gov; Commr CAROLYN W. COLVIN (acting).

Tennessee Valley Authority: 400 West Summit Hill Dr., Knoxville, TN 37902-1499; tel. (865) 632-2101; e-mail tvainfo@tva.gov; internet www.tva.gov; f. 1933; Chair. WILLIAM SANSOM; CEO and Pres. WILLIAM (BILL) D. JOHNSON.

United States Agency for International Development (USAID): Ronald Reagan Bldg, 1300 Pennsylvania Ave, NW, Washington, DC 20523-0016; tel. (202) 712-4810; fax (202) 216-3524; e-mail pinquiries@usaid.gov; internet www.usaid.gov; f. 1961; Admin. Dr RAJIV SHAH.

United States Consumer Product Safety Commission: 4330 East-West Hwy, Bethesda, MD 20814-4408; tel. (301) 504-7923; fax (301) 504-0124; e-mail info@cpsc.gov; internet www.cpsc.gov; f. 1972; Chair. and Commr INEZ MOORE TENENBAUM; Exec. Dir KENNETH HINSON.

United States International Trade Commission: 500 E St, SW, Washington, DC 20436; tel. (202) 205-2000; fax (202) 205-2338; e-mail webmaster@usitc.gov; internet www.usitc.gov; f. 1916; Chair. IRVING WILLIAMSON.

United States Postal Service: 475 L'Enfant Plaza, SW, Washington, DC 20260-0010; tel. (202) 268-2000; fax (202) 268-4860; internet www.usps.com; f. 1970; Chair. MICKEY D. BARNETT; Postmaster-Gen. and CEO PATRICK R. DONAHOE.

United States Trade and Development Agency (USTDA): 1000 Wilson Blvd, Suite 1600, Arlington, VA 22209-3901; tel. (703) 875-4357; fax (703) 875-4009; e-mail info@ustda.gov; internet www.ustda.gov; f. 1961; Dir LEOCADIA I. ZAK.

State Governments

(with expiration date of Governors' current term of office; legislatures at January 2013)

Alabama: Governor ROBERT J. BENTLEY (Rep.—Jan. 2015); Senate: Dem. 11, Rep. 23, Ind. 1; House: Dem. 39, Rep. 64, Vacant 2.

Alaska: Governor SEAN R. PARNELL (Rep.—Dec. 2014); Senate: Dem. 7, Rep. 13; House: Dem. 15, Rep. 25.

Arizona: Governor JAN BREWER (Rep.—Jan. 2015); Senate: Dem. 13, Rep. 17; House: Dem. 24, Rep. 36.

Arkansas: Governor MIKE BEEBE (Dem.—Jan. 2015); Senate: Dem. 14, Rep. 21; House: Dem. 49, Rep. 51.

California: Governor EDMUND G. (JERRY) BROWN (Dem.—Jan. 2015); Senate: Dem. 26, Rep. 12, Vacant 2; Assembly: Dem. 54, Rep. 26.

Colorado: Governor JOHN HICKENLOOPER (Dem.—Jan. 2015); Senate: Dem. 19, Rep. 16; House: Dem. 36, Rep. 29.

Connecticut: Governor DANIEL P. (DAN) MALLOY (Dem.—Jan. 2015); Senate: Dem. 22, Rep. 14; House: Dem. 99, Rep. 52.

Delaware: Governor JACK MARKELL (Dem.—Jan. 2017); Senate: Dem. 13, Rep. 8; House: Dem. 27, Rep. 14.

Florida: Governor RICK SCOTT (Rep.—Jan. 2015); Senate: Dem. 14, Rep. 26; House: Dem. 46, Rep. 74.

Georgia: Governor NATHAN DEAL (Rep.—Jan. 2015); Senate: Dem. 18, Rep. 38; House: Dem. 60, Rep. 119, Ind. 1.

Hawaii: Governor NEIL ABERCROMBIE (Dem.—Dec. 2014); Senate: Dem. 24, Rep. 1; House: Dem. 44, Rep. 7.

Idaho: Governor C. L. (BUTCH) OTTER (Rep.—Jan. 2015); Senate: Dem. 7, Rep. 28; House: Dem. 13, Rep. 57.

Illinois: Governor PATRICK J. QUINN, III (Dem.—Jan. 2015); Senate: Dem. 40, Rep. 19; House: Dem. 71, Rep. 47.

Indiana: Governor MICHAEL PENCE (Rep.—Jan. 2017); Senate: Dem. 13, Rep. 37; House: Dem. 31, Rep. 69.

Iowa: Governor TERRY BRANSTAD (Rep.—Jan. 2015); Senate: Dem. 26, Rep. 23, Ind. 1; House: Dem. 47, Rep. 53.

Kansas: Governor SAMUEL D. BROWNBACK (Rep.—Jan. 2015); Senate: Dem. 9, Rep. 31; House: Dem. 35, Rep. 90.

Kentucky: Governor STEVEN L. BESHEAR (Dem.—Dec. 2015); Senate: Dem. 14, Rep. 22, Ind. 1, Vacant 1; House: Dem. 55, Rep. 45.

Louisiana: Governor BOBBY JINDAL (Rep.—Jan. 2016); Senate: Dem. 15, Rep. 24; House: Dem. 45, Rep. 58, Ind. 2.

Maine: Governor PAUL LEPAGE (Rep.—Jan. 2015); Senate: Dem. 19, Rep. 15, Ind. 1; House: Dem. 89, Rep. 58, Ind. 4.

Maryland: Governor MARTIN O'MALLEY, Jr (Dem.—Jan. 2015); Senate: Dem. 35, Rep. 12; House: Dem. 98, Rep. 43.

Massachusetts: Governor DEVAL L. PATRICK (Dem.—Jan. 2015); Senate: Dem. 36, Rep. 4; House: Dem. 131, Rep. 29.

Michigan: Governor RICK SNYDER (Rep.—Jan. 2015); Senate: Dem. 12, Rep. 26; House: Dem. 51, Rep. 59.

Minnesota: Governor MARK B. DAYTON (Democratic Farmer Labor Party—Jan. 2015); Senate: Dem. 39, Rep. 28; House: Dem. 73, Rep. 61.

Mississippi: Governor PHIL BRYANT (Rep.—Jan. 2016); Senate: Dem. 21, Rep. 30, Vacant 1; House: Dem. 58, Rep. 63, Vacant 1.

Missouri: Governor JEREMIAH W. (JAY) NIXON (Dem.—Jan. 2017); Senate: Dem. 10, Rep. 24; House: Dem. 53, Rep. 110.

Montana: Governor STEVE BULLOCK (Dem.—Jan. 2017); Senate: Dem. 23, Rep. 27; House: Dem. 37, Rep. 63.

Nebraska: Governor DAVE HEINEMAN (Rep.—Jan. 2015); Legislature: unicameral body comprising 49 members elected on a non-partisan ballot and classed as senators.

Nevada: Governor BRIAN SANDOVAL (Rep.—Jan. 2015); Senate: Dem. 11, Rep. 10; Assembly: Dem. 27, Rep. 15.

New Hampshire: Governor MAGGIE HASSAN (Dem.—Jan. 2015); Senate: Dem. 11, Rep. 13; House: Dem. 221, Rep. 179.

New Jersey: Governor CHRIS CHRISTIE (Rep.—Jan. 2014); Senate: Dem. 24, Rep. 16; Assembly: Dem. 48, Rep. 32.

New Mexico: Governor SUSANA MARTÍNEZ (Rep.—Jan. 2015); Senate: Dem. 25, Rep. 17; House: Dem. 38, Rep. 32.

New York: Governor ANDREW M. CUOMO (Dem.—Jan. 2015); Senate: Dem. 30, Rep. 32; Assembly: Dem. 99, Rep. 51.

North Carolina: Governor PAT MCCRORY (Rep.—Jan. 2017); Senate: Dem. 18, Rep. 32; House: Dem. 43, Rep. 77.

North Dakota: Governor JACK DALRYMPLE (Rep.—Jan. 2017); Senate: Dem. 13, Rep. 33, Vacant 1; House: Dem. 23, Rep. 71.

Ohio: Governor JOHN KASICH (Rep.—Jan. 2015); Senate: Dem. 10, Rep. 23; House: Dem. 39, Rep. 60.

Oklahoma: Governor MARY FALLIN (Rep.—Jan. 2015); Senate: Dem. 12, Rep. 36; House: Dem. 29, Rep. 72.

Oregon: Governor JOHN KITZHABER (Dem.—Jan. 2015); Senate: Dem. 16, Rep. 14; House: Dem. 34, Rep. 26.

Pennsylvania: Governor TOM CORBETT (Rep.—Jan. 2015); Senate: Dem. 23, Rep. 27; House: Dem. 93, Rep. 110.

Rhode Island: Governor LINCOLN D. CHAFEE (Ind.—Jan. 2015); Senate: Dem. 32, Rep. 5, Ind. 1; House: Dem. 69, Rep. 6.

South Carolina: Governor NIMRATA (NIKKI) HALEY (Rep.—Jan. 2015); Senate: Dem. 18, Rep. 28; House: Dem. 46, Rep. 73, Ind. 5.

South Dakota: Governor DENNIS DAUGAARD (Rep.—Jan. 2015); Senate: Dem. 7, Rep. 28; House: Dem. 17, Rep. 53.

Tennessee: Governor BILL HASLAM (Dem.—Jan. 2015); Senate: Dem. 7, Rep. 26; House: Dem. 28, Rep. 70, Ind. 1.

Texas: Governor RICK PERRY (Rep.—Jan. 2015); Senate: Dem. 12, Rep. 19; House: Dem. 55, Rep. 95.

Utah: Governor GARY R. HERBERT (Rep.—Jan. 2017); Senate: Dem. 5, Rep. 24; House: Dem. 14, Rep. 61.

Vermont: Governor PETER SHUMLIN (Dem.—Jan. 2015); Senate: Dem. 22, Rep. 6, Ind. and others 2; House: Dem. 96, Rep. 45, Ind. and others 9.

Virginia: Governor ROBERT F. MCDONNELL (Rep.—Jan. 2014); Senate: Dem. 20, Rep. 20; House: Dem. 31, Rep. 67, Ind. 1, Vacant 1.

Washington: Governor JAY INSLEE (Dem.—Jan. 2017); Senate: Dem. 26, Rep. 23; House: Dem. 55, Rep. 43.

West Virginia: Governor EARL RAY TOMBLIN (Dem.—Jan. 2017); Senate: Dem. 25, Rep. 9; House: Dem. 54, Rep. 46.

Wisconsin: Governor SCOTT WALKER (Rep.—Jan. 2015); Senate: Dem. 15, Rep. 18; Assembly: Dem. 39, Rep. 60.

Wyoming: Governor MATTHEW MEAD (Rep.—Jan. 2015); Senate: Dem. 4, Rep. 26; House: Dem. 8, Rep. 52.

Political Organizations

Communist Party USA (CPUSA): 235 West 23rd St, 8th Floor, New York, NY 10011; tel. (212) 989-4994; fax (212) 229-1713; e-mail cpusa@cpusa.org; internet www.cpusa.org; f. 1919; mems in all 50 states, organized in over 40 states; Nat. Chair. SAM WEBB; Exec. Vice-Chair. JARVIS TYNER.

Constitution Party: 23 North Lime St, POB 1782, Lancaster, PA 17602; tel. (717) 390-1993; fax (717) 299-5115; e-mail webmaster@constitutionparty.com; internet constitutionparty.com; f. 1991 as US Taxpayers' Party; adopted present name in 1999; right-wing; working to restore constitutionally limited govt; Nat. Chair. FRANK FLUCKIGER; Sec. CINDY REDBURN; Treas. JAMES (JIM) HEADINGS.

Democratic National Committee: 430 South Capitol St, SE, Washington, DC 20003; tel. (202) 863-8000; fax (202) 863-8174; internet www.democrats.org; f. 1848; Nat. Chair. DEBBIE WASSERMAN SCHULTZ; Sec. ALICE TRAVIS GERMOND; Treas. ANDREW TOBIAS.

The Green Party of the United States: 1623 Connecticut Ave, NW, POB 57065, Washington, DC 20037; tel. (202) 319-7191; fax (202) 289-5260; e-mail office@gp.org; internet www.gp.org; f. 2001; Sec. BUDD DICKINSON; Treas. JEFF TURNER.

Libertarian Party: 2600 Virginia Ave, NW, Suite 200, Washington, DC 20037; tel. (202) 333-0008; fax (202) 333-0072; e-mail info@lp.org; internet www.lp.org; f. 1971; advocates individual freedom, smaller govt and fewer taxes; Nat. Chair. GEOFFREY NEALE; Sec. DAVID BLAU; Treas. TIM HAGAN.

Prohibition National Committee: POB 212, Needemore, Pennsylvania, PA 17238; tel. (303) 237-4947; e-mail tdavis@prohibitionparty.org; internet www.prohibitionparty.org; f. 1869; opposes the manufacture and sale of alcoholic drinks; opposes abortion, drug abuse and euthanasia; Nat. Chair. TOBY DAVIS; Exec. Sec. JAMES HEDGES.

La Raza Unida Party (Partido Nacional La Raza Unida): POB 13, San Fernando CA 91340; tel. (818) 365-6534; e-mail Organize@pnlru.org; internet www.pnlru.org; f. 1970; aims to achieve self-determination and greater govt representation for Latinos through electoral processes; 4 state groups, 100 local groups; Nat. Chair. XENARO G. AYALA.

Reform Party of the USA: POB 660675, Dallas, TX 75266; tel. (972) 275-9297; e-mail info@reformparty.org; internet www.reformparty.org; f. 1996; advocates reform of political system and ethical govt; Nat. Chair. DAVID COLLISON.

Republican National Committee: 310 First St, SE, Washington, DC 20003; tel. (202) 863-8500; fax (202) 863-8820; e-mail info@gop.com; internet www.gop.com; f. 1854; Chair., Nat. Cttee REINCE PRIEBUS; Co-Chair. SHARON DAY; Sec. DEMETRA DEMONTE; Treas. TONY PARKER.

Social Democrats, USA: POB 16161, Pittsburgh, PA 15242; tel. (614) 263-0982; e-mail info@socialistcurrents.org; internet www .socialdemocrats.org; f. 1972 following split from the Socialist Party USA (fmrly the Socialist Party of America, f. 1901); relaunched in 2008 following a hiatus; Nat. Co-Chair. RICK D'LOSS, CRAIG MILLER; Sec. and Treas. GLENN KING.

Socialist Party USA: A. J. Muste Bldg, 339 Lafayette St, Suite 303, New York, NY 10012; tel. and fax (212) 982-4586; e-mail natsec@sp-usa.org; internet socialistparty-usa.org; f. 1972 following split from the Socialist Party of America (f. 1901); Co-Chair. STEPHANIE CHOLENSKY, WILLIAM WHARTON; Nat. Sec. GREG PASON; 1,800 mems.

Socialist Workers Party: 306 West 37th St, 10th Floor, New York, NY 10018; tel. (212) 736-2540; fax (212) 244-4274; e-mail swpno@mac.com; f. 1938; communist; Nat. Sec. JACK BARNES.

Diplomatic Representation

EMBASSIES IN THE USA

Afghanistan: 2341 Wyoming Ave, NW, Washington, DC 20008; tel. 483-6410; fax 483-6488; e-mail press@embassyofafghanistan.org; internet www.embassyofafghanistan.org; Ambassador EKLIL HAKIMI.

Albania: 2100 S St, NW, Washington, DC 20008; tel. (202) 223-4942; fax (202) 628-7342; e-mail info@albanianembassy.org; internet www .albanianembassy.org; Ambassador GILBERT GALANXHI.

Algeria: 2118 Kalorama Rd, NW, Washington, DC 20008; tel. (202) 265-2800; fax (202) 986-5906; e-mail mail@algeria-us.org; internet www.algeria-us.org; Ambassador ABDALLAH BAALI.

Andorra: 2 United Nations Plaza, 27th Floor, New York, NY 10017; tel. (212) 750-8064; fax (212) 750-6630; Ambassador NARCIS CASAL DE FONSDEVIELA.

Angola: 2100–2108 16th St, NW, Washington, DC 20009; tel. (202) 785-1156; fax (202) 822-9049; e-mail angola@angola.org; internet www.angola.org; Ambassador ALBERTO DO CARMO BENTO RIBEIRO.

Antigua and Barbuda: 3216 New Mexico Ave, NW, Washington, DC 20016; tel. (202) 362-5122; fax (202) 362-5225; e-mail embantbar@aol.com; Ambassador DEBORAH MAE LOVELL.

Argentina: 1600 New Hampshire Ave, NW, Washington, DC 20009-2512; tel. (202) 238-6401; fax (202) 332-3171; internet www .embassyofargentina.us; Ambassador CECILIA NAHÓN.

Armenia: 2225 R St, NW, Washington, DC 20008; tel. (202) 319-1976; fax (202) 319-2982; e-mail armpublic@speakeasy.net; internet www.armeniaemb.org; Ambassador TATOUL MARKARIAN.

Australia: 1601 Massachusetts Ave, NW, Washington, DC 20036-2273; tel. (202) 797-3000; fax (202) 797-3168; internet www.usa .embassy.gov.au; Ambassador KIM BEAZLEY.

Austria: 3524 International Court, NW, Washington, DC 20008-3035; tel. (202) 895-6700; fax (202) 895-6773; e-mail obwas@sysnet .net; internet www.austria.org; Ambassador HANS PETER MANZ.

Azerbaijan: 2741 34th St, NW, Washington, DC 20008; tel. (202) 337-3500; fax (202) 337-5911; e-mail azerbaijan@azembassy.com; internet azembassy.com; Ambassador ELIN SULEYMANOV.

Bahamas: 2220 Massachusetts Ave, NW, Washington, DC 20008; tel. (202) 319-2660; fax (202) 319-2668; e-mail bahemb@aol.com; Chargé d'affaires a.i. FREDDIE CLEVELAND TUCKER.

Bahrain: 3502 International Dr., NW, Washington, DC 20008; tel. (202) 342-1111; fax (202) 362-2192; e-mail ambsecretary@bahrainembassy.org; internet www.bahrainembassy.org; Ambassador HOUDA ERZA EBRAHIM NONOO.

Bangladesh: 3510 International Dr., NW, Washington, DC 20008; tel. (202) 244-0183; fax (202) 244-2771; e-mail bdootwash@bdembassyusa.org; internet www.bdembassyusa.org; Ambassador AKRAMUL QADER.

Barbados: 2144 Wyoming Ave, NW, Washington, DC 20008; tel. (202) 939-9200; fax (202) 332-7467; e-mail washington@foreign.gov .bb; Ambassador JOHN BEALE.

Belarus: 1619 New Hampshire Ave, NW, Washington, DC 20009; tel. (202) 986-1604; fax (202) 986-1805; e-mail usa@belarusembassy .org; internet www.belarusembassy.org; Chargé d'affaires a.i. OLEG KRAVCHENKO.

Belgium: 3330 Garfield St, NW, Washington, DC 20008; tel. (202) 333-6900; fax (202) 333-3079; e-mail washington@diplobel.org; internet www.diplobel.us; Ambassador JAN MATTHYSEN.

Belize: 2535 Massachusetts Ave, NW, Washington, DC 20008; tel. (202) 332-9636; fax (202) 332-6888; e-mail ebwreception@aol.com; internet www.embassyofbelize.org; Ambassador NESTOR MENDEZ.

Benin: 2124 Kalorama Rd, NW, Washington, DC 20008; tel. (202) 232-6656; fax (202) 265-1996; e-mail info@beninembassyus.org; internet www.beninembassy.us; Ambassador SÈGBÉ CYRILLE OGUIN.

Bolivia: 3014 Massachusetts Ave, NW, Washington, DC 20008; tel. (202) 483-4410; fax (202) 328-3712; e-mail webmaster@bolivia-usa

.org; internet www.bolivia-usa.org; Chargé d'affaires a.i. FREDDY BERSATTI TUDELA.

Bosnia and Herzegovina: 2109 E St, NW, Washington, DC 20037; tel. (202) 337-1500; fax (202) 337-1502; e-mail info@bhembassy.org; internet www.bhembassy.org; Ambassador JADRANKA NEGODIC.

Botswana: 1531–1533 New Hampshire Ave, NW, Washington, DC 20036; tel. (202) 244-4990; fax (202) 244-4164; e-mail sekgwa@ botswanaembassy.org; internet www.botswanaembassy.org; Ambassador TEBELELO MAZILE SERETSE.

Brazil: 3006 Massachusetts Ave, NW, Washington, DC 20008-3634; tel. (202) 238-2805; fax (202) 238-2827; e-mail ambassador@ brasilemb.org; internet www.brasilemb.org; Ambassador MAURO LUIZ IECKER VIEIRA.

Brunei: 3520 International Court, NW, Washington, DC 20008; tel. (202) 237-1838; fax (202) 885-0560; e-mail info@bruneiembassy.org; internet www.bruneiembassy.org; Ambassador Dato Paduka HAJI YUSOF HAJI ABDUL HAMID.

Bulgaria: 1621 22nd St, NW, Washington, DC 20008; tel. (202) 387-0174; fax (202) 234-7973; e-mail office@bulgaria-embassy.org; internet www.bulgaria-embassy.org; Ambassador ELENA POPTODOR-OVA.

Burkina Faso: 2340 Massachusetts Ave, NW, Washington, DC 20008; tel. (202) 332-5577; fax (202) 667-1882; e-mail ambawdc@ verizon.net; internet www.burkina-usa.org; Ambassador SEYDOU BOUDA.

Burundi: 2233 Wisconsin Ave, NW, Suite 212, Washington, DC 20007; tel. (202) 342-2574; fax (202) 342-2575; e-mail burundiembassy@erols.com; internet www.burundiembassy-usa .org; Ambassador ANGELE NIYUHIRE.

Cambodia: 4530 16th St, NW, Washington, DC 20011; tel. (202) 726-7742; fax (202) 726-8381; e-mail cambodian_embassydc@hotmail .com; internet www.embassyofcambodia.org; Ambassador HEM HENG.

Cameroon: 2349 Massachusetts Ave, NW, Washington, DC 20008; tel. (202) 265-8790; fax (202) 387-3826; e-mail cdm@ambacam-usa .org; internet www.ambacam-usa.org; Ambassador JOSEPH FOE-ATANGANA.

Canada: 501 Pennsylvania Ave, NW, Washington, DC 20001; tel. (202) 682-1740; fax (202) 682-7726; e-mail washington-im-enquiry@ international.gc.ca; internet www.canadainternational.gc.ca/ washington; Ambassador GARY DOER.

Cape Verde: 3415 Massachusetts Ave, NW, Washington, DC 20007; tel. (202) 965-6820; fax (202) 965-1207; e-mail ambacvus@sysnet.net; internet www.virtualcapeverde.net; Ambassador MARIA DE FÁTIMA LIMA DA VEIGA.

Central African Republic: 1618 22nd St, NW, Washington, DC 20008; tel. (202) 483-7800; fax (202) 332-9893; e-mail centralafricwashington@yahoo.com; Ambassador STANISLAS MOUSSA-KEMBE.

Chad: 2401 Massachusetts Ave, NW, Washington, DC 20008; tel. (202) 462-4009; fax (202) 265-1937; e-mail info@chadembassy.us; internet chadembassy.us; Ambassador MAITINE DJOUMBE.

Chile: 1732 Massachusetts Ave, NW, Washington, DC 20036; tel. (202) 785-1746; fax (202) 659-9624; e-mail embassy@embassyofchile .org; internet www.chile-usa.org; Ambassador FELIPE BULNES SERRANO.

China, People's Republic: 3505 International Pl., NW, Washington, DC 20522; tel. (202) 495-2000; fax (202) 495-2138; e-mail chinaembassy_us@fmprc.gov.cn; internet www.china-embassy.org; Ambassador CUI TIANKAI.

Colombia: 2118 Leroy Pl., NW, Washington, DC 20008; tel. (202) 387-8338; fax (202) 232-8643; e-mail embassyofcolombia@ colombiaemb.org; internet www.colombiaemb.org; Ambassador CARLOS URRUTIA.

Comoros: 866 United Nations Plaza, Suite 418, New York, NY 10017; tel. (212) 750-1637; fax (212) 750-1657; e-mail comun@undp .org; Ambassador KAAMBI ROUBANI.

Congo, Democratic Republic: 1726 M St, NW, Suite 601, Washington, DC 20036; tel. (202) 234-7690; fax (202) 234-2609; e-mail ambassade@ambardcusa.org; internet www.ambardcusa .org; Ambassador FAIDA MITIFU.

Congo, Republic: 4891 Colorado Ave, NW, Washington, DC 20011; tel. (202) 726-5500; fax (202) 726-1860; e-mail info@embassyofcongo .org; Ambassador SERGE MOMBOULI.

Costa Rica: 2114 S St, NW, Washington, DC 20008; tel. (202) 234-2945; fax (202) 265-4795; e-mail embassy@costarica-embassy.org; internet www.costarica-embassy.org; Ambassador META SHANON FIGUERES BOGGS.

Côte d'Ivoire: 2424 Massachusetts Ave, NW, Washington, DC 20008; tel. (202) 797-0300; fax (202) 204-3967; e-mail info@ ambacotedivoireusa.org; internet www.ambaci.us; Ambassador DAOUDA DIABATE.

Croatia: 2343 Massachusetts Ave, NW, Washington, DC 20008-2803; tel. (202) 588-5899; fax (202) 588-8936; e-mail washington@ mvep.hr; internet www.croatiaemb.org; Ambassador JOŠKO PARO.

Cuba: 'Interests section' in the Embassy of Switzerland, 2630 16th St, NW, Washington, DC 20009; tel. (202) 797-8518; fax (202) 797-0606; e-mail informacion1@sicuw.org; internet embacu.cubaminrex .cu/Default.aspx?tabid=8803; Counsellor JORGE ALBERTO BOLAÑOS SUÁREZ.

Cyprus: 2211 R St, NW, Washington, DC 20008; tel. (202) 462-5772; fax (202) 483-6710; e-mail info@cyprusembassy.net; internet www .cyprusembassy.net; Chargé d'affaires a.i. OLYMPIA NEOCLEOUS.

Czech Republic: 3900 Spring of Freedom St, NW, Washington, DC 20008; tel. (202) 274-9100; fax (202) 966-8540; e-mail washington@ embassy.mzv.cz; internet www.mzv.cz/washington; Ambassador PETR GANDALOVIČ.

Denmark: 3200 Whitehaven St, NW, Washington, DC 20008-3616; tel. (202) 234-4300; fax (202) 328-1470; e-mail wasamb@um.dk; internet www.ambwashington.um.dk; Ambassador PETER TAKSOE-JENSEN.

Djibouti: 1156 15th St, NW, Suite 515, Washington, DC 20005; tel. (202) 331-0270; fax (202) 331-0302; Ambassador ROBLÉ OLHAYE.

Dominica: 3216 New Mexico Ave, NW, Washington, DC 20016; tel. (202) 364-6781; fax (202) 364-6791; e-mail embdomdc@aol.com; Ambassador HUBERT JOHN CHARLES.

Dominican Republic: 1715 22nd St, NW, Washington, DC 20008; tel. (202) 332-6280; fax (202) 265-8057; e-mail embassy@us.serex.gov .do; internet www.domrep.org; Ambassador ANIBAL DE CASTRO.

Ecuador: 2535 15th St, NW, Washington, DC 20009; tel. (202) 234-7200; fax (202) 667-3482; e-mail embassy@ecuador.org; internet www.ecuador.org; Ambassador NATHALIE CELY.

Egypt: 3521 International Court, NW, Washington, DC 20008; tel. (202) 895-5400; fax (202) 244-4319; e-mail Embassy@egyptembassy .net; internet www.egyptembassy.net; Ambassador MOHAMED MOS-TAFA MOHAMED TAWFIK.

El Salvador: 1400 16th St, NW, Suite 100, Washington, DC 20036; tel. (202) 265-9671; fax (202) 232-3763; e-mail correo@elsalvador.org; internet www.elsalvador.org; Ambassador RUBEN IGNACIO ZAMORA RIVAS.

Equatorial Guinea: 2020 16th St, NW, Washington, DC 20009; tel. (202) 518-5700; fax (202) 518-5252; Chargé d'affaires a.i. ROMAN OBAMA EKUA.

Eritrea: 1708 New Hampshire Ave, NW, Washington, DC 20009; tel. (202) 319-1991; fax (202) 319-1304; e-mail embassyeritrea@ embassyeritrea.org; internet www.embassyeritrea.org; Chargé d'affaires a.i. BERHANE SOLOMON.

Estonia: 2131 Massachusetts Ave, NW, Washington, DC 20008; tel. (202) 588-0101; fax (202) 588-0108; e-mail embassy.washington@mfa .ee; internet www.estemb.org; Ambassador MARINA KALJURAND.

Ethiopia: 3506 International Dr., NW, Washington, DC 20008; tel. (202) 364-1200; fax (202) 587-0195; e-mail info@ethiopianembassy .org; internet www.ethiopianembassy.org; Ambassador GIRMA BIRRU GEDA.

Fiji: 2000 M St, NW, Suite 710, Washington, DC 20036; tel. (202) 466-8320; fax (202) 466-8325; e-mail info@fijiembassydc.com; internet www.fijiembassydc.com; Ambassador WINSTON THOMPSON.

Finland: 3301 Massachusetts Ave, NW, Washington, DC 20008; tel. (202) 298-5800; fax (202) 298-6030; e-mail sanomat.was@formin.fi; internet www.finland.org; Ambassador RITVA KOUKKU-RONDE.

France: 4101 Reservoir Rd, NW, Washington, DC 20007; tel. (202) 944-6000; fax (202) 944-6166; e-mail info@ambafrance-us.org; internet www.ambafrance-us.org; Ambassador FRANCOIS M. DELAT-TRE.

Gabon: 2034 20th St, NW, Suite 200, Washington, DC 20009; tel. (202) 797-1000; fax (202) 983-1994; Ambassador MICHAEL MOUSSA-ADAMO.

The Gambia: Georgetown Plaza, 2233 Wisconsin Ave, NW, Suite 240, Washington, DC 20007; tel. (202) 785-1399; fax (202) 342-0240; e-mail info@gambiaembassy.us; internet www.gambiaembassy.us; Ambassador ALIEU MOMODOU NGUM.

Georgia: 2209 Massachusetts Ave, NW, Washington, DC 20008; tel. (202) 387-2390; fax (202) 387-0864; e-mail embgeo.usa@mfa.gov.ge; internet www.usa.mfa.gov.ge; Ambassador ARCHIL GEGESHIDZE.

Germany: 4645 Reservoir Rd, NW, Washington, DC 20007-1998; tel. (202) 298-4000; fax (202) 298-4249; internet www.germany.info; Ambassador NIELS PETER GEORG AMMON.

Ghana: 3512 International Dr., NW, Washington, DC 20008; tel. (202) 686-4520; fax (202) 686-4527; e-mail info@ghanaembassy.org; internet www.ghanaembassy.org; Ambassador DANIEL OHENE AGYE-KUM.

Greece: 2217 Massachusetts Ave, NW, Washington, DC 20008; tel. (202) 939-1300; fax (202) 939-1324; e-mail greece@greekembassy.org; internet www.mfa.gr/washington; Ambassador CHRISTOS PANAGOPOULOS.

Grenada: 1701 New Hampshire Ave, NW, Washington, DC 20009; tel. (202) 265-2561; fax (202) 265-2468; internet www.grenadaembassyusa.org; Ambassador GILLIAN MARGARET SUSAN BRISTOL.

Guatemala: 2220 R St, NW, Washington, DC 20008; tel. (202) 745-4952; fax (202) 745-1908; e-mail embestadosunidos@minex.gob.gt; Ambassador JOSÉ FRANCISCO VILLAGRÁN DE LEÓN.

Guinea: 2112 Leroy Pl., NW, Washington, DC 20008; tel. (202) 986-4300; fax (202) 986-3800; Ambassador BLAISE CHERIF.

Guinea-Bissau: POB 33813, Washington, DC 20033-3813; tel. and fax (301) 947-3958; embassy operations suspended since 2007; Ambassador (vacant).

Guyana: 2490 Tracy Pl., NW, Washington, DC 20008; tel. (202) 265-6900; fax (202) 232-1297; e-mail guyanaembassydc@verizon.net; Ambassador BAYNEY RAM KARRAN.

Haiti: 2311 Massachusetts Ave, Washington, DC 20008; tel. (202) 332-4090; fax (202) 745-7215; e-mail amb.washington@diplomatie.ht; internet www.haiti.org; Ambassador PAUL ALTIDOR.

Holy See: 3339 Massachusetts Ave, NW, Washington, DC 20008; tel. (202) 333-7121; fax (202) 337-4036; e-mail nuntiususa@nuntiususa.org; Apostolic Nuncio CARLO MARIA VIGANÒ (Titular Archbishop of Ulpiana).

Honduras: 3007 Tilden St, NW, Suite 4-M, Washington, DC 20008; tel. (202) 966-2604; fax (202) 966-9751; e-mail embassy@hondurasemb.org; internet www.hondurasemb.org; Ambassador JORGE RAMÓN HERNÁNDEZ ALCERRO.

Hungary: 3910 Shoemaker St, NW, Washington, DC 20008; tel. (202) 362-6730; fax (202) 966-8135; e-mail informacio.was@mfa.gov.hu; internet www.washington.gov.hu; Ambassador GYÖRGY SZAPÁRY.

Iceland: House of Sweden, Suite 509, 2900 K St, NW, Washington, DC 20007-1704; tel. (202) 265-6653; fax (202) 265-6656; e-mail icemb.wash@utn.stjr.is; internet www.iceland.org/us; Ambassador GUDMUNDUR ARNI STEFANSSON.

India: 2107 Massachusetts Ave, NW, Washington, DC 20008; tel. (202) 939-7000; fax (202) 265-4351; e-mail info2@indiagov.org; internet www.indianembassy.org; Ambassador NIRUPAMA RAO.

Indonesia: 2020 Massachusetts Ave, NW, Washington, DC 20036-1084; tel. (202) 775-5200; fax (202) 775-5365; e-mail information@embassyofindonesia.org; internet www.embassyofindonesia.org; Ambassador DINO PATTI DJALAL.

Iran: 'Interests section' in the Embassy of Pakistan, 2209 Wisconsin Ave, NW, Washington, DC 20007; tel. (202) 965-4990; fax (202) 965-1073; e-mail requests@daftar.org; internet www.daftar.org; Dir ALI JAZINI.

Iraq: 3421 Massachusetts Ave, NW, Washington, DC 20007; tel. (202) 742-1600; fax (202) 462-5066; e-mail admin@iraqiembassy.us; internet www.iraqiembassy.us; Ambassador JABIR HABEB HEMAIDAWI.

Ireland: 2234 Massachusetts Ave, NW, Washington, DC 20008; tel. (202) 462-3939; fax (202) 232-5993; e-mail embirlus@aol.com; internet www.embassyofireland.org; Ambassador MICHAEL COLLINS.

Israel: 3514 International Dr., NW, Washington, DC 20008; tel. (202) 364-5500; fax (202) 364-5566; e-mail info@washington.mfa.gov.il; internet www.israelemb.org; Ambassador MICHAEL OREN.

Italy: 3000 Whitehaven St, NW, Washington, DC 20008; tel. (202) 612-4400; fax (202) 518-2151; e-mail stampa.washington@esteri.it; internet www.ambwashingtondc.esteri.it; Ambassador CLAUDIO BISOGNIERO.

Jamaica: 1520 New Hampshire Ave, NW, Washington, DC 20006; tel. (202) 452-0660; fax (202) 452-0036; e-mail dcm@jamaicaembassy.org; internet www.embassyofjamaica.org; Ambassador STEPHEN VASCIANNIE.

Japan: 2520 Massachusetts Ave, NW, Washington, DC 20008-2869; tel. (202) 238-6700; fax (202) 238-2184; e-mail jicc@embjapan.org; internet www.us.emb-japan.go.jp; Ambassador KENICHIRO SASAE.

Jordan: 3504 International Dr., NW, Washington, DC 20008; tel. (202) 966-2664; fax (202) 966-3110; e-mail hkjembassydc@jordanembassyus.org; internet www.jordanembassyus.org; Ambassador ALIA HATOUGH BOURAN.

Kazakhstan: 1401 16th St, NW, Washington, DC 20036; tel. (202) 232-5488; fax (202) 232-5845; e-mail zakh.embusa@verizon.net; internet www.kazakhembus.com; Ambassador KAIRAT UMAROV.

Kenya: 2249 R St, NW, Washington, DC 20008; tel. (202) 387-6101; fax (202) 462-3829; e-mail information@kenyaembassy.com; internet www.kenyaembassy.com; Ambassador ELKANAH ODEMBO ABSALOM.

Korea, Republic: KORUS House, 2370 Massachusetts Ave, NW, Washington, DC 20008; tel. (202) 939-5600; fax (202) 797-0595; e-mail webmaster@dynamic-korea.com; internet www.dynamic-korea.com; Ambassador CHOI YOUNG-JIN.

Kosovo: 1101 30th St, NW, Suite 330/340, Washington, DC 20007; tel. (202) 380-3581; fax (202) 380-3628; e-mail embassy.usa@ks-gov.net; Ambassador AKAN ISMAILI.

Kuwait: 2940 Tilden St, NW, Washington, DC 20008; tel. (202) 966-0702; fax (202) 966-0517; e-mail kio@kuwait-info.org; Ambassador Sheikh SALEM ABDULLAH JABER AS-SABAH.

Kyrgyzstan: 2360 Massachusetts Ave, NW, Washington, DC 20008; tel. (202) 449-9822; fax (202) 386 7550; e-mail consul@kgembassy.org; internet www.kgembassy.org; Ambassador MUKTAR DJUMALIEV.

Laos: 2222 S St, NW, Washington, DC 20008; tel. (202) 332-6416; fax (202) 332-4923; e-mail laoemb@verizon.net; internet www.laoembassy.com; Ambassador SENG SOUKHATHIVONG.

Latvia: 2306 Massachusetts Ave, NW, Washington, DC 20008; tel. (202) 328-2840; fax (202) 328-2860; e-mail embassy.usa@mfa.gov.lv; internet www.latvia-usa.org; Ambassador ANDRIS RAZANS.

Lebanon: 2560 28th St, NW, Washington, DC 20008; tel. (202) 939-6300; fax (202) 939-6324; e-mail info@lebanonembassyus.org; internet www.lebanonembassyus.org; Ambassador ANTOINE CHEDID.

Lesotho: 2511 Massachusetts Ave, NW, Washington, DC 20008; tel. (202) 797-5533; fax (202) 234-6815; e-mail lesothoembassy@verizon.net; internet www.lesothoemb-usa.gov.ls; Ambassador ELIACHIM MOLAPI SEBATANE.

Liberia: 5201 16th St, Washington, DC 20011; tel. (202) 723-0437; fax (202) 723-0436; e-mail info@liberiaemb.org; internet www.embassyofliberia.org; Ambassador JEREMIAH SULUNTEH.

Libya: Liaison Office, 2600 Virginia Ave, NW, Suite 705, Washington, DC 20037; tel. (202) 944-9601; fax (202) 944-9606; e-mail libya@libyanbureaudc.org; internet www.libyanbureaudc.org; Chief of Office ALI SULEIMAN AUJALI.

Liechtenstein: 2900 K St, NW, Suite 602B, Washington, DC 20007; tel. (202) 331-0590; fax (202) 331-3221; e-mail info@embassyli.org; internet www.liechtensteinusa.org; Ambassador CLAUDIA FRITSCHE.

Lithuania: 2622 16th St, NW, Washington, DC 20009; tel. (202) 234-5860; fax (202) 328-0466; e-mail info@ltembassyus.org; internet www.ltembassyus.org; Ambassador ŽYGIMANTAS PAVILIONIS.

Luxembourg: 2200 Massachusetts Ave, NW, Washington, DC 20008; tel. (202) 265-4171; fax (202) 328-8270; e-mail luxembassy.was@mae.etat.lu; internet washington.mae.lu; Ambassador JEAN-LOUIS WOLZFELD.

Macedonia: 2129 Wyoming Ave, NW, Washington, DC 20008; tel. (202) 667-0501; fax (202) 667-2131; e-mail usoffice@macedonianembassy.org; internet www.macedonianembassy.org; Ambassador Dr ZORAN JOLEVSKI.

Madagascar: 2374 Massachusetts Ave, NW, Washington, DC 20008; tel. (202) 265-5525; fax (202) 265-3034; e-mail malagasy.embassy@verizon.net; internet www.madagascar-embassy.org; Chargé d'affaires a.i. VELOTIANA R. RAOBELINA.

Malawi: 1029 Vermont Ave, NW, Suite 1000, Washington, DC 20005; tel. (202) 721-0270; fax (202) 721-0288; e-mail info@malawiembassy-dc.org; internet www.malawiembassy-dc.org; Ambassador STEPHEN DICK TENNYSON MATENJE.

Malaysia: 3516 International Court, NW, Washington, DC 20008; tel. (202) 572-9700; fax (202) 572-9882; e-mail malwashdc@kln.gov.my; internet www.kln.gov.my/web/usa_washington; Ambassador OTHMAN BIN HASHIM.

Maldives: 800 Second Ave, Suite 400E, New York, NY 10017; tel. (212) 599-6195; fax (212) 661-6405; Ambassador AHMED SAREER.

Mali: 2130 R St, NW, Washington, DC 20008; tel. (202) 332-2249; fax (202) 332-6603; e-mail info@maliembassy.us; internet www.maliembassy.us; Ambassador AL MAAMOUN BABA LAMINE KEITA.

Malta: 2017 Connecticut Ave, NW, Washington, DC 20008; tel. (202) 462-3611; fax (202) 387-5470; e-mail maltaembassy.washington@gov.mt; internet www.mfa.gov.mt; Chargé d'affaires a.i. DENNIS GRECH.

Marshall Islands: 2433 Massachusetts Ave, NW, Washington, DC 20008; tel. (202) 234-5414; fax (202) 232-3236; e-mail info@rmiembassyus.org; internet www.rmiembassyus.org; Ambassador CHARLES R. PAUL.

Mauritania: 2129 Leroy Pl., NW, Washington, DC 20008; tel. (202) 232-5700; fax (202) 319-2623; e-mail info@mauritaniaembassy.us; internet mauritaniaembassy.us; Ambassador MOHAMED LEMINE EL HAYCEN.

Mauritius: 1709 N St, NW, Washington, DC 200036; tel. (202) 244-1491; fax (202) 966-0983; e-mail mauritius.embassy@verizon.net; Ambassador SOMDUTH SOBORUN.

Mexico: 1911 Pennsylvania Ave, NW, Washington, DC 20006; tel. (202) 728-1600; fax (202) 728-1698; e-mail mexembusa@sre.gob.mx; internet www.sre.gob.mx/eua; Ambassador EDUARDO MEDINA-MORA.

Micronesia: 1725 N St, NW, Washington, DC 20036; tel. (202) 223-4383; fax (202) 223-4391; e-mail admin@fsmembassydc.org; internet www.fsmembassydc.org; Ambassador ASTERIO TAKESY.

Moldova: 2101 S St, NW, Washington, DC 20008; tel. (202) 667-1130; fax (202) 667-2624; e-mail washington@mfa.md; internet www.sua.mfa.md; Ambassador IGOR MUNTEANU.

Monaco: 3400 International Dr., NW, Suite 2K-100, Washington, DC 20008-3006; tel. (202) 234-1530; fax (202) 244-7656; e-mail embassy@monacodc.org; internet www.monaco-usa.org; Ambassador GILLES ALEXANDRE NOGHÈS.

Mongolia: 2833 M St, NW, Washington, DC 20007; tel. (202) 333-7117; fax (202) 298-9227; e-mail esyam@mongolianembassy.us; internet www.mongolianembassy.us; Ambassador ALTANGEREL BUL-GAAGIIN.

Montenegro: 1610 New Hampshire Ave, NW, Washington, DC 20009; tel. (202) 234 6108; fax (202) 234 6109; e-mail usa@mfa.gov.me; Ambassador SRÐAN DARMANOVIĆ.

Morocco: 1601 21st St, NW, Washington, DC 20009; tel. (202) 462-7979; fax (202) 265-0161; e-mail aafifi@moroccous.com; internet dcusa.themoroccanembassy.com; Ambassador MOHAMED RACHAD BOUHLAL.

Mozambique: 1525 New Hampshire Ave, NW, Washington, DC 20036; tel. (202) 293-7146; fax (202) 835-0245; e-mail embamoc@aol.com; internet www.embamoc-usa.org; Ambassador AMELIA MATOS SUMBANA.

Myanmar: 2300 S St, NW, Washington, DC 20008-4089; tel. (202) 332-3344; fax (202) 332-4351; e-mail pyi.thayar@verizon.net; internet www.mewashingtondc.com; Ambassador THAN SWE.

Namibia: 1605 New Hampshire Ave, NW, Washington, DC 20009; tel. (202) 986-0540; fax (202) 986-0443; e-mail info@namibiaembassyusa.org; internet www.namibianembassyusa.org; Ambassador MARTIN ANDJABA.

Nauru: 800 Second Ave, New York, NY 10017; tel. (212) 937-0074; fax (212) 937-0079; Ambassador MARLENE INEMWIN MOSES.

Nepal: 2131 Leroy Pl., NW, Washington, DC 20008; tel. (202) 667-4550; fax (202) 667-5534; e-mail info@nepalembassyusa.org; internet www.nepalembassyusa.org; Ambassador SHANKAR PRASAD SHARMA.

Netherlands: 4200 Linnean Ave, NW, Washington, DC 20008; tel. (202) 244-5300; fax (202) 362-3430; e-mail was@minbuza.nl; internet www.netherlands-embassy.org; Ambassador RUDOLF SIMON BEKINK.

New Zealand: 37 Observatory Circle, NW, Washington, DC 20008; tel. (202) 328-4800; fax (202) 667-5227; e-mail info@nzemb.org; internet www.nzembassy.com/usa; Ambassador MICHAEL MOORE.

Nicaragua: 1627 New Hampshire Ave, NW, Washington, DC 20009; tel. (202) 939-6570; fax (202) 939-6545; e-mail nicaraguan.embassy@embanic.org; Ambassador FRANCISCO OBADIAH CAMPBELL HOOKER.

Niger: 2204 R St, NW, Washington, DC 20008; tel. (202) 483-4224; fax (202) 483-3169; e-mail infos@embassyofniger.org; internet www.embassyofniger.org; Ambassador MAMAN SAMBO SIDIKOU.

Nigeria: 3519 International Court, NW, Washington, DC 20008; tel. (202) 986-8400; fax (202) 362-6541; e-mail babalola@nigeriaembassyusa.org; internet www.nigeriaembassyusa.org; Ambassador ADEBOWALE IBIBAPO ADEFUYE.

Norway: 2720 34th St, NW, Washington, DC 20008; tel. (202) 333-6000; fax (202) 337-0870; e-mail emb.washington@mfa.no; internet www.norway.org; Ambassador WEGGER CHRISTIAN STRØMMEN.

Oman: 2535 Belmont Rd, NW, Washington, DC 20008; tel. (202) 387-1980; fax (202) 745-4933; e-mail info@omaninfo.us; internet omanembassy.net; Ambassador HUNAINA SULTAN AHMED AL-MUGHAIRY.

Pakistan: 3517 International Court, NW, Washington, DC 20008; tel. (202) 243-6500; fax (202) 686-1534; e-mail info@embassyofpakistanusa.org; internet www.embassyofpakistanusa.org; Ambassador SHERRY RAHMAN.

Palau: 1701 Pennsylvania Ave, NW, Suite 400, Washington, DC 20006; tel. (202) 452-6814; fax (202) 452-6281; e-mail info@palauembassy.com; internet www.palauembassy.com; Ambassador HERSEY KYOTA.

Panama: 2862 McGill Terrace, NW, Washington, DC 20008; tel. (202) 483-1407; fax (202) 483-8413; e-mail info@embassyofpanama.org; internet www.embassyofpanama.org; Ambassador MARIO ERNESTO JARAMILLO CASTILLO.

Papua New Guinea: 1779 Massachusetts Ave, NW, Suite 805, Washington, DC 20036; tel. (202) 745-3680; fax (202) 745-3679; e-mail info@pngembassy.org; internet www.pngembassy.org; Chargé d'affaires a.i. ELIAS RAHUROMO WOHENGU.

Paraguay: 2400 Massachusetts Ave, NW, Washington, DC 20008; tel. (202) 483-6960; fax (202) 234-4508; e-mail secretaria@embaparusa.gov.py; internet www.embaparusa.gov.py; Ambassador FERNANDO ANTONIO PFANNL CABALLERO.

Peru: 1700 Massachusetts Ave, NW, Washington, DC 20036; tel. (202) 833-9860; fax (202) 659-8124; e-mail webadmin@embassyofperu.us; internet www.peruvianembassy.us; Ambassador HAROLD FORSYTH MEJIA.

Philippines: 1600 Massachusetts Ave, NW, Washington, DC 20036-2274; tel. (202) 467-9300; fax (202) 467-9417; e-mail information@philippineembassy-usa.org; internet www.philippineembassy-usa.org; Ambassador JOSÉ CUISIA, Jr.

Poland: 2640 16th St, NW, Washington, DC 20009; tel. (202) 234-3800; fax (202) 328-6271; e-mail polemb.info@earthlink.net; internet www.polandembassy.org; Ambassador RYSZARD SCHNEPF.

Portugal: 2012 Massachusetts Ave, NW, Washington, DC 20036; tel. (202) 350-5400; fax (202) 462-3726; e-mail info@embassyportugal-us.org; Ambassador NUNO FILIPE ALVES SALVADOR E BRITO.

Qatar: 2555 M St, NW, Washington, DC 20037-1305; tel. (202) 274-1600; fax (202) 237-0061; e-mail info@qatarembassy.net; internet www.qatarembassy.net; Ambassador MOHAMED ABDULLAH M. AL-RUMAIHI.

Romania: 1607 23rd St, NW, Washington, DC 20008; tel. (202) 232-4846; fax (202) 232-4748; e-mail office@roembus.org; internet washington.mae.ro; Ambassador ADRIAN COSMIN VIERITA.

Russia: 2650 Wisconsin Ave, NW, Washington, DC 20007; tel. (202) 298-5700; fax (202) 298-5735; e-mail russianembassy@mindspring.com; internet www.russianembassy.org; Ambassador SERGEI I. KISLYAK.

Rwanda: 1714 New Hampshire Ave, NW, Washington, DC 20009; tel. (202) 232-2882; fax (202) 232-4544; e-mail rwandaembassy@rwandaembassy.org; internet www.rwandaembassy.org; Ambassador JAMES KIMONYO.

Saint Christopher and Nevis: 3216 New Mexico Ave, NW, Washington, DC 20016; tel. (202) 686-2636; fax (202) 686-5740; e-mail info@embskn.com; internet www.embassy.gov.kn; Ambassador JACINTH LORNA HENRY-MARTIN.

Saint Lucia: OECS Bldg, 3216 New Mexico Ave, NW, Washington, DC 20016; tel. (202) 364-6792; fax (202) 364-6723; e-mail eofsaintlu@aol.com; Ambassador SONIA MERLYN JOHNNY.

Saint Vincent and the Grenadines: 3216 New Mexico Ave, NW, Washington, DC 20016; tel. (202) 364-6730; fax (202) 364-6736; e-mail mail@embvsg.com; internet www.embvsg.com; Ambassador LA CELIA PRINCE.

Samoa: 800 Second Ave, Suite 400J, New York, NY 10017; tel. (212) 599-6196; fax (212) 599-0797; e-mail samoa@un.int; Ambassador AL'IOAIGA FETURI ELISAIA.

San Marino: 1711 N St, NW, 2nd Floor, Washington, DC 20036; tel. (202) 223-2418; fax (202) 223-2585; e-mail smrassistant@gmail.com; Ambassador PAOLO RONDELLI.

São Tomé and Príncipe: 1211 Connecticut Ave, NW, Suite 300, Washington, DC 20036; tel. (202) 775-2075; fax (202) 775-2077; e-mail stp@un.int; Ambassador (vacant).

Saudi Arabia: 601 New Hampshire Ave, NW, Washington, DC 20037; tel. (202) 342-3800; fax (202) 944-5983; e-mail info@saudiembassy.net; internet www.saudiembassy.net; Ambassador ADEL BIN AHMED AL-JUBEIR.

Senegal: 2112 Wyoming Ave, NW, Washington, DC 20008; tel. (202) 234-0540; fax (202) 332-6315; Ambassador CHEIKH NIANG.

Serbia: 2134 Kalorama Rd, NW, Washington, DC 20008; tel. (202) 332-0333; fax (202) 332-3933; e-mail info@serbiaembusa.org; internet www.serbiaembusa.org; Ambassador VLADIMIR PETROVIĆ.

Seychelles: 800 Second Ave, Suite 900C, New York, NY 10017; tel. (212) 972-1785; fax (212) 972-1786; Ambassador MARIE-LOUISE CECILE POTTER.

Sierra Leone: 1701 19th St, NW, Washington, DC 20009; tel. (202) 939-9261; fax (202) 483-1798; e-mail info@embassyofsierraleone.net; internet www.embassyofsierraleone.net; Ambassador BOCKARI KORTU STEVENS.

Singapore: 3501 International Pl., NW, Washington, DC 20008; tel. (202) 537-3100; fax (202) 537-0876; e-mail singemb_was@sgmfa.gov.sg; internet www.mfa.gov.sg/washington; Ambassador ASHOK KUMAR MIRPURI.

Slovakia: 3523 International Court, NW, Washington, DC 20008; tel. (202) 237-1054; e-mail emb.washington@mzv.sk; internet www.mzv.sk/washington; Ambassador PETER KMEC.

Slovenia: 2410 California St, NW, Washington, DC 20008; tel. (202) 386-6610; fax (202) 386-6633; e-mail vwa@gov.si; internet www.washington.embassy.si; Ambassador ROMAN KIRN.

Solomon Islands: 800 Second Ave, Suite 400L, New York, NY 10017; tel. (212) 599-6192; fax (212) 661-8925; e-mail simny@solomons.com; Ambassador COLIN D. BECK.

South Africa: 3051 Massachusetts Ave, NW, Washington, DC 20008; tel. (202) 232-4400; fax (202) 265-1607; e-mail info@saembassy.org; internet www.saembassy.org; Ambassador EBRAHIM RASOOL.

South Sudan: 1233 20th St, NW, Suite 602, Washington, DC 20036; tel. (202) 293-7940; fax (202) 293-7941; e-mail njgile@gossmission.org; internet www.gossmission.org; Ambassador AKEC KHOC ACIEW KHOC.

Spain: 2375 Pennsylvania Ave, NW, Washington, DC 20037; tel. (202) 452-0100; fax (202) 833-5670; e-mail emb.washington@maec.es; internet www.maec.es/subwebs/embajadas/washington; Ambassador RAMON GIL-CASRES SATRUSTEGUI.

Sri Lanka: 2148 Wyoming Ave, NW, Washington, DC 20008; tel. (202) 483-4025; fax (202) 232-7181; e-mail slembassy@slembassyusa.org; internet www.slembassyusa.org; Ambassador JALIYA WICKRAMASURIYA.

Sudan: 2210 Massachusetts Ave, NW, Washington, DC 20008; tel. (202) 338-8565; fax (202) 667-2406; e-mail info@sudanembassy.org; internet www.sudanembassy.org; Chargé d'affaires a.i. EMAD MIRGHANI ALTOHAMY.

Suriname: 4301 Connecticut Ave, NW, Suite 460, Washington, DC 20008; tel. (202) 244-7488; fax (202) 244-5878; e-mail esuriname@covad.net; internet www.surinameembassy.org; Ambassador SUBHAS MUNGRA.

Swaziland: 1712 New Hampshire Ave, NW, Washington, DC 20009; tel. (202) 234-5002; fax (202) 234-8254; e-mail swaziland@compuserve.com; Ambassador ABEDNIGO MANDLA NTSHANGASE.

Sweden: 2900 K St, NW, Washington, DC 20007; tel. (202) 467-2600; fax (202) 467-2699; e-mail ambassaden.washington@foreign.ministry.se; internet www.swedenabroad.com/washington; Ambassador JONAS HAFSTRÖM.

Switzerland: 2900 Cathedral Ave, NW, Washington, DC 20008; tel. (202) 745-7900; fax (202) 387-2564; e-mail was.vertretung@eda.admin.ch; internet www.swissemb.org; Ambassador MANUEL SAGER.

Syria: 2215 Wyoming Ave, NW, Washington, DC 20008; tel. (202) 232-6316; fax (202) 265-4585; e-mail info@syrembassy.net; internet www.syrianembassy.us; Chargé d'affaires a.i. MOUNIR KOUDMANI.

Tajikistan: 1005 New Hampshire Ave, NW, Washington, DC 20037; tel. (202) 223-6090; fax (202) 223-6091; e-mail tajikistan@verizon.net; internet www.tjus.org; Ambassador NURIDDIN SHAMSOV.

Tanzania: 1232 22nd St, NW, Washington, DC 20037; tel. (202) 939-6125; fax (202) 797-7408; e-mail ubalozi@tanzaniaembassy-us.org; internet www.tanzaniaembassy-us.org; Chargé d'affaires a.i. LILY LETAWO MUNANKA.

Thailand: 1024 Wisconsin Ave, NW, Washington, DC 20007; tel. (202) 944-3600; fax (202) 944-3611; e-mail thaiembdc@thaiembdc.org; internet www.thaiembdc.org; Ambassador CHAIYONG SATJIPANON.

Timor-Leste: 4201 Connecticut Ave, NW, Suite 504, Washington, DC 20008; tel. (202) 966-3202; fax (202) 966-3205; e-mail info@timorlesteembassy.org; internet www.timorlesteembassy.org; Ambassador CONSTÂNCIO DA CONCEIÇÃO PINTO.

Togo: 2208 Massachusetts Ave, NW, Washington, DC 20008; tel. (202) 234-4212; fax (202) 232-3190; e-mail info@togoembassy.us; internet www.togoembassy.us; Ambassador LIMBIYE EDAWE KADANGHA BARIKI.

Tonga: 250 East 51st St, New York, NY 10022; tel. (917) 369-1025; fax (917) 369-1024; Ambassador SONATANE TU'AKINAMOLAHI TAUMOEPEAU TUPOU.

Trinidad and Tobago: 1708 Massachusetts Ave, NW, Washington, DC 20036; tel. (202) 467-6490; fax (202) 785-3130; e-mail embttgo@erols.com; internet www.bordeglobal.com/ttembassy; Ambassador Dr NEIL PARSON.

Tunisia: 1515 Massachusetts Ave, NW, Washington, DC 20005; tel. (202) 862-1850; fax (202) 862-1858; internet www.tunconsusa.org; Ambassador MOKHTAR CHAOUACHI.

Turkey: 2525 Massachusetts Ave, NW, Washington, DC 20008; tel. (202) 612-6700; fax (202) 612-6744; e-mail contact@turkishembassy.org; internet www.washington.emb.mfa.gov.tr; Ambassador NAMIK TAN.

Turkmenistan: 2207 Massachusetts Ave, NW, Washington, DC 20008; tel. (202) 588-1500; fax (202) 280-1003; e-mail turkmen@mindspring.com; internet www.turkmenistanembassy.org; Ambassador MERET B. ORAZOV.

Tuvalu: 800 Second Ave, Suite 400D, New York, NY 10017; tel. (212) 490-0534; fax (212) 937-0692; e-mail tuvalu@onecommonwealth.org; Ambassador AUNESE MAKOI SIMATI.

Uganda: 5911 16th St, NW, Washington, DC 20011; tel. (202) 726-7100; fax (202) 726-1727; e-mail info@ugandaembassyus.org; internet www.ugandaembassy.com; Chargé d'affaires a.i. ALFRED NNAM.

Ukraine: 3350 M St, NW, Washington, DC 20007; tel. (202) 333-0606; fax (202) 333-0817; e-mail mail@ukremb.com; internet www.mfa.gov.ua/usa; Ambassador OLEKSANDR MOTSYK.

United Arab Emirates: 3522 International Court, NW, Suite 400, Washington, DC 20008; tel. (202) 243-2400; fax (202) 243-2432; e-mail info@uaeembassy-usa.org; internet www.uae-embassy.org; Ambassador YOUSEF AL OTAIBA.

United Kingdom: 3100 Massachusetts Ave, NW, Washington, DC 20008; tel. (202) 588-6500; fax (202) 588-7850; e-mail britishembassyenquiries@gmail.com; internet ukinusa.fco.gov.uk; Ambassador Sir PETER JOHN WESTMACOTT.

Uruguay: 1913 Eye St, NW, Washington, DC 20006; tel. (202) 331-1313; fax (202) 331-8142; e-mail uruwashi@uruwashi.org; internet www.uruwashi.org; Ambassador JUAN CARLOS PITA ALVARIZA.

Uzbekistan: 1746 Massachusetts Ave, NW, Washington, DC 20036-1903; tel. (202) 887-5300; fax (202) 293-6804; e-mail info@uzbekistan.org; internet www.uzbekistan.org; Ambassador ILHOMJON T. NEMATOV.

Venezuela: 1099 30th St, NW, Washington, DC 20007; tel. (202) 342-2214; fax (202) 342-6820; e-mail despacho@venezuela-us.org; internet www.embavenez-us.org; Chargé d'affaires a.i. ANGELO AGUSTIN RIVERO SANTOS.

Viet Nam: 1233 20th St, NW, Suite 400, Washington, DC 20036; tel. (202) 861-0737; fax (202) 861-0917; e-mail info@vietnamembassy.us; internet www.vietnamembassy-usa.org; Ambassador NGUYEN QUOC CUONG.

Yemen: 2319 Wyoming Ave, NW, Washington, DC 20008; tel. (202) 965-4760; fax (202) 337-2017; e-mail information@yemenembassy.org; internet www.yemenembassy.org; Chargé d'affaires a.i. ADEL ALI AHMED SUNAINI.

Zambia: 2419 Massachusetts Ave, NW, Washington, DC 20008; tel. (202) 265-9717; fax (202) 332-0826; e-mail embzambia@aol.com; internet www.zambiaembassy.org; Ambassador PALAN MULONDA.

Zimbabwe: 1608 New Hampshire Ave, NW, Washington, DC 20009; tel. (202) 332-7100; fax (202) 483-9326; e-mail info33@zimbabwe-embassy.us; internet www.zimbabwe-embassy.us; Ambassador Dr MACHIVENYIKA TOBIAS MAPURANGA.

Judicial System

The Supreme Court is the only Federal Court established by the Constitution. It is the highest court in the nation, comprising a Chief Justice and eight Associate Justices. The Supreme Court has discretionary appellate jurisdiction over disputes concerning the Constitution or federal law.

The USA is divided into 94 federal judicial districts, with at least one district in each state. The 94 districts are organized into 12 judicial circuits, in each of which there is one Court of Appeals. The Court of Appeals for the Federal Circuit has nation-wide specialized jurisdiction. Federal Courts hear cases involving federal law, cases involving participants from more than one state, cases involving crimes committed in more than one state, and civil or corporate cases that cross state lines. Federal District Courts are the courts of first instance for most federal suits.

Each state has a judicial system structured similarly to the Federal system, with a Supreme Court and subsidiary courts, to deal with cases arising under State Law. These courts have jurisdiction in most criminal and civil actions. Each state has its own bar association of lawyers and its own legal code.

Supreme Court of the United States
Supreme Court Bldg, 1 First St, NE, Washington, DC 20543; tel. (202) 479-3000; fax (202) 479-2971; internet www.supremecourtus.gov.

Appointments, which are for life or until voluntary retirement, are made by the President, subject to confirmation by the US Senate.

Chief Justice: JOHN G. ROBERTS, Jr (appointed 2005).

Associate Justices: ANTONIN SCALIA (1986), ANTHONY M. KENNEDY (1988), CLARENCE THOMAS (1991), RUTH BADER GINSBURG (1993), STEPHEN G. BREYER (1994), SAMUEL A. ALITO, Jr (2006), SONIA SOTOMAYOR (2009), ELENA KAGAN (2010).

United States Courts of Appeal
Administrative Office of the US Courts, Washington, DC 20544; tel. (202) 502-2600; internet www.uscourts.gov.

Federal Circuit: RANDALL RAY RADER (Chief Judge).

District of Columbia Circuit: DAVID B. SENTELLE (Chief Judge).

First Circuit (Maine, Massachusetts, New Hampshire, Rhode Island, Puerto Rico): SANDRA L. LYNCH (Chief Judge).

Second Circuit (Connecticut, New York, Vermont): DENNIS JACOBS (Chief Judge).

Third Circuit (Delaware, New Jersey, Pennsylvania, Virgin Islands): THEODORE A. MCKEE (Chief Judge).

Fourth Circuit (Maryland, North Carolina, South Carolina, Virginia, West Virginia): WILLIAM B. TRAXLER, Jr (Chief Judge).

Fifth Circuit (Louisiana, Mississippi, Texas): SUSAN M. CHEHARDY (Chief Judge).

Sixth Circuit (Kentucky, Michigan, Ohio, Tennessee): ALICE M. BATCHELDER (Chief Judge).

Seventh Circuit (Illinois, Indiana, Wisconsin): FRANK H. EASTERBROOK (Chief Judge).

Eighth Circuit (Arkansas, Iowa, Minnesota, Missouri, Nebraska, North Dakota, South Dakota): WILLIAM J. RILEY (Chief Judge).

Ninth Circuit (Alaska, Arizona, California, Guam, Hawaii, Idaho, Montana, Nevada, Northern Mariana Islands, Oregon, Washington): ALEX KOZINSKI (Chief Judge).

Tenth Circuit (Colorado, Kansas, New Mexico, Oklahoma, Utah, Wyoming): MARY BECK BRISCOE (Chief Judge).

Eleventh Circuit (Alabama, Florida, Georgia): JOEL F. DUBINA (Chief Judge).

FEDERAL COURTS OF SPECIAL JURISDICTION

United States Court of Federal Claims: 717 Madison Pl., NW, Washington, DC 20005; tel. (202) 357-6400; internet www.uscfc.uscourts.gov; f. 1982 as the United States Claims Court to succeed the original Court of Claims; renamed as above in 1992; primarily, has jurisdiction over financial claims against the Federal Government in excess of US $10,000; Chief Judge EMILY C. HEWITT.

United States Court of International Trade: 1 Federal Plaza, New York, NY 10278-0001; tel. (212) 264-2800; fax (212) 264-1085; internet www.cit.uscourts.gov; f. 1980 to succeed the United States Customs Court; has jurisdiction over civil disputes arising from US customs and international trade laws; Chief Judge DONALD C. POGUE.

United States Tax Court: 400 Second St, NW, Washington, DC 20217; tel. (202) 521-0700; internet www.ustaxcourt.gov; jurisdiction over Federal tax disputes; Chief Judge MICHAEL B. THORNTON.

Religion

Christianity is the predominant religion. The largest single denomination is the Roman Catholic Church. Other major groups in terms of membership are the Baptist, Methodist, Lutheran and Orthodox churches. Numerous other beliefs are represented, the largest in terms of adherents being Judaism, Islam and Buddhism.

CHRISTIANITY

National Council of the Churches of Christ in the USA: 475 Riverside Dr., Suite 880, New York, NY 10115-0050; tel. (212) 870-2025; fax (212) 870-3112; e-mail webmaster@ncccusa.org; internet www.ncccusa.org; f. 1950; an ecumenical org. of 35 Protestant and Orthodox denominations, representing 100,000 congregations of c. 45m. mems; Pres. Rev. PEG CHEMBERLIN; Gen. Sec. Rev. Dr MICHAEL KINNAMON.

The Anglican Communion

The Episcopal Church in the USA: 815 Second Ave, New York, NY 10017; tel. (212) 716-6000; fax (212) 697-5892; e-mail pboffice@episcopalchurch.org; internet www.episcopalchurch.org; f. 1607; mem. of the Worldwide Anglican Communion and World Council of Churches; 7,200 parishes and missions; 2.4m. mems (2008); Presiding Bishop Most Rev. KATHARINE JEFFERTS SCHORI; Exec. Officer and Sec. Rev. Dr GREGORY S. STRAUB.

The Baptist Church

In 2008 there were an estimated 36.1m. Baptists in the USA.

American Baptist Association (ABA): 4605 North State Line Ave, Texarkana, TX 75503; tel. (903) 792-2783; fax (903) 792-8128; e-mail bssc@abaptist.org; internet www.abaptist.org; f. 1905; 1,867 churches; 280,973 mems (2000); Pres. JAMES A. CRAIN.

American Baptist Churches in the USA (ABCUSA): POB 851, Valley Forge, PA 19482-0851; 588 North Gulph Rd, King of Prussia, PA 19406; tel. (610) 768-2000; fax (610) 768-2275; e-mail cathy.brubaker@abc-usa.org; internet www.abc-usa.org; f. 1907; mem. of the World Council of Churches; 5,283 churches (2011); 1.3m. mems (2011); Gen. Sec. Rev. Dr A. ROY MEDLEY.

Conservative Baptist Association of America: 3686 Stagecoach Rd, Unit F, Longmont, CO 80504-5660; tel. (303) 827-3583; fax (303) 317-8147; e-mail info@cbamerica.org; internet www.cbamerica.org; f. 1947; 1,200 churches; 200,000 mems; Nat. Network Facilitator Rev. STAN RIEB.

General Association of Regular Baptist Churches (GARBC): 1300 North Meacham Rd, Schaumburg, IL 60173-4806; tel. (888) 588-1600; fax (847) 843-3757; internet www.garbc.org; 1,330 churches; 245,636 mems (2000); Nat. Rep. Rev. JOHN GREENING.

National Baptist Convention, USA: 1700 Baptist World Center Dr., Nashville, TN 37207; tel. (615) 228-6292; fax (615) 262-3917; e-mail president@nationalbaptist.com; internet www.nationalbaptist.com; f. 1880; mem. of the World Council of Churches; 9,000 churches; 5.0m. mems; Pres. Dr JULIUS R. SCRUGGS; Gen. Sec. Dr CALVIN McKINNEY.

Southern Baptist Convention (SBC): 901 Commerce St, Nashville, TN 37203-3629; tel. (615) 244-2355; fax (615) 782-8684; e-mail cr@sbc.net; internet www.sbc.net; f. 1845; 45,727 churches; 16.1m. mems (2010); Pres. and CEO Dr FRANK S. PAGE.

The Lutheran Church

In 2008 there were an estimated 8.7m. Lutherans in the USA.

Association of Free Lutheran Congregations: 3110 E Medicine Lake Blvd, Plymouth MN 55441; tel. (763) 545-5631; fax (763) 545-0079; e-mail president@aflc.org; internet www.aflc.org; 44,500 mems (2010); Pres. Rev. ELDEN NELSON.

Evangelical Lutheran Church in America: 8765 West Higgins Rd, Chicago, IL 60631; tel. (773) 380-2700; fax (773) 380-1465; e-mail bishop@elca.org; internet www.elca.org; f. 1988; mem. of the World Council of Churches; 10,448 churches; 4.5m. mems (2010); Presiding Bishop Rev. MARK STEPHEN HANSON; Sec. DAVID D. SWARTLING.

Lutheran Church—Missouri Synod: 1333 South Kirkwood Rd, St Louis, MO 63122-7295; tel. (314) 965-9000; fax (314) 822-8307; e-mail president@lcms.org; internet www.lcms.org; f. 1847; 6,150 churches; 2.4m. mems (2010); Pres. Dr MATTHEW C. HARRISON; Sec. Dr RAYMOND HARTWIG.

Wisconsin Evangelical Lutheran Synod: 2929 N Mayfair Rd, Milwaukee, WI 53222; tel. (414) 256-3888; fax (414) 256-3899; e-mail mark.schroeder@sab.wels.net; internet www.wels.net; 389,545 mems (2010); Pres. Rev. MARK SCHROEDER.

The Methodist Church

In 2008 there were an estimated 11.4m. Methodists and Wesleyans in the USA.

African Methodist Episcopal Church (AMEC): 500 Eighth Ave South, Nashville, TN 37203; tel. (615) 254-0911; fax (615) 254-0912; e-mail cio@ame-church.com; internet www.ame-church.com; f. 1816; mem. of the Churches Uniting in Christ and World Council of Churches; 4,174 churches; 2.5m. mems (1999); Gen. Sec. Dr JEFFERY B. COOPER.

African Methodist Episcopal Zion Church: 3225 Sugar Creek Rd, POB 32843, Charlotte, NC 28269; tel. (704) 599-4630; e-mail admin@amez.org; internet www.amez.org; f. 1796; mem. of the Churches Uniting in Christ; 3,236 churches; 1.4m. mems (2003); Gen. Sec. Rev. Dr W. ROBERT JOHNSON, III.

United Methodist Church: POB 320, Nashville, TN 37202; e-mail umc@umcom.org; internet www.umc.org; f. 1968; mem. of the Churches Uniting in Christ and World Council of Churches; 34,892 churches; 8.2m. mems (2003); President of Council of Bishops Bishop LARRY M. GOODPASTER; Exec. Sec. NEIL IRONS.

The Orthodox Churches

Members of Eastern Orthodox churches numbered an estimated 824,000 in 2008.

Antiochian Orthodox Christian Archdiocese of North America (Greek Orthodox Patriarchate of Antioch and all the East): 358 Mountain Rd, POB 5238, Englewood, NJ 07631-5238; tel. (201) 871-1355; fax (201) 871-7954; e-mail archdiocese@antiochian.org; internet www.antiochian.org; f. 1895; mem. of the World Council of Churches; 210 churches; 82,374 mems (2000); Primate Metropolitan PHILIP (Saliba); Auxiliaries Bishop ANTOUN (Khouri), Bishop BASIL (Essey), Bishop JOSEPH (Zehlaoui), Bishop ALEXANDER (Mufarrij), Bishop JOHN (Abdalah), Bishop ANTHONY (Michaels), Bishop NICHOLAS.

Armenian Apostolic Church of America: *Eastern Prelacy:* 138 East 39th St, New York, NY 10016; tel. (212) 689-7810; fax (212) 689-7168; e-mail email@armenianprelacy.org; internet www.armenianprelacy.org; *Western Prelacy:* 6252 Honolulu Ave, Suite 100, La Crescenta, CA 91214; tel. (818) 248-7737; fax (818) 248-7745; e-mail prelacy@aol.com; internet www.westernprelacy.org; f. 1887; mem. of the World Council of Churches; 38 churches; 23,200 mems (2000); Prelate (Eastern Prelacy) Archbishop OSHAGAN CHOLOYAN; Prelate (Western Prelacy) Archbishop MOUSHEGH MARDIROSIAN.

Armenian Church of America: *Eastern Diocese:* 630 Second Ave, New York, NY 10016; tel. (212) 686-0710; fax (212) 779-3558; e-mail primate@armenianchurch.net; internet www.armenianchurch.net; *Western Diocese:* 3325 North Glenoaks Blvd, Burbank, CA 91504; tel. (818) 558-7474; fax (818) 558-6333; e-mail info@armenianchurchwd.com; internet www.armenianchurchwd.com; f. 1889; mem. of the World Council of Churches; 89 churches; 45,800 mems (2000); Primate (Eastern Diocese) Archbishop KHAJAG BARSAMIAN; Primate (Western Diocese) Archbishop HOVNAN DERDERIAN.

Greek Orthodox Archdiocese of America: 8–10 East 79th St, New York, NY 10075; tel. (212) 570-3500; fax (212) 774-0251; e-mail archdiocese@goarch.org; internet www.goarch.org; f. 1921 as Greek Orthodox Archdiocese of North and South America; mem. of the World Council of Churches; 540 churches; 1.5m. mems (2008); Primate Archbishop DEMETRIOS; Chancellor Bishop ANDONIOS (of Phasiane).

Orthodox Church in America: POB 675, Syosset, NY 11791-0675; tel. (516) 922-0550; fax (516) 922-0954; e-mail info@oca.org; internet www.oca.org; f. 1794; fmrly Russian Orthodox Greek Catholic Church of North America; mem. of the World Council of Churches; 750 churches; 103,000 mems (2009); Primate Metropolitan JONAH; Chancellor Archpriest JOHN JILLIONS.

The Albanian, Bulgarian, Coptic, Romanian, Russian, Serbian, Syrian and Ukrainian Orthodox Churches are also represented.

The Presbyterian Church

In 2008 there were an estimated 4.7m. adherents of Presbyterian Churches.

Presbyterian Church in America: 1700 North Brown Rd, Lawrenceville, GA 30043-8143; tel. (678) 825-1000; fax (678) 825-1001; e-mail ac@pcanet.org; internet www.pcanet.org; f. 1973; 1,455 churches (2010); 300,000 mems; Moderator HARRY L. REEDER, III; Stated Clerk Dr L. ROY TAYLOR.

Presbyterian Church (USA): 100 Witherspoon St, Louisville, KY 40202-1396; tel. (502) 569-5000; fax (502) 569-8080; e-mail presbytel@pcusa.org; internet www.pcusa.org; f. 1983; mem. of the Churches Uniting in Christ and World Council of Churches; 11,100 churches; 2.4m. mems (2007); Moderator NEAL PRESA; Stated Clerk GRADYE PARSONS.

The Roman Catholic Church

In 2008 there were 194 dioceses, including 34 archdioceses, with some 57.2m. members.

United States Conference of Catholic Bishops: 3211 Fourth St, NE, Washington, DC 20017-1194; tel. (202) 541-3000; fax (202) 541-3322; internet www.usccb.org; f. 2001 by merger of the Nat. Conference of Catholic Bishops (f. 1966) and US Catholic Conference (f. 1966); Pres. Most Rev. TIMOTHY M. DOLAN (Archbishop of New York); Gen. Sec. Rev. Mgr RONNY E. JENKINS.

Archbishops

Anchorage: ROGER L. SCHWIETZ.
Atlanta: WILTON D. GREGORY.
Baltimore: WILLIAM EDWARD LORI.
Boston: Cardinal SÉAN PATRICK O'MALLEY.
Chicago: Cardinal FRANCIS E. GEORGE.
Cincinnati: DENNIS M. SCHNURR.
Denver: SAMUEL J. AQUILA.
Detroit: ALLEN HENRY VIGNERON.
Dubuque: JEROME G. HANUS.
Galveston-Houston: Cardinal DANIEL N. DiNARDO.
Hartford: HENRY J. MANSELL.
Indianapolis: (vacant).
Kansas City in Kansas: JOSEPH F. NAUMAN.
Los Angeles: Cardinal JOSÉ HORACIO GÓMEZ.
Louisville: JOSEPH E. KURTZ.
Miami: THOMAS WENSKI.
Milwaukee: JEROME E. LISTECKI.
Mobile: THOMAS JOHN RODI.
Newark: JOHN JOSEPH MYERS.
New Orleans: GREGORY M. AYMOND.
New York: TIMOTHY M. DOLAN.
Oklahoma City: PAUL STAGG COAKLEY.
Omaha: GEORGE J. LUCAS.
Philadelphia: Cardinal CHARLES J. CHAPUT, STEFAN SOROKA (Ukrainian, Byzantine Rite).
Pittsburgh: WILLIAM CHARLES SKURLA.
Portland in Oregon: JOHN G. VLAZNY.

Saint Louis: ROBERT J. CARLSON.
Saint Paul and Minneapolis: JOHN CLAYTON NIENSTEDT.
San Antonio: GUSTAVO GARCÍA-SILLER.
San Francisco: SALVATORE J. CORDILEONE.
Santa Fe: MICHAEL J. SHEEHAN.
Seattle: JAMES PETER SARTAIN.
Washington: Cardinal DONALD W. WUERL.

Other Christian Churches

Assemblies of God: The General Council, 1445 North Boonville Ave, Springfield, MO 65802-1894; tel. (417) 862-2781; fax (417) 862-0133; e-mail generalsecretary@ag.org; internet www.ag.org; f. 1914; 810,000 mems in 2008; Gen. Supt GEORGE O. WOOD; Gen. Sec. JAMES T. BRADFORD.

Christian Church (Disciples of Christ) in the USA and Canada: 130 East Washington St, POB 1986, Indianapolis, IN 46206-1986; tel. (317) 635-3100; fax (317) 635-3700; e-mail news@cm.disciples.org; internet www.disciples.org; f. 1804; 3,754 congregations (2008); 691,160 mems (2008); mem. of the Churches Uniting in Christ and World Council of Churches; Gen. Minister and Pres. Rev. Dr SHARON E. WATKINS.

Christian Reformed Church in North America: 2850 Kalamazoo Ave, SE, Grand Rapids, MI 49560; tel. (616) 241-1691; fax (616) 224-0803; e-mail crcna@crcna.org; internet www.crcna.org; f. 1857; Calvinist; 1,084 churches (2011); 255,700 mems (2011) (USA and Canada); Exec. Dir JOEL BOOT (interim).

Church of Christ: POB 472, Independence, MO 64051-0472; tel. (816) 833-3995; fax (816) 833-0210; e-mail cofctl@sbcglobal.net; internet www.churchofchrist-tl.org; f. 1830; Sec. Council of Apostles DUANE E. ELY; Gen. Church Sec. HARVEY E. SEIBEL.

Church of Christ, Scientist: 210 Massachusetts Ave, Boston, MA 02115; tel. (617) 450-2000; fax (617) 450-3554; e-mail info@churchofchristscientist.org; internet www.tfccs.com; f. 1879; 2,400 congregations world-wide; Pres. CHET MANCHESTER.

Church of God in Christ: Mason Temple, 930 Mason St, Memphis, TN 38126; tel. (901) 947-9300; fax (901) 947-9327; e-mail laity@cogic.org; internet www.cogic.org; f. 1907; 15,300 churches; 5.5m. mems (1991); Presiding Bishop CHARLES EDWARD BLAKE, Sr.

Church of Jesus Christ of Latter-day Saints (Mormon): 50 East North Temple, Salt Lake City, UT 84150; tel. (801) 240-1000; fax (801) 240-2033; internet www.lds.org; f. 1830; 12,112 wards and brs (congregations) in USA; c. 3.2m. mems in USA (2008); Pres THOMAS S. MONSON, HENRY B. EYRING, DIETER F. UCHTDORF.

Church of the Nazarene: 17001 Prairie Star Parkway, Lenexa, KS 66220; tel. (913) 577-0500; fax (913) 577-0848; e-mail gensec@nazarene.org; internet www.nazarene.org; f. 1908; 28,130 congregations; 2.1m. mems (2012); Gen. Sec. DAVID P. WILSON.

Friends United Meeting: 101 Quaker Hill Dr., Richmond, IN 47374-1980; tel. (765) 962-7573; fax (765) 966-1293; e-mail info@fum.org; internet www.fum.org; f. 1902; Quaker; mem. of the World Council of Churches; 44,000 mems (USA and Canada); Gen. Sec. COLIN SAXTON.

Jehovah's Witnesses: 25 Columbia Heights, Brooklyn, NY 11201-2483; tel. (718) 560-5000; internet www.jw.org; f. 1879; 12,494 congregations; c. 1.9m. mems (2008); Pres. DAN ADAMS.

Mariavite Old Catholic Church—Province of North America: 2803 10th St, Wyandotte, MI 48192-4994; tel. and fax (734) 281-3082; e-mail mariaviteocc@hotmail.com; f. 1930; 158 churches; 356,920 mems; Prime Bishop Most Rev. Archbishop MICHAŁ MARIA LUDWIK JABŁOŃSKI.

Reformed Church in America: 475 Riverside Dr., 18th Floor, New York, NY 10115; tel. (212) 870-3071; fax (212) 870-2499; e-mail questions@rca.org; internet www.rca.org; f. 1628; Calvinist; mem. of the World Council of Churches; 1,000 churches (USA and Canada); 170,000 mems; Pres. TOM SMITH; Gen. Sec. TOM DeVRIES.

Seventh-day Adventists: 12501 Old Columbia Pike, Silver Spring, MD 20904-6600; tel. (301) 680-6400; fax (301) 680-6464; e-mail info@nad.adventist.org; internet www.nadadventist.org; f. 1863; 5,413 churches; 938,000 mems in 2008; Pres. DANIEL R. JACKSON; Sec. G. ALEXANDER BRYANT.

United Church of Christ: 700 Prospect Ave, Cleveland, OH 44115; tel. (216) 736-2100; fax (216) 736-2103; e-mail guessb@ucc.org; internet www.ucc.org; f. 1957; mem. of the Churches Uniting in Christ and World Council of Churches; 5,633 churches; 736,000 mems in 2007; Gen. Minister and Pres. Rev. GEOFFREY A. BLACK.

United Pentecostal Church International (UPCI): 8855 Dunn Rd, Hazelwood, MO 63042; tel. (314) 837-7300; fax (314) 837-7304; e-mail info@upci.org; internet www.upci.org; f. 1945 by merger of the Pentecostal Church, Inc, and Pentecostal Assemblies of Jesus Christ; 4,358 churches (USA and Canada); c. 600,000 mems; Gen. Supt Rev. Dr DAVID K. BERNARD; Gen. Sec. JERRY JONES.

BAHÁ'Í FAITH

At October 2010 there were an estimated 168,647 adherents of the Bahá'í faith in the mainland USA.

National Spiritual Assembly of Bahá'ís of the United States: Public Affairs Office, 1320 19th St, NW, Suite 701, Washington, DC 20036; tel. (202) 833-8990; fax (202) 833-8988; e-mail BahaisUS@usbnc.org; internet www.bahai.us; f. 1844 in Persia (Iran); Chair. ROBERT HENDERSON; Sec. KENNETH E. BOWERS.

BUDDHISM

In 2008 there were an estimated 1.2m. Buddhists in the USA.

Buddhist Association of the United States (BAUS): Chuang Yen Monastery, 2020 Route 301, Carmel, NY 10512; tel. (845) 225-1445; fax (845) 225-1485; internet www.baus.org; f. 1964; Pres. Ven. JI-XING.

Buddhist Churches of America (BCA): 1710 Octavia St, San Francisco, CA 94109; tel. (415) 776-5600; fax (415) 771-6293; e-mail bcahq@pacbell.net; internet buddhistchurchesofamerica.org; f. 1899; Hongwanji-ha Jodo Shinshu denomination; over 60 ind. temples; 16,000 mems (2011); Bishop Rev. KODO UMEZU; Pres. RON MURAKAMI.

HINDUISM

In 2008 there were an estimated 582,000 Hindus in the USA.

Ramakrishna-Vivekananda Center: 17 East 94th St, New York, NY 10128; tel. (212) 534-9445; fax (212) 828-1618; e-mail rvcenternewyork@gmail.com; internet www.ramakrishna.org; f. 1933; teachings based on the system of Vedanta; Minister and Spiritual Leader SWAMI YUKTATMANANDA.

ISLAM

In 2008 there were an estimated 1.5m. Muslims in the USA.

Council of Masajid of United States (CMUS): 213 Patriots Path, Edison, NJ 08817; tel. (732) 985-3304; fax (732) 572-0486; e-mail dawud11@comcast.net; f. 1978; educational agency representing 650 local groups; Pres. DAWUD ASSAD.

Islamic Center of New York: 1711 Third Ave, New York, NY 10029-7303; tel. (212) 722-5234; fax (212) 722-5936; internet www.icnyu.org; f. 1966; Dir KHALID LATIF.

Islamic Information Center: 529 14th St, Suite 1292, Washington, DC 20045; tel. (202) 347-6405; fax (202) 347-6406; internet www.islamicinformationcenter.org; f. 2002; provides accurate information on Islam to Muslims and non-Muslims; Chair. Imam SYED NAQVI.

JUDAISM

In 2008 there were an estimated 6.5m. Jews in North America.

American Jewish Congress: 115 East 57 St, Suite 11, New York, NY 10022; tel. (212) 879-4500; fax (212) 758-1633; e-mail contact@ajcongress.org; internet www.ajcongress.org; f. 1918; 50,000 mems; Pres. JACK ROSEN; Chair. RICHARD S. GORDON.

Central Conference of American Rabbis: 355 Lexington Ave, New York, NY 10017; tel. (212) 972-3636; fax (212) 692-0819; e-mail info@ccarnet.org; internet www.ccarnet.org; f. 1889; organized rabbinate of Reform Judaism; 1,840 mems; Pres. Rabbi JONATHAN STEIN.

The Rabbinical Assembly: 3080 Broadway, New York, NY 10027; tel. (212) 280-6000; fax (212) 749-9166; e-mail info@rabbinicalassembly.org; internet www.rabbinicalassembly.org; f. 1901; 1,700 mems; Exec. Vice-Pres. Rabbi JULIE SCHONFELD.

Union of Orthodox Jewish Congregations of America: 11 Broadway, New York, NY 10004; tel. (212) 563-4000; fax (212) 564-9058; e-mail info@ou.org; internet www.ou.org; f. 1898; 1,000 affiliated congregations representing c. 1.0m. mems; Chair. STEPHEN J. SAVITSKY; Exec. Vice-Pres. Rabbi STEVEN WEIL.

Union for Reform Judaism: 633 Third Ave, New York, NY 10017-6778; tel. (212) 650-4000; fax (212) 650-4169; e-mail urj@urj.org; internet urj.org; f. 1873 as the Union of American Hebrew Congregations; present name adopted 2003; more than 900 affiliated congregations representing c. 1.5m. mems; Pres. Rabbi RICK JACOBS; Sr Vice-Pres. Rabbi DANIEL FREELANDER.

United Synagogue of Conservative Judaism: 820 Second Ave, New York, NY 10017-4504; tel. (212) 533-7800; fax (212) 353-9439; e-mail info@uscj.org; internet www.uscj.org; f. 1913; c. 700 affiliated congregations in North America representing c. 1.5m. mems; Pres. RICHARD SKOLNIK; Sec. RICHARD HELFAND.

SIKHISM

In the mid-2000s there were an estimated 200,000 Sikhs in the USA.

Sikh Information Centre: POB 392, Lathrop, CA 95330; e-mail info@sikhinformationcentre.org; internet www.sikhinformationcentre.org.

The Press

In 2012, according to the Audit Bureau of Circulations, 22 daily newspapers had circulations (Mon.–Fri.) of over 250,000 print copies (excluding branded editions). Among the largest of these, in order of daily circulation (Mon.–Fri.), were *The Wall Street Journal, USA Today, New York Times, Los Angeles Times, New York Daily News, San Jose Mercury News, New York Post, Washington Post, Chicago Sun-Times* and *Chicago Tribune*.

In 2011, according to the Newspaper Association of America (NAA), there were 1,382 daily newspapers, with a total circulation of 44.4m. copies per day. The Sunday edition is an important feature of US newspaper publishing. In 2011 there were 900 Sunday newspapers, with a total circulation of some 48.5m. In 2008 there were 6,253 weekly newspapers.

PRINCIPAL NEWSPAPER GROUPS

Advance Publications, Inc: 950 Fingerboard Rd, Staten Island, NY 10305-1453; tel. (212) 286-2860; fax (718) 981-1456; internet www.advance.net; Chair. and CEO SAMUEL I. (SI) NEWHOUSE, Jr; Pres. DONALD E. NEWHOUSE; interests in cable television and internet news websites; owns Condé Nast Publications, Parade Publications, Fairchild Publications and American City Business Journals, among others.

American Community Newspapers (ACN): 14875 Landmark Blvd, Suite 110, Dallas, TX 75254; tel. (972) 628-4080; fax (972) 801-3203; e-mail scarr@acnpapers.com; CEO and Pres. DICK FRANKS; 100 publs (86 newspapers, incl. the Sun Newspapers group, and 14 speciality publs); combined circ. c. 1.4m.

Block Communications, Inc (BCI): 405 Madison Ave, Suite 2100, Toledo, OH 43604; tel. (419) 724-6212; fax (419) 724-6167; e-mail info@blockcommunications.com; internet www.blockcommunications.com; f. 1900; Chair. ALLAN J. BLOCK; 2 daily newspapers, *The Pittsburgh Post-Gazette* and *The Toledo Blade*; also owns 2 cable cos, 5 television stations and a telephone co; interests in security, cable construction and advertising.

The Copley Press, Inc: 7776 Ivanhoe Ave, La Jolla, CA 92037; tel. (858) 454-0411; fax (858) 729-7629; internet www.copleynewspapers.com; f. 1928; Chair., Pres. and CEO DAVID C. COPLEY; 9 daily newspapers, incl. *The San Diego Union-Tribune*, 8 weekly newspapers and 1 bi-weekly newspaper; owns the Copley News Service syndicate (f. 1955).

Cox Media Group: 6205 Peachtree Dunwoody Rd, Atlanta, GA 30328; tel. (678) 645-0000; fax (678) 645-5002; e-mail brian.cooper@coxinc.com; internet www.coxmediagroup.com; f. 1898; Pres. DOUG FRANKLIN; 8 daily newspapers, incl. *The Atlanta Journal-Constitution*, and 16 weekly newspapers; combined weekday circ. 1.2m., combined Sun. circ. 1.6m.; also owns 15 broadcast television stations, 1 local cable channel, 86 radio stations and more than 100 digital services.

Dow Jones & Co Inc: 1 World Financial Center, 200 Liberty St, New York, NY 10281; tel. (212) 416-2000; fax (212) 416-3478; internet www.dowjones.com; f. 1882; acquired by News Corporation in December 2007; Chair. RUPERT MURDOCH; CEO LEX FENWICK; publs incl. *The Wall Street Journal*, the weekly financial magazine *Barron's* and the monthly *Far Eastern Economic Review*; also incl. the community newspaper subsidiary:

Dow Jones Local Media Group (ONI): POB 580, Middletown, NY 10940; tel. (845) 341-1100; e-mail dwaterman@ottaway.com; internet www.dowjoneslmg.com; f. 1936 as Ottaway Newspapers; merged with Dow Jones in 1970; present name adopted 2009; Exec. Chair. PATRICK J. PURCELL; 8 daily and 15 weekly newspapers; over 20 other publs; daily print circ. 282,000, Sun. circ. 316,000 (Oct. 2008).

Freedom Communications, Inc: 17666 Fitch, Irvine, CA 92614-6022; tel. (949) 253-2300; fax (949) 474-7675; e-mail info@link.freedom.com; internet www.freedom.com; Chair. JAMES D. DUNNING, Jr; Pres. and CEO MITCHELL STERN; 33 daily newspapers, incl. *The Orange County Register*, and 77 weekly publs; combined weekday circ. c. 1m.; owns 8 television stations.

Gannett Co Inc: 7950 Jones Branch Dr., McLean, VA 22107-0150; tel. (703) 854-6000; fax (703) 854-2046; e-mail gcishare@gannett.com; internet www.gannett.com; f. 1906; Chair. MARJORIE MAGNER; Pres. and CEO GRACIA C. MARTORE; 84 daily newspapers, incl. *USA Today, Detroit Free Press* and *The Arizona Republic*, c. 850 non-daily publs; combined weekday circ. 7.2m. (of which c. 2.1m. *USA Today*); owns 23 television stations broadcasting to 20m. households; owns and operates Newsquest Media Group (United Kingdom).

Hearst Corpn: Hearst Tower, 12th Floor, 300 West 57th St, New York, NY 10019; tel. (212) 649-4190; fax (212) 649-2108; e-mail lbagley@hearst.com; internet www.hearst.com; acquired Prime Time, Inc (publr, San Antonio region, Texas) in late 2006; acquired *Connecticut Post* and 7 Connecticut weekly newspapers, and assumed control of 3 daily newspapers, in mid-2008; Chair.

GEORGE R. HEARST, Jr; CEO FRANK A. BENNACK, Jr; 15 daily newspapers, incl. the *Houston Chronicle* and *San Francisco Chronicle*, and 49 weekly newspapers; 14 monthly magazines incl. *Good Housekeeping*, *Cosmopolitan*, *O, The Oprah Magazine* and *Redbook*; owns or operates 29 television stations, broadcasting to 18% of the US market, and 2 radio stations; interests in cable networks, interactive media, business information publishing and real estate.

Lee Enterprises: 201 North Harrison St, Davenport, IA 52801-1939; tel. (563) 383-2100; e-mail information@lee.net; internet www.lee.net; f. 1890; Chair., Pres. and CEO MARY E. JUNCK; 46 daily newspapers (jt interest in further 4 dailies) and more than 300 weekly newspapers and speciality publs; combined weekday circ. 1.5m., combined Sun. circ. 1.2m.; interests in publishing and purchasing and distribution of raw materials.

The McClatchy Co: 2100 Q St, Sacramento, CA 95816-6899; tel. (916) 321-1855; fax (916) 321-1869; e-mail ptira@mcclatchy.com; internet www.mcclatchy.com; acquired Knight Ridder Inc in 2006; established 10 foreign news bureaux in that year; sold largest daily, the *Star Tribune*, to Avista Capital Partners (New York) in 2007; Chair. KEVIN S. MCCLATCHY; Pres. and CEO PATRICK J. TALAMANTES; 30 daily newspapers, incl. the *Miami Herald*, and community newspapers.

Media General, Inc: 333 East Franklin St, Richmond, VA 23219; tel. (804) 649-6000; e-mail etucker@mediageneral.com; internet www.mediageneral.com; Chair. J. STEWART BRYAN, III; Pres. and CEO GEORGE L. MAHONEY (designate); 21 daily newspapers, incl. *The Tampa Tribune*, *Richmond Times-Dispatch* and *Winston-Salem Journal*, as well as c. 200 weekly newspapers and other publs; owns 18 network-affiliated television stations.

MediaNews Group: 101 West Colfax Ave, Suite 1100, Denver, CO 80202; tel. (303) 954-6360; fax (303) 954-6320; e-mail contact@medianewsgroup.com; internet www.medianewsgroup.com; CEO JOHN PATON; Chair. WILLIAM DEAN SINGLETON; Pres. JEFF BAIRSTOW; 54 daily newspapers, incl. *The Denver Post*; combined weekday circ. 2.3m., combined Sun. circ. 2.5m.; owns a television station in Anchorage, AK, and radio stations in Texas.

New York Times Co: 620 Eighth Ave, New York, NY 10018; tel. (212) 556-1234; internet www.nytco.com; Chair. ARTHUR O. SULZBERGER, Jr; Pres. and CEO JANET L. ROBINSON; 18 daily newspapers incl. *New York Times*, *The International Herald Tribune* and *The Boston Globe*; owns c. 50 websites; sold Broadcast Media Group to Oak Hill Capital Partners in May 2007.

E. W. Scripps Co: 312 Walnut St, 2800 Scripps Center, Cincinnati, OH 45202; POB 5380, Cincinnati, OH 45201; tel. (513) 977-3000; fax (513) 977-3024; e-mail corpcomm@scripps.com; internet www.scripps.com; Pres. and CEO RICHARD A. BOEHNE; 15 newspapers; owns the Scripps Howard News Service syndicate, 10 television stations, and 6 cable and satellite programming networks.

Tribune Co: 435 North Michigan Ave, Chicago, IL 60611; tel. (312) 222-9100; fax (312) 222-4760; e-mail gweitman@tribune.com; internet www.tribune.com; f. 1847; subsidiary of Tribune Co; merged with the Times Mirror Co in 2000; Tribune Co acquired by private investor in Dec. 2007; filed for Chapter 11 bankruptcy protection in Aug. 2010; Chair. SAMUEL ZELL; Pres. and CEO EDDY HARTENSTEIN; 8 daily newspapers incl. the *Chicago Tribune*, the *Los Angeles Times*, the *Baltimore Sun* and the Spanish-language newspaper *Hoy*; over 130 other publs; combined weekday circ. 2.3m., combined Sun. circ. 3.4m.; operates 23 television stations.

PRINCIPAL DAILY AND SUNDAY NEWSPAPERS

Alabama

Birmingham News: 2201 Fourth Ave North, POB 2553, Birmingham, AL 35203; tel. (205) 325-4444; fax (205) 325-3345; e-mail tscarritt@bhamnews.com; internet www.bhamnews.com; f. 1888; Publr PAM SIDDALL; Editor THOMAS SCARRITT; circ. Mon. to Fri. 103,729, Sat. 100,384, Sun. 173,187.

Huntsville Times: 2317 South Memorial Parkway, Huntsville, AL 35801-5623; tel. (256) 532-4400; fax (256) 532-4213; e-mail thehuntsvilletimes@htimes.com; internet www.htimes.com; f. 1910; Publr BOB LUDWIG; Editor KEVIN WENDT; circ. Mon. to Fri. 44,725, Sat. 44,345, Sun. 68,092.

Montgomery Advertiser: 425 Molton St, Montgomery, AL 36104; tel. (334) 262-1611; fax (334) 261-1521; e-mail editor@montgomeryadvertiser.com; internet www.montgomeryadvertiser.com; f. 1829 as *The Planter's Gazette*; subsidiary of Gannett Co, Inc, international news and information co (McLean, VA); Publr SAMUEL MARTIN; Exec. Editor WANDA S. LLOYD; circ. Mon. to Sat. 32,847, Sun. 44,010.

Press-Register: 401 North Water St, POB 2488, Mobile, AL 36602; tel. (251) 219-5632; fax (334) 219-5794; e-mail newsroom@press-register.com; internet www.press-register.com; f. 1813; Pres. and Publr RICKY R. MATTHEWS; Editor and Vice-Pres. MIKE MARSHALL; circ. Mon. to Fri. 82,088, Sat. 77,344, Sun. 103,373.

Alaska

Anchorage Daily News: POB 149001, Anchorage, AK 99514-9001; tel. (907) 257-4305; fax (907) 257-4544; e-mail newsroom@adn.com; internet www.adn.com; f. 1946; Pres. and Publr PATRICK DOYLE; Senior Vice-Pres. and Editor PAT DOUGHERTY; circ. Mon. to Fri. 43,725, Sat. 40,956, Sun. 47,029.

Arizona

Arizona Daily Star: 4850 South Park Ave, POB 26807, Tucson, AZ 85726-6807; tel. (520) 573-4215; fax (520) 573-4200; e-mail jhumenik@azstarnet.com; internet www.azstarnet.com; f. 1877; Publr and Editor JOHN M. HUMENIK; Man. Editor TERI HAYT; circ. Mon. to Fri. 96,682, Sat. 116,010, Sun. 154,715.

Arizona Republic: 200 East Van Buren St, POB 2244, Phoenix, AZ 85002; tel. (602) 444-8000; fax (800) 699-0732; e-mail comments@azcentral.com; internet www.azcentral.com/arizonarepublic; f. 1890; subsidiary of Gannett Co, Inc (McLean, VA) news group; Pres. and Publr JOHN ZIDICH; Vice-Pres. and Exec. Editor RANDY LOVELY; circ. Mon. to Fri. 321,600, Sat. 347,134, Sun. 538,579.

Arkansas

Democrat-Gazette: 121 East Capitol Ave, POB 2221, Little Rock, AR 72203; tel. (501) 378-3400; fax (501) 372-4765; e-mail ffellone@arkansasonline.com; internet www.arkansasonline.com; f. 1819; morning; Publr WALTER E. HUSSMAN, Jr; Man. Editor DAVID BAILEY; circ. Mon. to Fri. 179,258, Sat. 177,147, Sun. 267,730.

California

Bakersfield Californian: 1707 Eye St, Bakersfield, CA 93301; tel. (805) 395-7500; fax (805) 395-7519; internet www.bakersfield.com; f. 1866; Publr and Chair. GINGER MOORHOUSE; Vice-Pres. and Exec. Editor JOHN ARTHUR; circ. Mon. to Fri. 42,374, Sat. 43,048, Sun. 50,205.

Daily Breeze: South Bay Tower, 21250 Hawthorne Blvd, Suite 170, Torrance, CA 90503; tel. (310) 540-5511; fax (310) 540-6272; e-mail newsroom@dailybreeze.com; internet www.dailybreeze.com; f. 1894; publ. by the Los Angeles Newspaper group (subsidiary of MediaNews Group); Mon. to Sat. evening, Sun. morning; Publr JACK KLUNDER; Editor CAROLINA GARCIA; circ. Mon. to Fri. 75,352, Sat. 66,223, Sun. 66,293.

Daily News: 21860 Burbank Blvd, Suite 200, Woodland Hills, POB 4200, CA 91367; tel. (818) 713-3000; fax (818) 713-0058; e-mail dnmetro@dailynews.com; internet www.dailynews.com; f. 1911; publ. by Los Angeles Newspaper Group; morning; Publr JACK KLUNDER; Editor CAROLINA GARCIA; circ. Mon. to Fri. 94,016, Sat. 93,489, Sun. 97,606.

Fresno Bee: 1626 E St, Fresno, CA 93786; tel. (559) 441-6111; fax (559) 441-6499; e-mail blumbye@fresnobee.com; internet www.fresnobee.com; f. 1922; Publr and Pres. WILLIAM H. FLEET; Senior Vice-Pres. and Exec. Editor BETSY LUMBYE; circ. Mon. to Fri. 107,501, Sat. 115,628, Sun. 154,873.

Investor's Business Daily: 12655 Beatrice St, Los Angeles, CA 90066; tel. (310) 448-6700; fax (310) 577-7301; e-mail ibdnews@investors.com; internet www.investors.com; f. 1984; morning; Publr WILLIAM J. O'NEILL; Editor-in-Chief WESLEY F. MANN; circ. Mon. to Fri. 156,269.

Los Angeles Times: 202 West First St, Los Angeles, CA 90012; tel. (213) 237-5000; fax (213) 237-7679; e-mail nancy.sullivan@latimes.com; internet www.latimes.com; f. 1881; Publr and CEO EDDY W. HARTENSTEIN; Editor DAVAN MAHARAJ; circ. Mon. to Fri. 616,575, Sat. 666,592, Sun. 952,761.

Modesto Bee: 1325 H St, POB 3928, Modesto, CA 95352; tel. (209) 578-2000; fax (209) 578-2207; e-mail ejohnston@modbee.com; internet www.modbee.com; f. 1884; Publr and Pres. ERIC JOHNSTON; Vice-Pres. and Editor MARK VASCHÉ; circ. Mon. to Fri. 59,783, Sat. 61,339, Sun. 72,795.

Oakland Tribune: 1970 Broadway, Suite 100, Oakland, CA 94621; tel. (510) 208-6300; fax (510) 208-6477; e-mail mreynolds@bayareanewsgroup.com; internet www.insidebayarea.com/oakland-tribune; f. 1874; publ. by Alameda Newspaper Group (subsidiary of MediaNews Group); Publr JOHN ARMSTRONG; Man. Editor PAMELA TURNTINE; circ. Mon. to Fri. 94,120, Sat. 85,170, Sun. 94,424 (2010).

Orange County Register: 625 North Grand Ave, POB 11626, Santa Ana, CA 92701-4347; tel. (877) 627-7009; fax (714) 796-3681; e-mail customerservice@ocregister.com; internet www.ocregister.com; Pres. and Publr TERRY HORNE; Editor KEN BRUSIC; circ. Mon. to Fri. 280,812, Sat. 253,057, Sun. 385,283.

Press Democrat: 427 Mendocino Ave, POB 569, Santa Rosa, CA 95402; tel. (707) 526-8570; fax (707) 521-5330; e-mail mcatherine.barnett@pressdemocrat.com; internet www.pressdemocrat.com;

f. 1857; Publr BRUCE W. KYSE; Exec. Editor CATHERINE BARNETT; circ. Mon. to Fri. 56,003, Sat. 57,397, Sun. 59,563.

The Press-Enterprise: 3450 14th St, POB 792, Riverside, CA 92501; tel. (951) 684-1200; fax (951) 368-9022; e-mail feedback@pe .com; internet www.pe.com; f. 1878; publ. by A. H. Belo Corpn; morning; Publr and CEO RONALD R. REDFERN; Editor NELS JENSEN; circ. Mon. to Fri. 131,872, Sat. 133,520, Sun. 156,545.

Press-Telegram: 300 Oceangate, Long Beach, CA 90844-0001; tel. (562) 435-1161; fax (562) 499-1277; e-mail bernice.romo@ presstelegram.com; internet www.presstelegram.com; Publr JACK KLUNDER; Editor CAROLINA GARCIA; circ. Mon. to Fri. 82,556, Sat. 68,314, Sun. 68,020.

Sacramento Bee: 2100 Q St, POB 15779, Sacramento, CA 95852; tel. (916) 321-1000; fax (916) 321-1109; e-mail cdell@sacbee.com; internet www.sacbee.com; f. 1857; Pres. and Publr CHERYL DELL; Sr Vice-Pres. and Editor JOYCE TERHAAR; circ. Mon. to Fri. 196,667, Sat. 211,169, Sun. 271,610.

San Bernardino Sun: 4030 North Georgia Blvd, San Bernardino, CA 92407; tel. (909) 889-9666; fax (909) 381-8741; e-mail fred .hamilton@inlandnewspapers.com; internet www.sbsun.com; f. 1894; part of Los Angeles Media Group; Publr FRED HAMILTON; Exec. Editor FRANK PINE; circ. Mon. to Fri. 56,456, Sat. 47,248, Sun. 62,536.

San Diego Union-Tribune: 350 Camino de la Reina, San Diego, CA 92108; tel. (619) 299-3131; fax (619) 293-1896; e-mail letters@ uniontrib.com; internet www.signonsandiego.com; f. 1868; acquired by private equity firm, Platinum Equity, in May 2009; Pres. and Publr EDWARD R. MOSS; Vice-Pres. and Editor JEFF LIGHT; circ. Mon. to Fri. 230,742, Sat. 323,821, Sun. 364,454.

San Francisco Chronicle: 901 Mission St, San Francisco, CA 94103; tel. (415) 777-1111; fax (415) 896-1107; e-mail letters@ sfchronicle.com; internet www.sfgate.com; f. 1865; subsidiary of Hearst Communications; Publr and Pres. FRANK J. VEGA; Exec. Vice-Pres. and Editor WARD H. BUSHEE; circ. Mon. to Fri. 229,176, Sat. 216,767, Sun. 296,874.

San Francisco Examiner: 71 Stevenson, 2nd Floor, San Francisco, CA 94105; tel. (415) 359-2868; fax (415) 359-2766; e-mail dhussey@ examiner.com; internet www.sfexaminer.com; f. 1887; publ. by Clarity Media Group; Publr JOHN WILCOX; Editor-in-Chief STEPHEN BUEL; circ. Mon. to Fri. 70,000, Sat. 90,000 (2008).

San Jose Mercury News: 750 Ridder Park Dr., San Jose, CA 95190-0001; tel. (408) 920-5000; fax (408) 288-8060; e-mail dbutler@ mercurynews.com; internet www.mercurynews.com; f. 1851; owned by MediaNews Group; Pres. and Publr MAC TULLY; Editor and Vice-Pres. DAVID J. BUTLER; circ. Mon. to Fri. 575,786, Sat. 492,485, Sun. 690,258.

Stockton Record: 530 East Market St, POB 900, Stockton, CA 95201; tel. (209) 943-6568; fax (209) 547-8186; e-mail newsroom@ recordnet.com; internet www.recordnet.com; f. 1895; publ. by Dow Jones & Co; Publr ROGER COOVER; Editor MIKE KLOCKE; circ. Mon. to Sat. 33,675, Sun. 49,326.

Colorado

Denver Post: 101 West Colfax Ave, Denver, CO 80202; tel. (303) 954-1010; fax (303) 820-1369; e-mail gmoore@denverpost.com; internet www.denverpost.com; f. 1892; Publr WILLIAM DEAN SINGLE-TON; Editor GREGORY MOORE; circ. Mon. to Fri. 401,120, Sat. 428,570, Sun. 595,363.

The Gazette: 30 South Prospect St, Colorado Springs, CO 80903; tel. (719) 632-5511; fax (719) 636-0202; e-mail opinion@gazette.com; internet www.gazette.com; f. 1872; Publisher DAN STEEVER; Editor and Vice-Pres. JEFF THOMAS; circ. Mon. to Fri. 70,021, Sat. 68,051, Sun. 84,661.

Connecticut

Connecticut Post: 410 State St, Bridgeport, CT 06604-4501; tel. (203) 333-0161; fax (203) 366-8158; e-mail edit@ctpost.com; internet www.ctpost.com; f. 1883; Pres. and Publr JOHN J. DEAUGUSTINE; Exec. Editor BARBARA T. ROESSNER; circ. Mon. to Fri. 48,701, Sat. 33,436, Sun. 73,283.

Hartford Courant: 285 Broad St, Hartford, CT 06115; tel. (860) 241-6200; fax (860) 520-6941; e-mail letters@courant.com; internet www.courant.com; f. 1764; Publr and CEO RICHARD GRAZIANO; Editor ANDREW JULIEN; circ. Mon. to Fri. 132,006, Sat. 138,195, Sun. 191,044.

New Haven Register: 40 Sargent Dr., New Haven, CT 06511; tel. (203) 789-5200; fax (203) 865-7894; e-mail mbrackenbury@ nhregister.com; internet www.nhregister.com; f. 1812; Publr TOM WILEY; Man. Editor MARK BRACKENBURY; circ. Mon. to Fri. 60,275, Sat. 37,720, Sun. 90,049.

Waterbury Republican-American: American-Republican, Inc, 389 Meadow St, POB 2090, Waterbury, CT 06722-2090; tel. (203)

574-3636; fax (203) 596-9277; e-mail ghanisek@rep-am.com; internet www.rep-am.com; f. 1844; morning; Publr WILLIAM J. PAPE, II; Exec. Editor JONATHAN F. KELLOGG; circ. Mon. to Fri. 42,673, Sat. 41,248.

Delaware

News Journal: POB 15505, Wilmington, DE 19850; tel. (302) 324-2500; fax (302) 324-2595; e-mail newsroom@newsjournal.com; internet www.delawareonline.com; f. 1871; publ. by Gannett Co Inc; Publr CURTIS W. RIDDLE; Exec. Editor DAVID LEDFORD; circ. Mon. to Fri. 83,210, Sat. 77,091, Sun. 122,200.

District of Columbia

Washington Post: 1150 15th St, NW, Washington, DC 20071; tel. (202) 334-6000; fax (202) 334-5693; internet www.washingtonpost .com; f. 1877; Chair. BOISFEUILLET JONES; Publr KATHARINE WEY-MOUTH; Exec. Editor MARCUS BRAUCHLI, Jr; Man. Editors ELIZABETH SPAYD, JOHN TEMPLE; circ. Mon. to Fri. 507,615, Sat. 470,311, Sun. 719,301.

Washington Times: 3600 New York Ave, NE, Washington, DC 20002-1947; tel. (202) 636-3000; fax (202) 832-2982; e-mail yourletters@washingtontimes.com; internet www.washingtontimes .com; f. 1982; sold in 2010 to News World Media Devt group; Editor ED KELLEY; circ. Mon. to Fri. 83,509, Sun. 43,889 (2010).

Florida

Daytona Beach News-Journal: 901 Sixth St, Daytona Beach, FL 32117; tel. (386) 252-1511; e-mail cory.lancaster@news-jrnl.com; internet www.news-journalonline.com; f. 1904; morning; Publr RON WALLACE; Exec. Editor PAT RICE; circ. Mon. to Fri. 68,055, Sat. 73,080, Sun. 88,685.

Diario Las Américas: 2900 NW 39th St, Miami, FL 33142; tel. (305) 633-3341; fax (305) 635-7668; e-mail cartas@diariolasamericas.com; internet www.diariolasamericas.com; f. 1953; Spanish; Publr and Editor HORACIO AGUIRRE; circ. Mon. to Sat. 42,473, Sun. 44,951 (2009).

Florida Times-Union: 1 Riverside Ave, Jacksonville, FL 32202; POB 1949, Jacksonville, FL 32231; tel. (904) 359-4111; fax (904) 359-4478; e-mail letters@jacksonville.com; internet jacksonville.com; f. 1864; Publr LUCY TALLEY; Editor FRANK DENTON; circ. Mon. to Fri. 107,921, Sat. 117,742, Sun. 159,216 (2010).

Florida Today: Cape Publs, Inc, POB 419000, Melbourne, FL 32941-9000; tel. (321) 242-3606; fax (321) 242-9550; e-mail letters@floridatoday.com; internet www.floridatoday.com; f. 1966; morning; Publr and Pres. JEFF KIEL; Exec. Editor BOB STOVER; circ. Mon. to Fri. 63,087, Sat. 67,421, Sun. 89,258.

Ledger: 300 West Lime St, POB 408, Lakeland, FL 33802; tel. (863) 802-7000; fax (863) 802-7809; e-mail lenore.devore@theledger.com; internet www.theledger.com; f. 1924; morning; Publr JEROME FERSON; Editor LENORE DEVORE; circ. Mon. to Fri. 47,274, Sat. 46,982, Sun. 70,096.

Miami Herald: 1 Herald Plaza, Miami, FL 33132-1693; tel. (305) 350-2111; fax (305) 376-5287; e-mail dwilson@miamiherald.com; internet www.miamiherald.com; f. 1910; Publr and Pres. DAVID LANDSBERG; Exec. Editor AMINDA MARQUES; circ. Mon. to Fri. 160,988, Sat. 121,432, Sun. 212,541.

News-Press: 2442 Dr Martin Luther King Jr Blvd, Fort Myers, FL 33901-3987; tel. (239) 335-0200; e-mail response@news-press.com; internet www.news-press.com; f. 1884; morning; Publr MEI-MEI CHAN; Exec. Editor TERRY EBERLE; circ. Mon. to Fri. 70,410, Sat. 78,203, Sun. 98,836.

Orlando Sentinel: 633 North Orange Ave, Orlando, FL 32801; tel. (407) 420-5000; fax (407) 420-5350; e-mail editor@orlandosentinel .com; internet www.orlandosentinel.com; f. 1876; morning; Publr HOWARD GREENBERG; Editor MARK RUSSELL; circ. Mon. to Fri. 173,576, Sat. 195,270, Sun. 288,328.

Palm Beach Post: 2751 South Dixie Hwy, West Palm Beach, FL 33405; tel. (561) 820-4100; fax (561) 820-4407; internet www .palmbeachpost.com; f. 1916; Publr and Exec. Editor TIM BURKE; circ. Mon. to Fri. 110,373, Sat. 110,458, Sun. 139,221.

Pensacola News Journal: POB 12710, Pensacola, FL 32591; tel. (850) 435-8500; fax (850) 435-8633; e-mail news@pnj.com; internet www.pnj.com; f. 1889; Publr KEVIN DOYLE; Exec. Editor RICHARD A. SCHNEIDER; circ. Mon. to Fri. 40,435, Sat. 36,645, Sun. 59,018.

Sarasota Herald-Tribune: 1741 Main St, Sarasota, FL 34236; tel. (941) 953-7755; fax (941) 957-5276; e-mail advocate@heraldtribune .com; internet www.heraldtribune.com; f. 1925; Interim Publr ALLEN PARSONS; Exec. Editor MIKE CONNELLY; circ. Mon. to Fri. 79,845, Sat. 80,547, Sun. 105,470.

Tampa Bay Times: 490 First Ave South, POB 1121, St Petersburg, FL 33701; tel. (727) 893-8111; fax (727) 893-8675; e-mail custserv@ sptimes.com; internet www.tampabay.com; f. 1884; division of Poynter Institute for Media Studies; fmrly *St Petersburg Times*, renamed as above 2012; Chair. and CEO PAUL TASH; Editor NEIL BROWN; circ. Mon. to Fri. 299,497, Sat. 256,135, Sun. 432,202.

Sun-Sentinel: 200 East Las Olas Blvd, Fort Lauderdale, FL 33301-2293; tel. (954) 356-4000; fax (954) 356-4559; e-mail emaucker@sun-sentinel.com; internet www.sun-sentinel.com; f. 1960; Publr HOWARD GREENBERG; Editor-in-Chief HOWARD SALTZ; circ. Mon. to Fri. 180,273, Sat. 207,300, Sun. 263,409 (2010).

Tampa Tribune: 200 South Parker St, Tampa, FL 33606; POB 191, Tampa, FL 33601; tel. (813) 259-7600; fax (813) 259-7676; e-mail lomoto@tbo.com; internet www.tampatrib.com; f. 1893; morning; Publr and Pres. DENISE E. PALMER; Exec. Editor RICHARD DUKE MAAS; circ. Mon. to Fri. 144,510, Sat. 136,275.

Georgia

Atlanta Journal-Constitution: 223 Perimeter Center Pkwy, Atlanta, GA 30346-2390; tel. (404) 526-5151; fax (404) 526-5746; e-mail insideajc@ajc.com; internet www.ajc.com; f. 1950; morning; Publr AMY GLENNON; Editor KEVIN RILEY; circ. Mon. to Fri. 174,251, Sat. 180,592, Sun. 402,602.

Augusta Chronicle: 725 Broad St, POB 1928, Augusta, GA 30903-1928; tel. (706) 724-0851; fax (706) 823-3345; internet chronicle.augusta.com; f. 1785; Morris Communications Co, LLC; Publr WILLIAM S. MORRIS, III; Exec. Editor ALAN ENGLISH; circ. Mon. to Fri. 55,444, Sat. 59,839, Sun. 71,057.

Macon Telegraph: 120 Broadway, Macon, GA 31208; POB 4167, Macon, GA 31208; tel. (478) 744-4200; fax (478) 744-4663; e-mail smarshall@macon.com; internet www.macon.com; f. 1826; Publr GEORGE MCCANLESS; Exec. Editor SHERRIE MARSHALL; circ. Mon. to Fri. 43,100, Sat. 42,650, Sun. 64,845.

Savannah Morning News: 1375 Chatham Parkway, Savannah, GA 31401; POB 1088, Savannah, GA 31402-1088; tel. (912) 236-9511; fax (912) 234-6522; internet www.savannahnow.com; f. 1850; Publr MICHAEL C. TRAYNOR; Exec. Editor SUSAN CATRON, Jr; circ. Mon. to Fri. 51,456, Sat. 49,030, Sun. 64,308.

Hawaii

Honolulu Star-Advertiser: Restaurant Row, 7 Waterfront Plaza, Suite 210, 500 Ala Moana, Honolulu, HI 96813; tel. (808) 529-4747; fax (808) 529-4750; e-mail webmaster@staradvertiser.com; internet www.staradvertiser.com; f. 1882; known as *Honolulu Star-Bulletin* until 2010 when it bought *Honolulu Advertiser* (f. 1856) and present name adopted; owned by Black Press Ltd; Pres. and Publr DENNIS FRANCIS; Editor FRANK BRIDGEWATER; circ. Mon. to Fri. 209,915, Sat. 153,044, Sun. 164,316.

Idaho

Idaho Statesman: 1200 North Curtis Rd, POB 40, Boise, ID 83707; tel. (208) 377-6200; fax (208) 377-6449; e-mail vgowler@idahostatesman.com; internet www.idahostatesman.com; f. 1864; Publr MIKE JUNG; Editor and Vice-Pres. VICKI S. GOWLER; circ. Mon. to Fri. 48,739, Sat. 50,510, Sun. 76,047.

Illinois

Chicago Sun-Times: 350 North Orleans St, 10th Floor, Chicago, IL 60654; tel. (312) 321-3000; fax (312) 321-3084; e-mail aherrmann@suntimes.com; internet www.suntimes.com; f. 1948; Publr JOHN BARRON; Editor-in-Chief JIM KIRK; circ. Mon. to Fri. 422,335, Sat. 277,300, Sun. 434,861.

Chicago Tribune: 435 North Michigan Ave, Chicago, IL 60611-4041; tel. (312) 222-4300; fax (312) 222-4674; internet www.chicagotribune.com; f. 1847; publ. by Chicago Tribune Co; 2 sister newspapers: *RedEye* and *Hoy Chicago*; Publr TONY HUNTER; Editor GEROULD KERN; circ. Mon. to Fri. 414,590, Sat. 315,267, Sun. 779,440.

Daily Herald: 155 East Algonquin Rd, POB 280, Arlington Heights, IL 60006; tel. (847) 427-4300; fax (847) 427-4608; e-mail jbaumann@dailyherald.com; internet www.dailyherald.com; f. 1872; owned by Paddock Publications Inc; Publr and CEO DOUG RAY; Sr Vice-Pres. and Editor JOHN LAMPINEN; circ. Mon. to Fri. 106,287, Sat. 104,535, Sun. 115,504 (2010).

Journal Star: 1 News Plaza, Peoria, IL 61643; tel. (309) 686-3000; fax (309) 686-3296; e-mail kmauser@pjstar.com; internet www.pjstar.com; f. 1855; Publr KEN MAUSER; Exec. Editor DENNIS ANDERSON; circ. Mon. to Fri. 63,024, Sat. 64,078, Sun. 72,607.

Pantagraph: 301 West Washington St, POB 2907, Bloomington, IL 61702-2907; tel. (309) 829-9000; fax (309) 829-9104; e-mail jgerke@pantagraph.com; internet www.pantagraph.com; f. 1837; Publr RICHARD JOHNSTON; Editor MARK PICKERING; circ. Mon. to Fri. 37,434, Sat. 33,674, Sun. 41,115.

Rockford Register Star: 99 East State St, Rockford, IL 61104; tel. (815) 987-1200; fax (815) 987-1365; internet www.rrstar.com; f. 1888; acquired by GateHouse Media from Gannett Co in 2007; Publr JOSH

TRUST; Exec. Editor MARK BALDWIN; circ. Mon. to Fri. 65,224, Sat. 40,429, Sun. 62,381.

State Journal-Register: 1 Copley Plaza, POB 219, Springfield, IL 62705-0219; tel. (217) 788-1300; fax (217) 788-1551; e-mail sjr@sj-r.com; internet www.sj-r.com; f. 1831; Publr RICHARD JOHNSTON; Exec. Editor BOB HEISSE; circ. Mon. to Fri. 44,722, Sat. 44,864, Sun. 47,668.

Indiana

Evansville Courier and Press: 300 East Walnut, POB 268, Evansville, IN 47713; tel. (812) 424-7711; fax (812) 422-8196; e-mail eccnewmedia@courierpress.com; internet www.courierpress.com; f. 1845; Publr and Pres. JACK PATE; Editor DAVID DIXON; circ. Mon. to Fri. 51,618, Sat. 52,489, Sun. 73,690.

Indianapolis Star: POB 145, Indianapolis, IN 46206-0145; tel. (317) 444-4000; fax (317) 633-1038; internet www.indystar.com; Publr and Pres. KAREN CROTCHFELT; Editor JEFF TAYLOR; circ. Mon. to Fri. 176,232, Sat. 166,757, Sun. 272,798.

Journal-Gazette: 600 West Main St, POB 88, Fort Wayne, IN 46801-0088; tel. (260) 461-8773; fax (219) 461-8648; e-mail jgnews@jg.net; internet www.journalgazette.net; f. 1863; publ. by Fort Wayne Newspapers; Publr JULIE INSKEEP; Editor CRAIG KLUGMAN; circ. Mon. to Fri. 49,173, Sat. 61,903, Sun. 90,682.

News-Sentinel: 600 West Main St, POB 100, Fort Wayne, IN 46802; tel. (260) 461-8324; fax (260) 461-8817; e-mail lmorris@news-sentinel.com; internet www.news-sentinel.com; f. 1833; publ. by Fort Wayne Newspapers; Publr MICHAEL J. CHRISTMAN; Editor KERRY HUBARTT; circ. Mon. to Fri. 16,812, Sat. 17,091.

Post-Tribune: 1433 East 83rd Ave, Merrillville, IN 46410; tel. (219) 648-3100; fax (219) 648-3249; internet www.post-trib.com; f. 1907; Publr LISA TATINA; Exec. Editor PAULETTE HADDIX; circ. Mon. to Fri. 46,140, Sat. 42,640, Sun. 45,230 (2010).

South Bend Tribune: 225 West Colfax Ave, South Bend, IN 46626; tel. (574) 235-6161; fax (574) 236-1765; e-mail sbtnews@sbtinfo.com; internet www.southbendtribune.com; f. 1872; Publr KIM WILSON; Exec. Editor TIM HARMON; circ. Mon. to Fri. 59,351, Sat. 64,640, Sun. 78,257.

The Times: 601 45th Ave, Munster, IN 46321; tel. (219) 933-3200; fax (219) 933-3249; e-mail subinfo@nwitimes.com; internet www.nwitimes.com; f. 1906; morning; Publr BILL MASTERSON, Jr; Exec. Editor WILLIAM NANGLE; circ. Mon. to Fri. 85,692, Sat. 82,767, Sun. 93,019.

Iowa

Cedar Rapids Gazette: 500 Third Ave, SE, Cedar Rapids, IA 52401; tel. (319) 398-8333; fax (319) 398-5846; e-mail lyle.muller@thegazette.com; internet thegazette.com; f. 1883; Publr TIM MCDOUGALL; Man. Editor ANNETTE SCHULTE; circ. Mon. to Fri. 49,076, Sat. 56,704, Sun. 62,799.

Des Moines Register: 715 Locust St, POB 957, Des Moines, IA 50306-0957; tel. (515) 284-8000; fax (515) 268-2504; e-mail letters@dmreg.com; internet www.desmoinesregister.com; f. 1849; Pres. and Publr LAURA HOLLINGSWORTH; Editor RICK GREEN; circ. Mon. to Fri. 101,915, Sat. 112,819, Sun. 211,762.

Quad-City Times: 500 East Third St, POB 3828, Davenport, IA 52801; tel. (563) 383-2200; fax (563) 383-2223; internet www.qctimes.com; f. 1855; division of Lee Enterprises, Inc; Publr GREG VEON; Exec. Editor JAN TOUNEY; circ. Mon. to Fri. 46,824, Sat. 43,753, Sun. 56,551.

Sioux City Journal: 515 Pavonia St, Sioux City, IA 51102; tel. (712) 293-4250; fax (712) 279-5059; e-mail bwalker@siouxcityjournal.com; internet www.siouxcityjournal.com; f. 1864; subsidiary of Lee Enterprises, Inc; Publr RON PETERSON; Editor MITCH PUGH; circ. Mon. to Sat. 32,502, Sun. 36,123.

Kansas

Topeka Capital-Journal: 616 SE Jefferson St, Topeka, KS 66607; tel. (785) 295-1111; fax (785) 295-1230; e-mail tomari.quinn@cjonline.com; internet www.cjonline.com; f. 1879; Publr GREGG A. IRELAND; Man. Editor TOMARI QUINN; circ. Mon. to Fri. 40,435, Sat. 40,713, Sun. 47,596.

Wichita Eagle: 825 East Douglas Ave, POB 820, Wichita, KS 67201-0820; tel. (316) 268-6000; fax (316) 269-6799; e-mail wenews@wichitaeagle.com; internet www.kansas.com; f. 1872; Publr and Pres. KIM NUSSBAUM; Editor SHERRY CHISENHALL; circ. Mon. to Fri. 67,250, Sat. 75,928, Sun. 98,275.

Kentucky

Courier-Journal: 525 West Broadway, Louisville, KY 40201-7431; POB 740031, Louisville, KY 40201; tel. (502) 582-4011; fax (502) 582-4200; e-mail cjletter@courier-journal.com; internet www.courier-journal.com; f. 1868; Publr and Pres. ARNOLD GARSON; Man.

Editor JEAN PORTER; circ. Mon. to Fri. 154,033, Sat. 145,820, Sun. 254,685.

Lexington Herald-Leader: 100 Midland Ave, Lexington, KY 40508-1999; tel. (859) 231-3100; e-mail pbaniak@herald-leader .com; internet www.kentucky.com; f. 1860; Pres. and Publr RUFUS FRIDAY; Editor and Vice-Pres. PETER BANIAK; circ. Mon. to Fri. 89,735, Sat. 92,626, Sun. 115,737.

Louisiana

Advocate: 7290 Bluebonnet Blvd, Baton Rouge, LA 70817; tel. (225) 383-1111; fax (225) 388-0371; e-mail support@theadvocate.com; internet theadvocate.com; f. 1904; morning; Publr DOUGLAS L. MANSHIP, Jr; Exec. Editor CARL REDMAN; circ. Mon. to Fri. 82,695, Sat. 85,416, Sun. 104,215.

The Times: 222 Lake St, POB 30222, Shreveport, LA 71101; tel. (318) 459-3200; e-mail agprice@gannett.com; internet www .shreveporttimes.com; f. 1872; subsidiary of Gannett Co, Inc; Pres. and Publr DONALD W. BAILEY; Exec. Editor AFRICA PRICE; circ. Mon. to Sat. 37,666, Sun. 51,297.

Times-Picayune: 3800 Howard Ave, New Orleans, LA 70125-1429; tel. (504) 822-7355; fax (504) 826-3700; e-mail pkovacs@ timespicayune.com; internet www.nola.com/t-p; f. 1880; Publr ASHTON PHELPS, Jr; Editor JIM AMOSS; circ. Mon. to Fri. 133,557, Sat. 132,178, Sun. 154,353.

Maine

Bangor Daily News: 491 Main St, POB 1329, Bangor, ME 04401; tel. (207) 990-8000; fax (207) 941-9476; e-mail bdnnews@ bangordailynews.net; internet www.bangordailynews.com; f. 1834; Publr RICHARD J. WARREN; Editor-in-Chief MICHAEL J. DOWD; circ. Mon. to Fri. 45,180, Sat. and Sun. 52,695.

Portland Press Herald: 1 City Center, 5th Floor, POB 1460, Portland, ME 04101-5009; tel. (207) 791-6320; fax (207) 791-6920; e-mail news@pressherald.com; internet www.pressherald.com; f. 1862; incorporates the *Maine Sunday Telegram* (circ. 76,015); Publr and Editor RICHARD L. CONNOR; Exec. Editor CLIFFORD SCHECHTMAN; circ. Mon. to Fri. 47,326, Sat. 44,358.

Maryland

Baltimore Sun: 501 North Calvert St, POB 1377, Baltimore, MD 21278; tel. (410) 332-6000; fax (410) 752-6049; e-mail customersatisfaction@baltsun.com; internet www.baltimoresun .com; f. 1837; Publr, Pres. and CEO TIMOTHY E. RYAN; Sr Vice-Pres. and Dir of Content MARY COREY; circ. Mon. to Fri. 179,574, Sat. 262,197, Sun. 332,305.

Massachusetts

Boston Globe: 135 Morrissey Blvd, POB 55819, Boston, MA 02205-5819; tel. (617) 929-2000; fax (617) 929-3192; e-mail comments@globe .com; internet bostonglobe.com; f. 1872; Publr CHRISTOPHER MAYER; Editor MARTIN D. BARON; circ. Mon. to Fri. 225,482, Sat. 223,623, Sun. 365,512.

Boston Herald: 1 Herald Sq., Boston, MA 02118; tel. (617) 426-3000; fax (617) 426-1896; e-mail letterstoeditor@bostonherald.com; internet www.bostonherald.com; f. 1825; Publr PATRICK PURCELL; Man. Editor JOE SCIACCA; circ. Mon. to Fri. 108,548, Sat. 85,398, Sun. 81,925.

Christian Science Monitor: 210 Massachusetts Ave, Boston, MA 02115; tel. (617) 450-2300; e-mail letters@csmonitor.com; internet www.csmonitor.com; f. 1908; publ. by The First Church of Christ, Scientist; Man. Publr JONATHAN WELLS; Man. Editor MARSHALL INGWERSON; circ. Mon. to Fri. 47,951 (2009).

Lowell Sun: 491 Dutton St, Lowell, MA 01853; tel. (978) 458-7100; fax (978) 970-4600; e-mail moneil@lowellsun.com; internet www .lowellsun.com; f. 1878; Mon. to Fri. evening, Sat. and Sun. morning; Publr and Pres. MARK O'NEIL; Editor JAMES CAMPANINI; circ. Mon. to Fri. 42,312, Sat. 32,495, Sun. 48,213.

Patriot Ledger: 400 Crown Colony Dr., POB 699159, Quincy, MA 02269-9159; tel. (617) 786-7000; fax (617) 786-7025; e-mail newsroom@ledger.com; internet www.patriotledger.com; f. 1837; mem. of the South of Boston Media Group; Mon. to Fri. evening, weekend; Publr RICK DANIELS; Editor CHAZY DOWALIBY; circ. Mon. to Fri. 38,537, Sat. and Sun. 45,479.

The Republican: 1860 Main St, Springfield, MA 01101; tel. (413) 788-1200; fax (413) 788-1301; e-mail garwady@repub.com; internet www.repub.com; f. 1824; fmrly *Sunday Republican*, merged with Union-News in 2003; Publr and CEO GEORGE ARWADY; Exec. Editor WAYNE E. PHANEUF; circ. Mon. to Fri. 55,449, Sat. 39,131, Sun. 100,058.

Worcester Telegram & Gazette: 20 Franklin St, POB 15012, Worcester, MA 01615-0012; tel. (508) 793-9100; fax (508) 767-9529; e-mail info@telegram.com; internet www.telegram.com; f. 1866;

Publr BRUCE GAULTNEY; Editor LEAH LAMSON; circ. Mon. to Fri. 74,563, Sat. 70,805.

Michigan

Detroit Free Press: 615 West Lafayette Blvd, Detroit, MI 48226; tel. (313) 222-6400; fax (313) 222-5981; e-mail cserv@dnps.com; internet www.freep.com; f. 1831; subsidiary of the Gannett Corpn, Inc; Mon. to Fri. morning, Sat. and Sun.; Publr and Editor PAUL ANGER; circ. Mon. to Fri. 232,696, Sat. 203,621, Sun. 668,332.

The Detroit News: 615 West Lafayette Blvd, Detroit, MI 48226-3197; tel. (313) 222-2300; fax (313) 496-5400; e-mail jon.wolman@ detnews.com; internet www.detroitnews.com; f. 1873; subsidiary co of MediaNews Group; Publr and Editor JONATHAN WOLMAN; Man. Editor DONALD W. NAUSS; circ. Mon. to Fri. 133,508, Sat. 116,993.

Flint Journal: 540 South Saginaw St, Flint, MI 48502-1925; tel. (810) 766-6100; fax (810) 767-7518; e-mail fj@flintjournal.com; internet www.flintjournal.com; f. 1876; Thur., Fri. and Sun. morning; Publr MATTHEW SHARP; Editor MARJORY RAYMER; circ. Tue., Thur. and Fri. 49,685, Sun. 66,622.

Grand Rapids Press: 155 Michigan St, NW, Grand Rapids, MI 49503-2302; tel. (616) 222-5818; e-mail dgaydou@grpress.com; internet www.mlive.com/grpress; f. 1890; Publr DAN GAYDOU; Editor PAUL M. KEEP; circ. Mon. to Fri. 68,865, Sat. 29,459, Sun. 149,667.

Kalamazoo Gazette: 316 South Kalamazoo Mall, Kalamazoo, MI 49007; tel. (269) 345-3511; fax (269) 345-0583; e-mail jstephanak@ kalamazoogazette.com; internet www.mlive.com/kgazette; f. 1883; Mon. to Fri. evening, Sat. and Sun. morning; Publr JAMES STEPHANAK; circ. Mon. to Fri. 27,994, Sat. 12,091, Sun. 61,292.

Lansing State Journal: 120 East Lenawee St, Lansing, MI 48919-0001; tel. (517) 377-1000; fax (517) 377-1298; e-mail publisher@lsj .com; internet www.lansingstatejournal.com; f. 1855; Pres. and Publr BRIAN PRIESTER; Exec. Editor MICHAEL HIRTEN; circ. Mon. to Fri. 41,330, Sat. 43,885, Sun. 65,904.

Oakland Press: 48 West Huron St, Pontiac, MI 48342; tel. (248) 332-8181; fax (248) 253-9986; e-mail glenn.gilbert@oakpress.com; internet www.theoaklandpress.com; f. 1843; Publr and Pres. JIM O'ROURKE; Exec. Editor GLENN GILBERT; circ. Mon. to Fri. 65,197, Sat. 58,651, Sun. 81,935.

Saginaw News: 100 South Michigan Ave, Saginaw, MI 48602; tel. (989) 776-9764; e-mail thenews@thesaginawnews.com; internet www.mlive.com/saginawnews; f. 1859; Tue, Thur., Fri. and Sun. morning; Publr MATTHEW SHARP; Exec. Editor JOHN P. HINER; circ. Tue. 23,064, Thur. 24,171, Fri. 23,828, Sun. 36,960.

Minnesota

Duluth News Tribune: 424 West First St, Duluth, MN 55802; tel. (218) 723-5281; fax (218) 723-5295; e-mail webteam@duluthnews .com; internet www.duluthnewstribune.com; f. 1869; morning; Publr KEN BROWALL; Editor ROBIN WASHINGTON; circ. Mon. to Fri. 40,305, Sat. 40,082, Sun. 62,468 (2007).

Star Tribune: 425 Portland Ave South, Minneapolis, MN 55488; tel. (612) 673-4000; fax (612) 673-4359; e-mail customerservice@ startribune.com; internet www.startribune.com; f. 1920; Publr MIKE KLINGENSMITH; Editor and Sr Vice-Pres. NANCY BARNES; circ. Mon. to Fri. 300,330, Sat. 263,608, Sun. 544,186.

St Paul Pioneer Press: 345 Cedar St, St Paul, MN 55101; tel. (651) 222-1111; fax (651) 228-5500; e-mail mburbach@pioneerpress.com; internet www.twincities.com; f. 1849; Publr GUY L. GILMORE; Vice-Pres. and Editor MIKE BURBACH; circ. Mon. to Fri. 205,171, Sat. 175,820, Sun. 270,811.

Mississippi

Clarion-Ledger: 201 South Congress St, Jackson, MS 39201; tel. (601) 961-7000; fax (601) 961-7211; e-mail publisher@clarionledger .com; internet www.clarionledger.com; f. 1954; Publr and Pres. LESLIE HURST; Editor BRIAN TOLLEY; circ. Mon. to Fri. 57,710, Sat. 58,472, Sun. 72,386.

Missouri

Kansas City Star: 1729 Grand Blvd, Kansas City, MO 64108; tel. (816) 234-4741; fax (816) 234-4467; e-mail mfannin@kcstar.com; internet www.kansascity.com; f. 1880; Publr MI-AI PARRISH; Editor MIKE FANNIN; circ. Mon. to Fri. 200,365, Sat. 204,489, Sun. 310,487.

News-Leader: 651 Boonville Ave, Springfield, MO 65806; tel. (417) 836-1100; fax (417) 837-1381; e-mail letters@news-leader.com; internet www.news-leader.com; f. 1933; morning; Publr LINDA RAMEY-GREIWE; Exec. Editor DAVID STOEFFLER; circ. Mon. to Sat. 35,531, Sun. 62,083.

St Louis Post-Dispatch: 900 North Tucker Blvd, St Louis, MO 63101; tel. (314) 657-8000; fax (314) 340-3139; e-mail generalmanager@stltoday.com; internet www.stltoday.com; f. 1878;

Pres. and Publr KEVIN MOWBRAY; Editor-in-Chief GILBERT BAILON; circ. Mon. to Fri. 187,992, Sat. 333,529, Sun. 333,529.

Montana

Billings Gazette: POB 36300, Billings, MT 59107; tel. (406) 657-1200; fax (406) 657-1208; e-mail mgulledge@billingsgazette.com; internet billingsgazette.net; f. 1885; Publr MIKE GULLEDGE; Editor STEVE PROSINSKI; circ. Mon. to Sat. 39,405, Sun. 44,937.

Nebraska

Lincoln Journal Star: Journal Star Printing Co, 926 P St, POB 81609, Lincoln, NE 68508; tel. (402) 475-4200; fax (402) 473-7291; e-mail jbechtel@journalstar.com; internet journalstar.com; f. 1867; morning; Publr JULIE BECHTEL; Editor DAVE BUNDY; circ. Mon. to Fri. 55,398, Sat. 52,088, Sun. 68,816.

Omaha World-Herald: 1334 Douglas St, Omaha, NE 68102-1122; tel. (402) 444-1000; fax (402) 345-0183; e-mail mike.reilly@owh.com; internet www.omaha.com; f. 1885; CEO and Publr TERRY KROEGER; Exec. Editor MIKE REILLY; circ. Mon. to Fri. 135,223, Sat. 130,934, Sun. 168,403.

Nevada

Las Vegas Review-Journal: 1111 West Bonanza Rd, POB 70, Las Vegas, NV 89125; tel. (702) 383-0211; fax (702) 383-4676; e-mail MHengel@reviewjournal.com; internet www.lvrj.com; f. 1908; Publr BOB BROWN; Editor MICHAEL HENGEL; circ. Mon. to Fri. 220,619, Sat. 151,093, Sun. 205,931.

Reno Gazette-Journal: POB 22000, Reno, NV 89520-2000; tel. (775) 788-6397; fax (775) 788-6458; e-mail letters@rgj.com; internet www.rgj.com; f. 1870; Publr JOHN MAHER; Exec. Editor BERYL LOVE; circ. Mon. to Fri. 43,095, Sat. 37,643, Sun. 53,562.

New Hampshire

New Hampshire Union Leader, New Hampshire Sunday News: Union Leader Corpn, 100 William Loeb Dr., POB 9555, Manchester, NH 03108-9555; tel. (603) 668-4321; fax (603) 668-0382; e-mail publisher@unionleader.com; internet www.unionleader.com; f. 1863 (*New Hampshire Union Leader*); f. 1946 (*New Hampshire Sunday News*); Pres. and Publr JOSEPH W. McQUAID; circ. Mon. to Fri. 44,665, Sat. 28,181, Sun. 62,740.

New Jersey

Asbury Park Press: 3601 Hwy 66, POB 1550, Neptune, NJ 07754-1550; tel. (732) 922-6000; fax (732) 918-4818; e-mail htowns@njpressmedia.com; internet www.app.com; f. 1879; Publr and Pres. THOMAS M. DONOVAN; Exec. Editor HOLLIS R. TOWNS; circ. Mon. to Fri. 98,032, Sat. 103,645, Sun. 150,646.

Courier-News: 92 East Main St, Suite 202, Somerville, NJ 08876-2319; internet www.mycentraljersey.com; f. 1884; Publr and Pres. WILLIAM C. HIDLAY; Man. Editor PAUL GRZELLA; circ. Mon. to Sat. 15,533, Sun. 20,165.

Courier-Post: 301 Cuthbert Blvd, POB 5300, Cherry Hill, NJ 08034; tel. (856) 663-6000; fax (856) 663-2831; e-mail thearon@courierpostonline.com; internet www.courierpostonline.com; f. 1875; Pres. and Publr TIM DOWD; Exec. Editor EUGENE E. WILLIAMS; circ. Mon. to Fri. 46,547, Sat. 52,800, Sun. 63,676.

Home News Tribune: 35 Kennedy Blvd, East Brunswick, NJ 08816; tel. (732) 246-5500; fax (732) 565-7208; e-mail hntmetro@thnt.com; internet www.mycentraljersey.com; f. 1879; Publr and Pres. WILLIAM C. HIDLAY; Exec. Editor PAUL GRZELLA; circ. Mon. to Sat. 29,648, Sun. 38,024.

Jersey Journal: 30 Journal Sq., Jersey City, NJ 07306; tel. (201) 653-1000; fax (201) 217-2455; e-mail jjletters@jjournal.com; internet www.jjournal.com; f. 1867; Publr KENDRICK ROSS; Editor JUDITH A. LOCORRIERE; circ. Mon. to Fri. 18,047, Sat. 20,809.

The Record: 150 River St, Hackensack, NJ 07601-7172; tel. (201) 646-4444; fax (201) 457-2520; e-mail scandale@northjersey.com; internet www.northjersey.com; f. 1895; Publr STEPHEN A. BORG; Editor and Vice-Pres. FRANK SCANDALE; circ. Mon. to Fri. 155,236, Sat. 143,218, Sun. 178,446.

Star-Ledger: 1 Star-Ledger Plaza, Newark, NJ 07102-1200; tel. (973) 392-4040; e-mail jdennan@starledger.com; internet www.nj.com/starledger; f. 1917; Publr RICHARD VEZZA; Editor KEVIN WHITMER; circ. Mon. to Fri. 278,940, Sat. 239,151, Sun. 413,472.

The Times: 500 Perry St, POB 847, Trenton, NJ 08605; tel. (609) 989-5454; fax (609) 394-2819; e-mail bmalone@njtimes.com; internet www.nj.com/times; f. 1882; Publr BRIAN S. MALONE; Man. Editor KRISTIN J. BUCCI; circ. Mon. to Fri. 35,217, Sat. 33,798, Sun. 39,423.

Trentonian: 600 Perry St, Trenton, NJ 08618; tel. (609) 989-7800; fax (609) 393-6072; e-mail editor@trentonian.com; internet www.trentonian.com; f. 1946; Publr WILLIAM T. (BILL) MURRAY; Editor

JOEY KULKIN (acting); circ. Mon. to Fri. 25,303, Sat. 21,811, Sun. 18,171.

New Mexico

Albuquerque Journal: Albuquerque Publishing Co, 7777 Jefferson St NE, Albuquerque, NM 87109; tel. (505) 823-3800; e-mail jangel@abqjournal.com; internet www.abqjournal.com; f. 1880; Publr T. H. LANG; Editor KENT WALZ; circ. Mon. to Fri. 109,516, Sat. 88,899, Sun. 109,516.

New York

Albany Times Union: Times Union, News Plaza, POB 15000, Albany, NY 12212; tel. (518) 454-5694; fax (518) 454-5628; e-mail jcrupi@timesunion.com; internet www.timesunion.com; f. 1856; Publr GEORGE HEARST, III; Exec. Editor REX SMITH; circ. Mon. to Fri. 66,507, Sat. 57,329, Sun. 129,275.

Buffalo News: 1 News Plaza, POB 100, Buffalo, NY 14240; tel. (716) 849-4444; fax (716) 856-5150; internet www.buffalonews.com; f. 1880; Publr STANFORD LIPSEY; Editor BRIAN CONNOLLY (acting); circ. Mon. to Fri. 147,085, Sat. 158,879, Sun. 233,069.

Daily Gazette: 2345 Maxon Rd Ext., Schenectady, NY 12308; POB 1090, Schenectady, NY 12301-1090; tel. (518) 374-4141; fax (518) 395-3089; e-mail gazette@dailygazette.com; internet www.dailygazette.com; f. 1894; Publr and Editor JOHN E. N. HUME, III; Man. Editor JUDITH PATRICK; circ. Mon. to Fri. 55,719, Sat. 55,508, Sun. 56,461.

Democrat and Chronicle: 55 Exchange Blvd, Rochester, NY 14614-2001; tel. (585) 232-7100; fax (585) 258-3027; e-mail editor@democratandchronicle.com; internet www.democratandchronicle.com; f. 1833; Pres. and Publr MICHAEL KANE; Editor KAREN MAGNUSON; circ. Mon. to Fri. 114,502, Sat. 128,050, Sun. 167,862.

Newsday: 235 Pinelawn Rd, Melville, NY 11747; tel. (631) 843-2700; fax (516) 843-2953; e-mail editor@newsday.com; internet www.newsday.com; f. 1940; Publr FRED GROSER; Editor DEBBIE KRENEK; circ. Mon. to Fri. 397,973, Sat. 383,295, Sun. 495,416.

Post-Standard: Clinton Sq., POB 4915, Syracuse, NY 13221-4915; tel. (315) 470-0011; fax (315) 470-3081; e-mail mconnor@syracuse.com; internet post-standard.com; f. 1829; Editor and Publr STEPHEN A. ROGERS; Exec. Editor MICHAEL J. CONNOR; circ. Mon. to Fri. 78,616, Sat. 80,618, Sun. 137,489.

Press & Sun-Bulletin: 33 Lewis Rd, Binghamton, NY 13905-1044; tel. (607) 798-1234; fax (607) 798-1113; internet www.pressconnects.com; f. 1985; Publr SHERMAN M. BODNER; Exec. Editor CALVIN STOVALL; circ. Mon. to Sat. 34,311, Sun. 50,970.

Times Herald-Record ('The Record'): 40 Mulberry St, POB 2046, Middletown, NY 10940; tel. (914) 341-1100; fax (914) 343-2170; e-mail dosenenko@th-record.com; internet www.recordonline.com; f. 1956; Publr JOE VANDERHOOF; Exec. Editor DEREK OSENENKO; circ. Mon. to Fri. 50,579, Sat. 51,110, Sun. 65,040.

New York City

New York Daily News: 450 West 33rd St, New York, NY 10001; tel. (212) 210-2100; fax (212) 682-4953; e-mail voicers@edit.nydailynews.com; internet www.nydailynews.com; f. 1919; Publr MORTIMER B. ZUCKERMAN; Editor-in-Chief COLIN MYLER; circ. Mon. to Fri. 579,636, Sat. 479,370, Sun. 660,918.

New York Post: 1211 Ave of the Americas, New York, NY 10036-8790; tel. (212) 930-8000; fax (212) 930-8540; e-mail letters@nypost.com; internet www.nypost.com; f. 1801; Publr PAUL V. CARLUCCI; Editor-in-Chief COL ALLAN; circ. Mon. to Fri. 555,327, Sat. 442,365, Sun. 434,392.

New York Times: 620 Eighth Ave, New York, NY 10018; tel. (212) 556-1234; e-mail public@nytimes.com; internet www.nytimes.com; f. 1851; Chair. and Publr ARTHUR OCHS SULZBERGER, Jr; Pres. and Gen. Man. SCOTT H. HEEKIN-CANEDY; Exec. Editor JILL E. ABRAMSON; circ. Mon. to Fri. 1,586,757, Sat. 1,550,696, Sun. 2,003,247.

Staten Island Advance: 950 Fingerboard Rd, Staten Island, New York, NY 10305; tel. (718) 981-1234; fax (718) 981-5679; e-mail silverstein@siadvance.com; internet www.statenislandadvance.com; f. 1886; Mon. to Sat. evening, Sun. morning; Publr CAROLINE DIAMOND HARRISON; Editor BRIAN J. LALINE; circ. Mon. to Fri. 35,997, Sat. 34,770, Sun. 45,426.

The Wall Street Journal: 1211 Ave of the Americas, New York, NY 10036; tel. (212) 416-2000; e-mail wsj.ltrs@wsj.com; internet www.wsj.com; f. 1889; publ. by Dow Jones & Co Inc; morning; Chair. M. PETER MCPHERSON; Exec. Editor ALAN MURRAY; circ. Mon. to Fri. 2,118,315, Sat. and Sun. 2,078,564.

North Carolina

Charlotte Observer: 600 South Tryon St, POB 32188-28232, Charlotte, NC 28202-1842; tel. (704) 358-5000; fax (704) 358-5036; e-mail opinion@charlotteobserver.com; internet www

.charlotteobserver.com; f. 1886; Publr and Pres. ANN CAULKINS; Editor RICK THAMES; circ. Mon. to Fri. 146,511, Sat. 167,221, Sun. 216,862.

Citizen-Times: 14 Ohenry Ave, POB 2090, Asheville, NC 28802; tel. (828) 252-5610; fax (828) 251-0585; e-mail news@citizen-times.com; internet www.citizen-times.com; f. 1870; morning; Publr and Pres. RANDY HAMMER; circ. Mon. to Fri. 30,111, Sat. 31,031, Sun. 30,111.

Fayetteville Observer: Fayetteville Publishing Co, 458 Whitfield St, POB 849, Fayetteville, NC 28302; tel. (910) 323-4848; fax (919) 486-3531; e-mail cbwell@fayobserver.com; internet www.fayobserver.com; f. 1816; morning; Publr CHARLES BROADWELL; Exec. Editor MIKE ARNHOLT; circ. Mon. to Fri. 49,163, Sat. 49,471, Sun. 59,263.

Greensboro News and Record: 200 East Market St, POB 20848, Greensboro, NC 27420-0848; tel. (336) 373-7000; fax (336) 373-7067; e-mail jeff.gauger@news-record.com; internet www.news-record.com; f. 1905; Publr and Pres. ROBIN SAUL; Editor JEFF GAUGER; circ. Mon. to Fri. 57,274, Sat. 57,162, Sun. 86,234.

News and Observer: 215 South McDowell St, POB 191, Raleigh, NC 27602; tel. (919) 829-4500; fax (919) 829-4872; internet www.newsobserver.com; f. 1872; Publr ORAGE QUARLES, III; Exec. Editor JOHN DRESCHER; circ. Mon. to Fri. 129,698, Sat. 135,923, Sun. 196,219.

Winston-Salem Journal: 418 North Marshall St, POB 3159, Winston-Salem, NC 27102-3159; tel. (336) 727-7211; fax (336) 727-4071; e-mail letters@wsjournal.com; internet www2.journalnow.com; Publr and Pres. JEFFREY GREEN; Man. Editor CAROL HANNER; circ. Mon. to Fri. 55,752, Sat. 56,449, Sun. 74,066.

North Dakota

The Forum: 101 Fifth St North, Fargo, ND 58102; tel. (701) 235-7311; fax (701) 241-5406; e-mail inforum@fccinteractive.com; internet www.inforum.com; f. 1878; Publr BILL M. MARCIL, Jr; Editor MATT VON PINNON; circ. Mon. to Fri. 45,332, Sat. 45,298, Sun. 50,374.

Ohio

Akron Beacon Journal: 44 East Exchange St, POB 640, Akron, OH 44308; tel. (330) 996-3000; fax (330) 996-3033; internet www.ohio.com; f. 1839; Publr ANDREA MATHEWSON; Editor BRUCE WINGES; circ. Mon. to Fri. 88,040, Sat. 104,809.

Canton Repository: 500 Market Ave South, Canton, OH 44711-2112; tel. (330) 580-8300; fax (330) 454-5610; e-mail don.detore@cantonrep.com; internet www.cantonrep.com; f. 1815; Publr CHRIS WHITE; Exec. Editor DONALD J. DETORE; circ. Mon. to Fri. 56,789, Sat. 53,386, Sun. 69,638.

Cincinnati Enquirer: 312 Elm St, Cincinnati, OH 45202; tel. (513) 721-2700; fax (513) 768-8340; e-mail cwashburn@enquirer.com; internet news.cincinnati.com; f. 1841; Publr and Pres. MARGARET E. BUCHANAN; Editor CAROLYN WASHBURN; circ. Mon. to Fri. 144,165, Sat. 153,990, Sun. 278,607.

Cleveland Plain Dealer: 1801 Superior Ave East, Cleveland, OH 44114-2198; tel. (216) 999-4800; fax (216) 999-6354; e-mail dasimmon@plaind.com; internet www.plaindealer.com; f. 1842; Pres. and Publr TERRANCE C. Z. EGGER; Editor DEBRA A. SIMMONS; circ. Mon. to Fri. 286,405, Sat. 278,014, Sun. 440,968.

Columbus Dispatch: 34 South Third St, Columbus, OH 43215; tel. (614) 461-5000; fax (614) 461-8793; e-mail letters@dispatch.com; internet www.dispatch.com; f. 1871; Pres. MICHAEL FIORILE; Editor BEN MARRISON; circ. Mon. to Fri. 136,023, Sat. 172,183, Sun. 264,802.

Dayton Daily News: 1611 South Main St, Dayton, OH 45409; tel. (937) 222-5700; fax (937) 225-7302; e-mail kriley@coxohio.com; internet www.daytondailynews.com; Publr MICHAEL JOSEPH; circ. Mon. to Fri. 93,425, Sat. 89,844, Sun. 154,896.

News-Herald: 7085 Mentor Ave, Willoughby, OH 44094; tel. (440) 951-0000; fax (440) 951-0917; e-mail lkessel@news-herald.com; internet www.news-herald.com; f. 1880; Mon. to Sat. evening, Sun. morning; Publr JEFF SUDBROOK; Exec. Editor TRICIA AMBROSE; circ. Mon. to Sat. 32,493, Sun. 36,295.

Toledo Blade: 541 North Superior St, Toledo, OH 43660; tel. (419) 724-6000; fax (419) 724-6166; e-mail luannsharp@theblade.com; internet www.toledoblade.com; f. 1835; Pres. and Gen. Man. JOSEPH ZERBEY; Exec. Editor KURT FRANCK; circ. Mon. to Fri. 94,215, Sat. 93,278, Sun. 127,953.

The Vindicator: 107 Vindicator Sq., POB 780, Youngstown, OH 44501-0780; tel. (330) 747-1471; fax (330) 747-6712; e-mail bjagnow@vindy.com; internet www.vindy.com; Publr BETTY H. BROWN JAGNOW; Editor TODD FRANKO; circ. Mon. to Fri. 45,012, Sat. 53,419, Sun. 60,205.

Oklahoma

Daily Oklahoman: 9000 North Broadway, POB 25125, Oklahoma City, OK 73125; tel. (405) 475-3311; fax (405) 475-3183; internet www.newsok.com; f. 1894; Publr CHRISTOPHER P. REEN; Editor KELLY D. FRY; circ. Mon. to Fri. 130,177, Sat. 111,497, Sun. 187,240.

Tulsa World: 315 South Boulder Ave, POB 1770, Tulsa, OK 74103; tel. (918) 581-8300; fax (918) 581-8353; e-mail letters@tulsaworld.com; internet www.tulsaworld.com; f. 1906; Publr ROBERT E. LORTON, III; Exec. Editor JOE WORLEY; circ. Mon. to Fri. 97,725, Sat. 107,316, Sun. 140,242.

Oregon

The Oregonian: 1320 SW Broadway, Portland, OR 97201-3469; tel. (503) 221-8327; fax (503) 294-4193; e-mail newsroom@oregonian.com; internet www.oregonlive.com; f. 1850; Publr N. CHRISTIAN ANDERSON, III; Editor PETER BHATIA; circ. Mon. to Fri. 247,833, Sat. 238,884, Sun. 306,712.

The Register-Guard: 3500 Chad Dr., POB 10188, Eugene, OR 97440-2188; tel. (541) 485-1234; fax (541) 683-7631; e-mail tony.baker@registerguard.com; internet www.registerguard.com; f. 1867; Publr and Editor TONY BAKER; circ. Mon. to Fri. 53,812, Sat. 57,163, Sun. 59,221.

Statesman Journal: 280 Church St, NE, POB 13009, Salem, OR 97309-3009; tel. (503) 399-6611; fax (503) 399-6706; e-mail letters@statesmanjournal.com; internet www.statesmanjournal.com; f. 1851; Publr and Pres. STEVE SILBERMAN; Exec. Editor BILL CHURCH; circ. Mon. to Fri. 36,946, Sat. 34,617, Sun. 45,218.

Pennsylvania

Bucks County Courier Times: 8400 Route 13, Levittown, PA 19057-5198; tel. (215) 949-4161; fax (215) 949-4177; e-mail pwalker@phillyburbs.com; internet www.phillyburbs.com; f. 1910; owned by Calkins Media Inc; Publr DALE LARSON; Exec. Editor PATRICIA S. WALKER; circ. Mon. to Fri. 41,672, Sun. 52,430.

Call Chronicle: POB 1260, Allentown, PA 18105; tel. (610) 820-6500; fax (610) 820-6693; f. 1921; Sun.; Publr GARY K. SHORTS; Exec. Editor LAWRENCE H. HYMANS; circ. 189,000.

The Morning Call: 101 North Sixth St, POB 1260, Allentown, PA 18105; tel. (610) 820-6502; fax (610) 820-6756; e-mail david.erdman@mcall.com; internet www.mcall.com; Publr and Pres. TIMOTHY E. RYAN; Editor and Vice-Pres. DAVID ERDMAN; circ. Mon. to Fri. 100,196, Sat. 76,098, Sun. 125,549.

Patriot-News: 812 Market St, Harrisburg, PA 17105; tel. (717) 255-8100; fax (717) 255-8456; internet www.patriot-news.com; f. 1854; Publr JOHN A. KIRKPATRICK; Exec. Editor DAVID NEWHOUSE; circ. Mon. to Fri.77,598, Sat. 72,768, Sun. 119,885.

Philadelphia Daily News: 400 North Broad St, POB 7788, Philadelphia, PA 19130; tel. (215) 854-5901; fax (215) 854-5910; e-mail dailynews.opinion@phillynews.com; internet www.philly.com; f. 1925; filed for Chapter 11 bankruptcy protection in Feb. 2009; bought by Philadelphia Media Networks in Sept. 2010; Publr GREGORY J. OSBERG; Man. Editor MICHAEL DAYS; circ. Mon. to Fri. 99,103, Sat. 63,092 (2010).

Philadelphia Inquirer: 400 North Broad St, POB 8263, Philadelphia, PA 19101; tel. (215) 854-2000; fax (215) 854-4974; e-mail swischnowski@phillynews.com; internet philly.newspaperdirect.com/epaper/viewer.aspx; f. 1829; filed for Chapter 11 bankruptcy protection in Feb. 2009; bought by Philadelphia Media Networks in Sept. 2010; Publr GREGORY J. OSBERG; Editor STAN WISCHNOWSKI; circ. Mon. to Fri. 325,291, Sat. 201,342, Sun. 517,310.

Pittsburgh Post-Gazette: 34 Blvd of the Allies, Pittsburgh, PA 15222; tel. (412) 263-1100; fax (412) 391-8452; e-mail ssmith@post-gazette.com; internet www.post-gazette.com; f. 1786; Chair., Publr and Editor-in-Chief JOHN ROBINSON BLOCK; Exec. Editor DAVID M. SHRIBMAN, Jr; circ. Mon. to Fri. 188,545, Sat. 163,608, Sun. 318,962.

Sunday News: Lancaster Newspapers, Inc, 8 West King St, POB 1328, Lancaster, PA 17608; tel. (717) 291-8811; fax (717) 399-6506; e-mail sunnews@lnpnews.com; internet www.lancasteronline.com/lol_pages/paper/sundaynews; f. 1923; Editor MARV ADAMS; circ. 97,538 (2010).

Tribune-Democrat: 425 Locust St, POB 340, Johnstown, PA 15907-0340; tel. (814) 532-5050; fax (814) 539-1409; e-mail eknopsnyder@tribdem.com; internet www.tribune-democrat.com; f. 1853; morning; Publr ROBIN QUILLON; Editor ERIC KNOPSNYDER; circ. Mon. to Fri. 32,623, Sat. 32,103, Sun. 35,741.

Rhode Island

Providence Journal: 75 Fountain St, Providence, RI 02902-0050; tel. (401) 277-7000; fax (401) 277-7346; e-mail pjnews@providencejournal.com; internet www.projo.com; f. 1829; publ. by

THE UNITED STATES OF AMERICA

Directory

Belo Corpn; Publr Howard G. Sutton; Exec. Editor Thomas E. Heslin; circ. Mon. to Fri. 114,013, Sat. 109,229, Sun. 122,377.

South Carolina

Greenville News: 305 South Main St, POB 1688, Greenville, SC 29602; tel. (864) 298-4100; fax (864) 298-4805; e-mail jpittman@greenvillenews.com; internet www.greenvilleonline.com; f. 1874; Publr Steven Brandt; Pres. and Exec. Editor John S. Pittman; circ. Mon. to Fri. 53,440, Sat. 55,247, Sun. 111,316.

The Post and Courier: 134 Columbus St, Charleston, SC 29403-4800; tel. (843) 577-7111; fax (843) 937-5579; e-mail publiceditor@postandcourier.com; internet www.charleston.net; f. 1803; Publr and Editor Willam E. Hawkins; circ. Mon. to Fri. 87,817, Sat. 79,886, Sun. 95,291.

The State: 1401 Shop Rd, POB 1333, Columbia, SC 29202; tel. (803) 888-5353; fax (803) 771-8639; e-mail stateeditor@thestate.com; internet www.thestate.com; f. 1891; acquired by the McClatchy Co in 2006; Publr Henry Haitz, III; Exec. Editor Mark Lett; circ. Mon. to Fri. 70,980, Sat. 68,551, Sun. 124,817.

South Dakota

Argus Leader: 200 South Minnesota Ave, Sioux Falls, SD 57104; tel. (605) 331-2200; fax (605) 331-2294; e-mail jzimmerm@argusleader.com; internet www.argusleader.com; f. 1881; Publr Randell Beck; Man. Editor Patrick Lalley; circ. Mon. to Sat. 32,192, Sun. 50,757.

Tennessee

Chattanooga Times-Free Press: 400 East 11th St, Chattanooga, TN 37403; tel. (423) 756-6900; fax (423) 757-6383; e-mail jtaylor@timesfreepress.com; internet www.timesfreepress.com; f. 1888; Pres. Jason Taylor; Man. Editor Alison Gerber; circ. Mon. to Fri. 75,336, Sat. 78,108, Sun. 103,186.

The Commercial Appeal: 495 Union Ave, Memphis, TN 38103; tel. (901) 529-2345; fax (901) 529-2522; internet www.commercialappeal.com; f. 1841; Pres. and Publr Joseph Pepe; Editor Chris Peck; circ. Mon. to Fri. 118,978, Sat. 92,385, Sun. 155,864.

Knoxville News-Sentinel: 2332 News Sentinel Dr., Knoxville, TN 37921-5731; tel. (865) 521-8181; fax (865) 342-8650; internet www.knoxnews.com; f. 1886; Publr Patrick J. Birmingham; Editor Jack McElroy; circ. Mon. to Fri. 98,381, Sat. 95,160, Sun. 124,225.

The Tennessean: 1100 Broadway St, Nashville, TN 37203; tel. (615) 259-8000; fax (615) 259-8093; e-mail customer@tennessean.com; internet www.tennessean.com; f. 1812; Publr Carol Hudler; Exec. Editor Maria de Varenne; circ. Mon. to Fri. 128,400, Sat. 133,390, Sun. 222,714.

Texas

Austin American-Statesman: 305 South Congress Ave, Austin, TX 78704; POB 670, Austin, TX 78767; tel. (512) 445-3500; fax (512) 445-3679; internet www.statesman.com; f. 1871; Publr Mike Joseph; Editor Debbie Hiott (acting); circ. Mon. to Fri. 125,305, Sat. 117,852, Sun. 183,717.

Beaumont Enterprise: 380 Main St, POB 3071, Beaumont, TX 77701-2331; tel. (409) 838-2897; fax (409) 838-2857; e-mail tkelly@hearstnp.com; internet www.beaumontenterprise.com; f. 1880; Publr Bill Offill, II; Editor Timothy M. Kelly; circ. Mon. to Sat. 23,669, Sun. 34,046.

Corpus Christi Caller-Times: 820 North Lower Broadway, POB 9136, Corpus Christi, TX 78469; tel. (361) 884-2011; fax (361) 886-3732; e-mail webmaster@caller.com; internet www.caller.com; f. 1883; Pres. and Publr Darrell Coleman; Vice-Pres. and Editor Shane Fitzgerald; circ. Mon. to Fri. 46,015, Sat. 44,426, Sun. 61,470.

Dallas Morning News: 508 Young St, Dallas, TX 75202; tel. (214) 977-8222; fax (214) 977-8319; e-mail bmong@dallasnews.com; internet www.dallasnews.com; f. 1885; publ. by Belo Corpn; Publr James M. Moroney, III; Editor Robert W. Mong, Jr; circ. Mon. to Fri. 405,349, Sat. 255,579, Sun. 702,848.

El Paso Times: 300 North Campbell St, El Paso, TX 79901; tel. (915) 546-6119; fax (915) 546-6415; e-mail bmoore@elpasotimes.com; internet www.elpasotimes.com; f. 1881; Publr Sergio Salinas; Editor Robert Moore; circ. Mon. to Fri. 70,450, Sat. 56,676, Sun. 91,972.

Fort Worth Star-Telegram: 400 West Seventh St, Fort Worth, TX 76102; tel. (817) 390-7761; fax (817) 390-7789; e-mail lnorder@star-telegram.com; internet www.star-telegram.com; f. 1909; Publr Gary Wortel; Exec. Editor Jim Witt; circ. Mon. to Fri. 195,455, Sat. 275,345, Sun. 228,269.

Houston Chronicle: 801 Texas Ave, Houston, TX 77002; POB 4260, Houston, TX 77210-4260; tel. (713) 362-7171; fax (713) 362-3575; e-mail viewpoints@chron.com; internet www.chron.com; f. 1901;

Publr Thomas A. Stephenson; Editor Jeff Cohen; circ. Mon. to Fri. 384,007, Sat. 357,722, Sun. 916,934.

Lubbock Avalanche-Journal: 710 Ave J, POB 491, Lubbock, TX 79401-1808; tel. (806) 762-8844; fax (806) 744-9603; e-mail terry.greenberg@lubbockonline.com; internet www.lubbockonline.com; f. 1900; Publr Stephen A. Beasley; Editor Terry Greenberg; circ. Mon. to Fri. 35,362, Sat. 35,393, Sun. 44,681.

San Antonio Express-News: 301 Ave E, San Antonio, TX 78205; tel. (210) 250-3000; fax (210) 250-3105; e-mail letters@express-news.net; internet www.mysanantonio.com; f. 1864; Publr John C. McKeon; Editor Mike Leary; circ. Mon. to Fri. 139,099, Sat. 143,649, Sun. 353,572.

Utah

Deseret News: 55 North 300 West, Salt Lake City, UT 84101; tel. (801) 236-6000; fax (801) 237-2121; e-mail rhall@desnews.com; internet www.deseretnews.com; f. 1850; Pres. and CEO Clark Gilbert; Man. Editor Richard D. Hall; circ. Mon. to Fri. 83,719, Sat. 88,533, Sun. 160,617.

Salt Lake Tribune: 90 South 400 West, Suite 700, Salt Lake City, UT 84101; tel. (801) 237-8742; fax (801) 257-8525; e-mail news@sltrib.com; internet www.sltrib.com; f. 1871; publ. by MediaNews Group; Publr Dean Singleton; Editor Nancy Conway; circ. Mon. to Fri. 110,546, Sat. 111,188, Sun. 140,628.

Standard-Examiner: 332 Standard Way, POB 12790, Ogden, UT 84412-2790; tel. (801) 625-4400; fax (801) 625-4508; e-mail ahowell@standard.net; internet www.standard.net; f. 1888; Publr Lee Carter; Man. Editor Dave Greiling; circ. Mon. to Fri. 63,233, Sat. 63,538, Sun. 71,428.

Vermont

Burlington Free Press: 191 College St, POB 10, Burlington, VT 05402-0010; tel. (802) 863-3441; fax (802) 660-1802; e-mail letters@burlingtonfreepress.com; internet www.burlingtonfreepress.com; f. 1827; Publr James Fogler; Exec. Editor Michael Townsend; circ. Mon. to Sat. 30,558, Sun. 38,380.

Virginia

Daily Press: 7505 Warwick Blvd, Newport News, VA 23607; tel. (757) 247-4600; fax (757) 245-8618; e-mail customerservice@dailypress.com; internet www.dailypress.com; f. 1896; Publr Digby A. Solomon; circ. Mon. to Fri. 57,642, Sat. 65,195, Sun. 90,811.

Richmond Times-Dispatch: 300 East Franklin St, POB 85333, Richmond, VA 23219; tel. (804) 649-6990; fax (804) 819-1216; e-mail letters@timesdispatch.com; internet www2.timesdispatch.com; f. 1850; Publr Thomas A. Silvestri; Editor Danny Finnegan; circ. Mon. to Fri. 108,559, Sat. 121,777, Sun. 162,769.

Roanoke Times: 201 West Campbell Ave, POB 2491, Roanoke, VA 24010-2491; tel. (540) 981-3211; fax (540) 981-3346; e-mail debbie.meade@roanoke.com; internet www.roanoke.com; Publr Debbie Meade; Editor Carole Tarrant; circ. Mon. to Fri. 78,663, Sat. 72,725, Sun. 92,084.

USA Today: 7950 Jones Branch Dr., McLean, VA 22108-0605; tel. (703) 276-3400; e-mail hzimmerman@usatoday.com; internet www.usatoday.com; f. 1982; Pres. and Publr Larry Kramer; Editor David Callaway; circ. Mon. to Fri. 1,829,099.

Virginian-Pilot: 150 West Brambleton Ave, POB 449, Norfolk, VA 23501-0449; tel. (757) 446-2000; fax (757) 446-2051; e-mail contactvp@pilotonline.com; internet www.pilotonline.com; f. 1876; Publr and Pres. David Mele; Editor Denis Finley; circ. Mon. to Fri. 142,476, Sat. 131,447, Sun. 176,705.

Washington

The Herald: 1213 California St, Everett, WA 98201; POB 930, Everett, WA 98206; tel. (425) 339-3435; fax (425) 339-3049; e-mail customersvc@heraldnet.com; internet www.heraldnet.com; f. 1891; Publr David Dadisman; Exec. Editor Neal Pattison; circ. Mon. to Fri. 46,481, Sat. 44,358, Sun. 50,795.

News Tribune: 1950 South State St, POB 11000, Tacoma, WA 98411; tel. (253) 597-8742; fax (253) 597-8451; e-mail karen.peterson@thenewstribune.com; internet www.thenewstribune.com; f. 1883; Pres. and Publr David A. Zeeck; Exec. Editor Karen Peterson; circ. Mon. to Fri. 83,199, Sat. 80,355, Sun. 97,812.

Seattle Times: 1120 John St, POB 70, Seattle, WA 98111-0070; tel. (206) 464-2111; fax (206) 464-2261; e-mail letters@seattletimes.com; internet seattletimes.nwsource.com; f. 1896; Publr Frank A. Blethen; Exec. Editor David Boardman; circ. Mon. to Fri. 253,742, Sat. 226,846, Sun. 346,991.

Spokesman-Review: 999 West Riverside, POB 2160, Spokane, WA 99210-2160; tel. (509) 459-5000; fax (509) 459-3815; e-mail editor@spokesman.com; internet www.spokesman.com; f. 1883; Publr

WILLIAM STACEY COWLES; Editor GARY GRAHAM; circ. Mon. to Fri. 69,161, Sat. 77,965, Sun. 87,694.

West Virginia

Charleston Daily Mail: 1001 Virginia St East, Charleston, WV 25301-2835; tel. (304) 348-1797; fax (304) 348-4847; e-mail dmnews@ dailymail.com; internet www.dailymail.com; f. 1973; evening; Publr and Editor NANYA FRIEND; Man. Editor BRAD MCELHINNY; circ. Mon. to Fri. 17,879.

Wisconsin

Green Bay Press-Gazette: 435 East Walnut St, POB 23430, Green Bay, WI 54305-3430; tel. (920) 431-8400; fax (920) 431-8499; e-mail jdye@greenbaypressgazette.com; internet www .greenbaypressgazette.com; f. 1915; bought by Gannett Co in 1980; Publr KEVIN CORRADO; Exec. Editor MIKE KNUTH; circ. Mon. to Fri. 41,767, Sat. 53,371, Sun. 66,514.

Milwaukee Journal Sentinel: 333 West State St, POB 371, Milwaukee, WI 53201; tel. (414) 224-2000; fax (414) 224-2047; e-mail jsedit@journalsentinel.com; internet www.jsonline.com; f. 1837; Publr ELIZABETH 'BETSY' BRENNER; Editor MARTIN KAISER; circ. Mon. to Fri. 185,710, Sat. 152,295, Sun. 328,475.

Post-Crescent: 306 West Washington St, POB 59, Appleton, WI 54911; tel. (920) 993-1000; fax (920) 733-1983; e-mail jmara@ postcrescent.com; internet www.postcrescent.com; f. 1920; Mon. to Sat. evening, Sun. morning; Publr GENIA LOVETT; Exec. Editor DAN FLANNERY; circ. Mon. to Fri. 38,244, Sat. 45,006, Sun. 55,274.

Wisconsin State Journal: 1901 Fish Hatchery Rd, POB 8060, Madison, WI 53713; tel. (608) 252-6100; fax (608) 252-6119; e-mail wsjcity@madison.com; internet www.madison.com/wsj; f. 1839; Publr WILLIAM K. JOHNSTON; Editor JOHN SMALLEY; circ. Mon. to Fri. 83,083, Sat. 82,973, Sun. 116,329.

Wyoming

Star-Tribune: 170 Star Lane, POB 80, Casper, WY 82602; tel. (307) 266-0500; fax (307) 266-0568; e-mail nathan.bekke@trib.com; internet www.trib.com; f. 1891; Publr NATHAN BEKKE; Man. Editor RON GULLBERG; circ. Mon. to Fri. 24,791, Sat. 21,171, Sun. 23,697.

SELECTED PERIODICALS

AARP The Magazine: 601 East St, NW, Washington, DC 20049; tel. (202) 434-3525; e-mail aarpmagazine@aarp.org; internet www.aarp .org/magazine; f. 1958 following merger of *My Generation* and *Modern Maturity*; publ. of the American Asscn of Retired Persons; 6 a year; general interest for the over-50s; Group Publr, Vice-Pres. and Publr JIM FISHMAN; Editor-in-Chief NANCY P. GRAHAM; circ. 22,528,478; AARP also publishes *AARP Bulletin* (11 a year, circ. 22,283,411) and *AARP Segunda Juventud* (quarterly, in Spanish and English).

Allure: 4 Times Sq., New York, NY 10036; tel. (212) 286-2860; fax (212) 286-4654; e-mail letters@allure.com; internet www.allure.com; f. 1991; publ. by Condé Nast Publs Inc; monthly; women's fashion and well-being; Vice-Pres. and Publr AGNES B. CHAPSKI; Editor-in-Chief LINDA WELLS; circ. 1,127,636.

American Baby: 375 Lexington Ave, 9th Floor, New York, NY 10017-5514; tel. (212) 499-2000; fax (212) 499-2038; internet www .parents.com/american-baby-magazine/; f. 1986; 10 a year; Publr RICHARD BERENSON; Editor ERIN CRAWFORD.

American Heritage: 416 Hungerford Dr., Suite 216, Rockville, MD 20850-4127; tel. (240) 453-0900; e-mail editor@americanheritage .com; internet www.americanheritage.com; f. 1949; 4 a year; US history; CEO EDWIN S. GROSVENOR; Publr ROBERT L. JENKINS; circ. 165,000; also publishes *American Heritage of Inventions and Technology* and quarterly African American history and culture magazine *American Legacy*.

The American Legion Magazine: 700 North Pennsylvania St, POB 1055, Indianapolis, IN 46206-1055; tel. (317) 630-1298; fax (317) 630-1280; e-mail magazine@legion.org; internet www.legion.org; f. 1919; publ. of *The American Legion*; monthly; Editor JEFF STOFFER; circ. 2,284,729.

American Rifleman: NRA Publications, 11250 Waples Mill Rd, Fairfax, VA 22030; tel. (703) 267-1329; e-mail publications@nrahq .org; internet www.americanrifleman.org; f. 1885; official journal of the Nat. Rifle Asscn; monthly; Editor-in-Chief MARK A. KEEFE, IV; circ. 1,696,922.

American Teacher: 555 New Jersey Ave, NW, Washington, DC 20001-2079; tel. (202) 879-4400; fax (202) 783-2014; e-mail online@ aft.org; internet www.aft.org; f. 1916; publ. by American Federation of Teachers; 6 a year; Editor ROGER S. GLASS; circ. 919,000 (2009).

Architectural Digest: 4 Times Sq., New York, NY 10036; tel. (212) 286-2860; fax (212) 286-6905; e-mail jayson_goldberg@archdigest .com; internet www.architecturaldigest.com; f. 1920; monthly;

Vice-Pres. and Publr GIULIO CAPUA; Editor-in-Chief MARGARET RUSSELL; circ. 819,155.

Arthritis Today: 1330 West Peachtree St, NW, Suite 100, Atlanta, GA 30309; tel. (404) 965-7635; e-mail atmail@arthritis.org; internet www.arthritistoday.org; f. 1987; publ. by the Arthritis Foundation; 6 a year; health and lifestyle magazine for sufferers of arthritis; Publr CINDY MCDANIEL; Editor-in-Chief MARCY O'KOON MOSS; circ. 680,622.

Auxiliary: American Legion Auxiliary, 8945 North Meridian St, Indianapolis, IN 46260; tel. (317) 569-4500; fax (317) 569-4502; e-mail alamagazine@alaforveterans.org; internet www .alaforveterans.org; publ. of the American Legion Auxiliary (ALA); fmrly *National News*, above name adopted 2009; quarterly; Editor STEPHANIE L. HOLLOWAY; circ. 743,147.

Barron's: 1211 Ave of the Americas, New York, NY 10036; tel. (212) 416-2000; e-mail online.editors@barrons.com; internet online .barrons.com; f. 1921; publ. by Dow Jones & Co, Inc, which was acquired by News Corpn in 2008; weekly; business and finance; Publr and Pres. GARY HOLLAND; Pres. and Editor EDWIN A. FINN, Jr; Man. Editor RICHARD RESCIGNO; circ. 302,714.

Better Homes and Gardens: 1716 Locust St, Des Moines, IA 50309-3023; tel. (515) 284-3000; fax (515) 284-3684; e-mail bhgeditor@meredith.com; internet www.bhg.com; f. 1922; publ. by Meredith Corpn; monthly; Vice-Pres. and Publr JAMES T. CARR; Editor-in-Chief GAYLE BUTLER; Exec. Editor KITTY MORGAN; circ. 7,617,038.

Bon Appétit: 4 Times Sq., 5th Floor, New York, NY 10036; tel. (212) 286-3535; e-mail askba@bonappetit.com; internet www.bonappetit .com; f. 1955; monthly; Vice-Pres. and Publr PAUL JOWDY; Editor-in-Chief ADAM RAPOPORT; circ. 1,541,469.

Boys' Life: 1325 West Walnut Hill Lane, POB 152079, Irving, TX 75015-2079; tel. (972) 580-2263; fax (972) 580-2079; e-mail boyslifemagazine@netbsa.org; internet boyslife.org; f. 1911; publ. by Boy Scouts of America; monthly; Publr J. WARREN YOUNG; Editor-in-Chief J. D. OWEN; circ. 1,136,142.

Bloomberg BusinessWeek: 1221 Ave of the Americas, 43rd Floor, New York, NY 10120; tel. (212) 512-2511; e-mail lou_tosto@ businessweek.com; internet www.businessweek.com; f. 1929; publ. by Bloomberg LP; weekly; business, finance and technology; Publr HUGH WILEY; Editor-in-Chief JOSH TYRANGIEL; circ. 993,267.

Car and Driver: 1585 Eisenhower Pl., Ann Arbor, MI 48108; tel. (734) 971-3600; fax (734) 971-9188; e-mail editors@caranddriver .com; internet www.caranddriver.com; f. 1956; publ. by Hachette Filipacchi Media US, Inc; Vice-Pres. and Publr JOHN C. DRISCOLL, Jr; Editor-in-Chief EDDIE ALTERMAN; circ. 1,212,555.

Catholic Digest: 1 Montauk Ave, Suite 200, POB 6015, New London, CT 06320-4967; fax (860) 572-0788; e-mail dconnors@ catholicdigest.com; internet www.catholicdigest.com; f. 1936; monthly; Publr KATHLEEN STAUFFER; Editor DAN CONNORS; circ. 283,548 (2008).

Condé Nast Traveler: 4 Times Sq., 14th Floor, New York, NY 10036-6561; tel. (212) 286-2860; fax (212) 286-2094; e-mail beth_lusko@condenast.com; internet www.cntraveler.com; f. 1954; monthly; Publr CHRIS MITCHELL; Editor-in-Chief KLARA GLOWCZEWSKA; circ. 807,160.

Congressional Digest: Congressional Digest Corpn, POB 240, Boyds, MD 20841-0240; tel. (301) 916-1800; fax (240) 599-7679; e-mail info@congressionaldigest.com; internet congressionaldigest .com; f. 1921; monthly; Publr PAGE B. ROBINSON THOMAS; Editors SARAH ORRICK, ANTHONY ZURCHER.

Consumer Reports: 101 Truman Ave, Yonkers, NY 10703-1057; tel. (914) 378-2000; fax (914) 378-2900; e-mail pressroom@consumer .org; internet www.consumerreports.org; f. 1936; publ. by the Consumers Union; monthly; Editor-in-Chief KIM KLEMAN; Man. Editor ROBERT TIERNAN; circ. 4,000,000.

Consumers Digest: Consumers Digest Communications, 520 Lake Cook Rd, Suite 500, Deerfield, IL 60015; tel. (847) 607-3000; e-mail postmaster@consumersdigest.com; internet www.consumersdigest .com; f. 1959; 6 a year; Publr RANDY WEBER; Editor RICH DZIERWA; circ. 1,200,000 (2010).

Cosmopolitan: 300 West 57th St, New York, NY 10019-3299; tel. (212) 649-3570; e-mail cosmo@hearst.com; internet www .cosmopolitan.com; f. 1886; monthly; women's interest; Publr DONNA KALAJIAN LAGANI; Editor-in-Chief JOANNA COLES; circ. 3,017,834.

Country Home: 1716 Locust St, Des Moines, IA 50309; tel. (515) 284-2015; e-mail countryhome@meredith.com; internet www .countryhome.com; f. 1979; publ. by Meredith Corpn; 10 a year; lifestyle; Publr ANTHONY IMPERATO; Editor-in-Chief CAROL SHEEHAN; circ. 1,271,782.

Country Living: 300 West 57th St, New York, NY 10019-3788; tel. (212) 649-3500; e-mail countryliving@hearst.com; internet www .countryliving.com; f. 1978; monthly; Vice-Pres. and Publr CHRIS ALLEN; Editor-in-Chief SARAH GRAY MILLER; circ. 1,641,000.

Discover: 275 Seventh Ave, 21st Floor, New York, NY 10011; tel. (212) 624-4800; fax (212) 624-4813; e-mail editorial@ discovermagazine.com; internet www.discovermagazine.com; f. 1980; publ. by Kalmbach Publishing Co; science and technology; Publr HENRY DONAHUE; Editor-in-Chief COREY S. POWELL; circ. 599,196.

Ebony: Johnson Publishing, 820 South Michigan Ave, Chicago, IL 60605-2191; tel. (312) 322-9200; fax (312) 322-0039; e-mail editors@ ebony.com; internet www.ebony.com; f. 1945; publ. by Johnson Publishing Co; monthly; African American general interest; Editor-in-Chief AMY DUBOIS BARNETT; Man. Editor TERRY GLOVER; circ. 1,255,542.

Elks Magazine: 2750 North Lakeview Ave, Chicago, IL 60614-1889; tel. (773) 755-4700; fax (773) 755-4790; e-mail annai@elks.org; internet www.elks.org/elksmag; f. 1922; 10 a year; publ. by the Benevolent and Protective Order of Elks of the United States of America; Publr and Editor CHERYL T. STACHURA; Man. Editor ANNA L. IDOL; circ. 960,000 (2008).

Elle: 1633 Broadway, 44th Floor, New York, NY 10019; tel. (212) 767-5800; fax (212) 767-5980; internet www.elle.com; f. 1985; publ. by Hachette Filipacchi Media US, Inc; monthly; women's fashion; Sr Vice-Pres. and Group Publishing Dir ROBIN DOMENICONI; Editor-in-Chief ROBERTA MYERS; circ. 1,121,529.

Endless Vacation: 360 Lexington Ave, 19th Floor, New York, NY 10017; tel. (212) 481-3452; fax (212) 213-1287; e-mail barbara.peck@ storyworldwide.com; internet www.endlessvacation.com; f. 1975; publ. by Resort Condominiums Int; 5 a year; Publr BRIAN BRUNO; Editor BARBARA PECK; circ. 1,845,297 (2009).

Entertainment Weekly: 135 West 50th St, 3rd Floor, New York, NY 10020; tel. (212) 522-5600; fax (212) 522-4482; e-mail letters@ew .com; internet www.ew.com/ew; f. 1990; Publr KARIN TRACY; Editor-in-Chief JOHN HUEY; circ. 1,781,934.

ESPN The Magazine: 19 East 34th St, New York, NY 10016; tel. (212) 515-1000; fax (212) 515-1275; e-mail ms_support@espn.go.com; internet insider.espn.go.com/insider/espn-the-magazine; f. 1998; fortnightly; subsidiary of Walt Disney DIS; men's sports and lifestyle; Editor-in-Chief CHAD MILLMAN; circ. 2,132,897.

Esquire: 300 West 57th St, 21st Floor, New York, NY 10019-3797; tel. (212) 649-4020; fax (212) 649-4303; e-mail esquire@hearst.com; internet www.esquire.com; f. 1933; monthly; Vice-Pres. and Publr KEVIN O'MALLEY; Editor-in-Chief DAVID GRANGER; circ. 721,399.

Essence: 135 West 50th St, 4th Floor, New York, NY 10020; tel. (212) 642-0600; fax (212) 921-5173; e-mail webmaster@essence-online .com; internet www.essence.com; f. 1970; monthly; African American general interest; Editor-in-Chief CONSTANCE C. R. WHITE; circ. 1,080,633.

Family Circle: 375 Lexington Ave, 9th Floor, New York, NY 10017-5514; tel. (212) 499-2000; fax (212) 499-6740; e-mail support@ familycircle.com; internet www.familycircle.com; f. 1932; publ. by Meredith Corpn; every 3 weeks; Publr CAREY WITMER; Editor-in-Chief LINDA FEARS; circ. 4,100,977.

FamilyFun: Disney FamilyFun Group, 244 Main St, Northampton, MA 01060; tel. (413) 585-0444; fax (413) 587-9335; e-mail support@ familyfun.com; internet familyfun.go.com; f. 1991; publ. by Disney Publishing Worldwide; monthly; general interest for families with young children; Editorial Dir ANN HALLOCK; Editor JON ADOLPH; circ. 1,985,827.

Family Handyman (Home Service Publications): 2915 Commers Dr., Suite 700, Eagan, MN 55121; tel. (651) 454-9200; fax (651) 994-2250; e-mail editors@thefamilyhandyman.com; internet www .familyhandyman.com; f. 1951; publ. by Reader's Digest Asscn, Inc; 10 a year; Editor-in-Chief KEN COLLIER; circ. 1,138,612.

Fast Company: 7 World Trade Center, New York, NY 10007-2195; tel. (212) 389-5300; fax (212) 389-5496; e-mail editor@fastcompany .com; internet www.fastcompany.com; f. 1995; monthly; acquired by Mansueto Ventures LLC in 2005; global business practice; Publr CHRISTINE OSEKOSKI; Editor-in-Chief ROBERT SAFIAN; circ. 759,898.

FHM: 110 Fifth Ave, New York, NY 10011; tel. (212) 201-6702; fax (212) 201-6965; e-mail andrew.ormson@emapmetrousa.com; internet www.fhmus.com; f. 2000; publ. by Emap Metro LLC; monthly; men's lifestyle, entertainment and fashion; Exec. Publr and Pres. DANA FIELDS; Editor-in-Chief SCOTT GRAMLING; circ. 1,250,275 (2006).

Field & Stream: 2 Park Ave, New York, NY 10016-5601; tel. (212) 779-5000; fax (212) 779-5114; e-mail fsletters@bonniercorp.com; internet www.fieldandstream.com; f. 1895; publ. by Bonnier Corpn; 11 a year; Publr ERIC ZINCZENKO; Editor ANTHONY LICATA; circ. 1,252,833.

Fitness: 125 Park Ave, New York, NY 10017; tel. (212) 557-6600; e-mail eric.schwarzkopf@meredith.com; internet www .fitnessmagazine.com; f. 1992; acquired by Meredith Corpn in 2005; women's health and fitness; Publr LEE SLATTERY; Editor-in-Chief BETTY WONG; circ. 1,501,244 (2011).

Food & Wine: 1120 Ave of the Americas, New York, NY 10036; tel. (212) 382-5600; fax (212) 382-5879; e-mail christina.r.grdovic@aexp .com; internet www.foodandwine.com; f. 1978; publ. by American Express Publishing Corpn; monthly; Publr CHRISTINA R. GRDOVIC; Editor-in-Chief DANA COWIN; circ. 947,855.

Forbes: 60 Fifth Ave, New York, NY 10011-8802; tel. (212) 620-2200; fax (212) 620-1875; e-mail readers@forbes.com; internet www.forbes .com; f. 1917; fortnightly; Pres. and Editor-in-Chief STEVE FORBES; Publr RICHARD KARLGAARD; circ. 923,848.

Fortune: 1271 Ave of the Americas, New York, NY 10020; tel. (212) 522-1212; fax (212) 522-0810; e-mail letters@fortune.com; internet money.cnn.com/magazines/fortune; f. 1930; Man. Editor ANDREW SERWER; circ. 846,965.

Game Informer: 724 North First St, 3rd Floor, Minneapolis, MN 55401; tel. (612) 486-6100; fax (612) 486-6101; e-mail andy@ gameinformer.com; internet www.gameinformer.com; f. 1991; owned by Sunrise Publs; monthly; computer gaming; Publr CATHY PRESTON; Editor-in-Chief ANDY MCNAMARA; circ. 8,169,524.

Glamour: 4 Times Sq., 16th Floor, New York, NY 10036; tel. (212) 286-2860; fax (212) 286-8336; e-mail letters@glamour.com; internet us.glamour.com; f. 1939; publ. by Condé Nast Publs Inc; monthly; Publr WILLIAM WACKERMANN; Editor-in-Chief CYNTHIA LEIVE; circ. 2,374,291.

Golf Digest: 20 Westport Rd, POB 850, Wilton, CT 06897; tel. (800) 438-0491; fax (203) 761-5135; e-mail editor@golfdigest.com; internet www.golfdigest.com; f. 1950; publ. by Condé Nast Publs Inc; monthly; Vice-Pres. and Publr THOMAS J. BAIR; Editor-in-Chief JERRY TARDE; circ. 1,677,098.

Golf Magazine: 2 Park Ave, New York, NY 10016-5601; tel. (212) 779-5000; fax (212) 779-5588; e-mail golfletters@golfonline.com; internet www.golf.com; f. 1959; publ. by Time Inc; monthly; Publr CHARLIE KAMMERER; Editor DAVID CLARKE; circ. 1,425,490.

Good Housekeeping: 300 West 57th St, New York, NY 10019-5288; tel. (212) 649-2000; fax (212) 265-3307; e-mail tellgh@ goodhousekeeping.com; internet www.goodhousekeeping.com; f. 1885; monthly; Publr PATRICIA HAEGELE; Editor-in-Chief ROSEMARY ELLIS; circ. 4,346,757.

GQ: 4 Times Sq., New York, NY 10036; tel. (212) 286-6410; fax (212) 286-7969; e-mail letters@gq.com; internet us.gq.com; f. 1957; publ. by Condé Nast Publs Inc; monthly; men's lifestyle; Vice-Pres. and Publr PETER HUNSINGER; Editor-in-Chief JIM NELSON; circ. 963,507.

Guideposts: 39 Seminary Hill Rd, Carmel, NY 10512; tel. (212) 929-1300; fax (212) 929-9574; e-mail gpeditors@guideposts.org; internet www.guideposts.org; f. 1945; monthly; other publs incl. *Positive Thinking Magazine* (10 a year, circ. 335,000), *Angels on Earth* (6 a year, circ. 600,000) and *Guideposts Sweet 16* (6 a year); personal and spiritual development; Publr AMY MOLINERO; Editor-in-Chief EDWARD GRINNAN; circ. 1,774,250.

HANDY: 12301 Whitewater Dr., Minnetonka, MN 55343; tel. (952) 988-7294; fax (952) 988-7486; e-mail lokrend@namginc.com; internet www.handymanclub.com; f. 1993; publ. by North American Media Group Inc; official publ. of the Handyman Club of America; 6 a year; home improvement; Publr GRAYLE HOWLETT; Editor-in-Chief LARRY OKREND; circ. 455,986.

Harper's Bazaar: 300 West 57th St, New York, NY 10019-3799; tel. (212) 903-5000; fax (212) 262-7101; e-mail joyannking@hearst.com; internet www.harpersbazaar.com; monthly; Publr VALERIE SALEMBIER; Editor-in-Chief GLENDA BAILEY; circ. 734,504.

Health: 2100 Lakeshore Dr., Birmingham, AL 35209; tel. (205) 445-6476; fax (205) 445-5123; e-mail health@timeinc.com; internet www .health.com; f. 1987; publ. by Southern Progress Corpn, a subsidiary of Time Inc; 10 a year; women's health and well-being; Publr and Vice-Pres. RENEE TULENKO; Editor-in-Chief ELLEN KUNES; circ. 1,363,862.

Highlights for Children: 803 Church St, Honesdale, PA 18431; tel. (570) 253-1080; fax (570) 251-7847; internet www.highlights.com; f. 1946; monthly; Editor-in-Chief CHRISTINE FRENCH CLARK; circ. 1,800,000 (2007).

Home: 1633 Broadway, 44th Floor, New York, NY 10019; tel. (212) 767-5518; e-mail homeeditor@hfnm.com; internet www.homemag .com; f. 1981; publ. by Hachette Filipacchi Media US Inc; 10 a year; home improvement and decoration; Vice-Pres. and Publr JOHN H. GRANT; Vice-Pres. and Editor-in-Chief DONNA SAPOLIN; circ. 828,630.

Hot Rod Magazine: 831 South Douglas St, El Segundo, CA 90245; e-mail hotrod@primedia.com; internet www.hotrod.com; f. 1948; monthly; Sr Vice-Pres. and Group Publr DOUG EVANS; Editor-in-Chief DAVID FREIBURGER; circ. 654,135.

House Beautiful: 300 West 57th St, 24th Floor, New York, NY 10019-5970; tel. (212) 903-5206; e-mail readerservices@ housebeautiful.com; internet www.housebeautiful.com; f. 1896; monthly; Publr KATE KELLY SMITH; Editor-in-Chief NEWELL TURNER; circ. 835,005.

Inc.: 7 World Trade Center, New York, NY 10007-2195; tel. (212) 389-5377; fax (212) 389-5393; e-mail mail@inc.com; internet www .inc.com; f. 1987; acquired by Mansueto Ventures LLC in 2005; monthly; small business resources and advice; Publr JOHN TEBEAU; Editor-in-Chief JANE BERENTSON; circ. 711,068.

In Style: 1271 Ave of the Americas, New York, NY 10020; tel. (212) 522-1212; internet www.instyle.com; f. 1994; publ. by Time Inc; celebrity, women's lifestyle and fashion; Man. Editor ARIEL FOXMAN; circ. 1,767,248.

In Touch Weekly: 270 Sylvan Ave, Englewood Cliffs, NJ 07632; tel. (201) 569-6699; fax (201) 569-3584; e-mail contactintouch@ intouchweekly.com; internet www.intouchweekly.com; f. 2002; publ. by Bauer Publishing USA; weekly; celebrity and entertainment; Publr MARK OLTARSH; Editor-in-Chief MICHELLE LEE; circ. 595,614.

Jane: 750 Third Ave, New York, NY 10017; tel. (212) 630-4192; e-mail carlos_lamadrid@condenast.com; internet www.janemag .com; f. 1992; publ. by Condé Nast Publications; monthly; women's lifestyle; Vice-Pres. and Publr CARLOS LAMADRID; Editor-in-Chief BRANDON HOLLEY; circ. 706,561 (2005).

Jet: Johnson Publishing, 820 South Michigan Ave, Chicago, IL 60605-2191; tel. (312) 322-9200; fax (312) 322-1082; internet jetmag.com; f. 1951; weekly; African American general interest; Editor-in-Chief MITZI MILLER; circ. 745,809.

Junior Scholastic: 557 Broadway, New York, NY 10012; tel. (212) 343-6100; fax (212) 343-6333; e-mail junior@scholastic.com; internet www2.scholastic.com; f. 1937; 18 a year; Editor LEE BAIER; circ. 615,000 (2010).

Kiplinger's Personal Finance: 1729 H St, NW, Washington, DC 20006-3904; tel. (202) 887-6400; fax (202) 331-8637; e-mail magazine@kiplinger.com; internet www.kiplinger.com; f. 1947; monthly; Editor JANET BODNAR; circ. 631,548.

Ladies' Home Journal: 125 Park Ave, New York, NY 10017-5599; tel. (212) 557-6600; fax (212) 455-1010; e-mail lhj@meredith.com; internet www.lhj.com; f. 1883; monthly; Publr JULIE PINKWATER; Editor-in-Chief SALLY LEE; circ. 3,205,302.

The Lion: 300 22nd St, Oak Brook, IL 60523-8842; tel. (630) 468-6729; fax (630) 571-1685; e-mail magazine@lionsclubs.org; f. 1918; 11 a year; business and professional; Editor JAY COPP; circ. 385,705.

Lucky: 4 Times Sq., 6th Floor, New York, NY 10036; tel. (212) 286-2860; fax (212) 286-4986; internet www.luckymag.com; f. 2000; publ. by Condé Nast Publs Inc; monthly; fashion and shopping; Vice-Pres. and Publr GINA SANDERS; Editor-in-Chief BRANDON HOLLEY; circ. 1,109,757.

Marie Claire: 300 West 57th St, 34th Floor, New York, NY 10019-1497; tel. (212) 649-5000; fax (212) 501-5050; e-mail marieclairepromo@hearst.com; internet www.marieclaire.com; f. 1994; monthly; Publr SUSAN D. PLAGEMANN; Editor-in-Chief ANNE FULENWIDER; circ. 988,418.

Martha Stewart Living: 11 West 42nd St, 25th Floor, New York, NY 10036; tel. (212) 827-8000; fax (212) 827-8204; e-mail mstewart@ marthastewart.com; internet www.marthastewart.com; f. 1991; publ. by Martha Stewart Living Omnimedia, Inc; monthly; lifestyle and general interest; Group Publr SALLY PRESTON; Editor-in-Chief PILAR GUZMÁN; circ. 2,082,348; other publs incl. *Everyday Food* (f. 2003, circ. 1,088,109).

Maxim: 1040 Ave of the Americas, New York, NY 10018; tel. (212) 302-2626; fax (212) 302-2631; e-mail editors@maximmag.com; internet www.maximonline.com; f. 1997; publ. by Alpha Media Group; monthly; men's lifestyle and general interest; circ. 2,518,827.

MediZine Healthy Living: 500 Fifth Ave, Suite 1900, New York, NY 10110; tel. (212) 695-2223; fax (212) 695-2936; e-mail requestinfo@medizine.com; internet www.remedyhealthmedia.com; f. 1994; quarterly; health and well-being; other publs incl. *Remedy* (f. 1995, circ. 2,400,000) and *Diabetes Focus* (f. 2003, circ. 1,500,000); Editorial Dir DIANE UMANSKY; circ. 3,650,000 (2009).

Men's Fitness: 4 New York Plaza, New York, NY 10004; tel. (212) 545-4800; fax (212) 685-9644; e-mail jkimmel@amilink.com; internet www.mensfitness.com; f. 1985; publ. by AMI/Weider Publs; 10 a year; men's health, fitness and lifestyle; Publr MARC RICHARDS; circ. 585,265.

Men's Health: 33 East Minor St, Emmaus, PA 18098; tel. (212) 808-1676; e-mail mhletters@rodale.com; internet www.menshealth.com; f. 1988; men's health and general interest; 10 a year; publ. by Rodale Inc; Vice-Pres. and Publr JACK ESSIG; Editor-in-Chief DAVID ZINCZENKO; circ. 1,918,387.

Men's Journal Magazine: 1290 Ave of the Americas, New York, NY 10104-0298; tel. (212) 484-1616; fax (212) 484-3429; e-mail letters@ mensjournal.com; internet www.mensjournal.com; f. 1992; publ. by Wenner Media, Inc; monthly; men's general interest and active lifestyle; Publr CHRIS MCLOUGHLIN; circ. 700,916.

Metropolitan Home: 1633 Broadway, 44th Floor, New York, NY 10019-6741; tel. (212) 767-5522; fax (212) 767-5636; e-mail metletters@hfnm.com; internet www.methome.com; f. 1981; publ. by Hachette Filipacchi Media US Inc; 10 a year; interior design and architecture; Publr DEBORAH BURNS; Editor-in-Chief DONNA WARNER; circ. 563,417.

Midwest Living: 1716 Locust St, Des Moines, IA 50309; tel. (515) 284-3000; fax (515) 284-2700; e-mail midwestliving@meredith.com; internet www.midwestliving.com; f. 1987; publ. by Meredith Corpn; 6 a year; lifestyle with focus on US Midwest; Publr BRIAN KIGHTLINGER; Editor-in-Chief GREG PHILBY; circ. 977,272.

Money: Time & Life Bldg, Rockefeller Center, New York, NY 10020; tel. (212) 522-1210; fax (212) 522-0970; e-mail managing_editor@ moneymail.com; internet money.cnn.com; f. 1972; monthly; Publr FRANK WALL; Man. Editor CRAIG MATTERS; circ. 1,908,509.

More: 125 Park Ave, New York, NY 10017-5529; tel. (212) 557-6600; fax (212) 455-1244; e-mail more@meredith.com; internet www.more .com; f. 1998; publ. by Meredith Corpn; 10 a year; women's lifestyle; Publr BRENDA SAGET DARLING; Editor-in-Chief LESLEY JANE SEYMOUR; circ. 1,316,751.

Motor Trend: 831 South Douglas St, El Segundo, CA 90245; tel. (323) 782-2220; internet www.motortrend.com; f. 1949; publ. by Primedia, Inc; monthly; Publr IRA GABRIEL; Editor-in-Chief EDWARD LOH; circ. 1,137,252.

National Enquirer: American Media, Inc, 4950 Communication Ave, Suite 100, Boca Raton, FL 3343; e-mail letters@ nationalenquirer.com; internet www.nationalenquirer.com; f. 1926; publ. by American Media Inc; weekly; Publr DAVID J. PECKER; Editor-in-Chief TONY FROST; circ. 596,166.

National Geographic Magazine: POB 98199, Washington, DC 20090-8199; tel. (202) 857-7500; fax (202) 828-6679; e-mail ngm@ nationalgeographic.com; internet ngm.nationalgeographic.com; f. 1888; monthly; Exec. Vice-Pres. and Publr CLAUDIA MALLEY; Editor-in-Chief CHRIS JOHNS; circ. 4,000,000.

The New Yorker: 4 Times Sq., New York, NY 10036-7448; tel. (212) 286-5400; fax (212) 286-4168; e-mail themail@newyorker.com; internet www.newyorker.com; f. 1925; publ. by Condé Nast Publs Inc; weekly; Publr LISA HUGHES; Editor DAVID REMNICK; circ. 1,043,792.

Newsweek: Newsweek Bldg, 251 West 57th St, New York, NY 10019-1894; tel. (212) 445-4000; fax (212) 445-5068; e-mail letters@ newsweek.com; internet www.thedailybeast.com/newsweek.html; f. 1933; weekly; Propr SIDNEY HARMAN; Editor-in-Chief TINA BROWN; circ. 1,527,156.

Nick Jr. Family Magazine: 1515 Broadway, 32nd Floor, New York, NY 10036; tel. (212) 654-6198; fax (212) 846-1907; internet www .nickjr.com; f. 1999; subsidiary of Viacom Int. Inc; monthly; parenting; Editor-in-Chief FREDDI GREENBERG; circ. 431,136 (2009).

North American Hunter: 12301 Whitewater Dr., Minnetonka, MN 55343; tel. (320) 846-6090; fax (320) 846-6092; e-mail rsundberg@ namginc.com; internet www.huntingclub.com; f. 1979; publ. by North American Media Group Inc; 8 a year; official publ. of the North American Hunting Club; hunting and conservation; Publr RICH SUNDBERG; Editor DAVE MAAS; circ. 648,238.

O, The Oprah Magazine: 300 West 57th St, New York, NY 10019-5915; tel. (212) 903-5366; fax (212) 903-5388; e-mail omail@hearst .com; internet www.oprah.com/omagazine; f. 2001; monthly; Vice-Pres. and Publr JILL SEELIG; Editor-in-Chief SUSAN CASEY; circ. 2,444,934.

Organic Gardening: 400 South 10th St, Emmaus, PA 18098; tel. (610) 967-7671; fax (610) 967-8963; e-mail ogdcustserv@rodale.com; internet www.organicgardening.com; f. 1942; publ. by Rodale, Inc; 6 a year; Publr CHRIS LAMBIASE; Editor-in-Chief ETHNE CLARKE; circ. 295,253.

Outdoor Life: 2 Park Ave, 10th Floor, New York, NY 10016-5601; tel. (212) 779-5316; fax (212) 779-5118; e-mail olletters@bonniercorp .com; internet www.outdoorlife.com; f. 1898; publ. by Bonnier Corpn; 10 a year; Editor-in-Chief TODD W. SMITH; Exec. Editor JOHN SNOW; circ. 753,394.

Outside: 400 Market St, Santa Fe, NM 87501; tel. (505) 989-7100; fax (505) 989-4700; e-mail letters@outsidemag.com; internet www .outsideonline.com; f. 1976 as *Mariah*; publ. by Mariah Media Inc; monthly; adventure travel and outdoor recreation; Vice-Pres. and Publr SCOTT PARMELEE; Editor-in-Chief CHRISTOPHER KEYES; circ. 686,623.

Parenting: 2 Park Ave, New York, NY 10016; tel. (212) 779-5000; internet www.parenting.com; f. 1987; publ. by Bonnier Corpn; monthly; other publs incl. *Babytalk* (f. 1935, circ. 2,000,000); Editor-in-Chief ANA CONNERY; Publr MARK WILDMAN; circ. 2,232,588.

Parents: 375 Lexington Ave, 10th Floor, New York, NY 10017-5514; tel. (212) 878-8700; fax (212) 986-2656; e-mail support@parents.com; internet www.parents.com; f. 1926; monthly; Publr DIANE NEWMAN; Editor-in-Chief DANA POINTS; circ. 2,058,281.

PC World: IDG Consumer and SMB, 501 Second St, San Francisco, CA 94107; tel. (415) 243-0500; fax (415) 442-1891; e-mail pcwletters@pcworld.com; internet www.pcworld.com; f. 1982; publ. by IDG Consumer and SMB, Inc, a subsidiary of International Data Group; monthly; computer technology; Sr Vice-Pres. and Publr MIKE KISSEBERTH; Editor JOHN PHILIPS; circ. 357,169.

People: Time & Life Bldg, 28th Floor, Rockefeller Center, 1271 Ave of the Americas, New York, NY 10020; tel. (212) 522-3347; fax (212) 522-0883; e-mail editor@people.com; internet www.people.com; f. 1974; publ. by Time Inc; weekly; celebrity and entertainment; Group Pres. PAUL CAINE; Man. Editor LARRY HACKETT; circ. 3,563,035.

Playboy: 680 North Lake Shore Dr., Chicago, IL 60611-4402; tel. (312) 751-8000; fax (312) 751-2818; e-mail edit@playboy.com; internet www.playboy.com/magazine-toc.html; f. 1953; monthly; men's interest; Publr LOUIS MOHN; Editor-in-Chief HUGH M. HEFNER; circ. 1,363,615.

Popular Mechanics: 300 West 57th St, New York, NY 10019-5899; tel. (212) 649-2000; e-mail popularmechanics@hearst.com; internet www.popularmechanics.com; f. 1902; monthly; Publr WILLIAM CONGDON; Editor-in-Chief JAMES B. MEIGS; circ. 1,234,691.

Popular Science: 2 Park Ave, 9th Floor, New York, NY 10016; tel. (212) 779-5000; fax (212) 779-5108; e-mail letters@popsci.com; internet www.popsci.com; f. 1872; publ. by Bonnier Corpn; monthly; Publr GREGG R. HANO; Editor MARK JANNOT; circ. 1,350,685.

Prevention: 400 South 10th St, Emmaus, PA 18098; tel. (610) 967-8045; fax (610) 967-9198; e-mail pvncustserv@rodale.com; internet www.prevention.com; f. 1950; publ. by Rodale Inc; monthly; Vice-Pres. and Editor-in-Chief DIANE SALVATORE; circ. 2,930,730.

Progressive Farmer: Lakeshore Park Plaza, 2204 Lakeshore Dr., Birmingham, AL 35209; tel. (205) 414-4700; fax (205) 414-4705; e-mail jodle@progressivefarmer.com; internet www.progressivefarmer.com; f. 1886; monthly; Publr JACK ODLE; Editor-in-Chief GREGG HILLYER; circ. 675,000 (2009).

Reader's Digest: Reader's Digest Rd, Pleasantville, NY 10570-7000; tel. (914) 238-1000; fax (914) 238-4559; e-mail letters@rd.com; internet www.rd.com; f. 1922; 10 a year; filed for Chapter 11 bankruptcy protection in Aug. 2009; Pres. ROBERT E. GUTH; Editor-in-Chief LIZ VACCARIELLO; circ. 5,577,717.

Real Simple: Time and Life Bldg, 1271 Ave of the Americas, New York, NY 10020; tel. (212) 522-1212; fax (212) 467-1396; internet www.realsimple.com; f. 2000; publ. by Time Inc; monthly, plus 2 special issues; women's lifestyle and general interest; Producer ANTIGONI GOURAS; Man. Editor KATHLEEN MURRAY HARRIS; circ. 2,031,596.

Redbook: 224 West 57th St, 6th Floor, New York, NY 10019-3796; tel. (212) 649-3450; fax (212) 581-8114; e-mail redbook@hearst.com; internet www.redbookmag.com; f. 1903; monthly; Vice-Pres. and Publr MARY E. MORGAN; Editor-in-Chief JILL HERZIG; circ. 2,222,177.

Road & Track: 1499 Monrovia Ave, Newport Beach, CA 92663-2752; tel. (949) 720-5300; fax (949) 631-2757; e-mail rtletters@hfmus.com; internet www.roadandtrack.com; f. 1947; monthly; Editor-in-Chief LARRY WEBSTER; circ. 608,266.

Rolling Stone: 1290 Ave of the Americas, 2nd Floor, New York, NY 10104-0298; tel. (212) 484-1616; fax (212) 484-3429; e-mail feedback@rollingstone.com; internet www.rollingstone.com; f. 1967; fortnightly; Publr JANN S. WENNER; Man. Editor WILL DANA; circ. 1,464,943.

Scholastic Parent & Child: 557 Broadway, New York, NY 10012; tel. (212) 343-6100; e-mail news@scholastic.com; internet classroommagazines.scholastic.com/products/parent-child; f. 1995; publ. by Scholastic Inc; 8 a year; Publr JEFF WELLINGTON; Editor-in-Chief NICK FRIEDMAN; circ. 1,339,040.

Scientific American: 415 Madison Ave, New York, NY 10017-1179; tel. (212) 451-8200; fax (212) 754-1138; e-mail editors@sciam.com; internet www.sciam.com; f. 1845; monthly; Vice-Pres. and Publr BRUCE BRANDFON; Editor-in-Chief MARIETTE DiCHRISTINA; circ. 486,293.

Scouting Magazine: 1325 West Walnut Hill Lane, POB 152079, Irving, TX 75015-2079; tel. (972) 580-2000; fax (972) 580-2079; e-mail scole@netbsa.org; internet www.scoutingmagazine.org; f. 1913; publ. by Boy Scouts of America; 6 a year; Publr J. WARREN YOUNG; Editor-in-Chief J. D. OWEN; Man. Editor SCOTT DANIELS; circ. 955,637.

SELF Magazine: 4 Times Sq., 5th Floor, New York, NY 10036; tel. (212) 286-2860; fax (212) 286-6174; e-mail comments@self.com; internet www.self.com; f. 1979; publ. by Condé Nast Publs Inc; monthly; Vice-Pres. and Publr LAURA McEWEN; Editor-in-Chief LUCY DANZIGER; circ. 1,528,583.

Seventeen: 300 West 57th St, New York, NY 10019-1798; tel. (212) 649-2000; e-mail mail@seventeen.com; internet www.seventeen.com; f. 1944; publ. by Hearst Corpn; monthly; Publr JAYNE JAMISON; Editor-in-Chief ANN SHOKET; circ. 2,025,299.

Shape: 1 Park Ave, 10th Floor, New York, NY 10016; tel. (212) 545-4800; fax (212) 252-1131; internet www.shape.com; f. 1981; publ. by American Media, Inc; women's health and fitness; Editor-in-Chief TARA KRAFT; circ. 1,635,933.

Sierra: 85 Second St, 2nd Floor, San Francisco, CA 94105; tel. (415) 977-5606; fax (415) 977-5794; e-mail sierra.mail@sierraclub.org; internet www.sierraclub.org/sierra; f. 1893; official publ. of the Sierra Club; 6 a year; adventure, nature and ecology; Editor-in-Chief CHRISTIAN FODAY SESAY; circ. 512,072.

SmartMoney: 1755 Broadway, 2nd Floor, New York, NY 10019; tel. (212) 765-7323; e-mail editors@smartmoney.com; internet www.smartmoney.com; f. 1992; jt venture of Dow Jones & Co, Inc and Hearst Corpn; Publr BILL SHAW; Editor-in-Chief JONATHAN DAHL; circ. 817,225.

Smithsonian Magazine: 420 Lexington Ave, Suite 2335, New York, NY 10170; tel. (212) 916-1300; fax (212) 986-4259; e-mail info@si.edu; internet www.smithsonianmag.com; f. 1970; monthly; Editor-in-Chief MICHAEL CARUSO; circ. 2,138,931.

Southern Living: 2100 Lakeshore Dr., Birmingham, AL 35209-6721; tel. (205) 877-6000; fax (205) 445-7523; internet www.southernliving.com; f. 1966; monthly; Vice-Pres. and Editor-in-Chief LINDSAY BEARMAN; circ. 2,841,331.

Sporting News: POB 420235, Palm Coast, FL 32142-0235; tel. (646) 424-2227; fax (646) 424-2232; e-mail ebaker@sportingnews.com; internet aol.sportingnews.com; f. 1886; acquired by American City Business Journals, Inc in 2006; 2 a month; Pres. and CEO WHITNEY SHAW; Editorial Dir JOHN D. RAWLINGS; circ. 507,313.

Sports Illustrated: 1271 Ave of the Americas, 33rd Floor, New York, NY 10020-1339; tel. (212) 522-1212; fax (212) 522-0475; internet sportsillustrated.cnn.com; f. 1954; weekly; Editor TERRY McDONNELL; circ. 3,204,945.

Star: 1 Park Ave, 3rd Floor, New York, NY 10016; tel. (212) 743-6523; fax (212) 532-0940; e-mail djackson@starmagazine.com; internet www.starmagazine.com; f. 1974; weekly; Editor-in-Chief DAVID PERREL; circ. 782,333.

Sunset Magazine: 80 Willow Rd, Menlo Park, CA 94025-3691; tel. (650) 321-3600; fax (650) 327-7537; e-mail sunset@customersvc.com; internet www.sunset.com; f. 1898; monthly; travel, home, garden, food and drink; Sr Vice-Pres. and Publr KEVIN LYNCH; Editor-in-Chief KITTY MORGAN; circ. 1,264,308.

TENNIS: 79 Madison Ave, 8th Floor, New York, NY 10016; tel. (212) 636-2700; fax (212) 636-2720; e-mail jwilliams@tennismagazine.com; internet www.tennis.com; f. 1965; acquired by Miller Publishing Group LLC in 1997; 8 a year; tennis, travel and lifestyle; Publr JEFF WILLIAMS; Editor ED McGROGAN; circ. 603,069.

This Old House: 135 West 50th St, 10th Floor, New York, NY 10020; tel. (212) 522-9465; fax (212) 522-9435; e-mail toh_letters@thisoldhouse.com; internet www.thisoldhouse.com; f. 1995; publ. by Time Inc; 10 a year; home improvement; Editor J. SCOTT OMELIANUK; circ. 966,817.

Time: Time & Life Bldg, Rockefeller Center, 1271 Ave of the Americas, New York, NY 10020-1393; tel. (212) 522-1212; fax (212) 522-0023; e-mail letters@time.com; internet www.time.com; f. 1923; weekly; Man. Editor RICHARD STENGEL; Deputy Man. Editor NANCY GIBBS; circ. 3,276,822.

Traditional Home: 125 Park Ave, New York, NY 10017; tel. (212) 557-6600; fax (212) 551-6914; e-mail traditionalhome@meredith.com; internet www.traditionalhome.com; f. 1978; publ. by Meredith Corpn; 8 a year; Publr BETH FUCHS BRENNER; Editor-in-Chief ANN OMVIG MAINE; circ. 870,825.

Travel & Leisure: 1120 Ave of the Americas, 10th Floor, New York, NY 10036-6770; tel. (212) 382-5600; fax (212) 768-1568; e-mail tlquery@amexpub.com; internet www.travelandleisure.com; f. 1971; monthly; Editor-in-Chief NANCY NOVOGROD; circ. 984,302.

TV Guide: 11 West 42nd St, New York, NY 10036; tel. (212) 852-7500; fax (212) 852-7323; internet www.tvguide.com; f. 1953; weekly; Sr Vice-Pres. and Publr PETE HAEFFNER; Editor-in-Chief DEBRA BIRNBAUM; circ. 2,010,879.

US News & World Report: 1050 Thomas Jefferson St, NW, Washington, DC 20007-3837; tel. (202) 955-2000; fax (202) 955-2685; e-mail letters@usnews.com; internet www.usnews.com; f. 1933; monthly; online only from Jan. 2011; Publr KERRY F. DYER; Chair. and Editor-in-Chief MORTIMER B. ZUCKERMAN; Editor BRIAN KELLY; circ. 1,269,260.

US Weekly: 1290 Ave of the Americas, 2nd Floor, New York, NY 10104-0298; tel. (212) 484-1616; fax (212) 484-4242; e-mail letters@usmagazine.com; internet www.usmagazine.com; f. 1977; weekly; Publr VICTORIA LASDON ROSE; Editor-in-Chief MICHAEL STEELE; circ. 1,977,251.

Vanity Fair: 4 Times Sq., 7th Floor, New York, NY 10036; tel. (212) 286-2860; fax (212) 286-4324; e-mail vfmail@vf.com; internet www.vanityfair.com; f. 1983; publ. by Condé Nast Publs Inc; monthly;

Publr EDWARD MENICHESCHI; Editor-in-Chief GRAYDON CARTER; circ. 1,193,267.

VFW Magazine: 406 West 34th St, Kansas City, MO 64111-2736; tel. (816) 756-3390; fax (816) 968-1169; e-mail info@vfw.org; internet www.vfw.org; f. 1912; 11 a year; Editor RICHARD K. KOLB; circ. 1,264,347.

VIA: POB 24502, Oakland, CA 94623; tel. (925) 279-2441; fax (925) 279-5654; e-mail viamail@viamagazine.com; internet www.viamagazine.com; f. 1917; publ. by the California State Automobile Asscn; 6 a year; travel, motoring, insurance; Editor-in-Chief ANNE MCSILVER; circ. 2,805,214 (2010).

VIBE: 215 Lexington Ave, New York, NY 10016; tel. (212) 231-7300; fax (212) 231-7400; internet www.vibe.com; f. 1993; acquired by InterMedia Partners in 2009; bi-monthly; urban music and culture; Publr JEFF MAZZACANO; Editor-in-Chief JERMAINE HALL; circ. 202,439.

Vogue: 4 Times Sq., 12th Floor, New York, NY 10036; tel. (212) 286-2810; fax (212) 286-8593; e-mail voguemail@aol.com; internet www.style.com/vogue; f. 1892; monthly; also publ. *Teen Vogue* (10 a year, circ. 1,029,336); Editor-in-Chief ANNA WINTOUR; circ. 1,222,373.

Weight Watchers Magazine: 11 Madison Ave, 17th Floor, New York, NY 10010; tel. (212) 589-2791; fax (212) 589-2600; e-mail customerservice@weightwatchers.com; internet www.weightwatchers.com; f. 1968; monthly; Publr ANDREW AMILL; Editor KATE GREER; circ. 1,340,649.

WHERE: c/o Morris Visitor Publications, 699 Broad St, Suite 500, Augusta, GA 30901; tel. (706) 821-6663; fax (706) 836-3596; e-mail editorial@wheretraveler.com; internet www.wheretraveler.com; f. 1936; monthly; int. visitor information; 23 regional edns; Group Publr JEFF LEVY; circ. 1,249,635.

Woman's Day: 1271 Ave of the Americas, 42 Floor, New York, NY 10020; tel. (212) 767-6000; e-mail womansday@hearst.com; internet www.womansday.com; f. 1931; owned by Hachette Filipacchi; 17 a year; women's general interest; Vice-Pres. and Publr GINGER SUTTON; Editor-in-Chief SUSAN SPENCER; circ. 3,449,662.

Woman's World: Bauer Publishing, 270 Sylvan Ave, Englewood Cliffs, NJ 07632; tel. (201) 569-6699; fax (201) 569-5303; e-mail mrichards@bauermediaus.com; f. 1981; publ. by Bauer Publishing USA; weekly; women's general interest; other publs include *First* (circ. 1,310,696), *J-14* (circ. 321,558) and *Life & Style Weekly* (circ. 344,113); Publr MARC RICHARDS; Editor-in-Chief STEPHANIE SAIBLE; circ. 1,262,468.

Working Mother: Bonnier Corpn, 2 Park Ave, 10th Floor, New York, NY 10016; tel. (212) 779-5000; fax (212) 219-7448; internet www.workingmother.com; f. 1978; publ. by Working Mother Media, Inc; lifestyle magazine with focus on working mothers; Pres. CAROL EVANS; Editorial Dir JENNIFER OWENS; circ. 754,541.

NEWS AGENCIES

Associated Press (AP): 450 West 33rd St, New York, NY 10001; tel. (212) 621-1500; fax (212) 621-1679; e-mail info@ap.org; internet www.ap.org; f. 1846; Chair. MARY JUNCK; Pres. and CEO GARY PRUITT; c. 1,700 newspaper mems in the USA, 5,000 broadcast mems and over 8,500 subscribers abroad.

Bloomberg: 731 Lexington Ave, New York, NY 10022; tel. (212) 318-2000; fax (212) 369-5000; internet www.bloomberg.com; f. 1981; provides business data, news and analytics; CEO DANIEL L. DOCTOR-OFF; Editor-in-Chief MATTHEW WINKLER.

Dow Jones News Service: 1155 Ave of the Americas, 7th Floor, New York, NY 10036; tel. (212) 416-2000; internet www.dowjones.com; parent co, Dow Jones & Co, acquired by News Corpn in 2008; CEO LES FENWICK; Editor-in-Chief ROBERT THOMSON.

Jewish Telegraphic Agency, Inc (JTA): 330 Seventh Ave, 17th Floor, New York, NY 10001; tel. (212) 643-1890; fax (212) 643-8498; e-mail info@jta.org; internet www.jta.org; f. 1917; world-wide coverage of Jewish news; offices in Washington, DC, and Jerusalem, Israel; Pres. DAVID J. RUDIS; Editor-in-Chief AMI EDEN.

Religion News Service: 529 14th St, National Press Bldg, NW, Suite 425, Washington, DC 20045; tel. (202) 463-8777; fax (202) 662-7154; e-mail info@religionnews.com; internet www.religionnews.com; f. 1934; Editor KEVIN ECKSTROM.

United Media (UM): 200 Madison Ave, 4th Floor, New York, NY 10016; tel. (212) 293-8500; fax (212) 293-8600; e-mail press@amuniversal.com; internet www.universaluclick.com; f. 1978; licensing and syndication of news features; owned by The E. W. Scripps Co; syndication management services transferred to Universal Uclick in 2011; Pres. and CEO DOUGLAS R. STERN.

United Press International (UPI): 1133 19th St, NW, Washington, DC 20036; tel. (202) 898-8000; fax (202) 898-8048; e-mail editorforms@upi.com; internet www.upi.com; f. 1907; Pres. NICHOLAS CHIAIA; Exec. Editor JOHN HENDEL; serves c. 1,000 newspaper clients world-wide.

NATIONAL ASSOCIATIONS

American Business Media: 675 Third Ave, Suite 415, 7th Floor, New York, NY 10017-5704; tel. (212) 661-6360; fax (212) 370-0736; e-mail info@abmmail.com; internet www.americanbusinessmedia.com; f. 1906; Chair. JEFF LAPIN; Pres. and CEO CLARK PETTIT; 205 mem. cos.

American Society of Magazine Editors (ASME): 810 Seventh Ave, 24th Floor, New York, NY 10019; tel. (212) 872-3700; fax (212) 906-0128; e-mail asme@magazine.org; internet magazine.org/asme; Pres. LUCY DANZIGER; Chief Exec. SID HOLT; 850 mems.

Audit Bureau of Circulations (ABC): 48 West Seegers Rd, Arlington Heights, IL 60005-3913; tel. (224) 366-6939; fax (224) 366-6949; e-mail kammi.altig@accessabc.com; internet www.accessabc.com; f. 1914; Chair. MERLE K. DAVIDSON; Pres. and Man. Dir MICHAEL J. LAVERY; over 4,000 mems.

Council of Literary Magazines and Presses (CLMP): 154 Christopher St, Suite 3C, New York, NY 10014-9110; tel. (212) 741-9110; fax (212) 741-9112; e-mail info@clmp.org; internet www.clmp.org; f. 1967; provides services to non-commercial US literary magazines and presses; Exec. Dir JEFFREY LEPENDORF; 347 mems.

MPA—The Association of Magazine Media: 810 Seventh Ave, 24th Floor, New York, NY 10019; tel. (212) 872-3700; e-mail mpa@magazine.org; internet www.magazine.org; f. 1919; fmrly Magazine Publishers of America; adopted present name in 2010; Chair. MICHAEL A. CLINTON; Pres. and CEO NINA B. LINK; 175 mem. cos and 100 assoc. mems.

  Publishers' Information Bureau: 810 Seventh Ave, New York, NY 10019; tel. (212) 872-3722; e-mail pib@magazine.org; internet www.magazine.org; f. 1945; part of MPA; tracks advertising carried by consumer magazines; 250 mem. publs; Pres. WAYNE P. EADIE.

National Newspaper Association: 309 S. Providence Rd, Columbia, MO 65203; tel. (573) 777-4980; fax (573) 777-4985; e-mail info@nna.org; internet www.nnaweb.org; f. 1885 as National Editorial Association; present name adopted 1964; Pres. REED ANFINSON; CEO TONDA RUSH; over 2,700 mems.

Newspaper Association of America: 4401 Wilson Blvd, Suite 900, Arlington, VA 22203-1867; tel. (571) 366-1000; fax (571) 366-1195; e-mail cheryl.sadowski@naa.org; internet www.naa.org; f. 1992; Chair. JAMES M. MORONEY, III; Pres. and CEO CAROLINE LITTLE; more than 2,000 mems in USA and Canada accounting for over 87% of US daily newspaper circulation.

The Newspaper Guild: 501 Third St, NW, Washington, DC 20001-2797; tel. (202) 434-7177; fax (202) 434-1472; e-mail guild@cwa-union.org; internet www.newsguild.org; f. 1933; journalists' org., organ of the Communications Workers of America trade union; Pres. BERNARD J. LUNZER; Admin. Dir TIMOTHY SCHICK; over 34,000 mems in the USA, Puerto Rico and Canada.

Periodical & Book Association of America Inc: 481 Eighth Ave, Suite 526, New York, NY 10001; tel. (212) 563-6502; fax (212) 563-4098; e-mail lscott@pbaa.net; internet www.pbaa.net; Pres. JAY ANNIS; Exec. Dir LISA W. SCOTT; 90 mems.

Publishers

Abaris Books: 70 New Canaan Ave, Norwalk, CT 06850; tel. (203) 838-8625; fax (203) 857-0730; e-mail abaris@abarisbooks.com; internet www.abarisbooks.com; f. 1973; division of Opal Publishing Corpn; scholarly, fine art reference, philosophy; Publr ANTHONY S. KAUFMANN; Man. Editor J. C. WEST.

Abbeville Press, Inc: 137 Varick St, New York, NY 10013; tel. (212) 366-5585; fax (212) 366-6966; e-mail abbeville@abbeville.com; internet www.abbeville.com; f. 1977; fine arts and illustrated books; Pres. and Publr ROBERT E. ABRAMS.

Abingdon Press: 201 Eighth Ave South, POB 801, Nashville, TN 37202-0801; tel. (615) 749-6290; fax (615) 749-6512; e-mail orders@abingdonpress.com; internet www.abingdonpress.com; an imprint of The United Methodist Publishing House (f. 1789); religious; Vice-Pres. TAMMY GAINES.

Abrams: 115 West 18th St, New York, NY 10011; tel. (212) 206-7715; fax (212) 519-1210; e-mail abrams@abramsbooks.com; internet www.abramsbooks.com; f. 1949; acquired by Times Mirror Co in 1966; 7 imprints incl. Abrams Books (art, photography, design, architecture), Stewart, Tabori & Chang (f. 1981, cooking, design, gardening, crafts, pets, health, sports, and popular culture), Amulet Books (f. 2004, youth fiction and non-fiction) and Abrams Image (f. 2006, music, humour, reference, photography, design and popular culture); owned by Groupe de la Martinière, France; Pres. and CEO MICHAEL JACOBS.

AFB Press: 2 Penn Plaza, Suite 1102, New York, NY 10001; tel. (212) 502-7651; fax (917) 210-3979; e-mail press@afb.net; internet www

Directory

.afb.org/store; publishing arm of the American Foundation for the Blind; books, journals, videos, and electronic materials on visual impairment for professionals, researchers and blind or visually impaired individuals and their families; Pres. and CEO CARL R. AUGUSTO; Dir and Editor-in-Chief NATALIE HILZEN.

Alfred Music Publishing Co, Inc: 16320 Roscoe Blvd, Suite 100, Van Nuys, CA 91410-0003; tel. (818) 892-2452; fax (818) 891-6252; e-mail info@alfred.com; internet www.alfred.com; f. 1922; educational music, methods and texts; Pres. MORTY MANUS; CEO STEVEN MANUS.

Andrews McMeel Publishing: c/o Simon & Schuster, Inc, 100 Front St, Riverside, NJ 08075; tel. (816) 932-6700; fax (816) 932-6706; e-mail licensing@amuniversal.com; internet www.andrewsmcmeel.com; f. 1970; humour, general trade; Chair. JOHN P. MCMEEL; Pres. and CEO HUGH T. ANDREWS.

Augsburg Fortress, Publishers: 100 South Fifth St, POB 1209, Minneapolis, MN 55440; tel. (612) 330-3300; fax (612) 330-3455; e-mail info@augsburgfortress.org; internet www.augsburgfortress.org; f. 1890; publishing arm of the Evangelical Lutheran Church in America; religious (evangelical Lutheran) non-fiction; includes Fortress Press and Sparkhouse imprints; Pres. and CEO BETH A. LEWIS.

August House Inc, Publishers: 3500 Piedmont Rd, NE Suite 310, Atlanta, GA 30305; tel. (404) 442-4420; fax (404) 442-4435; e-mail ahinfo@augusthouse.com; internet www.augusthouse.com; f. 1979; Southern regional, history, humour and folklore; CEO STEVE FLOYD.

B&H Publishing Group: 127 Ninth Ave North, Nashville, TN 37214-0143; tel. (615) 251-5614; fax (615) 251-2701; e-mail miriam.evans@bhpublishinggroup.com; internet www.bhpublishinggroup.com; f. 1891; fmrly Broadman & Holman Publrs; present name adopted in 2006; religious (Protestant), fiction, non-fiction, reference and juvenile; Pres. SELMA WILSON; Publr DAVID SHEPHERD.

Baker Publishing Group: 6030 East Fulton Rd, Ada, MI 49301; tel. (616) 676-9185; fax (616) 676-9573; e-mail media@bakerbooks.com; internet www.bakerpublishinggroup.com; f. 1939; imprints incl. Bethany House (Christian fiction, q.v.), Baker Books (non-fiction for lay Christians), Baker Academic (scholarly, Christian), Brazos Press (Protestant and evangelical, Roman Catholic and Eastern Orthodox), Chosen Books (f. 1971, evangelical and charismatic Christian non-fiction), and Revell (Christian fiction and non-fiction); Pres. DWIGHT BAKER.

Ballantine Publishing Group: 1540 Broadway, New York, NY 10036; tel. (212) 572-2713; fax (212) 572-4912; e-mail bfi@randomhouse.com; internet www.randomhouse.com/rhpg; f. 1952; division of Random House Inc; fiction, non-fiction, reprints; Publr LIBBY MCGUIRE.

Barnes and Noble Books: POB 111, Lyndhurst, NJ 07071; tel. (800) 962-6177; fax (212) 559-6910; e-mail customerservice@bn.com; internet www.barnesandnoble.com; f. 1873; division of Rowman & Littlefield, Inc; educational and general; Chair. LEONARD RIGGIO; CEO WILLIAM J. LYNCH.

Barron's Educational Series, Inc: 250 Wireless Blvd, Hauppauge, NY 11788; tel. (631) 434-3311; fax (631) 434-3723; e-mail barrons@barronseduc.com; internet www.barronseduc.com; f. 1945; general non-fiction, educational and juvenile; Chair. and CEO MANUEL H. BARRON; Pres. and Publr ELLEN SIBLEY.

Beacon Press: 25 Beacon St, Boston, MA 02108; tel. (617) 742-2110; fax (617) 723-3097; e-mail lriviere@beacon.org; internet www.beacon.org; f. 1854; dept of the Unitarian Universalist Asscn; world affairs, religion and general non-fiction; Dir HELENE ATWAN.

R. R. Bowker LLC: 630 Central Ave, New Providence, NJ 07974; tel. (888) 269-5372; fax (888) 286-1090; e-mail info@bowker.com; internet www.bowker.com; f. 1872; reference and bibliography; Pres. and CEO ANNIE CALLANAN.

Branden Books, Inc: POB 812094, Wellesley, MA 02482; tel. (781) 734-2046; fax (781) 790-1056; e-mail branden@brandenbooks.com; internet www.brandenbooks.com; f. 1909 as The Four Seasons Press; art, music, classics, fiction and non-fiction; Pres. MARGARET CASO; Editor and Treas. ADOLPH CASO.

George Braziller, Inc: 277 Broadway, Suite 708, New York, NY 10007; tel. (212) 260-9256; fax (212) 260-1902; e-mail editorial@georgebraziller.com; internet www.georgebraziller.com; f. 1955; art, fiction and non-fiction; Pres. and Editor MICHAEL BRAZILLER.

Brookings Institution Press: 1775 Massachusetts Ave, NW, Washington, DC 20036-2103; tel. (202) 797-6000; fax (202) 536-3623; e-mail bibooks@brookings.edu; internet www.brookings.edu; f. 1927; economics, govt, foreign policy; Dir ROBERT L. FAHERTY.

Cambridge University Press: 32 Ave of the Americas, New York, NY 10013-2473; tel. (212) 924-3900; fax (212) 691-3239; e-mail information@cup.org; internet www.cambridge.org/us; scholarly; CEO PETER PHILLIPS; Man. Dir (Americas) MICHAEL PELUSE.

Catholic University of America Press: 620 Michigan Ave, NE, Washington, DC 20064; tel. (202) 319-5052; fax (202) 319-4985; e-mail cua-press@cua.edu; internet cuapress.cua.edu; f. 1939; scholarly; Dir and Editor-in-Chief TREVOR LIPSCOMBE.

Caxton Press: 312 Main St, Caldwell, ID 83605; tel. (208) 647-6465; fax (208) 459-7450; e-mail sgipson@caxtonpress.com; internet www.caxtonpress.com; f. 1903; Western Americana; Vice-Pres. and Publr SCOTT GIPSON.

Columbia University Press: 61 West 62nd St, New York, NY 10023; tel. (212) 459-0600; fax (212) 459-3678; e-mail cup_books@columbia.edu; internet www.columbia.edu/cu/cup; f. 1893; trade, educational, scientific and reference; Pres. and Dir JAMES D. JORDAN.

Concordia Publishing House (CPH): 3558 South Jefferson Ave, St Louis, MO 63118-3968; tel. (800) 325-3040; fax (800) 490-9889; e-mail order@cph.org; internet www.cph.org; f. 1869; publishing arm of the Lutheran Church—Missouri Synod; religious (Lutheran) children's books, devotionals and curriculum music; Pres. and CEO BRUCE G. KINTZ.

Cornell University Press: Sage House, 512 East State St, POB 250, Ithaca, NY 14850; tel. (607) 277-2338; fax (607) 277-2374; e-mail cupressinfo@cornell.edu; internet www.cornellpress.cornell.edu; f. 1869; scholarly, non-fiction; imprints incl. Comstock Publishing Associates, ILR Press and Fall Creek Books; Dir JOHN G. ACKERMAN.

CQ Press: 2300 N St, NW, Suite 800, Washington, DC 20037; tel. (202) 729-1900; fax (202) 729-1403; e-mail ahigginbotham@cqpress.com; internet www.cqpress.com; f. 1945; fmrly Congressional Quarterly Books; division of Sage Publications (q.v.); business, education and govt; directories; Pres. and Publr JOHN A. JENKINS.

The Creative Co: 123 South Broad St, POB 227, Mankato, MN 56001; tel. (507) 388-6273; fax (507) 388-2746; e-mail info@thecreativecompany.us; internet www.thecreativecompany.us; f. 1932; juvenile; Pres. TOM PETERSON.

F. A. Davis Co: 1915 Arch St, Philadelphia, PA 19103; tel. (215) 568-2270; fax (215) 568-5065; e-mail info@fadavis.com; internet www.fadavis.com; f. 1879; medical, nursing and allied health textbooks; Pres. ROBERT H. CRAVEN, Jr.

Dover Publications, Inc: 31 East Second St, Mineola, NY 11501; tel. (516) 294-7000; fax (516) 742-1401; internet www.doverpublications.com; f. 1941; trade, reprints, scientific, classics, language, arts and crafts; Pres. PAUL NEGRI.

Dufour Editions, Inc: 124 Byers Rd, POB 7, Chester Springs, PA 19425-0007; tel. (610) 458-5005; fax (610) 458-7103; e-mail info@dufoureditions.com; internet www.dufoureditions.com; f. 1949; literature, political science, humanities, music and history; Pres. CHRISTOPHER MAY.

Duke University Press: POB 90660, Duke University, Durham, NC 27708-0660; tel. (888) 651-0122; fax (888) 651-0124; e-mail bpublicity@dukepress.edu; internet www.dukepress.edu; f. 1921; scholarly; Dir STEVE COHN.

Duquesne University Press: 600 Forbes Ave, Pittsburgh, PA 15282; tel. (412) 396-6610; fax (412) 396-5984; e-mail dupress@duq.edu; internet www.dupress.duq.edu; f. 1927; scholarly; Dir SUSAN WADSWORTH-BOOTH; Production Editor KATHY MEYER.

Ediciones Universal: POB 450353, Miami, FL 33245-0353; tel. (305) 642-3234; fax (305) 642-7978; e-mail ediciones@ediciones.com; internet www.ediciones.com; f. 1965; Spanish-language fiction and non-fiction; Man. JUAN MANUEL SALVAT.

Elsevier: 11830 Westline Industrial Dr., St Louis, MO 63146; tel. (314) 453-6198; fax (314) 453-7095; e-mail usbkinfo@elsevier.com; internet www.elsevier.com; f. 1962; division of Reed Elsevier Group PLC; health sciences imprints incl. Butterworth-Heinemann (f. 1975, technology, medicine and management), Churchill Livingstone (f. 1972, medicine), Hanley & Belfus (f. 1984, medical textbooks and reference materials), Mosby (f. 1906, textbooks and reference materials on medicine, nursing, allied health and veterinary medicine), and W. B. Saunders Co (f. 1888, medicine); science and technology imprints incl. Academic Press (science, technology and business), Architectural Press (architecture), Focal Press (media technology), and Morgan Kaufmann (f. 1984, computing); CEO RON MOBED.

Encyclopaedia Britannica, Inc: 331 North La Salle St, Chicago, IL 60654; tel. (800) 621-3900; fax (800) 344-9624; e-mail international@eb.com; internet www.eb.com; f. 1768; encyclopaedias, atlases, dictionaries; Chair. JACOB E. SAFRA; Pres. JORGE CAUZ.

Farrar, Straus and Giroux, Inc (FSG): 18 West 18th St, New York, NY 10011; tel. (212) 741-6900; fax (212) 633-9385; e-mail fsg.publicity@fsgbooks.com; internet us.macmillan.com/fsg.aspx; f. 1946; acquired by Holtzbrinck Publrs, LLC in 1994; imprints incl. Hill and Wang (f. 1956), Faber and Faber, Inc, and North Point Press; literature, international fiction, history, current affairs and science; Pres. JONATHAN GALASSI.

Fordham University Press: 2546 Belmont Ave, University Box L, Bronx, NY 10458-5172; tel. (718) 817-4795; fax (718) 817-4785; e-mail bkaobrien@fordham.edu; internet www.fordhampress.com; f. 1907; scholarly; Dir FREDRIC NACHBAUR.

W. H. Freeman & Co, Publishers: 41 Madison Ave, 37th Floor, New York, NY 10010; tel. (212) 576-9400; fax (212) 689-2383; e-mail international@whfreeman.com; internet www.whfreeman.com; f. 1946; part of Holtzbrinck Publrs, LLC; textbooks; Pres. ELIZABETH WIDDICOMBE.

Samuel French, Inc: 45 West 25th St, New York, NY 10010; tel. (212) 206-8990; fax (212) 206-1429; e-mail info@samuelfrench.com; internet www.samuelfrench.com; f. 1830; plays; Pres. and CEO NATE COLLINS.

Gale Cengage Learning: 27500 Drake Rd, Farmington Hills, MI 48331-3535; tel. (248) 669-4253; fax (248) 669-8064; e-mail lindsay.brown@cengage.com; internet gale.cengage.com; f. 1954; division of Cengage Learning; reference; Exec. Vice-Pres. and Publr FRANK MENCHACA.

Garland Science Publishing, Inc: 270 Madison Ave, New York, NY 10016; tel. (917) 351-7100; fax (212) 947-3027; e-mail info@garland.com; internet www.garlandscience.com; f. 1969; part of the Taylor & Francis Group; biology and chemistry textbooks; Vice-Pres. DENISE SCHANCK.

Genealogical Publishing Co: 3600 Clipper Mill Rd, Suite 260, Baltimore, MD 21211; tel. (410) 837-8271; fax (410) 752-8492; e-mail info@genealogical.com; internet www.genealogical.com; f. 1959; genealogy, immigration studies, heraldry and local history; Pres. MICHAEL TEPPER.

The K. S. Giniger Co, Inc: 1045 Park Ave, New York, NY 10028; tel. and fax (212) 369-6692; f. 1965; general non-fiction; Pres. KENNETH S. GINIGER.

Greenwood Publishing Group, Inc: 88 Post Rd West, POB 5007, Westport, CT 06881; tel. (203) 226-3571; fax (203) 222-1502; e-mail webmaster@greenwood.com; internet www.abc-clio.com; f. 1967; division of Reed Elsevier Group PLC; comprises Greenwood Press (reference), Heinemann (f. 1978, educational, teaching, professional development), Praeger Publrs (f. 1949, academic and general-interest non-fiction) and Libraries Unlimited (educational and reference); business reference and non-fiction; Pres. WAYNE SMITH.

Grove/Atlantic, Inc: 841 Broadway, 4th Floor, New York, NY 10003-4793; tel. (212) 614-7850; fax (212) 614-7886; e-mail info@groveatlantic.com; internet www.groveatlantic.com; f. 1993 by merger of Grove Press and Atlantic Monthly Press (f. 1917); fiction, non-fiction, biography, history, social sciences, poetry; Pres. MORGAN ENTREKIN.

Hachette Book Group USA: 237 Park Ave, New York, NY 10017; tel. (212) 522-8700; fax (212) 522-2067; e-mail customer.service@hbgusa.com; internet www.hachettebookgroup.com; f. 2006 following acquisition of Time Warner Book Group by Hachette Livre (France); wholly owned subsidiary of Lagardère SCA; divisions incl. Little, Brown and Co (f. 1837, fiction and non-fiction), Grand Central Publishing (f. 1970 as Warner Books, paperbacks, reprints, business, fiction and non-fiction) and Twelve; Chair. and CEO DAVID YOUNG.

HarperCollins Publishers: 10 East 53rd St, New York, NY 10022; tel. (212) 207-7000; fax (212) 207-7759; e-mail orders@harpercollins.com; internet www.harpercollins.com; f. 1817; subsidiary of News Corpn; imprints incl. Amistad, Avon (f. 1941, romantic fiction), Avon A, Caedmon, Collins (general reference), Rayo (Latino culture) and William Morrow (f. 1926, fiction and non-fiction); fiction, non-fiction, religious, children's, medical, general; Pres. and CEO BRIAN MURRAY.

Harvard University Press: 79 Garden St, Cambridge, MA 02138; tel. (617) 495-2800; fax (401) 531-2801; e-mail contact_hup@harvard.edu; internet www.hup.harvard.edu; f. 1913; classics, fine arts, philosophy, science, medicine, law, literature, political science, religion, history and govt; Dir WILLIAM P. SISLER.

Hastings House/Daytrips Publishers: POB 908, Winter Park, FL 32790-0908; tel. (407) 339-3600; fax (407) 339-5900; e-mail hastings_daytrips@earthlink.net; internet www.hastingshousebooks.com; f. 1936; travel; Publr PETER LEERS.

Holiday House, Inc: 425 Madison Ave, New York, NY 10017; tel. (212) 688-0085; fax (212) 421-6134; e-mail info@holidayhouse.com; internet www.holidayhouse.com; f. 1935; juvenile; Pres. JOHN H. BRIGGS, Jr.

Holmes & Meier Publishers, Inc: POB 943, Teaneck, NJ 07666; tel. (201) 833-2270; fax (201) 833-2272; e-mail info@holmesandmeier.com; internet www.holmesandmeier.com; f. 1969; imprints incl. Africana Publishing Co (f. 1969); history, political science, area studies, Africana, Judaica, foreign literature in translation, college texts and scholarly; Publr MIRIAM H. HOLMES.

Hoover Institution Press: 434 Galvez Mall, Stanford University, Stanford, CA 94305-6010; tel. (650) 723-3373; fax (650) 723-8626; e-mail hooverpress@stanford.edu; internet www.hooverpress.org; f. 1962; scholarly; Assoc. Dir ERYN WITCHER.

Houghton Mifflin Harcourt: 222 Berkeley St, Boston, MA 02116; tel. (617) 351-5000; fax (617) 351-1125; e-mail corporate.communications@hmhpub.com; internet www.hmco.com; f. 1919 as Harcourt; owned by Education Media and Publishing Group; fmrly Houghton Mifflin Riverdeep Group PLC; changed name in December 2007; general and educational; Pres. and CEO LINDA K. ZECHER.

Indiana University Press: 601 North Morton St, Bloomington, IN 47404-3797; tel. (812) 855-8817; fax (812) 855-8507; e-mail iupress@indiana.edu; internet www.iupress.indiana.edu; f. 1950; trade and scholarly non-fiction; Dir JANET RABINOWITCH.

Infobase Publishing: 132 West 31st St, 17th Floor, New York, NY 10001; tel. (212) 896-4269; fax (917) 339-0323; e-mail custserv@factsonfile.com; internet www.infobasepublishing.com; f. 1941; acquired by Veronis Suhler Stevenson in 2005; imprints incl. Facts On File Inc (f. 1941), Ferguson Publishing (f. 1907, children's reference), Chelsea House Publrs, Bloom's and World Almanac; educational, reference and electronic and digital products; Pres. and CEO MARK MCDONNELL.

International Universities Press, Inc: 59 Boston Post Rd, Madison, CT 06443; tel. (203) 245-4000; fax (203) 245-0775; e-mail info@iup.com; internet www.iup.com; f. 1943; publrs of PsychoSocial Press; psychology, psychiatry, medicine, social sciences and journals; Pres. Dr MARGARET AZARIAN.

Tahrike Tarsile Qur'ān, Inc: 80-08 51st Ave, Elmhurst, NY 11373-0115; tel. (718) 446-6472; fax (718) 446-4370; e-mail read@koranusa.org; internet www.koranusa.org; f. 1978; Koran and Islamic religious texts; Pres. AUN ALI KHALFAN.

Jewish Publication Society: 2100 Arch St, 2nd Floor, Philadelphia, PA 19103; tel. (215) 832-0600; fax (215) 568-2017; e-mail jewishbook@jewishpub.org; internet www.jewishpub.org; f. 1888; Judaica; CEO BARRY L. SCHWARTZ; Man. Editor CAROL HUPPING.

Johns Hopkins University Press: 2715 North Charles St, Baltimore, MD 21218-4363; tel. (410) 516-6900; fax (410) 516-6968; e-mail kk@press.jhu.edu; internet www.press.jhu.edu; f. 1878; social and physical sciences, humanities, health sciences, economics, literary criticism, history; Dir KATHLEEN KEANE.

Kappa Map Group: 6198 Butler Pike, Blue Bell, PA 19422; tel. (386) 873-3010; fax (386) 873-3011; e-mail customerservice@americanmap.com; internet www.universalmap.com; f. 2010; brands include Universal Map, American Map, Mapsco, Hagstrom and ADC; maps, atlases, cartography; Pres. JERRY KILLIAN.

Kendall Hunt Publishing Co: 4050 Westmark Dr., POB 1840, Dubuque, IA 52004-1840; tel. (563) 589-1000; fax (563) 589-1046; e-mail orders@kendallhunt.com; internet www.kendallhunt.com; f. 1944; business and educational; Pres. CHAD CHANDLEE.

Krieger Publishing Co: 1725 Krieger Dr., Malabar, FL 32950; tel. (321) 724-9542; fax (321) 951-3671; e-mail info@krieger-pubishing.com; internet www.krieger-publishing.com; f. 1970; space technology, adult education, history and natural sciences; Pres. DONALD E. KRIEGER.

Little, Brown and Company: 237 Park Ave, New York, NY 10017; tel. (212) 522-8700; fax (212) 522-2067; e-mail publicity@littlebrown.com; internet www.hachettebookgroup.com; f. 1837; part of Hachette Book Group USA (q.v.); imprints include Back Bay Books, Bulfinch, Mulholland Books and Reagan Arthur Books; fiction and non-fiction; Publr MICHAEL PIETSCH.

Loyola Press: 3441 North Ashland Ave, Chicago, IL 60657; tel. (773) 281-1818; fax (773) 281-0885; e-mail marketing@loyolapress.com; internet www.loyolapress.com; f. 1912; owned by the Society of Jesus, Chicago Province; religious (Roman Catholic) education and language, religious trade and arts; Publr PAUL BRIAN CAMPBELL; Pres. TERRY LOCKE.

McGraw-Hill Companies, Inc: POB 182604, Columbus, OH 43272; tel. (877) 833-5524; fax (614) 759-3749; e-mail customer.service@mcgraw-hill.com; internet www.mcgraw-hill.com; f. 1888; information texts and services for business, industry, govt and the general public; Chair., Pres. and CEO HAROLD MCGRAW, III.

Melville House Publishing: 145 Plymouth St, Brooklyn, NY 11201; tel. (718) 722-9204; fax (718) 722-9205; e-mail info@mhpbooks.com; internet mhpbooks.com; f. 2001; fiction, poetry and non-fiction; Publrs DENNIS LOY JOHNSON, VALERIE MERIANS.

Merriam-Webster Inc: 47 Federal St, POB 281, Springfield, MA 01102; tel. (413) 734-3134; fax (413) 731-5979; e-mail jwithgott@merriam-webster.com; internet www.merriam-webster.com; f. 1831; subsidiary of Encyclopaedia Britannica, Inc; dictionaries, reference; Pres. and Publr JOHN M. MORSE.

Michigan State University Press: Manly Miles Bldg, Suite 25, 1405 South Harrison Rd, East Lansing, MI 48823-5245; tel. (517) 355-9543; fax (517) 432-2611; e-mail msupress@msu.edu; internet msupress.msu.edu; f. 1947; scholarly; Dir GABRIEL DOTTO.

The MIT Press: 55 Hayward St, Cambridge, MA 02142-1493; tel. (617) 253-5646; fax (617) 258-6779; e-mail niav@mit.edu; internet mitpress.mit.edu; f. 1932; computer sciences, architecture, design, linguistics, economics, philosophy, general science, neuroscience, cognitive science and engineering; Dir ELLEN W. FARAN.

Moody Publishers: 820 North LaSalle Blvd, Chicago, IL 60610; tel. (312) 329-2101; fax (312) 329-4157; e-mail pressinfo@moody.edu; internet www.moodypublishers.org; f. 1894; publishing division of Moody Bible Institute (f. 1886); religious; Vice-Pres., Publications GREG THORNTON.

National Academy Press (NAP): 500 Fifth St, NW, POB 285, Washington, DC 20055; tel. (202) 334-3180; fax (202) 334-2793; e-mail customer_service@nap.edu; internet www.nap.edu; f. 1863; division of Nat. Academy of Sciences; scientific and technical reports, abstracts, bibliographies, catalogues; Dir BARBARA KLINE POPE.

National Learning Corpn: 212 Michael Dr., Syosset, NY 11791; tel. (516) 921-8888; fax (516) 921-8743; e-mail info@passbooks.com; internet www.passbooks.com; f. 1967; professional and vocational study guides; Pres. MICHAEL P. RUDMAN.

New Directions Publishing Corpn: 80 Eighth Ave, New York, NY 10011; tel. (212) 255-0230; fax (212) 255-0231; e-mail editorial@ndbooks.com; internet www.ndpublishing.com; f. 1936; modern literature, poetry and criticism; Pres. BARBARA EPLER.

New York University Press: 838 Broadway, 3rd Floor, New York, NY 10003-4812; tel. (212) 998-2575; fax (212) 995-3833; e-mail information@nyupress.org; internet www.nyupress.org; f. 1916; scholarly and non-fiction; Dir STEVE MAIKOWSKI.

Nicholas Brealey Publishing: Intercultural Press, 20 Park Plaza, Suite 610, Boston, MA 02116; tel. (617) 523-3801; fax (617) 523-3708; e-mail info@nicholasbrealey.com; internet www.nicholasbrealey.com; f. 1992; business, economics, psychology, travel and cross-culture; Pres. NICHOLAS BREALEY.

Northwestern University Press: 629 Noyes St, Evanston, IL 60208-4210; tel. (847) 491-2046; fax (847) 491-8150; e-mail nupress@northwestern.edu; internet www.nupress.northwestern .edu; f. 1958; scholarly and trade; Dir JANE BUNKER.

W. W. Norton & Co Inc: 500 Fifth Ave, New York, NY 10110; tel. (212) 354-5500; fax (212) 869-0856; e-mail srothbard@wwnorton .com; internet www.wwnorton.com; f. 1923; college textbooks, paperbacks, fiction and non-fiction; Pres. DRAKE MCFEELY.

Nova Science Publishers: 400 Oser Ave, Suite 1600, Hauppauge, NY 11788-3619; tel. (631)231-7269; fax (631)231-8175; e-mail nova .main@novapublishers.com; internet www.novapublishers.com; f. 1985; science, medicine, political science, European and Asian studies, security studies; Pres. NADYA GOTSIRIDZE-COLUMBUS.

Ocean Publishing: POB 1080, Flagler Beach, FL 32136-1080; tel. (386) 517-1600; e-mail publisher@oceanpublishing.org; internet www.oceanpublishing.org; f. 2002; environment, nature; Publr FRANK GROMLING.

The Ohio State University Press: 180 Pressey Hall, 1070 Carmack Rd, Columbus, OH 43210-1002; tel. (614) 292-6930; fax (614) 292-2065; e-mail info@osupress.org; internet www.ohiostatepress .org; f. 1957; scholarly; Dir MALCOLM LITCHFIELD.

Ohio University Press: 19 Circle Dr., The Ridges, Athens, OH 45701-2979; tel. (740) 593-1154; fax (740) 593-4536; e-mail cunningh@ohio.edu; internet www.ohiou.edu/oupress; f. 1964; scholarly and regional studies; Editorial Dir GILLIAN BERCHOWITZ.

Open Court Publishing Co: 70 East Lake St, Suite 800, Chicago, IL 60601; tel. (312) 701-1720; fax (312) 701-1728; e-mail opencourt@caruspub.com; internet www.opencourtbooks.com; f. 1887; philosophy and general non-fiction; Pres. JASON PATENAUDE.

Orbis Books: Price Bldg, POB 302, Maryknoll, NY 10545-0302; tel. (914) 941-7636; fax (914) 941-7005; e-mail orbisbooks@maryknoll .org; internet www.orbisbooks.com; f. 1970; owned by the Catholic Foreign Mission Society of America (Maryknoll); theology, religion and social concerns; Publr ROBERT ELLSBERG.

Oxford University Press, Inc: 198 Madison Ave, New York, NY 10016; tel. (212) 726-6000; fax (212) 677-1303; e-mail custserv.us@oup.com; internet www.oup.com/us; f. 1896; non-fiction, trade, religious, reference, college textbooks, medical and music; Pres. NIKO PFUND; Man. Dir TIM BARTON.

Paladin Press: Gunbarrel Tech Center, 7077 Winchester Circle, Boulder, CO 80301-3505; tel. (303) 443-7250; fax (303) 442-8741; e-mail service@paladin-press.com; internet www.paladin-press .com; f. 1970; imprints incl. Sycamore Island Books and Flying Machines Press; military science and history; Chair. and Pres. PEDER C. LUND.

Paragon House: 1925 Oakcrest Ave, Suite 7, St Paul, MN 55113-2619; tel. (651) 644-3087; fax (651) 644-0997; e-mail paragon@paragonhouse.com; internet www.paragonhouse.com; f. 1982; academic non-fiction, university texts; Pres. GORDON L. ANDERSON.

Pearson Education: 1 Lake St, Upper Saddle River, NJ 07458; tel. (201) 236-7000; e-mail communications@pearsoned.com; internet www.pearsoned.com; imprints incl. Addison-Wesley, Allyn & Bacon, FT Prentice Hall, Scotts Foreman, Benjamin Cummings and Longman; educational; CEO JOHN FALLON.

Penguin Group (USA) Inc: 375 Hudson St, New York, NY 10014; tel. (212) 366-2000; fax (212) 366-2666; internet us.penguingroup .com; f. 1996 by merger between Penguin Books USA and the Putnam Berkley Group; imprints incl. Ace Books (f. 1953, science fiction), Alpha (f. 1991, general reference), Avery (f. 1976, health, self-help, diet, and fitness), Berkley (f. 1955, mass-market and trade paperback), Dutton (f. 1852, fiction and non-fiction), Gotham (f. 2001, nonfiction), HP Books (automotive, photography, gardening, health and child care), Hudson Street Press (f. 2003, hardcover non-fiction), Jeremy P. Tarcher (f. 1976, non-fiction), NAL (f. 1948, paperback fiction), Penguin (f. 1936, paperback), Plume (f. 1970, paperback), Portfolio (f. 2001, business), Putnam (f. 1838, fiction and non-fiction), Riverhead (f. 1994, fiction), Sentinel (f. 2003, conservative), and Viking (f. 1925, fiction and non-fiction); CEO DAVID SHANKS; Pres. SUSAN PETERSEN KENNEDY.

Pennsylvania State University Press: University Support Bldg I, Suite C, 820 North University Dr., University Park, PA 16802-1003; tel. (814) 865-1327; fax (814) 863-1408; e-mail info@psupress .org; internet www.psupress.org; f. 1956; scholarly non-fiction; Dir PATRICK H. ALEXANDER.

Presbyterian Publishing Corpn (PPC): 100 Witherspoon St, Louisville, KY 40202-1396; tel. (502) 569-5081; fax (502) 569-5113; e-mail customer_service@presbypub.com; internet www.ppcbooks .com; f. 1938; publishing arm of the Presbyterian Church (USA); imprints incl. Geneva Press (religious trade) and Westminster John Knox Press (f. 1938, non-denominational Christian, modern religious and scholarly); Pres. and Publr MARC LEWIS.

Princeton University Press: 41 William St, Princeton, NJ 08540; tel. (609) 258-4900; fax (609) 258-6305; e-mail webmaster@press .princeton.edu; internet press.princeton.edu; f. 1905; scholarly; Dir PETER J. DOUGHERTY; Editor-in-Chief BRIGITTA VAN RHEINBERG.

Quite Specific Media Group Ltd: 7373 Pyramid Pl., Hollywood, CA 90046; tel. (323) 851-5797; fax (323) 851-5798; e-mail info@quitespecificmedia.com; internet www.quitespecificmedia.com; f. 1967; costume, design, fashion and performing arts; Publr RALPH PINE.

Rand McNally: 9855 Woods Dr., Skokie, IL 60076; tel. (847) 329-8100; fax (800) 934-3479; e-mail kconkey@reynoldsgroup.com; internet www.randmcnally.com; f. 1856; maps, atlases, travel guides and educational; Pres. and CEO DAVE MUSCATEL.

Random House, Inc: 1745 Broadway, New York, NY 10019; tel. (212) 782-9000; fax (212) 572-8026; internet www.randomhouse .com; f. 2003 by merger of the Random House Trade Group and Ballantine Books Group; imprints incl. Random House Publishing Group (f. 1925, originals, reprints, paperbacks, juvenile, series, textbooks), Ballantine Books (f. 1952, hardcover, trade and mass-market paperback), Crown Publishing Group, Knopf Doubleday (f. 1915, fiction and non-fiction), Random House Audio Publishing, Random House Children's Books, and Random House Information (reference and non-fiction); Chair. and CEO MARKUS DOHLE; Pres. and Publr GINA CENTRELLO.

Reader's Digest Association: Reader's Digest Rd, Pleasantville, NY 10570-7000; tel. (914) 238-1000; fax (914) 238-4559; internet www.rd.com; f. 1922; reference and non-fiction; Pres. and CEO ROBERT GUTH.

Rizzoli International Publications: 300 Park Ave South, 3rd Floor, New York, NY 10010-5399; tel. (212) 387-3400; fax (212) 387-3535; e-mail comments@rizzoliusa.com; internet www.rizzoliusa .com; f. 1975; division of RCS Media Group (Italy); fine arts, performing arts, architecture; Pres. and CEO MARCO AUSENDA; Vice-Pres. and Publr CHARLES MIERS.

Routledge: 711 3rd Ave, 8th Floor, New York, NY 10017; tel. (212) 216-7800; fax (212) 563-2269; e-mail info@taylorandfrancis.com; internet www.routledge.com; f. 1977; imprint of Taylor & Francis Group (q.v.); scholarly, professional, trade, humanities, social sciences; Pres. EMMETT DAGES.

Rutgers University Press: 100 Joyce Kilmer Ave, Piscataway, NJ 08854; tel. (732) 445-7762; fax (732) 445-7039; e-mail jwi@rutgers .edu; internet rutgerspress.rutgers.edu; f. 1936; trade, scholarly and regional; Dir MARLIE WASSERMAN.

William H. Sadlier Inc: 9 Pine St, New York, NY 10005-1002; tel. (212) 227-2120; fax (212) 267-8696; e-mail BDingerJr@sadlier.com; internet www.sadlier.com; f. 1832; textbooks; Pres. WILLIAM SADLIER DINGER, Jr.

St Martin's Press Inc: 175 Fifth Ave, New York, NY 10010; tel. (212) 674-5151; fax (212) 420-9314; e-mail webmaster@stmartins .com; internet us.macmillan.com/smp.aspx; f. 1952; part of Holtzbrinck Publrs, LLC; general, scholarly, college textbooks, trade and mass-market; Pres. JOHN SARGENT.

Scarecrow Press, Inc: 4501 Forbes Blvd, Suite 200, Lanham, MD 20706; tel. (301) 459-3366; fax (301) 429-5748; e-mail customercare@rowman.com; internet www.scarecrowpress.com; f. 1950; subsidiary of Rowman & Littlefield, Inc; music, film, theatre, reference, textbooks, library and information science; Publr and Editorial Dir EDWARD KURDYLA.

Scholastic, Inc: 557 Broadway, New York, NY 10012; tel. (212) 343-6100; fax (212) 343-6930; e-mail customerservice@scholastic.com; internet www.scholastic.com; f. 1920; children's periodicals, textbooks, educational materials; Chair., Pres. and CEO RICHARD ROBINSON.

Simon & Schuster, Inc: 1230 Ave of the Americas, New York, NY 10020; tel. (212) 698-7000; fax (212) 698-7007; internet www.simonsays.com; f. 1924; part of the CBS Group; trade, juvenile, reference, educational, business and professional; imprints include Aladdin Paperbacks (juvenile fiction), Free Press (politics, history, religion, business, fiction), Howard Books (f. 1969, religion, gift books), Pocket Books (f. 1939, fiction), and Scribner (f. 1846, fiction); Pres. and CEO CAROLYN REIDY.

Peter Smith Publisher, Inc: 5 Lexington Ave, Gloucester, MA 01930-3915; tel. (978) 525-3562; fax (978) 525-3674; reprints; Pres. MARY ANN LASH.

Southern Illinois University Press: 1915 University Press Dr., Carbondale, IL 62901-4323; 1915 University Press Dr., SIUC Mail Code 6806, Carbondale, IL 62902-6806; tel. (618) 453-2281; fax (618) 453-1221; e-mail ladkins@siu.edu; internet www.siupress.com; f. 1953; scholarly non-fiction; Dir BARBARA MARTIN.

Springer US: 233 Spring St, New York, NY 10013; tel. (212) 460-1500; fax (212) 460-1575; e-mail service-ny@springer.com; internet www.springer.com; f. 1964; part of Springer Science+Business Media; divisions include Springer Healthcare, Humana Press and Apress; scientific, technical and medical; CEO DERK HAANK.

Stanford University Press: 1450 Page Mill Rd, Palo Alto, CA 94304-1124; tel. (650) 723-9434; fax (650) 725-3457; e-mail info@www.sup.org; internet www.sup.org; f. 1925; Dir ALAN P. HARVEY.

State University of New York Press: 22 Corporate Woods Blvd, 3rd Floor Albany, NY 12211-2504; tel. (518) 472-5000; fax (518) 472-5038; e-mail info@sunypress.edu; internet www.sunypress.edu; f. 1966; scholarly and general interest; Co-Dirs DONNA DIXON, JAMES PELTZ.

Sterling Publishing Co, Inc: 387 Park Ave South, New York, NY 10016; tel. (212) 532-7160; fax (212) 213-2495; e-mail publicity@sterlingpub.com; internet www.sterlingpub.com; f. 1949; subsidiary of Barnes and Noble, Inc; imprints incl. Lark Crafts and Hearst Books; non-fiction and illustrated; Pres. MARCUS LEAVER; Publr JASON PRINCE.

Syracuse University Press: Suite 110, 621 Skytop Rd, Syracuse, NY 13244-5290; tel. (315) 443-5534; fax (315) 443-5545; e-mail supress@syr.edu; internet www.syracuseuniversitypress.syr.edu; f. 1943; scholarly; Dir ALICE RANDEL PFEIFFER.

Taplinger Publishing Co Inc: POB 175, Marlboro, NJ 07746; tel. (305) 256-7880; fax (305) 256-7816; e-mail taplingerpub@yahoo.com; f. 1955; general fiction and non-fiction; Pres. LOUIS STRICK.

Taylor & Francis Group: 270 Madison Ave, New York, NY 10016; tel. (212) 216-7800; fax (212) 564-7854; e-mail info@taylorandfrancis.com; internet www.taylorandfrancis.com; f. 1972; division of Informa PLC; imprints incl. CRC Press (f. 1913, reference, science, engineering and medicine), Psychology Press (q.v.), Garland Science Publishing (f. 1969, molecular biology, immunology and protein science textbooks), Routledge (q.v.), and Taylor & Francis Books (f. 1972, academic, science and reference); CEO ROGER HORTON.

Charles C. Thomas, Publisher: 2600 South First St, Springfield, IL 62794-9265; tel. (217) 789-8980; fax (217) 789-9130; e-mail books@ccthomas.com; internet www.ccthomas.com; f. 1927; textbooks and reference on education, medicine, psychology and criminology; Pres. MICHAEL P. THOMAS.

Tuttle Publishing: Airport Business Park, 364 Innovation Dr., North Clarendon, VT 05759-9436; tel. (802) 773-8930; fax (802) 773-6993; e-mail info@tuttlepublishing.com; internet tuttlepublishing.com; f. 1948; part of the Periplus Publishing Group; the Far East, particularly Japan, languages, art, crafts, martial arts, culture, juvenile, cookery; Publr ERIC OEY.

United Nations Publications: National Book Network, 15200 NBN Way, POB 190, Blue Ridge Summit, PA 17214; tel. (888) 254-4286; fax (800) 338-4550; e-mail unpublications@nbnbooks.com; internet unp.un.org; f. 1946; world and national economies, international trade, social questions, human rights and international law; Chief of Section CHRISTOPHER WOODTHORPE.

University of Alabama Press: POB 870380, Tuscaloosa, AL 35487-0380; tel. (205) 348-5180; fax (205) 348-9201; e-mail sgriffit@uapress.ua.edu; internet www.uapress.ua.edu; f. 1945; scholarly; Dir CURTIS L. CLARK.

University of Alaska Press: 794 University Ave, Suite 220, POB 756240, Fairbanks, AK 99775; tel. (907) 474-5831; fax (907) 474-5502; e-mail fypress@uaf.edu; internet www.uaf.edu/uapress; f. 1967; scholarly regional non-fiction, history, anthropology of the circumpolar north; Dir JOAN BRADDOCK.

University of Arizona Press: 355 South Euclid Ave, Suite 103, Tucson, AZ 85719; tel. (520) 621-1441; fax (520) 621-8899; e-mail uapress@uapress.arizona.edu; internet www.uapress.arizona.edu; f. 1959; scholarly, popular, regional and non-fiction; Dir KATHRYN CONRAD (acting).

University of Arkansas Press: McIlroy House, 105 N McIlroy Ave, Fayetteville, AR 72701; tel. (479) 575-3246; fax (479) 575-6044; e-mail cmoss@uark.edu; internet www.uapress.com; f. 1980; humanities, regional studies, natural history, African American studies, Middle Eastern studies, poetry, civil rights studies and American history; Dir LAWRENCE J. MALLEY.

University of California Press: 2120 Berkeley Way, Berkeley, CA 94704-1012; tel. (510) 642-4247; fax (510) 643-7127; e-mail askucp@ucpress.edu; internet www.ucpress.edu; f. 1893; academic and scholarly; Dir ALISON MUDDITT.

University of Chicago Press: 1427 East 60th St, Chicago, IL 60637; tel. (773) 702-7700; fax (773) 702-9756; e-mail publicity@press.uchicago.edu; internet www.press.uchicago.edu; f. 1891; scholarly and general; Dir GARRETT KIELY.

University of Georgia Press: 330 Research Dr., Athens, GA 30602-4901; tel. (706) 369-6130; fax (706) 369-6131; e-mail books@ugapress.uga.edu; internet www.ugapress.org; f. 1938; academic, scholarly, poetry, fiction, non-fiction and literary trade; Dir LISA BAYER.

University of Hawaii Press: 2840 Kolowalu St, Honolulu, HI 96822; tel. (808) 956-8255; fax (808) 988-6052; e-mail uhpbooks@hawaii.edu; internet www.uhpress.hawaii.edu; f. 1947; Asian, Pacific and Hawaiian studies; Dir WILLIAM H. HAMILTON.

University of Illinois Press: 1325 South Oak St, Champaign, IL 61820-6903; tel. (217) 333-0950; fax (217) 244-8082; e-mail uipress@uillinois.edu; internet www.press.uillinois.edu; f. 1918; scholarly and trade; Dir WILLIS G. REGIER.

University of Massachusetts Press: East Experiment Station, 671 North Pleasant St, POB 429, Amherst, MA 01004-0429; tel. (413) 545-2217; fax (413) 545-1226; e-mail info@umpress.umass.edu; internet www.umass.edu/umpress; f. 1963; scholarly; Dir BRUCE G. WILCOX.

University of Michigan Press: 839 Greene St, Ann Arbor, MI 48104-3209; tel. (734) 764-4388; fax (734) 615-1540; e-mail dshafer@umich.edu; internet www.press.umich.edu; f. 1930; academic, textbooks and paperbacks; Dir JOHN WILKIN.

University of Minnesota Press: 111 Third Ave South, Suite 290, Minneapolis, MN 55401-5250; tel. (612) 627-1970; fax (612) 627-1980; e-mail ump@umn.edu; internet www.upress.umn.edu; f. 1925; scholarly and general; Dir DOUGLAS M. ARMATO.

University of Missouri Press: 2910 LeMone Blvd, Columbia, MO 65201; tel. (573) 882-7641; fax (573) 884-4498; e-mail upress@umsystem.edu; internet press.umsystem.edu; f. 1958; scholarly; to cease operations by 2013; Editor-in-Chief CLAIR WILLCOX.

University of Nebraska Press: 1111 Lincoln Mall, Lincoln, NE 68588-0630; tel. (402) 472-3581; fax (402) 472-6214; e-mail pressmail@unl.edu; internet www.nebraskapress.unl.edu; f. 1941; scholarly and general; Dir DONNA SHEAR.

University of New Mexico Press: 1717 Roma NE, Albuquerque, NM 87106; tel. (505) 277-2346; fax (505) 277-3495; e-mail unmpress@unm.edu; internet www.unmpress.com; f. 1929; scholarly and regional studies; Dir JOHN W. BYRAM.

University of North Carolina Press: 116 South Boundary St, Chapel Hill, NC 27514-3808; tel. (919) 966-3561; fax (919) 966-3829; e-mail uncpress@unc.edu; internet www.uncpress.unc.edu; f. 1922; biography, regional and scholarly; Dir JOHN SHERER.

University of Notre Dame Press: 310 Flanner Hall, Notre Dame, IN 46556; tel. (574) 631-6346; fax (574) 631-8148; e-mail undpress.1@nd.edu; internet www.undpress.nd.edu; f. 1949; humanities and social sciences; Man. Dir HARV HUMPHREY (acting).

University of Oklahoma Press: 2800 Venture Dr., Norman, OK 73069-8216; tel. (405) 325-2000; fax (405) 364-5798; e-mail presscs@ou.edu; internet www.oupress.com; f. 1928; scholarly; Dir B. BYRON PRICE.

University of Pennsylvania Press: 3905 Spruce St, Philadelphia, PA 19104-4112; tel. (215) 898-6261; fax (215) 898-0404; e-mail custserv@pobox.upenn.edu; internet www.pennpress.org; f. 1890; scholarly; Dir ERIC HALPERN.

University of Pittsburgh Press: Eureka Bldg, 3400 Forbes Ave, 5th Floor, Pittsburgh, PA 15260; tel. (412) 383-2456; fax (412) 383-2466; e-mail press@pitt.edu; internet www.upress.pitt.edu; f. 1936; scholarly; Dir CYNTHIA MILLER.

University of South Carolina Press: 718 Devine St, Columbia, SC 29208; tel. (803) 777-5245; fax (800) 868-0740; e-mail lmack@mailbox.sc.edu; internet www.sc.edu/uscpress; scholarly and regional studies; Dir JONATHAN HAUPT.

University of Tennessee Press: Conference Center Bldg, 600 Henley St, Suite 110, Knoxville, TN 37996-4108; tel. (865) 974-3321; fax (865) 974-3724; e-mail custserv@utk.edu; internet www .utpress.org; f. 1940; scholarly, regional, and literary fiction; Dir SCOT DANFORTH.

University of Texas Press: POB 7819, Austin, TX 78713-7819; tel. (512) 471-7233; fax (512) 232-7178; e-mail utpress@uts.cc.utexas .edu; internet www.utexas.edu/utpress; f. 1950; general, scholarly non-fiction; Dir DAVID HAMRICK.

University of Utah Press: J. Willard Marriott Library, Suite 5400, 295 South 1500 East, Salt Lake City, UT 84112-0860; tel. (801) 585-9786; fax (801) 581-3365; e-mail peter.delafosse@utah.edu; internet www.uofupress.com; f. 1949; scholarly, regional; Dir GLENDA COTTER.

University of Virginia Press: POB 400318, Charlottesville, VA 229034-4318; tel. (434) 924-3468; fax (434) 982-2655; e-mail lrb6c@ virginia.edu; internet www.upress.virginia.edu; f. 1963; scholarly, literary criticism, women's studies, political science and African studies; Dir MARK H. SAUNDERS (interim).

University of Washington Press: 4333 Brooklyn Ave, POB 50096, Seattle, WA 98145-5096; tel. (206) 543-4050; fax (206) 543-3932; e-mail uwpress@u.washington.edu; internet www.washington.edu/ uwpress; f. 1920; general, scholarly, non-fiction and reprints; Dir NICOLE F. MITCHELL.

University of Wisconsin Press: 1930 Monroe St, 3rd Floor, Madison, WI 53711-2059; tel. (608) 263-1110; fax (608) 263-1132; e-mail uwiscpress@uwpress.wisc.edu; internet www.wisc.edu/ wisconsinpress; f. 1936; scholarly and trade; Dir SHEILA LEARY.

University Press of America, Inc: 4501 Forbes Blvd, Suite 200, Lanham, MD 20706; tel. (301) 459-3366; fax (301) 429-5748; e-mail customercare@rowman.com; internet www.univpress.com; f. 1975; scholarly; Vice-Pres. JULIE KIRSCH.

University Press of Florida: 15 North West 15th St, Gainesville, FL 32611-2079; tel. (352) 392-1351; fax (352) 392-0590; internet www .upf.com; f. 1945; general, scholarly, regional; Dir MEREDITH MORRIS-BABB.

University Press of Kansas: 2502 Westbrooke Circle, Lawrence, KS 66045-4444; tel. (785) 864-4154; fax (785) 864-4586; e-mail upress@ku.edu; internet www.kansaspress.ku.edu; f. 1946; scholarly; Dir FRED M. WOODWARD.

University Press of Kentucky: 663 South Limestone St, Lexington, KY 40508-4008; tel. (606) 257-8400; fax (606) 323-1873; e-mail smwrin2@email.uky.edu; internet www.kentuckypress.com; f. 1943; non-fiction, scholarly and regional; Dir STEPHEN M. WRINN.

University Press of Mississippi: 3825 Ridgewood Rd, Jackson, MS 39211-6492; tel. (601) 432-6205; fax (601) 432-6217; e-mail press@mississippi.edu; internet www.upress.state.ms.us; f. 1970; scholarly, non-fiction and regional; Dir LEILA W. SALISBURY.

University Press of New England: 1 Court St, Lebanon, NH 03766; tel. (603) 448-1533; fax (603) 448-7006; e-mail upneweb@ dartmouth.edu; internet www.upne.com; f. 1970; scholarly; Dir MICHAEL P. BURTON.

Vanderbilt University Press: 2301 Vanderbilt Pl., POB 351813, Nashville, TN 37235-1813; tel. (615) 322-3585; fax (615) 343-8823; e-mail vupress@vanderbilt.edu; internet www .vanderbiltuniversitypress.com; f. 1940; scholarly and trade; Dir MICHAEL AMES.

Wayne State University Press: Leonard N. Simons Bldg, 4809 Woodward Ave, Detroit, MI 48201-1309; tel. (313) 577-6120; fax (313) 577-6131; e-mail jane.hoehner@wayne.edu; internet wsupress .wayne.edu; f. 1941; scholarly; Dir JANE HOEHNER.

Westview Press: 2465 Central Ave, Boulder, CO 80301; tel. (303) 444-3541; e-mail westview.press@perseusbooks.com; internet www .westviewpress.com; social sciences, humanities and science textbooks; f. 1975; part of the Perseus Books Group; Publr MARCUS BOGGS.

Wiley-Blackwell: 111 River St, Hoboken, NJ 07030-5774; tel. (201) 748-6000; fax (201) 748-6088; e-mail info@wiley.com; internet www .wiley.com; f. 1807; fmrly John Wiley and Sons, Inc; name changed as above in 2007; higher education, scientific, technical, medical, professional and trade; imprints include CliffsNotes; Chair. PETER B. WILEY; Pres. and CEO STEPHEN M. SMITH.

H. W. Wilson Co: 950 University Ave, Bronx, NY 10452; tel. (718) 588-8400; fax (718) 590-1617; e-mail custserv@hwwilson.com; internet www.ebscohost.com/wilson; f. 1898; reference and indices; part of EBSCO Publishing; Pres. and CEO TIM COLLINS.

Wolters Kluwer Health: 323 Norristown Rd, Suite 200, Ambler, PA 19002; tel. (215) 646-8700; internet www.wolterskluwerhealth.com; division of Wolters Kluwer (Netherlands); medical and scientific reference; imprints incl. Lippincott, Williams & Wilkins (f. 1792, dentistry, science, human and veterinary medicine); Pres. and CEO BOB BECKER.

Yale University Press: POB 209040, New Haven, CT 06520-9040; tel. (203) 432-0960; fax (203) 432-0948; e-mail marketing@yale.edu; internet yalepress.yale.edu/yupbooks; f. 1908; trade and scholarly; Dir JOHN DONATICH.

GOVERNMENT PUBLISHING HOUSE

Government Printing Office: 732 North Capitol St, NW, Washington, DC 20401; tel. (202) 512-1800; fax (202) 512-2104; e-mail contactcenter@gpo.gov; internet www.gpo.gov; Public Printer DAVITA VANCE-COOKS (acting).

ORGANIZATIONS AND ASSOCIATIONS

American Booksellers' Association (ABA): 200 White Plains Rd, Suite 600, Tarrytown, NY 10591; tel. (914) 591-2665; fax (914) 591-2720; e-mail info@bookweb.org; internet www.bookweb.org; f. 1900; 2,500 mems; Pres. BECKY ANDERSON; CEO OREN TEICHER.

Association of American University Presses, Inc: 28 West 36th St, Suite 602, New York, NY 10018; tel. (212) 989-1010; fax (212) 989-0275; e-mail info@aaupnet.org; internet www.aaupnet.org; f. 1937; 125 mems; Exec. Dir PETER J. GIVLER.

The Children's Book Council, Inc: 54 West 39th St, 14th Floor, New York, NY 10018; tel. (212) 966-1990; fax (212) 966-2073; e-mail cbc.info@cbcbooks.org; internet www.cbcbooks.org; f. 1945; 75 mems; Chair. NANCY FERESTEN; Exec. Dir ROBIN ADELSON.

Florida Publishers Association, Inc: POB 916383, Longwood, FL 32791-6383; tel. and fax (836) 647-5951; e-mail fpabooks@gmail.com; internet www.floridapublishersassociation.com; f. 1983; fmrly Nat. Asscn of Independent Publrs; 150 mems; Pres. CHRIS ANGERMANN.

Independent Book Publishers' Association (IBPA): 1020 Manhattan Beach Blvd, Suite 204, Manhattan Beach, CA 90266; tel. (310) 546-1818; fax (310) 546-3939; e-mail info@ibpa-online.org; internet www.ibpa-online.org; f. 1983 as Publishers' Marketing Asscn; over 4,000 mem. publrs; Pres. FLORRIE BINFORD KICHLER; Exec. Dir TERRY NATHAN.

Independent Publishers Group: 814 North Franklin St, Chicago, IL 60610; tel. (312) 337-0747; fax (312) 337-5985; e-mail frontdesk@ ipgbook.com; internet www.ipgbook.com; f. 1971; CEO CURT MATTHEWS.

Music Publishers Association of the US: 243 Fifth Ave, Suite 236, New York, NY 10016; tel. (212) 327-4044; e-mail admin@mpa .org; internet www.mpa.org; f. 1895; 80 mems; Pres. KATHLEEN MARSH.

Publishers Group West (PGW): 1700 Fourth St, Berkeley, CA 94710; tel. (510) 528-1444; fax (510) 528-3444; e-mail info@pgw.com; internet www.pgw.com; f. 1976; subsidiary of Publishers Group Worldwide; Vice-Pres. International Sales CHITRA BOPADIKAR.

Small Press Distribution: 1341 Seventh St, Berkeley, CA 94710-1409; tel. (510) 524-1668; fax (510) 524-0852; e-mail spd@spdbooks .org; internet www.spdbooks.org; f. 1969; distributes exclusively independently published literature; Exec. Dir JEFFREY LEPENDORF.

Small Publishers Association of North America (SPAN): 1618 West Colorado Ave, Colorado Springs, CO 80904; tel. (719) 475-1726; fax (719) 471-2182; e-mail span@spannet.org; internet www.spannet .org; f. 1996 to promote the profile and interests of independent publrs and authors; Exec. Dir SCOTT FLORA; over 1,000 mems.

Broadcasting and Communications

REGULATORY AUTHORITY

Federal Communications Commission (FCC): 445 12th St, SW, Washington, DC 20554; tel. (202) 418-0200; fax (202) 418-0232; e-mail fccinfo@fcc.gov; internet www.fcc.gov; f. 1934; regulates interstate and foreign communications by radio, television, wire and cable; Chair. JULIUS GENACHOWSKI; Man. Dir DAVID B. ROBBINS.

TELECOMMUNICATIONS

In 2011 there were an estimated 290.3m. mobile telephone subscribers and 85.6m. broadband internet subscribers.

Principal Telecommunications Networks

AT&T, Inc (American Telegraph and Telephone): 175 East Houston St, San Antonio, TX 78205; tel. (212) 387-5400; fax (212) 226-4935; internet www.att.com; f. 1885; bought by SBC Communications in 2005 and present name adopted; merged with the BellSouth Corpn in Dec. 2006, and acquired full ownership of Cingular Wireless; second largest telecommunications network in USA, with more than 150m. customers, incl. 103.3m. mobile subscribers (Dec. 2011); a planned merger with T-Mobile USA was cancelled in Dec. 2011; Chair., Pres. and CEO RANDALL L. STEPHENSON; 256,420 employees (Dec. 2011).

CenturyLink: 100 CenturyTel Dr., Monroe, LA 71203; tel. (318) 388-9000; fax (318) 340-5520; e-mail steve.davis@centurylink.com; internet www.centurylink.com; f. 1930 as CenturyTel, Inc; renamed as above following merger with EMBARQ in 2009; merged with Qwest Communications International, Inc in April 2011; third largest telecommunications company in the USA; operates around 7m. access lines in 33 states; more than 2.3m. broadband customers; Pres. and CEO GLEN F. POST, III; Exec. Vice-Pres. and COO KAREN A. PUCKETT.

Comcast Corpn: One Comcast Center, 1500 Market St, Philadelphia, PA 19103; tel. (215) 286-1700; e-mail corporate _communications@comcast.com; internet www.comcast.com; f. 1963 as American Cable Systems; renamed as above in 1969; acquired AT&T Broadband in 2002; acquired part of Adelphia Communications in 2006; acquired NBC Universal in 2011; 22.3m. cable customers in 39 states and the District of Columbia, 18.1m. broadband internet customers, 9.3m. voice customers (Dec. 2011); Chair. and CEO BRIAN L. ROBERTS.

Frontier Communications Corpn: 3 High Ridge Park, Stamford, CT 06905-1390; tel. (203) 614-5600; fax (203) 614-4602; e-mail frontier@frontiercorp.com; internet www.frontier.com; f. 1935; fmrly Citizens Communications Co; name changed as above in 2008; acquisition of Commonwealth Telephone Enterprises completed in 2007; bought Verizon West Virginia in 2010; Chair. and CEO MAGGIE WILDEROTTER; Pres. and COO DANIEL McCARTHY.

SES AMERICOM: 4 Research Way, Princeton, NJ 08540-6684; tel. (609) 987-4000; fax (609) 987-4517; e-mail info.americom@ ses-americom.com; f. 1975; fmrly GE American Communications, Inc; Pres. and CEO ROBERT BEDNAREK.

T-Mobile USA, Inc: 12920 South East 38th St, POB 53410, Bellevue, WA 98015-53410; internet www.t-mobile.com; f. 2002; US operating entity of T-Mobile International AG, owned by Deutsche Telekom AG (Germany); mobile cellular communications; planned merger with MetroPCS Wireless, Inc in 2013; fourth largest telecommunications network in USA, with 33.6m. customers; Pres. and CEO JOHN LEGERE; 36,000 employees.

Verizon Communications: 140 West St, 29th Floor, New York, NY 10007; tel. (800) 621-9900; internet www.verizon.com; f. 2000 by merger of Bell Atlantic Corpn and GTE Corpn; divisions include Verizon Business, fmrly MCI, Inc; largest telecommunications co in USA; 140.3m. landlines in service; Chair. and CEO LOWELL C. McADAM.

Associations

Telecommunications Industry Association (TIA): 1320 N Courthouse Rd, Suite 200, Arlington, VA 22201; tel. (703) 907-7700; fax (703) 907-7727; e-mail membership@tiaonline.org; internet www.tiaonline.org; f. 1988; trade association; represents the global information and communications technology (ICT) industries; Pres. GRANT SEIFFERT.

United States Telecom Association (USTelecom): 607 14th St, NW, Suite 400, Washington, DC 20005; tel. (202) 326-7300; fax (202) 315-3603; e-mail membership@ustelecom.org; internet www .ustelecom.org; broadband association; Pres. and CEO WALTER B. McCORMICK, Jr; Chair. JEFF GARDNER.

UTC—Utilities Telecom Council: 1901 Pennsylvania Ave, 5th Floor, NW, Washington, DC 20006; tel. (202) 872-0030; fax (202) 872-1331; e-mail utc@utc.org; internet www.utc.org; f. 1948; name changed from United Telecom Council in 2007; non-profit asscn representing telecommunications and information interests of public utilities, natural gas pipelines and other infrastructure cos and their strategic business partners; Pres. and CEO BILL MORONEY; Vice-Pres. (Operations) KATHLEEN FITZPATRICK.

BROADCASTING

Radio

Principal Domestic Networks

CBS RADIO: 40 West 57th St, New York, NY 10019; tel. (212) 846-3939; internet www.cbsradio.com; f. 1928; fmrly Infinity Broadcasting; division of CBS Corpn; owns CBS Radio Network serving more than 1,500 radio stations; operates 130 radio stations; Pres. and CEO DAN MASON.

Cumulus Media Networks: 13725 Montfort Dr., Dallas, TX 75240; tel. (972) 991-9200; fax (214) 991-1071; e-mail Richard.Denning@ cumulus.com; internet www.cumulusmedianetworks.com; f. 1944; fmrly Citadel Media Networks; name changed as above in 2011 following merger with Cumulus Media; fmrly wholly owned subsidiary of The Walt Disney Company; ABC Radio Business, as a spin-off concern of The Walt Disney Co, merged with a wholly owned subsidiary of Citadel Broadcasting Corpn in June 2007; 4,000 affiliated radio stations broadcasting 5 full service line networks; Chair., Pres. and CEO LEWIS W. DICKLEY, Jr.

Clear Channel Radio: 200 East Basse Rd, San Antonio, TX 78209; tel. (210) 822-2828; e-mail lisacdollinger@clearchannel.com; internet www.clearchannel.com/radio; c. 800 radio stations; in July 2008 Clear Channel Communications (parent co) merged with a wholly owned subsidiary corpn of CC Media Holdings, Inc, the latter becoming overarching parent co; Pres. JOHN HOGAN; CEO BOB PITTMAN.

Dial Global, Inc: Candler Tower, 220 W 42nd St, New York, NY 10036; tel. (212) 419-2926; e-mail bschaffer@cjpcom.com; internet www.dialglobal.com; completed merger with Westwood One, Inc in Oct. 2011; owned by Triton Media Group; largest domestic outsource provider, producing 200 radio programmes and providing services to around 7,000 radio stations; produces and distributes national news, sports, talk, music and special event programmes, in addition to local news, sports, weather and other information programming; operates CBS Radio News, CNBC Business Radio, MarketWatch and NBC News Radio networks; Chair. NEAL SCHORE; Man. Dirs SPENCER BROWN, DAVID LANDAU, KEN WILLIAMS.

National Public Radio (NPR): 635 Massachusetts Ave, NW, Washington, DC 20001; tel. (202) 513-2300; fax (202) 513-3329; e-mail achristopher@npr.org; internet www.npr.org; f. 1970; private, non-profit corpn providing programmes and support facilities to over 800 mem. stations nation-wide; also operates a global programme distribution service by radio, cable and satellite; Chair. DAVE EDWARDS; Pres. and CEO GARY E. KNELL.

Principal External Radio Services

American Forces Network Broadcast Center (AFN-BC): AFN Broadcast Center, 23755 Z St, Riverside, CA 92518; tel. (951) 413-2319; fax (951) 413-2227; e-mail larry.sichter@dma.mil; internet www.myafn.net; f. 1942; operated by Defense Media Activity, US Dept of Defense; provides encrypted US radio and TV programming in English exclusively to US military and Dept of Defense civilian personnel in 175 countries and aboard US Navy ships; Exec. Dir DAVID GEBHARDT (AFN Broadcast Center); Dir ANDREAS FRIEDRICH (AFRTS) (acting).

RFE/RL, Inc (Radio Free Europe/Radio Liberty): 1201 Connecticut Ave, NW, Suite 400, Washington, DC 20036; tel. (202) 457-6900; fax (202) 457-6992; e-mail zvanersm@rferl.org; internet www.rferl.org; f. 1950; private, non-profit corpn financed by Congress via the Broadcasting Board of Governors (BBG); broadcasts to 21 countries incl. Russia, Iran, Iraq, Afghanistan, Pakistan and the republics of Central Asia; c. 1,000 hours weekly in 28 languages; Chair. DENNIS MULHAUPT; Pres. and CEO STEVEN W. KORN.

Voice of America: 330 Independence Ave, SW, Washington, DC 20237; tel. (202) 203-4959; fax (202) 203-4960; e-mail askvoa@ voanews.com; internet www.voanews.com; f. 1942; govt-funded; broadcasts c. 1,500 hours weekly in 45 languages to all areas of the world via radio, television and the internet; serves more than 1,200 local affiliate stations and networks (radio, television and cable); Dir DAVID ENSOR; Exec. Editor STEVE REDISCH.

Television

Principal Networks

ABC, Inc (American Broadcasting Co, Inc): 77 West 66th St, 3rd Floor, Suite 100, New York, NY 10023; tel. (212) 456-7777; fax (212) 456-2795; e-mail netaudr@abc.com; internet abc.go.com; f. 1953; subsidiary of the Walt Disney Co since 1996; 10 owned and 226 affiliated stations; production through Touchstone Television, and Disney television content distribution through Buena Vista Television; Pres., Disney-ABC Television Group ANNE SWEENEY; Pres., ABC-owned television stations REBECCA CAMPBELL.

C-SPAN (Cable-Satellite Public Affairs Network): 400 North Capitol St, Suite 650, Washington, DC 20001; tel. (202) 737-3220; fax (202) 737-3323; e-mail viewer@c-span.org; internet www.c-span.org; f. 1979; private, non-profit public service; earns its operating revenues through licence fees paid by cable and satellite systems offering the network to their customers; Exec. Chair. BRIAN LAMB; Co-CEO SUSAN SWAIN, ROBERT KENNEDY.

CBS Television Network (Columbia Broadcasting System Television Network): 51 West 52nd St, New York, NY 10019-6188; tel. (212) 975-4321; internet www.cbs.com; f. 1928; subsidiary of CBS Corpn; serves more than 200 affiliated stations; parent CBS Corpn subsidiary, CBS Television Stations Group, operates 39 stations, incl. 21 CBS, 11 The CW, 3 MyNetworkTV and 4 independents; CBS Corpn Pres. and CEO LESLIE MOONVES; Chair. SUMNER REDSTONE.

CNN (Cable News Network): 1 CNN Center, POB 105366, Atlanta, GA 30348; tel. (404) 827-1700; fax (404) 827-1993; e-mail public .information@turner.com; internet www.cnn.com; subsidiary of Turner Broadcasting, Inc., part of Time Warner; Pres. JIM WALTON; Exec. Vice-Pres. and Man. Editor MARK WHITAKER.

FOX Broadcasting Co: 10201 West Pico Blvd, Los Angeles, CA 90035; tel. (310) 369-3716; fax (310) 969-3300; e-mail gaude.paez@fox

.com; internet www.fox.com; f. 1986; subsidiary of News Corpn; more than 900 cable affiliations; Chair. KEVIN REILLY; COO JOE EARLEY.

NBC Universal Television Stations: 30 Rockefeller Plaza, New York, NY 10112; tel. (212) 664-4444; fax (212) 664-5830; e-mail feedback@nbcuni.com; internet www.nbcuni.com; f. 1926; subsidiary of NBC Universal; 51% stake in NBC Universal acquired by Comcast Corpn (q.v.) in 2011; 27 owned and over 200 affiliated stations; CEO, NBC Universal STEPHEN B. BURKE; Pres., NBC-owned television stations VALARI DOBSON STAAB.

PBS (Public Broadcasting Service): 2100 Crystal Dr., Arlington, VA 22202; tel. (703) 739-5000; fax (703) 739-0775; e-mail cjohnson@pbs .org; internet www.pbs.org; f. 1969; non-profit-making; financed by private subscriptions and federal govt funds; owned and operated by the 356 public US television stations under 168 educational non-commercial licensees; Pres. and CEO PAULA KERGER; COO MICHAEL JONES.

Time Warner Cable, Inc (TWC): 290 Harbor Dr., Stamford, CT 06902-6732; tel. (203) 364-8203; fax (203) 328-0690; internet www .timewarnercable.com; cable television system serving c. 14.6m. subscribers in 28 states; 85.2% owned by Time Warner, Inc, following legal and structural separation of the two cos in March 2009; Chair. and CEO GLENN A. BRITT; Pres., Time Warner Cable Media JOAN GILLMAN.

Univision Network: 605 Third Ave, 12th Floor, New York, NY 10158-0180; tel. (212) 455-5200; fax (212) 867-6710; internet www .univision.com; f. 1961; subsidiary of Univision Communications, Inc; acquired by Broadcasting Media Partners, Inc, a group of private equity investors, in March 2007; Spanish-language television network; Pres., Univision Networks CESAR CONDE; Pres., Univision Television Group KEVIN CUDDIHY.

Associations

National Association of Broadcasters (NAB): 1771 N St, NW, Washington, DC 20036; tel. (202) 429-5300; fax (202) 429-4199; e-mail nab@nab.org; internet www.nab.org; f. 1922; trade asscn of radio and TV stations and networks; 8,300 mems; Pres. and CEO GORDON H. SMITH.

National Cable and Telecommunications Association (NCTA): 25 Massachusetts Ave, NW, Suite 100, Washington, DC 20001-1413; tel. (202) 222-2300; e-mail rstoddard@ncta.com; internet www.ncta.com; f. 1952 as Nat. Cable Television Asscn; represents cable operators for over 90% of customers and over 200 cable programme networks; internet and digital telephone service provider; c. 3,100 mems; Chair. GLENN A. BRITT; Pres. and CEO MICHAEL POWELL.

Finance

BANKING

There are two main types of banks in the USA: federally chartered banks (or national banks; often designated National Associations—NA) and state-chartered banks (or state banks). National banks operate under US federal law and are supervised by the Office of the Comptroller of the Currency (see below). Membership of the Federal Reserve System is mandatory for national banks. State banks operate under state law and are regulated by the relevant state banking authority. Membership of the Federal Reserve System is optional for state banks.

Since 1956 bank holding companies—corporations that control one or more banks—have become significant elements in the US banking system. The proportion of banks owned by holding companies increased from 62% in 1984 to almost 84% in 2007. In 2010 there were some 4,784 bank holding companies.

During much of the 20th century US banks were prohibited from opening branches or acquiring subsidiaries in states other than those in which they were based. From the 1980s many states introduced legislation to enable regional interstate banking operations. Federal legislation enacted in 1994 (the Riegle-Neal Interstate Banking and Branching Efficiency Act) permitted adequately capitalized bank holding companies to acquire banks in other states, and, from 1997, authorized interstate mergers between qualified banks, subject to state laws. Further federal legislation permitting the operation of interstate branch banking networks and the provision of non-banking financial services was enacted in 1999.

Federal Reserve System

The Federal Reserve System, founded in 1913, comprises the Board of Governors, the Federal Open Market Committee, the Federal Advisory Council, the Consumer Advisory Council, the Thrift Institutions Advisory Council, the 25 branches of the 12 Federal Reserve Banks, together with all member banks.

The Board of Governors is composed of seven members appointed by the President of the USA with the advice and consent of the Senate.

The Reserve Banks are empowered to issue Federal Reserve notes fully secured by the following assets, alone or in any combination: (i) Gold certificates; (ii) US Government and agency securities; (iii) other eligible assets as described by statute; and (iv) Special Drawing Rights certificates. The Reserve Banks may discount paper for depository institutions and make properly secured advances to depository institutions. Federal Reserve Banks were established by Congress as the operating arms of the nation's central banking system. Many of the services performed by this network for depository institutions and for the Government are similar to services performed by banks and thrifts for business customers and individuals. Reserve Banks hold the cash reserves of depository institutions and make loans to them. They move currency and coin into and out of circulation, and collect and process millions of cheques each day. They provide banking services for the Treasury, issue and redeem government securities on behalf of the Treasury, and act in other ways as fiscal agent for the US Government. The Banks also take part in the primary responsibility of the Federal Reserve System, the setting of monetary policy, through participation on the Federal Open Market Committee.

In March 2004 some 2,900 commercial banks were members of the Federal Reserve System.

Federal Reserve: 20th St and Constitution Ave, NW, Washington, DC 20551; tel. (202) 452-3000; fax (202) 452-3819; internet www .federalreserve.gov.

Board of Governors

Chairman: BEN S. BERNANKE.

Vice-Chairman: JANET L. YELLEN.

Governors: ELIZABETH A. DUKE, DANIEL K. TARULLO, SARAH BLOOM RASKIN, Dr JEREMY C STEIN, JEROME H. POWELL.

Secretary of the Board: ROBERT DEV. FRIERSON.

Federal Reserve Banks

There are 12 Federal Reserve districts, identified by the city in which each head office is located. The states of Alaska and Hawaii are included in the San Francisco district; the San Francisco Bank also serves American Samoa, Guam and the Northern Mariana Islands. The New York district is responsible for Puerto Rico and the US Virgin Islands. Reserve Bank Presidents, the banks' chief executive officers, are appointed for concurrent five-year terms.

Federal Reserve Districts

	Chairman	President
Boston	Kirk A. Sykes	Eric S. Rosengren
New York	Emily K. Rafferty	William C. Dudley
Philadelphia	Jeremy Nowak	Charles I. Plosser
Cleveland	Richard K. Smucker	Sandra Pianalto
Richmond	Linda D. Rabbitt	Jeffrey M. Lacker
Atlanta	Thomas I. Barkin	Dennis P. Lockhart
Chicago	Jeffrey A. Joerres	Charles L. Evans
St Louis	Ward M. Klein	James B. Bullard
Minneapolis	Mary K. Brainerd	Narayana Kocherlakota
Kansas City	Barbara Mowry	Esther L. George
Dallas	Herbert D. Kelleher	Richard W. Fisher
San Francisco	Patricia E. Yarrington	John C. Williams

The Federal Deposit Insurance Corporation

The Federal Deposit Insurance Corporation (FDIC—see Independent Agencies; f. 1933) promotes confidence in the financial system by providing insurance coverage for deposits in banks and thrift institutions. In addition, the FDIC has supervisory power over state banks that are not members of the Federal Reserve System, and serves as a secondary regulator for all national and Federal Reserve System-member banks. At 18 April 2013 there were 6,035 FDIC-insured commercial banks in the 50 states and the District of Columbia. At that time a total of 970 national savings institutions were insured by the FDIC. The Office of Thrift Supervision (OTS) was established in 1989, as part of the Department of Treasury, to regulate all federally chartered and many state-chartered thrift institutions, which include savings banks, and savings and loan institutions. The Dodd-Frank Wall Street Reform and Consumer Protection Act of 2010 provided for the abolition of the OTS. From July 2011 responsibility for regulating savings and loan holding companies, state savings associations and other thrift institutions was transferred to the Federal Reserve, the FDIC and the Office of the Comptroller of the Currency, respectively.

The Office of the Comptroller of the Currency

The Office of the Comptroller of the Currency (OCC) has primary supervisory authority over all national banks, federal savings associations, and the federal branches and agencies of foreign banks. In December 2011 there were 2,036 institutions under the supervision of the OCC.

Office of the Comptroller of the Currency: 400 7th St, SW, Washington, DC 20219; tel. (202) 874-5000; e-mail publicaffairs3@ occ.treas.gov; internet www.occ.gov; f. 1863; Comptroller THOMAS J. CURRY.

Principal Commercial Banks

(cap. = total capital and reserves; dep. = deposits; m. = million; amounts in US dollars)

In general, only banks with a minimum of $2,000m. deposits are listed. In states where no such bank exists, that with the largest deposits is listed.

Alabama

Regions Bank: 1900 Fifth Ave North, Birmingham, AL 35203; tel. (205) 326-5300; fax (205) 326-7779; internet www.regions.com; f. 1928; cap. 0.1m., res 20,430.3m., dep. 108,492.0m. (Dec. 2011); Chair. ERNEST W. DEAVENPORT, Jr; Pres. and CEO O. B. GRAYSON HALL, Jr.

Arizona

National Bank of Arizona: 6001 North 24th St, Phoenix, AZ 85016; tel. (602) 235-6000; internet www.nbarizona.com; f. 1984; 100% owned by Zions Bancorporation; cap. 309.5m., dep. 3,737.0m. (Dec. 2010); Chair. JOHN GISI; Pres. and CEO KEITH MAIO.

California

California Bank and Trust: 11622 El Camino Real, Suite 200, San Diego, CA 92130; tel. (858) 793-7400; fax (858) 793-7438; internet www.calbanktrust.com; f. 1998; cap. 265.2m., res 986.9m., dep. 9,193.9m. (Dec. 2011); Pres. and CEO DAVID BLACKFORD.

City National Bank: 400 Roxbury Dr. North, Beverly Hills, CA 90210; tel. (310) 888-6000; fax (310) 888-6045; e-mail contact@cnb .com; internet www.cnb.com; f. 1954; cap. 90.0m., res 994.4m., dep. 20,475.9m. (Dec. 2011); Chair. and CEO RUSSELL GOLDSMITH; Pres. CHRISTOPHER J. WARMUTH; 45 brs.

Union Bank NA: 400 California St, 1st Floor, San Francisco, CA 94104; tel. (415) 765-3434; fax (415) 765-3507; e-mail Investor .Relations@uboc.com; internet www.unionbank.com; f. 1996; fmrly Union Bank of California NA; name changed as above in 2008; cap. 604.6m., res 5,798m., dep. 65,286.4m. (Dec. 2011); Pres. and CEO MASASHI OKA; 323 brs.

WestStar Bank: 180 Montgomery St, San Francisco, CA 94104; tel. (415) 765-4800; fax (415) 434-3470; e-mail john.stafford@ bankofthewest.com; internet www.bankofthewest.com; f. 1874; owned by BancWest Corpn; cap. 0.006m., dep. 46,328.9m. (Dec. 2010); Chair. and CEO J. MICHAEL SHEPHERD; Pres. and COO MAURA MARKUS; 663 brs.

Colorado

FirstBank: 12345 West Colfax Ave, Lakewood, CO 80215; tel. (303) 237-5000; e-mail banking@efirstbank.com; internet www.efirstbank .com; f. 1963; cap. 7.0m., dep. 9,487.3m. (Dec. 2010); Pres. and CEO JOHN IKARD; more than 140 brs in 3 states.

Connecticut

Citizens Bank, Connecticut: 237 Main St, Middletown, CT 06457; tel. (860) 638-4411; fax (860) 638-4444; e-mail intbank@citizensbank .com; internet www.citizensbank.com; f. 1996; a division of RBS Citizens NA since 2007; dep. 4,205.8m., total assets 4,617.0m. (Dec. 2006); Pres. RICHARD M. BARRY; 48 brs.

Florida

Northern Trust NA: 700 Brickell Ave, Miami, FL 33131; tel. (305) 372-1000; fax (305) 789-1106; internet www.northerntrust.com; f. 1982; cap. 34.1m., dep. 10,986.7m. (Dec. 2010); Chair., Pres. and CEO FREDERICK H. WADDELL.

Ocean Bank: 780 Northwest 42nd Ave, Miami, FL 33126; tel. (305) 569-5000; e-mail obmail@oceanbank.com; internet www.oceanbank .com; f. 1982; cap. 8.5m., res 151.5m., dep. 3,056.2m. (Dec. 2011); Pres. and CEO A. ALFONSO MACEDO; 21 brs.

Georgia

SunTrust Bank: 303 Peachtree St, POB 4418, Atlanta, GA 30302-4625; tel. (800) 786-8787; fax (404) 588-7094; e-mail Michelle .Brewington@SunTrust.com; internet www.suntrust.com; f. 1891; assumed all SunTrust Banks 2000; cap. 21.6m., res 14,125m., dep. 129,833.2m. (Dec. 2011); Chair. and CEO WILLIAM H. ROGERS, Jr; 1,694 brs in 12 states.

Hawaii

Bank of Hawaii: 111 South King St, Honolulu, HI 96813; tel. (808) 538-4171; fax (808) 694-4826; e-mail info@boh.com; internet www .boh.com; f. 1897; cap. 14.9m., res 646.2m., dep. 10,599.9m. (Dec. 2011); Chair. and CEO PETER S. HO.

First Hawaiian Bank: 999 Bishop St, Honolulu, HI 96813; tel. (808) 525-6340; fax (808) 525-8182; e-mail bfarias@fhb.com; internet www .fhb.com; f. 1858; cap. 16.2m., res 1,617.5m., dep. 12,165.6m. (Dec. 2011); Chair. and CEO DONALD G. HORNER.

Illinois

First Midwest Bank: 1 Pierce Pl., Suite 1500, Itasca, IL 60143; tel. (630) 875-7450; fax (630) 875-7369; e-mail Investor.Relations@ firstmidwest.com; internet www.firstmidwest.com; cap. 40.0m., res 664m., dep. 6,529.2m. (Dec. 2011); Pres. and CEO MICHAEL L. SCUDDER; 100 brs.

BMO Harris Bank: 111 West Monroe St, 12th Floor, Chicago, IL 60603; tel. (312) 461-2121; fax (312) 293-4780; internet www4 .harrisbank.com; f. 1882 as N. W. Harris & Co; present name adopted 2011; owned by BMO Financial Group (Canada); cap. 504.3m., res 11,227.9m., dep. 75,624.6m. (Dec. 2011); Chair. DAVID A. GALLOWAY; Pres. and CEO WILLIAM A. DOWNE; 280 brs in 3 states.

Northern Trust Co: 50 South LaSalle St, Chicago, IL 60603; tel. (312) 630-6000; internet www.northerntrust.com; f. 1889; cap. 3.6m., res 2,347.8m., dep. 84,041.7m. (Dec. 2011); Pres. and CEO FREDERICK H. WADDELL.

Indiana

Ameriana Bank: 2118 Bundy Ave, POB H, New Castle, IN 47362-1048; tel. (765) 529-2230; e-mail jerry.gassen@ameriana.com; internet www.ameriana.com; f. 1890; total assets 426.4m., dep. 381.8m. (Dec. 2010); Chair. MICHAEL E. KENT; Pres. and CEO JEROME J. GASSEN.

Iowa

United Bank of Iowa: 501 2nd St, Ida Grove, IA 51445-1384; tel. (712) 364-3393; fax (712) 364-3293; e-mail info@unitedbk.com; internet www.unitedbk.com; f. 1932 as Ida County State Bank, present name adopted 1996; 100% owned by Ida Grove Bancshares, Inc; cap. 0.2m., dep. 1,003.2m. (Dec. 2010); Chair. and CEO KENNETH L. VAN KEKERIX.

Kentucky

First Capital Bank of Kentucky: 293 N. Hubbards Lane, Louis-ville, KY 40207; tel. (502) 895-5040; e-mail localroots@fcbok.com; internet www.fcbok.com; f. 1996; cap. 1.7m., dep. 392.4m. (Dec. 2010); Chair., Pres. and CEO H. DAVID HALE.

Louisiana

Whitney Bank: 228 St Charles Ave, New Orleans, LA 70130; tel. (504) 586-7456; fax (504) 586-7466; internet www.whitneybank.com; f. 1883; acquired by Hancock Holding Co in 2012; cap. 0.5m., res 1,783.1m., dep. 11,630m. (Dec. 2011); Pres. JOSEPH S. EXNICIOS; 150 brs in 5 states.

Maryland

Provident Bank of Maryland: 114 East Lexington St, Baltimore, MD 21202-1725; tel. (410) 281-7000; fax (410) 277-2768; internet www.provbank.com; f. 1951; cap. 30.0m., dep. 5,675.6m. (Dec. 2007); Chair. and CEO PETER MARTIN.

Massachusetts

Citizens Bank, Massachusetts: 28 State St, Boston, MA 02109; tel. (617) 725-5500; fax (617) 725-5877; e-mail intbank@citizensbank .com; internet www.citizensbank.com; f. 1825; a division of RBS Citizens NA since 2007; dep. 30,403.2m., total assets 35,276.0m. (Dec. 2006); Chair., Pres. and CEO ROBERT E. SMYTH.

Michigan

Citizens Bank: 328 South Saginaw St, Flint, MI 48502-2401; tel. (810) 766-7500; internet www.citizensbanking.com; f. 1871; cap. 454.2m., res 578.6m., dep. 7,451.9m. (Dec. 2011); Chair. JAMES L. WOLOHAN; Pres. and CEO CATHLEEN H. NASH; 219 brs.

Minnesota

US Bank NA: 800 Nicollet Mall, Minneapolis, MN 55402; tel. (612) 303-0799; fax (612) 973-0838; e-mail international.banking@usbank .com; internet www.usbank.com; f. 1853; fmrly Firstar Bank NA, present name adopted in Aug. 2001; cap. 18.2m., res 13,172.1m., dep. 236,091.5m. (Dec. 2011); Chair., Pres. and CEO RICHARD K. DAVIS; 3,085 brs.

Mississippi

Trustmark National Bank: 248 East Capitol St, POB 291, Jackson, MS 39201; tel. (601) 208-5111; fax (601) 949-2387; e-mail Trustmark@custhelp.com; internet www.trustmark.com; f. 1889; cap. 13.4m., res 685.3m., dep. 7,410.1m. (Dec. 2011); Chair., Pres. and CEO RICHARD G. HICKSON.

Missouri

Commerce Bank NA: 1000 Walnut St, POB 419248, Kansas City, MO 64141-6248; tel. (816) 234-2000; fax (800) 892-7100; e-mail mymoney@commercebank.com; internet www.commercebank.com; f. 1865; cap. 10.2m., res 1,129.4m., dep. 16,805.3m. (Dec. 2011); Chair., Pres. and CEO DAVID W. KEMPER.

Montana

First Interstate BancSystem Inc: 401 North 31st St, POB 30918, Billings, MT 59101; tel. (406) 255-5000; e-mail investor.relations@fib .com; internet www.fibk.com; f. 1968; cap. 50.0m., res 415.8m., dep. 5,827.2m. (Dec. 2011); Chair. THOMAS W. SCOTT; Pres. and CEO ED GARDING.

Nebraska

First National Bank of Omaha: 1620 Dodge St, Omaha, NE 68197; tel. (402) 341-0500; internet www.firstnational.com; f. 1857; cap. 8.5m., res 696.7m., dep. 10,746.6m. (Dec. 2011); Chair. BRUCE R. LAURITZEN; Pres. DANIEL K. O'NEILL; 37 brs.

New Hampshire

Citizens Bank, New Hampshire: 875 Elm St, Manchester, NH 03101; tel. (603) 634-7418; fax (603) 634-7481; e-mail intbank@ citizensbank.com; internet www.citizensbank.com; f. 1853; a division of RBS Citizens NA since 2007; cap. 0.8m., dep. 9,250.3m. (Dec. 2006); Pres. CATHLEEN SCHMIDT; 76 brs.

New Jersey

Provident Bank: 830 Bergen Ave, POB 17, Jersey City, NJ 07306-4599; tel. (201) 333-1000; e-mail ken.wagner@providentnj.com; internet www.providentnj.com; cap. 0.5m., dep. 5,937.8m. (Dec. 2010); Chair., Pres. and CEO CHRISTOPHER MARTIN.

New York

American Express Bank Ltd: American Express Tower, 23rd Floor, 200 Vesey St, New York, NY 10285-2300; tel. (212) 640-5000; fax (212) 693-1721; internet www.americanexpress.com; f. 1919; cap. 121.0m., dep. 12,992.0m. (Dec. 2006); Chair. and CEO KENNETH I. CHENAULT.

Bank of New York Mellon: 1 Wall St, New York, NY 10286; tel. (212) 495-1784; fax (212) 495-1398; e-mail comments@bankofny.com; internet www.bnymellon.com; f. 1784; renamed as above after merger of Bank of New York Co and Mellon Financial Corpn in 2007; cap. 1,135.0m., res 8,324m., dep. 213,640m. (Dec. 2011); Pres., Chair. and CEO GERALD L. HASSELL.

Bank of Tokyo–Mitsubishi UFJ: 1251 Ave of the Americas, New York, NY 10020-1104; tel. (212) 782-4000; internet www.bk.mufg.jp; f. 1919; cap. 132.9m., dep. 2,549.9m. (Dec. 2010); Chair. KATSUNORI NAGAYASU; Pres. NOBUYUKI HIRANO.

Citibank NA: 399 Park Ave, New York, NY 10022; tel. (212) 559-1000; fax (212) 223-2681; internet www.citibank.com; f. 1812; cap. 751.0m., res 128,369m., dep. 882,541m. (Dec. 2011); CEO EUGENE M. MCQUADE.

Deutsche Bank Trust Company Americas: 60 Wall St, New York, NY 10005; tel. (212) 250-2500; internet www.db.com/usa; f. 1903; fmrly Bankers' Trust Co, present name adopted April 2002; cap. 2,127m., res 612m., dep. 34,143m. (Dec. 2011); CEO, Americas (vacant).

HSBC USA, Inc: 452 Fifth Ave, New York, NY 10018; tel. (212) 525-5000; internet www.us.hsbc.com; f. 1999 following acquisition of Marine Midland Bank by Hongkong & Shanghai Banking Corpn; acquired Republic National Bank of New York in 2000; cap. 2.0m., dep. 153,750.5m. (Dec. 2010); Pres., Chair. and CEO IRENE DORNER.

JP Morgan Chase Bank National Asscn: 270 Park Ave, New York, NY 10017-2070; tel. (212) 270-6000; fax (212) 349-0990; e-mail patrick.linehan@jpmorgan.com; internet www.chase.com; f. 1982 as Chase Manhattan Bank USA; merged with Bank One Corpn in 2004; present name adopted 2005; cap. 1,785.0m., res 80,751m., dep. 1,190,738m. (Dec. 2011); Chair. and CEO JAMES DIMON.

M&T Bank Corpn: 1 M & T Plaza, Buffalo, NY 14203; tel. (716) 842-4200; fax (716) 842-5839; internet www.mtb.com; f. 1856; Mfrs' and Traders' Trust Co; cap. 120.6m., dep. 55,657.0m. (Dec. 2010); Chair. and CEO ROBERT G. WILMERS; Pres. MARK J. CZARNECKI; 736 brs.

Trustco Bank: POB 1082, Schenectady, NY 12301-1082; tel. (518) 377-3311; internet www.trustcobank.com; f. 1902; cap. 29.4m., res 105.8m., dep. 3,735.9m. (Dec. 2011); Chair., Pres. and CEO ROBERT J. MCCORMICK.

United States Trust Co: 114 West 47th St, New York, NY 10036; tel. (212) 852-1000; fax (212) 995-5642; e-mail info@trust.com; internet www.ustrust.com; f. 1853; cap. 15.0m., dep. 9,585.5m. (Dec. 2006); Chair. and CEO JEFFREY S. MAURER.

North Carolina

Bank of America NA: 100 North Tryon St, Charlotte, NC 28255; tel. (401) 865-7948; internet www.bankamerica.com; f. 1904; cap. 3,020.0m., res 144,181.3m., dep. 1,077,176.8m. (Dec. 2011); Chair. CHARLES HOLLIDAY, Jr; Pres. and CEO BRIAN T. MOYNIHAN.

Wachovia Bank NA: 301 South College St, Suite 4000, Charlotte, NC 28288-0013; tel. (704) 374-1246; internet www.wachovia.com; f. 1866; merged with Wells Fargo Bank in 2008; cap. 455.0m., dep. 549,062.0m. (Dec. 2008).

Ohio

Fifth Third Bank: 38 Fountain Square Plaza, Cincinnati, OH 45263; tel. (513) 579-5300; internet www.53.com; f. 1853; cap. 4.5m., res 11,961.7m., dep. 89,689.1m. (Dec. 2011); Pres. GREG D. CARMICHAEL; CEO KEVIN T. KABAT; 361 brs.

FirstMerit Bank NA: 106 S Main St, Akron, OH 44308; tel. (330) 384-7201; fax (330) 384-7008; e-mail customerservice@firstmerit .com; internet www.firstmerit.com; f. 1845; cap. 57.6m., res 619.9m., dep. 11,497.6m. (Dec. 2011); Chair. and CEO PAUL G. GREIG.

Huntington National Bank: 41 South High St, Columbus, OH 43287; tel. (614) 480-4685; fax (614) 480-5284; e-mail international@ huntington.com; internet www.huntington.com; f. 1866; cap. 40.0m., res 5,423.1m., dep. 44,300.3m. (Dec. 2011); Chair., Pres. and CEO STEVEN D. STEINOUR.

KeyBank NA: 127 Public Sq., Cleveland, OH 44114-1306; tel. (216) 689-5580; fax (216) 689-3683; e-mail KeyExpress@keybank.com; internet www.key.com; f. 1849; cap. 50.0m., res 5,711.7m., dep. 64,214.8m. (Dec. 2011); Chair. and CEO BETH E. MOONEY.

National City Bank: 1900 East Ninth St, POB 94750, Cleveland, OH 44114-3484; tel. (216) 575-2000; fax (216) 575-9263; internet www.nationalcity.com; f. 1845; acquired by PNC in 2008; cap. 7.3m., dep. 121,790.3m. (Dec. 2008); Chair., Pres. and CEO PETER E. RASKIND; c. 1,300 brs.

Oklahoma

BancFirst: Suite 200, 101 North Broadway, POB 26788, Oklahoma City, OK 73102; tel. (405) 270-1000; internet www.bancfirst.com; cap. 40.9m., res 76.8m., dep. 4,893.4m. (Dec. 2011); CEO DAVID RAINBOLT; Pres. DAVID HARLOW.

BOKF NA: Bank of Oklahoma Tower, POB 2300, Tulsa, OK 74192; tel. (918) 588-6010; fax (918) 588-6026; internet www .bankofoklahoma.com; f. 1933; wholly owned subsidiary of BOK Financial Corpn; fmrly Bank of Oklahoma NA; name changed as above in 2011; cap. 82.5m., res 1,160.6m., dep. 19,171.3m. (Dec. 2011); Chair. GEORGE B. KAISER; Pres. and CEO STANLEY A. LYBARGER; 56 brs.

Oregon

The Commerce Bank of Oregon: 1211 South West Fifth Ave, Suite 1250, Portland, OR 97204; tel. (503) 548-1000; fax (503) 548-1050; e-mail CustomerService@tcboregon.com; internet www .tcboregon.com; f. 2005; cap. 20.7m., dep. 55.0m. (Dec. 2010); Pres. and CEO LARRY OGG.

Pennsylvania

PNC Bank, NA: 1 PNC Plaza, 225 Fifth Ave, Pittsburgh, PA 15222-2707; tel. (412) 762-2021; internet www.pnc.com; f. 1959; merged with National City Bank in Dec. 2008; cap. 740.1m., res 24,302.7m., dep. 197,343m. (Dec. 2011); Chair. and CEO JAMES E. ROHR; Pres. WILLIAM S. DEMCHAK; 854 brs.

Rhode Island

Citizens Bank, Rhode Island: 1 Citizens Plaza, Providence, RI 02903; tel. (401) 454-7096; internet www.citizensbank.com; f. 1996;

cap. 1.0m., res 15,834.1m., dep. 75,690.2m. (Dec. 2011); Pres. ELLEN ALEMANY; 78 brs.

South Carolina

Carolina First Bank: 104 South Main St, Poinsett Plaza, 10th Floor, POB 1029, Greenville, SC 29602; tel. (864) 255-7900; fax (864) 241-1565; e-mail customerassistance@carolinafirst.com; internet www.carolinafirst.com; cap. 7.9m., dep. 10,558.8m. (Dec. 2009); part of The South Financial Group; Pres. and CEO H. LYNN HARTON; 110 brs.

South Dakota

Citibank (South Dakota) NA: 701 East 60th St, North, POB 6000, Sioux Falls, SD 57117; tel. (605) 331-2626; internet www.citibank.com; f. 1981; cap. 113.0m., dep. 114,614.2m. (Dec. 2010); Gen. Sec. DAVID L. ZIMBECK; Pres. KENDALL E. STORK.

Wells Fargo Bank NA: 101 North Phillips Ave, Sioux Falls, SD 57104; tel. (605) 575-6900; fax (605) 575-4815; e-mail ipb@wellsfargo.com; internet www.wellsfargo.com; f. 1960 as Wells Fargo Bank American Trust Co; fmrly Norwest Bank South Dakota NA, present name adopted in 2004; cap. 519.0m., res 104,095m., dep. 905,653m. (Dec. 2011); Pres. and CEO JOHN G. STUMPF; 3,000 brs.

Tennessee

First Tennessee Bank NA: 165 Madison Ave, 9th Floor, POB 84, Memphis, TN 38103; tel. (800) 489-4040; internet www.firsttennessee.com; f. 1864; subsidiary of First Horizon National Corpn; cap. 367.3m., res 1,714.6m., dep. 16,402.1m. (Dec. 2011); Chair., Pres. and CEO BRYAN JORDAN; 183 brs.

Texas

Frost Bank: 100 West Houston St, POB 1600, San Antonio, TX 78296; tel. (210) 220-4011; internet www.frostbank.com; f. 1899; cap. 8.5m., res 1,200.9m., dep. 16,846.8m. (Dec. 2011); Chair. and CEO RICHARD W. EVANS, Jr.

Virginia

Chevy Chase Bank, FSB: 7926 Jones Branch Dr., McLean, VA 22101; internet www.chevychasebank.com; f. 1955; merged with Capital One in July 2009; total assets 15,106.6m. (Sept. 2007); Pres. ROBERT D. BROEKSMIT, II.

Washington

Washington Trust Bank: 717 West Sprague Ave, POB 2127, Spokane, WA 99210-2127; tel. (509) 353-4204; fax (509) 358-3590; internet www.watrust.com; f. 1902; cap. 7.5m., res 110.5m., dep. 3,522.4m. (Dec. 2011); Chair. and CEO PETER F. STANTON; Pres. JOHN E. HEATH.

Wisconsin

Tri City National Bank: 6400 South 27th St, Oak Creek, WI 53154; tel. (414) 761-1610; fax (414) 761-2019; internet www.tcnb.com; f. 1963; cap. 2.8m., dep. 1,026.6m. (Dec. 2010); Chair., Pres. and CEO RONALD PUETZ.

Co-operative Bank

CoBank: 5500 South Quebec St, Greenwood Village, CO 80111; tel. (800) 542-8072; e-mail webmaster@cobank.com; internet www.cobank.com; f. 1933; provides loan finance and domestic and international banking services for agricultural and farmer-owned co-operatives; merged with U.S. AgBank in 2012; cap. 2,220.1m., dep. 51,911.3m. (Dec. 2009); Chair. EVERETT DOBRINSKI; Pres. and CEO ROBERT B. ENGEL.

Trade Bank

Export-Import Bank of the United States (Ex-Im Bank): 811 Vermont Ave, NW, Washington, DC 20571; tel. (202) 565-3946; fax (202) 565-3931; e-mail info@exim.gov; internet www.exim.gov; f. 1934; independent agency since 1945; cap. subscribed by the US Treasury; finances and facilitates US external trade, guarantees payment to US foreign traders and banks, extends credit to foreign governmental and private concerns; cap. 1,000.0m. (Sept. 2012); Chair. and Pres. FRED P. HOCHBERG; Inspector-Gen. OSVALDO LUIS GRATACOS MUNET.

BANKING ASSOCIATIONS

There is a State Bankers Association in each state.

American Bankers Association: 1120 Connecticut Ave, NW, Washington, DC 20036; tel. (202) 663-5000; fax (202) 828-4547; e-mail custserv@aba.com; internet www.aba.com; f. 1875; Chair. MATTHEW H. WILLIAMS; Pres. and CEO FRANK KEATING.

BAFT-IFSA: 1120 Connecticut Ave, NW, 5th Floor, Washington, DC 20036; tel. (202) 663-7575; fax (202) 663-5538; e-mail info@baft-ifsa.com; internet www.baft-ifsa.com; f. 1921; fmrly Bankers' Association for Finance and Trade (BAFT); merged with International Financial Services Asscn (IFSA) Jan. 2010 to form BAFT-IFSA; affiliated to the American Bankers Asscn; Chair. JEREMY J. O'B. WILSON; CEO TOD R. BURWELL.

Bank Administration Institute (BAI): 115 South LaSalle St, Suite 3300, Chicago, IL 60603-3801; tel. (312) 683-2464; fax (312) 683-2373; e-mail info@bai.org; internet www.bai.org; f. 1924; Chair. LEWIS C. FISCHER; Pres. and CEO DEBORAH L. BIANUCCI.

Conference of State Bank Supervisors (CSBS): 1129 20th St, NW, 9th Floor, Washington, DC 20036; tel. (202) 296-2840; fax (202) 296-1928; e-mail csmith@csbs.org; internet www.csbs.org; f. 1902 as the National Association of Supervisors of State Banks; changed name as above in 1971; organization of banking regulators; Chair. GREG GONZALES; Pres. and CEO JOHN RYAN.

Independent Community Bankers of America: 1615 L St, NW, Suite 900, Washington, DC 20036; tel. (202) 659-8111; fax (202) 659-3604; e-mail info@icba.org; internet www.icba.org; f. 1930; Chair. JEFFREY L. GERHART; Pres. and CEO CAMDEN R. FINE; c. 5,000 mems.

Mortgage Bankers Association of America: 1717 Rhode Island Ave, NW, Suite 400, Washington, DC 20036; tel. (202) 557-2700; internet www.mortgagebankers.org; f. 1914; Chair. MICHAEL W. YOUNG; Pres. and CEO DAVID H. STEVENS; 2,400 mems.

PRINCIPAL STOCK EXCHANGES

Chicago Stock Exchange: 1 Financial Pl., 440 South LaSalle St, Chicago, IL 60605; tel. (312) 663-2222; fax (312) 663-2721; e-mail info@chx.com; internet www.chx.com; f. 1882; Chair. MICHAEL H. KERR; CEO DAVID A. HERRON; 445 mems.

Nasdaq Stock Market LLC: 1 Liberty Plaza, 165 Broadway, New York, NY 10006; tel. (212) 401-8700; internet www.nasdaq.com; f. 1998 by the American Stock Exchange and the Nat. Asscn of Securities Dealers (NASD); incorporated the Boston Stock Exchange in 2008; world-wide electronic trading market; Chair. MERIT E. JANOW; CEO ERIC W. NOLL.

National Stock Exchange SM (NSX): 440 South LaSalle St, Suite 2600, Chicago, IL 60605; tel. (312) 786-8803; fax (312) 939-7239; internet www.nsx.com; f. 1885; fmrly Cincinnati Stock Exchange, name changed as above in Nov. 2003; Chair. JAMES M. ANDERSON; CEO JOSEPH S. RIZZELLO.

NYSE Euronext (New York Stock Exchange Euronext): 11 Wall St, New York, NY 10005; tel. (212) 656-3000; fax (212) 656-5549; internet www.nyse.com; f. 1792; incorporated the American Stock Exchange in 2009; Chair. JAN-MICHIEL HESSELS; Dir and CEO DUNCAN L. NIEDERAUER; 2,800 mems.

Philadelphia Stock Exchange (NASDAQ OMX PHLX): Stock Exchange Bldg, 1900 Market St, Philadelphia, PA 19103; tel. (215) 496-5000; fax (215) 496-5460; internet www.nasdaqtrader.com; f. 1790; acquired by NASDAQ OMX Group, Inc in 2008; Pres. THOMAS A. WITTMAN; 505 mems.

INSURANCE
Principal Companies

Acacia Life Insurance Co: 7315 Wisconsin Ave, Bethesda, MD 20814-3202; tel. (301) 280-1000; fax (310) 280-1161; internet www.unificompanies.com; f. 1869; part of UNIFI Mutual Holding Co; life and health; Pres. and CEO JOANN M. MARTIN.

Allstate Corpn: POB 12055, 1819 Electric Rd SW, Roanoke, VA 24018; tel. (708) 402-5000; fax (708) 402-2351; e-mail ceo@allstate.com; internet www.allstate.com; f. 1931; property and casualty, life, fire, indemnity; Chair., Pres. and CEO THOMAS J. WILSON.

American Family Insurance Group: 6000 American Pkwy, Madison, WI 53783-0001; tel. (608) 249-2111; internet www.amfam.com; f. 1927; life and annuities through subsidiary, American Family Life Insurance Co; property and casualty through eight other subsidiaries; Chair. and CEO JACK C. SALZWEDEL; Pres. and COO DANIEL R. SCHULTZ.

American Family Life Assurance Co of Columbus (AFLAC): 1932 Wynnton Rd, Columbus, GA 31999; tel. (706) 596-3493; e-mail news@aflac.com; internet www.aflac.com; f. 1955; life and health; Chair. and CEO DANIEL P. AMOS; Pres. and COO PAUL S. AMOS, II.

American General Life and Accident Insurance Co: POB 4373, Houston, TX 77210; tel. (800) 231-3655; fax (713) 831-3028; internet www.americangeneral.com; f. 1900; wholly owned subsidiary of American International Group, Inc (AIG); Pres. and CEO JIM MALLON.

American National Insurance Co: 1 Moody Plaza, Galveston, TX 77550-7999; tel. (409) 763-4661; fax (409) 763-4545; e-mail customerservice@anico.com; internet www.anico.com; f. 1905; operating in 50 states, the District of Columbia, Puerto Rico and

American Samoa; life and health, annuities, property and casualty, credit insurance and pension plan services; Chair. and CEO ROBERT L. MOODY, Sr; Pres. and COO JAMES E. POZZI.

American United Life Insurance Co: 1 American Sq., POB 368, Indianapolis, IN 46206-0368; tel. (317) 285-2364; fax (317) 285-1931; internet www.oneamerica.com; f. 1877; part of OneAmerica Financial Partners, Inc; owned by American United Mutual Insurance Holding Company (AUMIHC); life and health, annuities; Pres. and CEO DAYTON H. MOLENDORP.

Americo Financial Life and Annuity Insurance Co: 300 West 11th St, POB 410288, Kansas City, MO 64141-0288; tel. (816) 391-2000; e-mail contactamerico@americo.com; internet www.americo.com; f. 1909; Chair. MICHAEL A. MERRIMAN; Pres. and CEO GARY L. MULLER.

Ameritas Life Insurance Corpn: 5900 O St, POB 81889, Lincoln, NE 68501-1889; fax (402) 467-7335; e-mail avlic@ameritas.com; internet www.ameritas.com; f. 1887 as Old Line Bankers Life Insurance Co of Nebraska (Bankers Life); adopted present name in 1988; part of UNIFI Mutual Holding Co; life and health; Chair., Pres. and CEO JOANN M. MARTIN.

Aon Corpn: Aon Center, 200 E Randolph St, Chicago, IL 60601; tel. 381-1000; e-mail david.prosperi@aon.com; internet www.aon.com; f. 1982; following the merger of Ryan Insurance Group with Combined International Corpn; Pres. and CEO GREGORY C. CASE.

Assurant: 1 Chase Manhattan Plaza, New York, NY 10005; tel. (212) 859-7000; fax (212) 859-5893; e-mail vera.carley@assurant.com; internet www.assurant.com; life and health; Chair. ELAINE D. ROSEN; Pres. and CEO ROBERT B. POLLOCK.

Auto-Owners Insurance Group: 6101 Anacapri Blvd, Lansing, MI 48917; tel. (517) 323-1200; fax (517) 323-8796; internet www.auto-owners.com; f. 1916; property and casualty through Auto-Owners Insurance Co and 4 other subsidiaries; life through Auto-Owners Life Insurance Co; Chair. and CEO JEFFREY HARROLD.

Aviva USA Group: 7700 Mills Civic Parkway, West Des Moines, IA 50266; tel. (515) 362-3600; fax (515) 557-2625; e-mail steven.carison@avivausa.com; internet www.avivausa.com; f. 1896 as AmerUS group; life and health, annuities; subsidiaries: Aviva Life and Annuity Co (Des Moines, IA), Aviva Life and Annuity Co (Woodbury, NY); acquired by Aviva PLC in 2006; Pres. and CEO CHRISTOPHER LITTLEFIELD.

AXA-Equitable, Inc: 1290 Ave of the Americas, New York, NY; tel. (212) 554-1234; fax (212) 262-9019; internet www.axa-equitable.com; f. 1859; subsidiary of AXA Financial, Inc; life and health, annuities; Chair. and CEO MARK PEARSON.

Baltimore Life Insurance Co: 10075 Red Run Blvd, Owings Mills, MD 21117-4871; tel. (410) 581-6600; fax (410) 581-6253; e-mail info@baltlife.com; internet www.baltlife.com; f. 1882; life and health; Chair. GERARD E. HOLTHAUS; Pres. and CEO DAVID K. FICCA.

W. R. Berkley Corpn: 475 Steamboat Rd, Greenwich, CT 06830; tel. (203) 629-3000; fax (203) 629-3073; e-mail khorvath@wrberkley.com; internet www.wrberkley.com; f. 1967; property and casualty through subsidiaries, divided into 5 business sectors: regional, reinsurance, specialty, alternative markets and international; Chair. and CEO WILLIAM R. BERKLEY; Pres. and COO W. ROBERT BERKLEY, Jr.

Berkshire Hathaway, Inc: 3555 Farnam St, Omaha, NE 68131; tel. (402) 346-1400; e-mail berkshire@berkshirehathaway.com; internet www.berkshirehathaway.com; general insurance through Berkshire Hathaway Group; life insurance through subsidiary, Medical Protective, in Fort Wayne, IN; Chair. and CEO WARREN E. BUFFETT.

CIGNA Group Insurance: 900 Cottage Grove Rd, Bloomfield, CT 06002; tel. (215) 761-1000; fax (215) 761-5588; internet www.cigna.com; f. 1982; part of CIGNA Corpn; life and health; Pres. and CEO DAVID M. CORDANI.

CNA Insurance: 333 South Wabash, Chicago, IL 60604; tel. (312) 822-5000; e-mail cna_help@cna.com; internet www.cna.com; part of Loews Corpn; property and casualty; Chair. and CEO THOMAS F. MOTAMED.

Combined Insurance Co of America (CICA): 1000 North Milwaukee Ave, Glenview, IL 60025; tel. (847) 953-2025; fax (847) 953-8070; e-mail Amy.Burrell-Tichy@combined.com; internet www.combinedinsurance.com; f. 1949; life and health; operates as Combined Life Insurance Co of New York in NY; acquired by the ACE Group in 2008; Pres. BRAD BENNETT.

CNO Financial Group, Inc: 11825 North Pennsylvania St, Carmel, IN 46032; tel. (317) 817-6100; internet www.cnoinc.com; f. 1979; fmrly Conseco, Inc; present name adopted in 2010; life and health; subsidiaries: Conseco Life Insurance Co (IN), Conseco Insurance Co (IL), Conseco Variable Insurance Co (TX), Conseco Health Insurance Co (AZ), Conseco Senior Health Insurance Co (PA), Bankers Life & Casualty Co (Chicago, IL); Chair. NEAL C. SCHNEIDER; CEO EDWARD J. BONACH.

Erie Insurance Group: 100 Erie Insurance Pl., Erie, PA 16530-1104; tel. (814) 451-5000; fax (814) 451-5060; internet www.erieinsurance.com; f. 1925; vehicle, home, commercial and life through network of independent agents; Chair. J. RALPH BORNEMAN, Jr; Pres. and CEO TERRENCE W. CAVANAUGH.

Farmers Insurance Group of Cos: 4680 Wilshire Blvd, Los Angeles, CA 90010-3807; tel. (213) 930-3200; fax (213) 932-3101; internet www.farmers.com; f. 1928; part of Farmers Group, Inc; owned by Zurich Financial Services; vehicle, home and life; operates in 41 states; subsidiaries: Farmers Insurance Exchange, Truck Insurance Exchange, Fire Insurance Exchange, Farmers New World Life Insurance Co (Mercer Island, WA); acquired Foremost Insurance Co (MI) in 2000; CEO JEFF DAILEY.

Federal Insurance Co: POB 1615, Warren, NJ 07061; tel. (908) 903-2000; internet www.chubb.com; CEO JOHN D. FINNEGAN.

Fidelity National Financial (FNF): 601 Riverside Ave, Jacksonville, FL 32204; tel. (888) 934-3354; internet www.fnf.com; principal subsidiaries: Fidelity National Title Group and Fidelity National Property and Casualty Insurance Group; Chair. WILLIAM P. FOLEY, II; CEO GEORGE P. SCANLON.

First American Financial Corpn: 1 First American Way, Santa Ana, CA 92707; tel. (714) 250-3000; e-mail corporate.communications@firstam.com; internet www.firstam.com; f. 1889; Chair. PARKER S. KENNEDY; CEO DENNIS J. GILMORE.

General American Life Insurance Co: 1 Madison Ave, New York, NY 10010-3681; tel. (212) 578-2211; fax (212) 689-1980; internet www.metlife.com; f. 1933; wholly owned subsidiary of MetLife, Inc; Chair., Pres. and CEO KEVIN EICHNER.

Genworth Financial, Inc: 6620 West Broad St, Richmond, VA 23230; tel. (804) 281-6000; e-mail contactus@genworth.com; internet www.genworth.com; f. 1871 as The Life Insurance Co of Virginia; life, long-term care, annuities; CEO MARTIN P. KLEIN (acting).

The Guardian Life Insurance Co of America: 7 Hanover Sq., New York, NY 10004; tel. (212) 598-8000; fax (212) 353-7034; e-mail marketcc@glic.com; internet www.guardianlife.com; f. 1860; life and health through 12 subsidiaries and affiliates; CEO SCOTT DOLFI.

Hanover Insurance Group, Inc: 440 Lincoln St, Worcester, MA 01653-0002; tel. (508) 855-1000; fax (508) 853-6332; e-mail abanek@hanover.com; internet www.hanover.com; f. 1852; fmrly operated as Allmerica Financial Life Insurance and Annuity Co, name changed as above in 2005; property and casualty; operates as The Hanover Insurance Co, and as Citizens Insurance Co of America in MI; Chair. MICHAEL P. ANGELINI; Pres. and CEO FREDERICK H. EPPINGER.

Hartford Financial Services Group, Inc: 1 Hartford Plaza, Hartford, CT 06115; tel. (860) 547-5000; internet www.thehartford.com; f. 1810; vehicle, home, life, flood, property and casualty, group benefits, group reinsurance; Chair., Pres. and CEO LIAM E. MCGEE.

John Hancock Life Insurance Co: 197 Clarendon St, POB 111, Boston, MA 02117; tel. (617) 572-6000; fax (617) 572-4539; e-mail investor_relations@manulife.com; internet www.johnhancock.com; f. 1862; owned by Manulife (Canada); Pres. and Gen. Man. MICHAEL DOUGHTY.

Kansas City Life Insurance Co: 3520 Broadway, Kansas City, MO 64111; tel. (816) 753-7000; fax (816) 753-4902; internet www.kclife.com; f. 1895; life and health; operates in 48 states and the District of Columbia; subsidiaries: Old American Insurance Co, Sunset Life Insurance Co of America; Chair., Pres. and CEO R. PHILIP BIXBY.

Kemper Corporation: 1 East Wacker Dr., Chicago, IL 60601; tel. (312) 661-4600; e-mail GetAnswers@kemper.com; internet kempercorporation.com; fmrly Unitrin Inc; changed name as above in 2011; life and health through Kemper Life & Health Insurance Group (5 subsidiaries); property and casualty through Kemper Property & Casualty Insurance Group (19 subsidiaries); 2 further subsidiaries and 5 affiliated cos; Chair., Pres. and CEO DONALD G. SOUTHWELL.

Liberty Mutual Group, Inc: 175 Berkeley St, Boston, MA 02116; tel. (617) 357-9500; fax (617) 350-7648; internet www.libertymutualgroup.com; f. 1912; subsidiaries: Liberty Life Assurance Co of Boston, Liberty Mutual Insurance Co, Liberty Mutual Fire Insurance Co and Employers Insurance Co of Wasusau; Pres. and CEO DAVID H. LONG.

Lincoln National Life Insurance Co: 350 Church St, Hartford, CT 06103; tel. (877) 275-5462; e-mail personalservicecenter@lfg.com; internet www.lfg.com; f. 1905; part of Lincoln National Corpn; life and health; Pres. and CEO DENNIS R. GLASS.

Manhattan Insurance Group: 10700 NW Freeway, Houston, TX 77092; tel. (860) 298-9343; fax (877) 626-4281; e-mail cservice@manhattanlife.com; internet www.manhattanlife.com; f. 1850; comprises Manhattan Life, Central United Life, Western United Life and Family Life Insurance; Chair. and CEO DAVID W. HARRIS.

Massachusetts Mutual Life Insurance Co (MassMutual): 1295 State St, Springfield, MA 01111-0001; tel. (413) 788-8411; fax (413) 744-6005; internet www.massmutual.com; f. 1851; part of Mass-

Mutual Financial Group; mutual life and health; Chair., Pres. and CEO ROGER W. CRANDALL.

Metropolitan Life Insurance Co (MetLife): 200 Park Ave, New York, NY 10166; tel. (212) 578-2211; fax (212) 689-1980; internet www.metlife.com; f. 1863; life and health; Chair., Pres. and CEO STEVEN A. KANDARIAN.

Minnesota Life Insurance Co: 400 Robert St North, St Paul, MN 55101; tel. (651) 665-3500; fax (651) 665-4488; e-mail john.hageman@securian.com; internet www.securian.com; f. 1880; affiliated to Securian Financial Group, Inc; life and health; Chair., Pres. and CEO ROBERT L. SENKLER.

Mutual of Omaha Insurance Co: Mutual of Omaha Plaza, Omaha, NE 68175; tel. (402) 342-7600; e-mail corporatesecretary@mutualofomaha.com; internet mutualofomaha.com; f. 1909; life and health; operating in 50 states, the District of Columbia, the US Virgin Is, Puerto Rico and Guam; Chair. and CEO DANIEL P. NEARY.

Nationwide Mutual Insurance Co: 1 Nationwide Plaza, Columbus, OH 43215-2220; tel. (614) 249-7111; e-mail casej6@nationwide.com; internet www.nationwide.com; f. 1925; property and casualty through 18 subsidiaries; life and retirement savings through 25 subsidiaries; also asset management and strategic investment; CEO STEVE RASMUSSEN.

New York Life Insurance Co: 51 Madison Ave, New York, NY 10010-1603; tel. (212) 576-7000; fax (212) 576-6794; e-mail infonyl@e-mail.com; internet www.newyorklife.com; f. 1845; life and health; Chair., Pres. and CEO THEODORE (TED) MATHAS.

The Northwestern Mutual Life Insurance Co: 720 East Wisconsin Ave, Milwaukee, WI 53202-4797; tel. (414) 271-1444; fax (414) 665-5739; internet www.nmfn.com; f. 1857; mutual life and health; Chair. and CEO JOHN E. SCHLIFSKE; Pres. GARY (SKIP) POLINER.

Pacific Life Insurance Co: 700 Newport Center Dr., Newport Beach, CA 92660-6397; tel. (949) 219-3011; fax (949) 219-7614; e-mail info@pacificlife.com; internet www.pacificlife.com; f. 1868; life, annuities and mutual funds; Chair., Pres. and CEO JAMES T. MORRIS; Exec. Vice-Pres. ADRIAN S. GRIGGS.

Penn Mutual Life Insurance Co: 600 Dresher Rd, Horsham, PA 19044; tel. (215) 956-8000; fax (215) 956-7699; internet www.pennmutual.com; f. 1847; Chair. ROBERT E. CHAPPELL; Pres. and CEO EILEEN MCDONNELL.

Phoenix Life Insurance Co: 1 American Row, POB 5056, Hartford, CT 06102-5056; tel. (860) 403-5000; e-mail webmaster@phoenixwm.com; internet www.phoenixwm.com; f. 1851; life and health, annuities; operating in all states, the District of Columbia, Puerto Rico, the US Virgin Is and Canada; Chair. THOMAS J. JOHNSON; Pres. and CEO JAMES D. WEHR.

Pioneer Mutual Life Insurance Co: 101 North 10th St, Fargo, ND 58108; tel. (701) 297-5700; e-mail CorporateCommunications.CorpComm@oneamerica.com; internet www.oneamerica.com; f. 1868; part of OneAmerica Financial Partners, Inc, owned by American United Mutual Insurance Holding Co (AUMIHC); life and health, annuities; Pres. and CEO DAYTON H. MOLENDORP.

Principal Financial Group, Inc: 711 High St, Des Moines, IA 50392; tel. (515) 247-5111; fax (515) 235-5491; e-mail houser.susan@principal.com; internet www.principal.com; f. 1879; life and health; Chair., Pres. and CEO LARRY D. ZIMPLEMAN.

The Progressive Group: 6300 Wilson Mills Rd, Mayfield Village, OH 44143; tel. (440) 461-5000; e-mail Leah_Knapp@progressive.com; internet www.progressive.com; f. 1937; part of The Progressive Corpn; Chair. PETER B. LEWIS; Pres. and CEO GLENN M. RENWICK.

Protective Life Insurance Co: 2801 Hwy 280 South, Birmingham, AL 35223-2488; tel. (205) 268-1000; e-mail eva.robertson@protective.com; internet www.protective.com; f. 1907; part of Protective Life Insurance Corpn; life and health; Chair., Pres. and CEO JOHN D. JOHNS.

The Prudential Insurance Co of America: 751 Broad St, Newark, NJ 07102-3714; tel. (973) 802-6000; fax (973) 802-7277; e-mail investor.relations@prudential.com; internet www.prudential.com; f. 1875; life and health; Chair. and CEO JOHN R. STRANGFELD.

QBE Insurance Group: Wall Street Plaza, 88 Pine Street, New York, NY 10005; tel. (212) 422-1212; fax (212) 422-1313; internet www.qbeusa.com; CEO DAVE DUCLOS.

SAFECO Corpn: Safeco Plaza, 4333 Brooklyn Ave, NE, Seattle, WA 98185-0001; tel. (206) 545-5000; fax (206) 548-7117; e-mail Brenda.Harrison@safeco.com; internet www.safeco.com; f. 1929; part of Liberty Mutual Group since 2008; subsidiaries: SAFECO Property and Casualty Insurance Cos, SAFECO Surety; Pres. MICHAEL HUGHES.

Security Mutual Life Insurance Co of New York: 100 Court St, POB 1625, Binghamton, New York, NY 13902-1625; tel. (607) 723-3551; e-mail hpalmer@smlny.com; internet www.smlny.com; f. 1886; life and health, annuities; operating in all states; Chair., Pres. and CEO BRUCE W. BOYEA.

StanCorp Financial Group: 900 5th Ave SW, Portland, OR 97204; tel. (503) 248-2700; fax (503) 321-7757; e-mail info@standard.com; internet www.standard.com; f. 1906; includes the Standard Insurance Company and Standard Life Insurance Co of New York; disability, group disability, group life, group dental, annuities; Chair., Pres. and CEO J. GREG NESS.

Standard Life Insurance Co of New York: 420 Lexington Ave, New York, NY 10170; tel. (212) 883-0030; e-mail getinfo@standard.com; internet www.standard.com; subsidiary of StanCorp Financial Group, Inc; group life, disability, dental; Sen. Vice-Pres. FLOYD CHADEE.

State Farm Insurance: 1 State Farm Plaza, Bloomington, IL 61710-0001; tel. (309) 766-2311; fax (309) 766-6169; internet www.statefarm.com; f. 1929; vehicle, fire, life and health insurance; Chair., Pres. and CEO EDWARD B. RUST, Jr.

State Life Insurance Co: 1 American Sq., POB 368, Indianapolis, IN 46206-0368; tel. (317) 681-5300; fax (317) 681-5492; internet www.oneamerica.com; f. 1894; part of OneAmerica Financial Partners, Inc, owned by American United Mutual Insurance Holding Company (AUMIHC); life and health, annuities; Chair., Pres. and CEO DAYTON H. MOLENDORP.

Teachers Insurance and Annuity Association-College Retirement Equities Fund (TIAA-CREF): 730 Third Ave, New York, NY 10017-3206; tel. (212) 916-6066; fax (212) 916-6088; e-mail trustees@tiaa-cref.org; internet www.tiaa-cref.org; f. 1918 (TIAA); f. 1952 (CREF); mutual life and health; Chair. RONALD L. THOMPSON; Pres. and CEO ROGER W. FERGUSON, Jr.

Thrivent Financial for Lutherans: 4321 North Ballard Rd, Appleton, WI 54919-0001; tel. (920) 734-5721; e-mail mail@thrivent.com; internet www.thrivent.com; life and health; Chair. KURT M. SENSKE; Pres. and CEO BRAD HEWITT.

Torchmark Corpn: 3700 South Stonebridge Dr., POB 8080, McKinney, TX 75070-8080; tel. (972) 569-4000; e-mail tmkir@torchmarkcorp.com; internet www.torchmarkcorp.com; life and health; principal subsidiaries: American Income Life Insurance Co (Waco, TX), First United American Life Insurance Co (Syracuse, NY), Globe Life And Accident Insurance Co (Oklahoma City, OK), Liberty National Life Insurance Co (Birmingham, AL), United American Insurance Co (McKinney, TX), United Investors Life Insurance Co (Birmingham, AL); Chair. MARK S. MCANDREW; CEO GARY L. COLEMAN, LARRY M. HUTCHISON.

Transamerica Corpn: 4333 Edgewood Rd NE, Cedar Rapids, IA 52499-0010; tel. (319) 355-8511; fax (415) 983-4234; e-mail cindy.nodorft@transamerica.com; internet www.transamerica.com; f. 1906; part of AEGON Insurance Group; life and health, annuities, reinsurance; subsidiaries: Transamerica Occidental Life Insurance Co, Transamerica Life Insurance Co, Transamerica Financial Life Insurance Co; Pres. JAMES MARTIN FLEWELLEN.

The Travelers Companies, Inc: 385 Washington St, Saint Paul, MN 55102; tel. (615) 310-7911; fax (651) 310-8204; internet www.travelers.com; f. 2004 as St Paul Travelers by merger of St Paul Coes and Travelers Property and Casualty Corpn; adopted current name in 2007; Chair. and CEO JAY S. FISHMAN; Pres. and COO BRIAN W. MACLEAN.

Union Central Life Insurance Co: 1876 Waycross Rd, POB 40888, Cincinnati, OH 45240; tel. (513) 595-2200; fax (513) 595-2559; internet www.unioncentral.com; f. 1867; subsidiary of Ameritas Life Insurance Corpn; life and health; Pres. and CEO JOANN M. MARTIN.

Unum Group: 1 Fountain Sq., Chattanooga, TN 37402; tel. (432) 294-1011; e-mail tawhite@unum.com; internet www.unumprovident.com; f. 1848; life and health; subsidiaries: Colonial Life Accident and Insurance Co, Paul Revere Life Insurance Co, Provident Life and Accident Insurance Co, Provident Life and Casualty Insurance Co, First Unum Insurance Co, and Unum Life Insurance Co of America; Chair. WILLIAM J. RYAN; Pres. and CEO THOMAS R. WATJEN.

USAA: McDermott Bldg, 9800 Fredericksburg Rd, San Antonio, TX 78288; internet www.usaa.com; f. 1922; property and casualty through seven subsidiaries: United Service Automobile Asscn, USAA Casualty Insurance Co, USAA General Indemnity Co, Garrison Property and Casualty Insurance Co, USAA County Mutual Insurance Co, USAA Texas Lloyd's Co and USAA Ltd; life and annuities through 2 subsidiaries: USAA Life Insurance Co and USAA Life Insurance Company of New York (Highland Falls, NY); Chair. Lt-Gen. (retd) JOHN H. MOELLERING; Pres. and CEO JOSUE (JOE) ROBLES, Jr.

Washington National Insurance Co: 11825 N Pennsylvania St, Carmel, IN 46032; internet www.washingtonnational.com; f. 1911; a subsidiary of CNO Financial Group; Pres. STEVEN M. STECHER.

Western & Southern Financial Group: 400 Broadway, Mail Station 90, Cincinnati, OH 45202; tel. (866) 832-7719; fax (513) 629-1220; internet www.westernsouthern.com; f. 1888; operating in 44 states; life and health; subsidiaries: Western and Southern Life

Insurance Co, Western-Southern Life Assurance Co, Columbus Life Insurance Co, Integrity Life Insurance Co, Lafayette Life Insurance Co; Chair., Pres. and CEO JOHN F. BARRETT.

Zenith National Insurance Corpn: 21255 Califa St, Woodland Hills, CA 91367; tel. (818) 713-1000; fax (818) 710-1860; e-mail corpcomm@thezenith.com; internet www.thezenith.com; holding co Zenith National Insurance Corpn, wholly owned subsidiary of Fairfax Financial Holdings Ltd; specializes in workers' compensation; subsidiary: ZNAT Insurance Co; Chair. STANLEY R. ZAX; Pres. and CEO JACK D. MILLER.

INSURANCE ORGANIZATIONS

American Council of Life Insurance (ACLI): 101 Constitution Ave, NW, Washington, DC 20001-2133; tel. (202) 624-2000; fax (202) 624-2319; e-mail Media@acli.com; internet www.acli.com; f. 1976; 400 mem. cos; Chair. TED MATHAS; Pres. and CEO DIRK KEMPTHORNE.

American Institute of Marine Underwriters (AIMU): 14 Wall St, 21st Floor, New York, NY 10005-2145; tel. (212) 233-0550; fax (212) 227-5102; e-mail aimu@aimu.org; internet www.aimu.org; f. 1898; 105 mems; Chair. ROBERT C. GALLAGHER; Pres. JAMES M. CRAIG.

American Insurance Association (AIA): 2101 L St, NW, Suite 400, Washington, DC 20037; tel. (202) 828-7100; fax (202) 293-1219; e-mail info@aiadc.org; internet www.aiadc.org; f. 1964; 300 mems; Pres. and CEO LEIGH ANN PUSEY.

Casualty Actuarial Society: 4350 North Fairfax Dr., Suite 250, Arlington, VA 22203; tel. (703) 276-3100; fax (703) 276-3106; e-mail office@casact.org; internet www.casact.org; f. 1914; 4,400 mems; Pres. PATRICIA TEUFEL; Exec. Dir CYNTHIA R. ZIEGLER.

LIMRA International: 300 Day Hill Rd, Windsor, CT 06095; tel. (860) 285-7787; fax (860) 298-9555; e-mail ctheroux@limra.com; internet www.limra.com; f. 1916; research and consultancy services for insurance cos; Chair. STEVEN FINCH; Pres. and CEO ROBERT A. KERZNER; 850 mems.

LOMA (Life Office Management Association): 2300 Windy Ridge Pkwy, Suite 600, Atlanta, GA 30339-8443; tel. (770) 951-1770; fax (770) 984-6417; e-mail askloma@loma.org; internet www.loma.org; f. 1924; 1,200 mem. cos; Pres. and CEO ROBERT A. KERZNER.

National Association of Health Underwriters (NAHU): 1212 New York Ave NW, Suite 1100, Washington, DC 20005; tel. (202) 552-5060; fax (202) 747-6820; e-mail info@nahu.org; internet www.nahu.org; Exec. Vice-Pres. and CEO JANET STOKES TRAUTWEIN.

National Association of Life Underwriters: 2901 Telestar Court, Falls Church, VA 22042-1205; tel. (703) 770-8100; e-mail membersupport@naifa.org; internet www.naifa.org; 108,000 mems; Pres. ROBERT O. SMITH; CEO SUSAN B. WATERS.

National Association of Mutual Insurance Cos (NAMIC): 3601 Vincennes Rd, POB 68700, Indianapolis, IN 46268-0700; tel. (317) 875-5250; fax (317) 879-8408; e-mail service@namic.org; internet www.namic.org; f. 1895; 1,400 mems; Chair. JERRY G. ZENKE; Pres. and CEO CHARLES M. CHAMNESS.

Reinsurance Association of America: 1445 New York Ave, NW, 7th Floor, Washington, DC 20005; tel. (202) 638-3690; fax (202) 638-0936; e-mail infobox@reinsurance.org; internet www.reinsurance.org; f. 1969; 35 mems; Chair. JAMES FEW; Pres. FRANKLIN W. NUTTER.

Trade and Industry

CHAMBER OF COMMERCE

US Chamber of Commerce: 1615 H St, NW, Washington, DC 20062-2000; tel. (202) 659-6000; fax (202) 463-5836; internet www.uschamber.com; f. 1912; mems: c. 3m. cos; over 100 US chambers of commerce in 91 countries; Pres. and CEO THOMAS J. DONOHUE; Chair. EDWARD B. RUST, Jr.

EMPLOYERS' ORGANIZATIONS

Chemicals

American Chemistry Council (ACC): 700 Second St, NE, Washington, DC 20002; tel. (202) 249-7000; fax (202) 249-6100; e-mail helpline@americanchemistry.com; internet www.americanchemistry.com; f. 1872; incl. the Plastics Division and Chlorine Chemistry Division; 136 mems; Pres. and CEO CALVIN M. DOOLEY; Chief of Staff DELL PERELMAN.

American Cleaning Institute (ACI): 1331 L St, NW, Suite 650, Washington, DC, 20005; tel. (202) 347-2900; fax (202) 347-4110; e-mail info@cleaninginstitute.org; internet www.cleaninginstitute.org; f. 1926; fmrly Soap and Detergent Asscn (SDA); c. 100 mems; Pres. and CEO ERNIE ROSENBERG.

American Pharmacists Association (APhA): 2215 Constitution Ave, NW, Washington, DC 20037; tel. (202) 628-4410; fax (202) 783-2351; e-mail scorbitt@aphanet.org; internet www.pharmacist.com; f. 1852; over 60,000 mems; Exec. Vice-Pres. and CEO THOMAS E. MENIGHAN.

Consumer Specialty Products Association (CSPA): 1667 K St, NW, Suite 300, Washington, DC 20006; tel. (202) 872-8110; fax (202) 223-2636; e-mail info@cspa.org; internet www.cspa.org; f. 1914; fmrly Chemical Specialities Manufacturers Asscn; around 240 mems; Pres. CHRISTOPHER CATHCART.

Drug, Chemical and Associated Technologies Association, Inc (DCAT): 1 Washington Blvd, Suite 7, Robbinsville, NJ 08691; tel. (609) 448-1000; fax (609) 448-1944; e-mail info@dcat.org; internet www.dcat.org; f. 1890; fmrly Drug, Chemical and Allied Trades Asscn; name changed as above in 2003; 350 mems; Pres. JOAN CONNOLLY; Exec. Dir MARGARET M. TIMONY.

The Fertilizer Institute (TFI): 425 Third St, SW, Suite 950, Washington, DC 20024; tel. (202) 962-0490; fax (202) 962-0577; e-mail webmaster@tfi.org; internet www.tfi.org; f. 1883 as National Fertilizer Asscn; adopted current name 1969; c. 300 mem. orgs; Pres. FORD B. WEST.

National Community Pharmacists Association (NCPA): 100 Daingerfield Rd, Alexandria, VA 22314; tel. (703) 683-8200; fax (703) 683-3619; e-mail info@ncpanet.org; internet www.ncpanet.org; f. 1898; fmrly Nat. Asscn of Retail Druggists; more than 23,000 mems; Chair. MARK RILEY; Pres. LONNY WILSON; CEO B. DOUGLAS HOEY.

Pharmaceutical Research & Manufacturers of America (PhRMA): 950 F St, NW, Suite 300, Washington, DC 20004; tel. (202) 835-3400; fax (202) 835-3414; internet www.phrma.org; f. 1958; 46 mems; Pres. and CEO JOHN J. CASTELLANI; Chair. of Bd JOHN LECHLEITER.

Society of Chemical Manufacturers and Affiliates (SOCMA): 1850 M St, NW, Suite 700, Washington, DC 20036-5810; tel. (202) 721-4100; fax (202) 296-8120; e-mail info@socma.com; internet www.socma.com; f. 1921; fmrly Synthetic Organic Chemical Manufacturers' Asscn; renamed as above in 2009; 300 mem. cos; Chair. DAVE HURDER; Pres. and CEO LARRY SLOAN.

Construction
(see also Electricity, and Engineering and Machinery)

American Institute of Constructors (AIC): 700 North Fairfax St, Suite 510, POB 26334, Alexandria, VA 22314; tel. (703) 683-4999; fax (703) 527-3105; e-mail admin@aicnet.org; internet www.professionalconstructor.org; f. 1971; 1,600 mems; Pres. TANYA MATTHEWS.

Associated Builders and Contractors, Inc (ABC): 4250 North Fairfax Dr., 9th Floor, Arlington, VA 22203-1607; tel. (703) 812-2000; e-mail gotquestions@abc.org; internet www.abc.org; f. 1950; 22,000 mems; Chair. ERIC REGELIN; Pres. and CEO MICHAEL D. BELLAMAN.

Associated General Contractors of America (AGC) (AGC of America): 2300 Wilson Blvd, Suite 400, Arlington, VA 22201; tel. (703) 548-3118; fax (703) 548-3119; e-mail info@agc.org; internet www.agc.org; f. 1918; more than 27,000 mems; Pres. JOSEPH H. JARBOE; Exec. Dir CAROLYN COKER.

Associated Specialty Contractors, Inc (ASC): 3 Bethesda Metro Center, Suite 1100, Bethesda, MD 20814; tel. (301) 657-3110; fax (301) 215-4500; e-mail dgw@necanet.org; internet www.assoc-spec-con.org; f. 1955 as the Council of Mechanical Specialty Contracting Industries, Inc; name changed in 1973; 9 mem. asscns; Pres. DANIEL G. WALTER; Chair. of Bd D. L. SMITH.

Building Stone Institute (BSI): POB 419, 5 Riverside Dr., Bldg 2, Chestertown, NY 12817; tel. (518) 803-4336; fax (518) 803-4338; e-mail barb@buildingstoneinstitute.org; internet www.buildingstoneinstitute.org; f. 1919; 218 mems; Pres. ROB TEEL; Exec. Vice-Pres. JANE BENNETT.

Construction Specifications Institute (CSI): 110 South Union St, Suite 100, Alexandria, VA 22314-3351; fax (703) 236-4600; e-mail csi@csinet.org; internet www.csinet.org; f. 1948; over 14,000 mems; Pres. GREGORY J. MARKLING; Exec. Dir and CEO WALTER T. MARLOWE.

Mechanical Contractors Association of America, Inc (MCAA): 1385 Piccard Dr., Rockville, MD 20850-4340; tel. (301) 869-5800; fax (301) 990-9690; e-mail mcaainfo@mcaa.org; internet www.mcaa.org; f. 1889; 2,500 mems; Pres. WILLIAM J. LYNCH; Exec. Vice-Pres. and CEO JOHN R. GENTILLE.

National Association of Home Builders of the US (NAHB): 1201 15th St, NW, Washington, DC 20005; tel. (202) 266-8200; fax (202) 266-8400; e-mail jhoward@nahb.org; internet www.nahb.org; f. 1942; 800 mem. asscns, over 140,000 mems; CEO GERALD M. HOWARD; Chair. of Bd BARRY RUTENBERG.

National Ready Mixed Concrete Association (NRMCA): 900 Spring St, Silver Spring, MD 20910; tel. (301) 587-1400; fax (301)

585-4219; e-mail info@nrmca.org; internet www.nrmca.org; f. 1930; 1,000 mems; Chair. DAVID ROBISON; Pres. ROBERT GARBINI.

National Tile Contractors Association (NTCA): 626 Lakeland East Dr., POB 13629, Jackson, MS 39236; tel. (601) 939-2071; fax (601) 932-6117; e-mail webmaster@tile-assn.com; internet www.tile-assn.com; f. 1947; Pres. DAN WELCH; Chair. of Bd NYLE WADFORD.

Plumbing-Heating-Cooling Contractors Association (PHCC): 180 South Washington St, POB 6808, Falls Church, VA 22046; tel. (703) 237-8100; fax (703) 237-7442; e-mail naphcc@naphcc.org; internet www.phccweb.org; f. 1883; 4,000 mems; Pres. DAVID DUGGER.

Tile Council of North America Inc (TCNA): 100 Clemson Research Blvd, Anderson, SC 29625; tel. (864) 646-8453; fax (864) 646-2821; e-mail info@tileusa.com; internet www.tileusa.com; f. 1945 as Tile Council of America; adopted current name in 2003; 130 mems; Exec. Dir ERIC ASTRACHAN.

US Green Building Council (USGBC): 2101 L St, NW, Suite 500, Washington, DC 20037; tel. (202) 828-7422; fax (202) 828-5110; e-mail info@usgbc.org; internet www.usgbc.org; 14,000 mem. orgs; Pres. and CEO S. RICHARD FEDRIZZI; Chair. of Exec. Cttee ELIZABETH J. HEIDER.

Electricity
(see also Construction, Electronics and Technology, Engineering and Machinery, and Trade and Industry—Utilities)

Edison Electric Institute (EEI): 701 Pennsylvania Ave, NW, Washington, DC 20004-2696; tel. (202) 508-5000; e-mail feedback@eei.org; internet www.eei.org; f. 1933; mems: over 240 industry suppliers and related orgs as assoc. mems; more than 80 int. affiliates; mems generate about 70% of electricity produced by US utilities; Chair. LEWIS HAY, III; Pres. THOMAS R. KUHN.

National Association of Electrical Distributors (NAED): 1181 Corporate Lake Dr., St Louis, MO 63132; tel. (314) 991-9000; fax (314) 991-3060; e-mail info@naed.org; internet www.naed.org; f. 1908; 2,900 mems; Pres. and CEO THOMAS NABER; Chair. CLARENCE MARTIN.

National Electrical Contractors Association (NECA): 3 Bethesda Metro Center, Suite 1100, Bethesda, MD 20814; tel. (301) 657-3110; fax (301) 215-4500; internet www.necanet.org; f. 1901; 4,200 mems; Pres. DENNIS F. QUEBE; CEO JOHN M. GRAU.

National Electrical Manufacturers Association (NEMA) (Association of Electrical and Medical Imaging Equipment Manufacturers): 1300 North 17th St, Suite 1752, Rosslyn, VA 22209; tel. (703) 841-3200; fax (703) 841-5900; e-mail webmaster@nema.org; internet www.nema.org; f. 1926; c. 430 mem. cos; Chair. DOMINIC J. PILEGGI; Pres. and CEO EVAN R. GADDIS.

Electronics and Technology

TechAmerica: North Bldg, Suite 600, 601 Pennsylvania Ave, NW, Washington, DC 20004; tel. (202) 682-9110; fax (202) 682-9111; e-mail anne.caliguiri@techamerica.org; internet www.techamerica.org; formed by the merger of AeA (fmrly American Electronics Asscn), Cyber Security Industry Alliance (CSIA), Information Technology Asscn of America (ITAA) and Government Electronics & Information Technology Asscn (GEIA); 1,000 mem. cos; Chair. PETER J. BONI; Pres. and CEO SHAWN OSBORNE.

Electronic Components Industry Association: 1111 Alderman Dr., Suite 400, Alpharetta, GA 30005; tel. (678) 393-9990; fax (678) 393-9998; internet www.eciaonline.org; f. 2011 by merger of the National Electronic Distributors Asscn (NEDA) and the Electronic Components Asscn (ECA); Chair. JOHN F. DENSLINGER; Pres. ROBIN B. GRAY, Jr.

Institute of Electrical and Electronics Engineers, Inc (IEEE): 445 Hoes Lane, Piscataway, NJ 08854-4141; tel. (732) 981-0060; fax (732) 562-6380; e-mail contactcenter@ieee.org; internet www.ieee.org; f. 1963; 415,989 mems; Pres. and CEO Dr GORDON W. DAY; Exec. Dir JAMES PRENDERGAST.

IPC (Association Connecting Electronics Industries): 3000 Lakeside Dr., Suite 309, Bannockburn, IL 60015; tel. (847) 615-7100; fax (847) 615-7105; e-mail mcgude@ipc.org; internet www.ipc.org; f. 1957; 3,325 mem. cos located in 64 countries; Chair. STEPHEN PUDLES; Pres. and CEO JOHN W. MITCHELL.

Telecommunications Industry Association (TIA): 2500 Wilson Blvd, Suite 300, Arlington, VA 22201; tel. (703) 907-7700; fax (703) 907-7727; e-mail tia@tiaonline.org; internet www.tiaonline.org; f. 1988; 319 mems; Chair. of Bd DAN PIGOTT; Pres. GRANT E. SEIFFERT.

Engineering and Machinery
(see also Electricity and Construction)

Air-Conditioning, Heating and Refrigeration Institute (AHRI): 2111 Wilson Blvd, Suite 500, Arlington, VA 22201; tel.

(703) 524-8800; fax (703) 562-1942; e-mail ahri@ahrinet.org; internet www.ahrinet.org; f. 2007 by merger of the Air-conditioning and Refrigeration Institute (ARI) and the Gas Appliance Mfrs Asscn (GAMA); 7 assoc. mems, more than 300 mems and 23 int. mems; Pres. and CEO STEPHEN R. YUREK.

American Council of Engineering Companies (ACEC): 1015 15th St, NW, 8th Floor, Washington, DC 20005-2605; tel. (202) 347-7474; fax (202) 898-0068; e-mail acec@acec.org; internet www.acec.org; f. 1909; more than 5,500 mem. cos; Chair. TED C. WILLIAMS; Pres. and CEO DAVID A. RAYMOND.

American Institute of Chemical Engineers (AIChE): 3 Park Ave, 19 Fl, New York, NY 10016-5991; tel. (203) 702-7660; fax (203) 775-5177; e-mail customerservice@aiche.org; internet www.aiche.org; f. 1908; over 40,000 mems from over 90 countries; Pres. DAVID ROSENTHAL; Exec. Dir JUNE C. WISPELWEY.

American Institute of Mining, Metallurgical and Petroleum Engineers, Inc: 12999 East Adam Aircraft Circle, Englewood, CO 80112; tel. (303) 325-5185; fax (303) (888) 702-0049; e-mail aime@aimehq.org; internet www.aimehq.org; f. 1871; 4 mem. socs representing over 145,000 mems world-wide; Pres. GEORGE LUXBACHER; Exec. Dir L. MICHELE LAWRIE-MUNRO.

American Society of Civil Engineers (ASCE): 1801 Alexander Bell Dr., Reston, VA 20191-4400; tel. (703) 295-6300; fax (703) 295-6333; e-mail webmaster@asce.org; internet www.asce.org; f. 1852; more than 140,000 mems world-wide; Pres. ANDREW W. HERRMANN; Exec. Dir PATRICK J. NATALE.

American Society of Heating, Refrigerating and Air-conditioning Engineers (ASHRAE): 1791 Tullie Circle, NE, Atlanta, GA 30329; tel. (404) 636-8400; fax (404) 321-5478; e-mail ashrae@ashrae.org; internet www.ashrae.org; f. 1894; 51,000 mems; Pres. THOMAS WATSON.

American Society of Naval Engineers, Inc: 1452 Duke St, Alexandria, VA 22314-3458; tel. (703) 836-6727; fax (703) 836-7491; e-mail asnehq@navalengineers.org; internet www.navalengineers.org; f. 1888; 5,000 mems; Pres. RONALD K. KISS; Exec. Dir Capt. (retd) DENNIS K. KRUSE.

Association of Coastal Engineers (ACE): c/o Angie Gross, Erickson Consulting Engineers, Inc, 7201 Delainey Ct, Sarasota, FL 34240; e-mail hugo@coastharborenq.com; internet www.coastalengineers.org; f. 1999; Pres. JOHN RAMSEY.

Association of Home Appliance Manufacturers (AHAM): 1111 19th St, NW, Suite 402, Washington, DC 20036; tel. (202) 872-5955; fax (202) 872-9354; e-mail info@aham.org; internet www.aham.org; f. 1915; 156 mem. orgs; Chair. ROBERT P. SCAGLIONE; Pres. JOSEPH M. McGUIRE.

AMT (The Association for Manufacturing Technology): 7901 Westpark Dr., McLean, VA 22102-4206; tel. (703) 893-2900; fax (703) 893-1151; e-mail amt@amtonline.org; internet www.amtonline.org; f. 1902; 370 mems; Chairs TIMOTHY B. DINING, RONALD J. MAGER; Pres. DOUGLAS K. WOODS.

Manufacturers Alliance/MAPI, Inc: 1600 Wilson Blvd, Suite 1100, 11th Floor, Arlington, VA 22209-2594; tel. (703) 841-9000; fax (703) 841-9514; e-mail info@mapi.net; internet www.mapi.net; f. 1933; more than 500 mem. cos; Pres. and CEO STEPHEN GOLD; Chair. of Exec. Cttee CARLOS M. CARDOSO.

Petroleum Equipment Institute (PEI): POB 2380, Tulsa, OK 74101-2380; tel. (918) 494-9696; fax (918) 491-9895; e-mail info@pei.org; internet www.pei.org; f. 1951; over 1,600 mems world-wide; Pres. JOEY CHEEK; Exec. Vice-Pres. ROBERT RENKES.

SAE International (Society of Automotive Engineers): 400 Commonwealth Dr., Warrendale, PA 15096-0001; tel. (724) 776-4841; fax (724) 776-0790; e-mail customerservice@sae.org; internet www.sae.org; f. 1905; 133,000 mems in 110 countries; Pres. FRANK O. KLEGON; CEO DAVID L. SCHUTT.

Society of Naval Architects and Marine Engineers (SNAME): 601 Pavonia Ave, Suite 400, Jersey City, NJ 07306-2907; tel. (201) 798-4800; fax (201) 798-4975; e-mail ccali-poutre@sname.org; internet www.sname.org; f. 1893; over 8,500 mems world-wide; Pres. EDWARD N. COMSTOCK; Exec. Dir ERIK W. SEITHER.

United Engineering Foundation (UEF): POB 70, Mount Vernon, VA 22121-0070; tel. (973) 244-2328; fax (973) 882-5155; e-mail engfnd@aol.com; internet www.uefoundation.org; f. 1914; umbrella org. of engineering socs, incl. the American Institute of Chemical Engineers (AIChE), the American Institute of Mining Engineers (AIME), the American Society of Civil Engineers (ASCE), the American Society of Mechanical Engineers, and the Institute of Electrical and Electronics Engineers (IEEE); Pres. DENNIS R. MARTENSON; Exec. Dir Dr DAVID L. BELDEN.

Food

American Bakers Association (ABA): 1300 I St, NW, Suite 700 West, Washington, DC 20005; tel. (202) 789-0300; fax (202) 898-1164; e-mail info@americanbakers.org; internet www.americanbakers

.org; f. 1897; Chair. of the Bd HOWARD R. ALTON, III; Pres. and CEO ROBB MACKIE.

American Beverage Association (ABA): 1101 16th St, NW, Washington, DC 20036-4803; tel. (202) 463-6732; fax (202) 659-5349; e-mail info@ameribev.org; internet www.ameribev.org; f. 1919; fmrly Nat. Soft Drink Asscn; 1,700 mems; Chair. TOM L. BENÉ; Pres. and CEO SUSAN K. NEELY.

American Council for Food Safety and Quality (DFA of California): 710 Striker Ave, Sacramento, CA 95834; tel. (916) 561-5900; fax (916) 561-5910; e-mail samk@agfoodsafety.org; internet agfoodsafety.org; f. 1908; agricultural asscn (dried fruit and tree nuts); 51 mems; Pres. and CEO SAM KEIPER.

American Farm Bureau Federation (FB): 600 Maryland Ave, SW, Suite 1000W, Washington, DC 20024; tel. (202) 406-3600; fax (202) 406-3602; e-mail jeanb@fb.org; internet www.fb.org; f. 1919; 50 mem. states and Puerto Rico; Pres. BOB STALLMAN; Exec. Vice-Pres. JULIE ANNA POTTS.

American Meat Institute: 1150 Connecticut Ave, NW, 12th Floor, Washington, DC 20036; tel. (202) 587-4200; fax (202) 587-4300; e-mail webmaster@meatami.com; internet www.meatami.com; f. 1906; 1,100 mems; Chair. LARRY ODOM; Pres. and CEO J. PATRICK BOYLE.

Commodity Markets Council (CMC): 1300 L St, NW, Suite 1020, Washington, DC 20005; tel. (202) 842-0400; fax (202) 789-7223; e-mail sanjeev.joshipura@commoditymkts.org; internet www .commoditymkts.org; f. 1930 as the National Grain Trade Council; reformed as 2 separate entities, CMC and the Transportation, Elevator, & Grain Merchants Asscn, in 2006; 40 mems; Chair. CHARLES P. CAREY; Pres. SANJEEV JOSHIPURA.

Distilled Spirits Council of the US, Inc (DISCUS): 1250 Eye St, NW, Suite 400, Washington, DC 20005; tel. (202) 628-3544; internet www.discus.org; f. 1973; 14 active mems and 23 affiliates; Pres. and CEO Dr PETER H. CRESSY.

Food Marketing Institute (FMI): 2345 Crystal Dr., Suite 800, Arlington, VA 22202; tel. (202) 452-8444; fax (202) 429-4519; e-mail fmi@fmi.org; internet www.fmi.org; f. 1977; 1,500 mem. cos; Chair. FREDERICK J. MORGANTHALL, II; Pres. and CEO LESLIE G. SARASIN.

Foodservice Sales and Marketing Association (FSMA): 1810-J York Rd, Suite 384, Lutherville, MD 21093; tel. (800) 617-1170; fax (888) 668-7496; e-mail info@fsmaonline.com; internet www .fsmaonline.com; f. 2003; Chair. of Bd STUART WOLFF; Pres. and CEO RICK ABRAHAM.

Grocery Manufacturers of America, Inc (GMA): 1350 I St, NW, Suite 300, Washington, DC 20005; tel. (202) 639-5900; fax (202) 639-5932; e-mail info@gmaonline.org; internet www.gmaonline.org; f. 1908; over 300 mem. cos; Chair. GARY M. RODKIN; Pres. and CEO PAMELA G. BAILEY.

International Foodservice Distributors Association (IFDA): 1410 Spring Hill Rd, Suite 210, McLean, VA 22102; tel. (703) 532-9400; fax (703) 538-4673; internet www.ifdaonline.org; f. 1906; over 140 mems; Chair. THOMAS A. ZATINA; Pres. and CEO MARK S. ALLEN.

National Association of Wheat Growers (NAWG): 415 Second St, NE, Suite 300, Washington, DC 20002-4993; tel. (202) 547-7800; fax (202) 546-2638; e-mail wheatworld@wheatworld.org; internet www.wheatworld.org; f. 1950; 21 affiliated mem. states; Pres. ERIK YOUNGGREN; CEO DANA PETERSON.

National Beer Wholesalers Association (NBWA): 1101 King St, Suite 600, Alexandria, VA 22314-2944; tel. (703) 683-4300; fax (703) 683-8965; e-mail info@nbwa.org; internet www.nbwa.org; f. 1938; more than 3,300 mem. distributor cos; Chair. STEVE LYTLE; Pres. and CEO CRAIG A. PURSER.

National Cattlemen's Beef Association (NCBA): 9110 East Nichols Ave, Suite 300, Centennial, CO 80112; tel. (303) 694-0305; fax (303) 694-2851; e-mail membership@beef.org; internet www .beefusa.org; f. 1898; 28,000 mems, plus 44 cattle asscns and 50 breed and industry asscns; Pres. J. D. ALEXANDER; CEO FORREST ROBERTS.

National Confectioners Association of the US (NCA): 1101 30th St, Suite 200, Washington, DC 20007; tel. (202) 534-1440; fax (202) 337-0637; e-mail info@candyusa.com; internet www.candyusa .com; f. 1884; includes Chocolate Mfrs Asscn; 340 mems; Chair. ROBERT M. SIMPSON, Jr; Pres. LAWRENCE T. GRAHAM.

National Dairy Council (NDC): 10255 West Higgins Rd, Suite 900, Rosemont, IL 60018; tel. (847) 803-2000; fax (847) 803-2077; e-mail ndc@dairyinformation.com; internet www .nationaldairycouncil.org; f. 1915; 600 mems; Exec. Vice-Pres. JEAN RAGALIE.

National Farmers (NFO): 528 Billy Sunday Rd, Suite 100, POB 2508, Ames, IA 50010; tel. (800) 247-2110; fax (866) 629-3976; e-mail nfo@nfo.org; internet www.nfo.org; f. 1955; c. 35,000 mems; Chair. PAUL OLSON.

National Farmers Union (NFU): 20 F St NW, Suite 300, Washington, DC 20001; tel. (202) 554-1600; fax (202) 554-1654; e-mail lkendall@nfudc.org; internet www.nfu.org; f. 1902; 250,000 mems; Pres. ROGER JOHNSON.

National Frozen and Refrigerated Foods Association (NFRA): 4755 Linglestown Rd, Suite 300, POB 6069, Harrisburg, PA 17112; tel. (717) 657-8601; fax (717) 657-9862; e-mail info@ nfraweb.org; internet www.nfraweb.org; f. 1945; over 400 mem. cos; Chair. JOHN LARSEN; Pres. and CEO H. V. (SKIP) SHAW, Jr.

National Grocers Association (NGA): 1005 North Glebe Rd, Suite 250, Arlington, VA 22201-5758; tel. (703) 516-0700; fax (703) 516-0115; e-mail info@nationalgrocers.org; internet www .nationalgrocers.org; f. 1982; 3,000 mems; Chair. JOSEPH SHERIDAN; Pres. and CEO PETER J. LARKIN.

National Meat Association (NMA): NMA East: 7757 Citation Dr., Marshall, VA 20115; NMA West: 1970 Broadway, Suite 825, Oakland, CA 94612; tel. (510) 763-1533; fax (510) 763-6186; e-mail staff@ nmaonline.org; internet www.nmaonline.org; f. 1946; over 600 mems; Chair. ROBERT REBHOLTZ; CEO BARRY CARPENTER.

North American Millers' Association (NAMA): 600 Maryland Ave, SW, Suite 825 West, Washington, DC 20024; tel. (202) 484-2200; fax (202) 488-7416; e-mail generalinfo@namamillers.org; internet www.namamillers.org; f. 1998; 43 mems and 28 assoc. mems; Chair. PAUL MAASS; Pres. MARY WATERS.

United Fresh Produce Association: 1901 Pennsylvania Ave, NW, Suite 1100, Washington, DC 20006; tel. (202) 303-3400; fax (202) 303-3433; e-mail united@unitedfresh.org; internet www.unitedfresh.org; f. 1904; fmrly United Fresh Fruit & Vegetable Asscn; 1,300 mems; Chair. DAVID W. KRAUZE; Pres. and CEO THOMAS E. STENZEL.

US Dairy Export Council (USDEC): 2101 Wilson Blvd, Suite 400, Arlington, VA 22201-3061; tel. (703) 528-3049; fax (703) 528-3705; e-mail info@usdec.org; internet www.usdec.org; f. 1995; 113 mems, incl. 55 processors, 25 trading cos and 32 allied industry orgs; Pres. THOMAS M. SUBER.

Wine and Spirits Wholesalers of America, Inc (WSWA): 805 15th St, NW, Suite 430, Washington, DC 20005; tel. (202) 371-9792; fax (202) 789-2405; e-mail Info@wswa.org; internet www.wswa.org; f. 1943; over 350 mem. cos; Chair. CHARLES MERINOFF; Pres. and CEO CRAIG WOLF.

Iron and Steel

American Hardware Manufacturers Association (AHMA): The William P. Farrell Bldg, 801 North Plaza Dr., Schaumburg, IL 60173; tel. (847) 605-1025; fax (847) 605-1030; e-mail info@ahma .org; internet www.ahma.org; f. 1901; 500 mems; Chair. DONALD D. DRAY; Pres. and CEO TIMOTHY S. FARRELL.

American Institute of Steel Construction (AISC): 1 East Wacker Dr., Suite 700, Chicago, IL 60601-1802; tel. (312) 670-2400; fax (312) 670-5403; e-mail ferch@aisc.org; internet www.aisc .org; f. 1921; Chair. DAVID HARWELL; Pres. ROGER E. FERCH.

American Iron and Steel Institute (AISI): 25 Massachusetts Ave, NW, Suite 800, Washington, DC 20001; tel. (202) 452-7100; e-mail webmaster@steel.org; internet www.steel.org; f. 1908; 26 mem. cos and 130 assoc. and affiliated mems; Chair. JOSEPH A. CARRABBA; Pres. and CEO THOMAS J. GIBSON.

Steel Founders' Society of America (SFSA): 780 McArdle Dr., Unit G, Crystal Lake, IL 60014; tel. (815) 455-8240; fax (815) 455-8241; e-mail monroe@sfsa.org; internet www.sfsa.org; f. 1902; 80 mems; Exec. Vice-Pres. RAYMOND W. MONROE.

Steel Manufacturers Association (SMA): 1150 Connecticut Ave, NW, Suite 715, Washington, DC 20036; tel. (202) 296-1515; fax (202) 296-2506; e-mail cipicchio@steelnet.org; internet www.steelnet.org; 36 North American mem. cos and 129 assoc. mem. cos; Chair. JOHN FERRIOLA; Pres. THOMAS A. DANJCZEK.

Leather
(see also Textiles)

Leather Industries of America (LIA): 3050 K St, NW, Suite 400, Washington, DC 20007; tel. (202) 342-8497; fax (202) 342-8583; e-mail info@leatherusa.com; internet www.leatherusa.com; f. 1917; 55 mems; Pres. JOHN WITTENBORN.

Travel Goods Association (TGA): 301 North Harrison St, Suite 412, Princeton, NJ 08540-3512; tel. (877) 842-1938; fax (877) 842-1938; e-mail info@travel-goods.org; internet www.travel-goods.org; f. 1938; 300 mems; Chair. JACK HOLODNICKI; Pres. MICHELE MARINI PITTENGER.

Lumber
(see also Paper)

American Forest & Paper Association (AF&PA): 1111 19th St, NW, Suite 800, Washington, DC 20036; tel. (202) 463-2700; e-mail info@afandpa.org; internet www.afandpa.org; f. 1993; more than 157 mems; Chair. ALEXANDER TOELDTE; Pres. and CEO DONNA HARMAN.

APA–The Engineered Wood Association: 7011 South 19th St, Tacoma, WA 98466-5333; tel. (253) 565-6600; fax (253) 565-7265; e-mail help@apawood.org; internet www.apawood.org; f. 1933 as Douglas Fir Plywood Asscn; later became American Plywood Asscn; adopted current name 1994; 152 mems; Chair. MARY JO NYBLAD; Pres. DENNIS HARDMAN.

Forest Resources Association Inc (FRA): 600 Jefferson Plaza, Suite 350, Rockville, MD 20852-1150; tel. (301) 838-9385; fax (301) 838-9481; e-mail dh@forestresources.org; internet www .forestresources.org; f. 1934; 1,300 mems; Chair. TOM NORRIS; Pres. DEB HAWKINSON.

National Lumber and Building Material Dealers Association (NLBMDA): 2025 M St, NW, Suite 800, Washington, DC 20036-3309; tel. (202) 367-1169; fax (202) 367-2169; e-mail info@dealer.org; internet www.dealer.org; f. 1915; more than 6,000 mem. cos; Chair. CALLY FROMME; Pres. and CEO MICHAEL O'BRIEN.

National Wooden Pallet and Container Association (NWPCA): 1421 Prince St, Suite 340, Alexandria, VA 22314-2805; tel. (703) 519-6104; fax (703) 519-4720; e-mail bscholnick@ palletcentral.com; internet www.palletcentral.com; f. 1946; 700 co mems in 28 countries; Chair. JAMES RUDER; Pres. SAM MCADOW (interim).

North American Wholesale Lumber Association (NAWLA): 3601 Algonquin Rd, Suite 400, Rolling Meadows, IL 60008; tel. (847) 870-7470; fax (847) 870-0201; e-mail info@nawla.org; internet www .lumber.org; f. 1893; over 650 mems; Chair. CHRIS BEVERIDGE; Pres. GARY F. VITALE.

Southern Forest Products Association (SFPA): 2900 Indiana Ave, Kenner, LA 70065-4605; tel. (504) 443-4464; fax (504) 443-6612; e-mail mail@spfa.org; internet www.sfpa.org; f. 1915; c. 180 mem. orgs; Corp. Sec. TAMI KESSLER.

Western Wood Products Association (WWPA): Yeon Bldg, 522 South West Fifth Ave, Suite 500, Portland, OR 97204-2122; tel. (503) 224-3930; fax (503) 224-3934; e-mail info@wwpa.org; internet www .wwpa.org; f. 1964; c. 65 mem. orgs; Pres. and CEO KEVIN BINAM.

Wood Products Manufacturers Association (WPMA): 175 State Rd East, POB 761, Westminster, MA 01473-0761; tel. (978) 874-5445; fax (978) 874-9946; e-mail woodprod@wpma.org; internet www .wpma.org; f. 1929; 664 mems; Exec. Dir PHILIP A. BIBEAU.

Metals and Mining
(see also Iron and Steel)

Aluminum Association, Inc: 1525 Wilson Blvd, Suite 600, Arlington, VA 22209; tel. (703) 358-2960; fax (703) 358-2961; e-mail lwilson@aluminum.org; internet www.aluminum.org; f. 1933; 82 mems; Pres. HEIDI BIGGS BROCK.

American Zinc Association (AZA): 1750 K St, NW, Suite 700, Washington, DC 20006; tel. (202) 223-2478; fax (202) 223-2479; e-mail info@zinc.org; internet www.zinc.org; f. 1990; 41 full, 149 affiliate and 52 assoc. mems; Exec. Dir GEORGE VARY.

ASM International: 9639 Kinsman Rd, Materials Park, OH 44073-0002; tel. (440) 338-5151; fax (440) 338-4634; e-mail customerservice@asminternational.org; internet asmcommunity .asminternational.org; f. 1913; fmrly the American Society for Materials; 36,000 mems world-wide; Pres. CHRISTOPHER BERNDT; Man. Dir STANLEY C. THEOBALD.

Copper and Brass Fabricators Council, Inc: 3050 K St, NW, Suite 400, Washington, DC 20007; tel. (202) 833-8575; fax (202) 342-8451; e-mail copbrass@kelleydrye.com; f. 1964; 20 mem. cos; Pres. and Gen. Counsel DAVID A. HARTQUIST.

Copper Development Association, Inc (CDA): 260 Madison Ave, New York, NY 10016; tel. (212) 251-7200; fax (212) 251-7234; e-mail questions@cda.copper.org; internet www.copper.org; f. 1962; 65 mems; Pres. and CEO ANDREW G. KIRETA, Sr.

Fabricators and Manufacturers Association, International (FMA): 833 Featherstone Rd, Rockford, IL 61107; tel. (815) 399-8700; fax (815) 484-7701; e-mail info@fmanet.org; internet www .fmanet.org; f. 1970; more than 2,300 mems; Chair. BRIAN KOPACK.

Manufacturing Jewelers and Suppliers of America, Inc (MJSA): 57 John L. Dietsch Sq., Attleboro Falls, MA 02763; tel. (401) 274-3840; fax (401) 274-0265; e-mail info@mjsa.org; internet www.mjsa.org; f. 1903; 1,400 mem. cos; Chair. DAVE MELESKI; Pres. and CEO DAVID W. COCHRAN.

Metal Powder Industries Federation (MPIF): 105 College Rd East, 1st Floor, Princeton, NJ 08540-6692; tel. (609) 452-7700; fax (609) 987-8523; e-mail info@mpif.org; internet www.mpif.org; f. 1944; 6 feds of 300 corp. mems; Pres. MATTHEW BULGER; Exec. Dir and CEO C. JAMES TROMBINO.

Mining and Metallurgical Society of America (MMSA): POB 810, Boulder, CO 80306-0810; tel. (303) 444-6032; e-mail contactmmsa@mmsa.net; internet www.mmsa.net; f. 1908; 340 mems; Exec. Dir BETTY L. GIBBS; Pres. MARK JORGENSEN.

National Mining Association (NMA): 101 Constitution Ave, NW, Suite 500 East, Washington, DC 20001-2133; tel. (202) 463-2600; fax (202) 463-2666; e-mail craulston@nma.org; internet www.nma.org; f. 1995; over 325 mem. cos; Pres. and CEO HAROLD P. QUINN, Jr.

Northwest Mining Association (NWMA): 10 North Post St, Suite 305, Spokane, WA 99201; tel. (509) 624-1158; fax (509) 623-1241; e-mail nwma_info@nwma.org; internet www.nwma.org; f. 1895; over 2,000 mems; Pres. RICHARD DELONG; Exec. Dir LAURA E. SKAER.

The Silver Institute: 1400 I St, NW, Suite 550, Washington, DC 20005; tel. (202) 835-0185; fax (202) 835-0155; e-mail info@ silverinstitute.org; internet www.silverinstitute.org; f. 1971; 24 mems; Pres. GEOFF BURNS; Exec. Dir and Sec. MICHAEL DIRIENZO.

Paper
(see also Lumber)

Association of Independent Corrugated Converters (AICC): 113 South West St, 3rd Floor, POB 25708, Alexandria, VA 22313; tel. (703) 836-2422; fax (703) 836-2795; e-mail info@aiccbox.org; internet www.aiccbox.org; mems: 603 box-makers, 480 associates; Chair. CHUCK FIENNING; Pres. A. STEVEN YOUNG.

NPTA Alliance: 401 North Michigan Ave, Suite 2200, Chicago, IL 60611-4267; tel. (312) 321-4092; fax (312) 673-6736; e-mail npta@ gonpta.com; internet www.gonpta.com; f. 1903; fmrly Nat. Paper Trade Asscn, Inc; restructured Sept. 2007 to operate under management of SmithBucklin Corpn; 2,000 mems; Chair. GREG SAVAGE; CEO KEVIN GAMMONLEY.

Paperboard Packaging Council (PPC): 1350 Main St, Suite 1508, Springfield, MA 01103-1670; tel. (413) 686-9191; fax (413) 747-7777; e-mail paperboardpackaging@ppcnet.org; internet www .ppcnet.org; f. 1929; unified with North American Packaging Asscn (NAPA) in 2010; Chair. STEVEN LEVKOFF; Pres. BEN MARKENS.

Petroleum and Fuel

American Association of Petroleum Geologists (AAPG): 125 West 15th St, POB 979, Tulsa, OK 74101-0979; tel. (918) 584-2555; fax (918) 560-2665; e-mail postmaster@aapg.org; internet www.aapg .org; f. 1917; 30,000 mems world-wide; Pres. EDWARD BEAUMONT; Exec. Dir DAVID CURTISS.

American Association of Petroleum Landmen (AAPL): 4100 Fossil Creek Blvd, Fort Worth, TX 76137-2791; tel. (817) 847-7700; fax (817) 847-7704; e-mail aapl@landman.org; internet www .landman.org; f. 1955; 16,000 mems and 45 affiliated asscns; Pres. JIM R. DEWBRE; Exec. Vice-Pres. MARTIN SCHARDT.

American Petroleum Institute (API): 1220 L St, NW, Washington, DC 20005-4070; tel. (202) 682-8000; e-mail mediacenter@api .org; internet www.api.org; f. 1919; over 400 corporate mems; Pres. and CEO JACK N. GERARD.

Association of Diesel Specialists (ADS): 400 Admiral Blvd, Kansas City, MO 64106; tel. (816) 285-0810; fax (847) 770-4952; e-mail info@diesel.org; internet www.diesel.org; more than 700 corp. and individual mems; Pres. CHUCK HESS; Exec. Dir DAVID FEHLING.

Coal Exporters' Association of the US, Inc: 101 Constitution Ave, NW, Suite 500, Washington, DC 20001-2133; tel. (202) 463-2600; fax (202) 463-2666; f. 1945; 35 mems; Exec. Dir MOYA PHELLEPS.

Independent Petroleum Association of America (IPAA): 1201 15th St, NW, Suite 300, Washington, DC 20005; tel. (202) 857-4722; fax (202) 857-4799; e-mail webmaster@ipaa.org; internet www.ipaa .org; f. 1929; 6,000 mems; Chair. VIRGINIA B. LAZENBY; Pres. and CEO BARRY RUSSELL.

National Ocean Industries Association (NOIA): 1120 G St, NW, Suite 900, Washington, DC 20005; tel. (202) 347-6900; fax (202) 347-8650; e-mail mkearns@noia.org; internet www.noia.org; f. 1972; over 275 mem. cos; Chair. BILL E. CHILES; Pres. RANDALL LUTHI.

National Petrochemical and Refiners' Association (NPRA): 1667 K St, NW, Suite 700, Washington, DC 20006; tel. (202) 457-0480; fax (202) 457-0486; e-mail info@npra.org; internet www .npradc.org; f. 1902; nearly 500 mems; Chair. JAMES MAHONEY; Pres. CHARLES T. DREVNA.

Petroleum Marketers Association of America (PMAA): 1901 North Fort Myer Dr., Suite 500, Arlington, VA 22209-1604; tel. (703) 351-8000; fax (703) 351-9160; e-mail info@pmaa.org; internet www .pmaa.org; 51 mem. asscns; Chair. STANLEY ROBERTS; Pres. DANIEL F. GILLIGAN.

Western States Petroleum Association (WSPA): 1415 L St, Suite 600, Sacramento, CA 95814; tel. (916) 498-7750; fax (916) 444-5745; internet www.wspa.org; f. 1907; 27 mem. cos; Pres. CATHERINE REHEIS-BOYD.

Printing and Publishing
(see also Publishers)

Association for the Suppliers of Printing, Publishing and Converting Technologies (NPES): 1899 Preston White Dr.,

Directory

Reston, VA 22091-4367; tel. (703) 264-7200; fax (703) 620-0994; e-mail npes@npes.org; internet www.npes.org; f. 1933; over 400 mem. cos; Chair. CHRISTOPHER PAYNE; Pres. RALPH J. NAPPI.

Binding Industries Association International (BIA): 200 Deer Run Rd, Sewickley, PA 15143-2600; tel. (412) 259-1806; fax (412) 259-1800; e-mail jgoldstein@printing.org; internet www.printing.org/bia; f. 1955; 300 mems; Chair. CHRIS ECKHART; Dir JUSTIN GOLDSTEIN.

National Association for Printing Leadership (NAPL): 1 Meadowlands Plaza, Suite 1511, East Rutherford, NJ 07073; tel. (201) 634-9600; fax (201) 634-0324; e-mail information@napl.org; internet www.napl.org; f. 1933; 2,876 assoc. mems; Chair. NIGEL WORME; Pres. and CEO JOSEPH P. TRUNCALE.

National Association of Printing Ink Manufacturers (NAPIM): 581 Main St, Suite 520, Woodbridge, NJ 07095-1104; tel. (732) 855-1525; fax (732) 855-1838; e-mail napim@napim.org; internet www.napim.org; f. 1917; 35 mems; Exec. Dir BRAD BERGEY.

Printing Industries of America, Inc/Graphic Arts Information Network (PIA/GATF): 200 Deer Run Rd, Sewickley, PA 15143; tel. (412) 741-6860; fax (412) 741-2311; e-mail printing@printing.org; internet www.printing.org; f. 1887 (PIA), 1924 (GATF); consolidated operations in 1999; more than 10,000 mem. cos; Chair. LAURA LAWTON-FORSYTH; Pres. and CEO MICHAEL MAKIN.

Public Utilities
(see also Trade and Industry—Utilities)

American Public Power Association (APPA): 1875 Connecticut Ave, NW, Suite 1200, Washington, DC 20009-5715; tel. (202) 467-2900; fax (202) 467-2910; e-mail appanet@appanet.org; internet www.appanet.org; f. 1940; over 2,000 mem. utilities; Chair. PHYLLIS CURRIE.

American Public Works Association (APWA): 2345 Grand Blvd, Suite 700, Kansas City, MO 64108-2625; tel. (816) 472-6100; fax (816) 472-1610; e-mail apwa@apwa.net; internet www.apwa.net; f. 1937; 29,000 mems; Pres. ELIZABETH TREADWAY; Exec. Dir PETER KING.

Rubber

Rubber Manufacturers Association (RMA): 1400 K St, NW, Suite 900, Washington, DC 20005; tel. (202) 682-4800; e-mail info@rma.org; internet www.rma.org; f. 1915; over 100 mem. cos; Pres. and CEO Dr CHARLES A. CANNON.

Stone, Clay and Glass Products

Glass Association of North America (GANA): 800 South West Jackson St, Suite 1500, Topeka, KS 66612-1200; tel. (785) 271-0208; fax (785) 271-0166; e-mail gana@glasswebsite.com; internet www.glasswebsite.com; f. 1994; 208 mems; Exec. Vice-Pres. WILLIAM M. YANEK.

National Glass Association (NGA): 1945 Old Gallows Rd, Suite 750, Vienna, VA 22182; tel. (703) 442-4890; fax (703) 442-0630; e-mail administration@glass.org; internet www.glass.org; f. 1948; c. 3,000 mem. cos; Chair. CHRIS MAMMEN; Pres. and CEO PHILIP J. JAMES.

National Sand, Stone and Gravel Association (NSSGA): 1605 King St, Alexandria, VA 22314; tel. (703) 525-8788; fax (703) 525-7782; e-mail info@nssga.org; internet www.nssga.org; f. 2001; Pres. and CEO JENNIFER JOY PINNIGER.

Textiles

American Apparel and Footwear Association (AAFA): 1601 North Kent St, Suite 1200, Arlington, VA 22209; tel. (703) 524-1864; fax (703) 522-6741; e-mail mrust@apparelandfootwear.org; internet www.apparelandfootwear.org; f. 2000 following merger of American Apparel and Manufacturers Asscn and Footwear Industries of America; Chair. RICK DARLING; Pres. and CEO KEVIN M. BURKE.

American Fiber Manufacturers Association, Inc (AFMA): 1530 Wilson Blvd, NW, Suite 690, Arlington, VA 22209; tel. (703) 875-0432; fax (703) 875-0907; e-mail afma@afma.org; internet www.fibersource.com; f. 1933; 34 mems; Pres. PAUL T. O'DAY.

National Council of Textile Organizations (NCTO): 1001 Connecticut Ave, NW, Suite 315, Washington, DC 20036; tel. (202) 822-8028; fax (202) 822-8029; e-mail info@ncto.org; internet www.ncto.org; f. 2004; 88 mem. cos; Chair. WILLIAM L. JASPER; Pres. CASS JOHNSON.

National Textile Association (NTA): 6 Beacon St, Suite 1125, Boston, MA 02108; tel. (617) 542-8220; fax (617) 542-2199; e-mail info@nationaltextile.org; internet www.nationaltextile.org; f. 1854; fmrly Northern Textile Asscn and Knitted Textile Asscn; adopted current name in 2002; over 200 mems; Chair. GEORGE W. SHUSTER; Pres. KARL SPILHAUS.

Tobacco

Tobacco Associates, Inc: 8452 Holly Leaf Dr., McLean, VA 22102-2225; tel. (703) 821-1255; fax (703) 821-1511; e-mail taw@tobaccoassociatesinc.org; internet www.tobaccoassociatesinc.org; f. 1947; Pres. KIRK WAYNE.

Tobacco Merchants Association of the United States (TMA): POB 8019, Princeton, NJ 08543-8019; tel. (609) 275-4900; fax (609) 275-8379; e-mail tma@tma.org; internet www.tma.org; f. 1915; 170 mems; Pres. FARRELL DELMAN.

Transport

Aerospace Industries Association of America, Inc (AIA): 1000 Wilson Blvd, Suite 1700, Arlington, VA 22209-3928; tel. (703) 358-1000; fax (703) 358-1012; e-mail alexis.allen@aia-aerospace.org; internet www.aia-aerospace.org; f. 1919; 158 mems and 219 assoc. mems; Chair. DAVID P. HESS; Pres. and CEO MARION C. BLAKEY.

Air Transport Association of America, Inc: see Civil Aviation—Associations.

Alliance of Automobile Manufacturers (Auto Alliance): 1401 Eye St, NW, Suite 900, Washington, DC 20005; tel. (202) 326-5500; fax (202) 326-5598; internet www.autoalliance.org; f. 1999; asscn of 12 car and light truck mfrs; Pres. and CEO MITCH BAINWOL.

American Bureau of Shipping: see Ocean Shipping—Associations.

American Bus Association: 111 K St, NE, 9th Floor, Washington, DC 20002; tel. (202) 842-1645; fax (202) 842-0850; e-mail abainfo@buses.org; internet www.buses.org; f. 1926; 3,300 mems; Chair. DOUG ANDERSON; Pres. and CEO PETER J. PANTUSO.

American International Automobile Dealers' Association (AIADA): 211 North Union St, Suite 300, Alexandria, VA 22314; tel. (703) 519-7800; fax (703) 519-7810; e-mail goaiada@aiada.org; internet www.aiada.org; f. 1970; 11,000 mems; Chair. RAY MUNGENAST; Pres. CODY LUSK.

American Public Transportation Association (APTA): 1666 K St, NW, Suite 1100, Washington, DC 20006; tel. (202) 496-4800; fax (202) 496-4324; e-mail info@apta.com; internet www.apta.com; f. 1882; 1,600 mems; Chair. GARY C. THOMAS; Pres. MICHAEL P. MELANIPHY.

American Railway Engineering and Maintenance of Way Association (AREMA): 10003 Derekwood Lane, Suite 210, Lanham, MD 20706; tel. (301) 459-3200; fax (301) 459-8077; e-mail chemely@arema.org; internet www.arema.org; f. 1997 by merger of three engineering support asscns—the American Railway Bridge and Building Asscn, the American Railway Engineering Asscn, and the Roadmasters and Maintenance of Way Asscn, in addition to functions of the Communications and Signal Division of the Asscn of American Railroads; 6,000 mems; Pres. and Chair. JAMES N. CARTER, Jr; Exec. Dir and CEO Dr CHARLES H. EMELY.

American Short Line and Regional Railroad Association: see Railways—Associations.

American Trucking Associations (ATA): 950 North Glebe Rd, Suite 210, Arlington, VA 22203-4181; tel. (703) 838-1700; fax (703) 838-1994; e-mail media@trucking.org; internet www.truckline.com; f. 1933; 37,000 mems; Chair. DAN ENGLAND; Pres. and CEO BILL GRAVES.

Association of American Railroads: see Railways—Associations.

Chamber of Shipping of America (CSA): see Ocean Shipping—Associations.

National Automobile Dealers Association (NADA): 8400 Westpark Dr., McLean, VA 22102-3522; tel. (703) 821-7000; e-mail nadainfo@nada.org; internet www.nada.org; f. 1917; nearly 16,000 mems; Chair. WILLIAM P. UNDERRINER; Pres. JOSEPH L. COWDEN (interim).

Owner/Operator Independent Drivers' Association of America (OOIDA): 1 North-West OOIDA Dr., Grain Valley, MO 64029; tel. (816) 229-5791; e-mail ooida@ooida.com; internet www.ooida.com; f. 1973; 160,972 mems; Pres. JIM JOHNSTON.

Shipbuilders Council of America (SCA): 655 15th St, NW, Suite 225, Washington, DC 20005; tel. (202) 347-5462; fax (202) 347-5464; e-mail belliott@balljanik.com; internet www.shipbuilders.org; f. 1921; absorbed the American Waterways Shipyard Conference (f. 1976) in 1999; 49 mem. cos and 81 supplier and affiliate mems; Pres. MATTHEW PAXTON.

Miscellaneous

American Advertising Federation (AAF): 1101 Vermont Ave, NW, Suite 500, Washington, DC 20005-6306; tel. (202) 898-0089; fax (202) 898-0159; e-mail aaf@aaf.org; internet www.aaf.org; f. 1967; 40,000 mems, 100 corp. mems; Chair. JOHN OSBORN; Pres. and CEO JAMES EDMUND DATRI.

American Association of Exporters and Importers (AAEI): 1050 17th St, NW, Suite 810, Washington, DC 20036; tel. (202) 857-8009; fax (202) 857-7843; e-mail hq@aaei.org; internet www.aaei.org; f. 1921; 1,200 mems; Chair. STEVE JOHNSEN; Pres. and CEO MARIANNE ROWDEN.

American Marketing Association (AMA): 311 South Wacker Dr., Suite 5800, Chicago, IL 60606; tel. (312) 542-9000; fax (312) 542-9001; e-mail info@ama.org; internet www.marketingpower.com; f. 1937; over 40,000 mems; Chair. JEROME D. WILLIAMS; CEO DENNIS L. DUNLAP.

ASAE & the Center for Association Leadership (American Society of Association Executives): ASAE & The Center Bldg, 1575 I St, NW, Washington, DC 20005-1103; tel. (202) 626-2723; fax (202) 371-8825; e-mail pr@asaecenter.org; internet www.asaecenter.org; f. 1920; more than 21,000 mems in more than 10,000 orgs; provides resources, education and advocacy; Chair. PETER J. O'NEIL; Pres. and CEO JOHN H. GRAHAM.

Association of Equipment Manufacturers (AEM): 6737 West Washington St, Suite 2400, Milwaukee, WI 53214-5647; tel. (414) 272-0943; fax (414) 272-1170; e-mail aem@aem.org; internet www.aem.org; f. 2002; more than 850 mem. cos; Chair. RUSSELL A. FOWLER; Pres. DENNIS SLATER.

Consumer Healthcare Products Association (CHPA): 900 19th St, NW, Suite 700, Washington, DC 20006; tel. (202) 429-9260; fax (202) 223-6835; e-mail efunderburk@chpa-info.org; internet www.chpa-info.org; f. 1881; more than 175 mem. and assoc. mem. cos; Chair. PAUL L. STURMAN; Pres. and CEO SCOTT M. MELVILLE.

Institute for Supply Management (ISM): 2055 East Centennial Circle, POB 22160, Tempe, AZ 85285-2160; tel. (408) 752-6276; fax (408) 752-7890; e-mail jkellerman@ism.ws; internet www.ism.ws; f. 1915; more than 40,000 mems; Chair. SIDNEY JOHNSON; CEO PAUL NOVAK.

Motion Picture Association of America, Inc (MPAA): 1600 Eye St, NW, Washington, DC 20006; tel. (202) 293-1966; fax (202) 296-7410; e-mail contactus@mpaa.org; internet www.mpaa.org; f. 1922; Chair. and CEO CHRISTOPHER J. DODD.

National Association of Manufacturers (NAM): 733 10th St, NW, Washington, DC 20001; tel. (202) 637-3000; fax (202) 637-3182; e-mail manufacturing@nam.org; internet www.nam.org; f. 1895; 11,000 mems; Chair. MARY VERMEER ANDRINGA; Pres. and CEO JAY TIMMONS.

National Association of Realtors (NAR): 430 North Michigan Ave, Suite 500, Chicago, IL 60611-4087; fax (312) 329-8960; e-mail infocentral@realtors.org; internet www.realtor.org; f. 1908; 1.3m. mems; Pres. MAURICE VEISSI; CEO DALE STINTON.

National Center for Manufacturing Sciences (NCMS): 3025 Boardwalk, Ann Arbor, MI 48108-3230; tel. (734) 995-0300; fax (734) 995-1150; e-mail bethb@ncms.org; internet www.ncms.org; f. 1986; Pres. and CEO RICHARD B. JARMAN; Chair. of Bd RALPH RESNICK.

National Cooperative Business Association (NCBA): 1401 New York Ave, NW, Suite 1100, Washington, DC 20005-2160; tel. (202) 638-6222; fax (202) 638-1374; e-mail info@ncba.coop; internet www.ncba.coop; f. 1916; 450 mems; Chair. WILSON BEEBE; Pres. and CEO LIZ BAILEY (interim).

National Retail Federation (NRF): 325 Seventh St, NW, Suite 1100, Washington, DC 20004-2802; tel. (202) 783-7941; fax (202) 737-2849; e-mail colemanr@nrf.com; internet www.nrf.com; f. 1911; merged with American Retail Federation in 1990 and incorporated Apparel Retailers of America in 1995; mems: more than 100 state, nat. and trade orgs; Chair. TERRY J. LUNDGREN; Pres. and CEO MATTHEW R. SHAY.

Personal Care Products Council: 1101 17th St, NW, Suite 300, Washington, DC 20036-4702; tel. (202) 331-1770; fax (202) 331-1969; e-mail publications@personalcarecouncil.org; internet www.personalcarecouncil.org; f. 1894; fmrly Cosmetic, Toiletry and Fragrance Asscn (CTFA); adopted current name 2007; more than 600 mem. cos; Chair. E. SCOTT BEATTIE; Pres. and CEO LEZLEE WESTINE.

Society of Manufacturing Engineers (SME): 1 SME Dr., Dearborn, MI 48128; tel. (313) 425-3000; fax (313) 425-3400; e-mail service@sme.org; internet www.sme.org; f. 1932 as Society of Tool Engineers; name changed as above in 1969; Pres. LAROUX K. GILLESPIE; Exec. Dir and CEO MARK C. TOMLINSON.

UTILITIES

Regulatory Authority

Federal Energy Regulatory Commission (FERC): 888 First St, NE, Washington, DC 20426; tel. (202) 502-8004; e-mail customer@ferc.gov; internet www.ferc.gov; independent regulatory commission; Chair. JON WELLINHOFF.

Electricity

American Electric Power (AEP): 1 Riverside Plaza, Columbus, OH 43215-2372; tel. (614) 716-1000; e-mail jsloat@aep.com; internet www.aep.com; f. 1906 as the American Gas and Electricity Co; present name adopted 1958; electricity supplier to Arkansas, Indiana, Kentucky, Louisiana, Michigan, Ohio, Oklahoma, Tennes-

see, Texas, Virginia and West Virginia; Chair. and CEO MICHAEL G. MORRIS; Pres. NICHOLAS K. AKINS.

American Public Power Association (APPA): 1875 Connecticut Ave, NW, Suite 1200, Washington, DC 20009-5715; tel. (202) 467-2900; fax (202) 467-2910; e-mail info@publicpower.org; internet www.appanet.org; f. 1940; asscn of local publicly owned electric utilities; c. 2,000 mem. utilities; Chair. PHYLLIS CURRIE; CEO MARK CRISSOM.

Association of Edison Illuminating Cos: 600 North 18th St, POB 2641, Birmingham, AL 35291-0992; tel. (205) 257-2530; fax (205) 257-2540; e-mail aeicdir@bellsouth.net; internet www.aeic.org; f. 1885; mems comprise 165 investor-owned public utilities, co-ops and municipal utility systems; Pres. THOMAS R. VOSS; Exec. Dir EARL B. PARSONS, Jr.

Edison Electric Institute: 701 Pennsylvania Ave, NW, Washington, DC 20004-2696; tel. (202) 508-5000; fax (202) 508-5759; e-mail news@eei.org; internet www.eei.org; f. 1933; mems comprise 184 investor-owned electric utility cos in the USA and 63 foreign mems; Chair. RICHARD C. KELLY; Pres. THOMAS R. KUHN.

Energy Telecommunications and Electrical Association (ENTELEC): 5005 West Royal Lane, Suite 116, Irving, TX 75063; tel. (888) 503-8700; fax (972) 915-6040; e-mail blaine@entelec.org; internet www.entelec.org; f. 1928 as the Petroleum Industry Electrical Asscn; changed name as above in 1978; 170 mems; Pres. MICHAEL BURT; Exec. Man. BLAINE SISKE.

National Rural Electric Co-operative Association: 4301 Wilson Blvd, Arlington, VA 22203; tel. (703) 907-5500; e-mail patrick.lavigne@nreca.coop; internet www.nreca.org; f. 1942; operates rural electric co-operative systems and public power distribution in 47 states; 900 mems; Pres. F. E. (WALLY) WOLSKI; CEO GLENN ENGLISH.

Gas

American Gas Association (AGA): 400 North Capitol St, NW, Suite 450, Washington, DC 20001; tel. (202) 824-7000; fax (202) 824-7115; e-mail ccussimanio@aga.org; internet www.aga.org; f. 1989; represents 195 local utility cos; Chair. LAWRENCE T. BORGARD; Pres. and CEO DAVE MCCURDY.

American Public Gas Association (APGA): 201 Massachusetts Ave, NE, Suite C-4, Washington, DC 20002; tel. (202) 464-2742; fax (202) 464-0246; e-mail mhager@apga.org; internet www.apga.org; f. 1961; promotes efficiency among public gas systems; 700 mem. utilities in 36 states; Chair. WADE STINSON; Pres. and CEO BERT KALISCH.

Gas Technology Institute (GTI): 1700 South Mount Prospect Rd, Des Plaines, IL 60018; tel. (847) 768-0500; fax (847) 768-0501; e-mail businessdevelopmentinfo@gastechnology.org; internet www.gastechnology.org; f. 1976; fmrly Gas Research Institute; 175 mems; Chair. RANDALL L. BARNARD; Pres. and CEO DAVID CARROLL.

Natural Gas Supply Association: 1620 Eye St, NW, Suite 700, Washington, DC 20006; tel. (202) 326-9300; fax (202) 326-9330; internet www.ngsa.org; f. 1967; monitors legislation and economic issues affecting natural gas producers; Pres. R. SKIP HORVATH.

Water

American Water Works Association: 6666 West Quincy Ave, Denver, CO 80235-3098; tel. (303) 794-7711; fax (303) 347-0804; e-mail custsvc@awwa.org; internet www.awwa.org; f. 1881; 57,000 mems; Pres. CHARLES F. ANDERSON; Exec. Dir DAVID B. LAFRANCE.

The Water Research Foundation: 6666 West Quincy Ave, Denver, CO 80235-3098; tel. (303) 347-6100; fax (303) 730-0851; e-mail Info@WaterRF.org; internet www.waterrf.org; f. 1966; Chair. ROY WOLFE; Exec. Dir ROBERT RENNER.

Association of Metropolitan Water Agencies: 1620 I St, NW, Suite 500, Washington, DC 20006; tel. (202) 331-2820; fax (202) 785-1845; e-mail info@amwa.net; internet www.amwa.net; f. 1981; 192 mems; Pres. PAT MULROY; Exec. Dir DIANE VANDE HEI.

National Association of Water Companies: 2001 L St, NW, Suite 850, Washington, DC 20036; tel. (202) 833-8383; fax (202) 331-7442; e-mail info@nawc.com; internet www.nawc.org; f. 1895; privately owned and operated water cos; 161 mems; Pres. LISA SPARROW; Exec. Dir MICHAEL DEANE.

National Rural Water Association: 2915 South 13th St, Duncan, OK 73533; tel. (580) 252-0629; fax (580) 255-4476; e-mail info@nrwa.org; internet www.nrwa.org; Pres. JOE LILES; CEO ROB JOHNSON.

TRADE UNIONS

In 2011 there were approximately 14.8m. union members in the USA, representing 11.8% of the civilian labour force.

Many trade unions based in the USA have members throughout North America. Approximately 25% of Canada's trade union members belong to unions having headquarters in the USA.

American Federation of Labor and Congress of Industrial Organizations (AFL-CIO): 815 16th St, NW, Washington, DC

20006; tel. (202) 637-5000; fax (202) 637-5058; internet www.aflcio
.org; f. 1955; Pres. RICHARD L. TRUMKA; Sec.-Treas. ELIZABETH SHULER;
Exec. Vice-Pres. ARLENE HOLT BAKER; 56 affiliated unions with total
membership of 11.5m. (2009).

Major AFL-CIO Affiliates
(with 500,000 members and over)

American Federation of Government Employees: 80 F St, NW,
Washington, DC 20001; tel. (202) 737-8700; fax (202) 639-6490;
e-mail comments@afge.org; internet www.afge.org; f. 1932; Nat.
Pres. J. DAVID COX; Sec.-Treas. EUGENE HUDSON, Jr; 600,000 mems.

**American Federation of State, County and Municipal
Employees (AFSCME):** 1625 L St, NW, Washington, DC 20036-
5687; tel. (202) 429-1000; fax (202) 429-1293; internet www.afscme
.org; f. 1936; Pres. LEE SAUNDERS; Sec.-Treas. LAURA REYES; 1.6m.
mems (2012).

American Federation of Teachers (AFT-AFL-CIO): 555 New
Jersey Ave, NW, Washington, DC 20001; tel. (202) 879-4400; fax
(202) 879-4556; internet www.aft.org; f. 1916; Pres. RANDI WEINGAR-
TEN; Sec.-Treas. LORRETTA JOHNSON; more than 1.5m. mems (2012).

Communications Workers of America: 501 Third St, NW,
Washington, DC 20001; tel. (202) 434-1100; fax (202) 434-1279;
internet www.cwa-union.org; f. 1939; Pres. LARRY COHEN; Sec.-
Treas. ANNIE HILL; over 700,000 mems (2012).

**International Association of Machinists and Aerospace
Workers (IAM):** 9000 Machinists Pl., Upper Marlboro, MD
20772-2687; tel. (301) 967-4500; fax (301) 967-4588; e-mail
websteward@goiam.org; internet www.goiam.org; f. 1888; Int. Pres.
R. THOMAS BUFFENBARGER; Gen. Sec.-Treas. ROBERT ROACH, Jr;
720,000 mems (2010).

International Brotherhood of Electrical Workers: 900 Seventh
St, NW, Washington, DC 20001; tel. (202) 833-7000; fax (202) 728-
7676; e-mail glenn_perusek@ibew.org; internet www.ibew.org;
f. 1891; Int. Pres. EDWIN D. HILL; Int. Sec.-Treas. SALVATORE J.
CHILIA; 675,000 mems (2012).

Laborers' International Union of North America (LIUNA):
905 16th St, NW, Washington, DC 20006; tel. (202) 737-8320; fax
(202) 737-2754; e-mail communications@liuna.org; internet www
.liuna.org; f. 1903; Pres. TERENCE M. O'SULLIVAN; Gen. Sec.-Treas.
ARMAND E. SABITONI; 500,000 mems (2012).

United Food and Commercial Workers International Union:
1775 K St, NW, Washington, DC 20006; tel. (202) 223-3111; internet
www.ufcw.org; f. 1979; Int. Pres. JOSEPH T. HANSEN; Int. Sec.-Treas.
ANTHONY M. PERRONE; 1.3m. mems.

United Mine Workers of America (UMWA): 18354 Quantico
Gateway Dr., Suite 200, Triangle, VA 22172-1179; tel. (703) 291-
2400; internet www.umwa.org; f. 1890; Int. Pres. CECIL E. ROBERTS;
Int. Sec.-Treas. DANIEL J. KANE.

**United Steel, Paper and Forestry, Rubber, Manufacturing,
Energy, Allied Industrial and Service Workers International
Union (USW)** (United Steelworkers): 5 Gateway Center, Pitts-
burgh, PA 15222; tel. (412) 562-2400; fax (412) 562-2445; e-mail
webmaster@usw.org; internet www.usw.org; f. 1936; incorporated
PACE International Union in 2005 and Independent Steelworkers
Union in 2007; created international union, Workers Uniting
(www.workersuniting.org), with Unite (United Kingdom) in 2008;
represents workers in the USA, Canada and the Caribbean; Int. Pres.
LEO W. GERARD; Int. Sec.-Treas. STAN JOHNSON; 850,000 mems (2007).

Major Independent Unions
(with 500,000 members and over)

American Nurses Association: 8515 Georgia Ave, Suite 400,
Silver Spring, MD 20910-3492; tel. (301) 628-5000; fax (301) 628-
5001; e-mail ana@ana.org; internet www.nursingworld.org; f. 1896;
publishes *The American Nurse* (6 a year) and *American Nurse Today*
(6 a year); Pres. KAREN A. DALEY; 51 constituent mem. state asscns
comprising 3.1m. mems.

Change to Win: 1900 L St, NW, Suite 900, Washington, DC 20036;
tel. (202) 721-0660; fax (202) 721-0661; e-mail info@changetowin.org;
internet www.changetowin.org; f. 2005 following split in the AFL-
CIO; Int. Pres. JOSEPH HANSEN; Sec.-Treas. JAMES P. HOFFA.

Affiliated unions include:

International Brotherhood of Teamsters: 25 Louisiana Ave,
NW, Washington, DC 20001; tel. (202) 624-6800; fax (202) 624-
6918; internet www.teamster.org; f. 1903; withdrew from AFL-
CIO in 2005; Gen. Pres. JAMES P. HOFFA; Gen. Sec.-Treas. KEN
HALL; 1.4m. mems.

Service Employees' International Union (SEIU): 1800 Massachusetts Ave, NW, Washington, DC 20036; tel. (202) 730-7000;
fax (202) 898-3304; e-mail media@seiu.org; internet www.seiu.org;
f. 1921; withdrew from AFL-CIO in 2005; Pres. MARY KAY HENRY;
Int. Sec.-Treas. ELISIO MEDINA; over 2.1m. mems (2012).

United Farm Workers: 29700 Woodford-Tehachapi Rd, POB 62,
Keene, CA 93531; tel. (661) 823-6151; e-mail execoffice@ufw.org;
internet www.ufw.org; f. 1962; Pres. ARTURO RODRIGUEZ; Sec.-
Treas. SERGIO GUZMAN.

**United Food and Commercial Workers International
Union:** 1775 K St, NW, Washington, DC 20006; tel. (202) 223-
3111; internet www.ufcw.org; f. 1979; Int. Pres. JOSEPH T. HANSEN;
Int. Sec.-Treas. ANTHONY M. PERRONE; 1.3m. mems.

National Education Association of the United States: 1201
16th St, NW, Washington, DC 20036-3290; tel. (202) 833-4000; fax
(202) 822-7974; internet www.nea.org; f. 1857; Pres. DENNIS VAN
ROEKEL; Sec.-Treas. REBECCA PRINGLE; 3.2m. mems.

Transport

Federal Transit Administration: East Bldg, 4th Floor, 1200 New
Jersey Ave, SE, Washington, DC 20590; tel. (202) 366-4043; e-mail
fta.adaassistance@dot.gov; internet www.fta.dot.gov; Admin.
PETER M. ROGOFF.

National Transportation Safety Board: 490 L'Enfant Plaza, SW,
6th Floor, Washington, DC 20594; tel. (202) 314-6000; internet www
.ntsb.gov; f. 1967; seeks to ensure that all types of transportation in
the USA are conducted safely; carries out studies and accident
investigations; Chair. DEBORAH A. P. HERSMAN; Man. Dir DAVID
MAYER.

Surface Transportation Board: 395 E St, SW, Washington, DC
20423-0001; tel. (202) 245-0245; fax (202) 565-9016; e-mail
STBHelp@stb.dot.gov; internet www.stb.dot.gov; f. 1995 to succeed
Interstate Commerce Commission; exercises regulatory authority
over domestic surface common carriers; jurisdiction extends over
rail, inland waterways and motorized traffic; Chair. DANIEL R.
ELLIOTT, III.

Transportation Security Administration (TSA): 601 South
12th St, Arlington, VA 20598; tel. (866) 289-9673; e-mail
tsa-contactcenter@dhs.gov; internet www.tsa.gov; f. 2001 to ensure
the security of the country's transport system against possible
terrorist attacks; 50,000 employees; Admin. JOHN S. PISTOLE.

RAILWAYS

In 2011 there were 222,999 km (138,565 miles) of Class I railroads in
the USA, including 76 km (47 miles) operated by Canadian railroad
companies. In 2010 Amtrak operated inter-city passenger services on
more than 34,000 km of track, some 70% of which were owned by
other railroad companies.

Federal Railroad Administration (FRA): Dept of Transportation, 1200 New Jersey Ave, SE, Washington, DC 20590; tel. (202) 493-
6024; fax (202) 493-6009; e-mail webmaster@fra.dot.gov; internet
www.fra.dot.gov; f. 1966; part of the Dept of Transportation;
formulates federal railway policies and administers and enforces
safety regulations; Admin. JOSEPH C. SZABO.

Principal Companies

Alaska Railroad Corpn: 327 West Ship Creek Ave, POB 107500,
Anchorage, AK 99510; tel. (907) 265-2300; fax (907) 265-2312; e-mail
public_comment@akrr.com; internet www.akrr.com; f. 1912; independent corpn owned by the State of Alaska; year-round freight
service and summer passenger service; operates 845 km of track;
Chair. LINDA LEARY; Pres. and CEO CHRISTOPHER AADNESEN.

Amtrak (National Railroad Passenger Corpn): 60 Massachusetts
Ave, NE, Washington, DC 20002; tel. (202) 906-3860; fax (202) 906-
3306; internet www.amtrak.com; f. 1970; govt-funded private corpn
operating intercity passenger services over 34,118 track-km in 46
states; carried 28.7m. passengers in 2009/10; Chair. THOMAS C.
CARPER; Pres. and CEO JOSEPH H. BOARDMAN.

BNSF Railway: 2650 Lou Menk Dr., Fort Worth, TX 76131-2830;
tel. (913) 551-4479; fax (913) 551-4285; e-mail steven.forsberg@bnsf
.com; internet www.bnsf.com; fmrly Burlington Northern Santa Fe
Corpn; freight services; 51,498 track-km; Chair. and CEO
MATTHEW K. ROSE; Pres. and COO CARL R. ICE.

Consolidated Rail Corpn (Conrail): 1717 Arch St, Suite 3210,
32nd Floor, Philadelphia, PA 19103; tel. (215) 209-2000; e-mail info@
conrail.com; internet www.conrail.com; f. 1976 by fed. govt merger of
6 bankrupt freight carriers; jtly owned by CSX (42%) and Norfolk
Southern (58%); switching and terminal railroad operating in 3
locations: Northern New Jersey, Southern New Jersey/Philadelphia,
and Detroit, MI; Pres. and COO RONALD L. BATORY.

CSX Transportation, Inc (Rail Transport): 500 Water St, Jacksonville, FL 32202; tel. (904) 359-3100; e-mail nbd@csx.com; internet

www.csx.com; f. 1980 by merger; operates 34,371 km of track (2005); Chair., Pres. and CEO MICHAEL J. WARD.

Kansas City Southern Railway Co: 427 West 12th St, Kansas City, MO 64105; tel. (816) 983-1303; e-mail dcarlson@kcsouthern .com; internet www.kcsouthern.com; Chair. and CEO MICHAEL R. HAVERTY; Pres. and CEO DAVID L. STARLING; operates 4,989 km of track.

Long Island Rail Road Co: Jamaica Station, Jamaica, NY 11435-4380; tel. (718) 558-7400; internet www.mta.info/lirr; f. 1834; operates 3,291 km of track (Dec. 2007); operated by the Metropolitan Transportation Authority—State of New York; Chair. JOSEPH LHOTA; Pres. HELENA WILLIAMS.

Norfolk Southern Corpn: NS Tower, 3 Commercial Pl., Norfolk, VA 23510-9219; tel. (757) 629-2600; fax (757) 664-5117; e-mail contactus@nscorp.com; internet www.nscorp.com; f. 1988; operates 37,600 miles of track (2008); Pres., Chair. and CEO CHARLES WICK MOORMAN.

Pan Am Railways: 1700 Iron Horse Park, North Billerica, MA 01862; tel. (978) 663-1130; e-mail customerservice@panamrailways .com; internet www.panamrailways.com; fmrly Guilford Rail System; name changed as above in 2006; Pres. DAVID FINK.

Union Pacific Railroad Co: 1400 Douglas St, Omaha, NE 68179; tel. (402) 544-5000; fax (402) 350-7362; internet www.up.com; f. 1897; division of Union Pacific Corpn; operates 52,143 km of track in 23 states; Chair. JAMES R. YOUNG; Pres. and CEO JOHN J. KORALESKI.

Associations

American Short Line and Regional Railroad Association (ASLRRA): 50 F St, NW, Suite 7020, Washington, DC 20001; tel. (202) 628-4500; fax (202) 628-6430; e-mail aslrra@aslrra.org; internet www.aslrra.org; f. 1913; 875 mems; operates and maintains 29% of US rail mileage; Pres. and Treas. RICHARD F. TIMMONS.

Association of American Railroads: 425 Third St, SW, Suite 1000, Washington, DC 20024; tel. (202) 639-2100; fax (202) 639-2286; e-mail preilly@aar.org; internet www.aar.org; f. 1934; membership represents virtually all major railroads in the USA, Canada and Mexico, as well as rail industry products and services; oversees 173,000 miles of track; Pres. and CEO EDWARD R. HAMBERGER.

ROADS

In 2010 there were 75,479 km (46,900 miles) of interstate highway, 1,953,509 km of other national highway system roads and 4,516,338 km of other roads. Road network kilometres in that year totalled 6,545,326, making it the world's second longest road network system.

Federal Highway Administration (FHWA): 1200 New Jersey Ave, SE, Washington, DC 20590; tel. (202) 366-4000; fax (202) 366-3244; internet www.fhwa.dot.gov; part of the Dept of Transportation; implements federal highway policy and promotes road safety; Admin. VICTOR M. MENDEZ.

National Highway Traffic Safety Administration (NHTSA): 1200 New Jersey Ave, SE, West Bldg, Washington, DC 20590; tel. (202) 366-9550; e-mail webmaster@nhtsa.dot.gov; internet www .nhtsa.dot.gov; f. 1970; part of the Dept of Transportation; Admin. DAVID L. STRICKLAND.

INLAND WATERWAYS

In 2009 there were some 40,749 km (25,320 miles) of navigable channels in the USA.

St Lawrence Seaway Development Corpn (SLSDC): US Dept of Transportation, 1200 New Jersey Ave, SE, W32-300, Washington, DC 20590; tel. (202) 366-0091; fax (202) 366-7147; e-mail tim .downey@dot.gov; internet www.greatlakes-seaway.com; responsible for the operations and maintenance of sections of the St Lawrence Seaway within the territorial limits of the USA; Admin. CRAIG H. MIDDLEBROOK (acting).

Principal Companies

American Commercial Lines, Inc: 1701 East Market St, Jeffersonville, IN 47130; tel. (812) 288-0100; e-mail aclinfo@aclines.com; internet www.aclines.com; f. 1915; operates barge services on the Mississippi and Ohio rivers and tributaries to the Gulf Intracoastal Waterway; fleet of more than 2,700 barges and 125 towboats; Pres. and CEO MARK K. KNOY.

Great Lakes Dredge & Dock Corpn: 2122 York Rd, Oak Brook, IL 60523; tel. (630) 574-3000; fax (630) 574-2909; internet www.gldd .com; f. 1890; dredging, marine construction and reclamation; operates tugboats, drillboats, carfloats, barges and dredges; 180 vessels; Chair. NATHAN D. LEIGHT; CEO JONATHAN W. BERGER.

Great Lakes Fleet, Inc: 212 South 37th Ave, Suite 200, Duluth, MN 55807; tel. (218) 723-2420; fax (218) 723-2455; e-mail sdelia@keyship .com; f. 1901 as Pittsburgh Steamship Division; acquired by

Canadian National Railway Co in 2004; operated by Keystone Shipping Co; Gen. Man. WILLIAM PETERSON; 8 vessels.

Associations

American Waterways Operators: 801 North Quincy St, Suite 200, Arlington, VA 22203; tel. (703) 841-9300; fax (703) 841-0389; e-mail amcculloch@vesselalliance.com; internet www.americanwaterways .com; f. 1944; over 400 mems; Pres. and CEO THOMAS A. ALLEGRETTI.

Lake Carriers' Association: 20325 Center Ridge Rd, Suite 720, Rocky River, OH 44116; tel. (440) 333-4444; fax (440) 333-9993; e-mail info@lcaships.com; internet www.lcaships.com; f. 1892; 18 mem. cos; Pres. JAMES H. I. WEAKLEY.

National Waterways Conference, Inc: 1100 North Glebe Rd, Suite 1010, Arlington, VA 22201; tel. (703) 224-8007; fax (866) 371-1390; e-mail info@waterways.org; internet www.waterways.org; f. 1960; org. advocating water resource policies; 200 mems; Chair. SYKES STURDIVANT; Pres. AMY W. LARSON.

OCEAN SHIPPING

At 31 December 2012 the flag registered fleet comprised 10,099 vessels, with a total displacement of 23.0m. grt, of which 1,027 were fishing vessels, 114 were general cargo carriers and 109 were gas tankers.

Federal Maritime Commission: 800 North Capitol St, NW, Washington, DC 20573; tel. (202) 523-5725; fax (202) 523-0014; e-mail secretary@fmc.gov; internet www.fmc.gov; f. 1961 to regulate the water-borne foreign commerce of the USA; comprises 5 Commrs; Chair. RICHARD A. LIDINSKY, Jr; Man. Dir RONALD D. MURPHY.

Maritime Administration: 1200 New Jersey Ave, SE, Washington, DC 20590; tel. (202) 366-5807; e-mail pao.marad@dot.gov; internet www.marad.dot.gov; promotes the US Merchant Marine; administers subsidy programmes to ship operators; Maritime Administrator DAVID T. MATSUDA.

Principal Ports

The three largest ports in the USA, in terms of traffic handled, are the Port of South Louisiana, handling 236.3m. short tons in 2010, Houston (227.1m. tons) and New York/New Jersey (139.2m. tons). Many other large ports serve each coast, 22 of them handling between 30m. and 70m. tons of traffic in 2010. The deepening of channels and locks on the St Lawrence–Great Lakes Waterway, allowing the passage of large ocean-going vessels, has increased the importance of the Great Lakes ports, of which the largest, Duluth-Superior, handled some 36.6m. tons in 2010.

Principal Companies

APL: 16220 North Scottsdale Rd, Suite 300, Scottsdale, AZ 85254; tel. (602) 586-4800; fax (602) 586-4861; e-mail global_marketing@apl .com; internet www.apl.com; f. 1848; serves east and west coasts of North America, Mexico, Caribbean Basin, Middle East and Far East; wholly owned subsidiary of Neptune Orient Lines (Singapore); 146 vessels; Pres. AIK MENG ENG.

Central Gulf Lines, Inc: 11 North Water St, Suite 18290, Mobile, AL 36602; tel. (251) 243-9110; fax (251) 243-9111; e-mail wildkm@ intship.com; internet www.intship.com/centralgulf; f. 1947; Vice-Pres. KEVIN M. WILD.

Chevron Shipping Co: 6001 Bollinger Canyon Rd, San Ramon, CA 94583-5177; tel. (925) 842-1000; internet www.chevron.com/ countries/usa; f. 1895; subsidiary of Chevron Corpn; world-wide tanker services; regional offices in Houston, London, United Kingdom, and Singapore; 39 tankers; Chair. and CEO JOHN S. WATSON.

Crowley Maritime Corpn: 555 12th St, Suite 2130, Oakland, CA 94607; tel. (510) 251-7500; fax (510) 251-7510; internet www.crowley .com; f. 1892; 280 vessels; Pres., Chair. and CEO THOMAS B. CROWLEY, Jr.

ETG Dorchester Ltd: 654 Madison Ave, New York, NY 10022; tel. (212) 813-9360; fax (212) 813-6390; e-mail info@etgglobal.com; internet www.etgglobal.com/Shipping.htm; 8 vessels; part of the Energy Transportation Group (ETG); provides LNG ship and shore management services; Chair. and CEO KIMBALL C. CHEN; Pres. and COO ALEX W. EVANS.

Horizon Lines: 4064 Colony Rd, Suite 200, Charlotte, NC; tel. (704) 973-7000; e-mail customercare@horizonlines.com; internet www .horizon-lines.com; f. 2001 as Horizon Services Group following restructuring of CSX Lines; 21 container ships; Chair. ALEX J. MANDI; Pres. and CEO SAM WOODWARD.

Matson Navigation Co: 555 12th St, Suite 700, Oakland, CA 94607; tel. (510) 628-4000; fax (510) 628-7380; e-mail general_info@matson .com; internet www.matson.com; f. 1901; container and other freight services between US west coast and Hawaii; container leasing world-wide; subsidiary of Alexander & Baldwin, Inc; 17 vessels; Pres. MATTHEW J. (MATT) COX.

Stolt-Nielsen USA, Inc: 800 Connecticut Ave, 4th Floor, East Norwalk, CT 06854; tel. (203) 838-7100; fax (203) 299-0067; internet www.stolt-nielsen.com; over 130 tankers; Chair. CHRISTER OLSSON; CEO NIELS G. STOLT-NIELSEN.

Waterman Steamship Corpn: 1 Whitehall St, New York, NY 10004; tel. (212) 747-8550; fax (212) 747-8588; e-mail waterman@intship.com; internet www.intship.com/waterman; f. 1919; owned by International Shipholding Corpn.

Associations

American Bureau of Shipping: 16855 Northchase Dr., Houston, TX 77060; tel. (281) 877-5800; fax (281) 877-5803; e-mail abs-worldhq@eagle.org; internet www.eagle.org; f. 1862; 814 mems; Chair. ROBERT D. SOMMERVILLE; Pres., CEO and COO CHRISTOPHER WIERNICKI.

American Maritime Congress: Hall of the States, Suite 800, 444 North Capitol St, NW, Washington, DC 20001; tel. (202) 347-8020; fax (202) 347-1550; e-mail diannelauer@americanmaritime.org; internet www.americanmaritime.org; f. 1977 as Joint Maritime Congress; adopted current name 1989; mems represent major US-flag ship-operating cos; Chair. MIKE JEWELL; Pres. Capt. LEE A. KINCAID.

Chamber of Shipping of America (CSA): 1730 M St, NW, Suite 407, Washington, DC 20036-4517; tel. (202) 775-4399; fax (202) 659-3795; e-mail omoore@knowships.org; internet www.knowships.org; fmrly American Institute of Merchant Shipping; 34 mem. cos; Pres. and CEO JOSEPH J. COX.

CIVIL AVIATION

Federal Aviation Administration: 800 Independence Ave, SW, Washington, DC 20591; tel. (202) 267-8738; fax (202) 267-5301; internet www.faa.gov; f. 1958; part of the Dept of Transportation; promotes safety in the air, regulates air commerce and assists in development of an effective national airport system; Administrator MICHAEL P. HUERTA (acting).

Principal Scheduled Companies

In 2012 there were 5,173 public-use airports in the USA. There were 117 registered air carriers operating in the USA in 2012; of these, 22 companies were classified as major carriers.

Alaska Airlines: 19300 International Blvd, POB 68900, Seattle, WA 98188; tel. (206) 433-3200; fax (206) 392-7750; internet www.alaskaair.com; f. 1932; scheduled passenger services to 59 cities in the USA, Canada and Mexico; Chair. WILLIAM S. AYER; Pres. and CEO BRADLEY D. TILDEN.

Horizon Air: 19521 Pacific Hwy South, Seattle, WA 98188; tel. (206) 431-3647; e-mail support@horizonair.com; internet www.horizonair.com; f. 1981; serves 47 cities in the USA, Canada and Mexico; Pres. GLENN JOHNSON.

American Airlines, Inc: POB 619616, Dallas/Fort Worth Airport, TX 75261-9616; tel. (817) 967-1234; fax (817) 962-4162; internet www.aa.com; f. 1934; coast-to-coast domestic routes, and services to Canada, Hawaii, Mexico, the Caribbean, South America, Europe and the Far East; acquired Trans World Airlines in 2001; Chair. and CEO THOMAS W. HORTON.

Continental Airlines, Inc: 1600 Smith St, POB 4607, Houston, TX 77002; tel. (713) 324-5152; fax (713) 324-2637; e-mail geninfo@coair.com; internet www.continental.com; f. 1934; serves 133 US destinations and 132 int. destinations; part of United Continental Holdings, Inc; Chair. GLENN F. TILTON; Pres. and CEO JEFFERY A. SMISEK.

Delta Air Lines, Inc: 1030 Delta Blvd, POB 20706, Atlanta, GA 30320-6001; tel. (404) 715-2600; internet www.delta.com; f. 1928; merged with Northwest Airlines in 2008; domestic and int. services to 351 destinations in 64 countries; CEO RICHARD H. ANDERSON; Pres. EDWARD BASTIAN.

Hawaiian Airlines, Inc: 3375 Koapaka St, G-350, Honolulu, HI 96819; tel. (808) 835-3700; fax (808) 835-3690; internet www.hawaiianair.com; f. 1929 as Inter-Island Airways Ltd; inter-island, US mainland and South Pacific services; Chair. LAWRENCE S. HERSHFIELD; Pres. and CEO MARK B. DUNKERLEY.

Southwest Airlines: 2702 Love Field Dr., POB 36611, Dallas, TX 75235-1647; tel. (214) 792-4000; internet www.southwest.com; f. 1971; scheduled services to 69 cities in 35 states; Pres., Chair. and CEO GARY KELLY.

United Airlines Corpn: POB 66100, Chicago, IL 60666; tel. (847) 700-9838; fax (847) 700-4081; internet www.united.com; f. 1931; domestic and int. services to over 200 destinations; part of United

Continental Holdings, Inc; Chair. GLENN F. TILTON; Pres. and CEO JEFFERY A. SMISEK.

US Airways, Inc: 4000 East Sky Harbor Blvd, Phoenix, AZ 85034; tel. (480) 693-0800; fax (480) 693-2300; internet www.usairways.com; f. 1939 as All-American Airways; merged with America West Airlines in 2005; scheduled passenger services to 208 destinations world-wide; Chair. and CEO DOUG PARKER; Pres. SCOTT KIRBY.

Associations

Airlines for America (A4A): 1301 Pennsylvania Ave, NW, Suite 1100, Washington, DC 20004-1707; tel. (202) 626-4000; fax (202) 626-4181; e-mail a4a@airlines.org; internet www.airlines.org; f. 1936; 13 US airlines mems, 1 non-US assoc. mem.; Chair. RICHARD H. ANDERSON; Pres. and CEO NICHOLAS E. CALIO.

National Air Carrier Association: 1000 Wilson Blvd, Suite 1700, Arlington, VA 22209; tel. (703) 358-8060; fax (703) 358-8070; internet www.naca.cc; f. 1962; 15 mems; Pres. A. OAKLEY BROOKS.

National Air Transportation Association (NATA): 4226 King St, Alexandria, VA 22302; tel. (703) 845-9000; fax (703) 845-8176; internet www.nata.aero; f. 1940; approx. 2,000 mems; Chair. JAMES P. SWEENEY; Pres. THOMAS L. HENDRICKS.

Regional Airline Association: 2025 M St, NW, Suite 800, Washington, DC 20036-3309; tel. (202) 367-1170; fax (202) 367-2170; e-mail raa@raa.org; internet www.raa.org; f. 1975; 34 mems; Chair. JIM RANKIN; Pres. ROGER COHEN.

Tourism

In 2012 there were an estimated 61.1m. foreign visitors to the USA, a decrease of 1.9% compared with the previous year. Receipts from tourism in 2012 (including passenger transport) were estimated to total some US $168,076m.

American Society of Travel Agents: 1101 King St, Suite 200, Alexandria, VA 22314; tel. (703) 739-2782; fax (703) 684-8319; e-mail askasta@asta.com; internet www.asta.org; f. 1931; Pres. and Chair. NINA MEYER; Vice-Pres. and Sec. JOHN LOVELL; over 20,000 mems.

Corporation for Travel Promotion (Brand USA): 1725 I St, NW, Washington, DC 20006; tel. (202) 822-2160; e-mail info@corporationfortravelpromotion.com; internet www.corporationfortravelpromotion.org; f. 2010; non-profit org. intended to promote the USA as a tourist destination; Chair. CAROLINE BETETA; Pres. and CEO CHRISTOPHER L. THOMPSON.

Office of Travel and Tourism Industries: International Trade Administration, US Dept of Commerce, 14th and Constitution Ave, NW, Rm 1003, Washington, DC 20230; tel. (202) 482-0140; fax (202) 482-2887; e-mail otti@trade.gov; internet tinet.ita.doc.gov; f. 1996; fed. govt agency; analyses data and develops policy; Dir ISABEL HILL.

US Travel Association: 1100 New York Ave, NW, Suite 450, Washington, DC 20005; tel. (202) 408-8422; fax (202) 408-1255; e-mail feedback@ustravel.org; internet www.ustravel.org; f. 2009 after merger between Travel Industry Asscn (f. 1941) and the Travel Business Roundtable; promotes increased travel to and within the USA through marketing initiatives, including the Discover America brand; Chair. ROSSI RALENKOTTER; Pres. ROGER DOW.

Defence

As assessed at November 2012, US armed forces totalled 1,520,100: army 600,450, air force 346,100, navy 332,800 and 199,550 marine corps; there was also a Coast Guard numbering 41,200 (not including civilians). At the same time active reservists totalled 810,350. Military conscription ended in 1973. The Strategic Air Command and Polaris nuclear submarines are equipped with nuclear weapons. The USA is a member of the North Atlantic Treaty Organization.

Defence expenditure: budgeted at US $676,700m. in 2012.

Chairman of the Joint Chiefs of Staff: Gen. MARTIN E. DEMPSEY.

Chief of Staff of the Army: Gen. RAYMOND T. ODIERNO.

Chief of Staff of the Air Force: Gen. NORTON A. SCHWARTZ.

Chief of Naval Operations: Adm. JONATHAN W. GREENERT.

Commandant of the Marine Corps: Gen. JAMES F. AMOS.

Commandant of the Coast Guard: Adm. ROBERT J. PAPP Jr.

Education

Education is primarily the responsibility of state and local governments, but some federal funds are available to help meet special needs at primary, secondary and higher education levels. Public education is free in every state. The period of compulsory education varies among states, but most states require attendance between the ages of seven and 16 years. In 2010/11 there were an estimated 34.6m. pupils enrolled in public primary schools and 14.9m. in public secondary schools. In 2009/10 private school enrolment was approximately 4.2m. at primary level and about 1.3m. at secondary level. In 2009/10 there were 4,495 degree-granting universities and colleges, with a total enrolment of an estimated 21m. students. Federal government expenditure on education (including training and employment programmes) was budgeted at an estimated US $139,200m. in 2012 (3.0% of total expenditure). Spending on education by state and local government in 2008/09 was $850,674m.

UNITED STATES COMMONWEALTH TERRITORIES

There are two US Commonwealth Territories, the Northern Mariana Islands, in the Pacific Ocean, and Puerto Rico, in the Caribbean Sea. A Commonwealth is a self-governing incorporated territory that is an integral part of, and in full political union with, the USA.

THE NORTHERN MARIANA ISLANDS

Introductory Survey

LOCATION, CLIMATE, LANGUAGE, RELIGION, FLAG, CAPITAL

The Commonwealth of the Northern Mariana Islands comprises 14 islands (all the Marianas except Guam) in the western Pacific Ocean, about 5,300 km (3,300 miles) west of Honolulu (Hawaii). The temperature normally ranges between 24°C (75°F) and 30°C (86°F) in June–November, but is generally cooler and drier from December to May. The average annual rainfall is about 2,120 mm (84 ins). English, Chamorro and Carolinian are the official languages. The population is predominantly Christian, mainly Roman Catholic. The national flag of the United States of America (q.v.) is used by the Northern Mariana Islands. Six islands, including the three largest (Saipan, Tinian and Rota), are inhabited; the principal settlement and the administrative centre are on Saipan.

CONTEMPORARY POLITICAL HISTORY

Historical Context

The islands that comprise the territory of the Northern Mariana Islands were first sighted by Europeans during the 1520s, and were claimed for Spain in 1565. They were sold to Germany in 1899, but control was transferred to Japan, which had taken the islands from Germany in 1914, by the League of Nations in 1921. During the Second World War the USA captured Saipan and Tinian from the Japanese, after fierce fighting in 1944, and the Northern Mariana Islands became a part of the Trust Territory of the Pacific Islands in 1947 (see the Marshall Islands).

In June 1975 the Northern Mariana Islands voted for separate status as a US Commonwealth Territory, and in March 1976 President Gerald Ford of the USA signed the Northern Marianas Commonwealth Covenant. In October 1977 US President Jimmy Carter approved the Constitution of the Northern Mariana Islands, which provided for the former Marianas District to be internally self-governing from January 1978. In December 1977 elections took place for a bicameral legislature, a Governor and a Lieutenant-Governor. The gubernatorial election was won by Carlos Camacho of the Democratic Party, who took office in January 1978. The islanders also elected a Resident Representative (known as the 'Washington Representative') to promote their interests in the federal legislature in Washington, DC.

Domestic Political Affairs

In early 1982, following his defeat in the election held in late 1981, Camacho was replaced as Governor by Pedro (Pete) Tenorio of the Republican Party. The Northern Marianas were formally admitted to US Commonwealth status in November 1986, after the ending of the Trusteeship in the territory. At the same time a proclamation issued by US President Ronald Reagan conferred US citizenship on the islands' residents.

At elections in late 1989 Republicans retained control of the governorship of the Northern Marianas and ousted a Democrat from the position of the islands' Resident Representative in Washington, DC. Lorenzo (Larry) De Leon Guerrero was elected Governor, following Pedro Tenorio's decision to resign. However, candidates of the Democratic Party won a majority of seats in the islands' House of Representatives.

Guerrero took office in January 1990. In December the UN Security Council voted to end the Trusteeship of the Northern Marianas, as well as that of two other Pacific Trust Territories. Although the decision to terminate the relationship had been taken in 1986, voting had been delayed. However, Governor Guerrero opposed the termination on the grounds that the new relationship would leave the islands subject to US law while remaining unrepresented in the US Congress.

At elections in late 1991 Republicans regained a majority in the islands' House of Representatives (which had been enlarged by three seats), and in the Senate the Republican Party increased the number of its representatives to eight. Republicans retained their majority at elections to the House of Representatives in 1993. However, in the gubernatorial election a Democrat, Froilan Tenorio, was successful; Jesús Borja was elected as Lieutenant-Governor. Juan N. Babauta remained as the Northern Marianas' Resident Representative in Washington, DC.

The territory's reputation was marred in April 1995 when the Government of the Philippines introduced a ban on its nationals accepting unskilled employment in the islands, owing to persistent reports of abuse and exploitation of immigrant workers. Meanwhile, the US Congress announced that it was to allocate US $7m. towards the enforcement of the islands' labour and immigration laws, following the publication of a report in late 1994 that alleged the repeated violations of these regulations, as well as widespread corruption among immigration officials and business leaders.

In May 1997 US President Bill Clinton informed Governor Tenorio of his intention to apply US immigration and minimum wage laws to the territory, stating that labour practices in the islands were inconsistent with US values. The territory's Government successfully lobbied the Republican majority in the US House of Representatives to reject legislation proposed in the previous month that would have equalized the minimum wage levels in the islands with that of the US mainland.

In January 1999 the Office of Insular Affairs of the US Department of the Interior published a report in which it concluded that the Government's attempts to eradicate abuses of labour and immigration laws had been unsuccessful. In particular, the islands' administration was deemed to have failed to reduce the territory's reliance on alien workers, to enforce US minimum wage laws and to curb evasions of trade legislation governing the export of garments to the USA. In the same month former employees of 18 US clothing retailers initiated legal action against the companies, which were accused of failing to comply with US labour laws in Saipan. In April 2000 a settlement was reached with the garment manufacturers, providing some US $8m. in compensation for the workers. The companies also agreed to conform to regulations established by an independent monitoring system in Saipan.

At the islands' legislative elections in November 1997 Republican candidates won 13 of the 18 seats in the House of Representatives and eight of the nine seats in the Senate. At the gubernatorial election, held concurrently, the incumbent Pedro Tenorio was successful, securing 46% of total votes. However, opponents of Tenorio subsequently initiated an unsuccessful legal challenge to his re-election on the grounds that his return to office constituted his third term as Governor, thereby violating the Constitution: this stated that a maximum of two gubernatorial terms could be served by any one individual, although the Constitution had been amended to include this provision only during the course of Tenorio's second term of office. Following legislative elections in November 1999, Democratic candidates held six of the 18 seats in the House of Representatives and two of the nine seats in the Senate.

In February 2000 the US Senate approved a bill granting permanent residency in the Northern Marianas to some 40,000 immigrant workers. However, the bill also included provisions for limiting the stay of all future guest workers. In December Governor Tenorio announced that he was to oppose the decision by the US Government to bring the Northern Marianas' labour and immigration laws under federal control, arguing that this would have a negative impact on the islands' economy. In May 2001, following intense lobbying by the Government of the Northern Marianas, the US Congress abandoned the bill. The issue of permanent residency for qualified immigrant workers re-emerged in 2007 with the introduction of minimum wage legislation (see below).

At legislative elections in November 2001 the Republican Party secured 12 seats in the House of Representatives, the Democratic Party five and the newly formed Covenant Party (founded by Benigno R. Fitial, hitherto a member of the Republican Party, to support his gubernatorial bid) one. The Republican Party won six seats in the Senate, the Democratic Party two and the Covenant Party one. At the concurrent gubernatorial election Juan Babauta, the Republican Party candidate and former Washington Representative, won a convincing victory, securing 42.8% of the votes cast, defeating Fitial who received 24.4%; Diego Benavente, the former Speaker of the House of Representatives, was elected Lieutenant-Governor.

In January 2002 the Supreme Court suspended deportation proceedings against an immigrant labourer working illegally in the Northern Marianas, after he appealed to the office of the UN High Commissioner for Refugees. The Court warned the Government that it might not be able to order the deportation of up to 10,000 of the Chinese, Sri Lankan and Bangladeshi workers in the Northern Marianas. In late 2002 the Government successfully resisted a further attempt by the US Administration to place the Northern Mariana Islands' immigration and labour legislation under direct federal control. In September 2003 the Northern Mariana Islands announced the conclusion of a new immigration co-operation agreement with the US Department of the Interior, which removed the right of overseas political refugees in the territory to seek asylum in the USA.

In May 2002 the issue of the Northern Marianas' working conditions was raised again by US Senator Edward Kennedy, who proposed a bill that would incrementally increase the minimum wage. In September seven further major US clothing retailers agreed to pay US $11.25m. in compensation to employees alleged to have suffered intolerable working conditions and poor rates of pay. The case was settled in April 2003, when a total of $20m. in compensation was ordered to be paid to the claimants. In June the Garment Oversight Board was established with the authority to withdraw certification of working conditions in factories supplying major US clothing companies. In March 2004 the Board decertified one of the 26 participating garment manufacturers. In April more than 400 garment workers were referred to the Division of Immigration for probable deportation as a result of their non-compliance with a Fair Labor Standards Act civil action against garment manufacturers. However, owing to unfavourable external circumstances (see Economic Affairs), in 2005 about a dozen garment factories ceased operations or reduced their work-force. In mid-2005 the minimum hourly wage in the Northern Marianas stood at $3.05, some 40% less than the rate prevailing on the US mainland. Legislation seeking to harmonize the minimum wage in the Northern Marianas with that of the USA was introduced in the US Senate in May. In July, after lobbying from the Government and the Saipan Chamber of Commerce, the Northern Marianas were excluded from minimum wage legislation that would have ensured equivalence with the US wage increase to $7.25 an hour. However, in January 2007 the Northern Marianas were finally included in the new legislation, while various tax concessions were provisionally approved to ease any losses incurred by small businesses as a result of the increase. The legislation also allowed qualified immigrant workers to apply for permanent residency. Nevertheless, strong opposition to the federal legislation remained, as more garment factories closed down (see Economic Affairs).

In May 2002 the Government froze the assets of the Bank of Saipan after the institution's former Chairman was arrested for allegedly attempting to defraud the bank of more than US $6.6m. The bank, which was reported to hold substantial uninsured US government deposits, was placed in receivership and remained closed for 11 months. Four defendants were convicted in relation to the case in June 2003.

At legislative elections in November 2003 the Covenant Party won nine of the 18 seats in the House of Representatives. The Republican Party secured seven seats, the Democratic Party one seat and an independent candidate one seat. The Covenant Party won three seats in the Senate, the Republican Party two and the Democratic Party one; three independent candidates were also elected.

Several instances of corruption in public office were reported in 2003; in April Senator Ricardo S. Atalig was found guilty of illegally employing relatives of another Senator, José M. de la Cruz (who was suspended from office following his own conviction in July). In August 2004 the chief financial officer of Tinian municipality, Romeo Atalig Diaz, was convicted in the first public corruption case lodged by the new anti-corruption unit of the Attorney-General's Office. However, the sentence imposed (fines totalling only US $2,800) was considered derisory by the local press.

At legislative elections held in November 2005 the Covenant Party won eight seats in the House of Representatives, the Republican Party seven seats, the Democratic Party two seats and an independent candidate one seat. The Covenant Party and the Republican Party each secured three seats in the Senate, the Democratic Party won two seats and one independent senator was elected. At the concurrent gubernatorial election Benigno Fitial of the Covenant Party and Timothy P. Villagomez, hitherto Vice-Speaker of the House, were narrowly elected Governor and Lieutenant-Governor, respectively, winning 28.0% of the valid votes cast. Independent Republican Heinz S. Hofschneider and David M. Apatang received 27.3%, while incumbent Governor Babauta and Lieutenant-Governor Diego Benavente garnered 26.7%.

In March 2006 Jack Abramoff, who was involved, along with other lobbyists and government officials, in transforming and impeding congressional action relating to the Northern Marianas (particularly with regard to the issue of the federal minimum wage—see above), was sentenced to five years and 10 months in prison on fraud and conspiracy charges, and ordered to pay restitution of more than US $21m. Abramoff and his law firm had reportedly received large sums of money from the Northern Marianas Government between 1995 and 2001.

Legislative elections were held in November 2007 to an enlarged House of Representatives. The Republican Party regained a majority in the House of Representatives, securing 12 of the 20 seats, while the Covenant Party won four seats, the Democratic Party one seat and independent candidates three seats. In the mid-term elections to the Senate, three incumbents (two independent candidates and one Covenant Party candidate) were re-elected to the three contested seats.

In August 2008 Lieutenant-Governor Timothy Villagomez was indicted for conspiracy, wire fraud and theft, along with Tony Guerrero, former executive director of the Commonwealth Utilities Corporation (CUC). Also indicted were the Lieutenant-Governor's sister, Joaquina V. Santos, and James Santos, his brother-in-law and the islands' Secretary of Commerce. Villagomez was alleged to have presided over a scheme to misappropriate federal funds by exaggerating the cost of financial transactions with the CUC. James Santos resigned from office shortly after the indictment. Villagomez resigned as Lieutenant-Governor following his conviction in April 2009; he was replaced by Eloy Inos, hitherto the Secretary of the Department of Finance.

At legislative elections on 7 November 2009 the Republican Party won nine seats in the House of Representatives, the Covenant Party seven seats and independent candidates four seats, while the Democratic Party failed to secure representation. Four Republican Party candidates and two independent candidates were elected to the six seats in the Senate that were contested. At the concurrent gubernatorial election Heinz Hofschneider of the Republican Party, along with his vice-gubernatorial candidate, Arnold Palacios, the Speaker of the House of Representatives, attracted the highest number of votes. However, owing to their failure to secure the stipulated 50% plus one of the votes, a second round of voting between Hofschneider and the second highest polling candidate, the incumbent Governor Fitial, was contested on 23 November, at which Fitial, along with running mate Eloy Inos, defeated Hofschneider and Palacios by 6,610 votes to 6,240. The terms of office of the Governor, Lieutenant-Governor and legislators elected in 2009 were exceptionally extended by an additional 12 months, so as to align future general elections with federal elections in the USA. A constitutional amendment stipulated that elections would henceforth be held only in even-numbered years, meaning that the next legislative elections would take place in November 2012, followed by the gubernatorial poll two years later.

Economic concerns were prevalent during 2010. Poor performances by the tourism and garment industries resulted in a significant decline in government revenues. As a result of the widening fiscal deficit, the Government was forced to implement a range of austerity measures, including reductions in the working hours of public sector workers, and, on a number of occasions during that year, employees were not paid on time. A constitutional amendment adopted in 2009 required a balanced budget to be approved by the Legislature before the start of each fiscal year, with failure to do so resulting in the suspension of all but 'essential' government services. Following the Legislature's failure to approve the national budget for 2010/11 by the stipulated deadline of 30 September 2010, Governor Fitial declared a state of emergency on 1 October, and most public services and the employment of some 1,400 'non-essential' government workers (as determined by Fitial) were temporarily suspended pending approval of the budget. The budget was finally signed into effect by Fitial on 9 October. Lieutenant-Governor Inos estimated that the 10-day impasse had saved the Government about US $750,000 in personnel costs.

Meanwhile, the Speaker, Froilan Tenorio, introduced a bill to the House of Representatives seeking to legalize the operation of casinos on Saipan. Casinos had been legalized on Rota and Tinian, in 2007 and 1989, respectively. Tenorio argued that legalizing casinos on Saipan was the Northern Marianas' last remaining hope to improve the declining economy. Despite the public having rejected proposals to legalize casinos on Saipan twice previously, in August 2010 the House of Representatives approved Tenorio's bill. The bill was rejected by the Senate in the following month, with opponents of the draft legislation noting that the casinos on Rota and Tinian had not proven to be significant revenue-generating projects. A new version of the bill was approved by the House of Representatives in November, but was again rejected by the Senate in March 2012.

A serious financial crisis in the Northern Marianas' public services led the Government to declare a state of emergency in its Retirement Fund, Commonwealth Utility Fund and Commonwealth Healthcare Corporation in mid-2012, amid mounting debts, resignations of senior staff and unpaid salaries, resulting partly from significant reductions in federal funding.

Ongoing economic concerns led to a protracted debate on the budget for 2012/13 during the second half of 2012. Proposals approved by the House of Representatives were amended by the Senate, the members of which feared that insufficient funds had been allocated to education and health provision. Following its rejection by the House of Representatives, and after further negotiations, a version of the amended budget was finally approved on 30 September, the day before the fiscal year commenced.

At legislative elections conducted on 6 November 2012 independent candidates took 12 of the 20 seats in the House of Representatives, while the Republican Party and the Covenant Party each won four seats. One Republican candidate and two independents were elected to the three seats in the Senate that were contested.

In September 2012, meanwhile, seven opposition members of the House of Representatives introduced a motion of impeachment against Governor Fitial. The action was significant in being the first time that such a motion had been proposed in any part of the US insular area. The motion contained 16 articles of impeachment, including allegations of irregularities in the awarding of government contracts, of neglect of duty in failing to make public appointments in a timely manner (critics complained that many senior posts, including that of a Supreme Court justice, remained vacant) and of improper conduct, most notably for procuring a massage from a federal inmate in 2010. Moreover, Fitial was accused of failing to dismiss the Attorney-General, Edward Buckingham, who had been charged with several offences in early 2012 and who had eventually resigned and fled the country in August in order to avoid prosecution. In mid-October the motion, which required the approval of 14 of the 20 members, was defeated by 10 votes to nine in the House of Representatives. However, at a subsequent vote on 11–12 February 2013 the motion, which had been expanded to include 18 articles of impeachment, was approved by 16 votes to four. Three days later the Senate approved the rules that would govern Fitial's forthcoming impeachment trial in the chamber, which was subsequently scheduled for early March. However, on 20 February Fitial submitted his resignation. Lieutenant-Governor Eloy Inos was sworn in as Governor on the same day, with Jude Hofschneider, hitherto President of the Senate, appointed to replace Inos.

Following his appointment, Governor Inos paid tribute to the people of the Northern Marianas for surviving 'a significant constitutional test', remarking that the management of the crisis was a sign of the islands' political maturity. He also acknowledged that the islands were confronted with substantial challenges, most notably their ongoing economic problems and continued reductions in federal funding.

Relations with the Federal Government

In early 2004 the Northern Marianas requested provision for the appointment of a non-voting delegate to the US Congress from the islands. (Unlike other US territories such as American Samoa and Guam, the Northern Marianas had continued to be represented in the federal legislature by the islands' Resident Representative in Washington, DC.) In May 2008 US President George W. Bush approved the Consolidated Natural Resources Act of 2008 (introduced by the Senate in March of that year and approved by both chambers in April), which created a non-voting delegate seat for the Northern Marianas in the US House of Representatives, as well as providing for the territory to be brought under federal immigration laws (subject to a transitional period scheduled to conclude on 31 December 2014). In November the congressional election was held to select the first delegate to represent the Northern Marianas in Washington. Gregorio Sablan, a former Democratic member of the islands' House of Representatives standing as an independent candidate, won the election with 2,474 votes, narrowly defeating his Republican rival, Pedro (Pete) Tenorio, who received 2,117 votes. Sablan rejoined the Democrats in February 2009 and was re-elected to a second two-year term in November 2010, receiving 4,896 votes and defeating three challengers, the most successful of whom was Joseph Camacho of the Covenant Party, who won 2,744 votes. In January 2011 the US House of Representatives voted to rescind the 'symbolic' voting rights of territorial delegates in the Committee of the Whole House on the State of the Union, a means by which the House was able to expedite consideration of certain legislation, particularly amendments. Sablan, together with the Delegates from American Samoa, Guam, the District of Columbia, Puerto Rico and the Virgin Islands, expressed staunch opposition to the revocation of the privilege, arguing that it 'excludes us from even symbolic representation in our Government'. Sablan was re-elected to serve a third term as Delegate to the US House of Representatives in November 2012, overwhelmingly defeating Republican Ignacia Demapan by 9,829 votes to 2,503.

Meanwhile, in September 2008 Governor Benigno Fitial filed legal proceedings against the US Government intended to prevent the implementation, scheduled for June 2009, of the so-called federalization process that would bring the Northern Marianas under federal

immigration legislation. Fitial submitted a request to the US District Court for a permanent injunction against the US Administration on the basis that federalization would violate aspects of the islands' right to self-government. Although this request ultimately failed, a resolution adopted by the islands' House of Representatives in February 2009 was successful in delaying the implementation of federalization until November. The transition to US immigration laws began as planned on 28 November.

In March 2011 a delegation of senators from the territory travelled to Washington, DC, to lobby the US Congress for changes to the islands' immigration regulations, particularly that foreign workers resident in the Northern Marianas for more than 10 years be granted the status of freely associated states' citizens. Discussions on the topic continued when a US congressional delegation made an official visit to Saipan in May. Draft legislation relating to immigration reform was introduced in the US Senate in April 2013. Governor Inos expressed the view that the legislation, which would allow foreigners who had worked legally in the territory since 2003 or earlier to apply for permanent residency, would be beneficial to the Northern Marianas' business community by facilitating the employment of foreign workers.

CONSTITUTION AND GOVERNMENT

Legislative authority is vested in the Northern Marianas Commonwealth Legislature, a bicameral body consisting of the Senate and the House of Representatives. There are nine senators, elected for four-year terms, and 20 members of the House of Representatives, elected for two-year terms. Executive authority is vested in the Governor, who is elected by popular vote for a four-year term. (Following the adoption of a constitutional amendment stipulating that elections should only be held in even-numbered years, the Governor and legislators elected in 2009 were exceptionally to serve an additional 12 months.) The Northern Marianas' first non-voting delegate to the US House of Representatives was elected in November 2008; previously, the territory had been represented in the federal legislature by a Resident Representative ('Washington Representative').

REGIONAL AND INTERNATIONAL CO-OPERATION

The Commonwealth of the Northern Mariana Islands is a member of the Pacific Community (see p. 422) and an associate member of the UN's Economic and Social Commission for Asia and the Pacific (ESCAP, see p. 31).

ECONOMIC AFFAIRS

The Commonwealth of the Northern Mariana Islands' gross national income (GNI) was estimated by the Bank of Hawaii to be US $696.3m. in 1999. GNI per head was estimated at $8,582. According to figures from the Secretariat of the Pacific Community, the population of the Northern Marianas decreased at an estimated average annual rate of 0.4% during 2005–12. The territory's gross domestic product (GDP) was estimated by the US Bureau of Economic Analysis to total $733m. in 2010, equivalent to $11,484 per head. Real GDP declined by 18.8% in 2009, but rose by 2.3% in 2010, according to chain linked methodologies. Total reported business gross revenue (BGR—a measure of total revenues generated by business transactions that provides an indicator of economic performance in the absence of GDP data, which the Northern Marianas Government does not publish) was recorded at $1,552m. in 2009.

Agriculture is concentrated in smallholdings, important crops being taro, sweet potatoes, coconuts, breadfruit, bananas and melons. Cattle-ranching is practised on Tinian. Vegetables, beef and pork are produced for export. There is little commercial fishing in the islands (the total catch was 267 metric tons in 2010), although there is a major transshipment facility at Tinian harbour. Agriculture (including forestry, fishing and mining) engaged 1.5% of the employed labour force, according to the census of 2000. Its commercial value as a sector is minimal, although FAO forecast that almost 23% of the total labour force would be engaged in the sector in mid-2013, largely at subsistence level. In 2002 the sector accounted for only 0.1% of BGR.

Industry (including manufacturing and construction) engaged 47.2% of the employed labour force in 2000. Manufacturing alone engaged 31.4% of payroll workers, according to a US economic survey of island areas conducted in 2007. The principal manufacturing activity has been the garment industry, which grew rapidly after its establishment in the mid-1980s to become the islands' leading export sector. Manufacturers benefited from US regulations that permitted duty-free and quota-free imports from the Commonwealth. Garment manufacturing accounted for 23.6% of BGR in 2002, and overall exports of garments were worth US $1,017m. in 2000. However, following the liberalization of trade regulations in January 2005, which allowed developing countries to export garments to the USA, more than a dozen garment factories closed down. By 2008 the value of exports of garments had declined to $145.8m. In February 2009 Saipan's two remaining garment factories were closed down, bringing an end to production on the islands. Other small-scale manufacturing activities include handicrafts and the processing of fish and copra. Construction is very closely related to the tourism industry and demand for additional hotel capacity.

Service industries dominate the economy, particularly tourism. In 2000 services (including utilities) engaged 51.3% of the employed labour force, and accounted for 29.2% of BGR. According to the 2007 US economic census of island areas, some 21% of payroll workers were employed in hotels and restaurants. Visitor numbers were estimated to have decreased from 370,091 in 2010 to 340,957 in 2011, before rising to 389,485 in 2012. Japan provided the majority (54%) of the islands' visitors in 2009. Other significant sources of tourists were the Republic of Korea (South Korea), Guam, the USA and the People's Republic of China. In 1995 a US company opened the territory's first casino on Tinian (gambling being prohibited on other islands). The Northern Marianas were expected to receive some US $12m. annually in revenue from this casino, and further large leisure industry developments were announced for Tinian in 2005. A second casino subsequently opened on Rota.

The Northern Marianas are dependent on imports, the value of which totalled US $267.2m. in 2000. The principal imports in that year were clothing (which accounted for 27.6% of the total), beverages, construction materials and automobiles and parts. In 1991 there was a trade deficit of $126.9m. Remittances from overseas workers and investments declined from $76.8m. in 2008 to $64.7m. in 2009.

The annual rate of inflation averaged 2.0% in 2000–09. Consumer prices increased by 2.3% in 2009. The rate of unemployment was estimated at 4.6% in 2003.

The Northern Mariana Islands have long benefited from their political association with the USA. However, the cessation of garment manufacturing (see above) was estimated to have resulted in a 36% decline in employment during 2004–08. Tourism thus became the main source of income on the islands. In mid-2011 it was reported that 2,800 tourists from Japan (the principal source of visitors to the island) and 1,500 from South Korea had cancelled their holiday bookings in response to the tsunami disaster in Japan two months previously, amid continuing fears of wider releases of radiation from a damaged nuclear power plant. However, the inauguration of new flights from the Shanghai and Guangzhou in the People's Republic of China in May 2011 provided a boost to the tourism industry. Visitor numbers from Russia and China were reported to have increased during 2012, while arrivals from both Japan and the USA continued to decline. The islands' economy was estimated to have contracted by an average of 4.2% per year between 2002 and 2007. Following a decline of 18.8% in 2009, real GDP increased by 2.3% in 2010, according to chain linked figures released by the US Bureau of Economic Analysis. In an attempt to reduce government expenditure, the House of Representatives approved a bill reducing the working hours of public sector employees in 2010. Further reductions in budgetary spending were implemented in 2011/12 and 2012/13, largely as a result of federal fiscal retrenchment. A decline in the population to an estimated 51,395 at mid-2012 (from 69,221 in April 2000) had serious implications for the economy, as a significant proportion of the annual federal grants received by the territory was based on the size of its population. It was hoped that, if approved, the draft legislation on immigration reform introduced in the US Senate in April 2013 (see Relations with the Federal Government) would help to address the long-standing problem of labour shortages for businesses in the territory.

PUBLIC HOLIDAYS

2014: 8 January (Commonwealth Day), 20 January (Martin Luther King Day), 17 February (Presidents' Day), 24 March (Covenant Day), 18 April (Good Friday), 26 May (Memorial Day), 4 July (Liberation Day), 1 September (Labor Day), 13 October (Commonwealth Cultural Day), 4 November (Citizenship Day), 11 November (Veterans' Day), 27 November (Thanksgiving Day), 8 December (Constitution Day), 25 December (Christmas Day).

Statistical Survey

Source: (unless otherwise stated): Department of Commerce, Central Statistics Division, POB 10007, Saipan, MP 96950; tel. 664-3000; fax 664-3001; internet www.commerce.gov.mp.

AREA AND POPULATION

Area: 457 sq km (176.5 sq miles). *By Island:* Saipan 120 sq km; Tinian 102 sq km; Rota 85 sq km; Pagan 48 sq km; Anatahan 32 sq km; Agrihan 30 sq km; Alamagan 11 sq km; Asuncion 7 sq km; Aguijan (Goat Is) 7 sq km; Sarigan 5 sq km; Guguan 4 sq km; Farallon de Pajaros 3 sq km; Maug 2 sq km; Farallon de Medinilla 1 sq km.

Population: 69,221 at census of 1 April 2000; 53,883 at census of 1 April 2010. *Mid-2013* (Secretariat of the Pacific Community estimate): 64,947 (Source: Pacific Regional Information System). *By Island* (2010 census): Saipan 48,220; Rota 2,527; Tinian (with Aguijan) 3,136; Northern Islands 0.

Density (at mid-2013): 142.1 per sq km.

Population by Age and Sex (Secretariat of the Pacific Community estimates at mid-2013): *0–14:* 16,852 (males 8,796, females 8,056); *15–64:* 45,357 (males 22,835, females 22,522); *65 and over:* 2,738 (males 1,266, females 1,472); *Total* 64,947 (males 32,897, females 32,050) (Source: Pacific Regional Information System).

Ethnic Groups (2000 census): Filipino 18,141; Chinese 15,311; Chamorro 14,749; part-Chamorro 4,383; Total (incl. others) 69,221.

Principal Towns (population at 2000 census): San Antonio 4,741; Garapan (capital) 3,588; Koblerville 3,543; San Vincente 3,494; Tanapag 3,318; Chalan Kanoa 3,108; Kagman 3,026. Source: Thomas Brinkhoff, *City Population* (internet www.citypopulation.de).

Births and Deaths (2002): Registered live births 1,289 (birth rate 17.4 per 1,000); Registered deaths 164 (death rate 2.2 per 1,000). *2009:* Live births 1,110; Deaths 176 (Source: UN, *Population and Vital Statistics Report*).

Employment (2000 census, persons aged 16 years and over): Agriculture, forestry, fisheries and mining 623; Manufacturing 17,398; Construction 2,785; Transport, communication and utilities 1,449; Trade, restaurants and hotels 9,570; Financing, insurance and real estate 1,013; Community, social and personal services 9,915; *Total employed* 42,753 (males 19,485, females 23,268); Unemployed 1,712 (males 888, females 824); *Total labour force* 44,465 (males 20,373, females 24,092). *2007* (US economic census, paid employment only, excl. public administration): Total employed 22,622 (Manufacturing 7,094; Wholesale and retail 3,642; Hotels and restaurants 4,772). *Mid-2013:* Agriculture, etc. 7,000; Total labour force 31,000 (Source: FAO).

HEALTH AND WELFARE

Key Indicators

Access to Water (% of persons, 2008): 98.

Access to Sanitation (% of persons, 2006): 94.

For sources and definitions, see explanatory note on p. vi.

AGRICULTURE, ETC.

Principal Crops (crops harvested for sale, '000 lb, 2007): Cassava 30.3; Taro 221.6; Yams 67.7; Sweet potatoes 352.3; Beans, yard long 40.2; Chinese cabbage 38.2; Cucumbers 93.8; Aubergines (Eggplant) 47.3; Pumpkins and squash 68.0; Watermelons 150.2; Bananas 146.9; Breadfruits 4.8; Papayas 50.7; Betel nuts 88.3; Coconuts 42.9; Ginger 1.5.

Livestock (2007): Cattle 1,395; Pigs 1,483; Goats 276; Poultry birds 12,390.

Livestock Products (sales of dozens, 2007): Hen eggs 195,510.

Fishing (metric tons, live weight, 2010): Total catch 267 (Parrotfishes 10; Skipjack tuna 147; Yellowfin tuna 15; Common dolphinfish 10; Scads 11; Other marine fishes 28). Source: FAO.

FINANCE

Currency and Exchange Rates: United States currency is used: 100 cents = 1 United States dollar (US $). *Sterling and Euro Equivalents* (31 December 2012): £1 sterling = US $1.578; €1 = US $1.319; US $100 = £63.37 = €75.79.

Federal Direct Expenditures (US $ million, year ending September 2010): Retirement and disability 33; Total (incl. others) 250 (Source: US Census Bureau, *Consolidated Federal Funds Report*).

Budget (US $ million, 2009): General fund revenue 154.7 (Taxes 112.6, Fees, charges and other revenues 30.0, Net transfers from other funds 12.1); Total expenditure 168.1.

Cost of Living (Consumer Price Index for Saipan; quarterly averages; base: 2000 = 100): All items 111.9 in 2007; 117.2 in 2008; 119.9 in 2009. Source: ILO.

Gross Domestic Product (US $ million in current prices): 851 in 2008; 725 in 2009; 733 in 2010 (Source: Bureau of Economic Analysis, US Department of Commerce).

Expenditure on the Gross Domestic Product (US $ million in current prices, 2010): Government consumption expenditure and gross investment 370; Personal consumption expenditure 531; Private fixed investment 26; *Total domestic expenditure* 927; Exports of goods and services 242; *Less* Imports of goods and services 436; *GDP in purchasers' values* 733 (Source: Bureau of Economic Analysis, US Department of Commerce).

EXTERNAL TRADE

Principal Commodities (US $ million): *Imports* (1997): Beverages 12.8; Tobacco 5.4; Automobiles (incl. parts) 42.1; Clothing 309.2; Total (incl. others) 836.2. *Exports* (2000): Total 1,000. *Value of Garment Exports* (US $ million): 486.5 in 2006; 307.6 in 2007; 145.8 in 2008.

Principal Trading Partners (US $ million, 1997): *Imports*: Guam 298.0; Hong Kong 200.5; Japan 118.3; Korea, Republic 80.6; USA 63.3; Total (incl. others) 836.2.

Sources: partly UN, *Statistical Yearbook for Asia and the Pacific* and *Statistical Yearbook*.

TRANSPORT

Road Traffic (registered motor vehicles, 2001): 17,900.

Shipping: *Registered Fleet* (2001): 1,029 vessels (791 fishing vessels); *Traffic* ('000 short tons, 1997): Goods loaded 184.1; Goods unloaded 425.9.

Civil Aviation (Saipan Int. Airport, year ending September 1999): 23,853 aircraft landings; 562,364 boarding passengers. *2010:* Passenger arrivals 422,542, Passenger departures 429,401. Source: Commonwealth Ports Authority.

TOURISM

Visitor Arrivals: 353,956 in 2009; 370,091 in 2010 (estimate); 340,957 in 2011 (estimate).

Visitor Arrivals by Country (2009): China, People's Republic (incl. Hong Kong) 29,814; Japan 191,111; Korea, Republic 89,132; USA (incl. Guam) 29,259; Total (incl. others) 353,956.

Tourism Receipts (US $ million): 407 in 1999; 430 in 2000; 225 in 2002 (approximate figure). Source: Bank of Hawaii, *Commonwealth of the Northern Mariana Islands Economic Report* (October 2003).

COMMUNICATIONS MEDIA

Radio Receivers (households with access, census of 2000): 10,684.

Television Receivers (estimate, 1995): 15,460 in use.

Telephones (main lines in use, 2010): 25,500.

Mobile Cellular Telephones (2004): 20,500 subscribers (Source: International Telecommunication Union).

EDUCATION

Pre-primary (2002/03, state schools, Headstart programme): 12 schools; 98 teachers; 606 pupils.

Primary (2002/03, state schools): 12 schools; 283 teachers; 5,849 students.

Secondary (2002/03, state schools): 9 schools; 248 teachers; 4,705 students.

Higher (2000/01): 1 college; 1,641 students (full- and part-time students).

Private Schools (2002/03): 18 schools; 186 teachers; 2,326 students.

Directory

The Government

(May 2013)

Governor: ELOY S. INOS (took office 20 Feb. 2013).

Lieutenant-Governor: JUDE U. HOFSCHNEIDER (took office 20 Feb. 2013).

DEPARTMENT SECRETARIES

Secretary of the Department of Finance: LARRISA LARSON.

Secretary of the Department of Community and Cultural Affairs: MELVIN FAISAO.

Secretary of the Department of Labor: GIL M. SAN NICOLAS.

Secretary of the Department of Lands and Natural Resources: ARNOLD I. PALACIOS.

Secretary of the Department of Public Lands: PEDRO A. TENORIO (acting).

Secretary of the Department of Public Works: MARTIN C. SABLAN (acting).

Secretary of the Department of Commerce: SIXTO K. IGISOMAR.

Commissioner of the Department of Public Safety: JAMES C. DELEON GUERRERO.

Commissioner of the Department of Corrections: RAMON C. MAFNAS.

GOVERNMENT OFFICES

Office of the Governor: Caller Box 10007, Capitol Hill, Saipan, MP 96950; tel. 664-2200; fax 664-2211; internet gov.mp.

Department of the Interior, Office of Insular Affairs (OIA): Field Office of the OIA, Dept of the Interior, POB 502622, Saipan, MP 96950; tel. 234-8861; fax 234-8814; e-mail jeff.schorr@pticom.com; internet http://www.doi.gov/oia/islands/cnmi.cfm; OIA representation in the Commonwealth; Field Representative JEFFREY SCHORR.

Department of Commerce: Caller Box 10007, Capitol Hill, Saipan, MP 96950; tel. 664-3000; fax 664-3067; e-mail info@commerce.gov.mp; internet www.commerce.gov.mp.

Department of Community and Cultural Affairs: 1347 Ascension Court, Capitol Hill, Saipan, MP 96950; tel. 664-2576; fax 664-2570; e-mail faisaom_dcca.deputysecretary@pticom.com.

Department of Corrections: Saipan.

Department of Finance: POB 5234, Capitol Hill, Saipan, MP 96950; tel. 664-1100; fax 664-1115; e-mail finance.edp@cnmiarra.net; internet www.cnmidof.net.

Department of Labor: POB 10007, Saipan, MP 96950; tel. 236-0900; fax 236-0991; e-mail webmaster@marianaslabor.net; internet www.marianaslabor.net.

Department of Lands and Natural Resources: POB 10007, Saipan, MP 96950; tel. 322-9830; fax 322-2633.

Department of Public Health: POB 500409 CK, 1 Hospital Way, Saipan, MP 96950; tel. 234-8950; fax 236-8756; e-mail joseph.kevin@dph.gov.mp; internet www.dph.gov.mp.

Department of Public Lands: POB 500380, Capitol Hill, Saipan, MP 96950; tel. 234-3751; fax 234-3755; e-mail dpl@dpl.gov.mp; internet www.dpl.gov.mp.

Department of Public Safety: Jose M. Sablan Bldg, POB 500791, Susupe, Saipan, MP 96950; tel. 664-9022; fax 664-9027; internet www.dps.gov.mp.

Department of Public Works: Caller Box 10007, Capitol Hill, Saipan, MP 96950; tel. 235-5827; fax 235-6346; e-mail dpwadmin@pticom.com; internet www.dpw.gov.mp.

Legislature

NORTHERN MARIANAS COMMONWEALTH LEGISLATURE

Legislative authority is vested in the Northern Marianas Commonwealth Legislature, a bicameral body consisting of the Senate and the House of Representatives. There are nine senators, elected for four-year terms, and 20 members of the House of Representatives, elected for two-year terms. The most recent legislative election was held on 6 November 2012. The Republican Party won four seats in the House of Representatives, the Covenant Party also won four seats and independent candidates twelve seats. Meanwhile, one Republican Party candidate and two independent candidates were elected to the three Senate seats that were contested.

Senate President: RALPH TORRES.

Speaker of the House: JOSEPH P. DELEON GUERRERO.

Commonwealth Legislature: CNMI Legislative Bureau, POB 500586, Capitol Hill, Saipan, MP 96950; tel. 664-8954; fax 322-6840; e-mail semanp@cnmileg.gov.mp; internet www.cnmileg.gov.mp.

CONGRESS

Since 2008 the Northern Mariana Islands have been able to elect a non-voting Delegate to the US House of Representatives. Gregorio K. C. Sablan won the first election for this position on 4 November 2008, standing as an independent, but became a Democrat in February 2009. He was re-elected to the post in November 2010 and again on 6 November 2012.

Delegate of the Northern Mariana Islands: GREGORIO K. C. SABLAN, POB 504879 Saipan, MP 96950; tel. 323-2647; fax 323-2649; e-mail kilili@mail.house.gov; internet sablan.house.gov.

Election Commission

Commonwealth Election Commission: POB 500470, Saipan, MP 96950-0470; tel. 664-8683; fax 664-8689; e-mail info@votecnmi.gov.mp; internet www.votecnmi.gov.mp; Chair. FRANCES SABLAN; Exec. Dir ROBERT A. GUERRERO.

Political Organizations

Covenant Party: c/o Commonwealth Legislature, Capitol Hill, Saipan, MP 96950; Chair. GREGORIO 'KACHUMA' CAMACHO.

Democratic Party of the Commonwealth of the Northern Mariana Islands, Inc: Saipan, MP 96950; tel. 234-7497; fax 233-0641; Pres. Dr CARLOS S. CAMACHO; Chair. LORENZO CABRERA.

Republican Party of the Northern Marianas: POB 500777, Saipan, MP 96950; tel. and fax 233-1288; e-mail dpwpio@vzpacifica.net; State Chair. DAVID ATTAO; Exec. Dir (vacant).

Judicial System

The judicial system in the Commonwealth of the Northern Mariana Islands (CNMI) consists of the Superior Court, the Commonwealth Supreme Court (which considers appeals from the Superior Court) and the Federal District Court. Under the Covenant, federal law applies in the Commonwealth, with some exceptions: for example, the CNMI is not part of the US Customs Territory, and it may enact its own taxation laws.

Commonwealth Supreme Court: POB 502165, Saipan, MP 96950; Chief Justice of the Commonwealth Supreme Court ALEXANDRO C. CASTRO.

Superior Court: POB 500307, Saipan, MP 96950; Presiding Judge ROBERT C. NARAJA.

Attorney-General: JOEY PATRICK SAN NICOLAS.

US Attorney: ALICIA GARRIDO LIMTIACO.

Public Defender: DOUGLAS HARTIG.

Religion

The population is predominantly Christian, mainly Roman Catholic. There are small communities of Episcopalians (Anglicans—under the jurisdiction of the Bishop of Hawaii, in the USA) and Protestants.

CHRISTIANITY

The Roman Catholic Church

The Northern Mariana Islands comprise the single diocese of Chalan Kanoa, suffragan to the archdiocese of Agaña (Guam). The Bishop participates in the Catholic Bishops' Conference of the Pacific, based in Suva, Fiji. At 31 December 2007 there were 43,000 adherents, including temporary residents, in the Northern Mariana Islands.

Bishop of Chalan Kanoa: (vacant), Bishop's House, Chalan Kanoa, POB 500745, Saipan, MP 96950; tel. 234-3000; fax 235-3002; e-mail diocese@pticom.com; internet www.dioceseofchalankanoa.com.

The Press

The weekly *Focus on the Commonwealth* is published in Guam, but distributed solely in the Northern Mariana Islands.

Marianas Observer: POB 502119, Saipan, MP 96950; tel. 233-3955; fax 233-7040; weekly; Publr JOHN VABLAN; Man. Editor ZALDY DANDAN; circ. 2,000.

Marianas Review: POB 501074, Saipan, MP 96950; tel. and fax 234-7160; f. 1979 as *The Commonwealth Examiner*; weekly; English and Chamorro; independent; Publr LUIS BENAVENTE; Editor RUTH L. TIGHE; circ. 1,700.

Marianas Variety: POB 6338, Tamuning 96931; tel. 234-9272; fax 234-9271; e-mail editor@mvariety.com; internet www.mvariety.com; Mon.–Fri.; English and Chamorro; independent; f. 1972; Publr ABED E. YOUNIS; Editor ZALDY DANDAN; circ. 8,000.

North Star: Chalan Kanoa, POB 500745, Saipan, MP 96950; tel. 234-3000; fax 235-3002; e-mail nstar@pticom.com; internet www.dioceseofchalankanoa.com; weekly; English and Chamorro; Roman Catholic; f. 1976; Publr Bishop TOMAS A. CAMACHO; Man. Editor Fr CELSO MAGBANUA, Jr; circ. 3,000.

Pacific Daily News (Saipan bureau): POB 500822, Saipan, MP 96950; tel. 234-6423; fax 234-5986; Publr LEE WEBBER; circ. 5,000.

Pacific Star: POB 505815 CHRB, Saipan, MP 96950; tel. 288-0746; fax 288-0747; weekly; Operational Man. NICK LEGASPI; circ. 3,000.

Pacifica: POB 502143, Saipan, MP 96950; monthly; Editor MIKE MALONE.

Saipan Tribune: CIC Centre, 2nd Floor, Beach Rd, Saipan; tel. 235-6397; fax 235-3740; e-mail editor.tribune@saipan.com; internet www.saipantribune.com; 2 a week; Publr LYNN KNIGHT; Editor JAYVEE L. VALLEJERA; circ. 3,500.

Broadcasting and Communications

TELECOMMUNICATIONS

Docomo Pacific Inc: Gualo Rai Commercial Center, Main Bldg, Gualo Rai, Middle Rd, Saipan; tel. 483-2273; fax 235-7640; e-mail service@guamcell.net; internet docomopacific.com/saipan; fmrly Saipan Cellular & Paging; name changed to SAIPANCELL Communications in 1992; present name adopted 2008; mobile cellular services; Pres. JAY SHEDD.

IT & E Overseas Inc: POB 500306 CK, Saipan, MP 96950; tel. 682-4483; fax 682-4555; internet www.pticom.com; fmrly Pacific Telecom Inc; name changed as above in 2009; mobile cellular and internet services; Pres. and CEO RICKY DELGADO.

BROADCASTING

Radio

Far East Broadcasting Co, Inc: POB 500209, Saipan, MP 96950; tel. 322-9088; fax 322-3060; e-mail info@febcintl.org; internet www.febcintl.org; f. 1946; non-commercial, religious broadcasts; Chair. Dr DOUGLAS PENNOYER; Field Dir ROBERT L. SPRINGER.

Inter-Island Communications, Inc: POB 500914, Saipan, MP 96950; tel. 234-7239; fax 234-0447; f. 1984; commercial; station KCNM-AM, or KZMI-FM in stereo; Gen. Man. HANS W. MICKELSON; Programme Dir KEN WARNICK; CEO ANGEL OCAMPO.

KRNM: POB 501250, Saipan, MP 96950; tel. 234-5498; fax 235-0915; f. 1994; operated by Marianas Educational Media Services Inc; educational programmes; Gen. Man. CARL POGUE.

Magic 100.3: Magic Studio, 1st Floor, Naru Bldg, Susupe; tel. 234-5929; fax 234-2262; e-mail Kwaw100.3@Magic100Radio.com; internet www.magic100radio.com; contemporary music; Man. Dir LEO JUN GANACIAS.

Sorensen Media Group: POB 10000, Saipan, MP 96950; tel. 235-7996; fax 235-7998; e-mail cdancoe@spbguam.com; based in Guam; 2 radio stations: Power 99 and The KAT 97.9; 1 free television service: ABC 7; Gen. Man. CURTIS DANCOE.

Television

KMCV-TV: POB 501298, Saipan, MP 96950; tel. 235-6365; fax 235-0965; f. 1992; 52-channel commercial station, with 8 pay channels, broadcasting 24 hours a day; US programmes and local and international news; 5,650 subscribers; Gen. Man. WAYNE GAMBLIN.

Marianas CableVision: POB 501298, Saipan, MP 96950; tel. 235-4628; fax 235-0965; e-mail mcv.service@saipan.com; internet www.mcvcnmi.com; 55-channel cable service provider, broadcasting US and Pacific Rim programmes; Pres. JOHN CRUIKSHANK; Gen. Man. MARK BIRMINGHAM.

Finance

BANKING

Bank of Guam (USA): POB 500678, Saipan, MP 96950; tel. 236-2700; fax 233-5003; internet www.bankofguam.com; Gen. Man. LARRY PHILIP; 5 brs.

Bank of Hawaii: Bank of Hawaii Bldg, Suite 100, Marina Heights Business Park, Chalan Pale Arnold Rd, Saipan, MP 96950; tel. 237-2900; fax 322-4210; internet www.boh.com; Man. JOHN SHEATHER; 2 brs.

Bank of Saipan: POB 500690, Saipan, MP 96950; tel. 235-6260; fax 235-6294; e-mail bankofsaipan@gtepacifica.net; internet www.bankofsaipan.com; dep. US $23m. (Dec. 2004); Pres. JON BARGFREDE; 4 brs.

City Trust Bank: Gualo Rai, POB 501867, Saipan, MP 96950; tel. 235-7701; fax 234-8664; e-mail citytrustbank@ctbsaipan.com; Asst Vice-Pres. and Acting Man. MARIA LOURDES JOHNSON.

First Hawaiian Bank: Gualo Rai Commercial Center, Middle Rd, Gualo Rai, Saipan 96950; tel. 235-3090; fax 236-8936; internet www.fhb.com; Area Man. JUAN LIZAMA.

Guam Savings and Loan Bank: POB 503201, Saipan, MP 96950; tel. 233-2265; fax 233-2227; Gen. Man. GLEN PEREZ.

INSURANCE

Allied Insurance/Takagi and Associates, Inc: PPP 602, Box 10000, Saipan, MP 96950; tel. 233-2554; fax 670-2553; Gen. Man. PETER SIBLY.

Aon Insurance: Aon Insurance Micronesia (Saipan) Inc, POB 502177, Saipan, MP 96950; tel. 234-2811; fax 234-5462; e-mail rod.rankin@aon.com.au; internet www.aon.com/saipan; Communications Officer RODNEY RANKIN.

Associated Insurance Underwriters of the Pacific, Inc: POB 501369, Saipan, MP 96950; tel. 234-7222; fax 234-5367; e-mail aiup@pticom.com; Gen. Man. MAGGIE GEORGE.

Calvo's Insurance Underwriters, Inc: Oleai Centre Bldg, Saipan, MP 96950; tel. 234-5690; fax 234-5693; e-mail ebuenaventura@calvos.com; internet www.calvosinsurance.com; f. 1930; affiliated to Chartis; Br. Man. ELI C. BUENAVENTURA.

Century Insurance (Tan Holdings Corpn): Century Insurance PMB 193, POB 10000, Saipan, MP 96950; tel. 234-0609; fax 234-1845; e-mail nel_matanguihan@cicspn.com; internet www.cicspn.com; Gen. Man. NEL MATANGUIHAN.

General Accident Insurance Asia Ltd (Microl Insurance): POB 502177, Saipan, MP 96950; tel. 234-2811; fax 234-5462; Man. Dir MICHAEL W. GOURLAY.

Marianas Insurance Co Ltd: POB 502505, Saipan, MP 96950-2505; tel. 234-5091; fax 234-5093; e-mail admin@marianasinsurance.com; internet www.marianasinsurance.com; f. 1989; Gen. Man. ROSALIA S. CABRERA.

Midland Insurance Underwriters, Inc: PMB 219, POB 10000, Capitol Hill, Saipan, MP 96950; tel. 235-3598.

Moylan's Insurance Underwriters (Int.), Inc: POB 500658, Saipan, MP 96950; tel. 234-6571; fax 234-8641; e-mail saipan@moylans.net; internet www.moylansinsurance.com; Branch Man. CATHY TENORIO.

Pacifica Insurance Underwriters Inc: POB 500168, Saipan, MP 96950; tel. 234-6267; fax 234-5880; e-mail piui@pacificains.com; internet www.pacificains.com; f. 1972; affiliated to Tokio Marine & Nichido Fire Insurance Co, Japan; Pres. NORMAN T. TENORIO.

Primerica Financial Services: POB 500964, Saipan, MP 96950; tel. 235-2912; fax 235-7910; Gen. Man. JOHN SABLAN.

Royal Crown Insurance: Royal Crown Bldg, Beach Road, Chalan LauLau, POB 10001, Saipan, MP 96950; tel. 234-2256; fax 234-2258.

StayWell Saipan, Inc: POB 502050, Saipan, MP 96950-2050; tel. 323-4260; fax 323-4263; e-mail saipan.office@staywellguam.com; internet www.staywellguam.com; Branch Man. ERIC PLINSKE.

Trade and Industry

GOVERNMENT AGENCY

Commonwealth Development Authority: POB 502149, Wakins Bldg, Gualo Rai, Saipan, MP 96950; tel. 234-6245; fax 235-7147; e-mail administration@cda.gov.mp; internet www.cda.gov.mp; govt lending institution; funds capital improvement projects and private enterprises; offers tax incentives to qualified investors; Chair. PEDRO I. ITIBUS; Exec. Dir MANUEL A. SABLAN.

CHAMBER OF COMMERCE

Saipan Chamber of Commerce: Chalan Kanoa, POB 500806 CK, Saipan, MP 96950; tel. 233-7150; fax 233-7151; e-mail saipanchamber@saipan.com; internet www.saipanchamber.com; Pres. DOUGLAS BRENNAN; Exec. Dir KYLE CALABRESE.

EMPLOYERS' ASSOCIATIONS

Association of Commonwealth Teachers (ACT): POB 5071, Saipan, MP 96950; tel. and fax 256-7567; e-mail cnmiteachers@netscape.net; supports the teaching profession and aims to improve education in state schools.

Saipan Garment Manufacturers' Association (SGMA): POB 10001, Saipan, MP 96950; tel. 235-7699; fax 235-7899; e-mail sgmaemy@vzpacifica.net; Exec. Dir (vacant).

UTILITIES

Commonwealth Utilities Corporation (CUC): POB 501220, Saipan, MP 96950; tel. 235-7025; fax 235-6145; e-mail cucedp@gtepacifica.net; internet www.cucgov.org; Exec. Dir ABE UTU MALAE.

TRADE UNION AND CO-OPERATIVES

International Brotherhood of Electrical Workers: c/o Micronesian Telecommunications Corpn, Saipan, MP 96950; local branch of US trade union based in Washington, DC.

The Mariana Islands Co-operative Association, and the Rota Producers and Tinian Producers Associations operate on the islands.

Transport

RAILWAYS

There have been no railways operating in the islands since the Japanese sugar industry railway, on Saipan, ceased operations in the Second World War.

ROADS

In 1991 there were 494 km (307 miles) of roads on the islands, 320 km (199 miles) of which are on Saipan. First grade roads constitute 135 km (84 miles) of the total, 99 km (62 miles) being on Saipan. There is no public transport, apart from a school bus system.

SHIPPING

The main harbour of the Northern Mariana Islands is the Port of Saipan, which underwent extensive renovation in the mid-1990s. There are also two major harbours on Rota and one on Tinian. Several shipping lines link Saipan, direct or via Guam, with ports in Japan, Asia, the Philippines, the USA and other territories in the Pacific.

Commonwealth Ports Authority (CPA): POB 501055, Saipan, MP 96950; tel. 237-6500; fax 234-5962; e-mail cpa.admin@pticom.com; internet www.cpa.gov.mp; Exec. Dir EDWARD DELEON GUERRERO.

Mariana Express Lines: POB 501937, CTS Bldg, Saipan, MP 96950; tel. 322-1690; fax 323-6355; e-mail desmond_aw@mariana-express.com; internet www.mariana-express.com; services between Saipan, Guam, Japan and Hong Kong; Man. DESMOND AW.

Saipan Shipping Co Inc (Saiship): Saiship Bldg, Charlie Dock, POB 500008, Saipan, MP 96950; tel. 322-9706; fax 322-3183; e-mail darlene_cabrera@saipanshipping.com; f. 1956; weekly service between Guam and Saipan, bi-weekly to Tinian and Rota; monthly services to Japan and Micronesia; Gen. Man. DARLENE CABRERA.

Westpac Freight: POB 2048, Puerto Rico, Saipan, MP 96950; tel. 322-8798; fax 322-5536; e-mail westpac@gtepacifica.net; services between Saipan, Guam and the USA; Man. MICHIE CAMACHO.

CIVIL AVIATION

Air services are centred on the main international airport, Isley Field, on Saipan. There are also airports on Rota and Tinian.

Continental Micronesia: POB 508778, A.B. Won Pat International Airport, Tamuning, GU 96911, Guam; tel. 647-6595; fax 649-6588; internet www.continental.com; f. 1968, as Air Micronesia, by Continental Airlines (USA), operations merged in 2010; name changed 1992; owned by United Continental Holdings; hub operations in Saipan and Guam; services throughout the region and to destinations in the Far East and mainland USA.

Freedom Air: POB 500239 CK, Saipan, MP 96950; tel. 234-8328; e-mail freedom@ite.net; internet www.freedomairguam.com; scheduled internal flights.

Tourism

Tourism is one of the most important industries in the Northern Mariana Islands, earning some US $225m. in 2002. In that year there were 4,313 hotel rooms. Most of the islands' hotels are Japanese-owned, and in 2009 more than 50% of tourists came from Japan. The Republic of Korea, the People's Republic of China and the USA are also important sources of tourists. A decline in visitors to the Northern Mariana Islands to 340,957 was reported in 2011; however, arrivals were estimated to have increased to 389,485 in 2012. The islands of Asuncion, Guguan, Maug, Managaha, Sarigan and Uracas (Farallon de Pajaros) are maintained as uninhabited reserves. Visitors are mainly attracted by the white, sandy beaches and the excellent diving conditions. There is also interest in the *Latte* or *Taga* stones (mainly on Tinian), pillars carved from the rock by the ancient Chamorros, and relics from the Second World War.

Hotel Association of the Northern Mariana Islands: POB 501983 CHRB, Saipan, MP 96950; tel. 233-6964; fax 233-1424; e-mail lynn_knight@tanholdings.com; internet www.saipanhotels.org; f. 1983; Chair. NICK NISHIKAWA.

Marianas Visitors Authority (MVA): POB 500861 CK, Saipan, MP 96950; tel. 664-3200; fax 664-3237; e-mail mva@mymarianas.com; internet www.mymarianas.com; f. 1976; responsible for the promotion and devt of tourism in the Northern Mariana Islands; Chair. MARIAN ALDAN-PIERCE; Man. Dir PERRY TENORIO.

Defence

The USA is responsible for the defence of the Northern Mariana Islands. The US Pacific Command is based in Hawaii (USA).

Education

School attendance is compulsory from six to 16 years of age. In 2002/03 there were 12 state primary schools, with a total of 5,849 pupils enrolled, and there were nine state secondary schools, with a total enrolment of 4,705 pupils. There was a total of 18 private schools, with a total enrolment of 2,326 pupils. There was one college of further education in 2000/01, with 1,641 students. Budgetary expenditure on education totalled US $49.6m. in 2000, equivalent to 22.0% of total government expenditure.

PUERTO RICO

Introductory Survey

LOCATION, CLIMATE, LANGUAGE, RELIGION, FLAG, CAPITAL

The Commonwealth of Puerto Rico comprises the main island of Puerto Rico, together with the small offshore islands of Vieques and Culebra and numerous smaller islets, lying about 80 km (50 miles) east of Hispaniola (Haiti and the Dominican Republic) in the Caribbean Sea. The climate is maritime-tropical, with an average annual temperature of 24°C (75°F) and a normal range between 17°C (63°F) and 36°C (97°F). The official languages are Spanish and English. Christianity is the dominant religion, and about 73% of the population are Roman Catholics. The flag (proportions 3 by 5) has five alternating red and white horizontal stripes of equal width, with a blue triangle, in the centre of which is a five-pointed white star, at the hoist. The capital is San Juan.

CONTEMPORARY POLITICAL HISTORY

Historical Context

Puerto Rico, also known as Borinquen (after the original Arawak Indian name Boriquen), was ruled by Spain from 1509 until 1898, when it was ceded to the USA at the conclusion of the Spanish–American War, and administered as an Unincorporated Territory of the USA. In 1917 Puerto Ricans were granted US citizenship, and in 1947 Puerto Rico obtained the right to elect its own Governor. A Constitution, promulgated in 1952, assigned Puerto Rico the status of a self-governing Commonwealth, or 'estado libre asociado', in its relation to the USA.

The Partido Popular Democrático (PPD) held a majority in both chambers of the legislature from 1944 until 1968, when, following a split within the party, the Partido Nuevo Progresista (PNP), an advocate of statehood, won the governorship and legislative control. This followed a plebiscite in 1967, when 61% of voters had ratified a continuation of Commonwealth status in preference to independence (1%) or incorporation as a state of the USA (39%). In the 1972 election the PPD, under the leadership of Rafael Hernández Colón, regained the governorship and legislative control from the PNP, only to lose them again in 1976. The victorious PNP was led by Carlos Romero Barceló, who became Governor.

Domestic Political Affairs

Romero Barceló, who had promised a referendum on statehood if re-elected for a further term in 1980, abandoned this plan following the election, in which he narrowly defeated former Governor Hernández Colón. The PPD, however, gained control of the legislature. The 1984 gubernatorial election was won by Hernández Colón by only 50,000 votes, with the PPD retaining substantial majorities in both legislative chambers. In 1985 Romero Barceló was succeeded as leader of the PNP by Baltasar Corrada del Río.

A gubernatorial election, held in November 1988, resulted in the re-election of Hernández Colón. Electoral participation was unusually high, at almost 90%.

The question of eventual independence for Puerto Rico has been a politically sensitive issue for over 50 years. With the PPD supporting the continuation and enhancement of Commonwealth status and the PNP advocating Puerto Rico's inclusion as a state of the USA, mainstream party encouragement of independence aims has come mainly from the Partido Independentista Puertorriqueño (PIP) and other left-wing groups. There are two small, and occasionally violent, terrorist factions, the Ejército Popular Boricua (Los Macheteros), which operates in Puerto Rico, and the Fuerzas Armadas de Liberación Nacional (FALN), functioning principally on the US mainland.

In the 1988 election campaign, Corrada del Río, whose campaign was endorsed by the successful US presidential candidate, George Bush, advocated the admission of Puerto Rico as the 51st state of the USA, while Hernández Colón reiterated the traditional PPD policy of 'maximum autonomy' for Puerto Rico 'within a permanent union with the USA'. President Bush's open support of the statehood option was criticized by Hernández Colón and the PPD. In 1989 Hernández Colón promised that a further plebiscite would be held. Although it was initially planned to hold this referendum in June 1991, in February the proposed legislation to make its result binding on the US Government failed to obtain sufficient support in the US Senate to allow it to proceed to full consideration by the US Congress.

In December 1991 the PPD Government held a referendum on whether to adopt a charter of 'democratic rights', which included guarantees of US citizenship regardless of future change in Puerto Rico's constitutional status, and the maintenance of Spanish as the official language. The proposal was rejected by a margin of 53% to 45%. This result was widely interpreted as an indication that the majority of voters wished to retain Puerto Rico's Commonwealth status. Hernández Colón resigned as leader of the PPD in February

1992. His successor, Victoria Muñoz Mendoza, was defeated in the November election by the PNP candidate, Pedro Rosselló.

Rosselló, who took office in January 1993, announced that a further plebiscite on Puerto Rico's future constitutional status would be held during the year. The referendum, which took place in November, resulted in a 48% vote favouring the retention of Commonwealth status, with 46% of voters supporting accession to statehood and 4% advocating full independence.

Rosselló was re-elected as Governor at elections held in November 1996. The PNP retained control of both chambers of the legislature.

In March 1998 the US House of Representatives narrowly approved legislation providing for a referendum to determine the island's future status. At the referendum, held in December, the Puerto Rican electorate rejected the statehood proposal by a margin of 50% to 47%. Rosselló described the result as a reflection of the PNP Government's decline in popularity over domestic issues.

Sila María Calderón of the PPD was elected Governor in November 2000, narrowly defeating Carlos Pesquera of the PNP. The PPD also secured a majority in both chambers in congressional elections.

Vieques

An extended period of public protest followed the accidental death, in April 1999, of a civilian security guard during routine US military exercises on the small offshore island of Vieques, the eastern section of which, covering a coastline of 32 km, was used by the US Navy as an ammunition testing range. With support from the PIP, groups of protesters promptly established camps on the firing range, compelling the US Navy temporarily to suspend these operations. Following extended negotiations between the Puerto Rican and US Governments, in January 2000 Rosselló and US President Bill Clinton announced that, in return for the resumption of naval exercises in which only dummy ammunition would be used, the US Administration would provide immediate development aid to Vieques of US $40m. This figure would rise to $90m. if residents of the island would agree in a referendum to allow the US Navy to resume live ammunition testing, in which event the Navy would undertake to leave Vieques permanently by 2003. In May 2000, prior to a proposed unilateral resumption of naval exercises (using dummy ammunition), protests on Vieques intensified, and several hundred federal government agents were sent to remove the protesters forcibly. The US Navy subsequently declared a 5-km land and sea 'security area' around the island.

Upon taking office in 2001, Governor Calderón announced her administration's repudiation of the agreement on military activity on Vieques signed in the previous year by Clinton and Rosselló. Military exercises on the island were resumed in April, despite legal challenges and protests. In June the new US President, George W. Bush, announced that the US Navy would end military activity on the island by May 2003. Meanwhile, Calderón announced plans for a referendum on US military activity on Vieques to be held in July 2001; it was subsequently cancelled by the US Congress, which ordered the US military to remain on Vieques until an alternative location was found. The US Congress claimed that on-going tests were necessary as part of the US-led 'war on terror' following the terrorist attacks on the USA in September. (A non-binding referendum had been held in July, in which 68% of voters were in favour of the immediate departure from the island of the US Navy.) Tests resumed in April 2002, amid protests from members of the PIP. The final scheduled bombing exercises took place in February 2003, and the US Navy withdrew from the island on 1 May. The last remaining base, at Ceiba, was closed on 31 March 2004. The firing range became a wildlife reserve.

The Acevedo Vilá Government

Legislative and gubernatorial elections were held in November 2004. Aníbal Acevedo Vilá of the ruling PPD won the gubernatorial election with 48.4% of the ballot, while the PNP's candidate, former Governor Rosselló, attracted 48.2%. In the concurrently held legislative election, the PNP won a majority of seats in both the Senate and the House of Representatives.

In March 2005 both houses of the legislature unanimously approved legislation providing for a referendum in July on whether to petition the US Congress and President Bush to agree to honour the results of a further plebiscite on how the island's future status should be decided, to be held before the end of 2006. However, the following month, Governor Acevedo Vilá vetoed the legislation on the grounds that it did not make sufficient provision for the option of a constituent assembly, instead of a popular, binding referendum, to decide on the eventual status of the island.

Also in March 2005, there was widespread opposition to the decision by the US Territorial District Court of Puerto Rico to impose the death sentence on two convicted murderers. Capital punishment had been banned in the territory in 1930, a decision that had been upheld in 2000 by a ruling of the Supreme Court of Puerto Rico.

However, the ruling was subsequently overturned by the US Court of Appeals, which found that Puerto Rico was subject to US federal law and that the death penalty was applicable in certain cases; this decision was upheld by the US Supreme Court. In April Acevedo Vilá wrote to the US Attorney-General requesting that the death penalty should not apply to residents of Puerto Rico. In May the jury serving on the trial moved to sentence the two men to life imprisonment.

In July 2005 Acevedo Vilá vetoed the proposed budget on the grounds that expenses were greater than income. The Government continued to operate using the previous year's budget. However, in April 2006 Acevedo Vilá announced that the budget was insufficient to provide for the Government's operating expenses until the end of the financial year (30 June) and that non-essential public sector services would be suspended from 1 May unless the legislature approved an emergency loan to fund the US $740m. shortfall, and the introduction of a 7% sales tax, to finance the loan repayments. The announcement prompted a protest march through San Juan in which more than 45,000 people participated. At a series of demonstrations in the capital, public sector employees demanded an early resolution to the impasse between the executive and the legislature. An emergency commission was established in May, composed of the Governor, members of the House of Representatives and banking agents. The initiative resulted in an agreement to secure a loan and to replace excise tax with a general sales and use tax of 5.5%, with revenue to be divided between federal and local government. However, owing to inaccurate phrasing, the legislation that was enacted on 13 May authorized a combined sales tax of 7%. A petition filed by PNP deputies in early November requesting the Supreme Court to uphold the intended rate of tax was rejected and the law took effect later that month.

In December 2005 a US presidential task force on the status of Puerto Rico recommended that Congress approve legislation for a two-stage plebiscite to be held in Puerto Rico within a year. In the first stage, the people of Puerto Rico would be given the option to continue as part of the Commonwealth or to seek a change in status. In the event that they chose the latter, a second vote would be held on whether to be incorporated as a state within the USA or become an independent country. Irrespective of the outcome, any decision would have to be approved mutually by the US Congress and the Government of Puerto Rico. While the PNP and the PIP welcomed the report, it was criticized by Governor Acevedo Vilá and the PPD because it omitted autonomy as an option. In January 2006 both houses of the Puerto Rican legislature approved legislation calling on Congress to act on the recommendations of the task force. A series of proposed laws consistent with the task force's findings was submitted to Congress throughout 2006, while a bill supported by Acevedo Vilá and the PPD was submitted in March 2007. The latter advocated that a constitutional convention choose one of three options: statehood, independence or a new or modified commonwealth status. The proposal provided for a referendum to be held on the recommended option, prior to its submission for debate in Congress.

Acevedo Vilá was the subject of corruption allegations in 2008 when an investigation by the Federal Bureau of Investigation (FBI) revealed details of improper campaign financing and tax fraud between 1999 and 2004. The Governor was charged in March 2008 on 19 criminal counts relating to the use of illegally obtained donations to eliminate campaign debts and to pay for family holidays and other personal expenses. Among a further 12 associates also indicted were four US businessmen and a Puerto Rican business owner, who were accused of obtaining government contracts in return for making campaign donations. Following a federal court trial, Acevedo Vilá was cleared of all charges in March 2009.

Gubernatorial and legislative elections were held on 4 November 2008. Luis Fortuño Burset of the PNP won 53% of the votes cast, defeating Acevedo Vilá, who attracted 41% of the ballot. The PNP also increased its representation in the Legislative Assembly at the expense of the PPD, securing a majority in both the Senate and the House of Representatives. Voter turn-out was recorded at 78%. Fortuño's running mate, Pedro Pierluisi Urrutia, succeeded him as Resident Commissioner in Washington, DC.

Fortuño in office

Upon taking office in January 2009, Governor Fortuño announced a series of measures aimed at reducing the fiscal deficit. These included controversial plans to reduce the public sector work-force by some 30,000 employees, as well as to introduce widespread outsourcing of government functions and increase certain taxes. In June an estimated 100,000 people marched through San Juan to protest against the job losses. In a further attempt at reducing government expenditure, in April 2010 Fortuño announced plans to reduce the number of seats in the House of Representatives from 51 to 39 and in the Senate from 27 to 17. The opposition PPD expressed concern at the proposals, which it claimed would undermine democracy in Puerto Rico by removing representation from areas that traditionally have shown strong support for the PPD.

Crime remained a concern for many Puerto Ricans. In early 2010 Fortuño announced that troops would accompany police in patrolling areas particularly affected by violent crime. In October 130 people, including some 75 police officers, 12 prison officials and three members of the National Guard, were arrested in Puerto Rico by the FBI in connection with alleged drugs offences. The police corruption scandal was the largest such incident ever recorded in Puerto Rico, and the FBI operation involved the deployment of over 700 federal agents from the USA. A report issued by the US Department of Justice in September 2011 criticized alleged corruption within the Puerto Rican police department and accused officers of perpetrating human rights abuses; Fortuño declared his commitment to further police reform. Also in that month the Governor revealed plans to establish a police task force to combat violent crime, while in November he announced additional police funding and an increase in officers' salaries. Nevertheless, the number of murders continued to rise, reaching a record 1,136 in 2011 (up from 983 in 2010); levels of impunity were also worryingly high. Recorded homicides declined to approximately 970 in 2012.

Rum dispute

Puerto Rico's relations with the neighbouring US Virgin Islands deteriorated in late 2009 following the decision by international drinks producer Diageo to relocate its production facilities for the Captain Morgan's brand of rum to the territory. The decision by the company, which was a major employer in Puerto Rico, was expected to result in some 350 direct and 5,000 indirect job losses in the territory. The authorities in Puerto Rico had accused the US Virgin Islands Government of misusing their share of the federal rum tax revenue to persuade Diageo to relocate to the islands. (Puerto Rico and the US Virgin Islands both benefit from the USA's 'cover over' programme, which redistributes 98% of rum excise duties collected in the USA to the two territories.) The US Virgin Islands denied the claim and asserted that Puerto Rico was conducting a campaign of misinformation against the territory. The dispute escalated during 2012, when some members of the Caribbean Community and Common Market (CARICOM) threatened to file a complaint with the World Trade Organization owing to concerns about the 'cover over' programme, which, they argued, constituted an illegitimate subsidization scheme. CARICOM claimed that the programme was distorting the regional market, leaving its members at a disadvantage. Nevertheless, the US Congress renewed the 'cover over' programme for a further two years in January 2013.

Recent developments: status referendum

In April 2010 the US House of Representatives voted in favour of a bill that would allow Puerto Ricans to determine their future relationship with the USA. It would provide for a referendum asking islanders if they wanted to change their political status. If the answer was no, eight years would elapse before the same question would be asked again. However, if the answer was yes, a second referendum would be held, offering a choice between statehood, independence or 'sovereignty in association with the United States'. Many observers, however, considered that it was unlikely that islanders, who were facing the imminent loss of important government subsidies and tens of thousands of jobs, would want to endanger their current relationship with the USA. The bill failed to receive approval by the US Senate during the 2009–11 congressional term and hence expired in January 2011. In March the US presidential task force on the status of Puerto Rico again recommended a two-stage referendum, and in June US President Barack Obama, while on an official visit to the island (the first by a US President since 1961), declared his support for another plebiscite. Consequently, Fortuño, who was in favour of statehood, ratified legislation in December providing for a referendum to be conducted on 6 November 2012. The status questions to be posed to the electorate remained broadly the same as those announced in 2010, but both questions would be asked simultaneously, thus obviating the need for a second referendum. US congressional and presidential approval would have to be secured before any change to the status quo could be legally enforced. Gubernatorial and legislative elections were also scheduled to take place on 6 November 2012. Fortuño had declared in June 2011 that he would seek re-election, while PPD President Alejandro García Padilla had been named as the opposition party's gubernatorial candidate.

An unrelated constitutional referendum was held on 19 August 2012. The electorate voted against proposals to reduce the size of the Legislative Assembly and to restrict bail rights under certain circumstances. In both cases, the 'no' vote represented approximately 55% of the ballot; turn-out was only 35.5%.

In the gubernatorial election, conducted in November 2012 as scheduled, García attracted 47.9% of the votes cast, narrowly defeating Fortuño, who garnered 47.0%. The PPD also performed well in the legislative polls, gaining control of 28 of the 51 seats in the House of Representatives and 18 of the 27 seats in the Senate. The remaining seats were secured by the PNP, with the exception of one Senate seat won by the PIP. Pierluisi was re-elected as Resident Commissioner in Washington, DC. In the concurrent status referendum, in which 1.7m. people participated, 54.0% of voters declared themselves to be dissatisfied with the territory's existing relationship with the

USA. Of the 1.3m. who answered the follow-up question, 61.2% supported a transition to statehood, 33.3% voted in favour of sovereign free association and 5.5% endorsed independence. (However, when taking the substantial number of blank votes into consideration, the statehood option only accounted for 45% of the ballot.) The referendum results were non-binding, and, with Puerto Rico's admission to the Union requiring the consent of a US Congress preoccupied with other matters, it was unclear whether any further progress on the statehood question would be made in the near future. The rate of participation by the electorate (in the elections and the referendum) was 78.2%. In April 2013 the US Administration requested financing from Congress of US $2.5m. to fund a further, binding, plebiscite on Puerto Rico's status.

CONSTITUTION AND GOVERNMENT

On 3 July 1950 the Congress of the United States of America adopted Public Law No. 600, which was to allow 'the people of Puerto Rico to organize a government pursuant to a constitution of their own adoption'. This Law was accepted by referendum in 1951. A new Constitution was drafted in which Puerto Rico was styled as a Commonwealth, or 'estado libre asociado', 'a state which is free of superior authority in the management of its own local affairs', though it remained in association with the USA. This Constitution, with its amendments and resolutions, was ratified by the people of Puerto Rico on 3 March 1952, and by the Congress of the USA on 3 July 1952. The Commonwealth of Puerto Rico was established on 25 July 1952. The Constitution may be amended by a two-thirds' vote of the Puerto Rican Legislature and by the subsequent majority approval of the electorate.

Executive power is vested in the Governor, elected for a four-year term by universal adult suffrage. The Governor is assisted by an appointed cabinet. Legislative power is held by the bicameral Legislative Assembly, comprising the Senate (with 27 members) and the House of Representatives (51 members). Additional members may be assigned in each chamber to ensure adequate representation of minority parties. The members of both chambers are elected by direct vote for four-year terms. The Resident Commissioner, also elected for a four-year term, represents Puerto Rico in the US House of Representatives, but is permitted to vote only in committees of the House. Puerto Ricans are citizens of the USA, but those resident in Puerto Rico, while eligible to participate in national party primary elections, may not vote in presidential elections.

REGIONAL AND INTERNATIONAL CO-OPERATION

Puerto Rico holds associate status in the UN Economic Commission for Latin America and the Caribbean (ECLAC, see p. 35) and has observer status in the Caribbean Community and Common Market (CARICOM, see p. 231). Puerto Rico declined to accept associate status in the Association of Caribbean States (see p. 459), formed in 1994, because of opposition by the US Government to the inclusion of Cuba. In 2001 Puerto Rico applied for associate membership of CARICOM; the USA criticized the move, emphasizing that it had authority over the island's foreign policy as long as Puerto Rico held Commonwealth status.

ECONOMIC AFFAIRS

In 2010, according to UN figures, Puerto Rico's gross national income was US $61,647m., equivalent to approximately $16,560 per head. During 2002–11, it was estimated, the population decreased at an average annual rate of 0.3%. According to UN figures, gross domestic product (GDP) per head increased, in real terms, by an average of 3.7% per year during 2002–11, while GDP decreased, in real terms, by an average of 0.6% per year over the same period. According to official figures, GDP decreased by an estimated 0.1% in 2010/11.

Agriculture, forestry and fishing contributed an estimated 0.7% of GDP in the fiscal year ending 30 June 2011, according to preliminary figures, and employed 1.6% of the working population in 2011/12. Dairy produce and other livestock products are the mainstays of the agricultural sector. The principal crops are fruits (principally plantains, bananas, pineapples and oranges) and coffee. Cocoa cultivation has been successfully introduced, and measures to improve agricultural land use included the replanting of some sugar-growing areas with rice and the cultivation of plantain trees on unproductive hill land. Commercial fishing is practised on a small scale. The GDP of the agricultural sector increased, in real terms, at an average rate of 6.2% per year between 2002 and 2011, according to UN estimates. Agricultural GDP declined by approximately 6.9% in 2010, and by a further 3.1% in 2011.

According to preliminary official figures, industry provided an estimated 52.0% of GDP in 2010/11 and employed 13.8% of the working population in 2011/12. According to UN estimates, industrial GDP declined, in real terms, at an average annual rate of 0.4% during 2002–11; industrial GDP increased by 0.9% in 2010, but decreased by 2.9% in 2011.

Puerto Rico has no commercially exploitable mineral resources, although deposits of copper and nickel have been identified. The

sector provided less than 0.1% of GDP in 2010/11, according to official estimates.

Manufacturing is a significant source of income, accounting for an estimated 48.5% of GDP in 2010/11 and employing 9.1% of the working population in 2011/12. The principal branch of manufacturing was chemical products, mainly drugs and medicines. Other important products were computers, electronic and electrical products and food products. The GDP of the manufacturing remained constant, in real terms, between 2002 and 2011, according to UN estimates. The sector increased by 1.3% in 2010, before declining by 3.6% in 2011. In 2011/12 total electricity production was 22,191m. kWh.

The construction sector contributed as estimated 1.4% of GDP in 2010/11, and engaged 4.7% of the employed labour force in 2011/12. Between 2002 and 2011, according to UN estimates, the GDP of the sector declined at an average annual rate of 4.4%. Construction GDP decreased by 7.7% in 2010, but increased by 12.1% in 2011.

Services provided an estimated 47.4% of GDP in 2010/11 and engaged 84.4% of the employed labour force in 2011/12 (including 22.2% employed by the Government). In real terms, the GDP of all service sectors declined at an average rate of 1.1% per year between 2002 and 2011; sectoral GDP declined by 1.4% in 2010, before increasing by 0.3% in 2011, according to UN estimates. Tourism is of increasing importance; in 2010/11 tourist arrivals were estimated at 4.2m. visitors (including 1.2m. excursionists), generating revenue totalling US $3,142.8m. Visitors from the US mainland comprised almost 85% of the total number of visitors (excluding excursionists) in 2010/11.

In 2009/10 there was a visible merchandise trade surplus of US $18,542.3m. and a surplus of $3,512.3m. on the current account of the balance of payments. In 2011/12 the principal source of imports was the USA (responsible for 42.6% of the total value of imports), which was also the principal market for exports (70.9% of the total). Other important trading partners included Belgium, Germany, Ireland, Japan and the US Virgin Islands. The principal imports in that year were chemicals and related manufactures (particularly pharmaceuticals and medicines), petroleum and coal products, manufactured food products, and computer and electronic products. The principal exports were manufactured chemical products (mainly pharmaceuticals and medicines), medical equipment and supplies and manufactured food products.

In 2010/11 there was a budget deficit of US $1,641.8m. (excluding other government fund financing). According to preliminary estimates, Puerto Rico's gross public debt at the end of the fiscal year to 30 June 2010 was an estimated $56,823.1m. The annual inflation rate averaged 1.9% in 2002–12. Consumer prices increased by an average of 1.4% in 2012. Puerto Rico is very densely populated, and unemployment was a persistent problem. The average rate of unemployment was estimated at 15.0% in 2011/12.

Economic growth has been inhibited by the lack of adequate infrastructure. Government programmes of industrial and taxation incentives, aimed at attracting investment, have generated growth in the manufacturing and services sectors, although the withdrawal by the USA of a number of important tax exemptions enjoyed by investors had a negative impact on the economy in recent years. The worsening global economic downturn, together with the already poor investment climate, exacerbated the economic situation in 2009. Governor Luis Fortuño declared a state of fiscal emergency, introducing austerity measures to reduce the fiscal deficit. A fiscal stimulus programme was also introduced, in the hope of boosting investor confidence. However, higher unemployment and a concomitant decline in receipts from income tax placed considerable strain on the budget. Economic activity was subdued throughout 2010 and the unemployment rate remained high, although most economic indicators registered modest improvements during 2011. According to official data, GDP declined by 0.1% in 2010/11, the fifth consecutive year of recession in the territory. The economy grew by an estimated 0.4% in 2011/12 and was projected to expand by 0.6% in 2012/13. With the territory's fiscal position continuing to cause concern, recently elected Governor Alejandro García Padilla announced further austerity measures in early 2013. The new Governor's first budget in April of that year proposed a fiscal plan to eliminate the budget deficit by 2016.

PUBLIC HOLIDAYS

2014: 1 January (New Year), 6 January (Epiphany), 13 January (Birthday of Eugenio María de Hostos), 20 January (Martin Luther King Day), 17 February (Presidents' Day), 22 March (Emancipation of the Slaves), 16 April (Birthday of José de Diego), 18 April (Good Friday), 26 May (Memorial Day), 4 July (US Independence Day), 21 July (Birthday of Luis Muñoz Rivera), 25 July (Constitution Day), 27 July (Birthday of José Celso Barbosa), 1 September (Labor Day), 13 October (Columbus Day), 11 November (Veterans' Day), 19 November (Discovery of Puerto Rico Day), 27 November (US Thanksgiving Day), 25 December (Christmas Day).

Statistical Survey

Source (unless otherwise stated): Puerto Rico Planning Board, POB 41119, San Juan, 00940-1119; tel. (787) 723-6200; internet www.jp.gobierno.pr.

Area and Population

AREA, POPULATION AND DENSITY

Area (sq km)	8,959*
Population (census results)	
1 April 2000	3,808,610
1 April 2010	3,725,789
Males	1,785,171
Females	1,940,618
Population (estimates at mid-year)†	
2011	3,989,133
2012	3,998,905
2013	3,674,209
Density (per sq km) at mid-2013	410.1

* 3,459 sq miles.
† Source: Population Division, US Census Bureau.

POPULATION BY AGE AND SEX
(population estimates at mid-2013)

	Males	Females	Total
0–14	346,794	330,221	677,015
15–64	1,147,495	1,247,748	2,395,243
65 and over	261,345	340,606	601,951
Total	1,755,634	1,918,575	3,674,209

Source: Population Division, US Census Bureau.

PRINCIPAL TOWNS
(population at 2010 census)

San Juan (capital) .	395,326	Caguas	142,893
Bayamón . . .	208,116	Guaynabo . . .	97,924
Carolina . . .	176,762	Arecibo	96,440
Ponce	166,327		

Source: Population Division, US Census Bureau.

BIRTHS, MARRIAGES AND DEATHS

	Registered live births		Registered marriages		Registered deaths	
	Number	Rate (per 1,000)	Number	Rate (per 1,000)*	Number	Rate (per 1,000)
2000	59,460	15.5	25,980	8.9	28,550	7.6
2001	55,983	14.6	28,598	7.4	28,794	7.5
2002	52,871	13.7	25,645	6.6	28,098	7.3
2003	50,803	13.1	25,236	6.5	28,356	7.3

* Rates calculated using estimates of population aged 15 years and over.
Source: Department of Health, Commonwealth of Puerto Rico.

2007 (preliminary): Births 46,744 (birth rate 11.9 per 1,000); Deaths 29,292 (death rate 7.4 per 1,000).

2008 (preliminary): Births 45,687 (birth rate 12.1 per 1,000); Deaths 29,024 (death rate 7.3 per 1,000).

2009 (preliminary): Births 44,080 (birth rate 12.1 per 1,000); Deaths 28,173 (death rate 7.3 per 1,000).

Source: Department of Health, Commonwealth of Puerto Rico.

Life expectancy (years at birth): 79.2 (males 75.2; females 83.1) in 2011 (Source: Pan American Health Organization).

ECONOMICALLY ACTIVE POPULATION
('000 persons aged 16 years and over)

	2009/10	2010/11	2011/12
Agriculture, forestry and fishing .	17	17	17
Manufacturing	102	99	99
Construction	54	47	51
Trade	240	241	240
Transportation, communication and other public utilities .	57	48	41
Finance, insurance and real estate	41	41	36
Services	330	344	358
Government	261	240	241
Total employed	1,103	1,077	1,085
Unemployed	210	204	191
Total labour force	1,313	1,281	1,276

Note: Totals may not be equal to the sum of components, owing to rounding.

Health and Welfare

KEY INDICATORS

Total fertility rate (children per woman, 2011)	1.8
Under-5 mortality rate (per 1,000 live births, 2011) . . .	8.8
Physicians (per 1,000 head, c. 2007)	2.2
Hospital beds (per 1,000 head, 2006)	3.1
Health expenditure (public, 2004): % of GDP	3.5

Source: mainly Pan American Health Organization.

For other sources and definitions see explanatory note on p. vi.

Agriculture

PRINCIPAL CROPS
('000 metric tons, FAO estimates)

	2009	2010	2011
Tomatoes	22.1	17.0	20.2
Pumpkins, squash and gourds .	13.5	11.6	11.6
Bananas	53.9	62.2	68.2
Plantains	77.9	81.1	90.5
Oranges	18.5	15.4	12.8
Guavas, mangoes and mangosteens	18.3	13.8	12.7
Pineapples	22.6	24.9	32.5
Coffee, green	5.8	3.6	4.5

Aggregate production (may include official, semi-official or estimated data): Total fruits (excl. melons) 207.8 in 2009, 218.0 in 2010, 237.4 in 2011; Total roots and tubers 12.9 in 2009, 13.0 in 2010, 12.7 in 2011; Total vegetables (incl. melons) 48.2 in 2009, 40.7 in 2010, 46.1 in 2011.

Source: FAO.

LIVESTOCK
('000 head, year ending September, FAO estimates)

	2009	2010	2011
Asses	2	2	2
Cattle	380.0	380.0	380.0
Sheep	6.3	6.3	6.3
Goats	3.3	3.3	3.3
Pigs	50.0	50.0	50.0
Horses	6.6	6.6	6.6
Chickens	13,200	14,000	14,500

Source: FAO.

LIVESTOCK PRODUCTS
('000 metric tons, FAO estimates)

	2009	2010	2011
Cattle meat	10.3	10.3	10.3
Pig meat	11.9	11.9	11.9
Chicken meat	52.2	55.0	58.0
Cows' milk	378.6	378.6	378.6
Hen eggs	12.0	11.7	11.7

Source: FAO.

Fishing

(metric tons, live weight)

	2008	2009	2010
Capture	1,793	1,702	1,898
Groupers	19	15	18
Snappers and jobfishes . .	374	329	419
Caribbean spiny lobster . .	142	139	148
Stromboid conchs	829	803	915
Aquaculture*	22	21	17
Tilapias*	10	5	3
Total catch*	1,815	1,723	1,915

* FAO estimates.

Source: FAO.

Industry

SELECTED PRODUCTS
(year ending 30 June)

	1995/96	1996/97	1997/98*
Distilled spirits ('000 proof gallons)	25,343	36,292	33,471

* Preliminary.

Electric energy (million kWh): 23,578.7 in 2009/10; 22,631.1 in 2010/11; 22,191.4 in 2011/12.

Cement ('000 metric tons): 1,550 in 2006; 1,390 in 2007; 1,300 in 2008 (Source: US Geological Survey).

Beer ('000 hl): 317 in 1997; 263 in 1998; 259 in 1999 (Source: UN, *Industrial Commodity Statistics Yearbook*).

Finance

CURRENCY AND EXCHANGE RATES

Monetary Units
United States currency: 100 cents = 1 US dollar (US $).

Sterling and Euro Equivalents (31 December 2012)
£1 sterling = US $1.578;
€1 = US $1.319;
US $100 = £63.37 = €75.79.

BUDGET
(US $ '000, general government operations, year ending 30 June)

Revenue*	2008/09	2009/10	2010/11
Income tax	5,191,042	5,109,313	4,749,942
Excise tax	1,118,283	1,145,538	2,106,784
Sales and use tax . . .	797,194	540,348	555,990
Other taxes	103,348	98,530	83,589
Charges for services . .	758,427	600,473	632,005
Intergovernmental transfers .	5,580,153	6,528,804	6,002,950
Interest	25,928	24,567	22,138
Other revenue	540,854	506,014	597,455
Total	14,115,229	14,553,587	14,750,853

Expenditure	2008/09	2009/10	2010/11
General government services . .	1,363,118	1,711,761	1,145,340
Public safety	2,071,001	2,207,228	2,044,398
Health	2,761,868	2,783,185	2,928,477
Public housing and welfare . .	3,428,546	3,553,699	3,734,850
Education	5,048,612	4,583,918	4,450,805
Economic development . . .	687,183	249,188	460,878
Intergovernmental transfers . .	425,418	418,458	429,702
Capital outlays	60,684	129,735	227,003
Principal on debt servicing . .	284,925	505,480	658,752
Interest	219,135	201,233	312,462
Total	16,350,490	16,343,885	16,392,667

* Excluding net financing (US $ '000): 2,773,115 in 2008/09; 2,678,629 in 2009/10; 1,938,050 in 2010/11.

Source: Department of the Treasury, Commonwealth of Puerto Rico.

COST OF LIVING
(Consumer Price Index; base: 2000 = 100)

	2008	2009	2010
Food (incl. beverages)	128.0	133.3	134.2
Fuel and light	159.7	149.0	146.2
Rent	117.3	120.3	121.1
Clothing (incl. footwear) . . .	73.0	74.2	72.4
All items (incl. others) . . .	127.6	128.0	131.1

2011: Food (incl. beverages) 137.5; All items (incl. others) 134.9.

2012: Food (incl. beverages) 140.2; All items (incl. others) 136.8.

Source: ILO.

NATIONAL ACCOUNTS
(US $ million at current prices, year ending 30 June)

Expenditure on the Gross Domestic Product

	2008/09	2009/10	2010/11*
Government final consumption expenditure	11,101.7	10,841.9	10,501.6
Private final consumption expenditure	55,533.1	57,170.1	58,889.6
Gross domestic investment . .	10,053.9	9,190.8	9,967.8
Net sales to the rest of the world	−14,090.6	−14,144.8	−15,252.8
Gross national product . .	62,598.1	63,058.0	64,106.2
Exports of goods and services . } *Less* Imports of goods and services . . . . . . }	32,771.7	34,089.3	34,650.8
GDP in purchasers' values .	95,369.8	97,147.3	98,757.0

* Preliminary.

Gross Domestic Product by Economic Activity

	2008/09	2009/10	2010/11*
Agriculture	567.1	707.2	670.2
Mining†	46.1	40.9	39.4
Manufacturing	43,872.2	46,553.7	47,987.9
Utilities	1,966.9	1,989.2	2,000.8
Construction	1,730.6	1,435.7	1,348.8
Transportation	894.9	910.1	907.2
Trade	7,312.8	7,433.2	7,547.8
Finance, insurance and real estate	17,748.9	17,710.9	17,578.1
Other services	11,702.9	12,242.3	12,585.5
Government	9,047.4	8,349.9	8,228.9
Sub-total	94,889.8	97,373.1	98,894.6
Statistical discrepancy . . .	480.0	−225.8	−137.7
Total	95,369.8	97,147.3	98,757.0

* Preliminary.
† Mining includes only quarries.

BALANCE OF PAYMENTS
(US $ million, year ending 30 June)

	2007/08	2008/09	2009/10*
Merchandise exports	68,551.0	66,077.6	67,558.5
Merchandise imports	−52,386.3	−48,285.6	−49,016.2
Trade balance	15,164.7	17,792.0	18,542.3
Exports of services	6,951.5	6,503.0	6,310.1
Imports of services	−4,903.5	−4,528.2	−4,600.8
Balance on goods and services	17,212.7	19,766.8	20,251.6
Other income received . . .	1,763.7	1,158.6	752.2
Other income paid	−33,703.7	−34,816.0	−34,858.6
Balance on goods, services and income	−14,727.4	−13,890.6	−13,854.8
Net transfers and interest . .	13,015.0	14,869.5	17,367.1
Current balance	−1,712.5	978.9	3,512.3
Net capital movements . . .	7,030.1	7,199.1	10,853.7
Overall balance	−5,317.7	−8,178.0	−14,366.0

* Preliminary.

External Trade

PRINCIPAL COMMODITIES
(US $ million, year ending 30 June)

Imports	2009/10	2010/11	2011/12
Mining products	407.4	424.1	604.8
Manufacturing products . .	38,517.3	42,250.6	44,284.8
Food	2,987.8	3,178.5	3,385.2
Products of petroleum and coal .	4,952.5	5,738.8	6,603.4
Chemical products . . .	18,066.1	20,022.9	20,573.5
Basic chemicals . . .	3,249.7	4,428.5	3,917.7
Pharmaceuticals and medicines	13,761.7	14,476.8	15,503.0
Machinery, except electrical .	1,039.4	1,048.6	1,183.5
Computer and electronic products	2,604.1	2,398.4	2,415.4
Transport equipment . . .	1,841.6	2,002.6	2,271.7
Motor vehicles	1,535.0	1,713.3	1,965.3
Miscellaneous manufacturing .	1,552.0	1,650.2	1,696.3
Total (incl. others)	40,810.1	44,670.6	46,574.6

Exports	2009/10	2010/11	2011/12
Manufacturing products . .	60,056.6	62,875.2	58,164.6
Food	3,611.3	3,980.4	3,670.4
Chemicals	46,536.0	48,763.7	44,488.3
Pharmaceuticals and medicines	42,492.7	43,224.0	40,848.0
Computer and electronic products	2,511.1	2,005.4	1,575.1
Computers and peripheral equipment	962.6	815.0	440.5
Electrical equipment, appliances and components	876.9	872.2	1,023.9
Miscellaneous manufacturing .	4,095.8	4,574.2	4,517.4
Medical equipment and supplies	4,053.1	4,539.9	4,481.6
Total (incl. others)	61,657.2	64,876.0	58,914.1

PRINCIPAL TRADING PARTNERS
(US $ million, year ending 30 June)

Imports	2004/05	2005/06	2006/07
Brazil	689.9	676.4	672.9
China, People's Republic . . .	n.a.	566.7	644.9
Dominican Republic	643.9	596.4	485.7
Germany	828.0	903.0	871.9
Ireland	7,716.8	7,950.2	9,492.6
Japan	1,554.8	1,834.9	1,661.3
Nigeria	n.a.	n.a.	903.4
Singapore	956.7	592.7	612.2
United Kingdom	524.5	513.4	n.a.
USA	19,133.7	21,502.9	22,662.4
US Virgin Islands	1,264.7	1,486.1	1,377.5
Total (incl. others)	38,905.2	42,629.5	45,265.8

Exports	2004/05	2005/06	2006/07
Belgium	1,335.5	1,464.1	2,013.9
Dominican Republic	845.2	887.0	987.6
France	693.5	410.2	358.8
Germany	544.5	635.5	2,046.3
Italy	414.9	216.3	n.a.
Japan	n.a.	458.3	526.6
Netherlands	1,800.6	2,356.7	2,763.8
Singapore	608.0	849.7	1,119.2
Spain	n.a.	n.a.	353.6
United Kingdom	749.2	693.8	935.0
USA	46,703.0	49,651.8	46,324.0
Total (incl. others)	56,543.2	60,118.7	60,010.8

2008/09: *Imports:* USA 19,069.1; Total (incl. others) 40,651.0. *Exports:* USA 43,543.9; Total (incl. others) 60,806.6.

2009/10: *Imports:* USA 20,895.5; Total (incl. others) 40,810.10. *Exports:* USA 41,989.2; Total (incl. others) 61,657.2.

2010/11: *Imports:* USA 20,579.1; Total (incl. others) 44,670.6. *Exports:* USA 45,872.7; Total (incl. others) 64,876.0.

2011/12: *Imports:* USA 19,837.1; Total (incl. others) 46,574.6. *Exports:* USA 41,798.0; Total (incl. others) 58,914.1.

Transport

ROAD TRAFFIC
(motor vehicles registered at 31 December)

	2004	2006*	2007
Passenger cars	2,210,998	2,341,820	2,421,055
Buses and coaches	3,308	3,503	3,698
Lorries (trucks) and vans . . .	36,063†	100,841	106,446
Motorcycles	31,770	91,082	115,865

* Data for 2005 were not available.
† Privately owned vehicles only.

Source: Federal Highway Administration, US Department of Transportation, *Highway Statistics*.

SHIPPING
(Port of San Juan, year ending 30 June)

	2007/08	2008/09	2009/10
Cruise passenger movements . .	1,496,853	1,236,121	1,185,780
Cruise ship calls	581	470	466
Cargo movements ('000 short tons)	9,395.9	8,272.9	7,949.0

Source: Puerto Rico Ports Authority.

CIVIL AVIATION
(year ending 30 June)

	2007/08	2008/09	2009/10
Luis Muñoz Marín International Airport			
Passenger movements ('000) .	n.a.	8,352.5	8,523.4
Freight (million lbs)	n.a.	445.9	413.9
Regional airports			
Passenger movements ('000) .	1,294.7	1,093.1	1,149.0
Freight (million lbs)	243.2	199.1	203.0

Source: Puerto Rico Ports Authority.

Tourism

(year ending 30 June)

	2008/09	2009/10	2010/11*
Total visitors ('000)	3,183.3	3,185.6	3,047.9
From USA	2,691.1	2,630.9	2,586.6
From US Virgin Islands . .	13.0	8.8	7.2
From elsewhere	479.2	545.9	454.1
Excursionists (incl. cruise passengers) . .	1,232.0	1,193.5	1,165.8
Expenditure (US $ million) . .	3,175.8	3,210.7	3,142.8

* Preliminary figures.

Communications Media

	2009	2010	2011
Telephones ('000 main lines in use)	905.7	890.8	826.1
Mobile cellular telephones ('000 subscribers)	2,712.2	2,934.0	3,108.4
Internet subscribers ('000) . .	512.4	575.9	568.1
Broadband subscribers ('000) . .	480.3	551.5	558.1

Source: International Telecommunication Union.

Education

(public education at late 2008 unless otherwise indicated)

	Institutes	Teachers	Enrolment
Elementary and secondary . .	1,511*	39,356	503,635
Post-secondary†	17‡	13,874§	68,584

* 2008/09.
† Excluding adult (enrolment 34,019) and vocational education.
‡ 2009/10.
§ Four-year full-time equivalent teaching staff.

Adult and vocational education: 80 institutes (private only); 33,463 students enrolled (public only).

Source: National Center for Education Statistics, US Department of Education.

Private education (accredited private institutions, 2010/11 unless otherwise indicated): Institutes 145 (2003/04); Pre-primary enrolment 26,320; Elementary and secondary enrolment 104,981; Post-secondary enrolment 29,690 (Source: Consejo General de Educacíon, San Juan).

Pupil-teacher Ratio (primary education, UNESCO estimate): 11.7 in 2009/10 (Source: UNESCO Institute for Statistics).

Adult literacy rate (UNESCO estimates): 90.4% (males 89.8%; females 91.0%) in 2010 (Source: UNESCO Institute for Statistics).

Directory

The Government

HEAD OF STATE

President: BARACK HUSSEIN OBAMA (took office 20 January 2009, re-elected 6 November 2012).

EXECUTIVE
(May 2013)

The Government is formed by the Partido Popular Democrático.

Governor: ALEJANDRO GARCÍA PADILLA (took office on 2 January 2013).

Secretary of State: DAVID BERNIER.

Secretary of Justice: LUIS SÁNCHEZ BETANCES.

Secretary of the Treasury: MELBA ACOSTA.

Secretary of Education: RAFAEL ROMÁN MELÉNDEZ.

Secretary of the Family: IDALIA COLÓN RONDÓN.

Secretary of Labour and Human Resources: VANCE THOMAS.

Secretary of Transportation and Public Works: MIGUEL TORRES DÍAZ.

Secretary of Health: FRANCISCO JOGLAR PESQUERA.

Secretary of Agriculture: MYRNA COMAS PAGÁN.

Secretary of Housing: RUBÉN RÍOS PAGÁN.

Secretary of Natural and Environmental Resources: CARMEN GUERRERO PÉREZ.

Secretary of Recreation and Sports: RAMÓN ORTA.

Secretary of Economic Development and Commerce: ALBERTO BACO BAGUÉ.

Secretary of Correction and Rehabilitation: JOSÉ NEGRÓN FERNÁNDEZ.

Attorney-General: OBDULIO MELÉNDEZ.

Resident Commissioner in Washington: PEDRO PIERLUISI URRUTIA.

Officials with Cabinet Rank

Secretary of the Interior: INGRID VILA BIAGGI.

Director of the Office of Management and Budget: CARLOS D. RIVAS QUIÑONES.

GOVERNMENT OFFICES

Office of the Governor: La Fortaleza, POB 9020082, PR 00902-0082; tel. (787) 721-7000; fax (787) 724-1472; e-mail secretariomail@ fortaleza.gobierno.pr; internet www.fortaleza.gobierno.pr.

Department of Agriculture: Avda Fernández Juncos 1309, 2°, Parada 19 1/2, PR 00908-1163; POB 10163, Santurce, PR 00909; tel. (787) 721-2120; fax (787) 723-8512; e-mail enegron@da.gobierno.pr; internet www.agricultura.gobierno.pr.

Department of Consumer Affairs: Edif. Norte, 4°, Avda José de Diego, Parada 22, Centro Gubernamental Minillas, San Juan, PR 00940-1059; POB 41059, Minillas Station, Santurce, PR 00940; tel. (787) 722-7555; fax (787) 726-5707; e-mail confidencia@daco .gobierno.pr; internet www.daco.gobierno.pr.

Department of Correction and Rehabilitation: Avda Teniente César González, esq. Calle Juan Calaf 34, Urb. Industrial Tres Monjitas, San Juan, PR 00917; POB 71308, Río Piedras, PR 00936; tel. (787) 273-6464; fax (787) 792-7677; internet www.ac .gobierno.pr.

Department of Economic Development and Commerce: Avda Roosevelt 355, Suite 401, San Juan, PR 00936-2350; POB 362350, Hato Rey, PR 00918; tel. (787) 758-4747; fax (787) 753-6874; internet www.ddec.gobierno.pr.

Department of Education: Avda Teniente César González, esq. Calaf, Urb. Industrial Tres Monjitas, Hato Rey, PR 00919-0759; POB 190759, San Juan, PR 00917; tel. (787) 759-2000; fax (787) 250-0275; internet www.de.gobierno.pr.

Department of the Family: POB 11398, Santurce, San Juan, PR 00910-1398; tel. (787) 294-4900; fax (787) 294-0732; internet www .familia.gobierno.pr.

Department of Health: Edif. A, Antiguo Hospital de Psiquiatría, Area Centro Médico, Río Piedras, San Juan, PR 00936-0184; POB 70184, Río Piedras, PR 00936; tel. (787) 274-7676; fax (787) 250-6547; e-mail webmaster@salud.gov.pr; internet www.salud.gov.pr.

Department of Housing: Edif. Juan C. Cordero, Avda Barbosa 606, Río Piedras, PR 00928-1365; Apdo 21365, San Juan, PR 00928-1365;

tel. (787) 274-2527; fax (787) 758-9263; e-mail mcardona@vivienda
.gobierno.pr; internet www.vivienda.gobierno.pr.

Department of Justice: Edif. Principal del Depto de Justicia, 11°,
Calle Olimpo, esq. Axtmayer, Parada 11, No 601, Miramar, San
Juan, PR 00902-0192; POB 9020192, San Juan, PR 00907; tel. (787)
721-2900; fax (787) 724-4770; e-mail aalamo@justicia.gobierno.pr;
internet www.justicia.gobierno.pr; incl. the Office of the Attorney-
General.

Department of Labour and Human Resources: Edif. Prudencio
Rivera Martínez, Avda Muñoz Rivera 505, Hato Rey, PR 00918; POB
191020, San Juan, PR 00919-1020; tel. (787) 754-5353; fax (787) 756-
1149; e-mail webmaster@dtrh.gobierno.pr; internet www.dtrh
.gobierno.pr.

Department of Natural and Environmental Resources: Carretera 8838, Km 6.3, Sector El Cinco, Río Piedras, PR 00906-6600;
POB 366147, San Juan, PR 00936; tel. (787) 999-2200; fax (787) 999-
2303; e-mail webmaster@drna.gobierno.pr; internet www.drna
.gobierno.pr.

Department of Recreation and Sports: Parque de Santurce,
Calle Los Angeles, San Juan, PR 00902-3207; POB 9023207, Santurce, PR 00909; tel. (787) 721-2800; fax (787) 728-0313; e-mail
mraffaele@drd.gobierno.pr; internet www.drd.gobierno.pr.

Department of State: Calle San José, esq. San Francisco, San
Juan, PR 00902-3271; Apdo 9023271, San Juan, PR 00901; tel. (787)
722-2121; fax (787) 725-7303; e-mail estado@gobierno.pr; internet
www.estado.gobierno.pr.

Department of Transportation and Public Works: Edif. Sur,
17°, Avda de Diego, Santurce, PR 00940-1269; POB 41269, Minillas
Station, Santurce, PR 00940; tel. (787) 722-2929; fax (787) 725-1620;
e-mail servciud@act.dtop.gov.pr; internet www.dtop.gov.pr.

Department of the Treasury: Edif. Intendente Ramírez, Parada 1,
Paseo Covandonga 10, San Juan, PR 00902-4140; POB 9024140, San
Juan, PR 00902; tel. (787) 722-0216; fax (787) 723-6213; e-mail
infoserv@hacienda.gobierno.pr; internet www.hacienda.gobierno
.pr.

Office of Management and Budget: POB 9023228, San Juan, PR
00902-3228; tel. (787) 725-9420; fax (787) 722-0299; internet www2
.pr.gov/agencias/OMB.

Office of the Resident Commissioner in Washington: POB
9023958, San Juan, PR 00901; tel. (787)723-6333; fax 787)729-
7738; internet www.pierluisi.house.gov.

Gubernatorial Election, 6 November 2012

Candidate	Votes	%
Alejandro García Padilla (PPD)	873,072	47.85
Luis G. Fortuño Burset (PNP)	858,361	47.04
Juan Dalmau Ramírez (PIP)	46,112	2.53
Rafael Bernabe (PPT)	17,545	0.96
Arturo Hernández (MUS)	10,154	0.56
Rogelio Figueroa García (PPR)	6,346	0.35
Total (incl. others)*	**1,824,764**	**100.00**

* Including 1,373 votes for write-in candidates, 4,291 blank votes and
7,510 invalid votes.

Legislature

LEGISLATIVE ASSEMBLY

Senate

President of the Senate: EDUARDO BHATIA GAUTIER.

Election, 6 November 2012

Party	Seats
Partido Popular Democrático	18
Partido Nuevo Progresista	8
Partido Independentista Puertorriqueño	1
Total	**27**

House of Representatives

Speaker of the House: JAIME PERELLÓ.

Election, 6 November 2012

Party	Seats
Partido Popular Democrático	28
Partido Nuevo Progresista	23
Total	**51**

Election Commission

Comisión Estatal de Elecciones de Puerto Rico (CEE): Edif.
Administrativo, Avda Arterial B 550, Hato Rey, San Juan, PR 00940-
5552; POB 19555, San Juan, PR 00919; tel. (787) 777-8682; fax 296-
0173; e-mail comentarios@cee.gobierno.pr; internet www.ceepur
.org; f. 1977; independent; Pres. HÉCTOR CONTY PÉREZ; Dir YVONNE
RIVERA PICORELLI.

Political Organizations

Frente Socialista: Buzón 69, POB 71325, San Juan, PR 00936; tel.
(787) 617-7105; e-mail fs@frentesocialistapr.org; internet www
.frentesocialistapr.org; f. 1990; mem. orgs incl. the Partido Revolucionario de los Trabajadores Puertorriqueños (PRTP—Los Macheteros) and Movimiento Socialista de Trabajadores

Movimiento Socialista de Trabajadores (MST): POB 123, Río
Piedras, PR 00123; e-mail info@bandera.org; internet www
.bandera.org; f. 1982 by merger of the Movimiento Socialista
Popular and Partido Socialista Revolucionario; pro-independence.

Movimiento Independentista Nacional Hostosiano (MINH):
Of. Central, Calle 25 NE 339, San Juan, PR 00920; tel. (787) 774-
8585; e-mail minhpuertorico@minhpuertorico.com.ar; internet
minhpuertorico.com.ar; f. 2004 by merger of the Congreso Nacional
Hostosiano and Nuevo Movimiento Independentista (fmr mems of
the Partido Socialista Puertorriqueño); pro-independence; Co-Pres
JOSÉ RIVERA SANTANA, HÉCTOR PESQUERA SEVILLANO.

Movimiento Unión Soberanista (MUS): POB 9023323, San
Juan, PR 00902-3323; tel. (787) 294-9142; fax (787) 294-9143;
e-mail info@muspr.org; internet muspr.org; f. 2012; pro-
independence; Pres MARÍA DE LOURDES GUZMÁN; Leader ARTURO
HERNÁNDEZ.

Partido Comunista de Puerto Rico: POB 13362, San Juan, PR
00908-3362; internet partidocomunistapr.org; f. 2001 as Refunda-
ción Comunista Puerto Rico, present name adopted 2010; Marxist-
Leninist; pro-independence.

Partido Independentista Puertorriqueño (PIP):
Avda Roosevelt 963, San Juan, PR 00920-2901; tel. (787) 782-
1430; fax (787) 782-2000; e-mail correopip@independencia.net;
internet www.independencia.net; f. 1946; advocates full independence for Puerto Rico as a socialist democratic republic; Leader RUBÉN
BERRÍOS MARTÍNEZ; Sec.-Gen. JUAN DALMAU RAMÍREZ; c. 6,000 mems.

Partido Nuevo Progresista (PNP): POB 1992, Fernández Zuncos
Station, San Juan 00910-1992; tel. (787) 289-2000; internet www
.pnppr.com; f. 1967; pro-statehood; Pres. LUIS G. FORTUÑO BURSET; c.
225,000 mems.

Partido Popular Democrático (PPD): Avda Constitución 403,
San Juan, PR 00906; POB 9065788, San Juan, PR 00906-5788; tel.
(787) 725-7001; e-mail info@ppdpr.net; internet ppdpr.net; f. 1938;
supports continuation and improvement of the present Commonwealth status of Puerto Rico; Pres. ALEJANDRO GARCÍA PADILLA; Vice-
Pres. BRENDA LÓPEZ DE ARRARÁS; c. 950,000 mems.

Partido del Pueblo Trabajador (PPT): POB 21042, San Juan, PR
00928; tel. (787) 374-8061; e-mail rescatapuertorico@gmail.com;
internet www.pueblotrabajador.org; f. 2010; Pres. ANNELIESSE
SÁNCHEZ.

Partido Puertorriqueños por Puerto Rico (PPR): Avda Ponce
de León 611, Hato Rey; tel. (787) 340-4476; e-mail contacto@
porpuertorico.com; internet www.porpuertorico.com; f. 2003, formally registered as political party in 2007; promotes citizen participation, sustainable devt and quality of life; Pres. ROGELIO FIGUEROA
GARCÍA.

Puerto Rican Republican Party: Suite 203, Avda Piñero 1629,
San Juan, PR 00920; tel. (787) 462-7474; internet www.goppr.org;
Pres. CARLOS MÉNDEZ MARTÍNEZ; Exec. Dir RICARDO APONTE.

Puerto Rico Democratic Party: American Airlines Bldg, 1509
Lopez Landrón, 10th Floor, POB 19328, San Juan, PR 00910-3939;
tel. (787) 721-6010; fax (787) 759-9075; internet www.democrats.org;
Chair. ROBERTO PRATS.

Judicial System

The judiciary is vested in the Supreme Court and other courts as may be established by law. The Supreme Court comprises a Chief Justice and up to nine Associate Justices, appointed by the Governor with the consent of the Senate. The lower judiciary consists of Superior and District Courts and Municipal Justices equally appointed.

There is also a US Federal District Court, the judges of which are appointed by the President of the USA. Judges of the US Territorial District Court are appointed by the Governor.

Supreme Court of Puerto Rico: POB 2392, Puerta de Tierra, San Juan, PR 00902-2392; tel. (787) 724-3551; fax (787) 725-4910; e-mail buzon@tribunales.gobierno.pr; internet www.tribunalpr.org; Chief Justice FEDERICO HERNÁNDEZ DENTON.

US District Court for the District of Puerto Rico: Clemente Ruiz-Nazario US Courthouse and Federico Degetau Federal Bldg, Avda Carlos Chardón 150, Hato Rey, PR 00918; tel. (787) 772-3011; fax (787) 766-5693; internet www.prd.uscourts.gov; Chief Judge AIDA M. DELGADO-COLÓN.

Religion

CHRISTIANITY

The Roman Catholic Church

Puerto Rico comprises one archdiocese and five dioceses. Some 73% of the population are Roman Catholics.

Bishops' Conference of Puerto Rico

POB 40682, San Juan, PR 00940-0682; tel. (787) 728-1650; fax (787) 728-1654; e-mail ceppr@coqui.net.

f. 1960; Pres. Mgr RUBÉN ANTONIO GONZÁLEZ MEDINA (Bishop of Caguas).

Archbishop of San Juan de Puerto Rico: Rt Rev. ROBERTO OCTAVIO GONZÁLEZ NIEVES, Arzobispado, Calle San Jorge 201, Santurce, POB 00902-1967; tel. (787) 725-4975; fax (787) 723-4040; e-mail cancilleria@arqsj.org.

Other Christian Churches

The Protestant churches active in Puerto Rico include the Episcopalian, Baptist, Presbyterian, Methodist, Seventh-day Adventist, Lutheran, Mennonite, Salvation Army and Christian Science.

Episcopal Church of Puerto Rico: POB 902, St Just, PR 00978; tel. (787) 761-9800; fax (787) 761-0320; e-mail iep@episcopalpr.org; internet www.episcopalpr.org; f. 1872; diocese of the Episcopal Church in the USA, part of the Anglican Communion; Leader Bishop Rt Rev. DAVID ANDRÉS ALVAREZ; 42,000 baptized mems.

Puerto Rico Council of Churches: Calle El Roble 54, Apdo 21343, Río Piedras, San Juan, PR 00928; tel. (787) 765-6030; fax (787) 765-5977; f. 1954 as the Evangelical Council of Puerto Rico; Pres. Rev. HÉCTOR SOTO; Exec. Sec. Rev. CRUZ A. NEGRÓN TORRES; 8 mem. churches.

BAHÁ'Í FAITH

Spiritual Assembly of the Bahá'ís of Puerto Rico: POB 11603, San Juan, PR 00910-2703; tel. (787) 763-0982; fax (787) 763-0982; e-mail bahaipr@prtc.net; internet www.bahaipr.org; f. 1972.

JUDAISM

There is a small Jewish community numbering around 2,500 adherents (less than 1% of the population).

Sha'are Zedek Synagogue-Community Center: Avda Ponce de León 903, Santurce, San Juan, PR 00907; tel. (809) 724-4157; fax (809) 722-4157; f. 1942; conservative congregation with 250 families; Rabbi GABRIEL FRYDMAN.

There is also a reform congregation with 60 families.

The Press

Puerto Rico has high readership figures for its few newspapers and magazines, as well as for mainland US periodicals. Several newspapers have a large additional readership among the immigrant communities in New York.

DAILIES

(m = morning; s = Sunday)

El Nuevo Día: Parque Industrial Amelia, Carretera 165, Guaynabo; POB 9067512, San Juan, PR 00906-7512; tel. (787) 641-8000; fax (787) 641-3924; e-mail laferre@elnuevodia.com; internet www .elnuevodia.com; f. 1970; Chair. and Editor MARÍA LUISA FERRÉ RANGEL; Pres. MARÍA EUGENIA FERRÉ RANGEL; Dir LUIS ALBERTO FERRÉ RANGEL; circ. 202,212 (m), 254,769 (s).

Primera Hora: Calle Génova A16, Extensión Villa Caparra, Guaynabo, PR 00965; POB 2009, Cataño, PR 00963-2009; tel. (787) 641-5454; fax (787) 641-4472; e-mail vozdelacalle@primerahora.com; internet www.primerahora.com; Pres. and Editor MARIA LUISA FERRE RANGEL; Dir LUIS ALBERTO FERRE RANGEL; Gen. Man. JUAN MARIO ÁLVAREZ CARTAÑA; circ. 133,483 (m), 92,584 (Sat.).

The San Juan Star: POB 364187, San Juan, PR 00936-4187; tel. (787) 782-4200; fax (787) 783-5788; internet www.thesanjuanstar .com; f. 1959; English; Pres. and Publr GERRY ANGULO; Gen. Man. SALVADOR HASBÚN; circ. 50,000.

El Vocero de Puerto Rico: Avda Constitución 206, San Juan, PR 00901; tel. (787) 721-2300; fax (787) 722-0131; e-mail opinion@vocero .com; internet www.vocero.com; f. 1974; Dir and Editor PETER W. MILLER; circ. 143,150 (m), 123,869 (Sat.).

PERIODICALS

BuenaVIDA: Avda Fernández Juncos 1700, San Juan, PR 00909; tel. (787) 728-3000; e-mail buenavidaedit@casiano.com; f. 1990 as *Buena Salud*; monthly; health and fitness; Editor ELENA MENÉNDEZ; circ. 61,000.

Caribbean Business: Avda Fernández Juncos 1700, San Juan, PR 00909-2938; POB 12130, San Juan, PR 00914-0130; tel. (787) 728-9300; fax (787) 726-1626; e-mail philipe@casiano.com; internet www .casiano.com/cb.php; f. 1973; weekly; business and finance; Man. Editor PHILIPE SCHOENE; circ. 45,000.

La Estrella de Puerto Rico: Edif. Roosevelt 140, Avda F. D. Roosevelt, Hato Rey, PR 00917; tel. (787) 754-4440; fax (787) 754-4457; e-mail hevia.rivera@periodicolaestrella.com; internet www.periodicolaestrella.com; f. 1983; weekly; Spanish and English; Editor-in-Chief FRANK GAUD; circ. 123,500.

Imagen: Avda Fernández Juncos 1700, Stop 25, San Juan, PR 00909-2999; tel. (787) 728-2350; fax (787) 728-7325; e-mail online@ imagen.pr; internet www.casiano.com/imagen.php; f. 1986; monthly; women's interest; Editor ANNETTE OLIVERAS; circ. 80,000.

¡Qué Pasa!: Loiza St Station, POB 6338, San Juan, PR 00914; tel. (787) 728-3000; fax (787) 728-1075; e-mail manoly@casiano.com; internet www.casiano.com/quepasa.php; f. 1948; every other month; English; publ. by Puerto Rico Tourism Co; official tourist guide; Editor RONALD FLORES; circ. 120,000.

Resonancias: Instituto de Cultura Puertorriqueña, Oficina de Publicaciones, Ventas y Mercadeo, POB 9024184, San Juan, PR 00902-4184; tel. (787) 724-4215; fax (787) 723-0168; e-mail revista@ icp.gobierno.pr; internet www.icp.gobierno.pr; f. 2000; 2 a year; Spanish; Puerto Rican and general culture and music; Editor GLORIA TAPIA; circ. 3,000.

Revista del Instituto de Cultura Puertorriqueña: Oficina de Publicaciones, Ventas y Mercadeo, POB 9024184, San Juan, PR 00902-4184; tel. (787) 721-0901; e-mail revista@icp.gobierno.pr; internet www.icp.gobierno.pr; f. 1958; 2 a year; Spanish; arts, literature, history, theatre, Puerto Rican culture; Editor GLORIA TAPIA; circ. 3,000.

La Semana: Calle Cristóbal Colón, esq. Ponce de León, Casilla 6537, Caguas 00726-6537; tel. (787) 743-5606; fax (787) 743-5500; e-mail editorial@periodicolasemana.net; internet www.lasemana.com; weekly; f. 1963; Spanish; regional interest; Gen. Man. MARJORIE M. RIVERA RIVERA.

La Torre: POB 23322, UPR Station, San Juan, PR 00931-3322; tel. (787) 758-0148; fax (787) 753-9116; e-mail ydef@hotmail.com; f. 1953; publ. by University of Puerto Rico; quarterly; literary criticism, linguistics, humanities; Editor YUDIT DE FERDINANDY; circ. 1,000.

El Visitante: POB 41305, San Juan, PR 00940-1305; tel. (787) 728-3710; fax (787) 268-1748; e-mail director@elvisitante.biz; internet www.elvisitante.net; f. 1975; weekly; Roman Catholic; Dir JAIME TORRES TORRES; Editor Rev. EFRAÍN ZABALA; circ. 59,000.

Publishers

Ediciones Huracán Inc: 874 Baldorioty de Castro, San Juan, PR 00925; tel. (787) 763-7407; fax (787) 753-1486; e-mail edhucan@ caribe.net; f. 1975; textbooks, literature, social studies, history; Pres. CARMEN RIVERA-IZCOA.

Editorial Cordillera, Inc: Of. 1A, Calle México 17, Hato Rey, PR 00917; tel. (787) 767-6188; fax (787) 767-8646; e-mail info@ editorialcordillera.com; internet www.editorialcordillera.com; f. 1962; Puerto Rican history, culture and literature, educational, trade; Pres. PATRICIA GUTIÉRREZ; Man. ADOLFO R. LÓPEZ.

Editorial Cultural Inc: POB 21056, Río Piedras, San Juan, PR 00928; tel. and fax (787) 765-9767; e-mail ventas@editorialculturalpr .com; internet editorialculturalpr.com; f. 1949; general literature and political science; Dir FRANCISCO M. VÁZQUEZ.

Instituto de Cultura Puertorriqueña: Oficina de Publicaciones, Ventas y Mercadeo, POB 9024184, San Juan, PR 00902-4184; tel.

(787) 724-4295; fax (787) 723-0168; e-mail tiendaicp@gmail.com; internet www.icp.gobierno.pr; f. 1955; literature, history, poetry, music, textbooks, arts and crafts; Dir GLORIA TAPIA RIOS.

University of Puerto Rico Press (EDUPR): POB 23322, UPR Station, Río Piedras, San Juan, PR 00931-3322; tel. (787) 250-0550; fax (787) 753-9116; e-mail info@laeditorialupr.com; internet www .laeditorialupr.com; f. 1947; general literature, children's literature, Caribbean studies, law, philosophy, science, educational; Exec. Dir JOSEPH R. ORTIZ-VALLADARES.

Broadcasting and Communications

TELECOMMUNICATIONS

Puerto Rico Telephone Co (PRTC): Avda Juan Ponce de León 562, Hato Rey; POB 360998, San Juan, PR 00936-0998; tel. (787) 782-8282; fax (787) 774-0037; internet www.telefonicapr.com; provides all telecommunications services in Puerto Rico; fmrly state-owned; acquired by America Móvil in 2007; Pres. and CEO ENRIQUE ORTIZ DE MONTELLANO RANGEL.

WorldNet: Centro Internacional de Mercadeo, 90 Carretera 165, Guaynabo, PR 00968-8059; tel. (787) 705-0505; fax (787) 277-0788; e-mail ventas@worldnetpr.com; internet www.worldnetpr.com; internet service provider; Pres. and CEO DAVID BOGATY.

Regulatory Authority

Junta Reglamentadora de Telecomunicaciones de Puerto Rico: Avda Roberto H. Todd 500, Parada 18, Santurce, San Juan, PR 00907-3981; tel. (787) 756-0804; fax (787) 756-0814; e-mail correspondencia@jrtpr.gobierno.pr; internet www.jrtpr.gobierno.pr; telecommunications regulator; Pres. SANDRA E. TORRES LÓPEZ.

BROADCASTING

The only non-commercial stations are the radio station and the two television stations operated by the Puerto Rico Department of Education. The US Armed Forces also operate a radio station and three television channels.

Asociación de Radiodifusores de Puerto Rico (Puerto Rican Radio Broadcasters' Asscn): POB 11208, San Juan, PR 00922; tel. (787) 783-8810; fax (787) 781-7647; e-mail radiodifusorespr@gmail .com; internet www.radiodifusorespr.com; f. 1947; Pres. ALAN CORALES VALLE; Exec. Dir JOSÉ A. RIBAS DOMINICCI; 102 mems.

WAPA TV: POB 362050, San Juan, PR 00936-2050; tel. (787) 792-4444; e-mail annie.berrios@wapa-tv.com; internet www.wapa.tv; owned by Intermedia Español; largest TV network in Puerto Rico; merger with WAPA Americas and Cinelatino (both based in the USA) announced in early 2013; Pres. and Gen. Man. JOE E. RAMOS.

Finance

(cap. = capital; res = reserves; dep. = deposits; brs = branches; amounts in US dollars)

BANKING

Government Bank

Banco Gubernamental de Fomento para Puerto Rico (BGF): Roberto Sánchez Vilella Government Centre, Avda de Diego, Stop 22, Santurce, PR 00907; POB 42001, San Juan, PR 00940-2001; tel. (787) 722-2525; fax (787) 721-1443; e-mail gdbpr@bgf.gobierno.pr; internet www.gdb-pur.com; f. 1942; independent govt agency; acts as fiscal (borrowing) agent to the Commonwealth Govt and its public corpns and provides long- and medium-term loans to private businesses; equity 2,450.6m., dep. 11,420.8m. (June 2009); Pres. JAVIER FERRER FERNÁNDEZ; Chair. DAVID CHAFEY, Jr.

Autoridad para el Financiamiento de la Vivienda de Puerto Rico: Edif. Juan C. Cordero, Avda Barbosa 606, Río Piedras, PR 00919-0345; POB 71361, San Juan, PR 00936-8461; tel. (787) 765-7577; fax (787) 620-3521; f. 1961; fmrly Banco y Agencia de Financiamiento de la Vivienda de Puerto Rico; present name adopted in 2001; subsidiary of the Government Development Bank for Puerto Rico; finance agency; helps low-income families to purchase houses; Exec. Dir JOSÉ A. SIERRA MORALES.

Commercial Banks

Banco Bilbao Vizcaya Argentaria Puerto Rico: Torre BBVA, 15°, Avda Muñoz Rivera 258, San Juan 00918; POB 364745, San Juan, PR 00936-4745; tel. (787) 777-2000; fax (787) 777-2999; internet www.bbvapr.com; f. 1967 as Banco de Mayagüez; taken over by Banco Occidental in 1979; merged with Banco Bilbao Vizcaya, S.A. in 1988; named changed from BBV Puerto Rico in 2000; cap. 166.0m., res, surplus and profits 380.0m., dep. 4,098.5m. (Dec. 2010); Pres. RAFAEL VARELA MARTÍNEZ; 65 brs.

Banco Popular de Puerto Rico: POB 362708, San Juan, PR 00936-2708; tel. (787) 724-3659; e-mail internet@bppr.com; internet www.bppr.com; f. 1893; cap. 7.0m., res 882.0m., dep. 21,021.0m. (Dec. 2012); Chair. and CEO RICHARD L. CARRIÓN; 195 brs.

Banco Santander Puerto Rico: Avda Ponce de León 207, Hato Rey, PR 00919; POB 362589, San Juan, PR 00936-0062; tel. (787) 759-7070; fax (787) 767-7913; e-mail jdiaz@bspr.com; internet www .santanderpr.com; f. 1976; cap. 183.7m., res 306.2m., dep. 5,936.6m. (Dec. 2012); Pres. and CEO JAVIER HIDALGO; Chair. GONZALO DE LAS HERAS; 67 brs.

Citibank NA: Avda Munoz Rivera 270, 6°, Hato Rey, PR 00918; tel. (787) 282-2201; internet www.latam.citibank.com/puertorico; Country Officer RAYMOND GATCLIFFE; 14 brs.

Doral Bank: Galería Paseos Mall, Grand Blvd Paseos, Suite 107, San Juan, PR 00926; tel. (787) 725-6060; fax (787) 725-6062; e-mail dbcw@doralbank.com; internet www.doralbank.com; cap. 20.0m., dep. 6,866.1m., assets 7,797.0m. (Dec. 2012); 90% investor-owned, through Doral Holdings Delaware, LLC; subsidiary of local bank holding co, Doral Financial Corpn, which completed buyout negotiations with financial group led by Bear Stearn Cos Inc (USA) in 2007; Pres. and CEO GLEN R. WAKEMAN; 37 brs.

FirstBank Puerto Rico: First Federal Bldg, Avda Ponce de León 1519, POB 9146, Santurce, PR 00908-0146; tel. (787) 760-8100; fax (787) 729-8139; internet www.firstbankpr.com; f. 1948, adopted current name in 1998; part of First BanCorp; cap. 487.6m., res 1,196.7m, dep. 9,952.8m. (Dec. 2011); Pres. AURELIO ALEMÁN; 45 brs.

Scotiabank de Puerto Rico: Plaza Scotiabank, Avda Ponce de León 273, esq. Calle Méjico, Hato Rey, PR 00918; POB 362230, San Juan, PR 00936-2230; tel. (787) 758-8989; fax (787) 766-7879; internet www.scotiabankpr.com; f. 1910; cap. 227.3m., res 297.8m., dep. 3,467.6m. (Dec. 2012); Chair. PETER CARDINAL; Pres. and CEO PETER BESSEY; 47 brs.

Savings Banks

Oriental Bank and Trust: Avda Fagot, esq. Obispado M-26, Ponce; tel. (787) 259-0000; fax (787) 259-0700; e-mail ofg@anreder.com; internet www.orientalonline.com; total assets 2,039m. (June 2001); Pres. and CEO JOSÉ ENRIQUE FERNÁNDEZ; Chair. JOSÉ J. GIL DE LAMADRID.

R & G Financial Corporation: POB 2510, Guaynabo, PR 00970; tel. (787) 766-6677; fax (787) 766-8175; internet www.rgonline.com; total assets 4,676m. (Dec. 2001); Pres. and CEO ROLANDO RODRÍGUEZ; Chair. JUAN AGOSTO-ALICEA.

Banking Organization

Puerto Rico Bankers' Association: Avda Ponce de León 208, Suite 1014, San Juan, PR 00918-1002; tel. (787) 753-8630; fax (787) 754-6022; e-mail info@abpr.com; internet www.abpr.com; Pres. AURELIO ALEMÁN; Vice-Pres. JOSÉ RAFAEL FERNÁNDEZ.

INSURANCE

Oficina del Comisionado de Seguros: B5 Calle Tabonuco, Suite 216, POB 356, Guaynabo, PR 00968 3029; tel. (787) 304-8686; fax (787) 273-6082; e-mail webmaster@ocs.gobierno.pr; internet www .ocs.gobierno.pr; regulatory authority for insurance sector; Commr RAMÓN L. CRUZ COLÓN.

Asociación de Compañías de Seguros de Puerto Rico: POB 363395, San Juan, PR 00936-3395; tel. (787) 793-4430; fax (787) 793-4447; internet www.acodese.com; Pres. JAIME J. GONZÁLEZ; Exec. Dir PERNAS IRAELIA.

Atlantic Southern Insurance Co: POB 362889, San Juan, PR 00936-2889; tel. (787) 767-9750; fax (787) 764-4707; e-mail executive@atlanticsouthern.com; internet www.atlanticsouthern .com; f. 1945; Pres. and CEO ALEXIS GONZÁLEZ.

Caribbean American Life Assurance Co: Scotiabank Plaza, Avda Ponce de León 273, Suite 1300, Scotiabank Plaza, San Juan, PR 00917; tel. (787) 250-6470; fax (787) 250-7680; e-mail customerservicepr@assurant.com; internet www.calac.com; owned by Assurant Solutions; Group Pres. and CEO S. CRAIG LEMASTERS; Pres. EDUARDO A. ARTHUR.

Cooperativa de Seguros Multiples de Puerto Rico: POB 363846, San Juan, PR 00936-3846; internet www .segurosmultiples.coop; general insurance; Pres. JUAN GONZÁLEZ FELICIANO.

FirstBank Insurance Agency, Inc: Avda Muñoz Rivera 1130, POB 9146, San Juan, PR 00908-0146; tel. (787) 292-4380; fax (787) 292-4355; e-mail seguros@firstbankpr.com; internet www .firstbankpr.com; f. 2003; owned by First BanCorp; Pres. VÍCTOR SANTIAGO.

MAPFRE Puerto Rico: Urb. Tres Monjitas Industrial, Avda Carlos Chardón 297, San Juan, PR 00918-1410; tel. (787) 622-7780; fax (787) 622-7775; e-mail customer_first@mapfrepr.com; internet www

.mapfrelife.com; f. 1920 as the Puerto Rican and American Insurance Co; comprises 4 insurance cos: MAPFRE PRAICO, MAPFRE Preferred Risk, MAPFRE Pan American, and MAPFRE Life; Pres. RAÚL COSTILLA; 28 brs.

National Insurance Co: POB 366107, San Juan, PR 00936-6107; tel. (787) 758-0909; fax (787) 756-7360; e-mail nic.sales@ nationalgrouppr.com; internet www.nicpr.com; f. 1961; subsidiary of National Financial Group; Chair., Pres. and CEO CARLOS M. BENÍTEZ, Jr.

Pan American Life Insurance Co: POB 364865, San Juan, PR 00936-4865; tel. (787) 620-1414; fax (787) 999-1250; e-mail CRMCPuertoRico@panamericanlife.com; internet www .panamericanlife.com; Regional Pres. JUAN A. ORTEGA.

Triple-S Salud: Avda Franklin D. Roosevelt 1441, San Juan, PR 00920; tel. (787) 774-6060; fax (787) 706-2833; e-mail servicioalcliente@ssspr.com; internet www.ssspr.com; bought Cruz Azul de Puerto Rico in 2009; health insurance provider; Pres. JESÚS R. SÁNCHEZ COLÓN.

Universal Insurance Group: Calle 1, Lote 10, 3°, Metro Office Park, Guaynabo; POB 2145, San Juan, PR 00922-2145; tel. (787) 793-7202; fax (787) 782-0692; internet www.universalpr.com; f. 1972; comprises Universal Insurance Co, Eastern America Insurance Agency and Caribbean Alliance Insurance Co; Chair. and CEO MONIQUE MIRANDA-MERLE.

Trade and Industry

DEVELOPMENT ORGANIZATION

Puerto Rico Industrial Development Co (PRIDCO): POB 362350, San Juan, PR 00936-2350; Avda Roosevelt 355, Hato Rey, San Juan, PR 00918; tel. (787) 758-4747; fax (787) 764-1415; internet www.pridco.com; public agency responsible for the govt-sponsored industrial devt programme; Exec. Dir ANTONIO MEDINA.

CHAMBERS OF COMMERCE

Chamber of Commerce of Puerto Rico: 100 Calle Tetuán, Viejo San Juan, PR 00901; POB 9024033, San Juan, PR 00902-4033; tel. (787) 721-6060; fax (787) 723-1891; e-mail camarapr@camarapr.net; internet www.camarapr.org; f. 1913; Pres. SALVADOR CALAF LEGRAND; Exec. Vice-Pres. EDGARDO BIGAS VALLADARES; 1,800 mems.

Chamber of Commerce of the South of Puerto Rico: 65 Calle Isabel, POB 7455, Ponce, PR 00732-7455; tel. (787) 844-4400; fax (787) 844-4705; e-mail camarasur@prtc.net; internet www .camarasur.org; f. 1885; Pres. ABEL E. MISLA VILLALBA; Exec. Dir HÉCTOR E. LÓPEZ PALERMO; 550 mems.

Chamber of Commerce of the West of Puerto Rico, Inc: Edif. Doral Bank, Of. 905, 101 Calle Méndez Vigo Oeste, POB 9, Mayagüez, PR 00680; tel. (787) 832-3749; fax (787) 832-4287; e-mail info@ ccopr.com; internet www.ccopr.com; f. 1962; Pres. JOSÉ A. JUSTINIANO; 300 mems.

Puerto Rico/United Kingdom Chamber of Commerce: 1509 Lopez Landron, Suite 1100, San Juan, PR 00911; tel. (877) 721-0160; fax (787) 721-7333; e-mail iancourt1@cs.com; internet users.bivapr .net/iancourt; Chair. Dr IAN COURT; 120 mems.

INDUSTRIAL AND TRADE ASSOCIATIONS

Asociación de Constructres de Hogares de Puerto Rico (ACH) (Home Builders' Association of Puerto Rico): Avda Ponce de León 1605, Condominium San Martín, Santurce, San Juan, PR 00909; tel. (787) 723-0279; internet www.constructorespr.com; Pres. ALEJANDRO BRITO; 150 mems.

Centro Unido de Detallistas de Puerto Rico (CUD) (Puerto Rico United Retailers Center): 501 Avda Muñoz Rivera, Hato Rey; tel. (787) 641-8405; fax (787) 641-8406; e-mail info@centrounido.com; internet www.centrounido.com; f. 1891; represents small and medium-sized businesses; Pres. ENID MONGE; 20,000 mems.

Compañía de Comercio y Exportación de Puerto Rico (CCE): Avda Chardón, POB 195009, San Juan, PR 00918; tel. (787) 294-0101; fax (787) 878-4630; internet www.comercioyexportacion.com; Dir FRANCISCO CHÉVERE.

Pharmaceutical Industry Association of Puerto Rico (PIA-PR): City View Plaza, Suite 407, Guaynabo, PR 00968; tel. (787) 622-0500; fax (787) 622-0503; e-mail contact@piapr.com; internet www .piapr.com; Man. Dir Dr ELSA SAAVEDRA-GARAY; Chair. CAMILO GÓMEZ; 19 mem. cos.

Puerto Rico Farm Bureau: Avda Ponce de León 1605, Suite 403, Condominium San Martín, San Juan, PR 00909-1895; tel. (787) 721-5970; fax (787) 724-6932; f. 1925; Pres. RAMÓN GONZÁLEZ; over 1,500 mems.

Puerto Rico Manufacturers' Association (PRMA) (Industriales Puerto Rico): Centro Internacional de Mercadeo, Torre II, Suite 702m, Carretera 165, Guaynabo, PR 00968; POB 195477, San Juan,

PR 00919-5477; tel. (787) 759-9445; fax (787) 756-7670; e-mail prma_info@prma.com; internet www.prma.com; Pres. PEDRO WATLINGTON; Exec. Vice-Pres. WILLIAM RIEFKOHL.

UTILITIES

Electricity

Autoridad de Energía Eléctrica (AEE): POB 364267, San Juan, PR 00936-4267; tel. (787) 521-3434; fax (787) 521-4120; e-mail prensa@prepa.com; internet www.prepa.com; f. 1979; govt-owned electricity corpn; monopoly on power transmission and distribution ended in 2009; installed capacity of 4,404 MW; Exec. Dir JOSUÉ A. COLÓN ORTIZ (acting).

TRADE UNIONS

American Federation of Labor–Congress of Industrial Organizations (AFL–CIO): POB 19689, San Juan, PR; tel. (787) 728-0300; fax (787) 728-0470; internet www.afl-cio.org; c. 60,000 mems.

Central Puertorriqueña de Trabajadores (CPT): POB 364084, San Juan, PR 00936-4084; tel. (787) 781-6649; fax (787) 277-9290; f. 1982; Leader VÍCTOR VILLALBA.

Federación de Trabajadores de Puerto Rico (FTPR-AFL/ CIO): Avda Ponce de León 1704, POB S-1648, San Juan, PR 00903; tel. (787) 728-0300; fax (787) 728-0470; e-mail ftpr@coqui .net; internet ftpr-aflcio.org; f. 1952; Pres. JOSÉ RODRÍGUEZ BÁEZ; Sec.-Treas. NÉSTOR SOTO LÓPEZ; 200,000 mems.

Transport

RAILWAYS

In 2004 a 17-km urban railway (Tren Urbano), capable of carrying some 300,000 passengers per day, was inaugurated in greater San Juan. The railway took eight years to build and cost some US $2,150m. In 2007 plans were announced for a light-rail line to connect the urban area of Caguas with the Tren Urbano system, at a cost of $450m. Work on the project was expected to begin by November 2013.

Alternativa de Transporte Integrado (ATI): San Juan; internet www.ati.gobierno.pr; govt agency; operates the Tren Urbano railway system.

ROADS

The road network totalled 26,856 km (16,687 miles) in 2010, of which 21,216 km were secondary roads, while 5,102 km were national roads. A modern highway system links all cities and towns along the coast and cross-country.

Autoridad de Carreteras: Centro Gobierno Roberto Sánchez Vilella, Edif. Sur Avda de Diego 328, POB 42007, Santurce, San Juan, PR 00940-2007; tel. (787) 721-8787; fax (787) 727-5456; internet www.dtop.gov.pr/carretera; f. 1965; regulatory authority; Exec. Dir RUBEN HERNÁNDEZ GREGORAT.

SHIPPING

There are 11 major ports on the island, the principal ones being San Juan, Ponce and Mayagüez. Other ports include Guayama, Guayanilla, Guánica, Yabucoa, Aguirre, Aguadilla, Fajardo, Arecibo, Humacao and Arroyo. San Juan, one of the finest and longest all-weather natural harbours in the Caribbean, is the main port of entry for foodstuffs and raw materials and for shipping finished industrial products. In 2009/10 it handled 7.9m. short tons of cargo. Under US cabotage laws all maritime freight traffic between the USA and Puerto Rico must be conducted using US-registered vessels. Passenger traffic is limited to tourist cruise vessels. Work on the US $84.4m. Port of the Americas megaport at Ponce was ongoing in 2013.

Autoridad de los Puertos: Calle Lindbergh, 64 Antigua Base Naval Miramar, San Juan, PR 00907; POB 362829, San Juan, PR 00936-2829; tel. (787) 723-2260; fax (787) 722-7867; e-mail webmaster@prpa.gobierno.pr; internet www.prpa.gobierno.pr; f. 1942 as the Autoridad de Transporte de Puerto Rico; present name adopted in 1955; manages and administers all ports and airports; Exec. Dir VÍCTOR SUÁREZ.

CIVIL AVIATION

There are two international airports on the island (Luis Muñoz Marín at Carolina, San Juan, and Rafael Hernández at Aguadilla) and nine regional airports. There are also six heliports. In 2013 plans to transfer the management of Luis Muñoz Marín airport to the private sector were under way. Southwest Airlines of the USA commenced direct flights to San Juan in April 2013.

Air Sunshine: POB 37698, San Juan, PR 00937; tel. (888) 879-8900; e-mail email@airsunshine.com; internet www.airsunshine.com;

f. 1982; private charters, and scheduled passenger and cargo services to other Caribbean destinations.

Tourism

An estimated 3.0m. tourists visited Puerto Rico in 2010/11. In addition, there were an estimated 1.2m. excursionists. Almost 85% of all tourist visitors were from the US mainland. Tourism revenue was estimated at US $3,143m. in 2010/11. In 2010 there were approximately 12,000 guest rooms.

Compañía de Turismo: Edif. La Princesa, 2 Paseo La Princesa, POB 9023960, San Juan, PR 00902-3960; tel. (787) 721-2400; fax (787) 722-6238; e-mail drodriguez2@prtourism.com; internet www .seepuertorico.com; f. 1970; Exec. Dir INGRID RIVERA ROCAFORT.

Puerto Rico Hotel & Tourism Association (PRHTA): Doral Bank Plaza, Calle Resolución 33, Suite 701- B, San Juan, PR 00920; tel. (787) 758-8001; fax (787) 758-8091; e-mail mtosses@prhta.org; internet www.prhta.org; more than 550 corporate mems; Chair. ISMAEL VEGA; Pres. and CEO CLARISA JIMÉNEZ.

Defence

The USA is responsible for the defence of Puerto Rico. In 2003 the US Navy withdrew from Puerto Rico closing its bases at Roosevelt Roads and on the island of Vieques. Puerto Rico has a paramilitary National Guard of some 11,000 men, which is funded mainly by the US Department of Defense. The National Guard has served under US command in Iraq and has also been deployed to support domestic police operations.

Education

The public education system is centrally administered by the Department of Education. Education is compulsory for children between six and 16 years of age. The 12-year curriculum, beginning at five years of age, is subdivided into six grades of elementary school, three years at junior high school and three years at senior high school. Vocational schools at the high-school level and kindergartens also form part of the public education system. Instruction is conducted in Spanish, but English is a required subject at all levels. In 2010 there were 894 elementary schools, attended by 299,746 pupils. There were 380 secondary schools in the same year, attended by 146,819 pupils. In 2004 there were 12 universities. The State University system consists of three principal campuses and six regional colleges. In 2010 the number of students enrolled in higher education was 96,893, of which nearly 30,000 were enrolled in private post-secondary institutions. Some 33,463 students were attending adult education courses in 2008. In 2011/12 US $2,228m. of general government expenditure was allocated to education (24.0% of total expenditure).

UNITED STATES EXTERNAL TERRITORIES

The External or Unincorporated Territories of the USA comprise the Pacific territories of American Samoa and Guam, the Caribbean territory of the US Virgin Islands, and a number of smaller islands.

AMERICAN SAMOA

Introductory Survey

LOCATION, CLIMATE, LANGUAGE, RELIGION, FLAG, CAPITAL

American Samoa comprises the seven islands of Tutuila, Ta'u, Olosega, Ofu, Aunu'u, Rose and Swains. They lie in the southern central Pacific Ocean, along latitude 14°S at about longitude 170°W, about 3,700 km (2,300 miles) south-west of Hawaii. The temperature normally ranges between 21°C (70°F) and 32°C (90°F), and the average annual rainfall is 5,000 mm (197 ins), the greatest precipitation occurring between December and March. English and Samoan, a Polynesian language, are spoken. The population is largely Christian, more than 50% being members of the Congregational Christian Church. The flag has a dark blue field, on which is superimposed a red-edged white triangle (with its apex at the hoist and its base at the outer edge of the flag), containing an eagle, representing the USA, grasping in its talons a yellow *fue* (staff) and *uatogi* (club), Samoan symbols of sovereignty. The capital is Pago Pago, on Tutuila (the officially designated seat of government is the village of Fagatogo).

CONTEMPORARY POLITICAL HISTORY

Historical Context

The Samoan islands were first visited by Europeans in the 1700s, but it was not until 1830 that missionaries from the London Missionary Society settled there. In 1878 the Kingdom of Samoa, then an independent state, gave the USA the right to establish a naval base at Pago Pago. The islands were also of interest to the United Kingdom and Germany, but the former withdrew in 1899, leaving the western islands for Germany to govern. The chiefs of the eastern islands ceded their lands to the USA in 1904, and the islands officially became an Unincorporated Territory of the USA in 1922.

Domestic Political Affairs

Until 1978 American Samoa was administered by a Governor, appointed by the US Government, with a legislature comprising the Senate and the House of Representatives. In November 1977 American Samoa's first gubernatorial election took place, and in January 1978 Peter Tali Coleman of the Republican Party, who had previously served in the position between 1956 and 1961, was inaugurated as the islands' first directly elected Governor. He was re-elected for a further term in November 1980, after three years in office instead of the prescribed four, in order to allow synchronization with mainland US elections in 1980. At the gubernatorial election of November 1984 A. P. Lutali of the Democratic Party was elected Governor and Eni Hunkin (who subsequently adopted the use of his chiefly name, Faleomavaega) became Lieutenant-Governor. Coleman was ineligible to stand for election to a third successive term as Governor, as legislation restricted tenure by any individual to two successive terms. In October 1986 a constitutional convention completed a comprehensive redrafting of the American Samoan Constitution. However, the draft revision had yet to be submitted to the US Congress in the early 21st century. In April 2004 it was announced that the Political Status Study Commission was to examine the territory's situation; the Commission concluded its investigations in 2006 and published a final report detailing its recommendations in January 2007. A series of constitutional conventions was subsequently held, most recently in mid-2010, at which proposed amendments to the Constitution were discussed—see below.

Meanwhile, American Samoa continued to be represented in the federal legislature by a non-voting delegate, the first election for this post having been held in 1981. The islands' Delegate was permitted to vote in committee but not on the floor of the US House of Representatives. In July 1988 the territory's Delegate in Washington, DC, Fofo Sunia, announced that he would not seek re-election, as he was under official investigation for alleged financial mismanagement. In October he received a prison sentence for fraud. Eni Faleomavaega replaced Sunia as American Samoa's Delegate to the US House of Representatives in November. At the gubernatorial election held concurrently Republican Peter Coleman was returned to office for a third term as Governor, and Galea'i Poumele replaced Faleomavaega as Lieutenant-Governor. However, at the next gubernatorial election conducted in November 1992 Peter Coleman was defeated by A. P. Lutali. At elections to the House of Representatives in November 1994 about one-third of those members seeking re-election were defeated. Faleomavaega was re-elected as non-voting Delegate.

Gubernatorial and legislative elections took place in November 1996. At a second round of voting the incumbent Lieutenant-Governor, the Democrat Tauese Sunia, was elected Governor with 51.3% of the votes cast, defeating Lealaifuaneva Peter Reid, Jr. Eni Faleomavaega was re-elected as Delegate to the US House of Representatives.

The decision in July 1997 by the Government of neighbouring Western Samoa to change the country's name simply to Samoa caused some controversy. Legislation approved in March 1998 by the territory's House of Representatives stated that American Samoa should not recognize the new name, which many islanders believed would undermine their own Samoan identity. Also in response to the change of name, legislation prohibiting citizens of the former Western Samoa from owning land in American Samoa was approved. Nevertheless, some rapprochement followed. In 2004 plans were announced for greater economic co-operation and a twice-weekly air link commenced. However, concerns were expressed at the decision of the Samoan Government in 2005 to require a permit and a passport from American Samoan citizens travelling to Samoa. In the following year the Samoan Government opened a consulate in American Samoa.

Meanwhile, in November 1998 Eni Faleomavaega was re-elected as the islands' Delegate to the US House of Representatives. At a gubernatorial election held in November 2000 Democrat Tauese Sunia was narrowly re-elected as Governor, receiving 50.7% of the votes cast, compared with 47.9% for the independent candidate, Senator Lealaifuaneva. At the US congressional elections, held concurrently, no candidate received the necessary 50% majority, Eni Faleomavaega winning 45.7% of the votes cast, compared with 30.3% for Gus Hannemann. A second round of polling took place on 21 November, when Faleomavaega was re-elected, with 61.1% of the vote.

In September 2001 the islands' Senate approved a resolution urging discussion with the US Government on the conferral of limited federal jurisdiction to the High Court of American Samoa, the only US territory without a sitting federal judge. A congressional public survey, conducted in the same month, registered wide popular support for a Federal Court and Public Prosecutor. At a meeting of the UN General Assembly in January 2002, the UN accepted American Samoa's request of May 2001 to be removed from the list of colonized territories. The Governor had sent a resolution to the UN Committee on Decolonization affirming American Samoa's wish to remain a US territory.

In September 2002 the territory's immigration procedures were amended to give the Attorney-General, rather than the Immigration Board, the ultimate authority to grant permanent residency status to aliens. The House of Representatives of American Samoa also approved a resolution to repeal legislation automatically conferring US citizenship in the territory to foreign parents. Meanwhile, in June a former president of the Amerika Samoa Bank (now ANZ Amerika Samoa Bank) was convicted of fraud for his involvement in a scheme in which US $75m. of investors' money had been misappropriated. Further allegations of corruption in the banking sector followed in 2004.

Elections for American Samoa's Delegate to the US House of Representatives took place in November 2002. Following a second round of voting, Faleomavaega secured an eighth term in office. In March 2003 Governor Tauese Sunia died while en route to Hawaii for medical treatment; Lieutenant-Governor Togiola Tulafono replaced him and appointed Faoa Aitofele Sunia, the late Governor's younger brother, as his deputy.

In December 2002 legislation was introduced that prohibited nationals of 23 countries deemed to present a terrorist threat from entering the territory, unless they were granted special permission. Opposition groups in Fiji expressed their displeasure at the inclusion of their country on the list, owing to its large Muslim population.

In March 2003 it was reported that the South Korean owner of the Daewoosa Samoa clothing factory, Kil Soo Lee, had been convicted by a US court of trafficking in humans. In July 2005 Lee was sentenced to 40 years' imprisonment. The mainly Vietnamese and Chinese factory employees had reportedly received very low wages, and their working conditions were described as appalling. The American Samoan High Court had previously ordered Daewoosa to pay workers US $3.5m. in compensation and fined the company an additional $290,000 in 2002.

At the gubernatorial election held in November 2004 incumbent Democrat Governor Togiola Tulafono was re-elected at a second round of voting, securing 55.7% of the vote to defeat Moega Lutu.

In October 2006 the minimum hourly wage for five industry categories was increased by between seven and nine cents. However, plans to raise the hourly rate for the cannery sector encountered strong opposition from the business community and from the Government itself, which argued that the decision would adversely affect companies' cost effectiveness. As the greatest source of revenue for the islands, the tuna-canning industry was able to exert significant pressure on wage levels. However, supporters of the decision pressed for a greater increase in order to attract and retain employees. Minimum wage legislation was brought under federal control in 2007, when it was envisaged that the minimum wage in the territory would increase to US $7.25 per hour by 2014. This rise was to be implemented in phases, with variations among industries.

Eni Faleomavaega was re-elected as Delegate to the US House of Representatives for an unprecedented 10th term in office in November 2006, narrowly defeating his closest rival, Aumua Amata Coleman.

None of the four gubernatorial candidates obtained the requisite 50% of the votes cast to secure office at an election in November 2008. At a second round of voting incumbent Governor Togiola Tulafono was re-elected with 6,590 votes, defeating Utu Abe Malae, who garnered 5,084 votes. In the concurrent legislative elections eight incumbents were re-elected. Eni Faleomavaega was re-elected for an 11th consecutive term as American Samoa's Delegate to the US House of Representatives. American Samoan voters also participated in a referendum on a proposed amendment to the Constitution (endorsed by the territory's House of Representatives in February), which would enable the Fono (legislature) to overrule the Governor's power of veto; however, this was defeated by a narrow margin of only 22 votes.

During a forum on the subject of constitutional change in March 2010 Governor Tulafono expressed his personal belief that American Samoa would benefit from the sort of relationship with the USA held by Palau under the latter's Compact of Free Association; the Governor noted that Palau's system of 'autonomous governance' allowed it to seek foreign aid, while American Samoa was able to seek only US funding, which, he argued, was an obstacle to the islands' development. A two-week constitutional convention was held in June–July, during which proposed amendments to the Constitution were discussed. The convention endorsed a series of proposals, including a new stipulation that members of the Fono should be US nationals of American Samoan ancestry, a proposal that provoked considerable censure owing to its perceived discriminatory and unconstitutional nature.

At a popular referendum held concurrently with legislative elections on 2 November 2010, the proposed amendments were rejected by a majority of voters: 7,410 voted against and 3,149 voted in favour of the changes. The handling of the referendum attracted considerable criticism; voters were given the option only to reject or to approve the entire list of proposed constitutional amendments, rather than to respond to each individual proposal. In the legislative poll, six new representatives were elected to the Fono. Meanwhile, in an election for American Samoa's Delegate to the US House of Representatives, held concurrently, Eni Faleomavaega was re-elected for a 12th consecutive term. Later that month US Secretary of State Hillary Clinton made a brief official visit to Pago Pago, during which she acknowledged the 'close relationship' between the USA and American Samoa, and expressed appreciation for the 'long and noble history of sacrifice' by American Samoans serving within the US military.

In January 2011 the US House of Representatives voted to rescind the 'symbolic' voting rights of territorial delegates in the 'Committee of the Whole House on the State of the Union', a means whereby the House was able to expedite consideration of certain legislation, particularly amendments. Faleomavaega joined with the Delegates from Guam, the Northern Mariana Islands, the District of Columbia, Puerto Rico and the Virgin Islands to express opposition to the revocation of the privilege, arguing that American Samoans 'fight and die in disproportionate numbers in defence of our nation' and that the revocation of the territorial delegates' symbolic voting rights 'dishonours their service and demeans their sacrifice'.

In November 2011 American Samoa was one of eight Pacific states and territories that jointly established the Polynesian Leaders Group (see p. 478), which was widely viewed as being intended to provide a counterweight to the Melanesian Spearhead Group. The first formal meeting of the Group, which pledged to enhance co-operation among its members across a wide range of fields, including trade and investment, education, climate change and health, was held in August 2012.

In July 2012 five American Samoans and a US-based non-governmental organization, the Samoan Federation of America, brought a legal challenge in the federal court in Washington, DC, claiming the right of American Samoans to US citizenship under the citizenship clause of the 14th amendment to the US Constitution. The US Government maintained that American Samoans are 'non-citizen nationals' of the USA but not US citizens.

In September 2012 Governor Tulafono proposed a legislative debate on the repeal of the death penalty in American Samoa. Tulafono argued that technical difficulties in implementing the punishment, together with the excessive costs associated with death penalty cases (estimated to total at least US $10m. for each case), meant that capital punishment in the territory was an empty threat with no deterrent value. He proposed the imposition of a life sentence for crimes such as murder, with a minimum of 40 years' imprisonment. Tulafono also introduced a debate on the introduction of a system of popular election for members of the Senate with an increased term of six years. The Governor stated that such a reform would assist the territory in achieving a greater measure of self-government. The House of Representatives approved the bill to repeal the death penalty in October, but it still required the approval of the Senate.

At a gubernatorial election held on 6 November 2012, at which Tulafono was constitutionally barred from seeking a third consecutive term, none of the candidates achieved the requisite 50% of the vote to secure office. At a second round of voting former President of the Senate and President of the Development Bank of American Samoa, Lolo Matalasi Moliga, defeated the incumbent Lieutenant-Governor, Faoa Aitofele Sunia, winning 52% of the votes cast. In the legislative poll, six new members were elected to the House of Representatives. Meanwhile, in the concurrent election for American Samoa's Delegate to the US House of Representatives, Eni Faleomavaega was re-elected, with 55% of the votes cast, for a 13th consecutive term. A proposed change to the Constitution, which would have enabled the Fono to override the Governor's legislative veto, was rejected in a referendum held alongside the elections.

Lolo Matalasi Moliga was sworn in as Governor, and Lemanu Peleti Mauga as Lieutenant-Governor, on 4 January 2013. Moliga appointed a Cabinet that included four women, and stated that his priorities included creating increased employment opportunities for American Samoans.

Corruption Issues

During the early 2000s several allegations of official corruption were made against government officials. In September 2002 the territory's intelligence agencies claimed that the Speaker of the House of Representatives, Tuanaitau Tuia, had used public funds to purchase a car and to finance private travel for his wife. In September 2003 an employee of the territory's Office of Procurement was allowed to return to work despite a recent conviction in an insurance fraud case. In the same month the Senate ordered an official investigation into contracts awarded by Tafua Faau Seumanutafa, the Chief Procurement Officer, and senior officials from the Department of Health and Social Security and the Department of Education. In May 2004 Seumanutafa pleaded guilty in the Hawaii Federal District Court to one count of conspiracy to defraud the US Government, in a case that also implicated senior officials from the Department of Health and Social Security and the Department of Education. In September the Senate Select Investigative Committee recommended that, while under investigation for alleged corruption, Lieutenant-Governor Faoa Aitofele Sunia have his name removed from the list of candidates for the forthcoming gubernatorial election. Governor Tulafono claimed that the charges were politically motivated.

Meanwhile, in February 2004 the US Federal Bureau of Investigation (FBI) began an investigation into the alleged misuse of US government funds. In March 2005 the FBI effected an unannounced search of the government offices in Pago Pago. In October Dr Sili K. Sataua and Patolo Mageo, the former Directors of the Education and Human Resources Departments, respectively, were sentenced in a federal court in Honolulu, Hawaii, to custodial sentences following their conviction on corruption charges. In September 2007 Lieutenant-Governor Faoa Aitofele Sunia and Senator Tulifua Tini Lam Yuen were detained on federal charges of fraud, bribery and obstruction in relation to business transactions involving the Department of Education. Their trial commenced in January 2010 in the US federal court in Washington, DC, but a mistrial was declared in the following month, owing to the jury's inability to reach a unanimous verdict, and criminal charges against both men were dismissed in April.

Natural Phenomena

The islands are vulnerable to adverse weather phenomena. In May 2003 severe flooding and landslides led to the deaths of five people, and in the following month US President George W. Bush declared American Samoa a federal disaster area. In January 2004 a state of emergency was declared when a cyclone damaged the islands. The USA allocated US $12.5m. towards the relief effort. In February 2005 Cyclone Olaf caused extensive damage to the territory's Manu'a islands. In October 2009 US President Barack Obama declared both American Samoa and Samoa a federal disaster area, following a tsunami, which had been caused by a massive submarine earthquake in the region of the Samoan islands; combined, the earthquake and tsunami resulted in 187 deaths (34 in American Samoa, 149 in Samoa and four in Tonga) and caused extensive damage to properties and infrastructure.

CONSTITUTION AND GOVERNMENT

Executive power is vested in the Governor, who is elected by popular vote and has authority that extends to all operations within the territory of American Samoa. The Governor has the power of veto with respect to legislation approved by the Fono (legislature). The Fono comprises the Senate and the House of Representatives, with a President and a Speaker presiding over their respective divisions. The Senate is composed of 18 members, elected, according to Samoan custom, from local chiefs, or Matai, for a term of four years. The House of Representatives consists of 20 members, who are elected by popular vote for a term of two years, and a non-voting delegate from Swains Island. The Fono meets twice a year, in January and July, for not more than 45 days, and at such special sessions as the Governor may call. The Governor, who serves a four-year term, has the authority to appoint heads of government departments with the approval of the Fono. The islands' non-voting Delegate to the US House of Representatives is elected every two years.

REGIONAL AND INTERNATIONAL CO-OPERATION

American Samoa is a member of the Pacific Community (see p. 422), and is an associate member of the UN's Economic and Social Commission for Asia and the Pacific (ESCAP, see p. 31). In November 2011 American Samoa was one of eight founding members of the Polynesian Leaders Group (see p. 478).

ECONOMIC AFFAIRS

In 2000, according to estimates by the American Samoa National Income and Product Accounts Task Force, American Samoa's gross national income (GNI), measured at constant 1999 prices, was about US $348.6m., equivalent to some $6,332 per head. Between 1973 and 1985, it was estimated, GNI increased, in real terms, at an average rate of 1.7% per year, with real GNI per head rising by only 0.1% per year. In 2010, according to estimates by the US Department of Commerce's Bureau of Economic Analysis, American Samoa's gross domestic product (GDP) was $615m. According to the World Bank, in 2002–11 the population increased by an average of 1.7% per year.

Agriculture, hunting, forestry and fishing are forecast to engage 23.3% of the total labour force in mid-2013, according to FAO estimates. According to estimates by the American Samoa National Income and Product Accounts Task Force, the sector (excluding fish-processing) accounted for 11.3% of GDP in 2002. Agricultural production provides little surplus for export. Major crops are coconuts, bananas, taro, pineapples, yams and breadfruit. Local fisheries are at subsistence level, but tuna-canning plants at Pago Pago process fish from US, Taiwanese and South Korean vessels. Canned tuna constituted 78.8% of export revenue in 2010/11, when earnings amounted to US $13.4m.

Within the industrial sector, manufacturing activities engaged 35.3% of the employed labour force in 2000. Fish-canning is the dominant industry; in 2001 some 70% of those employed in these factories were guest workers from Samoa (formerly Western Samoa). According to official estimates, basic employment in fish-processing increased from 1,300 workers in 1975 to 4,546 in 2005. According to estimates by the American Samoa National Income and Product Accounts Task Force, fish-processing accounted for 22.3% of GDP in 2002. Other manufacturing activities include garment-manufacturing, meat-canning, handicrafts, dairy-farming, orchid-farming, and the production of soap, perfume, paper products and alcoholic beverages. The construction sector engaged 6.4% of the employed labour force in 2000.

Service industries engage a majority of the employed labour force in American Samoa (55.2% in 2000), and the sector contributed 51.5% of GDP in 2002, according to estimates by the American Samoa National Income and Product Accounts Task Force. The Government, supported by federal government grants, engaged 27.7% of all employed workers in 2010, according to official estimates. The development of the tourism industry has been hindered by the

cost and paucity of air services. The number of tourist arrivals declined from 44,158 in 2000 to 21,929 in 2011. Of those, 43.0% were from Samoa, while 29.9% originated from the USA and 12.8% from New Zealand.

In 2005/06 American Samoa recorded a visible trade deficit of US $140.7m. Most of American Samoa's trade is conducted with the USA, which purchased almost all exports and supplied 54.4% of total imports (excluding government purchases and cannery goods) in 2010/11. Other significant sources of imports in that year included New Zealand, the Republic of Korea, Fiji and Samoa. Principal imports in 2010/11 included food, miscellaneous manufactured articles, construction materials, and machinery and transport equipment. The principal exports were canned tuna and fish meal.

A fiscal surplus of US $2.6m. was recorded in the year to September 2010. The annual rate of inflation averaged 5.4% in 2008–11. Consumer prices increased by 8.1% in 2011. An estimated 10.5% of the total labour force were unemployed in 2003.

Economic development has been hindered by the islands' remote location and limited infrastructure. A controversial minimum wage structure, whereby American Samoa's minimum hourly rates of pay were considerably lower than those of the mainland USA, was largely attributed to the presence of two tuna-canning plants, which together provided employment for almost one-half of the islands' labour force, thus exerting substantial influence over the setting of wage levels. However, the remit of US minimum wage legislation was extended to American Samoa from 2007, although the implementation of the minimum wage increase was subsequently postponed until September 2010. The closure of the COS Samoa Packing plant in 2009, which resulted in the loss of about 2,000 jobs, together with retrenchment at the other tuna cannery, StarKist Samoa, had a major impact on the economy. However, the sale of the COS plant to a US company, TriMarine, led to the resumption of fish-processing operations in 2011. The company opened a major cold storage facility in Atu'u in April 2013 and expected to begin construction in May of a sea wall enabling the establishment of a new tuna cannery. Furthermore, by mid-2011 the work-force of StarKist had been expanded to more than 2,000, supported by government tax concessions. A budget of US $455m. was approved for 2012/13, and the Government announced several measures aimed at stimulating the economy. These included the planting of 2,000 cocoa trees in an effort to revive the export of the commodity and the introduction of a Comprehensive Economic Development Strategy, which focused on developing transport infrastructure, agriculture and tourism in the Manu'a islands.

PUBLIC HOLIDAYS

2014: 1 January (New Year's Day), 20 January (Martin Luther King Day), 17 February (Presidents' Day), 17 April (Flag Day, commemorating the first raising of the US flag in American Samoa), 26 May (Memorial Day), 4 July (Independence Day), 1 September (Labor Day), 13 October (Columbus Day), 11 November (Veterans' Day), 27 November (Thanksgiving Day), 25 December (Christmas Day).

Statistical Survey

Source (unless otherwise indicated): Statistics Division, Department of Commerce, Pago Pago, AS 96799; tel. 633-5155; fax 633-4195; internet www.spc.int/prism/Country/AS/ASindex.html.

AREA AND POPULATION

Area: 201 sq km (77.6 sq miles); *By Island* (sq km): Tutuila 137; Ta'u 46; Ofu 7; Olosega 5; Swains Island (Olohenga) 3; Aunu'u 2; Rose 1.

Population: 57,291 (males 29,264, females 28,027) at census of 1 April 2000; 55,519 at census of 1 April 2010. *Mid-2013* (Secretariat of the Pacific Community estimate) 68,329 (Source: Pacific Regional Information System). *By Island* (2010 census): Western district 31,329; Eastern district 23,030; Manu'a District (Ta'u, Olosega and Ofu islands) 1,143; Swains Island (Olohenga) 17.

Density (at mid-2013): 339.9 per sq km.

Population by Age and Sex (Secretariat of the Pacific Community estimates at mid-2013): *0–14:* 22,972 (males 11,906, females 11,066); *15–64:* 41,966 (males 21,376, females 20,590); *65 and over:* 3,391 (males 1,579, females 1,812); *Total* 68,329 (males 34861, females 33,468) (Source: Pacific Regional Information System).

Ethnic Groups (2000 census): Samoan 50,545; part-Samoan 1,991; Asian 1,631; Tongan 1,598; Total (incl. others) 57,291.

Principal Towns (population at 2010 census): Tafuna 7,945; Nu'uuli 3,955; Pago Pago (capital) 3,656; Ili'ili 3,195; Pava'ia'i 2,450; Aua 2,077.

Births, Marriages and Deaths (2011): Registered live births 1,287 (birth rate 19.3 per 1,000); Registered marriages 191 (marriage rate 2.9 per 1,000); Registered deaths 283 (death rate 4.2 per 1,000).

Life Expectancy (years at birth, 2011): 74.2 (males 71.3; females 77.3).

Economically Active Population (persons aged 16 years and over, 2000 census): Agriculture, hunting, forestry, fishing and mining 517; Manufacturing 5,900; Construction 1,066; Trade, restaurants and hotels 2,414; Transport, storage, communications and utilities 1,036; Financing, insurance, real estate and business services 311; Community, social and personal services 5,474; *Total employed* 16,718 (males 9,804, females 6,914); Unemployed 909 (males 494, females 415); *Total labour force* 17,627 (males 10,298, females 7,329) (Source: US Department of Commerce, *2000 Census of Population and Housing*). *2003* (estimates): Total employed 14,319; Unemployed 1,681; Total labour force 16,000 (Source: US Department of State). *2005* (official estimates): Basic employment 8,428 (Fish-processing 4,546, Government employment—supported by federal grants 3,282, Other 600); Non-basic employment 8,916; Total employment 17,344. *Mid-2013* (estimates): Agriculture, etc. 7,000; Total labour force 30,000 (Source: FAO).

AGRICULTURE, ETC.

Principal Crops ('000 metric tons, 2011, FAO estimates): Coconuts 6.9; Taro 8.8; Bananas 0.7.

Livestock (year ending September 2011, FAO estimates): Pigs 10,500; Cattle 110; Chickens 40,000.

Livestock Products (metric tons, 2011, FAO estimates): Pig meat 315; Chicken meat 24; Cows' milk 26; Hen eggs 45.

Fishing (metric tons, live weight, 2010): Total catch 5,261 (Albacore 3,947; Yellowfin tuna 469; Wahoo 125; Bigeye tuna 491).

Source: FAO.

INDUSTRY

Production (2009, estimated production): Electric energy 202 million kWh. Source: UN Industrial Commodity Statistics Database.

FINANCE

Currency and Exchange Rates: United States currency is used: 100 cents = 1 United States dollar (US $). *Sterling and Euro Equivalents* (31 December 2012): £1 sterling = US $1.578; €1 = US $1.319; US $100 = £63.37 = €75.79.

Federal Direct Expenditures (US $ million, year ending September 2010): Retirement and disability payments 61; Grants 408; Total (incl. others) 515 (Source: US Census Bureau, *Consolidated Federal Funds Report*).

Budget (US $ '000, year ending September 2010): *Revenue:* Taxes 58,933; Licences and permits 1,003; Intergovernmental 183,753; Charges for services 7,587; Fines and fees 2,616; Total (incl. others) 267,357. *Expenditure:* General government 79,398; Public safety 17,722; Public works 26,863; Health and recreation 27,065; Education and culture 78,517; Economic development 23,103; Capital projects 7,858; Debt-servicing 4,192; Total 264,718.

Cost of Living (Consumer Price Index; base: October–December 2007 = 100): All items (excl. rent) 110.9 in 2009; 116.2 in 2010; 125.6 in 2011.

Gross Domestic Product (US $ million at current prices): 609 in 2008; 714 in 2009; 615 in 2010 (Source: Bureau of Economic Analysis, US Department of Commerce).

Expenditure on the Gross Domestic Product (US $ million at current prices, 2010): Government consumption expenditure and gross investment 325; Personal consumption expenditure 412; Private fixed investment 22; Change in private inventories –7; *Total domestic expenditure* 752; Exports of goods and services 366; *Less* Imports of goods and services 502; *GDP in purchasers' values* 615 (Source: Bureau of Economic Analysis, US Department of Commerce).

Gross Domestic Product by Economic Activity (US $ million at current prices, 2002): Agriculture and fishing (excl. fish-processing) 54.3; Fish-processing 107.3; Wholesale and retail trade 36.6; Government services 100.0; Other services 111.3; Other non-services 71.9; *Total* 481.4. Note: Recorded accounts are not available; figures represent the findings of the American Samoa National Income and Product Accounts Task Force, established to produce reliable economic statistics for the territory.

EXTERNAL TRADE

Principal Commodities (US $ million, year ending September 2011): *Imports* (excl. government purchases and cannery goods):

Food 86.0 (Fish 28.3; Frozen meat 5.7); Fuel and oil 3.1; Textiles and clothing 4.7 (Wearing apparel 3.5); Machinery and transport equipment 21.2 (Road motor vehicles and parts 10.8; Ship parts 6.6); Miscellaneous manufactured articles 69.4 (Tin plates 12.7); Construction materials 27.0; Total (incl. others) 215.2. *Exports:* Total exports 17.0 (Canned tuna 13.4; Fish meal 3.6).

Principal Trading Partners (US $ million, year ending September 2011): *Imports* (excl. government purchases and cannery goods): Australia 4.6; China, People's Republic 4.3; Fiji 16.3; Japan 1.5; Korea, Republic 16.5; New Zealand 25.0; Papua New Guinea 1.9; Samoa 10.8; Singapore 1.1; USA 117.0; Total (incl. others) 215.2. *Exports:* Total 17.0 (almost entirely to the USA).

TRANSPORT

Road Traffic ('000 registered motor vehicles, year ending September 2011): Passenger cars 8.8; Total 9.4.

International Sea-borne Shipping (freight traffic, '000 metric tons, year ending September 2011): Goods loaded 82; Goods unloaded 417.

Civil Aviation (Pago Pago Int. Airport, year ending September 2011): Flights 3,511; Passengers (excl. transit) 134,760 (Boarding 68,782, Disembarking 65,978); Transit 1,211; Freight and mail loaded 4,740,000 lb; Freight and mail unloaded 5,354,000 lb.

TOURISM

Tourist Arrivals by Country (2011): Australia 910; New Zealand 2,805; Philippines 307; Samoa 9,439; Tonga 368; United Kingdom 121; USA 6,548; Total (incl. others) 21,929.

Tourism Receipts (US $ million): 9 in 1996; 10 in 1997; 10 in 1998.

Source: World Tourism Organization.

COMMUNICATIONS MEDIA

Telephones ('000 main lines in use, 2010): 9.8.

Mobile Cellular Telephones (2010): 20,053 subscribers.

Source: International Telecommunication Union.

EDUCATION

Pre-primary (2011 unless otherwise indicated): 32 schools (2007); 140 teachers (2006); 1,923 pupils.

Primary (2011 unless otherwise indicated): 33 schools (2007); 481 teachers (2009); 11,542 pupils.

Secondary (2011 unless otherwise indicated): 12 high schools (2007); 219 teachers (2009); 5,108 pupils.

Higher (2011): American Samoa Community College 2,042 students.

Source: American Samoa Department of Education.

Directory

The Government
(May 2013)

Governor: Lolo Matalasi Moliga (took office 4 Jan. 2013).

Lieutenant-Governor: Lemanu Peleti Mauga (took office 4 Jan. 2013).

GOVERNMENT OFFICES

Governor's Office: A. P. Lutali Executive Office Bldg, Pago Pago, AS 96799; tel. 633-4116; fax 633-2269; internet www.americansamoa.gov.

Department of the Interior, Office of Insular Affairs (OIA): Field Office of the OIA, Dept of the Interior, POB 1725, Pago Pago, AS 96799; tel. 633-2800; fax 633-2415; internet www.interior.gov/oia/islands/american-samoa.cfm; Field Representative Lydia Faleafine Nomura.

Hawaii Office of the American Samoa Government: Amerika Samoa Office, 1427 Dillingham Blvd, Suite 210, Honolulu, HI 96817, USA; tel. (808) 847-1998; fax (808) 845-3420; e-mail hawaii.office@as.gov; Dir Afimutasi Gus Hannemann, Jr.

Department of Administrative Services: American Samoa Government, Executive Office Bldg, Utulei, Pago Pago, AS 96799; tel. 633-4156; fax 633-1841; e-mail das@as.gov; Dir Eliki Afalava.

Department of Agriculture: American Samoa Government, Executive Office Bldg, Utulei, Pago Pago, AS 96799; tel. 699-9272; fax 699-4031; e-mail gurrpete@yahoo.com; Dir PETER GURR.

Department of Commerce: American Samoa Government, Executive Office Bldg, 2nd Floor, POB 1147, Utulei, Pago Pago, AS 96799; tel. 633-5155; fax 633-4195; e-mail lelei.peau@noaa.gov; internet www.doc.as; Dir LELEI PEAU.

Department of Education: American Samoa Government, Executive Office Bldg, Utulei, Pago Pago, AS 96799; tel. 633-5237; fax 633-4240; e-mail philoj@doe.as; internet www.doe.as; Dir VAITINASA SALU HUNKIN-FINAU.

Department of Homeland Security: POB 4567, Pago Pago, AS 96799; tel. 633-2827; fax 633-2979; e-mail mrsala@americansamoa .gov; Dir UTUALII IUNIASOLUA TULUI SAVUSA.

Department of Human Resources: American Samoa Government, Executive Office Bldg, Utulei, Pago Pago, AS 96799; tel. 633-4485; fax 633-1139; e-mail sonnythompson@samoatelco.com; Dir LE'I SONNY THOMPSON.

Department of Human and Social Services: American Samoa Government, Pago Pago, AS 96799; tel. 633-7506; fax 633-7449; e-mail jsuisala@dhss.as; internet www.dhss.as; Dir Dr MEKI SOLOMONA TAEAOAFUA.

Department of Legal Affairs: American Samoa Government, Executive Office Bldg, Utulei, Pago Pago, AS 96799; tel. 633-4163; fax 633-1838; e-mail attygeneral.americansamoa@gmail.com; Dir Attorney-General AFOA MOEGA LUTU.

Department of Marine and Wildlife Resources: American Samoa Government, Executive Office Bldg, Utulei, Pago Pago, AS 96799; tel. 633-4456; fax 633-5944; e-mail marine@americansamoa .gov; Dir RUTH S. MATAGI-TOFIGA.

Department of Parks and Recreation: American Samoa Government, Pago Pago, AS 96799; tel. 699-9614; fax 699-4427; e-mail parks@americansamoa.gov; Dir PILI GAOTEOTE.

Department of Public Health: American Samoa Government, Pago Pago, AS 96799; tel. 633-4606; fax 633-5379; e-mail eponausuia .dog@gmail.com; Dir TUILEAMA NUA.

Department of Public Information: American Samoa Government, Pago Pago, AS 96799; tel. 633-4191; fax 633-1044; e-mail public .info@as.gov; Dir SINIVA ANOA'I.

Department of Public Safety: American Samoa Government, Pago Pago, AS 96799; tel. 633-1111; fax 633-7296; e-mail commissioner@as.gov; Dir WILLIAM E. HALECK.

Department of Public Works: American Samoa Government, Pago Pago, AS 96799; tel. 699-9921; fax 699-9913; e-mail faleosina@asgdpw.org; Dir FALEOSINA VOIGT.

Department of Samoan Affairs: American Samoa Government, Pago Pago, AS 96799; tel. 633-5201; fax 633-5590; e-mail lefitipese@ yahoo.com; Dir LEFITI A. PESE.

Department of Treasury: American Samoa Government, Executive Office Bldg, Utulei, Pago Pago, AS 96799; tel. 633-4155; fax 633-4100; e-mail treasury@as.gov; Dir FALEMA'O M. PILI.

Department of Youth and Women's Affairs: American Samoa Government, Executive Office Bldg, Utulei, Pago Pago, AS 96799; tel. 633-2836; fax 633-2875; e-mail youthandwomen@ americansamoa.gov; Dir PA'U FUIAVAILIILI ROY TAITO AUSAGE.

Environmental Protection Agency: American Samoa Government, Executive Office Bldg, Utulei, Pago Pago, AS 96799; tel. 633-2304; fax 633-5801; e-mail toafa.vaiagae@asepa.gov; internet asepa .gov; Dir FA'AMAO ASALELE.

Office of Planning and Budget: Executive Office Bldg, AP Lutali, 3rd Floor, Pago Pago AS 96799; tel. 633-4201; fax 633-1148; e-mail budget@as.gov; Dir CATHERINE D. SAELUA.

Office of Port Administration: American Samoa Government, Pago Pago, AS 96799; tel. 633-4251; fax 633-5281; e-mail pa@as.gov; Dir Dr CLAIRE TUIA POUMELE.

Office of Procurement: American Samoa Government, Tafuna, AS 96799; tel. 699-1170; fax 699-2387; e-mail op@as.gov; Dir SAPI MA'O-ENA (acting).

Office of Property Management: American Samoa Government, Pago Pago, AS 96799; tel. 699-6505; fax 699-6535; e-mail pm@as.gov; Dir MOAMOANIUA INO VITALE.

Office of Protection and Advocacy: POB 3937, Pago Pago, AS 96799; tel. 633-2441; fax 633-7286; e-mail tineimalepeai@yahoo.com; Dir TINEI MALEPEAI.

Office of the Public Defender: American Samoa Government, Executive Office Bldg, 3rd Floor, Utulei, Pago Pago, AS 96799; tel. 633-1286; fax 633-4745; e-mail public.defender@as.gov; Dir RUTH RISCH.

Legislature

FONO

Senate

The Senate has 18 members, elected, according to Samoan custom, from local chiefs (*Matai*) for a term of four years. The last election took place on 6 November 2012.

President: GAOTEOTE PALAIE GAOTEOTE.

House of Representatives

The House has 20 members who are elected by popular vote for a term of two years, and a non-voting delegate from Swains Island. The last election took place on 6 November 2012.

Speaker: SAVALI TALAVOU ALE.

CONGRESS

Since 1980 American Samoa has been able to elect, for a two-year term, a Delegate to the Federal Congress, who may vote in committee but not on the floor of the House of Representatives. At the election to the post on 6 November 2012, incumbent Congressman Eni F. Hunkin Faleomavaega was re-elected for a 13th two-year term.

Delegate of American Samoa: ENI F. HUNKIN FALEOMAVAEGA, US House of Representatives, 2422 Rayburn House Office Bldg, Washington, DC 20515, USA; tel. (202) 225-8577; fax (202) 225-8757; e-mail faleomavaega@mail.house.gov; internet www.house .gov/faleomavaega.

Election Commission

Government Election Office: POB 3970, Pago Pago, AS 96799; tel. 699-3571; fax 699-3574; e-mail info@americansamoaelectionoffice .org; internet www.americansamoaelectionoffice.org; Chief Election Officer FIATAUIAULAVA SAUNI (acting).

Political Organizations

While the USA's Democratic Party and the Republican Party have local chapters in American Samoa, most politicians in the territory remain non-partisan.

Judicial System

The judicial system of American Samoa consists of the High Court, presided over by the Chief Justice and assisted by an Associate Justice (appointed by the Secretary of the Interior), and a local judiciary in the District and Village Courts. The judges for these local courts are appointed by the Governor, subject to confirmation by the Senate of the Fono. The High Court consists of three Divisions: Appellate, Trial, and Land and Titles. The Appellate Division has limited original jurisdiction and hears appeals from the Trial Division, the Land and Titles Division and from the District Court when it has operated as a court of record. The Trial Division has general jurisdiction over all cases. The Land and Titles Division hears cases involving land or *Matai* titles.

The District Court hears preliminary felony proceedings, misdemeanours, infractions (traffic and health), civil claims less than US $3,000, small claims, Uniform Reciprocal Enforcement of Support cases, and *de novo* trials from Village Courts. The Village Courts hear matters arising under village regulations and local customs.

High Court: Pago Pago, AS 96799; tel. 633-1261; fax 633-1318; e-mail hcourt@samoatelco.com; Chief Justice MICHAEL KRUSE; Assoc. Justice LYLE L. RICHMOND.

Office of the Attorney-General: 3rd Floor, A. P. Lutali Executive Office Bldg, Utulei Village, POB 7, Pago Pago; tel. 633-4163; fax 633-4964; e-mail attygeneral.americansamoa@gmail.com; Attorney-General AFOA L. S. LUTU (designate).

Village Court: Pago Pago, AS 96799; tel. 633-1102; Judge FAISIOTA TAUANU'U.

Religion

The population is largely Christian, more than 50% being members of the Congregational Christian Church and about 20% being Roman Catholics.

CHRISTIANITY

American Samoa Council of Christian Churches: c/o CCCAS Offices, POB 1537, Pago Pago, AS 96799; f. 1985; 6 mem. churches; Pres. (vacant); Gen. Sec. Rev. ENOKA L. ALESANA (Congregational Christian Church in American Samoa).

The Roman Catholic Church

American Samoa comprises the single diocese of Samoa-Pago Pago, suffragan to the archdiocese of Samoa-Apia and Tokelau. At 31 December 2007 there were 15,000 adherents in the islands. The Bishop participates in the Catholic Bishops' Conference of the Pacific, based in Suva, Fiji.

Bishop of Samoa-Pago Pago: Rev. JOHN QUINN WEITZEL, Diocesan Pastoral Center, POB 596, Fatuoaiga, Pago Pago, AS 96799; tel. 699-1402; fax 699-1459; e-mail quinn@samoatelco.com.

The Anglican Communion

American Samoa is within the diocese of Polynesia, part of the Church of the Province of New Zealand. The Bishop of Polynesia is resident in Fiji.

Protestant Churches

Congregational Christian Church in American Samoa (CCCAS): POB 1537, Pago Pago, AS 96799; tel. 699-9810; fax 699-1898; e-mail cccasgs@samoatelco.com; internet www.efkas.org; f. 1980; 39,000 mems (incl. congregations in New Zealand, Australia and USA) in 2011; Chair. Rev. LEATULAGI T. FAALEVAO.

Other active Protestant groups include the Baptist Church, the Christian Church of Jesus Christ, the Methodist Church, Assemblies of God, Church of the Nazarene and Seventh-day Adventists. The Church of Jesus Christ of Latter-day Saints (Mormons) is also represented.

The Press

American Samoa Tribune: 5 a week; circ. 4,500 (2006).

News Bulletin: Department of Public Information, American Samoa Government, Pago Pago, AS 96799; tel. 633-5490; daily (Mon.–Fri.); English; non-commercial; Editor PHILIP SWETT; circ. 1,800.

Samoa Journal and Advertiser: POB 3986, Pago Pago, AS 96799; tel. 633-2399; weekly; English and Samoan; Editor MICHAEL STARK; circ. 3,000.

Samoa News: POB 909, Pago Pago, AS 96799; tel. 633-5599; fax 633-4864; e-mail webmaster@samoanews.com; internet www.samoanews.com; owned by Osini Faleatasi Inc dba Samoa News; 6 a week; English and Samoan; Publr VERA M. ANNESLEY; circ. 6,000.

Broadcasting and Communications

TELECOMMUNICATIONS

American Samoa Telecommunications Authority: Box M, Pago Pago, AS 96799; tel. 633-1126; internet www.astca.net; provider of fixed telephone lines, mobile telecommunications and internet services; Exec. Dir ALEKI SENE, Sr.

Blue Sky Communications: 478 Laufou Shopping Center, Pago Pago, AS 96799; tel. 699-2759; fax 699-6593; e-mail webmaster@bluesky.as; internet www.bluesky.as; mobile telecommunications and internet services provider; Pres. and CEO ADOLFO MONTENEGRO.

BROADCASTING

Radio

KSBS-FM (Island 92): POB 793, Pago Pago, AS 96799; tel. 633-7000; fax 622-5727; e-mail info@ksbsfm92.com; internet www.ksbsfm92.com; commercial; Gen. Man. ESTHER PRESCOTT.

V103: POB 6758, Pago Pago, AS 96799; tel. 633-7793; fax 633-4493; e-mail thepeople@wvuv.com; internet www.wvuv.com; fmr govt-administered station leased to Radio Samoa Ltd in 1975; commercial; English and Samoan; 24 hours a day; Gen. Man. JOEY CUMMINGS.

Television

KVZK-TV: POB 3511, Pago Pago, AS 96799; tel. 633-4191; fax 633-1044; e-mail kvzk@americansamoa.gov; f. 1964; govt-owned; non-commercial; English and Samoan; broadcasts 18 hours daily on 2 channels; Dir PAOLO SIVIA SIVIA; Chief Eng. JEFFREY ALWIN.

Malama TV: Malama Communications, Inc, POB AB, Pago Pago 96799; tel. 699-5999; fax 699-6006; e-mail news@malama.tv; internet malama.solupress.com.

PCS-TV: POB U, Pago Pago, AS 96799; tel. 699-6853; e-mail pcstv11@yahoo.com; operates Channel 11; Owner BILL HYMAN.

Finance

(cap. = capital; dep. = deposits; m. = million; amounts in US dollars)

BANKING

Commercial Bank

ANZ Amerika Samoa Bank: POB 3790, Pago Pago, AS 96799; tel. 633-1151; fax 633-5057; internet www.anz.com.au/americansamoa; f. 1979; fmrly Amerika Samoa Bank; joined ANZ group in April 2001; Man. TERESE SALUMBIDES; 3 brs.

Development Bank

Development Bank of American Samoa: POB 9, Pago Pago, AS 96799; tel. 633-4031; fax 633-1163; e-mail dbasinfo@dbas.org; internet www.dbas.org; f. 1969; govt-owned and non-profit-making; Pres. JASON BETHAM (acting).

INSURANCE

American International Underwriters (South Pacific) Ltd: Pago Pago, AS 96799; tel. 633-4845.

Mark Solofa, Inc: POB 3149, Pago Pago, AS 96799; tel. 699-5902; fax 699-5904; e-mail marksalofainc@yahoo.com.

National Pacific Insurance Ltd: Centennial Bldg, POB 1386, Pago Pago, AS 96799; tel. 633-4266; fax 633-2964; e-mail contact@npipago.as; f. 1977; Country Man. JASON THOMAS.

Oxford Pacific Insurance Management: POB 1420, Pago Pago, AS 96799; tel. 633-4990; fax 633-2721; e-mail progressive_oxford@yahoo.com; f. 1977; represents major international property and life insurance cos; Pres. GREG F. DUFFY.

South Seas Financial Services Corporation: POB 1448, Pago Pago, AS 96799; tel. 633-7896; fax 633-7895; e-mail ssfs@samoatelco.com.

Trade and Industry

DEVELOPMENT ORGANIZATIONS

American Samoa Development Corporation: Pago Pago, AS 96799; tel. 633-4241; f. 1962; financed by private Samoan interests.

American Samoa Economic Advisory Commission: Pago Pago; Chair. JOHN WAIHEE.

Department of Commerce: see Government Offices; Dir FALESEU ELIU PAOPAO.

CHAMBER OF COMMERCE

Chamber of Commerce of American Samoa: POB 2446, Pago Pago, AS 96799; tel. 699-4814; fax 699-1878; e-mail info@amsamoachamber.com; internet www.amsamoachamber.com; 1979; Chair. DAVID ROBINSON.

UTILITIES

American Samoa Power Authority: POB PPB, Pago Pago, AS 96799; tel. 699-1234; fax 699-4329; internet www.aspower.com; supplies water and electricity throughout the islands; also manages sewer and solid waste collection; Chair. FONOTI PERELINI; Exec. Dir UTE ABE MALAE.

Transport

ROADS

There are about 150 km (93 miles) of paved and 200 km (124 miles) of secondary roads. Non-scheduled commercial buses operate a service over 350 km (217 miles) of main and secondary roads. There were some 9,400 registered motor vehicles in the islands in 2010/11.

SHIPPING

There are various passenger and cargo services from the US Pacific coast, Japan, Australia (mainly Sydney) and New Zealand that call at Pago Pago, which is one of the deepest and most sheltered harbours in the Pacific. Inter-island boats provide frequent services between Samoa and American Samoa.

Pacific Shipping Services: POB 4922, Pago Pago, AS 96799; tel. 633-0266; fax 633-0267; operated by Polynesia Shipping.

PM&O Line: Suite 202, Fagatogo Sq., POB 5023, Pago Pago, AS 96799; tel. 633-4527; fax 633-4530; e-mail paige@blueskynet.as; f. 1978.

Samoa Pacific Shipping: Samoan Sports Bldg, 1 Main St, Fagatogo, POB 1417, Pago Pago, AS 96799; tel. 633-4665; fax 699-4667;

e-mail spsi@samoatelco.com; internet www.hamburgsud.com; f. 1988; Gen. Man. VA'A UITUALAGI.

CIVIL AVIATION

There is an international airport at Tafuna, 11 km (7 miles) from Pago Pago, and smaller airstrips on the islands of Ta'u and Ofu. International services are operated by Hawaiian Airlines and Polynesian Blue.

Inter Island Airways: 4929 Airport Rd, Hangar 2, POB 4929, Pago Pago Intl Airport, Pago Pago, AS 96799; tel. 699-7100; e-mail info@ interislandair.com; internet www.interislandair.com; f. 1993; scheduled and charter passenger and cargo services from Pago Pago to the Manu'a Islands and Samoa; Pres. ALEX SENE, Jr; Dir of Operations VILIAME LOMALOMA.

Samoa Aviation: POB 280, Pago Pago Int. Airport, Pago Pago, AS 96799; tel. 699-9106; fax 699-9751; f. 1986; operates service between Pago Pago and Samoa, Tonga and Niue; Pres. ANDRE LAVIGNE.

Tourism

The tourism industry is encouraged by the Government, but its development has been impeded by the cost and paucity of air services. A total of 21,929 tourists visited the islands in 2011. The majority of tourists came from Samoa, the USA and New Zealand.

American Samoa Visitors Bureau: POB 4240, Pago Pago, AS 96799; tel. 699-9805; fax 699-9806; e-mail info@americansamoa .travel; internet www.americansamoa.travel; Exec. Dir DAVID VAEAFE.

Pago Pago Visitors Association (PPVA): f. 2004; Pres. TOM DRABBLE.

Defence

The USA is responsible for the defence of American Samoa. The US Pacific Command is based in Hawaii, but the territory receives regular naval visits and assistance in surveillance of its waters.

Education

The Government's early childhood education division provides facilities for all children between three and five years of age. Education is compulsory for children between six and 18 years of age. The education system is based on the US pattern of eight years' attendance at an elementary school and four years' enrolment at a high school. In 2011 there were 11,542 pupils enrolled in primary education and 5,108 at secondary level. In 2007 there were 33 primary schools and 12 secondary schools. The American Samoa Community College had 2,042 students in 2011.

GUAM

Introductory Survey

LOCATION, CLIMATE, LANGUAGE, RELIGION, FLAG, CAPITAL

Guam is the southernmost and largest of the Mariana Islands, situated about 2,170 km (1,350 miles) south of Tokyo (Japan) and 5,300 km (3,300 miles) west of Honolulu (Hawaii, USA). The temperature normally ranges between 24°C (75°F) and 30°C (86°F) in June–November, but it is generally cooler and drier from December to May. The average annual rainfall is about 2,000 mm (79 ins). English is the official language, but Japanese and Chamorro, the local language, are also spoken. The principal religion is Christianity, the majority of the population being Roman Catholics. The national flag of the United States of America (q.v.) is used by Guam. The capital is Hagåtña (formerly Agaña).

CONTEMPORARY POLITICAL HISTORY

Historical Context

Members of a Spanish expedition, led by the Portuguese navigator Fernão Magalhães (Ferdinand Magellan), were the first Europeans to discover Guam, visiting the island in 1521. Guam was claimed by Spain in 1565, and the first Jesuit missionaries arrived three years later. The native Micronesian population is estimated to have declined from 100,000 in 1521 to fewer than 5,000 in 1741, owing largely to a combination of aggression by the Spaniards and exposure to imported diseases. The intermarrying of Micronesians, Spaniards and Filipinos resulted in the people now called Chamorros. Guam was ceded to the USA after the Spanish–American War of 1898. In 1941, during the Second World War, Guam was invaded by Japanese troops, but following fierce fighting the island was recaptured by US forces in 1944.

Guam became an Unincorporated Territory of the USA, under the jurisdiction of the US Department of the Interior, in 1950. The island continued to be administered by an appointed Governor. However, in 1970 the population of Guam chose its first directly elected Governor, Carlos Camacho of the Republican Party, and in 1972 a new law gave Guam the right to elect one Delegate to the US House of Representatives in Washington, DC. The Delegate was permitted to vote in committee but not on the floor of the House. In 1976, in a referendum held on the island, it was determined that Guam should maintain its close links with the USA, but that negotiations should be held to improve the island's status. In a further referendum, conducted in 1982, in which only 38% of eligible voters participated, the status of a Commonwealth, in association with the USA, was the most favoured of six options, being supported by 48% of voters. In 1987, in a referendum on the provisions of a draft law aimed at conferring the status of Commonwealth on the territory, voters approved the central proposal, while rejecting articles empowering the Guam Government to restrict immigration and granting the indigenous Chamorro people the right to determine the island's future political status. In a further referendum later in the year, both outstanding provisions were approved. Negotiations between the Guam Com-

mission on Self-Determination and the USA subsequently continued.

Domestic Political Affairs

Having won the gubernatorial election held in late 1974, Ricardo Bordallo of the Democratic Party took office in January 1975. Bordallo was replaced as Governor in early 1979 by the Republican Paul McDonald Calvo, but he returned to the position in 1983, serving until January 1987. In February 1987 Bordallo was found guilty of charges of bribery, extortion and conspiracy to obstruct justice, and was sentenced to 30 years' imprisonment (later reduced to nine years) in April. In November Bordallo's wife, Madeleine, was elected to replace him as Senator (as the chamber's members were known) in the Guam Legislature. In October 1988 Ricardo Bordallo won an appeal and his sentence was cancelled. Bordallo was liable for imprisonment in the USA on charges of obstruction and attempting to influence witnesses, but in January 1990 he committed suicide. Madeleine Bordallo was the Democratic candidate at the gubernatorial election of November, when Republican Joseph Ada, who had replaced her husband as Governor in 1987, was re-elected. Concurrent elections to the Guam Legislature resulted in a Democratic majority of one seat.

At legislative elections in November 1992 the Democrats increased their representation to 14 of the 21 seats, while the Republicans secured only seven. Robert Underwood, the Democratic candidate, was elected as the island's Delegate to the US House of Representatives, replacing the Republican Ben Blaz.

In January 1994 the US Congress approved legislation providing for the transfer of 3,200 acres of land on Guam from federal to local control. This was a significant achievement for the Government of Guam, which had campaigned for the return of 27,000 acres (20% of Guam's total area), appropriated by US military forces after the Second World War. However, Chamorro rights activists claimed that land should be transferred to the original landowners rather than to the Government of Guam.

At the gubernatorial election held in November 1994 the Democratic candidate, Carl Gutierrez, defeated his Republican opponent, Tommy Tanaka, while Madeleine Bordallo was elected as Lieutenant-Governor. Legislative elections held concurrently resulted in a Democratic majority, with candidates of the party securing 13 seats, while the Republicans won eight. Robert Underwood was re-elected unopposed as Delegate to the US House of Representatives.

It was reported in 1995 that US President Bill Clinton had appointed a team of Commonwealth negotiators to review the draft Guam Commonwealth Act. In 1997 the Guam Commission on Self-Determination was replaced by the Guam Commission on Decolonization, headed by the Governor. A plebiscite on the political status of Guam was originally scheduled for November 2000 but was subsequently deferred, to coincide with the island's legislative and presidential elections scheduled for November 2004. However, in May 2004 legislation was drafted that would postpone the referendum until the number of Chamorro voters registered by the Guam Elections Committee had reached the requisite 50%.

At elections in November 1996 Republican members regained a majority in the Guam Legislature, winning 11 seats, while Democratic candidates secured 10 seats. In a concurrent referendum, voters approved a proposed reduction in the number of Senators from 21 to 15 (effective from November 1998) and plans to impose an upper limit (2.5% of total budgetary expenditure) on legislative expenses. However, a proposal to restrict the number of terms that Senators could seek to serve in the Legislature was rejected by voters. The island's Delegate to the US House of Representatives, Robert Underwood, was re-elected unopposed.

In June 1998 Underwood secured approval from the US authorities to change the spelling of Guam's capital from Agaña to Hagåtña. The change was effected in order to reflect more accurately the original Chamorro language name for the town.

Underwood was re-elected as Guam's Delegate to the US House of Representatives in November 1998. Concurrent gubernatorial and legislative elections resulted in the return to office of incumbent Governor Carl Gutierrez and of Lieutenant-Governor Madeleine Bordallo. (In December former Governor Joseph Ada alleged that Gutierrez's victory had been achieved by fraudulent means, and later in the month a Guam court invalidated the election result and ordered that a new poll be held. However, in February 1999 the Superior Court of Guam found that there had been no electoral malpractice, and confirmed the appointments of Gutierrez and Bordallo.) In elections to the 15-member Legislature, 12 candidates of the Republican Party and three candidates of the Democratic Party were elected as Senators. Underwood was re-elected as Guam's Delegate to the US House of Representatives in November 2000, winning 78.1% of the votes cast. At concurrent legislative elections, eight candidates of the Republican Party and seven candidates of the Democratic Party were successful.

Underwood secured the Democratic nomination for the gubernatorial election of November 2002, but was defeated at the poll by the Republican candidate, Felix P. Camacho, who received 55.4% of the votes cast. Madeleine Bordallo was designated Guam's Delegate to the US House of Representatives. Nine Democratic candidates were elected to the Legislature, while the Republican party's representation decreased to six seats. Governor Camacho pledged to halt the widely perceived rise in corruption and misallocation of public funds on Guam.

Also in November 2002, the US Congress approved the Guam War Claims Review Commission Act, which provided for the creation of a body to investigate events that had followed the island's occupation by Japanese forces during the Second World War. Furthermore, the Commission was to determine whether the USA had offered the islanders sufficient compensation for their mistreatment prior to Guam's liberation in 1944. The War Claims Review Commission, appointed in September 2003, acknowledged the hardship and suffering of the people of Guam, their 'courageous loyalty to the USA' and the inequality in compensation payments with regard to similar claims. In January 2013 the Guam World War II Loyalty Recognition Act was reintroduced; earlier versions of the legislation had previously been approved by the US House of Representatives (in May 2007 and February 2009), but had not been passed by the Senate. At April 2013 the proposed legislation remained outstanding.

In July 2003, in response to the high costs incurred by a typhoon recovery programme, Delegate Madeleine Bordallo introduced a bill to amend the Organic Act of Guam (see Constitution and Government). The legislation attempted to empower the US Secretary of the Interior to waive Guam's outstanding federal debt, in order to offset social costs caused by migration to Guam from Compact of Free Association countries (see the Marshall Islands). The measure was defeated, although the amended Compact of Free Association signed in December approved some US $14m. to offset Guam's migration costs and erased $157m. of debt owed to the US federal Government. New legislation seeking to amend the Organic Act of Guam, in order to grant the territory greater autonomy from the US federal Government, was submitted to the Guam Legislature in February 2006, and Governor Camacho announced his intention to restart negotiations on some $60.5m. of debt relief for Guam.

At the legislative election held in November 2004 the Republican party secured a majority, winning nine of the 15 seats in the Guam Legislature. At a concurrently held plebiscite, a proposal to legalize casinos on the island was rejected.

Meanwhile, numerous investigations into allegations of official corruption were conducted. In April 2003 a former Republican Senator and gubernatorial candidate, Tommy Tanaka, pleaded guilty to charges of misprision of felony relating to his alleged involvement in a fraudulent government contract. In the same month Joseph Mafnas, a former chief of the Guam police department, was indicted on forgery charges. In March 2004 former Governor Carl Gutierrez was tried for the misappropriation of public funds, although all but two minor charges against him were dismissed in April. Further charges of theft by deception and official misconduct against Gutierrez were dismissed in September, although he stood trial in June 2005 for alleged improper dealings relating to the island's retirement fund. He was acquitted of all charges in the

following month, and in August announced his intention to contest the next gubernatorial election. In December 2005 new corruption charges connected to the retirement fund were filed against Gutierrez, and in January 2006 further charges relating to his administration of the Guam Memorial Hospital were brought against him; however, none of these charges resulted in a conviction.

In an important decision in January 2006, the US House of Representatives approved an amendment to grant limited voting rights to the Delegate from Guam. Although the Delegate would be unable to vote on the final passage of legislation, the ruling would permit the island's envoy to cast a vote in the Committee of the Whole House on the State of the Union, a means by which the House expedites consideration of certain legislation, particularly amendments. The decision was expected to allow for more effective lobbying on the part of Guam's Delegate to Washington, DC, and the promotion of the islanders' views within the federal system. However, in January 2011 the Republican-controlled House of Representatives voted to rescind the 'symbolic' voting rights of territorial delegates. Madeleine Bordallo joined with the Delegates from American Samoa, the Northern Mariana Islands, the District of Columbia, Puerto Rico and the Virgin Islands to express opposition to the revocation of the privilege, arguing that it rendered the House 'less transparent and less responsive to the American people'.

Meanwhile, legislative and gubernatorial elections took place in November 2006. Felix P. Camacho secured a second term as Governor, defeating Robert Underwood. Michael W. Cruz was elected Lieutenant-Governor, replacing Kaleo Moylan. Madeleine Bordallo secured a third term as Delegate to the US House of Representatives. The Republicans retained control of the Guam Legislature, albeit with a decreased majority, winning eight seats, compared with the Democrats' seven.

On 4 November 2008 legislative elections were held at which the Democrats won 10 of the 15 seats in the Guam Legislature. The Democrats' increased majority was largely attributed to the party's opposition to the legalization of gambling in Tamuning, an initiative that appeared to be widely unpopular with the electorate. At a concurrent poll, Madeleine Bordallo won a fourth term as Delegate to the US House of Representatives.

US Secretary of State Hillary Clinton paid a brief visit to Guam in October 2010 during a two-week official tour of the Asia-Pacific region. During her stay, Clinton met with Governor Camacho and other local officials and pledged her support for a proposal to waive visa requirements for Chinese and Russian nationals in a bid to boost Guam's tourism industry.

Meanwhile, in September 2010 Edward (Eddie) Calvo, with Ray Tenorio as his running mate, was elected as the Republicans' candidate for the forthcoming gubernatorial election. Incumbent Governor Camacho was constitutionally barred from seeking re-election to a third term in office. The Democrats' gubernatorial nomination was secured by the sole candidate, former Governor Carl Gutierrez. Following a very closely contested poll, which took place on 2 November, the election commission voted unanimously to recount all of the ballots. Eddie Calvo, the son of former Governor Paul McDonald Calvo, was subsequently declared Governor, securing 20,066 votes (50.25% of the total) to Gutierrez's 19,579 (49.03%). In the legislative poll, nine Democrats and six Republicans were elected. Madeleine Bordallo secured re-election to a fifth successive term as Delegate to the US House of Representatives.

Draft legislation providing for the election of two Guam representatives to the US Senate was introduced in the Guam Legislature by Senator Frank Blas, Jr, in January 2011. However, the proposed legislation was deemed unconstitutional, since only members of the federal union of the USA were entitled to send representatives to the Senate, and the bill did not proceed beyond the committee stage.

In June 2011 Governor Eddie Calvo raised the issue of self-determination in a speech to the UN Special Committee on Decolonization in New York, USA. The speech, delivered on Calvo's behalf by his sister, claimed that Guam's Chamorro people had been unable to reach their full potential because of the territory's political status. In a formal letter to US President Barack Obama in September, Calvo expressed his desire to seek self-determination for the territory, whether in the form of free association, statehood or full independence. Also that month, the Commission on Decolonization was convened for the first time in around a decade; members of the Commission voted to hold regular meetings henceforth.

At legislative elections held on 6 November 2012 Democrats won nine seats in the Guam Legislature and Republicans six. Madeleine Bordallo was re-elected for a sixth consecutive term as Delegate to the US House of Representatives, defeating Frank Blas, Jnr, with 58.0% of the votes cast.

Guam attracted international attention in mid-February 2013, following a violent incident in which three Japanese nationals were killed in a tourist area of the island. A suspect was subsequently apprehended and charged with three counts of murder and 11 of attempted murder. However, it was feared that the incident might harm the island's important tourism industry, which had registered record visitor numbers totalling more than 1.3m. in 2012, of whom more than 70% were from Japan.

In late February 2013 Governor Eddie Calvo visited Washington, DC, for official discussions with President Obama and other members of his Administration, notably on the impact of reduced federal budgetary expenditure on the military in Guam, and once again requested that the US authorities waive visa requirements for Chinese nationals in order to stimulate the Guam economy, particularly the tourism industry.

Strategic Military Significance

Guam remains of vital strategic importance to the USA. In 2001 the US Army announced plans to move some combat weaponry and equipment from Europe to storage bases in Guam, as well as in Taiwan and Hawaii, USA. During 2004–05 the US Air Force stationed several of its B-52 and B-2 bombers on Guam, following the construction of a new hangar on the island. Notwithstanding the concerns of some anti-war and Chamorro rights activists, the increased military presence on Guam was welcomed as a source of new investment and employment. Rights activists continued to express their opposition after plans were revealed to relocate 8,000 US marines and their families from US bases in Japan, including the Futenma base in the Japanese city of Ginwan on the island of Okinawa, to Guam, as part of a broader agreement on the redeployment of US forces; the Futenma base itself was to be relocated within Okinawa, to the nearby city of Nago. An agreement on the relocation of troops to Guam was concluded in May 2006, and funding of some US $6,000m. for the move was approved by the Japanese legislature in the following year. The US Government was to provide $4,000m. for the realignment. The relocation of troops, the implementation of which was expected to require as many as 15,000 skilled workers, was scheduled to begin in 2010, with a target completion date of 2014.

However, a change of leadership in the Japanese Government in September 2009 threatened to disrupt the process. Shortly after his inauguration, Prime Minister Yukio Hatoyama antagonized US officials by suggesting that his administration would conduct a review of the relocation pact. However, in May 2010 Hatoyama stated that the Government would, after all, implement the 2006 agreement. Hatoyama's apparent vacillation over the issue precipitated his resignation from the premiership in June. His replacement as Prime Minister, Naoto Kan, pledged his support for the controversial policy on Okinawa to which his predecessor had been obliged to adhere. However, a number of points of contention, including the extent of Japan's financial responsibility for the relocation of troops, remained unresolved. In May 2011 the Japanese Government announced that it was to suspend payment of US $3,000m. towards the relocation, and in the following month the US authorities confirmed that the bidding process for construction contracts associated with the project had been suspended indefinitely and that the 2014 deadline had been abandoned. However, a further change in the premiership in Japan resulted in a commitment to the pact by newly installed Prime Minister Yoshihiko Noda and confirmation that funding of $3,930m. would be made available for the project in the following financial year. Following a decision in February 2012 to separate the issues of the transfer of US troops and the relocation of the base, at the end of April, prior to a visit to the USA by Noda, agreement was reached on the transfer of some 5,000 US marines from Okinawa to Guam; a further 4,000 would be relocated to other US bases in the Pacific.

Guam's strategic significance was brought to international attention in March 2013, when the Democratic People's Republic of Korea (North Korea) threatened to launch attacks against the Republic of Korea (South Korea) and US military bases in the Pacific, including on Guam. The threats were made amid tensions regarding joint military exercises by South Korean and US forces and the intensification of sanctions against North Korea by the UN Security Council after it conducted out a nuclear weapons test in February. The US Government responded in April by announcing that it would deploy an US $800m. advanced missile defence system (Terminal High Altitude Area Defence System) on Guam within a few weeks (rather than in 2015, as previously expected) as a 'precautionary move' to strengthen its presence in the region.

The Environment and Natural Phenomena

In March 1998 delegates from several Pacific island nations and territories met in Hawaii to discuss methods of controlling the increasing population of brown tree snakes in Guam. The venomous reptile, which was accidentally introduced to the island (probably from the Solomon Islands) after the Second World War, had been responsible for frequent power cuts (as it was able to ascend electricity poles and short-circuit the lines), as well as for major environmental problems, notably the decimation of native bird, rodent and reptile populations. The US Geological Survey estimated the density of tree snakes on Guam to be roughly 13,000 per sq mile (nearly 5,020 per sq km) of forested land. By 2004 a team of 25 full-time snaketrappers and nine dog handlers was capturing an estimated 6,000

tree snakes annually at Guam's five main ports (air and sea), but in September of that year plans were announced to reduce funding to this programme by nearly one-half. Also in September, the US House of Representatives approved the Brown Tree Snake Control and Eradication Act, which allocated US $104m. of federal funds towards the elimination of Guam's snake population, and further funding was authorized by the US Senate in October and in subsequent years. In mid-2012 the authorities dropped large numbers of mice laced with a substance toxic from helicopters in an attempt to attract and kill the snakes, which were acknowledged to have had a significant negative economic, as well as ecological, impact on the island.

The island remained vulnerable to the impact of extreme weather formations. The island was declared a federal disaster area following Typhoon Chata'an in July 2002 and Supertyphoon Pongsona in December, which left some 35,000 islanders homeless. The US Government granted US $10m. towards the recovery effort.

CONSTITUTION AND GOVERNMENT

Guam is governed under the Organic Act of Guam of 1950, which gave the island statutory local power of self-government. Its inhabitants are citizens of the USA, although they are not permitted to vote in national elections. Guam's non-voting Delegate to the US House of Representatives is elected every two years. Executive power is vested in the Governor, who is elected by popular vote every four years. The heads of the executive departments are appointed by the Governor, with the consent of the Guam Legislature. The Legislature comprises 15 members, known as Senators, who are elected by popular vote every two years. It is empowered to enact legislation on local matters, including taxation and fiscal appropriations.

REGIONAL AND INTERNATIONAL CO-OPERATION

Guam is a member of the Pacific Community (see p. 422) and an associate member of the UN's Economic and Social Commission for Asia and the Pacific (ESCAP, see p. 31).

ECONOMIC AFFAIRS

In 2000, according to estimates by the Bank of Hawaii, Guam's gross national income (GNI), at current prices, was US $2,772.8m., equivalent to $16,575 per head. Between 1988 and 1993, it was estimated, GNI increased, in real terms, at an average rate of some 10% per year. GNI increased by 3.9% in 1994. Gross island product (GIP—the official measure of the territory's economic performance) was officially estimated at some $3,700m. in 2005, equivalent to almost $22,700 per head, while gross domestic product (GDP) was estimated at $4,577m. in 2010 by the US Department of Commerce's Bureau of Economic Analysis. In 2002–11, according to World Bank figures, the population increased at an average annual rate of 1.4%.

Agriculture (including forestry, fishing and mining) engaged only 0.2% of the employed labour force in 2012. The principal crops cultivated on the island include watermelons, coconuts, cucumbers, gherkins, bananas, runner beans, aubergines (eggplants), squash, tomatoes and papaya. Livestock reared includes pigs, goats and poultry. The fishing catch (excluding aquaculture) totalled an estimated 420 metric tons in 2010, according to FAO.

The industrial sector accounted for some 15% of GDP in 1993. According to official figures, in 1995 construction contributed 12.6% of GIP. Manufacturing industries, including textile and garment production and boat-building, engaged 2.7% of the employed labour force in 2012. Construction, which engaged 10.6% of the employed labour force in that year, is the dominant industrial activity, and this sector is closely related to the development of the tourism industry.

Service industries dominate the economy, engaging 86.5% of the employed labour force in 2012. The federal and territorial Governments together employed 25.5% of workers at that time. According to official estimates, the services sector contributed 69.2% of GIP in 1995. Tourism is Guam's most important industry. Some 1,159,800 tourists visited the island in 2011, when 77.1% of visitors were from Japan; visitor arrivals reportedly rose by more than 12% in 2012, to exceed 1.3m.

The territory consistently records a visible trade deficit, and in 2010 this amounted to US $86.7m. Major imports in 2011 included food and non-alcoholic beverages, plastics, leather and paper (particularly travel goods and handbags), transportation and parts (notably motor cars), miscellaneous manufactured goods, home appliances and equipment, and men's and women's apparel. The principal exports in 2011 were motor cars, fish, plastics, leather and paper, and construction materials. Singapore supplied 34.2% of total imports in 2002. Japan purchased 26.6% of the island's exports in 2011. Other important trading partners include Germany, Hong Kong, the Federated States of Micronesia, the Republic of Korea, the Philippines, Singapore, Taiwan and Palau. Guam is a low-duty port, and is an important distribution point for goods destined for Micronesia. Re-exports constitute a high proportion of Guam's exports, major commodities being petroleum and petroleum products, iron and steel scrap, and eggs.

In the year ending September 2011 there was a deficit of US $125.3m. on the general fund budget. Expenditure by the US federal Government in Guam totalled $2,012m. in 2009/10. The Government's total debt stood at $326.7m. at the end of the financial year 2003/04. The average annual rate of inflation was 5.2% in 2002–12. Consumer prices increased by 3.1% in 2012. Guam's unemployment rate averaged 11.5% in 2012.

Guam continues to receive considerable financial support from the USA, particularly in the area of defence. The proposed relocation of US marines and their families from the Japanese island of Okinawa to Guam (see Contemporary Political History), and the USA's planned development of a global hub for intelligence, surveillance and reconnaissance at Andersen air force base on Guam, were crucial to the island's strategic planning. Despite US President Barack Obama's allocation of US $566m. to military construction projects on Guam in the 2010/11 budget, concerns from within the US Congress about increasing costs, together with frequent changes of administration in Japan, led to a delay in the implementation of the relocation project. The perceived lack of clarity over the situation had a negative impact on Guam's economy in 2011, with the unemployment rate increasing to an estimated 15.6% in November of that year, although it had decreased to 10.9% by the end of 2012. In April 2012 the USA and Japan agreed to transfer some 5,000 US troops from Japan to Guam (rather than the 8,000 originally envisaged); a further 4,000 would be relocated to other US bases in the Pacific. The tourism sector was adversely affected by the tsunami disaster in Japan (which provides the overwhelming majority of Guam's visitors) in March 2011. However, assisted by the introduction of new direct flights from Taiwan and Palau, the weakness of the US currency and the removal of immigration requirements from Russian visitors, visitor numbers reportedly reached a record 1.3m. in 2012, revealing an urgent need for increased tourist accommodation on the island.

PUBLIC HOLIDAYS

2014: 1 January (New Year's Day), 20 January (Martin Luther King Day), 17 February (Presidents' Day), 3 March (Guam Discovery Day), 18 April (Good Friday), 26 May (Memorial Day), 4 July (US Independence Day), 21 July (Liberation Day), 1 September (Labor Day), 13 October (Columbus Day), 2 November (All Souls' Day), 11 November (Veterans' Day), 27 November (Thanksgiving Day), 8 December (Immaculate Conception), 25 December (Christmas Day).

Statistical Survey

Sources (unless otherwise stated): Guam Bureau of Statistics and Plans, PO Box 2950, Hagåtña; tel. 472-4201; fax 477-1812; internet www.bsp.guam.gov.

AREA AND POPULATION

Area: 541 sq km (209 sq miles).

Population: 154,805 (males 79,181, females 75,624) at census of 1 April 2000; 159,358 at census of 1 April 2010. *Mid-2013* (Secretariat of the Pacific Community estimate): 202,033 (Source: Pacific Regional Information System).

Density (at mid-2013): 373.4 per sq km.

Population by Age and Sex (Secretariat of the Pacific Community estimates at mid-2013): *0–14:* 51,718 (males 26,690, females 25,028); *15–64:* 135,592 (males 71,401, females 64,191); *65 and over:* 14,723 (males 7,071, females 7,652); *Total* 202,033 (males 105,162, females 96,871) (Source: Pacific Regional Information System).

Ethnic Groups (2000 census): Chamorro 57,297; Filipino 40,729; White 10,509; Other Asian 9,600; part-Chamorro 7,946; Chuukese 6,229; Total (incl. others) 154,805.

Regions (population at 2010 census): North 85,167; Central 48,755; South 25,436.

Principal Localities (population according to 2010 census designations): Dededo 6,386; Apotgan 5,928; Mangilao 5,805; Liguan 5,735; Mataguac 5,520; Y Papao 5,370; Adacao 4,184; Barrigada 4,058; Hagåtña (capital) 1,051.

Births, Marriages and Deaths (2011): Registered live births 3,298 (birth rate 20.7 per 1,000); Registered marriages 1,579 (marriage rate 9.9 per 1,000); Registered deaths 842 (death rate 5.3 per 1,000).

Life Expectancy (years at birth, estimates): 78.3 (males 75.3; females 81.6) in 2011.

Economically Active Population (persons aged 16 years and over, excl. armed forces, 2012): Agriculture, forestry, fishing and mining 140; Manufacturing 1,660; Construction 6,540; Transport,

storage and utilities 4,670; Wholesale and retail trade 14,050; Finance, insurance and real estate 2,520; Public administration 15,790; Education, health and social services 16,470; *Total employed* 61,840; Unemployed 8,060; *Total labour force* 69,900. Source: Guam Department of Labor.

AGRICULTURE, ETC.

Principal Crops (metric tons, 2011, FAO estimates): Coconuts 52,000; Roots and tubers 2,600; Cucumbers and gherkins 353; Watermelons 1,810; Other melons 344; Bananas 331.

Livestock (head, year ending September 2011, FAO estimates): Chickens 200,000; Pigs 5,200; Goats 700.

Livestock Products (metric tons, 2011, FAO estimates): Chicken meat 12; Pig meat 156; Hen eggs 910.

Fishing (metric tons, live weight, 2010): Common dolphinfish 48; Skipjack tuna 146; Other marine fishes 95; Total capture (incl. others) 291; Mozambique tilapia 75; Milkfish 35; Total aquaculture (incl. others) 129; *Total catch* 420.

Source: FAO.

INDUSTRY

Electric Energy (million kWh, estimates): 1,879 in 2007; 1,870 in 2008; 1,868 in 2009. Source: UN Industrial Commodity Statistics Database.

FINANCE

Currency and Exchange Rates: US currency is used. For details, see section on the Northern Mariana Islands.

Federal Direct Expenditures (US $ million, year ending September): 1,533 (Defence 789) in 2008; 1,396 (Defence 567) in 2009; 2,012 (Defence 1,093) in 2010. Source: US Census Bureau, *Consolidated Federal Funds Report.*

General Fund Budget (US $ million, year ending September 2011): *Revenue:* Taxes 485.0 (Income tax 282.3, Gross receipts 200.0, Other 2.7); Licences, fees and permits 5.7; Use of money and property 0.2; Total (incl. others) 552.4. *Expenditure:* General government 75.9; Public order 84.9; Public health 13.8; Community services 20.1; Recreation 2.8; Individual and collective rights 38.7; Public education 210.0; Economic development 3.6; Debt service 56.6; Total (incl. others) 677.7.

Cost of Living (Consumer Price Index; annual averages, base: October–December 2007 = 100): All items 109.2 in 2010; 112.8 in 2011; 116.3 in 2012.

Gross Domestic Product (US $ million at current prices): 4,335 in 2008; 4,542 in 2009; 4,577 in 2010 (Source: Bureau of Economic Analysis, US Department of Commerce).

Expenditure on the Gross Domestic Product (US $ million at current prices, 2010): Government consumption expenditure and gross investment 2,951; Personal consumption expenditure 2,838; Private fixed investment 233; *Total domestic expenditure* 6,022; Exports of goods and services 675; *Less* Imports of goods and services 2,120; *GDP in purchasers' values* 4,577 (Source: Bureau of Economic Analysis, US Department of Commerce).

Gross Island Product by Economic Activity (US $ million, 1995): Construction 379.02; Trade 622.86; Public administration 965.97; Other services 486.94; Other non-services 544.61; *Total* 2,999.40.

EXTERNAL TRADE

Principal Commodities (US $ million, 2011): *Imports f.o.b.:* Food and non-alcoholic beverages 252.0 (Water, containing sugar 23.9); Alcoholic beverages 27.7; Home appliances, equipment, etc. 53.9 (Wrist watches, pocket watches and others 27.9); Transportation and parts 124.5 (Motor cars 92.9; Vehicles for transport of goods 13.2); Construction materials 36.8; Men's and women's apparel 49.7 (Suits, ensembles and jackets for boys 25.4; Suits, ensembles, blouses, jackets and dresses 19.8); Plastics, leather and paper 248.9 (Travel goods, handbags, etc. 66.8); Miscellaneous manufactured imports 107.5 (Perfumes and toilet waters 28.1); Total 901.0. *Exports (excl. re-exports) f.o.b.:* Food and non-alcoholic beverages 10.9 (Fish—fresh, chilled, frozen and preserved 10.0); Home appliances, equipment, etc. 2.1 (Wrist watches, pocket watches and others 1.5); Transportation and parts 15.6 (Motor cars 11.9); Construction materials 3.2 (Iron and steel 0.6; Aluminium waste, scraps, tubes and fittings 1.2); Plastics, leather and paper 3.4 (Travel goods, handbags, etc. 1.2); Miscellaneous manufactured imports 6.7 (Articles of jewellery 1.7); Total (incl. others) 43.2.

Principal Trading Partners: *Imports* (US $ '000, 2002): Australia 9,770; Hong Kong 36,240; Japan 96,450; Korea, Republic 9,688; New

Zealand 5,520; Philippines 1,437; Singapore 180,076; Total (incl. others) 527,000 (Source: UN, *Statistical Yearbook for Asia and the Pacific*). *Exports* (incl. re-exports, US $ million, 2011): Germany 3.8; Hong Kong 4.1; Japan 11.7; Korea, Republic 1.4; Micronesia, Federated States 9.5; Palau 1.9; Philippines 3.7; Singapore 4.4; Taiwan 0.5; Total (incl. others) 44.0.

TRANSPORT

Road Traffic (registered motor vehicles, 2011): Private cars 72,649; Taxis 216; Buses 720; Goods vehicles 26,560; Motorcycles 2,987; Total (incl. others) 109,842. Source: Department of Revenue and Taxation, Government of Guam.

International Sea-borne Shipping (estimated freight traffic, '000 revenue tons, 2011): Goods loaded 205.7; Goods unloaded 1,272.4; Goods transshipped 474.1. *Flag Registered Fleet* (at 31 December 2012): Total vessels 6; Total displacement ('000 grt) 3.4 (Source: Lloyd's List Intelligence—www.lloydslistintelligence.com).

Civil Aviation (Guam International Airport): *Passengers* (year ending May 2011): Arrivals 1,284,203; Departures 1,264,243; Transit 175,181. *Cargo* (metric tons, 2011): Unloaded 13,253; Loaded 5,840. *Mail* (metric tons, 2011): Incoming 4,313; Outgoing 1,134. *Aircraft Movements* (year ending May 2011): 46,030. Source: Guam International Airport Authority.

TOURISM

Foreign Tourist Arrivals ('000): 1,052.9 in 2009; 1,197.4 in 2010; 1,159.8 in 2011.

Tourist Arrivals by Country of Residence ('000, 2011): Japan 893.7; Korea, Republic 149.1; Philippines 10.0; Taiwan 45.1; USA 61.3; Total (incl. others) 1,159.8.

Tourism Receipts (US $ million): 2,361 in 1998; 1,908 in 1999. Source: World Tourism Organization.

COMMUNICATIONS MEDIA

Telephones (2010): 65,500 main lines in use.

Mobile Cellular Telephones (2008, estimate): 98,000 subscribers.

Internet Users (2009): 90,000.

Broadband Subscribers (2010): 3,000.

Source: International Telecommunication Union.

EDUCATION

Institutions (2008/09): Primary (incl. kindergarten, grades 1–8) 44 (public 29, private 15); Secondary (grades 9–12) 11 (public 5, private 6).

Teachers (2005/06): Primary 1,917 (public 1,405, private 512); Secondary 1,108 (public 470, private 638).

Enrolment (2010/11): Kindergarten (grades 1–5) 18,446 (public 13,774, private 3,599, military 1,073); Primary (grades 6–8) 9,688 (public 7,279, private 1,909, military 500); Secondary (grades 9–12) 12,239 (public 9,506, private 2,251, military 482); High school (graduates) 2,145 (public 1,547, private 504, military 94); Guam Community College 2,542; University of Guam 3,639.

Sources: Department of Education, Guam Community College, Office of Insular Affairs, *Guam Statistical Yearbook*; University of Guam.

Directory

The Government

(May 2013)

Governor: EDDIE BAZA CALVO (Republican—took office 3 Jan. 2011).

Lieutenant-Governor: RAY TENORIO (Republican—took office 3 Jan. 2011).

GOVERNMENT DEPARTMENTS

Government departments are located throughout the island.

Office of the Governor: POB 2950, Hagåtña, GU 96932; tel. 472-8931; fax 477-4826; e-mail governor@mail.gov.gu; internet governor .guam.gov.

Department of the Interior, Office of Insular Affairs (OIA): Hagåtña, GU 96910; tel. 472-7279; fax 472-7309; internet www .interior.gov/oia/islands/guam.cfm; Desk Officer ANGELA WILLIAMS (based in Washington, DC).

Department of Administration: POB 884, Hagåtña, GU 96932; tel. 475-1101; fax 475-6788; e-mail doadir@mail.gov.gu; internet www.doa.guam.gov; Dir BENITA MANGLONA.

Department of Agriculture: 163 Dairy Rd, Mangilao, GU 96913; tel. 734-3942; fax 734-6569; internet www.agriculture.guam.gov; Dir MARIQUITA TAITAGUE.

Department of Chamorro Affairs: POB 2950, Hagåtña, GU 96910; tel. 475-4278; fax 475-4227; internet www.dca.guam.gov; Pres. JOSEPH A. CAMERON.

Department of Corrections: POB 3236, Hagåtña, GU 96932; tel. 735-4131; fax 473-7009; internet www.doc.guam.gov; Dir JOSÉ A. SAN AGUSTIN.

Department of Education: POB DE, Hagåtña, GU 96932; tel. 475-0462; fax 472-5003; e-mail nbunderwood@gdoe.net; internet www .gdoe.net; Supt TALING M. TAITANO (acting).

Department of Integrated Services for Individuals with Disabilities: Suite 702, 238 Archbishop F. C. Flores St, Pacific News Bldg, Hagåtña, GU 96910; tel. 475-4646; fax 477-2892; e-mail benito .servino@disid.guam.gov; internet www.disid.guam.gov; Dir BENITO S. SERVINO.

Department of Labor: 414 West Soledad Ave, GCIC Bldg, Hagåtña, GU 96910; tel. 475-7000; fax 475-7045; e-mail connent@ ite.net; internet www.dol.guam.gov; Dir GEORGE SANTOS.

Department of Land Management: POB 2950, Hagåtña, GU 96932; tel. 649-5263; fax 649-5383; e-mail dlmdir@dlm.guam.gov; internet dlm.guam.gov; Dir MONTE MAFNAS.

Department of Mental Health and Substance Abuse: tel. 647-5330; fax 649-6948; e-mail info@guamdmhsa.com; internet dmhsa .guam.gov; Dir REY VEGA (acting).

Department of Military Affairs: 430 Army Dr., Bldg 300, Barrigada; tel. 735-0406; fax 649-8775; internet dma.guam.gov; Dir Maj.-Gen. BENNY M. PAULINO.

Department of Parks and Recreation: 490 Chalan Palasyo, Agaña Heights, GU 96910; tel. 475-6296; fax 477-0997; e-mail parks@ns.gov.gu; internet www.dpr.guam.gov; Dir PETER CALVO (acting).

Department of Public Health and Social Services: 123 Chalan Kareta, Route 10, Mangilao, GU 96913-6304; tel. 735-7166; fax 734-2105; internet dphss.guam.gov; Dir JAMES GILLAN.

Department of Public Works: 542 North Marine Dr., Tamuning, GU 96913; tel. 646-3131; fax 649-6178; e-mail joanne.brown@dpw .guam.gov; internet www.dpw.guam.gov; Dir CARL DOMINGUEZ.

Department of Revenue and Taxation: POB 23607, Guam Main Facility, GU 96921; tel. 635-1835; fax 633-2643; e-mail pinadm@ revtax.gov.gu; internet www.guamtax.com; Dir JOHN P. CAMACHO.

Department of Youth Affairs: POB 23672, Guam Main Facility, GU 96921; tel. 735-5010; fax 734-7536; e-mail adonis.mendiola@dya .guam.gov; internet dya.guam.gov; Dir ADONIS J. MENDIOLA.

Legislature

GUAM LEGISLATURE

The Guam Legislature has 15 members, known as Senators, who are directly elected by popular vote for a two-year term. At the election of 6 November 2012 the Democratic Party secured nine seats and the Republicans six. The 32nd Guam Legislature was inaugurated on 7 January 2013.

Speaker: JUDITH WON PAT.

CONGRESS

Guam elects a non-voting Delegate to the US House of Representatives. At an election on 6 November 2012 the Democratic candidate, Madeleine Z. Bordallo, was re-elected for a sixth term as Delegate.

Delegate of Guam: MADELEINE Z. BORDALLO, 2441 Rayburn HOB, Washington, DC 20515, USA; tel. (202) 225-1188; fax (202) 226-0341; e-mail madeleine.bordallo@mail.house.gov; internet www.house .gov/bordallo.

Election Commission

Guam Election Commission: Guam Capital Investment Corpn Bldg, 414 West Soledad Ave, Suite 200, Hagåtña 96910; tel. 477-9791; fax 477-1895; e-mail director@gec.guam.gov; internet www.gec .guam.gov; Chair. JOSEPH F. MESA; Exec. Dir MARIA PANGELINAN.

Political Organizations

The territory has a two-party system, comprising local chapters of the US Democratic Party and Republican Party. However, at the local level, non-partisan candidates may seek election.

Judicial System

Attorney-General: LEONARDO M. RAPADAS.

US Attorney: ALICIA GARRIDO LIMTIACO.

Supreme Court of Guam: Suite 300, Guam Judicial Center, 120 West O'Brien Dr., Hagåtña, GU 96910; tel. 475-3162; fax 475-3140; e-mail justice@guamsupremecourt.com; internet www.justice.gov .gu/supreme.html; Chief Justice F. PHILIP CARBULLIDO.

District Court of Guam: US Courthouse, 4th Floor, 520 West Soledad Ave, Hagåtña, GU 96910; tel. 473-9180; fax 473-9118; e-mail judith_hattori@gud.uscourts.gov; internet www.gud.uscourts.gov; judge appointed by the President of the USA; the court has the jurisdiction of a federal district court and of a bankruptcy court of the USA in all cases arising under US law; appeals may be made to the Court of Appeals for the Ninth Circuit and to the US Supreme Court; Chief Judge FRANCES TYDINGCO-GATEWOOD; Magistrate Judge JOAQUIN V. E. MANIBUSAN.

Superior Court of Guam: 120 West O'Brien Drive, Hagåtña, GU 96910; tel. 475-3544; fax 477-3184; internet www.guamcourts.org/ superior.html; judges are appointed by the Governor of Guam for an initial 7-year term and are thereafter retained by popular vote; the Superior Court has jurisdiction over cases arising in Guam other than those heard in the District Court; Presiding Judge ALBERTO C. LAMORENA, III.

There are also Probate, Traffic, Domestic, Juvenile and Small Claims Courts.

Religion

The majority of the population are Roman Catholic, but there are also members of the Episcopal (Anglican) Church, the Baptist churches and the Seventh-day Adventist Church. There are small communities of Muslims, Buddhists and Jews.

CHRISTIANITY

The Roman Catholic Church

Guam comprises the single archdiocese of Agaña. The Archbishop participates in the Catholic Bishops' Conference of the Pacific, based in Suva, Fiji, and the Federation of Catholic Bishops' Conferences of Oceania, based in Wellington, New Zealand.

At 31 December 2007 there were 141,177 adherents in Guam.

Archbishop of Agaña: Most Rev. ANTHONY SABLAN APURON, Chancery Office, Cuesta San Ramón 196B, Hagåtña, GU 96910; tel. 472-6116; fax 477-3519; e-mail archbishop@mail.archdioceseofagana .com; internet www.archdioceseofagana.com.

BAHÁ'Í FAITH

National Spiritual Assembly: POB Box BA, Hagåtña, GU 96932; tel. 472-9100; fax 472-9101; e-mail bahaioffice@marianas.bahai.org; internet marianas.bahai.org; mems resident in 19 localities in Guam and 10 localities in the Northern Mariana Islands.

The Press

NEWSPAPERS AND PERIODICALS

Bonita: POB 11468, Tumon, GU 96931; tel. 632-4543; fax 637-6720; f. 1998; monthly; Publr IMELDA SANTOS; circ. 3,000.

Directions: POB 27290, Barrigada, GU 96921; tel. 635-7501; fax 635-7520; f. 1996; monthly; Publr JERRY ROBERTS; circ. 3,800.

Guam Business: POB 3191, Hagåtña, GU 96932; tel. 649-0883; fax 649-8883; e-mail glimpses@glimpsesofguam.com; internet www .guambusinessmagazine.com; f. 1983; quarterly; Publr MAUREEN N. MARATITA; Man. Editor FRANK WHITMAN; circ. 2,600.

Hospitality Guahan: POB 8565, Tamuning, GU 96931; tel. 649-1447; fax 649-8565; e-mail info@ghra.org; internet www.ghra.org; f. 1996; quarterly; circ. 3,000.

Marianas Business Journal: POB 3191, Hagåtña, GU 96932; tel. 649-0883; fax 649-8883; e-mail glimpses@glimpsesofguam.com; internet www.mbjguam.net; f. 2003; fortnightly; Publr MAUREEN N. MARATITA; Editor PATRICIA SHOOK; circ. 3,000.

Pacific Daily News and Sunday News: POB DN, Hagåtña, GU 96932; tel. 472-1736; fax 472-1512; e-mail cblas@guampdn.com; internet www.guampdn.com; f. 1950; Publr RINDRATY LIMTIACO; Man. Editor DAVID CRISOSTOMO; circ. 28,520 (weekdays), 26,237 (Sunday).

The Pacific Voice: POB 2553, Hagåtña, GU 96932; tel. 472-6427; fax 477-5224; f. 1950; Sun.; Roman Catholic; Gen. Man. TEREZO MORTERA; Editor Rev. Fr HERMES LOSBANES; circ. 6,500.

TV Guam Magazine: 237 Mamis St, Tamuning, GU 96911; tel. 646-4030; fax 646-7445; f. 1973; weekly; Publr DINA GRANT; Man. Editor EMILY UNTALAN; circ. 15,000.

NEWS AGENCY

United Press International (UPI) (USA): POB 1617, Hagåtña, GU 96910; tel. 632-1138; Correspondent DICK WILLIAMS.

Broadcasting and Communications

TELECOMMUNICATIONS

DOCOMO Pacific: 219 S Marine Dr., Century Plaza Bldg, 2nd Floor, Suite 206, Tamuning, GU 96911; tel. 688-2273; internet www .docomopacific.com; f. 1992; fmrly Guamcell; wireless telephone services.

Guam Educational Telecommunication Corporation (KGTF): POB 21449, Guam Main Facility, Barrigada, GU 96921; tel. 734-2207; fax 734-3476; e-mail kgtf12@teleguam.net; internet www.kgtf .org.

Guam Telephone Authority: 624 North Marines Corps Dr., POB 9008, Tamuning, GU 96913; tel. 644-4482; fax 649-4821; e-mail ask@ gta.net; internet www.gta.net; acquired by TeleGuam Holdings LLC in Dec. 2004; provider of fixed telephone lines, mobile telecommunications and internet services; CEO and Pres. ROBERT HAULBROOK.

BROADCASTING

Radio

K-Stereo: 1868 Halsey Dr., Piti, GU 96915; tel. 477-9448; fax 477-6411; e-mail ksto@ite.net; operates on FM 24 hours a day; Pres. and Gen. Man. EDWARD H. POPPE.

KOKU-FM: 424 West O'Brien Drive, Julale Center, Hagåtña, GU 96910; tel. 477-5658; fax 472-7663; e-mail marketing@hitradio100 .com; operates on FM 24 hours a day; Pres. KURT S. MOYLAN.

KPRG FM: KPRG, UoG Station Mangilao, GU 96923; tel. 734-8930; fax 734-2958; e-mail marketing.kprg@gmail.com; internet www .kprgfm.com; operated by the Guam Educational Radio Foundation; news and music; Gen. Man. CHRIS HARTIG.

Radio Guam (KUAM): 600 Harman Loop, Dededo, GU 96912; tel. 637-5826; fax 637-9865; e-mail generalmanager@kuam.com; internet www.kuam.com; f. 1954; operates on AM and FM 24 hours a day; Pres. PAUL M. CALVO; Gen. Man. JOEY CALVO.

Sorensen Media Group: Suite 800, 111 Chalan Santo Papa, Hagåtña, GU 96910; tel. 477-5700; fax 477-3982; e-mail rex@ spbguam.com; internet www.pacificnewscenter.com; f. 1981; privately owned; Chair. and CEO REX SORENSEN.

Trans World Radio Pacific (TWR): POB CC, Hagåtña, GU 96932; tel. 477-9701; fax 477-2838; e-mail ktwr@twr.org; internet www .guam.net/home/twr; f. 1975; broadcasts Christian programmes on KTWR and 1 medium-wave station, KTWG, covering Guam and nearby islands, and operates 5 short-wave transmitters reaching most of Asia, Africa and the Pacific; Chair. THOMAS J. LOWELL; Pres. LAUREN LIBBY; Station Dir MICHAEL DAVIS.

Television

Guam switched from analogue to digital television broadcasting in 2009.

KGTF—TV: POB 21449 Guam Main Facility, Barrigada, GU 96921; tel. 734-3476; fax 734-5483; e-mail kgtf12@kgtf.org; internet www .kgtf.org; f. 1970; cultural, public service and educational programmes; Gen. Man. SAM MABINI; Operations Man. BENNY T. FLORES.

KTGM—TV: 692 Marine Dr., Tamuning 96911; tel. 649-8814; fax 649-0371.

KUAM—TV: 600 Harmon Loop, Dededo, Hagåtña, GU 96912; tel. 637-5826; fax 637-9865; e-mail generalmanager@kuam.com; internet www.kuam.com; f. 1956; operates channels 8 and 11; News Dir SABRINA SALAS.

Finance

(cap. = capital; res = reserves; dep. = deposits; m. = million; brs = branches; amounts in US dollars)

BANKING

Commercial Banks

Allied Banking Corpn (Philippines): Suite 104, Bejess Commercial Bldg, 719 South Marine Dr., Tamuning, GU 96913; tel. 649-5001; fax 649-5002; e-mail abcguam@kuentos.guam.net; Sr Man. SERAFIN B. AGDAGDAG; 1 br.

ANZ Guam Inc: 424 West O'Brien Dr., 112 Julale Shopping Center, Hagåtña, GU 96910; tel. 479-9000; fax 479-9092; internet www.anz .com/guam; mem. of ANZ Group; fmrly Citizens Security Bank

(Guam) Inc, name changed as above in 2009; cap. 8.6m., res 5.6m., dep. 246m. (Dec. 2011); CEO JOHN W. WADE; 4 brs.

Bank of Guam: 111 Chalan Santo Papa, Hagåtña, GU 96910; tel. 472-5300; fax 477-5454; e-mail customerservice@bankofguam.com; internet www.bankofguam.com; f. 1972; cap. 1.8m., dep. 1,048.4m. (Dec. 2011); Chair. LOURDES A. LEON GUERRERO; Exec. Vice-Pres. WILLIAM D. LEON GUERRERO; 12 brs.

Bank of Hawaii (USA): 134 West Soledad Ave, Hagåtña, GU 96910; tel. 479-3500; fax 479-3893; internet www.boh.com; Exec. Vice-Pres. RONALD CANNOLES; 3 brs.

BankPacific, Ltd: 151 Aspinall Ave, Hagåtña, GU 96910; tel. 472-6704; fax 477-1483; e-mail philipf@bankpacific.com; internet www.bankpacific.com; f. 1954; Pres. and CEO PHILIP J. FLORES; Exec. Vice-Pres. MARK O. FISH; 4 brs in Guam; 1 br. in Palau; 1 br. in Northern Mariana Islands.

Citibank NA (USA): 402 East Marine Corps Dr., Hagåtña, GU 96910; tel. 477-2484; fax 477-9441; internet www.citibank.com/guam; Country Man. AGUSTIN DAVALOS; 2 brs.

First Commercial Bank (Taiwan): POB 2461, Hagåtña, GU 96932; tel. 472-6864; fax 477-8921; e-mail fcbgu@ite.net; Gen. Man. JENN-HWA WANG; 1 br.

First Hawaiian Bank (USA): Compadres Mall 562, Harmon Loop Rd, Dededo, GU 96912; tel. 632-9381; fax 637-9686; internet www.fhb.com; Regional Man. LAURA-LYNN DACANAY; 3 brs.

HSBC Ltd: POB 27c, Hagåtña, GU 96932; tel. 647-8588; fax 646-3767; CEO GUY N. DE B. PRIESTLEY; 2 brs.

Metropolitan Bank and Trust Co: 665 South Marine Drive, Tamuning, GU 96911; tel. 649-9555; fax 649-9558; e-mail mbguam@metrobank.com.ph; f. 1975; Sen. Man. JOSEPHINE M. PAPELERA.

Union Bank of California (USA): 194 Hernan Cortes Ave, POB 7809, Hagåtña, GU 96910; tel. 477-8811; fax 472-3284; Man. KINJI SUZUKI; 2 brs.

INSURANCE

American National Insurance Co: POB 3340, Hagåtña, GU 96910; tel. 477-9600.

Chung Kuo Insurance Co: GCIC Bldg, Suite 707, 414 West Soledad Ave, Hagåtña, GU 96910; tel. 477-7696; fax 477-4788; e-mail chungkuo@ite.net; internet www.cki.com.tw.

Midland National Life Insurance Co: Winner Bldg, Suite 20N, Tamuning, GU 96911; tel. 649-0330; internet www.mnlife.com; f. 1906 as Dakota Mutual Life Insurance Company; name changed as above in 1925.

Moylan's Insurance Underwriters, Inc: Suite 102 Julale Shopping Center, 424 West O'Brien Dr., Hagåtña, GU 96910; tel. 477-8613; fax 477-1837; e-mail agana@moylans.net; internet www.moylansinsurance.com; Pres. KURT S. MOYLAN; CEO CESAR GARCIA.

Nanbo Insurance: 434 West O'Brien Dr., Hagåtña, GU 96910; tel. 477-9754; internet www.nanbo.com.

Pioneer Pacific Financial Services, Inc of Guam: POB EM, Hagåtña, GU 96910; tel. 477-6400.

Trade and Industry

DEVELOPMENT ORGANIZATION

Guam Economic Development Authority (GEDA): Guam International Trade Center Bldg, Suite 511, 590 South Marine Dr., Tamuning, GU 96913; tel. 647-4332; fax 649-4146; e-mail help@investguam.com; internet www.investguam.com; f. 1965; Administrator KARL A. PANGELINAN.

CHAMBER OF COMMERCE

Guam Chamber of Commerce: Ada Plaza Center, Suite 101, 173 Aspinall Ave, POB 283, Hagåtña, GU 96932; tel. 472-6311; fax 472-6202; e-mail gchamber@guamchamber.com; internet www.guamchamber.com.gu; f. 1924; Chair. DAVID J. JOHN; Pres. DAVID P. LEDDY.

EMPLOYERS' ORGANIZATION

The Employers' Council: 718 North Marine Dr., Suite 201, East-West Business Center, Upper Tumon, GU 96913; tel. 649-6616; fax 649-3030; e-mail tecinc@teleguam.net; internet www.guamemployers.org; f. 1966; private, non-profit asscn providing management devt training and advice on personnel law and labour relations; Exec. Dir ANDREW P. ANDRUS.

UTILITIES

Electricity

Guam Energy Office: 548 North Marine Corps Dr., Tamuning, GU 96913; tel. 646-4361; fax 649-1215; e-mail lucybk@teleguam.net; internet www.guamenergy.com; Dir PETE CALVO.

Guam Power Authority: POB 2977, Hagåtña, GU 96932; tel. 648-3000; fax 649-3290; e-mail webmaster@guampowerauthority.com; internet www.guampowerauthority.com; f. 1968; autonomous govt agency; supplies electricity throughout the island; Gen. Man. JOAQUIN FLORES.

Water

Guam Waterworks Authority: 578 North Marine Corps Dr., Tamuning, GU 96913-4111; tel. 647-2603; fax 646-2335; e-mail heidi@guamwaterworks.org; internet www.guamwaterworks.org; Gen. Man. MARTIN L. ROUSH.

TRADE UNIONS

Many workers belong to trade unions based in the USA such as the American Federation of Government Employees and the American Postal Workers' Union.

Guam Federation of Teachers (GFT): Local 1581, POB 2301, Hagåtña, GU 96932; tel. 735-4390; fax 734-8085; e-mail mrector@gftunion.com; internet www.gftunion.com; f. 1965; affiliate of American Federation of Teachers; Pres. MATT RECTOR; 2,000 mems.

Guam Hotel and Restaurant Association: POB 8565, Tamuning, GU 96931; tel. 649-1447; fax 649-8565; e-mail president@ghra.org; internet www.ghra.org; 37 mem. restaurants and hotels; Pres. MARY P. TORRE.

Transport

In September 2008 the Government announced that the sum of US $25m. was to be allocated to the creation of a mass transit network on the island, to accommodate the projected rise in the population that would result from the relocation of thousands of US marines to Guam.

ROADS

There are 885 km (550 miles) of public roads, of which some 675 km (420 miles) are paved. A further 685 km (425 miles) of roads are classified as non-public, and include roads located on federal government installations. In February 2009 a US $140m. project to upgrade the island's road network was announced. In the same month the US Government announced that it was committing $1,000m. to fund a new road to link US military facilities in northern and southern Guam. The works were expected to be completed by 2014.

SHIPPING

Apra, on the central western side of the island, is one of the largest protected deep-water harbours in the Pacific. Plans for the modernization of the port were under way in 2009.

Port Authority of Guam: 1026 Cabras Highway, Suite 201, Piti, GU 96925; tel. 477-5931; fax 477-4445; e-mail webmaster@portguam.com; internet www.portguam.com; f. 1975; govt-operated port facilities; Gen. Man. JOANNE BROWN.

Ambyth, Shipping and Trading, Inc: 1026 Cabras Highway, Piti, GU 96915; tel. 477-7250; fax 472-1264; e-mail ops@ambyth.guam.net; internet www.ambyth.com; agents for all types of vessels and charter brokers; Pres. ALFRED LAM; Gen. Man. ANDREW MILLER.

COAM Trading Co Ltd: PAG Bldg, Suite 110, 1026 Cabas Highway, Piti, GU 96925; tel. 477-1737; fax 472-3386.

Dewitt Moving and Storage: Suite 100, 165-1, Guerrero St, Tamuning, GU 96913; tel. 648-1800; fax 648-0034; e-mail ezdewitt@dewittguam.com; internet www.dewittguam.com; CEO JOHN BURROWS.

Guam Shipping Agency: POB GD, Hagåtña, GU 96932; tel. 477-7381; fax 477-7553; Gen. Man. H. KO.

Interbulk Shipping (Guam) Inc: Bank of Guam Bldg, Suite 502, 111 Chalan Santo Papa, Hagåtña, GU 96910; Man. S. GYSTAD.

Maritime Agencies of the Pacific Ltd: 1026 Cabras Highway, Piti, GU 96925; tel. 477-8500; fax 477-5726; e-mail rehmapship@kuentos.guam.net; f. 1976; agents for fishing vessels, cargo, dry products and construction materials; Pres. ROBERT E. HAHN.

Pacific Navigation System: POB 7, Hagåtña, GU 96910; f. 1946; Pres. KENNETH T. JONES, Jr.

Seabridge Micronesian, Inc: 1026 Cabras Highway, Suite 114, Piti, GU 96925; tel. 477-7345; fax 477-6206; e-mail plblas@ite.net; Gen. Man. PAUL L. BLAS.

Tucor Services: 180 Guerrero St, Harmon Industrial Park, POB 6128, Tamuning, GU 96911; tel. 646-6947; fax 646-6945; e-mail boll@tucor.com; general agents for numerous dry cargo, passenger and steamship cos; Pres. MICHELLE BOLL.

CIVIL AVIATION

Guam is served by A. B. Won Pat International Airport.

Guam International Airport Authority: POB 8770, Tamuning, GU 96931; tel. 646-0300; fax 646-8823; e-mail lizb@guamairport.net; internet www.guamairport.com; Chair. EDWARD UNTALAN; Exec. Man. MARY C. TORRES.

Asia Pacific Airlines (APA): POB 24858, Guam Main Facility, Barrigada, Guam 96921; fax 647-8440; e-mail info@flyapa.com; internet www.flyapa.com; f. 1999; affiliate of Tan Holdings Corpn (Commonwealth of the Northern Mariana Islands); cargo; serving Guam, Hawaii (USA), Hong Kong, Marshall Islands, Federated States of Micronesia, Palau and the Philippines.

Freedom Air: POB 1578, Hagåtña, GU 96932; tel. 647-8359; fax 646-7488; e-mail freedom@ite.net; internet www.freedomairguam.com; f. 1974; Man. Dir JOAQUIN L. FLORES, Jr.

United Continental Airlines: POB 8778, Tamuning, GU 96931; tel. 645-8182; internet www.unitedcontinentalholdings.com; f. 1968, as Air Micronesia, by Continental Airlines (USA); officially became United Continental as a result of the merger between United Airlines and Continental Airlines; hub operations in Guam and Saipan (Northern Mariana Islands); services throughout the region and to destinations in the Far East and the mainland USA; Pres. CHARLES DUNCAN.

Tourism

Tourism is the most important industry on Guam. Visitor arrivals totalled 1,159,800 in 2011 and reportedly exceeded 1.3m. in 2012. Most visitors are from Japan, the Republic of Korea, the USA and Taiwan. The majority of Guam's hotels are situated in, or near to, Tumon, where amenities for entertainment are well developed.

Numerous sunken wrecks of aircraft and ships from Second World War battles provide interesting sites for divers. There were 8,471 hotel rooms on Guam in 2006.

Guam Visitors Bureau: 401 Pale San Vitores Rd, Tumon, GU 96913; tel. 646-5278; fax 646-8861; e-mail guaminfo@visitguam.org; internet www.visitguam.org; Chair. MARK BALDYGA; Gen. Man. KARL PANGELINAN.

Defence

Guam is an important strategic military base for the USA. In 2004 a new hangar for B-52 and B-2 bombers was completed. In February 2012 the US Government announced plans to spend an estimated US $21,100m. to expand its military presence in Guam, and in April it was agreed that some 5,000 US marines would be transferred to Guam from US bases in Japan at an unspecified future date. In April 2013 the US Government announced that it would deploy an advanced missile defence system on Guam within a few weeks. As assessed at November 2012, a total of 4,300 members of the US Pacific Command were stationed on Guam, in addition to a US naval base and an airbase.

Education

School attendance is compulsory from six to 16 years of age. There were 44 kindergarten and primary schools (29 public, 15 private) and 11 secondary schools (five public, six private) operating on the island in 2008/09. In 2010/11 total enrolment at kindergarten schools amounted to 18,446 students; the comparable figures for primary and secondary schools were 9,688 and 12,239 students, respectively. Enrolment in tertiary education has expanded in recent years, with 2,542 students enrolled at the Guam Community College and 3,639 students enrolled at the University of Guam for 2010/11. Government expenditure on public education was US $210m. in 2010/11 (equivalent to 31% of total expenditure).

THE UNITED STATES VIRGIN ISLANDS

Introductory Survey

LOCATION, CLIMATE, LANGUAGE, RELIGION, FLAG, CAPITAL

The United States Virgin Islands consists of three main inhabited islands (St Croix, St Thomas and St John) and about 50 smaller islands, mostly uninhabited. They are situated at the eastern end of the Greater Antilles, about 64 km (40 miles) east of Puerto Rico in the Caribbean Sea. The climate is tropical, although tempered by the prevailing easterly trade winds. The temperature averages 26°C (79°F), with little variation between winter and summer. The humidity is low for the tropics. English is the official language, but Spanish and Creole are also widely used. The people of the US Virgin Islands are predominantly of African descent. There is a strong religious tradition, and most of the inhabitants are Christians, mainly Protestants. The flag (proportions 2 by 3) is white, with a modified version of the US coat of arms (an eagle holding an olive branch in one foot and a sheaf of arrows in the other, with a shield, comprising a small horizontal blue panel above vertical red and white stripes, superimposed), between the letters V and I, in the centre. The capital is Charlotte Amalie, on the island of St Thomas.

CONTEMPORARY POLITICAL HISTORY

Historical Context

The Virgin Islands, originally inhabited by Carib and Arawak Indians, were discovered by Europeans in 1493. The group subsequently passed through English, French, and Dutch control, before the western islands of St Thomas and St John, colonized by Denmark after 1670, and St Croix, purchased from France in 1733, became the Danish West Indies. In 1917 these islands, which are strategically placed in relation to the Panama Canal, were sold for US $25m. by Denmark to the USA. They now form an Unincorporated Territory of the USA. Residents of the US Virgin Islands are US citizens, but cannot vote in presidential elections, if resident in the islands. The US Virgin Islands is represented in the US House of Representatives by one popularly elected Delegate, who is permitted to vote only in committees of the House.

Domestic Political Affairs

The inhabitants of the islands were granted a measure of self-government by the Organic Act, as revised in 1954, which created the elected 15-member Senate. Since 1970 executive authority has been vested in the elected Governor and Lieutenant-Governor. In the first gubernatorial election, in 1970, the Republican incumbent, Melvin Evans, retained office. In 1974 Cyril E. King, leader of the Independent Citizens' Movement (a breakaway faction of the Democratic Party), was elected Governor. On King's death in 1978, the former Lieutenant-Governor, Juan Luis, was elected Governor. He was returned to power in the 1982 election. The governorship passed to the Democratic Party with the election of Alexander Farrelly in 1986. Farrelly was re-elected Governor in 1990, and in the 1994 elections was succeeded by an Independent, Dr Roy Schneider. The governorship was regained by a Democrat, Charles Turnbull, in the 1998 elections. Turnbull was re-elected to the post in 2000 and 2002. The Democrats retained the governorship in 2006, with the election of John deJongh, Jr (Turnbull was constitutionally precluded from standing for a third consecutive term of office).

In February 2005 a 7,000-signature petition was submitted to the US Congress by residents of St Croix, in support of making the island a separate US External Territory from St Thomas and St John. Organizers of the petition claimed that such a move would generate more federal funding for the island, which was affected by a higher unemployment rate than the other two islands, despite being the location for one of the world's largest petroleum refineries. In May the Territorial Government brought a court case against the owners of the Hovensa LLC oil refinery (see Economic Affairs) and the defunct St Croix Alumina plant for contaminating the sole groundwater supply on St Croix. Both companies had reached an agreement with the US Environmental Protection Agency (EPA) in 2001 to clean up petroleum spillages; according to the EPA, some 2m. gallons of petroleum leaked into the local aquifer between 1978 and 1991.

In May 2007 the territory's Delegate to Congress, Donna M. Christensen, presented legislation for the institution of a Chief Financial Officer in the territory to function as an independent arbiter upon government fiscal policy. It was hoped that the new legislation would encourage greater co-operation between the Governor and Legislative Assembly towards reducing the fiscal deficit, and would facilitate and enhance the transparency of financial policy. A number of financial scandals earlier in the year had foregrounded the necessity of financial services regulatory reform: in May former director of the Department of Planning and Natural Resources Division of Environmental Protection Hollis L. Griffin was given a custodial sentence at the federal court in Atlanta, Georgia, after being convicted of conspiring to defraud the islands' Government of US \$1.4m. Furthermore, an economic development programme, implemented by the Territorial Government, that permitted firms operating in the islands to reduce their tax payments by up to 90%, was discovered to have been exploited in March, when four people were charged with tax evasions amounting to \$74m. In February the US Inland Revenue Service announced that the financial affairs of 8,500 high-salaried residents of the US Virgin Islands would be subjected to increased scrutiny. In April Alric Simmonds, Deputy Chief of Staff to erstwhile Governor Turnbull, was indicted on charges of embezzlement, conversion of government property and grand larceny. He was sentenced to eight years' imprisonment in the following year.

Combating crime was a stated objective of Governor deJongh's administration. An anti-crime initiative was announced in February 2007; measures included an increase in the size of the police force and establishment of a forensic facility. Specialized police professionals from external US police jurisdictions were also to be drafted in to support and instruct existing personnel. A previous scheme, the Blue Lightning Marine unit (based on St Thomas), was to be reinstated to address the problems of guns- and drugs-trafficking and illegal immigrant incursions through coastal patrols. In March 2008 deJongh submitted legislation to abolish the Drug Enforcement Bureau and to redirect funding to the police department, which had proved to be more successful in targeting drugs-trafficking. Despite the enhanced crime prevention measures, the murder rate continued to rise, reaching a record 66 in 2010 (from 56 in 2009). The number of recorded murders declined to 48 in 2011, before increasing again, to 59, in 2012.

Constitutional review

Since 1954 there have been five attempts to redraft the Constitution to give the US Virgin Islands greater autonomy. Each draft has, however, been rejected by a referendum. The US Government has expressed the view that it would welcome reform, if approved by the residents, as long as it was economically feasible and did not affect US national security. A non-binding referendum on the islands' future status in 1993 produced support of 80% for retaining the islands' existing status, with 14% favouring full integration with the USA and 5% advocating the termination of US sovereignty. The result of the referendum was, however, invalidated by the low turnout: only 27% of registered voters took part, falling short of the 50% participation required for the referendum to be valid. Subsequent legislation to create a constitutional convention was presented to the US Virgin Islands Senate, and in 2000 a committee of the US House of Representatives began consideration of a range of measures to enlarge the scope of local self-government in the territory. In November 2004 Governor Turnbull approved legislation allowing the creation of a further constituent assembly to redraft the Constitution.

Progress towards formulating a new constitution for the territory was furthered in July 2007, when a Fifth Constitutional Convention was assembled to commence work upon the drafting of a new document. A final draft would require the approval of two-thirds of all convention delegates before being put before the Governor for approval. The Governor was then legally obliged to present the document to the US Congress for scrutiny and, ultimately, presidential approval, after which the amended draft would put to a referendum. The Convention presented a proposed constitution for consideration by the Governor in June 2009. Governor deJongh objected to several clauses in the document, claiming that it did not recognize the supremacy of the US Constitution, and was therefore invalid. In particular, he opposed proposals that the Governor and Lieutenant-Governor be native or ancestral Virgin Islanders and that native or ancestral citizens be granted property tax exemptions, as well as a provision allowing only native or ancestral Virgin Islanders the right to vote on constitutional amendments. In spite of his objections, the constitution was forwarded to the US Congress, which began discussion of the document in March 2010. However, the charter was rejected by Congress in June on the grounds that certain provisions within the document were in contravention of the US Constitution and federal law. Concerns were specifically raised over the benefits that would be bestowed upon native or ancestral citizens and the failure of the draft constitution to acknowledge US sovereignty over the islands. Congress requested that the Fifth Constitutional Convention review and modify the clauses in question. The Convention was convened in early October 2012 and amendments to the charter were approved later that month, although some observers questioned whether the correct procedures had been followed. A referendum on the proposed constitution was not expected to be held until at least 2014.

Elections in 2010 and 2012

John deJongh was re-elected as Governor in an election held on 2 November 2010, attracting 56.3% of the votes cast. Kenneth Mapp, an independent and the only other candidate, received 43.6% of the ballot. Donna Christensen was re-elected as the territory's Delegate to the US Congress. Governor deJongh was inaugurated on 6 January 2011; he reiterated his commitment to addressing crime and boosting economic activity on the islands.

Christensen was re-elected on 6 November 2012. In concurrent elections to the territorial Senate, the Democratic Party gained control of 10 seats, independent candidates won four and the remaining seat was secured by the Independent Citizens' Movement.

Recent developments: rum dispute

In November 2010 a rum distillery was inaugurated in St Croix that would supply the international drinks producer Diageo with rum for its Captain Morgan brand. The project was part of an agreement reached between the Government and Diageo in 2009: the US Virgin Islands authorities agreed to finance construction of the plant in return for receiving an estimated US \$3,000m. in additional excise revenue over the 30-year duration of the contract. A similar accord with drink producer Fortune Brands was reached in October: the Government would meet the necessary costs in expanding and improving the company's Cruzan Rum distillery on the islands in exchange for a guarantee that the rum producer would maintain a presence in the territory for 30 years. The Puerto Rican Government protested against Diageo's decision to relocate to the US Virgin Islands, claiming that the Virgin Islands had misappropriated federal excise taxes collected on rum revenues to persuade the company to move to the territory, a claim the Government vehemently denied. (The US Virgin Islands and Puerto Rico benefit from the USA's 'cover over' programme, which redistributes 98% of rum excise duties collected in the USA to the two territories.) The dispute escalated during 2012, when some members of the Caribbean Community and Common Market (CARICOM) threatened to file a complaint with the World Trade Organization owing to concerns about the 'cover over' programme, which, they argued, constituted an illegitimate subsidization scheme. CARICOM claimed that the programme was distorting the regional market, leaving its members at a disadvantage.

CONSTITUTION AND GOVERNMENT

The Government of the US Virgin Islands is organized under the provisions of the Organic Act of the Virgin Islands, passed by the US Congress in 1936 and revised in 1954 and 1984. Executive power is vested in the Governor, elected for four years by universal suffrage. Legislative power is vested in a unicameral, 15-member body.

REGIONAL CO-OPERATION

A memorandum of understanding was signed in September 2010 by the US Virgin Islands and the Organisation of Eastern Caribbean States. The agreement envisaged greater co-operation in the areas of security, economic development, disaster management and environmental protection.

ECONOMIC AFFAIRS

According to estimates by the US Bureau of Economic Analysis, the islands' gross domestic product (GDP) in 2010 was US \$4,498m., equivalent to about \$43,853 per head. GDP increased, in real terms, at an average rate of 1.3% per year during 2002–10. In 2002–10 the population decreased at an average annual rate of 0.4%. GDP declined by 5.9% in 2009, but increased by 2.9% in 2010.

Most of the land is unsuitable for large-scale cultivation, but tax incentives have encouraged the growing of vegetables, fruit and cereals, which are produced for local consumption. The islands are heavily dependent on links with the US mainland. There are no known natural resources, and, because of limited land space and other factors, the islands are unable to produce sufficient food to satisfy local consumption. Most goods are imported, mainly from the mainland USA. According to the 2000 census figures, 0.7% of the economically active population were engaged in agriculture, forestry, fishing and mining. According to FAO estimates, however, the sector engaged around 18.4% of the labour force in mid-2013.

Industry (including construction and mining) engaged some 9.2% of the non-agricultural labour force in 2011, according to official figures. The manufacturing and the construction and mining sectors each employed 4.6% of the employed labour force in 2011. The main branch of manufacturing is petroleum refining.

Services (including public administration) employed some 90.8% of the non-agricultural labour force in 2011, according to official figures, of which about 28.1% were employed in public administration. Tourism, which is estimated to account almost 30% of GDP, is the mainstay of the islands' income and employment, and provides the major source of direct and indirect revenue for other service sectors (including trade and transport). The emphasis is on the visiting cruise ship business and the advantages of duty-free products for tourist visitors. In 2012 visitor arrivals (including excursionists and cruise passengers) totalled 2.6m.; in 2010 visitor expenditures amounted to US $1,012.5m.

Until 2012 St Croix had one of the world's largest petroleum refineries, Hovensa LLC (a joint venture between the US oil company Amerada Hess and Petróleos de Venezuela, SA), which had a production capacity of almost 500,000 barrels per day. Its closure in February 2012, in response to declining demand, would adversely affect the territory's economy. Storage of oil was to continue at the site. In April 2013 Hovensa and the US Virgin Islands Government reached agreement on the terms of the sale of the refinery to any prospective buyer. Hovensa also agreed to make fuel available to those living on the islands until 2019. Efforts have been made to introduce labour-intensive and non-polluting manufacturing industries. Rum is an important product; in 2010 Diageo inaugurated a distillery that was expected to produce 20m. proof gallons annually. In 2009 the Government also agreed to fund expansion of the existing Cruzan Rum distillery. Federal excise taxes collected on rum exports to the USA (the so-called 'cover over' programme) returned $133.9m. of revenue in 2011; the 'cover over' programme was renewed for a further two years in January 2013.

In 2012 there was a projected budget deficit of $67m. In 2005/06 the islands' debt amounted to some $1,150m., equivalent to $10,272 per head. The average rate of unemployment stood at 11.7% in 2012.

In 2011 the islands recorded a merchandise trade deficit of US $659.2m. In that year the USA provided 12.7% of imports and took 82.6% of exports. Venezuela was also a major source of imports. Of total exports to the USA in 2011, some 78.8% were refined petroleum products. Crude petroleum accounted for 74.0% of the islands' total imports in that year.

Owing to the islands' heavy reliance on imported goods, local prices and inflation are higher than on the mainland, and the islands' economy was dependent on that of the USA. The economy, particularly the tourism and construction sectors, was adversely affected by the global economic downturn from 2009, while lower tax receipts put government finances under strain. According to the US Bureau of Economic Analysis, real GDP contracted by 0.4% in 2008 and by a further 5.9% in 2009. Nevertheless, the economy grew by 2.9% in 2010, supported mainly by the oil refining sector, and by an estimated 3.1% in 2011; tourist numbers rose in both years. With the budget deficit projected to rise to $90m. in 2011/12, legislation was adopted in 2011 to reduce public sector salaries by 8% and a voluntary retirement scheme was also introduced. The Senate rejected a further wage reduction bill in December, prompting the Government to implement a programme of civil service retrenchment. Meanwhile, the closure of the Hovensa LLC refinery, the territory's main employer, in February 2012 resulted in the loss a significant source of government receipts and over 2,000 jobs. The unemployment rate reached 13.7% in February 2013, up from 8.8% 12 months earlier. The Government was involved in efforts to find a new buyer for the refinery in early 2013. The rum 'cover over' programme with the federal USA, which had assumed even greater significance following the closure of the refinery, was renewed for two years by the US Congress in January 2013. Meanwhile, additional austerity measures were introduced in February. Real GDP contracted by an estimated 2.1% in 2012, but was projected to grow by 4.8% in 2013.

PUBLIC HOLIDAYS

2014: 1 January (New Year's Day), 6 January (Three Kings' Day), 20 January (Martin Luther King Day), 17 February (Presidents' Day), 31 March (Transfer Day), 18–21 April (Easter), 26 May (Memorial Day), 16 June (Organic Act Day), 3 July (Danish West Indies Emancipation Day), 4 July (US Independence Day), 26 July (Hurricane Supplication Day), 1 September (Labor Day), 13 October (Columbus Day/Puerto Rico Friendship Day), 20 October (Virgin Islands Thanksgiving Day), 1 November (Liberty Day), 11 November (Veterans' Day), 27 November (US Thanksgiving Day), 25 December (Christmas).

Statistical Survey

Sources (unless otherwise stated): Office of Public Relations, Office of the Governor, Charlotte Amalie, VI 00802; tel. (340) 774-0294; fax (340) 774-4988; Bureau of Economic Research, Dept of Economic Development and Agriculture, 1050 Norre Gade No. 5, Suite 301, Charlotte Amalie, VI 00802; POB 6400, Charlotte Amalie, VI 00804; tel. (340) 774-8784; e-mail dhazell@usviber.org; internet www.usviber.org.

AREA AND POPULATION

Area: 347.1 sq km (134 sq miles): St Croix 215 sq km (83 sq miles); St Thomas 80.3 sq km (31 sq miles); St John 51.8 sq km (20 sq miles).

Population: 108,612 (males 51,684, females 56,748) at census of 1 April 2000; 106,405 at census of 1 April 2010. *By Island* (2010 census): St Croix 50,601, St Thomas 51,634, St John 4,170 (Source: US Census Bureau). *Mid-2013* (UN estimate): 108,300. (Source: UN, *World Population Prospects: The 2010 Revision*).

Density (at mid-2013): 312.0 per sq km.

Population by Age and Sex ('000, UN estimates at mid-2013): *0–14:* 20,928 (males 10,775, females 10,153); *15–64:* 69,336 (males 32,523, females 36,813); *65 and over:* 18,036 (males 7,880, females 10,156); *Total* 108,300 (males 51,178, females 57,122) (Source: UN, *World Population Prospects: The 2010 Revision*).

Principal Towns (population at 2010 census): Charlotte Amalie (capital) 10,354; Christiansted 2,433; Frederiksted 859. Source: US Census Bureau.

Births and Deaths (2006, preliminary): Registered live births 1,431 (birth rate 13.2 per 1,000); Registered deaths 629 (death rate 5.8 per 1,000) (Source: US National Center for Health Statistics). *2011:* Birth rate 11.4 per 1,000; Death rate 7.2 per 1,000 (Source: Pan American Health Organization).

Life Expectancy (years at birth, estimates): 79.3 (males 76.3; females 82.6) in 2011. Source: Pan American Health Organization.

Employment (persons aged 16 years and over, 2000 census): Agriculture, forestry, fishing, hunting and mining 324; Manufacturing 2,754; Construction 4,900; Wholesale trade 912; Retail trade 6,476; Transportation, warehousing and utilities 3,321; Information 931; Finance, insurance, real estate, rental and leasing 2,330; Professional, scientific, management, administrative and waste management services 3,058; Educational, health, and social services 6,742; Arts, entertainment, recreation, accommodation and food services 7,351; Public administration 4,931; Other services 2,535; *Total employed* 46,565 (Source: US Bureau of the Census). *2011* (number of waged and salaried jobs, official figures): Construction and mining 2,036; Manufacturing 2,047; Transportation, warehouses and utilities 1,498; Wholesale and retail trade 6,753; Financial activities 2,362; Leisure and hospitality 7,222; Information 804; Other services 9,324; Federal government 964; Territorial government 11,563; Total 44,573. *Economically Active Population* (civilians only, annual averages, 2011): Total employed 46,121, Unemployed 4,608; Total labour force 50,729.

HEALTH AND WELFARE

Total Fertility Rate (children per woman, 2011): 1.8.

Under-5 Mortality Rate (per 1,000 live births, 2010): 9.8.

Physicians (per 1,000 head, 2003): 1.47.

Hospital Beds (per 1,000 head, 1996): 18.7.

Source: Pan American Health Organization.

For definitions, see explanatory note on p. vi.

AGRICULTURE, ETC.

Livestock (2011, FAO estimates): Cattle 8,200; Sheep 3,250; Pigs 2,650; Goats 4,100; Chickens 40,000.

Fishing (metric tons, live weight, 2010): Total catch (all capture) 857 (FAO estimate) (Groupers 47; Snappers, jobfishes, etc. 97; Grunts, sweetlips, etc. 33; Parrotfishes 104; Triggerfishes, durgons, etc. 53; Caribbean spiny lobster 111; Stromboid conchs 254).

Source: FAO.

INDUSTRY

Production ('000 metric tons, unless otherwise indicated, 2002, estimates): Jet fuels 1,745; Motor spirit (petrol) 2,654; Kerosene 91; Gas-diesel (distillate fuel) oil 5,725; Residual fuel oils 3,550; Liquefied petroleum gas 164; Electric energy (2008) 1,078 million kWh. Source: UN, *Industrial Commodity Statistics Yearbook* and Database.

FINANCE

Currency and Exchange Rates: 100 cents = 1 United States dollar (US $). *Sterling and Euro Equivalents* (31 December 2012): £1 sterling = US $1.578; €1 = US $1.319; US $100 = £63.37 = €75.79.

Budget (US $ million, 2011): Operating budget 793.4 (Net revenues from taxes, duties and other sources 587.6); Rum excise taxes (Federal remittance) 133.9; Direct Federal expenditures n.a.

Cost of Living (Consumer Price Index; base: 2009 = 100): All items 104.0 in 2010; 113.4 in 2011.

Gross Domestic Product (US $ million at current prices): 4,255 in 2008; 4,248 in 2009; 4,498 in 2010 (Source: Bureau of Economic Analysis, US Department of Commerce).

EXTERNAL TRADE

Total Trade (US $ million): *Imports:* 10,289.9 in 2009; 12,153.9 in 2010; 13,972.7 in 2011. *Exports:* 9,728.3 in 2009; 11,929.5 in 2010; 13,313.5 in 2011. Note: The main import is crude petroleum (10,340.9m. in 2011), while the principal exports are refined petroleum products (10,486.1m. in 2011).

Trade with the USA (US $ million): *Imports:* 1,139.3 in 2009; 1,548.9 in 2010; 1,767.6 in 2011. *Exports:* 8,495.3 in 2009; 9,992.5 in 2010; 10,994.8 in 2011.

TRANSPORT

Road Traffic (registered motor vehicles, 2011): 75,585.

Shipping: *Freight Imports* ('000 metric tons) 1,056 in 2002; 879 in 2003; 979 in 2004. *Cruise Ship Arrivals:* 680 in 2010; 698 in 2011; 667 in 2012. *Passenger Arrivals:* 1,858,946 in 2010; 2,008,991 in 2011; 1,904,468 in 2012.

Civil Aviation (visitor arrivals): 691,558 in 2010; 678,961 in 2011; 737,681 in 2012.

TOURISM

Visitor Arrivals ('000): 2,550.5 in 2010 (arrivals by air 691.6, cruise ship passengers 1,858.9); 2,688.0 in 2011 (arrivals by air 679.0, cruise ship passengers 2,009.0); 2,642.2 in 2012 (arrivals by air 737.7, cruise ship passengers 1,904.5).

Visitor Receipts (US $ million, 2010): Total receipts 1,012.5 (tourists 678.2, excursionists 334.3).

COMMUNICATIONS MEDIA

Telephones (2010): 75,800 main lines in use.

Mobile Cellular Telephones (2009): 80,300 subscribers.

Internet Users (2009): 30,000.

Broadband Subscribers (2010): 9,100.

Source: International Telecommunication Union.

EDUCATION

Pre-primary (1992/93, unless otherwise indicated): 62 schools; 121 teachers; 4,714 students (2000).

Elementary (1992/93, unless otherwise indicated): 62 schools; 790 teachers (public schools only); 11,728 students (2005).

Secondary: 541 teachers (public schools only, 1990); 5,022 students (2005).

Higher Education: 266 teachers (2003/04); 2,610 students (2004).

Sources: UNESCO, *Statistical Yearbook*; US Bureau of the Census.

Directory

The Government

HEAD OF STATE

President: BARACK HUSSEIN OBAMA (took office 20 January 2009, re-elected 6 November 2012).

EXECUTIVE
(May 2013)

The Government is formed by the Democratic Party of the Virgin Islands.

Governor: JOHN DEJONGH, Jr (took office 1 January 2007, re-elected 2 November 2010).

Lieutenant-Governor: GREGORY R. FRANCIS.

Commissioner of Agriculture: LOUIS E. PETERSON, Jr.

Commissioner of Education: Dr LAVERNE TERRY.

Commissioner of Finance: ANGEL DAWSON, Jr.

Commissioner of Health: DARICE PLASKETT.

Commissioner of Human Services: CHRISTOPHER FINCH.

Commissioner of Labor: ALBERT BRYAN, Jr.

Commissioner of Licensing and Consumer Affairs: WAYNE L. BIGGS, Jr.

Commissioner of Planning and Natural Resources: ALICIA BARNES.

Commissioner of Police: RODNEY F. QUERRARD, Sr (acting).

Commissioner of Property and Procurement: LYNN A. MILLIN MADURO.

Commissioner of Public Works: DARRYL SMALLS.

Commissioner of Sports, Parks and Recreation: ST CLAIRE N. WILLIAMS.

Commissioner of Tourism: BEVERLY NICHOLSON-DOTY.

Attorney-General: VINCENT FRAZER.

US Virgin Islands Delegate to the US Congress: DONNA M. CHRISTENSEN.

GOVERNMENT OFFICES

Office of the Governor: Government House, 21–22 Kongens Gade, Charlotte Amalie, VI 00802; tel. (340) 774-0001; fax (340) 693-4309; e-mail contact@governordejongh.com; internet www.governordejongh.com.

Office of the Lieutenant-Governor: Government Hill, 18 Kongens Gade, Charlotte Amalie, VI 00802; tel. (340) 774-2991; fax (340) 774-6953; internet www.ltg.gov.vi.

Department of Agriculture: Estate Lower Love, Kingshill, St Croix, VI 00850; tel. (340) 778-0997; fax (340) 778-7977; e-mail lpeters@uvi.edu; internet www.vifresh.com/.

Department of Education: 1834 Kongens Gade, Charlotte Amalie, VI 00802-6746; tel. (340) 774-0100; fax (340) 779-7153; e-mail ideas@doe.vi; internet www.doe.vi.

Department of Finance: GERS Bldg, 2nd Floor, 76 Kronprindsens Gade, Charlotte Amalie, VI 00802; tel. (340) 774-4750; fax (340) 776-4028; e-mail aedawson@dof.gov.vi; internet www.usvifinance.info.

Department of Health: 1303 Hospital Ground Suite 10, Charlotte Amalie, St Thomas, VI 00802; tel. (340) 774-9000; fax (340) 777-4001; e-mail julia.sheen@usvi-doh.org; internet www.healthvi.org.

Department of Human Services: Knud Hansen Complex, Bldg A, 1303 Hospital Ground, Charlotte Amalie, VI 00802; tel. (340) 774-0930; fax (340) 774-3466; internet www.dhs.gov.vi.

Department of Justice: GERS Bldg, 2nd Floor, 34–38 Kronprindsens Gade, Charlotte Amalie, VI 00802; tel. (340) 774-5666; fax (340) 774-9710; e-mail vfrazer@doj.vi.gov; internet doj.vi.gov.

Department of Labor: 53A–54AB Kronprindsens Gade, St Thomas, VI 00803-2608; tel. (340) 776-3700; fax (340) 774-5908; e-mail customersupport@vidol.gov; internet www.vidol.gov.

Department of Licensing and Consumer Affairs: Property & Procurement Bldg, 1 Sub Base, Rm 205, Charlotte Amalie, St Thomas, VI 00802; tel. (340) 774-3130; fax (340) 776-0675; e-mail dlcacommissioner@dlca.gov.vi; internet www.dlca.gov.vi.

Department of Planning and Natural Resources: Cyril E. King Airport, Terminal Bldg, 2nd Floor, Suite 6, 8100 Lindberg Bay, St Thomas, VI 00802; tel. (340) 774-3320; fax (340) 775-5706; e-mail robertmathes@dpnr.gov.vi; internet www.dpnr.gov.vi.

Department of Police: Alexander Farrelly Criminal Justice Center, Charlotte Amalie, St Thomas, VI 00802; tel. (340) 774-2211; fax (340) 715-5517; e-mail police.commissioner@vipd.gov.vi; internet www.vipd.gov.vi.

Department of Property and Procurement: Property & Procurement Bldg No. 1, 3rd Floor, Sub Base, Charlotte Amalie, VI 00802; tel. (340) 774-0828; fax (340) 774-9704; e-mail lmillin@pnpvi.org.

Department of Public Works: Bldg No. 8, Sub Base, Charlotte Amalie, VI 00802; tel. (340) 776-4844; fax (340) 774-5869; e-mail darryl.smalls@dpw.vi.gov.

Department of Sports, Parks and Recreation: Property & Procurement Bldg No. 1, Sub Base, 2nd Floor, Rm 206, Charlotte Amalie, VI 00802; tel. (340) 774-0255; fax (340) 774-4600; e-mail info@dspr.vi; internet www.dspr.vi.

Department of Tourism: POB 6400, St Thomas, VI 00804; tel. (340) 774-8784; fax (340) 774-4390; e-mail info@usvitourism.vi; internet www.visitusvi.com.

Legislature

LEGISLATIVE ASSEMBLY

Senate

President of the Senate: SHAWN-MICHAEL MALONE.

Election, 6 November 2012

Party	Seats
Democratic Party	10
Independent Citizens' Movement	1
Independent	4
Total	**15**

Election Commission

Election Board: Election Systems of the Virgin Islands, POB 1499, Kingshill, St Croix, VI 00851-1499; tel. (340) 773-1021; fax (340) 773-4523; e-mail electionsys@unitedstates.vi; internet www.vivote.gov; Supervisor of Elections JOHN ABRAMSON, Jr; brs on St Thomas and St John.

Political Organizations

Democratic Party of the Virgin Islands: POB 8507, St Thomas, VI 00801; tel. (340) 775-9675; internet www.democrats.org; affiliated to the Democratic Party of the USA; Chair. EMMETT HANSEN, III.

Independent Citizens' Movement (The ICM Party, VI): POB 305188, St Thomas, VI 00803-5188; tel. (340) 772-9524; f. 1968; Chair. Sen. TERRENCE NELSON.

Republican Party of the Virgin Islands: 6067 Questa Verde, Christiansted, St Croix, VI 00820-4485; tel. (340) 332-2579; e-mail info@virepublicanwomen.com; internet www.vigop.com; f. 1948; affiliated to the Republican Party of the USA since 1952; Chair. HERBERT SCHOENBOHM; Exec. Dir WARREN COLE.

Judicial System

Supreme Court of the Virgin Islands: No. 161B, Crown Bay, St Thomas, VI 00802; tel. (340) 774-2237; fax (340) 774-2258; e-mail administrative.services@visupremecourt.org; internet www.visupremecourt.org; f. 2007; assumed jurisdiction for all appeals formerly administered by the Superior Court; highest local appellate body, established to administer justice independently of the US federal justice system; judges are appointed by the Governor; Chief Justice RHYS S. HODGE.

Superior Court of the Virgin Islands: Alexander A. Farrelly Justice Center, 5400 Veteran's Dr., St Thomas, VI 00802; tel. (340) 774-6680; fax (340) 776-9889; e-mail court.administrator@visuperiorcourt.org; internet www.visuperiorcourt.org; f. 1976 as the Territorial Court of the Virgin Islands; name officially changed in 2004; jurisdiction over all local civil actions and criminal matters; court in St Croix also; judges are appointed by the Governor; Presiding Judge DARRYL DEAN DONOHUE.

US Federal District Court of the Virgin Islands: Division of St Thomas/St John: 5500 Veteran's Dr., Charlotte Amalie, St Thomas, VI 00802-6424; Division of St Croix: 3013 Estate Golden Rock, Christiansted, St Croix, VI 00820-4355; tel. (340) 774-0640; fax (340) 774-1293; internet www.vid.uscourts.gov; jurisdiction in civil, criminal and federal actions; judges are appointed by the President of the USA with the advice and consent of the Senate; Chief Judge CURTIS V. GOMEZ.

Religion

The population is mainly Christian. The main churches with followings in the islands are Baptist, Roman Catholic, Episcopalian, Lutheran, Methodist, Moravian and Seventh-day Adventist. There is also a small Jewish community, numbering around 900 adherents.

CHRISTIANITY

The Roman Catholic Church

The US Virgin Islands comprises a single diocese, suffragan to the archdiocese of Washington, DC, USA. Some 28% of the population are Roman Catholics.

Bishop of St Thomas: Most Rev. HERBERT A. BEVARD, Bishop's Residence, 29A Princesse Gade, POB 301825, Charlotte Amalie, VI 00803-1825; tel. (340) 774-3166; fax (340) 774-5816; e-mail chancery@islands.vi; internet www.catholicvi.com.

The Anglican Communion

Episcopal Diocese of the Virgin Islands: Bishop: Rt Rev. AMBROSE GUMBS, POB 7488, St Thomas, VI 00801; tel. (340) 776-1797; fax (340) 777-8485; internet www.episcopalvi.org.

The Press

St Croix This Week: POB 11199, St Thomas, VI 00801-4199; tel. (340) 774-2500; fax (340) 776-1466; e-mail sttw@viaccess.net; internet www.stcroixthisweek.com; monthly; comprises the *St Thomas/St John This Week* and *St Thomas This Week Cruise Edn*; Publr FRANCES NEWBOLD; Man. Editor SUSAN WALL.

St John Sun Times: 5000 Estate Enighed, POB 123, St John, VI 00830; tel. (340) 201-8700; e-mail info@stjohnsuntimes.com; internet www.stjohnsuntimes.com; 6 a year; lifestyle magazine; Publr and Editor ELLA ANDERSON.

St John Tradewinds: The Marketplace, Office Suites II, Office 104, POB 1500, Cruz Bay, St John, VI 00831; tel. (340) 776-6496; fax (340) 693-8885; e-mail info@tradewinds.vi; internet www.stjohntradewindsnews.com; f. 1972; weekly; Publr MALINDA NELSON; circ. 2,500.

Virgin Islands Daily News: 9155 Estate Thomas, VI 00802; tel. (340) 774-8772; fax (340) 776-0740; e-mail letters@dailynews.vi; internet www.virginislandsdailynews.com; f. 1930; acquired from Innovative Communication Corpn by Times-Shamrock Communications, USA in 2008; morning; Publr JASON ROBBINS; Exec. Editor J. LOWE DAVIS; circ. 15,000.

Virgin Islands Source: St Thomas; tel. (340) 777-8144; fax (340) 777-8136; e-mail visource@gmail.com; internet www.visource.com; f. 1998; comprises the *St Thomas Source*, *St Croix Source* and *St John Source*; daily; digital; Publr SHAUN A. PENNINGTON.

Broadcasting and Communications

TELECOMMUNICATIONS

Broadband VI: POB 26304, Christiansted, VI 00824; tel. 719-2943; e-mail office@broadband.VI; internet www.broadband.vi; internet service provider.

Innovative Telephone: Bjerget House, POB 1730, St Croix, VI 00821; tel. (340) 779-9999; fax (340) 777-7701; e-mail webmaster@iccvi.com; internet www.innovativetelephone.com; f. 1959 as Virgin Islands Telephone Corpn (Vitelco); acquired by Innovative Communication Corpn in 1987; present name adopted in 2001; provides telephone services throughout the islands; launched internet service, Innovative PowerNet, in 1999; Vice-Pres. JENNIFER MATAR-ANGAS-KING.

Innovative Wireless: 4006 Estate Diamond, Christiansted, St Croix, VI 00820; fax (340) 778-6011; internet www.vitelcellular.com; f. 1989 as VitelCellular; subsidiary of Innovative Communication Corpn; mobile cellular telecommunications; Man. Dir BEULAH JONIS.

BROADCASTING

Radio

WDHP 1620 AM, WRRA 1290 AM, WAXJ 103.5 FM: 79A Castle Coakley, Christiansted, St Croix, VI 00820; tel. (340) 719-1620; fax (340) 778-1686; e-mail wrra@islands.vi; internet www.reefbroadcasting.com; operated by Reef Broadcasting, Inc; commercial; broadcasts to the US and British Virgin Islands, Puerto Rico and the Eastern Caribbean; Owner and Gen. Man. HUGH PEMBERTON.

WEVI (Power 101.7 WeVi-FM): 2C Hogensborg, Frederiksted, St Croix, VI 00840; POB 892, Christiansted, VI 00821; tel. (340) 719-9384; e-mail aw@frontlinemissions.org; internet www.wevifm.net; operated by FrontLine Missions International, Inc; non-commercial; Christian programming; English, Spanish and Creole/Patois.

WGOD: 22A, Estate Dorothea, POB 305012, Charlotte Amalie, St Thomas, VI 00803; tel. (340) 774-4498; fax (340) 777-9978; internet wgodradio.org; operated by Moody Broadcasting Network, USA; commercial; Christian religious programming; Pres. Rev. REYNALD CHARLES; Gen. Man. MARIE RHYMER-MARTIN.

WIUJ: POB 2477, St Thomas, VI 00803; e-mail information@wiuj.com; internet www.wiuj.com; operated by V. I. Youth Development Radio, Inc; non-commercial; educational and public service programmes; Gen. Man. LEO MORON.

WJKC (Isle 95-FM), WMNG (Mongoose), WVIQ (Sunny): 5020 Anchor Way, POB 25680, Christiansted, St Croix, VI 00824; tel. (340) 773-0995; fax (340) 770-9093; e-mail jkc@viradio.com; f. 1982; commercial; Gen. Man. JONATHAN K. COHEN.

WSTA (Lucky 13): 121 Sub Base, POB 1340, St Thomas, VI 00804; tel. (340) 774-4500; fax (340) 776-1316; e-mail nfo@wsta.com; internet www.wsta.com; f. 1950; acquired by Ottley Communications Corpn in 1984; commercial; Owner and Gen. Man. ATHNIEL C. OTTLEY.

WVGN: 8000 Nisky Centre, Suite 714, St Thomas, VI 00802; tel. (800) 275-6437; e-mail info@wvgn.org; internet www.wvgn.org; f. 2002; operated by Caribbean Community Broadcasting Co; non-commercial; news and public affairs programming; affiliated to NBC, USA; Gen. Man. KEITH BASS.

WVWI (Radio One), WVJZ (Jamz), WWKS (Kiss), WIVI (Hitz) (Ackley Media Group Stations): POB 302179, St Thomas, VI 00803-2179; tel. (340) 776-1000; fax (340) 776-5357; e-mail info@amg.vi; internet www.amg.vi; f. 1962; acquired from Knight Quality Stations by Ackley Media Group in 2006; commercial; Pres. and CEO GORDON P. ACKLEY.

WZIN FM (The Buzz): Nisky Mall Center, PMB 696, St Thomas, VI 00802; tel. (340) 776-1043; e-mail cristy@buzzrocks.com; operated by Pan Caribbean Broadcasting, Inc; commercial; Gen. Man. ALAN FRIEDMAN.

Television

Innovative Cable Television (St Croix, St Thomas, St John): 4006 Estate Diamond, Christiansted, St Croix, VI 00820; POB 6100, St Thomas, VI 00804; fax (340) 778-6011; e-mail info@iccvi.com; internet www.innovativecable.com; f. 1997 following acquisition of St Croix Cable TV (f. 1981); subsidiary of Innovative Communication Corpn; acquired Caribbean Communication Corpn in 1998; comprises TV2 (f. 2000); broadcasts to 7 Caribbean islands and France; Vice-Pres. JENNIFER MATARANGAS-KING.

WSVI-TV8 (Channel 8): Sunny Isle Shopping Center, POB 6000, Christiansted, St Croix, VI 00823; tel. (340) 778-5008; fax (340) 778-5011; e-mail channel8@wsvitv.com; internet www.wsvi.tv; f. 1965; operated by Alpha Broadcasting Corpn; affiliated to ABC, USA; 1 satellite channel and 1 analogue translator.

WTJX-TV (Public Television Service): POB 808, St Croix, VI 00820; tel. (340) 773-3337; fax (340) 773-4555; e-mail pphipps@wtjxtv.org; internet www.wtjxtv.org; f. 1968; educational and public service programmes; affiliated to PBS, USA; broadcasts on 1 terrestrial and 4 digital (cable) channels; broadcasts to the US and British Virgin Islands and Puerto Rico; Chair. RAÚL CARRILLO; Exec. Dir OSBERT POTTER.

Finance

(cap. = capital; res = reserves; dep. = deposits; brs = branches; amounts in US dollars)

BANKING

Banco Popular of the Virgin Islands: 193 Altona and Welgunst, Charlotte Amalie, VI 00802; tel. (340) 693-2702; fax (340) 693-2782; e-mail internet@bppr.com; internet www.bancopopular.com; Pres. and CEO RICHARD L. CARRIÓN; 8 brs.

Bank of Nova Scotia (Scotiabank): 214C Altona and Welgunst, POB 420, Charlotte Amalie, VI 00804; tel. (340) 774-0037; fax (340) 693-5994; e-mail lawrence.aqui@scotiabank.com; internet www.usvi.scotiabank.com; Vice-Pres. and Country Man. LAWRENCE AQUI; 10 brs.

Bank of St Croix: POB 24240, Gallows Bay, St Croix 00824; tel. (340) 773-8500; fax (340) 773-8508; e-mail info@bankofstcroix.com; internet www.bankofstcroix.com; f. 1994; cap. 2.7m., dep. 98.2m. (Dec. 2012); CEO JAMES BRISBOIS; 1 br.

FirstBank VI: POB 309600, St Thomas, VI 00803; tel. (866) 695-2511; fax (340) 776-1313; internet www.firstbankvi.com; acquired First Virgin Islands Federal Savings Bank in 2000 and Virgin Islands Community Bank in 2008; Regional Pres. and CEO AURELIO ALEMÁN-BERMUDEZ; 2 brs.

Virgin Islands Community Bank: 12–13 King St, Christiansted, St Croix, VI 00820; tel. (340) 773-0440; fax (340) 773-4028; internet www.vibank.org/vicbank.html; acquired by FirstBank of Puerto Rico in Jan. 2008; Pres. and CEO MICHAEL J. DOW; 3 brs.

INSURANCE

A number of mainland US companies have agencies in the Virgin Islands.

Trade and Industry

GOVERNMENT AGENCY

US Virgin Islands Economic Development Authority: Government Development Bank Bldg, 5055 Norre Gade No. 5, POB 305038, St Thomas, VI 00803; tel. (340) 714-1700; internet www.usvieda.org; semi-autonomous body comprising Government Devt Bank, Economic Devt Commission, Industrial Park Devt Corpn, Small Business Devt Agency and the Enterprise Zone programme; offices in St Thomas and St Croix; Chair. ALBERT BRYAN, Jr; CEO PERCIVAL CLOUDEN.

CHAMBERS OF COMMERCE

St Croix Chamber of Commerce: 3009 Orange Grove, Suite 12, Christiansted, St Croix, VI 00820; tel. (340) 718-1435; fax (340) 773-8172; e-mail info@stxchamber.org; internet www.stxchamber.org; f. 1924; Pres. STUART LOGAN; Exec. Dir MICHAEL DEMBECK; 300 mems.

St Thomas-St John Chamber of Commerce: 6–7 Dronningens Gade, POB 324, Charlotte Amalie, VI 00804; tel. (340) 776-0100; fax (340) 776-0588; e-mail chamber@islands.vi; internet www.usvichamber.com; Pres. SEBASTIANO PAIEWONSKY CASSINELLI; Exec. Dir JOSEPH S. AUBAIN; c. 700 mems.

UTILITIES

Regulatory Authority

Virgin Islands Energy Office: 4101 Estate Mars Hill, Frederiksted, St Croix, VI 00840; tel. (340) 713-8436; fax (340) 772-0063; e-mail don.buchanan@eo.vi.gov; internet www.vienergy.org; f. 1974; Dir KARL KNIGHT.

Electricity and Water

Virgin Islands Water and Power Authority (WAPA): POB 1450, Charlotte Amalie, VI 00804-1450; tel. (340) 774-3552; fax (340) 774-3422; internet www.viwapa.vi; f. 1964; public corpn; manufactures and distributes electric power and desalinated sea water; Chair. JUANITA R. YOUNG; CEO HUGO HODGE, Jr; c. 55,000 customers.

Transport

ROADS

The islands' road network totals approximately 855.5 km (531.6 miles).

SHIPPING

The US Virgin Islands are a popular port of call for cruise ships. The bulk of cargo traffic is handled at a container port on St Croix. A passenger and freight ferry service provides frequent daily connections between St Thomas and St John and between St Thomas and Tortola (British Virgin Islands). A US $150m. marina restoration project on St Thomas, completed in 2006, included provision for 'mega-yacht' docking facilities in addition to conventional moorings.

Virgin Islands Port Authority: Administrative Bldg 8074, Lindberg Bay, POB 301707, St Thomas, VI 00803-1707; tel. (340) 774-1629; fax (340) 774-0025; e-mail info@viport.com; internet www.viport.com; f. 1968; semi-autonomous govt agency; maintains, operates and develops marine and airport facilities; Chair. BEVERLY NICHOLSON-DOTY; Exec. Dir KENN HOBSON.

CIVIL AVIATION

There are airports on St Thomas and St Croix, and an airfield on St John. Seaplane services link the three islands. The runways at Cyril E. King Airport, St Thomas, and Henry E. Rohlsen Airport, St Croix, can accommodate intercontinental flights. In 2011 Air Canada and JetBlue began weekly non-stop flights to St Thomas and St Croix. The Government also planned a weekly charter service to St Croix, which was expected to begin in October 2013.

Seaborne Airlines: 1210 Watergut, Christiansted, St Croix, VI 00820; tel. 773-6442; fax 773-8798; e-mail customerservice@seaborneairlines.com; internet www.seaborneairlines.com; Pres. GARY FOSS; CEO OMER ERSELCUK.

Tourism

The islands have a well-developed tourism infrastructure, offering excellent facilities for fishing, yachting and other aquatic sports. A National Park covers about two-thirds of St John. There were 4,948 guest rooms in 2009, 3,809 of which were in hotels. In 2012 there were some 2.6m. visitors to the islands, of whom 737,650 were stop-over tourists, mainly from the USA, and 1.9m. were cruise ship passengers. Visitor expenditure amounted to US $1,012.5m. in 2010.

St Croix Hotel and Tourism Association: POB 24238, Christiansted, St Croix, VI 00824; tel. (340) 773-7117; fax (340) 773-5883; e-mail info@stcroixhotelandtourism.com; internet www.stcroixhotelandtourism.com; Pres. JULIE PRINTY.

US Virgin Islands Department of Tourism: c/o Office of Film Promotion, POB 6400, St Thomas, VI 00804; tel. (340) 774-8784; fax (340) 774-4390; internet www.visitusvi.com; Commr BEVERLY NICHOLSON-DOTY.

US Virgin Islands Hotel and Tourism Association: POB 2300, Charlotte Amalie, St Thomas, VI 00803; tel. (340) 774-6835; fax (340) 774-4993; e-mail info@virgin-islands-hotels.com; internet usvihta.com; Chair. TRUDIE PRIOR; Pres. LISA HAMILTON.

Defence

The USA is responsible for the defence of the United States Virgin Islands.

Education

The public education system in the US Virgin Islands comprises a State Education Agency and two Local Education Agencies, serving the St Thomas/St John District and the St Croix District. Education is compulsory up to the age of 16 years. It generally comprises eight years at primary school and four years at secondary school. There are two high schools, three middle schools and 13 elementary schools in St Thomas/St John District, while the district of St Croix has two high schools, three middle schools, 10 elementary schools and an alternative and a vocational school. In 2009 there were 15,493 students enrolled at public elementary and secondary schools, while in 2008 a total of 6,907 students were enrolled at private schools. The University of the Virgin Islands, with campuses on St Thomas and St Croix, had 2,602 full- and part-time students in 2009. The proposed budget for 2010/11 allocated US $40.9m. in federal funds to the Department of Education.

OTHER UNITED STATES TERRITORIES

Baker and Howland Islands

The Baker and Howland Islands lie in the Central Pacific Ocean, about 2,575 km (1,600 miles) south-west of Honolulu, Hawaii; they comprise two low-lying coral atolls without lagoons, and are uninhabited. Both islands were mined for guano in the late 19th century. Settlements, known as Meyerton (on Baker) and Itascatown (on Howland), were established by the USA in 1935, but were evacuated during the Second World War, owing to Japanese air attacks. The islands are National Wildlife Refuges, and since 1974 have been administered by the US Fish and Wildlife Service. In January 2009 President George W. Bush established by proclamation the Pacific Remote Islands Marine National Monument, which included Baker and Howland Islands. The islands are administered by the US Department of the Interior, US Fish and Wildlife Service, Refuge Complex Office, POB 50167, Honolulu, Hawaii 96850; internet www.fws.gov.

Jarvis Island

Jarvis Island lies in the Central Pacific Ocean, about 2,090 km (1,300 miles) south of Hawaii. It is a low-lying coral island and is uninhabited. The island was mined for guano in the late 19th century. A settlement, known as Millersville, including a weather station for the benefit of trans-Pacific aviation, was established by the USA in 1935, but was evacuated during the Second World War. In January 2009 Jarvis Island became part of the Pacific Remote Islands Marine National Monument (see above). The island is a National Wildlife Refuge and is administered by the US Department of the Interior, US Fish and Wildlife Service (see Baker and Howland Islands for details).

Johnston Atoll

Johnston Atoll lies in the Pacific Ocean, about 1,319 km (820 miles) west-south-west of Honolulu, Hawaii. It comprises Johnston Island, Sand Island (uninhabited) and two man-made islands, North (Akua) and East (Hikina), with a total area of 2.6 sq km (1 sq mile). Johnston Atoll was designated a Naval Defense Sea Area and Airspace Reservation in 1941, and is closed to public access. In 1985 construction of a chemical weapons disposal facility began on the atoll, and by 1990 it was fully operational. In 1989 the US Government agreed to remove artillery shells containing more than 400 metric tons of nerve gas from the Federal Republic of Germany, and destroy them on Johnston Island. In late 1991, following expressions of protest to the US Government by the nations of the South Pacific Forum (now Pacific Islands Forum), together with many environmental groups, a team of scientists visited the chemical disposal facility to monitor the safety and environmental impact of its activities. In May 1996 it was reported that all nerve gases stored on the atoll had been destroyed. However, 1,000 tons of chemical agents remained contained in landmines, bombs and missiles at the site. In December 2000 it was announced that the destruction of the remaining stock of chemical weapons had been completed (the original deadline for the destruction of 40,000 weapons stored on the island had been August 1995). The closure and decontamination of the facility was completed in 2004; in June of that year all military personnel left and control of the atoll was transferred to the US Fish and Wildlife Service. In March 2005 the Department of Defense announced the termination of the Air Force mission in Johnston Atoll. A facility capable of performing atmospheric tests of nuclear weapons remains operational on the atoll. The atoll had an estimated population of 173 in 1990, although this increased to approximately 1,000, mainly military, personnel during weapons disposal operations in previous years. In January 2009 Johnston Atoll became part of the Pacific Remote Islands Marine National Monument (see Baker and Howland Islands). Johnston Atoll falls under the jurisdiction of the Department of the Interior, US Fish and Wildlife Service (see Baker and Howland Islands for details). Operational control is the responsibility of the US Air Force. Permission to land on Johnston Island must be obtained from the US Air Force. The residing military commander of Johnston Island acts as the agent for the Defense Threat Reduction Agency.

Kingman Reef

Kingman Reef lies in the Pacific Ocean, about 1,500 km (925 miles) south-west of Hawaii, and comprises a reef and shoal measuring about 8 km (5 miles) by 15 km (9.5 miles). In 2000 administrative control was transferred from the US Navy to the Department of the Interior. In 2001 the waters around the reef were designated a National Wildlife Refuge, under the jurisdiction of the US Fish and Wildlife Service (see Baker and Howland Islands for details). In January 2009 Kingman Reef became part of the Pacific Remote Islands Marine National Monument (see Baker and Howland Islands).

Midway Atoll

Midway Atoll lies in the northern Pacific Ocean, about 1,850 km (1,150 miles) north-west of Hawaii. A coral atoll, it comprises Sand Island, Eastern Island and several small islets within the reef, and has a total area of about 5 sq km (2 sq miles). The islands had a population of 2,200 in 1983, but by 1990 this had declined to 13. Since the transfer of the islands' administration from the US Department of Defense to the Department of the Interior in October 1996, limited tourism is permitted. There is a National Wildlife Refuge on the territory, which is home to many species of birds. In March 2011 it was reported that thousands of seabirds, including albatrosses and other endangered species, had been killed by the tsunami that followed the powerful earthquake of the east coast of Japan. A study of Midway Atoll by the US Geological Survey, concluded in April 2013, indicated that rising sea levels resulting from climate change could inundate low-lying Pacific islands far earlier than had previously been estimated, predicting, for example, that more than 90% of Eastern Island would be submerged if sea levels rose by 2 m (6.6 ft). The islands are administered by the US Department of the Interior, US Fish and Wildlife Service (see Baker and Howland Islands for details).

Navassa Island

Navassa Island lies in the Caribbean Sea, about 160 km (100 miles) south of Guantánamo Bay, Cuba, and 65 km (40 miles) west of Haiti. It is a raised coral island with a limestone plateau and has an area of 5.2 sq km (2 sq miles). The island is uninhabited. Navassa became a US Insular Area in 1857, and was mined throughout the late 19th century, under the Navassa Phosphate Co. All mining activities were terminated in 1898. In 1996 the US Coast Guard ceased operations of the island's lighthouse, and in January 1997 the Office of Insular Affairs (under the control of the US Department of the Interior) assumed control of the island. A research expedition undertaken in mid-1998 revealed the presence of numerous undiscovered plant and animal species, many of which were thought to be unique to the island. Visits to the island and its surrounding waters were subsequently prohibited, pending further assessment of the island's environment. In December 1999 administrative responsibility for Navassa passed wholly to the US Department of the Interior, US Fish and Wildlife Service (see Baker and Howland Islands for details); however, control over political matters was retained by the Office of Insular Affairs.

Palmyra Atoll

Palmyra Atoll lies in the Pacific Ocean, about 1,600 km (1,000 miles) south of Honolulu, Hawaii. It comprises some 50 low-lying islets, has a total area of 100 ha, is uninhabited and is privately owned. Since 1961 the territory has been administered by the US Department of the Interior. In mid-1996 it was announced that the owners (the Fullard-Leo family in Hawaii) were to sell the atoll to a US company, which, it was believed, planned to establish a nuclear waste storage facility in the territory. The Government of neighbouring Kiribati expressed alarm at the proposal, and reiterated its intention to seek the reinclusion of the atoll within its own national boundaries. However, in June one of the Hawaiian Representatives to the US Congress proposed legislation in the US House of Representatives to prevent the establishment of such a facility, and a US government official subsequently announced that the atoll would almost certainly not be used for that purpose. Palmyra was purchased by The Nature Conservancy (internet www.nature.org) in December 2000. Designated a National Wildlife Refuge, the lagoons and surrounding waters within the 12 nautical mile zone of US territorial seas were transferred to the US Fish and Wildlife Service (see Baker and Howland Islands for details) in January 2001; the US Fish and Wildlife Service subsequently undertook negotiations to purchase part of the 680 acres of emergent lands owned by The Nature Conservancy. In November 2005 an international team of scientists joined with The Nature Conservancy to establish a new station on the Palmyra Atoll in order to undertake environmental research. In January 2009 Palmyra became part of the Pacific Remote Islands Marine National Monument (see Baker and Howland Islands). In 2012 the US Fish and Wildlife Service and The Nature Conservancy successfully concluded a project to eradicate non-native black rats from Palmyra Atoll, as part of a wider effort to restore the atoll's ecological balance.

Wake Island

Wake Island lies in the Pacific Ocean, about 2,060 km (1,280 miles) east of Guam. It is a coral atoll comprising the three islets of Wake, Wilkes and Peale, with an area less than 8 sq km (3 sq miles). The Republic of the Marshall Islands, some 500 km (310 miles) south of Wake, has exerted a claim to the atoll (called Enenkio by the Micronesians), which is a site of great importance for the islands' traditional chiefly rituals. Plans by a US company, announced in 1998, to establish a large-scale nuclear waste storage facility on the atoll were condemned by environmentalists and politicians in the region and subsequently abandoned. In August 2006 Hurricane Loke severely damaged much of the island's infrastructure. The US Air Force had previously evacuated all 188 residents. In January 2009 Wake Island became part of the Pacific Remote Islands Marine National Monument (see above, under Baker and Howland Islands). The Office of Insular Affairs of the US Department of the Interior is responsible for the civil administration of Wake Island, but activities on the atoll have been managed since 1972 by the US Department of Defense, Department of the Air Force (Pacific Air Forces), The Pentagon, Washington, DC 20330; tel. (202) 694-6061; fax (703) 696-7273; internet www.af.mil.

URUGUAY

Introductory Survey

LOCATION, CLIMATE, LANGUAGE, RELIGION, FLAG, CAPITAL

The Eastern Republic of Uruguay lies on the south-east coast of South America, with Brazil to the north and Argentina to the west. The climate is temperate, with an average temperature of 14°C–16°C (57°F–61°F) in winter and 21°C–28°C (70°F–82°F) in summer. The language is Spanish. There is no state religion but Roman Catholicism is predominant. The national flag (proportions 2 by 3) has nine horizontal stripes (five white and four blue, alternating), with a square white canton, containing a yellow sun with 16 alternating straight and wavy rays, in the upper hoist. The capital is Montevideo.

CONTEMPORARY POLITICAL HISTORY

Historical Context

After independence, gained in 1825, domestic politics in Uruguay became dominated by two parties: the Colorados ('reds' or Liberals) and the Blancos ('whites' or Conservatives, subsequently also known as the Partido Nacional). Their rivalry resulted in frequent outbreaks of civil war in the 19th century: the names derive from the flags of the 1836 civil war. During 1880–1958 the governing Partido Colorado was led by the Batlle family. Owing to the progressive policies of José Batlle y Ordóñez, Colorado President in 1903–07 and in 1911–15, Uruguay became the first welfare state in Latin America. During 1951–66 the presidency was in abeyance, being replaced by a collective leadership.

Domestic Political Affairs

In December 1967 Jorge Pacheco Areco assumed the presidency. His period in office was notable for massive increases in the cost of living, labour unrest and the spectacular exploits of the Tupamaro urban guerrilla movement. In 1972 Pacheco was succeeded by Juan María Bordaberry Arocena, a Colorado, who won the presidential election in November 1971. The army took complete control of the campaign against the Tupamaros, and by late 1973 had suppressed the movement. Military intervention in civilian affairs led, in 1973, to the closure of the Congreso (Congress) and its replacement by an appointed 25-member Council of State (subsequently increased to 35 members). The Partido Comunista and other left-wing groups were banned; repressive measures, including strict press censorship, continued. In September 1974 army officers were placed in control of the major state-owned enterprises.

President Bordaberry was deposed by the army in June 1976 because of his refusal to countenance any return to constitutional rule. In July the recently formed Council of the Nation elected Aparicio Méndez Manfredini to the presidency for five years. Despite the Government's announcement that there would be a return to democracy, persecution of opponents continued.

President Méndez introduced constitutional amendments, known as Institutional Acts, to consolidate the internal situation and to create a 'new order'. By 1980 severe economic problems made the army anxious to return executive responsibility to civilian politicians. However, a new proposed constitution, under which the armed forces would continue to be involved in all matters of national security, was rejected by voters in a plebiscite in November. The military leadership was therefore forced to amend the draft document in consultation with leaders of the recognized political parties, and in September 1981 a retired army general, Gregorio Alvarez Armellino, was appointed President during the transition period to full civilian government.

The Government's reluctance to permit greater public freedom and to improve observance of human rights caused serious unrest throughout 1983. Popular discontent was further aroused by the rapid deterioration of the economy and by the effect of the end of military rule in Argentina. In August the authorities suspended all public political activity and reserved the right to impose a new constitution without consultation, insisting, however, that the original electoral timetable would be maintained.

The political opposition responded by threatening to boycott the elections and by uniting with proscribed groups to hold a national day of protest. In September the first organized labour protest for 10 years was supported by 500,000 workers.

Political agitation increased during 1984, and the Government threatened to postpone the November elections unless the political parties agreed to its proposals for constitutional reform. Tensions increased in June, following the return from exile and subsequent arrest of Ferreira Aldunate, the proposed presidential candidate of the Partido Nacional. Following talks between the Government, the Partido Colorado and the Unión Cívica (a Christian democratic party), in which the parties obtained several important concessions, including the right to engage in political activity, in August the parties (with the exception of the Partido Nacional) agreed to the Government's proposals. The Government confirmed that elections would take place, and all restrictions on political activity were withdrawn.

At elections in November 1984 the Partido Colorado, led by Dr Julio María Sanguinetti Cairolo, secured a narrow victory. Sanguinetti was inaugurated on 1 March 1985, as was a Government of national unity, incorporating representatives of the other parties. Concurrently, various outlawed organizations, including the Partido Comunista, were legalized. All political prisoners were released under an amnesty law later in the month. The new Government announced its commitment to reversing the economic recession; however, its efforts to address the crisis were hampered by frequent industrial stoppages.

A major political issue in 1986 was the investigation into alleged violations of human rights by the armed forces during the military dictatorship. In August the Government proposed legislation that would offer an amnesty for all military and police personnel accused of this type of crime, in accordance with a pact made with the armed forces. In October the draft legislation was rejected by opposition parties, but in December a revised law (the Ley de Caducidad, or Statute of Limitations Law) was approved, which brought an end to current military trials and made the President responsible for any further investigations. The law was widely opposed and a campaign was initiated to organize a petition containing the signatures of at least 25% of the registered electorate, as required by the Constitution, in order to force a referendum on the issue. The campaign was supported principally by human rights groups, trade unions and the centre-left coalition, the Frente Amplio (FA). A referendum duly took place in April 1989, at which a total of 53% of the votes were cast in favour of maintaining the amnesty law.

The presidential and legislative elections in November 1989 resulted in victory (for the first time since 1962) for the Partido Nacional. However, the Partido Nacional failed to obtain an overall majority in the Congreso, thus compelling President-elect Luis Alberto Lacalle to seek support from a wider political base. In March 1990 an agreement was concluded between the two principal parties, whereby the Partido Colorado undertook to support proposed legislation on economic reform, in return for the appointment of four of its members to the Council of Ministers.

Labour unrest intensified during the early 1990s. The trade union confederation, the Plenario Intersindical de Trabajadores—Convención Nacional de Trabajadores (PIT—CNT), organized a series of general strikes to demand wage increases and in opposition to government austerity measures and privatization plans. Opposition from within the ruling coalition to the planned sale of state enterprises also became apparent. In September, none the less, the privatization legislation was narrowly approved by the Congreso. In response, the opposition FA, with the support of another political organization, Nuevo Espacio, and the trade unions, began a campaign to overrule the legislature by way of a referendum. In October 1992, in a special poll, some 30% of the electorate voted for a full referendum to be held on the partial amendment of the Government's privatization legislation. At the referendum, held in December, 72% of voters supported the proposal for a partial repeal of the legislation. The vote was also widely recognized as a vote of censure against the President's economic policy, and in particular his determination to keep public sector wage increases to a minimum.

Emergence of a third political force

The presidential and legislative elections in November 1994 were notable for the emergence of a third political force to rival the traditional powers of the Partido Nacional and the Partido Colorado. The Encuentro Progresista (EP—a predominantly left-wing alliance principally comprising the parties of the FA, as well as dissidents of the Partido Nacional and other minor parties) secured 31% of the votes in the presidential poll, as did the Partido Nacional, while the Partido Colorado won a narrow victory, with 33% of the vote. Sanguinetti, the leading presidential candidate of the Partido Colorado, was pronounced President-elect. In early 1995 the Partido Colorado established a governability pact with the Partido Nacional, providing for a coalition Government.

In July 1995 the Government and the opposition reached an agreement on the reform of the electoral system. Under the existing system, known as the Ley de Lemas, parties were permitted to present more than one presidential candidate, with the leading candidate in each party assuming the total number of votes for candidates in that party. According to the proposed reform, each party would present one candidate, selected by means of an internal election, and, in the event of no candidate securing an absolute majority, a second round of voting would be conducted. In October 1996 President Sanguinetti finally secured the necessary two-thirds' support in the legislature for the reform. The amendments were approved by voters in a plebiscite held in December, and came into effect in January 1997.

In May 1997 some 20,000 civilians staged a rally in the capital to demand that the Government and the armed forces provide information on the whereabouts of as many as 140 people who had 'disappeared' during the military dictatorship. In December President Sanguinetti issued a decree that granted an amnesty to 41 former army officers who had been dismissed from service during the dictatorship, owing to their political beliefs. In May 1999 some 15,000 people participated in a further march in support of demands that the authorities account for the disappearance of friends and relatives during the military dictatorship.

Election of Batlle

The presidential and legislative elections of October 1999 confirmed the end of the traditional dominance of the Partido Colorado and the Partido Nacional. The Encuentro Progresista—Frente Amplio (EP—FA) became the largest single party in both the Cámara de Representantes (Chamber of Representatives) and the Cámara de Senadores (Senate). The Partido Colorado largely maintained its representation, while support for the Partido Nacional declined considerably. Tabaré Ramón Vázquez Rosas, a former Mayor of Montevideo and the candidate of the EP—FA, won 39% of the vote, compared with 31% for Batlle, representing the Colorados. However, Batlle defeated Vázquez in a second round of voting in November, aided by the support of the Partido Nacional. Following his inauguration on 1 March 2000, President Batlle appointed a new Council of Ministers, comprising members of the Partido Colorado and the Partido Nacional.

Batlle committed himself to resolving the issue of the 'disappeared', in marked contrast to his predecessor, Sanguinetti, who had consistently resisted pressure to investigate their fate. In August 2000 Batlle announced the formation of a commission, composed of representatives from the Government, the opposition, the Church and the victims' families, to investigate the fate of 164 people who 'disappeared' during the military dictatorship. The unexpected dismissal in January 2001 of Gen. Juan Geymonat, Commander-in-Chief of the Armed Forces, was interpreted as a first step in a military reform programme. In October 2002 the Commission reported its preliminary findings that 26 of the 33 'disappeared' Uruguayan citizens under its investigation had been murdered by Argentine and Uruguayan military officers.

Against a background of ongoing economic recession, the Batlle administration encountered opposition to its policies from organized labour groups. In June 2000 a general strike was organized by the PIT—CNT to demand increased action on unemployment and more finance for education and health care, as well as to protest against emergency legislation, approved that month, which would allow the partial privatization of some public services. A more widespread strike was held in December.

Financial crisis

The financial crisis in neighbouring Argentina of December 2001–January 2002 caused additional economic hardship in Uruguay, with continued rural unrest and political and trade union opposition to the austerity measures introduced by the Government. In May the Argentine Government's imposition of severe restrictions on bank withdrawals prompted many Argentine citizens holding assets in Uruguay to access their funds, precipitating a crisis in Uruguay's financial system. In June the Government was forced to abandon exchange rate controls in order to maintain the peso uruguayo's competitiveness against the devalued Argentine and Brazilian currencies. However, by late July, following a 30% decline in the peso's value in relation to the US dollar, and amid rising concerns over the viability and transparency of the banking sector, substantial numbers of Uruguayans also began to withdraw their deposits. In an attempt to avert a financial collapse, the Government instructed all banking institutions in Uruguay to close for four days and introduced emergency economic measures, which included an increase in taxation on salaries and pensions. Three state-owned banks were placed under direct government administration, and restrictions were imposed on their customers' access to long-term foreign exchange deposits. The Government successfully sought an immediate loan of US $1,500m. from the USA to prevent a severe deterioration in international reserves and in November agreement was reached with the IMF on stand-by loans totalling some $2,800m. Nevertheless, as a result of the financial crisis, in late July Alberto Bensión, the Minister of Economy and Finance, was forced to resign. He was succeeded by Alejandro Atchugarry, a prominent member of the Partido Colorado.

The financial crisis led to a greater willingness within the Partido Nacional to reconsider its association with the Partido Colorado. In November 2002 the Partido Nacional terminated discussions on a new governability pact between the two parties, removed its five ministers from the Government and withdrew from the ruling coalition, leaving the FA as the largest political bloc in the Congreso.

In August 2003 a series of strikes was held by public sector workers to protest at the Government's reform programme, in particular at plans to increase private sector participation in the economy. In June the EP—FA gained parliamentary approval for a referendum to be held on the proposed partial privatization of the state-run fuel, cement and alcohol monopoly, the Administración Nacional de Combustible, Alcohol y Portland. In the plebiscite, held in December, some 62% voted to repeal the controversial legislation; the high level of opposition was widely interpreted as a further expression of public dissatisfaction with the Batlle administration.

The Vázquez presidency, 2005–10

At the presidential election in October 2004 Tabaré Vázquez, the candidate of the EP—FA—Nueva Mayoría (as the grouping became known until late 2005, when it was renamed the FA), won the presidency in the first round of voting, with 50.7% of the ballot. His nearest rival, Jorge Larrañaga, the Partido Nacional candidate, obtained some 34.1% of the votes. The EP—FA—Nueva Mayoría coalition also made gains in the concurrent legislative elections, winning a majority in both chambers. The Partido Colorado's representation fell sharply, while the Partido Nacional became the second largest party in both chambers. A referendum was concurrently held on whether the water industry should remain under state control; 64.5% of those voting were in favour of retaining the status quo.

President Vázquez took office on 1 March 2005. The new administration initially received cross-party support for its economic policies (in addition to the support already pledged for its policies on education and foreign affairs), but both opposition parties withdrew their support for the Government's economic policies in mid-March in protest at their allocation of positions on the governing bodies of state banks, companies and quasi-autonomous agencies, which, they considered, fell short of the number traditionally allocated to members of the opposition.

The new Minister of National Defence, Azucena Berruti, announced that the Government had begun investigations into the 'disappearances' that had occurred during the years of military rule. In August 2005 the heads of Uruguay's armed forces submitted to the President a report admitting the kidnap, torture and murder of political dissidents, and purportedly detailing the whereabouts of their remains. Information in the report led to the exhumation in November of the bodies of two dissidents murdered by members of the air force. Earlier that month Vázquez had proposed legislation seeking to amend the 1986 amnesty law in order to facilitate prosecution of members of the military for human rights abuses committed during military rule. In December 35 unidentified corpses were exhumed from a cemetery in a town near the Brazilian border.

The investigation of human rights abuses continued during 2006–07. In May 2006 six former Uruguayan military officers were arrested in connection with the 'disappearance' in 1976 of María Claudia García, the daughter of the Argentine poet Juan Gelman, following an extradition request from Argentina. The arrests represented the first occasion on which any individuals had faced legal action for their alleged role in the torture and murder of dissidents during the military repression. In November 2006 former President Bordaberry and his then Minister of Foreign Affairs, Juan Carlos Blanco, were charged with the abduction and murder of four opponents of the authorities in 1976. Furthermore, in February 2007 a former officer of senior rank in the Uruguayan military was arrested in Brazil on charges relating to the murders of three dissidents in 1976, as well as the 'disappearance' of García. In December former President Alvarez was charged, along with two army captains, with the forced disappearance of up to 40 dissidents in 1978, during which time he was Commander-in-Chief of the Army. Alvarez's arrest was facilitated by legislation, adopted in September 2006, which established that acts of forced disappearance were considered to be ongoing, and were therefore not excluded from prosecution by the amnesty law. Alvarez was found guilty of the murder of 37 people and sentenced to 25 years' imprisonment in October 2009. Former President Bordaberry received a 30-year prison sentence in February 2010, having been convicted of the murder of two opposition supporters and of the 'disappearance' of nine others, although he died in 2011. The Inter-American Court of Human Rights ruled in February of that year that the Uruguayan state was responsible for the 'disappearance' of García and urged the Government to prosecute those involved. In January 2012 García's daughter received some US $500,000 in compensation from the state.

In November 2008 the FA party delegation nominated the outspoken and flamboyant José (Pepe) Mujica (a senator and erstwhile Tupamaro guerrilla), of the Movimiento de Participación Popular (MPP), as the coalition's official candidate for the presidential election due in October 2009. Meanwhile, in April the legislature approved plans to hold a referendum (concurrently with the presidential and legislative elections) to reform the Constitution in order to allow Uruguayan emigrants to vote in elections from 2014. It was estimated that as many as 600,000 Uruguayans lived abroad, the majority of whom were believed to be supporters of the FA. A referendum to consider whether to repeal the Ley de Caducidad was also to be held concurrently, following the presentation of some 325,000 signatures (far exceeding the requisite 250,000) to the Congreso in April 2009. In March the FA had won a non-binding vote in the Congreso declaring the amnesty law unconstitutional, and in October, considering the case of the alleged murder in 1974 of an opponent of the military Government, the Supreme Court also ruled that the law was unconstitutional.

Mujica in office

The FA narrowly retained its majority in both chambers of the Congreso in the legislative elections, which were held on 25 October 2009, securing 50 of the 99 seats in the Cámara de Representantes and 16 in the 30-seat Cámara de Senadores. The Partido Nacional won 30 seats in the lower chamber and nine in the upper, while the Partido Colorado increased its representation to 17 and five seats, respectively. The Partido Independiente obtained the remaining two seats in the Cámara de Representantes. In the concurrent presidential election, Mujica secured 48.0% of the votes cast, followed by Lacalle, again the Partido Nacional's candidate, with 29.1%, and Pedro Bordaberry of the Partido Colorado, with 17.0%. Two other candidates contested the election, in which 89.9% of the electorate participated. Mujica defeated Lacalle in a second round of voting on 29 November, winning 52.4% of the ballot. A turn-out of 89.2% was recorded. Mujica's victory was partly attributed to the popularity of outgoing President Vázquez and to the strong performance of the economy under the latter's FA administration. During the electoral campaign Mujica had pledged to continue Vázquez's moderate left-wing policies.

In the two referendums conducted on 25 October 2009, both initiatives were rejected by the electorate: 63.1% voted against permitting emigrants to vote in elections from 2014 and 52.6% opposed a repeal of the Ley de Caducidad. None the less, the Supreme Court's ruling earlier that month (see The Vázquez presidency, 2005–10), that the amnesty law was unconstitutional, set a significant precedent for future cases concerning human rights abuses allegedly committed during the military dictatorship.

Mujica was inaugurated as President on 1 March 2010. He declared that his priorities would be to improve education, to eradicate extreme poverty, to guarantee energy supplies, to maintain security and to reduce bureaucracy in public administration. Ministerial positions in the new Government were divided among the various constituent parties of the FA, with the majority of the more strategic portfolios, including the interior, foreign affairs and national defence, allocated to the MPP.

The FA suffered a defeat in the regional elections conducted in May 2010. The ruling coalition managed to gain control of only five of the 19 contested departments (including the key administration of Montevideo), while the Partido Nacional won 12 and the Partido Colorado two.

A corruption scandal within the navy was exposed in August 2010, involving the disappearance of around US $7m. Most of the funds had ostensibly been used to purchase naval vessels, but these ships were subsequently found to be non-existent. The Government acted promptly to address the structural inadequacies within the navy that had facilitated these so-called 'phantom purchases', and legal action commenced against some 25 senior naval officers, including a former naval commander. A further scandal erupted in September 2011 when it emerged that Uruguayan navy personnel deployed in Haiti as part of a UN peace-keeping mission had allegedly sexually assaulted a Haitian man. The subsequent outrage that this incident generated in Haiti prompted Mujica to make an official apology and was also believed to have been a factor behind the UN Security Council's decision, in October, to reduce the size of the mission.

Throughout the second half of 2010 the country was disrupted by widespread industrial action, primarily led by public sector workers appealing for improved salaries and conditions. The labour unrest culminated in November, when 12 different trade unions declared strikes. However, public opinion surveys showed that the majority of the population opposed the strike action, and Mujica's high approval ratings allowed him to resist the unions' demands.

Mujica implemented his first cabinet reorganization in July 2011. Jorge Venegas was appointed as Minister of Public Health, replacing Daniel Olesker, who became the new Minister of Social Development, while later that month Eleuterio Fernández Huidobro received the national defence portfolio. The ministers responsible for tourism and housing were both replaced in mid-2012. Susana Muñiz was named as the new Minister of Public Health in February 2013 following the resignation of Venegas.

Mónica Xavier of the centre-left Partido Socialista del Uruguay was elected as FA President in May 2012, indicating the rising influence of the moderate wing of the coalition. It was widely expected that former President Vázquez, who remained popular nationally and was regarded as a unifying figure within the often discordant ruling alliance, would stand as the FA's candidate in the 2014 presidential election.

In an effort to address popular concerns about rising crime rates, the Government presented a series of security proposals in June 2012. Most notably, the administration announced its intention to legalize the marijuana industry, which would be overseen by government officials, with revenues redirected towards drug rehabilitation initiatives. Advocates claimed that the elimination of the underground marijuana market would reduce criminal activity associated with the illegal drugs trade. However, the proposals proved to be controversial, domestically and internationally, and a lack of public support prompted Mujica to suspend the legislative process in December.

In mid-October 2012 Uruguay became the second country in Latin America (after Cuba) to legalize abortion, after the Senado approved a law allowing for termination in the first 12 weeks of pregnancy. This followed endorsement of the proposal, by 50 votes to 49, by the Cámara de Representantes in the previous month. Passage of the law provoked fierce opposition from many quarters, not least from the opposition Partido Nacional, which began a campaign to collect enough signatures (52,000, equivalent to 2% of the electorate) to trigger a referendum on the issue. In late March 2013 the Partido Nacional submitted 67,000 signatures to the electoral court, which had 45 days to verify the signatures. If the petition was ruled to be valid, a non-binding referendum on the issue would be held within a futher 45 days.

Recent developments: amnesty law

In November 2010 the Supreme Court again declared the Ley de Caducidad unconstitutional, while later that month, in an unprecedented move against a serving officer in the military, Gen. Miguel Dalmao was charged in connection with the alleged murder of left-wing activist Nibia Sabalsagaray in 1974. Meanwhile, despite the results of the October 2009 referendum and fervent opposition from the Partido Nacional and the Partido Colorado, in September 2010 the FA proposed a reinterpretation of several key clauses within the Ley de Caducidad, which would effectively invalidate the law and facilitate the resumption of legal action against those accused of committing human rights abuses during the military dictatorship. This proposal was adopted by the Cámara de Representantes in October and by the Cámara de Senadores in April 2011, but in a final ballot in May the lower chamber narrowly rejected the bill after a member of the FA abstained. Nevertheless, in October the Congreso approved legislation recognizing the violations of human rights committed by the armed forces during the years of military rule as crimes against humanity. This landmark law allowed victims to circumvent the Ley de Caducidad, since under the terms of the amnesty bill those accused of crimes against humanity would not be granted immunity from prosecution. Consequently, legal proceedings against the alleged perpetrators of these abuses commenced later that month. The opposition condemned the legislation, arguing that it undermined the will of the electorate, as expressed in the results of past plebiscites on the repeal of the Ley de Caducidad. Following a legal challenge, the Supreme Court controversially rejected the law in February 2013, adjudging it to be unconstitutional.

Foreign Affairs

In 1991 the Governments of Argentina, Brazil, Paraguay and Uruguay agreed to create a common market of the 'Southern Cone' countries, the Mercado Común del Sur (Mercosur, see p. 439). The Treaty of Asunción allowed for the dismantling of trade barriers between the four countries, and entered full operation in 1995. Uruguay repeatedly criticized protectionist measures introduced by Argentina and Brazil, arguing that they were damaging to the Uruguayan economy and violated Mercosur's free trade principles. In June 2012 Uruguay, Argentina and Brazil voted to suspend Paraguay from Mercosur following the impeachment, under questionable circumstances, of Paraguayan President Fernando Lugo Méndez earlier that month. The three nations also voted in favour of admitting Venezuela to the organization, a process that was formalized in July.

Relations with Argentina were strained from 2005, when a Finnish company began construction of a cellulose plant in the Uruguayan city of Fray Bentos near the River Uruguay, which separates the two countries. The Argentine Government expressed concerns over the environmental impact of this plant and of a further mill scheduled to be built nearby. In January 2006 Argentine demonstrators blocked the three bridges spanning the river in protests that were tolerated by the Argentine authorities, drawing condemnation from the Uruguayan Government. Demonstrations, attended by some 10,000 people claiming that the project would cause serious environmental damage, continued in the Argentine city of Gualeguaychú. The dispute escalated in May when the Argentine Government initiated proceedings at the International Court of Justice (ICJ) on the grounds that the project would contravene the 1975 Statute of the River Uruguay. The ICJ declined to order the suspension of construction of the mills in July, but in January 2007 also rejected a request by the Government of Uruguay to order Argentina to end the ongoing blockade between the two countries. Uruguay had claimed that Argentina's protests had caused a loss of revenue of some US $800m., much of this in the form of lost earnings from tourism. Bilateral relations improved slightly in April following mediation by Spain, as a result of which both countries declared their willingness to reach a resolution to the impasse. None the less, in November President Vázquez authorized the recently inaugurated mill to begin production, provoking condemnation from Argentina, and temporarily closed the border between the countries in anticipation of violent protests. Argentine demonstrations continued to impede cross-border traffic in 2008. The ICJ issued its ruling on the dispute in April 2010, concluding that Uruguay had breached its procedural obligations under the Statute of the River Uruguay to inform Argentina of its plans for the construction of the mills, but had not violated its environmental obligations. The Court rejected Argentina's request for the dismantling of the plant in operation

and for compensation for alleged damage to its economy. The demonstrators finally ended their blockade in June. The signing by both nations in November of a technical agreement on monitoring pollution levels in the River Uruguay signified a mutually satisfactory conclusion to the dispute. Uruguay and Argentina signed multiple economic agreements in March and August 2011.

In 2007 Uruguay and the USA signed a trade and investment framework, regarded as a step towards eventual free trade agreement negotiations.

CONSTITUTION AND GOVERNMENT

Uruguay is a republic comprising 19 departments. Under the 1966 Constitution, executive power is held by the President, who is directly elected by universal adult suffrage for a five-year term. The President is assisted by the Vice-President and the appointed Council of Ministers. Legislative power is vested in the bicameral Congreso, comprising the Cámara de Senadores (Senate) and the Cámara de Representants (Chamber of Representatives), also directly elected for five years. The President, the Vice-President, the Senators (who number 31, including the Vice-President, who is automatically allocated a seat as President of the Cámara de Senadores) and the 99 Deputies are elected nationally. Judicial power is exercised by the five-member Supreme Court of Justice and by tribunals and local courts.

REGIONAL AND INTERNATIONAL CO-OPERATION

Uruguay is a member of the Inter-American Development Bank (see p. 341), of the Asociación Latinoamericana de Integración (see p. 370), of the Sistema Económico Latinoamericano (see p. 462), of the Mercado Común del Sur (Mercosur, see p. 439), of the Organization of American States (see p. 404), and of the Community of Latin American and Caribbean States (see p. 475), which was formally inaugurated in December 2011. In December 2004 Uruguay was one of 12 countries that were signatories to the agreement creating the South American Community of Nations (Comunidad Sudamericana de Naciones), intended to promote greater regional economic integration. A treaty for the community—referred to as the Union of South American Nations (Unión de Naciones Suramericanas) from 2007—was initialled in 2008, with full functionality of economic union tentatively scheduled for 2019.

Uruguay was a founder member of the UN in 1945. As a contracting party to the General Agreement on Tariffs and Trade, Uruguay joined the World Trade Organization (see p. 444) on its establishment in 1995.

ECONOMIC AFFAIRS

In 2011, according to estimates by the World Bank, Uruguay's gross national income (GNI), measured at average 2009–11 prices, was US $39,956m., equivalent to $11,860 per head (or $14,740 per head on an international purchasing-power parity basis). During 2002–11, it was estimated, the population increased at an average annual rate of 0.2%, while gross domestic product (GDP) per head increased, in real terms, by an average of 5.1% per year. Overall GDP increased, in real terms, at an average annual rate of 5.3% in 2002–11; according to official preliminary figures, GDP increased by 3.9% in 2012.

Agriculture (including forestry and hunting) contributed 7.6% of GDP in 2012, according to preliminary official figures. Some 10.9% of the labour force was employed in the sector in mid-2013, according to FAO estimates. The principal crops are rice, sugar cane, wheat, barley, potatoes, sorghum and maize. Livestock-rearing, particularly sheep and cattle, is traditionally Uruguay's major economic activity. Food and live animals provided 33.4% of export revenues in 2011, while exports of crops and vegetable products provided a further 24.6% in the same year. Agricultural GDP increased at an average annual rate of 1.2% per year in 2005–12; sectoral GDP increased by 12.2% in 2011, before decreasing by 1.3% in 2012.

Industry (including mining, manufacturing, construction and power) contributed 24.4% of GDP in 2012, according to preliminary official figures, and employed 21.5% of the working population in 2003. Industrial GDP increased at an average annual rate of 3.4% in 2005–12; industrial GDP declined by 0.7% in 2011, but increased by 3.7% in 2012.

Uruguay has few mineral resources and no proven hydrocarbon reserves. Accordingly, mining and quarrying (including fishing) only contributed 0.4% of GDP in 2012, and employed 0.1% of the working population in 2003. Apart from the small-scale extraction of building materials, industrial minerals and semi-precious stones, there has been little mining activity, although gold deposits are currently being developed. The GDP of the mining sector increased at an average annual rate of 12.3% in 2005–12; mining GDP declined by 9.4% in 2011, but increased by 15.5% in 2012.

Manufacturing contributed 13.4% of GDP in 2012, according to preliminary official figures, and employed 14.6% of the working population in 2003. The principal branches of manufacturing were food products, beverages and tobacco, chemicals, metal products, machinery and equipment, and textiles, clothing and leather products. Manufacturing GDP increased at an average annual rate of 3.5% in 2005–12. Manufacturing GDP increased by 1.6% in 2012.

Construction contributed 9.9% of GDP in 2012, according to preliminary official figures, and employed 6.7% of the working population in 2003. Construction GDP increased at an average annual rate of 6.1% in 2005–12; the sector expanded by 18.7% in 2012.

Energy is derived principally from hydroelectric power (59.4% of total electricity production in 2009). A further 31.1% of energy was derived from petroleum in 2009. There were two natural gas pipelines in operation between Uruguay and Argentina, with a total operating capacity of 184.9m. cu ft per day. Imports of mineral fuels and lubricants comprised 21.1% of the value of total imports in 2011. In 2005 Venezuela agreed to supply Uruguay with petroleum on preferential terms for the next 25 years.

The services sector contributed 68.0% of GDP in 2012, according to preliminary official figures, and engaged 73.9% of the working population in 2003. Tourism is a significant source of foreign exchange, earning a provisional US $2,187m. in 2011 (excluding passenger transport). The GDP of the services sector increased at an average annual rate of 6.7% in 2005–12, according to provisional figures. The GDP of the services sector increased by 4.9% in 2012.

In 2011 Uruguay recorded an estimated visible merchandise trade deficit of US $1,383.5m., and there was a deficit of $1,442.0m. on the current account of the balance of payments. In 2011 the principal source of imports was Brazil (19.4%); other major suppliers were Argentina, the People's Republic of China and the USA. Brazil was also the principal market for exports (20.4%) in that year; the other major recipients were Argentina, China and Russia. The main exports in 2011 were live animals and animal products; crops and vegetable products; wood, charcoal, cork, etc.; plastic and plastic products; and chemical products. The principal imports in that year were mineral products; machinery, appliances and related products; chemical products; transport equipment; plastic and plastic products; and food industry products.

In 2011 there was a budgetary deficit of 11,004m. pesos uruguayos, equivalent to some 1.2% of GDP. Uruguay's general government gross debt was 457,804m. pesos uruguayos in 2010, equivalent to 57.9% of GDP. At the end of 2010 Uruguay's total external debt was US $11,347m., of which $9,704m. was public and publicly guaranteed debt. In that year, the cost of servicing long-term public and publicly guaranteed debt and repayments to the IMF was equivalent to 12.4% of the value of exports of goods, services and income (excluding workers' remittances). According to the ILO, the average annual rate of inflation was 8.5% in 2002–12. Consumer prices increased by 7.7% in 2012, according to official figures. Some 6.1% of the labour force was unemployed in 2012.

Uruguay fared relatively well in the wake of the international financial crisis, with real GDP expanding by 8.9% in 2010. This impressive performance was driven by increased domestic economic activity, a recovery in demand and prices for Uruguayan exports, and an upsurge in tourist numbers. The 6.6% growth recorded in 2011 was again supported by increasing exports, tourist arrivals and domestic demand. Nevertheless, rising inflation (8.9% in that year) was a concern. Additional employment opportunities were generated by the construction of a new US $1,900m. pulp mill, which commenced in May. The mill represented the largest foreign investment project in Uruguay's history and was forecast to transform the country into a cellulose exporter of international significance. Uruguay's removal in 2011 from the Organisation for Economic Co-operation and Development's (OECD) 'grey list', comprising nations that had failed to sign a sufficient number of tax-sharing agreements with OECD member states, was another positive development. Owing to the unstable international economic climate, real GDP growth decelerated to 3.9% in 2012, although levels of domestic consumption remained strong. Measures to control the high rate of inflation were only moderately successful. The Supreme Court's rejection of a new land tax on large estates, which had been anticipated to generate $60m. annually, to fund vital infrastructural upgrades, was a set-back for the Government in early 2013. The IMF expected the economy to expand by 4.0% in 2013.

PUBLIC HOLIDAYS

2014: 1 January (New Year's Day), 6 January (Epiphany), 3–4 March (Carnival), 14–18 April (Holy Week), 21 April (for Landing of the 33 Patriots), 1 May (Labour Day), 19 May (for Battle of Las Piedras), 19 June (Birth of José Artigas), 18 July (Constitution Day), 25 August (National Independence Day), 13 October (for Discovery of America and Battle of Sarandí), 2 November (All Souls' Day), 25 December (Christmas Day).

Statistical Survey

Sources (unless otherwise stated): Instituto Nacional de Estadística, Río Negro 1520, 11100 Montevideo; tel. 2902 7303; internet www.ine.gub.uy; Banco Central del Uruguay, Avda Juan P. Fabini, esq. Florida 777, Casilla 1467, 11100 Montevideo; tel. 2908 5629; fax 2902 1634; e-mail info@bcu.gub.uy; internet www.bcu.gub.uy; Cámara Nacional de Comercio y Servicios del Uruguay, Edif. Bolsa de Comercio, Rincón 454, 2°, Casilla 1000, 11000 Montevideo; tel. 2916 1277; fax 2916 1243; e-mail info@cncs.com.uy; internet www.cncs.com.uy.

Area and Population

AREA, POPULATION AND DENSITY

Area (sq km)	
Land area	175,016
Inland water	1,199
Total	176,215*
Population (census results)	
May–July 2004†	3,241,003
1–30 September 2011‡	
Males	1,577,416
Females	1,708,461
Total	3,285,877
Density (per sq km) at 2011 census	18.8

* 68,037 sq miles.
† Excluding adjustment for underenumeration.
‡ Excluding 437 persons classified as homeless.

POPULATION BY AGE AND SEX
(population at 2011 census)

	Males	Females	Total
0–14	365,546	349,419	714,965
15–64	1,027,701	1,079,485	2,107,186
65 and over	184,169	279,557	463,726
Total	**1,577,416**	**1,708,461**	**3,285,877**

DEPARTMENTS
(population at 2011 census)*

	Area (sq km)	Population	Density (per sq km)	Capital
Artigas . .	11,928	73,378	6.2	Artigas
Canelones . .	4,536	520,187	114.7	Canelones
Cerro Largo . .	13,648	84,698	6.2	Melo
Colonia . .	6,106	123,203	20.2	Colonia del Sacramento
Durazno . .	11,643	57,088	4.9	Durazno
Flores . .	5,144	25,050	4.9	Trinidad
Florida . .	10,417	67,048	6.4	Florida
Lavalleja . .	10,016	58,815	5.9	Minas
Maldonado . .	4,793	164,300	34.3	Maldonado
Montevideo . .	530	1,319,108	2,488.9	Montevideo
Paysandú . .	13,922	113,124	8.1	Paysandú
Río Negro . .	9,282	54,765	5.9	Fray Bentos
Rivera . .	9,370	103,493	11.0	Rivera
Rocha . .	10,551	68,088	6.5	Rocha
Salto . .	14,163	124,878	8.8	Salto
San José . .	4,992	108,309	21.7	San José de Mayo
Soriano . .	9,008	82,595	9.2	Mercedes
Tacuarembó .	15,438	90,053	5.8	Tacuarembó
Treinta y Tres .	9,529	48,134	5.1	Treinta y Tres
Total . . .	175,016†	3,286,314	18.8	

* Total includes 437 homeless persons classified by department, but not enumerated by main census.
† Land area only.

PRINCIPAL TOWNS
(population at 2011 census)

Montevideo (capital)	1,318,755		Maldonado . . .	62,590
Salto	104,011		Tacuarembó . .	54,755
Paysandú . . .	76,412		Melo	51,830
Las Piedras . .	71,258		Mercedes . . .	41,974
Rivera	64,465			

BIRTHS, MARRIAGES AND DEATHS*

	Registered live births		Registered marriages		Registered deaths	
	Number	Rate (per 1,000)	Number	Rate (per 1,000)	Number	Rate (per 1,000)
2004	50,052	15.2	13,123	4.0	32,222	9.8
2005	46,944†	14.2†	13,075	4.0	32,319†	9.8†
2006	47,410†	14.2†	12,415	3.7	31,056†	9.4†
2007	47,373	14.3	12,771	3.8	33,706†	10.3†
2008	47,484	14.2	12,180	3.7	31,363	9.4
2009	47,152	14.1	11,080	3.3	32,179	9.6
2010	47,420	14.1	10,629	3.2	33,474	10.0
2011	46,699	14.2	9,604	2.9	n.a.	n.a.

* Data are tabulated by year of registration rather than by year of occurrence and have not been adjusted to take account of the most recent census.
† Preliminary.

Life expectancy (years at birth): 76.4 (males 72.9; females 80.1) in 2011 (Source: World Bank, World Development Indicators database).

ECONOMICALLY ACTIVE POPULATION
(ISIC major divisions, '000 persons aged 14 years and over, urban areas)

	2001	2002	2003
Agriculture, hunting, forestry and fishing	45.4	43.7	46.9
Mining and quarrying . . .	1.3	1.2	1.2
Manufacturing (incl. electricity, gas and water) . . .	167.1	154.2	151.1
Construction	87.9	77.4	69.6
Trade, restaurants, hotels and repair of vehicles and household goods	240.8	228.9	225.4
Transport, storage and communications	66.8	62.4	61.1
Financing, insurance, real estate and business services . . .	97.4	96.5	91.0

—continued	2001	2002	2003
Public administration and defence, compulsory social security . .	85.1	86.9	91.2
Education	57.2	62.2	61.6
Health and social work . . .	72.5	76.7	76.7
Community, social and personal services	56.2	52.2	54.8
Private households with employed persons	98.5	96.0	100.9
Sub-total	—	—	1,031.7
Activities not adequately defined .	—	—	0.3
Total employed	1,076.2	1,038.3	1,032.0
Males	617.7	597.9	589.7
Females	458.5	440.4	442.3
Unemployed	193.2	211.3	208.5
Total labour force	1,269.4	1,250.1	1,240.5

Source: ILO.

2007 ('000 persons aged 14 years and over, estimates): Total employed 1,482; Unemployed 149; Total labour force 1,631 (males 913, females 718).

Mid-2013 ('000, estimates): Agriculture, etc. 184; Total labour force 1,687 (Source: FAO).

Health and Welfare

KEY INDICATORS

Total fertility rate (children per woman, 2010)	2.1
Under-5 mortality rate (per 1,000 live births, 2010) . . .	11
HIV/AIDS (% of persons aged 15–49, 2009)	0.5
Physicians (per 1,000 head, 2002)	3.7
Hospital beds (per 1,000 head, 2006)	2.9
Health expenditure (2009): US $ per head (PPP)	1,099
Health expenditure (2009): % of GDP	8.4
Health expenditure (2009): public (% of total)	65.3
Total carbon dioxide emissions ('000 metric tons, 2008) . .	8,327.8
Carbon dioxide emissions per head (metric tons, 2008) . .	2.5
Human Development Index (2011): ranking	48
Human Development Index (2011): value	0.783

For sources and definitions, see explanatory note on p. vi.

Agriculture

PRINCIPAL CROPS
('000 metric tons)

	2009	2010	2011
Wheat	1,844.4	1,300.7	1,470.3*
Rice, paddy	1,287.2	1,148.7	1,643.0
Barley	464.1	186.4	210.7*
Maize	269.8	529.1	286.2
Oats	54.4	42.9*	48.5*
Sorghum	324.2	138.0	123.4
Potatoes	102.3	114.7	90.2
Sweet potatoes*	72.0	72.5*	74.0
Sugar cane	296.5	313.3	314.0*
Sunflower seed	50.6	9.1	3.9
Tomatoes	37.0	31.6	30.6*
Onions, dry	25.6	17.5	17.3*
Carrots and turnips . . .	22.5	18.3	19.6*
Soybeans (Soya beans) . .	1,028.6	1,816.8	1,541.0
Oranges	130.1	154.2	135.2
Tangerines, mandarins, clementines and satsumas . .	92.8	121.5	93.4
Lemons and limes	42.0	37.7	38.2
Apples	58.8	52.2	73.4
Pears	13.3	18.7	14.8
Peaches and nectarines . .	19.1	23.0	22.6*
Grapes	87.5	110.3	126.2

* FAO estimate(s).

Aggregate production ('000 metric tons, may include official, semi-official or estimated data): Total cereals 4,247.9 in 2009, 3,348.9 in 2010, 3,785.5 in 2011; Total fruits (excl. melons) 457.8 in 2009, 532.2 in 2010, 522.8 in 2011; Total vegetables (incl. melons) 168.5 in 2009, 148.1 in 2010, 153.0 in 2011.

Source: FAO.

LIVESTOCK
('000 head, year ending September)

	2009	2010	2011
Cattle	12,490	11,800*	11,808*
Sheep	8,662	7,710	7,474
Pigs	200	210	220
Horses	393	399	405†
Chickens†	17,000	16,500	17,500

* Unofficial figure.
† FAO estimate(s).
Source: FAO.

LIVESTOCK PRODUCTS
('000 metric tons)

	2009	2010	2011
Cattle meat	491.2	524.0	479.0*
Sheep meat	32.7	31.6*	32.0†
Pig meat	17.3	18.4	20.9
Chicken meat†	72.8	69.2	85.3
Cows' milk	1,871.6	1,820.8	2,057.0
Hen eggs	52.5	52.5	52.5†
Wool, greasy	41.1	34.7*	34.7†

* Unofficial figure.
† FAO estimate(s).
Source: FAO.

Forestry

ROUNDWOOD REMOVALS
('000 cubic metres, excl. bark)

	2009	2010	2011
Sawlogs and veneer logs	1,020	1,547	1,779
Pulpwood	5,146	7,841	6,207
Other industrial wood*	14	14	14
Fuel wood	2,210	2,430	2,430
Total*	8,390	11,832	10,430

* FAO estimates.
Source: FAO.

SAWNWOOD PRODUCTION
('000 cubic metres, incl. railway sleepers)

	2009	2010	2011
Coniferous (softwood)	102	131	128
Broadleaved (hardwood)	162	215	248
Total	264	346	376

Source: FAO.

Fishing

('000 metric tons, live weight)

	2008	2009	2010
Capture	108.8	81.5	74.2
Argentine hake	34.1	29.0	33.9
Striped weakfish	11.0	6.4	5.5
Whitemouth croaker	27.2	23.7	15.4
Castaneta	4.4	1.0	0.6
Rays, stingrays and mantas	1.9	1.3	1.1
Argentine shortfin squid	10.9	1.6	2.4
Aquaculture	0.0	0.0	0.0
Total catch	110.7	81.5*	74.2*

* FAO estimate.

Note: Figures exclude aquatic mammals, recorded by number rather than by weight. The number of South American fur seals and sea lions caught was: 63 in 2008; 82 in 2009; 80 in 2010.
Source: FAO.

Mining

('000 metric tons unless otherwise indicated)

	2008	2009	2010*
Gold (kg)	2,182	1,690	1,736
Gypsum*	1,150	1,150	1,150
Feldspar (metric tons)	2,500	2,500	2,500

* Estimates.
Source: US Geological Survey.

Industry

SELECTED PRODUCTS
('000 metric tons unless otherwise indicated)

	2008	2009	2010
Raw sugar	7	10	n.a.
Wine	79.9	61.8	65.0*
Motor spirit (petrol, '000 barrels)†	1,850	1,850	1,850
Kerosene ('000 barrels)†	100	100	100
Distillate fuel oils ('000 barrels)†	8,500	8,500	8,500
Residual fuel oils ('000 barrels)†	3,650	3,650	3,650
Cement (hydraulic)†	600	600	600
Electric energy (million kWh)	8,769	8,838	n.a.

* FAO estimate.
† US Geological Survey estimates.

2011 (FAO estimate): Wine 65.0.

Sources: FAO; US Geological Survey; UN Industrial Commodity Statistics Database.

Finance

CURRENCY AND EXCHANGE RATES

Monetary Units
100 centésimos = 1 peso uruguayo.

Sterling, Dollar and Euro Equivalents (31 December 2012)
£1 sterling = 30.612 pesos;
US $1 = 19.399 pesos;
€1 = 25.595 pesos;
1,000 pesos uruguayos = £32.67 = $51.55 = €39.07.

Average Exchange Rate (pesos per US $)
2010   20.059
2011   19.314
2012   20.311

Note: On 1 March 1993 a new currency, the peso uruguayo (equivalent to 1,000 former new pesos), was introduced.

CENTRAL GOVERNMENT BUDGET*
(million pesos uruguayos)

Revenue	2009	2010	2011
Tax revenue	144,880	165,536	189,838
Taxes on income, profits, etc.	36,049	41,162	46,845
Individual taxes	16,613	18,930	—
Corporate taxes	2,847	948	—
Taxes on property	10,552	11,361	12,724
Domestic taxes on goods and services	88,160	100,751	115,412
General sales, take-over or value-added tax	73,977	83,341	—
Taxes on international trade and transactions	4,330	5,338	6,754
Taxes on leisure activities	65	71	78
Other taxes and rates	5,724	6,853	7,210
Non-tax revenue	9,559	10,898	13,091
Transfers	6,066	6,470	6,011
Other income	2,284	2,464	2,689
Total	162,789	185,368	211,629

Expenditure	2004	2005	2006
General public services . . .	23,204	25,519	28,230
Government administration .	13,444	15,058	16,290
Defence	4,376	4,660	5,187
Public order and safety . . .	5,385	5,801	6,753
Special and community services .	37,148	38,747	58,271
Education	11,873	12,573	14,392
Health	6,521	7,135	8,654
Social security and welfare . .	16,817	17,109	32,375
Housing and community amenities	1,259	1,371	2,029
Recreational, cultural and religious affairs	679	559	821
Economic affairs and services .	3,353	5,931	6,435
Fuel and energy	186	179	194
Agriculture, fishing, forestry and hunting	1,421	2,033	1,584
Mining and mineral resources .	253	273	275
Transport and communications .	2,530	2,728	3,725
Other economic services . .	964	718	657
Debt-servicing and governmental transfers	22,805	20,322	24,289
Total	**88,510**	**90,519**	**117,225**

* Figures represent the consolidated accounts of the central Government, which include social security revenue and expenditure.

Total expenditure: 178,543 in 2009; 196,597 in 2010; 222,633 in 2011.

General government finances (consolidated accounts of general government, million pesos uruguayos, cash basis, 2011): *Revenue:* Total 250,377. *Expenditure:* Total 255,520.

INTERNATIONAL RESERVES
(US $ million at 31 December)

	2010	2011	2012
Gold	12	13	14
IMF special drawing rights . .	378	377	378
Reserve position in the IMF . .	97	146	155
Foreign exchange	7,168	9,765	13,058
Total	**7,655**	**10,301**	**13,605**

Source: IMF, *International Financial Statistics.*

MONEY SUPPLY
(million pesos uruguayos at 31 December)

	2010	2011	2012
Currency outside depository corporations	29,516.1	35,034.1	39,486.5
Transferable deposits	126,702.7	151,576.9	163,838.9
Other deposits	182,433.3	213,244.3	231,589.7
Securities other than shares . .	2,354.2	2,501.1	4,650.3
Broad money	**341,006.3**	**402,356.4**	**439,565.4**

Source: IMF, *International Financial Statistics.*

COST OF LIVING
(Consumer Price Index for Montevideo; base: December 2010 = 100)

	2011	2012
Food and beverages	109.3	121.0
Housing	111.1	117.6
Clothing and footwear	103.5	108.9
Transport	109.7	113.4
Communications	100.2	99.8
All items (incl. others)	**108.9**	**117.3**

NATIONAL ACCOUNTS
('000 million pesos uruguayos at current prices, preliminary figures)

Expenditure on the Gross Domestic Product

	2010	2011	2012
Government final consumption expenditure	101,240.4	118,235.6	137,531.0
Private final consumption expenditure	526,404.5	609,224.4	696,090.5
Increase in stocks	−5,897.0	3,379.7	−8,899.9
Gross fixed capital formation . .	150,413.0	170,385.9	223,644.3
Total domestic expenditure .	**772,160.9**	**901,225.6**	**1,048,365.9**
Exports of goods and services . .	211,859.6	244,227.5	266,216.7
Less Imports of goods and services	204,794.8	248,603.7	300,704.7
GDP in market prices . . .	**779,225.6**	**896,849.4**	**1,013,877.8**
GDP at constant 2005 prices .	**562,768.3**	**599,520.7**	**623,113.9**

Gross Domestic Product by Economic Activity

	2010	2011	2012
Agriculture, hunting and forestry .	50,062.9	69,186.1	69,325.5
Fishing and mining	3,589.5	3,881.5	4,784.8
Manufacturing	96,471.6	103,242.7	122,392.1
Electricity, gas and water . . .	25,412.6	17,840.2	5,818.2
Construction	54,803.1	64,661.5	90,366.2
Trade, restaurants and hotels .	113,849.9	135,634.2	150,262.0
Transport, storage and communications	55,784.5	62,293.5	67,751.2
Finance and insurance . . .	34,372.1	39,823.5	47,345.9
Real estate and business services .	117,361.8	136,641.6	161,186.1
Public administration and defence; compulsory social security . .	40,851.4	46,986.4	54,140.8
Other community, social and personal services	105,494.4	122,197.1	139,871.4
Sub-total	**698,053.9**	**802,388.5**	**913,244.2**
Less Financial intermediation services indirectly measured .	20,710.4	23,645.5	28,535.9
Gross value added in basic prices	**677,343.5**	**778,743.0**	**884,708.3**
Taxes, less subsidies, on products .	101,882.2	118,106.5	129,169.5
GDP in market prices . . .	**779,225.6**	**896,849.4**	**1,013,877.8**

BALANCE OF PAYMENTS
(US $ million)

	2009	2010	2011
Exports of goods	6,391.8	8,031.4	9,306.9
Imports of goods	−6,895.7	−8,557.6	−10,690.4
Balance on goods	**−503.9**	**−526.2**	**−1,383.5**
Exports of services	2,245.4	2,576.4	3,394.7
Imports of services	−1,315.3	−1,552.6	−2,013.9
Balance on goods and services	**426.3**	**497.6**	**−2.8**
Primary income received . . .	531.6	454.6	493.1
Primary income paid	−1,544.5	−1,933.1	−2,058.5
Balance on goods, services and primary income	**−586.7**	**−981.0**	**−1,568.1**
Secondary income received . .	175.9	175.0	177.0
Secondary income paid . . .	−37.8	−57.0	−50.9
Current balance	**−448.6**	**−863.0**	**−1,442.0**
Capital account (net)	—	—	—
Direct investment assets . . .	−90.4	157.7	28.8
Direct investment liabilities . .	1,602.6	2,191.1	2,177.2
Portfolio investment assets . .	−706.7	−1,340.6	1,164.7
Portfolio investment liabilities .	−114.6	686.5	818.7
Other investment assets . . .	−1,465.1	352.3	1,032.3
Other investment liabilities . .	1,957.0	−980.3	−1,812.2
Net errors and omissions . . .	852.7	−565.3	596.8
Reserves and related items .	**1,586.9**	**−361.5**	**2,564.3**

Source: IMF, *International Financial Statistics.*

External Trade

PRINCIPAL COMMODITIES
(US $ million)

Imports c.i.f.	2009	2010*	2011*
Food industry products; beverages, tobacco, alcohol and vinegars	388.5	472.9	639.3
Mineral products	1,708.7	1,745.2	2,263.6
Mineral fuels, petroleum and petroleum products	1,684.3	1,699.7	1,699.7
Chemicals and related products	850.2	1,148.1	1,392.7
Fertilizers	156.4	249.5	249.5
Plastics and plastic products; rubber and manufactures thereof	441.7	641.0	768.1
Plastics and plastic products	340.4	456.0	456.0
Textiles and textile manufactures	286.2	373.0	496.3
Base metals and metal manufactures	312.8	383.6	492.1
Machinery and appliances, electrical materials, audio-visual recording and reproducing apparatus	1,331.5	1,636.7	1,887.0
Boilers, etc., machinery and apparatus	803.6	963.9	963.9
Transport equipment	603.8	1,026.4	1,196.4
Automobiles, tractors, cycles, parts and accessories	591.6	957.4	957.4
Total (incl. others)	6,906.7	8,621.8	10,726.4

Exports f.o.b.	2009	2010*	2011*
Live animals and animal products	1,788.8	2,157.3	2,659.8
Chilled beef products	212.2	263.4	320.0
Frozen beef products	736.5	833.5	972.0
Fish, crustaceans, molluscs and preparations thereof	168.7	172.8	218.6
Dairy products and birds' eggs	382.5	541.2	733.5
Crops and vegetable products	1,456.2	1,717.6	1,958.3
Rice	459.0	386.0	472.3
Food industry products; beverages, tobacco, alcohol and vinegars	152.0	201.2	250.2
Mineral products	90.3	227.7	87.1
Chemicals and related products	292.5	339.1	414.0
Plastics and plastic products; rubber and manufactures thereof	257.2	346.2	439.2
Pelts, skins, hides and products thereof	190.5	235.7	275.4
Hides and leathers	169.9	211.4	246.4
Wood, charcoal, cork, etc. and products thereof	334.1	473.2	520.5
Textiles and textile manufactures	243.1	301.8	378.6
Total (incl. others)	5,404.8	6,724.9	7,963.0

* Provisional.

PRINCIPAL TRADING PARTNERS
(US $ million)

Imports c.i.f.	2009	2010	2011
Argentina	1,628.3	1,468.9	2,003.8
Brazil	1,459.8	1,578.1	2,082.4
Canada	27.0	81.9	37.7
Chile	99.6	117.2	135.1
China, People's Republic	819.1	1,123.8	1,438.8
France (incl. Monaco)	82.7	136.7	186.7
Germany	167.6	198.0	257.8
India	47.5	68.6	115.7
Iran	0.8	12.8	20.7
Italy	119.2	160.9	148.4
Japan	73.2	94.6	96.0
Korea, Republic	52.5	100.2	204.1
Mexico	97.5	173.3	243.8
Russia	255.8	272.2	137.8
Spain	83.4	151.4	154.6
United Kingdom	52.4	71.5	125.2
USA	563.7	855.2	1,100.6
Venezuela	523.6	660.1	398.9
Total (incl. others)	6,906.7	8,621.8	10,726.4

Exports f.o.b.	2009	2010	2011
Argentina	346.6	573.5	588.4
Brazil	1,098.1	1,421.8	1,624.5
Canada	36.7	35.8	41.7
Chile	81.0	120.5	139.2
China, People's Republic	235.1	363.8	531.8
France (incl. Monaco)	28.2	31.3	41.2
Germany	158.3	237.8	303.2
Iran	25.4	42.3	56.6
Israel	60.2	78.0	118.0
Italy	115.1	144.2	158.4
Japan	5.1	8.8	10.1
Mexico	134.8	124.1	163.0
Netherlands	121.2	126.0	147.8
Paraguay	85.3	159.8	191.8
Russia	217.6	351.6	395.2
Spain	150.9	178.7	200.3
United Kingdom	141.7	108.6	121.7
USA	177.3	194.5	244.3
Venezuela	186.7	246.7	313.9
Total (incl. others)	5,404.8	6,724.9	7,963.0

Transport

RAILWAYS
(traffic)

	2002	2003	2004
Passenger-km (million)	8	11	11
Net ton-km (million)	178	188	297

Source: UN, *Statistical Yearbook*.

ROAD TRAFFIC
(motor vehicles in use at 31 December)

	1995	1996	1997
Passenger cars	464,547	485,109	516,889
Buses and coaches	4,409	4,752	4,984
Lorries and vans	41,417	43,656	45,280
Road tractors	12,511	14,628	15,514
Motorcycles and mopeds	300,850	328,406	359,824

Source: International Road Federation, *World Road Statistics*.

2009: Passenger cars and vans 600,191; Coaches and minibuses 8,100; Lorries and road tractors 60,314; Motorcycles and mopeds 691,840.

SHIPPING
Flag Registered Fleet
(at 31 December)

	2010	2011	2012
Number of vessels	90	91	90
Total displacement ('000 grt) . .	101.8	97.5	102.3

Source: Lloyd's List Intelligence (www.lloydslistintelligence.com).

CIVIL AVIATION
(traffic)

	2007	2008	2009
Kilometres flown (million) . .	8	9	8
Passengers carried ('000) . .	524	613	564
Passenger-km (million) . .	926	1,047	982
Total ton-km (million) . . .	83	99	93

Source: UN, *Statistical Yearbook*.

Tourism

ARRIVALS BY NATIONALITY*

	2008	2009	2010
Argentina	1,025,574	1,150,492	1,261,516
Brazil	300,791	263,414	376,894
Chile	39,236	41,106	53,194
Germany	16,499	18,450	19,102
Italy	17,267	16,098	16,603
Mexico	14,778	13,026	14,370
Paraguay	27,708	34,347	36,672
Peru	12,396	11,722	13,673
Spain	32,332	31,082	31,531
United Kingdom	14,397	14,963	15,737
USA	68,369	67,223	62,428
Total (incl. others)	1,997,884	2,098,780	2,407,676

* Figures refer to arrivals at frontiers of visitors from abroad, including Uruguayan nationals permanently resident elsewhere.

Total arrivals: 2,857,000 in 2011 (provisional).

Tourism receipts (US $ million, excl. passenger transport): 1,312 in 2009; 1,496 in 2010; 2,187 in 2011 (provisional).

Source: World Tourism Organization.

Communications Media

	2009	2010	2011
Telephones ('000 main lines in use)	953.4	962.2	964.9
Mobile cellular telephones ('000 subscribers)	4,111.6	4,437.2	4,757.4
Internet subscribers ('000) . .	319.3	374.9	455.2
Broadband subscribers ('000) . .	300.8	367.5	455.2

Source: International Telecommunication Union.

Education

(2008 unless otherwise indicated)

	Institutions	Teachers	Students
Pre-primary	1,412	4,089	109,654
Primary	2,396	19,143	342,498
Secondary: general	457	25,168*†	218,436
Secondary: vocational	131	n.a.	70,110
University and equivalent institutions*‡	6	7,723	72,100

* Public education only.
† 2003.
‡ 2005.

Pupil-teacher ratio (primary education, UNESCO estimate): 14.0 in 2008/09 (Source: UNESCO Institute for Statistics).

Adult literacy rate (UNESCO estimates): 98.1% (males 97.6%; females 98.5%) in 2010 (Source: UNESCO Institute for Statistics).

Directory

The Government

HEAD OF STATE

President: José Alberto Mujica Cordano (took office on 1 March 2010).
Vice-President: Danilo Astori (AU).

COUNCIL OF MINISTERS
(May 2013)

A coalition of the Movimiento de Participación Popular (MPP), the Asamblea Uruguay (AU), the Partido Comunista de Uruguay (PCU), the Partido Socialista del Uruguay (PS), the Vertiente Artiguista (VA), Corriente de Acción y Pensamiento-Libertad (CAP-L), the Alianza Progresista (AP) and one Independent.

Minister of the Interior: Eduardo Bonomi Varela (MPP).

Minister of Foreign Affairs: Luis Leonardo Almagro Lemes (MPP).

Minister of National Defence: Eleuterio Fernandez Huidobro (CAP-L).

Minister of Social Development: Daniel Olesker (PS).

Minister of Economy and Finance: Fernando Lorenzo (AU).

Minister of Industry, Energy and Mining: Roberto Kreimerman (PS).

Minister of Livestock, Agriculture and Fishing: Tabaré Aguerre (Ind.).

Minister of Tourism and Sport: Liliam Kechichián (AP).

Minister of Transport and Public Works: Enrique Pintado (AU).

Minister of Labour and Social Security: Eduardo Brenta (VA).

Minister of Education and Culture: Ricardo Ehrlich (MPP).

Minister of Public Health: Susana Muñiz (PCU).

Minister of Housing, Territorial Regulation and the Environment: Francisco Beltrame (MPP).

Director of the Planning and Budget Office: Gabriel Frugoni (MPP).

Secretary to the Presidency: Homero Guerrero.

Pro-Secretary to the Presidency: Diego Cánepa.

MINISTRIES

Office of the President: Casa de Gobierno, Plaza Independencia 710, Torre Ejecutiva, 1° y 2°, 11000 Montevideo; tel. 2150 2647; fax 2917 1121; e-mail sci@presidencia.gub.uy; internet www .presidencia.gub.uy.

Ministry of Economy and Finance: Colonia 1089, 3°, 11100 Montevideo; tel. 2712 2910; fax 2712 2919; e-mail seprimef@mef .gub.uy; internet www.mef.gub.uy.

Ministry of Education and Culture: Reconquista 535, 9°, 11000 Montevideo; tel. 2916 1174; fax 2916 1048; e-mail centrodeinformacion@mec.gub.uy; internet www.mec.gub.uy.

Ministry of Foreign Affairs: Edif. Nuevo Colonia 1206, Palacio Santos, Avda 18 de Julio 1205, 11100 Montevideo; tel. 2902 1010; fax 2902 1349; e-mail webmaster@mrree.gub.uy; internet www.mrree .gub.uy.

Ministry of Housing, Territorial Regulation and the Environment: Zabala 1432, esq. 25 de Mayo, 11000 Montevideo; tel. 2917 0710; fax 2916 3914; e-mail ministro@mvotma.gub.uy; internet www .mvotma.gub.uy.

Ministry of Industry, Energy and Mining: Paysandú s/n, esq. Avda Libertador Brig. Gral Lavalleja, 4°, Montevideo; tel. 2900 0231; fax 2900 0291; e-mail ministro@miem.gub.uy; internet www.miem .gub.uy.

Ministry of the Interior: Mercedes 993, 11100 Montevideo; tel. 2152 4000; fax 2902 3142; e-mail unicom@minterior.gub.uy; internet www.minterior.gub.uy.

Ministry of Labour and Social Security: Juncal 1511, 4°, Planta Baja, 11000 Montevideo; tel. 2916 2681; fax 2916 2966; e-mail consultas@mtss.gub.uy; internet www.mtss.gub.uy.

Ministry of Livestock, Agriculture and Fishing: Avda Constituyente 1476, 1°, 11200 Montevideo; tel. 2412 6326; fax 2418 4051; e-mail ministro@mgap.gub.uy; internet www.mgap.gub.uy.

Ministry of National Defence: Edif. General Artigas, Avda 8 de Octubre 2628, Montevideo; tel. 2487 2828; fax 2481 4833; e-mail rrpp .secretaria@mdn.gub.uy; internet www.mdn.gub.uy.

Ministry of Public Health: Avda 18 de Julio 1892, 11100 Montevideo; tel. 2400 0101; fax 2408 5360; e-mail comunicaciones@msp .gub.uy; internet www.msp.gub.uy.

Ministry of Social Development: Avda 18 de Julio 1453, esq. Dr Javier Barrios Amorín, 2°, 11200 Montevideo; tel. and fax 2400 0302; e-mail ministra@mides.gub.uy; internet www.mides.gub.uy.

Ministry of Tourism and Sport: Rambla 25 de Agosto 1825, esq. Yacaré s/n, 11000 Montevideo; tel. 2188 5100; fax 2916 2487; e-mail webmaster@mintur.gub.uy; internet www.mintur.gub.uy.

Ministry of Transport and Public Works: Rincón 561, 11000 Montevideo; tel. 2915 8333; fax 2916 2883; e-mail difusion@mtop.gub .uy; internet www.mtop.gub.uy.

Planning and Budget Office: Plaza Independencia 710, Torre Ejecutivo, 11000 Montevideo; tel. 2150 3581; fax 2209 9730; e-mail direccion@opp.gub.uy; internet www.opp.gub.uy.

President and Legislature

PRESIDENT

Election, 25 October and 29 November 2009

Candidate	First round % of vote	Second round % of vote
José Alberto Mujica Cordano (Frente Amplio)	47.96	52.39
Luis Alberto Lacalle de Herrera (Partido Nacional)	29.07	43.51
Pedro Bordaberry Herrán (Partido Colorado)	17.02	—
Pablo Mieres Gómez (Partido Independiente)	2.49	—
Raúl Rodríguez da Silva (Asamblea Popular)	0.67	—
Invalid votes	2.79	4.10
Total	100.00	100.00

CONGRESO

Cámara de Senadores
(Senate)

President: Vice-Pres. DANILO ASTORI.

Election, 25 October 2009

Party	Seats
Frente Amplio	16
Partido Nacional	9
Partido Colorado	5
Total*	30

* An additional seat is reserved for the Vice-President, who sits as President of the Senate.

Cámara de Representantes
(Chamber of Representatives)

President: GERMÁN CARDOSO.

Election, 25 October 2009

Party	Seats
Frente Amplio	50
Partido Nacional	30
Partido Colorado	17
Partido Independiente	2
Total	99

Election Commission

Corte Electoral: Ituzaingó 1467, Montevideo; tel. 2915 8950; fax 2916 5088; e-mail corelect@adinet.com.uy; internet www .corteelectoral.gub.uy; f. 1967; Pres. Dr RONALD HERBERT.

Political Organizations

Asamblea Popular: Avda Daniel Fernández Crespo 1910 bis, esq. La Paz, Montevideo; tel. 2929 0861; e-mail prensaasambleapopular@ gmail.com; internet www.asambleapopular.webcindario.com; f. 2008; extreme left-wing; mems include:

Movimiento de Defensa de los Jubilados: Leader HÉCTOR MORALES.

Movimiento 26 de Marzo: Durazno 1118, 11200 Montevideo; tel. 2902 3903; e-mail siempre26m@gmail.com; internet m26demarzo .blogspot.in; f. 1971; socialist; Pres. EDUARDO RUBIO; Sec.-Gen. FERNANDO VÁZQUEZ.

Partido Comunista Revolucionario: tel. 099962411 (mobile); e-mail pcruruguay@yahoo.com; internet www.pcr.org.uy; Sec.-Gen. RICARDO COHEN.

Partido Humanista: Durazno 1602, entre Lorenzo Carnelli y Minas, Montevideo; tel. 098001969 (mobile); e-mail partidohumanistauy@gmail.com; internet partidohumanistauy .jimdo.com; f. 1984; Leader DANIEL ROCCA.

Frente Amplio (FA): Colonia 1367, 2°, 11100 Montevideo; tel. 2902 6666; e-mail comunicacion@frenteamplio.org.uy; internet www .frenteamplio.org.uy; f. 1971; left-wing grouping; Pres. MÓNICA XAVIER; mems include:

Alianza Progresista 738 (AP): Colonia 1831, Montevideo; tel. and fax 2401 6365; e-mail a738@adinet.com.uy; internet alianza738.com.uy; f. 1998; left-wing; Leader RODOLFO NIN NOVOA.

Asamblea Uruguay (AU): Carlos Quijano 1273, Montevideo; tel. 2903 2121; fax 2924 1147; e-mail info@2121.org.uy; internet www .2121.org.uy; f. 1994; left; Leader DANILO ASTORI.

Corriente de Acción y Pensamiento-Libertad (CAP-L): Batoví 2169, esq. Nicaragua, Montevideo; tel. 2929 1740; e-mail 7373@caplibertad.org.uy; internet www.caplibertad.org.uy; f. 2007; Leader ELEUTERIO FERNÁNDEZ HUIDOBRO.

Frente Izquierda de Liberación (FIDEL): Mercedes 1244, Montevideo; tel. 2908 7530; e-mail contacto@fidel.com.uy; internet www.fidel.com.uy; f. 1962; socialist; Sec.-Gen. DOREEN IBARRA.

Movimiento de Liberación Nacional (MLN)—Tupamaros: Tristán Narvaja 1578, 11200 Montevideo; tel. 2409 2298; fax 2409 9957; e-mail mln@chasque.apc.org; internet www.chasque.net/ mlnweb; f. 1962; radical socialist; during 1962–73 the MLN, operating under its popular name of the Tupamaros, conducted a campaign of urban guerrilla warfare until it was defeated by the military in 1973; following the return to civilian rule, in 1985, the MLN announced its decision to abandon its armed struggle; legally recognized in 1989; part of the MPP; Sec.-Gen. JULIO MARENALES.

Movimiento de Participación Popular (MPP): Mercedes 1368, 11200 Montevideo; tel. 2908 8900; fax 2903 2248; e-mail info@mppuruguay.org.uy; internet www.mpp.org.uy; f. 1989; grouping of left-wing parties incl. MLN—Tupamaros; Leader LUCÍA TOPOLANSKY.

Nuevo Espacio: Eduardo Acevedo 1615, 11200 Montevideo; tel. 2402 6990; fax 2402 6989; e-mail internacionales@nuevoespacio .org.uy; internet www.nuevoespacio.org.uy; f. 1994; social-democratic; allied to the FA since Dec. 2002; moderate left-wing; Leader RAFAEL MICHELINI; Sec. EDGARDO CARVALHO.

Partido Comunista de Uruguay (PCU): Fernández Crespo 2098, 11100 Montevideo; tel. 2924 2697; fax 2901 1050; e-mail partidocomunista@adinet.com.uy; internet www.pcu.org.uy; f. 1920; Sec.-Gen. EDUARDO LORIER; c. 42,000 mems.

Partido Demócrata Cristiano (PDC): Aquiles Lanza 1318 bis, 11100 Montevideo; tel. 2903 0704; fax 2902 1044; e-mail pdc@chasque.net; internet www.pdcuruguay.uy; f. 1962; fmrly Unión Cívica del Uruguay; allied to the Alianza Progresista 738; Pres. Dr HÉCTOR LESCANO; Sec.-Gen. JUAN ANDRÉS ROBALLO.

Partido Socialista del Uruguay (PS): Casa del Pueblo, Soriano 1218, 11100 Montevideo; tel. 2901 3344; fax 2908 2548; e-mail info@ps.org.uy; internet www.ps.org.uy; f. 1910; Pres. REINALDO GARGANO; Sec.-Gen. YERÚ PARDIÑAS.

Partido por la Victoria del Pueblo (PVP): Mercedes 1469, esq. Tacuarembó, Montevideo; tel. 2402 0370; e-mail info@pvp.org.uy; internet www.pvp.org.uy; f. 1975 in Buenos Aires, Argentina; left-wing; Sec.-Gen. PABLO ANZALONE; Spokesperson ANGEL VERA.

Vertiente Artiguista (VA): San José 1191, 11200 Montevideo; tel. 2900 0177; e-mail vertiente@vertiente.org.uy; internet www.vertiente.org.uy; f. 1989; left-wing; Leader ENRIQUE RUBIO.

Partido Colorado: Andrés Martínez Trueba 1271, 11100 Montevideo; tel. 2409 0180; e-mail info@partidocolorado.com.uy; internet www.partidocolorado.com.uy; f. 1836; Sec.-Gen. MARTHA MONTANER; factions include:

Foro Batllista: Col. 1243, 11100 Montevideo; tel. 2903 0154; e-mail info@forobatllista.com.uy; internet www.forobatllista.com.uy; Leader Dr JULIO MARÍA SANGUINETTI CAIROLO.

Vanguardia Batllista: Casa de Vanguardia, Paysandú 1333, entre Ejido y Curiales, Montevideo; tel. 2902 7779; e-mail albertoscavarelli@yahoo.com; internet www.scavarelli.com; f. 1999; Sec.-Gen. Dr ALBERTO SCAVARELLI.

Partido Independiente: Avda 18 de Julio 2015, Montevideo; tel. 2402 0120; e-mail info@partidoindependiente.org; internet www.partidoindependiente.org.uy; Leader PABLO MIERES GÓMEZ.

Partido Nacional (Blanco): Juan Carlos Gómez 1384, Montevideo; tel. 2916 3831; fax 2916 3758; e-mail partidonacional@partidonacional.com.uy; internet www.partidonacional.com.uy; f. 1836; Exec. Pres. LUIS ALBERTO HEBER FONTANA; factions within the party include:

Alianza Nacional: Avda de las Leyes, Montevideo; tel. 2402 2020; fax 2209 7898; e-mail info@alianzanacional.com.uy; internet alianzanacional.com.uy; Leader JORGE LARRAÑAGA.

Concordia Nacional 747: Avda 18 de Julio 2139, esq. Juan Paullier, Montevideo; tel. 2401 4320; internet www.concordianacional.com.uy.

Consejo Nacional Herrerista: internet www.herrerismo.com.uy; Leader LUIS ALBERTO LACALLE DE HERRERA.

Desafío Nacional: Leader JUAN ANDRÉS RAMÍREZ.

Partido del Sol: Peatonal Yi 1385, 11000 Montevideo; tel. 2900 1616; fax 2900 6739; e-mail partidodelsol@adinet.com.uy; internet www.partidodelsoluruguay.org; ecologist, federal, pacifist; Leader HOMERO MIERES.

Unión Cívica: Montevideo; tel. 2900 5535; e-mail info@unioncivica.org; internet unioncivica.org.uy; f. 1912; recognized Christian Democrat faction, split from the Partido Demócrata Cristiano in 1980; Leader ALDO LAMORTE.

Diplomatic Representation

EMBASSIES IN URUGUAY

Argentina: Cuareim 1470, 11800 Montevideo; tel. 2902 8166; fax 2900 8408; e-mail eurug@mrecic.gov.ar; internet www.eurug.mrecic.gov.ar; Ambassador MIGUEL DANTE DOVENA.

Bolivia: Dr Prudencio de Peña 2469, entre Campbell y Ponce, Casilla 11600, 11300 Montevideo; tel. 2708 3573; fax 2708 0066; e-mail embouy@adinet.com; Chargé d'affaires a.i. JAVIER JIMÉNEZ PINAYA.

Brazil: Blvd Artigas 1328, 11300 Montevideo; tel. 2707 2119; fax 2707 2086; e-mail montevideu@brasemb.org.uy; internet www.brasil.org.uy; Ambassador JOÃO CARLOS DE SOUZA-GOMES.

Canada: Plaza Independencia 749, Of. 102, 11100 Montevideo; tel. 2902 2030; fax 2902 2029; e-mail mvdeo@international.gc.ca; internet www.canadainternational.gc.ca/uruguay; Ambassador CLAIRE POULIN.

Chile: 25 de Mayo 575, entre Juan Carlos Gómez e Ituzaingo, Montevideo; tel. 2916 4090; fax 2916 4083; e-mail echileuy@netgate.com.uy; internet chileabroad.gov.cl/uruguay; Ambassador PATRICIO PRADEL.

China, People's Republic: Miraflores 1508, esq. Pedro Blanes Viale, Carrasco, Casilla 18966, Montevideo; tel. 2601 6126; fax 2601 8508; e-mail embchina@adinet.com.uy; internet uy.china-embassy.org; Ambassador YAN BANGHUA.

Colombia: Edif. Tupí, Juncal 1305, 18°, esq. Buenos Aires, 11000 Montevideo; tel. 2916 1592; fax 2916 1594; e-mail embajada@colombia.com.uy; internet www.colombia.com.uy; Ambassador ALEJANDRO BORDA.

Costa Rica: Roque Graseras 740, entre Solano Antuña y Juan María Pérez, Casilla 12242, Montevideo; tel. 2711 6408; fax 2712 0872; e-mail embarica@adinet.com.uy; Chargé d'affaires a.i. CAROLINA JIMÉNEZ CASTAÑEDA.

Cuba: Cristóbal Echevarriarza 3471, Montevideo; tel. 2623 2803; fax 2623 2805; e-mail emcuburu@adinet.com.uy; internet embacu.cubaminrex.cu/uruguay; Ambassador CARMEN ZILIA PÉREZ MAZÓN.

Dominican Republic: Tomás de Tezanos 1186, entre Arturo Prat y Miguel Grau, 11300 Montevideo; tel. 2628 7766; fax 2628 9655; e-mail embajadomuruguay@adinet.com.uy; Ambassador DANIEL GUERRERO TAVERAS.

Ecuador: Juan María Pérez 2810, Montevideo; tel. 2711 0448; fax 2710 2492; e-mail embajadaecuador@netgate.com.uy; Ambassador EMILIO IZQUIERDO MIÑO.

Egypt: Avda Brasil 2663, 11300 Montevideo; tel. 2709 6412; fax 2708 0977; e-mail embassy.montevideo@mfa.gov.eg; Ambassador SAMI MAHMOUD ALI SALEM.

El Salvador: Arq. Raúl Lerena Acevedo 1453, Punta Gorda, 11300 Montevideo; tel. 2613 4143; fax 2619 9473; e-mail embasauy@dedicado.net.uy; Ambassador CARLOS ABARCA GÓMEZ.

France: Avda Uruguay 853, Casilla 290, 11100 Montevideo; tel. 2705 0000; fax 2705 0110; e-mail ambafranceuruguay@gmail.com; internet www.ambafranceuruguay.org; Ambassador JEAN-CHRISTOPHE POTTON.

Germany: La Cumparsita 1435, Plaza Alemania, Casilla 20014, 11200 Montevideo; tel. 2902 5222; fax 2902 3422; e-mail info@montevideo.diplo.de; internet www.montevideo.diplo.de; Ambassador Dr HEINZ PETERS.

Greece: Blvd José G. Artigas 1231, 11600 Montevideo; tel. 2408 9224; fax 2402 0360; e-mail gremb.mvd@mfa.gr; internet www.mfa.gr/montevideo; Ambassador LOUIS-ALKIVIADIS ABATÍS.

Guatemala: Costa Rica 1538, Carrasco, Montevideo; tel. and fax 2601 2225; fax 2601 4057; e-mail embaguate-uruguay@minex.gob.gt; Ambassador ROBERTO LEVA RAPELA.

Holy See: Blvd Artigas 1270, Casilla 1503, 11300 Montevideo (Apostolic Nunciature); tel. 2707 2016; fax 2707 2209; e-mail nuntius@adinet.com.uy; Apostolic Nuncio Most Rev. ANSELMO GUIDO PECORARI (Titular Archbishop of Populonia).

Iran: Blvd Artigas 531, Montevideo; tel. 2711 6657; fax 2711 6659; e-mail embajada.iran@adinet.com.uy; Chargé d'affaires a.i. SIYAVOSH SALIMI.

Israel: Blvd Artigas 1585, 11200 Montevideo; tel. 2400 4164; fax 2409 5821; e-mail info@montevideo.mfa.gov.il; internet montevideo.mfa.gov.il; Ambassador DORI GOREN.

Italy: José Benito Lamas 2857, Casilla 268, 11300 Montevideo; tel. 2708 4916; fax 2708 4148; e-mail ambasciata.montevideo@esteri.it; internet www.ambmontevideo.esteri.it; Ambassador MASSIMO ANDREA LEGGERI.

Japan: Blvd Artigas 953, 11300 Montevideo; tel. 2418 7645; fax 2418 7980; e-mail embjapon@adinet.com.uy; internet www.uy.emb-japan.go.jp; Ambassador KENICHI SAKUMA.

Korea, Republic: Edif. World Trade Center, Avda Luis Alberto de Herrera 1248, Torre 2, 10°, Montevideo; tel. 2628 9374; fax 2628 9376; e-mail koemur@gmail.com; internet ury.mofat.go.kr; Ambassador CHOI YEON-CHOONG.

Lebanon: Avda General Rivera 2278, Montevideo; tel. 2408 6640; fax 2408 6365; e-mail embliban@adinet.com.uy; Chargé d'affaires a.i. JIMMY ZAKHIA DOUAIHY.

Mexico: 25 de Mayo 512/514, esq. Treinta y Tres, 11100 Montevideo; tel. 2916 6034; fax 2916 6098; e-mail embajada-mexico@embamex.com.uy; internet embamex.sre.gob.mx/uruguay; Chargé d'affaires a.i. ARMANDO VIVANCO CASTELLANOS.

Nicaragua: Calle Sarandi 669, Montevideo; tel. 2916 2175; e-mail embanic.uy@gmail.com; Chargé d'affaires a.i. MAURIZIO GELLI.

Panama: Juan Benito Blanco 3388, Montevideo; tel. 2623 0301; fax 2623 0300; e-mail empanuru@netgate.com.uy; Ambassador DIGNA M. DONADO F.

Paraguay: García Cortina 2365, Montevideo; tel. 2710 6774; fax 2711 8326; e-mail embapur@gmail.com; Chargé d'affaires a.i. RICARDO CABALLERO AQUINO.

Peru: Obligado 1384, 11300 Montevideo; tel. 2707 6862; fax 2707 7793; e-mail embamontevideo@embaperu.org.uy; Ambassador AIDA DEL CARMEN JESÚS NARANJO MORALES.

Portugal: Avda Dr Francisco Soca 1128, Apto 701, 11300 Montevideo; tel. 2708 4061; fax 2709 6456; e-mail embport@montevideu

.dgaccp.pt; internet www.embajadadeportugalmontevideo.com; Chargé d'affaires a.i. ANTÓNIO JOSÉ ALVES DE CARVALHO.

Qatar: Plaza Independencia 759, 11100 Montevideo; tel. 2902 0111; fax 2902 0131; e-mail Montevideo@mofa.gov.qa; Chargé d'affaires a.i. ALI AL-NEAMA.

Romania: Echevarriarza 3452, Casilla 12040, 11000 Montevideo; tel. 2622 0135; fax 2622 0685; e-mail ambromvd@adinet.com.uy; Ambassador GHEORGHE PETRE.

Russia: Blvd España 2741, 11300 Montevideo; tel. 2708 1884; fax 2708 6597; e-mail embaru@montevideo.com.uy; internet www .uruguay.mid.ru; Ambassador SERGUEY N. KOSHKIN.

South Africa: Dr Gabriel Otero 6337, Carrasco, 11300 Montevideo; tel. 2601 7591; fax 2600 3165; e-mail montevideo.general@foreign .gov.za; Ambassador ZENANI MANDELA-DLAMINI (resident in Argentina).

Spain: Avda Libertad 2738, 11300 Montevideo; tel. 2708 6010; fax 2708 3291; e-mail emb.montevideo@maec.es; internet www.maec.es/ embajadas/montevideo; Ambassador ROBERTO VARELA FARIÑA.

Switzerland: Ing. Federico Abadie 2936/40, 11°, Casilla 12261, 11300 Montevideo; tel. 2711 5545; fax 2711 5031; e-mail vertretung@mtv.rep.admin.ch; internet www.eda.admin.ch/ montevideo; Ambassador HANS-RUEDI BORTIS.

United Kingdom: Marco Bruto 1073, Casilla 16024, 11300 Montevideo; tel. 2622 3630; fax 2622 3650; e-mail ukinuruguay@gmail .com; internet ukinuruguay.fco.gov.uk; Ambassador BEN LYSTER-BINNS.

USA: Lauro Muller 1776, 11200 Montevideo; tel. 2418 7777; fax 2418 8611; e-mail webmastermvd@state.gov; internet uruguay .usembassy.gov; Ambassador JULISSA REYNOSO.

Venezuela: Iturriaga 3589, esq. Tomás de Tezanos, Puerto Buceo, Montevideo; tel. 2622 1262; fax 2628 2530; e-mail despacho@ embvenezuelauy.org; internet www.embvenezuelauy.org; Ambassador JULIO RAMÓN CHIRINO RODRÍGUEZ.

Judicial System

The Supreme Court of Justice comprises five members appointed at the suggestion of the executive, for a period of five years. It has original jurisdiction in constitutional, international and admiralty cases, and hears appeals from the appellate courts, of which there are seven, each with three judges.

Cases involving the functioning of the state administration are heard in the ordinary Administrative Courts and in the Supreme Administrative Court, which consists of five members appointed in the same way as members of the Supreme Court of Justice.

In Montevideo there are 19 civil courts, 10 criminal and correctional courts, 19 courts presided over by justices of the peace, three juvenile courts, three labour courts and courts for government and other cases. Each departmental capital, and some other cities, have a departmental court; each of the 224 judicial divisions has a justice of the peace.

The administration of justice became free of charge in 1980, with the placing of attorneys-at-law in all courts to assist those unable to pay for the services of a lawyer.

Suprema Corte de Justicia: Pasaje de los Derechos Humanos 1310, Montevideo; tel. 2900 1041; fax 2902 3500; e-mail secruibal@ poderjudicial.gub.uy; internet www.poderjudicial.gub.uy; Pres. JORGE RUIBAL PINO.

Tribunal de lo Contencioso Administrativo (Supreme Administrative Court): Mercedes 961, 11100 Montevideo; tel. 2901 3090; fax 2908 0539; e-mail epineyrua@tca.gub.uy; internet www.tca.gub.uy; Pres. Dr ALFREDO GÓMEZ TEDESCHI.

Religion

Under the Constitution, the Church and the State are declared separate and toleration for all forms of worship was proclaimed. Roman Catholicism predominates.

CHRISTIANITY

Federación de Iglesias Evangélicas del Uruguay: Avda 8 de Octubre 3324, 11600 Montevideo; tel. and fax 2487 5907; e-mail fieu@ dcd.com.uy; internet www.chasque.net/obra/skontakt.htm; f. 1956; eight mem. churches; Pres. OSCAR BOLIOLI; Sec. OBED BODYAJIAN.

The Roman Catholic Church

Uruguay comprises one archdiocese and nine dioceses. Some 71% of the population are Roman Catholics.

Bishops' Conference

Conferencia Episcopal Uruguaya, Avda Uruguay 1319, 11100 Montevideo; tel. 2900 2642; fax 2901 1802; e-mail ceusecre@adinet.com .uy; internet www.iglesiauruguaya.com.

f. 1972; Pres. Rt Rev. CARLOS MARÍA COLLAZZI IRAZÁBAL (Bishop of Mercedes).

Archbishop of Montevideo: Most Rev. NICOLÁS DOMINGO COTUGNO FANIZZI, Arzobispado, Treinta y Tres 1368, Casilla 356, 11000 Montevideo; tel. 2915 8127; fax 2915 8926; e-mail info@arquidiocesis.net; internet www.arquidiocesis.net.

The Anglican Communion

Uruguay constitutes a diocese in the Province of the Southern Cone of America. The presiding Bishop of the Iglesia Anglicana del Cono Sur de América is the Bishop of Northern Argentina.

Bishop of Uruguay: Rt Rev. MIGUEL TAMAYO ZALDÍVAR, Centro Diocesano, Reconquista 522, Casilla 6108, 11000 Montevideo; tel. 2915 9627; fax 2916 2519; e-mail mtamayo@netgate.com.uy; internet www.uruguay.anglican.org.

Other Churches

Iglesia Adventista del Séptimo Día (Seventh Day Adventist Church): Mateo Vidal 3211, 11600 Montevideo; tel. 2481 0173; e-mail contact@adventistas.org.uy; internet iglesiaadventista.org .uy; f. 1893; 4,000 mems.

Iglesia Evangélica Metodista en el Uruguay (Evangelical Methodist Church in Uruguay): San José 1457, 11200 Montevideo; tel. 2413 6552; fax 2413 6554; e-mail iemu@adinet.com.uy; internet www .gbgm-umc.org/iemu; f. 1878; 1,193 mems (1997); Pres. Rev. OSCAR BOLIOLI.

Iglesia Evangélica Valdense (Waldensian Evangelical Church): Avda 8 de Octubre 3039, 11600 Montevideo; tel. and fax 2487 9406; e-mail ievm@internet.com.uy; f. 1952; 13,000 mems; Pastor HUGO ARMAND PILÓN.

Iglesia Pentecostal Unida Internacional en Uruguay (United Pentecostal Church International in Uruguay): Helvecia 4032, Piedras Blancas, 12200 Montevideo; tel. 2513 3618; e-mail lrodrigu@montevideo.com.uy; internet members.tripod.com/ ~lrodrigu; Pastor LUIS RODRÍGUEZ.

Primera Iglesia Bautista (First Baptist Church): Avda Daniel Fernández Crespo 1741, Casilla 5051, 11200 Montevideo; tel. 2409 8744; fax 2409 4356; e-mail piebu@adinet.com.uy; f. 1911; 314 mems; Pastor LEMUEL J. LARROSA.

Other denominations active in Uruguay include the Iglesia Evangélica del Río de la Plata and the Iglesia Evangélica Menonita (Evangelical Mennonite Church).

BAHÁ'Í FAITH

National Spiritual Assembly of the Bahá'ís: Blvd Artigas 2440, 11600 Montevideo; tel. 2487 5890; fax 2480 2165; e-mail bahai@multi .com.uy; f. 1938; mems resident in 140 localities.

The Press

DAILIES

Montevideo

El Diario Español: Cerrito 551–555, Casilla 899, 11000 Montevideo; tel. 2915 9481; fax 2915 7389; e-mail marcelo.reinante@ eldiarioespanol.com.uy; f. 1905; morning (except Monday); newspaper of the Spanish community; Editor MARCELO REINANTE; circ. 20,000.

Diario Oficial: Avda 18 de Julio 1373, Montevideo; tel. 2908 5042; fax 2902 3098; e-mail impo@impo.com.uy; internet www.impo.com .uy; f. 1905; bi-weekly; publishes laws, official decrees, parliamentary debates, judicial decisions and legal transactions; Dir-Gen. GONZALO REBOLEDO.

El Observador: Cuareim 2052, 11800 Montevideo; tel. 2924 7000; fax 2924 8698; e-mail elobservador@observador.com.uy; internet www.observa.com.uy; f. 1991; morning; Dir RICARDO PEIRANO; Chief Editor GABRIEL PREYRA; circ. 26,000.

El País: Zelmar Michelini 1287, 4°, 11100 Montevideo; tel. 2902 0115; fax 2902 0464; e-mail cartas@elpais.com.uy; internet www .elpais.com.uy; f. 1918; morning; supports the Partido Nacional; Dir GONZALO ROSADILLA; Editor MARTÍN AGUIRRE REGULES; circ. 106,000.

La República: Avda Gral Garibaldi 2579, 11600 Montevideo; tel. 2487 3565; fax 2487 3824; e-mail secretaria1@diariolarepublica.net; internet www.larepublica.com.uy; f. 1988; morning; Editor GUSTAVO CARABAJAL; Gen. Man. VALENTIN ACOSTA; circ. 25,000.

Ultimas Noticias: Paysandú 1179, 11100 Montevideo; tel. 2902 0452; fax 2902 4669; e-mail redaccion@ultimasnoticias.com.uy; internet www.ultimasnoticias.com.uy; f. 1981; evening (except Sat.); owned by Impresora Polo; Dir ALVARO GIZ; circ. 25,000.

Florida

El Heraldo: Independencia 824, 94000 Florida; tel. 4352 2229; fax 4352 4546; e-mail elheraldo@elheraldo.com.uy; internet www.diarioelheraldo.com.uy; f. 1919; morning; independent; Dir ALVARO RIVA REY; circ. 20,000.

Maldonado

Correo de Punta del Este: Edif. del Virrey, Casi 33 Sarandí, 20000 Maldonado; tel. and fax 4223 5633; e-mail info@correodepuntadeleste.com; internet correodepuntadeleste.com; f. 1993; morning; Editor MARCELO GALLARDO; circ. 2,500.

Paysandú

El Telégrafo: Avda 18 de Julio 1027, 60000 Paysandú; tel. 4722 3141; fax 4722 7999; e-mail correo@eltelegrafo.com; internet www.eltelegrafo.com; f. 1910; morning; independent; Dir FERNANDO A. BACCARO; circ. 9,000.

Salto

El Pueblo: Avda 18 de Julio 151, entre Artigas y Rivera, Salto; tel. 4733 4133; e-mail dipueblo@adinet.com.uy; internet www.diarioelpueblo.com.uy; f. 1959; morning; Dir ADRIANA MARTÍNEZ.

PERIODICALS

Brecha: Avda Uruguay 844, 11100 Montevideo; tel. 2902 5042; fax 2902 0388; e-mail brecha@brecha.com.uy; internet www.brecha.com.uy; f. 1985; weekly; politics, current affairs; Dir GABRIEL PAPA; Editor-in-Chief ROBERTO LÓPEZ BELLOSO; circ. 8,500.

Búsqueda: Avda Uruguay 1146, 11100 Montevideo; tel. 2902 1300; fax 2902 2036; e-mail info@busqueda.com.uy; internet www.busqueda.com.uy; f. 1972; weekly (Thurs.); independent; politics and economics; Dir CLAUDIO PAOLILLO; circ. 25,000.

Charoná: Gutiérrez Ruiz 1276, Of. 201, Montevideo; tel. 2908 6665; e-mail administracion@charona.com; internet www.charona.com; f. 1968; fortnightly; children's; Dir SERGIO BOFFANO; circ. 25,000.

Crónicas Económicas: Avda Libertador Brig.-Gen. Lavalleja 1532, Montevideo; tel. 2900 4790; fax 2902 0759; e-mail cronicas@netgate.com.uy; internet www.cronicas.com.uy; f. 1981; weekly; independent; business and economics; Dirs JULIO ARIEL FRANCO, WALTER HUGO PAGÉS, JORGE ESTELLANO.

El Derecho Digital: Montevideo; tel. 2409 9643; e-mail administracion@elderechodigital.com.uy; internet www.elderechodigital.com.uy; legal; Dir LUIS FERNANDO IGLESIAS; Editor FERNANDO VARGAS.

El Diario Medico: Avda 18 de Julio 1485, 2°, Montevideo; tel. and fax 2408 3797; e-mail eldiariomedico@eldiariomedico.com.uy; internet www.eldiariomedico.com.uy; f. 1997; health; Dir ELBIO D. ALVAREZ.

Guambia: Rimac 1576, 11400 Montevideo; tel. and fax 2613 2703; e-mail info@guambia.com.uy; internet www.guambia.com.uy; f. 1983; monthly; satirical; Dir and Editor ANTONIO DABEZIES.

La Justicia Uruguaya: Avda 25 de Mayo 555, Apto 404, 11000 Montevideo; tel. 2915 7587; fax 2915 9721; e-mail lajusticiauruguaya@lju.com.uy; internet www.lajusticiauruguaya.com.uy; f. 1940; bimonthly; jurisprudence; Dirs EDUARDO ALBANELL MARTINO, ADOLFO ALBANELL MARTINO (Editor); circ. 3,000.

Marketing Directo: Guaná 2237 bis, 11200 Montevideo; tel. 9961 6758; fax 2408 7221; e-mail cieccweb@adinet.com.uy; internet www.coaching.edu.uy; f. 1988; monthly; Dir EDGARDO MARTÍNEZ ZIMARIOFF; circ. 9,500.

Opinar: Río Negro 1192/60, Montevideo; tel. 099686125 (mobile); e-mail cgarcia@opinar.com; internet www.opinar.com.uy; communist; Dir TABARÉ VIERA DUARTE; Editor CÉSAR GARCÍA ACOSTA.

Patria: Montevideo; e-mail semanariopatria@gmail.com; internet www.patria.com.uy; weekly; organ of the Partido Nacional; right-wing; Dir LUIS A. HEBER; Editor Dr JOSÉ LUIS BELLANI.

Propiedades: Yaguaron 1407, Of. 1203, Montevideo; tel. 2711 8384; fax 2712 1674; e-mail redaccion@revistapropiedades.com.uy; internet www.revistapropiedades.com.uy; f. 1987; construction and real estate; Dir JULIO C. VILLAMIDE.

Uruguay Natural: Ibiray 2293, 11300 Montevideo; tel. 2711 4900; fax 2712 3421; e-mail info@uruguaynatural.com.uy; internet www.uruguaynatural.com.uy; tourism; Pres. JAVIER SANTOMÉ SOSA DIAS; Dir FERNANDO ROJO SANTANA.

Voces: Chaná 2389, Montevideo; tel. 2401 8298; e-mail voces@voces.com.uy; internet www.voces.com.uy; political, social, economic and cultural; Editor ALFREDO GARCÍA.

PRESS ASSOCIATIONS

Asociación de Diarios y Periódicos del Uruguay (ADYPU): Río Negro 1308, 6°, 11100 Montevideo; f. 1922; Pres. GUILLERMO SCHECK.

Asociación de la Prensa Uruguaya: San José 1330, Montevideo; tel. and fax 2901 3695; e-mail apu@adinet.com.uy; internet www.apu.org.uy; f. 1944; Pres. DANIEL LEMA; Sec.-Gen. RÚBEN HERNÁNDEZ.

Publishers

Cemar Editorial: Martin C. Maritinez 1664, 11200 Montevideo; tel. 2401 9137; fax 2409 7261; e-mail info@cemar.com.uy; internet www.cemar.com.uy; general non-fiction; Dir MERCEDES RIPOLL.

CENCI—Uruguay (Centro de Estadísticas Nacionales y Comercio Internacional): Juncal 1327D, Of. 1603, Casilla 1510, 11000 Montevideo; tel. 2915 2930; fax 2915 4578; e-mail cenci@cenci.com.uy; internet www.cenci.com.uy; f. 1956; economics, statistics; Dir KENNETH BRUNNER.

Ediciones de la Banda Oriental: Gaboto 1582, 11200 Montevideo; tel. 2408 3206; fax 2409 8138; e-mail info@bandaoriental.com.uy; internet www.bandaoriental.com.uy; f. 1961; general literature; Man. Dir ALCIDES ABELLA.

Ediciones HUM (Casa Editorial Hum): Jackson 1111, 11200 Montevideo; tel. and fax 2410 3936; e-mail info@casaeditorialhum.com; internet www.casaeditorialhum.com; f. 2005; Dir MARTÍN FERNÁNDEZ.

Ediciones Trilce: Durazno 1888, 11200 Montevideo; tel. 2412 7662; fax 2412 7722; e-mail trilce@trilce.com.uy; internet www.trilce.com.uy; f. 1985; science, politics, history; Dir PABLO HARARI.

Ediciones Urano: Uruguay 1579, 11200 Montevideo; tel. 2402 8469; fax 2408 5293; e-mail infour@edicionesurano.com; internet www.edicionesurano.com; subsidiary of Ediciones Uranos, Spain; alternative medicine, health and lifestyle; Dir REINALDO RODRÍGUEZ.

Editorial Agropecuaria Hemisferio Sur: Buenos Aires 335, Casilla 1755, 11000 Montevideo; tel. 2916 4515; fax 2916 4520; e-mail editorial@hemisferiosur.com; internet www.hemisferiosur.com; f. 1951; agronomy and veterinary science; Dir MARGARITA PERI.

Editorial Arca: Ana Monterroso de Lavalleja 2231, Montevideo; tel. 2409 7514; fax 2409 9788; e-mail arcaeditorial@adinet.com.uy; internet www.arcaeditorial.com; f. 1963; general literature, social science and history; Man. Dir GABRIELA MÁRQUEZ.

Editorial Océano del Uruguay, SA: Salvador Ferrer Serra 1966, 11200 Montevideo; tel. and fax 2403 6090; e-mail gbosca@oceanouruguay.com; internet www.oceanouruguay.com; subsidiary of Grupo Océano, Spain; Dir-Gen. GUSTAVO BOSCA.

Editorial Sudamericana Uruguaya, SA (Random House Mondadori): Yaguarón 1568, 11100 Montevideo; tel. 2901 3668; e-mail ventas@rhm.com.uy; internet www.rhm.com.uy; general fiction and non-fiction; Dir LUIS SICA.

Fundación de Cultura Universitaria: 25 de Mayo 568, Casilla 1155, 11000 Montevideo; tel. 2916 1152; fax 2915 1103; e-mail administrador@fcu.com.uy; internet www.fcu.com.uy; f. 1968; law and social sciences; Pres. Dr MARCELO VIGO.

Granica Ediciones: Scoseria 2639, 11300 Montevideo; tel. 2712 4857; fax 2712 4858; e-mail granica.uy@granicaeditor.com; internet www.granicaeditor.com; general non-fiction; Dir DIEGO SIMÓN.

Librería Linardi y Risso: Juan Carlos Gómez 1435, 11000 Montevideo; tel. 2915 7129; fax 2915 7431; e-mail libros@linardiyrisso.com.uy; internet www.linardiyrisso.com.uy; f. 1944; general; Man. Dirs ALVARO RISSO, ANDRÉS LINARDI.

A. Monteverde & Cía, SA (Editorial Monteverde): Treinta y Tres 1475, Casilla 371, 11000 Montevideo; tel. 2915 2939; fax 2915 2012; e-mail monteverde@monteverde.com.uy; internet www.monteverde.com.uy; f. 1879; educational; Man. Dir TERESITA MUSSINI.

Mosca Hermanos SA: Avda 18 de Julio 1578, 11300 Montevideo; tel. 2409 3141; fax 2408 8059; e-mail mosca@mosca.com.uy; internet www.mosca.com.uy; f. 1888 as Librería La Popular; changed name as above in 1947; general; Pres. SILVIA HERNÁNDEZ.

Psicolibros Waslala: Mercedes 1673, Montevideo; tel. 2400 3808; fax 2403 0332; e-mail lperez@psicolibroswaslala.com; internet www.psicolibroswaslala.com; f. 1997; psychology; Dir LOURDES PÉREZ.

Vintén Editor: Hocquart 1771, 11804 Montevideo; tel. 2209 0223; internet vinten-uy.com; f. 1980; poetry, theatre, history, art, literature.

PUBLISHERS' ASSOCIATION

Cámara Uruguaya del Libro: Colón 1476, Casilla 102, 11000 Montevideo; tel. 2916 7628; fax 2916 9374; e-mail gerencia@camaradellibro.com.uy; internet www.camaradellibro.com.uy; f. 1944; Pres. ALVARO RISSO; Man. CRISTINA APPRATTO.

Broadcasting and Communications

REGULATORY AUTHORITY

Unidad Reguladora de Servicios de Comunicaciones (URSEC): Uruguay 988, 11100, Montevideo; tel. 2902 8082; fax 2900 5708; e-mail webmaster@ursec.gub.uy; internet www.ursec .gub.uy; regulates broadcasting, telecommunications and postal sectors; Pres. GABRIEL LOMBIDE; Gen. Man. GONZALO BALSEIRO GIGLIO.

TELECOMMUNICATIONS

Administración Nacional de Telecomunicaciones (ANTEL): Complejo Torre de las Telecomunicaciones, Guatemala 1075, Montevideo; tel. 2928 0000; e-mail antel@antel.com.uy; internet www .antel.com.uy; f. 1974; state-owned; Pres. CAROLINA COSSE; Gen. Man. HORACIO ANDRÉS TOLOSA.

Claro: Avda General San Martin 2460, Montevideo; tel. 2201 1500; e-mail webmaster@claro.com.uy; internet www.claro.com.uy; owned by América Móvil, SA de CV (Mexico); fmrly CTI Móvil; name changed as above in 2008; mobile telephone services; Gen. Man. HORACIO ALVARELLOS.

Dedicado, SA: Plaza Independencia 755, 10°, Torre Radisson Victoria Plaza, Montevideo; tel. 2901 1010; fax 2900 9923; e-mail info@dedicado.com; internet www.dedicado.com.uy; internet services provider; CEO ARTURO VARGAS.

Movistar Uruguay (Telefónica Móviles de Uruguay): Avda Francisco Soca 1444, 11200 Montevideo; tel. 9570 2611; fax 2402 2395; internet www.movistar.com.uy; f. 2005; owned by Telefónica Móviles, SA (Spain); mobile telephone services; Pres. PABLO DE SALTERAIN.

BROADCASTING

Radio

El Espectador: Río Branco 1481, 11100 Montevideo; tel. 2902 3531; fax 2908 3192; e-mail ventas@espectador.com.uy; internet www .espectador.com; f. 1923; commercial; Gen. Man. ESTELA BARTOLIC.

FM del Sol: Plaza Independencia 753, Of. 201, 2°, Montevideo; tel. 2903 2225; e-mail marketing@fmdelsol.com; internet www.fmdelsol .com.

Radio Carve: Mercedes 973, 11100 Montevideo; tel. 2902 6162; fax 2902 0126; e-mail carve@sadrep.com.uy; internet www.carve850 .com.uy; f. 1928; commercial; Dir HÉCTOR CARLOS VERA.

Radio Montecarlo: Avda 18 de Julio 1224, 1°, 11100 Montevideo; tel. 2901 4433; fax 2901 7762; e-mail cx20@radiomontecarlo.com.uy; internet www.radiomontecarlo.com.uy; f. 1924; commercial; Dir DANIEL ROMAY.

Radio Sarandí: Enriqueta Compte y Riqué 1250, 11800 Montevideo; tel. 2208 2612; fax 2203 6906; e-mail direccion@sarandi690 .com.uy; internet www.radiosarandi.com.uy; f. 1931; commercial; Pres. RAMIRO RODRÍGUEZ VALLAMIL RIVIERE.

Radio Universal: Avda 18 de Julio 1220, 3°, 11100 Montevideo; tel. 2903 2222; fax 2902 6050; e-mail info@22universal.com; internet www.22universal.com; f. 1929; commercial; Pres. OSCAR IMPERIO.

Radiodifusión Nacional SODRE: Sarandí 430, 11000 Montevideo; tel. 2916 1933; fax 2916 1934; e-mail dirradio@sodre.gub.uy; internet www.sodre.gub.uy; f. 1929; state-owned; operates Radio Clásica 650 AM, Radio Uruguay 1050 AM, Emisora del Sur 94.7 FM and Babel 97.1 FM; Dir SERGIO SACOMANI.

Television

The Uruguayan Government holds a 10% stake in the regional television channel Telesur, which began operations in 2005 and is based in Caracas, Venezuela.

Canal 4 Monte Carlo: Paraguay 2253, 11800 Montevideo; tel. 2924 4444; fax 2924 7929; e-mail webmontecarlotv@montecarlotv.com.uy; internet www.canal4.com.uy; f. 1961; Dir HUGO ROMAY SALVO.

SAETA TV—Canal 10: Dr Lorenzo Carnelli 1234, 11200 Montevideo; tel. 2410 2120; fax 2400 9771; internet www.canal10.com.uy; f. 1956; Pres. JORGE DE FEO.

SODRE (Servicio Oficial de Difusión Radiotelevisión y Espectáculos): Blvd Artigas 2552, 11600 Montevideo; tel. 2480 6448; fax 2480 8515; e-mail direccion@tveo.com.uy; internet www.sodre.gub.uy; f. 1963; Pres. FERNANDO BUTAZZONI.

Teledoce Televisora Color—Canal 12: Enriqueta Compte y Riqué 1276, 11800 Montevideo; tel. 2208 3555; fax 2203 7623; e-mail latele@teledoce.com; internet www.teledoce.com; f. 1962; Gen. Man. (vacant).

Tevé Ciudad: Javier Barrios Amorín 1460, Montevideo; tel. 2400 1908; fax 2402 9369; e-mail griselda.diaz@imm.gub.uy; internet www.teveciudad.com; f. 1996; state-owned; Gen. Dir GRISELDA DÍAZ LARREA.

Association

Asociación Nacional de Broadcasters Uruguayos (ANDEBU): Carlos Quijano 1264, 11100 Montevideo; tel. 2902 1525; fax 2908 0037; e-mail info@andebu.org; internet www.andebu.org; f. 1933; represents private radio and television broadcasters; 101 mems; Pres. RAFAEL INCHAUSTI; Sec. GABRIEL SILVA.

Finance

BANKING

(cap. = capital; res = reserves; dep. = deposits; m. = million; brs = branches; amounts in pesos uruguayos, unless otherwise indicated)

State Banks

Banco Central del Uruguay: Avda Juan P. Fabini 777, Casilla 1467, 11100 Montevideo; tel. 2908 5629; fax 2902 1634; e-mail info@ bcu.gub.uy; internet www.bcu.gub.uy; f. 1967; note-issuing bank, also controls private banking; cap. 10,027.0m., res 4,529.0m., dep. 193,431.0m. (Dec. 2009); Pres. MARIO BERGARA DUQUE; Dir WASHINGTON RIBEIRO.

Banco Hipotecario del Uruguay (BHU): Avda Daniel Fernández Crespo 1508, Montevideo; tel. 2409 0000; fax 2409 0782; e-mail info@ bhu.net; internet www.bhu.net; f. 1892; state mortgage bank; in 1977 assumed responsibility for housing projects in Uruguay; cap. 28,700m., res 15,457.2m., dep. 10,850.2m. (Dec. 2011); Pres. ANA SALVERAGLIO.

Banco de la República Oriental del Uruguay (BROU): Cerrito y Zabala 351, 11000 Montevideo; tel. 2915 0157; fax 2916 2064; e-mail broupte@adinet.com.uy; internet www.brounet.com.uy; f. 1896; cap. 18,029.5m., res -218.5m., dep. 205,967.5m. (Dec. 2011); Pres. FERNANDO CALLOIA RAFFO; Gen. Man. DANIEL GARCÍA AZPIROZ; 117 brs.

Principal Commercial Banks

Banco Bilbao Vizcaya Argentaria Uruguay SA (BBVA): 25 de Mayo 401, esq. Zabala, 11000 Montevideo; tel. 2916 1444; fax 2916 2821; internet www.bbva.com.uy; f. 1968; fmrly Unión de Bancos del Uruguay, and later Banesto Banco Uruguay, SA and Banco Francés Uruguay, SA; adopted current name in 2000 following merger with Banco Exterior de América, SA; bought Crédit Uruguay Banco SA in April 2011; cap. 3,827.9m., res –43.4m., dep. 46,056.6m. (Dec. 2010); Exec. Pres. RAFAEL GONZÁLEZ MOYA; 14 brs.

Banque Heritage (Uruguay): Rincón 530, 11000 Montevideo; tel. 2916 0177; fax 2916 0241; e-mail banqueheritage@heritage.com.uy; internet www.heritage.com.uy; f. 1981 as Surinvest Casa Bancaria; name changed to Banco Surinvest in 1991; present name adopted 2011; owned by Banque Heritage (Switzerland); cap. 368.1m., res 60.4m., dep. 2,448m. (Dec. 2011); Gen. Man. GRACIELA REYBAUD.

Discount Bank (Latin America), SA: Rincón 390, 11000 Montevideo; tel. 2916 4848; fax 2916 0890; e-mail mensajes@discbank.com .uy; internet www.discbank.com.uy; f. 1978; owned by Israel Discount Bank of New York (USA); cap. 46m., res 942.1m., dep. 16,108.3m. (Dec. 2010); Pres. and Chair. EHUD ARNON; Dir and Gen. Man. JORGE LEONEL PÉREZ FERNÁNDEZ; 13 brs.

HSBC Bank (Uruguay), SA: Ituzaingó 1389, 11000 Montevideo; tel. 2915 3395; fax 2916 0125; e-mail contacto@hsbc.com.uy; internet www.hsbc.com.uy; f. 1995; owned by HSBC Bank PLC (United Kingdom); cap. 1,686.9m., res 160.5m., dep. 18,109m. (Dec. 2011); CEO VIRGINIA SUÁREZ.

Nuevo Banco Comercial, SA (NBC): Misiones 1399, 11000 Montevideo; tel. 2140 1300; fax 2140 1185; e-mail servicioalcliente@nbc .com.uy; internet www.nbc.com.uy; f. 2003 by merger of Banco Comercial, Banco La Caja Obrera and Banco de Montevideo; fmrly state-owned, privatized in 2006; cap. 3,349m., res 920m., dep. 28,931.5m. (Dec. 2011); Pres. CARLOS GONZALEZ TABOADA; Gen. Man. HORACIO ENRIQUE CORREGE; 48 brs.

Santander Uruguay: Julio Herrera y Obes 1365, Casilla 888, 11100 Montevideo; tel. 2903 1073; fax 2902 5011; internet www.santander .com.uy; f. 1952 as ABN AMRO Bank Uruguay; bought by Grupo Santander (Spain) in 2008; cap. 6,702.6m., res 1,200.2m., dep. 68,592.3m. (Dec. 2010); Dir JORGE JOURDAN; 38 brs.

Development Bank

Banco Bandes Uruguay: Sarandí 402, 111000, Montevideo; tel. 2916 0100; fax 2915 3904; internet www.bandes.com.uy; owned by Banco de Desarrollo Económico y Social (BANDES) of Venezuela; cap. 934m., res –357.2m., dep. 4,621.6m. (Dec. 2011); Gen. Man. REINIER JOSÉ PARRA.

Credit Co-operative

Federación Uruguaya de Cooperativas de Ahorro y Crédito (FUCAC): Blvd Artigas 1472, Montevideo; tel. and fax 2708 8888; e-mail info@fucac.com.uy; internet www.fucac.com.uy; f. 1972; Pres. CARLOS NEGRO; Gen. Man. JAVIER HUMBERTO PI LEÓN.

Bankers' Association

Asociación de Bancarios del Uruguay (Bankers' Association of Uruguay—AEBU): Camacuá 575, Montevideo; tel. 2916 1060; e-mail secprensa@aebu.org.uy; internet www.aebu.org.uy; f. 1945; 7 mem. banks; Pres. GUSTAVO PÉREZ.

STOCK EXCHANGE

Bolsa de Valores de Montevideo: Edif. Bolsa de Comercio, Misiones 1400, 11000 Montevideo; tel. 2916 5051; fax 2916 1900; e-mail info@bvm.com.uy; internet www.bvm.com.uy; f. 1867; 75 mems; Pres. IGNACIO ROSPIDE.

INSURANCE

Banco de Seguros del Estado: Avda Libertador 1465, Montevideo; tel. 2908 9303; fax 2901 7030; e-mail info@bse.com.uy; internet www .bse.com.uy; f. 1912; state insurance org.; all risks; Pres. MARIO CASTRO; Gen. Man. RAÚL ONETTO.

Chartis Uruguay: Colonia 993, 1°, Montevideo; tel. 2900 0330; fax 2908 4552; e-mail chartis.uruguay@chartisinsurance.com; internet www.chartisinsurance.com; f. 1996; all classes; Gen. Man. JORGE FERRANTE.

Compañía de Seguros Aliança da Bahia Uruguay, SA (Brazil): Río Negro 1394, 7°, Montevideo; tel. 2902 1086; fax 2902 1087; e-mail alianca@aliancadabahia.com; internet www.aliancadabahia.com; f. 1995; transport; Gen. Man. BERNARDO VIVO.

Mapfre Uruguay (Spain): Juncal 1385, esq. Plaza Independencia, Montevideo; tel. 2915 5555; fax 2915 7305; e-mail vida@mapfre.com .uy; internet www.mapfre.com.uy; f. 1995; general.

MetLife Seguros de Vida, SA (USA): Avda 18 de Julio 1738, Montevideo; tel. 2403 3939; fax 2403 3938; e-mail atencion .clientes@metlife.com.uy; internet www.metlife.com.uy; f. 1996 as Alico Cía de Seguros de Vida; bought by MetLife in 2010; life.

Porto Seguro, Seguros del Uruguay SA (Brazil): Blvd Artigas 2025–2033, Montevideo; tel. 2402 8000; fax 2402 7355; e-mail admin@portoseguro.com.uy; internet www.portoseguro.com.uy; f. 1995; car and property; Pres. LEANDRO SUÁREZ.

RSA Uruguay (United Kingdom): Edif. RSA, Peatonal Sarandí 620, Montevideo; tel. 2917 0505; fax 2917 0490; internet www.royalsun .com.ar/rsauy_site; f. 1997; fmrly known as Royal & SunAlliance; life and property; Gen. Man. ESTEBAN PIGNANELLI.

Surco Seguros: Blvd Artigas 1320, Montevideo; tel. 2709 0089; fax 2707 7313; e-mail surco@surco.com.uy; internet www.surco.com.uy; f. 1995; insurance co-operative; all classes; Pres. SERGIO FUENTES; Gen. Man. ANDRÉS ELOLA.

L'Union de Paris Cía Uruguaya de Seguros, SA: Misiones 1549, 11000, Montevideo; tel. 2916 0850; fax 2916 0847; e-mail lunion@ lunion.com.uy; internet www.lunion.com.uy; f. 1897 as L'Union IARD; present name adopted 2004; part of HDI Seguros group from April 2011; general; Gen. Man. GABRIEL PENNA.

INSURANCE ASSOCIATION

Asociación Uruguaya de Empresas Aseguradoras (AUDEA): Edif. Torre del Congreso, Of. 1501, Avda 8 de Octubre 2355, Montevideo; tel. 2408 7735; fax 2916 5991; e-mail audea@adinet .com.uy; internet www.audea.org.uy; Pres. ANDRÉS ELOLA; Gen. Man. MAURICIO CASTELLANOS.

Trade and Industry

GOVERNMENT AGENCIES

Administración Nacional de Combustibles, Alcohol y Portland (ANCAP): Payasandú y Avda del Libertador Brig.-Gen. Lavalleja, 11100 Montevideo; tel. 2902 0608; fax 2902 1136; e-mail webmaster@ancap.com.uy; internet www.ancap.com.uy; f. 1931; deals with transport, refining and sale of petroleum products, and the manufacture of alcohol, spirits and cement; tanker services, also river transport; Pres. RAÚL SENDIC; Sec.-Gen. MIGUEL A. TATO.

Oficina de Planeamiento y Presupuesto de la Presidencia de la República: Plaza Independencia 710, 11000 Montevideo; tel. 2487 2110; fax 2209 9730; e-mail direccion@opp.gub.uy; internet www.opp.gub.uy; f. 1967; responsible for the implementation of devt plans; co-ordinates the policies of the various ministries; advises on the preparation of the budget of public enterprises; Dir GABRIEL FRUGONI; Sub-Dir JERÓNIMO ROCA.

Uruguay XXI (Instituto de Promoción de Inversiones y Exportaciones de Bienes y Servicios): Rincón 518/528, 11100 Montevideo; tel. 2915 3838; fax 2916 3059; e-mail info@uruguayxxi.gub.uy; internet www.uruguayxxi.gub.uy; f. 1996; govt agency to promote economic investment and export; Exec. Dir ROBERTO VILLAMIL; Gen. Man. ALVARO INCHAUSPE.

DEVELOPMENT ORGANIZATIONS

Corporación Nacional para el Desarrollo (CND): Rincón 528, 7°, Casilla 977, 11000 Montevideo; tel. 2916 2800; fax 2915 9662; e-mail cnd@cnd.org.uy; internet www.cnd.org.uy; f. 1985; national devt corpn; mixed-capital org.; obtains 60% of funding from state; Pres. ADRIANA RODRÍGUEZ; Vice-Pres. PABLO GUTIÉRREZ.

Asociación Nacional de Micro y Pequeños Empresarios (ANMYPE): Miguelete 1584, Montevideo; tel. 2924 1010; e-mail info@anmype.org.uy; internet www.anmype.org.uy; promotes small businesses; f. 1988; Pres. JULIO DURANTE; Sec. GUILLERMO SABELLA.

Asociación Nacional de Organizaciones No Gubernamentales Orientadas al Desarrollo: Avda del Libertador 1985, esq. 202, Montevideo; tel. and fax 2924 0812; e-mail anong@anong.com .uy; internet www.anong.org.uy; f. 1992; umbrella grouping of devt NGOs; Pres. ANA LAURA SCARENZIO; Sec. MARCELO VENTOS.

Centro Interdisciplinario de Estudios sobre el Desarrollo, Uruguay (CIEDUR): Avda 18 de Julio 1645-1647, 11200 Montevideo; tel. and fax 2408 4520; e-mail ciedur@ciedur.org.uy; internet www.ciedur.org.uy; f. 1977; devt studies and training; Pres. ALMA ESPINO; Exec. Sec. ALFREDO BLUM.

Fundación Uruguaya de Cooperación y Desarrollo Solidario (FUNDASOL) (Uruguayan Foundation for Supportive Co-operation and Development): Blvd Artigas 1165, esq. Maldonado, 11200 Montevideo; tel. 2400 2020; fax 2408 1485; e-mail consultas@ fundasol.org.uy; internet www.fundasol.org.uy; f. 1979; Pres. EDUARDO PIETRA; Gen. Man. JORGE NAYA.

CHAMBERS OF COMMERCE

Cámara de Industrias del Uruguay (Chamber of Industries): Avda Italia 6101, 11500 Montevideo; tel. 2604 0464; fax 2604 0501; e-mail ciu@ciu.com.uy; internet www.ciu.com.uy; f. 1898; Pres. WASHINGTON BURGHI; Gen. Man. MIGUEL VILARIÑO.

Cámara Mercantil de Productos del País (Chamber of Commerce for Local Products): Avda General Rondeau 1908, 1°, 11800 Montevideo; tel. 2924 0644; fax 2924 4701; e-mail info@ camaramercantil.com.uy; internet www.camaramercantil.com.uy; f. 1891; 180 mems; Pres. CHRISTIAN BOLZ; Gen. Man. GONZALO GONZÁLEZ PIEDRAS.

Cámara Nacional de Comercio y Servicios del Uruguay (National Chamber of Commerce): Edif. Bolsa de Comercio, Rincón 454, 2°, Casilla 1000, 11000 Montevideo; tel. 2916 1277; fax 2916 1243; e-mail info@cncs.com.uy; internet www.cncs.com.uy; f. 1867; 1,500 mems; Pres. ALFONSO VARELA; Man. Dr CLAUDIO PIACENZA.

EMPLOYERS' ORGANIZATIONS

Asociación de Importadores y Mayoristas de Almacén (Importers' and Wholesalers' Asscn): Edif. Bolsa de Comercio, Of. 317/319, Rincón 454, 11000 Montevideo; tel. 2915 6103; fax 2916 0796; e-mail fmelissari@nidera.com.uy; f. 1926; 52 mems; Pres. FERNANDO MELISSARI.

Asociación Rural del Uruguay (ARU): Avda Uruguay 864, 11100 Montevideo; tel. 2902 0484; fax 2902 0489; e-mail aru@netgate.com .uy; internet www.aru.com.uy; f. 1871; 1,800 mems; Pres. MANUEL LUSSICH TORRENDEL; Gen. Man. Dr GONZALO ARROYO FACELLO.

Federación Rural: Avda 18 de Julio 965, 1°, 11100 Montevideo; tel. 2900 4791; fax 2900 5583; e-mail fedrural@gmail.com; internet www .federacionrural.org.uy; f. 1915; 2,000 mems; Pres. MIGUEL SANGUINETTI.

Unión de Exportadores del Uruguay (Uruguayan Exporters' Asscn): Avda Uruguay 917, 1°, esq. Convención, 11100 Montevideo; tel. 2901 0105; fax 2916 5967; e-mail info@uniondeexportadores.com; internet www.uniondeexportadores.com; Pres. ALEJANDRO BZUROVSKI; Exec. Sec. TERESA AISHEMBERG.

UTILITIES

Electricity

Administración Nacional de Usinas y Transmisiones Eléctricas (UTE): Palacio de la Luz, Paraguay 2431, 10°, 11100 Montevideo; tel. 2200 3424; fax 2203 7082; e-mail ute@ute.com.uy; internet www.ute.com.uy; f. 1912; autonomous state body; sole purveyor of electricity until 1997; Pres. GONZALO CASARAVILLA; Gen. Man. HÉCTOR GONZÁLEZ.

Gas

Conecta: Avda Giannattasio, Km 20, 800 Ciudad de la Costa, Canelones, Montevideo; tel. 2682 6817; fax 2600 6732; internet www.conecta.com.uy; gas distribution; Dir FRANCISCO LLANO.

MontevideoGas: Plaza Independencia 831, 10°, 11000 Montevideo; tel. 2901 7454; e-mail mlcoitino@montevideogas.com.uy; internet www.montevideogas.com.uy; gas producers and service providers; Pres. CLOVIS CORREA; Gen. Man. PEDRO BORGES.

Water

Aguas de la Costa: Calle 1 y 20, La Barra, Maldonado; tel. 4277 1930; fax 4277 1932; e-mail adlcosta@adinet.com.uy; internet www.aguasdelacosta.com.uy; subsidiary of Aguas de Barcelona (Spain); management of water supply in Maldonado Dept; Pres. MILTON MACHADO; Gen. Man. GERMÁN ALVAREZ.

Obras Sanitarias del Estado (OSE): Carlos Roxlo 1275, 11200 Montevideo; tel. 2400 1151; fax 2408 8069; e-mail info@ose.com.uy; internet www.ose.com.uy; f. 1962; processing and distribution of drinking water, sinking wells, supplying industrial zones of the country; Pres. JORGE MILTON EDUARDO MACHADO LENS.

TRADE UNION

Plenario Intersindical de Trabajadores—Convención Nacional de Trabajadores (PIT—CNT): Jackson 1283, 11200 Montevideo; tel. 2409 6680; fax 2400 4160; e-mail pitcnt@adinet.com.uy; internet www.pitcnt.org.uy; f. 1966; org. comprising 83 trade unions, 17 labour federations; 320,000 mems; Exec. Sec. JUAN CASTILLO.

Transport

Dirección Nacional de Transporte: Rincón 575, 5°, 11000 Montevideo; tel. and fax 2915 7933; e-mail infodnt@dnt.gub.uy; internet www.dnt.gub.uy; co-ordinates national and international transport services; Gen. Man. FELIPE MARTÍN.

RAILWAYS

Administración de los Ferrocarriles del Estado (AFE): Avda Rondeau 1921, esq. Lima, Montevideo; tel. 2924 3924; e-mail secretariogeneral@afe.com.uy; internet www.afe.com.uy; f. 1952; state org.; 3,002 km of track connecting all parts of the country; connections with the Argentine and Brazilian networks; passenger services ceased in 1988; passenger services linking Montevideo with Florida and Canelones were resumed in 1993; Pres. ALEJANDRO ORELLANO; Gen. Man. JOSÉ NUNES.

ROADS

In 2008 Uruguay had an estimated 8,696 km of motorways (forming the densest motorway network in South America), connecting Montevideo with the main towns of the interior and the Argentine and Brazilian frontiers. There was also a network of approximately 40,000 km of paved roads under departmental control.

Corporación Vial del Uruguay, SA: Rincón 528, 5°, 11000 Montevideo; tel. 2916 2680; fax 2917 0114; e-mail cvu@cnd.org.uy; internet www.cvu.com.uy; road construction agency; 100% owned by Corporación Nacional para el Desarrollo; Pres. ADRIANA RODRÍGUEZ; Gen. Man. RICHARD SERVAN.

INLAND WATERWAYS

There are about 1,600 km of navigable waterways, which provide an important means of transport.

Nobleza Naviera, SA: Avda General Rondeau 2257, Montevideo; tel. 2924 3222; fax 2924 3769; e-mail nobleza@deambrosi.com.uy; internet www.noblezanaviera.com; operates cargo services on the River Plate, and the Uruguay and Paraná rivers; Pres. TABARÉ VÁZQUEZ; Gen. Man. JORGE RAZQUÍN.

SHIPPING

There are 13 sea ports in the country. At December 2012 the flag registered fleet comprised 90 vessels, totalling 102,342 grt.

Administración Nacional de Puertos (ANP): Rambla 25 de Agosto de 1825, No 160, Montevideo; tel. 2915 1441; fax 2916 1704; e-mail presidencia@anp.com.uy; internet www.anp.com.uy; f. 1916; national ports admin; Pres. ALBERTO DÍAZ; Gen. Mans OSVALDO TABACCHI, SCHUBERT MENDÉZ.

Grupo Christophersen, SA: Rincón 550, Puerta Baja, Casilla 295, 11000 Montevideo; tel. 2916 0109; fax 2916 9243; e-mail chris@christophersen.com.uy; internet www.christophersen.com.uy; f. 1892; owns four shipping cos: Transportes Fluviales Fray Bentos, Tramaco, Magrausa and Newlar; Pres. JORGE FERNÁNDEZ BAUBETA.

Mediterranean Shipping Co (MSC Uruguay): 1365 Andes, 13°, 11100 Montevideo; tel. 2902 2935; fax 2902 9155; e-mail distribution@mscuy.mscgva.ch; internet www.mscuruguay.com; f. 1999; Man. Dir ROBERTO GONZALÉZ FACAL.

Navegación Atlántica Uruguay: Rambla 25 de Agosto de 1825, No 508, 5°, 11100 Montevideo; tel. 2917 2005; e-mail navemvd@nave.com.uy; represents Niver Lines Shipping Co and Wan Hai Lines; freight services to South America, the Mediterranean and the Far East; Man. JUAN TABORELLI.

Prefectura Nacional Naval: Edif. Comando General de la Armada, 4°, Rambla 25 de Agosto de 1825 s/n, esq. Maciel, Montevideo; tel. 2915 2210; fax 2916 0022; e-mail premo_imdg@armada.mil.uy; internet mercanciaspeligrosas.com.uy; f. 1829; maritime supervisory body, responsible for rescue services, protection of sea against pollution, etc.; Sec.-Gen. Rear-Adm. OSCAR DEBALI DE PALLEJA.

CIVIL AVIATION

Civil aviation is controlled by the Dirección General de Aviación Civil and the Dirección General de Infraestructura Aeronáutica. The main airport is at Carrasco, 21 km from Montevideo, and there are also airports at Paysandú, Rivera, Salto, Melo, Artigas, Punta del Este and Durazno. The state-owned airline PLUNA was dissolved in July 2012.

Aeromás, SA (MaxAir, SA): Avda de las Américas 5120, Montevideo; tel. 2604 6359; e-mail aeromas@aeromas.com; internet www.aeromas.com; private hire, cargo, and air ambulance flights; internal mass transit services to Salto, Paysandú, Rivera, Tacuarembó and Artigas; f. 1983; Dir DANIEL DALMÁS.

Tourism

The sandy beaches and woodlands on the coast and the grasslands of the interior, with their variety of fauna and flora, provide the main tourist attractions. About 55% of tourists came from Argentina and 13% from Brazil in 2009. Uruguay received an estimated 2.9m. visitors in 2011, while tourism revenues totalled a provisional US $2,187m. in that year.

Asociación Uruguaya de Agencias de Viajes (AUDAVI): Río Branco 1407, Of. 205, 11100 Montevideo; tel. 2901 2326; fax 2902 1972; e-mail audavi@netgate.com.uy; internet www.audavi.com.uy; f. 1951; 100 mems; Pres. SERGIO BAÑALES.

Cámara Uruguaya de Turismo: San José 942, 2°, Of. 4, 11200 Montevideo; tel. and fax 2900 0453; internet camtur.com.uy; f. 1993; Pres. LUIS BORSARI.

Uruguay Natural: Rambla 25 de Agosto de 1825, esq. Yacaré, Montevideo; tel. 2188 5100; e-mail webmaster@mintur.gub.uy; internet www.uruguaynatural.com; f. 2003; state-run tourism promotion agency; Dir-Gen. BENJAMÍN LIBEROFF.

Defence

As assessed at November 2012, Uruguay's Armed Forces consisted of 24,650 volunteers between the ages of 18 and 45, who contract for one or two years of service. There was an army of 16,250, a navy of 5,400 and an air force of 3,000. There were also paramilitary forces numbering 800.

Defence Budget: an estimated 9,550m. pesos uruguayos in 2013.

Commander-in-Chief of the Army: Lt-Gen. PEDRO AGUERRE SIQUEIRA.

Commander-in-Chief of the Navy: Adm. RICARDO GIAMBRUNO.

Commander-in-Chief of the Air Force: Brig.-Gen. WASHINGTON R. MARTÍNEZ.

Education

All education, including university tuition, is provided free of charge. Education is officially compulsory for six years between six and 14 years of age. Primary education begins at the age of six and lasts for six years. Secondary education, beginning at 12 years of age, lasts for a further six years, comprising two cycles of three years each. In 2008 primary enrolment included 99% of children in the relevant age-group (males 99%, females 98%), while the equivalent ratio for secondary enrolment was 70% (males 66%, females 73%). The programmes of instruction are the same in both public and private schools and private schools are subject to certain state controls. There are four universities in Uruguay, including the state Universidad de la República. In 2013 35,629m. pesos uruguayos of general government expenditure was allocated to the Administración Nacional de Educación Pública.

UZBEKISTAN

Introductory Survey

LOCATION, CLIMATE, LANGUAGE, RELIGION, FLAG, CAPITAL

The Republic of Uzbekistan is located in Central Asia. It is bordered by Kazakhstan to the north, Turkmenistan to the south-west, Kyrgyzstan to the east, Tajikistan to the south-east and Afghanistan to the south. The climate is marked by extreme temperatures and low levels of precipitation. Summers are long and hot with average temperatures in July of 32°C (90°F); daytime temperatures often exceed 40°C (104°F). During the short winter there are frequent severe frosts, and temperatures can fall as low as −38°C (−36°F). The official language is Uzbek. Islam is the predominant religion. Most Uzbeks are Sunni Muslims, principally of the Hanafi school, although there are small communities of Salafis; Sufism is relatively well established in southern Uzbekistan. There are also Orthodox Christians among the Slavic communities. The national flag (proportions 1 by 2) consists of five unequal horizontal stripes of (from top to bottom) light blue, red, white, red and light green, with a white crescent and 12 white stars near the hoist on the top stripe. The capital is Tashkent (Toshkent).

CONTEMPORARY POLITICAL HISTORY

Historical Context

Soviet power was first established in parts of Uzbekistan in November 1917. In April 1918 the Turkestan Autonomous Soviet Socialist Republic (ASSR), covering a vast region in Central Asia, was proclaimed, but Soviet forces withdrew against opposition from the local *basmachi* movement, the White Army and a British expeditionary force. Soviet power was re-established in September 1919, although armed opposition continued until the early 1920s. The khanates of Buxoro (Bukhara) and Xiva (Khiva) became nominally independent Soviet republics in 1920, but by 1924 they had been incorporated into the Turkestan ASSR. On 27 October 1924 the Uzbek Soviet Socialist Republic (SSR) was established (until 1929 it included the Tajik ASSR—now Tajikistan). In May 1925 the Uzbek SSR became a constituent republic of the Union of Soviet Socialist Republics (USSR). In 1936 Qoraqalpog'iston (Karakalpakstan) was transferred from the Russian Federation to the Uzbek SSR, retaining its status as a nominally autonomous viloyat (oblast or region).

The National Delimitation of the Central Asian republics of 1924–25 established an Uzbek nation-state for the first time. Literacy rose from 3.8% in 1926 to 52.5% in 1932. Muslim establishments were closed, and clergy were persecuted.

Under the first two Five-Year Plans (1928–38), however, there was considerable economic growth, aided by the immigration of skilled workers from within the USSR. Although economic expansion, which began in the 1930s, continued after the Second World War, most Uzbeks continued to lead a traditional rural lifestyle, affected only by the huge increase in the amount of cotton grown in the republic.

Environmental problems, particularly the dessication of the Aral Sea, and the status of the Uzbek language were among the concerns on which Uzbekistan's first independent political movement, Unity (Birlik), campaigned in the late 1980s. The movement remained unregistered and was unsuccessful in the 1989 elections to the USSR's Congress of People's Deputies; nevertheless, its political campaigning led to the adoption of legislation declaring Uzbek to be the official language of the republic in October of that year.

Following legislative elections on 18 February 1990 (which Unity was not permitted to contest), the 500-seat Uzbekistani Supreme Soviet (Supreme Council—legislature) became dominated by the Communist Party of the Uzbek SSR (CPU). The new Supreme Soviet convened in March and elected Islam Karimov, the First Secretary (leader) of the CPU, to the newly created post of executive President.

Domestic Political Affairs

In April 1991 Uzbekistan agreed, with eight other Soviet republics, to sign a new Union Treaty to reconstitute the USSR. However, on 19 August, the day before the signing was to take place, there was an attempt to stage a coup by conservative communists in Moscow, the Russian and Soviet capital. President Karimov only expressed his opposition to the coup once it became clear that it had failed. On 31 August an extraordinary session of the Supreme Soviet voted to declare an independent Republic of Uzbekistan. The CPU voted to dissociate itself from the Communist Party of the Soviet Union, and in November restructured itself as the People's Democratic Party of Uzbekistan (PDPU), still under Karimov's leadership.

On 21 December 1991 Karimov and 10 other republican leaders agreed to dissolve the USSR and establish the Commonwealth of Independent States (CIS, see p. 251). On 29 December a direct presidential election was held in Uzbekistan, at which Karimov won a reported 86% of votes cast. His sole rival (winning 12% of the votes) was Muhammad Salih, the leader of the Freedom (Erk) party, an offshoot of Unity. At a concurrent referendum, 98.2% of participants voted to endorse Uzbekistan's independence.

Under Karimov's leadership, there was widespread repression of opposition groups. A new Constitution, adopted on 8 December 1992, enshrined the concept of state secularism, and included formal provisions for a democratic multi-party system, freedom of expression and the observance of human rights (which were largely disregarded, in practice). It also provided for the establishment of a new, smaller legislature, the 250-member Oliy Majlis (Supreme Assembly), following elections due to be held in 1994. On the day of the adoption of the new Constitution three leading opposition members were seized by Uzbekistani security police in the Kyrgyzstani capital, Bishkek, and charged with sedition. One day later Unity was banned. Media regulation was intensified: in mid-1993 the Government ordered all newspapers and periodicals to re-register with the State Committee for the Press, permitting registration only to organs of the state and government. Only the PDPU and its ally, Progress of the Fatherland (PF), were permitted to register for the elections to the Oliy Majlis. At the elections, held on 25 December 1994 (with further rounds of voting, where required, on 8 and 22 January 1995), the PDPU won 69 of the 250 seats, and the PF secured 14. The remaining 167 deputies elected had been nominated by local councils rather than by political parties; some 120 of these deputies were PDPU members, and thus the party's domination of the Majlis was retained. Some 94% of eligible voters were reported to have participated in the elections.

In January 1995 Karimov announced that the formation of blocs in the Oliy Majlis was to be permitted. In February a new political party, the Justice Social Democratic Party of Uzbekistan (Adolat), was registered, and immediately declared its intention to establish such a parliamentary faction. A referendum held in March produced a 99.6% vote in favour of extending Karimov's presidential term, originally scheduled to end in 1997, until 2000. In June 1995 two new political formations, both of which were pro-Government, were officially registered: the National Revival Democratic Party (Milliy Tiklanish) and the People's Unity Movement (Xalq Birligi). In December O'tkir Sultonov, hitherto the Minister of Foreign Economic Relations, replaced Abdulkhashim Mutalov as Prime Minister. In June 1996 Karimov resigned from his position as Chairman of the PDPU. In December 1996 the Oliy Majlis approved a new law on political parties, which prohibited the organization of parties on a religious or ethnic basis and compelled prospective parties to prove that they had 5,000 members drawn from a majority of Uzbekistan's administrative regions.

In late 1997 there was an upsurge of violence, attributed to groups of Islamist activists, in the densely populated Farg'ona (Fergana) valley in eastern Uzbekistan. In November the deputy head of the administration of Namangan Viloyat (region), in the valley, was assassinated, and in December four police officers were killed; government troops arrested hundreds of suspects. The Government's campaign against Islamist militancy intensified in early 1998. In February the Ministry of Foreign Affairs appealed to the Pakistani Government to extirpate military training camps in that country, where Uzbeks were allegedly being trained in dissident activities. (Pakistan denied the existence of any such camps.) In May the Oliy Majlis adopted legislation that severely limited the activities of religious organizations. During May–July several suspected militant Islamists were sentenced to terms of imprisonment, and a member of an Islamist organization was sentenced to death, following his conviction for the murder of five people and for his role in the training of militants in Afghanistan. In January 1999 five men were found guilty of attempting to overthrow the Government and establish an Islamist state. Meanwhile, in June 1998 new legislation was adopted banning the purchase, sale or exchange of land.

In February 1999 a series of bombs exploded in the centre of Tashkent, killing an estimated 15 people. Following the trial, in June, of 22 people suspected of involvement in the bomb attacks, six of the accused were sentenced to death, and the other defendants received lengthy prison sentences. In August six members of the banned Freedom party were given prison sentences of between eight and 15 years for their involvement in the bombings. In November the Tashkent region was infiltrated by a group of about 15 armed militants, who shot three police officers and three civilians. (It was alleged that the group, who were subsequently killed by security forces, had been trained in the separatist Chechen Republic, Russia, and had entered Uzbekistan from Kyrgyzstan.) Following the violence, Karimov appealed to the Organization for Security and Co-operation in Europe (OSCE, see p. 397) to assist Uzbekistan in combating international terrorism.

At elections to the Oliy Majlis, held on 5 and 19 December 1999, the PDPU obtained 48 seats, more than any other party, while non-partisan local council nominees obtained a total of 110 seats. The rate of voter participation at the first round was reported to be some 93.5%. The OSCE had sent only a limited number of observers to the elections, since all of the parties participating were pro-Government, two opposition parties having been prevented from contesting.

President Karimov secured 91.9% of the votes cast at the presidential election held on 9 January 2000, according to official figures, overwhelmingly defeating his sole opponent, Abdulkhafiz Jalolov of the PDPU. Karimov was inaugurated for another five-year term on 22 January. Both the OSCE and the US Government criticized the election (in which 95% of the registered electorate were reported to have participated) as undemocratic.

The trial of a further 12 people accused of involvement in the bomb attacks of February 1999 opened in October 2000. In November the spiritual leader of the proscribed Islamic Movement of Uzbekistan (IMU), Tohir Yuldosh, and his field commander, Jumaboy Hojiyev (known as Juma Namangoniy), were sentenced to death *in absentia*. The remaining 10 defendants (including, *in absentia*, Salih) were sentenced to between 12 and 20 years' imprisonment. In June 2001 10 further Islamist militants were reported to have received prison sentences for attempting to overthrow the Government.

The perceived threat of militant Islamist movements intensified in the latter half of 2001, following the suicide attacks in the USA on 11 September (see the USA), and Uzbekistan's decision to co-operate with the USA in its attempts to form an international coalition to combat the al-Qa'ida organization of Osama bin Laden (elements of which were harboured by the Taliban militia in Afghanistan). It was widely believed that Karimov expected to secure strategic benefits from such co-operation, notably the suppression of the IMU and the moderation of international criticism of his Government's position on economic reforms and human rights. There were frequent allegations of the torture and arrest of suspected members of the IMU and Hizb-ut-Tahrir al-Islami (Hizb-ut-Tahrir—the Party of Islamic Liberation), a clandestine, transnational organization, which sought to re-establish a caliphate, apparently solely through peaceful means, and which was alleged to enjoy significant support in Uzbekistan and neighbouring countries, particularly in the Farg'ona valley. In October an estimated 5,000–7,000 members of the IMU (which both the UN and the USA identified as a terrorist organization) were reported to be fighting alongside Taliban forces in Afghanistan.

Constitutional revision

On 27 January 2002 a referendum took place to seek approval for proposed constitutional amendments. Some 91.6% of the electorate participated, of whom 93.7% approved the reorganization of the legislature on a bicameral basis, while 91.8% endorsed the extension of the presidential term from five to seven years. The amendments also prescribed that elections to all offices of state were henceforth to be held in December in the year in which the term of office expired, thereby further extending Karimov's presidential mandate by 11 months, until December 2007.

In April 2003 the Oliy Majlis approved constitutional amendments permitting the redistribution of authority within the Government, with effect from the next legislative elections and endorsed a law granting former Presidents both lifelong immunity from prosecution and permanent membership of the Senat (Senate), the new upper legislative chamber. On 11 December the Oliy Majlis confirmed the appointment of Shavkat Mirziyoyev, who had substantial experience in the agricultural sector, as Prime Minister. His predecessor, Sultonov became a Deputy Prime Minister, with responsibility for the energy, petroleum and chemicals sectors.

On 28–29 March 2004 three police officers were killed in two shooting incidents in Tashkent; on 29 March two bombings, seemingly by suicide bombers, in a market in the city resulted in further casualties. It was also reported that 10 people had been killed and 26 injured after bombs exploded in an apartment block, which police alleged was being used as a base for the manufacture of explosives, in Buxoro. On 30 March security forces carried out a raid in Tashkent, during which at least 16 suspected militant Islamists and three police officers were killed. A further bomb attack on 1 April killed one person and prompted the Government temporarily to close the country's land borders. By July some 85 people suspected of involvement in the attacks had been arrested. In August 15 of the accused were sentenced to between six and 18 years' imprisonment; in October a further 23 militants were sentenced to between three and 18 years' imprisonment. In July 2005 another 20 men were given gaol sentences for their involvement in the attacks. Meanwhile, in July 2004 seven people were killed as a result of suicide bomb attacks in Tashkent outside the Israeli and US embassies and outside the Office of the Prosecutor-General. President Karimov accused Hizb-ut-Tahrir of responsibility for the bombings.

Elections to the Qonunchilik palatasi (Legislative Chamber), the 120-seat lower chamber of the new bicameral legislature, were held on 26 December 2004, with a second round of voting on 9 January 2005 in the 58 constituencies in which no candidate had obtained an absolute majority of votes cast. All five parties permitted to participate in the elections supported Karimov. (Three opposition parties—Unity, Freedom and the Free Peasants' Party—had been denied permission to present candidates.) The Movement of Entrepreneurs and Businessmen—Liberal Democratic Party of Uzbekistan, established in late 1993 and led by Muhammadjon Ahmadjonov, obtained 41 seats. The PDPU obtained 28 seats, the Self-Sacrificers' National Democratic Party 18, the National Revival Democratic Party 11 and the Justice Social Democratic Party 10. The rate of voter participation at the first round was an estimated 85.1%. Several ministerial changes were effected in late 2004 and early 2005. On 14 January 2005 President Karimov announced the appointment of 16 members of the Senat, and regional council members elected a further 84 senators on 17–20 January. The inaugural session of the chamber took place on 27 January.

Violence in Andijon

Political tensions intensified in early 2005, particularly in the Farg'ona valley, as a result of dissatisfaction at widespread poverty, and discontent at restrictions on trade and on the freedom of association. From February daily peaceful protests took place outside a court in the town of Andijon, where 23 local business executives had been brought to trial on charges of belonging to a prohibited Islamist organization, Akramiya, which was alleged to have broken away from Hizb-ut-Tahrir. All 23 denied the charges brought against them. In the early hours of 13 May, several days before the trial was due to conclude, a group of armed men stormed the gaol in Andijon, and released as many as 2,000 prisoners, including the 23 alleged members of Akramiya. Armed rebels took control of the regional administration building in the city later that day, and several thousand people gathered in the main square, protesting against both the trial of the alleged militants and economic difficulties. Heavily armed state security forces entered Andijon and opened fire on the demonstrators, killing large numbers of people. Protests continued in Andijon later in the month, and unrest was reported in Qorasuv, on the border with Kyrgyzstan southeast of Andijon, although state forces subsequently recaptured the town. Meanwhile, Kyrgyzstan reported that it had registered more than 500 Uzbekistani refugees in the immediate aftermath of the violence in Andijon.

President Karimov rejected requests by the international community for an independent investigation into the events in Andijon. In July 2005 the Prosecutor of Andijon Viloyat announced that 187 people had been killed as a result of the violence; in contrast, independent reports claimed that as many as 1,000 people had been killed. In September the Office of the Prosecutor-General issued a report stating that foreign-based Islamists had staged the violence, and claiming that earlier in the year Kyrgyzstan-based instructors had trained some 70 militant Islamists in terrorist techniques. In August Karimov approved a decree abolishing capital punishment, with effect from 1 January 2008.

In September 2005 the First Deputy Prosecutor-General suggested that 'external forces' had instructed Western journalists to publish false information about the events in Andijon in the foreign media. Individuals and organizations that provided accounts undermining the credibility of the Government's version of events were subject to official harassment, including, in some cases, expulsion from the country or imprisonment. In October the European Union (EU, see p. 281) imposed sanctions on Uzbekistan (including a ban on travel to EU states by officials suspected of involvement in the shooting of civilians in Andijon, and an embargo on armaments), owing to the Government's refusal either to permit an international investigation into events at Andijon or to bring those who had perpetrated the killings to trial. (These sanctions were extended in November 2006 and again in May 2007.) By December 2005 more than 150 people had been imprisoned for their involvement in the Andijon protests; in November the USA and the Office of the UN High Commissioner for Human Rights expressed concern that some of the convicted defendants had not been permitted a fair trial, and about the alleged use of torture. In February 2006 the Government approved a resolution that made journalists deemed to be interfering in internal affairs or insulting Uzbekistani citizens liable to prosecution. In March the authorities requested that the UN High Commission for Refugees vacate its offices in Uzbekistan.

Meanwhile, frequent government and security personnel changes continued to be effected. In June 2005 the First Deputy Head of the Military Intelligence Directorate, Lt-Col Sanjar Ismoilov, was arrested on suspicion of spying for Russia; he was sentenced to 20 years' imprisonment in January 2006. In November 2005 Karimov dismissed the Minister of Defence, Qodir G'ulomov, who was subsequently succeeded by Ruslan Mirzayev. (G'ulomov was given a five-year suspended prison sentence in July 2006 for offences committed during his term of office.) In December 2005 the Minister of Internal Affairs, Zokirjon Almatov—whom the EU held responsible for overseeing the violent repression of the protests in Andijon—resigned, citing ill health. He was succeeded in January 2006 by Bahodir Matlyubov.

In March 2007 the Qonunchilik palatasi approved legislation (initially proposed by President Karimov) recognizing the existence of parliamentary factions, each of which was hitherto to be consulted by the President before the appointment of a Prime Minister or a regional hokim (regional governor). Provision was made for parliamentary factions to designate themselves as officially forming the role of opposition (although no faction subsequently did so), while the responsibilities of President and Prime Minister were more strictly defined than hitherto. The new provisions, which some observers suggested might be intended to bring about the eventual introduction of a parliamentary system of government, were to enter into effect from January 2008. In September 2007 the Central Election Commission announced that a presidential election was to take place on 23 December. Karimov subsequently confirmed that he would contest the election, despite a constitutional provision restricting the President to two consecutive terms in office.

On 23 December 2007 Karimov was re-elected President, receiving some 88.1% of votes cast (the other three candidates permitted to contest the election were all considered to be loyal to Karimov); the rate of voter participation was officially recorded as 90.6%. An observer mission from the Office for Democratic Institutions and Human Rights of the OSCE stated that the poll had failed to meet democratic standards. At the end of December Karimov appointed Rustam Azimov (the incumbent Minister of Finance) additionally as First Deputy Prime Minister, responsible for the Economic Sector and Foreign Economic Relations. In January 2008, following the removal of the Speaker of the lower legislative chamber, Erkin Halilov, for abuse of office, Dilorom Tashmuhamedova (who had contested the presidential election

as a candidate of the Justice Social Democratic Party) was elected to the post. In April a prominent poet and human rights activist, Yusuf Juma, was sentenced to five years' imprisonment for resisting arrest, after he staged a protest against the detention of one of his sons. (Juma was released in May 2011.) In June 2008 Ahmadjon Odilov, a former opposition figure who had been imprisoned in 1984, was released. In September Karimov dismissed Ruslan Mirzayev as Minister of Defence; he was succeeded by Qobul Berdiyev. As part of a government reorganization effected in July 2009, the hitherto Minister of the Economy, Botir Xo'jayev, became a Deputy Prime Minister, and was succeeded in his former position by Sunatilla Bekenov.

Meanwhile, in October 2008 EU foreign ministers formally ended the travel ban on Uzbekistani officials (which had been suspended since October 2007), citing improvements in the observance of human rights in Uzbekistan. In October 2009 the EU rescinded the armaments embargo that had been in force since 2005, while expressing continuing concerns at the human rights situation in the country; prominent human rights organizations criticized the decision.

The 2009 legislative elections

Legislative elections were held on 27 December 2009, with a second round of voting in 39 constituencies on 10 January 2010. In accordance with a revised version of the electoral law, approved in 2008, the Ecological Movement of Uzbekistan automatically received 15 seats in the Qonunchilik palatasi; the four remaining parties participating in the elections were supporters of the Karimov regime. The rate of participation by the electorate at the first round was 87.8%. The Movement of Entrepreneurs and Businessmen—Liberal Democratic Party of Uzbekistan obtained 53 seats, the PDPU 32, the National Revival Democratic Party 31 and the Justice Social Democratic Party 19.

In July 2010 G'ulomjon Ibragimov was appointed Deputy Prime Minister, responsible for Geology, Fuel and Energy and the Chemical, Petrochemical and Metallurgical Industries, in place of Ergash Shaismatov. In October Bekenov was succeeded as Minister of the Economy by Ravshan G'ulomov. Meanwhile, concerns about freedom of expression in Uzbekistan were heightened, when an Uzbekistani freelance journalist, Abdumalik Boboev, who worked as a correspondent for the US state-funded Voice of America radio service, was tried on various charges including slander and the dissemination of materials harmful to social stability. The USA placed diplomatic pressure upon Uzbekistan to release Boboev without charge, and, although the criminal code provided for imprisonment for the charges on which Boboev was convicted later in October, he was instead fined 18.1m. sum. In December Vladimir Norov was dismissed as Minister of Foreign Affairs; he was succeeded by Elyor G'aniyev, who retained his existing post as Deputy Prime Minister, responsible for Foreign Economic Activities, the Attraction of Foreign Investment and the Localization of Production, while his former concurrent position as Minister of Foreign Economic Relations, Investment and Trade was allocated to Galina Saidova. In January 2011 the Minister of Culture and Sports, Anvar Jabborov, was dismissed, following allegations that he had permitted corrupt practices to occur within his ministry.

In March 2011 the Oliy Majlis approved two items of draft legislation concerning the constitutional balance of powers, which had been presented by President Karimov in November 2010. The proposals provided, respectively, for presidential powers to be transferred to the Chairman of the Senate in the event of the incapacity of the head of state, and for prime ministerial candidates to be nominated by the leader of the party with the greatest number of legislative deputies. The legislature, moreover, was to be granted the right to undertake votes of no confidence in the Government. Some observers described these measures—which ostensibly strengthened the legislature at the expense of the executive—as representing an assertion of Karimov's authority, in particular over that of the incumbent Prime Minister.

In early June 2011 Elmira Basithanova was appointed Deputy Prime Minister, Chairman of the Committee of Women of Uzbekistan, succeeding Faroda Akbarova. Later in the month Tursunali Kuziyev was appointed Minister of Culture and Sports, which position had remained vacant following the dismissal of Jabborov. Also in June the Minister of Justice, Ravshan Muxitdinov, was appointed to the position of a senior state adviser; he was subsequently succeeded in his ministerial position by Nig'matilla Yo'ldoshev. In July Saidova became Minister of the Economy, replacing Ravshan G'ulomov, who was appointed as Minister of Economic Relations, Investment and Trade, while Temir Shirinov was appointed Minister of National Education, replacing Avazjon Marahimov. Political developments in November were interpreted by some observers as further evidence of President Karimov's consolidation of his authority at the expense of Prime Minister Mirziyoyev. In early November Botir Xo'jayev was removed from his post as Deputy Prime Minister and appointed First Deputy Minister of the Economy, while Botir Zokirov succeeded him in his former post. The hokim of Farg'ona Viloyat, Hamid Nematov, was also dismissed. Later that month, reports emerged that Muxitdinov, after being dismissed as presidential adviser in September, had been arrested in connection with corruption investigations. (Muxitdinov, who had been widely considered a close ally of Mirziyoyev, was sentenced to 15 years' imprisonment on corruption-related charges in February 2012.)

Recent developments: constitutional change

In December 2011 the Senat approved a constitutional amendment reducing the President's term of office from seven years to five. In January 2012 Elyor G'aniyev was dismissed as Deputy Prime Minister and Minister of Foreign Affairs, responsible for Foreign Economic Activities, the Attraction of Foreign Investment and the Localization of Production, and was instead appointed Minister of Foreign Economic Relations, Investment and Trade, replacing G'ulomov. In March the Oliy Majlis voted in favour of rescheduling the next presidential election, which had been scheduled for December 2014, ostensibly so that it would not coincide with elections to the Qonunchilik palatasi also due to be held in that month. Instead, the presidential election was to take place in 2015, 90 days after the official results of the legislative elections had been published.

In July 2012 the Government suspended the operating licence of the Uzbekistani subsidiary, Uzdunrobita (MTS-O'zbekiston), of Russian mobile telephone operator Mobile Telesystems (MTS), and arrested several senior officials, including its acting director, Radik Dautov, on suspicion of malpractice. Following the reported intervention of the Russian Government, Dautov, a Russian national, was released in early August and permitted to return to Russia. Meanwhile, on 4 August the Oliy Majlis adopted legislation that banned the establishment of foreign military bases on Uzbekistani territory and the country's membership of military alliances. Later that month President Karimov dismissed Abdulla Aripov as Deputy Prime Minister, responsible for Education, Health, Social Welfare, Information Systems and Telecommunications. Adxam Ikramov, the hitherto Minister of Health was subsequently appointed as Deputy Prime Minister, responsible for Culture, Education, Health and Social Welfare, and was succeeded in his former position by Anvar Alimov. In September a court in Tashkent ordered the confiscation of assets, totalling US $700m., belonging to Uzdunrobita, and sentenced four officials to three-year suspended sentences, following the company's failure to pay fines imposed for tax evasion. In early November a court revoked the confiscation of assets, but ordered Uzdunrobita to pay $600m. in compensation, after the Russian authorities seized an apartment in Moscow belonging to Karimov's daughter, Gulnora Karimova. Uzdunrobita announced bankruptcy in January 2013, owing to its inability to pay the $600m. penalty. In March government officials and Karimova both publicly denied reports published on opposition websites that Karimov had suffered a heart attack; however, the rumours prompted speculation regarding his potential successor.

Foreign Affairs

Regional relations

Uzbekistan's closest relations are with the neighbouring Central Asian republics—Kazakhstan, Kyrgyzstan, Tajikistan and Turkmenistan. In September 1997 a Central Asian peacekeeping battalion participated, with troops from the USA and other countries, in military manoeuvres, which were held in Uzbekistan and elsewhere in the region under the auspices of the 'Partnership for Peace' (see p. 383) programme of military co-operation of the North Atlantic Treaty Organization (NATO). (Uzbekistan had joined the programme in 1994.) In November 2008, however, the Eurasian Economic Community (EURASEC, see p. 461) officially confirmed that it had been informed of Uzbekistan's decision to suspend its membership of the organization.

Uzbekistan was a member, alongside the People's Republic of China, Kazakhstan, Kyrgyzstan, Russia and Tajikistan, of the Shanghai Five, founded in 1996 to address border disputes, and

acceded to that organization's successor, the Shanghai Cooperation Organization (SCO, see p. 478), signing the Shanghai Convention on Combating Terrorism, Separatism and Extremism. The organization subsequently established a regional anti-terrorism centre, located in Tashkent.

In June 2006 it was announced that Uzbekistan had commenced participation in the Collective Security Treaty Organization (CSTO, see p. 474), the successor organization to the CIS Collective Security Treaty (from which Uzbekistan had withdrawn in March 1999). In March 2008 the Oliy Majlis officially approved Uzbekistan's full membership of the CSTO (which also comprised Armenia, Belarus, Kazakhstan, Kyrgyzstan, Russia and Tajikistan). In June 2012 Uzbekistan announced the suspension of its membership of the CSTO; the decision was attributed by many observers to continued disputes with neighbouring states over energy and water supplies. Uzbekistan's membership was formally ended at a CSTO summit meeting held in Moscow, in December.

In October 1998 Uzbekistan and Kazakhstan signed a Treaty of Eternal Friendship and agreed on a seven-year programme of bilateral economic co-operation. In November 2001 the two countries signed a treaty demarcating most of their common border. However, the demarcation of certain areas, including the villages of Bagys and Turkestanets, remained unresolved. The majority of citizens in Bagys were ethnic Kazakhs, and it had been hoped that the land, hitherto leased to Uzbekistan, would be returned to Kazakhstan following independence. In December residents declared an 'Independent Kazakh Republic of Bagys', and elected a president and legislature. The Uzbekistani security forces subsequently arrested a number of activists, and in April 2002 it was reported that troops had barricaded the villages. In September a new agreement delimiting the Kazakhstani–Uzbekistani border was signed by the countries' Presidents. However, at the end of 2002 Uzbekistan closed its border with Kazakhstan. The creation of a working group to finalize the demarcation of the border was announced in August 2003. However, following the arrests of Kazakhstani citizens in connection with a series of bombings in Uzbekistan in mid-2004, in January 2005 representatives from the Uzbekistani Ministry of Defence reportedly announced that they considered Kazakhstan to be a potential military adversary and a base for armed groups opposed to the Uzbekistani regime. In the same month the Uzbekistani authorities announced proposals for the demolition of settlements along the border, apparently in response to cross-border smuggling. Demonstrations in February by residents demanding compensation for the destruction of their homes were met with a promise from the hokim of Tashkent Viloyat that an assessment of property values in the village would be conducted with the view of providing the residents with compensation. In March President Karimov and the President of Kazakhstan, Nursultan Nazarbayev, agreed to establish a working group to create a future free trade zone.

Relations with Kyrgyzstan worsened in September 2000, when Uzbekistani government forces planted land-mines along the Kyrgyzstani–Uzbekistani border, apparently without having informed Kyrgyzstan, in order to prevent insurgents from entering Uzbekistan. Although it was announced in June 2001 that the mines were to be removed, there were claims in September that the laying of mines was continuing. As a result, the Kyrgyzstani legislature refused to ratify an agreement with Uzbekistan on arms supplies. Relations were again strained in mid-2005, when the Kyrgyzstani Government refused to return a large number of refugees who had fled there from Uzbekistan following the violence in Andijon in May (see Domestic Political Affairs). In July more than 400 refugees were deported from Kyrgyzstan to Romania, which Uzbekistan condemned as a violation of international law, while there were subsequent reports that refugees repatriated to Uzbekistan had been tortured. In August Uzbekistan annulled a bilateral agreement to supply natural gas to Kyrgyzstan. In the following month Uzbekistan issued a report accusing Kyrgyzstan of having permitted extremist Islamists to use bases in the latter country to foment unrest in Andijon. In August 2006 Kyrgyzstan deported some of the Andijon refugees to Uzbekistan. In early 2007 a bilateral agreement providing for visa-free travel between the two countries took effect. However, further tensions developed in mid-2009, when Uzbekistan began digging trenches in disputed areas along the joint border, ostensibly to prevent incursions by militants. During an outbreak of inter-ethnic violence in southern regions of Kyrgyzstan, following the uprising there in April 2010, ethnic Uzbeks were targeted, and several hundred were killed. Uzbekistan unilaterally closed its border with Kyrgyzstan in April, and the border remained officially closed until October 2011.

In January 2013 Kyrgyzstani border guards clashed with (predominantly ethnic Tajik) residents of the Uzbekistani exclave of Sokh, which is surrounded by Kyrgyzstani territory, in a dispute over the installation of power transmission lines to a border post. Local residents temporarily took a number of Kyrgyzstani citizens hostage, after which the Kyrgyzstani authorities imposed a retaliatory blockade of the exclave. The incident prompted concerns of increased tensions in the border areas of the Farg'ona valley. In March discussions between Uzbekistani and Kyrgyzstani officials on border issues were conducted in Tashkent.

In September 2000 Turkmenistan and Uzbekistan signed a treaty demarcating their 1,867-km border. In December 2002 Turkmenistani special forces entered the Uzbekistani embassy in the Turkmenistani capital, Aşgabat, purportedly in order to investigate reports that it was harbouring Boris Shikhmuradov, whom the Turkmenistani authorities blamed for an assassination attempt against that country's President, Saparmyrat Niyazov. Uzbekistan's ambassador to Turkmenistan was subsequently declared *persona non grata*, on the grounds that he had offered support to Shikhmuradov. The Uzbekistani authorities denied the allegations and reacted with hostility; open confrontation rapidly led to the deployment of troops from both countries along their mutual border, and an associated increase in border security. In November 2004 Presidents Karimov and Niyazov met for their first presidential summit in more than four years, in Buxoro, where they signed three bilateral agreements, which included simplifying regulations concerning cross-border travel for residents of border zones (where cross-border smuggling and related shooting incidents had become problematic in recent years), and a framework for sharing regional water resources. The Presidents declared that all bilateral issues had been resolved, and in January 2005 Uzbekistan appointed a new ambassador to Turkmenistan. President Karimov made an official visit to Turkmenistan in October 2007, meeting the President installed earlier in that year, Gurbanguly Berdymuhamedov.

Uzbekistan dispatched troops to Tajikistan in 1992, as part of a CIS peace-keeping contingent, and tightened border controls with Tajikistan in an attempt to prevent the civil conflict in that country from extending into Uzbekistan (see Tajikistan). In August 1997 Uzbekistan agreed to act as one of the guarantors of a peace accord reached between the Tajikistani Government and opposition forces two months earlier. During a visit to Uzbekistan in January 1998 President Imamali Rakhmonov (later Rakhmon) of Tajikistan met Karimov, and the two leaders expressed their opposition to religious extremism. In August 1999 the Uzbekistani Government accused Tajikistan of allowing militant groups to operate from its territory. From August 2000 armed Islamist militants made a series of incursions into the section of the Farg'ona valley in Uzbekistan from Tajikistan, and entered into conflict with government forces. By September, however, the remaining militants were reported to have been killed by government troops. In the mean time, Uzbekistan, which had begun laying land-mines along its border with Tajikistan from mid-2000, in an effort to prevent cross-border incursions by Islamist insurgents, officially informed Tajikistan of its actions only in May 2001, although relations subsequently improved. The continued influx of illegal drugs from Tajikistan also threatened relations. President Rakhmonov met President Karimov in Uzbekistan in December; while no border agreement was reached, it was announced that the crossing between the Penjakent district in Tajikistan and Samarqand Viloyat, in Uzbekistan, was to reopen. In 2002 the Presidents of Tajikistan and Uzbekistan agreed on the demarcation of more than 85% of the two countries' shared borders.

Tajikistani-Uzbekistani relations deteriorated sharply following the suspension at the beginning of 2009 of Turkmenistan's electricity exports to Tajikistan, in response to the failure of Tajikistan and Uzbekistan to agree a transit rate. Tajikistan accused Uzbekistani state utility Uzbekenergo of interrupting deliveries of Turkmenistani electricity, and threatened to limit the amount of water flowing downstream to Uzbekistan, in order to maintain levels in its reservoirs (Tajikistan is a principal supplier of water to Uzbekistan). An additional matter of contention between the two countries was the planned construction of a hydroelectric plant at Roghun, in central Tajikistan, which was strongly opposed by Uzbekistan, owing to concerns regard-

ing the potential impact of the project on its own water supplies. Later in January Karimov and Russian President Dmitrii Medvedev issued a joint declaration, stating that any hydro-engineering projects with transboundary implications were required to meet international laws and standards. However, in February Karimov unexpectedly announced that Uzbekistan was prepared to reconsider its opposition to the project, provided that international auditors verified its viability. (In May 2012 the World Bank ordered construction on the Roghun hydroelectric project to be suspended, pending an ecological impact study.) In February 2009 First Deputy Prime Minister Azimov visited Tajikistan to attend the first bilateral high-level commission meeting in seven years; it was reported that negotiations resulted in agreement on a debt repayment schedule, and on a protocol regarding a reservoir in northern Tajikistan, although a number of fundamental issues remained unresolved. In March an agreement was reached between the national airlines of Uzbekistan and Tajikistan on the resumption of direct flights (suspended since 1992) between Tashkent and the Tajikistani capital, Dushanbe. However, relations with Tajikistan again deteriorated from late 2009, as rail traffic from Uzbekistan into Tajikistan (including non-military supplies being sent to the US-led troops in Afghanistan) was repeatedly disrupted. The Tajikistani Prime Minister, Oqil Oqilov, accused Uzbekistan of deliberately causing delays in transit, but Uzbekistan maintained that the cause of the delays was purely technical. However, in April 2010 it was reported that a spokesperson for the Uzbekistani state railways company had announced that the Government had issued a secret decree ordering the prevention of the passage of Tajikistani transit cargo through Uzbekistan. Moreover, in early 2010 a series of protests was organized in various cities in Uzbekistan, seemingly with official endorsement, ostensibly to protest against pollution allegedly being produced at the Tajikistani state-owned Talco aluminium plant in Tursunzade, western Tajikistan, and in late July some 1,400 people participated in a demonstration in Surxondaryo Viloyat organized by the Ecological Movement of Uzbekistan (a quasi-state organization with reserved parliamentary representation since the previous year) against the pollution from the plant.

Relations with Tajikistan remained strained in 2011. In November an explosion at a bridge disabled the railway line connecting Termez, near the Uzbekistani–Afghan border, with Qurghonteppa in south-western Tajikistan. The Uzbekistani authorities described the explosion as a terrorist attack. However, since this explosion did not hinder the provision of non-military supplies to US-led troops in Afghanistan, and the Uzbekistani authorities had apparently taken no action by early 2012 to repair the damage, speculation arose that the event had been deliberately orchestrated by Uzbekistan's authorities in order to disrupt the flow of goods and people between Tajikistan and Uzbekistan. In early 2013 the Uzbekistani authorities announced plans for the construction of a new railway that would bypass Tajikistan.

Relations with Russia have been intermittently strained by concerns regarding Uzbekistan's ethnic Russian population (which constituted an estimated 5.5% of the population in 1996). Uzbekistan has repeatedly refused to grant dual citizenship to its Russian minority, and since independence many thousands of these Russians have emigrated. In October 1998 Russia, Uzbekistan and Tajikistan signed a pact offering mutual military assistance, especially against 'the threat of religious extremism'; at the same time Russia and Uzbekistan signed a number of inter-governmental agreements. Uzbekistan forged closer relations with Russia in 2005, as the relations of both Uzbekistan and Russia with Western countries notably worsened, and in November Karimov and the Russian President, Vladimir Putin, signed a bilateral agreement providing for co-operation in trade and security, the use of military facilities and efforts to combat drugs-trafficking and terrorism. The two countries also agreed to provide support to the other in the event that one of them came under attack. In January 2009 Russian President Medvedev undertook a state visit to Uzbekistan to discuss issues of bilateral co-operation. Uzbekistan provided assurances that it would only export gas by way of Russia, and offered to increase the volume of gas to be allocated for purchase by Russia to an annual quota of 31,000m. cu m, after Russia agreed that the purchases would be made at market rates; additionally, the Russian energy company LUKoil was to invest some US $5,000m. in Uzbekistan's gas sector over the following seven years. In April 2010 President Karimov visited Moscow, where he again met Medvedev. In June 2012 Putin (who had returned to the Russian presidency) made an official visit to Tashkent; upon meeting with Karimov, the two Presidents signed a memorandum of understanding on Uzbekistan's membership of a CIS free trade area (which had been formally established under an agreement signed by eight other member states in October 2011), as well as a joint declaration of Uzbekistan's strategic partnership with Russia. Karimov met Putin for further discussions in Moscow in April 2013.

Following the suicide attacks in the USA in September 2001, and the commencement of US-led military action in Afghanistan, in October Uzbekistan began to deploy troops on the Uzbekistani–Afghan border. The Uzbekistani Government was reluctant to accept refugees from Afghanistan, even though 1.5m. of them were ethnic Uzbeks, citing security concerns. Initially, the Government also refused to open the border to allow humanitarian aid to reach Afghanistan. However, following the military successes of the anti-Taliban forces in November, the Government opened the 'Friendship Bridge', the only transit point into Afghanistan, in the following month. At an official summit of the heads of the Central Asian states in Tashkent in December, the leaders declared their support for the new Afghan Interim Administration, which was established following the defeat of the Taliban regime. In March 2002 the leaders of Uzbekistan and Afghanistan pledged jointly to combat terrorism and the drugs trade. In March 2013 it was announced that three Afghan militants had been killed after attacking an Uzbekistani border patrol, prompting further border security concerns; however, Afghanistan's border police commander claimed that the three nationals had been shot by Uzbekistani guards on Afghan territory.

Other external relations

Relations with the USA improved noticeably in the late 1990s, and during a visit to Tashkent in April 2000 the US Secretary of State had affirmed the USA's willingness to assist Uzbekistan in combating the spread of Islamist extremism. Following the suicide attacks on the USA of 11 September 2001, relations improved further. Uzbekistan's decision to support the US-led 'coalition against global terrorism' was of great strategic importance to the USA, which hoped to benefit from access to the country's transportation facilities. In late September the Uzbekistani Government confirmed that US military aircraft had landed at an airfield near Tashkent. In early October Uzbekistan and the USA signed a co-operation agreement, whereby Uzbekistan agreed to make its airbases available for use in humanitarian and 'search-and-rescue' operations during the US-led aerial bombardment of targets in Afghanistan. The USA also agreed that it would enter into urgent negotiations should Uzbekistan's security be threatened. In November Uzbekistan and the USA signed a number of agreements pledging to improve bilateral relations and to increase economic co-operation. Further bilateral agreements on political, economic and military co-operation were signed in January and March 2002, and Karimov visited the USA in March.

Following the violence in Andijon in May 2005, the USA urged Uzbekistan to allow an international inquiry to be undertaken. In June a US Department of State spokesperson stated that witnesses had reported the killing of hundreds of civilians by Uzbekistani government forces. Uzbekistan subsequently imposed restrictions on the USA's use of the Qarshi-Khanabad ('K-2') military base, which had been used by the USA since October 2001 to support military and other operations in Afghanistan; Uzbekistan also proposed that the USA withdraw from the airbase. In July 2005 the SCO issued a statement demanding that deadlines be imposed on the use of military bases in Central Asia by Western countries for operations in Afghanistan. Later in the month, following discussions with the USA, Uzbekistan renounced the agreement under which the USA was permitted to use the Qarshi-Khanabad airbase, and the last US military aircraft left the base in November. In April 2009 Uzbekistan signed an agreement with the USA allowing the use of Uzbekistani territory for the transit of non-military supplies to Afghanistan. In mid-August the Uzbekistani Minister of Defence and the head of US Central Command signed a bilateral agreement on military educational exchanges and training. The US Secretary of State, Hillary Clinton, visited Tashkent in December 2010, whereupon she signed an agreement on scientific and technical co-operation between the USA and Uzbekistan. In early 2012 the USA agreed to recommence provision of military aid to Uzbekistan, in exchange for Uzbekistan's continued co-operation as a transit country for supplies destined for US troops in Afghanistan. US Assistant Secretary of State Robert Blake

made an official visit to Uzbekistan in August (increasing speculation that the adoption by the Oliy Majlis of legislation prohibiting the establishment of foreign military bases on Uzbekistani territory—see Domestic Political Affairs—was intended to provide the Government with a better bargaining position). In early 2013 negotiations were underway regarding Uzbekistan's part in the impending withdrawal of the NATO-led International Security Assistance Force in Afghanistan. In February the United Kingdom announced an agreement under which Uzbekistan was to receive £450,000 of military equipment in exchange for the use of its railways and airspace in the British withdrawal from Afghanistan. Human rights organizations criticized a visit by the Uzbekistani Minister of Foreign Affairs, Abdulaziz Kamilov, to Washington, DC, USA, in March, where he met US Secretary of State John Kerry for discussions, citing ongoing human rights violations in Uzbekistan.

CONSTITUTION AND GOVERNMENT

Under the terms of the Constitution of 8 December 1992, Uzbekistan is a secular, democratic presidential republic. The directly elected President is head of state and also holds supreme executive power. The presidential term of office was extended from five years to seven years in April 2002, but in December 2011 the term was again reduced to five years, with effect from after the presidential election due in 2014. The Government (Cabinet of Ministers) is subordinate to the President, who appoints the Prime Minister, Deputy Prime Ministers and Ministers (subject to the approval of the legislature). The highest legislative body is the bicameral Oliy Majlis. The Majlis may be dissolved by the President (with the approval of the Constitutional Court). The Oliy Majlis comprises the 150-member lower chamber, the Qonunchilik palatasi (Legislative Chamber), whose members are directly elected for a five-year term, except for 15 seats that are reserved for members of the Ecological Movement of Uzbekistan. The upper chamber, the Senat (Senate), is composed of 84 members indirectly elected by regional Council members and 16 citizens appointed by the President. Judicial power is independent of government. Judges of higher courts (the Constitutional Court, the Supreme Court and the High Economic Court) are nominated by the President and confirmed by the Oliy Majlis. Uzbekistan is divided into 12 Viloyats (regions), the city of Toshkent (Tashkent), and one sovereign republic (Qoraqalpog'iston).

REGIONAL AND INTERNATIONAL CO-OPERATION

Uzbekistan is a member of the Commonwealth of Independent States (CIS, see p. 251), the Shanghai Cooperation Organization (SCO, see p. 478), the Economic Cooperation Organization (ECO, see p. 274) and the Organization for Security and Co-operation in Europe (OSCE, see p. 397).

Uzbekistan joined the UN in 1992. The country has observer status at the World Trade Organization (WTO, see p. 444).

ECONOMIC AFFAIRS

In 2011, according to the World Bank, Uzbekistan's gross national income (GNI), measured at average 2009–11 prices, was US $44,232m., equivalent to $1,510 per head (or $3,440 per head on an international purchasing-power parity basis). During 2002–11, it was estimated, the population increased by an annual average of 1.7%, while gross domestic product (GDP) per head increased, in real terms, at an average annual rate of 6.0%. Overall GDP increased, in real terms, by an average of 7.7% per year in 2002–11. According to the World Bank, growth was 8.3% in 2011.

In 2011, according to the Asian Development Bank (ADB, see p. 214), agriculture (including forestry) contributed 19.1% of GDP; the agricultural sector employed 19.8% of the working population in mid-2013, according to FAO estimates. Some 60% of the country's land is covered by desert and steppe, while the remainder comprises fertile valleys watered by two major river systems. The massive irrigation of arid areas has greatly increased production of the major crop, cotton, but has caused devastating environmental problems, particularly the desiccation of the Aral Sea. Uzbekistan is among the five largest producers of cotton in the world, and the crop accounted for 27.5% of the value of total exports in 2000. Other major crops include grain, rice, vegetables and fruit. Since independence the Government has striven to reduce the area under cultivation for cotton in order to produce more grain. Private farming was legalized in 1992, and by 1996 more than 98% of agricultural production originated in the non-state sector. According to World

Bank figures, during 2002–11 agricultural GDP increased, in real terms, at an average annual rate of 6.2%. Agricultural GDP increased by 4.0% in 2011.

According to the ADB, industry (including mining, manufacturing, utilities and construction) contributed 32.6% of GDP in 2011. It provided 13.2% of total employment in 2005. According to World Bank figures, during 2002–11 industrial GDP increased by an average of 5.4% annually, in real terms. Sectoral GDP increased by 5.0% in 2011.

Uzbekistan is well endowed with mineral deposits, in particular gold, natural gas, petroleum and coal. At the end of 2011 Uzbekistan had sufficient proven recoverable reserves of natural gas to maintain output at 2011 levels for a little over 28 years, and enough petroleum for over 19 years. There are large reserves of silver, copper, lead, zinc and tungsten, and Uzbekistan is one of the world's largest producers of uranium and gold. In 2010 some 2,830 metric tons of uranium ore was produced; all uranium mined is exported. The Murantau mine, in the Qizilkum desert, was reportedly the world's largest single open-cast gold mine, and produced a reported 74% of Uzbekistan's estimated output in 2003. In 2004 Oxus Gold and the Uzbekistani Government officially opened a further gold-mining complex in Amantaytau, 30 km from the Murantau mine. Each party had a 50% share in the mine, which had estimated reserves of some 1,400 tons.

The manufacturing sector contributed 8.6% of GDP in 2011, according to the World Bank. Significant investment has been directed to the expansion of the raw-materials processing industry. According to the World Bank, manufacturing GDP grew at an average annual rate of 3.0% in 2002–11. Sectoral GDP increased by 3.0% in 2011.

The construction sector contributed 6.6% of GDP in 2011, according to the ADB. The sector employed some 7.5% of the working population in 2000, according to official figures.

Uzbekistan is self-sufficient in natural gas, crude petroleum and coal, and became a net exporter of crude petroleum in 1995. Energy products accounted for 4.2% of the value of imports in 2000. The opening of two petroleum refineries, which had a total refining capacity of 173,000 barrels per day, significantly increased Uzbekistan's hydrocarbons capacity. In 2009 75.1% of electricity was generated by natural gas and 18.7% by hydroelectric power.

According to the ADB, the services sector contributed 48.3% of GDP in 2011. It employed 57.7% of the working population in 2005. According to World Bank figures, during 2002–11 the GDP of the services sector increased, in real terms, at an average annual rate of 9.9%. Services GDP increased by 10.5% in 2011.

In 2007, according to preliminary IMF figures, Uzbekistan recorded a visible merchandise trade surplus of US $2,296m., and there was a surplus of $4,267m. on the current account of the balance of payments. In 2011 the principal source of imports was Russia (accounting for 21.7% of the total value of imports). Other major suppliers were the Republic of Korea, the People's Republic of China and Kazakhstan. Russia was also the main market for exports in that year (accounting for 29.3% of the total value of exports); other important purchasers were Kazakhstan, China, Turkey and Afghanistan. The principal exports in 2000 were cotton fibre, energy products, metals and food products. The main imports in that year were machinery and equipment, chemicals and plastics, food products and metals. By 2000 trade with republics of the former USSR represented only about 35% of Uzbekistan's total trade, compared with some 83% in 1990.

In 2011, according to the ADB, Uzbekistan's overall budget surplus (including extrabudgetary operations) was 335,000m.

sum (equivalent to 0.4% of GDP). Uzbekistan's general government gross debt was 7,076,249m. sum in 2011, equivalent to 9.1% of GDP. At the end of 2010 Uzbekistan's total external debt was US $7,404m., of which $3,426m. was public and publicly guaranteed debt. Inflation declined at an annual average annual rate of 1.9% in 2002–11, according to ADB figures. Consumer prices increased by 7.3% in 2011. According to the ADB, in 2011 some 13,000 people (0.1% of the economically active population) were registered as unemployed, although the actual level of unemployment was believed to be considerably higher.

Uzbekistan's economy, in which the extraction of mineral resources and the production of cotton are both integral, expanded significantly during the 2000s. In the mid-2000s numerous initiatives to increase the output of natural gas were announced; in 2004 the Russian state-controlled natural gas company Gazprom and the Uzbekistani company Uzneftgazkurilish agreed a 15-year production-sharing agreement at the Shakhpakhty gas and condensate field. In 2006 Uzbekistan signed a production-sharing agreement with Gazprom for three further natural gas fields. In 2008 the Government created a free industrial-economic zone in Navoiy Viloyat, offering tax and customs preferences to foreign investors. Although the country attracted considerable investment interest, the poor business environment remained a concern (in 2012 Uzbekistan ranked only 170th of 176 countries in the Corruption Perceptions Index, published by the German-based non-governmental organization, Transparency International). Remittances from nationals living in Russia contributed an estimated 16.3% of GDP in 2012. In December 2011 the World Bank concluded a new Country Partnership Strategy with Uzbekistan, providing for financial assistance during 2012–15. In June a memorandum of understanding was signed on Uzbekistan's membership of a Commonwealth of Independent States free trade area (which had been formally established under an agreement signed by eight other member states in 2011). According to official figures, the value of Uzbekistan's energy exports increased by 81% in 2012, after the Uzbekistani section of a natural gas pipeline linking Turkmenistan and the People's Republic of China was completed in that year and exports to China commenced in August; however, domestic consumers continued to suffer from severe energy shortages, and a rise in domestic gas prices from April 2013 was announced. Sustained GDP growth of more than 8% was projected by the IMF for 2012 and the current account was in surplus in that year. In early 2013 the Uzbekistani authorities introduced a number of measures that were designed to prevent the depletion of foreign exchange reserves, including the imposition of prohibitive customs regulations on imports and of a ban on the sale of cash foreign currency; critics predicted that the new restrictions would result in dramatic increases in the price of domestic commodities and a rise in illicit trade.

PUBLIC HOLIDAYS

2014: 1 January (New Year's Day), 14 January (Defenders of the Native Land Day), 8 March (International Women's Day), 21 March (Navruz Bairam, Spring Holiday), 9 May (Memorial and Respect Day), 28 July* (Ruza Hayit, Id al-Fitr or end of Ramadan), 1 September (Independence Day), 1 October (Teachers' and Instructors' Day), 4 October* (Kurban Hayit, Id al-Adha or Feast of the Sacrifice), 8 December (Constitution Day).

*These holidays are dependent on the Islamic lunar calendar and may vary by one or two days from the dates given.

Statistical Survey

Principal source (unless otherwise indicated): The State Committee of the Republic of Uzbekistan on Statistics, 100077 Tashkent, Mustaqillik maydoni 63; tel. (71) 150-50-01; fax (71) 150-50-88; e-mail Gks@stat.uz; internet www.stat.uz.

Area and Population

AREA, POPULATION AND DENSITY

Area (sq km)	447,400*
Population (census results)†	
17 January 1979	15,389,307
12 January 1989	
Males	9,784,156
Females	10,025,921
Total	19,810,077
Population (official estimates of annual averages)	
2011	29,123,400
2012	29,555,400
2013	29,993,500
Density (per sq km) for 2013	67.0

* 172,740 sq miles.
† Figures refer to *de jure* population. The *de facto* total at the 1989 census was 19,905,158. A 'mini census' based on a sample 10% per cent of the population was conducted in April 2011 in order to improve the accuracy of official annual population estimates.

POPULATION BY AGE AND SEX
(UN estimates at mid-2013)

	Males	Females	Total
0–14	4,051,343	3,904,634	7,955,977
15–64	9,546,479	9,676,611	19,223,090
65 and over	521,506	697,587	1,219,093
Total	14,119,328	14,278,832	28,398,160

Source: UN, *World Population Prospects: The 2010 Revision.*

POPULATION BY ETHNIC GROUP
(1996, rounded estimates)

	%
Uzbek	80.0
Russian	5.5
Tajik	5.0
Kazakh	3.0
Karakalpak	2.5
Tatar	1.5
Others	2.5
Total	100.0

Source: Ministry of Health, Tashkent.

ADMINISTRATIVE DIVISIONS
(1996, rounded figures, official estimates)

	Area (sq km)	Population	Density (per sq km)	Capital city (with population)
Sovereign Republic:				
Qoraqalpog'iston .	165,600	1,400,000	8.5	Nukus (236,700)
Viloyats				
Andijon . . .	4,200	1,899,000	452.1	Andijon (303,000)
Buxoro . . .	39,400	1,384,700	35.2	Buxoro (263,400)
Farg'ona . .	6,800	2,597,000	381.9	Farg'ona (214,000)
Jizzax . . .	20,500	910,500	44.4	Jizzax (127,200)
Namangan . .	7,900	1,862,000	235.7	Namangan (341,000)
Navoiy . . .	110,800	767,500	6.9	Navoiy (128,000)
Qashqadaryo .	28,400	2,029,000	71.4	Qarshi (177,000)
Samarqand . .	16,400	2,322,000	141.6	Samarqand (366,000)
Sirdaryo . .	5,100	648,100	127.1	Guliston (54,000)
Surxondaryo .	20,800	1,676,000	80.6	Termiz (95,000)
Tashkent* . .	15,300	4,450,000	290.9	Tashkent (2,100,000)
Xorazm . . .	6,300	1,200,000	190.5	Urgench (135,000)
Total	447,400	23,145,800	51.7	

* Including Tashkent city, which subsequently assumed a separate administrative status.

Source: Government of Uzbekistan.

PRINCIPAL TOWNS
(estimated population at 1 January 2001)

Tashkent (the capital) . . .	2,137,218		Farg'ona . . .	183,037
Namangan . . .	391,297		Margilan . . .	149,646
Samarqand . . .	361,339		Chirchik . . .	141,742
Andijon	338,366		Urgench	138,609
Buxoro	237,361		Navoiy	138,082
Nukus	212,012		Jizzax	131,512
Qarshi	204,690		Termiz	116,467
Qoqand	197,450		Olmaliq	113,114

Source: UN, *Demographic Yearbook.*

Mid-2011 ('000, incl. suburbs, UN estimate): Tashkent 2,227 (Source: UN, *World Urbanization Prospects: The 2011 Revision*).

BIRTHS, MARRIAGES AND DEATHS

	Registered live births		Registered marriages		Registered deaths	
	Number	Rate (per 1,000)	Number	Rate (per 1,000)	Number	Rate (per 1,000)
2005 . .	533,500	20.3	184,000	7.0	140,600	5.4
2006 . .	555,900	20.9	208,500	7.8	139,600	5.3
2007 . .	608,900	22.6	254,200	9.4	137,400	5.1
2008 . .	646,100	23.9	250,200	9.2	138,800	5.1
2009 . .	651,300	23.7	272,100	10.0	133,600	4.9
2010 . .	634,800	22.7	292,300	10.4	138,400	4.9
2011 . .	626,900	21.5	289,000	9.9	144,600	5.0

Note: Numbers are rounded to the nearest 100 persons.

Life expectancy (years at birth): 68.3 (males 65.2; females 71.5) in 2011 (Source: World Bank, World Development Indicators database).

EMPLOYMENT

(annual averages, '000 persons)

	1998	1999	2000
Agriculture*	3,467	3,213	3,083
Industry†	1,114	1,124	1,145
Construction	573	640	676
Transport and communications	362	370	382
Trade and catering‡	717	735	754
Other services	1,976	2,042	2,042
Housing, public utilities and personal services	235	240	246
Health care, social security, physical culture and sports	502	538	567
Education, culture and art	1,073	1,094	1,120
Banking and insurance	50	48	51
General administration	111	122	126
Information and computer services	.5	—	—
Total (incl. others)	**8,800**	**8,885**	**8,983**

* Including forestry.
† Comprising manufacturing (except printing and publishing), mining and quarrying, electricity, gas, water, logging, and fishing.
‡ Including material and technical supply.

Source: Center for Economic Research, Tashkent, *Uzbek Economic Trends*.

2011 ('000 persons): Total employed 11,919 (Agriculture 3,240, Industry 1,564, Other 7,115) (Source: Asian Development Bank).

Total employed ('000 persons): 11,328 in 2009; 11,628 in 2010; 11,919 in 2011 (Source: Asian Development Bank).

Unemployed ('000 persons registered): 20 in 2009; 16 in 2010; 13 in 2011 (Source: Asian Development Bank).

Mid-2013 ('000, estimates): Agriculture, etc. 2,658; Total labour force 13,439 (Source: FAO).

Health and Welfare

KEY INDICATORS

Total fertility rate (children per woman, 2010)	2.4
Under-5 mortality rate (per 1,000 live births, 2010)	52
HIV/AIDS (% of persons aged 15–49, 2009)	0.1
Physicians (per 1,000 head, 2009)	2.6
Hospital beds (per 1,000 head, 2009)	4.6
Health expenditure (2009): US $ per head (PPP)	177
Health expenditure (2009): % of GDP	5.9
Health expenditure (2009): public (% of total)	45.3
Access to water (% of persons, 2010)	87
Total carbon dioxide emissions ('000 metric tons, 2008)	124,905.4
Carbon dioxide emissions per head (metric tons, 2008)	4.6
Human Development Index (2011): ranking	115
Human Development Index (2011): value	0.641

For sources and definitions, see explanatory note on p. vi.

Agriculture

PRINCIPAL CROPS

('000 metric tons)

	2009	2010	2011
Wheat	6,637.7	6,730.4	6,526.7
Rice, paddy	194	207	120
Barley*	210	170	145
Maize	231	232	256
Sorghum*	20	18	15
Potatoes	1,525	1,630	1,824
Broad beans, horse beans, dry*	11	10	9
Sunflower seed*	13	12	12
Safflower seed†	3	3	3
Sesame seed†	17	16	14
Seed cotton	3,420	3,443	2,980
Cabbages and other brassicas*	486	540	595
Tomatoes*	2,110	2,347	2,585
Cucumbers and gherkins*	350	390	430
Onions, dry*	795	884	975
Garlic*	49	55	60
Carrots and turnips*	995	1,107	1,220

—continued	2009	2010	2011
Watermelons	1,071	1,182	1,295
Apples*	635	712	779
Pears*	65	73	80
Apricots*	292	325	356
Sweet cherries*	67	75	82
Peaches and nectarines*	82	92	101
Plums and sloes*	70	78	85
Grapes	900	987	1,090
Tobacco, unmanufactured†	16	11	11
Jute†	21	20	19

* Unofficial figures.
† FAO estimates.

Aggregate production ('000 metric tons, may include official, semi-official or estimated data): Total cereals 7,358 in 2009, 7,416 in 2010, 7,114 in 2011; Total roots and tubers 1,525 in 2009, 1,630 in 2010, 1,824 in 2011; Total vegetables (incl. melons) 6,776 in 2009, 7,529 in 2010, 8,289 in 2011; Total fruits (excl. melons) 2,443 in 2009, 2,698 in 2010, 2,961 in 2011.

Source: FAO.

LIVESTOCK

('000 head at 1 January)

	2009	2010	2011
Horses	175	181	187
Cattle	8,025	8,511	9,094
Camels*	17	20	20
Pigs*	92	92	94
Sheep†	11,405	12,157	12,917
Goats†	2,154	2,281	2,424
Chickens†	29,100	34,820	37,250
Turkeys†	400	450	480

* FAO estimates.
† Unofficial figures.

Source: FAO.

LIVESTOCK PRODUCTS

('000 metric tons)

	2009	2010	2011
Cattle meat*	622.7	665.3	763.0
Sheep meat*	93.4	100.0	115.0
Pig meat*	20.0	21.0	24.0
Chicken meat*	25.0	27.0	30.7
Cows' milk*	5,732.4	6,120.0	6,712.2
Goats' milk*	46.2	48.5	53.2
Hen eggs*	148.7	170.9	192.3
Other poultry eggs*	3.9	4.4	5.0
Honey†	2.0	3.3	3.0
Wool, greasy	25.0	26.5	28.7

* Unofficial figures.
† FAO estimates.

Source: FAO.

Fishing

(metric tons, live weight)

	2008	2009	2010*
Capture	2,731	6,051	4,078
Common carp	630	1,636	1,100
Crucian carp	10	289	200
Roach	504	481	320
Silver carp	309	607	400
Aquaculture*	4,100	5,162	6,654
Common carp	600*	855	950
Crucian carp*	30	40	60
Grass carp (White amur)	250*	618	800
Silver carp	3,100*	3,504	4,500
Bighead carp*	50	50	80
Total catch*	**6,831**	**11,213**	**10,732**

* FAO estimate(s).

Source: FAO.

Mining

(metric tons unless otherwise indicated)

	2008	2009	2010
Coal ('000 metric tons)* . . .	3,092	3,553	3,102
Crude petroleum ('000 metric			
tons)†	2,533	2,331	1,866
Natural gas ('000 million cu m) .	68	65	59
Copper ore‡‖	92,000	92,000	92,000
Molybdenum ore‖‡	500	500	500
Silver ore (kilograms)‖ . . .	74,648	52,876	59,097
Gold (kilograms)‡‖	85,000	90,000	90,000
Kaolin ('000 metric tons)‡ . . .	5,500	5,500	5,500
Fluorspar‡	90	90	90
Uranium ore (metric tons)‖ . .	2,757	2,865	2,830

* Including lignite and brown coal.
† Including gas condensate.
‡ Estimated production.
‖ Figures refer to the metal content of ores.

Source: US Geological Survey.

Crude petroleum ('000 metric tons): 4,455 in 2009; 3,649 in 2010; 3,585 in 2011 (Source: BP, *Statistical Review of World Energy*).

Natural gas (excl. flared or recycled, million cu m): 60,000 in 2009; 59,638 in 2010; 57,014 in 2011 (Source: BP, *Statistical Review of World Energy*).

Industry

SELECTED PRODUCTS
('000 metric tons unless otherwise indicated)

	2009	2010	2011
Flour	1,270.1	1,217.3	1,470.8
Sugar (granulated)	275.1	286.1	322.7
Beer ('000 hectolitres)	1,811.2	2,500.0	n.a.
Vodka and other spirits ('000			
hectolitres)	943.5	959.3	1,136.6
Cigarettes, etc. (million) . . .	12,747	13,949	n.a.
Cotton yarn	145.5	185.8	n.a.
Knitwear articles ('000 pieces) .	33,968	50,500	68,000
Sulphuric acid	954.6	1,189.7	n.a.
Chemical fertilizers	1,073.2	1,134.6	1,171.7
Motor spirit (petrol)	1,621.9	1,443.6	1,308.2
Gas-diesel (distillate fuel) oils .	1,302.3	1,125.1	n.a.
Residual fuel oils	498.6	n.a.	n.a.
Lubricating oils	278.5	n.a.	260.3
Kerosene	405.7	372.8	n.a.
Cement	6,852.8	6,871.7	6,698.0
Window glass ('000 sq m) . . .	10,267.1	12,599.4	n.a.
Finished steel	731.7	691.6	709.9
Refrigerators and freezers (units) .	17,421	18,893	19,140
Motor cars	205,011	217,700	221,400
Buses	1,317	1,268	964
Tractors	2,737	2,539	n.a.
Tractor cultivators	1,852	n.a.	n.a.
Electric energy (million kWh) . .	50,000	51,700	52,400

Finance

CURRENCY AND EXCHANGE RATES

Monetary Units
100 teen = 1 sum.

Sterling, Dollar and Euro Equivalents (30 November 2012)
£1 sterling = 3,161.6 sum;
US $1 = 1,969.0 sum;
€1 = 2,556.9 sum;
10,000 sum = £3.16 = $5.08 = €3.91.

Average Exchange Rate (sum per US $)
2010   1,589.3
2011   1,719.2

CONSOLIDATED BUDGET
('000 million sum)

Revenue	2006	2007*	2008†
Tax revenue	4,365	5,870	6,791
Taxes on incomes and profits .	1,293	1,758	2,002
Taxes on property	276	349	438
Taxes on goods and services .	2,623	3,470	4,104
VAT	1,142	1,682	2,001
Excises	881	1,017	1,170
Customs duties	173	293	248
Other budget revenue	333	522	317
Social security contributions . .	1,253	1,761	2,650
Road fund and other extra-			
budgetary revenue	273	355	412
Education development tax . .	233	365	431
Grants	62	50	30
Total	6,519	8,922	10,632

Expenditure‡	2006	2007*	2008†
Socio-cultural expenditure . .	2,169	2,906	3,910
Social safety net	1,735	2,283	3,400
Low-income support . . .	366	397	620
Pension and employment fund .	1,369	1,886	2,780
Pension fund	1,335	1,841	2,726
Employment fund	35	45	54
Economy	594	678	915
Public authorities and			
administration	124	176	243
Public investment	532	627	847
Interest expenditure	74	172	103
Other expenditure in the budget .	879	1,138	1,078
Road fund	204	270	349
Extra-budgetary expenditure			
financed by grants	62	50	30
Statistical discrepancy . . .	—	155	—
Total	6,374	8,455	10,875

* Preliminary.
† Projected.
‡ Excluding net lending ('000 million): 40 in 2006; 48 in 2007 (preliminary); −90 in 2008 (projected).

Source: IMF, *Republic of Uzbekistan: 2008 Article IV Consultation-Staff Report; Public Information Notice on the Executive Board Discussion; and Statement by the Executive Director for the Republic of Uzbekistan* (July 2008).

2009 ('000 million sum): Total revenue 10,840; Total expenditure 10,764 (Source: Asian Development Bank).

2010 ('000 million sum): Total revenue 13,597; Total expenditure 13,387 (Source: Asian Development Bank).

2011 ('000 million sum): Total revenue 17,061; Total expenditure 16,726 (Source: Asian Development Bank).

INTERNATIONAL RESERVES
(US $ million at 31 December)

	2002	2003	2004
Gold (national valuation) . . .	505.8	558.0	418.5
IMF special drawing rights . .	1.1	0.1	0.0
Foreign exchange	709.8	1,101.2	1,728.0
Total	1,215.0	1,659.3	2,146.5

Total reserves (US $ million at 31 December): 412.7 in 2009; 405.4 in 2010.

Source: Asian Development Bank.

MONEY SUPPLY
('000 million sum at 31 December)

	2006	2007	2008
Currency outside banks . . .	1,495	2,048	2,528
Demand deposits at deposit money banks	491	1,061	1,415
Total money	1,986	3,109	3,943

Source: Asian Development Bank.

COST OF LIVING
(Consumer Price Index; base: previous year = 100)

	2009	2010	2011
Food	104.4	104.8	103.5
Other goods	105.0	105.3	108.3
All items	107.8	107.6	107.3

Source: Asian Development Bank.

NATIONAL ACCOUNTS
('000 million sum at current prices)

Expenditure on the Gross Domestic Product

	2009	2010	2011
Final consumption expenditure.	31,722.4	40,436.4	51,572.4
Households			
Non-profit institutions serving households	24,083.4	30,565.2	39,768.7
General government . . .	7,639.0	9,871.2	11,803.7
Gross capital formation . . .	14,786.9	16,568.3	19,443.3
Gross fixed capital formation .	13,998.9	17,036.6	20,738.7
Acquisitions, less disposals, of valuables	788.0	−468.3	−1,295.4
Changes in inventories . .			
Total domestic expenditure .	46,509.3	57,004.7	71,015.7
Exports of goods and services .	17,275.6	20,668.1	25,726.7
Less Imports of goods and services	14,409.3	15,284.5	18,991.8
GDP in market prices . .	49,375.6	62,388.3	77,750.6

Gross Domestic Product by Economic Activity

	2009	2010	2011
Agriculture and forestry . .	9,200.0	11,226.0	13,685.2
Mining and quarrying . . .			
Manufacturing	11,651.1	14,882.5	18,632.0
Electricity, gas and water . .			
Construction	3,335.7	4,033.5	4,714.2
Trade	4,381.1	5,781.4	6,863.4
Transport and communications	5,721.9	7,181.9	9,129.9
Finance			
Public administration . . .	10,321.6	13,566.1	18,622.9
Other services			
GDP at factor cost . . .	44,611.4	56,671.4	71,647.6
Indirect taxes			
Less Subsidies	4,764.2	5,716.9	6,103.0
GDP in purchasers' values .	49,375.6	62,388.3	77,750.6

Source: Asian Development Bank.

BALANCE OF PAYMENTS
(US $ million)

	2005	2006	2007*
Exports of goods f.o.b.	4,757	5,615	8,026
Imports of goods f.o.b.	−3,310	−3,841	−5,730
Trade balance	1,446	1,774	2,296
Export of services	659	775	965
Import of services	−790	−828	−1,007
Balance on goods and services	1,315	1,721	2,254
Income (net)	−24	41	62
Current transfers (net) . . .	658	1,171	1,951
Current balance	1,949	2,933	4,267
Capital account (net)	31	−116	−104
Foreign direct and portfolio investment (net)	88	195	739
Existing public and publicly guaranteed debt (net) . . .	−241	−347	−213
Commercial non-guaranteed debt (net)	34	43	273
Foreign assets of commercial banks (net)	—	−290	−433
Other capital and statistical discrepancy	−1,093	−854	−2,430
Adjustment	—	—	56
Overall balance	768	1,564	2,155

* Preliminary figures.

Source: IMF, *Republic of Uzbekistan: 2008 Article IV Consultation-Staff Report; Public Information Notice on the Executive Board Discussion; and Statement by the Executive Director for the Republic of Uzbekistan* (July 2008).

External Trade

PRINCIPAL COMMODITIES
(US $ million)

Imports f.o.b.	1998	1999	2000
Chemicals and plastics . . .	407.2	363.0	399.5
Metals	303.6	245.4	253.5
Machinery and equipment . .	1,553.7	1,393.5	1,044.1
Food products	512.2	408.1	361.1
Energy products	16.3	66.6	112.7
Total (incl. others)	3,288.7	3,110.7	2,696.4

Exports f.o.b.	1998	1999	2000
Cotton fibre	1,361.0	883.7	897.1
Chemicals and plastics . . .	51.7	101.8	93.4
Metals	180.7	138.9	216.7
Machinery and equipment . .	146.6	103.2	111.8
Food products	111.9	206.7	176.4
Energy products	277.8	371.5	335.2
Total (incl. others)	3,528.2	3,235.8	3,264.7

Source: Center for Economic Research, Tashkent, *Uzbek Economic Trends*.

2009 (US $ million, official estimates): Total imports 9,438.3; Total exports 11,771.3.

2010 (US $ million, official estimates): Total imports 9,175.8; Total exports 13,023.4.

2011 (US $ million, official estimates): Total imports 10,509.9; Total exports 15,027.2.

PRINCIPAL TRADING PARTNERS
(US $ million)

Imports	2009	2010	2011
Belarus	143.5	112.6	133.6
Brazil	181.6	231.6	299.8
China, People's Republic	1,562.4	1,252.0	1,294.5
France	70.3	86.3	134.0
Germany	417.0	442.6	517.6
India	101.6	123.8	137.6
Italy	147.8	134.8	172.8
Japan	124.0	106.0	147.1
Kazakhstan	793.5	997.1	1,097.6
Korea, Republic	1,125.8	1,457.6	1,485.6
Latvia	104.8	53.6	117.5
Russia	2,190.7	1,988.0	2,282.8
Turkey	267.1	244.8	277.4
Turkmenistan	60.7	148.5	285.7
Ukraine	834.9	378.2	485.9
USA	221.1	132.1	177.6
Total (incl. others)	9,438.3	9,175.8	10,509.9

Exports	2009	2010	2011
Afghanistan	703.8	655.6	797.7
China, People's Republic	489.0	931.8	1,302.2
France	119.3	88.6	220.3
Iran	538.0	595.4	378.4
Kazakhstan	513.7	886.5	1,673.2
Korea, Republic	102.6	164.0	142.5
Kyrgyzstan	136.3	105.2	94.2
Russia	2,257.2	4,154.8	4,405.5
Singapore	67.5	171.2	70.0
Switzerland	1,586.1	45.8	16.2
Tajikistan	143.5	120.7	119.0
Turkey	406.9	722.5	910.2
Turkmenistan	125.0	120.7	168.6
Ukraine	691.1	184.5	180.0
USA	146.6	51.3	72.2
Total (incl. others)	11,771.3	13,023.4	15,027.2

Transport

RAILWAYS
(traffic)

	2009	2010	2011
Passengers carried (million)	14	15	15
Passenger-km (million)	2,609	2,920	3,039
Freight carried (million metric tons)	66	57	60
Freight ton-km (million)	24,200	22,200	22,533

CIVIL AVIATION
(traffic on scheduled services)

	2009	2010	2011
Passengers carried ('000)	1,500	1,900	2,200
Passenger-km (million)	4,919	5,768	6,246
Freight carried ('000 metric tons)	15	29	31
Total ton-km (million)	104	168	162

Kilometres flown (million): 44 in 2007; 45 in 2008; 45 in 2009 (Source: UN, *Statistical Yearbook*).

Tourism

FOREIGN VISITOR ARRIVALS
('000, incl. excursionists)

Region of origin	2007	2008	2009
Africa	2.0	2.5	0.1
Americas	8.0	8.0	6.5
East Asia and the Pacific	442.7	578.6	649.3
Europe	370.4	385.2	333.2
Middle East	50.0	55.0	66.8
South Asia	30.0	40.0	158.8
Total	903.1	1,069.3	1,214.7

Total foreign visitor arrivals ('000): 975 in 2010.

Tourism receipts (US $ million, excl. passenger transport): 64 in 2008; 99 in 2009; 121 in 2010.

Source: World Tourism Organization.

Communications Media

	2009	2010	2011
Telephones ('000 main lines in use)	1,856.6	1,863.6	1,927.7
Mobile cellular telephones ('000 subscribers)	16,417.9	20,952.0	25,441.8
Internet subscribers ('000)	2,737.3	n.a.	n.a.
Broadband subscribers ('000)	88.7	89.1	147.8

Source: International Telecommunication Union.

Education

(2011/12 unless otherwise indicated)

	Schools	Teachers	Students
Pre-primary	4,978	55,218	52,515
Primary	} 9,763*	416,188	{ 1,905,693†
Secondary:			
general			5,715,100‡
teacher training	5.	2,027	26,358
vocational	1,052‡	7,900†	214,500†
Higher	63§	18,400†	263,600§
Universities	20†	n.a.	131,100†

* Including 20 evening schools.
† 1994/95.
‡ 2006.
§ 2004.

Sources: UNESCO, *Statistical Yearbook*, and Center for Economic Research, Tashkent.

Pupil-teacher ratio (primary education, UNESCO estimate): 15.6 in 2010/11 (Source: UNESCO Institute for Statistics).

Adult literacy rate (UNESCO estimates): 99.4% (males 99.6%; females 99.2%) in 2010 (Source: UNESCO Institute for Statistics).

Directory

The Government

HEAD OF STATE

President of the Republic: ISLAM KARIMOV (elected by Supreme Soviet 24 March 1990; term of office extended by popular referendum 26 March 1995; re-elected 9 January 2000 and 23 December 2007; inaugurated 16 January 2008).

CABINET OF MINISTERS
(May 2013)

Prime Minister: SHAVKAT MIRZIYOYEV.

First Deputy Prime Minister, Minister of Finance, responsible for Macroeconomic Development, Structural Economic Transformation and Integrated Regional Development: RUSTAM AZIMOV.

Deputy Prime Minister, Chairman of the State Committee for Architecture and Construction, responsible for Municipal Services, Transport, Capital Works and the Construction Industry: BOTIR ZOKIROV.

Deputy Prime Minister, responsible for Geology, Fuel and Energy and the Chemical, Petrochemical and Metallurgical Industries: G'ULOMJON IBRAGIMOV.

Deputy Prime Minister, Chairman of O'zavtosanoat Joint-Stock Co, responsible for the Development of Mechanical Engineering, the Electro-technical and Aviation Industries, and the Standardization of Production: ULUG'BEK ROZUKULOV.

Deputy Prime Minister, responsible for Culture, Education, Health and Social Welfare: ADXAM IKRAMOV.

Deputy Prime Minister, responsible for Information Systems and Telecommunications: (vacant).

Deputy Prime Minister, Chairman of the Committee of Women of Uzbekistan: ELMIRA BASITHANOVA.

Minister of the Economy: GALINA SAIDOVA.

Minister of Labour and Social Protection: AKTAM XAITOV.

Minister of Culture and Sports: MINXAJIDIN XODJIMATOV.

Minister of Internal Affairs: BAHODIR MATLYUBOV.

Minister of Foreign Affairs: ABDULAZIZ KAMILOV.

Minister of Foreign Economic Relations, Investment and Trade: ELYOR G'ANIYEV.

Minister of Defence: QOBUL BERDIYEV.

Minister of Higher and Specialized Secondary Education: BAXODIR XODIYEV.

Minister of National Education: ULUG'BEK INOYATOV.

Minister of Agriculture and Water Resources: ZAFAR RUZIEV.

Minister of Justice: NIG'MATILLA YO'LDOSHEV.

Minister of Health: ANVAR ALIMOV.

Minister of Emergency Situations: TURSINXON XUDAYBERGANOV.

Note: The Constitution provides for the Chairman of the Council of Ministers of the Republic of Qoraqalpog'iston to serve as an ex officio member of the Cabinet of Ministers of the Republic of Uzbekistan. Since March 2006 this position has been held by BAXODIR YANGI-BOYEV. The following are also members of the Cabinet of Ministers: the Chairman of the State Tax Committee, the Chairman of the State Customs Committee and the Chairmen of the State Committees for: Privatization, Demonopolization and the Development of Competition; Geology and Mineral Resources; Statistics; Architecture and Construction; Land Resources, Geodesy, Cartography and the State Cadastre; the Protection of the Environment; and Communications, Informatization and Telecommunications Technologies.

MINISTRIES

Office of the President: 100163 Tashkent, O'zbekiston shoh ko'ch. 43; tel. (71) 239-54-04; fax (71) 239-53-25; e-mail presidents_office@press-service.uz; internet www.press-service.uz.

Office of the Cabinet of Ministers: 100078 Tashkent, Mustaqillik maydoni 5; tel. (71) 239-82-95; fax (71) 239-84-63; internet www.gov.uz.

Ministry of Agriculture and Water Resources: 100004 Tashkent, A. Navoiy ko'ch. 4; tel. (712) 241-00-42; fax (712) 244-23-97; e-mail info@agro.uz; internet www.agro.uz.

Ministry of Culture and Sports: 100159 Tashkent, Mustaqillik maydoni 5; tel. (71) 139-83-31; fax (71) 139-46-11; e-mail minister@mcs.uz; internet uz.mcs.uz.

Ministry of Defence: 100000 Tashkent, Ak. Abdullaev ko'ch. 100; tel. (71) 269-82-43; fax (71) 268-48-67.

Ministry of the Economy: 100003 Tashkent, O'zbekiston shoh ko'ch. 45A; tel. (71) 232-63-20; fax (71) 232-63-72; e-mail info@mineconomy.uz; internet www.mineconomy.uz.

Ministry of Emergency Situations: 100084 Tashkent, Yunusobod tumani, Kichik xalka yo'li 4; tel. (71) 239-16-85; fax (71) 150-62-99; e-mail it@mchs.gov.uz; internet www.mchs.gov.uz.

Ministry of Finance: 100008 Tashkent, Mustaqillik maydoni 5; tel. (71) 233-70-73; fax (71) 244-56-43; e-mail iyuldashev@mf.uz; internet www.mf.uz.

Ministry of Foreign Affairs: 100029 Tashkent, O'zbekiston shoh ko'ch. 9; tel. (71) 233-64-75; fax (71) 239-15-17; e-mail info@tiv.uz; internet www.mfa.uz.

Ministry of Foreign Economic Relations, Investment and Trade: 100029 Tashkent, Shevchenko ko'ch. 1; tel. and fax (71) 238-51-00; e-mail secretary@mfer.uz; internet www.mfer.uz.

Ministry of Health: 100011 Tashkent, A. Navoiy ko'ch. 12; tel. (71) 242-16-91; fax (71) 244-10-33; e-mail info@minzdrav.uz; internet www.minzdrav.uz.

Ministry of Higher and Specialized Secondary Education: 100095 Tashkent, 2-Chimboy ko'ch. 96; tel. and fax (71) 246-01-95; e-mail devonxona@edu.uz; internet www.edu.uz.

Ministry of Internal Affairs: 100029 Tashkent, Yu. Rajaby ko'ch. 1; tel. (71) 233-66-46; fax (71) 233-38-82; e-mail info@mvd.uz; internet www.mvd.uz.

Ministry of Justice: 100047 Tashkent, Sayilgoh ko'ch. 5; tel. (71) 233-13-05; fax (71) 233-48-44; e-mail info@minjust.gov.uz; internet www.minjust.uz.

Ministry of Labour and Social Protection: 100100 Tashkent, A. Avloniy ko'ch. 20A; tel. and fax (71) 239-41-12; e-mail info@mexnat.uz; internet www.mexnat.uz.

Ministry of National Education: 100078 Tashkent, Mustaqillik maydoni 5; tel. (71) 239-17-35; fax (71) 239-42-14; e-mail press@mno.uz; internet www.uzedu.uz.

President

Presidential Election, 23 December 2007

Candidate	Votes	%
Islam Karimov (Movement of Entrepreneurs and Businessmen—Liberal Democratic Party of Uzbekistan)	13,008,357	88.10
Asliddin Rustamov (People's Democratic Party of Uzbekistan)	468,064	3.17
Dilorom Tashmuhamedova (Justice Social Democratic Party of Uzbekistan)	434,111	2.94
Akmal Saidov (Independent)	420,815	2.85
Total*	**14,765,444**	**100.00**

* Including 434,097 invalid votes (2.94% of the total).

Legislature

The Oliy Majlis (Supreme Assembly) is a bicameral legislative body, comprising the 100-member upper chamber, the Senat (Senate), and the 150-member lower chamber, the Qonunchilik palatasi (Legislative Chamber).

Qonunchilik palatasi
(Legislative Chamber)

100035 Tashkent, Bunyedkor ko'ch. 1; tel. (71) 239-87-07; fax (71) 239-41-51; e-mail info@parliament.gov.uz; internet www.parliament.gov.uz.

Speaker: DILOROM H. TASHMUHAMEDOVA.

General Election, 27 December 2009 and 10 January 2010

Parties and groups	Seats
Movement of Entrepreneurs and Businessmen—Liberal Democratic Party of Uzbekistan . . .	53
People's Democratic Party of Uzbekistan . .	32
National Revival Democratic Party of Uzbekistan (Milliy Tiklanish)	31
Justice Social Democratic Party of Uzbekistan (Adolat)	19
Total*	150

* Including 15 seats reserved for members of the Ecological Movement of Uzbekistan.

Senat
(Senate)

100029 Tashkent, Mustaqillik maydoni 6; tel. (71) 238-26-66; fax (71) 238-29-01; e-mail info@senat.uz; internet www.senat.uz.

Of the 100 members of the chamber, 84 members are indirectly elected by regional Council members and 16 are appointed by the President of the Republic. Following the indirect elections of senators, conducted on 20–22 January 2010, the presidential appointees to the Senat were announced on 22 January.

Speaker: ILGIZAR M. SOBIROV.

Election Commission

Central Election Commission (O'zbekiston Respublikasi Markaziy Saylov Kommissiyasi): 100078 Tashkent, Mustaqillik maydoni 6; tel. and fax (71) 239-15-72; internet www.elections.uz; mems approved by the Oliy Majlis; Chair. MIRZO-ULUG'BEK E. ABDUSALOMOV.

Political Organizations

Following Uzbekistan's independence, the ruling People's Democratic Party of Uzbekistan (PDPU) took increasingly repressive measures against opposition parties. The Movement of Entrepreneurs and Businessmen—Liberal Democratic Party of Uzbekistan, which effectively succeeded the PDPU as the 'party of power' in the 2000s (although the PDPU continued to play a substantial role in national life), continued to implement similarly restrictive policies. From February 2004 the minimum membership requirement for parties was increased from 5,000 to 20,000 people. The Ecological Movement of Uzbekistan, founded in 2008, has had a reserved allocation of 15 seats in the Oliy Majlis since late 2009. Since independence a number of opposition elements have been based abroad, particularly in Russia.

Ecological Movement of Uzbekistan (O'zbekiston Ekologik Harakati): 100027 Tashkent, Bunyodkor ko'ch. 1A; tel. (71) 227-44-95; fax (71) 245-96-32; e-mail info@eco.uz; internet www.eco.uz; f. 2008; holds legal entitlement to 15 reserved seats in the Oliy Majlis; Chair. BORIY B. ALIXONOV.

Free Peasants' Party (Ozod Dehqonlar partiyasi—Ozod Dehqonlar): 100000 Tashkent; f. 2003; denied registration; Exec. Sec. of Political Council NIGORA HIDOYATOVA; Ideological Leader BABUR MALIKOV (in USA).

Freedom Democratic Party of Uzbekistan (O'zbekiston Erk Demokratik Partiyasi—Erk): 100055 Tashkent, Ipakchi ko'ch. 38; tel. (71) 220-65-30; e-mail admin@uzbekistanerk.org; internet www.uzbekistanerk.com; f. 1990; banned in 1993; Chair. MUHAMMAD SALIH (in Norway).

Justice Social Democratic Party of Uzbekistan ('Adolat' Sotsial Demokratik Partiyasi—Adolat): 100043 Tashkent, Shark tongi ko'ch. 23; tel. (71) 288-46-64; e-mail info@adolat.uz; internet www.adolat.uz; f. 1995; advocates respect of human rights, improvement of social justice and consolidation of democratic reform; supports President Karimov; Pres. ISMOIL SAIFNAZAROV; 82,000 mems (2012).

Movement of Entrepreneurs and Businessmen—Liberal Democratic Party of Uzbekistan (Tadbirkorlar va Ishbilarmonlar Harakati—O'zbekiston Liberal Demokratik Partiyasi—O'zlidep): 100015 Tashkent, Mirobod tumani, Nukus ko'ch. 73A; tel. (71) 255-92-90; fax (71) 255-62-11; e-mail uzlidep@intal.uz; internet www.uzlidep.uz; f. 2003; supports President Karimov; Chair. MUXAMMADYUSUF M. TESHABAEV; 161,758 members (Aug. 2009).

National Revival Democratic Party of Uzbekistan (O'zbekiston Milliy Tiklanish Demokratik Partiyasi—Milliy Tiklanish): 100129 Tashkent, A. Navoiy ko'ch. 30; tel. (71) 239-45-77; fax (71) 239-45-53; e-mail uzmtdpmk@mail.ru; internet www.mt.uz; f. 1995; supports

President Karimov; merged with Self-Sacrificers' National Democratic Party 2008; Leader AXTAM TURSUNOV; 124,223 mems (Jan. 2012).

People's Democratic Party of Uzbekistan (O'zbekiston Xalq demokratik partiyasi): 100029 Tashkent, Mustaqillik maydoni 5/3; tel. (71) 239-83-11; fax (71) 239-48-73; e-mail info@xdp.uz; internet www.xdp.uz; f. 1991; successor of Communist Party of the Uzbek SSR; Chair. of Bd LATIF GULYAMOV; 346,800 mems (Jul. 2009).

Unity People's Movement Party ('Birlik' Xalq Harakati Partiyasi—Birlik): c/o Andijon Viloyat, Shahrihan, A. Ikromov ko'ch. 2; tel. (74) 342-19-00; e-mail postmaster@harakat.net; internet www.birlik.net; f. 1988; leading opposition group, banned in 1992; registered as a social movement; refused registration as a political party 2004; Co-Chair. Prof. ABDURAKHIM PULAT, PULATJAN AHUNOV.

The transnational militant Islamist **Hizb-ut-Tahrir al-Islami (Party of Islamic Liberation)** was believed to operate in Uzbekistan. As in neighbouring states, the organization was proscribed in Uzbekistan.

Diplomatic Representation

EMBASSIES IN UZBEKISTAN

Afghanistan: 100000 Tashkent, Kichik Beshyog ko'ch. 79; tel. (71) 140-41-34; fax (71) 140-41-33; e-mail afgemuz@mail.tps.uz; Ambassador MUHAMMAD SODIQ DAUDZAI.

Algeria: 100000 Tashkent, Beshog'aynilar ko'ch. 46; tel. (71) 281-55-65; fax (71) 120-61-80; Ambassador RAMDANE MEKDOUD.

Azerbaijan: 100000 Tashkent, Sharq Tongi ko'ch. 25; tel. (71) 273-61-67; fax (71) 273-26-58; e-mail sefiruz@gmail.com; internet www.azembassy.uz; Ambassador HUSEYN GULIYEV.

Bangladesh: 100015 Tashkent, Vasit Vaxidov ko'ch. 33; tel. (71) 254-04-21; fax (71) 120-67-11; e-mail mission.tashkent@mofa.gov.bd; internet www.bangladeshembtashkent.uz; Ambassador MOHAMMED IMRAN.

Belarus: 700047 Tashkent, Ya. G'ulomov ko'ch. 75; tel. (71) 120-75-11; fax (71) 120-72-53; e-mail uzbekistan@mfa.gov.by; internet www.uzbekistan.mfa.gov.by; Ambassador IGOR S. SOKOL.

Bulgaria: 100031 Tashkent, Rakatboshi ko'ch. 52; tel. (71) 258-48-88; fax (71) 120-33-73; e-mail embassy.tashkent@mfa.bg; internet www.mfa.bg/embassies/uzbekistan; Chargé d'affaires VOLODYA C. NEYKOV.

China, People's Republic: 100047 Tashkent, Ya. G'ulomov ko'ch. 79; tel. (71) 233-80-88; fax (71) 233-47-35; e-mail chinaemb@bcc.com.uz; internet uz.china-embassy.org; Ambassador YU HONGJUN.

Czech Republic: 100041 Tashkent, Navnixol ko'ch. 6; tel. (71) 120-60-71; fax (71) 120-60-75; e-mail tashkent@embassy.mzv.cz; internet www.mzv.cz/tashkent; Ambassador HYNEK PEJCHA.

Egypt: 100115 Tashkent, Okilov ko'ch. 10/53; tel. (71) 120-50-08; fax (71) 120-50-09; e-mail tashkent.embassy@mfa.gov.eg; Ambassador ABD AL-KADIR AL-HASHSHAB MUHAMMAD.

France: 100041 Tashkent, Istiqbol ko'ch. 25; tel. (71) 233-53-82; fax (71) 233-62-10; e-mail presse@ambafrance-uz.org; internet www.ambafrance-uz.org; Ambassador FRANÇOIS GAUTHIER.

Georgia: 100170 Tashkent, Polkovnik A. Muxitdinov ko'ch. 6; tel. (71) 262-62-43; fax (71) 262-91-39; e-mail tashkent.emb@mfa.gov.ge; internet www.uzbekistan.mfa.gov.ge; Ambassador GIORGI KUBLASHVILI.

Germany: 100017 Tashkent, Sh. Rashidov ko'ch. 15, POB 4337; tel. (71) 120-84-40; fax (71) 120-84-50; e-mail info@taschkent.diplo.de; internet www.taschkent.diplo.de; Ambassador ARISTID EMIL FENSTER.

Holy See: 100000 Tashkent, Musakhanov ko'ch. 80/1; tel. and fax (71) 233-70-25; Apostolic Nuncio IVAN JURKOVIČ (Titular Archbishop of Corbavia) (resident in Moscow, Russia).

India: 100052 Tashkent, Qarabuloq ko'ch. 15; tel. (71) 140-09-83; fax (71) 140-09-99; e-mail pol.tashkent@mea.gov.in; internet www.indembassy.uz; Ambassador GITESH SARMA.

Indonesia: 100000 Tashkent, Ya. G'ulomov ko'ch. 73; tel. (71) 232-02-36; fax (71) 233-05-13; e-mail unitkom@kbri-tashkent.go.id; internet www.kbri-tashkent.go.id; Ambassador ASRUCHIN MOHAMAD.

Iran: 100007 Tashkent, Parkent ko'ch. 20; tel. (71) 268-64-65; fax (71) 140-07-61; e-mail iriemuz@hotmail.com; Ambassador ALI MARDONIY FARD.

Israel: 100000 Tashkent, A. Qaxxor ko'ch. 3; tel. (71) 140-75-00; fax (71) 140-75-55; e-mail operator@tashkent.mfa.gov.il; internet embassies.gov.il/tashkent; Ambassador HILLEL NEUMAN.

Italy: 100017 Tashkent, Yusuf Xos Xojib ko'ch. 40; tel. (71) 252-11-19; fax (71) 220-66-06; e-mail segreteria.tashkent@esteri.it; internet www.ambtashkent.esteri.it; Ambassador RICCARDO MANARA.

Japan: 100047 Tashkent, S. Azimov ko'ch., 1-tor 28; tel. (71) 120-80-60; fax (71) 120-80-77; internet www.uz.emb-japan.go.jp; Ambassador FUMIHIKO KATO.

Jordan: 100000 Tashkent, Dipvilla, Farxod ko'ch. 9; tel. (71) 274-24-79; fax (71) 140-11-44; e-mail jordanembuzb@mail.ru; Ambassador MUHAMMAD NUR OTHMAN YOUSEF BALKAR.

Kazakhstan: 100015 Tashkent, Chexov ko'ch. 23; tel. (71) 252-16-54; fax (71) 252-16-50; e-mail info@kazembassy.uz; internet www.kazembassy.uz; Ambassador BORIBAI JEKSEMBIN.

Korea, Democratic People's Republic: 100000 Tashkent, Usmon Nosir ko'ch. 95A; tel. (71) 250-59-44; fax (71) 250-27-99; Ambassador WON RYONG SOP.

Korea, Republic: 100029 Tashkent, Afrosiyob ko'ch. 7; tel. (71) 252-31-51; fax (71) 140-02-48; e-mail uzkoremb@mofat.go.kr; internet uzb.mofat.go.kr; Ambassador CHON DE-WAN.

Kuwait: 100000 Tashkent, Batumskaya ko'ch. 2; tel. (71) 120-58-88; fax (71) 120-84-96; Ambassador KHALAF BUDHAIR.

Kyrgyzstan: 100000 Tashkent, X. Samatova ko'ch. 30; tel. (71) 237-47-94; fax (71) 220-72-94; e-mail erkindik@sarkor.uz; Ambassador EMILBEK UZAKBAEV.

Latvia: 100000 Tashkent, A. Lashkarbegi ko'ch. 16A; tel. (71) 237-22-15; fax (71) 120-70-36; e-mail embassy.uzbekistan@mfa.gov.lv; Ambassador IGORS APOKINS.

Malaysia: 100031 Tashkent, M. Yaqubova ko'ch. 28–30; tel. (71) 256-30-27; fax (71) 252-30-71; e-mail maltskent@kln.gov.my; internet www.kln.gov.my/web/uzb_tashkent; Ambassador ABDUL AZIZ BIN HARUN.

Oman: Tashkent, ko'ch Mohlaroyim 49; tel. (71) 1400533; fax (71) 1400529; e-mail tashkent@mofa.gov.om; Ambassador MUHAMMAD BIN SAID BIN MUHAMMAD AL-LAVATI.

Pakistan: 100115 Tashkent, Kichik Xalqa Yo'li ko'ch. 15; tel. (71) 248-86-49; fax (71) 120-49-21; e-mail pareptashkent@gmail.com; internet www.mofa.gov.pk/uzbekistan; Ambassador MOHAMMAD WAHEED-UL-HASAN.

Poland: 100084 Tashkent, Firdavsiy ko'ch. 66; tel. (71) 120-86-50; fax (71) 120-86-51; e-mail taszkent.amb.sekretariat@msz.gov.pl; internet www.taszkent.polemb.net; Ambassador MARIAN PRZEŹDZIECKI.

Romania: 100000 Tashkent, Rejametov ko'ch. 44A; tel. (71) 252-63-55; fax (71) 120-75-67; e-mail romanian_embassy@sarkor.uz; internet taskent.mae.ro; Ambassador ROMEO STANCIU.

Russia: 100015 Tashkent, Nukus ko'ch. 83; tel. (71) 120-35-04; fax (71) 120-35-09; e-mail embassy@russia.uz; internet www.russia.uz; Ambassador VLADIMIR L. TYURDENEV.

Saudi Arabia: 100000 Tashkent, Bobur ko'ch. 3 A; tel. (71) 281-51-01; fax (71) 152-61-06; e-mail uzemb@mofa.gov.sa; Ambassador ABD AL-RAHMAN BIN ABDULLAH AL-SHIA.

Slovakia: 100070 Tashkent, Kichik Beshyog ko'ch. 38; tel. (71) 120-68-52; fax (71) 120-68-51; e-mail emb.tashkent@mzv.sk; internet www.tashkent.mfa.sk; Chargé d'affaires a.i. ROMAN HAUSER.

Switzerland: 100070 Tashkent, Sh. Rustaveli ko'ch., tupik 1/4; tel. (71) 120-67-38; fax (71) 120-62-59; e-mail tas.vertretung@eda.admin.ch; internet www.eda.admin.ch/tashkent; Ambassador NICOLAS BRÜHL.

Tajikistan: 100000 Tashkent, A. Kaxxor ko'ch., 6-chi tor, 61; tel. (71) 254-99-66; fax (71) 254-89-69; e-mail tajembuz@mfa.tj; internet www.tajikistan.uz; Ambassador MUZAFFAR HUSEINOV.

Turkey: 100000 Tashkent, Ya. G'ulomov ko'ch. 87; tel. (71) 113-03-00; fax (71) 113-03-33; e-mail embassy.tashkent@mfa.gov.tr; internet tashkent.emb.mfa.gov.tr; Ambassador MEHMET SERTAÇ SÖNMEZAY.

Turkmenistan: 100000 Tashkent, Afrosiab ko'ch. 19; tel. (71) 256-94-02; fax (71) 256-94-03; Ambassador SHIRI SHIRIYEV.

Ukraine: 100000 Tashkent, Ya. G'ulomov ko'ch. 68; tel. (71) 233-52-80; fax (71) 233-10-89; e-mail emb_uz@mfa.gov.ua; internet uzbekistan.mfa.gov.ua; Ambassador YURII V. SAVCHENKO.

United Kingdom: 100000 Tashkent, ul. Ya. G'ulomov ko'ch. 67; tel. (71) 120-15-00; e-mail brit@emb.uz; internet ukinuzbekistan.fco.gov.uk; Ambassador GEORGE EDGAR.

USA: 100093 Tashkent, Moyqurg'on ko'ch. 3, Yunusobod District; tel. (71) 120-54-50; fax (71) 120-63-35; e-mail tashkentinfo@state.gov; internet uzbekistan.usembassy.gov; Ambassador GEORGE A. KROL.

Viet Nam: 100000 Tashkent, Sh. Rashidov ko'ch. 100; tel. (71) 235-64-93; fax (71) 120-62-65; e-mail vnemb.uz@mofa.gov.vn; internet www.vietnamembassy-uzbekistan.org/vi; Ambassador LE MANH LUAN.

Judicial System

Supreme Court (O'zbekiston Respublikasi Oliy sud): 100000 Tashkent, A. Qodiriy ko'ch. 1; tel. (71) 239-02-74; internet www.supcourt.uz; Chair. BURITOSH M. MUSTAFAEV.

Office of the Prosecutor-General: 100000 Tashkent, Ya. G'ulomov ko'ch. 66; tel. (71) 233-20-66; Prosecutor-Gen. RASHIDJON H. QODIROV.

Constitutional Court (Konstitutsiyaviy sud): 100087 Tashkent, Mustaqillik maydoni 6; tel. (71) 239-80-20; fax (71) 239-86-36; e-mail interconcourt@sarkor.uz; Chair. (vacant); Dep. Chair. BAKHTIYAR MIRBABAEV.

Supreme Economic Court (Oliy Xo'jalik Sudi): 100097 Tashkent, Cho'ponota ko'ch. 6; tel. (71) 273-89-84; fax (71) 273-84-78; e-mail economical-court@sarkor.uz; internet www.economical-court.uz; Chair. DILMURAD A. MIRZAKARIMOV.

Religion

Legislation adopted in May 1998 severely restricts the activities of religious organizations.

The most widespread religion in Uzbekistan is Islam; the majority of ethnic Uzbeks are Sunni Muslims of the Hanafi school, but the number of Salafi communities is increasing. Most ethnic Slavs in Uzbekistan are adherents of Orthodox Christianity.

State Committee for Religious Affairs: 100159 Tashkent, Mustaqillik 5; tel. and fax (71) 239-17-63; e-mail info@religions.uz; internet www.religions.uz; f. 1992; Chair. ARTIKBEK YUSUPOV.

ISLAM

Muslim Board of Uzbekistan (O'zbekiston Musulmonlari Idorasi): 100002 Tashkent, Zarkainar ko'ch. 103, Madrese 'Barakhan'; tel. (71) 240-39-33; fax (71) 240-08-31; internet www.muslim.uz; f. 1943 (as Muslim Board of Central Asia and Kazakhstan, covering the Kazakh, Kyrgyz, Tajik, Turkmen and Uzbek SSRs); Chair. Chief Mufti USMONXON OLIMOV.

CHRISTIANITY

Roman Catholic Church

The Church is represented in Uzbekistan by an Apostolic Administration, established in April 2005. There were an estimated 4,000 adherents at 31 December 2008.

Apostolic Administrator: Most Rev. JERZY MACULEWICZ (Titular Bishop of Nara), 100047 Tashkent, Musahanov ko'ch. 80/1; tel. (71) 233-70-25; fax (71) 233-70-35; e-mail adm.ap@mail.ru; internet catholic.uz.

Russian Orthodox Church (Moscow Patriarchate)

Metropolitanate of Tashkent and Central Asia (Moscow Patriarchate)—Orthodox Church of Central Asia: 100047 Tashkent, S. Azimov ko'ch. 22/3D; tel. (71) 233-33-21; fax (71) 236-79-39; e-mail church@albatros.uz; internet www.pravoslavie.uz; Metropolitan of Tashkent and Central Asia VIKENTII (MORAR); has jurisdiction over Kyrgyzstan, Tajikistan and Uzbekistan.

JUDAISM

Chief Rabbi: Rabbi DAVID GUREVICH, 100100 Tashkent, Shohzhahon ko'ch. 30; tel. (71) 252-59-78; fax (71) 220-64-31; e-mail jewish@jewish.uz; internet www.jewish.uz.

The Press

The publications listed below are in Uzbek, unless otherwise stated.

REGULATORY AUTHORITY

Uzbek Agency for Press and Information (O'zAAA) (O'zbekiston Aloqa Va Axborotlashtirash Agentligi): 100011 Tashkent, Navoiy ko'ch. 28A; tel. (71) 238-41-07; fax (71) 239-87-82; e-mail info@aci.uz; internet aci.uz; f. 2002; Gen. Dir HAKIM A. MUKHITDINOV.

PRINCIPAL NEWSPAPERS

XXI ASR (21st Century): 100000 Tashkent, Nukus ko'ch. 73A; tel. and fax (71) 281-40-17; fax (71) 215-63-80; e-mail axborotXXIasr@yahoo.com; internet www.21asr.uz; f. 2003; weekly; Chief Editor MIRODIL ABDURAHMONOV.

Adolat (Justice): 100000 Tashkent, Matbuotchilar ko'ch. 32; tel. and fax (71) 236-53-14; fax (71) 233-40-86; e-mail gazeta@adolat.uz; internet www.adolat.uz; f. 1995; organ of the Justice Social Democratic Party of Uzbekistan (Adolat) (q.v.); weekly; Editor XUDOYOR MAMATOV; circ. 9,657.

Biznes-vestnik Vostoka (Business Herald of the East): 100029 Tashkent, Buxoro ko'ch. 26; tel. (71) 232-27-30; fax (71) 236-00-55; e-mail bvv-info@mail.ru; f. 1991; 2 a week; in Russian; economic and financial news; also weekly English edition, *BVV Business Report*; circ. 8,000.

Ekonomicheskoye Obozreniye (Economic Survey): 100070 Tashkent, Usman Nosir ko'ch., 1 tupik, 5; tel. (71) 150-02-02; fax (71) 361-45-48; e-mail review@cer.uz; internet www.review.uz; f. 1998; monthly; economics, politics, civil society, finance.

Inson va Qonun (Person and Law): 100047 Tashkent, Sayilgoh ko'ch. 5; tel. (71) 233-95-31; e-mail info@press-iq.uz; internet www.minjust.uz/uz/group.scm?groupId=4146; weekly; organ of the Ministry of Justice (q.v.); Editor-in-Chief KO'CHQOR NORQOBIL.

Ma'rifat (Enlightenment): 100000 Tashkent, Matbuotchilar ko'ch. 32; tel. (71) 233-50-55; e-mail mariat@ars-inform.uz; internet www.marifat.uz; f. 1931; 2 a week; in Uzbek and Russian; Editor KHALIM SAIDOV; circ. 33,000 (2006).

Mulkdor (The Proprietor): 100083 Tashkent, Buyuk Turon ko'ch. 41; tel. (71) 239-21-96; f. 1994; weekly; Editor-in-Chief MIRODIL ABDURAKHMANOV; circ. 10,000.

Novosti Uzbekistani (News of Uzbekistan): 100000 Tashkent, Babur ko'ch. 4; tel. (71) 215-62-59; fax (71) 255-41-25; e-mail novosti.uz@mail.ru; internet www.nuz.uz; independent; in Russian; Chief Editor BAKHODYR YULDASHEV.

Novyi Vek (New Age): 100060 Tashkent, Movarounnaxr ko'ch. 19; tel. (71) 233-48-55; fax (71) 233-76-84; f. 1992; fmrly *Kommercheskii Vestnik* (Commerical Herald); in Russian; weekly; Editor VALERII NIYAZMATOV; circ. 22,000.

O'zbekiston Adabiyoti va San'ati (Literature and Art of Uzbekistan): 100000 Tashkent, Matbuotchilar ko'ch. 32; tel. (71) 233-52-91; e-mail uzas@bc2.uz; f. 1956; weekly; organ of the Union of Writers of Uzbekistan; Editor SADULLO HAKIMOV; circ. 9,400 (2011).

O'zbekiston ovozi/ Golos Uzbekistana (Voice of Uzbekistan): 100000 Tashkent, Matbuotchilar ko'ch. 32; tel. (71) 236-55-17; fax (71) 233-72-83; e-mail info@uzbekistonovozi.uz; internet www.uzbekistonovozi.uz; f. 1918; Uzbek and Russian edns; organ of the People's Democratic Party of Uzbekistan; Editor-in-Chief SAFAR OSTONOV.

Postda/ Na postu: 100029 Tashkent, Yu. Rajaby ko'ch. 1; tel. (71) 231-33-88; fax (71) 232-05-51; e-mail postda08@mail.ru; f. 1930; in Uzbek and Russian; military; weekly; Editor Z. NEMATOV.

Pravda Vostoka (Truth of the East): 100000 Tashkent, Matbuotchilar ko'ch. 32; tel. (71) 236-57-12; fax (71) 233-70-98; e-mail pvbox@mail.ru; internet www.pv.uz; f. 1917; 5 a week; in Russian; organ of the Cabinet of Ministers; Editor ABBASKHAN USMANOV; circ. 16,000.

Savdogar (The Trader): 100000 Tashkent, Buyuk Turon ko'ch. 41; tel. (71) 233-34-55; f. 1992; economy and commerce; Editor MUHAMMAD ORAZMETOV; circ. 17,000.

Sport: 100167 Tashkent, E. Bobohon ko'ch. 67A; tel. (71) 244-17-37; fax (71) 244-06-69; f. 1932; Editor HAYDAR AKBAROV; circ. 8,490.

Toshkent Haqiqati/ Tashkentskaya Pravda (Tashkent Truth): 100000 Tashkent, Matbuotchilar ko'ch. 32; tel. (71) 233-64-95; fax (71) 233-58-85; internet www.th.uz; f. 1954; 2 a week; Uzbek and Russian edns; Editor FATKHIDDIN MUKHITDINOV; circ. 19,000 (Uzbek edn), 6,400 (Russian edn).

Turkiston (Turkestan): 100083 Tashkent, Matbuotchilar ko'ch. 32; tel. (71) 233-95-97; f. 1925 as *Yash Leninchy* (Young Leninist), renamed as above 1992; 2 a week; organ of the Kamolot Asscn of Youth of Uzbekistan; Editor GAFAR KHATOMOV; circ. 8,000 (2010).

UzReport: 100000 Tashkent, Buxoro ko'ch. 26; tel. (71) 232-27-29; fax (71) 236-00-55; e-mail info@corp.uzreport.com; internet www.uzreport.com; online only; in Uzbek, Russian and English; business, economics; f. 1999.

Vatanparvar (The Patriot): 100000 Tashkent, Ak. Abdullaev ko'ch. 100; tel. (71) 269-82-43; fax (71) 269-82-28; f. 1992; fmrly *Frunzevets* (Supporter of Frunze); publ. by Ministry of Defence (q.v.); weekly.

Xalk So'zi/ Narodnoye Slovo (People's Word): 100000 Tashkent, Matbuotchilar ko'ch. 32; tel. (71) 233-15-22; e-mail info@narodnoeslovo.uz; internet www.narodnoeslovo.uz; f. 1991; Uzbek and Russian edns; 5 a week (Uzbek), weekly (Russian); organ of the Oliy Majlis and the Cabinet of Ministers; Editor ABBASKHON USMANOV; circ. 41,580 (Uzbek edn), 12,750 (Russian edn).

Xamkor/ Delovoi Partner/ Business Partner: 100084 Tashkent, Amir Temir ko'ch. 107A; tel. (71) 138-59-77; fax (71) 138-58-23; f. 1990; weekly; Uzbek, Russian and English edns; circ. 4,735.

Xurriiat (Freedom): 100000 Tashkent; tel. (71) 244-25-06; fax (71) 244-36-16; e-mail amir@uzpac.uz; f. 1996; weekly; independent; circ. 5,000.

Zerkalo XXI (Mirror XXI): 100000 Tashkent, Babur ko'ch. 4; tel. (71) 255-41-25; e-mail novosti.uz@mail.ru; internet www.zerkalo21.uz; f. 2000; in Russian; independent; suspended publication for financial reasons in Nov. 2011; Chief Editor BAKHODYR YULDASHEV.

PRINCIPAL PERIODICALS

Erk (Freedom): 100055 Tashkent, Ipakchi ko'ch. 38; tel. (71) 220-65-30; e-mail erkgazetasi@yahoo.com; organ of Freedom Democratic Party of Uzbekistan (Erk) (q.v.); f. 1991; 4 a month; Uzbek and Russian edns; circ. 5,300 (2007).

Fan va turmush/ Nauka i Zhizn Uzbekistana (Science and Life): 100047 Tashkent, Ya. G'ulomov ko'ch. 70; tel. (71) 235-06-38; fax (71) 234-48-67; e-mail shuhrat@astrin.uz; internet www.fvat.uz; f. 1933 as *Sosialistik ilm va Texnika* (Socialist Science and Technology); every 2 months; Uzbek and Russian edns; publ. by the Fan (Science) Publishing House; popular scientific; Editor Prof. SHUHRAT A. EGAMBERDIEV; circ. 20,000.

Guliston: 100000 Tashkent, Buyuk Turon ko'ch. 41; tel. (71) 236-78-90; f. 1925; present name adopted 1967; every 2 months; socio-political, literary; Editor-in-Chief AZIM SUYUN; circ. 4,000.

Gulxan (Bonfire): 100129 Tashkent, Navoiy ko'ch. 30; tel. (71) 236-78-85; f. 1929; monthly; illustrated juvenile fiction; Editor ASHURALI DZHURAEV; circ. 26,000.

Guncha (Small Bud): 700129 Tashkent, Navoiy ko'ch. 30; tel. (71) 236-78-80; e-mail guncha_2010@bk.ru; internet www.guncha.uz; f. 1958; monthly; illustrated; for pre-school-age children; Editor DILFUZA SHOMALIKOVA; circ. 35,000.

Ijtimoij fikr/ Obshchestvennoe mneniye. Prava Cheloveka (Public Opinion. Human Rights): 100029 Tashkent, Mustaqilliq maidoni 5/3; tel. (71) 239-84-29; fax (71) 239-85-48; e-mail info@ijtimoiy-fikr.uz; internet www.ijtimoiy-fikr.uz; f. 1998; 4 a year; in Uzbek, Russian and English; publ. by the Republican Centre for the Study of Public Opinion and National Human Rights Centre; Editor AMAL H. SAIDOV.

Jahon Adabiyoti (World Literature): 100129 Tashkent, Navoiy ko'ch. 30; tel. (71) 244-41-60; fax (71) 244-41-61; f. 1997; monthly; Editor MUPRIYRAT MUPZAEB; circ. 2,000.

Oila va zhamiiat (Family and Society): 100129 Tashkent, Navoiy ko'ch. 30; tel. and fax (71) 139-40-12; e-mail womancomitet@mail.ru; internet www.womancomitet.narod.ru; f. 1991; weekly; publ. by Women's Committee of Uzbekistan.

San'at (Art): 100029 Tashkent, Mustaqilliq maidoni 2; tel. (71) 239-44-51; fax (71) 239-44-86; e-mail bientash@globalnet.uz; internet sanat.orexca.com; f. 1997; 4 a year; publ. by Academy of the Arts of Uzbekistan; Uzbek, Russian and English edns; illustrated journal about the arts and crafts; Editor-in-Chief JULIYA SYRTSOVA.

Saodat (Happiness): 100083 Tashkent, Buyuk Turon ko'ch. 41; tel. (71) 233-68-10; f. 1925; 8 a year; women's popular; Editor OIDIN KHAJIYEVA; circ. 70,000.

Sikhat-salomatlik (Health): 100000 Tashkent, Parkent ko'ch. 51; tel. (71) 268-17-54; f. 1990; every 2 months; Editor DAMIN A. ASADOV; circ. 36,000.

Tafakkur (Contemplation): 100000 Tashkent, Movaraunnakhr ko'ch.; f. 1994; 4 a year; literary; organ of the (state-controlled) Republican Committee for Spirituality and Enlightenment; Editor-in-Chief ERKIN A'ZAM.

NEWS AGENCIES

Jahon (World) Information Agency: 100029 Tashkent, O'zbekiston shoh ko'ch. 9; tel. (71) 233-65-91; fax (71) 220-64-43; e-mail aajahon@mfa.uz; internet jahon.mfa.uz; information agency of Ministry of Foreign Affairs; Dir ABROR GULYAMOV.

Press-UZ.info: Tashkent; e-mail admin@press-uz.info; internet www.press-uz.info; f. 2005; independent; news from Uzbekistan, Central Asia and Russia, in Uzbek, Russian and English.

Uzbekistan National News Agency (UzA): 100000 Tashkent, Buyuk Nuron ko'ch. 41; tel. (71) 233-16-22; fax (71) 233-24-45; internet www.uza.uz; Dir MAMATSKUL KHAZRATSKULOV.

Publishers

Uzbek Agency for Press and Information: 100129 Tashkent, A. Navoiy ko'ch. 30; tel. (71) 244-32-87; fax (71) 244-14-84; e-mail uzapi@uznet.net; internet www.uzapi.gov.uz; f. 2002; mass media, press and information exchange; printing, publishing and distribution of periodicals; CEO AMANULLA YUNUSOV.

Chulpon (Morning Star) Publishers: 100129 Tashkent, A. Navoiy ko'ch. 30; tel. (71) 244-10-45; fax (71) 244-30-94; e-mail chulpan@sarkor.uz; internet www.chulpan.uz; Dir RUSTAM ZAPAROV.

Fan (Science) Publishers: 100047 Tashkent, Ya. G'ulomov ko'ch. 70/102; tel. (71) 233-69-61; scientific books and journals; Dir N. T. KHATAMOV.

Gafur Gulom Publishing House: 100129 Tashkent, A. Navoiy ko'ch. 30; tel. (71) 244-22-53; fax (71) 241-35-47; f. 1957; fiction, the arts; books in Uzbek, Russian and English; Dir MIZROB M. BURONOV; Editor-in-Chief NAZIRA J. JURAYEVNA.

O'qituvchi (Teacher) Publishing-Printing and Creative House: 100129 Tashkent, A. Navoiy ko'ch. 30; tel. and fax (71) 244-26-89; f. 1936; literary textbooks, education manuals, popular science, juvenile; Dir R. O. MIRZAYEV.

O'zbekiston Milliy Entsiklopediyasi (Uzbekistan National Encyclopedias): 100129 Tashkent, A. Navoiy ko'ch. 30; tel. (71) 244-34-38; fax (71) 244-24-91; e-mail uzme@ensiklopediya.uz; internet www .ensiklopediya.uz; f. 1997; encyclopedias, dictionaries and reference books; Dir N. TUKHLIYEV.

O'zbekiston (Uzbekistan) Publishing and Printing Creative House: 100129 Tashkent, A. Navoiy ko'ch. 30; tel. (71) 244-34-01; fax (71) 244-38-10; e-mail aptpk@ars-inform.uz; f. 2004; politics, economics, law, history, art, illustrated, manuals and textbooks for schools and higher educational institutes; Dir ZAIR T. ISADJANOV; Editor-in-Chief SHOMUXITDIN SH. MANSUROV.

Yozuvchi (Writer) Publishers: 100129 Tashkent, A. Navoiy ko'ch. 30; tel. (71) 244-29-97; f. 1990; Dir M. U. TOICHIYEV.

Broadcasting and Communications

TELECOMMUNICATIONS

The dominant fixed-line telephone network services provider in Uzbekistan is the state-owned Uzbektelecom, while Beeline and East Telecom also provide fixed-line telephone services. Beeline and Coscom (the latter under the brand name Ucell) are the major providers of mobile telecommunications services. The licence to operate of Russian-owned MTS-O'zbekiston, formerly a major provider of mobile telecommunications services, was suspended in July 2012. In 2011 there were 1.9m. fixed telephone lines and 25.4m. subscriptions to mobile telephone services in the country.

Communications and Information Agency of Uzbekistan (O'zbekiston Aloqa va Axborotlashtirish Agentligi): 100011 Tashkent, A. Navoiy ko'ch. 28A; tel. (71) 238-41-07; fax (71) 239-87-82; e-mail info@aci.uz; internet www.aci.uz; Dir-Gen. HAKIM A. MUKHITDINOV.

Beeline: 100000 Tashkent, Buxoro ko'ch. 1; tel. (71) 233-33-30; fax (71) 232-12-22; internet www.beeline.uz; f. 1996; fmrly Daewoo Unitel; absorbed provider of digital and other fixed-line telephony services Buzkom in 1999; subsidiary of VympelKom-Bilain (Russia) (q.v.); mobile cellular telecommunications; more than 1m. subscribers (2007); ANDREI SAFRONYUK.

Coscom: 100031 Tashkent, V. Vaxidov ko'ch. 118; tel. (71) 252-15-51; fax (71) 220-72-65; e-mail inform@coscom.uz; internet www.ucell .uz; f. 1996; 94% owned by TeliaSonera; provides mobile cellular telecommunications under the brand name 'Ucell'; Gen. Dir OGUZ MEMIGUVEN.

East Telecom: 100027 Tashkent, Afrosiyob ko'ch. 28/14; tel. (71) 150-01-17; fax (71) 150-01-02; e-mail info@etc.uz; internet www.etc .uz; provides digital fixed-line telecommunications services; Gen. Dir AN CHAE KUN.

Uzbektelecom: 100000 Tashkent, Amir Temur ko'ch. 24; tel. (71) 233-42-59; fax (71) 236-01-88; e-mail uinfo@uztelecom.uz; internet www.uztelecom.uz; f. 2000; provides local, regional and international telecommunications services; partial privatization pending; Gen. Dir MAHSUM M. MAHMUDOV.

BROADCASTING

State Television and Radio Broadcasting Company of Uzbekistan (Uzteleradio): 100011 Tashkent, A. Navoiy ko'ch. 69; tel. (71) 244-13-32; fax (71) 244-81-06; e-mail info@mtrk.uz; internet www.mtrk.uz; local broadcasts, as well as relays from Egypt, France, India, Japan, Russia and Turkey; Chair. ALISHER KHUJAYEV.

Finance

(cap. = capital; res = reserves; dep. = deposits; m. = million; amounts in Uzbek sum, unless otherwise stated; brs = branches)

BANKING

A reform of the banking sector was begun in 1994. A two-tier system was introduced, consisting of the Central Bank and about 30 commercial banks. An association of commercial banks was established in 1995 to co-ordinate the role of commercial banks in the national economy. At the end of 2002 there were reported to be 35 banks in Uzbekistan, of which 13 were under private ownership.

Central Bank

Central Bank of the Republic of Uzbekistan: 100001 Tashkent, O'zbekiston shoh ko'ch. 6; tel. and fax (71) 252-57-39; e-mail webmaster@cbu.st.uz; internet www.cbu.uz; f. 1991; Chair. of Bd FAIZULLA M. MULLAJONOV.

State Commercial Bank

National Bank for Foreign Economic Activity of the Republic of Uzbekistan (NBU) (O'zbekiston Respublikasi Tashqi Iqtisodiy Faoliyat Milliy Banki): 100047 Tashkent, Oxunbabaev ko'ch. 23; tel. (71) 233-62-87; fax (71) 232-01-72; e-mail webmaster@central.nbu .com; internet new.nbu.com; f. 1991; cap. 623,867m., res 11,696m., dep. 3,692,937m. (Dec. 2011); Chair. SAIDAKHMAT B. RAKHIMOV; 92 brs.

State Joint-Stock Commercial Banks

Asaka—Specialized State Joint-Stock Commercial Bank: 100015 Tashkent, Nukus ko'ch. 67; tel. (71) 120-81-11; fax (71) 120-86-91; e-mail contact@asakabank.com; internet www .asakabank.com; f. 1995; cap. 377,242m., res 21,324m., dep. 2,508,128m. (Dec. 2011); 66.7% owned by Ministry of Finance; Chair. KAHRAMON T. ARIPOV; 27 brs.

Ipoteka Commercial Mortgage Bank: 100000 Tashkent, Mustaqillik ko'ch. 17; tel. (71) 233-11-22; fax (71) 232-13-23; e-mail info@ ipotekabank.uz; internet www.ipotekabank.uz; f. 2005 by merger of UzJilSberBank and Zaminbank; cap. 61,889.3m., res 34,376.0m., dep. 702,768.4m. (Dec. 2010); Chair. of Bd ABDURASUL ABDULLAYEV; 38 brs.

Other Banks

Agrobank: 100096 Tashkent, Mukimi ko'ch. 43; tel. (71) 120-88-33; fax (71) 120-88-18; e-mail headoffice@agrobank.uz; internet www .agrobank.uz; f. 1995; cap. 151,142.7m., res 6,727.6m., dep. 1,168,813.9m. (Dec. 2011); fmrly Paxta Bank; present name adopted 2009; Chair. ABDURAXMAT BOYMURATOV; 185 brs.

Aloqabank: 100047 Tashkent, Amir Temur ko'ch. 4; tel. (71) 232-83-73; fax (71) 233-47-10; e-mail info@aloqabank.uz; internet www .alokabank.uz; f. 1995; cap. 62,041.3m., dep. 375,571m., total assets 478,894.2m. (Dec. 2011); Chair. XURSHID MIRZAHIDOV; 14 brs, 22 sub-brs (2012).

HamkorBank: 170111 Andijon, Babura ko'ch. 85; tel. (74) 224-76-88; fax (74) 224-73-83; e-mail info@hamkorbank.uz; internet www .hamkorbank.uz; f. 1991; Chair. SHAHRUH HAKIMOV; 25 brs.

Ipak Yuli Bank (Silk Road Bank): 100017 Tashkent, Kodiriy ko'ch. 2; tel. (71) 120-00-09; fax (71) 120-34-43; e-mail info@ipakyulibank .com; internet www.ipakyulibank.com; f. 2000; cap. 37,373.4m., res –441.6m., dep. 535,754.1m. (Dec. 2011); Chair. of Bd RUSTAMBEK R. RAHIMBEKOV.

Microkreditbank: 100096 Tashkent, Lutfiy ko'ch. 14; tel. (71) 273-28-11; fax (71) 273-05-89; e-mail office@mikrokreditbank.uz; internet www.mikrokreditbank.uz; f. 2006; micro-credit bank; Chair. JAMSHED SAYFIDDINOV.

O'zsanoatqurilishbank (Uzpromstroibank) (Uzbek Industrial and Construction Bank): 100000 Tashkent, Shaxrisab ko'ch. 3; tel. (71) 120-45-01; fax (71) 233-34-26; e-mail info@uzpsb.uz; internet www .uzpsb.uz; f. 1922; cap. 161,227.6m., res –5,306.9m., dep. 1,826,142.2m. (Dec. 2011); Chair. of Managing Bd ABDURASUL N. ABDULLAEV; 44 brs.

Qishloq Qurilish Bank (Rural Construction Bank): 100060 Tashkent, Lahuti ko'ch. 38; tel. and fax (71) 133-42-25; f. 2009 on basis of Galla Bank.

Savdogarbank: 100060 Tashkent, S. Barak ko'ch. 78; tel. (71) 281-30-29; fax (71) 256-56-71; internet www.savdogarbank.uz; Chair. MURSURMON N. NURMAMATOV.

Trustbank: 100038 Tashkent, A. Navoiy ko'ch. 7; tel. (71) 244-76-22; fax (71) 244-76-61; e-mail info@trustbank.uz; internet www .trustbank.uz; f. 1994; cap. 16,711.7m., dep. 344,524.5m., total assets 384,451.8m. (Dec. 2010); Chair. ILHOM F. SOLIYEV; 2 brs.

Turonbank: 100011 Tashkent, Abay 4A; tel. (71) 700-55-55; fax (71) 244-25-81; e-mail info@turonbank.uz; internet www.turonbank.uz; f. 1990; cap. 26,521.6m., res 365.9m., dep. 417,964.3m. (Jan. 2011); Chair. of Bd DANIYOR B. ARIFJANOV; 18 brs.

Uzbekistan-Turkish UT Bank: 100043 Tashkent, Bunyodkor ko'ch. 15B; tel. (71) 273-83-25; fax (71) 220-63-62; e-mail utbank@ utbk.com; internet www.utbank.uz; f. 1993; 50% owned by Paxta Bank, 50% owned by Türkiye Cumhuriyeti Ziraat Bankası (Agricultural Bank of the Turkish Republic); cap. 9,252.3m., res 7,699.3m., dep. 118,551.7m. (Dec. 2010); Chair. AZIM TANGIRBERDIEV.

INSURANCE

Ark Sugʻurta: 100000 Tashkent, Pushkin koʻch. 88; tel. (71) 267-73-19; fax (71) 267-70-28; e-mail info@arksugurta.uz; internet www.arksugurta.uz; f. 1991; life and non-life; Dir-Gen. ZAFAR O. TURSUNOV.

INGO Uzbekistan: 100128 Tashkent, Kunaev koʻch. 112; tel. (71) 150-99-99; fax (71) 150-01-01; e-mail info@ingo.uz; internet www.ingo.uz; f. 2005; present name adopted 2008; 90% owned by InVestPolis (Russia); non-life; Dir-Gen. RUSTAM TURAEV.

Ishonch: 100027 Tashkent, Xojaev koʻch. 1 A; tel. and fax (71) 238-69-65; e-mail info@ishonch-iic.uz; internet www.ishonch-iic.uz; f. 1996; life and non-life; Dir-Gen. MIRSHAMSIDDIN M. XIKMATILLAEV.

Kalofat: 100000 Tashkent, Mustaqillik maydoni 5, 9th Floor; tel. (71) 233-26-98; fax (71) 233-38-49; internet www.kalofatdask.uz; f. 1997; life and non-life; Dir-Gen. SHERALI B. IMAMOV.

Oʻzbekinvest (Uzbekinvest) National Export–Import Insurance Co: 100017 Tashkent, Istiqlol koʻch. 49; tel. (71) 235-78-01; fax (71) 235-94-09; e-mail office@uzbekinvest.uz; internet www.insurance.uz; f. 1994, restructured 1997; jt venture with American International Group (AIG—USA); cap. US $60m.; Dir-Gen. FAKH-RITDIN SAIDAKHMEDOV.

Temir Yoʻllari Sugʻurta: 100047 Tashkent, Amir Temur koʻch. 4; tel. and fax (71) 233-88-60; e-mail mail@tys.uz; internet www.tys.uz; f. 2002; owned by Oʻzbekiston Temir Yoʻllari (Uzbekistan State Railway Co); non-life; Dir-Gen. SUNNAT UMAROV.

COMMODITY EXCHANGE

Tashkent Republican Commodity and Raw Materials Exchange: 100003 Tashkent, Oʻzbekiston shoh koʻch. 53; tel. (71) 239-83-77; fax (71) 239-83-92; Chair. of Bd NABIHON S. SAMATOV.

STOCK EXCHANGE

Tashkent Republican Stock Exchange (UZSE) (Respublika Fond Birjasi 'Toshkent'): 100047 Tashkent, Buxoro koʻch. 10; tel. (71) 236-07-40; fax (71) 233-32-31; e-mail info@uzse.uz; internet www.uzse.uz; f. 1994; Chair. BAKHTIYOR I. KHUDOYAROV.

Trade and Industry

GOVERNMENT AGENCIES

Foreign Investment Agency: 100077 Tashkent, Buyuk Ipak Yuli koʻch. 75; tel. (71) 268-77-05; fax (71) 267-07-52; e-mail afi@mail.uznet.net; Gen. Dir SHAZIYATOV S. SHOAZIZ.

State Committee for Demonopolization and the Development of Competition (Oʻzbekiston Respublikasi Monopoliadan Chiqarish va Raqobatni Rivojlantirish Davlat Qoʻmitasi): 100011 Tashkent, A. Navoiy koʻch. 18A; tel. (71) 239-15-42; e-mail devonhona@antimon.uz; internet www.antimon.uz; Chair. BAIMUROD S. ULASHOV (acting).

State Committee for the Management of State Property (State Property Committee): 100003 Tashkent, Oʻzbekiston shoh koʻch. 55; tel. (71) 239-44-46; fax (71) 259-20-37; e-mail ves@gki.uz; internet www.gki.uz; f. 1994; Chair. DILSHOD O. MUSAEV.

CHAMBER OF COMMERCE

Chamber of Commerce and Industry of Uzbekistan (Oʻzbekiston Respublikasi Savdo-Sanoat Palatasi): 100047 Tashkent, Buxoro koʻch. 6; tel. (71) 150-60-00; fax (71) 150-60-09; e-mail info@chamber.uz; internet www.chamber.uz; f. 1996; present name adopted 2004; Chair. ALISHER SHAIHOV.

STATE HYDROCARBONS COMPANY

Uzbekneftegaz (Uzbekistani Petroleum and Natural Gas Co): 100047 Tashkent, Akhunbabayev koʻch. 21; tel. (71) 233-57-57; fax (71) 236-77-71; e-mail nhk@uzneftegaz.uz; internet www.uzneftegaz.uz; f. 1999; national petroleum and gas corpn; Dir SHOKIR N. FAYZULLAEV.

TRADE UNIONS

Federation of Trade Unions of Uzbekistan: 100000 Tashkent; Chair. of Council KHULKAR JAMALOV.

Transport

RAILWAYS

There were 4,227 km of track in 2010, of which 674 km were electrified.

Oʻzbekiston Temir Yoʻllari (Uzbekistan State Railway Co): 100060 Tashkent, T. Shevchenko koʻch. 7; tel. (71) 299-72-16; fax (71) 233-69-24; e-mail gajk@uzrailway.uz; internet www.uzrailway.uz; f. 1994; state-owned joint-stock co; Chair. of Bd ACHILBAY J. RAMATOV.

Toshkent metropoliteni (Tashkent Metro): 100027 Tashkent, Oʻzbekiston shoh koʻch. 93A; tel. (71) 239-89-32; fax (71) 233-66-81; e-mail metro@sarkor.uz; f. 1977; four lines with total length of 39 km, further extension under construction; Chair. M. A. ODILOV.

ROADS

In 2010 the total length of the road network was estimated at 183,000 km.

CIVIL AVIATION

There is an international airport at Tashkent.

Uzbekistan Airways (Uzbekiston Havo Yollari): 100061 Tashkent, A. Timur koʻch. 51; tel. (71) 140-47-50; fax (71) 140-48-18; e-mail info@uzairways.com; internet www.uzairways.com; f. 1992; Dir-Gen. VALERIY TYAN.

Tourism

The country has more than 4,000 historical monuments, many of which are associated with the ancient 'Silk Road'. Uzbekistan received an estimated 975,000 foreign visitors in 2010, when tourism receipts (excluding passenger transport) totalled US $121m.

Uzbektourism: 100047 Tashkent, Xorazm koʻch. 47; tel. (71) 233-54-14; fax (71) 233-80-68; e-mail info@uzbektourism.uz; internet www.uzbektourism.uz; f. 1992; Chair. ZAHID L. XAKIMOV.

Defence

As assessed at November 2012, active armed forces numbered some 48,000, comprising an army of 24,500, an air force of 7,500 and 16,000 joint troops. There were also paramilitary forces numbering up to 20,000 (comprising a 1,000-strong National Guard attached to the Ministry of Defence and up to 19,000 troops attached to the Ministry of Internal Affairs). Compulsory military service lasts for 12 months. In July 1994 Uzbekistan joined the North Atlantic Treaty Organization (NATO) 'Partnership for Peace' programme.

Defence Expenditure: Budgeted at an estimated 2,440,000m. sum in 2011.

Joint Chief of Staff of the Armed Forces: Maj.-Gen. V. MAHMU-DOV.

Education

In the 1990s a greater emphasis on Uzbek history and literature was introduced in the education system. In 2006 some 89.2% of pupils were educated in Uzbek. Primary education, beginning at seven years of age, lasts for four years. Secondary education, beginning at 11 years of age, lasts for seven years, comprising a first cycle of five years and a second cycle of two years. In 2010/11 enrolment at primary schools included 90% of children in the relevant age-group. In 2008/09 secondary enrolment included 92% of children in the relevant age-group. In 2006 some 5.7m. pupils were enrolled in general secondary schools. A total of 263,600 students were enrolled at 63 institutions of higher education in 2004. The 2006 budget allocated 1,285,078.5m. sum (29.8% of total budgetary expenditure) to education.

VANUATU

Introductory Survey

LOCATION, CLIMATE, LANGUAGE, RELIGION, FLAG, CAPITAL

The Republic of Vanuatu comprises an irregular archipelago of 83 islands in the south-west Pacific Ocean, lying about 1,000 km (600 miles) west of Fiji and 400 km (250 miles) north-east of New Caledonia. The group extends over a distance of about 1,300 km (808 miles) from north to south. The islands have an oceanic tropical climate, with a season of south-east trade winds between May and October. Winds are variable, with occasional cyclones for the rest of the year, and annual rainfall ranges from 2,300 mm (90 ins) in the south and 3,900 mm (154 ins) in the north. In Port Vila, in the centre of the group, mean temperatures vary between 22°C (72°F) and 27°C (81°F). The national language is Bislama, ni-Vanuatu pidgin. There are many Melanesian languages and dialects. English, French and Bislama are the official languages. Most of the inhabitants (about 80%) profess Christianity, of which a number of denominations are represented. The national flag (proportions 3 by 5) consists of two equal horizontal stripes, red above green, on which are superimposed a black-edged yellow horizontal 'Y' (with its base in the fly) and, at the hoist, a black triangle containing two crossed yellow mele leaves encircled by a curled yellow boar's tusk. The capital is Port Vila, on the island of Efate.

CONTEMPORARY POLITICAL HISTORY

Historical Context

During the 19th century the New Hebrides (now Vanuatu) were settled by British and French missionaries, planters and traders. The United Kingdom and France established a Joint Naval Commission for the islands in 1887. The two countries later agreed on a joint civil administration, and in 1906 the territory became the Anglo-French Condominium of the New Hebrides (Nouvelles-Hébrides). Under this arrangement, there were three elements in the structure of administration: the British National Service, the French National Service and the Condominium (Joint) Departments. Each power was responsible for its own citizens and other non-New Hebrideans who chose to be 'ressortissants' of either power. Indigenous New Hebrideans were not permitted to claim either British or French citizenship. This resulted in two official languages, two police forces, three public services, three courts of law, three currencies, three national budgets, two resident commissioners in Port Vila (the capital) and two district commissioners in each of the four districts.

Domestic Political Affairs

In mid-July 1980 agreement was reached between the two Condominium powers and the President of the Vanua'aku Pati (VP, Our Land Party—founded in 1972 as the New Hebrides National Party), Father Walter Lini, and the New Hebrides became independent within the Commonwealth, under the name of Vanuatu, on 30 July. The first President was the former Deputy Chief Minister, George Kalkoa, who adopted the surname Sokomanu ('leader of thousands'), although the post was largely ceremonial. Lini became Prime Minister.

At a general election in November 1983, the VP retained a majority in Parliament, taking 24 of the 39 seats in the Representative Assembly (representing a loss of two seats from the previous election held in November 1979). Sokomanu remained as President and Lini as Prime Minister. Sokomanu resigned as President in February 1984, after pleading guilty in court to the late payment of road taxes, but he was re-elected in the following month. Parliament was expanded to 46 seats for the general election held in December 1987. Of these, the VP won 26 seats, the Union of Moderate Parties (UMP) 19 and the Fren Melanesia Pati one. Lini retained the premiership. Following the election, the Secretary-General of the VP, Barak Sope, unsuccessfully challenged Lini for the party presidency, but later accepted a portfolio in the Council of Ministers.

In May 1988 a government decision to abolish a local land corporation, which had been a principal source of patronage for Sope, prompted a demonstration in Port Vila by Sope's supporters. Serious rioting ensued, in which one person was killed. Lini accused Sope of being instrumental in provoking the riots, and subsequently dismissed him from the Council of Ministers. In July Sope and four colleagues resigned from the VP, and were subsequently dismissed from Parliament at Lini's behest. In addition, 18 members of the UMP were dismissed after they had boycotted successive parliamentary sessions in protest against the expulsions. In September Sope and his colleagues formed a new political party, the Melanesian Progressive Pati (MPP), and in October the VP expelled 128 of its own members for allegedly supporting the new party. In October the Court of Appeal ruled as unconstitutional the dismissal from Parliament of Sope and his colleagues, and reinstated them, but upheld the expulsion of the 18 members of the UMP. In November Sope resigned from Parliament, citing loss of confidence in its Speaker. In December President Sokomanu dissolved Parliament and announced that Sope would act as interim Prime Minister, pending a general election scheduled for February 1989. Lini immediately denounced Sokomanu's actions, and the Governments of Australia, New Zealand and Papua New Guinea refused to recognize the interim Government. The islands' police force remained loyal to Lini, and later in December 1988 Sokomanu, Sope and other members of the interim Government were arrested and charged with treason. In 1989 Sokomanu was sentenced to six years' imprisonment, and Sope and the then leader of the parliamentary opposition, Maxime Carlot Korman, received five-year terms, for seditious conspiracy and incitement to mutiny. However, representatives of the International Commission of Jurists, who had been present at the trials, criticized the rulings, and in April the Court of Appeal overruled the original judgment, citing insufficient evidence for the convictions. Fred Timakata, the former Minister of Health, replaced Sokomanu as President in January 1989.

The removal of Walter Lini and subsequent events

Following the approval in August 1991 of a motion of no confidence in Lini as party President at the VP's congress, Donald Kalpokas, hitherto Secretary-General of the VP, was unanimously elected to replace him. In September a motion of no confidence in the premiership of Lini was narrowly approved in Parliament, and Kalpokas was elected Prime Minister. Subsequently, Lini, with the support of a substantial number of defectors from the VP, formed the National United Party (NUP). At a general election in December, the UMP secured 19 seats, while the VP and NUP each won 10 seats, the MPP four, and Tan Union, Fren Melanesia and Nagriamel one each. The leader of the UMP, Maxime Carlot Korman, was appointed Prime Minister, and a coalition Government was formed by the UMP and the NUP.

At a presidential election in February 1994, neither the UMP's candidate, Father Luc Dini, nor Father John Bani, who was supported by the opposition, attained the requisite two-thirds of the total votes cast. The election was rescheduled for March. The VP subsequently agreed to vote with the ruling UMP, in return for a guaranteed role in a future coalition government. As a result of this agreement, the UMP's candidate, Jean-Marie Leye, was elected to the presidency with 41 votes. The VP subsequently withdrew its support for the UMP when Carlot refused to offer the party more than one ministerial post.

In May 1994 the 'breakaway' members of the NUP who had remained in their ministerial posts, Sethy Regenvanu, Edward Tabisari and Cecil Sinker, were expelled from the party. They subsequently formed a new grouping, the People's Democratic Party (PDP), and later in that month signed an agreement with the UMP to form a new coalition Government, the third since the election of December 1991. The UMP-PDP coalition held a total of 26 legislative seats.

In October 1994 the Supreme Court granted the Government a restraining order against further actions by the President, pending the hearing of an application to the Supreme Court to overrule several of the President's recent decisions. Members of the Government and judiciary had become increasingly alarmed by Leye's exercise of his presidential powers, which had included orders to free 26 criminals and to appoint a convicted criminal as police commissioner.

At a general election held in November 1995, 20 of the 50 seats in the newly enlarged Parliament were won by the Unity Front coalition, the anglophone grouping led by Donald Kalpokas, which incorporated the VP, the MPP, the Tan Union and the NUP; the UMP secured 17 seats. A period of intense political manoeuvring followed the election, as the two main parties sought to form coalitions with other members in an attempt to secure a parliamentary majority. The situation was compounded by the emergence of two factions within the UMP, one comprising the supporters of Carlot and another led by Serge Vohor (the party's President). The Carlot faction of the UMP and the Unity Front both sought the political allegiance of the NUP. The latter's decision to accept the offer of a coalition with the UMP effectively excluded the Unity Front (the grouping with the largest number of seats) from the Government, and, in protest, its members boycotted the opening of Parliament in December, thus preventing a vote on the formation of a new government taking place. At a subsequent parliamentary session, Vohor was elected as Prime Minister, despite continuing allegations of irregularities in the election of senior members of the Government.

In February 1996 seven dissident UMP members of Parliament proposed a motion of no confidence in Vohor, supported by 22 other opposition members. However, Vohor announced his resignation as Prime Minister, thus preventing the vote from taking place. Carlot was subsequently elected as the new premier.

In July 1996 a report published by the national ombudsman revealed a serious financial scandal, involving the issuing of 10 bank guarantees with a total value of US $100m. The Minister of Finance, Barak Sope, who had issued the guarantees in April, had been persuaded by an Australian financial adviser, Peter Swanson, that the scheme could earn the country significant revenue. Swanson, who left Vanuatu after securing the guarantees, was subsequently traced and charged with criminal offences relating to his dealings with Sope. (In February 1998 the Supreme Court found Swanson guilty on seven charges arising from the scandal, sentencing him to 18 months' imprisonment.) Carlot, meanwhile, rejected demands for his resignation for his compliance with the scheme and resisted considerable pressure to dismiss Sope and the Governor of the Reserve Bank of Vanuatu. In the following month, however, Sope was dismissed following his defection to the opposition.

In an attempt to restore a measure of political stability, Carlot appealed for reconciliation among the various political groups in the country in August 1996 and invited members of the opposition to join the Government. The opposition responded by reiterating its demand for Carlot's resignation, and in September a motion of no confidence in the Government was approved and Vohor was elected Prime Minister. Vohor's coalition Government comprised the pro-Vohor faction of the UMP, the NUP, the MPP, Tan Union and Fren Melanesia. A new Council of Ministers, in which Sope was appointed Deputy Prime Minister, was announced in October.

Also in October 1996 a dispute over unpaid allowances, dating from 1993, led members of the 300-strong Vanuatu Mobile Force (VMF—the country's paramilitary force) briefly to abduct the President and Deputy Prime Minister to demand a settlement. Both Leye and Sope expressed sympathy for the VMF members. Sope was replaced as Deputy Prime Minister by Donald Kalpokas, and Father Walter Lini was appointed Minister of Justice. Following a further incident in November 1996 in connection with the pay dispute, in which an official from the Department of Finance was abducted and allegedly assaulted, Lini ordered the arrest of more than one-half of the members of the VMF. About 30 members were detained and charged with criminal offences. In June 1999 18 VMF members were charged with the kidnapping of a number of government officers in 1996; one was convicted.

In March 1997 a memorandum of agreement was signed between the VP, the NUP and the UMP, the three parties of the newly formed governing coalition. However, the defection in May of five NUP members of Parliament, including two cabinet ministers, to the VP led to the party's expulsion from the Government. As a result, a new coalition, comprising the UMP, the MPP, Tan Union and Fren Melanesia, was formed. The nomination of the new Council of Ministers was controversial, owing to the appointment of Sope to the position of Deputy Prime Minister and Minister of Commerce, Trade and Industry.

In September 1997 Vohor dismissed Willie Jimmy from his position as Minister of Finance, apparently owing to a dispute between Jimmy and the Prime Minister over the latter's decision to remove several areas of responsibility from the finance portfolio. The dispute intensified the disunity within the UMP, which had now come to comprise three factions, led respectively by Vohor, Carlot and Jimmy. In November Carlot filed a motion of no confidence in Vohor's Government. When Vohor attempted to withdraw all proposed legislation in order to prevent debate on the motion, Leye announced the dissolution of Parliament. However, the Supreme Court revived the parliamentary session in December. The matter was referred to the Court of Appeal, which in January 1998 ordered the immediate dissolution of Parliament. Following Leye's announcement of a forthcoming general election, Carlot announced the formation of the Vanuatu Republikan Pati (VRP).

The Governments of Donald Kalpokas and Barak Sope

At a general election held on 6 March 1998, the VP won 18 of the 52 seats in the newly enlarged Parliament, while the UMP secured 12 seats, the NUP 11, the MPP six, the John Frum Movement two, the VRP one, and independent candidates the remaining two. In mid-March the VP and the NUP agreed to form a coalition Government, with the support of Carlot (the VRP's sole representative) and one independent member. At the end of the month Donald Kalpokas was elected Prime Minister, defeating Vohor. Kalpokas also assumed three ministerial portfolios, including foreign affairs, while Lini, who was appointed to the revived post of Deputy Prime Minister, also became Minister of Justice and Internal Affairs.

In June 1998 Parliament approved a new 'leadership code'. Regarded as a crucial element in ensuring greater accountability and transparency in public life, the code defined clear guidelines for the conduct of state officials (including a requirement that all public figures submit an annual declaration of assets to Parliament), and laid down strict penalties for those convicted of corruption.

In October 1998 Kalpokas expelled the NUP from the governing coalition, following reports that the party's leader, Lini (who died in February 1999), had organized a series of meetings with prominent members of the opposition, with the aim of forming a new coalition government that would exclude the VP. NUP ministers were largely replaced by members of the UMP faction led by Jimmy; one ministerial post was allocated to the John Frum Movement. In March 1999 Father John Bani was chosen by the electoral college to succeed Jean-Marie Leye as President of Vanuatu.

The governing coalition was threatened in August 1999 by a decision by the National Council of the UMP to oppose participation in the Government. The Council issued a directive to the 17 members of Jimmy's faction to resign from the Kalpokas administration. Following their refusal to comply with the directive, the National Council acted to suspend the members in October. However, later in that month the suspensions were overruled by the Supreme Court. The two factions of the UMP had previously attempted reunification, but negotiations had stalled over the demands of Vohor's faction for two of the four ministerial positions held by Jimmy's faction. (The UMP achieved reunification in November 2000.)

The Government's majority in Parliament was eliminated at the end of August 1999, when three of four by-elections were won by opposition parties. In November the Government boycotted Parliament to avoid a proposed vote of no confidence by opposition parties against the Kalpokas administration. However, the subsequent defection to the opposition of an independent representative, followed by that of the Minister of Health, forced the resignation of Kalpokas prior to a motion of no confidence on 25 November. The Speaker, Edward Natapei, announced his resignation shortly afterwards, and Paul Ren Tari of the NUP was elected as his replacement. The leader of the MPP, Barak Sope, was elected to lead a new Government the same day; he secured 28 votes compared with the 24 votes gained by Natapei as the newly appointed President of the VP. Sope formed a coalition Government, comprising the MPP, the NUP, the Vohor faction of the UMP, the VRP and the John Frum Movement. The new Council of Ministers included Vohor as Minister of Foreign Affairs and Carlot as Minister of Lands and Mineral Resources, both of whom, with Sope, had been the subject of critical reports by the ombudsman.

In May 2000 Parliament approved controversial legislation (the Public Services Amendment Bill and the Government Amendment Bill) giving the Government direct power to appoint and dismiss public servants. The opposition criticized the changes, claiming that they contravened the principles of the

Comprehensive Reform Programme (a range of economic measures supported by the Asian Development Bank—ADB, see p. 214). President John Bani subsequently referred both pieces of legislation to the Supreme Court, which, in August, ordered that he approve them. The ADB reacted strongly to this development, arguing that it allowed for political bias in the public sector, and threatened to withhold further funds from Vanuatu. The bank's stance served to perpetuate an ongoing dispute between the organization and the Vanuatu Government, which had often expressed the view that the bank imposed harsh conditions in return for its finance. Also in August Deputy Prime Minister Reginald Stanley resigned, following his alleged involvement in a serious assault on two people and in causing criminal damage to property while under the influence of alcohol. He was replaced by the Minister of Trade Development, James Bule.

In September 2000 the opposition leader, Edward Natapei, invited the Vohor faction of the UMP to join the opposition and form a new government. Vohor declined, stating that his priority was the stability of the current Government. The resignation of a VP member in October prevented the success of a motion of no confidence in the Prime Minister.

The Government of Edward Natapei

In January 2001 three members of the UMP resigned from the party, further reducing the Government's majority. The Government's problems intensified in March after the withdrawal of the UMP from the ruling coalition. Opposition attempts to vote on a motion of no confidence were delayed as Sope initiated legal action against the motion, and the Speaker, Paul Ren Tari, refused to allow the vote while legal action was pending. The Chief Justice, however, ordered the vote to proceed, and, after further postponements by the Speaker, the Sope Government was voted out of office in April. A new Government, led by Edward Natapei of the VP, was elected. The incoming administration, a coalition of the VP and UMP, was duly sworn in; Vohor was appointed Deputy Prime Minister. In May Parliament held an extraordinary session to debate a motion to remove Ren Tari as Speaker owing to his conduct during the political crisis. Ren Tari responded by suspending Natapei, along with five other cabinet ministers, for breaching parliamentary procedure. Despite an order by the Chief Justice that they be allowed to return to Parliament to continue the extraordinary session, Ren Tari refused to open the legislature while he appealed to the Supreme Court against the order. In response, Ren Tari and his two deputies were arrested and charged with sedition. A new Speaker, Donald Kalpokas, President of the UMP, was elected, thus reducing Natapei's majority in Parliament to one. In September a motion of no confidence tabled by Sope against the ruling coalition was defeated.

In March 2002 Parliament was dissolved after the Supreme Court ruled that its four-year term had expired. Natapei remained in charge of an interim Government until the general election, scheduled for early May. Also in March it was announced that the newly established People's Progressive Party (PPP) and Fren Melanesia were to form a coalition with the ruling NUP to contest the forthcoming election. It was reported that the general election was to be monitored by an independent group of observers. The future of the Comprehensive Reform Programme was widely perceived to be the main issue in the electoral campaign.

The general election was held on 2 May 2002; a record 138 of the 327 candidates stood as independents. The UMP won 15 of the 52 seats in the new Parliament and the VP 14. However, in accordance with the terms of the coalition agreement, the VP was permitted to nominate the next Prime Minister. The new Government was formed in June, with Natapei as Prime Minister. In July former Prime Minister Sope was convicted of fraud and sentenced to three years' imprisonment, having been convicted of forging two government-supported Letters of Guarantee, worth US $23m., during his premiership.

In August 2002, following the controversial appointment of Mael Apisai as Vanuatu's new police commissioner, disaffected police officers staged a raid during which they arrested Apisai, Attorney-General Hamilton Bulu and 14 other senior civil servants on charges of seditious conspiracy. Following an investigation, the charges were abandoned owing to a lack of evidence. Prime Minister Natapei subsequently assumed the police and VMF portfolios from the Minister of Internal Affairs, Joe Natuman, in what was thought to be an attempt to distance Natuman from some members of the police force, with whom he had reportedly become too closely involved. Later in the month members of the paramilitary VMF surrounded the police headquarters in Port Vila to serve arrest warrants on 27 of those who had been involved in the raid, including the acting police commissioner, Holis Simon, and the commander of the VMF, Api Jack Marikembo. Shortly afterwards, in an attempt to bring an end to hostilities, the Government signed an agreement with representatives from the police department and the VMF during a traditional Melanesian reconciliation ceremony. The police officers involved, who had been suspended from their posts, were reinstated, the police and the VMF undertook to make no further arrests, and it was agreed that Apisai's appointment would be reviewed by a newly appointed police services commission. At the same time it was decided that the allegations of conspiracy that had been brought against the 15 officials initially arrested would be considered by the judicial authorities. A new acting police commissioner, Lt-Gen. Arthur Coulton, was then appointed.

In October 2002 it was announced that the charges against 18 of those arrested in connection with the August raid would be abandoned, leaving eight senior officers to face trial on charges of mutiny and incitement to mutiny. In December four of these police officers were found guilty by the Supreme Court on charges of mutiny, incitement to mutiny, kidnapping and false imprisonment and were given suspended two-year prison sentences. In the same month police intervened to prevent former Prime Minister Sope from reclaiming his seat in Parliament, claiming that this was nullified by his conviction for fraud in July, despite the granting of a pardon in November by President Bani. The pardon, which Bani stated that he had made on the grounds of Sope's poor health, provoked widespread public opposition and led the Government to announce the appointment of a commission of inquiry to investigate the President's decision. However, at a by-election in November 2003, Sope was re-elected to the seat left vacant as a result of his conviction for fraud.

In April 2003 the election of Ham Lini (brother of Walter Lini, the late founder of the NUP) as President of the NUP led to the signing of a Memorandum of Understanding (MOU) inviting that party to join the coalition Government. A subsequent attempt to propose a motion of no confidence in the Government led Natapei to remove the UMP from the ruling coalition in November. The party was replaced in the coalition by members of the NUP, the PPP, the Green Confederation Party and independents. Continued instability within the coalition prompted three further cabinet reorganizations during the first three months of 2004.

In April 2004 former Speaker Alfred Maseng Nalo was sworn in as Vanuatu's new President, having defeated 31 other candidates during four rounds of voting. However, it was subsequently revealed that Maseng was serving a suspended prison sentence, having been convicted of misappropriation and receiving property dishonestly, and in May the Supreme Court ruled that he should be removed from office; Kalkot Mataskelekele was elected in his stead in August. Meanwhile, pre-empting a vote of no confidence against the Government, which held a minority of seats in Parliament, the Council of Ministers dissolved Parliament in June.

The Governments of Serge Vohor and Ham Lini

A general election was held on 6 July 2004, at which no single party won an overall majority and 25 new members were elected, including many independent candidates. However, the validity of the election was jeopardized by an incident on Tanna in which ballot boxes en route to Port Vila for processing were ambushed and burnt. More than 40 people were arrested in connection with the incident, including the acting Minister of Finance, Jimmy Nickelim of the VP. In late July Serge Vohor was elected Prime Minister, defeating Ham Lini by 28 votes to 24. A Council of Ministers composed of five political groups and several independents was appointed shortly afterwards. However, the stability of the new administration was threatened by rumours of shifting allegiances and reports that several members were being persuaded to cross the floor of Parliament. Despite these suggestions, an opposition motion of no confidence in the new Government, proposed in September, was defeated, with Vohor's administration securing the support of 31 of the 52 members. Further doubts over Vohor's ability to continue as Prime Minister were raised when the country's police commissioner attempted to arrest him on charges of contempt, following comments made in Parliament accusing the Chief Justice, Vincent Lunabeck, of being unduly influenced by a desire to please foreign interests. However, the Supreme Court dismissed the charges against Vohor in an appeal.

The Prime Minister became the focus of further serious controversy in November 2004 when he announced the establishment of diplomatic relations with Taiwan. The announcement, which Vohor defended by claiming that Taiwan's assistance was necessary to cover the budget deficit, was made only weeks after the Prime Minister had made an official visit to the People's Republic of China during which he had reiterated Vanuatu's allegiance to that country. The Council of Ministers, which had not given the necessary approval of the agreement with Taiwan, responded by demanding that Vohor renounce recognition of Taiwan or dismiss the entire cabinet. Controversy increased following reports that Vohor had assaulted the Chinese ambassador when questioned over the legitimacy of the Taiwanese flag flying in Port Vila. A parliamentary vote of no confidence in Vohor in December was approved by 35 votes to 14. Ham Lini was elected Prime Minister and subsequently appointed a cabinet that included five former ministers who had withdrawn their support for and voted against Vohor.

Lini's Government reversed the policy of the previous administration regarding Taiwan, and in July 2005 the Minister for Home Affairs made an official visit to China to sign a co-operation agreement providing for technical, logistical and financial support for the Vanuatu Police Force. Lini effected a cabinet reorganization in the same month. Further changes to the Council of Ministers reflected the decision of five opposition members to join the Green Confederation Party, led by the Minister of Finance, Moana Carcasses Kalosil. Their defection resulted in the Green Confederation Party becoming Lini's most significant partner in the governing coalition. In a further cabinet reorganization in November, Moana Carcasses was replaced as Minister of Finance by Willie Jimmy, hitherto Minister of Lands, Geology and Mines. In a further reallocation of portfolios announced in March 2006, Dunstan Hilton replaced Barak Sope as Minister of Agriculture, following reports that the former Prime Minister had been conducting negotiations aimed at attempting to oust Lini from office. In the same month the Prime Minister defeated a motion of no confidence presented by the opposition.

In late 2006 activists of the Vete association, which comprised inhabitants of Tongoa, vandalized unoccupied government buildings in Port Vila to publicize their campaign for land ownership rights. Vete claimed that, prior to the declaration of areas of the capital as public land, no customary owner had been named. In December it was reported that members of Vete were occupying several empty government buildings. In March 2007 allegations of witchcraft, following the death of a woman, led to civil unrest in outlying areas of Port Vila, with migrants from two islands engaging in violence that resulted in three fatalities and some 150 arrests. A two-week state of emergency was declared. The conflict provoked renewed public debate about internal migration in Vanuatu.

In May 2007 the Minister of Agriculture, Forestry and Fisheries, Marcellino Pipite, was dismissed, having been accused of disloyalty to the Government; he was replaced by Donna Brounie. Following further cabinet changes in June, the VP was removed from the governing coalition and replaced by the UMP, the President of which, former premier Vohor, was appointed Minister of Infrastructure and Public Utilities. The VP had reportedly allied itself with the UMP in the latter's attempt to oust the Government in a motion of no confidence, but the UMP subsequently retracted the motion. Vohor himself was dismissed in July, allegedly having been involved in an altercation with a government official. At the same time, the Deputy Prime Minister and Minister for Foreign Affairs and External Trade, Sato Kilman, and the Minister of Sports and Youth Development, Dunstan Hilton, both of the PPP, were removed from office owing to allegations of fraud (in August Hilton was reported to have been charged in a fraud case involving funds misappropriated from the National Bank of Vanuatu). The VP rejoined the Government, and its members were allocated major portfolios including that of home affairs. The former Prime Minister and VP President, Edward Natapei, assumed the role of Deputy Prime Minister and resumed the infrastructure and public utilities portfolios.

Natapei's return to office

A general election took place on 2 September 2008. About one-third of the incumbent members of Parliament lost their seats at the poll, including Barak Sope, the former Prime Minister, and Willie Jimmy, hitherto the Minister of Finance. The VP won 11 of the 52 seats, the largest representation in Parliament, followed by the NUP with eight seats, the UMP with seven and the VRP,

also with seven. On 22 September Edward Natapei, the leader of the VP, was elected Prime Minister after obtaining 27 parliamentary votes, while Maxime Carlot Korman, the leader of the VRP, received 25. The former Minister of Foreign Affairs and External Trade, George Wells, was elected as Speaker of Parliament. Natapei appointed outgoing Prime Minister Ham Lini as his Deputy Prime Minister. Within days of its formation Carlot led a motion of no confidence against the Natapei administration. However, before the motion could be presented to Parliament, in early October the Prime Minister effected a cabinet reorganization, in order to accommodate three members of the UMP, including party President Serge Vohor, who returned to his former position as Minister of Infrastructure and Public Utilities. The Natapei Government was thus able to defeat the subsequent motion of no confidence by 31 votes to 20. In March 2009 former Deputy Prime Minister Sato Kilman replaced Carlot as Leader of the Opposition.

In June 2009 Speaker George Wells was expelled from the NUP after accusing James Bule, the Minister of Trade and Commerce and a fellow member of the NUP, of misappropriating funds intended for copra farmers. Wells then joined the opposition, along with three other members of the legislature. In the same month the opposition parties brought a motion of no confidence against the Government, citing the allegedly missing copra subsidies. Before the motion was debated Harry Iauko (a VP member who had reportedly been voting with the opposition) was appointed Minister of Lands, Geology and Mines, and the Supreme Court declared invalid the election (in the previous September) of four members of Parliament (including the Minister of Foreign Affairs and External Trade, Bakoa Kaltonga), in response to a petition by Barak Sope alleging that the four had bribed and threatened voters. The Government defeated the motion of no confidence (by 28 votes to 18). Parliament then voted to remove Wells from the office of Speaker, and he was replaced by Carlot.

President Mataskelekele's term of office expired in August 2009. In September, in the third round of the ensuing presidential election, Iolu Abbil Johnson (who had held office as the minister responsible for internal affairs shortly after independence) was successful, defeating 14 other candidates. In November, anticipating another motion of no confidence, Natapei reorganized the Council of Ministers, bringing opposition members, from the Green Confederation Party and from the PPP, into the Government to replace members of the NUP and VRP. Ham Lini was replaced as Deputy Prime Minister by Sato Kilman, who was also appointed Minister of External Trade, while Moana Carcasses Kalosil became the new Minister of Internal Affairs. The Minister of Lands, Geology and Mines, Harry Iauko, was removed from office following allegations of malpractice concerning sales of land. Later in November the Speaker, Carlot, declared that Natapei had forfeited his parliamentary seat, because he had been absent from three consecutive sittings without giving written notice. In early December, however, the Chief Justice ruled that Carlot's decision had been unconstitutional and had no legal effect. Later in December a vote of no confidence in the Government (the fifth since Natapei took office in September 2008) was defeated. After rejecting on technical grounds several attempts by the Government to remove him from the office of Speaker, in January 2010 Carlot resigned, and his predecessor, George Wells, was re-elected to the office.

In April 2010, at the VP Congress, Natapei's leadership was challenged by Iauko, and the party was reported to have split into two rival factions. The formation of a new political party, the Land and Justice Party, was announced in November. Led by Ralph Regenvanu, the new party aimed primarily to protect customary land ownership and to address the issue of foreign ownership of local businesses.

On 2 December 2010 Natapei was ousted from the premiership in a parliamentary vote of no confidence; 31 of the 52 parliamentary members voted in support of the motion, which was reported to have been filed in response to Natapei's attempted suspension from Parliament of five opposition legislators, as well as his failure to agree to Fiji's assumption of the rotating chairmanship of the Melanesian Spearhead Group (see Foreign Affairs). Natapei was replaced by Deputy Prime Minister Kilman.

The Kilman Government

The composition of a new coalition Government was announced on 7 December 2010; Ham Lini was appointed Deputy Prime Minister and Minister of Trade; George Wells assumed responsibility for foreign affairs, relinquishing the position of Speaker (to which post Maxime Carlot Korman was subsequently re-elected), and Moana Carcasses Kalosil was allocated the finance portfolio. In mid-December the opposition filed a motion of no confidence in Kilman's Government. During Prime Minister Kilman's absence from the country, Deputy Prime Minister Lini dismissed Willie Lop, the newly appointed Minister of Internal Affairs, and replaced him with Dunstan Hilton, hitherto the Minister of Justice and Social Affairs; the justice portfolio was reallocated to Alfred Carlot. Before the opposition's motion of no confidence could be debated, Kilman effected a further cabinet reorganization on 21 December, this time incorporating members of the UMP within the coalition Government; new appointments included that of UMP President Serge Vohor, who became Minister of Infrastructure and Public Utilities, while Minister of Justice and Social Affairs Alfred Carlot was among the recent appointees removed from office.

A report accusing Harry Iauko of involvement in corruption during his tenure as Minister of Lands, Geology and Mines was submitted to Prime Minister Kilman by the former Director-General of the Ministry in January 2011; a number of other senior officials of the ministry were also incriminated. Kilman was reported to have offered assurances that the allegations would be fully investigated and appropriate action taken if the accused were found to have committed any wrongdoing. Transparency International urged the Vanuatu Government to appoint a Commission of Inquiry to examine comprehensively the claims made in the report.

In February 2011 Vohor, Minister of Education Charlot Salwai (the Vice-President of the UMP) and Minister of Agriculture, Quarantine, Forestry and Fisheries Marcellino Pipite (the VRP Secretary-General) resigned in protest against the failure of Kilman to allocate additional cabinet posts to the UMP and the VRP. Pre-empting a parliamentary vote of no confidence in his administration, Kilman effected a further cabinet reorganization later in February. While the UMP declared its intention to rejoin the opposition, Pipite returned to the Government as Minister of Education; Harry Iauko was transferred to the public utilities portfolio. A few days later the opposition, no longer commanding sufficient support to oust Kilman, withdrew its motion of no confidence against the premier. Some members of the opposition claimed that the Government had bribed a number of parliamentary members into withdrawing support for the motion.

In March 2011 Ralph Regenvanu, who had been appointed Minister of Lands and Natural Resources in February, was transferred to the justice portfolio and replaced by Alfred Carlot. Also in March Marc Neil-Jones, publisher of the *Daily Post* newspaper, was physically assaulted in his workplace by several men who he claimed were led by Minister of Public Utilities Iauko; Iauko later admitted having stormed into Neil-Jones's office, stating that he had been angered by articles printed in the *Daily Post* alleging his involvement in fraudulent land deals. Iauko was charged with assault in April.

On 24 April 2011 the Government of Kilman was removed from office following the approval of a parliamentary motion of no confidence by 26 votes to 25. Serge Vohor was thus returned to the premiership, six years after his removal from office. On the following day the incoming Prime Minister announced the composition of the new Council of Ministers; Joshua Kalsakau of the VLP was appointed Deputy Prime Minister, while assuming concurrent responsibility for the portfolios of infrastructure and public utilities, and Joe Natuman, who had been responsible for the foreign affairs portfolio during the premiership of Natapei, was returned to that post.

However, Vanuatu's political upheavals continued. On 13 May 2011 the Court of Appeal overruled Vohor's election as Prime Minister and reinstated Kilman in the post, upholding the latter's appeal against the legitimacy of his removal from office. Kilman had contended that his removal by a simple majority was unconstitutional, arguing that an absolute majority (a minimum of 27 of the 52 parliamentary members' votes, i.e. one more than Vohor had received) was required. Having secured the support of 27 members, Kilman was able to defeat a subsequent parliamentary motion of no confidence. The reinstated Prime Minister appointed Alfred Carlot as his Minister of Foreign Affairs, and Steven Kalsakau of the UMP replaced Carlot as Minister of Lands and Natural Resources.

In response to the Court of Appeal's ruling, Natapei lodged an appeal against the legitimacy of the appointment of Prime Minister Kilman in December 2010, on the grounds that the Speaker had failed to conduct a parliamentary vote to elect the new premier by secret ballot, as stipulated by the Constitution, since Kilman's candidacy had been unopposed. In mid-June 2011 the Court upheld Natapei's appeal, ruling that the appointment of Kilman had indeed been unconstitutional, and designated Natapei as interim Prime Minister, pending a parliamentary vote to appoint a permanent successor. The Council of Ministers was also replaced on an interim basis by those ministers who had been in government at the time of Natapei's removal from office in December 2010. Shortly thereafter Natapei, who confirmed that he would not contest the election to the premiership, appointed six new ministers to the interim Council of Ministers, including Patrick Crowby as Minister of Internal Affairs.

The parliamentary vote to elect a new Prime Minister was due to have been held on 23 June 2011; however, the vote was postponed following the boycotting of the session by Natapei and his supporters, amid claims that Kilman and his camp had offered bribes to a number of legislators in an attempt to obtain their allegiance in the forthcoming ballot. Kilman denied the allegations. In the event, the vote proceeded on 26 June, when Kilman defeated his sole rival, Vohor, by 29 votes to 23. On the following day Kilman reinstated his former Council of Ministers.

At the end of June 2011, three days after his reinstatement as Minister of Public Utilities, Harry Iauko was convicted on charges pertaining to the assault in March of Marc Neil-Jones, having pleaded guilty, and was fined US $150; additional charges of unlawful assembly, unlawful entry and criminal trespass against the minister had been withdrawn. The perceived lenience of the punishment meted out to Iauko elicited widespread criticism from regional and international media groups. Seven other men were also convicted of involvement in the attack on the *Daily Post* publisher and were fined up to $1,000.

The Government attracted further controversy in July 2011, when the Minister of Co-operatives and Ni-Vanuatu Business Development, Don Ken, was arrested for drunken and disorderly behaviour. Ken was subsequently alleged to have attempted to intimidate journalists who had reported on the case. Demands by the opposition that Kilman dismiss the minister were ignored.

In September 2011 Maxime Carlot Kilman was dismissed as Speaker after a motion of no confidence filed against him by Prime Minister Kilman was approved in a parliamentary vote boycotted by the opposition. PPP Vice-President Dunstan Hilton was elected as the new Speaker, prompting concern in some quarters of a further concentration of power within the Kilman camp.

In January 2012 Kilman dismissed Minister of Justice Ralph Regenvanu in what was widely interpreted as a response to the latter's decision in November 2011 to vote against ratification of Vanuatu's accession to the World Trade Organization—see Foreign Affairs. Charlot Salwai was appointed in Regenvanu's stead. Willie Reuben Abel was dismissed as Minister of Health in March 2012, but reappointed to the post in April. Meanwhile, in February the UMP expelled Minister of Justice Salwai, together with Minister of Lands and Natural Resources Steven Kalsakau, for having joined the Kilman Government in defiance of the party line. Salwai and Kalsakau retained their seats in Parliament, as independent legislators.

In September 2012 Minister of Foreign Affairs Alfred Carlot and Minister of Education Marcelino Pepite were accused of unlawfully embarking on a vessel prior to a customs inspection. The vessel in question had subsequently been seized by the authorities owing to suspicions that its crew had been engaged in a variety of illegal activities, including smuggling and fraud. Carlot and Pepite denied any wrongdoing. Also in that month, an investigation commenced into allegations that Kalsakau had fraudulently divested state land to his associates.

Recent developments: the 2012 election and the collapse of the Kilman administration

A general election was held on 30 October 2012. The VP won eight of the 52 seats in Parliament, while the PPP secured six, the UMP five, and the NUP and the Graon mo Jastis Pati (Land and Justice Party) four each. The Green Confederation Party, the Reunification Movement for Change, the Iauko Group and Nagriamel all took three seats, and the MPP and the Natatok Indigenous People's Democratic Party each garnered two. Other smaller groupings obtained five seats, and four independent candidates also gained parliamentary representation. The rate of participation by the electorate was 63.2%. Sato Kilman was re-elected as Prime Minister on 19 November, winning 29 votes in the legislature, compared with 23 for Edward Natapei; George

Wells was again selected as Speaker of Parliament. Another coalition Government was duly formed, with Ham Lini appointed as Deputy Prime Minister, Alfred Carlot receiving the foreign affairs portfolio and Charlot Salwai designated as Minister of Finance. A motion of no confidence in the new Government, sponsored by the opposition, was defeated on 10 December. Moreover, in February 2013 the Supreme Court rejected an appeal against Kilman's electoral eligibility. The petitioner, Willie Jimmy, had claimed that Kilman had been indebted to the state at the time of the poll, a violation of electoral rules.

A further motion of no confidence was filed in mid-March 2013. Fearing that he lacked the necessary parliamentary support to survive the vote, Kilman resigned the premiership on 21 March. Moana Carcasses Kalosil, the leader of the Green Confederation Party, was elected as Kilman's successor on 23 March, and established a new coalition Government, comprising representatives of eight parties and one independent. Most notably, VP President Natapei became Deputy Prime Minister, Minister of Foreign and External Affairs, and Minister of Trade, and Jimmy was named as Minister of Finance. Philip Boedoro of the VP was elected as Speaker in early April, following the resignation of Wells (prior to a planned vote on a motion of no confidence against him). Later that month Ralph Regenvanu, who had been allocated the lands portfolio, officially requested that staff in his ministry surrender any leases over state land that they had obtained from his predecessor, Kalsakau, as investigations continued into a controversial programme of preferential access to state land allegedly established by the latter. Jimmy was dismissed from the Council of Ministers in May, following allegations that he had been colluding with the opposition. Maki Simelum, the Minister of Justice and Social Welfare, was appointed as his replacement, with Silas Yatan assuming Simelum's former duties.

Foreign Affairs

Regional relations

In March 1988 Vanuatu signed an agreement with Papua New Guinea and Solomon Islands to form the Melanesian Spearhead Group (MSG), which aimed to preserve Melanesian cultural traditions and to lobby for independence from French rule for New Caledonia. In 1994 the MSG concluded an agreement providing for the gradual establishment of a free trade area encompassing the three countries. Fiji joined the group in 1996. In March 2007 the members of the MSG adopted a formal constitution at a meeting in Vanuatu. A diplomatic dispute arose in July 2010 when ni-Vanuatu Prime Minister Edward Natapei, the outgoing chairman of the MSG, refused to agree to Fiji's scheduled assumption of the rotating chairmanship and cancelled a planned meeting of the Group at which the transfer of leadership was due to have taken place; Natapei argued that the MSG was founded on democratic ideals and that allowing Fiji's unelected Prime Minister, Frank Bainimarama, to chair the Group would thus be an affront to its core principles. However, Fiji was permitted to assume the chairmanship following the ousting from office of Natapei in December (see Domestic Political Affairs), and incoming premier Sato Kilman expressed his determination to improve relations between Vanuatu and Fiji. In response to severe flooding in Fiji in early 2012, in March the Vanuatu Government donated 5m. vatu to the Fijian authorities to assist with the ongoing disaster relief operation.

An MOU signed between Vanuatu and Solomon Islands in March 2011 provided for the recruitment by the former of nursing staff from the latter in a bid to combat a persistent shortage of nursing staff within Vanuatu. Both countries pledged their commitment further to enhance co-operation in health and other services.

Like other small Pacific island nations, Vanuatu has a close relationship with Australia and New Zealand, which are important trading partners and sources of financial and technical assistance. In April 2009 the Australian Minister for Trade, Simon Crean, visited Vanuatu for discussions with the Government regarding the negotiation of a free trade agreement, known as PACER Plus, by Australia, New Zealand and the Pacific islands. The Vanuatu Government was reported to be supportive of the proposed agreement, although in December the Governor of the Reserve Bank of Vanuatu, Odo Tevi, suggested that such an agreement would be disadvantageous to Vanuatu's producers. In May of the same year Vanuatu and Australia concluded a development partnership agreement. During 2009 Australia and New Zealand both committed funds for road construction and maintenance in Vanuatu, and for the provision of free primary education from the 2010 school year. A tax information exchange agreement was signed by Vanuatu and Australia in April 2010. In July of that year Australia's Governor-General, Quentin Bryce, visited Vanuatu to attend celebrations intended to commemorate the 30th anniversary of Vanuatu's accession to independence. In March 2012 Kalvau Kaloris arrived in Canberra to commence work as Vanuatu's first resident High Commissioner in the Australian capital. Meanwhile, in October 2011 Vanuatu and New Zealand signed a Joint Commitment for Development, one of the principal goals of which was to boost economic performance in the Pacific nation through private sector development, especially in rural areas.

In April 2012 relations between Vanuatu and Australia were strained by a diplomatic row arising from an alleged breach of diplomatic protocol on the part of the Australian authorities; while passing through Sydney airport en route to Israel, Prime Minister Kilman and his delegation were stopped and obliged to fill in customs and immigration forms. Furthermore, once the paperwork had been completed, the Australian police arrested Kilman's private secretary, Clarence Marae, on charges of alleged fraud. In response to this perceived disrespectful treatment of the premier, in May the Government of Vanuatu expelled a contingent of Australian federal police officers from Port Vila, where they had been conducting a police training programme as part of a long-term Australian initiative to support Pacific states, and closed down their liaison office. The Australian authorities expressed their disappointment at this action, stating that the ejection of the police officers constituted 'self-inflicted damage'. Nevertheless, following bilateral discussions, it was announced in February 2013 that the Australian police officers would be permitted to return to Vanuatu.

China is an important provider of development assistance (despite a temporary rift over Vanuatu's recognition of Taiwan in 2004—see Domestic Political Affairs). In September 2009 China provided a new jointly owned fish-processing plant near Port Vila, and this was expected to allow Vanuatu's economy to benefit from fish caught within its territorial waters but hitherto processed elsewhere. Two Chinese naval vessels docked at Port Vila in August 2010, the first time that Chinese ships had visited Vanuatu; the four-day 'goodwill visit' was intended to enhance bilateral military relations. In October Vanuatu halted the issuing of visas in China after claims that ni-Vanuatu passports were being sold on the black market in that country, for around US $5,000 each. Henceforth, Chinese nationals seeking a visa for travel to Vanuatu would have to apply directly to the ni-Vanuatu authorities. Following the Government's failure to achieve its targeted revenue of $132m. for 2011, in December of that year it was announced that China and the European Union (EU, see p. 281) were to fund the $8m. budgetary shortfall.

Vanuatu has repeatedly reaffirmed its support for dialogue on the issue of the desire for independence of the Indonesian province of Papua. In June 2010 the Vanuatu legislature adopted a motion appealing for the International Court of Justice (ICJ) to investigate the legality of the region's incorporation within Indonesia in the 1960s.

Other external relations

Vanuatu has had an uneasy relationship with France, the former joint colonial power, and the French ambassador to Vanuatu was expelled twice owing to bilateral disputes during the 1980s—in 1981 and again in 1987. However, Maxime Carlot Korman, Vanuatu's first francophone Prime Minister, made an official visit to France in May 1992, and the two countries fully restored diplomatic relations in October. Improved relations with France were confirmed in 1993 with the signing of a bilateral co-operation agreement. In mid-1995 the Carlot Government was virtually alone in the region in failing to condemn France's resumption of nuclear tests in French Polynesia. The opposition criticized the Government's stance as not reflecting the views of the vast majority of ni-Vanuatu. In 2006, during a 'France-Oceania' meeting of regional leaders, the Governments of France and Vanuatu and the administration of New Caledonia concluded a tripartite agreement on co-operation. Under this agreement, assistance to Vanuatu during 2009 included the provision of improved television transmitters and a new sound system for the Parliament building. A long-standing disagreement over the sovereignty of the small, uninhabited Matthew and Hunter islands, situated between Vanuatu and New Caledonia, caused renewed controversy in January 2010, when the Minister of Internal Affairs, Moana Carcasses Kalosil, was criticized by opposition politicians for suggesting that France and Vanuatu should establish a condominium over the islands. The Maritime

Zone Amendment Act, approved by the Vanuatu legislature in June, referred to Matthew and Hunter islands as 'within and part of the sovereign state of the Republic of Vanuatu'. In December Prime Minister Edward Natapei warned that if France were not prepared to open a dialogue over ownership of the disputed islands Vanuatu would be forced to refer the matter to the ICJ.

In February 2009 a government delegation travelled to the US city of New York for a meeting of the UN Economic and Social Council (ECOSOC, see p. 25) to present a case against recommendations that Vanuatu's status be raised from that of Least Developed Country (LDC) to Developing Country. The change in status would lead to the loss of a number of economic privileges, including special treatment in areas such as trade and foreign aid. However, ECOSOC recommended against Vanuatu's graduation to a Developing Country owing to doubts over the sustainability of its progress, and at mid-2013 Vanuatu still retained LDC status. In March 2009 the Government re-entered negotiations on its accession to the World Trade Organization (WTO, see p. 444), initiated in 1995 but subsequently suspended. In May 2011 the WTO Working Party on Vanuatu's accession approved the country's accession arrangements, which were officially adopted later that month. Following the approval of the agreement by the Vanuatu legislature in November and its ratification by the President in June 2012, Vanuatu's membership of the organization was formalized on 24 August. There had been some opposition to the agreement, centred primarily on concerns regarding the Government's perceived lack of consultation with the public about the implications of WTO membership, the benefits of which continued to be questioned by some local non-governmental organizations. Meanwhile, in March 2011 Vanuatu hosted the Pacific Regional Conference on Climate Change, organized by the European Commission and supported by the Pacific Islands Forum (see p. 426).

CONSTITUTION AND GOVERNMENT

Vanuatu is a republic. Under the 1980 Constitution, legislative power is vested in the unicameral Parliament, with 52 members who are elected by universal adult suffrage for four years. The President is the head of state, elected for a five-year term by an electoral college consisting of Parliament and the Presidents of the Regional Councils. Executive power is vested in the Council of Ministers, appointed by the Prime Minister and responsible to Parliament. The Prime Minister is elected by and from members of Parliament. Judicial power is exercised by Magistrates' and Island Courts and the Supreme Court. The Court of Appeal is constituted by two or more judges of the Supreme Court sitting together. The six provincial authorities are Malampa, Penama, Sanma, Shefa, Tafea and Torba.

REGIONAL AND INTERNATIONAL CO-OPERATION

Vanuatu is a member of the Pacific Community (see p. 422), the Pacific Islands Forum (see p. 426), the Asian Development Bank (ADB, see p. 214) and the UN's Economic and Social Commission for Asia and the Pacific (ESCAP, see p. 31). The country is a signatory of the South Pacific Regional Trade and Economic Agreement (SPARTECA, see p. 427) and of the Lomé Conventions and the successor Cotonou Agreement (see p. 334) with the European Union (EU, see p. 281). Vanuatu is also a member of the Melanesian Spearhead Group, along with Fiji, Papua New Guinea and Solomon Islands; a free trade agreement concluded by members grants most favoured nation status for all trading transactions.

Vanuatu joined the UN in 1981 and is a member of the Commonwealth and the Organisation Internationale de la Francophonie (La Francophonie). The country formally acceded to the World Trade Organization (WTO, see p. 444) in August 2012.

ECONOMIC AFFAIRS

In 2011, according to estimates by the World Bank, Vanuatu's gross national income (GNI), measured at average 2009–11 prices, was US $705m., equivalent to $2,870 per head (or $4,500 per head on an international purchasing-power parity basis). During 2002–11, it was estimated, the population increased at an average annual rate of 2.6%, while gross domestic product (GDP) per head rose, in real terms, by an average of 2.2% per year. Overall GDP grew, in real terms, at an average annual rate of 4.8% in 2002–11, expanding by 4.3% in 2011, according to the UN. According to the Asian Development Bank

(ADB, see p. 214), however, GDP increased by 1.4% in 2011 and by 2.0% in 2012.

The agricultural sector (including forestry and fishing) contributed 21.5% of GDP in 2011, according to UN figures, compared with some 40% in the early 1980s. About 28.8% of the employed labour force was engaged in agricultural activities in mid-2013, according to FAO estimates. Coconuts, cocoa and coffee are grown largely for export. In 2011 coconut oil provided 26.5% of total export earnings and copra 17.7%. Yams, taro, cassava, breadfruit and vegetables are cultivated for subsistence purposes. Cattle, pigs, goats and poultry are the country's principal livestock, and beef is a significant export commodity. The forestry industry is also important, with timber having become a major export item. The Government derives substantial revenue from the sale of fishing rights to foreign fleets. In October 2005 the Government and the People's Republic of China signed an agreement that provided for the financing of the establishment of a new fish-processing plant near Port Vila. The facility would also be available for processing other products for export, such as beef. According to UN figures, the GDP of the agricultural sector increased at an average annual rate of 2.8% in 2002–11; the sector's GDP rose by 4.3% in 2011.

The industrial sector (including manufacturing, utilities and construction) contributed 10.8% of GDP in 2011, according to UN figures, although only 3.5% of the employed labour force were engaged in the sector in 1989. In 2002–11 the GDP of the industrial sector increased at an average annual rate of 5.1%; industrial GDP grew by 4.3% in 2011.

Manufacturing, which, according to the UN, contributed 3.3% of GDP in 2011, is mainly concerned with the processing of agricultural products. The country's first kava extraction plant (for the manufacture of beverages) was opened in 1998. However, in 2001 a ban was imposed on kava imports by several countries in Europe, owing to health concerns. In 2002–11, according to UN figures, the GDP of the manufacturing sector decreased at an average annual rate of 0.4%; in 2011, however, manufacturing GDP expanded by 4.3%.

Various mineral deposits have been identified. These include manganese on the island of Efate, and there are reserves of gold, copper and petroleum around the islands of Malekula and Espiritu Santo. In March 2006 an agreement was signed by the Vanuatu Government to allow a Swiss-US company to extract manganese and to export the commodity.

According to UN figures, construction activity alone contributed 5.5% of GDP in 2011. During 2002–11 construction GDP increased at an average annual rate of 10.9%; the sector grew by 4.3% in 2011.

Electricity generation is largely thermal. Long-term plans focus on the potential of renewable resources. Imports of mineral fuels comprised 18.3% of the value of total imports in 2011.

The economy depends heavily on the services sector, which accounted for 67.7% of GDP in 2011, according to UN figures. Tourism, 'offshore' banking facilities and a shipping registry, providing a 'flag of convenience' to foreign-owned vessels, make a significant contribution to the country's income. In 2011 a total of 248,898 foreign tourists visited Vanuatu, including 154,938 cruise ship arrivals. Revenue from tourism was estimated at US $142m. in 2007. According to UN figures, in 2002–11 the GDP of the services sector increased at an average annual rate of 5.4%; services GDP expanded by 4.3% in 2011.

In 2011 Vanuatu recorded a visible merchandise trade deficit of US $172.7m. and there was a deficit of $54.6m. on the current account of the balance of payments. In 2011 the principal sources of imports were Australia (providing 29.9% of total imports); other major suppliers were Singapore, New Zealand and Fiji. In that year the principal destination for exports was New Zealand (accounting for 11.4% of the total); other major purchasers were Australia, New Caledonia and Japan. The principal imports in 2011 were machinery and transport equipment, food and live animals, and mineral fuels and lubricants. Coconut oil copra and kava were the main export commodities in 2011.

An overall budget deficit of 1,632m. vatu, equivalent to 2.3% of GDP, was recorded in 2011, according to the ADB. Australia, New Zealand, France, the United Kingdom and Japan are significant sources of development assistance. In 2012/13 Australia budgeted for aid of $A59.8m. In 2011/12 development assistance from New Zealand was projected at $NZ20.0m. Vanuatu's external debt totalled US $111m. at the end of 2010. In that year the cost of debt-servicing was estimated to be equivalent to 1.4% of the value of exports of goods and services. The annual rate of inflation averaged 2.7% in 2002–11.

Consumer prices increased by 1.4% in 2012, according to the ADB. According to official figures, the rate of unemployment stood at 9.7% in 2009.

Vanuatu's economic development has been curtailed by the slow pace of reform, weak infrastructure and dependence on the agricultural sector, which is vulnerable to adverse weather conditions. Another important factor is the relatively high rate of population growth: in the early 21st century the country's GDP per head was estimated to be below the level of the mid-1980s. Opportunities for overseas employment have traditionally been limited. Since 2007, however, the establishment of schemes permitting Pacific islanders to work in the New Zealand and Australian horticultural industries have provided wider opportunities for ni-Vanuatu. A major challenge for successive governments has been the need to address the problem of hardship in rural areas, where access to basic services has remained very limited. Despite the deterioration in global economic conditions, GDP growth was maintained in 2008–10, largely owing to the steady performance of the tourism sector. In 2011 tourist arrivals by air decreased, and the rate of overall GDP growth slowed to 1.4%, according to the ADB, notwithstanding strong expansion in agricultural exports and the construction sector. The economy expanded for the 10th consecutive year in 2012, by 2.0%, bolstered by an upturn in visitor numbers, although the agricultural and construction sectors both declined in that year. The rate of inflation, which had averaged just 0.8% in 2011, rose to 1.4% in 2012. Vanuatu's accession to the World Trade Organization (WTO, see p. 444) in August 2012 was expected to lead to the country's closer integration into the global economy and to yield major benefits in the longer term. An acceleration of GDP growth, to 3.2%, was projected for 2013, while the rate of inflation was forecast to increase further, to 2.5%.

PUBLIC HOLIDAYS

2014: 1 January (New Year's Day), 21 February (Father Walter Lini Day), 5 March (Custom Chief's Day), 18 April (Good Friday), 21 April (Easter Monday), 1 May (Labour Day), 29 May (Ascension Day), 24 July (Children's Day), 30 July (Independence Day), 15 August (Assumption), 6 October (for Constitution Day), 29 November (Unity Day), 25 December (Christmas Day), 26 December (Family Day).

Statistical Survey

Source (unless otherwise indicated): National Statistics Office, Ministry of Finance and Economic Management, PMB 9019, Port Vila; tel. (678) 22110; fax (678) 24583; e-mail stats@vanuatu.com.vu; internet www.spc.int/prism/country/vu/stats.

AREA AND POPULATION

Area: 12,190 sq km (4,707 sq miles); *By Island* (sq km): Espiritu Santo 4,010; Malekula 2,024; Efate 887; Erromango 887; Ambrym 666; Tanna 561; Pentecost 499; Epi 444; Ambae 399; Vanua Lava 343; Gaua 315; Maewo 300.

Population: 186,678 at census of 16 November 1999; 234,023 (males 119,090, females 114,933) at census of 16 November 2009. *Mid-2013* (Secretariat of the Pacific Community estimate): 264,652 (Source: Pacific Regional Information System). *By Island* (mid-1999, official estimates): Espiritu Santo 31,811; Malekula 19,766; Efate 43,295; Erromango 1,554; Ambrym 7,613; Tanna 26,306; Pentecost 14,837; Epi 4,706; Ambae 10,692; Vanua Lava 2,074; Gaua 1,924; Maewo 3,385. Source: partly Pacific Regional Information System.

Density (mid-2013): 21.7 per sq km.

Population by Age and Sex (Secretariat of the Pacific Community estimates at mid-2013): *0–14:* 97,671 (males 50,825, females 46,846); *15–64:* 156,737 (males 79,107, females 77,630); *65 and over:* 10,244 (males 5,238, females 5,006); *Total* 264,652 (males 135,170, females 129,482) (Source: Pacific Regional Information System).

Principal Towns (population at 2009 census): Port Vila (capital) 44,039; Luganville (Santo) 13,156.

Births and Deaths (annual averages, 2005–10, UN estimates): Birth rate 30.4 per 1,000; Death rate 5.1 per 1,000. Source: UN, *World Population Prospects: The 2010 Revision*.

Life Expectancy (years at birth): 71.1 (males 69.1; females 73.2) in 2011. Source: World Bank, World Development Indicators database.

Economically Active Population (census of May 1989): Agriculture, forestry, hunting and fishing 40,889; Mining and quarrying 1; Manufacturing 891; Electricity, gas and water 109; Construction 1,302; Trade, restaurants and hotels 2,712; Transport, storage and communications 1,030; Financing, insurance, real estate and business services 646; Community, social and personal services 7,891; *Sub-total* 55,471; Activities not adequately defined 11,126; *Total labour force* 66,597 (males 35,692, females 30,905). *2009 Census* (persons aged 15 to 64 years): Subsistence farmers 41,877; Total employed (incl. others) 42,295; Unemployed (seeking work) 4,518; Total labour force 46,813 (males 28,217, females 18,596). *Mid-2013:* Agriculture, etc. 40,000; Total labour force 139,000 (Source: FAO).

HEALTH AND WELFARE

Key Indicators

Total Fertility Rate (children per woman, 2010): 3.9.

Under-5 Mortality Rate (per 1,000 live births, 2010): 14.

Physicians (per 1,000 head, 2008): 0.1.

Hospital Beds (per 1,000 head, 2008): 1.7.

Health Expenditure (2009): US $ per head (PPP): 210.

Health Expenditure (2009): % of GDP: 4.9.

Health Expenditure (2009): public (% of total): 89.8.

Access to Water (% of persons, 2010): 90.

Access to Sanitation (% of persons, 2010): 57.

Total Carbon Dioxide Emissions ('000 metric tons, 2008): 91.7.

Carbon Dioxide Emissions Per Head (metric tons, 2008): 0.4.

Human Development Index (2011): ranking: 125.

Human Development Index (2011): value: 0.617.

For sources and definitions, see explanatory note on p. vi.

AGRICULTURE, ETC.

Principal Crops ('000 metric tons, 2011, FAO estimates): Coconuts 398.6; Roots and tubers 43.8; Vegetables and melons 11.3; Bananas 10.7; Groundnuts, with shell 2.6; Maize 0.8.

Livestock ('000 head, year ending September 2011, FAO estimates): Cattle 160; Pigs 92; Goats 20; Horses 3; Chickens 810.

Livestock Products (metric tons, 2011, FAO estimates): Cattle meat 2,500; Pig meat 3,468; Chicken meat 1,150; Cows' milk 3,300; Hen eggs 1,000.

Forestry ('000 cu m, 2011, FAO estimates): *Roundwood Removals* (excl. bark): Sawlogs and veneer logs 28; Fuel wood 91; Total 119. *Sawnwood Production* (all broadleaved, incl. railway sleepers): Total 14.

Fishing ('000 metric tons, live weight, 2010): Marine fishes 43.6 (Skipjack tuna 24.0; Yellowfin tuna 2.6; Bigeye tuna 4.3; Albacore 12.6); Marine crustaceans 250.0; Total catch (incl. others) 97.8.

Source: FAO.

FINANCE

Currency and Exchange Rates: Currency is the vatu. *Sterling, Dollar and Euro Equivalents* (31 October 2012): £1 sterling = 148.203 vatu; US $1 = 91.960 vatu; €1 = 119.484 vatu; 1,000 vatu = £6.75 = $10.87 = €8.37. *Average Exchange Rate* (vatu per US $): 106.74 in 2009; 96.91 in 2010; 89.47 in 2011.

Budget (million vatu, 2011): *Revenue:* Tax revenue 11,563; Other current revenue 1,198; Capital assets 4; Total 12,765, excluding grants from abroad (2,436). *Expenditure:* Current expenditure 15,527; Capital expenditure 1,305; Total 16,832. Source: Asian Development Bank.

International Reserves (US $ million at 31 December 2011): IMF special drawing rights 2.29; Reserve position in IMF 3.83; Foreign exchange 167.67; *Total* 173.79. Source: IMF, *International Financial Statistics*.

Money Supply (million vatu at 31 December 2011): Currency outside depository corporations 4,886; Transferable deposits 17,528; Other deposits 34,874; *Broad money* 57,288. Source: IMF, *International Financial Statistics*.

Cost of Living (Consumer Price Index; base: 2005 = 100): All items 129.8 in 2009; 133.1 in 2010; 134.3 in 2011. Source: ILO.

Gross Domestic Product (million vatu at constant 2006 prices): 56,652 in 2009; 57,898 in 2010; 60,388 in 2011.

Expenditure on the Gross Domestic Product (million vatu at current prices, 2011): Government final consumption expenditure 10,835; Private final consumption expenditure 43,271; Gross fixed capital formation 22,974; Increase in stocks 799; Statistical discrepancy –518; *Total domestic expenditure* 77,361; Exports of goods and services 34,747; *Less* Imports of goods and services 42,495; *GDP in purchasers' values* 69,613. Source: UN Statistics Division, National Accounts Main Aggregates Database.

Gross Domestic Product by Economic Activity (million vatu at current prices, 2011): Agriculture, forestry and fishing 13,724; Mining, manufacturing and utilities 3,386 (Manufacturing 2,115); Construction 3,493; Wholesale, retail trade, restaurants and hotels 13,635; Transport, storage and communications 7,563; Other activities 21,962; *Total gross value added* 63,763; Net taxes on products 5,850 (figure obtained as a residual); *GDP in purchasers' values* 69,613. Source: UN Statistics Division, National Accounts Main Aggregates Database.

Balance of Payments (US $ million, 2011): Exports of goods 60.2; Imports of goods –232.9; *Trade balance* –172.7; Exports of services and income 293.5; Imports of services and income –186.8; *Balance on goods, services and income* –66.0; Current transfers received 13.3; Current transfers paid –1.8; *Current balance* –54.6; Capital account (net) 21.3; Direct investment (net) –51.2; Portfolio investment (net) –0.5; Other investments (net) –4.6; Net errors and omissions 11.5; *Overall balance* –78.1. Source: Asian Development Bank.

EXTERNAL TRADE

Principal Commodities (million vatu, 2011): *Imports c.i.f.* (excl. imports for re-export): Food and live animals 5,537; Beverages and tobacco 1,038; Mineral fuels, lubricants, etc. 4,964; Chemicals 2,855; Basic manufactures 3,566; Machinery and transport equipment 5,542; Miscellaneous manufactured articles 2,820; Total (incl. others) 27,062. *Exports f.o.b.* (excl. re-exports): Cocoa 247; Copra 1,065; Beef 516; Timber 65; Coconut oil 1,592; Shells 30; Kava 762; Total (incl. others) 6,012.

Principal Trading Partners (million vatu, 2011): *Imports c.i.f.* (excl. imports for re-export): Australia 8,092; Fiji 1,686; France 875; Japan 696; New Zealand 3,103; Singapore 4,928; Total (incl. others) 27,062. *Exports f.o.b.* (excl. re-exports): Australia 679; European Union countries 181; Japan 317; New Caledonia 342; New Zealand 686; Total (incl. others) 6,012.

TRANSPORT

Road Traffic ('000 motor vehicles in use, 2001, estimates): Passenger cars 2.6; Commercial vehicles 4.4. Source: UN, *Statistical Yearbook*.

Shipping: *Flag Registered Fleet* (at 31 December 2012): Number of vessels 646; Total displacement ('000 grt) 3,362.1 (Source: Lloyd's List Intelligence—www.lloydslistintelligence.com). *International Sea-borne Freight Traffic* ('000 metric tons, 1990, estimates): Goods loaded 80; Goods unloaded 55 (Source: UN, *Monthly Bulletin of Statistics*).

Civil Aviation (traffic on scheduled services, 2009): Kilometres flown (million) 3; Passengers carried ('000) 112; Passenger-km (million) 227; Total ton-km (million) 22 (Source: UN, *Statistical Yearbook*). *2010:* Passengers carried ('000) 336 (Source: World Bank, World Development Indicators database).

TOURISM

Foreign Tourist Arrivals: 98,650 in 2009; 97,180 in 2010; 93,960 in 2011. Note: Figures refer to arrivals by air only; arrivals from cruise-ships were: 129,793 in 2009; 140,468 in 2010; 154,938 in 2011.

Tourist Arrivals by Country of Residence (2011): Australia 57,843; New Caledonia 11,376; New Zealand 11,399; Other Pacific 3,397; Europe 5,265; North America 1,922; Total (incl. others) 93,960.

Tourism Receipts (US $ million, incl. passenger transport): 104 in 2005; 109 in 2006; 142 in 2007 (Source: World Tourism Organization).

COMMUNICATIONS MEDIA

Telephones (2011): 6,200 main lines in use.

Mobile Cellular Telephones (2011): 137,000 subscribers.

Internet Subscribers (2011): 2,000.

Broadband Subscribers (2011): 300.

Source: International Telecommunication Union.

EDUCATION

Pre-primary (2009/10 unless otherwise indicated): 252 schools (1992); 822 teachers; 11,264 pupils.

Primary (2009/10 unless otherwise indicated): 374 schools (1995); 1,931 teachers; 41,834 pupils.

Secondary (2009/10 unless otherwise indicated): 27 schools (1995); 591 teachers (2002); 20,256 students.

Tertiary (2002): 2,124 students.

Secondary (Teacher Training): 1 college (1989); 13 teachers (1983); 124 students (1991).

Pupil-teacher Ratio (primary education, UNESCO estimate): 21.7 in 2009/10 (Source: UNESCO Institute for Statistics).

Adult Literacy Rate (UNESCO estimates): 82.6% (males 84.3%; females 80.8%) in 2010 (Source: UNESCO Institute for Statistics).

Directory

The Government

HEAD OF STATE

President: IOLU ABBIL JOHNSON (appointed 2 September 2009).

COUNCIL OF MINISTERS
(May 2013)

The Government includes members of the of the Green Confederation Party (GC), the Vanuatu Republikan Pati (VRP), the Union of Moderate Parties (UMP), the People's Progressive Party (PPP), the Vanua'aku Pati (VP), the Vanuatu Liberal Democratic Party (VLDP), the Melanesian Progressive Pati (MPP) and the Graon mo Jastis Pati (Land and Justice Party), as well one independent (Ind.).

Prime Minister: MOANA CARCASSES KALOSIL (GC).

Deputy Prime Minister, Minister of Foreign and External Affairs, and Minister of Trade: EDWARD NIPAKE NATAPEI (VP).

Minister of Tourism and Commerce: MARCELLINO PIPITE (VRP).

Minister of Infrastructure and Public Utilities: ESMON SAE (MPP).

Minister of Internal Affairs: PATRICK CROWBY (UMP).

Minister of Justice and Social Welfare: SILAS YATAN (GC).

Minister of Agriculture, Livestock, Forestry, Fisheries and Biosecurity: DAVID TOSUL (PPP).

Minister of Health: SERGE VOHOR (UMP).

Minister of Education: BOB LOUGHMAN (VP).

Minister of Finance: MAKI SIMELUM (VP).

Minister of Lands, Geology, Mines, Energy and Water Resources: RALPH REGENVANU (Graon mo Jastis Pati).

Minister of Youth Development and Sports: TONY WRIGHT (UMP).

Minister of Planning and Climate Change Adaptation: THOMAS LAKEN (Ind.).

MINISTRIES AND DEPARTMENTS

Prime Minister's Office: PMB 9053, Port Vila; tel. 22413; fax 26301; internet www.governmentofvanuatu.gov.vu.

Deputy Prime Minister's Office: PMB 9056, Port Vila; tel. 27045; fax 27832.

Ministry of Agriculture, Livestock, Forestry, Fisheries and Biosecurity: PMB 9039, Port Vila; tel. 23406; fax 26498.

Ministry of Education: PMB 9028, Port Vila; tel. 22309; fax 24569.

Ministry of Finance: PMB 9058, Port Vila; tel. 23032; fax 27937.

Ministry of Foreign and External Affairs: PMB 9051, Port Vila; tel. 27045; fax 27832.

Ministry of Health: PMB 9042, Port Vila; tel. 22545; fax 26113.

Ministry of Infrastructure and Public Utilities: PMB 9057, Port Vila; tel. 22790; fax 27714.

Ministry of Internal Affairs: PMB 9036, Port Vila; tel. 22252; fax 27064.

Ministry of Justice and Social Welfare: PMB 9036, Port Vila; tel. 22252; fax 27064.

Ministry of Lands, Geology, Mines, Energy and Water Resources: PMB 9090, Port Vila; tel. 22892; fax 27708; e-mail molvanuatu@gmail.com; internet www.mol.gov.vu.

Ministry of Planning and Climate Change Adaptation: Port Vila.

Ministry of Trade, Commerce and Tourism: PMB 9056, Port Vila; tel. 25674; fax 25677.

Ministry of Youth Development and Sports: POB 9006, Port Vila; tel. 25298; fax 26879.

Legislature

PARLIAMENT

Speaker: PHILIP BOEDORO.

General Election, 30 October 2012

Party	Seats
Vanua'aku Pati (VP)	8
People's Progressive Party (PPP)	6
Union of Moderate Parties (UMP)	5
Graon mo Jastis Pati	4
National United Party (NUP)	4
Nagriamel	3
Green Confederation Party	3
Reunification Movement for Change (RMC)	3
Iauko Group	3
Melanesian Progressive Pati (MPP)	2
Natatok Indigenous People's Democratic Party (NIPDP)	2
Others	5
Independents	4
Total	**52**

Election Commission

Vanuatu Electoral Commission: PMB 033, Port Vila; tel. 23914; fax 26681; Principal Electoral Officer LIONEL KALUAT (acting).

Political Organizations

Graon mo Jastis Pati (Land and Justice Party): POB 1189, Port Vila; e-mail ralph@graonmojastis.org; internet www.graonmojastis .org; f. 2010; aims to protect customary land ownership and to address issue of foreign ownership of local businesses; President RALPH REGENVANU.

Green Confederation Party: POB 538, Port Vila; tel. 7778069; e-mail moanakalosil6@gmail.com; f. 2001; est. by breakaway group of the UMP; Leader MOANA CARCASSES KALOSIL.

Melanesian Progressive Pati (MPP): POB 39, Port Vila; tel. 23485; fax 23315; f. 1988; est. by breakaway group of the VP; Chair. BARAK SOPE; Sec.-Gen. GEORGES CALO.

National Community Association Party (NCAP): Port Vila; f. 1996; advocates land reform.

National United Party (NUP): Port Vila; f. 1991; est. by supporters of Walter Lini, following his removal as leader of the VP; Pres. HAM LINI; Leader WILLIE TITONGOA.

People's Democratic Party (PDP): Port Vila; f. 1994; est. by breakaway faction of the NUP.

People's Progressive Party (PPP): Port Vila; f. 2001; Pres. SATO KILMAN; Sec.-Gen. WILLIE LOP.

Tu Vanuatu Kominiti: Port Vila; f. 1996; espouses traditional Melanesian and Christian values; Leader HILDA LINI.

Union of Moderate Parties (UMP): POB 698, Port Vila; f. 1980; Pres. SERGE VOHOR; Vice-Pres. CHARLOT SALWAI.

Vanua'aku Pati (VP) (Our Land Party): POB 472, Port Vila; tel. 22584; f. 1971; est. as the New Hebrides National Party; advocates 'Melanesian socialism'; Pres. EDWARD NATAPEI; First Vice-Pres. IOLU ABBIL JOHNSON; Sec.-Gen. SELA MOLISA.

Vanuatu Labour Party (VLP): Port Vila; f. 1986; trade union-based; Leader JOSHUA KALSAKAU.

Vanuatu Progressive Development Party: Epi; f. 2011; promotes devt in rural sector; Pres. ROBERT BOHN; Sec.-Gen. PETER MAWA.

Vanuatu Republikan Pati (VRP): Port Vila; f. 1998; est. by breakaway faction of the UMP; Pres. MARCELLINO PEPITE.

The following political organizations won seats at the 2012 general election: Nagriamel (Pres. THITAM GOISET, Spokesman JEFF PATUN-VANU), Iauko Group (Pres. HARRY IAUKO), Natatok Indigenous People's Democratic Party (Pres. ALFRED CARLOT), Reunification Movement for Change, People's Service Party, Vanuatu National Party and the Vanuatu Liberal Democratic Party (Pres. WILLIE JIMMY).

The groupings Namangie Aute, Tan Union (Leader VINCENT BULE-KONE) and Fren Melanesia (Leader ALBERT RAVUTIA) represent rural interests on the islands of Espiritu Santo and Malekula. The John Frum Movement represents interests on the island of Tanna.

Diplomatic Representation

EMBASSIES AND HIGH COMMISSIONS IN VANUATU

Australia: Winston Churchill Ave, POB 111, Port Vila; tel. 22777; fax 23948; e-mail australia_vanuatu@dfat.gov.au; internet www .vanuatu.highcommission.gov.au; High Commissioner JEREMY BRUER.

China, People's Republic: PMB 9071, Rue d'Auvergne, Nambatu, Port Vila; tel. 23598; fax 24877; e-mail publicinfo@chinese-embassy .com.vu; internet vu.china-embassy.org; Ambassador XIE BOHUA.

France: Kumul Highway, POB 60, Port Vila; tel. 28700; fax 28701; e-mail ambafra@vanuatu.com.vu; internet www.ambafrance-vu .org; Ambassador MICHEL DJOKOVIC.

New Zealand: La Casa d'Andrea e Luciano, Rue Pierre Lamy St, POB 161, Port Vila; tel. 22933; fax 22518; e-mail kiwi@vanuatu.com .vu; internet www.nzembassy.com/vanuatu; High Commissioner BILL DOBBIE.

Judicial System

The Supreme Court has unlimited jurisdiction to hear and determine any civil or criminal proceedings, and is the court of first instance in constitutional matters. It consists of the Chief Justice, appointed by the President of the Republic after consultation with the Prime Minister and the leader of the opposition, and three other judges, who are appointed by the President of the Republic on the advice of the Judicial Service Commission. The Court of Appeal is constituted by two or more judges of the Supreme Court sitting together.

Magistrates' Courts have limited jurisdiction to hear and determine any civil or criminal proceedings. Island Courts have been established in several local government regions, and are constituted when three justices are sitting together to exercise civil or criminal jurisdiction, as defined in the warrant establishing the court. A magistrate nominated by the Chief Justice acts as Chairman. The Island Courts are competent to rule on land disputes.

In 2001 legislation was introduced to establish a new Land Tribunal, in order to expedite the hearing of land disputes. The tribunal was to have three levels, and no cases were to go beyond the tribunal and enter either the Supreme Court or the Island Courts.

Supreme Court: PMB 041, rue de Querios, Port Vila; tel. 22420; fax 22692; Chief Justice VINCENT LUNABEK.

Public Prosecutor: KAYLEEN TAVOA.

Office of the Attorney-General: PMB 9048, Port Vila; tel. 22362; e-mail cngui@vanuatu.gov.vu; Attorney-General ISHMAEL KALSA-KAU.

Religion

Most of Vanuatu's inhabitants profess Christianity. Presbyterians form the largest Christian group (with about one-half of the population being adherents), followed by Roman Catholics and Anglicans.

CHRISTIANITY

Vanuatu Christian Council: POB 13, Luganville, Santo; tel. 03232; f. 1967; est. as New Hebrides Christian Council; 5 mem. churches, 2 observers; Chair. Rt Rev. JAMES LIGO; Sec. SHEM TEMA.

The Roman Catholic Church

Vanuatu forms the single diocese of Port Vila, suffragan to the archdiocese of Nouméa (New Caledonia). At 31 December 2007 there were an estimated 32,500 adherents in the country. The Bishop participates in the Catholic Bishops' Conference of the Pacific, based in Fiji.

Bishop of Port Vila: JOHN BOSCO BAREMES, Evêché, POB 59, Port Vila; tel. 22640; fax 25342; e-mail catholik@vanuatu.com.vu.

The Anglican Communion

Anglicans in Vanuatu are adherents of the Church of the Province of Melanesia, comprising eight dioceses: Vanuatu (which also includes New Caledonia), Banks and Torres and six dioceses in Solomon Islands. The Archbishop of the Province is the Bishop of Central Melanesia, resident in Honiara, Solomon Islands. In 1985 the Church had an estimated 16,000 adherents in Vanuatu.

Bishop of Vanuatu: Rt Rev. JAMES LIGO, Bishop's House, POB 238, Luganville, Santo; tel. 37065; fax 36331; e-mail comdov@vanuatu .com.vu.

Bishop of Banks and Torres: Rt Rev. NATHAN TOME, Bishop's House, POB 19, Sola, Torba Province; tel. and fax 38520.

Protestant Churches

Presbyterian Church of Vanuatu (Presbitirin Jyos long Vanuatu): POB 150, Port Vila; tel. 27184; fax 23650; f. 1948; 56,000 mems (1995); Moderator Pastor OBED MOSES; Assembly Clerk Pastor FAMA RAKAU.

Other denominations active in the country include the Apostolic Church, the Assemblies of God, the Churches of Christ in Vanuatu and the Seventh-day Adventist Church.

BAHÁ'Í FAITH

National Spiritual Assembly of the Bahá'ís of Vanuatu: POB 1017, Port Vila; tel. 22419; e-mail nsavanuatu@vanuatu.com.vu; f. 1953; Sec. CHARLES PIERCE; mems resident in 233 localities.

The Press

Hapi Tumas Long Vanuatu: POB 1292, Port Vila; tel. 23642; fax 23343; quarterly tourist information; English; Publr MARC NEIL-JONES; circ. 12,000.

Pacific Island Profile: Port Vila; f. 1990; monthly; general interest; English and French; Editor HILDA LINI.

Port Vila Presse: Raffea House, 1st Floor, POB 637, Port Vila; tel. 22200; fax 27999; e-mail marke@presse.com.vu; internet www .presse.com.vu; f. 2000; daily; English and French; Publr MARKE LOWEN; Editor RICKY BINIHI.

Vanuatu Daily Post: POB 1292, Port Vila; tel. 23111; fax 24111; e-mail tpost@vanuatu.com.vu; internet www.dailypost.vu; daily; English; Publr MARC NEIL-JONES; Editor ROYSON WILLIE; circ. 2,000.

Vanuatu Weekly: PMB 049, Port Vila; tel. 22999; fax 22026; f. 1980; weekly; govt-owned; Bislama, English and French; circ. 1,700.

Vanuatu Wikli Post: f. 2008; weekly; Bislama; Editor RICKY BINIHI.

Viewpoints: Port Vila; weekly; newsletter of Vanuaaku Pati; Editor PETER TAURAKOTO.

Wantok Niuspepa: POB 1292, Port Vila; tel. 23642; fax 23343.

Broadcasting and Communications

REGULATORY AUTHORITY

Telecommunications and Radio Communications Regulator: PMB 3547, Port Vila, Efate; tel. 27621; fax 27440; e-mail enquiries@ trr.vu; internet www.trr.vu; f. 2008; oversees telecommunications, radio communications and related sectors; Head RONALD BOX.

TELECOMMUNICATIONS

Digicel Vanuatu Ltd: PMB 9103, Ellouk Plateau, Port Vila; tel. 5556000; fax 27865; e-mail customercarevanuatu@digicelgroup .com; internet www.digicelvanuatu.com; f. 2008; CEO PAUL STAFFORD.

Telecom Vanuatu Ltd (TVL): POB 146, Port Vila; tel. 22185; fax 22628; e-mail customercare@tvl.net.vu; internet www.tvl.vu; f. 1989; national and international telecommunications and internet services; CEO CATHERINE RUMILLAT.

BROADCASTING

Radio

Vanuatu Broadcasting and Television Corpn (VBTC): PMB 9049, Port Vila; tel. 22999; fax 22026; internet www.vbtc.com.vu; fmrly Government Media Services, name changed in 1992; Gen. Man. FRED VUROBARAVU; Chair. CHRISTIAN BIHU.

Radio Vanuatu: PMB 9049, Port Vila; tel. 23615; fax 22026; f. 1966; govt-owned; broadcasts in English, French and Bislama; Dir JOE BOMAL CARLO.

Television

Vanuatu Broadcasting and Television Corpn (VBTC): see Radio

Television Blong Vanuatu: Port Vila; f. 1993; govt-owned; French-funded; broadcasts for 6 hours daily in French and English; Gen. Man. CLAUDE CASTELLY; Programme Man. GAEL LE DANTEC.

Finance

(cap. = capital; res = reserves; dep. = deposits; brs = branches; amounts in vatu unless otherwise indicated)

BANKING

Central Bank

Reserve Bank of Vanuatu: PMB 9062, Port Vila; tel. 23333; fax 24231; e-mail rbvinfo@rbv.gov.vu; internet www.rbv.gov.vu; f. 1981; est. as Central Bank of Vanuatu; name changed as above in 1989; govt-owned; cap. 100.0m., res 673.5m. (Dec. 2008); Gov. (vacant).

National Bank

National Bank of Vanuatu: POB 249, Rue de Paris, Port Vila; tel. 22201; fax 27227; e-mail info@nbv.vu; internet www.nbv.vu; f. 1991; est. upon assumption of control of Vanuatu Co-operative Savings Bank; govt-owned; cap. 600m., dep. 10,649m. (Dec. 2011); Chair. SILAS CHARLES HAKWA; Man. Dir BOB HUGHES; 25 brs.

Foreign Banks

ANZ Bank (Vanuatu) Ltd: PMB 9003, Lini Highway, Port Vila; tel. 26355; fax 22230; e-mail vanuatu@anz.com; internet www.anz.com/ vanuatu; f. 1971; CEO SHANE FREEMAN; brs in Port Vila and Luganville.

European Bank Ltd (USA): International Bldg, Fr Walter Lini Highway, POB 65, Port Vila; tel. 27700; fax 22884; e-mail info@ europeanbank.net; 'offshore' and private banking; cap. US $0.75m., res US $1.25m., dep. US $44.76m. (Dec. 2008); Chair. THOMAS MONTGOMERY BAYER; Pres. ROBERT MURRAY BOHN.

Westpac Banking Corporation (Australia): Lini Highway, Port Vila; tel. 22084; fax 24773; e-mail westpacvanuatu@westpac.com.au; internet www.westpac.vu; Man. R. B. WRIGHT; 2 brs.

Financial Institutions

The Vanuatu Financial Centre Association: POB 1128, Port Vila; tel. 23410; fax 23405; e-mail VFCA@vanuatu.com.vu; internet www.fca.vu; f. 1980; group of banking, legal, accounting and trust cos administering 'offshore' banking and investment; Chair. MARK STAFFORD; Sec. THOMAS BAYER.

Vanuatu Financial Services Commission (VFSC): Bougainville St, PMB 9023, Port Vila; tel. 22247; fax 22242; e-mail info@vfsc.vu; internet www.vfsc.vu; f. 1993; statutory body; regulation and supervision of non-banking financial services; Commr GEORGE ANDREWS.

INSURANCE

Pacific Insurance Brokers: POB 229, Port Vila; tel. 23863; fax 23089.

QBE Insurance (Vanuatu) Ltd: La Casa D'Andrea Bldg, POB 186, Port Vila; tel. 22299; fax 23298; e-mail info.van@qbe.com; Gen. Man. BARRY J. BAILEY.

Trade and Industry

GOVERNMENT AGENCY

Vanuatu Investment Promotion Authority: PMB 9011, Port Vila; tel. 24096; fax 25216; e-mail ataritambe@vanuatu.gov.vu; internet www.investinvanuatu.com; fmrly the Vanuatu Investment Board, name changed as above in 2000; CEO SMITH TEBU.

CHAMBER OF COMMERCE

Chamber of Commerce and Industry of Vanuatu: POB 189, Port Vila; tel. 27543; fax 27542; e-mail vancci@vanuatu.com.vu; internet www.vanuatuchamber.org; Pres. JACQUES NIOTEAU.

MARKETING BOARD

Vanuatu Commodities Marketing Board: POB 268, Luganville, Santo; f. 1982; sole exporter of major commodities, including copra, kava and cocoa; Chair. JACK LOWANI; Gen. Man. GABRIEL ARUBANI.

UTILITIES

Utilities Regulatory Authority: Port Vila, Efate; tel. 23335; internet www.ura.gov.vu; f. 2008; regulates electricity and water supply; Pres. JOHNSON NAVITI MARAKIPULE.

Union Electrique du Vanuatu (Unelco Vanuatu Ltd): POB 26, rue Winston Churchill, Port Vila; tel. 22211; fax 25011; e-mail unelco@unelco.com.vu; f. 1939; private org. contracted for the generation and supply of electricity in Port Vila, Luganville, Tanna and Malekula, and for the supply of water in Port Vila; fully owned subsidiary of GDF Suez, France; Dir-Gen. JEAN FRANÇOIS BARBEAU.

TRADE UNIONS

Vanuatu Council of Trade Unions (VCTU): POB 287, Port Vila; tel. 26903; fax 23679; e-mail carlo@vanuatu.com.vu; Pres. OBED MASINGIOW; Sec.-Gen. EPHRAIM KALSAKAU.

Transport

ROADS

There are about 1,070 km of roads, of which 54 km, mostly on Efate Island, are sealed.

SHIPPING

The principal ports are Port Vila and Luganville. Various shipping lines operate services to Vanuatu. At the end of 2012 the flag registered fleet comprised 646 vessels, with a total displacement of 3,362,111 grt. A shipping registry, based in Singapore, provides a 'flag of convenience' to foreign-owned vessels.

Vanuatu Maritime Authority: POB 320, Marine Quay, Port Vila; tel. 23128; fax 22949; e-mail iantchichine@vma.com.vu; domestic and international ship registry, maritime safety regulator; Commissioner of Maritime Affairs JOHN T. ROOSEN; Chair. LENNOX VUTI.

Ports and Harbour Department: PMB 9046, Port Vila; tel. 22339; fax 22475; e-mail nhamish@vanet.com; Harbour Master Capt. LUKE BEANDI; Dir NORRIS HAMISH.

Burns Philp (Vanuatu) Ltd: POB 27, Port Vila.

Ifira Shipping Agencies Ltd: POB 68, Port Vila; tel. 22929; fax 22052; f. 1986; Man. Dir CLAUDE BOUDIER.

Sami Ltd: Kumul Highway, POB 301, Port Vila; tel. 24106; fax 23405.

South Sea Shipping: POB 84, Port Vila; tel. 22205; fax 23304.

Vanua Navigation Ltd: POB 44, Port Vila; tel. 22027; f. 1977; est. by the Co-operative Federation and Sofrana Unilines; Chief Exec. GEOFFREY J. CLARKE.

CIVIL AVIATION

The principal airports are Bauerfield (Efate, for Port Vila) and Pekoa (Espiritu Santo, for Luganville), both of which service international flights. There are airstrips on all Vanuatu's principal islands, and also an international airport at White Grass on Tanna.

Civil Aviation Authority: PMB 9068, Port Vila; tel. 23301; fax 23783; e-mail civav@vanuatu.com.vu; Dir JOSEPH NEIL (acting).

Air Vanuatu: Air Vanuatu House, 3rd Floor, Rue de Paris, Port Vila; tel. 23838; fax 23250; e-mail sales@airvanuatu.com.vu; internet www.airvanuatu.com; f. 1981; govt-owned national carrier since 1987; regular services between Port Vila and Sydney, Brisbane and Melbourne (Australia), Nadi (Fiji), Nouméa (New Caledonia), Auckland (New Zealand) and Honiara (Solomon Islands); CEO JEAN-PAUL VIRELALA.

Dovair: Port Vila; privately owned; operates domestic services.

Tourism

Tourism is an important source of revenue. Visitors are attracted by the islands' scenery and rich local customs. There were some 120 hotels and guest houses in 2003, providing more than 1,300 rooms. In 2011 foreign visitor arrivals (including cruise-ship passengers) totalled 248,898. The majority of visitors by air in that year were from Australia, New Zealand and New Caledonia. Receipts from tourism totalled some US $142m. in 2007. The development of the tourism industry has hitherto been concentrated on the islands of Efate, Espiritu Santo and Tanna, but other islands are also being promoted.

Vanuatu Hotels and Resorts Association: POB 5151, Port Vila; tel. 22040; fax 27579; internet www.vanuatuhotelsandresortsassociation.com; Chair. TONY PITTAR; Sec. DAVE CROSS.

Vanuatu Tourism Office: Lini Highway, POB 209, Port Vila; tel. 22685; fax 23889; e-mail tourism@vanuatu.com.vu; internet www.vanuatutourism.com; Gen. Man. ANNIE NIATU; Chair. NOEL FAIONALAVE.

Defence

Upon Vanuatu's achievement of independence in 1980, a defence pact with Papua New Guinea was signed. A 300-strong paramilitary force, the Vanuatu Mobile Force, exists. In 2003 Vanuatu sent 50 defence personnel to join the Australian-led regional intervention force in Solomon Islands. In 2007 the Government allocated 1,087m. vatu for defence, equivalent to 11.1% of total expenditure.

Education

In 2009 the central Government launched a policy to provide free primary education from the following year. The policy, which was made possible with financial assistance from Australia and New Zealand, was in response to evidence that many children were denied access to education because their parents could not afford school fees. At 2007 it was estimated that 87% of children between the ages of six and 11 were enrolled at primary institutions. In 2010 enrolment in pre-primary schools included 41% of children in the relevant age-group, while the comparable ratio for secondary education was 47%. Secondary education begins at 12 years of age, and comprises a preliminary cycle of four years and a second cycle of three years. In 2009/10 there were 41,834 pupils enrolled in primary schools (which numbered 374 in 1995) and 20,256 pupils attended the country's secondary schools (which numbered 27 in 1995). Vocational education and teacher-training are also available.

An extension centre of the University of the South Pacific was opened in Port Vila in 1989. Students from Vanuatu can also receive higher education at the principal faculties of that university (in Suva, Fiji), in Papua New Guinea, or in France.

In 2004 the country's first pre-school (the Vila North Model Pre-School) was opened. The pre-school, which had been built with funding of 5.6m. vatu from the European Union, was to have a staff of four teachers and was expected to serve as a centre for training other pre-school teachers.

The 2007 budget allocated 2,542m. vatu to education (26.1% of total expenditure by the central Government).

THE VATICAN CITY

(THE HOLY SEE)

Introductory Survey

LOCATION, CLIMATE, LANGUAGE, RELIGION, FLAG

The State of the Vatican City is situated entirely within the Italian capital, Rome, on the right bank of the Tiber river. It covers an area of 0.44 sq km (0.17 sq miles). The climate is Mediterranean, with warm summers and mild winters (see Italy). Italian and Latin are the official languages. Roman Catholicism is the official religion. The state flag, which is square, consists of two vertical stripes of yellow and white, with the papal coat of arms superimposed on the white stripe.

HISTORY

For a period of nearly 1,000 years, dating roughly from the time of Charlemagne to the year 1870, the Popes ruled much of the central Italian peninsula, including the city of Rome. During the process of unification, the Kingdom of Italy gradually absorbed these States of the Church, the process being completed by the entry into Rome of King Victor Emmanuel's troops in September 1870. From 1860 to 1870 many attempts had been made to induce the Pope, Pius IX, to surrender his temporal possessions. However, since he regarded them as a sacred trust from a higher power, to be guarded on behalf of the Church, he refused to do so. After the entry of the Royal Army into Rome, he retired to the Vatican, from where no Pope emerged again until the ratification of the Lateran Treaty of 11 February 1929. By the Law of Guarantees of May 1871, Italy attempted to stabilize the position of the Papacy by recognizing the Pope's claim to use of the Palaces of the Lateran and the Vatican, the Papal villa of Castelgandolfo, and their gardens and annexes, and to certain privileges customary to sovereignty. This unilateral arrangement was not accepted by Pius IX, and his protest against it was repeated constantly by his successors.

In 1929 two agreements were made with the Italian Government—the Lateran Treaty and the Concordat. By the terms of the Lateran Treaty, the Holy See was given exclusive power and sovereign jurisdiction over the State of the Vatican City, which was declared neutral and inviolable territory. Financial compensation was also given for the earlier losses. Under the Concordat, Roman Catholicism became the state religion of Italy, with special privileges defined by law. The new Italian Constitution of 1947 reaffirmed adherence to the Lateran Treaty. In December 1978 the two sides agreed on a draft plan for a new Concordat, under which Catholicism would cease to be the official Italian state religion and most of the Catholic Church's special privileges in Italy would be removed. The revised version was signed in February 1984.

In 1917 the first legal code, the Code of Canon Law (Codex Iuris Canonici), was devised for the Catholic Church. In 1963 a pontifical commission was inaugurated to investigate possible reforms to the law, and in 1981 the Pope received more than 70 cardinals and bishops who had prepared the new code's 1,752 rules. Revisions included a reduction in the number of cases meriting excommunication and a general relaxing of penalties, with increased emphasis on the importance of the laity within the Church. The code was ratified in January 1983, and came into force in November.

In October 1978 Cardinal Karol Wojtyła (then Archbishop of Kraków, Poland) became the first non-Italian Pope since the 16th century, taking the name John Paul II. Security surrounding the Pontiff was tightened considerably after an attempt on his life in May 1981 and another in May 1982. An Italian parliamentary inquiry, which published its findings in March 2006, concluded that the 1981 attempt was orchestrated by the former USSR.

In April 1984 Pope John Paul II announced a major reorganization of offices in the Roman Curia, including the delegation of most of his responsibility for the routine administration of the Vatican City to the Secretariat of State. In July 1988 a number of reforms to the Curia were introduced. These consolidated the power of the Secretariat of State, as well as reorganizing some of the Congregations and Pontifical Commissions.

In February 1987 Italian judges issued a warrant for the arrest of Archbishop Paul Marcinkus, the Chairman of the Istituto per le Opere di Religione (IOR or 'Vatican Bank'), and two other bank officials for alleged involvement in the fraudulent bankruptcy of the Banco Ambrosiano in Milan, which collapsed in 1982. In July 1987, however, the Italian Supreme Court cancelled the warrants, stating that the Vatican stood outside Italian jurisdiction and that, according to the Lateran Treaty, Italy did not have the right to interfere in the affairs of the central organs of the Roman Catholic Church. In March 1989 the Vatican announced a wide-ranging reorganization of the IOR, abolishing the post of Chairman and appointing a commission of five cardinals, nominated by the Pope, to preside over the bank, assisted by a committee of financial experts. Archbishop Marcinkus retired from papal service in October 1990.

In March 1998 the Vatican released its long-awaited 'definitive statement' condemning anti-Semitism and anti-Judaism, and repenting for Roman Catholic passivity during the Nazi Holocaust. However, a number of high-ranking Jewish officials expressed disappointment at the document and demanded an explicit apology for the attitude of Pope Pius XII (who held the papacy during 1939–58) and the Roman Catholic Church's failure to speak out, at the time, against Nazi atrocities. In March 2000 the Pope made a comprehensive and unprecedented plea for forgiveness for the 'past sins of the Church', including racial and ethnic discrimination and Christian mistreatment of minorities, women and native peoples.

In February 2001 the Constitution, dating back to the Lateran Treaty of 1929, was replaced by a new Fundamental Law incorporating a number of constitutional amendments made over the years. The Fundamental Law clarified the distinction between the legislative, executive and judicial branches of the Vatican.

Following a lengthy period of ill health, Pope John Paul II died on 2 April 2005 at the age of 84. Only St Peter and Pius IX, in the mid-19th century, had enjoyed longer papacies. More than 3m. people visited the Vatican City in the period between the death of John Paul II and his funeral, which took place on 8 April and was attended by around 200 world leaders. By the time of his death, John Paul II had canonized 482 saints (more than all his predecessors combined since the 16th century), performed 1,338 beatifications and created 232 cardinals.

On 19 April 2005, at a conclave attended by 115 of the 117 cardinals of voting age (under 80 years old), Cardinal Joseph Ratzinger of Germany was elected as the new Supreme Pontiff, taking the name Benedict XVI. Ratzinger, who was aged 78 years, was hitherto the Dean of the College of Cardinals, the Prefect of the Congregation for the Doctrine of the Faith and President of the International Theological Commission and of the Pontifical Biblical Commission. The inauguration of the 265th Roman pontiff took place on 24 April. Benedict XVI subsequently reappointed the officials of the Roman Curia, who had, according to custom, ceased to hold their offices on the death of John Paul II. In his first addresses as Pope, Benedict pledged to continue his predecessor's attempts to improve ties with other Christian denominations and with other religions.

In early 2006 it was reported that the Pope had decided to stop using one of his nine official titles, that of Patriarch of the West; this was regarded as a gesture of reconciliation towards the Orthodox churches. On 24 March Benedict appointed 15 new cardinals; notable among the appointees was Joseph Zen Ze-kiun, Bishop of Hong Kong and an outspoken critic of the Chinese Government.

In September 2006 Cardinal Angelo Sodano retired as Secretary of State and was replaced by Cardinal Tarcisio Bertone, hitherto Archbishop of Genoa, Italy, while Cardinal Edmund Szoka was replaced as President of the Pontifical Commission for the Vatican City State and of the Governorate of the Vatican City

State by Archbishop Giovanni Lajolo. Archbishop Dominique Mamberti assumed Lajolo's previous post as Secretary of State for Relations with States (in effect the minister responsible for foreign affairs).

In January 2009 it was announced that legislation enacted in Italy would henceforth not automatically be incorporated into Vatican law, as had hitherto been the case; instead, each law would be considered on an individual basis prior to adoption. The Vatican stated that the decision had been motivated by the number and instability of Italian laws, as well as their increasing 'contrast with the inviolable principles of the Church'.

In June 2010 it was reported that Cardinal Crescenzio Sepe, the Archbishop of Naples, was under investigation for an allegedly corrupt property transaction, made in 2004, while he was Prefect of the Congregation for the Evangelization of Peoples (commonly known as Propaganda Fide, the shorter version of its former title); Sepe had been removed from his post as Prefect in 2006, and a new Prefect, Cardinal Ivan Dias, had been appointed by Pope Benedict with a mandate to introduce more transparent management of the large property assets used to finance the work of Propaganda Fide. In September 2010 the President of the IOR, Ettore Gotti Tedeschi, and the bank's Director-General, Paolo Cipriani, were placed under investigation, following the seizure by the Italian financial authorities of €23m. that had been deposited in an Italian bank for onward transfer: the transaction allegedly failed to comply with Italian regulations intended to prevent money-laundering. The Vatican Secretariat of State issued a statement expressing complete confidence in the two officials, and declaring that the problem was due to a misunderstanding. It pointed out that the Vatican had been making efforts to achieve greater financial transparency, and to comply with international standards, as stipulated by the Organisation for Economic Co-operation and Development (OECD, see p. 388), in order to combat money-laundering and the financing of terrorism. In late December Pope Benedict announced the creation of a new Financial Information Authority (FIA) to supervise the Vatican's financial operations and to ensure compliance with international regulations on financial transparency and the prevention of illegal transactions. New Vatican legislation on the prevention of money-laundering, the financing of terrorism, fraud and counterfeiting, which had been agreed in a Monetary Convention concluded with the European Union (EU, see p. 281) in December 2009, came into effect at the beginning of April 2011. The sum of €23m. that had been confiscated in 2010 was released by the Italian authorities in May 2011. Nevertheless, in March 2012 the Vatican appeared for the first time on the US Department of State's list of countries vulnerable to money-laundering. Following a unanimous vote of no confidence by the IOR's board of directors in May, Tedeschi was forced to stand down from his post as President of the bank; the board claimed that Tedeschi had failed adequately to perform his official duties, while Tedeschi himself countered that he had been dismissed as punishment for seeking to introduce greater transparency in the IOR's transactions.

In June 2010 Pope Benedict announced the creation of the Pontifical Council for Promoting the New Evangelization, to be presided over by Archbishop Salvatore (Rino) Fisichella, with the aim of countering what was perceived to be the increasingly secular nature of society in Western developed countries. In July a Swiss bishop, Kurt Koch, was nominated as the President of the Pontifical Council for Promoting Christian Unity. In November 24 new cardinals were created (including Bishop Koch). The late Pope John Paul II was beatified in a ceremony on 1 May 2011. In October Archbishop Giuseppe Bertello, hitherto the Apostolic Nuncio (diplomatic representative) to Italy, was appointed President of the Pontifical Commission for the Vatican City State and of the Governorate of the Vatican City State.

In October 2010, meanwhile, the European Commission recommended investigations (originally begun in 2005) into the exemption from taxation of church-owned property in Italy, following an official complaint by the Italian political party Radicali Italiani that the exemption contravened EU regulations on unfair competition. In February 2012 the Italian Government announced that it would remove the tax-exempt status of church-owned property that was not used for religious purposes, thereby raising an estimated €720m. annually.

In March 2012 the Vatican announced that a criminal investigation was under way concerning the unauthorized release to the Italian media, over the previous two months, of confidential documents: they included a letter to the Pope from Archbishop Carlo Maria Vigano, who had served as Secretary-General of the Governorate of the Vatican City State in 2009–11, alleging corrupt practices in the awarding of Vatican contracts. Other documents allegedly revealed disagreements among Vatican officials as to how the IOR should comply with international banking regulations. In April 2012 a commission comprising three cardinals was also appointed by the Pope to investigate the affair. In the following month the Pope's butler, Paolo Gabriele, was arrested in connection with the leaked documents. In October Gabriele was convicted of stealing thousands of confidential papers from the Pope, photocopying them and divulging their content to an Italian journalist (who had subsequently published a controversial book detailing alleged corruption, infighting and scandals within the Vatican), and was sentenced to 18 months' imprisonment. A computer expert, Claudio Sciarpelletti, was convicted in November for acting as Gabriele's accomplice in the crime and received a suspended sentence of two months.

In an unexpected development, following an announcement earlier in the month, on 28 February 2013 Pope Benedict XVI, who was 85 years old, became the first incumbent to resign from the papacy for nearly 600 years, citing poor health and his increasing inability adequately to fulfil his role. After his abdication Benedict XVI (who did not revert to his name of birth) was to be known as 'Pope emeritus' and retained the honorific title of 'His Holiness'. During the *interregnum* (also known as 'sede vacante'), the former Pope's duties were carried out by Cardinal Tarcisio Bertone, the Secretary of the Secretariat of State and Chamberlain of the Apostolic Chamber.

On 13 March 2013, at a conclave attended by 115 of the 117 cardinals of voting age, Cardinal Jorge Mario Bergoglio of Argentina was elected as the new Supreme Pontiff, taking the name Francis. Bergoglio, who was aged 76 years, was hitherto the Archbishop of Buenos Aires. His appointment was of particular historic import in that he was the first Jesuit pontiff, the first from the Americas and the first from the southern hemisphere. The inauguration of the 266th Roman pontiff, who was widely considered a doctrinal conservative but also a potential reformist, took place on 19 March. Of especial note was the attendance of Patriarch Bartholomew I of Constantinople at the inauguration, the first time that a leader of the Eastern Orthodox church had participated in this ceremony. In one of his first addresses as Pope, Francis demanded 'decisive action' in the fight against sexual abuse by priests. (Cardinal Keith O'Brien of Scotland, United Kingdom, had declined to participate in the papal conclave in March in the wake of allegations of past inappropriate behaviour with junior clergy members—some of which charges he subsequently admitted to.) In mid-April Pope Francis appointed a multinational committee of eight cardinals (only one of whom was from the Vatican itself) and one bishop, which was to act as an advisory body regarding the proposed restructuring of the Roman Curia; the first meeting of the committee was scheduled to be held in October. In the mean time, Pope Francis reappointed the officials of the Roman Curia on an interim basis.

Foreign Affairs

Pope Paul VI (who held the papacy from 1963–78) became the first Pope to make official visits outside Italy for over a century, undertaking nine tours on six continents from 1964. Pope John Paul II continued this policy, making more than 100 foreign visits during his papacy, and in 1984 he inaugurated World Youth Day, held annually in a different country. The Vatican's prominence in international affairs increased from the late 1980s. In July 1989 diplomatic relations with Poland, severed in 1945, were restored. The Vatican had hitherto maintained no diplomatic relations with Eastern European governments under communist rule, except for Yugoslavia. During the early 1990s diplomatic relations were restored or established with many former communist states, including with the USSR in 1990. In 1992 full diplomatic relations were restored, after more than 120 years of discord, between the Vatican and Mexico. In December 1993 the Vatican and Israel signed a mutual-recognition agreement, which led to the establishment of full diplomatic ties and the exchange of ambassadors in September 1994. Meanwhile, in February 1994 the Vatican established diplomatic relations with Jordan, in an apparent move to strengthen links with the Arab world to counterbalance its recent recognition of Israel. Similarly, in October of that year the Vatican instituted 'official relations' with the Palestine Liberation Organization.

Diplomatic relations between the Vatican and the People's Republic of China had been severed in 1951 following the communists' accession to power in Beijing. In August 1999 China vetoed plans for Pope John Paul II to visit Hong Kong later that year, owing to the Vatican's diplomatic ties with Taiwan. In January 2000 the state-controlled Chinese Patriotic Catholic Association (CPCA, which is not recognized by the Vatican) in Beijing ordained five bishops in a ceremony coinciding with official papal ordinations in the Vatican City. Relations further deteriorated following the Pope's announcement in September 2000 that he was to canonize 120 Western and Chinese Catholics killed in China between 1648 and 1930. However, in October 2001 Pope John Paul II issued an apology to China for the sins committed by Christians against the country; an appeal was also made for diplomatic relations between the two states to be restored. Informal talks recommenced in early 2003, but were adversely affected by the outspoken anti-Government stance of Hong Kong's Bishop (later Cardinal), Joseph Zen Ze-kiun. Following the accession of Benedict XVI, there appeared to be a growing emphasis on the need to improve Sino-Vatican relations, although the ordination of a series of bishops by the CPCA in April and May 2006 provoked criticism from the Pope. In July 2007 an open letter addressed to Chinese Catholics on behalf of the Pope called for 'respectful and constructive' relations. In September the Vatican approved the ordination of a bishop by the CPCA, allaying fears that efforts toward reconciliation would be undermined by the death earlier that month of a Vatican-appointed bishop, John Han Dingxiang, while in detention by the Chinese authorities. In November 2010 the ordination of a bishop by the CPCA (the first for almost five years) was described by the Holy See as harmful to relations, and in July 2011 another bishop was excommunicated after being ordained without papal authority; however, two bishops were subsequently ordained—one in November 2011 and the other in April 2012—with the approval of both the Pope and the Chinese authorities.

In February 2000 the Vatican and the Palestinian (National) Authority signed an historic agreement on joint interests, which appealed for a peaceful solution, through dialogue, to the Israeli–Palestinian conflict, and called for an internationally guaranteed special statute for the city of Jerusalem that safeguarded freedom of religion and conscience. The Israeli Government criticized the accord as representing unwelcome 'interference' by the Vatican in the ongoing Middle East peace talks. In early 2000 the Pope undertook a millennial pilgrimage to some of the principal biblical sites of the Middle East, visiting Egypt in February (the first visit by a pontiff to that country) and Israel, Jordan and the West Bank in March. Pope John Paul II's six-day visit to the politically volatile Holy Land constituted the first papal visit to that region for 36 years. In 2002 an agreement was signed by the Vatican and the Turkish Government, promoting religious dialogue between Muslims and Christians.

In mid-2001 Pope John Paul II undertook visits to Greece and Syria, the first by a Roman pontiff since the division of Christianity into eastern and western churches. During his visit to Greece, the Pope attempted to heal the historic rift between the Roman Catholic and Orthodox churches by presenting an apology to the Orthodox community for wrongs committed over the centuries by the Roman Catholic Church. The Pope, despite not being granted the consent of the Russian Orthodox Patriarch, also visited Ukraine, where he called for an end to the 1,000-year schism between Roman Catholicism and the Orthodox Church in Ukraine and, by extension, the Russian Orthodox Church. The leaders of the Orthodox Church in Ukraine refused to meet the Pope, although his visit attracted much popular support. Tensions between the Roman Catholic Church and the Russian Orthodox Church increased in February 2002 when the Vatican announced that the four apostolic administrations in Russia (officially considered to be temporary) had become dioceses. This move was interpreted by representatives of the Russian Orthodox Church as the establishment of an alternative church within the country, and a few days later a visit to Russia by the Head of the Pontifical Council for the Promotion of Christian Unity, Cardinal Walter Kasper, was cancelled by the Russian Orthodox Church.

In November 2002 John Paul II became the first pontiff to address the Italian Parliament, symbolically closing the Vatican's territorial dispute with Italy. His speech advocated institutional recognition by the EU of Europe's Christian heritage. This followed an ultimately unsuccessful call in October for Christianity to be enshrined in the proposed EU constitution. In June 2004 John Paul II publicly criticized the lack of reference to Christianity in the approved text of the EU constitutional treaty. In 2007 Pope Benedict XVI criticized the Italian Govern-

ment for its plans to give homosexual and unmarried couples equal legal status with married couples.

During late 2002 and early 2003 Pope John Paul II was prominent in opposing the prospect of US-led military intervention to remove the regime of Saddam Hussain in Iraq, urging a diplomatic resolution to the crisis. Papal envoys were sent to Baghdad, Iraq, and Washington, DC, USA. This was followed in March 2003 by an historic five-day meeting with a delegation from Israel's Chief Rabbinate.

Pope John Paul II visited Switzerland in June 2004, where it was announced that diplomatic relations, which had been severed in 1873, were to be restored. In July 2004 the Pope issued a joint statement with Patriarch Bartholomew I of Constantinople, the Orthodox Patriarch in Istanbul, Turkey, confirming their commitment to dialogue between the Roman Catholic and Orthodox churches.

Tensions between the Vatican and the Muslim world increased in September 2006 after Benedict XVI delivered a lecture at the University of Regensburg, Germany, in the course of which he quoted a medieval Byzantine emperor as saying that the Prophet Muhammad had contributed only 'evil and inhuman' things to the world. The Pope's remarks provoked widespread protest in Muslim countries. Benedict later apologized for causing offence, stating that the quotation did not reflect his personal belief. In November Benedict visited Turkey, where he was praised by Muslims for facing Mecca while praying in the Blue Mosque in Istanbul. He also held a joint service with Patriarch Bartholomew I, a gesture that was regarded as an attempt to heal the divisions between the Roman Catholic and Greek Orthodox churches. In May 2007 it was announced that the Pontifical Council for Inter-Religious Dialogue was to be restored, thereby reversing a decision in March 2006 to place it under the direction of the Pontifical Council for Culture. (The decision to downgrade the Council, which had previously been led by an expert on Islamic affairs, had been criticized by Muslim leaders.) King Abdullah ibn Abd al-Aziz Al Sa'ud of Saudi Arabia visited the Vatican in November 2007 for talks with the Pope, representing the first ever meeting between a Saudi monarch and a pontiff. In March 2008 Benedict XVI received a delegation of Muslim religious leaders, following the publication in October 2007 of an open letter to the Pope, in which 138 Muslim leaders had urged increased co-operation between Roman Catholic and Muslim religious leaders. In November 2008 the Vatican hosted a three-day conference of Roman Catholic and Muslim scholars, at which the Pope urged political and religious leaders to work together to protect the freedom of conscience and of worship. In January 2011 Egypt temporarily recalled its ambassador to the Vatican, after Pope Benedict had condemned recent violent attacks on Christians in Egypt and Iraq and urged the respective Governments to adopt measures to protect religious minorities. In July, following a visit to the Pope by the Malaysian Prime Minister, the Holy See and Malaysia established diplomatic relations, and in February 2013 formal diplomatic ties were created with the newly independent South Sudan. In May 2013 the recently installed Tawadros II became the first Pope of the Coptic Orthodox Church of Egypt to visit the Vatican for 40 years. During his six-day visit the Coptic leader discussed with Pope Francis the increasing incidence of violent attacks against the Christian minority in Egypt.

Relations between the Holy See and Israel have frequently been strained, despite continued efforts to resolve disputes (most notably concerning Pius XII's attitude to the Holocaust) since the establishment of diplomatic relations in 1993. In January 2009 the decision of Benedict XVI to rehabilitate four bishops who had been excommunicated in 1988 provoked severe criticism from world leaders and jeopardized efforts to improve relations with Israel, owing to the fact that one of the bishops, Richard Williamson, had denied the existence of gas chambers at the Nazi concentration camps. The Vatican subsequently claimed that Benedict XVI had not been aware of Williamson's views, and stipulated that he recant them before resuming his appointment as a bishop. In May 2009 Pope Benedict XVI spent five days in Israel and the West Bank. In a speech in Tel-Aviv, the Pope condemned anti-Semitism as 'totally unacceptable' and, during a visit to the Yad Vashem Holocaust museum in Jerusalem, he repudiated denial of the Holocaust. However, he was criticized by a number of Israeli political leaders for failing to express sufficient remorse for the Nazi persecution of the Jews.

From the 1980s the Vatican was obliged to confront growing scandal over allegations of the sexual abuse of children by clergy in many countries, over several previous decades. The scandal was compounded by the fact that, in many cases, senior clergy had been aware of the allegations but had simply transferred the perpetrators to a different post. In November 2001 Pope John Paul II issued an apology to victims of sexual abuse perpetrated by members of the Catholic clergy. In January 2002 new regulations were published by the Vatican, outlining the appropriate method of dealing with cases of alleged sexual abuse, notably against children, by members of the clergy. However, in mid-2002 it was revealed that Cardinal Bernard Law, the Archbishop of Boston, Massachusetts, USA, had protected a number of priests who faced accusations of sexual misconduct against children. Hundreds of priests in the USA resigned or were subsequently suspended or sued in the wake of more than 200 allegations of sexual abuse. A 'zero tolerance' policy adopted by the US Conference of Catholic Bishops in June was subsequently rejected by the Vatican; a somewhat altered charter, which provided for the eventual dismissal of any priests found guilty of sexual abuse by a church tribunal, was accepted by the Vatican in December. Cardinal Law resigned in that month.

In 2010 the Vatican was subject to renewed pressure following a series of allegations of sexual abuse of children perpetrated by clergy, notably in Belgium, Ireland, Germany and the USA. The issue caused outrage in Ireland following the publication in November 2009 of the findings of an official inquiry into abuse in the Archdiocese of Dublin in 1975–2004, which had led to the resignation of four bishops. In March 2010 the Pope was personally implicated in a number of abuse scandals for the first time, following various allegations that, as Archbishop of Munich and subsequently as Prefect of the Congregation for the Doctrine of the Faith, he had failed to take disciplinary action against priests in Germany and the USA accused of abusing children. In June the creation was announced of an Apostolic Visitation (an investigation at the most senior level) to Ireland concerning abuse; the investigation's report, issued in March 2012, found that those who should have exercised vigilance had often failed to do so effectively. In July 2011 the Irish Prime Minister, Enda Kenny, was scathingly critical of the Church's conduct; the Apostolic Nuncio in Ireland was recalled and later replaced. In May, meanwhile, the Pope instructed all dioceses to draw up rules (to be sent to the Vatican for review within one year) on the prompt reporting to the police of allegations of child abuse, in accordance with local legislation. In February 2012 the Pope convened a meeting of bishops from more than 100 countries, together with the heads of 32 religious orders, to discuss the prevention and detection of the sexual abuse of children by clergy.

CONSTITUTION AND GOVERNMENT

The State of the Vatican City came into existence with the Lateran Treaty of 1929. The Holy See (a term designating the papacy, i.e. the office of the Pope, and thus the central governing body of the Roman Catholic Church) is a distinct, pre-existing entity. Both entities are subjects of international law. On 22 February 2001 a new Basic Law replaced the former Constitution dating back to the 1929 Lateran Treaty.

The Vatican City State is under the temporal jurisdiction of the Pope, the Supreme Pontiff elected for life by a conclave comprising members of the Sacred College of Cardinals. The Pope holds all legislative, executive and judicial power. Legislative power is vested in the Pontifical Commission for the Vatican State, which comprises a Cardinal President and six other cardinals, nominated by the Pope for a five-year period. Executive power is vested in the President of the Pontifical Commission (who is also, ex officio, the President of the Governorate of the Vatican City State), who is assisted by a Secretary-General. The State Councillors, including one General Councillor and seven other Councillors, are nominated by the Pope for a five-year period, and assist in the drawing-up of laws and report to the Pontifical Commission. Judiciary power is vested in a number of Tribunals and the Apostolic Penitentiary, which exercise their judicial authority in the name of the Pope. The Pontiff exclusively retains the right to grant pardons and amnesties.

REGIONAL AND INTERNATIONAL CO-OPERATION

The Holy See has permanent observer status at a number of international organizations, including the UN, the World Trade Organization (WTO, see p. 444) and the Council of Europe (see p. 260).

ECONOMIC AFFAIRS

The official population of the Vatican City was 793 at March 2011, comprising 572 citizens of the Vatican City (including non-residents) and 221 resident non-citizens; the total resident population was 444. Its inhabitants are of many nationalities, representing the presence of the Roman Catholic Church throughout the world. The papal guards, who numbered 86 in 2011, are of Swiss nationality.

The Vatican City has no agricultural land and no industry. For its income, the Holy See/Vatican City State is chiefly reliant on four sources: the Istituto per le Opere di Religione (IOR or 'Vatican Bank', see History); interest on its financial investments; receipts from tourism, including profits from the Vatican museums and from the sale of postage stamps, publications and souvenirs; and voluntary contributions, known as 'Peter's Pence' (Obolo di San Pietro), which are used for philanthropic purposes such as charities and emergency assistance. The euro is used as currency, and the Vatican City issues its own euro coins.

No official annual accounts for the Holy See were published until 1979, when an annual budgetary deficit of US $20.1m. was revealed (the budget of the Holy See covers the costs of the Roman Curia, the diplomatic missions around the world and the various communications outlets). The deficit continued to increase in subsequent years until 1991, when a peak of $87.5m. was reached. In April of that year a meeting was held in the Vatican, attended by representatives of bishops' conferences throughout the world, which discussed ways of reducing the deficit through systematic contributions from local dioceses. The deficit declined in 1992, and small surpluses were returned for the remainder of the 1990s. After annual deficits in 2001–03, surpluses were again recorded in the following three years, followed by deficits in 2007–09. In 2010 the expenditure of the Holy See totalled €235.3m. and revenues totalled €245.2m., resulting in a budget surplus of €9.9m. ($12.0m.). However, largely owing to high personnel and communications costs combined with adverse market conditions (notably poor returns on its real estate holdings) and despite an increase in donations from dioceses and religious orders, the Holy See recorded another budget deficit, of €14.9m. ($18.4m.), in 2011; expenditure totalled €263.7m. and revenue €248.8m. In that year, 'Peter's Pence' contributions (not included in the consolidated budget of the Holy See) rose by 3%, compared with 2010, to reach €69.7m. The Vatican City State, of which one of the main functions is the management of the Vatican museums, Vatican post office and Sistine Chapel, and which is a separate and autonomous administration from the Holy See (and therefore has a separate budget), reported a profit of €21.8m. in 2011, largely attributed to an increase in income—to €91.3m.—from visitors to the Vatican museums.

At December 2011 a total of 2,832 people were employed in the Vatican City. In addition to staffing costs, principal destinations for expenditure are the Vatican Radio, the Vatican Television Centre and *L'Osservatore Romano*, the Vatican newspaper; these media outlets regularly incur substantial losses. Furthermore, the establishment of new diplomatic missions from the late 1980s onwards entailed considerable capital expenditure for the papacy.

The IOR is reported to have consistently returned an operating profit, although much of the revenue generated by it in the 1980s was used to repay the creditors remaining from the collapse of Banco Ambrosiano in 1982. New legislation concerning greater transparency in financial transactions, in compliance with international standards, came into effect in April 2011. Following the failure of the IOR fully to implement EU safeguards against money-laundering by the stipulated deadline of 1 January 2013, the Italian central bank temporarily suspended all bank card payments in the Vatican from that date; the suspension was lifted in the following month following an agreement allowing for the provision of card payment services by a Swiss financial company.

Directory

Government

THE GOVERNMENT OF THE VATICAN CITY STATE

Head of State

His Holiness Pope FRANCIS (elected 13 March 2013).

Pontifical Commission for the Vatican City State

Cardinal GIUSEPPE BERTELLO (President).
Cardinal GIOVANNI BATTISTA RE.
Cardinal JEAN-LOUIS TAURAN.
Cardinal ANTONIO MARIA VEGLIÒ.
Cardinal ATTILIO NICORA.
Cardinal LEONARDO SANDRI.
Cardinal DOMENICO CALCAGNO.

State Councillors

Prof. CESARE MIRABELLI (General Councillor).
There are seven additional councillors.

Governorate of the Vatican City State

President: Archbishop GIUSEPPE BERTELLO.
Secretary-General: Most Rev. GIUSEPPE SCIACCA (Titular Archbishop of Victoriana).
Vice-Secretary-General: (vacant).

THE SUPREME PONTIFF

His Holiness Pope Francis (Jorge Mario Bergoglio), Bishop of Rome, Vicar of Christ, Successor of the Prince of the Apostles, Supreme Pontiff of the Universal Church, Primate of Italy, Archbishop and Metropolitan of the Province of Rome, Sovereign of the Vatican City State, Servant of the Servants of God, acceded on 13 March 2013 as the 266th Roman pontiff.

THE SACRED COLLEGE OF CARDINALS AND THE ROMAN CURIA

Members of the Sacred College of Cardinals are created by the Pope. The cardinals are divided into three orders: Bishops, Priests and Deacons. Under the decree of November 1970, *Ingravescentem Aetatem*, only cardinals under 80 years of age have the right to enter the conclave for the election of the Pope. Cardinals who reside in Rome, Italy, as the Pope's immediate advisers are styled Cardinals 'in Curia'. The Roman Curia acts as the Papal court and the principal administrative body of the Church. The College of Cardinals derives from the Church's earliest days. In March 1973 Pope Paul VI announced that the number of cardinals permitted to participate in the conclave would be limited to 120. This was increased to 135 by Pope John Paul II in February 2001. At 12 March 2013, as the conclave to elect the successor to Benedict XVI began, there were 207 cardinals, of whom 115 participated in the conclave (two cardinals of voting age did not take part). In early April 2013 there were 205 cardinals. There are six Cardinal Bishops, who are in titular charge of suburban sees of Rome. The order of Cardinal Bishops also includes the additional four Cardinals of Patriarchal Sees of Oriental Rites. Cardinal Priests occupy titular churches in Rome founded soon after Christianity originated. The administration of the Church's affairs is undertaken through the Secretariat of State and the Council for the Public Affairs of the Church, under the Cardinal Secretary of State, and through a number of Congregations, each under the direction of a cardinal or senior member of the Church, as well as through Tribunals, Offices, Commissions and Secretariats for special purposes.

The 'Apostolic Constitution' (*Regimini Ecclesiae Universae*), published in August 1967 and effective from 1 March 1968, reformed the Roman Curia. Among the changes were the creation of new organs and the restructuring of the Secretariat of State. In 1969 the Congregation of Rites was divided into two Congregations—one for Divine Worship and the other for the Causes of Saints. The Congregation for the Discipline of the Sacraments and the Congregation for Divine Worship were amalgamated in 1975, but separated again in 1984.

In July 1988 further reforms of the Curia were introduced. The Secretariat of State was divided into two sections: the first section dealing with 'General Affairs' and the second 'Relations with States'. The Congregation for Divine Worship was again amalgamated with the Congregation for the Discipline of the Sacraments.

Members in order of precedence:

Cardinal Bishops

ANGELO SODANO (Italy—Titular Bishop of Albano and of Ostia and Dean of the College of Cardinals).
ROGER ETCHEGARAY (France—Titular Bishop of Porto-Santa Rufina and Vice-Dean of the College of Cardinals).
GIOVANNI BATTISTA RE (Italy—Titular Bishop of Sabina-Poggio Mirteto).
FRANCIS A. ARINZE (Nigeria—Titular Bishop of Velletri-Segni).
TARCISIO BERTONE (Italy—Titular Bishop of Frascati, Secretary of the Secretariat of State and Chamberlain of the Apostolic Chamber).
JOSÉ SARAIVA MARTINS (Portugal—Titular Bishop of Palestrina).

Cardinal Bishops of Patriarchal Sees of Oriental Rites

NASRALLAH PIERRE (BOUTROS) SFEIR (Lebanon).
EMMANUEL III DELLY (Iraq).
ANTONIOS NAGUIB (Egypt).
BÉCHARA BOUTROS RAÏ (Lebanon—Maronite Patriarch of Antioch).

Cardinal Priests

PAULO EVARISTO ARNS (Brazil).
WILLIAM WAKEFIELD BAUM (USA).
MARCO CÉ (Italy).
FRANCISZEK MACHARSKI (Poland).
MICHAEL MICHAI KITBUNCHU (Thailand).
ALEXANDRE DO NASCIMENTO (Angola).
GODFRIED DANNEELS (Belgium).
THOMAS STAFFORD WILLIAMS (New Zealand).
JOACHIM MEISNER (Germany—Archbishop of Cologne).
DURAISAMY SIMON LOURDUSAMY (India).
MIGUEL OBANDO BRAVO (Nicaragua).
RICARDO JAMIN VIDAL (Philippines).
HENRYK ROMAN GULBINOWICZ (Poland).
JOZEF TOMKO (Slovakia).
PAUL JOSEPH JEAN POUPARD (France).
FRIEDRICH WETTER (Germany).
SILVANO PIOVANELLI (Italy).
ADRIANUS JOHANNES SIMONIS (Netherlands).
BERNARD FRANCIS LAW (USA—Archpriest of the Patriarchal Liberian Basilica of Santa Maria Maggiore).
GIACOMO BIFFI (Italy).
EDUARDO MARTÍNEZ SOMALO (Spain).
ACHILLE SILVESTRINI (Italy).
JOSÉ FREIRE FALCÃO (Brazil).
ALEXANDRE JOSÉ MARIA DOS SANTOS (Mozambique).
GIOVANNI CANESTRI (Italy).
SIMON IGNATIUS PIMENTA (India).
EDWARD BEDE CLANCY (Australia).
EDMUND CASIMIR SZOKA (USA).
LÁSZLÓ PASKAI (Hungary).
CHRISTIAN WIYGHAN TUMI (Cameroon—Archbishop of Douala).
EDWARD IDRIS CASSIDY (Australia).
NICOLÁS DE JESÚS LÓPEZ RODRÍGUEZ (Dominican Republic —Archbishop of Santo Domingo).
FIORENZO ANGELINI (Italy).
ROGER MICHAEL MAHONY (USA—Archbishop of Los Angeles).
CAMILLO RUINI (Italy).
JÁN CHRYZOSTOM KOREC (Slovakia).
HENRI SCHWÉRY (Switzerland).
MILOSLAV VLK (Czech Republic).
CARLO FURNO (Italy).
JULIUS RIYADI DARMAATMADJA (Indonesia).
JAIME LUCAS ORTEGA Y ALAMINO (Cuba—Archbishop of San Cristóbal de la Habana).
GILBERTO AGUSTONI (Italy).
EMMANUEL WAMALA (Uganda).

WILLIAM HENRY KEELER (USA).

JEAN-CLAUDE TURCOTTE (Canada).

RICARDO MARÍA CARLES GORDÓ (Spain).

ADAM JOSEPH MAIDA (USA—Superior of the Cayman Islands).

VINKO PULJIĆ (Bosnia and Herzegovina—Archbishop of Vrhbosna, Sarajevo).

JUAN SANDOVAL IÑIGUEZ (Mexico—Archbishop of Guadalajara).

ERSILIO TONINI (Italy).

JORGE ARTURO AUGUSTIN MEDINA ESTÉVEZ (Chile).

DARÍO CASTRILLÓN HOYOS (Colombia).

JAMES FRANCIS STAFFORD (USA).

SALVATORE DE GIORGI (Italy).

SERAFIM FERNANDES DE ARAÚJO (Brazil).

ANTONIO MARÍA ROUCO VARELA (Spain—Archbishop of Madrid).

DIONIGI TETTAMANZI (Spain).

POLYCARP PENGO (Tanzania—Archbishop of Dar-es-Salaam).

CHRISTOPH SCHÖNBORN (Austria—Archbishop of Vienna).

NORBERTO RIVERA CARRERA (Mexico—Archbishop of Mexico City).

FRANCIS EUGENE GEORGE (USA—Archbishop of Chicago).

MARIAN JAWORSKI (Ukraine).

JĀNIS PUJATS (Latvia—Archbishop of Rīga).

AGOSTINO CACCIAVILLAN (Italy).

SERGIO SEBASTIANI (Italy).

ZENON GROCHOLEWSKI (Poland—Prefect of the Congregation for Catholic Education and Grand Chancellor of the Pontifical Gregorian University).

CRESCENZIO SEPE (Italy—Archbishop of Naples).

JORGE MARÍA MEJÍA (Argentina).

WALTER KASPER (Germany).

IVAN DIAS (India).

GERALDO MAJELLA AGNELO (Brazil—Archbishop of São Salvador de Bahia).

PEDRO RUBIANO SÁENZ (Colombia).

THEODORE EDGAR MCCARRICK (USA).

DESMOND CONNELL (Ireland).

AUDRYS JUOZAS BAČKIS (Lithuania—Emeritus Archbishop of Vilnius).

FRANCISCO JAVIER ERRÁZURIZ OSSA (Chile—Archbishop of Santiago de Chile).

JULIO TERRAZAS SANDOVAL (Bolivia—Archbishop of Santa Cruz de la Sierra).

WILFRID FOX NAPIER (South Africa—Archbishop of Durban).

ÓSCAR ANDRÉS RODRÍGUEZ MARADIAGA (Honduras—Archbishop of Tegucigalpa).

BERNARD AGRÉ (Côte d'Ivoire).

JUAN LUIS CIPRIANI THORNE (Peru—Archbishop of Lima).

FRANCISCO ALVAREZ MARTÍNEZ (Spain).

CLÁUDIO HUMMES (Brazil).

JOSÉ DA CRUZ POLICARPO (Portugal—Patriarch of Lisbon).

SEVERINO POLETTO (Italy).

CORMAC MURPHY-O'CONNOR (United Kingdom).

EDWARD MICHAEL EGAN (USA).

LUBOMYR HUSAR (Ukraine—Archbishop-Major of Kyiv-Halyč, Byzantine Ukrainian Rite).

KARL LEHMANN (Germany—Bishop of Mainz).

ROBERTO TUCCI (Italy).

ANGELO SCOLA (Italy—Archbishop of Milan).

ANTHONY OLUBUNMI OKOGIE (Nigeria).

BERNARD LOUIS AUGUSTE PANAFIEU (France).

GABRIEL ZUBEIR WAKO (Sudan—Archbishop of Khartoum).

CARLOS AMIGO VALLEJO (Spain).

JUSTIN FRANCIS RIGALI (USA—Archbishop of Philadelphia).

KEITH MICHAEL PATRICK O'BRIEN (United Kingdom).

EUSÉBIO OSCAR SCHEID (Brazil).

ENNIO ANTONELLI (Italy—President of the Pontifical Council for the Family).

PETER KODWO APPIAH TURKSON (Ghana—President of the Pontifical Council for Justice and Peace).

TELESPHORE PLACIDUS TOPPO (India—Archbishop of Ranchi).

GEORGE PELL (Australia—Archbishop of Sydney).

JOSIP BOZANIĆ (Croatia—Archbishop of Zagreb).

JEAN-BAPTISTE PHAM MINH MÂN (Viet Nam—Archbishop of Ho Chi Minh City).

PHILIPPE XAVIER IGNACE BARBARIN (France—Archbishop of Lyon).

PÉTER ERDŐ (Hungary—Archbishop of Esztergom-Budapest).

MARC OUELLET (Canada—Prefect of the Congregation for Bishops and President of the Pontifical Commission for Latin America).

AGOSTINO VALLINI (Italy—Vicar-General of His Holiness for the Diocese of Rome and Archpriest of the Lateran Patriarchal Archbasilica).

JORGE LIBERATO UROSA SAVINO (Venezuela—Archbishop of Caracas—Santiago de Venezuela).

GAUDENCIO BORBON ROSALES (Philippines—Archbishop of Manila).

JEAN-PIERRE BERNARD RICARD (France—Archbishop of Bordeaux).

ANTONIO CAÑIZARES LLOVERA (Spain—Prefect of the Congregation for Divine Worship and the Discipline of the Sacraments).

NICHOLAS CHEONG JIN-SUK (Republic of Korea).

SEAN PATRICK O'MALLEY (USA—Archbishop of Boston).

STANISŁAW DZIWISZ (Poland—Archbishop of Kraków).

CARLO CAFFARRA (Italy—Archbishop of Bologna).

JOSEPH ZEN ZE-KIUN (Hong Kong).

SEÁN BAPTIST BRADY (Ireland—Archbishop of Armagh).

LLUÍS MARTÍNEZ SISTACH (Spain—Archbishop of Barcelona).

ANDRÉ ARMAND VINGT-TROIS (France—Archbishop of Paris).

ANGELO BAGNASCO (Italy—Archbishop of Genoa).

THÉODORE-ADRIEN SARR (Senegal—Archbishop of Dakar).

OSWALD GRACIAS (India—Archbishop of Mumbai).

FRANCISCO ROBLES ORTEGA (Mexico—Archbishop of Monterrey).

DANIEL NICHOLAS DINARDO (USA—Archbishop of Galveston-Houston).

ODILO PEDRO SCHERER (Brazil—Archbishop of São Paulo).

JOHN NJUE (Kenya—Archbishop of Nairobi).

ESTANISLAO ESTEBAN KARLIC (Argentina).

MEDARDO JOSEPH MAZOMBWE (Zambia).

RAÚL EDUARDO VELA CHIRIBOGA (Ecuador).

LAURENT MONSENGWO PASINYA (Democratic Republic of the Congo—Archbishop of Kinshasa).

PAOLO ROMEO (Italy—Archbishop of Palermo).

DONALD WILLIAM WUERL (USA—Archbishop of Washington, DC).

RAYMUNDO DAMASCENO ASSIS (Brazil—Archbishop of Aparecida).

KAZIMIERZ NYCZ (Poland—Archbishop of Warsaw).

ALBERT MALCOLM RANJITH PATABENDIGE DON (Sri Lanka—Archbishop of Colombo).

REINHARD MARX (Germany—Archbishop of Munich and Freising).

JOSÉ MANUEL ESTEPA LLAURENS (Spain).

GEORGE ALENCHERRY (India—Archbishop of Ernakulam).

THOMAS CHRISTOPHER COLLINS (Canada—Archbishop of Toronto).

DOMINIK JAROSLAV DUKA (Czech Republic—Archbishop of Prague).

WILLEM JACOBUS EIJK (Netherlands—Archbishop of Utrecht).

GIUSEPPE BETORI (Italy—Archbishop of Florence).

TIMOTHY MICHAEL DOLAN (USA—Archbishop of New York).

RAINER MARIA WOELKI (Germany—Archbishop of Berlin).

JOHN TONG HON (Hong Kong).

LUCIAN MUREŞAN (Romania—Archbishop-Major of Făgăraş şi Alba Iulia).

BASELIOS CLEEMIS (ISAAC) THOTTUNKAL (India—Archbishop Major of Trivandrum).

JOHN OLORUNFEMI ONAIYEKAN (Nigeria—Archbishop of Abuja).

RUBÉN DARÍO SALAZAR GÓMEZ (Colombia—Archbishop of Bogotá).

LUIS ANTONIO GOKIM TAGLE (Philippines—Archbishop of Manila).

Cardinal Deacons

JEAN-LOUIS TAURAN (France—President of the Pontifical Council for Inter-Religious Dialogue).

RENATO RAFFAELE MARTINO (Italy).

FRANCESCO MARCHISANO (Italy).

JULIÁN HERRANZ CASADO (Spain—President of the Disciplinary Commission of the Roman Curia).

JAVIER LOZANO BARRAGÁN (Mexico).

ATTILIO NICORA (Italy—President of the Administration of the Patrimony of the Apostolic See).

GEORGES MARIE MARTIN COTTIER (Switzerland).

STANISŁAW KAZIMIERZ NAGY (Poland).

WILLIAM JOSEPH LEVADA (USA).

FRANC RODÉ (Slovenia).

ANDREA CORDERO LANZA DI MONTEZEMOLO (Italy).

ALBERT VANHOYE (France).

LEONARDO SANDRI (Argentina—Prefect of the Congregation for the Oriental Churches).

GIOVANNI LAJOLO (Italy—President of the Governorate of the Vatican City State, President of the Pontifical Commission for Vatican City State).

PAUL JOSEF CORDES (Germany).

ANGELO COMASTRI (Italy—President of the Fabric of St Peter).

STANISŁAW RYŁKO (Poland—President of the Pontifical Council for the Laity).

RAFFAELE FARINA (Italy).

GIOVANNI COPPA (Italy).

ANGELO AMATO (Italy—Prefect of the Congregation for the Causes of Saints).

ROBERT SARAH (Guinea—President of the Pontifical Council 'Cor Unum').

FRANCESCO MONTERISI (Italy—Archpriest of the Patriarchal Basilica of San Paolo Fuori-le-Mura).

RAYMOND LEO BURKE (USA—Prefect of the Apostolic Signatura).

KURT KOCH (Switzerland—President of the Pontifical Council for Promoting Christian Unity).

PAOLO SARDI (Italy—Vice-Chamberlain Emeritus of the Apostolic Chamber).

MAURO PIACENZA (Italy—Prefect of the Congregation for the Clergy).

VELASIO DE PAOLIS (Italy—President of the Prefecture for the Economic Affairs of the Holy See).

GIANFRANCO RAVASI (Italy—President of the Pontifical Council for Culture).

ELIO SGRECCIA (Italy).

WALTER BRANDMÜLLER (Germany).

DOMENICO BARTOLUCCI (Italy).

FERNANDO FILONI (Italy—Prefect of the Congregation for the Evangelization of Peoples).

MANUEL MONTEIRO DE CASTRO (Portugal—Major Penitentiary of the Apostolic Penitentiary).

SANTOS ABRIL Y CASTELLÓ (Spain—Vice-Chamberlain of the Apostolic Chamber).

ANTONIO MARIA VEGLIÒ (Italy—President of Pontifical Council for the Pastoral Care of Migrants and Itinerant People).

GIUSEPPE BERTELLO (Italy—President of the Governatorate of Vatican City State).

FRANCESCO COCCOPALMERIO (Italy—President of the Pontifical Council for Legislative Texts).

JOÃO BRÁZ DE AVIZ (Brazil—Prefect of the Congregation for Institutes of Consecrated Life and Societies of Apostolic Life).

EDWIN FREDERICK O'BRIEN (USA).

DOMENICO CALCAGNO (Italy—President of the Administration of the Patrimony of the Apostolic See).

GIUSEPPE VERSALDI (Italy—President of the Prefecture for the Economic Affairs of the Holy See).

PROSPERO (STANLEY) GRECH (Malta).

KARL JOSEF BECKER (Germany).

JAMES MICHAEL HARVEY (USA).

THE ROMAN CURIA

Secretariat of State: Palazzo Apostolico Vaticano, 00120 Città del Vaticano; tel. (06) 69883913; fax (06) 69885255; e-mail vati026@relstat-segstat.va; Sec. of State Cardinal TARCISIO BERTONE.

First Section—General Affairs: Segreteria di Stato, 00120 Città del Vaticano; tel. (06) 69883438; fax (06) 69885088; e-mail vati023@genaff-segstat.va; Asst Sec. of State Most Rev. GIOVANNI ANGELO BECCIU (Titular Archbishop of Roselle).

Second Section—Relations with States: Segreteria di Stato, 00120 Città del Vaticano; tel. (06) 69883014; fax (06) 69885364; e-mail vati032@relstat-segstat.va; Sec. Most Rev. DOMINIQUE MAMBERTI (Titular Archbishop of Sagona).

Congregations

Congregation for the Doctrine of the Faith: Piazza del S. Uffizio 11, 00120 Città del Vaticano; tel. (06) 69895911; fax (06) 69883409; e-mail cdf@cfaith.va; internet www.doctrinafidei.va; f. 1542; concerned with questions of doctrine and morals; examines questions of faith and morals and gives a judgement on them; Prefect Archbishop

GERHARD LUDWIG MÜLLER; Sec. Most Rev. LUIS FRANCISCO LADARIA FERRER (Titular Archbishop of Thibica).

Congregation for the Oriental Churches: Palazzo del Bramante, Via della Conciliazione 34, 00193 Rome, Italy; tel. (06) 69884281; fax (06) 69884300; e-mail cco@orientchurch.va; f. 1862; exercises jurisdiction over all persons and things pertaining to the Oriental Rites; Prefect Cardinal LEONARDO SANDRI; Sec. Most Rev. ANTONIO CYRIL VASIL (Titular Archbishop of Ptolemais in Libya).

Congregation for Divine Worship and the Discipline of the Sacraments: Palazzo delle Congregazioni, Piazza Pio XII 10, 00193 Rome, Italy; tel. (06) 69884005; fax (06) 69883499; considers all questions relating to divine worship, liturgy and the sacraments; Prefect Cardinal ANTONIO CAÑIZARES LLOVERA; Sec. Most Rev. ARTHUR ROCHE.

Congregation for the Causes of Saints: Palazzo delle Congregazioni, Piazza Pio XII 10, 00193 Rome, Italy; tel. (06) 69884247; fax (06) 69881935; e-mail vati335@csaints.va; concerned with proceedings relating to beatification and canonization; Prefect Cardinal ANGELO AMATO (Titular Archbishop of Sila); Sec. Most Rev. MARCELLO BARTOLUCCI (Titular Archbishop of Mevania).

Congregation for the Bishops: Palazzo delle Congregazioni, Piazza Pio XII 10, 00193 Rome, Italy; tel. (06) 69884217; fax (06) 69885303; e-mail vati076@cbishops.va; designed for the preparation of matters for the erection and division of dioceses and the election of Bishops and for dealing with Apostolic Visitations; Prefect Cardinal MARC OUELLET; Sec. Most Rev. LORENZO BALDISSERI (Titular Archbishop of Diocletiana).

Congregation for the Evangelization of Peoples: Palazzo di Propaganda Fide, Piazza di Spagna 48, 00187 Rome, Italy; tel. (06) 69879299; fax (06) 69880118; e-mail segreteria@propagandafide.va; exercises ecclesiastical jurisdiction over missionary countries; Prefect Cardinal FERNANDO FILONI (Cardinal-Deacon of Nostra Signora di Coromoto in San Giovanni di Dio); Sec. Most Rev. SAVIO HON TAI-FAI (Titular Archbishop of Sila).

Congregation for the Clergy: Palazzo delle Congregazioni, Piazza Pio XII 3, 00193 Rome, Italy; tel. (06) 69884151; fax (06) 69884845; e-mail clero@cclergy.va; internet www.clerus.org; has jurisdiction over the life and discipline of the clergy and its permanent formation; parishes, chapters, pastoral and presbyteral councils; promotes catechesis and the preaching of the Word of God; deals with economic questions related to the compensation of the clergy and the patrimony of the Church; Prefect Cardinal MAURO PIACENZA (Titular Archbishop of Victoriana); Sec. Most Rev. CELSO MORGA IRUZUBIETA.

Congregation for Institutes of Consecrated Life and for Societies of Apostolic Life: Palazzo delle Congregazioni, Piazza Pio XII 3, 00193 Rome, Italy; tel. (06) 69884128; fax (06) 69884526; e-mail vati059@ccscrlife.va; promotes and supervises practice of evangelical counsels, according to approved forms of consecrated life, and activities of societies of apostolic life; Prefect Most Rev. JOÃO BRÁZ DE AVIZ; Sec. Most Rev. JOSÉ RODRÍGUEZ CARBALLO (Titular Archbishop of Bellicastrum).

Congregation for Catholic Education: Palazzo delle Congregazioni, Piazza Pio XII 3, 00193 Rome, Italy; tel. (06) 69884167; fax (06) 69884172; e-mail cec@cec.va; f. 1588; concerned with the direction, temporal administration and studies of Catholic universities, seminaries, schools and colleges; Prefect Cardinal ZENON GROCHOLEWSKI; Sec. Archbishop ANGELO VINCENZO ZANI.

Tribunals

Apostolic Penitentiary: Palazzo della Cancelleria, Piazza della Cancelleria 1, 00186 Rome, Italy; tel. (06) 69887526; fax (06) 69887557; e-mail reggente@penitenzieria.va; internet www.penitenzieria.va; Major Penitentiary Cardinal MANUEL MONTEIRO DE CASTRO; Regent Rt Rev. KRZYSZTOF JÓZEF NYKIEL.

Supreme Tribunal of the Apostolic Signatura: Palazzo della Cancelleria, Piazza della Cancelleria 1, 00120 Città del Vaticano; tel. (06) 69887520; fax (06) 69887553; e-mail apost.segnatura@tribsgna.va; Prefect Cardinal RAYMOND LEO BURKE; Sec. Rt Rev. FRANS DANEELS.

Tribunal of the Roman Rota: Palazzo della Cancelleria, Piazza della Cancelleria 1, 00186 Rome, Italy; tel. (06) 69887502; fax (06) 69887554; Dean Mgr PIO VITO PINTO.

Pontifical Councils

Pontifical Council for the Laity: Piazza S. Calisto 16, 00153 Rome, Italy; tel. (06) 69869300; fax (06) 69887214; e-mail pcpl@laity.va; advises and conducts research on lay apostolic initiatives; Pres. Cardinal STANISŁAW RYŁKO (Titular Archbishop of Novica); Sec. Rt Rev. JOSEF CLEMENS (Titular Bishop of Segerme).

Pontifical Council for Promoting Christian Unity: Via della Conciliazione 5, 00193 Rome, Italy; tel. (06) 69884083; fax (06) 69885365; e-mail office1@chrstuni.va; f. 1960; Pres. Cardinal KURT KOCH; Sec. Rt Rev. BRIAN FARRELL (Titular Bishop of Abitinae).

Pontifical Council for the Family: Piazza S. Calisto 16, 00153 Rome, Italy; tel. (06) 69887243; fax (06) 69887272; e-mail pcf@family .va; internet www.familia.va; Pres. Most Rev. VINCENZO PAGLIA; Sec. Rt Rev. JEAN LAFFITTE (Titular Bishop of Entrevaux).

Pontifical Council for Justice and Peace: Piazza S. Calisto 16, 00153 Rome, Italy; tel. (06) 69879911; fax (06) 69887205; e-mail pcjustpax@justpeace.va; promotes social justice, human rights, peace and development in needy areas; Pres. Cardinal PETER KODWO APPIAH TURKSON; Sec. Rt Rev. MARIO TOSO (Titular Bishop of Bisarcio).

Pontifical Council 'Cor Unum': Cor Unum, Via della Conciliazione 5, 00193 Rome, Italy; tel. (06) 69889411; fax (06) 69887301; e-mail corunum@corunum.va; f. 1971; cares for the needy, promotes human fellowship; Pres. Cardinal ROBERT SARAH.

Pontifical Council for the Pastoral Care of Migrants and Itinerant People: Piazza S. Calisto, 00120 Città del Vaticano; tel. (06) 69887193; fax (06) 69887111; e-mail office@migrants.va; f. 1970; Pres. (vacant); Sec. Most Rev. JOSEPH KALATHIPARAMBIL (Titular Bishop of Calicut).

Pontifical Council for Health Pastoral Care: Via della Conciliazione 3, 00193 Rome, Italy; tel. (06) 69883138; fax (06) 69883139; e-mail opersanit@hlthwork.va; Pres. Most Rev. ZIGMUNT ZIMOWSKI; Sec. Fr JEAN-MARIE MATE MUSIVI MUPENDAWATU (Priest of Butembo-Beni).

Pontifical Council for Legislative Texts: Palazzo delle Congregazioni, Piazza Pio XII 10, 00193 Rome, Italy; tel. (06) 69884008; fax (06) 69884710; e-mail vati100@legtxt.va; f. 1984; publishes *Communicationes* journal twice yearly; Pres. Most Rev. FRANCESCO COCCOPALMERIO (Titular Archbishop of Coeliana); Sec. Rt Rev. JUAN IGNACIO ARRIETA OCHOA DE CHINCHETRU (Titular Bishop of Civitate).

Pontifical Council for Inter-Religious Dialogue: Via della Conciliazione 5, 00193 Rome, Italy; tel. (06) 69884321; fax (06) 69884494; e-mail dialogo@interrel.va; f. 1964; Pres. Cardinal JEAN-LOUIS TAURAN; Sec. Fr MIGUEL ÁNGEL AYUSO GUIXOT.

Pontifical Council for Culture: Via della Conciliazione 5, 00193 Rome, Italy; tel. (06) 69893811; fax (06) 69887368; e-mail cultura@ cultura.va; internet www.cultura.va; f. 1982; merged with Pontifical Council for Dialogue with Non-Believers in 1993; promotes understanding and dialogue between the Church, people from the field of learning, artists and non-believers; Pres. Cardinal GIANFRANCO RAVASI; Sec. BARTHÉLEMY ADOUKONOU.

Pontifical Council for Social Communications: Via della Conciliazione 5, 00120 Città del Vaticano; tel. (06) 69891800; fax (06) 69891840; e-mail pccs@pccs.va; internet www.pccs.va; f. 1948; examines the relationship between the media and religious affairs; manages radio, TV, film and photographic work in the Vatican; Pres. Most Rev. CLAUDIO MARIA CELLI (Titular Archbishop of Cluentum).

Pontifical Council for Promoting the New Evangelization: Via della Conciliazione 5, 00193 Rome, Italy; tel. (06) 69869500; fax (06) 69869521; internet www.annusfidei.va; f. 2010; Pres. Most Rev. SALVATORE (RINO) FISICHELLA (Titular Archbishop of Vicohabentia); Sec. Most Rev. JOSÉ OCTAVIO RUIZ ARENAS.

Pontifical Commissions and Committees

Pontifical Commission for the Cultural Heritage of the Church: Via della Conciliazione 5, 00193 Rome, Italy; tel. (06) 69885640; fax (06) 69884621; e-mail beniculturali@beniculturali .va; f. 1988; Pres. Cardinal GIANFRANCO RAVASI (Titular Archbishop of Villamagna in Proconsulari).

Pontifical Biblical Commission: Palazzo del Sant'Uffizio 11, 00120 Città del Vaticano; tel. (06) 69895974; e-mail vati419@cfaith .va; Prefect Archbishop GERHARD LUDWIG MÜLLER.

Pontifical Commission of Sacred Archaeology: Palazzo del Pontificio Istituto di Archeologia Cristiana, Via Napoleone III 1, 00185 Rome, Italy; tel. (06) 4465610; fax (06) 4467625; e-mail pcas@ arcsacra.va; Pres. Cardinal GIANFRANCO RAVASI.

Pontifical Commission 'Ecclesia Dei': Palazzo della Congregazione per la Dottrina della Fede, Piazza del S. Uffizio 11, 00193 Rome, Italy; tel. (06) 69885213; fax (06) 69883412; e-mail eccdei@ecclsdei .va; Pres. Archbishop GERHARD LUDWIG MÜLLER.

Pontifical Commission for Latin America: Palazzo di San Paolo, Via della Conciliazione 1, 00193 Rome, Italy; tel. (06) 69883131; fax (06) 69884260; e-mail pcal@latinamer.va; Pres. Cardinal MARC OUELLET.

International Theological Commission: Palazzo della Congregazione per la Dottrina della Fede, Piazza del S. Uffizio 11, 00193 Rome, Italy; tel. (06) 69895971; internet www.vatican.va/ roman_curia/congregations/cfaith/cti_index_it.htm; Pres. Archbishop GERHARD LUDWIG MÜLLER.

Pontifical Committee for International Eucharistic Congresses: Palazzo S. Calisto 16, 00120 Città del Vaticano; tel. (06) 69887366; fax (06) 6987154; e-mail eucharistcongress@org.va; f. 1881; Pres. Most Rev. PIERO MARINI (Titular Archbishop of Martirano).

Pontifical Committee of Historical Sciences: Palazzo delle Congregazioni, Piazza Pio XII 3, 00120 Città del Vaticano; tel. (06) 69884618; fax (06) 69873014; e-mail addetto@historia.va; Pres. Mgr BERNARD ARDURA; Sec. Rev. Prof. COSIMO SEMERARO.

Archives of the Second Vatican Council: c/o Archivio Segreto Vaticano, 00120 Città del Vaticano; tel. (06) 69883314; fax (06) 69885574; e-mail asv@asv.va; Dir Rt Rev. SERGIO PAGANO (Titular Bishop of Celene).

Commission for Lawyers: Palazzo della Cancelleria, Piazza della Cancelleria 1, 00186 Rome, Italy; tel. (06) 69887523; fax (06) 698887557; f. 1988; Pres. Cardinal RAYMOND LEO BURKE.

Disciplinary Commission of the Roman Curia: Palazzo delle Congregazioni, Piazza Pio XII 10, 00120 Città del Vaticano; tel. (06) 69884008; fax (06) 69884710; Pres. Rt Rev. GIORGIO CORBELLINI.

Offices

Apostolic Chamber: Palazzo Apostolico, 00120 Città del Vaticano; tel. (06) 69883554; Chamberlain of the Holy Roman Church Cardinal TARCISIO BERTONE; Vice-Chamberlain Most Rev. PIER LUIGI CELATA (Titular Archbishop of Doclea).

Administration of the Patrimony of the Apostolic See: Palazzo Apostolico, 00120 Città del Vaticano; tel. (06) 69893403; fax (06) 69883141; e-mail apsa-ss@apsa.va; f. 1967; Pres. Cardinal DOMENICO CALCAGNO; Sec. Most Rev. LUIGI MISTÒ.

Labour Office of the Apostolic See: Via della Conciliazione 1, 00193 Rome, Italy; tel. (06) 69884449; fax (06) 69883800; e-mail ulsa1@ulsa.va; Pres. Rt Rev. GIORGIO CORBELLINI (Titular Bishop of Abula); Dir Dott. MASSIMO BUFACCHI.

Prefecture for the Economic Affairs of the Holy See: Palazzo delle Congregazioni, Largo del Colonnato 3, 00193 Rome, Italy; tel. (06) 69884263; fax (06) 69885011; e-mail rmpaess@econaffr.va; f. 1967; Pres. Archbishop GIUSEPPE VERSALDI; Sec. Bishop LUCIO ANGEL VALLEJO BALDA.

Prefecture of the Papal Household: 00120 Città del Vaticano; tel. (06) 69883114; fax (06) 69885863; f. 1967; responsible for domestic administration and organization; Prefect Most Rev. GEORG GÄNSWEIN (Titular Archbishop of Urbs Salvia); Regent PAOLO DE NICOLÒ (Titular Bishop of Mariana in Corsica).

Office of the Liturgical Celebrations of the Supreme Pontiff: Palazzo Apostolico, 00120 Città del Vaticano; tel. (06) 69883253; fax (06) 69885412; Master Mgr GUIDO MARINI.

Central Statistical Office of the Church: Palazzo Apostolico, 00120 Città del Vaticano; tel. (06) 69883493; fax (06) 69883816; e-mail vformenti@statistica.va; Dir Mgr VITTORIO FORMENTI.

Holy See Press Office: Via della Conciliazione 54, 00120 Città del Vaticano; tel. (06) 698921; fax (06) 69892426; internet www.vatican .va; Dir Fr FEDERICO LOMBARDI; Vice-Dir Fr CIRO BENEDETTINI.

Pontifical Administration of the Patriarchal Basilica of San Paolo Fuori-le-Mura: 00120 Città del Vaticano; tel. (06) 69880800; fax (06) 69880803; e-mail spbasilica@org.va; Archpriest Cardinal JAMES MICHAEL HARVEY (Titular Archbishop of Memphis).

Diplomatic Representation

DIPLOMATIC MISSIONS IN ROME ACCREDITED TO THE HOLY SEE

Albania: Via Ottaviano 43, Scala B, 2°, Int. 3, 00192 Rome, Italy; tel. (06) 39733150; fax (06) 39730415; e-mail embassy.vatican@mfa.gov .al; internet www.albava.org; Ambassador RROK LOGU.

Angola: Palazzo Odescalchi, Piazza dei Santi Apostoli 81, 00187 Rome, Italy; tel. (06) 69190650; fax (06) 69788483; Ambassador ARMINDO FERNANDES DO ESPÍRITO SANTO VIEIRA.

Argentina: Via del Banco di Santo Spirito 42, 00186 Rome, Italy; tel. (06) 68801701; fax (06) 6879021; e-mail essed@mrecic.gov.ar; Ambassador JUAN PABLO CAFIERO.

Australia: Corso Vittorio Emanuele II 349, 00186 Rome, Italy; tel. (06) 686261; fax (06) 68626111; e-mail holysee.embassy@dfat.gov.au; internet www.holysee.embassy.gov.au; Ambassador JOHN MCCARTHY.

Austria: Via Reno 9, 00198 Rome, Italy; tel. (06) 853725; fax (06) 8543058; e-mail heiliger-stuhl-ob@bmeia.gv.at; Ambassador ALFONS KLOSS.

Belgium: Via Giuseppe de Notaris 6A, 00197 Rome, Italy; tel. (06) 3224740; fax (06) 3226042; e-mail romeholysee@diplobel.fed.be; internet www.diplomatie.be/vaticanfr; Ambassador CHARLES GHISLAIN.

Benin: Via Giosué Carducci 2, 00187 Rome, Italy; tel. (06) 42016782; fax (06) 42004007; e-mail ambasciata.beninss@gmail.com; Ambassador COMLANVI THÉODORE LOKO.

Bolivia: Via di Porta Angelica 15, Int. 2, 00193 Rome, Italy; tel. (06) 68802035; fax (06) 58179562; e-mail embolvat@rdn.it; Ambassador CARLOS FEDERICO DE LA RIVA GUERRA.

Bosnia and Herzegovina: Piazzale Clodio 12, Int. 19, 00195 Rome, Italy; tel. (06) 39742411; fax (06) 39742484; e-mail embvavat@tin.it; Ambassador SLAVICA KARAČIĆ.

Brazil: Via della Conciliazione 22, 00193 Rome, Italy; tel. (06) 6875252; fax (06) 6872540; e-mail embaixada@vatemb.it; Ambassador ALMIR FRANCO DE SÀ BARBUDA.

Bulgaria: Via di Porta Angelica 63, 00193 Rome, Italy; tel. (06) 6875717; fax (06) 6865233; e-mail embassy.vatican@mfa.bg; internet www.mfa.bg/embassies/vatican; Chargé d'affaires a.i. STEFAN BONCHEV.

Cameroon: Via Gregorio VII 58, 00165 Rome, Italy; tel. and fax (06) 39376429; e-mail ambacamsaintsiege@yahoo.fr; Ambassador ANTOINE ZANGA.

Canada: Palazzo Pio, Via della Conciliazione 4D, 00193 Rome, Italy; tel. (06) 68307316; fax (06) 68806283; e-mail vatcn@international.gc.ca; internet www.canadainternational.gc.ca/holy_see-saint_siege; Chargé d'affaires a.i. JON ALLEN.

Chile: Piazza della Città Leonina 9, 00193 Rome, Italy; tel. (06) 6861232; fax (06) 6874992; e-mail echileva@uni.net; Ambassador FERNANDO ZEGERS SANTA CRUZ.

Colombia: Via Cola di Rienzo 285/4B, 00192 Rome, Italy; tel. (06) 3211681; fax (06) 3211703; e-mail estasede@minrelext.gov.co; Ambassador GERMÁN CARDONA GUTIÉRREZ.

Congo, Democratic Republic: Via del Castro Pretorio 28/2, 00185 Rome, Italy; tel. (06) 4465829; e-mail missionrdcvaticantrois@gmail.com; Ambassador JEAN-PIERRE HAMULI MUPENDA.

Costa Rica: Largo Ecuador 6, 00198 Rome, Italy; tel. and fax (06) 80660390; e-mail embcr.vaticano@iol.it; Ambassador FERNANDO FELIPE SÁNCHEZ CAMPOS.

Côte d'Ivoire: Via Montevideo 2A, Int. 3, 00198 Rome, Italy; tel. (06) 6877503; fax (06) 6867925; e-mail ambaco.va@hotmail.it; Ambassador JOSEPH TEBAH-KLAH.

Croatia: Via della Conciliazione 44, 00193 Rome, Italy; tel. (06) 6877000; fax (06) 6877003; e-mail croemb.vatican@mvepei.hr; internet va.mfa.hr; Ambassador FILIP VUČAK.

Cuba: Via Aurelia 137/12B, 00165 Rome, Italy; tel. (06) 39366680; fax (06) 636685; e-mail embajada@cubassede.com; Ambassador EDUARDO DELGADO BERMÚDEZ.

Cyprus: Piazza Farnese 44, Scala A, Int. 1, 00186 Rome, Italy; tel. (06) 6865758; fax (06) 68803756; e-mail embcyprusholysee@tin.it; Ambassador GEORGIOS F. POULIDES.

Czech Republic: Via Crescenzio 91B, Int. 1, 00193 Rome, Italy; tel. (06) 6874694; fax (06) 6879731; e-mail vatican@embassy.mzv.cz; internet www.mzv.cz/vatican; Ambassador PAVEL VOŠALÍK.

Dominican Republic: Via di Porta Angelica 63, 00193 Rome, Italy; tel. and fax (06) 6864084; e-mail embajadasrdssomgre@gmail.com; Ambassador VICTOR GRIMALDI CÉSPEDES.

Ecuador: Via di Porta Angelica 63, 00193 Rome, Italy; tel. (06) 6897179; fax (06) 68892786; e-mail eecusatasede@mmrree.gob.ec; Ambassador LUIS DOSITEO LATORRE TAPIA.

Egypt: Piazza della Città Leonina 9, 00193 Rome, Italy; tel. (06) 6865878; fax (06) 6832335; e-mail ambegyptvatican@tiscali.it; Ambassador MAHMOUD MEKKI.

El Salvador: Via Domenico Cimarosa 18, Scala 3, Int. 17, 00198 Rome, Italy; tel. (06) 8540538; fax (06) 85301131; e-mail embasalssede@iol.it; Ambassador MANUEL BARRERA ROBERTO LÓPEZ.

France: Villa Bonaparte, Via Piave 23, 00186 Rome, Italy; tel. (06) 42030900; fax (06) 42030968; e-mail ambfrssg@tin.it; internet www.france-vatican.org; Ambassador BRUNO JOUBERT.

Gabon: Piazzale Clodio 12, 00195 Rome, Italy; tel. (06) 39745043; fax (06) 39038876; Ambassador FIRMIN MBOUTSOU.

Georgia: Via Emilia 25, 00187 Rome, Italy; tel. and fax (06) 45472787; e-mail vatican.emb@mfa.gov.ge; internet vatican.mfa.gov.ge; Ambassador KETEVAN BAGRATION-MUKHRANBATONI.

Germany: Via di Villa Sacchetti 4–6, 00197 Rome, Italy; tel. (06) 809511; fax (06) 80951227; internet www.vatikan.diplo.de; Ambassador Dr REINHARD SCHWEPPE.

Greece: Via Giuseppe Mercalli 6, 00197 Rome, Italy; tel. (06) 8070786; fax (06) 8079862; e-mail gremb.vat@mfa.gr; Ambassador GEORGIOS PAPADOPOULOS.

Guatemala: Piazzale Gregorio VII 65A, 00165 Rome, Italy; tel. (06) 6381632; fax (06) 39376981; e-mail embsantasede@minex.gob.gt; Ambassador ALFONSO ROBERTO MATTA FAHSEN.

Haiti: Via de Villa Patrizi 5B, 00161 Rome, Italy; tel. (06) 44242749; fax (06) 44236637; e-mail haitistsiege@virgilio.it; Ambassador CARLHENRI GUITEAU.

Honduras: Via Boezio 45, 00192 Rome, Italy; tel. and fax (06) 6876051; e-mail honvati@fastwebnet.it; Ambassador ALEJANDRO EMILIO VALLADARES LANZA.

Hungary: Piazza Girolamo Fabrizio 2, 00161 Rome, Italy; tel. (06) 4402167; fax (06) 4402312; e-mail mission.vat@mfa.gov.hu; Ambassador GÁBOR GYŐRIVÁNYI.

Indonesia: Via Marocco 10, 00144 Rome, Italy; tel. (06) 59290049; fax (06) 54221292; e-mail info@indonesiavatican.it; internet www.indonesiavatican.it; Ambassador BUDIARMAN BAHAR.

Iran: Via Bruxelles 57, 00198 Rome, Italy; tel. (06) 8552494; fax (06) 8547910; Ambassador MUHAMMAD TAHER RABBANI.

Iraq: Via della Camilluccia 355, 00135 Rome, Italy; tel. (06) 30111140; fax (06) 35506416; e-mail iraqivaticano@libero.it; Ambassador HABEEB HADI AL-SADR.

Israel: Via Michele Mercati 12, 00197 Rome, Italy; tel. (06) 36198690; fax (06) 36198590; e-mail ambasec-vat@holysee.mfa.gov.il; internet vatican.mfa.gov.il; Ambassador Dr ZION EVRONY.

Italy: Palazzo Borromeo, Viale delle Belle Arti 2, 00196 Rome, Italy; tel. (06) 3264881; fax (06) 3201801; e-mail amb.scv@esteri.it; Ambassador FRANCESCO MARIA GRECO.

Japan: Via Virgilio 30, 00193 Rome, Italy; tel. (06) 6875828; fax (06) 68807543; e-mail japanemb.holysee@va.mofa.go.jp; Ambassador HIDEKAZU YAMAGUCHI.

Korea, Republic: Via della Mendola 109, 00135 Rome, Italy; tel. (06) 3314505; fax (06) 3314522; e-mail holysee@mofat.go.kr; Ambassador THOMAS HAN HONG-SOON.

Lebanon: Via di Porta Angelica 15, 00193 Rome, Italy; tel. (06) 6833512; fax (06) 6833507; e-mail amb.libano@tin.it; Ambassador GEORGES CHAKIB AL-KHOURI.

Libya: Via Orazio 31B, 00193 Rome, Italy; tel. (06) 68803614; fax (06) 68801590; Chargé d'affaires a.i. MUHAMMAD ARIBI.

Lithuania: Via Giulia 66, 00186 Rome, Italy; tel. (06) 89165962; fax (06) 68809596; e-mail amb.va@urm.lt; internet va.mfa.lt; Ambassador IRENA VAIŠVILAITĖ.

Luxembourg: Via della Pisana 1111, 00163 Rome, Italy; tel. (06) 656121; fax (06) 65612679; e-mail jean-paul.muller@mae.etat.lu; Ambassador JEAN-PAUL SENNINGER.

Macedonia, former Yugoslav Republic: Via di Porta Cavalleggeri 143, 00165 Rome, Italy; tel. (06) 635878; fax (06) 634826; e-mail vatican@mfa.gov.mk; Ambassador GJOKO GJORGJEVSKI.

Mexico: Via Ezio 49/3, 00192 Rome, Italy; tel. (06) 3230360; fax (06) 3230361; e-mail embamex-s.sede@mclink.it; internet embamex.sre.gob.mx/vaticano; Ambassador HÉCTOR FEDERICO LING ALTAMIRANO.

Monaco: Largo Nicola Spinelli 5, 00198 Rome, Italy; tel. (06) 8414357; fax (06) 8414507; e-mail ambmonacovat@alice.it; Ambassador JEAN-CLAUDE MICHEL.

Montenegro: Via Crescenzio 97/III, 00193 Rome, Italy; tel. (06) 68134897; fax (06) 68130569; e-mail ambmont.vat@hotmail.it; Ambassador ANTUN SBUTEGA.

Morocco: Via delle Fornaci 203, 00165 Rome, Italy; tel. (06) 39388398; fax (06) 6374459; e-mail sifamavat@marocco.191.it; Chargé d'affaires a.i. NOUREDDINE BELABBES.

Netherlands: Via Michele Mercati 12, 00197 Rome, Italy; tel. (06) 32286206; fax (06) 32286272; e-mail vat@minbuza.nl; Ambassador JOSEPH WETERINGS.

Nicaragua: Via Luigi Luciani 42/1A, 00197 Rome, Italy; tel. (06) 32600265; fax (06) 3207249; e-mail embanicsantasede@tin.it; Ambassador JOSÉ CUADRA CHAMORRO.

Nigeria: Borgo Santo Spirito 16, 3°, Int. 5, 00193 Rome, Italy; tel. (06) 68392018; fax (06) 68307355; e-mail chancery@nigerianholysee.org; Ambassador FRANCIS CHUKWUEMEKA OKEKE.

Panama: Largo di Torre Argentina 11/28, 00186 Rome, Italy; tel. (06) 68809764; fax (06) 68809812; e-mail santasede@ambasciatapanama.191.it; Ambassador DELIA CÁRDENAS CHRISTIE.

Paraguay: Via Ugo Bartolomei 23B, Int. 1, 00136 Rome, Italy; tel. (06) 39751368; fax (06) 39745063; e-mail embapar.vaticano@mre.gov.py; Chargé d'affaires a.i. CARLOS VERA AGUILERA.

Peru: Via di Porta Angelica 63, Int. 6, 00193 Rome, Italy; tel. (06) 68308535; fax (06) 6896059; e-mail embaperuva@tin.it; Chargé d'affaires a.i. JOSÉ MARIANO DE COSSÍO RIVAS.

Philippines: Via Paolo VI 29, 00193 Rome, Italy; tel. (06) 68308020; fax (06) 6834076; e-mail embholysee@philvatican.it; Ambassador MERCEDES TUASON.

Poland: Via dei Delfini 16, Int. 3, 00186 Rome, Italy; tel. (06) 6990958; fax (06) 6990978; e-mail watykan.amb.sekretariat@msz.gov.pl; Ambassador HANNA SUCHOCKA.

Portugal: Villa Lusa, Via S. Valentino 9, 00197 Rome, Italy; tel. (06) 8091581; fax (06) 8077585; e-mail embportugalvatican@tiscalinet.it; Ambassador ANTÓNIO CARLOS CARVALHO DE ALMEIDA RIBEIRO.

Romania: Via Panama 92, 00198 Rome, Italy; tel. (06) 8541802; fax (06) 8554067; e-mail ambvatican@libero.it; internet vatican.mae.ro; Ambassador BOGDAN TĂTARU-CAZABAN.

Russia: Via della Conciliazione 10, 00193 Rome, Italy; tel. (06) 6877078; fax (06) 6877168; e-mail russsede@libero.it; Ambassador ALEXANDER AVDEYEV.

San Marino: Via Fogliano 6, Int. 2, 00199 Rome, Italy; tel. (06) 87860646; fax (06) 86205910; e-mail amb-sanmarino@libero.it; Ambassador Dr SANTE CANDUCCI.

Senegal: Via dei Monti Parioli 101, 00197 Rome, Italy; tel. (06) 3218892; fax (06) 3203624; e-mail ambasenevati@virgilio.it; Ambassador FÉLIX OUDIANE.

Serbia: Via dei Monti Parioli 20, 00197 Rome, Italy; tel. (06) 3223076; fax (06) 3204530; e-mail amb.serbia.vatican@ambroma.com; Ambassador MIRKO V. JELIĆ.

Slovakia: Via dei Colli della Farnesina 144, 00135 Rome, Italy; tel. (06) 36715234; fax (06) 36715237; e-mail emb.vatican@mzv.sk; internet www.mzv.sk/vatikan; Ambassador JOZEF DRAVECKÝ.

Slovenia: Via della Conciliazione 10, 00193 Rome, Italy; tel. (06) 6833009; fax (06) 68307942; e-mail vva@gov.si; Ambassador MAJA MARIJA LOVRENČIČ SVETEK.

Spain: Palazzo di Spagna, Piazza di Spagna 57, 00187 Rome, Italy; tel. (06) 6784351; fax (06) 6784355; e-mail emb.santasede@mae.es; internet www.maec.es/embajadas/santasede; Ambassador EDUARDO GUTIÉRREZ SÁENZ DE BURUAGA.

Taiwan (Republic of China): Via della Conciliazione 4D, 00193 Rome, Italy; tel. (06) 68136206; fax (06) 68136199; e-mail taiwan@embroc.it; internet www.taiwanembassy.org/va; Ambassador CHALERMPOL THANCHITT.

Timor-Leste: Via Cavour 285, 5°, Int. 10, 00184 Rome, Italy; tel. (06) 47824537; fax (06) 47883366; e-mail servicio.administracao@embtimorvaticano.it; Chargé d'affaires a.i. ARMINDO PEDRO SIMOES.

Turkey: Via Lovanio 24/1, 00198 Rome, Italy; tel. (06) 85508601; fax (06) 85508660; e-mail ambasciata.santasede@mfa.gov.tr; Ambassador KENAN GÜRSOY.

Ukraine: Via G. Bessarione 8, Int. 3, 00165 Rome, Italy; tel. (06) 39378800; fax (06) 39375884; e-mail emb_va@mfa.gov.ua; internet www.mfa.gov.ua/vatican; Ambassador TETIANA IZHEVSKA.

United Kingdom: Via XX Settembre 80A, 00187 Rome, Italy; tel. (06) 42204000; fax (06) 42204205; e-mail holysee@fco.gov.uk; internet www.ukinholysee.fco.gov.uk; Ambassador NIGEL BAKER.

USA: Villa Domiziana, Via delle Terme Deciane 26, 00153 Rome, Italy; tel. (06) 46743428; fax (06) 5758346; e-mail vaticaninfo@mail.usembassy.it; internet vatican.usembassy.gov; Chargé d'affaires a.i. MARIO MESQUITA.

Uruguay: Via Antonio Gramsci 9, Int. 14, 00197 Rome, Italy; tel. (06) 3218904; fax (06) 3613249; e-mail uruvati@tin.it; Ambassador DANIEL EDGARDO RAMADA PIENDIBENE.

Venezuela: Via Antonio Gramsci 14, 00197 Rome, Italy; tel. (06) 3225868; fax (06) 36001505; e-mail evidano@iol.it; Chargé d'affaires a.i. HÉCTOR J. PÉREZ ROMERO.

Ecclesiastical Organization

The organization of the Church consists of:
(1) Patriarchs, Archbishops and Bishops in countries under the common law of the Church.
(2) Abbots and Prelates 'nullius dioceseos'.
(3) Vicars Apostolic and Prefects Apostolic in countries classified as Missionary and under Propaganda, the former having Episcopal dignity.

The population of the world adhering to the Roman Catholic faith, according to official estimates, was 1,166m. at 31 December 2008.

Among the Pope's official titles until early 2006, when Pope Benedict XVI decided no longer to use it, was that of Patriarch of the West. There are five other Patriarchates of the Latin Rite—Jerusalem, the West Indies, the East Indies, Lisbon and Venice. The Eastern Catholic Churches each have Patriarchs: Alexandria for the Coptic Rite; Babylon for the Chaldean Rite; Cilicia for the Armenian Rite; and Antioch for the Syrian, Maronite and Melkite Rites.

At 31 December 2009 there were 2,812 residential sees—13 patriarchates, four senior archbishoprics, 539 metropolitan archbishoprics, 77 archbishoprics and 2,179 bishoprics. Of the 2,086 titular sees (92 metropolitan archbishoprics, 91 archbishoprics and 1,903 bishoprics), 1,086 are filled by bishops who have been given these titles, but exercise no territorial jurisdiction. Other territorial divisions of the Church include 48 prelacies, 11 territorial abbacies, 24 exarchates of the Eastern Church, 35 military ordinariates, 83 apostolic vicariates, 41 apostolic prefectures, nine apostolic administrations and nine missions 'sui iuris'. In January 2011 the Personal Ordinariate of Our Lady of Walsingham was established to accommodate former Anglican clergy and adherents in England and Wales.

The Press

Acta Apostolicae Sedis: Periodical Dept, Libreria Editrice Vaticana, 00120 Città del Vaticano; tel. (06) 69883529; fax (06) 69884716; e-mail mariasic2@publish.va; internet www.libreriaeditricevaticana.com; f. 1909; official bulletin issued by the Holy See; monthly, with special editions on special occasions; the record of Encyclicals and other Papal pronouncements, Acts of the Congregations and Offices, nominations, etc.; circ. 6,000.

Annuario Pontificio: Libreria Editrice Vaticana, Via del Tipografia, 00120 Città del Vaticano; tel. (06) 69883493; fax (06) 69885088; e-mail segreteria.lev@lev.va; official yearbook edited by Central Statistical Office; Dir Mgr VITTORIO FORMENTI.

L'Osservatore Romano: Tipografica Vaticana, Via del Pellegrino, 00120 Città del Vaticano; tel. (06) 69883461; fax (06) 69883675; e-mail ornet@ossrom.va; internet www.vatican.va/news_services/or/home_ita.html; f. 1861; an authoritative daily newspaper in Italian; its special columns devoted to the affairs of the Holy See may be described as semi-official; the news service covers religious matters and, in a limited measure, general affairs; weekly editions in English, French, German, Italian, Portuguese and Spanish; monthly editions in Polish; Editor-in-Chief GIOVANNI MARIA VIAN; circ. (Italian daily) 20,000.

Pro Dialogo: Via della Conciliazione 5, 00193 Rome, Italy; tel. (06) 69884321; fax (06) 69884494; e-mail dialogo@interrel.va; 3 a year; publ. by the Pontifical Council for Inter-Religious Dialogue.

Statistical Yearbook of the Church: Central Statistical Office of the Church, Palazzo Apostolico, 00120 Città del Vaticano; tel. (06) 69883493; fax (06) 69883816; e-mail vformenti@statistica.va; Dir Mgr VITTORIO FORMENTI.

NEWS AGENCY

Agenzia FIDES: Palazzo 'de Propaganda Fide', 00120 Città del Vaticano; tel. (06) 69880115; fax (06) 69880107; e-mail fides@fides.va; internet www.fides.org; f. 1927; handles news of missions throughout the world and publishes a weekly bulletin in 6 languages (circ. 3,000), provides a daily news service by e-mail; Dir LUCA DE MATA.

Publishers

Biblioteca Apostolica Vaticana: Cortile del Belvedere, 00120 Città del Vaticano; tel. (06) 69879411; fax (06) 69884795; e-mail bav@vatlib.it; internet www.vaticanlibrary.va; f. 1451; philology, classics, history, catalogues; Librarian of the Holy Roman Church Archbishop JEAN-LOUIS BRUGUÈS.

Libreria Editrice Vaticana: Via della Posta, 00120 Città del Vaticano; tel. (06) 69884834; fax (06) 69884716; e-mail lev@publish.va; internet www.libreriaeditricevaticana.com; f. 1926; religion, philosophy, literature, art, Latin philology, history; Pres. Mgr GUISEPPE SCOTTI; Dir Rev. GIUSEPPE COSTA.

Tipografia Vaticana (Vatican Press): Via della Tipografia, 00120 Città del Vaticano; tel. (06) 69883506; fax (06) 69884570; e-mail tipvat@tipografia.va; f. 1587; religion, theology, education, juveniles, natural and social sciences; publishes *Acta Apostolicae Sedis* and *L'Osservatore Romano*; Dir-Gen. Rev. ELIO TORRIGIANI.

Broadcasting and Communications

RADIO

Radio Vaticana was founded in 1931 and is situated within the Vatican City. A transmitting centre, inaugurated by Pius XII in 1957, is located at Santa Maria di Galeria, about 20 km north-west of the Vatican. Under a special treaty between the Holy See and Italy, the site of this centre, which covers 420 ha, enjoys the same extra-territorial privileges as are recognized by international law for the diplomatic headquarters of foreign states.

The station operates an all-day service, normally in 40 languages, but with facilities for broadcasting liturgical and other religious services in additional languages, including Latin.

The purpose of Radio Vaticana is to broadcast papal teaching, to provide information on important events in the Roman Catholic Church, to express the Catholic point of view on problems affecting religion and morality, and, above all, to form a continuous link between the Holy See and Roman Catholics throughout the world.

Radio Vaticana: Palazzo Pio, Piazza Pia 3, 00120 Città del Vaticano; tel. (06) 69883551; fax (06) 69884565; e-mail sedoc@vatiradio .va; internet www.vaticanradio.org; f. 1931; Dir-Gen. Rev. Fr FEDERICO LOMBARDI; Tech. Dir SANDRO PIERVENANZI; Admin. Dir ALBERTO GASBARRI; Dir of Programmes Rev. Fr ANDREJ KOPROWSKI.

TELEVISION

Centro Televisivo Vaticano (CTV) (Vatican Television Centre): Via del Pellegrino, 00120 Città del Vaticano; tel. (06) 69885467; fax (06) 69885192; e-mail ctv@ctv.va; f. 1983; produces and distributes programmes about the Pope and the Vatican City; Pres. Archbishop CLAUDIO MARIA CELLI; Dir-Gen. Rev. Fr FEDERICO LOMBARDI.

Finance

Financial Information Authority (FIA): 00120 Città del Vaticano; f. 2010; est. by Pope Benedict XVI as an autonomous and independent body; supervises adherence to international regulations to prevent money-laundering and the financing of terrorism; responsible for co-operation with foreign authorities; Chair. Cardinal ATTILIO NICORA; Dir RENE BRUELHART.

Istituto per le Opere di Religione (IOR): 00120 Città del Vaticano; tel. (06) 69883354; fax (06) 69883809; e-mail dige@sistonet .org; f. 1887; renamed in 1942; oversees the distribution of capital designated for religious works; it takes deposits from religious bodies and Vatican residents; governed by a Board of Superintendence comprising 5 financial experts, overseen by a commission of 5 cardinals; Pres. ERNST VON FREYBERG; Dir-Gen. PAOLO CIPRIANI; Commission mems Cardinals TARCISIO BERTONE, JEAN-LOUIS TAURAN, ODILO PEDRO SCHERER, TELESPHORE PLACIDUS TOPPO, DOMENICO CALCAGNO.

Lay Employees' Association

In 1989 Pope John Paul II agreed to establish a Labour Council to settle any disputes between the Holy See and its lay employees.

Associazione Dipendenti Laici Vaticani (Association of Vatican Lay Workers): Via della Posta, 00120 Città del Vaticano; tel. (06) 69885343; fax (06) 69884400; f. 1979; formally recognized by the Holy See in 1993; aims to safeguard the professional, legal, economic and moral interests of its members; Sec.-Gen. ALESSANDRO CANDI; 320 mems.

Transport

There is a small railway (863 m), which runs from the Vatican into Italy. It began operating in 1934 and now carries supplies and goods. There is also a heliport used by visiting heads of state and Vatican officials.

VENEZUELA

Introductory Survey

LOCATION, CLIMATE, LANGUAGE, RELIGION, FLAG, CAPITAL

The Bolivarian Republic of Venezuela lies on the north coast of South America, bordered by Colombia to the west, Guyana to the east and Brazil to the south. The climate varies with altitude from tropical to temperate; the average temperature in Caracas is 21°C (69°F). The language is Spanish. There is no state religion, but some 88% of the population is Roman Catholic. The national flag (proportions 2 by 3) has three horizontal stripes of yellow, blue and red, with eight five-pointed white stars, arranged in an arc, in the centre of the blue stripe. The state flag has, in addition, the national coat of arms (a shield bearing a gold wheatsheaf in the first division, a panoply of swords, an indigenous bow and arrow quiver, a machete, flags and a lance in the second, and a white running horse in the base, flanked by branches of laurel and palm and with two cornucopias at the crest) in the top left-hand corner. The capital is Caracas.

CONTEMPORARY POLITICAL HISTORY

Historical Context

Venezuela was a Spanish colony from 1499 until 1821 and, under the leadership of Simón Bolívar, achieved independence in 1830. The country was governed principally by dictators until 1945, when a military-civilian coup replaced Isaías Medina Angarita with Rómulo Betancourt as head of a revolutionary junta. Col (later Gen.) Marcos Pérez Jiménez seized power in December 1952 and took office as President in 1953. He remained in office until 1958, when he was overthrown by a military junta under Adm. Wolfgang Larrazábal. Betancourt was elected President in the same year.

Domestic Political Affairs

A new Constitution was promulgated in 1961. Three years later President Betancourt became the first Venezuelan President to complete his term of office. Dr Raúl Leoni was elected President in December 1963. Supporters of former President Pérez staged an abortive military uprising in 1966. Dr Rafael Caldera Rodríguez became Venezuela's first Christian Democratic President in 1969. He achieved some success in stabilizing the country politically and economically, although political assassinations and abductions continued into 1974. At elections in 1973 Carlos Andrés Pérez Rodríguez, candidate of Acción Democrática (AD), was chosen to succeed President Caldera. The new Government invested heavily in agriculture and industrial development, creating a more balanced economy, and also undertook to nationalize important sectors. The presidential election of 1978 was won by the leader of the Partido Social-Cristiano (Comité de Organización Política Electoral Independiente—COPEI), Dr Luis Herrera Campíns. In 1981 a deteriorating economic situation provoked social unrest and a succession of guerrilla attacks. At a presidential election in 1983, the AD candidate, Dr Jaime Lusinchi, was elected.

At elections conducted in December 1988, AD candidate Pérez became the first former President to be re-elected. However, the AD lost its overall majority in the Congreso Nacional (National Congress). President Pérez implemented a series of adjustments designed to halt Venezuela's economic decline. These measures provoked rioting throughout the country in February. The Government introduced a curfew and suspended various constitutional rights in order to quell the disturbances, but it was estimated that some 246 people had died during the protests. In March the curfew was revoked, and all constitutional rights were restored, after wages had been increased and the prices of some basic goods were frozen.

In May 1989 popular opposition to the Government's austerity programme became co-ordinated by the country's largest trade union, the Confederación de Trabajadores de Venezuela (CTV), which organized a 24-hour general strike (the first for 31 years) in favour of pro-labour reforms. In May 1991 a controversial new labour law came into effect, providing for a severance benefit scheme and a social security system. In the second half of that year a series of widespread and often violent demonstrations and strikes were staged to protest against monthly increases in the price of petrol, or to demand, *inter alia*, wage increases, the reintroduction of price controls on basic goods, and the suspension of planned public sector redundancies.

On 4 February 1992 an attempt by rebel army units to overthrow the President was defeated by armed forces loyal to the Government. The rebels, identified as members of the Movimiento Bolivariano Revolucionario 200 (MBR-200), attempted to occupy the President's office, the Miraflores palace, and his official residence, but were forced to capitulate. Simultaneous rebel action in the cities of Maracay, Valencia and Maracaibo ended when one of the leaders of the coup, Lt-Col Hugo Chávez Frías, broadcast an appeal for their surrender. More than 1,000 soldiers were arrested, and 33 officers were subsequently charged. A number of constitutional guarantees were immediately suspended, and press and television censorship was imposed to exclude coverage of Chávez, who had received considerable passive popular support. The rebels' stated primary reasons for staging the insurrection were the increasing social divisions and uneven distribution of wealth resulting from government economic policy, and widespread corruption in public life. Immediately following the attempted coup Pérez authorized a 50% increase in the minimum wage. He also announced plans to bring forward a US $4,000m. social project, aimed at improving health care, social welfare and education.

In March 1992 Pérez announced the suspension of increases in the price of petrol and electricity, and the reintroduction of price controls on a number of basic foodstuffs and medicine. Full constitutional rights were finally restored in April. Nevertheless, widespread protests against government austerity measures and alleged official corruption continued.

On 27 November 1992 a further coup attempt, reported to have been instigated by members of MBR-200, was suppressed by forces loyal to the Government. A statement by the imprisoned Lt-Col Chávez, transmitted from a captured government-owned television station, urged Venezuelans to stage public demonstrations in support of the rebels. Principal air force bases were seized, and rebel aircraft attacked the presidential palace and other strategically important installations. The Government introduced a state of emergency and suspended the Constitution. Sporadic fighting continued into the following day, but by 29 November order had been restored and some 1,300 rebel members of the armed forces had been arrested. Popular discontent with the Government was reflected further in regional and municipal elections held in December, which resulted in significant gains for COPEI.

In May 1993 an extraordinary joint session of the Congreso Nacional voted to endorse a Supreme Court ruling that sufficient evidence existed for Pérez to be prosecuted on corruption charges. The charges concerned allegations that Pérez, and two former government ministers, had embezzled US $17m. from a secret government fund. Pérez was subsequently suspended from office. On 5 June the Congreso Nacional elected Ramón José Velásquez, an independent senator, as interim President. In August the Congreso Nacional approved legislation enabling Velásquez to introduce urgent economic and financial measures by decree in order to address the growing economic crisis. In late August a special session of the Congreso Nacional voted in favour of the permanent suspension from office of Pérez, regardless of the outcome of any legal proceedings.

1993 elections

The presidential and legislative elections of December 1993 proceeded peacefully. Dr Rafael Caldera Rodríguez, the candidate of the newly formed Convergencia Nacional (CN), was elected President (having previously held office in 1969–74). However, the CN secured only minority representation in the Congreso Nacional. In February 1994 the AD and COPEI established a pact using their combined majority representation in the Congreso Nacional in order to gain control of the major legislative committees. Also in February, in an attempt to consolidate relations with the armed forces, Caldera initiated proceedings providing for the release and pardon of all those charged with involvement in the 1992 coup attempts.

In June 1994 the Government announced that it was to assume extraordinary powers, in view of the deepening economic crisis and the virtual collapse of the banking sector. Six articles of the Constitution were suspended; these concerned guarantees including freedom of movement, freedom from arbitrary arrest, and the right to own property and to engage in legal economic activity. The Government also announced the introduction of price controls and a single fixed exchange rate. Caldera also issued a decree placing the financial system under government control. In July the Congreso Nacional voted to restore five of the six suspended constitutional guarantees. Despite protests, the Government promptly reintroduced the suspensions. Later that month, however, the legislature endorsed emergency financial measures, including an extension of price controls and the strengthening of finance sector regulation. Full constitutional guarantees were finally restored in July. In September 1997 the Congreso Nacional approved an enabling law that conferred extraordinary powers on President Caldera to enact legislation by decree, in order to facilitate the implementation of emergency economic measures designed to reduce the huge fiscal deficit and to accelerate social security reforms.

The legislative elections of November 1998 were won by the Polo Patriótico, an alliance of small, mainly left-wing parties led by the Movimiento V República (MVR). The MVR was led by the leader of the attempted coup of February 1992, Lt-Col Chávez; its electoral success was widely considered to reflect the popular rejection of apparent corruption in the country's major political parties.

Hugo Chávez elected President, 1998

In the light of the MVR's success in the legislative poll, prior to the 1998 presidential election the AD and COPEI withdrew their support for their respective candidates and united in support of independent candidate Henrique Salas Römer, hoping to forestall the loss of their long-standing political predominance. However, Chávez, who styled himself as a radical left-wing populist, was elected President on 6 December.

Chávez immediately announced plans for elections to a Constituent Assembly to draft a new constitution, and asked the Congreso Nacional to pass a new enabling law to allow him to implement an extensive restructuring of public administration and a comprehensive economic recovery programme. Chávez was inaugurated as President on 2 February 1999. At the end of February he announced details of an ambitious emergency social improvement plan to rehabilitate public property and land through voluntary civil and military action. Such pledges (together with a promise that the armed forces would not be used against the civilian population) prompted a series of rural and urban public land occupations, none of which was forcibly ended.

In April 1999 the Congreso Nacional approved the enabling law. On 25 April a national referendum, organized to ascertain levels of popular support for the convening of a Constituent Assembly and the regulations governing the election of such a body, demonstrated 82% support for the Assembly and 80% support for Chávez's proposals for electoral procedures. Elections to the National Constituent Assembly (ANC) in July resulted in outright victory for the Polo Patriótico. The ANC was formally inaugurated and by late August had assumed most functions of the opposition-controlled Congreso Nacional; the Congreso itself was put into recess indefinitely. In response, the opposition accused the Government of establishing a de facto dictatorship. Chávez justified the control of the legislature, executive and judiciary as necessary in order to eradicate corruption and implement social reforms. A Judicial Emergency Commission was also appointed in August with the task of investigating the notoriously corrupt judicial system. (By November 200 judges had been dismissed or suspended.) In September the ANC and the Congreso Nacional signed an agreement of political coexistence that guaranteed the full functioning of the legislative branch from 2 October until a new constitution entered into force.

The draft of the new Constitution was signed by the ANC on 19 November 1999 and was approved by 71% of the popular vote in a referendum held on 15 December. The 350-article Constitution, which renamed the country the Bolivarian Republic of Venezuela, was promulgated on 30 December. It extended the President's term from five to six years, eliminated the Senado, permitted more state intervention in the economy, reduced civilian supervisory powers over the military, guaranteed the

Government's oil monopoly and strengthened minority rights. The Constitution also promoted public participation by giving the electorate the right to remove elected officials from office by referendum and to annul all but a handful of key laws with an absolute majority. The monitoring of such election processes was to be carried out by an independent National Electoral Council (Consejo Nacional Electoral—CNE). The Congreso Nacional was officially dissolved on 4 January 2000.

New elections for the President, governors, legislators and mayors, as stipulated under the new Constitution, were scheduled for May 2000. The ANC was dissolved in January after it formally delegated its powers to a newly created 21-member Legislative Commission, which was designated as an interim body until the formation of a new Asamblea Nacional (National Assembly). On 25 May, three days before voting was scheduled to take place, the Tribunal Supremo de Justicia (Supreme Tribunal of Justice) suspended the elections, citing technical faults with the electronic voting system. Elections for the President, national legislators and governors were eventually held on 30 July, separate from the local elections, which were postponed until December. Despite the weak economic situation, popular support for the President, especially from the poorest sections of society, remained strong: Chávez won 60% of the valid votes cast, compared with the 38% of the ballot polled by Francisco Arias Cárdenas. In the concurrent legislative elections, the ruling MVR secured a majority in the new, 165-seat Asamblea Nacional.

In November 2000 Chávez's powers were further enhanced when the Asamblea Nacional approved a new enabling law, allowing the President to decree, without legislative debate, a wide range of laws (in areas including public finance and land reform) for one year. In the same month the legislature also approved controversial legislation that assigned the power to appoint important government posts, such as Attorney-General, Ombudsman (Defensor del Pueblo) and senior judges, to a 15-member congressional committee that was dominated by members of the ruling party.

In November 2001 the opposition-controlled CTV allied itself with the country's largest business association, Fedecámaras (Federación Venezolana de Cámaras y Asociaciones de Comercio y Producción), to demand a nation-wide general strike. Fedecámaras was protesting against a recently decreed series of 49 laws; these measures included land reform legislation allowing the Government to expropriate land it deemed unproductive, and a hydrocarbons law, which increased royalties on the petroleum industry. The CTV objected to the hydrocarbons law, claiming that it threatened foreign investment and jobs.

In early 2002 Chávez appointed to his Council of Ministers several co-conspirators in the 1992 military coup attempt. The cabinet reorganization was interpreted by many as a move to the left that would increase political instability. In February four military officials, in separate statements, publicly demanded that Chávez resign, leading to further anti-Government protests and counter-demonstrations in support of the Government. In the same month, in the face of increasing economic uncertainty, the Government abandoned the fixed currency exchange regime and allowed the bolívar to float freely, in an attempt to halt mass capital flight.

In March 2002 business leaders, trade union leaders and representatives of the Catholic Church signed a pact calling for, *inter alia*, the installation of a government of national unity. At the same time, industrial unrest continued to escalate. Following the appointment of a new management board of the state petroleum company Petróleos de Venezuela, SA (PDVSA), several thousand PDVSA managers marched through Caracas in protest, claiming that the appointments were politically motivated. On 9 April a 48-hour general strike was organized by the CTV and Fedecámaras. It was subsequently announced that the strike would continue indefinitely, and on 11 April more than 150,000 people marched on the presidential palace to demand Chávez's resignation. In the subsequent clashes outside the Miraflores palace between protesters, government supporters and the security forces, 20 people were killed and more than 100 injured.

Failed coup of April 2002

On 12 April 2002 a group of senior military officers announced that President Chávez had resigned amid allegations that pro-Government loyalists had fired on opposition protesters. It later emerged that Chávez had, in fact, refused to resign and that, in effect, a military coup had taken place. The military conspirators appointed Pedro Carmona, the President of Fedecámaras, as interim President, while Chávez was held incommunicado. On assuming power, Carmona dissolved the Asamblea Nacional and the Tribunal Supremo de Justicia and pronounced Chávez's Bolivarian Constitution to be null and void. The removal from office by the military of an elected head of state was immediately condemned by many Governments in the region; however, by contrast, the US Administration of George W. Bush blamed the crisis on Chávez and refused to call his ousting from power a coup. Thousands of pro-Chávez and pro-democracy supporters took to the streets to demand Chávez's reinstatement, while many senior military officers also expressed their continued loyalty to the deposed President. In the face of threats by officers loyal to Chávez to attack the presidential palace, Carmona resigned; Vice-President Diosdado Cabello was sworn in as interim President on 13 April. Chávez returned to the Miraflores palace within hours and, in a televised ceremony, resumed his presidential powers, less than two days after he was ousted.

On reassuming the presidency, as a gesture of reconciliation, Chávez announced the resignation of the disputed PDVSA board of directors. He also declared that there would be no persecution of those who had supported his removal from office. Nevertheless, Carmona and 100 military personnel were arrested. (Carmona escaped from house arrest and was subsequently granted asylum in Colombia.) In late April 2002 the Asamblea Nacional approved the establishment of a Truth Commission to investigate the events surrounding the coup attempt. (In 2004 eight people were convicted and sentenced to prison terms of between three and six years for their roles in the uprising.)

The country's political and economic situation continued to deteriorate in mid-2002. In October the opposition and its allies in the CTV and Fedecámaras called a widely observed one-day strike. On 23 October a group of 14 senior military officers, many of whom had been involved in April's failed coup, declared themselves in rebellion against the Chávez Government, occupying a square in eastern Caracas, where they were joined by hundreds of opposition activists. More than 100 junior officers later also expressed their rejection of Chávez's policies and joined the protest. All of the officers involved were subsequently dismissed from the armed forces. In an attempt to find a constitutional solution to the ongoing political crisis, 12 representatives of the opposition and the Government began round-table discussions, sponsored by the Organization of American States (OAS, see p. 404), in early November. The talks failed to make any immediate progress, however, and in late November the opposition, the CTV and Fedecámaras announced that a general strike would be held from 2 December to force President Chávez to call fresh elections or submit to a referendum. The general strike lasted a further nine weeks. The majority of large businesses and international companies observed the stoppage, although small shopkeepers and public transport continued to operate throughout.

In January 2003 President Chávez suspended trading in the national currency, the bolívar, in response to the economic crisis. Early the following month it was announced that the bolívar was to be pegged to the US dollar, and that price controls were to be introduced on basic food items. Although the Government refused to negotiate on the issue of early elections, discussions between the two sides, suspended at the start of the strike, resumed in late January. The opposition, which had combined under the Coordinadora Democrática (CD) grouping, presented an estimated 4m. signatures in support of early elections. In mid-February the Government and opposition representatives signed an agreement to seek to reduce political tension in Venezuela. This was immediately thrown into question, however, when the following day police arrested the President of Fedecámaras, Carlos Fernández Pérez, on charges including treason, relating to his role in organizing the strike. A warrant was also issued for his fellow strike leader, the President of the CTV, Carlos Ortega, who went into hiding and later obtained political asylum in Costa Rica. In March an appeals court ordered the release without charge of Fernández Pérez, ruling that there was no evidence against him.

Presidential recall referendum

In May 2003, following further OAS-sponsored negotiations, the Government and opposition finalized an agreement that a referendum on the Chávez Government could be held if the opposition succeeded in collecting 2.4m. signatures in support of a vote. The signatures were acquired and submitted, but in early September the CNE ruled that the petition was not valid, as some of the signatures had been collected more than six months before the date on which a referendum could be held. Furthermore, in

late September the CNE issued a new and more stringent set of referendum guidelines, which stipulated that, in the case of a binding presidential recall referendum, a President would then only be removed from office if a greater proportion of the electorate voted against him than had supported him in the most recent election (in the case of Chávez in the 2000 ballot, this would be greater than 59.7% of the vote). Also, if there were insufficient valid signatures collected (20% of the electorate, equivalent to some 2.4m. voters), no further recall petitions would be permitted during that President's term of office.

In October 2003 the CD presented a new recall referendum request to the CNE. In response, the MVR announced that it intended to compile more than 40 recall petitions on opposition deputies and state governors. The CNE ruled that any recall referendums would be restricted to members of the Asamblea Nacional and federal Government. The CNE was scheduled to announce the validity of both sets of petitions by the end of December. However, a series of technical problems and doubts over the validity of some petitions led to delays, provoking civil unrest in which eight protesters were killed in February 2004. Finally, in June the CNE ruled that the number of valid signatures collected was sufficient to force a presidential recall referendum. The Government accepted this ruling, and the poll was duly held on 15 August. The motion to recall the President was defeated, with 59% of the valid votes cast against Chávez's removal from office. The rate of participation was 70% of the electorate. Despite assertions by international observers that the ballot had been conducted fairly, the CD disputed the result. In September the CNE rejected the CD's appeal against the referendum result, citing a lack of evidence.

In January 2005 President Chávez signed a decree initiating a 90-day review process into both the level of productivity on privately owned land and into the validity of its ownership. Local authorities were granted powers to expropriate estates deemed unproductive by the review for redistribution to landless farmers. In January 2006 the Government took control of 32 oilfields under private operation, in accordance with its policy of revising all private sector contracts for hydrocarbon exploitation in order to give the government-owned PDVSA a majority stake.

At elections to the Asamblea Nacional in December 2005 the ruling MVR secured an overwhelming number of seats. The government victory was primarily owing to the boycott of the ballot by the main opposition parties. As a result, voter participation was estimated at just 25%. However, observers from the European Union (EU, see p. 281) and the OAS declared the elections to be free and transparent.

The Government announced further measures under its so-called Bolivarian social reform programme in early 2006. In March it was stated that 150,000 new homes were to be built during the year to begin to address the housing crisis among impoverished sectors of society. In April a programme costing US $24m. to extend basic services to some 77,000 people living in rural areas was announced. Moreover, in November new measures aimed at widening access to higher education and providing dental care for the poor were introduced. The Government's ongoing revision of its hydrocarbons operations also continued. In April the state assumed control of seven oilfields operated by foreign petroleum companies, five of which were relinquished under legislation introduced in 2001 and two of which were retaken without the agreement of the companies currently operating the sites. Further amendments to the hydrocarbon laws, approved in May 2006, provided for an increase in royalties required from foreign companies operating Venezuelan oilfields.

Re-election of Chávez, 2006

At the presidential election held on 3 December 2006 Chávez was decisively re-elected with 62.9% of the vote. The opposition's unity candidate, Manuel Rosales Guerrero, the Governor of Zulia, secured 36.9% of the votes cast. Observers from the EU declared themselves to be generally satisfied with the conduct of the election and praised the high rate of participation (some 75% of registered voters took part). The victory was seen as a strong endorsement of the Government's Bolivarian programme of social reform, and of Chávez himself. Shortly after the election it was announced that the MVR was to be dissolved and replaced by a new political organization, the Partido Socialista Unido de Venezuela (PSUV), which was intended to unite the various left-wing parties allied to the Government. In January 2007 the Asamblea Nacional approved a wide-ranging enabling law granting the President powers to legislate by decree for a period of 18 months in 11 areas, including the reform of state institutions and public services. The law was intended, in particular, to facilitate one of the stated priorities of the new administration, the return to state ownership of privatized industries. To this end, in February the Government agreed the terms of the purchase of shares in Electricidad de Caracas, and in May it bought a majority share in the telecommunications concern Compañía Anónima Nacional Telefónos de Venezuela. In June PDVSA gained control of petroleum operations in the Orinoco Belt by acquiring majority stakes in four joint ventures with foreign companies. Two further companies refused to renegotiate their contracts with PDVSA, and the projects in which they were involved came under full state ownership.

The Government's announcement in December 2006 that it would not renew the broadcasting licence of Radio Caracas Televisión (RCTV), Venezuela's oldest television station, upon its expiry in May 2007 was condemned by numerous international media organizations. Chávez cited the station's support for the brief coup of 2002 and the anti-Government bias of its news reporting as reasons for the decision. The station duly ceased broadcasting in May; however, RCTV recommenced broadcasting via cable in July by means of its US-based subsidiary, RCTV International.

In August 2007 Chávez presented the Asamblea Nacional with a proposal to amend 33 articles of the 1999 Constitution. The most significant of the amendments would have removed the restriction limiting the President to two consecutive terms in office—allowing him to be re-elected indefinitely—and increased the presidential term from six to seven years. The revised Constitution would, *inter alia*, have abolished the autonomy of the central bank and placed the country's international reserves under government control, defined a political role for the armed forces, and reduced the maximum working day from eight to six hours. In November the Asamblea Nacional approved Chávez's proposed amendments, along with a further 36 proposed by the legislature. A referendum was held on 2 December on the two sets of amendments, both of which were rejected. Gen. Raúl Isaías Baduel, a former close ally of Chávez who had retired as Minister of National Defence in July, had been prominent in his opposition to the reforms, claiming that it would have amounted to a coup. (Baduel was arrested in April 2009 on corruption charges; he claimed that his detention was politically motivated. Nevertheless, he was convicted of corruption in May 2010 and received an eight-year prison term.)

In April 2008 Chávez announced that the Government would take control of the cement industry in Venezuela, in order to guarantee supplies for state housing construction programmes. Majority stakes in two of the three main cement companies were purchased in August; however, in the same month, following its failure to negotiate a take-over of the Venezuelan operations of the Mexican firm Cemex, the Government seized and expropriated the firm's plants and offices by force.

In May 2008 Chávez enacted a law on intelligence and counter-intelligence by decree. The new legislation was criticized by the opposition and human rights organizations, in particular for an article that established prison terms of up to four years for any person who refused to co-operate with the intelligence services. In response, the President repealed the law. On 31 July Chávez made further use of the enabling law—just before it was scheduled to expire—to promulgate 26 decrees, many of which introduced measures that had been included in the proposed constitutional reforms rejected in 2007. Several of the new laws increased state control over the economy, notably in the area of food security.

More than 65% of the registered electorate voted in municipal and gubernatorial elections in November 2008, representing the highest turn-out ever recorded in local elections. Although PSUV candidates were elected to governorships in 17 of the 22 contested states, the opposition's gain of three of the most populous states, in addition to the two it already held, was seen as a significant challenge to the pro-Chávez hegemony across the country.

In December 2008 Chávez initiated another attempt to remove the restriction on presidential re-election, asking PSUV members to gather signatures in support of the necessary constitutional amendment. In an effort to widen support for the initiative, in January 2009 the President proposed that term limits should be abolished for all popularly elected offices, including governors, mayors and deputies. Later in that month the Asamblea Nacional approved, subject to referendum, Chávez's proposed amendments to five articles of the Constitution that would enable re-election to all posts. A referendum was duly held on 15 February, at which the amendments were approved by 55% of the valid votes cast. Some 70% of the electorate participated in the poll. Immediately after the result was announced, Chávez confirmed his intention to stand in the presidential election due to take place in 2012.

In March 2009, following an investigation begun at Chávez's request, the Attorney-General issued an arrest order against Manuel Rosales, who was accused of having embezzled public funds while he was Governor of Zulia. The opposition leader denied the charges, which he denounced as politically motivated, and fled to Peru, claiming that the Venezuelan judicial system would not afford him a fair trial.

Further nationalization moves

In February 2009 Chávez ordered the National Guard to take control of all rice-processing plants to ensure that they complied with pricing regulations. In early March Chávez announced the expropriation of a rice mill belonging to the US multinational corporation Cargill, accusing it of failing to meet production quotas, and threatened other food producers with nationalization. In March the Asamblea Nacional approved legislation allowing the President to reassume the administration of strategic infrastructure, including ports, airports and roads, from state governments (to which control had been devolved in 1999). Chávez subsequently ordered the armed forces to take control of three major ports—Puerto Cabello, Guamache and Maracaibo—and an airport, all in states governed by the opposition. Furthermore, in April the Asamblea Nacional approved a law allowing the President to appoint a Head of Government of the Capital District (comprising the largest of Caracas's five municipalities), to whom most of the budget hitherto assigned to the metropolitan authority would be transferred. The new arrangements were widely regarded as being intended to diminish the authority of the recently elected opposition Mayor of the metropolitan district, Antonio Ledezma. In May the Government began the nationalization of all companies providing services to the petroleum and gas industry, taking control of terminals and boats on Lake Maracaibo; several steel and iron companies were also brought under state control in that month.

In June 2009 a total of 14 opposition parties, including the AD, COPEI, the pro-Chávez Por la Democracia Social (PODEMOS) and Primero Justicia (PJ), announced the formation of an alliance, the Mesa de Unidad Democrática (MUD).

The announcement in July 2009 that 34 radio stations were to be closed and more than 130 investigated for their alleged failure to comply with regulations was condemned by opposition politicians and others, who accused the Government of infringing the right to freedom of speech. The closure of a further 29 stations on similar grounds was announced in September. The Government rejected accusations that media organizations deemed to be critical of it were being specifically targeted. Meanwhile, various official investigations were initiated into the private cable television channel Globovisión, which frequently criticized the Government.

The Asamblea Nacional approved new electoral reforms in August 2009; the MUD claimed that the legislation favoured the ruling PSUV. Changes included a reduction in the number of deputies to be elected by proportional representation, a provision permitting two different political parties to nominate the same candidate (once as an individual and once through a party list), and the revision of electoral districts. Later that month controversial legislation on education was also adopted. Opponents of the new law, which excluded religious teaching from the curriculum and centralized state control over education, claimed that it promoted the 'indoctrination' of pupils with socialist ideology, although the Minister of Education, Héctor Navarro, insisted that it would provide equal access to education for all citizens. A few days later legislation allowing the seizure of unused or underused land or buildings for 'social purposes' was approved.

Legislation was approved in October 2009 according legal status to the Bolivarian National Militia, formed by the President in 2008, thus allowing it to be allocated budget funds. The Militia, in which foreigners were permitted to serve, was expected to provide logistical support for the next legislative elections. In December a new national police force, the Bolivarian National Police, was launched and the salaries of police officers increased substantially as part of an effort to reduce crime levels. Meanwhile, the Government assumed control of a total of eight private banks in November and December, citing liquidity deficiencies and administrative irregularities. In January 2010 Chávez unexpectedly announced a devaluation of the bolívar, with the introduction of a secondary rate of exchange for non-essential goods, in an attempt to increase revenues from oil exports and stimulate domestic production.

Several government changes were effected in January 2010, following the resignations of Vice-President Carrizalez and Yuvirí Ortega, the Minister of the Environment (and Carrizalez's wife). There was speculation that the resignation of Carrizalez had been prompted by his disagreement with a decision temporarily to suspend the broadcasting licences of six cable television channels, including RCTV International, after they refused to transmit state announcements and presidential speeches, as required under media regulations. The suspension prompted protests in several cities, including Mérida, where two students were killed and more than 20 police officers injured in violent clashes. Elías José Jaua Milano assumed Carrizales's vice-presidential post in addition to his existing position as Minister of Agriculture and Lands. Meanwhile, Chávez announced the creation of a peasant militia force, within the Bolivarian National Militia, which was to operate within rural areas. Chávez also promulgated legislation aimed at decentralizing powers from state and municipal administrations to local 'communal councils'. In accordance with this, the Consejo Federal de Gobierno (Federal Council of Government—comprising ministers, local governors and mayors, and communal council members) was established in May. The opposition criticized these measures, claiming that they would instead reinforce central authority and undermine the power and resources of elected local officials.

Guillermo Zuloaga, President of the private television station Globovisión, was charged with illegal business practices in June 2010, in relation to his operation of two motor vehicle companies. Zuloaga, who subsequently fled to the USA, claimed that this accusation was motivated by the authorities' disapproval of Globovisión's anti-Government programming. Later that month the Government seized the Banco Federal, presided over by Nelson Mezerhane, another Globovisión senior executive, owing to alleged violations of banking regulations, and in the process the state procured the bank's minority shareholding in Globovisión. Legislation was adopted in August that prohibited banks from investing in media companies. Globovisión received a US $2m. fine in October 2011 for purportedly breaching broadcasting regulations. Preliminary legal proceedings against Globovisión commenced at the Supreme Tribunal of Justice in March 2012 following the non-payment of the fine, which Globovisión regarded as an attempt to force it into bankruptcy. In June, after being subjected to an asset freeze, Globovisión reluctantly agreed to pay the penalty.

Towards the 2012 elections

Elections to the Asamblea Nacional were held on 26 September 2010. The PSUV maintained its legislative dominance, with 98 seats, but the opposition MUD registered a strong performance, securing 65 seats; the remaining two seats were won by Patria Para Todos. Turn-out was recorded at 66.5%. Although the PSUV and the MUD attracted virtually the same number of votes, modifications to constituency boundaries and the voting system (implemented earlier in the year) ensured that the ruling party obtained more seats. Nevertheless, the PSUV still lost ground to the opposition, principally because of public concern over the ailing economy, crime and electricity rationing.

In December 2010 a new enabling law, conferring decree powers upon the President for one-and-a-half years, was adopted. Chávez claimed that this was necessary to allow him to respond effectively to the widespread flooding in several regions, but these new powers also gave him the ability to advance his legislative agenda without the approval of the new Asamblea Nacional, which was inaugurated in January 2011, prompting opposition condemnation. The Asamblea's position was further weakened by the introduction of new rules limiting the number of times that the legislature would be convened and restricting the length of speeches, allegedly to increase efficiency. Meanwhile, a flurry of legislation was approved by the outgoing Asamblea, including controversial laws to regulate radio, television and internet output, which critics claimed would be used to suppress anti-Government media outlets. Although Chávez's initial decrees were solely related to the flooding, in August he used his new powers to nationalize the gold sector, while in April 2012 he unilaterally removed government spending limits, a move denounced by the MUD as unconstitutional.

Chávez revealed in June 2011 that he had been diagnosed with cancer and had received treatment in Cuba. After making multiple trips to Cuba throughout mid-2011 for further medical treatment, in October Chávez asserted that he had fully recovered, although there was widespread speculation, exacerbated by the paucity of reliable information on the President's condition, that he was still seriously ill. Moreover, Chávez's prolonged absences from Venezuela had raised serious legal questions, since, according to some interpretations of the Constitution, the Vice-President should have temporarily assumed the presidency while Chávez was incapacitated. The Government announced two major poverty reduction initiatives in December, targeting children and the elderly, respectively, while in the following month details of another social programme, to reduce unemployment and underemployment, were presented. The MUD accused Chávez of spending recklessly to boost his popularity among low-income voters prior to the upcoming presidential election. However, in February 2012 Chávez underwent surgery in Cuba to remove another cancerous growth, with several rounds of radiotherapy also required, bringing into doubt his ability to conduct a strenuous re-election campaign. Nevertheless, government officials reiterated that the poll would go ahead as scheduled. Earlier in February Henrique Capriles Radonski, the Governor of Miranda and a member of PJ, had been elected as the MUD's presidential candidate.

In an effort to address the deteriorating security situation, in November 2011 Chávez announced the deployment of some 3,500 National Guard troops to high-crime areas. Unofficial data indicated that the 2011 murder rate had reached a record level and that impunity was widespread. In January 2012 the Asamblea Nacional adopted legislation to combat organized crime and terrorism, although the opposition expressed concern that the enhanced surveillance powers granted to the security forces could be misused. Also in that month, Gen. Henry Rangel Silva was appointed as the new Minister of Defence. Chávez presented details of a new anti-crime programme in June. Nevertheless, the homicide rate rose again in 2012.

In April 2012 Chávez established an 'anti-coup command', an ill-defined military structure tasked with preventing the ouster of his regime, and in May he appointed the five members of the Council of State, a new advisory body to the President.

Chávez gave a positive assessment of his health in May 2012, and both he and Capriles were formally registered as presidential candidates in June. The pre-election period was marred by occasional outbreaks of political violence, the worst case being a shooting incident in September in which three opposition supporters lost their lives. Chávez significantly increased government spending during 2012, while the MUD expressed dissatisfaction with the state-run media's partisan coverage of the campaign.

At the presidential election, which took place on 7 October 2012, Chávez was re-elected for a fourth term, attracting 55.1% of the ballot, compared with 44.3% for Capriles. The rate of participation by the electorate was recorded at 80.5%. In mid-October Chávez reorganized the Council of Ministers and appointed Nicolás Maduro Moros, the Minister of Foreign Affairs, as Vice-President; Adm. Diego Molero Bellavia became Minister of Defence later that month, and former Vice-President Jaua received the foreign affairs portfolio in January 2013.

The PSUV secured an overwhelming victory in gubernatorial elections conducted on 16 December 2012, gaining control of 20 of the country's 23 states and leaving the MUD with just three governorships. Capriles was re-elected as Governor of Miranda. The voter participation rate was approximately 54%.

Recent developments: the death of Chávez and election of Maduro

Chávez travelled to Cuba in December 2012 for further cancer-related surgery, but it was revealed in early January 2013 that a post-operation lung infection had left the President gravely ill. He was consequently unable to attend his inauguration ceremony, which had been scheduled to take place on 10 January, leaving the country in a constitutionally ambiguous state. The Asamblea Nacional, in which the PSUV held a majority of seats, voted to allow Chávez to be sworn in by the supreme court at a later, unspecified date. The opposition argued that such a move was unconstitutional, and that if Chávez did not take office as scheduled, fresh elections must be called within 30 days. The Supreme Tribunal of Justice endorsed the Asamblea's decision to delay the inauguration, declaring that the ceremony was not essential before a new presidential term could begin. Chávez returned to Venezuela in February, but died on 5 March. Seven days of mourning were declared in the country. On 8 March Maduro was officially pronounced interim President, pending a fresh election that was to be arranged within 30 days, although questions were advanced regarding the constitutionality of his assumption of the presidency. Capriles was again nominated as the MUD's presidential candidate.

Maduro garnered 50.78% of the votes cast in the presidential poll, held on 14 April 2013, and thus secured a narrow victory over Capriles, who obtained 48.95%. Turn-out was 79.7%. Capriles disputed the validity of the results, alleging widespread irregularities in the voting process. He demanded a full recount of all ballot papers. Following several days of violent unrest in the capital, during which eight people lost their lives, on 18 April the CNE agreed to a recount of all electronic votes. This fell short of the full recount insisted on by Capriles, but quelled tensions in the country. The audit was expected to take at least 30 days. Nevertheless, regional leaders endorsed the results on 19 April, and Maduro took office later that day. A new Council of Ministers, which included many members of the previous administration, was installed on 22 April. Among the new appointments Nelson Merentes Díaz was designated as Minister of Finance, Gen. Miguel Rodríguez Torres was placed in charge of the Ministry of Interior Relations, Justice and Peace, while Jorge Arreaza Montserrat had earlier been named as Vice-President. On 2 May Capriles submitted to the Supreme Tribunal of Justice an appeal against the entire electoral process, requesting that the results of the 14 April be annulled and a fresh ballot take place.

Foreign Affairs

Regional relations

In 1982 Venezuela refused to renew the 1970 Port of Spain Protocol, which declared a 12-year moratorium on the issue of Venezuela's claim to a large area of Guyana to the west of the Essequibo river. In 1985 Venezuela and Guyana requested UN mediation in an attempt to resolve their dispute over the Essequibo region. A UN mediator was appointed in 1989; however, negotiations remained deadlocked. The dispute resurfaced in 1999 when Guyana granted offshore oil concessions in the disputed waters to foreign oil firms, and in October of that year President Hugo Chávez renewed Venezuela's claim to the Essequibo region. In 2004 Chávez met his Guyanese counterpart, Bharrat Jagdeo; although no progress was made on resolving the dispute, the Venezuelan Government indicated its willingness to 'authorize' Guyanese mineral exploration in the Essequibo region. In 2005 Guyana signed the PetroCaribe energy accord with Venezuela, granting Guyana preferential terms for purchasing Venezuelan petroleum. In July 2010 Chávez and Jagdeo concluded a number of trade agreements and agreed to restart UN-mediated negotiations on their territorial dispute, which had been in abeyance since 2007. However, tensions re-emerged in September 2011, when Guyana appealed to the UN Commission on the Limits of the Continental Shelf to increase the extent of its maritime boundaries. Guyana controversially granted further offshore oil concessions in June 2012.

Venezuela has a territorial dispute with Colombia concerning maritime boundaries in the Gulf of Venezuela. In 1989 an agreement was reached with Colombia on the establishment of a border commission to negotiate a settlement for the territorial dispute. In 1990 both countries signed the San Pedro Alejandrino document, pledging to implement the commission's proposals. Periodic incursions into Venezuelan territory by Colombian combatants and criminal elements continually strained relations with Colombia. Despite agreements signed by both countries in 1997 and 2000 to increase co-operation in policing the border area, clashes between the Venezuelan military and Colombian guerrillas were frequent. In November 2000 Colombia briefly recalled its ambassador to Venezuela after a representative of the Fuerzas Armadas Revolucionarias de Colombia—Ejército del Pueblo (FARC) was allowed to speak in the Venezuelan Asamblea Nacional. In a public demonstration of amity, in 2004 Chávez met his Colombian counterpart Alvaro Uribe in Cartagena, Colombia, to discuss border security and economic co-operation. However, relations were severely strained following the arrest by the Colombian authorities of Rodrigo Granda Escobar, the supposed international spokesperson of the FARC, at the end of the year. It was subsequently alleged by the Venezuelan Government that Granda, although ultimately arrested in Cúcuta, Colombia, was first kidnapped in Caracas by Venezuelan and Colombian agents in the pay of the Colombian Government and with the collusion of US intelligence services; the Uribe and US Governments denied any involvement. The Venezuelan ambassador to Colombia was recalled in

January 2005 and restrictions on trade and passage between the two countries were imposed by the Chávez Government. Following an expression of regret by the Colombian Government in January and a visit to Caracas by President Uribe in February, relations between the two countries were normalized.

In August 2007 Uribe engaged Chávez in negotiating with FARC leaders in respect of the release of hostages held by the guerrilla group. However, Uribe abruptly cancelled Chávez's mediation attempt in November, accusing him of making contact with senior Colombian military officers against his orders; nevertheless, the Venezuelan President's subsequent role in securing the release of two of the hostages in January 2008 led to a slight improvement in relations. Chávez strongly condemned Uribe following Colombia's incursion into Ecuadorean territory in March, during which time a senior FARC commander was killed; in response to the incident Chávez ordered the closure of the Venezuelan embassy in the Colombian capital, Bogotá, and sent troops to the Colombian border. Uribe subsequently alleged that evidence gathered during the raid indicated that Chávez had aided the FARC; however, formal diplomatic relations were swiftly restored after Chávez mediated a rapprochement between Uribe and the Ecuadorean President, Rafael Correa Delgado. In June, in a reversal of his previous declarations in support of the rebels, Chávez publicly urged the FARC to end its armed struggle and release all its remaining hostages. However, relations between Venezuela and Colombia deteriorated in July 2009 after it emerged that Colombia was negotiating an agreement with the USA (signed in October) to allow US troops access to its military bases. Tensions increased later that month, when the Colombian Vice-President accused Venezuela of supplying weapons to the FARC, prompting Chávez to sever diplomatic relations with Colombia and threaten to halt imports of Colombian goods. In November, following the signature of the agreement between Colombia and the USA, which the Venezuelan Government claimed represented a threat to Venezuela's security, Chávez ordered the deployment of 15,000 troops at the border with Colombia, citing increased violence by Colombian paramilitary groups. Increasingly aggressive rhetoric from Chávez subsequently prompted Colombia to lodge an official complaint with the UN Security Council. Critics of Chávez accused him of orchestrating the diplomatic row in order to deflect attention from domestic difficulties. In July 2010, at an OAS summit meeting, Colombian officials publicly accused the Venezuelan Government of providing shelter to large numbers of FARC guerrillas. Chávez immediately dismissed these claims and severed diplomatic relations with Colombia. However, tensions eased in August following the inauguration of new Colombian President Juan Manuel Santos Calderón, who took a more conciliatory stance towards Venezuela. During their first meeting, in August, Chávez and Santos agreed to restore diplomatic relations and establish a number of joint committees to discuss economic and security concerns. A second round of constructive talks in November resulted in the signing of several economic accords, and an agreement on combating cross-border drugs-trafficking was concluded in January 2011. Further economic co-operation agreements were signed by Chávez and Santos in April and November, while in May joint mediation efforts by the two leaders resulted in a major breakthrough in the political crisis in Honduras. A Venezuelan government official participated in peace talks between the FARC and the Santos administration during 2012–13.

Following his election in 1998, President Chávez announced that his administration would seek greater integration in large regional organizations such as the Caribbean Community and Common Market (CARICOM, see p. 231) and the Southern Common Market (Mercado Común del Sur—Mercosur, see p. 439). In September 2005 Chávez launched PetroCaribe, an initiative to promote energy integration and offer preferential prices for petroleum in the Caribbean region. Venezuela was admitted to Mercosur in 2006, but its entry was subject to ratification by the group's existing members, and Paraguay's legislature consistently refused to approve Venezuela's accession. However, in late June 2012 Argentina, Brazil and Uruguay voted to suspend Paraguay from Mercosur following the impeachment, under questionable circumstances, of Paraguayan President Fernando Lugo Méndez earlier that month. The three nations, taking advantage of Paraguay's temporary exclusion from Mercosur decision-making processes, acted swiftly to facilitate Venezuela's formal accession to the organization, which was completed on 31 July. Paraguay objected vehemently to this move and unsuccessfully appealed to the Tribunal

Permanente de Revisión del Mercosur. Venezuela, meanwhile, strongly criticized Lugo's impeachment, regarding it as a coup. Paraguay subsequently alleged that Maduro had attempted to interfere with the impeachment process, and in early July diplomatic relations were suspended.

President Chávez made closer relations with Cuba a priority, and in 2000 Chávez and the Cuban Head of State, Fidel Castro, signed a co-operation agreement allowing the export of oil to Cuba on preferential terms. From 2003 improved relations between the two countries led to increased Cuban assistance for the Government's social welfare programmes, and Venezuela continued to support Cuba's integration into regional trade associations. In December 2009 Venezuela and Cuba signed a series of accords on economic co-operation, reportedly worth some US $3,200m., which notably granted Venezuela increased involvement in petroleum exploration off the Cuban coast. The preferential oil export deal, signed in 2000, was extended in 2010 for another 10 years. Further joint co-operation agreements, valued at approximately $1,300m., were concluded in June 2011. President Maduro affirmed his administration's commitment to the bilateral relationship during a visit to Cuba in April 2013; multiple co-operation accords were also signed.

Other external relations

Relations between Venezuela and the USA (the main purchaser of Venezuelan crude petroleum) deteriorated markedly following the election of Chávez in 1998. In 2000 Chávez refused to authorize US drugs-surveillance flights over Venezuela. The President's close relationship with Fidel Castro led to further estrangement from the USA. Bilateral relations further deteriorated after the US Administration refused to condemn the short-lived military ousting of Chávez in April 2002. Relations with the USA remained hostile during the 2000s, owing in large part to Chávez's outspoken rhetoric against US 'imperialism'. In April 2005 Venezuela suspended its military exchange programmes with the USA. In August of that year Chávez suspended co-operation with the US Drug Enforcement Agency (DEA), following its repeated criticism of Venezuela's counternarcotics policies. Chávez accused DEA agents of spying on Venezuela and the US Government responded by 'decertifying' Venezuela for non-compliance in fulfilling its obligations to combat the trade in illegal drugs. None the less, in January 2006 Venezuela agreed to renew some co-operation with the DEA, although US agents from the organization were not to be allowed on Venezuelan territory. Meanwhile, from 2005 members of the Government, including President Chávez, repeatedly alleged that the USA was planning to invade Venezuela in order to secure its supply of petroleum; the USA dismissed the allegation as unsubstantiated and accused Chávez of seeking to destabilize the region by expanding its military capability. During 2006 the Venezuelan Government continued to strengthen its armed forces, purchasing weapons and military aircraft from Russia. In March the US authorities announced an embargo on all commercial arms sales to Venezuela. The US Government continued to express concern regarding Venezuela's close relations with countries including Cuba, Libya and Iran, with whose Government Chávez publicly stated his commitment to co-operate in the field of nuclear energy. In September 2008 Venezuela expelled the US ambassador, Patrick Duddy, and recalled its own ambassador from the USA, in solidarity with Bolivia, which had just carried out a similar action as part of an ongoing dispute.

The US Administration of Barack Obama sought to improve bilateral relations, and in June 2009 US-Venezuelan diplomatic relations were formally resumed. However, the agreement signed by the USA and Colombia in October of that year, granting the US military access to seven Colombian bases (see above), strained bilateral relations. In the previous month US Secretary of State Hillary Clinton had expressed concern about Venezuelan weapons purchases, following the conclusion of a new arms agreement between Venezuela and Russia (see below) during a tour by Chávez of several countries, including Libya and Iran. Venezuela demonstrated increased co-operation with the USA during mid-2010 by extraditing a number of alleged drugstraffickers. However, relations were strained by a dispute over the USA's designated ambassador to Venezuela, Larry Palmer. Chávez expressed dissatisfaction in August at Palmer's recent criticism of the Venezuelan armed forces and the policies of the Venezuelan Government, and Chávez officially protested against Palmer's nomination as ambassador. This position was reiterated in December, when Chávez stated that Palmer would be ejected if he attempted to enter Venezuela. Later that month, in retaliation, the US authorities rescinded the visa of the Venezuelan ambassador to the USA. As a penalty for allegedly trading with Iran, in May 2011 the Obama Administration announced sanctions against PDVSA, provoking strong condemnation from the Venezuelan Government. In September further US sanctions were imposed, targeting four Chávez-affiliated officials accused of providing support to the FARC; Venezuela again censured the US action.

Tensions between Venezuela and the USA remained high following Maduro's assumption of the presidency in March 2013. Maduro asserted that the USA had been plotting to destabilize Venezuela, and two US diplomatic personnel were ejected from the country in March, with the USA swiftly reciprocating.

President Chávez has sought to strengthen Venezuela's alliance with Russia. Chávez visited Russia in July 2008 to sign co-operation agreements in the fields of energy and defence. Russian President Dmitrii Medvedev paid a return visit to Venezuela in November (the first by a Russian leader), and promised Russian assistance to enable Venezuela to build its first nuclear power plant. During a visit to Russia in September 2009, Chávez announced that Venezuela would recognize the separatist Georgian territories of Abkhazia and South Ossetia as independent sovereign states (becoming only the third country to do so after Russia and Nicaragua), while the Russian Government agreed to loan Venezuela some US $2,200m. for the purchase of tanks and missiles. An accord on joint petroleum exploration in Venezuelan territory was also signed. Further bilateral agreements, again mainly in the areas of energy and defence, were signed in April 2010. Chávez travelled to Russia in October, during another controversial foreign tour that included visits to Iran, Libya, Syria and Belarus. A preliminary agreement on the construction of a nuclear power plant in Venezuela was signed; however, the Venezuelan Government cancelled this project in 2011, following the serious damage caused to two nuclear plants in Fukushima, Japan, by a devastating tsunami in March. Economic and military deals valued at some $8,000m. were concluded with Russia in October.

Chávez was notable as one of the few world leaders in 2011 to support publicly Libyan leader Col Muammar al-Qaddafi during his regime's violent attempts to suppress anti-Government protests, and was critical of the subsequent UN-supported military intervention in Libya, in which the USA played a prominent role. Chávez also openly endorsed the internationally discredited Syrian regime of Lt-Gen. Bashar al-Assad, which had orchestrated a similar campaign of violence against anti-Government elements.

CONSTITUTION AND GOVERNMENT

Venezuela is a federal republic comprising 23 states, a Capital District and 72 Federal Dependencies. Under the Constitution, which was promulgated on 30 December 1999, legislative power is held by the unicameral Asamblea Nacional (National Assembly). Executive authority rests with the President. The President is elected for six years by universal adult suffrage. The President has extensive powers, and is assisted by a Council of Ministers. Each state has a directly elected executive governor and an elected legislature. Judicial power is exercised by the Supreme Tribunal of Justice (Tribunal Supremo de Justicia) and by the other tribunals.

REGIONAL AND INTERNATIONAL CO-OPERATION

Venezuela is a member of the Inter-American Development Bank (see p. 341), of the Latin American Integration Association (Asociación Latinoamericana de Integración, see p. 370), of the Latin American Economic System (Sistema Económico Latinoamericano, see p. 462) and of the Organization of American States (OAS, see p. 404). Venezuela became a full member of the Southern Common Market (Mercado Común del Sur—Mercosur, see p. 439) in July 2012. In December 2004 Venezuela was one of 12 countries that were signatories to the agreement creating the South American Community of Nations (Comunidad Sudamericana de Naciones). A treaty for the community—renamed the Union of South American Nations (Unión de Naciones Suramericanas) in 2007—was initialled in 2008, with full functionality of economic union tentatively scheduled for 2019. In April 2006 the Venezuelan, Cuban and Bolivian heads of state signed a trade agreement, which became known as the Bolivarian Alliance for the Peoples of our America (Alianza Bolivariana para los Pueblos de Nuestra América—ALBA), intended to be an alternative to the stalled Free Trade Area of the Americas, advanced by the USA. A new monetary unit, the Sistema Unico de Compensación Regional (Sucre), intended to be used for electronic payments between ALBA member states, was introduced from 2010, initially just between Venezuela and Cuba. Venezuela is a member of the Community of Latin American and Caribbean States (see p. 475), which was formally inaugurated in December 2011. In July 2012 President Chávez announced his intention to withdraw Venezuela from the OAS Inter-American Court of Human Rights owing to a series of disputes with that body.

Venezuela was a founder member of the UN in 1945. As a contracting party to the General Agreement on Tariffs and Trade, Venezuela joined the World Trade Organization (WTO, see p. 444) on its establishment in 1995. Venezuela is also a member of the Organization of the Petroleum Exporting Countries (see p. 418).

ECONOMIC AFFAIRS

In 2011, according to estimates by the World Bank, Venezuela's gross national income (GNI), measured at average 2009–11 prices, was US $349,054m., equivalent to $11,920 per head (or $12,620 per head on an international purchasing-power parity basis). During 2002–11, it was estimated, the population increased by an annual average of 1.7%, while gross domestic product (GDP) per head decreased, in real terms, at an average of 2.9% per year. Overall GDP increased, in real terms, by an average annual rate of 4.7% in 2002–12; according to preliminary government figures, GDP increased by 5.6% in 2012.

According to the World Bank, agriculture (including hunting, forestry and fishing) contributed an estimated 4.2% of GDP in 2007. The sector engaged 7.8% of the employed labour force in 2012. The principal crops are sugar cane, bananas, maize, rice, plantains, oranges, sorghum and cassava. Cattle are the principal livestock. According to the World Bank, agricultural GDP increased by an estimated annual average of 2.2% during 2002–10; the sector's GDP decreased, in real terms, by 1.4% in 2010.

Industry (including mining, manufacturing, petroleum-related activities, construction and power) contributed a preliminary 25.9% of GDP and engaged 21.4% of the employed labour force in 2012. According to official estimates, industrial GDP rose by an annual average of 4.0% during 2002–12. Sectoral GDP increased by a preliminary 6.2% in 2012.

Mining and quarrying (including petroleum and petroleum-related activities) contributed a preliminary 11.9% of GDP in 2012, but mining and quarrying engaged only 1.2% of the employed labour force in that year. Petroleum and petroleum-related products provided 93.1% of export revenues in 2010. At the end of 2011 proven reserves totalled 296,500m. barrels. Production averaged 2.7m. barrels per day in 2011. As well as large reserves of petroleum, Venezuela has substantial deposits of natural gas, coal, diamonds, gold, zinc, copper, lead, silver, phosphates, manganese and titanium. The GDP of the mining sector declined by an estimated average of 1.2% per year in 2002–12; the sector increased, in real terms, by a preliminary 5.2% in 2011, but declined by a preliminary 6.2% in 2012.

Manufacturing contributed a preliminary 14.7% of GDP and engaged approximately 11.4% of the employed labour force in 2012. The most important sectors were food products, transport equipment, industrial chemicals and iron and steel. According to official estimates, manufacturing GDP increased by an annual average of 3.2% during 2002–12. The sector's GDP increased, in real terms, by a preliminary 1.8% in 2012.

Construction contributed a preliminary 8.4% of GDP in 2012 and engaged approximately 8.3% of the employed labour force in that year. Sectoral GDP increased by an annual average of 6.0% during 2002–12; it increased, in real terms, by a preliminary 4.8% in 2011 and by a further preliminary 16.6% in 2012.

Energy is derived principally from domestic supplies of petroleum and coal, and from hydroelectric power. Hydroelectric power provided 72.0% of electricity production in 2010, according to the US Energy Information Administration, with thermal generation supplying the remainder. Imports of mineral fuels comprised 0.9% of the total value of merchandise imports in 2010.

The services sector contributed a preliminary 62.6% of GDP and engaged some 70.8% of the employed labour force in 2012.

The sector increased by an annual average of 6.5% in 2002–12. Sectoral GDP increased, in real terms, by a preliminary 8.1% in 2012.

In 2011 Venezuela recorded a visible merchandise trade surplus of US $46,452m., and there was a surplus of $27,325m. on the current account of the balance of payments. In 2010 the principal source of imports (30.5%) was the USA; other major suppliers were the People's Republic of China and Brazil. The USA was also the principal market for exports; other major purchasers were China and Colombia. Venezuela's acession to the Mercado Común del Sur (Mercosur) in 2012 was expected to lead to an increase in trade with fellow member countries. The principal exports in 2010 were mineral fuels, lubricants and related materials (93.4%). The principal imports in 2010 were machinery and transport equipment (38.4%), chemicals, food and live animals, basic manufactures and miscellaneous manufactured articles.

There was a general budgetary deficit of 105,382.9m. bolívares fuertes in 2010. Venezuela's general government gross debt was 408,788m. bolívares in 2010, equivalent to 40.2% of GDP. Venezuela's total external debt was US $55,572m. at the end of 2010, of which $37,086m. was public and publicly guaranteed debt. In that year, the cost of servicing long-term public and publicly guaranteed debt and repayments to the IMF was equivalent to 8.8% of the value of exports of goods, services and income (excluding workers' remittances). The average annual rate of inflation was 19.0% in 2008–12. Consumer prices increased by an annual average of 21.1% in 2012. An estimated 8.7% of the labour force were unemployed in January–June 2012, according to government figures.

Venezuela's economy is largely dependent on the petroleum sector and is therefore particularly vulnerable to fluctuations in global oil prices. The administration of Hugo Chávez did little to diversify the economy away from oil, exports of which accounted for some 95% of export revenues. The Government consolidated its policy of increased state intervention by progressively nationalizing, *inter alia*, parts of the hydrocarbons, electricity, telecommunications, transport, banking, construction and agricultural sectors. This policy, however, deterred investment. From mid-2008 international oil prices suffered serious decreases, and as a result the economy contracted in 2009. In January 2010, in an effort to increase oil revenues and stimulate domestic production, the bolívar was devalued and a dual exchange rate system introduced. Although the economy benefited from rising oil prices during 2010, real annual GDP contracted by 1.5%. High inflation remained a problem, and another currency devaluation in January 2011 generated additional inflationary pressure. The price of Venezuelan oil reached a record high during 2011, significantly boosting the country's export receipts and thus facilitating additional public spending. This stimulus led to a resurgence in economic activity, particularly in the construction sector, and real GDP expanded by 4.2% in 2011. However, foreign investment inflows were negligible and high inflation continued to present a serious challenge; price controls, introduced in November in an effort to address this latter problem, proved to be ineffective. Economic growth of an estimated 5.6% was achieved in 2012. Oil prices remained very high during that year, while inflation declined. Moreover, government spending was increased prior to the elections of late 2012, resulting in greater construction activity. However, the administration's expansionary fiscal stance placed additional pressure on public finances, and in February 2013 the currency was devalued again. Nicolás Maduro, who took office as President in April following the death of Chávez in the previous month, was expected to continue the previous Government's policies. The IMF projected that real GDP would grow by 3.3% in 2013.

PUBLIC HOLIDAYS

2014: 1 January (New Year's Day), 3–4 March (Carnival), 17 April (Maundy Thursday), 18 April (Good Friday), 19 April (Declaration of Independence), 1 May (Labour Day), 24 June (Battle of Carabobo), 5 July (Independence Day), 24 July (Birth of Simón Bolívar and Battle of Lago de Maracaibo), 12 October (Day of Indigenous Resistance), 25 December (Christmas).

Statistical Survey

Sources (unless otherwise stated): Instituto Nacional de Estadística (formerly Oficina Central de Estadística e Informática), Edif. Fundación La Salle, Avda Boyacá, Caracas 1050; tel. (212) 782-1133; fax (212) 782-2243; e-mail ocei@platino.gov.ve; internet www.ine.gov.ve; Banco Central de Venezuela, Avda Urdaneta, esq. de las Carmelitas, Caracas 1010; tel. (212) 801-5111; fax (212) 861-0048; e-mail mbatista@bcv.org.ve; internet www.bcv.org.ve.

Area and Population

AREA, POPULATION AND DENSITY

Area (sq km)	916,445*
Population (census results)	
30 October 2001†	23,054,210
1 September 2011	
Males	13,549,752
Females	13,678,178
Total	27,227,930
Density (per sq km) at 2011 census	29.7

* 353,841 sq miles.

† Excluding Indian jungle population, enumerated at 183,143 in a separate census of indigenous communities in 2001. Also excluding adjustment for underenumeration, estimated at 6.7%.

POPULATION BY AGE AND SEX
(population at 2011 census)

	Males	Females	Total
0–14	3,788,616	3,568,158	7,356,774
15–64	9,034,671	9,215,986	18,250,657
65 and over	726,465	894,034	1,620,499
Total	13,549,752	13,678,178	27,227,930

ADMINISTRATIVE DIVISIONS
(population at 2011 census)

	Area (sq km)	Population	Density (per sq km)	Capital
Capital District .	433	1,943,901	4,489.4	Caracas
Amazonas . . .	177,617	146,480	0.8	Puerto Ayacucho
Anzoátegui . .	43,300	1,469,747	33.9	Barcelona
Apure	76,500	459,025	6.0	San Fernando
Aragua . . .	7,014	1,630,308	232.4	Maracay
Barinas . . .	35,200	816,264	23.2	Barinas
Bolívar . . .	240,528	1,413,115	5.9	Ciudad Bolívar
Carabobo . .	4,650	2,245,744	483.0	Valencia
Cojedes . . .	14,800	323,165	21.8	San Carlos
Delta Amacuro .	40,200	165,525	4.1	Tucupita
Falcón . . .	24,800	902,847	36.4	Coro
Guárico . . .	64,986	747,739	11.5	San Juan de los Morros
Lara	19,800	1,774,867	89.6	Barquisimeto
Mérida . . .	11,300	828,592	73.3	Mérida
Miranda . . .	7,950	2,675,165	336.5	Los Teques
Monagas . . .	28,900	905,443	31.3	Maturín
Nueva Esparta .	1,150	491,610	427.5	La Asunción
Portuguesa . .	15,200	876,496	57.7	Guanare
Sucre . . .	11,800	896,291	76.0	Cumaná
Táchira . . .	11,100	1,168,908	105.3	San Cristóbal
Trujillo . . .	7,400	686,367	92.8	Trujillo
Vargas . . .	1,497	352,920	235.8	La Guaira
Yaracuy . . .	7,100	600,852	84.6	San Felipe
Zulia . . .	63,100	3,704,404	58.7	Maracaibo
Federal Dependencies .	120	2,155	18.0	—
Total	916,445	27,227,930	29.7	—

PRINCIPAL TOWNS
(city proper, estimated population at 1 July 2000)

Caracas (capital) .	1,975,787	Mérida	230,101
Maracaibo . . .	1,764,038	Barinas . . .	228,598
Valencia	1,338,833	Turmero . . .	226,084
Barquisimeto . .	875,790	Cabimas . . .	214,000
Ciudad Guayana .	704,168	Baruta . . .	213,373
Petare	520,982	Puerto la Cruz . .	205,635
Maracay . . .	459,007	Los Teques . .	183,142
Ciudad Bolívar . .	312,691	Guarenas . . .	170,204
Barcelona . .	311,475	Puerto Cabello . .	169,959
San Cristóbal . .	307,184	Acarigua . . .	166,720
Maturín . . .	283,318	Coro	158,763
Cumaná	269,428		

Mid-2011 ('000, incl. suburbs, UN estimate): Caracas 3,242 (Source: UN, *World Urbanization Prospects: The 2011 Revision*).

BIRTHS, MARRIAGES AND DEATHS*

	Registered live births		Registered marriages		Registered deaths	
	Number	Rate (per 1,000)	Number	Rate (per 1,000)	Number	Rate (per 1,000)
2004 . .	637,799	22.3	74,103	2.8	110,946	5.0
2005 . .	665,997	22.0	86,093	3.2	110,301	5.0
2006 . .	646,225	21.8	89,772	3.2	115,348	5.1
2007 . .	615,371	21.5	93,003	3.4	118,594	5.1
2008 . .	581,480	21.3	93,741	3.4	124,062	4.4
2009 . .	593,845	20.9	94,870	3.3	123,530	4.4
2010 . .	591,303	20.6	94,977	3.3	130,597	4.3
2011 . .	615,132	21.0	103,004	3.5	136,803	4.7

* Figures for numbers of births and deaths exclude adjustment for under-enumeration. Rates are calculated using adjusted data.

Life expectancy (years at birth): 74.3 (males 71.4, females 77.4) in 2011.

ECONOMICALLY ACTIVE POPULATION
(labour force survey at January–June, '000 persons aged 15 years and over)*

	2010	2011	2012
Agriculture, hunting, forestry and fishing	985	982	950
Mining and quarrying	118	131	148
Manufacturing	1,353	1,365	1,382
Electricity, gas and water . . .	56	61	58
Construction	1,058	1,052	1,010
Wholesale and retail trade, restaurants and hotels . . .	2,792	2,826	2,915
Transport, storage and communications	1,092	1,134	1,115
Financing, insurance, real estate business services	630	680	670
Community, social and personal services	3,711	3,755	3,916
Sub-total	11,795	11,986	12,164
Activities not adequately defined .	30	19	44
Total employed	11,827	12,005	12,209
Unemployed	1,141	1,158	1,166
Total labour force	12,968	13,163	13,375
Males	7,893	7,998	8,096
Females	5,075	5,164	5,279

* Figures exclude members of the armed forces.

Source: ILO.

Health and Welfare

KEY INDICATORS

Total fertility rate (children per woman, 2010)	2.5
Under-5 mortality rate (per 1,000 live births, 2010) . .	18
HIV/AIDS (% of persons aged 15–49, 2005)	0.7
Physicians (per 1,000 head, 2001)	1.94
Hospital beds (per 1,000 head, 2007)	1.3
Health expenditure (2009): US $ per head (PPP) . . .	734
Health expenditure (2009): % of GDP	6.0
Health expenditure (2009): public (% of total)	40.0
Access to water (% of persons, 2010)	92
Access to sanitation (% of persons, 2010)	91
Total carbon dioxide emissions ('000 metric tons, 2008) . .	169,532.7
Carbon dioxide emissions per head (metric tons, 2008) . .	6.1
Human Development Index (2011): ranking	73
Human Development Index (2011): value	0.735

For sources and definitions, see explanatory note on p. vi.

Agriculture

PRINCIPAL CROPS
('000 metric tons)

	2009	2010*	2011*
Rice, paddy	1,194.0	1,250.0	1,422.6
Maize	1,803.6	2,145.0	2,250.0
Sorghum	370.0*	451.8	479.4
Potatoes	499.2	511.0	544.4
Cassava (Manioc)	491.6	496.6	505.3
Yautia (Cocoyam)	83.0	84.9	90.3
Yams	90.9	115.3	102.1
Sugar cane	8,907.7	8,907.7	8,907.7
Coconuts	160.8†	157.0	160.0
Oil palm fruit	325.0*	325.0	325.0
Cabbages and other brassicas .	100.0*	109.2	115.5
Tomatoes	200.0*	202.0	195.9
Chillies and peppers, green . .	100.0*	110.0	100.5
Onions, dry	270.0*	300.3	298.2
Carrots and turnips . . .	210.0*	203.4	218.2
Watermelons	170.0*	172.0	174.9
Cantaloupes and other melons .	190.0*	390.1	410.4
Bananas	400.0*	413.2	415.7
Plantains	480.0*	477.6	488.9
Oranges	380.0*	390.1	410.4
Tangerines, mandarins, etc. . .	70.0*	75.4	71.3
Lemons and limes	55.0*	51.6	56.9
Guavas, mangoes and mangosteens	65.0*	74.2	77.3
Avocados	75.0*	73.1	81.6
Pineapples	360.0*	378.7	419.8
Papayas	130.0*	133.4	125.6
Coffee, green	70.0*	71.8	69.1

* FAO estimate(s).
† Unofficial figure.

Aggregate production ('000 metric tons, may include official, semi-official or estimated data): Total cereals 3,368 in 2009, 3,847 in 2010, 4,152 in 2011; Total roots and tubers 1,213 in 2009, 1,262 in 2010, 1,295 in 2011; Total vegetables (incl. melons) 1,460 in 2009, 1,522 in 2010, 1,537 in 2011; Total fruits (excl. melons) 2,234 in 2009, 2,295 in 2010, 2,377 in 2011.

Source: FAO.

LIVESTOCK
('000 head, year ending September, FAO estimates)

	2009	2010	2011
Horses	510	515	518
Asses	440	440	440
Mules	72	72	72
Cattle	17,000	17,250	17,350
Pigs	3,350	3,385	3,450
Sheep	570	575	580
Goats	1,420	1,450	1,480
Chickens	116,000	117,000	118,000

Source: FAO.

LIVESTOCK PRODUCTS
('000 metric tons)

	2009	2010	2011
Cattle meat	482.0	492.0	494.5
Pig meat	165.0	168.1	172.1
Chicken meat	809.0	819.0	827.0
Cows' milk	2,200.0	2,294.4	2,294.4
Hen eggs	160.0	159.8	159.8

Source: FAO.

Forestry

ROUNDWOOD REMOVALS
('000 cubic metres, excl. bark)

	2009	2010	2011
Sawlogs, veneer logs and logs for sleepers	1,428*	445	336
Pulpwood*	920	920	920
Fuel wood*	4,011	4,055	4,089
Total*	6,359	5,420	5,345

* FAO estimate(s).

Source: FAO.

SAWNWOOD PRODUCTION
('000 cubic metres, incl. railway sleepers)

	2006	2007	2008*
Coniferous (softwood)	538	598	670
Broadleaved (hardwood) . . .	300	250	280
Total	838	848	950

* Unofficial figures.

2009–11: Production assumed to be unchanged from the year 2008 (FAO estimates).

Source: FAO.

Fishing

('000 metric tons, live weight)

	2008	2009	2010
Capture*	296.3	288.5	274.4
Freshwater fishes*	7.7	7.6	7.6
Sea catfishes	2.1	2.1*	2.1*
Round sardinella	36.2	35.0*	35.0*
Skipjack tuna	28.7	21.6	10.8
Yellowfin tuna	25.7	31.5	30.8
Marine crabs*	0.7	0.7	0.7
Ark clams	71.0	68.5*	68.5*
Aquaculture	18.8	14.8	18.4*
Whiteleg shrimp	16.0	10.5	13.0*
Total catch*	315.0	303.3	292.8

* FAO estimate(s).

Note: Figures exclude crocodiles, recorded by number rather than by weight. The number of spectacled caimans caught was: 15,489 in 2008; 16,246 in 2009; 10,989 in 2010.

Source: FAO.

Mining

('000 metric tons unless otherwise indicated)

	2009	2010	2011
Hard coal	8,792	8,793	8,792*
Crude petroleum† . . .	149,900	142,500	139,600
Natural gas (million cu m)‡ . .	28,700	28,500	28,000*
Iron ore: gross weight* . . .	14,900	14,900	14,900
Iron ore: metal content* . . .	15,200	14,000	17,000
Nickel ore (metric tons)§ . . .	10,400	10,400*	10,400*
Bauxite	4,267	2,500	4,500*
Gold (kg)§	11,880	12,000	12,000*
Phosphate rock	400	400	400*
Salt (evaporated)*	350	350	350
Diamonds (carats): Gem . .	6,000	6,000	6,000*
Diamonds (carats): Industrial .	9,000	9,000	9,000*

* Estimated production.
† Source: BP, *Statistical Review of World Energy*.
‡ Figures refer to the gross volume of output: estimated marketed production (in million cu m) was: 24,800 in 2009; 24,900 in 2010; 24,900 in 2011.
§ Figures refer to the metal content of ores and concentrates.

Source (unless otherwise indicated): US Geological Survey.

Industry

PETROLEUM PRODUCTS
('000 barrels)

	2004	2005	2006
Motor spirit (petrol)	131,929	75,000	85,000
Kerosene	179	120	120
Jet fuel	29,412	32,000	32,000
Distillate fuel oils	109,555	109,000	109,000
Residual fuel oils	101,481	90,000	90,000

2007–11: Figures assumed to be unchanged from 2006 (estimates).

Source: US Geological Survey.

SELECTED OTHER PRODUCTS
('000 metric tons unless otherwise indicated)

	2009	2010	2011
Raw sugar*	650	n.a.	n.a.
Cement†‡	8,500	8,000	7,700
Crude steel†	3,808	2,207	2,200‡
Aluminium†	561	335	380‡
Electric energy (million kWh)*	123,447	n.a.	n.a.

* Source: UN Industrial Commodity Statistics Database.
† Data from US Geological Survey.
‡ Estimate(s).

Finance

CURRENCY AND EXCHANGE RATES

Monetary Units
100 céntimos = 1 bolívar fuerte.

Sterling, Dollar and Euro Equivalents (31 December 2012)
£1 sterling = 6,769 bolívares fuertes;
US $1 = 4.289 bolívares fuertes;
€1 = 5.659 bolívares fuertes;
10 bolívares fuertes = £1.47 = $2.33 = €1.77.

Average Exchange Rate: From 1 March 2005 to 8 January 2010 the national currency was pegged to the US dollar at a fixed rate of US $1 = 2.147 bolívares fuertes. From 8 January 2010, when the currency was devalued, a dual fixed rate of US $1 = 2.6 bolívares fuertes for some essential goods (including foods and medicines), and US $1 = 4.3 bolívares fuertes for others, was established

Note: Venezuela adopted a new currency, the bolívar fuerte, equivalent to 1,000 of the former currency, on 1 January 2008; this became the sole legal tender from the end of June of the same year. Some of the relevant historical data in this survey continue to be presented in terms of Venezuelan bolívares.

CENTRAL GOVERNMENT BUDGET
(million bolívares fuertes, preliminary figures)

Revenue	2007	2008	2009
Tax revenue	78,945.8	90,706.5	94,274.7
Petroleum revenue . . .	19,958.5	17,834.2	12,944.1
Non-petroleum revenue . .	58,987.3	72,872.3	81,330.7
Non-tax revenue	62,387.5	75,391.8	57,250.7
Petroleum revenue . . .	51,624.5	64,598.0	40,286.8
Non-petroleum revenue . .	10,763.0	10,793.8	16,964.0
Total revenue	141,333.4	166,098.3	151,525.5

Expenditure*	2007	2008	2009
General public services . . .	15,589.8	22,588.1	20,232.6
Defence	11,522.1	9,639.8	9,173.3
Public order and safety . .	3,193.7	10,161.7	12,138.5
Education	24,591.8	33,581.4	40,099.9
Health	6,625.9	11,029.6	11,789.5
Social security and welfare . .	14,714.2	20,115.0	25,352.5
Housing and community . .	6,541.4	3,781.1	4,383.0
Recreational, cultural and religious	1,632.3	2,547.3	2,280.7
Fuel and energy	80.5	3,170.3	671.3
Agriculture, forestry, fishing and hunting	1,437.3	4,759.3	5,837.3
Mining, manufacturing and construction	3,545.0	10,040.2	10,291.8
Transportation and communication	685.3	540.6	680.2
Other expenditures	36,302.7	42,178.5	44,204.1
Total expenditure	126,462.1	174,132.8	187,134.6

* Including net lending (million bolívares fuertes): 524.8 in 2007; 1,441.2 in 2008; 2,973.3 in 2009.

General Government Budget (consolidated accounts of central government, Petróleos de Venezuela S.A., non-financial public enterprises, Venezuelan social security institute and deposit and guarantee fund, million bolívares fuertes, preliminary figures): *Total revenue:* 173,870.0 in 2009; 215,722.5 in 2010; *Total expenditure and net lending:* 235,302.5 in 2009; 321,105.4 in 2010.

CENTRAL BANK RESERVES
(US $ million at 31 December)

	2009	2010	2011
Gold (national valuation) . .	13,297	16,363	19,959
IMF special drawing rights . .	3,511	3,449	3,438
Reserve position in IMF . .	505	496	494
Foreign exchange	17,687	9,192	5,998
Total	35,000	29,500	29,889

Source: IMF, *International Financial Statistics*.

MONEY SUPPLY
(million bolívares fuertes at 31 December)

	2009	2010	2011
Currency outside banks . .	28,573	36,409	46,193
Demand deposits at commercial banks	188,939	262,094	417,043
Total (incl. others)	225,199	305,158	475,087

Source: IMF, *International Financial Statistics*.

COST OF LIVING
(Consumer Price Index; base: 2008 = 100)

	2010	2011	2012
Food	170.1	221.0	275.8
All items (incl. others) . . .	156.2	197.0	238.5

Source: ILO.

NATIONAL ACCOUNTS
('000 million bolívares at constant 1997 prices, preliminary)

Expenditure on the Gross Domestic Product

	2010	2011	2012
Final consumption expenditure .	48,984.6	51,145.5	54,656.6
Households			
Non-profit institutions serving households . . . . }	38,974.0	40,542.3	43,389.9
General government . . .	10,010.5	10,603.2	11,266.7
Gross capital formation . .	20,348.1	23,439.6	29,079.2
Gross fixed capital formation .			
Acquisitions, *less* disposals, of valuables }	16,925.9	17,665.5	21,783.0
Changes in inventories* . .	3,422.2	5,774.1	7,296.2
Total domestic expenditure .	69,332.7	74,585.1	83,735.8
Exports of goods and services .	7,825.8	8,190.9	8,321.4
Less Imports of goods and services	21,351.0	24,637.6	30,648.1
GDP in market prices . .	55,807.5	58,138.3	61,409.1

* Including statistical discrepancy.

Gross Domestic Product by Economic Activity

	2010	2011	2012
Petroleum-related activities .	6,554.3	6,593.1	6,682.7
Non-petroleum activities . .	45,639.3	47,905.2	51,522.3
Mining and quarrying . .	265.0	278.5	261.2
Manufacturing	8,095.5	8,405.2	8,555.5
Electricity and water . . .	1,258.9	1,322.1	1,372.6
Construction	4,018.5	4,209.4	4,907.1
Wholesale and retail trade; repair of motor vehicles, motorcycles and personal and household goods . .	5,243.2	5,585.1	6,096.1
Transport and storage . .	1,940.9	2,052.5	2,187.8
Communications	3,560.8	3,820.2	4,086.5
Financial intermediation and insurance	2,269.8	2,541.5	3,392.8
Real estate, renting and business activities . . .	5,485.3	5,678.9	5,917.7
Community, social and personal services . . .	3,243.6	3,430.3	3,684.3
Government services . . .	6,798.4	7,171.5	7,543.4
Others*	3,459.6	3,410.0	3,517.3
Sub-total	52,193.6	54,498.3	58,205.0
Less Financial intermediation services indirectly measured .	2,512.4	2,849.8	3,873.9
Gross value added in basic prices	49,681.3	51,648.5	54,331.1
Taxes on products . . . }			
Less Subsidies on products . . }	6,126.3	6,489.6	7,078.0
GDP in market prices . .	55,807.5	58,138.3	61,409.1

* Including agriculture and hotels and restaurants.

BALANCE OF PAYMENTS
(US $ million)

	2009	2010	2011
Exports of goods	57,599	65,741	92,649
Imports of goods	−39,619	−38,581	−46,197
Balance on goods . . .	17,980	27,160	46,452
Exports of services . . .	2,231	1,861	2,025
Imports of services . . .	−10,751	−11,080	−12,742
Balance on goods and services	9,460	17,941	35,735
Primary income received . .	2,263	1,921	2,076
Primary income paid . . .	−5,397	−7,223	−9,990
Balance on goods, services and primary income . . .	6,326	12,639	27,821
Secondary income received .	532	491	454
Secondary income paid . .	−823	−1,059	−950

—*continued*	2009	2010	2011
Current balance	6,035	12,071	27,325
Capital account (net) . . .	—	−211	—
Direct investment assets . .	−1,328	−2,239	−88
Direct investment liabilities .	−3,046	777	5,226
Portfolio investment assets .	4,321	−221	−173
Portfolio investment liabilities .	5,384	2,658	2,644
Other investment assets . .	−24,465	−27,210	−43,043
Other investment liabilities .	5,814	8,749	7,879
Net errors and omissions . .	−3,522	−2,313	−3,783
Reserves and related items .	−10,807	−7,939	−4,013

Source: IMF, *International Financial Statistics*.

External Trade

PRINCIPAL COMMODITIES
(US $ million)

Imports f.o.b.	2008	2009	2010
Food and live animals . . .	6,764.3	5,493.1	4,314.0
Cereals and cereal preparations .	1,489.6	1,041.2	945.8
Chemicals and related products	6,496.0	6,629.2	6,577.0
Medicinal and pharmaceutical products	1,813.5	2,361.9	2,823.4
Medicaments (incl. veterinary) .	1,408.5	1,841.5	2,015.5
Basic manufactures . . .	7,212.8	5,749.0	3,937.6
Textile yarn, fabrics, etc. . .	1,470.4	1,266.0	633.1
Machinery and transport equipment	18,487.1	13,296.1	12,409.8
Machinery specialized for particular industries . . .	2,617.4	2,079.8	1,715.9
General industrial machinery equipment and parts . . .	3,593.3	2,975.8	2,235.3
Office machines and automatic data processing machines . .	1,414.5	1,023.2	650.9
Telecommunications and sound recording and reproducing equipment	3,159.1	2,019.9	1,598.7
Telecommunications equipment parts and accessories . .	2,550.1	1,626.0	1,301.9
Transmission apparatus for radio-telephony, radio-telegraphy, etc. . . .	1,898.1	1,161.3	979.9
Transmission apparatus incorporating reception apparatus	1,884.7	1,158.2	977.1
Other electrical machinery, apparatus, etc.	2,769.5	2,217.5	2,094.9
Road vehicles	3,101.1	1,056.9	983.1
Passenger motor vehicles (except buses)	1,138.6	65.1	297.4
Miscellaneous manufactured articles	5,895.3	4,295.4	3,540.1
Articles of apparel and clothing accessories	1,641.4	851.4	606.0
Total (incl. others)	47,450.1	38,676.6	32,342.9

Exports f.o.b.	2008	2009	2010
Mineral fuels, lubricants and related materials	78,199.5	54,232.2	62,541.1
Petroleum, petroleum products and related materials . . .	77,882.2	54,201.8	62,330.3
Crude petroleum	61,005.6	35,844.0	44,156.6
Basic manufactures . . .	2,874.6	1,445.9	1,951.0
Iron and steel	1,703.6	904.8	1,085.1
Total (incl. others)	83,477.8	56,583.1	66,962.7

Source: UN, *International Trade Statistics Yearbook*.

PRINCIPAL TRADING PARTNERS
(US $ million)

Imports f.o.b.	2008	2009	2010
Argentina	1,152.2	873.9	923.5
Bolivia	401.7	351.2	396.4
Brazil	4,275.5	3,396.4	3,180.5
Canada	807.2	539.4	485.0
Chile	1,213.3	877.8	555.2
China, People's Republic	4,527.5	4,034.5	3,593.3
Colombia	6,903.4	4,417.6	1,424.2
Ecuador	557.2	616.8	880.9
France (incl. Monaco)	486.4	423.2	512.8
Germany	1,420.1	1,258.5	1,212.3
Italy	1,172.0	1,018.9	755.4
Japan	764.5	624.5	449.6
Korea, Republic	557.0	320.2	231.6
Mexico	2,202.9	1,461.1	1,445.6
Netherlands	362.2	390.2	260.5
Netherlands Antilles	78.3	787.5	142.2
Panama	1,018.4	930.7	737.9
Peru	961.3	541.3	527.1
Spain	953.2	794.8	882.7
Switzerland-Liechtenstein	307.4	343.3	345.0
United Kingdom	397.2	377.8	356.8
USA	12,651.3	10,545.4	9,866.0
Total (incl. others)	47,450.1	38,676.6	32,342.9

Exports f.o.b.	2008	2009	2010
Brazil	1,808.3	112.7	272.5
Canada	141.6	35.6	84.2
Chile	1,167.4	26.4	61.1
China, People's Republic	270.3	304.0	719.4
Colombia	929.6	424.3	591.4
Germany	1,452.6	57.9	74.1
Netherlands	1,193.1	108.2	196.5
Netherlands Antilles	13,198.1	17.0	30.1
Spain	1,603.4	41.0	115.6
United Kingdom	1,190.4	3.1	26.3
USA	26,750.5	491.1	970.9
Total (incl. others)	83,477.8	56,583.1	66,962.7

Source: UN, *International Trade Statistics Yearbook*.

Transport

RAILWAYS
(traffic)

	1994	1995	1996
Passenger-km (million)	31.4	12.5	0.1
Net ton-km (million)	46.8	53.3	45.5

Net ton-km (million): 54 in 1997; 79 in 1998; 54 in 1999; 59 in 2000; 81 in 2001; 32 in 2002; 12 in 2003; 22 in 2004.

Source: UN, *Statistical Yearbook*.

ROAD TRAFFIC
('000 motor vehicles in use)

	2002	2003	2004
Passenger cars	2,092	2,173	2,466
Commercial vehicles	615	630	677

Source: UN, *Statistical Yearbook*.

2007 ('000 motor vehicles in use): Passenger cars 2,952,129; Buses and coaches 40,440; Lorries and vans 1,051,443 (Source: IRF, *World Road Statistics*).

SHIPPING

Flag Registered Fleet
(at 31 December)

	2010	2011	2012
Number of vessels	274	283	297
Total displacement ('000 grt)	1,220.9	1,191.7	1,472.4

Source: Lloyd's List Intelligence (www.lloydslistintelligence.com).

CIVIL AVIATION
(traffic on scheduled services)

	2004	2005	2006
Kilometres flown (million)	64	65	59
Passengers carried ('000)	5,495	5,767	5,121
Passenger-km (million)	2,803	2,947	2,649
Total ton-km (million)	250	265	239

Source: UN, *Statistical Yearbook*.

2010: Passengers carried ('000) 5,881 (Source: World Bank, World Development Indicators database).

Tourism

ARRIVALS BY NATIONALITY

	2008	2009	2010
Argentina	26,055	24,601	24,801
Brazil	58,539	42,813	47,968
Canada	25,870	18,165	21,002
Chile	15,424	13,175	10,563
Colombia	77,417	61,659	49,333
France	23,026	19,739	22,418
Germany	37,719	27,040	22,009
Italy	52,131	45,926	36,928
Mexico	17,405	15,624	12,824
Netherlands	17,651	10,528	11,337
Peru	26,720	24,069	19,331
Portugal	19,466	17,268	13,857
Spain	66,649	62,848	47,137
Trinidad and Tobago	14,870	12,223	19,368
United Kingdom	27,180	17,119	11,261
USA	86,982	76,059	61,376
Total (incl. others)	744,709	615,188	518,711

Total arrivals ('000, provisional): 551 in 2011.

Tourism receipts (US $ million, excl. passenger transport): 917 in 2008; 990 in 2009; 739 in 2010.

Source: World Tourism Organization.

Communications Media

	2009	2010	2011*
Telephones ('000 main lines in use)	6,866.7	7,082.9	7,332.1
Mobile cellular telephones ('000 subscribers)	28,123.6	27,880.1	28,782.0
Internet subscribers ('000) . .	1,517.7	1,800.6*	2,038.5
Broadband subscribers ('000) .	213.1	231.7	1,815.5

* Preliminary.

Source: International Telecommunication Union.

Education

(2003/04)

	Institutions	Teachers	Students*
Pre-school	14,857†	59,178	984,224
Basic education:			
grades 1–6	17,521†	172,322	3,449,579
grades 7–9	4,667†	109,437	1,383,891
Further education:			
general . . . . . . }	3,362† {	56,458	501,243
professional		8,844	68,372
Adult education	2,402	43,660	506,301
Special needs	1,999	8,723	317,687
Universities	48	51,459	626,837
Other higher	120‡	30,664	447,513‡

* Excluding students in out-of-school education: 720,726 in 2003/04.

† Data may be duplicated for institutions where education is offered at more than one level. The total number of pre-school, basic and further educational establishments in 2003/04 was 24,634.

‡ Estimate.

Sources: Ministry of Education, Caracas; National Council of Universities, Caracas.

2009/10 (UNESCO estimates): *Teachers:* Pre-primary 108,424; Primary 284,602; Secondary 333,245 (Source: UNESCO Institute for Statistics).

2010/11 (UNESCO estimates): *Pupils:* Pre-primary 1,287,156; Primary 3,466,230; Secondary 2,287,393 (Source: UNESCO Institute for Statistics).

Pupil-teacher ratio (primary education, UNESCO estimate): 12.1 in 2009/10 (Source: UNESCO Institute for Statistics).

Adult literacy rate (UNESCO estimates): 95.5% (males 95.7%; females 95.4%) in 2009 (Source: UNESCO Institute for Statistics).

Directory

The Government

HEAD OF STATE

President of the Republic: NICOLÁS MADURO MOROS (took office 19 April 2013).

Executive Vice-President: JORGE ALBERTO ARREAZA MONTSERRAT.

COUNCIL OF MINISTERS
(May 2013)

The Government is formed by the Partido Socialista Unido de Venezuela (PSUV).

Minister of Foreign Affairs: ELÍAS JAUA MILANO.

Minister of the Interior Relations and Justice: Gen. MIGUEL RODRÍGUEZ TORRES.

Minister of Agriculture and Lands: IVÁN GIL.

Minister of Finance: NELSON JOSÉ MERENTES DÍAZ.

Minister of Health: ISABEL ITURRIA.

Minister of Planning: JORGE A. GIORDANI.

Minister of Science, Technology and Innovation: MANUEL FERNÁNDEZ.

Minister of Energy and Petroleum: RAFAEL DARÍO RAMÍREZ CARREÑO.

Minister of Electric Energy: JESSE CHACÓN ESCAMILLO.

Minister of Defence: Adm. DIEGO ALFREDO MOLERO BELLAVIA.

Minister of Commerce: ALEJANDRO ANTONIO FLEMING CABRERA.

Minister of Labour and Social Security: MARÍA CRISTINA IGLESIAS.

Minister of Food: FÉLIX OSORIO.

Minister of Education: MARYANN HANSON FLORES.

Minister of Tourism: ANDRÉS IZARRA.

Minister of University Education: PEDRO CALZADILLA.

Minister of Housing and Habitat: RICARDO MOLINA PEÑALOZA.

Minister of the Environment: DANTE RIVAS QUIJADA.

Minister of Communes and Social Protection: REINALDO ITURRIZA.

Minister of Communication and Information: ERNESTO VILLEGAS POLJAK.

Minister of Sport: ALEJANDRA BENÍTEZ.

Minister of Culture: FIDEL BARBARITO.

Minister of Indigenous Peoples: ALOHA NÚÑEZ.

Minister of Women's Affairs and Gender Equality: ANDREÍNA TARAZÓN.

Minister of Land Transport: JUAN GARCÍA TOUSSAINTT.

Minister of Industries: RICARDO JOSÉ MENÉNDEZ PRIETO.

Minister of the Penitentiary System: IRIS VARELA.

Minister of Air and Water Transport: Maj.-Gen. HEBERT GARCÍA PLAZA.

Minister of Public Banking: RODOLFO MARCO TORRES.

Minister of the Office of the Presidency and Government Management: Adm. CARMEN TERESA MELÉNDEZ.

Minister of Youth: HÉCTOR RODRÍGUEZ CASTRO.

MINISTRIES

Ministry of Agriculture and Lands: Avda Urdaneta, entre esq. Platanal a Candilito, a media cuadra de la Plaza la Candelaria, Parroquia la Candelaria, Caracas; tel. (212) 509-0347; e-mail pda2007@mat.gob.ve; internet www.mat.gob.ve.

Ministry of Air and Water Transport: Avda Francisco de Miranda, Torre Pequiven, 12°, Municipio Chacao, Caracas 1010; tel. (212) 274-5458; fax (212) 263-2570; e-mail ccmpptaa@gmail.com; internet www.mpptaa.gob.ve.

Ministry of Communes and Social Protection: Edif. INCE, Avda Nueva Granada, Apdo 10340, Caracas 1040; tel. (212) 603-2396; internet www.mpcomunas.gob.ve.

Ministry of Communication and Information: Torre Ministerial, 9° y 10°, Avda Universidad, esq. el Chorro, Caracas 1010; tel. (212) 505-3322; e-mail contactenos@minci.gob.ve; internet www.minci.gob.ve.

Ministry of Culture: Edif. Archivo General de la Nación, Avda Panteón Foro Libertador, Caracas; tel. (212) 509-5681; e-mail mppc@mincultura.gob.ve; internet www.mincultura.gob.ve.

Ministry of Defence: Edif. 17 de Diciembre, planta baja, Base Aérea Francisco de Miranda, La Carlota, Caracas; tel. (212) 908-

1264; fax (212) 237-4974; e-mail noiralith.gil@mindefensa.gov.ve; internet www.mindefensa.gob.ve.

Ministry of Education: Edif. Sede del MPPE, Mezzanina, esq. de Salas a Caja de Agua, Parroquia Altagracia, Caracas 1010; tel. (212) 596-4111; e-mail atencionsocial@me.gob.ve; internet www.me.gob.ve.

Ministry of Electric Energy: Avda Vollmer, Urb. San Bernardino, Municipio Libertador, Caracas 1010; tel. (212) 502-2650; internet www.mppee.gob.ve.

Ministry of Energy and Petroleum: Edif. Petróleos de Venezuela, Torre Oeste, Avda Libertador con Avda Empalme, La Campiña, Porroquia El Recreo, Caracas; tel. (212) 708-7581; fax (212) 708-7598; e-mail atencionalpublico@menpet.gob.ve; internet www.menpet.gob.ve.

Ministry of the Environment: Torre Sur Plaza, 25°, Centro Simón Bolívar, Caracas 1010; tel. (212) 408-1111; internet www.minamb.gob.ve.

Ministry of Finance: Edif. Ministerio de Finanzas, esq. Carmelitas, Avda Urdaneta, Caracas 1010; tel. (212) 802-1000; internet www.mppef.gob.ve.

Ministry of Food: Edif. Las Fundaciones, Avda Andrés Bello, Caracas; tel. (212) 395-7474; e-mail oirp@minpal.gob.ve; internet www.minpal.gob.ve.

Ministry of Foreign Affairs: Torre MRE, al lado del Correo de Carmelitas, Avda Urdaneta, Caracas 1010; tel. (212) 806-4400; fax (212) 861-2505; e-mail web.master@mre.gov.ve; internet www.mre.gov.ve.

Ministry of Health: Edif. Sur, 8°, Avda Baralt, Centro Simón Bolívar, El Silencio, Caracas 1010; tel. (212) 408-0033; fax 483-2560; e-mail mpps@mpps.gob.ve; internet www.mpps.gob.ve.

Ministry of Housing and Habitat: Avda Francisco de Miranda, antigua sede de INAVI, Municipio Chacao, Caracas 1010; tel. (212) 266-8625; fax (212) 265-4644; internet www.mvh.gob.ve.

Ministry of Indigenous Peoples: Antiguo Edif. Sudeban, Avda Universidad, esq. Traposos, 8°, Caracas 1010; tel. (212) 543-1599; fax (212) 543-3100; e-mail atencionlindigena@minpi.gob.ve; internet www.minpi.gob.ve.

Ministry of Industries: Caracas.

Ministry of Interior Relations and Justice: Edif. Ministerio, esq. de Platanal, Avda Urdaneta, Caracas 1010; tel. (212) 506-1101; fax (212) 506-1559; e-mail webmaster@mij.gov.ve; internet www.mpprij.gob.ve.

Ministry of Labour and Social Security: Torre Sur, 5°, Centro Simón Bolívar, Caracas 1010; tel. (212) 481-1368; fax (212) 483-8914; internet www.mintra.gov.ve.

Ministry of Land Transport: Torre MTT, Avda Francisco de Miranda, Municipio Chacao, Caracas; tel. (212) 201-5515; internet www.mtc.gob.ve.

Ministry of the Office of the Presidency and Government Management: Palacio de Miraflores, final Avda Urdaneta, esq. de Bolero, Caracas; tel. (212) 806-3111; fax (212) 806-3229; e-mail dggcomunicacional@presidencia.gob.ve; internet www.presidencia.gob.ve.

Ministry of the Penitentiary System: Caracas; internet www.mppsp.gob.ve.

Ministry of Planning and Finance: Edif. Ministerio de Finanzas, esq. Carmelitas, Avda Urdaneta, Caracas 1010; tel. (212) 802-1000; internet www.mppef.gob.ve.

Ministry of Public Banking: Caracas.

Ministry of Science, Technology and Innovation: Torre Ministerial, Avda Universidad, esq. El Chorro, La Hoyada, Caracas; tel. (212) 555-7410; fax (212) 555-7504; e-mail mcti@mcti.gob.ve; internet www.mct.gob.ve.

Ministry of Sport: Sede Principal, Avda Teheran, Urb. Montalbán, La Vega, Caracas 1020; tel. (212) 443-2682; fax (212) 443-3224; e-mail nororiente@mindeporte.gob.ve; internet www.mindeporte.gob.ve.

Ministry of Tourism: Edif. Mintur, Avda Francisco de Miranda con Avda Principal de la Floresta, Municipio Chacao, Caracas; tel. (212) 208-4651; e-mail auditoria@mintur.gob.ve; internet www.mintur.gob.ve.

Ministry of Commerce: Torre Oeste de Parque Central, entrada por el Nivel Lecuna, Avda Lecuna, Caracas 1010; tel. (212) 509-6861; fax (212) 574-2432; e-mail ministro@milco.gob.ve; internet www.mincomercio.gob.ve.

Ministry of University Education: Torre Ministerial, 1°–7°, Avda Universidad, esq. el Chorro, Caracas 1010; tel. (212) 596-5270; fax (212) 569-5261; e-mail webmaster@mppeu.gob.ve; internet www.mppeu.gob.ve.

Ministry of Women's Affairs and Gender Equality: Torre Este, 4°, Parque Central, Avda Lecuna, Caracas; e-mail minmujer@minmujer.gob.ve; internet www.minmujer.gob.ve.

Ministry of Youth: Avda Andrés Bello, Centro Andrés Bello, Torre Oeste, Mezzanina 2°, Caracas; e-mail despacho@mppj.gob.ve; internet www.minjuventud.gob.ve.

State Agencies

Consejo de Defensa de la Nación (Codena): Edif. 2, 2°, Fuerte Tiuna, Caracas; tel. (212) 690-3222; e-mail secodena@codena.gob.ve; internet www.codena.gob.ve; national defence council; Sec.-Gen. Gen. VIVIAM ANTONIO DURÁN GARCÍA.

Contraloría General de la República (CGR): Edif. Contraloría, Avda Andrés Bello, Guaicaipuro, Caracas 1050; tel. (212) 508-3656; e-mail dict@cgr.gob.ve; internet www.cgr.gob.ve; national audit office for Treasury income and expenditure, and for the finances of the autonomous institutes; Comptroller-Gen. (vacant).

Defensoría del Pueblo: Edif. Defensoría del Pueblo, 8°, Avda México, Plaza Morelos, Los Caobos, Caracas; tel. (212) 575-4703; fax (212) 575-4467; e-mail prensadefensoria@hotmail.com; internet www.defensoria.gob.ve; acts as an ombudsman and investigates complaints between citizens and the authorities; Ombudsman GABRIELA DEL MAR RAMÍREZ.

Procuraduría General de la República: Paseo Los Ilustres con Avda Lazo Martí, Santa Mónica, Caracas; tel. (212) 597-3300; e-mail webmaster@pgr.gov.ve; internet www.pgr.gob.ve; Procurator-Gen. CILIA FLORES.

President

Election, 14 April 2013

Candidates	Votes	% of total
Nicolás Maduro Moros (Partido Socialista Unido de Venezuela) . .	7,575,506	50.78
Henrique Capriles Radonski (Mesa de Unidad Democrática)	7,302,641	48.95
Others	38,910	0.26
Total valid votes*	14,917,057	100.00

* In addition, there were 66,691 blank or spoiled votes.

Legislature

ASAMBLEA NACIONAL
(National Assembly)

President: DIOSDADO CABELLO RONDÓN.

First Vice-President: DARÍO VIVAS VELÁSCO.

Second Vice-President: BLANCA ROSA EEKHOUT GÓMEZ.

General Election, 26 September 2010

Party	Seats
Partido Socialista Unido de Venezuela (PSUV) . .	98
Mesa de Unidad Democrática (MUD)	65
Patria para Todos (PPT)	2
Total	165

Governors

STATES
(May 2013)

Amazonas: LIBORIO GUARULLA.

Anzoátegui: ARISTÓBULO ISTÚRIZ.

Apure: RAMÓN CARRIZALEZ.

Aragua: TARECK EL AISSAMI.

Barinas: ADÁN CHÁVEZ FRÍAS.

Bolívar: FRANCÍSCO JOSÉ RANGEL GÓMEZ.

Carabobo: FRANCISCO AMELIACH ORTA.

Cojedes: ERIKA FARÍAS.

Delta Amacuro: LIZETA HERNÁNDEZ.

Falcón: STELLA LUGO DE MONTILLA.

Guárico: RAMÓN RODRÍGUEZ CHACÍN.

Lara: HENRI FALCÓN FUENTES.

Mérida: ALEXIS RAMÍREZ.

Miranda: HENRIQUE CAPRILES RADONSKI.

Monagas: YELITZE SANTAELLA.
Nueva Esparta: CARLOS MATA FIGUEROA.
Portuguesa: WILMAR CASTRO SOTELDO.
Sucre: LUIS ACUÑA.
Táchira: JOSÉ GREGORIO VIELMA MORA.
Trujillo: HENRY RANGEL SILVA.
Vargas: JORGE LUIS GARCÍA CARNEIRO.
Yaracuy: JULIO LEÓN HEREDIA.
Zulia: FRANCISCO ARIAS CÁRDENAS.

FEDERAL DISTRICT

Caracas: ANTONIO LEDEZMA.

Election Commission

Consejo Nacional Electoral (CNE): Edif. Sede del Consejo Nacional Electoral, Centro Simón Bolívar, Frente a la Plaza Caracas, Caracas; tel. (212) 408-5200; fax (212) 576-5603; internet www.cne .gov.ve; f. 2002; Pres. TIBISAY LUCENA RAMÍREZ.

Political Organizations

Mesa de Unidad Democrática (MUD): Caracas; internet www .unidadvenezuela.org; f. 2008; opposition coalition; Exec. Sec. RAMÓN GUILLERMO AVELEDO; comprises the following parties.

Acción Democrática (AD): Casa Nacional Acción Democrática, Calle Los Cedros, La Florida, Caracas 1050; internet www .acciondemocratica.org.ve; f. 1936 as Partido Democrático Nacional; adopted present name and obtained legal recognition in 1941; social democratic; Pres. ISABEL CARMONA DE SERRA; Sec.-Gen. HENRY RAMOS ALLUP.

Alianza Bravo Pueblo: Caracas; e-mail alianzabravopueblo@ gmail.com; opposition; merged with Visión Emergente in 2010; Pres. RICHARD BLANCO (acting); Sec.-Gen. EDWIN LUZARDO.

Avanzada Progresista: Caracas; f. 2012; dissidents from PODEMOS, Patria Para Todos, Gente Emergente and the PSUV; Pres. HENRI FALCÓN; Sec.-Gen. ISMAEL GARCÍA.

La Causa Radical (La Causa R): Santa Teresa a Cipreses, Residencias Santa Teresa, 2°, Ofs 21 y 22, Caracas; tel. (212) 545-7002; internet lacausarbolivar.com; f. 1971; radical democratic; Leader ANDRÉS VELÁSQUEZ; Sec.-Gen. DANIEL SANTOLO.

Movimiento al Socialismo (MAS): Quinta Alemar, Avda Valencia, Las Palmas, Caracas 1050; tel. (212) 793-7800; fax (212) 761-9297; e-mail asamblea07@cantv.net; internet www.masvenezuela .com.ve; f. 1971 by PCV dissidents; opposition democratic socialist party; Pres. NICOLÁS SOSA; Sec.-Gen. FELIPE MUJICA.

Partido Social-Cristiano (Comité de Organización Política Electoral Independiente) (COPEI): El Bosque, Avda Principal El Bosque, cruce con Avda Gloria Quinta Cujicito, Chacao, Caracas; tel. (212) 731-4746; fax (212) 731-4953; e-mail info@ copeivenezuela.com; internet www.copeivenezuela.com; f. 1946; Christian democratic; Pres. ROBERTO ENRÍQUEZ; Sec.-Gen. EDUARDO VELASCO.

Primero Justicia: Edif. Primero Justicia, 3ra Transversal, entre Avda 4 y Avda Luis Guillermo Villegas Blanco, Urb. Los Palos Grandes, Caracas; tel. (212) 285-8391; e-mail pjelhaltillo@cantv .net; internet www.primerojusticia.org.ve; f. 2000; Nat. Co-ordinator JULIO ANDRÉS BORGES; Nat. Sec. TOMÁS GUANIPA.

Un Nuevo Tiempo (UNT): Edif. Montral, Avda Principal de Las Palmas, Municipio Libertador, Caracas; tel. (212) 425-1239; e-mail prensa@partidounnuevotiempo.org; internet www.partido unnuevotiempo.org; f. 2005; Exec. Pres. OMAR BARBOZA; Exec. Sec. ALFONSO MARQUINA.

Voluntad Popular: Edif. Menegrande, 5°, Of. 51, Avda Francisco de Miranda, Urb. Los Palos Grandes, Miranda, Caracas 1060; tel. (212) 740-7441; e-mail reinaldo.diaz@gmail.com; internet www .voluntadpopular.com; f. 2004; registered as a political party in 2011; Nat. Co-ordinator LEOPOLDO LÓPEZ.

Movimiento Demócrata Liberal (MDL): Quinta El Encuentro, 1°, Avda de Santa Eduvigis, entre 5a y 6a Transversal, Caracas; tel. (212) 442-3956; fax (212) 471-3856; e-mail info@democrataliberales .org; internet www.democrataliberales.org; liberal opposition party; Political Dirs MARCO POLESEL, ENIO DAZA.

Movimiento Electoral del Pueblo (MEP): Calle Buenos Aires, Urb. Los Caobos, Parroquia El Recreo Municipio Libertador, Caracas 1050; tel. (212) 793-4135; internet www.mep.com.ve; f. 1967 by left-wing AD dissidents; 100,000 mems; Pres. ANDRÉS LUCIANO LARA OJEDA; Sec.-Gen. WILMER JOSÉ NOLASCO.

Movimiento Republicano (MR): Edif. Yetesa, Of. 1, Avda Libertador, con Avda Principal Las Palmas, Caracas; tel. (212) 693-2937; e-mail elrepublicano.ve@gmail.com; f. 1997; Pres. CARLOS PADILLA; Sec.-Gen. MANUAL RIVAS.

Movimiento Tupamaro (Tendencia Unificada para Alcanzar el Movimiento de Acción Revolucionario): Caracas; internet www .tupamaro.org.ve; Sec.-Gen. JOSÉ TOMÁS PINTO.

Organización Renovadora Auténtica: Caracas; internet oraporvenezuela.org; f. 1987; Pres. LUIS REYES CASTILLO.

Partido Comunista de Venezuela (PCV): Edif. Cantaclaro, Calle Jesús Faría, esq. de San Pedro a San Francisquito, Parroquia San Juan, Caracas; tel. (212) 484-0061; fax (212) 481-9737; internet www .pcv-venezuela.org; f. 1931; Pres. PEDRO EUSSE; Sec. OSCAR FIGUERA.

Partido Socialista Unido de Venezuela (PSUV): Calle Lima, cruce con Avda Libertador, Los Caobos, Caracas; tel. (212) 782-3808; fax (212) 782-9720; e-mail contacto@psuv.org.ve; internet www.psuv .org.ve; f. 2007; successor party to the Movimiento V República; promotes Bolivarian revolution; Pres. DIOSDADO CABELLO (acting).

Patria Para Todos (PPT): Calle Montevideo, Quinta Plaza, Calle Maripérez, Plaza Venezuela, Caracas; tel. (212) 578-3098; fax (212) 577-4545; e-mail partidoppt@gmail.com; internet www .patriaparatodos.com.ve; f. 1997; breakaway faction of La Causa Radical; revolutionary humanist party; Nat. Sec.-Gen. RAFAEL UZCÁTEGUI.

Por la Democracia Social (PODEMOS): Caracas; f. 2001 by dissident mems of MAS (q.v.); Leader DIDALCO BOLÍVAR.

Proyecto Venezuela (PRVZL): Edif. El Nacional, 2°, De Puente Nuevo a Puerto Escondido, El Silencio, Caracas; f. 1998; humanist party; supported the MUD in the 2012 presidential election; Leader HENRIQUE SALAS RÖMER; Sec.-Gen. CARLOS BERRIZBEITIA.

Unidad Democrática: Caracas; contested the 2012 presidential election as a separate entity to the MUD; Leader REINA SEQUERA.

OTHER ORGANIZATIONS

Comité de Familiares Víctimas de los Sucesos de Febrero y Marzo de 1989 (COFAVIC): Edif. El Candil, 1°, Of. 1-A, Avda Urdaneta, Esq. El Candilito, Apdo 16150, Caracas; tel. (212) 572-9631; fax (212) 572-9908; e-mail cofavic@cofavic.org; internet www .cofavic.org; f. 1989 as an asscn of relatives of those who had died in demonstrations of Feb.–March; promotes human rights and democracy; Exec. Dir LILIANA ORTEGA.

Súmate: Torre A, 5°, Avda Francisco de Miranda, Centro Plaza, Urb. Los Palos Grandes, Caracas; tel. (212) 285-4562; e-mail prensa@ sumate.org; internet www.sumate.org; f. 2002; opposition grouping promoting citizens' rights; Co-ordinator (Distrito Capital) CAROLINA REYES.

Diplomatic Representation

EMBASSIES IN VENEZUELA

Algeria: 8a Transversal con 3a Avda, Quinta Azahar, Urb. Altamira, Caracas 1062; tel. (212) 263-2092; fax (212) 261-4254; e-mail ambalgcar@cantv.net; Ambassador RACHID BLADEHANE.

Argentina: Edif. Fedecámaras, 3°, Avda El Empalme, El Bosque, Apdo 569, Caracas; tel. (212) 731-3311; fax (212) 731-2659; e-mail evene@mrecic.gov.ar; internet evene.mrecic.gov.ar; Ambassador CARLOS ALBERTO CHEPPI.

Austria: Edif. Torre D&D, Piso PT, Of. PTN, Avda Orinoco, entre Mucuchíes y Perijá, Urb. Las Mercedes, Apdo 61381, Caracas 1060-A; tel. (212) 999-1211; fax (212) 993-2753; e-mail caracas-ob@bmeia .gv.at; internet www.aussenministerium.at/caracas; Ambassador GERHARD MAYER.

Barbados: Edif. Los Frailes, 5°, Of. 501, Avda Principal de Chuao, Chuao, Apdo 68829, Caracas 1060; tel. (212) 992-0545; fax (212) 991-0333; e-mail caracas@foreign.gov.bb; Ambassador SANDRA PHILLIPS.

Belarus: Quinta Campanera, 3a Transversal (Calle Aveledo) con Avda 7, Urb. Los Chorros, Municipio Sucre, Caracas 1071; tel. (212) 239-2760; fax (212) 239-0419; e-mail venezuela@belembassy.org; internet venezuela.mfa.gov.by; Ambassador OLEG PAFEROV.

Belgium: 10a Transversal con 9a Transversal, Apdo del Este 61550, Altamira, Caracas 1060; tel. (212) 263-3334; fax (212) 261-1333; e-mail caracas@diplobel.fed.be; internet www.diplomatie.be/ caracas; Ambassador JEAN-PAUL WARNIMONT.

Bolivia: Edif. Los Llanos, 1°, Avda Francisco Zolano, esq. San Gerónimo, Zabana Grande, Caracas; tel. (212) 263-3015; fax (212) 261-3386; e-mail embaboliviaven@hotmail.com; internet www .embajada-boliviana-venezuela.com; Chargé d'affaires a.i. JORGE ALVARADO RIVAS.

Brazil: Avda Mohedano con Calle Los Chaguaramos, Centro Gerencial Mohedano, 6°, La Castellana, Caracas 1060; tel. (212) 918-

6000; fax (212) 261-9601; e-mail brasembcaracas@cantv.net; internet caracas.itamaraty.gov.br; Ambassador JOSÉ ANTONIO MAR-CONDES DE CARVALHO.

Canada: Edif. Embajada de Canadá, Avda Francisco de Miranda con Avda Sur, Altamira, Apdo 62302, Caracas 1060-A; tel. (212) 600-3101; fax (212) 261-8741; e-mail crcas@international.gc.ca; internet www.canadainternational.gc.ca/venezuela; Ambassador PAUL GIB-BARD.

Chile: Edif. Torre La Noria, 10°, Of. 10A, Paseo Enrique Eraso, Urb. Las Mercedes, Caracas; tel. (212) 992-3378; fax (212) 992-0614; e-mail echileve@cantv.net; internet chileabroad.gov.cl/venezuela; Ambassador MAURICIO UGALDE BILBAO.

China, People's Republic: Avda Orinoco con Calle Monterrey, Urb. Las Mercedes, Municipio Baruta, Caracas; tel. (212) 993-1171; fax (212) 993-5685; e-mail chinaemb_ve@mfa.gov.cn; internet ve.china-embassy.org; Ambassador ZHAO RONGXIAN.

Colombia: Torre Credival, 11°, 2A Calle de Campo Alegre con Avda Francisco de Miranda, Apdo 60887, Caracas; tel. (212) 216-9596; fax (212) 261-1358; e-mail ecaracas@minrelext.gov.co; internet www.embajadaenvenezuela.gov.co; Ambassador (vacant).

Costa Rica: Edif. For You, 11°, Avda San Juan Bosco, entre 1a y 2a Transversal, Urb. Altamira, Chacao, Apdo 62239, Caracas; tel. (212) 267-1104; fax (212) 265-4660; e-mail embaricavene@yahoo.com.mx; Ambassador NAZARETH AVENDAÑO SOLANO.

Cuba: Calle Roraima, entre Río de Janeiro y Choroní, Chuao, Caracas 1060; tel. (212) 991-6661; fax (212) 993-5695; e-mail ministroconsejero@embajadacuba.com.ve; internet www.cubadiplomatica.cu/venezuela; Ambassador ROGELIO POLANCO FUENTES.

Dominican Republic: Edif. Argentum, Ofs 1 y 2, 2a Transversal, entre 1a Avda y Avda Andrés Bello, Los Palos Grandes, Caracas 1060; tel. (212) 283-3709; fax (212) 283-3965; e-mail embajada_dominicana@hotmail.com; Ambassador ADONAIDA MEDINA.

Ecuador: Edif. Bancaracas, 8°, Of. 8-01, Avda Principal de la Castellana con 2da Transversal, Apdo 62124, Caracas 1060; tel. (212) 265-0801; fax (212) 264-6917; e-mail embve.ecuador@mppre.gob.ve; Ambassador LEONARDO ARÍZAGA.

Egypt: Calle Caucagua con Calle Guaicaipuro, Quinta Maribel, Urb. San Román, Municipio Baruta, Apdo 49007, Caracas 1042-A; tel. (212) 992-6259; fax (212) 993-1555; e-mail embassy.caracas@mfa.gov.eg; internet www.mfa.gov.eg/Caracas_Emb; Ambassador ALI SALEH MOURAD.

El Salvador: Avda Nicolás Copérnico, Quinta Cuscatlán, Urb. Valle Arriba, Sector Los Naranjos, Municipio Baruta, Miranda, Caracas; tel. (212) 991-4472; fax (212) 959-3920; e-mail embasalve@cantv.net; internet embajadavenezuela.rree.gob.sv; Ambassador ROMÁN ANTONIO MOYORGA QUIROZ.

France: Calle Madrid con Avda Trinidad, Las Mercedes, Apdo 60385, Caracas 1060; tel. (212) 909-6500; fax (212) 909-6630; e-mail infos@francia.org.ve; internet www.ambafrance-ve.org; Ambassador JEAN-MARC LAFORET.

The Gambia: 4a Avda con 8a Transversal, Quinta La Paz, Urb. Los Palos Grandes, Chacao, Caracas; tel. (212) 285-2554; fax (212) 285-6250; Ambassador BALA GARBA JAHUMPA.

Germany: Torre La Castellana, 10°, Avda Eugenio Mendoza, cruce con Avda José Angel Lamas, La Castellana, Apdo 2078, Caracas 1010-A; tel. (212) 219-2500; fax (212) 261-0641; e-mail info@caracas.diplo.de; internet www.caracas.diplo.de; Ambassador WALTER LINDNER.

Greece: Quinta Maryland, Avda Principal del Avila, Alta Florida, Caracas 1050; tel. (212) 730-3833; fax (212) 731-0429; e-mail gremb.car@mfa.gr; Ambassador ANASTASSIOS PETROVAS.

Grenada: Avda Norte 2, Quinta 330, Los Navajos del Cafetal, Caracas; tel. (212) 985-5461; fax (212) 985-6391; e-mail egrenada@cantv.net; Chargé d'affaires a.i. MATTEW SIMON.

Guatemala: Avda de Francisco de Miranda, Torre Dozsa, 1°, Urb. El Rosal, Caracas; tel. (212) 952-5247; fax (212) 954-0051; e-mail embaguat@cantv.net; Ambassador ERICK ROBERTO MOLINA SANDOVAL.

Guyana: Quinta 'Roraima', Avda El Paseo, Prados del Este, Apdo 51054, Caracas 1050; tel. (212) 977-1158; fax (212) 976-3765; e-mail embaguy@cantv.net; Ambassador GEOFFREY DA SILVA.

Haiti: Quinta Flor 59, Avda Las Rosas, La Florida, Caracas; tel. (212) 730-7220; fax (212) 730-4605; Ambassador LESLY DAVID.

Holy See: Avda La Salle, Los Caobos, Apdo 29, Caracas 1010-A (Apostolic Nunciature); tel. (212) 781-8939; fax (212) 793-2403; e-mail nunapos@cantv.net; Apostolic Nuncio Most Rev. PIETRO PAROLIN (Titular Archbishop of Acquapendente).

Honduras: Edif. Banco de Lara, 8°, Of. B2, Avda Principal de la Castellana con 1a Transversal de Altamira, La Castellana, Apdo

68259, Caracas; tel. (212) 264-0606; fax (212) 263-4379; e-mail honduven@cantv.net; Chargé d'affaires a.i. FERNANDO SUÁREZ LOVO.

India: Quinta Tagore, No. 12, Avda San Carlos, La Floresta, Apdo 61585, Caracas; tel. (212) 285-7887; fax (212) 286-5131; e-mail info@embindia.org; internet www.embindia.org; Ambassador SMITA PURUSHOTTAM.

Indonesia: Quinta 'Indonesia', Avda El Paseo, con Calle Maracaibo, Prados del Este, Apdo 80807, Caracas 1080; tel. (212) 976-2725; fax (212) 976-0550; e-mail kbricaracas1@yahoo1.com; internet www.kemlu.go.id/caracas; Ambassador PRIANTI GAGARIN DJATMIKO SINGGIH.

Iran: Quinta Ommat, Calle Kemal Atatürk, Urb. Valle Arriba, Apdo 68460, Caracas; tel. (212) 992-3575; fax (212) 992-9989; e-mail embairanve@cantv.net; Ambassador HOJATTOLAH SOLTANI.

Iraq: Quinta Babilonia, Avda Nicolás Copérnico con Calle Los Malabares, Urb. Valle Arriba, Caracas; tel. (212) 993-3446; fax (212) 993-0819; e-mail crcemb@iraqmfamail.com; Ambassador TAHA AL ABASSI.

Italy: Edif. Atrium PH, Calle Sorocaima, entre Avdas Tamanaco y Venezuela, El Rosal, Apdo 3995, Caracas 1060; tel. (212) 952-7311; fax (212) 952-4960; e-mail ambcaracas@esteri.it; internet www.ambcaracas.esteri.it; Ambassador PAOLO SERPI.

Jamaica: Edif. Los Frailes, 5°, Calle La Guairita, Urb. Chuao, Caracas 1062; tel. (212) 916-9055; fax (212) 991-5708; e-mail embjaven@cantv.net; Ambassador SHARON WEBER.

Japan: Edif. Bancaracas, 10°, Avda San Felipe con 2a Transversal, La Castellana, Caracas; tel. (212) 261-8333; fax (212) 261-6780; e-mail ajapon@genesisbci.net; internet www.ve.emb-japan.go.jp; Ambassador TETSUO SHIOGUCHI.

Korea, Republic: Avda Francisco de Miranda, Centro Lido, Torre B, 9°, Ofs 91-B y 92-B, El Rosal, Caracas; tel. (212) 954-1270; fax (212) 954-0619; e-mail venezuela@mofat.go.kr; internet ven.mofat.go.kr; Ambassador KIM JOO-TECK.

Kuwait: Quinta El-Kuwait, Avda Las Magnolias con Calle Los Olivos, Los Chorros, Caracas; tel. (212) 235-3864; fax (212) 238-1752; e-mail caracas@mofa.gov.kw; Ambassador MARZOUK AL SHABO.

Lebanon: Edif. Embajada del Líbano, Prolongación Avda Parima, Colinas de Bello Monte, Calle Motatán, Caracas 1041; tel. (212) 751-5943; fax (212) 753-0726; e-mail emblibano@cantv.net; internet www.lebanonembassy.org.ve; Ambassador ELÍAS LEBBOS.

Malaysia: Centro Profesional Eurobuilding, 6°, Ofs 6D-G, Calle La Guairita, Apdo 65107, Chuao, Caracas 1060; tel. (212) 992-1011; fax (212) 992-1277; e-mail malcaracas@kln.gov.my; internet www.kln.gov.my/perwakilan/caracas; Ambassador MAHINDER SINGH.

Mexico: Edif. Forum, Calle Guaicaipuro con Principal de las Mercedes, 5°, El Rosal, Chacao, Apdo 61371, Caracas; tel. (212) 952-5777; fax (212) 952-3003; e-mail embvenezuela@sre.gob.mx; internet embamex.sre.gob.mx/venezuela; Chargé d'affaires a.i. EDUARDO MARTINEZ CURIEL.

Netherlands: Edif. San Juan, 9°, Avda San Juan Bosco con 2a Transversal de Altamira, Caracas; tel. (212) 276-9300; fax (212) 276-9311; e-mail car@minbuza.nl; internet venezuela.nlambassade.org; Ambassador JOHANNES GERARDUS VAN VLOTEN DISSEVELT.

Nicaragua: Avda El Paseo, Quinta Doña Dilia, Prados del Este, Caracas; tel. (212) 977-3289; fax (212) 977-3973; e-mail spoveda@cancilleria.gob.ni; Ambassador RAMÓN ENRIQUE LEETS CASTILLO.

Nigeria: Calle Chivacoa cruce con Calle Taría, Quinta Leticia, Urb. San Román, Apdo 62062, Chacao, Caracas 1060-A; tel. (212) 993-1520; fax (212) 993-7648; e-mail embnig@cantv.net; Ambassador CHARLES NDUKA ONIANWA.

Panama: Edif. Los Frailes, 6°, Calle La Guairita, Chuao, Apdo 1989, Caracas; tel. (212) 992-9093; fax (212) 992-8107; e-mail empanve@cantv.net; Ambassador PEDRO PEREIRA.

Peru: Edif. San Juan, 5°, Avda San Juan Bosco con 2a Transversal, Altamira, Caracas; tel. (212) 264-1483; fax (212) 265-7592; e-mail leprucaracas@cantv.net; Ambassador (vacant).

Philippines: 5a Transversal de Altamira, Quinta Filipinas, Altamira, Municipio Chacao, Caracas 1060; tel. (212) 266-4725; fax (212) 266-6443; e-mail caracas@embassyph.com; Ambassador JOCELYN BATOON-GARCÍA.

Poland: Quinta Ambar, Calle Nicolás Copérnico, Sector Los Naranjos, Valle Arriba, Apdo 62293, Chacao, Caracas; tel. (212) 991-1461; fax (212) 992-2164; e-mail ambcarac@cantv.net; internet www.caracas.polemb.net; Ambassador PIOTR KASZUBA.

Portugal: Torre La Castellana, 3°, Avda Eugénio Mendoza, cruce con Calle José Angel Lamas, Urb. La Castellana, Caracas 1062; tel. (212) 263-2529; fax (212) 267-9766; e-mail caracas@mne.pt; Ambassador MÁRIO ALBERTO LINO DA SILVA.

Qatar: Avda Principal Lomas El Mirador, Quinta Alto Claro, Municipio Baruta, Caracas; tel. (212) 993-7925; fax (212) 993-

2917; e-mail qatarven@cantv.net; Ambassador RASHID MUBARAK AL-KUWARI.

Romania: 4a Avda de Altamira, entre 8a y 9a Transversales, Quinta Guardatinajas 49-19, Chacao, Caracas; tel. (212) 261-9480; fax (212) 263-5697; e-mail secretariat.amb@gmail.com; Chargé d'affaires a.i. EMIL GHIŢULESCU.

Russia: Quinta Soyuz, Calle Las Lomas, Las Mercedes, Apdo 60313, Caracas; tel. (212) 993-4395; fax (212) 993-6526; e-mail rusemb@cantv.net; internet www.venezuela.mid.ru; Ambassador VLADIMIR F. ZAEMSKY.

Saudi Arabia: Calle Andrés Pietri, Quinta Makkah, Los Chorros, Caracas 1071; tel. (212) 239-0290; fax (212) 239-6494; e-mail veemb@mofa.gov.sa; Ambassador ABDELRAHMAN BIN ABDULAZIZ BIN SULAIMAN ABANAMY.

South Africa: Edif. Atrium, PH-1A, Sorocaima con Avda Venezuela, Urb. El Rosal, Chacao, Apdo 2613, Caracas 1064; tel. (212) 952-0026; fax (212) 952-0277; e-mail embajador.caracas@foreign.gov.za; Ambassador BHEKI WISDOM GILA.

Spain: Avda Mohedano entre 1a y 2a Transversal, La Castellana, Apdo 62297, Caracas; tel. (212) 263-2855; fax (212) 261-0892; e-mail emb.caracas@maec.es; internet www.maec.es/embajadas/caracas; Ambassador ANTONIO PÉREZ-HERNÁNDEZ.

Sudan: Caracas; Ambassador ABDURRAHMAN AHMED KLALID SHARFI.

Suriname: 4a Avda entre 7a y 8a Transversal, Quinta 41, Altamira, Caracas; Apdo 61140, Chacao, Caracas; tel. (212) 261-2724; fax (212) 263-9006; e-mail emsurl@cantv.net; Ambassador SAMUEL PAWIRO-NADI.

Switzerland: Centro Letonia, Torre Ing-Bank, 15°, Avda Eugenio Mendoza y San Felipe, La Castellana, Apdo 62555, Chacao, Caracas 1060-A; tel. (212) 267-9585; fax (212) 267-7745; e-mail car.vertretung@eda.admin.ch; internet www.eda.admin.ch/caracas; Ambassador MARKUS-ALEXANDER ANTONIETTI.

Syria: Avda Casiquiare, Quinta Damasco, Colinas de Bello Monte, Caracas; tel. (212) 753-5375; fax (212) 751-6146; Ambassador GHASSAN SULEIMAN ABBAS.

Trinidad and Tobago: Quinta Poshika, 3a Avda entre 7 y 8 Transversales, Altamira, Municipio Chacao, Caracas; tel. (212) 261-5796; fax (212) 261-9801; e-mail embassytt@cantv.net; Ambassador ANTHONY DAVID EDGHILL.

Turkey: Calle Kemal Atatürk, Quinta Turquesa 6, Valle Arriba, Apdo 62078, Caracas 1060-A; tel. (212) 991-0075; fax (212) 992-0442; e-mail turkishemb@cantv.net; internet karakas.be.mfa.gov.tr; Ambassador MUHSIN TUĞRUL KILIÇASLAN.

United Kingdom: Torre La Castellana, 11°, Avda Principal La Castellana, Caracas 1061; tel. (212) 263-8411; fax (212) 267-1275; e-mail britishembassy@internet.ve; internet ukinvenezuela.fco.gov.uk; Ambassador CATHERINE ELIZABETH NETTLETON.

USA: Calle Suapure con Calle F, Urb. Colinas de Valle Arriba, Caracas 1080; tel. (212) 975-6411; fax (212) 975-6710; e-mail embajada@state.gov; internet caracas.usembassy.gov; Chargé d'affaires a.i. KELLY KEIDERLING.

Uruguay: Torre Seguros Altamira, 4°, Of. D y E, 4a Avda de los Palos Grandes, Apdo 60366, Caracas 1060-A; tel. (212) 285-3549; fax (212) 286-6777; e-mail uruvene@cantv.net; internet www.uruvene.com; Ambassador OSCAR MILTON RAMOS FERNÁNDEZ.

Viet Nam: 9a Transversal, entre 6a y 7a Avdas, Quinta Las Mercedes, Urb. Altamira, Chacao 1060-025, Caracas; tel. (212) 635-7402; fax (212) 264-7324; e-mail embavive@yahoo.com.vn; internet www.vietnamembassy-venezuela.org; Ambassador NGO TIEN DUNG.

Judicial System

The judicature is headed by the Supreme Tribunal of Justice, which replaced the Supreme Court of Justice after the promulgation of the December 1999 Constitution. The judiciary is divided into penal, civil and mercantile judges; there are military, juvenile, labour, administrative litigation, finance and agrarian tribunals. In each state there is a superior court and several secondary courts which act on civil and criminal cases. A number of reforms to the judicial system were introduced under the Organic Criminal Trial Code of 1998. The Code replaced the inquisitorial system, based on the Napoleonic code, with an adversarial system in July 1999. In addition, citizen participation as lay judges and trial by jury was introduced, with training financed by the World Bank.

SUPREME TRIBUNAL OF JUSTICE

The Supreme Tribunal comprises 32 judges appointed by the Asamblea Nacional for 12 years. It is divided into six courts, each with three judges: political-administrative, civil, constitutional, electoral, social and criminal. When these act together the court is in full session. It has the power to abrogate any laws, regulations or other acts of the executive or legislative branches conflicting with the Constitution. It hears accusations against members of the Government and high public officials, cases involving diplomatic representatives and certain civil actions arising between the state and individuals.

Tribunal Supremo de Justicia: Final Avda Baralt, esq. Dos Pilitas, Foro Libertador, Caracas 1010; tel. (212) 801-9178; fax (212) 564-8596; e-mail cperez@tsj.gov.ve; internet www.tsj.gov.ve; Pres. GLADYS GUTIÉRREZ ALVARADO.

President of the Constitutional Court: GLADYS GUTIÉRREZ ALVARADO.

President of the Court of Civil Cassation: YRIS ARMENIA PEÑA DE ANDUEZA.

President of the Court of Penal Cassation: DEYANIRA NIEVES BASTIDAS.

President of the Court of Social Cassation: LUIS EDUARDO FRANCESCHI GUTIÉRREZ.

President of the Electoral Court: FERNANDO VEGAS TORREALBA.

President of the Political-Administrative Court: EMIRO ROSAS GARCÍA.

Prosecutor-General: LUISA ORTEGA DÍAZ.

Religion

Roman Catholicism is the religion of the majority of the population, but there is complete freedom of worship.

CHRISTIANITY

The Roman Catholic Church

For ecclesiastical purposes, Venezuela comprises nine archdioceses, 24 dioceses and three Apostolic Vicariates. There are also apostolic exarchates for the Melkite and Syrian Rites. Some 85% of the population are Roman Catholics.

Latin Rite

Bishops' Conference

Conferencia Episcopal de Venezuela, Prolongación Avda Páez, Montalbán, Apdo 4897, Caracas 1010; tel. (212) 471-6284; fax (212) 472-7029; e-mail prensa@cev.org.ve; internet www.cev.org.ve.

f. 1985; statutes approved in 2000; Pres. Most Rev. UBALDO RAMÓN SANTANA SEQUERA (Archbishop of Maracaibo).

Archbishop of Barquisimeto: Most Rev. ANTONIO JOSÉ LÓPEZ CASTILLO, Arzobispado, Venezuela con Calle 29 y 30 Santa Iglesia Catedral, Nivel Sótano, Barquisimeto 3001; tel. (251) 231-3446; fax (251) 231-3724; e-mail arquidiocesisdebarquisimeto@hotmail.com.

Archbishop of Calabozo: MANUEL FELIPE DÍAZ SÁNCHEZ, Arzobispado, Calle 4, No 11–82, Apdo 954, Calabozo 2312; tel. (246) 871-0483; fax (246) 871-2097; e-mail el.real@telcel.net.ve.

Archbishop of Caracas (Santiago de Venezuela): Cardinal JORGE LIBERATO UROSA SAVINO, Arzobispado, Plaza Bolívar, Apdo 954, Caracas 1010-A; tel. (212) 542-1611; fax (212) 542-0297; e-mail arzobispado@cantv.net.

Archbishop of Ciudad Bolívar: Most Rev. ULISES ANTONIO GUTIÉRREZ REYES, Arzobispado, Avda Andrés Eloy Blanco con Calle Naiguatá, Apdo 43, Ciudad Bolívar 8001; tel. (285) 654-4960; fax (285) 654-0821; e-mail arzcb@cantv.net.ve.

Archbishop of Coro: Most Rev. ROBERTO LÜCKERT LEÓN, Arzobispado, Calle Federación esq. Palmasola, Apdo 7342, Coro; tel. (268) 251-7024; fax (268) 251-1636; e-mail dioceco@reaccium.ve.

Archbishop of Cumaná: Most Rev. DIEGO RAFAEL PADRÓN SÁNCHEZ, Arzobispado, Calle Bolívar 34 con Catedral, Apdo 134, Cumaná 6101-A; tel. (293) 431-4131; fax (293) 433-3413; e-mail dipa@cantv.net.

Archbishop of Maracaibo: Most Rev. UBALDO RAMÓN SANTANA SEQUERA, Arzobispado, Calle 95, entre Avdas 2 y 3, Apdo 439, Maracaibo; tel. (261) 722-5351; fax (261) 721-0805; e-mail ubrasan@hotmail.com.

Archbishop of Mérida: Most Rev. BALTAZAR ENRIQUE PORRAS CARDOZO, Arzobispado, Avda 4, Plaza Bolívar, Apdo 26, Mérida 5101-A; tel. (274) 252-5786; fax (274) 252-1238; e-mail arquimer@latinmail.com.

Archbishop of Valencia: Most Rev. REINALDO DEL PRETTE LISSOT, Arzobispado, Avda Urdaneta 100-54, Apdo 32, Valencia 2001-A; tel. (241) 858-5865; fax (241) 857-8061; e-mail arqui_valencia@cantv.net.

Melkite Rite

Apostolic Exarch: Rt Rev. GEORGES KAHHALÉ ZOUHAÏRATY, Iglesia San Jorge, Final 3a Urb. Montalbán II, Apdo 20120, Caracas; tel. (212) 472-5367; fax (212) 443-0131; e-mail georgeskhhale@cantv.net.

Syrian Rite

Apostolic Exarch: HIKMAT BEYLOUNI, Parroquia Nuestra Señora de la Asunción, 1A Calle San Jacinto, Apdo 11, Maracay; tel. (243) 235-0821; fax (243) 235-7213.

The Anglican Communion

Anglicans in Venezuela are adherents of the Episcopal Church in the USA, in which the country forms a single, extra-provincial diocese attached to Province IX.

Bishop of Venezuela: Rt Rev. ORLANDO DE JESÚS GUERRERO, Avda Caroní 100, Apdo 49-143, Colinas de Bello Monte, Caracas 1042-A; tel. (212) 753-0723; fax (212) 751-3180; e-mail iglanglicanavzla@cantv.net.

Protestant Churches

Convención Nacional Bautista de Venezuela: Avda Santiago de Chile 12–14, Urb. Los Caobos, Caracas 1050; Apdo 61152, Chacao, Caracas 1060-A; tel. (212) 782-2308; fax (212) 781-9043; e-mail cnbv@telcel.net.ve; internet www.cnbv.org.ve; f. 1951; Pres. Rev. IVÁN MARTÍNEZ; Dir-Gen. Rev. ALEXANDER MONTERO.

Iglesia Evangélica Luterana en Venezuela: Apdo 68738, Caracas 1062-A; tel. and fax (212) 264-1868; e-mail ielv.venezuela@gmail.com; internet ielv.tripod.com; Pres. GUILLERMINA CHAPARRO; 1,950 mems.

JUDAISM

Confederación de Asociaciones Israelitas de Venezuela: Avda Washington, al lado del Hotel Avila, San Bernardino, Caracas; tel. (212) 551-0368; fax (212) 551-0377; e-mail caiv.org@gmail.com; internet www.caiv.org; f. 1966; federation of 5 Jewish orgs; Pres. DAVID BITTAN OBADIA; Exec. Dir JACQUELINE FLUGELMAN.

ISLAM

Mezquita Sheikh Ibrahim bin-Abdulaziz bin-Ibrahim: Calle Real de Quebrada Honda, Los Caobos, Caracas; tel. (212) 577-7382; f. 1994; Leader OMAR KADWA.

BAHÁ'Í FAITH

National Spiritual Assembly of the Bahá'ís: Colinas de Bello Monte, Apdo 49133, Caracas; tel. and fax (212) 751-7669; e-mail aenbaven@telcel.net.ve; internet www.bci.org/venezuela; f. 1961; mems resident in 954 localities.

The Press

PRINCIPAL DAILIES

Caracas

Diario 2001: Edif. Bloque DeArmas, 2°, final Avda San Martín cruce con Avda La Paz, Caracas; tel. (212) 406-4111; fax (212) 443-4961; e-mail contacto@dearmas.com; internet www.2001.com.ve; f. 1973; Dir JAVIER CONDE; Editor-in-Chief WILFER PULGARÍN.

Meridiano: Edif. Bloque DeArmas, final Avda San Martín cruce con Avda La Paz, Caracas 1010; tel. (212) 406-4040; fax (212) 442-5836; e-mail opina@dearmas.com; internet www.meridiano.com.ve; f. 1969; morning; sport; Dir RAMÓN NAVARRO; Editor-in-Chief HUMBERTO GALARZA.

El Mundo: Edif. Cadena Capriles, 2°, Final Avda Rómulo Gallegos con calle 4 de La Urbina, Apdo 1073, Caracas; tel. (212) 240-9911; fax (212) 240-9478; e-mail olugo@cadena-capriles.com; internet www.elmundo.com.ve; f. 1958; morning; independent; economics and business; Pres. MIGUEL ANGEL CAPRILES LÓPEZ; Dir OMAR LUGO.

El Nacional: Avda Principal de Los Cortijos de Lourdes con 3a Transversal, Caracas 1071-A; tel. (212) 203-3243; fax (212) 203-3158; e-mail contactenos@el-nacional.com; internet www.el-nacional.com; f. 1943; morning; right-wing; independent; Pres. and Editor MIGUEL HENRIQUE OTERO.

TalCual: Edif. Menegrande, 5°, Of. 51, Avda Francisco de Miranda, Caracas; tel. (212) 286-7446; fax (212) 232-7446; e-mail tpetkoff@talcualdigital.com; internet www.talcualdigital.com; f. 2000; evening; right-wing; Editor-in-Chief TEODORO PETKOFF.

Ultimas Noticias: Edif. Torre de la Prensa, 3°, Plaza del Panteón, Parroquia Altagracia, Apdo 1192, Caracas; tel. (212) 596-1911; fax (212) 596-1433; e-mail edrangel@cadena-capriles.com; internet www.ultimasnoticias.com.ve; f. 1941; morning; independent; Dir ELEAZAR DÍAZ RANGEL; Editor-in-Chief ERYS WILFREDO ALVARADO.

El Universal: Edif. El Universal, Avda Urdaneta, esq. de Animas, Apdo 1909, Caracas; tel. (212) 505-2314; fax (212) 505-3710; e-mail consejoeditorial@eluniversal.com; internet www.eluniversal.com; f. 1909; morning; Dir ANDRÉS MATA OSORIO; Chief Editor ELIDES ROJAS.

Vea: Edif. San Martín, Sótano Uno, Parque Central, Caracas 1010; tel. (212) 578-3639; fax (212) 578-3031; e-mail webmaster@diariovea.com.ve; internet www.diariovea.com.ve; f. 2003; morning; left-wing; Dir SERVANDO GARCÍA PONCE; Editor-in-Chief ANGELIO PÉREZ.

Barcelona

El Norte: Avda Intercomunal Jorge Rodríguez, Sector Las Garzas, Grupo UP, entre el Banco Exterior y el BOD, Barcelona; tel. (281) 286-2484; e-mail fmartinez@elnorte.com.ve; internet www.elnorte.com.ve; f. 1989; morning; Exec. Dir FERNANDO MARTÍNEZ; Editor MEURY MANZANO.

Barquisimeto

El Impulso: Edif. El Impulso, Calle Juan Carmona, Urb. El Parque, Apdo 2 y 602, Barquisimeto; tel. (251) 256-1111; fax (251) 256-1129; e-mail reaccion@elimpulso.com; internet www.elimpulso.com; f. 1904; morning; independent; Dir JUAN M. CARMONA P.; Editor-in-Chief JOSÉ A. OCANTO.

El Informador: Edif. El Informador, Carrera 21, esq. Calle 23, Barquisimeto; tel. (251) 231-1811; fax (251) 231-0624; e-mail informatica@elinformador.com.ve; internet www.elinformador.com.ve; f. 1968; morning; Dir-Gen. MAURICIO GÓMEZ SIGALA.

Ciudad Bolívar

El Expreso: Edif. El Expreso, Paseo Gáspari con Calle Democracia, Ciudad Bolívar 8001; tel. and fax (285) 632-3246; e-mail info@diarioelexpreso.com.ve; internet www.diarioelexpreso.com.ve; f. 1969; morning; independent; Dir and Editor LUIS ALBERTO GUZMÁN ALFONZO.

Maracaibo

Panorama: Avda 15, No 95-60, Apdo 425, Maracaibo; tel. (261) 725-6888; fax (261) 725-6911; e-mail panorama@panorama.com.ve; internet www.panorama.com.ve; f. 1914; morning; independent; Pres. PATRICIA PINEDA; Editorial Dir MARÍA INÉS DELGADO.

Maracay

El Aragüeño: Calle 3a Oeste con Avda 1 Oeste, Urb. Ind. San Jacinto, Maracay; tel. (243) 235-9018; fax (243) 235-7866; e-mail diarioelaragueno@gesindoni.com; internet www.elaragueno.com.ve; f. 1972; morning; Pres. GIUSEPPE SINDONI; Editor ROSELYS PEÑA.

El Periodiquito: Calle Páez Este 178, Maracay; tel. (243) 237-7776; fax (243) 233-6987; e-mail redaccion@elperiodiquito.com; internet www.elperiodiquito.com; f. 1986; Dir JORGE ALBORNOZ; Editor RAFAEL RODRÍGUEZ RONDÓN.

El Siglo: Edif. El Siglo, Avda Bolívar Oeste 244, La Romana, Maracay; tel. (243) 554-9265; fax (243) 554-5154; e-mail informaciones@elsiglo.com.ve; internet www.elsiglo.com.ve; f. 1973; morning; independent; Pres. TULIO CAPRILES MENDOZA.

Puerto la Cruz

El Tiempo: Edif. Diario El Tiempo, Avda Municipal 153, Puerto La Cruz; tel. (281) 260-0600; fax (281) 260-0660; e-mail ediaz@eltiempo.com.ve; internet www.eltiempo.com.ve; f. 1958; independent; Dir GIOCONDA DE MÁRQUEZ; Editor EDDER DÍAZ.

San Cristóbal

Diario La Nación: Edif. La Nación, Calle 4 con Carrera 6 bis, La Concordia, Apdo 651, San Cristóbal; tel. (276) 346-4263; fax (276) 346-5051; e-mail lanacion@lanacion.com.ve; internet www.lanacion.com.ve; f. 1968; morning; independent; Editor JOSÉ RAFAEL CORTEZ.

El Tigre

Antorcha: Edif. Antorcha, Avda Francisco de Miranda, El Tigre; tel. (283) 235-2383; fax (283) 235-3923; e-mail webmaster@diarioantorcha.com; internet www.diarioantorcha.com; f. 1954; morning; independent; Pres. and Editor ANTONIO BRICEÑO AMPARÁN.

Valencia

El Carabobeño: Edif. El Carabobeño, Avda Universidad, Urb. La Granja, Naguanagua, Valencia; tel. (241) 867-2918; fax (241) 867-3450; e-mail redaccion@el-carabobeno.com; internet www.el-carabobeno.com; f. 1933; morning; Dir EDUARDO ALEMÁN PÉREZ; Editor-in-Chief CAROLINA GONZÁLEZ.

Notitarde: Edif. Carabobo, Avda Boyacá, entre Navas Spínola y Flores, Apdo 1958, Valencia; tel. (241) 850-1666; fax (241) 850-1534; e-mail redaccion@notitarde.com; internet www.notitarde.com; f. 1976; evening; Dir LAURENTZI ODRIOZOLA ECHEGARAY; Editor-in-Chief LUIS BORJAS.

SELECTED PERIODICALS

Automóvil de Venezuela: Avda Caurimare, Quinta Expo, Colinas de Bello Monte, Caracas 1050; tel. (212) 751-1355; fax (212) 751-1122; e-mail ortizauto@gmail.com; internet www.automovildevenezuela.com; f. 1961; monthly; automotive trade; Editor MARÍA A. ORTIZ; circ. 6,000.

Business Venezuela: Torre Credival, Avda de Campo Alegre, Apdo 5181, Caracas 1010-A; tel. (212) 263-0833; fax (212) 263-2060; e-mail yrojas@venamcham.org; internet www.bvonline.com.ve; every 2 months; business and economics journal in English; published by the Venezuelan-American Chamber of Commerce and Industry; Dir YUSMERRY ROJAS; Editor-in-Chief CARLOS TEJERA.

ComputerWorld Venezuela: Apdo 76276, Caracas 1071; tel. (212) 976-7423; fax (212) 416-9144; e-mail cwv@computerworld.net.ve; internet www.cwv.com.ve; Dir and Editor CLELIA SANTAMBROGIO.

Dinero: Torre Sur, 1°, Centro Comercial El Recreo, Avda Casanova, Sabana Grande, Caracas 1050; tel. (212) 750-5011; fax (212) 750-5005; e-mail mcastillo@gep.com.ve; internet www.dinero.com.ve; monthly; business and finance; Dir SALVATORE LOMONACO.

Nueva Sociedad: Edif. IASA, 6°, Of. 606, Plaza La Castellana, Apdo 61712, Caracas; tel. (212) 265-9975; fax (212) 267-3397; e-mail nuso@nuso.org; internet www.nuso.org; f. 1972; Latin American affairs; Dir SVENJA BLANKE; Editor PABLO STEFANONI.

Producto: Torre Sur, 8°, Ofs 8-1 y 8-2, Centro Comercial El Recreo, Avda Venezuela, Caracas 1050; tel. (212) 750-5011; fax (212) 750-5005; e-mail mcastillo@producto.com.ve; internet www.producto.com.ve; f. 1983; monthly; business; Editor ERNESTO LOTITTO; circ. 18,000.

Quinto Día: Avda Principal de Los Ruíces con Avda Romúlo Gallegos, Residencia Los Almendros, Nivel Mezzanina, Of. 5, Los Ruíces, Caracas; tel. (212) 237-9809; fax (212) 239-2955; e-mail acarrera@quintodia.net; internet www.quintodia.net; weekly; current affairs; Dir CARLOS CROES.

La Razón: Edif. Valores, Sótano A, Avda Urdaneta, esq. de Urapal, Apdo 16362, La Candelaria, Caracas; tel. (212) 578-3143; fax (212) 578-2397; e-mail larazon@internet.ve; internet www.larazon.net; weekly, Sun.; independent; Dir PABLO LÓPEZ ULACIO.

La Red: Urb. Vista Alegre, Calle 7, Quinta Luisa Amelia, Caracas; tel. (212) 472-0703; fax (212) 471-7749; e-mail info@lared.com.ve; internet www.lared.com.ve; f. 1996; information technology; Editor LUIS MANUEL DÁVILA.

Ronda: Edif. Bloque DeArmas, final Avda San Martín cruce con Avda La Paz, Caracas 1020; tel. (212) 406-4018; fax (212) 406-4158; e-mail jmiranda@dearmas.com; internet www.bloquedearmas.com/ronda.asp; fortnightly; celebrities and entertainment; Dir JENNIFER MIRANDA; Editor-in-Chief YINESKA PARRA.

Sic: Edif. Centro de Valores, esq. de Luneta, Centro Gumilla, Caracas; tel. (212) 564-9803; fax (212) 564-7557; e-mail sic@gumilla.org; internet www.gumilla.org; f. 1938; Compañía de Jesús; monthly; liberal Jesuit publ; Dir WILFREDO GONZÁLEZ.

Tendencia: Torre Tendencia, 5°, Of. 5A, Avda El Milagro 2, Sector Gonzaga, Maracaibo; tel. (261) 743-7674; fax (261) 742-0960; e-mail info@tendencia.com; internet www.tendencia.com; every 2 months; lifestyle; Dir ROSANNA BERNARDONI; Editor ANA BRACHO.

Variedades: Edif. Bloque DeArmas, 6°, final Avda San Martín cruce con Avda La Paz, Caracas 1020; tel. (212) 406-4111; fax (212) 406-4112; e-mail mrodriguez@dearmas.com; internet www.bloquedearmas.com/variedades.asp; f. 1963; monthly; women's interest; Dir LAVINIA MUÑOZ; circ. 35,000.

VenEconomía: Edif. Gran Sabana, 1°, Avda Abraham Lincoln 174, Blvr de Sabana Grande, Caracas 1050; tel. (212) 761-8121; fax (212) 762-8160; e-mail editor@veneconomia.com; internet www.veneconomia.com; f. 1982; weekly and monthly edns; Spanish and English; business, economic and political issues; Editor ROBERT BOTTOME.

PRESS ASSOCIATIONS

Bloque de Prensa Venezolano (BEV): Edif. El Universal, 5°, Of. C, Avda Urdaneta, Caracas; tel. (212) 561-7704; fax (212) 561-9409; e-mail contacto@bloquedeprensavenezolano.com; internet www.bloquedeprensavenezolano.com; assen of newspaper owners; Pres. Dr DAVID NATERA FEBRES; Sec.-Gen. LUISA CHIOSSONE.

Colegio Nacional de Periodistas (CNP): Casa Nacional del Periodista, 3°, Avda Andrés Bello, Caracas; tel. and fax (212) 781-7601; e-mail colegiodeperiodistasjdn@yahoo.com; internet www.cnpven.org; journalists' asscn; Pres. SILVIA ALEGRETT; Sec.-Gen. DELVALLE CANELÓN.

PRESS AGENCY

Agencia Venezolana de Noticias (AVN): Torre Lincoln, 7°, Sabana Grande, Caracas; tel. (212) 572-6543; fax (212) 781-2711; internet www.avn.info.ve; Pres. FREDDY FERNÁNDEZ.

Publishers

Armitano Editores, CA: Edif. Centro Industrial Boleita Sur, 4a Transversal de Boleita, Apdo 50853, Caracas 1070; tel. (212) 234-2565; fax (212) 234-1647; e-mail armiedit@telcel.net.ve; internet www.armitano.com; art, architecture, ecology, botany, anthropology, history, geography; Pres. ERNESTO ARMITANO.

Colegial Bolivariana, CA (Ediciones Co-Bo): Edif. COBO, 1°, Avda Diego Cisneros (Principal), Los Ruices, Apdo 70324, Caracas 1071-A; tel. (212) 239-1433; fax (212) 239-6502; e-mail ventas@co-bo.com; internet www.co-bo.com.ve; f. 1961; general, educational; Dir FABRICIO ACERO.

Ediciones Ekaré: Edif. Banco del Libro, Avda Luis Roche, Altamira Sur, Caracas 1062; tel. (212) 264-7615; fax (212) 263-3291; e-mail editorial@ekare.com.ve; internet www.ekare.com; f. 1978; children's literature; Pres. CARMEN DIANA DEARDEN; Exec. Dir MARÍA FRANCISCA MAYOBRE.

Ediciones IESA: Edif. IESA, 3°, final Avda IESA, San Bernardino, Apdo 1640, Caracas 1010-A; tel. (212) 555-4504; e-mail comunicacionesiesa@iesa.edu.ve; internet www.iesa.edu.ve/publicaciones/ediciones; f. 1984; economics, business; Pres. FRANCISCO SANÁNEZ.

Ediciones Universitarias Venezolanas, SA (EDUVEN): Edif. Atenev, 1°, Calle Segundaria, Urb. Lebrun, Petare; tel. and fax (212) 256-7237; e-mail eduvensa@cantv.net; internet www.eduven.com.ve; f. 1989; Pres. JOSÉ ANTONIO NAVARRO GISBERT; Gen. Man. CARMEN TERESA ALDANA D'SANTIAGO.

Editorial Biosfera: Avda Chama, Quinta Coral, Colinas de Bello Monte, Apdo 50634, Caracas 1050; tel. (212) 751-9119; fax (212) 751-9320; e-mail julio@editorialbiosfera.com; internet www.editorialbiosfera.com; f. 1978; academic and cultural; Pres. SERAFIN MAZPARROTE.

Editorial Medica Panamericana: Edif. Polar, Of. 6-c, 6°, Torre Oeste, Plaza, Caracas; tel. (212) 793-2857; fax (212) 793-5885; e-mail info@medicapanamericana.com.ve; internet www.medicapanamericana.com.ve; health and medicine; Gen. Man. MARÍA ROSALES.

Editorial Océano de Venezuela y Ocelibros: Edif. El Candor, Calle 8, entre calles 4 y 5, Zona Industrial La Urbina, Caracas; tel. (212) 242-0508; fax (212) 242-0516; e-mail info@oceano.com.ve; internet www.oceano.com.ve; Dir-Gen. JOSÉ FARRES.

Editorial Romor: Avda El Cortijo, Quinta El León 21, Urb. Los Rosales, Caracas; tel. (212) 633-0933; fax (212) 632-6355; e-mail mercadeo.caracas@editorialromor.com.ve; internet www.editorialromor.com.ve; Gen. Man. CARLOS CASTILLO.

Fondo Editorial Fundarte (Fundación para la Cultura y las Artes): Edif. Tajamar, Avda Lecuna, Parque Central, Apdo 17559, Caracas 1015-A; tel. (212) 577-8343; fax (212) 571-0320; e-mail informatica@fundarte.gob.ve; internet www.fundarte.gob.ve; f. 1975; literature, history; Pres. FREDDY ÑÁÑEZ; Dir ROBERTO LOVERA DE SOLA.

Fundación Biblioteca Ayacucho: Centro Financiero Latino, 12°, Ofs 1, 2 y 3, Avda Urdaneta, Animas a Plaza España, Apdo 14413, Caracas 1010; tel. (212) 561-6691; fax (212) 564-5643; e-mail biblioayacucho@cantv.net; internet www.bibliotecaayacucho.gob.ve/fba; f. 1974; indigenous literature; Pres. HUMBERTO MATA; Exec. Dir LUIS EDGAR PÁEZ.

Fundación Bigott: Casa 10–11, Calle El Vigia, Plaza Sucre, Centro Histórico de Petare, Caracas 1010-A; tel. (212) 205-7111; fax (212) 272-0120; e-mail contacto@fundacionbigott.com; internet www.fundacionbigott.com; f. 1981; Venezuelan traditions, environment, agriculture; Gen. Man. KARINA ZAVARCE.

Fundación Editorial Salesiana: Avda Andrés Bello, Paradero a Salesianos 6, La Candelaria, Apdo 369, Caracas; tel. (212) 571-6109; fax (212) 574-9451; e-mail gerenciales@cantv.net; internet www.salesiana.com.ve; f. 1960; education; Pres. LUCIANO STÉFANI; Gen. Man. JAIME GARCÍA.

Magenta Ediciones: Edif. Rupi, 2°, Of. 21, Calle El Recreo con Avda Casanova, El Recreo, Caracas 1050; tel. (212) 762-5420; fax (212) 832-3171; e-mail magenta@magentaediciones.com; internet www.magentaediciones.com; f. 2006; general; Editorial Dir BLANCA STREPPONI.

Monte Avila Editores Latinoamericana, CA: Centro Simón Bolívar, La Torre Norte, 22°, El Silencio, Caracas; tel. (212) 482-2850; fax (212) 482-0472; e-mail editorial@monteavila.gob.ve; internet www.monteavila.gob.ve; f. 1968; general; Pres. CARLOS NOGUERA; Exec. Dir NELCI MARIN.

Vadell Hermanos Editores, CA: Edif. Golden, Avda Sur 15, esq. Peligro a Pele el Ojo, Sótano, La Candelaria, Caracas; tel. (212) 572-3108; fax (212) 572-5243; e-mail edvadell1@gmail.com; internet www.vadellhermanos.com; f. 1973; science, social sciences; Gen. Man. MANUEL VADELL GRATEROL.

PUBLISHERS' ASSOCIATION

Cámara Venezolana del Libro: Centro Andrés Bello, Torre Oeste, 11°, Of. 112-O, Avda Andrés Bello, Caracas 1050-A; tel. (212) 793-1347; fax (212) 793-1368; e-mail direccion_ejecutiva@cavelibro.org; internet www.cavelibro.org; f. 1969; Pres. YOLANDA DE FERNÁNDEZ; Exec. Dir DALILA DA SILVA.

Broadcasting and Communications

TELECOMMUNICATIONS

AT&T Venezuela: Edif. Centro Banaven, Avda La Estancia A, Chuao, Caracas 1060; internet www.att.com.

Compañía Anónima Nacional Teléfonos de Venezuela (CANTV): Edif. NEA, 20, Avda Libertador, Caracas 1010-A; tel. (212) 500-3016; fax (212) 500-3512; e-mail amora@cantv.com.ve; internet www.cantv.com.ve; privatized in 1991; renationalized in 2007; Pres. MANUEL FERNÁNDEZ.

> **Movilnet:** Edif. NEA, 20, Avda Libertador, Caracas 1010-A; tel. (202) 705-7901; e-mail info@movilnet.com.ve; internet www.movilnet.com.ve; f. 1992; mobile cellular telephone operator; owned by CANTV; 6.3m. subscribers (June 2006); Pres. MANUEL FERNÁNDEZ.

Digitel TIM: Caracas; tel. (212) 280-5902; fax (212) 280-5943; e-mail 0412empres@digitel.com.ve; internet www.digitel.com.ve; f. 2000; mobile cellular telephone operator; owned by Telecom Italia, Italy; 2.4m. subscribers (June 2006); Pres. OSWALDO CISNEROS.

Inter: Urb. Chuao, Centro Ciudad Comercial Tamanaco (CCCT), Nivel C2, Caracas; internet www.inter.com.ve; f. 1996 as Intercable; changed name as above in 2007; cable, internet and telecommunications services; CEO EDUARDO STIGOL.

Movistar: Edif. Parque Cristal, Torre Oeste, Avda Francisco Miranda, 14°, Los Palos Grandes, Caracas 1062; tel. (582) 201-8200; internet www.movistar.com.ve; f. 2005; subsidiary of Telefónica Móviles (Spain); 6.5m. subscribers (June 2006); Pres. PEDRO CORTEZ.

NetUno: Edif. Insenica II, planta baja, Calle 7, La Urbina, Caracas; tel. (212) 710-0404; e-mail atccaracas@netuno.net; internet www.netuno.net; f. 1995; voice, data and video transmission services; Pres. GILBERT MINIONIS.

Telecom Venezuela: Torre Fondo Común, 5°, Avda Andrés Bello, Caracas; tel. (212) 393-2931; e-mail eauverana@cvgtelecom.com.ve; internet www.telecom.gob.ve; f. 2004 as CVG Telecomunicaciones, CA; present name adopted Aug. 2007; state-owned telecommunications co; Pres. KAI CHEN; Man. EVELYN RANGEL.

Telecomunicaciones Gran Caribe: Caracas; f. 2007; owned by Telecom Venezuela (60%) and Transbit of Cuba (40%); construction and operation of 1,550 km fibre-optic cable connecting La Guaira (Venezuela) and Siboney (Cuba); Pres. WILFREDO MORALES.

Regulatory Authority

Comisión Nacional de Telecomunicaciones (CONATEL): Avda Veracruz con Cali, Edif. Conatel, 6°, Las Mercedes, Municipio Baruta, Caracas 1060; tel. (212) 909-0493; fax (212) 993-6122; e-mail conatel@conatel.gob.ve; internet www.conatel.gob.ve; regulatory body for telecommunications; Dir-Gen. PEDRO ROLANDO MALDONADO MARÍN.

BROADCASTING

Radio

Radio Nacional de Venezuela (RNV): Final Calle Las Marías, entre Chapellín y Country Club, La Florida, Caracas 1050; tel. (212) 730-6022; fax (212) 731-1457; e-mail infornv@rnv.gob.ve; internet www.rnv.gov.ve; f. 1936; state broadcasting org.; 15 stations; Pres. DESIRÉ SANTOS AMARAL.

Television

Government Stations

Telesur (Televisora del Sur): Edif. Telesur, Calle Vargas con Calle Santa Clara, Urb. Boleíta Norte, Caracas; tel. (212) 600-0202; e-mail contactenos@telesurtv.net; internet www.telesurtv.net; f. 2005; jtly owned by Govts of Venezuela (51%), Argentina (20%), Cuba (19%) and Uruguay (10%); regional current affairs and general interest; Pres. Lt (retd) ANDRÉS IZARRA; Vice-Pres. ARAM AHARONIAN.

Televisora Venezolana Social—Canal 2 (TVes): Quinta Thaizza, Avda Principal Augusto César Sandino con 10a Transversal, Maripérez, Municipio Libertador, Caracas; tel. (212) 781-8069; e-mail info@tves.com.ve; internet tvestv.blogspot.com; f. May 2007 to replace private channel RCTV (q.v.); govt-owned; Pres. LIL RODRÍGUEZ.

Venezolana de Televisión (VTV)—Canal 8: Edif. VTV, Avda Principal Los Ruices, Caracas; tel. (212) 207-1220; fax (212) 239-8102; e-mail web@vtv.gob.ve; internet www.vtv.gob.ve; f. 1964; 26 relay stations; Vice-Pres. VANESSA DAVIES.

ViVe TV (Visión Venezuela): Edif. Biblioteca Nacional, AP-4, final Avda Panteón, Foro Libertador, Altagracia, Caracas; tel. (212) 505-1611; e-mail webmaster@vive.gob.ve; internet www.vive.gob.ve; f. 2003; govt-run cultural channel; Pres. RICARDO MÁRQUEZ.

Private Stations

Corporación Venezolana de Televisión (Venevisión)—Canal 4: Edif. Venevisión, final Avda La Salle, Colinas de los Caobos, Apdo 6674, Caracas; tel. (212) 708-9224; fax (212) 708-9535; e-mail mponce@venevision.com.ve; internet www.venevision.net; f. 1961; privately owned; Pres. GUSTAVO CISNEROS.

Globovisión—Canal 33: Quinta Globovisión, Avda Los Pinos, Urb. Alta Florida, Caracas; tel. (212) 730-2290; fax (212) 731-4380; e-mail info@globovision.com; internet www.globovision.com; f. 1994; 24-hour news and current affairs channel; Pres. GUILLERMO ZULOAGA; Dir-Gen. (vacant).

Meridiano Televisión: Caracas; e-mail opina@dearmas.com; internet www.meridiano.com.ve; f. 1997; sports programming; Pres. MARTÍN DE ARMAS; Dir-Gen. JUAN ANDRÉS DAZA.

Radio Caracas Televisión (RCTV): Edif. RCTV, Dolores a Puente Soublette, Quinta Crespo, Caracas; tel. (212) 401-2222; fax (212) 401-2647; e-mail marriaga@rctv.net; internet www.rctv.net; f. 1953; fmrly broadcast on terrestrial channel as Radio Caracas Televisión—Canal 2; ceased broadcasting in May 2007; subsidiary RCTV International (based in Miami, FL, USA) recommenced broadcasting in Venezuela via cable in July 2007; broadcasting licence of RCTV Internacional temporarily suspended in Jan. 2010; Pres. MARCEL GRANIER.

Televén—Canal 10 (Televisión de Venezuela): Edif. Televén, 4a Transversal con Avda Rómulo Gallegos, Urb. Horizonte, Apdo 1070, Caracas; tel. (212) 280-0011; fax (212) 280-0204; e-mail aferro@televen.com; internet www.televen.com; f. 1988; privately owned; Pres. OMAR CAMERO ZAMORA.

Televisora Andina de Mérida (TAM)—Canal 6: Edif. Imperador, Entrada Independiente, Avda 6 y 7, Calle 23, Mérida 5101; tel. and fax (274) 251-0660; f. 1982; regional channel; Pres. Most Rev. BALTAZAR ENRIQUE PORRAS CARDOZO.

VALE TV (Valores Educativos Televisión)—Canal 5: Quinta VALE TV, final Avda La Salle, Colinas de los Caobos, Caracas 1050; tel. (212) 793-9215; fax (212) 708-9743; e-mail info@valetv.com; internet www.valetv.com; f. 1998; Pres. JORGE CARDENAL L. UROSA SAVINO.

Zuliana de Televisión—Canal 30: Edif. 95.5 América, Avda 11 (Veritas), Maracaibo; tel. (265) 641-0355; fax (265) 641-0565; e-mail elregionalredac@iamnet.com; Pres. GILBERTO URDANETA FIDOL.

Zuvisión: Maracaibo; f. 2007; regional channel for the state of Zulia; Pres. RAFAEL URDANETA.

Regulatory Authorities

Cámara Venezolana de la Industria de Radiodifusión: Avda Antonio José Istúriz Transversal 3, Urb. La Castellana, Caracas 1060; tel. (212) 261-1651; fax (212) 261-4783; e-mail camradio@camradio.org.ve; internet www.camradio.org; Pres. ENZA CARBONE; Exec. Dir JESÚS R. SARCOS.

Cámara Venezolana de Televisión por Suscripción: Edif. Banco Venezolano de Crédito, Avda Londres con Avda Principal de Las Mercedes, Caracas; tel. and fax (212) 993-7553; e-mail cavetesu@gmail.com; internet www.cavetesu.org.ve; f. 1995; regulatory body for private stations; Pres. ALEXANDER ELORRIAGA.

Finance

(cap. = capital; res = reserves; dep. = deposits; m. = million;
brs = branches; amounts in bolívares fuertes unless otherwise
indicated)

BANKING

Regulatory Authorities

Corporación de la Banca Pública (CBP): Caracas; f. 2009 to oversee all state-owned financial institutions; Supt EDGAR HERNÁNDEZ BEHRENS.

Superintendencia de Bancos (SUDEBAN): Edif. Centro Empresarial Parque del Este, Avda Francisco de Miranda, Urb. La Carlota, Municipio Sucre del Estado Miranda, Apdo 6761, Caracas; tel. (212) 280-6933; fax (212) 238-2516; e-mail sudeban@sudeban.gob.ve; internet www.sudeban.gob.ve; regulates banking sector; Supt EDGAR HERNÁNDEZ BEHRENS.

Central Bank

Banco Central de Venezuela: Avda Urdaneta, esq. de Carmelitas, Caracas 1010; tel. (212) 801-5111; fax (212) 861-0048; e-mail info@bcv.org.ve; internet www.bcv.org.ve; f. 1940; bank of issue and clearing house for commercial banks; granted autonomy 1992; controls international reserves, interest rates and exchange rates; res 18,892.0m., dep. 83,303.7m. (Dec. 2009); Pres. and Chair. EDMÉE BETANCOURT DE GARCÍA (designate); 2 brs.

Commercial Banks

Banco del Caribe, CA: Edif. Banco del Caribe, 1°, Dr Paúl a esq. Salvador de León, Apdo 6704, Carmelitas, Caracas 1010; tel. (212) 505-5103; fax (212) 562-0460; e-mail producto@bancaribe.com.ve; internet www.bancaribe.com.ve; f. 1954; cap. 201m., res 455.4m., dep. 19,554.4m. (Dec. 2011); Pres. MIGUEL IGNACIO PURROY; Exec. Pres. JUAN CARLOS DAO; 109 brs.

Banco Caroní: Edif. Multicentro Banco Caroní, Vía Venezuela, Puerto Ordaz, Estado Bolívar; tel. (286) 950-5200; fax (286) 920-0995; e-mail contactenos.caroni@bancocaroni.com.ve; internet www.bancocaroni.com.ve; cap. 526.8m., res 441.3m., dep. 8,803.2m. (Dec. 2011); Pres. ARÍSTIDES MAZA TIRADO.

Banco de Comercio Exterior (Bancoex): Central Gerencial Mohedano, 1°, Calle Los Chaguaramos, La Castellana, Caracas 1060; tel. (212) 265-1433; fax (212) 265-6722; e-mail exporte@bancoex.gob.ve; internet www.bancoex.gob.ve; f. 1997 principally to promote non-traditional exports; state-owned; cap. 825.4m., res 206.7m. (Dec. 2010); Pres. EYILDE MARGARITA GRACIA.

Banco Exterior, CA—Banco Universal: Edif. Banco Exterior, 1°, Avda Urdaneta, esq. Urapal a Río, Candelaria, Apdo 14278, Caracas 1011-A; tel. (212) 501-0211; fax (212) 501-0745; e-mail lperez@bancoexterior.com; internet www.bancoexterior.com; f. 1958; cap. 223.3m., res 312.4m., dep. 20,995.8m. (Dec. 2011); Chair. LUIS ENRIQUE FRANCESCHI; Exec. Pres. RAÚL BALTAR ESTÉVEZ; 106 brs.

Banco Guayana, CA: Edif. Los Bancos, Avda Guayana con Calle Caura, Puerto Ordaz, Bolívar; e-mail bguayana06@cantv.net; f. 1955; state-owned; cap. 158m., res 27.5m., dep. 2,476m. (Dec. 2011); Pres. OSCAR EUSEBIO JIMÉNEZ AYESA; Exec. Pres. BERNARDO KABCHE.

Banco Industrial de Venezuela, CA: Torre Financiera BIV, Avda Las Delicias de Sabana Grande, cruce con Avda Francisco Solano López, Caracas 1010; tel. (212) 952-4051; fax (212) 952-6282; e-mail webmaster@biv.com.ve; internet www.biv.com.ve; f. 1937; 98% state-owned; took over Banco de Inversión Industrial de Venezuela in Sept. 2011; cap. 9,840m., res 278,645m., dep. 8,600,674m. (Dec. 2006); Pres. RODOLFO PORRO ALETTI; 60 brs.

Banco Occidental de Descuento Banco Universal, CA: Calle 77, esq. Avda 17, Maracaibo 4001, Apdo 695, Zulia; tel. (261) 759-3011; fax (261) 594-9811; e-mail atclient@bodinternet.com; internet www.bodinternet.com; f. 1957; transferred to private ownership in 1991; cap. 629.7m., res 381.3m., dep. 15,233.8m. (Dec. 2010); Pres. VÍCTOR J. VARGAS IRAUSQUIN; Exec. Pres. TOMÁS NIEMBRO CONCHA; 17 brs.

Banco de Venezuela, SA: Torre Banco de Venezuela, 16°, Avda Universidad, esq. Sociedad a Traposos, Apdo 6268, Caracas 1010-A; tel. (212) 501-3333; fax (212) 501-2570; e-mail bancodevenezuela@banvenez.com; internet www.bancodevenezuela.com; f. 1890; nationalized in July 2009; cap. 364.7m., res 1,361m., dep. 47,861.6m. (Dec. 2010); Pres. RODOLFO C. MARCO TORRES; 367 brs.

Banesco Banco Universal, CA: Edif. Banesco, 12°, Avda Guaicaipura con Avda Principal de Las Mercedes, Caracas; tel. (212) 952-4972; fax (212) 952-7124; e-mail atclient@banesco.com; internet www.banesco.com; cap. 1,250m., res 2,059.4m., dep. 109,055.2m. (Dec. 2012); Chair. JUAN CARLOS ESCOTET RODRÍGUEZ; Exec. Pres. LUIS JUAN CARLOS ESCOTET RODRÍGUEZ; 455 brs.

BBVA Banco Provincial, SA: Centro Financiero Provincial, 27°, Avda Vollmer con Avda Este O, San Bernadino, Apdo 1269, Caracas 1011; tel. (212) 504-5098; fax (212) 574-9408; e-mail calidad@provincial.com; internet www.provincial.com; f. 1952; 55.14% owned by Banco Bilbao Vizcaya Argentaria, 26.27% owned by Grupo Polar; cap. 1,078.3m., res 1,907.4m., dep. 58,699.7m. (Dec. 2011); Pres. LEÓN HENRIQUE COTTIN; Exec. Pres. PEDRO RODRÍGUEZ SERRANO.

Bicentenario Banco Universal: Avda Venezuela, El Rosal, Chacao, Miranda; tel. (212) 958-5113; fax (212) 901-6920; e-mail irene.mora@bicentenariobu.com; internet www.bicentenariobu.com; f. 2009 by merger of Banco Bolívar, Banco Confederado, Banfoandes and Banco Central; BaNorte incorporated in Jan. 2010; state-owned; Pres. DARÍO ENRIQUE BAUTE DELGADO.

Corp Banca, CA Banco Universal: Torre Corp Banca, Plaza la Castellana, Chacao, Caracas 1060; tel. (212) 206-3333; fax (212) 206-4950; e-mail calidad@corpbanca.com.ve; internet www.corpbanca.com.ve; f. 1969; fmrly Banco Consolidado, current name adopted in 1997; cap. 40.0m., res 85.3m., dep. 9,635.3m. (Dec. 2010); CEO JOSÉ OMAR GUEVARA; 114 brs.

Mercantil CA Banco Universal: Edif. Mercantil, 35°, Avda Andrés Bello 1, San Bernardino, Apdo 789, Caracas 1010-A; tel. (212) 503-1111; fax (212) 503-1075; e-mail mercan24@bancomercantil.com; internet www.bancomercantil.com; f. 1925; cap. 268.1m., res 465.6m., dep. 59,580.1m. (Dec. 2011); Pres. Dr GUSTAVO A. VOLLMER; 273 brs.

Venezolano de Crédito, SA—Banco Universal: Edif. Banco Venezolano de Crédito, Avda Alameda, San Bernadino, Caracas 1011; tel. (212) 806-6111; fax (212) 541-2757; e-mail info@venezolano.com; internet www.venezolano.com; f. 1925 as Banco Venezolano de Crédito, SACA; name changed as above in 2001; cap. 330.6m., res 226.3m., dep. 7,507.2m. (Dec. 2011); Pres. Dr OSCAR GARCÍA MENDOZA; 95 brs in Venezuela and abroad.

Development Banks

Banco de Desarrollo Económico y Social de Venezuela (BANDES): Torre Bandes, Avda Universidad, Traposos a Colón, Caracas 1010; tel. (212) 505-8010; fax (212) 505-8030; e-mail apublicos@bandes.gov.ve; internet www.bandes.gov.ve; state-owned; Pres. EDMÉE BETANCOURT DE GARCÍA.

Banco del Pueblo Soberano, CA: Edif. El Gallo de Oro, Gradillas a San Jacinto Parroquia Catedral, Caracas; tel. (212) 505-2800; fax (212) 505-2995; e-mail abarrera@bancodelpueblo.gob.ve; internet www.bancodelpueblo.gob.ve; f. 1999; microfinance; Pres. LEONARDO JOSÉ RODRÍGUEZ BASTARDO.

Banco del Sur: Caracas; e-mail atencionalcliente@delsur.com.ve; internet www.delsur.com.ve; f. 2007 by Govts of Argentina, Bolivia, Brazil, Ecuador, Paraguay, Uruguay and Venezuela; regional devt bank; brs in Buenos Aires (Argentina) and La Paz (Bolivia); cap. 116.4m., res 34.9m., dep. 1,619.4m. (Dec. 2009); Pres. CÉSAR NAVARRETE.

Fondo de Desarrollo Microfinanciero (FONDEMI): Edif. Sudameris, 2°, Avda Urdaneta con Fuerzas Armadas, esq. Plaza España, Caracas 1030; tel. (212) 287-7611; fax (212) 287-7658; e-mail fondemi@fondemi.gob.ve; internet www.fondemi.gob.ve; f. 2001; microfinancing devt fund; Pres. WILLY CASANOVA; Gen. Man. DANY MACAYO.

Banking Association

Asociación Bancaria de Venezuela: Torre Asociación Bancaria de Venezuela, 1°, Avda Venezuela, El Rosal, Caracas; tel. (212) 951-4711; fax (212) 951-3696; e-mail abvinfo@asobanca.com.ve; internet www.asobanca.com.ve; f. 1959; 49 mems; Pres. LUIS A. ESCOTET; Exec. Dir LARRY M. FERNÁNDES.

STOCK EXCHANGE

Bolsa de Valores de Caracas, CA: Edif. Atrium, Nivel C-1, Calle Sorocaima entre Avdas Tamanaco y Venezuela, Urb. El Rosal, Apdo 62724-A, Caracas 1060-A; tel. (212) 905-5511; fax (212) 952-2640; e-mail bvc@bolsadecaracas.com; internet www.bolsadecaracas.com; f. 1947; 63 mems; Pres. MANUEL ALONSO REBAREDA; Gen. Man. JUAN CARLOS DA SILVA.

INSURANCE

Supervisory Board

Superintendencia de Seguros: Edif. Torre del Desarollo, P. H., Avda Venezuela, El Rosal, Chacao, Caracas 1060; tel. (212) 905-1611; fax (212) 953-8615; e-mail sudeseg@sudeseg.gob.ve; internet www.sudeseg.gob.ve; Supt JOSÉ LUÍS PÉREZ.

Principal Insurance Companies

Adriática, CA de Seguros: Edif. Adriática de Seguros, Avda Andrés Bello, esq. de Salesianos, Caracas; tel. (212) 571-5702; fax

(212) 571-0812; e-mail adriatica@adriatica.com.ve; internet www
.adriatica.com.ve; f. 1952; Pres. BARTOLOMÉ RUGGIERO IMBRIACO; Gen.
Man. TOBÍAS CARRERO NÁCAR.

Avila, CA de Seguros: Edif. Torre Británica de Seguros, P. H., Avda
José Felix Sosa, Urb. El Dorado, Altamira, Chacao, Caracas; tel.
(212) 238-2470; fax (212) 239-9743; f. 1936; Pres. RAMÓN RODRÍGUEZ;
Gen. Man. WILLIAM CARRILLO.

Bolivariana de Seguros: Caracas; f. 2010; state-owned; Pres.
JESÚS TOVAR JIMÉNEZ.

Carabobo, CA de Seguros: Edif. Mene Grande, 7°, Avda Francisco
de Miranda, Urb. Los Palos Grandes, Caracas; tel. (212) 286-9229;
fax (212) 620-7320; e-mail info@seguroscarabobo.com; internet www
.seguroscarabobo.com; f. 1955; Pres. PAUL FRAYND; Gen. Man.
ANDRÉS HERNÁNDEZ.

Mapfre La Seguridad, CA de Seguros: Calle 3A, frente a La Torre
Express, La Urbina Sur, Apdo 473, Caracas 1010; tel. (212) 213-8000;
fax (212) 204-8751; e-mail tucontactomapfre@mapfre.com.ve;
internet www.mapfre.com.ve; f. 1943; owned by Seguros Mapfre
(Spain); Pres. ARISTÓBULO BAUSELA.

La Occidental, CA de Seguros: Edif. Seguros Occidental, Avda 4
(Bella Vista) esq. con Calle 71, No 10126, Maracaibo, Zulia; tel. (261)
200-2222; fax (261) 200-2292; e-mail clientes@laoccidental.com;
internet www.laoccidental.com; f. 1956; Pres. TOBÍAS CARRERO
NÁCAR; Dir CARLOS MONÍZ ROCHA.

La Oriental, CA de Seguros: Torre Oriental de Seguros, Avda
Venezuela, entre Calle Sojo y Avda Sorocaima, Urb. El Rosal,
Chacao, Caracas 1060; tel. (212) 905-9999; fax (212) 905-9652;
internet www.laoriental.com; f. 1975; Pres. GONZALO LAURÍA ALCALÁ.

Seguros Los Andes, CA: Edif. Central, 5°, Avda San Felipe, entre
1a y 2a Transversal, La Castellana, Caracas; tel. (276) 266-5020; fax
(276) 340-2596; internet www.seguroslosandes.com; Pres. RAMÓN
RODRÍGUEZ.

Seguros Caracas de Liberty Mutual, CAV: Torre Seguros Caracas C-4, Centro Comercial El Parque, Avda Francisco de Miranda,
Los Palos Grandes, Caracas; tel. (212) 209-9111; fax (212) 209-9556;
e-mail informatica@seguroscaracas.com; internet www
.seguroscaracas.com; f. 1943; Pres. ROBERTO SALAS; Regional Man.
ANDRÉS VERROCCHI.

Seguros Catatumbo, CA: Edif. Seguros Catatumbo, Avda 4 (Bella
Vista), No 77–55, Apdo 1083, Maracaibo; tel. (261) 700-5555; fax (261)
216-0037; e-mail mercado@seguroscatatumbo.com; internet www
.seguroscatatumbo.com; f. 1957; cap. 9,300m. (2003); Pres. ERNESTO
PINEDA HERNÁNDEZ; Dir-Gen. RAFAEL ARRAGA HUERTA.

Seguros Constitución: Torre Constitución, Avda Venezuela, entre
Avda Lazo Martí y Calle Mohedano, El Rosal, Caracas; tel. (212)
957.9800; internet www.segurosconstitucion.com; Pres. OMAR JESÚS
FARÍAS LUCES.

Seguros Horizante: Avda Francisco de Miranda, Torre la Primera,
Chacao, Miranda; tel. (212) 750-9080; e-mail marian.guevara@
seguroshorizonte.com; internet www.seguroshorizonte.gob.ve;
f. 1956; Pres. JIMMY LENÍN GUZMÁN PINTO.

Seguros Mercantil, CA: Edif. Seguros Mercantil, Avda Libertador
con calle Andrés Galarraga, Chacao, Caracas; tel. (212) 276-2000; fax
(212) 276-2001; e-mail cat@segurosmercantil.com; internet www
.segurosmercantil.com; f. 1988; acquired Seguros Orinoco in 2002;
Pres. ALBERTO BENSHIMOL; Gen. Man. MARÍA SILVIA RODRÍGUEZ FEO.

Seguros Nuevo Mundo, SA: Torre Nuevo Mundo, Avda Luis Roche
con 3a Transversal, Urb. Altamira, Apdo 2062, Caracas; tel. (212)
201-1111; fax (212) 201-1428; e-mail jesus.heredia@nuevomundo
.com.ve; internet www.nuevomundo.com.ve; f. 1856; cap. 100m.
(2003); Pres. RAFAEL PEÑA ALVAREZ; Sec. JUAN CARLOS TRIVELLA.

Seguros La Previsora, CNA: Torre La Previsora, Avda Abraham
Lincoln, Sábana Grande, Caracas; tel. (212) 709-1555; fax (212) 709-
1976; internet www.previsora.com; f. 1914; nationalized in Dec.
2009; Pres. ALBERTO QUINTANA; Exec. Vice-Pres. JUAN CARLOS
MALDONADO.

Seguros Venezuela, CA: Edif. Seguros Venezuela, 8° y 9°, Avda
Francisco de Miranda, Urb. Campo Alegre, Caracas; tel. (212) 901-
7111; fax (212) 901-7218; e-mail servicio.cliente@segurosvenezuela
.com; internet www.segurosvenezuela.com; f. 1948; part of American
International group; Exec. Pres. ENRIQUE BANCHIERI ORTIZ.

Universitas de Seguros, CA: Edif. Impres Médico, 2°, Avda
Tamanaco, El Rosal, Caracas; tel. (212) 951-6711; fax (212) 901-
7506; e-mail tbarrera@universitasdeseguros.com; internet www
.universitasdeseguros.com; cap. 6,500m; Pres. CÉSAR AUGUSTO
BOLÍVAR.

Insurance Association

Cámara de Aseguradores de Venezuela: Torre Taeca, 2°, Avda
Guaicaipuro, Urb. El Rosal, Apdo 3460, Caracas 1010-A; tel. (212)
952-4411; fax (212) 951-3268; e-mail rrpp@camaraseg.org; internet

www.camaraseg.org; f. 1951; 42 mems; Pres. JOSE MIGUEL REYES;
Exec. Pres. ALESIA RODRIGUÉZ PARDO.

Trade and Industry
GOVERNMENT AGENCIES

Comisión de Administración de Divisas (CADIVI): Antiguo
Edif. PDVSA Servicios, 6°, Avda Leonardo Da Vinci, Los Chaguaramos, Caracas; tel. (212) 606-3904; fax (212) 606-3026; e-mail info@
cadivi.gov.ve; internet www.cadivi.gob.ve; f. 2003; regulates access
to foreign currency; Pres. MANUEL BARROSO.

Corporación Venezolana de Guayana (CVG): Edif. General, 2°,
Avda La Estancia, Apdo 7000, Chuao, Caracas; tel. (212) 992-1813;
fax (212) 993-4306; e-mail presidenciaccs@cvg.com; internet www
.cvg.com; f. 1960 to organize devt of Guayana area, particularly its
metal ore and hydroelectric resources; Pres. JOSÉ SALAMAT KHAN
FERNÁNDEZ (Minister of Basic Industry and Mining); 15 subsidiaries;
18,000 employees.

Instituto Nacional de Tierras (INTI): Quinta La Barranca, Calle
San Carlos, Urb. Vista Alegre, Caracas; tel. (212) 471-0222; fax (212)
576-2201; internet www.inti.gob.ve; f. 1945 as Instituto Agrario
Nacional; present name adopted in 2001; authorized to expropriate
and redistribute idle or unproductive lands; Pres. JUAN CARLOS LOYO.

Instituto Nacional de la Vivienda: Torre Inavi, Avda Francisco de
Miranda, Chacao, Caracas; tel. (212) 206-9279; e-mail comunica@
inavi.gov.ve; internet www.inavi.gob.ve; f. 1975; administers govt
housing projects; Pres. PABLO CANDIDA MOSQUERA; Gen. Man.
NEPTALI FERNÁNDEZ.

Mercal, CA: Edif. Torres Seguros Orinoco, Avda Fuerzas Armadas,
esq. Socarras, Caracas; tel. (212) 564-3856; e-mail fosorio@correo
.mercal.gob.ve; internet www.mercal.gob.ve; responsible for marketing agricultural products; fmrly Corporación de Mercadeo
Agrícola; Pres. Lt-Col FÉLIX OSORIO GUZMÁN.

**Servicio Autónomo Nacional de Normalización, Calidad,
Metrología y Reglamentos Técnicos (SENCAMER):** Avda Libertador, Centro Comercial los Cedros, Caracas; tel. (212) 703-2005;
e-mail juan.gallegos@sencamer.gob.ve; internet www.sencamer.gob
.ve; responsible for proposing, organizing and implementing quality
and metrology laws; Pres. AMANDA CAMACHO.

Superintendencia de Inversiones Extranjeras (SIEX): Edif. La
Perla, esq. La Bolsa a Mercaderes, 3° y 5°, Capitolio, Caracas 1010;
tel. (212) 483-6666; fax (212) 484-4368; e-mail siexdespacho@cantv
.net; internet www.siex.gob.ve; f. 1974; supervises foreign investment in Venezuela; Supt MANUEL FIGUEROA.

DEVELOPMENT ORGANIZATIONS

Fonden (Fondo de Desarrollo Nacional): Edif. Sede Ministerio del
Poder Popular para las Finanzas, 1°, Avda Urdaneta, Esq. de
Carmelitas, Caracas; tel. (212) 802-1213; e-mail fondensa@mppf
.gob.ve; internet www.fonden.gob.ve; f. 2005; govt investment
agency; Pres. Minister of Planning and Finance ; Exec. Sec. CLAUDIA
DÍAZ GUILLÉN.

Fondo para el Desarrollo Agrario Socialista (FONDAS): Edif.
FONDAFA, esq. Salvador de León a Socarras, La Hoyada, Caracas;
tel. (212) 542-3570; fax (212) 542-5887; internet www.fondas.gob.ve;
f. 1974; devt of agriculture, fishing and forestry; Pres. RICARDO JAVIER
SÁNCHEZ.

**Instituto de Desarrollo de la Pequeña y Mediana Industria
(INAPYMI):** Torre Británica, 14°, 15°, 16° y planta baja, Avda José
Felix Sosa, Altamira Sur, Caracas; tel. (212) 276-9511; e-mail
zcarrillo@inapymi.gob.ve; internet www.inapymi.gob.ve; f. 2001;
govt agency; promotes the devt of small and medium-sized industries; Pres. PATRICIA FEBLES MONTES; Exec. Dir ZAIDA MARÍA
CARRILLO.

CHAMBERS OF COMMERCE AND INDUSTRY

**Federación Venezolana de Cámaras y Asociaciones de
Comercio y Producción (Fedecámaras):** Edif. Fedecámaras,
Avda El Empalme, Urb. El Bosque, Apdo 2568, Caracas; tel. (212)
731-1711; fax (212) 730-2097; e-mail presidencia@fedecamaras.org
.ve; internet www.fedecamaras.org.ve; f. 1944; 307 mems; Pres.
JORGE BOTTI; Gen. Man. GILBERTO DELGADO G.

Cámara de Comercio, Industria y Servicios de Caracas: Edif.
Cámara de Comercio de Caracas, 8°, Avda Andrés Eloy Blanco 215,
Los Caobos, Caracas; tel. (212) 571-3222; fax (212) 571-0050; e-mail
servicios@lacamaradecaracas.org.ve; internet www.lacamarade
caracas.org.ve; f. 1893; 650 mems; Pres. FERNANDO ESEVERRI; Exec.
Dir VÍCTOR MALDONADO.

**Cámara Venezolano-Americana de Industria y Comercio
(Venamcham):** Torre Credival, 10°, Of. A, 2a Avda Campo Alegre,
Apdo 5181, Caracas 1010-A; tel. (212) 263-0833; fax (212) 266-3437;

e-mail venam@venamcham.org; internet www.venamcham.org; f. 1950; Pres. CARLOS HENRIQUE BLOHM; Gen. Man. CARLOS TEJERA.

EMPLOYERS' ORGANIZATIONS

Asociación de Comerciantes e Industriales del Zulia (ACIZ): Edif. Los Cerros, 9°, Calle 77 con Avda 3c, Apdo 91, Maracaibo, Zulia; tel. (261) 91-7064; fax (261) 92-0907; e-mail info@aciz.org; f. 1941; traders and industrialists; Pres. DANIEL HÓMEZ.

Asociación Nacional de Cultivadores de Algodón (ANCA) (National Cotton Growers' Association): Edif. Portuguesa, Avda Los Pioneros, Sector Aspiga-Acarigua; tel. (255) 621-5111; fax (255) 621-4368; e-mail anca@asoanca.com; Pres. CONCEPCIÓN QUIJADA G.

Asociación Nacional de Industriales Metalúrgicos y de Minería de Venezuela (AIMM): Centro Empresarial Senderos, 3°, Ofs 302 y 303A, Avda Principal Los Cortijos de Lourdes, 2a Transversal, Sucre, Caracas 1071; tel. and fax (212) 237-5169; e-mail aimmv@cantv.net; internet www.aimm-ven.org; metallurgy and mining; Pres. JORGE ROIG; Exec. Dir MARÍA GRACIELA FERREIRA.

Asociación Textil Venezolana: Edif. Textilera Gran Colombia, Calle el Club 8, Los Cortijos de Lourdes, Caracas; tel. (212) 238-1744; fax (212) 239-4089; e-mail asociaciontextilvenezolana@gmail.com; f. 1957; textiles; Pres. DAVID FIHMAN; 68 mems.

Asociación Venezolana de Exportadores (AVEX): Centro Comercial Concresa, Of. 435, 2°, Prados del Este, Avda Río Caura, Baruta, Caracas; tel. (212) 979-5042; fax (212) 979-4542; e-mail asistentedepresidencia@avex.com.ve; internet www.avex.com.ve; Pres. ALBA GUEVARA; Gen. Man. MARÍA ISABEL SÁEZ.

Cámara Petrolera: Torre Domus, 3°, Of. 3A, Avda Abraham Lincoln con Calle Olimpo, Sábana Grande, Caracas; tel. (212) 794-1222; fax (212) 794-0068; e-mail informacion.web@camarapetrolera.org; internet www.camarapetrolera.org; f. 1978; asscn of petroleum-sector cos; Pres. MAURICIO CANARD MENDOZA; Exec. Dir ELOISA LÓPEZ.

Confederación Nacional de Asociaciones de Productores Agropecuarios (FEDEAGRO): Edif. Casa de Italia, planta baja, Avda La Industria, San Bernardino, Caracas 1010; tel. (212) 571-4035; fax (212) 573-4423; e-mail fedeagro@fedeagro.org; internet www.fedeagro.org; f. 1960; agricultural producers; 133 affiliated asscns; Pres. PEDRO RIVAS ISMAYEL.

Confederación Venezolana de Industriales (CONINDUSTRIA): Edif. CIEMI, Avda Principal de Chuao, Caracas 1061; tel. (212) 991-2116; fax (212) 991-7737; e-mail conindustria@conindustria.org; internet www.conindustria.org; asscn of industrialists; Pres. CARLOS LARRAZABAL; Exec. Pres. ISMAEL PÉREZ VIGIL.

Federación Nacional de Ganaderos de Venezuela (FEDENAGA): Avda Urdaneta, Centro Financiero Latino, 18°, Ofs 18-2 y 18-4, La Candelaria, Caracas; tel. (212) 563-2153; fax (212) 564-7273; e-mail fedenagat@cantv.net; internet www.fedenaga.org; f. 1962; cattle owners; Pres. MANUEL CIPRIANO HEREDIA C.

STATE HYDROCARBONS COMPANIES

PDVSA Petróleo SA: Edif. Petróleos de Venezuela, Torre Este, Avda Libertador, La Campiña, Apdo 169, Caracas 1010-A; tel. (212) 708-4743; fax (212) 708-4661; e-mail saladeprensa@pdvsa.com; internet www.pdvsa.com; f. 1975; responsible for petrochemical sector since 1978 and for devt of coal resources in western Venezuela since 1985; in 1997 the 3 operating branches (Lagoven, SA, Maraven, SA and Corpoven, SA) were reintegrated to form PDVSA Petróleo y Gas; in 2001 gas-related activity passed to PDVSA Gas; state-owned, under control of the Ministry of Energy and Petroleum; Pres. RAFAEL DARÍO RAMÍREZ CARREÑO (Minister of Energy and Petroleum); Vice-Pres. of Exploration and Production EULOGIO DEL PINO; Vice-Pres. of Refining ASDRÚBAL CHÁVEZ; the following are subsidiaries of PDVSA:

Bariven, SA: Edif. PDVSA Los Chaguaramos, 6°, Avda Leonardo Da Vinci, Urb. Los Chaguaramos, Apdo 1889, Caracas 1010-A; tel. (212) 606-4060; fax (212) 606-2741; handles the petroleum, petrochemical and hydrocarbons industries' overseas purchases of equipment and materials.

Corporación Venezolana del Petróleo (CVP): Edif. Pawa, Calle Cali con Avda Veracruz, Las Mercedes, Caracas; f. 1960, reformed 2003; responsible for PDVSA's negotiations with other petroleum cos.

Deltaven, SA: Edif. PDVSA Deltaven, Avda Principal de La Floresta, La Floresta, Caracas 1060; tel. (212) 208-1111; f. 1997; markets PDVSA products and services within Venezuela.

Intevep, SA: Centro de Investigación y Apoyo Tecnológico, Edif. Sede Central, Urb. Santa Rosa, Sector El Tambor, Los Teques, Apdo 76343, Caracas 1070-A; tel. (212) 330-6011; fax (212) 330-6448; f. 1973 as Fundación para la Investigación de Hidrocarburos y Petroquímica; present name adopted in 1979; research and devt br. of PDVSA.

Palmaven: Avda Principal de la Urbina, Torre Olimpia, 7°, Caracas; tel. (212) 204-4511; sustainable devt agency of PDVSA; Man. Dir EDDIE RAMÍREZ.

PDV Marina: Edif. Petróleos de Venezuela Refinación, Suministro y Comercio, Torre Oeste, 9°, Avda Libertador, La Campiña, Apdo 2103, Caracas 1010-A; tel. (212) 708-1111; fax (212) 708-2200; f. 1990; responsible for the distribution, by ship, of PDVSA products.

PDVSA Gas: Edif. Sucre, Avda Francisco de Miranda, La Floresta, Caracas; tel. (212) 208-6212; fax (212) 208-6288; e-mail messina@pdvsa.com; f. 1998; gas exploration and extraction; Pres. WUILMAN PAREIRA.

Pequiven (Petroquímica de Venezuela, SA): Zona Industrial Municipal Sur, Avda 73, con Calle 79B, Valencia, Carabobo; tel. (241) 839-4665; e-mail deinterespequiven@pequiven.com; internet www.pequiven.com; f. 1956 as Instituto Venezolano de Petroquímica; became Pequiven in 1977; involved in many joint ventures with foreign and private Venezuelan interests for expanding petrochemical industry; active in regional economic integration; an affiliate of PDVSA from 1978 until 2005; thereafter state-owned, under Ministry of Energy and Petroleum; Pres. SAUL AMELIACH.

UTILITIES

Electricity

Corporación Eléctrica Nacional (Corpoelec): Edif. Centro Eléctrico Nacional, Avda Sanz, Urb. El Marqués, Sucre, Caracas; tel. (212) 280-8111; internet www.corpoelec.gob.ve; f. 2007; generation, transmission, distribution and marketing of electric power and energy; incorporated Edelca, La Nueva Electricidad de Caracas, ENELVEN, ENELCO, ENELBAR, CADAFE, GENEVAPCA, ELEBOL, ELEVAL, Seneca, ENAGAS, TURBOVEN into one corpn in 2010; state-owned; Chair. (vacant); Dir (Generation) (vacant); Dir (Distribution) JOAQUIN OSORIO; Dir (Commercial) JAVIER ALVARADO OCHOA.

CADAFE (Compañía de Administración y Fomento Eléctrico): Edif. Centro Eléctrico Nacional, 14°, Avda Sanz, Urb. El Marqués, Sucre, Caracas; tel. (212) 280-8583; fax (212) 280-8667; e-mail dirgestion@cadafe.com.ve; internet www.cadafe.com.ve; f. 1958; electricity transmission.

La Electricidad de Caracas (EDC): Edif. La Electricidad de Caracas, Avda Vollmer, Urb. San Bernadino, Apdo 2299, Caracas 1010-A; tel. (212) 502-2111; e-mail info@edc-ven.com; internet www.laedc.com.ve; supplies electricity to Caracas.

Electrificación del Caroní, CA (Edelca): Edif. General, planta baja, Avda La Estancia, Chuao, Caracas; tel. (212) 950-2111; fax (212) 950-2808; e-mail asuntos-publicos@edelca.com.ve; internet www.edelca.com.ve; supplies some 70% of the country's electricity.

Enelbar (Energía Eléctrica de Barquisimeto): Edif. Sede, Avda Francisco de Miranda, Carora, Barquisimeto; tel. (251) 239-4050; internet www.enelbar.com.ve.

Enelco (Energía Eléctrica de la Costa Oriental): Edif. Suminstro, Calle Rosario 32, Urb. La Rosa, Cabimas, Miranda; tel. (264) 370-5555; e-mail atencionalcliente@enelco.com.ve; internet www.enelco.com.ve; electricity services to the eastern coast of the Lago de Maracaibo region.

Enelven (Energía Eléctrica de Venezuela): Calle 77, entre Avda 10 y 11, Maracaibo; tel. (261) 790-3800; e-mail asuntospublicos@enelven.com.ve; internet www.enelven.gob.ve.

Gas

ENAGAS (Ente Nacional del Gas): Calle Panamá con Avda Libertador, 8°, Urb. Los Caobos, Caracas; tel. (212) 706-6654; fax (212) 706-6471; e-mail presidencia@enagas.gov.ve; internet www.enagas.gob.ve; f. 1999; subsidiary of Corpoelec; Pres. JORGE LUIS SÁNCHEZ.

Water

Hidroven: Edif. Hidroven, Avda Augusto César Sandino con 9a Transversal, Maripérez, Caracas; tel. (212) 781-4778; fax (212) 781-6424; e-mail ngamboa@cantv.net; internet www.hidroven.gov.ve; national water co; owns Hidroandes, Hidrocapital, Hidrocaribe, Hidrofalcon, Hidrolago, Hidrollanos, Hidropaez, Hidrosuroeste, Aguas de Monagas, Aguas de Ejido, Hidrolara, Aguas de Anaco, Aguas de Cojedes, Aguas de Mérida, Aguas de Apure, Aguas de Yaracuy, Aguas de Portuguesa; Pres. CRISTÓBAL FRANCISCO ORTIZ; Vice-Pres. FRANCISCO DURÁN.

Compañía Anónima Hidrológica de la Región Capital (Hidrocapital): Edif. Hidrocapital, Avda Augusto César Sandino con 9a Transversal, Maripérez, Caracas; tel. (212) 793-1638; fax (212) 793-6794; internet www.hidrocapital.com.ve; f. 1992; operates water supply in Federal District and states of Miranda and Vargas; Pres. ALEJANDRO ANTONIO HITCHER MARVALDI.

TRADE UNIONS

Confederación de Trabajadores de Venezuela (CTV) (Confederation of Venezuelan Workers): Edif. José Vargas, 17°, Avda Este 2, Los Caobos, Caracas; tel. (212) 574-1049; e-mail ctv@ctv.org.ve; internet www.ctv.org.ve; f. 1936; principally active in public sector; Chávez Govt disputes legitimacy of election of CTV leadership; Pres. CARLOS ALFONSO ORTEGA CARVAJAL; Sec.-Gen. MANUEL JOSÉ COVA FERMÍN; 26 regional and 57 industrial feds.

Unión Nacional de Trabajadores (UNT): f. 2003; pro-Govt federation; Nat. Co-ordinator MARCELA MÁSPERO.

Transport

RAILWAYS

In 2006 a 41.4-km railway line from Caracas to Cúa was opened. A 173.7-km railway line linking Puerto Cabello and Acarigua was also in operation. In 2011 a line linking Puerto Cabello and La Encrucijada in the centre of the country was completed and was expected to commence operations in 2012, as was a 468-km line connecting Anaco and Tinaco. Other lines under construction included a 252.5-km line connecting San Juan de los Moros and San Fernando de Apure; a 44.3-km line linking Acarigua and Turén; and a 201-km line between Chaguaramas and Cabruta.

CA Metro de Caracas: Multicentro Empresarial del Este, Edif. Miranda, Torre B, 7°, Avda Francisco de Miranda, Calle Los Maristas, Apdo 61036, Caracas; tel. (212) 206-7111; fax (212) 266-3346; e-mail sugerencias@metrodecaracas.com.ve; internet www .metrodecaracas.com.ve; f. 1976 to supervise the construction and use of the underground railway system; services began in 1983; state-owned; Pres. HAIMAN EL TROUDI.

Ferrocarril de CVG Bauxilum—Operadora de Bauxita: Edif. Administrativo, Avda Fuerzas Armadas, Zona Industrial Matanzas, Ciudad Guayana, Bolívar; tel. (286) 950-6271; fax (286) 950-6270; e-mail asuntos.publicos@bauxilum.com.ve; internet www.bauxilum .com; f. 1989; state-owned; operates line linking Los Pijiguaos with river Orinoco port of Gumilla (52 km) for transporting bauxite; Pres. JOSÉ CHINA.

Instituto de Ferrocarriles del Estado (IFE): Edif. Torre Británica de Seguros, 7° y 8°, Avda José Félix Sosa, Urb. Altamira, Chacao, Caracas 1062-A; tel. (212) 201-8736; fax (212) 201-8902; e-mail tlopez@ife.gob.ve; internet www.ife.gob.ve; state co; Pres. FRANKLIN PÉREZ COLINA.

ROADS

In 2006 there were an estimated 96,200 km of roads, of which 32,300 km were paved. Responsibility for road maintenance generally lies with state governments; however, legislation adopted in 2009 allowed the central Government to take control of motorways and major roads, as well as ports and airports.

INLAND WATERWAYS

Instituto Nacional de Canalizaciones: Edif. INC, Calle Caracas, al lado de la Torre Diamen, Chuao, Caracas; tel. (212) 908-5106; fax (212) 959-6906; e-mail atencionalciudadano@incanal.gov.ve; internet www.incanal.gov.ve; f. 1952; semi-autonomous institution; Vice-Pres. NELSON FREDYS MARIÑA MULLER.

SHIPPING

There are 13 major ports, 34 petroleum and mineral ports and five fishing ports. The main ports for imports are La Guaira, the port for Caracas, and Puerto Cabello, which handles raw materials for the industrial region around Valencia. Maracaibo is the chief port for the petroleum industry. Puerto Ordaz, on the Orinoco River, was also developed to deal with the shipments of iron from Cerro Bolívar. At December 2012 the flag registered fleet comprised 297 vessels, totalling 1,472,351 grt, of which 34 were gas tankers and 34 were fishing vessels.

Consolidada de Ferrys, CA (CONFERRY): Edif. Conferry, Planta Baja, Of. Comercial, Avda Terranova con Llano Adentro, Porlamar, Isla de Margarita; tel. (295) 263-9878; fax (295) 263-8372; internet www.conferry.com; f. 1970; ferry services to Margarita island; Dir ROSSANA GONZÁLEZ.

Instituto Nacional de los Espacios Acuáticos (INEA): Edif. INEA, Avda Orinoco, entre Calles Perijá y Mucuchies, Urb. Las Mercedes, Municipio Baruta, Caracas; tel. (212) 909-1430; fax (212) 909-1431; internet www.inea.gob.ve; f. 2001; supervises marine and related activities; Pres. JORGE MIGUEL SIERRALTA.

PDV Marina: Edif. Sede Administrativa del Centro de Refinación Paraguaná, 2°, Ala 2, Of. 21, Comunidad Cardón, Falcón; tel. (269) 240-9215; fax (269) 240-9112; e-mail angolamd@pdvsa.com; f. 1990;

shipping subsidiary of Venezuela's state oil company PDVSA; Pres. FERNANDO CAMEJO ARENAS.

Scat, CA: Edif. Scat, Avda Juan Bautista Arismendi, Isla de Margarita; tel. (295) 274-5882; fax (295) 274-1525; e-mail contacto@scatca.com; internet www.scatca.com; operates in Puerto del Guamache.

Transpapel, CA: Edif. Centro, 11°, Of. 111, Centro Parque Boyaca, Avda Sucre, Los Dos Caminos, Apdo 61316, Caracas 1071; tel. (212) 283-8366; fax (212) 285-7749; e-mail nmaldonado@cantv.net; f. 1985; Man. Dir ERNESTO VILLASMIL.

CIVIL AVIATION

There are two adjacent airports 13 km from Caracas: Maiquetía for domestic and Simón Bolívar for international services. There are 11 international airports.

Regulatory Authority

Instituto Nacional de Aeronáutica Civil: Torre Británica, 2°–8°, Avda José Félix Sosa, Urb. Altamira Sur, Chacao, Caracas 1060; tel. (212) 267-5031; e-mail contacto@inac.gob.ve; internet www.inac.gob .ve; f. 2005; Pres. FRANCISCO JOSÉ PAZ FLEITAS; Dir GRISEL PEDRAZA.

National Airlines

Aeropostal (Alas de Venezuela): Torre Polar Oeste, 22°, Avda Paseo Colón, Plaza Venezuela, Los Caobos, Caracas 1051; tel. (212) 708-6211; fax (212) 782-6323; e-mail corporativa@aeropostal.com; internet www.aeropostal.com; f. 1933; privatized in 1996, acquired by Venezuelan/US consortium Corporación Alas de Venezuela; domestic services and flights to destinations in the Caribbean, South America and the USA; Pres. and CEO LUIS GRATEROL CARABALLO.

Aserca Airlines: Edif. Aserca Airlines, Avda Andrés Eloy Blanco, Calle 137-C, Urb. Prebo I, Valencia; tel. (241) 237-111; fax (241) 220-210; e-mail rsv@asercaairlines.com; internet www.asercaairlines .com; f. 1968; domestic services and flights to Caribbean destinations; Pres. SIMEÓN GARCÍA; Dir-Gen. ROBERTO JORGEZ.

Consorcio Venezolano de Industrias Aeronáutica y Servicios Aéreos, SA (CONVIASA): Aeropuerto Internacional de Maiquetía, Edif. Sector 6.3, Avda Intercomunal, Adyacente a Tránsito Terrestre, Maiquetia; tel. (212) 303-7332; e-mail mercadeo@conviasa.aero; internet www.conviasa.aero; f. 2004; state-owned; Pres. NICOLÁS SEIJAS ARRIETA.

LASER (Línea Aérea de Servicio Ejecutivo Regional, CA): Torre Bazar Bolívar, 8°, Avda Francisco de Miranda, El Marqués, Caracas; tel. (212) 202-0100; fax (212) 235-8359; internet www.laser.com.ve; f. 1994; scheduled and charter passenger and cargo services to domestic and international destinations; Pres. INOCENCIO ALVAREZ.

Línea Turística Aereotuy, CA: Edif. Gran Sábana, 5°, Blvd de Sábana Grande, Apdo 2923, Carmelitas, Caracas 1050; tel. (212) 761-6231; fax (212) 762-5254; e-mail tuysales@etheron.net; internet www.tuy.com; f. 1982; operates on domestic and international routes; Pres. JUAN CARLOS MÁRQUEZ.

Santa Barbara Airlines (SBA): Edif. Tokay, 3°, Calle 3-B, La Urbina, Caracas; tel. (212) 204-4400; fax (212) 242-3260; e-mail atc@ sbairlines.com; internet www.sbairlines.com; f. 1995; domestic and international services; Pres. ORLAN VILORIA.

Tourism

In 2011 Venezuela received an estimated 551,000 tourists. Receipts from tourism in 2010 amounted to a provisional US $739m. An estimated 90% of tourists visit the island of Margarita, while only 20% of tourists visit the mainland.

Asociación Venezolana de Agencias de Viajes y Turismo (AVAVIT): Avda 6, entre 6 y 7, Transversal, Quinta 17, Altamira, Caracas; tel. (212) 261-1845; fax (212) 261-0821; e-mail turvspecialtours@cantv.net; internet www.avavit.com; Pres. MARÍA LUCILA BELTRÁN.

Instituto Nacional de Turismo (INATUR): Edif. MINTUR, Avda Francisco de Miranda, con Avda Ppal de La Floresta, Municipio Chacao, Caracas; tel. (212) 208-4651; fax (212) 208-4652; e-mail inatur@inatur.gob.ve; internet www.inatur.gob.ve; f. 2001; govt tourism devt agency; Pres. ALEJANDRO FLEMING; Exec. Dir DAVID RIVAS.

Venezolana de Turismo, SA (VENETUR): Centro Empresarial Centro Plaza, Torre B, 16°, Los Palos Grandes, Caracas; tel. (212) 208-4812; fax (212) 208-8160; e-mail sugurencias@venetur.gob.ve; internet www.venetur.gob.ve; govt tourism promotion agency; Gen. Man. ANTONIO J MORILLO P.

Defence

As assessed at November 2012, the armed forces numbered 115,000 men: an army of 63,000, a navy of 17,500 (including an estimated 7,000 marines), an air force of 11,500 and a National Guard of 23,000. In October 2009 legal status was accorded to a fifth unit of the armed forces, the Bolivarian National Militia, and in February 2010 the creation was announced within the National Militia of a peasant force. There was also an army reserve numbering 8,000. Military service is selective and the length of service varies by region for all services. The President is Commander-in-Chief of the Armed Forces.

Defence Budget: 21,300m. bolívares in 2012.

Commander-General of the National Guard: Maj.-Gen. JUAN FRANCISCO ROMERO FIGUEROA.

Commander-General of the Navy: Adm. DIEGO ANTONIO GUERRA BARRETO.

Commander-General of the Army: Maj.-Gen. CARLOS ANTONIO ALCALÁ CORDONES.

Commander-General of the Air Force: Maj.-Gen. JOSÉ GREGORIO PÉREZ ESCALONA.

Commander-General of the Bolivarian National Militia: Maj.-Gen. GUSTAVO ENRIQUE GONZÁLEZ LÓPEZ.

Education

Primary education in Venezuela is free and compulsory between the ages of six and 15 years. Secondary education begins at the age of 15 years and lasts for a further two years. In 2009/10 enrolment at primary schools included 93% of children in the relevant age-group, while the equivalent ratio for secondary enrolment was 72% (males 68%; females 76%). In 2003/04 there were 48 universities. In 2003 the Government, with assistance from Cuba, initiated Misión Robinson, a project intended to eradicate illiteracy and innumeracy. Expenditure by the central Government on education was projected at an estimated 47,913m. bolívares in 2012.

VIET NAM

Introductory Survey

LOCATION, CLIMATE, LANGUAGE, RELIGION, FLAG, CAPITAL

The Socialist Republic of Viet Nam is situated in South-East Asia, bordered to the north by the People's Republic of China, to the west by Laos and Cambodia, and to the east by the South China Sea. The climate is humid during both the hot summer and the relatively cold winter, and there are monsoon rains in both seasons. Temperatures in Hanoi are generally between 13°C (55°F) and 33°C (91°F). The language is Vietnamese. The principal religion is Buddhism. There are also Daoist, Confucian, Hoa Hao, Caodaist and Christian (mainly Roman Catholic) minorities. The national flag (proportions 2 by 3) is red, with a large five-pointed yellow star in the centre. The capital is Hanoi.

CONTEMPORARY POLITICAL HISTORY

Historical Context

Cochin-China (the southernmost part of Viet Nam) became a French colony in 1867. Annam and Tonkin (central and northern Viet Nam) were proclaimed French protectorates in 1883. Later all three were merged with Cambodia and Laos to form French Indo-China. Throughout the French colonial period, but especially after 1920, nationalist and revolutionary groups operated in Viet Nam, the best organized of which was the Vietnamese Revolutionary Youth League, founded by Ho Chi Minh. The League was succeeded in 1930 by the Communist Party of Indo-China, also led by Ho Chi Minh.

In September 1940 Japanese forces began to occupy Viet Nam, although (Vichy) France retained administrative authority, and in June 1941 the nationalists formed the Viet Nam Doc Lap Dong Minh Hoi (Revolutionary League for the Independence of Viet Nam), or Viet Minh. In March 1945 French control was ended by a Japanese coup. Following Japan's surrender in August, Viet Minh forces entered Hanoi, and on 2 September the new regime proclaimed independence as the Democratic Republic of Viet Nam (DRV), with Ho Chi Minh as President. The Communist Party, formally dissolved in 1945, continued to be the dominant group within the Viet Minh Government. In March 1946, after French forces re-entered Viet Nam, an agreement between France and the DRV recognized Viet Nam as a 'free' state within the French Union. However, the DRV Government continued to seek complete independence. Negotiations with France broke down, and full-scale hostilities began in December 1946.

In March 1949 the French established the State of Viet Nam in the South. Meanwhile, in the North the Viet Minh was dissolved in 1951, and the Communists formed the Dang Lao Dong Viet Nam (Viet Nam Workers' Party), with Ho Chi Minh as Chairman of the Central Committee. After the defeat of French forces at Dien Bien Phu in May 1954, terms for a cease-fire were settled in Geneva, Switzerland. Agreements signed in July provided for the provisional partition of Viet Nam into two military zones, with French forces south of latitude 17°N and DRV forces in the north. Later in 1954 the French withdrew from South Viet Nam. Ngo Dinh Diem became Prime Minister of the State of Viet Nam, and in 1955, following a referendum, proclaimed himself President of the Republic of Viet Nam. He thereby deposed Bao Dai, Emperor of Viet Nam from 1932 until his forced abdication in 1945, who had become Head of the State of Viet Nam in 1949. (The former Emperor died in exile in France in 1997.) Ngo Dinh Diem refused to participate in elections envisaged by the Geneva agreement. In the DRV Ho Chi Minh was succeeded as Prime Minister by Pham Van Dong in 1955, but remained head of state and party Chairman.

Domestic Political Affairs

The anti-communist regime in the South was opposed by former members of the Viet Minh, who became known as the Viet Cong. Ngo Dinh Diem was overthrown by a coup in November 1963, and a series of short-lived military regimes held power until June 1965, when some stability was restored by the National Leadership Committee, with Lt-Gen. Nguyen Van Thieu as Chairman and Air Vice-Marshal Nguyen Cao Ky as Prime Minister. In 1967 Gen. Nguyen Van Thieu was elected President, with Marshal Nguyen Cao Ky as Vice-President; in 1971, after a division with the latter, the President was re-elected unopposed.

From 1959 the DRV actively assisted the insurgent movement in South Viet Nam, supporting the establishment there of the communist-dominated National Liberation Front (NLF) in December 1960. In 1961 the USA joined the war on the side of the anti-communist regime in the South, later bombing the North extensively from 1965 to 1968. In November 1968 peace talks between the four participants in the Viet Nam War began in Paris, France, but remained deadlocked as the fighting continued. In June 1969 the NLF formed the Provisional Revolutionary Government (PRG) in the South. Ho Chi Minh died in September 1969: he was succeeded as head of state by Ton Duc Thang, while political leadership passed to Le Duan, First Secretary of the Viet Nam Workers' Party since 1960.

In 1972 PRG and North Vietnamese forces launched a major offensive in South Viet Nam, and US bombing of the North was renewed with greater intensity. In January 1973 a peace agreement was finally signed in Paris, providing for a cease-fire in the South, the withdrawal of US forces, the eventual peaceful reunification of the whole country, and US aid to the Government in the North to assist in reconstruction. US troops withdrew, and in December 1974 combined PRG and North Vietnamese forces began a final offensive, taking the southern capital, Saigon, in April 1975. By May the new regime was in complete control of the South. While South Viet Nam, under the PRG, remained technically separate from the DRV, effective control of the whole country passed to Hanoi.

In July 1976 the country's reunification was proclaimed under the name of the Socialist Republic of Viet Nam, and Saigon was renamed Ho Chi Minh City. A new Government was appointed, dominated by members of the former Government of the DRV but including some members of the PRG. In December Le Duan was appointed General Secretary of the Communist Party of Viet Nam (CPV—formerly the Viet Nam Workers' Party). President Ton Duc Thang died in March 1980. A new Constitution was adopted in December of that year. Truong Chinh was appointed President of the Council of State (head of state) in July 1981, but real power remained with Le Duan, until his death in July 1986, whereupon he was succeeded as General Secretary of the CPV by Truong Chinh.

At the Sixth Communist Party Congress, held in December 1986, the country's three most senior leaders, Truong Chinh, Pham Van Dong and Le Duc Tho, announced their retirement from the party Political Bureau (Politburo). Truong Chinh and Pham Van Dong retained their respective posts as President of the Council of State and Chairman of the Council of Ministers (Prime Minister) until 1987, and Le Duc Tho continued to wield considerable political influence until his death in October 1990. The 1986 Congress appointed Nguyen Van Linh, a long-standing party official, as General Secretary of the Party.

In February 1987 an extensive government reorganization involved the dismissal of 12 ministers, as well as the merger or restructuring of several ministries, apparently with a view to the implementation of economic reforms. An election to the National Assembly took place in April. There were 829 candidates for the 496 seats (compared with 613 candidates at the previous election). In June the new Assembly elected Vo Chi Cong and Pham Hung, both former Vice-Chairmen of the Council of Ministers, to the posts of President of the Council of State and Chairman of the Council of Ministers, respectively. Although a veteran of the struggle with the South, and reputedly a strict conservative, Pham Hung gave his support to the programme of economic reform, referred to as *doi moi* (renovation), initiated by Nguyen Van Linh. The new liberalism of the regime was demonstrated by the release in September of 480 political prisoners from 're-education' camps, as part of an amnesty for more than 6,600 prisoners on the anniversary of independence from France in 1945. In February 1988 more than 1,000 political prisoners were released. In March Pham Hung died. The Council of State appointed Vo Van Kiet, a Vice-Chairman of the Council of Ministers and the Chairman of the State Commission for Planning, as acting Chairman of the Council of Ministers.

At the meeting of the National Assembly in June 1988, members from the South took the unprecedented step of nominating the reformist Vo Van Kiet to oppose the Central Committee's more conservative candidate, Do Muoi (ranked third in the Politburo), in the election for the chairmanship of the Council of Ministers. Do Muoi was elected to the position, but Vo Van Kiet received unexpectedly strong support. Despite his reputation, Do Muoi declared his commitment to the advancement of reform. Widespread dissatisfaction with the condition of the economy led to the removal of hundreds of cadres from government posts in a 'purification' of the party. In an attempt to improve international relations, and thus secure much-needed Western aid, Viet Nam amended its Constitution in December, removing derogatory references to the USA, the People's Republic of China, France and Japan. In March 1989 a reorganization of senior economic ministers adjusted the balance further towards reform and strengthened the position of Nguyen Van Linh.

Municipal elections to provincial and district councils took place in November 1989, in which candidates who were not members of the CPV were allowed to participate for the first time. In December the National Assembly approved legislation imposing new restrictions on the press: the appointment of editors became subject to government approval, and journalists were required to reveal sources of information on request. Open dissension towards CPV policy also became a criminal offence.

In the second half of 1990 the Government dismissed or brought charges against more than 18,000 officials, in an attempt to eradicate corruption. In December the Central Committee produced draft political and economic reports, reaffirming the party's commitment to socialism and to the process of economic liberalization, which were to be submitted to the next Party Congress. In the same month Bui Tin, the deputy editor of the official organ of the CPV, *Nhan Dan*, criticized government policy. He was subsequently expelled from the Politburo and dismissed as deputy editor. Following a request by the Central Committee for public comment on the reports, in early 1991 the party journal, *Tap Chi Cong San* (Communist Review), published articles by prominent intellectuals that severely criticized the reports and questioned the effectiveness of the socialist system. The CPV subsequently increased surveillance of dissidents and instructed the press to publish retaliatory articles condemning party critics. In June the Communist Party Congress approved the reports. It elected Do Muoi to replace Nguyen Van Linh as General Secretary of the Party; seven members of the Politburo were removed from their posts, including Nguyen Van Linh, although he, together with Pham Van Dong and the President of the Council of State, Vo Chi Cong, remained in the Central Committee in an advisory capacity. At a session of the National Assembly held in late July and early August, the reformist Vo Van Kiet was elected to replace Do Muoi as Chairman of the Council of Ministers.

A new draft Constitution was published in December 1991 and, after being reviewed in public discussions, was adopted by the National Assembly in April 1992. Like the previous (1980) Constitution, it emphasized the central role of the CPV; however, the new document stipulated that the party must be subject to the law. While affirming adherence to a state-regulated socialist economy, the new Constitution guaranteed protection for foreign investment in Viet Nam, and permitted foreign travel and overseas investment for Vietnamese. Land was to remain the property of the State, although the right was granted to procure long-term leases, which could be inherited or sold. The National Assembly was to be reduced in number, but was to have greater power. The Council of State was to be replaced by a single President as head of state, to be responsible for appointing (subject to the approval of the National Assembly) a Prime Minister and senior members of the judiciary. The new Constitution was to enter into effect after the July 1992 general election.

The ninth National Assembly, 1992–97

In July 1992 a total of 601 candidates contested 395 seats in the National Assembly. Almost 90% were members of the CPV: although independent candidates (i.e. not endorsed by the Viet Nam Fatherland Front—the grouping of mass organizations, such as trade unions, affiliated to the CPV) were for the first time permitted to seek election, in the event only two were deemed to qualify, and neither was elected.

At the first session of the ninth National Assembly, in September 1992, the conservative Gen. Le Duc Anh (a member of the Politburo and a former Minister of Defence) was elected to the new post of executive President. Vo Van Kiet was appointed

Prime Minister (the equivalent of his former post) by the Assembly in October. Only four ministers, all of whom had been implicated in corruption scandals, were not reappointed. In January 1994 four new members were appointed to the Politburo, including the Minister of Foreign Affairs, Nguyen Manh Cam, and 20 new members (all under the age of 55) were elected to the CPV's Central Committee. In June the National Assembly approved a labour law that guaranteed the right to strike (providing that the 'social life of the community' was not adversely affected). Strikes followed in some southern provinces, and in August the first incident of industrial action in Hanoi was reported. At the fourth Congress of the Fatherland Front, in August, a new, 200-member Central Committee was elected. Elections to provincial and district councils took place during December 1994.

Meanwhile, there was no tolerance of political dissent, and a series of convictions of pro-democracy activists was reported during 1993–95, including two former prominent members of the CPV, Do Trung Hieu and Hoang Minh Chinh, who in November 1995 were sentenced to custodial terms on charges of damaging national security after criticizing government policy. In October 1995 the National Assembly adopted an extensive civil code (drafted over a period of 10 years), guaranteeing the rights of the individual and enshrining existing rights concerning land usage and inheritance of property.

In April 1996 the Vice-Chairman of the National Assembly was dismissed from the Politburo and from the CPV; it was reported that he had been accused of treason in connection with the Viet Nam War. In June the Congress elected a new, 170-member Central Committee and an expanded (19-member) Politburo. A five-member Standing Board, which included Do Muoi, Le Duc Anh and Vo Van Kiet, was created. In November 12 ministers were dismissed in an extensive reorganization of the Government (as the Council of Ministers had become known under the 1992 Constitution).

In December 1996 the Politburo issued a directive requiring the establishment of CPV cells in all foreign-invested enterprises. In January 1997 an unprecedentedly high-profile corruption case was brought to trial: the case involved former senior officials of Tamexco (an import-export company owned by the CPV), along with officials from Vietcombank (the state foreign trade bank) and the financial sector. The 20 defendants were accused of a range of financial crimes, principally embezzlement of socialist property. In late January four death sentences were pronounced, together with one sentence of life imprisonment, two suspended sentences and a combined total of 103 years' imprisonment for the remaining defendants. In February a judge of the Supreme People's Court was sentenced to two years' imprisonment, having been found to have abused a position of influence for personal gain, and was thus the first member of Viet Nam's judiciary to be convicted of corruption.

In May 1997 substantial amendments to the criminal code were approved by the National Assembly in respect of corruption, bribery, child abuse and drugs-trafficking. The acceptance of bribes in excess of 50m. đông, and possession of 5 kg of opium or 100 g of heroin, became crimes punishable by death or life imprisonment; increased penalties were introduced for first-time offenders in cases of corruption. In the same month a group of 22 people, including police, customs and border officials, stood trial for drugs-trafficking: all were convicted, with eight sentenced to death and eight to life imprisonment. In July, following what was reported as Viet Nam's first terrorism trial, two people were sentenced to death, and three others to life imprisonment, having been convicted of involvement in a bomb attack in Ho Chi Minh City in October 1994. Official reports stated that the defendants were members of the National Resistance Front for the Restoration of Viet Nam, which was alleged to have issued death threats to foreign nationals who had established businesses in Viet Nam.

The 10th National Assembly, 1997–2002

Elections to the 10th National Assembly took place on 20 July 1997. A record 663 candidates contested 450 seats (expanded from 395 seats). Under a modified selection process, 112 non-CPV members registered as potential candidates. However, following rigorous screening procedures, only 11 independent ('self-nominated') candidates qualified to contest the elections, of whom three secured seats in the Assembly. Do Muoi was among senior figures who did not seek re-election, and, in total, fewer than one-third of the members of the outgoing Assembly returned to office. At the first session of the new National Assembly in September, Tran Duc Luong, hitherto a Deputy

Prime Minister, was elected as President in succession to Le Duc Anh, who, owing to continued ill health, did not seek re-election. The Assembly subsequently endorsed the appointment of Nguyen Thi Binh as Vice-President, Nong Duc Manh as Chairman of the National Assembly Standing Committee, and Phan Van Khai as Prime Minister. (Vo Van Kiet had also stepped down.) A cabinet reorganization was approved at the end of September: the new administration included an increased number of Deputy Prime Ministers, each of whom held a wide portfolio of responsibilities.

In December 1997 Le Kha Phieu, a member of the new Standing Board and widely seen as a conservative, was elected to succeed Do Muoi as General Secretary of the Central Committee of the CPV. At the same time Do Muoi, Le Duc Anh and Vo Van Kiet resigned from the Politburo; all three were subsequently appointed as advisers to the Central Committee. Four new members were elected to the Politburo, and in January 1998 the election by the Politburo of a new Standing Board, comprising Le Kha Phieu, Tran Duc Luong, Phan Van Khai, Nong Duc Manh and Pham The Duyet, was announced. The new appointments were widely perceived to reflect the consolidation of the conservative tendency within the leadership, to the detriment of reformists, among them the Prime Minister.

In March 1998 the CPV announced that during 1997 it had disciplined and expelled some 18,000 members, and sentenced 469 to terms of imprisonment. Further members of the party were reported to have been disciplined over corruption-related offences in July 1998. In the same month more than 30 people were sentenced to gaol terms for their involvement in violent unrest in the northern province of Thai Binh in mid-1997, during which hundreds of farmers had protested against local corruption and taxes.

In a general amnesty announced by the Government to mark Viet Nam's National Day on 2 September 1998, more than 5,000 prisoners, including four of the country's most prominent dissidents—Doan Viet Hoat, Nguyen Dan Que, Thich Quang Do and Thich Tue Sy—were released from detention (although the liberation of at least two of the dissidents was reported to be dependent upon their immediate exile from Viet Nam). In October amnesty was granted to a further 2,630 prisoners. In the same month the former editor-in-chief of *Doanh Nghiep*, Nguyen Hoang Linh, was convicted of 'abusing freedom and democratic rights to violate the interests of the State', following the publication in his newspaper of articles detailing alleged government corruption; Linh was sentenced to more than 12 months' imprisonment, but, having already been detained for that length of time while awaiting trial, was released almost immediately. Following a visit to Viet Nam, also in October, to investigate assertions made by the Vietnamese authorities that greater freedom of religious expression was being afforded in the country, the Special Rapporteur on religious intolerance of the UN Commission on Human Rights, Abdelfattah Amor, stated that his investigation had been obstructed by government officials and that he had been prevented from meeting key religious dissidents.

In January 1999 the CPV leadership announced that it had expelled Gen. (retd) Tran Do from the party in response to his explicit criticism of the establishment. His expulsion caused renewed speculation about party divisions, and also set the precedent for the continued suppression of political dissent. In March a prominent writer and geophysicist, Nguyen Thanh Giang, whose critiques of the CPV were reported to have been widely disseminated both within Viet Nam and abroad, was arrested on the grounds of 'propagandizing against the socialist regime'; he was released in May, but reportedly remained under house arrest. In September the trial opened of 24 members of the dissident People's Action Party, charged with 'exiting the country illegally for the purpose of undermining the people's administration'; all 24 defendants were subsequently convicted and sentenced to terms of imprisonment ranging from two to 20 years.

The issue of corruption remained a major source of concern for the CPV. The trial of 74 people accused of smuggling (more than one-half of whom were reported to be former government officials) opened in March 1999, with two of the defendants later being sentenced to death, and the remainder to terms of imprisonment. In May 77 businessmen, bankers and government officials appeared in court charged with the fraudulent procurement of state loans; in August six of the defendants were sentenced to death (although two of these subsequently had their sentences commuted to life imprisonment), and the remainder to

various terms of imprisonment. In December Deputy Prime Minister Ngo Xuan Loc was dismissed from the Cabinet following his implication in a corrupt land deal related to a private sector project. However, in April 2000 he was reinstated to a government post and resumed responsibility for the sectors related to the accusations against him, prompting speculation as to the credibility of the Government's commitment to eliminate corruption. In September 2001 eight officials were tried on charges of fraud in Hanoi in connection with the land deal. One businessman received a 20-year prison sentence; the remaining defendants were either released or sentenced to prison terms of nine months or less.

The Ninth Party Congress was held in April 2001, and resulted in the election of a new 150-member Central Committee, 15-member Politburo and nine-member Secretariat. Nong Duc Manh was appointed General Secretary, replacing Le Kha Phieu, who had resigned under pressure from the Central Committee, after being accused of using military intelligence against party members and of slowing the pace of reforms. Nong Duc Manh, who was rumoured to be the illegitimate son of Ho Chi Minh, was the first ethnic Tay to attain such a senior position. Some 84 members of the previous Central Committee were re-elected. President Tran Duc Luong and Prime Minister Phan Van Khai retained their party posts, but former President Le Duc Anh, former Prime Minister Vo Van Kiet and former General Secretary Do Muoi lost their positions as senior advisers to the Central Committee upon the abolition of the posts. In June 2001 Nguyen Van An, a member of the Politburo, was elected to the chairmanship of the National Assembly, succeeding Nong Duc Manh. In December the National Assembly approved several constitutional amendments, including one allowing politicians to instigate mid-term votes of no confidence if they considered any minister to be performing unsatisfactorily.

Meanwhile, in March 2001 the authorities denounced a Catholic priest, Father Nguyen Van Ly, for writing to the US Congress and urging it not to ratify a bilateral trade agreement, owing to human rights abuses in Viet Nam. In October Nguyen Van Ly was sentenced to 15 years in prison after a court convicted him of undermining national unity and contravening a detention order. (His sentence was reduced by five years in July 2003 and by a further five years in June 2004, and in February 2005 he was released from prison, having been granted amnesty. However, he was imprisoned again in March 2007—see The 11th National Assembly, 2002–07.) Exiled Vietnamese Buddhist leaders also claimed that their followers in Viet Nam were routinely harassed. In September 2001 Ho Tan Anh, leader of the Buddhist Youth Movement, burnt himself to death in protest at the restrictions that had been imposed upon his organization. It was reported in January 2002 that the CPV had approved a decree authorizing the police to destroy publications that had not been approved by the party. Books written by several leading dissidents, including Gen. Tran Do, had subsequently been destroyed.

In March 2002 the CPV decided that it would formally permit its members to engage in private business, indicating the Government's desire to encourage the expansion of the role of the private sector within the economy. In the same month the Politburo was reported to have established a special investigation into allegations that more than 50 government officials had colluded in organized crime. Several of those accused were reported to have accepted bribes to protect a gang whose alleged leader, Truong Van Cam, known as Nam Cam, was undergoing investigation on murder charges. As the investigation proceeded, more than 100 government officials and an estimated 50 police officers were implicated; two members of the Central Committee (the Director-General of the state radio station Voice of Viet Nam, Tran Mai Hanh, and Pham Sy Chien) were expelled from the CPV in July owing to their involvement. In November the Deputy Minister of Public Security, Maj.-Gen. Haong Ngoc Nhat, was dismissed from his position and demoted in rank, owing to his alleged complicity. In January 2003 the director of the Economic Commission of the Politburo, Truong Tan San, became the most senior member of the CPV to be punished in relation to the investigation; he was formally reprimanded for 'dereliction of duty' during his tenure as secretary of the party in Ho Chi Minh City in 1996–2000. Meanwhile, in May 2002 59 people charged with embezzling state assets and violating commercial law in connection with the Chinese-owned Viet Hoa bank were found guilty of the charges against them; 43 were sentenced to prison terms, while the remainder were given suspended sentences.

The 11th National Assembly, 2002–07

Elections to the 11th National Assembly took place on 19 May 2002. The 498 seats available were contested by 759 candidates, only 13 of whom were independent. Non-CPV candidates won 51 seats and independents two, the remainder being secured by party members. In July and August the newly elected National Assembly held its first session, during which significant reorganizations of both the Standing Committee and the Cabinet were approved. Three new ministries were created as part of the extensive reorganization, in which Vu Khoan, the former Minister of Trade, was promoted to the position of Deputy Prime Minister. President Tran Duc Luong, Prime Minister Phan Van Khai and the Chairman of the National Assembly, Nguyen Van An, were all formally re-elected to their posts, while Truong My Hoa succeeded Nguyen Thi Binh as Vice-President.

At the Seventh Plenum of the Central Committee of the CPV held in January 2003, a resolution intended to increase the party's control over religious affairs was approved. In February the trial of Nam Cam and 154 other defendants on a number of charges, including murder, organized gambling, bribery, drugs-trafficking and extortion, began in Ho Chi Minh City. Among the defendants were 21 former state and government officials. In June Nam Cam was convicted of all the charges against him and sentenced to death, while a number of other defendants were also found guilty, including Tran Mai Hanh, who received a 10-year prison term, and Pham Sy Chien, who was to serve a six-year sentence; five were given death sentences. In June 2004 Nam Cam and four of his co-defendants were executed by firing squad, the death sentence of the fifth having been commuted to life imprisonment.

In November 2003 the trial opened in Hanoi of two former junior agriculture ministers, Nguyen Thien Luan and Nguyen Quang Ha, together with La Thi Kim Oanh, the former director of a company controlled by the Ministry of Agriculture and Rural Development, and five other officials, on embezzlement charges. The opening of the trial was televised as part of the Government's ongoing campaign to combat corruption. In December all those tried were found guilty of the charges against them. La Thi Kim Oanh was sentenced to death, while the remaining defendants received prison sentences. In June 2004 the National Assembly approved the dismissal of the Minister of Agriculture and Development, Le Huy Ngo, on the grounds that he had failed adequately to monitor his subordinates and organizations under his administration in connection with the embezzlement case; he was replaced by Cao Duc Phat.

Meanwhile, the suppression of dissent continued unabated, with the imposition of prison terms on a number of pro-democracy activists during 2002–04. Prominent convictions included that in March 2003 of the dissident Nguyen Dan Que, who had been released from prison five years previously, having spent over 18 years in detention; Nguyen was rearrested after publishing an essay on the internet concerning Viet Nam's control of the media. (In July 2004 Nguyen was sentenced to a 30-month prison term, but he was released in February 2005 under a government amnesty—see below.)

In April 2003 Prime Minister Phan Van Khai held talks with Thich Huyen Quang, leader of the anti-Government Unified Buddhist Church of Viet Nam, who had been held under house arrest since the group was proscribed almost 20 years previously. In May Thich Huyen Quang was permitted to meet with his deputy, Thich Quang Do, for only the third time in 21 years. In June Thich Quang Do was released from house arrest, two months before the end of his two-year sentence. In November both the US House of Representatives and the European Parliament approved resolutions condemning the continuing official repression of non-recognized religious organizations in Viet Nam and appealing for the release of Thich Huyen Quang. In March 2004 police arrested four members of the Mennonite Church, which was not officially recognized by the Government, after scuffles broke out when a number of Mennonites attempted to photograph police officers who were posted outside the headquarters of the Church. In June Nguyen Hong Quang, the Secretary-General of the Mennonite Church in Viet Nam, was also arrested for his involvement in the incident, and a sixth church member was detained the following month. In November Nguyen Hong Quang was sentenced to three years' imprisonment for preventing officials from carrying out their duties, while the five other defendants received custodial sentences of between nine months and two years.

In July 2004 the Minister of Posts and Telecommunications, Do Trung Ta, issued new regulations aimed at controlling access to the internet by allowing internet service providers to suspend contracts with cafés that allowed customers to view pornographic websites or those deemed to threaten national security. In August a special police unit was established to combat internet crime and prevent the spread of banned materials. In November the National Assembly approved new legislation on national security, which stipulated the principles of security policy and the powers and responsibilities of the agencies in charge of national security. The implementation in the same month of an Ordinance on Beliefs and Religions was condemned by a coalition of non-recognized Protestant churches; the new law, while upholding the right of citizens to freedom of religious belief, decreed that only state-authorized clergy be entitled to preach (and only within defined territorial jurisdictions), and also provided for the suspension of religious activities that were deemed to jeopardize national security, public order or national unity. In February 2005 it was reported that the Government had issued a decree allowing outlawed Protestant churches to operate if they renounced connections to the United Front for the Liberation of Oppressed Races (FULRO—a guerrilla unit that had close links with the US military and the Central Intelligence Agency during the Viet Nam War).

Details emerged in September 2004 of a major corruption scandal in which local textile companies had been allegedly obliged to pay large bribes to trade officials in order to secure export quotas to the USA. Some 19 people were subsequently arrested in connection with the case; the most prominent of these was Deputy Minister of Trade Mai Van Dau, who was charged with abuse of power and dismissed from the Government in November. Mai Van Dau's trial was conducted in March 2007: the former Deputy Minister of Trade was convicted of receiving bribes and sentenced to 14 years' imprisonment (subsequently reduced to 12 years), while 12 other defendants received sentences ranging from one year to 17 years.

In January 2005 the Government announced that 8,323 prisoners, including six political dissidents and 33 foreigners, were to be released in an amnesty to mark Tet (the lunar New Year). In March, however, the Government issued a decree that increased restrictions on demonstrations and banned unauthorized gatherings. It was reported that the decree required the approval in advance of all gatherings not organized by the CPV or state organs. In November the National Assembly ratified a long-awaited Anti-Corruption Law, which required all officials and their close relatives to disclose fully their assets. There was considerable scepticism as to how effectively this would be enforced, especially in view of the protection given to the authorities by state control of the media. In the previous month the deputy head of the State Inspectorate's department of economic inspection, Luong Cao Khai, was arrested, following allegations that he had accepted bribes and had abused his position to provide relatives with employment; in November 2007 he was convicted of the charges against him and sentenced to 21 years' imprisonment, while two other former senior officials from the State Inspectorate received shorter custodial terms for accepting bribes.

In April 2006 the Minister of Transport and Communications, Dao Dinh Binh, tendered his resignation from the Cabinet, following allegations concerning an apparent misappropriation of state funds by staff members within his ministry. It was claimed that officials had stolen money allocated to construction projects and had accepted numerous bribes. Dao Dinh Binh announced that he would accept full responsibility for the actions of those employed in his ministry. The Deputy Minister of Transport and Communications, Nguyen Viet Tien, was arrested in connection with the embezzlement of state funds. In August 2007 eight people were sentenced to between seven and 13 years' imprisonment for their involvement in the scandal, while a ninth defendant received a suspended two-year term. Criminal charges against Nguyen Viet Tien were withdrawn in March 2008.

The 10th CPV Congress was held in April 2006, during which elections were held for a new 160-member Central Committee, 14-member Politburo and eight-member Secretariat. Nong Duc Manh was retained as General Secretary of the Party; five other members of the previous Politburo also secured re-election. President Tran Duc Luong, Prime Minister Phan Van Khai and Chairman of the National Assembly Standing Committee, Nguyen Van An, all announced that they were to resign, thus allowing a younger generation of officials to assume prominent positions within the party leadership. The Congress reaffirmed its commitment to socialism, announced its aim of Viet Nam achieving the status of a developed country by 2020 and adopted the Report and Five-Year Plan of Action on Socio-economic Development Goals for 2006–10. In June 2006, at its annual session, the National Assembly formally approved the resignations of Tran Duc Luong, Phan Van Khai and Nguyen Van An. Phan Van Kai's nominee, Nguyen Tan Dung, was confirmed as Prime Minister, while Nguyen Minh Triet succeeded Tran Duc Luong as President. Nguyen Phu Trong was elected Chairman of the National Assembly Standing Committee. Soon after, a cabinet reorganization was approved: among the new appointees were Truong Vinh Trong as Deputy Prime Minister and Lt-Gen. Phung Quang Thanh as Minister of National Defence, while Deputy Prime Minister Pham Gia Khiem took additional charge of the foreign affairs portfolio.

In October 2006 the Central Steering Committee for Corruption Prevention and Control, chaired by Nguyen Tan Dung, was created to oversee and co-ordinate national anti-corruption operations, and was afforded the power to suspend government officials for unlawful practices. In November the Government was reported to have established a department to address the issue of corruption, as part of the General Directorate of Police, with links to the Ministry of Public Security.

Meanwhile, in August 2006 thousands of prisoners were freed under an amnesty to commemorate National Day in the following month. In November seven people, three of them US nationals, were convicted on terrorism charges and sentenced to 15 months' imprisonment. In the same month the USA's decision to remove Viet Nam from its list of 'countries of particular concern' in relation to religious freedom provoked criticism from the dissident Thich Quang Do. Although the decision recognized the country's progress towards greater religious freedom, reports of cases against dissidents continued: in March 2007 the Catholic priest Father Nguyen Van Ly was convicted of disseminating information against the State and sentenced to eight years' imprisonment. None the less, relations between the Vietnamese Government and the Roman Catholic Church were improving. In January 2007 Nguyen Tan Dung became the first Vietnamese Prime Minister to visit the Vatican, where he held talks with Pope Benedict XVI, and in March a delegation from the Vatican visited Viet Nam to discuss the possibility of establishing full diplomatic relations. Moreover, during 2007 the Government's Committee for Religious Affairs granted operating licences to several additional religions, including the Mennonite Church, the Baptist Church and the Bahá'í faith.

The 12th National Assembly, 2007–11

Elections to the 12th National Assembly held on 20 May 2007 were contested by 875 candidates, including 30 independents. Of the 493 deputies elected, only one was an independent, while a further 42 were non-CPV members. A high turn-out, of 99.6%, was recorded. The first session of the newly elected National Assembly commenced in July. Nguyen Minh Triet, Nguyen Tan Dung and Nguyen Phu Trong were all re-elected to their respective positions as President, Prime Minister and Chairman of the National Assembly Standing Committee, while Nguyen Thi Doan succeeded Truong My Hoa as Vice-President. In August the National Assembly endorsed a cabinet reorganization, which included a reduction in the number of ministries from 26 to 22 and the appointment of Hoang Trung Hai and Nguyen Thien Nhan, both relatively young and with economic backgrounds, as additional Deputy Prime Ministers (joining Nguyen Sinh Hung, Pham Gia Khiem and Truong Vinh Trong), with Nguyen Thien Nhan also remaining Minister of Education and Training. The incumbent Ministers of National Defence, Public Security, Finance and Foreign Affairs all remained in the Cabinet, while new appointees were allocated responsibility for some of the less strategic portfolios. A reduction in the term of the 12th National Assembly from five years to four years was also approved.

Meanwhile, hundreds of peasant farmers from the Mekong River Delta protested in Ho Chi Minh City in July 2007 against the seizure of their land and alleged abuse of legislation on land usage by local government officials; a smaller demonstration also took place in Hanoi. Deputy Prime Minister Truong Vinh Trong urged local leaders to conduct a swift investigation into the farmers' complaints.

An apparent intensification of government efforts to suppress dissident activity became evident from mid-2007, with a series of reported arrests of pro-democracy activists. In May several activists were convicted of spreading propaganda intended to undermine the State, including two human rights lawyers, Nguyen Van Dai and Le Thi Cong Nhan, who were sentenced to terms of five years and four years, respectively; both were also

to serve four years and three years under house arrest subsequent to their release from prison. The sentence of both lawyers was reduced by one year on appeal in November. (Le Thi Cong Nhan and Nguyen Van Dai were released, as scheduled, in March 2010 and March 2011, respectively, and placed under house arrest.)

In July 2008 thousands of people attended the funeral of Thich Huyen Quang, the leader of the outlawed Unified Buddhist Church of Viet Nam. The authorities, under international pressure, had permitted the ceremony to proceed despite having earlier condemned the dissident's supporters as 'extremist elements disguised as Buddhist monks'. In October the mayor of Hanoi, Nguyen The Thao, appealed for the dismissal of the Archbishop of Hanoi, Joseph Ngo Quang Kiet, amid a dispute over two pieces of land in the capital that the Church claimed to own. Church officials asserted that the State had illegally confiscated the land in 1954 after independence from France and that they had documentation proving continuing church ownership of the land; for its part, the Government stated that the land had been officially signed over to the city authorities in 1962 and that the disputed areas were now public parks. In March 2009 seven Roman Catholics, who had taken part in demonstrations in Hanoi in August and September in the previous year to protest against the Government's alleged confiscation of the land, received suspended prison sentences of between 12 and 15 months on charges of public order offences and damage to public property. (Ngo Quang Kiet tendered his resignation as Archbishop in early 2010, with effect from May of that year, amid speculation that the Vietnamese Government had made his relinquishment of the post a precondition for establishing full diplomatic relations with the Vatican.)

In October 2008 an investigative journalist, Nguyen Viet Chien, who worked for the daily newspaper *Thanh Nien*, was sentenced to two years' imprisonment, after being found guilty of 'abusing freedom and democratic rights' during his investigation into the 2006 government corruption case involving the Ministry of Transport and Communications. Another journalist, Nguyen Van Hai of the daily *Tuoi Tre*, was sentenced to two years' re-education without detention on the same charges. Although the Vietnamese press remained generally deferential to the authorities, the Government's treatment of the two journalists prompted unprecedented criticism from the Vietnamese media on the grounds that it would discourage further action against corruption. The issue of government corruption came to the fore again in January 2009 when the former Deputy Chief of the Government Office, Vu Dinh Thuan, was charged with embezzlement and abuse of power. Vu Dinh Thuan had been in charge of the so-called Project 112, a flawed plan to computerize Viet Nam's administrative system that had been abandoned in April 2007, and, together with the project secretary, Luong Cao Son, was alleged to have misappropriated some 1,000m. dông of allocated funds. Both men were convicted in January 2010; Vu Dinh Thuan was sentenced to five years' imprisonment on charges of 'abuse of power', while Luong Cao Son, who was deemed to have been the main instigator of the crime, was sentenced to a six-year prison term, as was Nguyen Thuy Ha, the director of an information and technology company. A further 20 defendants were also convicted of involvement in the scandal, and received sentences of between 18 months' probation and 30 months' imprisonment.

Further convictions of dissidents during 2009–11 included that of prominent human rights lawyer Le Cong Dinh, who in January 2010 was convicted of subversion, together with three other pro-democracy activists, having been found to have colluded with 'Vietnamese reactionary groups and hostile forces in exile'; Le Cong Dinh, who had been arrested in June 2009 after writing an article in which he had questioned government plans for a bauxite mining operation by a Chinese company in the Central Highlands region, was sentenced to five years' imprisonment, while his three co-defendants received prison terms ranging from five to 16 years. Other prominent convictions included those of Tran Anh Kim, a former army officer who had confessed to joining the outlawed Democratic Party of Viet Nam, on charges of 'working to overthrow the people's administration', for which he was sentenced to five-and-a-half years' imprisonment in December 2009, and of Vi Duc Hoi, a former member of the CPV who had been expelled from the party in 2007 after urging democratic reforms, on the charge of disseminating propaganda against the State following appeals for the introduction of political pluralism, for which he was imprisoned for eight years (to be followed by five years under house arrest) in January 2011.

Meanwhile, following repeated pleas by Western governments and international human rights organizations, Father Nguyen Van Ly was released from prison in March 2010, having been granted a one-year suspension of his sentence owing to the deteriorating state of his health. Despite the launching of campaigns by a number of rights groups, including Amnesty International, to prevent the return to prison of Father Nguyen, he was taken into custody again in July 2011 to serve the remainder of his sentence, amid claims by the Vietnamese authorities that he had been distributing anti-Government material.

In its annual global report published in January 2011, Human Rights Watch urged the US Government to return Viet Nam to its list of 'countries of particular concern' with regard to religious freedoms, alleging that the Vietnamese Government continued to harass peaceful worshippers of religions other than those officially recognized by the State. In February prominent human rights activist Nguyen Dan Que was again arrested, on charges of 'directly violating the stability and strength of the people's government', after posting a message on an internet forum in which he urged opponents of the Government to stage a popular revolution akin to those that had successfully overthrown the respective regimes of Tunisia and Egypt earlier in the year. Following widespread criticism from local and international rights organizations, including Amnesty International, the pro-democracy dissident, who had appealed for 'a new, free, democratic, humane and progressive Viet Nam', was released on bail a few days later. Three US citizens of Vietnamese origin, all members of the outlawed US-based Viet Tan (Vietnam Reform Party—the stated aim of which was to promote democratic reform in Viet Nam through peaceful means, although it was branded a terrorist organization by the Vietnamese state media), were arrested in Ho Chi Minh City in March after attending a peaceful protest against state corruption and land rights; all three were released without charge by the end of the month. In April Cu Huy Ha Vu, a prominent dissident whose father had been a cabinet minister during the presidency of Ho Chi Minh, was sentenced to seven years' imprisonment (to be followed by a three-year period of house arrest) upon his conviction on charges of disseminating anti-State propaganda; Cu Huy Ha Vu had advocated an end to communist rule and the establishment of a multi-party system. An appeal lodged subsequently against his sentence was rejected in August.

Meanwhile, the 11th CPV Congress was held in January 2011, during which a new 175-member Central Committee (with an additional 25 alternate members), a 14-member Politburo and a 10-member Secretariat were elected. The inclusion within the new Central Committee of a higher proportion of representatives from provincial areas engendered some hope that the issue of growing income disparity between urban and rural areas across Viet Nam might be afforded greater prominence during the coming five-year period. Prime Minister Nguyen Tan Dung was reappointed to the Politburo, as was Truong Tan Sang (a member of the Politburo since 1996). Truong Tan Sang secured the most senior position within the Politburo ahead of Prime Minister Nguyen, amid concerns about the latter's management of the economy, thus preparing the way for Truong Tan Sang's formal confirmation as President at the inaugural session of the new National Assembly, which was due to be convened in July 2011 (see The 13th National Assembly). Seven other members of the previous Politburo were also re-elected. Nguyen Phu Trong was elected General Secretary of the Party, in place of Nong Duc Manh, who had previously announced his resignation from the position; Nguyen Phu Trong relinquished his previous position as Chairman of the National Assembly Standing Committee. Four new members were elected to the Secretariat. During the Congress, national strategies on socio-economic development for 2011–20, and on political policies and tasks for 2011–15, were adopted; party leaders acknowledged that the issue of public corruption and abuse of power had significantly constrained the pace of national development and needed effectively to be addressed to ensure strong economic performance.

The 13th National Assembly

Elections for the 500 seats of the 13th National Assembly (for the period 2011–16) were held on 22 May 2011. Of the 827 candidates, 15 were independent candidates, while a further 117 were non-CPV members. None the less, more than 90% of incoming legislators were reported to be members of the CPV; 42 non-party candidates, including four independents, were elected. Some 122 seats were secured by female candidates, while 78 seats were won by candidates from ethnic minority groups. The inaugural session of the new National Assembly was convened in mid-July. A few days later the Assembly formally elected Truong Tan Sang as President, in place of the retiring Nguyen Minh Triet. In his inaugural address to the legislature, President Truong Tan Sang pledged to work towards facilitating the development of Viet Nam into an industrialized and modernized country by 2020. On the following day Nguyen Tan Dung and Nguyen Thi Doan were duly reconfirmed as Prime Minister and Vice-President, respectively, while Nguyen Sinh Hung was appointed as the new Chairman of the National Assembly.

Prime Minister Nguyen Tan Dung's new Cabinet was approved by the National Assembly in August 2011. The 26-member Cabinet comprised 15 new ministers, the majority of whom were known supporters of Nguyen Tan Dung; the new appointees included Pham Binh Minh, who was named Minister of Foreign Affairs; Nguyen Thai Binh, who was awarded the home affairs portfolio; and Vuong Dinh Hue, who was designated as Minister of Finance in place of Vu Van Ninh, who was in turn promoted to the position of deputy premier, together with Nguyen Xuan Phuc, hitherto Director of the Government Office. Nguyen Thien Nhan and Hoang Trung Hai remained deputy premiers, while Gen. Phung Quang Thanh and Ha Hung Cuong retained responsibility for the national defence and justice portfolios, respectively.

Meanwhile, in early May 2011 thousands of ethnic Hmong protesters staged a rare demonstration in the north-western province of Dien Bien, appealing for greater autonomy, land rights and religious freedoms. The unrest, which the authorities alleged to have been fomented by 'external elements', was quashed after several days, following the deployment of troops to the vicinity. It was claimed later that month that around 63 Hmong had been killed during the suppression of the protests. Although the Government acknowledged that some Hmong had died, it denied the use of excessive force, insisting that the deaths had been as a result of 'unhygienic conditions'. At the end of May seven pro-democracy activists and land rights campaigners, of whom several were alleged to be members of the outlawed Viet Tan, were sentenced to prison terms ranging between two and eight years upon their conviction on charges of 'working to overthrow the people's administration'. In August four of the seven dissidents lodged appeals against their sentences. Earlier in August Pham Minh Hoang, a French-Vietnamese professor, was sentenced to a three-year prison term upon his conviction on the charge of attempting to overthrow the Government. Pham Minh Hoang had been arrested for writing articles in his personal internet journal ('blog') in which he had criticized aspects of Vietnamese society and had appealed for democratic reforms. During his trial, Pham admitted to having joined Viet Tan, but maintained that he had become a member in France, where Viet Tan was not a proscribed organization, and stressed that his writings had not been intended to undermine the Government. At the end of August the Government announced that 10,535 prisoners (including 11 foreign nationals and five prisoners convicted of national security violations) were to be released in an amnesty to mark National Day on 2 September.

Reports emerged in September 2011 that nine senior executives of the state-owned ship-building company Vinashin, which in December 2010 had defaulted on debts of US $4,500m., had been arrested on suspicion of violating government regulations that had led to the accumulation of the massive debt. Pham Thanh Binh, former Chairman of Vinashin, was among those detained. A report issued in March 2012 by a government-appointed team of inspectors determined that 16 former Vinashin officials were implicated in the financial debacle, while the Ministries of Transport, of Finance and of Home Affairs were deemed to have failed to administer the shipping firm's activities with due care. At the end of March Pham Thanh Binh was sentenced to 20 years' imprisonment, while a further eight officials received custodial terms of between three and 19 years. Meanwhile, in October 2011 Huynh Thi Huyen Nhu, a senior official of the Vietnam Joint Stock Commercial Bank for Industry and Trade (VietinBank), was arrested on charges of misappropriating some 4,000,000m. dông; a further 16 people were subsequently also taken into custody on suspicion of involvement in the embezzlement.

Following continued disputes over land rights, in January 2012 a farmer, Doan Van Vuon, who had refused to relinquish his land in a village near the northern town of Haiphong, used home-made explosive devices and shotguns in an attempt to prevent police from evicting him. In April some 2,000 members of the security forces forcibly evicted protesting farmers from a disputed area of land in northern Hung Yen province, near Hanoi, which a private company was seeking to develop; the farmers complained that they had received inadequate compensation from the authorities for the loss of land. (In April 2013 a Haiphong court sentenced Doan Van Vuon to five years' imprisonment for injuring several police officers during the seizure of his land, while three of his relatives received terms of between two and five years.)

Recent developments: banking crisis

In August 2012 Nguyen Duc Kien, a prominent businessman and one of the founders of the Asia Commercial Joint Stock Bank (ACB), was arrested by police on charges of violating state regulations on economic management. The chief executive of the ACB, Ly Xuan Hai, resigned from his post, and was arrested a few days later, and the bank's Chairman and Vice-Chairmen also tendered their resignations. Amid ensuing public alarm, large numbers of depositors withdrew funds from the ACB, and the central bank, the State Bank of Viet Nam, was obliged to support it with funds of some 17,000,000m. dồng. In September, moreover, the former Chairman of Vietnam National Shipping Lines, Duong Chi Dung, was arrested abroad and extradited to Viet Nam on charges of financial mismanagement. The resignation of the Chairman of the state-owned Sacombank also necessitated the extension of rescue funds from the State Bank in November. Following a two-week meeting in October, the CPV Central Committee announced that the Politburo had apologized for its failure to prevent corruption among some party members, and pledged that economic reforms would be undertaken. During a televised parliamentary debate in November, Prime Minister Nguyen Tan Dung rejected demands for his resignation made by a deputy, who accused him of responsibility for the economic crisis. On 22 November, however, the National Assembly adopted a resolution under which elected officials, including the President and the Prime Minister, were to be subject to annual parliamentary votes of confidence from 2013.

Meanwhile, in September 2012 three internet bloggers belonging to a group known as the Free Journalists' Club, notably including Nguyen Van Hai (who had remained in detention since late 2008—see The 12th National Assembly, 2007–11), were convicted of anti-state propaganda by a court in Ho Chi Minh City; Nguyen Van Hai was sentenced to 12 years' imprisonment, while terms of four and 10 years were imposed on the other two defendants. (The mother of one of the defendants had died in July, after setting fire to herself in protest against the trial of her daughter.) In October two musicians received sentences of six years' and four years' imprisonment for writing songs critical of the Government. A further 14 dissident bloggers, who had contributed to the online site Vietnam Redemptorist News, were sentenced to between three and 13 years' imprisonment in January 2013 on charges of having connections with Viet Tan, and of having received training and funding abroad for anti-Government activities. In February a court in southern Phu Yen province convicted 22 alleged members of a dissident group that had issued documents critical of the regime of planning to overthrow the Government; the group's leader was sentenced to life imprisonment, while other defendants received custodial terms of between 10 and 17 years.

Political Refugees, Economic Migrants and Ethnic Unrest

During the late 1970s regional tensions increased over the growing number of Vietnamese refugees (particularly ethnic Chinese) arriving in Thailand and other nearby countries. In 1979 more than 200,000 fled Viet Nam, and in July an international conference was convened in Geneva to discuss the situation. The Orderly Departure Programme, sponsored by the office of the UN High Commissioner for Refugees (UNHCR, see p. 69), whereby Viet Nam agreed to legal departures, was negotiated, and by the end of 1988 about 140,000 people had left the country in this way. However, illegal departures continued, and the increasing reluctance of Western countries to provide resettlement opportunities led to a meeting in Malaysia in March 1989, at which representatives of 30 nations were present and a comprehensive programme of action was drafted. Members of the Association of Southeast Asian Nations (ASEAN, see p. 218) subsequently ceased to accept refugees for automatic resettlement and planned to institute a screening procedure to distinguish genuine refugees from economic migrants. A similar procedure had been in effect since June 1988 in Hong Kong, and an agreement had been signed in November, whereby Viet

Nam agreed to accept voluntary repatriation of refugees from Hong Kong, funded by UNHCR and the United Kingdom, with UN supervision to protect the returning refugees from punitive measures by the Vietnamese Government.

In June 1989 a UN-sponsored conference adopted the so-called Comprehensive Action Plan that had been drafted in March, introducing the desired screening procedures to distinguish political refugees from economic migrants (who might be forcibly repatriated if efforts to secure their voluntary return proved unsuccessful). In July 1990 the USA accepted in principle the 'involuntary' repatriation of refugees classed as economic migrants who did not actively oppose deportation. In September the United Kingdom, Viet Nam and UNHCR reached an agreement whereby the Vietnamese Government would no longer refuse refugees who had been repatriated 'involuntarily'. In May 1992 the United Kingdom and Viet Nam signed an agreement providing for the compulsory repatriation of all economic migrants from Hong Kong. In 1991–95 some 66,132 Vietnamese were voluntarily repatriated, while an additional 1,562 were forcibly returned. In January 1996 ASEAN member states, including Viet Nam, agreed that all Vietnamese residing in South-East Asian refugee camps (apart from those in Hong Kong) would be repatriated by the end of June of that year. (China had already indicated that all Vietnamese refugees in Hong Kong should be returned prior to the transfer of the territory to Chinese sovereignty in June 1997.) In March 1996 UNHCR announced that it would suspend funding of Vietnamese refugee camps from the end of June. In April a new initiative, proposed by the US Government in an effort to accelerate the repatriation programme, whereby refugees who returned to Viet Nam would be eligible to apply for settlement in the USA under a new screening process, was received with caution by the Vietnamese authorities. By February 1997 Malaysia, Singapore, Indonesia and Thailand had closed their camps, following the repatriation of all Vietnamese refugees from those countries, leaving Hong Kong as the only South-East Asian country with a significant number (12,000 in November 1996). In December 1996 repatriates were prohibited from engaging in any type of political activity, and from January 1997 anti-communist activists and critics of the Government were banned from returning to Viet Nam. In mid-June the main Vietnamese detention centre in Hong Kong was closed. However, the scheduled repatriation of all remaining Vietnamese (estimated at some 1,600 people qualifying as refugees and 700 non-refugees) before the end of the month was not achieved. In July 1999 Hong Kong announced that the Vietnamese who remained in the territory—estimated to number around 1,400, some classed as refugees, others as 'stateless' persons—would be given permanent residency in Hong Kong; the last remaining camp for Vietnamese refugees in Hong Kong was closed in May 2000.

Ethnic violence broke out in the Central Highland provinces of Gia Lai and Dak Lak in February 2001, as local hill minorities (known as Montagnards) protested against perceived injustices caused by the migration of ethnic Vietnamese from the densely populated coastal regions and by the deforestation resulting from the establishment of coffee plantations. Some 5,000 protesters in the provincial capitals of Pleiku and Buon Ma Thuot, respectively, attacked state offices and blocked roads, while demanding autonomy, freedom to practise their Protestant religion, the return of ancestral lands confiscated for use as coffee plantations and the right to preserve their traditional way of life. The Vietnamese authorities deployed troops, riot police, water cannon and helicopters to quell the unrest, and injuries were reported on both sides. Some 20 people were arrested in connection with instigating the violence. The Ministry of Public Security accused the US-based Montagnard Foundation of organizing the violence, stating that several of those arrested were former members of the guerrilla unit FULRO. In September 14 Montagnards received sentences of between six and 12 years' imprisonment for participating in the protests. In October a further six men were convicted of distributing propaganda and inciting ethnic unrest in the city of Buon Ma Thuot during the disturbances.

Following the unrest in the Central Highlands, many Montagnards fled over the border into Cambodia, where they were accommodated in two camps situated in the provinces of Mondol Kiri and Ratanak Kiri. By December 2001 the camps housed 805 refugees, who sought a supervised return to the Highlands, accompanied by a guarantee that they would be given permission to reoccupy their ancestral lands. In January 2002 Viet Nam and Cambodia signed a joint repatriation agreement with UNHCR, and in February 15 refugees left the camps to return to their home in Kon Tum province. Later in the same month the Vietnamese Government criticized UNHCR for the delay in the repatriation of the refugees (of whom there were now more than 1,000). A deadline of 30 April 2002 for the completion of the repatriation process had been imposed. The programme was later suspended, as UNHCR claimed that by imposing the deadline the Government was undermining the voluntary nature of returns. In March UNHCR announced its withdrawal from the agreement, owing to the frequent intimidation of both refugees and UN staff at the camps. Following the termination of the agreement, the US Government stated that it was prepared to offer asylum to the refugees who remained in Cambodia. The Cambodian Government announced in April that, while it would authorize the resettlement of the Montagnard refugees in the USA, it planned to close down the camps housing the refugees and cease its provision of asylum within one month. A critical report issued by the international organization Human Rights Watch in the same month warned of further violence in the Central Highlands if the Government continued to implement its repressive policies towards ethnic minorities.

In November 2002 it was alleged that the Government had executed three Montagnards in the previous month, reportedly owing to their involvement in the violence of February 2001. In December 2002 a further eight people were convicted of charges of undermining national unity, having allegedly aided people attempting to leave the region following the violence. In May 2003 15 Montagnards were convicted of causing social disorder during the protests of February 2001 and sentenced to lengthy prison terms.

Following the repression of a rally held by Montagnards in the Central Highland province of Dak Lak in April 2004, in protest against land confiscation and religious persecution, there was a further influx of Montagnards into Cambodia. Human Rights Watch claimed that at least 10 Montagnards had been killed, although the Vietnamese Government insisted that only two people had died. In May Human Rights Watch reported that the Vietnamese authorities had arrested a number of Montagnard church leaders, as well as Montagnards with relatives in the USA. In August nine Montagnards, who were alleged to be former members of the FULRO, were convicted of fomenting disorder and undermining national unity during the demonstrations of February 2001 and thereafter. They were sentenced to prison terms of between five and 12 years.

In January 2005 UNHCR and the Governments of Cambodia and Viet Nam signed an agreement on the resettlement to third countries or the repatriation to Viet Nam of some 750 Montagnards in Cambodia. The Vietnamese Government guaranteed that returnees would not be punished, discriminated against or prosecuted for their departure. In March the first group of 43 Montagnards who had opted for repatriation returned to Viet Nam; by that time a further 297 had decided to accept resettlement in third countries, including the USA, Finland and Canada. In December 2010 the Cambodian Government ordered UNHCR to close its centre for Montagnard refugees in Phnom Penh, the Cambodian capital, by 1 January 2011, insisting that there was no reason for the refugees' continued stay in Cambodia, citing Viet Nam's economic progress and absence of armed conflict in Montagnard areas. The Cambodian Government subsequently agreed to an extension to the deadline, until 15 February, in order to allow more time to resettle or repatriate the 62 Montagnards remaining at the centre; the final inmates were repatriated to Viet Nam on 16 February.

Foreign Affairs

Regional relations

Relations with Kampuchea (known as Cambodia until 1976 and again from 1989) deteriorated during 1977, and in December Viet Nam launched a major offensive into eastern Kampuchea. Sporadic fighting continued, and in December 1978 Viet Nam invaded Kampuchea in support of elements opposed to the regime of the Khmers Rouges. By January 1979 the Government of Pol Pot had been overthrown and a pro-Vietnamese regime was installed. The invasion prompted much international criticism, and in February Chinese forces launched a punitive attack across the border into Viet Nam. Peace talks began in April but made little progress, and in March 1980 they were suspended by China. In 1984 Chinese and Vietnamese troops engaged in heavy fighting, accusing each other of persistent border violations. Throughout 1986 and 1987 further armed clashes between Vietnamese and Chinese soldiers occurred on the Sino-

Vietnamese border. Both sides denied responsibility for initiating the attacks. In early 1988 the tension between the two countries was exacerbated by the re-emergence of conflict over the Spratly Islands in the South China Sea, when the Vietnamese Government alleged that China had dispatched warships to the islands. (For many years the sovereignty of the islands had been contested, not only by Viet Nam and China, which engaged in military conflict over the issue in 1974, but also by the neighbouring states of Brunei, Malaysia, the Philippines and Taiwan.)

In March 1984 Viet Nam agreed in principle that it would eventually withdraw its troops from Kampuchea, and in August 1985 it was announced that all Vietnamese troops would be withdrawn by 1990. An eight-point peace plan, proposed by Kampuchean resistance leaders in March 1986 (involving the installation of a quadripartite government in Kampuchea, to be followed by UN-supervised elections), was rejected by Viet Nam. Viet Nam's urgent need of Western aid, together with increasing pressure from the USSR, prompted an announcement in May 1988 that Viet Nam would withdraw 50,000 (of an estimated total of 100,000) troops from Kampuchea by the end of the year. The Vietnamese military high command left Kampuchea in June, placing the remainder of the Vietnamese forces under Kampuchean control.

In April 1989 the Vietnamese Government and the Heng Samrin regime in Kampuchea declared that Vietnamese troops would withdraw by September even if a political settlement had not been reached, on condition that military assistance to the three other Kampuchean factions also ceased by that date. China responded that it would halt military aid to the Khmers Rouges only after a complete withdrawal of Vietnamese troops had been verified. The Vietnamese Government claimed that the withdrawal of troops had been completed by the end of September. However, the absence of a UN commission to verify the troops' departure led to claims by the Government-in-exile of Democratic Kampuchea that a number of troops remained in the country, while ASEAN, China and the USA initially refused to recognize the alleged withdrawal. In July 1990 the USA finally acknowledged that all troops had been withdrawn.

In September 1990 secret negotiations took place between Viet Nam and China, during which the Vietnamese endorsed a new UN Security Council agreement to resolve the conflict in Cambodia (q.v.). It was widely believed that the Chinese had promised an improvement in Sino-Vietnamese relations in exchange for Vietnamese support for the UN plan. In October 1991 Viet Nam was a signatory to a peace agreement whereby an interim Supreme National Council was established in Cambodia, representing all four factions there, as a prelude to the holding of UN-supervised elections. The agreement allowed immediate progress towards ending Viet Nam's diplomatic and economic isolation. During 1992–93 there were several massacres of civilians of Vietnamese origin living in Cambodia. In January 1995 the First Prime Minister of Cambodia, Prince Norodom Ranariddh, visited Viet Nam for discussions. In January 1996 it was reported that Cambodian troops had opened fire in a southern border area; Cambodia subsequently claimed that Vietnamese forces had made incursions into Cambodian territory. Discussions between Vietnamese and Cambodian government officials on the border issue took place in April and May, and in March 1997 Viet Nam and Cambodia signed an agreement on bilateral co-operation in combating crime.

In 2000 security officials from Viet Nam and Cambodia signed a number of agreements aimed at combating drugs-trafficking and strengthening border controls. In November 2005 Viet Nam and Cambodia signed a supplementary border treaty to an existing one concluded in 1985; under the new agreement, the demarcation of the border between the two countries was to be finalized by the end of 2008. However, owing to technical problems, such as unclear maps drawn up during colonial times, and to flooding, work on demarcation progressed slowly and it was announced that the projected date for its completion had been postponed until 2012. (The two countries nevertheless failed to complete the process of demarcation by the revised deadline of June 2012.) In May 2008 a new body, the Vietnam-Laos-Cambodia Economic Cooperation and Development Association, was established in Hanoi. Relations were further strengthened in December 2009 by the signing of bilateral co-operation agreements on power generation, industry, mining and maritime transport. In March 2010 a new 70-km road extending from the Vietnamese province of Gia Lai, in the Central Highlands region, to the Cambodian province of Ratanak Kiri was opened to traffic. At a tripartite ministerial meeting on anti-narcotics co-operation held in December, Viet Nam, Cambodia and Laos agreed to intensify co-operation in order to combat the circulation, production, farming and smuggling of drugs within the three countries. In June 2011 the Cambodian Government signed an agreement with the Laotian and Vietnamese Governments that provided for the establishment of a trilateral economic development zone. In March 2013 the Vietnamese Minister of National Defence, Gen. Phung Quang Thanh, and his Cambodian counterpart signed a defence co-operation plan in Ho Chi Minh City. At a bilateral conference held in Ho Chi Minh City in April, Vietnamese and Cambodian officials further agreed to conduct joint maritime patrols in the Gulf of Thailand.

Meanwhile, following the conclusion of the Cambodian peace agreement in October 1991, Vo Van Kiet and Do Muoi paid an official visit to China in November, during which normal diplomatic relations were restored and agreements were concluded on trade and on border affairs. Further agreements were signed in March 1992 on the resumption of transport and communications links (severed in 1979), and on the reopening of border posts. In May 1992 Viet Nam protested to China when the latter unilaterally granted exploration rights to a US petroleum company in an area of the South China Sea regarded by Viet Nam as part of its continental shelf; several more protests were lodged later in the year over the presence of Chinese vessels in disputed areas. In November the Chinese Premier, Li Peng, made an official visit to Viet Nam (the first visit by a Chinese head of government since 1971): new agreements on economic, scientific and cultural co-operation were signed, and the two Governments agreed to accelerate negotiations on disputed territory that had begun in the previous month. In October 1993 Viet Nam and China concluded an agreement to avoid the use of force when resolving territorial disputes. In November 1994 the two countries agreed to co-operate in seeking an early resolution to all border disputes. During an official visit by Do Muoi to China in November 1995, it was agreed that rail links between the two countries would be restored (they were subsequently reopened in February 1996). In April 1996 the state-owned petroleum company, Petrovietnam, signed a joint exploration contract with a US enterprise that covered part of the South China Sea where the Chinese Government had granted exploration rights in May 1992. In May 1996 China agreed to abide by the UN Convention on the Law of the Sea (UNCLOS), which provided for international arbitration, but at the same time announced a new delineation of its sea border, attracting criticism from Viet Nam and other nations in the region.

In March 1997 Chinese vessels entered Vietnamese waters around the disputed Spratly Islands and were believed to be carrying out exploratory activities. China defended its actions, declaring a legitimate claim to the territory. In April China agreed to hold talks with Viet Nam over the issue; however, China withdrew the vessels before the discussions took place, stating that its operation in the area had been completed. In October 1998 Phan Van Khai made an official visit to China, during which it was agreed that Viet Nam and China would increase efforts to reach a settlement on their various border disputes; in November, however, Viet Nam reiterated its territorial claim to the disputed Spratly Islands. In December 1999 a formal border treaty was signed by Viet Nam and China. Vietnamese leaders travelled to China in June 2000 to attend an ideological symposium on methods of introducing market reforms without incurring any loss of political control. The visit was regarded as a major improvement in bilateral relations, and was followed by a second symposium in Hanoi in November. The two countries also made further progress in delineating their mutual land border, which took effect from July 2000, and finalized their border in the Gulf of Tonkin in late December, the latter agreement demarcating their economic and fishing zones. Chinese military delegations visited Viet Nam in July 2000 and February 2001 to enhance military co-operation, and President Tran Duc Luong visited China in December 2000 and 2001. In February 2002 Chinese President Jiang Zemin paid an official visit to Viet Nam, his second since the restoration of normal bilateral relations in 1991. His visit coincided with campaigns mounted by several dissidents expressing concern over the agreements that had been signed to demarcate the Sino-Vietnamese border. An ongoing dispute over fishing rights in the Gulf of Tonkin prevented the ratification of any agreement to delineate the shared maritime boundary. In April 2002 it was reported that the two countries had begun demarcating their land border. In November of that year, following an ASEAN

summit meeting attended by China, a declaration was issued outlining a code of conduct to be observed by those countries contesting the Spratly Islands. However, China strongly opposed Viet Nam's decision, in March 2004, to allow tourists to visit the Spratly Islands, claiming that the tours infringed its territorial sovereignty.

Viet Nam and China accelerated efforts to delineate their border in early 2005, and an 11th round of talks was held on the issue in Hanoi in February and March. In October Viet Nam and China agreed to conduct joint military patrols of the Gulf of Tonkin. Later that month Chinese President Hu Jintao made a three-day state visit to Viet Nam, during which he met with President Tran Duc Luong and General Secretary of the Central Committee of the CPV Nong Duc Manh. Bilateral relations were discussed, as were issues of regional and international concern, and both countries pledged to work together to promote mutual trust and encourage further bilateral co-operation. President Nguyen Minh Triet visited China in May 2007, holding talks with Hu Jintao and Premier Wen Jiabao. Several agreements on co-operation were signed during the visit, including nine economic accords. Notably, a joint working group was established to formulate a five-year plan for the further development of bilateral economic and trade co-operation. Border issues were also addressed, with Presidents Nguyen and Hu pledging to complete the demarcation of the 1,350-km land border in 2008 and to accelerate negotiations on the delineation of boundaries in the Gulf of Tonkin.

However, the territorial dispute in the South China Sea continued to provoke tensions, and in July 2007 a Chinese naval vessel fired on Vietnamese fishing boats near the Spratly Islands, sinking one boat; one fisherman died in the incident and several others were injured. In November, moreover, Viet Nam protested after China conducted naval exercises near the Paracel Islands, and in the following month Vietnamese students demonstrated outside China's embassy in Hanoi and its consulate in Ho Chi Minh City, following reports that China was to create a new municipality incorporating the Spratly and Paracel Islands. In July 2008 Viet Nam announced that it intended to continue with a joint petroleum exploration project with ExxonMobil in disputed waters in the South China Sea, despite a warning from China to the US energy company to cancel the agreement. In December the Chinese and Vietnamese Governments announced that, following four days of negotiations in Hanoi, the demarcation of the land border had been completed as scheduled. Three formal border agreements were signed by the two countries in November 2009 and took effect in July 2010: a protocol on border demarcation and landmark-planting; an agreement on border management regulations; and an agreement on border-gates and their management. Both countries hailed the implementation of the agreements as the formal conclusion to the 36-year land border dispute and an important 'milestone' in bilateral relations; an agreement to form a joint land border committee was also announced.

In commemoration of the 60th anniversary of the establishment of diplomatic relations, the year 2010 was designated as the 'China-Viet Nam Friendship Year'. However, relations continued to be impeded by ongoing tensions over the disputed Spratly and Paracel Islands. In June a Chinese tourism development plan incorporating the disputed islands was denounced by the Vietnamese Government, which restated its belief that Viet Nam held 'indisputable sovereignty' over both archipelagos. In July the two countries agreed to address 'properly' their maritime territorial issues, as well as to expand political, economic, trade and cultural ties, and to enhance co-operation on regional and international issues. However, in August the Vietnamese Government issued a demand that China 'immediately cease violating Viet Nam's sovereignty . . . in the East Sea' in response to reports that Chinese vessels had, since May, been conducting oil and gas exploration activities off the coast of Tri Ton Island, part of the Paracel Islands. Tensions were significantly exacerbated by the arrest in mid-September of nine Vietnamese fishermen in the South China Sea by the Chinese authorities; following forthright demands from the Vietnamese Government, the fishermen were released in mid-October. The first direct flights between Ho Chi Minh City and Beijing were inaugurated in December; it was hoped that the new route would facilitate an expansion in bilateral trade and tourism.

An escalation of the maritime dispute was evident from mid-2011. Following a series of alleged incursions into Vietnamese territorial waters by Chinese vessels in the South China Sea, from early June anti-China protests were staged outside the

Chinese embassy in Hanoi and also in Ho Chi Minh City, as well as at Chinese embassies in a number of foreign countries, including the USA and the United Kingdom. China, meanwhile, accused Viet Nam of 'gravely violating' its sovereignty and cautioned it to cease all 'invasive activities' after a clash in mid-June between a Chinese fishing boat and a Vietnamese oil exploratory vessel, which the Chinese authorities alleged had been operating in its territorial waters. Tensions were further exacerbated a few days later when Viet Nam conducted live-fire military exercises in the South China Sea; while the Vietnamese Government insisted the exercises were 'routine', Chinese state media denounced the drill as a 'military show of force to defy Beijing'. At a meeting of ASEAN ministers responsible for foreign affairs, also attended by Chinese representatives, on Bali, Indonesia, in July, an agreement was reached providing for the establishment of a code of conduct to defuse tensions over competing territorial claims in the South China Sea. In the following month the Vietnamese Government ordered that anti-China protests, which had continued to be staged on a weekly basis since June, be halted. The respective vice-ministers responsible for foreign affairs of Viet Nam and China in October signed a bilateral agreement pledging to seek solutions to the ongoing maritime dispute based on UNCLOS, and providing for, *inter alia*, twice-yearly meetings to discuss issues pertaining to the dispute.

In April 2012 the Chinese authorities released 21 Vietnamese fishermen who had been detained since early March on the grounds that they had fished illegally near the Paracel Islands. On 21 June the National Assembly adopted legislation reaffirming Viet Nam's sovereignty over the Paracel and Spratly Islands, prompting strong criticism from the Chinese Government. Later that month Viet Nam protested after the Chinese National Offshore Oil Corporation invited bids for exploration rights in areas regarded by Viet Nam as being within its maritime zone. In December the Vietnamese Government announced that it was to conduct new maritime patrols to prevent foreign vessels from fishing in its territorial waters, and formally protested at the alleged sabotage of a Vietnamese oil exploration operation by Chinese boats; in the same month further anti-China protests (which were dispersed by the police) were staged in Hanoi and Ho Chi Minh City. Bilateral tensions again increased in March 2013, when the Vietnamese Government claimed that a Chinese patrol boat had fired on, and set alight, a Vietnamese fishing vessel near the Paracel Islands, formally protesting to China about the incident; the Chinese authorities insisted that the action had been justified on the grounds the Vietnamese vessel had been operating illegally in Chinese waters (and subsequently claimed that no weapons had been used against the vessel). In April the Chinese Government announced that tourists were to be permitted to visit the Paracel Islands as part of Chinese territory.

The Cambodian peace agreement of 1991 allowed Viet Nam to initiate closer relations with ASEAN member states: Vo Van Kiet visited Indonesia, Thailand and Singapore in late 1991 and Malaysia, Brunei and the Philippines in early 1992; agreements on economic co-operation were concluded with these countries, including guarantees of protection for future investment by them in Viet Nam. In July 1992 Viet Nam signed the ASEAN agreement (of 1976) on regional amity and co-operation, and in July 1995 became a full member of the organization. In September 1992 an agreement was signed with Singapore on the mutual provision of 'most favoured nation' trading status. In April 1995 Viet Nam, Thailand, Laos and Cambodia signed an agreement providing for the establishment of the Mekong River Commission (see p. 462), which was to co-ordinate the sustainable development of the resources of the Lower Mekong River basin. In October 1997 Viet Nam and Thailand reached an agreement to demarcate their maritime boundary, following a series of incidents between Vietnamese and Thai fishing vessels. In December 1998 Viet Nam hosted the sixth summit meeting of the heads of state and government of the ASEAN grouping of countries. During 2000 Viet Nam reaffirmed sovereignty over the Spratly and Paracel Islands, but reassured ASEAN that it was committed to a peaceful solution to the territorial dispute through multilateral negotiations. It was hoped that the declaration of November 2002, which established a code of conduct to be adhered to by the claimants of the islands, would provide such a solution. Vietnamese and Laotian officials held several meetings during the course of 2000, and Viet Nam provided assistance to Laos in its fight against ethnic Hmong rebels. In November 2001 President Tran Duc Luong held talks with President Gloria Macapagal Arroyo while on an official visit to the Philippines.

The two countries agreed to the enhancement of economic relations and to co-operation in trade, investment and tourism. In February 2002 the Prime Minister met with the premiers of Cambodia and of Laos in Ho Chi Minh City. The three countries agreed to promote co-operation in the development of tourism and infrastructure within the 'development triangle'. In February 2004 the first joint meeting of the cabinets of Viet Nam and Thailand took place. During the meeting, several co-operation agreements were signed concerning various social and economic issues. Prime Minister Phan Van Khai paid a four-day visit to Singapore (the largest foreign investor in Viet Nam) in March, during which a comprehensive co-operation framework document was signed. Following the announcement also in March that Viet Nam intended to allow tourists to begin visiting the Spratly Islands, the first tour took place in April, despite opposition from other claimants to the disputed islands. In May Viet Nam announced that it was renovating a disused runway on one of the islands to further its tourism plans.

As part of efforts to strengthen relations with other ASEAN member states, particularly in the area of economic co-operation, Vietnamese Prime Minister Nguyen Tan Dung visited Brunei, Indonesia, Myanmar, the Philippines and Singapore in August 2007. In February 2008 Viet Nam, Cambodia and Laos concluded a draft agreement on defining the intersection point of their borders. In the following month Viet Nam ratified the new ASEAN Charter, which codified the principles and purposes of the Association and had been signed in November 2007 at the 13th summit meeting in Singapore. Viet Nam initially opposed the inclusion of a human rights mechanism in the Charter, but later agreed to the provision. Viet Nam assumed the annually rotating chair of ASEAN in January 2010. An agreement committing the respective legislative bodies of Viet Nam and Indonesia to increased collaboration and visit exchanges was signed in the Indonesian capital, Jakarta, in March. During a visit to Hanoi by Philippine President Benigno Aquino in October, Aquino and Vietnamese President Nguyen Minh Triet concluded a number of agreements, including separate memorandums of understanding (MOUs) on defence and education. At a five-nation regional summit meeting held in Cambodia in November 2010, Viet Nam, Cambodia, Laos, Myanmar and Thailand signed the Phnom Penh Declaration, which was intended to improve regional co-operation in numerous fields of activity, including agriculture, industry and the energy sector, the environment, investment and trade facilitation, transport, tourism and public health.

In January 1992 a Japanese government mission visited Viet Nam to negotiate the repayment of Vietnamese debts, and in November Japan (which—although a principal trading partner—had hitherto imposed a ban on official economic co-operation) began to provide financial assistance to Viet Nam. By the end of the 2000s Japan was the largest source of official development assistance to Viet Nam. During 2000 Viet Nam and Japan also strengthened their defence links, with the aim of promoting regional security. In May 2008 Viet Nam and Japan signed a co-operation agreement on the use of nuclear energy, under the terms of which Japan pledged to help Viet Nam to prepare and plan for the introduction of nuclear energy. During a visit to Hanoi by Japanese Prime Minister Naoto Kan in October 2010, Vietnamese premier Nguyen Tan Dung thanked Kan for Japan's continued financial contribution to Viet Nam's economic and social development. In a joint statement the two leaders underscored the importance of ongoing bilateral co-operation in the fields of, *inter alia*, energy and climate change, and noted that the Vietnamese Government had decided to choose Japan as its partner in the proposed construction of two reactors at a second planned nuclear plant in Viet Nam's Ninh Thuan province; however, no formal agreement to this end was reported to have been signed. The statement also revealed that the two countries had agreed to co-operate in the exploration for, and the mining, development and production of, rare earth minerals within Viet Nam that were vital to the manufacture of high-technology merchandise. Amid further tensions in the South China Sea (see above), in April 2013 Viet Nam's army Chief of General Staff, Do Ba Ty, visited Japan; it was agreed that the two states would conduct bilateral discussions on maritime security in the following month, with the aim of strengthening defence co-operation.

Relations with the USA

Following discussions on the normalization of bilateral relations, in July 1988 Viet Nam agreed in principle to the resettlement of former political detainees in the USA or elsewhere. In early 1991 a US representative was stationed in Hanoi to supervise inquiries into US soldiers 'missing in action' MIA, the first official US presence in Viet Nam since 1975. In April 1991 the USA proposed a four-stage programme for the resumption of normal diplomatic relations with Viet Nam, principally conditional on Vietnamese co-operation in reaching a diplomatic settlement in Cambodia and in accounting for the remaining MIA. Following the conclusion of the peace agreement on Cambodia in October, Viet Nam made a plea for the removal of the US economic embargo, and in November discussions on the establishment of normal trade relations began. In early 1992 the US Government agreed to provide humanitarian aid for Viet Nam, but refused to end the economic embargo, reiterating that relations would not fully return to normal until after the UN-supervised elections in Cambodia, due to take place in early 1993. The embargo was renewed for another year in September 1992, although in December the US Government announced that US companies would now be allowed to open offices and sign contracts in Viet Nam, in anticipation of a future removal of the embargo. In July 1993 the new administration of President Bill Clinton revoked the US veto on assistance from the IMF and the World Bank for Viet Nam. In September the USA permitted US companies to take part in projects in Viet Nam that were financed by international aid agencies. The trade embargo was finally removed in February 1994.

In January 1995 Viet Nam and the USA signed an agreement permitting the two countries to establish liaison offices in each other's capitals (these were opened immediately) and which resolved a long-standing dispute concerning former US diplomatic properties seized by the Vietnamese authorities in 1975. The establishment of full diplomatic relations was announced in July 1995. In May 1996 Clinton formally ended Viet Nam's official classification as a combat zone. In March 1997 military relations were established between the two countries. In April Douglas Peterson was appointed as the first US ambassador to Viet Nam, and in May Le Van Bang was formally appointed the first Vietnamese ambassador to the USA. In June Madeleine Albright became the first US Secretary of State to visit the country since the end of the Viet Nam War. During a visit to Washington, DC, in November by the Vietnamese Minister of Planning and Investment, an agreement was signed to promote greater economic co-operation. This was facilitated in March 1998, when Clinton signed a waiver to the 'Jackson-Vanik amendment' to 1974 US trade legislation, which restricted trade with communist countries. (In August 1999 the US House of Representatives voted in favour of an extension of the waiver of the amendment for Viet Nam.) In September 1998 the Vietnamese Deputy Prime Minister and Minister of Foreign Affairs, Nguyen Manh Cam, made an official visit to the USA. In July 1999 Viet Nam and the USA reached agreement in principle on the establishment of normal trade relations. Madeleine Albright made another official visit to Viet Nam in September. In March 2000 the US Secretary of Defense, William Cohen, made the first visit to Viet Nam by a US Secretary of Defense since the end of the Viet Nam War.

Although in early 2000 the US Government continued to refuse to acknowledge the responsibility of the chemical defoliant Agent Orange, sprayed in large quantities over areas of Viet Nam by the USA during the Viet Nam War, for widespread health problems (including birth defects) among the Vietnamese, Cohen, during his visit in March, reportedly indicated that the US Government would be willing to conduct joint research with the Vietnamese Government into the effects of the chemical. In May the US House of Representatives approved a resolution calling for the release of all political and religious prisoners in Viet Nam, a motion that was criticized as 'impudent interference' by Viet Nam. A landmark bilateral trade agreement between the USA and Viet Nam was signed in Washington, DC, in 2000, preparing the way for an increase in exports to, and investment from, the USA. The agreement was subject to an annual review by the US Congress. US President Bill Clinton made a highly significant visit to Viet Nam in November; however, his calls for greater freedoms were rebuffed by General Secretary Le Kha Phieu, who defended the socialist system. In March 2001 Viet Nam accused US-based groups of fomenting the recent unrest in the Central Highlands (see Political Refugees, Economic Migrants and Ethnic Unrest). In April a helicopter carrying nine Vietnamese and seven US citizens, searching for the remains of MIA, crashed in the highlands, killing all on board. At that time some 1,498 US servicemen and 300,000 Vietnamese remained unaccounted for in Viet Nam.

Following the September 2001 attacks on the USA, the Vietnamese Government expressed its support for the US-led 'war on terror'. In October the severe penalty imposed on the dissident Roman Catholic priest Father Nguyen Van Ly (see Domestic Political Affairs) accelerated the passage of the Viet Nam Human Rights Act through the US House of Representatives. The act was intended to make US non-humanitarian aid to Viet Nam conditional upon the improvement of its human rights record, thus antagonizing the Vietnamese Government; however the act was subsequently blocked and never voted on in the Senate. (The act was reintroduced and approved again by the US House of Representatives in July 2004, but subsequently stalled in the Senate. The House of Representatives adopted another version of the act in September 2007.) In November 2001 the National Assembly finally ratified the bilateral trade agreement, marking the complete restoration of normal relations between the two countries. In March 2002 Vietnamese and US scientists attended an unprecedented joint conference in Hanoi, at which the effects of Agent Orange were discussed. As a result, the two countries formally agreed to conduct joint research into the effects of the defoliant. However, relations with the USA threatened to deteriorate once more when the US Government expressed its concern for the safety of refugees returning to the Central Highlands from Cambodia. In March 2002, following the collapse of Viet Nam's agreement with UNHCR, the USA offered asylum to those refugees who remained in Cambodia. In the same month relations were further strained when the US Government issued a critical report on Viet Nam's human rights record.

In early 2003 the Vietnamese Government condemned the US-led campaign to oust the regime of Saddam Hussain in Iraq. However, in November relations improved when Minister of National Defence Lt-Gen. Pham Can Tra visited Washington, DC, and held talks with US Secretary of Defense Donald Rumsfeld. In the same month a US frigate spent four days in the port of Ho Chi Minh City, the first visit to Viet Nam by a US warship since the end of the Viet Nam War in 1975. In December 2003 an aviation agreement was signed with the USA, enabling direct flights between the two countries for the first time; the first US flight arrived in Ho Chi Minh City in December 2004. During a visit to Viet Nam in February 2004 Adm. Thomas Fargo, head of the US Pacific Command, reportedly became the first foreign official to visit the naval base at Da Nang. In January, meanwhile, an independent organization, the Vietnam Association for Victims of Agent Orange, submitted a lawsuit to the US Federal Court, on behalf of three Vietnamese people who had been affected by the defoliant, against the US companies that were responsible for its manufacture. In March 2005, however, the US Federal Court dismissed the lawsuit, ruling that there was no legal basis for the claims of the plaintiffs. In February 2008 an appeal against the judgment was rejected. The Vietnam Association for Victims of Agent Orange condemned the decision and announced its intention to file an appeal with the US Supreme Court.

In September 2004 the US Secretary of State designated Viet Nam as a 'country of particular concern' under the International Religious Freedom Act for particularly severe violations of religious freedom. (Viet Nam was removed from the list in November 2006.) The Department of State again urged the Vietnamese Government to release prisoners detained for their religious beliefs and to reopen churches closed in the Central Highlands. The designation was denounced by the Vietnamese Government, which lodged an official protest with the US Government. In June 2005 Prime Minister Phan Van Khai, accompanied by a delegation of government officials, made an official state visit to the USA (becoming the most senior Vietnamese official to visit the USA since the end of the Viet Nam War). During his visit, he held discussions with US President George W. Bush on Viet Nam's application to join the World Trade Organization (WTO, see p. 444), human rights, religious freedom and corporate development. In May 2006 the two countries signed a bilateral trade agreement, marking the final stage of Viet Nam's accession to the WTO. US Secretary of Defense Rumsfeld's visit to Viet Nam in June was followed by a visit from President Bush in November. In December the US Congress approved legislation permitting 'permanent normal trade relations' with Viet Nam, and in February 2007 the Bush Administration approved funding of US $400,000 towards a $1m. study into the decontamination of its former base in Da Nang.

In June 2007 Nguyen Minh Triet became the first Vietnamese head of state to visit the USA since the end of the Viet Nam War.

Nguyen held talks with President Bush during the visit, and several bilateral economic agreements were signed, including a Trade and Investment Framework Agreement (TIFA). However, while the two Presidents were meeting, hundreds of protesters, including many Vietnamese exiles, demanded the release of Vietnamese political prisoners. The first ministerial-level meeting on the TIFA took place in Washington, DC, in December, focusing on Viet Nam's implementation of its WTO commitments, following its accession to that organization in January, as well as measures to expand bilateral trade and investment relations. In June 2008 Prime Minister Nguyen Tan Dung visited the USA, where he and Bush agreed to launch negotiations on a potential bilateral investment agreement; the first round of negotiations was held in Washington, DC, in December, followed by a second round in Hanoi in July 2009 (although the talks were reported subsequently to have stalled). In early August 2010 the 15th anniversary of the restoration of normal diplomatic relations was commemorated by a port visit to Viet Nam by a US war vessel, a visit that reflected burgeoning military links between the two countries, which held their first senior-level defence dialogue in mid-August. Meanwhile, during a visit to Hanoi in the previous month, US Secretary of State Hillary Clinton stated that resolution of the dispute over ownership of the Spratly Islands was 'pivotal' to regional stability, as well as to US and Vietnamese national interests, and offered US mediation in efforts to resolve the issue; however, the offer provoked an irate response from the Chinese Government, which accused the US Administration of interference in regional affairs. Following the escalation of the maritime dispute in mid-2011 (see Regional relations), the US Administration urged restraint on all sides and appealed for the holding of urgent talks to broker a diplomatic resolution.

In its annual report for 2012, published in March of that year, the US Commission on International Religious Freedom (USCIRF), a US federal agency, noted a marked deterioration in the human rights situation within Viet Nam since the country's removal in November 2006 from the US Department of State's list of 'countries of particular concern' with regard to violations of religious freedoms. The USCIRF alleged that during 2011 alone at least 33 peaceful dissidents, including political reform advocates, pro-democracy activists and those protesting against religious freedom restrictions, had been imprisoned by the authorities, and recommended that Viet Nam be redesignated as a 'country of particular concern'. The USCIRF repeated this recommendation in its annual report for 2013.

In June 2012 US Secretary of Defense Leon Panetta visited Viet Nam, following a defence conference in Singapore, where he had announced that about 60% of the USA's total naval fleet would be based in the Asia-Pacific region; Panetta and Minister of National Defence Gen. Phung Quang Thanh signed an agreement allowing the search for MIA remains to proceed in three previously restricted areas. During a visit to Viet Nam in July, however, US Secretary of State Clinton expressed further criticism of Viet Nam's human rights record, especially in relation to the restriction of free speech (following the detention of three internet bloggers—see Domestic Political Affairs). In August the US military officially commenced a programme to reduce Agent Orange contamination in Vietnamese territory, beginning at Da Nang International Airport; it was announced that the US Administration was to provide US $41m. towards the operation. Following pressure from the US Administration, in January 2013 the Vietnamese authorities released and deported Nguyen Quoc Quan, a US national of Vietnamese origin, who had been detained without trial since the previous April on charges of subversive activities and membership of US-based opposition movement Viet Tan.

Relations with Russia

Following the dissolution of the USSR at the end of 1991, the Vietnamese Government pursued close relations with its successor states, particularly Russia. In June 1994 Vo Van Kiet visited Russia, Ukraine and Kazakhstan to discuss economic and defence co-operation issues. In February 1997 Russia announced plans further to develop its defence links with Viet Nam, and in November of that year the Russian Prime Minister, Viktor Chernomyrdin, paid an official visit to Viet Nam; Tran Duc Luong made a reciprocal visit to Russia in August 1998. The Russian Deputy Prime Minister, Viktor Khristenko, visited Viet Nam in July 2000 to discuss Russian involvement in oil and gas development, and Viet Nam's outstanding 11,000m. rouble Soviet-era debt. Agreement on the latter was reached in September, when it was arranged that Viet Nam would repay Russia

US $1,700m. over 23 years, mostly in the form of business concessions. In February–March 2001 the Russian President, Vladimir Putin, became the first Russian (or Soviet) head of state to visit Viet Nam. The two countries agreed to strengthen co-operation in economic, energy, and military and defence matters, and proclaimed a new 'strategic partnership'. In May 2002 control of the former Soviet naval base at Cam Ranh Bay, in central Viet Nam, was formally transferred to the Vietnamese Government, two years ahead of the agreed date.

In May 2004 President Tran Duc Luong visited Russia and held talks with President Putin on bilateral relations, focusing particularly on expanding economic co-operation. In April 2007 Russia and Viet Nam reached agreement in principle on reducing barriers to bilateral trade, and in June the two countries initialled an MOU on Russia's bid for accession to the WTO, which Viet Nam had joined in January 2007. Trade and investment were also the main areas of discussion during visits by Prime Minister Nguyen Tan Dung to Russia, the Czech Republic and Poland in September. During a state visit to Russia in October 2008, President Nguyen Minh Triet stressed that Viet Nam wished to increase co-operation with Russia in all areas, including the media, education, and the oil and gas sectors; Nguyen Minh Triet's proposal to establish a joint Vietnamese-Russian university was welcomed by his Russian counterpart. During a visit to Moscow in December 2009, Prime Minister Nguyen Tan Dung announced that Viet Nam had reached a US $2,000m. agreement to purchase submarines from Russia. During a visit to Hanoi by Russian President Dmitrii Medvedev in October 2010, an agreement was signed on the construction, by the state-owned Russian Atomic Energy Corp, of Viet Nam's first nuclear power plant, to be located in Ninh Thuan province. In November 2011 it was announced that Russia was to extend an $8,000m. loan to Viet Nam for the construction of the plant, which was due to commence in 2014, with completion of the first of the two 1,200-MW reactors scheduled by 2020. Meanwhile, the delivery of four Russian fighter jets purchased by Viet Nam was completed in June 2011. A further 16 fighter jets were supplied to Viet Nam by Russia during 2012. The Russian Minister of Defence, Sergei Shoigu, visited Viet Nam in March 2013, when the agreement on the sale and servicing of Russian submarines was finalized; it was reported that the possibility of the resumed use of facilities at Cam Ranh Bay by the Russian navy was also discussed.

Other external relations

In the late 1990s Viet Nam developed closer links with India, ostensibly because of mutual concerns about China. The Indian Minister of Defence visited Viet Nam in March 2000 and signed a wide-ranging defence agreement that would allow Viet Nam to train the Indian army in jungle warfare and counter-insurgency methods, and India to assist in the modernization of the Vietnamese military. The two countries also agreed to take action to combat piracy in the South China Sea. The Indian Minister of External Affairs, Jaswant Singh, and Prime Minister Atal Bihari Vajpayee made separate visits to Viet Nam in November 2000 and January 2001, respectively, and agreed to co-ordinate their positions in the Non-aligned Movement (see p. 477), South-South Co-operation and regional forums. India's Oil and Natural Gas Company became an investor in Viet Nam's Nam Con Son gas field in 2000, and India pledged some US $238m. of investment in the Vietnamese petroleum and gas industries. In September 2001 the Minister of Foreign Affairs, Nguyen Dy Nien, visited India, and in March 2002 Vice-President Nguyen Thi Binh also visited the country to discuss the possibility of closer bilateral co-operation. Relations were further strengthened in July 2007 by a state visit to India by Prime Minister Nguyen Tan Dung, during which a joint declaration was signed on the establishment of a 'strategic partnership' between India and Viet Nam, covering bilateral co-operation in the areas of politics, the economy, security, defence, culture, science and technology. In March 2008 the Vietnamese Minister of Public Security, Le Hong Anh, and the Indian Minister of Home Affairs, Shivraj Patil, signed an MOU on bilateral co-operation in combating international terrorism and drugs-trafficking. The Indian President, Pratibha Devisingh Patil, held talks with President Nguyen Minh Triet regarding the expansion of economic relations between the two countries during her first official visit to Viet Nam in November 2008. Defence links were bolstered by the visit to India of the Vietnamese Minister of National Defence, Gen. Phung Quang Thanh, in November 2009. In May 2010 the two countries announced an agreement to create a joint committee to promote co-operation in, *inter alia*, trade, investment and technology. The Viet Nam-India Business Forum was launched in mid-2011. During a visit to India in October, President Truong Tan Sang addressed a meeting of the Forum, pledging to facilitate the creation of favourable conditions for Indian enterprises to invest in Viet Nam; Truong also signed a number of trade and security pacts, including an agreement providing for enhanced co-operation in oil exploration in the South China Sea, with the Indian Prime Minister, Manmohan Singh. In January 2013 Indian Vice-President Mohammad Hamid Ansari met Vietnamese government leaders during an official visit to Hanoi, when a further agreement on increased co-operation in a number of areas, including national defence, was signed.

In October 1990 the European Community (EC, now the European Union—EU, see p. 281) announced the restoration of diplomatic relations with Viet Nam. The EU-Vietnam Joint Commission, a forum for senior-level discussions on political and economic developments in the EU and Viet Nam, was established in 1996; continuing to meet once every two years, the Commission was convened in Brussels, Belgium, in October 2011. Meanwhile, in June 2008 the first session of negotiations on a comprehensive Partnership and Co-operation Agreement (PCA) between Viet Nam and the EU took place in Brussels. A further eight rounds of negotiations had been held by September 2010, following which a draft agreement was initialled by both sides in October. During a visit to Hanoi in April 2012, the EU Commissioner for Trade, Karel De Gucht, announced that the EU and Viet Nam had completed the necessary procedures required to launch formal talks on a bilateral free trade agreement; consequently, in June the final PCA was signed, and negotiations on the free trade agreement officially commenced. In April 2013 the European Parliament adopted a resolution demanding that the Vietnamese Government cease human rights violations, including political intimidation, arbitrary arrests and unfair trials (citing the conviction of a number of internet bloggers under legislation restricting freedom of expression—see Domestic Political Affairs), in addition to religious persecution and land confiscation. In the same month the International Federation for Human Rights urged the EU to suspend the free trade agreement discussions with Viet Nam in order to assess the potential impact of an accord on the rights of the country's domestic workers and farmers.

In February 1993 the French President, François Mitterrand, made an official visit to Viet Nam (the first Western head of state to do so since the country's reunification). In October 2002 President Tran Duc Luong paid the first visit to France by a Vietnamese leader since the establishment of diplomatic relations with that country in 1973. French President Jacques Chirac made an official visit to Viet Nam in October 2004, attending the fifth biennial Asia-Europe Meeting, which took place in Hanoi. Several agreements on bilateral co-operation were signed during the visit, and that Chirac pledged his country's support for Viet Nam's (ultimately successful) bid to join the WTO. In April 2013 the French Minister of Foreign Trade, Nicole Bricq, made a three-day visit to Viet Nam, during which she attended a bilateral business forum (France was in 2012 the second largest European investor in Viet Nam, after the Netherlands).

Prime Minister Nguyen Tan Dung visited Germany, Ireland and the United Kingdom in March 2008, agreeing with his counterparts in the three countries to strengthen bilateral co-operation in a range of areas. During a visit to the United Kingdom in September 2010, the Vietnamese Deputy Prime Minister and Minister of Foreign Affairs, Pham Gia Khiem, and the British Secretary of State for Foreign and Commonwealth Affairs, William Hague, signed a Strategic Partnership Agreement. Direct air passenger services between Viet Nam and the United Kingdom commenced in December 2011. In January 2013 Nguyen Phu Trong made the first official visit by a CPV General Secretary to the United Kingdom, where he met Prime Minister David Cameron for discussions; the two leaders issued a joint statement welcoming increased bilateral co-operation since the signing of the Strategic Partnership.

CONSTITUTION AND GOVERNMENT

The 1992 Constitution declares the supremacy of the Communist Party. Legislative power is vested in the National Assembly, which has 500 members and is elected for a five-year term by universal adult suffrage. The President, elected by the National Assembly from among its members, is the head of state and Commander-in-Chief of the armed forces. The President nominates a Prime Minister (from among the members of the National Assembly, and subject to their approval), who forms a government (again, subject to ratification by the National Assembly). The country is divided into provinces and municipalities, which are subordinate to the central government. Local government is entrusted to locally elected People's Councils.

REGIONAL AND INTERNATIONAL CO-OPERATION

Viet Nam is a member of the Association of Southeast Asian Nations (ASEAN, see p. 218), the Asia-Pacific Economic Co-operation (APEC, see p. 208), the Asian Development Bank (ADB, see p. 214), the UN's Economic and Social Commission for Asia and the Pacific (ESCAP, see p. 31) and the Mekong River Commission (see p. 462).

Viet Nam became a member of the UN in 1977, and was admitted to the World Trade Organization (WTO, see p. 444) in 2007. Viet Nam is also a member of the International Labour Organization (ILO, see p. 142) and the Non-aligned Movement (see p. 477).

ECONOMIC AFFAIRS

In 2011, according to estimates by the World Bank, Viet Nam's gross national income (GNI), measured at average 2009–11 prices, was US $110,907m., equivalent to $1,260 per head (or $3,260 per head on an international purchasing-power parity basis). During 2002–11, it was estimated, the population increased at an average annual rate of 1.1%, while gross domestic product (GDP) per head grew, in real terms, by an average of 6.0% per year. According to figures from the Asian Development Bank (ADB), overall GDP increased, in real terms, at an average annual rate of 7.2% in 2002–11; GDP rose by 5.0% in 2012.

In 2011, according to the ADB, agriculture (including forestry and fishing) contributed 22.0% of GDP; according to official figures, the sector engaged 47.1% of the employed labour force in 2012. The staple crop is rice. Viet Nam is also a major producer of coffee; this commodity accounted for 4.2% of export revenue in 2007. Other important cash crops include sugar cane, groundnuts, cashew nuts, rubber, tea and cotton. Exports of wood and wood products increased from US $1,943m. in 2006 to $2,404m. in 2007, when they accounted for 5.3% of total export earnings. Livestock-rearing and fishing are also important. In 2007 marine products accounted for some 8.3% of export revenues. According to figures from the ADB, agricultural GDP increased at an average annual rate of 3.6% in 2002–11; the sector's GDP expanded by 2.7% in 2012.

According to the ADB, industry (comprising manufacturing, mining and quarrying, construction and utilities) contributed 40.3% of GDP in 2011. In 2012, according to official figures, the industrial sector engaged 21.2% of the employed labour force. According to figures from the ADB, industrial GDP increased at an average annual rate of 8.5% in 2002–11. The sector's GDP expanded by 4.5% in 2012.

In 2011, according to the ADB, mining and quarrying contributed 11.0% of GDP. According to official figures, the mining sector engaged only 0.6% of the employed labour force in 2012. Viet Nam's principal mineral exports are petroleum and coal. Tin, zinc, iron, antimony, chromium, natural phosphates, bauxite and gold are also mined. Significant reserves of offshore natural gas were discovered in 1993. In 2010 exports of mineral fuels accounted for 11.0% of total merchandise exports. According to figures from the ADB, mining GDP increased at an average annual rate of 1.3% in 2002–11. Mining GDP decreased by 0.1% in 2011.

Manufacturing, according to the ADB, contributed 19.4% of GDP in 2011, and, according to official figures, accounted for 13.8% of employment in 2012. Manufacturing activities include food-processing, textiles, footwear, chemicals and electrical goods. Manufacturing GDP increased at an average annual rate of 10.0% in 2002–11, according to figures from the ADB. The sector's GDP expanded by 4.5% in 2012.

According to the ADB, construction contributed 6.4% of GDP in 2011. In 2012, according to official figures, the sector engaged 6.4% of the employed labour force. According to figures from the ADB, construction GDP increased at an average annual rate of 8.1% in 2002–11. The sector's GDP declined by 1.0% in 2011, but rose by 2.1% in 2012.

Energy is derived principally from natural gas, which in 2009 accounted for 43.4% of the total electricity produced. Other significant sources are hydroelectric power (36.0%) and coal (18.0%). In 2010 imports of mineral fuels accounted for 9.6% of the value of total merchandise imports. In February 2009 Viet

Nam's first petroleum refinery, at Dung Quat, became operational. Construction of a 2,400-MW nuclear power plant in Ninh Thuan province was due to commence in 2014, funded by a loan from Russia; the first of two planned reactors at the plant was scheduled to be completed by 2020.

The services sector, according to the ADB, contributed 37.7% of GDP in 2011; in 2012, according to official figures, the sector engaged 31.7% of the employed labour force. Tourism is an important source of foreign exchange; receipts from tourism totalled a provisional US \$5,620m. in 2011. The number of tourist arrivals rose from 6.0m. in 2011 to 6.8m. in 2012. According to figures from the ADB, the GDP of the services sector increased by an average of 7.5% per year in 2002–11. The sector's GDP rose by 6.4% in 2012.

In 2011 Viet Nam recorded a visible merchandise trade deficit of US \$450m. However, there was a surplus on the current account of the balance of payments of \$236m. in that year. In 2011 the People's Republic of China was Viet Nam's principal source of imports, supplying 25.5% of total imports; other major sources were the Republic of Korea, Singapore, Japan and Thailand. The principal market for exports in that year was the USA (which accounted for 19.1% of total exports); other important purchasers were Japan, China and the Republic of Korea. The principal exports in 2010 were miscellaneous manufactured articles, food and live animals, machinery and transport equipment, basic manufactures and mineral fuels. In that year the principal imports were machinery and transport equipment, basic manufactures, chemicals and related products, mineral fuels, food and live animals, inedible crude materials (except fuels) and miscellaneous manufactured articles.

In 2011 a budget deficit of an estimated 65,000,000m. dông, equivalent to 2.6% of GDP, was recorded. Viet Nam's total external debt was estimated by the ADB at US \$32,501m. in 2010; in 2011 the cost of servicing the debt was equivalent to 3.5% of the value of exports of goods and services. According to the International Labour Organization, the annual rate of inflation averaged 9.1% in 2002–10. According to the ADB, the rate of inflation averaged 18.6% in 2011 and 9.2% in 2012. In 2012, according to official figures, 1.7% of the labour force were unemployed.

The process of *doi moi* (renovation) was initiated in 1990 with the objective of transforming Viet Nam's centralized economy into a market-orientated system. Viet Nam's accession to the World Trade Organization (WTO, see p. 444) in January 2007 greatly improved the country's investment potential. After four years of negotiations, in June 2012 a comprehensive Partnership and Co-operation Agreement was signed between Viet Nam and the European Union (see p. 281), and negotiations on a free trade agreement officially commenced. However, owing to the deterioration in global economic conditions, foreign direct investment in Viet Nam declined from 2008. The Vietnamese Government affirmed its commitment to its programme of 'equitization', under which the number of state-owned enterprises was to be reduced by about one-half, to 690, by 2015 and to 200 by 2020, through full or partial privatization. From late 2010, however, revelations of corruption and mismanagement within state-owned enterprises, notably two shipping groups, prompted increasing public discontent. In August 2012 the arrest of a senior member of the Asia Commercial Joint Stock Bank (see Domestic Political Affairs) severely affected depositor confidence, necessitating rescue financing by the central bank. Amid a severe shortage of credit resulting from the unsustainable level of debt in the banking sector, more than 100,000 local businesses closed in 2011 and 2012, and a further 13,000 in the first quarter of 2013, according to government figures. In May 2013 the authorities planned to establish a debt asset management company, with starting capital of US \$24m., which was to issue bonds to finance the acquisition of debt; at that time non-performing loans in the banking sector were officially estimated at the equivalent of \$7,800m., or 6% of total outstanding loans (although other sources indicated that the actual level was considerably higher). Analysts criticized the proposed government measures to address banking debts as slow and inadequate, while reform of the management of state-owned enterprises was regarded as a priority. Following several currency devaluations, the authorities had succeeded in reducing the inflation rate (which had reached more than 20% at the end of 2011) to 6%–7% by early 2013; however, the worsening crisis in the banking sector had resulted in estimated growth of only 5% in 2012 (the lowest rate since 1999), and was expected further to deter foreign investment during 2013.

PUBLIC HOLIDAYS

2014: 1 January (New Year's Day), 30 January (Eve of Tet, lunar New Year)*, 31 January–5 February (Tet, lunar New Year)*, 9 April (Hung Kings Day)*, 30 April (Liberation of Saigon), 1 May (Labour Day), 2 September (National Day).

* Varies according to the lunar calendar.

Statistical Survey

Sources (unless otherwise stated): General Statistics Office of Viet Nam, 2 Hoang Van Thu, Ba Dinh District, Hanoi; tel. (4) 7332997; e-mail banbientap@gso.gov .vn; internet www.gso.gov.vn; Communist Party of Viet Nam, 1 Hoang Van Thu, Hanoi; e-mail cpv@hn.vnn.vn; internet www.cpv.org.vn.

Area and Population

AREA, POPULATION AND DENSITY

Area (sq km)	330,958*
Population (census results)	
1 April 1999	76,323,173
1 April 2009	
Males	42,413,143
Females	43,433,854
Total	85,846,997
Population (UN estimates at mid-year)†	
2011	88,791,995
2012	89,730,273
2013	90,656,548
Density (per sq km) at mid-2013	273.9

* 127,783 sq miles.
† Source: UN, *World Population Prospects: The 2010 Revision*.

POPULATION BY AGE AND SEX
(UN estimates at mid-2013)

	Males	Females	Total
0–14	10,577,670	10,099,373	20,677,043
15–64	32,008,300	32,427,159	64,435,459
65 and over	2,275,783	3,268,263	5,544,046
Total	44,861,753	45,794,795	90,656,548

Source: UN, *World Population Prospects: The 2010 Revision*.

ADMINISTRATIVE DIVISIONS
(official population estimates at 2011)

	Area (sq km)	Population ('000)	Density (per sq km)
Red River Delta	21,068.1	19,999.3	949.3
Hanoi	3,328.9	6,699.6	2,012.6
Vinh Phuc	1,236.5	1,014.6	820.5
Bac Ninh	822.7	1,060.3	1,288.8
Quang Ninh	6,102.4	1,163.7	190.7
Hai Duong	1,656.0	1,718.9	1,038.0
Haiphong	1,523.4	1,878.5	1,233.1
Hung Yen	926.0	1,150.4	1,242.3
Thai Binh	1,570.0	1,786.0	1,137.6
Ha Nam	860.5	786.9	914.5
Nam Dinh	1,651.4	1,833.5	1,110.3
Ninh Binh	1,390.3	906.9	652.3
North East	57,849.6	8,467.8	146.4
Ha Giang	7,914.9	746.3	94.3
Cao Bang	6,707.9	515.0	76.8
Bac Kan	4,859.4	298.7	61.5
Tuyen Quang	5,867.3	730.8	124.6
Lao Cai	6,383.9	637.5	99.9
Yen Bai	6,886.3	758.6	110.2
Thai Nguyen	3,531.7	1,139.4	322.6
Lang Son	8,320.8	741.2	89.1
Bac Giang	3,844.0	1,574.3	409.5
Phu Tho	3,533.4	1,326.0	375.3
North West	37,414.8	2,822.7	75.4
Dien Bien	9,562.9	512.3	53.6
Lai Chau	9,068.8	391.2	43.1
Son La	14,174.4	1,119.4	79.0
Hoa Binh	4,608.7	799.8	173.5
North Central Coast	51,461.1	10,145.6	197.2
Thanh Hoa	11,131.9	3,412.6	306.6
Nghe An	16,493.7	2,942.9	178.4
Ha Tinh	5,997.2	1,229.3	205.0
Quand Binh	8,065.3	853.0	105.8
Quang Tri	4,739.8	604.7	127.6
Thua Thien-Hué	5,033.2	1,103.1	219.2
South Central Coast	33,205.7	7,151.6	215.4
Da Nang	1,285.4	951.7	740.4
Quang Nam	10,438.4	1,435.0	137.5
Quang Ngai	5,153.0	1,221.6	237.1
Binh Dinh	6,050.6	1,497.3	247.5
Phu Yen	5,060.6	871.9	172.3
Khanh Hoa	5,217.7	1,174.1	225.0
Central Highlands	54,641.0	5,282.0	96.7
Kon Tum	9,689.6	453.2	46.8
Gia Lai	15,536.9	1,322.0	85.1
Dak Lak	13,125.4	1,771.8	135.0
Dak Nong	6,515.6	516.3	79.2
Lam Dong	9,773.5	1,218.7	124.7
South East	34,769.1	16,640.1	478.6
Ninh Thuan	3,358.3	569.0	169.4
Binh Thuan	7,812.9	1,180.3	151.1
Binh Phuoc	6,871.5	905.3	131.7
Tay Ninh	4,039.7	1,080.7	267.5
Binh Duong	2,694.4	1,691.4	627.7
Dong Nai	5,907.2	2,665.1	451.2
Ba Ria-Vung Tau	1,989.5	1,027.2	516.3
Ho Chi Minh City	2,095.6	7,521.1	3,589.0
Mekong River Delta	40,548.2	17,330.9	427.4
Long An	4,492.4	1,449.6	322.7
Tien Giang	2,508.3	1,682.6	670.8
Ben Tre	2,360.6	1,257.8	532.8
Tra Vinh	2,341.2	1,012.6	432.5
Vinh Long	1,496.8	1,028.6	687.2
Dong Thap	3,377.0	1,673.2	495.5
An Giang	3,536.7	2,151.0	608.2
Kien Giang	6,348.5	1,714.1	270.0
Can Tho	1,409.0	1,200.3	851.9
Hau Giang	1,602.5	769.2	480.0
Soc Trang	3,311.6	1,303.7	393.7
Bac Lieu	2,468.7	873.3	353.7
Ca Mau	5,294.9	1,214.9	229.4
Total	330,957.6	87,840.0	265.4

PRINCIPAL TOWNS
(excl. suburbs, estimated population at mid-1992)

Ho Chi Minh City (formerly Saigon)	3,015,743*	Nam Dinh		171,699
Hanoi (capital)	1,073,760	Qui Nhon		163,385
Haiphong	783,133	Vung Tau		145,145
Da Nang	382,674	Rach Gia		141,132
Buon Ma Thuot	282,095	Long Xuyen		132,681
Nha Trang	221,331	Thai Nguyen		127,643
Hué	219,149	Hong Gai		127,484
Can Tho	215,587	Vinh		112,455
Cam Pha	209,086			

* Including Cholon.

Source: UN, *Demographic Yearbook*.

Mid-2010 (incl. suburbs, '000 persons, UN estimates): Ho Chi Minh City 6,189; Hanoi 2,809 (refers to urban population in city districts); Can Tho 902; Haiphong 889; Da Nang 805 (Source: UN, *World Urbanization Prospects: The 2011 Revision*).

Mid-2011 (urban population in city districts, UN estimate): Hanoi 2,955,130 (Source: UN, *World Urbanization Prospects: The 2011 Revision*).

BIRTHS AND DEATHS
(annual averages, UN estimates)

	1995–2000	2000–05	2005–10
Birth rate (per 1,000)	19.0	17.2	17.2
Death rate (per 1,000)	5.8	5.3	5.2

Source: UN, *World Population Prospects: The 2010 Revision*.

Life expectancy (years at birth): 75.1 (males 73.1; females 77.1) in 2011 (Source: World Bank, World Development Indicators database).

ECONOMICALLY ACTIVE POPULATION
('000 persons aged 15 years and over, averages at mid-year)

	2010	2011	2012
Agriculture, forestry and fishing	24,279.0	24,362.9	24,359.0
Mining and quarrying	275.6	279.1	294.2
Manufacturing	6,645.8	6,972.6	7,122.8
Power and utilities	247.6	245.9	255.3
Construction	3,108.0	3,221.1	3,300.5
Wholesale and retail trade; repair of motor vehicles, motor cycles and personal and household goods	5,549.7	5,827.6	6,296.8
Hotels and restaurants	1,711.0	1,995.3	2,201.0
Transport, storage and communications	1,674.1	1,683.5	1,784.9
Financial intermediation	254.5	301.1	312.5
Scientific activities and technology	217.5	220.2	246.8
Real estate, renting and business activities	286.8	316.9	376.7
Public administration and defence; compulsory social security	1,569.6	1,542.2	1,619.8
Education and training	1,673.4	1,731.8	1,829.4
Health and social work	437.0	480.8	469.1
Recreational, cultural and sporting activities	232.4	250.1	257.2
Community, social and personal service activities and private households with employed persons	886.5	920.9	973.0
Total employed	49,048.5	50,352.0	51,699.0
Unemployed	1,344.4	1,046.4	882.3
Total labour force	50,392.9	51,398.4	52,581.3
Males	25,897.0	26,468.2	26,980.5
Females	24,495.9	24,930.2	25,600.7

Health and Welfare

KEY INDICATORS

Total fertility rate (children per woman, 2010)	1.8
Under-5 mortality rate (per 1,000 live births, 2010) . . .	23
HIV/AIDS (% of persons aged 15–49, 2009)	0.4
Physicians (per 1,000 head, 2008)	1.2
Hospital beds (per 1,000 head, 2009)	3.1
Health expenditure (2009): US $ per head (PPP)	204
Health expenditure (2009): % of GDP	6.9
Health expenditure (2009): public (% of total)	37.5
Access to water (% of persons, 2010)	95
Access to sanitation (% of persons, 2010)	76
Total carbon dioxide emissions ('000 metric tons, 2008) . .	127,384.2
Carbon dioxide emissions per head (metric tons, 2008) . .	1.5
Human Development Index (2011): ranking	128
Human Development Index (2011): value	0.593

For sources and definitions, see explanatory note on p. vi.

Agriculture

PRINCIPAL CROPS
('000 metric tons)

	2009	2010	2011
Rice, paddy	38,950	40,006	42,332
Maize	4,372	4,607	4,684*
Potatoes†	388	395	449
Sweet potatoes	1,211	1,319	1,391
Cassava (Manioc)	8,531	8,596	9,876
Sugar cane	15,608	16,162	17,465
Beans, dry†	173	185	217
Cashew nuts, with shell . . .	1,166	1,242	1,272
Soybeans (Soya beans) . . .	215	299	266
Groundnuts, with shell . . .	511	487	466
Coconuts	1,129	1,162	1,189
Cabbages and other brassicas† .	745	805	775
Onions, dry†	315	339	318
Watermelons†	440	388	468
Bananas†	1,428	1,490	1,523
Oranges	694	729	746†
Guavas, mangoes and mangosteens	554	580	596
Pineapples†	500	522	533
Coffee, green	1,058	1,106	1,168
Tea	186	198	207
Tobacco, unmanufactured . .	40	57	58†
Natural rubber	711	752	812

* Unofficial figure.
† FAO estimate(s).

Aggregate production ('000 metric tons, may include official, semi-official or estimated data): Total cereals 43,324 in 2009, 44,614 in 2010, 47,018 in 2011; Total roots and tubers 10,130 in 2009, 10,309 in 2010, 11,715 in 2011; Total vegetables (incl. melons) 9,064 in 2009, 8,976 in 2010, 10,321 in 2011; Total fruits (excl. melons) 6,162 in 2009, 6,428 in 2010, 6,573 in 2011.

Source: FAO.

LIVESTOCK
('000 head, year ending September)

	2009	2010	2011
Horses	102.2	93.1	88.1
Cattle	6,103.3	5,808.3	5,436.6
Buffaloes	2,886.6	2,877.0	2,712.0
Pigs	27,627.7	27,373.1	27,056.0
Goats	1,375.1	1,288.4	1,267.8
Chickens	200,000	218,201	225,820
Ducks	72,566	68,633	96,780

Source: FAO.

LIVESTOCK PRODUCTS
('000 metric tons)

	2009	2010	2011
Cattle meat	263.4	278.9	287.2
Buffalo meat*	105.6	105.4	99.3
Pig meat	3,035.9	3,036.4	3,098.9
Chicken meat	528.5	456.6	512.0†
Duck meat*	79.2	74.8	105.0
Cows' milk	278.2	306.7	345.4
Buffaloes' milk*	33.0	32.0	32.0
Hen eggs*	273	321	345
Silkworm cocoons* . . .	2.2	2.5	2.5

* FAO estimates.
† Unofficial figure.

Source: FAO.

Forestry

ROUNDWOOD REMOVALS
('000 cubic metres, excl. bark)

	2009	2010	2011
Sawlogs, veneer logs and logs for sleepers*	2,450	2,850	2,750
Pulpwood	2,500*	3,000	3,100
Other industrial wood . . .	900*	850	850
Fuel wood	22,000*	21,500	20,400
Total*	27,850	28,200	27,100

* FAO estimate(s).

Source: FAO.

SAWNWOOD PRODUCTION
('000 cubic metres, incl. railway sleepers, FAO estimates)

	2009	2010	2011
Total (all broadleaved) . . .	5,000	5,800	6,000

Source: FAO.

Fishing

('000 metric tons, live weight)

	2008	2009	2010
Capture*	2,136.3	2,280.5	2,420.8
Freshwater fishes . . .	178.7	177.4	182.5*
Marine fishes	1,437.8	1,530.5	1,632.0*
Prawns and shrimps . .	113.3	138.7	146.7
Cephalopods	227.7	246.5*	262.0†
Aquaculture*	2,462.5	2,556.1	2,671.8
Freshwater fishes* . . .	1,417.2	1,252.2	1,328.6
Giant tiger prawns . .	324.6	316.0	333.0*
Marine molluscs . . .	170.0*	165.0	165.0*
Total catch*	4,598.8	4,836.6	5,092.6

* FAO estimate(s).

Note: Figures exclude aquatic plants ('000 metric tons, all aquaculture, FAO estimates): 36 in 2008; 34 in 2009; 35 in 2010.

Source: FAO.

Mining

('000 metric tons unless otherwise indicated)

	2008	2009	2010
Crude petroleum ('000 barrels) .	109,291	119,968	109,753
Natural gas (million cu m)* . .	7,499	8,010	9,240
Coal (anthracite)	39,777	44,078	44,011
Chromium ore—gross weight . .	55.9	37.1	40.0
Ilmenite—gross weight† . . .	710	699	912
Gold (kg)†	3,000	3,000	3,500
Kaolin†	650	650	650
Barite (metric tons)	80,000	70,000	85,000
Phosphate rock:			
gross weight	2,101	2,047	2,268
P₂O₅ content†	630	614	680
Salt (unrefined)	717	679	1,057

P_2O_5 content†

* Gross production.
† Estimates.

Source: US Geological Survey.

Industry

SELECTED PRODUCTS

('000 metric tons unless otherwise indicated)

	2009	2010	2011*
Raw sugar	1,103.2	1,141.5	1,204.0
Beer (million litres) . . .	2,007.5	2,420.2	2,650.6
Cigarettes ('000 million packets) .	4.8	5.1	5.5
Fabrics	1,187.3	1,176.9	1,294.8
Chemical fertilizers . . .	2,360	2,411	2,397
Insecticides	75.4	73.6	74.2
Soap	845.4	815.6	763.5
Cement	48,800	55,800	59,000
Crude steel	6,531.4	7,910.5	7,527.7
Paint	254.4	292.6	344.5
Footwear (million pairs) . .	45.4	50.3	52.8
Ready-made clothes (million			
pieces)	2,776.5	2,604.5	2,890.9
Electric energy (million kWh) .	80,643	91,722	101,309

* Preliminary figures.

Finance

CURRENCY AND EXCHANGE RATES

Monetary Units
100 xu = 1 new dông.

Sterling, Dollar and Euro Equivalents (28 September 2012)
£1 sterling = 33,722.6 dông;
US $1 = 20,828.0 dông;
€1 = 26,930.6 dông;
100,000 new dông = £2.97 = $4.80 = €3.71.

Average Exchange Rate (new dông per US $)
2009   17,065.1
2010   18,612.9
2011   20,509.8

Note: The new dông, equivalent to 10 former dông, was introduced in September 1985.

BUDGET
('000,000 million dông)

Revenue (incl. grants)	2005	2006	2007*
Tax revenue	166.2	210.3	231.4
Corporate income tax . . .	71.7	100.8	99.0
Individual income tax . .	4.2	5.2	6.1
Tax on the transfer of properties	2.8	3.4	3.8
Value-added tax (VAT) . . .	45.7	54.8	78.9
Excises	15.7	17.1	17.1
Taxes on international trade .	23.6	26.3	23.8
Other taxes	2.3	2.8	2.7
Non-tax and capital revenue . .	48.5	50.3	47.5
Fees and charges	21.0	23.1	23.1
Income from natural resources .	21.9	20.2	19.9
Capital revenues	0.9	1.5	0.8
Grants	2.3	3.6	3.0
Total	**217.1**	**264.2**	**281.9**

Expenditure (cash basis)†	2005	2006	2007*
Current expenditure	155.0	181.5	221.3
General administrative services	16.8	19.0	24.8
Economic services	12.8	15.0	16.3
Social services	77.3	91.4	97.3
Education	29.1	33.8	38.1
Health	10.7	12.7	14.7
Social subsidies	23.6	28.7	26.8
Other services (incl. defence) .	13.8	16.3	17.8
Interest on public debt . . .	7.0	8.9	11.7
Capital expenditure	72.0	86.1	99.5
Total	**226.9**	**267.6**	**320.7**

* Forecasts.
† Excluding off-budget investment expenditure ('000,000 million dông): 39.4 in 2005; 33.7 in 2006; 39.4 in 2007 (forecast).

Source: IMF, *Vietnam: Statistical Appendix* (December 2007).

2009 ('000 billion dông): *Revenue:* Tax revenue 373 (Oil revenues 61, Non-oil tax revenues 312); Non-tax and capital revenues 72; Total 445 (excl. grants 8). *Expenditure:* Government expenditure 349; Net acquisition of non-financial assets 223; Total 572 (Source: IMF—see below).

2010 ('000 billion dông, estimates): *Revenue:* Tax revenue 477 (Oil revenues 69, Non-oil tax revenues 408); Non-tax and capital revenues 69; Total 547 (excl. grants 5). *Expenditure:* Government expenditure 434; Net acquisition of non-financial assets 221; Total 655 (Source: IMF—see below).

2011 ('000 billion dông, estimates): *Revenue:* Tax revenue 615 (Oil revenues 111, Non-oil tax revenues 504); Non-tax and capital revenues 82; Total 697 (excl. grants 7). *Expenditure:* Government expenditure 557; Net acquisition of non-financial assets 212; Total 769 (Source: IMF, *Vietnam: Staff Report for the 2012 Article IV Consultation*—July 2012).

INTERNATIONAL RESERVES
(US $ million at 31 December)

	2009	2010	2011
Gold (market valuation) . . .	356.1	459.6	506.4
IMF special drawing rights . .	419.7	412.5	411.5
Foreign exchange	16,027.4	12,054.1	13,127.6
Total	**16,803.2**	**12,926.2**	**14,045.5**

Source: IMF, *International Financial Statistics*.

MONEY SUPPLY
('000 million dông at 31 December)

	2009	2010	2011
Currency outside banks . . .	293,225	337,949	370,992
Demand deposits at banks . .	271,988	287,503	315,128
Total money	**565,213**	**625,451**	**686,120**

Source: IMF, *International Financial Statistics*.

COST OF LIVING
(Consumer Price Index; base: previous year = 100)

	2009	2010	2011
Food	108.7	110.7	126.5
Beverages and tobacco	109.6	108.2	111.7
Clothing (incl. footwear) . . .	108.9	106.9	112.1
Household goods	108.5	105.4	108.8
Housing and construction . . .	103.5	114.7	119.7
Education	105.7	110.4	123.2
All items (incl. others) . . .	106.9	109.2	118.6

NATIONAL ACCOUNTS
('000 million dông at current prices)

Expenditure on the Gross Domestic Product

	2009	2010	2011
Government final consumption expenditure	104,540	129,313	164,323
Private final consumption expenditure	1,102,279	1,317,588	1,630,143
Increase in stocks	59,800	65,810	81,538
Gross fixed capital formation . .	572,526	704,401	745,494
Total domestic expenditure .	1,839,144	2,217,112	2,621,498
Exports of goods and services . .	1,132,688	1,535,816	2,205,858
Less Imports of goods and services	1,304,350	1,739,363	2,312,711
Sub-total	1,667,481	2,013,565	2,514,645
Statistical discrepancy	−9,093	−32,651	20,363
GDP in purchasers' values .	1,658,389	1,980,914	2,535,008
GDP at constant 1994 prices .	516,566	551,609	584,073

Gross Domestic Product by Economic Activity

	2009	2010	2011
Agriculture, forestry and fishing .	346,786	407,647	558,284
Mining and quarrying	165,310	215,090	279,934
Manufacturing	333,166	389,807	491,778
Electricity, gas and water . . .	58,592	70,006	86,076
Construction	110,255	139,162	162,620
Trade	244,933	289,089	369,618
Transport, storage and communications	72,412	85,392	101,247
Finance	31,617	37,404	47,569
Public administration . . .	128,904	149,647	188,342
Other community, social and personal services	166,414	197,670	249,540
Total	1,658,389	1,980,914	2,535,008

Source: Asian Development Bank.

BALANCE OF PAYMENTS
(US $ million)

	2009	2010	2011
Exports of goods	57,096	72,237	96,906
Imports of goods	−64,703	−77,373	−97,356
Balance on goods	−7,607	−5,136	−450
Exports of services	5,766	7,460	8,879
Imports of services	−8,187	−9,921	−11,859
Balance on goods and services	−10,028	−7,597	−3,430
Primary income received . . .	753	456	395
Primary income paid . . .	−3,781	−5,020	−5,414
Balance on goods, services and primary income	−13,056	−12,161	−8,449
Secondary income (net) . . .	6,448	7,885	8,685
Current balance	−6,608	−4,276	236
Direct investment assets . . .	−700	−900	−950
Direct investment liabilities . .	7,600	8,000	7,430
Portfolio investment assets . .	−199	−13	348
Portfolio investment liabilities .	128	2,383	1,064
Other investment assets . . .	−4,803	−7,063	−6,402
Other investment liabilities . .	5,146	3,794	4,900
Net errors and omissions . . .	−9,029	−3,690	−5,475
Reserves and related items .	−8,465	−1,765	1,151

Source: IMF, *International Financial Statistics*.

External Trade

SELECTED COMMODITIES
(distribution by SITC, US $ million)

Imports c.i.f.	2008	2009	2010
Food and live animals	4,525	4,631	6,225
Beverages and tobacco	269	342	293
Crude materials (inedible) except fuels	4,006	3,389	4,622
Mineral fuels, etc.	12,330	7,497	8,140
Animal and vegetable fats, and oils	636	482	682
Chemicals and related products .	10,298	10,225	12,491
Basic manufactures . . .	20,113	17,777	22,450
Machinery and transport equipment	22,425	21,908	24,714
Miscellaneous manufactured goods	3,384	3,315	4,256
Total (incl. others)	80,714	69,949	84,839

Exports f.o.b.	2008	2009	2010
Food and live animals	12,164	11,515	13,433
Beverages and tobacco	191	238	301
Crude materials (inedible) except fuels	2,492	1,928	3,374
Mineral fuels, etc.	12,751	8,507	7,980
Chemicals and related products .	1,450	1,270	1,882
Basic manufactures . . .	6,398	5,226	8,486
Machinery and transport equipment	7,368	7,399	11,476
Miscellaneous manufactured goods	19,409	20,112	25,169
Total (incl. others)	62,685	57,096	72,237

2011 (preliminary): Total imports 106,750; Total exports 96,906.

PRINCIPAL TRADING PARTNERS
(US $ million)

Imports c.i.f.	2009	2010	2011
China, People's Republic . . .	16,441	20,019	31,997
Hong Kong	826	860	6,524
India	1,635	1,762	2,623
Indonesia	1,546	1,909	2,590
Japan	7,468	9,016	10,563
Korea, Republic	6,976	9,761	14,906
Malaysia	2,505	3,413	3,802
Singapore	4,248	4,101	11,255
Thailand	4,514	5,602	7,684
USA	3,009	3,767	4,775
Total (incl. others)	69,949	83,365	125,723

Exports f.o.b.	2009	2010	2011
Australia	2,277	2,704	2,925
China, People's Republic . . .	4,909	7,309	10,098
Germany	1,885	2,373	4,161
Japan	6,292	7,728	10,532
Korea, Republic	2,065	3,092	4,622
Malaysia	1,682	2,093	2,880
Netherlands	1,335	1,688	1,615
Philippines	1,462	1,642	n.a.
Singapore	2,076	2,121	1,508
United Kingdom	1,329	1,682	2,152
USA	11,356	14,238	16,777
Total (incl. others)	57,196	69,820	87,936

Note: Data reflect the IMF's direction of trade methodology and, as a result, the totals may not be equal to those presented for trade in commodities.

Source: Asian Development Bank.

Transport

RAILWAYS
(traffic)

	2009	2010	2011*
Passengers carried (million) . .	11.1	11.2	11.9
Passenger-km ('000 million) . .	4.1	4.4	4.6
Freight carried (million metric tons)	8.2	7.9	7.2
Freight ton-km ('000 million) .	3.9	4.0	4.1

* Preliminary figures.

ROAD TRAFFIC

	2009	2010	2011*
Passengers carried (million) . .	1,761.0	2,011.1	2,326.8
Passenger-km ('000 million) . .	61.5	69.2	78.7
Freight carried (million metric tons)	513.6	587.0	663.9
Freight ton-km ('000 million) .	31.6	36.2	40.2

* Preliminary figures.

Commercial vehicles ('000 in use): 49.4 in 1998; 57.8 in 1999; 69.9 in 2000 (Source: UN, *Statistical Yearbook*).

INLAND WATERWAYS

	2009	2010	2011*
Passengers carried (million) . .	151.3	157.5	172.6
Passenger-km ('000 million) . .	3.0	3.2	3.6
Freight carried (million metric tons)	137.7	144.2	157.2
Freight ton-km ('000 million) .	31.2	31.7	36.6

* Preliminary figures.

SHIPPING

Flag Registered Fleet
(at 31 December)

	2010	2011	2012
Number of vessels	1,122	1,153	1,181
Total displacement ('000 grt) . .	4,164.7	4,252.7	4,382.3

Source: Lloyd's List Intelligence (www.lloydslistintelligence.com).

International Sea-Borne Shipping
(freight traffic)

	2009	2010	2011*
Freight carried (million metric tons)	55.8	61.6	64.7
Freight ton-km ('000 million) .	132.1	145.5	142.6

* Preliminary figures.

CIVIL AVIATION
(domestic and international traffic on scheduled services)

	2009	2010	2011*
Passengers carried (million) . .	10.9	14.2	15.6
Passenger-km (million) . . .	16,507.6	21,162.0	23,476.0
Freight carried ('000 metric tons).	139.6	190.1	199.2
Freight ton-km (million) . . .	316.6	426.8	449.0

* Preliminary figures.

Tourism

TOURIST ARRIVALS BY COUNTRY OF RESIDENCE

Country	2010	2011	2012
Australia	278,155	289,762	289,844
Cambodia	254,553	423,440	331,939
China, People's Republic . . .	905,360	1,416,804	1,428,693
France	199,351	211,444	219,721
Japan	442,089	481,519	576,386
Korea, Republic	495,902	536,408	700,917
Malaysia	211,337	233,132	299,041
Taiwan	334,007	361,051	409,385
Thailand	222,839	181,820	225,866
USA	430,993	439,872	443,826
Total (incl. others)	5,049,855	6,014,032	6,847,678

Source: Viet Nam National Administration of Tourism.

Tourism receipts (US $ million, excl. passenger transport): 3,050 in 2009; 4,450 in 2010; 5,620 in 2011 (provisional) (Source: World Tourism Organization).

Communications Media

	2009	2010	2011
Telephones ('000 main lines in use)	17,427.4	14,374.4	10,174.8
Mobile cellular telephones ('000 subscribers)	98,224.0	111,570.2	127,318.0
Broadband subscribers ('000) . .	3,214.2	3,669.3	3,838.2

Internet subscribers ('000): 6,700 in 2008.

Source: International Telecommunication Union.

Education

(2011/12 unless otherwise indicated)

	Institutions	Teachers ('000)	Students (million)
Pre-primary	13,174	174.0	3.3
Primary	15,337	366.0	7.1
Lower secondary	10,243	312.0	4.9
Upper secondary	2,350	150.1	2.8
Universities and colleges . . .	419	84.2	2.2

Pupil-teacher ratio (primary education, UNESCO estimate): 19.9 in 2009/10 (Source: UNESCO Institute for Statistics).

Adult literacy rate (UNESCO estimates): 93.2% (males 95.3%; females 91.1%) in 2010 (Source: UNESCO Institute for Statistics)

Directory

The Government

HEAD OF STATE

President: TRUONG TAN SANG (appointment approved by the 12th National Assembly on 25 July 2011).

Vice-President: NGUYEN THI DOAN.

CABINET
(May 2013)

The Cabinet is formed by Dang Cong San Viet Nam (the Communist Party of Viet Nam).

Prime Minister: NGUYEN TAN DUNG.

Deputy Prime Ministers: NGUYEN THIEN NHAN, HOANG TRUNG HAI, NGUYEN XUAN PHUC, VU VAN NINH.

Minister of Foreign Affairs: PHAM BINH MINH.

Minister of National Defence: Gen. PHUNG QUANG THANH.

Minister of Public Security: TRAN DAI QUANG.

Minister of Justice: HA HUNG CUONG.

Minister of Finance: VUONG DINH HUE.

Minister of Labour, War Invalids and Social Affairs: PHAM THI HAI CHUYEN.

Minister of Health: NGUYEN THI KIM TIEN.

Minister of Education and Training: PHAM VU LUAN.

Minister of Culture, Sports and Tourism: HOANG TUAN ANH.

Minister of Construction: TRINH DINH DUNG.

Minister of Transport: DINH LA THANG.

Minister of Home Affairs: NGUYEN THAI BINH.

Minister of Agriculture and Rural Development: CAO DUC PHAT.

Minister of Industry and Trade: VU HUY HOANG.

Minister of Planning and Investment: BUI QUANG VINH.

Minister of Science and Technology: NGUYEN QUAN.

Minister of Natural Resources and the Environment: NGUYEN MINH QUANG.

Minister of Information and Communications: NGUYEN BAC SON.

Chief Government Inspector: HUYNH PHONG TRANH.

Minister, Chairman of the Committee for Ethnic Minority Affairs: GIANG SEO PHU.

Minister, Chairman of the Government Office: VU DUC DAM.

MINISTRIES AND COMMITTEES

Ministry of Agriculture and Rural Development: 2 Ngoc Ha, Ba Dinh District, Hanoi; tel. (4) 38468161; fax (4) 38454319; e-mail webmaster@agroviet.gov.vn; internet www.agroviet.gov.vn.

Ministry of Construction: 37 Le Dai Hanh, Hai Ba Trung District, Hanoi; tel. (4) 39760271; fax (4) 39762153; e-mail boxaydung@moc .gov.vn; internet www.moc.gov.vn.

Ministry of Culture, Sports and Tourism: 2 Hoa Lu, Hanoi; tel. (4) 39439915; fax (4) 39439009; e-mail phongthongtin@cinet.gov.vn; internet www.cinet.gov.vn.

Ministry of Education and Training: 49 Dai Co Viet, Hai Ba Trung District, Hanoi; tel. (4) 38692397; fax (4) 38694085; e-mail bogddt@moet.edu.vn; internet www.moet.gov.vn.

Ministry of Finance: 28 Tran Hung Dao, Hoan Kiem District, Hanoi; tel. (4) 22202828; fax (4) 22208091; e-mail support@mof.gov .vn; internet www.mof.gov.vn.

Ministry of Foreign Affairs: 1 Ton That Dam, Ba Dinh District, Hanoi; tel. (4) 37992000; fax (4) 38231872; e-mail banbientap@mofa .gov.vn; internet www.mofa.gov.vn.

Ministry of Health: 138A Giang Vo, Ba Dinh District, Hanoi; tel. (4) 62732273; fax (4) 38464051; e-mail byt@moh.gov.vn; internet www .moh.gov.vn.

Ministry of Home Affairs: 8 Ton That Thuyet, Cau Giay District, Hanoi; tel. (4) 39764116; fax (4) 39781005; e-mail websitemaster@ moha.gov.vn; internet www.moha.gov.vn.

Ministry of Industry and Trade: 54 Hai Ba Trung, Hoan Kiem District, Hanoi; tel. (4) 22202222; fax (4) 22202525; e-mail bbt@moit .gov.vn; internet www.moit.gov.vn.

Ministry of Information and Communications: 18 Nguyen Du, Hanoi; tel. (4) 39435602; fax (4) 38263477; e-mail banbientap@mic .gov.vn; internet mic.gov.vn.

Ministry of Justice: 60 Tran Phu, Ba Dinh District, Hanoi; tel. (4) 37332802; fax (4) 38431431; e-mail banbientap@moj.gov.vn; internet www.moj.gov.vn.

Ministry of Labour, War Invalids and Social Affairs: 12 Ngo Quyen, Hoan Kiem District, Hanoi; tel. (4) 38248913; fax (4) 38248036; e-mail lasic@molisa.gov.vn; internet www.molisa.gov.vn.

Ministry of National Defence: 7 Nguyen Tri Phuong, Ba Dinh District, Hanoi; tel. (69) 534223; fax (69) 532090.

Ministry of Natural Resources and the Environment: 83 Nguyen Chi Thanh, Dong Da District, Hanoi; tel. (4) 38343911; fax (4) 37736892; e-mail baotainguyenmoitruong@gmail.com; internet www.monre.gov.vn.

Ministry of Planning and Investment: 6B Hoang Dieu, Ba Dinh District, Hanoi; tel. (4) 38433360; fax (80) 48473; e-mail banbientap@ mpi.gov.vn; internet www.mpi.gov.vn.

Ministry of Public Security: 44 Yet Kieu, Hoan Kiem District, Hanoi; tel. (4) 38226602; fax (4) 39420223; internet www.mps.gov.vn.

Ministry of Science and Technology: 113 Tran Duy Hung, Cau Giay District, Hanoi; tel. (4) 39437056; fax (4) 39439733; e-mail bbt@ most.gov.vn; internet www.most.gov.vn.

Ministry of Transport: 80 Tran Hung Dao, Hoan Kiem District, Hanoi; tel. (4) 39424015; fax (4) 39423291; internet www.mt.gov.vn.

Committee for Ethnic Minority Affairs: 80 Phan Dinh Phung, Ba Dinh District, Hanoi; tel. (4) 37333511; fax (4) 38230235; internet www.cema.gov.vn.

Government Inspection Committee: 29D Tran Thai Tong, Cau Giay District, Hanoi; tel. (80) 43490; fax (80) 48493; e-mail ttcp@ thanhtra.gov.vn; internet www.thanhtra.gov.vn.

NATIONAL DEFENCE AND SECURITY COUNCIL

President: TRUONG TAN SANG.

Vice-President: NGUYEN TAN DUNG.

Members: NGUYEN SINH HUNG, TRAN DAI QUANG, PHUNG QUANG THANH, PHAM BINH MINH.

Legislature

QUOC HOI
(National Assembly)

Elections for the 13th National Assembly were held on 22 May 2011. More than 90% of the new Assembly's 500 legislators were reported to be members of the Communist Party. Of these, people from ethnic minority groups won 78 seats and women 122 seats. Also elected were 42 non-party candidates, including four independents.

Standing Committee

Chairman: NGUYEN SINH HUNG.

Vice-Chairmen: UONG CHU LUU, NGUYEN THI KIM NGAN, TONG THI PHONG, HUYNH NGOC SON.

Political Organizations

COMMUNIST PARTY

Dang Cong San Viet Nam (Communist Party of Viet Nam—CPV): 1A Hung Vuong, Hanoi; e-mail dangcongsan@cpv.org.vn; internet www.cpv.org.vn; f. 1976; ruling party; fmrly the Viet Nam Workers' Party (f. 1951 as the successor to the Communist Party of Indo-China, f. 1930); Cen. Cttee of 175 full mems and 25 alternate mems elected at 11th National Congress held in Jan. 2011; 14-mem. Politburo and 4-mem. Secretariat elected (see below); 3.6m. mems; Gen. Sec. of Cen. Cttee NGUYEN PHU TRONG.

Political Bureau (Politburo)

Members: LE HONG ANH, NGO VAN DU, NGUYEN TAN DUNG, LE THANH HAI, NGUYEN SINH HUNG, DINH THE HUYNH, PHAM QUANG NGHI, TONG THI PHONG, NGUYEN XUAN PHUC, TRAN DAI QUANG, TO HUY RUA, TRUONG TAN SANG, Gen. PHUNG QUANG THANH, NGUYEN PHU TRONG.

Secretariat

Members: TRUONG HOA BINH, HA THI KHIET, NGO XUAN LICH, NGUYEN THI KIM NGAN.

OTHER POLITICAL ORGANIZATIONS

Ho Chi Minh Communist Youth Union: 62 Ba Trieu, Hanoi; tel. (4) 62631874; fax (4) 62631875; e-mail bqt.twd@gmail.com; internet doanthanhnien.vn; f. 1931; 4m. mems; First Sec. NGUYEN DAC VINH.

People's Action Party (PAP): POB 4752, San Jose, CA 95150-4752, USA; e-mail tnhd2010@gmail.com; internet www.dndhd.org; Chair. NGUYEN SI BINH.

Viet Nam Fatherland Front: 46 Trang Thi, Hanoi; tel. (4) 9287401; e-mail ubmttqvn@mattran.org.vn; internet www.mattran.org.vn; f. 1930; replaced the Lien Viet (Viet Nam National League), the successor to Viet Nam Doc Lap Dong Minh Hoi (Revolutionary League for the Independence of Viet Nam) or Viet Minh; in 1977 the original org. merged with the National Front for the Liberation of South Viet Nam and the Alliance of National, Democratic and Peace Forces in South Viet Nam to form a single front; 200-mem. Cen. Cttee; Pres. Presidium of Cen. Cttee HUYNH DAM; Gen. Sec. NONG DUC MANH.

Vietnam Women's Union (VWU): 39 Hang Chuoi, Hanoi; tel. (4) 9713436; fax (4) 9713143; internet hoilhpn.org.vn; f. 1930; 13m. mems; Pres. NGUYEN THI THANH HOA.

Diplomatic Representation

EMBASSIES IN VIET NAM

Algeria: 13 Phan Chu Trinh, Hanoi; tel. (4) 38253865; fax (4) 38260830; e-mail ambalghanoi@ambalgvn.org.vn; internet www.ambalgvn.org.vn; Ambassador CHÉRIF CHIKHI.

Argentina: Sentinel Place, 41A Ly Thai To, Hoan Kiem, Hanoi; tel. (4) 38315262; fax (4) 38315577; e-mail eviet@mrecic.gov.ar; internet www.eviet.mrecic.gob.ar; Ambassador ALBERTO J. KAMINKER.

Australia: 8 Dao Tan, Ba Dinh District, Hanoi; tel. (4) 37740100; fax (4) 37740111; e-mail austemb@fpt.vn; internet www.vietnam.embassy.gov.au; Ambassador HUGH BORROWMAN.

Austria: Prime Centre, 8th Floor, 53 Quang Trung, Hai Ba Trung District, Hanoi; tel. (4) 39433050; fax (4) 39433055; e-mail hanoi-ob@bmeia.gv.at; internet www.bmeia.gv.at/botschaft/hanoi; Ambassador Dr GEORG HEINDL.

Bangladesh: Vuon Dao Compound, Villa D6B-05, 675 Lac Long Quan, Tay Ho District, Hanoi; tel. (4) 37716625; fax (4) 37716628; e-mail bdoothn@netnam.org.vn; internet www.bangladeshembassy.vn; Ambassador SUPRADIP CHAKMA.

Belarus: 66 To Ngoc Van, Tay Ho District, Hanoi; tel. (4) 38290494; fax (4) 37197125; e-mail vietnam@mfa.gov.by; internet www.vietnam.mfa.gov.by; Ambassador VALERIY E. SADOKHO.

Belgium: Hanoi Towers, 9th Floor, 49 Hai Ba Trung, Hanoi; tel. (4) 39346179; fax (4) 39346183; e-mail Pub.Hanoi@diplobel.fed.be; internet www.diplomatie.be/hanoi; Ambassador BRUNO ANGELET.

Brazil: Villa D6-07, 14 Thuy Khue, Tay Ho District, Hanoi; tel. (4) 38432544; fax (4) 38432542; e-mail vetbrem@vnn.vn; internet hanoi.itamaraty.gov.br; Ambassador VITÓRIA ALICE CLEAVER.

Brunei: Villa 8 and 9, 44/8 Van Bao, Van Phuc Diplomatic Quarter, Ba Dinh District, Hanoi; tel. (4) 7262001; fax (4) 7262010; e-mail hanoi.vietnam@mfa.gov.bn; Ambassador Dato Paduka Haji MAHADI BIN WASLI.

Bulgaria: Van Phuc Quarter, 5 Nui Truc, Hanoi; tel. (4) 38452908; fax (4) 38460856; e-mail embassy.hanoi@mfa.bg; internet www.mfa.bg/embassies/vietnam; Chargé d'affaires STOYAN PETKOV.

Cambodia: 71A Tran Hung Dao, Hanoi; tel. (4) 8253788; fax (4) 9423225; e-mail camemb.vnm@mfa.gov.kh; Ambassador HUL PHANY.

Canada: 31 Hung Vuong, Hanoi; tel. (4) 37345000; fax (4) 37345049; e-mail hanoi@international.gc.ca; internet www.canadainternational.gc.ca/vietnam; Ambassador DEBORAH CHATSIS.

Chile: Villa C8–D8, 14 Thuy Khue, Tay Ho District, Hanoi; tel. (4) 39351147; fax (4) 38430762; e-mail embajada1@chile.org.vn; internet chileabroad.gov.cl/vietnam; Ambassador FERNANDO URRUTIA CONCHA.

China, People's Republic: 46 Hoang Dieu, Hanoi; tel. (4) 38453736; fax (4) 38232826; e-mail eossc@hn.vnn.vn; internet vn.chineseembassy.org; Ambassador KONG XUANYOU.

Cuba: 65A Ly Thuong Kiet, Hanoi; tel. (4) 9424775; fax (4) 9422426; e-mail embacuba@fpt.vn; internet embacuba.cubaminrex.cu/vietnam; Ambassador FREDESMÁN TURRÓ GONZÁLEZ.

Czech Republic: 13 Chu Van An, Hanoi; tel. (4) 38454131; fax (4) 38233996; e-mail hanoi@embassy.mzv.cz; internet www.mfa.cz/hanoi; Ambassador MARTIN KLEPETKO.

Denmark: 19 Dien Bien Phu, Hanoi; tel. (4) 38231888; fax (4) 38231999; e-mail hanamb@um.dk; internet www.ambhanoi.um.dk; Ambassador JOHN NIELSEN.

Egypt: 63 To Ngoc Van, Quang An, Tay Ho District, Hanoi; tel. (4) 8294999; fax (4) 8294997; e-mail arabegypt@ftp.vn; Ambassador MUHAMMAD R. K. EL-TAIFY.

Finland: Central Bldg, 6th Floor, Suite 63, 31 Hai Ba Trung, Hanoi; tel. (4) 38266788; fax (4) 38266766; e-mail sanomat.han@formin.fi; internet www.finland.org.vn; Ambassador KIMMO LÄHDEVIRTA.

France: 57 Tran Hung Dao, Hanoi; tel. (4) 39445700; fax (4) 39445717; e-mail ambafrance.hanoi@diplomatie.gouv.fr; internet www.ambafrance-vn.org; Ambassador JEAN-NOËL POIRIER.

Germany: 29 Tran Phu, Hanoi; tel. (4) 38453836; fax (4) 38453838; e-mail info@hanoi.diplo.de; internet www.hanoi.diplo.de; Ambassador JUTTA FRASCH.

Greece: 28 Thanh Nien, Ba Dinh District, Hanoi; tel. (4) 37152254; fax (4) 37152253; e-mail gremb.han@mfa.gr; Ambassador ROSE IEREMIA.

Hungary: Daeha Business Centre, 12th Floor, 360 Kim Ma, Ba Dinh District, Hanoi; tel. (4) 37715714; fax (4) 37715716; e-mail mission.hoi@kum.hu; internet www.mfa.gov.hu/kulkepviselet/vn; Ambassador ESZTER TORDA.

India: 58–60 Tran Hung Dao, Hanoi; tel. (4) 38244990; fax (4) 38244998; e-mail embassyindia@fpt.vn; internet www.indembassy.com.vn; Ambassador RANJIT RAE.

Indonesia: 50 Ngo Quyen, Hanoi; tel. (4) 38253353; fax (4) 38259274; e-mail komhan@hn.vnn.vn; internet www.deplu.go.id/hanoi; Ambassador MAYERFAS.

Iran: 54 Tran Phu, Ba Dinh District, Hanoi; tel. (4) 8232068; fax (4) 8232120; e-mail embiri@fpt.vn; internet www.iranembassy.org.vn; Ambassador HOSSEIN ALVANDI-BEHINEH.

Iraq: 66 Tran Hung Dao, Hanoi; tel. (4) 39424141; fax (4) 39424055; e-mail hanemb@iraqmfamail.com; internet www.mofamission.gov.iq/vnm; Ambassador FARIS ABD AL-KARIM ZAARAWI.

Ireland: Sentinel Place, 2nd Floor, 41A Ly Thai To, Hoan Kiem District, Hanoi; tel. (4) 39743291; fax (4) 39743295; e-mail irishembassyhanoi@dfanet.ie; internet www.embassyofireland.vn; Ambassador DAMIEN COLE.

Israel: 68 Nguyen Thai Hoc, Dong Da, Hanoi; tel. (4) 38433140; fax (4) 38435760; e-mail info@hanoi.mfa.gov.il; internet hanoi.mfa.gov.il; Ambassador MEIRAV EILON SHAHAR.

Italy: 9 Le Phung Hieu, Hoan Kiem District, Hanoi; tel. (4) 38256256; fax (4) 38267602; e-mail ambasciata.hanoi@esteri.it; internet www.ambhanoi.esteri.it; Ambassador LORENZO ANGELONI.

Japan: 27 Lieu Giai, Ba Dinh District, Hanoi; tel. (4) 38463000; fax (4) 38463043; e-mail soumuhan@vnn.vn; internet www.vn.emb-japan.go.jp; Ambassador YASUAKI TANIZAKI.

Korea, Democratic People's Republic: 25 Cao Ba Quat, Hanoi; tel. (4) 8453008; fax (4) 8231221; e-mail emb.dprk@hn.vnn.vn; Ambassador KIM CHANG IL.

Korea, Republic: Daeha Business Centre, 4th Floor, 360 Kim Ma, Ba Dinh District, Hanoi; tel. (4) 38315111; fax (4) 38315117; e-mail koreambviet@mofat.go.kr; internet vnm-hanoi.mofa.go.kr; Ambassador HA CHAN-HO.

Kuwait: Hilton Hanoi Opera Hotel, Dang Thai Than, Hoan Kiem District, Hanoi; tel. (4) 9330609; fax (4) 9330611; e-mail hanoi@mofa.gov.kw; Chargé d'affaires a.i. OSAMA AL-OBAID.

Laos: 22 Tran Binh Trong, Hai Ba Trung, Hanoi; tel. (4) 9424576; fax (4) 8228414; internet www.embalaohanoi.gov.la; Ambassador SOMPHONE SICHALENNE.

Libya: A3 Van Phuc Residential Quarter, Kim Ma, Hanoi; tel. (4) 8453379; fax (4) 8454977; e-mail libpbha@yahoo.com; Secretary SALEM ALI SALEM DANNAH.

Malaysia: 43–45 Dien Bien Phu, Ba Dinh District, Hanoi; tel. (4) 37343836; fax (4) 37343832; e-mail malhanoi@kln.gov.my; internet www.kln.gov.my/web/vnm_hanoi; Ambassador Datuk AZMIL MOHD ZABIDI.

Mexico: 14 Thuy Khue, T-11, Hanoi; tel. (4) 38470948; fax (4) 38470949; e-mail embvietnam@sre.gob.mx; internet www.sre.gob.mx/vietnam; Ambassador GILBERTO LIMON ENRIQUEZ.

Mongolia: Villa 6, Van Phuc Diplomatic Quarter, Hanoi; tel. (4) 38453009; fax (4) 38454954; e-mail mongembhanoi@vnn.vn; Ambassador DORJIIN ENKHBAT.

Morocco: 9 Chu Van An, Ba Dinh District, Hanoi; tel. (4) 37345586; fax (4) 37345589; e-mail embamaroc-hanoi@vnn.vn; Ambassador EL HOUCINE FARDANI.

Myanmar: 298A Kim Ma, Hanoi; tel. (4) 38453369; fax (4) 38452404; e-mail mevhan@fpt.vn; internet www.mofa.gov.mm/myanmarmissions/vietnam.html; Ambassador THET OO.

Netherlands: Daeha Office Tower, 6th Floor, 360 Kim Ma, Ba Dinh District, Hanoi; tel. (4) 38315650; fax (4) 38315655; e-mail han@minbuza.nl; internet www.hollandinvietnam.org; Ambassador JOZEF WILLEM SCHEFFERS.

New Zealand: 5th Floor, 63 Ly Thai To, Hanoi; tel. (4) 38241481; fax (4) 38241480; e-mail nzembassy.hanoi@mft.net.nz; internet www.nzembassy.com/viet-nam; Ambassador HAIKE MANNING.

Norway: Hanoi Tower, 8th Floor, 42 Hai Ba Trung, Hanoi; tel. (4) 39748900; fax (4) 39743301; e-mail emb.hanoi@mfa.no; internet www.norway.org.vn; Ambassador STÅLE TORSTEIN RISA.

Pakistan: 44/2 Van Bao, Van Phuc Diplomatic Quarter, Hanoi; tel. (4) 37262251; fax (4) 37262253; e-mail parepvietnam@yahoo.com; internet www.mofa.gov.pk/vietnam; Ambassador (vacant).

Panama: 17F, 191 Ba Trieu, Hai Ba Trung, Hanoi; tel. (4) 9365213; e-mail empanviet@yahoo.com; Ambassador EDUARDO ANTONIO YOUNG VIRZI.

Philippines: 27B Tran Hung Dao, Hanoi; tel. (4) 39437873; fax (4) 39435760; e-mail hnpe2000@gmail.com; internet www.hanoipe.org; Ambassador JERRIL G. SANTOS.

Poland: 3 Chua Mot Cot, Hanoi; tel. (4) 38452027; fax (4) 38236914; e-mail hanoi.amb.sekretariat@msz.gov.pl; internet www.hanoi.msz.gov.pl; Ambassador ROMAN IWASZKIEWICZ.

Qatar: 43 Tran Hung Dao, Hoan Kiem District, Hanoi; tel. (4) 39430222; fax (4) 39440148; e-mail hanoi@mofa.gov.qa; Ambassador MUHAMMED JABER ABDULLAH AL-SULAITI.

Romania: 5 Le Hong Phong, Hanoi; tel. (4) 38452014; fax (4) 38430922; e-mail romambhan@fpt.vn; Chargé d'affaires a.i. VALERIU ARTENI.

Russia: 191 La Thanh, Hanoi; tel. (4) 38336991; fax (4) 38336995; e-mail rusemb.vietnam@gmail.com; internet www.vietnam.mid.ru; Ambassador ANDREI GRIGORIEVICH KOVTUN.

Saudi Arabia: 42A Tran Phu, Ba Dinh District, Hanoi; tel. (4) 37264373; fax (4) 37264374; e-mail viemb@mofa.gov.sa; Ambassador SALAH AHMAD SARHAN.

Singapore: 41–43 Tran Phu, Hanoi; tel. (4) 38489168; fax (4) 38489178; e-mail singemb_han@sgmfa.gov.sg; internet www.mfa.gov.sg/hanoi; Ambassador NG TECK HEAN.

South Africa: Central Bldg, 3rd Floor, 31 Hai Ba Trung, Hanoi; tel. (4) 9362000; fax (4) 9361991; e-mail admin.hanoi@foreign.gov.za; Ambassador K. R. MAGAU.

Spain: 4 Le Hong Phong, Ba Dinh District, Hanoi; tel. (4) 37715207; fax (4) 37715206; e-mail Emb.Hanoi@maec.es; internet www.maec.es/subwebs/embajadas/hanoi; Ambassador FERNANDO CURCIO RUI-GÓMEZ.

Sri Lanka: 55B Tran Phu, Ba Dinh District, Hanoi; tel. (4) 37341894; fax (4) 37341897; e-mail slembvn@fpt.vn; internet www.slembvn.org; Ambassador KALAHE GAMAGE IVAN AMARASINGHE.

Sweden: 2 Nui Truc, Ba Dinh District, Hanoi; tel. (4) 37260400; fax (4) 38232195; e-mail ambassaden.hanoi@foreign.ministry.se; internet www.swedenabroad.com/hanoi; Ambassador CAMILLA MEL-LANDER.

Switzerland: Central Office Bldg, 15th Floor, 44B Ly Thuong Kiet, Hanoi; tel. (4) 39346589; fax (4) 39346591; e-mail han.vertretung@eda.admin.ch; internet www.eda.admin.ch/hanoi; Ambassador ANDREJ MOTYL.

Thailand: 63–65 Hoang Dieu, Hanoi; tel. (4) 38235092; fax (4) 38235088; e-mail thaihan1@fpt.vn; internet www.thaiembassy.org/hanoi; Ambassador ANUSON CHINVANNO.

Turkey: 44B Ly Thuong Kiet, Hoan Kiem District, Hanoi; tel. (4) 38222460; fax (4) 38222458; e-mail embassy.hanoi@mfa.gov.tr; internet hanoi.emb.mfa.gov.tr; Ambassador AHMET AKIF OKTAY.

Ukraine: 6B Le Hong Phong, Ba Dinh District, Hanoi; tel. (4) 37344484; fax (4) 37344497; e-mail emb_vn@mfa.gov.ua; internet www.mfa.gov.ua/vietnam; Ambassador OLEKSIY SHOVKOPLIAS.

United Arab Emirates: 44/3 Van Bao, Van Phuc Diplomatic Quarter, Ba Dinh District, Hanoi; tel. (4) 37264545; fax (4) 37262020; e-mail hanoi@mofa.gov.ae; internet uaeembassy.vn; Ambassador Sheikh AHMED ALI AL-MUALLA.

United Kingdom: Central Bldg, 4th Floor, 31 Hai Ba Trung, Hanoi; tel. (4) 39360500; fax (4) 39360561; e-mail behanoi02@vnn.vn; internet www.gov.uk/government/world/vietnam; Ambassador Dr ANTHONY STOKES.

Uruguay: 407 Au Co, Tay Ho District, Hanoi; tel. (4) 37188047; fax (4) 37188049; CARLOS IRIGARAY.

USA: 7 Hang La, Ba Dinh District, Hanoi; tel. (4) 38505000; fax (4) 38505120; e-mail hanoiac@state.gov; internet vietnam.usembassy.gov; Ambassador DAVID SHEAR.

Venezuela: 368 Lac Long Quan, Tay Ho District, Hanoi; tel. (4) 7588891; fax (4) 7588893; e-mail embavenezhanoi@yahoo.com; Ambassador JORGE JOSÉ RONDÓN UZCÁTEGUI.

Judicial System

The Supreme People's Court in Hanoi is the highest court and exercises civil and criminal jurisdiction over all lower courts. The Supreme Court may also conduct trials of the first instance in certain cases. There are People's Courts in each province and city which exercise jurisdiction in the first and second instance. Military courts hear cases involving members of the People's Army and cases involving national security. In 1993 legislation was adopted on the establishment of economic courts to consider business disputes. The observance of the law by ministries, government offices and all citizens is the concern of the People's Procuracy, under a Supreme People's Procuracy. The Chief Justice of the Supreme People's Court and the Procurator-General of the Supreme People's Procuracy are elected by the National Assembly, on the recommendation of the President.

Supreme People's Court: 48 Ly Thuong Kiet, Hanoi; Chief Justice TRUONG HOA BINH.

Supreme People's Procuracy: 44 Ly Thuong Kiet, Hanoi; tel. (4) 438255058; fax (4) 438255400; e-mail htqt@vks.gov.vn; internet www.vksndtc.gov.vn; Procurator-General NGUYEN HOA BINH.

Religion

Traditional Vietnamese religion included elements of Indian and all three Chinese religions: Mahayana Buddhism, Daoism and Confucianism. Its most widespread feature was the cult of ancestors, practised in individual households and clan temples. Various Buddhist sects belong to the 'new' religions of Caodaism and Hoa Hao. The Protestant and Roman Catholic Churches are also represented. In 2007 operating licences were granted to several additional religious groups, including the Mennonite Church, the Baptist Church and the Bahá'í faith.

BUDDHISM

In the North a Buddhist organization, grouping Buddhists loyal to the Democratic Republic of Viet Nam, was established in 1954. In the South the United Buddhist Church was formed in 1964, incorporating several disparate groups, including the 'militant' An-Quang group (mainly natives of central Viet Nam), the group of Thich Tam Chau (mainly northern emigrés in Saigon) and the southern Buddhists of the Xa Loi temple. In 1982 most of the Buddhist sects were amalgamated into the state-approved Viet Nam Buddhist Church (which comes under the authority of the Viet Nam Fatherland Front). The number of adherents was estimated at 10m. in 2005, approximately 12% of the total population. The Unified Buddhist Church of Viet Nam is an anti-Government organization.

Viet Nam Buddhist Church: e-mail trisu@phattuvietnam.net; internet www.phattuvietnam.net; Pres. Exec. Council Most Ven. THICH TRI TINH; Gen. Sec. THICH MING CHAU.

Unified Buddhist Church of Viet Nam: Leader Patriarch THICH QUANG DO.

CAODAISM

Formally inaugurated in 1926, this is a syncretic religion based on spiritualist seances with a predominantly ethical content, but sometimes with political overtones. There are 13 different sects, of which the most politically involved (1940–75) was that of Tay Ninh. Another sect, the Tien Thien, was represented in the National Liberation Front from its inception. There were an estimated 2.4m. adherents in 2005, resident mainly in the South.

Leader: Cardinal THAI HUU THANH.

CHRISTIANITY

In 2005 the number of Christian adherents represented an estimated 7.2% of the total population.

The Roman Catholic Church

The Roman Catholic Church has been active in Viet Nam since the 17th century, and since 1933 has been led mainly by Vietnamese priests. Many Roman Catholics moved from North to South Viet Nam in 1954–55, but some remained in the North. The total number of adherents was estimated at 6,089,223 in December 2007, representing 6.9% of the population. For ecclesiastical purposes, Viet Nam comprises three archdioceses and 23 dioceses.

Bishops' Conference

Conférence Episcopale du Viet Nam, 22 Tran Phu, Khank Hoa, Nha Trang; tel. (58) 822842; fax (58) 815494; e-mail vptk.hdgm@gmail.com.

f. 1980; Pres. Most Rev. PIERRE NGUYEN VAN NHON (Bishop of Da Lat).

Archbishop of Hanoi: Most Rev. PIERRE NGUYEN VAN NHON, Archevêché, 40 Pho Nha Chung, Hanoi; tel. (4) 8254424; fax (4) 9285073; e-mail ttgmhn@hn.vnn.vn.

Archbishop of Ho Chi Minh City: Cardinal JEAN-BAPTISTE PHAM MINH MÂN, Archevêché, 180 Nguyen Dinh Chieu, Ho Chi Minh City 3; tel. (8) 9303828; fax (8) 9300598.

Archbishop of Hué: Most Rev. ETIENNE NGUYEN NHU THE, Archevêché, 37 Phan Dinh Phung, Hué; tel. (54) 824937; fax (54) 833656; e-mail tgmhue@dng.vnn.vn.

Committee for Solidarity of Patriotic Vietnamese Catholics: 59 Trang Thi, Hanoi; Pres. Rev. VUONG DINH AI.

The Protestant Church

Introduced in 1920 with 500 adherents; the total number was estimated at 500,000 in 2005.

HOA HAO

A new manifestation of an older religion called Buu Son Ky Huong, the Hoa Hao sect was founded by Nguyen Phu So in 1939. There were an estimated 1.6m. adherents in 2005.

ISLAM

The number of Muslims was estimated at 65,000 in 2005.

The Press

The Ministry of Information and Communication supervises the activities of newspapers, news agencies and periodicals.

DAILIES

Hanoi

Le Courrier du Viet Nam: 33 Le Thanh Tong, Hanoi; tel. (4) 38252096; fax (4) 38258368; e-mail courrier@vnagency.com.vn; internet lecourrier.vnagency.com.vn; French; publ. by the Viet Nam News Agency; Editor-in-Chief HOANG LAN HUONG.

Dan Tri (Intellectual People's Standard): 2/48 Giang Vo, Dong Da District, Hanoi; tel. (4) 37366491; fax (4) 37366490; e-mail dantri@dantri.com.vn; internet www.dantri.com.vn; f. 1982, fmrly known as *Tin Tuc* (News); publ. by the Viet Nam News Agency; afternoon; Vietnamese; Editor-in-Chief HUY HOAN PHAM.

Hanoi Moi (New Hanoi): 44 Le Thai To, Hoan Kiem District, Hanoi; tel. (4) 38253067; fax (4) 39287445; e-mail webmaster@hanoimoi.com.vn; internet www.hanoimoi.com.vn; f. 1976; organ of Hanoi Cttee of the Communist Party of Viet Nam; Editor HO QUANG LOI; circ. 35,000.

Lao Dong (Labour): 52B Nguyen Thi Dinh, Trung Hoa, Cau Giay, Hanoi; tel. (4) 35562295; fax (4) 35562275; e-mail webmaster@laodong.com.vn; internet www.laodong.com.vn; f. 1929; organ of the Viet Nam General Confederation of Labour; Editor-in-Chief VUONG VAN VIET; circ. 80,000.

Nhan Dan (The People): 71 Hang Trong, Hoan Kiem District, Hanoi; tel. (4) 38254231; fax (4) 38255593; e-mail toasoan@nhandan.org.vn; internet www.nhandan.org.vn; f. 1946; official organ of the Communist Party of Viet Nam; Editor-in-Chief THUAN HUU; circ. 220,000.

Nong Nghiep Viet Nam (Viet Nam Agriculture): 1059 Hongha, Hoan Kiem, Hanoi; tel. (4) 38256492; fax (4) 38252923; e-mail baonnvn@hn.vnn.vn; internet www.nongnghiep.vn; f. 1987; fmrly a weekly publ; Editor-in-Chief LE MAI SON.

Quan Doi Nhan Dan (People's Army): 7 Phan Dinh Phung, Hanoi; tel. (4) 37471748; fax (4) 37474913; e-mail dientubqd@gmail.com; internet www.qdnd.vn; f. 1950; organ of the armed forces; Editor NGUYEN LE PHUC; circ. 80,000.

Thanh Nien: 248 Cong Quynh, District 1, Ho Chi Minh City; tel. (8) 39255738; fax (8) 39255901; e-mail admin@thanhniennews.com; internet www.thanhniennews.com; f. 1986; English; Chief Editor NGUYEN QUANG THONG.

Viet Nam Economic Times: 96 Hoang Quoc Viet, Cau Giay District, Hanoi; tel. (4) 37552060; fax (4) 37552046; e-mail editor@vneconomy.vn; internet vneconomy.vn; f. 1994; in Vietnamese (with monthly edn in English); Editor-in-Chief Prof. DAO NGUYEN CAT; Dep. Editor-in-Chief NGUYEN THI VAN ANH; circ 38,900.

Viet Nam News: 11 Tran Hung Dao, Hanoi; tel. (4) 39332316; fax (4) 39332311; e-mail vnnews@vnagency.com.vn; internet vietnamnews.vnanet.vn; f. 1991; English; publ. by the Viet Nam News Agency; Editor-in-Chief TRAN MAI HUONG; circ. 60,000.

Ho Chi Minh City

Sai Gon Giai Phong (Liberated Saigon): 399 Hong Bang, Ward 14, District 5, Ho Chi Minh City; tel. (8) 39294092; fax (8) 39294083; e-mail sggponline@sggp.org.vn; internet www.sggp.org.vn; f. 1975; organ of Ho Chi Minh City Cttee of the Communist Party of Viet Nam; Editor-in-Chief TRAN THE TUYEN; circ. 100,000.

Saigon Times: 35 Nam Ky Khoi Nghia, District 1, Ho Chi Minh City; tel. (8) 38295936; fax (8) 38294294; e-mail sgt@thesaigontimes.vn; internet www.thesaigontimes.vn; f. 1991; Vietnamese and English; business issues; Editor-in-Chief TRAN THI NGOC HUE.

PERIODICALS

Dai Doan Ket (Great Unity): 66 Ba Trieu, Hanoi; tel. (4) 38228303; fax 38228547; e-mail toasoan@baodaidoanket.com.vn; internet www.daidoanket.vn; f. 1977; weekly; organ of the Viet Nam Fatherland Front; Editor DINH DUC LAP.

Dau Tu: 47 Quan Thanh, Ba Dinh, Hanoi; tel. (4) 38450537; fax (4) 38235281; e-mail baodautu.vn@gmail.com; internet www.baodautu.vn; 3 a week; business newspaper publ. in Vietnamese; Editor-in-Chief Dr NGUYEN ANH TUAN; circ. 50,000.

Dau Tu Chung Khoan: 47 Quan Thanh, Ba Dinh, Hanoi; tel. (4) 98450537; fax (4) 38430969; e-mail tinnhanhchungkhoan@vir.com.vn; internet www.tinnhanhchungkhoan.vn; weekly; stock market news publ. in Vietnamese; Editor-in-Chief Dr NGUYEN ANH TUAN; circ. 50,000.

Giao Duc Thoi Dai (People's Teacher): 29B Ngo Quyen, Hoan Kiem District, Hanoi; tel. (4) 39369800; fax (4) 39345611; e-mail gdtddientu@gmail.com; internet www.gdtd.vn; f. 1959; weekly; organ of the Ministry of Education and Training; Chief Editor Dr NGUYEN DANH BINH.

Giao Thong-Van Tai (Communications and Transport): 1 Nha Tho, Hoan Kiem, Hanoi; tel. (4) 9286763; fax (4) 8255387; e-mail toasoan@giaothongvantai.com.vn; internet giaothongvantai.com.vn; f. 1962; weekly (Thur.); organ of Ministry of Transport; Editor NGUYEN VAN LUU; circ. 30,000.

Hoa Hoc Tro (Pupils' Flowers): 5 Hoa Ma, Hanoi; tel. (4) 8211065; internet www.hoahoctro.vn; weekly; Chief Editor NGUYEN HUY LOC; circ. 150,000.

Khoa Hoc Ky Thuat Kinh Te The Gioi (World Science, Technology and Economy): 5 Ly Thuong Kiet, Hanoi; tel. (4) 8252931; f. 1982; weekly.

Khoa Hoc va Doi Song (Science and Life): 70 Tran Hung Dao, Hanoi; tel. (4) 8253427; f. 1959; weekly; Editor-in-Chief TRAN CU; circ. 30,000.

Nghe Thuat Dien Anh (Cinematography): 65 Tran Hung Dao, Hanoi; tel. (4) 8262473; f. 1984; fortnightly; Editor DANG NHAT MINH.

Nguoi Cong Giao Viet Nam (Vietnamese Catholic): 59 Trang Thi, Hanoi; tel. (4) 8256242; f. 1984; weekly; organ of the Cttee for Solidarity of Patriotic Vietnamese Catholics; Editor-in-Chief SO CHI.

Nguoi Dai Bieu Nhan Dan (People's Deputy): 35 Ngo Quyen, Hanoi; tel. (4) 08046231; fax (4) 08046659; e-mail ndbnd@hn.vnn.vn; f. 1988; bi-weekly; disseminates resolutions of the National Assembly and People's Council; Editor-in-Chief HO ANH TAI; circ. 2m.

Nguoi Hanoi (The Hanoian): 19 Hang Buom, Hanoi; tel. (4) 8255662; f. 1984; Editor VU QUAN PHUONG.

Nha Bao Va Cong Luan (The Journalist and Public Opinion): 59 Ly Thai To, Hanoi; tel. (4) 8253609; fax (4) 8250797; f. 1985; monthly review; organ of the Viet Nam Journalists' Asscn; Editor-in-Chief PHAN DUOC TOAN; circ. 40,000.

Outlook: 11 Tran Hung Dao, Hanoi; tel. (4) 8222884; fax (4) 9424908; e-mail vnnews@vnagency.com.vn; internet vietnamnews.vnanet.com.vn; f. 2002; monthly news magazine; Editor-in-Chief TRAN MAI HUONG; circ. 6,000.

Phu Nu (Woman): Vietnam Women's Union, International Relations Dept, 39 Hang Chuoi, Hanoi; e-mail VWUnion@netnam.org.vn; f. 1997; fortnightly; women's magazine; circ. 100,000.

Phu Nu Thu Do (Capital Women): 72 Quan Su, Hanoi; tel. (4) 8247228; fax (4) 8223989; f. 1987; weekly; magazine of the Hanoi Women's Union; Editor-in-Chief MAI THUC.

Phu Nu Viet Nam (Vietnamese Women): 39 Hang Chuoi, Hanoi; tel. (4) 8253500; weekly; magazine of the Vietnam Women's Union; Editor-in-Chief PHUONG MINH.

Suc Khoe Va Doi Song (Health and Life): 138A Giang Vo, Ba Dinh District, Hanoi; tel. (4) 38461684; fax (4) 38443144; e-mail tranyenchau@gmail.com; internet suckhoedoisong.vn; f. 1961; weekly; published by the Ministry of Health; Editor-in-Chief TRAN SI TUAN; circ. 45,000.

Tap Chi Cong San (Communist Review): 28 Tran Binh Trong Thanh, Hanoi; tel. (4) 9429753; fax (4) 9429754; e-mail baodientu@tccs.org.vn; internet www.tapchicongsan.org.vn; f. 1955 as *Hoc Tap*; fortnightly; political and theoretical organ of the Communist Party of Viet Nam; Editor-in-Chief Dr VU VAN PHUC; circ. 50,000.

Tap Chi Nghiên Cuu Van Hoc (Literature Research Magazine): 20 Ly Thai To, Hanoi; tel. (4) 8252895; e-mail tcvapmail@vnn.vn;

monthly; published by the Institute of Literature; Editor-in-Chief PHAN TRONG THUONG.

Tap Chi San Khau (Theatre Magazine): 51 Tran Hung Dao, Hanoi; tel. (4) 9434423; fax (4) 9434293; e-mail trongkhoi@hn.vnn.vn; f. 1973; monthly; Editor NGO THAO.

Tap Chi Tac Pham Van Hoc: 65 Nguyen Du, Hanoi; tel. (4) 8252442; f. 1987; monthly; organ of the Viet Nam Writers' Asscn; Editor-in-Chief NGUYEN DINH THI; circ. 15,000.

Tap Chi Tu Tuong Van Hoa (Ideology and Culture Review): Hanoi; f. 1990; organ of the Central Committee Department of Ideology and Culture; Editor PHAM HUY VAN.

The Thao Van Hoa (Sports and Culture): 5 Ly Thuong Kiet, Hanoi; tel. (4) 8267043; fax (4) 8264901; f. 1982; weekly; Editor-in-Chief NGUYEN HUU VINH; circ. 100,000.

The Thao Viet Nam (Viet Nam Sports): 5 Trinh Hoai Duc, Hanoi; tel. (4) 35625457; fax (4) 35625455; e-mail baottvn@yahoo.com; internet www.thethaovietnam.com.vn; f. 1968; weekly; Editor HOANG DUR.

Thieu Nhi Dan Toc (The Ethnic Young): 5 Hoa Ma, Hanoi; tel. (4) 9317133; bi-monthly; Editor PHAM THANH LONG; circ. 60,000.

Thieu Nien Tien Phong (Young Pioneers): 5 Hoa Ma, Hanoi; tel. (4) 39713133; fax (4) 38215710; e-mail toasoan@thieunien.vn; internet www.thieunien.vn; 3 a week; Editor VU QUANG VINH; circ. 210,000.

Thoi Bao Kinh Te Viet Nam: 175 Nguyen Thai Hoc, Hanoi; tel. (4) 8452411; fax (4) 8432755; f. 1993; 2 a week; Editor-in-Chief PAVEF DAONGUYENCAT; circ. 37,000.

Thoi Trang Tre (New Fashion): 12 Ho Xuan Huong, Hanoi; tel. (4) 8254032; fax (4) 8226002; f. 1993; monthly; Editor VU QUANG VINH; circ. 80,000.

Thuong Mai (Commerce): 100 Lo Duc, Hanoi; tel. (4) 8263150; f. 1990; weekly; organ of the Ministry of Industry and Trade; Editor TRAN NAM VINH.

Tien Phong (Vanguard): 15 Ho Xuan Huong, Hanoi; tel. (4) 8264031; fax (4) 8225032; f. 1953; 4 a week; organ of the Ho Chi Minh Communist Youth Union and of the Forum of Vietnamese Youth; Editor DUONG XUAN NAM; circ. 165,000.

Van Hoa (Culture and Arts): 26 Dien Bien Phu, Hanoi; tel. (4) 8257781; f. 1957; fortnightly; Editor PHI VAN TUONG.

Van Nghe (Arts and Letters): 17 Tran Quoc Toan, Hanoi; tel. (4) 8264430; f. 1949; weekly; organ of the Vietnamese Writers' Union; Editor HUU THINH; circ. 40,000.

Van Nghe Quan Doi (Army Literature and Arts): 4 Ly Nam De, Hanoi; tel. (4) 8254370; f. 1957; monthly; Editor NGUYEN TRI HUAN; circ. 50,000.

Viet Nam Business Forum: 9 Dao Duy Anh, 4th Floor, Dong Da District, Hanoi; tel. (4) 35743985; fax (4) 35743063; e-mail vbfhn@hn.vnn.vn; internet vibforum.vcci.com.vn; f. 1995; weekly magazine in English; publ. by the Viet Nam Chamber of Commerce and Industry; Editor-in-Chief DOAN DUY KHUONG.

Viet Nam Courier: 5 Ly Thuong Kiet, Hanoi; tel. (4) 8261847; fax (4) 8242317; weekly; English; publ. by the Viet Nam News Agency; Editor-in-Chief NGUYEN DUC GIAP.

Viet Nam Cultural Window: 46 Tran Hung Dao, Hanoi; tel. (4) 38253841; fax (4) 38269578; e-mail vncw@hn.vnn.vn; f. 1998; every 2 months; English; Dir TRAN DOAN LAM.

Viet Nam Investment Review (VIR): 47 Quan Thanh, Ba Dinh, Hanoi; tel. (4) 38450537; fax (4) 38457937; e-mail vir.hn@vir.com.vn; internet www.vir.com.vn; f. 1990; weekly; business newspaper publ. in English; Editor-in-Chief Dr NGUYEN ANH TUAN; circ 40,000.

Vietnam Pictorial: 11 Tran Hung Dao, Hanoi; tel. (4) 39332303; fax (4) 39332291; e-mail vietnamvnp@gmail.com; f. 1954; monthly online, in Vietnamese, English, French, Chinese, Japanese, Spanish and Russian; fmrly Viet Nam Review; Editor-in-Chief NGUYEN THANG; circ. 138,000.

Viet Nam Renovation: Hanoi; f. 1994; quarterly magazine on reform of the agricultural sector; in Vietnamese, Chinese and English.

Viet Nam Social Sciences: 27 Tran Xuan Soan, Hanoi; tel. (4) 9784578; fax (4) 9783869; e-mail 21.6.tapchikhxh@fpt.vn; f. 1984; every 2 months; publ. in English and Vietnamese; organ of Viet Nam Social Academy; Editor-in-Chief Dr LE DINH CUC.

Vietnamese Studies: 46 Tran Hung Dao, Hanoi; tel. (4) 38253841; fax (4) 38269578; e-mail thegioi@hn.vnn.vn; internet www.thegioipublishers.com.vn; f. 1964; quarterly; English and French edns; Dir and Chief Editor Dr TRAN DOAN LAM.

NEWS AGENCY

Viet Nam News Agency (VNA): 79 Ly Thuong Kiet, Hoan Kiem District, Hanoi; tel. (4) 38255443; fax (4) 38252984; e-mail btk@vnanet.vn; internet www.vnanet.vn; f. 1945; mem. of Organization of Asian and Pacific News Agencies; Gen. Dir TRAN MAI HUONG.

PRESS ASSOCIATION

Viet Nam Journalists' Association (VJA): 59 Ly Thai To, Hanoi; tel. (4) 39386270; fax (4) 38250797; e-mail hnbvietnam@gmail.com; internet www.vja.org.vn; f. 1950; asscn of editors, reporters and photographers working in the press, radio, television and news agencies; 17,000 mems (2008); Pres. NGUYEN CHU NHAC; Vice-Pres. HA MINH HUE.

Publishers

Am Nhac Dia Hat (Music) Publishing House: 61 Ly Thai To, Hoan Kiem District, Hanoi; tel. (4) 8256208; f. 1986; produces cassettes, videocassettes, books and printed music; Dir PHAM DUC LOC.

Cong An Nhan Dan (People's Public Security) Publishing House: 167 Mai Hac De, Hai Ba Trung District, Hanoi; tel. (4) 8260910; f. 1981; cultural and artistic information, public order and security; Dir PHAM VAN THAM.

Giao Thong Van Tai (Communications and Transport) Publishing House: 80B Tran Hung Dao, Hanoi; tel. (4) 39423346; fax (4) 38224784; e-mail nxbgtvt@fpt.vn; f. 1983; managed by the Ministry of Transport; 350 titles annually; Dir LE TU GIANG.

Khoa Hoc Va Ky Thuat (Science and Technology) Publishing House: 70 Tran Hung Dao, Hanoi; tel. (4) 39423172; fax (4) 8220658; e-mail nxbkhkt@hn.vnn.vn; internet www.nxbkhkt.com.vn; f. 1960; scientific and technical works, guide books, dictionaries, popular and management books; Dir PHAM VAN DIEN.

Khoa Hoc Xa Hoi (Social Sciences) Publishing House: 61 Phan Chu Trinh, Hanoi; tel. (4) 8255428; f. 1967; managed by the Institute of Social Science; Dir Dr NGUYEN DUC ZIEU.

Kim Dong Publishing House: 55 Quang Trung, Hanoi; tel. (4) 39434730; fax (4) 38229085; e-mail kimdong@hn.vnn.vn; internet www.nxbkimdong.com.vn; f. 1957; children's; managed by the Ho Chi Minh Communist Youth Union; Dir PHAM QUANG VINH; Dir PHAM QUANG VINH.

Lao Dong (Labour) Publishing House: 54 Giang Vo, Hanoi; tel. (4) 8515380; f. 1945; translations and political works; managed by the Viet Nam Gen. Confed. of Labour; Dir LE THANH TONG.

My Thuat (Fine Arts) Publishing House: 44B Hamlong, Hanoi; tel. (4) 39449076; fax (4) 39436133; e-mail ngandangminh@yahoo.com.vn; f. 1987; managed by the Plastic Arts Workers' Asscn; Dir NGAN DANG THI BICH.

Nha Xuat Ban Giao Duc (Education) Publishing House: 81 Tran Hung Dao, Hanoi; tel. (4) 38220801; fax (4) 39422010; e-mail vanphong@nxbgd.vn; internet www.nxbgd.vn; f. 1957; managed by the Ministry of Education and Training; Dir NGO TRAN AI; Editor-in-Chief NGUYEN QUY THAO.

Nha Xuat Ban Hoi Nha Van (Writers' Association) Publishing House: 65 Nguyen Du, Hoan Kiem District, Hanoi; tel. and fax (4) 8222135; f. 1957; managed by the Vietnamese Writers' Asscn; Editor-in-Chief NGO VAN PHU.

Nong Nghiep (Agriculture) Publishing House: DH 14, Phuong Mai Ward, Dong Da District, Hanoi; tel. (4) 8523887; f. 1976; managed by the Ministry of Agriculture and Rural Devt; Dir DUONG QUANG DIEU.

Phu Nu (Women) Publishing House: 16 Alexandre De Rhodes, Hanoi; tel. (4) 8294459; f. 1957; managed by the Vietnamese Women's Union; Dir TRAN THU HUONG.

Quan Doi Nhan Dan (People's Army) Publishing House: 25 Ly Nam De, Hanoi; tel. (4) 8255766; managed by the Ministry of National Defence; Dir DOAN CHUONG.

San Khau (Theatre) Publishing House: 51 Tran Hung Dao, Hanoi; tel. (4) 8264423; f. 1986; managed by the Stage Artists' Asscn; Dir NGO THE NGOC.

Su That (Truth) Publishing House: 24 Quang Trung, Hanoi; tel. (4) 8252008; fax (4) 8251881; f. 1945; Marxist-Leninist classics, politics and philosophy; managed by the Communist Party of Viet Nam; Dir TRAN NHAM.

Thanh Nien (Youth) Publishing House: 270 Nguyen Dinh Chieu, District 3, Hanoi; tel. and fax (4) 8222612; f. 1954; managed by the Ho Chi Minh Communist Youth Union; Dir BUI VAN NGOI.

The Duc The Thao (Physical Education and Sports) Publishing House: 7 Trinh Hoai Duc, Hanoi; tel. (4) 8256155; f. 1974; managed by the Ministry of Culture, Sports and Tourism; Dir NGUYEN HIEU.

The Gioi Publishers: 46 Tran Hung Dao, Hanoi; tel. (4) 38253841; fax (4) 38269578; e-mail thegioi@hn.vnn.vn; internet www.thegioipublishers.com.vn; f. 1957; foreign language publs; managed by the Ministry of Culture, Sports and Tourism; Dir and Chief Editor Dr TRAN DOAN LAM.

Thong Ke (Statistics) Publishing House: 86–98 Thuy Khe, Hanoi; tel. (4) 38471483; fax (4) 38473714; e-mail nxbthongke@hn.vnn.vn; internet www.nxbthongke.com.vn; f. 1980; managed by the Gen. Statistics Office; Dir TRAN HUU THUC.

Van Hoa (Culture) Publishing House: 43 Lo Duc, Hanoi; tel. (4) 8253517; f. 1971; managed by the Ministry of Culture, Sports and Tourism; Dir QUANG HUY.

Van Hoc (Literature) Publishing House: 19 Nguyen Truong To, Ba Dinh, Hanoi; tel. (4) 8294783; fax (4) 8294781; f. 1948; managed by the Ministry of Culture, Sports and Tourism; Dir NGUYEN VAN CU.

Xay Dung (Building) Publishing House: 37 Le Dai Hanh, Hanoi; tel. (4) 8268271; fax (4) 8215369; f. 1976; managed by the Ministry of Construction; Dir NGUYEN LUONG BICH.

Y Hoc (Medicine) Publishing House: 4 Le Thanh Ton, Phan Chu Trinh, Hoan Kiem District, Hanoi; tel. (4) 8255281; e-mail xuatbanyhoc@netnam.vn; managed by the Ministry of Health; Dir HOANG TRONG QUANG.

PUBLISHERS' ASSOCIATION

Viet Nam Publishers' Association (Hoi Xuat Ban Viet Nam): Lo 2, B15, My Dinh 1, Tu Liem District, Hanoi; tel. and fax (4) 62872645; e-mail thuytp1803@gmail.com; Pres. NGUYEN KIEM.

Broadcasting and Communications

TELECOMMUNICATIONS

Board of the Technical and Economic Programme on Information Technology: 39 Tran Hung Dao, Hanoi; e-mail nyenet@itnet.gov.vn; Gen. Dir Dr DO VAN LOC.

FPT Telecom: FPT Bldgs, Lot 2, Duong Pham Hung, Cau Giay, Hanoi; tel. (4) 73002222; fax (4) 73008889; internet www.fpt.vn; f. 1997; fixed–line telephone services; Chair. TRUONG DINH ANH.

GTEL Mobile (Beeline VN): 280B Lac Long Quan, Hanoi; tel. (4) 37674846; fax (4) 37674854; e-mail DVKH@beeline.vn; internet beeline.vn; f. 2008; mobile cellular telephone services; Dir-Gen. MICHAEL SASCHA CLUZEL.

Hanoi Telecommunications Co (Hanoi Telecom): 2 Chua Boc, Dong Da District, Hanoi; tel. (3) 35729833; fax (4) 35729834; e-mail info@hanoitelecom.com; internet www.hanoitelecom.com; f. 2005; cellular telephone service provider; Chair. PHAM NGOC LANG.

Saigon Post and Telecommunications Service Corpn: 199 Dien Bien Phu, Binh Thanh District, Ho Chi Minh City; tel. (8) 54040608; fax (8) 54040609; e-mail info@spt.vn; internet www.spt.vn; f. 1995; partially state-owned; nation-wide post and telecommunications services; Chair. TRAN THI NGOC BINH; Dir-Gen. HOANG SI HOA.

Viet Nam Military Electronics and Telecommunications Corpn (Viettel): 1 Giang Van Minh, Ba Dinh District, Hanoi; tel. (4) 62556789; fax (4) 62996789; e-mail gopy@viettel.com.vn; internet www.viettel.com.vn; f. 1998; offers range of post and telecommunication services, including cellular, 3G, telephone and broadband internet services; took over EVN Telecom in 2011; CEO TONG VIET TRUNG.

Viet Nam Posts and Telecommunications Corpn (VNPT): VNPT Bldg, 57 Huynh Thuc Khang, Dong Da District, Hanoi; tel. (3) 35775104; fax (3) 37741093; e-mail vnpt_website@vnpt.com.vn; internet www.vnpt.com.vn; f. 1995; state-owned communications co; plans to merge MobiFone and VinaPhone were under way in May 2012; Viet Nam Post (VNPost) was to begin operations as an independent company on Jan. 2013; Chair. PHAM LONG TRAN; Pres. and CEO VU TUAN HUNG.

Viet Nam Mobile Telecommunication Services Co (Mobi-Fone): Lot VP1, Yen Hoa Ward, Cau Giay District, Hanoi; tel. (4) 37831733; e-mail webmaster@mobifone.com.vn; internet www.mobifone.com.vn; f. 1993; mobile cellular telephone service provider; Dir PHAM NGOC MINH.

Viet Nam Telecommunication Services Co (VinaPhone): 1 Nam Thanh Cong, Lot A, Dong Da District, Hanoi; tel. (4) 8358816; fax (4) 7731745; internet www.vinaphone.com.vn; f. 1996; provides mobile cellular telephone services; Man. Dir LAM HOANG VINH.

Regulatory Authority

Viet Nam Telecommunications Authority (VNTA): VNTA Bldg, Yen Hoa, Cau Giay, Hanoi; tel. (4) 39436608; fax (4) 39436607; e-mail vnta@mic.gov.vn; internet www.vnta.gov.vn; f. 2011; Dir-Gen. PHAM HONG HAI.

RADIO

Voice of Viet Nam (VOV): 58 Quan Su, Hanoi; tel. (4) 8255694; fax (4) 8265875; e-mail toasoan@vovnews.vn; internet www.vov.org.vn; f. 1945; 4 domestic channels in Vietnamese; 2 foreign service channels in English, Japanese, French, Khmer, Laotian, Spanish, Thai, Cantonese, Mandarin, Indonesian, Vietnamese and Russian; Dir-Gen. Dr NGUYEN DANG TIEN.

TELEVISION

Viet Nam Television (VTV): 43 Nguyen Chi Thanh, Hanoi; tel. (4) 8354992; fax (4) 8350882; e-mail webmaster@vtv.org.vn; internet www.vtv.org.vn; television was introduced in South Viet Nam in 1966 and in North Viet Nam in 1970; broadcasts from Hanoi (via satellite) to the whole country, the Asia region, Western Europe and North America; Vietnamese, French, English, Russian, Chinese; Pres. TRAN BINH MINH.

Vietnam Multimedia Corpn (Vietnam Television Corpn—VTC): 18 Duong Tam Trinh, Phuong Minh Khai, Hai Ba Trung, Hanoi; e-mail vtcvod@vtc.vn; internet www.vtc.com.vn; controlled by the Ministry of Information and Communication; Dir TAN THAI MINH.

Finance

(cap. = capital; res = reserves; dep. = deposits; m. = million; brs = branches; amounts in new dông unless otherwise indicated)

BANKING

In 2012 the Vietnamese banking system comprised five state-owned commercial banks, four joint venture banks, 50 foreign bank branches and 35 joint stock commercial banks. In 2010 Viet Nam had 1,016 local credit funds, supervised by the Central People's Credit Fund. The Vietnam Bank for the Poor, established in 1995, was renamed the Vietnam Bank for Social Policies in 2003. It provides subsidized credit. From March 2006 foreign banks were for the first time allowed to offer a full range of banking services.

Central Bank

State Bank of Viet Nam: 49 Ly Thai To, Hanoi; tel. (4) 39343327; fax (4) 39349569; e-mail webmaster@sbv.gov.vn; internet www.sbv.gov.vn; f. 1951; central bank of issue; provides a national network of banking services and supervises the operation of the state banking system; Gov. NGUYEN VAN BINH; 61 brs and sub-brs.

State Banks

Bank for Investment and Development of Vietnam (BIDV): BIDV Tower, 35 Hang Voi, Hoan Kiem District, Hanoi; tel. (4) 22205544; fax (4) 22200399; e-mail info@bidv.com.vn; internet www.bidv.com.vn; f. 1957; cap. 12,947,563m., res 10,017,416m., dep. 283,997,625m. (Dec. 2011); Chair. TRAN BAC HA; CEO PHAN DUC TU.

Housing Bank of Mekong Delta (MHB): 9 Vo Van Tan, District 3, Ho Chi Minh City; tel. (8) 39302501; fax (8) 39302506; e-mail webmaster@mhb.com.vn; internet www.mhb.com.vn; f. 1997; cap. 3,062,152m., res 40,882m., dep. 38,236,664m. (Dec. 2011); Chair. HUYNH NAM DUNG; 44 brs.

Joint Stock Commercial Bank for Foreign Trade of Viet Nam (Vietcombank): 198 Tran Quang Khai, Hanoi; tel. (4) 9343137; fax (4) 8269067; e-mail webmaster@vietcombank.com.vn; internet www.vietcombank.com.vn; f. 1963; authorized to deal in foreign currencies and all other international banking business; undergoing equitization in mid-2005; cap. 19,743,205m., res 3,374,025m., dep. 281,339,741m. (Dec. 2011); Chair. NGUYEN HOA BINH; Dir-Gen. NGUYEN PHUOC THANH; 23 brs.

Vietnam Bank for Agriculture and Rural Development (VBARD): 36 Nguyen Co Thach, My Dinh, Tu Liem, Hanoi; tel. (4) 8313717; fax (4) 8313719; e-mail webmaster@agribank.com.vn; internet www.agribank.com.vn; f. 1988; cap. 21,160,111m., res 10,220,145m., dep. 418,113,096m. (Dec. 2011); Chair. NGUYEN NGOC BAO; Gen. Dir KIEU TRONG TUYEN; 2,200 brs.

Vietnam Joint Stock Commercial Bank for Industry and Trade (VietinBank): 108 Tran Hung Dao, Hoan Kiem, Hanoi; tel. (4) 39421030; fax (4) 39421032; internet www.vietinbank.vn; f. 1987; fmrly Industrial and Commercial Bank of Viet Nam (Incombank); authorized to receive personal savings, extend loans, issue stocks and invest in export-orientated cos and jt ventures with foreign interests; cap. 20,229,722m., res 3,720,535m., dep. 318,811,955m. (Dec. 2011); Chair. PHAM HUY HUNG; Gen. Dir NGUYEN VAN THANG; 150 brs.

Joint-Stock and Other Banks

Asia Commercial Joint Stock Bank (ACB): 442 Nguyen Thi Minh Khai, District 3, Ho Chi Minh City; tel. (8) 39290999; fax (8) 38399885; e-mail acb@acb.com.vn; internet www.acb.com.vn; f. 1993; Chair. TRAN HUNG HUY; Pres. DO MINH TOAN.

Indovina Bank Ltd: 46–50 Pham Hong Thai, District 1, Ho Chi Minh City; tel. (8) 38224995; fax (8) 38230131; e-mail support@indovinabank.com.vn; internet www.indovinabank.com.vn; f. 1990; jt venture of Cathay United Bank (Taiwan) and VietinBank; also has brs in Hanoi, Haiphong, Binh Duong, Can Tho and Dong Nai; cap. US $165m., res $15.1m., dep. $580.5m. (Dec. 2011); Chair. ROGER MING HSIEN LEE; Gen. Dir JAN YEI FONG; 9 brs.

Maritime Commercial Joint Stock Bank: 88 Lang Ha, Dong Da District, Hanoi; tel. (4) 37718989; fax (4) 37718899; e-mail msb@msb.com.vn; internet www.msb.com.vn; f. 1991; cap. 8,000,000m., res 811,277m., dep. 83,686,679m. (Dec. 2011); Chair. LE THI LIEN; Gen. Dir TRAN ANH TUAN; 9 brs.

Phuong Nam Commercial Joint-Stock Bank (Southern Bank): 279 Ly Thuong Kiet, District 11, Ho Chi Minh City; tel. (8) 38663890; fax (8) 38663891; e-mail icsc@southernbank.com.vn; internet www.southernbank.com.vn; f. 1993; cap. 3,212,480m., res 208,875m., dep. 45,445,292m. (Dec. 2011); Chair. MACH THIEU DUC.

Sacombank (Saigon Thuong Tin Commercial Joint-Stock Bank): 266–268 Nam Ky Khoi Nghia, Ward 8, District 3, Ho Chi Minh City; tel. (8) 39320420; fax (8) 39320424; e-mail info@sacombank.com.vn; internet www.sacombank.com.vn; f. 1991; became the first bank to list on the Securities Trading Centre in July 2006; cap. 10,740,625m., res 1,848,250m., dep. 105,532,549m. (Dec. 2011); Chair. PHAM HUU PHU; CEO PHAN HUY KHANG.

Saigon Bank for Industry and Trade: 2C Pho Duc Chinh, District 1, Ho Chi Minh City; tel. (8) 39143183; fax (8) 39143193; e-mail webadmin@saigonbank.com.vn; internet www.saigonbank.com.vn; cap. 2,460,000m., res 270,840m., dep. 12,390,365m. (Dec. 2010); specializes in trade and industry activities; Chair. NGUYEN PHUC MINH; Dir-Gen. TRAN THI VIET ANH; 32 brs.

Shinhan Bank Vietnam Ltd (Korea): 100 Nguyen Thi Minh Khai, Ward 6, District 3, Ho Chi Minh City; tel. (8) 38291581; fax (8) 38291583; internet www.shinhan.com.vn; est. following the merger of Shinhanvina Bank with Shinhan Bank in 2011; cap. 4,560,225m., res 321,500.5m. (Dec. 2011); Gen. Dir HONG MAN KI.

Southeast Asia Commercial Joint Stock Bank (SeABank): 25 Tran Hung Dao, Hoan Kiem, Hanoi; tel. (4) 39448688; fax (4) 39448689; e-mail contact@seabank.com.vn; internet www.seabank.com.vn; f. 1994; cap. 5,334,711m., res 101,165m., dep. 94,517,522m. (Dec. 2011); Chair. NGUYEN THI NGA.

VID Public Bank: Prime Bldg Centre, 7th Floor, 53 Quang Trung, Hanoi; tel. (4) 39438999; fax (4) 39439005; e-mail vidservice@vnn.vn; internet www.vidpublicbank.com.vn; f. 1992; jt venture between Bank for Investment and Devt of Viet Nam and Public Bank Bhd (Malaysia); commercial bank; cap. US $20m. (2001); Chair. TRAN ANH TUAN (acting); Gen. Dir KONG CHEE FIRE; 7 brs.

Vietnam Export-Import Commercial Joint-Stock Bank (Vietnam Eximbank): Vincom Centre, 8th Floor, 72 Le Thanh Ton and 45A Ly Tu Trong, Ben Nghe Ward, District 1, Ho Chi Minh City; tel. (8) 38210056; fax (8) 38216913; e-mail website@eximbank.com.vn; internet www.eximbank.com.vn; f. 1989; est. as Vietnam Export Import Bank; present name adopted 1992; authorized to undertake banking transactions for the production and processing of export products and export-import operations; cap. 12,355,229m., res 1,287,536m., dep. 138,560,061m. (Dec. 2011); Chair. LE HUNG DUNG; Dir-Gen. TRUONG VAN PHUOC; 124 brs and offices.

Viet Nam Technological and Commercial Joint-Stock Bank (Techcombank): 70–72 Ba Trieu, Hoan Kiem District, Hanoi; tel. (4) 39446368; fax (4) 39446362; internet www.techcombank.com.vn; cap. 8,788,079m., res 1,059,566m., dep. 140,057,459m. (Dec. 2011); Chair. HO HUNG ANH; Gen. Dir SIMON MORRIS.

VinaSiam Bank: 2 Pho Duc Chinh, District 1, Ho Chi Minh City; tel. (8) 38210630; fax (8) 38210585; e-mail vsb@vsb.com.vn; internet www.vinasiambank.com; f. 1995; jt venture between Bank for Agriculture and Rural Devt, Siam Commercial Bank (Thailand) and Charoen Pokphand Group (Thailand); cap. US $20.0m., res. $1.1m., dep. $37.2m. (Dec. 2005); Chair. TIET VAN THANH; Gen. Man. TSE HONG.

VP Bank (Viet Nam Commercial Joint-Stock Bank for Private Enterprises): 8 Le Thai To, Hoan Kiem District, Hanoi; tel. (4) 39288869; fax (4) 39288867; e-mail customercare@vpb.com.vn; internet www.vpb.com.vn; cap. 5,050,000m., res 152,749m., dep. 54,999,726m. (Dec. 2011); Chair. NGO CHI DUNG; Gen. Dir NGUYEN DUC VINH.

STOCK EXCHANGES

Hanoi Stock Exchange (HNX): 81 Tran Hung Dao, Hoan Kiem, Hanoi; tel. (4) 39360750; fax (4) 39347818; e-mail marketinfo@hnx.vn; internet www.hnx.vn; f. 2005; est. as Hanoi Securities Trading Centre; renamed as above 2009; 395 listed stocks (Sept. 2012); CEO TRAN VAN DZUNG.

Ho Chi Minh Stock Exchange: 16 Vo Van Kiet, District 1, Ho Chi Minh City; tel. (8) 38217713; fax (8) 38217452; e-mail hotline@hsx.vn; internet www.hsx.vn; f. 2000; fmrly Securities Trading Centre; name changed as above in 2007; 305 listed stocks (Sept. 2012); Chair. TRAN DAC SINH; Gen. Dir PHAN THI TUONG TAM.

Supervisory Body

State Securities Commission: 164 Tran Quang Khai, Hanoi; tel. (4) 39340750; fax (4) 39340739; e-mail banbientap@ssc.gov.vn; internet www.ssc.gov.vn; f. 1997; responsible for developing the capital markets, incl. the establishment of a stock exchange; 13 mems; Chair. BANG VU.

INSURANCE

In September 2006 there were 22 insurance companies operating in the country.

Aon Vietnam Ltd: Vietcombank Tower, Suites 1403–07, 14th Floor, 198 Tran Quang Khai, Hoan Kiem District, Hanoi; tel. (4) 38260832; fax (4) 38243983; e-mail vu_my_lan@aon-asia.com; internet www.aon.com/vietnam; f. 1993; fmrly Inchibrok Insurance; Man. Dir VU MY LAN.

Bao Long (Nha Rong Joint-Stock Insurance Co): 185 Dien Bien Phu, Dakao Ward, District 1, Ho Chi Minh City; tel. (8) 8239219; fax (8) 8239223; internet www.nharonginsurance.com; Dir TRAN VAN BINH.

Bao Minh Insurance Co (Ho Chi Minh City Insurance Co): 26 Ton That Dam, District 1, Ho Chi Minh City; tel. (8) 38294180; fax (8) 38294185; e-mail baominh@baominh.com.vn; internet www.baominh.com.vn; f. 1994; non-life; Chair. and CEO VINH DUC TRAN; Gen. Dir LE VAN THANH.

Baoviet (Viet Nam Insurance Co): 35 Hai Ba Trung, Hoan Kiem District, Hanoi; tel. (4) 38262774; fax (4) 38257188; e-mail bvvn@baoviet.com.vn; internet www.baoviet.com.vn/bvvn.asp; f. 1965; property and casualty, personal accident, liability and life insurance; total assets 8,817,000m. dông (2004); Chair. LE QUANG BINH; CEO TRAN TRONG PHUC.

Dai-ichi Life Insurance Co of Vietnam Ltd: Saigon Riverside Office Center, 3rd Floor, 2A–4A Ton Duc Thang, District 1, Ho Chi Minh City; tel. (8) 38291919; fax (8) 38293131; e-mail info@dai-ichi-life.com.vn; internet www.dai-ichi-life.com.vn; f. 2007; Chair. and CEO TAKASHI FUJII.

Manulife (Vietnam) Ltd: Manulife Plaza, 75 Hoang Van Thai, Tan Phu Ward, District 7, Ho Chi Minh City; tel. (8) 54166888; fax (8) 54161818; e-mail manulifevn_info@manulife.com; internet www.manulife.com.vn; f. 1999; fmrly Chinfon-Manulife Life Insurance Co Ltd; first wholly foreign-owned life insurance co to operate in Viet Nam; Gen. Dir CARL GUSTINI.

Petrolimex Joint-Stock Insurance Co (PJICO Insurance): 532 Lang Ha, Dong Da District, Hanoi; tel. (4) 37760867; fax (4) 37760868; e-mail pjico@petrolimex.com.vn; internet www.pjico.com.vn; f. 1995; non-life insurance; Chair. NGUYEN VAN TIEN; Gen. Dir NGUYEN ANH DUNG.

PetroVietnam Insurance Joint Stock Corpn (PVI): 154 Nguyen Thai Hoc, Ba Dinh District, Hanoi; tel. (4) 37335588; fax (4) 37336284; e-mail contact@pvi.com.vn; internet www.pvi.com.vn; f. 1996; non-life insurance; Chair. NGUYEN ANH TUAN; Gen. Dir BUI VAN THUAN.

Viet Nam International Assurance Co (VIA): Sun Red River Bldg, 6th Floor, 23 Phan Chu Trinh, Hoan Kiem District, Hanoi; tel. (4) 39330704; fax (4) 39330706; e-mail hn@via.com.vn; internet www.via.com.vn; f. 1996; jt venture co, 51% owned by Baoviet, 49% owned by Tokio Marine and Nichido Fire Insurance Co (Japan); non-life insurance and reinsurance for foreign cos; Marketing Man. VU THI KIM CHI.

INSURANCE ASSOCIATION

Association of Vietnamese Insurers: 8th Floor, 141 Le Duan, Hanoi; tel. (4) 39412063; fax (4) 39422601; internet www.avi.org.vn; Chair. TRINH QUANG TUYEN.

Trade and Industry

GOVERNMENT AGENCIES

State Financial and Monetary Council (SFMC): f. 1998; established to supervise, review and resolve matters relating to national financial and monetary policy.

Vietrade (Viet Nam Trade Promotion Agency): 20 Ly Thuong Kiet, Ba Dinh District, Hanoi; tel. (4) 39347628; fax (4) 39344260; e-mail vietrade@vietrade.gov.vn; internet www.vietrade.gov.vn; part of the Ministry of Industry and Trade; responsible for state management, co-ordination and implementation of trade and trade-related investment promotion and development activities; Dir-Gen. Do Thang Hai.

Vinacontrol Group Corp: 54 Tran Nhan Tong, Hanoi; tel. (4) 39433840; fax (4) 39433844; e-mail vinacontrolvn@hn.vnn.vn; internet www.vinacontrol.com.vn; f. 1957; brs in all main Vietnamese ports and trade centres; controls quality and volume of exports and imports and transit of goods, and conducts inspections, sampling and testing of deliveries and production processes; price, assets and enterprise valuation, marine survey, damage survey, claim settling and adjustment; Chair. Bui Duy Chinh; Gen. Dir Mai Tien Dung; 600 employees.

CHAMBER OF COMMERCE

VCCI (Viet Nam Chamber of Commerce and Industry): 9 Dao Duy Anh, 4th Floor, Hanoi; tel. (4) 35742022; fax (4) 35742020; e-mail webmaster@vcci.com.vn; internet www.vcci.com.vn; f. 1963; offices throughout Viet Nam; promotes business and investment between foreign and Vietnamese cos; organizes exhibitions, provides information etc.; represents foreign applicants for patents and trade mark registration; helps domestic and foreign businesses to settle disputes by negotiation or arbitration; Pres. and Chair. Dr Vu Tien Loc; Sec.-Gen. Pham Gia Tuc; assoc. orgs: Viet Nam Int. Arbitration Centre, Viet Nam General Average Adjustment Cttee, Advisory Bd.

Viet Nam International Arbitration Centre (VIAC): 9 Dao Duy Anh, 6th Floor, Dong Da District, Hanoi; tel. (4) 35744001; fax (4) 35743001; e-mail viac-vcci@hn.vnn.vn; internet www.viac.org.vn; f. 1993; adjudicates in disputes concerning both domestic and international economic relations.

INDUSTRIAL AND TRADE ORGANIZATIONS

AFIEX (An Giang Agriculture and Foods Import-Export Joint Stock Co): 25/40 Tran Hung Dao, My Thoi Ward, Long Xuyen City, An Giang Province; tel. (76) 932985; fax (76) 932981; e-mail xnknstpagg@hcm.vnn.vn; internet www.afiex.com.vn; f. 1990; mfr and sale of agricultural products; Dir Pham Van Bay.

Agrex Saigon (Agricultural Products and Foodstuffs Export Co): 58 Vo Van Tan, District 3, Ho Chi Minh City; tel. (8) 39303186; fax (8) 38725194; e-mail tt-agr@hcm.fpt.vn; internet www.agrexsaigon.com.vn; f. 1976; exports agricultural produce, coffee, frozen foods and aquatic products; imports agricultural and industrial materials, machinery and equipment, and consumer goods; Gen. Dir Le Thi My Linh; 1,200 employees.

Agrimex (Viet Nam National Agricultural Products Corpn): 173 Hai Ba Trung, District 3, Ho Chi Minh City; tel. (8) 8241049; fax (8) 8291349; e-mail agrimex@hcm.fpt.vn; f. 1956; imports and exports agricultural products; Gen. Dir Nguyen Bach Tuyet.

Airimex (General Civil Aviation Import-Export and Forwarding Co): 414 Nguyen Van Cu, Gia Lam, Long Bien District, Hanoi; tel. (4) 38271939; fax (4) 38271925; e-mail contact@airimex.vn; internet www.airimex.vn; f. 1989; imports and exports aircraft, spare parts and accessories for aircraft and air communications; Gen. Dir Pham Doa Hong.

Artexport–Vietnam (Viet Nam Handicrafts and Art Articles Export-Import Joint Stock Co): 2A Pham Su Manh, Hanoi; tel. (4) 38266576; fax (4) 38259275; e-mail ducquantri@artexport.com.vn; internet www.artexport.com.vn; f. 1964; deals in craft products and art articles; Gen. Dir Do Van Khoi.

B12 Petroleum Co: Cai Lan, Bay Chay Sub-District, Ha Long City, Quang Ninh Province; tel. (33) 846360; fax (33) 846349; internet www.b12petroleum.com.vn; distribution of petroleum products; Dir Vu Ngoc Hai.

Barotex (Viet Nam Investment and Trading Joint Stock Co): 100 Thai Thinh, Dong Da District, Hanoi; tel. (4) 38573428; fax (4) 38573036; e-mail info@barotex.com.vn; internet www.barotex.com.vn; f. 1971; specializes in art and handicrafts made from natural materials, sports shoes, ceramic and lacquer wares, gifts and other housewares, fibres, agricultural and forest products; Gen. Dir Ta Quoc Toan.

Bim Son Cement Co: Badinh, Bimson Town, Thanh Hoa Province; tel. (37) 3824242; fax (37) 3824046; e-mail ktkh_bs@yahoo.com; internet www.ximangbimson.com.vn; mfr of cement; Dir Nguyen Nhu Khue.

Binh Tay Import-Export Joint Stock Co (BITEX): 110–112 Hau Giang, District 6, Ho Chi Minh City; tel. (8) 9604325; fax (8) 9602478; e-mail bitexvn@bitexvn.com; trade in miscellaneous goods; Dir Nguyen Van Thien.

Centrimex (Viet Nam National General Import-Export Corpn): 247 Giang Vo, Dong Da District, Hanoi; tel. (58) 8512986; fax (58) 8512974; e-mail centrimexhn@fpt.vn; internet www.centrimexhn.com.vn; f. 1986; exports and imports goods for 5 provinces in the south-central region of Viet Nam; Gen. Dir Hoang Dinh Dung.

Coalimex (Vinacomin Coal Import-Export Joint Stock Co): 47 Quang Trung, Hanoi; tel. (4) 9423166; fax (4) 9422350; e-mail coalimex@fpt.vn; internet www.coalimex.com.vn; f. 1982; exports coal, imports mining machinery and equipment; Gen. Dir Pham Hong Khanh.

Cocenex (Central Production Import-Export Corpn): 80 Hang Gai, Hanoi; tel. (4) 8254535; fax (4) 8294306; f. 1988; Gen. Dir Bui Thi Thu Huong.

Coffee Supply, Processing and Materials Co: 38B Nguyen Bieu, Nha Trang City, Khanh Hoa Province; tel. (58) 21176; coffee mfr.

Cokyvina (Post and Telecommunication Equipment Import-Export Service Corpn): 178 Trieu Viet Vuong, Hai Ba Trung, Hanoi; tel. (4) 39781323; fax (4) 39782368; e-mail info@cokyvina.com.vn; internet www.cokyvina.com.vn; f. 1987; imports and exports telecom equipment, provides technical advice on related subjects, undertakes authorized imports, jt ventures, jt co-ordination and co-operation on investment with foreign and domestic economic orgs; Dir Nguyen Kim Ky.

Constrexim (Viet Nam Construction Investment and Export-Import Holdings Corpn): 39 Nguyen Dinh Chieu, Hai Ba Trung, Hanoi; tel. (4) 2812000; fax (4) 7820176; e-mail constrexim@fpt.vn; internet www.constrexim.com.vn; f. 1982; exports and imports building materials, equipment and machinery; undertakes construction projects in Viet Nam and abroad, and production of building materials with foreign partners; also involved in investment promotion and project management, real estate development, and human resources development and training; Gen. Dir Do Manh Vu.

Culturimex (State Enterprise for the Export and Import of Works of Art and other Cultural Commodities): 22B Hai Ba Trung, Hanoi; tel. (4) 8252226; fax (4) 8259224; e-mail namson@fpt.vn; f. 1988; exports cultural items and imports materials for the cultural industry; Gen. Dir Nguyen Lai.

Dau Tieng Rubber Corpn: Dau Tieng Townlet, Dau Tieng District, Binh Duong Province; tel. (650) 561479; fax (650) 561789; e-mail vanphong@caosudautieng.com.vn; internet www.caosudautieng.com.vn; f. 1981; govt-owned; planting, processing and export of natural rubber; Man. Dir Tien Duc Nguyen.

Epco Ltd (Export Import and Tourism Co Ltd): 1 Nyuyen Thuong Hien, District 3, Ho Chi Minh City; tel. (8) 8324392; fax (8) 8324744; f. 1986; processes seafood; tourism and hotel business; Gen. Dir Nguyen Loc Ri.

Foodcosa (Food Co Ho Chi Min City): 57 Nguyen Thi Minh Khai, District 1, Ho Chi Minh City; tel. (8) 39309184; fax (8) 39304552; e-mail info@foodcosa.vn; internet www.foodcosa.vn; mfr and distributor of food products (rice, instant noodles, porridge, sauces, biscuits); Dir Ngo Van Tan; 3,500 employees.

Forexco Quang Nam (Quang Nam Forest Products Export Joint Stock Co): Xa Dien Ngoc, Dien Ban District, Quangnam Province; tel. (510) 3944073; fax (510) 3843619; e-mail forexcoqnam@dng.vnn.vn; internet forexco.com.vn; f. 1986; mfr and exporter of furniture and other wood products; Gen. Dir Pham Phu Thong.

Garmex Saigon (Saigon Garment Manufacturing Import-Export Co): 236/7 Nguyen Van Luong, Ward 17, Go Vap District, Ho Chi Minh City; tel. (8) 39844822; fax (8) 39844746; e-mail gmsg@hcm.fpt.vn; internet www.garmexsaigon-gmc.com; f. 1993; garment production and export; Pres. Le Quang Hung; Man. Dir Nguyen An.

Genecofov (General Co of Foods and Services): 64 Ba Huyen Thanh Quan, District 3, Ho Chi Minh City; tel. (8) 9325366; fax (8) 9325428; e-mail gecofov@hcm.fpt.vn; f. 1956; import and export of food products, handicrafts and ceramics, garage services, vehicle trading; under the Ministry of Trade; Dir To Van Phat.

Generalexim (Viet Nam National General Export-Import Corpn): 46 Ngo Quyen, Hoan Kiem, Hanoi; tel. (4) 38264009; fax (4) 38259894; e-mail gexim@generalexim.com.vn; internet www.generalexim.com.vn; f. 1981; export and import on behalf of production and trading organizations, also garment processing for export and manufacture of toys; Gen. Dir Hoang Tuan Khai.

Generalimex (General II Import-Export Joint Stock Co): 212/1 Nguyen Trai, District 1, Ho Chi Minh City; tel. (8) 62907517; fax (8) 62907518; e-mail generalimex@generalimex.com.vn; internet www.generalimex.com.vn; exports of agricultural products and spices, imports of machinery, vehicles, chemicals and fertilizers; Gen. Dir Nguyen Van Hoang.

Haprosimex (Hanoi General Production and Import-Export Company): Km 11, National Highway 1A, Van Dien, Hanoi; tel. (4) 8618341; fax (4) 8615390; e-mail business@hapro.com.vn; internet www.hapro.com.vn; specializes in handicrafts, textiles, clothing and agricultural and forestry products; Gen. Dir Nguyen Minh Tuan.

Hatien 1 Cement Joint Stock Co: 360 Ben Chuong Dong, P. Cau Kho, District 1, Ho Chi Minh City; tel. (8) 38368363; fax (8) 38361278; e-mail hatien1@hatien1.com.vn; internet www.hatien1.com.vn; mfr of cement; Dir Nguyen Ngoc Anh.

Hatien Cement Co No 2: Kien Luong Town, Ha Tien, Kien Giang Province; tel. (77) 53004; fax (77) 53005; e-mail xmht2@vnn.vn; internet www.xmht2.com; mfr of cement; Dir Nguyen Manh.

Haugiang Petrolimex (Haugiang Petrol and Oil Co): 21 Cach Mang Thang 8, Can Tho City, Can Tho Province; tel. (71) 21657; fax (71) 12746; distributor of fuel; Dir TRINH MANG THANG.

Hoang Thach Cement Co: Minh Tan Hamlet, Kinh Mon, Hai Duong; tel. (32) 3821092; fax (32) 3821098; e-mail contact@ ximanghoangthach.com; internet www.ximanghoangthach.com.vn; sale of construction materials; Dir NGOC BINH DAO.

Intimex Import-Export Corpn: 96 Tran Hung Dao, Hanoi; tel. (4) 39423529; fax (4) 39424250; e-mail intimex@hn.vnn.vn; internet www.intimexco.com; f. 1979; exports mainly agricultural products and processed items; imports mainly consumer goods, motorcycles and raw materials, machinery and equipment for the construction industry; Chair. NGUYEN THI NGA; Gen. Dir HOANG HOANG HANH.

Lefaso (Viet Nam Leather and Footwear Asscn): 160 Hoang Hoa Tham, Tay Ho, Hanoi; tel. (4) 37281560; fax (4) 37281561; e-mail hhdg@hn.vnn.vn; internet www.lefaso.org.vn; f. 1990 to promote external trade relations, to provide technical support and technological training and to disseminate market information; Chair. NGUYEN DUC THUAN; Gen. Sec. NGUYEN THI TONG.

Machinoimport (Viet Nam Machinery and Spare Parts Co): 8 Trang Thi, Hoan Kiem, Hanoi; tel. (4) 8253703; fax (4) 8254050; e-mail machinokhdt@hn.vnn.vn; internet www.machinoimport.com .vn; f. 1956 as Vietnam National Machinery Export-Import Corpn; reorganized in 2003; controlled by Ministry of Industry and Trade; imports and exports machinery, spare parts and tools; consultancy, investment, jt venture, and manufacturing services; comprises 12 cos; Chair. NGUYEN TRAN DAT; Gen. Dir TRAN DUC TRUONG.

Marine Supply (Marine Technical Materials Import-Export and Supplies): 276A Da Nang, Ngo Quyen, Haiphong; tel. (31) 847308; fax (31) 845159; f. 1985; imports and exports technical materials for marine transportation industry; Dir PHAN TRANG CHAN.

Mecanimex (Viet Nam National Mechanical Products Export-Import Co): 37 Trang Thi, Hoan Kiem District, Hanoi; tel. (4) 8257459; fax (4) 9349904; e-mail mecahn@fpt.vn; internet mecanimex.com.vn; exports and imports mechanical products and hand tools; Gen. Dir TRAN BAO GIOC.

Nafobird (Viet Nam Forest and Native Birds, Animals and Ornamental Plants Export-Import Enterprises): 64 Truong Dinh, District 3, Ho Chi Minh City; tel. (8) 8290211; fax (8) 8293735; f. 1987; exports native birds, animals and plants, and imports materials for forestry; Dir VO HA AN.

Naforimex (Hanoi Forest Products Export-Import and Production Corpn): 19 Ba Trieu, Hoan Kiem District, Hanoi; tel. (4) 8261255; fax (4) 8259264; e-mail naforimexhanoi@fpt.vn; f. 1960; imports chemicals, machinery and spare parts for the forestry industry and water supply network; exports oils, forest products, gum benzoin and resin; CEO NGUYEN BA HUNG.

Nitagrex (Ninh Thuan Agricultural Products Import-Export Co): 158 Bac Ai, Do Vinh Ward, Phan Rang Thap Cham, Ninh Thuan Province; tel. (68) 888779; fax (68) 888842; e-mail nitagrex@hcm.vnn .vn; internet www.nitagrex.com.vn; f. 1999; production and export of agricultural products; import of consumer goods, transport vehicles and agricultural materials and equipment; Gen. Dir DAO VAN CHAN.

Packexport (Viet Nam National Packaging Technology and Import-Export Co): 31 Hang Thung, Hanoi; tel. (4) 8262792; fax (4) 8269227; e-mail packexport-vn@vnn.vn; f. 1976; manufactures packaging for domestic and export demand, and imports materials for the packaging industry; Gen. Dir TRINH LE KIEU.

Petec Trading and Investment Corpn: 194 Nam Ky Khoi Nghia, District 3, Ho Chi Minh City; tel. (8) 39303633; fax (8) 39305686; e-mail petectonghop@hcm.vnn.vn; internet www.petec.com.vn; f. 1981; imports equipment and technology for oil drilling, exploration and oil production; exports crude petroleum, rice, coffee and agricultural products; invests in silk, coffee, financial and transport sectors; Chair. and CEO NGUYEN MINH TRUC.

Petrol and Oil Co (Zone 1): Duc Gliang Town, Gia Lam, Hanoi; tel. (4) 8271400; fax (4) 8272432; sales of oil and gas; Dir PHAN VAN DU.

Petrolimex (Viet Nam National Petroleum Corpn): 1 Kham Thien, Dong Da District, Hanoi; tel. (4) 38512603; fax (4) 38519203; e-mail xttm@petrolimex.com.vn; internet www.petrolimex.com.vn; f. 1956; import, export and distribution of petroleum products and liquefied petroleum gas; Chair. NGUYEN THANH SON; Dir-Gen. BUI NGOC BAO.

Petrolimex Saigon Petroleum Co (Zone 2): 15 Le Duan, District 1, Ho Chi Minh City; tel. (8) 8292081; fax (8) 8222082; sales of petroleum products; Dir TRAN VAN THANG.

Petrovietnam (Viet Nam Oil and Gas Corpn): 18 Lang Ha, Ba Dinh, Hanoi; tel. (4) 38252526; fax (4) 38265942; e-mail info@pvn.vn; internet www.petrovietnam.com.vn; f. 1975; exploration and production of petroleum and gas; Chair. DINH LA THANG; Pres. and CEO PHUNG DINH THUC.

Saigon Beer Alcohol Beverage Corpn (Sabeco): 6 Hai Ba Trung, Ben Nghe District, Ho Chi Minh City; tel. (8) 38294083; fax (8) 38296856; e-mail biasaigon@sabeco.com.vn; internet www.sabeco .com.vn; producer of beer; Pres. NGUYEN ANH DZUNG.

Seaco (Sundries Electric Appliances Co): 64 Pho Duc Chinh, District 1, Ho Chi Minh City; tel. (8) 8210961; fax (8) 8210974; deals in miscellaneous electrical goods; Dir MAI MINH CUONG.

Seaprodex Hanoi (Hanoi Sea Products Export-Import Co): 20 Lang Ha, Dong Da, Hanoi; tel. (4) 38345678; fax (4) 38354125; e-mail seahn@seaprodexhanoi.com.vn; internet www.seaprodexhanoi.com .vn; Dir LE CONG DUC.

Seaprodex Saigon (Ho Chi Minh City Sea Products Import-Export Corpn): 87 Ham Nghi, District 1, Ho Chi Minh City; tel. (8) 38214186; fax (8) 39142236; e-mail info@seaprodexsg.com; internet www .seaprodexsg.com; f. 1978; exports frozen and processed sea products; imports machinery and materials for fishing and processing; Gen. Dir NGUYEN DUY DUNG.

SJC (Saigon Jewellery Co): 115 Nguyen Cong Tru, District 1, Ho Chi Minh City; tel. (8) 39144056; fax (8) 39144057; e-mail info@sjc.com .vn; internet www.sjc.com.vn; f. 1988; manufacturing, processing and trading of gold, gemstones, silver and jewellery; Man. Dir DO CONG CHINH.

Technimex JSC (Technology Import-Export Joint Stock Company): 70 Tran Hung Dao, Hoan Kiem District, Hanoi; tel. (4) 7519423; fax (4) 3778220; e-mail technimex@hn.vnn.vn; internet www .technimexvn.com; f. 1982 under the name Viet Nam Technology Import-Export Corpn; name changed as above in 2001; exports and imports machines, equipment, instruments, etc.; Dir NGUYEN HUY BINH.

Technoimport (Viet Nam National Complete Equipment and Technics Import-Export Corpn): 16–18 Trang Thi, Hanoi; tel. (4) 38254974; fax (4) 38254059; e-mail technohn@netnam.vn; internet technoimport.vn; f. 1959; imports and exports equipment, machinery, transport equipment, spare parts, materials and various consumer commodities; exports products by co-investment and jt-venture enterprises; provides consulting services for trade and investment, transport and forwarding services; acts as import-export brokering and trading agents; Gen. Dir VU CHU HIEN.

Terraprodex (Corpn for Processing and Export-Import of Rare Earth and Other Specialities): 35 Dien Bien Phu, Hanoi; tel. (4) 8232010; fax (4) 8256446; f. 1989; processing and export of rare earth products and other minerals; Dir TRAN DUC HIEP.

Thanglong Minerals and Metals Co Ltd: 127 Khuat Duy Tien, Hanoi; tel. (4) 35535218; fax (4) 35532669; e-mail thanglong@ thanglongcastiron.com; internet www.thanglongcastiron.com; fmrly Viet Nam National Minerals Export Import Corpn; exports cast iron products; imports pig iron and crude steel; Gen. Dir LE THI MINH.

Tocontap Saigon (Saigon Sundries Export-Import Joint Stock Co): 35 Le Quy Don, District 3, Ho Chi Minh City; tel. (8) 39325687; fax (8) 39325963; e-mail info@tocontapsaigon.com; internet www .tocontapsaigon.com; f. 1956; imports and exports apparel, agricultural products, art and handicrafts and sundries; Gen. Dir LE THI THANH HUONG.

Tracimexco (Transport Investment Co-operation and Import-Export Corpn): 22 Phan Dinh Giot, Ward 2, Tan Binh District, Ho Chi Minh City; tel. (8) 8442247; fax (8) 8445240; e-mail tralico@hn .vnn.vn; internet www.tracimexco.com.vn; fmrly Vietranscimex; exports and imports specialized equipment and materials for transportation and communication; Gen. Dir PHAM QUANG VINH.

Vama (Viet Nam Automobile Manufacturers' Association): Sun Red River Bldg, 6th Floor, Phan Chu Trinh Ward, Hoan Kiem District, Hanoi; tel. (4) 38331282; fax (4) 38331750; e-mail vama.office@gmail .com; internet www.vama.org.vn; f. 2000; 18 mems; Chair. LAURENT CHARPENTIER.

Vasep (Viet Nam Asscn of Seafood Exporters and Producers): Lot 218A, 6 An Kanh, An Phu Ward, District 2, Ho Chi Minh City; tel. (8) 62810432; fax (8) 62810450; e-mail vasep@fpt.vn; internet www .vasep.com.vn; f. 1998; exports seafood products; provides essential market information to Viet Nam's seafood industry; organizes and implements activities designed to develop and promote the industry; Chair. TRAN THIEN HAI.

Vegetexco (Viet Nam National Vegetables and Fruit Export-Import Corpn): 2 Pham Ngoc Thach, Dong Da District, Hanoi; tel. (4) 5744592; fax (4) 8523926; e-mail vegetexcovn@fpt.vn; internet www.vegetexcovn.com.vn; f. 1971; exports fresh and processed vegetables and fruit, spices and flowers, and other agricultural products; imports vegetable seeds and processing materials; Gen. Dir LE VAN ANH.

Vicem (Viet Nam Cement Industry Corpn—Vinacement): 228 Le Duan, Dong Da District, Hanoi; tel. (4) 8512425; fax (4) 8512778; e-mail banbt@vinacement.com.vn; internet www.vicem.vn; f. 1980; manufactures and exports cement and clinker; Chair. LE VAN CHUNG; Gen. Dir NGUYEN NGOC ANH.

Viet Nam Dairy Products JS Company (VINAMILK): 10 Tan Trao, Ward Tan Phu, District 7, Ho Chi Minh City; tel. (8) 54155555;

fax (8) 54161226; e-mail vinamilk@vinamilk.com.vn; internet www
.vinamilk.com.vn; f. 1976; producer of dairy products; Dir MAI KIEU
LIEN.

Vietnam Rubber Group: 236 Nam Ky Khoi Nghia, District 3, Ho
Chi Minh City; tel. (8) 9327857; fax (8) 9327341; merged with
Rubexim (rubber export-import corpn) in 1991; fmrly known as
GERUCO; manages and controls the Vietnamese rubber industry,
including the planting, processing and trading of natural rubber and
rubber wood products; also imports chemicals, machinery and spare
parts for the industry; Chair. TRAN NGOC THANH; Dir-Gen. LE QUANG
THUNG.

Vietrans (Viet Nam National Foreign Trade Forwarding and Warehousing Corpn): 13 Ly Nam De, Hoan Kiem District, Hanoi; tel. (4)
38457417; fax (4) 38455829; e-mail info@vietrans.com.vn; internet
vietrans.com.vn; f. 1970; agent for forwarding and transport of
exports and imports, diplomatic cargoes and other goods, warehousing, shipping and insurance; Gen. Dir THAI DUY LONG.

Viettronimex (Viet Nam Electronics Import-Export Corpn): 74–76
Nguyen Hue, District 1, Ho Chi Minh City; tel. (8) 8298201; fax (8)
8294873; e-mail vtr@hcm.vnn.vn; internet viettronimex.com.vn;
f. 1981; imports and exports electronic goods; Dir NGUYEN HUU
THINH.

Vigecam (Viet Nam General Corpn of Agricultural Materials): 16
Ngo Tat To, Dong Da District, Hanoi; tel. and fax (4) 37478890; e-mail
info@vigecam.vn; internet www.vigecam.vn; exports and imports
agricultural products; Gen. Dir TRAN VAN KANH.

Viglacera (Viet Nam Glass and Ceramics Corpn): 16–17 Viglacera
Bldg, 1 Thang Long, Ward Me Tri, Tu Liem, Hanoi; tel. (4) 5536660;
fax (4) 5536671; e-mail vgc@hn.vnn.vn; internet www.viglacera.com
.vn; f. 1974; mfr of building materials; Gen. Dir NGUYEN ANH TUAN.

Vimedimex II (Vimedimex Medi-Pharma Joint Stock Co): 602/45D
Dien Bien Phu, Ward 22, Binh Thanh District, Ho Chi Minh City; tel.
(8) 38990164; fax (8) 38990165; e-mail info@vietpharm.com.vn;
internet www.vietpharm.com.vn; f. 1984; exports and imports
medicinal and pharmaceutical materials and products, medical
instruments; Gen. Dir NGUYEN TIEN HUNG.

Vimico (Viet Nam National Minerals Corpn): 562 Nguyen Van Cu,
Gia Lam District, Hanoi; tel. (4) 8770010; fax (4) 8770006; e-mail
vimico@hn.vnn.vn; internet www.vimicovn.com; Chair. VU XUAN
KHOAT; Gen. Dir NGO VAN TROI.

Vinacafe (Viet Nam National Coffee Import-Export Corpn): 211–
213 Tran Huy Lieu, Ward 8, Phu Nuan District, Ho Chi Minh City;
tel. (8) 54495514; fax (8) 54495513; e-mail vinacafe@hn.vnn.vn;
internet www.vinacafe.com.vn; f. 1995; state-owned; exports coffee,
and imports equipment and chemicals for coffee production; Chair.
Dr DOAN DINH THIEM.

Vinachem (Viet Nam National Chemical Corpn): 1A Trang Tien,
Hoan Kiem District, Hanoi; tel. (4) 38240551; fax (4) 38252995;
e-mail info@vinachem.com.vn; internet www.vinachem.com.vn;
f. 1969; production, import and export of chemicals and fertilizers;
Chair. NGUYEN QUOC TUAN; Pres. and CEO NGUYEN DINH KHANG.

Vinachimex (Viet Nam National Chemicals Import-Export Corpn):
4 Pham Ngu Lao, Hanoi; tel. (4) 8256377; fax (4) 8257727; f. 1969;
exports and imports chemical products, minerals, rubber, fertilizers,
machinery and spare parts; Dir NGUYEN VAN SON.

Vinacomin (Viet Nam National Coal-Mineral Industries Group):
226 Le Duan, Dong Da District, Hanoi; tel. (4) 5180141; fax (4)
8510724; e-mail info@vinacomin.vn; internet www.vinacomin.vn;
f. 2005; est. following merger of Vietnam Coal Corpn and Vietnam
Minerals Corpn; subsidiaries include Vinacomin Port Co; coal and
bauxite mining, shipbuilding, automobile manufacturing, tourism,
financing, and power generation in thermal power plants; Gen. Dir
TRAN XUAN HOA.

Vinafilm (Viet Nam Film Import, Export and Film Service Corpn):
73 Nguyen Trai, Dong Da District, Hanoi; tel. (4) 8244566; f. 1987;
export and import of films and videotapes; film distribution; organization of film shows and participation of Vietnamese films in international film festivals; Gen. Man. NGO MANH LAN.

Vinafimex (Viet Nam National Agricultural Produce and Foodstuffs
Import and Export Corpn): 58 Ly Thai To, Hanoi; tel. (4) 8255768; fax
(4) 8255476; e-mail fime@hn.vnn.vn; internet www.vinafimex.com
.vn; f. 1984; exports cashews, peanuts, coffee, rubber and other
agricultural products, and garments; imports malt, fertilizer,
insecticide, seeds, machinery and equipment, etc.; Pres. NGUYEN
TOAN THANG; Gen. Dir NGUYEN VAN THANG.

Vinafood Hanoi (Hanoi Food Import-Export Co): 6 Ngo Quyen,
Hoan Kiem District, Hanoi; tel. (4) 8256771; fax (4) 8258528; f. 1988;
exports rice, maize, tapioca; imports fertilizers, insecticides, wheat
and wheat flour; Dir NGUYEN DUC HY.

Vinalivesco (Vietnam National Livestock Corpn): 519 Minh Khai,
Hai Ba Trung District, Hanoi; tel. (4) 38621814; fax (4) 38623645;
e-mail vilico@vilico.vn; internet vilico.vn; f. 1996; imports and

exports animal and poultry products, animal feeds and other agro-
products, and foodstuffs; Gen. Dir NGUYEN VAN KHAC.

Vinapimex (Viet Nam Paper Corpn): 25A Ly Thuong Kiet, Hanoi;
tel. (4) 8260143; fax (4) 8260381; f. 1995; production and marketing of
paper; Pres. and CEO VO SY DONG.

Vinaplast (Viet Nam Plastics Corpn): 300B Nguyen Tat Thanh,
District 4, Ho Chi Minh City; tel. (8) 39453301; fax (8) 39453298;
e-mail vinaplast@vinaplast.com.vn; internet www.vinaplast.com
.vn; f. 1976; import and export of products for plastic processing
industry; production and trade of plastic products; Gen. Dir NGUYEN
KHAC LONG.

Vinasteel (Viet Nam National Steel Corpn): D2 Ton That Tung,
Dong Da District, Hanoi; tel. (4) 8525537; fax (4) 8262657; distributor
of metal products; Dir NGO HUY PHAN.

Vinataba (Viet Nam National Tobacco Corpn): 25A Ly Thuong Kiet,
Hoan Kiem District, Hanoi; tel. (4) 8265778; fax (4) 8265777; internet
www.vinataba.com.vn; mfr of tobacco products; Chair. NGUYEN THAI
SINH; Gen. Dir NGUYEN NAM HAI.

Vinatea (Viet Nam National Tea Development Investment and
Export-Import Co): 92 Vo Thi Sau, Hanoi; tel. (4) 6226990; fax (4)
6226991; e-mail info@vinatea.com.vn; internet www.vinatea.com
.vn; exports tea, imports tea-processing materials; Gen. Dir NGUYEN
THIEN TOAN.

Vinatex (Viet Nam National Textile and Garment Corpn): 25 Ba
Trieu, Hoan Kiem District, Hanoi; tel. (4) 38257700; fax (4)
38262269; e-mail vinatexhn@vinatex.com.vn; internet www
.vinatex.com; f. 1995; imports raw material, textile and sewing
machinery, spare parts, accessories, dyestuffs; exports textiles,
ready-made garments, carpets, jute, silk; Gen. Dir VU DUC GIANG.

Vitas (Viet Nam Tea Association): 92 Vo Thu Sau, Hai Ba Trung
District, Hanoi; tel. (4) 36250908; fax (4) 36251801; e-mail vitas@fpt
.vn; internet www.vitas.org.vn; f. 1988; promotes the trading and
marketing of tea products; offers advice and information, both to the
Govt and to farmers, regarding development schemes and policies;
Chair. and Pres. NGUYEN VAN THU.

Vocarimex (National Co for Vegetable Oils, Aromas, and Cosmetics
of Viet Nam): 58 Nguyen Binh Khiem, District 1, Ho Chi Minh City;
tel. (8) 8294513; fax (8) 8290586; e-mail vocar@hcm.vnn.vn; internet
www.vocarimex.com; f. 1976; producing and trading vegetable oils,
oil-based products and special industry machinery; packaging;
operating port facilities; Gen. Dir DO NGOC KAI.

Xunhasaba (Viet Nam State Corpn for Export and Import of Books,
Periodicals and other Cultural Commodities): 32 Hai Ba Trung,
Hanoi; tel. (4) 38262989; fax (4) 38252860; e-mail xunhasaba@hn
.vnn.vn; internet www.xunhasaba.com.vn; f. 1957; exports and
imports books, periodicals, postage stamps, greetings cards, calendars and paintings; Dir HA TRIEU KIEN.

UTILITIES
Electricity

Electricity of Viet Nam (EVN): 18 Tran Nguyen Han, Hanoi; tel.
(4) 2201371; fax (4) 2201369; e-mail vp@evn.com.vn; internet www
.evn.com.vn; produces, transmits and distributes electrical power;
Chair. DAO VAN HUNG; Pres. and CEO PHAM LE TANH.

Power Co No 1 (PC1): 20 Tran Nguyen Han, Hoan Kiem, Hanoi; tel.
(4) 8255074; fax (4) 8244033; e-mail anhdn@pc1.com.vn; manages
the generation, transmission and distribution of electrical power in
northern Viet Nam; Dir DO VAN LOC.

Power Co No 3 (PC3): 315 Trung Nu Vuong, Hai Chau District, Da
Nang; tel. (511) 621028; fax (511) 625071; f. 1975; manages the
generation, transmission and distribution of electrical power in
central Viet Nam; Gen. Dir TA CANH.

Southern Power Corpn (EVN SPC): 72 Hai Ba Trung, District 1,
Ho Chi Minh City; tel. (8) 22200350; fax (8) 22200352; fmrly Power Co
No 2; reorg. and renamed as above in early 2010; manages the
distribution of electrical power in southern Viet Nam; Gen. Dir
NGUYEN THANH DUY.

Water

Hanoi Water Business Co: 44 Yen Phu, Hanoi; tel. (4) 8293179; fax
(4) 8294069; f. 1954; responsible for the supply of water to Hanoi and
its 5 urban and 2 suburban districts; Dir-Gen. NHU HAI NGUYEN.

Saigon Water Corpn (SAWACO): 1 Cong Truong Quoc Te, District
3, Ho Chi Minh City; tel. (8) 38291974; fax (8) 38241644; e-mail
hcmcwater@hcm.vnn.vn; internet www.sawaco.com.vn; f. 1966;
govt-owned; manages the water services and water construction
works of Ho Chi Minh City; Gen. Dir DINH PHU TRAN.

CO-OPERATIVES

Viet Nam Co-operative Alliance (VCA): 77 Nguyen Thai Hoc, Ba
Dinh District, Hanoi; tel. (4) 8431689; fax (4) 8431883; e-mail admin@

vca.org.vn; internet www.vca.org.vn; f. 1993; fmrly Viet Nam Co-operatives Council; Pres. DAO XUAN CAN.

TRADE UNIONS

Tong Lien doan Lao dong Viet Nam (Vietnam General Confederation of Labour): 82 Tran Hung Dao, POB 627, Hanoi; tel. (4) 9421794; fax (4) 9423781; e-mail doingoaitld@hn.vnn.vn; internet www.congdoanvn.org.vn; f. 1929; merged in 1976 with the South Viet Nam Trade Union Fed. for Liberation; 6m. mems; 20 affiliated unions; Pres. DANG NGOC TUNG; Vice-Pres. NGUYEN HOA BINH.

Transport

RAILWAYS

Viet Nam had a railway network of 2,347 km in 2010. Plans to construct a new rail link between Hanoi and Ho Chi Minh City, which would reduce the journey time from 29 hours to less than 10 hours, were postponed in mid-2010, owing to concerns over the cost. In 2008 construction commenced of a metro system in Ho Chi Minh City. The 19.7-km route was due for completion in 2014.

Duong Sat Viet Nam (DSVN) (Viet Nam Railways): 118 Le Duan, Hanoi; tel. (4) 8220537; fax (4) 9422866; e-mail dsvn@vr.com.vn; internet www.vr.com.vn; 2,347 km of main lines (2010); routes are: Hanoi–Ho Chi Minh City, Hanoi–Haiphong, Hanoi–Dong Dang, Hanoi–Lao Cai, Hanoi–Thai Nguyen, Thai Nguyen–Kep–Bai Chay; Chair. and Gen. Dir Dr NGUYEN HUU BANG.

ROADS

In 2010 there were an estimated 160,089 km of roads, of which 13,554 km were highways and 31,575 km were secondary roads. In 2006 an upgrade of National Highway No. 2, linking An Giang province in Viet Nam to Takeo province in Cambodia, was completed. In early 2012 the Government announced a project to expand and upgrade the 1,446-km Hanoi-Can Tho section of the 2,300-km National Highway No. 1; the project, which was estimated to cost some US $6,000m. was scheduled for completion in late 2016.

SHIPPING

The principal port facilities are at Haiphong, Da Nang and Ho Chi Minh City. At the end of 2012 the Vietnamese flag registered fleet numbered 1,181 vessels (including 786 general cargo carriers, 109 tank ships, 108 bulk carriers and nine gas tankers), with a combined displacement totalling 4,382,320 grt.

Transport and Chartering Corpn (Vietfracht): 74 Nguyen Du, Hai Ba Trung, Hanoi; tel. (4) 38228915; fax (4) 39423679; e-mail vfhan@vietfracht.com.vn; internet www.vietfracht.com.vn; f. 1963; ship broking, chartering, ship management, shipping agency, international freight forwarding; logistic and consultancy services, import-export services; Pres. TRAN VAN QUY; Gen. Dir NGO XUAN HONG.

Viet Nam National Shipping Lines (Vinalines): Ocean Park Bldg, 1 Dao Duy Anh, Phuong Mai Quarter, Dang Da District, Hanoi; tel. (4) 35770825; fax (4) 35770850; e-mail vnl@vinalines.com.vn; internet www.vinalines.com.vn; f. 1996; 27 subsidiaries and 36 associated companies; import and export of maritime materials and equipment, shipping agency and repair, construction, hotels, tourism, warehousing and logistics services; Chair. NGUYEN NGOC HUE; Pres. and CEO NGUYEN CANH VIET.

Viet Nam Ocean Shipping Agency Corporation (VOSA Corpn): Unit 801, Harbour View Tower, 35 Nguyen Hue, District 1, Ho Chi Minh City; tel. (8) 39141490; fax (8) 39140423; e-mail vosagroup@hcm.vnn.vn; internet www.vosagroup.com; f. 1957; fmrly the Viet Nam Ocean Shipping Agency; controlled by Vinalines; in charge of merchant shipping; arranges ship repairs, salvage, passenger services, air and sea freight forwarding services; offices throughout Viet Nam; Chair. PHAM MANH CUONG; Dir-Gen. VU XUAN TRUNG.

Viet Nam Ocean Shipping Joint Stock Co (VOSCO) (Cong Ty Van Tai Duong Bien Viet Nam): 215 Lach Tray St, Ngo Quyen District, Haiphong; tel. (31) 3731090; fax (31) 3731007; e-mail pid@vosco.vn; drycargo@vosco.vn; internet www.vosco.com.vn; f. 1970; state-owned; Chair. and CEO VU HUU CHINH.

Viet Nam Sea Transport and Chartering Co (Vitranschart): 428 Nguyen Tat Thanh, Ward 18, District 4, Ho Chi Minh City; tel. (8) 39404271; fax (8) 39404711; e-mail vtc-hcm@vitranschart.com.vn; internet www.vitranschart.com.vn; Dir TRUONG DINH SON.

Viet Nam Shipbuilding Industry Group (Vinashin): 172 Ngo Quyen, Hanoi; tel. (4) 37711212; fax (4) 37711535; e-mail contact@vinashin.com.vn; internet www.vinashin.com.vn; f. 1972; shipbuilding and ship repair, marine transport and trade services; Chair. NGUYEN HONG TRUONG; Gen. Dir VU ANH TUAN.

CIVIL AVIATION

Viet Nam's principal airports are Tan Son Nhat International Airport (located 6 km north of Ho Chi Minh City) and Noi Bai International Airport (Hanoi), which handle both overseas and domestic traffic. A third international airport is located at Da Nang, and an international terminal was inaugurated at Can Tho in January 2011, following the upgrading of that airport's facilities. In 2004 plans were announced for the construction of a new international airport at Long Thang, in Dong Nai province; work on the three-stage project was expected to commence in 2015. When operational, the airport would have an initial capacity of 25m. a year. A total of three new airports were under development in 2012, and in late 2006 there were 20 domestic airports in Viet Nam, including Ca Mau, Con Son, Chu Lai and Nha Trang.

Jetstar Pacific Airlines: 112 Hong Ha, Tan Binh District, Ho Chi Minh City; tel. (8) 38450092; fax (8) 38450085; internet www.jetstar .com/vn/vi/index.aspx; f. 1991; fmrly Pacific Airlines; present name adopted 2008; 70% owned by Viet Nam Airlines and 30% owned by Qantas (Australia); operates low-cost domestic flights; CEO LE LONG HA.

Viet Nam Airlines: 200 Nguyen Son, Long Bien District, Hanoi; tel. (4) 38320320; fax (4) 38722375; internet www.vietnamairlines.com; fmrly the Gen. Civil Aviation Admin. of Viet Nam, then Hang Khong Viet Nam; privatization plans mooted; operates domestic passenger services from Hanoi and from Ho Chi Minh City to the principal Vietnamese cities, and international services to 18 countries; Chair. PHAM VIET THANH; Pres. and CEO PHAM NGOC MINH.

VietJet Air: 60A Truong Son St, Tan Binh District, Ho Chi Minh City; tel. (4) 37281828; fax (4) 37281838; internet www.vietjetair .com; f. 2011; operates low-cost passenger services on nine domestic routes; plans to expand operations to international destinations in South-East Asia; CEO NGUYEN DUC TAM.

Tourism

Tourist arrivals increased by 13.9% in 2012, to reach 6.8m. Of these, the largest proportion was from the People's Republic of China (20.9%); other important sources of visitors included the Republic of Korea, Japan and the USA. Revenue from tourism totalled a provisional US $5,620m. in 2011.

Viet Nam National Administration of Tourism (VNAT): 80 Quan Su, Hanoi; tel. (4) 39422070; fax (4) 39424115; e-mail titc@ vietnamtourism.gov.vn; internet www.vietnamtourism.com; f. 1960; Dir-Gen. NGUYEN VAN TUAN.

Hanoi Tourism Service Co (HANOI TOSERCO): 273 Kim Ma, Hanoi; tel. (4) 7262626; fax (4) 7262571; e-mail hanoitoserco@hn.vnn .vn; internet www.tosercohanoi.com; f. 1988; manages the devt of tourism, hotels and restaurants in the capital, and other services incl. staff training; Dir TRAN TIEN HUNG.

Tong Cong ty Du lich Sai Gon (Saigon Tourist Holding Co): 23 Le Loi, District 1, Ho Chi Minh City; tel. (8) 38292291; fax (8) 38243239; e-mail saigontourist@sgtourist.com.vn; internet www.saigon-tourist .com; f. 1975; holding co controlling 11 tour operators, 56 hotels, 10 resorts and 24 restaurants; Gen. Dir TRAN HUNG VIET.

Defence

As assessed at November 2012, the total strength of the armed forces was an estimated 482,000: army 412,000; navy 40,000; air force 30,000. Men are subject to a two-year minimum term of compulsory military service between 18 and 35 years of age. Paramilitary forces number in excess of 5m. and include the urban People's Self-Defence Force and the rural People's Militia. Border defence troops number an estimated 40,000.

Defence Expenditure: Budgeted at US $3,330m. for 2012.

Commander-in-Chief of the Armed Forces: TRUONG TAN SANG.

Chief of General Staff (Army): Sr Lt-Gen. DO BA TY.

Commander of the Navy: Adm. NGUYEN VAN HIEN.

Education

Primary education, which is compulsory, begins at six years of age and lasts for five years. Secondary education, beginning at the age of 11, lasts for up to seven years, comprising a first cycle of four years and a second cycle of three years. In 2011 enrolment in primary schools included 99% of children in the relevant age-group, while enrolment in secondary schools included an estimated 65% of children in the relevant age-group in 2002. According to preliminary official figures, in 2011/12 a total of 3.3m. pupils attended pre-primary institutions, at which 174,000 teachers were employed. In the same year a total of 7.1m. pupils attended primary schools, at which 366,000 teachers were employed; and 7.7m. students were enrolled in secondary level institutions, at which 462,100 teachers

were employed. In 1989 Viet Nam's first private college since 1954, Thang Long College, was opened in Hanoi to cater for university students. In 2011/12 2.2m. students were enrolled at 419 universities and colleges, at which 84,200 teachers were employed. The adult literacy rate was 93.2% in 2010. Of total planned budgetary expenditure by the central Government in 2012, US $274m. (20% of total expenditure) was allocated to education. The Government also announced that $16.3m. would be allocated to education development until 2020.

YEMEN

Introductory Survey

LOCATION, CLIMATE, LANGUAGE, RELIGION, FLAG, CAPITAL

The Republic of Yemen is situated in the south of the Arabian peninsula, bounded to the north by Saudi Arabia, to the east by Oman, to the south by the Gulf of Aden, and to the west by the Red Sea. The islands of Perim and Kamaran at the southern end of the Red Sea, the island of Socotra, at the entrance to the Gulf of Aden, and the Kuria Muria islands, near the coast of Oman, are also part of the Republic. The climate in the semi-desert coastal strip is hot, with high humidity and temperatures rising to more than 38°C (100°F); inland, the climate is somewhat milder, with cool winters and relatively heavy rainfall in the highlands. The eastern plateau slopes into desert. The language is Arabic. The population is almost entirely Muslim, and mainly of the Sunni Shafi'a sect. The national flag (proportions 2 by 3) has three equal horizontal stripes, of red, white and black. The capital is San'a.

CONTEMPORARY POLITICAL HISTORY

Historical Context

The Republic of Yemen was formed in May 1990 by the amalgamation of the Yemen Arab Republic (YAR) and the People's Democratic Republic of Yemen (PDRY). The YAR (from 1967 also known as North Yemen) had formerly been a kingdom. When Turkey's Ottoman Empire was dissolved in 1918, the Imam Yahya, leader of the Zaidi community, was left in control. In 1948 Yahya was assassinated in a palace coup, when power was seized by forces opposed to his feudal rule. However, Yahya's son, Ahmad, defeated the rebel forces to become Imam. In 1958 Yemen and the United Arab Republic (Egypt and Syria) formed a federation called the United Arab States, though this was dissolved in 1961. The Imam Ahmad died in September 1962 and was succeeded by his son, Muhammad. Less than a week later army officers, led by Col (later Marshal) Abdullah al-Sallal, removed the Imam and proclaimed the YAR. Civil war ensued between royalist forces, supported by Saudi Arabia, and republicans, aided by Egyptian troops. The republicans prevailed and Egyptian forces withdrew in 1967. In November President Sallal was deposed by a Republican Council.

The People's Republic of Southern Yemen, comprising Aden and the former Protectorate of South Arabia, was formed on 30 November 1967. Aden had been under British rule since 1839, and the Protectorate was developed by a series of treaties between the United Kingdom and local leaders. Prior to the British withdrawal, two rival factions, the National Liberation Front (NLF) and the Front for the Liberation of Occupied South Yemen, fought for control. The Marxist NLF eventually prevailed and assumed power as the National Front (NF). The country's first President, Qahtan al-Sha'abi, was forced out of office in June 1969, when a Presidential Council, led by Salem Rubayi Ali, took power. Muhammad Ali Haitham became Prime Minister. In November 1970, on the third anniversary of independence, the country was renamed the PDRY. In May 1971 a provisional Supreme People's Council (SPC) was established as the national legislature. In August Haitham was replaced as Prime Minister by Ali Nasser Muhammad. Following the introduction of repressive measures against dissidents by the Government after independence, more than 300,000 Southern Yemenis fled to the YAR. Backed by Saudi Arabia and Libya, many of the refugees joined mercenary organizations, aimed at the overthrow of the Marxist regime in Southern Yemen, and conducted cross-border raids.

Intermittent fighting, beginning in early 1971, flared into open warfare between the two Yemens in October 1972, with the YAR receiving aid from Saudi Arabia and the PDRY being supplied with Soviet arms. A cease-fire was arranged in the same month, under the auspices of the League of Arab States (the Arab League, see p. 372), and soon afterwards both sides agreed to the union of the two Yemens within 18 months. The union was not, however, implemented.

Domestic Political Affairs

On 13 June 1974 a 10-member Military Command Council (MCC) seized power in the YAR, under the leadership of the pro-Saudi Lt-Col Ibrahim al-Hamadi. Mohsin al-Aini was appointed Prime Minister, but was replaced by Abd al-Aziz Abd al-Ghani in January 1975. An unsuccessful pro-royalist coup was reported in August. Al-Hamadi subsequently attempted to reduce the influence of the USSR, and endeavoured to re-equip the army with US weapons, making use of financial assistance from Saudi Arabia. In October 1977, however, al-Hamadi was killed by unknown assassins in San'a. Another member of the MCC, Lt-Col Ahmad bin Hussain al-Ghashmi, took over as Chairman, and martial law was imposed. In February 1978 the MCC appointed a Constituent People's Assembly, and in April the Assembly elected al-Ghashmi President of the Republic. The MCC was then dissolved.

In June 1978 the proposed union of the two Yemens was seriously hampered when President al-Ghashmi of the YAR was assassinated by a bomb carried in the suitcase of a PDRY envoy. In the following month the Constituent People's Assembly elected a senior military officer, Lt-Col (later Gen., and subsequently Field Marshal) Ali Abdullah Saleh, as President of the YAR. During recriminations that followed the assassination, Rubayi Ali of the PDRY was deposed and executed by opponents within the ruling party, which had been known as the United Political Organization—National Front (UPO—NF) since its merger with two smaller parties in October 1975. The Prime Minister, Ali Nasser Muhammad, became interim Head of State. Two days after the overthrow of Rubayi Ali, it was announced that the UPO—NF had agreed to form a Marxist-Leninist 'vanguard' party. At the constituent congress of this Yemen Socialist Party (YSP), held in October 1978, Abd al-Fattah Ismail, who favoured uncompromising Marxist policies, became Secretary-General. A new SPC was elected in December and appointed Ismail to be Head of State. In April 1980 Ali Nasser Muhammad replaced Ismail as Head of State, Chairman of the Presidium of the SPC and Secretary-General of the YSP, while retaining the post of Prime Minister; his posts were confirmed at an extraordinary congress of the YSP in October.

Renewed fighting broke out between the YAR and the PDRY in February and March 1979, when the National Democratic Front (NDF), an alliance of disaffected YAR politicians, won the support of the PDRY and began a revolt. Later in the same month, however, at a meeting between the North and South Yemeni heads of state in Kuwait, arranged by the Arab League, an agreement was signed pledging unification of the two states. Following a series of meetings, in December 1981 the two sides signed a draft Constitution for a unified state and established a joint YAR/PDRY Yemen Council to monitor progress towards unification. NDF forces rebelled again in 1982, but they were defeated and forced over the border into the PDRY.

In May 1983 President Saleh submitted his resignation at an extraordinary meeting of the Constituent People's Assembly, declaring his intention to nominate himself for a presidential election. His five-year term of office was due to end in July. However, he was nominated and unanimously re-elected by the Assembly for a further five-year term. Elections to the Assembly itself, scheduled for early 1983, were postponed.

In the PDRY, President Muhammad relinquished the post of Prime Minister in February 1985, nominating the Minister of Construction, Haidar Abu Bakr al-Attas, as his successor (while retaining his other senior posts). The former President, Abd al-Fattah Ismail, returned from exile in the USSR in the same month, and was reappointed to the Secretariat of the YSP's Central Committee. At the party's third General Congress, in October, President Muhammad was re-elected to the posts of Secretary-General of the YSP and of its Political Bureau for a further five years. However, his control over the party was weakened by the enlargement of the Political Bureau from 13 members to 16 (including his rival, Ismail), and by an increase in membership of the Central Committee from 47 to 77, to incorporate a number of his critics.

On 13 January 1986 President Muhammad attempted to eliminate his opponents in the Political Bureau: his personal guard opened fire on six members who had assembled for a meeting with the President. Three were killed, and three escaped, including Ismail (who was, however, officially declared to have been killed in subsequent fighting). Muhammad was reported to have left Aden for his tribal stronghold in Abyan province, to the east of the city. In Aden itself, rival elements of the armed forces fought for control, causing widespread destruction, and the conflict quickly spread to the rest of the country, despite diplomatic efforts by the USSR. Apparently prompted by reports of massacres by President Muhammad's supporters, the army intervened decisively, turning back pro-Muhammad tribesmen from Abyan who were advancing on Aden. On 24 January al-Attas, the Prime Minister, who had been abroad when the troubles began, was named by the YSP Central Committee as head of an interim administration in Aden, and Muhammad was stripped of all his party and state posts; he reportedly fled to Ethiopia. An estimated 5,000 people died in the conflict. A new Government of the PDRY was formed in February. Al-Attas was confirmed as President, Chairman of the Presidium of the SPC and Secretary-General of the YSP Political Bureau. The former Deputy Prime Minister and Minister of Fisheries, Dr Yasin Said Numan, was named as Prime Minister. The new Council of Ministers contained only three members of the previous Government. In March a general amnesty was proclaimed, inviting supporters of Muhammad to return from the YAR, where some 10,000 of them had sought refuge. In October a general election took place for a 111-member SPC. Al-Attas was unanimously elected Chairman of the YSP. In December the Supreme Court sentenced Muhammad to death, *in absentia*, for treason; 34 other men received the same sentence, although it was only carried out in five cases.

In July 1988 the first general election took place in the YAR for 128 seats in the new 159-member Consultative Council, which replaced the non-elected Constituent People's Assembly. The remaining 31 seats were filled by presidential decree. More than 1m. people registered to vote and more than 1,200 candidates contested the poll. Approximately 25% of the elective seats were won by candidates sympathetic to the Muslim Brotherhood, a militant Islamist organization. Later in the month President Saleh was re-elected by the Consultative Council for a third five-year term, winning 96% of the votes. Al-Ghani was reappointed Prime Minister.

Yemeni unification

The first session of the joint YAR/PDRY Yemen Council (which had been established in 1981) was held in San'a in August 1983 and discussed the state of progress towards unification. A joint committee on foreign policy met for the first time in March 1984 in Aden. In July 1986 Presidents Saleh of the YAR and al-Attas of the PDRY met for the first time in Libya to discuss unification. In May 1988 the Governments of the YAR and the PDRY agreed to withdraw troops from their mutual border and to create a demilitarized zone, covering an area of 2,200 sq km, between Marib and Shabwah, where they intended to carry out joint projects involving exploration for petroleum. In November Saleh and the Secretary-General of the Central Committee of the YSP, Ali Salim al-Baid, signed an agreement providing for the unification of the two states. On 1 December 1989 a draft Constitution for the unified state was published: it was to be ratified by both countries within six months, and was subsequently to be approved by a referendum.

The first joint meeting of the two Councils of Ministers was held in San'a in January 1990 and resulted in restrictions on travel between the two countries being rescinded. In February President Saleh held talks with King Fahd of Saudi Arabia, who pledged his official support for the unification of the YAR and the PDRY. However, opposition to unification developed in the YAR in early 1990. The Muslim Brotherhood, which believed that *Shari'a* (Islamic) law should be enshrined in the Constitution of the unified state (as in the YAR Constitution), condemned the draft Constitution, which was based principally, but not solely, on *Shari'a* law, and advocated a boycott of the referendum on the Constitution. In the PDRY, meanwhile, there were demonstrations by women, who feared that the increasing influence of Islamist militancy might jeopardize their freedom, and demanded that their existing rights in the secular Republic be guaranteed in the new Constitution.

In May 1990 the armed forces of the YAR and the PDRY were declared to be technically dissolved, prior to their unification, and it was announced that they were to be withdrawn from their respective capitals to designated military zones. In the same month a draft law embodying the freedom of the press was signed. The unification of the YAR and the PDRY was proclaimed on 22 May, six months ahead of the agreed deadline, apparently in order to counter the threat to the unification process posed by disruption in the north of the YAR. The unification agreement had been ratified on the previous day by both countries' legislatures. The new country was to be known as the Republic of Yemen, with San'a as its political capital and Aden its economic and commercial centre. President Saleh of the YAR became President of the new state, while al-Baid was elected Vice-President. The President of the PDRY, al-Attas, became Prime Minister, leading a transitional coalition Council of Ministers with 39 members, of whom 20 were from the YAR (members of the General People's Congress—GPC—a broad grouping of supporters of President Saleh) and 19 from the PDRY (all members of the YSP, under the continued leadership of al-Baid). A five-member Presidential Council (chaired by Saleh) was formed, together with a 45-member advisory council. The two legislatures were amalgamated to form the House of Representatives, pending elections to be held after a 30-month transitional period; an additional 31 members, including opponents of the YAR and PDRY governments, were nominated by Saleh. The Yemeni Congregation for Reform (al-Islah), an Islamic grouping with considerable support in the House of Representatives, was regarded as the most influential of the more than 30 new political parties reported to have formed since unification by September.

In May 1991 the people of Yemen voted in a referendum on the Constitution for the unified state. Religious fundamentalists and sympathizers, including al-Islah members, had urged a boycott of the referendum, owing to the proposed role of Islam. Those who participated in the referendum approved the new Constitution by a large majority, although less than 50% of the electorate registered to vote. Members of al-Islah and other opposition groups claimed that irregularities in the voting procedure had invalidated the result.

Deteriorating economic conditions prompted domestic unrest during late 1991 and 1992. At legislative elections held on 27 April 1993, an estimated 4,730 candidates contested the 301 elective seats in the House of Representatives, of whom approximately 30% were affiliated to political parties. International observers were largely satisfied with the conduct of the elections. The GPC secured 123 of the 300 seats for which results were announced. Al-Islah won 62 seats, and the YSP 56, with independents securing 47 of the remaining seats. In May the GPC and YSP agreed to merge, thereby creating a single political group with an overall majority in the new House of Representatives. The subsequent election of al-Islah's leader, Sheikh Abdullah bin Hussain al-Ahmar, as Speaker of the House was regarded as a concession to his party, the influence of which had been weakened by the merger. At the end of May, however, a new coalition Government was announced, including representatives of all three leading parties. Al-Attas was reappointed Prime Minister.

In August 1993 al-Baid ceased to participate in the political process and withdrew from San'a to Aden. This followed a visit by the YSP leader to the USA, apparently without the approval of President Saleh, for talks with the US Vice-President, Al Gore. Al-Baid claimed that Saleh had made no attempt to halt the numerous armed attacks by northern officials on southerners, and claimed that as many as 150 YSP members had been assassinated since unification. He also protested at what he perceived to be the increasing marginalization of the south, particularly with regard to the distribution of petroleum revenues. In October the House of Representatives elected a new five-member Presidential Council, and later in the month the Council, in the absence of al-Baid, re-elected Saleh as its Chairman, and, accordingly, as President of the Republic of Yemen, for a further four-year term. Al-Baid was unanimously re-elected as Vice-President, but was not sworn in.

In September 1993 al-Baid, who remained in Aden, submitted an 18-point programme of conditions for his return to San'a, which was accepted by President Saleh in December. In January 1994, following Jordanian mediation, representatives of the main political parties signed a 'Document of Pledge and Agreement' designed to resolve the crisis. In February Saleh and al-Baid signed the document, which contained certain security guarantees, as well as providing for a degree of decentralization, and for a review of the Constitution and of the country's economic policies. Nevertheless, both leaders remained active in mustering support for their positions throughout the region. At the same time there were reports of clashes between the armed forces of the former YAR and the PDRY (which had failed to integrate since unification).

Civil war and the declaration of the Democratic Republic of Yemen

In March 1994 Saleh and al-Baid held talks in Oman, but at the end of the month al-Baid refused to attend a meeting of the Presidential Council, which he had boycotted since August 1993. At the end of April 1994 the First Deputy Prime Minister, Hassan Muhammad Makki, was wounded during an assassination attempt in San'a. A series of pitched battles followed between battalions stationed in the territory of their former neighbour. On 5 May President Saleh declared a 30-day state of emergency, and dismissed al-Baid from his position as Vice-President, together with four other southern members of the Government, including Salim Muhammad. On the same day missile attacks were launched against economic and military targets, including San'a, Aden and other main airports. On 9 May Saleh announced that al-Attas had been replaced as Prime Minister by the Minister of Industry, Muhammad Said al-Attar, and that the Minister of Petroleum and Minerals had also been replaced. By this time fighting had become concentrated around Aden, and along the former north–south frontier. Several thousand southern reservists were mobilized, as the forces of the former YAR attempted to isolate and capture Aden. Meanwhile, President Saleh rejected appeals for a negotiated settlement to the civil war, and demanded that al-Baid surrender.

On 22 May 1994, the fourth anniversary of the unification of Yemen, al-Baid, in a televised address, declared the independence of a new Democratic Republic of Yemen (DRY), with Aden as its capital. He also announced the formation of a Presidential Council, with himself as President and Abd al-Rahman al-Jifri, the leader of the League of the Sons of Yemen (LSY), as Vice-President. The composition of the Council reflected al-Baid's need to achieve a consensus of the different political and tribal groups of the former PDRY. Saleh denounced the secession as illegitimate, and offered an amnesty to all in the PDRY who rejected it, with the exception of 16 YSP leaders (including al-Baid).

At the beginning of June 1994, with the northern army attacking Aden on three fronts to the north and east of the city, the UN Security Council adopted Resolution 924, demanding a cease-fire and the resumption of dialogue in Yemen, and ordering the dispatch of a UN commission of inquiry to the region. Although welcomed by the authorities in Aden, the resolution was initially rejected by the Government in San'a, which urged the Arab League to support the unity of Yemen. Subsequently, however, the San'a Government declared itself positively disposed towards the resolution.

On 1 June 1994 the House of Representatives voted to extend the state of emergency for a further 30 days. On the following day al-Baid announced the composition of a DRY Government, in which al-Attas was to be Prime Minister and Minister of Finance. As northern forces made further territorial gains around Aden, it was reported that al-Baid had transferred his centre of operations to Mukalla, east of Aden. On 7 July Aden came under the control of Saleh's troops. Many of the southern secessionist leaders fled to neighbouring Arab states, and it was officially announced that the civil war had ended. Al-Baid was believed to have requested political asylum in Oman. In March 1998 al-Baid, al-Attas and three other rebel leaders were sentenced to death *in absentia*.

According to official sources, 931 civilians and soldiers were killed, and 5,000 wounded, in the civil war, although this was generally regarded as a conservative estimate. President Saleh immediately undertook measures to consolidate his position and bring stability to the country, ending the state of emergency and reiterating the general amnesty; by August 1994, when the amnesty expired, more than 5,000 Yemenis had returned to the country. In the same month, in an attempt to undermine the strength of southern military units loyal to the YSP, Saleh announced that party membership would no longer be permitted within the armed forces. In September, moreover, Saleh introduced amendments to the Constitution intended to strengthen his position further: the Presidential Council was abolished, and in future the President would be elected by universal suffrage. *Shari'a* would also serve as the basis of all legislation. On 1 October Saleh was re-elected President; he appointed Abd al-Rabbuh Mansur al-Hadi as his deputy, and Abd al-Aziz Abd al-Ghani (hitherto a member of the Presidential Council) as

Prime Minister. In the new Council of Ministers, members of the GPC retained the key portfolios, the YSP was denied representation and al-Islah was rewarded for its allegiance during the civil war by the allocation of nine ministerial posts. In a reorganization of the Council of Ministers in June 1995, the GPC increased its share of portfolios at the expense of independents, leading to a Government composed entirely of GPC and al-Islah members. Also in June Saleh was re-elected Chairman of the GPC at the party's first general assembly since 1988.

In July 1994 UN-sponsored negotiations between the Yemeni leadership and the secessionists proved inconclusive. President Saleh announced that any further discussions would have to be conducted in Yemen, effectively terminating dialogue, as the YSP leaders remained in exile. In August a faction of the YSP in Yemen declared itself the new party leadership. In October, nevertheless, exiled leaders of the YSP announced the formation of a coalition, the National Opposition Front, which included former Prime Minister al-Attas and Abd al-Rahman al-Jifri, leader of the LSY. The role of the YSP in Yemeni politics subsequently diminished considerably.

Developments following the civil war

The economic repercussions of the civil war on the population were significant, particularly in the south. During March and April 1995, following the devaluation of the riyal (YR) and the doubling of the price of fuel, demonstrators clashed with police in Aden, San'a and Dhamar, resulting in three deaths and more than 50 arrests. The activities of militant Islamists, meanwhile, posed an additional threat to internal stability. In September 1994, meanwhile, some 20 people were reportedly killed in clashes with the security forces in Abyan province, following the destruction of three Muslim saints' shrines by Islamists who deemed them idolatrous.

The results of elections, conducted on 27 April 1997, demonstrated a decisive victory for the GPC, which increased its parliamentary representation from 123 to 187 seats. Al-Islah secured 53 seats (compared with 62 in 1993), and independent candidates won 54 seats. The remaining seats were shared between Nasserite and Baathist parties. The GPC's position was further consolidated by the stated intention of 39 newly elected independent deputies to demonstrate parliamentary allegiance to the GPC.

Al-Ghani presented his Government's resignation in May 1997. Two days later Faraj Said bin Ghanim, a political independent, was appointed Prime Minister. All but four of the new ministers were GPC members. In April 1998 bin Ghanim resigned; the Deputy Prime Minister and Minister of Foreign Affairs, Abd al-Karim al-Iryani, was appointed Prime Minister, announcing his new Government in May. A substantial increase in the price of petrol and basic foodstuffs in June led to public demonstrations in which more than 50 people died. In September a series of explosions in Yemen was attributed by the Government to 'foreign elements'.

The suppression of lawlessness, which had been exacerbated by the widespread ownership of weapons dating from the period of internal unrest, was a persistent domestic problem in the late 1990s. A number of bomb explosions and armed kidnappings, frequently of tourists, attracted international attention during 1997–2000, including the seizing of 16 foreign tourists in December 1998, four of whom were later killed during an attempt to release them. Yemen was criticized for failing to warn foreign embassies of an increased terrorist threat to tourists and for its precipitate use of force to free the hostages. In May 1999 three of the kidnappers, who belonged to the Islamic Aden-Abyan Army, a small extremist Islamist movement, were sentenced to death. Two of the death sentences were later commuted to life imprisonment, and in October the leader of the Islamic Aden-Abyan Army, Zein al-Abidine al-Mihdar, was executed. His was the first execution under legislation, enacted in August 1998, providing for the use of capital punishment in kidnapping cases. In August 1999 eight British citizens and two Algerians, who were reported to have links to the Islamic Aden-Abyan Army, were found guilty of plotting terrorist attacks on British targets in Aden, receiving sentences of up to seven years' imprisonment. (In October 2002 the Islamic Aden-Abyan Army attacked a French supertanker, the *Limburg*, off the coast of Yemen. A spokesman for the group declared the attack, which killed a crew member, to be revenge for the execution of al-Mihdar.)

On 23 September 1999 the first direct presidential election was held in Yemen. Saleh was re-elected, winning 96.3% of the votes; his only opponent was Najib Qahtan al-Sha'bi, a member of the GPC who stood as an independent. The election, which was boycotted by the YSP, was criticized for its lack of a credible candidate to oppose President Saleh.

In October 2000 a suicide bomb attack on a US destroyer, the USS *Cole*, in Aden harbour, as a result of which 17 US naval personnel were killed, was linked by many commentators to the escalating crisis in the Middle East. The Yemeni authorities responded by arresting several Islamist militants, including leading members of Islamic Jihad from Yemen, Egypt, Algeria and other Arab states. The USA blamed agents of Osama bin Laden, the Saudi-born fundamentalist Islamist believed at that time to be based in Afghanistan, for the attack, and claimed to have evidence that the two suicide bombers were Saudi nationals. Only days after the USS *Cole* bombing, the British embassy in San'a was the target of an attack, although it was unclear as to whether the two incidents were linked. (In July 2001 four Yemenis were found guilty of plotting and orchestrating the embassy bombing, and sentenced to between four and 15 years' imprisonment.)

In November 2000 Yemen and the USA signed an anti-terrorism agreement whereby the Yemeni authorities agreed to allow the US Federal Bureau of Investigation to assist in investigations into the USS *Cole* explosion, and to extradite any persons accused of involvement in terrorism against foreign targets. It was announced in the following month that investigations into the bombing had been completed and that six Yemeni nationals would stand trial in early 2001. In January, however, the Yemeni Government agreed to a postponement of the trial, following a request by US officials for more time to gather additional evidence. A further two Yemenis entering the country from Afghanistan were detained in February; another three suspects were reportedly arrested in April. In November a Yemeni newspaper published claims that the individual suspected of planning the attack had subsequently sought refuge in Afghanistan. The man was named as Muhammad Omar al-Harazi, and was also believed to have been one of the principal organizers of the 1998 attacks on the US embassies in Kenya and Tanzania. In February 2002 it was reported that the trial of eight of the suspects in the bombing of the USS *Cole* had been postponed at the request of the US authorities because of the possibility that new information about the case would be obtained during interrogation of al-Qa'ida (see Foreign Affairs) and Taliban prisoners captured by US military forces in Afghanistan in late 2001. Two senior al-Qa'ida operatives believed to have been responsible for planning the attack on the USS *Cole* were arrested by US forces and Pakistani police in November 2002 and April 2003, respectively. In April 10 of the Yemenis accused of involvement in the USS *Cole* attack escaped from a high-security prison; two of the fugitives were captured in May, and charged with the murder of US military personnel. The remaining eight, in addition to one further suspect, were reportedly captured in March 2004. In September two men (a Yemeni and a Saudi) were sentenced to death for their role in the attack. Four other Yemeni nationals received prison sentences of between five and 10 years. In February 2005 an appeal court ruling upheld one of the death sentences, but commuted the other to 15 years in prison and reduced the sentence of one of the other men from eight to five years.

In January 2001 the formation of a new opposition grouping, the Opposition Co-ordination Council, was announced in Yemen. The bloc, which included the YSP, was created in anticipation of the forthcoming municipal elections, Yemen's first since unification, which were held on 20 February. A national referendum was held concurrently on proposed amendments to the Constitution that would extend the President's term of office from five to seven years and the mandate of the House of Representatives from four to six years, abolish the right of the President to issue decree laws when parliament was not in session, and provide for the creation of a 111-member Consultative Council. According to official sources, 77.5% of voters endorsed the constitutional changes. There were claims of electoral irregularities and harassment of opposition candidates, and violent clashes were reported (principally between supporters of the GPC and those of al-Islah) in which, according to certain sources, up to 45 people were killed. The elections were boycotted by some opposition parties and were criticized by human rights groups, which claimed that the President and the GPC were seeking to consolidate their dominant position at the expense of further democratization.

In March 2001 President Saleh dismissed Prime Minister al-Iryani and declared the formation of a new Government, to be led by the former Deputy Prime Minister and Minister of Foreign Affairs, Abd al-Qadir Bajammal. The new Council of Ministers was composed exclusively of GPC members and included Yemen's first female minister. In April the President elected a new Consultative Council, which for the first time included three female politicians.

The 2003 parliamentary election and the 2006 presidential poll

In early 2003 22 political parties were registered for a parliamentary election, which was held on 27 April. The GPC recorded another decisive victory, winning 228 of the 301 seats, while al-Islah secured 47 seats, independents 14 and the YSP seven. (Final results were published following three by-elections held in July.) Voter turn-out was a reported 76% of the electorate. The European Union (EU, see p. 281) expressed its satisfaction with the elections, but the US-based National Democratic Institute for International Affairs claimed that the electoral process was flawed, citing instances of under-age voting, ballot-buying and inappropriate behaviour by security forces. Opposition parties threatened to boycott the new parliament after widespread claims of ballot-rigging, fraud and intimidation. None the less, on 10 May the President reappointed Bajammal as Prime Minister. Bajammal's new Council of Ministers included 17 new appointees, although the key portfolios of defence, the interior, petroleum and mineral resources, and foreign affairs remained unchanged.

Meanwhile, also in May 2003 President Saleh declared an amnesty for five exiled southern secessionist leaders who had been sentenced to death *in absentia* in 1998. In June 2003 the House of Representatives endorsed a government proposal that Yemen's counter-terrorism organization should become a separate department overseen by the Ministry of the Interior; the resources allocated to the unit were also increased. In July security forces killed six suspected Islamist militants during an operation in Abyan province, where alleged members of the Islamic Aden-Abyan Army had taken refuge after attacking a military detachment.

In June 2004 the Director of the Ministry of Religious Endowments and Guidance stated that the authorities would not allow Islamist parties to share control over state-controlled mosques and use them as platforms to preach extremism. Firm measures would be taken against imams who preached opposition to the Government and incited worshippers to violence. Later that month the Council of Ministers ordered the closure of all unlicensed religious schools in an effort to combat extremism, and stated that an extensive review of religious education in public schools was urgently needed to ensure that teaching about Islam advocated moderation.

As part of efforts to combat violence and extremism, the Government stated in 2003 that it had spent over US $32m. since 2002 purchasing weapons on sale on the open market and seeking to persuade ordinary citizens to sell their weapons to the authorities. (According to the Government, 60m.–80m. guns were owned by the country's population, which numbered some 19m.) An initiative endorsed by President Saleh to prevent the public from carrying firearms resulted in riots in February 2005, in which five people died in northern Yemen. Saudi Arabia had recently complained to Yemen over reports of the smuggling of arms into the kingdom, and in 2004 began the construction of a 'separation wall' along the Saudi–Yemeni border (see Foreign Affairs).

A series of kidnappings in late 2005 and 2006 further undermined Yemen's image abroad. Meanwhile, in July 2005 at least 39 people were killed in severe riots in San'a, Aden and several other towns in protest against the Government's decision to remove subsidies on fuel and the consequent doubling in the price of petroleum products. The GPC accused opposition parties of instigating the riots after they publicly criticized the price increases. The opposition denied the allegations and condemned the killing of civilians by security forces. At the end of July the Government announced a partial reduction in fuel prices.

President Saleh was re-elected as Chairman of the GPC in December 2005. In February 2006 Saleh effected a comprehensive reorganization of the Council of Ministers, which was increased in size, to 34 members (including two new female ministers). The ministers in charge of the key portfolios of defence, oil, finance and planning were all removed from their posts; however, the Minister of the Interior, Maj.-Gen. Dr Rashad Muhammad al-Alimi, who had been under pressure following the escape of 23 suspected al-Qa'ida sympathizers (including Jamal al-Badawi, who had been convicted for the bombing of the USS *Cole* in 2000) from a San'a prison earlier in the month, was promoted to Deputy Prime Minister. The President claimed that the changes would add new impetus to the process of economic and political reform, although the opposition suggested that the reorganization was targeted at strengthening the regime before the forthcoming presidential and municipal elections.

The presidential election was held on 20 September 2006, with turn-out estimated at approximately 65% of the 9.2m. registered voters. As widely predicted, Saleh, who had rescinded a statement made in July 2005 that he would not seek re-election, was chosen to serve another seven-year term, attracting 77.2% of the total ballot, according to official results published by the Supreme Commission for Elections and Referendums (SCER). Saleh's primary opponent, Faisal bin Shamlan of the Joint Meeting Parties (JMP—a recently formed opposition bloc comprising five Islamist and leftist parties, including the YSP, al-Islah and the al-Haq party), garnered 21.8% of the ballot, although Shamlan's supporters rejected the results, claiming that he had received at least 40% of all votes; three other candidates each won less than 0.5% of the total number of votes cast. The SCER acknowledged that tens of thousands of votes had been discounted owing to 'voter error'; however, the Minister of Foreign Affairs, Abu Bakr al-Kurbi, denied claims of electoral fraud. (One week prior to the polls at least 51 people died, and more than 230 were injured, during a stampede at an election campaign rally for the incumbent Saleh.) EU election observers reported that the presidential and municipal elections had been conducted in a reasonably free and fair manner, but identified a number of problems, particularly with regard to voter registration and the use of state resources to promote the ruling party. The JMP agreed to accept the election results on the condition that the Government enter into negotiations on electoral reform.

Security concerns and postponement of the 2009 legislative election

In September 2006 the Ministry of the Interior announced that security forces had foiled two co-ordinated suicide attacks intended to destroy oil facilities in Marib and Hadramout. Security guards identified vehicles laden with explosives at both locations, and destroyed the vehicles before they reached their intended targets, killing all four assailants and one security guard. In November a militant Islamist group calling itself al-Qa'ida in Yemen issued a statement via the internet in which it claimed responsibility for the attempted bombings.

A presidential decree was issued in March 2007 appointing Ali Muhammad Mujawar, hitherto Minister of Electricity, as Prime Minister, to replace Bajammal, whose dismissal was reported to be the result of weak anti-corruption policies. A new Council of Ministers, in which the key portfolios remained unchanged, was formed in April.

In July 2007 a suicide bomber drove an explosives-laden car into a convoy of tourist vehicles in Marib, killing eight Spanish tourists and two local drivers. Several arrests were made in connection with the attack. (An al-Qa'ida-affiliated group, Jund al-Yaman—Soldiers of Yemen—later claimed responsibility for the attack, as well as the killing of two Belgian tourists and their Yemeni driver in Hadramout in January 2008.) By mid-2007 just seven of the 23 suspected al-Qa'ida sympathizers who had escaped from prison in February 2006—including Nasir al-Wuhayshi (reported to be the new leader of al-Qa'ida in Yemen)—remained at large, the rest having surrendered to the authorities or been arrested or killed. In August three al-Qa'ida militants were killed by Yemeni security forces. Al-Badawi surrendered to the Yemeni authorities in October. In November 32 people were found guilty of planning the attacks on oil facilities in Marib and Hadramout in September 2006 and sentenced to prison terms of between two and 15 years; six of those convicted, including al-Wuhayshi, had been tried *in absentia*, while four other defendants were acquitted owing to a lack of evidence.

Clashes between government forces and al-Houthi rebels continued in Saada in early 2008 (see The Al-Houthi Rebellion), resulting in deaths on both sides, while further demonstrations against poor living standards and the perceived marginalization of the south took place in Aden and other southern towns, degenerating into rioting in Aden, Lahij and al-Dali from March. Tensions were further exacerbated by a series of attacks and bomb explosions, mainly targeting Western interests, including a grenade attack believed to have been aimed at the US embassy

in San'a in March. In April the US embassy announced that it was evacuating all non-essential personnel from the country.

Gubernatorial elections were held for the first time on 17 May 2008, governors having hitherto been appointed by the President. The electorate consisted of almost 7,500 elected members of local councils in the 20 governorates and the capital, with the Ministry of Local Administration reporting a turn-out of 87%. With the JMP opting to boycott the elections, the GPC secured the mayoralty of San'a and all governorships except three that were won by independent candidates, in al-Baida, Marib and al-Jawf. However, the election result in al-Jawf was subsequently overturned by the Government, amid allegations that the successful candidate had links to al-Houthi militants; an alternative Governor, selected by the Government, was appointed in June. Immediately following the gubernatorial elections, President Saleh effected a reorganization of the Council of Ministers, in which Rashad al-Alimi, hitherto Deputy Prime Minister and Minister of the Interior, was allocated the newly expanded post of Deputy Prime Minister for Defence and Security Affairs. Mutahar al-Masri, Governor of Saada, was appointed Minister of the Interior, and there were changes to a further seven cabinet posts.

The failure of the Government and the opposition to reach agreement on electoral reform led to an escalating political crisis in 2008. The opposition, dissatisfied with the Government's apparent reluctance to introduce promised revisions, refused to participate in the appointment of new commissioners to the SCER, which was due to review voter registration lists. Despite lengthy negotiations throughout 2007–08, in August 2008 an electoral reform bill was rejected by the GPC-dominated House of Representatives; the Government blamed the JMP's refusal to participate in the SCER for the rejection. A new SCER, formed without opposition involvement, appointed 35,000 teachers to sub-committees tasked with undertaking a comprehensive revision of the voter registry, beginning in November. However, as opposition parties appealed for a boycott of the registration process, which they claimed was illegitimate, sub-committees were hindered in their activities by protests in most governorates, and there were reports of attacks on committee members. Violent clashes between police and protesters intensified throughout November, and numerous opposition activists were reportedly arrested. In late November the House of Representatives voted to delay the forthcoming municipal elections, which had been due to be held in April 2009. Meanwhile, the Government continued to insist that the legislative polls would proceed as scheduled, urging the opposition parties to participate. However, in February 2009, after negotiations between the Government and the JMP, the House of Representatives voted overwhelmingly to postpone the elections until 27 April 2011, in order to allow sufficient time, it was hoped, for agreement to be reached on reform of the electoral system.

Increasing civil unrest in the southern provinces and militant activity

Demonstrations organized in the southern provinces by supporters of the so-called Southern Movement (an increasingly separatist group led by former military officers) once again escalated into violent clashes with security forces from January 2009. In an effort to suppress media coverage of the conflict in the south, the Ministry of Information issued a directive in May banning the publication of any material deemed harmful to national unity. Seven newspapers were ordered to suspend operations, and existing copies of their publications were seized by the authorities.

An increase in militant Islamist activity in Yemen prompted growing domestic and international concern from 2008. Observers speculated that successful counter-terrorism operations in neighbouring Saudi Arabia were resulting in the migration of al-Qa'ida-affiliated groups into Yemen. Militant activity in that year included an attack on the US embassy in San'a in mid-September, during which a car bomb was detonated outside the premises before armed militants attacked the heavily fortified building from a second car. Responsibility for the attack, in which at least 16 people were killed, was initially claimed by an organization calling itself Islamic Jihad in Yemen. Six men were arrested in October on suspicion of membership of the terrorist cell responsible for the US embassy bombing and the subsequent issuing of threats to attack other embassies in San'a. Of the six suspects detained, three were released, while the remaining three were found guilty of offences including espionage and fraud in March 2009; two of those convicted were sentenced to three and five years' imprisonment, respectively, the third receiving the death penalty. Meanwhile, Khalid Abd al-Nabi, reported to be the leader of the Islamic Aden-Abyan Army, was arrested in August 2008.

The first detainee at the US military detention camp at Guantánamo Bay, Cuba, to be convicted by a US military court was a Yemeni citizen. Salim Hamdan, who had worked as a driver for Osama bin Laden, was found guilty in August 2008 of providing material support for terrorism and sentenced to five-and-a-half years' imprisonment. The strategic importance of Yemen as a base for jihadist activity in the region was underlined in January 2009, when, in video footage posted on the internet, al-Qa'ida announced the merger of its Saudi Arabian and Yemeni operations, forming an entity known as al-Qa'ida in the Arabian Peninsula (AQAP). The authorities in Yemen responded by strengthening their counter-terrorism operations and increasing security co-operation with Saudi Arabia. In July six suspected AQAP militants were sentenced to death in a Yemeni court, while another 10 suspects, including four Syrians and a Saudi national, were sentenced to terms of imprisonment of up to 15 years; the militants were convicted of perpetrating 13 attacks in Yemen over two years, including the murder of two Belgian tourists in January 2008 and the attack on the US embassy in March of that year. Meanwhile, further attacks and kidnappings continued to be reported throughout 2009, including a suicide bombing at a popular tourist site at Shibam, in Hadramout, which claimed the lives of four tourists from the Republic of Korea (South Korea) tourists and a Yemeni guide in March.

Fuelled by the Government's rejection of its demands, and harsh repression of its activities, the Southern Movement gained considerable momentum in 2009, as the formerly disparate grouping began to coalesce into a unified political movement with significant popular support and an overtly separatist agenda. From April there was growing tension in the region as several demonstrations, attended by thousands of protesters, escalated into violent clashes with the security forces. Up to 16 people were killed, including 10 security officers, and more than 30 injured in violent clashes involving armed separatists and security forces following an unauthorized political rally in Zinjibar, in the southern Abyan province, in July 2009.

Large anti-Government demonstrations, at which the flag of the former PDRY was increasingly visible, continued during the latter part of 2009. Five people were killed in clashes between demonstrators and security forces at a rally in Ataq, in Shabwa province, on 25 November. Following reports of the murder of two civilians of northern Yemeni origin, the Government initiated a major clampdown on separatist activity, arresting around 200 separatist supporters in Aden and banning public demonstrations to mark the anniversary of the British withdrawal from Aden and southern Yemeni independence scheduled for 30 November.

On 17 December 2009 security forces, supported by air-strikes, launched a raid on an alleged AQAP training camp in Abyan province. According to official sources, more than 30 militants were killed and 17 captured in the operation. (However, in March 2010 a parliamentary committee reported that 42 civilians, predominantly women and children, had been killed in the raid. The Government issued an apology and resolved to pay compensation to the families of those killed.) While there was no consensus on the extent of any co-operation between AQAP and militant groups active in Yemen's northern and southern regional conflicts, most observers concluded that AQAP was likely to be exploiting the widespread political instability in order to expand its influence in the country. In mid-December the US authorities repatriated six Yemeni detainees from Guantánamo Bay; however, more than 90 Yemeni nationals remained in detention in the US facility.

Renewed civil unrest erupted in the south in February 2010 following the proclamation of a new campaign of demonstrations and civil disobedience to achieve independence. Large protests were held in Abyan, al-Dali, Lahij and Hadramout provinces to coincide with a regional donors' conference on Yemen, taking place under the auspices of the Cooperation Council for the Arab States of the Gulf (the Gulf Cooperation Council—GCC, see p. 255) in Riyadh, Saudi Arabia, at the end of that month. Security forces used tear gas and live ammunition in an effort to curtail the demonstrations. The unrest grew more violent in the following months, with increasing reports of armed attacks by separatist militants, bomb explosions in public buildings, kidnappings and mass arrests of demonstrators. Much of the unrest centred on al-Dali, where 30 separatist prisoners escaped from prison following a bomb attack in early April, and where a

general strike shut down all business activity in the city in mid-April.

Meanwhile, a failed attempt by a Nigerian jihadist to detonate explosives aboard a passenger aircraft in Detroit, Michigan, USA, on 25 December 2009 provoked renewed international concern about Yemen's reputation as a safe haven for Islamist militant groups. Omar Farouk Abdulmutallab had studied Arabic in San'a during 2004–05, and had reportedly been trained and equipped by AQAP during a second visit to Yemen in 2009. On 28 December AQAP claimed responsibility for the attempted bombing, stating that the mission had been instigated to avenge US support for recent security operations against jihadists in Yemen. In early January 2010 the authorities in the USA and the United Kingdom announced plans to fund a special counter-terrorism unit within Yemen's police force. Shortly after the announcement, the embassies of the USA, the United Kingdom and France in San'a were temporarily closed, following reports of direct threats from AQAP. Reports that the US Administration was preparing for direct military intervention in Yemen were denied by the Government in San'a. Yemeni security forces launched a series of operations against suspected AQAP militants that month.

In April 2010 the British ambassador to Yemen narrowly avoided injury when a suicide bomber targeted his convoy in San'a. The attacker himself was killed and three other people were injured in the incident, which prompted the temporary closure of the British embassy. The Yemeni Ministry of the Interior attributed the attack to AQAP. Following the provision of US intelligence, 30 foreign nationals domiciled in Yemen, some of whom had links to the San'a Institute for the Arabic Language, where Abdulmutallab had studied, were arrested in June. In the same month Hamza Saleh al-Dayan, one of 23 prisoners who had escaped from a San'a gaol in February 2006, surrendered to the authorities; al-Dayan was thought to have been responsible for a number of violent attacks, including that perpetuated against Spanish tourists in July 2007.

Concerns about the threat posed to international security by elements within Yemen were exacerbated in August 2010 when two Yemeni nationals were arrested on board a flight from Chicago, Illinois, USA, to Amsterdam, Netherlands; the two men were alleged to have been conducting a trial run of a planned terrorist attack, after a number of suspicious items were discovered in their hand luggage. In October two Chicago-bound air freight packages containing bombs, which had originated in Yemen, were intercepted at airports in the United Kingdom and Dubai, United Arab Emirates. The foiled attack, which was discovered with the assistance of Saudi intelligence, was attributed to AQAP, with Ibrahim Asiri, a Saudi citizen who was reported to have entered Yemen in mid-2006 and subsequently to have become a member of AQAP, named by the US authorities as the suspected bomb maker. President Saleh declared that Yemen was 'determined to continue fighting terrorism and al-Qa'ida in co-operation with its partners' but warned the Administration of US President Barack Obama against interference in Yemen's internal affairs by targeting al-Qa'ida operatives within Yemen in drone attacks. The US Government continued to deny any involvement in such attacks. Also in October a grenade attack on a British embassy vehicle in the capital, and a separate incident in which a French national was fatally shot and a British national seriously injured at the compound of Austrian oil company OMV, further fuelled concerns about the targeting of Westerners and Western interests in Yemen.

The arrest on unknown charges of Hassan Baoum, a prominent leader of the Southern Movement, sparked angry protests in al-Dali and several other southern towns in November 2010. (Baoum was subsequently freed but detained again in February 2011 with his son before their eventual release in December.) Protesters tried to break into a prison in al-Dali, while four soldiers were injured when a military checkpoint in the town was attacked. In January 2011 it was reported that 178 members of the Yemeni security forces had been killed and 852 others injured by AQAP militants or the Southern Movement during 2010.

Increasing opposition disaffection, and popular protests

An amendment to the electoral law, which stipulated that the SCER be composed of judges, rather than parliamentary delegates as had hitherto been the case, was approved by the GPC-dominated legislature in December 2010, prompting members of the opposition to stage a sit-in protest in parliament amid claims that the Government and its allies had 'put an end to the national dialogue' and were engaged in a 'conspiracy' against efforts towards meaningful political reform. Some members of the opposition threatened to boycott the postponed legislative elections, due to be held on 27 April 2011. In mid-December 2010 the Government underscored its commitment to the staging of elections as scheduled, with or without opposition participation. However, in March 2011 the SCER announced that the elections were again to be postponed, until later in the year, to allow additional time for electoral rolls to be revised. Meanwhile, in January 2011 Saleh, to the consternation of the opposition, proposed a constitutional amendment that would allow him to stand for re-election at the presidential election in 2013.

In mid-January 2011 protests erupted in Yemen, seemingly inspired by recent popular demonstrations in Tunisia that had precipitated the ouster of President Zine al-Abidine Ben Ali. Several thousand people participated in a demonstration within the grounds of San'a University to demand the removal from power of President Saleh. A female activist, Tawakel Karman, who was reported to have organized the protest, was arrested. Saleh subsequently pledged to step down as President upon the expiry of his second term in 2013, and dismissed widespread speculation that he planned to transfer power to his son. Saleh announced a series of measures intended to pacify critics of the Government, including the reduction by one-half of the rate of income tax, an increase in public sector wages and controls on price inflation. However, further protests were staged in various locations around the capital and elsewhere in the country in late January, at which tens of thousands of demonstrators chanted anti-Government slogans, and appealed for an end to corruption and ineffective economic policies.

Addressing an emergency session of the legislature shortly before a planned 'day of rage', organized by the political opposition and civil society groups, in early February 2011, President Saleh reiterated his pledge to seek neither to extend his term of office beyond 2013 nor to pass power to his son. He urged the opposition to halt all planned protests, rallies and sit-ins, and also announced a series of welfare reforms and tax relief measures. While the opposition welcomed the President's pledges, the 'day of rage' proceeded as planned on the following day, with an estimated 20,000 protesters amassing in the streets of the capital to reject publicly Saleh's offer, and to demand his immediate resignation. Thousands of pro-Government demonstrators also gathered in the capital, to pledge their support to Saleh; clashes were reported between the two camps of supporters and at least 20 people were arrested. There were widespread reports of the use of force by the authorities in their efforts to disperse crowds of anti-Government protesters in the capital and elsewhere, and in mid-February 2011 the first fatalities since the start of the protests were reported. In early March at least 80 people were injured when the authorities opened fire on protesters outside San'a University; one person subsequently died of his injuries.

Meanwhile, in mid-February 2011 an offer by President Saleh to hold talks at which 'legitimate' demands would be heard was rejected by the opposition, which stated its refusal to enter into negotiations until the Government desisted from using excessive force against protesters. In early March Saleh announced proposals for a transition to a parliamentary system of government, pledging to hold a popular referendum on the issue later in the year; however, the overture was rapidly dismissed by the opposition, and protesters continued to demand the President's immediate resignation. Later that month four journalists working for US media were arrested and deported; no official reason was given for their removal from the country, but, with only a few foreign journalists remaining in Yemen at that time, it was feared that the authorities were preparing for a violent escalation of efforts to suppress the anti-Government protests. Also in mid-March the Governor of Marib was seriously injured while trying to disperse a crowd of demonstrators outside the local government headquarters. On 14 March the Minister of Endowments and Religious Guidance, Hamoud al-Hitar, was removed from office; Hamoud Muhammad Abad, hitherto Minister of Youth and Sports, was appointed to replace him.

On 18 March 2011 52 protesters were killed and hundreds of others were wounded when unidentified gunmen in civilian clothes opened fire from rooftops on a large group of protesters as they observed morning prayers at their encampment in 'Change Square' outside San'a University; the security forces denied any involvement in the incident, as did local citizens, who were blamed by the Government. Later that day President Saleh declared a state of emergency, for a period of 30 days, and

announced the creation of a committee of inquiry to investigate the massacre, as well as other incidents that had led to fatalities during the protests. In the days that followed, an increasing number of defections from the GPC, including those of senior army commanders, was reported, precipitating violent clashes between defecting military personnel and forces remaining loyal to Saleh. Other prominent defectors included the Minister of Human Rights, Huda Abd al-Latif al-Ban, the Minister of Tourism, Nabil Hassan al-Faqih, and a number of diplomats, including the Yemeni ambassador to the UN. Saleh's declaration of emergency rule was approved by parliament, by 160 votes to four, on 23 March, although there was some controversy over the conduct of the vote was conducted. Meanwhile, on 20 March Saleh dismissed the Council of Ministers, although Prime Minister Mujawar and his administration were requested to remain in office on an interim basis.

On 24 March 2011 President Saleh was reported to have accepted a five-point plan for the transition of power proposed by the opposition that envisaged the formation of a government of national unity and a committee to draft a new constitution, the holding of a constitutional referendum, the implementation of new electoral legislation, and the staging of parliamentary and presidential elections, all by the end of the year. However, in advance of mass rival rallies organized by anti-Government protesters and Saleh's supporters on the following day, the President stated that, while he was prepared to hand over power, he would do so only to 'safe hands' and urged his supporters to 'stand firm', suggesting that he did not in fact intend to observe the opposition-proposed transition plan. Meanwhile, on 29 March 150 people were killed and around 80 others injured following explosions at a munitions factory in the southern town of Jaar; the authorities attributed responsibility for the incident to AQAP.

From early April 2011 the GCC member states initiated diplomatic efforts to bring an end to the ongoing impasse between President Saleh and the opposition. In a statement released on 7 April, Qatari Prime Minister Sheikh Hamad bin Jasim bin Jaber Al Thani announced that the GCC hoped to finalize a deal that would provide for the transfer of power to Vice-President Maj.-Gen. (latterly Field Marshal) Abd al-Rabbuh Mansur al-Hadi at the head of an interim government, while offering guarantees of safe protection for Saleh and his family. However, Saleh dismissed the proposal as an attempt to interfere in Yemeni affairs. In mid-April a number of those who had defected from the ruling party, reportedly including al-Ban and al-Faqih, formed a new political group, the Justice and Development Bloc, to oppose violence against the protesters.

In late April 2011 the GCC proposed a new mediation plan, under the terms of which both sides would agree to the immediate cessation of protests and Saleh, who would be offered immunity from prosecution, would step down within one month of signing the accord, having appointed an opposition leader to head a national unity government that would prepare for a presidential election within two months of Saleh's resignation; members of the GPC would account for one-half of the new government, members of the opposition JMP coalition would comprise 40%, while the remaining 10% would comprise members of non-affiliated political groupings. Saleh formally accepted the proposal, as did members of the opposition; however, following Saleh's subsequent refusal to sign the agreement, the Qatari Government withdrew from the GCC delegation later that month. In mid-May it was announced that a similar agreement had been reached. Representatives of the opposition parties duly signed the agreement, as did some members of the GPC, but Saleh again subsequently declined to follow suit, insisting that any agreement involving his vacating power would result in Yemen degenerating into a 'failed state'. Consequently, the GCC suspended its mediation efforts at the end of that month.

Meanwhile, following the announcement in May 2011 that Sheikh Sadeq al-Ahmar, the leader of the powerful Hashid tribal federation, had defected to the opposition, a marked escalation in violence became evident. A cease-fire declared between government and opposition forces on 29 May had little discernible effect; on the following day around 50 protesters were killed and hundreds more injured when government forces moved in to dismantle an opposition encampment erected in the main square in Taiz. It was reported that AQAP, capitalizing on the ongoing fighting between government and opposition forces, had seized control of Zinjibar during that month. This prompted an intensification from June of drone attacks against suspected AQAP targets in Yemen, for which the Yemeni Government continued officially to claim responsibility. Nevertheless, a number of deadly attacks attributed to AQAP militants were reported that month, including a raid on government buildings in Houta, in which three security guards were killed, and an attack on a prison in Mukalla, in which around 40 prisoners, of whom the majority were Islamic militants, were reported to have escaped.

The resignation of President Saleh and the presidential election of 2012

On 3 June 2011 President Saleh was seriously injured when a bomb exploded within the presidential compound in San'a; three security guards were killed and several senior government officials (including the Prime Minister and the Speaker of the legislature) were injured in the attack, responsibility for which was widely attributed to fighters loyal to Sheikh Sadeq al-Ahmar. On the following day Saleh was evacuated to Riyadh for medical treatment, relinquishing control on an interim basis to Vice-President al-Hadi, although Saleh's two sons, Ahmed and Khaled Saleh, both of whom were serving as army commanders, were believed to have retained control of the capital. News of Saleh's departure from Yemen was celebrated by the protesters, and precipitated a series of further demonstrations demanding an official end to the Saleh administration and the departure from the country of his sons.

In a recorded address broadcast on national television on 7 July 2011, President Saleh made his first public appearance since being injured. In his address, Saleh insisted that the ongoing political impasse would be resolved by dialogue alone and blamed 'terrorist elements' for the attack on his presidential compound. On 16 July members of the opposition proclaimed a 17-member transitional council that was intended to succeed Saleh and pledged to draft a new constitution. On the following day a 'day of rage' was staged by the opposition.

In mid-August 2011 the Deputy Minister of Information stated that President Saleh, who had been released from hospital earlier that month (although he remained at that time in Riyadh), did not object to transferring power to Vice-President al-Hadi, but cautioned that if the opposition continued their violent protests Saleh would remain in power until the expiry of his term in 2013. A few days later former Prime Minister al-Ghani died from injuries sustained during the attack on the presidential compound.

Meanwhile, at least nine government troops were killed and more than 20 others injured when a suspected AQAP militant drove a vehicle laden with explosives into an army checkpoint in Aden on 25 July. At the end of that month the Government acknowledged that around 40 pro-Government tribespeople had been accidentally killed in recent air-strikes targeting AQAP interests and personnel in southern Yemen. Efforts to halt the progress of AQAP continued, with the Government claiming to have killed a large number of militants during August and September, including 36 suspected AQAP members in air-strikes in Zinjibar and the Arkoub region in mid-August.

A new transition proposal approved by the GPC in early September 2011, under the terms of which President Saleh would formally transfer his powers to Vice-President al-Hadi over a three-month period, was rejected by the JMP. On 23 September state television unexpectedly announced that Saleh had returned to Yemen. On the same day almost 1m. protesters were estimated to have gathered in San'a for the largest anti-Government rally to be held thus far. On the following day, in his first public address since returning to Yemen, Saleh stated that he had authorized al-Hadi to engage in dialogue with the JMP with a view to signing the GCC-brokered agreement providing for a transfer of power following the staging of an early presidential election. However, the opposition remained sceptical about the sincerity of Saleh's pledges and continued to demand his immediate resignation. Meanwhile, some 50 protesters had been killed by government forces in 'Change Square' since the start of the month.

On 27 September 2011 the Minister of Defence, Brig.-Gen. Muhammad Nasser Ahmad Ali, escaped an apparent assassination attempt when a vehicle laden with explosives drove into his convoy travelling in Aden. The killing on 30 September of Anwar al-Awlaki in a drone attack in al-Jawf was welcomed by both the Yemeni and US Governments. Al-Awlaki was suspected of involvement in the foiled plot to bomb Chicago-bound freight aircraft in October 2010.

On 21 October 2011 the UN Security Council unanimously approved Resolution 2014, which condemned the human rights violations allegedly committed by the Yemeni authorities during

their efforts to curb the pro-democracy protesters, appealed for the immediate cessation of attacks against civilians, demanded that the authorities allow the fundamental rights of peaceful assembly and expression to be exercised, and urged all parties to commit to a peaceful transition of power based on the GCC's proposals. On the following day the Yemeni Government stated that it was ready to 'deal positively' with the terms of the resolution. However, further fatalities continued to be reported, particularly in San'a and Taiz, in the weeks that followed. In early November the Government stated that it was engaged in dialogue with the JMP with regard to implementation of the GCC agreement. On 18 November hundreds of thousands of Yemeni gathered at demonstrations in San'a and a number of other locations across the country to condemn government violence against civilians, particularly women and children, and appealed for Saleh and other members of the regime to be tried for crimes against humanity. Meanwhile, on 14 November three French aid workers who had been kidnapped in Yemen in late May by suspected AQAP militants, who had subsequently demanded a ransom of US $12m., were released unharmed following Omani mediation. It was not clear whether the ransom had been paid.

On 23 November 2011, nearly 11 months after the initial outbreak of anti-Government protests, President Saleh signed the GCC-brokered agreement in Riyadh. Under the terms of the accord, Saleh was to relinquish his constitutional powers on 23 December, although he was to retain the title of President until a successor was chosen at an early presidential election to be held in February 2012 (with the new President due to remain in office for a two-year transitionary period prior to the staging of both presidential and parliamentary elections in 2014); power was to be transferred in the interim to Vice-President al-Hadi, while Saleh and his family were to be granted immunity from prosecution. The development was widely welcomed by the international community, including the USA and the EU; however, although the announcement of Saleh's resignation was met with jubilation in the capital, many protesters remained critical of the immunity afforded to Saleh.

On 7 December 2011 Vice-President al-Hadi approved the formation of a new interim Government, comprising members of the GPC and the JMP, and headed by Muhammad Salem Basindwa, a former Minister of Foreign Affairs and a prominent opposition leader, as Prime Minister. Abu Bakr al-Kurbi and Brig.-Gen. Muhammad Nasser Ahmad Ali were retained as Minister of Foreign Affairs and Minister of Defence, respectively, while notable new appointments included those of Abd al-Qader Qahtan as Minister of the Interior and Sakhr Ahmed al-Wajih as Minister of Finance.

Despite the appointment of the interim Government, the violence continued, particularly in Taiz, where a number of fatalities were reported throughout December 2011; the signing of a cease-fire agreement by the Governor of Taiz and opposition officials on 3 December appeared largely to be ignored. A number of mass demonstrations were staged in San'a and other cities during the month, at which hundreds of thousands of Yemeni reiterated demands for Saleh and other senior members of the outgoing administration to face criminal prosecution for civilian deaths arising from the authorities' violent crackdown on the anti-Government protest movement.

Nevertheless, in early January 2012 the Council of Ministers endorsed draft legislation awarding immunity from prosecution to Saleh, in line with the terms of the GCC-brokered agreement, as well as to anyone who had worked with Saleh 'in all the state's civil, military and security apparatuses' during his 33-year presidency, and referred the bill for parliamentary approval. However, following severe criticism of the draft legislation, including from the UN High Commissioner for Human Rights, Navi Pillay, who stressed that granting immunity to those accused of gross human rights violations would contravene international law, the bill was amended in mid-January so as to restrict the provision of immunity to Saleh's associates in 'political cases' only. The amended bill was formally approved by the House of Representatives on 21 January, on which day it also nominated Vice-President al-Hadi as its candidate for the forthcoming presidential election. On the following day Saleh left Yemen for Oman en route to the USA for medical treatment, but vowed to return. At the end of January the Minister of Information, Ahmed Ali al-Amrani, survived an apparent assassination attempt, when unidentified gunmen opened fire on the car in which he was travelling in San'a.

Amid ongoing violent clashes between pro-democracy protesters and forces loyal to Saleh, as well as between pro-Government fighters and al-Houthi rebels in the north, and between the authorities and AQAP militants (which continued to exploit weakened central government control to expand its hold over the south), there were widespread fears that the presidential election might be postponed. However, in the event, the poll was conducted, as scheduled, on 21 February 2012, despite the designation of the date as a 'day of civil disobedience' by the Southern Movement. At least nine people were killed in electoral violence, which forced the early closure of a number of polling stations in Aden. However, voting in the capital was conducted for the most part in a calm and orderly manner. Turn-out was reported to have been relatively high, at around 65% of the registered electorate. Al-Hadi's uncontested candidacy for the presidency was approved by 99.8% of the valid votes cast, and on 25 February he was officially sworn in as President, pledging to preserve the country's unity and territorial integrity as well as to address the issues of chronic poverty and internal displacement. A separate inauguration ceremony on 27 February, organized by the GPC and attended by Saleh (who had affirmed his intention to remain as Chairman of the GPC), was boycotted by members of the JMP, who branded the ceremony as an act of 'heresy' and warned al-Hadi against appearing alongside Saleh in public for the sake of national unity. Meanwhile, hours after al-Hadi was sworn into office on 25 February, a suicide bombing outside the presidential palace in Mukalla, for which AQAP subsequently claimed responsibility, was reported to have killed 26 people.

A number of kidnappings in the first half of 2012 included that of Abdullah al-Khalidi, the Saudi deputy consul in Aden, who was abducted outside his residence in the city. The kidnapping followed that of Saeed al-Maliqi, the First Secretary at the Saudi embassy in San'a, in April 2011 (al-Maliqi had been released unharmed in the following month). Plans for al-Khalidi's release in August were abandoned after his captors reportedly doubled their ransom demand.

In early April 2012 al-Hadi effected a reorganization of senior military posts in an apparent effort to remove from office a number of Saleh loyalists. Gen. Muhammad Saleh al-Ahmar, Saleh's half-brother and commander of the air force, was among those dismissed. Members of the air force forced the closure of San'a International Airport in protest at al-Ahmar's dismissal, while al-Ahmar himself refused to stand down and threatened to shoot down any aircraft using the airport unless he was reinstated (al-Ahmar finally agreed to step down at the end of that month). Meanwhile, in mid-March, on the first anniversary of the killing of 52 protesters in 'Change Square', the Ministry of Human Rights announced that at least 2,000 people (including more than 120 children) had been killed during the year-long uprising, a figure far higher than that previously estimated by a number of human rights groups.

Recent developments: President al-Hadi's first year in office

On 4 March 2012 an assault was carried out by Ansar Al-Sharia (an off-shoot of al-Qa'ida) on a military base near Zinjibar resulting in the deaths of nearly 200 soldiers and in dozens being captured. The following month, following appeals from soldiers' families and tribal mediation, 73 soldiers were released. A further attack on a military post on 7 May killed at least 30 personnel. This last incident occurred the day after a US-led drone attack resulted in the death of two al-Qa'ida operatives, including Fahd al-Quso, one of those responsible for the bombing of the USS *Cole* in 2000. On 21 May, in the capital, 96 soldiers were killed in a suicide bomb attack at a military parade rehearsal. The incident was believed to have been a failed assassination attempt against the Minister of Defence, Brig.-Gen. Muhammad Nasser Ahmad Ali, and resulted in the removal from office of several security and intelligence officers. Meanwhile, government forces, with the help of local militias, were conducting a fierce military assault in Abyan province to win back the cities taken by AQAP the previous year; Lowder was the first to fall, on 18 May, with Jaar and Zinjibar following suit on 13 June and the last stronghold, Azzan, being abandoned by AQAP four days later.

President al-Hadi's administration won significant backing by the international community on 12 June 2012, when the UN Security Council issued Resolution 2051 demanding an end to all actions aimed at undermining the national unity government and confirming the UN's commitment to the implementation of the transition process. None the less, AQAP continued its assault against the Government's security apparatus over the ensuing months: on 18 June Maj.-Gen. Salem Ali al-Quton, commander of the southern military district, was assassinated in a suicide attack in Aden; while on 11 July 10 cadets were killed in a bombing at a police academy in San'a. Suspected US drone attacks continued to target militants, most notably AQAP's second-in-command, Saeed al-Shihri, who died in Hadramout province on 10 September. (Drone attacks were estimated to have killed 53 people in 2012, against 18 deaths recorded in the previous year.)

In early August 2012, in an attempt to curb the influence of Saleh, and in accordance with the GCC-brokered transition agreement, President al-Hadi began the process of restructuring of Yemen's armed forces by significantly reducing the number of units of the élite Republican Guard under the command of Saleh's son, Ahmad Saleh. The following week, on 14 August, Ahmad Saleh led members of the Republican Guard in an attack on the interior ministry; government troops subsequently gained control of the building and 62 pro-Saleh troops were arrested. On 7 September tens of thousands of demonstrators gathered in San'a to demand the prosecution of Ali Abdullah Saleh following his appearance earlier in the week at a GPC gathering. Further restructuring of Yemen's security apparatus occurred after another unsuccessful attempt was made on the life of the Minister of Defence on 11 September 2012, in which 12 people were killed. Al-Hadi subsequently replaced, among others, the heads of military intelligence and national security, and made some minor changes to the Government. Later in the month it was announced that a panel had been established to investigate alleged human rights abuses during the uprising in 2011—a move which some hoped might pave the way for the prosecution of Saleh and his relatives.

At a conference held in Aden in late September 2012, prominent Southern Movement leader Hassan Baoum rejected what he termed the 'occupation' of the south, and declared the start of a 'peaceful struggle' for independence. However, former Vice-President of the PDRY al-Baid, having announced that he was return to Yemen from exile, boycotted the conference. On 1 December a largely peaceful rally involving thousands across the south of the country was held to mark the 45th anniversary of the end of British rule and to demand independence from the north.

On 11 November 2012 Tareq al-Fadhli, influential tribal leader and prominent member of the separatist movement, was placed under house arrest in Aden. Al-Fadhli had long been suspected of links to al-Qa'ida and had returned to his home town of Zinjibar after a period of absence following the forced withdrawal of AQAP militants from towns in the south in June. At the end of November Abu Osama al-Abi, one of the leaders of AQAP, was arrested in Zinjibar. Terrorist incidents and reprisals against AQAP continued to take place in Yemen throughout the last months of 2012, one of the most significant events being the assassination of a Saudi diplomat and his Yemeni bodyguard in Sana'a on 28 November.

In addition to military and security personnel being targeted by insurgents, an increasing number of incidents of sabotage to oil and gas pipelines occurred in Yemen towards the end of 2012. On 3 December a major army offensive was launched in Marib province against tribal militias suspected of attacks on the main pipeline running from the east of the country to an export facility on the Red Sea. Two tribesmen were killed in the attack. Several days later some 17 officers were killed in an ambush while visiting the pipeline; officials believed that AQAP was responsible for the attack which resulted in subsequent clashes between tribesmen and AQAP as local militias attempted to find those responsible for the ambush. On 24 December clashes occurred in Marib province between the Yemeni army and tribesmen suspected of being responsible for the sabotage which, according to official figures, had cost the Government more than US $1,000m. in lost revenues in the course of 2012. Three days later the army took control of the area; around 15 people had been killed in the violence. Despite military activity in the area renewed attacks on the pipeline were launched in early 2013.

On 13 December 2012 President al-Hadi's reorganization of the military suffered a setback when Ahmad Saleh refused to transfer long-range missiles from the possession of the Republican Guard to the defence ministry. The son of the former President finally acquiesced, however, after a further series of military decrees issued by al-Hadi six days later, which effectively abolished the Republican Guard by merging the disparate elements of the military into four branches. The move also resulted in the removal of all generals loyal to former President Saleh and created a separate Missile Group, to be brought under al-Hadi's direct command. (Ahmad Saleh was subsequently named commander of a military region.)

Kidnappings of westerners continued to be a problem throughout 2012, culminating in the abduction of an Austrian and a Finnish couple on a busy street in the capital on 21 December. In January 2013 it was reported that the three hostages were being held by AQAP in Bayda province, having been sold to the militants by their abductors. At the end of that month Yemeni forces embarked on a offensive against those suspected of holding the hostages, during which a suicide car bomb killed at least 10 soldiers at a checkpoint in the region. On 31 January the military suspended their attack (which so far had claimed the lives of around 65 soldiers and militants) to allow for local tribesmen to secure their release. On 23 February the Austrian hostage, Dominik Neubauer, appeared in a video posted on the internet appealing to the Austrian Government to save his life by meeting his captors' ransom demand. Four days later Neubauer's parents in turn issued an appeal for their son's release. In early May it was reported that the hostages had been freed, following mediation by Oman.

The separatist Southern Movement gained momentum in Yemen in early 2013. Despite being offered one-half of the seats at the upcoming national dialogue conference (which had as its aim the drafting a new constitution and the preparation for general elections in February 2014), on 13 January 2013 tens of thousands of separatists gathered in rallies in several cities ostensibly to mark 'Reconciliation Day', in memory of the conflict that erupted in the PDRY in 1986. On 30 January two policemen were killed in Aden by suspected secessionists; another officer and a civilian died in the ensuing gun fight. In addition to violence between protesters and police in Aden, clashes occurred in early February between AQAP and pro-Government forces attempting to drive them out of the mountainous stronghold of Al Maraksha, in Abyan province. In early March President al-Hadi rejected efforts by clerics and tribal leaders to broker a truce with AQAP on the grounds that the militants must first lay down their arms.

Relations between separatists and the Yemeni authorities worsened after a pregnant woman was accidentally shot dead in Aden on 10 February 2013 during fighting between police and protesters demanding the release of prisoners arrested during the recent unrest. Meanwhile, thousands of pro-democracy supporters gathered in San'a to celebrate the second anniversary of the start of the anti-Saleh uprising. Following the threat of sanctions by the UN Security Council against Ali Salim al-Baid, on 18 February a major faction of the Southern Movement agreed to participate in the national dialogue conference scheduled for the following month. However, two days later two separatist leaders, Qaeem Askar and Hussain bin Shoaib, were arrested ahead of planned rival rallies to mark the first anniversary of the ouster of President Saleh. On 22 February, when thousands of supporters of President al-Hadi gathered in the capital to celebrate his election one year earlier, clashes broke out between pro-Government forces and armed separatists. The ensuing violence spread across the south of the country in the following days and resulted in at least nine deaths, prompting the President to make his first visit to the region since his inauguration. On 27 February separatists agreed to suspend their campaign of civil disobedience on the condition that if their demands were not met they would resume on 1 March; these included the removal from office of the governor of Aden and its central security chief. Despite the release of Askar and Shoaib, the violence resumed; three activists were killed in the week leading up to the national dialogue conference. A general strike was held in Aden on 16 March at the instigation of al-Baid. The conference commenced as scheduled on 18 March but without the participation of several hardline factions, including that led by al-Baid, who demanded that the dialogue be held in a neutral country.

In early March 2013 it was announced that two security chiefs from the Saleh regime, one of them the former President's nephew, would appear in court at the trial of the nine AQAP suspects accused of the bombing in San'a in May 2012, although it was unclear whether they would be charged or merely give testimony. The two had refused to attend the trial in February and had subsequently had their assets frozen. In April President al-Hadi issued a series of decrees finalizing the restructuring of the armed forces. The Republican Guard, formerly led by Ahmad Saleh, was subsumed into a larger élite force, while several new regional and unit commanders were appointed. Moreover,

Ahmad Saleh himself was appointed as Yemen's ambassador to the United Arab Emirates.

The Al-Houthi Rebellion

In June 2004 violent clashes took place in the mountainous north-western province of Saada between the security forces and supporters of a militant Zaidi cleric, Hussain al-Houthi, leader of Al-Shabab al-Mo'men (Believing Youth). The authorities alleged that al-Houthi's movement had formed its own militia near the border with Saudi Arabia and had launched attacks against government buildings and mosques in Saada. Although the group appeared to be motivated by opposition to the USA and Israel and to have a militant Islamist agenda, it was not thought to have links with al-Qa'ida. Reports estimated that al-Houthi had some 3,000 armed supporters, of whom some 200–300 had been killed since the conflict began, with hundreds of rebels wounded or arrested. In September al-Houthi himself was killed by members of the security forces. However, renewed fighting broke out with followers of the cleric in April 2005; five Yemeni soldiers and eight members of Al-Shabab al-Mo'men were understood to have been killed. On 12 April it was reported that the conflict had decreased in intensity and that government forces were seeking al-Houthi's relatives, in particular his brother, Abd al-Malik al-Houthi, and his father, Badr al-Din al-Houthi, who were believed to have acceded to the leadership of the movement. After several months of relative peace, fighting broke out again in November when two days of conflict reportedly left 16 rebels and eight government soldiers dead.

Renewed violence broke out in the province of Saada in early 2007, with a series of clashes between insurgents led by Abd al-Malik al-Houthi and government forces. President Saleh issued an ultimatum, warning of a full military campaign against the rebels if they did not surrender their weapons, and thousands of additional troops were subsequently deployed to the region.

Following mediation by Qatar, in June 2007 the Government and the leaders of the al-Houthi rebellion reached a cease-fire agreement, which, among other conditions, required Abd al-Malik al-Houthi, two of his brothers and another rebel leader to move to the Qatari capital, Doha, for an unspecified period of exile. However, later that month it was reported that the rebel leaders remained in Saada and that insurgents were continuing to attack government troops in the province. The rebels had apparently issued a new set of demands, most notably the return of the body of Hussain al-Houthi. The cease-fire was breached in October, when at least three armed rebels and one soldier were killed in clashes resulting from the rebels' refusal to surrender their weapons. Four soldiers died in further fighting later that month after al-Houthi supporters reportedly attacked a police station.

With the security situation in Saada deteriorating further, the Qatari Government renewed its efforts at mediation, and in February 2008 a document was signed outlining measures for the implementation of the initial agreement reached in June 2007. In mid-February 2008 it was reported that hostilities had ceased and that the rebels had freed two military commanders who had been captured in January. Furthermore, by early March the Government had released 376 detainees arrested in connection with the rebellion. However, the Government subsequently accused the rebels of violating the cease-fire agreement and of killing a detainee whom they had recently abducted, and sporadic violence resumed. In April Abd al-Malik al-Houthi asserted that efforts to implement the peace agreement had failed, owing to the Government's refusal to withdraw its forces from the areas in which they were deployed during the conflict with the rebels. A few days later further clashes resulted in the deaths of eight al-Houthi insurgents and three soldiers. In May at least 15 people were killed and up to 60 injured in a bombing at a mosque frequented by military personnel in Saada. Abd al-Malik al-Houthi denied claims of his followers' involvement in the incident.

In July 2008 President Saleh announced that the conflict with the al-Houthi militants had ended, adding that the combatants were engaged in constructive dialogue. Despite this pronouncement, there were continued reports of sporadic violence in the region. In August Abd al-Malik al-Houthi was reported to have accepted the President's 10-point proposal for a final settlement of the conflict, which was believed to encompass most of the terms of the Qatari-mediated agreement of 2007. In September 2008 the Government established a Saada Reconstruction Fund and announced a four-year strategy to rehabilitate the war-ravaged province. In addition to the hundreds of fatalities caused by the fighting, thousands of people had been displaced, many of whom were living in poor conditions in makeshift refugee camps. Several international non-governmental organizations, including Médecins sans frontières, endeavoured to bring medical and other humanitarian aid into affected areas, although all reported severe difficulties in delivering aid, mainly owing to ongoing instability.

During the first half of 2009 the truce in Saada province appeared increasingly fragile, amid reports of clashes between government and rebel forces. Furthermore, al-Houthi representatives alleged that the Government was sending substantial military reinforcements into the area in preparation for a new offensive. Renewed fighting erupted in July; at least seven Yemeni soldiers were killed during rebel attacks on army bases in Saada province. In early August al-Houthi militants ousted government troops from several towns and seized control of a strategic military post on the highway linking Saada with San'a. On 11 August the Government launched 'Operation Scorched Earth', a campaign of intensive aerial, missile and artillery strikes against insurgent positions in the region. Dozens of militants and civilians were reportedly killed during the opening days of the campaign, as rebel strongholds came under heavy bombardment from jet fighters and tanks. According to the office of the UN High Commissioner for Refugees (UNHCR), an estimated 35,000 people were displaced during the first two weeks of the operation. On 21 August President Saleh issued a cease-fire proposal that required the rebels to accept six conditions for peace: the release of all civilian and military prisoners; withdrawal from occupied areas and reinstatement of local government control; the reopening of roads and clearing of checkpoints and landmines; the surrender of weapons and equipment seized during the conflict; the cessation of incursions into Saudi territory; and a commitment to abide by the Constitution. The al-Houthi leadership rejected the proposed terms.

Official sources reported on 23 August 2009 that at least 100 rebels, including two senior commanders, had been killed during an anti-insurgent operation in the Harf Sufyan district of Amram province, to the south of Saada. At the beginning of September a cease-fire initiative proposed by the rebels was flatly rejected by the Government, and intensive ground operations and air-strikes continued. President Saleh subsequently alleged that the rebels were receiving financial support from groups within Iran and from supporters of Iraqi Shi'a cleric Moqtada al-Sadr. Conversely, al-Houthi representatives increasingly complained of Saudi Arabian collaboration in the Government's campaign, claiming that Yemeni troops had been granted access to Saudi territory in order to outflank rebel positions. It was reported in mid-September that more than 85 civilians had been killed when Yemeni forces launched air-strikes against a refugee camp in Harf Sufyan, provoking widespread condemnation from international human rights groups. On 20 September government forces repelled a rebel assault on their headquarters in Saada; more than 140 al-Houthi militants were reportedly killed in the battle. Nevertheless, despite vast advantages in troop numbers and equipment, the Government's goal of securing a swift and decisive victory looked increasingly uncertain. (During 'Operation Scorched Earth' the Government reportedly deployed up to 40,000 troops to the region, as well as mobilizing numerous irregular tribal militias.)

In October 2009 Yahya Badr al-Din al-Houthi, an exiled parliamentary deputy and a brother of the rebellion's leader, having been stripped of his parliamentary immunity, was placed on trial, *in absentia*, on charges of fomenting rebellion. Yahya was convicted of involvement in the rebellion in April 2010 and sentenced to 15 years' imprisonment; however, he remained in exile in Germany. Meanwhile, at the end of October 2009 the authorities apprehended an Iranian-crewed vessel reportedly transporting a shipment of weapons to the al-Houthi rebels.

In early November 2009, following an exchange of gunfire between al-Houthi militants and Saudi border guards, in which at least one guard was killed, Saudi Arabia launched a campaign of air-strikes and ground offensives against rebel targets in the Saudi-Yemeni border region. In mid-November Saudi Arabia enforced a naval blockade along Yemen's northern coast to prevent the supply of weapons and fighters to the rebel movement. The Saudi intervention exacerbated the already serious humanitarian crisis in north-western Yemen: in mid-November there were reported to be in excess of 170,000 internally displaced people in the region, with aid agencies reporting difficulties in delivering humanitarian supplies, while thousands of people were also evacuated from villages on the Saudi Arabian

side of the border; furthermore, reports indicated that the air-strikes had claimed a high number of civilian fatalities.

Despite incurring heavy casualties while under sustained attack from government forces to the south and Saudi forces in the border areas, the militants continued a campaign of guerrilla warfare. On 22 December 2009 Saudi Arabia announced the end of major combat operations, stating that full control of the border region had been regained. At that time 73 Saudi troops had been killed and 26 were missing since the commencement of the operation in early November. A truce offered to the Saudi authorities by the rebels, who stated that all fighters had been withdrawn from the kingdom's territory, was rejected in mid-January 2010. Although heavy fighting between government forces and the militants persisted, a truce based on recognition of the six-point agenda proposed by the Government in August 2009 was initiated on 11 February 2010. Nevertheless, sporadic violent incidents had continued to be reported throughout 2010 and into 2011, and in April 2011 the fragile cease-fire was broken when al-Houthi rebels, the leadership of which had previously expressed its support for the anti-Government protest movement that emerged from early 2011, seized control of Saada, causing the local Governor to flee. Intermittent clashes between al-Houthi rebels and tribespeople loyal to President Saleh continued to be reported throughout 2011 and into 2012. In January 2012 at least 46 people were reported to have been killed and dozens others injured in fighting between al-Houthi-led Shi'a rebels and Sunni Salafi gunmen in the north-western governorate of Hajjah. In the following month Abd al-Malik al-Houthi appealed for the creation of a 'civil state' in which political forces respected the will of the Yemeni people, and urged a boycott of the presidential election to be held on 21 February. In early June he agreed to join the national dialogue on establishing political stability in the country.

Foreign Affairs

Relations with Saudi Arabia

The Governments of Yemen and Saudi Arabia held negotiations concerning the demarcation of their common border during 1992–94; however, in December 1994 Yemen accused Saudi Arabia of trespassing on Yemeni territory and alleged that three of its soldiers had been killed during clashes earlier in that month. Further clashes were reported in January 1995 following the failure of the two countries to renew the 1934 Ta'if agreement (renewable every 20 years), which delineated their existing frontier. Intense mediation by Syria culminated in a joint statement in mid-January 1995, in which Yemen and Saudi Arabia pledged to cease all military activity in the border area. It was subsequently announced that the demarcation of the disputed border would be undertaken by a joint committee. In February the Yemeni and Saudi Governments signed a memorandum of understanding that reaffirmed their commitment to the Ta'if agreement and provided for the establishment of six joint committees to delineate the land and sea borders and develop economic and commercial ties. In June President Saleh led a high-ranking delegation to Saudi Arabia, constituting the first official visit to that country since February 1990.

Friction between Yemen and Saudi Arabia over border claims was revived in 1997, and in May 1998 it was reported that Saudi Arabia had occupied an uninhabited island in the Red Sea regarded by Yemen as within its national boundaries. In the same month Saudi Arabia sent a memorandum to the UN stating that it did not recognize the 1992 border agreement between Yemen and Oman and claiming that parts of the area involved were Saudi Arabian territory. The Saudi objection to the accord was widely believed to be related to its attempts to gain land access to the Arabian Sea, via a corridor between Yemen and Oman, which it had thus far been denied in its negotiations with Yemen. In July 1998 Yemen submitted a memorandum to the Arab League refuting the Saudi claim to the land, and stating that the Saudi protests contravened the Ta'if agreement signed by that country. In the same month three Yemeni troops were killed during fighting with a Saudi border patrol on the disputed island of Duwaima in the Red Sea; Saudi Arabia claimed its actions on the island were in self-defence and that, under the Ta'if agreement, three-quarters of the island belonged to Saudi Arabia.

Despite reported clashes in the border area during 1999, relations continued to improve. In June 2000, at a ceremony in the Saudi capital, Riyadh, the Saudi Arabian and Yemeni ministers responsible for foreign affairs signed a final border treaty demarcating their joint land and sea border. The treaty incorporated both the 1934 Ta'if agreement and the 1995 MOU, although it failed to define the eastern section of the Saudi–Yemeni land frontier. The two countries also agreed to further economic, commercial and cultural ties, and each pledged not to permit its territory to be used as a base for political or military aggression against the other. Renewed tensions surfaced in early 2004 after the Saudi Government began construction of a 'separation wall' along the border that some considered to be in violation of the border treaty of June 2000. The construction of the wall reflected unease on the part of the Saudis regarding the capacity of the Yemeni authorities to maintain their own border security. In June 2006 the Saudi and Yemeni ministers responsible for internal affairs signed an agreement on the final demarcation of their shared border.

Following the formation of AQAP in early 2009 (see Domestic Political Affairs), the Saudi Arabian authorities became increasingly concerned about the concentration of militant Islamist activity in ungoverned areas of Yemen. President Saleh held talks on regional security issues and bilateral relations with King Abdullah ibn Abd al-Aziz Al Sa'ud in Riyadh in June 2009. A failed attempt to assassinate the Saudi security chief, Prince Muhammad ibn Nayef, in Jeddah, Saudi Arabia, in August was attributed to AQAP. The growing lawlessness in Yemen's northern border region during 2009, exacerbated by the al-Houthi conflict, led to a significant expansion of Saudi military capacity in the region, which culminated in a military campaign against northern Yemeni rebels from November (see The Al-Houthi Rebellion). A meeting of the Saudi-Yemeni Co-operation Council in Riyadh in March 2010 led to the signing of a number of agreements concerning Saudi-funded energy, health, education and humanitarian projects in Yemen. Following the eruption of anti-Government protests in Yemen from January 2011, Saudi Arabia was swift to lend its support to the GCC-brokered transition agreement intended to facilitate the transfer of power from Saleh to a transitional administration.

Other external relations

An agreement on the long-disputed former PDRY–Omani border was signed in San'a in October 1992 and ratified in December. Demarcation was completed in June 1995. Oman withdrew an estimated 15,000 troops from the last of the disputed territories on the Yemeni border in July 1996, in accordance with the 1992 agreement. In May 1997 officials from both countries signed the demarcation maps at a ceremony in Muscat, Oman. In January 2004 the two countries signed an agreement on their sea border during wider discussions over the establishment of a joint free trade zone.

Following the suicide attacks apparently perpetrated by Osama bin Laden's al-Qa'ida network against New York and Washington, DC, USA, on 11 September 2001, the Yemeni Government arrested a number of suspected Islamist militants and froze the assets of individuals and organizations deemed to have links with al-Qa'ida. In December up to 30 people (including about 19 soldiers) were reportedly killed during clashes in the central Marib governorate, when local residents apparently fought to prevent the Yemeni security forces from arresting a group of alleged militants. (President Saleh had, during a visit to Washington, DC, in November, been presented with a list of suspected al-Qa'ida members residing in Yemen.) In January 2002 the US embassy in San'a was closed amid fears of an imminent terrorist attack; two grenades were thrown at the building in March, although no injuries were reported. Despite increasing popular resentment towards US activities in the Middle East among Yemenis, President Saleh continued to co-operate with the USA over anti-terrorism initiatives, and in November an unmanned US aircraft killed six men in northern Yemen believed to have links with al-Qa'ida. In December three US missionaries were murdered by a Yemeni who confessed to having links with bin Laden's network.

In February 2002 President Saleh was reported to have warned the US Government that a US-led attack on the regime of Saddam Hussein in Iraq, as part of its 'war on terror', would jeopardize the continued support of its traditional allies in the Arab region. However, Saleh was careful to emphasize his own ongoing efforts to persuade the Iraqi authorities to accept the return of UN weapons inspectors. When the US-led military campaign commenced in Iraq in March 2003, some 30,000 protesters, some of them armed, marched on the US embassy in San'a. In June the Director of the US Federal Bureau of Investigation, Robert Mueller, met Saleh in Aden to discuss further co-operation on security and intelligence. In November Muhammad Hamdi al-Ahdal, who, according to the USA, had been among the

20 most significant al-Qa'ida members still at large, was captured by security forces; al-Ahdal was suspected of having organized the bombings of the USS *Cole* in 2000 and the French petroleum tanker the *Limburg* in 2002. Another reported senior al-Qa'ida operative, who had apparently survived a US attempt to assassinate him in 2002, was arrested by security forces in March 2004.

In March 2004 Yemen welcomed the signing of an interim constitution in Iraq, describing it as a step towards Iraq recovering its sovereignty, but continued to press for the USA and its allies to withdraw their forces from the country. In August the Minister of Foreign Affairs confirmed that Yemen was preparing a peace-keeping force for Iraq under mandates from the Arab League and the UN, but would only send the troops should the US-led coalition forces withdraw from Iraq. Discussions held between Saleh and US President George W. Bush in May 2007, during a visit by the Yemeni President to Washington, DC, focused on efforts to combat terrorism and developments in the Middle East, as well as bilateral relations. In September 2008 the US embassy in San'a was the target of another violent attack, in which at least 16 people were killed, although no embassy staff were reported to have been injured in the incident.

Media reports in December 2010 claimed that the USA had launched four clandestine cruise missile strikes in the previous 12 months, which had killed 40 suspected terrorists but had also claimed the lives of more than 200 civilians. The online release by the WikiLeaks organization of a series of leaked classified US diplomatic cables from late 2010 appeared to indicate the existence of an agreement whereby the Administration of US President Barack Obama offered covert military support to target suspected terrorists in Yemen in exchange for the Yemeni Government claiming responsibility for the air-strikes in order to shield the US Administration from external criticism, and revealed that the USA had provided emergency supplies of weapons as well as intelligence to support Saudi military action against al-Houthi rebels (see The Al-Houthi Rebellion) in late 2009, despite a denial of any military involvement at the time by the US Department of State.

During a visit to San'a in January 2011, the first visit to the Yemeni capital by a US Secretary of State in two decades, Hillary Clinton stressed that the issue of AQAP militants operating in Yemen was an 'urgent concern' for the Obama Administration and declared that the Administration sought to 'broaden dialogue' and enhance bilateral ties beyond those of a military nature. In March US Secretary of Defence Robert Gates noted his 'concern' about the authorities' handling of the anti-Government protest movement but stressed that it was not his place to discuss Yemeni internal affairs. However, US rhetoric in response to widespread reports of the excessive use of force to quell the protesters became increasingly firm and outspoken, and US media reported in early April that the Obama Administration had told Yemeni officials that Saleh's position had become 'untenable'. From June drone attacks widely believed to have been launched by the USA against suspected AQAP targets in Yemen intensified, amid concerns over the militant group's growing stronghold over southern regions of the country; however, the Yemeni Government continued officially to claim that the attacks were launched by its air force. The eventual signing in November by Saleh of the GCC-brokered transition plan that provided for the transfer of his constitutional powers to Vice-President al-Hadi in the following month, and the successful staging of the presidential election in February 2012, were strongly welcomed by the Obama Administration, with the US President affirming that the developments represented an important step forward in Yemen's democratic transition process; Obama also pledged US support for the efforts of the incoming administration of President al-Hadi to address the urgent political, economic, social and humanitarian challenges confronting the country.

In May 2007 the staging of a demonstration intended to protest against perceived Iranian and Libyan interference in Yemeni domestic affairs was prevented by the Ministry of the Interior, provoking outrage among, in particular, many in Saada, who were angered by alleged Iranian and Libyan support for those rebels loyal to al-Houthi who were thought to be responsible for much of the violence in that region. A few days previously Yemen had recalled its ambassadors from both countries. The Iranian and Libyan Governments both denied any involvement in the rebellion in Saada and sought to ease tensions with Yemen. Later in May the Libyan leader dispatched an envoy to San'a to deliver a letter to President Saleh expressing support for the Yemeni

Government's efforts to quash the insurgency, and in July Muhammad Reza Baqeri, the Iranian Deputy Foreign Minister for Arab and African Affairs, visited Yemen in an effort to improve bilateral relations. However, in November 2008 Rashad al-Alimi, Yemen's Deputy Prime Minister for Defence and Security Affairs, alleged that al-Houthi militants were receiving training and support from Iran. Two Yemeni citizens were convicted in April 2009 of spying for Iran and sentenced to death. The intensification of the Government's conflict with the al-Houthi militants from August led to increased tensions with Iran. Reports that the security authorities had apprehended an Iranian shipment of arms destined for the rebels, in October, were vehemently denied by the Iranian authorities. Trial proceedings against a further four Yemenis, accused of spying for Iran on behalf of the al-Houthi movement, commenced in April 2010; the defendants denied the charges against them and alleged that they had been tortured while in police custody. The trial of three further Yemenis on charges of spying for Iran commenced in February 2011. In April US intelligence officials claimed that Iran was attempting to assist the opposition in Yemen and Bahrain, apparently following the interception of communications between prominent opposition figures in both countries and Iranian officials. Iran denied the allegations of interference in Yemeni and Bahraini internal affairs. In October 2012 the Yemeni Ministry of Defence claimed to have dismantled an organization involved in espionage against Yemen that included among its number Iranian citizens (as well as Syrians and Yemenis). Two months later President Abd al-Rabbuh Mansur al-Hadi accused Iran of supporting the secessionist Southern Movement. Relations between the two countries were further strained in early 2013 when a ship carrying weapons and explosives was intercepted in the Arabian Sea. Iran denied claims by the Yemeni authorities that the shipment, destined for the al-Houthi militants, came from Iran. On 15 February the UN Security Council warned against attempts by foreign countries to destabilize the Yemeni regime with weapons shipments.

President Saleh sought to mediate in the dispute that arose between rival Palestinian political factions the Islamic Resistance Movement (Hamas) and Fatah after Hamas had seized control of the Gaza Strip in June 2007. In March 2008 the Yemeni President brokered a reconciliation agreement, the San'a Declaration, which was signed by the two organizations (see the chapter on the Palestinian Territories). The launch of Israel's military offensive against Hamas targets in the Gaza Strip in late December 2008 led to angry demonstrations throughout Yemen. Protesters angered by Egypt's perceived support for Israel stormed the Egyptian consulate in Aden, causing serious damage. President Saleh attended the Arab Economic, Social and Development Summit in Kuwait in January 2009, at which he presented proposals for the formation of a union of Arab states.

From the mid-1990s President Saleh increasingly sought to widen the range of Yemen's international contacts, particularly in relation to aid and co-operation agreements. Saleh made a state visit to the People's Republic of China in February 1998, during which extensive agreements were negotiated for Yemen to receive technical and economic assistance. In early 2000 Saleh made official visits to Canada, the USA, Italy and Iran; at the same time Yemen repeatedly denied reports that it had had secret contacts with Israel and that it was seeking to normalize relations with that country. At a meeting held in London, United Kingdom, in November 2006, international donors pledged some US $5,000m. in development assistance for Yemen; however, the IMF noted in August 2010 that only a small portion of this pledged amount had been disbursed hitherto. Meanwhile, in August 2007 Yemen signed a 10-year development partnership agreement with the United Kingdom. In February 2011 the British Government announced that it was almost to double its aid to Yemen from £46.7m. in 2011 to £90m. by 2015, on the condition that Yemen meet a series of targets, including the holding of free and fair elections and the promotion of economic reforms; a British government spokesperson identified Yemen as 'a major priority for British aid' and expressed the hope that the planned increase would facilitate a move towards 'a more stable and prosperous future' for the Middle Eastern country, while also suggesting that the Saleh administration needed to do more to counter the threat posed to domestic and international security by AQAP and other terrorist elements within Yemen. Following the relinquishment by Saleh of his constitutional powers in December 2011, and the successful staging of an election to

choose a permanent successor to the erstwhile President in February 2012, the British Secretary of State for Foreign and Commonwealth Affairs, William Hague, issued a statement welcoming the election of al-Hadi, which he hailed as a 'key milestone in Yemen's transition' and urged the interim Government to begin the process of national reconciliation immediately. The British Government pledged an additional £15.4m. in humanitarian aid for 2012, in recognition of the scale of the humanitarian needs of the Yemeni population in the aftermath of the protracted political crisis.

CONSTITUTION AND GOVERNMENT

A draft Constitution for the united Republic of Yemen, based on that endorsed by the Yemen Arab Republic (YAR) and the People's Democratic Republic of Yemen (PDRY) in December 1981, was published in December 1989; it was approved by a popular referendum held on 15–16 May 1991. Legislative power is vested in the House of Representatives, with 301 members directly elected by universal adult suffrage. Under the revised Constitution, the President of the Republic (head of state) was to be elected directly by voters for a period of seven years, renewable once, while the President appointed a Council of Ministers, headed by a Prime Minister. Following the signing in November 2011 of an agreement providing for the transfer of power from President Ali Abdullah Saleh to Vice-President Maj.-Gen. (latterly Field Marshal) Abd al-Rabbuh Mansur al-Hadi, and the subsequent election to the presidency of al-Hadi in February 2012, the new President was to oversee the drafting of a new constitution in advance of presidential and parliamentary elections scheduled to be held in 2014.

REGIONAL AND INTERNATIONAL CO-OPERATION

Yemen is a member of the League of Arab States (the Arab League, see p. 372) and is currently pursuing membership of the Cooperation Council for the Arab States of the Gulf (the Gulf Cooperation Council—GCC, see p. 255). Since unification in 1990, Yemen has been represented at the UN as a single member. (The Yemen Arab Republic joined the organization in September 1947, and the People's Democratic Republic of Yemen in December 1967.) The country has observer status at the World Trade Organization (WTO, see p. 444), membership of which organization was applied for in 2000. It also participates in the Organization of Islamic Cooperation (OIC, see p. 413).

ECONOMIC AFFAIRS

In 2011, according to estimates by the World Bank, Yemen's gross national income (GNI), measured at average 2009–11 prices, was US $26,419m., equivalent to $1,070 per head (or $2,180 per head on an international purchasing-power parity basis). During 2002–11, it was estimated, the population increased at an average annual rate of 3.1%, while gross domestic product (GDP) per head decreased, in real terms, by an average of 0.5% per year. According to official estimates, overall GDP increased, in real terms, at an average annual rate of 2.4% in 2002–11; GDP grew by 6.8% in 2010, but declined by some 15.3% in 2011.

Agriculture (including forestry and fishing) contributed an estimated 14.0% of GDP in 2011, and the sector engaged 35.1% of the working population in 2005/06. According to FAO estimates, however, the sector is to be engaged by some 35.8% of the total labour force in mid-2013. The principal cash crops are coffee, cotton and fruits. Subsistence crops include sorghum, potatoes, wheat and millet. However, cultivation of the amphetamine-like narcotic qat has displaced other crops in many areas. Livestock-rearing (particularly in the east and north) and fishing are also important activities. Official estimates indicated an average annual growth rate of 6.0% in 2002–11; real agricultural GDP increased by an estimated 2.8% in 2011.

Industry (including mining, manufacturing, construction and power) contributed an estimated 39.7% of GDP in 2011, and 18.5% of the working population were employed in the sector in 2005/06. According to official estimates, industrial GDP decreased at an average annual rate of 2.4% in 2001–10; industrial GDP grew by an estimated 8.0% in 2010, but decreased by 22.0% in 2011.

Mining and quarrying contributed an estimated 28.1% of GDP in 2011, and employed only 0.4% of the working population in 2005/06. Yemen's proven petroleum reserves totalled 2,670m. barrels at the end of 2011, sufficient to maintain production at that year's levels for more than 32 years. Petroleum production averaged 228,400 barrels per day (b/d) during 2011. The value of exports of petroleum and petroleum products accounted for 88.4% of the value of total exports in 2009. There are also significant reserves of natural gas: proven reserves at the end of 2011 were 479,000m. cu m. Salt and gypsum are also exploited on a large scale. It was announced in late 2008 that the country's first gold mine was to be established at Haddah, on the border with Saudi Arabia. In addition, there are deposits of copper, lead, zinc, sulphur and molybdenum. The GDP of the mining sector decreased at an estimated average annual rate of 6.5% in 2002–11; real mining GDP expanded by 4.0% in 2010, but contracted by 18.6% in 2011, according to official estimates.

The manufacturing sector contributed an estimated 6.0% of GDP in 2011; in 2005/06 some 5.5% of the working population were employed in the sector. The most important branches of manufacturing are food-processing, petroleum-refining, construction materials (particularly cement and iron and steel), paper and paper products, and traditional light industries (including textiles, leather goods and jewellery). Production of liquefied natural gas (LNG) commenced in October 2009. According to official estimates, manufacturing GDP increased at an average annual rate of 1.4% in 2002–11; the sector's real GDP increased by 5.5% in 2010, but decreased by 26.5% in 2011.

Construction contributed an estimated 5.0% of GDP in 2011, and employed 12.1% of the working population in 2005/06. The real GDP of the sector increased at an estimated average annual rate of 8.7% in 2002–11; construction GDP grew by some 17.2% in 2010, but declined by 24.6% in 2011, according to official estimates.

Some domestic energy requirements are served by locally produced petroleum, but the country is somewhat reliant on fuel imports (particularly petroleum from other producers in the region). Imports of fuel and energy comprised 20.9% of the value of total imports in 2009. The northern and southern electricity grids were linked in 1997.

The services sector contributed an estimated 46.3% of GDP in 2011, and employed 46.4% of the working population in 2005/06. A free trade zone at Aden was inaugurated in May 1991. Security concerns have undermined Yemen's attractiveness as a destination for tourism and investment. The real GDP of the services sector increased at an estimated average annual rate of 4.6% in 2002–11; real services GDP expanded by 7.5% in 2010, but contracted by 19.5% in 2011, according to official estimates.

In 2011 Yemen recorded a visible merchandise trade deficit of US $413.7m., and there was a deficit of $1,663.1m. on the current account of the balance of payments. In 2011 the principal source of imports (15.9%) was the United Arab Emirates; other major suppliers were Saudi Arabia, Switzerland, the Netherlands, the People's Republic of China and the USA. In that year China was the main export destination (32.3%). Other important export markets were Thailand, India, the Republic of Korea and Saudi Arabia. The principal exports in 2011 were mineral fuels and lubricants (86.3%), and food and live animals. The main imports in that year were mineral fuels and lubricants, food and live animals (especially cereals and cereal preparations), machinery and transport equipment, basic manufactures, and chemical and related products.

A preliminary budget deficit of YR 272,000m. was recorded in 2010. Yemen's general government gross debt was YR 2,788,200m. in that year, equivalent to 40.9% of GDP. Total external debt at the end of 2010 was estimated to be US $6,324m., of which $5,933m. was public and publicly guaranteed debt. In that year the cost of servicing long-term public and publicly guaranteed debt and repayments to the IMF was equivalent to 2.8% of the value of exports of goods, services and income (excluding workers' remittances). The annual rate of inflation averaged 12.0% in 2002–11, according to ILO figures; consumer prices increased by 13.0% in 2010 and by 19.5% in 2011. The rate of unemployment was estimated at 17.8% of the labour force in 2010.

Following the election of Abd al-Rabbuh Mansur al-Hadi to the presidency in February 2012 (see Contemporary Political History), the IMF approved a US $93.8m. emergency loan to support Yemen in its recovery from the political unrest of the previous year, which had affected most major economic sectors in the country, including oil, tourism, and national and international investments, as well as foreign exchange. The loan was intended primarily to maintain macroeconomic stability and to safeguard foreign exchange reserves, while allowing for a concomitant increase in capital and social expenditure. The Fund stressed that support from the international donor community was 'necessary if sustainable growth and tangible progress in combating poverty were to be achieved. Despite a period of relative stability during 2012 and a number of relief campaigns from international donors (in particular Saudi Arabia), by the latter half of that year Yemen was undergoing a humanitarian crisis, with almost 1m. children thought to be suffering from acute malnutrition. In January 2013 the UN Development Programme launched its annual Yemen Humanitarian Response Plan, which estimate that Yemen required US $716m. of outside financial assistance in that year, compared with $585m. the previous year. Although continued attacks on oil and gas pipelines throughout 2012 had a significant impact on Yemen's energy output, by the end of that year economic activity was showing signs of recovery. A decline in the rate of inflation (to 5.5% in November 2012, from some 25% in October 2011), and the stabilization of the exchange rate resulted in the reduction of interest rates by the Central Bank in October 2012 from 20% to 18%. In 2013 diversification of Yemen's economy, which was in part effected in 2009 by the commencement of production of liquefied natural gas, continued to be regarded as a priority. Further measures to be taken to strengthen the economy included a reduction in both energy subsidies (amounting to around 8% of GDP at the start of 2013), and the public sector wage bill (which accounted for more than 10% of GDP). The IMF forecast the overall rate of GDP growth to contract by 1.9% in 2012, although a return to positive growth, at a rate of 4.4%, was projected for 2013.

PUBLIC HOLIDAYS

2014: 1 January (New Year's Day), 13 January* (Mouloud, Birth of the Prophet), 1 May (Labour Day), 22 May (National Day of the Republic—Unification Day), 28 June* (Ramadan begins), 28 May* (Id al-Fitr, end of Ramadan), 26 September (National Day—Establishment of the Yemen Arab Republic), 4 October (Id al-Adha, Feast of the Sacrifice), 14 October (Revolution Day), 24 October* (Muharram, Islamic New Year), 30 November (Independence Day—Establishment of the People's Republic of Southern Yemen).

* These holidays are dependent on the Islamic lunar calendar and may vary by one or two days from the dates given.

Statistical Survey

Sources (unless otherwise indicated): Republic of Yemen Central Statistical Organization, POB 13434, San'a; tel. (1) 250619; fax (1) 250664; e-mail csoi@y.net.ye; internet www.cso-yemen.org; Central Bank of Yemen, POB 59, Ali Abd al-Mughni St, San'a; tel. (1) 274314; fax (1) 274360; e-mail cbyh@y.net.ye; internet www.centralbank.gov.ye.

Area and Population

AREA, POPULATION AND DENSITY

Area (sq km)	536,869*
Population (census results)	
16 December 1994†	14,587,807
16 December 2004‡	
Males	10,036,953
Females	9,648,208
Total	19,685,161
Population (UN estimates at mid-year)§	
2011	24,799,877
2012	25,569,263
2013	26,358,020
Density (per sq km) at mid-2013	49.1

* 207,286 sq miles.
† Excluding adjustment for underenumeration.
‡ Population is *de jure*.
§ Source: UN, *World Population Prospects: The 2010 Revision*.

POPULATION BY AGE AND SEX
(UN estimates at mid-2013)

	Males	Females	Total
0–14	5,854,879	5,623,487	11,478,366
15–64	7,102,922	7,088,773	14,191,695
65 and over	309,791	378,168	687,959
Total	13,267,592	13,090,428	26,358,020

Source: UN, *World Population Prospects: The 2010 Revision*.

PRINCIPAL TOWNS
(population at 1994 census)

San'a (capital) . .	954,448		Hodeida	298,452
Aden	398,294		Mukalla	122,359
Taiz	317,571		Ibb	103,312

Source: UN, *Demographic Yearbook*.

Mid-2011 ('000, incl. suburbs, UN estimate): San'a 2,419 (Source: UN, *World Urbanization Prospects: The 2011 Revision*).

BIRTHS, MARRIAGES AND DEATHS
(annual averages, UN estimates)

	1995–2000	2000–05	2005–10
Birth rate (per 1,000)	42.7	39.9	38.6
Death rate (per 1,000)	10.2	8.3	7.0

Source: UN, *World Population Prospects: The 2010 Revision*.

Registered births: 271,269 in 2009; 318,936 in 2010; 239,980 in 2011.

Registered deaths: 31,914 in 2009; 28,494 in 2010; 23,662 in 2011.

Marriages (2002, estimate): 10,934 (Source: UN, *Demographic Yearbook*).

Life expectancy (years at birth): 65.5 (males 64.0, females 67.0) in 2011 (Source: World Bank, World Development Indicators database).

EMPLOYMENT
(persons aged 15 years and over, 2005/06)

	Males	Females	Total
Agriculture, hunting and forestry .	1,260,796	113,797	1,374,593
Fishing	31,506	—	31,506
Mining and quarrying	14,225	735	14,959
Manufacturing	200,339	21,799	222,138
Electricity, gas and water . . .	18,466	308	18,773
Construction	485,048	816	485,864
Trade, restaurants and hotels .	641,117	9,697	650,814
Transport, storage and communications	235,681	3,796	239,477
Hotels and Restaurants . . .	72,992	1,063	74,054
Finance, insurance and real estate	37,368	2,539	39,907
Education	196,594	49,535	246,129
Health and social welfare . . .	38,146	16,763	54,909
Personal and social services . .	72,163	5,282	77,445
Public administration and defence	436,802	16,730	453,532
Private households with employed persons	15,196	8,106	23,302
Sub-total	3,756,438	250,967	4,007,404
Unspecified	73,363	68,679	142,043
Total	3,829,801	319,646	4,149,447

Mid-2013 (estimates in '000): Agriculture, etc. 2,390; Total labour force 6,684 (Source: FAO).

Health and Welfare

KEY INDICATORS

Total fertility rate (children per woman, 2010)	5.2
Under-5 mortality rate (per 1,000 live births, 2010) . . .	77
HIV/AIDS (% of persons aged 15–49, 2003)	0.1
Physicians (per 1,000 head, 2009)	0.3
Hospital beds (per 1,000 head, 2010)	0.7
Health expenditure (2009): US $ per head (PPP) . . .	139
Health expenditure (2009): % of GDP	5.5
Health expenditure (2009): public (% of total)	26.5
Access to water (% of persons, 2010)	55
Access to sanitation (% of persons, 2010)	53
Total carbon dioxide emissions ('000 metric tons, 2008) . .	23,384.5
Carbon dioxide emissions per head (metric tons, 2008) . .	1.0
Human Development Index (2011): ranking	154
Human Development Index (2011): value	0.462

For sources and definitions, see explanatory note on p. vi.

Agriculture

PRINCIPAL CROPS
('000 metric tons)

	2009	2010	2011*
Wheat	222	265	278
Barley	23	40	38
Maize	56	89	89
Millet	62	111	131
Sorghum	312	507	603
Potatoes	278	303	368
Chick-peas	51	51*	57
Sesame seed	24	25	28
Seed cotton	25	25	29
Tomatoes	251	262	253
Cucumbers and gherkins . . .	16	17*	18
Chillies and peppers, green . .	21	22*	22
Onions, dry	216	224	237
Garlic	4	4*	5
Beans, green	4	4	5

—continued	2009	2010	2011*
Carrots and turnips	15	16*	19
Okra	23	24*	24
Watermelons	172	189	187
Cantaloupes and other melons .	32	35	34
Bananas	132	133	136
Oranges	113	122†	127
Tangerines, mandarins, etc. .	22	22†	23
Grapes	129	166	167
Mangoes, mangosteens and			
guavas	405	401	472
Dates	57	58	60
Papayas	25	26	21
Coffee, green	19	19	20
Tobacco, unmanufactured . .	23	23	20

* FAO estimate(s).
† Unofficial figure.

Aggregate production ('000 metric tons, may include official, semi-official or estimated data): Total cereals 674 in 2009, 1,013 in 2010, 1,139 in 2011; Total roots and tubers 278 in 2009, 304 in 2010, 369 in 2011; Total vegetables (incl. melons) 820 in 2009, 868 in 2010, 887 in 2011; Total fruits (excl. melons) 981 in 2009, 1,031 in 2010, 1,112 in 2011.

Source: FAO.

LIVESTOCK
('000 head, year ending September)

	2009	2010	2011*
Horses	2†	2†	2
Asses*	500	500	500
Cattle	1,567	1,605	1,610
Camels	384	403†	405
Sheep	9,087	9,206	9,250
Goats	8,883	9,016	9,050
Chickens*	58,000	60,000	60,000

* FAO estimates.
† Unofficial figure.

Source: FAO.

LIVESTOCK PRODUCTS
('000 metric tons)

	2009	2010	2011*
Cattle meat	96.7	107.5	109.9
Sheep meat	30.7	34.3	36.0
Goat meat	31.6	35.0	37.0
Chicken meat	139.7	144.1	149.7
Camels' milk*	19.0	19.4	19.4
Cows' milk	291.1	301.3*	301.3
Sheep's milk	42.1	43.0*	43.0
Goats' milk	52.3	53.5*	53.5
Hen eggs	58.6†	60.6†	60.6
Wool, greasy	7.6†	7.7†	7.7

* FAO estimate(s).
† Unofficial figure.

Source: FAO.

Forestry

ROUNDWOOD REMOVALS
('000 cubic metres, excl. bark, estimates)

	2009	2010	2011
Total (all fuel wood)	425	441	441

Source: FAO.

Fishing

('000 metric tons, live weight of capture)

	2008	2009	2010
Demersal percomorphs* . . .	8.1	11.6	15.1
Indian oil sardine	17.7	21.1*	24.5*
Yellowfin tuna	13.7	14.8*	15.9*
Pelagic percomorphs*	34.0	40.4	46.9
Sharks, rays and skates, etc. . .	5.5	8.6*	12.0
Cuttlefish and bobtail squids . .	6.0	11.5*	17.0
Total catch (incl. others)* . .	127.1	159.0	191.1

* FAO estimate(s).

Source: FAO.

Mining

('000 metric tons unless otherwise indicated)

	2008	2009	2010
Crude petroleum	14,866	14,426	14,173
Natural gas (million cu m)* . .	29,632	14,412	20,000†
Salt	65	65	75†
Gypsum (crude)	100	100	100†

* Gross production.
† Estimate.

2011: Crude petroleum ('000 metric tons) 10,766.

Sources: BP, *Statistical Review of World Energy*; US Geological Survey.

Industry

SELECTED PRODUCTS
('000 barrels unless otherwise indicated)

	2008	2009	2010
Mineral water (million litres) .	401*	n.a.	n.a.
Soft drinks (million litres) . .	270*	n.a.	n.a.
Cigarettes (million packets) . .	215*	n.a.	n.a.
Liquefied petroleum gas ('000			
metric tons)	758	735	736
Motor spirit	5,110	5,110	5,110*
Kerosene	4,052	4,052	4,052*
Distillate fuel oils	7,775	7,775	7,775*
Residual fuel oils	3,723	14,750	14,750*
Cement ('000 metric tons) . .	2,111	2,118	3,500
Paints ('000 litres)	47,551*	n.a.	n.a.
Plastic bags (metric tons) . .	39,768*	n.a.	n.a.
Electric energy (million kWh) .	6,546	6,749	7,755

* Estimated figure.

2011: Electric energy (million kWh) 6,206.

Source: partly US Geological Survey.

Finance

CURRENCY AND EXCHANGE RATES

Monetary Units
100 fils = 1 Yemeni riyal (YR).

Sterling, Dollar and Euro Equivalents (31 December 2012)
£1 sterling = YR 339.10;
US $1 = YR 214.89;
€1 = YR 283.53;
YR 1,000 = £2.95 = $4.65 = €3.53.

Average Exchange Rate (YR per US $)
2010   219.590
2011   213.800
2012   214.351

Note: The exchange rate of US $1 = YR 9.76, established in the YAR in 1988, remained in force until February 1990, when a new rate of $1 = YR 12.01 was introduced. Following the merger of the two Yemens in May 1990, the YAR's currency was adopted as the currency of the unified country. In March 1995 the official exchange rate was amended from YR 12.01 to YR 50.04 per US dollar. The rate has since been adjusted. From mid-1996 data refer to a market-determined exchange rate, applicable to most private transactions.

CENTRAL GOVERNMENT BUDGET

(YR '000 million)

Revenue*	2008	2009	2010†
Oil and gas	1,456.3	715.8	1,120.3
Exports	837.3	349.4	598.3
Domestic revenues	619.0	366.4	522.0
Non-oil revenues	522.3	562.7	632.7
Tax revenues	371.4	409.5	449.7
Non-tax revenues	150.9	153.2	183.0
Total	1,978.6	1,278.5	1,753.0

Expenditure	2008	2009	2010†
Current expenditure	1,866.5	1,478.2	1,733.7
Civil wages and salaries	578.0	569.4	589.9
Materials and services	192.4	199.2	214.6
Interest	125.9	124.6	162.7
Domestic	115.0	113.9	147.7
Foreign	10.9	10.7	15.0
Transfers and subsidies	940.4	555.5	733.9
Current transfers	175.1	158.4	171.8
Subsidies	765.3	397.1	562.1
Other current expenditure	29.8	29.5	32.6
Capital development expenditure	300.4	269.8	261.6
Net lending	54.7	75.9	54.8
Total	2,221.6	1,823.9	2,050.1

* Excluding grants received (YR '000 million): 14.2 in 2008; 27.6 in 2009; 25.1 in 2010 (preliminary).
† Preliminary figures.

INTERNATIONAL RESERVES

(US $ million at 31 December)

	2009	2010	2011
Gold (national valuation)	57.4	74.4	82.4
IMF special drawing rights	313.6	280.5	253.9
Foreign exchange	6,622.0	5,587.8	4,195.0
Total	6,993.0	5,942.7	4,531.3

Source: IMF, *International Financial Statistics*.

MONEY SUPPLY

(YR million at 31 December)

	2009	2010	2011
Currency outside banks	532,372	547,284	777,407
Demand deposits at commercial banks	165,915	175,592	162,300
Total money (incl. others)	758,561	786,560	993,031

Source: IMF, *International Financial Statistics*.

COST OF LIVING

(Consumer Price Index; base: 2000 = 100)

	2008	2009	2010
Food	323.2	331.4	381.3
Rent	189.5	198.1	230.3
Clothing	141.6	151.7	154.4
All items (incl. others)	249.1	258.3	292.0

2011: All items 349.0.

Source: ILO.

NATIONAL ACCOUNTS

(YR million at current prices)

National Income and Product

	2008	2009*	2010†
Domestic factor incomes	6,269,146	5,617,865	6,749,512
Consumption of fixed capital	401,871	357,608	395,928
Gross domestic product (GDP) at factor cost	6,671,017	5,975,472	7,145,440
Indirect taxes, *less* subsidies	−598,745	−277,916	−419,769
GDP in purchasers' values	6,072,272	5,697,556	6,725,671
Factor income from abroad (net)	−360,983	−219,232	−353,792
Gross national product (GNP)	5,711,289	5,478,324	6,371,879
Less Consumption of fixed capital	401,871	357,608	395,928
National income in purchasers' values	5,309,418	5,120,716	5,975,951
Other transfers from abroad (net)	410,540	287,927	442,396
National disposable income	5,719,958	5,408,644	6,418,347

Expenditure on the Gross Domestic Product

	2008	2009*	2010†
Government final consumption expenditure	819,710	826,645	886,613
Private final consumption expenditure	4,018,275	4,281,535	4,899,780
Changes in stocks	466,746	29,244	−11,782
Gross fixed capital formation	1,067,345	1,142,324	1,344,701
Total domestic expenditure	6,372,076	6,279,748	7,119,312
Exports of goods and services	2,033,922	1,419,177	2,032,053
Less Imports of goods and services	2,333,726	2,001,369	2,425,694
GDP in purchasers' values	6,072,272	5,697,556	6,725,671
GDP at constant 2000 prices	2,561,890	2,672,684	2,854,039

2011 (preliminary estimates): Government final consumption expenditure 945,539; Private final consumption expenditure 4,573,171; Changes in stocks 205,420; Gross fixed capital formation 886,444; *Total domestic expenditure* 6,610,574; Exports of goods and services 2,118,762; *Less* Imports of goods and services 2,230,261; *GDP in purchasers' values* 6,499,075; *GDP at constant 2000 prices* 2,417,472.

Gross Domestic Product by Economic Activity

	2008	2009*	2010†
Agriculture, hunting, forestry and fishing‡	605,928	727,505	815,855
Mining and quarrying . . .	1,939,485	1,137,604	1,599,586
Manufacturing	341,377	389,056	440,462
Electricity, gas and water . .	41,283	46,225	53,226
Construction	275,576	322,225	386,868
Trade, restaurants and hotels .	1,008,629	1,138,650	1,303,949
Transport, storage and communications	677,769	749,638	823,577
Finance, insurance, real estate and business services . . .	471,472	470,563	539,694
Government services . . .	604,435	595,015	627,818
Other community, social and personal services . . .	52,762	57,843	61,700
Private non-profit services and services to households . .	4,625	5,305	5,938
Sub-total	6,023,341	5,639,629	6,658,672
Import duties (net) . . .	48,931	57,927	66,999
GDP in purchasers' values .	6,072,272	5,697,556	6,725,671

* Provisional.
† Preliminary estimates.
‡ Including production of qat.

2011 (preliminary estimates): Agriculture, hunting, forestry and fishing (incl. production of qat) 896,695; Mining and quarrying 1,802,362; Manufacturing 382,199; Electricity, gas and water 47,418; Construction 318,607; Trade, restaurants and hotels 1,048,248; Transport, storage and communications 675,383; Finance, insurance, real estate and business services 482,021; Government services 709,072; Other community, social and personal services 52,582; Private non-profit services and services to households 4,910; Sub-total 6,419,496; Import duties (net) 79,579; GDP in purchasers' values 6,499,075.

BALANCE OF PAYMENTS
(US $ million)

	2009	2010	2011
Exports of goods	5,855.0	7,649.8	8,662.2
Imports of goods	−7,867.8	−8,700.5	−8,248.4
Balance on goods	−2,012.8	−1,050.7	413.7
Exports of services	1,237.2	1,611.7	1,247.9
Imports of services	−2,132.8	−2,348.5	−2,273.1
Balance on goods and services	−2,908.5	−1,787.5	−611.5
Primary income received . .	115.0	54.5	53.3
Primary income paid . . .	−1,286.3	−1,771.6	−2,604.9
Balance on goods, services and primary income . . .	−4,079.8	−3,504.6	−3,163.1
Secondary income received . .	1,628.3	1,837.5	1,549.6
Secondary income paid . . .	−113.4	−57.7	−49.6
Current balance	−2,564.9	−1,724.8	−1,663.1
Capital account (net) . . .	—	88.4	—
Direct investment liabilities . .	129.2	−93.3	−712.8
Portfolio investment assets . .	−13.5	−358.1	114.5
Other investment assets . .	−574.9	61.3	38.4
Other investment liabilities . .	142.1	−209.1	−252.6
Net errors and omissions . .	1,589.6	674.7	354.7
Reserves and related items .	−1,292.4	−1,561.0	−2,121.0

Source: IMF, *International Financial Statistics*.

External Trade

PRINCIPAL COMMODITIES
(distribution by SITC, YR '000 million)

Imports c.i.f.	2009	2010	2011
Food and live animals	464.2	521.6	597.7
Cereal and cereal preparations . .	248.7	252.0	308.8
Wheat and meslin	148.9	154.9	205.7
Rice	61.5	54.1	50.5
Sugars, sugar preparations and honey .	55.6	78.6	111.5
Mineral fuels and lubricants . .	391.3	496.2	633.3
Petroleum and petroleum products . .	389.2	489.9	627.2
Animal and vegetable oils and fats .	22.0	69.6	41.8
Chemicals and related products .	128.9	154.5	140.1
Basic manufactures	250.2	284.7	201.0
Iron and steel	110.5	112.9	61.5
Machinery and transport equipment	431.4	438.1	312.3
Machinery specialized for particular industries	64.3	64.1	45.2
General industrial machinery, equipment and parts	55.6	54.5	42.9
Road vehicles	178.9	195.6	124.7
Passenger motor vehicles (excl. buses)	120.1	138.3	88.6
Miscellaneous manufactured articles	123.3	77.3	65.8
Total (incl. others)	1,861.7	2,095.1	2,037.4

Exports f.o.b.*	2009	2010	2011
Food and live animals	68.5	93.4	101.3
Fish and fish preparations	36.8	47.1	51.9
Mineral fuels and lubricants . . .	1,129.3	1,274.2	1,314.4
Petroleum and petroleum products . .	1,021.7	992.4	984.6
Petroleum oils and oils obtained from bituminous minerals, crude . .	94.2	120.9	61.7
Chemicals and related products .	14.7	22.9	49.2
Machinery and transport equipment	29.4	32.0	26.8
Road vehicles	11.7	8.3	9.5
Total (incl. others)	1,270.1	1,457.8	1,523.8

* Including re-exports.

PRINCIPAL TRADING PARTNERS
(distribution by SITC, YR '000 million)

Imports c.i.f.	2009	2010	2011
Argentina	26.5	29.3	33.8
Australia	62.4	38.9	38.4
Brazil	60.8	83.4	72.7
Canada	19.6	11.8	1.8
China, People's Republic . . .	152.4	144.1	121.4
Egypt	29.4	42.9	40.0
France (incl. Monaco)	35.6	56.4	46.9
Germany	38.6	34.4	25.7
India	60.5	61.6	93.1
Italy	18.4	29.2	14.1
Japan	31.7	39.2	17.7
Korea, Republic	24.5	24.0	16.0
Kuwait	84.3	82.3	85.7
Malaysia	39.0	74.6	46.8
Netherlands	66.7	132.1	157.9
Oman	36.8	45.3	37.2
Pakistan	16.3	19.2	27.8
Russia	18.6	16.1	15.7
Saudi Arabia	138.7	173.8	212.6
Singapore	27.0	21.1	30.8
Switzerland-Liechtenstein . .	102.3	24.0	174.5
Thailand	41.5	41.5	31.1
Turkey	72.1	63.5	49.3
United Arab Emirates	321.1	399.8	323.7
United Kingdom	26.0	27.5	23.9
USA	119.6	106.0	102.3
Total (incl. others)	1,861.7	2,095.1	2,037.4

Exports f.o.b.*	2009	2010	2011
Belgium	0.9	1.2	20.5
China, People's Republic	318.5	312.7	491.5
Egypt	5.0	9.4	15.0
France (incl. Monaco)	3.4	5.6	6.7
Greece	—	27.4	14.0
India	255.6	475.3	202.3
Japan	60.6	9.5	20.4
Korea, Republic	6.6	60.3	119.3
Kuwait	20.0	16.0	4.5
Malaysia	1.0	35.2	0.8
Netherlands	6.6	5.3	7.9
Saudi Arabia	38.5	58.7	86.2
Singapore	85.8	142.3	20.8
Somalia	11.7	20.4	15.0
South Africa	82.5	0.1	0.4
Switzerland-Liechtenstein	3.6	0.1	5.7
Thailand	231.8	50.8	271.5
United Arab Emirates	87.4	126.1	62.1
United Kingdom	2.7	10.8	27.9
USA	1.2	27.6	59.2
Viet Nam	5.4	6.1	12.1
Total (incl. others)	1,270.1	1,457.8	1,523.8

* Including re-exports.

Transport

ROAD TRAFFIC
(vehicles in use at 31 December)

	1994	1995	1996
Passenger cars	227,854	229,084	240,567
Buses and coaches	2,712	2,835	3,437
Goods vehicles	279,154	279,780	291,149

2004: Private cars 285,335; Taxi cars 36,371; Buses 22,214; Lorries 127,213; Motorcycles 64,845.

Source: IRF, *World Road Statistics*.

SHIPPING

Flag Registered Fleet
(at 31 December)

	2010	2011	2012
Number of vessels	41	41	40
Total displacement ('000 grt)	221.9	221.9	221.0

Source: Lloyd's List Intelligence (www.lloydslistintelligence.com).

International Sea-borne Freight Traffic
('000 metric tons, unless otherwise indicated, excluding dhows)

	2009	2010	2011
Vessels called (number)	2,831	2,813	2,152
Dry cargo:*			
goods loaded	400	487	377
goods unloaded	7,006	8,298	6,341
Oil products:			
goods loaded	5,064	5,026	3,832
goods unloaded	11,481	10,933	9,029

* Excluding livestock and vehicles.

CIVIL AVIATION
(traffic on scheduled services)

	2007	2008	2009
Kilometres flown (million)	22	24	24
Passengers carried ('000)	1,039	1,065	1,051
Passenger-km (million)	3,041	3,029	3,015
Total ton-km (million)	344	315	307

Source: UN, *Statistical Yearbook*.

2010: Passengers carried ('000) 1,134 (Source: World Bank, World Development Indicators database).

Tourism

TOURIST ARRIVALS

	2009	2010	2011
Africa	16,418	20,257	15,719
Djibouti	7,169	8,636	3,852
Ethiopia	6,711	9,359	8,134
Sudan	3,190	4,494	2,852
Americas	25,493	28,006	18,275
Asia	n.a.	64,292	38,068
India	n.a.	26,112	13,251
Pakistan	n.a.	7,681	5,350
Europe	43,493	32,057	13,380
France	6,141	5,567	2,724
Germany	4,257	4,559	1,235
Italy	2,749	2,003	791
United Kingdom	13,844	10,949	4,704
Middle East	296,906	390,112	301,631
Egypt	14,293	18,204	8,855
Iraq	3,447	3,271	2,669
Jordan	7,880	9,069	7,600
Oman	46,098	49,659	38,497
Saudi Arabia	163,000	235,412	198,823
Syria	10,792	14,668	12,876
United Arab Emirates	22,438	21,681	10,904
Total (incl. others)	433,921	536,020	387,498

Tourism receipts (US $ million): 903 in 2009; 1,161 in 2010; 780 in 2011.

Communications Media

	2009	2010	2011
Telephones ('000 main lines in use)	997	1,046	1,075
Mobile cellular telephones ('000 subscribers)	8,313	11,085	11,668
Internet subscribers ('000)	456	582	n.a.
Broadband subscribers ('000)	54	84	109

Source: International Telecommunication Union.

Education

(2010/11)

	Schools	Teachers	Males	Females	Total
			Students		
Pre-primary	485	1,999	16,143	13,713	29,856
Primary	12,376	120,339	2,667,272	1,989,118	4,656,390
Secondary	331	6,891	382,708	232,883	615,591
Higher	34	10,649	188,097	80,958	296,055

Pupil-teacher ratio (primary education, UNESCO estimates): 30.8 in 2009/10 (Source: UNESCO Institute for Statistics).

Adult literacy rate (UNESCO estimates): 63.9% (males 81.2%; females 46.8%) in 2010 (Source: UNESCO Institute for Statistics).

Directory

The Government

HEAD OF STATE

President: Field Marshal ABD AL-RABBUH MANSUR AL-HADI (took office 25 February 2012).

COUNCIL OF MINISTERS
(May 2013)

Prime Minister: MUHAMMAD SALEM BASINDWA.

Minister of Local Administration: ALI MUHAMMAD AL-YAZIDI.

Minister of Planning and International Co-operation: MUHAMMAD AL-SA'ADI.

Minister of the Interior: ABD AL-QADER QAHTAN.

Minister of Finance: SAKHR AHMED AL-WAJIH.

Minister of Oil and Minerals: HISHAM SHARAF.

Minister of Social Affairs and Labour: AMAT AL-RAZZAK ALI HAMAD.

Minister of Human Rights: HOURIAH AHMED MASHHOUR.

Minister of Transport: WA'ED ABDULLAH BATHIB.

Minister of Information: AHMED ALI AL-AMRANI.

Minister of Foreign Affairs: ABU BAKR AL-KURBI.

Minister of Expatriate Affairs: MUJAHID AL-QUHALI.

Minister of Electricity: SALEH HASAN SUMAI.

Minister of Legal Affairs: MUHAMMAD AHMED AL-MIKHLAFI.

Minister of Religious Endowments and Guidance: HAMOUD MUHAMMAD ABAD.

Minister of Culture: ABDULLAH AUBAL MANDHOUQ.

Minister of Agriculture and Irrigation: FARID AHMED MUJAWAR.

Minister of Industry and Trade: SAAD AL-DIN ALI BIN TALIB.

Minister of Public Health and Population: AHMED QASSIM AL-ANSI.

Minister of Education: ABD AL-RAZZAQ YAHYA AL-ASHWAL.

Minister of Fisheries: AWADH SAAD AL-SOCATRI.

Minister of Justice: MURSHED ALI AL-ARASHANI.

Minister of Higher Education and Scientific Research: YAHYA AL-SHU'AIBI.

Minister of Technical Education and Vocational Training: ABD AL-HAFEZ NOMU'AN.

Minister of Tourism: QASIM SALLAM.

Minister of the Civil Service and Social Security: NABIL SHAMSAN.

Minister of Telecommunications and Information Technology: AHMED OBAID BIN DAGHR.

Minister of Defence: Brig.-Gen. MUHAMMAD NASSER AHMAD ALI.

Minister of Public Works and Highways: OMAR ABDULLAH AL-KURSHUMI.

Minister of Water and the Environment: ABDO RAZZAZ SALEH KHALED.

Minister of Youth and Sports: MUAMMAR AL-ERYANI.

Minister of State for Parliament and Shoura Council Affairs: RASHAD AHMAD AL-RASSAS.

Minister of State for Cabinet Affairs: JAWHARAH HAMOUD THABET.

Minister of State: SHAIF EZI SAGHIR.

Minister of State: HASAN AHMED SHARAF AL-DIN.

MINISTRIES

Ministry of Agriculture and Irrigation: POB 2805, San'a; tel. (1) 282962; fax (1) 289509; internet www.agricultureyemen.com.

Ministry of Civil Service and Social Security: POB 1992, San'a; tel. (1) 282404; fax (1) 283592.

Ministry of Culture: San'a; tel. (1) 235461; fax (1) 251557; e-mail moc@y.net.ye; internet www.mocyemen.com.

Ministry of Defence: POB 1399, San'a; tel. (1) 252374; fax (1) 252378.

Ministry of Education: San'a; tel. (1) 274548; fax (1) 274555; e-mail moetele@yemen.net.ye; internet www.moe.gov.ye.

Ministry of Electricity: POB 11422, San'a; tel. (1) 326191; fax (1) 326214; e-mail yempec@y.net.ye.

Ministry of Expatriate Affairs: San'a; tel. (1) 402643; fax (1) 400710; e-mail info@iayemen.org; internet www.iayemen.org.

Ministry of Finance: POB 190, San'a; tel. (1) 260365; fax (1) 263040; e-mail support@mofyemen.net; internet www.mof.gov.ye.

Ministry of Fisheries: San'a; tel. (1) 268583; fax (1) 263182.

Ministry of Foreign Affairs: POB 1994, San'a; tel. (1) 276612; fax (1) 286618; e-mail mofa1@mofa.gov.ye; internet www.mofa.gov.ye.

Ministry of Higher Education and Scientific Research: San'a.

Ministry of Human Rights: San'a.

Ministry of Industry and Trade: POB 22210, San'a; tel. (1) 252345; fax (1) 252337; e-mail info@moitye.net; internet www.moit.gov.ye.

Ministry of Information: POB 3040, San'a; tel. (1) 274011; fax (1) 282004; e-mail yemen-info@y.net.ye.

Ministry of the Interior: POB 4991, San'a; tel. (1) 274147; fax (1) 332511; e-mail moi@yemen.net.ye; internet www.moi.gov.ye.

Ministry of Justice: San'a.

Ministry of Legal Affairs: POB 1192, San'a; tel. (1) 402213; fax (1) 402695; e-mail legal@y.net.ye; internet www.legalaffairs.gov.ye.

Ministry of Local Administration: POB 2198, San'a; tel. (1) 252532; fax (1) 251513; internet www.molayemen.com.

Ministry of Oil and Minerals: POB 81, San'a; tel. (1) 202306; fax (1) 202314; e-mail mom@y.net.ye; internet www.mom.gov.ye.

Ministry of Planning and International Co-operation: POB 175, San'a; tel. (1) 250713; fax (1) 250662; e-mail kamalmasoud@hotmail.com; internet www.mpic-yemen.org.

Ministry of Public Health and Population: POB 274160, San'a; tel. (1) 252193; fax (1) 252247; e-mail his@moh.gov.ye; internet www.mophp-ye.org.

Ministry of Public Works and Highways: San'a; tel. (1) 262602; fax (1) 262609; e-mail info@mpwh-ye.net; internet www.mpwh-ye.net.

Ministry of Religious Endowments and Guidance: San'a.

Ministry of Social Affairs and Labour: San'a; tel. (1) 274921; fax (1) 262806.

Ministry of State for Cabinet Affairs: San'a.

Ministry of State for Parliament and Shoura Council Affairs: San'a.

Ministry of Technical Education and Vocational Training: POB 25235, San'a; tel. (1) 406287; fax (1) 469043; e-mail mtevt@yemen.net.ye; internet www.mtevt.info.

Ministry of Telecommunications and Information Technology: San'a.

Ministry of Tourism: POB 5607, San'a; tel. (1) 570821; fax (1) 570823; e-mail tourism@yementourism.com; internet www.yementourism.com/gov.

Ministry of Transport: POB 2781, San'a; tel. (1) 260903; fax (1) 260901; e-mail mot@yemen.net.ye; internet www.mot.gov.ye.

Ministry of Water and the Environment: San'a; tel. (1) 418290; fax (1) 418282; internet www.mweye.org.

Ministry of Youth and Sports: POB 2414, San'a; tel. (1) 472901; fax (1) 472900; e-mail hamod.obad@yahoo.com.

President and Legislature

PRESIDENT

In accordance with an agreement between President Field Marshal Ali Abdullah Saleh and representatives of the opposition signed in Riyadh, Saudi Arabia, in late November 2011, Saleh transferred his constitutional powers to his Vice-President, Maj.-Gen. (latterly Field Marshal) Abd al-Rabbuh Mansur al-Hadi, on 23 December 2011, while retaining the title of President for a further three months. On 21 February 2012 an early presidential election took place, at which al-Hadi was the sole candidate. At the election, al-Hadi's candidacy was approved by 99.8% of participating voters. He was officially sworn into office on 25 February.

LEGISLATURE

House of Representatives

POB 623, San'a; tel. (1) 272761; fax (1) 276099; e-mail parliament.SG@y.net.ye.

Speaker: YAHYA ALI AL-RA'EI.

General Election, 27 April 2003

Party	Seats*
General People's Congress (GPC)	228
Yemeni Congregation for Reform (al-Islah) . . .	47
Independents	14
Yemen Socialist Party (YSP)	7
Nasserite Unionist Popular Organization	3
Arab Socialist Baath Party	2
Total	**301**

* Includes the results of three by-elections held in July 2003.

Election Commission

Supreme Commission for Elections and Referendums (SCER): POB 15491, San'a; tel. (1) 202345; fax (1) 402685; e-mail scer@y.net.ye; internet www.scer.org.ye; f. 1992; Chair. MUHAMMAD HUSSEIN HAIDAR AL-HAKIMI.

Political Organizations

In the former PDRY the Yemen Socialist Party (YSP) was the only legal political party until December 1989, when the formation of opposition parties was legalized. There were no political parties in the former YAR. The two leading parties that emerged in the unified Yemen were the General People's Congress and the YSP. During 1990 an estimated 30–40 further political parties were reported to have been formed, and in 1991 a law regulating the formation of political parties was approved. Following the civil war from May to July 1994, President Saleh excluded the YSP from the new Government formed in October. There were 22 registered political parties in April 2003.

General People's Congress (GPC): San'a; e-mail gpc@y.net.ye; internet www.almotamar.net; f. 1982; a broad grouping of supporters of President Saleh; Chair. Field Marshal ALI ABDULLAH SALEH; Sec.-Gen. ABD AL-LATIF AL-ZAYANI.

Al-Haq: San'a; f. 1995; conservative Islamic party; operates within the JMP opposition coalition; Sec.-Gen. HASSAN MUHAMMAD ZAID.

Joint Meeting Parties (JMP): San'a; f. 2006 as a coalition of five parties incl. al-Haq, al-Islah and the YSP; a sixth party, the Arab Socialist Baath Party, joined in 2008; Chair. SULTAN AL-SAMI.

League of the Sons of Yemen (Rabitat Abna' al-Yemen—RAY): Aden; e-mail services@ray-party.org; internet www.ray-party.org; f. 1951; represents interests of southern tribes; Chair. OMAR ABDULLAH AL-JIFRI; Sec.-Gen. MOHSIN MUHAMMAD BIN FAREED.

Nasserite Unionist Popular Organization: Aden; tel. (1) 536497; e-mail alwahdawinet@hotmail.com; internet www.alwahdawi.net; f. 1989 as a legal party; operates within the JMP opposition coalition; Sec.-Gen. SULTAN AL-ATWANI.

National Opposition Council: San'a; a coalition of eight small opposition parties.

Yemen Socialist Party (YSP): San'a; f. 1978 to succeed the United Political Organization—National Front (UPO—NF); fmrly Marxist-Leninist 'vanguard' party based on 'scientific socialism'; has Political Bureau and Cen. Cttee; mem. of the JMP opposition coalition; Chair. YASIN SAID NO'MAN.

Yemeni Congregation for Reform (al-Islah): POB 23090, San'a; tel. (3) 131001; fax (1) 383879; e-mail info@al-islah.net; internet www.al-islah.net; f. 1990 by mems of the legislature, other political figures and tribal leaders; seeks constitutional reform based on Islamic law; a leading mem. of the JMP opposition coalition; Chair. Sheikh MUHAMMAD ALI AL-YADOUMI; Sec.-Gen. ABD AL-WAHAB AL-ANISI.

Other parties in Yemen include the **Arab Socialist Baath Party**; the **Federation of Popular Forces**; the **Liberation Front Party**; the **Nasserite Democratic Party**; the **National Democratic Front**; the **National Social Party**; the **Popular Nasserite Reformation Party**; the **Social Green Party**; the **Yemen League**; the **Yemeni Unionist Congregation Party**; and the **Yemeni Unionist Rally Party**

Diplomatic Representation

EMBASSIES IN YEMEN

Algeria: POB 509, 67 Amman St, San'a; tel. (1) 206350; fax (1) 209688; e-mail ambalg-sa-ye@y.net.ye; Ambassador ABDELWAHAB ABU ZAHER.

Bulgaria: POB 1518, Asr, St 4, Residence 5, San'a; tel. (1) 208469; fax (1) 207924; e-mail embassy.sanaa@mfa.bg; internet www.mfa.bg/embassies/yemen; Ambassador BORIS BORISOV.

China, People's Republic: POB 482, az-Zubairy St, San'a; tel. (1) 275337; fax (1) 275341; e-mail chinaem@y.net.ye; internet ye.china-embassy.org; Ambassador CHANG HUA (designate).

Cuba: POB 15256, St 6B, Blk 9, House 3, Safia Zone, nr Amman St, San'a; tel. (1) 442321; fax (1) 442322; e-mail embacubayemen@y.net.ye; Ambassador BUENAVENTURA REYES ACOSTA.

Djibouti: POB 3322, 6 Amman St, San'a; tel. (1) 445236; fax (1) 445237; e-mail youssouf@y.net.ye; Ambassador MOHAMMED HERSI.

Egypt: POB 1134, Gamal Abd al-Nasser St, San'a; tel. (1) 275948; fax (1) 274196; Ambassador ASHRAF AQAL.

Eritrea: POB 11040, Western Safia Bldg, San'a; tel. (1) 209422; fax (1) 214088; Ambassador MOUSA YASSIN SHEIKH ALDDIN.

Ethiopia: POB 234, Al-Hamadani St, San'a; tel. (1) 208833; fax (1) 213780; e-mail ethoembs@y.net.ye; Ambassador ATO HASSEN ABDELLA.

France: POB 1286, cnr Sts 2 and 21, San'a; tel. (1) 268888; fax (1) 269160; e-mail sanaa@ambafrance-ye.org; internet www.ambafrance-ye.org; Ambassador FRANCK GELLET.

Germany: POB 2562, Hadda, San'a; tel. (1) 413174; fax (1) 413179; e-mail info@sanaa.diplo.de; internet www.sanaa.diplo.de; Ambassador HOLGER GREEN.

India: POB 1154, Bldg 12, Djibouti St, San'a; tel. (1) 441251; fax (1) 441257; e-mail indiaemb@y.net.ye; internet www.eoisanaa.com.ye; Ambassador AUSAF SAYEED.

Indonesia: POB 19873, Bldg 16, Beirut St, Haddah, San'a; tel. (1) 427210; fax (1) 427212; e-mail indosan@y.net.ye; Ambassador NOUR AL-AULIA'A.

Iran: POB 1437, Haddah St, San'a; tel. (1) 413552; fax (1) 414139; e-mail iriranemb@y.net.ye; Ambassador MAHMOUD ALI ZADA.

Iraq: POB 498, South Airport Rd, San'a; tel. (1) 440184; fax (1) 440187; e-mail snaemb@iraqmofamail.net; Ambassador (vacant).

Italy: POB 1152, Haddah St No. 131, San'a; tel. (1) 432587; fax (1) 432590; e-mail ambasciata.sanaa@esteri.it; internet www.ambsanaa.esteri.it; Ambassador LUCIANO GALLI.

Japan: POB 817, Haddah Area, San'a; tel. (1) 423700; fax (1) 417850; e-mail info@ye.emb-japan.go.jp; internet www.ye.emb-japan.go.jp; Ambassador KATSUYOSHI HAYASHI.

Jordan: POB 2152, Hadat Damascus St, San'a; tel. (1) 413276; fax (1) 414516; e-mail sanaa@fm.gov.jo; Ambassador SULEIMAN GHWEIRI.

Korea, Democratic People's Republic: POB 1209, al-Hasaba, Mazda Rd, San'a; tel. (1) 232340; Ambassador CHANG MYONG SON.

Korea, Republic: POB 5005, San'a; tel. (1) 431801; fax (1) 431806; e-mail yemen@mofat.go.kr; internet yem.mofat.go.kr/eng/af/yem/main; Ambassador PARK KYU-OCK.

Kuwait: POB 3746, South Ring Rd, San'a; tel. (1) 268876; fax (1) 268875; Ambassador FAHD SAAD SAEED AL-MAI'A.

Lebanon: POB 38, St 12, San'a; tel. (1) 203959; fax (1) 201120; e-mail lebem@y.net.ye; Ambassador (vacant).

Libya: POB 1506, Ring Rd, St 8, House 145, San'a; Secretary of Libyan Brotherhood Office MUSTAFA HWAIDI.

Malaysia: POB 16157, San'a; tel. (1) 429781; fax (1) 429783; e-mail malsanaa@kln.gov.my; internet www.kln.gov.my/perwakilan/yemen; Ambassador ABDULLAH FAIZ ZAIN.

Mauritania: POB 19383, No. 6, Algeria St, San'a; tel. (1) 264188; fax (1) 215926; Ambassador MUHAMMAD MAHFOUZ OULD AL-QADI.

Morocco: POB 3181, Faj Attan, Hay Assormi, ave Beyrouth, San'a; tel. (1) 426628; fax (1) 426627; e-mail sifama_sanaa@hotmail.com; Ambassador MUHAMMAD HAMMA.

Netherlands: POB 463, off 14th October St, San'a; tel. (1) 421800; fax 417280; e-mail saad@minbuza.nl; internet yemen.nlembassy.org; Ambassador J. VERHEUL.

Oman: POB 6163, 14th October St, al-Gala Quarter, Bldg 2, Khormaskar, San'a; tel. (1) 208874; fax (1) 204586; e-mail sanaa@mofa.gov.om; Ambassador ABDULLAH BIN HAMAD AL-BADI.

Pakistan: POB 2848, Ring Rd, off Haddah St, San'a; tel. (1) 248814; fax (1) 248866; e-mail pakembassy@yemen.net.ye; internet www.pakistanembassyyemen.com; Ambassador Dr IRFAN YUSUF SHAMI.

Qatar: POB 19717, San'a; tel. (1) 304640; fax (1) 304645; e-mail sanaa@mofa.gov.qa; Ambassador JASIM BIN ABD AL-AZIZ AL-BUAINAIN.

Russia: POB 1087, 26 September St, San'a; tel. (1) 278719; fax (1) 283142; e-mail remb@y.net.ye; internet www.rusemb-ye.org; Ambassador SERGEI KOZLOV.

Saudi Arabia: POB 1184, Zuhara House, Hadda Rd, San'a; tel. (1) 240429; Ambassador ALI BIN MUHAMMAD AL-HAMDAN.

Somalia: POB 101, San'a; tel. (1) 208864; e-mail webmaster@somaligov.net; internet www.yemen.somaligov.net; Ambassador AHMED OMAR HAMIIDI.

Spain: POB 7108, San'a; tel. (1) 429899; fax (1) 429893; e-mail emb .sanaa@maec.es; Ambassador FRANCISCO JAVIER HERGUETA GARNICA.

Sudan: POB 2561, 82 Abou al-Hassan al-Hamadani St, San'a; tel. (1) 265170; fax (1) 265234; Ambassador AWAD HUSSEIN RIZIQ.

Syria: POB 494, Hadda Rd, Damascus St 1, San'a; tel. (1) 414891; Ambassador (vacant).

Tunisia: POB 2561, Diplomatic Area, St 22, San'a; tel. (1) 471845; fax (1) 471840; Ambassador JAMAL AL-JUWEILI.

Turkey: POB 18371, San'a; tel. (1) 432890; fax (1) 434828; e-mail embassy.sanaa@mfa.gov.tr; internet sanaa.emb.mfa.gov.tr; Ambassador FAZLI ÇORMAN.

United Arab Emirates: POB 2250, Ring Rd, San'a; tel. (1) 248777; fax (1) 248779; e-mail sanaa@mofa.gov.ae; internet uae-embassy.ae/embassies/ye; Ambassador ABDULLAH MATAR AL-MAZROUEI.

United Kingdom: POB 1287, 938 Thaher Himiyar St, East Ring Rd, San'a; tel. (1) 308114; fax (1) 302454; e-mail BritishEmbassySanaa@fco.gov.uk; internet ukinyemen.fco.gov.uk; Ambassador NICHOLAS HOPTON.

USA: POB 22347, Sa'awan St, Sheraton Hotel District, San'a; tel. (1) 7552000; fax (1) 303182; e-mail passanaa@state.gov; internet yemen .usembassy.gov; Ambassador GERALD M. FEIERSTEIN.

Judicial System

Yemen's Constitution guarantees the independence of the judiciary and identifies Islamic law (*Shari'a*) as the basis of all laws.

Yemen is divided into 20 governorates in addition to the Capital Secretariat of San'a (a municipality), each of which is further divided into districts. Each district has a Court of First Instance in which all cases are heard by a single magistrate. Appeals against decisions of the Courts of First Instance are referred to a Court of Appeal. Each governorate has a Court of Appeal with four divisions: Civil, Criminal, Matrimonial and Commercial, each of which consists of three judges.

The Supreme Court of the Republic, which sits in San'a, rules on matters concerning the Constitution, appeals against decisions of the Courts of Appeal and cases brought against members of the legislature. The Supreme Court has eight divisions, each of which consists of five judges.

Supreme Judicial Council: The Supreme Judicial Council supervises the proper function of the courts, and its Chairman is the President of the Republic; Chief of Supreme Judicial Council Dr ALI NASSER SALEM.

Religion

ISLAM

The majority of the population are Muslims. Most are Sunni Muslims of the Shafi'a sect, except in the north-west of the country, where Zaidism (a moderate sect of the Shi'a order) is the dominant persuasion.

CHRISTIANITY

The Roman Catholic Church

Apostolic Vicariate of Southern Arabia: POB 54, Abu Dhabi, United Arab Emirates; tel. (2) 4461895; fax (2) 4465177; e-mail info@ccsarabia.org; internet www.ccsarabia.org; f. 1889 as Apostolic Vicariate of Arabia; renamed as above, following reorganization in 2011; responsible for a territory comprising the UAE, Oman and Yemen, with an estimated 650,000 Roman Catholics (31 December 2010); Vicar Apostolic PAUL HINDER (Titular Bishop of Macon, Georgia, resident in the UAE); Vicar-Gen. Most Rev. LENNIE CONNULLY.

The Anglican Communion

Within the Episcopal Church in Jerusalem and the Middle East, Yemen forms part of the diocese of Cyprus and the Gulf. The Anglican congregations in San'a and Aden are entirely expatriate; the Bishop in Cyprus and the Gulf is resident in Cyprus, while the Archdeacon in the Gulf is resident in Bahrain.

HINDUISM

There is a small Hindu community.

The Press

Legislation embodying the freedom of the press in the unified Republic of Yemen was enacted in May 1990. The lists below include publications that appeared in the YAR and the PDRY prior to their unification in May 1990.

DAILIES

Al-Ayyam: POB 648, al-Khalij al-Imami, Crater, Aden; tel. (2) 255170; fax (2) 255692; e-mail editor@al-ayyam-yemen.com; internet www.al-ayyam.info; f. 1958; Editor HISHAM BASHRAHEEL.

Al-Jumhuriya: Taiz Information Office, Taiz; tel. (4) 216748; Arabic; Deputy Editor ZAID MUHAMMAD AL-GHABIRI; circ. 100,000.

Al-Rabi' 'Ashar Min Uktubar (14 October): POB 4227, Crater, Aden; f. 1968; not publ. on Sat; Arabic; Editorial Dir FAROUQ MUSTAFA RIFAT; Chief Editor MUHAMMAD HUSSAIN MUHAMMAD; circ. 20,000.

Al-Sharara (The Spark): POB 4227, Crater, Aden; Arabic; circ. 6,000.

Al-Thawra (The Revolution): POB 2195, San'a; tel. (1) 262626; fax (1) 274139; e-mail contact@althawranews.net; internet www .althawranews.net; Arabic; govt-owned; Editor MUHAMMAD AL-ZORKAH; circ. 110,000.

PERIODICALS

Almotamar Net: San'a; tel. (1) 208934; fax (1) 402983; e-mail editing@almotamar.net; internet www.almotamar.net; online news organ of the General People's Congress; Editor-in-Chief ABD AL-MALIK AL-FUAIDI.

Attijarah (Trade): POB 3370, Hodeida; tel. (3) 213784; fax (3) 211528; e-mail hodcci@y.net.ye; monthly; Arabic; publ. by Hodeida Chamber of Commerce.

Al-Balagh: San'a; tel. (1) 280581; fax (1) 280584; internet www .al-balagh.net; Arabic; weekly; Editor ABDULLAH IBRAHIM.

Al-Bilad (The Country): POB 1438, San'a; weekly; Arabic; centre-right; Editor-in-Chief ABD AL-MALIK AL-FAISHANI.

Dar al-Salam (Peace): POB 1790, San'a; tel. (1) 272946; f. 1948; weekly; Arabic; political, economic and general essays; Editor ABDULLAH MUKBOOL AL-SICGUL.

Al-Hares: Aden; fortnightly; Arabic; publ. by Ministry of the Interior; circ. 8,000.

Al-Hikma (Wisdom): POB 4227, Crater, Aden; monthly; Arabic; publ. by the Writers' Union; circ. 5,000.

Al-Mithaq (The Charter): San'a; weekly; organ of the Gen. People's Congress.

Al-Ra'i al-'Am (Public Opinion): POB 293, San'a; tel. (1) 253785; fax (1) 223378; e-mail alraialaam2002@yahoo.com; internet www .alraialaam.com.ye; weekly; independent; Editor KAMAL ALUFI.

Ray: Aden; tel. (1) 400532; internet www.ray-yem.com; Arabic; organ of League of the Sons of Yemen.

Al-Risalah: POB 55777, 26 September St, Taiz; tel. (4) 214215; fax (4) 221164; e-mail alaws@y.net.ye; f. 1968; weekly; Arabic; publ. by Assalam Trading Houses.

Al-Sahwa (Awakening): POB 11126, Hadda Rd, San'a; tel. (1) 247892; fax (1) 269218; e-mail aa230317@yahoo.com; internet www.alsahwa-yemen.net; weekly; publ. by Yemeni Congregation for Reform (al-Islah); Editor-in-Chief MUHAMMAD YOUSUFI.

Sawt al-Yemen (Voice of Yemen): POB 302, San'a; weekly; Arabic.

Al-Shoura: POB 15114, San'a; tel. (1) 251106; fax (1) 251104; e-mail shoura@y.net.ye; internet www.y.net.ye/shoura; circ. 15,000.

Al-Thawry (The Revolutionary): POB 4227, Crater, Aden; internet www.althawry.org; weekly, on Sat.; Arabic; organ of Cen. Cttee of Yemen Socialist Party.

26 September: POB 17, San'a; tel. (1) 262626; fax (1) 274139; e-mail 26sept@yemen.net.ye; internet www.26september.info; armed forces weekly; Editor-in-Chief ALI AL-SHATIR; circ. 25,000.

Al-Wahda al-Watani (National Unity): Al-Baath Printing House, POB 193, San'a; tel. (1) 77511; f. 1982; fmrly Al-Omal; monthly; Editor MUHAMMAD SALEM ALI; circ. 40,000.

Al-Wahdawi: POB 13010, San'a; tel. (1) 536497; e-mail alwahdawinet@hotmail.com; internet www.alwahdawi.net; weekly; organ of Nasserite Unionist Popular Org.

Yemen Observer: POB 19183, San'a; tel. (1) 505466; fax (1) 260504; e-mail contact@yobserver.com; internet www.yobserver.com; f. 1996; twice-weekly; English; publ. by Yemen Observer Publishing House; Editor-in-Chief ZAID AL-ALAYA'A.

Yemen Post: POB 15531, San'a; tel. (1) 000202; fax (1) 539268; e-mail editor@yemenpost.net; internet www.yemenpost.net; f. 2007; English; weekly; Editor-in-Chief HAKIM AL-MASMARI.

The Yemen Times: POB 2579, Hadda St, San'a; tel. (1) 268661; fax (1) 268276; e-mail yementimes@yementimes.com; internet www

.yementimes.com; f. 1990; Mon. and Thur.; English; privately owned; Editor-in-Chief NADIA AL-SAQQAF; circ. 30,000.

Yemen Today: POB 19183, San'a; tel. (1) 248444; fax (1) 260504; e-mail info@yemen-today.com; internet www.yemen-today.com; f. 2007; monthly; English; politics and current affairs; publ. by Yemen Observer Publishing House; Man. Editor DAVID MACDONALD.

Yemeni Women: POB 4227, Crater, Aden; monthly; circ. 5,000.

PRESS ASSOCIATION

Yemeni Journalists Syndicate: San'a; internet yemenjournalist .org; Chair. YASSIN AL-MASOUDI; Sec.-Gen. MARWAN AL-DAMMAJ.

NEWS AGENCY

Yemen News Agency (SABA): Five Story Office Bldg and Printing Plant, al-Jama'ah al-Arabia St, al-Hasaba, San'a; tel. (1) 252944; fax (1) 251586; e-mail info@sabanews.net; internet www.sabanews.net; f. 1990 by merger of Saba News Agency and Aden News Agency following reunification of Yemen; mem. of the Fed. of Arab News Agencies and of the Non-Aligned News Agencies; Editor-in-Chief NASR TAHA MUSTAFA.

Publishers

Armed Forces Printing Press: POB 17, San'a; tel. (1) 274240; publishes *26 September*.

14 October Corpn for Printing, Publishing, Distribution and Advertising: POB 4227, Crater, Aden; under control of the Ministry of Information; publs include *Al-Rabi' 'Ashar Min Uktubar*; Chair. AHMAD AL-HUBAISHI.

Al-Thawrah Corpn: POB 2195, San'a; fax (1) 251505; Chair. M. R. AL-ZURKAH.

Yemen Observer Publishing House: POB 19183, San'a; tel. (1) 248444; fax (1) 260504; e-mail contact@yobserver.com; internet www .yobserver.com; f. 1996; publs include *Yemen Observer* and *Yemen Today*; Publr FARIS ABDULLAH SANABANI.

PUBLISHERS' ASSOCIATION

Yemeni Publishers' Association: f. 2008; Man. Dr NABIL ABADI.

Broadcasting and Communications

TELECOMMUNICATIONS

HiTs-Unitel (Y): San'a; tel. (700) 700111; internet www.y-gsm.com; f. 2007; provides mobile telephone services; Chair. NADER KALAI; CEO IMAD HAMAD.

MTN Yemen: POB 4562, San'a; e-mail ashahidi@mtn.com.ye; internet www.mtn.com.ye; f. 2000 as Spacetel Yemen; renamed as above in 2006, following merger of MTN Group Ltd with Investcom LLC; provides mobile services; CEO RAED AHMAD.

Public Telecommunications Corpn: POB 17045, Airport Rd, al-Jiraf, San'a; tel. and fax (1) 331109; e-mail ptc@yemen.net.ye; internet www.ptc.gov.ye; state-owned; Dir-Gen. MUHAMMAD AL-KASSOUS.

Yemen International Telecommunications Co (TeleYemen): POB 168, al-Tahreer Area, San'a; tel. (1) 7522000; fax (1) 270848; e-mail teleyemen@y.net.ye; internet www.teleyemen.com.ye; f. 1990 as a jt venture with Cable and Wireless PLC (United Kingdom); wholly owned by Public Telecommunications Corpn since 2003; provides fixed-line, mobile and internet services; CEO HESHAM AL-ALAILI.

Yemen Mobile Co: San'a; internet www.yemenmobile.com.ye; f. 2004 as a subsidiary of Yemen Int. Telecommunications Co (TeleYemen); initial public offering of 45% of shares in 2006; provides mobile services; Chair. ALI NAJI NASRI; CEO SADEK MUHAMMAD MOUSLEH; 1.9m. subscribers (2009).

Yemen Co for Mobile Telephony (SabaFon): POB 18550, San'a; e-mail website@sabafon.com; internet www.sabafon.com; f. 2001; shareholders include Al-Ahmar Group For Trade, the Iran Foreign Investment Co and Batelco (Bahrain); provides mobile services; Chair. Sheikh HAMID AL-AHMAR; CEO TARIK AL-HAIDARY.

BROADCASTING

Yemen Radio and Television Corpn: POB 2182, San'a; tel. (1) 230654; fax (1) 230761; e-mail info@yemenradio.net; internet www .yemenradio.net; state-controlled; operates two television channels and eight regional radio stations for San'a, Taiz, Mukalla, Aden, Lahij, Sayoun, Hodeida and Abyan; Chair. ABDULLAH AL-ZALAB; Gen. Man. AHMAD T. SHAYANY.

Finance

(cap. = capital; res = reserves; dep. = deposits; m. = million; brs = branches; amounts in Yemeni riyals unless otherwise indicated)

BANKING

Central Bank

Central Bank of Yemen: POB 59, Ali Abd al-Mughni St, San'a; tel. (1) 274314; fax (1) 274360; e-mail cbyh@y.net.ye; internet www .centralbank.gov.ye; f. 1971; merged with Bank of Yemen in 1990; cap. 6,000m., res 275,871m., dep. 773,681m. (Dec. 2009); Gov. MUHAMMAD AWAD BIN HUMAM; Dep. Gov. MUHAMMAD AL-RUBIDI; 20 brs.

Principal Banks

Co-operative and Agricultural Credit Bank (CACBANK): POB 2015, Banks Complex, al-Zubairy St, San'a; tel. and fax (1) 250009; e-mail info@cacbank.com.ye; internet www.cacbank.com.ye; f. 1976; cap. 11,000m., res 310m., dep. 212,861m. (Dec. 2011); Chair. MEHDAR ABDULLAH AL-SAGGAF; 54 brs.

International Bank of Yemen YSC: POB 4444, 106 al-Zubairy St, San'a; tel. (1) 407000; fax (1) 407020; e-mail info@ibyemen.com; internet www.ibyemen.com; f. 1980; commercial bank; 75% private Yemeni interests; 25% foreign shareholders; cap. 8,000m., res 1,950m., dep. 168,712m. (Dec. 2010); Chair. HAYEL A. HAQ BESHER (acting); Gen. Man. AHMAD T. N. AL-ABSI; 19 brs.

Islamic Bank of Yemen for Finance and Investment: POB 18452, Mareb Yemen Insurance Co Bldg, al-Zubairy St, San'a; tel. (1) 206117; fax (1) 206116; internet www.islbank.com; f. 1996; savings, commercial, investment and retail banking; cap. 3,568m., res 1,449m., dep. 12,616m. (Dec. 2009); Chair. ABD AL-KAREM AL-ASWADI; Man. Dir KHALED AL-DUSARI; 5 brs.

National Bank of Yemen: POB 5, Arwa Rd, Crater, Aden; tel. (2) 253753; fax (2) 252325; e-mail nby.ho@y.net.ye; internet www .nbyemen.com; f. 1970 as Nat. Bank of South Yemen; reorg. 1971; 100% state-owned; cap. 10,000m., res 3,554m., dep. 92,125m. (Dec. 2010); Chair. AHMED OBAID AL-FADHLI; Gen. Man. ESAM ALAWI AL-SAKKAF; 28 brs.

Shamil Bank of Yemen and Bahrain: POB 19382, Haddah St, San'a; tel. (1) 411847; fax (1) 411848; e-mail shamilbank@y.net.ye; internet www.sbyb.net; f. 2002; cap. 6,000m., res 136m., dep. 22,586m. (Dec. 2010); Chair. AHMAD ABUBAKER OMER BAZARA; Gen. Man. SAEED MUHAMMAD BAZARA.

Tadhamon International Islamic Bank: POB 2411, al-Saeed Commercial Bldg, al-Zubairy St, San'a; e-mail tib@y.net.ye; internet www.tiib.com; f. 1995 as Yemen Bank for Investment and Devt; became Tadhamon Islamic Bank in 1996; name changed as above in 2002; cap. 20,000m., res 29,113m., dep. 323,016m. (Dec. 2010); Chair. ABD AL-GABBAR HAYEL SAID; Man. Dir SHAWKI AHMED HAYEL; 21 brs.

Yemen Bank for Reconstruction and Development (YBRD): POB 541, 26 September St, San'a; tel. (1) 270483; fax (1) 271684; e-mail ybrdho@y.net.ye; internet www.ybrd.com.ye; f. 1962; 51% state-owned; 49% owned by public shareholders; cap. 10,000m., res 4,225m., dep. 111,158m. (Dec. 2010); Chair. HUSSAIN FADHL MUHAMMAD HARHARA; Gen. Man. ABD AL-NASER NOMAN AL-HAJ; 43 brs.

Yemen Commercial Bank (YCB): POB 19845, al-Rowaishan Bldg, al-Zubairy St, San'a; tel. (1) 277224; fax (1) 277291; e-mail info@ycb .com.ye; internet www.ycb.com.ye; f. 1993; cap. 6,926m., res 619m., dep. 83,361m. (Dec. 2010); Board Dir Sheikh MUHAMMAD BIN YAHYA AL-ROWAISHAN; Exec. Pres. and Gen. Man. AYED AL-MASHNI; 13 brs.

INSURANCE

Aman Insurance Co (YSC): POB 1133, al-Zubairy St, San'a; tel. (1) 202106; fax (1) 209452; e-mail akil@amaninsurance-ye.com; internet www.y.net.ye/amaninsurance; all classes of insurance; Chair. MUHAMMAD ABDULLAH AL-SUNIDAR; Man. Dir AKIL AL-SAKKAF.

Mareb Yemen Insurance Co: POB 2284, al-Zubairy St, San'a; tel. (1) 206111; fax (1) 206118; e-mail maryinsco74@y.net.ye; internet www.marebinsurance.com.ye; f. 1974; all classes of insurance; cap. 150m.; Chair. and CEO ALI MUHAMMAD HASHIM; Gen. Man. ALI ABD AL-RASHID.

Saba Yemen Insurance Co: POB 19214, Ishaq Bldg, al-Zubairy St, San'a; tel. (1) 240908; fax (1) 240943; e-mail saba-ins@y.net.ye; internet www.saba-insurance.com; f. 1990; all classes of insurance; cap. 400m. (Jan. 2006); Chair. Sheikh MUHAMMAD BIN YAHIAH AL-ROWAISHAN; Man. Dir MUHAMMAD HUSSEIN ZAWIYAH.

Trust Yemen Insurance and Reinsurance Co: POB 18392, San'a; tel. (1) 425007; fax (1) 412570; e-mail trust-yemen@y.net.ye; internet www.trustgroup.net/Main; f. 1995; all classes of insurance; Chair. ALI DHIB; Gen. Man. HUSSAIN AYYOUB.

United Insurance Co: POB 1883, al-Saeed Commercial Bldg, 2nd Floor, al-Zubairy St, San'a; tel. (1) 555555; fax (1) 214012; e-mail uuicyemen@uicyemen.com; internet www.uicyemen.com; f. 1981; general and life insurance; cap. 400m. (2005); Chair. AHMAD SAID; Gen. Man. TAREK A. HAYEL SAID.

Al-Watania Insurance Co (YSC): POB 15497, al-Kasr St, San'a; tel. (1) 272874; fax (1) 272924; e-mail alwatania-ins@y.net.ye; internet www.alwataniains.com; f. 1993; all classes of insurance; cap. 100m. (2005); Exec. Chair. YOUSUF ABD AL-WADUD SAID.

Yemen General Insurance Co (SYC): POB 2709, YGI Bldg, 25 Algiers St, San'a; tel. (1) 442489; fax (1) 442492; e-mail ygi-san@y.net .ye; internet www.yginsurance.com; f. 1977; all classes of insurance; cap. 500m. (2005); Chair. ABD AL-GABBAR THABET; Gen. Man. BAKIR AL-MUNSHI.

Yemen Insurance Co: POB 8437, San'a; tel. (1) 272806; fax (1) 274177; e-mail sanaa@yemenins.com; internet yemenins.com; f. 1990; all classes of insurance; cap. 100m.; Chair. MUHAMMAD MUBARAK ADHBAN; Gen. Man. KHALID BASHIR TAHIR.

Yemen Insurance and Reinsurance Co: POB 456, Aden; tel. (2) 54286; fax (2) 57336; e-mail yireico@y.net.ye; f. 1969; Lloyd's Agents; cap. 5m.; Gen. Man. HUSSAIN AL-HADDAD.

Trade and Industry

GOVERNMENT AGENCIES

General Investment Authority (GIAY): POB 19022, Hadda St, San'a; tel. (1) 434312; fax (1) 434314; e-mail investinyemen.gov .ye; internet www.investinyemen.gov.ye; f. 1992; promotes and facilitates strategic investment in Yemen; Chair. SALEH MUHAMMAD SAID AL-ATTAR.

Yemen Economic Corpn: POB 1207, San'a; tel. (1) 262501; fax (1) 262508; e-mail yeco@yeco.biz; internet www.yeco.biz; f. 1973; promotes and facilitates investment and development across various sectors of the economy; Gen. Man. ALI MUHAMMAD AL-KUHLANI.

DEVELOPMENT ORGANIZATIONS

Agricultural Research and Extension Authority: POB 87148, Dhamar; tel. (6) 423913; fax (6) 423914; e-mail area@yemen.net.ye; internet www.area.gov.ye; Chair. Dr ISMAIL A. MUHARRAM.

Social Fund for Development (SFD): POB 15485, Fij Attan, San'a; tel. (1) 449669; fax (1) 449670; e-mail sfd@sfd-yemen.org; internet www.sfd-yemen.org; f. 1997; autonomous devt agency, governed by a bd of dirs representing the Govt, non-governmental orgs and the private sector, chaired by the Prime Minister.

Tihama Development Authority: POB 3792, Doreihemy Rd, Hodeida; e-mail arcechodeida@y.net.ye; agricultural devt agency under the supervision of the Ministry of Agriculture and Irrigation; Chair. MUHAMMAD YAHIA AL-GASHAM.

Yemen Free Zone Public Authority: POB 5842, Aden; tel. (2) 241210; fax (2) 221237; e-mail yfzpa@y.net.ye; internet www .yemenfreezone.com; f. 1991; supervises creation of a free zone for industrial investment; Vice-Chair. ABD AL-GALIL SHAIF AL-SHAIBI.

CHAMBERS OF COMMERCE

Chamber of Commerce and Industry—Aden: POB 473, Crater 101, Aden; tel. (2) 251104; fax (2) 255446; e-mail cciaden@yemen.net .ye; internet www.adenchamber.org; f. 1886; 9,000 mems; Chair. MUHAMMAD OMER BAMASHMUS; Dir-Gen. KHALIL TAHA KHALIL.

Federation of Chambers of Commerce: POB 16992, San'a; tel. (1) 232445; fax (1) 221765; e-mail moh-saeed@fycci.org; internet www.fycci.org; Chair. MUHAMMAD ABDO SAID AN'AM; Dir-Gen. MUHAMMAD AL-MAITAMI.

Hadramout Chamber of Commerce and Industry: POB 8302, Main St, Mukalla City, Hadramout; tel. (5) 353258; fax (5) 303437; e-mail hdramoutchamber@y.net.ye; Chair. OMER A. R. BAJARASH.

Hodeida Chamber of Commerce: POB 3370, 20 al-Zubairy St, Hodeida; tel. (3) 217401; fax (3) 211528; e-mail hodcci@y.net.ye; f. 1960; 6,500 mems; cap. YR 10m.; Dir NABIL AL-WAGEEH.

Ibb Chamber of Commerce and Industry: POB 70004, Ibb; tel. (4) 404868; fax (4) 403893.

Saadah Chamber of Commerce and Industry: POB 3754-2566, Saadah; tel. (7) 521524; fax (7) 513671; Chair. MUHAMMAD R. JARMAN.

San'a Chamber of Commerce and Industry: Airport Rd, al-Hasabah St, POB 195, San'a; tel. (1) 232361; fax (1) 232412; e-mail sanaacomyemen@y.net.ye; f. 1959; over 35,000 mems; Chair. HASSAN AL-KABOUS; Gen. Man. MUHAMMAD AL-MAHALLA.

Taiz Chamber of Commerce and Industry: POB 5029, Chamber St, Taiz; tel. (4) 210580; fax (4) 212335; e-mail taizchamber@y.net.ye; internet www.taizchamber.com; f. 1962; 5,600 mems; Chair. AHMED HAYEL SAID; Dir MOFID A. SAIF.

Thamar Chamber of Commerce and Industry: POB 87010, Thamar; tel. (5) 502200; fax (6) 501191.

STATE ENTERPRISES

While the Government is committed to privatization in all areas of trade and industry, there are still numerous state-owned enterprises:

General Corpn for Foreign Trade and Grains: POB 710, San'a; tel. (1) 202361; fax (1) 209511; f. 1976; Dir-Gen. ABD AL-RAHMAN AL-MADWAHI.

General Corpn for Manufacturing and Marketing of Cement: POB 1920, San'a; tel. (1) 215691; fax (1) 263168; Chair. AMIN ABD AL-WAHID AHMAD.

National Co for Foreign Trade: POB 90, Crater, Aden; tel. (2) 42793; fax (2) 42631; f. 1969; incorporates main foreign trading businesses (nationalized in 1970) and arranges their supply to the National Co for Home Trade; Gen. Man. AHMAD MUHAMMAD SALEH (acting).

National Co for Home Trade: POB 90, Crater, Aden; tel. (2) 41483; fax (2) 41226; f. 1969; marketing of general consumer goods, building materials, electrical goods, motor cars and spare parts, agricultural machinery, etc.; Man. Dir ABD AL-RAHMAN AL-SAILANI.

National Dockyards Co: POB 1244, Hedjuff, Aden; tel. (2) 244503; fax (2) 241681; f. 1969; maintenance and repair of ships and vessels; marine engineering; Man. Dir ABDULLAH ALI MUHAMMAD.

Yemen Drug Co for Industry and Commerce (YEDCO): POB 40, San'a; tel. (1) 370210; fax (1) 370209; e-mail yedco@y.net.ye; import, maufacture and distribution of pharmaceutical products, chemicals, medical supplies, baby foods and scientific instruments; Chair. MUHAMMAD AL-KOHLANI; Gen. Man. MUHAMMAD ALI AL-KADIR.

Yemen Trading and Construction Co: POB 1092, San'a; tel. (1) 264005; fax (1) 240624; e-mail ytcc@y.net.ye; f. 1979; initial cap. YR 100m.; Gen. Man. GHASSAN AMIN KASSIM.

STATE HYDROCARBONS COMPANIES

General Corpn for Oil and Mineral Resources: San'a; f. 1990; state petroleum co; Pres. AHMAD BARAKAT.

Ministry of Oil and Minerals: POB 81, San'a; tel. (1) 202306; fax (1) 202314; e-mail mom@y.net.ye; internet www.mom.gov.ye; responsible for the refining and marketing of petroleum products, and for prospecting and exploitation of indigenous hydrocarbons and other minerals; subsidiaries include:

Aden Refinery Co: POB 3003, Aden 110; tel. (2) 376214; fax (2) 376600; e-mail info@arc-ye.com; internet www.arc-ye.com; f. 1952; operates petroleum refinery; capacity 8.6m. metric tons per year; operates two general tankers and one chemical tanker; Exec. Dir FATHI SALEM ALI; Refinery Man. MUHAMMAD YESLAM.

Petroleum Exploration and Production Authority (PEPA): POB 7196, Haddah St, San'a; tel. (1) 442630; fax (1) 442632; e-mail pepa-expo.com@y.net.ye; internet www.pepa.com.ye; f. 1990; manages petroleum concessions; Chair. NASSER ALI AL-HOMADY.

Safer Exploration and Production Operations Co: POB 481, San'a; tel. (1) 416080; e-mail webmaster@sepocye.com; internet www.sepocye.com; f. 1997; operation of Marib/Al-Jawf Blk 18 since 2005; Exec. Man. MUHAMMAD HUSSAIN AL-HAJ.

Yemen Co for Investment in Oil and Minerals: POB 11993, San'a; tel. (1) 203925; fax (1) 203923; e-mail yicom@y.net.ye; internet www.yicom.net; promotes investment in new exploration areas; supervises operators in several exploration blocks; Exec. Gen. Man. Eng. ALI AL-KADI.

Yemen Gas Co: al-Raqas St, San'a; internet www.yemengasco .com; f. 1993 as Gen. Gas Corpn; renamed as above 1996; 100% govt-owned; production and distribution of LPG; Deputy Dir NAJEEB AL-OUD.

Yemen General Oil and Gas Corporation: POB 19137, San'a; tel. (1) 446857; fax (1) 446417; e-mail info@yogc.com.ye; internet www.yogc.com.ye; f. 1996; Exec. Dir ABD AL-KADER SHAEA.

Yemen National Oil Co: POB 5050, Ma'alla, Aden; importer and distributor of petroleum products; Gen. Man. MUHAMMAD ABD HUSSEIN.

Yemen Oil Refinery Co: POB 15203, San'a; tel. and fax (1) 218962; e-mail info@yorco.net; internet www.yorco.net; f. 1996; operates petroleum refinery at Marib; Gen. Man. Eng. MUSAD AHMAD AL-SUBARI.

Yemen Petroleum Co: tel. (1) 444046; fax (1) 447691; internet www.ypcye.com; f. 1961; responsible for marketing of oil in domestic market; Exec. Dir OMAR MUHAMMAD ISMAIL AL-ARHABI.

Yemen LNG Co Ltd: POB 15347, San'a; tel. (1) 438000; fax (1) 428042; e-mail pr@yemenlng.com; internet www.yemenlng.com; f. 2005; shareholders include Total SA (France—39.62%), Hunt Oil (USA—17.22%), Yemen Gas Co (16.73%), SK Corpn (Repub. of

Korea—9.55%); operates a two-train LNG plant in Marib region; Chair. AMIR SALIM AL-AIDAROUS (Minister of Oil and Minerals); Gen. Man. JOEL FORT.

UTILITIES
Electricity

Public Electricity Corpn: POB 178, Airport Rd, San'a; tel. (1) 328141; fax (1) 328150; e-mail ypecnt@y.net.ye; Man. Dir ABD AL-MONIM MUTAHAR.

Water

General Authority for Rural Water Supply Projects (GARWSP): San'a; govt agency responsible for water supply in rural areas.

National Water Resources Authority (NWRA): POB 8944, Amran St, al-Hassaba, San'a; tel. (1) 231733; e-mail info@nwra-yemen.org; internet www.nwra-yemen.org; govt agency responsible for management of water resources; Chair. SALEM HASSAN BASHUEB.

National Water and Sewerage Authority (NWSA): POB 104, San'a; tel. (1) 250158; fax (1) 251536; e-mail NWSA@y.net.ye; govt agency responsible for water supply in urban areas.

TRADE UNIONS

General Confederation of Workers: POB 1162, Ma'alla, Aden; f. 1956; affiliated to WFTU; 35,000 mems; Pres. RAJEH SALEH NAJI; Gen. Sec. ABD AL-RAZAK SHAIF.

Trade Union Federation: San'a; Pres. ALI SAIF MUQBIL.

Transport

RAILWAYS
There are no railways in Yemen.

ROADS
In 1996 Yemen had a total road network of 64,725 km, including 5,234 km of main roads and 2,474 km of secondary roads. In 2006 there were an estimated 73,200 km of roads; some 13.7% of the road network was paved.

General Corpn for Roads and Bridges: POB 1185, al-Zubairy St, Asir Rd, San'a; tel. (1) 202278; fax (1) 209571; e-mail gcrb@y.net.ye; responsible for maintenance and construction.

Yemen Land Transport Co: POB 279, Taiz St, San'a; tel. (1) 262108; fax (1) 263117; f. 1961; incorporates fmr Yemen Bus Co and all other public transport of the fmr PDRY; oversees provision of public transport; scheduled for privatization; Chair. YAHYA AHMED AL-KOHLANI; Gen. Man. SALEH ABDULLAH ABD AL-WALI.

SHIPPING
Aden is the main port. Aden Main Harbour has 28 first-class berths. In addition, there is ample room to accommodate vessels of light draught at anchor in the 18-ft dredged area. There is also 800 ft of cargo wharf accommodating vessels of 300 ft length and 18 ft draught. Aden Oil Harbour accommodates four tankers of 57,000 metric tons and up to 40 ft draught. A long-term concession to operate Aden Container Terminal and nearby Ma'alla Container Terminal, in partnership with the Gulf of Aden Port Corporation, was signed by Dubai Ports World, of the United Arab Emirates, in late 2005 and came into effect in November 2008, incorporating an estimated US $220m. upgrade programme; this was expected to increase the annual capacity from 700,000 containers in 2007 to 1.5m. containers by 2012. Total container throughput at Aden was 265,459 20-ft equivalent units in 2009. Hodeida port, on the Red Sea, also handles a considerable amount of traffic. The port of Bal Haf has been developed to accommodate natural gas liquefaction and export facilities; shipments commenced in late 2009. Al-Mukalla port, in Hadramout province, is an important regional centre for trade, fishing and shipbuilding. Plans to develop a new industrial port at Dhabah, also in Hadramout, were announced in 2009.

At 31 December 2012 Yemen's flag registered fleet comprised 40 vessels, with a combined displacement of some 220,977 grt, of which one was a fish carrier and six were general cargo ships.

Regulatory and Port Authorities

Maritime Affairs Authority: POB 1443, San'a; tel. (2) 221581; fax (2) 221448; e-mail maa-headoffice@y.net.ye; internet www.maa-yemen.net; f. 1990 as Public Corpn for Maritime Affairs; renamed as above 2001; protection of the marine environment; registration of ships; implementation of international maritime conventions; Capt. ABDULLAH IBRAHIM ABKAR AL-NEGRI.

Yemen Arabian Sea Ports Corpn: POB 50793, al-Mukalla, Hadramout; tel. (5) 305560; fax (5) 303508; e-mail info@portofmukalla.com; internet www.portofmukalla.com; management and supervision of ports at al-Mukalla and Socotra; Chair. ABD AL-HAFEDH AL-QUAITI.

Yemen Gulf of Aden Ports Corpn: POB 1316, Tawahi, Aden; tel. (2) 202666; fax (2) 203521; e-mail info@portofaden.net; internet www.portofaden.net; f. 1888; management and supervision of Port of Aden and other ports in the western Gulf of Aden; Chair. Capt. MUHAMMAD ISHAQ; Port Officer Capt. SHAKEEB M. ABD AL-WAHED.

Yemen Red Sea Ports Corpn: Hodeidah; tel. (3) 211603; fax (3) 211561; e-mail chairman@portofhodeidah.com; internet www.portofhodeidah.com; management and supervision of the Port of Hodeidah as the main port and ports of Mokha and Saleef as secondary ports.

Principal Shipping Companies

Atlas Shipping and Transport Co Ltd: POB 3182, Hodeida; tel. (3) 202053; fax (3) 202057; e-mail atlas@atlasye.com; internet www.atlasye.com; f. 1998; subsidiary of Al-Hadha Group; shipping agents, cargo, bunkering.

Al-Bukari Shipping Co Ltd: POB 3358, Hodeida; tel. (3) 222888; fax (3) 211741; e-mail bukari@y.net.ye; internet www.bukarishipping.com; f. 1978; shipping agents, stevedoring, cargo, bunkering; Man. Dir SULEIMAN H. AL-BUKARI.

Elkirshi Shipping and Stevedoring Co: POB 3813, al-Hamdi St, Hodeida; tel. (3) 204448; fax (3) 241199; operates at ports of Hodeida, Mocha and Salif; Contact FATHI ALI MUHAMMAD.

Gulf of Aden Shipping Co: POB 1439, Tawahi, Aden; tel. (2) 271080; fax (2) 237912; e-mail almansoob@y.net.ye; internet www.almansoob.com.ye; f. 1990; cargo operations, arranges crew changes, bunkers and repairs; Operations Man. MUHAMMAD ADAM.

Hodeida Shipping and Transport Co Ltd: POB 3337, Hodeida; tel. (3) 228543; fax (3) 228533; e-mail hodship_1969@y.net.ye; internet www.hodship.aden.com.ye; f. 1969; shipping agents, stevedoring, Lloyd's agents; clearance, haulage, land transportation, cargo and vessel surveys; Gen. Man. HASSAN A. KASSIM.

Middle East Shipping Co Ltd (Mideast): POB 3700, Hayel Saeed Bldg, al-Tahreer St, Hodeida; tel. (3) 203977; fax (3) 203910; e-mail mideast@mideastshipping.com; internet www.mideastshipping.com; f. 1962; Chair. ABD AL-WASA HAYEL SAID; Gen. Man. AHMAD GAZEM SAID; brs in Mocha, Aden, Taiz, Mukalla, San'a, Salif, Ras Isa, al-Shihr.

National Shipping Co: POB 1228, Steamer Point, Aden; tel. 733553888 (mobile); fax (2) 202644; e-mail natship@y.net.ye; shipping, bunkering, clearing and forwarding, and travel agents; Dir-Gen. MOHSEN SALEM BIN BREIK.

Saba Shipping and Stevedoring Co Ltd: POB 3378/3173, Meena St, Hodeida; tel. (3) 226628; fax (3) 211588; e-mail sabaship@y.net.ye; internet www.sabashipping.com; f. 1983; shipping agents, stevedoring, cargo, bunkering.

CIVIL AVIATION
There are six international airports—San'a International (13 km from the city), Aden Civil Airport (at Khormaksar, 11 km from the port of Aden), al-Ganad (at Taiz), Mukalla (Riyan), Seyoun and Hodeida. Work on the third and final phase of a US $500m. expansion of San'a international airport was initially expected to be completed in 2009, but was subsequently delayed.

Civil Aviation and Meteorology Authority: POB 1042, San'a; tel. (1) 274717; fax (1) 274718; e-mail hasconst@cama.gov.ye; internet www.cama.gov.ye; supervisory body for civil aviation and meteorology affairs; Chair. HAMED AHMAD FARAG.

Felix Airways: Al-Hasaba St, Airport Rd, San'a; tel. (1) 252992; fax (1) 252989; e-mail hassan.thabet@felixairways.com; internet www.felixairways.com; f. 2008; 75% owned by Islamic Corpn for the Devt of the Private Sector, 25% by Yemen Airways; low-cost carrier providing domestic services from San'a and Aden and regional services to the United Arab Emirates, Oman, Saudi Arabia and Djibouti; CEO Eng. MUHAMMAD ABDULLAH AL-ARASHA; Chair. Sheikh SALEH AL-AWAJI.

Yemen Airways (Yemenia): POB 1183, Airport Rd, San'a; tel. (1) 232400; fax (1) 252991; e-mail info@yemenia.com; internet www.yemenia.com; f. 1961 as Yemen Airlines; nationalized as Yemen Airways Corpn 1972; present name adopted 1978; merged with airlines of fmr PDRY in 1996; owned 51% by Yemeni Govt and 49% by Govt of Saudi Arabia; scheduled for privatization; supervised by a ministerial cttee under the Ministry of Transport; internal services and external services to more than 30 destinations in the Middle East, Asia, Africa, Europe and the USA; Chair. and CEO ABD AL-KALEK S. AL-KADI; Man. Dir ABD AL-AZIZ AL-HAZMI.

Tourism

Yemen boasts areas of beautiful scenery, a favourable climate, and towns of historic and architectural importance. UNESCO has named San'a, Shibam and Zabid as World Heritage sites because of their cultural significance; in 2008 the Socotra Archipelago was added to the list of World Heritage sites as a natural landmark. However, the growth of tourism has, in recent years, been hampered by political instability, with a number of foreign tourists being victims of fatal attacks and kidnappings. In 2011 some 387,498 tourists visited Yemen; tourism receipts totalled US $780m. in that year.

Association of Yemen Tourism and Travel Agencies: San'a; e-mail ysaleh@y.net.ye; internet www.aytta.org.ye; f. 1996; Chair. YAHYA M. A. SALEH.

General Authority of Tourism: POB 129, San'a; tel. (1) 252319; fax (1) 252317; e-mail gtda@gtda.gov.ye; internet www.gtda.gov.ye; Chair. MUTAHAR TAQI.

Yemen Tourism Promotion Board: POB 5607, 48 Amman St, San'a; tel. (1) 251033; fax (1) 251034; e-mail ytpb@yementourism.com; internet www.yementourism.com; f. 1999; Exec. Dir AHMAD AL-BIEL.

Defence

The armed forces of the former YAR and the PDRY were officially merged in May 1990, but by early 1994 the process had not been completed and in May civil war broke out between the forces of the two former states, culminating in victory for the North. In October former President Saleh announced plans for the modernization of the armed forces, which would include the banning of party affiliation in the security services and armed forces, and in March 1995 the full merger of the armed forces was announced.

Supreme Commander of the Armed Forces: President Field Marshal ABD AL-RABBUH MANSUR AL-HADI.

Chief of the General Staff: Brig.-Gen. AHMAD ALI AL-ASHWAL.

Chief of the Air Force: Gen. RASHED NASIR ALI AL-JANAD.

Defence Budget (2013): YR 357,000m.

Military Service: Two years.

Total Armed Forces (as assessed at November 2012): 66,700: army 60,000; navy 1,700; air force 3,000; air defence 2,000.

Paramilitary Forces (as assessed at November 2012): an estimated 50,000-strong Ministry of the Interior Force, at least 20,000 tribal levies, and a coast guard of about 1,200.

Education

Primary education in Yemen is compulsory from the age of six and lasts for six years. Secondary education, beginning at 13, lasts for a further six years. In the 2009/10 academic year enrolment at primary schools included 78% of children in the relevant age-group (boys 85%; girls 70%). In the same year enrolment at secondary schools included 40% of students in the appropriate age-group (males 49%; females 31%). In 2009/10 a total of 26,044 pupils were in pre-primary education, and 4,402,679 pupils attended primary institutions. There were 574,899 pupils in secondary education in that year, while 266,096 students were enrolled at public and private universities. In 2010 public expenditure on education amounted to an estimated YR 279,000m., equivalent to 19% of total government spending. A Basic Education Development project, for which the World Bank provided a loan of US $65m., aims to increase enrolment in primary schools to 85% over 40 years.

ZAMBIA

Introductory Survey

LOCATION, CLIMATE, LANGUAGE, RELIGION, FLAG, CAPITAL

The Republic of Zambia is a land-locked state in southern central Africa, bordered to the north by Tanzania and the Democratic Republic of the Congo, to the east by Malawi and Mozambique, to the south by Zimbabwe, Botswana and Namibia, and to the west by Angola. The climate is tropical, modified by altitude, with annual average temperatures ranging from 18°C to 24°C (65°F–75°F). The official language is English. The principal African languages are Nyanja, Bemba, Tonga, Lozi, Lunda and Luvale. Christians comprise an estimated 50% of the population and are roughly divided between Protestants and Roman Catholics. A sizeable proportion of the population follow traditional animist beliefs. Most Asians are Muslims, although some are Hindus. The national flag (proportions 2 by 3) is green, with equal red, black and orange vertical stripes in the lower fly corner, and an orange eagle in flight in the upper fly corner. The capital is Lusaka.

CONTEMPORARY POLITICAL HISTORY

Historical Context

In 1924 control of Northern Rhodesia was transferred from the British South Africa Company to the Government of the United Kingdom. In 1953 the protectorate united with Southern Rhodesia (now Zimbabwe) and Nyasaland (now Malawi) to form the Federation of Rhodesia and Nyasaland. In 1962, following a campaign of civil disobedience organized by the United National Independence Party (UNIP), in support of demands that Northern Rhodesia be granted independence, the British Government introduced a new Constitution, which provided for a limited African franchise. In December 1963 the Federation was formally dissolved. Northern Rhodesia, which was henceforth known as Zambia, became an independent republic within the Commonwealth on 24 October 1964, with the leader of UNIP, Dr Kenneth Kaunda, as the country's first President.

Following its accession to power, the Kaunda administration supported African liberation groups operating in Southern Rhodesia (then known as Rhodesia) and Mozambique; repeated clashes along the border with both countries were reported, while incidents of internal political violence, particularly in the Copperbelt region, also occurred. In December 1972 Zambia was declared a one-party state. Kaunda, the sole candidate, was re-elected to the presidency in 1978, 1983 and 1988.

Domestic Political Affairs

In May 1990 Kaunda announced that a popular referendum on the subject of multi-party politics would take place in October, and that supporters of such a system (which Kaunda and UNIP opposed) would be permitted to campaign and hold public meetings. Accordingly, in July the Movement for Multi-party Democracy (MMD), an unofficial alliance of political opponents of the Government, was formed. The MMD, which was led by a former government minister, Arthur Wina, and the Chairman of the Zambian Congress of Trade Unions (ZCTU), Frederick Chiluba, swiftly gained widespread public support. Later in July Kaunda announced that the referendum was to be postponed until August 1991, to facilitate the registration of a large section of the electorate. In September 1990, however, following proposals by Kaunda that a multi-party political system be reintroduced, that multi-party elections be organized by October 1991, that the national referendum be abandoned, and that a commission be appointed to revise the Constitution, the National Council of UNIP endorsed plans for multi-party legislative and presidential elections, and accepted the recommendations of a parliamentary committee regarding the restructuring of the party.

In December 1990 constitutional amendments were adopted that permitted the formation of other political associations to contest the forthcoming elections. The MMD was subsequently granted official recognition. In early 1991 several prominent members of UNIP resigned from the party and declared their support for the MMD, while the ZCTU officially transferred allegiance to the MMD. Several other opposition movements were also established.

In June 1991 the constitutional commission presented a series of recommendations, including the creation of the post of Vice-President, the expansion of the National Assembly to 150 members and the establishment of a constitutional court. Kaunda accepted the majority of the proposals, which were subsequently submitted for approval by the National Assembly. However, the MMD rejected the draft and announced that it would boycott the forthcoming elections if the proposals were accepted. In July Kaunda agreed to suspend the review of the draft Constitution in the National Assembly pending further negotiations. Subsequent discussions between the MMD and UNIP resulted in the establishment of a joint commission to revise the draft Constitution. In late July Kaunda conceded to opposition demands that ministers be appointed only from the National Assembly and that proposals for a constitutional court be abandoned. A provision granting the President the power to impose martial law was also rescinded.

On 2 August 1991 the National Assembly formally adopted the new Constitution. At the UNIP congress in the same month Kaunda was unanimously re-elected as President of the party. Kaunda also announced the dissociation of the armed forces from UNIP; senior officers in the armed forces were subsequently obliged to retire from the party's Central Committee. In September Kaunda officially dissociated UNIP from the State.

On 31 October 1991 Chiluba, with 75.8% of votes cast, defeated Kaunda in the presidential election. In the concurrent legislative elections, the MMD secured 125 seats in the National Assembly, while UNIP won the remaining 25 seats; only four members of the previous Government were returned to the National Assembly. On 2 November Chiluba was inaugurated as President. He appointed Levy Mwanawasa as Vice-President and Leader of the National Assembly, and formed a new Cabinet. Chiluba subsequently initiated a major restructuring of the civil service and of parastatal organizations, as part of efforts to reverse the country's significant economic decline and eradicate widespread corruption among officials.

Divisions within the MMD became apparent in August 1993, when 15 prominent members (11 of whom held seats in the National Assembly) resigned from the party: they accused the Government of protecting corrupt cabinet ministers and of failing to respond to numerous reports linking senior party officials with the illegal drugs trade. Their opposition to the Government was consolidated later in the month by the formation of a new political group, the National Party (NP). In November Chiluba appointed a commission to revise the Constitution; it was announced that the draft document was to be submitted for approval by a Constituent Assembly, and subsequently by a national referendum. At partial elections for 10 of the 11 vacated seats in the National Assembly, which took place in November 1993 and April 1994, the MMD regained five seats, while the NP secured four and UNIP took one. The remaining seat was secured by UNIP at a by-election in December. Meanwhile, in July 1994 Mwanawasa resigned as Vice-President, citing long-standing differences with Chiluba, and was subsequently replaced by Brig.-Gen. Godfrey Miyanda.

In June 1995 some members of the Constitutional Review Commission rejected a final draft of the Constitution, objecting, in particular, to restrictions on the independent press, and on public gatherings and demonstrations; they claimed that the four members of the Commission who had prepared the draft had taken payments from the Government, and accused the Chairman of complicity with the authorities. Later that month, however, the draft Constitution was submitted for approval. At the end of June Kaunda was re-elected President of UNIP and announced his intention of seeking re-election to the state presidency, despite provisions in the draft Constitution that effectively debarred his candidature. In October the Minister for Legal Affairs announced that Kaunda had not officially relinquished Malawian citizenship until 1970 (and had therefore governed illegally for six years), and that he had not obtained Zambian citizenship through the correct procedures. However, following widespread reports that the authorities intended to deport Kaunda, the Government ordered security forces to suspend investigations into the former President's citizenship (apparently owing to fears of civil unrest).

In January 1996 seven opposition parties, including UNIP and the NP, established an informal alliance to campaign in favour of democratic elections and the establishment of a Constituent Assembly to approve the draft Constitution by a process of national consensus. Opposition parties subsequently demanded that the Government abandon the draft Constitution and negotiate with them regarding electoral reform. Later that month UNIP deputies withdrew from a parliamentary debate on the draft, which was subsequently approved by a large majority in the National Assembly. On 28 May the Constitution was officially adopted by Chiluba. In early June Western donor governments suspended aid to Zambia, in protest at the constitutional provisions that effectively precluded Kaunda from contesting the presidency, who announced that he intended to defy the ban.

Chiluba's second term

In August 1996 Chiluba and Kaunda met for discussions, as part of a programme of dialogue between the Government and opposition parties. The Government made minor concessions regarding the conduct of forthcoming elections, including assurances that votes would be counted at polling stations and that the Electoral Commission (appointed by Chiluba) would be independent. In mid-October 1996 Chiluba dissolved the National Assembly and announced that presidential and legislative elections would take place on 18 November. UNIP, still dissatisfied with the electoral system, announced its intention to boycott the elections and organize a campaign of civil disobedience; by early November a further six political parties had also decided to boycott the elections. There was widespread criticism of the voter registration process, in which fewer than one-half of the estimated 4.6m. eligible voters had been listed.

Despite appeals for a postponement, the elections were held as planned, and Chiluba and the MMD were returned to power by a large majority. In the presidential election Chiluba defeated the four other candidates with 72.5% of the valid votes cast. His nearest rival (with only 12.5%) was Dean Mung'omba of the Zambia Democratic Congress (ZADECO). The MMD secured 131 of the 150 seats in the National Assembly, the NP won five, and ZADECO and Agenda for Zambia each obtained two, with independent candidates taking the remaining 10 seats.

Chiluba was inaugurated for a second presidential term on 21 November 1996. Amid demands for his resignation and for fresh elections to be held, Chiluba dissolved the Cabinet and placed the military on alert at the end of the month. In early December a new Government was appointed, although the main portfolios remained largely unchanged.

Political tension increased in the second half of 1997 and in August Kaunda and Roger Chongwe, the leader of the Liberal Progressive Front, were shot and wounded (Chongwe seriously) when the security forces opened fire on an opposition gathering in Kabwe, north of Lusaka. Kaunda's subsequent allegation that the shooting was an assassination attempt organized by the Government was strongly denied by Chiluba. On 28 October rebel army officers briefly captured the national television and radio station from where they proclaimed the formation of a military regime. The attempted coup was swiftly suppressed by regular military units. Allegations by Kaunda that the Government had orchestrated the coup in order to be in a position to detain prominent members of the opposition appeared to be confirmed by Chiluba's declaration of a state of emergency on 29 October, providing for the detention for 28 days without trial of people suspected of involvement in the attempted coup.

Chiluba carried out an extensive cabinet reshuffle in early December 1997. Observers interpreted the transfer to lesser cabinet posts of Miyanda and of Benjamin Mwila, hitherto the Minister of Defence, as an attempt to forestall the emergence of potential rivals to Chiluba within the MMD. Lt-Gen. Christon Tembo, hitherto the Minister of Mines and Mineral Development, replaced Miyanda as Vice-President.

On 25 December 1997 there was widespread domestic and international concern expressed following Kaunda's arrest and imprisonment under emergency powers. On the following day Kaunda was placed under house arrest at his home in Lusaka. In mid-February 1998 he was formally notified that he was to stand trial for 'misprision of treason', on the grounds that he had failed to report in advance to the authorities details allegedly known to him of the attempted coup of October 1997. Meanwhile, in late January 1998 the National Assembly voted to extend the state of

emergency for a further three months; Chiluba eventually revoked the state of emergency on 17 March, following pressure from external donors. Also in March, Chiluba effected a minor cabinet reshuffle, most notably dismissing the Minister of Finance and Economic Development, Ronald Penza. In April 80 people who were being detained in connection with the attempted coup, including Kaunda and Mung'omba, were committed to summary trial in the High Court. Kaunda was released from detention in June, after charges against him were withdrawn, apparently owing to lack of evidence.

In November 1998 Penza was murdered at his home by a gang of masked men. Shortly afterwards five of the six suspects were shot dead by police officers, who claimed the motive for Penza's murder was robbery, although it was reported that nothing had been stolen. The police action, and Chiluba's subsequent approval of legislation providing for Zambia's intelligence service to be armed, were of considerable concern to human rights organizations. In December Mung'omba was granted bail, as no witnesses had provided evidence against him since his detention on charges of treason following the failed coup attempt of October 1997.

At the end of March 1999 the High Court delivered its judgment in a case concerning Kaunda's citizenship, declaring him to be a stateless person. The following day Kaunda appealed to the Supreme Court against the ruling, and later that day he escaped a reported assassination attempt, when a group of armed men opened fire on his car. In April five opposition parties, including the AZ and ZADECO, formed a new alliance, the Zambia Alliance for Progress (ZAP). However, the authorities refused to register the ZAP on the grounds that its constituent parties had not been dissolved. In August ZADECO formally announced its dissolution, thus effectively losing its parliamentary seat.

In September 1999 59 soldiers were sentenced to death for their part in the failed coup, most of whom subsequently launched an appeal against their convictions. In December 2003 the Supreme Court upheld the death sentences imposed on 44 of the soldiers, but in February 2004 President Mwanawasa commuted these to gaol terms of 10–20 years.

In March 2000 Kaunda announced his resignation as President of UNIP and his retirement from active politics. In May Francis Nkhoma, a former governor of the Bank of Zambia, was elected to replace Kaunda as President of UNIP, while Kaunda's son, Tilyenji, became the party's new Secretary-General.

In May 2000 the Minister of the Environment and Natural Resources and MMD National Treasurer, Benjamin Mwila, announced that he intended to stand in the presidential election scheduled for 2001; Chiluba had previously prohibited members of his Cabinet from publicly discussing their potential candidacy for the presidency upon the expiry of the two terms permitted to him by the Constitution. Mwila was subsequently dismissed from the Government and expelled from the MMD. In July Mwila and a number of other MMD members formed a new political movement, the Republican Party (RP); Mwila reiterated his intention to seek election to the presidency. The RP merged with the ZAP in February 2001, Mwila becoming leader of the new movement, known as the Zambia Republican Party (ZRP).

In early 2001 a number of prominent figures in the MMD publicly advocated Chiluba's election to a third presidential term, despite such an event being prohibited by the Constitution. Opposition parties and some leading MMD members (including Tembo) demanded that Chiluba announce that he would not seek re-election. In April, amid increasing controversy, a convention of the MMD approved a motion removing the stipulation that the party's President should serve a maximum of two five-year terms. Tembo, Miyanda and seven other ministers expressed their opposition to the convention's decision and were expelled from the party. In April Tilyenji Kaunda was elected as the President of UNIP.

In May 2001 a motion to impeach Chiluba for misconduct, proposed by two MMD deputies, was signed by more than one-third of the members of the National Assembly. The following day Chiluba announced that he would not seek re-election and dissolved the Cabinet. A new Cabinet was appointed some days later, with the ministers who had opposed Chiluba all being replaced—Tembo was succeeded as Vice-President by Enoch Kavindele. In July the recently established Forum for Democracy and Development (FDD) won a by-election in Lusaka, occasioned by the resignation of Tembo after his expulsion from the MMD; violent confrontations between rival supporters from the MMD and FDD were reported. Meanwhile, Miyanda had established a further opposition party, the Heritage Party (HP).

The MMD adopted former Vice-President Mwanawasa as its presidential candidate in August 2001. In September Michael Chilufya Sata resigned as Minister without Portfolio and as National Secretary of the MMD, in protest at Mwanawasa's nomination. He subsequently formed a new political party, the Patriotic Front (PF). In October Tembo was elected as President of the FDD and as that party's candidate in the forthcoming presidential election.

The 2001 elections

The presidential and legislative elections took place on 27 December 2001. On 1 January 2002 (the scheduled date for the announcement of the election results) violent confrontations took place between anti-Government demonstrators and the security forces in Lusaka and Kitwe, amid allegations that the MMD had engaged in electoral fraud and voter intimidation. Mwanawasa was officially declared President the following day, with 29.2% of the valid votes cast, narrowly defeating Anderson Mazoka, the leader of the United Party for National Development (UPND, established in 1998), who secured 27.2%, while Tembo won 13.2% and Tilyenji Kaunda 10.1%. The MMD secured 69 of the 150 elective seats in the National Assembly (and subsequently all eight of the seats nominated by the President); the UPND won 49 seats. Other parties to gain legislative representation were UNIP (with 13 seats), the FDD (12 seats), the HP (four seats), and the PF and the ZRP (one seat each); one independent candidate was also elected.

Although the MMD held only 77 of the 158 seats in the National Assembly, Mwanawasa refused to form a coalition with any of the opposition parties to ensure a working majority, and appointed a new Cabinet in early January, retaining many ministers from the previous administration.

In July 2002 the National Assembly voted to remove Chiluba's immunity from prosecution to allow his trial on charges of corruption to proceed. In February 2003 the Supreme Court ruled that Chiluba's immunity could not be restored, and a few days later he was arrested and charged with stealing more than US $2m. of public funds while President.

In August 2003 Chiluba, who had been released on bail following his arrest in February, was rearrested and charged with the theft of US $29.7m. while in office. In December two concurrent trials of Chiluba commenced. The former President was reportedly arraigned on 264 charges of stealing a total of some $40m., in collaboration, in some instances, with other former government officials. In March 2004 Nevers Mumba, Vice-President since May 2003, announced that about 150 former government officials and businessmen linked to Chiluba's administration were under investigation in connection with the theft of public funds. By January 2005 the charges against Chiluba had been reduced to six counts of theft of some $488,000. In November 2006 a magistrates' court ruled that Chiluba was not medically fit to stand trial and ordered the release of his passport so that he could undergo treatment in South Africa. In August 2009 Chiluba was formally cleared of all charges, with a judge ruling that the funds he was accused of embezzling could not be traced to government sources. Meanwhile, a civil case against Chiluba (which had been initiated in the United Kingdom by Minister for Legal Affairs George Kunda) concluded in May 2007; Chiluba was found guilty of embezzling $46m. of public funds and was ordered to return the stolen money. However, in August 2010 the Zambian High Court dismissed the British judgment as legally unenforceable within Zambia, prompting criticism from the PF and US officials. The Government's subsequent failure to appeal against the High Court ruling raised doubts about the authorities' willingness to address high-level corruption. In December the High Court acquitted Regina Chiluba, the wife of the former President, of corruption, overruling a 2009 judgment that declared her guilty of embezzling state funds. Frederick Chiluba died of a heart attack in June 2011.

Mwanawasa re-elected

Mwanawasa secured a second presidential term on 28 September 2006, with 43.0% of the votes cast. Sata, the populist candidate of the PF, took 29.4%, while Hakainde Hichilema of the opposition United Democratic Alliance (UDA) coalition, won 25.3%. Voter turn-out was estimated at 70.8%. Sata alleged electoral fraud, claiming that as many as 400,000 votes appeared not to have been counted in areas where he had expected to win support. Clashes between PF supporters and the security forces broke out in Lusaka when the Electoral Commission of Zambia (ECZ) announced that Sata had fallen from first place to third in interim vote counts. The subsequent violence, which lasted two days, and allegations of irregularities contrasted with the voting on election day, which international observers proclaimed took place in a generally efficient and transparent manner. In concurrently held parliamentary elections, the MMD took 72 seats, the PF won 43 and the UDA secured 26. Voting in two constituencies was postponed until 26 October, owing to the deaths of candidates. Mwanawasa was in sworn in as President on 3 October 2006 and a new Cabinet was announced a few days later.

Banda replaces Mwanawasa

Following President Mwanawasa's death on 19 August 2008, Vice-President Rupiah Banda was appointed as acting head of state, as stipulated in the Constitution, and was subsequently selected by the MMD to contest the presidential election, which was to be held on 30 October. (The successful candidate would serve the remainder of Mwanawasa's presidential term, which was to expire in October 2011.) At the election, Banda narrowly defeated Sata, again representing the PF, winning 40.6% of the votes to Sata's 38.6%; Hichilema took third place in the ballot with 20.0% of the votes cast. Despite Sata's allegations of vote-rigging, African Union (AU, see p. 191) monitors declared the election to be free and fair. On 1 November 2008 police used tear gas to suppress a demonstration in Lusaka organized by Sata's supporters. In mid-November 38 people were arrested when violent protests broke out in the city of Kitwe, apparently in response to the arrest of Frank Bwalya, a priest and manager of a Catholic radio station that had been critical of Banda's Government.

Meanwhile, Banda was sworn in as President on 2 November 2008 and later that month he appointed a new Cabinet in which George Kunda, Minister of Justice since 2001, was appointed to the vice-presidency while retaining responsibility for the justice portfolio.

In late 2009 disaffected members of the UPND formed the Alliance for Democracy and Development (ADD), under the interim presidency of Douglas Shing'andu.

In May 2010 Katele Kalumba was found guilty of corruption while serving as Minister of Finance and National Planning (1999–2002) and received a five-year gaol term. Former Minister of Defence George Mpombo was imprisoned for two months in August after being convicted of failing to honour a cheque that he had written in December 2009; the PF accused Banda of exerting pressure on the judiciary to ensure the conviction of Mpombo, a prominent critic of the President.

In January 2011 violent clashes erupted in Western Province between the police and demonstrators demanding greater autonomy and even the complete secession of the region from Zambia. (The lands comprising Western Province, formerly known as Barotseland, had been autonomous before being incorporated into the Zambian state at independence.) At least 19 deaths were reported, and the authorities detained nearly 125 protesters, some of whom were charged with treason. Banda accused the demonstrators of fomenting disunity within the state, but commentators noted that a lack of government investment in the poverty-ridden Western Province had acted as a catalyst for the unrest.

Recent developments: the 2011 elections

Presidential, legislative and local elections took place on 20 September 2011. In the presidential contest, Sata secured 42.9% of the votes cast, defeating Banda (36.2%), Hichilema of the UPND (18.5%) and the ADD's Charles Milupi (1.0%). The rate of participation by the electorate was recorded at 53.7%. Sata's PF won 60 elective seats in the concurrent parliamentary polls, while the MMD obtained 55, the UPND 28, independent candidates three, and the ADD and the FDD one each; the remaining two seats were left vacant. The MMD won the majority of local government mandates, with 547, compared to 528 for the PF and 259 for the UPND. European Union monitors reported that in general the polls had been free, fair and peaceful. Sata assumed the presidency on 23 September, thereby ending 20 consecutive years of MMD rule; his inaugural Cabinet notably included Guy Scott, who was appointed as Zambia's first white Vice-President.

In accordance with a campaign pledge vigorously to combat high-level corruption, upon taking office President Sata dismissed a number of senior officials within the police force, the Anti-Corruption Commission and various parastatal organizations. In November 2011 Austin Liato, the former Minister of

Labour and Social Security in the Banda administration, was arrested after being found in possession of some US $400,000 of allegedly stolen funds; his trial commenced in January 2012, and in April he received a two-year prison sentence. Also in April, former Minister of Communications and Transport Dora Siliya was charged with abuse of office, while Liato and Ronnie Shikapwasha, an erstwhile Minister of Information and Broadcasting Services, were accused of the same offence in July 2012 and January 2013, respectively. Meanwhile, an international warrant was issued in January 2012 for the arrest of Henry Banda, the former President's son, who was wanted for questioning over alleged corrupt practices, and in May Rupiah Banda's eldest son, Andrew, was detained and charged in relation to suspected financial irregularities. In mid-March 2013 the National Assembly authorized the revocation of former President Banda's immunity from prosecution, and he was arrested later that month on suspicion of misappropriating funds from a petroleum deal; further corruption charges against Banda were announced in April.

Meanwhile, in September 2011 President Sata granted a pardon to 28 activists who had been imprisoned for their involvement in the January protests in Western Province; a commission of inquiry was also formed to investigate the unrest. In February 2012 the commission issued its report, criticizing the draconian police response to the demonstrations and recommending the reinstatement of the 1964 Barotseland Agreement, which had guaranteed a level of autonomy for the region until its abrogation in 1969. However, Sata rejected this proposal owing to fears that other provinces would also demand increased powers of self-government.

Sata established a constitutional review commission in November 2011. It was expected that, after public consultations, the commission would submit a draft constitution to the President in 2013, following which a national referendum on the proposed charter would be held.

In a highly controversial move, in mid-March 2012 the Registrar of Societies announced the dissolution of the MMD and the nullification of its seats in the National Assembly, on the grounds that the former ruling party had allegedly neglected to pay any registration duties since 1993. The MMD denied any wrongdoing and declared that it would launch a legal challenge against the ruling, which it denounced as an 'assault on democracy'. In June 2012 the High Court rescinded the deregistration order against the MMD, regarding it as a 'disproportionate' punishment. Meanwhile, in March Banda resigned as MMD President; Nevers Mumba was elected as his successor in May. The PF, the MMD and the UPND each garnered one seat in by-elections conducted on 6 July. Sata effected a cabinet reorganization shortly thereafter, with the most notable change being the appointment of Edgar Lungu as Minister of Home Affairs. Mumba announced in mid-July that all MMD members serving in Sata's administration would be expelled from the party, prompting the MMD's Isaac Banda to resign as minister responsible for mines. Conversely, Steven Masumba, a deputy government minister, resigned from the MMD, and in the consequent by-election held in November he was re-elected to the National Assembly as a member of the PF. The MMD's poor performance in the recent by-elections left the party with 51 seats, resulting in the loss of its status as the official opposition, and in December a faction of the MMD attempted to eject Mumba from the party. Mumba was arrested later that month for allegedly holding an unauthorized meeting with his supporters, and in January 2013 he was charged with abuse of office and financial mismanagement in connection with his former role as ambassador to Canada (2009–11). Also in January, the Supreme Court revoked two of the MMD's legislative seats due to alleged irregularities during the election; following by-elections in April 2013, one seat was awarded to the PF and the UPND gained control of the other. The PF won two further by-elections in March, although a PF official was killed during the pre-election period in Livingstone in what was thought to have been a politically motivated attack. Hichilema—who, in two separate incidents in August 2012 and January 2013, had been arrested and charged with, respectively, disseminating false information about the PF and defaming President Sata—was detained again, on suspicion of fomenting the violence. (The defamation charges were withdrawn in April.)

Wynter Kabimba was appointed to the justice portfolio in September 2012, while Effron Lungu became Minister of Foreign Affairs in February 2013.

Foreign Affairs

In 1986 South African troops launched attacks on alleged bases of the African National Congress of South Africa (ANC) in Zambia; a number of foreigners and Zambian citizens were subsequently arrested in Zambia on suspicion of spying for South Africa. In August of that year Zambia undertook to impose economic sanctions against South Africa, and the South African Government retaliated by temporarily enforcing trade restrictions on Zambia. Further attacks on ANC targets took place during 1987–89. During the 1980s President Kaunda's support for the Governments of Angola and Mozambique resulted in attacks on Zambian civilians by Angolan rebels (with assistance from the Governments of South Africa and the USA) and by Mozambican rebels (also allegedly supported by South Africa). In September 1992 the Governments of Zambia and Angola signed a security agreement providing for common border controls. In early 1996 Zambia contributed some 1,000 troops to the UN Angola Verification Mission. Zambia consistently denied allegations, made by the Angolan Government in 1997–98, that it was providing military and logistical support to the Angolan rebel movement, União Nacional para a Independência Total de Angola (UNITA).

In early 1999, however, tension between Zambia and Angola intensified as the accusations resurfaced and a bomb severely damaged the Angolan embassy in Lusaka. In April, however, relations appeared to have improved, when both countries were reported to have signed an agreement aimed at resolving their differences. In June the Zambian and Angolan Governments signed a further agreement, which provided for the reactivation of the joint permanent commission on defence and security. In December it was reported that Angolan jets had bombed Zambian territory in pursuit of UNITA rebels, and in January 2000 it was announced that some 21,000 Angolan refugees had entered Zambia since October 1999. During January–February 2000 UNITA rebels carried out a series of raids on Zambian villages, which prompted Chiluba to announce that he would not permit UNITA troops to operate from Zambia. In February, following the convention of the joint permanent commission on defence and security, both sides resolved to strengthen measures against UNITA forces operating in the common border area.

In February 2001 the Governments of Zambia, Angola and Namibia agreed to establish a tripartite mechanism for political and security co-operation in an attempt to improve security on their joint borders. However, armed Angolans raided three Zambian villages close to the border in November, reportedly abducting some 100 Zambians and subsequently killing seven of them; Zambian forces claimed to have killed 10 Angolans in retaliation. Reports in the Zambian press attributed the attacks on the villages to the Angolan armed forces, which admitted occupying UNITA bases in the area, but claimed to have observed UNITA rebels crossing the border shortly before the attacks. In January 2002 there were 218,154 Angolan refugees in Zambia; by January 2012, according to the office of the UN High Commissioner for Refugees (UNHCR), that figure had been reduced to 20,970. Due to the improved security environment in Angola, the refugee status of Angolans in Zambia was rescinded in June. UNHCR had increased its efforts to repatriate the remaining Angolans still sheltering in Zambia, while the Zambian Government permitted approximately 10,000 former refugees to settle permanently in Zambia.

In early March 1997 the Zambian Government appealed for international assistance in coping with the influx of refugees fleeing the civil conflict in Zaire (now the Democratic Republic of the Congo—DRC); by March some 6,000 Zairean refugees had arrived in Zambia. In January 1998 Zambia and the DRC agreed to establish a joint permanent commission on defence and security. During late 1998 and early 1999 the Zambian Government was involved in regional efforts to find a political solution to the conflict in the DRC, after a rebellion was mounted against the Government in August 1998; President Chiluba was appointed to co-ordinate peace initiatives on the crisis by the Southern African Development Community (SADC, see p. 434) and the Organization of African Unity (OAU, now the AU, see p. 191). Meanwhile, thousands of Congolese entered Zambia, fleeing the renewed fighting, prompting the Government to appeal to the international community for immediate assistance to cope with the refugees, who, by then, reportedly numbered more than 30,000. At a summit held in Lusaka during June–July 1999 a cease-fire document was formulated, providing for the withdrawal of foreign forces from the DRC and for political reform in the country. The accord was signed by the President of the DRC and the leaders of the five other countries involved in the conflict in July, and by rebel leaders in August. In March 2004 it was reported that more than 1,000 DRC nationals had entered Zambia, fleeing renewed fighting between government and rebel forces in south-eastern DRC. At the end of 2006 there were more than 64,000 refugees living in UNHCR refugee camps in Zambia, of whom 43,788 were from the DRC. In addition, UNHCR estimated that a further 75,000 refugees (including 49,000 Angolans) had settled among the Zambian population. According to UNHCR, over 7,000 refugees from the DRC were repatriated between May and December 2007, and almost 10,000 returned home in 2008. In October 2008 Zambia closed its border to refugees arriving from the DRC, owing to heavy fighting in the east of the country. By January 2012 the number of DRC refugees in Zambia had declined to 12,020.

Relations with Zimbabwe deteriorated following the disputed presidential election in that country in March 2008. Mwanawasa, in his capacity as Chairman of SADC, had been highly critical of the conduct of Zimbabwean President Robert Mugabe's ZANU—PF and had proposed the postponement of the second round of polling in view of the worsening situation in Zimbabwe. Mwanawasa also denounced the outcome of the run-off as undemocratic and unacceptable; however, his forthright stance was not endorsed by most other SADC leaders. The installation of a power-sharing government in Zimbabwe in February 2009 resulted in an improvement in relations.

In February 2007 Chinese President Hu Jintao announced new investment worth US $800m. in Zambia after talks in Lusaka with President Mwanawasa. The two leaders stated that a special economic zone would be created in Zambia's copper-mining area in Chambishi, north of Lusaka, where Chinese firms could operate without paying import or value-added taxes. Part of Zambia's bilateral debt to the People's Republic of China was also written off. Further economic accords were concluded in early 2010, and additional funding was pledged by China in August in support of a large-scale power project. Chinese investment in Zambia during 2010 totalled over $1,000m. and was forecast to exceed $2,000m. in 2011. However, China's increasing economic presence within Zambia also led to accusations that Chinese business owners were exploiting the local labour force. Miners protesting against low salaries and dangerous working conditions at Collum coal mine in the south of the country were allegedly fired upon by the mine's Chinese managers in October 2010, resulting in injuries being sustained by 11 workers. Two Chinese nationals were subsequently arrested and accused of attempted murder. The shootings caused widespread public outrage, and President Banda was forced to appeal for calm amid rising anti-Chinese sentiments. The murder charges were withdrawn by the authorities in April 2011, reportedly following the payment of compensation to the injured miners. Although Sata had been critical of China's involvement in the local economy while in opposition, once in office he declared his support for Chinese investment, but emphasized that Chinese firms must comply with Zambian labour regulations. A Chinese supervisor was murdered by workers at the Collum facility during further wage-related unrest in August 2012. The Government rescinded Collum's operating licences in February 2013, citing safety concerns.

CONSTITUTION AND GOVERNMENT

Under the provisions of the Constitution, which was formally adopted in May 1996, Zambia is a multi-party state. Executive power is vested in the President, who is the constitutional Head of State. Legislative power is vested in a National Assembly, which comprises 158 members, of whom 150 are elected by universal adult suffrage, and eight nominated by the President. The President and the National Assembly are elected simultaneously by universal adult suffrage for a five-year term. The maximum duration of the President's tenure of office is limited to two five-year terms. The President governs with the assistance of a Vice-President and a Cabinet, whom he appoints from members of the National Assembly. The Constitution also provides for a 27-member House of Chiefs, which represents traditional tribal authorities. Each of Zambia's nine provinces has a minister, who is appointed by the President. In September 2009 the National Constitutional Conference approved an increase in the number of members of the National Assembly from 158 to 280. Also approved was a proposal to have 240 of those members elected by simple majority, 30 members elected by proportional representation and a maximum of 10 nominated by the President.

REGIONAL AND INTERNATIONAL CO-OPERATION

Zambia is a member of the African Union, of the Southern African Development Community (see p. 434) and of the Common Market for Eastern and Southern Africa (see p. 241).

Zambia became a member of the UN in 1964. As a contracting party to the General Agreement on Tariffs and Trade, Zambia joined the World Trade Organization (WTO, see p. 444) on its establishment in 1995. Zambia participates in the Group of 77 (G77, see p. 461) developing countries.

ECONOMIC AFFAIRS

In 2011, according to estimates by the World Bank, Zambia's gross national income (GNI), measured at average 2009–11 prices, was US $15,619m., equivalent to $1,160 per head (or $1,490 per head on an international purchasing-power parity basis). During 2002–11, it was estimated, the population increased at an average annual rate of 2.6%, while gross domestic product (GDP) per head grew, in real terms, by an average of 3.3% per year. Overall GDP increased, in real terms, at an average annual rate of 6.0% in 2002–11; growth in 2011 was 5.9%.

Agriculture (including forestry and fishing) contributed 19.3% of GDP in 2011, according to the African Development Bank (AfDB). According to the 2000 census, 71.6% of those employed were engaged in the sector. However, in 2006 only 11.7% of those in paid employment were engaged in agriculture. According to FAO, some 61.4% of the labour force were estimated to be employed in the sector in mid-2013. The principal crops are sugar cane, maize, cassava, cotton, wheat, sweet potatoes and groundnuts. Millet, rice, sorghum, tobacco, sunflower seeds and horticultural produce are also cultivated. Cattle-rearing remains important. During 2002–11, according to the World Bank, agricultural GDP increased by an average of 3.8% per year; agricultural GDP rose by 0.1% in 2010 and by 24.9% in 2011.

Industry (including mining, manufacturing, construction and power) contributed 36.4% of GDP in 2011, according to the AfDB, and engaged 22.7% of all those in paid employment in 2006. According to the World Bank, industrial GDP grew at an average annual rate of 8.1% in 2002–11; industrial GDP increased by 10.8% in 2010, but decreased by 4.7% in 2011.

In 2011 mining and quarrying contributed 3.5% of GDP, according to the AfDB, and engaged 5.5% of those in paid employment in 2006. Exports of copper contributed 68.1% of the value of total exports in 2011. Output of copper ore increased from 514,000 metric tons in 2006 to 820,000 tons in 2010, but decreased to 524,000 metric tons in 2011. Cobalt is also an important export, while coal, gold, emeralds, amethyst, limestone and selenium are mined as well. In addition, Zambia has reserves of phosphates, fluorspar and iron ore. During 2002–06, according to the IMF, mining GDP increased by an estimated average of 8.1% per year. Mining GDP grew by 1.3% in 2011, according to the AfDB.

According to the AfDB, manufacturing contributed 8.1% of GDP in 2011. The sector engaged 11.6% of those in paid employment in 2006. The principal manufacturing activities are food-processing, the smelting and refining of copper and other metals, vehicle assembly, petroleum-refining, and the production of fertilizers, explosives, textiles, bottles, batteries, bricks and copper wire. During 2002–11, according to the World Bank, manufacturing GDP increased at an average annual rate of 4.6%; manufacturing GDP rose by 5.4% in 2010, but declined by 0.7% in 2011.

Construction contributed 21.7% of GDP in 2011, according to the AfDB. The sector engaged only 3.0% of those in paid employment in 2006. During 2002–06, according to the IMF, construction GDP increased at an average annual rate of 19.4%. Sectoral GDP grew by 7.2% in 2011, according to the AfDB.

Energy is derived principally from hydroelectric power (99.7% in 2009), in which Zambia is self-sufficient. Imports of mineral fuels accounted for 10.6% of the value of merchandise imports in 2011. In an effort to address the problem of power shortages and expand availability of electricity, the construction was planned of three new hydroelectric plants during 2009–15, for which a financing requirement of some US $1,200m. was anticipated.

In 2011, according to the AfDB, the services sector contributed 44.3% of GDP. The sector engaged 65.6% of those in paid employment in 2006. According to the World Bank, the GDP of the services sector increased by an average of 6.2% per year in 2002–11; services GDP grew by 10.9% in 2011.

In 2011 Zambia recorded a visible merchandise trade surplus of US $2,217.6m., and there was a surplus of $69.1m. on the current account of the balance of payments. In 2012 the principal source of imports (providing 33.7% of the total) was South Africa; other major suppliers were the Republic of the Congo, the People's Republic of China and Kuwait. The principal market for exports in that year was Switzerland-Liechtenstein (accounting for 42.3% of the total); other significant purchasers were the People's Republic of China and South Africa. The principal export in 2012 was copper, which accounted for 68.1% of the total. The principal imports in that year were boilers and machinery, mineral fuels and lubricants, vehicles other than railway, and electrical and electronic equipment.

In 2010 there was an overall budgetary deficit of K2,386,000m. A budgetary deficit of K2,796,000m. was projected by the IMF in 2011 and K4,302,000m. in 2012. Zambia's general government gross debt was K24,237,517m. in 2011, equivalent to 26.0% of GDP. Zambia's total external debt was US $3,689m. at the end of 2010, of which $1,309m. was public and publicly guaranteed debt. In that year, the cost of servicing long-term public and publicly guaranteed debt and repayments to the IMF was equivalent to 1.9% of the value of exports of goods, services and income (excluding workers' remittances). In 2002–12 the average annual rate of inflation was 12.3%. Consumer prices increased by 4.1% in 2012.

Zambia's economy successfully withstood the negative impact of the global economic slowdown, which resulted in lower copper prices from late 2008 and job losses in the industry. Increased production in the mining and agricultural sectors during late 2009, combined with the recovery of copper prices, led to GDP expansion of 6.4% in that year, according to the IMF. Rising demand for copper prompted a significant increase in output during 2010, while the agricultural sector enjoyed another year of robust production; buoyant activity in the construction and tourism sectors was also reported. Furthermore, there was a strong resurgence in levels of foreign direct investment (FDI) throughout 2010, with the manufacturing and mining industries attracting most of this capital, and the IMF estimated that GDP grew by 7.6% during the year. The mining and agricultural sectors remained vibrant in 2011, driving real GDP growth of 6.6%. The copper industry benefited from record high prices and robust levels of FDI, and both production and exports of the metal rose during 2011. The Patriotic Front administration, which took office in September, pledged to focus on alleviating poverty, and the new Government's first budget included an increase in mining royalties to fund additional social expenditure and the extension of the country's agricultural subsidy programme. Economic growth accelerated to 7.3% in 2012. Although copper production and prices declined in that year, revenues from the mining sector increased sharply because of the new royalty regime, and there was also an upturn in copper exports. The Government's fiscal stance remained expansionary. With large-scale investment in the copper industry continuing and copper prices expected to remain high, Zambia's near-term prospects were encouraging, and the IMF forecast further real GDP growth, of 8.2% in 2013.

PUBLIC HOLIDAYS

2014: 1 January (New Year's Day), 8 March (International Women's Day), 11 March (Youth Day), 18 April–21 April (Easter), 1 May (Labour Day), 25 May (African Freedom Day, anniversary of OAU's foundation), 1 July (Unity Day), 7 July (Heroes' Day), 4 August (Farmers' Day), 24 October (Independence Day), 25 December (Christmas Day).

Statistical Survey

Source (unless otherwise indicated): Central Statistical Office, POB 31908, Lusaka; tel. (21) 1211231; internet www.zamstats.gov.zm.

Area and Population

AREA, POPULATION AND DENSITY

Area (sq km)	752,612*
Population (census results)	
25 October 2000	9,885,591
15 October 2010	
Males	6,454,647
Females	6,638,019
Total	13,092,666
Population (UN estimates at mid-year)† . . .	
2011	13,474,960
2012	13,883,575
2013	14,314,515
Density (per sq km) at mid-2013	19.0

* 290,585 sq miles.
† Source: UN, *World Population Prospects: The 2010 Revision*; estimates not adjusted to take account of 2010 census.

POPULATION BY AGE AND SEX
(UN estimates at mid-2013)

	Males	Females	Total
0–14	3,366,639	3,331,560	6,698,199
15–64	3,619,241	3,561,780	7,181,021
65 and over	193,640	241,655	435,295
Total	7,179,520	7,134,995	14,314,515

Source: UN, *World Population Prospects: The 2010 Revision*.

PROVINCES
(2010 census)

	Area	Population	Density
Central	94,394	1,307,111	13.8
Copperbelt	31,328	1,972,317	63.0
Eastern	69,106	1,592,661	23.0
Luapula	50,567	991,927	19.6
Lusaka	21,896	2,191,225	100.1
Northern*	147,826	1,817,481	12.3
North-Western	125,826	727,044	5.8
Southern	85,283	1,589,926	18.6
Western	126,386	902,974	7.1
Total	752,612	13,092,666	17.4

* Including 711,657 persons enumerated in districts which were separated into the new province of Muchinga in 2011.

PRINCIPAL TOWNS
(population at 2000 census)

Lusaka (capital) .	1,084,703	Lundazi . . .	236,833
Kitwe	376,124	Petauke . . .	235,879
Ndola	374,757	Choma . . .	204,898
Chipata . . .	367,539	Solwezi . . .	203,797
Chibombo . . .	241,612	Mazabuka . . .	203,219

Mid-2011 (incl. suburbs, UN estimate): Lusaka 1,802,470 (Source: UN, *World Urbanization Prospects: The 2011 Revision*).

BIRTHS AND DEATHS
(annual averages, UN estimates)

	1995–2000	2000–05	2005–10
Birth rate (per 1,000) . . .	44.6	44.4	44.5
Death rate (per 1,000) . . .	19.6	19.6	16.7

Source: UN, *World Population Prospects: The 2010 Revision.*

Life expectancy (years at birth): 49.0 (males 48.5; females 49.4) in 2011 (Source: World Bank, World Development Indicators database).

EMPLOYMENT
(Usually active population aged 12 years and over at 2000 census)

Agriculture, hunting, forestry and fishing	2,014,028
Mining and quarrying	36,463
Manufacturing	77,515
Electricity, gas and water	11,016
Construction	36,790
Wholesale and retail trade; restaurants and hotels . .	190,354
Transport, storage and communications	53,736
Financial, insurance, real estate and business services . .	29,151
Community, social and personal services	363,375
Total	**2,812,428**

Source: ILO.

2006 (persons in paid employment, labour force survey, January): Agriculture, forestry and fishing 56,139; Mining and quarrying 26,253; Manufacturing 55,709; Electricity and water 12,399; Construction 14,343; Wholesale and retail trade 65,012; Transport and communications 19,378; Finance and insurance 54,032; Public administration 176,062; *Total* 479,327 (Source: IMF, *Zambia: Statistical Appendix*, January 2008).

Mid-2013 ('000, estimates): Agriculture, etc. 3,483; Total labour force 5,677 (Source: FAO).

Health and Welfare

KEY INDICATORS

Total fertility rate (children per woman, 2010)	6.3
Under-5 mortality rate (per 1,000 live births, 2010) . . .	111
HIV/AIDS (% of persons aged 15–49, 2009)	13.5
Physicians (per 1,000 head, 2006)	0.1
Hospital beds (per 1,000 head, 2010)	2.0
Health expenditure (2009): US $ per head (PPP) . . .	90
Health expenditure (2009): % of GDP	6.2
Health expenditure (2009): public (% of total)	58.6
Access to water (% of persons, 2010)	61
Access to sanitation (% of persons, 2010)	48
Total carbon dioxide emissions ('000 metric tons, 2008) . .	1,888.5
Carbon dioxide emissions per head (metric tons, 2008) . .	0.2
Human Development Index (2011): ranking	164
Human Development Index (2011): value	0.430

For sources and definitions, see explanatory note on p. vi.

Agriculture

PRINCIPAL CROPS
('000 metric tons)

	2009	2010	2011
Wheat	195.5	172.3	153.8*
Rice, paddy	41.9	51.7	46.1†
Maize	1,887.0	2,795.5	2,496.4
Millet	49.0	48.0	38.0*
Sorghum	21.8	27.7	24.8*
Potatoes	21.3	22.9	21.2*
Sweet potatoes	200.5	252.9	236.6
Cassava (Manioc)	1,160.9	1,151.7	1,266.3*
Sugar cane*	3,500	3,500	3,500
Soybeans (Soya beans) . . .	40*	41*	13†
Groundnuts, with shell . . .	121	164	175*
Sunflower seed	33.7	26.4	28.0†
Seed cotton*	136	107	114
Onions, dry*	28.5	29	37.8
Tomatoes*	25.0	26.0	19.7
Tobacco, unmanufactured* . .	65.7	59.3	60.3

* FAO estimate(s).
† Unofficial figure.

Aggregate production ('000 metric tons, may include official, semi-official or estimated data): Total cereals 2,197 in 2009, 3,098 in 2010, 2,761 in 2011; Total pulses 28 in 2009, 27 in 2010, 30 in 2011; Total roots and tubers 1,383 in 2009, 1,428 in 2010, 1,524 in 2011; Total vegetables (incl. melons) 330 in 2009, 366 in 2010, 418 in 2011; Total fruits (excl. melons) 118 in 2009, 112 in 2010, 111 in 2011.

Source: FAO.

LIVESTOCK
('000 head, year ending September, FAO estimates)

	2009	2010	2011
Cattle	3,038	3,100	3,000
Sheep	210	220	225
Goats	2,100	2,200	2,300
Pigs	712	715	718
Chickens	33,000	35,000	36,000

Source: FAO.

LIVESTOCK PRODUCTS
('000 metric tons, FAO estimates)

	2009	2010	2011
Cattle meat	68.0	74.4	67.2
Pig meat	23.1	22.9	23.1
Chicken meat	40.0	42.5	43.0
Cows' milk	87.0	88.5	88.5
Hen eggs	45.0	49.5	54.0
Cattle hides	8.9	10.0	8.8

Source: FAO.

Forestry

ROUNDWOOD REMOVALS
('000 cubic metres, FAO estimates)

	2009	2010	2011
Sawlogs, veneer logs and logs for sleepers	245	245	245
Other industrial wood	1,080	1,080	1,080
Fuel wood	8,978	9,119	9,249
Total	**10,303**	**10,444**	**10,574**

Source: FAO.

SAWNWOOD PRODUCTION
('000 cubic metres, incl. railway sleepers, FAO estimates)

	1995	1996	1997
Coniferous (softwood)	300	230	145
Broadleaved (hardwood) . . .	20	15	12
Total	320	245	157

1998–2011: Figures assumed to be unchanged from 1997 (FAO estimates).

Source: FAO.

Fishing

('000 metric tons, live weight)

	2008	2009	2010
Capture	79.4	84.7	76.4
Dagaas	7.9	10.0	7.8
Other freshwater fishes . . .	71.5	74.7	68.6
Aquaculture	5.6	8.5	10.3
Three-spotted tilapia . . .	2.0	3.1	3.7
Total catch	85.0	93.2	86.7

Note: Figures exclude crocodiles, recorded by number rather than weight. The number of Nile crocodiles caught was: 28,197 in 2008; 43,655 in 2009; 23,717 in 2010.

Source: FAO.

Mining

(estimates)

	2009	2010	2011
Coal ('000 metric tons)	200	200	220
Copper ore ('000 metric tons)* .	557	540	524
Cobalt ore (metric tons)* . . .	4,900	5,700	6,600
Amethysts ('000 kilograms) . .	1,400	1,300	1,000

* Figures refer to the metal content of ore.

Source: US Geological Survey.

Industry

SELECTED PRODUCTS
('000 metric tons unless otherwise indicated)

	2009	2010	2011
Cement	880	1,127	1,200
Copper (unwrought): smelter . .	334	490	511
Copper (unwrought): refined . .	414	530	516
Cobalt (refined, metric tons) . .	1,271	1,092	1,100
Raw sugar	323	n.a.	n.a.
Electric energy (million kWh) .	10,308	n.a.	n.a.

Sources: US Geological Survey; UN Industrial Commodity Statistics Database.

Finance

CURRENCY AND EXCHANGE RATES

Monetary Units
100 ngwee = 1 Zambian kwacha (K).

Sterling, Dollar and Euro Equivalents (30 November 2012)
£1 sterling = 8,383.39 kwacha;
US $1 = 5,221.02 kwacha;
€1 = 6,780.01 kwacha;
10,000 Zambian kwacha = £1.19 = $1.92 = €1.47.

Average Exchange Rate (Zambian kwacha per US $)
2009   5,046.11
2010   4,797.14
2011   4,860.67

Note: On 23 January 2012 it was announced that the kwacha was to be rebased, with existing currency denominations divided by 1,000; the newly redenominated currency was formally introduced on 1 January 2013, and both old and new denominations were to circulate during a transitional period until 30 June 2013, after which the old currency would cease to be legal tender.

CENTRAL GOVERNMENT BUDGET
(K '000 million)

Revenue	2010	2011*	2012*
Tax revenue	12,700	18,018	17,481
Income tax	6,914	10,655	8,665
Excise taxes	1,377	1,665	1,953
Value-added tax (VAT) . . .	3,160	3,973	4,725
Customs duty	1,250	1,725	2,139
Non-tax revenue	1,109	1,501	2,727
Total†	13,809	19,519	20,208

Expenditure	2010	2011*	2012*
Expense	15,073	18,680	19,382
Compensation of employees .	6,325	7,402	9,600
Goods and services	3,272	4,754	3,768
Interest payments	1,370	1,082	1,664
Subsidies	1,897	2,837	1,393
Intergovernmental transfers .	1,098	1,433	1,806
Social benefits	194	977	1,047
Other	917	195	104
Net acquisition of non-financial assets	2,512	5,085	7,811
Fiscal Measures	—	—	–843
Total	17,584	23,765	26,350

* Projections.
† Excluding grants received (K '000 million): 1,389 in 2010; 1,450 in 2011 (projection); 1,840 in 2012 (projection).

Source: IMF, *Zambia: Staff Report for the 2012 Article IV Consultation* (July 2012).

INTERNATIONAL RESERVES
(excl. gold, US $ million at 31 December)

	2009	2010	2011
IMF special drawing rights . .	637.6	625.2	617.8
Foreign exchange	1,254.4	1,468.5	1,706.2
Total	1,892.1	2,093.7	2,324.0

Source: IMF, *International Financial Statistics*.

MONEY SUPPLY
(K '000 million at 31 December)

	2009	2010	2011
Currency outside depository corporations	1,579.6	2,229.5	2,790.3
Transferable deposits	7,517.1	10,039.9	11,535.6
Other deposits	4,700.2	5,647.1	7,478.8
Broad money	13,796.9	17,916.5	21,804.8

Source: IMF, *International Financial Statistics*.

COST OF LIVING
(Consumer Price Index; low-income group; base: 2000 = 100)

	2001	2002	2003
Food (incl. alcohol and tobacco) .	118.9	151.1	184.5
Clothing and footwear	120.5	139.4	168.8
Fuel and rent	121.4	145.1	176.5
All items (incl. others) . . .	121.4	148.4	180.1

Food (incl. alcohol and tobacco): 384.3 in 2010; 403.2 in 2011; n.a. in 2012.

All items: 419.6 in 2010; 456.0 in 2011; 474.6 in 2012.

Source: ILO.

NATIONAL ACCOUNTS
(K '000 million at current prices)

Expenditure on the Gross Domestic Product

	2009	2010*	2011*
Government final consumption expenditure	11,651	12,738	15,410
Private final consumption expenditure	37,532	37,982	45,953
Changes in inventories . . .	946	1,165	1,410
Gross fixed capital formation .	12,646	16,553	20,027
Total domestic expenditure .	62,775	68,438	82,800
Exports of goods and services .	22,624	36,329	43,953
Less Imports of goods and services	20,783	27,101	32,788
GDP in purchasers' values .	64,616	77,667	93,964

Gross Domestic Product by Economic Activity

	2009	2010*	2011*
Agriculture, hunting, forestry and fishing	13,461	15,642	18,229
Mining and quarrying . . .	1,682	2,838	3,289
Manufacturing	6,017	6,771	7,611
Electricity, gas and water . .	1,780	2,202	2,913
Construction	11,819	15,704	20,484
Wholesale and retail trade, restaurants and hotels . . .	11,453	13,043	14,940
Transport and communications .	2,355	3,076	3,571
Finance and insurance, real estate and business services . . .	9,206	11,051	12,873
Public administration and defence	1,647	1,733	2,639
Other services	5,002	6,416	7,697
Sub-total	64,423	78,475	94,246
Less Imputed bank service charge	2,922	3,876	4,416
Indirect taxes, less subsidies . .	3,114	3,068	4,134
GDP in purchasers' values .	64,616	77,667	93,964

* Provisional.

Source: African Development Bank.

BALANCE OF PAYMENTS
(US $ million)

	2009	2010	2011
Exports of goods	4,319.1	7,413.6	8,671.8
Imports of goods	−3,413.4	−4,709.9	−6,454.2
Balance on goods	905.7	2,703.7	2,217.6
Export of services	240.9	310.9	375.2
Import of services	−705.4	−939.7	−1,193.0
Balance on goods and services	441.2	2,074.9	1,399.7
Primary income received . . .	4.5	8.4	11.1
Primary income paid	−424.2	−1,371.4	−1,573.5
Balance on goods, services and primary income	21.5	711.9	−162.7
Secondary income received . .	255.5	242.4	273.3
Secondary income paid . . .	−37.0	−39.2	−41.5

—*continued*	2009	2010	2011
Current account	239.9	915.1	69.1
Capital account (net)	237.3	149.7	119.0
Direct investment assets . . .	−269.6	−1,095.4	−1,150.2
Direct investment liabilities . .	694.8	1,729.3	1,981.7
Portfolio investment liabilities .	−74.9	73.6	47.7
Financial derivatives and employee stock options (net)	219.6	225.7	124.1
Other investment assets . . .	−1,578.0	−3,288.4	−1,654.6
Other investment liabilities . .	834.3	1,210.3	563.0
Net errors and omissions . . .	−64.4	−66.6	−5.6
Reserves and related items .	239.1	−146.7	94.3

Source: IMF, *International Financial Statistics*.

External Trade

PRINCIPAL COMMODITIES
(distribution by HS, US $ million)

Imports c.i.f.	2010	2011	2012
Fertilizers	190.8	329.7	308.8
Plastics and articles thereof . .	156.6	228.3	265.2
Mineral fuels and lubricants . .	618.1	532.7	949.4
Crude petroleum oils . . .	508.8	335.4	557.2
Electrical, electronic equipment .	247.7	467.8	505.0
Boilers, machinery, etc. . . .	865.9	1,302.4	1,530.6
Iron and steel and products thereof	163.1	267.7	355.6
Pharmaceutical products . . .	115.0	139.3	206.9
Vehicles other than railway, tramway	373.8	616.0	888.5
Total (incl. others)	5,320.8	7,177.8	8,938.7

Exports f.o.b.	2010	2011	2012
Cereals	37.2	195.9	425.1
Copper and articles thereof . .	5,417.5	6,769.7	6,487.9
Pearls, precious stones, metals, coins, etc.	67.1	128.9	288.0
Ores, slag and ash	523.6	202.8	71.8
Total (incl. others)	7,200.3	9,000.9	9,524.0

Source: Trade Map-Trade Competitiveness Map, International Trade Centre, www.intracen.org/marketanalysis.

PRINCIPAL TRADING PARTNERS
(US $ million)

Imports c.i.f.	2010	2011	2012
China, People's Repub. . . .	289.7	706.3	883.3
Congo, Democratic Repub. . .	1,268.7	1,330.4	0.0
Congo, Republic	0.0	0.1	1,288.7
Egypt	15.0	29.2	95.1
Finland	36.8	83.7	46.8
Germany	54.0	58.6	113.8
India	144.4	248.1	310.0
Japan	84.8	150.6	246.5
Kenya	64.6	130.3	287.5
Kuwait	508.7	335.8	560.5
Singapore	41.7	93.1	56.7
South Africa	1,829.5	2,562.7	3,014.2
Sweden	48.5	88.7	98.7
United Arab Emirates . . .	116.7	241.2	223.5
United Kingdom	105.9	189.8	223.7
USA	72.5	98.2	252.2
Zimbabwe	72.0	87.4	94.5
Total (incl. others)	5,320.8	7,177.8	8,938.7

Exports f.o.b.	2010	2011	2012
Belgium	72.4	84.8	89.3
China, People's Repub.	1,455.4	1,504.6	1,836.3
Congo, Democratic Repub.	333.5	584.1	0.0
Malawi	102.7	119.6	189.6
Namibia	19.6	36.5	154.8
South Africa	657.8	838.4	859.6
Switzerland-Liechtenstein	3,673.5	4,402.9	4,026.5
Tanzania	31.8	75.3	101.4
United Arab Emirates	176.2	87.5	229.4
United Kingdom	134.8	333.1	316.4
Zimbabwe	120.6	242.5	437.4
Total (incl. others)	7,200.3	9,000.9	9,524.0

Source: Trade Map-Trade Competitiveness Map, International Trade Centre, www.intracen.org/marketanalysis.

Transport

ROAD TRAFFIC
(estimates, '000 motor vehicles in use at 31 December)

	1994	1995	1996
Passenger cars	123	142	157
Lorries and vans	68	74	81

2007: Passenger cars 131; Buses 4; Lorries and vans 76; Motorcycles 7.

2008: Passenger cars 167; Buses 6; Lorries and vans 92; Motorcycles 7.

Source: IRF, *World Road Statistics*.

CIVIL AVIATION
(traffic on scheduled services)

	2006	2007	2008
Kilometres flown (million)	2	2	2
Passengers carried ('000)	59	62	63
Passenger-km (million)	19	20	20
Total ton-km (million)	2	2	2

Source: UN, *Statistical Yearbook*.

Tourism

TOURIST ARRIVALS BY NATIONALITY

	2008	2009	2010
Australia	14,517	16,316	10,430
South Africa	95,415	84,413	144,980
Tanzania	106,284	81,288	121,275
United Kingdom	46,516	53,370	50,958
USA	33,870	49,451	29,521
Zimbabwe	226,428	171,232	171,806
Total (incl. others)	811,775	709,948	815,164

Tourism receipts (US $ million, excl. passenger transport): 148 in 2008; 98 in 2009; 125 in 2010.

Source: World Tourism Organization.

Communications Media

	2009	2010	2011
Telephones ('000 main lines in use)	90.3	118.4	85.7
Mobile cellular telephones ('000 subscribers)	4,406.7	5,447.0	8,164.6
Internet subscribers ('000)	17.8	17.3	14.8
Broadband subscribers ('000)	10.7	10.3	7.6

Source: International Telecommunication Union.

Education

(2009/10 unless otherwise indicated)

	Institutions	Teachers	Students
Primary	4,221*	49,987	2,899,131
Secondary	n.a.	29,887	747,935
Tertiary	n.a.	n.a.	24,553†

* 1998 figure.
† 1999/2000 estimate.

Source: UNESCO Institute for Statistics.

Pupil-teacher ratio (primary education, UNESCO estimate): 58.0 in 2009/10 (Source: UNESCO Institute for Statistics).

Adult literacy rate (UNESCO estimates): 71.2% (males 80.7%; females 61.7%) in 2010 (Source: UNESCO Institute for Statistics).

Directory

The Government

HEAD OF STATE

President: MICHAEL CHILUFYA SATA (took office 23 September 2011).

THE CABINET
(May 2013)

President: MICHAEL CHILUFYA SATA.

Vice-President: GUY L. SCOTT.

Minister of Finance: ALEXANDER BWALYA CHIKWANDA.

Minister of Justice: WYNTER MUNACAAMBWA KABIMBA.

Minister of Defence: GEOFFREY B. MWAMBA.

Minister of Home Affairs: EDGAR LUNGU.

Minister of Health: Dr JOSEPH KASONDE.

Minister of Foreign Affairs: EFFRON LUNGU.

Minister of Agriculture and Livestock: ROBERT SICHINGA.

Minister of Information and Broadcasting Services: KENNEDY SAKENI.

Minister of Commerce, Trade and Industry: EMMANUEL T. CHENDA.

Minister of Local Government and Housing: EMERINE KABANSHI.

Minister of Mines, Energy and Water Development: YAMFWA MUKANGA.

Minister of Tourism and the Arts: SYLVIA T. MASEBO.

Minister of Labour and Social Security: FACKSON SHAMENDA.

Minister of Education, Science, Vocational Training and Early Education: Dr JOHN T. N. PHIRI.

Minister of Lands, Natural Resources and Environmental Protection: WYLBER SIMUUSA.

Minister of Community Development, Mother and Child Health: Dr JOSEPH KATEMA.

Minister of Transport, Works, Supply and Communications: CHRISTOPHER YALUMA.

Minister of Gender and Child Development: INONGE WINA.

Minister of Youth and Sport: CHISHIMBA KAMBWILI.

Minister of Chiefs and Traditional Affairs: Prof. NKANDU LUO.

There were, in addition, 38 Deputy Ministers. The Attorney-General is also a member of the Cabinet.

MINISTRIES

Office of the President: POB 30135, Lusaka 10101; tel. (21) 1260317; fax (21) 1254545; internet www.statehouse.gov.zm.

Office of the Vice-President: Lusaka.

Ministry of Agriculture and Livestock: Mulungushi House, Independence Ave, Nationalist Rd, POB RW50291, Lusaka; tel. (21) 1213551.

Ministry of Chiefs and Traditional Affairs: Lusaka.

Ministry of Commerce, Trade and Industry: 9th and 10th Floor, Nasser Rd, POB 31968, Lusaka 10101; tel. (21) 1228301; fax (21) 1226984; internet www.mcti.gov.zm.

Ministry of Community Development, Mother and Child Health: Fidelity House, POB 31958, Lusaka; tel. (21) 1228321; fax (21) 1225327.

Ministry of Defence: POB 31931, Lusaka; tel. (21) 1252366.

Ministry of Education, Science, Vocational Training and Early Education: Civic Center Area, Plot 89, cnr Mogadishu and Chimanga Rds, POB 50093, Lusaka 10101; tel. (21) 1250855; fax (21) 1250760; internet www.moe.gov.zm.

Ministry of Finance: Finance Bldg, POB 50062, Lusaka; tel. (21) 1252121; fax (21) 1251078; e-mail info@mofnp.gov.zm; internet www.mofnp.gov.zm.

Ministry of Foreign Affairs: POB RW50069, Lusaka; tel. (21) 1252718; fax (21) 1222440.

Ministry of Gender and Child Development: Lusaka; tel. (21) 1253513.

Ministry of Health: Ndeke House, POB 30205, Lusaka; tel. (21) 1253040; fax (21) 1253344; internet www.moh.gov.zm.

Ministry of Home Affairs: POB 32862, Lusaka; tel. (21) 1213505.

Ministry of Information and Broadcasting Services: Independence Ave, POB 51025, Lusaka; tel. and fax (21) 1235410; internet www.mibs.gov.zm.

Ministry of Justice: Fairley Rd, POB 50106, 15101, Ridgeway, Lusaka; tel. (21) 1228522.

Ministry of Labour and Social Security: Lusaka.

Ministry of Lands, Natural Resources and Environmental Protection: POB 50694, Lusaka; tel. (21) 1252288; fax (21) 1250120; internet www.ministryoflands.gov.zm.

Ministry of Local Government and Housing: Church Rd, POB 50027, Lusaka; tel. (21) 1250528; fax (21) 1252680; e-mail ps@mlgh.gov.zm; internet www.mlgh.gov.zm.

Ministry of Mines, Energy and Water Development: Chilufya Mulenga Rd, POB 31969, 10101 Lusaka; tel. (21) 1235323; fax (21) 1235346.

Ministry of Tourism and the Arts: POB 30055, Lusaka; tel. (21) 1223930.

Ministry of Transport, Works, Supply and Communications: Fairley Rd, POB 50065, Lusaka; tel. (21) 151444; fax (21) 151795; internet www.mct.gov.zm.

Ministry of Youth and Sport: Lechwe House, Freedom Way, POB 32186, Lusaka; tel. (21) 1212020; internet www.mlss.gov.zm.

President and Legislature

PRESIDENT

Presidential Election, 20 September 2011

Candidate	Votes	% of votes
Michael Chilufya Sata (PF)	1,170,966	42.85
Rupiah Banda (MMD)	987,866	36.15
Hakainde Hichilema (UPND)	506,763	18.54
Charles Milupi (ADD)	26,270	0.96
Others	40,797	1.49
Total	**2,732,662**	**100.00**

NATIONAL ASSEMBLY

Speaker: Dr PATRICK MATIBINI.
General Election, 20 September 2011

Party	Seats
Patriotic Front (PF)	60
Movement for Multi-party Democracy (MMD)	55
United Party for National Development (UPND)	28
Independents	3
Alliance for Democracy and Development (ADD)	1
Forum For Democracy and Development (FDD)	1
Total	**148***

* Voting in two constituencies did not take place.

House of Chiefs

The House of Chiefs is an advisory body which may submit resolutions for debate by the National Assembly. There are 27 Chiefs, four each from the Northern, Western, Southern and Eastern Provinces, three each from the North-Western, Luapula and Central Provinces, and two from the Copperbelt Province.

Election Commission

Electoral Commission of Zambia (ECZ): Elections House, Haile Selassie Ave, POB 50274, Longacres, Lusaka; tel. (21) 1253155; fax (21) 1253884; e-mail elections@electcom.org.zm; internet www.elections.org.zm; f. 1996; independent; Chair. IRENE C. MAMBILIMA; Dir PRISCILLA MULENGA ISAAC.

Political Organizations

Agenda for Change (AfC): POB 37119, Lusaka; e-mail agenda@zambia.co.zm; f. 1995; Pres. Prof. HENRY KYAMBALESA; Nat. Chair. DARROH P. CHOONGA.

Alliance for Democracy and Development (ADD): Plot 6592, Nationalist Rd, opp. UTH Filter Clinic, POB 36792, Lusaka; tel. 977822902 (mobile); e-mail admin@add-zambia.org; f. 2009; Pres. CHARLES MILUPI; Nat. Chair. AMOS NAKALONGA; Sec.-Gen. STAFFORD LIZU (acting).

Citizens Democratic Party (CDP): POB 37277, Lusaka; tel. 975642011 (mobile); fax 967052011 (mobile); e-mail citizens@thecitizensdemocraticparty.com; internet www.thecitizensdemocraticparty.com.

Heritage Party (HP): POB 51055, Lusaka; f. 2001 by expelled mems of the MMD; Pres. Brig.-Gen. GODFREY MIYANDA.

Movement for Multi-party Democracy (MMD): POB 30708, Lusaka; tel. (21) 1250177; fax (21) 1252329; e-mail mmd@zamtel.zm; internet www.mmdzam.org; f. 1990; registration suspended in March 2012; Pres. (vacant); Nat. Sec. Maj. RICHARD KACHINGWE.

National Democratic Focus: Lusaka; f. 2006 to contest the presidential election; Acting Chair. NEVERS MUMBA (RP).

All Peoples' Congress Party (APC): Lusaka; f. 2005 by fmr mems of the FDD; Pres. WINRIGHT K. NGONDO.

Party for Unity, Democracy and Development (PUDD): Lusaka; f. 2004 by fmr mems of the MMD; Pres. (vacant).

Reform Party (RP): Lusaka; f. 2005 by fmr mems of the MMD; Pres. NEVERS MUMBA; Nat. Chair. EVA SANDERSON; Sec.-Gen. CLEMENT MICHELO.

Zambia Democratic Conference (ZADECO): Lusaka; f. 1998 as the Zambia Democratic Congress Popular Front by fmr mems of the Zambia Democratic Congress; disbanded in 1999; reformed after 2001 election by fmr mems of the ZAP; Pres. Rev. Dr DAN PULE.

Zambia Republican Party (ZRP): Lusaka; f. 2001 by merger of the Republican Party (f. 2000) and the Zambia Alliance for Progress (f. 1999); Gen. Sec. SILVIA MASEBO; Nat. Chair. BEN KAPITA.

National Party (NP): POB 37840, Lusaka 10101; tel. (21) 18491431; e-mail nationalparty1993@yahoo.com; f. 1993; by fmr mems of the MMD; promotes human rights; Pres. Rev. RICHARD KAMBULU; Sec.-Gen. NDANISO BANDA.

National Restoration Party (NAREP): Plot 2386, Tuleteka Rd, off Makishi Rd, Fairview, Lusaka; tel. 966102016 (mobile); e-mail info@newzambia.org; internet www.newzambia.org; f. 2009; Pres. ELIAS CHIPIMO, Jr; Sec.-Gen. Bishop JAVAN KAMANGA (acting).

Patriotic Front (PF): Farmers House, POB 320015, Lusaka; tel. 96768080 (mobile); fax (21) 1228661; internet www.pf.com.zm; f. 2001 by expelled mems of the MMD; Pres. MICHAEL CHILUFYA SATA; Sec.-Gen. WYNTER MUNACAAMBWA KABIMBA.

United Democratic Alliance (UDA): Kenneth Kaunda House, Cairo Rd, Lusaka; f. 2006 to contest that year's elections; Nat. Chair. TILYENJI KAUNDA (FDD).

Forum for Democracy and Development (FDD): POB 35868, Lusaka; f. 2001 by expelled mems of the MMD; Pres. EDITH NAWAKWI; Chair. SIMON ZUKAS.

United National Independence Party (UNIP): POB 30302, Lusaka; tel. (21) 1221197; fax (21) 1221327; f. 1959; sole legal party 1972–90; Pres. TILYENJI KAUNDA; Nat. Chair. KEN KAIRA.

United Party for National Development (UPND): POB 33199, Lusaka; internet www.upnd.org; f. 1998; incl. fmr mems of the Progressive People's Party and Zambia Dem. Party; Pres. HAKAINDE HICHILEMA.

Diplomatic Representation

EMBASSIES AND HIGH COMMISSIONS IN ZAMBIA

Angola: Plot 108, Great East Rd, Northmead, POB 31595, 10101 Lusaka; tel. (21) 1134764; fax (21) 1221210; Ambassador BALBINA MALHEIROS DIAS DA SILVA.

Botswana: 5201 Pandit Nehru Rd, Diplomatic Triangle, POB 31910, 10101 Lusaka; tel. (21) 1250555; fax (21) 1250804; High Commissioner TUELONYANA DITLHABI-OLIPHANT.

Brazil: 4 Manenekela Road, Woodlands, Lusaka; tel. (21) 1252171; fax (21) 1253203; e-mail brasemblusaca@iconnect.zm; Ambassador JOSAL LUIZ PELLEGRINO.

China, People's Republic: Plot 7430, United Nations Ave, Long-acres, POB 31975, 10101 Lusaka; tel. (21) 1251169; fax (21) 1251157; e-mail chinaemb_zm@mfa.gov.cn; internet zm.chineseembassy.org; Ambassador ZHOU YUXIAO.

Congo, Democratic Republic: Plot 1124, Parirenyatwa Rd, POB 31287, 10101 Lusaka; tel. and fax (21) 1235679; Ambassador JOHNSON WA BINANA.

Cuba: 5574 Mogoye Rd, Kalundu, POB 33132, 10101 Lusaka; tel. (21) 1291308; fax (21) 1291586; e-mail ambassador@iconnect.zm; internet www.cubadiplomatica.cu/zambia; Ambassador CARIDAD PÉREZ GONZÁLEZ.

Denmark: 5219 Haile Selassie Ave, POB 50299, Lusaka; tel. (21) 1254277; fax (21) 1254618; e-mail lunamb@um.dk; internet www .zambia.um.dk; Chargé d'affaires PETER JUL LARSEN.

Egypt: Plot 5206, United Nations Ave, Longacres, POB 32428, Lusaka 10101; tel. (21) 1250229; fax (21) 1252213; Ambassador SALAH EL-DIN ABDEL SADEK.

Finland: Haile Selassie Ave, opp. Ndeke House, Longacres, POB 50819, 15101 Lusaka; tel. (21) 1251988; fax (21) 1253783; e-mail sanomat.lus@formin.fi; internet www.finland.org.zm; Ambassador PERTTI ANTTINEN.

France: Mpile Bldg, 74 Independence Ave, POB 30062, 10101 Lusaka; tel. (21) 1251322; fax (21) 1254475; e-mail cad .lusaka-amba@diplomatie.gouv.fr; internet www.ambafrance-zm .org; Ambassador MARIE-ANNICK BOURDIN.

Germany: Plot 5209, United Nations Ave, POB 50120, 15101 Ridgeway, Lusaka; tel. (21) 1250644; fax (21) 1254014; e-mail info@lusaka.diplo.de; internet www.lusaka.diplo.de; Ambassador BERND FINKE.

Holy See: 283 Los Angeles Blvd, POB 31445, 10101 Lusaka; tel. (21) 1251033; fax (21) 1250601; e-mail nuntius@coppernet.zm; Apostolic Nuncio Most Rev. JULIO MURAT (Titular Archbishop of Orange).

India: 1 Pandit Nehru Rd, POB 32111, 10101 Lusaka; tel. (21) 1253159; fax (21) 1254118; e-mail hoc.lusaka@mea.gov.in; internet www.hcizambia.com; High Commissioner ASHOK KUMAR.

Ireland: 6663 Katima Mulilo Rd, Olympia Park, POB 34923, 10101 Lusaka; tel. (21) 1290650; fax (21) 1290482; e-mail iremb@zamnet .zm; internet www.embassyofireland.co.zm; Ambassador TONY COTTER.

Italy: Plot 5211, Embassy Park, Diplomatic Triangle, POB 50497, Lusaka; tel. (21) 1250781; fax (21) 1254929; e-mail ambasciata .lusaka@esteri.it; internet www.amblusaka.esteri.it; Ambassador Dr PIER MARIO DACCO.

Japan: Plot 5218, Haile Selassie Ave, POB 34190, 10101 Lusaka; tel. (21) 1251555; fax (21) 1254425; e-mail jez@zamtel.zm; internet www .zm.emb-japan.go.jp; Ambassador AKIO EGAWA.

Kenya: 5207 United Nations Ave, POB 50298, 10101 Lusaka; tel. (21) 1250722; fax (21) 1253829; e-mail highcommissioner@ kenyamission.org.zm; internet www.kenyamission.org.zm; High Commissioner Dr KIPYEGO CHELUGET.

Libya: 251 Ngwee Rd, off United Nations Ave, Longacres, POB 35319, 10101 Lusaka; tel. (21) 1253055; fax (21) 1251239; Ambassador KHALIFA OMER SWIEXI.

Malawi: 31 Bishops Rd, Kabulonga, POB 50425, Lusaka; tel. (21) 1265768; fax (21) 1265765; e-mail mhcomm@iwayafrica.com; High Commissioner Dr CHRISSIE MUGHOGHO.

Mozambique: Kacha Rd, Plot 9592, POB 34877, 10101 Lusaka; tel. (21) 1220333; fax (21) 1220345; e-mail embamoc.zambia@minec.gov .mz; High Commissioner (vacant).

Namibia: 30B Mutende Rd, Woodlands, POB 30577, 10101 Lusaka; tel. (21) 1260407; fax (21) 1263858; e-mail namibia@coppernet.zm; High Commissioner SALOMON WITBOOI.

Netherlands: 5208 United Nations Ave, POB 31905, 10101 Lusaka; tel. (21) 1253819; fax (21) 1253733; e-mail lus@minbuza.nl; internet www.netherlandsembassy.org.zm; Ambassador ARDI STOIOS-BRAKEN.

Nigeria: 5203 Haile Selassie Ave, Diplomatic Triangle, Longacres, POB 32598, Lusaka; tel. (21) 1229860; fax (21) 1223791; High Commissioner SIFAWU MOMOH.

Norway: cnr Birdcage Walk and Haile Selassie Ave, Plot No. 245/61, Longacres, POB 34570, 10101 Lusaka; tel. (21) 1252188; fax (21) 1253915; e-mail emb.lusaka@mfa.no; internet www.norway.org.zm; Ambassador ARVE OFSTAD.

Russia: Plot 6407, Diplomatic Triangle, POB 32355, 10101 Lusaka; tel. (21) 1252120; fax (21) 1253582; Ambassador (vacant).

Saudi Arabia: 27BC Leopards Hill Rd, Kabulonga, POB 34411, 10101 Lusaka; tel. (21) 1266861; fax (21) 1266863; e-mail saudiemb@ uudial.zm; Ambassador HASSAN ATTAR.

Serbia: Independence Ave 5216, POB 33379, 10101 Lusaka; tel. (21) 1250235; fax (21) 1253889; e-mail serbianemb.lusaka@gmail.com; internet lusaka.mfa.gov.rs; Chargé d'affaires a.i. DJORDJE LUKIC.

Somalia: G3/377A Kabulonga Rd, POB 34051, Lusaka; tel. (21) 1262119; Ambassador (vacant).

South Africa: D26, Cheetah Rd, Kabulonga, Private Bag W369, Lusaka; tel. (21) 1260999; fax (21) 1263001; e-mail sahcadmin@ samnet.zm; High Commissioner MOSES MABOKELA CHIKANE.

Sudan: 31 Ng'umbo Rd, Longacres, POB RW179X, 15200 Lusaka; tel. (21) 1252116; fax (21) 1252448; e-mail sudemblsk@hotmail.com; Ambassador MOHAMED BALILA.

Sweden: Haile Selassie Ave, POB 50264, 10101 Lusaka; tel. (21) 1251711; fax (21) 1254049; e-mail ambassaden.lusaka@foreign .ministry.se; internet www.swedenabroad.com/lusaka; Ambassador LENA NORDSTRÖM.

Tanzania: Ujamaa House, Plot 5200, United Nations Ave, POB 31219, 10101 Lusaka; tel. (21) 1253222; fax (21) 1254861; e-mail tzreplsk@zamnet.zm; High Commissioner JUSTA NYANGE (acting).

United Kingdom: Plot 5210, Independence Ave, POB 50050, 15101 Ridgeway, Lusaka; tel. (21) 1423200; fax (21) 1423291; internet ukinzambia.fco.gov.uk; High Commissioner JAMES THORNTON.

USA: cnr Independence and United Nations Aves, POB 31617, Lusaka; tel. (21) 1250955; fax (21) 1252225; e-mail irclusaka@ state.gov; internet zambia.usembassy.gov; Ambassador MARK CHARLES STORELLA.

Zimbabwe: 11058 Haile Selassie Ave, Longacres, POB 33491, 10101 Lusaka; tel. (21) 1254012; fax (21) 1227474; e-mail zimzam@ coppernet.zm; Ambassador LOVEMORE MAZEMO.

Judicial System

The judicial system of Zambia comprises a Supreme Court, a High Court, two Industrial Relations Courts, Subordinate Courts and Local Courts. The Supreme Court, consisting of a Chief Justice, a Deputy Chief Justice and seven other judges (or any such number of judges as may be prescribed by an Act of Parliament), is the final court of appeal and has the final say in all matters, including interpretation of the Constitution. The Chief Justice is also an ex officio judge of the High Court. The High Court hears appeals from the Subordinate Courts. It has jurisdiction to supervise any civil or criminal proceedings before any Subordinate Court or any Court-martial, and may make such orders, issue such writs and give such direction as it may consider appropriate for ensuring that justice is duly administered by them. The Local Courts deal primarily with customary law, but they also have limited criminal jurisdiction.

Supreme Court: Independence Ave, POB 50067, Ridgeway, Lusaka; tel. (21) 1251330; fax (21) 1251743; internet www .judiciary.gov.zm; Chief Justice LOMBE CHIBESAKUNDA; Deputy Chief Justice FLORENCE MUMBA (acting).

High Court: Lusaka; consists of the Chief Justice and 19 other judges.

Attorney-General: MUMBA MALILA.

Religion

CHRISTIANITY

Council of Churches in Zambia: CCZ Ecumenical Centre, Plot 377A, Bishops Rd, Kabulonga, POB 30315, Lusaka; tel. (21) 1267738; fax (21) 1267740; e-mail info@ccz.org.zm; internet www.ccz.org.zm; f. 1945; Pres. Rev. MOSES LUCAS MWALE (Brethren in Christ Church); Gen. Sec. SUZANNE MEMBE MATALE; 22 mem. churches and 19 affiliate mem. orgs.

The Anglican Communion

Anglicans are adherents of the Church of the Province of Central Africa, covering Botswana, Malawi, Zambia and Zimbabwe. The Church comprises 15 dioceses, including five in Zambia. There are an estimated 80,000 adherents in Zambia.

Archbishop of the Province of Central Africa and Bishop of Northern Zambia: Rt Rev. ALBERT CHAMA, POB 20798, Kitwe; tel. (21) 2223264; fax (21) 2224778; e-mail dionorth@zamnet.zm.

Bishop of Central Zambia: Rt Rev. DEREK G. KAMUKWAMBA, POB 70172, Ndola; tel. (21) 2612431; fax (21) 2615954; e-mail adcznla@zamnet.zm.

Bishop of Eastern Zambia: Rt Rev. WILLIAM MUCHOMBO, POB 510154, Chipata; tel. and fax (21) 6221294; e-mail dioeastzm@zamnet.zm.

Bishop of Luapula: Rt Rev. ROBERT MUMBI, POB 710210, Mansa, Luapula.

Bishop of Lusaka: Rt Rev. DAVID NJOVU, Bishop's Lodge, POB 30183, Lusaka; tel. (21) 1264515; fax (21) 1262379; e-mail angdiolu@zamnet.zm.

Protestant Churches

At mid-2000 there were an estimated 2.7m. Protestants in Zambia.

African Methodist Episcopal Church: Carousel Bldg, Lumumba Rd, POB 36628, Lusaka; tel. 955708031; fax (21) 1225067; Presiding Elder Rev. PAUL KAWIMBE; 440 congregations, 880,000 mems.

Baptist Church: Lubu Rd, POB 30636, Lusaka; tel. (21) 1253620.

Baptist Mission of Zambia: Baptist Bldg, 3062 Great East Rd, POB 50599, 15101 Ridgeway, Lusaka; tel. (21) 1222492; fax (21) 1227520; internet bmoz.org.

Brethren in Christ Church: POB 630115, Choma; tel. (21) 3320228; fax (21) 3320127; e-mail biccz@zamtel.zm; internet www .bic.org; f. 1906; Bishop Rev. T. HAMUKANG'ANDU; 180 congregations, 19,526 mems.

Evangelical Lutheran Church in Zambia: Plot No. 145-4893, Mpezeni Rd, POB 37701, 10101 Lusaka; tel. 97787584 (mobile); fax (21) 1224023; e-mail elcza_head@yahoo.com; Senior Pastor Rev. ALFRED CHANA; 2,210 mems (2010).

Reformed Church in Zambia: POB 38255, Lusaka; tel. (21) 1295369; e-mail info@rczsynod.co.zm; internet www.rczsynod.co .zm; f. 1899; African successor to the Dutch Reformed Church mission; Synod Moderator Rev. MOSES LUCAS MWALE; 147 congregations, 400,000 mems.

Seventh-day Adventist Church: Plot 9221, cnr Burma Rd and Independence Ave, POB 36010, Lusaka; tel. and fax (21) 1254036; e-mail lcsdac@zamnet.zm; internet www.lcsdac.net.zm; f. 1905; Pres. Dr CORNELIUS MULENGA MATANDIKO; Sec. HARRINGTON SIMUI AKOMBWA; 534,126 mems.

United Church of Zambia: Synod Headquarters, Nationalist Rd at Burma Rd, POB 50122, Lusaka; tel. (21) 1250641; fax (21) 1252198; e-mail uczsynod@zamnet.zm; f. 1965; Synod Bishop Rev. MUTALE MULUMBWA; Gen. Sec. PEGGY KABONDE; c. 3m. mems.

Other denominations active in Zambia include the Assemblies of God, the Church of Christ, the Church of the Nazarene, the Evangelical Fellowship of Zambia, the Kimbanguist Church, the Presbyterian Church of Southern Africa, the Religious Society of Friends (Quakers) and the United Pentecostal Church. At mid-2000 there were an estimated 2m. adherents professing other forms of Christianity.

The Roman Catholic Church

Zambia comprises two archdioceses and nine dioceses. The number of adherents in the country is equivalent to some 30% of the total population.

Bishops' Conference

Catholic Secretariat, Unity House, cnr Freedom Way and Katunjila Rd, POB 31965, 10201 Lusaka; tel. (21) 1262613; fax (21) 1262658; e-mail zec@zamnet.zm.

f. 1984; Pres. Rt Rev. LUNGU GEORGE COSMOS ZUMAIRE (Bishop of Chipata).

Archbishop of Kasama: Most Rev. IGNATIUS CHAMA, Archbishop's House, POB 410143, Kasama; tel. (21) 4221248; fax (21) 4222202; e-mail archkasa@zamtel.zm.

Archbishop of Lusaka: Most Rev. TELESPHORE GEORGE MPUNDU, 41 Wamulwa Rd, POB 32754, 10101 Lusaka; tel. (21) 1255973; fax (21) 1255975; e-mail adlarch@zamnet.zm.

ISLAM

There are about 10,000 members of the Muslim Association in Zambia.

Supreme Islamic Council of Zambia: Lusaka; Pres. SUZYO ZIMBA.

BAHÁ'Í FAITH

National Spiritual Assembly: Sekou Touré Rd, Plot 4371, Private Bag RW227X, Ridgeway 15102, Lusaka; tel. and fax (21) 1254505; f. 1952; Sec.-Gen. MARGARET K. LENGWE; mems resident in 1,456 localities.

The Press

DAILIES

The Post: 36 Bwinjimfumu Rd, Rhodespark, Private Bag E352, Lusaka; tel. (21) 1231092; fax (21) 1229271; e-mail post@post.co.zm; internet www.postzambia.com; f. 1991; privately owned; Editor FRED M'MEMBE; circ. 29,000.

The Times of Zambia: Kabelenga Ave, POB 70069, Ndola; tel. and fax (21) 2614469; e-mail times@zamtel.zm; internet www.times.co .zm; f. 1943; govt-owned; English; Man. Editor GODFREY MALAMA; circ. 25,000.

Zambia Daily Mail: Zambia Publishing Company, POB 31421, Lusaka; tel. (21) 1225131; fax (21) 1225881; internet www.daily-mail .co.zm; f. 1968; govt-owned; English; Man. Editor ISAAC CHIPAMPE; circ. 40,000.

PERIODICALS

The Challenge: Mission Press, Chifubu Rd, POB 71581, Ndola; tel. (21) 2680456; fax (21) 2680484; e-mail info@missionpress.org; internet www.missionpress.org; f. 1999; quarterly; English; social, educational and religious; Roman Catholic; edited by Franciscan friars; Dir Fr MATTHEW MUMBA; circ. 5,000.

Chipembele Magazine: POB 30255, Lusaka; tel. (21) 1251630; fax (21) 1251630; e-mail wecsz@coppernet.zm; internet www .conservationzambia.org; f. 1953; 2 a year; publ. by Wildlife Conservation Soc. of Zambia; circ. 3,000 annually; Editor ADAM GOULDING.

Farming in Zambia: POB 50197, Lusaka; tel. (21) 1213551; f. 1965; quarterly; publ. by Ministry of Agriculture and Livestock; Editor L. P. CHIRWA; circ. 3,000.

Icengelo: Lusaka; internet icengelo.com; Bemba language.

Imbila: POB RW20, Lusaka; tel. (21) 1217254; e-mail mambue2002@zanis.org.zm; f. 1953; monthly; publ. by Zambia Information Services; Bemba; Editor ALFRED M ZULU; circ. 20,000.

Intanda: POB RW20, Lusaka; tel. (21) 1219675; f. 1958; monthly; publ. by Zambia Information Services; Tonga; Editor J. SIKAULU; circ. 6,000.

Konkola: Zambia Consolidated Copper Mines Ltd, PR Dept, POB 71505, Ndola; tel. (21) 2640142; f. 1973 as *Mining Mirror*; monthly; English; Editor G. MUKUWA; circ. 30,000.

The Lowdown: Lusaka; internet www.lowdown.co.zm; f. 1995; monthly; English; Editor HEATHER CHALCRAFT.

Lukanga News: POB 919, Kabwe; tel. (21) 5217254; publ. by Zambia Information Services; Lenje; Editor J. H. N. NKOMANGA; circ. 5,500.

National Mirror: Multimedia Zambia, 15701 Woodlands, POB 320199, Lusaka; tel. (21) 1263864; fax (21) 1263050; f. 1972; fortnightly; news, current affairs and foreign affairs; publ. by Multimedia Zambia; Editor SIMON MWANZA; circ. 40,000.

Ngoma: POB RW20, Lusaka; tel. (21) 1219675; monthly; Lunda, Kaonde and Luvale; publ. by Zambia Information Services; Editor B. A. LUHILA; circ. 3,000.

Speak Out!: POB 70244, Ndola; tel. (21) 2612241; fax (21) 2620630; e-mail speakout@zamnet.zm; f. 1984; six a year; Christian; aimed at youth readership up to 35 years; Man. Editor CONSTANTIA TREPPE; circ. 25,000.

The Sportsman: POB 31762, Lusaka; tel. (21) 1214250; f. 1980; monthly; Man. Editor Sam Sikazwe; circ. 18,000.

Sunday Times of Zambia: Kabelenga Ave, POB 70069, Ndola; tel. (21) 1614469; fax (21) 2617096; e-mail times@zamtel.zm; internet www.times.co.zm/sunday; f. 1965; owned by UNIP; English; Man. Editor Arthur Simuchoba; circ. 78,000.

Workers' Voice: POB 20652, Kitwe; tel. (21) 2211999; f. 1972; fortnightly; publ. by Zambia Congress of Trade Unions.

Youth: POB 30302, Lusaka; tel. (21) 1211411; f. 1974; quarterly; publ. by UNIP Youth League; Editor-in-Chief N. Anamela; circ. 20,000.

Zambia Government Gazette: POB 30136, Lusaka; tel. (21) 1228724; fax (21) 1224486; f. 1911; weekly; English; official notices.

NEWS AGENCY

Zambia News and Information Services (ZANIS): Mass Media Complex, 2nd Floor, Alick Nkhata Rd, POB 50020, Lusaka; tel. (21) 1255255; fax (21) 125163; e-mail zana@zamnet.zm; internet www.zana.gov.zm; f. 2005 through merger of Zambia News Agency (ZANA) and Zambia Information Services (ZIS).

PRESS ASSOCIATIONS

Press Association of Zambia (PAZA): Bishops Rd, Multi-Media Centre, POB 37065, Lusaka; tel. (21) 1263595; fax (21) 1263110; f. 1983; Pres. Andrew Sakala; Vice-Pres. Amos Chanda.

Zambia Media Council (ZAMEC): Lusaka; f. 2012; Chair. Paul Mususu.

Zambia Union of Journalists: POB 30394, Lusaka; tel. (21) 1227348; fax (21) 1221695; e-mail zuj.zambia@yahoo.com; Pres. Anthony Mulowa; Sec.-Gen. Bob Sianjalika.

Publishers

Africa: Literature Centre, POB 21319, Kitwe; tel. (21) 2210765; fax (21) 2210716; general, educational, religious; Dir Jackson Mbewe.

African Social Research: Institute of Economic and Social Research, University of Zambia, POB 32379, Lusaka; tel. (21) 1294131; fax (21) 1253952; social research in Africa; Editor Mubanga E. Kashoki.

Bookworld Ltd: Plot 10552, off Lumumba Rd, POB 31838, Lusaka; tel. (21) 1230606; fax (21) 1230614; e-mail bookworld@realtime.zm; f. 1991.

Daystar Publications Ltd: POB 32211, Lusaka; f. 1966; religious; Man. Dir S. E. M. Pheko.

Directory Publishers of Zambia Ltd: Mabalenga Rd, POB 30963, Lusaka; tel. (21) 1257133; fax (21) 1257137; e-mail dpz@coppernet.zm; f. 1958; trade directories; Gen. Man. W. D. Wratten.

Multimedia Zambia: Woodlands, POB 320199, Lusaka; tel. and fax (21) 1261193; f. 1971; religious and educational books, audio-visual materials; Exec. Dir Eddy Mupeso.

University of Zambia Press (UNZA Press): POB 32379, 10101 Lusaka; tel. (21) 1292269; fax (21) 1253952; f. 1938; academic books, papers and journals.

Zambia Educational Publishing House: Chishango Rd, POB 32708, 10101 Lusaka; tel. (21) 1222324; fax (21) 1225073; f. 1967; educational and general; Man. Dir Beniko E. Mulota.

GOVERNMENT PUBLISHING HOUSES

Government Printer: POB 30136, Lusaka; tel. (21) 1228724; fax (21) 1224486; official documents and statistical bulletins.

Zambia Information Services: POB 50020, Lusaka; tel. (21) 1219673; state-controlled; Dir Benson Sianga.

PUBLISHERS' ASSOCIATION

Booksellers' and Publishers' Association of Zambia: POB 31838, Lusaka; tel. (21) 1222647; fax (21) 1225195; Chair. Ray Munamwimbu; Sec. Basil Mbewe.

Broadcasting and Communications

TELECOMMUNICATIONS

In 2011 there were three providers of mobile telephone services in Zambia. ZAMTEL also provides fixed-line telephone services. At the end of 2011 there were 8,164,553 mobile telephone subscribers and 85,727 fixed-line telephone subscribers in the country.

Airtel Zambia Ltd: Nyerere Rd, Woodlands, POB 320001, Lusaka; tel. (21) 1250707; e-mail customerservice.zm@zain.com; internet africa.airtel.com/zambia; f. 1997 as ZamCell Ltd; fmrly Celtel Zambia, subsequently Zain Zambia, present name adopted 2010; mobile cellular telephone operator; Man. Dir Fayaz King; c. 500,000 subscribers.

MTN (Zambia) Ltd: Plot 1278, Lubuto Rd, Rhodespark, POB 35464, Lusaka; tel. 966750750 (mobile); fax 966257732 (mobile); e-mail mtn@mtnzambia.co.zm; internet www.mtnzambia.co.zm; f. 1997 as Telecel (Zambia) Ltd; acquired by MTN Group, South Africa, in 2005; mobile cellular telecommunications provider; CEO Abdul Ismail; 152,000 subscribers (2006).

Zambia Telecommunications Co Ltd (ZAMTEL): Zamtel House, POB 37000, Lusaka; tel. (21) 1333152; fax (21) 1256622; e-mail zamtel@zamtel.zm; internet www.zamtel.zm; operates fixed-line network and Cell-Z cellular network (f. 1995); Chair. and Acting CEO Dr Mupanga Mwanakatwe.

Regulatory Authority

Zambia Information and Communications Technology Authority (ZICTA): Plot 4909, cnr Independence and United Nations Aves, POB 36871, Lusaka; tel. (21) 1241236; fax (21) 1246701; e-mail info@zicta.zm; internet www.zicta.zm; f. 1994; fmrly Zambian Communications Authority, present name adopted 2009; Dir-Gen. Margaret Mudenda.

BROADCASTING

Zambia National Broadcasting Corpn: Mass Media Complex, Alick Nkhata Rd, POB 50015, Lusaka; tel. (21) 1252005; fax (21) 1254013; e-mail lukundosa@yahoo.com; internet www.znbc.co.zm; f. 1961; state-owned; two national radio stations (Radio 1 and Radio 2) and one line-of-rail station (Radio 4); television broadcasts along the line of rail, from Livingstone to Chililabombwe; services in English and seven Zambian languages; Dir-Gen. Joe Chilaizya.

Radio

Breeze FM: POB 511178, Chipata; tel. (21) 6221175; fax (21) 6221823; e-mail news@breezefmchipata.com; internet breezefmchipata.com; f. 2003; Nyanja and English; community-based commercial radio; broadcasts to the Eastern Province; signal is also received in parts of north-west Malawi and border areas of Tete Province in Mozambique; Man. Dir Mike Daka.

Educational Broadcasting Services: Headquarters: POB 50231, Lusaka; tel. (21) 1251724; radio broadcasts from Lusaka; audio-visual aids service from POB 50295, Lusaka; Controller Michael Mulombe.

Radio Chikaya: POB 530290, Lundazi; tel. (6) 480080; e-mail rchikaya@zamtel.zm.

Radio Chikuni: Private Bag E702, POB 660239, Monze; tel. and fax (32) 50708; e-mail chikuni@sat.signis.net; internet www.chikuniradio.org.

Radio Icengelo: Plot 5282, Mwandi Cres., Riverside, POB 20694, Kitwe; tel. (2) 220478; fax (2) 229305; e-mail radioice@mail.zamtel.zm; Man. Rev. Fr Nicholas Mubanga.

Radio Maria: POB 510307, Chipata; tel. and fax (21) 6221154; e-mail info.zam@radiomaria.org; internet www.radiomaria.org; f. 1999; Dir Mwanza Gabriel Kwaku.

Radio Phoenix: Private Bag E702, Lusaka; tel. (21) 1223581; fax (21) 1226839; e-mail rphoenixinfo@gmail.com; internet www.radiophoenixzambia.com; commercial radio station; Chair. Errol T. Hickey.

Yatsani Radio: Leopards Hill Rd, Bauleni Catholic Church, POB 320147, Lusaka; tel. (21) 1261082; fax (21) 1265842; internet yatsani.com; f. 1999; owned by the Archdiocese of Lusaka; Roman Catholic religious community; broadcasts to Lusaka; Dir Most Rev. Medardo Joseph Mazombwe (Archbishop of Lusaka).

Television

Educational Broadcasting Services: (see Radio).

Muvi Television: Plot No. 17734, Nangwenya Rd, POB 33932, Lusaka; tel. (21) 1253171; fax (21) 1257351; e-mail frontoffice@muvitv.com; internet www.muvitv.com; Man. Dir Steve Nyirenda.

Finance

(cap. = capital; auth. = authorized; res = reserves; dep. = deposits; m. = million; br(s). = branch(es); amounts in kwacha)

BANKING

In 2010 there were 18 commercial banks, 24 microfinance institutions and one development bank in Zambia.

Central Bank

Bank of Zambia: Bank Sq., Cairo Rd, POB 30080, 10101 Lusaka; tel. (21) 1228888; fax (21) 1225652; internet www.boz.zm; f. 1964; bank of issue; cap. 10,020m., res 317,538m., dep. 5,460,206m. (Dec. 2009); Gov. and Chair. Dr MICHAEL M. GONDWE; br. in Ndola.

Commercial Banks

Finance Bank Zambia Ltd: 2101 Chanik House, Cairo Rd, POB 37102, 10101 Lusaka; tel. (21) 1229733; fax (21) 1227290; e-mail fbz@financebank.co.zm; internet www.financebank.co.zm; f. 1986 as Leasing Finance Bank Ltd; name changed as above 1988; cap. 3,630m., res 9,320m., dep. 823,894m. (Dec. 2006); Man. Dir and CEO BARKAT ALI; 33 brs and 10 agencies.

National Savings and Credit Bank: Plot 248B, Cairo Rd, POB 30067, Lusaka; tel. (21) 1227534; fax (21) 1223296; e-mail natsave@zamnet.zm; internet www.natsave.co.zm; f. 1972; state-owned; Chair. FRANK NGAMBI; Man. Dir CEPHAS CHABU.

Zambia National Commercial Bank PLC (ZANACO): POB 33611, Plot 33454 Cairo Rd, Lusaka; tel. (21) 1228979; fax (21) 1223106; e-mail support@zanaco.co.zm; internet www.zanaco.co.zm; f. 1969; 50.8% govt-owned; cap. 11,550m., res 189,142m., dep. 2,296,000m. (Dec. 2009); Chair. Dr MUTUMBA BULL LAWANIKA; Man. Dir MARTYN H. SCHOUTEN; 41 brs.

Foreign Banks

Bank of China (Zambia) Ltd (China): Amandra House, Ben Bella Rd, POB 34550, Lusaka; tel. (21) 1235349; fax (21) 1235350; e-mail service_zm@bank-of-china.com; f. 1997; Chair. PING YUE; Gen. Man. HONG XINSHENG.

Barclays Bank Zambia PLC (United Kingdom): Kafue House, Cairo Rd, POB 31936, Lusaka; tel. (21) 1228858; fax (21) 1226185; e-mail barclays.zambia@barclays.com; internet www.africa.barclays.com; f. 1971; cap. 91,109m., res 247,794m., dep. 2,857,304m. (Dec. 2009); Chair. JACOB SIKAZWE; Man. Dir SAVIOUR CHIBIYA; 5 brs.

Citibank Zambia Ltd (USA): Citibank House, Cha Cha Cha Rd, POB 30037, Southend, Lusaka; tel. (21) 1229025; fax (21) 1226264; internet www.citibank.co.zm; f. 1979; cap. 1,000.0m., res 23,655.7m., dep. 1,100,772.6m. (Dec. 2009); Man. Dir JOYCE-ANN WAINAINA; 1 br.

Ecobank Zambia: 22768 Thabo Mbeki Rd, POB 30705, Lusaka; tel. (21) 1250056; fax (21) 1250171; e-mail ecobankzm@ecobank.com; internet www.ecobank.com; Chair. PETRONELLA N. MWANGALA; Man. Dir CHARITY LUMPA.

Indo-Zambia Bank (IZB): Plot 6907, Cairo Rd, POB 35411, Lusaka; tel. (21) 1224653; fax (21) 1225090; e-mail izb@zamnet.zm; internet www.izb.co.zm; f. 1984; cap. 15,000.0m., res 38,591.9m., dep. 767,161.3m. (March 2010); Chair. ORLENE Y. MOYO; Man. Dir CYRIL PATRO; 9 brs.

Stanbic Bank Zambia Ltd: Woodgate House, 6th Floor, Cairo Rd, POB 32111, Lusaka; tel. (21) 1229285; fax (21) 1225380; e-mail stanbic@zamnet.zm; internet www.stanbicbank.co.zm; f. 1971; wholly owned by Standard Bank Investment Corpn; cap. 7,700m., res 172,526m., dep. 2,160,400m. (Dec. 2009); Chair. V. CHITALU; Man. Dir L. F. KALALA; 7 brs.

Standard Chartered Bank Zambia PLC: Standard House, Cairo Rd, POB 32238, Lusaka; tel. (21) 1229242; fax (21) 1225337; internet www.standardchartered.com/zm; f. 1971; 90% owned by Standard Chartered Holdings (Africa) BV, Netherlands; 10% state-owned; cap. 2,048m., res 23,657m., dep. 2,589,288m. (Dec. 2009); Chair. GEORGE SOKOTA; Man. Dir MIZINGA MELU; 16 brs.

Development Bank

Development Bank of Zambia: Development House, Katondo Rd, POB 33955, Lusaka; tel. (21) 1228576; fax (21) 1222821; e-mail projects@dbz.co.zm; internet www.dbz.co.zm; f. 1973; 99% state-owned; total assets 64,111m. (Dec. 2005); Chair. NAMUKULO MUKUTU; Man. Dir ABRAHAM MWENDA; 2 brs.

Banking Association

Bankers' Association of Zambia: POB 34810, Lusaka; tel. (21) 1234255; fax (21) 1233046; e-mail bazsecretariat@coppernet.zm; Chair. MIZINGA MELU.

STOCK EXCHANGE

Lusaka Stock Exchange (LuSE): Exchange Bldg, 3rd Floor, Central Park, Cairo Rd, POB 34523, Lusaka; tel. (21) 1228391; fax (21) 1225969; e-mail info@luse.co.zm; internet www.luse.co.zm; f. 1994; Chair. FRIDAY NDHLOVU; Gen. Man. BEATRICE NKANZA.

INSURANCE

In 2010 there were 15 licensed insurance companies in Zambia: two reinsurance companies, eight general insurance companies and five long-term insurance companies.

African Life Assurance Zambia: Mukuba Pension House, 4th Floor, Dedan Kimathi Rd, POB 31991; tel. (21) 1225452; fax (21) 1225435; e-mail customercare@african-life.com.zm; f. 2002; life insurance; CEO STEVE WILLIAMS.

Goldman Insurance Ltd: Zambia National Savings and Credit Bank Bldg, 2nd Floor, Cairo Rd, Private Bag W395, Lusaka; tel. (21) 1235234; fax (21) 1227262; e-mail goldman@zamnet.zm; internet www.goldman.co.zm; f. 1992; CEO M. N. RAJU.

Madison Insurance Co Ltd: Plot 255, Kaleya Rd, Roma, POB 37013, Lusaka; tel. (21) 1295311; fax (21) 1295320; internet www.madisonzambia.com; f. 1992; general and micro-insurance; Chair. DAVID A. R. PHIRI; Man. Dir LAWRENCE S. SIKUTWA.

NICO Insurance Zambia Ltd (NIZA): 1131 Parirenyatwa Rd, Fairview, POB 32825, Lusaka; tel. (21) 1222862; fax (21) 1222863; e-mail nicozam@zamnet.zm; internet www.nicomw.com/zambia; f. 1997; subsidiary of NICO Group, Malawi; general insurance; Chair. JOHN MWANAKATWE; Gen. Man. TITUS KALENGA.

Professional Insurance Corpn Zambia Ltd (PICZ): Finsbury Park, Kabwe Roundabout, POB 34264, Lusaka; tel. (21) 1227509; fax (21) 1222151; e-mail customerservice@picz.co.zm; internet www.picz.co.zm; f. 1992; Chair. R. L. MATHANI; Man. Dir ASHOK CHAWLA.

Zambia State Insurance Corpn Ltd: Premium House, Independence Ave, POB 30894, Lusaka; tel. (21) 1229343; fax (21) 1222263; e-mail zsic@zsic.co.zm; internet www.zsic.co.zm; f. 1968; transfer to private sector pending; Chair. ALBERT WOOD; Man. Dir IRENE MUYENGA.

ZIGI Insurance Co Ltd: Mukuba Pension House, 5th Floor, POB 37782, Lusaka; tel. (21) 1226835; fax (21) 1231564; e-mail zigi@zamnet.zm; f. 1998; Chair. and CEO SAVIOUR H. KONIE.

Regulatory Authority

Pensions and Insurance Authority: Private Bag 30X, Ridgeway, Lusaka; tel. (21) 1293533; fax (21) 1293530; e-mail pia@pia.org.zm; internet www.pia.org.zm; f. 2005; Registrar MARTIN LIBINGA.

Trade and Industry

GOVERNMENT AGENCIES

Food Reserve Agency (FRA): Plot 7419, Manda Rd Light Industrial Area, POB 34054, Lusaka; tel. (21) 286097; fax (21) 1286096; e-mail fra@fra.org.zm; internet www.fra.org.zm; f. 1996; Exec. Dir LOVEJOY MALAMBO.

Zambia Development Agency (ZDA): Privatisation House, Nasser Rd, POB 30819, Lusaka; tel. (21) 1220177; fax (21) 1225270; e-mail info@zda.org.zm; internet www.zda.org.zm; f. 2006 by merger of the Zambia Privatisation Agency, the Zambia Investment Centre, the Export Board of Zambia, the Zambia Export Processing Zones Authority and the Small Enterprises Development Board; Dir-Gen. and CEO ANDREW CHIPWENDE.

Zambia Environmental Management Agency (ZEMA): cnr Church and Suez Rds, POB 35131, Lusaka; tel. (21) 1254023; fax (21) 1254164; tel. www.zema.org.zm.

Zambia Revenue Authority: Lusaka; internet www.zra.org.zm; f. 1994; Dir-Gen. WISDOM NEKAIRO.

DEVELOPMENT ORGANIZATION

Industrial Development Corpn of Zambia Ltd (INDECO): Indeco House, Buteko Place, POB 31935, Lusaka; tel. (21) 1228026; fax (21) 1228868; f. 1960; auth. cap. K300m.; taken over by the Nat. Housing Authority in May 2005; Chair. R. L. BWALYA; Man. Dir S. K. TAMELÉ.

CHAMBERS OF COMMERCE

Zambia Association of Chambers of Commerce and Industry: Great East Rd, Showgrounds, POB 30844, Lusaka; tel. (21) 1252483; fax (21) 1253020; e-mail secretariat@zacci.co.zm; internet www.zambiachambers.org; f. 1938; Pres. GEOFFREY SAKULANDA; CEO PRISCA M. CHIKWASHI; 16 district chambers, 11 trade assocs, 48 corporate mems.

Member chambers and associations include:

Chamber of Mines of Zambia: POB 22100, Kitwe; tel. (21) 2214122; f. 1941 as Northern Rhodesia Chamber of Mines; replaced by the Copper Industry Service Bureau 1965–2000; represents mining employers; 19 mems; Pres. NATHAN CHISHIMBA; Gen. Man. FREDERICK BANTUBONSE.

Zambia Association of Manufacturers: POB 30036, Lusaka; tel. (21) 1242780; fax (21) 1222912; e-mail babbar@zamnet.zm; f. 1985; Chair. CHANCE KABAGHE; 180 mems.

INDUSTRIAL AND TRADE ASSOCIATIONS

Tobacco Board of Zambia (TBZ): POB 31963, Lusaka; tel. (21) 1288995; fax (21) 1287118; e-mail tbz@zamnet.zm; promotes, monitors and controls tobacco production; CEO AVEN MUVWENDE.

Zambia Farm Employers' Association (ZFEA): Farmers' Village, Lusaka Agricultural and Commercial Showgrounds, POB 30395, Lusaka; tel. (21) 1252649; fax (21) 1252648; e-mail znfu@zamnet.zm; Chair. R. DENLY; 350 mems.

Other associations include: the Bankers' Asscn of Zambia; the Cotton Asscn of Zambia; the Environmental Conservation Asscn of Zambia; the Insurance Brokers' Asscn of Zambia; the Kapenta Fishermen Asscn; the National Aquaculture Asscn of Zambia; the National Council for Construction; the Poultry Asscn of Zambia; the Tobacco Asscn of Zambia; the Wildlife Producers' Asscn of Zambia; the Young Farmers' Clubs of Zambia; the Zambia Asscn of Clearing and Forwarding; the Zambia Asscn of Manufacturers; the Zambia Coffee Growers' Asscn; the Zambia Export Growers' Asscn; and Zambian Women in Agriculture.

EMPLOYERS' ORGANIZATION

Zambia Federation of Employers (ZFE): Olympia Extension, Mberere Rd, POB 31941, Lusaka; tel. (21) 1295969; fax (21) 1295781; e-mail zfe@zamnet.zm; internet www.zfe.co.zm; f. 1966; Pres. ALFRED MASUPHA.

UTILITIES

Electricity

Copperbelt Energy Corpn PLC (CEC): Private Bag E835, Postnet No. 145, Chindo Rd, Kabulonga, Lusaka; tel. (21) 1261647; fax (21) 1261640; e-mail info@cec.com.zm; internet www.cecinvestor.com; f. 1997 upon privatization of the power div. of Zambia Consolidated Copper Mines; privately owned co supplying power generated by ZESCO to mining cos in the Copperbelt; Exec. Chair. HANSON SINDOWE.

ZESCO (Zambia Electricity Supply Corpn) Ltd: Stand 6949, Great East Rd, POB 33304, Lusaka; tel. (21) 1226084; fax (21) 1222753; e-mail mchisela@zesco.co.zm; internet www.zesco.co.zm; f. 1970; state-owned; Chair. KWALELA LAMASWALA; Man. Dir CYPRIAN CHITUNDU.

CO-OPERATIVE

Zambia Co-operative Federation Ltd: Co-operative House, Cha Cha Cha Rd, POB 33579, Lusaka; tel. (21) 2220157; fax (21) 2222516; f. 1973; agricultural marketing; supply of agricultural chemicals and implements; cargo haulage; insurance; agricultural credit; auditing and accounting; property and co-operative devt; Chair. B. TETAMASHIMBA; Man. Dir G. Z. SIBALE.

TRADE UNION

Zambia Congress of Trade Unions (ZCTU): National Center, Solidarity House, POB 31146, Lusaka; tel. (21) 1260016; fax (21) 1266680; e-mail zctu@microlink.zm; f. 1965; Pres. LEONARD HIKAUMBA; Sec.-Gen. ROY MWABA; c. 350,000 mems (2012).

Transport

RAILWAYS

The total length of railways in Zambia was 2,162 km (including 891 km of the Tanzania–Zambia railway) in 2000. There are two major railway networks: the Zambia Railways network, which traverses the country from the Copperbelt in northern Zambia and links with the National Railways of Zimbabwe to provide access to South African ports, and the Tanzania–Zambia Railway (Tazara) network, linking New Kapiri-Mposhi in Zambia with Dar es Salaam in Tanzania. In August 2010 a 27-km railway line linking Chipata with Mchinji, Malawi, was inaugurated. There were plans to link Mulobezi with the Namibian railway system.

Tanzania–Zambia Railway Authority (Tazara): POB T01, Mpika; Head Office: POB 2834, Dar es Salaam, Tanzania; tel. (21) 4370684; fax (21) 4370228; f. 1975; operates passenger and freight services linking New Kapiri-Mposhi, north of Lusaka, with Dar es Salaam in Tanzania, a distance of 1,860 km, of which 891 km is in Zambia; jtly owned and administered by the Govts of Tanzania and Zambia; Chair. SALIM H. MSOMA; Man. Dir AKASHAMBATWA MBIKUSITA-LEWANIKA.

Zambia Railways Ltd: cnr Buntungwa St and Ghana Ave, POB 80935, Kabwe; tel. (21) 5222201; fax (21) 5224411; f. 1967; Acting Man. Dir MUYENGA ATANGA.

ROADS

In 2001 there was a total road network of 91,440 km, including 4,222 km of main roads and 8,948 km of secondary roads. The main arterial roads run from Beitbridge (Zimbabwe) to Tunduma (the Great North Road), through the copper-mining area to Chingola and Chililabombwe (hitherto the Zaire Border Road), from Livingstone to the junction of the Kafue river and the Great North Road, and from Lusaka to the Malawi border (the Great East Road). In 1984 the 300-km BotZam highway linking Kazungula with Nata, in Botswana, was formally opened. A 1,930-km main road (the TanZam highway) links Zambia and Tanzania.

Road Development Agency: POB 50003, Lusaka; tel. (21) 1253801; fax (21) 1253404; e-mail rda_hq@roads.gov.zm; internet www.rda.org.zm; f. 2002; fmrly Dept of Roads; CEO ERASMUS CHILUNDIKA.

CIVIL AVIATION

In 2011 there were four designated international airports in Zambia, at Lusaka, Ndola, Livingstone and Mfuwe.

Department of Civil Aviation: Block 26A, Independence Ave, Ridgeway, POB 5013, Lusaka; tel. (21) 1251861; fax (21) 1251841; e-mail aviation@coppernet.zm; internet www.dca.com.zm.

National Airports Corpn Ltd (NACL): Airport Rd, 10101 Lusaka; tel. (21) 1271313; fax (21) 1271048; e-mail nacl@zamnet.zm; internet www.lun.aero; f. 1973; air cargo services; Man. Dir ROBINSON MISITALA.

Proflight Zambia: Site 15B, Private Hangars, Lusaka International Airport, POB 30536, Lusaka; tel. (21) 1271032; fax (21) 1271139; e-mail reservations@proflight-zambia.com; internet www.proflight-zambia.com; f. 2004; Chair. TONY IRWIN.

Zambezi Airlines: Petroda House, 2nd Floor, Great East Rd, Rhodes Park, POB 35470, Lusaka; tel. (21) 1257606; fax (21) 1257631; e-mail info@flyzambezi.com; internet www.flyzambezi.com; f. 2008; Chair. Dr MAURICE JANGULO; CEO DON MACDONALD.

Tourism

Zambia's main tourist attractions, in addition to the Victoria Falls, are its wildlife, unspoilt scenery and diverse cultural heritage; there are 19 national parks and 36 game management areas. In 2010 815,164 tourists visited Zambia; tourism receipts totalled US $125m. in that year.

Tourism Council of Zambia: 55–56 Mulungushi International Conference Centre, POB 36561, Lusaka; tel. (21) 1291788; fax (21) 1290436; e-mail secretariat.tcz@iconnect.zm; internet www.tcz.org.zm; f. 1997; Exec. Dir VICTOR INAMBWAE.

Zambia National Tourist Board: Century House, Lusaka Sq., POB 30017, Lusaka; tel. (21) 1229087; fax (21) 1225174; e-mail zntb@zambiatourism.org.zm; internet www.zambiatourism.com; Chair. ERROL HICKEY; Man. Dir CHANDA CHARITY LUMPA.

Defence

As assessed at November 2012, Zambia's armed forces officially numbered about 15,100 (army 13,500 and air force 1,600). Paramilitary forces numbered 1,400. There was also a reserve of 3,000. Military service is voluntary. There is also a National Defence Force, responsible to the Government. In 2012 some 30 Zambian troops were stationed abroad, attached to UN missions in Africa; of these, 26 were serving as observers.

Defence Expenditure: Estimated at K1,650,000m. for 2012.

Commander of the Army: Lt-Gen. PAUL MIHOVA.

Commander of the Air Force: Lt-Gen. ANDREW SAKALA.

Education

Primary education, which is compulsory, begins at seven years of age and lasts for seven years. Secondary education, beginning at the age of 14, lasts for a further five years, comprising a first cycle of two years and a second of three years. According to UNESCO estimates, in 2008/09 91% of children (90% of boys; 92% of girls) in the relevant age group attended primary schools, while enrolment at secondary schools included 46% of children (51% of boys; 42% of girls) in the relevant age group. There are two universities: the University of Zambia at Lusaka, and the Copperbelt University at Kitwe, which had a combined total of some 16,655 students in 2010. There are 14 teacher training colleges. The 2011 budgetary allocation for the education sector was equivalent to 18.6% of the overall government budget.

ZIMBABWE

Introductory Survey

LOCATION, CLIMATE, LANGUAGE, RELIGION, FLAG, CAPITAL

The Republic of Zimbabwe is a land-locked state in southern Africa, with Mozambique to the east, Zambia to the north-west, Botswana to the south-west and South Africa to the south. The climate is tropical, modified considerably by altitude. Average monthly temperatures range from 13°C (55°F) to 22°C (72°F) on the Highveld, and from 20°C (68°F) to 30°C (86°F) in the low-lying valley of the Zambezi river. The rainy season is from November to March. The official languages are English, Chi-Shona and SiNdebele. About 55% of the population are Christians. A large number of the African population follow traditional beliefs, while the Asian minority comprises both Muslims and Hindus. The national flag (proportions 1 by 2) has seven equal horizontal stripes, of green, gold, red, black, red, gold and green, with a white triangle, bearing a red five-pointed star on which a gold 'Great Zimbabwe bird' is superimposed, at the hoist. The capital is Harare.

CONTEMPORARY POLITICAL HISTORY

Historical Context

In 1923 responsibility for Southern Rhodesia (now Zimbabwe) was transferred from the British South Africa Company to the Government of the United Kingdom, and the territory became a British colony. It had full self-government (except for African interests and some other matters) under an administration controlled by European settlers. African voting rights were restricted.

In 1953 the colony united with two British protectorates, Northern Rhodesia (now Zambia) and Nyasaland (now Malawi), to form the Federation of Rhodesia and Nyasaland. A new Constitution, which ended most of the United Kingdom's legal controls and provided for a limited African franchise, came into effect in November 1962. At elections in December the Prime Minister, Sir Edgar Whitehead, lost power to the Rhodesian Front (RF), a coalition of white opposition groups committed to maintaining racial segregation. The leader of the RF, Winston Field, became Prime Minister.

As a result of pressure from African nationalist movements in Northern Rhodesia and Nyasaland, the Federation was dissolved in December 1963. African nationalists were also active in Southern Rhodesia: Joshua Nkomo formed the Zimbabwe African People's Union (ZAPU), which was declared an unlawful organization in September 1962. ZAPU split in July 1963, and a breakaway group, led by the Rev. Ndabaningi Sithole, formed the Zimbabwe African National Union (ZANU) in August. Robert Mugabe became Secretary-General of ZANU.

In April 1964 Field was succeeded as Prime Minister of Southern Rhodesia by his deputy, Ian Smith. The new regime rejected British conditions for independence, including acceptance by the whole Rhodesian population and unimpeded progress to majority rule. In August ZANU was banned. After Northern Rhodesia became independent as Zambia in October, Southern Rhodesia became generally (although not officially) known as Rhodesia. On 5 November 1965 a state of emergency (to be renewed annually) was declared, and on 11 November Smith made a unilateral declaration of independence (UDI) and proclaimed a new Constitution, naming the country Rhodesia. The British Government regarded Rhodesia's independence as unconstitutional and illegal, and no other country formally recognized it. The United Kingdom terminated all relations with Rhodesia, while the UN applied economic sanctions. Both ZAPU and ZANU took up arms against the RF regime.

Following a referendum in June 1969, Rhodesia was declared a republic in March 1970. The 1969 Constitution provided for a bicameral Legislative Assembly, comprising a 23-member Senate and a 66-member House of Assembly (50 Europeans and 16 Africans). The President had only formal powers, and Smith remained Prime Minister. The RF won all 50 European seats in the House of Assembly in 1970, 1974 and 1977.

In November 1971 the British and Rhodesian Governments agreed on draft proposals for a constitutional settlement, subject to their acceptability to the Rhodesian people 'as a whole'. In December the African National Council (ANC), led by Bishop Abel Muzorewa, was formed to co-ordinate opposition to the plan. However, in December 1974 the Rhodesian Government and leaders of four nationalist organizations (including ZAPU, ZANU and the ANC) agreed the terms of a cease-fire, conditional on the release of African political detainees and on the convening of a constitutional conference in 1975. The African organizations agreed to unite within the ANC, with Muzorewa as President. Mugabe opposed the incorporation of ZANU into the ANC, and in mid-1975 left Rhodesia for neighbouring Mozambique, where he took control of ZANU's external wing, and challenged Sithole's leadership of the party. In September the ANC split into rival factions, led by Muzorewa and Nkomo. Constitutional talks between the Government and the Nkomo faction began in December 1975, but were abandoned in March 1976. In September, under pressure from South Africa, Smith announced his Government's acceptance of proposals leading to majority rule within two years. In late 1976 representatives of the RF, the African nationalists and the British Government met to discuss the transition to majority rule. The nationalists were led by Muzorewa, Sithole, Nkomo and Mugabe (by then the recognized leader of ZANU). Nkomo and Mugabe adopted a joint position as the Patriotic Front (PF).

In January 1977 Angola, Botswana, Mozambique, Tanzania and Zambia (the 'front-line' states) declared their support for the PF. Smith rejected British proposals for an interim administration, and received a mandate from the RF to repeal racially discriminatory laws and to seek agreement with such African factions as he chose. In November Smith accepted the principle of universal adult suffrage, and talks on an internal settlement were initiated with Muzorewa's United African National Council (UANC), Sithole's faction of the ANC and the Zimbabwe United People's Organization, led by Chief Jeremiah Chirau. These talks led to the signing of an internal settlement on 3 March 1978, providing for an interim power-sharing administration to prepare for independence on 31 December. The proposals were rejected by the PF and by the UN Security Council. In May 1978 the newly created Executive Council, consisting of Smith, Sithole, Muzorewa and Chirau, ordered the release of all political detainees in an attempt to bring about a cease-fire.

In January 1979 a 'majority rule' Constitution, with entrenched safeguards for the white minority, was approved by the House of Assembly and endorsed by a referendum of European voters. In April elections to the new House of Assembly (the first by universal adult suffrage) were held in two stages: for 20 directly elected European members (chosen by non-African voters only) and then for 72 African members (chosen by the whole electorate). The UANC emerged as the majority party, with 51 seats, while the RF won all 20 seats for whites. In May the new Parliament elected Josiah Gumede as President. Muzorewa became Prime Minister of the country (renamed Zimbabwe Rhodesia) in June. In accordance with the Constitution, Muzorewa formed a government of national unity, including European members (Smith became Minister without Portfolio). However, international recognition was not forthcoming, and UN sanctions remained in force.

New impetus for a lasting and internationally recognized settlement followed the Commonwealth Conference in Zambia in August 1979. In September a Rhodesian Constitutional Conference in London, United Kingdom, was attended by delegations under Muzorewa and the joint leaders of the PF. The PF reluctantly agreed to special representation for the whites under the proposed new Constitution, which was eventually accepted by both parties. On 11 December the Zimbabwe Rhodesia Parliament voted to renounce independence and to revert to the status of a British colony, as Southern Rhodesia. Illegal rule ended on the following day, when Parliament was dissolved, the President, Prime Minister and Cabinet resigned, and the British-appointed Governor, Lord Soames, was vested with full executive and legislative authority for the duration of the transition to legal independence. The United Kingdom immediately revoked economic sanctions.

Lord Soames ended the ban on the two wings of the PF (ZAPU and ZANU) and ordered the release of most of the detainees who were held under the 'emergency powers' laws. Elections to a new House of Assembly proceeded in February 1980 at which Mugabe's ZANU—PF emerged as the largest single party, winning 57 of the 80 African seats; Nkomo's PF—ZAPU took 20 seats and the UANC only three. In a separate poll of white voters, the RF secured all 20 reserved seats. The new state of Zimbabwe became legally independent, within the Commonwealth, on 18 April, with Rev. Canaan Banana as President (with largely ceremonial duties) and Mugabe as Prime Minister, at the head of a coalition Government.

By May 1984 the RF, now restyled the Republican Front, retained only seven of the 20 seats reserved for whites, the remaining 13 being held by independents. In July the RF was renamed the Conservative Alliance of Zimbabwe (CAZ), and opened its membership to all races.

Domestic Political Affairs

There were several outbreaks of violence prior to a general election in June–July 1985. ZANU—PF was returned to power with an increased majority, winning 63 of the 79 'common roll' seats in the House of Assembly (and an additional seat at a by-election in August). ZAPU won 15 seats, retaining its traditional hold over Matabeleland, and ZANU—Sithole took a single seat. Of the 20 seats reserved for whites, 15 were secured by the CAZ. However, the CAZ was not represented in the new Cabinet.

During mid-1985 a large number of ZAPU officials were detained for questioning about dissident activity in Matabeleland. The failure, in August 1987, of talks aimed at uniting ZANU and ZAPU led to renewed rebel activity, whereupon the Government took steps to prevent ZAPU from functioning effectively. Furthermore, ZANU declined to endorse seven ZAPU-nominated candidates for the parliamentary seats made vacant in September by the abolition of seats reserved for whites (see below). In December Mugabe and Nkomo finally signed an agreement of unity, which was ratified by both parties in April 1988. In January 1988 Nkomo was appointed as one of the Senior Ministers in the President's Office, and two other ZAPU officials were given government posts. Following the unity agreement, there was a significant improvement in the security situation in Matabeleland. However, the state of emergency remained in force, owing to incursions into eastern Zimbabwe by the Mozambican rebel movement, the Resistência Nacional Moçambicana (Renamo, see Foreign Affairs).

Two major constitutional reforms were enacted during 1987. In September the reservation for whites of 20 seats in the House of Assembly and 10 seats in the Senate was abolished, as permitted by the Constitution, subject to a majority vote in the House. In October the 80 remaining members of the House of Assembly elected 20 candidates, who were nominated by ZANU, including 11 whites, to fill the vacant seats in the House of Assembly until the next general election. In the same month Parliament approved the replacement of the ceremonial presidency by an executive presidency. The post of Prime Minister was to be incorporated into the presidency. President Banana (who, as the only candidate, had been sworn in for a second term of office as President in April 1986) retired in December 1987, and at the end of that month Mugabe (the sole candidate) was inaugurated as Zimbabwe's first executive President.

In December 1989 ZANU and ZAPU merged to form a single party, named the Zimbabwe African National Union—Patriotic Front (ZANU—PF). The united party aimed to establish a one-party state with a Marxist-Leninist doctrine. Mugabe was appointed President of ZANU—PF.

Presidential and parliamentary elections were held concurrently in March 1990; at these elections legislation approved in late 1989 came into effect, abolishing the Senate and increasing the number of seats in the House of Assembly from 100 to 150 (of which 120 were to be directly elected; 12 were to be allocated to presidential nominees, 10 to traditional Chiefs and eight to provincial governors). Mugabe won nearly 80% of all votes cast at the presidential election and at the parliamentary elections ZANU—PF secured 117 of the 120 elective seats in the House of Assembly. In August 1990 the state of emergency was finally revoked.

In March 1992 the House of Assembly approved legislation (the Land Acquisition Act) that permitted the compulsory acquisition of land by the Government; this was intended to facilitate the redistribution of land ownership from Europeans (who owned about one-third of farming land in early 1992) to Africans. In May 1993 the Government published a list of properties

allotted for transfer to the State under the Act, provoking a strong protest from the white-dominated Commercial Farmers' Union (CFU). The High Court subsequently ruled against three white farmers who had attempted to prove that the confiscation of their land was unconstitutional. A lack of available funds impeded the progress of the Government's land resettlement programme.

ZANU—PF won an overwhelming victory at legislative elections in April 1995, receiving more than 82% of the votes cast and securing 118 of the 120 elective seats in the House of Assembly (55 of which were uncontested). The remaining two elective seats were taken by ZANU—Ndonga (formerly ZANU—Sithole). Following the allocation of nominated and reserved seats, ZANU—PF controlled 148 of the total 150 seats. However, only 54% of the electorate voted, and the elections were boycotted by eight opposition groups.

Mugabe retained the presidency at an election in March 1996, winning 92.7% of the votes cast, although turn-out was again low. In October it was announced that ZANU—PF was abandoning Marxism-Leninism as its guiding principle. In August the Government had announced that the independence war veterans (an increasingly powerful lobby) would be awarded a number of substantial, unbudgeted benefits.

Land resettlement

In October 1997 Mugabe announced that the pace of the land resettlement programme would be accelerated, declaring that the constitutional right of white commercial farmers to receive full and fair compensation for confiscated land would not be honoured and (unsuccessfully) challenging the United Kingdom, in its role as former colonial power, to take responsibility for assisting them. A list of 1,503 properties to be reallocated forthwith was published in November. In January 1998, however, the IMF stipulated on an assurance from the Mugabe administration that it would respect the Constitution during the land resettlement procedure as a condition for the release of financial assistance; such an assurance was eventually given in March, when it was announced that 120 farms would be acquired in the near future in exchange for full and fair compensation. In August Mugabe introduced the second phase of the programme, to resettle 150,000 families on 1m. ha of land each year for the next seven years. Under pressure from Western donors, the Government agreed to reduce its plans, and was restricted to using 118 farms that it had already been offered. In November, however, 841 white-owned farms were ordered to be confiscated by the State: compensation was to be deferred. Pressure exerted by the IMF in light of a forthcoming release of aid brought an assurance from Mugabe that his administration would not break agreements for a gradual land reform programme; however, at the end of March 1999 the President contravened the agreement when he announced a new plan to acquire a further 529 white-owned farms. Mugabe accused the USA and the United Kingdom of 'destabilizing' Zimbabwe through their alleged control over the IMF, which was delaying financial assistance to the country. In May the Government agreed a plan that aimed to resettle 77,700 black families on 1m. ha by 2001. Some of this land was to come from the 118 farms that had already been offered. The remainder would be the result of uncontested acquisitions under the Government's reduced list of 800 farms for compulsory purchase. The plan was to be partially funded by the World Bank, and was broadly accepted by the white landowners' association.

Meanwhile, labour unrest escalated in December 1997, when a general strike was organized by the Zimbabwe Congress of Trade Unions (ZCTU), in protest at the imposition by the Government of three unpopular new taxes in order to finance the provision of benefits to war veterans; the authorities capitulated, withdrawing two of the taxes immediately. Shortly after the demonstrations had subsided, Morgan Tsvangirai, the Secretary-General of ZCTU, was attacked in his office by unknown assailants. The weak Zimbabwe currency and soaring food prices aggravated the nation-wide mood of discontent. In January 1998 riots erupted in most of the country's urban areas in protest at rises in the price of maize meal, the staple food. In response Mugabe agreed to withdraw the most recent price increase. However, the army was deployed to suppress the disturbances and was authorized to open fire on protesters; nine people were reportedly killed and some 800 rioters were arrested.

In March 1999 Mugabe appointed a commission of inquiry to make recommendations for a new constitution. An international constitutional conference was held in November, but several experts suspected that the draft constitution had already been written, and that they had been invited primarily to give the process global credibility. In late November a document bearing no relation to that prepared by the 400-member constitutional commission, a drafting committee overseen by ZANU—PF having deleted crucial clauses (particularly relating to the reduction of the President's powers and the introduction of a parliamentary system), was declared to have been 'adopted by acclamation', despite vigorous protests. In January 2000 Mugabe announced that a referendum on the new constitution would take place on 12–13 February. Confusion before the polls over such issues as eligibility to vote and the location of polling stations was believed by the opposition to have been orchestrated by ZANU—PF to maximize Mugabe's chances of victory. Despite fears that a lack of supervision of the ballot had led to widespread irregularities on ZANU—PF's part, 54.6% of the 26% of the electorate who participated in the polls voted to reject the draft constitution. The level of participation was highest in urban areas where support for the recently formed opposition party, the Movement for Democratic Change (MDC), led by Tsvangirai, was strong.

The Government embarked on a campaign to restore its popularity prior to the June 2000 legislative elections. Illegal occupations of white-owned farms by black 'war veterans' (many of whom, too young to have taken part in the war of independence, were suspected of having been paid to participate), which began in late February, were rumoured to have been organized by the Government in an attempt to regain support through the land issue. Mugabe repeatedly denied that his administration was behind the occupations, but made no secret of his support for them. The international community condemned the Government's increasingly militant stance, which also extended to the treatment of the opposition, in particular the MDC, which was subjected to a campaign of intimidation and aggression. In May Mugabe signed a law allowing the seizure of 841 white-owned farms without compensation and the following month a list was published of 804 farms that were to be confiscated.

Prior to legislative elections, which took place on 24–25 June 2000, there were reports of violence towards observers, and a UN team, dispatched to co-ordinate the polls, was recalled following obstruction by the Government. The authorities also refused to permit the accreditation of some 200 foreign monitors. ZANU—PF secured 48.6% of the votes cast and 62 of the 120 elective seats in the House of Assembly, the MDC won 47.0% of the ballot and 57 seats, while ZANU—Ndonga received one seat. There were reports of widespread irregularities in the polls, which international observers declared not to have been free and fair.

Shortly after the legislative elections, Mugabe announced that some 500 additional white-owned farms would be appropriated for resettlement. In December 2000 a court ruling upheld previous opinions that declared the appropriation of white-owned farms without compensation payments to be unlawful; Mugabe announced that sufficient white-owned land had been appropriated for resettlement, but repeated his assertion that he would not accept court-imposed impediments to any further land-reform measures. Negotiations between the Government and farmers' representatives resumed in January 2001.

International isolation

In March 2001 the Commonwealth announced that it would send a delegation comprising the foreign ministers of Australia, Barbados and Nigeria to Zimbabwe for discussions with the Government. Mugabe refused to meet the delegation, however, claiming that the decision had been inspired by the United Kingdom. Similar criticisms were made of an attempt by the European Union (EU, see p. 281) to establish a dialogue with Zimbabwe regarding its record on human rights. In early June Mugabe urged war veterans to intensify the occupation of white-owned farms, and in the following days attacks against such farms throughout the country were reported to have increased, causing the death of at least one farm worker. The Zimbabwean Government criticized US and British media coverage of the events, and in mid-June it imposed restrictions on journalists visiting the country. Later that month the Government listed a further 2,030 farms for compulsory acquisition, and in August the Minister of Lands, Agriculture and Rural Development announced the Government's intention to appropriate 8.3m. ha of commercial farmland. Further unrest occurred later that month in the north of the country, where approximately 100 white-owned farms were reported to have been evacuated following attacks by war veterans.

In early September 2001 a meeting of Commonwealth ministers was convened in Abuja, Nigeria, to discuss Mugabe's land resettlement programme; it was agreed that illegal farm seizures would cease and that international donors would compensate white farmers for the distribution of their land to landless black families. The agreement was broadly supported by both ZANU—PF and the MDC. By the end of September, however, more than 20 new farm invasions were reported to have taken place, resulting in several deaths, and talks between the Government and the CFU collapsed. Mugabe's intention to disregard the terms of the Abuja agreement became apparent in early October, when he ordered the Supreme Court to recognize the land reform programme as legal, reversing the ruling of December 2000; widespread criticism was directed at the Government for its manipulation of the judiciary. Commonwealth ministers and officials visited Zimbabwe later in October 2001 to monitor the Government's adherence to the Abuja agreement, but failed to persuade the Government to comply with its terms. State repression intensified in November, when the Government amended the Land Act by decree. According to the revised legislation, any farm issued with a 'notice of acquisition' would become the property of the State with immediate effect; previously, a farm owner had been served 90 days' notice.

International concern regarding the situation in Zimbabwe intensified at the end of 2001. South African President Thabo Mbeki expressed doubts as to whether conditions were suitable for a free and fair presidential election (scheduled to be held in March 2002), and the Commonwealth Ministerial Action Group on the Harare Declaration warned the Zimbabwean Government that it risked suspension from the organization unless it ended violent land seizures and political intimidation of the media and opposition groups. Despite Zimbabwe's growing isolation, in January 2002 further controversial legislation, aimed at suppressing opposition to Mugabe, was introduced: the Public Order and Security Bill prohibited the publication of documents that incited public disorder or undermined the security services, and banned public gatherings that incited rioting; the General Laws Amendment Bill prohibited foreign and independent missions from monitoring the elections, and forbade voter education (the Bill was repealed by the Supreme Court in February, following a challenge from the MDC); and the Access to Information Bill made it an offence for foreign news services to report from Zimbabwe unless authorized by the Zimbabwean Government. The EU finally imposed so-called 'smart' sanctions on Zimbabwe in mid-February, after the leader of its electoral observer mission was expelled from the country. The sanctions included an embargo on the sale of arms to Zimbabwe, the suspension of €128m. of aid scheduled to be disbursed during 2002–07, and the freezing of the assets of 19 Zimbabwean officials, including Mugabe, who were also prohibited from visiting any EU state; the USA imposed similar measures several days later. In July the EU applied the sanctions to a further 53 people, including all cabinet members. The EU extended sanctions for a further 12 months in February 2003, although Mugabe attended the Franco-African summit in Paris, France, later that month. The USA also extended its sanctions to more than 70 senior officials in March.

The presidential election took place on 9–10 March 2002, but voting was extended to 11 March by the High Court, in response to a request from the MDC. Mugabe was declared the winner on 13 March, with 56.2% of the valid votes cast; Tsvangirai secured 42.0%. Independent observers were divided in their judgement of whether the election was free and fair; most observers from African countries declared the election result legitimate, while the Norwegian delegation (the only European representatives) and independent Zimbabwean observers condemned the result and reported widespread electoral fraud and intimidation of the electorate and of observers by members of ZANU—PF. The MDC claimed that a number of its agents had been abducted from certain polling stations and detained by the police. (Tsvangirai mounted a legal challenge to have the results declared null and void; however, after a protracted case, the High Court eventually ruled against him in 2005 and the Supreme Court dismissed his application in February 2006.)

Prior to the presidential election the Commonwealth had nominated the Nigerian President, Olusegun Obasanjo, Mbeki and the Australian Prime Minister, John Howard, to consider the conduct of the election and to formulate the organization's response. Mbeki and Obasanjo visited Zimbabwe following the election and urged Mugabe and the MDC to form a government of national unity; however, the MDC refused to co-operate unless the election was reheld. The Commonwealth suspended Zimbabwe from meetings of the organization for one year in mid-March 2002, stating that the election result had been undermined by politically motivated violence and that conditions did not permit the free will of the electorate to be expressed. (The suspension was extended for a further nine months in March 2003.) Immediately after the election the Government enacted the Access to Information and Protection of Privacy Act, which required all journalists reporting in Zimbabwe to be approved by the State. In April 2002 the National Constitutional Assembly (NCA—an opposition grouping formed in 1997) organized demonstrations in support of demands for a new constitution and a re-run of the presidential election; more than 80 demonstrators were arrested. Violence directed at supporters of the MDC, allegedly committed by ZANU—PF supporters, intensified following the election and more than 50 people were reported to have been killed between the election and the end of April.

Land seizures also escalated, and in March 2002 the Government listed almost 400 white-owned farms for compulsory acquisition, bringing the area scheduled for redistribution to the black population to around 85% of total commercial farmland. In June Mugabe issued an order listing some 2,900 white-owned farms for seizure; farmers were obliged to cease working their land in June, or face up to two years' imprisonment, and to leave their properties by August. Some 860 farmers had vacated their properties by the deadline, while 1,700 refused to leave. (Around 300 had left their farms temporarily to avoid confrontation.) In a speech in August Mugabe stated that white farmers who were 'loyal' to the Government had the option of staying, although later that month it was reported that almost 200 farmers had been arrested for refusing to leave their properties, while others had gone into hiding. In September the Land Acquisition Act was amended to allow the eviction of white farmers within seven days, as opposed to the 90 days previously required.

Opposition to Mugabe

In April 2002 ZANU—PF and the MDC engaged in talks in an effort to end the political crisis, but negotiations collapsed in the following month when ZANU—PF withdrew, citing the MDC's petition to the High Court seeking to overturn the election results, which ZANU—PF regarded as unlawful. In February 2003, following their arrest the previous year, the trial of Tsvangirai and two other senior MDC officials for allegedly plotting to assassinate Mugabe began in Harare. In March the MDC led a 'mass action' against the Government, aimed at forcing it to repeal what the party called repressive legislation and to release political prisoners; the Government claimed that the MDC had detonated bombs in Kadoma, south-west of Harare, and it was reported that up to 500 members of the opposition had been arrested and many more driven from their homes and beaten. In June Tsvangirai was arrested at the conclusion of further demonstrations against the Government organized by the MDC, reportedly in connection with statements he had made in May; he was released on bail later in June.

In September 2003 the closure of *The Daily News*, owing to the failure of its publisher to register with the Government's Media and Information Commission (MIC), provoked international condemnation. A court ruling that the newspaper should be allowed to resume publication, pending the result of an application that it had made to register with the MIC, was initially disregarded by the police. Publication of *The Daily News* did subsequently resume, despite the refusal of the MIC to grant it a licence, but was suspended again in February 2004 when the Supreme Court confirmed that its unlicensed appearance was illegal. (By early 2005 four newspapers had been closed under the Access to Information and Protection of Privacy Act: *The Daily News*, the *Daily News on Sunday*, *The Tribune* and *The Weekly Times*. However, *The Daily News*, along with four other newspapers, was awarded a new operating licence in May 2010 and began publishing again in early 2011.)

The decision, taken at a meeting of Commonwealth Heads of Government held in Abuja, Nigeria, in December 2003, to extend Zimbabwe's suspension from the organization indefinitely, until the country had restored democracy and the rule of law, confirmed the existence of a rift between African Commonwealth members and their Western counterparts. The 12 members from southern Africa criticized the decision, and Mbeki claimed that other Commonwealth members had failed to understand the question of land ownership in Zimbabwe and that they were mistaken in their belief that the presidential election held in Zimbabwe in 2002 had been unfair. Zimbabwe, for its part, announced its decision to withdraw from the Commonwealth shortly before the conclusion of the Heads of Government meeting.

In January 2004, giving evidence for the first time in his trial for treason, Tsvangirai denied that he had ever plotted to assassinate President Mugabe or to overthrow the Government. Tsvangirai was acquitted of the assassination charges in mid-October 2004; the outstanding treason charge was finally dropped in August 2005. Meanwhile, in February 2004 the EU renewed sanctions imposed upon the Mugabe regime, extending the travel ban and assets freeze to cover a total of 95 Zimbabwean officials, and in March the USA imposed a further series of sanctions on Zimbabwe, notably targeting government-owned enterprises.

According to provisional results of the legislative elections held on 31 March 2005, Mugabe's ruling ZANU—PF party won 78 of the 120 seats available, taking 56.4% of the vote. The opposition MDC took 41 seats, with 42.1% of the votes cast. Under the Constitution, the President could allocate 12 seats in the House of Assembly to candidates of his choosing and appoint the eight provincial governors; a further 10 seats were reserved for tribal chiefs, also loyal to Mugabe. The overall results therefore gave ZANU—PF a two-thirds' majority in the Assembly, which would allow Mugabe to amend the Constitution. International observers from the African Union (AU, see p. 191) and the Southern African Development Community (SADC, see p. 434) endorsed the results; observers from the Commonwealth, the EU and the USA were not invited, owing to their perceived hostility towards the Mugabe Government. The Governments of Malawi, Mozambique, South Africa and Zambia were among those who accepted the elections as free and fair; however, the results were dismissed by Australia, the EU and the USA. (The observers from the AU later reversed their opinion and called for investigations into allegations of electoral fraud.) The MDC contested the results, citing electoral irregularities in 76 out of the 120 constituencies, and claimed that it should, in fact, have won 94 seats. In mid-April the MDC released a report alleging that some 134,000 people had been turned away from polling stations and that ballot boxes had been filled with votes for ZANU—PF after the polls had closed. The MDC filed petitions at the Electoral Court challenging the results in 13 constituencies. Meanwhile, the outgoing Minister responsible for Land Reform and Resettlement, John Nkomo, announced that white farmers who had lost their farms during the resettlement programme would be compensated for the value of assets and improvements but not for the land itself, which the Government maintained was the responsibility of the United Kingdom. It was estimated that the white population in Zimbabwe had fallen from 200,000 in 2000 to around 25,000 at March 2005; of these some 500 were farmers.

In May 2005 the Government launched Operation Murambatsvina ('Sweep Away the Rubbish'), which targeted black market trading—principally in foreign currency and fuel—and 'general lawlessness'. The MDC claimed that it was a punitive action against the urban poor who had voted against ZANU—PF in the elections in March. Shanty towns were razed to the ground in Harare and other major cities. The operation attracted widespread international condemnation and, according to the UN, approximately 700,000 people were made homeless; however, the Government refused offers of humanitarian aid. In June President Mugabe announced that some Z.$3,000,000m. was to be spent on new housing and commercial premises under a three-year redevelopment programme entitled Operation Garikai/Hlalani Kuhle. (In September 2006 the human rights organization Amnesty International reported that the Government had not met its housing obligations as just 3,325 new homes had been built, while 92,460 had been demolished.) In late 2005 Vice-President Joyce Mujuru announced the official end of Operation Murambatsvina and appealed for humanitarian aid.

In August 2005 the House of Assembly approved legislation that provided for a number of changes to the Constitution and that was also to conclude the land redistribution programme: courts would no longer be able to hear appeals on land acquisition and once listed for appropriation land would immediately become state property. Under the bill it became a criminal offence for Zimbabweans to endorse sanctions or military action against their country, and the Zimbabwe Electoral Commission (ZEC) was established in place of the Electoral Supervisory Commission. In addition, the legislation provided for the reintroduction of a 66-member Senate (abolished in 1990) as the second chamber of the legislature; senatorial elections were held in November 2005. The MDC was deeply divided over the issue of participating in the elections. Tsvangirai opposed electoral participation, advocating mass protests and 'democratic resistance'; however, a faction led by the party's Secretary-General, Welshman Ncube, fielded 26 candidates. ZANU—PF won 43 of the 50 elected seats, receiving 73.7% of the vote; MDC candidates took the remaining seven seats, with 20.3% of the vote. The MDC effectively split in two, with a 'pro-Senate' faction electing Arthur Mutumbara as its leader in February 2006. The rump of the party re-elected Tsvangirai as its President in March.

Financial decline

In March 2006 the IMF postponed a decision to expel Zimbabwe after the country repaid US $120m. of its debt to the fund and pledged to clear its remaining obligations by November. In December the IMF recommended sharp reductions in public spending to lower inflation (the annual rate was recorded as 1,594% in January 2007) as well as the reform of exchange rates, the liberalization of price controls, the removal of restrictions on current account payments and the strengthening of private property rights. In August 2006 the Reserve Bank of Zimbabwe unexpectedly devalued the Zimbabwe dollar by 59.3%, and removed three zeros from the currency in an attempt to stem both corruption and hyperinflation. In June the People's Republic of China had signed an agreement worth $1,300m. with Zimbabwe to help relieve an acute shortage of energy. In exchange for chrome from Zimbabwe, Chinese companies agreed to build new coal mines and three thermal power stations in the Zambezi valley on the Zambian border.

Between November 2006 and February 2007 more than 31,000 people were arrested in a major police crackdown, known as Operation Chikorokoza Chapera ('The End of Illegal Gold Dealings'). With the rate of unemployment reportedly standing at more than 80%, many Zimbabweans had turned to gold- or diamond-prospecting following the collapse of commercial agriculture. In February the Government had announced that the last white farmers, numbering some 400, could remain on their land long enough to harvest their crops, even though the deadline to leave had passed.

In mid-February 2007 police used tear gas and water cannons to prevent an MDC rally from proceeding in Harare, despite the organization having obtained a High Court order allowing the rally to take place. In late February anti-Government protesters took control of Budiriro township in Harare for several hours, setting up roadblocks of boulders and burning tyres. Political tensions intensified further when Tsvangirai was arrested in mid-March, along with five other members of the MDC, after riot police violently dispersed a 'Save Zimbabwe' prayer meeting in Harare's Highfield township. One activist was killed by the police and Tsvangirai suffered severe injuries while in police custody. The Government stated that the rally breached a recently introduced three-month ban on political gatherings. The incident provoked widespread international condemnation. Following an SADC summit in Dar es Salaam, Tanzania, in late March, it was announced that Mbeki had agreed to mediate between the MDC and the Zimbabwean Government; however, there were further reports of the mistreatment of MDC activists in police custody, provoking renewed opposition protests and repeated calls for Mugabe to relinquish the presidency. Nevertheless, in April ZANU—PF declared that Mugabe would stand as the party's candidate in the 2008 presidential election.

In June 2007 constitutional amendments were proposed that would allow the legislative elections to be brought forward to coincide with the presidential election in 2008, harmonizing the presidential and parliamentary terms of office. The proposals also contained provisions for amendments to the structure of the House of Assembly and the Senate. The MDC opposed the proposals, which would, *inter alia*, allow the House of Assembly to nominate a new President should the incumbent stand down; under the existing structure, new elections would be required if the presidency were vacated. The MDC continued to be weakened by divisions between party members and in July 2007 it was announced that the two factions planned to field separate candidates in the presidential and legislative elections. Meanwhile, South African-led mediation between the MDC and ZANU—PF faltered amid worsening political and economic conditions.

The 2008 elections

On 30 October 2007 a number of changes to the Constitution were officially adopted. With effect from the 2008 elections, the House of Assembly was to be enlarged to comprise 210 directly elected members, while the total number of members of the Senate was to be increased to 93. Of these, 60 were to be directly elected, five were to be nominated by the President and 10 seats were reserved for provincial governors; the remaining 18 were to include the President and the Deputy President of the Council of Chiefs and 16 traditional Chiefs. The presidential term was reduced to five years. However, talks between ZANU—PF and the opposition failed to produce any agreement on electoral procedures and negotiations continued.

In January 2008 Mugabe confirmed that presidential and legislative elections would be held concurrently on 29 March, prompting complaints from the opposition, which continued to demand further electoral and constitutional reforms. The MDC announced that it was to organize a mass protest against the Government's decision not to delay elections, claiming that Mugabe had reneged on agreements reached during the earlier talks mediated by Mbeki. In February Simba Makoni, a senior member of ZANU—PF who had served as Minister of Finance and Economic Development in 2000–02, announced his intention to challenge Mugabe for the presidency; Makoni was later expelled from the ruling party.

Presidential and legislative elections took place as scheduled on 29 March 2008. The faction of the MDC led by Tsvangirai (MDC—T) secured 99 of the 210 seats in the House of Assembly, while ZANU—PF took 97 seats; the MDC faction led by Mutambara (MDC—M) obtained 10 seats. However, no immediate announcement was made regarding the outcome of the presidential poll. Widespread irregularities were reported and observers expressed concern that the delay in releasing official results was allowing the ruling party to manipulate ballot papers. A recount of the legislative votes in 23 constituencies—the majority of which had been awarded to the MDC after the first count—commenced in mid-April. Following completion of the recount, the ZEC confirmed that the original results remained unchanged. In mid-May it was reported that ZANU—PF had filed legal petitions challenging the results in 53 constituencies, while the MDC had challenged the election of 52 deputies. Provisional results of the senatorial elections indicated that ZANU—PF had secured 30 of the 60 directly elected seats in the upper chamber; the MDC—T took 24 seats, while the MDC—M won six.

On 2 May 2008 the ZEC released results of the disputed presidential election, according to which Tsvangirai secured 47.9% of the votes cast, while Mugabe took 43.2%. Makoni was placed third with 8.3%. As no candidate secured the requisite 50% of the votes, a second round of voting was to be conducted. Following an alleged campaign of violent intimidation of MDC supporters by ZANU—PF loyalists, Tsvangirai refused to confirm his participation in the run-off. On 10 May, however, Tsvangirai, who had temporarily relocated to South Africa, announced that he would take part in the second round. Nevertheless, the Chairman of the ZEC expressed doubt that the run-off would take place within three weeks of the declaration of the election results, as stipulated by the Electoral Law, and in mid-May it was announced that the second round would take place on 27 June. Tsvangirai withdrew his candidacy shortly before the election, claiming that he was unwilling to ask his supporters to vote amid the increasing violence in which some 80 MDC members were reported to have been killed. On 23 June the UN Security Council issued a statement condemning the actions of ZANU—PF and ruled that a free and fair ballot would be 'impossible'. The UN Secretary-General, Ban Ki-Moon, expressed his support for the postponement of the second round; however, the run-off proceeded as scheduled with Mugabe as the sole candidate. On 29 June the ZEC announced that Mugabe had secured 85.5% of votes cast in the second round of voting, and he was sworn in for a sixth term as President. However, turn-out was low and the MDC claimed that ZANU—PF had coerced people to vote.

The Interparty Political Agreement

Following an AU summit held in Sharm el-Sheikh, Egypt, on 29 June–1 July 2008, African leaders failed to condemn the result of the presidential election, instead appealing to Mugabe and Tsvangirai to enter into negotiations to establish a government of national unity; by contrast, Western observers insisted that Mugabe should be removed from power and that financial assistance to Zimbabwe would be dependent on the formation of a government led by Tsvangirai. The AU's stance also appeared divided as it later emerged that several members, including Nigeria and Senegal, wished to see a government formed on the basis of the results of the first round of the election, won by Tsvangirai. In August Lovemore Moyo of the MDC was elected Speaker of the House of Assembly, strengthening that party's position. Following protracted negotiations involving SADC mediation, a power-sharing agreement was concluded in September. Under the terms of the Interparty Political Agreement (IPA), Mugabe was to remain as President with executive authority and would chair the 31-member Cabinet (which would evaluate and adopt all government policies and approve all international agreements) and the National Security Council, while Tsvangirai would be appointed Prime Minister, also with executive authority, and would chair the Council of Ministers, which was to consist of all ministers from the Cabinet and would 'ensure that the Prime Minister properly discharges his responsibility to oversee the implementation of the work of government and assesses the implementation of Cabinet decisions'. The IPA also stipulated that there would be no reversal of the land redistribution policy. Meanwhile, in mid-March 2008 Mugabe had signed a controversial indigenization law requiring 51% of all companies operating in Zimbabwe to be owned by black Zimbabweans. The legislation also banned mergers and restructuring of businesses unless the majority share was owned by black interests.

Further lengthy negotiations regarding the composition of the Cabinet followed, again mediated by Mbeki and SADC, and in early February 2009 the House of Assembly and the Senate approved a number of transitional amendments to the Constitution. These confirmed the arrangements agreed under the IPA and also stipulated the division of senior roles among the three signature parties. Mugabe and/or ZANU—PF was to nominate two Vice-Presidents, while provision was made for the appointment of two Deputy Prime Ministers, one from the MDC—T and one from the MDC—M. On 11 February Tsvangirai was inaugurated as Prime Minister and Thokozani Khupe and Arthur Mutambara were sworn in as First and Second Deputy Prime Ministers, respectively. A 35-member Cabinet was installed on 13 February, with ZANU—PF allocated a total of 17 posts, including Mumbengegwi, who retained the foreign affairs portfolio, and Chinamasa who remained Minister of Justice and Legal Affairs. Emmerson Mnangagwa was named Minister of Defence. The MDC—T had 15 representatives in the Government, most notably Tendai Biti as Minister of Finance and Elton Mangoma as Minister of Economic Planning and Development. The MDC—M held three portfolios. ZANU—PF and the MDC—T shared responsibility for the Ministry of Home Affairs; Kembo Mohadi was nominated for ZANU—PF, while Giles Mutsekwa represented the MDC—T in that ministry. Shortly before the inauguration ceremony, the designated Deputy Minister of Agriculture, Roy Bennett, of the MDC—T, was arrested and charged with treason. His detention delayed proceedings and threatened to undermine the projected image of unity within the Government, which was already viewed by many analysts with extreme suspicion. In early March the Supreme Court ordered his release on bail.

In April 2009 Mugabe's commitment to the power-sharing arrangement was called into question when he unilaterally announced that the ZANU—PF-controlled Ministry of Transport would absorb the functions hitherto carried out by the Minister of Information and Communications Technology, Nelson Chamisa of the MDC—T. Earlier that month the Government adopted a 100-day renewal plan aimed at improving ties with Western nations, in particular the USA and the United Kingdom. The Government also pledged to restore human rights, address security concerns, stabilize the economy, adopt a new constitution and review media legislation that prevented independent local and international media from operating freely within Zimbabwe. In early April it was announced that the Government had appointed a 25-member parliamentary committee to supervise the process of drafting a new constitution, which would include nation-wide consultation; it was envisaged that the new document would then be submitted for approval at a national referendum.

During June 2009 Tsvangirai visited the USA and several European states, in an effort to secure financial support for economic reconstruction. It was reported that US President Barack Obama had pledged only US $73m. in conditional aid to Zimbabwe and expressed continued concerns over democracy and human rights in the country. In total, only about $150m. in humanitarian and transitional assistance had been pledged to Zimbabwe, reflecting the international community's lack of confidence in the reconciliation process, in view of the delays in the implementation of the IPA. In July a constitutional convention in Harare degenerated into clashes between ZANU—PF and MDC delegates, which were suppressed by special police; the convention was resumed on the following day, under police supervision. In August Joseph Msika, a Vice-President in the Government and ZANU—PF, died, after becoming ill in June. (In December he was succeeded in both posts by John Nkomo, hitherto Minister of State in the President's Office.)

In September 2009 a high-level EU delegation visited Zimbabwe for the first time since the imposition of sanctions; senior EU officials indicated that further progress was required in ending human rights violations in the country before the removal of sanctions. In October a court in Mutare ruled that Bennett be returned to prison; Tsvangirai subsequently announced that the MDC would suspend participation in government meetings until the resolution of Bennett's detention and a number of other outstanding issues within the power-sharing arrangements. Although Bennett was again released on bail two days later, his trial, on charges of funding the purchase of armaments, began in early November. Tsvangirai agreed to end the MDC boycott of government meetings, following the intervention of SADC (with new South African President Jacob Zuma succeeding Mbeki as the principal mediator); however, the MDC issued an ultimatum that Mugabe implement the power-sharing agreement fully within 30 days to avert the collapse of the Government. Meanwhile, in late October Manfred Nowak, the UN Special Rapporteur on Torture, announced that he would recommend action against Zimbabwe, after he was detained on arrival at Harare airport and deported. At the end of 2009 a Zimbabwean Farmers' rights group, Justice for Agriculture, stated that the seizure of farms, which often involved attacks on white farmers, had increased dramatically since the establishment of the coalition Government in February, and were frequently perpetrated by senior members of ZANU—PF, and political and military officials. Reports of further illegal occupations of white-owned farms continued throughout 2010 and 2011.

In early 2010 ongoing negotiations between ZANU—PF, the MDC—T and the MDC—M on power-sharing issues were reported to be at an impasse, while the programme to draft a new constitution had been suspended owing to lack of funding. In February the EU issued a statement extending the sanctions in force against Zimbabwe for a further year, citing lack of progress in implementing the IPA (although the Union had ended restrictive measures against some officials and corporations previously associated with Mugabe's administration). In early March President Obama also announced the extension of travel and financial restrictions against Mugabe and other officials for a further year. Later that month Zuma continued mediation efforts in Harare to resolve the impasse between the government parties; however, Mugabe demanded the removal of all sanctions prior to any concessions and rejected the MDC's demands, which were, principally, for Bennett's inauguration as Deputy Minister of Agriculture, the allocation of five provincial governorships to the MDC, and the replacement of the Governor of the central bank and the Attorney-General. At the end of March Mugabe inaugurated the country's first Human Rights Commission, chaired by a former senior Commonwealth official, and a new Electoral Commission; under the terms of the IPA, elections had been scheduled to take place by September.

Also in March 2010 Mugabe's controversial indigenization law, which required companies operating in Zimbabwe to transfer 51% of their shareholdings to black Zimbabweans within five years, entered into force. The MDC—T's opposition to the legislation exacerbated the existing tensions within the Government. Critics argued that the indigenization programme acted as a huge deterrent to investors, a claim supported during 2010 by the low levels of investment recorded and the withdrawal of several foreign-owned firms from the country. In March 2011 the Government ordered foreign companies, under the threat of expulsion, to begin implementing the indigenization legislation. This first phase was mainly focused on multinational mining operations, but the programme was broadened in mid-2012 to encompass most sectors of the economy. By early 2013 many foreign-owned firms had agreed to comply with the indigenization regulations, while negotiations between the Government and other corporations were ongoing. However, much uncertainty remained regarding the financial compensation arrangements for the affected companies.

Meanwhile, Bennett was acquitted of all charges by the High Court in May 2010, and the Supreme Court subsequently upheld this judgment. However, following the initiation of further legal action, Bennett fled to South Africa in September, and his seat in the Senate was declared vacant in April 2011. Tsvangirai effected a reorganization of MDC—T cabinet ministers in June 2010; most notably, Theresa Makone became the MDC—T's representative in the shared Ministry of Home Affairs.

Supported by EU funding, a nation-wide public consultation scheme regarding the drafting of the new constitution began in the same month. However, the outreach campaign was disrupted by escalating political violence (predominantly directed against MDC—T followers), which Tsvangirai accused ZANU—PF of orchestrating. Further divisions between the two parties were created by Mugabe's unilateral moves throughout the year to appoint high-ranking public officials. Mugabe rejected Tsvangirai's demands to be consulted on the appointments and claimed that his actions had been lawful. In late 2010 Mugabe began publicly to advocate the holding of new elections in 2011, and he was announced as ZANU—PF's presidential candidate in December. However, with the constitutional drafting process running behind schedule, and limited progress reported on other vital political reforms, it appeared unlikely that the legal framework necessary to guarantee free and fair elections would be in place by 2011. Tsvangirai vehemently opposed a fresh ballot governed by existing legislation since it was weighted unfairly in ZANU—PF's favour and pledged to boycott a poll conducted under these circumstances.

In January 2011 Welshman Ncube, the Minister of Industry and Commerce, replaced Arthur Mutambara as leader of the MDC—M. The EU and the USA renewed their existing sanctions against Zimbabwe for one year in February and March, respectively. The EU criticized the slow pace of reform and continuing politically motivated violence. Zimbabwe attracted further international censure in February, when 46 people were arrested and accused of treason for holding a meeting to discuss the popular uprisings in Tunisia and Egypt that had resulted in the overthrow of the long-standing Presidents of those nations earlier in the year. The police claimed that those arrested were planning a similar revolt to unseat Mugabe, an allegation rejected by the detainees. In the following month 40 of those charged were released on the grounds of insufficient evidence, but in March 2012 the remaining six detainees, including a former MDC—T deputy, were found guilty of 'inciting public violence' and fined; Tsvangirai condemned the convictions. Meanwhile, Elton Mangoma, the MDC—T Minister of Energy and Power Development and a close associate of Tsvangirai, was detained by the police in March 2011 and charged with corruption. The MDC—T criticized the arrest, while Mangoma's lawyer claimed that his client was an innocent victim of a 'harassment campaign' organized by ZANU—PF; Mangoma was exonerated in June. Under pressure from ZANU—PF, in March the Supreme Court, citing a procedural violation, annulled the 2008 vote that had resulted in the MDC—T's Lovemore Moyo assuming the politically significant position of Speaker of the House of Assembly. Nevertheless, Moyo was re-elected to the post later that month, in spite of alleged attempts by ZANU—PF to distort the vote by bribing MDC—T deputies. Numerous violent attacks against members of the MDC—T and the MDC—M were reported throughout 2011 with militant groups aligned with ZANU—PF suspected of perpetrating the assaults. Mugabe's public appeals for an end to political violence and his support for a cross-party code of conduct appeared to have little substantive impact.

Vice-President Mujuru's husband, Gen. (retd) Solomon Mujuru, a prominent figure within ZANU—PF and viewed as a potential successor to Mugabe, died in a house fire in August 2011, prompting rumours that he had been murdered by his political rivals. An inquiry into Mujuru's death, conducted during January–February 2012, proved inconclusive.

In an unusual move indicative of the growing frustration within SADC, in April 2011 the regional bloc criticized Mugabe, indirectly, for hindering the implementation of the IPA and for fomenting violence against his political opponents. Nevertheless, Zimbabwe's three governing parties drafted an electoral 'roadmap' in that month, which envisaged that polls would be held during 2012 following a constitutional referendum and the compilation of a new electoral register; a final roadmap agreement was signed in July 2011. Mugabe, at the age of 87 and reportedly in ill health, was reconfirmed as ZANU—PF's presidential nominee in December. However, by early 2012, with the constitutional drafting process advancing more slowly than expected and the referendum scheduled for August at the earliest, it seemed improbable that fair elections could be organized before 2013. Mugabe's repeated threats to call early elections, irrespective of the status of the new constitution, were firmly rejected by Tsvangirai and the Zuma administration in South Africa. The EU renewed most of its sanctions against Zimbabwe in February 2012, although some restrictions were rescinded in July and February 2013. All of the USA's sanctions remained in place throughout 2012.

Mangoma was re-arrested in October 2012 in connection with offensive remarks that he had allegedly made against Mugabe. In December Mugabe was again selected as ZANU—PF's presidential candidate. Vice-President Nkomo died of cancer in January 2013; it was reported in the domestic media that his successor would not be named until after the elections.

Recent developments: towards a new constitution

After lengthy cross-party discussions, the draft constitution was finally completed in July 2012. However, in the following month ZANU—PF declared its dissatisfaction with the document, citing, *inter alia*, the proposed limitations on presidential authority. None the less, in January 2013 further dialogue yielded a mutually satisfactory charter, which received legislative approval in February, and a national referendum was scheduled to be conducted in March. The final draft of the constitution notably restricted the President to a five-year term, renewable only once; loosened presidential control over parliament and the judiciary; removed the executive's legislative veto and unilateral powers of decree; and deprived future Presidents of legal immunity upon leaving that office. In addition, the premiership was to be abolished, some government competencies were to be decentralized and the House of Assembly was to be expanded to include 60 female deputies. Civil rights and the neutrality of the security forces were guaranteed. The new constitution also provided for the establishment of a Constitutional Court, an anti-corruption body, and a peace and reconciliation commission. Capital punishment was to be retained, but with new restrictions on its imposition, while Mugabe's redistributive land reforms were formalized.

Notwithstanding an upturn in politically motivated violence and arrests during early 2013, the constitutional referendum was held peacefully on 16 March, with the new charter being endorsed by 94.5% of participants. Voter turn-out was approximately 55%. SADC monitors expressed satisfaction with the conduct of the plebiscite. The EU withdrew most of its sanctions against Zimbabwe on 25 March in recognition of this major democratic advance, although the USA declined to echo this gesture. It was anticipated that presidential and legislative elections would take place during the second half of 2013. In early May the two houses of Parliament began debating the Constitution of Zimbabwe Amendment Bill. Subject to approval by two-thirds of the members of both houses, the Bill would then become effective upon the assent of President Mugabe.

Foreign Affairs

Regional relations

Zimbabwe severed diplomatic relations with South Africa in September 1980 and subsequently played an important role in international attempts to stabilize southern Africa and to end apartheid in South Africa. South Africa is believed to have been responsible for intermittent attacks during the 1980s against the then banned African National Congress of South Africa (ANC) in Zimbabwe. The two countries re-established diplomatic relations following the holding of the first democratic elections in South Africa in April 1994, and in March 1997 a mutual defence co-operation agreement was concluded. Relations deteriorated in 1998, owing to South Africa's opposition to Zimbabwe's military intervention in the civil war in the Democratic Republic of the Congo (DRC—see below). Relations were also strained from 1999, owing to Zimbabwe's increasingly negative economic and political circumstances. By May 2000 the increasingly turbulent land reform situation in Zimbabwe had adversely affected South Africa's economy, prompting Mbeki to appeal to foreign donors to fund the transfer of white-owned land to black farmers. Following his election in May 2009, South African President Jacob Zuma succeeded Mbeki as the Chairman of SADC and principal mediator in negotiations between the government parties in Zimbabwe. The South African authorities began repatriating undocumented Zimbabweans in October 2011 following the expiry of an immigration normalization deadline in July. Unofficial estimates put the number of Zimbabwean nationals residing illegally in South Africa at over 1m.

During the 1980s and early 1990s Zimbabwe provided support to the Mozambican Government against Renamo rebels; in late 1992–early 1993, under the terms of the peace agreement in Mozambique (q.v.), Zimbabwean troops, who had been stationed in Mozambique since 1982, were withdrawn. During the mid-1990s a group of armed Zimbabwean dissidents, the

Chimwenjes, were reportedly active in western Mozambique. In January 1996 the Mozambican Government announced its intention to expel the rebels, and in January 1997 an accord was signed by representatives of Mozambique and Zimbabwe on the co-ordination of activities against the rebels. Plans for the repatriation of some 145,000 Mozambican refugees were announced in March 1993; this scheme, co-ordinated by the Office of the UN High Commissioner for Refugees, was completed by May 1995.

Following an SADC summit in Harare in August 1998, the Zimbabwean Government dispatched troops and arms to the DRC to support the regime of President Laurent-Désiré Kabila against advancing rebel forces. However, in early 2000 the Zimbabwean Government was reportedly unable to pay allowances to its troops fighting in the region, owing to the critical shortage of foreign currency. Public opinion was further turned against the continuation of the conflict in February when heavy rains and a cyclone struck eastern Zimbabwe. There was a desperate shortage of helicopters, which were needed to bring aid to those affected, owing to their deployment in the DRC. The war also caused tensions between Zimbabwe and the IMF, the latter suspending assistance partly because of Zimbabwe's false accounting of expenses relating to the conflict. Following a number of positive developments in the lengthy peace process between the DRC Government and the rebels, the last Zimbabwean troops, from an initial deployment of around 11,000, withdrew from the DRC in October 2002. Zimbabwean soldiers were expected to be redeployed to the DRC in mid-2013 as part of a regional 'intervention brigade', which had been authorized in March under UN Security Council Resolution 2098. The brigade was to be overseen by the UN Organization Stabilization Mission in the DRC (MONUSCO) and was tasked with suppressing militant groups operating in eastern DRC.

In March 2004, at the international airport in Harare, the Zimbabwean authorities detained 70 men alleged to be involved in a plot to overthrow the Government of Equatorial Guinea, after impounding the aircraft in which 67 of them had travelled from South Africa. South African government officials suggested that the suspected mercenaries had landed in Harare en route to Equatorial Guinea in order to collect weapons, although the company that had chartered the aircraft insisted that the men had stopped to obtain mining-related supplies before flying to Burundi and the DRC to work as security guards. Later that month the 70 defendants appeared in a prison court near Harare, charged with a number of offences, including conspiring against the Government of Equatorial Guinea and violating immigration laws. In June Zimbabwe and Equatorial Guinea agreed to open embassies in their respective capitals and it was reported that President Mugabe had agreed to extradite the 70 men accused of involvement in the coup plot in exchange for petroleum to the value of US $1,200m. Simon Mann, a South African-based British security consultant and the alleged leader of the coup plot, was convicted in September of attempting illegally to procure weapons and was sentenced to seven years' imprisonment (subsequently reduced to four) in Zimbabwe. At the completion of that sentence in 2007, the Equato-Guinean authorities sought to extradite Mann in order to undergo further legal proceedings. That request was granted by a Zimbabwean judge in May and in early February 2008 Mann was transported to custody in Equatorial Guinea.

Other external relations

Relations between the United Kingdom and Zimbabwe remained strained throughout 2000 and 2001. In September 2002 tensions increased when Mugabe criticized the British Prime Minister, Tony Blair, for his part in imposing EU sanctions on Zimbabwe and for interfering in the country's domestic politics; later that month the Government informed British diplomats that they could not leave Harare without permission from the Ministry of Foreign Affairs. In November Mugabe imposed a ban on senior British officials, including Blair, from travelling to Zimbabwe; the measure was taken in response to the United Kingdom's introduction of a requirement for Zimbabwean nationals to apply for a visa in order to visit that country. Blair's successor as British Prime Minister, Gordon Brown, boycotted a summit of EU and African states held in Lisbon, Portugal, in December 2007, in opposition to Mugabe's attendance. Relations between the United Kingdom and Zimbabwe deteriorated further following the disputed presidential election of 2008. In June 2009 Prime Minister Tsvangirai visited the United Kingdom, in an effort to secure financial assistance, meeting Prime Minister Brown, who (in common with other European government leaders) was reluctant to extend large-scale funds in view of lack of progress in the power-sharing agreement.

Iranian President Mahmoud Ahmadinejad made a controversial visit to Zimbabwe in April 2010. During his trip a series of bilateral co-operation accords were signed and Mugabe pledged his support for Iran's contentious nuclear power plans. However, the MDC—T labelled Ahmadinejad's presence in Zimbabwe a 'scandal' and boycotted the discussions amid fears that closer ties with Iran would damage relations with Western nations. Iran approved a €40m. loan for Zimbabwe in July to support a variety of economic development schemes in the country.

CONSTITUTION AND GOVERNMENT

Under the terms of the 1980 Constitution (as subsequently amended), legislative power is vested in the President and a bicameral Parliament, consisting of a House of Assembly and a Senate. The House of Assembly comprises 210 members, who are directly elected by universal adult suffrage. Members of the House of Assembly serve for five years. The Senate comprises 93 members, 60 of whom are directly elected by universal adult suffrage (six in each of the 10 Provinces), five are appointed by the President, 10 are provincial governors, two are the President and the Deputy President of the Council of Chiefs and 16 are traditional Chiefs. Members of the Senate serve for five years.

Following the unanimous approval of the Zimbabwe Amendment (No. 19) Bill by the House of Assembly and the Senate on 5 February 2009, certain transitional amendments were made to the 1980 Constitution, pertaining to the Interparty Political Agreement signed on 15 September 2008. These stated that the President, the Prime Minister and the Cabinet shall all exercise executive authority. The Office of the President shall continue to be occupied by Robert Gabriel Mugabe, who chairs the Cabinet and the National Security Council and formally appoints the Vice-Presidents, the Prime Minister, the Deputy Prime Ministers, ministers and deputy ministers. Following consultation with the Vice-Presidents, the Prime Minister and the Deputy Prime Ministers, he also allocates ministerial portfolios. The Office of the Prime Minister shall be occupied by Morgan Tsvangirai, who chairs the Council of Ministers (which is a subset of the larger Cabinet and which acts as a liaison office) and is Deputy Chairperson of the Cabinet. There shall be two Vice-Presidents nominated by the President and/or the Zimbabwe African National Union—Patriotic Front (ZANU—PF). There shall be two Deputy Prime Ministers, one from the Movement for Democratic Change—Tsvangirai (MDC—T) and one from the Movement for Democratic Change—Mutambara (MDC—M). Provision is made for the nomination of ministers and deputy ministers by ZANU—PF, the MDC—T and the MDC—M. The President shall, at his discretion, appoint five persons to the existing positions of presidential senatorial appointments. An additional six appointed senatorial posts shall be created and filled by persons appointed by the President, four of whom shall be nominated by MDC—T and two by the MDC—M. The Cabinet, *inter alia*, evaluates and adopts all government policies and the consequential programmes, and approves all international agreements. The Council of Ministers, which consists of all ministers from the Cabinet, ensures that the Prime Minister properly discharges his responsibility to oversee the implementation of the work of government and assesses the implementation of decisions made by the Cabinet.

A new draft constitution was approved by referendum on 16 March 2013 and was awaiting presidential promulgation in May.

REGIONAL AND INTERNATIONAL CO-OPERATION

Zimbabwe is a member of the Southern African Development Community (see p. 434), which aims to promote closer economic integration among its members, and also belongs to the Common Market for Eastern and Southern Africa (see p. 241).

Zimbabwe became a member of the UN in 1980 and was admitted to the World Trade Organization (WTO, see p. 444) in 1995. Zimbabwe participates in the Group of 15 (G15, see p. 461) and the Group of 77 (G77, see p. 461) developing countries. Zimbabwe joined the Commonwealth (see p. 244) in 1980, but was suspended from the organization in 2002 and announced its withdrawal in 2003.

ECONOMIC AFFAIRS

In 2011, according to the World Bank, Zimbabwe's gross national income (GNI), measured at average 2009–11 prices, was

US \$8,110m., equivalent to \$640 per head. During 2002–11, it was estimated, the population increased at an average annual rate of 0.1%, while gross domestic product (GDP) per head decreased, in real terms, by an average of 3.8% per year. Overall GDP decreased, in real terms, at an average annual rate of 3.7% in 2002–11, according to the World Bank; GDP rose by 9.3% in 2011.

Agriculture (including forestry and fishing) contributed 15.5% of GDP in 2011 and engaged 65.9% of the employed labour force in that year. According to FAO estimates, the sector was estimated to employ 54.3% of the total labour force in mid-2013. The principal cash crops are tobacco (which accounted for an estimated 21.5% of export earnings in 2012), maize, cotton, coffee and sugar. In addition, wheat, soybeans and groundnuts are cultivated. Beef production was traditionally an important activity; however, at December 2004 the Cattle Producers' Association reported that the commercial beef herd numbered fewer than 125,000 head of cattle, down from 1.4m. in 2000. Agricultural output has declined significantly since the farm invasions that took place from the late 1990s (see Contemporary Political History). According to the World Bank, in 2002–11 agricultural GDP declined by an average of 5.0% per year. Agricultural GDP increased by 13.9% in 2011.

Industry (including mining, manufacturing, construction and power) contributed 36.0% of GDP in 2011 and engaged 9.1% of the employed labour force in the same year. During 2002–11, according to the World Bank, industrial GDP decreased at an average annual rate of 1.1%. Industrial GDP increased by 11.1% in 2011.

Mining (including utilities) contributed 11.7% of GDP and engaged 2.0% of the employed labour force in 2011. Nickel, gold (much of which is illegally smuggled out of the country) and asbestos are the major mineral exports. Chromium ore, copper, silver, platinum, emeralds, lithium, tin, iron ore, cobalt, magnesite, niobium, tantalum, limestone, phosphate rock, coal and diamonds are also mined. In October 1999 the discovery of significant diamond deposits in Zimbabwe was announced; in 2003 Rio Tinto opened Zimbabwe's second diamond mine, at Murowa, near Zvishavane. In 2011 Anglo American Platinum opened a new platinum mine at Unki, on the Great Dyke; the Unki Mine, which was expected to become the country's second largest platinum producer, is located on top of one of the world's largest deposits of the precious metal. Zimbabwe also has large reserves of kyanite and smaller reserves of zinc and lead. Mining GDP increased by 13.2% in 2010 and by 25.1% in 2011.

Manufacturing contributed 17.9% of GDP in 2011 and engaged 5.0% of the employed labour force in that year. The most important sectors, measured by gross value of output, are beverages and tobacco, chemicals, textiles, food-processing and metals (mainly ferrochrome and steel). According to the Confederation of Zimbabwe Industries, 840 manufacturing companies closed between 2000 and 2003. During 2002–11, according to the World Bank, manufacturing GDP decreased by an average of 3.9% per year. Manufacturing GDP increased by 2.0% in 2011.

Construction contributed 0.9% of GDP and engaged 1.9% of the employed labour force in 2011. According to the UN, construction GDP decreased by an average of 0.2% per year during 2002–11. It increased by 14.1% in 2010 and by 6.2% in 2011.

In 2009 53.3% of Zimbabwe's electricity production was derived from hydroelectric power, and 46.4% from coal. Imports of mineral fuels comprised an estimated 21.0% of the value of total imports in 2012. In 2007 the supply of electricity to households was rationed to four hours per day, and frequent power cuts were reported in subsequent years.

The services sector contributed 48.5% of GDP in 2011 and engaged 25.0% of the employed labour force in that year. During 2002–11, according to the World Bank, the GDP of the services sector decreased at an average annual rate of 3.0%. Services GDP increased by 6.7% in 2011.

In 2011, according to IMF estimates, Zimbabwe had a visible merchandise trade deficit of US \$3,066m. and there was a deficit of \$3,427m. on the current account of the balance of payments. In 2012 South Africa was the principal source of imports (providing 42.9% of the total); other major sources of imports were the United Kingdom, the USA, Zambia and the People's Republic of China. South Africa was also the principal market for exports (taking 69.0% of the total) in that year; the other major purchasers were the United Arab Emirates and

Mozambique. The principal exports in 2012 were pearls, precious stones, metals, coins; tobacco and manufactured tobacco substitutes; nickel and nickel articles; ores, slag and ash; and cotton. The main imports in that year were mineral fuels, oils and distillation products, vehicles, nuclear reactors, boilers and electrical machinery, chemicals, cereals, prepared foodstuffs, and base metals.

In 2011 there was an estimated budgetary deficit of US \$302m. The budget was projected to be balanced at US \$4,000m. in 2012. Zimbabwe's general government gross debt was Z.\$4,205m. in 2010, equivalent to 56.2% of GDP. At the end of 2010 Zimbabwe's external debt totalled US \$5,016m., of which US \$3,686m. was public and publicly guaranteed debt. In 2009 external debt was estimated to be equivalent to 103% of GDP. The annual rate of inflation averaged 478.2% in 2000–07, according to ILO. By October 2008 the year-on-year rate of inflation had reached 231m.%; however, following the declaration in January 2009 of a number of foreign currencies (including the US dollar, the euro, the British pound sterling, the South African rand and the Botswana pula) as legal tender in Zimbabwe, consumer prices were reported to have declined by 3.1%. Consumer prices increased at an average annual rate of 3.6% during 2010–12; inflation was 3.8% in 2012. According to official figures, 10.7% of the total labour force were unemployed in 2011.

From 1999 the Zimbabwean economy entered a period of significant decline, and by the late 2000s the country was suffering hyperinflation, extremely high levels of unemployment, and a chronic shortage of foreign exchange to finance essential imports. In 2008 hyperinflation increased to an extent that the Zimbabwe dollar became virtually worthless, contributing to widespread food shortages. Real GDP contracted by 18.3% in that year, according to the IMF. In January 2009 the authorities legalized the use of selected foreign currencies in the country in order to combat the spiralling inflation. Consumer prices subsequently fell steadily and financial conditions improved. Efforts by new Prime Minister Morgan Tsvangirai in June to secure international aid for economic reconstruction met with only limited success, owing to continuing doubts on the part of the US and European governments concerning the implementation of the power-sharing agreement (although in September the IMF provided funds of US \$400m.). A reported increase in attacks against white farmers and landowners during 2009 presented a continued deterrent to foreign investment. Despite this, according to IMF data, real GDP grew by 6.3% in that year. In February 2010 the IMF restored Zimbabwe's voting rights (which had been suspended in 2003); the Fund stated that, although Zimbabwe was henceforth eligible to use resources from its General Resources Account, it would not be able to access support under the facility until it settled arrears of \$140m. to its Poverty Reduction and Growth Trust. Legislation to reform the Reserve Bank of Zimbabwe, the policies of which had been widely held responsible for contributing to the hyperinflation, was approved in April 2010. Real GDP grew by 9.6% in that year, according to the IMF. The economy was buoyed by the recovery of international commodity markets, which had driven up the prices of key Zimbabwean exports such as gold and platinum, while clement weather conditions had led to a resurgence in agricultural production (particularly in the tobacco sector). However, the country's enormous debt burden was restricting development and the slow pace of political reform meant that donors were still unwilling to commit significant funding to the Government. There were also indications that the entry into force in March of contentious indigenization legislation, which involved the phased transfer of 51% of all company shareholdings to black Zimbabweans, had dampened inflows of foreign direct investment. Meanwhile, the Government was hindered in its attempts to commence potentially lucrative exports of diamonds from the country's Marange fields owing to its failure to secure full accreditation through the Kimberley Process Certification Scheme (KPCS) because of allegations that the military forces controlling the fields had committed extensive human rights abuses. Limited trading was allowed to proceed from July 2010, and, despite opposition from human rights groups, the KPCS finally approved diamond exports from Marange in November 2011 (an earlier KPCS endorsement had been rejected by Western nations in June owing to ongoing concerns). The IMF estimated that real GDP rose by 9.4% in 2011, once again supported by high commodity prices and growth in the mining and agricultural sectors. The approval of loans totalling some \$700m. by the People's Republic of China in March was also a positive development. However, economic growth decelerated to 5.0% in

2012: drought conditions had a negative impact on agricultural activity in that year, while mineral output was lower than expected; growth was also impeded by the continuing implementation of the indigenization programme, ongoing political instability, the precarious fiscal situation and the weakness of the global economy. The IMF projected real GDP expansion of 6.0% in 2013.

PUBLIC HOLIDAYS

2014: 1 January (New Year's Day), 18 April (Independence Day and Good Friday), 19 April–21 April (Easter), 1 May (Workers' Day), 25 May (Africa Day, anniversary of OAU's foundation), 11 August (Heroes' Day), 12 August (Defence Forces National Day), 22 December (National Unity Day), 25–26 December (Christmas).

Statistical Survey

Source (unless otherwise stated): Zimbabwe National Statistics Agency, 20th Floor Kaguvi Building, Cnr Fourth St/Central Ave, PO Box CY 342, Causeway, Harare; tel. (4) 706681; fax (4) 728529; internet www.zimstat.co.zw.

Area and Population

AREA, POPULATION AND DENSITY

Area (sq km)	390,757*
Population (census results)	
17 August 2002	11,631,657
18 August 2012 (preliminary)	
Males	6,234,931
Females	6,738,877
Total	12,973,808
Density (per sq km) at 2012 census	33.2

* 150,872 sq miles.

POPULATION BY AGE AND SEX
(UN estimates at mid-2013)

	Males	Females	Total
0–14	2,481,943	2,468,171	4,950,114
15–64	3,869,977	3,951,081	7,821,058
65 and over	241,001	315,749	556,750
Total	**6,592,921**	**6,735,001**	**13,327,922**

Note: Estimates not adjusted to take account of results of 2012 census.

Source: UN, *World Population Prospects: The 2010 Revision.*

PROVINCES
(population at 2012 census, preliminary)

	Area (sq km)	Population	Density (per sq km)
Bulawayo	479	655,675	1,368.8
Harare	872	2,098,199	2,406.2
Manicaland	36,459	1,755,000	48.1
Mashonaland Central	28,347	1,139,940	40.2
Mashonaland East . .	32,230	1,337,059	41.5
Mashonaland West . .	57,441	1,449,938	25.2
Masvingo	56,566	1,486,604	26.3
Matabeleland North .	75,025	743,871	9.9
Matabeleland South .	54,172	685,046	12.6
Midlands	49,166	1,622,476	33.0
Total	**390,757**	**12,973,808**	**33.2**

PRINCIPAL TOWNS
(population at 2012 census, preliminary)

Harare (capital) .	1,468,767	Chinhoyi (Sinoia) .	79,368
Bulawayo . . .	655,675	Marondera . . .	
Chitungwiza . .	354,472	(Marandellas) . .	62,120
Mutare (Umtali) .	188,243	Zvishavane . . .	
Gweru (Gwelo) .	158,233	(Shabani) . .	45,325
Kwekwe (Que Que) .	100,455	Hwange (Wankie) .	37,602
Kadoma (Gatooma) .	90,109	Redcliff	35,924
Masvingo . . .	88,554		

BIRTHS AND DEATHS
(annual averages, UN estimates)

	1995–2000	2000–05	2005–10
Birth rate (per 1,000) . . .	31.5	29.7	29.4
Death rate (per 1,000) . . .	14.5	17.5	15.1

Source: UN, *World Population Prospects: The 2010 Revision.*

2011: Birth rate 29.0 per 1,000; Death rate 12.7 per 1,000 (Source: African Development Bank).

Life expectancy (years at birth): 51.2 (males 52.0; females 50.4) in 2011 (Source: World Bank, World Development Indicators database).

ECONOMICALLY ACTIVE POPULATION
(sample survey, persons aged 15 years and over, 1999)

	Males	Females	Total
Agriculture, hunting, forestry and fishing	1,215,661	1,584,839	2,800,500
Mining and quarrying . . .	46,946	3,367	50,313
Manufacturing	283,090	94,667	377,757
Electricity, gas and water . . .	10,158	n.a.	10,158
Construction	98,908	6,659	105,567
Trade, restaurants and hotels .	154,198	178,341	332,539
Transport, storage and communications	93,289	8,288	101,577
Financing, insurance, real estate and business services . . .	100,425	20,749	121,174
Community, social and personal services	320,020	258,505	578,525
Sub-total	**2,322,695**	**2,155,415**	**4,478,110**
Activities not adequately defined .	63,052	124,286	187,338
Total employed	**2,385,747**	**2,279,701**	**4,665,448**
Unemployed	187,142	110,669	297,811
Total labour force	**2,572,889**	**2,390,370**	**4,963,259**

2011 (labour force survey, '000 persons aged 15 years and over): Agriculture, hunting, forestry and fishing 3,573.9; Mining and quarrying 107.7; Manufacturing 269.8; Electricity, gas and water 13.1; Construction 101.8; Trade, restaurants and hotels 545.1; Transport, storage and communications 106.7; Financing, insurance, real estate and business services 135.5; Public administration 70.8; Education 167.3; Health 67.2; Other services 264.9; *Sub-total* 5,423.8; Activities not adequately defined 7.2; *Total employed* 5,431.0; *Unemployed* 652.7; *Total labour force* 6,083.8 (males 2,895.7, females 3,188.1).

Mid-2013 (estimates in '000): Agriculture, etc. 3,274; Total labour force 6,029 (Source: FAO).

Health and Welfare

KEY INDICATORS

Total fertility rate (children per woman, 2010)	3.3
Under-5 mortality rate (per 1,000 live births, 2010) . . .	80
HIV/AIDS (% of persons aged 15–49, 2009)	14.3
Physicians (per 1,000 head, 2004)	0.2
Hospital beds (per 1,000 head, 2006)	3.0
Health expenditure (2007): US $ per head (PPP)	20
Health expenditure (2007): % of GDP	8.9
Health expenditure (2007): public (% of total)	46.3
Access to water (% of persons, 2010)	80
Access to sanitation (% of persons, 2010)	40
Total carbon dioxide emissions ('000 metric tons, 2008) . .	9,075.8
Carbon dioxide emissions per head (metric tons, 2008) . .	0.7
Human Development Index (2011): ranking	173
Human Development Index (2011): value	0.376

For sources and definitions, see explanatory note on p. vi.

Agriculture

PRINCIPAL CROPS
('000 metric tons)

	2009	2010	2011
Wheat*	40	50	44
Barley*	58	67	65
Maize	700†	1,192	1,328*
Millet	40	51	58*
Sorghum	70*	74	94*
Potatoes*	51	58	54
Cassava (Manioc)*	216	204	225
Beans, dry	34*	22	26*
Sugar cane*	3,100	3,100	3,100
Soybeans (Soya beans) . . .	90†	57	80†
Groundnuts, with shell . . .	79†	106	93†
Sunflower seed	15†	12	15†
Oranges*	61	79	98
Bananas*	106	109	95
Coffee, green†	1	2	3*
Tea*	17	20	18
Tobacco, unmanufactured* . .	85	110	112
Cotton lint*	80	38	90

* FAO estimate(s).
† Unofficial figure(s).

Aggregate production ('000 metric tons, may include official, semi-official or estimated data): 911 in 2009, 1,437 in 2010, 1,592 in 2011; Total roots and tubers 270 in 2009, 266 in 2010, 281 in 2011; Total vegetables (incl. melons) 182 in 2009; 208 in 2010, 228 in 2011; Total fruits (excl. melons) 221 in 2009, 242 in 2010, 246 in 2011.

Source: FAO.

LIVESTOCK
('000 head, year ending September, FAO estimates)

	2009	2010	2011
Horses	28.0	28.0	28.0
Asses	112	112	112
Cattle	5,030	5,040	5,060
Sheep	380	375	365
Pigs	630	635	640
Goats	2,895	2,703	2,650
Chickens	32,500	33,000	34,000

Source: FAO.

LIVESTOCK PRODUCTS
('000 metric tons, FAO estimates)

	2009	2010	2011
Cattle meat	104.1	99.6	102.0
Goat meat	12.9	13.1	13.0
Pig meat	31.2	31.4	31.5
Chicken meat	61.9	62.1	63.3
Cows' milk	389	396	396
Hen eggs	30	30	30

Source: FAO.

Forestry

ROUNDWOOD REMOVALS
('000 cubic metres, excl. bark, FAO estimates)

	2009	2010	2011
Sawlogs, veneer logs and logs for sleepers	445	335	335
Pulpwood	81	8	8
Other industrial wood . . .	112	175	175
Fuel wood	8,626	8,709	8,788
Total	9,264	9,227	9,306

Source: FAO.

SAWNWOOD PRODUCTION
('000 cubic metres, incl. railway sleepers, FAO estimates)

	2008	2009	2010
Coniferous (softwood) . . .	254	254	163
Broadleaved (hardwood) . . .	14	14	14
Total	268	268	177

2011: Production assumed to be unchanged from 2010 (FAO estimates).

Source: FAO.

Fishing

('000 metric tons, live weight, FAO estimates)

	2008	2009	2010
Capture	10.5	10.5	10.5
Tilapias	1.0	1.0	1.0
Other freshwater fishes . . .	1.6	1.6	1.6
Dagaas	7.8	7.9	7.9
Aquaculture	2.6	2.7	2.7
Tilapias	2.6	2.7	2.7
Total catch	13.1	13.2	13.2

Note: Figures exclude aquatic animals, recorded by number rather than weight. The number of Nile crocodiles caught was: 81,554 in 2008; 62,101 in 2009; 104,731 in 2010.

Source: FAO.

Mining

('000 metric tons unless otherwise indicated)

	2008	2009	2010*
Asbestos	11	5	2
Chromium ore	442.6	193.7	510.0
Coal	1,947	1,750*	2,400
Cobalt ore (metric tons)†	28	39	60
Copper ore‡	2.8	3.6	4.7
Gold (kilograms)	3,579	4,965	9,100
Iron ore	3	n.a.	n.a.
Limestone	50*	40*	50
Magnesite (metric tons)	2,549	449	n.a.
Nickel ore (metric tons)	6,354	4,858	6,200
Phosphate rock	21.1	20.0*	63.0
Silver (kilograms)	150*	200*	400

* Estimate(s).
† Figures include metal content of compounds and salts and may include cobalt recovered from nickel-copper matte.
‡ Figures refer to the metal content of ores and concentrates.

Source: US Geological Survey.

Industry

SELECTED PRODUCTS
('000 metric tons unless otherwise indicated)

	2008	2009	2010
Coke (metallurgical)	112	43	20*
Cement*	400	700	800
Ferro-chromium	145.4	72.2	146.0*
Crude steel*	10	14	14
Refined copper—unwrought (metric tons)	3,072	4,000*	4,545
Refined nickel—unwrought (metric tons)	13,700*	5,000*	4,039

* Estimate(s).

Source: US Geological Survey.

Raw sugar ('000 metric tons): 446 in 2006; 349 in 2007; 291 in 2008 (Source: UN Industrial Commodity Statistics Database).

Electric energy (net production, million kWh): 8,472.9 in 2010; 9,019.2 in 2011; 8,962.7 in 2012.

Finance

CURRENCY AND EXCHANGE RATES

Monetary Units
100 cents = 1 Zimbabwe dollar (Z.$).

Sterling, US Dollar and Euro Equivalents (31 December 2008)
£1 sterling = Z.$7,143,221.60;
US $1 = Z.$4,900,000.00;
€1 = Z.$6,819,326.81;
Z.$10,000 = £0.0014 = US $0.0020 = €0.0015.

Average Exchange Rate (Z.$ per US dollar)
2008   6,723,052,073

Note: On 1 August 2008 a redenomination of the Zimbabwe dollar was introduced whereby 10,000m. of the former currency was revalued at 1 dollar. In January 2009, in order to address the diminishing value of the national currency, a number of foreign currencies (including the US dollar, the euro, the British pound sterling, the South African rand and the Botswana pula), were also declared legal tender in Zimbabwe. A further massive redenomination of the Zimbabwe dollar was announced in February (whereby 1,000,000m. of the former currency was to be revalued at 1 dollar), but in April of the same year legal use of the national currency was effectively suspended until further notice. Foreign currencies (specifically those of Botswana, the Euro Zone, South Africa, the United Kingdom and the USA) are currently in use.

BUDGET
(US $ million, estimates)

Revenue*	2010	2011†	2012‡
Tax revenue	2,074	2,660	3,253
Personal income tax	428	588	670
Corporate income tax	256	296	362
Other direct taxes	168	188	343
Customs	340	333	400
Excise	165	307	330
Value-added tax	689	912	1,108
Other taxes	28	36	40
Non-tax revenue	124	110	148
Additional mineral revenue	—	151	600
Budget grants	1	—	—
Total	2,199	2,921	4,000

Expenditure	2010	2011†	2012‡
Current expenditure	1,779	2,750	3,200
Salaries and wages	784	1,126	1,365
Pensions and benefits	279	691	916
Interest payments	176	198	18
Foreign	176	198	18
Grants and transfers	178	195	302
Other current expenditure	362	539	599
Capital expenditure§	593	473	800
Total	2,372	3,223	4,000

* Excluding off-budget grants received (excl. food aid, US $ million): 587 in 2010; 460 in 2011 (estimate); 519 in 2012 (budgeted figure).
† Estimates.
‡ Budgeted figures.
§ Including net lending.

Source: IMF, *Zimbabwe: Staff Report for the 2012 Article IV Consultation* (September 2012).

INTERNATIONAL RESERVES
(US $ million at 31 December)

	2012
Gold (national valuation)	1.2
IMF special drawing rights	143.0
Reserve position in IMF	0.5
Foreign exchange	430.9
Total	575.6

Source: IMF, *International Financial Statistics*.

MONEY SUPPLY
(Z.$ '000 million at 31 December)

	2005	2006	2007
Currency outside banks	9,876	228,064	73,075
Demand deposits at deposit money banks	34,048	404,965	350,999
Total money (incl. others)	44,746	636,799	425,445

Note: The value of the Zimbabwe dollar has not been adjusted retrospectively to reflect subsequent redenominations.

Source: IMF, *International Financial Statistics*.

COST OF LIVING
(Consumer Price Index; base: December 2008 = 100)

	2010	2011	2012
Food and non-alcoholic beverages	90.5	94.1	98.5
Beverages and tobacco	100.9	105.9	112.5
Clothing and footwear	80.2	81.4	82.1
Rent and electricity	115.6	120.7	135.0
Health	93.0	92.7	94.2
Transport	106.0	113.9	116.1
Education	110.6	115.0	125.7
Recreation and culture	100.6	100.8	101.5
All items (incl. others)	94.9	98.2	101.9

NATIONAL ACCOUNTS
(US $ million at current prices)

Expenditure on the Gross Domestic Product

	2009	2010	2011*
Government final consumption expenditure	988.5	2,238.2	2,889.9
Private final consumption expenditure	5,390.2	5,903.4	8,694.1
Gross capital formation . . .	929.2	1,808.5	2,271.3
Total domestic expenditure	7,307.9	9,950.1	13,855.3
Exports of goods and services .	2,302.8	2,689.2	3,555.7
Less Imports of goods and services	3,477.4	5,206.0	8,545.6
GDP in purchasers' values .	6,133.2	7,433.3	8,865.4

Gross Domestic Product by Economic Activity

	2009	2010	2011*
Agriculture, hunting, forestry and fishing	1,038.4	1,157.2	1,222.1
Mining and quarrying	475.2	716.8	920.7
Manufacturing	953.4	1,166.5	1,409.1
Electricity and water	275.8	355.3	432.1
Construction	32.6	57.8	70.6
Trade, restaurants and hotels .	615.8	734.6	749.7
Transport, storage and communications	853.8	908.5	1,084.6
Finance, insurance and real estate	332.0	367.3	671.3
Public administration	186.4	291.6	321.4
Education	209.0	303.2	423.0
Health	87.3	101.5	134.5
Domestic services	35.2	38.7	39.1
Other services	297.1	347.4	391.5
Sub-total	5,392.0	6,546.4	7,869.6
Less Imputed bank service charges	22.1	35.6	50.3
GDP at factor cost	5,369.9	6,510.7	7,819.4
Indirect taxes, less subsidies . .	763.4	922.6	1,046.1
GDP in purchasers' values .	6,133.2	7,433.3	8,865.4

* Preliminary data.

BALANCE OF PAYMENTS
(US $ million)

	2009	2010	2011*
Exports of goods f.o.b.	1,613	3,317	4,496
Imports of goods f.o.b.	−3,213	−5,162	−7,562
Trade balance	−1,600	−1,844	−3,066
Non-factor services (net) . . .	−266	−449	−645
Balance on goods and services	−1,866	−2,293	−3,711
Investment income (net) . . .	−419	−421	−519
Balance on goods, services and income	−2,285	−2,714	−4,230
Private transfers (net)	926	573	803
Current balance	−1,359	−2,141	−3,427
Official transfers (net)	391	231	210
Direct investment (net) . . .	105	123	373
Portfolio investment (net) . . .	67	63	38
Long-term capital (net) . . .	−101	−2	769
Short-term capital (net) . . .	241	90	327
IMF special drawing rights liabilities	520	100	—
Net errors and omissions . . .	−103	860	959
Overall balance	−239	−677	−751

* Estimates.

Source: IMF, *Zimbabwe: Staff Report for the 2012 Article IV Consultation* (September 2012).

External Trade

PRINCIPAL COMMODITIES
(distribution by HS, US $ million)

Imports f.o.b.	2010	2011	2012
Food products	464.3	526.6	587.4
Cereals	292.8	352.0	466.2
Animal, vegetable fats and oils, cleavage products, etc. . .	153.4	222.2	223.8
Prepared foodstuffs; beverages, spirits and vinegar; tobacco, etc. . . .	379.3	450.1	513.0
Mineral products	966.2	1,289.4	1,573.9
Mineral fuels, oils and distillation products; mineral waxes, etc. .	939.6	1,255.4	1,532.1
Chemicals and related products	569.2	2,592.8	973.2
Fertilizers	149.8	2,031.4	330.7
Plastics, rubbers and articles thereof	227.4	305.9	316.3
Base metals and articles of base metal	418.4	474.5	389.2
Machinery and mechanical appliances and electrical equipment, etc.	992.5	992.4	1,034.9
Boilers, general industrial machinery, equipment and parts	529.1	581.4	641.4
Electrical machinery and equipment; sound and television recorders and reproducers . .	463.4	411.0	393.5
Vehicles, vessels, aircraft and other transport equipment .	1,088.9	1,077.9	1,121.7
Vehicles other than railway, tramway	1,081.8	1,065.8	1,107.5
Total (incl. others)	5,864.7	8,596.4	7,484.0

Exports f.o.b.	2010	2011	2012
Prepared foodstuffs; beverages, spirits and vinegar; tobacco, etc. . . .	549.9	792.0	967.2
Tobacco and manufactured tobacco substitutes	477.5	717.4	826.6
Mineral products	392.7	441.1	451.9
Ores, slag and ash	310.5	363.6	367.3
Pulp of wood, paper and paperboard	573.3	404.6	10.9
Printed books, newspapers, pictures etc.	559.3	393.2	0.1
Textiles and textile articles .	171.9	277.4	240.9
Cotton	162.5	269.1	233.3
Pearls, precious stones, metals, coins, etc.	669.1	717.3	1,436.3
Base metals and articles of base metal	655.7	659.2	502.0
Iron and steel	204.5	117.5	134.2
Nickel and nickel articles . . .	440.7	528.6	352.5
Total (incl. others)	3,204.2	3,516.6	3,839.3

PRINCIPAL TRADING PARTNERS
(US $ million)

Imports f.o.b.	2010	2011	2012
Botswana	215.9	204.1	112.9
China, People's Repub. . . .	319.7	371.4	354.5
Germany	69.1	84.2	66.7
India	65.5	168.4	150.4
Japan	29.1	40.3	93.2
Kuwait	317.1	800.6	152.7
Malawi	43.9	88.8	44.0
Mauritius	74.8	122.2	38.0
Mozambique	165.5	169.0	177.5
South Africa	2,820.5	4,833.1	3,207.2
United Arab Emirates . .	147.9	70.2	86.9
United Kingdom	158.6	188.2	1,262.7
USA	744.5	589.1	558.2
Zambia	146.4	217.9	492.3
Total (incl. others)	5,864.7	8,596.4	7,484.0

Exports f.o.b.	2010	2011	2012
Belgium	60.5	60.0	47.6
Botswana	27.6	36.2	48.3
China, People's Repub. . . .	237.3	185.9	85.0
Germany	46.4	32.0	16.0
Italy	76.9	59.5	41.0
Mozambique	90.9	128.2	278.4
Singapore	30.5	49.4	1.4
South Africa	1,773.7	2,395.6	2,649.4
United Arab Emirates . .	329.0	208.9	481.9
United Kingdom	96.4	33.1	2.0
Zambia	68.0	75.4	85.1
Total (incl. others)	3,204.2	3,516.6	3,839.3

Transport

RAIL TRAFFIC
(National Railways of Zimbabwe, including operations in Botswana)

	1998	1999	2000
Total number of passengers ('000).	1,787	1,896	1,614
Revenue-earning metric tons hauled ('000)	12,421	12,028	9,422
Gross metric ton-km (million) .	9,248	8,962	6,953
Net metric ton-km (million) . .	4,549	4,375	3,326

ROAD TRAFFIC
('000 motor vehicles in use, estimates)

	1998	1999	2000
Passenger cars	540	555	573
Commercial vehicles	37	38	39

2007 (motor vehicles in use at 31 December): Passenger cars 1,214,137; Buses and coaches 15,566; Vans and lorries 186,790; Motorcycles and mopeds 108,961 (Source: IRF, *World Road Statistics*).

CIVIL AVIATION
(traffic on scheduled services)

	2007	2008	2009
Kilometres flown (million) . .	11	11	11
Passengers carried ('000) . . .	255	264	262
Passenger-km (million) . . .	711	727	703
Total ton-km (million) . . .	78	81	79

Source: UN, *Statistical Yearbook*.

Passengers carried ('000): 302 in 2010 (Source: World Bank, World Development Indicators database).

Tourism

VISITOR ARRIVALS BY NATIONALITY

	2008	2009	2010
Australia and New Zealand . .	20,201	33,041	37,708
Botswana	147,780	183,212	114,718
Canada and USA	37,754	48,809	60,514
Malawi	63,597	108,103	67,291
Mozambique	118,117	110,058	131,653
South Africa	936,727	912,244	1,368,238
Zambia	346,344	230,198	168,722
Total (incl. others)	1,955,597	2,017,264	2,239,165

Tourism receipts (US $ million, excl. passenger transport): 294 in 2008; 523 in 2009; 634 in 2010.

Source: World Tourism Organization.

Communications Media

	2009	2010	2011
Telephones ('000 main lines in use)	385.1	379.0	356.0
Mobile cellular telephones ('000 subscribers)	2,991.0	7,700.0	9,200.0
Internet subscribers ('000) . .	99.7	121.0	54.0
Broadband subscribers ('000) . .	29.1	33.0	34.0

Source: International Telecommunication Union.

Education

(2002/03 unless otherwise indicated)

	Institutions*	Teachers	Students
Pre-primary	n.a.	19,588	448,124
Primary	4,699	64,001†	2,445,520†
Secondary	1,539	33,964	831,488†
Tertiary	n.a.	4,081‡	94,611‡

* 1998 figures.
† 2005/06.
‡ 2009/10.

Source: mainly UNESCO Institute for Statistics.

Pupil-teacher ratio (primary education, UNESCO estimate): 38.2 in 2005/06 (Source: UNESCO Institute for Statistics).

Adult literacy rate (UNESCO estimates): 92.2% (males 94.7%; females 89.9%) in 2010 (Source: UNESCO Institute for Statistics).

Directory

The Government

HEAD OF STATE

President: ROBERT GABRIEL MUGABE (took office 31 December 1987; re-elected March 1990, 16–17 March 1996, 9–11 March 2002 and 27 June 2008).

THE CABINET
(May 2013)

The Cabinet comprises representatives of the Zimbabwe African National Union—Patriotic Front (ZANU—PF), the Movement for Democratic Change—Tsvangirai (MDC—T) and the Movement for Democratic Change—Mutambara (MDC—M).

Vice-President (ZANU—PF): (vacant).

Vice-President (ZANU—PF): JOYCE MUJURU.

Prime Minister (MDC—T): MORGAN RICHARD TSVANGIRAI.

First Deputy Prime Minister (MDC—T): THOKOZANI KHUPE.

Second Deputy Prime Minister (MDC—M): ARTHUR MUTAMBARA.

Minister of Agriculture, Mechanisation and Irrigation Development (ZANU—PF): JOSEPH MADE.

Minister of Constitutional and Parliamentary Affairs (MDC—T): ERIC MATINENGA.

Minister of Defence (ZANU—PF): EMMERSON MNANGWAGWA.

Minister of Economic Planning and Development (MDC—T): TAPIWA MASHAKADA.

Minister of Education, Sports and Culture (MDC—M): DAVID COLTART.

Minister of Energy and Power Development (MDC—T): ELTON MANGOMA.

Minister of the Environment and Natural Resources (ZANU—PF): FRANCIS NHEMA.

Minister of Finance (MDC—T): TENDAI BITI.

Minister of Foreign Affairs (ZANU—PF): SIMBARASHE MUMBENGEGWI.

Minister of Health and Child Welfare (MDC—T): HENRY MADZORERA.

Minister of Higher and Tertiary Education (ZANU—PF): I. STANISLAUS GORERAZVO MUDENGE.

Minister of Home Affairs (ZANU—PF): KEMBO MOHADI.

Minister of Home Affairs (MDC—T): THERESA MAKONE.

Minister of Industry and Commerce (MDC—M): WELSHMAN NCUBE.

Minister of Information and Communications Technology (MDC—T): NELSON CHAMISA.

Minister of Justice and Legal Affairs (ZANU—PF): PATRICK ANTHONY CHINAMASA.

Minister of Labour and Social Welfare (MDC—T): PAULINE GWANYANYA MPARIWA.

Minister of Lands and Rural Resettlement (ZANU—PF): HERBERT MURERWA.

Minister of Local Government and Urban and Rural Development (ZANU—PF): Dr IGNATIUS MORGAN CHIMINYA CHOMBO.

Minister of Media, Information and Publicity (ZANU—PF): WEBSTER SHAMU.

Minister of Mines and Mining Development (ZANU—PF): OBERT MPOFU.

Minister of National Housing and Social Amenities (MDC—T): GILES MUTSEKWA.

Minister of Public Service (MDC—T): LUCIA MATIBENGA.

Minister of Public Works (MDC—T): JOEL GABUZA.

Minister of Regional Integration and International Co-operation (MDC—M): PRISCILLA MISIHAIRABWI.

Minister of Science and Technology (MDC—T): HENERI DZINOTYIWEI.

Minister of Small and Medium Enterprises and Co-operative Development (ZANU—PF): SITHEMBISO NYONI.

Minister of State Enterprises and Parastatals (MDC—T): GORDON MOYO.

Minister of State for National Security in the President's Office (ZANU—PF): SYDNEY SEKERAMAYI.

Minister of State for Presidential Affairs (ZANU—PF): DIDYMUS MUTASA.

Minister of State in the Prime Minister's Office (MDC—T): JAMESON TIMBA.

Minister of State in the Prime Minister's Office (MDC—T): SEKAI MASIKANA HOLLAND.

Minister of Tourism and the Hospitality Industry (ZANU—PF): WALTER MZEMBI.

Minister of Transport and Infrastructural Development (ZANU—PF): NICHOLAS GOCHE.

Minister of Water Resources (MDC—T): SAMUEL SIPEPA NKOMO.

Minister of Women's Affairs, Gender and Community Development (ZANU—PF): OLIVIA MUCHENA.

Minister of Youth Development, Indigenization and Empowerment (ZANU—PF): SAVIOR KASUKUWERE.

In addition, there are 20 deputy ministers, 10 from ZANU—PF, nine from the MDC—T and one from the MDC—M.

The Constitution provides for the Attorney-General to serve as an ex officio member of the Cabinet.

MINISTRIES

Office of the President: Munhumutapa Bldg, Samora Machel Ave, Private Bag 7700, Causeway, Harare; tel. (4) 707091.

Office of the Vice-Presidents: Munhumutapa Bldg, Samora Machel Ave, Private Bag 7700, Causeway, Harare; tel. (4) 707091.

Ministry of Agriculture, Mechanisation and Irrigation Development: Ngungunyana Bldg, 1 Borrowdale Rd, Private Bag 7701, Causeway, Harare; tel. (4) 700596; fax (4) 734646; internet www.moa.gov.zw.

Ministry of Constitutional and Parliamentary Affairs: Harare.

Ministry of Defence: Defence House, cnr Kwame Nkruma and 3rd Sts, Harare; tel. (4) 700155; fax (4) 727501; internet www.mod.gov.zw.

Ministry of Economic Planning and Development: New Complex Bldg, Government Composite Offices, cnr 3rd St and Samora Machel Ave, Harare; e-mail moed@gta.gov.zw; internet www.mofed.gov.zw.

Ministry of Education, Sports and Culture: Ambassador House, Union Ave, POB CY121, Causeway, Harare; tel. (4) 734051; fax (4) 707599; internet www.moesc.gov.zw.

Ministry of Energy and Power Development: Chaminuka Bldg, Private Bag 7758, Causeway, Harare; tel. (4) 733095; fax (4) 797956; e-mail energy@gta.gov.zw; internet www.energy.gov.zw.

Ministry of the Environment and Natural Resources: Kaguvi Bldg, 12th Floor, cnr 4th St and Central Ave, Private Bag 7753, Causeway, Harare; tel. (4) 701681; fax (4) 252673; e-mail metlib@zarnet.ac.zw; internet www.met.gov.zw.

Ministry of Finance: Blocks B, E and G, Composite Bldg, cnr Samora Machel Ave and Fourth St, Private Bag 7705, Causeway, Harare; tel. (4) 738603; fax (4) 792750; internet www.mofed.gov.zw.

Ministry of Foreign Affairs: Munhumutapa Bldg, Samora Machel Ave, POB 4240, Causeway, Harare; tel. (4) 727005; fax (4) 705161; internet www.zimfa.gov.zw.

Ministry of Health and Child Welfare: Kaguvi Bldg, Fourth St, POB CY198, Causeway, Harare; tel. (4) 730011; fax (4) 729154; internet www.mohcw.gov.zw.

Ministry of Higher and Tertiary Education: Government Composite Bldg, cnr Fourth St and Samora Machel Ave, Union Ave, POB UA275, Harare; tel. (4) 796440; fax (4) 790923; e-mail thesecretary@mhet.ac.zw; internet www.mhet.ac.zw.

Ministry of Home Affairs: Mukwati Bldg, 11th Floor, cnr Fourth St and Livingstone Ave, Private Bag 7703, Causeway, Harare; tel. (4) 703641; fax (4) 707231; e-mail moha@gvt.co.zw; internet www.moha.gov.zw.

Ministry of Industry and Commerce: Mukwati Bldg, Fourth St, Private Bag 7708, Causeway, Harare; tel. (4) 702731; fax (4) 729311; internet www.miit.gov.zw.

Ministry of Information and Communications Technology: Linquenda House, Baker Ave, POB CY825, Causeway, Harare; tel. (4) 703894; fax (4) 707213.

Ministry of Justice and Legal Affairs: New Government Complex, cnr Samora Machel Ave and 4th St, Private Bag 7751, Causeway, Harare; tel. (4) 774620; fax (4) 772999; internet www.justice.gov.zw.

Ministry of Labour and Social Welfare: Harare.

Ministry of Lands and Rural Resettlement: Block 2, Makombe Complex, cnr Harare St and Herbert Chitepo, Harare; tel. (4) 797325; internet www.lands.gov.zw.

Ministry of Local Government and Urban and Rural Development: Mukwati Bldg, Fourth St, Private Bag 7755, Causeway, Harare; tel. (4) 7282019; fax (4) 708493; internet www.mlgvturd.gov.zw.

Ministry of Media, Information and Publicity: Harare.

Ministry of Mines and Mining Development: ZIMRE Centre, 6th Floor, cnr Leopold Takawira St and Kwame Nkrumah Ave, Private Bag 7709, Causeway, Harare; tel. (4) 777022; fax (4) 777044; e-mail minsec@technopark.co.zw; internet www.mines.gov.zw.

Ministry of National Housing and Social Amenities: Kaguvi Bldg, 6th Floor, cnr 4th St and Central Ave, Private Bag 7780, Causeway, Harare; tel. (4) 790948.

Ministry of Public Service: Compensation House, cnr Central Ave and Fourth St, Private Bag 7707, Causeway, Harare; tel. (4) 790871; fax (4) 794568; e-mail mpslsw@gta.gov.zw; internet www.pslsw.gov.zw.

Ministry of Public Works: Harare.

Ministry of Regional Integration and International Co-operation: Harare.

Ministry of Science and Technology: Livingstone House, 17th Floor, 48 Samora Machel Avenue, Harare; tel. (4) 727579; fax (4) 734986; internet www.mstd.gov.zw.

Ministry of Small and Medium Enterprises and Co-operative Development: Linquenda House, cnr Nelson Mandela and First Sts, Private Bag 7740, Causeway, Harare; tel. (4) 731003; fax (4) 731879; e-mail info@msmed.gov.zw; internet www.msmed.gov.zw.

Ministry of State Enterprises and Parastatals: Harare.

Ministry of Tourism and the Hospitality Industry: Harare.

Ministry of Transport and Infrastructural Development: Kaguvi Bldg, 4th Central Ave, POB 595, Causeway, Harare; tel. (4) 252396; fax (4) 726661; e-mail angiekaronga@yahoo.co.uk; internet www.transcom.gov.zw.

Ministry of Water Resources: Kurima House, 8th Floor, cnr Nelson Mandela Ave and Fourth St, Private Bag CY 7767, Harare; tel. (4) 700596; fax (4) 738165; internet www.water.gov.zw.

Ministry of Women's Affairs, Gender and Community Development: Kaguvi Bldg, 8th Floor, cnr Fourth St and Central Ave, Harare; tel. (4) 708389; internet www.women.gov.zw.

Ministry of Youth Development, Indigenization and Empowerment: ZANU—PF Bldg, Private Bag 7762, Causeway, Harare; tel. (4) 734691; fax (4) 732709; e-mail mydgec@zarnet.ac.zw; internet www.mydgec.gov.zw.

PROVINCIAL GOVERNORS
(May 2013)

Bulawayo: CAIN MATHEMA.

Harare: DAVID KARIMANZIRA.

Manicaland: CHRISTOPHER MUSHOHWE.

Mashonaland Central: MARTIN DINHA.

Mashonaland East: AENEAS CHIGWEDERE.

Mashonaland West: FABER CHIDARIKIRE.

Masvingo: TITUS MALULEKE.

Matabeleland North: THOKOZILE MATHUTHU.

Matabeleland South: ANGELINE MASUKU.

Midlands: JAISON MACHAYA.

President and Legislature

PRESIDENT

Presidential Election, First Round, 29 March 2008

Candidate	Votes	% of valid votes
Morgan Tsvangirai	1,195,562	47.87
Robert Gabriel Mugabe	1,079,730	43.24
Simba Herbert Makoni	207,470	8.31
Langton Towungana	14,503	0.58
Total	**2,497,265**	**100.00**

Presidential Election, Second Round, 27 June 2008, provisional results

Candidate	Votes	% of valid votes
Robert Gabriel Mugabe	2,150,269	90.21
Morgan Tsvangirai*	233,000	9.78
Total†	**2,383,629**	**100.00**

* Tsvangirai announced his withdrawal from the second round of voting on 22 June; however, the Zimbabwe Election Commission stated that the Constitution necessitated that the run-off take place and Tsvangirai's name remained on the ballot papers.
† Excludes 131,481 spoiled ballots.

HOUSE OF ASSEMBLY

Speaker: LOVEMORE MOYO.

General Election, 29 March 2008, provisional results

Party	Votes	% of votes	Seats
MDC—Tsvangirai	1,041,176	42.99	99
ZANU—PF	1,110,649	45.86	97
MDC—Mutambara	202,259	8.35	10
Independents	54,254	2.24	1
Others	13,635	0.56	—
Total	**2,421,973**	**100.00**	**207***

* Voting was postponed in three constituencies, owing to the deaths of candidates.

SENATE

Speaker: EDNA MADZONGWE.

General Election, 29 March 2008, provisional results

Party	Seats
ZANU—PF	30
MDC—Tsvangirai	24
MDC—Mutambara	6
Total	**60***

* In addition to the 60 directly elective seats, five are held by nominees of the President, 10 by provincial governors, two by the President and the Deputy President of the Council of Chiefs and 16 by traditional Chiefs.

Election Commission

Zimbabwe Electoral Commission (ZEC): Mahachi Quantum Bldg, 1 Nelson Mandela Ave, PMB 7782, Causeway, Harare; tel. (4) 770340; fax (4) 781903; e-mail inquiry@zec.org.zw; internet www.zec.org.zw; f. 2005; the President appoints eight members, four of whom must be women, and also the Chair. in consultation with the Judicial Service Commission and the Committee on Standing Rules and Orders for a six-year term; superseded and replaced the Electoral Supervisory Commission (abolished Aug. 2005); responsible for establishing constituency boundaries, voter registration and conducting elections; Chair. RITA MAKARAU.

Political Organizations

Christian Democratic Party: Leader WILLIAM GWATA.

Mavambo Kusile Dawn (MKD): Harare; internet www.mavambokusiledawn.org; f. 2009; Leader SIMBA MAKONI.

Movement for Democratic Change—Mutambara (MDC—M): 11 Creswick Rd, Hillside, Harare; tel. (4) 747071; e-mail a.mutambara@mdczim.com; internet www.mdczim.net; f. 2005; Pres. Prof. WELSHMAN NCUBE; Sec.-Gen. PRISCILLA MISIHAIRABWI-MUSHONGA.

Movement for Democratic Change—Tsvangirai (MDC—T): Harvest House, 6th Floor, cnr Angwa St and Nelson Mandela Ave, Harare; tel. (4) 770708; fax (4) 780302; e-mail mdcnewsbrief@gmail.com; internet www.mdc.co.zw; f. 2005; allied to Zimbabwe Congress of Trade Unions; Pres. MORGAN TSVANGIRAI; Sec.-Gen. TENDAI BITI.

Mthwakazi Liberation Front: Office 9, Solomon Bldg, cnr Raymond and Rockey Sts, Yeoville, Johannesburg, South Africa; f. 2010; secessionist movement; Leader PAUL SIWELA.

United People's Party (UPP): f. 2006; Leader DANIEL SHUMBA.

Zimbabwe African National Union—Ndonga (ZANU—Ndonga): POB UA525, Union Ave, Harare; tel. and fax (4) 481180; f. 1977; breakaway faction from ZANU, also includes fmr mems of United African Nat. Council; supports free market economy; Nat. Chair. REKETAI MUSHIWEKUFA SEMWAYO; Sec.-Gen. EDWIN C. NGUWA.

Zimbabwe African National Union—Patriotic Front (ZANU—PF): cnr Rotten Row and Samora Machel Ave, POB 4530, Harare; tel. (4) 753329; fax (4) 774146; internet www.zanupf.org.zw; f. 1989 by merger of PF—ZAPU and ZANU—PF; Pres. ROBERT GABRIEL MUGABE; Vice-Pres SIMON VENGAYI MUZENDA, JOHN NKOMO; Nat. Chair. SIMON KHAYA MOYO.

Zimbabwe African People's Union (ZAPU): 18 Jason Ziyaphapha Moyo St, Bulwayo; tel. 342654987 (mobile); fax 234567890 (mobile); e-mail info@zapu.org; internet www.zapu.org; f. 1961; merged into ZANU—PF in 1987; re-established 2008; Pres. Dr DUMISO DABENGWA; Sec.-Gen. Dr RALPH MGUNI.

Zimbabwe Development Party: Harare; Leader KISINOTI MUKWAZHE.

Zimbabwe Integrated Programme: f. 1999; seeks economic reforms; Pres. Prof. HENEDI DZINOCHIKIWEYI.

Zimbabwe People's Democratic Party: POB 4001, Harare; e-mail mail@zpdp.org; f. 1991; Sec.-Gen. DUDLEY GURA.

Zimbabwe Progressive People's Democratic Party: Harare; Leader TAFIRENYIKA MUDAVANHU.

Zimbabwe Youth in Alliance: Leader MOSES MUTYASIRA.

Diplomatic Representation

EMBASSIES IN ZIMBABWE

Algeria: 8 Pascoe Ave, Belgravia, Harare; tel. (4) 791773; fax (4) 701125; e-mail offambalch@utande.co.zw; internet www.algerianembassy-harare.org; Ambassador LAZHAR SOUALEM.

Angola: 26 Speke Ave, POB 3590, Harare; tel. (4) 770075; fax (4) 770077; Ambassador FILIPE PEDRO HENDRICK VAAL NETO.

Australia: 1 Green Close, Borrowdale, Harare; POB 4541, Harare; tel. (4) 852471; fax (4) 870566; e-mail zimbabwe.embassy@dfat.gov.au; internet www.zimbabwe.embassy.gov.au; Ambassador MATTHEW NEUHAUS.

Botswana: 22 Phillips Ave, Belgravia, POB 563, Harare; tel. (4) 729551; fax (4) 721360; Ambassador GLADYS KOKORWE.

Brazil: 16 Prestwood Lane, Borrowdale, POB 2530, Harare; tel. (4) 861912; fax (4) 861254; e-mail brasemb.harare@itamaraty.gov.br; internet www.itamaraty.gov.br; Ambassador RAUL DE TAUNAY.

Canada: 45 Baines Ave, POB 1430, Harare; tel. (4) 252181; fax (4) 252186; e-mail hrare@international.gc.ca; internet www.canadainternational.gc.ca/zimbabwe; Ambassador LISA STADELBAUER.

China, People's Republic: 58 Golden Stairs Rd, Mount Pleasant, POB 4749, Harare; tel. (4) 332760; fax (4) 334716; e-mail chinaemb_zw@mfa.gov.cn; internet www.chinaembassy.org.zw; Ambassador LIN LIN.

Congo, Democratic Republic: 5 Pevensey Rd, Highlands, POB 2446, Harare; tel. (4) 481172; fax (4) 796421; e-mail harare@embadrcongo.co.zw; internet www.embadrcongo.co.zw; Ambassador MAWAMPANGA MWANA NANGA.

Cuba: 5 Phillips Ave, Belgravia, POB A1196, Harare; tel. (4) 790126; fax (4) 707998; e-mail cuba.embassy@cubanembassy.co.zw; internet www.cubadiplomatica.cu/zimbabwe; Ambassador ENRIQUE ANTONIO PRIETO LÓPEZ.

Czech Republic: 4 Sandringham Dr., Alexandra Park, GPO 4474, Harare; tel. (4) 700636; fax (4) 792950; e-mail embassy@czeharare.com; internet www.mzv.cz/harare; Chargé d'affaires PETR STARÝ.

Egypt: 7 Aberdeen Rd, Avondale, POB A433, Harare; tel. (4) 303445; fax (4) 303115; Ambassador BASSEM KHALIL.

Ethiopia: 14 Lanark Rd, Belgravia, POB 2745, Harare; tel. (4) 701514; fax (4) 701516; e-mail emb@ecoweb.co.zw; Ambassador ADBI DALAL MOHAMMED.

France: 3 Princess Dr., Newlands, POB 1378, Harare; tel. (4) 776118; fax (4) 776780; e-mail web.harare@diplomatie.gouv.fr; internet www.ambafrance-zw.org; Ambassador FRANÇOIS PONGE.

Germany: 30 Ceres Rd, Avondale, POB A1475, Harare; tel. (4) 308655; fax (4) 303455; e-mail botschaft_harare@gmx.de; internet www.harare.diplo.de; Ambassador HANS GNODTKE.

Ghana: 11 Downie Ave, Belgravia, POB 4445, Harare; tel. (4) 700982; fax (4) 707076; e-mail ghanaembassy@zol.co.zw; Ambassador JAMES OKOE NAADJIE.

Greece: 8 Deary Ave, Belgravia, POB 4809, Harare; tel. (4) 793208; fax (4) 703662; e-mail grembha@ecoweb.co.zw; Ambassador CHRISTOS SALAMANIS.

Holy See: 5 St Kilda Rd, Mount Pleasant, POB MP191, Harare (Apostolic Nunciature); tel. (4) 744547; fax (4) 744412; e-mail nunzim@zol.co.zw; Apostolic Nuncio Most Rev. GEORGE KOCHERRY (Titular Archbishop of Othona).

India: 12 Natal Rd, Belgravia, POB 4620, Harare; tel. (4) 795955; fax (4) 795958; e-mail ambassador@embindia.org.zw; Ambassador JAITENDRA KUMAR TRIPATHI.

Indonesia: 3 Duthie Ave, Belgravia, POB CY69, Causeway, Harare; tel. (4) 251799; fax (4) 796587; e-mail indohar@ecoweb.co.zw; internet www.indonesia-harare.org; Ambassador EDDY POERWANA.

Iran: 8 Allan Wilson Ave, Avondale, POB A293, Harare; tel. (4) 726942; Ambassador (vacant).

Italy: 7 Bartholomew Close, Greendale North, POB 1062, Harare; tel. (4) 498190; fax (4) 498199; e-mail ambasciata.harare@esteri.it; internet www.ambharare.esteri.it; Ambassador STEFANO MOSCATELLI.

Japan: Social Security Centre, 4th Floor, cnr Julius Nyerere Way and Sam Nujoma St, POB 2710, Harare; tel. (4) 250025; fax (4) 250111; internet www.zw.emb-japan.go.jp; Ambassador YONEZO FUKUDA.

Kenya: 95 Park Lane, POB 4069, Harare; tel. (4) 704820; fax (4) 723042; Ambassador Prof. JOHN ABDUBA.

Korea, Democratic People's Republic: 102 Josiah Chinamano Ave, Greenwood, POB 4754, Harare; tel. (4) 724052; Ambassador AN HUI JONG (resident in South Africa).

Kuwait: 1 Bath Rd, Avondale, POB A485, Harare; Ambassador ABDALLAH JUMA ABDALLAH AL-SHARHAN.

Libya: 124 Harare St, POB 4310, Harare; tel. (4) 728381; Ambassador (vacant).

Malawi: 9–11 Duthie Rd, Alexandra Park, POB 321, Harare; tel. (4) 798584; fax (4) 799006; e-mail malahigh@africaonline.co.zw; Ambassador JANE NGINERIWA KAMBALANE.

Malaysia: 40 Downie Ave, Avondale, POB 5570, Harare; tel. (4) 334413; fax (4) 334415; e-mail malharare@kln.gov.my; Ambassador (vacant).

Mozambique: 152 cnr Herbert Chitepo Ave and Leopold Takawira St, POB 4608, Harare; tel. (4) 253871; fax (4) 253875; e-mail emba@embamoc.org.zw; Ambassador PEDRO JOÃO DE AZEVEDO DAVANE.

Netherlands: 2 Arden Rd, Highlands, POB HG601, Harare; tel. (4) 776701; fax (4) 776700; e-mail har@minbuza.nl; Ambassador BARBARA JOZIASSE.

Nigeria: 36 Samora Machel Ave, POB 4742, Harare; tel. (4) 253900; fax (4) 253877; e-mail ngrharamb@yahoo.com; internet www.nigeriaharare.co.zw; Ambassador ADEKUNLE OLADOKUN ADEYANJU.

Norway: 5 Lanark Rd, Belgravia, POB A510, Avondale, Harare; tel. (4) 252426; fax (4) 252430; e-mail emb.harare@mfa.no; internet www.norway.org.zw; Ambassador INGEBJØRG STØFRING.

Pakistan: 11 Van Praagh Ave, Milton Park, POB 3050, Harare; tel. (4) 762018; fax (4) 794264; e-mail pahichar@yahoo.com; Ambassador ZAHID A. KHAN JATOI.

Portugal: 12 Harvey Brown Ave, Milton Park, Harare; tel. (4) 253023; fax (4) 253637; e-mail embport@harare.dgaccp.pt; Chargé d'affaires a.i. MARIA INÊS DE ALMEIDA COROA.

Romania: 105 Fourth St, POB 4797, Harare; tel. (4) 700853; e-mail romemb@cybersatafrica.com; Chargé d'affaires a.i. FLORICĂ BARBU.

Russia: 70 Fife Ave, POB 4250, Harare; tel. (4) 701957; fax (4) 795932; e-mail russianembassy@zol.co.zw; internet www.zimbabwe.mid.ru; Ambassador OLEG YU OSINTSEV.

South Africa: 7 Elcombe Rd, Belgravia, POB A1654, Harare; tel. (4) 760404; fax (4) 749657; e-mail admin@saembassy.co.zw; Ambassador VUSI MAVIMBELA.

Spain: 16 Phillips Ave, Belgravia, POB 3300, Harare; tel. (4) 250740; fax (4) 795261; e-mail emb.harare@mae.es; Ambassador (vacant).

Sudan: 4 Pascoe Ave, Harare; tel. (4) 700111; fax (4) 703450; e-mail sudan@africaonline.co.zw; internet www.sudaniharare.org.zw; Ambassador ELSIDDIEG ABDALA.

Sweden: 32 Aberdeen Rd, Avondale, POB 4110, Harare; tel. (4) 302636; fax (4) 302236; e-mail ambassaden.harare@foreign.ministry.se; internet www.swedenabroad.com/harare; Ambassador LARS RONNÅS.

Switzerland: 15 Fleetwood Rd, Alexandra Park, POB 3440, Harare; tel. (4) 745682; fax (4) 745465; e-mail har.vertretung@eda.admin.ch; internet www.eda.admin.ch/harare; Ambassador ALEXANDER WITTWER.

Tanzania: Ujamaa House, 23 Baines Ave, POB 4841, Harare; tel. (4) 792714; fax (4) 792747; e-mail tanrep@icon.co.zw; Ambassador ADADI RAJABU.

United Kingdom: 3 Norfolk Rd, Mount Pleasant, POB 4490, Harare; tel. (4) 338800; fax (4) 338829; e-mail ukinfo.harare@fco .gov.uk; internet ukinzimbabwe.fco.gov.uk/en; Ambassador DEBORAH BRONNERT.

USA: 172 Herbert Chitepo Ave, POB 3340, Harare; tel. (4) 250593; fax (4) 796488; e-mail hararepas@state.gov; internet harare .usembassy.gov; Ambassador DAVID BRUCE WHARTON.

Zambia: Zambia House, cnr Union and Julius Nyerere Aves, POB 4698, Harare; tel. (4) 773777; Ambassador NDIYOI MULIWANA MUTITI.

Judicial System

The legal system is Roman-Dutch, based on the system which was in force in the Cape of Good Hope on 10 June 1891, as modified by subsequent legislation. The court system comprises a Supreme Court, a High Court, an Administrative Court, Magistrates' Courts and Labour Courts. The Supreme Court is the final court of appeal and hears appeals from the High Court, the Labour Courts and the Administrative Court. It sits as a court of first instance in constitutional cases. As well as hearing appeals from the subordinate courts, the High Court has full, original and unlimited jurisdiction over all persons and matters in Zimbabwe. Below the High Court are Magistrates' Courts with both civil and criminal jurisdiction presided over by full-time professional magistrates. The Customary Law and Local Courts Act, adopted in 1990, abolished the village and community courts and replaced them with customary law and local courts, presided over by chiefs and headmen; in the case of chiefs, jurisdiction to try customary law cases is limited to those where the monetary values concerned do not exceed Z.$1,000 and in the case of a headman's court Z.$500. Appeals from the Chiefs' Courts are heard in Magistrates' Courts and, ultimately, the Supreme Court. All magistrates now have jurisdiction to try cases determinable by customary law.

Supreme Court: Harare; has original jurisdiction in matters in which an infringement of Chapter III of the Constitution defining fundamental rights is alleged; consists of the Chief Justice, a Deputy Chief Justice and such other judges of the Supreme Court, being not less than two, as the President may deem necessary; Chief Justice GODFREY CHIDYAUSIKU; Deputy Chief Justice LUKE MALABA.

High Court: Harare; consists of the Chief Justice, the Judge President, and such other judges of the High Court as may from time to time be appointed; Judge Pres. GEORGE CHIWESHE.

Attorney-General: JOHANNES TOMANA.

Religion

AFRICAN RELIGIONS

Many Zimbabweans follow traditional beliefs.

CHRISTIANITY

About 55% of the population are Christians.

Zimbabwe Council of Churches: 128 Mbuya Nehanda St, POB 3566, Harare; tel. (4) 772043; fax (4) 773650; e-mail zcc@africaonline .co.zw; f. 1964; Pres. Rt Rev. Dr WILSON SITSHEBO; Gen. Sec. DENSEN MAFIYANI; 24 mem. churches, nine assoc. mems.

The Anglican Communion

Anglicans are adherents of the Church of the Province of Central Africa, covering Botswana, Malawi, Zambia and Zimbabwe. The Church comprises 15 dioceses, including five in Zimbabwe. The current Archbishop of the Province is the Bishop of Northern Zambia.

Bishop of Central Zimbabwe: Rt Rev. ISHMAEL MUKUWANDA, POB 25, Gweru; tel. (54) 21030; fax (54) 21097; e-mail diocent@telconet.co .zw.

Bishop of Harare: Rt Rev. CHAD NICHOLAS GANDIYA, 9 Monmouth Rd, Avondale, Harare; tel. (4) 308042; e-mail diohrecpca@ecoweb.co .zw.

Bishop of Manicaland: JULIUS TAWONA MAKONI, 113 Herbert Chitepo St, Mutare; tel. (20) 64194; fax (20) 63076; e-mail diomani@syscom.co.zw; internet www .anglicandioceseofmanicaland.co.zw.

Bishop of Masvingo: Rt Rev. GODFREY TOANEZVI, POB 1421, Masvingo; tel. (39) 362536; e-mail anglicandiomsv@comone.co.zw.

Bishop of Matabeleland: Rt Rev. CLEOPHAS LUNGA, POB 2422, Bulawayo; tel. (9) 61370; fax (9) 68353; e-mail clunga@aol.com.

The Roman Catholic Church

For ecclesiastical purposes, Zimbabwe comprises two archdioceses and six dioceses. The number of adherents is equivalent to an estimated 10% of the total population.

Zimbabwe Catholic Bishops' Conference (ZCBC)
Catholic Secretariat, Causeway, 29 Selous Ave, POB 8135, Harare; tel. (4) 705368; fax (4) 705369; internet www.zcbc.co.zw. f. 1969; Pres. Most Rev. ROBERT C. NDLOVU (Archbishop of Harare).

Archbishop of Bulawayo: Most Rev. ALEX THOMAS KALIYANIL, cnr Lobengula St and 9th Ave, POB 837, Bulawayo; tel. (9) 63590; fax (9) 60359; e-mail archdbyo@mweb.co.zw.

Archbishop of Harare: Most Rev. ROBERT C. NDLOVU, Archbishop's House, 66 Fifth St, POB CY330, Causeway, Harare; tel. (4) 727386; fax (4) 721598; e-mail hrearch@zol.co.zw.

Other Christian Churches

At mid-2000 there were an estimated 4.8m. adherents professing other forms of Christianity.

Dutch Reformed Church in Zimbabwe (Nederduitse Gereformeerde Kerk): 35 Samora Machel Ave, POB 503, Harare; tel. (4) 774738; fax (4) 774739; e-mail pvanvuuren@mango.zw; f. 1895; 11 congregations in Zimbabwe and two in Zambia; Chair. Rev. PIETER F. J. VAN VUUREN; Sec. Rev. J. HAASBROEK; 1,245 mems.

Evangelical Lutheran Church: 7 Lawley Rd, POB 2175, Bulawayo; tel. (9) 254991; fax (9) 254993; e-mail elczhead@mweb.co.zw; f. 1903; Sec. Rt Rev. L. M. DUBE; 150,000 mems (2009).

Greek Orthodox Church: POB 2832, Harare; tel. (4) 744991; fax (4) 744928; e-mail zimbabwe@greekorthodox-zimbabwe.org; internet www.greekorthodox-zimbabwe.org; f. 1968; Archbishop SERAPHIM KYKKOTIS.

Methodist Church in Zimbabwe: POB CY71, Causeway, Harare; tel. (4) 250523; fax (4) 723709; e-mail methodistconn@zol.co.zw; f. 1891; Presiding Bishop Rev. SIMBARASHE SITHOLE; Sec. of Conference Rev. AMOS NDHLUMBI.

United Congregational Church of Southern Africa: 40 Jason Moyo St, POB 2451, Bulawayo; tel. (9) 63686; internet www.uccsa .org.za/zimbabwe-synod; Chair. Rev. B. MATHEMA (acting); Sec. Rev. MAJAHA NTHLIZIYO.

United Methodist Church: POB 3408, Harare; tel. (4) 704127; f. 1890; Bishop of Zimbabwe EBEN NHIWATIWA; 45,000 mems.

Among other denominations active in Zimbabwe are the African Methodist Church, the African Methodist Episcopal Church, the African Reformed Church, the Christian Marching Church, the Church of Christ in Zimbabwe, the Independent African Church, the Presbyterian Church (and the City Presbyterian Church), the United Church of Christ, the Zimbabwe Assemblies of God and the Ziwezano Church.

JUDAISM

The Jewish community numbered 897 members at 31 December 1997; by 2006 that number had fallen to around 300.

Zimbabwe Jewish Board of Deputies: POB 1954, Harare; tel. (4) 702507; fax (4) 702506; Pres. P. STERNBERG; Sec. E. ALHADEFF.

BAHÁ'Í FAITH

National Spiritual Assembly: POB GD380, Greendale, Harare; tel. (4) 495945; fax (4) 744611; internet www.bahai.co.zw; Nat. Sec. DEREK SITHOLE; f. 1970; mems resident in 57 clusters.

The Press

DAILIES

The Chronicle: 9th Ave and George Silundika St, POB 585, Bulawayo; tel. (9) 888871; fax (9) 888884; e-mail editor@chronicle .co.zw; internet www.chronicle.co.zw; f. 1894; publ. by govt-controlled co Zimpapers; circulates throughout south-western Zimbabwe; English; Editor ITAI MUSENGEYI; circ. 25,000 (2004).

The Daily News: 18 Sam Nujoma St and cnr Speke Ave, Harare; tel. (4) 753027; fax (4) 753024; internet www.dailynews.co.zw; publ. by Associated Newspapers of Zimbabwe; English; publ. suspended Sept. 2003; Editor NQOBILE NYATHI; CEO SAM SIPEPA NKOMO; Chair. STRIVE MASIYIWA; circ. c. 80,000 (2003).

The Herald: POB 396, Harare; tel. (4) 795771; fax (4) 700305; internet www.herald.co.zw; f. 1891; publ. by govt-controlled co Zimpapers; English; Editor INNOCENT GORE; circ. c. 60,000 (2006).

The Insider: 12 Penwith Court, Jason Moyo St, Bulawayo; tel. (11) 789-759; e-mail charlesrukuni@insiderzim.com; internet www .insiderzim.com; f. 1990; digital newsletter; news and current affairs; Editor and Publr CHARLES RUKUNI.

NewsDay: Harare; tel. (4) 773839; e-mail newsday@zimind.co.zw; internet www.newsday.co.zw; f. 2009; owned by ZimInd Publrs (Pvt) Ltd; Editor-in-Chief VINCENT KAHIYA.

ZIMBABWE

The Zimbabwe Mail: e-mail editor@thezimbabwemail.com; internet www.thezimbabwemail.com; f. 2011; Exec. Chair. LEIGHTON MUSHANINGA; Man. Editor NKULULEKO NDLOVU.

WEEKLIES

Financial Gazette: Coal House, 5th Floor, cnr Nelson Mandela Ave and Leopold Takawira St, Harare; tel. (4) 781571; fax (4) 781578; e-mail schamunorwa@fingaz.co.zw; internet www.fingaz.co.zw; f. 1969; publ. by ZimInd Publrs (Pvt) Ltd; affiliated to the ZANU—PF party; Editor-in-Chief SUNSLEEY CHAMUNORWA; Gen. Man. JACOB CHISESE; circ. c. 40,000 (2004).

Indonsakusa/Ilanga: c/o CNG, POB 6520, Harare; tel. (4) 796855; fax (4) 703873; publ. by Community Newspaper Group; distributed in north and south Matabeleland; circ. c. 10,000.

Kwayedza: POB 396, Harare; tel. (4) 795771; fax (4) 791311; internet www.kwayedza.co.zw; publ. by govt-controlled co Zimpapers; f. 1985; ChiShona; Editor GERVASE M. CHITEWE; circ. c. 15,000 (2003).

Manica Post: POB 960, Mutare; tel. (20) 61212; fax (20) 61149; internet www.manicapost.com; f. 1893; publ. by govt-controlled co Zimpapers; English; Editor PAUL MAMBO; circ. 15,000 (2004).

Mashonaland Guardian/Telegraph: c/o CNG, POB 6520, Harare; tel. (4) 796855; fax (4) 703873; publ. by Community Newspaper Group; distributed in Mashonaland; circ. c. 10,000.

Masvingo Mirror: POB 1214, Masvingo; tel. (39) 64372; fax (39) 64484; independent; Editor NORNA EDWARDS.

Masvingo Star: 2–3 New Market Centre, R. Tangwena Ave, POB 138, Masvingo; tel. and fax (39) 63978; English; distributed in Masvingo province; Editor (vacant); circ. c. 10,000.

Midlands Observer: POB 533, Kwekwe; tel. (55) 22248; fax (55) 23985; e-mail nelson_mashiri@yahoo.com; f. 1953; weekly; English; Editor R. JARIJARI; circ. 20,000.

The Standard: 1st Block, 3rd Floor, Ernst and Young Bldg, 1 Kwame Nkrumah Ave, POB 661730, Kopje, Harare; tel. (4) 773930; fax (4) 798897; internet www.thestandard.co.zw; f. 1997; publ. by ZimInd Publrs (Pvt) Ltd; Sun.; Chair. TREVOR NCUBE; Editor NEVANJI MADANHIRE; circ. 42,000 (2004).

Sunday Mail: POB 396, Harare; tel. (4) 795771; fax (4) 700305; internet www.sundaymail.co.zw; f. 1935; publ. by govt-controlled co Zimpapers; English; Chair. THOMAS SITHOLE; Editor WILLIAM CHIKOTO; circ. 110,000 (2004).

Sunday News: POB 585, Bulawayo; tel. (9) 540071; fax (9) 540084; f. 1930; publ. by govt-controlled co Zimpapers; English; Editor BREZHNEV MALABA; circ. 30,000 (2004).

The Times: c/o CNG, POB 6520, Harare; tel. (4) 796855; fax (4) 703873; f. 1897; fmrly *The Gweru Times*; distributed in Mashonaland; English; circ. c. 5,000.

uMthunywa (The Messenger): 9th Ave and George Silundika St, POB 585, Bulawayo; tel. (9) 880888; fax (9) 888884; e-mail advertising@chronicle.co.zw; internet www.umthunywa.co.zw; f. 2004; SiNdebele; publ. by govt-controlled co Zimpapers; Editor BHEKITHEMBA J. NCUBE.

The Vanguard: Zimbabwe National Students' Union, 21 Wembley Cres., Eastlea, Harare; tel. (4) 788135; e-mail zinasu@gmail.com; publ. by the Zimbabwe Nat. Students' Union.

Zimbabwe Independent: Zimind Publishers (Pvt) Ltd, Suites 23/24, 1 Union Ave, POB BE1165, Belvedere, Harare; e-mail trevorn@mg.co.za; internet www.theindependent.co.zw; f. 1996; publ. by ZimInd Publrs (Pvt) Ltd; English; Chair. TREVOR NCUBE; Editor DUMISANI MULEYA; circ. 30,500 (2005).

The Zimbabwean: POB 248, Hythe, SO45 4WX, United Kingdom; tel. (23) 8084-8694; e-mail feedback@thezimbabwean.co.uk; internet www.thezimbabwean.co.uk; f. 2005; independent; publ. in the United Kingdom and South Africa; focus on news in Zimbabwe and life in exile; Publr and Editor WILF MBANGA.

Zimbabwean Government Gazette: POB 8062, Causeway, Harare; official notices; Editor L. TAKAWIRA.

PERIODICALS

The Agenda: Information Department, 348 Herbert Chitepo Ave, Harare; tel. (4) 736338; fax (4) 721146; e-mail info@nca.org.zw; internet www.nca.org.zw; f. 1997; publ. by the Nat. Constitutional Assembly; quarterly; civil rights issues.

Chaminuka News: POB 650, Marondera; f. 1988; publ. by Community Newspaper Group; fortnightly; English and ChiShona; Editor M. MUGABE; circ. c. 10,000.

Indonsakusa: Hwange; f. 1988; monthly; English and SiNdebele; Editor D. NTABENI; circ. 10,000.

Masiye Pambili (Let Us Go Forward): POB 591, Bulawayo; tel. (9) 75011; fax (9) 69701; e-mail tcdept@citybyo.co.zw; f. 1964; 2 a year; English; Editor M. NYONI; circ. 25,000.

Moto (Fire): POB 890, Gweru; tel. (54) 24886; fax (54) 28194; e-mail mot@hnetzim.wn.apc.org; f. 1959; monthly; publ. by govt-controlled co Zimpapers; banned in 1974; relaunched in 1980 as a weekly newspaper, then in magazine format in 1982; Roman Catholic; Editor SYDNEY SHOKO; circ. 22,000.

Mukai-Vukani Jesuit Journal for Zimbabwe: Jesuit Communications, 37 Admiral Tait, Malborough, POB A949, Avondale, Harare; tel. (4) 309623; fax (4) 744284; e-mail gmambipiri@gmail.com; internet www.jescom.co.zw; 4–6 a year; Catholic; Editor GIFT MAMBIPIRI; circ. 2,500.

New Farmer: Herald House, cnr George Sikundika and Sam Nujoma Sts, POB 55, Harare; tel. (4) 708296; fax (4) 702400; e-mail advertising@chronicle.co.zw; internet www.newfarmer.co.zw; f. 2002; publ. by govt-controlled co Zimpapers; weekly; English; Editor GEORGE CHISOKO.

The Outpost: POB HG106, Highlands; tel. (4) 700171; fax (4) 703631; e-mail theoutpostmag@yahoo.com; f. 1911; publ. of the Zimbabwe Republic Police; monthly; English; Editor RESISTANT NCUBE; circ. c. 45,000 (2012).

Railroader: National Railways of Zimbabwe, cnr Fife St and 10th Ave, POB 596, Bulawayo; tel. (9) 363716; fax (9) 363502; f. 1952; publ. by Nat. Railways of Zimbabwe; monthly; Editor M. GUMEDE; circ. 10,000.

Southern African Political and Economic Monthly (SAPEM): Southern Africa Political Economy Series Trust, 2–6 Deary Ave, Belgravia, POB MP111, Mt Pleasant, Harare; tel. (4) 252962; fax (4) 252964; f. 1987; monthly; publ. by the SAPES Trust; incorporating *Southern African Economist*; Editor-in-Chief KHABELE MATLOSA; circ. 16,000.

Trends: 9th Ave and George Silundika St, POB 585, Bulawayo; tel. (9) 880888; fax (9) 888884; e-mail advertising@chronicle.co.zw; internet www.zimtrends.co.zw; f. 2003; monthly; English; leisure and entertainment; Editor EDWIN DUBE.

The Worker: ZCTU, Chester House, 9th Floor, Speke Ave and Third St, POB 3549, Harare; tel. (4) 794742; fax (4) 728484; e-mail info@zctu.co.zw; publ. by the Zimbabwe Congress of Trade Unions; News Editor BRIGHT CHIBVURI.

Zambezia: University of Zimbabwe Publications, POB MP203, Mount Pleasant, Harare; tel. (4) 303211; fax (4) 333407; e-mail uzpub@admin.uz.ac.zw; internet www.uz.ac.zw/publications; publ. by the Univ. of Zimbabwe; 2 a year; humanities and general interest; Editor Dr ZIFIKILE MAKWAVARARA.

Zimbabwe Agricultural Journal: Dept of Research and Specialist Services, 5th St, Extension, POB CY594, Causeway, Harare; tel. (4) 704531; fax (4) 728317; f. 1903; 6 a year; Editor R. J. FENNER; circ. 2,000.

The Zimbabwe Farmer: POB 1683, Harare; tel. (4) 736836; fax (4) 749803; monthly; fmrly *Tobacco News*; present name adopted in 2003; publ. by Thomson Publs; Editor D. MILLER; circ. 2,000.

Zimbabwe National Army Magazine: Ministry of Defence, Defence House, cnr Kwame Nkruma Ave and 3rd St, Harare; tel. (4) 700316; f. 1982; 4 a year; Dir of Communications Col LIVINGSTONE CHINEKA; circ. 5,000.

Zimbabwean Travel: Herald House, cnr George Sikundika and Sam Nujoma Sts, POB 55, Harare; tel. (4) 708296; fax (4) 702400; e-mail advertising@chronicle.co.zw; internet www.zimtravel.com; f. 2003; publ. by govt-controlled co Zimpapers; monthly; English; Editor NOMSA NKALA.

NEWS AGENCY

NewZiana (Pvt) Ltd: Mass Media House, 19 Selous Ave, POB CY511, Causeway, Harare; tel. (4) 251754; fax (4) 794336; internet www.newziana.co.zw; f. 1981 as Zimbabwe Inter-Africa News Agency; present name adopted in 2003; owned by govt-controlled co Multimedia Investment Trust (fmrly Zimbabwe Mass Media Trust); operates 10 community newspapers; CEO MUNYARADZI MATANYAIRE.

Publishers

Amalgamated Publications (Pvt) Ltd: POB 1683, Harare; tel. (4) 736835; fax (4) 749803; f. 1949; trade journals.

The Argosy Press: POB 2677, Harare; tel. (4) 755084; magazine publrs; Gen. Man. A. W. HARVEY.

Baobab Books (Pvt) Ltd: POB 567, Harare; tel. (4) 665187; fax (4) 665155; general, literature, children's.

College Press Publishers (Pvt) Ltd: 15 Douglas Rd, POB 3041, Workington, Harare; tel. (4) 754145; fax (4) 754256; f. 1968; educational and general; Man. Dir B. B. MUGABE.

5085

Harare Publishing House: Chiremba Rd, Hatfield, Harare; tel. (4) 570342; f. 1982; Dir Dr T. M. SAMKANGE.

HarperCollins Publishers Zimbabwe (Pvt) Ltd: Union Ave, POB UA201, Harare; tel. (4) 721413; fax (4) 732436; Man. S. D. MCMILLAN.

Longman Zimbabwe (Pvt) Ltd: POB ST125, Southerton, Harare; tel. (4) 62711; fax (4) 62716; f. 1964; general and educational; Man. Dir N. L. DLODLO.

Munn Publishing (Pvt) Ltd: POB UA460, Union Ave, Harare; tel. (4) 481048; fax (4) 7481081; Man. Dir I. D. MUNN.

Southern African Printing and Publishing House (SAPPHO): 109 Coventry Rd, Workington, POB MP1005, Mount Pleasant, Harare; tel. (4) 621681; fax (4) 666061; internet www.zimmirror.co .zw; Editor-in-Chief Dr IBBO MANDAZA.

University of Zimbabwe Publications: University of Zimbabwe, POB MP203, Mount Pleasant, Harare; tel. (4) 303211; fax (4) 333407; e-mail uzpub@admin.uz.ac.zw; internet www.uz.ac.zw/publications; f. 1969; Dir MUNANI SAM MTETWA.

Zimbabwe Newspapers (1980) Ltd (Zimpapers): POB 55, Harare; tel. (4) 704088; fax (4) 702400; e-mail theherald@zimpapers.co .zw; internet www.herald.co.zw; f. 1981; 51% state-owned; publ. the newspapers *The Herald, The Sunday Mail, The Manica Post, The Chronicle, The Sunday News, Kwayedza, Umthunywa* and *The Southern Times* (based in Namibia); and magazines incl. *Zimbabwean Travel, Trends Magazine* and *New Farmer Magazine*; Chair. HERBERT NKALA; Group CEO JUSTIN MUTASA.

ZPH Publishers (Pvt) Ltd: 183 Arcturus Rd, Kamfinsa, GD510, Greendale, Harare; tel. (4) 497548; fax (4) 497554; e-mail tafi@zph.co .zw; internet www.zphpublishers.com; f. 1982 as Zimbabwe Publishing House Ltd; Chair. BLAZIO G. TAFIREYI.

Broadcasting and Communications

TELECOMMUNICATIONS

In 2011 there were three providers of mobile telephone services and one provider of fixed-line telephone services in Zimbabwe.

Econet Wireless Zimbabwe: Econet Park, 2 Old Mutare Rd, Msasa, POB BE1298, Belvedere, Harare; tel. (4) 486121; fax (4) 486120; e-mail enquiry@econet.co.zw; internet www.econet.co.zw; f. 1998; mobile cellular telecommunications operator; Chair. TAWANDA NYAMBIRAI; CEO DOUGLAS MBOWENI.

Net.One Ltd: POB CY579, Causeway, Harare; tel. (4) 707138; e-mail marketing@netone.co.zw; internet www.netone.co.zw; f. 1998; state-owned; mobile cellular telecommunications operator; Chair. CALLISTUS NDLOVU; CEO REWARD KANGAI.

Telecel Zimbabwe: 148 Seke Rd, Graniteside, POB CY232, Causeway, Harare; tel. (4) 748321; fax (4) 748328; e-mail info@telecelzim.co .zw; internet www.telecel.co.zw; f. 1998; 60% owned by Telecel Globe and 40% owned by Empowerment Corpn; mobile cellular telecommunications operator; Chair. JAMES MAKAMBA; CEO FRANCIS MAWINDI.

TelOne: Runhare House, 107 K. Nkrumah Ave, POB CY331, Causeway, Harare; tel. (4) 798111; fax (4) 700474; e-mail web-master@ telone.co.zw; internet www.telone.co.zw; state-owned; sole fixed-line telecommunications operator; Man. Dir HAMPTON MHLANGA.

Regulatory Authority

Posts and Telecommunication Regulatory Authority (POTRAZ): Block A, Emerald Park, 30 The Chase, Mt Pleasant, POB MP843, Harare; tel. (4) 333032; fax (4) 333041; e-mail the .regulator@potraz.gov.zw; internet www.potraz.gov.zw; fmrly Post and Telecommunications Corpn; Chair. DAVIDSON CHIROMBO; Dir-Gen. CHARLES MANZI SIBANDA.

BROADCASTING

There are four govt-controlled radio stations (National FM, Power FM, Radio Zimbabwe and Spot FM) and one television station. Radio Voice of the People was established as an alternative to state broadcasting. In June 2012 the country's first commercial radio station, Star FM, began broadcasting. An independent radio station, SW Radio Africa, broadcasts to Zimbabwe from London, United Kingdom. Since 2003 Voice of America has broadcast a weekday news and entertainment programme (Studio 7) from the USA in ChiShona, English and SiNdebele.

Regulatory Authority

Zimbabwe Media Commission: Harare; f. 2009 to introduce media reforms; Chair. GODFREY MAJONGA.

Radio

Feba Radio: 69 Central Ave, POB A300, Avondale, Harare; tel. (4) 708207; e-mail info@feba.co.zw; internet www.feba.co.zw; Nat. Dir KURAI MADZONGA.

Star FM: Harare; f. 2012; broadcasts in Harare and Bulawayo; Gen. Man. ADMIRE TADERERA.

Voice of the People (VOP): POB 5750, Harare; tel. (4) 707123; e-mail voxpop@ecoweb.co.zw; internet www.vopradio.co.zw; f. 2000 by fmr ZBC staff; broadcasts one hour per day; relayed by Radio Netherlands transmitters in Madagascar; news and information in ChiShona, SiNdebele and English; Chair. DAVID MASUNDA; Exec. Dir JOHN MASUKU.

Zimbabwe Broadcasting Corpn: Broadcasting Center, Pocket Hill, POB HG444, Highlands, Harare; tel. and fax (4) 498940; e-mail edward.ndamba@zbc.co.zw; internet www.zbc.co.zw; f. 1957; programmes in English, ChiShona, SiNdebele and 14 minority languages, incl. Chichewa, Venda and Xhosa; broadcasts a general service (mainly in English), vernacular languages service, light entertainment, and educational programmes; Registry Supervisor EDWARD NDAMBA.

Television

Zimbabwe Broadcasting Corpn: (see Radio).

The main broadcasting centre is in Harare, with a second studio in Bulawayo. ZBC-TV is broadcast 24 hours per day, while a second channel (ZBC Channel 2) was launched in May 2010.

Finance

(cap. = capital; res = reserves; dep. = deposits; m. = million; br(s). = branch(es); amounts in Zimbabwe dollars unless otherwise indicated)

BANKING

In 2010 there were 15 commercial banks, six merchant banks, three discount houses and four building societies in Zimbabwe. In August 2012 it was announced that commercial banks and merchant banks operating in Zimbabwe were required to have a minimum capital of US $100m., while discount houses were required to have a minimum capital of US $60m. Institutions were expected to be 100% compliant with these requirements by 30 June 2014.

Central Bank

Reserve Bank of Zimbabwe: 80 Samora Machel Ave, POB 1283, Harare; tel. (4) 703000; fax (4) 707800; e-mail rbzmail@rbz.co.zw; internet www.rbz.co.zw; f. 1964 as Reserve Bank of Rhodesia; bank of issue; cap. 2m., res 89,161,333m., dep. 471,625,968m. (Dec. 2007); Gov. Dr GIDEON GONO.

Commercial Banks

Barclays Bank of Zimbabwe Ltd: Barclays House, cnr First St and Jason Moyo Ave, POB 1279, Harare; tel. (4) 758281; fax (4) 752913; e-mail barmkt@africaonline.co.zw; internet www.barclays .com/africa/zimbabwe; f. 1912; commercial and merchant banking; cap. 1,000m., res 18,123m., dep. 125,836m. (Dec. 2004); Chair. Dr ROBBIE MATONGO MUPAWOSE; 44 brs.

CBZ Bank Ltd (CBZ): Union House, 60 Kwame Nkrumah Ave, POB 3313, Harare; tel. (4) 748050; e-mail info@cbz.co.zw; internet www.cbz.co.zw; state-owned; f. 1981 as Bank of Credit and Commerce Zimbabwe Ltd; renamed Commercial Bank of Zimbabwe Ltd in 1991; present name adopted 2005; Chair. L. ZEMBE; CEO Dr J. P. MANGUDYA; 60 brs.

FBC Bank Ltd: FBC Centre, Marketing and Public Relations Division, 45 Nelson Mandela Ave, POB 1227, Harare; tel. (4) 783204; fax (4) 783440; e-mail info@fbc.co.zw; internet www.fbc.co .zw/bank; f. 1997; cap. 1,000m., res 11,035,000m., dep. 39,946,000m. (Dec. 2007); Chair. DAVID W. BIRCH; Man. Dir JOHN MUSHAYAVANHU.

Kingdom Bank Ltd: 3rd Floor, Karigamombe Centre, 53 Samora Machel Ave, POB CY 3205, Harare; tel. (4) 749400; fax (4) 755201; e-mail kmb@kingdom.co.zw; internet www.kingdom.co.zw; f. 1997; res US $20.4m., dep. US $46.7m. (Dec. 2009); CEO LYNN MUKONOWESHURO.

Stanbic Bank Zimbabwe Ltd: Stanbic Centre, 1st Floor, 59 Samora Machel Ave, POB 300, Harare; tel. (4) 759471; fax (4) 751324; e-mail zimbabweinfo@stanbic.com; internet www .stanbicbank.co.zw; f. 1990 as ANZ Grindlays Bank; acquired by Standard Bank Investment Corpn in 1992; total assets US $201,387 (Dec. 2009); Chair. S. MOYO; Man. Dir JOSHUA TAPAMBGWA; 16 brs.

Standard Chartered Bank Zimbabwe Ltd: Mutual Centre, 2nd Floor, POB 373, Harare; tel. (4) 52852; fax (4) 752609; internet www .standardchartered.com/zw; f. 1983; cap. US $0.8m., res US $26.5m., dep. US $26.5m. (Dec. 2009); Chair. H. P. MKUSHI; CEO WASHINGTON MATSAIRA; 28 brs.

ZB Bank Ltd: ZB House, 10th Floor, 46 Speke Ave, POB 3198, Harare; tel. (4) 757535; fax (4) 757497; e-mail info@zb.co.zw; internet www.zb.co.zw; f. 1951; subsidiary of ZB Financial Holdings Ltd; cap. 102m., res 178,293m., dep. 821,214m. (Sept. 2004); Chair. ZVINE-CHIMWE RUVINGA CHURU; COO RONALD MUTANDAGAYI; 38 brs.

Development Banks

African Export-Import Bank (Afreximbank): Eastgate Bldg, 3rd Floor, Gold Bridge (North Wing), Second St, POB 1600, Causeway, Harare; tel. (4) 729751; fax (4) 729756; e-mail info@afreximbank.com; internet www.afreximbank.com; Pres. and Chair. J. L. EKRA.

Infrastructure Development Bank of Zimbabwe (IDBZ): 99 Rotten Row, Harare; tel. (4) 750171; fax (4) 774225; e-mail enquiries@zdb.co.zw; internet www.idbz.co.zw; f. 2005, to replace Zimbabwe Development Bank; CEO CHARLES CHIKAURA.

Merchant Banks

African Banking Corpn of Zimbabwe Ltd (ABC): ABC House, 1 Endeavour Cres., Mount Pleasant Business Park, Mount Pleasant, POB 2786, Harare; tel. (4) 369260; fax (4) 369939; e-mail abczw@africanbankingcorp.com; internet www.africanbankingcorp.com; f. 1956 as Rhodesian Acceptances Ltd; name changed to First Merchant Bank of Zimbabwe Ltd in 1990; merged with Heritage Investment Bank in 1997; present name adopted in 2002; subsidiary of ABC Holdings Ltd, Botswana; Chair. O. M. CHIDAWU; Man. Dir F. M. DZANYA; 1 br.

MBCA Bank Ltd: Old Mutual Centre, 14th Floor, cnr Third St and Jason Moyo Ave, POB 3200, Harare; tel. (4) 701636; fax (4) 708005; e-mail mbcabank@mbca.co.zw; internet www.mbca.co.zw; f. 1956; a mem of the Nedbank Goup; total assets US $192m. (Jun. 2012); Chair. V. W. ZIREVA; Man. Dir Dr CHARITY C. JINYA.

NMB Bank Ltd: Unity Court, 4th Floor, cnr Union Ave and First St, POB 2564, Harare; tel. (4) 759651; fax (4) 759648; e-mail enquiries@nmbz.co.zw; internet www.nmbz.co.zw; f. 1993; fmrly Nat. Merchant Bank of Zimbabwe; cap. 0.3m., res 8,017m., dep. 51,128m. (Dec. 2006); Chair. TENDAYI MUNDAWARARA; Group CEO JAMES MUSHORE; 10 brs.

Standard Chartered Merchant Bank Zimbabwe Ltd: Standard Chartered Bank Bldg, cnr Second St and Nelson Mandela Ave, POB 60, Harare; tel. (4) 708585; fax (4) 725667; f. 1971; Chair. BARRY HAMILTON; Man. Dir EBBY ESSOKA.

Tetrad Investment Bank: Block 5, 1st Floor, Arundel Office Park, Norfolk Rd, Mt Pleasant, Harare; tel. (4) 704271; fax (4) 338400; internet www.tetrad.co.zw; f. 1995; Chair. A. S. CHATIKOBO; Man. Dir E. E. CHIKAKA.

Discount Houses

African Banking Corpn Securities Ltd: 69 Samora Machel Ave, POB 3321, Harare; tel. (4) 752756; fax (4) 790641; fmrly Bard Discount House Ltd; Chair. N. KUDENGA; Man. Dir D. DUBE.

The Discount Co of Zimbabwe (DCZ): 70 Park Lane, POB 3424, Harare; tel. (4) 705414; fax (4) 731670; Man. Dir PETER MUKUNGA.

Intermarket Discount House: Unity Court, 5th Floor, Union Ave, POB 3290, Harare.

National Discount House Ltd: MIPF House, 5th Floor, Central Ave, Harare; tel. (4) 700771; fax (4) 792927; internet www.ndh.co.zw; Chair. EDWIN MANIKAI; Man. Dir LAWRENCE TAMAYI.

Banking Organizations

Bankers' Association of Zimbabwe (BAZ): Kuwana House, 4th Floor, Union Ave and First St, POB UA550, Harare; tel. (4) 728646; f. 1992; Pres. JOHN MUSHAYAVANHU; Dir SIJABULISO T. BIYAM.

Institute of Bankers of Zimbabwe: Centre Block, Second Floor, Suite 13, 1 Union Ave, POB UA521, Harare; tel. (4) 752474; fax (4) 750281; e-mail info@iobz.co.zw; internet www.iobz.co.zw; f. 1973; Chair. S. MALABA; Pres. STEVE GWASIRA; Dir T. BIYAM; 7,000 mems.

STOCK EXCHANGE

Zimbabwe Stock Exchange: Chiyedza House, 5th Floor, cnr First St and Kwame Nkrumah Ave, POB UA234, Harare; tel. (4) 736861; fax (4) 791045; f. 1946; Chair. G. MHLANGA; CEO EMMANUEL MUNYUKWI.

INSURANCE

Export Credit Guarantee Corpn of Zimbabwe (Pvt): 6 Earles Rd, Alexandra Park, POB CY2995, Causeway, Harare; tel. and fax (4) 744644; e-mail ecgc@telco.co.zw; internet www.ecgc.co.zw; f. 1999 as national export credit insurance agency; also provides export finance guarantee facilities; 100% owned by Reserve Bank of Zimbabwe; Chair. J. A. L. CARTER; Man. Dir RAPHAEL. G. NYADZAYO.

Credit Insurance Zimbabwe (Credsure): Credsure House, 69 Sam Nujoma St, POB CY1584, Causeway, Harare; tel. (4) 706101; fax (4) 706105; e-mail headoffice@credsure.co.zw; export credit insurance; Man. Dir BRIAN HILLEN-MOORE.

Fidelity Life Assurance of Zimbabwe (Pvt) Ltd: 66 Julius Nyerere Way, POB 435, Harare; tel. (4) 750927; fax (4) 751723; f. 1977; 52% owned by Zimre Holdings Ltd; pensions and life assurance; Chair. J. P. MKUSHI; Man. Dir SIMON B. CHAPAREKA.

NICOZ Diamond: Insurance Centre, 30 Samora Machel and Leopold Takawira Ave, POB 1256, Harare; tel. (4) 704911; fax (4) 704134; e-mail enquiries@nicozdiamond.co.zw; internet www.nicozdiamond.co.zw; f. 2003 by merger of National Insurance Co of Zimbabwe and Diamond Insurance of Zimbabwe; Chair. PHINEAS S. CHINGONO; Man. Dir GRACE MURADZIKWA.

Old Mutual PLC: POB 70, Highlands, Harare; tel. (4) 308400; fax (4) 308467; e-mail info@oldmutual.co.zw; internet www.oldmutual.co.zw; f. 1845; life and general insurance, asset management and banking services; Chair. M. J. LEVETT; CEO J. H. SUTCLIFFE.

ZB Life Assurance Ltd: ZB Life Towers, 77 Jason Moyo Ave, POB 969, Harare; tel. (4) 708800; fax (4) 708894; e-mail info@zblife.co.zw; internet www.zb.co.zw/life-assurance.html; f. 1964 as Intermarket Life Assurance; subsidiary of ZB Financial Holdings Ltd, which also owns ZB Reinsurance; Man. Dir AMBROSE G. CHINEMBIRI.

Zimnat Lion Insurance Co Ltd: Zimnat House, cnr Nelson Mandela Ave and Third St, POB CY1155, Causeway, Harare; tel. (4) 707581; fax (4) 793441; e-mail enquiries@zimnatlion.co.zw; internet www.zimnatlion.co.zw; f. 1998 by merger of Zimnat Insurance Co Ltd and Lion of Zimbabwe Insurance; merged with AIG Zimbabwe in 2005; short-term insurance; Chair. NYAJEKA BOTHWELL; Man. Dir ELISHA K. MOYO.

Trade and Industry

GOVERNMENT AGENCIES

Industrial Development Corpn of Zimbabwe (IDC): 93 Park Lane, POB CY1431, Causeway, Harare; tel. (4) 706971; fax (4) 250385; e-mail pr@idc.co.zw; internet www.idc.co.zw; f. 1963; state investment agency; Gen. Man. MICHAEL NDUDZO.

State Enterprises Restructuring Agency (SERA): Cecil House, 1st Floor, cnr Jason Moyo Ave and Third St, Private Bag 7728, Causeway, Harare; tel. (4) 729164; fax (4) 726317; e-mail communications@sera.co.zw; internet www.sera.co.zw; f. 1999 as Privatisation Agency of Zimbabwe; name changed as above in 2005; CEO ANDREW N. BVUMBE.

Zimbabwe Investment Authority (ZIA): Investment House, 109 Rotten Row, POB 5950, Harare; tel. (4) 757931; fax (4) 773843; e-mail info@zia.co.zw; internet www.zia.co.zw; f. 2007 by merger of Zimbabwe Investment Centre and the Export Processing Zones Authority; promotes domestic and foreign investment; CEO RICHARD MBAIWA.

ZimTrade: 904 Premium Close, Mt Pleasant Business Park, POB 2738, Harare; tel. (4) 369330; fax (4) 369244; e-mail info@zimtrade.co.zw; internet www.zimtrade.co.zw; f. 1991; national trade development and promotion org.; Chair. J. SIZIBA; CEO SITHEMBILE PRISCILLA PILIME.

DEVELOPMENT ORGANIZATIONS

Alternative Business Association (ABA): Stand No. 15295, cnr First St and Eighth Cres., Sunningdale, Harare; tel. (4) 589625; fax (4) 799600; f. 1999 to address urban and rural poverty; programme areas include: agriculture, micro-mining, cross-border trade, micro-enterprise devt and micro-finance; Dir ISRAEL MABHOU.

Indigenous Business Development Centre (IBDC): Pocket Bldg, 1st Floor, Jason Moyo Ave, POB 3331, Causeway, Harare; tel. (4) 748345; f. 1990; Pres. BEN MUCHECHE; Sec.-Gen. ENOCH KAMUSHINDA.

Indigenous Business Women's Organisation (IBWO): 73B Central Ave, POB 3710, Harare; tel. (4) 702076; fax (4) 614012; Pres. JANE MUTASA.

Zimbabwe Human Rights NGO Forum: Blue Bridge, 8th Floor, Eastgate, POB 9077, Harare; tel. (4) 250511; fax (4) 250494; e-mail admin@hrforum.co.zw; internet www.hrforumzim.com; f. 1998; provides legal and 'psycho-social' assistance to the victims of organized violence; comprises 16 mem. orgs.

Zimbabwe Women's Bureau: 43 Hillside Rd, POB CR 120, Cranborne, Harare; tel. (4) 747809; fax (4) 707905; e-mail zwbtc@africaonline.co.zw; f. 1978; promotes entrepreneurial and rural community devt; Dir MAVIS MADAURE.

CHAMBERS OF COMMERCE

Manicaland Chamber of Industries: 6 St Helens Dr., POB 92, Mutare; tel. (20) 64909; e-mail czimtre@zol.co.zw; internet www.czi .co.zw; f. 1945; Pres. KUMBIRAI KATSANDE; 60 mems.

Mashonaland Chamber of Industries: 31 J. Chinamano Ave, POB 3794, Harare; tel. (4) 772763; fax (4) 750953; f. 1922; Pres. CHESTER MHENDE; 729 mems.

Matabeleland Chamber of Industries: 104 S. Parirenyatwa St, POB 2317, Bulawayo; tel. (9) 60642; fax (9) 60814; e-mail czibyo@zol .co.zw; f. 1931; Pres. Dr RUTH LABODE; 75 mems (2003).

Midlands Chamber of Industries: POB 213, Gweru; tel. (54) 2812; Pres. Dr BILL MOORE; 50 mems.

Zimbabwe National Chamber of Commerce (ZNCC): ZNCC Business House, 42 Harare St, POB 1934, Harare; tel. (4) 749335; fax (4) 750375; e-mail info@zncchq.co.zw; internet www.zncc.co.zw; f. 1983; represents small and medium businesses; Pres. OSWELL BINHA; CEO ANDREW MATIZA; 2,500 mems; 8 brs.

INDUSTRIAL AND TRADE ASSOCIATIONS

Chamber of Mines of Zimbabwe: Stewart House, North Wing, 4 Central Ave, POB 712, Harare; tel. (4) 702841; fax (4) 707983; e-mail info@chamines.co.zw; internet www.chamberofminesofzimbabwe .com; f. 1939 by merger of the Rhodesian Chamber of Mines (Bulawayo) and Salisbury Chamber of Mines; Pres. WINSTON CHITANDO; CEO J. B. R. CHIKOMBERO.

Confederation of Zimbabwe Industries (CZI): 31 Josiah Chinamano Ave, POB 3794, Harare; tel. (4) 251490; fax (4) 252424; e-mail cmsileya@czi.co.zw; internet www.czi.co.zw; f. 1923; Pres. KUMBIRAYI KATSANDE; CEO CLIFFORD M. SILEYA.

Specialized affiliate trade associations include:

CropLife Zimbabwe: POB MP712, Mount Pleasant, Harare; tel. (4) 487211; fax (4) 487242; e-mail graeme.reid@bayer.co.zw; internet www.croplifeafrica.org; fmrly Agricultural Chemical Industry Asscn; Chair. MAX MAKUVISE.

Furniture Manufacturers' Association: c/o CZI, 31 Josiah Chinamano Ave, POB 3794, Harare; Pres. MATT SNYMAN.

Zimbabwe Association of Packaging: 17 Coventry Rd, Workington, Harare; tel. (4) 753800; fax (4) 882020.

Construction Industry Federation of Zimbabwe: Conquenar House, 256 Samora Machel Ave East, POB 1502, Harare; tel. (4) 746661; fax (4) 746937; e-mail cifoz@comone.co.zw; Pres. GILBERT MATIKA; CEO MARTIN CHINGAIRA; c. 460 mems.

Grain Marketing Board (GMB): Dura Bldg, 179–187 Samora Machel Ave, POB CY77, Harare; tel. (4) 701870; fax (4) 251294; e-mail marketing@gmbdura.co.zw; internet www.gmbdura.co.zw; f. 1931; responsible for maintaining national grain reserves and ensuring food security.

Indigenous Petroleum Group of Zimbabwe (IPGZ): Harare; f. 2004 following split from Petroleum Marketers' Asscn of Zimbabwe; Chair. HUBERT NYAMBUYA; represents 68 importers.

Minerals Marketing Corpn of Zimbabwe (MMCZ): 90 Mutare Rd, Msasa, POB 2628, Harare; tel. (4) 487200; fax (4) 487161; e-mail administrator@mmcz.co.zw; internet www.mmcz.co.zw; f. 1982; sole authority for marketing of mineral production (except gold); Chair. J. MACHOBA (acting); Gen. Man. MASIMBA CHANDAVENGERWA (acting).

Petroleum Marketers' Association of Zimbabwe (PMAZ): 142 Samora Machel Ave, Harare; tel. (4) 797556; represents private importers of petroleum-based products; Chair. GORDON MUSARIRA.

Timber Council of Zimbabwe: Conquenar House, 256 Samora Machel Ave, POB 3645, Harare; tel. (4) 746645; fax (4) 746013; Exec. Dir MARTIN DAVIDSON.

Tobacco Association of Zimbabwe (TAZ): Harare; CEO WILFRED NHEMWA.

Tobacco Growers' Trust (TGT): POB AY331, Harare; tel. (4) 781167; fax (4) 781722; f. 2001; manages 20% of tobacco industry foreign exchange earnings on behalf of Reserve Bank of Zimbabwe; affiliated orgs include Zimbabwe Tobacco Asscn and Zimbabwe Farmers' Union; Chair. WILFANOS MASHINGAIDZE; Gen. Man. ALBERT JAURE.

Tobacco Industry and Marketing Board: POB 10214, Harare; tel. (4) 613310; fax (4) 613264; internet www.timb.co.zw; f. 1936; Chair. NJODZI MACHIRORI; CEO ANDREW MATIBIRI.

Tobacco Trade Association: c/o 4–12 Paisley Rd, POB ST180, Southerton, Harare; tel. (4) 773858; fax (4) 773859; f. 1948; represents manufacturers and merchants.

Zimbabwe National Traditional Healers' Association (ZINATHA): Red Cross House, 2nd Floor, Rm 202, 98 Cameron St, POB 1116, Harare; tel. and fax (11) 606771; f. 1980; certifies and oversees traditional healers and practitioners of herbal medicine through the Traditional Medical Practitioners Council; promotes indigenous methods of prevention and treatment of HIV/AIDS; Pres. Prof. GORDON CHAVUNDUKA; 55,000 mems (2004).

Zimbabwe Tobacco Association (ZTA): 108 Prince Edward St, POB 1781, Harare; tel. (4) 796931; fax (4) 791855; e-mail fctobacco@ zta.co.zw; internet fctobacco.com; f. 1928; represents growers; Pres. ADRIAN SWALES; CEO RODNEY AMBROSE; c. 5,500 mems.

EMPLOYERS' ASSOCIATIONS

Commercial Farmers' Union (CFU): Agriculture House, cnr Adylinn Rd and Marlborough Dr., Marlborough; POB WGT390, Westgate, Harare; tel. (4) 309800; fax (4) 309849; e-mail aisd3@cfu .co.zw; internet www.cfuzim.org; f. 1942; Pres. CHARLES TAFFS; CEO HENDRIK W. OLIVIER; 1,200 mems.

Cattle Producers' Association (CPA): Agriculture House, cnr Adylinn Rd and Marlborough Dr., Marlborough; POB WGT390, Westgate, Harare; tel. and fax (4) 309837; e-mail livestock@cfuzim .org; Chair. MARYNA ERASMUS.

Crops Association: Agriculture House, cnr Adylinn Rd and Marlborough Dr., Marlborough; POB WGT390, Westgate, Harare; tel. (4) 309843; fax (4) 309850; e-mail copa@cfu.co.zw; comprises the Commercial Oilseeds Producers' Asscn, the Zimbabwe Cereal Producers' Asscn and the Zimbabwe Grain Producers' Asscn; Chair. DENNIS LAPHAM; Man. (Crops) GEORGE HUTCHISON; represents c. 800 producers.

National Association of Dairy Farmers: Agriculture House, cnr Adylinn Rd and Marlborough Dr., Marlborough; POB WGT390, Westgate, Harare; tel. (4) 309800; fax (4) 309837; e-mail livestock@cfuzim.org; f. 1953; Chair. PETRUS ERASMUS; CEO ROB J. VAN VUUREN; 174 mems.

Zimbabwe Association of Tobacco Growers (ZATG): Agriculture House, cnr Adylinn Rd and Marlborough Dr., Marlborough; POB WGT390, Westgate, Harare; f. 2001; Pres. JULIUS NGORIMA; CEO CANAAN RUSHIZHA; 1,500 mems.

Zimbabwe Poultry Association (Commercial Poultry Producers' Association): Agriculture House, cnr Adylinn Rd and Marlborough Dr., Marlborough; POB WGT390, Westgate, Harare; tel. (4) 309800; fax (4) 309849; Chair. PETER DRUMMOND; represents c. 200 producers.

Employers' Confederation of Zimbabwe (EMCOZ): Stewart House, 4 Central Ave, 2nd Floor, POB 158, Harare; tel. (4) 739647; fax (4) 739630; e-mail emcoz@emcoz.co.zw; Pres. DAVID GOVERE; Exec. Dir JOHN W. MUFUKARE.

Horticultural Promotion Council (HPC): 12 Maasdorp Ave, Alexandra Park; POB WGT290, Westgate, Harare; tel. (4) 745492; fax (4) 745480; Chief Exec. BASILIO SANDAMU; represents c. 1,000 producers.

Export Flower Growers' Association of Zimbabwe (EFGAZ): 12 Maasdorp Ave, Alexandra Park; POB WGT290, Westgate, Harare; tel. (4) 725130; fax (4) 795303; e-mail exflower@icon.co.zw; Dir MARY DUNPHY; c. 300 mems.

National Employment Council for the Construction Industry of Zimbabwe: St Barbara House, Nelson Mandela Ave and Leopold Takawira St, POB 2995, Harare; tel. (4) 773966; fax (4) 773967; CEO STANLEY R. MAKONI; represents over 19,000 mem. cos (2002).

Timber Producers' Federation (TPF): Fidelity Life Centre, 4th Floor, H. Chitepo St, POB 1736, Mutare; tel. and fax (20) 60959; e-mail lmubaiwa@mweb.co.zw; CEO LOYD MUBAIWA.

Zimbabwe Building Contractors' Association: Caspi House, Block C, 4 Harare St, Harare; tel. (4) 780411; represents small-scale building contractors; CEO CONCORDIA MUKODZI.

Zimbabwe Commercial Farmers' Union (ZCFU): 53 Third St, Mutare; tel. (20) 67163; fmrly Indigenous Commercial Farmers' Union; Pres. TREVOR GIFFORD; Dir JOHN MAUTSA; represents c. 11,000 black farmers (2003).

Zimbabwe Farmers' Union (ZFU): POB 3755, Harare; tel. (4) 704763; fax (4) 700829; Pres. SILAS HUNGWE; Exec. Dir KWENDA DZAVIRA; represents c. 200,000 small-scale black farmers (2002).

Zimbabwe Progressive Farmers' Union: Harare; Pres. NICHOLAS KAPUNGU.

UTILITIES

Electricity

Rural Electrification Agency (REA): Office 720, 7th Floor, Megawatt House, 44 Samora Machel Ave, Private Bag 250A, Harare; tel. (4) 770666; fax (4) 707667; e-mail emidzi@zesa.co.zw; internet www .rea.co.zw; f. 2002; manages the Rural Electrification Fund to expand and accelerate the electrification of rural areas; Chair. Dr SYDNEY ZIKUZO GATA; CEO EMMANUEL MIDZI.

ZESA Holdings (Pvt) Ltd: 25 Samora Machel Ave, POB 377TA, Harare; tel. (4) 774508; fax (4) 774542; e-mail pr@zesa.net; internet www.zesa.co.zw; f. 2002 following restructure of Zimbabwe Electricity Supply Authority; operates one hydroelectric and four thermal power stations; CEO JOSH CHIFAMBA; dependable generation capacity of 1,700 MW.

Zimbabwe Electricity Transmission Co (ZETCO): Electricity Centre, 8th Floor, 25 Samora Machel Ave, POB 1760, Harare; tel. (4) 774508; fax (4) 756179; e-mail zetconews@zetco.co.zw; internet www.zetco.org; f. 2002; develops, operates and maintains transmission infrastructure; Man. Dir (vacant).

Zimbabwe Electricity Regulatory Commission (ZERC): Century Towers, 14th Floor, 45 Samora Machel Ave, POB CY2585, Causeway, Harare; tel. (4) 780010; fax (4) 250696; e-mail admin@zerc .co.zw; internet www.zerc.co.zw; f. 2004 to oversee the unbundling from ZESA of the Zimbabwe Power Co, the Zimbabwe Electricity Transmission Co and the Zimbabwe Electricity Distribution Co; Dir-Gen. MAVIS CHIDZONGA.

Oil

National Oil Company of Zimbabwe (Pvt) Ltd (NOCZIM): NOCZIM House, 100 Leopold Takawira St, POB CY223, Causeway, Harare; tel. (4) 748543; fax (4) 748525; responsible for importing liquid fuels; Chair. CHARLES CHIPATO; Man. Dir ZVINECHIMWE CHURA.

Water

Zimbabwe National Water Authority (ZINWA): POB CY1215, Causeway, Harare; tel. and fax (4) 793139; e-mail mtetwa@utande.co .zw; f. 2001; fmrly Dept of Water, privatized in 2001; construction of dams, water supply, resources planning and protection; Chief Exec. ALBERT MUYAMBO.

TRADE UNIONS

Zimbabwe Congress of Trade Unions (ZCTU): Chester House, 9th Floor, Speke Ave and Third St, POB 3549, Harare; tel. (4) 794742; fax (4) 728484; internet www.zctu.co.zw; f. 1981 by merger of the African Trade Union Congress, the Nat. African Trade Union Congress, the Trade Union Congress of Zimbabwe, the United Trade Unions of Zimbabwe, the Zimbabwe Fed. of Labour and the Zimbabwe Trade Union Congress; co-ordinating org. for trade unions; Pres. GEORGE NKIWANE; Sec.-Gen. JAPHET MOYO; c. 70,000 mems (2007).

Zimbabwe Federation of Trade Unions (ZFTU): Makombe Complex, Causeway, Harare; f. 1996 as alternative to ZCTU; 23 affiliated unions (2006); Gen. Sec. ADAMS VERENGA.

Transport

RAILWAYS

In 2008 the rail network totalled 2,583 km, of which 313 km was electrified. Trunk lines run from Bulawayo south to the border with Botswana, connecting with the Botswana railways system, which, in turn, connects with the South African railways system; north-west to the Victoria Falls, where there is a connection with Zambia Railways; and north-east to Harare and Mutare connecting with the Mozambique Railways' line from Beira. From a point near Gweru, a line runs to the south-east, making a connection with the Mozambique Railways' Limpopo line and with the Mozambican port of Maputo. A connection runs from Rutenga to the South African Railways system at Beitbridge. A 320-km line from Beitbridge to Bulawayo was opened in 1999. In 2010 plans were announced for the construction of a railway line in northern Zimbabwe running to the border with Zambia, which would eventually be linked with the southern Zambian town of Kafue.

National Railways of Zimbabwe (NRZ): cnr Fife St and 10th Ave, POB 596, Bulawayo; tel. (9) 363716; fax (9) 363502; internet www.nrz .co.zw; f. 1899; reorg. 1967; privatization under way; Chair. KHOTSO DUBE; Gen. Man. Air Commodore MIKE TICHAFA KARAKADZAI.

ROADS

In 2002 the road system in Zimbabwe totalled an estimated 97,267 km; some 18,481 km of the total network was paved. In December 2005 tollgates were introduced at the borders to raise funds to maintain the road network.

CIVIL AVIATION

AirZim operates an effective monopoly over air travel and transport within Zimbabwe. International and domestic air services connect most of the larger towns.

Civil Aviation Authority of Zimbabwe (CAAZ): Harare Int. Airport Terminal, Level 3, New Terminal Bldg, Private Bag CY7716, Causeway, Harare; tel. (4) 585073; fax (4) 585100; e-mail ais@caaz.co.zw; internet www.caaz.co.zw; f. 1999; operates eight airports incl. Harare Int. Airport and Joshua Mqabuko Nkomo Int. Airport (fmrly Bulawayo Airport); CEO DAVID CHAWOTA.

Air Zimbabwe (Pvt) Ltd (AirZim): POB AP1, Harare Airport, Harare; tel. (4) 575111; fax (4) 575068; internet www.airzimbabwe .com; f. 1967; scheduled domestic and international passenger and cargo services to Africa, Australia and Europe; plans were announced in April 2006 to separate operations, creating the new cos Air Zimbabwe Technical, Air Zimbabwe Cargo, Nat. Handling Services and Galileo Zimbabwe, in addition to Air Zimbabwe; Chair. JONATHAN KADZURA; CEO INNOCENT MAVHUNGA (acting).

Tourism

The principal tourist attractions are the Victoria Falls, the Kariba Dam, and the Hwange Game Reserve and National Park. Zimbabwe Ruins, near Fort Victoria, and World's View, in the Matapos Hills, are also of interest. There is climbing and trout-fishing in the Eastern Districts, around Umtali. In 2010 some 2.34m. tourists visited Zimbabwe; revenue from tourism totalled US $634m. in that year.

Zimbabwe Tourism Authority (ZTA): Samora Machel Ave, POB CY286, Causeway, Harare; tel. (4) 752570; fax (4) 758826; e-mail info@ztazim.co.zw; internet www.zimbabwetourism.co.zw; f. 1984; promotes tourism domestically and from abroad; Chair. EMMANUEL FUNDIRA; CEO KARIKOGA KASEKE.

Associations licensed by the ZTA include:

Safari Operators' Association of Zimbabwe (SOAZ): 18 Walter Hill Ave, Eastlea, Harare; tel. and fax (4) 702402; e-mail soaz@mweb.co.zw; internet www.soaz.net; f. 1973 as Zimbabwe Association of Tourist and Safari Operators; present name adopted 2006; Chair. EMMANUEL FUNDIRA.

Defence

As assessed at November 2012, total armed forces numbered about 29,000: 25,000 in the army and 4,000 in the air force. Paramilitary forces comprised a police force of 19,500 and a police support unit of 2,300.

Defence Expenditure: Budgeted at Z.$130,000m. in 2013.

Commander-in-Chief of the Armed Forces: Pres. ROBERT GABRIEL MUGABE.

Head of the Armed Forces: Lt-Gen. CONSTANTINE CHIWENGA.

Commander of the Zimbabwe National Army: Lt-Gen. PHILLIP V. SIBANDA.

Education

Primary education, which begins at six years of age and lasts for seven years, is free and has been compulsory since 1987. Secondary education begins at the age of 13 and lasts for six years, comprising a first cycle of four years and a second cycle of two years. According to UNESCO estimates, in 2005/06 enrolment at primary schools included 90% of children in the relevant age-group (males 89%; females 91%), while the comparable ratio for secondary enrolment was just 38% of children (males 39%; females 37%) in the same school year. In 2009/10 some 94,611 students were enrolled in tertiary institutions. There are two state-run universities: the University of Zimbabwe, which is located in Harare, and the University of Science and Technology, at Bulawayo. There are also two private universities, Africa University in Mutare and Solusi University in Figtree. Education was allocated Z.$6,800,000m. by the central Government in the budget for 2005, equivalent to 24.7% of total expenditure for that year.

INDEX OF TERRITORIES IN VOLUMES I AND II

INDEX OF TERRITORIES IN VOLUMES I AND II

INDEX OF TERRITORIES IN VOLUMES I AND II